Who's Who of American Women®

Who'sWho of American Women®

2007

MARQUIS
Who'sWho®

890 Mountain Avenue, Suite 4
New Providence, NJ 07974 U.S.A.
www.marquiswhoswho.com

Who'sWho of American Women®

Marquis Who's Who

For information, contact:
Marquis Who's Who®
890 Mountain Avenue, Suite 4
New Providence, New Jersey 07974
908-673-1001; www.marquiswhoswho.com

Library of Congress Catalog Card Number	50-58231	
International Standard Book Number	0-8379-0434-X	(Classic Edition)
International Standard Book Number	0-8379-0435-8	(Deluxe Edition)
International Standard Serial Number	0083-9841	

Manufactured in the United States of America.

Table of Contents

Preface

Marquis Who's Who is proud to present the 2006-2007 edition of *Who's Who of American Women.* This 26th edition includes a special supplement—*Difference Makers 2006*—paying tribute to several women of particular distinction and interest.

Though not all biographees can be emphasized in such a manner, this edition is filled with the valuable biographical profiles of more than 40,000 women. Each listing provides you with critical biographical information, including educational background, family history, work history, civic activity, memberships, honors and awards. In many cases hobbies and special interests are also listed.

Looking back on the history of this publication, it is clear that the role of women in American society has changed dramatically in the years since our first edition, back in 1958. While the first version was heavily populated by women involved in volunteer, civic and "club" activities, this version features Supreme Court Justices, Cabinet members, CEOs, astronauts, self-made billionaires, and leading figures in virtually all fields of endeavor.

Factors such as position, noteworthy accomplishments, visibility, and prominence in a field are all taken into account in making selections for the book. Final decisions concerning inclusion or exclusion are made following extensive discussion, evaluation, and deliberation.

Biographical information is gathered in a variety of manners. In most cases, we invite our biographees to submit their biographical details. In many cases, though, the information is collected independently by our research and editorial staffs, which use a wide assortment of tools to gather complete, accurate, and up-to-date information.

To help you more effectively use this volume, we have provided special indexes, which give you the opportunity to reference our biographees by geographic location (state and city) and by professional title.

While the Marquis Who's Who editors exercise the utmost care in preparing each biographical sketch for publication, in a publication involving so many profiles, occasional errors may appear. Users of this publication are urged to notify the publisher of any issues so that adjustments can be made.

All of the profiles featured in *Who's Who of American Women* are available on *Who's Who on the Web* (www.marquiswhoswho.com) through a subscription. At the present time, subscribers to *Who's Who on the Web* have access to all of the names included in all of the Marquis Who's Who publications as well as many new biographies that will appear in upcoming publications.

We sincerely hope that this volume will be an indispensable reference tool for you. We are always looking for ways to better serve you and welcome your ideas for improvements. In addition, we continue to welcome your Marquis Who's Who nominations. *Who's Who of American Women* and all Marquis Who's Who publications pay tribute to those individuals who make significant contributions to our society. It is our honor and privilege to present their profiles to you.

Key Information

[1] SCHAFFER, STACY LYNN, [2] elementary school educator; **[3]** b. Skokie, Ill., Feb. 16, 1958; **[4]** d. Barry and Lorraine (Lebovitz) Lutz; **[5]** m. Bennett Shaffer, June 12, 1985; **[6]** children: Brandon, Bret, Alison. **[7]** Student U. Ill. Chgo, 1976-78; BE Nat. Louis U., 1980, MEd, 1984. **[8]** Cert. elem. tchr., Ill., learning disabilities. **[9]** Tchr. Edison Elem Sch., Skokie, 1980-81, primary tchr. learning disabilities, 1982—1987; ass't. supt. Learning Disabilities curriculum Skokie elementary schs., 1987—1998; supt., 1998— **[10]** tchr. remedial reading Madison Elem. Sch., Skokie, summers, 1980, 81, cons., lectr. in field. **[11]** Author: Beginning Reading Series for grades K-2, 1994; contbr. articles to profl. jours., mags., 2nd edit., 2001 **[12]** Vol. MADD, Am. Cancer Soc. **[13]** Capt. USAFR, 1985—2001; **[14]** Recipient Good Apple award. 1992. **[15]** Mem. NEA, Ill. Tchrs. Assn., Ill. Coun. Learning Disabilites (bd. dirs. 1989—), Internat. Reading Assn., Phi Beta Kappa. **[16]** Democrat. **[17]** Jewish. **[18]** Running, pottery. **[19]** Home: 1842 Willow Ln **[20]** Office: 22 Alexander Ave *

KEY

[1]	Name
[2]	Occupation
[3]	Vital statistics
[4]	Parents
[5]	Marriage
[6]	Children
[7]	Education
[8]	Professional certifications
[9]	Career
[10]	Career-related
[11]	Writings and creative works
[12]	Civic and political activities
[13]	Military
[14]	Awards and fellowships
[15]	Professional and association memberships, clubs and lodges
[16]	Political affiliation
[17]	Religion
[18]	Achievements information
[19]	Home address
[20]	Office address
[*]	Researched by Marquis Who's Who

Table of Abbreviations

The following abbreviations and symbols are frequently used in this book.

**An asterisk following a sketch indicates that it was researched by the Marquis Who's Who editorial staff and has not been verified by the biographee.*

A

A Associate (used with academic degrees only)
AA, A.A. Associate in Arts, Associate of Arts
AAAL American Academy of Arts and Letters
AAAS American Association for the Advancement of Science
AACD American Association for Counseling and Development
AACN American Association of Critical Care Nurses
AAHA American Academy of Health Administrators
AAHP American Association of Hospital Planners
AAHPERD American Alliance for Health, Physical Education, Recreation, and Dance
AAS Associate of Applied Science
AASL American Association of School Librarians
AASPA American Association of School Personnel Administrators
AAU Amateur Athletic Union
AAUP American Association of University Professors
AAUW American Association of University Women
AB, A.B. Arts, Bachelor of
AB Alberta
ABA American Bar Association
ABC American Broadcasting Company
AC Air Corps
acad. academy, academic
acct. accountant
acctg. accounting
ACDA Arms Control and Disarmament Agency
ACHA American College of Hospital Administrators
ACLS Advanced Cardiac Life Support
ACLU American Civil Liberties Union
ACOG American College of Ob-Gyn
ACP American College of Physicians
ACS American College of Surgeons
ADA American Dental Association
a.d.c. aide-de-camp
adj. adjunct, adjutant
adj. gen. adjutant general
adm. admiral
adminstr. administrator
adminstrn. administration
adminstrv. administrative
ADN Associate's Degree in Nursing
ADP Automatic Data Processing
adv. advocate, advisory
advt. advertising
AE, A.E. Agricultural Engineer
A.E. and P. Ambassador Extraordinary and Plenipotentiary
AEC Atomic Energy Commission
aero. aeronautical, aeronautic
aerodyn. aerodynamic
AFB Air Force Base
AFL-CIO American Federation of Labor and Congress of Industrial Organizations
AFTRA American Federation of TV and Radio Artists
AFSCME American Federation of State, County and Municipal Employees
agr. agriculture
agrl. agricultural
agt. agent
AGVA American Guild of Variety Artists
agy. agency
A&I Agricultural and Industrial
AIA American Institute of Architects
AIAA American Institute of Aeronautics and Astronautics
AIChE American Institute of Chemical Engineers
AICPA American Institute of Certified Public Accountants
AID Agency for International Development
AIDS Acquired Immune Deficiency Syndrome
AIEE American Institute of Electrical Engineers
AIM American Institute of Management
AIME American Institute of Mining, Metallurgy, and Petroleum Engineers
AK Alaska
AL Alabama
Ala. Alabama
ALA American Library Association
alt. alternate
Alta. Alberta
A&M Agricultural and Mechanical
AM, A.M. Arts, Master of
Am. American, America
AMA American Medical Association
amb. ambassador
A.M.E. African Methodist Episcopal
Amtrak National Railroad Passenger Corporation
AMVETS American Veterans of World War II, Korea, Vietnam
ANA American Nurses Association
anat. anatomical
ANCC American Nurses Credentialing Center
ann. annual
ANTA American National Theatre and Academy
anthrop. anthropological
AP Associated Press
APA American Psychological Association
APGA American Personnel Guidance Association
APHA American Public Health Association
APO Army Post Office
apptd. appointed
Apr. April
apt. apartment
AR Arkansas
ARC American Red Cross
arch. architect
archeol. archeological
archtl. architectural
Ariz. Arizona
Ark. Arkansas
ArtsD, ArtsD. Arts, Doctor of
arty. artillery
AS American Samoa
AS Associate in Science
ASCAP American Society of Composers, Authors and Publishers
ASCD Association for Supervision and Curriculum Development
ASCE American Society of Civil Engineers
ASHRAE American Society of Heating, Refrigeration, and Air Conditioning Engineers
ASME American Society of Mechanical Engineers
ASNSA American Society for Nursing Service Administrators
ASPA American Society for Public Administration
ASPCA American Society for the Prevention of Cruelty to Animals
assn. association
assoc. associate
asst. assistant
ASTD American Society for Training and Development
ASTM American Society for Testing and Materials
astron. astronomical
astrophys. astrophysical
ATLA Association of Trial Lawyers of America
ATSC Air Technical Service Command
AT&T American Telephone & Telegraph Company
atty. attorney
Aug. August
AUS Army of the United States
aux. auxiliary
Ave. Avenue
AVMA American Veterinary Medical Association
AZ Arizona
AWHONN Association of Women's Health Obstetric and Neonatal Nurses

B

B. Bachelor
b. born
BA, B.A. Bachelor of Arts
BAgr, B.Agr. Bachelor of Agriculture
Balt. Baltimore
Bapt. Baptist
BArch, B.Arch. Bachelor of Architecture

BAS, B.A.S. Bachelor of Agricultural Science
BBA, B.B.A. Bachelor of Business Administration
BBB Better Business Bureau
BBC British Broadcasting Corporation
BC, B.C. British Columbia
BCE, B.C.E. Bachelor of Civil Engineering
BChir, B.Chir. Bachelor of Surgery
BCL, B.C.L. Bachelor of Civil Law
BCLS Basic Cardiac Life Support
BCS, B.C.S. Bachelor of Commercial Science
BD, B.D. Bachelor of Divinity
bd. board
BE, B.E. Bachelor of Education
BEE, B.E.E. Bachelor of Electrical Engineering
BFA, B.F.A. Bachelor of Fine Arts
bibl. biblical
bibliog. bibliographical
biog. biographical
biol. biological
BJ, B.J. Bachelor of Journalism
Bklyn. Brooklyn
BL, B.L. Bachelor of Letters
bldg. building
BLS, B.L.S. Bachelor of Library Science
BLS Basic Life Support
Blvd. Boulevard
BMI Broadcast Music, Inc.
BMW Bavarian Motor Works (Bayerische Motoren Werke)
bn. battalion
B.&O.R.R. Baltimore & Ohio Railroad
bot. botanical
BPE, B.P.E. Bachelor of Physical Education
BPhil, B.Phil. Bachelor of Philosophy
br. branch
BRE, B.R.E. Bachelor of Religious Education
brig. gen. brigadier general
Brit. British, Brittanica
Bros. Brothers
BS, B.S. Bachelor of Science
BSA, B.S.A. Bachelor of Agricultural Science
BSBA Bachelor of Science in Business Administration
BSChemE Bachelor of Science in Chemical Engineering
BSD, B.S.D. Bachelor of Didactic Science
BSEE Bachelor of Science in Electrical Engineering
BSN Bachelor of Science in Nursing
BST, B.S.T. Bachelor of Sacred Theology
BTh, B.Th. Bachelor of Theology
bull. bulletin
bur. bureau
bus. business
B.W.I. British West Indies

C

CA California
CAA Civil Aeronautics Administration
CAB Civil Aeronautics Board
CAD-CAM Computer Aided Design–Computer Aided Model
Calif. California
C.Am. Central America
Can. Canada, Canadian
CAP Civil Air Patrol
capt. captain
cardiol. cardiological
cardiovasc. cardiovascular
CARE Cooperative American Relief Everywhere
Cath. Catholic
cav. cavalry
CBC Canadian Broadcasting Company
CBI China, Burma, India Theatre of Operations
CBS Columbia Broadcasting Company
C.C. Community College
CCC Commodity Credit Corporation
CCNY City College of New York
CCRN Critical Care Registered Nurse
CCU Cardiac Care Unit
CD Civil Defense
CE, C.E. Corps of Engineers, Civil Engineer
CEN Certified Emergency Nurse
CENTO Central Treaty Organization
CEO chief executive officer
CERN European Organization of Nuclear Research
cert. certificate, certification, certified
CETA Comprehensive Employment Training Act
CFA Chartered Financial Analyst
CFL Canadian Football League
CFO chief financial officer
CFP Certified Financial Planner
ch. church
ChD, Ch.D. Doctor of Chemistry
chem. chemical
ChemE, Chem.E. Chemical Engineer
ChFC Chartered Financial Consultant
Chgo. Chicago
chirurg. chirurgical
chmn. chairman
chpt. chapter
CIA Central Intelligence Agency
Cin. Cincinnati
cir. circle, circuit
CLE Continuing Legal Education
Cleve. Cleveland
climatol. climatological
clin. clinical
clk. clerk
C.L.U. Chartered Life Underwriter
CM, C.M. Master in Surgery
CM Northern Mariana Islands
CMA Certified Medical Assistant
cmty. community
CNA Certified Nurse's Aide
CNOR Certified Nurse (Operating Room)
C.&N.W.Ry. Chicago & North Western Railway
CO Colorado
Co. Company
COF Catholic Order of Foresters
C. of C. Chamber of Commerce
col. colonel
coll. college
Colo. Colorado
com. committee
comd. commanded
comdg. commanding
comdr. commander
comdt. commandant
comm. communications
commd. commissioned
comml. commercial
commn. commission
commr. commissioner
compt. comptroller
condr. conductor
Conf. Conference
Congl. Congregational, Congressional
Conglist. Congregationalist
Conn. Connecticut
cons. consultant, consulting
consol. consolidated
constl. constitutional
constn. constitution
constrn. construction
contbd. contributed
contbg. contributing
contbn. contribution
contbr. contributor
contr. controller
Conv. Convention
COO chief operating officer
coop. cooperative
coord. coordinator
CORDS Civil Operations and Revolutionary Development Support
CORE Congress of Racial Equality
corp. corporation, corporate
corr. correspondent, corresponding, correspondence
C.&O.Ry. Chesapeake & Ohio Railway
coun. council
CPA Certified Public Accountant
CPCU Chartered Property and Casualty Underwriter
CPH, C.P.H. Certificate of Public Health
cpl. corporal
CPR Cardio-Pulmonary Resuscitation
C.P.Ry. Canadian Pacific Railway
CRT Cathode Ray Terminal
C.S. Christian Science
CSB, C.S.B. Bachelor of Christian Science
C.S.C. Civil Service Commission
CT Connecticut
ct. court
ctr. center
ctrl. central
CWS Chemical Warfare Service
C.Z. Canal Zone

D

D. Doctor
d. daughter
DAgr, D.Agr. Doctor of Agriculture
DAR Daughters of the American Revolution
dau. daughter
DAV Disabled American Veterans
DC, D.C. District of Columbia
DCL, D.C.L. Doctor of Civil Law
DCS, D.C.S. Doctor of Commercial Science
DD, D.D. Doctor of Divinity
DDS, D.D.S. Doctor of Dental Surgery
DE Delaware

Dec. December
dec. deceased
def. defense
Del. Delaware
del. delegate, delegation
Dem. Democrat, Democratic
DEng, D.Eng. Doctor of Engineering
denom. denomination, denominational
dep. deputy
dept. department
dermatol. dermatological
desc. descendant
devel. development, developmental
DFA, D.F.A. Doctor of Fine Arts
D.F.C. Distinguished Flying Cross
DHL, D.H.L. Doctor of Hebrew Literature
dir. director
dist. district
distbg. distributing
distbn. distribution
distbr. distributor
disting. distinguished
div. division, divinity, divorce
divsn. division
DLitt, D.Litt. Doctor of Literature
DMD, D.M.D. Doctor of Dental Medicine
DMS, D.M.S. Doctor of Medical Science
DO, D.O. Doctor of Osteopathy
docs. documents
DON Director of Nursing
DPH, D.P.H. Diploma in Public Health
DPhil, D.Phil. Doctor of Philosophy
D.R. Daughters of the Revolution
Dr. Drive, Doctor
DRE, D.R.E. Doctor of Religious Education
DrPH, Dr.P.H. Doctor of Public Health, Doctor of Public Hygiene
D.S.C. Distinguished Service Cross
DSc, D.Sc. Doctor of Science
DSChemE Doctor of Science in Chemical Engineering
D.S.M. Distinguished Service Medal
DST, D.S.T. Doctor of Sacred Theology
DTM, D.T.M. Doctor of Tropical Medicine
DVM, D.V.M. Doctor of Veterinary Medicine
DVS, D.V.S. Doctor of Veterinary Surgery

E

E, E. East
ea. eastern
E. and P. Extraordinary and Plenipotentiary
Eccles. Ecclesiastical
ecol. ecological
econ. economic
ECOSOC Economic and Social Council (of the UN)
ED, E.D. Doctor of Engineering
ed. educated
EdB, Ed.B. Bachelor of Education
EdD, Ed.D. Doctor of Education
edit. edition
editl. editorial
EdM, Ed.M. Master of Education
edn. education
ednl. educational
EDP Electronic Data Processing
EdS, Ed.S. Specialist in Education
EE, E.E. Electrical Engineer
E.E. and M.P. Envoy Extraordinary and Minister Plenipotentiary
EEC European Economic Community
EEG Electroencephalogram
EEO Equal Employment Opportunity
EEOC Equal Employment Opportunity Commission
E.Ger. German Democratic Republic
EKG Electrocardiogram
elec. electrical
electrochem. electrochemical
electrophys. electrophysical
elem. elementary
EM, E.M. Engineer of Mines
EMT Emergency Medical Technician
ency. encyclopedia
Eng. England
engr. engineer
engring. engineering
entomol. entomological
environ. environmental
EPA Environmental Protection Agency
epidemiol. epidemiological
Episc. Episcopalian
ERA Equal Rights Amendment
ERDA Energy Research and Development Administration
ESEA Elementary and Secondary Education Act
ESL English as Second Language
ESPN Entertainment and Sports Programming Network
ESSA Environmental Science Services Administration
ethnol. ethnological
ETO European Theatre of Operations
Evang. Evangelical
exam. examination, examining
Exch. Exchange
exec. executive
exhbn. exhibition
expdn. expedition
expn. exposition
expt. experiment
exptl. experimental
Expy. Expressway
Ext. Extension

F

F.A. Field Artillery
FAA Federal Aviation Administration
FAO Food and Agriculture Organization (of the UN)
FBA Federal Bar Association
FBI Federal Bureau of Investigation
FCA Farm Credit Administration
FCC Federal Communications Commission
FCDA Federal Civil Defense Administration
FDA Food and Drug Administration
FDIA Federal Deposit Insurance Administration
FDIC Federal Deposit Insurance Corporation
FE, F.E. Forest Engineer
FEA Federal Energy Administration
Feb. February
fed. federal
fedn. federation
FERC Federal Energy Regulatory Commission
fgn. foreign
FHA Federal Housing Administration
fin. financial, finance
FL Florida
Fl. Floor
Fla. Florida
FMC Federal Maritime Commission
FNP Family Nurse Practitioner
FOA Foreign Operations Administration
found. foundation
FPC Federal Power Commission
FPO Fleet Post Office
frat. fraternity
FRS Federal Reserve System
FSA Federal Security Agency
Ft. Fort
FTC Federal Trade Commission
Fwy. Freeway

G

G-1 (or other number) Division of General Staff
GA, Ga. Georgia
GAO General Accounting Office
gastroent. gastroenterological
GATE Gifted and Talented Educators
GATT General Agreement on Tariffs and Trade
GE General Electric Company
gen. general
geneal. genealogical
geod. geodetic
geog. geographic, geographical
geol. geological
geophys. geophysical
geriat. geriatrics
gerontol. gerontological
G.H.Q. General Headquarters
GM General Motors Corporation
GMAC General Motors Acceptance Corporation
G.N.Ry. Great Northern Railway
gov. governor
govt. government
govtl. governmental
GPO Government Printing Office
grad. graduate, graduated
GSA General Services Administration
Gt. Great
GTE General Telephone and Electric Company
GU Guam
gynecol. gynecological

H

HBO Home Box Office
hdqs. headquarters
HEW Department of Health, Education and Welfare
HHD, H.H.D. Doctor of Humanities
HHFA Housing and Home Finance Agency
HHS Department of Health and Human Services
HI Hawaii
hist. historical, historic

HM, H.M. Master of Humanities
HMO Health Maintenance Organization
homeo. homeopathic
hon. honorary, honorable
Ho. of Dels. House of Delegates
Ho. of Reps. House of Representatives
hort. horticultural
hosp. hospital
HS, H.S. High School
HUD Department of Housing and Urban Development
Hwy. Highway
hydrog. hydrographic

I

IA Iowa
IAEA International Atomic Energy Agency
IATSE International Alliance of Theatrical and Stage Employees and Moving Picture Operators of the United States and Canada
IBM International Business Machines Corporation
IBRD International Bank for Reconstruction and Development
ICA International Cooperation Administration
ICC Interstate Commerce Commission
ICCE International Council for Computers in Education
ICU Intensive Care Unit
ID Idaho
IEEE Institute of Electrical and Electronics Engineers
IFC International Finance Corporation
IGY International Geophysical Year
IL Illinois
Ill. Illinois
illus. illustrated
ILO International Labor Organization
IMF International Monetary Fund
IN Indiana
Inc. Incorporated
Ind. Indiana
ind. independent
Indpls. Indianapolis
indsl. industrial
inf. infantry
info. information
ins. insurance
insp. inspector
insp. gen. inspector general
inst. institute
instl. institutional
instn. institution
instr. instructor
instrn. instruction
instrnl. instructional
internat. international
intro. introduction
IRE Institute of Radio Engineers
IRS Internal Revenue Service
ITT International Telephone & Telegraph Corporation

J

JAG Judge Advocate General
JAGC Judge Advocate General Corps
Jan. January
Jaycees Junior Chamber of Commerce
JB, J.B. Jurum Baccalaureus
JCB, J.C.B. Juris Canoni Baccalaureus
JCD, J.C.D. Juris Canonici Doctor, Juris Civilis Doctor
JCL, J.C.L. Juris Canonici Licentiatus
JD, J.D. Juris Doctor
jg. junior grade
jour. journal
jr. junior
JSD, J.S.D. Juris Scientiae Doctor
JUD, J.U.D. Juris Utriusque Doctor
jud. judicial

K

Kans. Kansas
K.C. Knights of Columbus
K.P. Knights of Pythias
KS Kansas
K.T. Knight Templar
KY, Ky. Kentucky

L

LA, La. Louisiana
L.A. Los Angeles
lab. laboratory
L.Am. Latin America
lang. language
laryngol. laryngological
LB Labrador
LDS Latter Day Saints
LDS Church Church of Jesus Christ of Latter Day Saints
lectr. lecturer
legis. legislation, legislative
LHD, L.H.D. Doctor of Humane Letters
LI, L.I. Long Island
libr. librarian, library
lic. licensed, license
L.I.R.R. Long Island Railroad
lit. literature
litig. litigation
LittB, Litt.B. Bachelor of Letters
LittD, Litt.D. Doctor of Letters
LLB, LL.B. Bachelor of Laws
LLD, L.L.D. Doctor of Laws
LLM, L.L.M. Master of Laws
Ln. Lane
L.&N.R.R. Louisville & Nashville Railroad
LPGA Ladies Professional Golf Association
LPN Licensed Practical Nurse
LS, L.S. Library Science (in degree)
lt. lieutenant
Ltd. Limited
Luth. Lutheran
LWV League of Women Voters

M

M. Master
m. married
MA, M.A. Master of Arts
MA Massachusetts
MADD Mothers Against Drunk Driving
mag. magazine
MAgr, M.Agr. Master of Agriculture
maj. major
Man. Manitoba
Mar. March
MArch, M.Arch. Master in Architecture
Mass. Massachusetts
math. mathematics, mathematical
MATS Military Air Transport Service
MB, M.B. Bachelor of Medicine
MB Manitoba
MBA, M.B.A. Master of Business Administration
MBS Mutual Broadcasting System
M.C. Medical Corps
MCE, M.C.E. Master of Civil Engineering
mcht. merchant
mcpl. municipal
MCS, M.C.S. Master of Commercial Science
MD, M.D. Doctor of Medicine
MD, Md. Maryland
MDiv Master of Divinity
MDip, M.Dip. Master in Diplomacy
mdse. merchandise
MDV, M.D.V. Doctor of Veterinary Medicine
ME, M.E. Mechanical Engineer
ME Maine
M.E.Ch. Methodist Episcopal Church
mech. mechanical
MEd., M.Ed. Master of Education
med. medical
MEE, M.E.E. Master of Electrical Engineering
mem. member
meml. memorial
merc. mercantile
met. metropolitan
metall. metallurgical
MetE, Met.E. Metallurgical Engineer
meteorol. meteorological
Meth. Methodist
Mex. Mexico
MF, M.F. Master of Forestry
MFA, M.F.A. Master of Fine Arts
mfg. manufacturing
mfr. manufacturer
mgmt. management
mgr. manager
MHA, M.H.A. Master of Hospital Administration
M.I. Military Intelligence
MI Michigan
Mich. Michigan
micros. microscopic, microscopical
mid. middle
mil. military
Milw. Milwaukee
Min. Minister
mineral. mineralogical
Minn. Minnesota
MIS Management Information Systems
Miss. Mississippi
MIT Massachusetts Institute of Technology
mktg. marketing
ML, M.L. Master of Laws
MLA Modern Language Association
M.L.D. Magister Legnum Diplomatic
MLitt, M.Litt. Master of Literature, Master of Letters
MLS, M.L.S. Master of Library Science
MME, M.M.E. Master of Mechanical Engineering

MN Minnesota
mng. managing
MO, Mo. Missouri
moblzn. mobilization
Mont. Montana
MP Northern Mariana Islands
M.P. Member of Parliament
MPA Master of Public Administration
MPE, M.P.E. Master of Physical Education
MPH, M.P.H. Master of Public Health
MPhil, M.Phil. Master of Philosophy
MPL, M.P.L. Master of Patent Law
Mpls. Minneapolis
MRE, M.R.E. Master of Religious Education
MRI Magnetic Resonance Imaging
MS, M.S. Master of Science
MS, Ms. Mississippi
MSc, M.Sc. Master of Science
MSChemE Master of Science in Chemical Engineering
MSEE Master of Science in Electrical Engineering
MSF, M.S.F. Master of Science of Forestry
MSN Master of Science in Nursing
MST, M.S.T. Master of Sacred Theology
MSW, M.S.W. Master of Social Work
MT Montana
Mt. Mount
MTO Mediterranean Theatre of Operation
MTV Music Television
mus. museum, musical
MusB, Mus.B. Bachelor of Music
MusD, Mus.D. Doctor of Music
MusM, Mus.M. Master of Music
mut. mutual
MVP Most Valuable Player
mycol. mycological

N

N, N. North
NAACOG Nurses Association of the American College of Obstetricians and Gynecologists
NAACP National Association for the Advancement of Colored People
NACA National Advisory Committee for Aeronautics
NACDL National Association of Criminal Defense Lawyers
NACU National Association of Colleges and Universities
NAD National Academy of Design
NAE National Academy of Engineering, National Association of Educators
NAESP National Association of Elementary School Principals
NAFE National Association of Female Executives
N.Am. North America
NAM National Association of Manufacturers
NAMH National Assn. for Mental Health
NAPA National Association of Performing Artists
NARAS National Academy of Recording Arts and Sciences
NAREB National Association of Real Estate Boards
NARS National Archives and Record Service
NAS National Academy of Sciences
NASA National Aeronautics and Space Administration
NASP National Association of School Psychologists
NASW National Association of Social Workers
nat. national
NATAS National Academy of Television Arts and Sciences
NATO North Atlantic Treaty Organization
NATOUSA North African Theatre of Operations, United States Army
nav. navigation
NB New Brunswick
NBA National Basketball Association
NBC National Broadcasting Company
NC, N.C. North Carolina
NCAA National College Athletic Association
NCCJ National Conference of Christians and Jews
ND, N.D. North Dakota
NDEA National Defense Education Act
NE Nebraska
NE, N.E. Northeast
NEA National Education Association
Nebr. Nebraska
NEH National Endowment for Humanities
neurol. neurological
Nev. Nevada
NF Newfoundland
NFL National Football League
Nfld. Newfoundland
NG National Guard
NH, N.H. New Hampshire
NHL National Hockey League
NIH National Institutes of Health
NIMH National Institute of Mental Health
NJ, N.J. New Jersey
NLRB National Labor Relations Board
NM New Mexico
N.Mex. New Mexico
No. Northern
NOAA National Oceanographic and Atmospheric Administration
NORAD North America Air Defense
Nov. November
NOW National Organization for Women
N.P.Ry. Northern Pacific Railway
nr. near
NRA National Rifle Association
NRC National Research Council
NS, N.S. Nova Scotia
NSC National Security Council
NSF National Science Foundation
NSTA National Science Teachers Association
NSW New South Wales
N.T. New Testament
NT Northwest Territories
nuc. nuclear
numis. numismatic
NV Nevada
NW, N.W. Northwest
N.W.T. Northwest Territories
NY, N.Y. New York
N.Y.C. New York City
NYU New York University
N.Z. New Zealand

O

OAS Organization of American States
ob-gyn obstetrics-gynecology
obs. observatory
obstet. obstetrical
occupl. occupational
oceanog. oceanographic
Oct. October
OD, O.D. Doctor of Optometry
OECD Organization for Economic Cooperation and Development
OEEC Organization of European Economic Cooperation
OEO Office of Economic Opportunity
ofcl. official
OH Ohio
OK Oklahoma
Okla. Oklahoma
ON Ontario
Ont. Ontario
oper. operating
ophthal. ophthalmological
ops. operations
OR Oregon
orch. orchestra
Oreg. Oregon
orgn. organization
orgnl. organizational
ornithol. ornithological
orthop. orthopedic
OSHA Occupational Safety and Health Administration
OSRD Office of Scientific Research and Development
OSS Office of Strategic Services
osteo. osteopathic
otol. otological
otolaryn. otolaryngological

P

PA, Pa. Pennsylvania
P.A. Professional Association
paleontol. paleontological
path. pathological
PBS Public Broadcasting System
P.C. Professional Corporation
PE Prince Edward Island
pediat. pediatrics
P.E.I. Prince Edward Island
PEN Poets, Playwrights, Editors, Essayists and Novelists (international association)
penol. penological
P.E.O. women's organization (full name not disclosed)
pers. personnel
pfc. private first class
PGA Professional Golfers' Association of America
PHA Public Housing Administration
pharm. pharmaceutical
PharmD, Pharm.D. Doctor of Pharmacy
PharmM, Pharm.M. Master of Pharmacy
PhB, Ph.B. Bachelor of Philosophy
PhD, Ph.D. Doctor of Philosophy

PhDChemE Doctor of Science in Chemical Engineering
PhM, Ph.M. Master of Philosophy
Phila. Philadelphia
philharm. philharmonic
philol. philological
philos. philosophical
photog. photographic
phys. physical
physiol. physiological
Pitts. Pittsburgh
Pk. Park
Pky. Parkway
Pl. Place
P.&L.E.R.R. Pittsburgh & Lake Erie Railroad
Plz. Plaza
PNP Pediatric Nurse Practitioner
P.O. Post Office
PO Box Post Office Box
polit. political
poly. polytechnic, polytechnical
PQ Province of Quebec
PR, P.R. Puerto Rico
prep. preparatory
pres. president
Presbyn. Presbyterian
presdl. presidential
prin. principal
procs. proceedings
prod. produced (play production)
prodn. production
prodr. producer
prof. professor
profl. professional
prog. progressive
propr. proprietor
pros. atty. prosecuting attorney
pro tem. pro tempore
PSRO Professional Services Review Organization
psychiat. psychiatric
psychol. psychological
PTA Parent-Teachers Association
ptnr. partner
PTO Pacific Theatre of Operations, Parent Teacher Organization
pub. publisher, publishing, published
pub. public
publ. publication
pvt. private

Q

quar. quarterly
qm. quartermaster
Q.M.C. Quartermaster Corps
Que. Quebec

R

radiol. radiological
RAF Royal Air Force
RCA Radio Corporation of America
RCAF Royal Canadian Air Force
RD Rural Delivery
Rd. Road
R&D Research & Development
REA Rural Electrification Administration
rec. recording
ref. reformed
regt. regiment
regtl. regimental
rehab. rehabilitation
rels. relations
Rep. Republican
rep. representative
Res. Reserve
ret. retired
Rev. Reverend
rev. review, revised
RFC Reconstruction Finance Corporation
RFD Rural Free Delivery
rhinol. rhinological
RI, R.I. Rhode Island
RISD Rhode Island School of Design
Rlwy. Railway
Rm. Room
RN, R.N. Registered Nurse
roentgenol. roentgenological
ROTC Reserve Officers Training Corps
RR Rural Route
R.R. Railroad
rsch. research
rschr. researcher
Rt. Route

S

S, S. South
s. son
SAC Strategic Air Command
SAG Screen Actors Guild
SALT Strategic Arms Limitation Talks
S.Am. South America
san. sanitary
SAR Sons of the American Revolution
Sask. Saskatchewan
savs. savings
SB, S.B. Bachelor of Science
SBA Small Business Administration
SC, S.C. South Carolina
SCAP Supreme Command Allies Pacific
ScB, Sc.B. Bachelor of Science
SCD, S.C.D. Doctor of Commercial Science
ScD, Sc.D. Doctor of Science
sch. school
sci. science, scientific
SCLC Southern Christian Leadership Conference
SCV Sons of Confederate Veterans
SD, S.D. South Dakota
SE, S.E. Southeast
SEATO Southeast Asia Treaty Organization
SEC Securities and Exchange Commission
sec. secretary
sect. section
seismol. seismological
sem. seminary
Sept. September
s.g. senior grade
sgt. sergeant
SHAEF Supreme Headquarters Allied Expeditionary Forces
SHAPE Supreme Headquarters Allied Powers in Europe
S.I. Staten Island
S.J. Society of Jesus (Jesuit)
SJD Scientiae Juridicae Doctor
SK Saskatchewan
SM, S.M. Master of Science
SNP Society of Nursing Professionals
So. Southern
soc. society
sociol. sociological
S.P.Co. Southern Pacific Company
spkr. speaker
spl. special
splty. specialty
Sq. Square
S.R. Sons of the Revolution
sr. senior
SS Steamship
SSS Selective Service System
St. Saint, Street
sta. station
stats. statistics
statis. statistical
STB, S.T.B. Bachelor of Sacred Theology
stblzn. stabilization
STD, S.T.D. Doctor of Sacred Theology
std. standard
Ste. Suite
subs. subsidiary
SUNY State University of New York
supr. supervisor
supt. superintendent
surg. surgical
svc. service
SW, S.W. Southwest
sys. system

T

TAPPI Technical Association of the Pulp and Paper Industry
tb. tuberculosis
tchg. teaching
tchr. teacher
tech. technical, technology
technol. technological
tel. telephone
Tel. & Tel. Telephone & Telegraph
telecom. telecommunications
temp. temporary
Tenn. Tennessee
Ter. Territory
Ter. Terrace
TESOL Teachers of English to Speakers of Other Languages
Tex. Texas
ThD, Th.D. Doctor of Theology
theol. theological
ThM, Th.M. Master of Theology
TN Tennessee
tng. training
topog. topographical
trans. transaction, transferred
transl. translation, translated
transp. transportation
treas. treasurer
TT Trust Territory
TV television
TVA Tennessee Valley Authority
TWA Trans World Airlines
twp. township
TX Texas

U

U., univ. University
UAW United Auto Workers
UCLA University of California at Los Angeles
UDC United Daughters of the Confederacy
U.K. United Kingdom
UN United Nations
UNESCO United Nations Educational, Scientific and Cultural Organization
UNICEF United Nations International Children's Emergency Fund
UNRRA United Nations Relief and Rehabilitation Administration
UPI United Press International
U.P.R.R. United Pacific Railroad
urol. urological
U.S. United States
U.S.A. United States of America
USAAF United States Army Air Force
USAF United States Air Force
USAFR United States Air Force Reserve
USAR United States Army Reserve
USCG United States Coast Guard
USCGR United States Coast Guard Reserve
USES United States Employment Service
USIA United States Information Agency
USMC United States Marine Corps
USMCR United States Marine Corps Reserve
USN United States Navy
USNG United States National Guard
USNR United States Naval Reserve
USO United Service Organizations
USPHS United States Public Health Service
USS United States Ship
USSR Union of the Soviet Socialist Republics
USTA United States Tennis Association
USV United States Volunteers
UT Utah

V

VA Veterans Administration
VA, Va. Virginia
vet. veteran, veterinary
VFW Veterans of Foreign Wars
VI, V.I. Virgin Islands
vice pres. vice president
vis. visiting
VISTA Volunteers in Service to America
VITA Volunteers in Technical Assistance
vocat. vocational
vol. volunteer, volume
v.p. vice president
vs. versus
VT, Vt. Vermont

W

W, W. West
WA Washington (state)
WAC Women's Army Corps
Wash. Washington (state)
WATS Wide Area Telecommunications Svc.
WAVES Women's Reserve, US Naval Reserve
WCTU Women's Christian Temperance Union
we. western
W. Ger. Germany, Federal Republic of
WHO World Health Organization
WI Wisconsin
W.I. West Indies
Wis. Wisconsin
WSB Wage Stabilization Board
WV West Virginia
W.Va. West Virginia
WWI World War I
WWII World War II
WY Wyoming
Wyo. Wyoming

X, Y

YMCA Young Men's Christian Association
YMHA Young Men's Hebrew Association
YM & YWHA Young Men's and Young Women's Hebrew Association
yr. year
YT Yukon Territory
YWCA Young Women's Christian Association

Z

zool. zoological

Alphabetical Practices

Names are arranged alphabetically according to the surnames, and under identical surnames according to the first given name. If both surname and first given name are identical, names are arranged alphabetically according to the second given name.

Surnames beginning with De, Des, Du, however capitalized or spaced, are recorded with the prefix preceding the surname and arranged alphabetically under the letter D.

Surnames beginning with Mac and Mc are arranged alphabetically under M.

Surnames beginning with Saint or St. appear after names that begin Sains, and are arranged according to the second part of the name, e.g., St. Clair before Saint Dennis.

Surnames beginning with Van, Von, or von are arranged alphabetically under the letter V.

Compound surnames are arranged according to the first member of the compound.

Many hyphenated Arabic names begin Al-, El-, or al-. These names are alphabetized according to each biographee's designation of last name. Thus Al-Bahar, Neta may be listed either under Al- or under Bahar, depending on the preference of the listee.

Also, Arabic names have a variety of possible spellings when transposed to English. Spelling of these names is always based on the practice of the biographee. Some biographees use a Western form of word order, while others prefer the Arabic word sequence.

Similarly, Asian names may have no comma between family and given names, but some biographees have chosen to add the comma. In each case, punctuation follows the preference of the biographee.

Parentheses used in connection with a name indicate which part of the full name is usually omitted in common usage. Hence, Chambers, E(lizabeth) Anne indicates that the first name, Elizabeth, is generally recorded as an initial. In such a case, the parentheses are ignored in alphabetizing and the name would be arranged as Chambers, Elizabeth Anne.

However, if the entire first name appears in parentheses, for example, Chambers, (Elizabeth) Anne, the first name is not commonly used, and the alphabetizing is therefore arranged as though the name were Chambers, Anne.

If the entire middle name is in parentheses, it is still used in alphabetical sorting. Hence, Belamy, Katherine (Lucille) would sort as Belamy, Katherine Lucille. The same occurs if the entire last name is in parentheses, e.g., (Brandenberg), Howard Keith would sort as Brandenberg, Howard Keith.

For visual clarification:

Smith, H(enry) George: Sorts as Smith, Henry George
Smith, (Henry) George: Sorts as Smith, George
Smith, Henry (George): Sorts as Smith, Henry George
(Smith), Henry George: Sorts as Smith, Henry George

Difference Makers 2006

Who's Who of American Women®

Marquis Who's Who is proud to present

"Difference Makers 2006,"

honoring ten women

whose contributions to America and the world

were of particular note in the past year.

The following Marquis Who's Who honorees represent a wide range of talents and contributions, from Supreme Court Justice Ruth Bader Ginsburg to comedienne and activist Ellen DeGeneres, from director of the Centers for Disease Control Julie Gerberding to groundbreaking journalist Katie Couric.

Of course, *Who's Who of American Women* is filled with thousands who have made a real difference in their fields, in their communities, and in the world.

We are always searching for leading women in all endeavors for future editions of *Who's Who of American Women* and encourage you to contact us with your nominations and suggestions.

We hope you enjoy reading these profiles.

NANCY BARRY

Former President, Women's World Banking

To paraphrase an old adage: Give a woman a fish and she'll eat for a day; teach a woman to fish and she'll eat for a lifetime.

Give a woman a small loan allowing her to invest in fishing equipment, and she'll make a profit, invest in her children's futures, pull her family out of poverty, shore up the local economy, and pay you back in a timely fashion—with interest. That is the basic philosophy behind Women's World Banking (WWB), a global institution of which Nancy Barry was president and CEO for 16 years.

WWB is a worldwide network of banks with a common goal of providing low-income women with financing, information, and markets. Formed in 1979, it is one of the premiere microfinance institutions in the world. For those unfamiliar with the concept of microfinance, the basic idea is that a bank provides poor people with small loans—perhaps \$50 to \$75—to improve their small businesses or enterprises. If they can pay it back, they qualify for slightly larger loans.

Traditionally, poor women have been egregiously underserved by the typical banking system. In many parts of the world, women are not permitted to open their own bank accounts or can only manage their finances if supervised by a male relative. Many are illiterate and cannot sign for loans. And many, although they generate revenue, have no control over their families' finances.

Too often, women are not thought of as active members of the economy, when in fact, Barry often points out, "in most developing countries, women are the farmers, the transporters, and the sellers." The WWB was formed when women from separate countries at the United Nations global conference on women got together and agreed that women need to be recognized as business people and to be provided access to the services that would enable their economic development.

WWB believes that poor women are a bank's best clients. Poor women typically pay borrowed money back at a rate far higher than wealthier borrowers. They are less likely to spend their borrowed money on risky ventures. And women, who often have to care for children and aging relatives, are vastly more likely to consider their families' long-term futures in their investment decisions, often putting their money into education and medicine. In short, Barry explains, "the best social investment that you can make in a country is investing in women."

When she assumed the presidency in 1990, microfinance was still a new and relatively untested concept, and WWB was still a fledgling organization. Although both the idea and the institution had met with initial success, critics dismissed them as passing fads with no long-term future. Over the years, Barry forced the world to take WWB seriously. Barry, who had abandoned a career at a more conventional institution to devote her energies to these revolutionary ideas, stated, "I left the World Bank because I think WWB is the future." According to a Harvard Business School study, between 1990 and 2005, WWB's aggregate portfolio grew to over \$8 billion, and its clientele grew from around 20,000 poor women to more than 18 billion households. Within the term of her tenure, many of the small, local affiliates of WWB in third-world countries became successful enough to become "real" banks, and the high payback rates and profits of such organizations encouraged companies such as Citibank and Deutsche Bank to adopt some of WWB's methods.

After 16 years as president and CEO of WWB, and after winning many awards and accolades for her amazing accomplishments, Nancy Barry was succeeded by Mary Ellen Iskenderian in late September 2006. When asked in the early years of her presidency about the driving beliefs of her organization, she replied: "We believe in the power of women, through their local institutions, to transform the earth." ■

SUSAN BERRESFORD

President, Ford Foundation

As the head of one of the most powerful and influential philanthropic organizations in the world, Susan Berresford has dedicated her life to helping others.

In over 30 years with the Ford Foundation (the last 10 as its president), Berresford has worked tirelessly to further the foundation's original charter to "strengthen democratic values, reduce poverty and injustice, promote international cooperation, and advance human achievement."

The Ford Foundation, based in New York City, provides loans and grants to programs and organizations throughout the world that focus on economic and community development, human rights, education, and arts and culture.

Berresford has spent her entire professional career in public service. After graduating from Radcliffe College in 1965 with a B.A. in American history, she immediately joined the Neighborhood Youth Corps as a program officer. In 1967, she spent a year working for the Manpower Career Development Agency.

Berresford's career at the Ford Foundation began in 1970 when she joined the foundation as project assistant in the national affairs division. In 1980, she was put in charge of women's programs and a year later was named vice president for U.S. and international affairs programs; in 1989, she became vice president of the worldwide programming division. Her responsibilities continued to increase at the Foundation, and in 1995, she became executive vice president and COO.

In 1996, she was elected the eighth president of the Ford Foundation, which placed her at the helm of one of the biggest and most respected foundations in the world.

In her tenure as president, Berresford has headed many programs and initiatives to better the lives of underprivileged people. These initiatives include funding of the International Center for Transitional Justice, creating an organization to sponsor individual artists, establishing a program to raise home ownership rates for low-income Americans, and starting a graduate fellowship program for poor students.

In recent years, the Ford Foundation has assisted the victims and individuals affected by the 9/11 terrorist attacks, the tsunami in Asia, and Hurricane Katrina. "I am proud," Berresford said, "that in difficult times, we quickly provided support to people in distress."

In addition to her accomplishments at the Ford Foundation, Berresford serves on several boards including the Council on Foundations, the Panel on the Nonprofit Sector, The Trilateral Commission, the European Foundation Centre's Governing Council, and the American Academy of Arts and Sciences. She is also chair of the United States Artists Board.

After spending 36 years at the Ford Foundation, Susan Berresford announced that she will be retiring as president in January 2008 to start a new chapter in her life. Though this will be her final year, she has no intention of slowing down and has a bold agenda for 2007. As far as the future is concerned, she is confident that the Ford Foundation will continue to thrive.

"Our Foundation, networked around the world and driven by ambitions for fairness, democratic practice, and excellence, will be important for decades to come. We are dedicated to the discovery of knowledge, the expression of ideas, and to principles of democratic decision-making and accountability. This is at the heart of our work and our charter." ■

KATIE COURIC

Journalist/Activist

On September 5, 2006, television broadcasting history was made when Katie Couric—the immensely popular television news personality—became the first woman solo anchor of a major television network's weekday evening newscast.

The role of anchor for the *CBS Evening News* is generally acknowledged as the most prestigious in television journalism. Couric follows in the footsteps of such journalism icons as Edward R. Murrow, Walter Cronkite, and Dan Rather. She is also the managing editor of the *CBS Evening News* and a contributor to *60 Minutes*; she will also anchor various primetime news specials.

Couric was exposed early in life to the world of journalism. Her father was a reporter with the *Atlanta Journal-Constitution*. She has described her childhood as "Leave it to Beaver." She wrote for the campus newspaper at the University of Virginia, and after getting her degree in American studies in 1979, Couric was hired as a desk assistant for the ABC News bureau in Washington, D.C. Over the next 10 years, she worked at various positions of increasing responsibility and scope, first at CNN, and then at local stations in Miami and Washington, D.C. While in D.C., as a reporter for WRC-TV, she earned both an Associated Press Award and an Emmy.

Her association with NBC News began in 1989 when she became deputy Pentagon correspondent. Over the next two years, she filled in for various people on a variety of roles at *Today*. Couric's long tenure as co-host of NBC's *Today* began in 1991. The ratings for the show had been floundering, but due to her personable style and journalistic talents, the ratings improved immediately.

By the time Couric left in May 2006, *Today* had been the number one morning news show for more than a decade. In her years at NBC, she interviewed five presidents, various world leaders, and major figures from industry, entertainment, and sports.

Among the accolades Couric has received are six Emmy Awards, the Sigma Delta Chi Award, the Edward R. Murrow Award, and UNICEF's Danny Kaye Humanitarian Award. She is also one of only five women to have been repeatedly ranked by *Time* magazine, including in 2006, when she was ranked among the world's most influential people.

While Couric has enjoyed enormous success as a journalist, her "proudest achievement" has been her role as a spokesperson for cancer awareness. Her husband, Jay Monahan, died in 1998 of colon cancer at the age of 42. Couric has since made colon cancer awareness a personal crusade. Since early detection of a person's colon cancer or pre-cancerous polyps can greatly increase the chance of survival, she has encouraged everyone to have colonoscopies performed on a regular basis.

She demonstrated her commitment by undergoing her own colonoscopy—on air—in 2000. Following this broadcast, there was a documented 20% increase in colonoscopies across the country. The increase became known as the "Katie Couric effect." Her series on colon cancer earned her the highly prestigious George Foster Peabody Award.

Katie Couric is the co-founder of the National Colorectal Cancer Research Alliance (NCCRA). In 2004, she played a key role in establishing the Jay Monahan Center for Gastrointestinal Health at NewYork-Presbyterian Hospital/Weill Cornell. Of this, she's particularly proud.

"Clearly this is precisely the kind of center we wish had existed when Jay was diagnosed," Couric said. "Having this comprehensive center full of compassionate caregivers all under one roof would have been a wonderful place for us to go. The opening was a bittersweet occasion, but the center is going to be incredibly helpful to thousands of families and what can be better than that?" ■

ELLEN DEGENERES

Comedienne/Activist

Before *Queer Eye for the Straight Guy*, *Queer as Folk*, *The L Word*, or even *Will & Grace*, there was *Ellen*.

A decade ago, Ellen DeGeneres made the brave decision to simultaneously "come out" as a lesbian in her public life and have her semi-autobiographical character "come out" on the sitcom *Ellen*. Her decision did far more than just change the face of television. It helped to change America forever.

Today, DeGeneres is one of the most powerful women in entertainment and has emerged as a leading advocate and spokesperson for the gay community. She hosts a highly popular talk show, *The Ellen DeGeneres Show*, and has been given the honor of hosting the 2007 Academy Awards, which will take place in February.

While DeGeneres insists that she came out of the closet as a way of dealing with her personal issues, the impact of her decision has affected the lives of countless others.

"I made a decision to come out because it was the right thing to do for my soul, for me as a person, and I realized that it was more important to fully embrace and not to feel one ounce of shame about myself," she said.

Even though this was a personal choice, it became a national phenomenon that sparked a popular "Come Out with Ellen" campaign. This attention culminated with the now iconic *Time* magazine cover, which boldly pronounced—"Yep, I'm Gay." Not everyone responded positively. Many conservative groups denounced DeGeneres' actions, and televangelist Jerry Falwell called her "Ellen Degenerate."

The public pressure eventually subsided, but after another year of episodes, DeGeneres' sitcom was ultimately cancelled because of a decline in ratings and the public's lack of interest in a show that was labeled by some critics as "too gay."

DeGeneres, who was born in Louisiana and grew up in a small town in northeast Texas, struggled with her sexuality during her high school years. After graduating from high school, she moved back to Louisiana and proceeded to work in a series of odd jobs. Shortly after, she embarked upon a career in comedy.

DeGeneres first gained national attention in 1986 when she was voted "Funniest Person in America" by Showtime. During her premier performance on *The Tonight Show Starring Johnny Carson*, she not only impressed the audience, she wowed the host. In a foreshadowing of future success, she was asked by Mr. Carson to sit on the coveted couch and have a chat. She was the first female comic to do so on the first appearance.

DeGeneres has since been asked to host the Emmy Awards three times; she hosted in November 2001, when she had the somber duty of helping America laugh after the events of 9/11. In 2005, she was again asked to host the Emmys, this time only three weeks after the tragedy of Hurricane Katrina.

Her daytime talk show is now entering its fourth season and has earned a total of 15 Daytime Emmy Awards, including three consecutive Outstanding Talk Show awards. DeGeneres has also had a series of successful books and comedy films.

Ellen DeGeneres still finds the time to support gay issues and speaks extensively at high schools and colleges. When she speaks, she tries to avoid global issues, concentrating instead on her own experiences.

"I am not representing every gay person...these are my thoughts and my feelings," she said. "[Gays] don't have a lifestyle. We have a life." ■

JULIE LOUISE GERBERDING

Director, CDC

For Dr. Julie Gerberding, organic chemistry was a breeze, biology was child's play, and public health was a passion.

The one course that nearly did her academic career in?

Gym!

"I was commuting to a larger school district, and I was so intent on trying to take as many classes as I could because my parents had to pay money to be able to do this that I didn't want to waste any of my curriculum time on things like physical education," she explained. "And so I just skipped it; I didn't sign up for it. Nobody noticed it for two years."

As the woman at the forefront of a major national campaign to battle obesity, this is more than just a little ironic—it's almost hilarious.

Needless to say, Gerberding made up her gym classes and finished her high school degree. She went on to have an exceptional academic career. She earned a B.A. in chemistry and biology and an M.D., both from Case Western Reserve University and received a master of public health degree from the University of California, Berkeley. Along the way, she became a member of Phi Beta Kappa and Alpha Omega Alpha, the medical honor society.

After beginning her career as a professor at the University of California, San Francisco (UCSF), Gerberding joined the Centers for Disease Control (CDC) in 1998 as director of the Division of Healthcare Quality and Promotion at the National Center for Infectious Diseases. Although she became the director of the CDC in July 2002, she continued her role at UCSF in the department of medicine while also teaching at Emory University.

As head of the CDC, Gerberding is responsible for a wide range of issues and initiatives, from bioterrorism to avian flu, from anthrax to tainted spinach. She is responsible for creating the Emergency Response Center, a state-of-the-art operations center in which scientists from around the world are able to share valuable information. Her contributions have earned her commendations from a variety of organizations, including recognition in 2005 as one of *Forbes* magazine's "100 Most Powerful Women" in the world.

But despite her many honors and achievements, Gerberding has retained an ability to enjoy a laugh at her own expense. Perhaps to atone for her inactivity in high school or maybe to align herself with her stated goal to address obesity in America, she makes an attempt to incorporate more walking into her daily routine at the CDC. She recounts one of the events of her first day:

"When I started as the director, I wanted to set a good example at CDC, so I took the staircase in the headquarters building. I got in it, and I climbed up five floors, and I couldn't get out. So one of my first phone calls was to my secretary to say, 'Help, I'm stuck in the staircase.' But since that time, we have initiated some additional plans to rehabilitate the staircases in the facility."

Dr. Julie Gerberding's position at the CDC allows her to not only understand the diseases and the disorders but also their impact on the community.

"Each day at CDC, we try to imagine a safer, healthier world," she said. "A world where infants are born healthy and cared for—so, as children, they can arrive at school safe, well-nourished, and ready to learn. A world in which teenagers have the information, motivation, and hope they need to make healthy choices about their lifestyles and behaviors. A world in which adults enjoy active and productive lives in safe communities where they can remain independent and engaged with family and friends throughout their senior years." ■

RUTH BADER GINSBURG

Supreme Court Justice

A determined and fearless advocate for women's rights, Ruth Bader Ginsburg has devoted her life to the fight for gender equality.

Over the last 50 years, she has been a frequent victim of gender discrimination, a leading advocate for gender equality, and an influential jurist who helped women make enormous gains in the battle for equal treatment.

As a student in the 1950s, Ginsburg almost invariably found herself in the position of being a trailblazer. After graduating first in her class and Phi Beta Kappa from Cornell University, Ginsburg was one of only nine women admitted to her class at Harvard Law School. Though the women admitted to the school had academic credentials at least as good as (and often better than) their male counterparts, women at Harvard Law School were clearly unwelcome. The dean of the law school told the women straight out that he resented the fact that they were occupying places in the law school that should have gone to men.

Even when Ginsburg earned Harvard's highest honor—a place on the *Law Review*—it remained clear that she wasn't being taken seriously.

Two years later, after graduating first in her class from Columbia University's School of Law, she couldn't get a job. While her male classmates had no problems getting multiple job offers from leading law firms from around the country, Ginsburg didn't get a single offer.

Collection, The Supreme Court Historical Society
Photographed by Steve Petteway, Supreme Court

Spurned by the law firms, Ginsburg first served a judicial clerkship and then entered academia. She was the first tenured woman law professor at Rutgers University and later served as a full professor at Columbia's School of Law.

During her time at Rutgers, she became involved with the New Jersey branch of the American Civil Liberties Union. Ginsburg litigated some of the earliest sexual discrimination cases, including several involving teachers whose jobs were threatened when they became pregnant.

In 1971, she was instrumental in preparing arguments in the *Reed v. Reed* gender discrimination case before the U.S. Supreme Court. In that case, the court struck down a state law that gave preference to men over women in naming administrators of estates.

In 1972, Ginsburg headed the historic Women's Rights Project, where she argued six sexual discrimination cases before the Supreme Court, winning five. She was general counsel of the ACLU from 1973 to 1980 and sat on its national board of directors from 1974 to 1980.

Though often viewed as a "feminist," Ginsburg feels that the elimination of gender discrimination is a benefit to all members of society. She has also been responsible for striking down laws that gave women an unfair advantage over men. "It is not women's liberation," she said. "It is women's and men's liberation."

Ginsburg's first judicial post was on the U.S. Court of Appeals for the D.C. Circuit. Appointed by Jimmy Carter, she served 13 years as an appellate court judge before President Bill Clinton nominated her to succeed retiring Justice Byron R. White.

Ginsburg has written the court's opinion in several key gender discrimination cases, but as one of the more liberal members of a conservative court she often finds herself writing dissents, including the dissent in the seminal *Bush v. Gore*, which ultimately gave the 2000 presidential election to George W. Bush.

One of Ginsburg's remaining disappointments is that the Equal Rights Amendment was never passed.

"Every constitution written since the end of World War II includes a provision that men and women are citizens of equal stature," she said. "Ours does not. I have three granddaughters. I'd like them to be able to take out their Constitution and say, 'Here is a basic premise of our system, that men and women are persons of equal citizenship stature.' But it's not in there." ■

MARY-CLAIRE KING

Geneticist/Activist

It's hard to pin a single title on Mary-Claire King...but it's simple to choose an adjective: remarkable.

King is a world-renowned cancer researcher, teacher, and political activist. She has spent a lifetime using her scientific genius not just for medical advances but for social change as well.

Her social activism nearly derailed what has been a lifetime of achievement. Her graduate studies were interrupted briefly when she dropped out to work as a consumer and social advocate for Ralph Nader.

Fortunately, she returned to school to continue her education. The rest, as they say, is history.

Though she initially entered graduate school to study mathematics, she was eventually convinced to switch to the field of genetics.

As a doctoral student, King compared the genetic makeup of humans to that of chimpanzees. Her groundbreaking research resulted in the then-stunning revelation that humans' and chimps' genomes are 99% identical.

While it had previously been assumed that humans and chimpanzees had genetically diverged over 15 million years ago, Dr. King's research indicated that humans and chimpanzees took different genetic paths a mere five million years ago.

King's work as a geneticist later focused on possible genetic links to certain forms of cancer. She was the first to find a direct connection between a specific gene and a pre-disposition to breast cancer. This research isolated the genetic marker on chromosome 17. This gene was later linked to several other inherited breast and ovarian cancers.

Armed with this knowledge, women from families with a history of breast cancer have availed themselves of earlier and more regular screening, and the result has been countless lives saved.

Dr. King's continued dedication to social, political, and human rights causes would lead her, in 1984, to Argentina. While there, she employed advanced DNA testing (involving mitochondrial sequencing) to identify the children of parents who had been murdered during the Argentinean civil war of the 1970s.

At the time, thousands of these children were either placed in orphanages or were adopted by military families. Thanks to King's groundbreaking work, over 60 of these orphans were re-united with their real families.

More recently, King's ability to positively identify individuals through mitochondrial DNA sequencing has been used to identify murdered war victims in Bosnia, Ethiopia, and Rwanda. This information will be used as evidence in international war crimes trials.

King's methodology was also used to identify the remains of victims of the September 11, 2001 terror attacks in New York City.

King's work continues to this day. She has been working on studies for the earliest and most effective cancer screening for women with family histories of breast and other forms of cancer. Her work has also led her to breakthroughs involving genetics and deafness, a pursuit that has led her to study deafness among Palestinians.

Dr. King has been elected to the Institute of Medicine (and its Council) and to the American Academy of Arts and Sciences. She has received the Clowes Award for Basic Research from the American Association for Cancer Research, the Jill Rose Award from The Breast Cancer Research Foundation, and numerous other awards. Most recently, in June 2006, King was awarded the Weizmann Women & Science Award and the Dr. A.H. Heineken Prize for Medicine.

Says King, "I think there are two keys to being creatively productive. One is not being daunted by one's fear of failure. The second is sheer perseverance." She is simply a remarkable person. ■

GAY MCDOUGALL

Champion of Women's and Minorities' Rights

Gay McDougall has spent a lifetime combating human rights violations, a battle that has taken her to virtually every corner of the globe. From Afghanistan to Liberia, from Burundi to Mongolia, McDougall has been a tireless advocate for social, sexual, and political justice.

McDougall currently serves as the United Nations' independent expert on minority issues, a post to which she was appointed in 2005. In her first year, McDougall has focused heavily on those she believes are the most disadvantaged—minority women.

"In every region and in every society, women are undervalued, face issues of personal insecurity because of violence in their homes and communities, and must wage a constant struggle for self-determination over their bodies and personal destinies," McDougall wrote in a statement issued in commemoration of International Women's Day. "However, some women's problems are compounded by their uniquely disadvantaged position in society as members of national, racial, ethnic, religious, or linguistic minorities. Across the full spectrum of rights, civil and political, economic, social and cultural, minority women are often the most disadvantaged from birth until death."

McDougall came to the United Nations with an impressive resume. She earned her law degree from Yale University and holds an LLM in public international law from the London School of Economics and Political Science.

Prior to her most recent post at the United Nations, McDougall spent 11 years as the executive director of Global Rights, a human rights advocacy group that partners with local activists to challenge injustice and to give them the tools to fight. She came to that position after having spent the previous 14 years battling against the apartheid system in South Africa. She was one of only five international members of the 16-member Independent Electoral Commission.

When Nelson Mandela cast his vote on the day of South Africa's first free elections, McDougall was at his side.

McDougall had also been no stranger to service at the United Nations. Her first post came in 1988, when she was elected to serve as an independent expert on the United Nations treaty body that oversees the International Convention on the Elimination of All Forms of Racial Discrimination (CERD). Eight years later, McDougall was elected to serve a four-year term as a member of the Commission on Human Rights' Sub-Commission on Promotion and Protection of Human Rights.

While working with the Commission on Human Rights, she also served as special rapporteur on the issue of systematic rape, sexual slavery, and slavery-like practices in armed conflict.

For her efforts, McDougall has garnered myriad honors, including a highly prestigious MacArthur Foundation "genius" Fellowship.

McDougall believes that while there have been improvements in the status of women in the world, the progress has been far from universal:

"True gender equality will only be achieved when it is achieved for all women, not simply the women in advantaged majority communities. And, the rights of ethnic, religious, and linguistic minorities will be realized only when the women of those communities enjoy fully their human rights." ■

SUSAN MURCOTT

Environmental Engineer

It is not the sophistication of the work of Susan Murcott that makes her so remarkable—it is the utter simplicity.

Murcott is a world-renowned expert in safe drinking water technology. A senior lecturer at the Massachusetts Institute of Technology (MIT), she has devoted her career to studying, teaching, and designing low-cost, clean-water solutions for developing countries.

Contaminated water is responsible for death and disease around the world. The World Health Organization estimates that about one billion people worldwide do not have access to clean water supply and about two million people a year die as a consequence—most of them under the age of five.

Polluted water leads to water-borne diseases, and women not only carry the water but carry the burden of caring for the sick. "This leaves women with little time for education and economic advancement," says Murcott.

Murcott's genius lies in creating technologies that are not only inexpensive, but can be made from materials readily available in just about every country. Her students have produced numerous designs for water treatment systems that could be produced from local materials for $20 or less.

She is the leader of an MIT graduate program with the Department of Civil and Environmental Engineering in which students travel worldwide to conduct fieldwork: testing water, evaluating clean water technology, creating new product designs, and analyzing business and implementation processes. Under Murcott's guidance, students work one-on-one with local residents at the grassroots level and document their results in their elaborate theses papers, which are then posted on the MIT Web site.

In 1997, engineering students approached Murcott and requested that international projects in water and sanitation be offered. The first offering was the 1998 project in chemically enhanced wastewater treatment in Brazil. Next was the Nepal Water Project in 1999. Since then, her students have worked in Nicaragua, Peru, the Dominican Republic, Kenya, Haiti, and now Ghana. In developing new water treatment systems, students look at the cost of treatment systems; how easy they are to produce, use, and maintain; and how easy their results are to interpret; they look at convenience, accuracy, skill-level requirements, and most importantly, user acceptance.

Under Murcott's guidance and tutelage, MIT students won a World Bank competition in which they were awarded $115,000 for developing the Kanchan Arsenic Filter™, which treats both microbial and arsenic contamination. In 2005, the Kanchan Arsenic Filter won the *Wall Street Journal* Innovation Technology Award. More than 3,000 units are currently in use, and it is estimated that 8,000 will be in use by 2007. Murcott and her engineering teams have been working with business students from the MIT Sloan School of Management to find a way to scale up worldwide production.

As well as being a world expert in safe water technologies, Murcott is a leading voice for sustainability in which factors such as longevity of natural systems, practicality of harvesting procedures, and long-term maintenance are considered of vital importance. She also runs her own consulting company, Ecosystems Engineering, which specializes in drinking water and wastewater projects.

Influenced by Buddhism, Murcott is the author of *First Buddhist Women: Songs and Stories from the Therigatha*, which she wrote in the 70s. Since then, she has authored numerous professional papers and lectures worldwide. Murcott says, "Like the 20th century search for a polio vaccine or the 21st century search for a cure for HIV/AIDS or cancer, the motivation driving household water treatment and safe storage research and development is a search for a common, social good, and an instatement of a basic human right." ■

RUTH J. SIMMONS

President, Brown University

Ruth J. Simmons, president of Brown University, had to break more than a few glass ceilings on the way to the top of the academic world. In 2001, Simmons became not only the first female president of Brown University, but also the first African American president of any Ivy League School.

Simmons received her bachelor of arts degree from Dillard University in New Orleans in 1967. She went on to study romance languages and literature at Harvard University, earning her Ph.D. in 1973. Most at home in the university setting, Simmons accepted teaching and research positions at various institutions, implementing profound changes at each juncture.

In 1993, as vice provost at Princeton University, she wrote the now famous "Report on Campus Race Relations," in which she urged several recommendations to ease campus discontent. Her report resulted in a number of initiatives at Princeton, including the development of a race relations working group. This caught the attention of other universities where similar initiatives were eventually established.

In 1995, Simmons became president of Smith College. She immediately worked with the women's studies program to create a journal focused on the concerns of minority women. As a result, *Meridians* was founded, a peer-reviewed, feminist, interdisciplinary journal that provides a forum for scholarship and creative work by and about women of color.

She also established an undergraduate engineering program that required students to take not only a demanding regimen of physics and math courses but also required them to study literature, history, analytic philosophy, and a foreign language. This innovation was profiled by *The New York Times* and gained national attention as the first engineering program to be offered at an all-women's college.

In 2001, Simmons left Smith College to become president of Brown University. Brown, like most U.S. institutions founded before 1865, bears undeniable ties to slavery. The Brown family's fortune was based, in no small part, on revenues from the slave trade. Always a simmering pot, the issue of reparations boiled over in renewed debate in the spring of 2001, when the university's student paper printed a full-page advertisement entitled "Ten Reasons Why Reparations for Slavery Is a Bad Idea—and Racist Too." During Simmons' tenure, in 2003, she formed the Steering Committee on Slavery and Justice, comprised of faculty members, students, and administrators to research Brown's involvement in slavery and recommend a course of action.

In October 2006, the committee released its recommendations, calling for the university to issue a public apology and to create a center for the study of slavery and justice, as well as other proposals. The recommendations will be discussed at a public forum before the university issues an official response. Simmons, a great-granddaughter of slaves, whose office in University Hall was built with the labor of slaves, says "The Committee deserves praise for demonstrating so steadfastly that there is no subject so controversial that it should not be submitted to serious study and debate."

Now that she is in a highly visible leadership position, Simmons hopes to motivate others to follow in her footsteps. Simmons explains her primary motivation: "If there is anything that I can bring to higher education, it is a constant reminder of the need to bring children from the margins to the center, constantly redefining the center so that our democracy remains strong."

With all her accomplishments, breaking boundaries herself—as well as positioning others to do so, Ruth J. Simmons remains consistently aware of a perspective larger than her own. Of her achievements, she simply states, "My ancestors are smiling." ■

Who'sWho of American Women®

AAHOLM, SHERRY A., delivery service executive; Attended, U. Wis., Green Bay. Info. tech. and transp. positions Schneider Nat./Schneider Logistics, Inc., Wis.; v.p. info. tech. GeoLogistics Americas Inc., Atlanta; joined FedEx Corp., 1999; v.p., CIO FedEx Logistics; now sr. v.p. express and freight solutions FedEx Services. Named one of The Premier 100 IT Leaders, Computerworld, 2005. Office: FedEx Corp 942 S Shady Grove Rd Memphis TN 38120

AAKER, MELISSA B., secondary school educator; b. Wilmar, Minn., June 11, 1970; d. Ronald Lowell and Mary Jean Ryks; m. Michael David Aaker, June 22, 1990; children: Nicholas, Erika. BS in English summa cum laude, St. Cloud U., Minn., 1992; MS in Ednl. Leadership, SW State U., Marshall, Minn., 1999. English instr. ACGC Sr. HS, Grove City, Minn., 1993—2002; comms. instr. Willmar Sr. HS, Minn., 2002—. Pvt. tutor, Willmar, 2003. Sunday sch. tchr. 1st Covenant Ch., Millmar, 1993, jr. high youth leader, 1998—2003, Club 56 drama dir., 2002—, small group leader, 2005—. Target Tchr. scholar, 1998. Mem.: Willmar Edn. Assn., Nat. Coun. Tchrs. English. Avocations: reading, writing, scrapbooks. Office: Willmar Sr HS 2701 30th St NE Willmar MN 56201

AARON, BARBARA ROBINSON, real estate broker; b. Washington, Sept. 19, 1941; d. Tremain Fisher and Margaret Coe (Edgerton) Robinson; m. John Marshall Aaron III, June 27, 1964; children: Anne Kimbrough, Jennifer Coe. BA in Econs., Duke U., 1963. Cert. residential broker. Investment assoc. Old Colony Trust Co., Boston, 1963-64; ednl. tester Pa. State U., State Coll., 1964-65; real estates salesperson Trans Indies Realty & Investment, Guaynabo, P.R., 1973-75; real estate saleswoman Wellborn Real Estate, Reston, Va., 1975-76; real estates saleswoman Worthington & Vincent, Falmouth, Mass., 1977-80; real estates salesperson Chimney House Real Estate, Reston, 1976-77, 80-83, real estate mgr., 1983-95; real estate broker, asst. mgr. Coldwell Banker Stevens, Realtors, Reston, 1995—. Mem. Nat. Assn. Realtors, Realtors Brokerage Coun., Va. Assn. Realtors, No. Va. Assn. Realtors (std. forms com. 1989—, profl. stds. com., strategic planning com., bd. dirs.), Greater Reston C. of C. (bd. dirs. 1990-97, pres. 1992-93). Office: Realtors 11890 Sunrise Valley Dr Reston VA 20191-3302

AARON, CYNTHIA G., judge; b. Mpls., May 3, 1957; d. Allen Harold and Barbara Lois (Perlman) A.; m. Craig D. Higgs, May 15, 1993. Student, Brandeis U., 1975-77; BA with honors and distinction, Stanford U., 1979; JD cum laude, Harvard U., 1984. Bar: Calif. 1984, U.S. Dist. Ct. (so. dist.) Calif. 1984, U.S. Ct. Appeals (9th cir.) 1984, U.S. Dist. Ct. (no. dist.) Calif. 1986, U.S. Dist. Ct. (ctrl. dist.) Calif. 1988, U.S. Supreme Ct. 1991. Rsch. asst. to Prof. Alan Dershowitz Law Sch. Harvard U., 1982-83; trial atty. Fed. Defenders San Diego, Inc., 1984-88; ptnr. Aaron & Cortez, 1988-94; U.S. magistrate judge U.S. Dist. Ct. (so. dist.) Calif., San Diego, 1994—. Instr. Nat. Inst. for Trial Advocacy, 1988—93; adj. prof. Calif. Western Sch. Law, San Diego, 1990—93; adj. prof. law sch. U. San Diego, 1993, 95. Bd. dirs. San Diego Vol. Lawyer Program, 2001—. Mem.: San Diego County Judges Assn. (bd. dirs., pres. 2001—02), Lawyers Club San Diego, City Club San Diego, Phi Beta Kappa. Office: US Dist Ct So Dist 940 Front St Ste 1185 San Diego CA 92101-8940

AARSVOLD-INDRELIE, JUDITH, psychologist; b. Rochester, Minn., Jan. 31, 1957; d. Jacob Henry and Lina Mae (Patterson) Aarsvold; m. Jeffrey A. Indrelie, June 28, 1980; children: Erin, Leah, Kirsten, Brit Jacob. BA in Psychology and Sociology cum laude, Winona State U., 1979; MA in Psychology, St. Mary's Coll., Winona, Minn., 1980. Lic. profl. counselor, Okla. 1986. Psychologist Luth. Social Services, Rochester, Minn., 1980-86; therapist Social Work Services Reynolds Army Community Hosp., Lawton, Okla., 1987-88; psychologist pvt. practice, 2000—. Bd. dirs. Minn. Council Unplanned Pregnancy and Parenthood, Mpls., St. Paul, 1984-86; mem. Minn. Council on Sudden Infant Death Syndrome, Mpls., 1984-86; coordinator Ft. Sill Army's Family Advocacy Program in Spouse Abuse, 1987-88. Developer Unmarried Parent Booklet, 1983. Mem. Sexuality Task Force Zumbro Luth. Ch., Rochester, 1984-86, tchr., 1985-86; parent liaison Rochester Montessori Sch., 1985-86; escort to Korea Luth. Social Service, Mpls., 1982, 85; bd. dirs. Women's Shelter for Battered Women and their Children, 1987-88; bd. mem. Faith Luth. Ch., Waconia, Minn., 1996-1998, chair social outreach com., 1996-1998. Mem. Sierra Club, Psi Chi. Clubs: Nature Conservancy. Democrat. Lutheran. Avocations: cross country skiing, aerobics, hiking, biking, camping. Home: 1204 Butternut Ln Waconia MN 55387-1252

AATRAPI, MARJANE, writer, illustrator; b. Rasht, Iran, 1969; arrived in Vienna, 1984, Strasbourg, arrived in Iran, 1989, arrived in Paris, 1994; married. Student, Lycee Francais, Tehran, Iran. Contbr. NY Times, The New Yorker, others. Author: Persepolis: The Story of an Iranian Childhood, 2003, Persepolis 2: The Story of a Return, 2004, Embroideries, 2005.

ABAJIAN, WENDY ELISSE, broadcast executive, writer; b. Selma, Calif., Mar. 16, 1955; d. Mesik Nishon and Blanche Peggy (Emerzian) A. AA, Kings River Community Coll., 1975; BA, Calif. State U., Fresno, 1978; MS, U. So. Calif., 1981, EdD, 1986. Instr., tchr. various sch. dists., Burbank, Fresno & L.A., Calif., 1981—; free-lance writer various corps., Los Angeles area, 1984—; pres., ind. producer Abhawk Prodns., Inc., Long Beach, Calif., 1986-91; ind. writer/producer for TV, cable and video, 1991—; owner, ednl. media cons./specialist Gold Giraffe, 1995—; ednl. therapist, 1999—; co-owner MediaDuo, Inc., 2000—. Contbr. articles to profl. jours. Active Statue of Liberty Ellis Island Found., 1984-99, Women Appointees Coun., Sacramento, 1988-93, Burbank Ctr. for Retarded; gubernatorial appointee to adv. bd. Lanterman State Hosp., 1986-93; gubernatorial appointee to bd. dirs. Protection and Advocacy, Inc., 1990-93. Fellow: U. S.C. Ednl. Grad. Orgn.; mem.: Assn. Ednl. Therapist (profl.), Film Adv. Bd. (mem. adv. bd.). Armenian. Apostolic. Office Phone: 818-845-3499. Personal E-mail: mediaduoinc@aol.com.

A-BAKI, IVONNE, ambassador; b. Guayaquil, Ecuador; m. Sammi A-Baki; children: Tatiana, Mohammed, Faisal. Grad., The Sorbonne, France, Harvard U. Amb. to U.S. Govt. of Ecuador, Washington, 1998—. Artist-in-residence Harvard U., 1991—98; advisor in Ecuador-Peru peace negotiations Pres. of Ecuador, 1998; dir. Conflict Mgmt. Group Harvard U. Represented in permanent collections in galleries and pvt. collections, Europe, N.Am., S.Am., Middle East. Office: Embassy of Ecuador 2535 15th St NW Washington DC 20009

ABARBANEL, GAIL, social services administrator, educator; b. L.A., Apr. 17, 1944; d. Sam and Sylvia (Cramer) A.; m. Stephen P. Klein, Jan. 31, 1975. BA magna cum laude, UCLA, 1966; MSW, U. So. Calif., 1968. Lic. clin. social worker. Clin. social worker Mental Health Agy., L.A., 1968-74; founder, dir. Rape Treatment Ctr. & Dept. Social Svcs. Santa Monica (Calif.) Hosp. Med. Ctr., L.A., 1974—. Cons., educator in field. Contbr. articles to profl. jours. Bd. dirs. Clare Found., 1975-77; atty. gen. task force Violence Against Women Act, 1995-00; mem. Calif. Campus Sexual Assault Task Force, 2003; active Am. Cancer Soc., 1975-79, Child Trauma Coun., 1978-81, Sr. Health Ctr., 1981-87, Mayor's Transition Team, 2005. Recipient Gov.'s Victim Svcs. award, 1985, Pub. Affairs award Coro Found., 1985, Woman of Year Leadership award YWCA, 1980, 82, Status of Women award AAUW, 1978, Nat. Outstanding Achievement award Am. Cancer Soc., 1977, Disting. Citizen award L.A. County Bar Assn., 1988, Humanitarian award Nat. Conf. Christians and Jews, 1987, Soc. for Clin. Social Work award, 1989, DOJ award for Outstanding Svc., on Behalf of Vibtims of Crime, Pres. of U.S., 1991, Woman of Distinction award Soroptimist Internat., 1992, Excellence in Profl. Achievement Alumni award, UCLA, 1994, Outstanding Corp. Citizen award Pub. Rels. Soc. Am. La. chpt., 1997, Calif. Sexual Assault Investigators Assn. award, 1999, Pathfinder award Women Lawyers Assn., 2004; named Outstanding Alumni, U. So. Calif., 1979, one of Heroes of 1988 L.A. mag. Fellow Soc. Clin. Social Work; mem. NASW (Agy of Yr. award 1977, Social Worker of Yr. award 1995), Nat. Orgn. for Victim Assitance (Exemplary Program award 1995), Nat. Coalition Against Sexual Assault, Nat. Orgn. Victims Assistance, Phi Beta Kappa, Pi Gamma Mu. Office: Santa Monica-UCLA Med Ctr 1250 16th St Santa Monica CA 90404-1249

ABATE, ANNE KATHERINE, librarian, consultant, educator; b. Cleve., Mar. 10, 1958; d. Frank M. and Cecelia (Homic) Abate; m. George S. Maley, May 17, 1980. HAB with honors, Xavier U., Cin., 1980; MSLS, U. Ky., 1986; PhD, Nova Southeastern U., Ft. Lauderdale, Fla., 1998. Asst. dept. head Kenton County Pub. Libr., Covington, Ky., 1985-87; asst. dir. Lloyd Libr. and Mus., Cin., 1987-88; libr. Dinsmore & Shohl, 1988-99; asst. prof. Xavier U., 1999—2000; mktg. dir. GovConnect, 2000—04; exec. dir. Greater Cin. Libr. Consortium, SWON Libraries, 2004—. Part time faculty Xavier U., Cin., 1997—, U. Ky., 1998—; mem. adj. faculty Nova Southeastern U., Ft. Lauderdale, Fla., 1999—; mem. adv. bd. West Pub. Corp., Eagan, Minn., 1992-95. Contbr. articles to profl. jours.; cons./author video package: Managing Emerging Technologies, 1994. Mem. Spl. Librs. Assn. (bd. dirs. 1997-99, chpt. pres. 1992-93, chair pub. rels. com. 1993-95), Am. Libr. Assn., Beta Phi Mu. Roman Catholic. Avocations: reading, cooking, world travel. Office: SWON Libraries 10815 Indeco Dr Ste 200 Cincinnati OH 45241 Office Phone: 513-751-4422. Business E-Mail: anne@swonlibraries.org.

ABATE, CATHERINE M., retired state legislator; b. Margate, NJ, Dec. 8, 1947; d. Joseph and Carolyn (Fiore) A.; m. Ronald E. Kliegerman, Oct. 28, 1978; 1 child, Kyle. BA, Vassar Coll., 1969; JD, Boston U., 1972. Bar: N.Y. 1973, U.S. Dist. Ct. (so. dist.) N.Y. 1976. Staff atty. Legal Aid Soc., NYC, 1972-74, 75-78, supervising atty., 1979-81, dir. tng., 1981-85, acting chairperson Gov.'s Taskforce Criminal Justice, 1983; chairperson NY State Platform Criminal Justice, 1984, NY Crime Victims Bd., 1988-90; exec. dep. commr. NY State Div. Human Rights, 1986-88; commr. NYC Dept. Probation, 1990-92, NYC Dept. Correction, 1992-94; mem. NY State Senate, Albany, 1995-98; pres., CEO Cmty. Healthcare Network, 1999—. Dist. leader Dem. Party, 1981-86; 1st vice chmn. county com. Dem. Party, N.Y. County; bd. dirs. Village Nursing Home, 1987-99; bd. mem. Naral, 1999—, Correctional Assn., 1999—, Eleanor Roosevelt Legacy Com., 2003, Citizen Action, 2001—; chair 2001—; pres. bd. Family Planning Advs., 2004—. Mem. Bar Assn. City N.Y. (criminal cts. com. 1982-86), Nat. Assn. Crime Victims Compensation Bd. (bd. dirs. 1989-90), Nat. Orgn. Italian-Am. Women (bd. dirs. 1986-2003, chief judge's CPL com., 1999—, prisoner legal svcs. com., 1999—). Roman Catholic. Avocation: tennis. Home: 303 Mercer St New York NY 10003-6706 Office Phone: 212-366-4500 ext. 262. Business E-Mail: cabate@chnnyc.org.

ABATEMARCO, TRACY J., lawyer; BA summa cum laude, SUNY, Albany, 1988; JD, Georgetown U., 1991. Bar: NY 1991, Conn. 1992, US Dist. Ct. So. Dist. NY, US Dist. Ct. Ea. Dist. NY. Ptnr. Wilson, Elser, Moskowitz, Edelman & Dicker LLP, NYC. Mem.: NY State Bar Assn., Phi Beta Kappa. Office: Wilson Elser Moskowitz Edelman & Dicker LLP 23rd Fl 150 E 42nd St New York NY 10017-5639 Office Phone: 212-490-3000 ext. 2613. Office Fax: 212-490-3038. Business E-Mail: abatemarcot@wemed.com.

ABBE, ELFRIEDE MARTHA, sculptor, graphics designer; b. Washington; d. Cleveland Jr. and Frieda (Dauer) A. Student, Art Inst. Chgo., 1937; B.F.A., Cornell U., 1940; postgrad., Syracuse U., 1947. Author and illustrator: books including The Plants of Virgil's Georgics, 1965; One-woman exhbns. include Carnegie-Mellon U., 1962, 69, Cornell U., 1963, Trinity Coll., Hartford, 1964, Arts Club of Washington, 1972, Cornell Club of N.Y., 1977, Copley Soc. Boston, 1978, Woods-Gerry Gallery, R.I. Sch. Design, 1983; represented in permanent collections Met. Mus. Art., Watson Library, Boston Mus. Fine Arts, Cin. Art Mus., Dumbarton Oaks, Washington, Houghton Library, Harvard U., Hunt Library, Carnegie-Mellon U., N.Y. Pub. Library, Rosenwald Collection Nat. Gallery, Kew Gardens Library, Royal Bot. Garden, Edinburgh, Nat. Library, Canberra, Australia; sculpture placed in Mann Library, Kroch Library and Morrison Hall, Cornell U., McGill U., N.Y. Bot. Gardens, Hunt Library, Pitts., Pres.'s Office, Keene (N.H.) State Coll., Herzog August Bibliothek, Wolfenbüttel, Fed. Republic Germany (bronze bust of founder), Abbe Mus., Bar Harbor, Maine (bronze bust of founder Dr. Robert Abbe). Recipient Gold medals Pen and Brush, N.Y.C., 1964, Margaret Sussman Meml. award 1987, Gold medals Nat. Arts Club, 1970, Gold medals Acad. Artists Assn., Springfield, Mass., 1976, Founders' Prize Pen and Brush, 1977; Bd. Dirs. award Salmagundi Club N.Y., 1978; Elliot Liskin award, 1979, Catherine Lorillard Wolfe Club award, 1993. Fellow Nat. Sculpture Soc. (Barrett-Colea prize 1984); mem. Nat. Soc. Mural Painters, Phi Kappa Phi.

ABBEY, HELEN, science educator; ScD, Johns Hopkins U. Prof. Johns Hopkins Sch. Medicine, Balt. Contbr. articles to profl. jours. Achievements include research in statistical methods for epidemiology and human genetics. Office: Johns Hopkins Sch Medicine E2004 Hygiene 725 N Wolfe St Baltimore MD 21205-2105 Fax: 410-955-0958. E-mail: habbey@jhsph.edu.

ABBEY, LINDA ROWE, artist, educator; d. Robert Bradford and Elizabeth Spencer Rowe; m. Bruce James Abbey, Aug. 23, 1969; 1 child, Jason James. AA, Piedmont Coll., Charlottesville, Va., 1986; BA, Hanover Coll., Hanover, Ind., 1966. Cert. tchg. N.J., 1969, Va., 1975. Tchg. english as a fgn. lang. Peace Corps, Bizerte, Tunisia, 1966—68; tchg. english to italian navy officers Shenker Inst., Rome, Italy, Taranto, Italy, 1969—69; fourth grade tchr. Princeton Regional Sch., Princeton, NJ, 1969—72; title I tchr. Charlottesville City Sch., Charlottesville, Va., 1974—89; artist self-employed, Syracuse, NY, 1990—. Watercolor tchr. to adults and children, Syracuse, NY, 1993—; watercolor tchr. Everson Mus. of Art, Syracuse, NY, 1997—2001; vol. artist McKinley Brighton Elem. Sch., Syracuse, NY, 1995—2004; judge of artwork for on my own time show Syracuse U., Syracuse, NY; founding mem. Pleiades, A Group Of Six To Eight Artists Who Exhibit Together, Syracuse, NY, 1998—. One-woman shows include Watermark Gallery, Balt., Md., Fox & Fowle, Architects, N.Y.C., Straun Art Gallery, Jacksonville, Ill., prin. works include painting of Syracuse U.'s chancellor's house (The Brochure received a bronze medal from the Coun. for Advancement and Support of Edn., 2001), prin. works include 12 paintings in a Plexi frame to raise money for Onandaga Park trees damaged in the 1998 Labor Day Storm, 1998—2000, exhibitions include AAUW Invitational Show, Skaneateles, N.Y., Edith Barrett Fine Arts Gallery, Utica Coll., Utica, N.Y., Veerhoff Gallery, Washington, SUNY Ints. of Tech., Utica/Rome, N.Y., Lagerquist Gallery, Atlanta, Ga., Artifice Gallery, Syracuse, N.Y., Gallery 210 Juried Exhbn., Fine Details Gallery, Skaneateles, N.Y., Kirkland Art Ctr., Ctrl. N.Y. Juried Show, Clinton, N.Y., Adirondacks Nat. Exhbn. of Am. Watercolors, Old Forge, N.Y., Delavan Gallery, Syracuse, NY, 2004, 2006, Represented in permanent collections, TV program. Organizer of art show for over 50 artists in neighborhood Art on the Porches, Syracuse, 2001—04. Recipient Golden Rule Award, JC Penny and McKinley Brighton Sch., Syracuse, NY, 1997, Best Watercolor, Delavan Award, Hon. Mention, Cazenova Caral Mus. Show, 1992, 1994, 1996, Second Pl. Watercolor, SUNY Inst. Tech., Regional Art Show, 2000; grantee John DeFrancisco N.Y. Arts and Cultural Grant Fund and Cultural Resources Coun., 2003, 2004. Mem.: Onondaga Art Guild (assoc.; sec. 1998—99, pres. 1999—2000).

ABBINANTE, VITA, sales executive, administrator; b. Chgo., Nov. 5, 1948; d. Michael and Madeline Abbinante; divorced; children: Maria Theresa Gehard, Valerie Gehard, Leslie Gehard. Grad., Selan Beauty Sch., Chgo., 1976, Coll. of DuPage, 1971. Pres., owenr Gehard Enterprises, Elmhurst, Ill., 1992-96; mfrs. rep. Widdes Mktg., Northbrook, Ill., 1996-98; v.p. Metaltech Mfg., Jamestown, N.Y., 1998—. Bd. dirs., sec.-treas. MMAC, Jamestown, N., 1998—, Eisenhauer Group, Lake Bluff, Ill., 1996—, Buck Sci., Schiller Park, Ill., 1994-96. Author: (poems) Words of Praise, 1984, Hearts of Fire, 1985; contbr. poetry to Am. Poetry Anthology, Am. Poetry Assn., Eternal Echoes. Mem. NAFE, Jamestown Bus. and Profl. Women's Club. Roman Catholic. Avocations: reading, boating, creative writing, horseback riding. Home: 10116 W Cermak Rd Westchester IL 60154-4511

ABBOTT, AMY P., design educator; d. ClarenceDee and Dee Plymale; m. Randall Abbott, June 23, 1973; 1 child, Chelsea. BA, Averett U., Danville, Va., 1976, BA, 1990; M of Libr. and Info. Sci., U. NC, Greensboro, 1995. Tchr. art Pittsylvania County Schs., Chatham, Va., 1976—84; coord. print shop Averett Coll., Danville, 1985—91; tchr. designer Danville C.C., 1991—. Office Phone: 434-797-8557.

ABBOTT, ANN AUGUSTINE, social worker, educator; b. Green Bay, Wis., July 6, 1943; d. Walter A. and Ethel D. Augustine. BS in Psychology, St. Norbert Coll., W. DePere, Wis., 1965; MSS in Social Work, Bryn Mawr Coll., 1969, PhD (NIMH fellow), 1977, postgrad. in higher edn. adminstrn., 1978. Acad. tutor, counselor Devereux Schs., Devon, Pa., 1965-67; psychol. clin. coord. Pa. State U., University Park, 1969-71; social worker Tidewater Mental Health Clinic, Williamsburg, Va., 1971-72; adj. prof. Pa. State U., King of Prussia, 1973-75; vis. lectr. C.C. of Phila., 1975-76; asst. prof. dir. social work, cmty. psychology Widener U., Chester, Pa., 1976-81, project dir. Univ. Yr. for Action, 1976-81, project cons. Adult Competency Tng. Grant, 1976-81; with sch. social work Rutgers U., Camden, 1981—2001, assoc. prof., 1987—2001, assoc. dean, 1993—2001; prof., MSW program dir. grad. social work dept. West Chester U., Pa., 2001—. Faculty fellow NIAAA/NIDA/OSAP, 1990-93. Tennis coach Nat. Jr. Tennis League, Phila., 1974-76; budget rev. bd. United Way, vice-chair allocations com., 1979-86; trustee Ins. Trust, 1995-98, chair, 1996-98. Vocation Rehab. Tng. grantee, 1964. Fellow Am. Orthopsychiat. Assn., Coll. Physicians of Phila.; mem. NASW (nat. bd. mem. region IV 1988-91, del. assembly rep. 1979-89, pres. Pa. state chpt. 1987-89, nat. pres.-elect 1992-93, nat. pres. 1993-95), Coun. on Social Work Edn. (commn. on accreditation 1997-2000), Am. Group Psychotherapy Assn., Internat. Fed. Social Workers (v.p. for N.Am. 1994-96). Home: PO Box 637 Villanova PA 19085-0637 Office: Grad Social Work Dept West Chester U Reynolds Hall West Chester PA 19383 Office Phone: 610-738-0351. Business E-Mail: aabbott@wcupa.edu.

ABBOTT, BARBARA GAYLE, academic administrator; d. Raymond A. and Barbara A. Moore; 1 child, Kyle M. EdD, N.Mex State U., Las Cruces, 2004. Lic. counselor N.Mex Counseling and Therapy. Dir. student support svcs. N.Mex Jr. Coll., Hobbs, 1999—. Disaster vol. ARC, Hobbs, 1988—2006. Mem.: Inst. of Noetic Scis. (assoc.). Office Phone: 505-492-2617.

ABBOTT, BARBARA LOUISE, artist, educator; b. San Francisco, Oct. 16, 1941; d. C. Paige and Mary Ellen Abbott; m. Edward Michael Seman, Nov. 21, 1964 (div. June 1980); children: Jill, Janet, Michael Paige. BFA, U. Utah, 1982; MFA, Ariz. State U., 1986. Prof. art Edinboro U. Pa., Edinboro, Pa., 1989—90, La. State U., Shreveport, La., 1990—96; prin., owner Abbott Art Studio, San Jose, Calif., 1996—. Prin. works include Quilt Kiosks, Shreveport, La., 1993, Great Blue Herons, Santa Cruz, Calif., 2000, Perro Feliz, San Jose, Calif., 2002, exhibitions include Award Winning Prints, Phila. Print Club, Phila., 1986, Marking Time: Making Space, South of Mkt. Cultural Ctr., San Francisco, 2001, book, Twice Descending, 1991. Fellow Fulbright-Hays fellowship, U.S. Govt., 1993. Home and Studio: 778 Crestview Drive San Jose CA 95117

ABBOTT, GINA, municipal government executive; b. Patuxent River, Md., Oct. 12, 1954; d. Ralph Orlando Pivero and Nancy Dinicola; m. Winthrop S. Abbott, Jr., Nov. 13, 1977 (dec. Aug. 1996). BSBA, U. Phoenix, 1989. Cert. profl. pub. buyer. From purchasing asst. to small order buyer Tex. Instruments, Colorado Springs, 1984-89; from buyer to procurement & contracts dir. El Paso County Govt., Colorado Springs, 1990—. Recipient cert. of achievement Fed. Emergency Mgmt. Assn. Mem. Nat. Inst. Govtl. Purchasing, Rocky Mtn. Govtl. Purchasing Assn. (v.p. 2001). Avocations: cooking, baking, travel, watching sports. Office: El Paso County Govt 27 E Vermijo Ave Colorado Springs CO 80903-2208 Home: 14 Anita Rd Colorado Springs CO 80906-3110

ABBOTT, ISABELLA AIONA, retired biology educator; b. Hana, Maui, Hawaii, June 20, 1919; d. Loo Yuen and Annie Patseu (Chung) Aiona; m. Donald P. Abbott, Mar. 3, 1943 (dec.); 1 dau., Ann Kaiue Abbott. AB, U. Hawaii, 1941; MS, U. Mich., 1942; PhD, U. Calif., Berkeley, 1950. Prof. biology Stanford U., 1972-82; G.P. Wilder prof. botany U. Hawaii, 1978-98, G.P. Wilder emerita prof. botany, 1998—. Vis. rsch. biologist and tchr., Japan and Chile. Co-author: (with G.J. Hollenberg) Marine Algae of Calif., 1976, La'au Hawaii, traditional Hawaiian uses of plants, 1992; contbr. articles to profl. jours. Co-recipient NY Bot. Garden award for best book in botany, 1978; recipient Merit award Bot. Soc. Am., 1995, G.M. Smith medal NAS, 1997, Wings Spl. Award for Ethnobotany Wings WorldQuest Women of Discovery Awards, 2006. Fellow AAAS; mem. Internat. Phycological Soc. (treas. 1964-68), Western Soc. Naturalists (sec. 1962-64, pres. 1977), Phycological Soc. Am., Brit. Phycological Soc., Hawaiian Bot. Soc. Office: U Hawaii Manoa Botany Dept 3190 Maile Way Honolulu HI 96822-2232

ABBOTT, LINDA JOY, stained glass artisan, educator, photographer; b. Hempstead, NY, Oct. 10, 1943; d. Edward Morton Brandstatter and Evalyne Manchik; divorced 1971; children: David Edward Black, Adam Michael Black. AAS in Design, SUNY at FIT, N.Y.C., 1963; Cert. paralegal, Tarrant County C.C., Fort Worth, Tex., 1983; student, Disney Inst. Wildlife Photog., 2000, N.Y. Inst. Photography, 2001. Fashion designer Alyssa/Little Craft, N.Y.C., 1963-65; bus. owner Virgin Islands Diving Sch., St. Thomas, V.I., 1972-76; stained glass artisan Creative Glass, Salt Lake City, 1978-81, Linda Abbott Glass Art, Willow Park, Tex., 1981-86; founder, stained glass artisan, instr. Crystal Rainbow Glass Studio, Dania, Fla., 1986-99; stained glass artisan Linda Abbott Glass Studio, 1999—; freelance photographer. Freelance calligrapher various colls., Covina, Calif., 1968—71; freelance artist, Lancaster, 1976—78; cons. various stained glass cos., 1989—; product cons. various stained glass equipment mfrs., 1994—; sem. instr. Internat. Art Glass Supplies Assn., 1994—, coord. seminars, chair, 1999; mem. steering com. Art Glass Am., Tampa, 1998; guest instr. MISC Studios nationwide, 1999—; webmaster Cert. Career Inst., Clearfield, Utah; instr. in field. Author: E-Magine This! Book One, 2002, That's A Wrap!!!, 2005; co-author: Hot & Wired, 1993, Some Things Fishy, 1993, Rainforest, 1994, Stargazing, 1995, Image is Everything, 1996; prodr. (video) Hot & Wired; contbr. articles to mags. in field. Recipient Best in Show award Calif. City Art Assn., 1978,

Glass Expo, Salt Lake City, 1982. Mem. So. Fla. Ferret Club, Internat. Art Glass Suppliers Assn. (com. chair 1996—), Internat. Stained Glass Designers Assn. (pres. 1995-99), Art Glass Guild Artisans (dir. 1996—), Art Glass Am. (founder), Ednl. Consumer Conf. Jewish. Avocations: scuba diving, white-water rafting, photography. Office Phone: 801-399-1818. Personal E-mail: linda@abbottglass.com.

ABBOTT, REBECCA PHILLIPS, art historian, consultant, photographer, director; b. Giessen, Germany, Jan. 10, 1950; d. Charles Leonard and Janet Alice (Praeger) Phillips. BA, Emory and Henry Coll., 1973; postgrad., Georgetown U., 1975, Am. U., 1982-88. Assoc. univ. registrar Am. U., Washington, 1977-81, assoc. dir. adminstrv. computing, 1981-84, dir. adminstrv. computing, 1984-88; dir. membership Nat. Mus. of Women in the Arts, Washington, 1988-89, dir., 1989-98; cons. in fine arts, 1998—. Fine arts photographer. Selected solo exhbns., Includes Anton Gallery, Public Places Private Views, 1992, The Wind, 1994, Canal Views, 1996, Burton Marinkovich Fine Art, Shadows at 18th and K, 1998; Selected group exhbns. includes The Annex Gallery, Metaphysical Landscapes,1989, Embassy of Japan: East Meets West, 1995, Nippon Gallery, Assimilations, 1997. Mem.: Coll. Art Assn., Mus. Art Table, Am. Assn. Mus. Personal E-mail: rphillipsabbott@netscape.net, rphillipsabbott@yahoo.com.

ABBOTT, REGINA A., neurodiagnostic technologist, consultant, business owner; b. Haverhill, Mass., Mar. 5, 1950; d. Frank A. and Ann (Drelick) A. Student, Pierce Bus. Sch., Boston, 1967-70, Seizure Unit Children's Hosp. Med. Ctr. Sch. EEG Tech., 1970-71. Registered electroneurodiagnostic technologist Advanced Fuller Sch. Massage Therapy, 2001, nat. cert. massage therapist Nat. Cert. Bd. Therapeutic Massage and Bodywork. Tech. dir. electrodiagnostic labs. Salem Hosp., 1972-76; lab. dir. clin. neurophysiology Tufts U. New Eng. Med. Ctr., Boston, 1976-78; clin. instr. EEG program Laboure Coll., Boston, 1977-81; adminstrv. dir. dept. Neurology Mt. Auburn Hosp., Cambridge, Mass., 1978-81; tech. dir. clin. neurophysiology Drs. Diagnostic Service, Virginia Beach, Va.; tech. dir. neurodiagnostic ctr. Portsmouth Psychiatric Ctr., 1981-87; founder, pres., owner Commonwealth Neurodiagnostic Services, Inc., 1986—, Hands on HealthCare, 2001—, Hands On-Site, LLC, 2004—. Co-dir. continuing edn. program EEG Tech., Boston, 1977-78; mem. adv. com. sch. neurodiagnostic tech. Laboure Coll., 1977-81, Sch. EEG Tech. Children's Hosp. Med. Ctr., Boston, 1980-81; assoc. examiner Am. Bd. Registration of Electroencephalographic Technologists, 1977-83; mem. guest faculty Oxford Medilog Co.; cons. Nihon Kohden Am., 1981-83; cons., educator Teca Corp., Pleasantville, N.Y., 1981-87; clin. evaluator Calif. Coll. for Health Scis., 1995—. Contbr. articles to profl. jours. EIL scholar, Poland/USSR, 1970; recipient Internat. Woman of Yr. award in bus. and sci. Internat. Biographical Ctr., London, 1993-94. Mem.: NAFE, Am. Soc. Electroneurodiagnostic Technologists, Am. Massage Therapy Assn. Avocations: running, art collecting, photography, reading, investing.

ABBOTT, SUSAN L., lawyer; b. Oct. 1968; BA in History, cum laude, Williams Coll., 1990; MA, Duke U., 1994; JD, Duke U. Law Sch., 1994. Bar: Mass., DC. Assoc. Williams & Connolly, Washington, 1995—99; sr. mgr. Wealth Transfer Solutions Practice PricewaterhouseCoopers, 1999—2000; joined Goodwin Procter LLP, Boston, 2000, assoc. Trusts & Estate Planning Practice, co-chair Nonprofit and Charitable Organizations Group. Mem. Boston Estate Planning Coun., Planned Giving Group of New England. Mem.: Boston Bar Assn., ABA. Office: Goodwin Procter LLP Exchange Place 53 State St Boston MA 02109 Office Phone: 617-570-1787. E-mail: sabbott@goodwinprocter.com.*

ABBOTT, VERNA RUTH, social studies educator; b. Shawnee, Okla., July 4, 1925; d. James Ivan and Gladys Beatrice (Bennett) Forston; m. Lowell Woodrow Abbott, June 25, 1946 (dec. June 1989); children: Carlin, Priscilla, Patricia. BS, East Tenn. State U., Johnson City, 1967. Cert. tchr. polit. sci., history and speech, Tenn. Broadcaster KGFF Radio, Shawnee, 1943-48, WNAD Radio, U. Okla., 1948-50; broadcaster women's TV show WJHL-TV, Johnson City, 1960; tchr., audio-visual coord. Dobyns-Bennett H.S., Kingsport, Tenn., 1966-93; mem. Bd. Edn., Kingsport City Schs., 1993—. Sponsor domestic exch. Dobyns-Bennett H.S., Kingsport, 1982-93. Author articles and essays. Liaison, Kingsport Bd. of Mayor and Aldermen, 1993-97; chmn. Kingsport Schs. Safety Coun., 1995—; mem. bd. distinction Tenn. Sch. Bds. Assn., 1999. Named Outstanding Sch. Bd. Mem., Tenn. Congress Parents and Tchrs., 1996-97. Mem. AAUW, DAR (program com. 1996), LWV, Ret. Tchrs. Assn. Baptist. Avocations: volunteering, speaking. Home: 4321 Stagecoach Rd Kingsport TN 37664-2137 Office: Kingsport City Schs 1701 E Center St Kingsport TN 37664-2608

ABBOTT-LYON, FRANCES DOWDLE, journalist, civic worker; b. Rome, Ga., Mar. 21, 1924; d. John Wesley and Lucille Elizabeth (Field) Dowdle; m. Jackson Miles Abbott, May 15, 1948; children: Medora Frances, David Field, Elizabeth Stockton, Robert Jackson; m. Archibald W. Lyon, Oct. 15, 1993. Student, Draughon's Bus. Coll., Columbia, SC. Feature writer, Mt. Vernon corr. Alexandria Gazette, Va., 1967-75; libr., rsch. assoc. Gadsby's Tavern Mus., Alexandria, 1977-99. Chmn. ann. George Washington Birthnight Ball, Mt. Vernon, 1974-82; sec. George Washington 250th Birthday Celebration Commn., 1979-82; steering com. Neighborhood Friends Hist. Mt. Vernon, 1988-92; chmn. publicity Waynewood Woman's Club, Waynewood Citizens Assn.; treas. Mt. Vernon Citizens Assn., 1967-82; dist. chmn. Mt. Vernon March of Dimes, 1960-62; sec. Waynewood Sch. PTA, 1962-64; tchr. 1st aid Girl Scouts U.S., 1964-65; den mother Cub Scouts, 1966; chmn. publicity Mt. Vernon Women's Rep. Club, 1955. Named Mrs. Waynewood by Cmty. Vote, 1969. Mem. DAR (registrar 1968-77, conservation chair 1992-98), The Nature Conservancy, SC Hist. Soc., Hat Ladies of Charleston. Episcopalian. Home: 1235 Colfax Ct Mount Pleasant SC 29466

ABBOTT-RYAN, PAT, painter, writer; b. Bloomington, Ind., Aug. 2, 1932; d. John Carl Abbott and Martha Louise Stone; m. James Herbert Ryan, June 7, 1955; 1 child, Pamela Louise. BA cum laude, U. Md., 1981. Coll. bd. mem. Mademoiselle Mag., N.Y.C., 1952. Exhibits chmn. Petersburg (Va.) Area Art League, 2000—04. Editor: Silver-Burdett Time/Life, 1967; assoc. editor: Detective Mag., 1960—62; contbr. columns in newspapers, chapters to books, articles to popular mags.; one-woman shows include Touchstone Gallery, Washington, 1985, Foundry Gallery, 1985, PAAL Gallery, Petersburg, Va., 1999, others, exhibited in group shows at Rawls Mus. Arts, Courtland, Va., 2000, 1708 Gallery, Richmond, Va., 2000, St. Paul's Ch. and St. Stephen's Ch., 2001, Zenith Gallery, Washington, 2002—03, Olde Towne Pet Resort, Springfield, Va., 2002—03, others. Scholar, Skowhegan (Maine) Sch. Painting & Sculpture, 1981. Mem.: Petersburg (Va.) Area Art League (bd. dirs. 2000—04). Home: 1221 Woodland Road Petersburg VA 23805 Personal E-mail: ryancqrt@msn.com.

ABBOUD, SABRA NATASHA, psychotherapist, psychology professor; b. Elmhurst, Ill., Aug. 30, 1972; d. George James Chechopoulos and Bette Sue Goessling; m. Raymond M. Abboud, May 18, 2002; 1 child, Rayna Angeline. BSc in Psychology, York Coll., 1994; MSc in Clin. Psychology, Millersville U., 2002; student, Phila. Coll. Osteo. Medicine, 2003—. Cert. Addictions Counselor Diplomat. Psychiat. technician York Hosp., Pa., 1994—95, crisis counselor, 1995—2000; grad asst. Millersville U. Women's Commn., Pa., 2000—02; substance abuse therapist New Insights, York, 2002—04; adj. prof. Harrisburg Area CC, 2004—. Intern, neuropsychiatry Hershey Hosp., 2002; intern, osteo. therapy Polly Rost & Assoc., Hershey, 2004; intern, neuropsychology Lancaster Gen. Hosp., 2005. Mem.: APA, Penn. Psychol. Assn. Avocations: knitting, flute, horseback riding, running.

ABDALLAH, CLAUDE, anesthesiologist; MD, St. Joseph U.; M in Pharmacology, 1993. Pediatric anesthesiologist Children's Nat. Med. Ctr., Washington, 2002—. Mem.: Am. Soc. Anesthesiology. Office Phone: 202-884-2407.

ABDELLAH, FAYE GLENN, retired public health service executive; d. H. B. and Margaret (Glenn) Abdellah. BS in Tchg., Columbia U., 1945, MA in Tchg., 1947, EdD, 1955; LLD (hon.), Case Western Res. U., 1967, Rutgers U., 1973; DSc in Nursing (hon.), U. Akron, 1978; DSc (hon.), Cath. U. Am., 1981; DSc in Public Svc. (hon.), Monmouth Coll., 1982; DSc (hon.), Ea. Mich U., 1987, U. Bridgeport, 1987, Georgetown U., 1989; D in Pub. Svc. (hon.), Am. U., 1987; LHD (hon.), Georgetown U., 1989, U. SC, 1991, D in Pub. Svc., 1991; D, Norwich U., Vt., 1996; D in Mil. Nursing (hon.), USUHS, 2002. RN NY, DC. Commd. officer USPHS, Rockville, Md., 1949, advanced through grades to rear adm., 1970, dep., Surgeon Gen., chief nurse officer, 1970—87, dep. Surgeon Gen., 1981—89, chief nursing edn. br., divsn. nursing, 1949—59, Surgeon Gen., 1989; chief rsch. grants br. Bur. Health Manpower Edn., NIH, HEW, Rockville, 1959—69; dir. Office Rsch. Tng. Nat. Ctr. for Health Svcs. R & D, Health Svcs. Mental Health Adminstrn., Rockville, 1969; acting dep. dir. Nat. Ctr. for Health Svcs. R & D, Rockville, 1971, Bur. Health Svcs. Rsch. and Evaluation, Health Resources Adminstrn., Rockville, 1973; dir. Office Long-Term Care, Office Asst. Sec. for Health, HEW, Rockville, 1973—80; exec. dir. Grad. Sch. Nursing Uniformed Svcs. U. Health Scis., Bethesda, Md., 1993—, founding dean, prof. emeritus, 2001—. Prof. nursing, Emily Smith chair U. SC, Columbia, 1990—91; dean, prof. Grad. Sch. Nursing, Uniformed Svcs. U. Health Scis., 1993—2002, founding dean, prof. emerita, 1993—2002. Author: Effect of Nurse Staffing on Satisfactions with Nursing Care, 1959, Patient Centered Approaches to Nursing, 1960, Better Patient Care Through Nursing Research, 1965, 2d edit., 1979, 3d edit., 1986, Intensive Care, Concepts and Practices for Clinical Nurse Specialists, 1969, New Directions in Patient Centered Nursing, 1972, Preparing Nursing Research for the 21st Century, 1994; contbr. articles to profl. jours. Named to TC Nursing Hall of Fame, Columbia U., 1999, Nat. Women's Hall of Fame, 2000; recipient Mary Adelaide Nutting award, 1983, Oustanding Leadership award, U. Pa., 1987, 1999, Disting. Svc. award, 1973—89, Surgeon Gen.'s medal and medallion, 1989, Achievement award in aging, Allied-Signal, 1989, Gustav O. Lienhard award, Inst. Medicine NAS, 1992, Breaking Ground in Women's Health award, 2001, G.W. "Sonny" Montgomery award, Dept. Vets. Affairs, 2002, Centennial award for Achievements in Nursing, Ohio State U., 1970. Fellow: Am. Acad. Nursing (charter, past v.p., pres.); mem.: AAAS, ANA (hon.), APA, Assn. Mil. Surgeons US, Douglas Soc., Phi Lambda Theta, Sigma Theta Tau (Disting. Rsch. Fellow award 1989, Nells Watt Lifetime Achievement Nursing award 2005). Achievements include established first military school of nursing at USUSH, 1993. Home: 3713 Chanel Rd Annandale VA 22003-2024

ABDO, LYNDA LEE, art director; b. Hollywood, Calif., Sept. 6, 1955; d. Carl Edward and Carol Jean (Bedford) Cons; children: Allexis, Athena. Degree with honors, West Valley Occupational Ctr., 1979; BA cum laude, Calif. State U., Northridge, 1985. Asst. art dir. Malibu Grand Prix, Warner Communications, Woodland Hills, Calif., 1979-85; prodn. artist CBS Studios; designer, illustrator Sulka Agy., Studio City, Calif.; designer Phil Mendez Animation Prodns., Burbank, Calif.; art dir. Shields & Yarnell, Encino, Calif.; merchandising designer Zak Designs, Disney, Universal Studios, Warner Bros., 1988-94; co-prodr. video Avio Prodns., 1995-97; computer art designer Ultra Glas Inc., 1997—2005. Hon. co-chmn. Nat. Bus. Adv. Coun. Recipient Parents Choice award, Parent's Choice Found., 1999, 2006. Democrat. Avocations: swimming, hiking, travel, feng shui. Home and Office: 22731 Schoolcraft St West Hills CA 91307-2612 Office Phone: 818-710-8108. E-mail: lynabdo@sbcglobal.net.

ABDOO, ELIZABETH A., lawyer; b. Apr. 1958; BA, JD, Georgetown U. Bar: 1987. Sr. v.p., asst. gen. counsel Orbital Sciences Corp., 1996—2001; sr. v.p., gen. counsel Host Marriott Corp., Bethesda, Md., 2001—03, corp. sec., 2001—, exec. v.p., gen. counsel, 2003—. Office: Host Marriott Corp 6903 Rockledge Dr Ste 1500 Bethesda MD 20817

ABDOO, ROSE MARIE, actor; b. Detroit, Nov. 28, 1962; d. Mary Abdoo; life ptnr. John Matta. BA in Comm., Mich. State U., East Lansing, 1984, MFA in Theater with honors, 1986. Actor: (solo performance) Get To the Part About Me (Female Solo Performer of Yr., LA Weekly, 2000); guest star Gilmore Girls, CW Network, That's So Raven, Disney Channel. Nominee Screen Actor's Guild award in motion picture for Good Night & Good Luck, Academy Awards, 2005. Mem.: Acad. TV Arts & Scis. (hon.).

ABDUL, PAULA (PAULA JULIE ABDUL), singer, dancer, choreographer; b. San Fernando, Calif., June 19, 1963; d. Harry and Lorraine A.; m. Emilio Estevez, Apr. 29, 1992 (div. 1994); m. Brad Beckerman, Oct. 14, 1996 (div. 1998). Student, Calif. State Univ., Northridge; studied tap, jazz with Joe Tramine, the Bella Lewitzky Co. Laker Girls head cheerleader, head choreographer L.A. Lakers basketball team; choreography for Jacksons singing group, Janet Jackson, ZZ Top, Arnold Schwarzenegger, Tom Hanks, The Tracey Ullman Show, others. Albums: Forever Your Girl, 1988, Shut Up and Dance, 1990, Spellbound, 1991, Head Over Heels, 1995; Actress (TV films) Junior High School, 1978, Touched By Evil, 1997, Amy Fuentes, The Waiting Game, 1998, Denise Walton, Mr. Rock 'n' Roll: The Alan Freed Story, 1999; (voice) Robots, 2005; choreographer (films) Private School, 1983, A Smoky Mountain Christmas, 1986, Dragnet, 1987, Can't Buy Me Love, 1987, The Running Man, 1987, Coming to America, 1988, Bull Durham, 1988, Action Jackson, 1988, Dance to Win, 1989, The Karate Kid Part III, 1989, She's Out of Control, 1989, The Doors, 1991, Jerry Maguire, 1996, American Beauty, 1999, Black Knight, 2001, The Master of Disguise, 2002, (TV series) The Tracy Ullman Show, 1987, (TV) The 17th Annual Am. Music Awards, 1990, 62nd Annual Academy Awards, 1990, (video) ZZ Top: Greatest Hits (Velcro Fly), 1992; singer, Side Out, 1990; exec. prodr. (video) Paula Abdul: Cardio Dance, 1998; judge American Idol, 2002-; guest appearahcess include: Top of the Pops, 1989, 1990, 1995, Spin City, 1998, The Wayans Bros., 1999, Sabrina, the Teenage Witch, 1999, Mad TV, 2002, The Bernie Mac Show, 2004, Fashion In Focus, 2005, Less Than Perfect, 2005, The Contender, 2005, "So You Think You Can Dance", 2005 and several others. Recipient Soul Train award for best video, 1989, best choreography, 1989, Am. Video Arts award choreographer of yr. 1990, Nat. Acad. Video Arts and Scis., 1987, Emmy awards: best choreography for the Tracy Ullman Show, 1988-89, Outstanding Achievement in Choreography for Am. Music Awards, 1990; MTV awards: best choreography, Janet Jackson's Nasty video, 1986, best female video, best dance video, best choreography in a video, best editing in a video for hit Straight Up, 1989, Am. Music awards: for choreography on ZZ Top's Velcro Fly video, 1987, Favorite Pop-Rock Female, 1990, 1992, Favorite Dance artist, 1990; People's Choice awards: Favorite Female Musical Performer, 1990, 1991; named to Nickelodeon's Kids Choice Hall of Fame; represented by star on Hollywood Blvd. Mailing: American Idol Fox Broadcasting PO Box 900 Beverly Hills CA 90213-0900

ABEE, ROSE ROONEY, school guidance counselor; b. Atlanta, Oct. 15, 1959; d. Donald Roe and Ann (Oster) Rooney; m. Richard Preston Abee, July 19, 1986. BS in Psychology, Presbyterian Coll., Clinton, S.C., 1981; MEd, U. S.C., 1988, Ednl. Specialist Degree in Counselor Edn., 1997. Cert. profl. educator S.C. Dept. Edn. Cert.; secondary sch. counselor; secondary sch. adminstrn. & supervision; nat. cert. counselor, nat. cert. sch. counselor Nat. Bd. Cert. Counselors. Guidance counselor Aiken (S.C.) County Schs., 1981—. Mem. SC Assn. for Counseling and Devel., S.C. Sch. Counselors Assn., Am. Sch. Counselors Assn., Nat. Edn. Assn., SC Edn. Assn., Aiken County Edn. Assn. Avocations: camping, boating. Home: 2147 Riverside Plantation Rd Jackson SC 29831-2924 Office: Jackson Middle Sch Atomic Rd Jackson SC 29831-9307

ABEL, BARBARA ELLEN, photographer; d. Robert and Virginia Buckley; m. Ernest Abel, Sept. 20; children: Jason Robert, Rebecca Abel Salama. BS in Edn., Salem State U., 1966; MA, SUNY, Amherst, 1980; student, Oakland C.C., 1994—2005. Tchr. Gloucester (Mass.) Pub. Sch., 1966—68, Oakland (Calif.) Pub. Sch., 1968—70, Toronto Pvt. Sch., 1970—71, Durham (N.C.) County Pub. Sch., 1971—73; substitute tchr. Amherst (N.Y.) Pub. Sch., 1973—75; pvt. reading specialist Amherst, 1980—83; rsch. asst. Rsch. Inst. Alcohol, Buffalo, 1983—85, Wayne State U., Detroit, 1985—95; pres. Babel's Dreamcatcher Photography, Inc., West Bloomfield, Mich., 1996—. Exhibitions include Bloomfield Art Assn., 1997 (1st pl. award), City Hall Gallery, Dearborn, Mich., 1997 (Best of Show award), 1998, Erector Sq. Gallery, New Haven, Conn., 1998 (Curator's Choice award), Stamford (Conn.) Art Assn., 1998, Masuer Mus. Art, Monroe, La., 0199 (Juror's award), Albercrombie Gallery, La., 1999 (Purchase award), Chautauqua Nat. Exhbn. Am. Art., 1999 (William S. Holmes award), Arts Coun. S.E., Mo., 1999 (Juror's award), Loudon House Gallery, Lexington, Ky., 1999, Paint Creek Ctr. Arts, Rochester, Mich., 1999, Janice Charach Epstein Gallery, West Bloomfield, 2000, Mem. Gallery, Soc. Contemporary Photography, Kansas City, 2000, Dennos Mus., Traverse City, Mich., 2000, Veridian Gallery, N.Y.C., 2000 (Show Competition All Media award), Rice/Polak Gallery, Provincetown, Mass., 2002, 2004—06, Air Gallery, N.Y.C., 2005, Brighton Mus., England, 2005. Pres. Maple West Sch. PTA, Williamsville, NY, 1984—85; vol. Bloomfield Hills Sch., Mich., 1986—94; vol. photographer calendar Mich. Humane Soc., Mich., 1995. Mem.: Women of Bloomfield (bd. mem. 2005—). Office Phone: 248-872-8513. Personal E-mail: abel55@comcast.net.

ABEL, ELIZABETH ANN, dermatologist; b. Hartford, Conn., Mar. 16, 1940; d. Frederick A. and Rose (Borovicka) Abel; m. Barton Lane; children: Barton F. Lane, Geoffrey Lane, Suzanne Lane Franklin. Student, Colby-Sawyer Coll., 1957-60; BS, Wash. Hosp. Ctr. Sch. Med. Tech., 1961, U. Md., 1965, MD cum laude, 1967. Diplomate Am. Bd. Dermatology. Intern San Francisco Gen. Hosp., 1967-68; resident in medicine, fellow in oncology U. Calif. Med. Ctr., San Francisco, 1968-69; resident in dermatology NYU Med. Ctr., 1969-72, chief resident, 1971-72, USPHS research trainee in immunology, 1972-73; dep. chief dept. dermatology USPHS Hosp., S.I., NY, 1973-74; instr. clin. dermatology Columbia U. Coll. Physicians and Surgeons, N.Y.C., 1974-75, Stanford (Calif.) U. Sch. Medicine, 1975-77, clin. asst. prof. dermatology, 1977-82, asst. prof. dermatology, 1982-90, clin. assoc. prof., 1990-96, clin. prof., 1996—. Asst. editor Jour. Am. Acad. Dermatology, 1993-98; mem. med. adv. bd. The Nat. Psoriasis Found., 1993-95. Contbr. articles to profl. sci. jours. Mellon Found. fellow, 1983, 87. Fellow Am. Acad. Dermatology; mem. N.Am. Clin. Dermatologic Soc., San Francisco Dermatologic Soc., Internat. Soc. Dermatology, Pacific Dermatologic Assn., Women's Dermatologic Soc., Noah Worcester Dermatologic Soc., Alpha Omega Alpha. Avocations: piano, golf, travel, reading. Office: 2660 Grant Rd Ste D Mountain View CA 94040-4315 Office Phone: 650-938-6244. Personal E-mail: eaabelmd@aol.com.

ABEL, FLORENCE CATHERINE HARRIS, social worker; b. Phila., Dec. 28, 1941; d. Wilber Fiske and Melda Elizabeth (Beitzel) Harris; m. David Lynn Abel, Jan. 22, 1983. BS, High Point U., NC, 1963; MSW, U. Md., 1972. Cert. social worker Acad. Cert. Social Workers, 1974, diplomate clin. social work Acad. Cert. Social Workers, 1985. Social work asst. Calvert County Dept. social Svcs., Prince Frederick, Md., 1964—69, Prince George's County Dept. Social Svc., Hyattsville, Md., 1969—71; social worker Md. Children's Aid and Family Svc., Towson, 1972—80, Crownsville Hosp. Ctr., Md., 1980—86; field instr. U. Md. Sch. Social Work, 1985—86; counselor Family Life Ctr., Columbia, Md., 1974—80; sec. bd. dirs. Christian Counseling Assocs., Columbia, 1978—90, family therapist, 1978—, social work supr., 1990—96. Chairperson Social Work Peer Rev. Com., 1982—83; cons. Contact Balt., 1974—79; mem. citizens adv. coun. N.W. Mental Health Balt. County, 1977—78; dir. Dayspring Counseling Svc., Bowie, Md., 1994—96. Author: The Beitzel Family: a History of the Descendants of John George Beitzel, 1986, The Shadow of His Hand: The Biography of Melda B. Harris, 1995. Mem. Faith at Work Team, Columbia, 1973—75, Calvert County Commn. on Aging, 1967—68, Evang. Women's Caucus, Washington, 1976—85, N.W. Coalition Social Agys., Balt. County, 1978; sec. local bd. adminstrn. Dayspring Wesleyan Ch., Bowie, Md., 1996; mem. at large Local Bd Adminstrn for Coll. Park Weslyan Ch., 2005—; v.p., treas., bd. dirs. Wheaton Animal Hosp., Inc., Kensington, Md. Mem.: NASW, Christian Assocs. for Psychol. Studies, Md. Conf. Social Concern, Assn. Cert. Social Workers, Nat. Register Clin. Social Workers, Am. Assn. Christian Counselors (charter mem.). Democrat. Wesleyan. Home: 120 Hedgewood Dr Greenbelt MD 20770-1611 Office: 9630 Santiago Rd Ste 101 Columbia MD 21045-3907 Personal E-mail: floabel_20770@yahoo.com.

ABEL, LAURA SORVETTI, retired literature and language educator; b. Oakland, Calif., Dec. 17, 1950; d. Lawrence Angelo and Rosalie Ruth Sorvetti; m. Dennis Michael Abel, Nov. 21, 1970; children: Stacy Nicole-(dec.), Lindsy Louise. BA in English, Calif. State U., Sacramento, 1988. Cert. secondary tchr. Calif. Tchr. Fairfield (Calif.) Unified Sch. Dist., 1990—92, Vacaville, Calif., 1992—2004. Pres. Vacaville (Calif.) Tchrs. Assn., 2000—04. Mem. state coun. tchrs. Calif. Teachers Assn., 1996—2004. Democrat. Roman Catholic. Home: 580 Kelsie Dr Waldport OR 97394-1902 Home Fax: 541-563-2051. Personal E-mail: 2beachbums@gmail.com.

ABELES, KIM VICTORIA, artist; b. Richmond Heights, Mo., Aug. 28, 1952; d. Burton Noel Wright and Frances Elizabeth (Sander) Hoffman. BFA in Painting, Ohio U., 1974; MFA in Studio Art, U. Calif., Irvine, 1980. Free-lance artist, L.A., 1975—. Lectr. varius schs. and art ctrs., 1980—; vis. disting. artist Calif. State U., Fullerton, 1985-87; assoc. prof. Calif. State U., Northridge, 1998—; artist-in-residence Art Mill, Czech Republic, 2005. Author, illustrator Crafts, Cookery and 'Country Living, 1976, Kim Abeles, 1988, Kim Abeles: Encyclopedia Persona, 1993, author, photographer: Impressions, 1979; co-author: Surface tension Problematics of Site, 2003; work featured in Artery, 1979, Pacific Poetry and Fiction Review, 1980, Fiction Internat., 1985; one-woman shows include U. Calif., Irvine, 1979—80, Mcpl. Art Gallery, LA, 1981, L.A. City Hall, 1982, Phyllis Kind Gallery, Chgo., 1983, Karl Bornstein Gallery, Santa Monica, Calif., 1983, 1985, 1987, Pepperdine U., Malibu, Calif., 1985, A.I.R. Gallery, N.Y.C., 1986, Chapman Coll., Orange, Calif., 1986, Mount St. Mary's Coll., L.A., 1987, Atlanta Pavilion, 1990, Calif. Mus. of Sci. and Industry, L.A., 1991, Laguna Art Mus. Satellite Gallery, Costa Mesa, Calif., 1991, Turner-Krull Gallery, L.A., 1992, Lawrence Miller Gallery, N.Y.C., 1992, Santa Monica Mus. Art, L.A., 1993, Nat. Mus. Fine Arts, Santiago, Chile, 1996, Mus. Modern Art, Rio de Janeiro, 1996, Cmplejo Cultural Recoleta, Buenos Aires, 1986, Centro Cutural Consolidado, Caracas, 1997, Cepa Gallery, Buffalo, 1998, A.R.T., Inc., N.Y.C., 1989, Contemporary Arts Ctr., Cin., 2000, Art Resources Transfer, N.Y.C., 2001, Intersection, San Francisco, 2001, Calif. Sci. Ctr., L.A., 2000—01, Coll. Environ. Design, Calif. Poly. U., Pomona, 2002, El Camino Coll., L.A., 2003, 2003, exhibitions include Mus. of Contemporary Art, L.A. County Mus. Art, Calif. African-Am. Mus., Allen Meml. Art Mus., Ohio, Represented in permanent collections Marriott Hotels, City of Pasadena, San Fernando Valley Constituent Svc. Ctr., Marvin Braude San Fernando Valley Constituent Svc. Ctr., Dept. Transp., L.A., Cmty. Magnet Sch., exhibited in group shows at Mus. Kampa, Czech Republic, Silpakorn U., Bangkok, 2002, Nat. History Mus., LA, 2005, Hanoi U. Fine Arts, Vietnam, 2005, Sun Valley Ctr. Arts, Idaho, 2006. Honored for Outstanding Student Rsch. & Creative Achievement U. Calif., 1979; recipient U.S. Steel award Exhbn. of the Associated Artists of pitts., 1977, Clean Air award Air Quality Mgmt. Dist., Calif., 1992; hand Hollow Found. fellow, 1984, Design Team fellow Panorama City Libr., Calif., 1992-93, J. Paul Getty Trust Fund for the Visual Arts fellow, 1994; Pollock-Krasner Found. grantee, 1990, Calif. Arts Coun. grantee, 1990, L.A. Cultural Affairs grantee, 1991, 95, 96, U.S. Info. Agy. grantee, 1995-97; commissioned by Panorama City Pub. Libr., L.A., 1993, Met. Transp. Authority, L.A., 1995, Dept. Transp., L.A., 2000; recipient Richard Neutra award for Profl. Excellence, 2001. Office Phone: 213-626-4623. Personal E-mail: kimabeles@earthlink.net.

ABELL, ANNA ELLEN, primary school educator; b. Phila., Nov. 24, 1945; d. Elwood George Daeche and Anna Pauline Pflaumer; m. DeLeon Abell, Aug. 24, 1974; children: Sara Abigail, Beth Ann, Rebecca Nöel. B in Music Edn., Westminster Choir Coll., 1967; postgrad., Assn. Christian Sch. Internat., Piscataway Unified Sch. Dist. Educator Piscataway (N.J.) Sch. Dist., 1967—74; pvt. music tchr. Orange Coast Christian Sch., San Clemente, Calif., 1982—89, 6th grade tchr., 1989—90; jr. high tchr. Dana Point (Calif.) Christian Sch., Calif., 1991—94; 5th grade tchr. Capo Beach Calvary Sch., Dana Point, 1994—98, kindergarten tchr., 1998—. Distbr. JuicePlus/NSA,

Dana Point, 2001—. Choral mem. Sanctuary Choir, San Clemente, Calif., 1990—; bell choir mem. Sounds of Bronze, San Clemente, Calif., 1992—. Mem.: Assn. Christian Schs. Internat. Republican. Presbyterian. Avocations: cooking, reading, health and nutrition.

ABELL, JOHANNA MATHIS, music educator; b. Franklin, N.C., Oct. 28, 1974; d. Emma (Siler) and Allen Kirk Mathis; m. Gregory Chapman Abell, Aug. 2, 1997. BS Edn. Instrumental Music, We. Carolina U., Cullowhee, N.C., 1998; postgrad., James Madison U., Harrisonburg, Va. Tchr. kindergarten Northampton County Pub. Schs., Jackson, NC, 1998—99; educator music, dir. band, dir. chorus, tchr. drama Jackson County Pub. Schools, Sylva, NC, 1999—2001; educator music Loudoun County Pub. Schools, Ashburn, Va., 2001—. Clinician Massanetta Springs, Harrisonburg, Va., 2004—05. Friends Music Dept. Scholarship, We. Carolina U., 1997—98. Mem.: Am. Orff-Schulwerk Assn. Office: Frances Hazel Reid Elem Sch 800 North King St Leesburg VA 20176 Personal E-mail: jabell@loudoun.k12.va.us.

ABELL, NANCY L., lawyer; b. LA, July 19, 1950; BA with honors, Pitzer Coll., 1972; JD, UCLA, 1979. Bar: Calif. 1979. Extern clk. to Hon. Shirley Hufstedler U.S. Ct. Appeals (9th cir.), 1978; ptnr. Paul, Hastings, Janofsky & Walker LLP, LA, 1986—, chairperson employment law dept. Bd. govs. Inst. Corp. Counsel, 1989—, chairperson, 1994-95; bd. advisors UCLA Sch. Law. Author: (with P.W. Cane) An Employer's Guide to the Americans with Disabilities Act, 1991, An Employer's Guide for Preparing Affirmative Action Programs. Bd. advisors UCLA Sch. Law. Fellow Coll. Labor and Employment Lawyers, Inc.; mem. ABA (mgmt. co-chair trial advocacy subcom., employee rights and responsibilities com., labor and employment law sect. 1991-94); Order of Barristers, Order of Coif. Office: Paul Hastings Janofsky & Walker LLP 515 S Flower St Fl 23 Los Angeles CA 90071-2300 Office Phone: 213-683-6162. Office Fax: 213-996-3162. Business E-Mail: nancyabell@paulhastings.com.

ABELL, NICOLE FORCHT, secondary school educator; d. Karen Bishop Forcht; m. James Michael Abell, July 5, 2003; 1 child, James William. BA in History, Greensboro Coll., N.C., 1997. Cert. secondary social studies edn. State of N.C., 1998. Tchr. Guilford County Schs., Greensboro, NC, 1998—. Student coun. advisor Page H.S., Greensboro, NC, 2000—. Office: WH Page HS 201 Alma Pinnix Dr Greensboro NC 27405 Office Phone: 336-370-8200.

ABELL, SARA NIGHTINGALE, music educator, musician; b. Toledo, Ohio, Apr. 28, 1952; d. Homer Scott and Alice (Walbolt) Nightingale; m. Ralph "Casey" Abell, May 10, 1986; children: Alison Margaret, Nathan Samuel. MusB, Bowling Green State U., 1974; MusM, Coll. Conservatory Music U. Cin., 1978, D in Music Edn., 1993. Elem. music tchr. Toledo Pub. Schs., 1974—76; music edn. tchg. asst. Coll.-Conservatory Music, U. Cin., 1976—78; elem. music tchr. Mt. Healthy Pub. Schs., Cin, 1979—84; tchr. pre-sch. music classes Musical Arts Ctr., Cin, 1980—82; music edn. tchg. asst. Coll.-Conservatory of Music U. Cin, 1983—86; pre-sch. music tchr. Little Lambs Children's Ctr., Columbus, Ohio, 1994—97; pre-sch. and elem. music tchr. Acad. Fine Arts, Highland Village, Tex., 1999—2002; dir. music Trinity Presbyterian Ch., Flower Mound, Tex., 2002—. Mem.: Tex. Music Educators Assn., Music Educators Nat. Conf., Sigma Alpha Iota (Denton Alumni chpt.), Ariel Club in Tex. Fedn. Women's Clubs.

ABELS, GUSTA J., artist, art and art history educator; b. N.Y.C., May 20, 1932; d. Max Emanuel and Selma G. Zuckerman; m. Robert Samuel Abels, Mar. 9, 1958; children: Julienne Claire Chevan, Margot Ellen. AB, Barnard Coll., 1954; MFA, Columbia U., 1956. Tchr. upper sch. art and art history Vail Deane Sch., New Providence, N.J., 1981-90; tchr. h.s. art history Wardlaw-Hartridge Sch., Edison, N.J., 1993-98; adj. prof. drawing and painting Seton Hall U., South Orange, N.J., 1992-98; instr. art history and painting Guilford Art Ctr., Conn., 1999—. Solo and group exhbns. of painting in galleries in N.J., N.Y.; works in pvt. collections. Chair Livingston (N.J.) Arts Coun., 1996-98; county committeeperson Dem. Party, Livingston, 1987-98. Fulbright scholar, Antwerp, Belgium, 1954-55. Mem. Art Students League N.Y. (life). Jewish. Home: 28A Harbour Vlg Branford CT 06405-4472 E-mail: gbabels@comcast.net.

ABER, ITA, artist, conservator, historian; b. Montreal, Can., Mar. 27, 1932; arrived in U.S., 1954; d. Tudick and Fannie (Zabitsky) Herchcovich; m. Joshua Aber, Dec. 8, 1954; children: Mindy Ann Barad, Judah David, Harry Asher. BA in Cultural Studies, Empire State Coll., Albany, N.Y., 1982; postgrad., Jewish Theol. Sem., N.Y.C. Asst. curator-history Hudson River Mus., Yonkers, NY, 1969-70; textile curator Jewish Mus., N.Y.C., 1971; guest curator Yeshiva U. Mus., N.Y.C., 1976, 82, 97; adj. curator of collection Park Ave Synagogue, N.Y.C., 1980—2003; guest curator 150th Anniversary, Mpls., 1985; curator Hebrew Home for Aged, Riverdale, NY, 1989-93. Bd. dirs. Judaica Mus., Riverdale, 1989—, guest curator, docent trainer Jewish ethnography & textiles, 2003. Author: (book) The Art of Judaic Needlework, 1979; editor: The Paper Pomegranate, 1976—80; contbr. articles to profl. jours., 55-yr. retrospective exhbn. and catalogue, 2001; dir.: (DVD) Spanier Arbeit Lives, 2005. Comm. cons. programming and fundraising PBS, Riverdale, 1964—66; bd. dirs. Textile Cons. Group, N.Y.C., AM. Friends Tel Aviv Mus., N.Y.C., 1970—72; mem. Landmarks Bd., Yonkers, 1991—94; founder Pomegranate Guild of Judaic Needlework, 1976—; campaign mgr. Reform Dems., Riverdale, 1965. Philip Morris grantee, Hudson River Mus., 1997, Pomegranate Guild, 2001, 2004. Mem.: Surface Design Assn., Bead Soc. N.Y., Internat. Soc. Jewish Art (bd. dirs. 1990—2003, v.p. 1997—98), Textile Study Group of NY, N.Y. Landmark Conservancy, Pomegranate Guilds U.S. and Can. Avocations: research, training museum docents, publishing, textile. Office Phone: 718-548-3355. Personal E-mail: mjaberesq@msn.com, itaaber@gmail.com.

ABERCROMBIE, EYDIE L., physiologist, consultant; b. Bakersfield, Calif., Oct. 30, 1955; d. James Robert Helms and Arrevia Bell Creekbaum; m. James J. Peter (div.); children: Anthony, Andrea; m. Delbert L. Abercrombie, Nov. 26, 1993; children: David, Shonda, Tara. AA in Behavioral Sci., Bakersfield C.C., Calif., 1975; BS cum laude, Calif. State U., Bakersfield, 1993; gerontology cert., L.A. Mission Coll., Sylmar, Calif., 1998; postgrad., U. Ark., Little Rock. CHES NCHEC, CEP ACSM, cert. exercise specialist AFAA, CLE Calif. State U., San Diego, ADC NCCAP. Health and fitness cons., Calif. and Ark., 1986—; coord., exercise physiologist Pacific Care of Calif., Cypress, Calif., 1993—97; dir. health edn. Bakersfield Family Med. Ctr., 1996—2000; COO Nat. Health Svc. Inc., Buttonwillow, Calif., 2000—02; adminstr., exercise physiologist Kern Rehab., Inc., Bakersfield, 2002—03; comty. health promotion specialist Ark. Dept. Health and Human Svcs. Divsn. Health, Harrison, 2003—. Mktg. dir., exec. bd. Healthy Mothers / Healthy Babies, Bakersfield, 2000—02; cons. Comty. Health Ctrs. Ark., Little Rock, 2004—06. Author: (exercise manual) Club Strength Instructor Training Manual, 2002, Improving Patients' Health through Exercise, 2004. Mem.: Nat. Commn. for Health Edn. Credentialing, Ark. Bd. Health Edn., Ark. Soc. Pub. Health Educators, Ark. Pub. Health Assn., Diamond City C. of C. (bd. dirs. 2005—06). Office: Ark Dept Health and Human Svcs Divsn Health 4815 W Markham Little Rock AR 72205

ABERNATHY, JENNIFER P., music educator; b. Naperville, Ill., Nov. 12, 1980; d. Beatrice J. and Robert P. Abernathy. AA, Lincoln Trail Coll., Robinson, Ill., 2000; MusB, Ea. Ill. U., Charleston, 2003. Dir. bands, choral dir. Hutsonville CUSD No. 1, Ill., 2003—05; dir. bands, kindergarten music tchr. Oblong CUSD No. 4, Ill., 2005—06; dir. bands Princeton H.S., Ill., 2006—. Named Outstanding Young Career Woman of the Yr., Crawford County Bus. and Profl. Women's Orgn., 2004. Mem.: NEA, Music Educator's Nat. Conf. Office Phone: 815-875-3308 ext. 250. Personal E-mail: jennabernathy@gmail.com.

ABERNATHY, KATHLEEN QUINN, lawyer, former commissioner; b. Louisville, June 5, 1956; m. Charles Abernathy, June 30, 1984; 1 child, Julia 1 stepchild, Charles Jr. BS magna cum laude, Marquette U., Milw., 1982; JD, Cath. U. Am. Columbus Sch. Law, Washington, 1984. Assoc. Kadison, Pfaelzer Woodard Quinn & Rossi, 1986—87, Thelen, Marrin, Johnson and Bridges, 1987—88; dir. fed. affairs COMSAT, 1988—90; spl. asst. to gen. counsel FCC, Washington, legal advisor to chmn. James H. Quello and Commr. Sherrie P. Marshall, 1992—93, commr., 2001—05; v.p. fed. regulatory AirTouch Comm., Inc., 1993—98; v.p. regulatory affairs U.S. West, Inc.; ptnr. Wilkinson Barker Knauer, 1999—2000; v.p. pub. policy BroadBank Office Comm., Inc., 2000—01; ptnr. Akin Gump Strauss Hauer & Feld LLP, Washington, 2006—. Adj. prof. Georgetown U. Law Ctr., Washington, Cath. U. Am., Washington; bd. dirs. Citizens Communications Co., 2006—. Named one of Most Powerful Women in TV, Electronic Media mag.; recipient Milestone award, Cath. U. Am. Columbus Sch. Law, 2001, Forerunner Accolade, Women in Cable and Telecom., 2002. Mem.: Washington Bar Assn., Fed. Comm. Bar Assn. (past pres.). Office: Akin Gump Strauss Hauer & Feld LLP Robert S Strauss Bldg 1333 New Hampshire Ave NW Washington DC 20036-1564*

ABERNETHY, IRENE MARGARET, civic worker, retired county official; b. Ord, Nebr., Mar. 28, 1924; d. Glen Dayton and Margaret Lillian (Jones) Auble; m. Don R. Abernethy, Aug. 8, 1954 (dec. Nov. 1980); children: Jill Adele Abernethy Johnson, Ted Verne (dec.). BA cum laude, Hastings Coll., 1946; postgrad., U. Nebr., 1950—53. Tchr. Ord H.S., 1946-50, Scottsbluff (Nebr.) H.S., 1950-55, Grand Island (Nebr.) Sr. H.S., 1961-62; mem. Hall County Bd. Suprs., Grand Island, 1979-98, chmn., 1984, 95; ret., 1998. Vice-chair Hall County Rep. Ctrl. Com., Grand Island, 1971-73; chair campaign Congresswoman Virginia Smith for Hall County, 1974-80; sr. v.p. Nebr. Rep. Founders Day, Lincoln, 1981; chair Gov.'s Juv. Justice Adv. Group, Lincoln, 1981-91; mem. Nebr. Commn. on Law Enforcement and Criminal Justice, Lincoln, 1970-91, Nebr. Commn. on Local Govt. Innovation and Restructuring, 1997-00; bd. dirs. Head Start, 1979-02, Hall County Leadership Tomorrow, 1990-94, Indsl. Found., 1991, College Park, 1991-98, Cmty. Help Ctr., 1991-96, Family Violence Coalition, 1993-02, Midland Area Agy. on Aging, 1993-95; adv. com. Region III Mental Health Bd., quality rev. team, 1996-99; active Nat. Coalition State Juvenile Justice Adv. Groups, 1981-91, Partners in Cmty. Planning, 1994-97, Grand Island Area Edn. 2000, Grand Island Bd. Edn., 1998-00; bd. dirs. task force on needs Heartland United Way, Hall County Hist. Soc., 2003-06. Named Woman of Yr., Grand Island Independent, 1980, Bus. and Profl. Woman, Grand Island, 1980, Beta Sigma Phi, 1982, Alpha Delta Kappa, 1982, 2000, Nebr. chpt. NASW, 1983, Merit Mother of Nebr., 2002, Nebr. Mother of Yr. Nebr. Mothers Assn., 2004; recipient Svc. to Mankind award Sertoma, 1983-84, recognition award PTA, 1988, Outstanding Cmty. Svc. award Rotary, 1985, Cmty. Leadership award Ak-Sar-Ben, 1995, Outstanding Alumni award Hastings Coll., 1996, Hall County Rep. Hall of Fame award, 1997, Disting. Citizenship award Grand Island Elks, 1997, cert. of appreciation Grand Island-Hall County Dept. Health, 1998, A.L. Carlisle Child Advocacy award Coalition for Juvenile Justice, 2001; honoree Nebr. Commn. on Status of Women, 1998, 2000; recipient Spirit of Youth award Girls and Boys Town, 2000, Ord H.S. Disting. Alumni award, 2004. Mem. LWV (local pres. 1962-64, state bd. dirs. 1965-69), AAUW (local pres. 1966-68, state bd. dirs. 1970-71), YWCA (local pres. 1974-75, Woman of Distinction award 1988), Nebr. Assn. County Ofcls. (pres. 1985, Pres.'s award for Disting. Leadership 1997, County Ofcl. of Yr. award 1998), Assn. Child Abuse Prevention, Grand Island Area C. of C. (bd. dirs. 1992-94, Disting. Svc. award 1999), Philanthropic Ednl. Orgn. (local pres. 1970-71), Rotary, Woodland Golf Club Ladies Assn. (champion 1961, 63, 64, local pres. 1963), Riverside Golf Club (champion 1969), Grand Island Woman's Club (past bd. dirs.), Pi Lambda Theta. Republican. United Methodist. Avocations: travel, music, photography, golf, spectator sports. Home: 707 S Blaine St Grand Island NE 68803-6146

ABERNETHY, SHARRON GRAY, language educator; b. Tishomingo, Miss., Mar. 22, 1945; d. Dennis F. Gray (deceased) and Lyda Waddell Gray; m. Elliott Lee Abernethy, Jr.; children: Damon, Ryan (Deceased). BA, Secondary Edn., U. North Ala., Florence, 1966; MA in Latin and Am. Studies, U. Ala., Tuscaloosa, 1971, PhD, 1982, EdS, 1976; cert., U. Carlos III, Madrid, 2000. Cert. ESADE Barcelona, Spain, 1999. Spanish/Latin Am. history tchr. Deshler H.S., Tuscumbia, Ala., 1966—68; Spanish/English tchr. Eastwood Jr. H.S., Tuscaloosa, 1968—68; rsch. asst. U. Ala., Tuscaloosa, 1969—70, tchg. asst., 1970—73, Spanish instr., 1977, Spanish prof. (part-time) Huntsville, 1988—90, 1994—96, Spanish prof., 1996—, departmental internat. internship coord., 2001—; Spanish/Am. history tchr Eastwood Jr. H.S., Tuscaloosa, 1973—76; Spanish prof. Miss. State U., Meridian, 1982—84; Spanish instr. Meridian H.S., 1982—85; owner Sir Speedy Printing franchise, Pittsburg, 1986—87, Huntsville, 1988—93; reviewer John Wiley & Sons, Inc., New York, NY, 2002—. Faculty advisor Phi Sigma Iota, Huntsville, 1997—; participant numerous confs./workshops on curricular and instrnl. improvement, 1999—. Vol. St. Jude's Children's Hosp., Memphis, 1977—78, Riley Hosp., Meridian, 1981—83; bd. dirs. Harris Home for Children, Huntsville, 1990—92; supporter/vol. Chi-Ho Home for Children, Huntsville, 1988—2001; mem./officer Huntsville West Kiwanis, Huntsville, 1988—94; chair Huntsville West Kiwanis/Chi-Ho Benefit Golf Tournament, Huntsville, 1990—93; leader Cub Scouts, Meridian, 1981—84; mem. Rep. Women, Huntsville, 1988—89; tchr., deacon, com. mem. adminstrn., stewardship, fin., hospitality, pastoral search coms., co-editor 1993 ch. history/dire First Presbyn. Ch., Huntsville, 1988—2002. Mem.: Naita (UAH liaison to North Ala. Internat. Trade Assn. 1999—, bd. dirs. 2003, 1999—), Exec. Women Internat. (VIP award 2001). Republican. Presbyterian. Avocations: piano, travel, golf, culinary arts.

ABEY, KATHY MICHELE, district representative, congressional caseworker; d. George Melvin Abey and Catherine Harrison-Abey Windsor; children: Loren Michele Crutchley, Michael Jarrod Horney, Casey Wade Horney, William Ryan. Cert. paralegal, Chesapeake Coll., 1988. Cert. compensation claims specialist U.S. Dept. of Labor. Asst. mgr. Hardees/ Imasco Foods, Inc, Stevensville, Md., 1984—87; legal asst. The Legal Aid Bur., Balt., 1988—95; hearings specialist Health Mgmt. Assocs., Balt., 1995—98; paralegal, legal asst. Conrad and Chirumbole, Gaithersburg, Md., 1998; hearings specialist Health Mgmt. Assocs./DEAP Program, Balt., 1998—2000; congl. caseworker, dist. rep. U.S. Ho. of Reps., Bel Air, Md., 2000—. Ptnr., coord. Svc. Learning Project Harford C.C., 2006. Vol. Libr. of Congress Vets. History Project, Washington, 2002; sec. Eric Rada Vocat. Scholarship Fund, Queenstown, Md., 1981—82; vol. photographer Chicamicomico Life Saving Sta., Rodanthe, NC, 2000; mem. client cmty. adv. bd. Legal Aid Bur., Balt., 1983—84; bd. dirs. Boy Scouts of Am. Troop 278, Stevensville, Md., 1990—94; sec. Queen Anne's County H.S. Football Boosters, Centreville, Md., 1998—2000, Queen Anne's County H.S. Athletic Bosters, 2000—01; pres. Queen Anne's County H.S. Football Boosters, 2000—01; mem., client adv. Dorchester County AIDS Found., Cambridge, 1998—2000; advisor Aberdeen Proving Ground Ordnance Mus. Found., 2004—05; mem. 90th ann. commoration com. Aberdeen Proving Grounds, 2006; vol. Retirees Coop., Ft. Meede, Md., 2006; bd. mem. Queen Anne's County Consumer Adv. Bd., Centreville, 1998—99; bd. trustees Ordnance Mus. Found., 2006—. Named Fair Grand Champion in Photography, Queen Anne County, 2003; recipient Vets. History Project citation, Gov., 2006. Republican. Methodist. Avocations: photography, reading, camping, music/theater, travel. Office Phone: 410-838-2517.

ABEYTA, JEANIE, secondary school educator; b. Las Vegas, N.Mex., Jan. 8, 1967; d. Manuel B. and Genevieve H. Alcon; m. John Paul Abeyta, Aug. 24, 1991; children: Angelica Marie, Elisa Janelle. BA, N.Mex. Highlands U., Las Vegas, MA, 2002. Tchr. Mora H.S., Mora, N.Mex., 1995—; instr. fitness Luna C.C., Las Vegas, 2004—. Girls basketball coach, recreation youth soccer coach Mora Middle Sch. Mem.: AAPHERD (mem. 2003—06). Roman Catholic. Avocations: weightlifting, reading, motorcycling, music, gardening. Office: Mora High School PO 180 Ranger Drive Mora NM 87732 Office Phone: 505-387-3122. Home Fax: 505-387-3121; Office Fax: 505-387-3121. Personal E-mail: jabeytaj@hotmail.com.

ABID, ANN B., art librarian; b. St. Louis, Mar. 17, 1942; d. Clarence Frederick and Luella (Niehaus) Bartelsmeyer; m. Amor Abid (div. 1969); children: Rod, Kady; m. Cleon R. Yohe, Aug. 10, 1974 (div.); m. Roldo S. Bartimole, Feb. 1, 1991. Cert. in Librarianship, Washington U., St. Louis, 1976. Asst. to libr. St. Louis Art Mus., 1963-68, libr., 1968-85; head libr. Cleve. Mus. Art, 1985—2004; ret., 2004. Vis. com. univ. librs. Case We. Res.U., 1987-90, co-chairperson, 1990. Co-author: Documents of Surrealism, 1918-1942, 1981, Planning for Automation of the Slide and Photograph Collections at the Cleveland Museum of Art: A Draft Marc Visual Materials Record, 1998; contbr. articles to profl. jours. Grantee Mo. Coun. Arts, 1978, Mo. Com. Humanities, 1980, Nat. Hist. Pubs. and Records Commn., 1981, Reinberger Found., 1987, Japan Found., 1996. Mem. ALA, Art Librs. Soc. N.Am. (chmn. mus.-type-of-libr. group nat. chpt. 1979-81, chmn. New Orleans 1980, nominating com. 1980, 84, Wittenborn awards com. 1981, 90, v.p., pres.-elect 1987-88, pres. 1988-89, past pres. 1989-90, chmn. N.Am. art libr. resources com. 1991-93, search com. new exec. dir. 1993-94. chmn. fin. com. 1996-98, presenter numerous papers, chmn. nominating com. 1999-2000, co-chair conf. program com. 1999-2000), Soc. Am. Archivists, Midwest Mus. Conf. (co-chmn. program com. ann. meeting 1982), Spl. Librs. Assn., Rsch. Librs. Group (shares exec. group 1996-98, shares participation com. 1997-99). E-mail: aabid@clevelandart.org, annaoh@adelphia.net.

ABINGTON ALEXIE, SUSAN EDITH, elementary school educator; b. Kans., Feb. 15, 1955; d. Richard William Abington Sr. and Edith Jewel (Sawyer) Abington; m. Joe Alexie, Aug. 11, 1979; children: Abington Angayarr Alexie, Sayer Nerluyaagaq Alexie. BA in Elem. Edn., U. Alaska, Fairbanks, 2000; attended, Mich. State U., E. Lansing, 1973—76, U. Minn., Mpls., 1978, Alaska Bible Coll., Glennallen, 1978—79. Elem. tchr. Southwest Region Schs., Togiak, Alaska, 2000—. Bible club tchr., vacation bible sch. tchr. Cmty. Ch., Togiak, 1996—. Avocations: reading, writing, hiking, camping. Home: PO Box 86 Togiak AK 99678

ABISH, CECILE, artist; b. N.Y.C. m. Walter Abish. B.F.A., Bklyn. Coll., 1953. Instr. art Queens Coll. Vis. artist U. Mass, Amherst, Cooper Union, Harvard U. Solo exhbns. include Newark Coll. Engring., 1968, Inst. Contemporary Art, Boston, 1974, U. Md., 1975, Alessandra Gallery, N.Y.C., 1977, Wright State U., Dayton, Ohio, 1978, Carpenter Ctr., Cambridge, Mass., 1979, Anderson Gallery, Va. Commonwealth U., Richmond, 1981, SUNY-Stony Brook, 1982, Ctr. for Creative Photography, Tucson, 1984, Books & Co., N.Y.C., 1996; group exhbns.: Detroit Inst. Art, 1969, Aldrich Mus. Art, 1971, 10 Bleecker St., N.Y.C., 1972, Lakeview Ctr. Arts, Peoria, Ill., 1972, Bykert Gallery, N.Y.C., 1971-74, Michael Walls Gallery, N.Y.C., 1975, Fine Arts Bldg. Gallery, N.Y.C., 1976, Mus. Modern Art, N.Y.C., 1976, Hudson River Mus., 1979, Atlanta Arts Festival, 1980, New Mus., N.Y.C., 1980, 81, Kuntsgebaude, Stuttgart, Fed. Republic Germany, 1981, Long Beach (Calif.) Mus., 1983, Edith C. Blum Art Inst., Bard Coll., Annandale-on-Hudson, N.Y., 1984, Mus. Modern Kunst, Vienna, Austria, 1985, U. R.I., Kingston, 1985, Art Defense Galleries, Paris, 1993, Architektur Zentrum, Vienna, 1993, Artists Space, N.Y.C., 1994, Islip Art Mus., N.Y., 1995, P.S. 1 Contemporary Art Ctr., N.Y., 1999; numerous commns.; represented in permanent collections; published photo works: Firsthand, 1978, Chinese Crossing, 1986, 99: The New Meaning, 1990. Nat. Endowment Arts fellow, 1975, 77, 80; CAPS fellow, 1975. Mem. Coll. Art Assn. Office: Cooper Station PO Box 485 New York NY 10276-0485

ABLES, LINDA BOMBERGER, biology professor; d. Tom John and Doris Faye Bomberger; 1 child, Zachary William. BS in Biology, U. West Fla., Pensacola, 1976, EdM in Adminstrn. and Supervision, 1980, MST in Biology, 1990. Cert. tchr. Nat. Bd. Profl. Tchg. Stds., 2001. Sci. instr. Pine Forest H.S., Pensacola, Fla., 1976—; prof. biology Pensacola Jr. Coll., 1990—. Primary leader People to People. Recipient Behren's award, Fla. Marine Sci. Educators Assn., 2005. Mem.: Escambia Tchr. Leadership Consortium. Office: Pine Forest High School 2500 Longleaf Drive Pensacola FL 32506 Office Phone: 850-941-6150 256.

ABLOW, ROZ KAROL (ROSELYN KAROL ABLOW), painter, curator; b. Allentown, Pa. BA, Bennington Coll., 1954; student, Boston U. Fellow Bunting Inst., 1988; instr. Newton Arts Ctr., Mass., 1989-92, New Arts Ctr., Newton, Mass., 1993-95. Curator New Arts Ctr., Newton, Mass., 1994. One-person shows at Amherst (Mass.) Coll., 1976, Impressions Gallery, Mass., 1979, Clark Gallery, Lincoln, Mass., 1984, Pine Manor Coll., Brookline, Mass., 1991, Miami U., Oxford, Ohio, 1995, Art Guild of Old Forge, NY, 2002; group shows include Smithsonian Traveling Exhbn., 1978-80, Fitchburg Art Mus., 1988, Bunting Inst., Radcliffe Coll., 1988, David Brown Gallery, Provincetown, Mass., 1988, Pratt Graphic Ctr. Internat. Monotype Show, 1989, Gallery 30, Burlingame, Calif., 1993, New Art Ctr., Newton, Mass., 1994, Pucker Gallery, 2004, 05, 06, others; represented in permanent collections Mobil Corp., Chemical Bank, NY, New Eng. Mutual Life Ins. Co., Boston, Conn. Gen. Life, Hartford, Sears, Roebuck & Co., Chgo., Philip Morris, NYC, Odell Assocs., Charlotte, NC, Conn. Gen. Life, Hartford, Broadway Crown Plaza Hotel, NY, Pucker Gallery, Boston, Boston Pub. Libr. Bunting Inst. fellow Radcliffe Coll., 1988; grantee Mass. Arts Lottery Coun., 1990-91. Address: Pucker Gallery Boston MA 02116 Office Phone: 617-734-3652.

ABNEY, DENISE ANN CARDIN, psychologist, researcher; b. Fall River, Mass., Dec. 20, 1955; d. Ernest Lucien and Theresa (Jusseaume) C. BS Psychology, Providence Coll., 1977; MS Edn., Purdue U., 1984; PhD Counseling, Psychology, Auburn U., 1992. Lic. psychologist, Ala., Tex. Psychology intern VA Med. Ctr., San Antonio, 1990—91, psychologist PCT Tuskegee, Ala., 1992—94, psychologist geriatrics Waco, Tex., 1994-95, psychologist PTSU, 1995—; psychologist geriat. Ctrl. Tex. Med. Ctr., Waco, 1995—; clin. mgr. geriat. svcs., psychologist Deer Oaks Mental Health Assocs., San Antonio, 1997—98; psychologist Kerrville divsn. South Tex. Vets. Health Care Sys., 1998—. Cons. to PTSD adv. com. Vietnam Vets. Am., Ala. State Coun., 1993-94 Contbr. articles to profl. jours Charter mem. U.S. Holacaust Meml. Mus.; mem. Nat. Audubon Soc., Arthritis Found., Lupus Found., Nature Conservancy Named Citizen of Yr. Vietnam Vets. Am., Ala. State Coun., 1994 Mem. APA (counseling and psychology of women sects.), Internat. Soc. for Traumatic Stress Studies, Phi Delta Kappa Avocations: reading, painting, travel. Home: 110 Creekside Ter Boerne TX 78006-5631 Office: South Tex Vets Health Care Sys Kerrville divsn MHC 116A 3600 Memorial Blvd Kerrville TX 78028

ABNEY, MARTHA MCEACHERN, music educator; b. Bremen, Ga., Dec. 6, 1957; d. James Sterling and Nancy Hughes McEachern; m. Jeffrey Robert Abney, June 8, 2002; children: Laura, Steve, Ginger, Sam, Ellen, Peter. B of Music Edn., West Ga. Coll., 1987, M of Music Edn., 1992. Tchr. music Bremen City Schs., Ga., 1987—98, Carroll County Schs., Villa Rica, 1998—, State U. West Ga., Carrollton, 1999—. Music dir. Bremen 1st United Meth. Ch., 1992—95, Tallapoosa 1st United Meth. Ch., 2005—. Mem.: Ga. Music Educators Assn., Am. Choral Dirs. Assn., Spirit Atlanta Alumni Assn. (assoc.). Republican. Methodist. Home: 34 Woodstream Ln Tallapoosa GA 30176 Office: Villa Rica High Sch 600 Rocky Branch Rd Villa Rica GA 30180 Office Phone: 770-459-5185. Business E-Mail: martie.abney@carrollcountyschools.com.

ABOUSSIE, MARILYN, retired judge; b. Wichita Falls, Tex., June 9, 1948; m. John A. Hay, Jr., Dec. 9, 1973; 1 child, John A. III. BA, Midwestern U., 1969; JD, U. Tex., 1974. Bar: Tex. 1974. Assoc. Foreman, Dyess, Prewett, Rosenberg & Henderson, Houston, 1974-76; pvt. practice San Angelo, Tex., 1976-78; ptnr. Smith, Davis, Rose, Finley & Hofmann, San Angelo, Tex., 1978-83; judge 340th Dist. Ct., San Angelo, 1983-86; justice Tex. Ct. Appeals, Austin, 1986-98, chief justice, 1998—2003; ret., 2003; sr. judge Tex., 2003—. Mem.: ABA, State Bar Assn. of Tex. Episcopalian. Office Phone: 325-659-9758.

ABRAHAM, BONDI CORINNE, artist; b. Van Nuys, Calif., Aug. 5, 1942; d. Henry Clayton Winters and Irene Perrick; m. Ronald Louis Abraham, Jan. 30, 1965. Exhibitions include Kaiser Ctr., Oakland, Calif., Walnut Creek Watercolor Soc., San Francisco Art Inst., Diablo Valley Coll., Walnut Creek Women's Ctr., Penhallow Galleries, Sacramento, Eastbay Watercolor Society

Member's Show, Acad. of Art, San Francisco, numerous private collections, nationally and internationally. Recipient Merit award, E. Bay Watercolor Soc. 17th Ann. Exhibit, 1984. Mem.: Calif. Watercolor Assn. (bd. dirs., membership dir. 2004—05). Office: 8683 Rawhide Ln Box 27 Wilton CA 95693

ABRAHAM, FRANCINE DINNEEN, sales executive, banker; b. Pitts., Jan. 9, 1946; d. Francis Joseph Dinneen and Margaret Mary McMillen; m. James Esber Abraham, Feb. 29, 2000; children: Patrick Ferraro, Amy Victoria Ferraro. BS in Bus. Mgmt., Point Pk. U., Pitts., 1983; MBA, Internat. U. San Diego, Mex., 1987. Sr. mgr. assoc. dir. Mellon Bank, Pitts., 1983; v.p. credit internat. ops. Ernst and Young, Pitts., 2000—06. Trustee Point Pk. U., Pitts., 1990—2006; bd. mem. FISA Found., Pitts., 2004—06, Pitts. Irish and Classical Theatre, Pitts., 2005—06, ARCS Found., Pitts., 2005—06. Mem.: EWC, Women and Girls Founs. Democrat. Avocations: reading, exercise, bicycling.

ABRAHAM, LYNNE M., district attorney; b. Phila., 1941; BA, Temple U., 1962, JD, 1965. Mem. reg. counsel's office U.S. Dept. HUD, 1965-67; asst. dist. atty. City and County of Phila., 1967-72, 73-74, dist. atty., 1991—; exec. dir. Phila. Redevel. Authority, 1972-73; legis. cons. Phila. County Coun., 1974-76; rsch. assoc. Ct. Common Please/Ct. Adminstr. of Pa., 1974-77; judge Phila. Mcpl. Ct., 1976-80, Ct. Common Pleas/Phila. County, 1980-91. Office: City and County of Phila 1421 Arch St Philadelphia PA 19102-1507

ABRAHAM, MELISSA E., psychologist; d. Jerrold and Harriet Abraham; m. Dost Ongur, Aug. 29, 2004. BA, Wellesley Coll., 1991; MSc, Harvard Sch. Pub. Health, 1997; PhD, Northwestern U., 2002. Clin. fellow Harvard Med. Sch./Mass. Gen. Hosp., Boston, 2001—05; staff psychologist Mass. Gen. Hosp., Boston, 2005—. Chair Ptnrs. Human Rsch. Com., Boston, 2004—; instr. Harvard Med. Sch., Boston, 2005—. Mem.: APA. Office: Mass General Hosp 15 Parkman St WAC 812 Boston MA 02114 Business E-Mail: mabraham2@partners.org.

ABRAHAMSEN, VALERIE, academic administrator; b. Norwood, Mass., Oct. 5, 1954; d. Frederick Henry and Ruth Eleanor A. BA, U. S.C., 1975; M Theol. Studies, Harvard U., 1977, ThD, 1986. Cert. secondary social studies tchr., Mass. Adminstr. Harvard U., Cambridge, Mass., 1986-89; exec. office mgr. Mass. Gen. Hosp., Boston, 1990-93; registrar, bursar MGH Inst. Health Professions, Boston, 1993—98; registrar and dir. Inst. Rsch. Lasell Coll., Newton, 1998—99; registrar Roxbury CC, Boston, 2000—02; registrar and assoc. dean Marlboro Coll., Vt., 2003—. Mem. adj. faculty Bunker Hill C.C., Boston, 1995—; vis. scholar Andover-Newton (Mass.) Theol. Sch., 1997-98; reviewer NEH, Washington, 1994-95; editor Fortress Press, Phila., 1977-79. Author: Women and Worship at Philippi, 1995; contbr. articles and revs. to profl. publs. Mem. anti-racism task force Episcopal Diocese Mass., Boston, 1993-2002, co-chmn. congl. resources and devel. com., 1995-96; mem. choir Cathedral Ch. of St. Paul, 1991-2003. Pfeiffer fellow Harvard Div. sch., 1979, 80; travel grantee Kittridge Found., 1990, Am. Coun. Learned Socs., 1995. Mem. Am. Acad. Religion, Soc. Bibl. Lit., Nat. Assn. Student Pers. Adminstrs. (state adv. bd. 1995-97), Am. Assn. Collegiate Registrars and Admissions Officers. Avocations: music, photography.

ABRAHAMSON, SHIRLEY SCHLANGER, state supreme court chief justice; b. NYC, Dec. 17, 1933; d. Leo and Ceil (Sauerteig) Schlanger; m. Seymour Abrahamson, Aug. 26, 1953; 1 son, Daniel Nathan. AB, NYU, 1953; JD, Ind. U., 1956; SJD, U. Wis., 1962. Bar: Ind. 1956, N.Y. 1961, Wis. 1962. Asst. dir. Legis. Drafting Research Fund, Columbia U. Law Sch., 1957-60; since practiced in Madison, Wis., 1962-76; mem. firm LaFollette, Sinykin, Anderson & Abrahamson, 1962-76; justice Wis. Supreme Ct., Madison, 1976-96, chief justice, 1996—. Bd. visitors Ind. U. Sch. Law, 1972-02, U. Miami Sch. Law, 1982-97, U. Chgo. Law Sch., 1988-92, Brigham Young U., Sch. Law, 1986-88, Northwestern U. Law Sch., 1989-94; chmn. Wis. Rhodes Scholarship Com., 1992-95; chmn. nat. adv. com. on ct.-adjudicated and ct.-ordered health care George Washington U. Ctr. Health Policy, Washington, 1993-95; mem. DNA adv. bd. FBI, U.S. Dept. Justice, 1995-2001; bd. dirs. Inst. Jud. Adminstrn., Inc., NYU Sch. Law; chair Nat. Inst. Justice's Commn. Future DNA Evidence, 1997-2001; prof. U. Wis. Sch. Law, 1966-92; v.p. Conference of Chief Justices, 2002-. Editor: Constitutions of the United States (National and State) 2 vols, 1962. Mem. study group program of rsch., mental health and the law John D. and Catherine T. MacArthur Found., 1988-96; mem. coun. fund for rsch. on dispute resolution Ford Found., 1987-91; bd. dirs. Wis. Civil Liberties Union, 1968-72; mem. ct. reform adv. panel Internat. Human Rights Law Group Cambodia Project, 1995-97. Recipient Dwight D. Opperman award, Am. Judicature Soc., 2004. Mem. ABA (coun., sect. legal edn. and admissions to bar 1976-86, mem. commn. on undergrad. edn. in law and the humanities 1978-79, standing com. on pub. edn. 1991-95, mem. commn. on access to justice/2000 1993-02, mem. adv. bd. Ctrl. and East European law initiative 1994-99, mem. consortium on legal svcs. and the public 1995-2001, vice-chair ABA Coalition for Justice 1997-2000), Wis. Bar Assn., Dane County Bar Assn., 7th Cir. Bar Assn., Nat. Assn. Women Judges, Am. Law Inst. (mem. coun. 1985-), Am. Philos. Soc., Am. Acad. Arts and Scis. Office: Wis Supreme Ct PO Box 1688 Madison WI 53702-1688*

ABRAHM, JANET LEE, hematologist, oncologist, educator, palliative care specialist; b. San Francisco, Mar. 14, 1949; d. Paul Milton and Helen Lesser Abrahm; m. David Rytman Slavitt, Apr. 16, 1978. Student, U. Calif., Berkeley, 1969; BA, U. Calif., San Francisco, 1970, MD, 1973. Diplomate in internal medicine, hematology and oncology Am. Bd. Internal Medicine; diplomate Am. Bd. Hospice and Palliative Medicine. Intern and resident medicine Mass. Gen. Hosp., Boston, 1973-75, hematology fellow, 1975-76; chief resident medicine Moffitt Hosp. U. Calif., San Francisco, 1976-77; hematology/oncology fellow Hosp. U. Pa., Phila., 1977-80; postdoctoral fellow medicine U. Pa., Phila., 1977-78, postdoctoral trainee medicine, 1977-80, asst. prof. medicine, 1980-86, Hosp. U. Pa. and VA Med. Ctr., Phila., 1986-89, assoc. prof. medicine, 1989-2000; attending physician Hosp. U. Pa., Phila., 1980-93; from staff physician to assoc. chief of staff, primary care and consultation medicine Phila. VA Med. Ctr., 1982—97, faculty scholar Project Death in Am., 1997—2000; med. dir. Wissahickon Hospice UPHS, 1998-2000; assoc. prof. medicine and anesthesia Harvard Med. Sch., 2001—; attending physician Dana-Farber Cancer Inst., Brigham and Women's Hosp., Boston, 2001—. Prin. investigator Palliative Care Fellowship Grant, 1996-2001, 03—; mem. concensus panel on End-of-Life Care, ACP, 1997—; chmn. adv. com. Cancer Care VA Dist. 4, 1987-90; sec. subspecialty bd. hematology Am. Bd. Internal Medicine, 1987-92, sec. SEP subcom. hematology, 1993-95; mem. tech. adv. group Cancer Care Region 1, 1990-95; med. oncology cons. cancer pain consultation panel Ctr. for Continuing Edn. U. Pa. Sch. Nursing, 1990-2000; mem. quality of life and cancer edn. com. Pa. Cancer Adv. Bd., 1994-97; mem. human resources coun. of VHA VISN, 1996-97, councillor Region 1, AVOCOM, 1996-97, TAPC mem., 2000-02, Am. Acad. Hospice and Palliative Medicine, 1999-, ACP, 2000-, others; attending physician Brigham and Women's Hosp., Boston, 2001—; dir. pain and palliative care program Dana-Farber Career Inst., Boston, 2001—. Author: Pain Management and Antiemetic Therapy in Hematologic Disorders in Hematology: Basic Principles and Practice, 1994, 2005, Anemia, Pain Management in Geriatric Secrets, 1996, 2000, 2004, A Physician's Guide to Pain and Symptom Management in Cancer Patients, 2000, 2d edit., 2005, Caring For Patients at the End of Life Clinical Oncology, 2004, Specialized Care of the Terminally Ill, In Cancer, Principles & Practices of Oncology, 2005; reviewer New Eng. Jour. Medicine, JAMA, Cancer, Archives Internal Medicine, Annals Internal Medicine, mem. editl. bd. Jour. Palliative Medicine, 2004—; contbr. numerous articles to profl. jours. Recipient Manual award Merck, 1973; Fife Medicine scholar, 1973. Fellow: ACP, Am. Acad. Hospice and Palliative Medicine (bd. dirs. 2002—); mem.: Am. Pain Soc., Am. Assn. Cancer Edn. (program com. 1993), Am. Soc. Clin. Oncology, Am. Soc. Clin. Hypnosis, Am. Soc. Hematology, Alpha Omega Alpha, Phi Beta Kappa. Home: 35 West St #5 Cambridge MA 02139 Office: Dana Farber Cancer Inst 44 Binney St Boston MA 02115 Office Phone: 617-632-6464. Business E-Mail: jabrahm@partners.org.

ABRAMOVIC, MARINA, artist; b. Belgrade, Yugoslavia, 1946; PhD (hon.), Art Inst. Chgo., 2004. Instr. Acad. Fine Arts, Novi Sad, 1973—75; visiting prof. Académie des Beaux-Arts, Paris, 1983, Hochschule der Kunst, Berlin, 1990—91, Hochschule für Bildende Kunst, Hamburg, 1992—96, prof. Braunschweig, 1997; artist in residence Atelier Calder, Saché, 2001. One-woman shows include Art must be Beautiful Artist must be Beautiful, Art Festival, Copenhagen, Denmark, 1975, Breathing out/Breathing in (with Ulay), Studenski Kulturni Centar, Belgrade, 1977, Charged Space (with Ulay), Brooklyn Mus., European Performance Series, NY, 1978, Rest Energy (with Ulay), ROSC 80, Dublin, 1990, Nightsea Crossing (with Ulay), Mus. Contemporary Art, Chgo., 1982, Die Mond der Sonne (with Ulay), The House, Santa Monica, 1987, The Lovers: The Great Wall Walk (with Ulay), The Great Wall China, 1988, Dragon Heads, Kunstmuseum, Bonn, Germany, 1992, Delusional (with Charles Atlas), Theater am Turin, Frankfurt, Germany, 1994, Cleaning the House, Sean Kelly Gallery, NY, 1995, The Biography, Schouwburg, Groningen, 1996, Balkan Baroque, Biennale di Venezia, Venice, Italy, 1997, Luminosity, Sean Kelly Gallery, NY, 1997, Artist Body-Pub. Body, Mus. Contemporary Art, Valencia, Spain, 1998, The House with the Ocean View, 2003 (NY Dance & Performance Award, 2003), Directions, Hirschhorn Mus. & Sculpture Garden, 2001, Moving Pictures, Soloman R. Guggenheim Mus., NY, 2002, exhibited in group shows at Whitney Biennial Exhbn., Whitney Mus. Am. Art, 2004. Recipient Niedersächsicher Kunstpreis, 2003. Mailing: c/o Solomon R Guggenheim Mus 1071 5th Ave New York NY 10128

ABRAMOWICZ, JANET, painter, print-maker; b. N.Y.C. children: Alex, Anna. BFA, Acad. di Belle Arti, Bologna, Italy, 1954, MFA, 1955. Teaching asst. to Giorgio Morandi Acad. di Belle Art, 1953-55; instr. dept. art and architecture U. Ill., 1955-57, Sch. Worcester, Mass., 1957-58; sr. lectr. fine arts Harvard U., Cambridge, Mass., 1971-91. Past lectr. on spl. exhibits Mus. Fine Arts, Boston; vis. artist Am. Acad. Rome, 1984-85, 94; fellow Japan Found., 1979-80; advisor Calcografia Nat., Rome, 1989-90; hon. fellow Acad. Clementina, Bologna, 1990—. Contbg. editor: Opera Grafiche di Morandi, 1990; contbr. articles to profl. jours. Sr. Fulbright fellow, 1977-79, 89, Rockefeller Found., 1989—, Am. Coun. Learned Socs. fellow, 1990, John Simon Guggenheim fellow, 1992. Democrat.

ABRAMS, JACKIE, artist, educator; b. N.Y.C., Jan. 19, 1949; d. Moe Werner and Eleanor Borhak; children: Dani Mariasha, Rina Rose Tobias. BS in Child Devel., U. Mass., Amherst, 1970, MEd in Humanistic Edn., 1973; studied ash basketry with Ben Higgins, Chesterfield, Mass., 1975. Staff Internat. Fiber Forum, Geelong, Australia, 2004. Chairperson North Country Basketmakers Guild, 1985—86, newsletter editor, 1986—88; founder, planning com. North Country Studio Workshops, Hanover, NH, 1990—2003, pres., 2001—03; juror Am. Craft Coun., 2001; curator Brookfield Craft Ctr., Conn., 2002; bd. trustees Am. Craft Coun., 2002—05; scribe Handweavers Guild Am., 2002; co-curator hanging com. Windham Art Gallery, Brattleboro, 2003—05; adv. coun. mem. Arrowmont Sch. Arts and Crafts, Gatlinburg, Tenn., 2004—. Represented in permanent collections League NH Craftsmen, Concord, Mich. State U. Mus., Lansing, Wustum Mus. Fine Arts, Racine, Wis., selected exhbn., The Works Gallery, Phila., 1998, 2001, Brookfield Craft Ctr., Conn., 1998, 2002, 2004, Gallery at Phil. Mus. Art, 1998, Am. Craft Enterprises, Balt., 1998, 1999, 2001, Am. Craft Expn., Evanston, Ill., 1998, 2000, 2001, Northeast Basketmakers Guild, Lexington, Mass., 1998, Creative Arts Workshop, New Haven, Conn., 1998, Washington Craft Show, DC, 1998, 1999, 2004, Arrowmont Sch. Arts and Crafts, 1999, 2001, 2003, 2005, Westchester Craft Show, NY, 1999, SOFA, Mobilia Gallery, Chgo., 1999, 2000, Crafts at the Castle, Boston, 1999, 2003, John Michael Kohler Arts Ctr., Treasures, Wis., 1999, 2000, 2001, Firehouse Gallery, Damariscotta, Maine, 1999, New Eng. Artists' Trust Congress Juried Show, New Haven, Conn., 1999, Guild.com, 1999—, Chester Gallery, Conn., 2000, Fountainhead Gallery, Seattle, 2000, Rutledge Gallery, Dayton, Ohio, 2000, Wustum Mus. Fine Arts, Racine, Wis., 2000, 2003, 2005, Am. Craft Coun., Balt., 2000, 2001, 2002, 2004, 2005, Phila. Mus. Art Craft Show, 2000, 2002, 2003, 2006, Smithsonian Craft Show, Washington, DC, 1997, 2000, 2002, delMano Gallery, LA, 2001, SOFA, Katie Gingrass Gallery, Chgo., 2001, 2002, 2003, 2004, NYC, 2005, 2006, Dane Gallery, Nantucket, Mass., 2001, Nat. Basketry Orgn., Abiquiu, N.Mex, 2002, 2005, Fiber Art Ctr., Amherst, 2002, NH Inst. Art, 2002, 2004, Handweavers Guild Am., Vancouver, Can., 2002, Boulder, Colo., 2004, Am. Art Co., Tacoma, Wash., 2002, 2003, 2005, Soc. Arts and Crafts, Boston, 2002, Ark. Art Ctr., 2002, U. Conn., Storrs, 2003, Windham Art Gallery, Brattleboro, 2003, 2005, 2004, The Carnegie, Cin., 2003, Craft Alliance, St. Louis, 2003, Yeiser Art Ctr., Paducah, Ky., 2003, Penland Gallery, NC, 2003, Allied Arts Assn. Gallery, Richland, Wash., 2004, Dairy Ctr. Arts, Boulder, 2004, Brookfield Craft Ctr., Conn., 2004, Gallery 205, Concord, 2004, Convergence, HGA, Boulder, 2004, Dairy Barn Arts Ctr., Athens, Ohio, 2004, Goldstein Mus. Design, Mpls., 2004, Grubbs Gallery, Easthampton, Mass., 2004, U. So. Maine, Gorham, 2005. Sunapee Fair com. League NH Craftsmen, Concord, 1983—85, bd. trustees, 1987—90; charter bd. mem. Vt. Crafts Coun., Montpelier, 1990—93; edn. com. Brattleboro Mus. Art, Vt., 2001—. Finalist Niche award, 2001; recipient Edith Grodin award, Annual Juried Exhibit, League NH Craftsmen, 1988, Janeway Fellowship award, Stratton Arts Festival, Vt., 1990, Juror's award of Distinction, 1995, Merit award for Outstanding Work of Art, Paper/Fiber XVII, Iowa City, 1994, Honorable Mention award, Am. Craft Enterprises, Balt., 2000, Craft Emergency Relief Fund Artist, CERF Life Boats, 2002, Third Place award, Small Expressions, Handweavers Guild Am., 2004; grantee, League NH Craftsmen, 1984, 1987; scholar, 1992, 1997; Study Grant, Vermont Arts Coun., 1995, Artist Devel. Grant, 1996, Opportunity Grant, 1999, 2003, 2005, Creation Grant, Vt. Arts Coun., 2001, Vt. Cmty. Found., 2002, Residency Grant, Cross Cultural Collaboratives, Ghana, West Africa, 2005. Avocations: gardening, walking, yoga, knitting, travel. Home: 21 Howard St Brattleboro VT 05301 Office Phone: 802-257-2688. Personal E-mail: jabrams@together.net. E-mail: jackie@jackieabrams.com.

ABRAMS, JANE ELDORA, artist; b. Eau Claire, Wis., Jan. 2, 1940; children: John, Joan. BS, U. Wis., Menomonie, 1962, MS, 1967; MFA, Ind. U., 1971. Regent's prof. U. N.Mex., Albuquerque, 1971-93, prof. emeritus, 1993—. One-woman show include Fine Arts Gallery, Ind. U., Bloomington, Ind., Nora Eccles Harrison Mus. of Art, Logan, Utah, 1989-90, Zimmerman/Saturn Gallery, Nashville, 1989, Marilyn Butler Fine Arts, Santa Fe, R.S. Levy Gallersy, Austin, 1988, Norman R. Eppink Gallery, Emporia (Kans.) State U., 1988, Kron/Reck Gallery, Albuquerque, 1987, Owings-Dewey Fine Art, Santa Fe, 1993, Charlotte Jackson Fine Art, Santa Fe, 1993, Robischon Gallery, Denver, 1993, Amarillo (Tex.) Mus. Art, 1995, Charlotte Jackson Fine Arts, 1995, and numerous others; exhibited in group shows at Albuquerque Mus., 1991, Robischon Gallery, Denver, 1989-90, Janus Gallery, Santa Fe, 1989, Lew Allen/Butler Gallery, N.Mex., Guadalajara, 1994, Mus. of N.Mex., Santa Fe, 1994, Ind. U. Art Mus, Bloomington, 1994. Grad. studies fellowship Ind. U., 1969, 70, rsch. fellowship, 1970; grantee Tamarind Inst., 1973, Roswell Mus. & Art Ctr., N.Mex., 1985-86, NEA, 1984, 94; recipient disting. alumni award Ind. U., 1991, U. Wis., 1992. Home: 7811 Guadalupe Trl NW Albuquerque NM 87107-6507 Office: U NMex Dept Art And History Albuquerque NM 87131-0001

ABRAMS, JOYCE D., artist; d. Harry and Diana (Goldman) Abrams. BFA, Cooper Union Coll., 1966; MFA, Columbia U., 1972. Prodn. mgr., film editor Sta. KQED-TV, San Francisco, 1968—70. Instr. CUNY, NYC, 1978—81, U. So. Maine, Gorham, 1987, Parson Sch. Design, NYC, 1989—91; curator Rockland Ctr. for the Arts, West Nyack, NY, 1991; vis. lectr. MIT, Boston Coll., Boston, 1980; cons. in field. Exhibited in group shows at The Nippon Club Gallery, NYC, 1982, First Women's Bank, 1983, Rockland Ctr. for the Arts, West Nyack, N.Y., 1985, Humphrey Fine Art, NYC, 1992, Marsh Gallery, Mt. Kisco, N.Y., 1994, Sharjah Art Mus., UAR, 2000, 2005, Ctr. for the Arts, Camden, N.J., 2005, AIR Gallery, NYC, 2002, 2004, 2005, 2006, Represented in permanent collections UCLA Anderson Sch. Bus., N.Y. Pub. Libr. Print Collection, NYC, Mus. Modern Art, Tokyo Ctrl. Mus., numerous cos., pvt. collections in Europe, U.S. and Japan. Fellow, MacDowell Colony, 1985, 1987, Corp. Yaddo, 1988; Creative Arts fellow, Japan Found., 2000. Mem.: NY Artists Equity Assn. Home: 100 W 94th St 24C New York NY 10025

ABRAMS, JULIE MARIE, counseling psychologist; b. Lower Marion, Pa., Aug. 26, 1962; d. Robert Marlow and Patricia Ann Abrams. BA in Psychology cum laude, Davidson Coll., 1984; MS, U. Fla., 1988, PhD, 1992. Intern in psychology Counseling Ctr. So. Ill. U., Carbondale, 1989-90; student counseling specialist sexual assault recovery svc. U. Fla., Gainesville, 1991-92, psychologist, 1992-94, interim coord., 1994-95, psychologist, 1995—. Peer edn. coord. U. Fla., Gainesville, Fla., 1995—2001, staff psychologist employee assistance program, 2001—. Contbr. articles to profl. jours. Crisis phone counselor Alachua County Crisis Ctr., Gainesville, 1985-86; mem. sexual battery com. City of Gainesville, 1988-89, 1991-99. Fellow U. Fla. Grad. Coun., 1984-85, O. Ruth McQuown, 1989-90. Office: U Fla Student Health Care Ctr PO Box 117500 Gainesville FL 32611-7500

ABRAMS, ROSALIE SILBER, retired state agency official; b. Balt., June 2, 1916; d. Isaac and Dora (Rodbell) Silber; 1 child, Elizabeth Joan. RN, Sinai Hosp.; postgrad., Columbia U.; BS, Johns Hopkins U., 1963, MA in Polit. Sci. Pub. health nurse USNR, 1945-46; bus. mgr. Sequoia Med. Group, Calif., 1946-47; asst. bus. mgr. Silber's Bakery, Balt., 1947-53; mem. Md. Ho. of Dels., 1967-70, Md. Senate, 1970-83, majority leader, 1978-82; chmn. Dem. Party of Md., 1978-83, chmn. fin. com., 1982-83; dir. Office on Aging, State of Md., 1983-95, ret., 1995. Chair World War II Meml. Commn., 1996-2000; mem. Balt. City Commn. on Aging, 1997—2000; host Outlook TV show, 1983-90; guest lectr., witness before congl. coms. Platform com. on nat. healthcare Dem. Nat., Com., 1979—; chmn. Md. Humane Practices Commn., 1978-83, mem., 1971-74; mem. New Coalition, 1979-83, State-Fed. Assembly Com. on Human Resources, 1977-83, Md. Comprehensive Health Planning Agy., 1972-75, Md. Commn. on Status of Women, 1968—, Am. Jewish Com. Chair Med. Supplies Com. for Needy and Elderly in Odessa, Ukraine; chair dept. human resources, dept. health and mental hygiene, transp., housing and cmty. devel., econ. and employment devel., Interagy. Com., 1984-95; bd. dirs. Sinai Hosp., Balt., 1973-2000, Balt. Jewish Coun., Cross Country Improvement Assn., 1969—2000, Fifth Dist. Reform Dems., 1967—2000; chmn. legis. com. Balt. Area Coun. on Alcoholism, 1973-75; mem. adv. bd. long term care project U. Md., Balt., 1986; mem. Md. Adv. Com. for Adult and Cmty. Svcs., 1984; mem. nat. adv. bd. Pre-Retirement Edn. Planning, 1986—93; mem. State Adv. Coun. on Nutrition, 1988—; spl. trustee Sheppard-Pratt Hosp., 1992-2000. With Nurse Corps USN, 1944-46. Recipient Louise Waterman Wise Cmty. Svc. award, 1969, award Am. Acad. Comprehensive Health Planning, 1971, Balt. News Am. award, Women of Distinction in Medicine, 1971, traffic safety award, Safety First Club of Md., 1971, ann London Scott Meml. award for legis. excellence, Md. chpt. NOW, 1975, Md. Nurses Assn., 1975, svc. award Balt. Area Coun. on Alcoholism, 1975, First Citizens award Md. Senate Pres., 1999, named to Md. Women's Hall of Fame, Md. Commn. for Women and Women Legislators of Md. Gen. Assembly, 1994, numerous others; 1st ann. Rosalie S. Abrams Firsts award awarded by Women Legislators of Md., 2004, Nursing Spectrum award, 2005. Mem. AAUW, AARP, Md. Order Women Legislators (pres. 1973-75), Nat. Conf. State Legislatures (human resources and urban affairs steering com. 1977-83), Nat. Legis. Conf. (human resources task force, intergovtl. rels. com. 1975-83), Md. Gerontol. Assn. (bd. dirs. 1984—), Nat. Fedn. Dem. Women, Am. Jewish Congress, Am. Soc. on Aging, Md. Gerontol. Assn., Sigma Theta Tau Nursing Soc., Balta City Hist. Soc. (trustee 2000—). Home: North Oaks 725 Mt Wilson Ln Apt 729 Baltimore MD 21208

ABRAMS, ROZ, newscaster; married; 2 children. BS in Sociology, Western Mich. U.; MA in Speech, U. Mich. Anchor KRON-TV, San Francisco, CNN; anchor/reporter WXIA-TV, Atlanta; with WABC-TV, NYC, 1986—2003, weekend anchor, gen. assignment reporter, anchor Eyewitness News at 5 PM, host program Making It; co-anchor 5pm and 11pm news WCBS-TV, NYC, 2004—. Editl. adv. bd. Making Waves Am. Women in Radio and TV, 2003—. Co-chair NY Reads Together. Recipient numerous awards including Centennial award for svc. and achievement in media Greater Harlem C. of C.

ABRAMS-COLLENS, VIVIEN, artist; b. Cleve. BFA, Carnegie-Mellon U.; MFA, Instituto Allende, San Miguel de Allende, Mex. Art tchr. Biblioteca Publica, San Miguel de Allende, Mex., 1969, Cleve. Mus. Art, 1971-72; instr. drawing Cuyahoga C.C., Cleve., 1974; design instr. Manhattanville Coll., Purchase, N.Y., 1985-86. Artist-in-residence Bennington (Vt.) Coll., 1980; vis. artist in painting SUNY, Purchase, N.Y., 1983; lectr. in field. One-woman shows include Akron (Ohio) Art Inst., 1976, The New Gallery Contemporary Art, Cleve., 1977, 80, Luise Ross Gallery, N.Y.C., 1984, Coup de Grâce Gallery, N.Y.C., 1992, 100 Church Street, N.Y.C., 1992, Lisa Stern Gallery, Mountainville, N.Y., 1993, Lycian Ctr. Galleries, Sugarloaf, N.Y., 1994, Mus. Hudson Highlands, Cornwall-on-Hudson, N.Y., 1995; selected group exhbns. include Butler Inst. Am. Art, Ohio, 1976, 77, Cleve. Mus. Art, 1976, 77, 79, 81, 84 (1st Prize in Painting 1981), Akron Inst. Art, 1977, Harbourfront Gallery, Toronto, 1978, Marilyn Pearl Gallery, N.Y.C., 1978, 82, Phoenix Mus. Art, 1979, Soho Ctr. Visual Artists, N.Y.C., 1979, Washington Sq. East Galleries, N.Y.C., 1980, Little Rock (Ark.) Art Mus., 1982, Steven Rosenberg Gallery, N.Y.C., 1983, Ericson Gallery, N.Y.C., 1983, Sculpture Ctr., N.Y.C., 1983, A.I.R. Gallery, N.Y.C., 1983, Aldrich Mus. Contemporary Art, Ridgefield, Conn., 1984, 86, 92, Luise Ross Gallery, 1984, Mus. of the Hudson Highlands, 1985, City Gallery, N.Y.C., 1987, Squibb Gallery, Princeton, N.J., 1988, Cleve. Inst. Art, 1988, Mansfield Art Ctr., Ohio, 1989, OIA Salon, N.Y.C., 1991, Middletown Art Ctr., 1994 (Oil/Acrylic award 1994), Dietrich Contemporary Arts, N.Y.C., 1994, Cleve. Ctr. for Contemporary Art, 1994, Mansfield (Ohio) Art Ctr., 1995; permanent collections include Cleve. Found., Cleve. Art Assn., The Currier Gallery Art, Home Ins. Co., We. Electric, J.P. Morgan & Co., Continental Corp., Progressive Ins. Co., Nat. City Bank Cleve., Sohio, Walter & Samuels, Inc., Columbus Mus. Arts & Scis., Cleve. Mus. Art, Aldrich Mus. Contemporary Art; commns. include AT&T Longlines. Mem. fellows exec. com. MacDowell Colony, 1982-85. Cleve. Found. grantee, 1976, Athena Found. grantee, 1984; Hand Follow Found. fellow, 1983, fellow MacDowell Colony, Peterborough, N.H., 1979, 81, 85; recipient 1st prize Cleve. Mus. Art 62nd May Show, 1981, award Middletown Art Ctr., 1994; named to Shaker Heights H.S. Hall of Fame, 1994. Office: 196 Mountain Rd Cornwall On Hudson NY 12520-1803 also: Newburgh Art Gallery 394 Broadway Newburgh NY 12550-5304

ABRAMS FINGER, IRIS DALE, retired elementary school educator; b. Ironton, Ohio, Jan. 22, 1939; d. Frank Abrams and Pearl (Moore) Schwab; m. Robert James Roderick, Sr., July 20, 1957 (div. Nov. 1971); children: Robert James Roderick Jr., Elizabeth Ann Roderick Travis; m. Henry Waterman Bromley, Jr., May 14, 1972 (div. June 1987); 1 child, Henry Waterman Bromley III; m. Grover Cleveland Finger, III, Apr. 1, 1989; stepchildren: Linda Hall, Adam Finger, Sara Mason. Degree in Early Childhood and Elem. Edn., U. South Fla.; degree in Design, Jackson Coll., Honolulu. Cert. mid. sch. math. tchr. TESLA and gifted edn. Children's libr. Ft. Myers (Fla.) Pub. Libr., 1955—57; workmen's compensation payroll adminstr. San Diego, 1964—66; permanent substitute tchr. Sigsbee Elem. Sch., Key West, Fla., 1968—70; part time libr. Danielson (Conn.) Libr., 1970—71; residential design Bateman Homes, Leigh Acres, Fla., 1971—72; structural steel designer So. Machine and Steel, Ft. Myers, 1972—73; dir. Ft. Myers Bus. Coll., 1973—77; structural prestress concrete designer Southland Prestress, Dean Steel and Kirby MaCumber Steel, 1977—83; tchr. Lee County Sch. Bd., Ft. Myers, 1983—2004, team leader, math. coach, 1983, 1994—95; with Bonita Spring Mid. Sch., 1994—96, equity coord., 1995—96; ret., 2004. Pres. PTA Key West, 1966—68, Fla. Art League, Ft. Myers, 1984—86; hosp. nurse ARC, 1964—66; med. evacuation Vietnam wounded Philippine Islands Subic Hosp.; mem. treasury Island Coast Uni-Serve; rep. Lee County Safety Com. Named to Wall of Tolerance, 2005, Wall at Justice Ctr., Montgomery, Ala., 2005; recipient Pres. Johnson People to People award and Plank award for Sch. Constrn., San Meguel, Philippines, 1960, Pres. Regan Achievement award, 1976. Mem.: NEA, Lee County Math. Coun., Fla. Math. Coun., Tchrs. Assn. Lee County, Fla. Tchrs. Profession, Am. Legion, Rep. Assembly, Navy

Wives and Navy Relief Soc., VFW Aux., Pioneer Club Ft. Myers, Phi Beta Kappa (program chmn., treas.), Alpha Delta Kappa. Republican. Methodist. Avocations: art, crafts, reading, travel, swimming.

ABRAMSON, JILL, newspaper publishing executive; AB in History and Lit., Harvard U., 1976. Stringer Time mag., 1974-76, Boston bur. mgr., reporter, 1976-77; with NBC News Election Unit, 1979-81; sr. writer Am. Lawyer, 1981-88; editor Legal Times, 1986-88; with New York Times, Washington, 1988—, Chernoff Silver, 1988-97; dep. bur. chief The Wall Street Jour., 1993-97; enterprise editor Washington bur. New York Times, 1997—2003, mng. editor, 2003—. Co-author: Where They Are Now: The Story of Women of Harvard Law 1974, 1976, Strange Justice, 1994. Recipient Matrix award for newspaper work, NY Women in Comm. Inc., 2006. Office: NY Times 229 W 43rd St New York NY 10036*

ABRAMSON, LESLIE HOPE, lawyer; b. Queens, NY, 1943; 1 child, Laine. Grad., Queens Coll.; JD, UCLA. Bar: Calif. 1970. Lawyer L.A. County Pub. Defender's Office, 1970—77; pvt. practice, 1977—. Co-author: (with Richard Flaste) The Defense is Ready: My Life in Crime, 1997. Recipient award for outstanding trial atty., Criminal Cts. Bar Assn., 1985. Mem.: Calif. Attys. for Criminal Justice (pres.). Office: PMB 4 122 A E Foothill Blvd Arcadia CA 91006

ABRAMSON, STEPHANIE W., retired advertising executive, lawyer; b. Dec. 24, 1944; BA, Radcliffe Coll., 1966; JD, NYU, 1969. Bar: N.Y. 1969. Mem. Morgan, Lewis & Bockius, N.Y.C.; exec. v.p. and gen. counsel Young & Rubicam Inc, N.Y.C, 1996—2001; legal officer, chief corp. devel. officer Heidrick & Struggles Internat. Inc., N.Y.C, 2001—03.

ABRECHT, MARY ELLEN BENSON, lawyer; b. Granby, Mass., Dec. 18, 1945; d. Donald Dean and Mary Ellen (Ballard) Benson; m. Gary Lorne Abrecht, Sept. 7, 1968; children: Karen Elizabeth, Rachel Benson. BA, Mt. Holyoke Coll., 1967; postgrad., Union Theol. Sem., 1967-68; cert. in adminstrn. of justice, Am. U., Washington, 1970; JD, Georgetown U., 1974. Bar: D.C. 1975, U.S. Dist. Ct. D.C. 1975, U.S. Ct. Appeals D.C. Cir. 1975, U.S. Supreme Ct. 1980. Police officer Met. Police, Washington, 1968-72, patrol sgt., 1972-75; asst. U.S. atty. U.S. Atty.'s Office, Washington, 1975-90, dep. exec. asst. U.S. atty., 1979-81, sr. asst. U.S. Atty. appellate divsn., 1983-86; spl. counsel U.S. Sentencing Commn., Washington, 1986-87; dep. chief appellate divsn. U.S. Atty.'s Office, 1987-88, tng. dir., 1989-90; assoc. judge Superior Ct., Washington, 1990—2003, trial judge in family divsn., 1990, 1991, 1996, 1999—2001, trial judge in criminal divsn., 1992-93, 96-98, trial judge in civil divsn., 1994-95, 2002, sr. judge, 2003—. Mem. juvenile justice adv. com. D.C. Govt., 1979-81. Co-author: The Making of a Woman Cop, 1976. Vice chmn. Rights of Children Forum, White House Conf. on Children, Washington,1970; mem. cmty. adv. bd. dirs. Project on Child Sexual Abuse, Children's Hosp., Washington, 1978-79. Recipient Spl. Achievement award Dept. Justice, 1980, 84. Mem. Coun. Ct. Excellence (bd. mem. 2002-), Bryant Inn of Am. Inns of Ct. (pres. 1997-99). Democrat. Episcopalian. Office: Superior Ct 500 Indiana Ave NW # 680 Washington DC 20001-2131

ABREU, SUE HUDSON, physician, retired military officer, health facility administrator, consultant; b. Indpls., May 24, 1956; d. M.B. Hudson and Wilma (Jones) Hudson Black. BS in Engring., Purdue U., 1978; MD, Uniformed Services U., 1982; grad., U.S. Army Command & Gen. Staff, 1988, Armed Forces Staff Coll., 1990. Commd. 2d lt. U.S. Army, 1978, advanced to col., 1999, ret., 2002; intern Walter Reed Army Med. Ctr., Washington, 1982-83, resident in diagnostic radiology, 1983-85, fellow in nuc. medicine, 1985-87, staff nuc. medicine physician, 1987-88; med. rsch. fellow Walter Reed Army Inst. Rsch., Washington, 1988-89; chief nuc. medicine svc. Womack Army Med. Ctr., Ft. Bragg, NC, 1990—96, chief dept. radiology, 1991-92, 96-98, med. dir. quality assurance, 1998-2001, asst. dep. commdr. clin. svcs., 2001—02; orgnl. and healthcare cons., 2002—. Nuc. medicine cons. to Army Surgeon Gen., 2000-2002; bd. dirs. Intersocietal Commn. for Accreditation Nuclear Medicine Labs., 2001-, sec. 2003-. Named Outstanding Interdisciplinary Engr., Purdue U., 2001; named one of Purdue Old Masters, 2004; named to Tri-Svc. ROTC Hall of Fame, Purdue U., 2004. Fellow Am. Coll. Nuclear Physicians (pres. 2001); mem. Soc. Nuc. Medicine, Soc. Women Engrs., Am. Soc. Nuclear Cardiology, U.S. Parachute Assn., Mortar Bd., Tau Beta Pi, Omicron Delta Kappa, Phi Kappa Phi., Sigma Gamma Tau. Avocations: calligraphy, parachuting. Home: 613 Saddlebred Ln Raeford NC 28376-5535 Office Phone: 910-875-4268. Personal E-mail: sueabreu@mindspring.com. E-mail: sha@sueabreu.com.

ABRIOLA, LINDA MARIE, civil engineer, environmental engineer; BS in Civil Engring., Drexel U., 1976; MS in Civil Engring., Princeton U., 1979, MA in Civil Engring., 1980, PhD in Civil Engring., 1983. Project engr. Procter and Gamble Mfg. Co., S.I., NY, 1976—78; rsch. asst. dept. civil engring. Princeton U., NJ, 1979—83, postdoctoral rschr. dept. civil engring., 1983—84; vis. assoc. prof. dept. petroleum engring. U. Tex., Austin, 1991; vis. scientist dept. geotech. engring. Universitat Politecnica de Cataluna, Barcelona, 1992; asst. prof. dept. civil and environ. engring. U. Mich., Ann Arbor, 1984—90, assoc. prof. dept. civil and environ. engring., 1990—96, prof., dir. Environ. and Water Resources Engring. Program, 1996—2003; dean engring., prof. civil and environ. engring. Tufts U., 2003—. Mem. environ. engring. com. USEPA Sci. Adv. Bd., 1990—96; mem. com. on groundwater clean-up alternatives NRC, 1991—94, mem. water sci and tech. bd., 1994—97; mem. sci. adv. com. Western Region Hazardous Substance Rsch. Ctr., 1995—. Contbr. articles to profl. jours. Recipient Presdl. Young Investigator award, NSF, 1985, Faculty award for Women Scientists and Engrs., 1991, Outstanding Educator award, Assn. for Women Geoscientists, 1996; Vis. Scientist's grant, Spanish Ministry of Edn. and Sci., 1992, Disting. Darcy lectr., Nat. Groundwater Assn., 1996. Fellow: Am. Acad. Arts and Sciences; mem.: Nat. Acad. Engring., Am. Geophys. Union (hydrology divsn. 1992—94), Assn. Environ. Engring. Profs. (bd. dirs. 1990—92). Office: Dean Engring Tufts U Medford MA 02155

ABRON, LILIA A., chemical engineer; b. Memphis, Mar. 8, 1945; d. Ernest and Bernice (Wise) A.; children: Fredeick, Ernest, David. BS in Chemistry, Lemoyne Coll., 1966; MS in Sanitary Engring., Washington U., 1968; PhD in Chem. Engring., U. Iowa, 1971. Profl. engr. Free lance cons., Washington, 1971-74; asst. prof. Howard U., Washington, 1974-81; chief environ. div. Delon Hampton & Assocs., Washington, 1975-78; pres., CEO Peer Cons., Rockville, Md., 1978—. Com. mem. Nat. Coun. Examiners, Clemson, S.C. Pres. Jack & Jill Am., Inc., D.C. Chpt., 1990-92; bd. dirs. Bapt. Home for Children, Washington. Recipient Women Owned Bus. Enterprise award DOT, 1988, Balti. Outstanding Minority Bus. award Fed. Exec. Bd., 1987; named Alumnus of Yr. Lemoyne Owen Coll., 1988. Fellow Am. Acad. Arts & Scis.; mem. AAAS, Water Environ. Fedn., Am. Soc. Civil Engrs., Am. Water Works Assn., Sigma Xi Office: PEER Cons 12300 Twinbrook Pkwy Ste 410 Rockville MD 20852-1650

ABSHER, DONNA ATKINS, textile designer; b. Ft. Ord, Calif., July 25, 1956; d. James Edward and Mary Ward (Shearin) Atkins; m. Glen Alan Downs, Jan. 2, 1982 (div. Nov. 1990); m. Robert Blair Martin, June 29, 1991 (div. 1998); 1 child, Parker James Blair Martin; m. Ray Grubb Absher, Oct. 20, 2002. AAS in Fashion Design, SUNY, 1977; BS in Textile Tech., NC State U., 1978. Head designer Chatham Mills, Pittsboro, NC, 1978; dept. mgr. JC Penney, Wilson, NC, 1982—85; house mem.'s asst. NC Legislature, Raleigh, 1985—86; dir. product devel. Doblin Fabrics, Morganton, NC, 1989—94; pres., CEO Martin Textiles, Ltd., Hickory, NC, 1994—. Freelance designer, stylist Carolina Mills, Hickory, 1995-97; automotive textile designer, CMI Industries, Elkin, NC, 1998-2000; design ops. mgr. Chatham-Borgstena Automotive Textiles, Mt. Airy, NC, 2001—04. Mem.: Overmountain Victory Trail Assn. Southern Baptist. Avocations: travel, choral singing. E-mail: donnaaa@earthlink.net.

ABSHER, ROBIN DAWN, security firm executive, private investigator; b. Concord, N.C., Dec. 28, 1971; d. Judy Kay Tinch and David Eugene Absher, Wayne Tinch (Stepfather) and Margaret Amy Absher (Stepmother); life ptnr. C. L. Crawford, Sept. 25, 1998. Student, U. Nev., 1990—91, Detective Tng. Inst., Calif., 2002—03. Dir., ptnr. Ultraimaging Corp., Henderson, Nev., 1998—. Mem.: Nev. State Firefighters' Assn. Inc., Nat. Police & Trooper Assn., Nev. Fraternal Order of Police. Office: Ultraimaging Corp 848 Wintersweet Rd Henderson NV 89015 Personal E-mail: eyessoblu30@aol.com. E-mail: ultraimagingcorp@aol.com.

ABTS, GWYNETH HARTMANN, retired dietician; b. Union, Ill., Oct. 31, 1923; d. William John and Olga Anna (Krause) Hartmann; m. Rufus Heath Jr., Apr. 6, 1942 (div. Dec. 1945); m. Harold Henry Abts, Feb. 14, 1948; children: Leigh, Michael, Patricia. BS, U. Ill., 1945; postgrad., U. Oreg., 1945-46, U. Ill., Elgin, 1957, No. Ill. U., 1966, 74, 82, 87. Registered dietitian, Ill., Lic. Ill. Dietitian. Clin. dietitian St. Joseph Hosp., Elgin, 1947; asst. dietitian French Hosp., San Francisco, 1948-50, Elgin State Hosp., 1950-58; dietary cons. Ill. Youth Commn., Springfield, 1958-70; food adminstr. Ill. Dept. of Corrections, Springfield, 1970-85. Mem. Food and Nutrition Cou. on Govt. Commodities, Springfield, 1980-85; bd. dirs. Ill. Nutrition Assn., Urbana, 1983. Pres. PTO, Geneva, 1972. McHenry County Home Econ. scholar U. Ill., 1941-45. Mem. Am. Dietetic Assn. (citizens ambassador program to Australia and New Zealand and China), Fox Valley Home Economists, West Suburban Dietetic Assn., AAUW. Lutheran. Avocations: quilting, cooking, duplicate bridge. Home: Apt 107 975 N 5th Ave Saint Charles IL 60174-1284

ABUDULMAJID, IMAN See IMAN

ABU-LUGHOD, JANET LIPPMAN, sociologist, educator; b. Newark, Aug. 3, 1928; d. Irving O. and Tessie Lippman; m. Ibrahim Abu-Lughod, Dec. 8, 1951 (div. 1992); children: Lila, Mariam, Deena, Jawad. BA, U. Chgo., 1947, MA, 1950; PhD (NSF fellow), U. Mass., 1966. Dir. research Am. Soc. Planning Ofcls., 1950-52; sociologist-cons. Am. Council to Improve Our Neighborhoods, 1953-57; asst. prof. sociology Am. U., Cairo, 1958-60, Smith Coll., 1963-66; assoc. prof. Northwestern U., Evanston, Ill., 1967-71, prof. sociology, urban affairs, 1971-87, dir. comparative urban studies program, 1974-77, dir. urban studies program, 1984-87; emerita, 1987; prof. sociology Grad. Faculty The New Sch. for Social Research, N.Y.C., 1986-98; dir. Rsch. Ctr. on Lower Manhattan, N.Y.C., 1988-91, chmn. dept. of sociology, 1990-92; emerita, 1999. Cons. UN, 1971—, UNESCO, 1979-80. Author: (with Nelson Foote, others) Housing Choices and Constraints, 1960, Cairo-1001 Years of the City Victorious, 1971, (with Richard Hay, Jr.) Third World Urbanization, 1977, Rabat: Urban Apartheid in Morocco, 1980, Before European Hegemony, 1989, Changing Cities, 1991, From Urban Village to East Village, 1994, New York, Chicago, Los Angeles, 1999, Sociology For the 21st Century, 1999; contbr. chpts. to books, articles, revs. to profl. jours.; also monographs. Radcliffe Inst. scholar, 1963-64; Ford Faculty fellow, 1971-72, Simon Guggenheim fellow, 1976-77, NEH fellow, 1977-78, ACLS fellow, 1994; Getty Sr. scholar, 1994-96; H.F. Guggenheim fellow, 1997-98; recipient Disting. Career award, Polit. Economy of the World Sys., 1999, Disting. Scholar award, Internat. Studies Assn., 2002. Mem. Internat. Sociol. Assn., Am. Sociol. Assn. (governing coun. 1994-97, Robert and Helen Lynd award for disting. career achievement in urban sociology 1999), Phi Beta Kappa.

ACCOUNTIUS, PATRICIA L., dietician, consultant; b. Lima, Ohio, Dec. 16, 1930; d. William Gerald and Margaret Lucille Accountius. BS, Miami U., Oxford, Ohio; M in Hosp. Adminstrn., Baylor U. Registered dietitian Commn. on Registration, Am. Dietetic Assn., lic. Tex. State Lic. Bd. Commd. officer U.S. Army, 1952, advanced through grades to col., 1972, ret., 1982, dietetic intern Walter Reed Army Med. Ctr. Washington, 1952—53, spl. project officer nutritional care directorate Walter Reed Army Med. Ctr., 1958—60, chief clin. dietetics br. Ryukyus Army Hosp. Okinawa, Japan, 1956—58, resident Letterman Army Med. Ctr. San Francisco, 1960—61, resident health care adminstr. Letterman Army Med. Ctr. Presidio, 1962, chief nutritional care divsn. U.S. Army Hosp. Fort Jay, NY, 1962—63, chief prodn. and svc. br. Brooke Army Med. Ctr. Fort Sam Houston, 1963—66, dietetic cons. 44th Med. Brigade Vietnam, 1966—67, chief nutrition care divsn., dir. dietetic intern Fitzsimons Gen. Hosp. Denver, 1967—69, chief nutritional care divsn. Walson Army Hosp. Ft. Dix, NJ, 1969—73, chief nutritional care directorate Walter Reed Army Med. Ctr. Washington, 1973—75, chief dietitian sect. and asst. chief army med. specialist corp. Office Surgeon Gen., 1974—78, chief army med. specialist corps divsn., dietetic staff advisor Health Svcs. Command Fort Sam Houston, 1978—82; vis. lectr. U. Md., 1973—75; mem. adv. coun. Miami U. Sch. Edn., 1975—77; tchg. assoc. nutrition edn. U. Tex., 1990—91; nutritionist long term care unit State of Tex. Pub. Health Region 6, 1991—98; cons. to exec. dir. Army Residence Cmty., 2001. Bd. dirs. Women in the Army Mus., Women in the Army Found. Decorated Legion of Merit with oak leaf cluster, Bronze star, Meritorious Svc. medal, Army Commendation medal with three oak leaf clusters; named to, Lima City Schs. Disting. Alumni Hall of Fame, 2002. Mem.: Mil. Ret. Officers Assn., San Antonio Ret. Officer Assn., Walter Reed Army Med. Ctr. Heritage Soc., Vietnam Women's Veterans, Nat. Mil. Officers Assn., San Antonio Mil. Officers Assn., Nat. Coun. on Aging, Bexar County Soc. on Aging, Tex. State Nutrition Coun. (past sec.), Nat. Clin. Nutrition Practice Group, San Antonio Gerontol. Nutrition Practice Group, Tex. State Gerontol. Nutrition Practice Group (past pres., treas.), Nat. Gerontol. Nutrition Practice Group, Nat. Cons. Dietitions in Health Care Facilities Practice Group, Tex. State Cons. Dietitions in Health Care Facilities Practice Group, San Antonio Cons. Dietitions in Health Care Facilities Practice Group, Am. Dietetic Assn., Tex. Dietetic Assn., San Antonio Dietetic Assn., Ret. Army Med. Specialists Corps Assn. (past treas), Nat. Women's Overseas Svc. League (sec.), Women's Overseas Svc. League (past v.p. San Antonio unit, sec. San Antonio unit), ARC Golden K Kiwanis Club and Found. (sec.), Am. Legion (adjutant, historian). Republican. Roman Catholic. Achievements include first military dietician in Vietnam. Avocations: RVing, cooking, gardening, dogs. Home: Apt 1105 7400 Crestway San Antonio TX 78239

ACETO, LISA M., management consultant; b. NYC, Apr. 12, 1980; d. John and Janet Aceto. BS, Cornell U., Ithaca, NY, 2002, M of Engring., 2003. Cons. Capgemini, NYC, 2003—05; sr. cons. Pittiglio Rabin Todd & McGrath, Stamford, Conn., 2005—. Office: Pittiglio Rabin Todd & McGrath 2 Stamford Plaza Stamford CT 06901 Office Phone: 917-232-5294. Personal E-mail: lisa.aceto@gmail.com. E-mail: laceto@prtm.com.

ACEVEDO, ELIZABETH MORRISON, special education educator; b. Kittanning, Pa., Apr. 22, 1938; d. Thomas L. and Ethel (Morrison) McKelvey; m. Ruben Acevedo, Oct. 11, 1963; children: Thomas B., Samantha Jo Acevedo-Fox, Holly Elizabeth. BA, Muskingum Coll., 1960; MS, Pepperdine U., 1980; postgrad., Claremont Grad. Sch., 1988-90, Azusa-Pacific U. Lifetime credentials in English and spl. edn., Calif., Pa.; credential in resource specialist, Calif.; cert. adminstr., Calif. Tchr. Armstrong Sch. Dist., Ford City, Pa., 1970-77, Glendora (Calif.) Unified Sch. Dist., 1979-80, resource specialist, 1980-97; adj. prof., field supervisor Grad. Sch. of Edn., Azusa-Pacific U., Azusa, Calif., 1997—. Cons. reading program The Acevedo Advantage, Glendora, 1986—. Contbr. articles to profl. jours. Bd. dirs. christian edn. Ch. Brethren, Glendora, 1989—. Grantee Claremont (Calif.) Grad. Sch., 1989. Mem. AAUW, ASCD, Calif. Assn. Resource Specialists, Pi Lambda Theta (membership com.). Democrat. Mem. Ch. Brethren. Avocations: reading, jogging, sewing, refinishing antique wood pieces. Home: 643 N Wabash Ave Glendora CA 91741-2116 E-mail: eacevedo@apu.edu.

ACHENBACH, LAURIE A., science educator; d. Herbert Ralph and Delores Mae Achenbach; m. Shane A. Williams, Oct. 18, 2003; 1 child, Natalie Ann Nickrent. BS, No. Mich. U., Marquette, 1982—84; PhD, U. Ill., Urbana, 1983—87. Prof. So. Ill. U., Carbondale, 1991—. Contbr. scientific papers. Fellow U. Fellowship, U. Ill., 1984-1986; scholar Bd. Control Scholarship, No. Mich. U., 1982-1984. Mem.: Am. Soc. Microbiology. Achievements include research in Microbial genetics and biodiversity. Office: So Ill U Dept of Microbiology MC6508 Carbondale IL 62901 Business E-Mail: laurie@micro.siu.edu.

ACHON, RAQUEL ANDREA, music educator, consultant; b. Ctrl. Preston, Cuba, May 5, 1927; arrived in U.S., 1947; d. Crescencio Gutierrez and Basilisa Semorile; m. David Achon, Dec. 25, 1957; 1 child, David. BA, Instituto Santiago, 1947; diploma, Martin Coll., 1949; BS in Arts, Peabody Coll., 1951. Pvt. music tchr., Downey, Calif., 1968—. Cons. in field. Editor: Celebrenos II, 1983, El Himnario, 1998, 1999. Pianist Crusader's Class, 2004; vice-chair, editor United Meth. Hymnal, 1989; pianist Downey (Calif.) United Meth. Ch., 1995. Named to Hall of Fame, Am. Coll. Musicians, 1990. Mem.: Am. Coll. Musicians. Republican. Methodist. Avocations: collecting angels, collecting boxes. Home: 12029 Gurley Ave Downey CA 90242

ACHTERMAN, GAIL LOUISE, lawyer; b. Portland, Oreg., Aug. 1, 1949; AB in Econs. with distinction, Stanford U., 1971; MS in Natural Resource Policy and Mgmt., U. Mich., 1975, JD cum laude, 1974. Bar: Oreg. 1974, U.S. Dist. Ct. Oreg. 1978, U.S. Supreme Ct. 1978, U.S. Ct. Appeals (fed. and 10th cirs.). Atty.-advisor U.S. Dept. Interior, 1975-78; asst. for natural resources Gov. Neil Goldschmidt, 1987-91; mem. Stoel Rives LLP, Portland, 1978-2000; dir. Inst. for Natural Resources, Oreg. State U., Corvallis, 2003—. Exec. dir. Deschutes Resources Conservancy, 2000—03; adj. prof. forest policy, Coll. Forestry Oreg. State U., 1991—. Mem. Oreg. Water Resources Commn., 1981-85, Gov.'s Growth Task Force, 1998; mem. pres.'s bd. advisors Oreg. State U., 2000—03, Oreg. Transp. Commn., 2000—. Mem. N.W. Environment Watch (bd. dirs.), Oregon Garden (bd. dirs.), Am. Leadership Forum, Oreg. Women's Forum, Portland C. of C. (bd. dirs. 1996-99). Office: Oreg State U INR Dirs Office 210 Strand Ag Hall Corvallis OR 97331-5712

ACIMAN, CAROLE V., lawyer; b. Cotonou, Rep. of Benin, 1964; Diploma, Maitrise, Université de Paris-Panthéon-Sorbonne, 1986; D.E.S.S., Université de Nanterre-Paris, 1988; LLM, NYU Sch. Law, 1990. Bar: N.Y. 1991, Second Cir., U.S. Dist. Ct., So. and Ea. Dists. N.Y. 1992, U.S. Supreme Ct. 1999. Counsel Hughes Hubbard & Reed LLP, New York. Trade adv. Govt. France; adj. asst. prof E-law Sch. Continuing and Profl. Studies, NYU; dir. Global Nomads Group, Inc.; Dir. Women's eNews; mem. adv. bd. Inst. Law, Sci. and Tech, Seton Hall Sch. Law. Mem. Internat. Adv. Bd. Taking it Global Youth Assn.; dir. Global Youth Action Network, Inc. Recipient Rising Star award, N.Y. County Lawyers' Assn., 1999, Women of the Future award, N.Y. Women's Agenda, 2000. Mem.: ABA (Sci & Tech. Sec. 1988—), Law Alumni Assn, NYU Sch. Law (dir.), Nat. Conf. Women's Bar Assn (dir., pres. 2005). Office: Greenberg Trawig LLP MetLife Bldg 200 Park Ave New York NY 10166 Office Phone: 212-801-9200. Business E-Mail: aciman@gtlaw.com.

ACKER, ANN E., lawyer; b. Chgo., July 21, 1948; BA magna cum laude, St. Mary's Coll., 1970; JD cum laude, Loyola U., 1973. Bar: Ill. 1973. Asst. corp. counsel City of Chgo.; partner Chapman and Cutler, Chgo. Fellow: Am. Bar Found.; mem.: Nat. Assoc. of Bond Lawyers, Chicago Bar Assoc., Amer. Bar Assoc. Office: Chapman and Cutler 111 W Monroe St Ste 1700 Chicago IL 60603-4006 Office Phone: 312-845-3710. Office Fax: 312-701-2361. Business E-Mail: acker@chapman.com.

ACKER, ROSE L., elementary school educator; b. Washington, May 10, 1945; d. Samuel L. and Bessie L. Acker. BA, Howard U., 1970; MA, U. D.C., 1979; EdD, George Washington U., 1994. Coord., instr. U. D.C., Washington; dictaphone transcriber editor NEA of Sch. Adminstrs., Washington; with U.S. Office Personnel Mgmt., Washington; sec.-adminstrv. aide H. Vogel Law Firm; educator D.C. Pub. Schs., Washington; counselor Fairfax County Pub. Sch., Ft. Belvoir Elem. Sch., Va. Recipient Regional Supts. Cert. of Merit, Outstanding Tchr. of Yr. award. Mem. LWV, Internat. Reading Assn., Am. Assn. Counseling and Devel., D.C. Alliance Sch. Educators, Nat. Coun. Negro Women (life), George Washington Alumni Assn., Delta Sigma Theta (life), Pi Lambda Theta, Chi Sigma Iota, Phi Delta Kappa (past pres., del., Bessie Gabbard Disting. award Leadership 2002-2003). Home: 1301 Delaware Ave SW Washington DC 20024-3911

ACKER, VIRGINIA MARGARET, nursing consultant; b. Madison, Wis., Aug. 11, 1946; d. Paul Peter and Lucille (Klein) A. Diploma in nursing, St. Mary's Med. Ctr., Madison, 1972; BSN, Incarnate Word Coll., San Antonio, 1976; MS in Health Professions, S.W. Tex. State U., 1980; postgrad., U. Tex., 1992-93. RN, Tex. Staff nurse St. Mary's Hosp., Milw., 1972-73, Kenosha (Wis.) Meml. Hosp., 1973-74, S.W. Tex. Meth. Hosp., San Antonio, 1974-75, Met. Gen. Hosp., San Antonio, 1975-76; instr. Bapt. Meml. Hosp. Sys. Sch. Nursing, San Antonio, 1976-83; DON, Meml. Hosp., Gonzales, Tex., 1983-84; instr., DON, Victoria Coll., Cuero, Tex., 1984-86; DON, Rocky Knoll Health Care Facility, Plymouth, Wis., 1986-87, Unicare Health Facilities, Milw., 1987-88; coord. nursing edn. St. Nicholas Hosp., Sheboygan, Wis., 1989-90; instr. U. Wis., Oshkosh, 1990-92, St. David's Hosp., Austin, Tex., 1992-95; coord. quality improvement Bailey Square Surgery Ctr., Austin, 1995-98; coord. regulation compliance South Austin Hosp., 1998—2003; program dir. Prevent Inc., 2003—05. Roman Catholic. Avocations: cross stitch, reading, camping, fishing. Home: PO Box 1514 Rockport TX 78351 Personal E-mail: virginia_acker@yahoo.com.

ACKERLY, WENDY SAUNDERS, construction company executive; b. Chgo., July 23, 1960; d. Robert S. Jr. and Linda Ackerly. BS in Atmospheric Sci., U. Calif., Davis, 1982; postgrad., U. Nev., Reno, 1985. Programmer U. Calif, Davis, 1982-83; cons. software Tesco, Sacramento, 1983; software engr. Bently Nev. Corp., Minden, Nev., 1984-85; mgr. computer scis. Jensen Electric Co., Reno, 1985-86, software engr. Cameron Park, Calif., 1986-89; sr. engr. Aerojet, Sacramento, 1989-96, test ops. specialist, 1996-98; dir. design and devel. Kerry King Constrn., Inc., 1998—, sec.-treas., 1991—. Mem. Nat. Space Soc., Planetary Soc., U.S. Tennis Assn., Calif. Aggie Alumni Assn. Republican. Avocations: tennis, hiking, travel, piano. Office: PO Box 269 Rescue CA 95672-0269

ACKERMAN, ARLENE, school system administrator; BA in Elem. Edn., Harris Stowe Tchrs. Coll.; MA in Ednl. Adminstrn. an dpolicy, Washington U.; MA in Edn., Harvard U., EdD in Adminstrn., Planning and Social Policy. Supt. Washington (D.C.) Pub. Schs., 1997—99, San Francisco United Sch. Dist., 1999—. Bd. mem. WestEd Regional Edn. Lab., 2003—; mem. Bay Area Sch. Reform Collaboration; program advisor BROAD-Urban Supts. Acad. Trustee San Francisco Fine Arts; bd. govs. San Francisco Symphony; active San Francisco Workforce Investment Bd. Recipient Apple for the Tchr. award, Iota Lambda Sorority. Disting. Alumni award, Harris Stowe Tchrs. Coll.; McDonnell Douglas fellow. Mem.: ASCD, Presdl. Commn. on Hist. Black Colls. and Univs., Nat. Assn. Black Sch. Educators, Coun. of the Great City Schs. (chair), Am. Assn. Sch. Adminstrs., Phi Delta Kappa. Office: 555 Franklin St San Francisco CA 94102

ACKERMAN, DEBORAH, lawyer; b. Santa Monica, CA, 1950; BA, So. Meth. U., 1972; JD, St. Mary's U., 1979. Ptnr. Oppenheimer, Rosenberg, Kelleher & Wheatley, 1979—87, Cauthorn & Tobin, 1987—88; asst. gen. counsel S.W. Airlines Co., Dallas, 1988—2001, v.p., gen. counsel, asst. sec., 2001—. Mem.: ABA. Office: Southwest Airlines Customer Rels PO Box 36647 1CR Dallas TX 75235-1647 also: Southwest Airlines 2702 Love Field Dr Dallas TX 75346 Office Phone: 214-792-4000. Office Fax: 214-792-5015.

ACKERMAN, DIANE, author, educator; b. Waukegan, Ill., Oct. 7, 1948; d. Sam and Marcia Molly (Tischler) Fink Student, Boston U., 1966-67; BA in English, Pa. State U., 1970; M.F.A., Cornell U., 1976, PhD, 1978. Editorial asst. Library Jour., N.Y.C., 1970; teaching fellow Cornell U., Ithaca, N.Y., 1971-78; asst. prof. U. Pitts., 1980—. Vis. writer-in-residence Coll. William and Mary, Williamsburg, Va., 1982-83, Ohio U., Athens, 1983; writer-in-residence Washington U., St. Louis, 1984—, dir. WRiting Programs, 1982—; vis. writer Columbia U., N.Y.C., 1986, NYU, 1986; mem. lit. panel N.Y. State Council on Arts, 1980—; mem. poetry panel Pa. Arts Council, 1980, Creative Artists Pub. Service Program, 1978; mem. adv. bd. Planetary Soc., 1980—; host (TV series) Mystery of the Senses. Author: (poetry) The Plantes: A Cosmic Pastoral, 1976, 80, Wife of Light, 1978, Lady Faustus, 1983, Jaguar of Sweet Laughter, 1990, I Praise My Destroyer, 1998, Animal Sense, 2003;

(prose memoir) Twilight of the Tenderfoot, 1980; (drama) Reverse Thunder, 1988; (nonfiction) On Extended Wings, 1985, A Natural History of the Senses, 1990, The Moon By Whale Light, and Other Adventures Among Bats, Penguins, Crocadilians and Whales, 1990, A Natural History of Love, 1994, The Rarest of the Rare, 1995, A Slender Thread, 1997, Deep Play, 1999, Cultivating Delight: A Natural History of My Garden, 2001; (children's nonfiction) Monk Seal Hideaway, 1995, Bats: Shadow's in the Nights, 1997; contbr. poetry and prose to various lit. jours. Recipient Black Warrior Rev. Poetry prize, 1981; Abbie Copps Poetry prize, 1974; Pushcart prize, 1983; Peter I.B. Lavan Poetry prize, 1985; CAPS creative writing fellow, 1980; Rockefeller fellow, 1974-75; Nat. Endowment Arts fellow, 1976, 85; Nat. Book Cir. Critics nomination, 1991; Wordsmith award, 1992; Literary Lion award N.Y. Pub. Libr., 1994. Mem. PEN, Author's Guild, Explorer's Club.

ACKERMAN, FELICIA NIMUE, philosophy educator, writer; b. Bklyn., June 23, 1947; d. Arthur and Zelda (Sondack) A. AB summa cum laude, Cornell U., 1968; PhD, U. Mich., 1976. Asst. prof. philosophy Brown U., Providence, 1974-79, assoc. prof., 1979-91, prof., 1991—. Vis. asst. prof. philosophy UCLA, 1976; vis. hon. lectr. logic and metaphysics U. St. Andrews, Scotland, 1983; sr. Fulbright lectr. Hebrew U., 1985. Contbr. articles and short stories to various mags. Recipient O. Henry award for short story pub. in Prize Stories, 1990; fellow Ctr. for Advanced Study in Behavioral Scis., NEH, 1988-89. Mem. ACLU, NAACP (asst. sec. Providence br.), Am. Philos. Assn., Amnesty Internat. Office: Brown U Dept Philosophy PO Box 1918 Providence RI 02912-1918 Office Phone: 401-863-3240. Business E-Mail: felicia_ackerman@brown.edu.

ACKERMAN, HELEN RUTH PENNER, psychologist; b. N.Y.C., Mar. 5, 1939; d. Isaac and Sylvia (Katz) Penner; m. Ross A. Ackerman, 1960; children: Eric, Ruth. B.A., Hofstra U., 1960; M.A., George Washington U., 1962; Ed.D., U. Md., 1967. Lic. psychologist, Fla. Psychiat. technician U. Md. Psychiat. Inst., Balt., 1960; psychology extern Springfield State Hosp., Sykesville, Md., 1961; tchr. Army Edn. Ctr., Bad Kissingen, W. Ger., 1961-63, lectr. U. Md. Schweinfurt Ctr., 1962-63; research psychologist Johns Hopkins U., Balt., 1965; asst. prof. Anne Arundel Community Coll., Arnold Md., 1968; psychologist Balt. County pub. schs., 1966-68, Mills Sch., Fort Lauderdale, Fla., 1968-69; cons. Hosp. Mgmt. and Planning Assocs., Miami, 1968-75; pvt. practice psychology, Ft. Lauderdale, 1975—; Md. psychol. cons. for Md. residents in Fla. institutions, 1979-83; psychol cons. Broward County (Fla.) pub. schs., 1980-83. U. Md. fellow, 1964-65. active numerous Plantation (Fla.) civic orgns., local Jewish community affairs, local sch. support groups. Mem. Am. Psychol. Assn. Contbr. numerous articles to profl. jours. Home: 5921 Almond Ter Fort Lauderdale FL 33317-2501 Office: 1020 SW 40th Ave Plantation FL 33317-4525 Office Phone: 954-791-6373.

ACKERMAN, JOYCE SHOHET, psychologist; b. Boston, Aug. 3, 1950; d. Robert and Jeanne (Prager) Shohet; m. Alan Harvey Ackerman, Dec. 27, 1970; children: Laura, Rachel. BS in Spl. Edn. and Elem. Edn., Boston U., 1971; MS in Edn., Lesley Coll., 1974; EdD in Counseling Psychology, U. No. Colo., 1981. Lic. psychologist, Colo.; cert. elem. tchr.; cert. tchr. grades K-12 emotionally disturbed, learning disabled and retarded. Intern Somerville (Mass.) Mental Health Clinic, 1971; learning disabilities specialist Somerville (Mass.) Pub. Schs., 1972; tchr. emotionally disturbed children Dedham (Mass.) Pub. Schs., 1972-74; edn. specialist, counselor Rough Rock (Ariz.) Demonstration Sch., 1975; chairperson dept. edn. and behavioral scis. Navajo C.C., Tsaile, Ariz., 1975-78; pvt. practice in psychology Greeley, Colo., 1981—. Adj. faculty in edn. and psychology Curry Coll., 1972, U. N.Mex., 1975, Aims C.C., Greeley, 1980-87; psychologist subcontractor Vietnam Vets. Counseling Program VA, 1983-86; provider, coord. mental health svcs. Peak Health Care, Greeley, Colo., 1986-89; cons. psychologist Progressive Care Rehab. Ctr., Greeley, 1986—, Family Recovery Ctr., North Colo. Med. Ctr., Greeley, 1986-89; head injury treatment team North Colo. Med. Ctr., Greeley, 1989-92, others. Bd. mem. Scott Elem. Sch. Adv. Bd., Greeley, 1982-85; mem. Women's Polit. Caucus, Greeley, 1983-87. Mem. APA, Colo. Psychol. Assn. (bd. mem. 1987-90, Pres.'s award 1989), Colo. Women Psychologists. Jewish. Avocations: biking, hiking, piano, reading. Office: 1750 25th Ave Greeley CO 80634-4943

ACKERMAN, VALERIE B., former sports association executive; b. Nov. 7, 1959; m. Charlie Rappaport; children: Emily, Sally. Grad., U. Va., 1981, UCLA Sch. Law, 1985. Assoc. Simpson, Thacher & Bartlett, N.Y.C.; staff atty. NBA, 1988, spl. asst. to commr., 1990-92, dir. bus. affairs, 1992—94, v.p. bus. affairs, 1994—96; pres. WNBA, 1996—2005. Bd. dirs. USA Basketball; exec. com. Naismith Meml. Basketball Hall of Fame. Trustee March of Dimes. Named to, GTE Acad. All-Am. Hall of Fame, 1999, Scholar Athlete Hall Fame, Inst. for Internat. Sport, 2003; recipient Disting. Alumna award, U. Va. Women's Ctr., 1997.

ACKERMANN, BARBARA BOGEL, counselor; b. Bay Shore, NY, Nov. 16, 1940; d. Charles Henry Jurgens and Marjorie (Stevens) Bogel; children: Erika, Stefan. BS in Polit. Sci., Ursinus Coll., 1962; MS in Counseling Edn., L.I. U., 1978, profl. diploma in counseling, 1982, postgrad., 1991. Lic. sch. adminstr., NY. Child protective worker Suffolk County Social Svc., NY, 1962-65; med. social worker St. Joseph's Hosp., Syracuse, NY, 1965-69; child protective worker Tallahassee Social Svc., Fla., 1967-68; RSVP coord. Suffolk County Ret. Sr. Vol. Program, 1975; sch. counselor Hampton Bays HS, NY, 1978-86; guidance dir., counselor Southold HS, NY, 1986—2002; ret. Treas. Human Understanding and Growth Seminars, Laurel, NY, 1987-89, bd. dirs., 1984-90. Alt. committeewoman Southold Town Rep. Com., 1976-83; deacon Presbyn. Ch., Mattituck, NY, 1977—. Named NY State HS Counselor of Yr., 1995, Educator of Yr. Suffolk Times, 2002-. Mem. East End Counselors Assn. (pres. 1982, bd. dirs. 1979—), LI Counselors Ann. Conf. (co-chairperson 1985, 94, 98), NY State Assn. for Counseling and Devel. (v.p. 1983-85, North Atlantic region rep. 1985-87), NY Counseling Assn., Am. Counseling Assn., Nat. Assn. Coll. Admission Counselors, Am. Sch. Counselor Assn., NY State Sch. Counselors Assn. (dist. gov. 1989-92), Southold Rotary (bd. dirs., pres. 2003-, asst. gov. Dist. 7260, 2005-, scholarship chmn., 2005-, Paul Harris fellow), Delta Kappa Gamma. Personal E-mail: back56@aol.com.

ACKERMANN, SUE ANN, mathematics educator; d. Robert and Yvonne Ackermann. BA, Calif. State U., Northridge, 1996. Tchr. Northridge Mid. Sch., 1998—. Contbr. articles to profl. jours. Mem.: NEA, Math. Assn. Am., Assn. Women in Math. Home: 7015 Tampa Ave Reseda CA 91335 Office: Northridge Mid Sch 17960 Chase St Northridge CA 91325 Office Phone: 818-885-8253. Business E-Mail: saa0224@lausd.k12.ca.us.

ACKERSON, BECKY LOUISE, literature and language educator; d. Robert Laurence and Jeanette Edith Ackerson. BA, Flagler Coll., 1996. Cert. tchr., gifted endorsement Fla. English tchr. Bartram Trail HS, Jacksonville, Fla., 1997—2002, Switzerland Point Mid. Sch., Jacksonville, 2002—. Vol. Habitat for Humanity, St. Augustine, 2005. Mem.: ASCD, Nat. Coun. Tchrs. English, Delta Kappa Gamma. Home: 312 Alcazar St Saint Augustine FL 32080 Office: Bartram Trail HS 2050 Roberts Rd Jacksonville FL 32259

ACKERSON, PATRICIA KATHLEEN FREIS, art educator, artist; b. Plainfield, N.J., Sept. 22, 1970; d. Peter Charles and Kathleen Claire Freis; m. Richard Stephen Ackerson, June 15, 1996. BFA in Illustration and Design, Marywood Coll., Scranton, Pa., 1993. Woodshop asst. K & S Marine Woodcraftsmen, Long Branch, NJ, 1988—90; designer / woodcrafter Long Br. Mfg. & Design, Long Branch, NJ, 1992—94; full-time asst. tchr. Metuchen-Edison YMCA, Metuchen, NJ, 1995—98, part-time asst. tchr., 1999—; art tchr. St. Francis Cathedral Sch., Metuchen, 1999—. Calligrapher, Edison, NJ, 1984—; custom-made craft designer, Edison, 1990—; freelance illustrator, Edison, 1990—; calligrapher NJ Polic Benevolent Assn. Contbr. program design St. Francis of Assisi Cathedral bull.; carbothello drawings/paintings, Barron Arts Ctr. Exhbn.; illustrator (calendar cover) St. Francis of Assisi Sch. calendar, calligrapher St. Francis of Assisi. Mem.: Nat. Mus. of Women in the Arts (hon.; mem. 2003—), Nat. Cath. Ednl. Assn. (assoc.; mem. 2003—). Roman Catholic. Avocations: reading, drawing, music, travel. Home: 61 Sixth St Edison NJ 08837 Office: St Francis Cathedral Sch 528 Main St Metuchen NJ 08840 Personal E-mail: pattifa@aol.com.

ACOBA, VALERIE LEE, performing arts educator; d. Thomas Gong and Geraldine Law Lee; m. Benjamin Vallesteros Acoba, Apr. 13, 1937; 1 child, Gwendolyn Acoba Moran. BA, U. of the Pacific, Stockton, Calif. Cert. secondary tchr. Calif. Tchr. drama, chair dept. performing arts Thomas Alva Edison H.S., Stockton, Calif., 1996—; tchr. children's theater Kid's Coll./San Joaquin Delta C.C., Stockton, Calif.; freelance choreographer/dir. Cmty. Theater, Stockton, Calif. Founder, artistic dir. Asian Am. Repertory Theatre, Stockton, Calif. Commr. Stockton Arts Commn., Calif. Recipient Susan B. Anthony award, City of Stockton. Mem.: Filipino Am. Nat. Hist. Soc., Chinese Cultural Soc. of Stockton. Home: 3650 N Merrimac Cir Stockton CA 95219 Office: Thomas Alva Edison HS 1425 S Center St Stockton CA 95206 Office Phone: 209-933-7425.

ACRA, REEM, apparel designer; b. Lebanon; Studied, Esmode Sch. of Design, Paris; grad., Fashion Inst. of Tech., NYC. Designer, owner Reem Acra Collection, NYC, 1995—, launched eveningwear collection, 2000. Work featured in InStyle, Town & Country, Vogue, Women's Wear Daily. Office: Reem Acra 16 E 34th St New York NY 10016 also: Reem Acra Salon 245 7th Ave New York NY 10016*

ACREE, WILMA KATHERYN, retired secondary school educator; b. Ripley, W.Va., July 16, 1942; d. Mote Jackson and Emma Roseanne (McHenry) Stanley; m. Frank H. Acree Sr., Sept. 26, 1975 (dec. Oct. 1990). BA in Edn., Glenville State Coll., 1965; MA in Edn., W.Va. U., 1971. Tchr. English Wood County Schs., Parkersburg, W.Va., 1965-97, ret., 1997. Adj. faculty mem. W.Va. U., Parkersburg, 1999—; presenter workshop W.Va. Writers' Conf., Ripley, 1995, 96. Author: About Bee Robbing and Other Things, 1995, Wilma Acree: Greatest Hits 1985-2000, 2001; contbr. poems in lit. publs.; editor children's poetry Gambit Lit. Mag., Parkersburg, W.Va., 1986. Citizen rep. Jackson Jr. H.S. Local Sch. Improvement Assn., Vienna, W.Va., 1997-2000; advisor Jackson Jr. H.S. Writers' Club, 1995-99; mem. adv. bd. Confluence lit. mag., Marietta (Ohio) Coll., 1996—, editor, 2000—. Mem. W.Va. Writers, Inc. (pres. 1997-99, 3rd pl. narrative poetry 1991), Ohio Valley Lit. Group (exec. dir. 1993—), Wood County Ret. Tchrs. Assn. Avocations: writing, reading, walking, dogs, computers. Home: 1024 28th St Vienna WV 26105-1475 Personal E-mail: wilmaacree@charter.net.

ACRES, JO DEVINE, literature and language educator; b. LA, Calif., Oct. 17, 1954; d. Charles Joseph and S. Ruth Devine; m. Gregory Ives Acres, July 29, 2000; children from previous marriage: Bradley B., Mason F. BLA in Comms., U. Alaska SE, Juneau, 1983; MA in English, U. Wash., Seattle, 1988; postgrad., Middlebury Coll., Vt., 1997—. Asst. prof. English Maui CC, Hawaii, 1989—90; assoc. prof. English U. Alaska SE, 1990—, chair humanities, 2005—. Office: U Alaska SE Humanities Dept 11120 Glacier Hwy Juneau AK 99801-8699

ACTON, ELIZABETH S., corporate financial executive; b. 1952; V.p. multinational banking group Continental Bank, Chgo.; exec. v.p. fin., CFO Ford Motor Credit Co., Dearborn, Mich.; v.p., treas. Ford Motor Co., Dearborn, Mich., 2000—02; exec. v.p., CFO Comerica Inc., Detroit, 2002—. Office: Comerica Tower at Detroit Ctr MC 3391 500 Woodward Ave Detroit MI 48226

ADA, ALMA FLOR, education educator, writer; b. Camagüey, Cuba, Jan. 3, 1938; came to U.S., 1970; d. Modesto Arturo Ada and Alma Lafuente; children: Rosalma, Alfonso, Miguel, Gabriel Zubizarreta. Diploma in Spanish studies, U. Complutence, Madrid, 1960; B of Humanities, U. Cath., Lima, Peru, 1963, PhD, 1965. Assoc. prof. Emory U., Atlanta, 1970-72; prof. Mercy Coll. Detroit, 1972-75; prof. Sch. Edn. U. San Francisco, 1976—2004, prof. emeritus, 2004—. Author: The Gold Coin (Christopher award 1991), My Name is María Isabel, 1993, The Unicorn of the West, 1994, Dear Peter Rabbit, 1994, Where the Flametrees Bloom, 1995, Gathering the Sun, 1997, Under the Royal Palms, 1998 (Pura Belpré award 2000), The Lizard and the Sun, 1997, The Malachite Palace, 1998, Yours Truly, Goldilocks, 2002, Three Golden Oranges, 1999, Friend Frog, 2000, With Love, Little Red Hen, 2003, I Love Saturdays.y domingos, 2003, Daniel's Mystery Egg, 2004, A pesar del amor, 2003, A Magical Encounter: Latino Children's Literature in the Classroom, 2003; co-author: Gateways to the Sun, 2001-03, Pio Peep: Spanish Nursery Rhymes, 2004, Mamá Goose: A Treasury of Nursery Rhymes in Spanish and English, 2005, Authors in the Classroom. A Transformative Education Experience, 2003, Tales Our Abuelitas Told, 2006, Celebrate Mardi Gras, 2006, Celebrate 4th of July, 2006, Alma For Ada and You, 2005, Stories Our Abuelitas Told, 2006. Recipient Ann. award L.A. Bilingual Dirs. Assn., 1993, Calif. State PTA Assn., Simon Weisenthal Mus. of Tolerance award, 1998, Gold medal Parenting Mag., 1998, Purá Belpré, 2000; scholar Radcliffe Inst. Harvard U., 1965-67; Fulbright scholar, 1966-68. Mem. Internat. Bd. Books for Young People, Nat. Assn. for Bilingual Edn., Calif. Assn. for Bilingual Edn. Office: U San Francisco Ignatian Heights San Francisco CA 94117 Office Phone: 415-383-8047. Personal E-mail: almaflorada@yahoo.com.

ADAIR, ELEANOR REED, environmental biologist; b. Arlington, Mass., Nov. 28, 1926; d. Kenneth Clarke and Margaret Reed; m. Robert Kemp Adair, June 21, 1952; children: Douglas, Margaret, James(dec.). BA, Mt. Holyoke Coll., 1948; MA, U. Wis., 1951, PhD, 1955. From rsch. asst. to lectr., sr. scientist Yale U., New Haven, 1960—. From asst. fellow to fellow John B. Pierce Lab., New Haven, 1966—96; cons. sci. adv. bd. EPA, 1983—89; sr. scientist Electromagnetic Radiation Effects, Air Force Rsch. Lab., Brooks AFB, Tex., 1996—2001, sr. scientist emeritus, 2001—. Editor: Microwaves & Thermoregulation, 1983; contbr. articles to profl. jours. Bd. dirs. Am. Himalayan Found., 1990—. Fellow: IEEE, APA, AAAS, N.Y. Acad. Scis., Am. Inst. Med. and Biol. Engring.; mem.: Bioelectromagnetics Soc. Avocations: birdwatching, gardening, Buddhism. Home: 50 Deepwood Dr Hamden CT 06517

ADAIR, IRMALEE TRAYLOR, social worker; b. Portsmouth, Ohio, Jan. 5, 1920; d. Finley Arving and Lora Alice (Nickell) Traylor; m. James Russell Adair; children: Jacqueline, Robert, Celeste, Marquita. AA in Social Work, Chipola Jr. Coll., 1980; BA in Social Work, U. West Fla., 1983; MSW, Fla. State U., 1985. Cert. gerontologist, community info. counselor. Sr. aide Guardian Office ESSH, Trevose, Pa.; interviewer, subcontractor Nat. Analysts, Phila.; social worker Hill House Manor, Bensalem, Pa.; ret. Mem. NASW, Fla. State U. Alumni Assn., U. West. Fla. Alumni Assn., Am. Assn. Retired Persons. Home: 2851 S Valley View 1060 Las Vegas NV 89102

ADAIR, MARY ROBERTS, special education educator; b. Johnstown, Pa., May 27, 1933; d. William Alexander and Catharine (Roberts) A. BA, Wellesley Coll., 1955; MEd, Pa. State U., 1961, PhD, 1966. Cert. elem. tchr., spl. edn. tchr., sch. psychologist. Elem. tchr. Ligonier (Pa.) Valley Schs., 1956-60; spl. edn. tchr. Westmoreland County schs., Greensburg, Pa., 1960-63; instr., asst. prof. Pa. State U., State Coll., Pa., 1965-70; pre-sch. dir. Ctr. County Assn. for Retarded Citizens, State Coll., 1968-70; asst. prof. Rutgers U., New Brunswick, NY, 1970-73; assoc. prof. to prof. spl. edn. Slippery Rock (Pa.) U., 1975—; prof. Edn. emerita, 1995. Psychologist Slippery Rock area schs., 1981-86. Contbr. articles to profl. publs. Prin. investigator U.S. Dept. Edn. Grant, 1986, 1989; team leader Right Whale Survey of Assoc. Scientists of Woods Hol Marineland, Fla. U.S. Dept. Edn. fellow, 1963-65. Avocations: travel, photography, hiking, digital imaging. Home: 16 Countryside Ln Lititz PA 17543-9579

ADAM, JUSTINE E., psychologist; b. Queens, NY, Apr. 14, 1961; d. Henry John Adam and Della May; m. Dominic John Altieri; 1 child, Christopher John Adam Altieri. BA, St. John's U., 1983; MA, NYU, 1986; MS in Edn., Pace U., 1990, D Psychology, 1992. Lic. psychologist N.Y. Staff therapist, intern Pederson Kegg, Huntington, NY, 1991—93; psychologist North Suffolk Mental Health Ctr., Smithtown, 1993—98, New Hope Guild (Steinway Child & Family Ctr), 1992—2003, pvt. practice, N.Y., 1991—. Contbr. scientific papers. Vol. Nassau County Psychol. Inst., Nassau County, 2004. Mem.: EMDIRA, APA, Nassau County Psychol. Assn. Avocations: bicycling, needlepoint, photography.

ADAMAK, M. JEANELLE, broadcast executive; b. Odessa, Tex., Aug. 18, 1952; d. E.W. and Jo Martin; m. Russell J. Adamak, July 19, 1973; children: Aaron, Ashley. BS in Mgmt./Telecom., Ind. Wesleyan U., 1995. Dir. devel. Odessa Coll., 1986-90; exec. v.p. WFYI TelePlex, Indpls., 1990—. Chair Exec. Women's Leadership Program, Indpls., 1994-96, Vol. Action Ctr. Com., Indpls., 1996—. Mem. Vol. Action Ctr., United Way, 1996-98; bd. dirs. YWCA, Indpls., 1995-99, Cmty. Svc. Coun.-United Way, Indpls., 1996—, Prevent Blindness, Ind., 1996-2000. Recipient Devel. award So. Ednl. Comm. Assn., 1988. Office: WFYI TelePlex 1401 N Meridian St Indianapolis IN 46202-2304 E-mail: jadamak@wfyi.org.

ADAMIEC, JEAN KRAUS, retired advertising executive; b. NYC; d. Henry Fred and Florence (Dulfer) Kraus; m. Robert John Adamiec, July 23, 1966 (dec. 2001); 1 child, Tracy Christine. BA, Syracuse U., NY; AS, Del. Co. CC, Media, Pa., 1987. Shopping editor, "What's New" editor Outdoor Life Mag., NYC, 1955—58; merchandising mgr. Field & Stream Mag., NYC, 1958—61; advt. promotions mgr. Internat. Sci. and Tech. Mag., NYC, 1961—63; merchandising mgr. True Mag., NYC, 1963—66; tchr. Taipei Am. Sch., Taiwan, 1966—68; tax preparer, cons. Paperworkers Union, Phila., 1995—97; estates executrix, fin. adminstr. Wallingford, Pa., 2001—. Mem.: Syracuse U. Alumni Assn., Newcomers & Neighbors, Phi Mu Alumnae Assn. Presbyterian. Avocations: travel, theater, investing, animal welfare. Home: 106 Brent Dr Wallingford PA 19086 Office Phone: 610-876-2962. Business E-Mail: jadamiec@usadatanet.net.

ADAMS, ALICE, sculptor; b. NYC, Nov. 16, 1930; d. Charles P. and Loretto G. (Tobin) Adams; m. William D. Gordy, Feb. 7, 1969; 1 child, Katherine Adams Gordy. Student, Adelphi Coll., 1948—50; BFA, Columbia U., 1953; postgrad. (French Govt. fellow), 1953—54; postgrad. Fulbright Travel grantee, L'Ecole Nat d'Art Decoratif, Aubusson, France, 1953—54. Lectr. Manhattanville Coll., Purchase, NY, 1960—79; instr. sculpture Sch. Visual Arts, 1980—87. One-woman shows include Hall Bromm Gallery, NYC, 1979, 1980, Lehman Coll. Gallery, 2000—01, exhibited in group shows at Whitney Mus. Am. Art, 1971, 1973, Indpls. Mus. Art, 1974, Nassau County Mus. Fine Arts, Roslyn, NY, 1977, Wave Hill, Riverdale, NY, 1979, Mus. Modern Art, NYC, 1984, Represented in permanent collections Weatherspoon Gallery U. NC, Greensboro, U. Nebr., Everson Mus., Syracuse, NY, Haags Gemetemuseum, The Hague, Netherlands, Am. Crafts Mus., NYC, Edwin I. Ulrich Mus., Wichita, prin. works include Bot. Garden, Toledo, Port Authority NY and NJ, Thomas Jefferson U., Phila., NYC Bd. Edn., State of Conn., Denver Internat. Airport, NYC Met. Transp. Authority, U. Tex., San Antonio, Broward County, Fla., U. Del., Newark, Montclair State U., Station NJ Transit, Vets. Meml. Home, Vineland, NJ; mem. design team Seattle Transit Project, St. Louis Metro-Link Project, Midland Metro, Brimingham, Eng., Charlotte Area Transit Sys., NC, 2003—05. Creative Artists Pub. Svc. grantee, 1973—74, 1976—77, Nat. Endowment Arts Artists grantee, 1978—79, AM. Acad. Arts and Letters grantee, 1984, Richard Florsheim grantee, 1999, Guggenheim fellow, 1981—82, Rockefeller Found. resident, Bellagio, Italy, 2002. Home: 3370 Fort Independence St Bronx NY 10463-4502 Office Phone: 718-543-4658.

ADAMS, AMANDA KELLEY, mathematics educator; b. Birmingham, Ala., June 19, 1975; d. John Roberson and Gwen Gibson Kelley; m. Michael Roy Adams, June 8, 1996. BS, Birmingham So. Coll., 1998. Math. tchr. Jefferson County Bd. Edn., Birmingham, 1998—. Mem. AEGIS Women's Club, Gardendale, Ala., 2005. Named Tchr. of Yr., Wal-Mart, North Jefferson County, 2005. Mem.: Nat. Coun. Tchrs. of Math., Zeta Tau Alpha. R-Consevative. Baptist. Office: Gardendale High Sch 850 Mt Olive Rd Gardendale AL 35071 Office Phone: 205-379-3600. Office Fax: 205-379-3645. Personal E-mail: mathmandi@yahoo.com. E-mail: aadams@jefcoed.com.

ADAMS, AMY (AMANDA JESSICA ADAMS), actress; b. Vicenza, Italy, Aug. 20, 1975; Actress (films) Drop Dead Gorgeous, 1999, Psycho Beach Party, 2000, The Chromium Hook, 2000, Cruel Intentions 2, 2000, The Slaughter Rule, 2002, Pumpkin, 2002, Serving Sara, 2002, Catch Me If You Can, 2002, The Last Run, 2004, Junebug, 2005 (Critics Choice award, best supporting actress, Broadcast Film Critic Assn., 2006, Nat. Soc. Film Critic award, best supporting actress, 2006, Best Supporting Female, Independent Spirit awards, 2006), Standing Still, 2005, The Wedding Date, 2005, Moonlight Serenade, 2006, Talladega Nights: The Ballad of Ricky Bobby, 2006, (TV series) Dr. Vegas, 2004—05.*

ADAMS, BARBARA, language educator, poet, writer; b. NYC, Mar. 23, 1932; d. David S. Block and Helen (Taxter) Block Tyler; m. Elwood Adams, June 6, 1952; (dec. 1993); children: Steven, Amy, Anne, Samuel. BS, SUNY, New Paltz, 1962, MA, 1970; PhD, NYU, 1981. Prof. English Pace U., N.Y.C., 1984—2000, dir. bus. comm., 1984—2001. Poet in residence Cape Cod Writers' Conf., 1988. Author: Double Solitaire, 1982, The Enemy Self: The Poetry & Criticism of Laura Riding, 1990, Hapax Legomena, 1990, Negative Capability, 1999 (1st Prize for Fiction); (poetry) The Ordinary Living, 2004; (play) God's Lioness and the Crow: Sylvia Plath and Ted Hughes, 2000; author numerous poems; contbr. articles to profl. jours. Recipient 1st prize for poetry NYU and Acad. Am. Poets, 1975, 1st prize for fiction Negative Capability contest, 1999; Penfield fellow NYU, 1977. Mem. PEN, Poetry Soc. Am., Poets and Writers. Home: 59 Coach Ln Newburgh NY 12550-3818

ADAMS, BARBARA, lawyer; b. Hutchinson, Kans., Nov. 17, 1951; d. Robert Thomas and MaryJane (Lewis) Adams; m. John B. Rosenthal, Apr. 22, 1983 (div. 1986); children: Anna Adams-Sarthou, Kari Torp, Sian Torp. BA, Smith Coll., 1973; JD, Temple U., 1978. Bar: Pa. 1978, US Dist. Ct. Ea. Dist. Pa. 1978, US Ct. Appeals 3rd Cir. 1978. Rsch. ofcl. Schuylkill County Office Tech. Assistance, Pottsville, Pa., 1974-75; mgr. First Valley Bank, Bethlehem, Pa., 1975-77; clk. Duane Morris LLP, Phila., 1977—78, assoc., 1978—85, ptnr., 1986—2005, chair firm fin. practice group; gen. counsel for Commonwealth of Pa., 2005—. Co-author booklet: Business Political Action in Pennsylvania, 1977; editor PABL Update newsletter, 1991-92. Coord. housing task force Rendell Transition Team, Phila., 1991-92; policy com. co-chair of housing Gov.-elect Rendell Transition Team, 2002; commr. Ind. Charter Commn. of City of Phila., 1992—94, Phila. Gas Commn., 1995-98; bd. mem. & sec. Phila. Neighborhood Enterprise, 1989-93; treas. Reading Terminal Market Corp., 1994-2001, bd. mem., 1997-2001; co-founder Pa. Energy Buyers Forum, 1997-, mem. mgmt. com., sec./treas.; bd. mem. Phila. Assn. Cmty. Devel. Corporations, 1998-, People's Emergency Ctr., 2003-. Mem. ABA (sect. pub. utility; charter mem. forum on affordable housing and cmty. devel. law), Pa. Bar Assn., Phila. Bar Assn. (bus. law sect.), Nat. Assn. Bond Lawyers, Pa. Assn. Bond Lawyers (bd. dirs. 1991-97). Avocations: interior decorating, travel, violin, yoga. Office: Office Gen Counsel 225 Main Capitol Harrisburg PA 17120

ADAMS, BETSY ANNE, principal; b. Phoenixville, Pa., Feb. 19, 1952; d. Garnet O. and Vera Warner Adams. BS, Lehigh U., 1973, MEd, 1978; EdD, U. Pa., 1990. Math tchr. Palisades HS, Kintnersville, Pa., 1973—81, asst. prin., 1981—83; asst prin. Plymouth Whitemarsh HS, Plymouth Meeting, Pa., 1983—85; prin. Tamaqua (Pa.) HS, 1985—93, Conrad Weiser HS, Robesonia, Pa., 1993—. Pres. Berks County Interscholastic Athletic Assn. Named HS Prin. of Yr. for Pa., 2001; named to Athletic Hall of Fame, Conrad Weiser HS.

ADAMS, BETTY SUE, mathematics educator; b. Kosciusko, Miss., Sept. 19, 1948; d. Zelma M. Worrell; m. Joe A. Adams, June 23, 1967; children: Susan Shirley, Jeffrey Mark. Cert. in Secretarial Tng., Holmes C.C., Goodman, Miss., 1967; BS, Miss. State U., Starkville, 1980, MEd, 1985. Sec.

Holmes C.C., Goodman, Miss., 1972—77; math. tchr. Kosciusko City Schs., Miss., 1980—85; math. instr. Holmes C.C., Ridgeland, Miss., 1985—. Adv. Phi Theta Kappa Holmes C.C., 1986—. Named Robert Giles Disting. Advisor, Phi Theta Kappa Internat. Honor Soc., 1995, Bennie Warren Outstanding Advisor, Miss./La. Region of Phi Theta Kappa, 1998; recipient Continued Excellence for Advisors, Phi Theta Kappa Internat. Honor Soc., 1996, 2001, Del. to N.I.S.O.D., Holmes C.C., 1992, H.E.A.D.W.A.E. award for Outstanding Faculty Mem., 1997, Coll. Yearbook Dedication, 2005—06. Mem.: Assn. Phi Theta Kappa Advisors, Miss. Collegiate Math. Assn. Home: 224 Timbermill Dr Madison MS 39110 Office: Holmes Community Coll 412 W Ridgeland Ave Ridgeland MS 39157 Office Phone: 601-605-3316. Business E-Mail: badams@holmescc.edu.

ADAMS, BRIANA ELIZABETH, elementary school educator; b. Huntington, W.Va., Sept. 26, 1977; d. Donald Edward and Diane Sue Caudill; m. Jody Adams, June 7, 2003. B of Elem. Edn., Morehead State U., 2000, M, 2006. Tchr. 4th grade Prichard Elem. Sch., Grayson, Ky., 2000—. Mem. Ky. Scoring Accuracy & Assurance Team, 2002—. Recipient Leadership award, Nat. Coun. Tchrs. English/Lang. Arts, 2003—04. Mem.: Ky. Edn. Assn. Home: 115 1/2 E 2nd St Grayson KY 41143 Office: Prichard Elem Sch 401 E Main St Grayson KY 41143

ADAMS, CAROL H., dean; d. Wilfred L. and Sadie Dean Hoskins; m. John W. Adams, Apr. 10, 1966; children: Craig J., Dina R. BA in Edn., Mich. State U., 1965; MS in Edn., CUNY, Queens, 1975. Tchr. K-6 N.Y.C. Bd. Edn., 1965—72; tech. cons. Green Leigh Assocs., N.Y.C., 1972—74; instr. tchr. edn. York Coll. CUNY, Jamaica, 1974—75; instr. SUNY Brockport, Rochester, 1975—77; prof. devel. edn. Monroe C.C., Rochester, 1977—91, acad. dean, 1991—. Cons. Greenleigh Assn., N.Y.C., 1972—74; cons. tchr. edn. Corning C.C., NY, 2003. Bd. dirs. YWCA, Rochester, 1989—; mem. steering com. AALDP United Way, Rochester, 1992—93; mem. adv. bd. youth/family project U. Rochester, 2000. Recipient Women's History award, Rochester City Sch. Dist., 1997, Chancellor's award for excellence, SUNY, 2000. Mem.: AAUW, Nat. Inst. Leadership Devel., Am. Assn. Women in Cmty. and Jr. Colls., Nat. Assn. Devel. Edn., The Links (v.p. 2002), Leaders League for Innovation, Phi Delta Kappa. Home: 106 Elmore Rd Rochester NY 14618 Office: Monroe Community Coll 1000 E Henrietta Rd Rochester NY 14623

ADAMS, CHERYL, newscaster; Grad., Marquette U. Coll. Journalism. Creator weekly news setment The Parent Place Sta. WXIN-TV, Indpls., anchor, 1994—. Nominee Emmy awards (5); recipient Outstanding Journalist award, Luth. Child and Family Svcs.; fellow, Casey Journalism Ctr. Children and Families, U. Md., 1997. Mem.: Indpls. Assn. Black Journalists.

ADAMS, CHERYL PALONIS, secondary school educator, dancer, choreographer; b. Detroit, Sept. 13, 1950; m. John Dobree Adams, Nov. 9, 1980; children: Jessica Miller, Cate Palonis. BA, Wayne State U., Detroit, 1973; MFA, U. Utah, Salt Lake City, 1976. Cert. movement analyst Md. Dance/advanced placement English tchr. Calvert HS, Prince Frederick, Md., 2000—. Choreographer/dancer So. Md. Modern Dance Collective, Mechanicsville, Md., 2004—; bd. dirs. Nat. Dance Edn. Orgn., Capitol Region Ednl. Dance Orgn. Avocations: travel, gardening, swimming, reading. Home: 10550 Old Mill Rd Lusby MD 20657 Office: Calvert HS 600 Dares Beach Rd Prince Frederick MD 20678 Office Phone: 410-535-7330. Personal E-mail: cpadams1@comcast.net.

ADAMS, CINDY, journalist; b. NYC, Apr. 24; d. Harry and Jessica (Sugar); m. Joey Adams, Feb. 14, 1952 (dec. Dec. 2, 1999). News commentator Sta. WABC-TV, N.Y.C., 1967-70; interviewer NBC-TV, 1970-73; dir., asst. to pres. Miss Universe, Inc., N.Y.C., 1970-77, Good Morning Am., 1996—98; columnist N.Y. Post, N.Y.C., 1981—. Interviewer of celebrities for Fox-TV's "A Current Affair", 1986-91, Lifetime Cable, 1991—; commentator fashion show Bonds for Israel, N.Y., 1970-85; lectr. Keedick Lectr. Service, N.Y., 1970-80. Author: Sukarno of Indonesia, 1965, Lee Strasberg: The Imperfect Genius of the Actor's Studio, 1980, Jolie Gabor, 1978, The Gift of Jazzy, 2003, Living a Dog's Life: Jazzy, Juicy and Me, 2005; co-author (with Susan Crimp): Iron Rose: The Story of Rose Fitzgerald Kennedy and Her Dynasty, 1995; contbr. articles to mags.; designer jewelry Cartier, N.Y. 1971. Avocation: travel. Office: NY Post 1211 Avenue Of The Americas New York NY 10036-8790*

ADAMS, CLARA I., academic administrator; BSc in Chemistry, Morgan State Coll., 1954; MSc in Chemistry, Iowa State Coll., 1957; PhD in Chemistry, U. Mass., 1970. Chemist Nat. Heart Inst. NIH, Bethesda, Md., 1957—59; asst. prof. chemistry Morgan State U., Balt., 1959—68, assoc. prof. chemistry, 1968—73, prof., chmn. chemistry dept., 1973—75, dean Sch. Grad. Studies, 1975—85, acting v.p. acad. affairs, 1985—86, v.p. acad. affairs, 1986—; tchg. fellow Smith Coll., Northampton, Mass., 1963—65. Mem. com. on minority grad. edn. Coun. Grad. Schs. in the U.S., regional rep. on bd. dirs., 1983—84, 1986—88; mem.-at-large exec. com. Northea. Assn. Grad. Schs., 1977—79, pres., 1979—81; mem. Accreditation Bd. Engring. and Tech. Mem. Md. State Legis./Univ. Coun. on Provision of Acad. Svcs. to Gen. Assembly, 1977—80; bd. dirs. Nat. Aquarium in Balt., 1977—82, v.p. bd. dirs., 1979—82. Named one of 100 Women Who Influence Balt., Balt. Mag., 1983; recipient Disting. Alumnus award, Morgan State U., 1976. Mem.: AAUP, AAAS, Mid. States Assn. Schs. and Colls., Commn. Higher Edn., Am. Assn. State Colls. and Univs., Am. Chem. Soc. Office: Morgan State U VP Acad Affairs 300 Truth Hall Baltimore MD 21251

ADAMS, CLARA WEBB, secondary school educator; b. Fort Knox, Ky., Aug. 11, 1965; d. Wesdie Lee and Jeanette Phelps Webb. BA, Western Ky. U., Bowling Green, 1988; MA in Edn., Western Ky. U., 1998. Cert. tchr. secondary edn. Ky., 1988. Spanish tchr. Reitz Meml. H.S., Evansville, Ind., 1988—90; tchr. Muhlenberg County Bd. of Edn., Powderly, Ky., 1990—. Cheerleader coach Muhlenberg South Mid. Sch., Greenville, Ky., 2005—, Muhlenberg North Mid. Sch., 1991—2004. Mem.: NEA (assoc.), Order Ea. Star (worthy matron 2005—06). Southern Baptist. Avocations: special effects makeup, cross stitch, singing, travel, movies. Home: 307 N Third St Apt #2 Central City KY 42330 Office: Muhlenberg North Middle School 1000 N Main St Greenville KY 42345 Office Phone: 270-338-3550. Office Fax: 270-338-2911. Personal E-mail: clara.adams@muhlenberg.kyschools.us.

ADAMS, CONSTANCE EWING, school psychologist, art therapist; b. Troy, N.Y., Oct. 15, 1946; d. Walter Duncan and Gabrielle Roberts (Solomon) Ewing; m. Robert Maurice Adams, Aug. 23, 1969; children: Karen Gayle, Louise Katherine, Robert Ewing. BA, Denison U., 1968; MA, Ft. Hays (Kans.) State U., 1977; MS, Ea. Ky. U., 1988; EdD, U. Ky., 1999. Cert. art therapist, sch. psychologist, Ky. Counselor High Plains Comprehensive Cmty. Mental Health Ctr., Hays, 1970-72, art therapist, 1974-75; instr. Ft. Hays State U., 1974-79; sch. psychologist Madison County Schs., Richmond, Ky., 1987—2002, dir. psychol. svcs., 2002—. Presenter in field; mem. adv. bd. Richmond Youth Svcs. Ctr., 1994—; mem.-at-large Sch. Psychology Coun., Ky. Dept. Edn., Frankfort, 1993-98; chmn. adv. coun. Clark Moores Youth Svcs. Ctr., 2001—. Paintings exhibited in one-woman show, other invitational and juried exhbns., 1975-79. Mem. Kans. Gov.'s Commn. on Criminal Adminstrn., Hays, 1975; chair, pers. dir. Friendship Home, Youth Care, Inc., Kans., 1970-77; responder Ky. Cmty. Crisis Respnse Team, 1993-. Mem. LWV (pres., bd. dirs. Hays chpt. 1970-79, bd. dirs., bull. editor, 2d v.p. Madison County chpt. 1980—), Nat. Assn. Sch. Psychologists (cert., Govtl. and Profl. Rels. award 1996), Am. Art Therapy Assn. (registered), Ky. Assn. for Psychology in Schs. (exec. coun. 1990—, program chair 1990-91, legis. chair 1991—, Ky. Sch. Psychologist of Yr. 1991), Ky. Assn. Sch. Adminstrs. Home: 390 Adams Ln Richmond KY 40475-8763 Office: Madison County Schs 707 N 2nd St Richmond KY 40475-1259

ADAMS, DIANE LORETTA, physician; b. St. Louis, Nov. 3, 1948; m. William McKinley Adams; children: Kareem McKinley, Dawn Caron, Akeem Michael. BS, Howard U., 1969; MD, N.J. Med. Sch., 1976; MPH, Johns Hopkins U., 1980, resident in gen. preventive medicine, 1980. Resident in family practice Howard U. Hosp., Washington, 1976-79; chief med. officer USCG Shipyard, Curtis Bay, Md., 1980-83, Bur. Engraving and Printing, Washington, 1983-85; med. officer St. Elizabeth Hosp., Washington, 1985-86; rsch. analyst Office Asst. Sec. Health, Rockville, Md., 1987-90; chief minority health svcs. rsch. program Agy. Health Care Policy and Rsch., Rockville, 1990-93; congl. fellow office of Congressman Louis Stokes U.S. Ho. of Reps., Washington, 1990; sr. med. adv. Agy. Health Care Policy and Rsch., Rockville, 1993-99, Agy. Healthcare Rsch. and Quality, Dept. Health/Human Svcs., 1999-2000, cons., 2000—; clin. assoc. prof. dept. phys. therapy U. Md., 1993—2000; dir. health policy, rsch. and profl. med. affairs Nat. Med. Assn., 2001—02. Cons. rep. AIDS Task Force, 1987-93; lectr. intensive bioethics Georgetown U. Kennedy Inst. Ethics, 1991; sr. health policy fellow, Ga. Ctr. Advanced Telecommns. Tech. Editor: Health Issues for Women of Color: A Cultural Diversity Perspective, 1995. Named to, Md. Women's Hall of Fame, 1997, Black Coll. Alumni Hall of Fame in Medicine, 2001, Women of Achievement in Md. History, 2002; recipient Adminstrs. Outstanding Cmty. Svc. award, Agy. Health Care Policy and Rsch., 1996. Mem.: APHA, Am. Coll. Preventive Medicine, Alpha Kappa Alpha (mem. internat. program com. 1998—2002, Outstanding Comt. Svc. award 1981—85). Avocation: equitation. Home: 17032 Barn Ridge Dr Silver Spring MD 20906-1106

ADAMS, DIEDRE SHOOK, science educator; b. Walterboro, SC, Apr. 14, 1954; d. Charles Davis and Marjorie H. Shook; m. Thomas McDaniel Adams, Dec. 22, 1989; children: Kyle Robert Gahagan, Shannon Kathleen Gahagan. BS, Coll. Charleston, 1976; MEd, Armstrong Atlantic, 1985. Cert. Math, Physics, Gen. Sci. Tchr. Ind. Tchr. Colleton County Schs., Walterboro, 1975—79, U.S. Army, Germany, 1979—84, Savannah-Chatham Schs., Ga., 1984—90, Dekalb County Schs., Atlanta, 1990—99, Vigo County Schs., Terre Haute, Ind., 1999—. Reviewer Holt Rhinehart Winston, 2004—05, Glenco, 2004—05, Rose Hulman Inst. Tech., Terre Haute, 2004—. Named Star Rising Tchr., Ga., 1998-1999; recipient Disting. Tchr. Del. award, Internat. Physics Soc., 1999, Guest Stephen Hawking Lecture award, 1999, Tchr. Excellence award, Vigo County, 2001-2002; Tchg. grant, 2001, 2002, 2003, 2004. Mem.: NEA, ISTA, VCTA (rep. 2003—05), ISMTA, MENSA. Luth. Avocations: hiking, camping, travel. Home: 60 S 24th St Terre Haute IN 47803 Office: W Vigo Mid Sch 4750 W Sarah Meyers Dr West Terre Haute IN 47885 Office Phone: 812-462-4361. Business E-Mail: dsa@vigoschools.net.

ADAMS, ELEANOR JUNE, medical/surgical nurse; b. N.Y.C., June 16, 1930; d. Joseph and Sophie (Zalenski) Bachmaier; children: Mary Ellen Hodapp, Mary Beth Young, Eileen Judge Meneley. BA, Coll. of White Plains, N.Y., 1952; AAS, Nassau Community Coll., Garden City, N.Y., 1967; BSN, SUNY, Stony Brook, 1972; postgrad., U. Ariz. RN. Asst. dir. nursing Kotzebue (Alaska) Dept. Pub. Health, 1984-85, Parker (Ariz.) Dept. Pub. Health, 1984-85; nurse med. ICU and cardiology dept. VA Med. Ctr., Sepulveda, Calif., 1986; oncology nurse Balboa Hosp., San Diego, 1986-87; evening charge nurse VA Med. Ctr., Tucson, 1987-97; RN, case mgr. Hospice of Valley, Phoenix, 1997—. Recipient Legend award, March of Dimes, 2005. Mem. Sigma Theta Tau Internat. Honor Soc. Nursing.

ADAMS, ELIZABETH HERRINGTON, banker; b. Tulsa, May 25, 1947; d. James Dillon and Helen (Allderdice) Herrington; m. Phillip Hollis Hackney, Mar. 5, 1977 (dec. Jan. 1990); m. Keith R. Adams, Sept. 4, 1993. Student, No. Ariz. U., 1965-67, 68-69. With Coldwater (Kans.) Nat. Bank, summers 1964-67, The Ariz. Bank, Phoenix, 1969, Flagstaff, 1970-71; asst. cashier The Wilmore (Kans.) State Bank, 1972—2001, The Coldwater Nat. Bank, 1974-83, cashier, ops. officer, 1984—; v.p. The Coldwater (Kans.) Nat. Bank, 1998—2002, sr. v.p., 2002—04, exec. v.p., 2005—. Bd. dirs. The Coldwater Nat. Bank., 1972-. Bd. dirs. Pioneer Lodge Nursing Home, Coldwater, 1984-89; mem. sch. site coun., 1993-94; life mem. Girl Scouts, chmn. Neighborhood Cookie Drive, 1991-95; bd. dirs., mem. strategic planning com. Wheatbelt Area Girl Scout Coun., 1994-96—; elder 1st Presbyn. Ch., Coldwater; Kans. Lung Assn. Vol. Spkrs. Bur., 1998—; mem. Ch. Session Bd., Coldwater, 1994-2000. Mem. Fin. Women Internat., Cmty. Bankers Assn. Kans. (membership com. 1991-94, INPAC com. 1992-93), Kans. Ind. Bankers (gen. svcs. com. 1986-87), PEO, Alpha Omicron Pi, Lake Coldwater Archtl. Rev. Bd. Republican. Avocation: music (pianist). Office: Coldwater Nat Bank PO Box 726 Coldwater KS 67029-0726

ADAMS, FRANCES GRANT, II, lawyer; b. Wheeling, W.Va., Nov. 30, 1955; d. Jack Richard and Frances Irene (Grant) A. BA, W.Va. U., 1976, JD, 1979; MA, Webster U., 1983. Bar: W.Va. 1979, U.S. Dist. Ct. (so. dist.) W.Va. 1979, U.S. Ct. Mil. Appeals 1979, U.S. Supreme Ct. 1988, D.C. 1989. Asst. staff judge advocate armament divsn. USAF, Eglin AFB, Fla., 1979-82, dep. staff judge advocate Keflavik, Iceland, 1982-83, staff judge advocate 71st Air Base Group Vance AFB, Okla., 1984-86, chief gen. torts sect. claims and tort litig. staff hdqrs. Washington, 1986-88, chief mgmt. and analysis br. claims and tort litig. divsn. Legal Svcs. Agy., 1988-92, sr. tort atty. tort claims and litig. divsn. Legal Svcs. Agy., 1992-97, chief internat. torts br., 1997—2005; atty. environ. law and litig. divsn., Legal Svcs. Agy. USAFR, USAF, Washington, 1992—99; atty. advisor Office of Gen. Counsel, Dept. Homeland Security, Washington, 2005—. Program chmn. Pentagon chpt. Fed. Bar Assn., 1989-90. Mem. DAR (chmn. procedures manual W.Va. chpt. 1989-92), Magna Carta Dames, Ancient and Honorable Arty. Co., Air Force Assn. (life), Ret. Officers Assn. (life). Avocations: photography, travel, farming, gardening. Office: Dept Homeland Security Office Gen Counsel Washington DC 20528

ADAMS, GABRIELLE, biologist; b. Mateszalka, Hungary; BSc, McMaster U., 1963; PhD, Carleton U., 1968. From postdoctoral fellow to rsch. officer Nat. Rsch. Coun. Canada, 1967-71; rsch. assoc. biology dept. Carleton U., 1971-75; with rsch. jour. Inst. Biol. Scis. Nat. Rsch. Coun. Can., 1975—93, dir. gen., 1993—. Office: Inst Biol Scis Bldg M54 1200 Montreal Rd Ottawa ON Canada K1A 0R6 E-mail: gabrielle.adams@nrc-cnrc.gc.ca.

ADAMS, GAIL HAYES, interior designer; b. Bronxville, NY, Nov. 18, 1944; d. Samuel Eugene and Kathryn Minnette (Hayes) Adams; m. Gilbert Johnson, Oct. 25, 1968; m. Jay Martin Goodfarb, Nov. 5, 1978. BS in Fine Arts, Ariz. State U., 1967. Interior designer Mehagians Furniture Galleries Co., Phoenix, 1967—79; pres., interior designer Gail Adams Interiors, LLC, Phoenix, 1979—. Active Phoenix Art Mus.; mem. interior design program adv. com. UCSD; mem. interior design adv. com. Scottsdale (Ariz.) C.C. Mem.: Nat. Coun. Interior Design Qualification (cert., nat. treas. 1987), Am. Soc. Interior Designers (cert., nat. pres. 1985, v.p. Rocky Mountain region 1981—82). Home and Office: 110 E San Miguel Ave Phoenix AZ 85012-1339 E-mail: gadams2B@aol.com.

ADAMS, HEIDI-CHRISTA, counselor; came to U.S., 1956; d. Gustav and Anna Rieger; m. Daniel Mark Adams, Aug. 17. 1981; 1 child, Anngela Christina. BS in Edn., U. Wis., Whitewater, 1976; MS in Edn. Psychology, U. Wis., Milw., 1980; EdD, Ariz. State U., 2000. German, French, Spanish tchr. Oshkosh (Wis.) Middle Sch., 1976-77; German, French tchr. Wauwatosa (Wis.) H.S., 1977-80; counselor Valley Luth. H.S., Phoenix, 1981-84, Chandler (Ariz.) H.S., 1984-92, Mesa (Ariz.) C.C., 1992—. Creator peervention program Mesa C.C., 1992—. Author: Peervention, 1994, Eliminating Self-Defeating Behaviors, 1994, Celebrate Multicultural Diversity Through Classroom Climate, 1991. Ariz. Dept. Edn. Consortium grantee Fund for the Improvement of Postsecondary End., 1994; recipient Educator award Ariz. Am. Legion Womens Aux., 1990, Mathew B. Juan award, 1989, Future Farmers Assn. award, 1990; named Innovator of Yr. Peervention Nat., 1987 Mem. Am. Counseling Assn., Am. Sch. Counselor Assn., Phi Kappa Phi. Avocations: quilting, writing, travel, walking, dance. Office: Mesa CC 1833 W Southern Ave Mesa AZ 85202-4822

ADAMS, INGRID G., federal government intelligence specialist; b. Washington, Oct. 11, 1959; d. Norbert Green and Marion Zeno Joseph; m. Keith Michael Adams, Mar. 1994 (div. Apr. 21, 1998); 1 child, Oliver; children: Ashaunta, Diondra, Dana Tumblin. BA magna cum laude in Psychology, So. U., 1983. Case worker Office Family Security State of La., Hahnville, La., 1984—87, supr. eligibility worker Thibodaux, La., 1987—88; import specialist U.S. Customs Svc., New Orleans, 1989—98; intelligence specialist Dept. Homeland Security, New Orleans, 1998—. Ind. assoc. Pre Paid Legal Svcs., Ada, Okla., 2003—; spkr. Green's Consulting Co., St. Rose, La., 2003. Mem. com. Curtis Johnson Campaign, St. Rose, 1999, Dems. for Mary Landreu, St. Rose, 1999; bd. dir. Dem. Women Orgn., 1998—2001. Mem.: Positive Women/Men of New Orleans, St. Charles Hist. Found., So. U. Alumni Assn. (2d v.p. 2001—03). Democrat. Baptist. Avocations: writing, singing, dance, stamp collecting/philately, reading. Home: 309 Turtle Creek Lane Saint Rose LA 70087 Office: Dept Homeland Security 423 Canal St Rm 242 New Orleans LA 70130

ADAMS, JANE, actress; b. Washington, Apr. 1, 1965; Diploma, Julliard Sch. Performances include (Broadway) The Crucible, 1991, I Hate Hamlet, 1991 (Outer Critics Cir. award best featured actress in a play, Theatre World award 1991), An Inspector Calls, 1994 (Antoinette Perry award 1994, Tony award best performance by an actress in a play 1994, Drama Desk award outstanding supporting actress in a play 1994), Enchanted April, 2003, Match, 2004; (off-Broadway) The Nice and the Nasty, Psychoneurotic Phantasies, Mutterschaft; (regional) Careless Love, Our Town, Love Diatribe, Greetings From Elsewhere Cabaret, Candide/Len Jenkin, Talking With, Camino Real, The Glass Menagerie, Resurrection Blues, 2006; (TV films) The Rising Son, 1990, From Where I Sit, 2000, Stone Cold, 2005; (TV series) Family Ties 1987, 89, Frasier, 2000, Citizen Baines, 2001, Law & Order: Criminal Intent, 2003; (film) Vital Signs, 1990, Light Sleeper, 1992, Mrs. Parker and the Vicious Circle, 1994, I Love Trouble, 1994, Father of the Bride II, 1995, Kansas City, 1996, Happiness, 1998, Day at the Beach, 1998, Music From Another Room, 1998, A Fish in the Bathtub, 1999, A Texas Funeral, 1999, Mumford, 1999, Songcatcher, 2000, Wonder Boys, 2000, The Anniversary Party, 2001, Orange County, 2002, Eternal Sunshine of a Spotless Mind, 2004, Lemony Snicket's A Series of Unforuntate Events, 2004, Last Holiday, 2006, The Sensation of Sight, 2006. Office: ICM care Lisa Loosemore 40 W 57th St Fl 16 New York NY 10019-4098*

ADAMS, JENNIFER, medical products executive; MBA, Northwestern Univ. Kellogg Sch. Mgmt., 1998. Office supplies sales; with Deerfield Med. Supplies, Chgo., Baxter Internat. Inc., Chgo., 1994—, v.p. sales, transfusion therapies, 2002—. Named one of 40 Under Forty, Crain's Bus. Chgo., 2005. Avocations: running sprint triathlons, running marathons. Office: Baxter Internat Inc One Baxter Pkwy Deerfield IL 60015-4625 Office Fax: 847-948-3642.*

ADAMS, JESSICA TEREACE, music educator, director; b. Claremore, Okla., Oct. 20, 1980; d. Larry Dwayne and Ellen Faye McBride; m. James Adams. B of Music Edn., U. Okla., 2004. Cert. tchr. Okla. Music educator Pawhuska (Okla.) Pub. Schs., 2004—; choir dir. First United Meth. Ch., Pawhuska, 2004—. Mem.: Sigma Alpha Iota. Democrat. Methodist. Avocations: poetry, sewing, golf, gardening, cooking. Office: Pawhuska High Sch 615 E 15th Pawhuska OK 74056 Office Phone: 918-287-1264.

ADAMS, JOEY LAUREN, actress; b. Little Rock, Jan. 6, 1971; Appeared in films Dazed and Confused, 1993, Coneheads, 1993, The Program, 1993, Sleep With Me, 1994, The Pros & Cons of Breathing, 1994, S.F.W., 1994, Mallrats, 1995, Drawing Flies, 1996, Bio-Dome, 1996, Michael, 1996, Chasing Amy, 1997 (Golden Globe award nominee 1998, Chgo. Film Critics Assn. award 1998), A Cool, Dry Place, 1998, Big Daddy, 1999, Bruno, 2000, Beautiful, 2000, Harvard Man, 2001, (voice) Dr. Dolittle 2, 2001, In the Shadows, 2001, Jay and Silent Bob Strike Back, 2001, Grand Champion, 2002, Beeper, 2002, The Big Empty, 2003, A Promise Kept, 2003; appeared in TV movies One the Edge, 2001, Remembering Charlie, 2003; appeared in tv series Top of the Heap, 1991, Vinnie & Bobby, 1992, Second Noah, 1996; guest tv appearances include Married with Children, 1987, Double Rush, 1995, Hercules, 1998, Dinner for Five, 2001, Stripperella, 2003.

ADAMS, JOYCE M., retired academic administrator; b. Dickinson, Tex., Dec. 21; d. Clarence L. and Effie R. Adams. BS, Prairie View A&M U., 1965; MS, Tex. Woman's U., 1978, PhD, 1996. RN Tex. Staff nurse M.D. Anderson Hosp., Houston, 1967—73; instr., prof. San Jacinto Coll., Houston, 1973—94, dept. chmn., 1994—98, assoc. dean, 1998—2003, dean program devel. instl. effectiveness and health careers, 2003—04; ret., 2004. V.p. Bd. of Vocat. Nurse Examiners for State of Tex. Bd. dirs. Eastwood Health Clinic, Houston, 1999—2003, Benevolent Mission Internat., Houston, 1994—2003; chair health com. Shalom Zone Mobile Health Ministries, Houston, 1998—2003. Mem.: ANA, Tex. Nurses Assn., Sigma Theta Tau. Home: 5434 Botany Lane Houston TX 77048 Personal E-mail: jadams0513@aol.com.

ADAMS, JULIE KAREN, psychologist; b. Portland, Oreg., Dec. 12, 1955; d. Allen Hays and Susanna Angelina (Meyers) A. B, Willamette U., 1977; M, Ctrl. Wash. U., 1982; cert. bus. adminstrn., U. Wash., 1986; D, Pacific U., 1992; MS, Columbia U., 2000. Lic. clin. psychologist; cert. counselor, sch. psychologist, Wash. Sch. psychologist Highline Sch. Dist., Seattle, 1987—90; psychology intern Elmcrest Psychiat. Hosp., Portland, Conn., 1990, clinician, 1991; rsch. asst. Yale U., New Haven, 1991; clinician Advanced Clin. Svcs., Seattle, 1991—93; postdoctoral fellow U. Wash., Seattle, 1991—93; acad. counselor Johns Hopkins U., Balt., 1993; behavior intervention specialist Edmonds Sch. Dist., Wash., 1993—94, Marysville Sch. Dist., Wash., 1994—99; instr. Seattle U., 1995—99. Guest spkr. in field to profl. assns., also Pacific U., U. Wash., U. Oreg., 1989—. Freelance writer: Psychology Today Mag., reporter: Wash. Psychologist Newsletter; contbr. (book chpt.) Women in Communication; contbr. articles to profl. jours. Mem. tng. com., kids week com., nursing home com., pub. policy com. Jr. League Seattle, 1988—, bd. dirs. 2004-05; health care rsrch. Wash. State Legis., Olympia, 1993; campaigner Bush for Pres., Seattle, 1988, 92; rsch. asst. to state senator Oreg. State Legis., Salem, 1985; press page nat. conv. Rep. Nat. Com., Detroit, 1980; student grad. v.p., faculty rep. com. Pacific U. Sch. Profl. Psychology, 1989-90 Mem. APA (health psychology com. student rep. 1992-93), Wash. Psychol. Assn. (coun. reps.), Wash. State Psychol. Assn. Coun., Soc. Profl. Journalists, Willamette U. Alumni Assn. (bd. dirs. 1983-88), Vols. for Outdoor Wash. (bd. dirs. 1986-87), City Club Seattle (membership com. 1986-88), Psi Chi, Beta Alpha Gamma Avocations: writing, skiing, history, reading, travel. Home: 9226 46th Dr NE Marysville WA 98270 Business E-Mail: ja365@columbia.edu.

ADAMS, KAREN V., elementary school educator; d. Jack L. and Carol Jeanne Oliver; m. Gregory Bruce Adams, Aug. 26, 1978; children: Jesse Eliot, Ethan Oliver, Claire Eleanore Rose. BS, Calif. Poly. U., San Luis Obispo, 1978; M Tchg., Ea. Oreg. U., La Grande, 1997; Endorsement ESOL, Lewis and Clark Coll., Portland, Oreg., 1999. Cert. Nat. Bd. Profl. Tchg., 2005, ESOL tchr. trainer Oreg., 2004, sheltered instrn. tchr. trainer Oreg., 2005. English lang. specialist Jefferson County Schs., Madras, Oreg., 1997—, dist. tchr. trainer, 2003—. Item writer English lang. proficiency assessment Oreg. Dept. Edn. and Lang. Learning Solutions, Eugene and Salem, 2003—06. Mem.: Oreg. Geographic Alliance, Delta Kappa Gamma (grantee, scholar 2004). Office: Westside Elem Sch 410 SW 4th St Madras OR 97741 Office Phone: 541-475-4820.

ADAMS, LAVONNE MARILYN BECK, critical care nurse, educator; b. Bridgeport, Conn., Feb. 22, 1965; d. Adolf and Hazel B. (Henderson) Beck. ASN, Kettering Coll. Med. Arts, 1985; BSN, Wright State U., 1988; MSN, Andrews U., 1992, PhD, 2003. CCRN. Staff nurse Kettering Med. Ctr., Ohio, 1985-89, resource staff nurse, 1989-95, instr. in nursing, 1989-92; asst. prof. nursing Kettering Coll. Med. Arts, 1992—99, Southwestern Adventist U., Keene, Tex., 1999—2003, assoc. prof., 2003—04; asst. prof. nursing Harris Coll. Nursing and Health Scis. Tex. Christian U., Ft. Worth, 2004—; PRN staff nurse Huguley Mem. Hosp., 2002—. Vol. Adventist Comty. Svcs.Disaster Response, 2004—, ARC, 2005—; active Southwestern Sym. Oratorio Chorus, 1999—. Mem.: Am. Assn. Critical Care Nurses, Pi Lambda Theta,

Sigma Theta Tau, Phi Kappa Phi. Avocations: music, travel. Home: 7000 Welch Ct Fort Worth TX 76133-6726 Office: Tex Christian U Harris Coll Nursing and Health Scis TCU Box 298620 Fort Worth TX 76129

ADAMS, LEOCADIA DONAT, secondary school educator, writer; b. Clinton, Mass., Oct. 9, 1947; d. Leokadia Marianna Donat; children: Erik Paul, Keith David. BS in Edn. and Vocat. Home Econs., Ctrl. Mo. State U., 1972, MA in Edn., Spl. Edn., Learning Disabilities, Emotionally Disturbed, 1987. Pre-sch. dir. La Petite Acad., Overland Park, Kans., 1973—74; vocat. home econ. instr. Martin Luther King Jr. H.S., Kansas City, Mo., 1974—75, Longfellow Elem., Kansas City, Mo., 1975—76; instr. needle arts, head dept. St. Teresa's Acad., Kansas City, Mo., 1976—83; owner The Light Ho., Kansas City, 1983—84; learning disabilities specialist. itinernant tchr. Kans. City Sch. Dist., 1985—86; learning disabilities specialist Westport Mid. Sch., Kansas City, 1986—89, SW H.S., Kansas City, 1989—90, Satchel Paige Elem. Sch., Kansas City, 1990—96, Chester R. Anderson Alternative Mid. Sch., Kansas City, 1997—99, Ctrl. Mid. Sch., 1999—2000; learning disabilities specialist, mentor tchr. Van Horn H.S., Independence, Mo., 2000—. Presenter in field. Author: (text book) Beginning to Advanced Sewing, (cookbook) Drink's On Me, 1994; prodr.: Poland's History and Culture, 1988—95; columnist: Clinton Item, guest columnist: Post Eagle; contbr. columns in newspapers. Zone coord., block capt. 49/63 Neighborhood Coalition, Kansas City, 1974—79, co-chmn. edn. com., 1974—75, chmn. govt. com., 1977; campaign mgr. Jim Dolan for State Rep., Kansas City, 1977—78; vol. Elect Ed Growney, Kansas City, 1978—88. Named to Wall of Freedom, Birmingham, Ala., Outstanding Am. Tchrs., 2005—06. Mem.: ASCD, Coun. Exceptional Children (mentor tchr.), Phi Delta Kappa. Roman Catholic. Avocations: reading, classical music, gourmet cooking, Polish studies, sewing. Office Phone: 816-418-4000 x0330. Personal E-mail: lodgia@sbcglobal.net.

ADAMS, LILIANA OSSES, music performer, harpist; b. Poznan, Poland, May 16, 1939; came to U.S., 1978, naturalized, 1990; d. Sylwester and Helena (Koswenda) O.; m. Edmund Pietryk, Sept. 4, 1965 (div. Aug. 1970); m. Bruce Meredith Adams, Feb. 3, 1978. MA, Music Acad. Poznan, Poland, 1971. Prin. harpist Philharm. Orch. of Szczecin, Poland, 1964-72, Imperial Opera and Ballet Orch., Tehran, Iran, 1972-78; pvt. music tchr. Riyadh, Saudi Arabia, 1979-81; soloist Austrian Radio, 1981-86; solo harpist, pvt. tchr. harp and piano Antioch, Calif., 1986—. Music cons. Schs. and Librs., Calif., 1991—. Contbr. articles to profl. jours. Mem. Am. Fedn. of Musicians, Am. Harp Soc., Music Tchrs. Assn. Calif., Internat. Soc. of Harpers, U.K. Harp Assn., Internat. Harp Ctr. (Switzerland). Home: PO Box 233 Antioch CA 94509-0023 E-mail: harpliliana@comcast.net.

ADAMS, LINDA HUNTER, humanities educator; b. Logan, Utah, Mar. 13, 1941; d. Milton Reed and Ferne Gardner Hunter; m. Charles Parley Adams, Apr. 1, 1969 (div. Oct. 0, 1975); children: Jennifer Lynne Grillone, Nathaniel Hunter. BA, Brigham Young U., Provo, Utah, 1963, MA in English, 1968. Tchr. South HS, Salt Lake City, 1963—65, Granite HS, Salt Lake City, 1968—69; assoc. prof. Brigham Young U., Provo, 1978—, dir. Coll. Humanities Publs. Ctr. Dir. McGraw-Hill Pub. Inst., Shippensburg, Pa., 1995—2002; pres. Assn. Mormon Letters, Salt Lake City; faculty advisor Life, the Universe, and Everything Sci. Symposium, Provo. Editor: (procs.) Association of Mormon Letters Proceedings, (journal) BYU Studies (Recognition for Editl. Svc. Award, 1992), Encyclia, journal of Utah Academy of Science, Arts, and Letters (Recognition for Editl. Svc. Award, 1993), Literature and Belief, Am. Viol. Soc. Jour., Benson Inst. Rev.; contbr. articles to profl. jours., chpt. to book;, author numerous books in field. Docent Crandall Print Mus., Provo, 2004; writer, editor Provo Hist. Sites Com., 2005; personal and family history advisor LDS Ch., Salt Lake City. Linda Hunter Adams Scholarship named in her honor, Intell, 2005—. Mem.: Tyndale Soc. (editor 1996—98), Mormon History Assn. Republican. Avocations: reading, travel, sewing, piano, hiking. Office: Brigham Young U 4040 JFSB Provo UT Office Phone: 801-422-3448. Business E-Mail: linda_adams@byu.edu.

ADAMS, LISA, lawyer; BS in Chemistry, Tex. State U., 1996; JD, New England Sch. Law, 1999. Bar: Mass. 1999, US Patent and Trademark Office, US Dist. Ct. (Dist. Mass.). Assoc. intellectual property practice group and life sciences practice group Nutter, McClennen & Fish LLP, Boston. Pro bono atty. Volunteer Lawyers for Arts Mass. Mem.: ABA, Am. Intellectual Property Law Assn., Boston Patent Law Assn. (sec. bd. governors, former chair pro bono com., activities com. and young lawyers com.). Office: Nutter McClennen & Fish LLP World Trade Center West 155 Seaport Blvd Boston MA 02210 Office Phone: 617-439-2550. Office Fax: 617-310-9550. E-mail: ladams@nutter.com.*

ADAMS, LUCILLE JOAN, psychotherapist, health administrator; b. Hartford, Conn., Apr. 2, 1933; d. Charles William and Catherine Therese (Messmer) A. AS, Hartford Coll. for Women, 1958; BA, Wheaton Coll., Norton, Mass., 1960; MSW, Smith Coll., 1962; cert. child psychotherapy, Chgo. Inst. Psychoanalysis, 1972. Diplomate clin. social work; lic. clin. social worker, Ill. Caseworker I and II Family Service of Milw., 1962-66; child therapist Lakeside Children's Ctr., Milw., 1966-69; social worker, clin. supr., dist. dir. Jewish Children's Bur., Chgo., 1969-89; psychotherapist Genesis Day Sch., Chgo., 1989-92; pvt. practice psychotherapy Inverness, 1989—93; psychotherapist Leyden Family Svc. and Mental Health Ctr., 1992-94; dept. head The Imperial, Chgo., 1992—98. Field instr. U. Chgo. Sch. Social Svc. Adminstrn., 1970-72, Loyola U. Chgo. Sch. Social Work, 1993-97; clin. instr. Smith Coll. Sch. Social Work, Northampton, Mass., 1979-81; faculty post-grad. edn. Inst. Psychoanalysis, Chgo., 1978-82. Contbr. articles to profl. jour. Mem. NASW (sec. 1965-66, cert. clin. social worker), Acad. Cert. Social Workers, Assn. Child Psychotherapists (sec. 1972-73), Photographic Soc. Am., Nature Camera Club of Chgo. (pres. 1994-97), North Shore Camera Club, Riverwoods Nature Photographic Soc. Avocations: nature photography, photojournalism. Office: The Imperial 1366 W Fullerton Ave Chicago IL 60614-2199 Home: 1100 Pembridge Dr Apt 345 Lake Forest IL 60045-4220

ADAMS, MARGARET BERNICE, retired museum official; b. Toronto, Ont., Can., Apr. 29, 1936; arrived in U.S., 1948, naturalized, 1952; d. Robert Russell and Kathleen Olive (Buffin) A.; m. Alberto Enrique Sánchez-Quiñonez, Nov. 30, 1956 (div. 1960). AA, Monterey Peninsula Coll., 1969; BA, San Jose State U., 1971; MA, U. Utah, 1972. Curator ethnic arts Civic Art Gallery, San Jose, Calif., 1971; staff asst. Utah Mus. Fine Arts, Salt Lake City, 1972; lectr., curator Coll. Seven, U. Calif., Santa Cruz, 1972-74; part-time educator Cabrillo Coll., Aptos, Calif., 1973, Monterey Peninsula Coll., 1973-84; dir. U.S. Army Mus., Presidio of Monterey, 1974-83; chief. mus. br. Ft. Ord Mil. Complex, 1983-88; ret., 1988. Guest curator Am. Indian arts Monterey Peninsula Mus. Art, 1975-88. Author: Indian Tribes of North America and Chronology of World Events in Prehistoric Pueblo Times, 1975, Historic Old Monterey, 1976; contbg. editor Indian Am., Writing on the Wall, WWII Patriotic Posters, 1987; contbr. articles to jours. Mem. Native Am. adv. panel AAAS, Washington, 1972-78; mem. rev. and adv. com. Project Media, Nat. Indian Edn. Assn., Mpls., 1973-78; working mem. Program for Tng. Am. Indian Counsellors in Alcoholism Counselling and Rehab. Programs, 1972-74; mem. hist. adv. com. Monterey County Bd. Suprs., 1987-89. Grad. fellow, dean's scholar U. Utah, 1972; dean's scholar Monterey Peninsula Coll., 1969, San Jose State U., 1971. Mem. Am. Anthrop. Assn., Am. Assn. Museums, Soc. Am. Archeology, Nat., Calif., Indian Edn. Assns.

ADAMS, MARILYN JAGER, developmental psychologist; b. Washington, Dec. 14, 1948; d. Raymond Eugene and Alva Verna (Sibley) Jager; m. Milton B. Adams Jr., Aug. 27, 1972; children: John Milton, Jocelyn Jager. BS in arts, sci., psychology with high honors, U. Md., 1966; MS, Brown U., 1968, PhD, 1975. Scientist Bolt Beranek & Newman, Cambridge, Mass., 1975-80, sr. scientist, 1980—2000; chief scientist Soliloquery Learning, 2000—. Assoc. scientist Ctr. for the Study of Reading, Champaign, Ill., 1978-92; mem. adv. bd. Nat. Assessment of Ednl. Progress on Reading, 1992; adj. prof. Ctr. Reading Rsch. Stavanger (Norway) Coll., 1992—; vis. prof. dept. cognitive and linguistic scis. Brown U., 1994-95; adv. panel Nat. Assessment of Literacy, 2000—. Author: Odyssey: A Curriculum for Thinking, 1986, Beginning to Read, 1990, Collections for Young Scholars, 1995, Pronwmic Awareness in Young Children, 1997; mem. editorial bd. Reading Rsch. Quar., 1978-91, Reading Tchr., 1988-92, Lang. Arts, 1990-92, Applied Psycholinguistics, 1991-2000, Memory & Cognition, 1993-2000. Corinna Borden Keene Rsch. fellow Brown U., 1974. Mem. Internat. Reading Assn., Am. Ednl. Rsch. Assn. (divsn. C, Sylvia Scribner award 1995), Am. Psychol. Assn., Am. Psychol. Soc., Psychonomic Soc., Soc. for Sci. Study of Reading (bd. dirs. 1993-95), Phi Beta Kappa, Sigma Xi, Psi Chi, Pi Mu Epsilon. Office: Soliloquery Learning 100 Fifth Ave Ste 410 Waltham MA 02451

ADAMS, MARTHA JEAN MORRIS, art educator, artist; d. Frank Elliott and Theodosia Ellen (Dever) Morris; m. John Hines Adams, Sr., Aug. 3, 1962; children: John Hines Jr., Jean Karole Adams Meares. BS in Edn., Elizabeth City State U., 1985. Art tchr. Hertford County Schs., Winton, NC, 1986—99, 2002—, Franklin County Schs., Louisburg, NC, 1999—2000, Vance County Schs., Henderson, NC, 2000—02. Mem. county-wide sch. improvement com. Hertford County Schs., Winton, 1993—94; program enhancement chmn. Riverview Elem., Murfreesboro, NC, 1994—96; mem. exec. bd. Profl. Educators N.C., Raleigh, 1993—2003. Vol. Spl. Olympics Riverview Elem., Ahoskie, NC, 1992—96; participant N.C. Ctr. for Advancement Tchg., Cullowhee, 1996, 1999; Sunday sch. tchr. Grantee, N.C. Arts Coun., 1993—94, U.S. Govt., 1995—97. Mem.: Nat. Art Edn. Assn. Baptist. Avocations: reading, cooking. Home: 103 Springlake Dr Murfreesboro NC 27855 Office: Ahoskie Elem Sch 200 N Talmage Ave Ahoskie NC 27910

ADAMS, MARY LOU, piano teacher; b. Feb. 22, 1934; BA, Goucher Coll., Balt., 1956; BMEd, Wichita State U., 1984. Nat. cert. music tchr. Historian Ctrl. Okla. Music Tchrs. Assn., Oklahoma City, 1985-90, notification chair, 1986—98, hospitality chair, 1999—2000. Tutor, Oklahoma City Literacy Coun., 1989-2003. Mem. Nat. Music Tchrs. Assn., Ctrl. Okla. Music Tchrs. Assn., Olahoma City Pianists Club, Ladies Music Club Oklahoma City. Home and Office: 6316 NW 83d St Oklahoma City OK 73132-4633 Office Phone: 405-721-5758. Personal E-mail: mladams866@aol.com.

ADAMS, MARY LOUISE, education educator, archivist; b. Troy, Mo., Oct. 15, 1919; d. Robert Andrews and Mary Louise (Harbaugh) A. AB, Harris Coll., 194l; MA, St. Louis U., l95l, PhD, l960; BA, Maryville U., 1980; M of Liberal Arts, Washington U., St. Louis., 1989. Tchr. St. Louis Pub. Schs., 1941-43; asst. prof. edn. St. Louis U., 1960-67; assoc. prof. edn. Maryville Coll., St. Louis, 1967-72, prof., 1972-89, prof. emeritus, 1989—. Resident scholar Radcliffe Coll.-Harvard U., Cambridge, Mass., 1980-82; hon. trustee St. Louis U. Arts and Sci. Alumni Bd. Dirs., 1989—. Bd. dirs. UNICEF, St. Louis, 1980-85; historian Gateway Waves, St. Louis, 1980—. Lt. comdr. USNR, 1943-73. Scholar Bleweit scholar, 1959—60. Mem. NEA, AAUP (local chpt. pres.), UN Assn., St. Louis Area Archivists Assn. (bd. dirs. 1986—), Enfant de Marie (prefect 1983-87), Mo. Hist. Assn., Assn. Alumnae Sacred Heart Acad., Cardinal Newman Assn., Friends St. Louis Art Mus., Res. Officers Assn., Landmarks Club, DuBourg Soc. St. Louis U., Alpha Sigma Nu, Gamma Phi Epsilon. Roman Catholic. Home: 3393 McKelvey Rd Ste 22F Bridgeton MO 63044-2544

ADAMS, NANCY D., elementary school educator; b. Denver, Colo., Feb. 9, 1948; d. John Armin and June Gerber; m. Charles Doug Adams, Oct. 31, 1970; 1 child, Donald I. Martin. BA, U. N.M., Albuquerque, 1966—72, MA, 1978—80, Edn. Specialist, 1982—83. Tchr. Los Lunas Schs., Los Lunas, N.Mex. Mem. N.Mex. German Shepherd Search & Rescue, 1970—82. Recipient Tchr. of Yr., Manzano Vista Mid. Sch., 2003—04. Avocations: backpacking, hiking, stain glass work. Home: 3924 Smit SE Albuquerque NM 87108

ADAMS, NANCY R., nurse, retired military officer; b. Rochester, N.Y., Apr. 20, 1945; BSN, Cornell U., 1968; MSN, Cath. U. Am., 1974; grad., U.S. Army War Coll., 1986. Advanced through grades to maj. gen. U.S. Army, 1991; comdr. William Beaumont Army Med. Ctr., S.W. Regional Med. Command; chief Army Nurse Corps; asst. surgeon gen. for pers. and comdr. U.S. Army Ctr. for Health Promotion and Preventive Medicine; lead agt. TRICARE Region VII U.S. Army; chief nurse Frankfurt Army Regional Med. Ctr., 1987—89; staff asst. profl. affairs and quality assurance Office of Asst. Sec. of Def., asst. inspector gen., dir. intensive care nursing course; nursing cons. Army Surgeon Gen., 1989—91; commd. Nurse Corps U.S. Army, 1991—95; commdg. gen. Tripler Army Med. Ctr., Hawaii, 1998—2002; sr. advisor to the dir. TRICARE Mgmt. Activity, 2002—04, north region dir., 2004—05. Decorated Legion of Merit, Meritorious Svc. medal; recipient Disting. Svc. medal, Defense Superior Svc. medal. Fellow: Am. Acad. Nursing; mem.: ANA, Am. Orgn. of Nurse Execs., Assn. of Mil. Surgeons of the U.S., Sigma Theta Tau. Home: 1920 S Ocean Dr Apt 1611 Fort Lauderdale FL 33316-3730 Personal E-mail: nradams2@aol.com.

ADAMS, PATTI JEAN, literature and language educator; b. Columbus, Ohio, Nov. 18, 1950; d. Mary Jane and James Berton Ridenour; children: Denise Tameron Snuggs, Leah Jane Dansby. AA, Brevard C.C., Cocoa, Fla., 1991; BS, U. Ctrl. Fla., Orlando, 1993. Tchr. Ctrl. Jr. H.S., Melbourne, Fla., 1993—97, Southlake Elem. Sch., Titusville, 1997—99, Titusville H.S., Fla., 1999—2005, reading tchr., 2005—. Sec. Kappa Gamma, Titusville, 2002—06; mem. choir United Meth. Ch., Titusville, 1984—2006. R-Liberal. Avocation: reading.

ADAMS, ROSE ANN, nonprofit administrator; b. McHenry, Ill., Apr. 4, 1952; d. Clemens Jacob and Marguerite Elizabeth (Freund) A. BS in Edn., Ill. State U., 1974; MEd, U. Ark., 1979. Supt., exec. dir. Clinton County Children's Services, Wilmington, Ohio, 1979-81; dir. ednl. and adult svcs. Bost Human Devel. Svcs., Ft. Smith, Ark., 1981-87; adminstrv. officer Cen. Ark. Devel. Coun., Benton, 1987; adminstrv. officer, interim Head Start dir., dir. resource devel. Community Orgn. Poverty Elimination Pulaski, Lonoke Counties, Little Rock, 1987-93; exec. dir. So. Early Childhood Assn., 1993-94; sr. cons. Earl Moore and Assocs., Little Rock, 1994-2000, exec. v.p., 1999-2000; exec. dir. Ark. Cmty. Action Agys. Assn., Little Rock, 2000—. Inaugural instr. U. Ark. Clinton Sch. Pub. Svc., 2005—. Coord. White House Conf. on Families, 1980; mem. Task Force Child Abuse; charter mem. Am. Lung Assn.; active Welfare adv. Bd., Clinton County, 1979—81; pres., v.p. Ark. Single Parent Scholarship Fund.; trustee Morris Found., Multiple Sclerosis Soc.; active Home Econs. Extension Svcs. Adv. Com., 1979—81; mem. adv. bd. U. Ark. Women's Ctr., 1979; chair Ark. Health Promotion Coalition; vice-chair Pulaski County Local Planning Group; chair Ark. Com. on Women's Concerns; mem. adv. com. Ark. Mentors; Ark. Hunger Coalition, 2001—. Named one of Outstanding Young Women of Am., 1982. Mem.: Am. Bus.Women's Assn. (Woman of Yr. Avant Garde chpt. 1992), U. Ark. (Little Rock) Alumni Assn. (bd. dirs., pres., v.p. 1999—2005). Avocations: antique collection, sports, music. Home: Sonata Trl # 1 Little Rock AR 72205-1632 Office: Ark Cmty Action Agys Assn Ste 1020 300 S Spring St Little Rock AR 72201 Office Phone: 501-372-0807. E-mail: radams@acaaa.org.

ADAMS, SARAH VIRGINIA, psychotherapist, family counselor; b. San Francisco, Oct. 23, 1955; d. Marco Tulio and Helen (Jorge) Zea; children: Mark Vincent, Elena Giselle, Johnathan Richard. BA, Calif. State U., Long Beach, 1978, MS in Psychology, 1980; MA in Psychology, Fuller Sem., Pasadena, 1996, MA in Christian Leadership, 1997; PsyD in Clin. Psychology, Fuller Sem., 2000. Lic. marriage, family, child counseling. Tutor math. and sci., Montebello, Calif., 1979-82; behavioral specialist Cross Cultural Psychol. Corp., L.A., 1979-80; psychol. asst. Legal Psychology, L.A., 1980-82, Eisner Psychol. Assocs., L.A., 1982-83; assoc. dir. Legal Psychodiagnosis and Forensic Psychology, L.A., 1982-83; adminstrv. dir. Diagnostic Clinic, Calif., 1983-85; dir. Diagnostic Clinic of West Covina, Calif., 1985-87; owner Adams Family Counseling Inc., Calif., 1987—; with Health Group Psychol. Svcs., 1994—; domestic violence counselor Baldwin Park Counseling, 1996—2001; battered wives counselor Wings, 1996—2002; facilitator, vol., 1995—; facilitator in domestic violence Redlands, 2002—; program dir. Alternative Choices Together Batterers Counselor, 2002—. Tchr. piano, Montebello, 1973-84; ins. agent Am. Mut. Life Ins., Des Moines, 1982-84; DV counselor Baldwin Park Counseling, 1996-2001, Wings-Shelter for Battered Wives, 1996-, ALternatives Choices Together, Treatment Ctr. Batterers, 2002-. Fellow Am. Assn. Marriage and Family Therapists, Am. Psychol. Assn.; mem. NAFE, Calif. Assn. Marriage and Family Therapists, Calif. State Psychol. Assn., Calif. Soc. Indsl. Medicine and Surgery, Western Psychol. Assn., Psi Chi, Pi Delta Phi. Republican. Roman Catholic. Avocations: piano, creative writing, drawing, collecting coins. Office: 260 S Glendora Ave Ste 107 West Covina CA 91790-3041 Personal E-mail: glenna@earthlink.net. Business E-Mail: drsarahadams48@yahoo.com.

ADAMS, SHARON BUTLER, minister, philosopher, researcher; b. Chgo., Oct. 30, 1949; d. Lionel Augustus and Clara Bernice Butler; m. Vernon McFadden Jr., June 13, 1968 (div. Oct. 1977); children: Vernon McFadden III, Aleceia Marie McFadden. Ordained min. African-Am. Universal Ministry. Engrng. technician Servitron, Baton Rouge, 1976—78; instr. Coml. Bus. Coll, Baton Rouge, 1978—80; project mgr. Minority Engrs. La., Baton Rouge, 1980—86; cleric adminstr. Baton Rouge African-Am. Cath. Cong., 1997—98, cleric adminstr., So. Region Baton Rouge, 1998—99; interim pastor Imani Temple, Baton Rouge, 1998—99; pastor Ch. of the Living God, Baton Rouge, 1999—2002. Advisor Kwanzaa celebration A-A Universal Apostolic Ministry, Baton Rouge, 1999—; dir. Females in Ministry, Baton Rouge, 1999—; spiritual adv. Jazz and Heritage Festival, New Orleans, 2001—; cons. NAACP, New Orleans, 2001; advisor La. Dept. of Environ. Quality, 1990; owner ADHD-Alarm, 2004—. Author to newspapers and jours. Panelist New Orleans Jazz & Heritage Festival, 2002, Jazz Festival, 2003; bd. dirs. Cmty. Devel. Project, Baton Rouge, 1998, La. Dem. Project, Baton Rouge, 2000. Recipient Kwanazz Celebration award, Mayor & Metr. Coun. of Baton Rouge, 2001. Mem.: Internat. Black Environ. & Econ. Justice, Soc. Am. Music. Avocation: reading, sewing, singing and playing musical instruments. Office Phone: 225-383-6479. E-mail: asharon@bellsouth.net.

ADAMS, SHIRLEY A., mathematics educator; b. Bellville, Tex., Sept. 17; d. Benjamin Cochran Rehms and Katie Bell; m. John William, Jr. Adams, July 13, 1973; children: Shawn, Jenna. BS, Sam Houston U., 1972. Cert. tchr. 7th and 8th grade tchr. Edna Jr. High, Tex., 1975—81; math. tchr. Karnack HS, Tex., 1981—82; algebra and trig tchr. Waskom HS, Tex., 1982—83; 8th grade math. tchr. A&M Consolidated Jr. HS, College Station, Tex., 1983—84; math. Jersey Village HS, Houston, 1984—85; algebra I, II tchr. Angleton HS, Tex., 1985—86, Brazoswood HS, Chute, Tex., 1986—91; pre-AP algebra II, pre-calculus tchr. Magnolia HS, Tex., 1991—. Mem.: Lambda Kappa Charter of Delta Kappa Gamma (pres. Magnolia and Mongomery area 2004—), Nat. Council for Tchrs. of Math. Republican. Baptist. Avocations: sports, cooking. Home: 18123 Patricia Ln Magnolia TX 77355

ADAMS, STEPHANIE LYNN, elementary school educator; b. Decatur, Ga., Mar. 10, 1978; d. James W. and Leona R. White; m. Jonathan N. White, Aug. 30, 2003. BA, Mercer U., Macon, Ga., 2000; MA in Tchg., Ga. State U., Milledgeville, 2005. Cert. tchg. Ga. Profl. Stds. Commn., 2005. Cancer control program mgr. Am. Cancer Soc., Vero Beach, Fla., 2000—02; ESL paraprofessional Conyers Mid. Sch., Ga., 2003—04; social studies tchr. Meml. Mid. Sch., Conyers, Ga., 2005—. Missions team mem. Rockdale Bapt. Ch., Conyers, 2004—06. Recipient Rose award, Am. Cancer Soc., 2002; Saul Wolpert scholar, Ga. State U., 2004—05. Mem.: Ga. Coun. for Social Studies. Baptist. Avocations: travel, reading. Office Phone: 770-922-0139.

ADAMS, SUSAN L., art educator; d. Leo Edward and Eleanor Gertrude (Yatko) Adams; 1 child, Adam Joseph Guzik. BA in Art, Wilkes U., Wilkes-Barre, Pa., 1978; MS in Edn. Adminstrn., U. Scranton, Scranton, Pa., 1985; postgrad., Pa. State U., University Park, 1991. Cert. Instrl. II Art, elemantry prin., asst. supt. Dist. mgr. Wilkes-Barre Times Leader, Tower City, Pa., 1978—79; HS art tchr. Williams Valley Sch. Dist., Tower City, Pa., 1980—86, elem. art tchr., 1986—. Bldg. com. Williams Valley Elem., Tower City, Pa., 1990—92; in svc. com. Williams Valley HS, Tower City, Pa., 1982—85; adj. prof. King's Coll., Wilkes Barre, Pa., 1988—96. Reviewer (edn. textbook) In the Classroom an Intro to Education, 1995. Den mother Tiger Cub Pack, Crressona, Pa., 2001—02; base coach Pirates Tee Ball, Crressona, Pa., 2001—02; catechist 2nd grade St. Patrick's ch., Pottsville, Pa., 2001—. Named Crayola Gold Star Tchr., 2006. Mem.: NEA, Kappa Delta Pi, Pi Lambda Theta. Democrat. Roman Catholic. Avocations: painting, photography, piano, interior decorating, gardening. Office: Williams Valley Elem 10400 State Rte 209 Tower City PA 17980

ADAMS, SUSAN LOIS, music educator; b. New Albany, Ind., July 27, 1946; d. Frank Mitchell, Sr. and Dorothy Stalker Adams. BA, Smith Coll., 1968; MS in Edn., Ind. U., 1970, postgrad., 1994. Cert. tchr. Ind. Tchr. Lafayette (Ind.) Sch. Corp., 1969—70, New Albany-Floyd County Consol. Sch. Corp., 1970—. Mem. editl. com. (hymnal) Chalice Hymnal, 1995; co-editor: (hymnal companion) Chalice Hymnal Worship Leaders' Companion, 1998. Elder Ctrl. Christina Ch., New Albany, 1996—98, Ctrl. Christian Ch., New Albany, 2000—02. Recipient Honored Laywoman, Commn. Women-Ind. Region Christian Ch., 1998. Mem.: Ind. Music Educators, Music Educators Nat. Conf., Nat. Assn. Disciple Musicians (pres. 1988, chair workshop 1989, 2001). Mem. Christian Ch. (Disciples Of Christ). Avocations: travel, reading.

ADAMS, SUSAN SEIGLER, music educator; b. Valparaiso, Fla., Apr. 17, 1953; d. Roberta Whitfield Seigler Moseley and Claude Milo Seigler; m. Michael S. Adams, June 30, 1984; children: Rachel Kathryn, John Michael. B of Music Edn., Valdosta State Coll., Ga., 1975; MEd, Augusta State Coll., Ga., 1980. Cert. tchr. Ga. Tchr. Wrens Elem. Sch., Ga., 1975—; min. of music Wrens Bapt. Ch., Ga. Mem.: PA of Ga. Educators, Callaway Family Assn., DAR (registrar 2004—06). Southern Baptist. Avocations: church activities, singing, walking. Office: Wrens Elem Hwy 17 N Wrens GA Office Phone: 706-547-2063. Personal E-mail: adamss@jefferson.k12.ga.us.

ADAMS, VALENCIA I., telecommunications industry executive; b. Atlanta; BBA, Ga. State U.; postgrad. in Mgmt., Columbia U., Emory U. COO consumer svcs. BellSouth Corp., Atlanta, v.p., chief diversity officer, 2002—. Former mem. adv. coun. to pres. BellSouth Telecom. Inc.; mentor BellSouth Mentor Exch. Program; trustee Ga. Coun. on Econ. Edn.; bd. dirs. BellSouth Found., Prevent Child Abuse Ga., Possible Woman Found. Chairperson Met. Atlanta United Way Campaign, 1998. Named Woman of Yr., Women Looking Ahead News Mag., 2004; recipient Jr. Achievement Vol. award, Gov. Ga., Bus. Assoc. of Yr. award, Am. Bus. Women's Assn. Mem.: Atlanta C. of C. (life).

ADAMS, VELMA M., assistant principal, consultant; b. Balt., Oct. 1, 1945; d. George and Anna Jones; m. Kenneth G. Adams, Jan. 5, 1946; 1 child, Mark. MusB in Edn., Howard U., 1968; MusM, Morgan State U., 1978; Profl. Cert. for Adminstrn. and Supervision, Queens Coll. Cert. bldg. and dist. adminstrn. N.Y., 1996. Choral and gen. music tchr. Balt. City Pub. Schs., 1968—80; vocal and gen. music tchr. Uniondale (N.Y.) Pub. Schs., 1980—99, asst. prin., 2000—; discipline supr. Lawrence Rd. Jr. High, Uniondale, 1999—2000. Second step character edn. trainer. Recipient Jenkins PTA award, PTA of Turtle Hook Mid. Sch., 1998. Mem.: ASCD, The Mid. Sch. Adminstr., Curriculum Audit Mgmt. Ctrs., Inc. (assoc.), Nassau Music Educators Assn. (life; pres.). Democrat. Episcopalian. Achievements include development of peer mediation program. Avocations: avid reader, mediation consultant, curriculum auditor, rehearsal and show pianist, computer enthusiast. Home: 71-24 Sutton Place #2 Fresh Meadows NY 11365 Office: Lawrence Rd Middle School 50 Lawrence Rd Hempstead NY 11550 Office Phone: 516-918-1503. Business E-Mail: vadams@uniondaleschools.org. E-mail: velmaa1@hotmail.com.

ADAMS, YOLANDA YVETTE, singer; b. Houston, Aug. 27, 1962; m. Timothy Crawford, Jr., 1997; 1 child, Taylor Ayanna Crawford. Singer: (albums) Just as I Am, 1988, Through the Storm, 1991, More Than a Melody, 1995, Shakin' the House, 1996, Yolanda Live in Washington, 1996, Battle is the Lord, 1996, Songs from the Heart, 1998, Mountain High.Valley Low,

1999 (Grammy award for Best Contemporary Soul Gospel Album, 1999), Christmas with Yolanda Adams, 2000, The Experience, 2001 (Grammy award for Best Contemporary Soul Gospel Album, 2001), Believe, 2001, Day by Day, 2005 (Grammy award, Best Gospel Song for Be Blessed, 2006). Recipient Image award for Outstanding Gospel Artist, NAACP, 2000—02, 2006, Image award for Outstanding Female Artist, 2001. Office: N-House Mgmt Inc Ste 220 4204 Bellaire Blvd Houston TX 77025 also: Atlantic Records Publicity Dept 1290 Ave of the Americas New York NY 10104 Office Phone: 832-778-6774. E-mail: yolanda@yolandaadams.com.*

ADAMS-COOPER, VERONICA LYNN, education educator, foundation administrator; d. Jerome Adams, Sr. and Helen Elizabeth (White) Adams; m. Anthony Phillip Cooper, Jan. 9, 1993. BS in Psychology, Grambling State U., La., 1989, BS in Sociology, 1990, MS in Criminal Justice, 1995; PhD in Pub. Adminstrn., Jackson State U., Miss., 2001. Pre-doctoral fellow Charles F. Kettering Found., Dayton, Ohio, 1999—2000; asst. prof. pub. adminstrn. Albany State U., Ga., 2002—. Cons. Found. for the Mid South, Jackson, 1998—99; skills trainee Nat. Congress for Cmty. Econ. Devel., Washington, 2000; pres., CEO The Estus Smith Vineyard Healing Found., Jackson, 2002—. Pres., CEO Abundant Life Cmty. Devel. Corp., Albany, Ga., 2005—; mem. Leadership Albany, 2005—; steering com. mem. Tools for Change, Albany, 2005—; mem. Abundant Life Fellowship Ch., Albany, 2003—. Recipient Friend in the Faculty award, Students Affairs Divsn., Albany State U., 2003—04, Appreciation for Inspiring, Motivating Leadership, POLS 2101 - Talented Tenth Class Mems., Albany State U., 2004; grantee, Coun. for Pub. Policy Edn., 2005—, City of Albany, 2002. Mem.: ASPA, Toastmasters Internat. (treas. 2006—), Pi Alpha Alpha Nat. Honor Soc. for Pub. Affairs and Adminstrn., Sigma Gamma Rho Sorority, Inc. Christian. Avocations: cultural heritage, gardening, motivational speaking. Office: Albany State Univ 504 College Dr Simmons Hall 314 Albany GA 31705 Office Phone: 229-420-1135. Office Fax: 229-430-7895. Business E-Mail: veronica.adams-cooper@asurams.edu.

ADAMS-CURTIS, LEAH E., academic administrator; b. Athens, Ga., Jan. 9, 1961; d. James N. and Margie Beatrice Adams; m. R. Craig Curtis, May 16, 1982; children: Anna C. Curtis, Galen R. Curtis. BS, Millsaps Coll., 1982; MS, Wash. State U., 1987, PhD, 1990. Instr. psychopharmacology/asst. to the chair Dept. of Basic Scis., U. Ill. Coll. Medicine, Peoria, 1993—95; asst. prof. pyschology Millikin U., Decatur, Ill., 1995—2001, assoc. prof. psychology, 2001—03; assoc. dean social scis. Ill. Ctrl. Coll., East Peoria, 2003—. Author: (article) Psychol. Reports, Jour. Comparative Psychology, Devel. Psychobiology, Jour. Life Scis., Italian Jour. Neurolotical Scis., The Physiologist, Brain Rsch. Bulletin, Annals of the N.Y. Academy Scis., Internat. Jour. Primatology, Folia Primatologica, Violence Against Women, Trauma, Violence and Abuse: A Rev. Jour., Psychology of Women Quar., Jour. Social Psychology, Jour. Interpersonal Violence, Am. Jour. Primatology, (jour. commentaries) Behavioral and Brain Scis., (book chpts.) 3 sci. vols., over 30 presentations at sci. confs. Mem.: Am. Assn. Women in Cmty. Colls., Am. Psychol. Soc., Brain and Behavioral Scis. (assoc.), Rotary Club (North Peoria). Achievements include Project Kaleidoscope, Faculty for the 21st Century. Office: Illinois Ctrl Coll 1 College Dr Peoria IL 61635

ADAMSON, JANE NAN, retired elementary school educator; b. Amarillo, Tex., Feb. 5, 1931; d. Carl W. and Lydie O. (Martin) Ray (dec.); 1 child, Dave R. Student, Eastfield Coll., Amarillo Coll., Richland Coll. Univ. Dallas, U. North Tex.; BS, West Tex. A&M U., Canyon, 1953; MEd, Tex. A&M U., Commerce, 1975; diploma, Inst. Children's Lit., 1991; cert., Bur. Edn. and Rsch., 1995; PhD, Am. Coll. Metaphys. Theology, 2000. Cert. elem. tchr., Tex. Tchr. Dallas Ind. Sch. Dist., ret. Avocations: music, travel, decorating, writing, dog training.

ADAMSON, LYNDA G., literature educator, writer; b. Erwin, NC, Aug. 22, 1945; d. Norman E. and Irma Smith Gossett; m. Frank M. Adamson Jr., Dec. 18, 1971; children: Frank M. III, Gregory T. BA, U. NC, 1967, MA, 1968; PhD, U. Md., 1981. Prof. English Prince George's Coll., Largo, Md., 1969—2001, chair lit. dept., 1986—87, chair English dept., 1995—2001, prof. emerita, 2001—. Creator travel study program Prince George's Coll. Author: (reference work) A Reference Guide to Historical Fiction for Children and Young Adults, 1987, Recreating the Past: A Guide to American and World Historical Fiction for Children and Young Adults, 1994, Literature Connections to American History, K-6, 1998, Literature Connections to American History, 7-12, 1998, Literature Connections to World History, K-6, 1998, Literature Connections to World History, 7-12, 1998, Notable Women in World History: A Guide to Biographies and Autobiographies, 1999, World Historical Fiction for Adults and Young Adults, 1999, American Historical Fiction Novels for Adults and Young Adults, 1999, Notable Women in American History: A Guide to Biographies and Autobiographies, 1999, Thematic Guide to the Modern American Novel, 2002, A Thematic Guide to Popular Nonfiction, 2006; contbr. articles to profl. jours. Editor dir. Woodmont Civic Assn., Arlington, Va.; vol. Arlington Ctrl. Libr.; choir Foundry United Meth. Ch., Washington, 1985—; sec., instr. Arlington Learning in Retirement Inst., 2002—04. Recipient Faculty Excellence award, Faculty Senate at Prince George's Coll., 1995; grantee, NEH, 1989, ALA, 1999—2000. Mem.: U.S. Bd. on Books for Young Adults, Internat. Rsch. in Children's Lit., Capitol Choices, Choral Arts Soc. Washington. Democrat. Methodist. Avocations: travel, music, miniatures, art. E-mail: ladamson@alumni.unc.edu.

ADAMSON, MARY ANNE, geographer, systems engineer, consultant; b. Berkeley, Calif., June 25, 1954; d. Arthur Frank and Frances Isobel Adamson; m. Richard John Harrington, Sept. 20, 1974. BA with highest honors, U. Calif., Berkeley, 1975, MA, 1976, postgrad., 1976-78. Cert. tchr. earth scis., Calif.; cert. cave rescue ops. and mgmt., Calif.; lic. EMT, Contra Costa (Calif.) County, 1983. Tchg. asst. dept. geography U. Calif., Berkeley, 1976; geographer, environ. and fgn. area analyst Lawrence Livermore Nat. Lab., Calif., 1978-83, cons. Calif., 1983-86; sys. engr. ESL, Sunnyvale, Calif., 1986-90; rsch. analyst, rsch. devel. and analysis Pacific Gas & Electric Co., San Francisco, 1990-93, asst. to gen. auditor internal audit dept., 1993—. Asst. editor Vulcan's Voice, 1982; contbr. articles to profl. jours. Staff mem. ARC/Am. Trauma Soc./Sierra Club Urgent Care and Mountain Medicine seminars, 1983-98; mem. bd. leadership team Asian Employee Assn., 2003-06. With USNR, 1983—, comdr., 1999—. Recipient Navy Achievement medal, 1992, Navy Commendation medal, 2003. Mem. Assn. Am. Geographers (life), Assn. Pacific Coast Geographers, Nat. Speleol. Soc. (geology, geography sects., sec., editor newsletter Diablo Grotto chpt. 1982-86), Toastmasters Internat. Club (adminstrv. v.p. Blue Monday Club 1991), Sierra Club (life), Nature Conservancy (life), U. Calif. Alumnae Assn., Phi Beta Kappa. Home: 4603 Lakewood St Pleasanton CA 94588-4342 Office: PG&E Corp Dept Internal Auditing 245 Market St San Francisco CA 94105-1702

ADAMS-PASSEY, SUELLEN S., retired elementary school educator; b. Cin. d. Raymond J. and Thelma P. (Munk)Sweany; m. Douglas Passey; children; Amy, Jacqueline, James, Sarah, Kristina, Zoya. BS in Edn., Kent State U. Cert. elem. tchr., Wash. Tchr. 4th and 5th grades Chgo. Jr. Sch., Elgin, Ill.; gen. dir., program developer Courtyard Theatre, Edmonds, Wash.; tchr. 4th grade Edmonds (Wash.) Dist. 15; tchr. 4th, 5th and 6th grades combination class Martha Lake Elem. Sch., Lynnwood, Wash.; founder Suellen Adams Sch. of Hope for Orphans, Armenia, 2003. Bd. dirs. Pub. Edn. Fund for Dist. 15, 1985-87; pres. Seattle Storytellers Guild, 1985-88; bd. dirs. Seattle Folklore Soc. 1998-2004, founder and chair, concert com. 1988-2002, dir. Crackerbarrel Mornings, 1982-87, co-chair, student subsidy program, 1989-2000, Seattle Opera Guild.

ADAMS-SALLUSTIO, PATRICIA JAYNE, elementary school educator; b. Chattanooga, Tenn., Dec. 4, 1939; d. Robert Mills and Mildred Louise Proctor; m. Duval Frank Sallustio, Jan. 22, 2002; children: Stephen Michael Adams, Christopher Noel Adams, Christina Louise Covert. BS, U. of Tenn., 1976—79, MEd, 1980—83; Ed.S., U. of Ala., 1998—99. Tchr. Dade County Mid. Sch., Trenton, Ga., 1980—83, Soddy Daisy H.S., Soddy Daisy, Tenn., 1983—89, Hawksbill H.S., Freeport, Grand Bahama, Bahamas, 1990—94, Sequastchie H.S., Dunlap, Tenn., 1994—95, Ringgold H.S., Ringgold, Ga., 1995—2003, Tequesta Trace Mid. Sch., Weston, Fla., 2003—. Owner New Horizons Ednl. Group, Freeport, Bahamas, 1991—94. Photography, graphics, watercolors, Southern Artists. Mem. Christ United Meth. Ch., Ft. Lauderdale, Fla., 2004—05. Recipient Tenn. Social Studies Tchr. of Yr., Tenn. Social Studies Assn., 1988. Mem.: NEA. D-Conservative. Methodist. Avocations: photography, writing, swimming, watercolor. Home: 2631 NW 5th Terrace Pompano Beach FL 33064 Office: Tequesta Trace Mid Sch Indian Trace Weston FL 33064 Address: 546 River St Chattanooga TN 37405 Personal E-mail: patriciaatarms.com.

ADANG, ROSEMARY, humanities educator; MA, U. Wash., Seattle, 1984—86. Faculty women's studies Highline CC, Des Moines, Wash., 1990—. Rep. Nat. Unitarian Universalist Svc. Com., Seattle, 2005—06. Mem.: Nat. Orgn. Women (bd. mem., Seattle chpt. 2004—06), Nat. Women's Studies Assn. D-Liberal.

ADATO, LINDA JOY, artist, educator; b. London, Oct. 24, 1942; d. John and Renee (Katz) Falber; m. Albert Adato, June 26, 1966; 1 child, Vanessa. Student, Hornsey Coll. Art, Eng., 1960—61; BA in Pictorial Arts, UCLA, 1966, MA in Art Edn., 1967. Adj. lectr. in art Manhattanville Coll., Purchase, NY, 1987—2000; printmaking tchr. Silvermine Sch. of Art, New Canaan, Conn., 1995—. Exhibitions include Achenbach Found. for Graphic Arts, Fine Arts Mus., San Francisco, 1987, Decordova Mus., Lincoln, Mass., 1990, Portland (Oreg.) Art Mus., 1994, Art Complex Mus., Duxbury, Mass., 1994, Newark Pub. Libr., 1994, Housatonic Mus. Art, Bridgeport, Conn., 1998, Old Print Shop, N.Y.C., 1998, 2002, De Cordova Mus., Lincoln, Mass., 1998-99; mem. travelling exhbn. Am. Print Alliance, 1998—, 5th Brit. Internat. Miniutre Print Exhbn., 2003-04, Boston U., 2005, 6th British Internat. Miniature Print Exhibition, 2006-, N.Y. Soc. Etchers and Instituto Cultural Peruano Norte Americano, Lima Peru, 2005, Hollar Soc. Gallery, Prague, Czech Republic, 2006, Silvermin Guild Art Ctr., 2006. Recipient anonymous prize for prints NAD, 1990, Karlene Cusick Purchase award Print Club Albany, 1995; William Meyerowitz Meml. award Audubon Artists, 1996, Atlantic Papers award 1997; purchase award Internat. Miniature Print Exhibit, Conn. Graphic Arts Ctr., 1997, Alice Pauline Schafer Meml. purchase award Print Club, Albany, 1998, Gold medal of Honor Audubon Artists, 2000, Ralph Fabri medal of Merit Audubon Artists, 2002, Art Students League of N.Y. award, Audubon Artists, 2003. Mem. Soc. Am. Graphic Artists (treas. 1995-2002, purchase award 1985). Home: 20 Pratt St New Rochelle NY 10801-4314 Personal E-mail: alada2@verizon.net.

ADATO, PERRY MILLER, documentary producer, director, writer; b. Yonkers, N.Y. d. Perry and Ida (Block) Miller; m. Neil M. Adato, Sept. 11, 1955; children: Laurie, Michelle. Student, Marshalov Sch. Drama, N.Y.C., New Sch. Social Rsch.; LHD (hon.), Ill. Wesleyan U., 1984. Film rsch. coord. CBS-TV Network, N.Y.C., 1959—64, prodr., 1964; assoc. prodr. NET, N.Y.C., 1964—68, prodr., dir., 1968—72, Sta. 13/WNET-TV (formerly NET), N.Y.C., 1972—92; writer Sta. 13/WNET-TV, N.Y.C., 1989, 1996—97, 1999—2001, prodr., dir., 1999—. Exec. prodr. Alvin H. Perlmutter Inc./Ind. Prodn. Fund, 1992-96; guest lectr. on film Harvard U., Columbia U., NYU, Yale U., U. Ill., others, 1970—; lectr. Fairfield (Conn.) U., 1974-75; film lectr. Smithsonian Assocs., Washington, 1997, 98, 99, 2001, 2003-04, 2005, Columbia (Md.) Festival of Arts, 1998, 99; mem. film award jury Am. Film Inst., Beverly Hills, Calif., 1974; judge film award Creative Artists Pub. Svc., N.Y.C., 1976; first chmn. UN Women in the Arts Film Com., 1976-77; pres. jury Montreal Internat. Festival Films on Art, 1990; mem. jury Pompidou Ctr., Paris Internat. Festival of Films on Art, 1994. Producer, dir.: (TV documentary films) Dylan Thomas: The World I Breathe, 1968 (Emmy award for outstanding achievement in cultural documentary 1968), Gertrude Stein: When This You See, Remember Me, 1970 (Montreal Festival Diplome d'Excellence 1970, Am. Film Festival Blue Ribbon award 1970, 2 Emmy nominations for outstanding direction and outstanding achievement in cultural documentary 1971), The Great Radio Comedians, 1972 (Am. Film Festival Red Ribbon award 1972), An Eames Celebration: Several Worlds of Charles and Ray Eames, 1973 (Chgo. Internat. Film Festival Silver Hugo award 1973, Am. Film Festival Red Ribbon award 1973), Mary Cassatt: Impressionist From Philadelphia, 1974 (Women in Communications Clarion award 1974), Georgia O'Keeffe, 1977 (Dirs. Guild Am. award for documentary achievement 1977-1st woman to receive any Dirs. Guild Am. award, NCCJ Christopher award 1978, Com. for Internat. Events Golden Eagle award 1978, Women in Communications Clarion award 1978, Alfred I. DuPont/Columbia U. citation 1978), Frankenthaler: Toward a New Climate, 1978 (Am. Film Festival Blue Ribbon award in fine arts 1979), Picasso: A Painter's Diary, 1980 (Dirs. Guild Am. award for directorial achievement in TV documentary 1980, Alfred I. DuPont/Columbia U. award for excellence in broadcast journalism 1980, Com. for Internat. Events Golden Eagle award 1980, Am. Film Festival Blue Ribbon award in fine arts 1980, Montreal Internat. Festival of Films on Art First prize for Best Biography of an Artist 1981), Carl Sandburg: Echoes and Silences, 1982 (Women in Communications Matrix award 1982, American Women in Radio and TV Pinnacle award for TV documentary 1982, Dirs. Guild Am. award for achievement in TV documentary 1983), Eugene O'Neill: A Glory of Ghosts, 1984-85, Broadcast, 1986 (Most Outstanding Achievement in TV Documentary award Dirs. Guild Am. 1986, Spl. Jury award San Francisco Film Festival 1985, Internat. Film and TV Festival of N.Y. Silver medal 1986); exec. producer (TV series) Women in Art, 1974-78, Art of the Western World, 1985-89; producer, dir., writer: A White Garment of Churches, 1989 (Clarion award 1990, Silver Plaque award Chgo. Internat. Film Festival 1990, Assn. Visual Comm. Silver Cindy award 1990); exec. prodr. rsch. and devel. 3 part series Asian Art, 1990-94; prodr., dir. Great Tales in Asian Art, 1994-96; writer Dream Journeys-Nature in East Asian Art, 1994-95; prodr. R & D Alfred Steiglitz, 1996-98, (working title) Writer, Alfred Steiglitz, 1996-98; prodr., dir., writer Alfred Steiglitz-The Eloquent Eye, 1999-2001 (Comm. Internat. Events Golden Eagle award 2002, Montreal Fest Films on Art selection 2002, film festival award for biog. Houston World Fest 2002). Hon. bd. dirs. Weston-Westport Arts Coun., Conn., 1981—89. Recipient Lifetime Achievement award in visual arts category, Westport (Conn.) Arts Coun., 1996, recipient film retrospective, Nat. Gallery Art, Washington, 1998, hon. award lifetime achievement, Montreal Internat. Festival Films Art, 2002; grantee, NEA, 1977—78, 1993, 2006, NEH, 1980, 1983, 1991, 1993, 1999, 2006; Poynter fellow, Yale U., 1976, Calhoun Coll. assoc. fellow, 1993—, subject tribute, Montreal Internat. Art Film Festival, 1990. Mem. Dirs. Guild Am., Writers Guild Am., N.Y. Women in Film and TV.

ADCOCK, MURIEL W., special education educator; b. Chgo. BA, U. Calif. Sonoma State, Rohnert Park, 1979. Cert. spl. edn. tchr., Calif., Montessori spl. edn. tchr. Tchr. The Concordia Sch., Concord, Calif., 1980-85; tchr., cons. Tenderloin Community Children's Ctr., San Francisco, 1985-86; adminstr. Assn. Montessori Internat.-USA, San Francisco, 1988, tchr., advisor, 1989—. Course asst. Montessori Spl. Edn. Inst., San Francisco, 1985-87, tchr. spl. edn., 1990, tchr. cons., 1991—, rschr. 1992—. U.S. mng. editor World Futures: The Jour. of Gen. Evolution, 2000—; contbr. articles to profl. jour. Sec. Internat. Forum World Affairs Coun., San Francisco, 1990-95, program chair, 1993-95, pres./founder Club of Budapest, U.S., 2000—. Mem. ASCD, Am. Orthopsychiat. Assn., Internat. Soc. Sys. Scientists, Internat. Sys. Inst., Assn. Montessori Internat., N.Am. Montessori Tchrs. Assn., Assn. Childhood Edn. Internat., Smithsonian Assocs., N.Y. Acad. Scis., Internat. Sys. Inst. Avocations: general evolutionary systems theory, sustainable development, human capacity building. Office: 4040 Civic Center Dr Ste 200 San Rafael CA 94903

ADCOX, MARY SANDRA, dietician, consultant; b. Portsmouth, Ohio, Dec. 4, 1939; d. Philip Henry and Bertha Mae (Hansgen) Riddinger; m. Steve Jordan Jr., Dec. 5, 1962 (dec. May 1972); 1 child, Michael Philip; m. Henry Lonzo Adcox Jr., Sept. 30, 1972. BS in Food and Nutrition, U. Cin., 1961; MEd, Tex. State U., 1984. Registered dietitian Commn. on Dietetic Registration. Rsch. dietitian U.S. Army Inst. Surg. Rsch., Ft. Sam Houston, 1964-65; chief dietitian Luth. Gen. Hosp., San Antonio, 1966-67; dir. dietetics Santa Rosa Med. Ctr., San Antonio, 1967-72, San Antonio Cmty. Hosp., 1972-75; adult edn. instr. San Antonio Coll., 1973-84; food svc. supr. San Antonio Ind. Sch. Dist., 1975-96, ret., 1996. Sch. food svc. cons., San Antonio, 1996-2004. Author: Dietetic Assistant Program, 1983, Diet Manual: San Antonio Community Hospital, 1st edit., 1973, Diet Manual: Santa Rosa Medical Center, 4th edit., 1969. Past den. leader Boy Scouts Am. 1st lt. U.S. Army, 1962—64. Mem. Am. Dietetic Assn., San Antonio Dietetic Assn., U. Cin. Alumni Assn., Tex. State U. Alumni Assn., San Antonio Area Ret. Tchrs. Assn., Delta Zeta. Baptist. Avocations: piano, organ, herb gardening. Home: 5503 Oo-Loo-Te-Ka Dr San Antonio TX 78218-5041

ADCOX, SEANNA MICHELLE, reporter; b. Galesburg, Ill., June 8, 1974; d. Larry Neil and Jonna Rae Adcox; m. William Layman Meacham, Apr. 26, 2003. BA in Mass Comm., Winthrop U., Rock Hill, S.C., 1996. Reporter/photographer The Cheraw Chronicle, Cheraw, SC, 1996—97, The Fort Mill Times, SC, 1997—98; reporter The Herald, Rock Hill, SC, 1998—2000, AP, Albany, NY, 2001—03; edn. reporter The Post and Courier, Charleston, SC, 2003—05; statehouse reporter AP, Columbia, SC, 2005—. Home: 519 Aiken Hunt Cir Columbia SC 29223-8421

ADCROFT, PATTI (PATRICE GABRIELLA ADCROFT), editor; b. Scranton, Pa., Apr. 15, 1954; d. Joseph Raymond and Patricia Ann (Ryan) Adcroft. BA In Mag. Journalism and Creative Writing, Syracuse U., 1976. Editor-in-chief Carbondale (Pa.) Miner Mid Valley Gazette, 1976—77; staff writer Good Housekeeping Mag., N.Y.C., 1978—80; mng. editor Family Media/Alive and Well, N.Y.C., 1980—81; freelance writer, editor N.Y.C., 1981—82; sr. editor CBS Mags. Family Weekly, N.Y.C., 1982—84, Omni Mag., N.Y.C., 1984—85, exec. editor, 1985—86, editor-in-chief, 1986—90, Seventeen Mag., 1998—2001; exec. editor Marie Claire, 2004—06; spl. projects editor Discover mag., 2006—. Vis. prof. Syracuse U., 1992—93. Editor-in-chief Omni Future Medical Almanac, 1987, NetGuide Mag., 1994—95, deputy editor InStyle Mag., 1995—98; author: (novels) Every Day Doughnuts; contbr. writer Arthur C. Clarke's 2019, 1986, Omni Book of Continuum, 1982. Bd. advisors SCI Ctr. for Advanced Studies in Mgmt. Wharton Sch., U. Pa. Roman Catholic. Office: Discover 90th Fifth Ave New York NY 10011*

ADDESSO, ANGELA JOYCE, school system administrator; m. Jack Anthony Addesso, Oct. 21, 1973; children: Adam Louis, Jack, Jr. Anthony. BS in Art and Art History, Herbert H. Lehman Coll., Bronx, 1983; MS in Edn., Herbert H. Lehman Coll., 1989; postgrad., Coll. of New Rochelle, N.Y., 1995. Cert. sch. adminstrn. and supervision N.Y. State Dept. Edn., 2003, dist. adminstr. N.Y. State Dept. Edn., 1995, art tchr. K-12 N.Y. State Dept. Edn., 1989, reading tchr. N.Y. State Dept. Edn., 1991. Art instr. Longfellow Elem. - Mt. Vernon C.S.D., NY, 1984—85; dist. wide humanities art coord./instr. Dist. Elem. Schools - Mt. Vernon C.S.D., Mount Vernon, NY, 1985—88; art instr. Mt. Vernon C.S.D. - Franko Mid. Sch., NY, 1988—90, Thornton Elem. Sch. - Mt. Vernon C.S.D., NY, 1990—99; adj. prof. - edn. Mercy Coll., Dobbs Ferry, NY, 1998—; dist. adminstr. for the arts Mt. Vernon C.S.D., Mount Vernon, NY, 1999—. Com. chairperson profl. devel. Mt. Vernon C.S.D., NY, 2004—. Exhibitions include Fried Eggs Mixed Media and other untitled works (Third Pl. - Rye Womans Club, RYE, NY, 2001). Adv. bd. Concordia Conservatory; coord. United Way, Mount Vernon, NY, 2004—06. Recipient Mosaic Award for Multi-Cultural Edn., Mt. Vernon C.S.D., 1992. Mem.: Phi Delta Kappa, Westchester Coalition for Arts Leadership Assn., Nat. Art Edn. Assn., N.Y.State Art Tchrs. Assoc. (sec., v.p., pres. 1998—2004, Region 7 Award for Outstanding Leadership 2001). Avocations: painting, museums, theater, exercise, travel. Home: 4 Sutton Pl Katonah NY 10536 Office: Mount Vernon City School District 165 N Columbus Ave Mount Vernon NY 10553 Office Phone: 914-665-5181. E-mail: aaddesso@mtvernoncsd.org.

ADDICOTT, BEVERLY JEANNE, retired elementary school educator; b. Youngstown, Ohio, Nov. 9, 1948; m. Gerald Leslie Addicott, Mar. 30, 1974; 1 child, Katherine Elizabeth. BS in Edn., Youngstown State U., 1971, cert. media specialist, 1978; cert. in ESL, 1995. Cert. tchr., Ohio, Fla. Tchr. Mathews Sch. Dist., Vienna, Ohio, 1972-75, media specialist, 1975-78, supr. media, 1978-79; media specialist Brevard County Schs., Melbourne, Fla., 1987-91, tchr., 1991—2000. Chef du jour Haven for Children, Melbourne, 1989-94; vol. Habitat for humanity, Melbourne, 1993, University Park PTO, Melbourne, 1989-2000. Mem. Melbourne Alumnae Panhellenic (chair fundraiser 1992), Jr. League of South Brevard (parent educator 1992-95). Avocations: cross-stitch, knitting, crocheting.

ADDIS, DEBORAH JANE, management consultant; b. Rahway, NJ, Jan. 29, 1950; d. Emmanuel and Stella (Oles) Addis; m. James Eldin Reed, Apr. 14, 1983. BA, Bowling Green State U., 1972; MA in Orgn., Mgmt. and Pub. Policy, Lesley U., Cambridge, Mass., 1992. cons. House Judiciary Com., Washington, 1999-2000. Pub. info. officer Dept. Transp., State of Ohio, 1972-73; dir. pub. info. and edn. Dept. Commerce, State of Ohio, 1973-75; press sec. Atty. Gen., State of Ohio, 1975-77; dep. press sec. Office of Gov., Commonwealth of Mass., Boston, 1978-79; sr. account exec. Miller Comms., Boston, 1979-80; v.p., prin. Addis & Reed Cons., Inc., Boston, 1981-91, pres., 1992—. Adj. faculty Lesley Coll. Grad. Sch., 1992-95; bd. dirs. Can. Inst. Internat. Affairs, Boston; cons. in field. Mng. editor The American Canada Watch, 1995-99; contbr. articles to profl. jours. and newspapers. Bd. govs. Women's City Club of Boston, 1982-85; pres. Asbestos Victims Campaign, Boston, 1987-90. Mem. New Eng.-Can. Bus. Coun. (bd. dirs. 1994-98), Inst. Mgmt. Cons. (bd. dirs. New Eng. chpt. 1988-89), Can. Inst. Internat. Affairs (bd. dirs. Boston br. 1967—), Mass. Audubon Soc., Harvard Club of Boston, Boston Athenaeum. Democrat. Avocations: photography, herpetology, hiking, travel, yoga. Home: 25 Holly Ln Brookline MA 02467-2156 Office: Addis & Reed Cons Inc PO Box 85 Chestnut Hill MA 02467 Business E-Mail: addis@addisreed.com.

ADDIS, ILANA BETH, obstetrician; b. 1971; BA, U. Chgo., 1992; MPH, U. Calif., 1996; MD, U. Ariz. Coll. Medicine, 1998. Cert. Obsterics and Gynecology. Assoc. dir. Divsn. Female Pelvic Medicine & Recovery Surgery; asst. prof., Obstetrics & Gynecology U. Ariz. Coll. Medicine. Mem. Planned Parenthood of Southern Ariz., Southern Ariz. Human Soc., Big Brothers/Big Sisters; vol. Shubitz refugee clinic. Named one of 40 Under 40, Tucson Bus. Edge, 2006; fellow Am. Coll. Obstetrics and Gynecology; women's health clinical rsch. fellowship, U. Calif. Mem.: Nat. Physicians Alliance, Am. Urogynecologic Assn. Office: University of Arizona College of Medicine PO Box 245017 1501 N Campbell Ave Tucson AZ 85724*

ADDIS, KAY TUCKER, newspaper editor; AB in English, Coll. of William and Mary, 1970. Editor The Virginian-Pilot, Norfolk, 1996—. Office: The Virginian-Pilot 150 W Brambleton Ave Norfolk VA 23510-2075 also: Virginian Pilot P O Box 449 Norfolk VA 23501-0449

ADDISON, ANNE SIMONE POMEX, television director, consultant, commentator; b. Antwerp, Belgium, Dec. 2, 1927; d. Eli and Mary Deborah (Rubinstein) Cleeman; m. Joseph B. Pomex, Mar. 6, 1947 (div. Apr. 1954); 1 child, Steven M.; m. John Addison, Sept. 1, 1966. BA, Barnard Coll., 1947; MA, Columbia U., 1952. Instr. Columbia U., N.Y.C., 1947-48; circulation dir. Ford Found., N.Y.C., 1952-58; assoc. dir. radio Broadcasting Found. Am., N.Y.C., 1958-60; dir., v.p. NET-WNET-13 TV, N.Y.C., 1960—, internat. dir., 1960—; cons., producers rep., pres. Communications Internat., N.Y.C. Cons. dept. culture U.S. Dept. of State, Washington, 1961; dir. Coll. Skills, N.Y.C.; bd. dirs. ednl. dept. Internat. Ctr. Photography, 1983, Bezalel Acad. Design and Architecture, 1994. Contbr. articles to profl. jours; producer TV dramas, dance and documentaries. Bd. dirs. Am. Friends of Hermitage, 1994. Recipient awards, medals for fostering understanding and cultural cooperation: Austria, Belgium, Holland, Israel, Italy and Brazil, Woman of Achievement award Broadcasting Industry, 1967; featured in N.Y. Times Mag., others. Mem. Am. Women in Radio and TV (1st v.p. 1972—), Am. Women in Communications, Women's Econ. Forum, NATAS, Lotos Club, Advt. of Am. Club. Office: 1035 5th Ave New York NY 10028-0135

ADDISON, LINDA LEUCHTER, lawyer, writer, commentator, columnist; b. Allentown, Pa., Nov. 25, 1951; d. Marcus and Sophie Theresa (Tisch) Leuchter; m. Max M. Addison, Sept. 10, 1977; 1 child, Alexandra Leuchter Addison. BA with honors, U. Tex., 1973, JD, 1976. Bar: Tex. 1976, U.S. Dist. Ct. (so. dist.) Tex. 1977, U.S. Dist. Ct. (no. dist.) Tex. 2000, U.S. Dist. Ct. (ea. dist.) Tex. 2003, U.S. Ct. Appeals (5th cir.) 1981, U.S. Ct. Appeals (fed. cir.) 2003, U.S. Supreme Ct. 2003. Assoc. Fulbright & Jaworski LLP, Houston, 1976—83, ptnr., 1984—, exec. com., tech. ptnr., 2002—. Expert on fed. and Tex. evidence. Author: Texas Practice Guide: Evidence, 2006; mng. editor Tex. Law Rev. 1975-76; contbr. chpt. to book, articles to profl. jours. Trustee U. Tex. Law Sch. Found., 1994-2006; mem. fed. jud. evaluation com. of Senators Hutchison and Cornyn, 1997-; exec. com. chancellor's coun. U. Tex. Sys., 1999-; bd. dirs. Holocaust Mus. Houston, 2001-; mem. Commn. of 125, U. Tex., Austin, 2003-04, vice chmn. mission task force centennial commn., 1981-83, mem. U.S. commn. preservation Am.'s heritage abroad U.S., 2006-; bd. visitors U. Tex. M.D. Anderson Cancer Ctr., U. Cancer Found., 2006-. Named a Woman on the Move, Tex. Exec. Women, 2000, Woman to Watch, Jewish Women Internat., 2002, Woman of Yr., United Way Tex. Gulf Coast, 2006; named an Hon. Barrister, U. Tex. Sch. Law Bd. Advs., 2000, Outstanding Young Lawyer of Houston, 1984-85; named one of Am.'s Top 50 Women Litigators, Nat. Law Jour., 2001, 100 Most Influential Lawyers in Am., 2006, Tex. Go To Litigators, Tex. Lawyer, 2002, Most Fascinating People in Houston, Friends of Tex. Med. Ctr. Libr., 2001, Best Lawyers in Am., Woodard and White, 2003—, Tex. Super Lawyers, Tex. Monthly, 2003, 04, 05, 500 Leading Litigators in Am., Lawdragon, 2006, 500 Leading litigators in Am., 2006; named to Chambers & Ptnrs. USA, 2004, 05, 06. Fellow: Tex. Bar Found. (life; trustee 2003—), Houston Bar Found. (life), Am. Bar Found. (life); mem.: ABA, Am. Bd. Trial Advs., World Internat. Patent Orgn. (arbitration and mediation ctr. domain name panel 2002—), Am. Intellectual Property Law Assn., Am. Arbitration Assn. (internat. panel 1992—, panel of neutrals, large complex case panel), Houston Young Lawyers Assn. (chmn. cont. legal edn. com. 1977—78, bd. dirs. 1978—81, Outstanding Chmn. award), Tex. Young Lawyers Assn. (bd. dirs. 1981—83), Houston Bar Assn. (chmn. cont. legal edn. com. 1981—82, mem. jud. evalns. com. 1982—83, Pres.'s award for outstanding svc. 1982), State Bar Tex. (chmn. bar jour. com. 1988—90, adminstr. rules evidence com. 1988—90, chmn. bar jour. com. 1991—99), Tex. Law Rev. Ex-Editors Assn. (life), Abbot, Friar Soc., United Way, deTocqueville Soc., Anti-Defamation League (bd. dirs. S.W. Region 1992—94), Omicron Delta Kappa. Office: Fulbright & Jaworski LLP 1301 McKinney St Ste 5100 Houston TX 77010-3095

ADDOR, LINA AL KAISSY, science educator; b. Sofia, Bulgaria, Jan. 13, 1975; arrived in U.S., 1992; d. Kais-Arif Al-Kaissy and Daniela Leseva Omcikus; m. Forrest Matthew Addor, Aug. 8, 2005. A in Liberal Arts/Sci., Dutchess CC, Poughkeepie, NY, 1996; BSc, Roger Williams U., Bristol, R.I., 1998; M in Tchg., SUNY, New Paltz, NY, 2002. Sci. tchr. Wallkill Ctrl. Sch., Wallkill, NY, 2002—. Student coun. advisor Wallkill CSD, Wallkill, NY, 2004—05, multicultural club advisor, 2002—. Mem.: NY State United Tchr., SUNY Alumni, Roger Williams Alumni. Democrat. Orthodox. Avocations: tennis, piano, dance.

ADDY, JO ALISON PHEARS, economist; b. Germany, May 2, 1951; d. William Phears and Paula Hubbard; m. Tralance Obuma Addy, May 25, 1979; children: Mantse, Miishe, Dwetri, Naakai. BA, Smith Coll., 1973; MBA, Adelphi U., 1975; postgrad., Stanford U., 1975—79; MPA, Harvard U., 2006. Econ. analyst Morgan Guaranty, N.Y.C., 1973—75; economist Young Profls. Program, World Bank, Washington, 1979—80; asst. v.p., internat. economist Crocker Bank, San Francisco, 1980—85; asst. v.p., economist for money markets 1st RepublicBank, Dallas, 1985—87; prin. SEGI Internat., Dallas, 1987—91; pres. Unimed Ventures, Inc., 1991—95; mng. dir. Alsweb Bus. Advantage, 2000—; mem. adv. bd. Plebys Internat. LLC, 2003—. Lectr. in field. Docent Bowers Mus.; vice chmn. St. John's Sch. Com.; pres. Saddle-back Valley chpt. Nat. Charity League. Office: 8 Palomino Trabuco Canyon CA 92679-4837 Business E-Mail: jo.addy@gmail.com.

ADEDEJI, SHARON LILLY, literature and language educator; b. York, Pa., Sept. 4, 1974; d. Elbert Graydon Jr. and Ricki Lila Lilly; m. Adebukola Taofeeq Adedeji, July 23, 1999; children: Alexander, Aeryn. BA, U. Md., College Park, 1996; MA in Leadership, Coll. Notre Dame, Balt., 2001. Cert. educator Towson U., Md., 1998, advanced profl. Md., adminstr. level I Nat. Bd. Profl. Tchg. Stds. Tchr. English Owings Mills H.S., Md., 1998—. Coach girl's lacrosse Owings Mills H.S., Md., 1999—2004, coach field hockey, 1999—2005, class advisor steering com., 1999—2005, journalism advisor Eagle's Eye and Eagle TV, 2004—, student govt. advisor, 2005—. Nominee Balt. County Excellence award, Owings Mills C. of C., 2002, 2004, 2006; recipient Student's Choice award, Music Dept. Owings Mills H.S., 2001, 2003, 2d pl. yearbook, Quill and Scroll, 2005. Mem.: NEA, Tchrs. Assn. Balt. County (Rookie Tchr. award 2002), Nat. Coun. Tchrs. English. Avocations: reading, writing, scrapbooks, bicycling, skiing. Office: Owings Mills HS 124 Tollgate Rd Owings Mills MD 21117

ADEKSON, MARY OLUFUNMILAYO, counselor, educator; b. Ogbomoso, Nigeria; came to U.S., 1988; d. Gabriel and Deborah Williams; children: Adedayo, Babatunde. BA in English and Am. Lit., Brandeis U., 1975; MEd in Guidance and Counseling, Obafemi Awolowo U., Ile-Ife, Nigeria, 1987; PhD, Ohio U., 1997. English tchr. Ctrl. Sch. Bd., Ibadan, Nigeria, 1968-88; acting prin. Abe Tech. Coll., Ibadan, Nigeria, 1978; coord. guidance svcs. Min. Edn., Ile-Ife, 1984-88; part-time lectr. Obafemi Awolowo U., Ile-Ife, 1986-88; vice prin. Olubuse Meml. HS, Ile-Ife, 1987-88; grad. asst. Ohio U., Athens, 1988-91. Vol. contract worker, trainer Careline, Tri-County Mental Health Ctr., Athens, 1988-92; vol. My Sister's Place, Athens, 1989, Good Works Athens, 1989, Montgomery County Hotline, 1994; contract worker Tri County Activity Ctr., Athens, 1989-92, therapist II Woodland Ctr., Gallipolis, Ohio, 1991-92; part-time lectr. U. Md., 1993, coord. tutorial svc.; dir. Christian Book Ctr., Ile-Ife; vol., part-time counselor DWI program Prince George's County Health Dept., Hyattsville, Md.; counselor Potomac Healthcare Found. Mountain Manor Treatment Program; adj. prof. Bowie (Md.) State U. Counseling Program, 1997-98; asst. prof. St. Bonaventure U., 1998-2004, assoc. prof. 2004-; faculty adviser Chi Sigma Iota, Phi Rho chpt. Author: Traditional Healers of Nigeria, 2004. Vol. Montgomery County Police Dept., 1993; mem. Alcohol and Other Drug Abuse Adv. Coun., Montgomery County, Md., 1994-98; mem. adv. com. Germantown (Md.) Libr., 1993-98; mem. Gaithersburg (Md.) City Adv. Com., 1993-98; chmn. bd. dirs. Faith Enterprises; bd. dirs. Faith Consultancy Group, Olean Cultural Dialogue Group, 1999—. Recipient Gold medal West African Athletic Assn., 1965; Internat. Peace scholar P.E.O., 1990-91, Wien Internat. scholar Brandeis U., 1973-75. Mem. ACA, Am. Mental Health Counselors Assn. Network on Children and Teens (membership chair 1991-92, chair 1993-98), Am. Assn. Counseling and Devel. (award for internat. grad. students 1990), Counseling Assn. Nigeria (planning com. 1986), Oyo State Nigeria Assn. Guidance Counselors (chmn. Oranmiyan local govt. area 1986-88), Chi Sigma Iota (program coord. Ohio U. chpt. 1990, faculty advisor Phi Rho chpt.). Avocations: meeting people from around the world, jogging, walking, playing tennis, reading. Business E-Mail: madekson@sbu.edu.

ADELMAN, BAYLA ANN, occupational therapist; b. Milw., Aug. 29, 1929; d. Barney Edward and Sadye Rachel Shimon; children: Scott, Boni, Shawn. BS in Occupational Therapy, U. So. Calif., L.A., 1951; MA in Counseling & Guidance, Calif. State U., Northridge, 1980. Cert. occupl. therapist U. So. Calif., 1952. Staff occupational therapist Wadsworth Hosp., L.A., 1952—54; dir. occupational therapy Compton Hosp., 1955—57; staff specialist Children's Spastic Soc., L.A., 1958—60; staff therapist Northridge Hosp., Northridge, 1970—75, Van Nuys Psychiat. Hosp., 1976—78, Tarzana Regional Med. Ctr., 1984—2001, JFK Meml. Hosp., Indio, 2002—04. Instr. Sherman Oaks Elem. Sch., Calif., 1971—73. Brownie leader Girl Scouts Am., 1960—61; Cub Scout leader Boy Scouts Am., 1967—69; mem. Desert Friends John Tracy Clinic Audiometrist, 2002—05, Brandies U. Nat. Women's Com., 1998—2005; campaign worker Dem. Club, Sherman Oaks, 1955—56. Mem.: Am. Occupational Therapy Assn. Avocation: golf. Home: 43 Blue River Dr Palm Desert CA 92211

ADELSON, GLORIA ANN, retired financial executive; b. Savannah, Ga., Aug. 3, 1944; d. Lee Roy and Edith Thelma (Horovitz) Schraibman; m. Joseph Harvey Adelson, Mar. 19, 1967 (dec.). BA in Polit. Sci., U. Fla., 1965; MA in Bus., Webster U., 1991. Cert. fin. def. mgr. Budget analyst U.S. Dept. Labor, Silver Spring, Md., 1967; mgmt. analyst U.S. Naval Supply Ctr., Charleston, S.C., 1967-69, budget analyst, 1969-70, head fin. mgmt. staff, 1970-73, head. ops. and maintenance br., 1973-75; mgmt. coord. officer So. Divsn. Naval Facilities Engring. Commd., Charleston, 1975-80, dir. budget br., 1980-85, dir. budget and programs divsn., 1985-88, dep. dir. programs and comptroller dept., 1988—2004; ret., 2004. Fin. sec., treas. Synagogue Emanu-El, Charleston, 1982-88, program chmn., 2002-2004; pres. Sisterhood Emanu-El, Charleston, 1993-94, 95-96; active patron com. Am. Cancer Soc., Charleston, 1989, 91, 95, 97; mem. fed. sector com. United Way, Charleston, 1991; bd. dirs. so. br. Women's League for Conservative Judaism, 1996-98, v.p., 1998-2002, pres., 2002-04, mem. Internat. bd. dirs., 2001—; mem. Trident Area Cmty. Excellence Comm. Team, 1995-99, examiner for quality awards, 1999; mem. Jewish cmty. rels. com. Charleston Jewish Fedn., 2004—; published fgn. interpreter's list S.C. World Trade Ctr, 1998, 99, 2001, 02. Mem. Am. Soc. Mil. Comptrs. (chmn. coms. Charleston chpt. 1987—, v.p. Navy, 1990-91, pres., 1991-92), Charleston C. of C. (Leadership Charleston 1997-98), Arthritis Found., Arthritis Vol. Adv. Comm. (co-chair arthritis support group). Avocations: reading, exercise. Home: 4 Berwick Cir Charleston SC 29407-3414 Personal E-mail: happygaa@bellsouth.net.

ADERHOLDT, TRACI EAVES, music educator; b. Rutherfordton, N.C., Mar. 3, 1964; d. Julian Bobby and Alice Faye (Waldrop) Eaves; m. James Lamar Aderholdt, June 17, 2000. B in Music Edn., U. N.C., 1986; M in Music Edn., Converse Coll., 1992. Drama tchr. Montgomery County Sch., Troy, NC, 1986—87; gen. music tchr. Shelby City Sch., Shelby, NC, 1987—2001, 2002—, Gaston County Sch., Gastonia, NC, 2001—02. Music dir. Greater Shelby Cmty. Theater, Shelby, 1988—95; pianist Cleve. County Choral Soc., Shelby, 1988—99, Eastside Bapt. Ch., Shelby, 1991—97, First Bapt. Ch., Kings Mt., NC, 1997—. Mem.: Am. Choral Dir. Assn. (SSA all-state coord. 1994—95), Music Educators Nat. Conf. Baptist. Avocations: antiques, painting, coin collecting/numismatics, drawing. Home: 357 Beattie Rd Kings Mountain NC 28086

ADESIYAN, HATTIE ROSE OLAGBEGI, education educator, consultant; b. Greenwood, Miss., May 10; d. Leroy and Tennessee (Mayfield) Williams; m. D.V.F. Olagbegi Adesiyan, Aug. 5, 1974 (div. Jan. 1985); children: Michael, Steve. BSc, Ind. Cen. U., 1967; MEd, Ohio U., 1968; PhD, Ohio State U., 1973. Cert. elem. tchr., Ind., Ohio; cert. sch. counselor, Ind., Ohio. Elem. tchr. Indpls. Pub. Schs., 1965-67; sys. engr. IBM, Inc., Upper Arlington, Ohio, 1968-69; reading specialist Columbus (Ohio) Pub. Schs., 1969-70; asst. prof. edn. Colgate U., Hamilton, NY, 1973-76; dir. tutorial and student adv. svcs. U. Lagos (Nigeria), 1975-76; dir. tchr. edn. Wabash Coll., Crawfordsville, Ind., 1977-80; asst. dean Sch. Gen. Studies, assoc. prof. edn. Purdue U.-Calumet, Hammond, Ind., 1981—2002, ret., 2002. Pres. Olagbegi, Adesiyan & Assoc., Indpls., 1987—; cons., reviewer Choice, N.Y.C., 1978-89; cons. Hammond Pub. Schs., 1991-98; bd. dirs. Hammond Edn. Found., 1988-92; reviewer Longman Pubs. and William C. Brown Pubs.; dir. Positive Mental Attitude Curriculum Devel. Project, 1992-2000. Contbr. articles, monographs to profl. publs. and Eric; cons. editor, mem. nat. editorial bd. Nat. Social Sci. Jour., 1988—. Mem. long range planning com. City of Hammond, 1988-90; chair rsch. grant com. Dr. Martin Luther King Meml. Com., Hammond, 1988-89; regional dir. Black Women in Midwest Rsch. Project, Hammond, 1984-85; speaker in field. Bd. dirs. N.W. Ind. Coalition for Edn., 1986-89, Cmty. Concerts Assn., 1987-89, Calumet Area YWCA, 1989-90, Hammond YMCA, 1992-94; mem. cmty. adv. bd. Merchantile Nat. Bank, Hammond, 1989-92. Fulbright fellow, 1987; Calumet Sch. Profl. Studies grantee, 1988, 91, NEH humanities scholar, 1978. Mem. NAACP, ASCD, Ind. Coalition of Blacks in Higher Edn. (instnl. rep. 1988), Colored Women's Federated Club (v.p. 1988-89, 92—), Tabitha Calyx Club. Republican. Avocations: golf, reading, travel, dance, folklore drama. Home: 5151 Pin Oak Dr Indianapolis IN 46254-1498 Office: 5151 Pin Oak Dr Indianapolis IN 46254

ADESSA, LORI, music educator; d. Donald and Emily Jantz; m. Anthony Adessa, May 22, 1983; 1 child, Dominique. BS in Music Therapy, Ind. U., Ft. Wayne, 1985. Registered music therapist Nat. Assn. Music Therapy, 1985, cert. tchr. Calif., 2003. Tchr. gen. music Crawford County Sch. Dist., Roberta, Ga., 1991—93, Mill Valley Sch. Dist., Calif., 1993—. Contract music therapist Wesleyan Retirement and Nursing Home, Georgetown, Tex., 1985—89; presenter in field. Active Big Bros./Big Sisters, Ft. Wayne, 1979—83; hospice vol. Hospice, Austin, Tex., 1987—89. Named Big Sister of Yr., Big Bros./Big Sisters, 1983; recipient Golden Bell Tchg. award. Mem.: Music Edn. Nat. Conf., Nat. Assn. Music Therapy. Office: Mill Valley School District 411 Sycamore Mill Valley CA 94941 Office Phone: 415-389-7700. Office Fax: 415-389-7773. Business E-Mail: millvalleyschooldistrict@marin.k12.ca.us.

ADICKES, SANDRA ELAINE, language educator, writer; b. N.Y.C., July 14, 1933; d. August Ernst and Edythe Louise (Oberschlake) A.; children: Delores, Lily, Cynthia. BA, Douglass Coll., 1954; MA, CUNY, 1964; PhD, NYU, 1977. Asst. registrar NYU, 1954-55; sec. McCann Erickson, J. Walter Thompson Cos., N.Y.C., 1955-60; English tchr. N.Y.C. Bd. Edn., 1960-70, 1980-88; instr. edn. N.Y.C. Tech. Coll., 1970-72; asst. prof. English S.I. C.C., N.Y.C., 1972-77; dir. project chance Bklyn. Coll., 1977-80; from assoc. prof. to prof. English Winona (Minn.) State U., 1988-98, prof. emerita, 1998—. Cons. Antioch Coll. N.Y.C., 1970; guest tutor London U., 1979. Author: The Social Quest, 1991, Legends of Good Women, 1992, To Be Young Was Very Heaven, 1997, The Legacy of a Freedom School, 2005; editor: By A Woman Writt, 1973; contbr. articles to profl. jours. Co-founder Tchrs'. Freedom Sch. Project, Miss., 1963-64, Tchrs'. Com. for Peace Vietnam, 1965-66. Named Woman of Yr. Nat. Assn. Negro Bus. Profl. Women, N.J., 1966. Mem. MLA, Midwest Modern Lang. Assn., Nat Coun. Tchrs. of English, Popular Culture Assn. Democrat. Home: 93 Renaissance Ln New Brunswick NJ 08901 E-mail: sadickes@eudoramail.com.

ADILETTA, DEBRA JEAN OLSON, mathematics professor; b. Gloucester, Mass., Oct. 1, 1959; d. Melvin Porter Jr. and Ruth Margaret (Dahlmer) Olson; m. Mark Anthony Adiletta, Aug. 25, 1984; children: Christopher Michael, Nichole Brianna, Mark Andrew. BA, Coll. of Holy Cross, Worcester, Mass., 1981; MBA, U. Rochester, N.Y., 1986. Systems analyst Eastman Kodak Co., Rochester, NY, 1981—85, infosystems specialist, 1985—86, personal computer area mgr., 1986—87, bus. analyst cons., 1987—90, info. sys. co-dir., 1990—92, bus. sys. specialist, 1992—2003; prof. math. Monroe CC, Rochester, 2004—. Seminar instr., Rochester, 1987. Fin. advisor Sts. Peter and Paul Ch., Rochester, 1985-86; div. chairperson United Way, Rochester, 1987. Mem. Assn. Systems Mgmt., Holy Cross Alumni Assn. (class agt. 1981—, sec. 1983-84, treas. 1984-88, v.p. 1988-90, pres. 1990-91, bd. dirs. 1992—). Avocations: snow and water skiing, horseback riding.

ADKERSON, DONYA LYNN, clinical counselor; b. Mattoon, Ill., Oct. 5, 1959; d. Edwin Dwayne and Sonya Jeanne (Abernathie) Adkerson; m. George Anthony Ferguson, May 20, 1990; children: Tiana Jo Berry-Jones, Thomas A.R. Ferguson. MA, So. Ill. U., Edwardsville, 1983. Outpatient dir. Children's Ctr. for Behavioral Devel., Centerville, Ill., 1983-90; pvt. practice psychotherapy Evaluation & Therapy Svc., Edwardsville, 1991-92; dir. Alternatives Counseling, Inc., 1993—; grant coord. Ill. Sex Offender Mgmt. Bd., 2003—05. Cons. St. Louis City Juvenile Ct., 1991-94, Covenant Children's Home, 1991-93, U. Ill., 1997-2000. Co-author: Adult Sexual Offender Assessment Packet, 1994. Founding mem. Ill. Assn. Treatment Sex Abusers, 1996—2001; pres. Ill. Network for Mgmt. Abusive Sexuality, 1991; clin. mem., exec. bd. Assn. Treatment of Sex Abusers, 1995—2000, chair orgn. and devel. com., 1996—2000; mem. ethics and stds. com., founding mem. Madison County Child Protection Task Force, 1999—; mem. 3d Jud. Cir. Family Violence steering com., 1996—, Adolescent Perpetrator Network, 1987—95; exec. bd. Arts League Players Theatre, Edwardsville, 1996—2005; former chmn. Metro-East Task Force on Sexual Offenders; mem. Madison County Child Protection task force, Am. Profl. Soc. on Abuse of Children, Ill. Sex Offender Mgmt. Bd. assessment and treatment subcoms.; bd. dirs. Ill. Assn. Treatment Sex Abusers, 2005. Mem. Ill. Counseling Assn., Ill. Mental Health Counselors Assn. Avocations: theater, water gardening. Office: Alternatives Counseling PO Box 639 88 S Main Glen Carbon IL 62034 Office Phone: 618-288-8085.

ADKINS, CATHERINE IRENE, secondary school educator, department chairman; d. Dean Duane and Doris Jean Fletcher; m. Gary Wayne Adkins, Aug. 14, 1982; 1 child, Kimberly Deane. BA, U. No. Iowa, Cedar Falls, Iowa, 1973. Cert. tchr. secondary English Iowa State Bd. Ednl. Examiners, 1973. Tchr. English Clinton (Iowa) Cmty. Schs., 1973—; chmn. Dept. English Clinton (Iowa) H.S., 2004—. Mentor Clinton (Iowa) Cmty. Schs., 1988—, mem. curriculum com. Mem.: PTA, NEA (bldg. rep. 2000, mem. exec. bd. 2000), Iowa State Edn. Assn., Clinton (Iowa) Edn. Assn. Avocations: walking, reading, travel. Office: Clinton High School 817 8th Avenue South Clinton IA 52732 Office Phone: 563-243-7540. Business E-Mail: cadkins@po-2.clinton.k12.ia.us.

ADKINS-REGAN, ELIZABETH KOCHER, biological psychology educator; b. Washington, July 12, 1945; d. Charles Peter and Dorothy Esther (Clay) Kocher; m. David Adkins, 1971 (div. 1973); m. Dennis Thomas Regan, 1980. BS, U. Md., 1967; PhD, U. Pa., 1971. Rsch. assoc. Bucknell U., Lewisburg, Pa., 1971-72, asst. prof., 1972-74, SUNY, Cortland, 1974-75; asst. prof. psychology/neurobiology and behavior Cornell U., Ithaca, N.Y., 1975-81, assoc. prof., 1981-88, prof., 1988—, assoc. dean, 1991—96, chair, 2001—05. Editl. bd. Hormones and Behavior, 1986—, Am. Naturalist, 2004-, Proceedings of the Royal Society, 2006-; cons. editor Journal Comparative Psychology, 1994-2001, Behavioral Neuroscience, 1998-2001; author Hormones and Animal Social Behavior; contbr. articles and book revs. to profl. jours., chpts. to books. Recipient sr. award NSF, 1986; Woodrow Wilson Found. hon. fellow, 1967, NSF grad. fellow, 1967-71, Fulbright scholar, 1986. Fellow AAAS, Animal Behavior Soc., Am. Psychol. Soc.; mem. Soc. Neurosci., Internat. Soc. Psychoneuroendocrinology, Phi Beta Kappa. Avocation: piano. Office: Cornell U Uris Hall Ithaca NY 14853-7601 Business E-Mail: er12@cornell.edu.

ADKISON, CHARLA S., biology educator; b. Opp, Ala., Nov. 4, 1950; d. Charlie R. and Frances A. Spears; m. Rodney N. Adkison, Feb. 2, 1974; 1 child, Alex C. BS in Biology, U. Montevallo, Ala., 1973; EdM with emphasis in Biology, Auburn at Montgomery, Ala., 1977. Tchr. sci. Kinston H.S., Ala., 1973—85; tchr. chemistry Enterprise H.S., 1986—89; instr. biology Enterprise - Ozark C.C., 1989—. Mem. biology academic comm. articulation com. State of Ala., 1997—; chair course of study Ala. Coll. Sys., 1997—, mem. post secondary adv. com. policy matters, 2000—. Participant Relay Life Coffee County, Enterprise, Ala., 1992—. Named Sci. Tchr. of Yr., Ala. Acad. Scis., 1985; recipient Predl. award Excellence in Sci. Tchg., 1985, Profl. Devel. award, Enterprise State Jr. Coll., 1999. Mem.: Ala. Edn. Assn., Enterprise Ozark C.C. Edn. Assn., Enterprise Literary Club, Phi Mu (pres. Kappa Chi chpt.). Home: 108 S Oak Ridge Dr Enterprise AL 36330 Office: Enterproze Ozark CC 600 Plz Dr Enterprise AL 36330

ADLER, AMY M., law educator; b. 1963; BA summa cum laude, Yale U., 1985, JD, 1990. Bar: NY 1993. Law clk. to Judge John M. Walker, Jr. US Ct. Appeals 2nd Cir., NYC, 1990—91; litig. assoc. Debevoise & Plimpton, NYC, 1992—94; fellow Freedom Forum Media Studies Ctr. Columbia U., 1994—95; asst. prof. law NYU Sch. Law, 1996—99, assoc. prof., 1999—2001, prof., 2001—. Office: NYU Sch Law Vanderbilt Hall Rm 314K 40 Washington Sq S New York NY 10012-1099 Office Phone: 212-998-6645. E-mail: adlera@juris.law.nyu.edu.

ADLER, FREDA SCHAFFER (MRS. G. O. W. MUELLER), criminologist, educator; b. Phila., Nov. 21, 1934; d. David and Lucia G. (de Wolfson) Schaffer; children by previous marriage: Mark, Jill, Nancy. BA, U. Pa., 1956, MA, 1968, PhD (fellow), 1971. Instr. dept. psychiatry Temple U., Phila., 1971; rsch. coord. Addiction Scis. Ctr., 1971—72; rsch. dir. sect. on drug and alcohol abuse Med. Coll. Pa., 1972—74, asst. prof. psychiatry, 1972—74; assoc. prof. criminal justice Rutgers U., Newark, 1974—79, prof., 1979—82, disting. prof., 1982—, acting dean grad. sch. criminal justice, 1986—87. Bd. dirs. Internat. Sci. and Profl. Adv. Coun. UN Programs in Crime Prevention and Criminal Justice; vis. fellow Yale U., 1976; cons. to Nat. Commn. on Marijuana and Drug Abuse, 1972-73, NYU Sch. Law, 1972-74; mem. faculty Nat. Jud. Coll., U. Nev., 1973—, Nat. Coll. Criminal Def. Lawyers and Pub. Defenders U. Houston, 1975; mem. adv. com. Gen. Fedn. Women's Clubs, 1975-77; UN rep. Internat. Prisoner Aid Assn., 1973-75, Centro Nat. di Prevenzione e Difesa Sociale, 1989—, Internat. Soc. Social Def., regional sec. gen., 1991—, bd. dirs.; sec. bd. dirs. Inst. for Continuous Study of Man, 1974-77, v.p., 1977—; adv. bd. Internat. Jour. Comparative and Applied Criminal Justice, 2005— Author: Sisters in Crime, 1975, The Incidence of Female Criminality in the Contemporary World, 1981, Nations Note Obsessed with Crime, 1983; co-author: A Systems Approach to Drug Treatment, 1975, Medical Lollypop, Junkie Insuline or what?, 1974, Criminology of Deviant Women, 1978, Outlaws of the Ocean, 1985, Criminology, 1991, 6th edit., 2007, Criminal Justice, 1993, 4th edit., 2006, Criminology and the Criminal Justice System, 1995, 5th edit., 2006, Criminal Justice: The Core, 1996, Kriminologia, 2000, Criminology and the Criminal Justice System: United States and Georgia, 2003; editor: Advances in Criminological Theory, 1987—; mem. editl. bd.: Criminology, 1971—73, Jour. Criminal Law and Criminology, 1982—, The American Sociologist, 1999—, Feminist Criminology, 2006; co-editor: Politics, Crime and the International Scene, 1972—, Revue Internationale de Droit Penal, 1974—, European Jour. Criminology, 2003—; assoc. editor: LAE Jour., 1977—85, cons. editor: Jour. Criminal Law and Criminology, mem. adv. bd.: Internat. Jour. Comparative and Applied Criminal Justice, 2005—; contbr. numerous articles on criminology and psychiatry to profl. jours. Bd. dirs. U. Pa. Alumnae Assn., 1974—77, The Police Found., 1996—2002. Recipient (with G.O.W. Mueller) Beccaria medal in Gold Deutsche Kriminologische Gesellschaft, 1979; fellow Max Planck Inst. Fgn. and Internat. Law and Criminology, 1984, Am. Soc. Criminology, 1994, Northeastern Criminal Inst. Assn., 2002; named Cecil H. and Ida Green Honors Prof., Tex. Christian U., 1998, Ind. U. Disting. Scholar of Crime, Law, and Justice, 1999, Excellence award minorities and women's sect. Acad. Criminal Justice Scis., 2001, 1st Disting. Criminology award U. Pa., 2006; Alumni award established in her honor Rutgers U. Sch. Criminal Justice, 2006. Fellow Am. Soc. Criminology (pres. 1994-95, Herbert Bloch award 1972, award Divsn. Internat. Criminology 2006); mem. Am. Sociol. Assn., Internat. Assn. Penal Law, U. Pa. Alumnae Assn. (bd. dirs. 1974-77), Chi Omega (award established in her name 2006). Home: 30 Waterside Plz Apt 37J New York NY 10010-2628 Office: Rutgers U Sch Criminal Justice 123 Washington St Newark NJ 07102-3094 Personal E-mail: freadler@nyc.rr.com, f-adler@cox.net.

ADLER, LOUISE DECARL, judge; b. 1945; BA, Chatham Coll., Pitts.; JD, Loyola U., Chgo. Bar: Ill., 1970, Calif., 1972. Practicing atty., San Diego, 1972-84; standing trustee Bankruptcy Ct. So. Dist. Calif., San Diego, 1974-79, chief bankruptcy judge, 1996—2001. Mem. editorial bd. Calif. Bankruptcy Jour., 1991-92. Fellow Am. Coll. Bankruptcy; mem. San Diego County Bar Assn. (chair bus. law study sect. 1979, fed. ct. com. 1983-84), Lawyers Club of San Diego (bd. dirs. 1972-73, treas. 1972-75, sec. 1972-74, v.p. 1974-75), San Diego Bankruptcy Forum (bd. dirs. 1989-92), Nat. Conf. Bankruptcy Judges (bd. dirs. 1989-91, sec. 1992-93, v.p. 1993-94, pres. 1994-95). Office: US Bankruptcy Ct 325 W F St Rm 2 San Diego CA 92101-6017 Office Phone: 619-557-5661.

ADLER, MARGOT SUSANNA, journalist, radio producer, radio correspondent, writer; b. Little Rock, Apr. 16, 1946; d. Kurt Alfred and Freyda (Nacque) A. BA, U. Calif., Berkeley, 1968; MS, Columbia U., 1970.

Newscaster Sta. WBAI-FM, N.Y.C., 1968-71, host talk show, 1972-90; chief Washington bur. Pacifica News Svc. Network; corr., prodr. All Things Considered, Morning Edit., Nat. Pub. Radio, N.Y.C., 1978—, host Justice Talking, 1999—. Instr. radio comms. Goddard Coll., Plainfield, Vt., 1977; instr. religion and ecology Inst. for Social Ecology, Vt., 1986-93. Author: Drawing Down the Moon, 1979, Heretic's Heart, 1997; co-prodr., dir. (radio drama) War Day, 1985; contbr. articles to prof. jours. Nieman fellow Harvard U., 1982. Mem. Phi Beta Kappa. Avocations: swimming, bird watching, science fiction. Home: 333 Central Park W New York NY 10025-7145 Office: Nat Pub Radio 801 2nd Ave Rm 701 New York NY 10017-4781 Office Phone: 212-878-1435. Business E-Mail: madler@npr.org.

ADLER, PEGGY ANN, writer, illustrator, consultant, protective services official; b. NYC, Feb. 10, 1942; d. Irving and Ruth Adler; children: Tenney Whedon Walsh, Avery Denison Walsh (Mrs. Adam I. Lapidus). Student, Bennington Coll., 1959—60, Columbia U., 1962. Illustrator, author children's books, 1958—; logistics and ticket sales and mgmt. the world premiere "Butch Cassidy and Sundance Kid", 1969; agt. Jan J. Agy., Inc., NYC, 1981-82; freelance talent scout Cuzzins Mgmt., NYC, 1982-83; personal mgmt. and pub. rels. cons. Madison, Conn., 1983-93. Rsch. assoc. Steve Fredericksen, Pvt. Investigator, Conn. and NY, 1990—96; investigative rschr., writer, lit. cons., 1986—; asst. investigator Ho. of Reps. October Surprise Task Force, Washington, 1992; pvt. investigator; child care provider, 1998—. Author (illustrator): The Adler Book of Puzzles and Riddles, 1962, The 2nd Adler Book of Puzzles and Riddles, 1963, Metric Puzzles, 1977, Math Puzzles, 1978, Geography Puzzles, 1979; author: Hakim's Connection, 1988; co-author: Skull and Bones: The Skeleton in Bush's Closet?, 1988; contbr. illustrator numerous books including Hot and Cold, 1959, Numbers New and Old, 1960, Reading Fundamentals for Teen-Agers, 1973, Do a Zoomdo, 1975, Pet Care, 1974, Caring for Your Cat, 1974; graphic designer: various book covers, posters, and logos; pub. rels. Sweetie, Baby, Cookie, Honey (Freddie Gershon), 1986, rschr. Passion and Prejudice: A Family Memoir (Sallie Bingham), 1989, The Village Voice, 1991, 1992, numerous others; contbr. The President's Private Eye: The Journey of Detective Tony U, from N.Y.P.D. to the Nixon White Ho., 1990; cons., rschr.: Bush's Boys Club: Skull and Bones, 1990; cons. Spy Saga (Philip H. Melanson), 1990; contbr. Lies of Our Times; licensee/story cons. 60 Minutes, 1991; cons., rschr.: London Sunday Times, 1991; contbr. The Independent London, 1994, 1995; rsch. assoc. for Ron Rosenbaum, I Stole the Head of Prescott Bush! More Scary Skull and Bones Tales (N.Y. Observer), 2000, Inside Skull and Bones' Secret Initiation Ritual (N.Y. Observer), 2001, cons. BBC Current Affairs, 2004. Founder Shoreline Youth Theatre, Inc., 1979, bd. dirs., 1979—81, mem. adv. bd., 1981—86; bd. dirs. Greens Condominium Assn. Branford, Conn., 1975—78, Arts Coun. Greater New Haven, 1971—73, Planned Parenthood Greater New Haven, 1972—73, Assassination Archives and Rsch. Ctr., Washington, 1990—96; v.p., bd. dirs. Pub. Info. Rsch., Washington, 1989; hon. mem. Forgotten Families; chmn. majority subcom. study com. 10 Killingworth Turnpike bldg., mem. charter revision commn. Town of Clinton, 1997—98, author, charter revisions, legal notice and ballot questions, 1998, mem. design adv. bd., 2000—, chmn. design adv. bd., 2003—05, mem. Clinton Landing study com., 2003—, charter revision commn., 2003—04, vice chmn., 2005—06, chmn., 2006—, author charter revisions; vol. Clinton Pub. Schs.; project dir. Clinton Village/Main St. Hist. Enhancement Project; mem. hist. dist. commn. Town of Clinton, 2001—06, vice chmn., 2005—06, constable, 2001—05, police commr., 2005—. Mem.: Police Commr.'s Assn. Conn., Conn. Soc. Genealogists Inc., Assn. Former Intelligence Officers (program coord. 1997—2004, bd. dirs. 1997—, pres. New Eng. chpt. 2001—03, ex officio 2004—, Gen. Richard G. Stilwell Chmn.'s award 2001), Rotary (mem. cancer relief fund com. Clinton chpt. 2006—), Duck Island Yacht Club (membership com. 1997—2000, social com. 1997—2004, Duck Stop 1997—2004, Don Dyson Corinthian award 1998). Home and Office: 5 Liberty St Clinton CT 06413

ADLIS, SUSAN ANNETTE, biostatistician; b. Mpls., Mar. 7, 1951; d. Paul and Miriam A. BA, Coll. St. Catherine, St. Paul, 1972; BS, U. Minn., Mpls., 1982, MS, 1987. Med. technologist U. Minn., Mpls., 1983-85, tchg. asst., 1985-87, rsch. asst., 1988-90; epidemiologist Minn. Dept. Health, Mpls., 1987-88; rsch. analyst Abbott Northwestern Hosp., Mpls., 1990-92; biostatistician Park Nicollet Inst., Mpls., 1992—. Mem. protocol rev. com. Health Sys. Minn., Mpls., 1993-98. Contbr. articles to profl. jours. Mem. AAAS, APHA, Am. Statis. Assn., Am. Soc. Clin. Lab. Scis., NY Acad. Scis. Achievements include research on health services and internal medicine. Office: Park Nicollet Inst 3800 Park Nicollet Blvd Minneapolis MN 55416-2527

ADOLPHSON, VANESSA, counseling administrator, educator, chemist; b. Bakersfield, Calif., Oct. 13, 1973; d. Juan A. and Elena L. Garza; m. David J. Adolphson, Apr. 28, 2001; children: Marissa E., Blake J. BS in Chemistry, Calif. State U. Bakersfield, 1996; MS in Sch. counseling, U. La Verne, 2000, MEd in Ednl. Mgmt., 2003. Sch. counselor Winterstein Adult Ctr., Sacramento, 2000—; counselor Stanford Home For Children, Sacramento, 1998—2000. Evening sch. adminstr. Winterstein Adult Ctr., Sacramento, 2001—. Activist Foster Youth Forum, Sacramento, 1998—2000. Mem.: Phi Sigma Sigma (life; jud. bd. 1994—95). D-Conservative. Roman Catholic. Avocations: travel, tennis, painting. Office: Winterstein Adult Center 900 Morse Ave Sacramento CA 95864 Office Phone: 916-971-7414. Personal E-mail: vangarza@hotmail.com. E-mail: vadolphson@sanjuan.edu.

ADOUR, COLLEEN MCNULTY, artist, educator; BFA in Studio Arts, cum laude, Syracuse U., 1980, postgrad. in MFA program in Studio Arts, 1980—84; grad. level ceramics, Alfred U., 1994; MFA in Art History, magna cum laude, SUNY, Binghamton, 2002. Daytime supr., art and music libr. Bartle Libr., SUNY, Binghamton, 2000—02; art tchr., lectr. Broome CC, SUNY, 2003—. Pub. info. mgr. Everson Mus. Art, Syracuse, NY, 1982—84. Notary pub. Dept. State, Divsn. Licensing Svcs., Albany, NY, 1998—; insp. of elections Broome County Bd. Elections, Binghamton, 1998—. Mem.: Binghamton U. Medieval and Renaissance Group (assoc.; v.p., treas. 2000—02). Office: Adour Art & Pottery PO Box 1196 Vestal NY 13850-1196

ADRI, (ADRI STECKLING COEN), fashion designer; b. St. Joseph, Mo. Student, Sch. Fine Arts, Washington U., St. Louis, Parson Sch. Design. With B.H. Wragge; owner, pres. Adri Studio, Ltd., NYC, 1983—. Critic Parsons Sch. Design, 1982—; with Claire McCardell in 2-person showing, Innovative Contemporary Fashion, Smithsonian Instn., Washington, 1971. Two-woman show (with Claire McCardell) Smithsonian Instn., Washington, 1972. Recipient Coty award, 1982, Internat. Best Five award, Tokyo, 1986. Office: 143 W 20th St 11th Fl New York NY 10011-3630

ADRIAN, BARBARA (MRS. FRANKLIN C. TRAMUTOLA), artist; b. NYC, July 25, 1931; d. Allen Isaac and Mildred (Brown) A.; m. Franklin C. Tramutola, July 26, 1972. Student, Art Students League, 1947-54, Hunter Coll., 1951, Columbia Sch. Gen. Study, 1952-54. Art cons. Doyle-Dane-Bernbach, advt. agy., 1960, A.H. Macy, N.Y.C., 1960-61, Saks Fifth Avenue, 1960, Black, Starr & Gorham, 1960; instr. art workshop Jamaica, NY, 1958-59; pvt. tchr. art, 1960—; instr. Art Students League, NY. One man shows, G. Gallery, 1957, San Juan, P.R., 1951, Grippi Gallery, N.Y.C., 1963, Banfer Gallery, N.Y.C., 1966, Eileen Kuhlik Gallery, 1973, Century Assn., N.Y.C., 1998; exhibited in group shows, G. Gallery, 1955-59, City Center Gallery, N.Y.C., 1954, N.Y.C. Festival, 1957, Portland (Maine) Mus., 1958, Workshop Gallery, N.Y.C., 1959, Grippi Gallery, 1960-63, Lane Gallery, Calif., 1962-63, Mus. Gallery, Lubbock, Tex., 1962-63, The Gallery, Norwalk, Ohio, 1962, Gallery 777, Plainview, L.I., N.Y., 1963, NAD, 1963, 81, Butler Art Inst., Youngstown, Ohio, 1963, Gallery Modern Art, N.Y.C., 1969, Child Hassam Fund Purchase Exhbn., N.Y.C., 1968, Orr's Gallery, San Diego, 1968, Pa. Acad. Fine Arts, Phila., 1980, Art Students League, N.Y.C., 1982, Norman A. Eppink Art Gallery, Emporia State U. (Kans.), 1983, Assn. of Bar of City of N.Y., 1986, Loyola Law Sch., L.A., 1986, Blanden Meml. Art Mus., Ft. Dodge, Iowa, 1986-87, Minn. Mus. Art, St. Paul, 1987, Sunrise Art Mus., Charleston, W.Va., 1987, Capricorn Gallery, Washington, Kenmore Gallery, Phila., Whitney Mus. Am. Art, Albrecht Art Mus., Minn. Mus. Art, St. Paul, Nat. Acad. Design, N.Y.C., 1991, 2003-04, Century Assn., N.Y.C., 2001-06, Babcock Gallery, N.Y.C., 2005; represented in permanent collections, Grippi Gallery, Summer Found., Butler Inst., McMay Mus., U. So. Ill., San Antonio, Corcoran Gallery, Washington, Assn. of Bar of City of N.Y., Loyola U. Law Sch., L.A., Blanden Meml. Art Mus., Ft. Dodge, Iowa, Minn. Mus. of Art, St. Paul, Sunrise Art Mus., Charleston, W.Va., Ark. Arts Ctr., Little Rock. Recipient Dorothy Lapham Ferriss award, 1983, Walker award, 1985, Spring Oil Exhbn. Forbes Inc. award, 1990, Elizabeth Morse Genius award, 1992. Mem. NAD (academician), Century Assn. Address: 420 E 64th St New York NY 10021-7853 Office Phone: 212-371-3598.

ADRIAN, JUDY, healthcare educator; b. Monroe, N.C., Aug. 17, 1965; m. Michael C. Adrian, Oct. 16, 1999. AS, Ctrl. Piedmont C.C., 1987; BS, Med. U. S.C., 1997. Registered respiratory therapist Nat. Bd. Respiratory Care, 1988, lic. neonatal pediatric specialist Nat. Bd. Respiratory Care, 2004. Respiratory therapist Bapt. Med. Ctr. Wake Forest U., Winston-Salem, NC, 1987—89; clin. instr. Stanly C.C., Albemarle, NC, 1991—92, dir. clin. edn., 1993—. Respiratory therapist Carolina Med. Ctr., Charlotte, NC, 1989—93. Named Faculty Mem. of Yr., Stanly C.C., 1998, Clin. Educator of Yr., N.W. AHEC, 2001; recipient Excellence in Tchg. award, Nat. Inst. Staff and Orgn. Devel., 1996, 1998, President's Choice award, Stanly C.C., 1998. Mem.: N.C. C.C. Faculty Assn., N.C. Assn. Respiratory Educators (sec. 1999—2006, treas. 1999—2006), N.C. Soc. Respriatory Care, Am. Assn. Respiratory Care, Lambda Beta. Office: Stanly Community College 141 College Drive Albemarle NC 28001

ADRIANOPOLI, BARBARA CATHERINE, librarian; b. Fort Dodge, Iowa, Jan. 27, 1943; d. Daniel Joseph and Mary Dolores (Coleman) Hogan; m. Carl David Adrianopoli, June 28, 1969; children: Carlin, Laurie. BS, Mundeline Coll., 1966; MLS, Rosary Coll., 1975; postgrad., Ozark Rsch. Inst., 1999—2000. Cert. in Pranic Healing and Dowsing Ozark Rsch. Inst. Dir. br. and extension svcs. Schaumburg Twp. (Ill.) Dist. Libr., 1979—. Mem. commn. Hoffman Estates History Mus., 2004, Ill. Libr. Assn. Cultural and Racial Diverstiy; co-chair Dorothy Brown Clk. of Cook County Cts. Adv. Com. on Women's Issues, 2002. Columnist local newspaper, 1995—, Sr. Connection, 2000—; contbr. articles to profl. jours. Mem. com. Schaumburg Twp. Disabled, 1981-95; historian Village of Hoffman Estates, 1986-99; adv. com. Hoffman Estates Sister Cities, 1996-98, Hoffman Estates History Commn., 2004—; asst. coach St. Viator H.S., 1999-2003; mem. adv. bd. Cmty. Nutrition Network, 1994—; organizer, mem. Northwest Corridor-St. Patrick's Day Parade com., 1986-2003; trainer A World of Difference Anti-Defamation League, 1994; mem. Com. For Choices For Success-Seminars For Young Women, 1996-2002; mem. Hoffman Estates Sr. and Disabled Commn., 2001; apptd. 8th Dist. State Dem. Com. Women, 2002-06; appt. to cultural and racial diversity com. Ill. Libr. Assns, 2006—. Recipient Hoffman Estates Citizen of Yr. award, VFW, 1995. Mem.: ALA, Ill. Libr. Assn. (mem. com. cultural and racial diversity 2006—). Home: 1105 Kingsdale Rd Hoffman Estates IL 60194-2378 Office: Schaumburg Twp Pub Libr 130 S Roselle Rd Schaumburg IL 60193 Personal E-mail: cadriano@sbcglobal.net.

ADRINE-ROBINSON, KENYETTE, art educator, poet, artist, photographer; b. Cleve., May 14, 1951; d. James Leroy Adrine and Beatrice (Jones) Johnson; (div. Aug. 1980); 1 child, Jua. BA, Kent State U., Ohio, 1976, MEd, 1980, M in Edn., 1985. Cert. spl. edn., developmentally handicapped and learning disabilities tchr., Ohio, Mich. Pub. info. specialist morale support activities U.S. Army, Wiesbaden, Fed. Republic of Germany, 1981-83, writer, editor pub. info. office Mainz, Fed. Republic of Germany, 1983-84; tchr. intern Positive Edn. Program, Cleve., 1984-85; tutor Glenville Presbyn. Ch., Cleve., 1985-86; mem. residential team, case mgmt. therapist Murtis H. Taylor Multi Svcs. Ctr., Cleve., 1985-86; resident photographer, tchr. Ann Arbor (Mich.) Art Assn., 1986; tchr. Cleve. Mcpl. Schs., 1986—, Juvenile Detention Ctr. Sch., Cleve. Bd. of Edn., 1987-91; instr. dept. Pan-African studies Kent State U., 1978—93; tchr. Child Mgmt. Program, Cleve., 1991. Pres. Kenyette Prodns., Cleve., 1976—; mem. Karamu House, Inc., Cleve., 1988-99, New Day Press, Inc., Cleve., 1989-99, artists in edn. program Ohio Arts Coun., Columbus, Ohio, 1989—; mem. Poets' and Writers' League of Greater Cleve., 1989—, trustee, 1991—; instr. Cleve. State Univs. First Coll., 1990; cons. Northeast Women's Pre-Release Ctr., Cleve., 1991; trustee New Day Press, 1991-99. Author: Thru Kenyette Eyes, 1978, Be My Shoo-Gar, 1987; editor: Black Image Makers, 1988, Love is a Child, 1992, The Ghetto in Me, 1994; author poems. Trustee Cmty. Christian Ch., Euclid, Ohio, 2001-05. With U.S. Army, 1969-71. Recipient Fela Sowande award Inst. for African Am. Affairs, 1976, Cert. of Recognition, Cuyahoga Spl. Edn. Svc. Ctr., 1988. Mem. Am. Fedn. Tchrs., Internat. Assn. Ind. Pubs., Verse Writers Guild Ohio (hon. mention 1988), Internat. Black Writers and Artists Assn., Urban Lit. Arts Workshop (treas. Cleve. chpt. 1988, pres. 1989-91), Kent State U. Alumni Assn. (life). Avocations: travel, music, photography, drumming, meeting with other writers. Home: 20131 Champ Dr Euclid OH 44117-2208 Office Phone: 216-671-0272. Personal E-mail: k_adrine@yahoo.com.

ADU, HELEN FOLASADE See SADE

AEHLERT, BARBARA JUNE, health facility administrator; b. San Antonio, June 17, 1956; d. Bobby Ray and Ronella Su (Light) Mahoney; m. Dean A. Aehlert, Sept. 6, 1980; children: Andrea, Sherri. AA in Nursing, Glendale (Ariz.) C.C., 1976; BS in Profl. Arts, St. Joseph's Coll., Windham, Maine, 1997. Cert. ACLS instr., BLS and PALS instr., emergency med. tng./paramedic instr. Gen. mgr. Hosp. Ambulance Svc., Phoenix, 1982-83; critical care nurse Samaritan Health Svcs., Phoenix, 1978-80, coord. patient transp., 1980-82, mgr. clin. programs, 1983-92; dir. emergency med. svcs. edn. EMS Edn. and Rsch., 1992-97; pres. S.W. EMS Edn. Inc., Glendale, Ariz., 1997—. EMS coord., City of Mesa Fire Dept., 2001-04. Author: ACLS Quick Review Study Guide, 2d edit., 2001, ACLS Quick Review Slide Set, 1994, ACLS Quick Review Study Cards, 2003, PALS Study Guide, 3d edit., 2006, ECGs Made Easy, 3d edit., 2006, ECGs Made Easy Lesson Plans, 1996, Mosby's Computerized Paramedic Test Generator, 1996, Aehlert's EMT Basic Study Guide, 1997, ECGs Made Easy Study Cards, 2003, Mosby's Comprehensive Pediatric Emergency Care, 2005. Republican.

AELION, C. MARJORIE, science educator; BS summa cum laude, U. Mass., 1980; MSCE, MIT, 1983; PhD, U. N.C., 1988. Park ranger Nat. Park Svc., Cape Cod Nat. Seashore, South Wellfleet, Mass., 1976-78; biologist, resource assessment divsn. Nat. Marine Fisheries, Woods Hole, Mass., 1978-84; rsch. asst. MIT, Cambridge, Mass., 1981-83, U. Mass.-Amherst, Amherst, Peru, 1983-84, U. N.C., Chapel Hill, 1986-88, tchg. asst., 1987; hydrologist U.S. Geol. Survey, Water Resources Divsn., Columbia, SC, 1988-91, faculty mem., 1991-97; asst. prof. dept. environ. health scis. U. S.C., Columbia, 1991-97, assoc. prof., 1997-2001, prof., 2001—. Presenter in field. Contbr. articles to profl. jours. Fulbright-Hayes scholar, 1980-81; Bd. Govs.' fellow U. N.C., 1984-86, Dissertation fellow, 1988, NSF fellow in engring., 1993; grantee U.S. EPA, 1991-93, Hazardous Waste Mgmt. Rsch. Fund, 1991-94, 99-2002, Nat. Geographic Soc., 1992, S.C. Dept. Health and Environ. Control and Hazardous Waste Mgmt. Rsch. Fund, 1991-94, U. S.C., 1993-94, NSF, 1993-00, 99—, NIEHS, 2005—; Fulbright scholar, 2002; grad. student travel grantee award U. N.C., 1988; Rsch. fellow Internat. Agrl. Ctr., The Netherlands, 2002. Mem. Am. Chem. Soc., Am. Soc. Microbiology, Assn. for Women in Sci. (sec. S.C. chpt. 1996-97, pres. S.C. chpt. 1997-98), Soc. Women Engrs., Soc. Environ. Toxicology and Chemistry, Phi Kappa Phi, Delta Omega. Office: U SC Environ Health Scis Dept Columbia SC 29208-0001

AESCHLIMANN, SOFIA LIZBETH, psychiatrist; b. Ponce, P.R., Mar. 24, 1974; d. Werner Edward Aeschlimann and Sofia Gladys Padilla; m. Mark William Philpott, June 16, 1996; 1 child, Ethan James Philpott. BS in Biology, Southwestern Adventist U.; MD, Loma Linda U., Lona Linda, Calif., 1999. Residency psychiatry UT Southwestern Med. Sch., Dallas, 2004; psychiatrist Woodland Med. Ctr., Cullman, Ala., 2004—06. Mem.: APA, Tex. Soc. Psychiatric, Alpha Omega Alpha. Christian. Avocations: piano, violin, reading, travel. Office: 900 W Mitchell St Arlington TX 76013

AFFINITO, MONA GUSTAFSON, psychologist; b. Bristol, Conn., Oct. 28, 1929; d. Carl Arthur and Jennie Alida (Anderson) Gustafson; m. Louis A. Affinito, Oct. 3, 1955 (div. Dec. 1976); children: Douglas Anthony, Lisa Marie Affinito Neun. BA, Conn. Coll., 1951; MA, Boston U., 1952, PhD, 1964. Lic. psychologist, Minn. Instr. Johnson (Vt.) State Coll., 1952-53, U. Vt., Burlington, 1953-55; mem. faculty So. Conn. State U., New Haven, 1959—, prof. psychology, 1969-87, prof. emeritus, 1987—, chmn. dept., 1974-80, dir. grad. program in psychology, 1982-84; pvt. practice Shorewood, Minn., 1995—2002, Chaska, Minn., 2002—; teaching faculty/supr. Eden Prairie (Minn.) Psychol. Resources, Eden Prairie, Minn., 1995—99; adj. fculty Alfred Adler Inst. Minn.; emeritus faculty Alfred Adler Grad. Sch., 2002—. Mem. staff New Haven Ctr. for Human Rels., 1976-80; psychologist Assocs. in Counseling and Therapy, New Haven, 1978-80; frequent lectr., workshop condr.; presenter in field. Author: When to Forgive, 1999; contbr. articles to profl. jours. Past pres. ch. women Christ Luth. Ch., Hamden, Conn. Mem. APA, Minn. Psychol. Assn., Minn. Women in Psychology. Office: 1359 White Oak Dr Chaska MN 55318-1401

AFFLECK, MARILYN, retired sociology educator; b. Logan, Utah, July 1, 1932; d. Clark B. and Velda (Bryson) A.; children: Michelle Alisa, Kimberly Kay, Lacey Dawn. BA, U. Okla., 1954; MA, Brigham Young U., 1957; PhD, UCLA, 1966. Instr. Ctrl. State Coll., Edmond, Okla., 1958—60; asst. prof. Fla. State U., Tallahassee, 1966—68; asst. prof. sociology U. Okla., Norman, 1968—70, assoc. prof., 1971—90, interim dean Grad. Coll., 1978—79, asst. dean, 1976—82. Editor Free Inquiry in Creative Sociology Jour., 1984-90. Recipient AMOCO Good Tchg. award U. Okla., 1974 Mem. Okla. Sociol. Assn. (pres. 1974-75), South Ctrl. Women's Studies Assn. (treas. 1979-83), Phi Beta Kappa. Democrat. Mem. Lds Ch. Home: 6395 Corky Dr NE Norman OK 73026-3135

AFTERMAN, JEAN, professional sports team executive; BA in History of Art, U. Calif., Berkeley, 1979; JD, U. San Francisco, 1991. Aide Don Nomura, 1994—99; pvt. practice, 1999—2001; asst. gen. mgr. N.Y. Yankees, Bronx, 2001—, v.p., 2003—. Office: NY Yankees Yankee Stadium E 161 St & River Ave Bronx NY 10451

AGAJANIAN, ANITA SHAKEH, lawyer; BA, Boston U., 1990; JD, U. Mich. Law Sch., 1995. Bar: Colo. 1995, Mass. 1997. Ptnr. DLA Piper, Boston, mem. diversity com., mem. winning women com. Bd. dirs. Boston Mcpl. Rsch. Bur.; mentor minority law students Boston Lawyers' Group. Mem.: Boston Bar Assn. (co-chair leasing com., Real Estate Sect.). Office: DLA Piper 26th Floor 33 Arch St Boston MA 02110-1447 Office Phone: 617-406-6058. Office Fax: 617-406-6158. E-mail: anita.agajanian@dlapiper.com.*

AGAJANIAN, GILDA, pianist; d. Oganes and Azatuhi A. BA, U. So. Calif., 1973, Grad. Study, 1974-76; Diploma, Am. Coll. of Musicians, Austin, Tex., 1981, Artist Diploma, 1984. Russian educator, Calif., 1976-81; music educator Gilda Agajanian Piano Studio, La Habra Heights, Calif., 1987—; profl. classical pianist Calif., 1985—; entrepreneur, ptnr. Aggie's Restaurants, Calif., 1981-89. Mem. Westshore Musicians Club (pres. 1992-95), Music Tchrs. Nat. Assn., Calif. Assn. Profl. Music Tchrs. (chmn. recitals 1992—), Dominant Club (sec. 1994-96), Nat. Guild of Piano Tchrs. Avocations: Slavic language and literature, exotic birds, horticulture, cats, dogs. Office: Gilda Agajanian Piano Studio 2039 N Cypress St La Habra Heights CA 90631

AGARD, EMMA ESTORNEL, psychotherapist; b. Bronx, N.Y. BA, Queens Coll.; MSW, Fordham U., 1962; cert. in Psychoanalytic Psychotherapy, Tng. Inst. for Mental Health, 1979; cert. in Child and Adolescent Psychotherapy, Postgrad. Ctr. for Mental Health, 1982. Supr. social work Foster Care Div., N.Y.C., 1968-72; asst. dir. Henry St. Settlement Urban Family Ctr., N.Y.C., 1972-74; tng. analyst, sr. supr. Tng. Inst. for Mental Health, N.Y.C., 1974—; pvt. practice psychotherapist N.Y.C., 1974—. Lectr. social work Columbia U., N.Y.C., 1977-90; adj. asst. prof. NYU, 1978-80; field instr. N.Y.C. Housing Authority, 1974-80; dist. dir., cons. Am. Consultation Ctrs., Bklyn. and N.Y.C., 1985—, dir. Park Slope br.; field instr. Sch. Social Svc. Fordham U., 1985—. Mem. Albemarle-Kenmore Neighborhood Assn., Bklyn., 1974—99. Fellow N.Y. State Soc. Clin. Social Work Psychotherapists (pres. Bklyn. chpt. 1988-91); mem. Profl. Soc. Tng. Inst. for Mental Health (sec.), Nat. Assn. Social Workers (diplomate), Acad. Cert. Social Workers, Nat. Coalition 100 Black Women, Delta Sigma Theta. Avocations: painting, tennis, yoga, swimming. Address: 109 E 36th St New York NY 10016-3447

AGEE, CLAUDIA, executive secretary, tax specialist; b. Selma, Ala., Nov. 11, 1939; d. Claude and M. Marie (McConico) Thomas; m. Cleveland Agee, Jr. (dec.); children: Debbie K., Danita McCary, Cleveland III(dec.), La Shondria, Ed'Kela, Mondena, Tocara, Lil Freddie, Mondeno. Student, Booker T. Washington, 1973, Birmingham Bapt. Bible Coll., 1989, Bessemer Tech., 1992; AA in Office Adminstrn., Bessemer State Tech. Coll., 1997. Bookkeeper, gen. mgr. Thomas Deli, Birmingham, Ala., AmSouth Corp. Revolving Credit Rsch., Birmingham; garment mgr. NLS, Birmingham; svc. clk., bookkeeper Minority Literacy Expo; office mgr., personal sec. Ross Gardner, ENT Specialist. Mem.: Bidders Orgn. (sec.), Order of Eastern Star (sec. Lodge 385), Zeta Phi Lambda (Beta Psi chpt. honoree 1976).

AGEE, NELLE HULME, retired art history educator; b. Memphis, May 22, 1940; d. John Eulice and Nelle (Ray) Hulme; m. Bob R. Agee, June 7, 1958; children: Denise, Robyn. Student, Memphis State U., 1971—72; BA, Union U., Jackson, Tenn., 1978; postgrad., Seminole Okla. Col., 1982, Okla Bapt. U., 1984; MEd, Ctrl. State U., Edmond, Okla., 1989. Cert. tchr. art, history Ky., Tenn., Okla. Offices svcs. supr. So. Bapt. Theol. Sem., Louisville, 1961—64; kindergarten tchr. Shively Heights Bapt. Ch., Louisville, 1965—70; editl. asst. Little Pubs., Memphis, 1973—75; tchr. art Humboldt HS, Tenn., 1978—82. Vis. artist-in schs. Tenn. Arts. Commn., Nashville, 1978, 81, 82; adj. prof. art history Seminole Col., Okla., 1985—86, 1989; asst. prof. art and edn. Okla. Bapt. U., 1989—98; spkr. art orgns, ch. groups; tchr. art workshops Humboldt City Sch. Sys.; tchr. Cultural Arts Day Camp, Jackson, Tenn., 1982. Exhibited in various shows. Nat. pres. ministers' wives conf. So. Bapt. Conv., 1988; vol. Mabee-Gerrer Mus., Shawnee; bd. dirs. Robert Dotson Foun., Mabee-Gerrer Mus., Family Resource Ctr., 1993—98; active vol. Salvation Army Aux., Shawnee. Recipient Disting. Classroom Tchr. award, Tenn. Edn. Assn., 1982. Mem.: Goals 2000, Alpha Delta Kappa, Delta Kappa Gamma. Republican. Baptist. Avocations: stained glass, pottery, travel. Home: 270 Asmport Rd Humboldt TN 38343

AGHDASHLOO, SHOHREH, actress; b. Tehran, Iran, May 11, 1952; m. Houshang Touzie, 1985; 1 child, Tara; m. Aydin Aghdashloo, 1972 (div. 1980). BA in Internat. Rels., 1984. Actor: (films) Shatranje bad, 1976, Gozaresh (The Report), 1977, Sootah Delaan, 1978, Guests of Hotel Astoria, 1989, Twenty Bucks, 1993, Maryam, 2000, Surviving Paradise, 2000, America So Beautiful, 2001, House of Sand and Fog, 2003 (best supporting actress award L.A. Film Critics Assn., 2003, best supporting actress award N.Y. Film Critics Cir., 2003, Ind. Spirit award for best supporting female, 2004, Acad. award nomination for best supporting actress, 2004), The Exorcism of Emily Rose, 2005, American Dreamz, 2006, X-Men: The Last Stand, 2006, The Lake House, 2006, (guest appearances): (TV series) Martin, 1993, "24", 2005.*

AGNE, PHYLLIS G., artist, educator; b. N.Y.C., May 20, 1932; d. John J. and Anna (Rosen) Gross; 1 child, Wendy Reed. Student, Art Students League, 1950-51; BA, Hunter Coll., CUNY, 1970; MFA, Columbia U., 1972. Lectr. Wagner Coll., Staten Island, N.Y., 1971-72, Fairleigh Dickinson U., Madison, N.J., 1972; assoc. prof. U. Conn., Waterbury, 1973-92. Vis. faculty fellow Yale U./Carnegie Mellon Inst. Solo exhbns. include Fulton Gallery, NYC,

1960, 1963, 1965, 1973, Mattatuck Mus., Waterbury, Conn., 1979, The Waterbury Club, 1986, Eierweiss Gallery, New Haven, Conn., 1992, Promenade Gallery, The Bushnell, Hartford, Conn., 1998, William Benton Mus., Storrs, 1996, others; group exhbns. include Conn. Women Artists New Haven, Norwich and Hartford, 1976-86, Discovery Mus., Bridgeport, Conn., 1987, 89, 93, Mattatuck Mus., 1993, Slater Meml. Mus., Norwich, 1986, 88, 89, New Haven Paint & Clay Club, Inc., 1980—, CUNY Grad. Ctr., N.Y.C., 1978, L'Atelier Gallery, Essex, Conn., 1985, Nat. Drawing Assn., N.Y.C., 1987, 1988, 1989, 1993, 1994, Galerie Triangle, Washington, 1988, Erector Sq. Gallery, New Haven, 1990, Aetna Gallery, Hartford, 1991, Inter Art Galerie Reich, Cologne, Germany, 1999-03, many others; represented in permanent collections William Benton Mus. Art Storrs, Conn., Slater Meml. Mus., Norwich, Conn., Mattatuck Mus., Waterbury, Conn., The Amity Art Found., Am. Brands, Anco Wood Specialties, Inc., The Delong Corp., The New Haven Paint and Clay Club, Tarlow, Levy, Harding and Droney, Mimi Kazon, Irena Urdang De Tour, and numerous pvt. collections. William Graf scholar Women's Trade Union League; U. Conn. Rsch. Found. grantee. Mem. Am. Artists Profl. League, Nat. Drawing Assn., Conn. Women Artists, New Haven Paint and Clay Club (v.p., archivist). Avocations: music, gardening.

AGNOR, KIMBERLY KEATTS, elementary school educator; b. Selma, Ala., Oct. 25, 1968; d. Burton Eugene Keatts, Jr. and Bettie Walker Keatts; children: Emilee Wanda, Carrie LeighAnn. BSc in Elem. Edn., Longwood U., Farmville, Va., 1990, MSc in Elem. Edn., 1996. Lic. tchr. Va. Tchr. Chesterfield (Va.) County Pub. Schs., 1990—96, Pittsylvania County Pub. Schs., Chatham, Va., 1996—97, Danville (Va.) City Schs., 1997—. Administrator summer sch. Danville (Va.) City Schs., 2005; lead tchr. Bonner Mid. Sch., Danville, 2004—. Organist Hillcrest Bapt. Ch., Danville, 1980—; treas. Coates Rec. Adv. Coun., Danville, 2004—06. Mem.: NCTM, Va. Assn. Gifted, Delta Kappa Gamma (sec. 2000—). Home: 109 Barrett St Danville VA 24541 Office: Bonner Mid Sch 300 Appollo Ave Danville VA 24540

AGOGINO, ALICE MERNER, computer scientist, mechanical engineer, educator; b. Albuerque, N.Mex., Dec. 1, 1952; married; 2 children. BS in Mech. Engring., U. N.Mex., 1975; MS in Mech. Engring., U. Calif. Berkeley, 1978; PhD in Engring. Econ. Systems, Stanford U., 1984. Registered Profl. Mech. Engr., Calif., 1978. Project engr. Dow Chem., Freeport, Tex., 1972-73; mech. engr. GE, San Jose and Sunnyvale, Calif., 1975-78, commercial specialist San Jose, Calif., 1978-79; systems analyst SRI Internat., Menlo Park, Calif., 1980; dir. Women-in-Engring. program U. Santa Clara, Calif., 1980-81; prin., engring. and mgmt. cons. firm Agogino Engring., 1979—; asst. prof., mech. engring. U. Calif., Berkeley, 1984—88, assoc. prof., mech. engring., 1988—92, dir., curriculum reform, synthesis coalition, 1990—94, prof. mech. engring., 1992—, co-chair, instructional tech. com. of the campus computing and communication policy bd., 1993—97, dir., synthesis coalition, 1994—97, assoc. dean spl. programs Coll. Engring., 1995—99, assoc. dean, instructional tech./distance learning, coll. engring., 1996—99, chair, instructional tech. com. of the campus computing and communication policy bd., 1997—2001, dir., Instructional Tech. Program, 1999—2001, faculty asst. to Exec. Vice Chancellor and Provost Carol Christ in Educational and Develop. Tech., 1999—2000, faculty asst. to Exec. Vice Chancellor and Provost Paul Gray, 2000—01, vice-chair, Faculty Academic Senate, Berkeley Divsn., 2004—05, chair, faculty academic senate, Berkeley Divsn., 2005—06, Roscoe and Elizabeth Hughes prof. mech. engring, 1998—. Spkr. in field; proposed reviewer NSF, U. Calif. Microelectronics Innovation and Computer Rsch. Opportunities (MICRO), Electric Power Rsch. Inst. (EPRI), Australian Science Fund, Canadian Nat, Sci. and Engring. Rsch. Coun. and Swedish Coun. Higher Edn.; mem. exec. com. Digital Media Innovation Initiative, U. Calif. Sys., 2000—02; mem. adv. bd. Nat. Digitial Libr. for Technological Literacy project, 2001—02, Jet Propulsion Lab, 2002—04; mem. Radcliffe Inst. for Advanced Study, MIT Corp. vis. com. in mech. engring.; mem. mfg. engring. lab. Nat. Inst. of Standards & Tech., 2004—05; mem. Women in Academic Sci. Engring. Com. of the Nat. Academies Com. on Sci., Engring., and Pub. Policy, 2005—06, Nat. Academies Bd. on Sci. Edn., 2005—; pres., Assn. of Academic Women U. Calif., Berkeley, 2001—03, chair, Studies in Engring., Sci., and Math. Edn., 2003—04, co-chair, working group, Berkeley Diversity Rsch. Intiative, 2005, co-chair, steering com., Berkeley Diversity Rsch. Initiative, 06, co-chair, U. Athletics Bd., 2005—06; and several others. Reviewer for: ASME Transactions, Journal of Optimization Theory and Applications, IEEE Transactions, IEEE Computer, AI in Engineering, Design, Analysis and Manufacturing, Research in Engineering Design, Journal of Intelligent Computing, ASEE Journal of Engineering Education, Engineering with Computers, and Advances in Engineering Software, and numerous technical confs.; mem. editl. review bd., Journal of Engineering Education, mem. editl. bd., Concurrent Engineering: Research and Applications, Research in Engineering Design; assoc. editor Artificial Intelligence in Engineering, Design, Analysis and Manufacturing. Chancellor's Hon. Fellow in Mech. Engring., U. Calif. Berkeley, 1977; recipient IBM Faculty Develop. award, 1985-86, Presdl. Young Investigator award NSF, 1985, Ralph R. Teetor Educator award Soc. Automotive Engrs., 1987, Young Mfg. Engr. Yr., Soc. Mfg. Engrs., 1987-88, Most Outstanding Alummnus, Dept. Mech. Engring., U. New Mexico, 1992, NSF Director's award for Disting. Tchg. Scholars, 2004; co-recipient Best Paper at the Conf. on AI Apllications, 1992, Best Paper award, Artificial Intelligence in Design Conf., 1996, John Wiley & Sons Premier Courseware award for Virtual Disk Drive Design Studio, 1997 Fellow AAAS (mem. electronics nominating com., sect. engring., 1994-95, chair, 1995, mem.-at-large engring. sect. 1996-2000, mem. com. on opportunities in sci., 1997-2003, chair sect. engring., 2001-02, retiring chair, 2002-03), Assn. for the Advancement of Women; mem. NSF (mem. proposal review adv. team, 1996-97, mem. adv. com. for engring., engring. doctorate, 1991-96, co-chair, 1996-97), ASME (chair Santa Clara Valley sect. 1981-82, dir. 1983-84, mem. program com. design for manufacture conf., 1997, bd. dir. Ctr. for Edn., 2004-06, co-recipeint, Xerox Best Paper award, 2004), IEEE(recipient Helen Plants award for Best Non-Traditional Session at Frontiers in Edn., 1998, co-recipient Robotics & Automation Soc. Best Paper award, 2005, NAE(mem. academic adv. bd., 1998-99, mem. com. on tech. literacy standards, 1997-2000, mem. com. engring. edn., 1999-2002, mem. Bernard M. Gordon prize for Innovation in Engring. and Tech. Edn. com., 2001-02, co-chair planning com. on engring. edn. for the yr. 2020, 1999-2000, vice-chair mech. engring. peer com., 2004-05, chair 2005-06), Am. Soc. Elec. Engrs.(mem. Fred Merryfield Design award com., 1993-96, mem. Wickenden award com., 1997-98, mem. women and minorities task force, 2001-02, co-recipient Best Paper award, 1997, Best Overall Paper award, 1998), European Acad. Sciences, Am. Assn. Artificial Intelligence, Assn. Computing Machinery, Soc. Women Engrs. (v.p. San Francisco Bay Area, 1979-80), Pi Tau Sigma (Academic Honor award, 1973, award for Excellence in Tchg., 1986), Tau Beta Pi, Phi Kappa Phi. Avocations: guitar, gardening, hiking, exploring. Office: U Calif 5136 Etcheverry Hall Mail Stop 1740 Berkeley CA 94720-1740 Office Phone: 510-642-6450. Office Fax: 510-643-5599. Business E-Mail: agogino@berkeley.edu, agogino@socrates.berkeley.edu.

AGOORA, LAMMIA HASSON, mathematics educator; arrived in U.S., 1972; d. Hasson Ali Agoora and Fathia Mohamed Yousuf. BA, We. Conn. State U., Danbury, 1985, MA in History, 1988; post grad., U. Bridgeport, Conn., 1989, EdD, 1997. Substitute tchr. Danbury Bd. Edn., Conn., 1986—92, tchr. math, 1992—; coord. EXCEL program Western Conn. State U., 1999—. Patricipant St. Jude Children's Hosp. Math-a-Thon, 1997—2000; mentor program Danbury Bd. Edn., Conn., 1997—, mentoring tchr., 2006—, mem. supt. adv. com., mem.prin. adv. com.; participant Delta Adminstrv. Aspirants Program. Mem.: NEA, Conn. Edn. Assn. Democrat. Avocation: running. Office: 2 Whitney Ave Danbury CT 06810-6209 Home: 11 Hoyt Ave Bethel CT 06801

AGOST, DALENE BETH, elementary school educator; b. Portland, Oreg., Nov. 9, 1960; d. Harold Dale DeWitz; m. Brett William Agost, Aug. 18, 1990; children: Taylor Marie, Dane William, Leah Grace. BA in Elem. Edn., Concordia U., Portland, 1983. Cert. tchr. Oreg. Tchrs. Stds. and Practices, 1983. Elem. tchr. Our Savior Luth. Sch., Aiea, Hawaii, 1983—88, Joseph Ln. Jr. H.S., Roseburg, Oreg., 1989—97; phys. edn. specialist Oreg. Trail Elem., Clackamas, Oreg., 1997—. Dance instr. (H.S. dance team) State Competition Routines (Fifth Pl. in State Competition, 1990). Tchr./instr. Camp Fire USA, Gresham, Oreg., 2002—05; tchr. Imanuel Luth. Ch., Portland, 2000—06. Mem.: Nat. Tchrs. Assn. (life). Democrat. Avocations: gardening, travel, piano, music. Office: Oregon Trail Elementary School 13895 SE 152nd Dr Clackamas OR 97015 Office Phone: 503-658-0365. Personal E-mail: agostd@nclack.k12.or.us.

AGOSTA, SUSAN MARIE, web site designer; b. Bronx, NY, Jan. 3, 1958; d. Hermann Alfred and Catherine Loretta Wacker; m. Paul Peter Agosta, Nov. 6, 1977; children: Melanie Marie Gasper, Paul Peter III, Nicole Marie. BS in Mgmt. and Computer Info. Sys., Park U., 1997. Sr. web developer CACI, Rosslyn, Va., 1997—. Team capt. local Relay for Life Am. Cancer Soc., Vienna, Va., 2005. Mem.: Mensa (assoc.). Republican. Roman Catholic. Avocation: stained glass. Home: 1423 Admiral Dr Woodbridge VA 22192 Office: CACI 1600 Wilson Blvd 14the Floor Rosslyn VA 22209 Office Phone: 703-558-0283. Office Fax: 703-875-3197. Personal E-mail: sueagosta@comcast.net.

AGOSTI, DEBORAH ANN, retired senior justice; BA cum laude, U. Toledo, 1973, JD, 1976. Bar: Nev., U.S. Supreme Ct. Dep. pub. defender Montgomery County, Ohio, 1977; sr. staff atty. Sr. Citizens Legal Assistance Program, Washoe County, 1977—79; dep. dist. atty., 1979—82; justice of the peace Reno Twp., Nev., 1982—85; dist. judge 2d Jud. Dist., Reno, 1985—99; justice Nev. Supreme Court, Carson City, 1999—2004, sr. justice, 2005—. Trustee Nat. Jud. Coll., 2001—, Pretrial Svcs. Resource Ctr., 1999—; co-chmn. jury improvement commn. Supreme Ct. of Nev., 2001—; mem., dean's adv. bd. U. Toledo Coll. Law. Chmn. Task Force to Revitalize Interest in Attendance at Washoe County Bar Meetings, 2001—. Named Outstanding Young Woman for State of Nev., 1983, One of Am.'s 100 Young Women of Promise, Good Housekeeping mag., 1985, Reno's Outstanding Woman for 1986, One of Three Outstanding Young Nevadans, Reno Jaycees, 1986, Outstanding Women Lawyer, No. Nev. Women Lawyer's Assn., 1993, Judge of Yr., Nev. Dist. Judge's Assn., 1989, Woman of Achievement, Nev. Women's Fund, 1998, Woman of Distinction, Nat. Assn. Women Bus. Owners-So. Nev. Chpt., 2004, One of Nev.'s First One Hundred Women Attys., Woman of Distinction, Soroptimists of Reno, 2005. Master: Bruce Thompson Inn of Ct.; mem.: No. Nev. Women Lawyers Assn., Nat. Assn. Women Judges, Soroptimists Internat. of Truckee Meadows (life mem., Woman of Distinction 2001). Office: Supreme Ct Nev 201 S Carson St Carson City NV 89701-4702 Office Phone: 775-684-1600. E-mail: dagosti@nvcourts.state.nv.us.

AGOSTO RIVERA, LUZ ESTHER, elementary school educator; b. San Juan, P.R., July 11, 1953; d. Felix and Isabel Agosto; m. Juan B. Soto, Apr. 12, 1971; children: Joel, Marisabel. Grad., U. del Turabo, Gurabo, P.R., 1978. Cert. tchr., P.R. Kindergarten tchr., Caguas, 1975-77; math. tchr. grades 3, 6 Canaboncito, P.R., 1977-78; math. tchr., 1978-80; sci. tchr. grade 6, 1980-81; elem. math. tchr., 1981-82; sci. tchr. grades 4, 6, 1982—. Counselor Sci. Fair, Caguas, 1992—, grad. class, 1989-94, judge Sci. Fair, 1992-95. Recipient Pres.'s award San Juan, P.R., 1993, AT&T award, 1994, State award, 1993, NSF grant, 1993, Presdl. award White House, 1994. Mem. Am. Chem. Soc., Tchrs. Sci. Soc., The Planetary Soc. Roman Catholic. Avocation: computers. Home: Residencial Bairoa J11 Calle Santa Maria Caguas PR 00725-1568

AGRESTA, DIANE MARIE, psychologist; b. Detroit, June 18, 1953; d. Dano Joseph and Dolores Marie Agresta; children: Laura, Claire. BS in Psychology, Wayne State U., Detroit, 1975; MS in Psychology, Ea. Mich. U., Ypsilanti, 1977; PhD in Psychology, Ctrl. Mich. U., Mt. Pleasant, 1983. Lic. psychologist Mich. Clin. asst. Lafayette Clinic, Detroit, 1974—75; staff psychologist Jackson-Hillsdale Cmty. Mental Health, Jackson, Mich., 1978—79; assoc. clin. psychologist U. Mass., Amherst, 1983; clin. psychologist Assoc. Counseling Svcs., Plymouth, Mich., 1983—87; dir. counseling svcs. Adrian Coll., Adrian, Mich., 1984—85; clin. psychologist Huron Valley Cons., Ann Arbor, Mich., 1984—88; clin. psychologist in pvt. practice Ann Arbor, 1988—. Bd. dirs., v.p., pub. chair Ann Arbor Civic Ballet Co., 2004—06. Doctoral fellow, Ctrl. Mich. U., 1980. Mem.: APA, Mich. Psychoanalytic Coun., Internat. Soc. for Study of Dissociation. Unitarian Universalist. Avocations: hiking, gardening, cooking, reading, needlecrafts. Office: 321 S Main St Ste 209 Ann Arbor MI 48104 Office Phone: 734-665-9890.

AGUADO, SANDRA, social studies educator; b. France, Jan. 7, 1973; d. Petar and Mirijana Fatovic; m. David Aguado. MA in Liberal Studies, Ramapo Coll. of N.J., Mahwah, 2006. Cert. social studies tchr. NJ., 1997. Social studies tchr. Bergenfield H.S., NJ, 1999—. Office: Bergenfield High School 80 S Prospect Ave Bergenfield NJ 07621

AGUAYO-TABOR, MARICRUZ ROCIO, secondary school educator; b. McAllen, Tex., Apr. 14, 1977; d. Jesus and Elvira Ledesma Aguayo; m. Charles Tabor, Dec. 16, 2006. BA in Anthropology, English and History, Brandeis U., Waltham, Mass., 1999; AM in History, Harvard U., Cambridge, Mass., 2001. Cert. tchr. Tex., 2002. Tchr. Liberal Arts Acad. of Austin, Tex., 2001—02; social studies dept. chair, tchr. Liberal Arts and Sci. Acad. of Austin, Tex., 2002—. Named L.B.J. Tchr. of the Yr., Lyndon Baines Johnson H.S., 2005; recipient Edith May Sliffe award, The Math. Assn. of Am., 2005, Outstanding Tchg. of the Humanities award, Humanities Tex., 2006; fellow Mellon fellow, Mellon Found., 1999. Mem.: Phi Beta Kappa (life), Phi Alpha Theta (life). Office: Liberal Arts & Science Academy of Austin 7309 Lazy Creek Dr Austin TX 78724 Office Phone: 512-841-3085. E-mail: mraguayo@austinisd.org.

AGUDO, MERCEDES ENGRACIA, psychiatrist; arrived in U.S., 1990; d. Isidoro Reyes and Pura Engracia Agudo. MD, U. Santo Tomas, Manila, Philippines, 1989; degree in psychiatry, Howard U. Hosp., Washington, 1996; degree in child and adolescent psychiatry, Med. Coll. Va., Richmond, 1998. Child, adolescent & adult psychiatrist pvt. solo. practice, Iligan City, Philippines, 1998—2002; faculty Mindanao State U., Iligan City, 1999—2002; child & adolescent psychiatrist Philhaven, Mt. Gretna, Pa., 2002—. Officer Rotary Club Maria Cristina, Iligan City, Philippines, 1998—2002; aux. mem. Legion of Mary, Hershey, Pa., 2003—; extraordinary eucharistic minister St. Joan of Arc Ch., Hershey, Pa., 2005—. Fellow: Am. Coll. Ethical Physicians, Am. Bd. Hosp. Physicians; mem.: APA. Roman Catholic. Avocations: piano, drawing, cooking, travel. Office: Philhaven 283 S Butler Rd Mount Gretna PA 17064 Personal E-mail: meagudo1@comcast.net.

AGÜERO-TORRES, IRENE BEATRIZ, language educator; b. Barquisimeto, Venezuela, Jan. 30, 1958; d. David Agüero Segura and Ana P. Torres Puerta de Agüero; m. M. A. Morgan; children: Chispa María, Pancho Ramón. BS cum laude, Northeastern U., 1987; MA, U. Mass., 1996. Cert. tchr. Mass., 2000. Instr. Spanish Phillips Acad., Andover, Mass., 1987—88; lectr. Spanish U. Mass., Amherst, 1988—93, Amherst (Mass.) Coll., 1989—93, Coll. of Holy Cross, Worcester, Mass., 1993—94, Tuft U., Medford, Mass., 1995—96, U. Mass., Boston, 1996, Wheelock Coll., Boston, 1994—2000, Brandeis U., Waltham, Mass., 1997—99; tchr. Spanish Walsh Mid. Sch., Framingham, Mass., 2000—06. Instr. Pine Tree Lang. Summer Camp, Inlet, NY, 1994. Integrating Women Studies Bibliography grantee, Northeastern U., 1986, Empowering Educators with Technology grantee, Mass., 2002. Mem.: Spanish Book Club (dir. 1999—). Avocations: reading, golf, tennis, music, cooking, photography.

AGUIAR, ELIZABETH JOAN, publishing executive, educator; b. Union City, Tenn., Nov. 16, 1954; d. John Roland and Doris Olson Beck; m. Albert Anthony Aguiar, Nov. 30, 1991; 1 stepchild, Cassandra Nicole. BA, Bowling Green State U., 1977; MA, George Washington U., 1979. Dean Coll. Undergraduate Bus. and Mgmt. U. Phoenix, 1993—99; assoc. v.p. acad. pub. Apollo Group, Inc., Phoenix, 1999—2001, v.p. acad. pub., 2001—. Mem. resource project team, chmn. bd. initiative, 2000—02. Author: (fiction) Big Book, 2002, Managing Service for Success, 1987, 1989; mem. editl. bd. Future mag., U. Phoenix Alumni Network, 2003—. Avocations: reading, art. Home: 1224 E Grandview Rd Phoenix AZ 85022 Office: Apollo Group Inc 4615 E Elwood St Phoenix AZ 85040 Office Phone: 480-557-1736. Office Fax: 480-921-4271. Business E-Mail: ejaguiar@apollogrp.edu.

AGUILAR, JULIA ELIZABETH, real estate company executive; b. Orgainal, Mex., Feb. 16, 1943; came to U.S., 1965; d. Felix and Leticia (Rodriguez) Vergara; m. Aaron Aguilar, Feb. 1, 1964; children: Juan Antonio, Elizabeth, Alex. Grad., San Fernando (Calif.) Adult Sch., 1980; Real Estate Assoc., Anthony Real Estate Sch., Sepulveda, Calif., 1985. Real estate assoc. ERA Rocking Horse Realty, San Fernando, 1986-98; owner Home Sweet Home Realty, San Fernando, 1998—. Author poetry, cooking recipes, song lyrics, 1996, Musical Poetry, 1997. Democrat. Roman Catholic. Avocations: writing, gardening, knitting, painting. Home: 626 Newton St San Fernando CA 91340-2107 Office: Home Sweet Home Realty 1000 N Maclay Ave San Fernando CA 91340-1326

AGUILAR, JULIA SHELL, publishing executive; BS in Sociology and Psychology, Va. Commonwealth U., MS in Social Work Adminstrn. Dir. human resources Times-Advocate, Escondido, Calif., 1982—84; v.p. human resources L.A. Daily News, 1984—87; dir. human resources John P. Scripps Newspapers, 1987—90; pres., then pub. San Luis Obispo (Calif.) County Telegram-Tribune, 1990—98; dir. mgmt. devel. E.W. Scripps Co., Cin., 1998—2000; gen. mgr. Knoxville (Tenn.) News-Sentinel, 2000—. Office: Knoxville News-Sentinel 2332 News Sentinel Dr PO Box 59038 Knoxville TN 37950-9038

AGUILAR, MIRIAM REBECCA, technology project manager; b. Torrance, Calif., Feb. 6, 1963; d. Samuel Conklin and Victoria Lizarraga Aguilar; children: Samantha Victoria Reed, Olivia Linda Reed. AA in Liberal Arts, L.A. Harbor Coll., 1984; BA in Anthropology Minor Art History, Colo. State U., 1998; M of Internat. Pub. Mgmt., Monterey Inst. of Internat. Studies, 2001. Cert. travel counselor Travel and Trade Career Inst. IT market analyst Kagan World Media, Carmel, Calif., 2000; tech. project mgr. CTB McGraw-Hill, Monterey, Calif., 2001—. Proposed design and devel. for creation of Internat. Lang. and Culture Meml. Mus. and Rsch. Ctr. World Trade Ctr. Author: (pub. project) Developing and Designing An Administrative Model for an International Language and Culture Museum and Research Center. Bd. dirs. internat. programs Internat. Lang. and Culture Found., Monterey, 1999. Mem.: Internat. Lang. and Culture Found. (life; bd. dirs. internat. programs 1999, treas. 2002). Avocations: reading, travel, gardening, research, yoga. Personal E-mail: miriama0246@yahoo.com.

AGUILERA, CHRISTINA, singer; b. Staten Island, NY, Dec. 18, 1980; d. Fausto Agilera and Shelly Kearns; m. Jordan Bratman, Nov. 19, 2005. Vocalist New Mickey Mouse Club, 1994-96; vocalist theme song for Disney animated film Mulan, 1998); (Albums) Christina Aguilera, 1999 (Grammy award, Best New Artist, 2000), My Kind of Christmas, 2000, Mi Reflejo, 2000, Just be Free, 2001, Stripped, 2002 (Grammy award, Best Female Pop Vocal Performance for song "Beautiful", 2003), Back to Basics, 2006; singles: What A Girl Wants, 1999, Come on Over Baby (All I Want Is You), 1999, Genie in a Bottle, 1999, The Christmas Song, 1999, (with Lil'Kim, Pink, Mya) Lady Marmalade, 2001 (Grammy award for Best Pop Collaboration with Vocals, 2002), Beautiful, 2003, Dirty, 2003, Ain't No Other Man, 2006; video: The Genie Gets Her Wish, 1999. Recipient ALMA award, best new artist, 1999, Best Female award, MTV Europe Music Awards, 2006. Office: c/o RCA Recods 1540 Broadway New York NY 10036*

AGUIRRE, SARAH K., lawyer; BA, Tex. A&M U., 1997; JD, U. Houston Law Ctr., 2001. Bar: Tex. 2001. Intern Tex. Dept. Commerce, Mexico City; jud. intern Staff of US Magistrate Marcia Crone, US Dist. Ct., So. Dist. Tex.; assoc. Baker Hostetler, Houston. Named a Rising Star, Tex. Super Lawyers mag., 2006. Mem.: Orgn. Women in Internat. Trade, Tex.-Mex. Bar Assn. Office: Baker Hostetler 1000 Louisiana Ste 2000 Houston TX 77002-5009 Office Phone: 713-646-1330. Office Fax: 713-751-1717. E-mail: saguirre@bakerlaw.com.*

AGUIRRE BATTY, MERCEDES, Spanish and English language educator, literature educator; b. Cd Juarez, Mex., Dec. 20, 1952; arrived in US, 1957; d. Alejandro M. and Mercedes (Peón) Aguirre; m. Hugh K. Batty, Mar. 17, 1979; 1 child, Henry B BA, U. Tex., El Paso, 1974, MA, 1977; PhD in edn., Capella U., 2005. Cert. online tchr., Calif. Instr. ESL Paso del Norte- Prep Sch., Cd Juarez, 1973-74; tchg. asst. ESL and English U. Tex., El Paso, 1974-77; instr. ESL English Lang. Svcs., Bridgeport, Conn., 1977-80; instr. Spanish and English, coord. modern lang. Sheridan (Wyo.) Coll., 1980—, pres. faculty senate, 1989-90; pres. faculty senate, chair dist. coun. No. Wyo. C.C. Dist., 1995-96. Planning com. No. Wyo. C.C. Dist., 1996-97; advanced placement faculty Spanish cons. Coll. Bd. Ednl. Testing Svc., 1996-99; adj. prof. Spanish, U. Autonoma Cd Juarez, 1975; adj. prof. Spanish and English, Sacred Heart U., Fairfield, Conn., 1977-80; spkr. in field Bd. dirs. Wyo. Coun. for the Humanities, 1988-92; translator county and dist. cts., Sheridan; vol. Wmen's Ctr.; translator Sheridan County Meml. Hosp.; del. Citizen Ambassador Program, People to People-India, 1996. NEH fellow, 1991-92; Wyo. State Dept. Edn. grant, 1991. Mem. MLA (del. assembly 1998-2000, 2004-), Wyo. Fgn. Lang. Tchrs. Assn. (pres. 1990-92), Am. Assn. Tchrs. Spanish and Portuguese (founder, 1st pres. Wyo. chpt. 1987-90), TESOL, Sigma Delta Mu (v.p. 1992-99, pres. 2000—), Sigma Delta Pi (Alpha Iota chpt. pres. 1974-75). Avocations: travel, reading, archaeology, languages, geography. Office: Sheridan Coll NWCCD 3059 Coffeen Ave Sheridan WY 82801-9133

AHEARN, ELIZABETH LOWE, performing arts educator; b. Oklahoma City., Oct. 8, 1963; d. James Benjamin and Linda Ann Lowe; m. Thomas Joseph Ahearn, May 27, 1989; children: Alexandra Nicole, Brandon Thomas. BFA, N.Y. U., N.Y.C., 1988, MFA, 1989. Asst. prof. Goucher Coll., Balt., 1990—91, 1993—2006, U. Wash., Seattle, 1991—93; instr. Carver Ctr. for Arts and Tech., 1994—2006. Curator, performer Eleanor King Centennial Concert, Balt., 2005; Exhibited in group shows at Balt. Mus. Art, 2006; contbr. articles to profl. jours. Mem. Jr. League, Balt., 1990—2004. Mem.: Corps de Ballet Internat., World Dance Americas, Pilates Method Alliance, Am. Coll. Dance Festival Assn. (bd. dis. 2005—). Home: 12845 Stone Eagle Rd Phoenix MD 21131 Office: Goucher Coll 1021 Dulaney Valley Rd Towson MD 21204 Office Phone: 410-337-6399. Office Fax: 410-337-6433. Business E-Mail: eahearn@goucher.edu.

AHEARN, GERALDINE, medical/surgical nurse, writer, poet; b. Bklyn., Aug. 14, 1950; d. Louis Principessa and Patricia Donato; m. James J. Ahearn, Aug. 13, 1972 (div. June 4, 2001); children: Alicia Danielle, Katherine Ann. AA, Suffolk County CC, Selden, NY, 1971; diploma in nursing, Ctrl. Islip State Hosp. Sch. Nursing, 1974. LPN, NY, Ariz., RN NY, Ariz., cert. CCRN, Am. Heart Assn., EKG technician, Am. Heart Assn., med. claims and billing, med. coding. RN Bayshore Hosp., NY, 1970—83, Farmingville Clinic, NY, 1986—87, Sachem Schs., Farmingville, 1988—93; hosp. CCRN cardiac care NY, 1978—83; hosp. CCRN severely disabled children NY, 1989—90; freelance writer Mesa, Ariz., 1993—. Instr. CPR ARC, Coram, NY, 1986—90, instr. first aid, 1986—90, instr. CPR, Bohemia, NY, 1986—90. Author: (book) Inspirations, 2001, Words to Live By, 2001, Life's Poetic Journey, 2002, (series) The Nurse in the Purse, Vol. 1, 2001, (book) From America's Future Leaders, 2005; contbr. poetry to anthologies. Leader Girl Scouts U.S., Farmingville, 1988—91; cmty. leader Am. Online, 2001—04; catechist Farmingville Ch., 1985—87. Republican. Roman Catholic. Avocation: gardening. Home and Office: 1015 S Val Vista Dr Apt 81 Mesa AZ 85204 Personal E-mail: hrt4angel@aol.com.

AHEARN, HOLLY ANDE, music educator; d. Hugh David and Edna Olive Ahearn. MusB in Vocal Music Edn., U. Mass., 1986; MusM in Voice performance, U. Conn., 1996. Cert. secondary music tchr. grades 5-12 Mass. Music tchr. 7-9 Holyoke (Mass.) Pub. Schs., 1987—88; choral dir. 6-8 Danvers (Mass.) Pub. Schs., 1988—89; music tchr. K-6 Claremont (N.H.) Pub. Schs., 1989—90, Quabbin Regional Sch. Dist., Barre, Mass., 1992—93;

choral dir., music tchr. 5-8 Lowell (Mass.) Pub. Schs., 1995—99; choral dir. 6-8 Burlington (Mass.) Pub. Schs., 1999—2000; choral dir., music tchr. K-8 Brookline (Mass.) Pub. Schs., 2000—. Adjudicator Mass. Music Educators' Assn., 1998—2005. Recipient Bd. Regents Honor scholarship, State of Mass., 1981—86, grad. assistantship, U. Conn., 1990—92, 1st pl. award profl. divsn., Conn. Chpt. Nat. Assn. Tchrs. Singing, 1996. Mem.: Am. Guild Mus. Artists, Music Educators Nat. Conf., Am. Choral Dirs.' Assn. Avocations: gardening, travel.

AHERN, JO ANN, diabetes clinical nurse specialist; b. Bridgeport, Conn., Mar. 22, 1951; d. Charles Cary and Mabel Rose (Donovan) Hickey; m. Brian Joseph Ahern, May 27, 1972; children: Sean, Jeremy, Abby ASN, U. Bridgeport, 1979, BSN, 1989; MSN, So. Conn. State U., 1993. Cert. diabetes educator; advanced practice RN. Staff nurse Children's Clin. Rsch. Ctr. Yale/New Haven Hosp., 1979—82, trial coord. Diabetes Control and Complications Trial, 1982—83, pediat. and adult diabetes nurse specialist, 1993—. Author, reviewer The Diabetes Educator jour., 1990—; mem. editl. bd. Diabetes Forecast Mag., Diabetes Care, 2005-07 Recipient Wittnauer Diabetes Educator award, 1997; named Nat. Nurse of Yr. Nursing Spectrum mag., 1998 Mem. Am. Diabetes Assn. (Conn. affiliate, symposia com. 1994, DCCT transl. task force 1993-94), Am. Assn. Diabetes Educators (bd. dirs. 1994-97), Conn. Assn. Diabetes Educators (v.p. 1993-94, chair profl. edn. 1989-98) Democrat. Roman Catholic. Avocations: walking, soccer, reading, tennis. Home: 530 Scenic Rd Orange CT 06477-2127 Office: Animas Corp New Haven CT 06519 Personal E-mail: jodiahnur@aol.com.

AHERN, MARGARET ANN, nun, nursing educator; b. Manchester, N.H., Nov. 23, 1931; d. Timothy Joseph and Helen Bridget (Kearns) Ahern. Diploma, Sacred Heart Hosp. Sch. Nursing, 1952; BSN, Mt. St. Mary Coll., 1957; MSN, Cath. U. Am., 1965. Entered Sisters of Mercy, Roman Cath. Ch., 1953. Staff nurse Sacred Heart Hosp., Manchester, 1954-57, oper. rm. supr., 1957-62, med.-surg. nursing instr., 1962-66, dir. Sch. Nursing, 1966-75, Cath. Med. Ctr., Manchester, 1975-79, dir. dept. edn. and mem. sr. mgmt., 1979-87; pres. Cath. Med. Ctr. Networks, Inc., Manchester, 1987-94; mng. dir. Optima Health Systems, Inc., Manchester, N.H., 1994-99, v.p. cmty. svcs. and mission integration, 1999—2003; parish nurse Cath. Med. Ctr., Manchester, 2003—. Contbr. articles to profl. jours. Chmn. bd. dirs. Health Edn. Consortium, 1977-89; bd. dirs. Vis. Nurse Assn., 1981-87; adv. bd. Hesser Coll., 1980-98, N.H. Vocat.-Tech. Coll., 1979-87; mem. United Health Systems Agy., 1977-83; mem. adv. coun. on continuing edn. St. Anselm Coll., 1978-89; mem. gen. chpt. Sisters of Mercy, 1968-70, 79-81, chmn. fin. bd., 1981-86, chmn. Bd. Consolidation and Arbitration, 1981-86, 1991—. Recipient Disting. Women Leaders award YWCA, 1986, Pres's. award Fidelity Health Alliance, 1992, Good Samaritan award Pastoral Counseling Svcs., 1998, Leadership award N.H. Hosp. Assn., 2000, Cmty. Svc. award Bi-State Primary Care Assn., 2005 Mem. ANA, N.H. Nurses Assn., Nat. League for Nursing, New Eng. Cath. Hosp. Assn., N.H. Heart Assn., Sigma Theta Tau (Leadership Recognition award Epsilon Tau chpt. 1989, Disting. Leaders award 1989). Democrat. Roman Catholic. Home: 96 River Rd Unit 411 Manchester NH 03104-2900

AHLERS, LINDA L., retail executive; BA, U. Wisc. Buyer, Target Stores Dayton Hudson Corp., 1977-83, divsn. mdse. mgr., Target Stores, 1983-85, dir. mdse. planning and control, 1985-88, v.p. mdse. planning and control, 1988, sr. v.p. Target Stores, 1988-95, exec. v.p. merchandising, dept. store divsn., 1995-96; pres., dept. store divsn. Dayton Hudson Corp. (now Marshall Field's), 1996—; bd. dirs. Dayton Hudson Corp., 1997—. Dir. Guthrie Theatre; mem. Com. of 200, Detroit Renaissance Bd., Minn. Women's Econ. Roundtable. Office: Target Corp 1000 Nicollet Mall Minneapolis MN 55403-2467

AHLM, JO LAVONNE, elementary school educator; b. Roswell, N.Mex., Mar. 4, 1963; d. James William and Peggy Jean (Eads) Suter; m. Lief August Ahlm, Jan. 1, 1988; children: Jamie LaVonne, Augusta Ruth. BS in Edn., N.Mex. State U., Las Cruces, 1996. Specialist early childhood U.S. Army, White Sands Missile Range, N.Mex., 1986—88; tchr. Bloomfield Mid. Sch., N.Mex., 1989—90, Chama Mid. Sch., N.Mex., 1996—98, Raton Mid. Sch., N.Mex., 1998—. Leader 4-H, Raton, N.Mex., 1989—2005. Avocation: genealogy. Office: Raton Mid Sch 500 S 3rd St Raton NM 87740-4199

AHLQUIST, JANET SUE, musician, music educator; b. Worland, Wyo. d. John Orrin Ahlquist and Thelma Evelyn Jorgensen; children: J. Kirk Roberts, Tracy Sandmann Roberts, Jon M. Roberts. MusB, Juilliard; artist diploma, Longy Sch. Music, 1985; M, Eastman Sch. Music, 1989, performer's cert., 1990. Accompanying asst. Eastman Sch. Music, Rochester, N.Y., 1988-90, tchng. asst., 1990; prof. music Casper (Wyo.) Coll., 1991-99. Dir. Humanities Festival 2000, Casper, 1999—; artistic. dir. Casper Chamber Music Soc., 1993-99; convention artist Music Tchrs. Nat. Assn., Casper, 1997. Performing artist (CDs): Soul of Russia, Piano Classics by Portuguese Masters, 1992. Faculty Senate mem. Casper Coll., 1992-94; mem. Women Studies, 1994-99, Coun. Fgn. Rels., 1996-99, Performing Arts Coalition, 1999. Recipient Gov.'s award Wyo. Arts Coun., gov., 1998, Performance prize French Piano Inst., 1997; Gulbenkian grant Gulbenkian Found., Am.-Portuguese Soc., 1987, Wyo. Arts Coun. grant 1992. Mem. Music Edrs. Nat. Assn., Music Tchrs. Assn., Coll. Music Soc., Performing Arts Coalition, Cultural Affairs Com. Avocations: bicycling, skiing, hiking. Home: PO Box 406 Meriden NH 03770-0406

AHMED, GAIL R., music educator; b. Martins Ferry, Ohio, Oct. 2, 1953; d. Edgar Milton and Margaret Elizabeth Horner; 1 child, Aisha. BA, West Liberty State Coll., 1975; MEd, U. Dayton, 1991. Cert. music profl. K-12. Music educator Edison Local Schs., Ironton, Ohio, 1975—77, Tipp City (Ohio) Schs., Tipp City, 1977—. Music dir. Tippecanoe Cmty. Band, Tipp City, 1979—; gen. music rep. Ohio Music Educator's Nat. Conf., Columbus, 1985—90; mem. gifted com. Tipp City Schs., 1999—2002; cons. curriculum devel. Dayton Islamic Sch., Beavercreek, 1997—98; dist. gen. music rep. Ohio Music Educator's Nat. Conf., Columbus, 1985—90; orchestral dir. Tippecanoe H.S. Mus., Tipp City, 2000—; presenter Lesson Plans that Work TRIAD OMEA State Conv., 1995. Dir. United Meth. Church Bell Choir, Tipp City, 1985—87. Grantee Environ. Edn. grantee, Miami County Park Dist., 2001—02. Mem.: NGAC, Music Educator's Nat. Conf. (dist. gen. music rep. 1985—90, Ohio chpt. dist. II treas. 2002—, 25-Yr. mem. 2001), Friends of Libr. Avocations: travel, music, needlecrafts, reading. Office: Tipp City Schs 90 S Tippecanoe D Tipp City OH 45371 Home: 535 Stonecress Dr Tipp City OH 45371-1216

AHMOSE, NEFERTARI A., journalism educator; b. Kingston, Jamaica, Oct. 3, 1951; arrived in U.S., 75; d. Cecil Alexander Rose and Florence Rhodian Daley. Student, L.A. Valley Coll., 1975. Journalist Jamaica Daily News, 1974—80; pub. African Expression, Bronx, NY, 1982—91; founder Wafrakan People Stock Exchange, 1982—; politician Wafrakan Polit. Party, Ensley, Ala., 1985—2001; founder Wafrakan U. in West, Bklyn., 1996—, Wafrakan Ins. Co., 1990—, Merkhutu Currency Kiafrafan Lang. Kiafrakan Corp. Leader Empress Afrikan Diasporan Nation, Queendom of Wafrakan. Author: Black Sovereign-The Black Alternative, 1992, Harmonization, Unification and Standardization in Afrikan Tribal Vernaculars into Kiafrakan Language-Dictionary and Grammar, 1996, Ki-Afrakan-English Exercise, 1997, Ki-Afrakan Grammar, 1996, Ki-Afrakan Dictionary, 1996, Incorp. Afrakan Standard Language, 1994, Sex Education for Youngsters, 1994, Kemet Calendar, 2000. Founder Royal Bank Wafrakan, Merkhutu Currency, Kemet-Kush (now Wafrakan Polit. Party), NY, 2000—. Mailing: PO Box 971 Bronx NY 10472 Office Phone: 718-601-9419. Personal E-mail: nefertari@kiaprakan.com.

AHN, SHI HYUN, professional golfer; b. Inchon, Korea, Sept. 15, 1984; Winner three events Apache Dream Tour, 2002; winner CJ Nine Bridges Classic, 2003. Mem. Korean Nat. Team, 2000—01. Recipient Louise Suggs Rolex Rookie of Yr., LPGA, 2004. Achievements include being the youngest internat. winner in LPGA history and sixth youngest winner in LPGA history. Avocation: quilting. Office: c/o LPGA 100 International Dr Daytona Beach FL 32124-1092*

AHRENDTS, ANGELA J., apparel executive; b. New Palestine, Ind., June 7, 1960; d. Richard and Jean Ahrendts; m. Greg Couch; children: Jennings, Summer, Angelina. Degree (hon.), Ball State U., 1993. Account exec. Damon Creations, 1981—83, Warnaco, Inc., 1983—85, nat. sales mgr., 1985—87, v.p. sales Geoffrey Beene knitware, pres. Pringle of Scotland divsn., sr. v.p. Valentino intimate apparel & Ungaro intimate apparel; v.p. mktg. & sales Carmelo Pomodoro Ltd., 1989—90, pres., 1990—91; v.p. merchandising Donna Karen Co., 1992, pres. Donna Karen Collection, 1992—96; v.p. gen. mdse. mgr. Henri Bendel, 1996—98; v.p. corp. merchandising and design Liz Claiborne, Inc., NYC, 1998—2000, sr. v.p. corp. merchandising, grp. pres., 2000—02, exec. v.p., 2002—06; CEO Burberry Grp. plc, London, 2006—. Bd. dirs. Burberry Grp. plc, 2006—. Named one of 50 Women to Watch, Wall St. Jour., 2005, 100 Most Powerful Women, Forbes mag., 2006; recipient Alumni Achievement award, Ball State U., 2003. Achievements include being featured in Time Magazine Style and Design Women in Fashion Power List, 2004. Office: Burberry Group plc 18-22 Haymarket SW1 4DQ England*

AHRENS, MARY ANN PAINOVICH, small business owner; b. Des Moines, Oct. 9, 1942; M. Duane Keith Ahrens, June 11, 1966; children: Angela Ann, Alycia Ann. Student, Am. Inst. Bus., 1966-67; BA in Bus. Mgmt. with honors, U. Northern Iowa, 1979. Sec., supr., tour guide Iowa State Edn. Assn., Des Moines, 1960-66; sec. Fairall & Co. Advt. and Pub. Relations, Des Moines, 1966-67; legal sec. Frundt & Hibbs, Blue Earth, Minn., 1967-69; sec., supr. Western State Coll., Gunnison, Colo., 1970-71; sales coord. Henke Mfg., Waverly, Iowa, 1981-82; pres., mgmt. trainer Ahrens & Affiliates, Waverly, 1982—. Co-author: (with others) (tng. manual) VOLT Training Manual Level 1, 1985, Iowa AAUW Branch Action Team Training, 1986; contbr. articles to profl. jours. Pres. Wartburg Coll. Cmty. Symphony, Inc., Waverly; chmn. City of Waverly Airport Commn., 1981-99, mem. adv. com. Iowa Dept. Transp. Aviation Sys. Plan, 1997-98; bd. dirs. Iowa Leadership Comm. Coun., 1990-92; chair Bremer County Dem. Ctrl. Com., 2005—; bd. dirs. AAUW-Iowa, 2005—; mem. adv. bd. Nat. 19th Amendment Soc. Mem. AAUW (pres. Waverly br. 1983-84, many other offices including selection to nat. VOLT tng. team 1985-88, project dir. Voices for Choices 1990-91, Iowa reproductive rights, ednl. tng. project 1990-91, tng. and devel. coord. Iowa bd. 1987-91, Iowa equity trainer 1993-95, pres.-elect Iowa divsn. 1991-92, pres. Iowa 1992-94, legal adv. fund bd. dirs. 1997-99, nat. bd. dirs. 1995-99, nat. nominating com. 2001-03), ASTD, Waverly Area Devel. Group (co-chair Project: LEAD); bd. dirs. Iowa Fedn. Women's Clubs (pres. 1974-76, 80-82, Bremer County pres. 1982-84, dir. 3d dist. 1978-80, chair state leadership divsn. 1980-84). Avocations: antiques, music, travel. Office: 222 5th Ave NW Waverly IA 50677-2536

AH SOON, MELANIE FRANCES KAWAMOTO, science educator; b. Honolulu, Sept. 21, 1967; d. Clarence Osamu and Jean Setsuko Kawamoto; m. Clyde Matagi Ah Soon, Mar. 15, 1997; children: Kalehua, Kauhi. BA, Chaminade U., Honolulu, 1990. Pvt. sch. cert. Hawaii. 7th and 8th grade tchr. St. Patrick Sch., Honolulu, 1993—, level coord., 1997—2006; tchr. 6th grade sci. Sacred Hearts Acad., 2006—. Mem.: Nat. Cath. Edni. Assn. (assoc.). Democrat. Roman Catholic. Office Phone: 808-734-5058. E-mail: melanieahsoon@yahoo.com.

AIELLO, JUDITH A., music educator; b. Newton, Iowa, Aug. 17, 1939; d. Delmar Harry Grosvenor and Helen Erdine Jacobs; m. Frank John Aiello, Aug. 13, 1966; children: Rose Helen, Dominic. BA, Vennard Coll., 1961; B in Music Edn., Drake U., 1963, M in Music Edn., 1966. Cert. educator, Iowa, N.Y., S.D. Piano tchr. St. John's Sch., Des Moines, 1962-63; ch. organist Luth. Ch., Des Moines, 1962-63; tchr. music K-8 Davis County Schs., Bloomfield, Iowa, 1963-65; tchr. music 3-6 Westchester County Schs., Port Chester, N.Y., 1966-67; staff accompanist U. S.D., Vermillion, 1968-69; tchr. music K-8 Vermillion Pub. Schs., 1975-94; pvt. piano tchr. Vermillion, 1995—. Organist St. Agnes Ch., Vermillion, 1980-2000; faculty piano, music Edn. Mt. Marty Coll., Yankton, SD, 2005—. Mem. Nat. Guild Am. Musicians, Music Tchrs. Nat. Assn., Federated Music Club (pres. 1990-99), Delta Kappa Gamma. Roman Catholic. Avocations: organizing bible study groups, gardening. Home: 30174 448th Ave Volin SD 57072-7021

AIELLO, KIMBERLY JEAN, surgeon; b. Batavia, N.Y., Feb. 4, 1957; d. Samuel C. and Mary E. Scime; m. Lawrence Joseph Aiello, Aug. 7, 1982; children: Amanda Catherine, Phillip Joseph. Cert. Surg. Tech., Niagara County C.C., Sanborn, N.Y., 1976. Surg. technologist DeGraff Meml. Hosp., North Tonawanda, NY, 1976—. Mem.: Assn. Surg. Technologists (cert.). Democrat. Roman Catholic. Avocations: reading, kickboxing, walking, cooking, sewing.

AIELLO, MARCIE JEANNE GRUENER, secondary school educator; b. Amherst, N.Y., Jan. 27, 1977; d. Michael H. and Christine A. Gruener. BS Bus. and Secondary Edn., Canisius Coll., 1999; MEd Curriculum and Instrn., Ashland U., 2002. Lic. tchr. Ohio, cert. NY. Computer and tech. tchr. Hamilton Twp. H.S., Columbus, Ohio, 1999—2005; computer, bus., info. tech. tchr. Gahanna Lincoln H.S., Ohio, 2005—.

AIELLO, THERESA, social sciences educator; b. N.Y.C., Jan. 7, 1947; d. Salvatore and Lucy Suozzo Aiello. BMus, Juilliard Sch., N.Y.C., 1968; MS in Music, Juilliard Sch., 1969; MSW, Hunter Coll., N.Y.C., 1979; PhD in Clin. Social Work, NYU, N.Y.C., 1993. LCSW. Freelance musician N.Y.C., 1964—79; supr., cons. Jewish Bd. Family and Children's Svcs., N.Y.C., 1985—, Family Cons. of Eastchester, Pelham Family Svcs., Nat. Inst. for Psychotherapy; assoc. prof. NYU Sch. Social Work, N.Y.C., 2000—, chair human behavior curriculum, 2004—. Author: Child and Adolescent Treatment for Social Work Practice, 1999, 2004; author: (co-editor) Love and Attachment; contbr. chapters to books. Recipient Disting. Tchr. medal, NYU, 2000; grantee Humanities Coun. Interdiscipline grantee, 2003, Jane Bram grant, 2005; scholar, Goddard scholar, 1996—97. Mem.: NASW, Soc. Adolescent Social Work, N.Y. State Clin. Soc. Office: New York University Sch of Social Work 1 Washington Sq N New York NY 10003 Office Phone: 212-998-5927. Business E-Mail: theresa.aiello@nyu.edu.

AIGEN, BETSY PAULA, psychotherapist; b. N.Y.C., Sept. 13, 1938; d. Abraham H. and Gertrude (Rosenblum) Wasserman; m. Ronald Aigen, Dec. 7, 1957 (div. Jan. 1979); m. Isadore Schumukler, June 20, 1982; children: Jennifer Loren, Samantha Devin. BA, New Sch. Social Research, 1971; MA, Columbia U., 1972; D of Psychology, Rutgers U., 1980. Group co-leader, asst. psychotherapist Inst. Rational Psychotherapy, N.Y.C., 1967-72; asst. course instr. Columbia U., N.Y.C., 1971-72; psychotherapist Mt. Carmel Guild, Englewood, NJ, 1980-82, SELF Edn. Learning and Feeling, N.Y.C., 1982—; founder, dir. Surrogate Mother Program, N.Y.C., 1985—. Cons. Police Chief Tng. Community Workshops Assn., N.Y.C., 1973-74, Richmond Fellowship Mental Health Halfway Houses, Eng. and U.S., 1970-75. Contbr. articles to profl. jours. Chmn. Tenants Com., N.Y.C., 1975-85; active Profl. Theatre, 1956-67. Mem. Nat. Orgn. Women, RESOLVE, Adoptive Parents Com., Am. Psychol. Assn., N.Y. St. Psychol. Assn., N.J. St. Psychol. Assn., N.Y. Assn. Feminist Therapists. (co-founder, charter), Am. Orgn. Surrogate Parenting Practitioners (founder, charter). Democrat. Jewish. Home: 220 W 93rd St Apt 10B New York NY 10025-7412 Office: Surrogate Mother Program Childbirth Cons Svcs 220 W 93rd St Apt 10B New York NY 10025-7412 Office Phone: 212-496-1070.

AIGNER, EMILY BURKE, Christian lay minister; b. Henrico, Va., Oct. 28, 1920; d. William Lyne and Susie Emily (Willson) Burke; m. Louis Cottrell Aigner, Nov. 27, 1936; children: Lyne, Betty, D. Muriel (dec.), Willson, Norman, William, Randolph, Dorothy. Cert. in Bible, U. Richmond, 1969; postgrad., So. Bapt. Sem. Extension, Nashville, 1987, Va. Commonwealth U., 1981; diploma in Bible, Liberty Home Bible Inst., 1992, masterlife grad., 1994. Deacon Four Mile Creek Bapt. Ch., Richmond, Va., 1972—, trustee, 1991, dir. Woman's Missionary Union, 1986-94, treas., 1984-89, dir. Sunday sch., 1969-78, 84-85, 1989-93. Spl. edn. tchr., 1993-99; acctg. tech., 1959-80; farm owner. Prodr. Dial-A-Devotion for pub. by telephone, 1978-85, 2003—. Solicitor ARC, Henrico County, 1947-49, induction ctr. vol., 1994-97; solicitor, United Givers' Fund, Henrico County, 1945-48; sec.-treas. soliciting funds Bible Edn. in Varina Sch., 1946-49; singer Bellwood Choir, Chesterfield County, Va., 1965-70; telephone counselor Richmond Contact, 1980-82, Am. Cancer Soc., Richmond, 1980-82; program chmn. Varina (Va.) Home Demonstration Club, 1950-53; worker Vol. Visitor Program Westport Convalescent Home, 1983-2000; vol. patient rep. Richmond Meml. Hosp., 1994-98, chaplain, 1996-97; jail min. Richmond City Jail, 1973—; lay minister to sr. adults Four Mile Creek Bapt. Ch., 2002—, chairperson bd. deacons, 2004—. Named Woman of Yr., Henrico Farm Bur., 1996. Mem. UDC, Am. Assn. Christian Counselors, Gideons Internat. (sec. Va. aux. 1977-80, 82-84, new mem. plan rep. 1981, 85, 91, 94, zone leader 1988-91, state cabinet rep. 1989-90, pres. Richmond N.E. Camp 1976-78, sec.-treas. 1980-82, 93, scripture sec. 1973-75, 87-89, v.p., 1997-98, chmn. Va. state widows com. 1993-97, pres. Richmond East Camp, 2000-02, 2005—), State Aux. (tng. leader, 2004), Henrico Farm Bur. (women's com. 1994—), Alpha Phi Sigma. Home: 9717 Varina Rd Richmond VA 23231-8428 Office Phone: 804-795-1406.

AIKEN, LISA ANNE, psychologist, author, lecturer; b. Balt., July 8, 1956; d. Sidney Herbert and Janet Betty (Segall) A.; m. Ira Michaels, Aug., 1992. BA in Psychology summa cum laude, Towson State Coll., 1975; MA in Clin. Psychology, Loyola U., Chgo., 1977, PhD in Clin. Psychology, 1979. Lic. psychologist. Psychologist, cons. liaison psychiatry North Cen. Bronx (N.Y.) Hosp., 1980-82; chief psychologist Lenox Hill Hosp., N.Y.C., 1982-89; pvt. practice N.Y.C., 1982—. Spkr. in field, 1988—; cons. Forest Hills Ind. Practice Assn., Queens, N.Y., 1989-92. Author: Why Me, God, 1996, Beyond Bashert: A Guide to Dating Marriage Enrichment, 1996, To Be a Jewish Woman, 1992, The Hidden Beauty of the Shema, 1997, Guide For The Romantically Perplexed, 2003, Tuning In, 2005; co-author: The Art of Jewish Prayer, 1991, What Your Unborn Baby Wants You To Know, 2001. Avocation: travel. Home: 7866 Seville Pl Apt 2303 Boca Raton FL 33433-6325

AIKENS, MARTHA BRUNETTE, park service administrator; b. Jayess, Miss., Aug. 23, 1949; d. Walter and Elnora La Doris (Bridges) A. BS in Social Sci., Alcorn State U., 1971; postgrad., George Williams Coll., 1974, Fla. Internat. U., 1977, George Washington U., 1979, Pa. State U., 1979, U. So. Calif., D.C. Ext., 1980. Social worker Pearl River County Devel. Corp., Picayune, Miss., 1971—72; environ. ednl. specialist Nat. Park Svc., Homestead, Fla., 1973—75, environ. ednl. coord., 1973—75, comm. specialist, 1976—78; park mgr. Bklyn., 1978—79, Dept. Interior's Mgmt. Program, 1979—80, St. Augustine, Fla., 1979—83, Washington, 1983—88; dir. tng. and employee development Nat. Park Svc., 2002—. Instr., cons. Coll. African Wildlife Mgmt., Tanzania, 1980, Fed. Law Enforcement Tng. Ctr., Glynco, Ga., 1983—, Stephen T. Mather Employee Devel. Ctr., Harper's Ferry, W.Va., 1988—91; supt. Independence Nat. Hist. Pk., Phila., 1991—2002; chair Nat. Pk. Svc. Women's Conf., New Orleans, 1991. Author: tchrs. guides on Everglades Nat. Park, 1973—76, park brochure, 1977; contbr. chapters to books chpts. to books. Active Dept. Interior's Partnership in Edn. Commn., Washington, 1983—, Fed. Interagy Commn. on Edn., Washington, 1983—, Nat. Park Svc. Employee Rels. Task Force, Washington, 1983—, 21st Century Task Force, 1988—, Salt River Bay Nat. Hist. Pk. and Ecol. Preserve Adv. Commn., 1993—, Strategic Planning Task Force, Atlanta, 1981—83, S.E. Regional Equal Opportunity Commn., Atlanta, 1982—83; bd. trustees Walnut St. Theatre, Phila., 1993—; bd. dirs. Peopling of Phila., 1993—; mem. Leading by Example, 1992—. Recipient Star 104.5 Woman of Yr. award, 1993, Image award, YWCA. Office: Dept Training & Employee Devel Nat Park Svc 1849 C St NW Washington DC 20240

AIKINS, CANDACE SUE, music educator, consultant; b. Pitts., Feb. 7, 1973; d. Ronald Leason and Bonnie Graham Aikihs. MusB, Grove City Coll., Pa., 1995; MusM, Carnegie Mellon U., Pitts., 1997. Ch. organist Vandergrift Presbyn. Ch., Pa., 1988—94; ch. organist, choir dir. Natrona Heights Presbyn. Ch., Pa., 1994—; tchr. music Ambridge HS, 1998, Moniteau Jr./Sr. HS, West Sunbury, 1999—2001, Valley HS, New Kensington, 2001—02, Highlands Sch. Dist., Natrona Heights, 2002—04; cons. music Mmacmillan/McGraw Hill, N.Y.C., 2004—. Fellow, Carnegie Mellon U., 1995. Mem.: Am. Guild Organists, Pa. Music Educators Assn., Music Educators Nat. Conf., Kappa Delta Pi. Republican. Presbyterian. Home: 127 E Adams Ave Vandergrift PA 15690

AIKMAN, ELFLORA ANNA K., senior citizens center administrator; b. Marion, Ill., July 21, 1929; d. John Frederick and Elsa Flora (Weber) Kaeser; m. Samuel Vick Aikman, Dec. 24, 1949; children: Vicki Ann Aikman Hayes, Vance J., Valerie Sue Aikman Henshaw, Samuel Vick III. Student, So. Ill. U., 1949, John A. Logan Coll., 1970, 80, 87, cert. food handler, 1984. Numerous positions, 1947-67; sec. Color-Craft Products, Detroit, 1967-69; admitting clk. Marion Meml. Hosp., 1969-70, appointed to task force, 1989—; co-owner, office mgr., decorating cons. House of Color, Marion, 1970-79; sec., bookkeeper, receptionist Mitchell-Hughes Funeral Home, Marion, 1979-80; receptionist Meredith Funeral Home, Marion, 1980—94; exec. dir. Marion Sr. Citizens Ctr., 1981—99. Co-designer, decorator Meredith Funeral Home; decorator Marion Meml. Hosp. Chapel, 1971, 77; sr. ctr. operator Emergency Assistance Pl., City of Marion; coord. Sr. Health Ins., Vol. Income Tax Assistance, Tax Counsel Elderly. Columnist: Marion Daily Republican, 1984; editor monthly newsletter The Yodler, 1984-99; columnist, contbr. Sr. World, 1987; prodr. program Sta. WGGH, 1989; columnist, contbr. newspaper Old Friends, 1989; author: Memories II, 2006. Founder Bethesda Home Waifs, Marion, 1948; pack officer Boy Scouts Am., Mt. Vernon, 1964—67; home rm. mother St. Clair, 1958—67, Mt. Vernon, 1958—67; chmn. Vols. to Arts, Mt. Vernon, 1966—67; library asst. Plymouth Middle Sch., 1968—69; mem. Marion Meml. Hosp. Aux., 1980—, Hearts Helping Hearts, Marion, 1987—2002, So. Ill. Easter Seal Soc., 1987; treas., Project Manna Marion Ministerial Alliance, 1985—97; mem. Greater Marion Area United Way, sec.; mem. adv. bd. So. Ill. Medicare Beneficiary; vol. Ill. Dept. of Insurance, 1982; sec. Greater Marion Area United Way; blood pressure check vol. Marion US Post Office, 1995—96; tornado vol. Ill. Dept. Ins., 1982; organist St. Clair, Mo., 1958—63, Myers Funeral Home, Mt. Vernon, 1964—67; jr. choir dir. St. Clair, 1958—63, Trinity Episcopal Ch., sr. choir dir., 1964—67; choir mem. United Ch. Christ, Plymouth, Mich., 1967—69; asst. organist Zion United Ch. of Christ, Marion, choir mem., Sunday sch. tchr., funeral coord., liturgist, mem. numerous ch. coms.; com. mem. Girl Scouts Am., Mt. Vernon, 1964—67, PTA, St. Clair, 1960—63, Williamson County Sesquicentennial Celebration, Ill., 1989. Recipient Svc. Plaque, Marion Recreation Dept. Bd., 1983, cert. award svc., Chautauqua Ill. Humanities Coun., 1986, cert. recognition for outstanding svc. to sr. citizens, 1995—99, cert. recognition, Modern Woodmen Am., Camp 3600, 1998, Mayors Svc. award, city of Marion, 1996, cert. recognition, AARP Tax Counsel Elder, IRS, plaque 40 yrs. svc. to music ministry, Zion UCC, 1999, Govs. award, Ill. Dept. on Aging, 2004, Sr. Health Ins. Program Coord. of Yr., State of Ill., 1998. Mem. Marion C. of C. (com. 1988), Marion S.A.L.T. (charter mem.), TRIAD (charter mem., treas.), Beta Sigma Phi. Avocations: crocheting, sewing, reading, playing piano and organ. Home: 1200 Abbey Ln Marion IL 62959

AILEEN-DONOHEW, PHYLLIS AUGUSTA, educational consultant; b. Cin., Aug. 27, 1948; d. Earl John and Mary Roth (Groh) Wilson; m. Robert Lewis Donohew, Oct. 19, 1998; children: Robert Lewis Donohew, Jr., Susan Kerry Schneider, John Patrick Donohew, Kimberly Aileen Braun, Kelly Augusta Chin-Yee, Kristopher Adam Braun. AA with high distinction, Somerset CC, Ky., 1993; BS summa cum laude, U. Ky., Lexington, 1995; MS in Comm., U. Ky., 1995, PhD in Higher Edn., 2003. Gen. office acctg. clk. sci. instruments divsn. Bendix Corp., Cin., 1966—71; ind. cons. pub. rels., devel., seminars Cin., 1971—95; comml./indsl. chem. specialist, ter. sales mgr. Phillips Supply Co., Cin., 1974—82; corp. exec., dist. sales mgr. Owens, Mpls., 1982—86; realtor, v.p., owner Ross and Lingrosso Realtors, Inc., Sarasota, Fla., 1986—90; interventionist, asst. early childhood cons. Pulaski

County Sch. Sys., Somerset, 1990—93; ind. scholar, rschr., cons., lectr. Mt. Sterling, Ky., 1995—. Grant adminstr. fed. part B, Kera at-risk programming, family literacy programming, parent and child edn. Pulaski County Schs., Somerset, 1990—93; cons. devel. and fund raising U. Ky. Coll. of Comm., Lexington, 1993—95; rsch. asst., devel., pub. rels. U. Ky. Appalachian Ctr., Lexington, 1993—95; adj. faculty orgnl. comms., cons. bus. and curriculum devel. Midway (Ky.) Coll., 1995—96; field interviewer U. Ky. Survey Rsch. Ctr., Lexington, 1995; rsch. asst. to dir. grad. studies U. Ky. Coll. of Edn., Lexington, 1996—99; prodr. conf. presentation The Charism of the Carmelite Cloistered; presenter papers in field. Author: (book chpt.) Women of Steel: Unsentimental Stories, (book chpt., conf. presentation) Etiology of Silence: Secrecy or Solitude-Five Women's Stories, Sounds of Silence: Women in Oppression from Victimization to Empowerment. Founding team mem. Archdiocese of Cin., 1977—78; retreat coord., educator Incarnation Parish, Sarasota, 1977—82; adv. bd. mem. Montgomery County Arts Coun., Mt. Sterling, 2004—05; adviser, spkr. Transitional Support for Displaced Homemakers, Somerset, 1991—94; coach, judge Nat. Forensic League, Sarasota, 1963—85. Recipient Lyman T. Johnson Grad. fellowship, U. Ky. Fellowship Bd., 1996—99, Commonwealth scholarship, U. Ky. Merit Bd., 1995, full acad. scholarship, Somerset C.C. Fin. Aid Bd., 1991—93, Disting. Svc. award, Mirror Student Newspaper Faculty Advisor, 1991—93. Fellow: U. of Ky. Fellows Soc. (life); mem.: Mt. Notre Dame H.S. (assoc.), U. of Ky. Alumni Assn. (assoc.), Ky. Comm. Assn. (assoc.; editl. bd. 1994—98), Ky. Vineyard Assn. (assoc.). Democrat. Roman Catholic. Avocations: reading, walking, cross stitch. Home: 1428 Lemon Bay Dr Englewood FL 34223 Office: 5488 Howards Mill Rd Mount Sterling KY 40353 Office Phone: 859-585-3673. Office Fax: 859-498-7496. Business E-Mail: aileen@uky.edu.

AILLONI-CHARAS, MIRIAM CLARA, interior designer, consultant; b. Veere, The Netherlands, July 31, 1935; arrived in US, 1958; d. Maurits and Elzina (De Groot) Taytelbaum; m. Dan Ailloni-Charas, Oct. 8, 1957; children: Ethan Benjamin, Orrin, Adam. Degree in Interiors, Pratt Inst., 1962; BSc, SUNY, Albany, 1978. Interior designer S.J. Miller Assocs., N.Y.C., 1960-63; interior design cons. Rye Brook, NY, 1963—88, 1990—2003; exec. v.p. Contract 2000 Inc., Port Chester, NY, 1988-90; interior design cons. Scottsdale, Ariz., 2003—. Treas. Temple Guild, Congregation Emanu-El, Rye, N.Y., 1979-88, co-chmn., 1988-96, chair, 1996-97, trustee, 1986-92. Recipient Cert. of Merit, U.S. Jaycees, 1962, March of Dimes, 1989, 91. Mem.: Westchester C. of C. (Area Devel. Coun. 1988—90), Westchester Assn. Women Bus. Owners (bd. of dir. 1988—93), Allied Bd. Trade, Am. Soc. Interior Designers, Nat.Trust of Hist. Preservation.

AIN, DIANTHA, poet, artist, educator; b. Middletown, N.Y., Jan. 21, 1930; d. Maynicke Munn Pattison and Rose Dorothy Dravis; m. Robert Arthur Ain, July 1, 1950; children: Robert Arthur, Judith Pattison, Elizabeth Dravis. Student, New Sch. for Social Rsch., N.Y.C., 1946—48, Inst. of Children's Lit., Redding Ridge, Conn., 1983. Vis. poet Edison Elem. Sch., Burbank, Calif., 1985—87; cons. on cultivating creativity in children K-6th grades, 1981—. Actor: (plays) Elizabeth the Queen, Pasadena Playhouse, 1949; (films) Girls School, 1949, A Life of Her Own, 1950; author (illustrator): (poetry book) What Do You Know About Succotash?, 1984; co-author (haiku): Grieving God's Way, 2004; Halku editor: Bereavement Mag., 2000—; composer: (musical score) The Melancholy King, Aesop Fables, A Gift of Love; contbr.: haiku Joyful Parenting, 2006. Recipient Cert. of Recognition, Calif. Legis. Assembly/Cathie Wright, 1987, Woman in History award, Simi Valley Unified Sch. Dist., 1986, Merit award, Leaders of Readers, Family Cir. Mag., 1987. Mem.: Acad. Am. Poets, Soc. of Children's Book Writers and Illustrators, Nat. League of Am. Pen Women (treas., pres., Woman of Achievement 1990). Avocations: classical piano, theater, flying.

AINES, LINDA DIANE, financial consultant; b. St. Leonard, N.B., Can., Aug. 12, 1947; came to U.S., 1962; d. Onesime and Liliane (Gauvin) Soucy; m. J. Peter Aines, Jr., Mar. 16, 1968 (div. Dec. 2001) BSBA summa cum laude, Ohio State U., 1976, MBA, 1978. Asst. to dir. fin. aid U. Hartford, West Hartford, 1969—74; pers. asst. Orient Devel. Inst., Ohio, 1975—76; assoc. dir. fin. United Way, Columbus, Ohio, 1977—78; coord. bus. planning Doody Co., Columbus, 1978—79; dir. fin. aid Coll. St. Joseph, Rutland, Vt., 1981—83; specialist cmty. resource devel. U. Vt. Extension Sys., Rutland, 1983—2002; internat. bus. cons., 2002—; owner Internat. Link Recruitment Svc., Brandon, Vt., 2004—. Coord. SBDC sm. bus. ctr. U. Vt., 1983-92, founder, coord. export assistance ctr., 1991-2002; judge Blue Chip Enterprise Initiative, 1990-95; mentor Women's Network for Entrepreneurship Tng., 1990-92; adv. panelist Entrepreneur's Project, 1990-91 Editor, pub.: Vermont Export Resource Guide, 1992-98. Mem. planning commn. Town of Sudbury, Vt., 1993-2000; chair Vt. Women 1987: Steps to Econ. Independence Conf., 1986-87; chair planning com. Vt. Wood Products Confs., 1995-99; founder Vermonters in Internat. Trade and Svcs., 1996-2002; mem. Nat. E-Team, 2000-02; bd. dirs. Vt. Coun. in World Affairs Mem. Rutland Bus. and Profl. Women (v.p. 1993-94, pres. 1994-95), Lake Champlain Regional C. of C. (export edn. com. 1993-96, project mgr. export edn. program 1995-96) Avocations: photography, skiing, hiking. Home and Office: Sudbury 158 Burr Pond Rd Brandon VT 05733

AINSWORTH, ELAINE MARIE, occupational therapist; b. Jamestown, N.Y., July 24, 1948; d. Ralph Marion and Martha Elaine (Dunn) Sorenson; m. Stephen Marshall Ainsworth, Jan. 17, 1970 (div. Aug. 1973). BS in Edn., Edinboro State Coll., 1971; MS in Occupl. Therapy, Columbia U., 1975; DEd, Pa. State U., 2004. Occupl. therapy staff Warren (Pa.) State Hosp., 1975-77, chief occupl. therapy staff, 1977; occupl. therapy staff Sheppard & Enoch Pratt Hosp., Towson, Md., 1978; pvt. practice Allentown, Pa., 1981-82; chief occupl. therapy dept. Cmty. Hosp. of Lancaster, Pa., 1982-86; asst. prof. Elizabethtown (Pa.) Coll., 1986-88, Alvernia Coll., Reading, Pa., 1996; chief occupl. therapy dept. Lebanon (Pa.) VA Med. Ctr., 1989-90; owner Elaine Ainsworth & Assocs., Lancaster, Pa., 1991-97; profl. adv. com. Cmty. Home Health Lancaster, 1997-99; instr. Pa. State U., Mont Alto, 1997—2006; occupl. therapist Del. Psychiat. Ctr., New Castle, Del., 2006—, chief dept. occupl. therapy, 2006—. Adv. bd. occupl. therapy dept. Alvernia Coll., Reading, Pa., 1995, Home Health Agy., Brethren Village, Lancaster, 1995--, Northwestern Home Health Care/Svcs. Agy., 1994-95; cons. Mental Health Mgmt., Alexandria, Va., 1985, Stairways Agy., Erie, Pa., 1976, Hamot Med. Ctr., Erie, 1976, W.C.A. Hosp., Jamestown, 1976; allied health Liaison Parkinson Support Group, Lancaster, 1983-86. Author: (with others) Core Curriculum for Home Health Care Nursing, 1993, 2d edit., 1995. Treas., bd. dirs. Orgn. for Responsible Care of Animals, Lancaster, 1988. Recipient scholarship Commonwealth of Pa., 1973-75. Mem. Am. Occupl. Therapy Assn., Pa. Occupl. Therapy Assn. (chair nominating com. 1980-81, 2000—, chair program com. state conf. 1982, exec. officer 2001—). Avocations: international travel, local historical research. Office: Delaware Psychiatric Ctr 1901 N DuPont Hwy New Castle DE 19720 Office Phone: 302-255-2917.

AINSWORTH, JOAN HORSBURGH, retired director; b. Cleve., Dec. 30, 1942; d. Donald Francis and Elaine Mildred Horsburgh; m. Richard B. Ainsworth Jr., Oct. 30, 1965; children: Richard B. III, Alison. BA, Wells Coll., 1965; MBA, Case Western Res. U., 1986. Cert. fund raising exec. Social worker San Diego County (Calif.) Welfare Dept., 1966-68; social worker, vol. coord. Washtenaw County (Mich.) Juvenile Ct., Ann Arbor, 1968-70; adminstrv. asst. to pres. Med. Ventures, Ltd., Cleve., 1985-86; dir. Project MOVE, Office of Mayor City of Cleve., 1986-89; dir. devel. and pres.'s programs Case Western Res. U., Cleve., 1989-97, dir. spl. gifts and prin. projects, 1997-98, dir. devel. Coll. Arts and Scis., 1998-2001, asst. dean for devel. Coll. Arts and Scis., 2001—04; sr. devel. officer Cleve. Mus. Art, 2006—. Trustee, v.p. Children's Aid Soc., Cleve., 1989-2004, pres., 1997-2004; trustee, chair devel. Project: LEARN, Cleve., 1990-96; past trustee, cmty. vol. Jr. League Cleve., Inc., 1971—; active Vol. Ohio, 1987-96; trustee Applewood Ctrs., 2000— Named Hon. Mayor, City of Cleve., 1989. Mem.: Coun. for Advancement and Support of Edn., Nat. Assn. Fundraising Profls. (cert, chair publicity Greater Cleve. chpt. 1994—96). Avocations: flying, tennis, boating, travel. Home: 2023 Lyndway Rd Cleveland OH 44121-4265 Office Phone: 216-707-6775.

AINSWORTH, SHARIE LYNN, athletic trainer, educator; d. Jack Oakley and Irene Glenn; children: Jennifer, James Ray. BS in Health, NW Okla. State U., Alva, 1984; postgrad., Okla. State U., 1987, postgrad., 1993. Cert. athletic trainer Okla., 1993. Health cluster career tech. tchr. Putnam City West HS, Oklahoma City, 2001—, head athletic trainer, 2001—. Named Athletic Trainer of Yr., 1999. Mem.: Okla. Edn. Assn., Okla. Athletic Trainers Assn., Nat. Athletic Trainers Assn., Profl. Women's Orgn. Avocations: reading, travel, sports. Office: Putnam City West HS 8500 NW 23 D Oklahoma City OK 73126

AITCHISON, ANNE CATHERINE, retired environmental activist; b. Pontiac, Mich., Dec. 27, 1939; d. Willard Francis and Elizabeth (Smith) Speer; m. Robert Terrington Aitchison, Aug. 10, 1963; children: Hannah, Guy, Will. MusB, U. Mich., 1963, MusM, 1965. Chair Naperville (Ill.) Area Recycling Ctr., 1980-89, exec. dir., 1989-93, Sun Shares, Durham, N.C., 1994-96; ret., 1996; cons. Rsch. Triangle Inst., Research Triangle Park, N.C., 1996—. Mem. Citizen's Solid Waste Adv. Com., Will County, Ill., 1989-90, Task Force on Solid Waste, Ill., 1989-90, Task Force on Degradable Plastic, Ill., 1990-91, Mayor's Adv. Com. on Plastic Recycling, Chgo., 1990, Chmn.'s Environ. Com., DuPage County, 1993; cons. cmty. recycling Rsch. Triangle Inst., Durham. Co-author: Resource Recycling, 1991, Environmental Policy for DuPage County, 1993. Founding mem. Naperville Chamber Winds, 1981—93; dir. DuPage Environ. Awareness Ctr., 1987—93; mem. Chmn.'s Environ. Commn., DuPage County, 1992—93, Durham County Solid Waste Adv. Bd., 1994—96; bd. dirs. Durham Symphony, 1994—2000, 2001—, mem. edn. outreach com., 1994—, pres., 2004—05; bd. dirs. Meals on Wheels, Durham, 1999—2005, pres. bd., 2001—02; bd. dirs., membership chmn. Friends of Durham Libr., 1999—2001. Named Individual Recycler of Yr. Keep Am. Beautiful, 1987, Outstanding Woman Leader YWCA, 1988. Mem. Ill. Recycling Assn. (co-pres. 1987-90, founding dir. 1980—, Pied Piper of Recycling 1989, founding mem. 25th anniversary award, 2005), Women in Waste, Ill. Environ. Coun. (bd. dirs. 1989-90), LWV (bd. dirs. Naperville chpt. 1977-93), Kiwanis (Disting. Svc. award 1987). Avocation: flute.

AITCHISON, BRIDGET MARY, theater educator, theater director; b. L.A., Feb. 27, 1969; d. James and Donna Jean Calcandis, Frederick Anthony Searles; children: Marion Donna Grace, Heather Margaret. Student, U. N.H., 1986—88; BA with honors, U. NSW, 1991; D in Creative Arts, U. Wollongong, NSW, 2001. Head faculty of drama Wesley Inst., Sydney, Australia, 1998—. Dir., facilitator Using Drama to Help Street Kids, 1996. Dir., prodr., writer (touring theatrical prodn.) Back From Nowhere, 2000 (Arts Contbn. cert. NSW Mental Health Assn., 2001, Mental Health Matters award, 2001); actor: 36 commls., TV shows, stage appearances; dir., prodr., artistic dir. BookMark, 1999, A Dry and Thirsty Land, 2000, Sacrifice and Remembrance, 2001; dir., prodr.: Runaways, 1997 (Queen's Trust award for Young Australians, 1996); author: Transformational Drama: Theatre for Community and Social Change, 2002; co-author: Youth Arts and Social Change, 2002; contbr. articles to profl. jours.; prodr., dir.: Bach's Easter Cantata No. 4, 2002; J.B., 2002; Why the Cross?, 2003; Watch This Space!, 2003. Pres. Students Against Drunk Driving, Manchester, NH, 1984—86; orientation counselor U. N.H., Durham, 1986—88; arts/youth worker/activist Sydney, 1995—2001. Recipient Queens Trust award for Young Australians, 1996. Mem.: AFTRA, SAG, MEAA, Australian Coll. Edn., Cultural Studies Assn. Australia, Drama Australia, Edn. Drama Assn. NSW, Australasian Drama Studies Assn. Avocations: violin, folk art, drama, chess, snorkeling. E-mail: bri@butterfly-b.com.

AIZEN, RACHEL K., clinical psychologist; b. Tel-Aviv; MA, U. Ill., 1968, PhD, 1970; postgrad. in clin. psychology, U. Mass., 1980-83. Lic. psychologist Mass., nat. cert. sch. psychologist. Asst. prof. Tel-Aviv U., 1972-73; psychologist Northampton (Mass.) State Hosp., 1971-72; clin. psychologist Amherst (Mass.) Sch. Sys., 1974—; pvt. practice, 1974—; intern VA Med. Ctr., Northampton, 1982-83; clin. psychologist Shieba Med. Ctr., Israel, 1985-86; fellow in neuropsychology Mass. Mental Health Hosp., Boston, 1987-88. Cons. psychologist Mass. Rehab., 1974—, various local agys. and cts. Cons. editor: Am. Psychologist, 1974; co-author: Psychological Counseling: Principles, Strategies and Intervention, 1990; contbr. articles to profl. jours. Mem.: NEA, APA (divisn. clin. and psychoanalysis), Nat. Assn. Sch. Psychologists. Avocations: travel, art. Office: 48 N Pleasant St Ste 204 Amherst MA 01002-1758

AJA-HERRERA, MARIE, fashion designer, educator; b. Bedford, Eng., Mar. 19, 1955; d. Henry and Ariadne Swiejkowski; m. Manny Anjel Aja-Herrera, Oct. 24, 1981. BA in Fashion, U. Ctrl. England, 1977; MA in Fashion/Textiles, Lodz U./Krakow U., Poland, 1980; MA in Design Studies, Ctrl. St. Martins, England, 1995; postgrad. cert. in Edn., U. London, 1981. Head fashion dept. Southend Coll. Essex U., 1981—84; head womenswear design (Byblos) Ghirombelli/Pacanina Modas/Santini S.A., Barcelona, Milan, London, 1984—88; head womenswear design Jefferson Internat. PLC, Hong Kong, 1988—89; sales exec., design & edn. coord. Lectra Sys., 1989; chair fashion design, chair fashion merchandising Am. Coll. in London, 1989—92; design dir. CAD, knitwear, textiles Jacques Vert PLC, 1992—95; dean faculty of art and design Am. U. Dubai, United Arab Emirates, 1995—96; head of design Twins/NIKE Enterprise PLC, 1996—97; chair fashion design Savannah Coll. Art & Design, Ga., 1997—. Cons. Herrera UK Ltd., 1982—95. Fellow: Soc. Artists & Designers (lic.); mem.: Textile Inst., Polish Union Artists, The Fashion Group Internat., Clothing & Footwear Inst. Avocations: horse riding, skiing, collecting antiques, travel. Office: Savannah Coll Art & Design HR-Clinard Hall Drayton St Savannah GA 31401-5644 Office Phone: 912-525-6661. Business E-Mail: mcajaher@scad.edu.

AJELLO, EDITH H., state legislator; b. Apr. 26, 1944; d. Kenneth Aaron and Rozella Christine (Ewoldt) Hanover; children: Linell, Aaron. BA, Bucknell U., 1966. Store mgr. V. George Rustigian Rugs, Inc., 1981-93, 94—; interim exec. dir. Vols. in Providence Schs., 1993; mem. R.I. Ho. of Reps., 1993—. Democrat. Home and Office: 29 Benefit St Providence RI 02904-2743 Business E-Mail: rep-ajello@rilin.state.ri.us.

AJZENBERG-SELOVE, FAY, physicist, researcher; b. Berlin, Feb. 13, 1926; came to U.S., 1940, naturalized, 1946; d. Mojzesz A. and Olga (Naiditch) A.; m. Walter Selove, Dec. 18, 1955. BS in Engring., U. Mich., 1946; MS, U. Wis., 1949, PhD, 1952; DSc (hon.), Smith Coll., 1995, Mich. State U., 1997, Haverford Coll., 1999—. Rsch. fellow Calif. Inst. Tech., 1952, 54; lectr. Smith Coll., 1952-53; cons., fellow MIT, Cambridge, 1952-53; from asst. prof. to rsch. assoc. prof. Boston U., 1953-57; mem. faculty Haverford Coll., 1957-70, prof. physics, 1962-70, acting chmn. dept. physics, 1967-69; rsch. prof. U. Pa., Phila., 1970-73, prof. physics, 1973—2005, prof. emeritus, 2005—, assoc. chmn., 1989-93. Vis. asst prof. Columbia, summer 1955, Nat. U. Mexico, summer 1955; lectr. U. Pa., 1957; cons. in field, 1962-63; vis. assoc. Calif. Inst. Tech., 1973-74; Exec. sec. com. physics faculties in colls. Am. Inst. Physics, 1962-65, mem. adv. com. manpower, 1963-68, adv. com. vis. scientists program, 1963-67; commr. Commn. on Coll. Physics, 1968-71; exec. sec. ad hoc panel on nuclear data compilations NAS-NRC, 1971-75; mem. Commn. on Nuclear Physics, Internat. Union Pure and Applied Physics, 1972-78, chairperson. 1978-81; mem. U.S. del. low energy nuclear physics to USSR, AEC, 1966; mem. Distinguished Faculty Awards Commn. Commonwealth of Pa., 1976; mem. nuclear sci. adv. com. Dept Energy-NSF, 1977-80; mem. numerical data adv. bd., assembly math. and phys. scis. NRC, 1977-79; lectr. U. Minn., 1994 Author: A Matter of Choice, Memoirs of a Female Physicist, 1994; editor: Nuclear Spectroscopy, vol. A and B, 1960; bd. editors Phys. Rev. C., 1981-83. Mem. Bower awards com. Franklin Nat. Meml., 1993. Recipient Christian R. and Mary F. Lindback award for disting. teaching, 1991, Nicholson medal for humanitarian svc. Am. Phys. Soc., 1999, 1st Disting. Alumni fellow in Physics, U. Wis., 2001; Smith-Mundt fellow, 1955; Guggenheim fellow, 1965-66. Fellow AAAS (mem. governing coun. 1974-80, mem. com. on coun. affairs 1977, 78), Am. Phys. Soc. (chairperson divsn. nuclear physics 1973-74); mem. AAUP, NRC (mem. phys. scis. panel, associateship program 1988-91), Am. Inst. Physics (mem. com. on pub. edn. and info. 1980-83), Phi Beta Kappa, Sigma Xi (nat. lectr. 1973-74). Home: 118 Cherry Ln Wynnewood PA 19096-1209 Office: U Pa Philadelphia PA 19104-6396 Business E-Mail: fay@pobox.upenn.edu.

AKABAS, SHEILA HELENE, social work educator; b. NYC, Apr. 24, 1931; d. Louis Arnold and Lillian (Lefrak) Epstein; m. Aaron Louis Akabas, Sept. 27, 1953; children: Myles, Seth, Miriam. BS, Cornell U., 1951; PhD, NYU, 1970. Assoc. dir. Just One Break, 1953—55; rsch. dir. mental health rehab. program Amalgamated Clothing & Textile Workers Union, 1963—69; rsch. dir. Ctr. for Social Policy and Practice in the Workplace Columbia U., N.Y.C., 1969—75, dir., 1975—, prof. Sch. Social Work, 1975—. Adv. bd. Work In Am. Inst., 1988—, N.Y. State Sch. Indsl. Labor Rels., Cornell U., 1989—, chair, 1992—93, 1993—94; dir. Mcpl. Employees Legal Svcs., 1973—83. Co-author: Mental Health Care in the World of Work, 1973, Disability Management, 1992; co-editor: Work, Workers & Work Organizations, 1982, Work and Well-Being, 1993; guest editor: Practice Digest issue, 1982; contbr. articles to jours.; editl. advisor: Employee Assistance, 1988—98, mem. editl. bd.: Jour. Disability Policy Studies, 1988—. Mem. Pres.'s Com. Employment of Persons with Disabilities, 1975—2001, chair med. and ins. com., 1988—94, exec. com., 1994—2001; mem. NIMH Manpower Demonstration Rev. Com., 1980—85, exec. com., 1994—98; mem. adv. workplace policy panel Nat. Inst. Drug Abuse, 1990—94; mem. Cornell U. Coun., 1971—86, 1988—92, 1994—; mem. adv. bd. Menninger Found. Rehab. Inst., 1984—88; mem. tech. adv. com. Dole Found., 1984—96, chair, 1992—96; mem. adv. bd. Washington Bus. Group on Health Inst. Rehab. and Disability Mgmt., 1985—98; fund rep. Cornell U. Class Assn.; bd. dirs. Cornell Hillel, 1997—; mem. N.Y. Statewide Ednl. Adv. Bd., 2000—; mem. adv. bd. N.Y. Work Exch., 2000—; active Temple B'nai Jeshurun, N.Y.C.; bd. dirs. Internat. Com. on Occupl. Mental Health, 1982—86, 1994—96, Westchester Symphony Orch., 1965—80. Recipient Rsch. in Rehab. award, 1982, Rehab. Project of Yr. award, NRA, 1992; fellow Switzer fellow, 1980, World Rehab. Fund, 1983, 1988; grantee, HHS, NIMH, Nat. Inst. Disability and Rehab. Rsch., U.S. Dept. Edn., 1985—, Nat. Inst. on Drug Abuse, others. Mem.: Coun. Social Work Edn., Hadassah (N.Y.C.). Office: Columbia University School Of Social Wor 1255 Amsterdam Ave New York NY 10027-5927 Business E-Mail: sa12@columbia.edu.

AKAIKE, HIROKO, music educator, conductor; arrived in U.S., 1997; d. Hiroshi and Etsuko Akaike. BMus in Edn., Kunitachi Coll. Music, Tokyo, 1995; MS in Music Performance, Shenandoah U., 1999, MS in Music, 2003. Lic. tchg. Va. Tutor, accompanist Shenandoah U., Winchester, Va., 1998—2003; substitute tchr. Winchester Pub. Sch., 2002—03; band, choir dir. Highland County Pub. Sch., Monterey, Va., 2003—. Pvt. piano, vocal instr., 1997—; pianist Wesleyan Fellowship Ch., Winchester, 1998—2003; asst. music dir., conductor Mary Washington Coll., Fredericksburg, Va., 1999; music dir. Highland County Arts Coun., Monterey, 2004—. Contbr. articles to newspaper. Musician West Minster Canterbury Nursing Home, Winchester, 1999—2003. Named Employee of Month, Highland County Pub. Schs., 2003; fellow, Shenandoah U., 1999—2003; scholar, Ikueikai, 1991—95, Kunitachi Coll. Music, 1991—95. Mem.: Conductors Guild, Va. Edn. Assn., Nat. Assn. Music Educators. Avocations: dance, reading. Office: Highland County High Sch PO Box 430 Monterey VA 24465 Office Phone: 540-468-2181. Personal E-mail: hakaike@yahoo.com.

AKBAR, SHAAKIRA NADIYA, elementary school educator; b. Chgo., Aug. 2, 1977; d. Naim and Renee Akbar; children: Jhari Anthony Hasaan, Jamillah Rena Anthony Niarra. BA, Spelman Coll., Atlanta, Ga., 1999; MEd, U. Fla., Gainesville, 2001; postgrad., Fla. Atlantic U., Boca Raton, 2002—05. Cert. prin. Fla., 2005. Tchr. 4th grade Westward Elem. Sch., West Palm Beach, Fla., 2001—04, tchr. 5th grade, chair dept., 2004—05; tchr. 5th grade lang. arts, high achiever magnet students Browns Mill Elem. Sch., Lithonia, Ga., 2005—. Mem.: Delta Sigma Theta. Avocations: travel, reading, learning.

AKHAVANHAIDARY, SEPIDEH, psychologist, educator; arrived in U.S., 1979; d. Nader and Fakhriran Akhavanhaidary; m. Mark John Souris, June 6, 2004; 1 child, Alexandra Asal. BA, U. Calif., L.A., Calif., 1989; MA, Pepperdine U., 1991, PhD in Psychology, 1995. Lic. psychologist Calif., 1997. Pvt. practice, L.A., 1997—; asst. prof. U. Calif., L.A., 1999—. From psychologist to dir. psychology tng. L.A. (Calif.) County Dept. Mental Health, 1997—2001, dir. psychology tng., 2003—04; chief psychol. svcs. L.A. (Calif.) County Chief Adminstrv. Office, 2004—. Mem.: APA, Psi Chi. Avocations: reading, writing, exercise, music. Office: Los Angeles County Chief Adminstrv Office 3333 Wilshire Blvd Ste 1000 Los Angeles CA 90010

AKI, ANGELA, singer; b. Tokushima, Shikoku, Japan, Sept. 15, 1977; BA, George Washington U. Signed to Sony Music Japan, 2005—, Tofu Records, Calif., 2006—. Singer: (albums) These Words, 2000, ONE, 2005, Home, 2006, Final Fantasy XII soundtrack, 2006, (songs) Kiss Me Good-Bye, 2006. Office: Tofu Records PO Box 5158 Santa Monica CA 90409 E-mail: info@tofurecords.com.*

AKIBA, LORRAINE HIROKO, lawyer; b. Honolulu, Dec. 28, 1956; d. Lawrence H. and Florence K. (Iwasa) Katsuyama. BS with honors, U. Calif., Berkeley, 1977; JD, U. Calif., San Francisco, 1981. Bar: Hawaii 1981, U.S. Dist. Ct. Hawaii 1981, U.S. Ct. Appeals (9th cir.) 1981, U.S. Supreme Ct. 1986. Dir. State of Hawaii Dept. Labor and Indsl. Rels., 1995—2000; ptnr. Cades, Schutte, Fleming & Wright, Honolulu, 1981—94, McCorriston Miller Mukai and MacKinnon LLP, Honolulu, 2000—. Lawyer rep. 9th Cir. Jud. Conf., 1991-94; mem., past treas. Hawaii Inst. for CLE, Honolulu, 1987—. Chairperson attys. divsn. Aloha United Way, Honolulu, 1991, 04, statewide chairperson, 1995; mem. State of Hawaii Environ. Coun., Honolulu, 1990-94, chair, 1992; mem. city and county Honolulu Transp. Commn., 2005-. Named one of Outstanding Young Women Am., 1985 Mem. ABA, Hawaii Bar Assn., Hawaii Women Lawyers Assn., Hawaii Women Lawyers Found. (pres. 1988-92), Honolulu Club, Phi Beta Kappa. Office: McCorriston Miller Mukai MacKinnon LLP PO Box 2800 Honolulu HI 96803-2800 Office Phone: 808-529-7300. Business E-Mail: akiba@m4law.com.

AKIL, HUDA, neuroscientist, educator, researcher; b. Damascus, Syria, May 19, 1945; came to U.S., 1968; d. Fakher and Widad (Al-Imam) A.; m. Stanley Jack Watson Jr., Dec. 21, 1972; children: Brendon Omar, Kathleen Tamara. BA, Am. U., Beirut, Lebanon, 1966, MA, 1968; PhD, UCLA, 1972. Postdoctoral fellow Stanford U., Palo Alto, Calif., 1974-78; from asst. prof. to prof. psychiatry and neuroscience U. Mich., Ann Arbor, 1979—, co-dir., sr. rsch. scientist Mental Health Rsch. Inst. Mem. adv. bd. Neurex Corp., Menlo Park, Calif., 1986—, Neurobiol. Techs., Inc., 1994-97; sec. Internat. Narcotics Rsch. Conf., 1990-94. Editor: (jour.) Pain and Headache: Neurochemistry of Pain, 1990; contbr. articles over 300 articles to profl. jours., 1971—2001. Recipient Pacesetter award Nat. Inst. Drug Abuse, 1993, Pasarow award Pasarow Found., 1994, Bristol-Myers Squibb award, 1998, Edward Sachar award Columbia U., 1998; Rockefeller scholar, Beirut, 1963-66; Alfred P. Sloan fellow, Stanford, Calif., 1974-78; grantee Nat. Inst. Drug Abuse, Washington, 1978—, NIMH, Washington, 1980—, Markey Found., U. Mich., 1988-97. Fellow Am. Acad. Arts & Scis., Am. Coll. Neuropsychopharmacology (pres. 1997-98), U. Mich. Soc. Fellows; mem. Inst. Medicine/NAS, Soc.for Neuroscience (pres. 2002-03). Achievements include first to produce physiological evidence for existence of naturally occurring opiate-like substances (endorphins) in brain; described phenomenon of stress-induced analgesia; described functions and regulation of endorphins in brain and pituitary gland; contributed to understanding of biological mechanisms of morphine tolerance and physical dependence; (with colleagues) cloned two main types of opiate receptors, described critical brain circuits relevant to stress and depression. Office: Mental Health Rsch Inst 205 Zina Pitcher Ann Arbor MI 48109-2214

AKIN, ANN FOSTER, special education educator; b. Danbury, Conn., Apr. 11, 1953; d. Thomas Joseph and Sarah Foster; m. Kent Brown Akin, Aug. 22, 1981; children: Hannah Kathleen, Nicholas Kent. BA in Psychology, Elem. Edn. and Edn. for Blind, Dominican Coll., 1976; EdM Edn. of Blind and

Visually Impaired, Boston Coll., 1981. Cert. tchr. for blind and partially seeing, elem. edn. N.Y., 1977. Itinerant tchr. for blind and visually impaired Bd. Coop. Ednl. Svcs., Ashville, NY, 1977—. Coord. religious edn. St. Mary's Ch., Mayville, NY. Mem.: AAUW, Coun. for Exceptional Children, Assn. for the Edn. and Rehab. Blind and Visually Impaired, Mayville-Chautauqua Lions Club (pres. 2003—), Eta Nu (pres. 1989—90).

AKIN, DONNA RAE, retired elementary school educator; b. Hobart, Ind., Aug. 20, 1945; d. Raymond Paul and Doris Mildred Vasil; m. William Gerald Akin, Mar. 28, 1970; 1 child, Renee K. Akin Youssef. BS in Edn., Ind. State U., 1967; MS in Edn., Ind. U., 1970. Elem. educator Merrillville (Ind.) Cmty. Sch., 1967—2001; ret. Adv. bd. Merrillville Prime-Time, 1992—94; mem. state bd. Prime-Time Com., Ind., 1994. Editor: (sch. newspaper) Fieler Fun-Times, 1989—2000 (1st pl., 1992). Sec. Ind. Ballet Theatre, N.W., 2001—02; moderator debates League of Women Voters, Crown Point, Ind., 1998—2000, sec., 2000—01. Mem.: AAUW (pres. 1993—95, state nominating com. 1999—2000, 2000—02, named gift honoree 1997), Trinity Oaks Women's Assn., Lake Lodge Eastern Star. Avocations: swimming, exercising. Home: 2131 Blue Beech Ct Trinity FL 34655

AKIN, LILLIE VIOLET, chemistry educator, writer, television personality, consultant; d. Frederick Allen and Myrtle Mae (Yahn) Tucker; m. Raymond Frederick Akin, May 27, 1957; children: Mark A., Angeleque Akin-Little, Robert A. BSc, U. Ark., 1957, Tex. Woman's U., 1958; MSc, U. Houston, 1963, U. Miss., 1976; postgrad., Princeton U., U. Calif., Berkeley, 1985—93. Ins. agent; dir. pub. rels.; v.p. Akin Manufactured Homes; chemistry educator Tupelo HS, Tupelo Christian Prep., Shannon Sr. HS, Houston Ind. Sch., Galveston Ind. Sch.; sci. cons. Delta Ed, NH. Chemistry educator U. So. Miss.; pres. Sci. Cons. Inc., Coronado, Calif.; co-dir. N.S.F. Chemistry Elem. Tchrs.; presenter in field. Author: (books) Chemistry on the Chep, Teaching High School Chemistry, (program) Chemistry that Teach. Vice chair Rep. Party, Lee County, Miss., nat. conv. del. Washington. Named a Nat. HS Chemistry Day Chair, Am. Chemistry Soc.; recipient Nat. Polymer Chemistry award; grant, NSF. Mem.: NSTA (nat. dir., regional dir.), Bldg. Presence Sci. (dir.), Am. Assn. U. Women (v.p.). Republican. Baptist. Avocations: music, drama, speech, horseback riding. Office: Delta Ed Ste 114 941 Orange Ave Coronado CA 92118 Office Phone: 619-961-7177.

AKIYAMA, KAREN N., elementary school educator; d. Yukito and Myrtle Nanbara; m. Alvin W. Akiyama, July 4, 1970. BEd, U. Hawaii Manoa, Honolulu, 1961, PhD, 1963, MEd, 1982. Flight attendant Pan Am., Honolulu, 1969—70; tchr. Hawaii State Dept. Edn., 1967—69, Lanai City, 1972—76, Eva Beach, 1976—. Recipient scholarship, Fulbright Found., 1967, 1977. Mem.: Phi Delta Kappa, Pi Lambda Theta. Avocations: flower arranging, origami, calligraphy.

AKOURIS, DIANNE FRANCES, school system administrator; b. Nenno, Wis., Aug. 19, 1940; d. Sylvester X. and Marcella H. Hefter; m. John G. Akouris, June 19, 1976. BS in Edn., Alverno Coll., Milw., 1969; MA in Reading, Northeastern Ill. U., Chgo., 1988. Cert. advanced study of supr. Nat. Louis U., 1992, elem. and secondary tchg. Ill. Tchr. Parochial Archdioceses of Chgo., 1959—64, 1966—85, St. Mary's Sch., Holly Springs, Miss., 1964—66, Cook County, Chgo., 1985; tchrs. aide Westnorthfield Elem. Sch. #31, Glenview, Ill., 1985—86; comm. tchr. Waukegan Pub. Sch. #60, Waukegan, Ill., 1986—87; tchr. Fremont Sch. Dist., Fremont, Ill., 1987—88, Waukegan Pub. Sch., Waukegan, Ill., 1988—2000, summer bridges coord., 2000; lead tchr., curriculum specialist Waukegan Pub. Schs., 2006—; facilitator Waukegan Tchrs. Acad., Waukegan, Ill., 2000—06, lead tchr., 2006—, curriculum specialist, 2006—. Coop. tchr. Barat Coll., Lake Forest, Ill., 1995, Lake Forest, 97, Nat. Louis U., Evanston, Ill., 1999. Presenter Ill. State Kindergarten Conf., Rosemont, Ill., 1992; moderator League of Women Voters, Libertyville, Ill., 1993, WKRS Radio Station, Waukegan, Ill., 1993; presenter Ill. Reading Coun., Columbus, Ohio, 2001. Nominee Golden Apple award, Golden Apple Found., 2000; recipient First Grant award, First Bank of Am., 1995, Excellence in Tchg., Classic Cheverlot of Waukegan, 2000. Mem.: Lake County Curriculum Resource Coun., Internat. Reading Assn., Assn. for Supervision and Curriculum Devel., Ill. Principals Assn. Avocations: gardening, reading, choir. Home: 2004 Sunset Ct Zion IL 60099 Office: Curriculum Dept Lincoln Ctr 1201 N Sheridan Rd Waukegan IL 60085 Office Fax: 847-360-5654. Business E-Mail: dakouris@waukeganschools.org.

ALAIGH, POONAM, health facility administrator; b. Nov. 19, 1964; MB BS, Lady Hardinge Med. Coll., New Delhi, 1987; MS in Health Care Policy and Adminstrn., SUNY, Stony Brook, 1997. Resident in internal medicine SUNY, Stony Brook, 1993, fellow in vascular medicine, 1994; assoc. med. dir. HMO of NYL Care, 1994-97; med. dir. Vytra Health Plans, Huntington Station, N.Y., 1998-2000; sr. med. dir. Glaxo Smithkline Pharms., Phila., 2000—. Fellow ACP. Office: 3 Franklin Plz Philadelphia PA 19102-1100

ALAIMO, TERRY M., financial consultant; b. Orange, N.J., Dec. 3, 1955; d. Louis Joseph and Julia Clara (Carlin) Mazziotto; m. Salvatore Alaimo, June 5, 1972 (div. Mar. 1975); 1 child, Roxanne. Student, William Patterson Coll., 1974-78. Organizer 1199 Nat. Union Health and Human Svc., N.Y.C., 1984-88; organizing coord. Pub. Employers Fedn., N.Y.C., 1988-89; organizer 1199 Nat. Union, N.Y.C., 1989-92, v.p., 1992-96; cons. S.I. (N.Y.) Amalgamated Transit Union, 1996-97, Svc. Employers Internat. Union, Washington, 1997, 1199 N.W., Seattle, 1997-99; fin. advisor Prudential Securities, 1999-2000, Montauk Securities, Paramus, N.J., 2000—. Coord. Dinkins for Mayor, S.I., 1990, 94, Albanese for Congress, S.I., 1992. Mem. Nat. Abortion Rights Action League. Democrat. Avocations: painting, writing, travel.

ALANAZI, JESSICA LANE, science educator; b. Morrilton, Ark., Dec. 23, 1975; d. David Albert and Dorothy Ann Lane; children: Byron, Noah. B, U. Ctrl. Ark., Conway, 2000; M, Capella U., Mpls., 2002. Tchr. English as 2d lang. U. Ark., Little Rock, 2001—02; tchr. 7th grade sci. Little Rock Sch. Dist., 2003—04; tchr. 5th grade sci. Pulaski Acad., 2004—06. Mem.: Nat. Sci. Tchrs. Assn.

ALANDER, VIRGINIA NICKERSON, retired student assistance coordinator; b. Springfield, Ill., Aug. 16, 1931; d. Carl Lee Nickerson and Zola Audrey Mitchell; m. Robert Huntley Alander, June 16, 1956 (dec. Nov. 1966); children: Dirk, Erik, Link. BS, U. Wis., 1953; MS, Ill. State U., 1973. Tchr. Elmhurst (Ill.) Jr. High, 1953-55, Woodruff High Sch., Peoria, Ill., 1955-56; vol. tchr. Kikongo Mission, Leopoldville, Belgian Congo, 1956-58; tchr., student asst. coord. Joliet West High Sch., Joliet, Ill., 1965-95, dir. Tiger Paws dance team, 1969-93; ret., 1995. Contbr. articles on organizing teams and motivation. Vice-chairperson Joliet Twp. High Sch. Found., 1995-99. Named to Ill. Drill Team Assn. Hall of Fame, Let's Cheer Mag. Hall of Fame, U.S. Cheerleading Assn. Hall of Fame. Mem. Ill. Drill Team Assn. (pres.). Lutheran. Avocations: travel, antiques, theater. Home: 23545 W Fern St Plainfield IL 60544-2323 E-mail: vnalander@comcast.net.

ALANIS, LORENA, elementary school educator; d. Victor Manuel and Cande Garcia; m. Emilio Alanis, Sept. 16, 2003; 1 child, Karen Belle. B in Sci. Bus. Mgmt., U. Tex., 2001, M in Edn. Counseling, Guidance, 2006. Office asst. LSAMP Office UTPA, Edinburg, Tex., 1999—2001; vault teller Wells Fago Bank, Pharr, Tex., 2002—03; kindergarten tchr. La Joya Ind. Sch. Dist., Mission, Tex., 2003—. Academic All-Am. scholar, U.S. Achieve. Acad., 2001. D-Liberal. Roman Cath. Avocations: travel, drawing, gardening, scrapbooks.

ALANIZ, THEODORA VILLARREAL, elementary school educator; b. Mercedes, Tex., Feb. 16, 1951; d. Alejandro and Maria (Villarreal) A. BS in Elem. Edn., Pan Am. U., 1979; MEd, Tex. A&I U., 1984; cert. in counseling, U. Tex., 1992. Cert. vocat. counselor, Level I and II lic. chem. dependency counselor, South Tex. C.C. Asst. tchr. Mercedes Ind. Sch. Dist., 1973-78; tchr. Pharr (Tex.)-San-Juan-Alamo Ind. Sch. Dist., 1979-91, Edcouch-Elsa (Tex.) Ind. Sch. Dist., 1991-93; counselor Donna Ind. Sch. Dist., 1993—. Census rep. Diocese of Brownsville, 1974-75; choir mem. Sacred Heart Ch., Mercedes, Tex., 1974-78, 3rd grade tchr., 1975-78; rep. Cancer Soc., Mercedes, 1980-81, Assn. Tex. and Profl. Educators to Pharr and Elsa Ind. Sch. Dists. Scholar Title VII Bilingual/Bicultural, 1978-79. Roman Catholic. Avocations: photography, pencil drawing, sight seeing. Address: RR 4 Box 161-c Mercedes TX 78570-9313

ALARIE-ANDERSON, PEGGY SUE, physician assistant; b. Flint, Mich., Feb. 8, 1957; d. Albert Joseph Jr. and Elizabeth Anna (Eksten) A.; m. John L. McAttee III, Oct. 3, 1980 (div. Aug. 1987); m. Donn P. Anderson, Aug. 23, 1997. AAS, Mott CC, 1983; BS, Mich. State U., 1988; MS, U. Detroit Mercy, Mich., 1994. Physician asst. supr. emergency rm. Hurley Med. Ctr., Flint, Mich., 1996—. Fellow Am. Acad. Physician Assts., Mich. Acad. Physician Assts.; mem. Soc. Emergency Physician Assts., Am. Acad. Surg. Physician Assts., Sigma Theta Tau. Avocations: dance (ballet, ballroom, tap, jazz). Home: 5072 Scott Rd Mount Morris MI 48458-9724 Office: Hurley Med Ctr 1 Hurley Plz Flint MI 48503-5902

ALAUPOVIC, ALEXANDRA VRBANIC, artist, educator; b. Slatina, Yugoslavia, Dec. 21, 1921; d. Joseph and Elizabeta (Papp) Vrbanic; m. Peter Alaupovic, Mar. 22, 1947; 1 child, Betsy. Student Bus. Sch., Zagreb, Yugoslavia, 1940-41, Acad. Visual Arts, Zagreb, Yugoslavia, 1944-48; postgrad. Acad. Visual Arts, Prague, Czechoslovakia, 1949, Art Sch., U. Ill., 1959-60; MFA, U. Okla., 1966; came to U.S., 1958. Sec., Arko Liquer & Yeast Factory and Distillery, Zagreb, 1941-44; instr. U. Okla., Norman, 1964-66; instr. three dimensional design sculpture Oklahoma City U., 1969-77, Okla. Sci. Found., Oklahoma City, 1969-75; one-woman shows at Okla. Art Ctr., Oklahoma City, U. Okla. Mus. Art, Norman, La Mandragore Internat. Galerie d'Art, Paris, 1984; exhibited art in group shows retrospective 50 yrs. Struggle, Growth and Whimsy, 1987-88, Okla. Art Ctr., Springfield (Mo.) Art Mus., Okla. U. Mus., Norman, 7th Ann. Temple Emanuel Brotherhood Arts Festival, Dallas, Salon des Nation, Paris, 1983; since statehood twevle Okla. artists Art. Mus., Okla. 1996; represented in permanent collections Okla. U. Art Mus., Okla. State Art Collection, Okla. Art Ctr., Mercy Health Ctr. Recipient Jacobson award U. Okla., 1964; hon. mention in sculpture Philbrook Art Ctr., Tulsa, 1967; 1st sculpture award Philbrook Art Ctr., Tulsa, 1970; biography included in Virginia Watson Jones' Contemporary American Women Sculptors, 1986, Jules and Nancy Heller's North American Women Artists of 20th Century, 1995; State of Okla. Art commemdation, 1996. Mem. Internat. Sculpture Center, Lausanne, Suisse, Prestige de la Peinture et de la Sculpture d'Aujourd'hui dans le Monde, 1992, Paris, 1995. Home and Office: 11908 N Bryant Ave Oklahoma City OK 73131-4823

ALBA, BENNY, artist; b. Columbus, Ohio, 1949; Student, Kent State U., Ohio, 1968—70; BA in Psychology, U. Mich., Ann Arbor, 1982. Artist in residence Mont. Artists Refuge, Basin, 2003. Artist-in-residence St. Charles Boy's Sch., Columbus, 1982-85, Mont. Artist Refuge, Basin, 2002; lectr. Columbus Cultural Arts Ctr., 1983-84, 93; presenter in field; panelist Calif. Inst. for Intergral Studies, San Francisco, 1995, panelist, Fire 2004, No. Calif. Enameling Guild, juror and award judge, Art Assn., Palo Alto, 2001, San Francisco Women Artists; award judge, Adobe Gallery, Castro Valley, Calif., 2003; juror Oakland (Calif.) Art Assn., Alameda Art Ctr., Calif.; panelist grants rev. Oakland City Arts Commn., 2005; lectr. Merced Coll., Calif., 1997 One-woman shows include Columbus Cultural Arts Ctr., 1993, Apprentice Alliance, San Francisco, 1994, Las Vegas Mus., Nev., 1994, Artist TV Access, San Francisco, 1993, Western Wyo. Coll., Rock Springs, 1994, A Gallery in the Clock Tower, San Francisco, 1994, Ctr. for Psychol. Studies, Albany, Calif., 1994, Idyllwild Sch. Music and Art, Calif., 1995, Merced Coll. Art Gallery, 1997, North Country Mus. of Art, Park Rapids, Minn., 1997, Martinez City Hall, Calif., 1996, Martinez Arts and Culture Com., 1998, Office of Sup. Contra County Ct., Martinez, 1997, State Bd., Sacramento, Calif., 1997, Saginaw Art Mus., Mich., 1998, Met. Transp. Co., Oakland, Calif., 1998, Commonwealth Club, San Francisco, 1998, San Francisco State U. Club, 1998, Zen Ctr., San Francisco, 1998, Hastings Coll. Law, 1999, U. Oreg., Eugene, 1999, Oakland Higher Edn. Ctr., 1999, The Arts Ctr., Jamestown, N.D., 2000, North Valley Arts Coun., Grand Forks, N.D., 2000, Lake Region Heritage Ctr., Devils Lake, N.D., 2000, Bismarck Art and Galleries Assn., N.D., Valley Art Ctr., Clarkston, Wash., 2000, Pacific Grove Art Ctr., Calif., 2000, Rogue C.C., Grants Pass, Oreg., 2000, Sedona Art Ctr., Ariz., 2000, ARC Gallery, Chgo., 2000, Napa City County Libr., 2000, East Bay Mcpl. Utilities Dist., 2002, Looking at the Sky, PARC, Xerox Corp., Palo Alto, Calif., 2004, U. Ala., Montgomery, 2003, Birnbaum's Broad Frame and Gallery, Missoula, Mont, 2003, Oakland City Arts Coun., Calif., 2005, exhibited in group shows at Mountain Art, Bernardville, NJ, 2002, Fredericksburg for Creative Arts, Va., 2002, Wenatchee Valley Coll., 2002, Alice Arts Ctr., Oakland, Calif., 2002, Central Mo. State U., 2002, San Pablo City Arts Gallery, Calif., 2003, Tex. Artists Mus., Port Arthur, Tex., 2002, San Pablo City Gallery, Calif., 2003, U. Calif., Berkeley, Calif., 2003, Kellog G. Calif. State Polytec, Pomona, Calif., 2003, State Polytech. U., 2003, 2004, U. Mont., Butte, 2003, Nicolet Coll. Art Gallery, Rhinelander, Wis., 2003, Coos Art Mus., Coos Bay, Wash., 2003, Wenatchee Valley Coll., Wenatchee, Wash., 2003, 2002, Phantom Galleries, San Jose, 2005, SOMAR, San Francisco, 2005, Alameda Art Ctr., 2005, Oakland Craft & Cultural Arts Gallery, 2005, Frank Bette Ctr. for the Arts, Alameda, 2005, Art in Embassies, Amb. Joseph Mussomeli, Phnom Pehn, Cambodia, 2006, Mon Dak Hist. and Art Soc., Sidney, Mont., 2006, Nicolet Coll. Art Gallery, Rhinelander, Wis., 2006, Sebastopol Ctr. for the Arts, Calif., 2006, Represented in permanent collections Nat. Mus. Women in Arts, Mint Mus., Charlotte, N.C., Ark. Arts Ctr., Little Rock, U. Mich. Mus. Art, Kalamazoo Inst. Arts, Greenpeace, Ulli Wachter, Germany, Las Vegas Art Mus., Ctr. for Psychol. Studies, Albany, Calif., Birmingham Mus. Art, Ala., Portland Art Mus., Oreg., Tyler Mus. Art, Tex., Canajoharie Libr., N.Y., others, Art in Embassies, Tashkent, Ubikistan. Bd. dirs. No. Calif. Women's Caucus for Art, 1991, sec. 1991-92, phone liaison, 1991-93, No. Calif. Enameling Guild, 2004; juror Oakland Art Assn., 2005, Alameda (Calif.) Art Ctr., 2005. Recipient Merit Award, S.F. Women Artist Gallery, CA., 1986, Lenore Miles Award, National Juried Show, NPVAG, Scottsbluff, NE., 1991, Dr. S. Mackoff Award, 28th Annual, Palm Springs Desert Mus., CA., 1997, Merit Award, Calif. Works Exhibition, CA State Fair, Sacramento, CA., 1999, Honorable Mention, Fredericksburg C for the C Arts, Fredericksburg, VA., 2001, Second Place, Gallery '76, Wenatchee Valley College, Wenatchee, Wash., 2003. Mem. Calif. Soc. Printmakers (v.p. 1999, pres. 2004, 05, 06), Calif. Enamaling Guild (bd. dirs. 2004). Studio: 4219 M L King Jr Way Oakland CA 94609-2321 Office Phone: 510-547-4512.

ALBA, JESSICA, actress; b. Pomona, Calif., Apr. 28, 1981; Actor: (films) Camp Nowhere, 1994, Venus Rising, 1995, P.U.N.K.S., 1999, Never Been Kissed, 1999, Idle Hands, 1999, Paranoid, 2000, The Sleeping Dictionary, 2003, Honey, 2003, Sin City, 2005 (Sexiest Performance, MTV Movie awards, 2006), Fantastic Four, 2005, Into the Blue, 2005; (TV films) Too Soon for Jeff, 1996; (TV series) Flipper, 1995—96, Dark Angel, 2000—02, (guest appearance) The Secret World of Alex Mack, 1994, Chicago Hope, 1996, Beverly Hills 90210, 1998, The Love Boat: The Next Wave, 1998, Entourage, 2004. Recipient Choice Hottie-Female, Teen Choice Awards, 2006, Choice Red Carpet Fashion Icon (Female), 2006.

ALBAGLI, LOUISE MARTHA, psychologist; b. Queens, N.Y., Jan. 15, 1954; d. Meyer Nathan and Leah (Bleier) Greenberg; m. Eli S. Albagli, July 31, 1977. BA in Psychology summa cum laude, CUNY, 1976; D of Clin. Psychology, Rutgers U., 1983. Cert. Reiki master. Clin. psychology intern Postgrad. Ctr. Mental Health, N.Y.C., 1980-81; staff psychologist Queens County Neuropsychiat. Inst., Jackson Heights, N.Y., 1981-83, Bklyn. Cmty. Counseling Ctr., 1981-84; sr. clin. psychologist Richard Hall Cmty. Mental Health Ctr., Bridgewater, NJ, 1984-86; pvt. practice Highland Park, NJ, 1985—2001; mem. adj. faculty Rutgers U., 1990-93; adj. faculty Montgomery Coll., Rockville, Md., 2006; ret., 2006. Jin Shin Jyutsu practitioner, 1995—; self-help tchr., 1996—; adj. faculty Montgomery Coll., Rockville, Md., 2006—. Mem. APA, Nat. Register Health Care Providers, Internat. Childbirth Edn. Assn., Phi Beta Kappa.

ALBAIN, KATHY S., oncologist; b. Monroe, Mich., June 4, 1952; d. James Jay and Elizabeth G. (Jakscy) A. BS in Chemistry summa cum laude, Wheaton Coll., 1974; MD, U. Mich., 1978. Diplomate Am. Bd. Internal Medicine, Am. Bd. Oncology. Instr. physical diagnosis U. Mich. Med. Sch., 1978; intern U. Ill. Med. Ctr., Chgo., 1978-79, resident in internal medicine, 1979-81, clin. instr. medicine, 1980-81; instr. in medicine U. Ill. Hosps. and Clinics, 1980-81; fellow dept. medicine sect. hematology/oncology U. Chgo. Med. Ctr./U. Chgo. Hosps. and Clinics, 1981-84; asst. prof. medicine Loyola U. Chgo. Strich Sch. Medicine, 1984-91, assoc. prof. medicine divsn. hematology/oncology, 1991—; attending physician Hines (Ill.) VA Hosp., 1984—, Loyola U. Chgo. Foster G. McGaw Hosp., 1984—. Co-investigator multidisciplinary lung cancer staging and rsch. group U. Chgo. and Michael Reese Hosp. Med. Ctrs., 1982-84; coord. ann. breast cancer screening program Sr. Ctr. LaGrange, Ill., 1985-91; mem. med. adv. bd. Y-Me Nat. Breast Cancer Orgn., 1987—; co-dir. Multidisciplinary Breast Care Ctr. Loyola U. Med. Ctr., 1991—, dir. Multidisciplinary Lung Cancer Evaluation Ctr., 1994—; mem. oncology med. adv. bd. Eli Lilly and Co., 1993—; co-investigator nat. surg. adjuvant breast and bowel project U. Chgo., 1982-84; mem. breast cancer com., breast cancer working group, lung cancer com., lung cancer working group S.W. Oncology Group, 1986—, mem. gynecol. cancer com. and working group, 1989—, sarcoma and brain coms., 1990—, chair com. on women's health, 1992—; mem. intergroup lung cancer working cadre Nat. Cancer Inst., 1993—, mem. breast cancer intergroup com. on correlative scis. Nat. Cancer Inst., 1995, mem. breast cancer intergroup chairs com., 1994—; clin. trials co-chair Sec. of HHS Nat. Breast Cancer Action Plan, 1993-94; mem. adv. panel State of Ill. Breast and Cervical Cancer Rsch. Fund, 1994—; charter mem. adv. com. on rsch. in women's health NIH, 1995—; mem. Early Breast Cancer Trialists' Collaborative Group, 1995—; mem. clin. trials working group Sec. of Health Nat. Breast Cancer Action Plan, 1995—; rschr., lectr., presenter in field. Reviewer jours. Cytometry, Breast Cancer Rsch. and Treatment, Cancer Rsch., Jour. Clin. Oncology, Cancer, Chest; contbr. articles to profl. publs. Mem. sr. choir Grace Luth. Ch., River Forest, Ill. Nat. Cancer Inst. fellowship tng. grantee, 1981-84, grantee Bristol-Myers, 1988-93, Squibb Mark Co., 1989, UpJohn Co., 1990, 92, Office Rsch. on Women's Health/Nat. Cancer Inst., 1992, 93-95, Nat. Cancer Inst., 1993—. Mem. ACP, Am. Assn. Cancer Rsch., Am. Fedn. Clin. Rsch., Am. Soc. Clin. Oncology, Internat. Assn. for Study of Lung Cancer, Christian Med. and Dental Soc. Home: 220 S Maple Ave Oak Park IL 60302-3031 Office: Loyola U Med Ctr Divsn Hematology/Oncology 2160 S 1st Ave Maywood IL 60153-3304

ALBANO, CHRISTINE GRACE, lawyer; BA, So. Meth. U., Dallas, 1993; JD, U. Mo., Kansas City, 1996. Bar: Tex. 1997. Assoc. Loughmiller & DePlaza, Dallas, 1997—98; staff atty. Legal Svcs. of North Tex., McKinney, 1998—2003; pvt. practice law McKinney, 2003—. Contbr. articles to profl. jours. Mem. Collin County Dems., McKinney, 2004—05, Planned Parenthood of North Tex., Plano, 2004—05. Named a Rising Star, Tex. Super Lawyers mag., 2006. Fellow: Am. Bar Found.; mem.: ABA (family law sect., gen. practice, solo and small firm sect.), State Bar of Tex. (family law and women and the law sects. 1997—), Grayson County Bar Assn., Frisco Bar Assn., Plano Bar Assn., Tex. Young Lawyers Assn. (dir. 2004—06, sec. 2006—, Presdl. award of merit for exemplary svc. to the bar and pub. 2003—05), Collin County Bench Bar Found. (bd. dirs. 2001—02, treas. 2002—04, bd. trustees 2002—06), Collin County Bar Assn. (mem. family law sect. 1999—, liaison to Collin County Young Lawyers Assn. 2003—05, Svc. Star award 1998—2001, Golden Chalice award 2004—05), Collin County Young Lawyers Assn. (bd. dirs. 2000—01, sec. 2001—02, treas. 2002—03, pres.-elect 2005—06, pres. 2006—, Outstanding Young Lawyer of Collin County 2001—02), Attys. Serving the Cmty., Phi Delta Phi, Chi Omega. Office: Law Office of Christine G Albano 201-1/2 E Virginia Ste 5 Mc Kinney TX 75069 Office Phone: 972-562-5884. E-mail: calbano@albanolaw.com.

ALBARADO, REBECCA HILL, elementary school educator; b. Langdale, Ala., Oct. 17, 1952; d. Benjamin Harvey and Annie Ruth (Taylor) Hill; m. Edward Joseph Albarado, July 1, 1990 (dec.); m. Madison Grover Blackwell (div.); 1 child, Adam. BS in Elem. Edn., U. West Ga., 1985, MEd, 1987. Payroll clk. Milliken, LaGrange, 1979—83; tchr. Troup County, LaGrange, Ga., 1985—91; historian Ctr. for Environ. Health, Charleston, SC, 1991—94; tchr. Troup County, West Pt., Ga., 1994—. Author: (book) A Story Worth Telling, 2005. Mem.: Profl. Assn. of Ga. Educators, Chattahoochee Hist. Soc. Avocations: reading, gardening, painting. Home: 86 Highland Dr West Point GA 31833 Business E-Mail: rhalba@knology.net.

ALBAUM, JEAN STIRLING, psychologist, educator; b. Beijing, Jan. 11, 1932; came to U.S., 1936; d. Richard Henry and Emma Bowyer (Lueders) Ritter; m. B. Taylor Stirling, Aug. 15, 1953 (div. 1965); 1 child, Christopher Taylor Stirling; m. Joseph H. Albaum; stepchildren: Thomas Gary, Lauren Jean. BA, Beloit (Wis.) Coll., 1953; MS, Danbury (Conn.) State U., 1964, U. La Verne, Calif., 1983; PhD, Claremont (Calif.) Grad. Sch., 1985. Lic. ednl. psychologist, Calif. Spl. edn. tchr. Charter Oak (Calif.) Sch. Dist., 1966-80; psychologist, coord. elem. counseling Claremont Sch. Dist., 1980—2002; pvt. practice in ednl. psychology Encino, Calif., 1987—2003. Clin. supr. marriage, family and child counselor interns Claremont Grad. Sch., 1987—2002; sr. adj. prof. U. La Verne, 1988—; oral commr. Bd. Behavioral Sci. Examiners, Sacramento, 1989—2001. Contbr. articles to profl. jours. Hostess L.A. World Affairs Coun., 1980—; pres. Woodley Homeowner's Assn., Encino, 1986-89. Grantee Durfee Found., 1986, 92. Mem. Am. Psychol. Assn., Calif. Assn. Marriage, Family and Child Therapists, Calif. Assn. Lic. Ednl. Psychologists. Avocations: travel, international relations, history, sailing, skiing. Office: Edn Ctr 2080 N Mountain Ave Claremont CA 91711-2643

ALBEE, GLORIA, playwright; b. Brockton, Mass., Apr. 26, 1931; d. Earl Fredric and Rita Marie (Walls) Albee; m. Leonard Goodman, Jan. 13, 1961 (div.); 1 child, Anna Albee Goodman. Student, Boston U., 1948-49, U. Wash., 1972-74, Sarah Lawrence Coll., 1975-76, Hunter Coll., 1986-92. Playwright: Medea, 1975, Helen of Sparta, 1991; plays produced include Medea, Nothing Personal, The Yellow Wallpaper. Recipient John Golden Theatre award Hunter Coll., 1986, Mary M. Fay award in poetry Hunter Coll., 1990, Honorable Mention award Jane Chambers Playwriting Award, 1994; Rockefeller Bros. Found. grantee; Nat. Arts Club Lit. scholar, 1990. Mem. Dramatists Guild. Home: 828 Blackwood Clementon Rd # 73 Clementon NJ 08021

ALBER, ORO LINDA, healthcare educator, consultant; b. Barranquilla, Colombia, Colombia, June 27, 1952; arrived in US, 1971; d. Cevastian Alcala and Ana Mendez; m. Charles Alber, Aug. 10, 1974; 1 child, jonathan. BA, St. Thomas U., Miami, 1986. Cert. HIV/AIDS. Tchr. spl. assignment Sch. Bd. Broward County, Ft. Lauderdale, Fla., 1981—91; sr. health educator Broward County Health Dept., Ft. Lauderdale, Fla., 1991—97, Vista Health Plans, Sunrise, Fla., 1999—2003; health educator Total Edn., Inc., Hollywood, Fla., 2003—. World refugee program adv. Sheridan Tech. Ctr., Hollywood, Fla., 2003—04; founder, dir. Total Edn., Inc., Hollywood, Fla., 2003—; health cons. Broward Career Inst., Pembroke Pines, Fla., 2003—06; lead ctr. field officer FEMA, West Palm Beach, Fla., 2005—. Prodr.: HIV/AIDS Edn., 1997. Nat. trainer Parent-Tchr. Assn, Chgo., 2005—; pres. Latin Am. Democrats, Broward County, Fla., 2000—. Recipient Employee of Year, Broward County Health Dept., 1995, Outstanding Adv. Mem. award, Broward County, 2005. Mem.: Hispanic Am. Alliance (bd. adv. 2002—). Democrat. Roman Catholic. Avocations: angels, wrist watches. Home: 141 NW 73rd Ave Pembroke Pines FL 33024 Personal E-mail: lindaalber@bellsouth.net.

ALBERS, DOLORES M., secondary school educator; b. Lander, Wyo., June 2, 1949; AA, Casper Coll., 1969; BS, U. No. Colo., 1972; postgrad., U. N.C., U. Wyo., Chadron State. Lic. massage therapist Utah. Physical edn. instr. for grades K-12, 6th and 8th grade sci. tchr. Bent County Sch. Dist. 2, McClave, Colo., 1972-75; physical edn./health instr. Sweetwater County Sch. Dist. # 2, Green River, Wyo., 1972—. Mem. phys. edn. coun. Mid. and Secondary Schs., 1999—2003, chmn. phys. edn. coun., 2002—03. Mem., chmn. Green

River Parks and Recreation Bd.; coord. Hoops for Heart; co-chmn. United Way Sweetwater County, 1999-2001. Named Tchr. of Yr., Ctrl. Dist., 1994—95, Nat. Assn. Sport and Phys. Edn., 1995. Mem. AAHPERD, AALR, ASCD/NFOIA, NEA, Wyo. Edn. Assn., Wyo. Assn. Health, Phys. Edn., Recreation and Dance (Tchr. of Yr. award 1994-95), Green River Edn. Assn., Nat. Assn. for Sport and Phys. Edn., Mid. and Secondary Sch. Phys. Edn. Coun. (chmn. 2002-03). Roman Catholic. Avocations: snowboarding, backpacking, woodworking, crewel, cross country skiing. Home: 1745 Massachusetts Ct Green River WY 82935-6229 Office: Green River HS 1615 Hitching Post Dr Green River WY 82935-5771 Office Phone: 307-872-4747.

ALBERS, SHERYL KAY, state legislator; b. Sauk County, Wis., Sept. 9, 1954; d. Marcus J. and Norma Gumz; 1 child, Joel Albert. BA, Ripon Coll., 1976; JD, U. Wis., 2004. Mem. children and families com. Wis. State Assembly, chmn. property rights/land mgmt. com. Assembly Rep. Caucus Wis., 1987-91; mem. Local Emergency Planning Com. Juneau County; mem. Joint Com. on Fin., 1996-2000; mem. Sauey Foun. Scholarship Com. Recipient Campbell award Sauk County Rep. Com., 1981, 90, Top 10 County award Wis. State Rep. Party, 1982, Pacesetter award Wis. Forage Coun., 1983, Bovay award Rep. Party Wis., 1990; named one of Outstanding Farmers Sauk County Farm Bur., 1982. Mem. Sauk County Farm Bur. (dir., treas. 1977-82), Sauk County Hist. Soc., Agrl. Bus. Coun. Wis., Kiwanis. Republican. Office: Hazelbaker and Assoc SC 3240 University Ave Ste 3 Madison WI 53704 Office Phone: 608-266-8531. Business E-Mail: Rep.Albers@legis.state.wi.us.

ALBERT, ELIZABETH FRANZ (MRS. HENRY B. ALBERT), investor, artist, conservationist; b. Chgo., Nov. 9, 1923; d. Herbert George and Louise Anders Franz; m. Henry Burton Albert, Oct. 24, 1964 (dec. July 1980). Student, Chevy Chase Jr. Coll., 1942. Investor stock market, real estate. Breeder several champion Miniature Poodles. Exhibitions include portraits, still life (various painting awards); contbr. biology textbook; editor: biology textbook. Former mem. Landmarks Preservation Coun. Chgo. Mem.: Am. Farmland Trust, Nat. Trust Hist. Preservation, Cousteau Soc. (founding mem.), Natural Resources Def. Coun., Environ. Def. Fund (Osprey Soc.), Nat. Mus. Women in the Arts (charter mem.), Chgo. Symphony Orch. Soc., Art Inst. Chgo. (life). Republican. Episcopalian. Achievements include design of a house in college within the architectural field; conservationist who campaigned against the herbicide Dacthal which causes lymphoma and Parkinson's Disease and is used by lawn care companies, home owners, farmers, and golf course greens keepers. Avocations: music, renovating houses, antiques, gardening, reading. Home: 316 Courtland Ave Park Ridge IL 60068

ALBERT, JANYCE LOUISE, human resources specialist, retired business educator, banker, consultant; b. Toledo, July 27, 1932; d. Howard C. And Glenola Mae (Masters) Blessing; m. John R. Albert, Aug. 7, 1954; children: John R., James H. Student, Ohio Wesleyan U., 1949-51; BA, Mich. State U., 1953; MS, Iowa State U., 1980. Asst. pers. mgr./tng. sup. Sears, Roebuck & Co., Toledo, 1953-56; tchr. adult edn. Tenafly Pub. Schs. (N.J.), 1966-70; pers. officer, tng. officer, tng. and edn. mgr. Iowa Dept. Transp., Ames, 1974-77; coll. recruiting coord. Rockwell Internat., Cedar Rapids, Iowa, 1977-79, engring. adminstrn. mgr., 1979-80; employee rels. and job evaluation analyst, recruiter Phillips Petroleum Co., Bartlesville, Okla., 1980-81; v.p., dir. pers. Rep. Bancorp, Tulsa, 1981-83; sr. v.p. and dir. human resources First Nat. Bank, Rockford, Ill., 1983-94; dir. bus. divsn. Rock Valley Coll., Rockford, Ill., 1994-99, ret., 1999; human resources cons. Furst Group, Rockford, 2000—04. Advisor to Nat. Profl. Secs. Assn.; mem. adv. com. Zion Devel. Corp., 1999-2002. Bd. dirs. Rocvale Children's Home, 1986-97, 99-2001, pres. 1991-94; bd. dirs. United Way of Ames, 1976-77; mem. employee svc. comm., Rockford Pub. Schs., 1988-92; acct. exec. United Way Rockford, 1993-98, acct. sec. head, 1996, allocations com., 2000-01; bd. dirs. Rockford Human Resources Cmty. Action Program; chair legis. com. Rockford Human Svcs. Dept., 1989-92; chair Rockford State of Ill. Job Svcs. Employers Coun., 1990-97; publicity chmn. Tenafly, NJ 300th Ann. Celebration, 1969; task force Rockford Bd. Edn., 1993-94; gala com. Janet Wattles Mental Health Ctr., 1990; deacon Collegiate Presbyn. Ch., Ames, 1972-75; adv. coun. Rockford YWCA, 1986, fund drive task force, 1998-99, co-chair YWCA Leader Luncheon, 1986-87; advisor Rockford chpt. ARC, 1991-04; mem. Mayor's Task Force for Rockford Project Self-Sufficiency, 1986-89, chmn. adv. coun., 1991; chair info. and referral com., bd. dirs. Contact, 1994-03; bd. dirs. Rockford Symphony Orch., 1992-95, sec. 1994-95; bd. dirs. Rockford Leadership Found., 1994-96; chair pers. com. Rockford Ctrl. Area Commn., 1997-99, v.p., bd. dirs.; fund drive taskforce Blackhawk Day Nursery, 1998-99; bd. dirs. Rock Valley Coll. Found., 2000-03, co-chmn. governance com., 2001-03; mem. session 1st Presbyn. Ch., Rockford, 2000-01, chair mktg. task force, 2003, mem. space allocation task force, 2004; ctrl. steering com. Ctr. for Learning in Retirement, 2000-01; bd. dirs. strategic planning com. Mendelssohn Ctr. Performing Arts, 2005-; co-chair pub. fund dr. Burpee Mus. Connecting Our Future, Rockford Art Mus., 2006-. Pres.'s scholar Mich. State U., 1951-53; recipient YWCA Kate O'Connor award for Women in Labor Force, 1984; named Bd. Mem. of Yr. Rockford Human Resources Community Action Program, 1992. Mem.: Ill. Consortium Internat. Travel (mentor The Netherlands 1997), Employee Benefits Assn. No. Ill. (mem. chmn.), Am. Soc. Pers. Adminstrn., Crusader Clin. Found. (bd. dirs. 1997—2003, v.p., bd. dirs. 2000, chmn. 2001—02, pres. bd. 2001—02), Rockford Pers. Assn. (adv. coun. 1983—91, co-chmn. programs 1985—86), Rockford C. of C. (leadership program 1989, Athena event com. 1990—2005, chmn. Rockford Athena chpt. 1991, pres. coun. 1991—94, internat. bus. coun. 1993—99, transp. com., human resources com., Nat. Athena Found. award 1991, Woman of Yr.), Rockford Network (past chair 1985—86, awards com. 1995—97), World Trade Coun. (bd. dirs. 1994—97), Womenspace (bd. dirs. 1993—95, mktg. com. 1993—99, awards com. 1995—98, adv. bd. 1996—2005), Rockford Panhellenic Coun. (sec. 1992—93, treas. 1993—94, v.p. 1994—95, pres. 1995—96, Woman of Yr. award 1994, Rockford Lifescape Sr. of Yr. award 1999), P.E.O., Rockford Rotary Internat. (mem. com. 1999—2003, chair steering com. 2000—01, co-chair mem. com. 2001—03, Svc. Above Self com. 2004—, bd. dirs. 2004—06, co-chair Rockford Acad. Event), Phi Kappa Phi, Alpha Gamma Delta, Sigma Epsilon. Home and Office: 5587 Thunderidge Dr Rockford IL 61107-1756 Fax: 815-282-8248. Office Phone: 815-877-8364. E-mail: janycealbert@hotmail.com.

ALBERT, KRISTEN ANN, music educator; b. Harrisburg, Pa., July 29, 1962; d. Charles Orth and Kathryn Johnson Froehlich; m. Douglas Lee Albert, Aug. 31, 2001. BS Edn., Millersville U., 1983; EdM, Shippensburg U., 1989; EdD in Ednl. Leadership, U. Del., 2006. Cert. instrnl. II Pa. Dept. Edn., 1983, specialist II Pa. Dept. Edn., 1989. Music specialist Warwick Sch. Dist., Lititz, Pa., 1984, Manheim Twp. Sch. Dist., Lancaster, Pa., 1984—89, guidance counselor, 1990—92, Hempfield Sch. Dist., Landisville, Pa., 1989—90; music specialist Lampeter-Strasburg Sch. Dist., Pa., 1992—2000; instr. music edn. West Chester U., Pa., 2001; asst. prof. music edn. West Chester U. Pa., 2001—, chmn. Dept. Music Edn., 2005—. Co-dir. Children's Choir Lancaster, 2000—05; guest condr. Kennett Symphony Children's Chorus, 2006—. Musician: Allegro: The Chamber Orch. Lancaster, 2001—; contbr. articles to profl. jours. ETeaching/eLearning grant, West Chester U., 2002, 2003. Mem.: ASCD, Am. Ednl. Rsch. Assn., Orgn. Am. Kodaly Educators, Am. Choral Dirs. Assn., Tech. Inst. Music Edn. (instr.), Music Educators Nat. Conf. Lutheran. Avocations: golf, reading, computers. Office: West Chester Univ Pa Swope Hall West Chester PA 19383

ALBERT, ROSALIE SNOW, secondary school educator, writer; b. Prentiss, Maine; d. James Linwood and Eleanor Rebecca (Averill) Snow; m. Bertrand Donald Albert, June 28, 1958; children: Daniel Bertrand, Rebecca Mae. BA in Spanish and French, U. Maine, 1951; postgrad., U. Fla., 1972-75. Life cert. secondary French and Spanish tchr., Mass. Sec. Head Travel Bur., Bangor, Maine, 1956-58; tchr. Montfort Sch., St. Agatha, Maine, 1965, Brewer (Maine) Jr. H.S., 1965-66; tchr., retreat leader Blessed Trinity Sch., Ocala, Fla., 1972-75; permanent substitute tchr., Augusta, Maine, 1968-71, Reading, Mass., 1971-72; tchr. French, Gate of Heaven Sch., Dallas, Pa., 1975—2001, eucharistic min., 1978—. Author: (juvenile) Whitey Wooly Lamb, 2001, The Sleepy Seed Fairy, 2003; contbr. poetry to anthology Nen. Grey Lady Assn., Bangor, 1951-53; bd. dirs. YWCA, Bangor, 1952-53; Cub Scout leader Boy Scouts Am., Augusta, 1968-70; leader Girl Scouts U.S.A., Reading, 1971-72; confirmation sponsor Gate of Heaven Ch., 1997, 99. Mem. Am. Assn. Tchrs. French, Nat. Cath. Edn. Assn., Altar and Rosary Soc., Delta Zeta. Avocations: writing, bridge, internet, letter writing. Home: Shrine Acres 3 Laurel Lane Dallas PA 18612 Office: Gate of Heaven Sch 40 Machell Ave Dallas PA 18612 E-mail: mrsa@epix.net.

ALBERT, SUSAN, mathematics educator; d. Anne Heatherington and William Frederick Albert. MA in Math. Edn., New Jersey City U., N.J., 2004. Tchr. Clifton Bd. Edn., NJ, 1999—2001, Parsippany-Troy Hills Bd. Edn., NJ, 2001—. Mem.: AMTNJ. Office: Parsippany Hills High Sch 20 Rita Dr Parsippany NJ 07054 Office Phone: 973-682-2815. Personal E-mail: salbert@pthsd.k12.nj.us.

ALBERT, SUSAN WITTIG, writer; b. Maywood, Ill., Jan. 2, 1940; d. John H. and A. Lucille (Franklin) Webber; m. William Albert, 1986; children by previous marriage: Robert, Robin, Michael. BA, U. Ill., 1967; PhD, U. Calif.-Berkeley, 1972. Instr. U. San Francisco, 1969—71; asst. prof. to assoc. prof. U. Tex., Austin, 1971—79; assoc. dean Grad. Sch., U. Tex., Austin, 1977—79; dean Sophie Newcomb Coll., New Orleans, 1979—81; dean of faculty. grad. dean S.W. Tex. State U., San Marcos, 1981—82, v.p. acad. affairs, 1982—86, prof. English, 1981—87. Founder Story Circle Network, Inc., 1997. Author: Work of Her Own, 1992, Writing From Life, 1996; author: (China Bayles novels) Thyme of Death, 1992, Witch's Bane, 1993, Hangman's Root, 1994, Rosemary Remembered, 1995, Rueful Death, 1996, Love Lies Bleeding, 1997, Chile Death, 1998, Lavender Lies, 1999, Mistletoe Man, 2000, Bloodroot, 2001, Indigo Dying, 2003, An Unthymely Death, 2003, A Dilly of a Death, 2004; author: Dead Man's Bones, 2005, Bleeding Hearts, 2006, The China Bayles Herbal Book of Days, 2006; author: (as Robin Paige with Bill Albert) Death at Bishop's Keep, 1994, Death at Gallows Green, 1995, Death at Daisy's Folly, 1997, Death at Devil's Bridge, 1998, Death at Rottingdean, 1999, Death at Whitechapel, 2000, Death at Epsom Downs, 2001, Death at Dartmoor, 2002, Death at Glamis Castle, 2003, Death in Hyde Park, 2004, Death at Blenheim Palace, 2005, Death on the Lizard, 2006; author: (Cottage Tales of Beatrix Potter novels) The Tale of Hill Top Farm, 2004, The Tale of Holly How, 2005, The Tale of Cuckoo Brow Wood, 2006; editor: With Courage and Common Sense: Memoirs from the Older Women's Legacy Circles, 2003; contbr. articles to profl. jours. Danforth grad. fellow, 1967—72. Home and Office: PO Box 1616 Bertram TX 78605 E-mail: china@tstar.net.

ALBERTI, JEAN MAE CLAIRE, clinical psychologist; b. Buffalo, Sept. 3, 1935; d. Anthony Aloysius and Mary Grace Agnes (Gervase) Alberti. BS, D'Youville Coll., 1957; EdM, U. Buffalo, 1962; PhD, SUNY, Buffalo, 1970; MS, George Williams Coll., 1984. Tchr. elem., Buffalo, 1957—65; grad. asst. univ. rschr. SUNY, Buffalo, 1965—68, dir. univ. rsch., 1968—72; asst. prof. med. edn. U. Ill. Med. Sch., Chgo., 1972—75; assoc. prof., dept. chair med. edn. U. Health Scis., Chgo. Med. Sch., 1975—80; dir. health edn. evaluation Chgo. Heart Assn., 1981—84; owner, clin. psychologist Alberti Psychol. Svcs., Glen Ellyn, Ill., 1981—. Cons., grant reviewer NIH, Heart Lung and Blood Inst., Arthritis, Metabolism and Digestive Diseases Inst., Washington, 1976-84; cons., evaluator Northwestern U. Arthritis Ctr., Chgo., 1984-88. Named Woman of Achievement, Women in Mgmt., Chgo. and Oak Brook, Ill., 1983. Mem. APA, Pi Lambda Theta (internat. v.p. 1969-73, internat. 1st v.p. 1973-77, internat. pres., 1977-81, Disting. Pi Lambda Thetan 1991, Scepter & Key award 2003). Unitarian Universalist. Office: Alberti Psychol Svcs Bldg 3 Ste 101 799 Roosevelt Rd Glen Ellyn IL 60137-5908

ALBERTI-CHAPPELL, ROXANA DEARING, psychologist; b. LA, June 8, 1945; d. George Arthur and Ollie (McMurtrey) Dearing; m. Robert Brian Chappell, Mar. 23, 1998; children: Anthony Wyatt Alberti, Luke Alexander Enrique Alberti. BA in English, Calif. State U., 1967, MA in Ednl. Psychology, 1972; PhD in Counseling Psychology, U. So. Calif., 1996. Standard lifetime tchg. Calif., 1972, cert. pupil pers. svcs. Calif., 1987, bilingual cert. competence Calif., 1990. Sch. tchr. LA Unified Sch. Dist., 1967—87, bilingual sch. psychologist, 1987—. Sabbath sch. tchr Seventh Day Adventist Ch., Northridge, Calif., 1980—87, sec. bd., 1984—87. Avocations: bicycling, hiking, dance.

ALBERTSON, SUSAN L., retired federal government official; b. Washington, Dec. 3, 1929; d. J. Mark and Alice (Myers) Albertson. BS, Purdue U., 1952; postgrad., George Washington U., 1956-58. Numerous profl. positions CIA, Washington, 1952-88; ret., 1988. Republican. Avocations: piano, cooking, swimming. Personal E-mail: alb606@aol.com.

ALBERTUS, ESTHER L., vice principal; b. Medford, Oreg., Apr. 3, 1953; d. Lewis R. Collins and Ruth C. Fackler - Collins; m. John C. Collins, June 4, 1977; children: Miranda Joy Powers, Melissa Dawn Scheer. BA, Simpson Coll., 1975; MEd, Ctrl. Wash. U., 2001. Cert. tchng. Wash. Banking officer Key Bank Puget Sound, Seattle, 1978—89; tchr. Lake Wash. Tech. Coll., Kirkland, Wash., 1989—93; vice prin., counselor So. Kitsap HS, Port Orchard, Wash., 1997—. Tchr. Bryman Coll., Seattle, 1994—97. Participating mem. Adv. Com., Port Orchard, 1997—2006; conf. chmn. Family Life Conf., Seattle, 1986—96; participating mem. Chapel Hill, Gig Harbor, Wash., 2004—06. Named Outstanding Educator, Target Corp, 2000, Employee of Month, South Kitsap, 2000. Mem.: Small Bus. Owners (assoc.). Achievements include curriculum devel. and instrn. Avocations: travel, bicycling. Office: S Kitsap HS 425 Mitchell Ave Port Orchard WA 98366 Office Phone: 360-874-5600. Business E-Mail: albertus@skitsap.wednet.edu.

ALBINO, JUDITH ELAINE NEWSOM, university president; b. Jackson, Tenn. m. Salvatore Albino; children: Austin, Adrian. BJ, U. Tex., 1967, PhD, 1973. V.p. acad. affairs and rsch. dean system grad. sch. U. Colo., Boulder, 1990-91; mem. faculty sch. dental medicine SUNY, Buffalo, 1972-90, assoc. provost, 1984-87, dean sch. arch. and planning, 1987-89, dean grad. sch., 1989-90; pres. U. Colo., Boulder, 1991-95, pres. emerita, prof. psychiatry, 1995-97; pres. Calif. Sch. Profl. Psychology Alliant Internat. U., San Francisco, 1997—2004; cons. Health Sci. Ctr., Univ. Colo., Denver, 2004—. Contbr. articles to profl. jours. Acad. Adminstrn. fellow Am. Coun. on Edn., 1983; grantee NIH. Fellow APA (treas., bd. dirs.); mem. Behavioral Scientists in Dental Rsch. (past pres.), Am. Assn. Dental Rsch. (bd. dirs.), Psychologists in Mgmt. (pres.). Mailing: Health Sciences Ctr Campus Box 8120 4200 E 9th Ave Denver CO 80262 Personal E-mail: judithalbino@comcast.net.

ALBRECHT, BETHANY JANE, counselor; b. Carson City, Nev., May 4, 1980; d. Arnold Jacob and Jane Sheridan Albrecht. BA in Anthropology, U. Nev., 2002; EdM in Counseling and Guidance-Cmty. Counseling, U. Hawaii Manoa, 2006. Mental health assoc. DREAMS, TFC, Juneau, Alaska, 2002—03, Juneau Youth Svcs., 2003; social worker, children's svcs. specialist II, child abuse investigator Office Children's Svcs., Juneau, 2003—04; mental health counselor-intern/adv. II Child and Family Svc., Ewa Beach, Hawaii, 2005—. Western Undergraduate Exch. scholar, U. Nev., Reno, 1999, 2000, 2001, 2002, Acad. scholar, U. Hawaii Manoa Coll. Edn., 2005, 2006, A.R. Iverson scholar, Hawaii Counseling Assn., 2005. Mem.: Chi Sigma Iota, Golden Key Internat. Honor Soc. (life). Avocations: hiking, hunting, kayaking, beach going, travel. Home: PO Box 33061 Juneau AK 99803 Office Phone: 808-847-4602. Personal E-mail: bethanysaddress@hotmail.com.

ALBRECHT, BEVERLY JEAN, special education educator; b. Dixon, Ill., Sept. 8, 1936; d. Harold Ivan Foster and Grace Gertrude Tracy Freed; m. Marvin Blackert Albrecht, Aug. 13, 1960; children: Bradley K., Brent D., Kimberly S. Albrecht Schluns. BS, Manchester Coll., North Manchester, Ind., 1958; MS, No. Ill. U., 1978. Cert. in elem. edn., educable mentally handicapped, learning disabled, supervision and early childhood edn., Ill. Kindergarten tchr. Sch. Dist. 300, Carpentersville, Ill, 1958-60; thcr. 5th grade Sch. Dist. 5, Sterling, Ill., 1960-61, 64-65, kindergarten tchr., 1962-64, substitute tchr., 1965-71, 97—; dir. nursery sch. Sterling YWCA, 1971-75; program dir. Ctr. for Human Devel., Sterling, 1975-76; family advocate Ill. Dept. Child and Family Svcs., Rock Falls, 1977-78; learning disablities and behavior disorders spl. edn. tchr. Sch. Dist. 289, Mendota, Ill., 1978-84, devel. pre-sch. tchr., 1984-89; clinician, case mgr., mental health provider Family Preservation Sinnissippi Ctrs. Inc., Sterling, 1989-97. Replication specialist PEECH project U. Ill., Champaign, 1985-88; supervisory faculty Ill. State U., Normal, 1983-85, Ill. Valley C.C., Oglesby 1985-89. Author: The Fosdick/Foster Annals, 2004. Participant Women's Health Initiative; chair coun. on edn. United Meth. Ch., Rock Falls, 1973—75, supt., tchr. ch. sch., 1968—88; host family Rock River Valley Internat. Fellowships, Sterling, 1975—2003; vol. Rock River Valley Hospice United Ch. Women's Bd., 1998—2002; vol. Pub. Action to Deliver Shelter, 1997—99; vol. tutor Ill. Cmty. Sch. Dist. #5, 1997. Spl. Edn. fellow Ill. Office of Pub. Instrn., 1966; name grant honoree United Meth. Women, Rock Falls. Republican. Avocations: tennis, golf, travel. Home: 3254 Mineral Springs Rd Sterling IL 61081-4107 E-mail: marvbev@essex1.com.

ALBRECHT, KATHE HICKS, art historian, visual resources manager; b. Ann Arbor, Mich., Aug. 21, 1952; d. Richard Brian and Mafalda (Brasile) Hicks; m. Mark Jennings Albrecht, July 20, 1973; children: Nicole, Alexander, Olivia. BA in Art History, UCLA, 1975; MA in Art History, Am. U., 1989. Slide libr. asst. Am. U., Washington, 1986—88, visual resources curator, 1991—; pres.-elect Visual Resources Assn., 2003, pres., 2004—06. Co-coord. Mus. Ednl. Site Licensing Project (Nat. Initiative Getty), 1994; mem. Conf. on Fair Use (Dept. of Commerce) VRA rep. to Digital Future Coalition, 1996—; mem. Nat. Initiative for a Networked Cultural Heritage, 1996-2003. Vol. Fairfax County Pub. Sch. Sys., 1980-2000; re-election com. Rep. Nat. Com., Washington, 1984; Rep. precinct worker Mason dist., 1980s. Grantee Am. U. (image processing, database devel.), 1995, 2003. Mem.: Visual Resources Assn. (pres. Mid-Atlantic region 1995—96, chair nat. membership com. 1995—97, chair intellectual property rights com. 1996—2000, pres. Mid-Atlantic region 2000—02, pres.-elect 2003—04, pres. 2004—06), Southeastern Coll. Art Conf., Am. Assn. Mus., Coll. Art Assn. Presbyterian. Avocation: antiques. Office: Am Univ 4400 Massachusetts Ave NW Washington DC 20016-8001 Office Phone: 202-885-1675. E-mail: kalbrec@american.edu.

ALBRECHT, REBEKAH S., mathematician, educator; b. Scranton, Pa. m. Thomas C. Albrecht; children: Thomas, Matthew, Stephen, Elizabeth, Mark, Andrew, Peter. BA in Math. and Secondary Edn., Marywood U., Scranton, Pa., 1975; MA in Math., West Chester U., Pa., 1978. Cert. in bibl. counseling Christian Counseling and Edn. Found., 2005. Tchr. East H.S., West Chester, 1978—79; faculty Broward County C.C., Ft. Lauderdale, Fla., 1979—80; adj. faculty Northeastern Christian Jr. Coll., Villanova, Pa., 1992, Delaware County C.C., Media, Pa., 2000—. Mem. Rep. Com. of Chester County, 1996—2002. Mem.: Christian Motorcyclists Assn. Presbyterian.

ALBRECHT, ROBERTA J., writer; b. Bronx, NY, May 27, 1945; d. Robert H. and Beverly (Burgess) Albrecht; m. David B. Richards, Aug. 13, 1983; m. Franklin D. Adams, Dec. 26, 1967 (div. Sept. 1980); 1 child, Emma Adams. MA in English, Stetson U., Deland, Fla., 1979; postgrad., NYU, 1993. Tchg. asst. Purdue U., West Lafayette, Ind., 1979—81, Marquette U., Milw., 1981—83; instr. freshman composition Concordia Coll., Wis., 1982—84, asst. prof. English Bronxville, NY, 1986—92, dir. honors program, 1991—92. Book reviewer Books and Coffee series Concordia Coll., 1990, dir. symposium study The Stronger, 88; spkr., presenter in field, 2001—05. Author: Going Around with God: Patterns of Motion in Donne's Holy Sonnets, 1986, The Virgin Mary as Alchemical and Lullian Reference in Donne, 2005; contbr. articles to profl. jours. Recipient Nonfiction Book award, Devonshire Pub. Co., 1986. Mem.: DAV, MLA, Eastern Paralyzed Vets. Assn., The John Donne Soc. Democrat. Lutheran. Avocations: travel, opera. Home: 3801 Hudson Manor Ter #7L Bronx NY 10463 Personal E-mail: robertalbrecht@verizon.net.

ALBRIGHT, CHRISTINE L., lawyer; b. June 21, 1951; BA with high distinction, U. Mich., 1973, JD magna cum laude, 1976. Bar: Ill. 1976, U.S. Dist. Ct. Ill. (no. dist.) 1976, Fla. 1985. Ptnr. Winston & Strawn LLP, Chgo., 1993—, head trusts and estates dept. Adj. prof. Northwestern U.; mem. charitable advisory coun. Ill. Atty. Gen.; mem. Estate Planning Coun., Chgo. Past dir. YWCA Met. Chgo. Fellow: Am. Coll. Trust and Estate Counsel (regent); mem.: ABA (chair-elect real property, probate and trust law sects.), Fla. Bar Assn., DC Bar Assn., Chgo. Bar Assn. (past chair trust law com.), Order of Coif. Office: Winston & Strawn LLP 35 W Wacker Dr Chicago IL 60601-9703 Office Phone: 312-558-5585. Office Fax: 312-558-5700. E-mail: calbright@winston.com.

ALBRIGHT, MADELEINE KORBEL, former secretary of state; b. Prague, Czechoslovakia, May 15, 1937; arrived in Am., 1950, naturalized, 1957; d. Josef and Anna (Speeglova) Korbel; m. Joseph Medill Patterson Albright, June 11, 1959 (div. 1983); children: Anne Korbel, Alice Patterson, Katharine Medill. BA with honors in Polit. Sci., Wellesley Coll., 1959; student, John's Hopkins U.; MA, Columbia U., 1968, cert.Russian Inst., 1968, PhD, 1976. Washington coord. Maine for Muskie, 1975-76; chief legis. asst. to Senator Edmund S. Muskie US Senate, 1976-78; mem. staff NSC, 1978-81, The White House, 1978-81; sr. fellow in Soviet and Eastern European Affairs Ctr. for Strategic and Internat. Studies, Ctr. for Strategic and Internat. Studies, 1981; fellow Woodrow Wilson Internat. Ctr. for Scholars, Washington, 1981-82; research prof. internat. affairs, dir. women in fgn. service Sch. Fgn. Service Georgetown U., 1982-93; pres. Ctr. for Nat. Policy, 1985-93; fgn. policy coord. Mondale for Pres. campaign, 1984, to Geraldine A. Ferraro, 1984; vice chmn. Nat. Dem. Inst. for Internat. Affairs, Washington, 1984-93; perm. rep. of the U.S. UN, N.Y.C., 1993-97; sec. US Dept. State, Washington, 1997-2001; founder & prin. The Albright Group LLC, Washington, 2001—; chair Nat. Dem. Inst., Washington, 2001—; Michael and Virginia Mortara Endowed prof. in practice of diplomacy Georgetown Sch. Fgn. Svc.; Disting. scholar William Davidson Inst., U. Mich. Bus. Sch. Sr. fgn. policy advisor Dukakis for Pres. Campaign, 1988 Author: Poland: The Role of the Press in Political Change, 1983, Madam Secretary: A Memoir, 2003; Co-author: (with Bill Woodward) The Mighty and the Almighty: Reflections on America, God, and World Affairs, 2006; contbr. articles to profl. jours., chpts. to books; (TV appearances) The Gilmore Girls, 2005 Bd. dirs. Beauvoir Sch., Washington, 1968-76, chmn., 1978-83; trustee Black Student Fund, 1969-78, 82-93, Dem. Forum, 1976-78, Williams Coll., 1978-82, Wellesley Coll., 1983-89; mem. exec. com. D.C. Citizens for Better Pub. Edn., 1975-76; bd. dirs. Washington Urban League, 1982-84, Atlantic Coun., 1984-93, Ctr. for Nat. Policy, 1985-93, Chatham House Fedn., 1986-88. Mem. Council Fgn. Relations, Am. Polit. Sci. Assn., Czechoslovak Soc. Arts and Scis. Am., Atlantic Council U.S. (dir.), Am. Assn. for Advancement Slavic Studies. Democrat. Office: The Albright Group LLC 901 15th St NW Ste 1000 Washington DC 20005 Office Phone: 202-842-7222. Office Fax: 202-354-3888.*

ALBRINK, MARGARET JORALEMON, medical educator; b. Warren, Ariz., Jan. 6, 1920; d. Ira Beaman and Dorothy (Rieber) Joralemon; m. Wilhelm Stockman Albrink, Sept. 16, 1944 (dec. July 1991); children: Frederick Henry, Jonathan Wilhelm, Peter Varick (dec. March 2003). BA in Psychology cum laude, Radcliffe Coll., 1941; MS in Physiol. Chemistry, Yale U., 1943, MD, 1946, MPH, 1951. Cert. Diplomate Am. Bd. Med. Examiners, Diplomate Am. Bd. Internal Medicine, Diplomate Am. Bd. Physician Nutrition Specialists. Intern New Haven (Conn.) Hosp., 1946—47; NIH postdoctoral fellow Yale U., New Haven, 1947—49, fellow pub. health, 1950—51, instr. medicine, 1952—58, asst. prof. medicine, 1958—61; assoc. prof. W.Va. U., Morgantown, 1961—66, prof. medicine, 1966—90, prof. emerita, 1990—, mem. grad. faculty, 1977—92; mem. med. and dental staff W.Va. U. Hosp., Morgantown, 1961—2000. Vis. scientist Donner Lab., U. Calif., Berkeley, 1993—; assoc. physician Grace-New Haven Cmty. Hosp., 1952-61; cons. nutrition study sect. NIH; vis. scholar U. Calif., Berkeley, 1977-78; established investigator Am. Heart Assn., 1958-63. Guest editor: Clinics in Endocrinology and Metabolism, 1976; guest editor Am. Jour. Clin. Nutrition, 1968, mem. editorial bd., 1963-68; mem. editorial adv. bd. Jour. Am. Coll.

Nutrition, 1988-89; reviewer jours.; contbr. articles, chpts. and abstracts to profl. jours. Recipient Rsch. Career award Nat. Heart, Lung and Blood Inst., 1963-90. Fellow: ACP, Am. Coll. Nutrition, Am. Heart Assn. (emeritus, fellow arteriosclerosis coun., fellow coun. epidemiology); mem.: LWV, ACLU, Am. Diabetes Assn. (epidemiology coun.), Am. Soc. Clin. Nutrition, Am. Soc. Clin. Investigation, Am. Fedn. Clin. Rsch., Phi Beta Kappa, Sigma Xi, Alpha Omega Alpha. Democrat. Avocations: music, archaeology, computers, nature conservation. Home: 817 Augusta Ave Morgantown WV 26501-6237 Office: WVa U Dept Medicine PO Box 9159 Morgantown WV 26506-9159 E-mail: mjalbrink@aol.com.

ALBRITTON, EVELYN MCDONALD, elementary school educator; d. Edward Lamar and Madge Sadie (Greene) McDonald; m. Gregg Wyatt Albritton (div.); 1 child, Jeremy Blane Polk. AA with honors, South Fla. C.C., Avon Park, 1977; BS magna cum laude, Fla. So. Coll., 1979; M in Ednl. Leadership, U. South Fla., 1998. Cert. early childhood elem. edn., ednl. leadership Fla. Tchr. North Wauchula Elem. Sch., 1979—88, Avon Elem. Sch., Avon Park, 1989—. Mem. tchr. of yr. com. Avon Elem., Avon Park, 2000—02. Mem.: NEA, Phi Kappa Phi. Avocations: antiques, garage sales, scrapbooks, reading. Office: Avon Elem Sch 705 W Winthrop Avon Park FL 33825

ALBU, JEANINE BREAZU, endocrinologist, educator; b. Ploiesti, Romania, Mar. 30, 1956; came to U.S., 1978; d. Haralamb and Paula Breazu; m. Peter E. Albu, May 25, 1977; children: Myra, Monica. Diploma, Inst. Medicine and Pharmacy, Bucharest, Romania, 1978; MD, Tel Aviv U., 1982. Diplomate Am. Bd. Internal Medicine, Am. Bd. Endocrinology and Metabolism. Resident in internal medicine Bronx (N.Y.)-Lebanon Hosp., 1982-85; fellow in endocrinology, metabolism and nutrition St. Luke's-Roosevelt Hosp., N.Y.C., 1985-87, jr. asst. attending physician, 1987-91, attending ambulatory care program, 1987-91, chief diabetes and endocrinology clinic, 1991—, asst. attending physician, 1991-1997, assoc. attending physician, 1997—. Assoc. clin. medicine Columbia U., N.Y.C., 1987-91, asst. prof. clin. medicine, 1991-95, asst. prof. medicine, 1995-2002; assoc. prof. clin. medicine, 2002—. Spl. editor Endocrine Practice, vol. I, 1995; reviewer Diabetes, Am. Jour. Physiology, Jour. Clin. Endocrinology Metabolism, Diabetes Care, Am. Jour. Clin. Nutrition, New Eng. Jour. Med., Internat. Jour. Obesity, Endocrinology; interviewed in TV and newspapers; contbr. articles to profl. jours. Recipient Clin. Investigator award NIH, 1993; Rsch. grantee NIH, 1988-2002, Genentech, 1990-97, Weight Watchers Found., 1993-95, St. Luke's Roosevelt Inst. Health Scis., 1993, WRISC, 1998-99, Novo Nordisk, 1998-99, Eli Lilly, 1999—, Pfizer, 1999—, Novartis, 2002, Anyliu Pharm., 2002—. Mem. ACP, AAAS, Am. Diabetes Assn. (Rsch. Career Devel. award 1992), Endocrine Soc., Am. Fedn. Clin. Rsch., N.Am. Assn. Study Obesity (fin. com. 1998—). Avocations: needlepoint, embroidery, hiking. Office: Saint Luke's Roosevelt Hosp 1111 Amsterdam Ave New York NY 10025-1716 E-mail: jbal@columbia.edu.

ALBUQUERQUE, HEATHER LYNNE, biology educator; b. Huntingdon, England, Aug. 17, 1971; d. Herman Houston and Charlotte Hallock Greenhaw; m. Oseas Coelho Albuquerque, Jan. 5, 1991; children: Christian Thomas, Gabriel Lucas. BSc, U. Okla., Norman, 1999. Cert. secondary tchr. Okla., 1999. Biology tchr. Garland H.S., Tex., 2000—. Tchr. Sunday sch. First Bapt. Ch., Garland, Tex., 2002—. Office: Garland HS 310 S Garland Ave Garland TX 75040

ALCON, SONJA L., retired medical social worker; b. Orange City, Iowa, Aug. 2, 1937; d. Albert Lee Gerard and Clarice Victoria (Brown) deBey; m. Richard J. Gebhardt, June 6, 1959; children: Russell Gebhardt, Cheryl Gebhardt, Kurt Gebhardt; m. George W. Ryan, Dec. 28, 1968; 1 child, Alanna Ryan (dec.); m. David E. Alcon, July 20, 1985. BA, Western Md. Coll./McDaniel Coll., 1959; MSW, U. Md., 1973. Caseworker Springfield State Hosp., Sykesville, Md., 1959-61; dir. social work dept. Hanover (Pa.) Gen. Hosp., 1966-96; ret., 1996. Staff Matthews Hallmark Store, Hanover, 1997—99, Hanover, 2002; sales assoc. BONTON Dept. Store, Hanover, 2003—05; field instr. Western Md. Coll., 1967—96, social work adv. coun., 1979—81, 1984—86; clin. assoc. prof. Sch. Social Work and Social Planning U. Md., 1987—92; cons. Golden Age Nursing Home, Hanover, 1973—76, Carlisle (Pa.) Hosp., 1974—78, Hanover Vis. Nurse Assn., 1977—83; emergency svcs. Mental Health Clinic, 1972; chmn. profl. adv. com. Vis. Nurses Assn. Hanover and Spring Grove, 1986—89; ind. beauty cons. Mary Kay, 1999—2000. Bd. dirs. Hospice of York, 1980—82, Hanover chpt. ARC, 1976—79, Adams-Hanover Mental Health, 1973—76; pres. Human Svcs. Orgn., 1980, v.p., 1985—86; adv. coun. Hanover Hospice, 1982—85; treas. Hanover Cmty. Progress Com., 1976—80; mem. Adams-Hanover Sheltered Workshop Com., 1968—70; bd. dirs. Hanover Cmty. Players, 1974—77, sec., 1982; organizer local chpt. Make Today County and Peemie Parent Support Group, 1979; initiator, co-trustee Children's Cardiac Fund, 1979—82; adv. bd. United Cerebral Palsy S. Ctrl. Pa., 1989—90; active YWCA, 1979—84, 1996—98; co-organizer Adams-Hanover chpt. Compassionate Friends, 1983; adminstr. Hanover Gen. Hosp. Spl. Needs Fund, 1986—96; mem. cmty. adv. com. Healthsouth Rehab. York, 1995—96; co-facilitator I Can Cope classes Am. Cancer Soc., 1989—92; active Cmty. Needs Coalition, 1990—96, S. Ctrl. Pa. Coalition Organ/Tissue Donation, 1994—98; mem. Case Mgmt. Network S. Ctrl. Pa., 1994—96; vol. Hanover Hosp.; adv. group Inst. Pastoral Care, 1976—77; adv. coun. Parents Anonymous, 1976—79, 1985—92; mem. vestry All Sts. Episcopal Ch., 1973—74, 1976—79, 1983—86, 1997, vestry sec., 1975, diocesan del. Ctrl. Pa., 1978, 1980—86, altar guild, 1968—86, 1992—93, treas. ch. women, 1979—83, ch. choir, soloist, 1975—; vol. Hanover Area Coun. Chs.; bd. dirs. Episcopal Home Shippensburg, 1979—85, Ea. Star Home, Warminster, Pa., Grand Ct. of Pa., 1995—98. Finalist YWCA Salute to Women, 1986, 1987; recipient York Daily Record Exceptional Citizen award, 1979, Recognition cert., Col. Richard McAllister chpt. DAR, 1980, Companion of the Temple award, Grand Encampment Knights Templar, 1999. Mem.: NASW, Acad. Cert. Social Workers, Hanover Hosp. Aux. (life), Pa. White Shrine Club (pres. 2002—03), Hanover Gen. Hosp. Aux. (life), Md. Alumni Assn. (bd. dirs. 1983), Hanover Hosp. Auxiliary (life), Elizabethtown Assembly, Westminster Assembly, Social Order of Beauceant (worthy pres. 1999, organizer, Elizabethtown Assembly 265, charter pres. 2000—01, supreme worthy preceptress 2003—04, supreme worthy 2d v.p. 2004—05, supreme worthy 1st v.p. 2005—06, worthy pres. 2006, supreme worth pres. 2006—), Order of White Shrine of Jerusalem (life; worthy high priestess 1994—95, watchman of shepherds 1999—2000, supreme worthy herald 1999—2000, material objective), Order of Amaranth (life; royal patron 1988—89, royal matron 1995—96, grand historian 1998—99, royal matron 1999—2000, grand standard bearer 2001—02, royal patron 2001—02, grand rep. to Eng. 2002—03, grand rep. Iowa 2005—06), Order Eastern Star (life; worthy matron 1985—86). Home: 6918 Seneca Ridge Dr York PA 17403

ALCORN, KAREN ZEFTING HOGAN, artist, educator, journalist; b. Hartford, Conn., Sept. 29, 1949; d. Edward C. and Doris V. (Anderson) Zefting; m. Wendell R. Alcorn, Apr. 12, 1985. BS, Skidmore Coll., 1971; MFA, Boston U., 1976. Secondary art tchr. Scituate (Mass.) High Sch., 1971-73, Milton (Mass.) High Sch., 1973-79; engr. VEDA, Inc., Arlington, Va., 1979-80; analyst, Info. Spectrum, Inc., Arlington, Va., 1980-82, Pacer Systems, Inc., Arlington, Va., 1982-84; dir. ops., mgr. tng. program Starmark Corp., Arlington, Va., 1984; sr. systems analyst VSE Corp., Arlington, Va., 1984-85; analyst, tech. writer Allen Corp., Las Vegas and Fallon, Nev., 1987-88; mem. faculty Western Nev. C.C., 1989, 97-2000; instr. Newport (R.I.) Art Mus., 1990-92; dir. North Tahoe (Calif.) Art Ctr. Dir. Artward Bound, 1994; instr. Sierra Nevada Coll., 1995-98; acting edn. dir., instr. Brewery Arts Ctr., 1996-97; columnist, writer Artifacts Mag., 1998-2000; dir. Art Gallery Western Nevada C.C., Carson City, 1999-2000; trustee Western Nev. C.C. Found., 2000-03; arts cons., Nev., 2004-. Exhibitions include Am. Artists Profl. League Grand. Nat., NYC, 1995, 1998, 2003, 2005, Nev. Biennial, 1996, Catharine Lorillard Wolfe Art Club, NYC, 1996, 2000, Nat. Oil and Acrylic Painters Soc., 1996, 1998, 2000, 2005, Nev. State Libr. and Archives, 1997, Salmagundi Club, NYC, 1997, 1998, 2000, 2002, 2005, Allied Artists Am., NYC, 1997, Butler Inst. Am. Art, Youngstown, Ohio, 2001, Audubon Artists Inc., 2001, Great Still Life Adventure II, 2002. Finalist, Artist's Mag., 1994; recipient Silver medal, Calif. Discovery Awards, 1994, Art Calendar Centerfold Contest award, 1999, Sarah Marshall and Ida Kaminski Meml. award, Salmagundi Club, 2000; grantee Sierra Arts Found., 1996. Fellow: Am. Artists Profl. League (Graphics award 1995, 1998, Pastel award 2003); mem.: Nat. Oil and Acrylic Painters Soc. (signature mem.). Address: 1788 Eagle Lake Dr Brevard NC 28712 E-mail: alcornart@att.net.

ALCOTT-JARDINE, SUSAN, artist, writer; b. L.A., June 7, 1940; d. William Kenneth and Hazel Stella (Pearson) Allin; m. Neal J. Jardine, 1996. Student, LA Harbor Coll., 1958—59, El Camino Coll., 1959—61, Calif. State U., 1961—64, Writers Guld Am. West, Inc., 1970—74, UCLA, 1993, U. Judaism, 2000—. Tchg. asst., lab. technician Calif. State U., LA, 1963—64; with Musifon, Inc., LA, 1965—69, Mickey Garrett & Assoc., LA, 1967—68; freelance reader Screen Gems TV, Burbank, Calif., 1972; corp. sec.-treas., adminstrv. asst., dir. Don Perry Enterprises, Inc., LA, 1969—80; owner Susan Alcott's Scribe Svcs. Ltd., Sherman Oaks, Calif., 1981—88; pub. rels. adminstr., editor, feature writer the Spl. Friends of Kenny Rogers Kenny Rogers Prodns. Inc., LA, 1981—87; with music pub. and copyright dept. Cooper, Epstein & Hurewitz, Beverly Hills, Calif., 1988—90; with Sta. KRCA-TV, Burbank, 1990—94, Fischbach, Perlstein, Lieberman & Yanny, LA, 1995—96; owner, fine artist ltd. edit. art prints Greendoor Edits., 1999—. Actress: theatres So. Calif., films, TV, commls; author: numerous poems; editor: Patterns, 1982; contbr. articles to popular mags.; Represented in permanent collections; lyricist: Nobody's Child. Recipient Writers Guild Found. award, 1972, Writers Guild Found. cert., 1974, Dorothy Daniels Hon. Writing award, Nat. League of Am. PEN Women, 1994, 1997, 1st place fiction, Nat. League Am. Pen Women-Simi Valley Br., 1988. Mem.: SAG, ASCAP, Nat. Writers Union (steering com. 1998—2000), Folk Art Soc. Am., Artist Co-Op 7, Friends of PEN Am. West. Office: PO Box 56839 Sherman Oaks CA 91413-1839 Office Phone: 818-906-9650. E-mail: susanajardine@greendooreditions.com.

ALDAHL, DEBORAH CAMPBELL, elementary school educator; b. Atlanta, Sept. 23, 1951; d. Ted Denson and Leonard Myrtle Beshers; children: James, Rachel Aldahl Heine. Student, U. Barcelona, Spain, 1978—79; BA, U. Calif., Irvine, 1981; Bilingual Cross Cultural Degree, U. So. Calif., L.A., 1984. Adminstrv. asst. Agy. for Internat.l Devel., Washington, 1983; tchr. L.A. Sch. Dist., 1984—. Mem.: Calif. Tchrs. Assn., Computer-User Educators, United Tchrs. L.A. (chpt. chair 1987—98). Democrat. Universal Unitarian. Avocations: reading, travel, weightlifting, dance. Home: 1516 Malcolm Ave Los Angeles CA 90024 Office: Cheremoya Ave Elem Sch 6017 Franklin Ave Los Angeles CA 90068 E-mail: alldoll51@yahoo.com.

ALDAVE, BARBARA BADER, lawyer, educator; b. Tacoma, Dec. 28, 1938; d. Fred A. and Patricia W. (Burns) Bader; m. Rafael Aldave, Apr. 2, 1966; children: Anna Marie Alkin, Anthony John. BS, Stanford U., 1960; JD, U. Calif., Berkeley, 1966. Bar: Oreg. 1966, Tex. 1982. Assoc. law firm, Eugene, Oreg., 1967-70; asst. prof. U. Oreg., 1970-73, prof. Eugene, 2000—; vis. prof. U. Calif., Berkeley, 1973-74; from vis. prof. to prof. U. Tex., Austin, 1974-89, co-holder James R. Dougherty chair for faculty excellence, 1981-82, Piper prof., 1982, Joe A. Worsham centennial prof., 1984-89, Liddell, Sapp, Zivley, Hill and LaBoon prof. banking fin. and comml. law, 1989; dean Sch. Law, prof. St. Mary's U., San Antonio, 1989-98, Ernest W. Clemens prof. corp. law, 1996-98; Loran L. Stewart prof. corp. law, dir., Ctr. for Law and Entrepreneurship U. Oreg. Sch. Law, 2000—. Vis. prof. Northeastern U., 1985-88, 98, Boston Coll. 1999-2000, Cornell U., 2002; ABA rep. to Coun. Inter-ABA, 1995-99; NAFTA chpt. 19 panelist, 1994-96. Pres. NETWORK, 1985-89; chair Gender Bias Task Force of Supreme Ct. Tex., 1991-94; bd. dirs. Tex. Alliance Children's Rights, Lawyer's Com. for Civil Rights Under Law of Tex., 1995-2000; nat. chair Gray Panthers, 1999-2003; pres. Portia Project, 2003—; vice chair Mex. Am. Cultured Ctr., 2003—. Recipient Tchg. Excellence award U. Tex. Student Bar Assn., 1976, Appreciation awards Thurgood Marshall Legal Soc. of U. Tex., 1979, 81, 85, 87, Tchg. Excellence award Chicano Law Students Assn. of U. Tex., 1984, Hermine Tobolowsky award Women's Law Caucus of U. Tex., 1985, Ethics award Kugle, Stewart, Dent & Frederick, 1988, Leadership award Women's Law Assn. St. Mary's U., 1989, Ann. Inspirational award Women's Advocacy Project, 1989, Appreciation award San Antonio Black Lawyers Assn., 1990, Spl. Recognition award Nat. Conv. Nat. Lawyers Guild, 1990, Spirit of the Am. Woman award J. C. Penney Co., 1992, Sarah T. Hughes award Women and the Law sect. State Bar Tex., 1994, Ann. Tchg. award Soc. Am. Law Tchrs., 1996, Legal Svcs. award Mexican-Am. Legal Def. and Ednl. Fund, 1996, Woman of Justice award NETWORK, 1997, Ann. Peacemaker award Camino a la Paz, 1997, Outstanding Profl. in the Cmty. award Dept. Pub. Justice, St. Mary's U., 1997, Charles Hamilton Houston award Black Allied Law Students Assn. St. Mary's U., 1998, Woman of Yr. award Tex. Women's Polit. Caucus, 1998, award Clin. Legal Edn. Assn., 1998, Lifetime Achievement award Jour. Law and Religion, 1998, Harriet Tubman award African-Am. Reflections, 2002. Mem.: ABA (com. on corp. laws, sect. banking and bus. law 1982—88, Latin Am. law initiative coun. 2004—), US-Mex. Bar Assn. (U.S. chair legal edn. com. 2005—, mem. legal edn. com. 2006—), Inter-Am. Bar Assn., Am. Bar Found. (life), Tex. Bar Found. (life), Stanford U. Alumni Assn., Order of Coif, Delta Theta Phi (Outstanding Law Prof award St. Mary's U. chpt. 1990, 1991), Omicron Delta Kappa, Iota Sigma Pi, Phi Delta Phi. Roman Catholic. Home: 86399 N Modesto Dr Eugene OR 97402-9031 Office: U Oreg Sch Law Eugene OR 97403-1221 Office Phone: 541-346-3985. Personal E-mail: balaw98@aol.com. Business E-Mail: aldave@law.uoregon.edu.

ALDEA, PATRICIA, architect; b. Bucharest, Romania, Mar. 18, 1947; came to U.S., 1976; d. Dan Jasmin Negreanu and Sonia (Friedgant) Philipp-Negreanu; m. Val O. Aldea, Feb. 17, 1971; 1 child, Donna-Dana. March, Ion Mincu, Bucharest, 1970. Registered architect, N.Y. Architect, project. mgr. The Landmark Preservation Inst., Bucharest, 1971-76; architect Edward Durell Stone Assn., N.Y.C., 1977-79; sr. assoc. architect, project mgr. Alan Lapidus P.C., N.Y.C., 1980-2001; assoc. project arch., mgr. HLW, N.Y.C., 2001—02; chief plan examiner DOB, N.Y.C., 2003—. Columnist Contemporanul art jour., 1969-73. Hist. landmarks study fellow Internationes Fed. Republic of Germany, 1974. Office: DOB 120-55 Queens Blvd Kew Gardens NY 11424

ALDEN, BETSY TURECKY, academic administrator, clergywoman; b. Washington, Sept. 12, 1942; d. John T. Alden and Mary Faison Covington; m. Mark Rutledge, Oct. 4, 1987; children: Katy Turecky, Rebecca Turecky-Moya, Joseph Turecky. BA, Colo. Coll., Colorado Springs, 1963; MA, Ind. U., Bloomington, 1966; MDiv (highest hons.), So. Meth. U., Dallas, 1978, D in Ministry, 1982. Faculty in English Eastfield CC, Dallas, 1970—78; dir. Dallas CC Ministry, 1978—84; nat. comm. dir. United Ministries in Edn., 1984—89; faculty in English TVI CC, Albuquerque, 1989—94; faculty, gen. honors program U. N.Mex, Albuquerque, 1994—96; svc. learning coord. Duke U., Durham, NC, 1997—. Mem. status/role of women com. United Meth. Ch., Dallas, 1976—84, cons. ministry in higher edn., Nashville, 1980—90; creator, dir. the praxis project Dallas Cmty. of Chs., 1980—85; cons., bd. mem. Nat. Partnership for Svc. Learning, N.Y.C., 1986—91; continuing edn. coord. N.Mex Conf. of Chs., Albuquerque, 1989—95; nat. self-devel. of people com. Presbyn. Ch. (PCUSA), Louisville, 1991—94; adj. prof. Hart leadership program Duke U., 1999—2006, student advisor/mentor, LEAPS. Author (creator, founder): (svc. learning program in higher edn.) Service-LearningThrough the Classroom (Campus Compact Svc. Learning award, 2006). Pres. Nat. Com. on Campus Ministry, Nashville, 1982—85. Recipient Outstanding Vol. Orgn. in Dallas, ARCO, 1984, Outstanding Woman in N.Mex, N.Mex. Gov., Commn. on Women, 1996, Sigmon award for Outstanding Contbn., N.C. Campus Compact, 2006. Fellow: Nat. Campus Ministry Assn. (program coord. 1989—95, GNOME-Outstanding Contbn. to the Field 1993). Democrat. Avocations: mentoring younger women, reading/discussion groups. Office: Duke Univ Box 90432 102 W Duke Durham NC 27708 Office Phone: 919-660-3199. Office Fax: 919-660-3049. Business E-Mail: alden@duke.edu.

ALDEN, DAWN MARGARETE, actor, choreographer, educator; b. New Brunswick, NJ, Oct. 19, 1964; d. Christel Kate Erika Neugebauer. MFA, U. Pitts., 1992. Cert. massage therapist Ill., 1995. Resident fight choreographer Footsteps Theatre, Chgo., 1993—98. Actor(founder, artistic director): (theatre company) Babes With Blades. Ex officio Babes With Blades, Chgo., 2003—06. Mem.: Internat. Order Sword and Pen, Ind. Fight Dirs. Guild, Women's Theater Alliance. Liberal. Pagan. Achievements include first female Resident Fight Choreographer for a theatre company in the Midwest (and possibly the country). Avocations: knitting, sewing, gardening, beading, triathlons. Home: 5920 N Paulina Chicago IL 60660-3238

ALDERMAN, AMY JOY SPIGEL, elementary school educator; b. Boston, May 16, 1961; d. Gerald David and Rosalind Natalie (Kisloff) Spigel; m. Wesley Lee Alderman, June 22, 1986; children: Adam Michael, Sara Elizabeth. BA, U. Mass., 1983. Cert. tchr. Mass., Tex. Tchr. Daniel Webster Elem. Sch., Dallas, 1983—88, T. C. Wilemon Elem. Sch., Waxahachie, Tex., 1991—97, E. B. Wedgeworth Elem. Sch., Waxahachie, 1997—99, Turner Mid. Sch., Waxahachie, 2000—. Chair lang. arts dept. Turner Mid. Sch., Waxahachie, 2000—01, chair math dept., 2005—, tchr. math., 2005—. Mem.: Newspapers in Edn., Assn. Tex. Profl. Educators. Avocations: assertive discipline, accelerated reading, philosophies. Home: 4230 Black Champ Rd Midlothian TX 76065

ALDERMAN, MINNIS AMELIA, psychologist, educator, small business owner; b. Douglas, Ga., Oct. 14, 1928; d. Louis Cleveland Sr. and Minnis Amelia (Wooten) A. AB in Music, Speech and Drama, Ga. State Coll., 1949; MA in Supervision/Counseling Psychology, Murray State U., 1960; postgrad., Columbia Pacific U., 1987. Tchr. music Lake County Sch. Dist., Umatilla, Fla., 1949—50; instr. vocal/instrumental music, dir. band, orch., choral Fulton County Sch. Dist., Atlanta, 1950—54; instr. English, speech, debate, vocal and instrumental music Elko County Sch. Dist., Wells, Nev., 1954—59, dir. drama, band, choral and orchestra, 1954—59; tchr. English and social studies Christian County Sch. Dist., Hopkinsville, Ky., 1960; instr. psychology, counselor critic prof. Murray State U., Ky., 1961—63, U. Nev., Reno, 1963—67; owner Minisizer Exercising Salon, Ely, Nev., 1969—71, Knit Knook, Ely, 1969—, Minimimeo, Ely, 1969—, Gift Gamut, Ely, 1977—; prof. dept. fine arts Wassuk Coll., Ely, 1986—91, assoc. dean, 1986—87, dean, 1987—90; counselor White Pine County Sch. Dist., Ely, 1960—68; dir. Child and Family Ctr. Ely Indian Tribe, 1988—93. Supr. testing Ednl. Testing Svc., Princeton, NJ, 1960-68, Am. Coll. Testing Program, Iowa, 1960-68, U. Nev., Reno, 1960-68; chmn. bd. White Pine Sch. Dist. Employees Fed. Credit Union, Ely, 1961-69; psychologist mental hygiene divsn. Nev. Pers., Ely, 1969-75, dept. employment secrity, 1975-80; sec.-treas. bd. dirs. Gt. Basin Enterprises, Ely, 1969-71; rep. Ely/East Ely Bus. Coun., 1997—; mem. Econ. Devel. Bd., 1998—; prof. Great Basin C.C., 1999—, pvt. instructor piano, violin, voice and organ, Ely, 1981—; spkr., presenter in field. Contbr. articles to profl. jours. Dir. Family Resource Ctr. (Great Basin Rural Nev. Youth Cabinet), 1996—; bd. dir. band Sacred Heart Sch., Ely, 1982-99; active Gov.'s Mental Health State Commn., 1963-65, Nev. Hwy. Safety Leaders Bd., 1979-82, Ely Shoshone Tribal Youth Camp, 1991-92, Elys Shoshone Tribal Unity Conf., 1991-92, Tribal Parenting Skills Coord., 1991, White Pine Overall Econ. Devel. Plan Coun., 1992-2005; bd. dir. White Pine County Sch. Employees Fed. Credit Union, 1961-68, pres., 1963-68; 2d v.p. White Pine Cmty. Concert Assn., 1965-67, pres., 1967, 85—, treas., 1975-79, dr. chmn., 1981-85; chmn. bd., 1984; bd. dir. United Way, 1970-76, White Pine chpt. ARC, 1978-82; mem. Gov.'s Commn. on Status Women, 1968-74, Gov.'s Nevada State Juvenile Justice Adv. Commn., 1992-94; dir. White Pine Cmty. Choir, 1962—, Ret. Sr. Vol. Program, 1973-74, White Pine Legis. Coalition, 2002—; sec.-treas. White Pine Rehab. Tng. Ctr. for Retarded Persons, 1973-75, White Pine County Juvenile Problems Cabinet, 1994—, Gt. Basin chpt. Nev. Employees Assn., 1970-76; chmn. adv. coun. White Pine Sr. Ctr., 2005—; mem. Gov.'s Commn. on Hwy. Safety, 1979-81, Gov's. Juvenile Justice Program; vice-chmn. Gt. Basin Health Coun., 1973-75, Home Ext. adv. Bd., 1977-80; vice-chmn. White Pine Coun. on Alcoholism and Drug Abuse, 1975-76, chmn., 1976-77, White Pine County Bus. Coun., 1998—; dir. White Pine Coalition; grants author 3 yrs. Indian Child Welfare Act, State Hist. Preservation, Fair and Recreation Bd. Centennial Fine Arts Ctr.; originator Cmty. Tng. Ctr. Retarded People, 1972, Ret. Sr. Vol. Program, 1973-74, Nutrition Program Sr. Citizens, 1974, Sr. Citizens Ctr., 1974, Home Repairs Sr. Citizens, 1974, Sr. Citizens Crafters Assns., 1976, Inst. Current World Affairs, 1989, Victims of Crime, 1990-92, grants author Family Resource Ctr., 1995; bd. dirs. Family coalition, 1990-92, Sacred Heart Parochial Sch., dir. band, 1982-2000; candidate diaconal ministry, 1982-93; invited performer Branson Jubilee Nat. Ch. Choir Festival, Mo., Ely Meth. Ch. Choir, 1960-84; choir dir., organist Sacred Heart Ch., 1984—; Precinct reporter ABC News, 1966; bd. dir. White Pine Juvenile Cabinet, 1993—, Ely/East Ely Bus. Coun., 1997—, Econ. Devel. Bd., 1998—; chmn. adv. coun. White Pine Sr. Ctr., 2005—; bd. White Pine C. of C., 2000—. Named scholar, Nat. Trust for Hist. Preservation, 2000; recipient Recognition rose, Alpha Chi State Delta Kappa Gamma, 1994, Recognition Rose, 2002, Perserving America's Treasures in the 21st Century, 2001; grantee, Nat. Trust for Historic Preservation, L.A., 2000. Fellow Am. Coll. Musicians, Nat. Guild Piano Tchrs.; mem. NEA (life), UDC, DAR, Nat. Fedn. Ind. Bus. (dist. chair 1971-85, nat. guardian coun. 1985—, state guardian coun. 1987—), AAUW (pres. Wells br. 1957-58, pres. White Pine br. 1965-66, 86-87, 89-91, 93—, bd. dir. 1965-87, rep. edn. 1965-67, implementation chair 1967-69, area advisor 1969-73, 89-91), Nat. Fedn. Bus. and Profl. Women (1st v.p. Ely chpt. 1965-66, pres. Ely chpt. 1966-68, 74-76, 85—, bd. dir. Nev. chpt., 1st v.p. Nev. Fedn. 1970-71, pres. Nev. chpt. 1972-73, nat. bd. dir. 1972-73), White Pine County Mental Health Assn. (pres. 1960-63, 78—), Mensa (supr. testing 1965—), White Pine C. of C. (bd. dirs. 2000—), White Pine Nuc. Waste Assn., Lincoln Hwy. Assn., Bus. Area Network Group, Delta Kappa Gamma (br. pres. 1968-72, 94-99, state bd. 1967—, chpt. parliamentarian 1974-78, 99—, state 1st v.p. 1967-69, state pres. 1969-71, nat. bd. 1969-71, state parliamentarian 1971-73, 95—, chmn. state nominating com. 1995-97, chmn. bylaws com. 2003—, workshop presenter aging, itelligence and learning, San Francisco, 1995), White Pine Knife and Fork Club (1st v.p. 1969-70, pres. 1970-71, bd. dirs.), Soc. Descs. Knights Most Noble Order of Garter, Nat. Soc. Magna Charta Dames, Delta Kappa Gamma (workshop presenter 1995). Office: PO Box 150457 Ely NV 89315-0457 Office Phone: 775-289-2116.

ALDERMAN, SHIRLEY M., insurance agent; b. Woodlawn, Va., July 13, 1944; d. Raymond G. and Pearl M. Stoneman; m. Edward E. Alderman, June 6, 1964 (div.); children: Sheila G. Puckett, Melanie D. Stone. Student, Nat. Bus. Coll., Roanoke, Va., 1963. Lic. property, casualty, health, life agt. 1974. Sec., bookkeeper, agt. Hanks Ins., Galax, Va., 1965—80, owner, pres., 1980—. Pres. TiA Inc., Galax, 1998—. Sec.-treas. Woodlawn Pentecostal Holiness Ch., Va., 2000. Office Phone: 276-236-2297.

ALDERSON, GLORIA FRANCES DALE, rehabilitation specialist; b. Rainelle, W.Va., May 11, 1945; d. Orval Rupert and Juanita Rose (Nelson) Dale; m. Grayson Raines Alderson, June 3, 1964; children: John Grayson, James Leslie ADN, U. Charleston; BS, W.Va. U. DON Charleston Area Med. Ctr., 1977—84; head nurse Eye & Ear Clinic, Charleston, 1981—84; owner, operator ABZ Nursing, Kanawha County, W.Va., 1983—87; rehab. specialist W.Va., 1983—. Bd. dirs. Profl. and Social Com. on Nursing Bd. dirs. Urban Politics Symposium, Charleston, 1978; election campaign mgr. Rep. Party, Charleston Bd. Regents scholar, W.Va. U., 1974-77; named Woman of Yr., Am. Biog. Assn., 1996-97, Internat. Ambassador with hon. title HE, Cambridge, Eng. and the Crown, 1998 Mem.: AAUW, Internat. Platform Assn., Internat. Soc. Poets (Nominee Poet of Yr. 1997), Am. Rehab. Profls., Am. Bd. Disability Analysts (life; cert., diplomate). Avocations: painting, writing. Home and Office: 1089 Highland Dr Saint Albans WV 25177-3675 Personal E-mail: GFA722@msn.com.

ALDERSON, KAREN ANN, librarian, private investigator; b. Caledonia, Minn., Aug. 2, 1947; d. Merle and Zelda A. BA, Upper Iowa U., 1968; MA, U. Denver, 1979. Lic. pvt. investigator. Libr. North Linn Community Sch. Dist., Coggon, Iowa, 1968-79; cataloger, acquisitions libr. Coll. of St. Mary, Omaha, 1982; tech. svcs., information libr. Mason City (Iowa) Pub. Libr.,

1982-86; free-lance libr. Marion, Iowa, 1986—98, Cedar Rapids, Iowa, 1998—; libr. Alburnett (Iowa) Cmty. Sch. Dist., 1995—. Del. Iowa Gov.'s pre-White House Conf. on Libr. and Info. Svcs., 1991. Named Find-A-Fellow Campaign winner AAUW Ednl. Found., 1988, 89; named Profl. Women's Network Woman of Yr., 1992. Mem. ALA, NEA (various local chpt. offices), AAUW, Iowa Libr. Assn., Iowa Assn. Pvt. Investigators, Alpha Delta Kappa, Iowa State Edn. Assn. Office: 4316 Lorcardo Dr NE # A Cedar Rapids IA 52402-2342

ALDOUS, CHARLA G., lawyer; b. Tex. 4 children. BA in Polit. Sci and History, Austin Coll., 1982; JD, So. Methodist U. Sch. Law, 1985. Bar: Tex., US Dist. Ct. (ea. dist.) Tex., US Dist. Ct. (no. dist.) Tex., Spl. counsel Baron & Budd, P.C., Dallas, 2005—. Named a Tex. Super Lawyer, 2003, 2004, 2005; named one of Best Lawyers in Dallas, D Magazine, 2001, 2003, 2005, Best Lawyers in Am., 2003—04, 2005—06, Top 100 Dallas/Ft. Worth Super Lawyers, Top 50 Female Tex. Super Lawyers. Mem.: Tex. Trial Lawyers Assn., Tex. Bar Found., State Bar Tex., Dallas Trial Lawyers Assn., Dallas Bar Assn., Assn. Trial Lawyers Am., Am. Bd. Trial Advocates (exec. com., Dallas Chpt.), ABA. Office: Baron & Budd PC Ste 1100 3102 Oak Lawn Ave Dallas TX 75219 Office Phone: 214-521-3605. Office Fax: 214-520-1181.

ALDREDGE, THEONI VACHLIOTIS, costume designer; b. Athens, Greece, Aug. 22, 1932; d. Gen. Athanasios and Meropi (Gregoriades) Vachliotis; m. Thomas E. Aldredge, Dec. 10, 1953. Student, Am. Sch., Athens, 1949—53, Goodman Theatre, Chgo.; LHD, De Paul U., 1985. Mem. design staff Goodman Theatre, 1951-53; head designer NY Shakespeare Festival, 1962—91. Designer numerous Broadway and off Broadway shows, ballet, opera, TV spls.; films include Girl of the Night, You're a Big Boy Now, No Way to Treat a Lady, Uptight, Last Summer, I Never Sang for My Father, Promise at Dawn, The Great Gatsby (Brit. Motion Picture Acad. award 1976), Network, The Cheap Detective, The Fury, The Eyes of Laura Mars (Acad. Sci. Fiction Films award), The Champ, Semi-Tough, The Rose, Monsignor, Annie, Ghostbusters, Moonstruck, We're No Angels, Stanley and Iris, Other People's Money, Night and the City, Addams Family Values, Milk Money, Mrs. Winterbourne, The Mirror Has Two Faces, The First Wives Club; over 100 Broadway shows include A Chorus Line (Theatre World award 1976), Annie (Tony award 1977), Barnum (Tony award 1979), Dream Girls, Woman of the Year, Onward Victoria, La Cage Aux Folles (Tony award 1984), 42d Street, A Little Family Business, Merlin, Private Lives, The Corn Is Green, The Rink, Blithe Spirit, Chess, Gypsy (1989 revival), Oh, Kay, The Secret Garden, Nick and Nora, High Rollers, Putting It Together, Annie Warbucks, The Flowering Peach, School for Scandal, Taking Sides, The Three Sisters, St. Louis Woman, The Best Man, "EFX" MGM Grand, Follies 2001 Revival, A Chorus Line 2006 Revival. Recipient Obie award for Disting. Svc. to Off-Broadway Theatre Village Voice, Maharam award for Peer Gynt, N.Y.C. Liberty medal, 1986, Career Achievement award Costume Designers Guild, 2000, DePaul U., 1999, TDF Irene Sharaff Lifetime Achievement award, 2002, numerous Drama Desk and Critic awards; inducted into Theatre Hall of Fame. Mem. United Scenic Artists, Costume Designers Guild, Acad. Motion Picture Arts Scis. (Oscar award Great Gatsby 1975).

ALDRICH, ANN, judge; b. Providence, June 28, 1927; d. Allie C. and Ethel M. (Carrier) A.; m. Chester Aldrich, 1960 (dec.); children: Martin, William; children by previous marriage: James, Allen; m. John H. McAllister III, 1986. BA cum laude, Columbia U., 1948; LLB cum laude, NYU, 1950, LLM, 1964, JSD, 1967. Bar: DC, NY 1952, Conn. 1966, Ohio 1973, US Supreme Ct. 1956. Rsch. asst. to mem. faculty NYU Sch. Law; atty. IBRD, 1952; atty., rsch. asst. Samuel Nakasian, Esq., Washington, 1952—53; gen. counsel's staff FCC, Washington, 1953—60; U.S. del. to Internat. Radio Conf., Geneva, 1959; practicing atty. Darien, Conn., 1961—68; assoc. prof. law Cleve. State U., 1968—71, prof., 1971—80; judge U.S. Dist. Ct. (no. dist.) Ohio, Cleve., 1980—. Bd. govs. Citizens' Comm. Ctr, Inc., Washington, litig. com.; instrn. com. Sixth Cir. Pattern Criminal Jury, 1986—. Mem. Fed. Bar Assn., Nat. Assn. of Women Judges, Fed. Communications Bar Assn., Fed. Judge Assn. Episcopalian. Office: US District Court Ste 17B 801 W Superior Ave Cleveland OH 44113-1829 Office Phone: 216-357-7200. Business E-Mail: ann_aldrich@ohnd.uscourts.gov.

ALDRICH, PATRICIA ANNE RICHARDSON, retired magazine editor; b. St. Paul, Apr. 6, 1926; d. James Calvin and Anna Catherine (Eskra) Richardson; m. Edwin Chauncey Aldrich, July 31, 1948; 1 son, Mason Calvin. Student, Stout Inst., 1944-45; BS in Journalism; scholar, Northwestern U., 1948. Editor Child's World News, The Child's World, Inc., Chgo., 1952-57; assoc. editor Home Life mag. Advt. Div., Inc., Chgo., 1957-71, editor, 1971-90, ret., 1990; pres. Aldrich Enterprises, Inc., Chgo. Mem. steering com., publicity chmn. Evanston Urban League, 1961-64. Democrat.

ALDRIDGE, MARY NAN, education educator; b. Edinburg, Tex., Oct. 4, 1931; d. Charles Edgar and Lillian Rimassa Koen; m. richard Lafayette Aldridge, June 6, 1952; children: Richard L. Jr., David H. Sr. AA, U. Tex., 1950; BS, Tex. A&M U., 1952, MS, 1954; degree in Edn., U. No. Iowa, 1971; PhD, Iowa State U., 1976. Cert. tchr. Tex., 1952, ednl. adminstr. Tex., 1954, Iowa, 1954, sch. counselor Tex., 1954. Tchr. elem. sch. and jr. H.S. Edinburg Weslaco Schs., Coll. Sta., Tex., 1951—66; assoc. prof., coord. tchr. edn. U. No. Iowa, Cedar Falls, Iowa, 1976—80, prof., coord. edn. program, 1980—91; prof. Sul Ross State U., Alpine, Tex., 1991—95, coord. counselor edn., 1991—95. Founder day care U. No. Iowa, Cedar Falls, 1970, faculty commencement marshall, 1976—91; presenter in field. Co-author: Methods and Materials, 1981; contbr. articles to profl. jours. Named Outstanding Mid. Level Educator, Iowa, 1989; recipient Outstanding Tchr. award, Coll. Sta. (Tex.) Lions, 1965, Disting. Svc. award, Iowa Assn. Supr. and Curriculum Devel., 1991. Mem.: United Daus. Confederacy (v.p. 1997—, sec. 1997—), Daus. Republic Tex. (pres. 1996—). Home: 407 E Harriet Ave Alpine TX 79830

ALDWIN, CAROLYN MAGDALEN, behavioral science educator; b. Montgomery, Ala., Sept. 6, 1953; d. Francis Joseph and Anne Frances (Tutak) A.; m. Michael Richard Levenson, June 11, 1983. BA, Clark U., 1974; PhD, U. Calif., San Francisco, 1982. Trainee fellow Nat. Inst. on Aging, 1977-80; postdoctoral fellow U. Calif., Irvine, 1982-84, lectr., 1984-85, prof., 1996—2004, asst. prof. human devel. Davis, 1990—92, assoc. prof., 1992—96; rsch. psychologist Dept. Veterans Affairs Out-Patient Clinic, Boston, 1985-90; prof., dept chair Oreg. State U., 2004—. Asst. prof. Sch. Pub. Health, Boston U., 1986-90, adj. asst. prof., 1990—, U. Calif., 2004—. Author: Stress, Coping and Development: An Integrative Approach, 1994; contbr. numerous articles to profl. jours. Recipient FIRST (First Ind. Rsch. Scientist Transition) award Nat. Inst. on Aging, 1989-94; Jonas T. Clark scholar, 1972-74. Fellow APA; mem. Gerontol. Soc. Am., Health Illness and Optimal Aging. Democrat. Avocations: bicycling, hiking, reading. Office: Oregon State Univ HDFS Corvallis OR 97330 Business E-Mail: carolyn.aldwin@oregonstate.edu.

ALEGRE, MARIA-LUISA, medical educator, researcher; BS in Med. Sciences, Free U. Brussels, Belgium, 1981, MD, 1985; PhD in Immunology, U. Chgo., 1993. Resident, internal medicine Free U. Brussels, Belgium, 1989, fellow, intensive care, 1995; fellow, immunology U. Chgo., 1998, asst. prof., dept. medicine, sect. rheumatology, mem. com. on immunology, mem. com. molecular medicine. Contbr. articles to profl. jours. Recipient Am.Soc. Transplantation/Wyeth Basic Scie. Career Develop. award, 2005. Office: Dept Medicine Sect Rheumatology U Chgo AMB NB005C (MC 0930) 5841 South Maryland Ave Chicago IL 60637 Office Phone: 773-834-4317. Office Fax: 773-834-4510. Business E-Mail: malegre@medicine.bsd.uchicago.edu.*

ALEMÁN, MARTHANNE PAYNE, environmental scientist, consultant; b. Houston, Dec. 3, 1938; d. Charles Franklin and Evelyn Inez (Dudley) Payne; m. Samuel Garza Alemán, July 5, 1968. BS in Landscape Arch. magna cum laude, Tex. A&M U., 1988; MS in Interdisciplinary Studies, Tex. Tech. U., 1989; PhD in Urban and Regional Sci., Tex. A&M U., 1995. Engring. aide City of Austin, 1966-69, Bryant-Curington Engrs., Austin, 1969-72; entrepreneur Rio Verde Farm, San Benito, Tex., 1972-83; rsch. asst. Tex. Tech. U., Lubbock, 1988-91, Tex. A&M U., College Station, 1993-94; cons. Rio Verde Land & Investment Corp., Calvert, Tex., 1995—. Sec./treas., bd. dirs. Tex. Avocado Growers Assn., Weslaco, 1979-83. Author: Soil Salinity in the Texas Lower Rio Grande Valley: Cause for Concern, 1987, Export-Driven Development of Soil and Water Resources: Barrier to Sustainable Development and Inducement to Desertification, 1995. Mem. and active participant Robertson County Hist. Commn., Calvert, 1980-83. Smithsonian Instn. intern, Washington, 1987, Presdl. scholar U.S. Fed. Register, 1993; recipient Nat. Collegiate Archtl. and Design award, U.S. Achievement Acad., Lexington, Ky., 1989. Mem. Am. Planning Assn., Soil and Water Conservation Soc. of Am. (vol. Heart of Tex. chpt., Waco, Tex.). Avocation: dog breeding. Office: Rio Verde Land and Investment Corp 201 E Browning Calvert TX 77837 Office Phone: 979-364-2631.

ALEMAN, SHEILA B., special education educator; b. Waverly, N.Y., May 8, 1956; d. Anthony J. and Mary A. (Wright) Niemira; m. Edwin A. Aleman, Oct. 7, 1978. BA, William Paterson Coll., Wayne, N.J., 1978, MEd, 1982, postgrad., 1992. Cert. tchr. of handicapped, supr., N.J. Tchr. of handicapped Paterson (N.J.) Pub. Schs., 1978—. Exec. prod. Paterson Edn. Assn. Cable Access, 1991—. Co-author: Special Education Report Card, 1985. Bd. dirs., mem. state com. Kids Voting-U.S.A., Paterson Edn. Found., 1995—. Named Tchr. of Yr., Gov.'s Tchr. Recognition Program, 1991-92. Mem. Paterson Edn. Assn. (exec. bd. 1991—, co-founder/co-chair spl. edn. com. 1993—). Democrat. Roman Catholic. Avocations: Japanese embroidery, reading. Home: 998 Primrose Ave Stroudsburg PA 18360-9665

ALEMANY, ELLEN R., bank executive; b. Dec. 27, 1955; MBA, Fordham U., 1980. With ops., structured trade, media & electronics depts. Chase Manhattan Bank, 1977—87; various positions including sr. lender media and electronics dept., head N.Y. Leveraged Capital Group, sr. credit officer, customer group exec. N.Am. Citibank, 1987—; chmn., CEO Citibank Internat. plc, exec. v.p. Comml. Bus. Group; pres., CEO CitiCapital, 2001—06; CEO, Global Transactions Services Citigroup Corp. & Investment Banking, NYC, 2006—. Bd. dirs. Citicorp USA Inc., Citicorp N. Am. Inc., Equipment Leasing Assn. Bd. dirs. March of Dimes, NYC, 2005—. Named one of 25 Most Powerful Women in Banking, US Banker mag., 2005. Mem.: Equipment Leasing and Fin. Found. (bd. mem., treas. 2004). Office: Citigroup Corp & Investment G 399 Park Ave New York NY 10103*

ALES, BEVERLY GLORIA RUSHING, artist; b. Laplace, La. d. William Pinckney and Clementine Marie (Madere) Rushing; m. Warren Vincent Ales (dec. June 1991); children: Merrick Vance Patrick, Sheryl Ann (dec.), Lori Patrice. Student, La State U., U. New Orleans. Office mgr. Nat. Auto Assn., New Orleans, 1957—58; cosmetician Labiche's Inc., New Orleans, 1958; art gallery owner, mgr. Gallery Toulouse, New Orleans, 1970—80, Village D'Artiste, Metairie, La., 1980—82; pvt. practice Metairie, 1982—2006. Past pres. Metairie Art Guild, Le Petit Art Guild, New Orleans, New Orleans Art Assn.; art tchr. East Jefferson H.S., T.H. Harris Mid. Sch., Magnolia Spl. Sch Author poetry Active Rep. Nat. Com., pres. East Jefferson Hosp. Aux.; bd. dir. Rep. Women's Club in Jefferson Parish; bd. dir., bd. parliamentarian Rep. Women of Jefferson Parish, 2005—, parliamentarian, 2000-2004; past pres. La Soc. De Femme, Metarie Recipient Great Lady award East Jefferson Hosp. Aux., 1990, Legion of Merit award 1995. Mem. Nat. Mus. Women in Arts (charter), Nat. Authors Registry, Internat. Soc. Poets (bd. dirs.), Heart Ambassadors (v.p.), World Trade Ctr Roman Catholic. Home: 1500 Melody Dr Metairie LA 70002-1924

ALESCHUS, JUSTINE LAWRENCE, retired real estate broker; b. New Brunswick, NJ, Aug. 13, 1925; d. Walter and Mildred Lawrence; m. John Aleschus, Jan. 23, 1949; children: Verdene Jan, Janine Kimberley, Joanna Lauren. Student, Rutgers U. Dept. sec. Am. Bapt. Home Mission Soc., N.Y.C., 1947-49; claims examiner Republic Ins. Co., Dallas, 1950-52; broker Damon Homes, L.I., 1960-72; pres. Justine Aleschus Real Estate, Smithtown, NY, 1975—2002; ret. Exclusive broker estate of Kenneth H. Leeds, L.I., N.Y., 1980-90; past pres. S.C. Real Estate Bd. Past pres. Nassau-Suffolk Coun. of Hosp. Aux, 1981-82; hon. mem. aux. St. Catherine of Siena, Smithtown, N.Y., past pres., hosp. adv. bd.; past pres. L.I. Coalition for Sensible Growth, Inc.; past v.p. Suffolk County coun. Boy Scouts Am. Mem. Sky Island Club (gov.), S.C. Citizen Police Acad. (alumni). Republican. Lutheran. Address: 2261 The Woods Dr East Jacksonville FL 32246 Personal E-mail: landauntjay@aol.com.

ALESSE, JUDITH, special education educator; b. N.Y.C., Apr. 16, 1953; d. Joseph and Rose Alesse. BA cum laude, Hofstra U., 1977; MS, Adelphi U., 1979. Cert. spl. edn. tchr. N.Y. Spl. edn. tchr. Malverne (N.Y.) Sch. dist., 1980—. V.p. Nassau Reading Coun., Nassau County, NY, 2001—. Office: HT Herber Mid Sch 75 Ocean Ave Malverne NY 11565

ALEWINE, BETTY, retired telecommunications executive; V.p. sales and marketing Comsat Internat., v.p. & gen. mgr., pres.; CEO, pres. Comsat (merged with Lockheed Martin), Bethesda, Md., 1996—2000; ret., 2000. Bd. dirs. Rockwell Internat. Corp., 2000. Dir. The Nat. Symphony Orchestra, The Brink's Co., NY Life Ins. Co., Rockwell Automation, 2000—. Mailing: The Brink's Co PO Box 18100 Richmond VA 23226-8100

ALEX, JOANNE DEFILIPP, elementary school educator; m. Joseph Alex; children: Jessica, Joel, Julianna. BA in Art and Edn., Colby Coll., 1976; grad./cert., Montessori Methods, 1982; MEd, U. Maine, 2001. Tchr., kindergarten, Montessori schs., various cities, 1979-83; founder, tchr. Montessori Sch., Stillwater, Maine, 1983—; instr. elem. sci. methods U. Maine, 2003. AMS Montessori intern supr., Univ. student tchr. placements (supr. tchr.); presenter numerous workshops and confs.; trained facilitator of Systematic Tng. for Effective Parenting; instr. parenting courses; ednl. cons.; facilitator Project Learning Tree, Project Wild, Project Aquatic, Project Wet workshops; coord 1st Maine Tchrs. Forum, 1998; tchr. cons., Nat. Geographic Soc., 1993-. Co-author: I Wonder What's Out There? A Vision of the Universe for Primary Classrooms, 2002. Selected to attend Nat. Geographic Soc. Summer Inst., 1993, Nat. Geographic Soc. Alliance Leadership Acad., 1999; named State Coord. Maine, Nat. Geographic Soc. Action 2003!, Outstanding Environ. Educator of Yr. (nat.), Am. Tree Found., 1994, Tchr. of Yr., Maine Audubon Soc., 1995, Maine Tchr. of Yr., 1998; recipient award for outstanding contbns. to child-care in Maine, 1996, Rudie Memmel Chpt. Vol. award Children's Internat. Summer Village, 2005; state finalist Presdl. Award for Excellence in Elem. Sci. Tchg., 2002, 04. Mem. Am. Montessori Soc. (cert. tchr.), Maine Montessori Assn. (treas.), Nat. Ctr. for Montessori Edn., Maine Geog. Alliance, Maine Tchr. of Yr. Assn. Avocations: biking, hiking, wild flowers, children's books, children's resources. Office: Stillwater Montessori Sch 1024 Stillwater Ave Unit 1 Old Town ME 04468-5112 Office Phone: 207-827-2404. E-mail: jalex1@adelphia.net.

ALEX, PAULA ANN, foundation administrator; b. New Haven, May 1, 1945; d. Ralph P. and Louise A. (Pesanelli) A. Student, Conn. Coll., 1962-64; diploma, U. Paris, Sorbonne, 1966; BA, Am. U., 1967; cert. bus. mgmt., NYU, 1978. Exec. asst. Olin Corp., Stamford, 1968-72, Wheelabrator-Frye, N.Y.C., 1973-75; account exec. SSC & B: Lintas, N.Y.C., 1976-82; account supr. Lawrence Charles Free & Lawson, N.Y.C., 1982—84; v.p. Advt. Ednl. Found., N.Y.C., 1985-88, exec. v.p., 1989—, mng. dir., bd. dirs., 1992—, CEO, 2003—. Mem. exec. com. Murray Hill Aux. Lenox Hill Hosp., N.Y.C. Mem. Am. Acad. Advt., Am. Advt. Fedn. Bd., Advt. Women N.Y. Avocations: southeast asian art, opera, riding. Office: Advt Ednl Found 220 E 42d St Ste 3300 New York NY 10017-5806 Office Phone: 212-986-8060. E-mail: pa@aef.com.

ALEXANDER, ALISON F., communication educator; b. Petersburg, W.Va., Oct. 21, 1949; d. Leason Robert and Ardella (Hevener) Alexander; m. James E. Owers, Feb. 6, 1946; children: Katharine, James. BA, Marshall U., Huntington, W.Va., 1971; MA, U. Ky., 1974; PhD, Ohio State U., 1979. Asst. prof. U. Mass., Amherst, 1979-85, assoc. prof. dept. communication, 1985—. Editor Jour. Broadcasting & Electronic Media; contbr. articles to profl. jours. Mem. Broadcast Edn. Assn., Speech Communication Assn. (div. officer 1983-89), Internat. Communication Assn., Eastern Communication Assn. (v.p.). Democrat.

ALEXANDER, ANNA MARGARET, artist, writer, educator; b. Greenville, Tex., Jan. 26, 1913; d. Samuel Jefferson and Elizabeth (Smith) Fooshee; m. Joseph C. Jake Alexander, Feb. 12, 1936 (dec. 1988); children: Joanna, Ellen Alexander Stein, Mardi. BA, Rice U., 1933. Cert. tchr. Tchr., Klein, Tex., 1933-38; fashion artist, writer, adv. mgr. Smart Shop, Houston, 1938-43; fashion artist, writer Kreeger's, New Orleans, 1943-45, Everitt Buelow Ralph Rupley, 1953-68; owner Ideas Ink, 1950—54; art tchr. Spring Branch, Houston, 1968-74. Founder Historic Outdoor Art Gallery, New Braunfels, Tex. Vol. literacy program, ch., hist. socs., sr. citizen groups, children's mus., food bank; leader, camp counselor Girl Scouts U.S.A., Houston, 1956-60; pres. Girl's Booster Club, Houston, 1966-68; bd. dirs. St. Francis Episc. Day Sch., 1965-70; Sunday sch. tchr. St. Francis Ch., Houston, 1958-62; active PTA. Mem. Advt. Club Houston, Univ. Women Houston, DAR, Colonial Dames New Braunfels, Garden Club, Ret. Tchrs. Assn., C. of C. Vis. Bur. (downtown design rev. commn., 45 Yrs. as Vol. award 1983), others. Avocations: ecology, church activities, gardening, volunteerism, travel. Home: 909 Allen Ave New Braunfels TX 78130-4903

ALEXANDER, ANNE A., sales consultant; b. Bartlesville, Okla., Aug. 22, 1927; d. Francis Willard and Cloe Gray Alexander; children: Josiah A. Turner, Kathleen Jane Turner, Christopher R. Turner, Dennis T. Wallace, Jennifer J. Wallace. Degree in Visual Art Edn., U. Kans., 1975, MA, 1980. Cert. tchr., Kans., Mo. Artist Hallmark Cards, Kansas City, 1963-64; art tchr. North Kansas City (Mo.) Schs., 1975-88; sales cons. Transworld Sys. Inc., Mission, Kans., 1991—. Pvt. artist and art tchr., Kansas City. Restored historic statues Old St. Mary's Ch., Kansas City, 1992—; one-woman shows include Parkville (Mo.) Art Gallery, 1986, Mo. Artists Invitational, Riverfront, Jefferson City, Mo., 1985 (award), Art in the Woods, Corporate Woods, Overland Park, Kans., 1982 (Purchase award), River Bend Art Show, Atchison, Kans., 1980 (1st pl. award); exhbns. in group shows include Cottonstone Gallery, Jefferson City, Mo., 1979; represented in pvt. collections throughout the U.S. Vol. Greater Kansas City Cmty., 1968—; bd. mem. Share, Kansas City, 1978-79, SafeHaven, Clay, Platte and Ray Counties, 1978-94, WomenSpeak Steering Com., Kansas City, 1994—, Forward Kansas City, 1994—; commr. Met. Commn. on Status of Women, Kansas City, 1980-82, Kansas City Mo. Human Rels. Commn., 1982-90, Mayor's Key to the City Commn., Kansas City, 1993-95; participant Women's Leadership Inst.-Avila, Kansas City, 1984, Consensus City Planning, Kansas City, 1994; chair Tri-County Domestic Violence Bd., Platte, Clay and Ray Counties, 1990-94; active Sosland Series, Kansas City Pub. Libr., 1998—; bd. govs. Citizen's Assn., Kansas City, 1999; mem. Gladstone (Mo.) Planning Commn., 2000—. Mem. Sales Profls. Internat. (bd. mem. 1996—, Rookie of the Yr. 1997). Episcopalian. Avocations: reading, gardening, advocate for women's issues, dining with friends. Office: Transworld Sys Inc 5799 Broadmoor St Ste 312 Mission KS 66202 Office Phone: 913-677-0020. Business E-Mail: annealexander@transworldsystems.com.

ALEXANDER, ASCENCION (CENCY) H., school psychologist, educator; b. Flagstaff, Ariz., Aug. 14, 1955; d. Paul Ruiz and Carmen Mayorga Lopez; m. Philip Mark Alexander, Oct. 10, 1987; children: Freddy, Danny. BS in Elem. Edn., No. Ariz. U., 1978, MA in Tchg. English as a Second Lang., 1986, MA in Sch. Psychology, 1994. Sch. Psychologist Ariz. Bd. Edn., 1994, Elem. Edn. Ariz. Bd. Edn., 1978, Bilingual Endorsement Ariz. Bd. Edn., 1978. 3rd, 4th grade tchr. Tucson Unified Sch. Dist. #1, 1978—79; 4th grade tchr. Roosevelt Sch. Dist., Phoenix, 1979—80, Kyrene Sch. Dist., Tempe, Ariz., 1980—81; substitute tchr. Flagstaff Unified Sch. Dist., Ariz., 1982—83; esl adult edn. tchr. Mesa Cmty. Schs., Mesa, Ariz., 1983—84; esl transitional lab tchr. Mesa Sch. Dist., Ariz., 1983—85; 4th grade tchr. Flagstaff Unified Sch. Dist., 1986—95; esl immersion program tchr. Mesa CC, Mesa, Ariz., 1984—84; grad. asst. No. Ariz. U., 1985—86; bilingual edn. safety svcs. coord. and instr. Coconino County, 1985—88; sch. psychologist intern Cartwright Sch. Dist., Phoenix, 1994—95; sch. psychologist Flagstaff Unified Sch. Dist., Flagstaff, 1995—96; bilingual sch. psychologist Phoenix Elem. Sch. Dist., 1996—97; dist. wide bilingual sch. psychologist Flagstaff Unified Sch. Dist., 1997—2000; contracting cons. bilingual sch. psychologist Self-Employed, Greater Phoenix Area, Ariz., 2000—. Beautification commn. mem. Beautification Commn., Flagstaff, Ariz., 1994—99; mem. Ministry of Mothers Sharing, Chandler, Ariz., 2004—05, Coconino Ctr. for the Arts, Flagstaff, Ariz., 1990—92. Raymond Found. scholar, Raymond Found., 1978-79. Mem.: NASP (life), Ariz. Assn. of Sch. Psychologists (life). Roman Catholic. Avocations: reading, estate sale shopping, decorating, walking, crafts. Office Phone: 480-802-2929.

ALEXANDER, BARBARA LEAH SHAPIRO, clinical social worker; b. St. Louis, May 6, 1943; d. Harold Albert and Dorothy Miriam (Leifer) Shapiro; m. Richard E. Alexander. B in Music Edn., Washington U., St. Louis, 1964; postgrad., U. Ill., 1964-66; MSW, Smith Coll., 1970; postgrad., Inst. Psychoanalysis, Chgo., 1971-73, grad., child therapy program, 1976-80; cert. therapist Sex Dysfunction Clinic, Loyola U., Chgo., 1975. Diplomate in Clin. Social Work. Rsch. asst., NIMH grantee Smith Coll., 1968-70; probation officer Juvenile Ct. Cook County, Chgo., 1966-68, 70; therapist Madden Mental Health Ctr., Hines, Ill., 1970-72; supr., therapist, field instr. U. Chgo., U. Ill. Grad. Schs. Social Work; therapist Pritzker Children's Hosp., Chgo., 1972-82; therapist, cons., also pvt. practice, 1973—; pres. On Good Authority, 1992—; intern Divorce Conciliation Svc., Circuit Ct. Cook County, 1976-77. Contbr. articles to profl. jours. Bd. dirs., Grant Park Concerts Soc.; sec. Art Resources in Teaching. Recipient Sterling Achievement award Mu Phi Epsilon, 1964. Mem. Nat. Fed. Soc. for Clin. Social Work (chmn. 20th ann. conf., exec. bd.), Ill. Soc. Clin. Social Work (pres. 1986-90, bd. dirs., chmn. svcs. to mems. com., dir. pvt. practitioners' referral service), Assn. Child Psychotherapists, Amateur Chamber Music Players Assn., Jewish Geneal. Soc., Smith Coll. Alumni Assn. (bd. dirs., v.p. 1992-94). Home and Office: 6 Horizon Ln Galena IL 61036-9258

ALEXANDER, BARBARA TOLL, financial consultant; b. Little Rock, Dec. 18, 1948; d. Lawrence Jesser and Geraldine Best (Proctor) Toll; m. Lawrence Allen Alexander, Jan. 25, 1969 (div. 1980); m. Thomas Beveridge Stiles, II, Mar. 7, 1981; stepchildren: Thomas B. Stiles III, Jonathan E. Stiles. BS, U. Ark., 1969, MS, 1970. Asst. v.p. Wachovia Bank & Trust Co., Winston-Salem, NC, 1972—77; security analyst Investors Diversified Services, Mpls., 1977—78; 1st v.p. Smith Barney Inc., N.Y.C., 1978—84; mng. dir. Salomon Bros., N.Y.C., 1984—91, Dillon Read & Co., 1992—97, UBS Securities, 1997—99, sr. advisor, 1999—2004. Bd. dirs. Centex Corp., mem. nominating com., mem. governing com.; bd. dirs. Harrah's Entertainment, Inc., chmn. audit com., chmn. fin. com.; bd. dirs. Freddie Mac, mem. fin. com., mem. capital deployment com., mem. mission com., mem. sourcing com., mem. tech. com.; bd. dirs. HomeAid Am., QUALCOMM Inc., 2006—, mem. audit com.; former chmn. policy adv. bd. Joint Ctr. for Housing Studies of Harvard U.; exec. fellow Harvard U.; former bd. mem. Burlington Resources, CRHplc, Homestore, Inc. Presbyterian. E-mail: barbara.alexander@cox.net.

ALEXANDER, CHRISTINA ANAMARIA, translator, performing company executive; b. Bucuresti, Romania, June 30; naturalized U.S. citizen, 1975. d. Peter Vladimir and Maria Nicolae (Suciu) A. BA, Old Dominion U., 1990, MA, 1992; PhD in Religion (hon.), Pacific Universal Life Ch., 1996; acctg. degree, Sch. Acctg. and Bookkeeping, Atlanta, 2000. Cert. natural health cons. Translator, interpreter Word for Word, Inc., Norfolk, Va., 1990—; exec. dir. KultureKastle, Virginia Beach, Va., 1996—. Instr. lang. Prague (Czech Republic) Lang. Sch., 1990-91; adj. faculty Old Dominion U., Norfolk, 1993; prof. humanities St. Petersburg Coll., Fla., 2006—; cons. pub. rels. High Frequency Wavelengths, N.Y.C., 1995-96; cons. V.A.C.A., Richmond, Va., 1995-96; internat. star Oriental Dance Festival of Finland, 2002; artist in residence Beaux Arts Gallery and Mus., St. Petersburg, Fla., 2004. Performing artist MARA Agy., Vienna, Austria, 1994, Joy Fund Theater,

Norfolk, 1996-97, Boys and Girls Club, Inc., Newport News, Va., 1997, M.E. Cox Ctr., Virginia Beach, 1997, Waterfront Arts Festival, Virginia Beach, 1997, Cox Comm., 1997, Pepsi Island Music Festival, 1999, Frequencia Latina Network Peru, 1999, Multicultural Alliance Va. World Bazaar, 2000, Opsail 2000, Norfolk, Va., MTV Sink or Swim Talent Show, 2001, City of Clearwater Players, 2004, Pinellas Opera League, 2005; internat. star dancer Oriental Dance Festival of Finland, 2001; creator, dancer, choreographer Secret of the Lost Treasure, 1997 (award 1997); dancer Mantra, 1997; guest star Frequencia Latina Network; cons. Va. Ballet Theater, 2000. Bd. dirs., rec. sec. Bay West Condominiums, 2001—02. Named Ms. Petite Va. Beach, 1996. Mem. Hampton Roads Cultural Alliance, Multicultural Alliance of Va., Virgina Beach C. of C. Avocations: skiing, travel, costume design, nutrition. Office: 2525 W Bay Dr Apt A23 Belleair Bluffs FL 33770-1986 Personal E-mail: christalx@juno.com.

ALEXANDER, DAWN JO, middle school educator; d. Eddie Belton and Rose Ann Alexander; m. Anthony D. Francis, May 17, 1996; children: Viloa Liberia Yetunde Dja Francis, Ida Tuareg Chinasa Dja Francis. BA, Hofstra U., Hempstead, N.Y, 1989; MEd, Mercer U., Atlanta, 2003. Cert. tchr. gifted Ga., tchr. support specialist Ga. Tchr. Dekalb County Schs., Decatur, Ga., 1996—; after sch. dir. Henderson Mid. Sch., Chamblee, Ga., 1998—. Initiate Jegna Collective, Lithonia, Ga., 2003—06. Named Exceptional Tchr. of the Yr., Spl. Edn. Dept., 2005—06; scholar Tchr. scholar, WEDD, 2000, TARGET Stores, 2000. Mem.: Ga. Assn. Educators, Profl. Assn. Ga. Educators (rep. 1996—2005), Alpha Kappa Alpha. Home: 3124 Stanford Cir Lawrenceville GA 30044 Office: Henderson Middle School 2830 Henderson Mill Rd Chamblee GA 30341 Office Phone: 678-874-2903. Personal E-mail: dawn_j_alexander@fc.dekalb.k12.ga.us. E-mail: hendersonmiddleschool@fc.dekalb.k12.ga.us.

ALEXANDER, EDNA M. DEVEAUX, elementary school educator; d. Richard and Eva (Musgrove) DeVeaux. BBA, Fla. A & M U., 1943; BS in Elem. Edn., Fla. A&M U., 1948; MS in Supervision and Adminstrn., U. Pa., 1954; cert., U. Madrid, 1961; postgrad., Dade Jr. Coll., U. Miami. Sec. Dunbar Elem. Sch., 1943-46, tchr., 194-55, Orchard Villa Elem., 1959-66; prin. A. L. Lewis Elem. Sch., 1955-57; reading specialist North Cen. Dist., 1966-69; tchr. L. C. Evans Elem. Sch., 1969-71. First black woman newscaster in Miami, Sta. WBAY, 1948. V.p. Fla. Coun. on Human Rels. Dade County, Coun. for Internat. Visitors Greater Miami; vice chmn. Cmty. Action Agy. Dade County; chmn. Dade County Minimum Housing Appeals Bd.; active Vol. Unltd. Project Nat. Coun. Negro Women; sponsor Am. Jr. Red Cross, Girl Scouts U.S.; trustee Fla. Internat. U. Found., 1974—79; mem. Jacksonville Symphony Assn. Guild Bd., Salvation Army Women's Aux., Jacksonville U. Friends of Libr. Bd.; past pres. Episcopal Churchwomen of Christ Ch., Miami; bd. dirs. YWCA. Named to Miami Centennial Women's Hall of Fame, 1996. Mem. AAUW (life, Edna M. DeVeaux Alexander fellowship named in her honor Miami br., del. seminar 1977), NEA (life), LWV, Fla. Edn. Assn., Classroom Tchrs. Assn., Dade County Edn. Assn. (chmn. pub. rels. com.), Dade County Reading Assn., Assn. for Childhood Edn., Internat. Reading Tchr. Assn., U. Pa. Alumni Assn., Alpha Kappa Alpha. Avocations: composing lyrics and music, gardening, travel, golf, photography. Home: 805 Blue Gill Rd Jacksonville FL 32218-3660

ALEXANDER, FAITH DOROTHY, retired training services executive; b. NYC, Aug. 1, 1933; d. Howard Phillip and Ruth Dorothy Rubinow; m. Fred John Dunne (dec.); children: John Dunne, Robert Dunne, Laurie Martin, Bonnie Hunter; m. Daniel Lee Alexander, Apr. 27, 2000. BA, MA, Columbia U. Sales promotion mgr. Aseptic Thermo Indicator Co., N. Hollywood, Calif., 1956—57; v.p. Dunne, Rogers, Dunne Advt. and Pub. Rels., LA, 1958—79, NYC, 1958—79; records supr., training officer Newport Beach Police Dept., Calif., 1980—86; records, info. svcs. command Riverside County Calif. Sheriff Dept., Calif., 1987—2000; cert. instr. Ben Clark Training Acad., 0187—1990; instr. Regional Training Ctr., San Diego, 1996—2003, Calif. Peace Officer Assn., Sacramento, 1996—2003; ret., 2000. Author: Early Childhood Education, Coast Guard Prodecures, 2003; co-editor: Calif. Police Recorder Mag. Pres. Barrance Elem. Sch. PTA, Covina, Calif., 1972—74; sec. Covina Valley PTA, 1974—75; pres. Sierra Vista Intermediate Sch. PTA, 1974—75; mem. Lake Elsinore Grand Prix Races, Calif., 1986; vol. Helmet Images, Riverside, Calif., 1988—2005; sec., mem. exec. bd. Urban League Formation Com., 1989—90; bd. dirs. Greater Riverside Area Urban League, 1990—93; commr. Riverside County Commn. Women, 1995—97; mem. vol. Homeland Security Dept., 2003—; mem. LA Rep. Ctrl. Com., 1974, Rep. Presdl. Task Force, 1981, 1989, 2003; chair Larry Smith for Sheriff of Riverside County, 1993, co-chair, 1998; chair Del Norte County Bush/Cheny Campaign, 2003; mem. vol. Del Norte County Elections Bd., 2003; life mem. Nat. Rep. Senatorial Com., 2006—; registrar of voters Del Norte County, 2006; vol. Faith EV Luth. Ch., Medford, Oreg., 2004—05; hon. chair House Majority Trust, 2006. Recipient 2000 Women of Achievement award, 1961, 1971, Wall of Tolerance award, 2003, Riverside Calif. Pub. Svc. award, 1999, Nat. Rep. Party Gold medal, 1992, 2004, Rep. Yr., 2003. Mem.: Crescent city Coast Guard Aux., Del Norte County Rep. Women, Calif. Dept. Edn. Task Force, Campfire Girls (bd. mem., vice chair 1972—74), Nat. PTA (Hon. Svc. 1961), Am. Records Mgmt. Assn., Calif. Peace Officer's Assn., Calif. Law Enforcement Assn. of Record Suprs. (life; state conf. chair 1978, pres. So. Chpt. 1988—90, state conf. dir. 1989, founder, pres. Inland chpt. 1992—95, state exec. bd. 1992—95, Hon. Svc. award 1991, 1996), Nat. Rep. Senatorial Com. (life). Republican. Avocations: theater, music, art, writing, travel. Personal E-mail: faithanddan@earthlink.net.

ALEXANDER, GAIL SUSAN, psychiatrist; m. Joel Feiner, May 30, 1992; children from previous marriage: Deirdre, Peter, Margo Murray. BA, Vassar Coll., 1961; MD, NYU, 1966; MPH, Yale Sch. Medicine, 1983. Dir. health svc. SUNY, NY, 1977—87; dir. outpatient child adolscent psychiatry St. Lukes-Roosevelt Hosp., NYC, 1991; dir. tng. child adolscent psychiatry U. Tex., Dallas, 1992—2000; psychiatrist pvt. practice, 2000—. Mem. edn. com. U. Tex. Southwest Med. Sch., Dallas, 1992—2000; mem. bd. examiners Am. Bd. Psychiatry and Neurology, 1998; clin. assoc. prof. psychiatry U. Tex. S.W. Med. Ctr., Dallas. Fellow: Am. Psychiat. Assn.; mem.: Acad. Child & Adolscent Psychiatry. Office: 12860 Hillcrest Rd #211 Dallas TX 75230 Office Phone: 972-980-9423.

ALEXANDER, HOPE, actor, educator, theater director; b. San Francisco, June 16, 1947; d. Leon and Mara Alexander; 1 child, Thorin. Actor Am. Conservatory Theatre, San Francisco, 1974—76; actor TV series The New WKRP in Cin., Studio City, Calif., 1991—92, Mystery Of Black Rose Castle, Hungary, 2000—00; artistic dir. The Co. Rep, North Hollywood, Calif., 2001—; actor Berkeley Repertory Theatre, Berkeley, Calif., 1980—85, Actor's Theatre of Lousiville, Louisville, South Coast Repertory Theatre, Costa Mesa, Calif., Shakespeare's People national tour. Artistic dir. OmniArt, Inc., Oakland, Calif., 1978—81; conservatory dir. Bay Area Actor's Lab., Oakland, 1978—81; tchr. Drama Studio of London, Berkeley, Calif., 1980—82, U. NC, Chapel Hill, 1982; tchr., dir. Am. Acad. Dramatic Arts, LA, 2006—. Dir.: (numerous theatrical prodns.) (Bay Area Drama Critic's Cir. Award, 1989); prodr.: (theatrical prodns.). Recipient Drama-Logue award for acting, Drama Critics, 1984, award, Bay Area Drama Critic's Cir., 1982, award for acting, Bay Area Theatre Critics Cir., 1986; intern, San Francisco Actor's Workshop, 1963—65, Lucy Stern tchg. fellow, Mills Coll., 1980. Mem.: NOW, ACLU. Achievements include development of emotional memory movement technique for actors. Avocations: travel, writing.

ALEXANDER, ICIE MAE, communications executive; b. Knoxville, Tenn., Apr. 10, 1933; d. Jasper J. and Gracie L. (Taylor) Casey; m. William C. Alexander, July 14, 1954 (dec. 1982); 1 child, Billie Jean. Diploma in Supr., Ohio State Extension Studies, 1972. Instr. printing Columbus (Ohio) State Inst., 1967—70; supr. Dept. Printing Columbus (Ohio) Devel. Ctr., 1970—89; loan officer Columbus (Ohio) State Sch. Fed. Credit Union, 1982—89; sec. Labor Union Columbus (Ohio) Devel. Ctr., 1983—86; pres. Internat. Tng. in Comm., Columbus, 2002—03. Treas. Corban Comm. Rsch. Coun., Columbus, 2001—03. Performer: (play) Black to the Truth, 2000. Mentor Cassady Elem. sch., Columbus, 2000—02, Granville T. Woods Sch., Columbus, 2003—; vol. receptionist Corban Commons Sr. Cmty., 2004—. Mem.: Mt. Calvery Bapt. Dist. Assn. (gen. sec. 2001, Dedicated Svc. award 2002), East Columbus (Ohio) Civic Assn., Columbus (Ohio) Inner City Lions (chmn. membership, chmn. program, co-chmn. audit com.), East Columbus (Ohio) Dem. Club (chmn. fundraising 1995—2003), Cmty. Svc. Club. Democrat. Baptist.

ALEXANDER, JACQUELINE PETERSON, retired librarian; b. N.Y.C., Aug. 28, 1928; d. Stephen Edgar and Anna (Boehm) Peterson; m. Lewis McElwain Alexander, Dec. 30, 1950; children: Louise, Lance. AB, Hunter Coll., 1949; MLS, U. R.I., 1972. Asst. editor Law of the Sea Inst. Procs., 1966—71; reference libr. U. R.I., Kingston, 1971; rsch. libr. Internat. Ctr. Marine Resource Devel., 1973—79, 1988—92; tech. libr., head books, periodicals divsn. Naval Underwater Sys. Ctr., Newport, RI, 1971—72; regional libr. U.S. Naval Edn. and Tng. Support Ctr., Groton, Conn., 1979—81; asst. chief acquisitions sect. Dept. Transp., 1983—84; libr. Edwards & Angell, Providence, 1984—88; pres. Offshore Cons., Inc., Wakefield, RI, 1992—96. Pres. South County Sr. Citizens Housing, 1974—82; active South Kingstown Citizens Adv. Bd., 1965—71; vol. AARP; vol. for tax aide, 1997—2003; vol. libr. Vis. Nurse Assn., 1992—95; bd. dirs., sec. South County Housing Improvement Found., 1966—83; bd. dirs. Washington County Vis. Nurse Assn., 1968—71. Mem.: R.I. Libr. Assn., Law Librs. New Eng., Internat. Assn. Marine Sci. Librs. and Info. Ctrs., Am. Assn. Law Librs., Beta Phi Mu. Home: 66 Beech Hill Rd Wakefield RI 02879-2524

ALEXANDER, JANE (JANE QUIGLEY), actress, theater educator, writer; b. Boston, Oct. 28, 1939; d. Thomas Bartlett and Ruth (Pearson) Quigley; m. Robert Alexander, July 23, 1962 (div. 1969); 1 child, Jason; m. Edwin Sherin, Mar. 29, 1975. Student, Sarah Lawrence Coll., 1957—59, U. Edinburgh, 1959—60; LHD, Wilson Coll., 1984; DFA (hon.), The Julliard Sch., 1994, N.C. Sch. Arts, 1994; PhD (hon.), U. Pa., 1995; DFA (hon.), The New Sch. Social Rsch., 1996; PhD (hon.), Duke U., Durham, N.C., 1996; LHD (hon.), The Coll. of Santa Fe, 1997; PhD, Sarah Lawrence Coll., 1998; DFA (hon.), Smith Coll., 1999, Pa. State U., 2000. Ind. TV, film and theatrical actress, 1962—; chmn. Nat. Endowment for Arts, Washington, 1993-97. Guest artist in residence Okla. Arts Inst., 1982, tchr. adult theatre workshop, 1984, 91, tchr. master class, 1990, Francis Eppes prof. Fla. State U., 2002-2004; bd. trustees Wildlife Conservation Soc., 1997—, Am. Bird Conservancy, 1995-98, The MacDowell Colony, 1997—, Arts Internat., 2000-2004. Author: (with Greta Jacobs) The Bluefish Cookbook, 6 edits., 1979-95; translator: (with Sam Engelstad) The Master Builder (Henrik Ibsen), 1978; Command Performance, An Actress in the Theater of Politics, 2000; appeared in prodns.: Charles Playhouse Boston, 1964-65, Arena Stage, Washington, 1965-68, 70—, Am. Shakespeare Festival; plays include Major Barbara, Mourning Becomes Electra, Merry Wives of Windsor, Stratford, Conn., summers 1971-72; Broadway prodns. include The Great White Hope, 1968-69 (Tony award 1969, Drama Desk award, Theatre World award), 6 Rms Riv Vu, 1972-73 (Tony nomination), Find Your Way Home, 1974 (Tony nomination), Hamlet, 1975, The Heiress, 1976, First Monday in October, 1978 (Tony nomination), Goodbye Fidel, 1980, Monday After the Miracle, 1982, Night of the Iguana, 1988, Shadowlands, 1990-91, The Visit, 1992 (Tony nomination), The Sisters Rosensweig, 1993 (Drama Desk award 1992-93, Tony award nomination, Obie award 1993), Honour (Tony nomination), 1998; also appeared in plays The Time of Your Life, Present Laughter, 1975, The Master Builder, 1977, Losing Time, 1980, Antony and Cleopatra, 1981, Hedda Gabler, 1981, Old Times, 1984, Approaching Zanzibar, 1989, Mystery of the Rose Bouquet, 1989, The Cherry Orchard, 2000, Mourning Becomes Electra, 2002, Rose and Walsh, 2003, Ghosts, 2003, What of the Night, 2005; appeared in films The Great White Hope, 1970 (Acad. award nomination), A Gunfight, 1970, The New Centurions, 1972, All the President's Men, 1976 (Acad. award nomination), The Betsy, 1978, Kramer vs. Kramer, 1979 (Acad. award nomination), Brubaker, 1980, Night Crossing, 1981, Testament, 1983 (Acad. award nomination), City Heat, 1984, Sweet Country, 1986, Square Dance, 1987, Glory, 1989, The Cider House Rules, 1999, Sunshine State, 2001, The Ring, 2002, Carry Me Home, 2003, Fur, 2006; appeared in TV films Welcome Home Johnny Bristol, 1971, Miracle on 34th Street, 1973, Death Be Not Proud, 1974, This Was the West That Was, 1974, Eleanor and Franklin, 1976 (Emmy nomination), Eleanor and Franklin: The White House Years, 1977 (Emmy nomination, TV Critics Circle award), Lovey, 1977, A Question of Love, 1978, Playing for Time, 1980 (Emmy award 1980), Calamity Jane: The Diary of a Frontier Woman, 1981, Dear Liar, 1981, Kennedy's Children, 1981, In the Custody of Strangers, 1982, When She Says No, 1983, Mountainview, 1989, Daughter of the Streets, 1990, A Marriage: Georgia O'Keeffe and Alfred Stieglitz, 1991; appeared in TV spls. A Circle of Children, 1977, Blood and Orchids, 1986, Calamity Jane, 1984 (Emmy nomination), Malice in Wonderland, 1985 (Emmy nomination), In Love and War, 1987, Open Admissions, 1988, A Friendship in Vienna, 1988, Stay the Night, 1992, The Jenifer Estess Story, 2001; appeared in TV series: Law and Order Spl. Victims Unit, 2000, (Emmy nomination); Intimate Portrait, Lifetime TV Biography, 1998, Warm Springs (TV), 2005 (Emmy award, outstanding supporting actress in a mini series or movie, 2005). Recipient Achievement in Dramatic Arts award St. Botolph Club, 1979, Israel Cultural award, 1982, Western Heritage Wrangler award, 1985, Helen Caldicott Leadership award, 1984, Living Legacy award Women's Internat. Ctr., San Diego, 1988, Environ. Leadership award Eco-Expo, 1991, Muse award N.Y. Women in Film, 1993, Torch of Hope award, 1992, Lectureship award NIH, 1994, Houseman award The Acting Co., 1994, medal UCLA, 1994, Outer Critics Circle award Disting. Voice in Theatre, 1994, Helen Hayes award Am. Express Tribute, 1994, Women of Achievement award Anti-Defamation League, 1994, Margo Jones award, 1995, Mass. Soc. award, 1995, N.Am. Mont Blanc de la Culture award, 1995, Common Wealth award, 1995, Creative Coalition: Christopher Reeve First Amendment award, 1998, Outstanding Leadership for Advancement in Arts, People for Am. Way, 1998, Lifetime Achievement award Americans for Arts and U.S. Conf. Mayors, 1999, Harry S. Truman award for pub. svc., Independence, Md., 1999; Woman of Achievement Award, San Antonio, 2000, Dirs. Guild Am. award, 2002, Web of Life award High Falls Film Festival, 2005; named to Theatre Hall of Fame, 1993. Mem. AFTRA, SAG, Actors Equity Assn., Acad. Motion Picture Arts and Scis., Acad. Arts and Scis., Actors Fund. Office: William Morris Agy c/o Samuel Liff 1325 Avenue of Americas New York NY 10019

ALEXANDER, JANET COOPER, law educator; b. 1946; BA in English Lit., with distinction, Swarthmore Coll., 1968; MA in English, Stanford U., 1973; JD, U. Calif., Berkeley, 1978. Bar: Calif. 1978, DC 1980, US Dist. Ct. Ctrl. Dist. Calif. 1978, US Dist. Ct. No. Dist. Calif. 1982, US Dist. Ct. Ea. Dist. Calif. 1985, US Supreme Ct. 1987. Jud. clk. to Hon. Shirley M. Hufstedler US Ct. Appeals 9th Cir., 1978—79; jud. clk. to Hon. Thurgood Marshall US Supreme Ct., 1979—80; assoc. Califano, Ross & Heineman, Washington, 1980—82, Morrison & Foerster, San Francisco, 1982—84, ptnr., 1984—87; assoc. prof. law Stanford Law Sch., Calif., 1987—94, prof. Calif., 1994—2002, Frederick I. Richman prof. Calif., 2002—, Justin M. Roach, Jr. faculty scholar Calif., 1998—2002; prin. investigator Stanford Ctr. on Conflict and Negotiation, 1994—2002. Vis. prof. Toin U. of Yokohama, Japan, 1998. Alumni coun. Swarthmore Coll., 2001—, exec. com., 2003—, co-chair coll. advisory and support com., 2003—, acting chair, 2003; leadership coun. Castilleja Sch., Palo Alto, Calif., 2002—, athletic coun., 2002—, sch. assn. bd., 2002—03, co-chair parent edn., 2002—03, lead parent rep., 2002—03. Mem.: Am. Assn. Law Schools (sections on civil procedure, fed. courts, women and the law). Office: Stanford Law Sch Crown Quadrangle 559 Nathan Abbott Way Stanford CA 94305-8610 Office Phone: 650-723-2892. Business E-Mail: jca@stanford.edu.

ALEXANDER, JESSIE ARONOW, anesthesiologist; b. Beaumont, Tex., May 19, 1957; MD, U. Tex. Health Sci. Ctr., 1984. Diplomate Am. Bd. Anesthesiology. Resident in anesthesiology Med. U. S.C., Charleston, 1984-87, fellow in obstet. anesthesiology, pain mgmt., 1987-88; staff anesthesiologist Cape Fear Valley Med. Ctr., Fayetteville, NC, 1989-98, Highsmith-Rainey Meml. Hosp., Fayetteville, 1988-98; pvt. practice Valley Anesthesia, P.A., Fayetteville, 1988-90; founding ptnr., sec. bd. dirs. Cumberland Anesthesia Assocs., P.A., Fayetteville, 1990-98; asst. prof. anesthesiology U. N.C., Chapel Hill, 1989-94; assoc. prof. divsn. anesthesia, symptom control and palliative care U. Tex. M.D. Anderson Cancer Ctr., Houston, 1998—2003; clin. prof. anesthesiology U. Tex. Health Sci. Ctr., San Antonio, 2003—. Lectr., author on dangers of nutraceuticals and on physician stress; owner art studio Alexander Studios. Contbr. articles to profl. jours.; exhibited art work in one-woman show, 2004. Active Fayetteville Area C. of C., 1988-98, Fayetteville Area Econ. Devel. Corp., 1996-98. Recipient 1st prize award Am. Soc. Anesthesiologists Art Exhbn., 1999, 2000. Mem. AMA, Am. Soc. Anesthesiologists, So. Med. Assn., N.C. Med. Soc., N.C. Soc. Anesthesiology (past pres.), Tex. Soc. Anesthesiologists, Tex. Med. Assn. (comms. com., legis. affairs com.). E-mail: jleak@houston.rr.com.

ALEXANDER, JOYCE MARY, illustrator; b. Pepin, Wis., Mar. 31, 1927; d. Colonel and Martha (Varnum) Yochem; m. Don Tocher, June 27, 1955 (div. 1962); m. Dorsey Potter Alexander, Nov. 1, 1963. Student, Coll. Arts and Crafts, 1946, Acad. of Art, 1961-62. Co-founder, owner Turtle's Quill Scriptorium Publishers, Berkeley, Calif., 1963—. Author: Thaddeus, 1972, Happy Bird Day, 1980; illustrator numerous books including: Soil and Plant Analysis, A Practical Guide for the Home Gardener, 1963, CAlifornia Farm and Ranch Law, 1967, Chinatown, A Legend of Old Cannery Row, 1968, The Sea: Excerpts from Herman Melville, 1969, Of Mice, 1966, David: Psalm Twenty-Four, 1970, Shakespeare: Selected Sonnets, 1974, The Blue-Jay Yarn, 1975, Psalm One Hundred Four, 1978, Messiah: Choruses from Handel's Messiah, 1985, A Flurry of Angels, Angels in Literature, 1986, Eleven Poems by Emily Dickinson, A Packet of Rhymes, 1989, Psalm Eight (A Nature Psalm), 1991, Poems, Emily Dickenson, 1992, Comfort Me With Apples-Excerpts From Literature Involving Food, 1993, Father William, 1994, Alice by Lewis Carroll, Excerpts from Alice in Wonderland, 1999; work represented in permanent collections Hunt Botan. Libr. at Carnegie-Mellon U. Republican. Office: Turtle's Quill Scriptorium PO Box 643 Mendocino CA 95460-0643

ALEXANDER, JUDITH ELAINE, psychologist; b. Worcester, Mass., Nov. 30, 1948; d. Frank E. and Winnona V. (Tracy) A.; divorced; children: Kimberly, Jenniferlyn. BS, Worcester State Coll., 1981; MA, Assumption Coll., Worcester, 1986; PsyD, Antioch New Eng., Keane, N.H., 1991. Lic. psychologist. Dir. mental health Indian Health Svc., Ft. Thompson, S.D., 1992-95; cons. self employed, 1995—99; psychologist VAMC, Dublin, Ga., 2001—03, Bur. Indian Affairs Ea. Navajo Agy., 2003—. Adj. faculty Mt. Wachusett C.C., Gardner, Mass., 1996, Western New Eng. Coll., 1996-2001. Contbr. articles to profl. jours. Mem. Indian Health Svc. Home: 2040 Yost Rd Toppenish WA 98948 Office Phone: 509-865-2102 ext. 238.

ALEXANDER, JUDY LYNNE, investor; d. Richard M. and Ursula J. Scott; 1 child, Darbi Lynne Gilbert. CFO Calculated Industries, Inc., Carson City, Nev., 1978—; pres. Aspen Chelsea, Inc., Colo., 1998—; v.p. Believe Productions, Inc., Denver, 2000—. Real estate investor, 1976—. Pres. Fred and Judy Alexander Found., Lake Tahoe, Nev., 1992—2006; mem. nat. coun. JazzAspen, 2002—06. Named Citizen of Yr., Vail Valley Found., 1999. Mem.: Vail Valley Found. Friends of Vail (assoc.), Game Creek Club Vail (assoc.), Aspen Mountain Club (assoc.), PGA West Golf Club (assoc.). Republican. Avocations: skiing, golf, hiking. Office: Calculated Industries Inc 4840 Hytech Dr Carson City NV 89706 Office Phone: 775-885-4900.

ALEXANDER, KAREN, museum staff member; m. Walter Alexander. Vice chmn. bd. trustees Art Inst. Chgo., vol. Dept. European Decorative Arts and Sculpture and Ancient Art. Office: Art Inst Chgo 111 S Michigan Ave Chicago IL 60603

ALEXANDER, LYNN See MARGULIS, LYNN

ALEXANDER, MARJORIE ANNE, artist, consultant; b. Chgo., Apr. 16, 1928; d. Alexander and Nancy Rebecca (Cordrey) Roberts; m. Harold Harman Alexander, June 13, 1948; children: Jeffrey C., Cassandra J., Peter B., Timothy C., Patrick J. Student, Wilson Jr. Coll., 1945-47; MFA in Painting, U. Ill., 1968, MA in Art Edn., 1972. cert. tchr. K-12, Ill., Minn. Graphic artist Barry Martin Studio, Rumson, NJ, 1963-65; instr. painting, drawing U. YMCA, Champaign, Ill., 1968-72; teaching asst. U. Ill., Urbana, 1968-72, rsch. assoc., 1972-76; instr. art Champaign High Sch., 1973-75, Urbana High Sch., 1976-80, Concordia Acad., St. Paul, 1982-84, U. Minn., Mpls., 1984-87, design, housing and apparel artist in residence St. Paul, 1984-88; craft cons. and educator tech. asstance program USAID, OAS, U. Minn., Kingston, Jamaica, 1986—. Design cons. J.A.M. Corp., Mpls., 1988—; tech. cons. OAS, Kingston, 1990-91, Blandin Found. grantee, Minn., 1989—; rsch. and product devel. agrl. unilization rsch. inst., 1992-95; tech. cons. Zabbaleen Paper Project, Assn. for the Protection of the Environment, Cairo, 1993—, St. Lucia Paper project Weyerhauser Found., 1994—, paper project YMCA, Jamaica, W.I., 1997—; co-curator Paper Trivia and Treasure exhibit Goldstein Mus. Design/U. Minn., St. Paul, 2000; guest lectr. Chonbuk Nat. U. S. Korea, 2005, 06; invited artist Oesterreiches Papiernagier Mus. Austria, 2006; guest lectr. Chonbok Nat. U., 2006. Works have appeared in more than 35 solo shows, 1960—, more than 80 invitational shows nationally and internationally, 1985—; work chosen for inclusion 1996 Internat. Calendar Papierfabak Schfufelen Lenningen, Germany; work chosen for poster paper exhibit Leopold-Hoesch Mus., Doren, Germany, 1999; traveling exhibit, Bavaria, Germany, Geneva; work chosen for exhibit Mus. Santa Maria Della Scala, Siena, Italy, 2003, Augsburg Coll. Mpls., 2003, Hist. Mus. Jeongju, South Korea, 2004; invited guest profl. designer Fashion Fair, Joenju, Korea, 2006; represented in permanent collections Imadate, Fukui, Japan, U. Ill., Weisman Art Mus., U. Minn., So. Cross U., NSW, Australia, Montclair (N.J.) Art Mus., Am. U, Cairo, Sori Arts Ctr., Jeonju, Mus. Louvre It or Leavie It, Mpls., others; co-author: Selected Papers, 1994, Handcrafted paper and Paper Products Made from Indigenous Plant Fibers, 1997; contbr. articles to profl. jours, columns to newspaper Vestry mem. St. John's Episcopal Ch., Champaign, 1975-78, St. Matthew's Episcopal Ch., St. Paul, 1989—. Recipient Celebrity award, Minn. State Fair, 1984, book First award, 1986, Honorable mention, 3d On/Off Paper Nat., Wis., 1984, 1st prize cmty. fine art exhibit, St. Paul, Minn., 2002, 2003; grantee, Blandin Found., U. Minn., 1989—90, OAS, 1990—91, Agrl. Utilization Rsch. Inst., 1992—95, Weyerhauser Found., 1997, Minn. Arts Bd., 1999. Mem.: Internat. Assn. Hand Papermakers and Paper Artists (pres. 2003—05), Nat. League Am. Penwomen (state v.p. 1994—96, Minn. art chair 2002—), Friends of Dard Hunter Paper Mus. (com. chair 1990—95, adv. bd. 2001—). Episcopalian. Avocations: swimming, cooking, theater, travel.

ALEXANDER, NANCY A., information technology manager, consultant; b. Kansas City, Kans., Mar. 31, 1957; d. Carl Glenn and Norma Louise Hanks; m. Steven Dale Alexander, May 20, 1981; 1 child, Anne Louise. AS in Computer Info. Systems summa cum laude, Kansas City C.C., 1989; BS in Computer Info. Systems with highest honors, Friends U., Wichita, Kans., 1999, MS in Mgmt. Info. Systems, 2001. Sec., a/c schedule control Trans World Airlines, Inc., Kansas City, Mo., 1976—79, coord. scheduling and planning group, 1979—80, planner, facilities and equipment engring., 1980—81, master planner, facilities and equipment programs, 1981—82, mgr., facilities and equipment programs, 1982—83; office mgr., info. tech. dir. Steven D. Alexander, Chtd., Overland Park, Kans., 1983—2004. Faculty adv. bd. Kansas City (Kans.) C.C., 1988—90; cons. Profl. Support, Inc., Shawnee, Kans., 1983—; real estate investor, 1978—; real estate agent, cons., 2002—. Software developer Legal Billing and Analysis System, 1989; author: Think of Your Future, 1992. Troop leader Girl Scouts Am., Shawnee, 1988—92; county coun. rep., project leader 4-H, Olathe, Kans., 1994—97, judge, 1995—97; youth group leader Master's Cmty. Ch., Kansas City, Kans., 1999—2001. Avocations: travel, racquetball, swimming, painting.

ALEXANDER, ROBERTA SUE, history professor; b. N.Y.C., Mar. 19, 1943; d. Bernard Milton and Dorothy (Linn) Cohn; m. John Kurt Alexander, 1964 (div. Sept. 1972); m. Ronald Burett Fost, May 7, 1977. BA, UCLA, 1964; MA, U. Chgo., 1966, PhD, 1974; JD, U. Dayton, 2000. Instr. Roosevelt U., Chgo., 1967-68; prof. U. Dayton, Ohio, 1969—. Author: North Carolina

Faces the Freedman: Race Relations During Presidential Reconstruction, 1985; mem. editl. bd. Cin. Hist. Soc., 1973—; contbr. chpt. to book and articles to law revs. Recipient summer stipend NEH, Washington, 1975, Tchg. Excellence and Campus Leadership award Sears-Roebuck Found, 1990, Tchg. Excellence in History award Ohio Acad. History, 1991, Michael and Elissa Cohen Writing award, 1999; fellow in residence NEH, 1976-77, fellow Inst. for Legal Studies, NEH, 1982, summer rsch. fellow U. Dayton, 1972, 74, 76, 80. Mem. Am. Hist. Assn., Orgn. Am. Historians, Am. Soc. Legal History, Midwest Assn. Prelaw Advisors (pres.), So. Hist. Soc., Mortar Bd., Am. Contract Bridge Assn. (life master 1983), Phi Beta Kappa, Phi Alpha Theta. Avocations: bridge, golf. Office: U Dayton Dept History Dayton OH 45469-0310 Home: 701 Ocean Club Pl Fernandina Beach FL 32034-6565 Fax: (937) 229-4298. E-mail: roberta.alexander@notes.udayton.edu.

ALEXANDER, SHIRLEY BIRDSALL, retired librarian; b. Wichita Falls, Tex., Nov. 16, 1932; d. Gilbert Alton Birdsall and Nova D. Graham; m. Cecil B. Alexander (dec.). BA, Harding Coll., Searcy, Ark., 1954; MS in Libr. Sci., La. State U., Baton Rouge, 1959. Secondary tchr. Great Lakes Christian Coll., Beamsville, Ont., Canada, 1955—57; ref. libr. La. State U. Law Libr., Baton Rouge, 1959—62; libr. dir. Harding Coll. Libr., Searcy, Ark., 1962—75; documents libr. Oakland U., Rochester, Mich., 1978—79; cataloger, libr. dir. Mich. Christian Coll., Rochester, 1980—86; cataloger, documents libr. Abilene Christian U., Abilene, Tex., 1986—94; ret., 1994. Mem.: ALA. Ch. Of Christ. Avocations: reading, travel, genealogy. Home: 909 Mnciples way Abilene TX 79602

ALEXANDER, SILVESTA, elementary school educator; b. Sulphur Springs, Tex., June 27, 1948; d. Dexter and Emma Jewel Clayton; m. Clyde Ray Alexander, July 18, 1970; children: Marlon, Ashanta, Keiston. BSc, East Tex. State U., Commerce, 1970, MSc, 1974; V.E.H. (hon.), Tex. Tech. U., Lubbock, 1977. Tchr. sci. and math. grade 5 Douglas Intermediate Sch., Sulphur Springs, Tex., 1998—. Tchr. Tex. State Tchr. Assn., Sulphur Springs. Mem. NAACP, Sulphur Springs, 2000—. Named Elem. Tchr. of Yr., Sulphur Springs, 1996—97, Most Influential African American, Sulphur Springs, Tex., 2006; recipient World Greatest Tchr. award, Class of 1979, Dr. Martin Luther King award, East Caney Bapt. Ch., Sulphur Springs, 2001. Office: Douglas Intermediate Sch 600 Calvert St Sulphur Springs TX 75482-3236

ALEXANDER, SUE, writer; b. 1933; Student, Drake U., Des Moines, Iowa, 1950—52, Northwestern U., Evanston, Ill., 1952—53. Writer. Author: Small Plays for You and a Friend, 1973, Nadir of the Streets, 1975, Peacocks Are Very Special, 1976, Witch, Goblin and Sometimes Ghost, 1976, Small Plays for Special Days, 1977, Marc the Magnificent, 1978, More Witch, Goblin and Ghost Stories, 1978, Seymour the Prince, 1979, Finding Your First Job, 1980, Whatever Happened to Uncle Albert? and Other Puzzling Plays, 1980, Witch, Goblin and Ghost in the Haunted Woods, 1981, Witch, Goblin and Ghost's Book of Things to Do, 1982, Nadia the Willful, 1983, Dear Phoebe, 1984, World Famous Muriel, 1984, Witch, Goblin and Ghost Are Back, 1985, World Famous Muriel and the Scary Dragon, 1985, Lila on the Landing, 1987, There's More-Much More, 1987, America's Own Holidays, 1988, World Famous Muriel and the Magic Mystery, 1990, Who Goes Out on Halloween?, 1990, Sara's City, 1995, What's Wrong Now, Millicent?, 1996, One More Time, Mama, 1999, Behold the Trees, 2001. Home and Office: 6846 McLaren Ave Canoga Park CA 91307-2525 E-mail: sue-a@sbcglobal.net.

ALEXANDER, VERA, dean, marine science educator; b. Budapest, Hungary, Oct. 26, 1932; came to U.S., 1950; d. Paul and Irene Alexander; div.; children: Graham Alexander Dugdale, Elizabeth Alexander. BA in Zoology, U. Wis., 1955, MS in Zoology, 1962; PhD in Marine Sci., U. Alaska, 1965; LLD, Hokkaido U., Japan, 1999. From asst. prof. to assoc. prof. marine sci. U. Alaska, Fairbanks, 1965-74, prof., 1974—, dean Coll. Environ. Scis., 1977-78, 80-81, dir. Inst. Marine Sci., 1979-93, acting dean Sch. Fisheries and Ocean Scis., 1987-89, dean, 1989—2004; asst. to provost Fisheries and Oceans Policy, 2004—. Mem. adv. com. to ocean scis. divsn. NSF, 1980-84, chmn. adv. com., 1983-84; mem. com. to evaluate outer continental shelf environ. assessment program Minerals Mgmt. Svc., Bd. Environ. Sci. and Tech. NRC, 1987-91, mem. com. on geophys. and environ. Data, 1993-98; mem. adv. com. Office Health and Environ. Rsch., U.S. Dept. Energy, Washington, 1987-90; vice chmn. Arctic Ocean Scis. Bd., 1988-89; commr. U.S. Marine Mammal Commn., 1995—; U.S. del. North Pacific Marine Sci. Orgn., 1991-2002, vice-chmn., 1999-2002, chmn., 2002—; bd. dirs. Western Regional Aquaculture Ctr.; mem. sci. adv. bd. NOAA, 1998-2004; mem. ocean rsch. adv. panel Nat. Oceans Leadership Coun., 1998-2002; mem. internat. steering com. Census of Marine Life, 1999—; mem. Pres.'s Panel on Ocean Exploration, 2000; pres. Arctic Rsch. Consortium U.S., 2003-; chmn. Internat. Com. Sigma Xi, 2004-. Editor: Marine Biological Systems of the Far North (W.L. Rey), 1989. Sec. Fairbanks Light Opera Theatre Bd., 1987-88; chair Rhodes Scholar Selection Com., Alaska, 1986-95; pres. Arctic Rsch. Consortium U.S., 2003—. Research grantee U. Alaska. Fellow AAAS, Arctic Inst. N.Am., Explorers Club (sec., treas. Alaska/Yukon chpt. 1987-89, 91-99, pres. 1990-91); mem. Am. Soc. Limnology and Oceanography, Am. Geophys. Union, Oceanography Soc., Am. Fisheries Soc., Nature Conservancy of Alaska (bd. dirs.), Rotary (pres. 1999-2000). Avocations: classical piano, horsemanship. Home: 3875 Geist Rd Ste E Fairbanks AK 99709 Office: U Alaska PO Box 707220 Fairbanks AK 99775 Office Phone: 907-474-5071. Business E-Mail: vera@sfos.uaf.edu.

ALEXANDER, VICKIE LYNN, music educator; b. Clovis, N.Mex., Sept. 21, 1953; d. Roy N. and Mary Inez Anderson; m. James Lee Alexander, Sept. 22, 1972. BS, Tex. Woman's U., Denton, Tex., 1991, MEd, 1998. Cert. elem. tchr. Tex., elem. music tchr. Tex., all level music tchr. Tex., early childhood edn. Tex., elem. reading tchr. Tex. Music tchr. Sanger Ind. Sch. Dist., Tex., 1993—. Recipient Superior Ratings, Nat. Piano Tchrs. Guild. Home: PO Box 595 Sanger TX 76266

ALEXANDER-CLARKE, MARSIA, artist; b. Valparaiso, Chile, June 30, 1939; d. Addison Miller Alexander and Solena Rose Detrich; m. Oscar Franklin Clarke, May 4, 1996. BA, Pk. Coll., 1962; MFA, Claremont U., 1974. Nominee AVA award, Southeastern Ctr. for Contemporary Art, 1981; Artist Residency scholar, McDowell Colony, Petersberg, NH, 1974, Individual artist grantee, City of Pasadena Cultural Affairs, 2001. Home: 266 Frost Ct Riverside CA 92507 Personal E-mail: marsiaa@charter.net.

ALEXANDRA, ALLISON MELISSA, artist, writer, educator; BA with honors, U. Calif.-Berkeley, 1987; student, Acad. Art U., 2005—. Cert. acupressure practitioner Acupressure Inst., 1996, hypnotherapist Inner Quest Awareness Ctr., 1996. Graphic asst. LA Parent Mag., 1988, East Bay Express, Oakland, Calif., 1988; art tchr. for emotionally challenged teens Berkeley Acad., Calif., 1990; freelance graphic artist Berkeley, 1995—96, Oakland, 1995—96; instr. Kaplan Ednl. Ctrs., El Paso, Tex., 1998—99; counselor Life Healing Ctr., Sante Fe, 2000; art tchr., asst. mgr. Santa Fe Children's Mus., 2000—01; freelance illustrator, designer, writer Tuscon, Ariz., 2004—. Freelance graphic artist. Exhibitions include Annual Cmty. Art Exhibit, Oakland, 1994—95, Las Cruces, 1999, one-woman shows include Oakland, 1996, exhibited in group shows at Artists So. N.Mex., Las Cruces, 1998, We. Nat. Parks Assn. Bldg., Tuscon, Ariz., 2004, Joel D. Valdez Main Pub. Libr., Tucson, Ariz., 2004, Rose Portrait, 1996, digital illustration, Reflections, 2003; contbr. illustrations to Sierra Club Canyon Echo; editor: Mandana Newsletter, 1996. Vol. tutor San Fernando Valley Child Guidance Clinic, Northridge, Calif., 1982—83; vol. art/natural sci. floors Oakland Mus., 1998; vol. graphic designer Santa Fe (N.Mex.) Vipassan Sangha, 2000, Our Town, Tuscon, 2003; vol. Santa Fe Children's Mus., 2000—01. Co-recipient Courtyard Design Illustration award, Southwestern Grad. Coll., 1996. Mem.: Soc. Illustrators, Graphic Artists Guild, Soc. Children's Books, Writers & Illustrators, Phi Theta Kappa. Avocations: cooking, music, hiking, travel. Mailing: PO Box 30912 Walnut Creek CA 94598 Office Phone: 925-324-9335. Home Fax: 925-932-6053. Personal E-mail: allisonalexandra@msn.com.

ALEXIADES-ARMENAKAS, MACRENE RENEE, dermatologist, scientist, researcher, educator, consultant; d. Gregory and Sophia Alexiades; m. Noel Anthony Armenakas, Oct. 26, 1996; children: Sophia Stella Armenakas, Anthony Emmanuel Armenakas. BA, Harvard U., 1989; MD, Harvard Med. Sch., 1997; PhD, Harvard U., 1997. Cert. MD, PhD, lic. medicine & surgery N.Y., 1998, medicine and surgery Conn., 2004, Greece, 2004, credentialed in medicine and surgery European Union, 2004, diplomate Am. Bd. Dermatology, 2002. Rschr. Harvard U., Cambridge, 1984—91, tutor supr., 1985—89, tchg. asst., 1990—97, doctorate rschr. Boston, 1991—97; intern medicine Lenox Hill Hosp., N.Y.C., 1997—98; Fulbright scholar U. Heraklion, Crete, Greece, 1989—90; resident dermatology NYU Sch. Medicine, N.Y.C., 1998—2000, chief resident dermatology, 2000—01; dir. rsch. & laser dermatology Laser & Skin Surgery Ctr. N.Y., 2001—03; attending physician Lenox Hill Hosp., N.Y.C., 2001—; pres., dir. dermatology & laser surgery Macrene Alexiades-Armenakas, MD, PhD, PC, 2003—; asst. clin. prof. Yale U. Sch. Medicine, 2003—; attending physician Yale/New Haven Hosp. Tutor supr. Harvard Bur. Study Coun., 1985—89; mem. MD/PhD program steering com. Harvard Med. Sch., 1993—94, mem. MD/PhD program retreat com., 1992—94, mem. minority recruitment com., 1992—95, mem. advanced biomed. scis. com., 1993—95, admissions interviewer com., 2002—. Editor: (jour.) Dermatologic Surgery, 2004—, The Harvard Polit. Rev., 1985—89; editor: (writer) The Biology Rev., 1986—89; mem. editl. bd.: The Harvard Crimson, 1985—89; author: abstracts, jour. articles, book chpts. Counselor rape crisis Response, Cambridge, 1988-89; counselor Harvard Med. Sch. peer counseling, 1990-92; yoga instr. Vanderbilt Hall Athletic Facility, Boston, 1990-92; vol. St. Francis House Soup Kitchen, 1990-94; solicitation coord. fundraising com. William Woodward Nursery Sch., 2001-02, chairperson, 2004-, bd. trustees, 2004-; mem. art com. The Chapin Sch., 2004-05, mem. Parents Assn., 2004-05. Recipient Husik prize, 2001, First Pl. award, Jour. Drugs in Dermatology Rsch. Competition, 2004; grantee, Nat. Eye Inst., 1995; scholar, Fulbright Found., 1989—90; Paul Dudley White scholar, Harvard U., 1991. Fellow: Hellenic Med. Soc.; mem.: Women's Dermatologic Soc., Am. Soc. Laser Medicine and Surgery, Dermatology Found., Am. Acad. Dermatology, Harvard Hellenic Soc. (founder), Mass. Med. Soc., Am. Soc. Dermatologic Surgery (chmn. rsch. com. 2004—, councilman edn. and rsch. com. 2004—, editor, columnist jour. 2005), Harvard Greek Club. Greek Orthodox Christian. Achievements include numerous scientific discoveries, inventions, and patents. Avocations: portraiture, sculpting, drawing, painting, skiing, yoga, photography. Office Phone: 212-570-2067. Office Fax: 212-861-7964. Business E-Mail: dralexiades@nyderm.org.

ALEXIS, GERALDINE M., lawyer; b. NYC, Nov. 3, 1948; d. William J. and Margaret Daly; m. Marcus Alexis, June 15, 1969; children: Marcus L., Hilary I., Sean C. BA, U. Rochester, 1971; MBA, JD, Northwestern U., 1976. Bar: Ill. 1976, Calif. 2001, U.S. Dist. Ct. (no. dist.) Calif. 1976, U.S. Dist. Ct. (no. dist.) Ill. 1976, U.S. Trial Bar 1985, U.S. Ct. Appeals (7th cir.) 1986, U.S. Ct. Appeals (5th cir.) 1996, U.S. Ct. Appeals (9th cir.) 2002. Law clk. to Hon. John F. Grady, justice U.S. Dist. Ct. (no. dist.) Ill., Chgo., 1976-77; assoc. Sidley & Austin, Chgo., 1977-79, 81-83, ptnr., 1983-2000; advisor U.S. Dept. Justice Office Legal Counsel, Washington, 1979-81; ptnr. McCutchen, Doyle, Brown & Enersen (now Bingham McCutchen LLP), San Francisco, 2001—. Mem.: ABA (co-chair fin. svcs. com. antitrust sect.). Democrat. Office: Bingham McCutchen LLP 3 Embarcadero Ctr San Francisco CA 94111

ALEXIS, TRACY L., project manager, project specialist, information technology manager, small business owner; b. Atlanta, Oct. 15, 1955; d. William Emanual and Hazel Harcourt Alexis; children: Karrie Crystallyn Mayes, Ryan Andrew McClelland. AA with high honors, Ga. Perimeter Coll., South Campus, 1981; BA magna cum laude, U. N.Mex, Albuquerque, 2003. Cert. Micropigmentation SofTap, Las Vegas Nev., 2005, permanent cosmetic technician SofTap, Las Vegas Nev., 2005. Exec. event coord./mgr. Global Player Events, Albuquerque, 1999—2006; strategic project mgr. Strategic & Learning Svcs., Inc., Albuquerque, 2005—. Author: Birth Announcement, 1979. Vol. Habitat for Humanity, Albuquerque, 1996—2003. Pell grantee, U. N.Mex, 2001-2003, Amigo Transfer scholar, 1999, Native scholar High Honors, Native Am. Scholarship and Rsch. Coun., 2000. Mem.: Phi Theta Kappa, Golden Key Internat., Psi Chi, Mortar Bd. Alumni (assoc.). Achievements include patents for Automatic Faucet Drip. Avocations: hiking, travel, fine dining, reading, gardening. Office: Strategic & Learning Svcs Inc 6100 Seagull Ln NE Ste B200 Albuquerque NM 87109 Office Phone: 866-827-3500. Personal E-mail: gpexecutive@att.net. Business E-Mail: talexis@slsinc.com.

ALF, MARTHA JOANNE, artist; b. Berkeley, Calif., Aug. 13, 1930; d. Foster Wise and Julia Vivian (Kane) Powell; m. Edward Franklin Alf, Mar. 17, 1951; 1 child, Richard Franklin. BA with distinction, San Diego State U., 1953, MA in Painting, 1963, jr. coll. teaching credential, 1969; MFA in Pictorial Arts, UCLA, 1970. Rsch. asst. Health and Welfare Assn., Seattle, 1956; tchg. asst. in drawing, instr. design San Diego State U., 1963; instr. drawing L.A. Valley Coll., 1970-73, El Camino Coll., Hawthorne, Calif., 1971; instr. drawing and painting L.A. Harbor Coll., Wilmington, Calif., 1971-75; instr. art UCLA Extension, 1971-79. Instr. contemporary art Brand Library Art Ctr., Glendale, Calif., 1973; vis. artist Calif. State Coll., Bakersfield, 1980; freelance art critic Artweek, Oakland, Calif., 1974-77; guest curator Lang Art Gallery, Scripps Coll., Claremont, Calif., 1974. Retrospective exhbn. Fellows Contemporary Art, LA Mcpl. Art Gallery, San Francisco Art Inst., 1984; exhibited in group shows at San Diego Mus. Art, 1964, 67-68, 70-71, 77-78, 83, Whitney Mus. Contemporary Art Biennial, 1975, Newport Harbor Art Mus., 1975, Marion Koogler McNay Art Inst., San Antonio, 1976, Long Beach Mus. Art, 1972, 82, 86, Am. Acad. Arts and Letters, NY, 1985, 96, Henry Art Gallery, U. Wash., Seattle, 1985, LA County Mus. Art, 1979, 82 (Kay Neilson award 1979), Womens Mus., Wash., 1994, Bakersfield Mus. Art, 1999, Santa Barbara Mus. Art, 2001, Calif. State U., LA, 2001, Laguna Beach Art Mus., 2001, San Jose Mus. Art, 2003-04, Pasadena Mus. Calif. Art, 2004, Contemporary Arts Ctr., New Orleans, 2004, Norton Mus. Art, West Palm Beach, Fla., 2004, Hudson River Mus., Yonkers, NY, 2004, Arcadiana Ctr. Arts, Lafayette, La., 2005, McDonough Mus. Arts, Youngstown State U., Ohio, 2005, Tucson Mus. Art, 2006; one-woman shows include John Berggruen Gallery, San Francisco, 1977, Forth Worth Art Mus., 1988, Susan Caldwell Gallery, NY, 1980, Dorothy Rosenthal Gallery, Chgo., 1982, Eloise Pickard Smith Gallery, Cowell Coll., U. Calif., Santa Cruz, 1983, Newspace Gallery, LA, 1976-85, 90-2004, Henry Gardiner Gallery, Palm Beach, 1986, Tortue Gallery, Santa Monica, 1986, Jan Baum Gallery, LA, 1988, Trabia Gallery, NY, 1990, 871 Fine Arts, San Francisco, 1991, Art Inst. So. Calif., Laguna Beach, Calif., 1991, Fresno Art Mus., 1992, Mt. San Antonio Coll., Walnut, Calif., 1993; represented in permanent collections LA County Mus. Art, Chem. Bank NY, Ga. Mus. Art., Israel Mus. Art, Jerusalem, LA County Mus. Art, McCrory Corp., NY, Metromedic Inc., LA, NY, San Diego Mus. Art, San Jose Mus., Santa Barbara Mus. Art, Southland Corp., Dallas, Spencer Mus. Art, U. Kans., Lawrence, Met. Mus. Art., NY, Phoenix Art Mus., Fresno Art Mus., Grand Rapids Art Mus., Orange County Mus. Art, Newport Beach, Calif., Palm Springs Desert Mus., Laguna Art Mus., U. Calif. Santa Barbara Art Gallery, Eli Broad Collection, Santa Monica, U. Va. Bayley Art Mus., Charlottesville. Nat. Endowment for Arts grantee, 1979, 89; recipient Richard Florsheim Art Fund award, 1996, Calif. Heritage Mus. print commn., 1998. Avocations: body building, walking, reading, bird study and videos. Home: 103 Brooks Ave Venice CA 90291-3254 Office Phone: 310-396-3031. Personal E-mail: alf1@earthlink.net.

ALFONSO, BERTA, computer engineer; b. Cuba; U.S. married; children: Victor, Sabrina. Student, Miami-Dade C.C.; BSEE, U. Miami. Design engr. NASA Kennedy Space Ctr., Fla. Office: NASA Kennedy Space Ctr Bldg K6-1200C Rm 1130 Kennedy Space Center FL 32899 Business E-Mail: alfonba@kscems.ksc.nasa.gov, berta.alfonso-1@ksc.nasa.gov.

ALFONSO-BICA, KRISTY LYNN, elementary school educator; b. Port Jefferson, NY, Jan. 6, 1979; d. Oswaldo and Patricia Alfonso; m. Giuseppe Alfonso, June 26, 2004. BA in Edn. with honors, SUNY, Geneseo, 2001; MA in Reading Edn. with honors, Dowling Coll., Oakdale, NY, 2005. Tchr. Pub. Sch. 171, Astoria, NY, 2001—02, Clayton Huey Elem. Sch., Center Moriches, NY, 2002—03, Fairview Sch., Corona, NY, 2003—. Religious educator St. Gerards Ch., Terryville, NY, 1997—2001. Recipient Gold award, Girl Scouts USA, 1997, Hon. award, United Fedn. Tchrs., 2002. Roman Catholic. Avocations: swimming, travel, horsebackriding, reading, writing. Office: PS 14 Fairview Sch 107-01 Otis Ave Corona NY Office Phone: 718 699 6071. Personal E-mail: elmo7979@aol.com.

ALFORD, CONSTANCE KEITH, recreational facility executive, artist; b. Louisville, Mar. 27, 1943; d. Jack Edwin Rogers and Constance Kennedy Moehlman; m. Prentiss Keith Alford, Sept. 4, 1965; children: Claiborne Kennedy, McKenna Caswell. AB, Randolph-Macon Woman's Coll., 1965; MA, U. Miss., Oxford, 1967, MFA, 1972. Art tchr. Clay County H.S., Green Cove Springs, Fla., 1965-66; art instr. U. Miss., Oxford, 1967-72, asst. prof. art, 1972-73; asst./assoc. prof. art Alcorn State U., Lorman, Miss., 1975-96; summer crafts counselor Camp Monterey, Tenn., 1984-95, camp dir., 1996—. Lectr. art Elizabeth Gaskell Coll., Manchester, Eng., 1972-73; bd. mem. Miss. Cultural Crossroads, Port Gibson, Miss., 1978-82, dir., cons. summer art for children, 1983-84; commn. panelist Miss. Arts Commn., Jackson, 1988; dir. Port Gibson Main St. Bd., 1991-98. Exhibited at La. World Fair Exposition, New Orleans, 1984; invitationals include Appalachian State U.-Catherine U. Smith Gallery, Boone, N.C., 1988; one-woman shows include N.E. La. U. Gallery, Monroe, 1993, MGCCC Gallery, Gautier, Miss., 2001; group shows include JCC Gallery, Ellisville, Miss., 1999, Bi-State Exhibit, Meridian, Miss., 1999, Miss. Art Colony Travelling Exhibit, 1984—, revolving art program, Miss. Gov.'s Mansion, 1989-90, others. Guest spkr. Alumnae Career Day, Randolph-Macon Woman's Coll., Lynchburg, Va., 1974; mem. Port Gibson Preservation Commn., 1992-98, chmn., 1994-98; mem. Claiborne County Preservation Commn., Port Gibson, 1992-98, v.p., 1996-98; participant, hostess Countryside Inst., Port Gibson, 1996. Recipient purchase award Peat Marwick, Jackson, 1987; Fulbright-Hays Tchr. Exch., Manchester, Eng., 1972-73. Mem. Miss. Art Colony (v.p. 1999—, bd. mem., 1st pl. 1984, Fontaine award Best in Workshop 1985, Marie Hull 1st place 1986, Top Purchase prize 1998, 1st place 1998, 2nd place 1999). Episcopalian. Avocation: collecting art. Home: 1208 Church St Port Gibson MS 39150-2610 E-mail: cm4keith@aol.com.

ALFORD, FRANCES HOLLIDAY, artist, retired special education educator; b. Houston, Tex., Oct. 1, 1945; d. Samuel and Nancy Hayes Holliday; m. John R. Alford Jr., Oct. 25, 1996. MEd, U. of Ariz., 1972. Cert. Tchr. Tex., 1980. Tchr. Tex. Pub. Schools, 1989—94. Trustee Huston-TillitsonU. Vol. U.S. Peace Corps, 1979—80; trustee The Congl. Ch. of Austin, Austin, Tex.; chair, director's cir., fund raising com. Nat. Peace Corps Assn., Washington, 2001—03; pres. Friends of Korea, Washington. Mem.: AAUW (assoc.), Coun. for Exceptional Children, Austin Area Textile Artists (assoc.), 1812 Club (assoc.). Non-Partisan. Protestant/ Congregational. Avocations: travel, art quilting, philanthrophy. Home: 8100 Hickory Creek Dr Austin TX 78735 Personal E-mail: francesholliday@aol.com.

ALFORD, RENEE MARIE, speech pathology/audiology services professional, educator; d. James, Jr. and Claudia Mae Alford, Aloysius (Stepfather) and Emily Patricia Chisley (Stepmother). BS in Speech and Lang. Pathology, U. DC, 1986, MS in Speech and Lang. Pathology, 1993. Cert. speech-lang. pathology Va., lic. speech/lang. disorders PreK-12 Va.; cert. early/primary edn. PreK-3 Va., devel. reading assessment Fairfax County Pub. Schs. Tchr. Fairfax County Pub. Schs., Alexandria, Va., 1990—, speech and lang. pathologist, 1990—2000, Chesapeake Ctr., Inc., Springfield, Va., 1998. Presenter mentoring program Fairfax County Pub. Schs., Alexandria, 2001—; presenter troops tchrs. program Old Dominion U., Ft. Belvior, Va., 2002—. Clinic team coord. Mid-Atlantic Pom and Dance Assn.; team coord. Mid Atlantic Poand Dance Assn. Named Outstanding Young Women of Am., 1988; scholar, U. DC, 1982, 1983; Dept. of Edn. Minority Tng. grantee, 1988—90. Mem.: Mid-Altantic Pomand Dance Assn. (team coord.), Am. Speech-Lang. Hearing Assn. (life cert. clin. competence in speech-lang. pathology), Nat. Allied Health Honor Soc., Delta Sigma Theta (life scholar 1984), Phi Delta Kappa (life). Avocations: dance choreography, pom pon coach. Personal E-mail: teachernva2000@aol.com.

ALFREY, MARIAN ANTOINETTE, retired education educator; b. Crab Orchard, Nebr., Dec. 5, 1925; d. Rollin Milton and Emma Antoinette (Schultz) S.; m. David Homer, Aug. 10, 1947; children: Gary David, Judith Ann. BS, U. Nebr., Lincoln, 1968; MA, U. No. Iowa, Cedar Falls, 1972. Permanent Profl. Cert. Tchr. Louisville (Nebr.) Schs., 1945-46, Tecumseh (Nebr.) Schs., 1946-47, North Loup (Nebr.) Schs., 1949-51, Malvern (Iowa) Schs., 1951-52, Beatrice Schs., 1967-68, Waterloo (Iowa) Community Schs., 1968-89. Active Waterloo Cmty. Schs., 1973-88. Mem. Covenant Hosp. Aux., 1989—, pres.; diplomat Waterloo C. of C., 1995, sec. Recipient Mayors' Vol. award, Mayors of Black Hawk County, 2000, Vol. Performance award, Cedar Valley Mayors, 2000. Mem. NEA, Nebr. Congress PTA (hon. life). Republican. Methodist. Home: 1925 Westchester Rd Apt 220 Waterloo IA 50701-4522

ALGOOD, LAURIE, performing arts educator; b. Ellwood City, Pa., Sept. 18, 1976; d. Leonard Henry Newton, Sr. and Mary Louise Newton; m. Michael Donovan Algood, Aug. 16, 2003. BA, Pa. State U., State College, 1998; postgrad., Am. U., Washington, 2001—03. Prof. dance Montgomery Coll., Rockville, Md., 2002—; tchr. dance Mus. Theater Ctr., Rockville, Md., 2002—. Choreographer Montgomery Coll., Rockville, Md., 2002—, Mus. Theater Ctr., Rockville, Md., 2002—; dir., choreographer Fairfield H.S. Mus., Pa., 2004—. Dir., choreographer (dance mus.) Turning Pointes, 2002. Mem. Humane Soc. U.S., Washington, People for the Ethical Treatment of Animals, Washington. Home: 113 Valley View Ct Boonsboro MD 21713 E-mail: mikeandlaurielagood@yahoo.com.

ALI, LAYLAH, artist; b. Buffulo, NY, 1968; BA in Studio Art & English Lit., Williams Coll., 1991; attended, Whitney Mus. Ind. Study Program, NY, 1991—92, Skowhegan Sch. Painting & Sculpture, Maine, 1993; MFA in Painting, Washington U., 1994. One-woman shows include, 303 Gallery, NY, 2005, Mus. Contemporary Art, Chgo., Inst. Contemporary Art, Boston, Albright-Knox Art Gallery, Buffalo, NY, 2003, Project 75, Mus. Modern Art, NY, 2002, Atlanta Coll. Art Gallery, Ga., 2002, Indpls. Mus. Art, Iowa, 2002, Inst. Contemporary Art, Boston, 2001, Yerba Buena Ctr. Arts, San Francisco, 2001, 303 Gallery, NY, 2000, MassMOCA, North Adams, Mass., 2000, Mus. Contemporary Art, Chgo., 1999, Miller Block Gallery, Boston, 1998, Hallwalls Contemporary Arts Ctr., Buffalo, NY, 1994, exhibited in group shows at The 10 Commandments, KW Inst. Contemporary Art, Berlin, 2004, Whitney Biennial Am. Art, Whitney Mus. Am. Art, NY, 2004, Material Witness, Mus. Contemporary Art, Cleve., 2004, Crosscurrents at Century's End, Henry Art Gallery, Seattle, 2003, me and more, Kunstmusuem Lucerne, Switzerland, 2003, Fault Lines: Contemporary African Art & Shifting Landscapes, Venice Biennale, Italy, 2003, Splat, Boom, Pow, Contemporary Art Mus., Houston, Tex., 2003, Comic Release: Negotiating Identity for a New Generation, Carnegie Mellon U., Pitts., 2002, Fantasyland, D'Amelio Terras, NY, 2002, Painting in Boston, DeCordova Mus. & Sculpture Park, Mass., 2002, First Person Singular, Seattle Art Mus., 2002, Against the Wall: Painting against the Grid, Surface, Frame, U. Pa., 2001, A Work in Progress, New Mus., NY, 2001, Premio Regione Piemonte, Palazzo Re Rebaudengo, Italy, 2001, Freestyle, Studio Mus. Harlem, NY, 2001, FRESH: The Altoids Curiously Strong Collection 1998 - 2000, New Mus., NY, 2001, Art on Paper, Weatherspoon Art Gallery, U. NC, 2000, Bizzarro World, Cornell Fine Arts Mus., Fla., 1999, The 1999 DeCordova Ann. Exhbn., Decordova Mus. & Sculpture Park, Mass., 1999, Collectors Collect Contemporary, Inst. Contemporary Art, Boston, 1999, No Place Rather than Here, 303 Gallery, NY, 1999, Selections Summer '98, Drawing Ctr., NY, 1998, Posing, Boston Ctr. Arts, 1998, Paradise 8, Exit Art, NY, 1998, Telling Tales, Atrium Gallery, U. Conn., 1998. Mailing: c/o 303 Gallery 525 West 22nd St New York NY 10011

ALI, SANDRA, announcer; b. Queens, N.Y. Grad. cum laude, Syracuse U.; M in Journalism, Northwestern U. Weekend anchor, reporter WTAJ-TV 10, Altoona, Pa.; anchor 6pm and 10pm WJBK Fox 2, Detroit, 2000—. Avocations: attending plays, reading. Office: WJBK Fox 2 PO Box 2000 Southfield MI 48037-2000

ALIANO, JOY CARYL, retired elementary school educator; b. N.Y.C., Mar. 13, 1944; d. Irving and Iris (Plavnick) Cofsky; m. John Anthony Aliano, Aug. 20, 1966; children: Catherine, Kelly. BS, CCNY, 1964; MA, NYU, N.Y.C., 1969. Cert. elem., reading tchr. N.Y. Salesperson Macy's, N.Y.C., 1960—61; proof reader, editor Plenum Pub., N.Y.C., 1964—66; tchr. N.Y.C. Bd. Edn., 1967—79; ret., 1979. Home: 790 Mervin Ct Baldwin NY 11510-4038

ALICEA, YVETTE, special education educator; b. Bronx, Aug. 27, 1962; d. Gregorio and Lucia Alicea; m. Leontitsis Eleftherios, Sept. 19, 1997. BA in Modern Langs., U. P.R., 1987; MS in Spl. Edn., CUNY, 1995. Cert. tchr. N.Y. Tchr. English José de Choudens, Arroyo, PR, 1983—84; tchr., asst. prin. St. Patrick's Bilingual Sch., Guayama, 1987—91; tchr. bilingual spl. edn. P.S. 26, N.Y.C. Bd. Edn., 1991—95; tchr. English Betsis Lang. Sch., Athens, Greece, 1996—99; tchr. spl. edn. P.S./M.S. 306, N.Y.C. Bd. Edn., 1999—2000, P.S. 46, N.Y. C. Bd. Edn., 2000—. Recipient Appreciation plaque, Parents Assn. of P.S. 26, Bronx, 1995. Avocations: reading, literature, movies. Home: 163 Timberwood Trail Chelsea AL 35043-9791

ALICUDO, LYNDA, management consultant; Mng. dir. Alicudo & Assoc., Herndon, Va. Bd. mem. Angels Network, Fairfax Area Christian Emergency Transition Services. Recipient Lifetime Achievement award, Heroine in Tech., Women in Tech., March of Dimes, 2005. Office: Alicudo & Assoc Ste 500 2325 Dulles Corner Blvd Herndon VA 20171*

ALIGA, OLIVIA R., music educator, choral director; b. Manila, Philippines, Sept. 8, 1951; d. Fernando Bellapaz Rocha and Thelma Reyes Rocha; m. Norman Asis Aliga, Apr. 24, 1976; children: Norman Vincent, Ferdinand Alphonse, Chester. AM in Music, Pilar Coll., Zamboanga City, Philippines; B of Music, U. Philippines, 1974, postgrad., Vandercook Coll. Music, Chgo. Cert. in Kindermusik. Mem. faculty Vallejo (Calif.) Conservatory of Music, 1982-83; music tchr. New Life Christian Sch., Middleton, Wis., 1983-86; choral dir. Lombard (Ill.) Chorale, 1986—. Music dir. Winfield Cmty. United Meth. Ch., 1988—, trustee, 1995—; bd. dirs. U. Philippines Club Am., Chgo., 1996—, music dir., 1999; music dir., vocal coach U. of the East Med. Chorale, Chgo., 1990-95. Pianist, performed to benefit Marklund Found., Chgo., 1997, and the U. Philippines Club Am., Chgo., 1991. Named to Filipino Am. Chicago Hall of Fame, 1999. Mem. Ill. Music Assn., Ill. State Music Tchrs. Assn., Ill. Philippine Med. Soc. Aux., Philippine Med. Assn. Chgo. Aux., U. PHilippines Club Am. (pres. 2003). Methodist. Avocations: raising orchids, flower arrangements, collecting stamps and coins.

ALIGARBES, SANDRA LYNNE, nurse; b. Pitts., Oct. 13, 1960; d. Ronald Dean and June Irene (Cooper) Cummings; m. Luwil Hobar Aligarbes, July 21, 1989. BA in Anthropology, Coll. William & Mary, 1984; MEd, Utah State U., 1993; ADN in Nursing, San Juan Coll., Farmington, N.Mex., 2005. Cert. tchr. N.Mex.; RN. Tchr. spl. edn. Cache County Schs., Providence, Utah, 1988, Aztec (N.Mex.) Mcpl. Schs., Aztec, N.Mex., 1988—89, Bloomfield (N.Mex.) Mcpl. Schs., 1989—91, Hawaii Unified Schs., Waipahu, 1991, Bloomfield (N.Mex.) Mcpl. Schs., 1991—92, 1994—98, Aztec (N.Mex.) Mcpl. Schs., Aztec, N.Mex., 1992—2005, San Juan Regional Med. Ctr., Farmington, N.Mex., 2005—. Cons. in field. Named Vol. of Yr. Assn. Retarded Citizens, 1982. Mem. ANA, Coun. Exceptional Children, Assn. Persons with Severe Handicaps. Avocations: needlecrafts, travel, reading.

ALINDER, MARY STREET, writer, educator; b. Bowling Green, Ohio, Sept. 23, 1946; d. Scott Winfield and McDonna Street; m. James Gilbert Alinder, Dec. 17, 1965; children: Jasmine, Jesse, Zachary. Student, U. Mich., 1964-65, U. N.Mex., 1966-68; BA, U. Nebr., 1976. Mgr. The Weston Gallery, Carmel, Calif., 1978-79; chief asst. Ansel Adams, Carmel, 1979-84; exec. editor, bus. mgr. The Ansel Adams Pub. Rights Trust, Carmel, 1984-87; freelance writer, lectr., curator, Gualala, Calif., 1989—; selector and writer biographies Focal Press Ency., 3d edit., 1993; ptnr. The Alinder Gallery, Gualala, 1990—; cultural expert U.S. State Dept., Guadalajara, Mexico, 2003. Curator Ansel Adams Centenial Celebration, 2002, Ansel Adams: 80th Birthday Retrospective, Friends of Photography, Carmel, Acad. Sci., San Francisco, Denver Mus. Natural History, Ansel Adams and the West, Calif. State Capitol, Sacto., 2001; co-curator One With Beauty, M.H. deYoung Meml. Mus., 1987, Ansel Adams: American Artist, The Ansel Adams Ctr., San Francisco; lectr. Nat. Gallery Art, Barbican Ctr., M.H. deYoung Meml. Mus., Stanford U., LA County Mus., U. Mich.; vis. artist and lectr. Nebr. Art Assn., 1997; Wallace Stegner meml. lectr. Peninsula Open Space Inst., Mountainview, Calif., 1998, Assn. Internat. Photographic Art Dealers, NYC, 1999, Cin. Art Mus., 2000, Eiteljorg Mus., Indpls., 2001, Internat. Wildlife Mus., Jackson Hole, 2003, Telluride Mountain Film Festival, Nev. Mus. Art, Reno, 2004, U. Tex., Austin, 2005, Manzanar Hist. Monument, 2006; Sierra Club Golden Keynote spkr.; faculty Stanford U., 2000. Author: Picturing Yosemite (Places), 1990, The Limits of Reality: Ansel Adams and Group f/64 (Seeing Straight), 1992, Ansel Adams, A Biography (Henry Holt), 1996, Mabel Dodge Luhan, 1997 (ViewCamera), Ansel Adams: Milestone, 2002; (with others) the Scribner Encyclopedia of American Lives, 1998; co-author: Ansel Adams: An Autobiography, 1985; co-editor: Ansel Adams: Letters and Images, 1988; columnist Coast and Valley Mag., 1993-98, Ansel Adams: Political Landscape, Focal Ency. Photography, 1993; political landscape (Civilization), 1999; contbr. articles to profl. jours., popular mags. Business E-Mail: alinders@mcn.org.

ALIOTO, ANGELA MIA, lawyer; b. San Francisco, Oct. 20, 1949; m. Adolfo Veronese (dec. Sept. 1990); children: Angela Veronese, Adolfo Veronese, Joseph Veronese, Gian-Paolo Veronese. BA, Lone Mountain Coll., 1971; JD, U. San Francisco, 1983. Lawyer Alioto and Alioto, San Francisco, 1980—; mem. bd. supr. City and County of San Francisco, 1989—97, pres. bd. supr., 1993—95. Candidate for mayor City of San Francisco, 1991, 2003; first vice-chair Calif. State Dem. Party, 1991—93; co-chair Calif. del. Dem. Nat. Conv., 1992; mem. Golden Gate Bridge Dist., Outer-Continental Shelf Bd. Control; vice-chair San Francisco County Transp. Authority; mem. San Francisco Mental Health Bd. Author: Straight to the Heart. Chair bd. dir. Nat. Shrine St. Francis Assisi. Mem.: Soc. Profl. Journalists, Am. Trial Lawyers Assn., Bar Assn. San Francisco, NAACP (life), Dante Soc. Am. Democrat. Roman Catholic. Office: Alioto & Alioto 700 Montgomery St San Francisco CA 94111

ALISON, ALLISON MERKLE, secondary school educator, lawyer; BA, Radford U., Va., 1984; JD, Pepperdine U., Malibu, Calif., 1987; MEd, Marymount U., Va. Bar: Calif. 1987, DC, Va.; cert. tchr. Va. Tchr. advance placement US history Stone Bridge H.S., Ashburn, Va., 2004—. Vol. Leadership in Law Camp, Leesburg, Va. Mem.: NEA (corr.). Office: Stone Bridge HS 43100 Hay Rd Ashburn VA 20147 Office Phone: 703-779-8900.

ALITO, MARTHA-ANN B., librarian; b. Ft. Knox, July 31, 1953; d. Bobby Gene and Barbara-Ann (Auwaerter) Bomgardner; m. Samuel A. Alito, Feb. 1985; 1 child, Philip Samuel. Student, Rutgers U., France, 1973-74; BA, U. Ky., 1975, MSL.S., 1977. Research asst. Info. for Bus., N.Y.C., 1977; reference librarian Neptune Pub. Library, N.J., 1977-79; librarian U.S. Atty. for Dist. N.J., Newark, 1979-82; head reference Main Library, Dept. Justice, Washington, 1982-83; library dir. Congl. Quar., Washington, 1983-87. Mem. Am. Assn. Law Librarians, Law Librarians Soc. Washington, Law Library Assn. Greater N.Y. Home: 14 Seymour St Caldwell NJ 07006-6111

ALKON, ELLEN SKILLEN, physician; b. LA, Apr. 10, 1936; d. Emil Bogen and Jane (Skillen) Rost; m. Paul Kent Alkon, Aug. 30, 1957; children: Katherine Ellen, Cynthia Jane, Margaret Elaine. BA, Stanford U., 1955; MD, U. Chgo., 1961; MPH, U. Calif., Berkeley, 1968. Diplomate Nat. Bd. Med. Examiners, Am. Bd. Pediat., Am. Bd. Preventive Medicine in Pub. Health. Chief sch. health Anne Arundel County Health Dept., Annapolis, Md., 1970-71; practice medicine specializing in pediat. Mpls. Health Dept., 1971-73, dir. MCH, 1973-75, commr. health, 1975-80; chief preventive and pub. health Coastal Region of Los Angeles County Dept. Health Svcs., 1980-81; chief pub. health West Area Los Angeles County Dept. Health Svcs., 1981-85; acting med. dir. pub. health Los Angeles County Dept. Health, 1986-87, med. dir. pub. health, 1987-93; med. dir. Coastal Cluster Health Ctrs. L.A. County Dept. Pub. Health Svcs., 1993-96, CEO, 1996-98, med. dir., 1998-2000; dir. Pub. Health Edn. in Medicine, 2000—. Adj. prof. UCLA Sch. Pub. Health, 1981—; adminstr. vis. nurses svc., Mpls., 1975-80. Fellow Am. Coll. Preventive Medicine, Am. Acad. Pediat.; mem. So. Calif. Pub. Health Assn. (pres. 1985-86, 04), Minn. Pub. Health Assn. (pres. 1978-79), Am. Pub. Health Assn., Calif. Conf. Local Health Officers (pres. 1990-91), Calif. Ctr. for Pub. Health Advocacy (pres. 2002-03), Calif. Acad. Preventive Medicine (pres. 1988-92, 2003-05), Delta Omega. Office: Los Angeles County DHS 241 N Figueroa St Rm 151 Los Angeles CA 90012 Office Phone: 213-250-8623. Business E-Mail: ealkon@ladhs.org.

ALLAM, HANNAH, journalist; b. 1978; Grad., U. Okla., 1999. Reporter St. Paul Pioneer Press, Minn., 1999—2003; bur. chief Knight Ridder, Baghdad, Iraq, 2003—05, Cairo, 2006—. Co-recipient Hal Boyle award, Overseas Press Club, 2006; recipient Journalist of Yr. award, Nat. Assn. Black Journalists, 2004, Journalism Excellence award, Knight Ridder, 2004. Office: Knight Ridder Washington Bur Ste 1000 700 12th St NW Washington DC 20005-3994 Office Phone: 202-383-6000. E-mail: hallam@krwashington.com.*

ALLAMAN, KATHRYN ANN, vice principal, mathematician; b. Sacramento, Calif., May 17, 1957; d. Clifford and Mildred Rowe; m. Marc Allaman; children: Ryan, Megan Philipps. BA in Math., Calif. State U., Sacramento, 1980, MA in Math. Edn., 1995. Cert. tchr. Calif., adminstrn. Calif. With Loretto HS, Sacramento, 1979—84, Center HS, Antelope, Calif., 1990—2005, Folsom HS, Calif., 2005—. Panel mem. SETRC (engrng. consortium), Sacramento, 2000—; adminstrv. rep. Design & Restructuring Team, Folsom, 2005—. Named County Tchr. of Yr., 2002. Mem.: ASCD, NCTM, Alpha Phi Sorority Alumni Assn. Avocations: tennis, travel. Office: Folsom HS 1655 Iron Pt Rd Folsom CA 95630 Business E-Mail: kallaman@fcusd.k12.ca.us.

ALLAMON, KAREN HENN, minister; b. Jackson, Mich., Aug. 1, 1958; d. Richard Leonard and Lujean Lirones Henn; m. Randall M. Allamon, Nov. 26, 1983; children: Matthew B., Lucas A. BFA, Webster U., 1992; MDiv, Princeton Theol. Sem., 1994—96, post grad, 2002—. Crisis Counselor Life Crisis Services - St. Louis, 1992. Pastor Barre Ctr. Presbyn. Ch., Albion, NY, 1996—; interim spiritual care coord. Hospice of Orleans County, Albion, NY, 1998—99; critical incident stress debriefer COVA, Albion, NY, 1998—; instr., worship, sacraments, preaching Presbytery of Genesse Valley, Rochester, NY, 2001—04. Presbyn. worship coord. Presbyn. of Genessee Valley, Rochester, NY, 2001—04. Cmty. leadership participant Albion Sch. Sys., NY, 1996—; mem. Ministirial Alliance, Albion, NY, 1996—; Legacy of Love endowment com. ARC of Orleans County, Albion, 2003—05; with Rural Opportunities Bd., 2005—. Recipient One of the Fastest Growing Congregations in the US: US Congl. Study, Eli Lilly Found., 2002, Excellence in Evangelism, Synod of the NE, Presbyn. Ch. (USA), 1998—99, Preaching prize, Princeton Theol. Sem., 1996, Bibl. Theology; Hebrew, Eden Theol. Sem., 1994; Synod Mission Partnership Grant: Leadership Devel., Synod of the NE, 2003. Mem.: Albion Area Ministirium (treas. 2002, v.p. 2003). Achievements include development of family systems leadership group for pastors. Office: Barre Center Presbyterian Church 4706 Oak Orchard Albion NY 14411 Personal E-mail: pastorkaren96@yahoo.com.

ALLAMONG, BETTY DAVIS, retired academic administrator; b. Morgantown, W.Va., Apr. 8, 1935; d. Lonnie R. and Jessie R. (Hoffman) Davis; m. Joseph K. Allamong, Sept. 12, 1954; 1 child, John Bradley. BS, W.Va. U., Morgantown, 1961, MA, 1964, PhD, 1971; student Inst. Ednl. Mgmt. program, Harvard U., Cambridge, Mass., 1984. Instr. biology Morgantown HS, 1961-67; instr. edn. W.Va. U., Morgantown, 1965-67, instr. biology, 1967-72; from asst. prof. to prof. Ball State U., Muncie, Ind., 1972-87, assoc. dean scis. and humanities, 1981-86, dean scis. and humanities, 1986-87; provost, v.p. acad. affairs Bloomsburg U., Pa., 1987-92; ret., 1992. Mem. Ind. Corp. Sci. & Tech., 1983—87. Co-author: Energy for Life, 1976; author: numerous lab. manuals; contbr. articles to profl. jours. Recipient Women of Achievement Edn. award, Women in Comm. Inc., 1981. Fellow: Ind. Acad. Sci. Home: 253 Pixler Hill Rd Morgantown WV 26508-9541

ALLAN, SUSAN, public health service officer; BA, Seattle Univ.; MD, JD, Harvard Univ.; MPH, Johns Hopkins Univ. Cert. Am. Bd. Preventive Medicine. Public health physician & med. supr. Arlington County Dept. Human Svc., Va., dir. public health svc. Va., 1987—2004; public health dir. Oreg. Dept. Human Svcs., Portland, 2004—. Fellow: Am. Coll. Preventive Medicine. Office: Public Health Dir 800 NE Oregon St Portland OR 97232

ALLARD, JUDITH LOUISE, secondary school educator; b. Rutland, Vt., Feb. 21, 1945; d. William Edward and Orilla Marion (Trombley) A. BA, U. Vt., 1967, MS, 1969. Nat. bd. cert. tchr. in adolescent and young adulthood sci., 1999. Tchr. math., sci. Edmunds Jr. H.S., Burlington, Vt., 1969-73, biology tchr., 1973-78, sci. dept. chair, 1975-78; biology tchr. Burlington (Vt.) H.S., 1978—2001, lead sci. tchr., 2001—05. Bd. dirs. Vt. Creative Imagination, Inc.; instr. U. Vt., Burlington, 1988-89, lectr., 2002—, St. Michaels Coll., Winooski, Vt., 2001-02; adviser Nat. Honor Soc., 1986—; mentor No. New Eng. Comentoring Network, 2002—05; leader Vt. Profl. Devel. Network, 2004—. Co-author Favorite Labs of Outstanding Tchrs., 1991. Active Amnesty Internat., 1985—; mem. Lake Champlain Com., Burlington, 1987—, Vt. Goals 2000 Panel, 1995—99, Vt. State Licensing Commn., 1995—96, Vt. Stds. Bd. for Profl. Educators, 1996—2002, co-vice chair, 2000—01, chmn., 2001—02; state bd. dirs. Odyssey of the Mind, 1986—98. Named Outstanding Vt. Educator, U. Vt., 1983, Outstanding Vt. Sci. Tchr., Sigma Xi Soc., 1984, Vt. Tchr. Yr., 1998, Outstanding Vt. Sci. Tchr., Vt. Acad. Sci. and Engring., 2000, Tandy Tech. scholar, 1990, Genentech Access Excellence fellow, 1995, 1996, Access Excellence Retro fellow, 1996, Tchr. of Yr., Biol. Scis. Curriculum Study, 2001; recipient Presdl. Sci. Tchg. award, NSF, 1983, Tech. award, Tandy, 1998, Siemens award for Advanced Placement, 2000. Mem. NEA (bd. dirs. Vt. chpt., 1990-98), Vt. Sci. Tchrs. Assn. (bd. dirs. 1980-92, treas. 1985-92), Burlington Profl. Stds. Bd. (chair 1991-2001), Parents and Friends of Edn. (trustee), Nat. Assn. Biology Tchrs. (dir. Vt. Outstanding Biology Tchr. award program 1977—, Outstanding Biology Tchr. award 1975), Assn. Presdl. Awardees in Sci., Phi Delta Kappa. Roman Catholic. Avocations: needlecrafts, fishing, music. Home: 221 Woodlawn Rd Burlington VT 05401-5722 Office Phone: 802-864-8411. Business E-Mail: jallard@bsdvt.org.

ALLARD, MARVEL JUNE, psychology educator, researcher; b. Detroit; d. Adrian Clarence and Marvel Claudia (Tremper) A.; m. James Donald Widmayer, Mar. 22, 1970 (div. Mar. 1982). AB, MA, PhD, Mich. State U. Rsch. assoc. Mich. State U., East Lansing, 1965-66; project dir., rsch. scientist Am. U., Washington, 1966-67; sr. staff Ops. Rsch., Inc., Silver Spring, Md., 1967-70; rsch. cons., 1970—; chair social and behavior sci., prof. psychology Worcester (Mass.) State Coll., 1973—2005, prof. emeritus, 2005. Adj. prof. Assumption Coll., 2005-; cons. Leasco Systems, Yankelovich Co., Assumption Coll., Framingham State Coll.; lectr., cons., examiner Internat. Baccalaureate Orgn.; internat. lectr. Internat. Edn. Programs. Editor: Understanding Diversity: Readings, Cases and Exercises, 1994, 2002, 2005; contbr. rsch. articles to profl. jours. Mem. Worcester County Hort. Soc.; bd. dirs. Girls, Inc., Worcester; pres., bd. trustees Worcester State Hosp. NSF fellow Mich. State U., 1959-64, Nat. fellow Assn. Am. Colls., 1985; scholar Mich. State U. and pvt. orgns., 1954-58, Phi Kappa Phi scholar Mich. State U.; named to Fulbright Sr. Specialist Roster. Mem. APA (site visitor, mem. undergrad. cons. svc.). Avocations: gardening, music, travel. Home and Office: 24 Curtis St Auburn MA 01501-3149 Office Phone: 508-791-0322. Business E-Mail: jualland@assumption.edu.

ALLBEE, TERESA JO, elementary school educator; b. Indpls., Sept. 20, 1961; d. Jack M. and Sally J. (Sipe) Roach; m. D. Scott Allbee, May 4, 1985; children: Justin, Joshua, Courtney. BA, North Cen. Coll., Naperville, Ill., 1984; postgrad., Northeastern Ill. U., Chgo. Cert. elem. educator. Tchr. Sipley Elem. Sch., Woodridge, Ill., summer 1985, Jane Addams Middle Sch., Bolingbrook, Ill., 1986-88, John R. Tibbott Elem. Sch., Bolingbrook, 1989-95, Indian Trace Elem. Sch., Weston, Fla., 1995—2000, Walter C. Young Mid. Sch., Pembroke Pines, Fla., 2000—. Mem. PEO. Home: 16311 NW 19th St Pembroke Pines FL 33028-1742 Office: Walter C Young Mid Sch 901 NW 129th Ave Pembroke Pines FL 33026

ALLBRIGHT, KARAN ELIZABETH, psychologist, consultant; b. Oklahoma City, Jan. 28, 1948; d. Jack Gahnal and Irma Lolene (Keesee) Allbright. BA, Okla. City U., 1970, MAT, 1972; PhD, U. So. Miss., Hattiesburg, 1981. Cert. nat. sch. psychologist, psychometrist, lic. psychologist Okla., Ark. Psychol. technician Donald J. Bertoch, PhD, Okla. City, 1973-76; asst. adminstr. Parents' Assistance Ctr., Okla. City, 1976-77; psychology intern Burwell Psycho-ednl. Ctr., Carrollton, Ga., 1980-81; staff psychologist Griffin Area Psychoednl. Ctr., Ga., 1981-85; clinic dir. Sequoyah County Guidance Clinic, Sallisaw, Okla., 1985-88; psychologist Baker Psychiat. Clinic, Ft. Smith, Ark., 1988-90; cons. Harbor View Mercy Hosp., 1988-90, Integris Bethany Med. Ctr., 1992-99; pvt. practice Okla. City, 1990—, Mercy Health Ctr., 1996—. Cons. Family Alliance (Parents Anonymous) Sequoyah County, 1985-88; lectr. various orgns.; bd. dir. workshops. Mem. Task Force to Prevent Child Abuse, Fayette County, Ga., 1984-85, Task Force on Family Violence, Spalding County, Ga., 1983-85, Oklahoma County Child Abuse Task Force, 2006; assoc. bd. dir. Lyric Theatre. Named to Outstanding Young Women in Am., 1980. Mem. APA, Okla. Psychol. Assn. Nat. Register Health Svc. Providers in Psychology, Okla. County Mental Health Assn., Okla. City Orch. League, Psi Chi, Delta Zeta (chpt. dir. 1970-72), Okla. City Mus. Art. Democrat. Presbyterian. Home: 3941 NW 44th St Oklahoma City OK 73112-2517 Office: Northwest Mental Health Assocs 3832 N Meridian Ave Oklahoma City OK 73112-2849 Office Phone: 405-949-9322.

ALLDREDGE, NOREEN S., librarian; b. Sacramento, Apr. 8, 1939; d. Harold and Cecelia (Doherty) Sunderland. BA, Mount St. Mary's Coll., L.A., 1961; MS, Columbia U., 1965; MA, Tex. A&M U., 1980. Film librarian N.Y. Pub. Library, N.Y.C., 1964-65; ref. librarian U. Nev., Reno, 1965-66, librarian Desert Rsch. Inst., 1966-70, circulation librarian, 1970-74, collection devel. librarian, 1974-76; asst. dir. Tex. A&M U., College Station, 1976-81; dean libraries Mont. State U., Bozeman, 1981—93; libr. Calif. State U., Hayward, 1993—2001. Accreditation visitor ALA, 1982-90, N.W. Assn. Schs. and Colls., 1985-02. Vol. Am. Hiking Soc., 1985-88; sr. assoc. U.S. Dept. Edn., 1990. Mem. ALA, Women Acad. Library Dirs., Am. Assn. Higher Edn. Home: 2203 Pinehurst Ct El Cerrito CA 94530-1881

ALLECTA, JULIE, lawyer; b. Worcester, Mass., Oct. 28, 1946; BA magna cum laude, U. N. Mex., 1973, MBA magna cum laude, 1977, JD, 1977. Bar: M. Mex. 1978, D.C. 1984, Calif. 1985, U.S. Supreme Ct., U.S. Ct. Appeals, fifth & tenth cir. Office gen. counsel SEC, Washington, 1977—81; ptnr. Paul, Hastings, Janofsky & Walker LLP, San Francisco. Editl. bd. Arlen Mutual Fund Handbook, Bd. IQ. Mem.: Am. Law Inst. ABA Com. Continuing Profl. Edn. (faculty mem.), Mutual Fund Dir. Forum (adv. dir.), ABA-Bus. Law Sect. (com. fed. regulation securities, sub. com. investment co. & investment advisers). Office: Paul Hastings Janofsky & Walker LLP 55 Second St 24th Floor San Francisco CA 94105 Office Phone: 415-856-7000. Office Fax: 415-856-7106. Business E-Mail: julieallecta@paulhastings.com.

ALLEN, ALANA S., not-for-profit developer; b. Atlanta, Sept. 11, 1978; BA in Sociology, Ga. State U., Atlanta, 2000. Tchr. math. Dekalb County Sch. Sys., Stone Mountain, Ga., 2001—05; coord. Cool Girls, Inc., Atlanta, 2005—. Recipient Shirley Chisolm/Malcolm X Award for Social Sciences, Ga. State U. Black Heritage Awards, 2000. Office: Cool Girls Inc 100 Edgewood Ave Ste 580 Atlanta GA 30303 Office Phone: 404-614-3440. Home Fax: 770-465-2831. E-mail: a.allen@thecoolgirls.org.

ALLEN, ALICE, communications and marketing executive; b. NYC, May 31, 1943; d. C. Edmonds and Helen (McCreery) A.; 1 child, Helen. Student, Conn. Coll., 1961. Pres. Alice Allen, Inc., N.Y.C., 1970—83; sr. v.p. Robert Marston, N.Y.C., 1983—84, Cunningham & Walsh, N.Y.C., 1984—86, Carl Byoir (acquired by Hill & Knowlton), N.Y.C., 1986; sr. v.p., dir. comms. and corp. mktg. Hill & Knowlton, N.Y.C., 1986—88; pres., owner Allen Comms. Group, Inc., N.Y.C., 1988—95, Alice Allen Comms., 1995—2003. Bd. dirs. Family Dynamics, N.Y.C., 1976-78, Veritas, 1980-85; v.p. Jr. League, N.Y.C., 1975-76; mem. adv. bd. Enterprise Found., 1992-2001. Mem. Pub. Rels. Soc. Am., Pub. Publicity Assn. (pres. 1969-71), Women's Media Group, Comm. Network. Office: Alice Allen Comms 320 E 72nd St New York NY 10021-4769

ALLEN, ANNETTE, minister; b. Helena, Ga., Apr. 27, 1962; d. Raymond and Nonie Mae Allen; m. Tigen R. Griffith (div.); children: Erick Raphael Griffith, Leah Charisse Griffith. Student, Medgar Evers Coll., Bklyn., 1983—85; cert., Inst. Biblical Studies, Lynchburg, Va., 2000; diploma, Liberty U., Lynchburg, 2004; DD, World Christianship Ministry, Fresno, Calif., 2004. Program asst. Nat. Coun. Ch. World Svc., N.Y.C., 1981—90; cmty. activist Clergy Inc., Bklyn., 1990—92; office mgr. United Ch. of Christ, N.Y.C., 1992—93; freelance writer Bklyn., 1993—96; metaphysician Lady Solomon, McRae, Ga., 1997—; min. New Hope Deliverance Ctr., McRae. Motivational spkr., Ga., 2000—. Author: War Between Two Minds, 2003. Founder New Hope HIV/AIDS Outreach Ctr., 2005. Republican. Home: Rte 1 Box 26C Mc Rae GA 31055 Home Fax: 229-868-5886. Personal E-mail: ladysolomon@planttel.net.

ALLEN, BARBARA ROTHSCHILD, retired psychology professor; d. Walter A. and Ruth Klein Friedman; m. George H. Rothschild Sr. (dec.); children: George H. Rothschild Jr., Deborah Rothschild; m. Alfred W. Wedel, Sept. 20, 1994 (dec. Nov. 28, 2003). BA in Psychology, Case Western U., 1945, MA in Psychology, 1946. Lic. Psychologist La., 1965. Psychol. asst. Ctrl. La. State Hosp., Pineville, 1955—58, 1960—62; assoc. prof. psychology La. State U., Alexandria, 1962—90. Co-author: Adolescence: Transition From Childhood to Maturity, 1972, 2d edit., 1978, Effective Elder Caregiving, 2006; contbr. articles to profl. jours. Parenting classes instr. Family Outreach, Georgetown, Tex., 1992—99; adv. bd. mem. La. Savings Assn., Lake Charles, 1976—89; family selection com. mem. Austin Habitat for Humanity, Tex., 2000—06. Nat. Sci. Found. grant, U. Calif., Berkeley, 1965, Beloit Coll., 1968, Philanthropic Edn. grant, La. State U., 1985, 2004. Mem.: AAUW (life; edn. v.p. 1995—96, br. pres. 1963, 1972). Avocations: writing, travel, bridge. Home: 40 NIH 35 Apt 12A2 Austin TX 78701

ALLEN, BEATRICE, music educator, pianist; b. N.Y.C., June 30, 1917; d. Samuel and Rose (Krell) Hyman; m. Eugene Murray Allen, Jan. 23, 1937; children: Marlene Allen Galzin, Julian Lewis. Student, NYU, 1933—36; diploma (scholar), Inst. Musical Arts, N.Y.C., 1939, postgrad. (scholar), 1939—40; diploma, Juilliard Grad. Sch., N.Y.C., 1943; BA magna cum laude, Cedar Crest Coll., 1980. Mem. faculty prep. div. Juilliard Sch. Music, N.Y.C., 1957—69, Moravian Coll., 1967—68, Northampton County Area CC, 1968—70, Manhattan Sch. Music, N.Y.C., 1969—89. Mem. founding faculty Cmty. Music Sch., Allentown, Pa., 1982—; artist-in-residence, condr. Tchrs. Workshop, Antioch Coll., Yellow Springs, Ohio, 1966; Bach lectr., recitals various univs.; concert appearances Town Hall, N.Y.C., Chautauqua, NY, others. Named Winner, NJ Artists contest, 1936. Mem.: Pa. Music Tchrs. Assn., Music Tchrs. Nat. Assn. (program chmn. Lehigh Valley chpt. 1981—82). Address: 580 Morningstar Lane Bethlehem PA 18018-6347

ALLEN, BELLE, management consulting firm executive, communications executive; b. Chgo. d. Isaac and Clara (Friedman) Allen., U. Chgo. Cert. conf. mgr. Internat. Inst. Conf. Planning and Mgmt., 1989. Reporter, spl. corr. The Leader Newspapers, Chgo., Washington, 1960—64; cons., v.p., treas., dir. William Karp Cons. Co. Inc., Chgo., 1961—79, chmn. bd., pres., treas.,

1979—; pres. Belle Allen Comm., Chgo., 1961—; nat. corr. CCA Press, 1990—. Apptd. pub. mem., com. on judicial evaluation Chgo. Bar Assn., 1998—; v.p., treas., bd. dirs. Cultural Arts Survey Inc., Chgo., 1965-79; cons., bd. dirs. Am. Diversified Rsch. Corp., Chgo., 1967-70; v.p., sec., bd. dirs. Mgmt. Performance Sys. Inc., 1976-77; cons. City Club Chgo., 1962-65, Ill. Commn. on Tech. Progress, 1965-67; hearing mem. Ill. Gov.'s Grievance Panel for State Employees, 1979—; hearing mem. grievance panel Ill. Dept. Transp., 1985—; mem. adv. governing bd. Ill. Coalition on Employment of Women, 1980-88; advisor, spl. program The President's Project Partnership, Washington, DC, 1980-88; bd. govs. fed. res. com., nominee consumer adv. coun. FRS, 1979-82; reporter CCA Press, 1990—; panel mem. Free Press vs. Fair Trial Nat. Ctr. Freedom of Info. Studies Loyola U. Law Sch., 1993, mem. planning com. Freedom of Info. awards, 1993; conf. chair The Swedish Inst. Press Ethics: How to Handle, 1993. Editor: Operations Research and the Management of Mental Health Systems, 1968; contbr. articles to profl. jours. Mem. campaign staff Adlai E. Stevenson II, 1952, 56, John F. Kennedy, 1960; founding mem. women's bd. United Cerebral Palsy Assn., Chgo., 1954, bd. dirs., 1954-58; pres. Dem. Fedn. Ill., 1958-61; pres. conf. staff Eleanor Roosevelt, 1960; mem. Welfare Pub. Rels. Forum, 1960-61; bd. dirs., mem. exec. com., chmn. pub. rels. com. Regional Ballet Ensemble, Chgo., 1961-63; bd. dirs. Soc. Chgo. Strings, 1963-64; mem. Ind. Dem. Coalition, 1968-69; bd. dirs. Citizens for Polit. Change, 1969; campaign mgr. aldermanic election 42d ward Chgo. City Coun., 1969; mem. selection com. Robert Aragon Scholarship, 1991; mem. planning com. mem. Hutchins Era reunion U. Chgo., 1995, 2000. Recipient Outstanding Svc. award United Cerebral Palsy Assn., Chgo., 1954, 55, Chgo. Lighthouse for Blind, 1986, Spl. Comms. award The White House, 1961, cert. of appreciation Ill. Dept. Human Rights, 1985, Internat. Assn. Ofcl. Human Rights Agys., 1985; selected as reference source Am. Bicentennial Rsch. Inst. Libr. Human Resources, 1973; named Hon. Citizen, City of Alexandria, Va., 1985; selected to be photographed by Bachrach nat. exhibit for Faces of Chicago, 1990. Mem. AAAS, NOW, AAAU, Affirmative Action Assn. (bd. dirs. 1981-85, chmn. mem. and programs com. 1981-85, pres. 1983—), Fashion Group (bd. dirs. 1981-83, chmn. Restrospective View of an Hist. Decade 1960-70, editor The Bull. 1981), Indsl. Rels. Rsch. Assn. (bd. dirs., chmn. pers. placement com. 1960-61), Sarah Siddons Soc., Soc. Pers. Adminstrs., Women's Equity Action League, Nat. Assn. Inter-Group Rels. Ofcls. (nat. conf. program 1959), Publicity Club Chgo. (chmn. inter-city rels. com. 1960-61, Disting. Svc. award 1968), Ill. C. of C. (cmty. rels. com., alt. mem. labor rels. com. 1971-74), Chgo. C. of C. and Industry (merit employment com. 1961-63), Internat. Press Club Chgo. (charter 1992—, bd. dirs. 1992—), Chgo. Press Club (chmn. women's activities 1969-71), U. Chgo. Club of Met. Chgo. (program com. 1993—, chair summer quarter programs 1994), Soc. Profl. Journalists (Chgo. Headline Club 1992—, regional conf. planning com. 1993, co-chair Peter Lisagor awards 1993, program com. 1992—), Assn. Women Journalists, Nat. Trust for Historic Preservation. Office: 111 E Chestnut St Ste 29J Chicago IL 60611

ALLEN, BERTRAND-MARC, lawyer; b. June 21, 1973; AB summa cum laude, Princeton Univ., 1995; JD, Yale Univ., 2002. Bar: Va. 2004. Law clk. U.S. Ct. Appeals (4th cir.), Alexandria, Va., 2002—03; law clk. to Hon. Anthony M. Kennedy U.S. Supreme Ct., Washington, 2003—04; assoc. Kellogg Huber Hansen Todd & Evans, Washington, 2004—. Contbr. articles in law jour. Mem.: N.Y. State Bar. Office: Kellogg Huber Hansen Todd & Evans Sumner Sq Suite 400 1615 M St NW Washington DC 20036

ALLEN, BESSIE MALVINA, music educator, organist; b. LaKemp, Okla., Oct. 14, 1918; d. Percy J. and Mary Allen (Hagler) Gheen; m. Edgar Charles Allen, Aug. 29, 1940 (dec. May 1981); children: Stanley Charles, Stephen Wayne. BA in English, Tex. Woman's U., 1939; MA in Music, W. Tex. State U., 1970. Cert. secondary edn. Tchr. English Balko (Okla.) High Sch. and Jr. High Sch., 1939-40; pvt. practice Phillips, Tex., 1950-85; tchr. music Frank Phillips Coll., Borger, Tex., 1960-63, 65-73, 76-85; pvt. practice Borger, 1997. Organist First Bapt. Ch., Borger, 1947-65, Faith Covenant Ch.-Ind., Borger, 1970-81, First Christian Ch., Borger, 1981-82, Faith Covenant Ch., Borger, 1982-2000. Active Nat. Rep. Senatorial Com., Washington, 1988-91; organist First United Meth. Ch., Borger, 2001—03. Recipient Presdl. Order of Merit, Nat. Rep. Senatorial Com., 1991; McCulley Organ scholar, W. Tex. State U., Canyon, 1969. Avocations: gardening, reading. Home and Office: 221 Inverness St Borger TX 79007-8215

ALLEN, BETTY (MRS. RITTEN EDWARD LEE III), mezzo-soprano; b. Campbell, Ohio, Mar. 17, 1930; d. James Corr and Dora Catherine (Mitchell) Allen; m. Ritten Edward Lee, III, Oct. 17, 1953; children: Anthony Edward, Juliana Catherine. Student, Wilberforce U., 1944-46; certificate, Hartford Sch. Music, 1953; pupil voice, Sarah Peck More, Zinka Milanov, Paul Ulanowsky, Carolina Segrera Holden; LHD (hon.), Wittenberg U., 1971; MusD (hon.), Union Coll., 1981; DFA (hon.), Adelphi U., 1990, Bklyn. Coll., 1991; LittD (hon.), Clark U., 1993; MusD (hon.), New Sch. Social Rsch., 1994. Mem. voice faculty Manhattan Sch. Music, 1969—; mem. faculty NC Sch. Arts, 1978-87, Phila. Mus. Acad., 1979, Curtis Inst. Music; mem. faculty to pres. emeritus Harlem Sch. Arts. Tchr. master classes Inst. Teatro Colon, 1985-86, Curtis Inst. Music, 1987—; exec. dir. Harlem Sch. Arts, 1979; vis. faculty Sibelius Akademie, Helsinki, Finland, 1976; mem. adv. bd. music panel Amherst Coll.; mem. music panel NY State Coun. of the Arts, Dept. State Office Cultural Presentations, Nat. Endowment Arts.; bd. dirs. Arts Alliance, Karl Weigl Found., Diller-Quaile Sch. Music, US Com. for UNICEF, Manhattan Sch. Music, Theatre Devel. Fund, Children's Storefront; mem. adv. bd. Bloomingdale House of Music; bd. vis. artists Boston U.; bd. dirs., mem. exec. com. Carnegie Hall, Nat. Found. for Advancement in the Arts; bd. dirs. Chamber Music Soc. of Lincoln Ctr., NYC Housing Authority Orch., Ind. Sch. Orch., NYC Opera Co., Joy in Singing, Arts & Bus. Coun.; mem. Mayor's adv. commn. Cultural Affairs. Appeared as soloist: Leonard Bernstein's Jeremiah Symphony, Tanglewood, 1951, Virgil Thomson's Four Saints in Three Acts, NYC and Paris, 1952, NYC Light Opera Co., 1954; recitalist, also soloist with major symphonies on tours including ANTA-State Dept. tours, Europe, North Africa, Caribbean, Can., US, S.Am., Far East, 1954-, S.Am. tour, 1968, Bellas Artes Opera, Mexico City, 1970; recital debut, Town Hall, NYC, 1958, ofcl. debuts, London, Berlin, 1958, formal opera debut, Teatro Colon, Buenos Aires, Argentina, 1964; US opera debut San Francisco Opera, 1966; NYC opera debut, 1973, Mini-Met. debut, 1973; Broadway debut in Treemonisha, 1975; opened new civic theaters in San Jose, Calif., and Regina, Sask., Can., concert hall, Lyndon Baines Johnson Libr., Austin, Tex., 1971; artist-in-residence, Phila. Opera Co.; appeared with Caramoor Music Festival, summer 1965, 71, Cin. May Festival, 1972, Santa Fe Opera, 1972, 75, Can. Opera Co., Winnipeg, Man., 1972, 77, Washington Opera Co., 1971, Tanglewood Festival, 1951, 52, 53, 67, 74, Oslo, The Hague, Montreal, Kansas City, Houston and Santa Fe operas, 1975, Saratoga Festival, 1975, Casals Festival, 1967, 68, 69, 76, Helsinki Festival, 1976, Marlboro Festival, 1967-74, numerous radio and TV performances, US, Can., Mex., Eng., Germany, Scandinavia; rec. artist, London, Vox, Capitol, Odeon-Pathe, Decca, Deutsche Grammophon, Columbia Records, RCA Victor records; represented US in Cultural Olympics, Mexico City, 1968. Recipient Marian Anderson award, 1953-54, Nat. Music League Mgmt. award, 1953, 52 St Am. Festival Duke Ellington Meml. award, 1989, Bowery award Bowery Bank, 1989, Harlem Sch. Arts award Harlem Sch. and Isaac Stern, 1990, Womans Day Celebration award St. Thomas Episcopal Ch., 1990, St. Thomas Ch. award St. Thomas Cath. Ch., 1990, Men's Day Celebration award St. Paul's Ch., 1990, Martell House of Segram award Avery Fisher Hall, 1990; named Best Singer of Season Critics' Circle, Argentina and Chile, 1959, Best Singer of Season Critics' Circle, Uruguay, 1961; Martha Baird Rockefeller Aid to Music grantee, 1953, 58; John Hay Whitney fellow, 1953-54; Ford Found. concert soloist grantee, 1963-64 Mem. NAACP, Urban League, Hartford Mus. Club (life), Am. Guild Mus. Artists, Actors Equity, AFTRA, Silvermine Guild Artists, Jeunesses Musicales, Gioventu Musicale, Student Sangverein Trondheim, Unitarian-Universalist Women's Fedn., Nat. Negro Musicians Assn. (life), Concert Artists Guild, Met. Opera Guild, Amherst Glee Club (hon. life), Union Coll. Glee Club (hon. life), Met. Mus. Art, Mus. Modern Art, Am. Mus. Natural Hist., Century Assn., Sigma Alpha Iota (hon.) Unitarian-Universalist. Clubs: Cosmopolitan, Second. Office: Harlem Sch Arts 645 St Nicholas Ave New York NY 10030-1098

ALLEN, CAROL MARIE, radiologic technologist; b. Alma, Ark., Nov. 4, 1941; d. Rhuel Teal and Blake Marie (Hickey) Edwards; m. Richard William Varney, Oct. 4, 1965 (dec. Mar. 1978); 1 stepchild, Mary Beth Varney; m. Michael Thomas Allen, Dec. 24, 1979; stepchildren: Richard Lawrence, Peter Michael, Nicola Susan. 2 yr. cert., Sparks Regional Med. Ctr.-Sch. Radiology, 1961. Cert. Am. Registry Radiologic Technologists, State Conn. Registry Radiologic Technologists, clin. densitometry Mass. Staff technologist Sparks Regional Med. Ctr., Ft. Smith, Ark., 1961—62, La Puente (Calif.) Hosp., 1962—64; asst. chief technologist La Harbor (Calif.) Hosp., 1964—67; traffic contr. Lawrence and Meml. Hosp., Pequot Treatment Ctr., New London, Conn., 1967—; clin. densitometry technologist L&M Pequot Treatment Ctr., 1998—2003, traffic controller, 2003—. Contbr. Critical Thinking Developing Skills in Radiography, 1999. Vol. ARC, Conn. Mem.: Am. Soc. for Radiologic Technologists, Internat. Soc. for Clin. Densitometry. Democrat. Avocations: gardening, antiques, reading. Home: 11 Route 165 Preston CT 06365-8414 Office: Lawrence & Meml Hosp 365 Montauk Ave New London CT 06320 also: Pequot Emergency Treatment Ctr 52 Hazelnut Hill Rd Groton CT 06340 Office Phone: 860-446-8265.

ALLEN, DEBORAH RUDISILL, clinical psychologist, educator; b. Port Chester, N.Y., Oct. 31, 1951; d. Stewart Ellwood and Sarah Louise (Rudisill) A.; m. Howard Schein, Nov. 24, 1984; children: Stevie Scarlett Schein, Zoe Susannah Schein. BA in Psychology summa cum laude, U. Vt., 1972; MA in Clin. Psychology, Mich. State U., 1974, PhD in Clin. Psychology, 1977. Lic. psychologist, Ill. Asst. prof. psychology Olin health svcs. and counseling ctr. Mich. State U., East Lansing, 1977-78; clin. counselor U. Ill., Urbana, 1978-88, asst. dir. counseling ctr., 1981-84, assoc. dir., 1984-88; pvt. practice psychology Champaign, Ill., 1979—. Contbr. articles to profl. jours.; co-author: (book) Giving Advice to Students: A Roadmap for College Professionals, 1987, (brochures) numerous self-help publs., 1984—. Mem. Am. Psychol. Assn., Phi Beta Kappa, Phi Kappa Phi, Psi Chi. Home: 401 W Nevada St Urbana IL 61801-4110 Office: Ste 202 1701 S Prospect Ave Champaign IL 61820-7054 Office Phone: 217-352-9207. Personal E-mail: deborahrallen@juno.com.

ALLEN, DENISE NEWBOLD, music educator; b. Salt Lake City, Apr. 25, 1963; d. Dennis Marlin and Deanna (Jeffery) Newbold; m. Gordon J. Allen, June 5, 1987; children: Bethany, Heidi, Andrew, Hayley, Darcy, Abigail AAS in Music, Ricks Coll., 1983; BA in Music, Utah State U., 1986; MA in Musicology, George Washington U., Washington, 1992. Asst. class piano instr. Ricks Coll., Rexburg, Idaho, 1982-83; pvt. piano instr. Utah State U. Youth Conservatory, Logan, 1983-86; music critic/reporter Utah Statesman, Utah State U., Logan, 1986; adj. piano faculty/resident advisor Idyllwild Sch. Music and the Arts, Calif., 1986-87; grad. asst. George Washington U., 1987-89; pvt. piano instr. Calif., Va., Utah, 1986—; instr. Kindermusik, South Jordan, Utah, 1991—, Musikgarten, 1995—. Mem. Music Tchrs. Nat. Assn. (cert. music tchr. 1994), Utah Music Tchrs. Assn. (treas. 1993-94), Am. Orff-Schulwerk Assn., Kindermusik Tchrs. Assn./Early Childhood Music and Movement Assn. (level 1 cert. 1993, level 2 cert. 1999) Mem. Lds Ch. Avocations: calligraphy, sewing, gardening, scrapbooks. Personal E-mail: gdallen@xmission.com.

ALLEN, DIANE BETZENDAHL, state legislator; b. Newark, Mar. 8, 1948; BA in Philosophy, Bucknell U., 1970. Pres. VidComm, Inc.; mem. N.J. Gen. Assembly, Trenton, 1996—98; dist. 7 mem. N.J. Senate, 1998—. Majority whip N.J. State Senate, 1998—2001, dep. rep. conf. leader, 2002—03, mem. transp. com., 2002—03, mem. sr. citizens com., 2002—05, mem. health and human svcs. com., 2002—05, mem. health and sr. svcs. com., 2003, Rep. conf. leader, 03, dep. minority leader, 2006—; mem. N.J. Coun. Armed Foces and Vet. Affairs, N.J. Human Rels. Coun.; chair tech. com. Commn. Bus. Efficiency Pub. Schools, Martin Luther King Commn. Republican. Address: NJ State Senate PO Box 098 Trenton NJ 08624-0098 Home: 11 W Broad St Burlington NJ 08016 Business E-Mail: SenAllen@njleg.org.

ALLEN, DONNA, mathematics educator; d. Betty Clarke; m. Lance Allen, Dec. 29, 1984; children: Courtney, Thomas. BS, Miss. State U., Starkville, 1983, MEd, 1984. Tchr. math. Southaven H.S., Miss., 1985—88, Madison-Ridgeland Acad., Miss., 1989—. Coord. Sun. sch. missions Broadmoor Bapt. Ch., Madison, 2006. Named STAR Tchr., Miss. Econ. Coun., 1990, 1997, 1998, 2001, 2004, 2005, Madison County H.S. Tchr. of Yr., Madison County C. of C., 1998, Tech. Outstanding Tchr. in Math., Tandy Corp., 1994, 1995, 1996, 1997, 1998; named to Who's Who Among Am. Tchrs., Who's Who, 1996, 2004. Mem.: Miss. Pvt. Sch. Edn. Assn., Miss. Coun. Tchrs. Math., Christian Educators Assn. Internat. Avocations: gardening, reading.

ALLEN, ELIZABETH ANN, writer; b. Ind., Oct. 8, 1934; d. Foster Leon Kindig and Margaret Louise Hammerel; children: Todd Sheetz, Douglas Sheetz, Robert Allen Jr., J. Phillip Allen, Mary A. Gibbs, Michael S. Editor Akron/Mentone News, Ind., 1962—77; mktg. dir. Akron Exch. State Bank, 1977—90; freelance writer, 1990—. Author: Born Again.But Still Wet Behind the Ears, 1979, Someone Has to Pop the Corn, 1981, From Ties to Technology, 1995, History of the Akron United Methodist Church, 2004. Sec., treas. Akron Town Bldg. Corp., Akron, Ind., 1987—, Akron Revitalization Com., 2003. Recipient state and nat. writing awards, Nat. Fedn. Press Women. Mem.: Women's Press Club Ind. (past pres.). Republican. Avocations: reading, philately, travel. Home: 801 E Walnut St Akron IN 46910

ALLEN, ELIZABETH MARESCA, marketing executive, telecommunications industry executive; b. Red Bank, NJ, Jan. 4, 1958; d. Paul William Michael and Roberta Gertrude (Abbes) Maresca; m. David D. Allen; 1 child, Brandon D. Student, Brookdale Community Coll., 1976-77; A Bus. Adminstrn., Tidewater C.C., 1988; BA in Bus. Mgmt., Va. Wesleyan Coll., 1997. Systems analyst Methods Rsch. Corp., Farmingdale, NJ, 1977-79; divsn. mgr. Abacus Comm. L.P., Va. Beach, Va., 1979—2003, dir. telecomm., dir. client svcs.; divsn. sales mgr. AmeriComm Direct Mktg., Chesapeake, 2003—06. V.p. Charlestowne Civic League, Virginia Beach, 1983—84, Plantation Lakes Homeowners Assn., Chesapeake, Va., 1992—; advisor Commonwealth Coll., Norfolk, 1984—91; commr. S. Norfolk Revitalization Commn., 1999—2001; v.p. Indian River HS Football Boosters, 2004—, pres., 2006—; del. Va. Rep. Conv., 1993—; mem. gov.'s coun. Rep. Nat. Com., 1997; bd. dirs. Arthritis Found., Norfolk, Va., 1986—90. Mem.: Williamsburg Area C. of C. (exhibit chmn. 1987), Hampton Roads C. of C. (com. chmn. 1985, 1989), Women's Network Hampton Roads (publicity chmn. 1988—91, chmn. publicity for Job Fair 1989). Republican. Roman Catholic. Avocations: tennis, Civil War history, collecting antiques, gardening. Office Phone: 757-622-2724.

ALLEN, FRANCES ELIZABETH, computer scientist; b. Peru, N.Y., Aug. 4, 1932; d. John Abram and Ruth Genevieve (Downs) A. BS, SUNY, Albany, 1954; MA, U. Mich., 1957; DSc (hon.), U. Alta., 1991. With IBM Rsch. Lab., Yorktown Heights, NY, 1957—2002, sr. tech. cons. to v.p. of solutions and services. Adj. assoc. prof. N.Y. U., 1970-72; mem. computer sci. adv. bd. NSF, 1972-75, cons., 1975-78; lectr. Chinese Acad. Scis., 1973, 77; IEEE disting. visitor, 1973-74; cons. prof. Stanford U., 1977-78; founder Parallel TRANslation Group (PTRAN); chancellor's disting. vis. lectr., U. Calif., Berkeley, 1988-89; mem. Stretch/HARVEST project.; pres. IBM Acad. Tech., 1995. IBM Corp. fellow (first women to be named this highest technical honor), 1989, Fellow Emeritus, 2002-; recipient fellow award Computer History Mus., 2000, Frances E. Allen Women in Tech. Mentoring award (first recipient-named in honor of), 2000, Grace Hopper Celebration of Women in Computing award, 2002, Augusta Ada Lovelace award, 2002, Anita Borg Technical Leadership award, 2004; named to Women In Tech. Internat. Hall of Fame, 1997. Fellow IEEE, Am. Acad. Arts and Scis., Assn. Computing Machinery (nat. lectr. 1972-73, SIGPLAN's Programming Languages Achievement award); mem. NAE Programming Sys. and Langs. (Paper award 1976), Am. Alpine Club, Alpine Club Can. Achievements include being the pioneer in the field of optimizing compilers. Avocation: hiking.*

ALLEN, FRANCES MICHAEL, publisher; b. Charlotte, N.C., Apr. 7, 1939; d. Thomas Wilcox and Lola Frances (Horne) A.; m. Joseph Taylor Lisenbee, Feb. 24, 1955 (div. 1957); 1 child, Leslie Autice., Abilene (Tex.) Christian Coll., 1954-56, Chico (Calif.) State U., 1957-59. Art dir. B&E Publs., L.A., 1963-65, editor, 1969-70; art dir. Tiburon Corp., Chgo., 1970-75; founder, editor Boxers, Internat., L.A., 1970-76; editor The Hound's Tale, 1974, Saints, Incorp., 1974-76; founder, editor Setters, Incorp., Costa Mesa, Calif., 1975-85; founder, owner Michael Enterprises, Midway City, Calif., 1976—; editor Am. Cocker Rev., Midway City, 1980-81; editor, pub. Am. Cocker Mag., 1981-99; editor, co-pub. Sporting Life, 1991; editor, pub. The Royal Spaniels, 1995—. Author: The American Cocker Book, 1989; editor, pub. The Royal Spaniels, 1995— (Dogs Writer's Assn. awards 1995, 96, 99); illustrator: The First Five Years, 1970, The Aftercare of the Ear, 1975, The Shenn Simplicity Collection, 1976, The Miniature Pinscher, 1967; prin. works include mag. and book covers for USA, most widely published show dog artist world wide, past 30 yrs. Recipient Dog World Award Top Producer, 5 times, 1966-88, 10-time winner and nominee Dog Writers Assn. Am., winner best breed publ. World Congress Pet Publs., Ukraine, 1995, winner Kirk Paper Co. award of excellence. Mem. Dog Writers Assn. Am. (life), Am. Spaniel Club (life). Republican. Mem. Ch. of Christ. Avocations: dog exhibiting, ballooning, photography, art. Home and Office: 14531 Jefferson St Midway City CA 92655-1030 Office Phone: 714-893-0053. E-mail: baliwck@socal.rr.com.

ALLEN, G. CHRISTY L. L., physics educator; b. Ft. Scott, Kans., Dec. 1, 1968; d. Stanley N. and Margaret G. (Steele) A. BS in Phys. Edn. and Biology, McPherson Coll., 1991; MS in Biomechanics, Kans. State U., 1994. Cert. tchr., Tex. Grad. tchg. asst. Kans. State U., Manhattan, 1991-94; tchr., coach Peaster (Tex.) Ind. Sch. Dist., 1993-94, Rains Ind. Sch. Dist., Emory, Tex., 1994—99; physics tchr., softball coach John Tyler HS, 1999—. Counselor Heart of Am. Camps, Salina, Kans., 1990-93; volleyball dir. Rains-Alba Volleyball Camps, Emory, 1994; health curriculum cons. Rains H.S., Emory, 1994-95; biology curriculum cons. Rains Ind. Sch. Dist., 1994-95. Cons. Rains Youth Sports Assn., Emory, 1994-95. Kans. State rsch. grantee, 1993. Mem. Women's Basketball Coaches Assn., Tex. Girl's Coaches Assn., Nat. Softball Coaches Assn., Sci. Tchrs. Assn. Tex., Classroom Tchrs., Fellow Christian Athletes (asst. dir. Rains chpt. 1994-95). Republican. Nazarene. Office: Rains Ind Sch Dist PO Box 247 Emory TX 75440-0247

ALLEN, GEMMA B., lawyer; b. Chgo., June 28, 1948; BS magna cum laude, Loyola U. Chgo., 1966; JD, U. Mich., 1969. Bar: Fla. 1970, Ill. 1972. With Pretzel & Stouffer, Chgo., 1990—99; ptnr., co-founder Ladden & Allen, Chgo., 2000—. Apptd. mem. Gov.'s Task Force on Child Support, Task Force on Attys. for Children, 1997—98; spkr. in field. Contbr. articles to profl. jours. Named one of 100 Most Influential Women, Crain's Chgo. Bus., 2004. Mem.: ABA (mem. family law sect.), Ill. State Bar Assn. (past chmn. family law com. mediation alternative dispute resolution, apptd. mem. family law sect. coun. 1996—99, co-chair model mediation act subcom.). Office: Ladden & Allen 55 W Monroe St Ste 3950 Chicago IL 60603 Office Phone: 312-853-3000. Office Fax: 312-201-1436.

ALLEN (IRVIN M.N.), GEORGIANNE LYDIA CHRISTIAN, writer, poet; b. Chgo., Apr. 30, 1943; d. George Aaron Irvin and Madeline Anandabai (Sobrian M.N.) Irvin Gordon, Earl Ovington Gordon (Stepfather); m. Ernest James Allen, Feb. 29, 1992; m. Hillard Roland Phillips, July 1, 1960 (div. June 16, 1977); children: Kellie Annette Phillips Mortley, Madeline Charlotte Phillips Kimmich, Matthew Roland Phillips. Secretarial cert., Chgo. Coll. Commerce, 1963; AA in Psychology, Southwestern Coll., Chula Vista, Calif., 1974; AS in Nursing, Mo. So. State Coll., Joplin, 1977; BSN, Pittsburg State U., Kans., 1979; clin. pastoral edn., St. Paul Sch. Theology and Ossawatomie State Hosp., Kans., 1984; MDiv, MRE, St. Paul Sch. of Theology, Kansas City, Mo., 1985; postgrad., Ga. State U., 2005. RN Mo., Ga., 1977; ordained to ministry Mo. West Conf., 1980; lic. practitioner Nambudripad Allergy Ellimination. Bd. dirs. United Meth. Ch. Black Meth. for Ch. Renewal, 1981—82; pastor Pitts Chapel United Meth. Ch., Springfield, Mo., 1984—85; founder, chairperson Matthew 25 Collaboration, Atlanta, 1998—99; pastor, CEO Ch. of the Creator Incarnate, Coverings, Creative Theol. Ministries, Stone Mountain, Ga., 1994—; nursing instr. Pacific Coast Coll., Chula Vista, Calif., 1990—91; mem. adv. bd. Nambudripad's Allergy Rsch. Found. Author: How to Study and Pass Tests (on line at Virtual University, www.vu.com), I Will Trust Him, Poetry of Faith, (book of poetry) Today (appeared in Poetry's Elite the Best Poets of 2000, 2000); composer: (songs) Atlanta, God Will See You Through, On this Our Wedding Day, The Gospel in Calypso, When I See a Rainbow et al.; prodr.: (radio broadcast) Creative Christian Living; prodr.: (motivational/relaxation cassette) How to Release Worry Anxiety and Stress; web site designer www.coverings.org:, author of poems. Participant Atlanta Taskforce for the Homeless, 1994—98; lectr. leadership classes Dekalb Hist. Soc., Decatur, Ga., 1999—2001; newsletter editor and organizer Stone Mountain Estates Cmty. Orgn., Ga., 2002—03; bd. dirs. Black Methodists for Ch. Renewal, 1981—82; chairperson Matthew 25 Collaboration, Atlanta, 1998—99; treas. Conf. Youth Coun. of Rock River Conf. of Meth. Episcopal Ch., 1959—60; designer, coord. Project Hope. Nominee Ga. Author Yr., Ga. Writers Assn., 2000; recipient Instr.'s Appreciation plaque, Nursing Students Pacific Coast Coll., 1991, Appreciation Cert., Bd. Dirs. Coverings Ministry, 1997, Internat. Poet of Merit award, Internat. Soc. Poets, 2000 - 2003; Betty Stephens Scholarship award for religious edn., St. Paul Sch. of Theology, 1980—81. Mem.: Sigma Theta Tau. Achievements include research in basis for harmonius race relations (100+ yrs) between residents of the Village of Stone Mountain, GA, former home of the Grand Imperial Wizard of the Ku Klux Klan, site of USAs largest Klan rallies; first African Am. woman to enter and grad. from both Mo. So. State Coll.'s Nursing Program and St. Paul Sch. of Theology. Avocations: travel, music (writing, playing and listening), sewing, writing, history. Home: 4965 Dantel Way Stone Mountain GA 30083 Office Phone: 770-469-6611.

ALLEN, GLORIA ANN, real estate broker, artist; b. Paterson, N.J., May 1, 1940; d. Victor and Anna (Nagorny) Borovoy; m. Byron Paul Allen, July 7, 1964 (div. Jan. 1986); children: Andreya Monica, Sarah Patricia. Student, Cir. in Sq. Acting Sch., N.Y.C., 1963-64; MA, Johns Hopkins U., Balt., 1962; MBA, Golden Gate U., San Francisco, 1986; art student, City Coll. of San Francisco, 2004—. Lic. real estate broker, Calif. Tchr. Elem. Sch., East Rutherford, N.J., 1963; social worker Bur. Child Welfare City of N.Y., 1964-68; social worker Dept. Social Svcs. City and County San Francisco, 1968-78; property mgr. San Francisco, 1981-91; broker assoc. Ritchie and Ritchie, San Francisco, 1992, Evans Pacific Realtor, San Francisco, 1993-94, Frank Howard Allen Realtors, San Francisco, 1994-97, Fred Sands City Properties, San Francisco, 1997-2001, Coldwell Banker, San Francisco, 2001—02, Merchant Real Estate Inc., 2003—. Fin. com. mem. St. Mary's Cathedral, San Francisco, 1993-94 Mem. Nat. Assn. Realtors, Nat. Network Comml. Real Estate Women (chief fin. officer 1987-89, co-chair facilities Nat. Conv. 1993). Democrat. Personal E-mail: gloriart8003@sbcglobal.net.

ALLEN, IRMA M., adult education educator; d. Henry Lemons and Mattie Robinson-Lemons; m. Ulysses Allen, Sept. 24, 1950; children: Wanda, Ulysses Jr., Walter, Richard, Eric, Janet Anderson. BS in Criminal Justice, San Jose State U., 1973. Cert. tchr. Calif. Substitute tchr. Monterey (Calif.) Unified Sch. Dist., 1972—73; correctional officer Fed. Correctional Instn., Dublin, Calif., 1975—77, GED tchr., 1977—95; adult edn. tchr. Milpitas (Calif.) Unified Sch. Dist., 1995—. Mem. St. James. A.M.E. Ch., San Jose, 1975—; chairperson St. James Outreach and Prison Ministry. Recipient cert. of appreciation, Fed. Correctional Instn., Dublin, 1976—2004, A.M.E. Ch., Oakland, 1999, Skyline Convalescent Hosp., San Jose, 2003—04. Mem.: Josephine Young Women's Missionary Soc. (v.p.), Southbay Mins., Wives and Widows (devotion dir., co-chairperson). Democrat. Methodist. Office: Milpitas Unified Sch Dist 1331 E Calaveras Milpitas St Milpitas CA 95035 Office Phone: 408-945-2341. Office Fax: 408-224-4257.

ALLEN, JANET LEE, special education educator; d. James Monroe and Clara Faye (Greiner) Crowder; m. Thomas Scott Allen, Aug. 11, 1973; children: Brian Alexander, Timothy Michael. BS in Edn., Emporia State U., 1974. Cert. tchr. Kans. From stenographer to trainmaster, various clk. positions Atchison, Topeka & Santa Fe Rlwy. Co., Kansas City, Kans., 1971—76; paraprofessional Shawnee Mission (Kans.) Sch. Dist., 1986—88, 2001—. ESL aide, 1997—2000. Cub scout leader Boy Scouts Am., Shawnee, 1985—89; vol. Project Finish Johnson County Libr., Merriam and Olathe, Kans., 1988; Sunday sch. tchr. St. Paul's United Meth., Lenexa, Kans., 1983—94. Named Outstanding Employee of Yr., Shawnee Mission Sch. Dist., 2002. Avocations: languages, reading, theater, travel. Office: Nieman Elem Sch 10917 W 67th St Shawnee Mission KS 66203 E-mail: jallen7779@hotmail.com.

ALLEN, JANICE FAYE CLEMENT, nursing administrator; b. Norfolk, Nebr., Aug. 19, 1946; d. Allen Edward and Hilda Bernice (Stange) Reeves; m. Roger Allen Clement, Oct. 6, 1968 (dec. July 1974); m. August H. Allen, Sept. 17, 1988. RN, Meth. Sch. Nursing, Omaha, 1967; BSN magna cum laude, Creighton U., 1978; MSN, U. Nebr., 1981. Cert. in nursing adminstrn., infection control. With Meth. Hosp., 1967-68, 72-83, asst. head nurse, 1974-77, staff devel. nurse, 1977-81, dir. staff adminstrv. svcs., 1981-83; pub. health nurse Wichita-Sedgwick County Health Dept., Wichita, Kans., 1970-72; dir. nursing Meth. Med. Ctr., St. Joseph, Mo., 1983-84; v.p. nursing and profl. svcs. Broadlawns Med. Ctr., Des Moines, 1984-93; dir. staff mgmt./infection control Ea. N.Mex. Med. Ctr., Roswell, 1993-2000; infection control practitioner Carl T. Hayden VA Med. Ctr., Phoenix, 2000—; faculty mem. U. Phoenix, 2002. Adj. clin. faculty nursing Drake U., Des Moines, 1986-93, adv. bd., 1984-93, Ctrl. Campus Practical Nursing, 1984-93; adv. bd. Des Moines Area C.C. Dist., 1987—, Des Moines Area C.C. Nursing Bd., 1987-93, Grandview Coll., 1988-93; assoc. Am. Coll. Healthcare Execs., Dept. Veteran Affairs VISN 18 Leadership Devel. Inst. Graduate, 2003. Mem.: ANA, Nat. Assn. for Healthcare Quality, Nurses Orgn. Vet. Affairs, N.Mex. Orgn. Nurse Execs., Assn. Infection Control and Epidemiology, Iowa Orgn. Nurse Execs. (treas. 1987, sec. 1989, pres.-elect 1993), Iowa League for Nursing (treas. 1987—89, pres. 1989), Colloquium Nursing Leaders Ctrl. Iowa, Ctrl. Iowa Nursing Leadership Conf. (pres. 1985), N.Mex. Nurses Assn., Altrusa of Roswell, Sigma Theta Tau (pres. Zeta Chi chpt. 1990—92). Home: 7380 W Remuda Dr Peoria AZ 85383 Office: Carl T Hayden VA Med Ctr 650 E Indian Sch Rd Phoenix AZ 85012 Office Phone: 602-277-5551. Business E-Mail: jan.allen@cox.net, jan.allen@va.gov.

ALLEN, JO LYNN, secondary school educator; d. Edward Sidney and Gertrude Allen. MA in Tchg., Converse Coll., Spartanburg, SC, 1960. Cert. secondary English tchr. SC. Tchr. James F. Byrnes HS, Duncan, SC, 1961—. Missions coord. Tucapau Bapt. Ch., 1980—2006. Pres. Associational Women's Missionary Union, Spartanburg, 1991—94. Named Tchr. of Yr., James F. Byrnes HS. Mem.: Delta Kappa Gamma (v.p.). Office Phone: 864-949-2355.

ALLEN, JOAN, actress; b. Rochelle, Ill., Aug. 20, 1956; m. Peter Friedman, Jan. 1, 1990; 1 child. Student, Ea. Ill. U., No. Ill. U. Founding mem. Steppenwolf Theatre Co., Chgo.; theater appearances include (debut) And A Nightingale Sang, N.Y.C. (Clarence Derwent award, Drama Desk award, Outer Critics Circle award 1984), Steppenwolf Theatre Co., also Hartford, 1983, The Marriage of Bette and Boo, N.Y. Shakespeare Festival, 1986, Burn This! (Tony awrd for Best Actress 1989) Mark Taper Forum, L.A., also NYC, 1987, The Heidi Chronicles, N.Y.C., 1988, 89; film appearances include Compromising Positions, 1985, Peggy Sue Got Married, 1986, Manhunter, 1986, Tucker: The Man and His Dream, 1988, In Country, 1989, Ethan Frome, 1993, Searching for Bobbie Fischer, 1993, Josh and S.A.M., 1993, Nixon, 1995 (Acad. award nominee for best supporting actress 1996), Mad Love, 1995, The Crucible, 1996, Ice Storm, 1997, Face/Off, 1997, Pleasantville, 1998, Veronica Guerin, 1999, All the Rage, 1999, When the Sky Falls, 2000, The Contender, 2000, Off the Map, 2003, The Notebook, 2004, The Bourne Supremacy, 2004, Yes, 2004, The Upside of Anger, 2005; TV appearances include The Twilight Zone, 1987, Am. Playhouse, PBS, 1987, Robert Frost, Voices and Visions, PBS, 1988, Fraiser, 1996, TV films All My Sons, 1986, The Room Upstairs, 1987, Without Warning: The James Brady Story, 1991, Say Goodnight, Gracie, PBS, TV miniseries Evergreen, 1985, The Mists of Avalon, 2001. Office: ICM care Brian Mann 8942 Wilshire Blvd Beverly Hills CA 90211-1934

ALLEN, JUDITH SYMA, art educator, artist; b. N.Y.C., Jan. 21, 1956; BA, Oberlin Coll., 1977; postgrad., Columbia U., 1978; MFA, Mills Coll., 1990. Asst. prof. photography Cornish Coll. of the Arts, Seattle, 1992—. Lectr. photography San Francisco State U., 1991, 92, Acad. Art Coll., San Francisco, 1991, 92, Calif. State Summer Sch. for Arts, Oakland, 1990, 91. One-woman shows include Lloyd Gallery, Spokane, Wash., 1982, New Performance Gallery, San Francisco, 1982; exhibited in group shows at Ctr. on Contemporary Art, Seattle, 1994, 95, Fisher Gallery, Seattle, 1993, 94, 95, 96, San Francisco Arts Commn. Gallery, 1991, Berkeley (Calif.) Art Ctr., 1991, Richmond (Calif.) Art Ctr., 1991, 86, San Francisco State U. Art Gallery, 1991, Intersection for Arts, San Francisco, 1990, 88, Bellevue (Wash.) Art Mus., 1994, Photographic Ctr. Northwest, 1997. Fellow Nat. Endowment for Arts, 1990-91; recipient Trefethen award Mills Coll., 1989, Betty Bowen Meml. Spl. Recognition award Seattle Art Mus., 1994. Mem. Soc. for Photographic Edn., Coll. Art Assn. Office: Cornish Coll of Arts 1501 10th Ave E Seattle WA 98102-4210

ALLEN, JULIE O'DONNELL, lawyer; BA, Stanford U., 1980; JD, U. Iowa, 1983. Bar: Iowa 1983, Ill. 1985, U.S. Dist. Ct. (no. dist.) Ill., U.S. Ct. Appeals (8th and 7th cirs.). Jud. clk. to Chief Judge Donald P. Lay, U.S. Ct. Appeals for 8th Circuit, 1983-84; assoc. Sidley & Austin, Chgo., 1985—, ptnr. Contbr. articles to law publs. Office: Sidley & Austin 1 S First National Plz Chicago IL 60603-2000 Fax: 323-853-7036. E-mail: jallen@sidley.com.

ALLEN, KAREN ALFSTAD, information technology executive; b. Wichita, Kans., Nov. 21, 1942; d. Harold Daniel and Myrtle (Creach) Keefer; m. Richard Allen, Dec. 16, 1962 (dec. 1994). AS, Oreg. Inst. of Tech., L.A., 1964; AA, Pasadena City, 1973; BS, Calif. State U., Pasadena City, 1974. Administra. asst. Transamerica, Los Angeles, 1974-75; v.p. Calif. Fed., Los Angeles, 1975-86; mgmt. cons. PriceWaterhouseCoopers, Los Angeles, 1986-90; mgr. large accounts J.D. Edwards, Denver, 1990-92; sr. v.p. Insecon Computer Sys., Encino, Calif., 1992—93; sr. project dir. MCI Systemhouse, Cerritos, Calif., 1995-98; delivery mgr. EDS, Cerritos, 1998-2000; chief info. officer Exult, Irvine, Calif., 2000—04, Hewitt Assocs., Newport Beach, Calif., 2004—. Vol. Youth Motivation Task Force, L.A., 1982—86, Huntington Libr., Big Wheel Soc., Children's Hosp. of Orange County Pabrinos, L.A.; bd. dirs. Polit. Action Com. Calif. Fed., L.A., 1984—86, Arcadia Arts Coun., 1993—2002. Recipient Honors Calif. State U., Los Angeles, 1974. Mem. Nat. Trust for Historic Preservation, Internat. Facility Mgmt., So. Calif. Emergency Assn., NAFE, NOW, U. Club L.A., Women's History Mus. Democrat. Home: 5161 Via Marcos Yorba Linda CA 93887 Office: Hewitt Assocs 100 Bayiew Cir Newport Beach CA 92660 Business E-Mail: karen.allen@hewitt.com.

ALLEN, KIMBERLY FERRICK, elementary school educator; b. Erie, Pa., Aug. 15, 1962; d. George Paul Ferrick and Barbara Jean Olszewski; m. Timothy Rand Allen, Nov. 25, 1995; children: Sydney Liane, Ryan Thomas. BA, Westminster Coll., New Wilmington, Pa., 1984. Tchr. Hanover County Pub. Sch., Ashland, Va., 2000—. Office: John M Gandy 201 Archie Cannon Dr Ashland VA 23005 Office Phone: 804-365-4640. Business E-Mail: kallen@hanover.k12.va.us.

ALLEN, LEATRICE DELORICE, psychologist; b. Chgo., July 15, 1948; d. Burt and Mildred Floy (Taylor) Hawkins; m. Allen Jr. Moore, July 30, 1965 (div. Oct. 1975); children: Chandra, Valarie, Allen; m. Armstead Allen, May 11, 1978 (div. May 1987). AA in Bus. Edn., Olive Harvey Coll., Chgo., 1975; BA in Psychology, Chgo. State U., 1977; M in Clin. Psychology, Roosevelt U., 1980; MS in Health Care Adminstrn., Coll. St. Francis, Joliet, Ill., 1993. Lic. clin. profl. counselor. Clk. U.S. Post Office, Chgo., 1967—72; clin. therapist Bobby Wright Mental Health Ctr., Chgo., 1979—80, Cmty. Mental Health Coun., Chgo., 1980—83, assoc. dir., 1983—. Cons. Edgewater Mental Health, Chgo., 1984—, Project Price, Chgo., 1980—83; victim svcs. coord. Cmty. Mental Health Coun., Chgo., 1986—87; mgr. youth family svcs. Mile Sq. Health Ctr., Chgo., 1987—88; coord. Evang. Health Sys., Oakbrook, Ill., 1988—93; adminstr. Human Enrichment Devel. Assn., Hazel Crest, Ill., 1993—96; bd. dirs. Ada S. McKinley, Chgo., Nat. Able Network, Chgo. Fellow, Menninger Found., 1985; scholar, Chgo. State U., 1976, Roosevelt U., 1978. Mem.: Chgo. Coun. Fgn. Rels., Chgo. Sexual Assault Svcs. Network (vice-chair, bd. dirs.), Soc. Traumatic Stress Studies (treatment innovations task force), Ill. Coalition Against Sexual Assault (del. 1985—), Nat. Orgn. for Victim Assistance, Am. Profl. Soc. on Abuse of Children. Avocations: aerobics, reading, theater, dining, making and collecting dolls. Office Phone: 773-434-5577. Personal E-mail: leatriceallen@sbcglobal.net. Business E-Mail: lallen@adasmckinley.org.

ALLEN, LINDA S., editor, writer; d. Jim J. and Barbara J. Holland; children: Amy L. Cason, Mandy S. Devich, Jeremy S., Ethan M. BS in Journalism/News Editl., U. Colo., Boulder, 1992. Electronics technician AT&T, Denver, 1973—83, master prodn. scheduling specialist, 1983—89; intern reporter Longmont Times-Call, Longmont, Colo., 1991—92; rschr. The NY Times-Rocky Mountain Bur., Denver, 1992—94; staff reporter The Stuart News, Fla., 1994—97; pub. info. officer Big Bros. Big Sisters of Martin County, Stuart, Fla., 1997—99; editor/writer LRP Publs., Palm Beach Gardens, Fla., 1999—. Author: (non-fiction) You Don't Know Jack: The Tale of a Father Once Removed, WaveMaker. Victim advisor Thornton/Northglenn Police Depts., Colo., 1989—94. Mem.: Fla. Press Assn. (assoc.). Liberal. Christian. Avocations: wilderness hiking/backpacking, downhill skiing, travel. Office Phone: 308-425-8815. Personal E-mail: lindaallen@comcast.net.

ALLEN, LOLA, insurance agent; b. Oakland, CA, Nov. 19, 1964; d. George William and Carol Annette (Goss) Davis. AA in bus., Laney Coll., 1996. Lic. insurance agent/notary pub., Calif. Comm. operator U.S. Army, 1985-90; tech. records U.S. Dept. HUD, San Francisco, 1990-92; account mgr. asst. Gallagher Heffernan Ins., San Francisco, 1992-94; account mgr. small bus. Calif. Insurance & Assocs., San Francisco, 1994-96; inside sales rep. Sweet & Baker Ins., San Francisco; special accounts mgr. Tanner Insurance Brokers, Pleasanton, Calif., 1997-99; account mgr. Crist, Fritschi & Paterson, Oakland, Calif., 1999—. COO, Aging Specialist & Assocs., Oakland, 1998—, Tri-Valley Ins. Profls. Editor: (newsletter) Tri-Valley Tribune, 1998-99. Vol. Safe Grad Nite, U.S. Army, 1988, S.F. Aids Found., San Francisco, 1996—. With U.S. Army, 1985-90. Mem. Tri-Valley Insurance Profls. (pres. 1999—, mem. Yr. 1998-99), Nat. Notary Assn. Avocations: reading, writing, cmty. work, sr. citizens. Office: Ins Personnel Svc 595 Market St #2520 San Francisco CA 94105-2802

ALLEN, LORI ANN, science educator; b. Redwood City, Calif., July 30, 1958; d. John Paul and Marilyn Joan (Barthes) Lucas; m. Wesley Scott Allen, Mar. 27, 1981; children: Melissa Dawn, Owen Ross. BS in Zoology, Okla. State U., 1980; MEd in Sci. Edn., U. Cen. Okla., 1987. Cert. tchr., Okla. Tchr. biology, phys. sci. Edmond (Okla.) Mid. High Sch., 1982-90; tchr. life sci., earth sci. Guthrie (Okla.) Jr. High Sch., 1990-93, Guthrie High Sch., 1993—. Mem. Nat. Sci. Tchrs. Assn., Nat. Assn. Biology Tchrs., Nat. Mid. Level Sci. Tchrs. Assn., Coun. Elem. Sci. Internat., Okla. Edn. Assn., Okla. Sci. Tchrs. Assn. Office: Guthrie HS 200 Crooks Dr Guthrie OK 73044-3746

ALLEN, MARILYN KAY, elementary school educator; b. Crawfordsville, Ind., Nov. 27, 1951; d. Donald Edward and Catherine D. (Sparks) Trosper; m. Gary Wayne Allen, June 10, 1973; children: Matthew, Daniel, Joseph, Sara. BA, Anderson U., Ind., 1974; gifted edn. endorsement, Purdue U., Lafayette, Ind., 1994; MEd, Ind. Wesleyan U., Marion, 1998. Tchg. asst. Western Boone Sch. Corp., Thorntown, Ind., 1986-89, tchr. Granville Wells Elem. Sch., 1989—. Sec. Granville Wells PTO, Jamestown, Ind., 1983-84, Jamestown Tri Area Libr., 1985-87, Western Boone Band Boosters, Thorntown, 1990-92; pres. children's primary sch. LDS Ch., Crawfordsville, 1984-85, pres. Relief Soc., 2005. Mem. NEA, Ind. Tchrs. Assn. (rep. 2000-), Western Boone Tchrs. Assn. (assn. rep. 1994-95). Avocations: cross stitch, reading, travel. Home: 8835 E 900 S Ladoga IN 47954-7246

ALLEN, MARILYN MYERS POOL, theater director, video specialist; b. Fresno, Calif., Nov. 2, 1934; d. Laurence B. and Asa (Griggs) Myers; m. Joseph Harold Pool, Dec. 28, 1955; children: Pamela Elizabeth, Victoria Anne, Catherine Marcia; m. Neal R. Allen, Apr. 1982. BA, Stanford U., 1955, postgrad., 1955—56, U. Tex., 1957—60, West Tex. State U., 1962—63, Odessa Coll., 1987—88. Free-lance radio and TV actress; adj. prof. theatre Midland Coll., 1997—98; dir. Globe Theater, Odessa, 1998, 2002; asst. mng. dir. Amarillo Little Theatre, 1964—66, mng. dir., 1966—68, Horseshoe Players, touring profl. theater, 1969—73; actress multi-media prodn. Palo Duro Canyon, 1971; dir. touring children's theatre, 1978—79; guest actress in Medea at Amarillo Coll., 1981; guest reciter Amarillo Symphony, 1972, Midland-Odessa Symphony, 1984. Pres. Tex. Non-Profit Theatres, 1972-74, 75-77, bd. dirs., 1988-91; 1st v.p. High Plains Ctr. for Performing Arts, 1969-73; adv. dept. fine arts Amarillo Coll., 1980-82; adv. Tex. Constnl. Revision Commn., 1973-75; adv. coun. U. Tex. Coll. Fine Arts, 1969-72; cmty. adv. com. for women Amarillo Coll., 1975-79; conv. program com. Am. Theatre Assn., 1978, program participant, 1978-80, bd. dirs., 1980-83; bd. dirs. Amarillo Found. Health and Sci. Edn., 1976-82, program v.p., 1979-81; bd. dirs. Domestic Violence Coun., 1979-82, March of Dimes, 1979-81, Tex. Panhandle Heritage Found., 1964-82, Friends of Fine Arts, West Tex. State U. (now West Tex. A&M U.), 1980-82, Amarillo Pub. Libr., 1980-82, Amarillo Symphony, 1981-82; publicity chmn. Midland Cmty. Theatre, 1984-87, bd. govs., 1986-92, sec., 1987-88, v.p., 1988-92; bd. dirs. Globe of the Great S.W., Odessa, 1998-2005, v.p. media, 2000-02, v.p. vols., 2002-05; active Mus. of S.W., Midland Arts Assembly; bd. dirs. Midland County Rep. Women, Ways and Means Ch., 1991, 1st v.p., 1992, publicity chair, 1994; mem. Midland County Redistricting com., 1991; cultural exch. del. from Midland, Tex., to Dong Ying, China, 1993; Tex. UIL one act play adjudicator, 1974-99; mem. N.W. Tex. Diocesan Mission Com., 2003-05; co-chmn. Companion Diocese Com., Spain, 2003—. Recipient cert. of appreciation Woman of Yr., Amarillo Bus. and Profl. Women's Club, 1966, Best Actress award for Hedda Gabler role Amarillo Little Theatre, 1965, Best Dir. award for Rashomon, 1967, 1st Pl. award for video spl. Tex. Press Conf., 1988, 1st Pl. award for news Tex. Press Conf., 1989, Disting. Svc. award Tex. Non-Profit Theatres, 1992; named Amarillo Woman of Yr., Beta Sigma Phi, 1980, Broadcaster of the Yr., Rocky Mountain Press Conf., 1988, Hamhock of Yr., Midland Cmty. Theatre, 1992, Outstanding Svc. award Midland Arts Assembly, 1992; Travel fellow AAUW, 1973, 78. Fellow Am. Assn. Cmty. Theatre (dir. 1969-72, 82-84, v.p. planning and devel. 1985-87, co-chair AACT/Fest '95), Internat. Amateur Theatre Assn. 23d World Congress (del. Monaco 1997); mem. USTA (sr. women's team sect. winner 1993, 94), S.W. Theatre Conf. (dir. 1973-76, 82-84, exec. com. 1982-84, Disting. Svc. award 1985), Tex. Theatre Coun. (dir. 1974-78, exec. com., pres. 1975-76), AAUW (br. pres. 1973-75, state chmn. cultural interests 1975-77, 86-88, state program v.p. 1977-79, state bd. dirs. 1984-88, program v.p. Midland 1988-89), Episc. Ch. Women (program v.p. Midland 1988-89, outreach chair 1996, 2005, program v.p., pres.-elect 1997-98, pres. 1999-2000), N.W. Tex. Deanery Ch., 2005-, Holy Trinity Vestry, 2006-, DAR (chpt. chaplain 1971-75, historian 1975-77), C. of C. (fine arts coun.), U.S. Tennis Assn. (sr. mixed doubles sect. winner 1999), U.S. Judo Assn., Symphony Guild, Amarillo Art Assn., Midland Symphony Guild (arrangements chmn. 1983-84), Act IX, Amarillo Law Wives Club (pres. 1976-77), Hamhocks (hon. life, v.p. 1985-86)

ALLEN, MARYON PITTMAN, former senator, clothing designer, journalist; b. Meridian, Miss., Nov. 30, 1925; d. John D. and Tellie (Chism) Pittman; m. Joshua Sanford Mullins, Jr., Oct. 17, 1946 (div. Jan. 1959); children: Joshua Sanford III, John Pittman, Maryon Foster; m. James Browning Allen, Aug. 7, 1964 (dec. June 1978). Student, U. Ala., 1944—47, Internat. Inst. Interior Design, 1970. Office mgr. for Dr. Alston Callahan, Birmingham, Ala., 1959-60; bus. mgr. psychiat. clinic U. Ala. Med. Center, Birmingham, 1960-61; life underwriter Protective Life Ins. Co., Birmingham, 1961-62; women's editor Sun Newspapers, Birmingham, 1962-64; v.p., ptnr. Pittman family cos., J.D. Pittman Partnership Co., J.D. Pittman Tractor Co., Emerald Valley Corp., Mountain Lake Farms, Inc., Birmingham; mem. U.S. Senate (succeeding late husband James B. Allen), 1978; dir. pub. rels. and advt. C.G. Sloan & Co. Auction House, Washington, 1981; feature writer Birmingham News, 1964; writer syndicated column Reflections of a News Hen, Washington, 1969—78; feature writer, columnist Maryon Allen's Washington, Washington Post, 1979—81; columnist McCall's Needlework Mag., 1993—. Owner The Maryon Allen Co. (Restoration/Design), Birmingham. Contbg. editor: So. Accents Mag., 1976—78. Mem. Ladies of U.S. Senate unit ARC, Former Mems. of Congress, Ala. Hist. Commn., Blair House Fine Arts Commn.; charter mem. Birmingham Com. of 100 for Women; mem. steering com. Ala. Gov.'s Mansion; trustee Children's Fresh Air Farm; trustee, deacon, elder Ind. Presbyn. Ch., Birmingham; Dem. Presdl. elector, Ala., 1968. Recipient 1st place award for best original column Ala. Press Assn., 1962, 63, also various press state and nat. awards for typography, fashion writing, food pages, also several awards during Senate service; sponsor, U.S. Navy Nuclear submarine, U.S.S. Birmingham, S.S.N. 695, launched Newport News, Va., 1977, commissioned 1978. Mem.: Nat. Press Club, 1925 F St. Club, 91st Congress Club, Congl. Club, Birmingham Country Club. Home and Office: Creekstone Cottage 1551 Creekstone Cir Birmingham AL 35243 Office Phone: 205-822-9266. E-mail: maryonallenco@aol.com.

ALLEN, MIA FLORENCE, health and physical education educator; b. Austell, Ga., May 20, 1974; d. Willie Mack and Linda Mae Clonts; children: Jada MaKayla, Naya Jenae. BS, Mid. Tenn. State U., Murfreesboro, 1996, Kennesaw State U., Ga., 2004; MEd, U. Phoenix, 2006. Cert. tchr. Ga. Fin. advisor Citigroup, Balt., 1998—2003; tchr. Fulton County Bd. Edn., Atlanta, 2004—. Volleyball and track coach Sandtown Mid. Sch., Atlanta, 2004—06. Home: 3004 Lonetree Point Douglasville GA 30135 Office Phone: 404-346-6500. Personal E-mail: allen_mia@yahoo.com.

ALLEN, NANCY SCHUSTER, librarian, director information resources; b. Buffalo, Jan. 10, 1948; d. Joseph E. and Margaret (Cormack) Schuster; m. Richard R. Allen, Sept. 2, 1967; children: Seth Cormack, Emily Margaret, Laura Jean. BA, U. Rochester, 1971, MA in Art History, 1973; MLS, Rutgers U., 1973. Asst. libr. Mus. Fine Arts, Boston, 1975-76, chief libr., 1976-95; reference libr. Medford (Mass.) Pub. Libr., 1973-75; Susan Morse Hilles dir. info. resources Mus. Fine Arts, Boston, 1995—. Lectr. Grad. Sch. Libr. and Info. Scis., Simmons Coll., Boston, 1984—; mem. preservation adv. group Rsch. Librs. Group, 1993—. Mem. art history scholarly adv. com. and joint task force Commn. on Preservation and Access, 1990-92. Mem. Art Libr. Soc. N.Am. (chmn. 1983-84), Soc. Am. Archivists, Rsch. Librs. Info. Network (chmn. art and architecture program com. 1985-88, mem. preservation adv. coun. 1993—), Internat. Fedn. Librs. (fin. officer sect. art librs. 1985-89), Fenway Librs. Online (v.p. 1987-89, pres. 1989-91), Rsch. Librs. Group (bd. dirs. 1995—). Office: Mus Fine Arts Dept Info Resources 465 Huntington Ave Boston MA 02115-5597

ALLEN, NORMA ANN, librarian, educator; b. Balt., Jan. 22, 1951; d. James Crawley and Thelma Agusta (Keaton) Ghee; children: Lamont Ricardo Ghee, Alissa S. Allen, Avery O. Allen. BA in Adminstrn. Mgmt., Sojourner Douglass Coll., Balt., 1987; MS in Instrnl. Tech., Towson State U., 1999. Instr. data processing PSI Inst., Balt., 1987-88; acquisition technician Social Security Adminstrn., Balt., 1987-89, reference librarian, 1989-91, acquisitions librarian, 1991—; librarian United Bapt. Membership Conv., Balt., 2002—. Instrnl. developer Computer Asst. Instrn., Towson U., 1995—; bus. computer tech. instr. Balt. City C.C., 2000—; freelance floral designer/arranger, freelance instr. basic writing skills and computer literacy; instr. bus. computer tech. Balt. City C.C., 2000—. Sec., bd. dirs. New Image Child Care Facility, Balt., 1992, chmn. bd. dirs., 2001-02; instr. active reading literacy program Enoch Pratt Libr., Balt., 1992; instr. United Missionary Bapt. Conv., 1997, libr., 2003. Multicultural scholar Towson U., 1995-96. Mem. ALA, Spl. Librs. Assn., Horizon User Group. Office: Social Security Adminstrn 6401 Security Blvd Rm 571 Baltimore MD 21235-0001 E-mail: norma.allen@ssa.gov.

ALLEN, PAMELA SMITH, retired psychologist, writer; b. Marianna, Fla., Dec. 19, 1943; d. Milton Clark Smith and Dora Bernadette Gordy; m. William Thomas Lassiter, Aug. 8, 1964 (div. 1972); 1 child, Kerry Lassiter Arnsten; m. George Young, 1974 (div. 1977); m. William Kelly, Feb. 11, 1979 (div. 1992); m. Lawrence Allen, Feb. 14, 2000 (div. Feb. 5, 2004); life ptnr. Lawrence Allen, 2005. BA, U. Fla., Gainesville, 1964; MEd, U. Fla., 1967, EdS, 1968; PhD, US Internat. U., San Diego, 1989. Lic. psychologist (inactive) Calif., marriage and family therapist (inactive) Calif., cert. pupil pers. svcs. plus psychology Calif., gen. elem. tchr. Calif. Spl. edn. tchr. Alachua County Schs., Gainesville, 1964—68, Duval County Schs., Jacksonville, Fla., 1969—70, sch. psychologist, 1970—72, spl. edn. tchr., 1972—73, Daniel Meml. Home, Jacksonville, 1973—74; 1st grade tchr. Valley Ctr. Schs., Valley Center, Calif., 1976—78; spl. edn. tchr. San Diego City Schs., 1978—79, sch. psychologist, 1979—2005; pvt. practice psychotherapist Escondido, Calif., 1990—92, Carlsbad, Calif., 1992—94. Adj. prof. US Internat. U., 1991—94; tchr. Camelrock Yoga Ctr., Valley Center, 2002—04; Tai Chi Chuan instr. Am. Universalist Temple of Divine Wisdom, Valley Center, 2005—, workshop presenter, 2004—05. Author: Enhancing Children's Creativity and Self Perceptions Through the Arts, 1989, Awakening to the Spirit Within: Eight Paths, 2004, (poetry) Unfolding, 1987; prodr.(with Barbara Morse): (game) Squnch Journey, 1993. Mem.: Inst. Noetic Scis., Assn. Rsch. and Enlightenment, Assn. Ret. Persons, Sierra Club. Personal E-mail: pmsmallen@yahoo.com.

ALLEN, PATRICIA J., library director; b. McLean County, Ky., Nov. 10, 1941; d. Richard Louis and Helen (Hancock) Jones; m. Jerry M. Mize, Mar. 19, 1960 (div. 1978); children: Martin P., Elizabeth M. Atherton; m. Lawrence A. Allen, Nov. 24, 1983 (div. 1985). Student, Murray (Ky.) State U., 1959-60; BA, Ky. Wesleyan Coll., 1962; MA, Western Ky. U., 1974; MLS, U. Ky., 1982; postgrad., U. N.C., 1983-84. Libr. pub. elem. schs., Daviess County, Ky., 1963-70; media specialist pub. elem., mid. and high schs. McLean County, Ky., 1970-78; head pub. svcs., assoc. prof. libr. sci. Ky. Wesleyan Coll., Owensboro, 1978-83; asst. dir. Evansville (Ind.) Vanderburgh County Pub. Libr., 1985-89; dir. Carmel (Ind.) Clay Pub. Libr., 1989-91, Sanibel (Fla.) Pub. Libr., 1991—. Mem. adj. faculty Western Ky. U., Bowling Green, 1977-78, Ind. U., Bloomington, 1988; workshop presenter Nursing Home Activities Dirs. Assn., Owensboro, Ky., 1981; cons. Ky. Dept. Librs. and Archives, Frankfort, 1982, Purchase (Ky.) Regional Libr. Sys., Murray, 1983, Henderson (Ky.) C.C. Libr., 1988. Editor: Emergency Handbook, 1987, Circulation Policies and Procedures, 1988, Sanibel Public Library Building Program Statement, 1992; contbr. article to profl. jours. Pres. Ret. Sr. Vol. Program Adv. Coun., Evansville, 1986-88; bd. dirs. Evansville Goodwill Industries, 1987-89. Named Outstanding Citizen of the Yr., Sanibel-Captiva Islands C. of C., 1995; Caroline M. Hewins scholar U. Ky., 1982, Margaret Ellen Kalp scholar U. N.C., 1983-84; hon. Ky. Col., 1981. Mem. ALA, Ky. Libr. Assn., Fla. Libr. Assn. (Transformer award 1996), Pub. Libr. Assn., Libr. Adminstrs. and Mgrs. Assn., S.W. Fla. Libr. Network (bd. dirs. 1997—, pres. 1999-2001), Zonta (bd. dirs. 1999-2001), Beta Phi Mu. Democrat. Baptist. Avocations: travel, walking, swimming, needlecrafts, reading. Office: Sanibel Pub Libr 770 Dunlop Rd Sanibel FL 33957-4016 E-mail: pallen@sanlib.org.

ALLEN, PATRICIA JEAN, graphics designer; b. Jersey City, Sept. 22, 1940; d. Joel Morris and Blanche Jeanne (de la Villebeuvre) Allen. BFA, Beaver Coll. Display artist Hahne's, Newark; v.p., assoc. design dir. Doremus & Co., N.Y.C. Judge DESI awards Graphic Design USA, N.Y.C. Mem.: Soc.

Illustrators (assoc.), Andy Award, Am. Inst. Graphic Arts, PIMNY, N.Y.C., Mead Library Ideas, Art Dirs. Club Chgo., Art Dirs. Club N.J., Type Dirs. Club, Art Dirs. Club Phila. (awards for design excellence). Home: 267 Laurel Ave Kearny NJ 07032-3630 Office: Doremus & Co 200 Varick St Fl 12 New York NY 10014-4810

ALLEN, PAULA SMITH, literature and language professor; b. Beckham County, Okla., Feb. 10, 1951; d. Emit Smith and Mildred Florence Bradley; m. Robert John Allen, Oct. 21, 1967; children: Sheila Marie, Jonathan David, Ana Lisa. MA in English Studies, W. Tex. State U., Canyon, 1990; PhD in Comparative Lit., Tex. Tech U., Lubbock, 1997. Tchr. Eagle Pass (Tex.) Ind. Sch. Dist., 1975—92; vis. prof. Angelo State U., San Angelo, Tex., 1997—98; prof. english S.E. Okla. State U., Durant, 1998—. Author: (monograph) Metamorphosis and the Emergence of the Feminine, (book chapter) Identity and the Teaching of Diversity, Summer's Lightning: Olive Senior's Jamaican Redemption. Mem. Westside Heritage Assn., Durant, Okla., 1999—2006. Mem.: Coll. English Assn., Nat. Coun. Tchrs. English. Democrat-Npl. Achievements include research in N.Am. and S.Am. literatures, education. Avocations: reading, writing, travel. Office: SE Okla State Univ 1405 N 4th Ave Durant OK 74701 Office Phone: 580-745-2592.

ALLEN, PINNEY L., lawyer; b. Marshalltown, Iowa, Jan. 26, 1953; d. Walker Woodrow and Doris (Pinney) A.; m. Charles C. Miller, III, Aug. 20, 1977; children: Linden, Doria. AB summa cum laude, Harvard U., 1976; JD cum laude, Harvard Law Sch., 1979. Bar: Ga., 1976; U.S. Tax Ct. 1984. Assoc. Alston & Bird, Atlanta, 1979-86; ptnr., co-chair, tax practice group Alston & Bird LLP, Atlanta, 1986—. Contbr. articles to profl. jours., 1981—. Mem. ABA, Nat. Soc. Accts. for Coops., Ga. Bar Assn., Atlanta Bar Assn., Atlant Tax Forum. Office: Alston & Bird 1 Atlantic Ctr 1201 W Peachtree St NW Atlanta GA 30309-3424 Office Phone: 404-881-7485. Office Fax: 404-881-7777. Business E-Mail: pallen@alston.com.

ALLEN, RENEE ANNETTE, application developer; d. Leo Fredrick and Mary Ann (Bollinger) Curran; m. Larry Don Allen, Apr. 19, 1980; children: Tammy Kaye, Christi Denice Hales. AAS, Tarrant County Coll., Fort Worth, Tex., 1984. Software engr. Policy Mgmt. Systems Corp., Ennis, Tex., 1984—85, Distributed Software Group, Fort Worth, 1985—89; owner/software engr. Double C Computer Co., Fort Worth, 1989—93; software engr. Randolph Data Systems, Fort Worth, 1993—97; IT devel. mgr. UICI, North Richland Hills, Tex., 1997—. Mem.: Mensa (life). Avocations: golf, travel, cake decorating.

ALLEN, ROBERTA, writer, photographer, conceptual artist; b. NYC, Oct. 6, 1945; d. Sol and Jeanette (Waldner) A. Student, Inst. Bellas Artes, Mex., 1971. Lectr. Corcoran Sch. Art, Washington, 1975, Kutztown State Coll., 1979, C.W. Post Coll., 1979. Instr. creative writing Parsons Sch. Design, N.Y.C., 1986; instr. The Writer's Voice, 1992—97, The New Sch., 1993—, Dept. Continuing Edn., NYU, 1993—99; Tennessee Williams fellow, writer-in-residence U. of the South, Sewanee, Tenn., 1998; adj. asst. prof. Columbia U. Sch. of the Arts, 1998—99, Eugene Lang. Coll., 2000. Author: Partially Trapped Lines, 1975, Pointless Arrows, 1976, Pointless Acts, 1977, Everything in The World There Is To Know Is Known By Somebody, But Not By the Same Knower, 1981, Amazon Dream, 1993; author: (fiction) The Daughter, 1992, The Dreaming Girl, 2000, The Traveling Woman, 1986, Certain People, 1997; author: (writing guide) Fast Fiction, 1997, The Playful Way to Serious Writing, 2002, (Personal Growth) The Playful Way to Knowing Yourself, 2003; one-woman shows include Galerie 845, Amsterdam, Netherlands, 1967, John Weber Gallery, N.Y.C., 1974—75, 1977, 1979, Inst. for Art and Urban Resources, 1977, 1980, Galerie Maier-Hahn, Dusseldorf, Germany, 1977, MTL Galerie, Brussels, 1978, C.W. Post Coll., Glenvale, N.Y., 1978, Galerie Walter Storms, Munich, 1981, Kunstforum, Stadt. Galerie in Lenbachhaus, 1981, Galeria Primo Piano, Rome, 1981, Perth Inst. Contemporary Arts, 1989, Art Resources Transfer, Inc., 2001, SUNY, Binghamton, 2001. Fellow, Va. Ctr. Creative Arts, 1985, 1994, 2005; McDowell Colony fellow, 1971—72, Yaddo fellow, 1983, 1987, 1993, LINE grantee, 1985. E-mail: robertaallen@mac.com.

ALLEN, ROSEMARY M., lawyer; b. 1948; BA, Ind. U., 1970; MEd, Boston U., 1979; JD, Northeastern U., 1986. Bar: Mass. 1987, RI 1995, US Ct. Appeals (1st Cir.). Law clk. to Hon. Bruce M. Selya US Ct. Appeals (1st Cir.), 1987; ptnr. Mintz, Levin, Cohn, Ferris, Glovsky & Popeo PC, Boston, coord., Intellectual Property Sect. Mem.: ABA, RI Bar Assn., Mass. Bar Assn., Boston Bar Assn. Office: Mintz Levin Cohn Ferris Glovsky & Popeo PC One Financial Center Boston MA 02111 Office Phone: 617-348-1601. Office Fax: 617-542-2241. Business E-Mail: rallen@mintz.com.

ALLEN, ROSETTA ROSETTA, elementary school educator; b. Asheville, NC, Aug. 6, 1973; d. Ernest Locke and Sheila Dianne Ramsey; m. Ronald Timothy Allen, Dec. 26, 1993; children: Isaac Timothy, Payton Ramsey. Student, U. NC, Asheville, 1991—95; BS in Elem. Edn., Austin Peay State U., Clarksville, Tenn., 1996. Cert. Nat. Bd. Tchr. Cert., 2001. Tchr. Yancey County Schs., Burnesville, NC, 1997—. Sec./treas. Bee Log Bapt. Ch., Burnsville, 1999—; bd. dirs. Edn. Found. Yancey County, Burnsville, 2001—02, Transition Team, Burnsville, 2004—. Named Tchr. of Yr., Yancey County Schs., 2001—02. Avocations: reading, fishing, piano, guitar. Home: 2617 Bald Mountain Rd Burnsville NC 28714

ALLEN, SHARON, accounting firm executive; B in acctg., U. Idaho, 1973, Ph.D (hon.) in adminstrv. sci., 2004. Mng. ptnr. Pacific Southwest practice Deloitte & Touche USA LLP, LA, 2003—, chmn. bd., 2003—. Mem. bd. United Way Greater LA; bd. mem. YMCA Met. LA; co-chair Nat. Campaign Com. Campaign for Idaho; bd. dirs. Malcolm Baldridge Found., Harvard U., John F. Kennedy Sch. Govt. Women's Leadership Coun.; chmn. bd. dirs. Independent Coll. So. Calif. (ICSC), 2003—; adv. bd. Coll. Bus. and Econ. Named Woman of the Yr., Fin. Woman's Assn., 2006; named one of Top 100 Most Influential People in 2003, Acctg. Today mag., 100 Most Powerful Women, Forbes Mag., 2006. Mem.: LA Area C. of C. (bd. mem.). Office: Deloitte & Touche USA LLP Two Calif Plz 350 S Grand Ave Ste 200 Los Angeles CA 90071-3492 Office Phone: 213-688-0800. Office Fax: 213-688-0100.

ALLEN, SHEILA W., dean; BS, DVM, Cornell U.; M in Vet. Clinical Pathology, U. Ga. Sch. Vet. Medicine, 1986. Diplomate Am. Coll. Vet. Surgeons. Intern small animal medicine and surgery U. Ga. Coll. Vet. Medicine, 1981, resident, faculty mem., 1986, head dept. small animal medicine and surgery, assoc. dean academic affairs, interim dean, 2005, dean, 2005—. Bd. dirs. Ga. Vet. Med. Assn. Mem.: European Coll. Vet. Surgeons (examination com.), Am. Coll. Vet. Med. Colleges (exec. com. chair, Assoc. Deans for Academic Affairs), Am. Coll. Vet. Surgeons (bd. regents, examination com., chair rsch. com., chair publications com.). Achievements include becoming the second female dean of a veterinary college in US. Office: Univ Ga College Vet Medicine Hodgson Oil Bldg Rm Ste 200N 286 Oconee St Athens GA 30602-4999 E-mail: sallen@vet.uga.edu.*

ALLEN, SHIRLEY JEANNE, humanities educator; b. Tyler, Tex., Dec. 19, 1941; d. Ralph Carnell and Theressa Gunzell Allen; m. George Taylor (div.). BA, Gallaudet U., Wash., DC, 1966; MA, Howard U., Wash., DC, 1972; EdD, U. Rochester, N.Y., 1992. Editl. clk. IRS, Wash., 1967; instr., dorm supr. Gallaudet U., 1968—73; prof. Rochester Inst. Tech., 1973—2001; ret., 2001. Bd. vis. Jarvis Christian Coll., Hawkins, Tex., 2000—. Named to Pioneer Hall of Fame, Jarvis Christian Coll., 1992. Mem.: Coun. Am. Instrs. of the Deaf, Nat. Black Deaf Advocates, Nat. Assn. Deaf. Baptist. Achievements include cover story in Jarvisonian Magazine, 2005. Avocations: reading, writing. Home: 9117 Vicksburg Ave Texas City TX 77591

ALLEN, SUSAN DIANE, educator; b. Ithaca, N.Y., Jan. 5, 1954; d. Bruce Richard and Judith Diane Schueler; m. Terrence Paul Allen, Aug. 6, 1977; children: Christopher Kirk, Justin Thomas. BS in Edn., SUNY, Fredonia, 1976; MS in Edn., SUNY, Buffalo, 1979; cert. in coaching, Batavia, 2006. Cert. permanent tchg. Dept. Edn. N.Y., 1979. Adminstrv. asst. Empire State Coll., Buffalo, 1977—78; tchr. Attica Ctrl. Sch., NY, 1978—. Advisor student coun. Attica Ctrl. Sch., 1978—, soccer coach, 1979—81, advisor yearbook, 1988—, varsity soccer coach, jr. varsity soccer coach, modified coach, 1997—; coord. United Schools In Action, Attica, 2001—. Bd. dirs. AYA, Attica, 1990—97, Angel Action, Perry, NY, 2000—06. Named Educator of Week, Channel 2, Buffalo, 2006, Citizen of Yr., Lion's Club, 2006; recipient Adult Vol. award, Wyo. County Youth Bd., 2002, Outstanding Orgn. for Youth award, 2004, Adult Vol. award, 2004. Mem.: Delta Kappa Gamma. Avocations: racquetball, reading, bicycling. Home: 3043 Dunbar Rd Attica NY 14011 Office: Attica Ctrl Sch 3338 E Main St Attica NY 14011 Office Phone: 585-591-0400. Business E-Mail: sallen@atticacsd.org.

ALLEN, SUZANNE, financial planning executive, insurance agent, writer, educator; b. Santa Monica, Calif., May 31, 1963; d. Raymond A. and Ethel Allen; m. Steve Milstein Roth, Dec. 27, 1992, (div. 2000). BA, U. Calif., Santa Cruz, 1986; MA in Edn., Calif. State U., L.A., 1990; postgrad., Art Ctr. Sch. Design, 1994—. Cert. tchr., Calif.; lic. real estate agt., Calif. Interviewer LA Times Newspaper, 1986-88; educator LA Unified Sch. Dist., 1987-90, Burbank Unified Sch. Dist., Calif., 1990-94, 1994—2000; ptnr. fin. svc. Roth & Assoc./NY Life, LA, 1993-2000; educator Pasadena Unified Sch. Dist., 2001—02; ptnr. fin. svc. Pacific Life Ins. Co.; v.p. Jarvis & Mandell LLC Estate Planning Svc., Mass. Mut. Ins. Co., 2001—; agt. Mass. Mut. Ins., Beverly Hills, Calif. Ptnr. Retirement Educators Fin. Svc.; agt.-cons. Frasier Fin. Group, 2001—02; bilingual program coord. Amadeo Spanish Lang. Enrichment Sch., 2004—. Model, actor:, 1998—; author: End of Days, 2001—, numerous poems, Gospel in the Air, 2005 (named Best Poems and Poets, Libr. Cong., 2005), (albums) Sound of Poetry, 2005. Mem. PTA, United Tchr. Pasadena, Civil War Trust; vol. SPCA/Humane Soc., 1999—; mem. Nat. Trust Hist. Preservation, Honor Roll mem.; bd. mem. Bungalow Heaven Neighborhood Assn.; hon. mem. Top Bus. Rep. Party for Sen. Tom Delany. Recipient 4 Silver Cups, Internat. Poet of Merit, 8 Bronze medals, Internat. Poets Soc., Piece of the Roof award, N.Y. Life Ins. Co. for Roth & Assocs., 1994, Nat. Leadership award, Nat. Rep. Congl. Com., 2003, Silver trophy Outstanding Achievement in Poetry, 2003, Silver trophy outstanding achievement in poetry, 2004, 2005. Mem.: NEA, Libr. of Congress, Nat. Soc. for Hist. Preservation, Burbank Tchrs. Union, U. Calif. Santa Cruz Alumni Assn., Internat. High IQ Soc., Abraham Lincoln Assn., Internat. Soc. Poets (hon.). Avocations: painting, jewelry designing, writing, weight training, quilting. Office: Michael's Agy Mass Mut Beverly Hills Office 1875 Century Park E # 1550 Los Angeles CA 90067 also: Jarvis And Mandell Llc 2321 Rosecrans Ave Ste 1280 El Segundo CA 90245-4933 Office Phone: 626-296-8479.

ALLEN, TERICE DIANN, music educator; b. Denton, Tex., Mar. 24, 1962; d. Norwood Raymond and Judith Diann Preto; m. Michael Lee Allen, July 6, 1985; children: Christopher Lee, Matthew Kendall. B in Music Edn., U. North Tex., Denton, 1985. Cert. tchr. Tex., Fla. Jr. youth orch. dir. North Tex. State U., Denton, 1984—85; orch. dir. Richardson Ind. Sch. Dist., Tex., 1985—89, Denton Ind. Sch. Dist., 1989—93; coach, dir. Tallahassee Symphony Youth Orch., 1995—2000; tchr. Fla. State U. Sch., Tallahassee, 1997—, head music dept., orch. dir., guitar instr., 2003—. Cellist Big Bend Cmty. Orch., Tallahassee, 2000—06, Allen Family Cello Quartet, Tallahassee, 1996—, Killearn United Meth. Ch. Orch., Tallahassee, 2002—. Orch. mem. Killearn United Meth. Ch., Tallahassee, 2002—06. Named Outstanding Am. Tchr., Nat. Honor Roll, 2005—06. Mem.: Tex. Orch. Dir. Assn., Fla. Orch. Assn., Fla. Music Educators Assn., Music Educators Nat. Conf. Avocations: reading, piano, cello. Office: Fla State U Sch 3000 School House Road Tallahassee FL 32311 Office Phone: 850-245-3700. Office Fax: 850-245-3737. Business E-Mail: tallen@mailer.fsu.edu.

ALLEN, TONI K., lawyer; b. NYC, Aug. 6, 1940; d. Irving M. and Mary (Sackler) Schoolman; m. Robert W. Clark III, July 22, 1985. AB, Wellesley Coll., 1960; LLB, NYU, 1964. Bar: NY 1964, DC 1972. Atty. Office of Irving M. Wall, Esquire, N.Y.C., 1964-68; gen. counsel, asst. to pres. Nat. Econ. Rsch. Assocs., N.Y.C., 1968-71; atty., advisor Postal Rate Commn., Washington, 1971-72; assoc. Wald, Harkrader & Ross, Washington, 1972-73, ptnr., 1974-85, Piper & Marbury LLP, Washington, 1986-98, chmn. environ. dept., 1991-94, mem. policy and mgmt. com., 1992-94, ptnr. emeritus, 1999—. Adj. fellow Hudson Inst., 2001—. Trustee Levine Sch. Music, Washington, 1981—2004, pres., 1991-96; co-chair exec. bd. Environ. Lawyer, 1994-96, Leadership Washington, 1996-97; bd. dirs., 2003—, vice chair United Way of the Nat. Capital Area, 2003—05, treas. 2005-06. Fellow Am. Bar Found.; mem. Order of Coif. Democrat. Avocations: sports, music, travel, cooking. E-mail: tka5640@aol.com.

ALLEN, VICKY, sales and marketing professional; b. Springfield, Pa., May 27, 1957; d. James Joseph and Ann Marie (Cifone) Cattafesta; m. James Francis DeLeone, Aug. 11, 1979 (div. 1982); m. Dennis Ronald Allen, June 30, 1990; children: Amber, Austen. BBA in Computer Sci., Temple U., 1979. Quality assurance Burroughs Corp., Downingtown, Pa., 1977, software QA, 1978, systems analyst, 1979-81; program analyst Crocker Internal Systems, San Jose, Calif., 1981-83; sr. systems analyst Avantek, Inc., Santa Clara, Calif., 1983-84; product mktg. program specialist Micro Focus, Palo Alto, Calif., 1984-96; OEM sales account mgr. Netscape Comms. Corp., Mountain View, Calif., 1996-99; mgr. Nortel Networks Strategic Relationships, 1999—2002; dir. inside sales Polycom, Milpitas, Calif., 2002—03; sales mktg. specialist Steel Eye Tech., Mountain View, Calif., 2003—04; sales territory mgr. telecomm. divsn. VeriSign, 2004—. Programmer cons. Fin. Group, Palo Alto, 1985-86. Active Sierra Club. Mem. Phi Sigma Sigma (sec. 1978-79). Democrat. Roman Catholic. Avocations: music, hiking, bicycling, walking. Office: Verisign 487 E Middlefield Rd Mountain View CA 94043 Office Phone: 650-426-3784. E-mail: squirlr1@yahoo.com.

ALLEN, VICTORIA TAYLOR, archivist; b. N.Y.C., June 22, 1942; d. Robert Grayson and Margaret (Seckel) Taylor; m. Ernest G. Allen, Dec. 28, 1985 (dec. Apr. 1989). BA in French, Mary Washington Coll./U. Va., 1964; MAT in English, Manhattanville Coll., 1979. Tchr. of French, Chatham Hall, Chatham, Va., 1965-73, Masters Sch., Dobbs Ferry, N.Y., 1973-79; tchr. English, Convent of the Sacred Heart, N.Y.C., 1979-86; archivist The Convent of the Sacred Heart, Greenwich, Conn., 1995—. Mem. adv. bd. Barat House, Manhattanville Coll., Purchase, N.Y., 1994—; mem. adv. bd. Open Door Health Ctr., Ossining, N.Y., 1986-90. Author; (booklet) Traditions and Customs of Sacred Heart Education, 1998. Roman Catholic. Avocations: photography, travel, cooking, gardening.

ALLENDE, ISABEL ANGELICA, writer; b. Chile, Aug. 2, 1942; d. Tomas and Francisca A.; m. Miguel Frias, 1962 (div. 1987); children: Paula (dec.), Nicolas; m. William Gordon, 1988. LLD (hon.), NYU, 1991; degree (hon.), U. Chile, 1991; LLD (hon.), Dominican Coll., 1994, Bates Coll., 1994; doctorate (hon.), Mills Coll., 2000, Lawrence U., 2000. Sec. FAO, Santiago, Chile, 1959-65; journalist Paula mag., Santiago, Chile, 1967-74, Mampato mag., Santiago, Chile, 1969-74; TV interviewer Canal 13/Canal 7, 1970-75; worked on movie newsreels, 1973-75; journalist El Nacional newspapers, Venezuela, 1975-84; adminstr. Colegio Marroco, Caracas, Venezuela, 1979-82. Lectr. U.S.A., Europe, and Latin Am., lit. workshops, U.S.A.; speaker, lectr. univs. and colls.; tchr. lit. U. Va., Charlottesville, Montclair (N.J.) Coll., U. Calif., Berkeley. Author: Civilice a su troglodita: los impertinentes de Isabel Allende, 1974, La casa de los espíritus, 1982 (pub. as The House of Spirits, 1985), La gorda de porcelana, 1984, De amor y de sombra, 1984 (pub. as Of Love and Shadows, 1987; L.A. Times Book prize nomination 1987), Eva Luna, 1987, Los cuentos de Eva Luna, 1990 (pub. as The Stories of Eva Luna, 1991), El plan infinito, 1991 (pub. as The Infinite Plan, 1993), Paula, 1995, Afrodita, 1997, Daughter of Fortune, 1999 (WILLA Lit. award 2000), Portrait in Sepia, 2001, City of the Beasts, 2002, Kingdom of the Golden Dragon, 2004, Forest of the Pygmies, 2005; Zorro, 2005 (Publishers Weekly Bestseller list, 2005); writer short stories for children and humor books, Chile, 1972-73, theater plays in Chile El Embajador, 1971, La Balada del Medio Pelo, 1973, Los Siete Espejos, 1974; contbr. articles to newspapers and mags. USA, Europe, Latin Am. Recipient Panorama Literario award (Chile), 1983, Grand Prix d'Évasion (France), 1984, Point de Mire (Belgium), 1985, XV Premio Internazionale I Migliori dell'Anno (Italy), 1987, Mulheres best fgn. novel award (Portugal), 1987, Before Columbus Found. award, 1988, Best Novel award (Mexico), 1985, Author of Yr. award (Germany), 1986, Freedom to Write Pen Club award, 1991, XLI Bancarella Lit. award (Italy), 1993, Ind. Fgn. Fiction award (Eng.), 1993, Brandeis U. Major Book Collection award, 1993, Critic's Choice award, 1996, Gabriela Mistral Recognition award (Chile), 1994, Chevalier dans l'Ordre des Arts et des Lettres award (France), 1994, Feminist of Yr. award Feminist Found., 1994, Read About Me Literary award, 1996, Books to Remember award ALA, 1996, Gift of Hope award, 1996, Harold Washington Lit. award, 1996, Malaparte award Amici di Capri, Italy, 1998, Donna Citta Di Roma Lit. award Italy, 1998, Dorothy and Lillian Gish prize, 1998, Sara Lee Frontrunner award, 1998, Woman of Yr. award GEMS, 1999, Donna Dell'Anno award, Italy, 1999; named Hon. Citizen of City of Austin, 1995, Mem. Academia de Artes y Ciencias (P.R.), 1995. Mem Acad. Devel. and Peace (Austria, hon.). Office: Carmen Balcells Diagonal 580 08021 Barcelona Spain

ALLENSON, JENNIFER LEIGH, elementary school educator; b. Santa Monica, Mar. 1, 1976; d. James Homer and Janice Catherine Pangburn; m. Matthew Stephen Allenson, Dec. 27, 2003. AA, Allan Hancock Coll., Santa Maria, 1996; BA, San Diego State U., 1999. Cert. tchr. Calif. State U., 2000. 8th grade tchr. Thomas Jefferson Mid. Sch., Madera, 2000—01, English reading tchr., 2001—02; composition/lit. tchr. Ralston Mid. Sch., Belmont, 2002—03, 2004—05, math. tchr., 2003—04, 2005—. Asst. youth pastor Orcutt Presbyn. Ch., 1994—95. Mem.: Phi Kappa Phi, Phi Beta Kappa. Avocations: reading, knitting, cooking.

ALLEN-SWARTTOUW, HEATHER LINDSEY, artist, art educator, writer; b. Concord, N.H., Feb. 1, 1963; d. Peter Herbert and Marion Lindsey (Butson) A. Cert. in lang. proficiency, Nanzan U., Nagoya, Japan, 1985; BFA, U. N.H., 1989; MFA, U. Mass., Dartmouth, 1992. Screenprinter N.H. Printwork, Greenland, 1989; color separator Roth Tec Engraving Corp., New Bedford, Mass., 1990; exhbn. tech. Childrens Mus., Dartmouth, Mass., 1990-91; emerging profl. artist residency Appalachian Ctr. for Crafts, Smithville, Tenn., 1993-95, workshop tchr., 1993-97; tchr. U. Mass., Darthmouth, 1991-93; workshop tchr. Quilt Surface Design Symposium, Columbus, Ohio, 1995-98, Arrowmont Sch. Art and Crafts, Gatlinburg, Tenn., 1996—; tchr. Penland (N.C.) Sch. Crafts, 1997—, Haystack Mt. Sch. Crafts, 2004—. V.p. Highland Rim Tenn. Assn. Craft Artists, Smithville, 1993-95; contbg. artist Art in Embassies Prog., 1996—. Author: Weaving Contemporary Rag Rugs, 1998; contbr. articles to craft mags. Big sister Big Brother Big Sister Prog., New Bedford, Mass., 1990-93. Recipient Spotlight '94 Handweavers Guild Am. award, Winston-Salem, N.C., Niche award Phila. Buyers Market, 1996; NEA Regional fellow So. Arts Fedn., Atlanta, 1995, artist fellow Tenn. Arts Commn., Nashville, 1995. Mem. Fiberarts Internat., Am. Craft Coun., Surface Design Assn., Highlands Craft Guild. Avocations: gardening, travel, color, cooking. Home and Office: 2 Grace Ave Asheville NC 28804-2503 Office Phone: 828-281-1778. E-mail: hallenstudio@earthlink.net.

ALLENTUCK, MARCIA EPSTEIN, English language educator, art history educator; b. N.Y.C., June 8, 1928; m. 1949; 1 child. BA, NYU, 1948; PhD, Columbia U., 1964; MA (hon.), Oxford U., 1975. Lectr. English Columbia U., N.Y.C., 1955-57, Hunter Coll., N.Y.C., 1957; from lectr. to prof. English CCNY, N.Y.C., 1959-88; prof. history of art Grad. Ctr. CUNY, N.Y.C., 1974-88, prof. emerita, 1988. Author: The Works of Henry Needler, 1961, Henry Fuseli: The Artist as Critic and Man of Letters, 1964, The Achievement of Isaac Bashevis Singer, 1969, John Graham's System and Dialectics of Art, 1971; contbr. articles to profl. jours. Morrison fellow AAUW, 1958-59, Howard fellow Brown U., 1966-67, Huntington Libr. fellow, 1968, 77, fellow Nat. Translation Ctr. U. Tex., 1968-69, Chapelbrook Found., 1970-72, Dumbarton Oaks Harvard U., 1972-73, sr. fellow NEH, 1973-74, vis. fellow Wolfson Coll. Oxford U., 1974—, fellow Brit. Acad. Newberry Libr., 1980, Murray rsch. fellow Radcliffe Coll., Harvard U., 1982, fellow Inst. Advanced Studies in the Humanities, Edinburgh (Scotland) U., 1984, rsch. fellow Swann Found., 1989—; vis. scholar Burrell Art Collection, Glasgow, Scotland, 1978, 88; Am. Philos. Soc. grantee, 1966-67. Fellow Royal Soc. Arts London; mem. MLA (del. assembly 1989—), Brit. Soc. Archtl. Historians, Milton Soc. Am., Augustan Reprint Soc., Soc. Archtl. Historians, Coll. Art Assn., Phi Beta Kappa. Home: 5 W 86th St Apt 12B New York NY 10024-3665

ALLER, MARGO FRIEDEL, astronomer; b. Springfield, Ill., Aug. 27, 1938; d. Jules and Claire (Cornick) Friedel; m. Hugh Duncan Aller, Aug. 17, 1964; 1 child, Monique Christine. BA, Vassar Coll., 1960; postgrad., Harvard U., 1961-62; MS, U. Mich., 1964, PhD, 1969. Mathematician programmer Smithsonian Astrophys. Obs., Cambridge, Mass., 1960-62; rsch. assoc. U. Mich., Ann Arbor, 1970-76, assoc. rsch. scientist, 1976-85, rsch. scientist, 1985—. Mem. users' com. Nat. Radio Astronomy Observatory, 1984—86. Mem. Internat. Union of Radio Sci., Am. Astron. Soc., Internat. Astron. Union, Sigma Xi. Avocation: skiing. Office: U Mich Dept Astronomy 817 Dennison Bldg Ann Arbor MI 48109-1042 Business E-Mail: mfa@umich.edu.

ALLEVI, ANGELA, pediatrician; Assoc. program dir. Nat. Capitol Consortium Pediatric Residency Program, Washington; asst. prof. pediatrics Thomas Jefferson U., Phila., A.I. DuPont Hosp. for Children, Wilmington. Served with USN, 2001—05. Recipient Leadership award (Young Physician), AMA Found., 2005. Mem.: Am. Acad. Pediatrics (exec. com. mem., sect. on young physicians). Office: Dept Pediatrics Thomas Jefferson Univ 833 Chestnut St Ste 300 Philadelphia PA 19107 Office Phone: 215-955-7800. E-mail: aallevi@nemours.org.*

ALLEY, KIRSTIE, actress; b. Wichita, Kans., Jan. 12, 1951; m. Parker Stevenson Dec. 22, 1983 (div. Dec. 1997); children: William True, Lillie. Student, U. Kans., Kans. State U. Actress: (stage prodns.) Cat on a Hot Tin Roof, Answers; (feature films) Star Trek II: The Wrath of Khan, 1982, Blind Date, 1984, Champions, 1984, Runaway, 1984, Summer School, 1987, Shoot to Kill, 1988, Look Who's Talking, 1989, Daddy's Home, 1989, One More Chance, 1990, Madhouse, 1990, Sibling Rivalry, 1990, Look Who's Talking Too, 1990, Look Who's Talking Now, 1993, Village of the Damned, 1995, It Takes Two, 1995, Sticks and Stones, 1996, For Richer of Poorer, 1997 (People's Choice award 1997), Deconstructing Harry, 1997 (People's Choice award 1997), Toothless, 1997, Drop Dead Gorgeous, 1999, The Mao Game, 1999, Back by Midnight, 2002; (TV mini-series) North and South Book I, 1985, North and South, Book II, 1986, The Last Don, 1997, The Last Don Part II, 1998 (Emmy nomination), Blonde, 2001, Salem Witch Trials, 2002; (TV movies) Sins of the Past, 1984, A Bunny's Tale, 1984, The Prince of Bel Air, 1985, Stark: Mirror Image, 1986, Infidelity, 1987, David's Mother, 1994 (Emmy award, Lead Actress - Special, 1994), Radiant City, 1996, Family Sins, 2004; (TV series) Masquerade, 1984-85, Cheers, 1987-1993 (Emmy award as Outstanding Lead Actress in a Comedy Series 1991); actress, exec. prodr.: Suddenly, 1996, Profoundly Normal, 2003; actress, co-prodr.: Nevada, 1997; prodr., actress: Veronica's Closet, 1997-2000; actress, writer, exec. prodr.: Fat Actress, 2005; TV appearances include The Match Game PM, 1979, The Hitchhiker, 1985, 87, Wings, 1993, Ink, 1997, Dharma & Greg, 2001, Without a Trace, 2004; spokesperson for Jenny Craig. Spokesperson for Narcanon Drug Rehab.; founder Ch. of Scientology, Mission of Wichita; involved with Fight for Kids. Recipient People's Choice award, 1998. Mem.: Gamma Phi Beta.

ALLEY, MARY LOU VANDE WOUDE, retired medical/surgical nurse; b. Sioux Center, Iowa, Mar. 23, 1942; d. Bert John Van Maanen and Gertrude Winters; m. Dallas Glen Alley, June 29, 2003; children: Michelle, Michael, Mark. RN, Meth. Hosp., Sioux City, 1963. Staff nurse Orange City (Iowa) Mcpl. Hosp., 1963—64, Hartley (Iowa) Cmty. Hosp., 1964—67, Mercy Hosp., Council Bluffs, Iowa, 1972—74, Jennie Edmunson Hosp., Council Bluffs, 1974—75; staff nurse, unit dir. Nebr. Med. Ctr., Omaha, 1975—2004; ret., 2004. Leader bible study United Meth. Ch., Council Bluffs. Methodis. Avocations: bible study, golf, reading, travel. Home: #9 Virginia Hills Rd Council Bluffs IA 51503 Personal E-mail: mvande5257@cox.net.

ALLEY, NANCY CORRIN, elementary school educator; b. Louisville, Ky., May 28, 1953; d. Ralph James and Ann Ellis Corrin; m. William Edward Alley, June 4, 1977. BA, Fla. So. Coll., Lakeland, 1975; MAT, East Tenn. State U., Johnson City, 1978. Profl. tchg. stds. bd. cert. Tchr. grades 3-4 Johnson County Sch. Dist., Dry Run, Tenn., 1978—80; art tchr. Fremont County Sch. Dist. 21, Ft. Washaki, Wyo., 1981—87; tchr. grades 2-6 Vail Sch. Dist., McCoy, Colo., 1988—90; kindergarten tchr. Vashan Island Sch. Dist., Vashan Island, Wash., 1990—93; tchr. kindergarten art, grades 3-4 Roaring Fork Sch. Dist., Glenwood Springs, Colo., 1993—2003; art tchr. Fremont County Sch. Dist. 25, Riverton, Wyo., 2003—. Contbr. articles mags. and publs. Named Dist. Tchr. of Yr., 1984, Wyo. Art Educator of Yr., 1988, Elem. Tchr. of Yr., Fremont County Sch. Dist. 25, 2005; recipient full scholarship, Getty Inst., 1987. Mem.: Phi Delta Kappa, Gamma Beta Phi. Methodist. Avocations: skiing, kayaking, hiking, painting, reading. Home: 2769 Sinks Canyon Rd Lander WY 82520

ALLINSON, DEBORAH LOUISE, economist; b. Providence, Oct. 30, 1950; d. Wayne Clinton and Barbara (Pearson) A.; m. Thomas J. Lamb, Apr. 27, 1973; children: Andrew Allinson Lamb, Michael Allinson Lamb, Peter Allinson Lamb, Emily Allinson Lamb. BA in Econs. cum laude, Tufts U., 1972. Rsch. asst. Wellington Mgmt., Boston, 1972-75, asst. v.p., 1975-78, v.p., 1978-89, sr. v.p., 1990-91, ptnr., 1991—. Bd. dirs. Wellington Trust Co., South Shore Conservatory of Music. Active Alexis de Tocqueville Coun. United Way. Mem. Nat. Assn. Bus. Economists, Boston Assn. Bus. Economists, Boston Econ. Club (pres. 1995, mem. exec. com.), Washington Nat. Econ. Club. Office: Wellington Mgmt 75 State St Boston MA 02109-1700 Home: 17 Martins Cove Rd Hingham MA 02043-1042 Office Phone: 617-951-5226.

ALLISON, ADRIENNE AMELIA, not-for-profit developer; b. Toronto, Ont., Can., Nov. 2, 1940; d. Harold Whitfield and Emmeline Amelia (Banister) Hedley; m. Stephen Vyvyan Allison, Jan. 2, 1960 (div. 1984); children: Mark Hedley, Myles Stephen, Alexander Andrew; m. Armin U. Kuder, Aug. 26, 1989 (div. 2002). BA, George Washington U., 1978; MA, Georgetown U., 1980; MPA, Harvard U., 1986. Social sci. analyst U.S. AID, Washington, 1980-85, project mgr., 1986-89, presdl. com. HIV epidemic, 1987-88; program dir. Centre for Devel. and Population Activities, 1988-91; v.p. Centre for Devel. and Population Activities, 1991-98; dir. maternal and neonatal health program Johns Hopkins Program in Reproductive Health, Balt., 1998—2001; ind. cons. Chevy Chase, Md., 2001—06. Adj. prof. George Washington U. Sch. Pub. Health; adj. prof. Bloomberg Sch. Pub. Health Johns Hopkins U., 1995—2005. Co-author: Vegetable Gardening in Bangladesh, 1975. Chair peace commn. Episcopal Diocese of Washington, 2002—06; mem. vestry St. Albans Parish, Washington, 1984—88. Mem.: APHA, Cosmos Club. Home: 8011 Glendale Rd Chevy Chase MD 20815-5902 Personal E-mail: adrienneaallison@aol.com.

ALLISON, AMY S., secondary school educator; b. Alpine, Tex., June 8, 1958; d. James Lafayette and Dorothy Buhler Crawford; m. James E. Allison Jr., Dec. 31, 1981; 1 child, James E. III. BS, Sul Ross State U., Alpine, 1980; M in Sci. Tchg., N.Mex Inst. Mining and Tech., Socorro, 1991. Cert. tchr. Ariz., Tex. Rsch. asst. SW Found. Biomed. Rsch., San Antonio, 1982—85; sci. educator Clark HS, San Antonio, 1985—93; secondary sci. educator, academic decathlon coach, tennis coach Desert View HS, Tucson, 1993—99; secondary sci. educator, academic decathlon coach Marfa (Tex.) HS, 1999—. Cons. U. Tex. Alliance For Edn./Project 2061, San Antonio, 1990—93, Psychol. Corp., San Antonio, 1992—93; chmn. North Ctrl. Outcome Accreditation/Desert View HS, Tucson, 1995—99; chem. hygiene officer Sunnyside Unified Sch. Dist., Tucson, 1996—99; site-based decision making com. Marfa HS, 2000—. Named Dist. Outstanding High Sci. Tchr., Northside Ind. Sch. Dist., 1992, Honored Educator, U. Ariz., 1997, Educator of Yr., Marfa C. of C., 2005; recipient Mayor's award (MESA), Mayor of Tucson, 1995; grantee, Tex. Learn and Serve, 2003, 2004. Avocations: reading, gardening, outdoor activities, motorcycling. Home: PO Box 1486 319 N Summer Marfa TX 79843 Office: Marfa HS PO Box T/ 300 N Gonzales Marfa TX 79843 Office Phone: 432-729-4252. Office Fax: 432-729-4053. Personal E-mail: amo6858@sbcglobal.net. E-mail: aallison@esc18.net.

ALLISON, ANNE MARIE, retired librarian; b. Oak Park, Ill., Oct. 3, 1931; d. Gerald Patrick and Anna Evelyn (Beam) Myers; m. James Dixon Alison, Aug. 28, 1954; children: Mark, Mary, Clare, Ruth, Edward. BA in French, St. Mary of the Woods Coll., 1951; postgrad., U. Fribourg, 1952-53; MLS, Rosary Coll., 1968. Asst. libr. Triton Coll., River Grove, Ill., 1967-68; asst. libr. tech. svcs. Moraine Valley Community Coll., Palos Hills, Ill., 1968-69; dir. learning resources, head libr. Coll. Lake County, Grayslake, Ill., 1969-71; asst. head catalog dept. Kent (Ohio) State U. Librs., 1971-73, head processing dept., 1973-79, asst. dir. libr. svcs., 1979-81; acting dir. Fla. Atlantic U. Libr., Boca Raton, 1980-81; asst. dir., head tech. svcs. Wayne State U. Librs., Detroit, 1981-83; dir. librs. U. Cen. Fla., Orlando, 1983-97, ret., 1997. Past chair, bd. dirs. Fla. Extension Libr., Tampa; bd. dirs. Ctr. for Libr. Automation, Gainesville, Fla., Cen. Fla. Holocaust Meml. Resource Ctr., Orlando; adj. prof. Libr. and Info. Sci., U. S. Fla., Tampa. Editor: OCLC: A National Library Network, 1979; contbr. articles to profl. jours. Arbitrator alternative dispute resolution program Better Bus. Bur. Cen. Fla., Maitland, 1985—; active Friends Winter Park Pub. Libr., Friends of Orlando Pub. Libr. Recognized for Outstanding Leadership in Edn. Cen. Fla. Ednl. Consortium for Women, 1990. Mem. ALA (chair profl. ethics com.), Fla. Libr. Assn., Fla. Assn. Coll. and Rsch. Librs. (pres. bd. dirs.). Avocations: fruit farming, collecting china. Office: U Cen Fla PO Box 25000 Orlando FL 32816-0001

ALLISON, ARLENE MARIE, elementary school educator; d. Richard and Judith Arlene Lasko; m. Scott Jeffery Allison, Sept. 26, 1998; children: Robert (Robby) Scott, Grace Marie, Jillian Rae. BA, Ohio No. U., Ada, 1997. Cert. elem. edn. Ohio, 1997. 8th grade health tchr. Ada Exempted Village Schs., 1998—99, Title I reading tchr., 2000—. Active PEO Chpt. O, Ada, Ohio, 1998—2006. Office: Ada Exempted Village School 435 Grand Ave Ada OH 45810 Office Phone: 419-634-2341. Business E-Mail: allisona@ada.k12.oh.us.

ALLISON, JOAN KELLY, music educator, pianist; b. Denison, Iowa, Jan. 25, 1935; d. Ivan Martin and Esther Cecelia (Newborg) K.; m. Guy Hendrick Allison, July 25, 1954 (div. Apr. 1973); children: David, Dana, Douglas, Diane. MusB, St. Louis Inst. of Music, 1955; MusM, So. Meth. U., 1976. Korrepetitor Corpus Christi (Tex.) Symphony, 1963-85; staff pianist Am. Inst. Mus. Studies, Graz, Austria, 1974-89; prof. Del Mar Coll., Corpus Christi, 1976—2002. Adj. prof. Del Mar Coll., 1959-75, 2006—, Corpus Christi State U., 1978-93, Tex. A&M U., Corpus Christi, 1993-2004; program dir. Corpus Christi Chamber Music Soc., 1986—; piano chmn. Corpus Christi Internat. Competition for Piano and Strings, 1987—; chmn. Del Mar Coll. Student Programs Com., 1986-88, 91-92, 94-95, 2001-02; chmn. radio com., S.Tex. Pub. Broadcasting Svc., Corpus Christi, 1987-88; asst. mus. dir. Little Theater, Corpus Christi, 1970-74; judge, Houston Symphony Auditions, 1988, S.C. Young Artist Competition, Columbia, 1990; freelance accompanist, 1955—, adjudicator, 1960—; v.p. united faculty Del Mar Coll., 1986-88; pianist with Del Mar Trio, 1965-95, Young Audiences, Inc., 1975-83; recital tours in U.S., Mex., Austria, 1954-88. Piano soloist, St. Louis Symphony, 1956, 57, Bach Festival Orch., St. Louis, 1955, Corpus Christi Symphony; recipient Artist Presentation award, Artist Presentation Soc., St. Louis, 1956; contbr. articles to profl. jours., including Internat. Piano Quar. Co-chmn. Mayor's Com. on Recycling, Corpus Christi, 1989-91; bd. dirs. Corpus Christi Symphony; adv. bd. Corpus Christi Concert Ballet; mem. steering com. cultural devel. plan City of Corpus Christi, 1995-96. Recipient Women in Careers award YWCA, 1985. Mem. Corpus Christi Music Tchrs. Assn., Liszt Soc. (contbr. to jour.). Avocations: foreign travel, water-skiing, hiking, acting in community theatre. Home: 4709 Curtis Clark Dr Corpus Christi TX 78411-4801 Personal E-mail: Jallison@the-i.net.

ALLISON, PAMELA A., mathematics educator; MEd, U. South Fla., Tampa, 1980. Cert. Nat. Bd. Profl. Tchg. Stds., 1999. Tchr., dept chair Middleton H.S., Tampa, 2003—. Finalist Dist. Tchr. of Yr., Hillsborough County, 2004—05. Mem.: Nat. Coun. Tchrs. Math. Office: Middleton High School 3814 N 22d Street Tampa FL 33610

ALLISON, SARAH AMANDA, art educator, consultant; b. Shreveport, La., Apr. 8, 1973; d. Rebecca Ellen and Robert Russell Yeager; m. Justin Williams Allison, Jan. 7, 2006. BA in Art Edn., La. State U., Shreveport, 1996; MA in Art, Northwestern State U., Natchitoches, La., 2001. Cert. tchr. La., 1996. Faculty art Tex. Christian U., Ft. Worth; art educator mid. and h.s. Shreveport, La., 1996—2001; tchg. fellow U. North Tex., Denton, 2001—05. Art edn. and disability cons., Fort Worth, Tex., 2001—; mem. adj. faculty Buffalo State Coll., 2005. Contbr. articles to profl. jours. Fellow Paine Webber fellow, Paine Webber Found., 1999, Marcus fellow, Edward and Betty Marcus Found., 2002—03; scholar Acad. Achievement award, U. of North Tex. Sch. of Visual Arts, 2001. Mem.: Tex. Art Edn. Assn., Nat. Art Edn. Assn. Office: Texas Christian University Box 298000 Fort Worth TX 76129 Office Phone: 817-257-7041. Personal E-mail: amandaallison2@gmail.com.

ALLMAN, MARGARET ANN LOWRANCE, counseling administrator; b. Carmel, Calif., June 2, 1938; d. Edward Walton and Rhoda Elizabeth (Patton) Lowrance; m. Jackie Howard Hamilton, Dec. 21, 1959 (div. May 1976); children: John Scott Hamilton, David Lee Hamilton, Dennis Lynn Hamilton; m. Jack Fredrick Allman, Dec. 22, 1977; stepchildren: John Frederick(dec.), James Paul, Jeffrey Lee. AA, Christian Coll., 1958; BA in Spanish, U. Mo., 1960, MEd, 1971, EdD, 1994. Tchr. Spanish Neosho (Mo.) HS, 1961-62, asst. prin., 1974-77; florist Wallflower Shop and Greenhouse, Joplin, Mo., 1962-69; dean girls Joplin Sr. HS, 1967-69; florist, bookkeeper Mueller's Garden Ctr., Columbia, Mo., 1969-71; instr. edn., asst. dean of students Columbia Coll., 1971-74; dir. guidance Am. Cmty. Sch., Buenos Aires, 1978-81; tchr. Spanish, psychology Ava (Mo.) HS, 1982-84; tchr. Spanish, social studies McDonald County HS, Anderson, Mo., 1984-88; counselor, acad. advisor Mo. So. State U., Joplin, 1988—2003. Cons. Mo. So. State Univ., 1990—; mem. internat. task force Mo. So. State Coll., 1994—96; mem. adv. bd. Adult Basic Edn., Joplin, 1992—2003; presenter Ctr. Applications Psychol. Type Internat. Conf., 1996. Named to Outstanding Young Women Am., 1972; recipient William D. Phillips Music award, 1st Christian Ch., Columbia, 1956. Mem.: Southwest Mo. Sch. Counselor Assn. (sec. 1994—97, v.p. 1992—94, 1999—2001, mem. governing bd., chmn. publs. and rsch. com. 1997—99), Mo. Sch. Counselor Assn., Phi Theta Kappa, Sigma Delta Pi, Phi Sigma Iota (romance lang., pres. 1959—60), Delta Eta Chi, Sigma Phi Gamma, Kappa Delta Pi. Avocations: music, photographer, sketch artist, needlecrafts, jewelry crafts. Home: 1214 Circle Dr Neosho MO 64850-1301 Office Phone: 417-451-7633. Personal E-mail: jfallman@sbcglobal.net.

ALLOTTA, JOANNE MARY, elementary school educator; b. Bklyn., Dec. 8, 1962; d. Joseph and Adela (Castagna) A.; m. Edward James Cirminiello, Mar. 23, 1991. BA in Child Study, St. Joseph's Coll., 1984; MS in Edn., Bklyn. Coll., 1987; postgrad., 1987-88; advanced cert., Bklyn. Coll. Cert. tchr., NY, sch. dist. adminstr., NY; provisional cert. sch. adminstr. and supr., NY. Tchr. Holy Family Sch., Bklyn., 1984—85; elem. tchr. Pub. Sch. 97, Bklyn., 1985—2001, cooperating tchr. for srs. majoring in edn., 1985—2001; curriculum writer for profl. devel. Sch. Dist. 21, N.Y.C., 1991—, program facilitator gifted program Bklyn., 2001—03; instrnl. literacy coach Pub. Sch. 95, 2003—04; asst. prin. Pub. Sch. 226, 2004—. Workshop presenter; reviewer N.Y.C. Bd. Edn., Bklyn, 1992; mem. task force com. N.Y. Partnership for Statewide Systems Change-Dist. 21, 1993-95; textbook reviewer grade 4 social studies Scott Forseman, 2002-03. Active Pub. Sch. 226 PTA, 1985-2001; fund raiser St. Jude's Children's Hosp., 1990-2001. Recipient Tchr. of Yr. award Phi Delta Kappa, 1994, Tchr. of Yr. award Pub. Sch. 97, 1999. Mem. ASCD, Am. Fedn. Tchrs., United Fedn. Tchrs., N.Y. State of United Tchrs., Coun. Sch. Suprs. and Adminstrs., Nat. Assn. Elem. Sch. Prins., Kappa Delta Pi. Roman Catholic. Avocations: reading, writing, needlepoint. Office: Pub Sch 226 6006 23rd Ave Brooklyn NY 11204

ALLRED, DAWN PETERMAN, adult education educator; b. Roscrea, Ireland, Aug. 15, 1952; arrived in U.S., 1958, naturalized; d. Eugene Vincent and Ruth Kavanaugh Peterman; children: Anne Kavanaugh, Brendan, James. BA in Speech and Comm., U. Mo., Columbia, 1973; MEd in Spl. Edn., U. Mo., St. Louis, 2000, PhD, 2005. Cert. tchr. Mo. Rschr. comm. divsn. Marshall Field & Co., Chgo., 1979; tchr. ESL Parkway Sch. Dist., Creve Coeur, Mo., 1977—78; tchr. grade 3, primary grade coord. Annunziata Sch., St. Louis, 1974—77; tchr. grades 4, 5, 6, 7 St. Justin the Martyr Sch., St. Louis, 1979—82; grad. tchg. fellow U. Mo., 2000—, instr. Coll. Edn., 2001—04, student tchr. supr., 2004. Mem. com. Qualitative Rsch. Conf., St. Louis, 2001—. Pres. PTA The Miriam Sch., Webster Groves, Mo., 1993—95; mem. govt. rels. com. Parkway Sch. Dist., Chesterfield, Mo., 2000—05; bd. dirs. Spl. Edn. Transition Adv. Bd., St. Louis, 2001—. Recipient Meritorious Svc. commendation, U. Mo., 2004, 2005, 2006. Mem.: Mo. Assn. on Higher Edn. and Disability, Learning Disabilities Assn. Mo., Assn. for Study Higher Edn., Equestrian Order of the Holy Sepulchre of Jerusalem, Kappa Delta Phi, Phi Kappa Phi. Roman Catholic. Avocations: travel, Irish history and culture, hiking. Business E-Mail: allredd@umsl.edu.

ALLRED, GLORIA RACHEL, lawyer; b. Phila., July 3, 1941; d. Morris and Stella Bloom; m. Peyton Bray; 1 child, Lisa; m. William Allred (div. Oct. 1987). BA, U. Pa., 1963; MA, NYU, 1966; JD, Loyola U., LA, 1974; JD (hon.), U. West LA, 1981. Bar: Calif. 1975, U.S. Dist. Ct. (ctrl. dist.) Calif. 1975, U.S. Ct. Appeals (9th cir.) 1976, U.S. Supreme Ct. 1979. Ptnr. Allred, Maroko, Goldberg & Ribakoff (now Allred, Maroko & Goldberg), LA, 1976—. Former host KABC TalkRadio, Los Angeles. Contbr. articles to profl. jours. Pres. Women's Equal Rights Legal Def. and Edn. Fund, LA, 1978—, Women's Movement Inc., LA. Recipient Commendation award City of LA, 1986, Mayor of LA, 1986, Pub. Svc. award Nat. Assn. Fed. Investigators, 1986, Vol. Action award Pres. of U.S., 1986, Women of Distinction award Nat. Coun. on Aging, 1994, The Judy Jarvis Meml. award, 2001; Named to Millennium Hall of Fame, Nat. Assoc. Women Bus. Owners, LA Chapter, 2000. Mem. ABA, Calif. Bar Assn., Nat. Assn. Women Lawyers, Calif. Women Lawyers Assn., Women Lawyers LA Assn., Friars (Beverly Hills, Calif.), Magic Castle Club (Hollywood, Calif.) Office: Allred Maroko & Goldberg 6300 Wilshire Blvd Ste 1500 Los Angeles CA 90048-5217 Office Phone: 323-653-6530.

ALLRED, MICKI KATHLEEN, music educator; b. Roosevelt, Utah, Aug. 7, 1976; d. McCord John and Kathleen Ruth Marshall; m. John Ned Allred, Sept. 12, 2002. BA, Weber State U., Ogden, Utah, 1998; MusM, U. Utah, Salt Lake City, 2001. Cert. tchg. Utah State Office Edn., 2003. Tchg. asst. U. Utah, Salt Lake City, 1998—2001; tchr. Allred Piano Studio, Roosevelt, Utah, 2002—; music tchr. East Elem. Sch., 2003—. Rep. Duchesne Educators Assn., Roosevelt, Utah, 2004—06. Scholar, Weber State U., 1994—98. Mem.: Utah Music Tchrs. Assn. (assoc.; chpt. pres. 1999—2001). Mem. Ch. Lds. Avocations: reading, swimming, travel. Home: 880 S 200 W 310-12 Roosevelt UT 84066 Office: Duchesne County Sch Dist 700 E 400 N Roosevelt UT 84066 Office Phone: 435-725-4671.

ALLSTEDT, NORA MARIE, music educator; b. Jacksonville, Fla., Aug. 4, 1965; d. Raymond Norman and Theresa Maria Allstedt. M in Music Edn., Valdosta State U., Ga., 1992. Band dir. Rocky Hill Elem. Sch., Exeter, Calif., 2001—04, Wilson Mid. Sch., Exeter, 2003—. Mem.: CBDA, TKMEA, IAJE, Music Educators Nat. Conf., Tau Beta Sigma (life), Sigma Alpha Iota (life). Home: 15040A Ivanhoe Dr Visalia CA 93292 Personal E-mail: nallstedt@msn.com.

ALLSTON, CHARITA CAPERS, music educator; d. Lloyd Sterling and Viretta Thomas Bond; children: Paul Capers Jr., Wayne Capers. AS in Music Edn., Essex County Coll.; BS in Voice, William Paterson Univ. Cert. tchg. cert. State of N.J. K-12. Acctg. tech. U.S. Postal Svc., Newark, 1973—91; choral instr. Orange Bd. of Edn., Orange, NJ, 1991—93, Elizabeth (N.J.) Bd. of Edn., 1993—99, Newark (N.J.) Newark Bd. of Edn., 1999—. Choir mem. R.P. Means Gospel Choir, 1975—99, M.A. Zimmerman Youth Choir, 1975—79, M.D. Birt AME Choir, 1977—92, Polyphonics Com. Ens., 1975—90; choir dir. Henry Tucker Male Chorus, 1977—84, rainbow Children's Choir, 1989—91, Chancellor Choir, 1989—91, St. Matthews Children's Choir, 1988—92, Angels of Zion Youth Choir, 1993—95, Allston/Shepard Gospel Music Works, 1991—2003, Park Ave. Christian Ch. Inspirational Choir and Crusaders For Christ, 1993—. Contbr. (vocals and piano for record album by Buddy Terry) Lean on Him; cinematographer: (organ and vocals for nat. TV) Dr. Albert Lewis Gospel Hour - Gospel Explosion; contbr. (organ and vocals for nat. TV) Bobby Jones Gospel Show: Black History Month Mass Concert; contbr. over 100 concerts and major events; contbr. US. Tennis Opening with Queen Latifah, 2000, in Going Home Celebration (Funeral) Lionel Hampton, 2002, Jubilation Choir N.J. Performing Arts, 2000, 02, Ray Charles Celebrates Christmas with the Voices of Jubilation, 2002, (CD) Launching Out Into the Deep, 2005. Recipient Charita C. Allston Resolution, City of Newark N.J., 1997, R.P. Means Adult Gospel Choir, 1997, Charita C. Allston Resolution for N.J. Performing Arts, City of Newark, N.J., 2003. Mem.: N.J. Music Edn. Assn., Newark Teachers Union, Nat. Assn. for Music Edn., Am. Fedn. of Musicians of US and Can. (Local 16). Personal E-mail: satindoucca@aol.com, callston@comcast.net.

ALLSUP, ROXANE CUELLAR, curriculum and instruction educator; b. Laredo, Tex., Feb. 26, 1968; d. Angel Arturo and Rosa Ramirez Cuellar; m. Christopher Bryan Allsup, July 28, 2001; children: Isabella Rose, Christopher Andrew. BS, Tex. A&M U., College Station, 1990, MEd, 1993, PhD, 2000. Cert. elem. edn. tchr., bilingual/ESL tchr., supr. Tex. Bilingual 2d grade tchr. Bryan Sch. Dist., Tex., 1991—94, bilingual resource specialist, 1995—96, 1997—98; asst. lectr., tchg. asst. Tex. A&M U., College Station, 1994—2000; vis. asst. prof. U. Houston, 2000—01; asst. prof. Tex. State U., San Marcos, 2001—. Cons., literacy coach Round Rock Sch. Dist., Tex., 2003—06; co-dir. bilingual edn. grant Tex. State U., San Marcos, 2005—06. Contbr. articles to profl. jours. Asst. chairperson multicultural awareness com. Bryan Sch. Dist., 1997—98; mem. San Marcos Sch. Dist., 2005—06. Bilingual Edn. fellowship, Tex. A&M U., 1994—97. Mem.: Tex. Assn. Bilingual Edn., Nat. Assn. Hispanic and Latino Studies, Nat. Assn. for Bilingual Edn., Phi Kappa Phi, Kappa Delta Pi. Roman Catholic. Avocation: spending time with my children. Office: Tex State Univ 601 University Dr San Marcos TX 78666 E-mail: rcuellar@txstate.edu.

ALLUMS, HENRIENE, elementary school educator; b. Jackson, Miss., July 30, 1945; d. Henry and Annie (Johnson) A. BA, Calif. State U., Long Beach, 1967; MA, U. San Francisco, 1978. Cert. elem., secondary tchr., Calif., ESL tchr., cross cultural, language and acad. devel. tchr. Tchr., grades 1-3 L.A. Unified Sch. Dist. Mem. Calif. Assn. bilingual Edn., Calig. Tchrs. English to Speakers of Other Langs., Internat. Reading Assn., Tchrs. English to Speakers of Other Langs. Home: 1522 E 123rd St Los Angeles CA 90059-2920

ALMEIDA, MICHELLE KATHLEEN, psychologist, educator; b. NYC, Aug. 23, 1967; d. Antonio Almeida and Victoria Cruz; m. Valentine Lopez, June 2, 1996; 1 child, Valentine Anthony. BA in Elem. Edn. summa cum laude, Bayamon Ctrl. U., Bayamon, PR, 1990; PhD in Clin. Psychology, Carlos Albizu U., San Juan, PR, 2006. Cert. tchr. PR Dept. Edn. Spanish tutor Bayamon Ctrl. U., PR, 1985—89; tchr. spl. edn. Strong Ednl. Ctr., Rio Piedras, 1989—94; prof. Ctr. Intensive Reviews, Toa Baja, 1990—92, ednl. coord., 1992—96; co-founder and exec. dir. Inst. Almeida, Inc., PR, 1996—. V.p. adv. bd. Empresas Afiliadas, Bayamon, 2000—. Author: Analytical Reasoning Review for the LSAT, 2001, Logical Reasoning Review for the LSAT, 2001, Rezonamiento Analitica - EXADEP, 2004. Vol. spl. edn. tchr. Parents' Assn. Handicapped Children of PR, San Juan, 1987—88. Named Most Successful Ex-Alumni, Pres. Bayamon Ctrl. U., 1998; named to Nat. Deans' List, Bayamon Ctrl. U., 1988—89, Distiguished Grad. Gallerty; recipient Academic Achievement award, Phi Delta Kappa, 1990. Mem.: ACA, APA, Stress and Anxiety Rsch. Soc. Office: Inst Almeida Inc PO Box 51466 Levittown Sta Toa Baja PR 00950-1466

ALMES, JUNE, retired education educator, librarian; b. Pitts., Feb. 14, 1934; d. Donald John Rowbottom and Marie Catherine (Linz) Douglas; widowed; children: Lawrence John, Douglas Alan. BS in Edn., Ind. U. of Pa., 1955; MLS, U. Pitts., 1969. Tchr. Shippensburg (Pa.) Area High Sch., 1964-68; assoc. prof. Lock Haven (Pa.) U., 1971-94; ret., 1990. Instr. Changsha U. Electric Power, Hunan, China, 1989-90, 95. Co-author: A Survey of the United Kingdom and the United States of America, 2004. Trustee Ross Pub. Libr., Lock Haven, 1975-88, community story programs, 1973-86; tutor Clinton City Literacy Found., Lock Haven, 1979; pres. Ea. Clinton Co. Democratic Women's Club, 2003—. Mem. Am. Assn. Sch. Librs., Pa. Assn. Sch. Librs., ACLU, Phi Kappa Phi, Phi Delta Kappa. Democrat. Avocations: bridge, reading, travel. Home: 228 East Hillside Dr Lock Haven PA 17745-1733 Personal E-mail: jalmes@lhup.edu.

ALMÉSTICA, JOHANNA LYNNETTE, mental health counselor, administrator; b. Ponce, P.R., Aug. 4, 1970; arrived in U.S., 1988; d. Joaquin Alméstica and Margarita Bracero. BA in Psychology, U. Mass. Boston, 1993; MS in counseling Psychology, Our Lady of Lake U., 1999. Counselor, case mgr. supr. Acute Treatment Ctr. Dimock Cmty. Health Ctr., Roxbury, Mass., 2000—. Mem.: APA. Roman Catholic. Avocation: reading. Office: Dimock Cmty Health Ctr Acute Treatment Ctr 41 Dimock St Roxbury MA 02119

ALMGREN, KANDEE ANN, language educator; b. Alva, Okla., July 10, 1972; d. Stanley Ray and Karen Ann Almgren. BA in Edn., Northwestern Okla. State U., Alva, 1995; MEd, U. Ctrl. Okla., Edmond, 2001. Cert. tchr. Okla. Dept. Edn., Nat. Bd. for Profl. Tchg. Standards. Tchr. English Arnett Pub. Schs., Okla., 1996—2000, Waynoka Pub. Schs., Okla., 2000—. Mem. bd. Wesley Found. at Northwestern Okla. State U., 2001—06. Mem.: Delta Kappa Gamma (sec. Chi chpt. 2004—06), Alpha Sigma Alpha (treas. Alva Alomnee chpt. 2003—06). Democrat. Methodist. Home: 715 Third Alva OK 73717

ALMON, LORIE, lawyer; b. NYC, Feb. 19, 1969; d. William Scott and Margaret Elise (Erickson) A. BA, U. Vt., 1991; JD, U. Va., 1994. Bar: N.Y. 1995, Conn., U.S. Dist. Ct. (so., ea. no. and we. dists.) NY, US Ct. of Appeals (2 and 3d cirs.). Asst. Corp. Counsel Office Corp. Counsel, NYC, 1994—98; co-mng. ptnr. Seyfarth Shaw, LLP, NYC, 1998—. Mem. regional bd. advisors Jumpstart. Named one of Top 40 Under 40 Lawyers, Nat. Law Jour., 2005. Mem. ABA, NYC Bar Assn., Soc. Human Resource Mgmt. Office: Seyfarth Shaw LLP 1270 Avenue Of The Americas Ste 2500 New York NY 10020-1801 Office Phone: 212-218-5517. Office Fax: 212-218-5526.

ALMOND, BEVERLY MCCULLOUGH, literature educator; d. Richard William and Louise Keylon McCullough; m. John Russell Almond, June 17, 1967; children: Brent McCullough, Bradley Alan, Bryan Jonathan, Brandon David. BA, Lyon Coll., Batesville, Ark., 1968; MA, U. Tex., San Antonio, Tex., 1989; student, Trinity Coll., Newburgh, Ind., 2005—. Music tchr. Wilbur Trimpe Jr. HS, Bethalto, Ill., 1968—70; grad. asst. U. Ark., Fayetteville, Ark., 1975; adult educator U.S. Army, Ft. Stewart, Ga., 1977—79; tutor Friends Abroad, Kadena AFB, Japan, 1983; bus. and tech. English instr. Ctrl. Tex. CC, Kadena AFB, Japan, 1984—85; counselor admissions Baylor U., Waco, Tex., 1989—92; English tchr. Am. Sch. RAF Alconbury, Huntington, England, 1992—95; chmn., dept. English Dominion and Trinity Christian Schs., Fairfax, Va., 1997—2000; prof. English and humanities Strayer U., Fredericksburg, Va., 2000—02; lectr. English U. Mary Washington, Fredericksburg, 2002—. Adj. prof. English Palo Alto C.C., San Antonio, 1989, Pikes Peak C.C., Colo. Springs, Colo., 1989—92. Contbr. articles to mags. Tutor Literacy Vols. Am., Rantoul, Ill., 1981—83; dir. choir Kadena Air Base Chapel USAF, Okinawa, Japan, 1984—85, dir. choir Alconbury Base Chapel, 1994—95. Mem.: Nat. Coun. Tchrs. English, Alpha Chi. Avocations: travel, walking, music. Office: Univ Mary Washington 1301 College Ave Fredericksburg VA 22401 Office Phone: 540-654-1547. Business E-Mail: balmond@umw.edu.

ALMORE-RANDLE, ALLIE LOUISE, special education educator, academic administrator; b. Jackson, Miss., Apr. 20; d. Thomas Carl and Theressa Ruth (Garrett) Almore; m. Olton Charles Randle, Aug. 3, 1974. BA, Tougaloo Coll., 1951; MS in Edn., U. So. Calif., L.A., 1971; EdD, Nova Southeastern U., 1997. Recreation leader Pasadena Dept. Recreation, Calif., 1954—58; demonstration tchr. Pasadena Unified Sch., 1956—63; cons. spl. edn. Temple City Sch. Dist., Calif., 1967; supr. tchr. edn. U. Calif., Riverside, 1971; tchr. spl. edn. Pasadena Unified Sch. Dist., 1955—70, dept. chair spl. edn. Pasadena H.S., 1972—98, adminstrv. asst. Pasadena H.S., 1993—98; ind. rep. Am. Comm. Network, Inc., 1997—. Supr. Evelyn Frieden Ctr., U. So. Calif., LA, 1970; mem. Coun. Exceptional Children, 1993—; ednl. cons. Shelby Renee Ednl. Ctr., Gardena, Calif., 2000—. Organizer Northwest Project, Camp Fire Girls, Pasadena, 1963; leader Big Sister Program, YWCA, Pasadena, 1966; organizer, dir. March on The Boys' Club, the Portrait of a Boy, 1966; organized Dr. Allie's Book Mobile Project, 2002; pub. souvenir jours. Women's Missionary Soc., Meth. Ch., State of Wash. to Mo.; mem. Ch. Women United, Afro-Am. Quilters L.A.; established Dr. Allie Louise Almore-Randle Scholarship Award, Pasadena H.S., 1998, Tougaloo Coll., 2005, First Meth. Ch., Pasadena, 2005, developer Econ. Devel. Fund, Inc., developer award; co-established Theressa Garrett Almore Music Scholarsip award Jackson State U., Jackson, Miss., 1989; charter mem. Cmty. Women of San Gabriel Valley, 1998, Women of Pasadena, 2002. Recipient Cert. of Merit, Pasadena City Coll., 1963, Outstanding Achievement award Nat. Coun. Negro Women, Pasadena, 1965, Earnest Thompson Seton award Campfire Girls, Pasadena, 1968, Spl. Recognition, Outstanding Cmty. Svc. award Tuesday Morning Club, 1967, Dedicated Svc. award AME Ch., 1983, Educator of Excellence award Rotary Club of Pasadena, 1993, Edn. award Altadena NAACP, 1994; named Tchr. of Yr., Pasadena Masonic Bodies, 1967, Woman of the Yr. Zeta Phi Beta, 1992, Commendation, City of Pasadena, 1998, Outstanding Educator, Phi Delta Kappa, 1998; Grad. fellow U. So. Calif., LA, 1970, recognition Uniformly Excellent Work and Exceptional Commitment and Dedication to Altadena/Pasadena Communities, Pasadena African Amer. Sch. Administr., 1998, Cert. Achievment award First AME Ch., 1998, Fran Cook Salute Great Inspiring Educator Award, United Tchr. of Pasadena, 1998; named Dr. Allie Louis Almore-Randle scholar in her honor Tougaloo Coll., Miss., 2005, First AME Ch., Pasadena, Calif., 2005. Mem. NAACP (life; bd. dirs., chmn. ch. workers com. 1955-63, Fight for Freedom award West Coast region 1957, Edn. award Altadena, Calif. chpt. 1994), ASCD, Calif. Tchrs. Assn., Calif. African Am. Geneal. Soc., Nat. Coun. Negro Women, African Pan Am. Doctoral Scholars, L.A. World Affairs Coun., Phi Delta Gamma (hospitality chair 1971—), U. So. Calif. Alumni Assn. (life), Tougaloo Coll. Nat. Alumni Assn. (life), Phi Delta Kappa, Alpha Kappa Alpha (life, membership com.), Phi Delta Phi (founder, organizer 1961), Phi Gamma Sigma. Democrat. Avocations: wedding director, photography, gardening, genealogy. Personal E-mail: akainger@sbcglobal.net.

ALMOUR, VICKI LYNN, elementary school educator; b. Oak Ridge, Tenn., May 22, 1954; d. Victor Glynnwood and Beverly Jane Harness; m. Gary Bruce Palmer, Sept. 5, 1981 (div. July 1989); m. Ralph Almour, Jan. 2, 1997; 1 child, Natasha Victoria. BA, East Tex. State U., 1976; MEd, Seattle U., 1989. Cert. tchr. ESL, history, gifted edn., early childhood edn., elem. edn., Tex. Tchr. elem. Killeen (Tex.) Ind. Sch. Dist., 1979—84, specialist ESL, 1994—99; specialist child devel. U.S. Dept. of Def., Seoul, Republic of Korea, 1984-86; specialist gifted edn. Clover Park Sch. Dist., Tacoma, 1987-92, Round Rock (Tex.) Ind. Sch. Dist., 2000—03, Leander (Tex.) Ind. Sch. Dist., 2004—05, Austin (Tex.) Ind. Sch. Dist., 2005—. Contbr. articles to mags. Recipient Outstanding ESL Tchr. award, Tex. TESOL, 1999. Mem. Tex. Assn. Talented and Gifted (staff devel. presenter 1997—, Awareness cert. 1998). Avocations: creative writing, aerobics, arts and crafts, travel, cultural studies. Home: 614 Thrush Dr Leander TX 78641-2963

ALMSTEAD, SHEILA LOUISE, art gallery owner; b. Albuquerque, Apr. 8, 1955; d. Laurence and Ida Seif Bair; m. Arlington J. Almstead (div.); children: Stacy Lynne Fusilier, Michael Laurence, Christopher James, Jason Andrew. BSW summa cum laude, Our Lady of the Lake U., San Antonio, 1991; MSW, Our Lady of the Lake U., 1992. Case mgr. III San Antonio State HOsp. & Bexar County Mental Health, 1991—97; dir. health care svcs. Brighton Gardens, San Antonio; owner Zingaro Home Accents, Glendale, Ariz., 2002—. Mem. select Edn. Reform Com., San Antonio, 1991; mental health cons. Monarch Apts., San Antonio, 1995; med. social worker Morningside Home Health, San Antonio, 1996—97. Vol. ct. adv. Ct. Apptd. Spl. Advs., San Antonio, 1989—91. Mem.: Alpha Chi, Phi Theta Kappa. Democrat. Agnostic. Avocations: theater, travel, music, reading, art. Office: Zingaro Home Accents 5746 W Glendale Ave Glendale AZ 85301

ALO, THERESA RENEÉ, secondary school educator, potter; b. Newark, Apr. 18, 1967; d. Joyce Patricia Alo. BFA, Alfred U., 1989; MA, Gallaudet U., 1994. Prof. pottery Charles County C.C. Mem. Am. Craft Coun. Subject of article in Ceramics Mag., 1993. Fine arts dept. chair North Point HS, Waldorf, Md. Named Best in Show Cerex Ceramic Show, N.J., 1993, 94, 95, 96. Mem. ASCD, The Potter's Guild, St. Mary's Art Assn., So. Md. Clay Artist Assn., Kappa Delta Pi. Home: Four Lee Ct Indian Head MD 20640-1103 Office: North Point HS 2500 Davis Dr Waldorf MD 20603

ALOFF, MINDY, writer; b. Phila., Dec. 20, 1947; d. Jacob and Selma (Album) A.; m. Martin Steven Cohen, June 16, 1968 (div. June 2000); 1 child, Ariel Nikiya. AB in English, Vassar Coll., 1969; MA in English, SUNY, Buffalo, 1972. Asst. prof. English U. Portland, Oreg., 1973-75; editor Encore Mag. of the Arts, Portland, 1977-80, Vassar Quar., Poughkeepsie, NY, 1980-88; dance critic New Republic, Bklyn., 1993—2001; cons. The George Balanchine Found., 2000—; editor Dance Critics Assn. Newsletter, 2003—06. Coord. Portland Poetry Festival, 1974—75; adj. assoc. prof. Barnard Coll., 2000—; lectr. Eugene Lang Coll., 2005—06. Author: (poems) Night Lights, 1979, (anthology) Dance Anecdotes, 2006; author essays and revs. theatrical dancing and lit. for NY Times Weekend, Book Rev. and Arts & Leisure, New Republic mag., Nation mag., Threepenny Rev., Dance mag., New Yorker mag., ann. Ency. Britannica, others. Recipient Whiting Writers award Mrs. Giles Whiting Found., N.Y.C., 1987; Woodrow Wilson Found. fellow, 1969, Woodburn fellow SUNY-Buffalo, 1972, Am. Dance Festival Dance Critics Inst. fellow, New London, Conn., 1977, John Simon Guggenheim Meml. Found. fellow, 1990. Mem. PEN Am. Ctr., Nat. Book Critics Circle (bd. dirs. 1988-91), Phi Beta Kappa. Personal E-mail: MindyAloff@aol.com.

ALONSO, MARIA CONCHITA, actress, singer; b. Cienfuegos, Cuba, June 29, 1957; arrived in U.S., 1982; d. Ricardo José and Conchita (Bustillo) Alonso. Owner Ambar Entertainment, Ambyth Prodns.; launced Soy fashion line, 2005. Appeared in films Moscow on the Hudson, 1984, A Fine Mess, 1986, Touch and Go, 1986, Extreme Prejudice, 1987, The Running Man, 1987, Colors, 1988, Vampire's Kiss, 1990, Predator II, 1990, Roosters, 1993, House of the Spirits, 1994, Caught, 1996, Caught, 1997, El Grito en el Cielo, 1997, Catherine's Grove, 1997, Acts of Betrayal, 1997, Knock out, 1998, Exposé, 1998, El Grito en el cielo, 1998, Dillinger in Paradise, 1999, Chain of Command, 2000, Knockout, 2000, The Code Conspiracy, 2001, Birth of Babylon, 2001, Blind Heat, 2002, The Company You Keep, 2003, Heart of America, 2003, Chasing Papi, 2003, Newton's Law, 2003, Return to Babylon, 2004, El Muerto, 2005, English as a Second Language, 2005, Smoke, 2005, Material Girls, 2006; appeared in numerous Venezuelan films and soap operas; TV films include Blood Ties, 1986, One of the Boys, 1989, Sudden Terror: The Hijacking of School Bus # 17, 1996, My Husband's Secret Life, 1998, A Vision of Murder: The Story of Donielle, 2000, Best Actress, 2000, High Noon, 2000, The Princess & the Barrio Boy, 2000; broadway plays: Kiss of the Spider Woman, 1995; recording artist, albums include: Maria Conchita, 1984 (Grammy award nomination for Best Latin Artist 1985), O ella o yo, 1985, Mirame, 1988, Imaginame, 1992, En Vivo-Mexico, 1992, Alejandra, 1994, De Coleccion, 1994, Boleros, 1996, Hoy and Siempre, 1997. Named Miss World Teenager, 1971, Miss Venezuela, 1975. Address: 8899 Beverly Blvd Los Angeles CA 90048-2412*

ALPERN, LINDA LEE WEVODAU, retired health agency administrator; b. Harrisburg, Pa., July 16, 1949; d. William Irvin Wevodau and Maretia Christine (Mills) Staley; m. Neil Stephen Alpern, Apr. 12, 1985; 1 child, Philip Wevodau. BS in Edn., Shippensburg U., Pa., 1971. Unit program coord. Pa. Div. Am. Cancer Soc., Harrisburg, 1973-75, unit exec. dir., 1975-76, div. svc. dir., 1976-81, div. med. affairs dir. Hershey, 1981-83; div. crusade dir. Md. Div. Am. Cancer Soc., Balt., 1983-87, div. v.p. for field ops., 1988, div. dep., exec. v.p. ops., 1988-95, divsn. chief oper. officer, 1995-96; sr. v.p. field ops. Mid-Atlantic divsn. Am. Cancer Soc., Balt., 1997—2003, sr. v.p. field ops. South Atlantic divsn., 2003—04; ret., 2004. Bd. dirs., sec. Cmty. Assn.; treas., v.p., pres. PTA; trustee Balt. Hebrew-Congregation Day Sch., 2000-03, mem. strategic planning com., 2004-05; bd. electors Balt. Hebrew Congregation, nominating com., 2001-03—. Democrat. Methodist. Avocations: photography, gardening, reading. Home: 4108 Colonial Rd Baltimore MD 21208-6042

ALPERT, ANN SHARON, retired insurance claims examiner; b. Indpls., Feb. 24, 1938; d. Oscar and Adele Alpert. BS in Edn., Ind. U., 1959. Tchr. Indpls. Pub. Schs., 1959-60; libr. George Fry & Assocs., Chgo., 1960-62, DeLeuw, Cather & Co., Chgo., 1962-65, Arthur Young & Co., CPAs, Chgo., 1965-74; statis. asst. Sargent & Lundy, Chgo., 1974-81, computer liaison agt., 1981-83, tech. editor, 1983-87; sales assoc. Jewelmaster, Inc., Chgo., 1987-88; claims processor Benefit Trust Life Ins. Co., 1988-90; claims examiner Ft. Dearborn Life Ins. Co., 1990-91, sr. disability claims examiner, 1991—; ret., 2002. Fellow: Life Mgmt. Inst. (assoc.).

ALPERT, SHIRLEY MARCIA, librarian; b. Pitts., Aug. 6, 1936; d. Arthur and Lillian (Goldberg) Forman; m. Norman Joseph Alpert, Dec. 25, 1956; children: Gary H., Andrea P. BA, Ariz. State U., 1958; MA, San Diego State U., 1980. Cert. elem. tchr., library media specialist, learning resources specialist. Librarian San Diego Unified Sch. Dist., 1973-84; learning resources specialist Northside Ind. Sch. Dist., San Antonio, Tex., 1985-87; librarian Hayward (Calif.) Unified Sch. Dist., 1988—. Mem. AAUW, Nat. Council Jewish Women, Women's Am. ORT, Tex. Library Assn., Calif. Media Library Edn. Assn. Lodges: Order Eastern Star. Democrat. Avocations: sailing, gourmet cooking, swimming. Home: 35810 Royal Sage Ct Palm Desert CA 92211-2755

ALSAPIEDI, CONSUELO VERONICA, psychoanalytic psychotherapist, consultant; b. N.Y.C., Nov. 9, 1927; d. Vernon Joseph Karram and Constance Agatha Taylor; m. John Romeo Alsapiedi, May 12, 1951; children: John Rino, Sharon Anne. BA, Seton Hill U., 1949; MSW, Fordham U., 1972; D Social Work, Psychoanalytic Inst. for Clin.Social Workers, N.Y.C., 1985. Lic. and cert. social worker, N.Y.; cert. alcoholism counselor, substance abuse counselor; bd. cert. diplomate, 1987. Case aide II, Cath. Charities, Bklyn., 1949-51, clin. social worker, 1963-70, clin. social worker rep. in Family Ct., 1965-70; inpatient and outpatient psychiat. social worker Office Mental Health, Queens Village, N.Y., 1972-95; pvt. practice psychoanalytic psychotherapy, N.Y.C., 1975—, Forest Hills, N.Y., 1989—. Ednl. lectr.; condr. workshops; psychotherapist staff outpatient psychotherapy svcs. A Family Ctr., Rosedale, NY, 1999—2002. Vol. Nat. Mental Health Assn., Albany, N.Y., 1994. Mem. N.Y. State Soc. for Clin. Social Work Psychotherapy (diplomate 1979—, sec.-rec. sec. 1985-99, membership chmn. 1989-90, pres. Queens chpt. 1986-88, rec. sec. 1992-99), Brain Injury Assn., Menninger Soc., Feudian Soc. Roman Catholic. Avocations: piano, music, ballet, art. Office: 71-36 110th St Ste 1K Forest Hills NY 11375-4838

ALSIP, CHERYL ANN, small business owner; b. Jersey City, Aug. 1, 1957; m. Manuel Edward Alsip, May 23, 1992 (dec. Oct., 1992); 1 child, Jeremy Tyler. Student, Bergen C.C., Paramus, N.J., 1979—82, Broward C.C., Coconut Creek, Fla., 1983—84; AS in Electronic Engring., NEC-Bauder, Ft. Lauderdale, Fla., 1988; AS in Acctg., Internat. Corr. Sch., Scranton, Pa., 1997. Various clerical positions, N.Y.C. and N.J., 1979-81; pers. mgr. Universal Merchandising, Inc., Clifton, N.J., 1981-82; store mgr. Travelers Transp. Inc. doing business as The Gift Shop, Deerfield Beach, Fla., 1983; gen. mgr. Travelers Transp. Inc. doing business as Budget Rent-A-Car, Pompano Beach, Fla., 1982-84; various office and technical positions Fla., 1985-91; ind. contractor Mary Kay, Pompano Beach, Fla., 1991-92; customer svc. rep. Taleigh, Inc., Boca Raton, Fla., 1992; tech. writer, technician various Fla. Cos., 1992-93; owner, operator CALA Distinctive Enterprises, Salcha, Alaska, 1992—2003; freelance writer, English editor Alaska, 1999-2000; desktop pub., editor CALA Distinctive Enterprises, 1992—2003; owner, operator, freelance writer CHAMA Enterprises, 2004—; grant rsch. and writing cons. Office Mgmt. and Prodecures. Commr. Boy Scouts of Am., 1992—; mem. Comty. Emergency Response Team, Pompano Beach, Fla., 1997-98—; vol. Aux. Police Dept., Pompano Beach, 1997-98; mem. CAP, 1996-2000; bd. dirs. Golden Valley Elec. Assn., Fairbanks, 2000-03; bd. dirs., mem., sec. Sacha Cmty. Coun., 2002-03. With U.S. Army, 1975-78. Mem. Internat. Soc. Cert. Electronic Technicians, Navy League of the U.S. Republican. Roman Catholic. Avocations: camping, handcrafts, reading. Home and Office: PO Box 140097 Salcha AK 99714-0097 Office Phone: 907-488-4310. Personal E-mail: camalsip@alaska.net.

ALSOP, MARIN, conductor, violinist, music director; b. NYC, Oct. 16, 1956; d. LaMar and Ruth A. Attended, Yale Univ., 1973—75; MusB, Julliard Sch., 1977, MusM, 1978. Debut with Symphony Space, NYC, 1984; founder, artistic dir. Concordia Chamber Orchestra, NYC, 1984; asst. condr. Richmond Symphony, Va., 1987; music dir. Eugene Symphony Orchestra, Oreg., 1989—96, Long Island Philharmonic, 1989—96, Cabrillo Music Festival, 1991, Colorado Symphony Orchestra, Denver, 1993—; principal guest condr. City of London Sinfonia, 1999—; principal condr. Bournemouth Symphony Orchestra, Poole, England, 2001—. Guest condr. San Francisco Symphony Orchestra, Boston Pops, Los Angeles Philharmonic Orchestra, 1991, City Ballet Orchestra, 1992; dir. Cabrillo Music Festival, Calif., 1991—; concertmaster Northeastern Pennsylvania Philharmonic, Scranton; founder, mem. String Fever (swing band), 1980—. Recipient Koussevitzky Conducting prize, Tanglewood Music Ctr., 1988, ASCAP award, CSO's Contemporary Music Festival, 2002—03, Conductor's award, Royal Philharmonic Soc., Artist of Yr., Gramophone, Classical Brit award, best female artist, 2005; MacArthur Fellow, John D. and Catherine T. MacArthur Found., 2005. Office: Bournemouth Symphony Orchestra 2 Seldown Lane Poole BH15 1UF England*

ALSTEENS, SUSETTE MARIE, English educator, athletic director; d. Jerry Ray and Shelby Jean Brandner; m. William Clarence Brandner, July 14, 1995; 1 child, Parker William. BS in Edn., U. Wis., LaCrosse, 1988. Tchr. H.S. English, Edgar Sch. Dist., Wis., 1988—90; tchr. H.S. English, athletic dir. Rib Lake Sch. Dist., Wis., 1990—95; tchr. H.S. English Belleville H.S., Wis., 1998—. Forensics dir., coach. Religious educator Holy Rosary Cath. Ch., Medford, Wis., 1993—95. Mem.: WADA. Roman Catholic. Office: Belleville Sch Dist PO Box 230 Belleville WI 53508 Office Phone: 608-424-1902 493.

ALSTON, ALYCE, diamond company executive; BA, So. Meth. Univ., Dallas; MBA, Pepperdine Univ., Calif. Writer to West Coast mgr. TV Guide Mag.; assoc. pub. Allure Mag.; pub. YM/Young & Modern/Gruner & Jahr, USA Pub., NYC, O, The Oprah Mag., 2000, W Mag., Fairchild Pubs., 2000—05; CEO De Beers LV USA, 2005—. Office: De Beers LV USA 703 Fifth Ave New York NY 10022*

ALSTON, BETTY B., retired elementary school educator; b. July 5, 1933; d. Buford B. and Ethel T. Bruner; m. Henry Clay Alston; children: Henry Clay Jr., Terry Venice. BS in Elem. Edn., Barber-Scotia Coll., 1955; postgrad., A&T State U., 1957, Appalachian State U., 1969. Tchr. Montgomery Bd. Edn., 1955—56, Stanly Bd. Edn., 1956—61, Kannapolis City Schs., 1961—63, Rowan County Bd. Edn., 1963—66, Mooresville City Schs., 1966—68, Charlotte-Mecklenburg Schs., 1968—93. Hon. mem. adv. coun. Internat. Biog. Ctr. Contbr. Invitation to Writing. Mem. 4-H Found., sec., 1987; mem. Democratic Women's Orgn., sec., 1983, second v.p., 1989, first v.p., 1991, pres., 1993; mem. exec. bd. Rep. Party, 2003; bd. trustees Barber-Scotia Coll., sec., 1995, bd. trustees, sec., 1995; mem. Cabarrus County Bd. Edn., chmn., 1993; adv. coun. Stonewall Jackson Tng. Sch., 1988, Cabarrus County Resource Dept. Correction, 1983; bd. mem. Cabarrus chpt. Am. Red Cross, 2000; mem. adv. bd. The Salvation Army, 2004. Named to People of 20th Century, Internat. Woman of Yr., 1000 World Leaders of Influence; recipient Disting. Alumni Citation of Yr. award, Barber-Scotia Coll., 1994, Cert. of Appreciation for Cmty. Support, N.C., 1988, Outstanding Svc. award, Truth Temple Ch., 1988, Plaque, Cabarrus County Dem. Party, 1987, Scroll of Honor for Edn. and Cmty. Svc., Omega Psi Phi, 1987, cert. for Cmty. Support, Optimist Club, 1986, Internat. Leaders in Achievement. Mem.: Cabarrus Regional C. of C. (life; pres.'s club 1994, ambassador 1996, adv. coun./coop. ext. 1993, Pres.'s Club Mem. of Yr. 1995, Internat. Woman of Yr. 2000), Lambda Upsilon Omega (Cert. of Outstanding Svc. 1991). E-mail: vhschule@netzero.com.

ALSTON, DEBBIE A., instructional technologist, educator; d. Evelyn E. and Kenneth E. Henke (Stepfather); m. Randal C. Alston, July 31, 1993; children: Jeremy M. Kissire, Benjamin M. Kissire. BS in Edn., U. Ctrl. Ark., Conway, 1990; MA in Edn., Curriculum and Tech., U. Phoenix, Ariz., 2005. Cert. tchr. Tex. Edn. Assn., 1993. Tchrs. aide South Conway County Sch. Dist., Morrilton, 1980—85, chpt. 1 reading tchr., 1980—85, 1990—92; basic skills tchr. Killeen Ind. Sch. Dist., Tex., 1990—92, 1992—93, fourth grade tchr., 1992—93, 1993—97, instrnl. technologist, 1993—; campus instrnl. technologist, lead trainer integrate Tex., 2006—. Campus chairperson United Way, Killeen, 2004—06. Nominee H.E.B. Excellence in Edn., H-E-B Food Stores, 2006; After Sch. grantee, Tex. Workforce, 2005-2006. Mem.: ASCD, Tex. Staff Devel. Coun., Internat. Soc. Tech. in Edn., Tex. Computer Edn. Assn. Home: 8714 Highland Trl Temple TX 76502 Office: Killeen Ind Sch Dist 200 North WS Young Llano TX 78643

ALSTON, JAMETTA O., lawyer; 1 child. Grad., Temple U.; JD, Howard U. Bar: D.C., RI 1987, Fed., Dist. and Cir. Cts. Asst. atty. gen. civil divsn., RI, 1993—2002; city solicitor Cranston, RI, 2002—. Mem. jud. nom. com., RI, 2003—; mem. exec. com. Edinburgh U.; gov. attys. com. women and minority involvement McGeorge U., 1985; spkr. in field. West Elmwood devel. Supreme Ct. com., 2003—; city solicitor Providence Shelter for Colored Children. Recipient Pro Bono award, Edinburgh, Scotland, 1989. Mem.: RI Bar Assn. (pres. 2004—, pres.-elect 2003). Office: 869 Park Ave Cranston RI 02910 Office Phone: 401-780-3133. Office Fax: 401-780-3179. E-mail: jalston@cranstonri.org.

ALSTROM, GAIL, Native American tribal leader; d. William and Hilda Alstrom; m. David Beans; children: Angelia, Ayden, Ronald, Madison. BA in psychology, Stanford U., 1994. YKHC ops. mgr. St. Mary's Subregional Clinic; pres. Yupiit of Andreafski Tribe. Office: Yupiit of Andreafski PO Box 80 Westdahl St Saint Marys AK 99658-0088 Office Phone: 907-438-2312. Office Fax: 907-438-2512.

ALT, BETTY L., sociology educator; b. Walsenburg, Colo., Nov. 12, 1931; d. Cecil R. and Mary M. (Giordano) Sowers; m. William E. Alt, June 19, 1960; 1 child, Eden Jeanette Alt Murrie. BA, Colo. Coll., 1960; MA, NE Mo. State U., 1968. Instr. sociology Indian Hills Community Coll., Centerville, Iowa, 1965-70; dept. chmn. Middlesex Community Coll., Bedford, Mass., 1971-75; instr. sociology Auburn U., Montgomery, 1975-76; div. chmn. Tidewater Community Coll., Virginia Beach, Va., 1976-80; program coord. Pikes Peak Community Coll., Woomera, Australia, 1980-83; instr. sociology Hawaii Pacific Coll., Honolulu, 1983-86, U. Md., Okinawa, Japan, 1987-88, Christopher Newport Coll., Newport News, Va., 1988-89, U. Colo., Colorado Springs, 1989-96, Colo. State U., Pueblo, 1992—. Co-author: Uncle Sam's Brides, 1990, Campfollowing: A History of the Military Wife, 1991, Weeping Violins: The Gypsy Tragedy in Europe, 1996, Slaughter in Cell House 3, 1997, Wicked Women, 2000, Black Soldiers-White Wars, 2002, Keeper of the Keys, 2003, Fleecing Grandma and Grandpa, 2004, Police Women: Life with The Badge, 2005, Following the Flag: Marriage and the Modern Military, 2006. Active Pueblo County Planning comm., Colo. Mem. AAUW, LWV, Pen Women, N.E. Mo. State U. Alumni Assn. (bd. dirs. 1993-97) Home: 2460 N Interstate 25 Pueblo CO 81008-9614 Office: Colo State U - Pueblo 2200 Bonforte Blvd Pueblo CO 81001-4901

ALT, CAROL A., actress, model, entrepreneur, writer; d. Anthony Ted and Muriel B. Alt; m. Ronald John Greschner, Nov. 21, 1983 (div. Mar. 12, 2001). Student, Hofstra U., LI, NY. Model Ford Models, NYC; actress Moress Nanas Hart Enterprises, LA; spokesperson QVC, Westchester, Pa. Reporter Fox News, 2002. Author: Eating In the Raw, 2004. Vol. Tribeca Performing Arts Ctr., NYC, MS, NYC, Am. Cancer Soc., NYC, Cerebral Palsy. With U.S. Army, 1978—79. Recipient Model Woman of Yr., CFDA, 1981, Female Model of Yr., 1986, Oscar Moda New Actress of Yr., Moda Mag., 1986, European Emmy, Berlosconi Group, 1987, Cert. of the Arts, European Artistic Cmty., 1988, European Emmy, Berlosconi Group, 1990, Mont Blanc award, 1991, Golden Box Office Ticket, Fedn. of European Theater Owners, 1993, European Emmy, Berlosconi Group, 1994. Avocations: amateur race car driver, interior decorating, marketing. Office: Just Simplicity c/o Assante 280 Park Ave New York NY 10010 Office Phone: 818-342-9800. Personal E-mail: altie1A@aol.com.

ALTEKRUSE, JOAN MORRISSEY, retired preventive medicine physician; b. Cohoes, NY, Nov. 15, 1928; d. William T. Dee and Agnes Kay (Fitzgerald) Morrissey; m. Ernest B. Altekruse, Dec. 17, 1950; children—Michael, Philip, Clifford, Lisa, Janice, Charles, Sean, Lowell, Patrick, E. Caitlin. AB, Vassar Coll., N.Y., 1949; MD, Stanford U., Calif., 1960; MPH, Harvard U., Cambridge, 1965; DPH, U. Calif., Berkeley, 1973; MPS, Loyola U., New Orleans, 1999. Cons., program dir. Calif. State Health Dept., 1966-69; vis. mem. faculty U. Heidelberg, Germany, 1970-72; med. dir. regional office Fla. State Health Dept., 1972-75; prof., dir. health adminstrn. Sch. Pub. Health, U. S.C., Columbia, 1975-77; prof. preventive medicine Univ. S.C. Sch. of Medicine, Columbia, 1975-94, chmn. dept., 1979-89, disting. prof. emerita, 1994—. Fellow, assoc. dir. Irish Peace Inst., U. Limerick, Ireland, 1990; vis. scholar Ctr. for Rsch. in Disease Prevention, Stanford U., 1992; women in medicine liaison officer Assn. Am. Med. Colls., 1980-94; mem. editl. bd. Aspen Publs. Mem. editl. bd. Family and Cmty. Health Jour., Jour. Cmty. Health; editl. adv. bd. VA Practitioner. Sr. docent chair, vol. bd. mem. Hunter Mus. Am. Art, Chattanooga, 1996—2002; activist in social justice, peace and health advocacy orgns. Lt. USMC, 1949—51, sr. surgeon USPHS, 1960—64, capt. USPHS. Recipient Adminstrn. award Women in Higher Edn., 1989, Achievement award S.C. Commn. on Women, 1990, Ann. award, 1991, Life Achievement award Emma Willard Sch., 1996; WHO travel fellow, Eng., 1974; grantee NIH, NCI, Ctr. for Disease Control, pvt. founds; recipient Alumni award of merit Harvard Sch. Pub. Health, 1997. Fellow: APHA (mem. emerita), Assn. Tchrs. Preventive Medicine (pres. 1986, Spl. Recognition award 1995), Am. Coll. Preventive Medicine; mem.: Nat. Bd. Med. Examiners (comprehensive test com. 1986—92), Am. Heart Assn. (SC affiliate pres. 1986, mem. nat. agenda planning com. 1987—89, women and minorities leadership com. 1989—92, Lifetime Achievement award 1992), Am. Bd. Med. Specialties, Am. Bd. Preventive Medicine (trustee 1983—92), Emma Willard Sch. Alumni Assn. (coun. mem. 2003—), Am. Womens Med. Assn., Harvard Sch. Pub. Health Alumni Assn. (pres. 1999—2001, leadership coun. 2003—06), Harvard Alumni Assn. (bd. dirs. 2001—03). Democrat. Roman Catholic. Personal E-mail: jaltekruse@yahoo.com.

ALTEMARA, MARIA CHRISTI STALEY, anthropologist, sociologist, educator; b. Washington, Pa., Dec. 10, 1971; d. Samuel Lee and Barbara Ann Staley; m. Ralph J. Altemara, Oct. 17, 1998. BA, Gannon U., Erie, Pa., 1993; MA, Calif. U. Pa., California, Pa., 1994. Prof. Robert Morris U., Moon Twp, Pa., 1993—, W.Va. U., Morgantown, 1994—; owner M.C. Altemara Travel & Tours, Charleroi, Pa., 2001—. D-Liberal. Avocations: travel, writing. Office Phone: 1-800-762-0097.

ALTENBERGER, CYNTHIA ANN, music educator; b. Chgo., Sept. 11, 1967; d. Charles Edward and Shirley Ruth Willard; m. Andrew J. Altenberger, Feb. 12, 2000; children: Jamie Jo, Emilie Ann, Abby Mae. BA in music edn. (cum laude with hons.), Western Ill. U., Macomb, 1989. Sch. accounts rep. KingMusic, Inc., Bradley, Ill., 1995—2000; adj. percussion instr. Olivet Nazarene U., Bourbonnais, Ill., 1996—99; percussion instr. Bradley-Bourbonnais Cmty. HS, Bradley, 1997—. Pit musician/percussionist Kankakee Valley Theatre, 1981—2004; musician/percussionist Kankakee Mcpl. Band, Ill., 1985—, bd. mem., 1999—2003; percussionist/musician Kankakee Valley Symphony Orch., Ill., 1995—2001; musician/percussionist Mallet Madness, Kankakee, 2003—06. Mem. praise band Calvary Bible Ch., Bradley, Ill., 1998—2006. Republican. Mem. Christian Ch. Avocations: travel, gardening, reading. Office: Bradley-Bourbonnais Cmty HS 700 W North St Bradley IL 60915 Office Phone: 815-937-3707 3723. Personal E-mail: cindya911@juno.com. Business E-Mail: caltenberger@bbchs.k12.il.us.

ALTENHOFEN, JANE ELLEN, federal agency administrator, auditor; b. Seneca, Kans., Sept. 4, 1952; d. Justin Leo and Marva Mae (Sextro) A.; m. John Dean Arnette, Sept. 12, 1975 (div. Mar. 1978). BBA cum laude, Wichita (Kans.) State U., 1973; MPA, Am. U., 1982; cert., Inst. Internal Auditors, 1986. Cert. internal auditor, cert. fraud examiner, cert. govt. fin. mgr. Auditor U.S. Gen. Acctg. Office, Kansas City, Kans., 1974-76, Honolulu, 1976-80, Washington, 1980-84, Fed. Emergency Mgmt. Agy., Washington, 1984-89; insp. gen. U.S. Internat. Trade Commn., Washington, 1989-99, Nat. Labor Rels. Bd., Washington, 1999—. Mem. Adopt a Grandparent Program, Wichita, 1973; vol. reading course work to blind students, Wichita, 1973; vol. Vis. Nurse Assn., Washington, 1986—; host, traveler, Wash. area rep. SERVAS, 1987—; commr. Adv. Neighborhood Commn., Washington, 1986-89; troop leader Girl Scouts U.S., Washington, 1983-85; foster home Washington Humane Soc., 1994—. Mem. Inst. Internal Auditors, Nat. Intergovtl. Audit Forum, Assn. Govt. Accouts, Nat. Assn. Cert. Fraud Examiners, Phi Kappa Phi, Pi Alpha Pi. Home: 507 2nd St SE Washington DC 20003-1928 Office: Nat Labor Rels Bd 1099 14th St NW Rm 9820 Washington DC 20570-0001

ALTER, ELEANOR BREITEL, lawyer; b. NYC, Nov. 10, 1938; d. Charles David and Jeanne (Hollander) Breitel; children: Richard B. Zabel, David B. Zabel. BA with honors, U. Mich., 1960; postgrad., Harvard U., 1960-61; LLB, Columbia U., 1964. Bar: N.Y. 1965. Atty., office of gen. counsel, ins. dept. State of N.Y., 1964-66; assoc. Miller & Carlson, N.Y.C., 1966-68, Marshall, Bratter, Greene, Allison & Tucker, N.Y.C., 1968-74, mem. firm, 1974-82, Rosenman & Colin, 1982-97, Kasowitz, Benson, Torres & Friedman, N.Y.C., 1997—. Fellow U. Chgo. Law Sch., 1988; adj. prof. law NYU Sch. Law, 1983-87; vis. prof. law U. Chgo., 1990-91, 93; lectr. in field. Mem. editl. bd. N.Y. Law Jour.; contbr. articles to profl. jours. Trustee Lawyers' Fund for Client Protection of the State of N.Y., 1983—, chmn., 1985—; bd. visitors U. Chgo. Law Sch., 1984-87. Mem. Am. Law Inst., Am. Coll. Family Trial Lawyers, N.Y. State Bar Assn., Assn. of Bar of City of N.Y. (libr. com. 1978-80, com. on matrimonial law 1977-81, 87-88, 2002-05, judiciary com. 1981-84, 94, 95, 96, exec. com. 1988-92), Am. Acad. Matrimonial Lawyers, Internat. Acad. Matrimonial Lawyers. Office: Kasowitz Benson Et Al 1633 Broadway New York NY 10019 Office Phone: 212-506-1760. Business E-Mail: ealter@kasowitz.com.

ALTER, MARIA POSPISCHIL, language educator; b. Vienna; came to U.S., 1947; d. Karl and Ludmilla (Von Adamovic) Pospischil; divorced; children: Assunta, Sylvia, Nora. BA, U. Okla., 1948, MA, 1950; PhD, U. Md., 1961. Instr., asst. prof. Howard U., Washington, 1955-66; asst. prof. Case Western U., Cleve., 1966-70; acad. cons. Am. Assn. Tchrs. German, Phila., 1970-73; prof. Villanova (Pa.) U., 1974—. Author: The Role of the Physicians in Schnitzler's and Corossa's Work, 1961, A Modern Case for German, 1971. Mem. Assn. German, Modern Lang. Assn. Home: 830 Montgomery Ave Bryn Mawr PA 19010-3343

ALTER, SHIRLEY JACOBS, jewelry store owner; b. Beaumont, Tex., June 23, 1929; d. Morris Louis and Helen (Dow) Jacobs; m. Nelson Tobias Alter, June 12, 1949; children: Dennis, Keith, Brian, Wendy. Student, U. Tex., Austin, 1950. Owner Alter's Gem Jewelry Co., Beaumont, 1950—. Pres. Nat. Coun. Jewish Women, Beaumont, 1965, 66, Sisterhood of Temple Emanuel, Beaumont, 1967, 68, Buckner Bapt. Benevolence Aux., Beaumont, 1970-72; bd. dirs. Temple Emanuel, pres. elect, 1994-96, pres. 1996-98; active Beaumont Music Commn., 1990; founder Beaumont Reach to Recovery, 1973; active BMW Drive for the Cure of breast cancer, 1997. Named Hero, Susan Komen Found., 1997. Democrat. Office: Alters Gem Jewelry 3155 Dowlen Beaumont TX 77706

ALTFEST, KAREN CAPLAN, diversified financial services company executive, director; b. Montreal, Que., Can. d. Philip and Betty (Gamer) Caplan; m. Lewis Jay Altfest; children: Ellen Wendy, Andrew Gamer. Tchr.'s diploma, McGill U.; BA cum laude, Hunter Coll., 1970, MA, 1972; PhD, CUNY, 1979. CFP, N.Y. V.p. L. J. Altfest & Co., Inc., N.Y.C., 1985—; dir. fin. planning program New Sch. Univ., N.Y.C., 1989—2005. Dir. CFP program Pace U., White Plains, N.Y., 1988-90. Author: Robert Owen, 1978, Keeping Clients for Life, 2001; co-author: Lew Altfest Answers Almost All Your Questions about Money, 1992; fin. columnist All You mag., 2004—; contbr. articles to fin. jours. Founding chmn. Yorkville Common Pantry, N.Y.C., 1980-84; v.p. PS 6 PTA, N.Y.C., 1991-92; bd. dirs. Temple Shaaray Tefila, 1993—. Named Planner of Month, Mut. Funds Mag., 2000; named one of 200 Best Fin. Planners in U.S., Worth Mag., 1996, 1997, 1998, Best Fin. Advisors, Med. Econs. Mag., 1998, 100 Top Advisors, Mut. Funds Mgrs., 2002, Best 100 Planners, Mut. Funds Mag., 2002, Top Wealth Mgrs. (firm), Bloomberg, 2004, 2005; recipient Cmty. Svc. award, Temple Shaaray Tefila, 1985; profile on cover, Fin. Planning Mag., 2001, Fin. Adv. Mag., 2006. Mem.: Fin. Planning Assn. N.Y. (pres. 2006), Women's Econ. Round Table, Fin. Women's Assn., Nat. Assn. Personal Fin. Advisors (chair N.E.-Mid Atlantic Conf. 1995, bd. dirs. N.E. region 1996—2003, v.p. 1997—99, pres. N.E.-Mid Atlantic region 1999—2001, chmn. 2001—03, Achievement cert. N.E. Region 1995, award for outstanding svc. to NE region 2001, 2003), Fin. Planning Assn. (bd. dirs. N.Y. chpt. 1994—99, bd. dirs. 2000—, dir. for pub. rels., pres. 2006, Dedicated Svc. cert. 1998, 1999, 2000, 2001, 2002, 2003, 2004, 2005), Assn. for Women's Econ. Devel., Assn. for Can. Studies in U.S., Nat. Assn. Women Bus. Owners (chmn. FOCUS 1993—95, bd. dirs.), CUNY PhD Alumni Assn. (v.p. 1982—84), Phi Alpha Theta. Achievements include featured on cover of Fin. Planning Mag., 2001. Office: LJ Altfest & Co Inc 425 Park Ave 24th Fl New York NY 10022 E-mail: karen@altfest.com.

ALTHERR, RITA JO, secondary school educator; b. Cleve., Mar. 3, 1952; d. William Thomas and Rosalind Josephine Boehnlein; m. Steve Charles Altherr; children: Sarah Beth, Amy Josephine. EdB, U. Mo., Columbia, 1974, EdM, 1975; Edn. Specialist, U. Mo., Kansas City, 1981. Cert. tchr. Mo., 1974. Academic interventions dir. Pk. Hill South H.S., Riverside, Mo., 1998—. Named Educator Ptnr. of Yr., Clay/Platte County Econ. Devel., 2000. Mem.: Pk. Hill NEA (first v.p. 1993—96). Office Phone: 816-587-7373.

ALTIER, JUDITH BARRETT, middle school educator; b. Cleve., June 16, 1945; d. John Joseph and Mary Rose (Maier) Barrett; m. Paul Kenneth Altier, Mar. 25, 1970 (dec. Apr. 1981); 1 child, Amanda Elizabeth. BS in Edn., Kent State U., 1967; cert. in reading, Calif. State U., Sacramento, 1988. Cert. tchr., Calif.; cert. reading specialist, Calif., Nat. Bd. Cert. English/Lang Arts early adolescents, 2002. English tchr. Shaw H.S., East Cleveland, Ohio, 1967-69; English tchr., asst. dept. chair comm., media coord. Armijo H.S., Fairfield, Calif., 1969-82; opportunity class English tchr. Mary Bird Continuation Sch., Fairfield, Calif., 1983-85; English tchr., dept. chair Sullivan Mid. Sch., Fairfield, Calif., 1985-90, Crystal Mid. Sch., Suisun, 1990—. Mem. dist. curriculum com. Fairfield-Suisun Unified Sch. Dist., 1986-94, English curriculum tchr., facilitator, 1989—. Mem. cmty. adv. bd. City of Fairfield, 1991-94. Mem. Calif. Reading Assn., Solano Reading Assn. Avocations: reading, gardening, writing. Home: 5041 Lynbrook Dr Fairfield CA 94534-3338 Office: Crystal Mid Sch 400 Whispering Bay Ln Suisun City CA 94585-2713

ALTIERE, LAUREN M., music educator, consultant; d. Charles and Jane McAlister; m. Michael P. Altiere, June 10, 1968 (dec. May 5, 1992); 1 child, Tamara Rae Miller. BA in Voice, Allegheny Coll., Meadville, Pa., 1968; ESL Certification, U. Phoenix, Ariz., 1998; M in Music Edn., Ctrl. Mo. State U., Warrensburg, 1978. Music specialist St. Joseph's Elem. Sch., Wichita, Kans., 1969—97, Yamaha Music Sch., Wichita, 1970—74, Carlton Jr. H.S., Derby, Kans., 1973—74, Windsor Pub. Sch., Mo., 1974—78, Massillon City Schs., Ohio, 1978—80, Shreveport City Schs., La., 1980—84, Dodge Elem. Sch., Wichita, 1985—95, Payne Elem. Sch., Wichita, 1995—97, Wilson Sch. Dist., Phoenix, 1997—. Music edn. cons. Yamaha Corp. Am., Buena Park, Calif., 1987—; chorus dir. Young Women in Harmony, Phoenix, 1990—. Avocation: singing with sweet adelines. Office: Wilson School District 415 N 30th St Phoenix AZ 85008 Office Phone: 602-683-2500.

ALTMAN, ADELE ROSENHAIN, radiologist; b. Tel Aviv, June 4, 1924; came to U.S., 1933, naturalized, 1939; d. Bruno and Salla (Silberzweig) Rosenhain; m. Emmett Altman, Sept. 3, 1944; children: Brian R., Alan L., Karen D. Diplomate Am. Bd. Radiology. Intern Queens Gen. Hosp., N.Y.C., 1949-51; resident Hosp. for Joint Diseases, N.Y.C., 1951-52, Roosevelt Hosp., N.Y.C., 1955-57; clin. instr. radiology Downstate Med. Ctr., SUNY, Bklyn., 1957-61; asst. prof. radiology N.Y. Med. Coll., N.Y.C., 1961-65, assoc. prof., 1965-68; assoc. prof. radiology U. Okla. Health Sci. Ctr., Oklahoma City, 1966-78; assoc. prof. dept. radiology U. N.Mex. Sch. Medicine, Albuquerque, 1978-85. Author: Radiology of the Respiratory System: A Basic Review, 1978; contbr. articles to profl. jours. Fellow Am. Coll. Angiology, N.Y. Acad. Medicine; mem. Am. Coll. Radiologist, Am. Roentgen Ray Soc., Assn. Univ. Radiologists, Radiol. Soc. N.Am., B'nai B'rith Anti-Defamation League (bd. dirs. N.Mex. state bd.), Hadassah Club.

ALTMAN, BETH LEE, social worker; b. Washington, July 2, 1952; d. Harry E. and Ada (Hurwich) A. AB (magna cum laude), Washington U., 1974; MSW, Cath. U., 1978. Lic. social worker, Md., D.C. Sr. counselor State Md. Juvenile Svcs. Adminstrn., Rockville, Md., 1974-85; clin. social worker Family Stress Clinic, Oxon Hill, Md., 1982-84; rschr. Chestnut Lodge Hosp., Rockville, 1985-92; clin. social worker, psychotherapist pvt. practice Washington, Washington, 1982—. Del Ward III Dem. Com., Washington, 1986—1990. Mem. NASW, Greater Washington Soc. for Clin. Social Work, Inst. Contemporary Pshychotherapy and Psychoanalysis, Assn. for Psychoanalytic Thought. Democrat. Jewish. Office: 910 17th St NW Ste 1015 Washington DC 20006 Office Phone: 202-775-0041.

ALTMAN, DOROTHY JEWELL, language educator; b. Gloversville, NY; d. Albert Edward and Irene Fitch Jewell; m. Eric H. Altman, May 10, 1969; children: Brian, Michael, Sara. BA magna cum laude, SUNY, Albany, 1963; MA English, CUNY, 1970; PhD, SUNY, Albany, 1979. Adj. instr. Ramapo Coll., Mahwah, NJ, 1979—80, Bergen CC, Paramus, NJ, 1980—94; gifted & talented coord. Rutherford Pub. Schs., NJ, 1994—96; instr. Bergen CC, 1996—2001, assoc. prof., 2002—. Mem.: N.J. Writing Alliance, N.E. Modern Lang. Assn., Two-Year Coll. Assn., Nat. Coun. Tchrs. English. Home: 10 Strawberry Ln Upper Saddle River NJ 07458 Office Phone: 201-493-3544. E-mail: daltman@bergen.edu.

ALTMAN, EDITH G., sculptor; b. Altenberg, Germany, May 23, 1931; arrived in U.S., 1939; BA, Wayne State U., 1949; student, Marygrove Coll., 1956-57. Instr. visual arts and printing project U. Omaha, 1984; asst. prof. painting, grad. advisor U. Chgo., 1984-85; vis. asst. prof. painting Sch. Art Inst. Chgo., 1985-86. Lectr. painting U. Ill., Columbia Coll., Oakton C.C., Chgo. One-woman shows include NAME Gallery, 1987, Spertus Mus. Gallery Contemporary Art, 1988, Rockford Art Mus., 1989, State of Ill. Mus. Gallery, Chgo., 1992, Loyola U. Fine Arts Gallery, 1993, Peace Mus., Chgo., 1993, Mitchell Mus., Ill., 1995, Minn. Mus. Am. Art, 1995, Lindeau Mus., Altenburg, Germany, 2001, Frauen Mus., Bonn, Germany, 2001, Contextual Cultural Ctr., Chgo., 2001, Natl. Museum of Szczecin, Poland, 2002-. Hyde Park Art Ctr., 2002. others; exhibited in group shows Art Inst. Chgo., 1975, 79, 81, 85, Mus. Contemporary Art, Chgo., 1976, 81, 83, 97, Acad. Kunst, Berlin, 1987, Barbicon Ctr., London, 1990, Knoxville Mus. Art, Tenn., 1998, N.J. State Mus., 1999, Okla. City Art Mus., 1999, Decordova Mus., 2000; represented in permanent collections Standard Oil Co., Mus. Contemporary Art, Chgo., 1997, State of Ill., Yale U. Mus., Holocaust Mus., Peace Mus., Gallery 312, Chgo., 2003; contbr. articles to profl. jours., newspapers. Named Art Matters fellow, 1994; Individual Artist fellow, Ill. Arts Coun., 1984, 1994, Internat. grantee, 2003, Individual Artist Fellow grantee, NEA, 1990—91. Mem. Chgo. Artist Coalition (founding mem., mem. com. artists rights, 1988). Home: 819 Foster St Apt 3s Evanston IL 60201-6144 Office Phone: 312-421-2881. E-mail: ealtman3@aol.com.

ALTMAN, ELLEN, librarian, educator; b. Pitts., Jan. 1, 1936; d. William and Catherine (Wall) Conley. AB, Duquesne U., 1957; MLS, Rutgers U., 1965, PhD, 1971. Instr., asst research prof. Rutgers U., 1965-67, 70-72; asst. prof. U. Ky., 1972-73, U. Toronto, 1974-76; assoc. prof. Ind. U., 1976-79; prof. Grad. Library Sch., U. Ariz., Tucson, 1979—. Cons. various research orgns., state libraries. Author: Performance Measures in Pub. Libraries, 1973, A Data Gathering and Instructional Manual for Performance Measures in Public Libraries, 1976, Local Public Library Administration, 1980; editor Pub. Librs., 1992—. Fulbright-Hayes sr. lectr., 1978 Mem. ALA, AAUP. Office: 1515 E 1st St Tucson AZ 85719-4505

ALTMAN, JOANNE D., psychology professor; d. Robert B. Altman and (Ann) Susan Altman-Sondak; m. Jack A. Kaplan, Aug. 2, 2003; 1 stepchild, Joel T. Kaplan. BA, Franklin and Marshall Coll., Lancaster, Pa., 1984; MA, Temple U., Phila., 1987, PhD, 1990; postgrad., John's Hopkins U., Balt., 1990—91. Adj. prof. Franklin and Marshall Coll., Lancaster, 1989; prof. Washburn U., Topeka, 1991—. Presenter in field. Contbr. articles to profl. jours. Recipient Ned N. Fleming Excellence in Tchg. award, Washburn U., 2003, Herrick award for Outstanding Svc., 2004. Fellow: Coun. Undergraduate Rsch. (councilor 2002); mem.: APA, Animal Behavior Soc., Am. Zoo and Aquaria, Internat. Soc. Comparative Psychology, Phi Kappa Phi (life; chpt. pres. 2003—05). Office: Washburn University 1700 College Ave Topeka KS 66621 Office Phone: 785-670-1568.

ALTMAN, SARAH BUSA, human services educator; b. Balt., Sept. 11, 1944; d. John and Neildre Busa; m. Arthur William Altman, Sept. 4, 1976; children: Christine McHone, Richard Gordineer, Janet Choitinihorn, Raymond, Nicholas. AAS in Recreation Leadership, Tri-County C.C., Murphy, NC, 1976; BS in Social Work, Western Carolina U., Cullowhee, NC, 1983, MAEd in Agy. Counseling, 1987. Lic. profl. counselor, clin. addiction specialist N.C., cert. nat. cert. counselor, master addiction counselor. Dir. partial hospitalization Smokey Mt. Mental Health, Cullowhee, NC, 1976—80; dir. new beginnings Western Carolina U., 1989—91; counselor Southwestern C.C., Sylva, 1986—91, instr. drug & alcohol, 1986—91, counselor student support svcs., 1986—91, instr. human svcs., 1991—. Pvt. practice counseling, Sylva, NC. Mem.: Am. Counseling Assn., Pi Gamma Mu. Office Phone: 828-586-4091 ext. 216. Business E-Mail: saltman@southwesterncc.edu.

ALTMANN, JEANNE, zoologist, educator; b. N.Y.C., Mar. 18, 1940; BA in Math., U. Alta., Can., 1962; MAT, Emory U., 1970; PhD, U. Chgo., 1979. Rsch. assoc., co-investigator U. Alta., Canada, 1963-65, Yerkes Regional Primate Rsch. Ctr., Atlanta, 1965-67, 69-70; rsch. assoc. dept. biology U. Chgo., 1970-85, assoc. prof. dept. ecology and evolution, 1985-89, prof., dept. ecology & evolution, 1989—98; rsch. curator, assoc. curator primates Chgo. Zool. Soc., 1985—; prof., dept. ecology & evolutionary biology Princeton U., NJ, 1998—, faculty assoc., Office of Population Rsch. NJ, 1999—. Hon. lectr. dept. zoology U. Nairobi, Africa, 1989-90; chair com. evolutionary biology U. Chgo., 1991—; bd. sci. dirs. Karisoke Rsch. Ctr., Rwanda, 1980-82, 86-89, acting chairperson, 1980; mem. biosocial perspectives on parent behavior and off-spring devel. com. Social Sci. Rsch. Coun., 1984-91; mem. adv. coun. dept. ecology and evolutionary biology Princeton (N.J.) U., 1991—; mem. rev. com. dept. zool. rsch. Nat. Zool. Park, Smithsonian Inst., Washington, 1992; mem. com. Internat. Ethol. Congress, 1992—; mem. vis. com. dept. anatomy and biol. anthropology Duke U., Durham, N.C., 1993; reviewer manuscripts various jours. Author: (with S. Altmann) Baboon Ecology: African Field Research, 1970, Baboon Mothers and Infants, 1980; editor: Animal Behaviour, 1978-82; consulting editor: Am. Jour. Primatology, 1981—; mem. editorial panel: Monographs in Primatology, 1982-90; mem. editorial bd. Bioscience, 1983-88, ISI Reviews in Animal Science, 1988, Human Nature, 1989-92, Internat. Jour. Primatology, 1990—, Am. Naturalist, 1991—; contbr. articles to profl. jours. Fellow Ctr. Advanced Study in Behavioral Scis., 1990-91. Fellow Animal Behavior Soc. (mem. exec. com 1978-82, 84-87, mem, nominating com. 1987-89, pres. 1985-86), Animal Behavior Soc.; mem. NSF (mem. sci. adv. panel psychobiology program 1983-86, mem. adv. panel for vis. professorships for women 1987, 88, mem. adv. panel conservation and restoration biology 1990, mem. task force behavioral, biol. and social scis. Looking Toward the 21st Century 1990-91, mem. adv. coun. directorate for social, behavioral and econ. scis. 1992—), Internat. Primatol. Soc. (v.p. conservation, mem. exec. com.). Home: 54 Hardy Dr Princeton NJ 08540-1211

ALTOMARE, ERICA VON SCHEVEN, psychologist; b. Trenton, NJ, Jan. 11, 1950; d. Eric Kurt and Lorraine (Seabridge) Von Scheven; m. Joseph E. Altomare, Aug. 14, 1971; children: Mikal Melissa, Damon Joseph, Reice Eric. RN, Helene Fuld Sch. Nursing, 1970; BSN, Clarion U., 1986; MA in Clin. Psychology, Edinboro U., 1988; PhD in Counseling Psychology, U. Pitts., 2001. Lic. psychologist; cert. clin. specialist in child and adolescent psychiatry and mental health nursing, cognitive behavioral therapist. Staff nurse N.Y. Hosp., N.Y.C., 1970-71; instr. Northeastern Hosp., Phila., 1971-74, Venango County Vocat. Tech. Sch., Oil City, Pa., 1974-81; psychology intern Meadville Mental Health Clinic, Pa., 1988-89; rsch. asst. Cleft Palate Clinic, Erie, Pa., 1987-89; psychotherapist, psychologist PSY Svcs., Titusville, Pa., 1989—96, asst. prof. psychology, 2001—. Instr. U. Pitts., 1989—96, rsch. asst. Pitt. Mother and Child Project, 1997—99, asst. prof., 2001—; psychology intern U. Buffalo Counseling Ctr., 2000—01; presenter, counselor Ctrs. N.Y. Conf., 2001. Contbr. articles to various prof. jours. Bd. dirs. Forest/Warren (Pa.) Mental Health Svcs., 1975-78, Forest/Warren Children Svcs., 1975-78, Tionesta (Pa.) Area Health Svcs., Inc., 1976-78, Western Pa. Behavioral Health Network, 1994—; producer Miss Crawford County Scholarship Pageant, Meadville, 1986-89; workshop presenter Titusville Area Hosp., 1989-91. Mem. APA (assoc.), AAUW, Learning Disabilities Assn. (adv. bd. 1993-2000), Pa. Psychol. Assn., N.W. Pa. Psychol. Assn., Soc. Rsch. in Children (writer, rsch. presenter 2003), Am. Cleft Palate Assn. (writer, rsch. presenter 1994), Charles F. Menninger Soc. Democrat. Avocations: travel, downhill skiing, racquetball, horseback riding. Home: 700 Rockwood Dr Titusville PA 16354-1244 Office: Univ Pitts Broadhurst Sci Ctr Titusville PA 16354 Office Phone: 814-827-4430. E-mail: altomar@pitt.edu.

ALTON, COLLEEN EDNA, education educator; b. Ventura, Calif., Mar. 17, 1959; d. Donald F. and Edna E. Mills; m. David S. Alton, Sept. 29, 1984; 1 child, Matthew C. BA, U. Calif., Irvine, 1981; diploma, Goldwest Police Acad., 1981; credential, U. Calif., Irvine, 1985; M, Pt. Loma U., 2006. Community svc. officer Irvine Police Dept., 1979-81, police officer, 1981-88; tchr. Chino (Calif.) Unified Sch. Dist., 1989—. Vol. Spl. Olympics, Ventura, County, 1974-77, Orange County, 1977-85; vol. rape crisis counselor Irvine Police Dept., 1981-85; coach China Uouth Softball, 1989-90; mem. PTA Chino, 1991—; libr. PTA-Butterfield Ranch Sch.; mem. Chins Corp. Challenge, 1989—; exec. bd. adminstr. officer West Valley Search and Rescue, 2000—; youth accountability bd., 2001—. Mem. Job's Daus. (queen 1977). Republican. Avocations: softball, basketball, marathon running, sailing, coaching sports. Office: Chino Unified Sch Dist 5130 Riverside Dr Chino CA 91710-4130

ALTSCHUL, B. J., public relations counselor; b. Jan. 28, 1948; d. Lemuel and Sylva (Behr) A. Student, Goucher Coll., 1965-67; BA, U. South Fla., 1970; MA, U. Md., 1995. Reporter St. Petersburg (Fla.) Times, 1973—74; dir. pub. rels. Valkyrie Press, Inc., St. Petersburg, 1974—77; founding editor Bay Life, Clearwater, Fla., 1977—79, Tampa Bay Monthly, Clearwater, 1977—79; mng. editor Fla. Tourist News, Tampa and Orlando, 1981; founder Capital Comms. of Tampa, 1981; owner, prin. b j Altschul & Assocs. (formerly Capital Comms. of Tampa), 1985—. Mgr. editl. and info. svcs. Va. Pt. Authority, Norfolk, 1985-88; dir. pub. rels. Va. Dept. Agr. and Consumer Svcs., Richmond, 1988-93; adj. faculty Old Dominion U., Norfolk, 1986-88, U. Richmond, 1990, 94, Washington Ctr. for Internships, 1995-96; mgr. pub. rels. U. Md. Biotech. Inst., 1997-99; lectr. dept. comm. U. Md., 1999-2001; asst. prof. Am. U., 2001—. Author: Cracker Cookin' & Other Favorites, 1984; contbg. author: Virginia: A Commonwealth Comes of Age, 1988. Bd. dirs. Pinellas County Big Bros.-Big Sisters, 1980-82, Fla. Folklore Soc., 1984-85. Mem. Fla. Motion Picture and TV Assn. (treas. 1976-78), Hampton Rds. C. of C. (co-chmn. pub. rels. Internat. Azalea Festival 1986, chmn. publs. 1987), Va. Conf. on World Trade (chmn. pub. rels. com.), Downtown Norfolk Devel. Corp. (chmn. urban living com.), Pub. Rels. Soc. Am. (chmn. Mid.-Atlantic Dist. 1988, chmn. govt. sect. 1989, bd. dirs., chmn. chpt. accreditation, chmn. Univ. Rels. Nat. Capital chpt. 2002-), Va. State Agy. Pub. Affairs Assn. (pres. 1990), Internat. Assn. Bus. Communicators (v.p. mem. svcs. Richmond chpt. 1996), Nat. Assn. Sci. Writers, D.C. Sci. Writers Assn. (bd. dirs. 2004—), Forum Agr. and Consumer Topics (founder, chmn. 1992), Sierra Club (mem. Montgomery County environ. edn. com. 2004—). Avocations: piano, sailing, music, traditional Irish set dancing. Office: b j Altschul & Assocs 14100 Beechvue Ln Silver Spring MD 20906 Personal E-mail: sunrises111@hotmail.com.

ALTSCHULER, MARJORIE, advertising executive; V.p., rsch. and account mgmt. dir. Foote, Cone & Belding, N.Y.C.; v.p., strategic planner, new bus. developer J. Walter Thompson Co., N.Y.C., 1990-94; sr. v.p., new bus. dir. McCann-Erickson Worldwide, N.Y.C., 1994-97, exec. v.p., new bus. dir., 1997—.

ALTSCHULER, RUTH PHYLLIS, realtor, secondary school educator; d. Morris and Sarah Dina Gass; m. Bruce Robert Altschuler, Oct. 27, 1974; children: Joan, Wendy, Cheryl. AA, San Antonio Coll., 1979; BS in English, Towson U., 1998; MA in English, Morgan State U., 2005. Cert. tchr. English grades 5-12 Md., lic. realtor Md. Pres. Cognitive Photonics, Ft. Meade, Md., 1989—90; dir. sales and mktg. Cobalt Rsch., Columbia, Md., 1997—99, CEO, 2001—03; tchr. English Prince George County Pub. Sch. Sys., Md., 1999, 2004—; instr. English writing Howard C.C., Columbia, 2000; tchr. English Balt. City Pub. Sch. Sys., 2001. Realtor Long and Foster Realtors, Columbia, 2002—04; lectr. English, Humanities Morgan State U., 2006. Stop smoking facilitator Am. Cancer Soc., San Antonio, 1979—80; troop leader Girl Scouts Am., Ft. Meade, Md., 1991; precinct chmn. Rep. Party Bexar County, San Antonio, 1976—82. Sgt. USAF, 1970—74. Named Outstanding Young Woman Am., Jaycees, 1981. Mem.: NEA, Acad. Am. Poets, Nat. Coun. English Tchrs., Golden Key. Jewish. Avocations: writing, sailing, singing, sewing, cooking. Office: Cobalt Rsch LLC PO Box 458 Simpsonville MD 21150-0458 Office Phone: 410-309-6089.

ALTURA, BELLA T., physiologist, educator; b. Solingen, Germany; came to U.S., 1948; d. Sol and Rosa (Brandstetter) Tabak; m. Burton M. Altura, Dec. 27, 1961; 1 child, Rachel Allison. BA, Hunter Coll., 1953, MA, 1962; PhD, CUNY, 1968. Instr. exptl. anesthesiology Albert Einstein Coll. Medicine, Bronx, 1970-74; asst. prof. physiology SUNY Health Sci Ctr., Bklyn., 1974-82, assoc. prof. physiology, 1982-97, rsch. prof. physiology, 1997—, rsch. prof. pharmacology, 1998—. Vis. prof. Beijing Coll. of Traditional Chinese Medicine, 1988, Jiangxi (China) Med. Coll., 1988, Tokyo U. Med. Sch., 1993, U. Brussels Esramé Hosp., 1995, Humboldt U.-Charité Hosp., 1995, Kagoshima U., Japan, 1995, U. Birmingham, England, 1996, Self Med. Def. Coll. Japan, 1996, Nat. Def. Med. Sch., Japan, 1996, Albert Szent Gyorgi

Med. U., Szeged, Hungary, 1997; mem. Nat. Coun. on Magnesium and Cardiovascular Disease, 1991—; cons. NOVA Biomedical, 1989—; Niche pharm. cons. Protina GmbH, Munich, 1992—96, Otsuka Pharm. Co., Japan, 1995—97, Roberts Pharm. Co., 1999—2000; v.p. for rsch. and diagnostics Bio-Def. Sys., Inc., 2005—; co-prin. investigator NIH, Nat. Heart, Lung and Blood Inst., NIMH, Nat. Inst. on Alcoholism and Alcohol Abuse. Contbr. over 700 articles to profl. jours. Fellowship NASA, 1966-67, CUNY, 1968; co-recipient Gold-Silver medal French Nat. Acad. Medicine, 1984, Silver medal Mayor of Paris, 1984, Seelig award for lifetime rsch. on magnesium, Am. Coll. Nutrition, 2002, Outstanding Inventor of Yr., SUNY, 2002, Seelig award for lifetime rsch. Gordon Rsch. Conf. on Magnesium, 2005. Mem. Am. Physiol. Soc., Am. Soc. Pharmacology and Exptl. Therapeutics, Am. Soc. for Magnesium Rsch. (founder, treas. 1984—), Hungarian Soc. Electrochemistry (hon. co-pres. 1995-96), Nat. Heart, Lung and Blood Inst., Nat. Inst. on Alcohol Abuse and Alcoholism, Phi Beta Kappa, Sigma Xi. Achievements include first measurement ionized magnesium with ion selective electrode in blood, serum and plasma in health and disease states; demonstration that substances of abuse can cause cerebrovasospasm and stroke. Office: SUNY Health Sci Ctr Box 31 450 Clarkson Ave Brooklyn NY 11203-2056 Office Phone: 718-270-2205. Business E-Mail: baltura@downstate.edu.

ALTUS, DEBORAH ELAINE, social sciences educator; d. William and Grace Altus; m. Jerrold T. Jost, Sept. 9, 1995; 1 child. PhD, U. Kans., Lawrence, 1988. Dir. Coop. Living Project. U. Kans., 1988—92, asst. rsch. prof. Gerontology Ctr., 1992—99, assoc. prof. Sch. Family Studies Manhattan, 1999—2000, adj. assoc. prof. dept. applied behavioral sci., 1999—; assoc. prof. dept. human svcs. Washburn U., Topeka, 2000—. Editl. bd. Communal Socs. Jour., Amana, Iowa; editl. rev. bd. Fellowship Intentional Cmty., Rutledge, Mo. Contbr. chapters to books, articles to profl. jours. Assoc. bd. mem. Fellowship for Intentional Cmty., Rutledge, Mo., 1993—94; mem. Nat. Shared Housing Task Force, 1993—95; Kans. coord. Postpartum Support Internat., Santa Barbara, Calif., 2001—03; mem. KS Arthritis Steering Com., Topeka, 2000—04; cmty. edn. adv. bd. mem. KU Med Ctr. on Aging, Kansas City, 2000—04; adv. com. mem. Kans. Elder Count, Kansas City, 2001—03; adv. bd. mem. Ctr. Aging KS State U., Manhattan, 2000—06; co-chair pub. engagement task force Living Initiatives for End of Life Care Project, Kans., 2001—06; mem. Kans. Mental Health & Aging Coalition, Topeka; chairperson Cultural Design Interest Grp. Assn. Behavior Analysis, Kalamazoo, 1989—92, treas. Behavioral Gerontolgy Interest Grp., 2002—04. Recipient Schiefelbusch Gerontology Rsch. Devel. award, U. Kans., 1992, Co-Investigator Evaluating Elder Cottage Housing grant, Nat. Inst. Aging, Co-Investigator Locating Wanderers with Dementia grant, 1998, Educator Hall of Fame award, N.Am. Students of Cooperation; grantee Merit Rsch. fellowship, Nat. Inst. Disability & Rehab. Rsch., 1994; Housing Coop. Rsch. grant, Commonwealth Ter. Coop., 1990, Increasing Ind. Functioning of Persons with Dementia grant, Alzheimer's Assn., 1998—99, Personal Actions to Health Intergenerational Project grant, Kans. Health Found., 1999—2000. Fellow: Gerontol. Soc. Am.; mem.: Internat. Communal Studies Assn. (bd. dirs.), Am. Soc. Aging, Communal Studies Assn. (pres. 2004—06), Assn. Gerontology in Higher Edn., Assn. Behavior Analysis, Postpartum Support Internat. Office: Washburn Univ Dept Human Svcs Topeka KS 66621 Office Fax: 785-670-1027. Business E-Mail: deborah.altus@washburn.edu.

ALTY, SALLY JOAN, elementary school educator; d. Wayne Sawin and Frances Elizabeth Linfield; m. Jeff Scott Alty, July 30, 1988; children: Jacob Scott, Amanda Kate. BS in Elem. Edn., Towson U., Balt., 1980. Cert. tchr. Fla., 1981. Mid. sch. sci. tchr. Wash. County Schs., Hagerstown, Md., 1980—81, Collier County Pub. Schs., Naples, Fla., 1981—. Choir Cmty. Congl. United Ch. of Christ, Naples, 1988—2003, Unity Ch., Naples, 2003—06. Named Collier County Tchr. of Yr., 1999. Avocations: singing, guitar, nature study, reading, crafts. Office: 14975 Collier Blvd Naples FL 34119 Office Phone: 239-377-4800.

ALUMBAUGH, JOANN MCCALLA, magazine editor; b. Ann Arbor, Mich., Sept. 16, 1952; d. William Samuel and Jean Arliss (Guy) McCalla; m. Lyle Ray Alumbaugh, Apr. 27, 1974; children: Brent William, Brandon Jess, Brooke Louise. BA, Ea. Mich. U., 1974. Cert. elem. tch., Mich. Assoc. editor Chester White Swine Record Assn., Rochester, Ind., 1974-77; prodn. editor United Duroc Swine Registry, Peoria, Ill., 1977-79; dir., pres. Nat. Assn. Swine Records, Macomb, Ill., 1979-82; free-lance writer, artist Ill. and Nat. Specific Pathogen Free Assn., Ind. producers, Good Hope, Emden, Ill., 1982-85; editor The Hog Producer Farm Progress Publs., Urbandale, Iowa, 1985-99; exec. editor Nebr. Farmer, Kans. Farmer, Mo. Ruralist, We. Beef Prodr., Beef Prodr., Farm & Fireside, 1999—2003; dir. comms. Farms.Com, 2003—. Family Living Program, Farm Progress Show, 1985-2004, Master Farm Homemaker Program, 1989-99; mem. U.S. Agrl. Export Devel. Coun., Washington, 1979-82, apptd. mem. Blue Ribbon Com. on Agr., 1980-81. Contbr. numerous articles to profl. jours. Precinct chmn. Rep. Party, Linden, Iowa, 1988; mem. Keep Improving Dist. Schs., Panora, Iowa, 1990-91; v.p. Sunday sch. com. Sunset Circle, United Meth. Ch., Linden, 1990-91; pres. PTA, Panorama Schs., Panora, 1993-94; coach Odyssey of Mind Program World Competition, 1994—. Mem.: Iowa Master Farm Homemakers (chair nat. farm homemakers planning com. 2005—06), Guthrie County Prok Prodrs., McDonough County and Ill. Porkettes (county pres. 1978—79, Belleringer award 1979), Nat. Pork Prodrs. Coun., Iowa Pork Prodrs. Assn. (legis. com. 1990—95, hon. master pork prodr.), U.S. Animal Health Assn., Am. Agrl. Editors Assn. (chmn. dist. svc. com. 1991, master writer 1997, pres.-elect 1998, pres. 1999, chmn. adv. coun. 1999—2002, trustee 2002—, co-chmn. comm. clinic, chmn. comms. clinic, co-chmn. internat. com. 2005—, World of Difference award 1995, Oscar in Agr. 1999), Internat. Platform Assn. Avocations: reading, painting, gardening. Home: 2644 Amarillo Ave Linden IA 50146-8029 Office: PigChamp Aspen Business Park 426 S 17th Ames IA 50010 Office Phone: 515-233-2551. E-mail: joann.alumbaugh@farms.com.

ALVARADO, GRACE, elementary school educator; b. Tempe, Ariz., Apr. 10, 1963; d. Joe and Rosa Martinez; m. Art Alvarado, July 16, 1988; children: Sabrina Renee, Arthur Jr., Rosa Armida, Alex Vicente. B in Elem. Edn., Ariz. State U., Tempe, 1986; M in Secondary Edn., No. Ariz. U., Flagstaff, 1991. Tchr. phys. edn. Andersen Elem. Sch., Chandler, Ariz., 1986—87, Glaveston/Frye Elem. Sch., 1987—88, Goodman Elem. Sch., 1988—. Coach basketball Goodman Elem. Sch., 1988—2006. Coord. sock hop/sock/can food dr. Chandler Sch. Dist., 1995—2006; coord. Lions club journey sight Goodman Sch., 1988—2000. Mem.: Ariz. Assn. Phys., Health Edn., Recreation and Dance (assoc.), Chandler Edn. Assn. (assoc.). Home: 2600 W Knox Rd Chandler AZ 85224 Office: Goodman Elementary School 2600 W Knox Rd Chandler AZ 85224 Office Phone: 480-812-6900. Home Fax: 480-812-6920; Office Fax: 480-812-6920. Personal E-mail: alvarado.grace@chandler.k12.az.us. E-mail: alvarado.grace@chandlerk12.az.us.

ALVARADO, LINDA G., construction executive; Doctorate (hon.), Dowling Coll. Pres., CEO Alvarado Constrn., Inc., Denver, 1976—. Owner Colorado Rockies franchise; corp. dir. 3M, Pepsi Bottling Group, Pitney Bowes and Lennox Industries. Chmn. bd. dirs. Denver Hispanic C. of C.; commrs. White House Initiative for Hispanic Excellence in Edn. Named Revlon Bus. Woman of Yr., 1996, Bus. Woman of Yr., U.S. Hispanic C. of C., 1996, 100 Most Influential Hispanics in Am., Hispanic Bus. Mag., others; recipient Nat. Minority Supplier Devel. Coun. Leadership award, 1996, Sara Lee Corp. Frontrunner award, 2001, Horatio Alger award, others; inducted into Nat. Women's Hall of Fame, Colo. Women's Hall of Fame. Office: Alvarado Construction 1266 Santa Fe Dr Denver CO 80204-3546

ALVAREZ, AIDA M., former federal agency administrator; b. Aguadilla, P.R., July 22, 1949; BA cum laude, Harvard U., 1971; LLD (hon.), Iona Coll., 1985. News reporter, anchor Metromedia TV, N.Y.C.; reporter N.Y. Post, N.Y.C.; mem. N.Y.C. Charter Revision Commn.; v.p. N.Y.C. Health and Hosps. Corp., 1984—85; investment banker 1st Boston Corp., N.Y.C., San Francisco, 1986-93; dir. Office Fed. Housing Enterprise Oversight, Washington, 1993-97; adminstr. Small Bus. Adminstrn., 1997-2001. Bd. dirs. Pacific Healthcare Systems, 2003—05, UnionBanCal Corp., 2004—, Wal-Mart Stores Inc., 2006—; diversity advisory bd. Deloitte & Touche LLP. Former mem. bd. dirs. Nat. Hispanic Leadership Agenda, N.Y. Cmty. Trust, Nat. civic League; former chmn. bd. Mcpl. Assistance Corp./Victim Svcs. Agy., N.Y.C.; N.Y. State chmn. Gore Presdl. Campaign, 1988; nat. co-chmn. women's com. Clinton Presdl. Campaign, 1992; mem. President's Econ. Transition Team, 1992. Recipient Front Page award, award for excellence AP, 1982, Emmy nomination for reporting guerrilla activities in El Salvador. Democrat.*

ALVAREZ, CONSUELO JACKELINE, science educator, researcher; d. Simon Bolivar and Maria Teresa Alvarez; m. Gary Alvarez, 1993; 1 child, Henry. D in Biochemistry and Pharmacy, Universidad Ctrl., Quito, 1988; PhD, U. Ill., Urbana-Champaign, 1996. Instr. Coll. Veterinarian Medicine, Quito, 1988—90; postdoctoral rschr. E. Tenn. State U., Johnson City, 1996, 1999—2000, Med. Coll. Va., Richmond, 2000—01; asst. prof. Universidad San Francisco de Quito, Quito, 1996—98; lectr. Longwood U., Farmville, Va., 2001—02, asst. prof., 2002—. Spanish tchr. Stepping Stones Childcare Ctr., Farmville, 2002—06. Translator, editor: spanish animations for biology textbooks. Teller, lector, eucharistic min. St. Theresa Cath. Ch., Farmville, 2001—. Fulbright-LASPAU scholar, 1990—96, Faculty R & D grantee, Longwood U., 2003, Genomics Edn. Matching grantee, LI-COR, 2004. Mem.: Med. Coll. Admission Test (chief health professions advisor 2004), Va. Acad. Scis., Genomic Consortium Active Tchg., RNA Soc. Achievements include design of a ribbon to use in the openning ceremony of the science building that represents an specific DNA molecule which afterwards is been used as a tool in classes; research to incorporate DNA microarray technique into undergraduate curriculum, not R1 institution. Avocations: sports, travel. Office: Longwood U 201 High St Farmville VA 23909 Office Phone: 434-395-2847. Office Fax: 434-395-2652. Business E-Mail: alvarezcj@longwood.edu.

ALVAREZ, JULIA, writer; b. NYC, 1950; m. Bill Eichner. Attended, Conn. Coll., Bread Loaf Sch. English, Middlebury Coll.; BA summa cum laude, Middlebury Coll., 1971; MFA, Syracuse U., 1975; LHD honoris causa (hon.), CUNY John Jay Coll., 1996; D (hon.), Union Coll., Schenectady, NY, 2004. Poet-in-the-schools, Ky., 1975—78, Del., 1975—78, NC, 1975—78; prof. creative writing and English Phillips Andover Acad., Mass., 1979—81, U. Vt., 1981—83, U. Ill., 1985—88; prof. English Middlebury (Vt.) Coll., 1988—98, writer-in-residence, 1998—; co-owner Café Alta Gracia fair trade organic coffee co., Dominican Republic; co-creator Fundación Alta Gracia Sch., Dominican Republic. Jenny McKean Moore vis. writer George Wash. U., 1984; nat. mem. coun. PEN Am. Ctr., 1997—99. Author: (novels) How the Garcia Girls Lost Their Accents, 1991 (selected as notable book Am. Libr. Assn., 1992, Pen Oakland/Josephine Miles award for multicultural viewpoint, 1991, one of 21 classics for 21st century NY Librarians, 1999), In the Time of Butterflies, 1994 (selected as notable book Am. Libr. Assn., 1994, finalist Nat. Book Critics Cir. award in fiction, 1995, one of Best Books for Young Adults YA Libr. Svcs. Assn., Am. Libr. Assn., 1995), The Other Side, 1995, YO!, 1997, Something to Declare, 1998, In the Name of Salomé, 2000 (One of top 10 books Latino.com, 2000), The Secret Footprints, 2000, How Tia Lola Came to Stay, 2001 (Parent's Guide to Children's Media Inc. outstanding book, 2001, Child Mag. Best Children's Book, 2001), A Cafecito Story, 2001 (Nebr. Book award for fiction, 2002), Before We Were Free, 2002 (Am. Libr. Assn. notable book, 2002, Am. Libr. Assn. Best Book for Young Adults, 2002, Américas award for Children's and Young Adult Lit. Consortium Latin Am. Studies Programs, 2002), Saving the World, 2006, (poetry) The Woman I Kept to Myself, Homecoming: New and Collected Poems. Named Woman of Yr., Latina Mag., 2000; recipient Benjamin T. Marshall Poetry Prize, Conn. Coll., 1968, 1969, prize, Acad. Am. Poetry, 1974, poetry award, La Reina Press, 1982, Third Woman Press award, first prize in narrative, 1986, award for younger writers, Gen. Elec. Found., 1986, syndicated fiction prize for "Snow" grant from Ingram Merrill Found., PEN, 1990, Josephine Miles award, PEN Oakland, 1991, Lit. Leadership award, Dominico-Am. Soc. of Queens, Inc., 1998, Fray Anton de Montesinos award, Alumni Assn. Univ. Santo Domingo, 2002, Sor Juana award, Mexican Fine Arts Mus., Chgo., 2002, Hispanic Heritage award in lit., Kennedy Ctr., Washington, 2002; grantee, Nat. Endowment Arts, 1987—88; creative writing fellow, Syracuse U., 1974—75, Robert Frost Poetry fellowship, Bread Loaf Writers' Conf., 1986, Kenan grant, Phillips Andover Acad., 1980, exhbn. grant, Vt. Arts Coun., 1984—85. Mem.: Latin Am. Writers' Inst., Poets & Writers, Associated Writing Programs, Acad. Am. Poets, Phi Beta Kappa, Sigma Tau Delta (hon.). Mailing: Susan Berghol Literary Svcs 17 W 10th St 5B New York NY 10011 Home: Weybridge VT Address: care Algonquin Books of Chapel Hill PO Box 2225 Chapel Hill NC 27515-2225*

ALVAREZ, OFELIA AMPARO, pediatrician, hematologist; b. Havana, Cuba, Mar. 29, 1958; BS, U. Puerto Rico, 1978, MD, 1982. Diplomate Nat. Bd. Med. Examiners, Am. Bd. Pediat., Sub-bd. Pediatric Hematology-Oncology. Pediat. resident U. Children's Hosp., San Juan, PR, 1982—85; fellow pediat. hematology, oncology Children's Hosp. L.A., 1985—88; asst. prof. pediat. Loma Linda U., Calif., 1988—95, assoc. prof., 1995—2000; assoc. prof. clin. pediats. U. Miami, 2001—, dir. pediat. sickle cell program. Chmn. instnl. rev. bd. U. Miami, 2004—. Contbr. articles to profl. jours. Clin. oncology fellow Am. Cancer Soc., 1985-86; named one of Best Doctors, 2005 Fellow: Am. Acad. Pediat.; mem.: Am. Soc. Hematology, Am. Soc. Pediat. Hematology/Oncology, Am. Soc. Clin. Oncology. Roman Catholic. Achievements include research in sickle cell disease. Office: Univ Miami Divsn Pediats Hematology Oncology Dept Pediats PO Box 016960 Miami FL 33101 E-mail: oalvarez2@med.miami.edu.

ALVAREZ-CORONA, MARTI, school psychologist, educator; b. Phoenix, Jan. 14, 1949; BA, Calif. State U., L.A., 1984; MA, Western N.Mex. U., 1992. ESL adult educator LA Unified Sch. Dist.; trilingual elem. edn. tchr. Glendale Sch. Dist., Ariz.; behavioral counselor St. Lukes Behavioral Ctr., Phoenix; cert. sch. psychologist Isaac Sch. Dist., Phoenix, 1994—. Recipient Silver Apple award Dial Corp. News Channel 3; featured in Phoenix mag., 1992, Ariz. Republic. Mem. APA, Am. Counseling Assn., Nat. Assn. Sch. Psychologists, Ariz. Assn. Sch. Psychology, Nat. Assn. Masters in Psychology.

ALVARIÑO DE LEIRA, ANGELES (ANGELES ALVARIÑO), biologist, oceanographer; b. El Ferrol, Spain, Oct. 3, 1916; came to U.S., 1958, naturalized, 1966; d. Antonio Alvariño-Grimaldos and Carmen Gonzalez Diaz-Saavedra; m. Eugenio Leira-Manso, Mar. 16, 1940; 1 child, Angeles. BS Letters and Humanities summa cum laude, U. Santiago de Compostela, Spain, 1933; M in Natural Scis., U. Madrid (now U. Complutense), 1941, Doctorate cert., 1951, DSc summa cum laude, 1967. Cert. biologist-oceanographer, 1951, Spanish Inst. Oceanography. Prof. biology Univ. Coll., El Ferrol, Spain, 1941-48; fishery rsch. biologist dept. Sea Fisheries Spain, 1948-52; histologist Superior Coun. Sci. Rsch., 1948-52; biologist, oceanographer Spanish Inst. Oceanography, 1952—57; biologist Scripps Inst. Oceanography-U. Calif. San Diego, LaJolla, 1958—69; fishery rsch. biologist Nat. Marine Fisheries Svc. S.W. Fisheries Sci. Ctr., NOAA, U.S. Dept. Commerce, La Jolla, 1970-87; emeritus scientist Nat. Marine Fisheries Svc. S.W. Fisheries Ctr., NOAA, U.S. Dept. Commerce, La Jolla, 1987—; assoc. prof. U. Nat. Autonomous Mexico, 1976, San Diego State U., 1979-82; rsch. assoc. U. San Diego, 1982—84. Vis. prof. Inst. Poly. Tech. Mexico, 1982—, U. Parana, Brazil, 1982. Author: Spain and the First Scientific Oceanic Expedition (1789-1794) Malaspina and Bustamante with the Corvettes "Descubierta" and "Atrevida", 2000, 2d deluxe edit., 2003; contbr. over 100 articles to profl. jours., chpts. to books; discovered 22 new species of oceanic animals and the indicator species for various oceanic currents, ocean dynamics, and the study of the biotic environment of fish spawning grounds, study of plankton predators and the impact in fisheries, bunch of plankton populations carried by ships into exotic oceanic areas and throughout interoceanic canals, studies on Chaetognatha and Siphonophora in all world oceans and of Hydromedusae in the Atlantic, Pacific and Indian oceans; studies on the reproductive processes in Chaetognatha, others. Brit. Coun. fellow, 1953-54, Fulbright fellow, 1956-57; NSF grantee, 1961-69, U.S. Office Navy grantee, 1958-69, Calif. Coop. Oceanic Fishery Investigations grantee, 1958-69, UNESCO grantee, 1979; recipient Great Silver Medal of Galicia, Spain, presented by King Juan Carlos and Queen Sofia of Spain, 1993. Fellow Am. Inst. Fishery Rsch. Biologists, Natural History Assn.; mem. Am. Assn. Rschrs. on Marine Scis. Achievements include discovery of biotic differences in the habitat of various fishes; sci. work on the fauna represented in about 100 color plates from specimens of plankton, fishes, turtles, birds. It includes a total of near 200 species collected along the South Atlantic and Pacific (up to Alaska, western Pacific Islands, the Philippines, Australia and back to Spain), during oceanic sci. expedition of 1789-1794 with specific identification, description, behavior and distribution; scientist in British, U.S., Mexican and Spanish research vessels in cruisers and expeditions in the Atlantic and Pacific Oceans. Home: 7535 Cabrillo Ave La Jolla CA 92037-5206

ALVES, CONSTANCE DILLENGER, special education educator; b. Richmond, Va., Sept. 17, 1956; d. George Stuart and Betty Jane (Westwood) Dillenger; m. Bruce Alves, June 28, 1980; 1 child, Caitlin. BA in Speech, Audiology, Mary Washington Coll., 1978; MEd in Deaf Edn., U. Va., 1980; postgrad., Gallaudet U., 1980. Cert. tchr., Va. Tchr. of hearing-impaired students Danville (Va.) Pub. Schs., 1980-90; tchr. of deaf Henrico County Schs., Richmond, Va., 1990—99; kindergarten tchr., 1999—2005; 1st grade tchr., 2005—. Adj. faculty Danville Community Coll., 1980-89; adj. faculty interpreter's program J. Sargeant Reynolds, Richmond, 1990—; interpreter for deaf Va. Dept. Deaf and Hard of Hearing, Richmond, 1988—; chmn. Together for the Hearing Impaired, Danville, 1981, 82, 86-87; mem. Danville Local Adv. Com., 1984-86; chmn. Com. for Devising Evaluation Criteria for Teaching Hearing Impaired, Danville, 1984; cons., hearing-impaired specialist Pittsylvania County Schs., Chatham, Va., 1980—. Career Ladder Status Mark Excellence in Tchg. award, Danville Pub. Schs. Evaluation Com., 1987-90; Va. Econ. Edn. award, Va. Ctr. Econ. Edn., 1999, 2005. Mem. NEA, Va. Edn. Assn., Va. Registry Interpreters for Deaf, Nat. Coun. on Edn. of Deaf (cert.). Home: 3612 Meadow Pond Ct Glen Allen VA 23060-2518

ALVILLAR-SPEAKE, THERESA, federal agency administrator; Grad., Calif. State U.; MBA, Golden Gate U. Asst. dir. program devel. minority bus. devel. agy. Dept. Commerce, 1991—93; mgr. small bus. and disabled vet. bus. enterprise programs State Calif. Dept. Transp.; exec. dir. Calif. Employment Devel. Dept., 1994—97, asst. dir. bus. rels., 1997—2000; dir. minority econ. impact & diversity US Dept. Energy, Washington, 2001—. Founder NEDA San Joaquin Valley. Office: Dept Energy Econ Impact and Diversity 1000 Independence Ave SW Washington DC 20585-0001

ALVING, BARBARA, federal agency administrator, hematologist; BS with highest distinction, Purdue U., 1967; MD cum laude, Georgetown U., 1972. Intern in internal medicine Georgetown U.; resident in internal medicine Johns Hopkins U. Hosp., fellow in hematology; rsch. investigator Divsn. Blood and Blood Products FDA; joined dept. hematology and vascular biology Walter Reed Army Inst. Rsch., 1980, chief dept. hematology and vascular biology, 1992—96; dir. med. oncology/hematology sect. Washington Hosp. Ctr., 1996—99; dir. extramural Divsn. Blood Diseases and Resources Nat. Heart, Lung, and Blood Inst., NIH, Bethesda, Md., 1999—2001, dep. dir., 2001—03, acting dir., 2003—05, dir. Women's Health Initiative, 2002—; acting dir. Nat. Ctr. Rsch. Resources, NIH, 2005—. Prof. medicine Uniformed Services U. Health Services, Bethesda. Master: ACP. Achievements include patents in field. Office: Nat Ctr Rsch Resources Democracy Plz One 9th Fl 6701 Democracy Blvd MSC 4874 Bethesda MD 20892-4872 also: Women's Health Initiative Program Office 2 Rockledge Ctr Ste 8093 6701 Rockledge Dr MS 7935 Bethesda MD 20892-7935 Office Phone: 301-496-5793. Office Fax: 301-402-0006. E-mail: alvingb@mail.nih.gov.*

ALWARD, RUTH ROSENDALL, nursing consultant; d. Henry Rosendall and Freda Jonkman; m. Samuel Alward, Jan. 17, 1976. RN, Butterworth Hosp. Sch. Nursing, Grand Rapids, Mich.; BSN summa cum laude, Hunter Coll./CUNY, N.Y., 1980; MA Tchrs. Coll., Columbia U., 1982, EdM, 1983, EdD, 1986. Sr. clin. nurse Wadsworth VA Hosp., L.A., 1966-68; exec. dir. nursing Care Corp, Grand Rapids, Mich., 1968-71; nursing cons. Humana Inc., Louisville, 1972-76; asst. prof., dir. nursing adminstrn. grad. prog. Hunter Coll., CUNY, N.Y.C., 1986-90; pres. Nurse Exec. Assocs., Inc., Washington, 1990—; series editor Delmar Pubs. Inc., Albany, 1993-96. Co-author: The Nurse's Shift Work Handbook, 1993, The Nurse's Guide to Marketing, 1991; contbr. articles to profl. jours.; mem. editorial adv. bd. Jour. of Nursing Adminstrn. Bd. dirs., past pres. James Lenox House Assn.; bd. dirs. IONA Sr. Svcs., 1998-2004. Mem. Nat. League Nursing (treas. D.C. chpt.), Am. Orgn. Nurse Execs., Sigma Theta Tau. Home and Office: 2011 N St NW Washington DC 20036-2301 Office Phone: 202-728-2956. E-mail: ruthalward@aol.com.

ALWARD, SARAH ANNE, mathematics educator; b. Rochester, N.Y., Mar. 1, 1980; d. Daniel Alan Schutt and Patricia Anita Mehlenbacher, John Mehlenbacher (Stepfather); m. Michael Robert Alward, Aug. 23, 2003. BA in Math. and Secondary Edn., SUNY, Geneseo, 2002; MS in Math., Sci. and Tech. Edn., St. John Fisher Coll., Rochester, 2006. Lic. tchr. math. 7-12 N.Y., 2002. Summer inst. teacher's asst. Rochester City Sch. Dist., 2001; summer inst. math. tchr. Gananda Ctrl. Sch. Dist., Macedon, NY, 2002; substitute tchr. Fairport Ctrl. Sch. Dist., NY, 2002, Brighton Ctrl. Sch. Dist., NY, 2002, Attica Ctrl. Sch. Dist., NY, 2002; math. tchr. Palmyra-Macedon Ctrl. Sch. Dist., NY, 2002—. Mem.: Assn. Math. Tchrs. N.Y. State, Nat. Coun. Tchrs. of Math. Independent. Avocations: scrapbooks, theater, movies, music. Office Phone: 315-597-3420. Personal E-mail: sarahalward@aol.com. E-mail: sarah.alward@palmaccsd.org.

AMADEI, DEBORAH LISA, librarian; b. Jersey City, June 13, 1952; d. Joseph and Thelma (Pugach) Irgon; m. Albert E. Amadei, July 19, 1987. BA, Northeastern U., 1975; MS, Pratt Inst., 1985. Cert. profl. librarian. Tech. libr. asst. Tracor Jitco, Dover, N.J., 1977-84, lead tech. libr. asst., 1984-85; sr. libr. East Orange (N.J.) Pub. Libr., 1986—. Mem. ALA, N.J. Libr. Assn. Avocations: writing, hiking, movies. Office: East Orange Pub Libr 21 S Arlington Ave East Orange NJ 07018-3804 Office Phone: 973-266-5204. E-mail: d_amadei@hotmail.com.

AMADIO, BARI ANN, metal fabrication executive, retired nurse; b. Phila., Mar. 26, 1949; d. Fred Deutscher and Celena (Lusky) Garber; m. Peter Colby Amadio, June 24, 1973; children: P. Grant, Jamie Blair. BA in Psychology, U. Miami, 1970; diploma in Nursing, Thomas Jefferson U., 1973, Johnston-Willis Sch. Nursing, 1974; BS in Nursing, Northeastern U., 1977; MS in Nursing, Boston U., 1978; JD, Quinnipiac Sch. Law, 1983. Faculty Johnston-Willis Sch. Nursing, Richmond, Va., 1974-75; staff, charge nurse Mass. Gen. Hosp., Boston, 1975-78; faculty New Eng. Deaconess, Boston, 1978-80, Lankenau Hosp. Sch. of Nursing, Phila., 1980-81; pres. Original Metals, Inc., Phila., 1985—, also bd. dirs. Owner Silver Carousel Antiques, Rochester, Minn. Treas. Women's Assn. Minn. Orch., Rochester, 1986-87, pres., 1987-89, life advisor, 1989—, editor newsnotes, 1985-87; mayor's coms. All Am. City Award Com., Rochester, 1984-88; bd. dirs. Rochester Civic League, 1988-94, pres.-elect, 1990-91, pres., 1991-92, Rochester Civic Theatre, 2005-06; pres. Rochester Friends of Mpls. Inst. Arts, 1989-90, Folwell PTA, 1990-91; state liaison Gateway, 1990-91; bd. dirs. Rochester Civic Theatre, 1993-99, 2003--, v.p., 1994-95, pres., 1995-96; Minn. site coord. Pew Charitable Trust's Project 540, 2002-05; program coord. Southeast Svc. Corp., 2006—. Recipient Joe Saidy award Rochester Civic Theatre, 1999, Mayor's Artistic and Cultural Achievement medal of honor, 2003. Mem.: NAFE, Nat. Assn. Food Equipment Mfrs., Zumbro Valley Med. Soc. Aux. (Rochester, fin. chmn. 1986—90, treas. 1988—90), Am. Soc. Law and Medicine, Rotary Club Rochester, Friends of Mayowood, Order of the Eastern Star (trustee), Sigma Theta Tau, Phi Alpha Delta. Avocations: fencing, painting, poetry, piano, squash.

AMADO, HONEY KESSLER, lawyer; b. Bklyn., July 20, 1949; d. Bernard and Mildred Kessler; m. Ralph Albert Amado, Oct. 24, 1976; children: Jessica Reina, Micah Solomon, Gabrielle Beth. BA in Polit. Sci., Calif. State Coll., Long Beach, 1971; JD, Western State U., Fullerton, Calif., 1976. Bar: Calif.

1977, U.S. Dist. Ct. (ctrl. dist.) Calif. 1981, U.S. Ct. Appeals (9th cir.) 1981, U.S. Supreme Ct. 1994. Pvt. practice, Beverly Hills, Calif., 1978—. Mem. family law exec. com. Calif. State Bar, 1987—91; lectr. in field. Contbr. articles to profl. jours.; mem. editl. bd. L.A. Lawyer mag., 1996—, articles coord., 1999-2000, chair, 2000-01. Mem. Com. Concerned Lawyers for Soviet Jewry, 1979-90; nat. v.p. Jewish Nat. Fund, 1995-97, 2002—; bd. dirs. Jewish Nat. Fund L.A., 1990-98, 2002—, Women's Alliance Israel; mem. pres.'s coun. Am. Jewish Com., 2002—; sec. L.A. region, bd. dirs., 1991-94, Am. Jewish Congress, Jewish Feminist Ctr., 1992-99, co-chair steering com., 1994-96; mem. Commn. on Soviet Jewry of Jewish Fedn. Coun. Greater L.A., 1977-83, chmn., 1979-81, commn. on edn., 1982-83, cmty. rels. com., 1979-83; mem. pres.'s coun. Am. Jewish Com. Nat. Coun., L.A., 2006—, bd. dirs., 2002—; co-chair Internat. Rels. Com. L.A. Region, 2003-04, chair internat. com., 2004-. Mem.: Calif. Ct. Appeal, Calif. State Bar, LA County Bar Assn. (family law sect., appellate cts. com. 1987—, chmn. subcom. to examine reorgn. Calif. Supreme Ct. 1990—94, judge pro tem panel 1985—95, appellate jud. evaluations com. 1989—, Dist. 2 settlement program 1996—), Beverly Hills Bar Assn. (family law mediators panel 1985—94), Calif. Women Lawyers (bd. govs. 1988—90, 1st v.p. 1989—90, jud. evaluations co-chair 1988—90). Democrat. Jewish. Office: 261 S Wetherly Dr Beverly Hills CA 90211-2515 Office Phone: 310-550-8214. Personal E-mail: hkaatty@earthlink.net.

AMADOR, ANNE, architect, composer; b. Racine, Wis., Apr. 29, 1958; d. Anthony s. and Marian A. Methenitis; m. Germán Amador, Jr., Aug. 20, 1983; children: Cristián Mateo, Isabel Celeste. BA, Rice U., 1980, MusB, 1995; MArch, U. Houston, 1983. Registererd arch., Tex.; registered interior designer, Tex. Intern arch. Sobel/Roth Archs., Houston, 1980-83, Ceria & Coupel, Houston, 1983-84; project arch. 3/D Internat., Houston, 1984-89, 91-93; interior arch. Gensler & Assocs., London, 1991; artistic dir. Chimney Rock Studios, Houston, 1993—. Vis. student St. Hilda's Coll., Oxford (Eng.) U., 1989-90. Composer (choral music) Satires of Circumstance, 1991 (Soc.for the Promotion of New Music award 1991), (choral) Whither Thou Goest, 1995, (choral/instrumental) Processional-St. Philip, 2000. Bd. dirs. St. Philip Child's Day In Presch., Houston, 1995—; deacon St. Philip Presbyn. Ch., Houston, 1999-01. Mem. Tanglewood Garden Club (com. mem.), Rice U. Bus. and Profl. Women (program chair 1995-96), Rice Design Alliance, The Shepherd Soc. Avocations: piano, running. Home: 1022 Chimney Rock Rd Houston TX 77056-2001 E-mail: anamador@msn.com.

AMALFE, CHRISTINE A., lawyer; b. Union, N.J., Dec. 21, 1960; d. Salvatore Thomas and Sandra (Boccalero) Amalfe; 3 children. BS, Seton Hall U., 1982; JD, Syracuse U., 1985. Bar: NJ 1985, US Dist. Ct. NJ 1985, NY 1986, US Dist. Ct. (so., ea. and no. dists.) NY 1986, US Ct. Appeals (3d cir.), 1986, US Supreme Ct., 2002. Sr. editor Syracuse Law Review, 1984—85; assoc. Gibbons, Del Deo, Dolan, Griffinger & Vecchione, Newark, 1985, dir., 1993—, dir. employment and labor dept., 2002, chair employment law dept., human resources gen. counsel. Adj. prof. legal writing and advocacy Seton Hall U. Sch. of Law, 1992—93. Mem. NJ Gender Parity Labor and Edn. Coun. Named one of 25 Women of Influence, NJ Biz mag., 2004; named to Com. on Character, Supreme Ct. NJ, 2000—03; recipient Salute to the Policy Makers, Exec. Women NJ, 2000. Mem.: Def. Rsch. Inst. (employment law com.), NJ State Bar Assn. (pro bono com. 1995—97), Essex County Bar Assn., NJ 300, Exec. Women NJ, Order of Coif, ABA (employment law section, EEO Com.). Office: Gibbons, Del Deo, Dolan, Griffinger & Vecchione One Riverfront Plaza Newark NJ 07102 Office Phone: 973-596-4829. Office Fax: 973-639-6230. Business E-Mail: camalfe@gibbonslaw.com.*

AMANO, IMELDA, school librarian; d. Conchita Corpuz; m. Rick Amano, July 19, 1991; 1 child, Kazumi. M in Info. Sci., U. Hawaii, Honolulu, 2002. Lic. tchr. Hawaii, 1987. Libr. Dept. Edn., Honolulu, 2003—, tchr. hs.s. Dancer Pearl Orient Dance Co., Gabing Pilipino, U. Hawaii. Docent Hawaii Plantation Village, Honolulu, 1993—2000. Grantee, Pub. Schs. Hawaii Found., 2000, 2002. Mem.: Hawaii Assn. Sch. Librs. (dir. of nominations, nat. libr. week chairperson 2004—06, exec. bd. mem. 2003—). Avocations: travel, dance, cooking, languages.

AMANPOUR, CHRISTIANE, news correspondent; b. London, Jan. 12, 1958; m. James Rubin, 1998; 1 child, Darius John Rubin. BA in Journalism, summa cum laude, Rhode Island U. Reporter, anchor, prodr. WBRU-Radio, Providence, 1981—82; asst. internat. assignment desk CNN, Atlanta, 1983, correspondent Frankfurt, West Germany, 1989, Kuwait, 1990; contbr. 60 Minutes CBS News, 1996—. Named Woman of Yr., Women in Cable and Telecommunications, NY Chpt., 1994; named one of 100 Most Powerful Women, Forbes mag., 2005—06; recipient News & Documentary Emmy, George Foster Peabody award, 1994, 1997, Courage in Journalism award, Worldfest-Houston Internat. Film Festival Gold award, Livingston award for young journalists, Breakthrough award, Women, Men and Media, 1991, Sigma Chi award, Edward R. Murrow award for disting. achievement in broadcast journalism, 2002. Fellow: Soc. of Profl. Journalists. Fluent in English and Farsi (Persian). Mailing: CNN One CNN Center Atlanta GA 30303*

AMAR, PAULA BRAM, psychologist, consultant; b. Pitts., Jan. 9, 1934; d. Samuel H. and Anne Levine; m. Harold Bram, Oct. 23, 1955 (div. June 1972); children: Aaron (dec.), Adam; m. Henri Amar, Mar. 16, 1975 (dec. Aug. 1980); m. Melvin J. Schwartz, Oct. 22, 1983. BA, Antioch Coll., 1956; postgrad., U. N.Mex., 1958-62; MS, Med. Coll. Pa., 1970, PhD, 1972. Lic. psychologist Pa., N.Mex.; diplomate Am. Bd. Adminstrv. Psychology. Psychotherapist Albuquerque Child Guidance, 1959-62, Devereaux Found., Devon, Pa., 1962-69; asst. prof. Jefferson Med. Coll., Phila., 1972-78; program adminstr. Jefferson Community Mental Health, Phila., 1973-79; dir. Ambler (Pa.) Psychol. Svcs., 1979-91; cons. Psychol. Svcs., Albuquerque, 1991—. Seminar leader Nat. YMCA, Washington, 1969-72, Stamford (Conn.) Health Agy., 1976, Save-Your-Heart Weekend, Stamford, 1977, Jefferson Med. Col., 1978, Sta. 12 Ask WHYY, 1979, Greater Phila. Claims Assn., 1979, Conf. of the Phila. Bar Assn., Diocesan Coun. and JCRA, 1979, FOP, Phila., 1979, HUD Mgrs., Columbia, Md., 1980, Pa. Pers. and Guidance Assn., Phila., 1980, McNeil Labs., Spring House, Pa., 1981, 83; examiner Biofeedback Cert. Inst. Am., 1984—. Editor: Biofeedback Soc. Am. Clin. Notes, 1981-85; contbg. editor to encys.; contbr. articles to profl. jours. Pres. Jewish Family Svc.; bd. dirs. Jewish Cmty. Ctr., Albuquerque; bd. mem. Albuquerque Open Space Alliance. Grantee The Schweppes Found., 1971, Nat. Heart Lung Inst., 1975, Jefferson Med. Coll., 1976. Fellow Phila. Soc. Clin. Psychologists, Am. Assn. for Behavior Therapy and Exptl. Psychiatry; mem. APA (mem. div. 38 health psychology), AAAS, Assn. for Applied Psychophysiology and Feedback (mem. clin. and rsch. divs., pres. 1992-93), Phila. Soc. Clin. Hypnosis, Pa. Biofeedback Soc., Biofeedback Soc. Am., Pa. Psychol. Assn. (pres. acad. div. 1979-80, conf. chair 1981, pres. clin. div. 1985), Phila. Soc. Clin. Psychologists, Jewish Family Svc. of Albuquerque, Anne Frank Inst. of Phila. Avocations: tennis, skiing, writing, hiking.

AMARA, LUCINE, vocalist; b. Hartford, Conn., Mar. 1, 1925; d. George and Adrine (Kazanjian) Armaganian; married, Jan. 7, 1961 (div. June 1964). Student, Music Acad. of West, 1947, U. So. Calif., 1949-50. Artistic dir. N.J. Assn. Verismo Opera, Ft. Lee. Tchr. master classes U.S., Mex., Can., Australia. Appeared at Hollywood Bowl, 1948, soloist, San Francisco Symphony, 1949-50; career includes over 1000 operatic performances; with Met. Opera, N.Y.C., from 1950, sang 800 performances, 9 new prodns., 5 opening nights, 57 radio broadcasts, 4 telecasts including appeared on Met. Opera: In Performance, 1982, 83, 84, 85, 86, 87, 88, 90, 91; recorded Pagliacci, 1951, 60; singer with New Orleans, Hartford, Pitts., Central City operas, 1952-54, appeared Glyndebourne Opera, 1954, 55, 57, 58, Edinburgh Festival, 1954, Aida, Terme Di Caracalla, Rome, 1954, also Stockholm Opera, N.Y. Philharm., St. Louis Civic Light Opera, 1955-56; has appeared in leading or title roles in several operas including: Tosca, Aida, Amelia in Un Ballo in Maschera, Turandot, Riverside Opera Assn., 1986, others; appeared with St. Petersburg (Fla.) Opera, Venezuela Philharm. Orch., 1988, 93; opera and concert tour, USSR, 1965, 91, Manila, 1968, Paris, Mex., 1966, Hong Kong and China, 1983, Yugoslavia, 1988; rec. artist, Columbia, RCA, Victor, Angel records, Met. Opera Record Club; albums include: Beethoven's Symphony No. 9, Leoncavallo's, I Pagliacci, Puccini's La Bohème, Verdi Requiem. Recipient 1st prize Atwater-Kent Radio Auditions, 1948; inducted to Acad. Vocal Arts Hall Fame, 1989. E-mail: lamara@nyc.rr.com.

AMARA, SUSAN, neuroscientist; BS, Stanford U.; PhD in physiology and pharmacology, U. Calif., San Diego, 1983. Sr. scientist Vollum Inst.; investigator Howard Hughes Med. Inst.; prof. Oreg. Health Sci. U.; Thomas Detre prof., chair, dept. neurobiology Pitts. Sch. Medicine, U. Pitts., 2003—. Mem.: Dana Alliance Brain Initiatives, Soc. Neurosci., NAS. Office: Univ Pitts Dept Neurobiology E1440 Biomedical Sci Tower 3500 Terrace Pittsburgh PA 15261 Business E-Mail: amaras@pitt.edu.*

AMARO, LETICIA, medical/surgical nurse; b. Santurce, P.R., Nov. 4, 1950; d. Edmund and Francisca (Luyanda) Rivera; m. Ernest Amaro, June 6, 1970; children: Ernest Jr., Nicolas, Daniel, Natalie Luz. Lic. practical nurse diploma, Helene Fuld Sch. Practical Nursing, N.Y.C., 1971; BSN magna cum laude, U. Sacred Heart, Santurce, 1986. cert. MSN in patient care adminstrn., Sacred Heart U., Conn., 2004, lic. RN in P.R., Conn. Nurse's aide Lenox Hill Hosp., N.Y.C.; med. asst. Presbyn. Health Ctr., Bklyn.; staff nurse St. George Hosp., Santurce; staff nurse med.-surg. and coronary units and dialysis, RN VA Med. Ctr., West Haven, Conn. E-mail: lamaro3@hotmail.com.

AMATANGEL, LISA, lawyer; BA magna cum laude, Tufts U., 1993; JD, Boston Coll. Law Sch., 1999. Bar: Mass. Law clk. to Hon. Mary M. Lisi US Dist. Ct. (Dist. RI); assoc. Litig. Dept. Wilmer, Cutler, Pickering, Hale and Dorr, LLP, Boston, 2001—. Office: Wilmer Cutler Pickering Hale and Dorr LLP 60 State St Boston MA 02109 Office Phone: 617-526-6643. Office Fax: 617-526-5000. E-mail: lisa.amatangel@wilmerhale.com.*

AMATANGELO, KATHLEEN DRISCOLL, interior designer, educator; d. Cassidy and Frances Driscoll; m. Nicholas S. Amatangelo, May 16, 1964; children: Amy Kathleen, Holly Megan. BA, Saint Joseph Coll., 1962; student, Manhattan Coll., NY, 1966—67, Fordham U., 1967—69, U. Santa Clara, 1972—73. Cert. tchr. Conn., 1962, NY, 1966. Tchr. english Kelly Jr. H.S., Norwich, Conn., 1962—63; intern White Ho. U.S. Govt., Washington, 1963—64; tchr. english Pulaski Sr. H.S., New Britain, Conn., 1964—66, Dobbs Ferry (N.Y.) H.S., 1966—72; designer residential KDA Interiors, San Mateo, Calif., 1975—79, designer contract Houston, 1979—87, Barrington, Ill., 1987—. Author: The Case for Sex Education, 1975; contbr. numerous poems to jours. Women's bd. Children's Home and Aid Soc., Chgo., 1996—2001. Named Top Fund Raiser, Houston (Tex.) Symphony, 1983; recipient Blue Ribbon award, Peony Soc. Am., 1992, Parents Coun. Exec. Bd. award, Washington U., 1996. Mem.: Pkwys. Found., The Sarah Siddons Soc. (mem. exec. bd. 2000—), Chgo. (Ill.) Zool. Soc. (women's bd. 2003—), Woman's Athletic Club Chgo. (tech. com. 2000—). Avocation: skiing. Office: KDA Interiors 12 Bellwood Rd Barrington IL 60010 Office Phone: 847-382-5558.

AMATO, DARIA U., critical care, medical, and surgical nurse; b. Kingston, N.Y., Mar. 11, 1954; d. Charles T. and Joan C. (Geary) A. Student, Spalding Coll., Louisville, 1975; AS in Nursing, Excelsior Coll., Albany, N.Y., 1980; BSN, Cath. U. Am., 1988, MS in Cardiovascular Nursing Mgmt., 1991. RN, N.Y., Ky., D.C., Va., Md.; cert. adult med.-surg. nurse, nursing adminstr., ANCC. Staff nurse cardiothoracic surgery ICU, surg. ICU, sr. clin. nurse emergency dept. Mt. Sinai Hosp. Med. Ctr., N.Y.C.; clin. instr. critical care Mt. Sinai Sch. Continuing Nursing Edn.; per diem night adminstrv. supr. Our Lady of Mercy Med. Ctr.-Pelham Bay Campus, Bronx, N.Y., staff nurse I and II med.-surg. unit; staff nurse III emergency room Washington Hosp. Ctr.; asst. prof. nursing Iona Coll., New Rochelle, N.Y.; night adminstrv. dir. nursing Children's Nat. Med. Ctr., Washington; emergency rm. clin. nurse Georgetown U. Hosp., Washington. Mem. PN faculty Harrison Ctr. YWCA, Washington; clin. nurse I, ER, Georgetown U. Hosp., charge nurse CNA testing; cons. Mary Kay Cosmetics; asst. prof. nursing, No. Va. C.C. Coord. Health Fair, Cath. U. Am., Washington, 1988, chmn., 1989; cons. curriculum devel. Word Alive Bible Coll. Mem. AACN, Nat. Assn. Cath. Nurses. E-mail: damato@nv.cc.va.us.

AMATO, DEBORAH DOUGLASS, aerospace engineer; b. Mo. d. Clyde and Wilma Douglass; m. Michael Amato, 1996. BS, MIT, 1994; MS, U. Md., 1998. Programmer Orbital Scis. Corp., Va., 1993; aerospace engr. NASA-Goddard Space Flight Ctr., Greenbelt, Md., 1993—. Mem.: AIAA. Avocations: music, swimming. Office: NASA Goddard Space Flight Ctr Greenbelt MD 20771-0001

AMATO, MICHELE AMATEAU, artist, educator; b. Flushing, N.Y., July 29, 1945; d. Harold Amateau and Ann (Resnick) A.; m. Albert Alhadeff, May 28, 1969 (div.); 1 child, Cara Judea; m. Don K. Schule, Nov. 22, 1978. BFA, Boston U., 1968; MFA, U. Colo., 1973. Chairperson, prof. of art Wichita (Kans.) State U., 1977-78; vis. prof. art Mpls. (Minn.) Coll. of Art and Design, 1978-79, U. Tex., San Antonio, 1982-83; curator of exhbns. Patrick Gallery, Austin, 1983-84; vis. artist U. Colo., Boulder, 1984-85; prof. art U. Tex., Austin, 1985; vis. artist East Carolina U., Greenville, N.C., 1986; prof. art S.W. Tex. State U., San Marcos, 1987-88; represented by Flatfile Contemporary Gallery, Chgo.; area head, prof. art Pa. State U. Sch. of Visual Arts, University Park, 1988—. Mem. editorial adv. bd. Collegiate Press, Alta Loma, Calif., 1990—. Mem. editorial bd. Ocular mag., 1972-79; art and dance columnist Straight Creek Jour., 1971-76, Boulder Daily Camera, 1971-74; exhibited in one-person shows Kornblee Gallery, NYC, 1975-78, 85, Mus. Contemporary Hispanic Art, 1989, Nahan Contemporary, NYC, 1990, Freedman Gallery, Albright Coll., 1991, Lyons Matrix Gallery, 1993; exhibited in group shows Cleve. State U., 1994, Dallas Internat. Art Expo., 1994, Chgo. Art Fair, 1994, Tokyo Art Expo, 1990-94, Acme Inc., LA, 2004, SUNY, Cortland, 1993; represented in permanent collections Chase Manhattan Bank, NYC, Denver Art Mus., Rose Art Mus., Brandeis U.; represented by Sandra Gering Gallery, NYC, Recipient New Forius Regional award, Nat. Endowment Arts, 1992; NEA fellow, 1988; rsch. grantee Pa. State U., 1989, travel grantee Pa. State U. Inst. for Arts and Humanistic Studies, 1991. Mem. Coll. Art Assn., Women's Caucus for Art. Democrat. Jewish. Home: 1721 Linden Hall Rd Boalsburg PA 16827-1720 Office: 102VAB Pa State U Sch Visual Arts University Park PA 16827

AMATO, ROSALIE, secondary school educator; b. Racalmuto, Agrigento, Sicily, June 3, 1920; came to U.S., 1923; d. Nicolo and Francesca (Macaluso) A. BS, Buffalo State U., 1964, MEd, 1968. Office supr. Wm. Hengerer Co. (Sibley's), Buffalo, N.Y., 1941-51; installation personnel Remington Rand, Dayton, Ohio, 1951-53; office supr., acctg. City of Buffalo, 1953-61; home econs. tchr. Buffalo Bd. Edn., 1964-70, supr. home econs. federally funded projects, 1971—. Vol. Civil Def., State of N.Y., 1953-58 (Cert. Pub. Service, 1958). Mem. Am. Home Econs. Assn. (area coord. 1973-75), Kappa Delta (treas. 1962-63), Phi Epsilon Omicron (pres. 1968-70). Roman Catholic. Avocations: art, design, concerts, opera, bowling. Home: 327 Colvin Ave Buffalo NY 14216-2338

AMAYA-THETFORD, PATRICIA, elementary school educator; b. Orange, Calif., Feb. 25, 1965; d. Guillermo Jimenez and Maria Angelina (Avalos) Mojarro; m. Elias Amaya, Oct. 22, 1988 (dec. Oct. 1993); children: Eliana Ashley, Hunter C.; m. Gary S. Thetford, June, 1999. BA in Spanish, U. Calif., Irvine, 1987; MS in Instrnl. Leadership Curr. & Instrn, Nat. U., 1998. Cert. elem. tchr., bilingual, cert. bilingual competence, Calif., 1989. Biliterate instrnl. asst. Franklin Elem. Sch., Santa Ana, Calif., 1986-89, bilingual tchr., 1989-91, Alcott Elem. Sch., Pomona, Calif., 1991-97, bilingual resource tchr., 1997—. Mem. ASCD, NEA, Calif. Tchrs. Assn., U. Calif.-Irvine Alumnae Assn., Calif. Assn. Bilingual Edn. Avocations: travel, reading, writing, collecting children's literature books. Home: 7415 Jola Drive Riverside CA 92506 Office: Alcott Elem Sch 1600 S Towne Ave Pomona CA 91766-5367

AMBADY, NALINI, social psychologist, educator, researcher; b. Calcutta, India; came to U.S., 1983; d. Shanker and Viji Ambady; m. Raj Marphatia, June 8, 1988; children: Maya Mallika, Leena Anupama. PhD, Harvard U., 1991. Asst. prof. Holy Cross Coll., Worcester, Mass., 1993-94, Harvard U., Cambridge, Mass., 1994-99, Ruth and John Hazel assoc. prof. social sci., 1999—2004; prof., social psychology Tufts U., Medford, Mass., 2004—. Recipient, Behavioral Sci. Rsch. prize AAAS, 1993, Presdl. Early Career award U.S. Govt., 1998, Excellence in Mentoring Award, Harvard U., 2000. Office: Tufts U The Psychology Bldg 490 Boston Ave Medford MA 02155 E-mail: naliniambady@tufts.edu.

AMBERG, DEBORAH ANN, lawyer; b. 1965; BA, U. Minn., 1987, JD cum laude, 1990. Bar: Minn. 1990. Staff atty. Allete, Inc., Duluth, Minn., 1990—98, sr. atty., 1998—2004, gen. counsel, v.p., corp. legal svcs. corp. sec., 2004—. Mem.: ABA, Minn. State Bar Assn., Minn. Women Lawyers. Office: Allete Inc 30 W Superior St Duluth MN 55802-2093 Office Phone: 218-723-3930. Office Fax: 218-723-3996. E-mail: damberg@allete.com.

AMBERS, ANN, bishop, educator; b. Brusly, La., Feb. 26, 1948; d. Fannie Mae Jones and Eddie Elmore, Sr., Oliver Jones, Jr. (Stepfather); m. Jackie Roy Ambers, Sept. 3, 1994; m. Lester Moore Jackson, Feb. 11, 1967 (dec. May 24, 1987); children: Gregory, Felita, Lindsey. B, Golden State Sch. Theology, 1989; M, Bell Grove Theol. Sem., 1993, DD (hon.), 1998. Cert. Ordination New St. Paul Missionary Bapt. Ch., 1988, Missionary Lic.-Exec. Sec. Nat. Bapt. Women Min. Conv., 1988. Substitute tchr. Iberia Parish Sch. Bd., New Iberia, La., 1998—; assoc. min. New St. Paul Missionary Bapt. Ch., Oakland, Calif., 1987—93; acctg. clk. Iberia Parish Sheriff's Dept., New Iberia, 1998—2000; pastor True Vine Full Gospel Ch., Oakland, 1990—93, Port Allen, La., 1993—; exec. sec. J. Bryant Aids Found., Oakland, 1991—93; exec. dir. True Vine Ministries, Oakland, 1988—93. Nat. pres. Nat. Bapt. Women Min. Conv., New Iberia, 2003; assoc. min. Union Bapt. Ch., Brusly, La., 1999—2003; state mission pres. La. Freewill Bapt. Assn., Baton Rouge, 1999—2003; nat. amb. #1 Nat. Bapt. Women Min. Conv., Berkeley, Calif., 1990—2003. Recipient Cert. Of Award, Nat. Bapt. Women Min. Conv., 1989, Cert. Of Honor, Alpha Tron Task Force, 1990, Alphatron Christian Task Force, 1990, Disting. Achievement Award, Greater Resurrection Bapt. Ch., 1996, Disting. Svc. award, J. Bryant Aids Found., 1991, Disting. Achievement Award, New St. Paul Missionary Bapt. Ch., 1988, Disting. Achievement, One True Vine Outreach Ministries, 1997.

AMBORN, JENNIFER, physical education educator; b. Dec. 31, 1975; MA, Midamerica Nazarene U., Olathe, Kans., 1998; MEd, North Ctrl. Coll., Naperville, Ill., 2000; postgrad., St. Louis U., 2000—. Grad. intern, athletic trainer North Ctrl. Coll., 1998—2000; asst. proff., program dir., athletic trainer Midamerica Nazarene U., 2000—. Recipient Al Ortaloni award of merit, NH Assn. Intercollegiate Athletics, 1997, Rsch. and Edn. Athletic Tng. Grad. award, 1998, Nat. Athletic Dirs. Cup, Sears, 1998; athletic tng. scholar, Swede-O, 1996. Mem.: Midamerica Athletic Trainers' Assn., Kans. Athletic Trainers' Soc., Nat. Athletic Trainers' Assn. Avocations: basketball, softball, volleyball, rollerblading, painting. Office: MidAmerica Nazarene U 2030 E College Way Olathe KS 66062

AMBROSE, ADELE D., communications executive; B in Journalism, U. Pitts. Joined Western Electric, 1978; sr. mgmt. positions pub. rels. AT&T Wireless Svcs., Inc., 1991—99, v.p. pub. rels., 1999—2001, exec. v.p. pub. rels. and investor comm., 2001—. Mem.: Arthur W. Page Soc. Office: AT&T Wireless Svcs Inc Bldg 1 7277 164th Ave NE Redmond WA 98052

AMBROSE, DONETTA W., federal judge; b. New Kensington, Nov. 5, 1945; m. J. Raymond Ambrose Jr., Aug. 19, 1972; 1 child. BA, Duquesne U., 1963-67, JD cum laude, 1967-70. Law clerk to Hon. Louis L. Manderino Commonwealth Ct. Pa., 1970-71, Supreme Ct. Pa., 1972; asst. atty. gen. Pa. Dept. Justice, 1972-74; pvt. practice atty. Ambrose & Ambrose, Kensington, Pa., 1974-81; asst. dist. atty. Westmoreland County, Pa., 1977-81; judge Ct. Common Pleas Westmoreland County, 1982-93, US Dist. Ct. (We. Dist.) Pa., Pitts., 1994—, chief judge. Resident advisor Duquesne U., 1967-70. Scholar Pa. Conf. State Trial Judges, 1992, State Justice Inst., 1993. Mem. ABA, Nat. Assn. Women Judges, Am. Judicature Soc., Pa. Bar Assn., Women's Bar Assn. Western Pa., Pa. Conf. State Trial Judges (sec. 1992-93), Westmoreland County Bar Assn., Italian Sons and Daus. Am., William Penn Fraternal Assn., New Kensington Women's Club, Delta Kappa Gamma. Office: US Courthouse Office 700 Grant St Rm 307 Pittsburgh PA 15219-1906

AMBROSE, JUDITH ANN, wedding planner; b. San Jose, Calif., Oct. 22, 1940; d. Howard Linse and Beula May (Russell) Shannon; m. James Paul Ambrose, Apr. 17, 1965; children: Sheryl Ann Beckey, James Paul Jr. BS, Salem Coll., Winston-Salem, NC, 1962; postgrad., Purdue U., 1963—64. Lic. home econs. tchr. Fla., NC. Home econs. tchr. Broward County, Ft. Lauderdale, Fla., 1962—67; owner Decorative Accents, Ft. Lauderdale, 1984—99; wedding coord. Christ Ch. United Meth., Ft. Lauderdale, 1990—2004. Home econs. curriculum dir. Broward County Schs., Ft. Lauderdale, 1965—66. Pres. Parent Tchr. Fellowship Westminster Acad., 1982—83; mem. resource group Children's Diagnostic and Treatment Ctr., Ft. Lauderdale, 1997—2003, bd. dirs., 2001—, sec. bd. dirs., 2003—, interim co-chair Sunflower Cir. of Friends, 2004; founder Friends of Jack & Jill Nursery, Ft. Lauderdale; organizer shoe fund for children in cmty. Christ Meth. Ch., 1992—; mem. Pres's Coun. Ft. Lauderdale, 1989; bd. dirs. Jack & Jill Nursery Sch., Ft. Lauderdale, 1974—2000; mem. Beaux Arts, 1986—90. Recipient Outstanding Cmty. Svc. award, Jr. League of Ft. Lauderdale, 1989, Golden Rule award, J C Penney, Ft. Lauderdale, 1995, Heart of the Cmty. Vol. of Yr. award, Children's Diagnostic and Treatment Ctr., Broward, Fla., 2002, 2005. Mem.: AAUW, Charity Guild (chmn. fall function 1992, publicity chmn. 1993—96, chmn. fall function 1997, pres. 1998—99, bd. dirs. 2001—03, rep. to Kids in Distress), Coral Ridge Jr. Women's Club (hon.; past pres., Clubwoman of Yr. 1975—76). Republican. Methodist. Avocations: growing orchids, volunteer work. Home: 4720 NE 25th Ave Fort Lauderdale FL 33308-4811

AMBROSE, LAUREN (LAUREN ANNE D'AMBRUOSO), actress; b. New Haven, Conn., Nov. 16, 1978; d. Frank and Annie Ambrose; m. Sam Handel, 2001. Attended, Conn. Ednl. Ctr. Arts, Tanglewood Inst., Boston U., Yale U.; classically trained opera singer. Actor(guest appearances): (TV series) Law & Order, 1992—98, Party of Five, 1999, Saving Graces, 1999, Six Feet Under, 2001—05 (Emmy nom. Supporting Actress Drama, 2003); (plays, off-Broadway) Soulful Scream of a Chosen Son, 1992; (plays, Nat. Theatre) Buried Child, 2004; (Broadway plays) Awake and Sing!, 2006; (films) In & Out, 1997, Can't Hardly Wait, 1998, Summertime's Calling Me, 1998, Psycho Beach Party, 2000, Swimming, 2000. Office: c/o United Talent Agency 9560 Wilshire Blvd Ste 500 Beverly Hills CA 90212*

AMBRUS, CLARA MARIA, physician; b. Rome, Dec. 28, 1924; arrived in U.S., 1949, naturalized, 1955; d. Anthony and Charlotte (Schneider) Bayer; m. Julian Lawrence Ambrus, Feb. 17, 1945; children: Madeline Ambrus Lillie, Peter, Julian, Linda Ambrus-Broenniman, Steven, Katherine Ambrus-Cheney, Charles. Student, U. Budapest, Hungary, 1943—47; MD, U. Zurich, Switzerland, 1949; postgrad., U. Paris, 1949; PhD, Jefferson Med. Coll., 1955. Diplomate Am. Bd. Clin. Chemists. Research asst. Inst. Histology, Embryology and Biology U. Budapest, 1943-45; demonstrator in pharmacology U. Budapest Med. Sch., 1946-47; asst. dept. pharmacology U. Zurich Med. Sch., 1947-49; asst. dept. therapeutic chemistry and virology Inst. Pasteur, Paris, 1949; asst. prof. pharmacology Phila. Coll. Pharmacy and Sci., 1950-52, assoc. prof., 1952-55; research assoc. Roswell Park Meml. Inst., Buffalo, 1955-58, sr. cancer research scientist, 1958-64, assoc. scientist, 1964-69, prin. cancer research scientist, 1969-85; prof. pharmacology State U. N.Y., Buffalo Med. and Grad. Schs., 1955—, assoc. prof. pediatrics, 1955-76, prof. pediatrics, 1976, research prof. ob-gyn, 1983—; chmn., founder, chief of R&D Hemex Inc., 1984—. Contbr. articles to med. and sci. jours. Trustee Nichols Sch., Buffalo, Cmty. Music Sch. Decorated lady comdr. Equestrian Order of the Holy Sepulchre of Jerusalem; named Outstanding

Woman of Western N.Y., Cmty. Adv. Coun., SUNY, Buffalo, 1980, Med. Woman of Yr., Buffalo Gen. Hosp., 2000; recipient award for excellence in clin. care, d'Youville Coll., 2004, George F. Koepf, MD award, Hauptman-Woodward Med. Rsch. Inst., Buffalo, 1997. Fellow: ACP, Internat. Soc. Hematology; mem.: Hungarian Acad. Sci. (fgn. mem.), Am. Med. Women's Assn., Buffalo Acad. Medicine, Am. Soc. Hematology, Am. Physiol. Soc., Am. Fedn. Clin. Rsch., Am. Soc. Cancer Rsch., Am. Soc. Pharmacology and Exptl. Therapeutics, Saturn Club, Clarksburg Country Club, Garrett Club, Sigma Xi. Home: 143 Windsor Ave Buffalo NY 14209-1020 also: West Hill Farm Boston NY 14025 Office: Buffalo Gen Hosp 100 High St Buffalo NY 14203-1154 Office Phone: 716-859-1512. Office Fax: 716-859-3659. Personal E-mail: jlambrus@netscape.net.

AMEEN, BETSY HARRISON, science educator, department chairman; b. Hopewell, Va., Feb. 15, 1953; d. Henry Pretlow and Bessie Richeson Harrison; m. David Bruce Ameen, Aug. 1, 1992. At, Longwood Coll., Farmville, Va, 1971—73, U. Va. Sch. Nursing, Charlottesville, 1973—74; BS, Va. Commonwealth U., Richmond, 1976. Cert. tchr. biology and gen. sci. edn. Va. Dept. Edn., 1976. Tchr. biology, life sci. and phys. sci. Clover Hill H.S. Chesterfield County Pub. Schs., Midlothian, Va., 1976—79; tchr. phys. sci. Swift Creek Mid. Sch. Chesterfield County Pub. Schs., 1979—. Chmn. sci. dept. Swift Creek Mid. Sch. Chesterfield County Pub. Schs., 1985—. Worship chmn. Wesley United Meth. Ch., Hopewell, Va., 1999—2001, chmn. Gruber cir., 2003—04, chmn. staff parish rels. com., 2003—04. Recipient Tchr. of Yr., Swift Creek Mid. Sch., 1994, Mid. Sch. Tchr. Disting. Svc. award, Am. Chem. Soc. (Va. sect.), 2002. Mem.: NEA, Chesterfield Edn. Assn., Va. Edn. Assn. Office: Swift Creek Mid Sch 3700 Old Hundred Rd Midlothian VA 23112 Office Phone: 804-739-6315. E-mail: betsy_ameen@ccpsnet.net.

AMENDT, MARILYN JOAN, personnel director; b. Marshalltown, Iowa, June 21, 1928; d. Floyd Wilford and Helen Mary (Scheid) Peterson; m. Virgil E. Amendt, Sept. 4, 1949 (div. Aug. 1971); children: Gregory F., Scott R., Brad A. AA, Stephens Coll., Columbia, Mo., 1948; postgrad., U. Mich., 1978, U. Wis., Superior, 1980-83. Cert. personnel mgr. Office mgr. S&O Products, Inc., Marshalltown, Iowa, 1961-71; life underwriter Lincoln Liberty Life Ins. Co., Marshalltown, Iowa, 1971-72; retail store mgr. Amy's Fashions, Marshalltown, Iowa, 1972-74, Maurices, Inc., Marshalltown, Iowa, 1974-76, corp. personnel dir. Duluth, Minn., 1976-84; sr. v.p., dir. human resources Ohrbach's, Inc., N.Y.C., 1984-87; dir. personnel adminstrn. AMCENA Corp., N.Y.C., 1987—91; pres., owner Success Strategies, Des Moines, 1992—. Lectr. U. Wis, Superior, 1981-82, U. Minn., Duluth, 1981-82. Founder, pres., bd. dirs. Mid-Iowa Sheltered Workshop, Marshalltown, 1968-76; mem. Hostess com. Duluth (Minn.) Day Luncheon, 1983; keynote speaker Am. Bus. Women's Day, Mpls. and Duluth, 1984, 85, 86, 90; bd. pres. Young Women's Resource Ctr., 1994-95, bd. dirs., Des Moines, 1992—. Mem. Am. Bus. Women's Assn. (dist. v.p. 1982, nat. v.p. 1983, nat. pres. 1984, woman of the yr. 1978, Top Ten Bus. Woman 2005), Beacon of Life (bd. mem. 2003-). Avocations: speaking, travel, sports, reading. Home: 2233 Country Club Blvd Des Moines IA 50325-8602

AMENTA, CAROLINE, travel agency executive; b. Tarrytown, N.Y., Sept. 30, 1928; d. Carmelo John and Rosaria (Cavalieri) Malandrino; m. Sebastian Amenta, Dec. 27, 1952; children— Paul, John, Frank. Student Wood Bus. Sch., N.Y.C., 1946-47. Office sec. Westinghouse Internat., N.Y.C., 1947-49, Polychrome Co. Inc., Yonkers, N.Y., 1949-52, N.Y. State Regional Health Office, White Plains, 1952-55; travel cons. McGregor Travel, White Plains, 1967-70; pres. ATC Travel, Inc., Tarrytown, 1970—; sec. PJF Properties Ltd., Tarrytown, 1984. Fellow Profl. Bus. Women (v.p. 1983-85). Roman Catholic. Avocations: swimming, reading, travel. Office: ATC Travel Inc 239 N Broadway Ste 3 Tarrytown NY 10591-2654 Office Phone: 914-631-8301. E-mail: caroline@atctravelinc.com.

AMERIAN, MARY LEE, physician; b. Burbank, Calif., May 15, 1956; d. Sam and Alice Anterasian; m. Roger Amerian, Aug. 11, 1979; children: Nicole, Danielle. BA, UCLA, 1979, MD, 1983. Pvt. practice, Santa Monica, Calif., 1987—; intern in internal medicine UCLA Sch. Medicine, 1983—84, resident in dermatology, 1984—87. Reipient Sandoz award Sandoa Pharm., 1983. Fellow Am. Acad. Dermatology, Am. Soc. Dermatol. Surgery; mem. Calif. Med. Assn., L.A. Med. Assn. Avocation: the arts. Office: 2336 Santa Monica Blvd Ste 209 Santa Monica CA 90404-2067

AMES, LOIS WINSLOW SISSON, social worker, educator, writer; b. Boston, Jan. 21, 1931; d. Winslow Chase and Lois (Barton) Sisson; m. Robert Webb Ames, Dec. 15, 1956 (div. Aug. 1969); children: Elisabeth Harriett Winslow, Adam Barton. AB, Smith Coll., 1952; AM in Psychiat. Social Work, U. Chgo., 1958. LICSW Mass., cert. social worker Acad. Cert. Social Workers, bd. cert. diplomate Nat. Registry Health Care Providers in Clin. Social Work, bd. cert. diplomate clin. social work Am. Bd. Examiners Clin. Social Work. Caseworker children's divsn. City of Chgo. Pub. Welfare Dept., 1953—56; intern Family Svc. Salvation Army, Chgo., 1956—57, Ill. Neuropsychiat. Inst., Chgo., 1957—58; child care worker Inst. for Juvenile Rsch., William Healy Residential Treatment Ctr., Chgo., 1957; psychiat. social worker Lake County Mental Health Clinic, Gary, Ind., 1958—59; pvt. clin. practice, 1958—; counselor Hyde Park Unitarian Cooperative Nursery Sch., Chgo., 1964—68; lower and middle sch. counselor U. Chgo. Lab. Schs., 1966—69; lectr. Northeastern U., Boston, 1969—77, asst. prof. Coll. Criminal Justice, 1970—77, coord. social welfare and social work practice curriculum, 1970—77, asst. dir. The Weekend Coll., 1969—70, dir. The Weekend Coll., 1970—72; lectr. psychiatry dept. psychiatry Harvard Med. Sch., Cambridge (Mass.) Hosp., 1982—; asst. editor Women's Page Tucson (Ariz.) Daily Citizen, 1952—53. Dir. The Cmty. Svc. Practicum, Boston, 1972—77; vis. lectr. Sch. Social Work Smith Coll., Northampton, Mass., 1975; mem. adv. com. career edn. Lincoln Sudbury (Mass.) Regional H.S., Sudbury, Mass., 1975—77; mem. adv. bd. Mass. Correctional Instn., Concord, Mass., 1977—82; pvt. psychotherapy cons., Cambridge and Sudbury, Mass.; lectr. psychiatry Harvard Med. Sch., Cambridge Hosp., Mass., 1982—. Editor (with L. Gray Sexton): Anne Sexton: A Self Portrait in Letters, 1977; mem. editl. bd.: Suicide and Life Threatening Behavior; contbr. chapters to books;, author poems and essays. Bd. mem. adv. bd. Franklin Pierce Coll., NH, 1982—85. Recipient Alumni Gold medal citation, U. Chgo., Sch. Social Svcs. Adminstrn., 1974, Affirmative Action cert appreciation, Northeastern U., 1976; rsch. fellow, State Ill. Mental Health Grant, 1956—57, Nat. Inst. Mental Health Grant, 1957—58, Ella Lyman Cabot Trust Grant, 1966, Ill. Arts Coun., 1967, U. Chgo. Lab. Schs., 1967. Mem.: NASW (registered social worker, diplomate in clin. social work), New Eng. Poetry Club (bd. mem. 1987—92). Home: 285 Marlborough Rd Sudbury MA 01776 Office Phone: 978-443-2601.

AMES, SANDRA CUTLER, secondary school educator; b. Putnam, Conn., Nov. 3, 1935; d. Loid C. and Sophie M. (Kowal) Cutler; m. David Crouse Ames, Oct. 28, 1955; children: Deborah Lee, Susan Lynn. BS, U. Conn., 1957, MS, 1959; postgrad., Ea. Conn. State U., 1965. Cert. elem. tchr., Conn. Tchr. elem. Killingly Ctrl. Sch., Dayville, Conn., 1959-88, tchr. K-4 resource math., testing coord., 1988—97; ret., 1997; substitute tchr., 1997—. Presenter math. workshops, Dayville, 1981—; co-chair Invention Conv., Dayville, 1987-90. Recipient Presdl. award in math. Fed. & State Bds. Edn., 1990, 93. Mem. Delta Kappa Gamma. Avocations: crafts, crocheting, knitting, decorating. Home: 235 Chase Rd Putnam CT 06260-2810

AMEZCUA, ESTHER HERNANDEZ, elementary school educator; b. Guadalajara, Jalisco, Mexico, Nov. 9, 1949; came to the U.S., 1961; d. Rodolfo (stepfather) and Guillermina (Hernandez) Sanchez; m. Juan Elizondo Amezcua, June 23, 1973; children: Juanguillermo Gabriel, Jaime Jose Vicente. BA, U. Calif., Davis, 1972. Life tchg. credential, Calif.; multicultural and bilingual credential. With Sacramento City Unified Sch., 1973—; intermediate tchr. William Land Elem., 1973-81, 83-93, primary tchr., 1981-83, 2002—; intermediate tchr., head tchr. Oak Ridge Elem., 1993-97, Caroline Wenzel Elem., 1997—2002. Head tchr. William Land Sch., Sacramento, 1976-83, 89-93, Oak Ridge Elem., Sacramento, 1993-94; mentor tchr. Sacramento Unified Sch. Dist., 1991-93. Vol. Short Term Emergency Assistance Ctr., Davis, Calif., 1990—; dance instr. ballet folklorico, Sacramento, 1990—; vol. tutor, Sacramento, 1993—. Named Educator of Yr. Yolo County, Mexican-Am. Concilio of Woodland, 1997. Mem. Hispanic Educators Sacramento, Calif. Tchrs. Assn., Sacramento City Tchrs. Assn. Democrat. Roman Catholic. Avocations: reading, crocheting, sightseeing, dance, family activities. Home: 3207 Monte Vista Pl Davis CA 95616-4932 Office: William Land Sch 2120 12th St Sacramento CA 95818 Office Phone: 916-264-4166. E-mail: amezcua20@yahoo.com.

AMGOTT, MADELINE, television producer, consultant; b. N.Y.C., Aug. 31, 1921; d. Samuel and Rose (Kanter) Barotz; m. David Karr, Sept. 5, 1942 (div. 1956); children: Andrew, Katharine Karr-Kaitin; m. Milton Amgott, Dec. 15, 1962; 1 child, Seth; 1 stepchild, Margo. BA cum laude, Bklyn. Coll., 1942. Feature coord. CBS News, N.Y.C., 1948—. Prodr. WNBC-TV Not for Women Only, CBS News 60 Minutes, Morning Show, 30 Minutes, Bill Moyers' Constitution Hours, Phil Donahue spl. documentary The Human Animal, Good Housekeeping A Better Way, Today Show, CNBC Home and Family Hour, Real Story, Hans Hofmann, Artist/Teacher, Teacher/Artist, PBS, 2003; cons. Times Mirror, N.Y.C., King Features Entertainment, TBM; bd. dirs. Am. Jour. Nursing Pub. Co., N.Y.C. Co-author: Teenage Gangs, 1957. Mem. West Pride, W. 86th St. Tenants Assn.; co-founder 168 W 68th St Tenants Assn.; mem. N.Y.C. Bicentennial Commn., 1987-89. Recipient Emmy Nat. Acad. TV Arts, 1981, 82, 83; Ohio State award, 1976, 78; Peabody award, 1976; Matrix award, 1976, award Greater Miami Film Festival, Internat. Film Festival of N.Y., others. Mem.: Women in Comm., Inc. Avocations: gardening, bicycling. Office Phone: 212-580-2421.

AMICK, DEBORAH ANNE, medical/surgical and women's health nurse; b. Glendale, Calif., Feb. 10, 1955; d. Edward Paul and Yvonne Marie (Dick) DeVreugd; m. Philip Jonathan Amick, Aug. 8, 1981; children: Scott, Jason, Stacey, Travis, Joyelle. AA, Long Beach City Coll., Calif., 1982; AS in Respiratory Therapy, Long Beach City Coll., 1976. Staff respiratory therapist Pacific Hosp. of Long Beach, 1975-86, staff nurse, 1982-86, Meml. Med. Ctr./Women's Hosp., Long Beach, 1983-86, St. Joseph's Med. Ctr., Stockton, Calif., 1988-94, maternal/child health nurse ICU, 1994—. Mem. Calif. Nurses Assn., Cert. Respiratory Therapy Tech. Assn.

AMIN, FARZANA, psychiatrist, researcher; b. Bahawalpur, Pakistan, Aug. 28, 1973; d. Mohammed and Rehana Amin. MBBS, MD, King Edward Med. Coll., Lahore, Pakistan, 1998. Lic. physician Mo., 2003. Med. officer ob.-gyn. Lady Willingdon Hosp., Lahore, Pakistan; med. officer Amin's Hosp., Bahawalpur, Pakistan; resident psychiatry St. Louis (Mo.) U. Hosp., 2003—06, chief resident Drpartment Psychiatry, 2005—. Editor: Cerebral Blood Flow Changes During Vagus Nerve Stimulation for Depression, Subacute and Chronic Brain Metabolic Change with Vagus Nerve Stimulation in Depression. Vol. program polio prevention Gov. Pakistan, 1994—95. Fellow, Stanford (Calif.) U., 2006—. Mem.: Clin. Trial Unit (corr.; rschr. 2003—06), Am. Acad. Child And Adolescent Psychiatry (corr.), Am. Psychiat. Assn. (corr.). Achievements include discovery of vagal nerve stimulation studies. Office Phone: 314-577-8728. Personal E-mail: boneyamin@yahoo.com.

AMM, SOPHIA JADWIGA, artist, educator; b. Czestochowa, Poland, June 13, 1932; arrived in Can., 1948, arrived in U.S., 1987; d. Romuald Witold and Jadwiga Wactawa (Kotowska) Sulatycki; m. Bruce Campbell Amm, Aug. 5, 1961; children: Alicia, Alexander, Christopher, Bruce Jr., Gregory. Diploma in nursing, Ont. Hosp., 1953; cert. in pub. health nursing, U. Toronto, Ont., Can., 1960; BFA with honors, York U., 1980; MFA, Norwich U., 2000. RN. Pvt. duty nurse Allied Registry, Toronto, 1954-56; asst. head nurse Reddy Meml. Hosp., Montreal, Que., Canada, 1957-59; pub. health nurse Dist. of Sudbury, Ont., Canada, 1960-62; pvt. duty nurse Gen. Hosp., Millinocket, Maine, 1962-66; counselor to new immigrants Ont. Welcome House, Toronto, 1982; vis. nurse St. Elizabeth Vis. Nurses Assn., Toronto, 1983-87; artist, tchr. YMCA, Appleton, Wis., 1994. Art rental and sales Art Gallery Hamilton, 1985—2003; condr. art workshops Very Spl. Arts Wis. festivals, 1989, 90, 92; artist resident Studios Midwest, Civic Art Ctr., Galesburg, Ill., 2003. One-woman shows include Bergstrom Mahler Mus., Neenah, Wis., 1991, Alfonse Gallery, Milw., 2001, exhibited in group shows at Harbourfront Exhbn. Gallery, Toronto, IDA Gallery, York U., 1980—81, 1986, Calumet Coll., York U., 1981, 1984, Simpson's Art Gallery, Toronto, 1984, Art Gallery Hamilton, Can., 1985—86, 2001, Pastel Soc. Can., Ottawa, 1985, Carnegie Gallery, Dundas, Can., 1986, Gallery 68, Burlington, Can., 1986, Del Bello Gallery, Toronto, 1986—93, Neville Pub. Mus., Green Bay, Wis., 1987—89 (Art Annual 3d pl award, 2004), 1992, 1994—97, Consilium Pl., Scarborough, Can., 1987, 1989, 1992—93, Charles A. Wustum Mus. Fine Arts, Racine, Wis., 1990—91, 1994, Gallery Ten, Rockford, Ill., 1992 (3d pl. award, 1992), 1994—95, New Vision Gallery, Marshfield, Wis., 1992, 2001, U. Wis. Gallery, Madison, 1992, 1994, Butler Inst. Am. Art, Youngstown, Ohio, 1993, Lakeland Coll., Wis., 1994, Alverno Coll., Milw., 1994, 1997, Ariz. State U., 1995, Bergstrom Mahler Mus., 1995—96 (1st pl. award, 1995, 3d pl. award, 1996, 1997), Appleton Art Ctr., 1995, 1996, 2002, 2003, 2004, 2005, Ctr. Visual Arts, Wausau, Wis., 1996, Marian Coll. Art, Fond du Lac, Wis., 1996, Anderson Art Ctr., Kenosha, Wis., 1997, Stage Gallery, Merrick, N.Y., 1997, 1998, Norwich U. Vt. Coll. Gallery, Montpelier, 1998—2000, T. W. Wood Gallery, 2000, Hendrickson Art Ctr., Waupaca, Wis. (Hon. Mention, 2000, 2002, 2004, 2005), West Bend Gallery, 2000, Art Quest Nat. Juried Exhbn., Ft. Smith, 2001, N.E. Exposure, Priebe Gallery Exhbn. (Jurors award, 2001), Fulton St. Gallery, Troy, N.Y., 2002, Paine Art Ctr., Oshkosh, Wis., 2002, 2003, Galesburg (Ill.) Civic Art Ctr., 2003, Hothouse Ctr., Chgo., 2003, St. Norbert's Coll., De Pere, Wis., 2003—05, Midwest Studios, Galesburg, Ill., 2003, Neville Pub. Mus., Green Bay Wis., 2004, Coventry Glass Gallery, Appleton Wis., 2004, Wis. Painters and Sculptor and Japanese Artists Exhbn., 2005, Roots Exhbn. at Acad. Arts and Letters, Madison, Wis., 2005, U. Wis. Union Gallery, 2005, Neville Pub. Mus., Green Bay, 2005, West Bend Gallery, 2005, Wis. and Japanese Artists Art Exhbn., 2005, Gallery Brocken, Tokyo, 2006. Vol. art tchr. children with disabilities, Appleton, 1988—89, disabled srs. Colony Oaks Nursing Home, Appleton, 1988—91. Recipient award of Excellence, North York (Can.) Arts Coun., 1982, 1986, Best in Show, Etobicoke (Can.) Arts Coun., 1982, 1987; Project grantee, Very Spl. Arts Wis., 1989. Mem.: Wis. Painters and Sculptors, Appleton Art Ctr., Nat. Mus. Women Arts. Roman Catholic. Avocations: golf, gardening. Home: 1109 N Briarcliff Dr Appleton WI 54915-2848 Personal E-mail: bamm@new.rr.com.

AMMAN, E(LIZABETH) JEAN, academic administrator; b. Hoyleton, Ill., July 13, 1941; d. James Kerr and Marie Fern (Schnake) White; m. Douglas Dorrance Amman, Aug. 12, 1962; children: Mark, Kirk, Jill, Drew, Gwen, Joyce. BA in English, Ill. Wesleyan U., 1963; MA in English, U. Cin., 1975. Cert. tchr., Ill. Tchr. lang. arts John Greer Jr. High Sch., Hoopeston, Ill., 1963-64, Pleasant Hill Sch., East Peoria, Ill., 1966-67; tchr. English, chmn. Am. studies Anderson Sr. High Sch., Cin., 1967-69; instr. English, No. Mich. U., Marquette, 1976-82, Ball State U., Muncie, Ind., 1982-86, adminstrv. intern, 1983-84, asst. to chmn. dept., 1984-86, adminstrv. asst., 1986, asst. to provost, coord. provost's lecture series, 1986—, exec. sec. student and campus life coun., 1986—2002. Editor: Provost's Lecture Series: Perspectives on Culture and Society, Vol. I, 1988, Vol. II, 1991, The Associator, 1983-86; flutist Muncie Westminster Orch., 1989-2004, Am.'s Hometown Band, 1991—, Baroque Consort, 1998—, East Ctrl. Ind. Chamber Orch., 2004— Mem. choir College Ave. Meth. Ch., Muncie, 1989—; fundraiser Delaware County Coalition for Literacy, 1989, 90; v.p. Cornerstone Ctr. Arts, 2005— Recipient recognition Black Student Assn., Ball State U., 1988, cert. of svc. for minority student devel., 1990, 91, 92. Mem. AAUW (pres. Muncie br. 1997-98, Ind. dir. programs 1999-2003, pres. elect Ind. chpt. 2003-04, pres. Ind. chpt. 2004—), Ind. Coll. English Assn. (editor 1983-85, exec. bd. 1983-86), P.E.O. (pres. Muncie 1985-87), Sigma Alpha Iota (v.p. 1994-97, pres. 1999-2000, Sword of Honor 1995), Kappa Delta (Ind. Kappa Delta of Yr. 1994, advisor 1992-95, collegiate province pres. 1995-98), Phi Kappa Phi. Democrat. Avocations: travel, reading, music. Home: 4305 Castleton Ct Muncie IN 47304-2476 Office: Ball State U 2000 W University Ave Muncie IN 47306-0002 Office Phone: 765-285-1333. Business E-Mail: jamman@bsu.edu.

AMMANN, MELADEE, music educator; d. Paul Robert and Dorothy Marilyn Smith; m. Bruce Thomas Ammann, Dec. 29, 1979; children: Lindsay, Brent. BA in Music, Anderson U., Ind., 1977. Music tchr. Monte Vista Elem. Sch., Phoenix, 1977—79, Elvira Elem. Sch., Tucson, 1980—84, San Marcos Elem. Sch., Chandler, Ariz., 1987—88, Laura B. Anderson Sch., Sioux Falls, SD, 1989—. Office: Laura B Anderson Elem Sch 1600 N Wayland Ave Sioux Falls SD 57103

AMMON, CAROL KAY, social worker; b. Albion, Nebr., Dec. 11, 1949; d. Arthur and Mary Susan (King) Fleming; children: Jennifer, Analisa. BA magna cum laude, Macalester Coll., 1970; MA, Stanford U., 1972; MSW, San Francisco State U., 1977. Lic. clin. social worker. Employment counselor Snelling & Snelling, Mpls., 1971; social worker Santa Clara Dept. Social Svcs., Calif., 1973-80; med. social worker Santa Clara Valley Med. Ctr., San Jose, Calif., 1980—. Vol. therapist Santa Clara County Cen. Mental Health Ctr., San Jose, 1979-80; vol. classroom aide Eisenhower Sch., Santa Clara, 1984-88, Girl Scout Bilingual Programs, 1988-98, classroom aide, 1984—, Brownie asst. to leader, Girl Scouts U.S., Santa Clara, 1986-87, scout leader 1987-89; pres. Holy Redeemer Luth. Ch. Coun., San Jose, 1986-88; mem. Macalester Coll. Alumni Admissions Com., 1976—-98 Nat. Fgn. Def. Lang. fellow, 1971-72. Mem. Nat. Assn. Social Workers (diplomate in clin. social work, qualified clin. social worker), Nat. Assn. Perinatal Social Workers (edn. chair 1993-2000, bd. mem. 1991-93, treas. 2004—; award for excellence 2006), Phi Beta Kappa. Avocations: swimming, yoga, gardening. Office: Santa Clara Valley Med Ctr 751 S Bascom Ave San Jose CA 95128-2604

AMMON, JENNIFER TUCKER, orthopedist, surgeon; d. Larry Kendall and Joanna Siebert Tucker; m. Philip Aaron Ammon, May 16, 2004. BS, Ctr. Coll., Danville, Ky., 1994; MS, U. Louisville, 1997, MD, 2002. Rsch. assoc. Allergy and Asthma Assn., Louisville, 1995; rsch. asst. Ctr. for Microcirculatory Rsch., Louisville, 1995—97; resident dept. orthopedic surgery U. Louisville, 2002—, rsch. resident dept. orthopedic surgery, 2003—04. Contbr. articles to profl. jours. Grantee, Fischer Ower Found., 2002—05. Mem.: PETA, Ky. Med. Soc., Am. Acad. Orthopedic Surgery, Ky. Humane Soc. Avocations: triathlon, equestrian. Office: Dept Orthopedic Surgery Ste 1003 210 E Grey St Louisville KY 40202

AMMONS, CAROL HAMRICK, psychologist, editor; b. Tampa, Fla., Feb. 22, 1927; d. Joe Fred and B. Carolyn (Patton) Hamrick; m. Robert Bruce Ammons, Aug. 26, 1999; children: Carl, Bruce, Douglas, Beth, Richard, Stephanie, Glenyss. BA, Hariette Sophie Newcomb Coll. for Women, 1947; MA, Tulane U., 1949; PhD, U. Ky., 1955. Lectr. U. Louisville, 1949-55; pvt. practice cons. psychologist Louisville, 1949—. Tchr. gigong, tai chi, chiuan. Co-editor Perceptual and Motor Skills, 1949—, Psychol. Reports, 1955—; contbr. numerous articles to profl. jours. Grantee U. Ky., Lexington, 1952-54, Tulane U., New Orleans, 1947-49. Mem. AAAS, Am. Psychol. Assn., N.Y. Acad. Scis., Am. Statistical Assn., Internat. Coun. Psychologists (sec. 1965-68), Sigma Xi. Home: 411 Keith Ave Missoula MT 59801-4410 Office: PO Box 9229 Missoula MT 59807-9229

AMON, CAROL BAGLEY, federal judge; b. 1946; BS, Coll. William and Mary, 1968; JD, U. Va., 1971. Bar: Va. 1971, D.C. 1972, N.Y. 1980. Staff atty. Communications Satellite Corp., Washington, 1971-73; trial atty. U.S. Dept. Justice, Washington, 1973-74; asst. U.S. atty. Ea. Dist. N.Y., 1974-86, U.S. magistrate, 1986-90, dist. ct. judge, 1990—. Recipient John Marshall award U.S. Dept. Justice, 1983. Mem. ABA (joint commn. evaluate model code judicial conduct 2004-05), Va. State Bar Assn., D.C. Bar Assn. (chair codes of conduct com. of jud. conf. 1998-2001). Office: US District Court 225 Cadman Plz E Brooklyn NY 11201-1818 Office Phone: 718-613-2410.

AMOS, BETTY GILES, food service executive, accountant; b. Lebanon, Mo., July 18, 1941; d. Clarence Edgar and Clara Mae (Gann) Giles; m. E.L. Amos, Sept. 18, 1959 (div. Oct. 1965); 1 child, Jeffrey Lee; m. Thomas R. Righetti, Jan. 2, 1983 (dec. Sept. 18, 2002). BBA magna cum laude, U. Miami, Coral Gables, Fla., 1973, MBA, 1976; D of Bus. Adminstrn. honoris causa, Johnson & Wales U., 1990. CPA, Fla. Sec. City of Lebanon, 1959-63; dept. head Empire Gas Co., Lebanon, 1963-68; fin. analyst asst. Biscayne Assocs., Ltd., Miami, Fla., 1968-73; investment mgr. Universal Restaurants Inc., Miami, 1973-77; pvt. practice acct., investment mgr. Miami, 1977-83; pres. The Abkey Cos., Miami, 1983—. Founder Mega Bank, Miami, 1983-94; mem. adv. com. Fuddruckers, Inc., Boston, 1986-2002. Trustee Miami Project, 1986-89, United Fund of Dade County, 1992—; pres. Humane Soc. Greater Miami, 1994-2000, bd. dirs., 1993-2000; mem. pres. coun. U. Miami, 1994—, mem. founder's soc., 1994—, bd. trustees, 1997—; mem. presdl. search com. U. Miami, 2000; mem. Orange Bowl Com., 2002—; dir. Wings Over Miami Aviation Mus., treas., 2002-03, pres., 2004—; bd. dirs. IVAX Corp., 2003—; mem. audit com. Miami-Dade County Sch. Bd., 2004—. Recipient Philip J. Romano Founders award, 1988. Mem. AICPA, Fla. Inst. CPAs, Am. Women's Soc. CPAs, Coconut Grove C. of C. (trustee 1988-2001), Nat. Assn. Women Bus. Owners (Outstanding Woman Bus. award 1993), U. Miami Alumni Assn. (nat. pres. 1999-2001), Iron Arrow, Internat. Women's Forum (bd. dirs. 2006—), Women of Tomorrow (bd. dirs. 2006—), Women's Exec. Leadership (adv. bd. 2005—). Republican. Avocations: skiing, water-skiing, scuba diving, tennis. Office: The Abkey Cos 9275 Coral Reef Dr Ste 107 Miami FL 33157 Home: 8206 SW 171 Ter Palmetto Bay FL 33157 Office Phone: 305-278-4422. Business E-Mail: bgamos@bellsouth.net.

AMOS, HELEN, hospital administrator; b. Mobile, Ala. BA, Mt. St. Agnes Coll., 1962; MS, U. Notre Dame, 1968; DHL (hon.), Coll. Misericordia, 1987, Coll. Notre Dame Md., 1999. Joined Sisters of Mercy. Provincial adminstr. Sisters of Mercy Province Balt.; pres. Sisters of Mercy of the Union; pres., CEO Mercy Med. Ctr., 1992—99; exec. chair Mercy Health Svcs. Bd. Trustees, 1999—. Bd. dirs. Mercy Ridge, St. Joseph Health Sys., Downtown Mgmt. Dist. Authority, Balt., The Greater Balt. Com., United Way Ctrl. Md., Md. Hosp. Assn., Loyola Coll. Md., St. Mary's Seminary, Balt., Archdiocesan Bd. Fin. Adminstrn., Balt. Named Women of Yr., Towsontowne Profl. Bus. Women Assn., Top 50 Women in Baltimore Mag. Most Powerful Women Issue, Md. Pub. TV Women of Triumph; named one of Md. Top 100 Women, Daily Record, 1997, 1999, 2001; named to Baltimore City Commn. of Women Hall of Fame; recipient Pro Ecclesia honor from Pope John Paul II, Sarah's Circle award, Women's Inst., Coll. Norte Dame. Office: Mercy Health Svcs Mercy Med Ctr 301 St Paul Pl Baltimore MD 21202

AMOS, JANETTE GARBEE, retired secondary school educator; b. Copperhill, Tenn., Mar. 31, 1940; d. Howard Frank and Martha (Porter) Garbee; m. William E. Amos, Dec. 14, 1961 (div. 1988); children: Leisl, Douglas. BA, Carson-Newman Coll., 1962. Tchr. Jeffersonville HS, Ind., 1962-66, 69-71, Am. Heritage sch., Ft. Lauderdale, Fla., 1981-86, Nova HS, Ft. Lauderdale, Fla., 1986-97; tchr. English to Spkrs. of Other Langs. Athens City Schs., Tenn., 1997—2005. Mem. Keith Meml. United Meth. Ch., Stephen ministry leader, choir mem., liturgical dance. Mem. NEA, Tchrs. of English to Spkrs. of Other Langs., Tenn. Tchrs. of English to Spkrs. of Other Langs. Democrat. Avocations: liturgical dance, music, hiking, camping, needle work. Home: 1002 Brentwood Dr Etowah TN 37331-1824

AMOS, LINDA K., academic administrator; b. Findlay, Ohio, Sept. 7, 1940; d. Blond G. and Dorotha (Brinkman) A. BS, Ohio State U., 1962, MS, 1964; EdD, Boston U., 1977. Asst. dean of baccalaureate affairs Boston U. Coll. Nursing, 1971-74, dean, prof., 1975-80, U. Utah Coll. Nursing, Salt Lake City, 1980—2000, dean, prof. emerita, 2006—; assoc. v.p. for health scis. U. Utah, Salt Lake City, 1998—2006, Dorthie & Keith Barnes presdl. chair, prof. nursing, prof. emerita, dean emerita Coll. Nursing, 2006—. Cons. Social Sci. Rsch. Inst., Boston; chmn. Commn. on Collegiate Nursing Edn., 1998-2000; bd. dirs. Univ. Health Network. Contbr. articles to profl. jours. Chmn. Presdl.

Commn. on Status of Women, U. Utah, 1995—99; bd. dirs. Utah Heart Assn.; trustee U. Utah Hosp. Served as cons. with USPHS. Named for Outstanding Contbns. to the Nursing Profession, Utah Citizen's League for Nursing, 1989, Linda K. Amos Atrium, U. Utah, 2005; recipient VA Chief Nurse award for promoting unity between edn. and practice, Lawrence and Delores Weaver Coll. Pharmacy Recognition award, 2002, Disting. Woman prize Salt Lake Jr. Assistance League, 2004, Client Achievement award, Utah AIA, 2005, Utah Owner of Yr. award Am. Gen. Contractors Utah, 2006; named Atrium in her honor, U. Utah, 2006. Fellow Am. Acad. Nursing (governing coun. 1986-90, selection com. 1995—98); mem. ANA, Am. Assn. Colls. of Nursing (pres. 1984-86, Sister Bernadette Armiger award 2000), Nat. Adv. Coun. on Nurse Tng., Utah Women's Forum, Internat. Women's Forum, Salt Lake City Rotary, Sigma Theta Tau (internat. nominating com. 1995-97, Mary Tolle Wright award for excellence in leadership 1991).

AMOS, MICHELLE, electronics engineer; d. Dunk and Dorothy Wright; m. John Amos; children: Alexandria, Austin. BSEE, So. U. A&M Coll., 1989. Electronics engr. NASA Kennedy Space Ctr. Vol. Engring. Week, Career Days. Avocations: African-American history, nutrition, leadership. Office: NASA Kennedy Space Ctr Bldg M7-0409 Rm 212 Kennedy Space Center FL 32899 Business E-Mail: michelle.amos-1@ksc.nasa.gov.

AMOS, SHIRLEYANN, mental health therapist, social worker; b. Hampton, Va., Oct. 14, 1953; d. Pink Amos Jr. and Pauline Amos; 1 child, John David Taylor. AS, Commonwealth Coll., Virginia Beach, Fla., 1991; BA in Psychology, U. Ctrl. Fla., 1998, MSW, 2001; PhD, Canbourne U., 2005. Enlisted USN, 1973; substance abuse counselor USN and Fla. Keys Meml. Hosp., Key West, 1984—88; advanced through grades to yeoman 1st class petty officer (air warfare) USN, 1980, ret., 1994, administrv. supr. various duty stas, 1980—88, substance abuse counselor Norfolk, Va., 1988—90; asst. investigator Dept. Children and Families, DeLand, Fla., 1998; vol., protective svcs. Ctr. for Drug Free Living, Orlando, Fla., 1999—2000; mental health therapist House Next Door, Deland, Fla., 2000—01. Co-author: Conduct Disorder: DSM-IV-TR in Action, 2001. Mem.: NASW, APA, Nat. Assn. Alcoholism and Drug Abuse Counselors, Disabled Am. Vets. Fla., Am. Legion, Psi Chi. Avocations: art, photography, genealogy, singing. Home: 2741 Coventry Rd Las Cruces NM 88011-0827 Personal E-mail: dr_sam@comcast.net.

AMOS, THERESA ANN, marketing professional; BA in Comm., U. Colo., Colorado Springs, 1985. Cert. sailing. Mktg. mgr. Subway Devel. Corp. San Diego, 1990—94; dir. bus. devel. and account supr. Janis Brown and Assocs., San Diego, 1996—99; dir. corp. mktg. Boxlot, San Diego, 1999—2001; dir. Marcom Bidland Sys., San Diego, 2001; v.p. bus. devel. and mktg. Computer Market Rsch., San Diego, 2001—02; v.p. comm. techs. The Dakota Group, San Diego; v.p. mktg. comm. Path Network Techs., San Diego, 2001—02; dir. comm. strategies Four Sq., San Diego, 2002—. Mem. adv. bd. Cmty. Options, San Diego, 2003; mem. adv. bd. cord blood options Stem Cell Consortium, Calif., 2003. Vol. Am.'s Cup, San Diego, 1992, Am. Diabetes Assn., San Diego, 1994. Mem.: NAFTA, AMA, Health Care Communicators, Nat. Acad. TV Arts and Scis., Am. Mktg. Assn., Nat. Home Builders Assn., Bldg. Industry Assn., Biocom. Avocations: sailing, running, bodybuilding, writing, dance. Office: Four Square 5205 Kearny Villa Way San Diego CA 92123

AMOS, TORI, musician, singer; b. N.C. d. Edison and Mary Ellen A. Student, Peabody Conservatory. Albums: Y Kant Tori Read, 1988, Little Earthquakes, 1992, Under the Pink, 1994 (Grammy nomination, Best Alternative Music Performance, 1995), Boys for Pele, 1996, From the Choirgirl Hotel, 1998, To Venus and Back, 1999, Strange Little Girls, 2001, Scarlet's Walk, 2002, Tales of a Librarian: Tori Amos Collection, 2003, The Beekeeper, 2005, A Piano: The Collection, 2006; author: (with Ann Powers) Tori Amos: Piece By Piece, 2005. Office: Atlantic Records 1290 Avenue Of The Americas New York NY 10104-0184

AMPOLA, MARY G., pediatrician, geneticist; b. Syracuse, NY, Nov. 2, 1934; d. Mariangelo and Filomena (Albanese) Giambattista; m. Vincent G. Ampola, Aug. 7, 1966 (dec. 2003); children: Leanna, David. BA cum laude, Syracuse U., 1956; MD, SUNY, Syracuse, 1960. Diplomate Am. Bd. Pediatrics. Intern George Washington Univ. Hosp., Washington, 1960-61; pediatric resident Children's Nat. Med. Ctr., Washington, 1961-63, chief resident in pediatrics, 1963-64; genetics fellow Children's Hosp. Med. Ctr., Boston, 1964-66; metabolic diseases fellow Mass. Gen. Hosp., Boston, 1966-67; cytogeneticist New Eng. Med. Ctr., Boston, 1967-69, dir. pediatric amino acid lab., 1969—, pediatrician, 1969—, acting chief clin. genetics divsn. dept. pediatrics, 1989-96, chief divsn. metabolism, dept. pediatrics, 1996—; from asst. to assoc. prof. pediatrics New Eng. Med. Ctr./Tufts U. Sch. Medicine, Boston, 1967-92, prof., 1992—2004; ret., 2004; provisional staff Neonatology Associates, PC, Atlanta. Chmn. PL-1 selection com. dept. pediat. New Eng. Med. Ctr., 1975—, chmn. residency com., 1981—87, mem. curriculum com., 1981—84, mem. hosp. quality assurance com., 1982—92, mem. residency com., 1987—98, bd. dirs. Ctr. Children Spl. Needs, 1987—2003; chmn. evaluation and promotions com. Tufts U. Sch. Medicine, 1998—. Editor: Early Detection and Management of Inborn Errors, 1976; author: Metabolic Diseases in Pediatric Practice, 1982; contbr. chpts. to books and articles to profl. jours. Named Alumna of Yr., SUNY Coll. Medicine, 1980. Fellow Am. Acad. Pediatrics (sect. genetics); mem. Am. Soc. Human Genetics, New Eng. Pediatric Soc. (sec.-treas. 1993—), Soc. Inherited Metabolic Disorders, Soc. Study Inborn Errors Metabolism, Phi Beta Kappa. Republican. Office: Neonatology Associates PC 5901 Peachtree Dunwoody Rd Atlanta GA 30338

AMRAM, LAURA, psychiatrist; b. Kzil-Orda, Kazahstan, Jan. 25, 1958; arrived in U.S., 1993; d. Rafael Ilyayev and Zinaida Ilyayeva; m. Yuriy Amram, Sept. 22, 1982; children: Michael, Ruzanna. Degree in physician asst. (hon.), Nursing Coll., Kzil-Orda, 1977; MD, Med. Inst., Andijan, 1983. Emergency rm. nurse City Hosp., Kzil-Orda, 1977; emergency med. techician Ambulance Svc., Andijan, 1979—83; intern Andijan Clin. Hosp., Andijan, 1984—85; neuropsychiatrist City Hosp., Andijan, 1985—93; med. asst. Premier Medicine PC, N.Y.C., 1996—2000; rsch. asst. Jamaica Med. Ctr., 2000—02; post grad. tng. Maimonides Med. Ctr., 2002—. Mem.: APA. Office Phone: 718-264-4473. Office Fax: 718-283-8567. Personal E-mail: amramlaura@yahoo.com.

AMRON, CORY M., lawyer; b. NYC; BA, U. Rochester, 1974; JD, Harvard U., 1977. Ptnr. Vorys, Sater, Seymour and Pease, LLP. Mem.: Commercial Real Estate Women Fellows of the Am. Bar Found. (state chair 2001—), Women's Bar Assn. DC (tres. 1982—83, mem., bd. dirs. 1994—97, Woman Lawyer Yr. 2004), Am. Bar Assn. (mem., Task Force Law Schools and Profession: Narrowing the Gap 1988—92, chair, Commn. Women Profession 1991—94, mem., Commn. Domestic Violence 1998—2002), Bar Assn. DC (chair, Young Lawyers Sect. 1983—84, mem., bd. dirs. 1985—87, mem., Out of Box Com., Sect. Legal Edn. 2001—), DC Bar (editor, DC Practical Manual 1985—87, chair, Commerical Real Estate Com. 1986—89, mem., Steering Com., Real Estate Housing and Land Use Sect. 1989—94, mem., Reproductive Cancer Task Force 1994—96). Office: Vorys Sater Seymour and Pease LLP 11th Fl 1828 L St NW Washington DC 20036-5109 Business E-Mail: cmamron@vssp.com.

AMSLER, GEORGEANN LUCILLE, publishing executive; b. Springfield, Mass., May 26, 1943; d. John Stephan Amsler and Lucille Adele Myshkowsky. Student, SUNY, Farmingdale, 1961—63. Lic. trade sch. instr. Tech. illustrator A.F. Michael Publ. Svcs., Massapequa, NY, 1961—63; box office treas. Westbury (N.Y.) Music Fair, 1966—69; adminstr. Barbizon Sch. Modeling, Garden City and Babylon, NY, 1969—73; bus./mktg. mgr. UTP div. Hearst Bus. Comm. Inc., Garden City, 1973—2002, dir. circulation, 1983—86, ret., 2002. Freelance model and actor; pvt. practice, 2002—. Mem.: Nat. Bus. Circulation Assn. (membership chmn.). Office: 645 Stewart Ave Garden City NY 11530-4709

AMSTADT, NANCY HOLLIS, retired language educator; b. Chgo., Ill., Mar. 1, 1932; d. James George and Agnes Green Hollis; m. Ervin Carl Amstadt, Dec. 27, 1952; children: Elaine, Joan, Steven, Carolyn. BA, De Paul U., 1952; MA, San Diego State U., 1966. English & history tchr. Sweetwater H.S. Dist., Chula Vista, Calif., 1957—59; tchr., counselor Santa Clara City Schs., Santa Clara, Calif., 1959—63; secondary English tchr. San Diego City Schs., San Diego, 1966—91; English instr. San Diego C.C., San Diego, 1993—95; ret., 1995. Chmn. dept. English Kearny H.S., San Diego, 1985—91. Exhibitions include San Diego Art Inst., 1984—2003. Mem. U.N. Gender Equity, San Diego, 2001—04; docent art gallery U. Calif., San Diego, 1998—2004; program dir. San Diego Mus. Art, San Diego, 1968—2003. Democrat. Avocations: tennis, women refugees, art history, classical music, Chinese exercise. Home: 1097 Alexandria Drive San Diego CA 92107

AMSTER, LINDA EVELYN, newspaper executive, consultant; b. NYC, May 21, 1938; d. Abraham and Belle Shirley (Levine) Meyerson; m. Robert L. Amster, Feb. 18, 1961 (dec. Feb. 1974). BA, U. Mich., 1960; M.L.S., Columbia U., 1968. Tchr. English Stamford High Sch., Conn., 1961-63; research librarian The Detroit News, 1965-67, The N.Y. Times, N.Y.C., 1967-69, supr. news research, 1969-74, news research mgr., 1974—2004, dir. news research, 2004—05; pvt. practice cons. N.Y., 2005—. Bd. dirs. Council for Career Planning, N.Y.C., 1982— Editor: The New York Times Passover Cookbook, 1999, Kill Duck Before Serving, 2002, The New York Times Jewish Cookbook, 2003, The New York Times Chicken Cookbook, 2005; contbr. articles to books, N.Y. Times and other publs. Mem. adv. com. N.Y.C. 100 Greater N.Y. Centennial Celebration. Mem.: Spl. Librs. Assn., Coffee House. Home: 336 Central Park W New York NY 10025-7111 Business E-Mail: liamst@nytimes.com.

AMSTERDAM, MILLICENT, manufacturing executive; Pres. MAF Mech. Svc. Corp., 1968—. Former bd. dirs. Long Island Ctr. for Bus. and Profl. Women, Advancement Commerce, Industry & Tech.; apptd. mem. Nassau County Panel for Home Improvement Industry. Recipient Small Bus Adv. Women in Bus. award, 1988. Mem.: Nat. Assn. Remodeling Industry, Long Island Builders Inst., Nat. Assn. Women in Constrn., Nat. Assn. Women Bus. Owners, Long Island Assn., Women Econ. Developers Long Island (bd. dirs.), Air Conditioning Contractors Am. (bd. dirs.).

AMSTUTZ, JULIE DENISE, elementary school educator; b. Nashville, Aug. 29, 1969; d. L.G. and Edith Virginia White; m. Bradley William Amstutz, July 15, 2000; children: Christopher Blake Williams, Rachel Elizabeth Williams, Madison Jeanee. AAS in Psychology and Sociology, Columbia State C.C., Columbia, Tenn., 1989; BS in Elem. Edn., Mid. Tenn. State U., Murfreesboro, 1992; MS in Curriculum and Instrn., Trevecca Nazarene U., Nashville, 2000. 1st grade tchr. Mt. Pleasant Christian Acad., Mt. Pleasant, Miss.; 5th grade tchr. Harding Acad., Cordova, Tenn.; 7th and 8th grade tchr. Dickson County Bd. of Edn., Dickson, Tenn., 1995—2000; 4th grade tchr. CMCSS, Clarksville, Tenn., 2000—03; acad. coach Clarksville-Montgomery County Bd. of Edn., Clarksville, Tenn., 2003—. Class facilitator Madison St. United Meth. Ch., Clarksville, Tenn., 2002—06. Mem.: ASCD (assoc.), NEA (assoc.), TASCD (assoc.), Tenn,. Edn. Assn. (assoc.), Phi Kappa Phi (assoc.). Achievements include development of Curriculum alignment for reading and lang. arts. Home: 2475 Outlaw Rd Woodlawn TN 37191 Office: CMCSS 621 Gracey Ave Clarksville TN 37040 Office Phone: 931-648-5695. Office Fax: 931-648-5695. Personal E-mail: julie.amstutz@cmcss.net.

AMUNDSON, BEVERLY CARDEN, artist; b. Kansas City, Kans., Dec. 31, 1937; d. Linton Franklin and Arlene Rose Carden; m. Jerry Warren Amundson; children: Sherry Camargo, Cynthia Harmison, Eric. Student, Kansas City Art Inst., 1955—58; studied with, Robert Byerley, Harry Fredman, Daniel Greene, Burton Silverman, Albert Handell and Anita Louise West. Freelance illustrator, designer, Kansas City, Mo., 1958—64; founding ptnr., dir. Amundson & Assoc. Art Studio, DBA The Amundson Group, Kansas City, Mo., 1964—2003, AGI Inc., Kansas City, Kans., 1994—, Taipei, 1994—, Hong Kong, 1994—, AGI Packaging Svcs. Ltd., Taipei, 1994—, Kansas City, Kans., 1999—, Hong Kong, 1999—. Lectr., cons. in field; pvt. lessons and workshops, Merriam, Kans. Work exhibited in shows and galleries nationwide. Com. worker Rep. Party, Merriam. Recipient numerous art awards; scholar Scholarship, Kansas City Art Inst., 1955—58. Master: Mid-Am. Pastel Soc.; mem.: Conn. Pastel Soc., Degas Pastel Soc., Kansas City Artist Coalition, Am. Soc. Classical Realism, Portrait Soc. Am. (charter), Nat. Pastel Soc. Am. (signature). Covenant Ch. Avocations: travel, textile weaving. Studio: 9903 West 70th Terrace Merriam KS 66203 Office: AGI Inc & AGI Packaging Svcs Home Offices 8008 Floyd Overland Park KS 66204

ANANIA, ANDREA, information technology executive; Grad., Queens Coll.; MBA, U. Pa. Various positions Unisys Corp., 1975—95; sr. v.p., divsn. sys. info. officer Cigna Corp., 1995—98, chief info. officer, 1998—, exec. v.p., chief info. officer Phila., 2001—.

ANASTACIA, (ANASTACIA LYN NEWKIRK), singer; b. Chgo., Ill., Sept. 17, 1973; Grad., Profl. Children's Sch. Of Manhattan. Former dancer Club MTV. Singer: (songs-single) I'm Outta Love, 2000, Not That Kind, 2000, One Day In Your Life, 2002, Left Outside Alone, 2004 (nominated for best song, MTV Europe Music Awards, 2004), (albums) Not That Kind, 2001, Freak of Nature, 2002, Anastacia, 2004; singer, performer (DVD Video) The Video Collection, 2002, One Day In Your Life, 2003, (DVD Video (single), 2002; singer: (TV) Party in the Park 2001, 2001, Double Bill, 2003, (films) Coyote Ugly, 2000, Chicago, 2002, (TV series) Um Anjo Caiu do Céu, 2001; composer, performer (TV) VH1 Divas Las Vegas, 2002, guest singer Elton John: One Night Only-Greatest Hits Live, 2001; performer: (TV) Pavarotti & Friends for Afghanistan, 2001, Nobel Peace Prize Concert, 2001, Danish Music Awards, 2001, Brit Awards, 2002, Royal Variety Performance, 2002, 95.8 Capital FM's Party in the Park for the Prince's Trust, 2004; presenter (TV) MTV Europe Music Awards, 2002, special guest appearences I Love the 80's, Tops of the Pops, 2000, 2001, 2004, Ally McBeal, 2001, Wetten, dass.?, 2002, 2004, and several others. Her trademark: rose-colored glasses. Address: Club Anastacia PO Box 7149 San Francisco CA 94120-7149

ANASTOLE, DOROTHY JEAN, retired electronics company executive; b. Akron, Ohio, Mar. 26, 1932; d. Helen (Sagedy) Dice; children: Kally, Dennis, Christopher. Student, De Anza Jr. Coll., Cupertino, Calif., 1969. Various secretarial positions in mfg., 1969-75; office mgr. Sci. Devices Co., Mountain View, Calif., 1975-76; exec. adminstrv. sec. corp. office Cezar Industries, Palo Alto, Calif., 1976-77; office and pers. mgr. AM Bruning Co., Mountain View, 1977-81; dir. employee rels. Consol. Micrographics, Mountain View, 1981-83; pers. mgmt. cons., 1983-84; mgr. adminstrn./employee rels. Mitsubishi Electronics Am., Inc., Sunnyvale, Calif., 1984-89, sr. mgr., 1989-91, corp.-nat. v.p., 1991-96, ret., 1996. Nat. adv. Field Philanthropy, 1992-96. Bd. dirs. Agnew State Hosp., San Jose, Calif., 1966-72, div. chmn. program mentally retarded, 1966-72, staff tutor, 1966-72; bd. dirs. Project Hired, Sunnyvale, 1991-93; bd. advisors The Senior Staff, 1994-96. Recipient Svc. award Agnew State Hosp., 1972.

ANAWALT, PATRICIA RIEFF, anthropologist, researcher; b. Ripon, Calif., Mar. 10, 1924; d. Edmund Lee and Anita Esto (Capps) Rieff; m. Richard Lee Anawalt, June 8, 1945; children: David, Katherine Anawalt Arnoldi, Harmon Fred. BA in Anthropology, UCLA, 1957, MA in Anthropology, 1971, PhD in Anthropology, 1975. Cons. curator costumes and textiles Mus. Cultural History UCLA, 1975-90, dir. Ctr. for Study Regional Dress, Fowler Mus. Cultural History, 1990—; trustee S.W. Mus., L.A., 1978-92; rsch. assoc. The San Diego Mus. Man, 1980—, UCLA Inst. Archaeology, 1994—. Trustee Archaeol. Inst. Am., U.S., Can., 1983-95, 98—; traveling lectr., 1975-86, 1994-2000, Pres.'s Lectureship, 1993-94, Charles E. Norton lectureship, 1996-97; cons. Nat. Geog. Soc., 1980-82, Denver Mus. Natural History, 1992-93; apptd. by U.S. Pres. to Cultural Property Adv. Com., Washington, 1984-93; fieldwork Guatemala, 1961, 70, 72, Spain, 1975, Sierra Norte de Puebla, Mex., 1983, 85, 88, 89, 91. Author: Indian Clothing Before Cortés: Mesoamerican Costumes from the Codices, 1981, paperback edit., 1990; co-author: The Codex Mendoza, 4 vols., 1992 (winner Archaeol. Inst. Am. 1994 James Wiseman Book award), The Essential Codex Mendoza, 1996; mem. editl. bd. Ancient Mesoamerica; contbr. articles to profl. jours. Adv. com Textile Mus., Washington, 1983-87. Grantee NEH, 1990, 96, J. Paul Getty Found. 1990, Nat. Geog. Soc., 1983, 85, 88, 89, 91, Ahmanson Found., 1996; Guggenheim fellow, 1988. Fellow Am. Anthrop. Assn.; mem. Centre Internat. D'Etude Des Textiles Anciens, Am. Ethnol. Soc., Soc. Am. Archaeology, Soc. Women Geographers (Outstanding Achievement award 1993), Textile Soc. Am. (bd. dirs. 1992-96, co-coord. 1994 biennial symposium). Avocations: ballet, reading, hiking. Office: Fowler Mus Cultural History Ctr Study Of Regional Dress Los Angeles CA 90095-0001 E-mail: panawalt@arts.ucla.edu.

ANCHIE, TOBY LEVINE, health facility administrator; b. New Haven, Conn., Jan. 21, 1944; d. Solomon and Mary (Karlins) Levine; m. Alonzo C. Moreland III; children from previous marriage: Michael D., Robert P. BSN, U. of Conn., 1966; MA in Edn. magna cum laude, Nor. Ariz. U., 1984. RN Ariz., Conn., Ga. Coord. spl. projects, nurse coord., adult day hosp. Barrow Neurol. Inst. of St. Joseph's Hosp. and Med. Ctr., Phoenix, 1984—87, mgr., 1987—92, mgr. adminstrv. and support svcs., neuroscis., 1992—94, mgr. rsch. adminstrn., 1994—97, dir. rsch. adminstrn., 1997—2000, exec. dir. R&D, 2000—. Cons.; presenter in field; faculty mem. U. Phoenix; adv. bd. mem. Myasthenia Gravis Assn.; adv. coun. mem. Office Disability Prevention Ariz. Dept. Health Svcs., strategic planning com. mem. Contbr. articles to profl. jours., chpts. in books. Mem.: NAFE, Ariz. Assn. Neurosci. Nurses, Assn. Clin. Rsch. Profls. (Ariz. chpt.), Soc. Rsch. Adminstrs., World Fedn. Splty. Nursing Orgn. (chair membership com. 1993—95), Am. Bd. Neurosci. Nursing (treas, 1995—96), Assn. Clin. Rsch. Profls. (continuing edn. com.), Am. Assn. Neurosci. Nurses (nominating com. 2003—06, bd. dirs., pres.). Home: 3112 S Los Feliz Dr Tempe AZ 85282-2854 Office Phone: 602-406-3178. E-mail: tanchie@chw.edu.

ANCKER-JOHNSON, BETSY, physicist, engineer, retired automotive executive; b. St. Louis, Apr. 29, 1927; d. Clinton James and Fern (Lalan) Ancker; m. Harold Hunt Johnson, Mar. 15, 1958; children: Ruth P. Johnson, David H. Johnson, Paul A. Johnson (dec.), Marti H. Johnson. BA in Physics with high honors (Pendleton scholar), Wellesley Coll., 1949; PhD in Exptl. Physics magna cum laude, U. Tuebingen, Germany, 1954; D.Sc. (hon.), Poly. Inst. N.Y., 1979, Trinity Coll., 1981, U. So. Calif., 1984, Alverno Coll., 1984; LL.D. (hon.), Bates Coll., 1980. Instr., jr. research physicist U. Calif., Berkeley, 1953-54; physicist Sylvania Microwave Physics Lab., 1956-58; mem. tech. staff RCA Labs., 1958-61; rsch. specialist Boeing Co., 1961-70, exec., 1970-73; asst. sec. U.S. Dept. Commerce for Sci. and Tech., 1973-77; dir. phys. rsch. Argonne Nat. Lab., Ill., 1977-79; v.p. for environ. activities GM, Warren, Mich., 1979-92. Affiliate prof. elec. engring. U. Wash., 1961-73; mem. Energy Rsch. Adv. Bd., 1983-87, adv. com. on inertial confinement fusion Dept. Energy, 1992-94, US Antarctic Safety Rev. Panel NSF, 1987-88; cons. Inland Steel Inc., 1991-96; adv. com. Rowan Sch. Engring., 1993-96; Regents vis. prof. U. Calif., Berkeley, 1988-89; founding dir. Acad. Medicine, Engring. and Sci. of Tex., 2004—. Contbr. articles to profl. jours. Mem. staff Inter-Varsity Christian Fellowship, 1954-56; mem. vis. com. elec. and computer divsn. MIT, U.S. Dept. Def. Sci. Bd.; mem. adv. bd. Stanford U. Sch. Engring., Fla. State U., Fla. A&M U., Congl. Caucus for Sci. and Tech.; trustee Wellesley Coll., 1971-77; chair bd. dirs. World Environ. Ctr., 1988-93, dir., 1988-99; founding trustee Johnson Scholarship Found., 1991-2001; founding dir. Work Place Influence, 1997—, dir. Enterprise Devel. Internat., 1992—; mem. faculty adv. coun. U. Tex. Sch. Engring., 1998—; bd. dirs. Tex. Environ. Forum, 2000-01. AAUW fellow, 1950-51; Horton Hollowell fellow, 1951-52; NSF grantee, 1967-72; recipient Chmn's. award Am. Assn. Engring. Socs., 1986, Award of Honor, Licensing Execs. Soc. Fellow AAAS, IEEE, Am. Phys. Soc. (councillor-at-large 1973-76); mem. NRC (bd. engring. edn. 1991-95, com. on women in sci. and engring. 1990-96, office sci. and engring. pers. adv. com. 1993-96), Nat. Acad. Engring. (councillor 1995-2001), Air Pollution Control Assn., Soc. Automotive Engrs. (bd. dirs. 1979-81); founding dir. Acad. Medicine, Engring. and Sci. Tex. (founding dir. 2004-, treas.-elect 2006-), Phi Beta Kappa, Sigma Xi Achievements include patents in field; being Top Ten World Master Swimmer. Business E-Mail: bancker-johnson@austin.rr.com.

ANCOLI-ISRAEL, SONIA, psychologist, researcher; b. Tel Aviv, Dec. 25, 1951; came to U.S., 1955. m. Andrew G. Israel; 2 children. BA, SUNY, Stony Brook, 1972; MA, Calif. State U., Long Beach, 1974; PhD, U. Calif., San Francisco, 1979. Lic. psychologist, Calif. Staff psychologist U. Calif. San Diego, La Jolla, 1979-84, asst. adj. prof., 1984-88, assoc. prof., 1988-94; prof., 1994—; assoc. dir. Sleep Disorders Ctr., VA Med. Ctr., San Diego, 1981-92, dir., 1992—. Author: All I Want Is a Good Night's Sleep, 1996; contbr. numerous articles to profl. jours. Mem. bd. mgrs. Jewish Cmty. Ctr., La Jolla, 1985-91; mem. exec. bd. Nat. Sleep Found., 1990-95. Recipient Robert E. Harris Meml. award, U. Calif., San Franicsco, 1978. Mem. AAAS, Am. Acad. Sleep Medicine, Sleep Rsch. Soc. (bd. dirs. 1993-96, pres. 2004-05), Soc. for Light Treatment and Biol. Rhythms (bd. dirs. 1994-97, pres. 2000—02), Gerontol. Soc. Am., N.Y. Acad. Sci. Business E-Mail: sancoliisrael@ucsd.edu.

ANCRUM, CHERYL DENISE, dentist; b. Bklyn., Sept. 28, 1958; d. Ida Jackson. BA in Psychology, Harvard U., 1980; DDS, Columbia U., 1986, MPH, 1989; postgrad., Rutgers U. Dentist. Credit analyst Hartford (Conn.) Nat. Bank, 1980-81; statis. coding instr., analyst Aetna Ins. Co., Hartford, 1981-82; dental asst. Gouverneur Hosp., N.Y.C., 1983; clk. typist Columbia Presbyn. Med. Ctr., N.Y.C., 1984-86; gen. practice resident Beth Israel Med. Ctr., N.Y.C., 1986-87; dental attending Montefiore Med. Ctr., Bronx, 1987-89; rsch. assoc., dentist North Ctrl. Bronx Hosp., 1989-90; dental dir. Manhattan Men's House of Detention, N.Y.C., 1989-97; pvt. practice, 1998—. Dental extern North Ctrl. Bronx. Hosp., 1985-86. Vol. St. John Episc. Hosp., Bklyn., 1974-75, Mt. Auburn Hosp., Cambridge, 1978, Harlem Hosp., N.Y.C., 1987-88; health adv. Harvard U., Cambridge, 1977-80; active Sutton for Mayor Campaign, Bklyn., 1977; mem. Girl Scouts U.S., Bklyn., 1969-75, Operation PUSH, Hartford, 1981-82, Hartford Black Women Network, 1980-82, Kuumba Singers, Harvard U., 1977-78, New Temple Singers, Cambridge, 1978-80; mem. tape commn. Bridge St. A.M.E. Ch., Bklyn., 1987-88; fin. sec. Flower Guild, Allen A.M.E. Church, Queens, 1994-97; bd. dirs. F.I.S.H. of Uniondale, 1991-96. A Better Chance scholar, 1973-76, Am. Fund for Dental Health scholar, 1982-84, Clark Found. scholar, 1983-86; selected profl. fellow AAUW, 1985-86; recipient Letter of Commendation, Columbia U., 1983, Applewhite award, 1984, William Bailey Dunning award, 1986, Lester R. Cain Pathology prize, 1986; named to Outstanding Young Women Am., 1983. Mem. ADA, Nat. Dental Assn. (rec. sec. 1998-2000), FDI World Dental Fedn., NY State Dental Soc., Acad. Gen. Dentistry, Am. Assn. Pub. Health Dentistry, Am. Profl. Practice Assn., Order Ea. Star (Elizabeth Moore chpt. sec. 1995-96), Delta Sigma Theta (Nassau alumnae chpt. journalist, 1992-96, 2d v.p., 1995-96). Democrat. Mem. African Methodist Episcopal Ch. Avocations: creative arts, writing, reading, music, skating. Office: 230 Hilton Ave Ste 203 Hempstead NY 11550-8116 Office Phone: 516-483-8375. Business E-Mail: cherlyancrumdds@verizon.net.

ANDEREGG, KAREN KLOK, business executive; b. Council Bluffs, Iowa; d. George J. and Hazel E. Klok; m. George F. Anderegg Jr., Aug. 27, 1970 (div. Dec. 1993); m. William Drake Rutherford, Jan. 2, 1994. BA, Stanford U., 1963. Copywriter Vogue Mag., NYC, 1963-72; copy editor Mademoiselle Mag., NYC, 1972-77, mng. editor, 1977-80; assoc. editor Vogue Mag., NYC, 1980-85; editor-in-chief Elle Mag., NYC, 1985-87; pres. Clinique USA, 1987-92; bus. cons. Portland, Oreg., 1993—. Bd. dirs. Oreg. Dental Svcs. Health Plans.

ANDERSEN, ELLEN MARIE, social worker; b. Kingman, Ariz., Jan. 25, 1948; d. William Franklin Cummings and Beatrice Ellen (Vanderberg) Kohlhase; m. Larry Harold Andersen, Feb. 16, 1973; children: Hans Harold, Anna Marie. Student, U. Puget Sound, 1966-68; BA, U. Oreg., 1970; MSW, U. Mich., 1972. Family services specialist Municipality of Anchorage,

1972-75; clinic coordinator River Bluffs Child Guidance Ctr., Council Bluffs, Iowa, 1975-78; social worker Bur. Indian Affairs, Anchorage, 1978, Indian Health Service, Anchorage, 1978-88; chief social svcs. Alaska Native Med. Ctr., Anchorage, 1988—2005, dir. continuum of care mgmt., 2005—. Active in child devel. and child health subjects, 1978—. Mem. Anchorage Child Abuse Bd., 1974-75. Health Careers grant March of Dimes, 1971-72. Mem. Nat. Assn. Social Workers (sec. Anchorage 1979-80, co-editor newsletter 1979-80), Acad. Cert. Social Workers (diplomate), Registry Clin. Social Workers (diplomate), Soc. Hosp. Social Work Dirs., Phi Beta Kappa. Avocations: ice skating, cross country skiing, movies, books. Office: Alaska Native Med Ctr 4315 Diplomacy Dr Anchorage AK 99508

ANDERSEN, JULIE B., elementary school educator; b. Salt Lake City, Mar. 19, 1958; d. Blaine T. and Colleen T. Busenbank; m. Steven N. Andersen, Sept. 15, 1978; children: Natalie, Rachel. BS in Elem. Edn., U. Utah, 1980; MEd in Ednl. Adminstrn., U. Utah, Salt Lake City, 1993. Cert. ESL. Tchr. Magna Elem., Utah, 1980—91, Lincoln Elem., Salt Lake City, 1991—92, James E. Moss Elem., Salt Lake City, 1992—98, Millcreek Elem., Salt Lake City, 1998—2005, Overlake Elem., Toole, Utah, 2005—. Registration, vol. Utah Dems., Bountiful, 1976—. Mem.: ASCD, Utah Edn. Assn., Toole Edn. Assn., Young Alumni Assn. U. Utah, Alpha Delta Kappa (chaplain 2004—). Avocations: aerobics, reading, gardening, skiing, swimming. Home: 1823 Jeri Dr Bountiful UT 84010

ANDERSEN, MARIANNE SINGER, psychologist; b. Baden nr. Vienna, Austria; came to U.S., 1940; naturalized, 1946; d. Richard L. and Jolanthe (Garda) Singer; 1 child, Richard Esten. BA, CUNY, 1950, MA, 1974; PhD, Fla. Inst. Tech., 1980. Rsch. assoc. Inst. for Rsch. in Hypnosis, N.Y.C., 1974-76, fellow in clin. hypnosis, 1976, dir. seminars, 1978-82, dir. edn., 1982—2005; psychotherapist specializing in hypnotherapy Morton Prince Ctr. for Hypnotherapy, dir. clin. svcs., 1981-82; dir. adminstrn. Internat. Grad. U., N.Y.C., 1974-77; pvt. practice psychotherapy, 1977—. Adminstrv. coordinator Internat. Grad. Sch. Behavior Sci., Fla. Inst. Tech., 1978; co-dir. The Melbourne Group, 1983—90; clin. instr. hypnotherapy Mt. Sinai Sch. Medicine, N.Y.C., 1996—; lectr. hypnosis and hypnotherapy to mental and phys. health profls., 1977—. Author: (with Louis Savary) Passages: A Guide for Pilgrims of the Mind, 1972; rsch. on treatment of obesity with hypnotherapy; book editor specializing in psychology and psychiatry including W.W. Norton Co., Sterling Pub. Co., E.P. Dutton Co., 1950-71. Fellow Soc. for Clin. and Exptl. Hypnosis; mem. APA, Internat. Soc. Clin. and Exptl. Hypnosis. Home: 60 W 57th St New York NY 10019-3909 Office Phone: 212-246-1790.

ANDERSEN, MARTHA S., biophysicist, researcher; BS in Physics, Ill. Inst. Tech., 1962; MS in Physics, U. Tenn., 1968; PhD in Biophysics with distinction, SUNY, 1976. Rsch. affiliate Roswell Park Cancer Inst., Buffalo, 1979—82, rsch. assoc., 1986—87; radiation physicist US Army Armament R&D Command, Dover, NJ, 1982—83; asst. prof. Erie CC, SUNY, Buffalo, 1983—; rsch. scientist SUNY, Buffalo, 1987—91. Contbr. articles to profl. jours. Fellow, NIH, 1977—80. Office: Erie Cmty Coll Dept Physics 121 Ellicott St Buffalo NY 14221 Office Phone: 716-851-1064.

ANDERSEN, NANCY, music educator, director; b. Douglas, Ariz., Jan. 19, 1969; d. L. LeGrand and Mary Anne Andersen. Degree in Psychology, U. Calif., Santa Barbara, 1990; credential Elem. Edn., Calif. State U., Fresno, 1992; Master's, The Boston Conservatory, 1996. K-12 music endorsement Nev., ESL tchg. credential Nat. U. Tchr. John Still Mid. Sch., Sacramento, 1996—97, Elitha Donner Elem. Sch., Elk Grove, Calif., 1997—99, Betsy Rhodes Elem. Sch., Las Vegas, 2001—03, Las Vegas Acad., 2003—. Com. mem. Calif. Arts Commn., Sacramento, 1994—96; instr. Sierra Nev. Arts Project, 1994—96. Recipient Rhodes scholar, U. Calif. Santa Barbara, 1989, Disting. Educator award, CCSD East Region, 2005, Pub. Servant Commendation, Mayor Oscar Goodman, Las Vegas, 2005. Mem.: Assn. for Music Edn., Am. Choral Dirs. Assn. Avocation: theater. Office: Las Vegas Academy 315 S 7th St Las Vegas NV 89101 E-mail: NAndersen@interact.ccsd.net.

ANDERSEN, SUSAN MARIE, psychologist, educator, director; b. Santa Monica, Calif., June 6, 1955; BA in Psychology with honors, U. Calif., Santa Cruz, 1977; PhD in Psychology, Stanford U., 1981. Lic. psychologist Calif., N.Y. Asst. prof. psychology U. Calif., Santa Barbara, 1981—87; assoc. prof. NYU, NYC, 1987—94, prof., 1994—, dir. grad. studies in psychology, 1993—97, 2000—02, dir. doctoral program in social psychology, 2005—. Dir. doctoral program social psychology, cons. Edn. Commn. of the States; Grantmaker Forum for Cmty. and Nat. Svc., Common Cents N.Y.; bd. dirs. Common Cents, N.Y.; grants panel, social and group processes rev. panel NIMH, 1992-94, 96, Integrative Grad. Edn. and Rsch. Tng. rev. panel NSF, 2003; other panels. Assoc. editor Jour. Social and Clin. Psychology, 1987-92; Social Cognition, 1993; Jour. Personality and Social Psychology: Attitudes and Social Cognition, 1994-95, Psychol. Rev., 1998-00, Self and Identity, 2004—; mem. editl. bd. Jour. Personality and Social Psychology, 1990-93, 00-01, Nouvelle Revue de Psychologie Sociale, 2002—; ad hoc reviewer Jour. Comm. Rsch., Jour. Consulting and Clin. Psychology, Jour. Exptl. Psychology: Learning, Memory & Cognition, Psychonomic Bull. and Rev., Jour. Exptl. Social Psychology, Jour. Personality, Jour. Rsch. in Personality, Motivation and Emotion, Personality and Social Psychology Bull., Psychology Bull., Psychology Rev., Psychol. Sci., NSF, Australian Social Sci. Rsch. Coun., Social Sci. and Human Rsch. Coun. Can., Brit. Jour. Clin. Psychology, Brit. Jour. Social Psychology, Jour. Abnormal Psychology; contbr. articles to profl. jours. Chair svc. learning task force White House Congl. Conf. on Character Bldg.; mem. rsch. and evaluation com. Character Edn. Partnership; rsch. adv. bd. Kellogg Found. Nat. Initiative on Cmty. Svc. in Edn.; Learning in Deed; edn. policy task force Inst. for Comm. Policy Studies, George Washington U.; mem. Russell Sage Found.'s Social Identity Consortium; bd. dirs. Common Cents, N.Y. Grantee NIMH, 1985-86, 92-98; sr. fellow Inst. for Comm. Policy Studies, George Washington U. Fellow: APA, Soc. Psychol. Study Social Issues, Soc. Personality and Social Psychology (mem. exec. com.), Am. Psychol. Soc.; mem.: Soc. Advancement of Socio Econ., Soc. Exptl. Social Psychology, Internat. Soc. Self and Identity. Office: Dept Psychology NY Univ 6 Washington Pl 7th Fl New York NY 10003-6603 Business E-Mail: susan.andersen@nyu.edu.

ANDERSON, ALLAMAY EUDORIS, health educator, home economist; b. N.Y.C., July 18, 1933; d. John Samuel and Charlotte Jane (Harrigan) Richardson; m. Edgar Leopold Anderson, Jr., Apr. 14, 1957 (div. Apr. 14, 1963); 1 child, David Lancelot; m. Diane Kay Swartz, July 19, 2003. B.A., Queens Coll., CUNY, 1975; profl. mgmt. cert. Adelphi U., 1978; M.S. in Edn., Fordham U., 1984. Mem. staff sch. food svc. dietitian Bd. Edn., N.Y.C., 1968-88; tchr. home and career skills Louis Armstrong Mid. Sch., 1988; spl. edn. tchr. Manhattan H.S., N.Y.C., 1989-95, coord AIDS resource, 1995, ret. 1995; profl. devel. cons., N.Y.C., 1978—; ptnr. Masiba Bldg. Corp., Corona, N.Y., 1975-82; adj. lectr. home econs. Queens Coll., 1987; owner AEA Devel. Svc., 1987-97; mem. exec. bd. Ssch. Edn. Alumni Assn., Fordham U., 1997—. Devel. coord. League for Better Cmty. Life, Inc., 1977; treas. exec. bd., 1970-76; officer N.Y.C. Cmty. Devel. Agy., 1980-83; mem. Kwanzaa Adv. Com. (P.R.) Urban Coalition, 1983, L.I. # 28 Episcopal Cursillo, 1991; vestry mem. youth ministries Grace Episcopal Ch., 1982-85, vestry mem., 1996-99; mem. NAACP (local Women's History Month honoree); asst. presiding ptnr. Dynamic Investors Club, 1996—; Bridges chairperson Srs. of Dorie Miller, 2003. Recipient Elmcor Cmty. Svc. award Elmcor Youth and Adult Activities, Inc., 1989, Alumni Achievement award Fordham U. Sch. Edn., 2000, Cmty. Svc. award N.Y. State United Tchrs., 2001, Concourse Village Br. Positive Image award Key Women Am., Inc., 2005. Mem. Assn. Fundraising Profls. (Greater N.Y. chpt.), Nat. Assn. Investment Clubs, Langston Hughes Libr. Action Com. (bd. dirs. 1987—, treas. 1989, Kwanza chair 1994-97), Queens Coll. Home Econs. Alumni Assn. (v.p., chmn. bylaws com. 1982), United Fedn. Tchrs. (Ret. Tchrs. chpt.), Negro Bus. and Profl. Women's Clubs (Profl. award 1998), Phi Delta Kappan (Fordham U. chpt.).

ANDERSON, AMY LEE, realtor; b. Tampa, Fla., July 24, 1950; d. Ernest William and Gloria June (Terrell) Denham; m. Arnold Albin Anderson Jr., Dec. 21, 1986; children: Melissa Lee, Nancy Marie. BA, U. Tampa, 1971. Lic. realtor Nat. Bd. Realtors. Sys. analyst Nat. CSS, Tampa, 1971-79; field analyst Digital Equipment Corp., Meriden, Conn., 1979-84; dir. nat. accounts Canaan Computer Corp., Stratford, Conn., 1984—92; realtor Prudential Carolinas Realty, Raleigh, N.C., 1992-95, Block & Assocs., Raleigh, 1995—97, Prudential Carolinas Realty, Raleigh, NC, 1997—2000, Midway Airlines, Raleigh, NC, 2001, Keller Williams Realty, Raleigh, NC, 2002—. Exec. staff Canaan Computer Corp., Stratford, 1987-92. Editor (manual) Corporate Policies, 1986; co-author: Start at the Top, 1989. Treas. PTA, Basking Ridge, N.J., 1989; advisor Tarheel Challenge Acad., Clinton, N.C., 1995; participant Paws Walk for Cancer, Raleigh, 1995. Mem. Data Processing Mgmt. Assn. (publicity com. 1978-92), Capital City Club (membership com. 1993—). Republican. Episcopalian. Avocations: needlecrafts, reading, landscaping, upholstering.

ANDERSON, ANITA A., secondary school educator; b. Winston-Salem, N.C., Sept. 13, 1938; d. Birden Dixon and Lovie Josephine McCoy; m. Clarence B. Crumpton (dec.); children: Clarence B., Victoria E.; m. William Webb (dec.); 1 child, William R.; m. William Wallace Parker, Sept. 8, 1992 (dec. June 1998); m. William G. Anderson, Mar. 27, 1999. BS in English and Social Studies, U. Detroit Mercy, Mich., 1973; MEd, Marygrove Coll., Detroit, 1974, cert. secondary adminstrn., 1994; computerized office cert., Acock Computerized Ctr., Athens, Ga., 1986; postgrad., Oakland U., Rochester, Mich., 1996—. Tchr., dept. head Western H.S., Las Vegas, Nev., 1974-76; tchr. reading, dir. learning ctr. Ecorse (Mich.) H.S., 1976-81; tchr., coord. reading Winston-Salem-Forsyth County Schs., 1981-87; tchr. math. Holt (Ala.) H.S., 1987-88; tchr. algebra and sci. Pontiac (Mich.) Pub. Schs., 1988—, self-esteem, self-awareness and peer rels. grant writr, 1989—. Self-esteem facilitator, substance abuse specialist Washington Mid. Sch., Pontiac, 1991—. Author: (tng. manual) Surving Societal Stressors, 1990. Bd. dirs. Fedn. Youth Svcs., Detroit, 1991—. Recipient Tech. of Yr. award N.C. Bd. Edn., 1994; grantee 1st of Am. Bank, Inc., 1994-95. Mem. AAUW, Internat. Reading Assn., Am. Bus. Women Assn., NAACP (life, bd. dirs. Detroit 1990—), Lions (bd. dirs. Detroit 1992—, sec.-editor 1993-95, Melvin Jones fellow 1997), Order Ea. Star (worthy matron 1996—), Daus. of Isis (dir. team I 1996-97), Gamma Phi Delta (life, internat. Greek queen 1979). Avocations: horticulture, travel, reading, drama, surfing the internet. Office: Washington Middle Sch 701 Menominee Rd Pontiac MI 48341-1544

ANDERSON, ANITA L., psychology professor; d. Wilson Anderson and Frankie Lavallis-Anderson; m. Ernest E. Haffner, Aug. 21, 1984; 1 child, Edwin C. Haffner. BA, U. Tex., San Antonio, 1985; MA, St. Mary's U., San Antonio, 1988; PhD, U. Wis., Milw., 1996. Grad. intern inpatient psychiatry Wilson Hall USAF Med. Ctr., San Antonio, 1987; grad. intern neuropsychol. assessment svcs. Brooke Army Med. Ctr., Fort Sam Houston, Tex., 1988; asst. to clinic coord. U. Wis., Milw., 1991—92; psychometric asst. Milw. Pub. Schs., 1993—94; pre-doctoral fellow clin. psychology Yale U. Sch. Medicine, New Haven, 1994—95; asst. prof. psychology U. Incarnate Word, San Antonio, 1998—, chairperson psychology dept., 2000—02. Mem.: APA, Nat. Social Sci. Assn., Assn. Black Psychologists, Phi Kappa Phi, Sigma Xi. Office: Univ Incarnate Word CPO 102 4301 Broadway San Antonio TX 78209 Office Phone: 210-829-3992. Office Fax: 210-829-3880.

ANDERSON, ANNETTE SHIREY, retired deaf education educator, educational consultant; b. Little Rock, May 1, 1940; d. Alton J. and Freida Elizabeth (Yarbrough) Shirey; m. Charles D. Thompson (dec. Apr. 1977). B.A., Centenary Coll., 1961; M. Communication Disorders, U. Okla., 1965. Council on Edn. of Deaf. Tchr., Pilot Sch. for Deaf, Dallas, 1965-68; supr. and curriculum coordinator Callier Hearing and Speech Center, Dallas, 1968-70; prin. W.Va. Schs. for Deaf and Blind, Romney, W.Va., 1970-80; asst. prof. deaf edn. tchr. tng. program U. Tulsa, 1980—95, ret. 1995; ednl. cons. to pub. sch. deaf edn. programs; mem. state adv. bd.; mem. Early Identification Task Force Com.; officer Okla. Council on Hearing Impaired. Mem. bd. March of Dimes; vol. worker United Way. Recipient Outstanding Faculty award U. Tulsa, 1981. Mem. Am. Conv. of Instrs. of Deaf, A.G. Bell Assn., Conf. Ednl. Adminstrs. Serving the Deaf (assoc.), Okla. Council on Hearing Impaired, Okla. Tchrs. of Hearing Impaired; Okla. Univ. Personnel Assn., Tulsa Speech and Hearing Assn. (bd. dirs. 1980—). Republican. Presbyterian. Home: 1064 Brookfield Pl Glendora CA 91741-6612 Office Phone: 626-852-0738. E-mail: eraasa@pocketmail.com.

ANDERSON, BARBARA ALLEN, alcohol/drug abuse services professional, archivist; b. Atlanta, Aug. 15, 1956; d. Cliff Cole and Jeanne Tiller Allen; m. Richard Jefferson Anderson, Oct. 20, 1984. BA, Shorter Coll., 1978; MCM, S.B.T.S., Louisville, 1981. Cert. addictions counselor, master's level addiction counselor, clin. supr. Asst. creative dir. Trilogy Entertainment Corp., Atlanta, 1984—89; spiritual dir. Breakthru Ho., Decatur, Ga., 1989—92; continuing care therapist SAFE Recovery Campus, Atlanta, 1990—93; continuing care assoc. Talbott Recovery Campus, Atlanta, 1993—95, continuing care coord., 1996, dir. continuing care, 1996—2003, dir. continuing care, ref. liaison, 2004—. World svc. del. AFG of Ga., Inc., Atlanta, 1995—97, area office bd. chmn., 1998—2000, archivist, 2001—. Vol. writer, editor Paths to Recovery, 1997, editor (newsletter) Talbott Times, 1997—99; contbr. articles to Talbott Times. Mem.: NAFE, Ga. Addiction Counselors Assn., Nat. Employee Assistance Profls. Assn., Nat. Assn. Alcohol and Drug Abuse Counselors. Avocations: music, tennis, writing, movies, crafts. Office: Talbott Recovery Campus 5448 Yorktowne Dr Atlanta GA 30349 Home: 4380 Veterans Memorial Hwy Lithia Springs GA 30122-1707 Office Phone: 678-251-3119. Personal E-mail: pianobarb@aol.com.

ANDERSON, BARBARA JEAN, biology professor; b. Evergreen Park, Ill., June 24, 1950; d. William Albert and Margery Jean Kleist; m. John Donald Anderson, Mar. 14, 1950; 1 child, Megan. BS of Edn. in Biology, Western Ill. U., Macomb, 1972, MS in Botany, 1977. Tchr. sci. Oak Lawn High Sch., Ill., 1973—79; prof. biology Coll. DuPage, Glen Ellyn, 1980—. Co-chair Nat. Sci. Ctr., Glen Ellyn, 1983—2006, chair biology faculty, 2004—06, biology liaison to dean, 2004—06. Vol. Eisenhower Hr. High Band Boosters, Darien, Ill., 1993—98, Fairview Sch. Recycling, 1989—93; product chmn. Girl Scouts Am., 1990—2002. Mem.: Ill. State Acad. Sci., Nat. Assn. Biology Tchrs., Nat. Sci. Tchrs. Assn. Presbyterian. Avocations: skiing, camping, gardening, bicycling. Office: Coll DuPage 425 Fawell Blvd Glen Ellyn IL 60137 Office Phone: 630-942-2347. Personal E-mail: agroouymom@aol.com.

ANDERSON, BARBARA MCCOMAS, lawyer; d. Ben C. Jr. and Elsa A. McComas; m. Roy Ryden Anderson Jr., Dec. 11, 1982; 1 child, Ryden McComas Anderson. BA, Trinity U., San Antonio, 1972; JD, U. Tex., 1978. Bar: Tex. 1978; cert. in estate planning and probate Tex. Bd. Legal Specialization. From assoc. to ptnr. Locke Purnell Rain Harrell, Dallas, 1978-97; of counsel Locke Liddell & Sapp, LLP, Dallas, 1997—2003; pvt. practice Dallas, 1997—. Fellow: Coll. of State Bar of Tex., Tex. Bar. Found., Am. Coll. Trusts and Estates Counsel; mem.: Tex. Acad. Probate and Trust Lawyers (charter, v.p., bd. dirs.), Dallas Bar Assn., Tex. Bar Assn. (chair real estate, probate and trust law sect. 2003—04). Avocations: reading mysteries, gardening. Office: PO Box 181147 Dallas TX 75218-8147

ANDERSON, BETTE (BONNIE) FERGUSON, music educator; b. June 28, 1948; d. Richard Allen and Bettie Parsons Ferguson; m. Michael Ratcliff Anderson, June 19, 1971; children: Bettie Michelle Anderson-Haigler(dec.), Richard Ratcliff. BME, Longwood U., Va., 1970. Cert. tchr. Va. Music tchr. Henrico Co. Schs., Richmond, Va., 1970—74; studio piano, pre-school music Richmond, Va., 1974—84; music tchr. The Steward Sch., Richmond, Va., 1984—. Home: 4115 Roundtree Rd Richmond VA 23294-5620 Business E-Mail: AndersonBonnie@stewardschool.org.

ANDERSON, CAROL LYNN, social worker, educator; b. LaPorte, Ind., Apr. 22, 1958; d. Paul Lewis and Marilee Anderson. BS summa cum laude, Ball State U., Muncie, Ind., 1983, BS, 1985; MSW, Ind. U., Indpls., 1986; D of Ministry, U. of Creation Spirituality/Wisdom U., Oakland, Calif., 2004. Cert. addictions counselor, social worker Acad. of Cert. Social Workers, lic. masters of social work. Counselor Adult and Child Mental Health Ctr., Indpls., 1986—88; counselor, program coord. Anderson Ctr. for Chem. Dependency, Ind., 1989—91; pvt. practice therapist Profl. Counseling Ctr. Ind., Anderson, 1990—91; chem. dependency counselor Phoenix Hall, Traverse City, Mich., 1991—95; clin. therapist, dual disorders specialist Great Lakes Cmty. Mental Health, Traverse City, Mich., 1995—2002; expert witness State of Mich., Dept. Consumer and Industry Svcs., Lansing, 2002—05; therapist, cons. Sarah's Cir., LLC, Traverse City, Mich., 1999—; counselor in behavioral health Murson Med. Ctr., Traverse City, Mich., 2002—; instr. social work Ferris State U., Big Rapids, Mich., 2005—. Founder, facilitator Dual Disorders Task Force, Traverse City, Mich., 1995—; guest spkr. Sarah's Cir., LLC, Traverse City, Mich., 1999—. Author: Where All Our Journeys End: Searching for the Beloved in Everyday Life, 2006. Commr. Traverse City Human Rights Commn., 1995—98; spokesperson, mem. com. Traverse City Campaign Against Discrimination, 2000—02; sex edn. adv. com. Traverse City Area Pub. Schs., 2005—. Mem.: Acad. of Cert. Social Workers, NASW. Democrat. Avocations: reading, sports, gardening, writing, drawing. Home: 2016 Chippewa St Traverse City MI 49686 Office: Sarah's Cir LLC PO Box 3052 Traverse City MI 49685 Office Phone: 231-632-5072. E-mail: sarahscirclellc@yahoo.com.

ANDERSON, CAROLE ANN, nursing educator, academic administrator; b. Chgo., Feb. 21, 1938; d. Robert and Marian (Harrity) Irving; m. Clark Anderson, Feb. 14, 1973; 1 child, Julie. Diploma, St. Francis Hosp., 1958; BS, U. Colo., 1962, MS, 1963, PhD, 1977. Group psychotherapist Dept. Vocat. Rehab., Denver, 1963-72; psychotherapist Prof. Psychiatry and Guidance Clinic, Denver, 1970-71; asst. prof., chmn. nursing sch. U. Colo., Denver, 1971-75; therapist, coordinator The Genessee Mental Health, Rochester, N.Y., 1977-78; assoc. dean U. Rochester, N.Y., 1978-86; dean, prof. Coll. Nursing Ohio State U., Columbus, 1986-2001, prof., 2001—, vice provost acad. and faculty offices, 2001—, interim dean grad. sch., 2005. Lectr. nursing sch. U. Colo., Denver, 1970-71; prin. investigator biomed. rsch. support grant, 1986-93, clin. rsch. facilitation grant, 1981-82; program dir. profl. nurse traineeship, 1978-86, advanced nurse tng. grant, 1982-85. Author: (with others) Women as Victims, 1986, Violence Toward Women, 1982, Substance Abuse of Women, 1982; editor Nursing Outlook, 1993-2002. Pres., bd. dirs. Health Assn., Rochester, 1984-86; mem. north sub area council Finger Lakes Health Systems Agy., 1983-86, longrange planning com., 1981-82; mem. Columbus Bd. Health; dir. Netcare Mental Health Ctr. Am. Acad. Nursing fellow. Mem. ANA, Ohio Nurses Assn., Am. Assn. Colls. Nursing (bd. dirs. 1992-94, pres.-elect 1994-96, pres. 1996-98), Sigma Theta Tau. Home: 406 W 6th Ave Columbus OH 43201-3137 Office: The OH State U Office Acad Affairs 203 Bricker Hall 190 N Oval Mall Columbus OH 43210-1358 Business E-Mail: anderson.32@osu.edu.

ANDERSON, CATHERINE M., consulting company executive; b. N.Y.C., Feb. 28, 1937; d. Edward Charles and Elizabeth (O'Shea) McElligott; m. Robert Brown Anderson, June 22, 1963; children: Mark Robert, Jennifer Elizabeth. BA, Rutgers U., 1959, MA, 1960. Staff asst. to pres. Chatham Coll., Pitts., 1960-61; instr. urban studies ctr. Rutgers U., New Brunswick, N.J., 1961-63; prin. urban renewal coord. City of Cleve., Cleve., 1963-64; regional admisions counselor Am. Inst. Fgn. Study, Pitts., 1964-74; chief planner, mgr. emergency ops. ctr. Allegheny County Govt., Pitts., 1975-79; dir. accreditation svcs. Energy Cons., Inc., Pitts., 1981-83; pub. involvement cons. Pitts., 1983—. Contbr. articles to profl. jours. Committeewoman Mt. Lebanon (Pa.) Mcpl. Dem. Com., 1970-85; active United Way Allegheny County, Pitts., mem. rev. com., 1980—, chmn. rev. com., 1986-89; bd. dirs. Mt. Lebanon Nature Conservancy, v.p., 1985-88, pres., 1988-92, v.p., 2004—; bd. dirs. Conservation Cons. Inc., 1983—, v.p., 1983-92, pres., 1992-95; bd. dirs. Pitts. chpt. Women's Transp. Seminar, v.p., 1992-94, pres. 1994-95; bd. dirs. Exec. Women's Coun. Greater Pitts., v.p., 1986-88; bd. dirs. Carnegie-Mellon U. Art Gallery, 1986-89, USC Citizens for Land Stewardship, 1997-99, Healthy Home Resources, v.p., 2004—. Recipient Robert L. Wells award Mt. Lebanon Nature Conservancy, 1991, Outstanding Svc. award Exec. Women's Coun., 1988; Eagleton Inst. Politics grad. fellow Rutgers U., 1960. Mem.: Women's Press Club Pitts., Women's Transp. Seminar (v.p. 1992—94, pres. 1994—95, nat. bd. dirs.), Exec. Women's Coun. (life; v.p. 1987—88, charter, Outstanding Svc. award 1988), Am. Soc. Hwy. Engrs. (sr.; bd. dirs. Pitts. chpt. 1998—, 1st v.p. 2005—, pres. 2006—, Pres.'s award Pitts. sect. 2001). Home and Office: 217 Thornberry Cir Pittsburgh PA 15234-1024 Office Phone: 412-854-3606. E-mail: kabob@adelphia.net.

ANDERSON, CATHY C., lawyer; BA, U. Mich.; JD, Loyola U. Dir. comml. law svcs. The Nutrasweet Co., 1986—92, dep. gen. counsel, asst. sec., 1992—95; exec. v.p., gen. counsel, sec. Alliant Foodservice, Inc., Deerfield, Ill., 1995—2003; sr. v.p., gen. counsel, sec. TruServ Corp., Chgo., 2003—. Affiliated with Georgetown U. Corp. Coun. Inst. Bd. dirs. Evanston-Northwestern Healthcare. Mem.: ABA, Chgo. Bar Assn. Office: TruServ Corp 8600 W Bryn Mawr Ave Chicago IL 60631-3505 Office Phone: 773-695-5000.

ANDERSON, CHERINE E., television and film production manager, special events planner, marketing executive; b. Kingston, Jamaica, Mar. 21; d. Percival and Joyce A. (Brown) A. BS, Fordham U., 1986. Community rels. assoc. N.Y.C. Pks. and Recreation Dept., 1986; employee activities coord. The Rockefeller Group, N.Y.C., 1986-87, employment interviewer, 1987-88; licensing coord. DC Comics-a Div. of Time-Warner, N.Y.C., 1988-90; employee rels. coord. ARC, N.Y.C., 1990; freelance spl. events planner N.Y.C., 1990—; auditor N.Y.C. Bd. Edn., 1991-94; affiliate mktg. mgr. Nickelodeon, Nick at Nite MTV Networks, 1996—; mktg. mgr. brand/franchise, movie and affiliate mktg. Nickelodeon. Prodn. mgr. Bklyn. Shakespeare Co., 1991—; assoc. producer Sports Desk Program-WNYE-FM, Bklyn., 1989-91; prodn. mgr. for film The Best Kept Secret, 1992; mng. dir. (13 week TV series) African Theatre and Drama Prodn., 1993; line producer and asst. dir. for film Angel Walk Prodn., 1993; v.p. ops. and prodn. mgmt. In Stitches Entertainment, 1994—. Contbr. articles to profl. jours. Bd. dirs. N.Y. Dist. Circle K - An Internat. Collegiate Svc. Orgn., N.Y.C., 1983-87; vol. mem. Vol. Svcs. for Children, 1986—. Named Disting. Sec. L.P. Merridew Award Circle K Internat., 1987, Outstanding Dist. Bd. Mem., 1987. Mem.: N.Y. Women in Film and TV, Nat. Assn. Minorities in Comm. (v.p. 2002, pres. 2003), Am. Mgmt. Assn. (cert. 1988, mgmt. cert. 1990). Democrat. Avocations: racquetball, theater, reading, travel, writing.

ANDERSON, CLAIRE W., gifted and talented educator; b. Albuquerque, May 22, 1930; d. Wentworth Henry and Clara Lea (Magruder) Corley; m. William James Young (div.); children: Gayle L. Mirkin, D. Young, Sherry B. Butler; m. Wallace L. Anderson. Student in Engring., U. Miss., 1946; BA, Rice U., 1951, postgrad., 1993; MEd, U. Houston, 1962, postgrad., 1963, Carnegie Mellon U., Tex. A&M, 1992. Cert. elem. and secondary tchr., early childhood, exceptional children tchr., Tex. Tchr. Golfcrest Elem. Shc., Houston, 1959-60, Montrose, Poe Elem. Sch., Houston, 1960-62, St. Mark's Private Sch., Houston, 1962-63; substitute teaching Spring Branch Ind. Sch. Dist., Houston, 1965-68; tchr. Meml. Hall, Houston, 1968-73; instr. English, math. Internat. Hispanic U., Houston, 1971-74; tchr. Dogan Elem. Sch., Houston, 1971-74, Lanier Mid. Sch., Houston, 1974-79, High Sch. Health Profl., Houston, 1979-90, Clifton Mid. Sch., Houston, 1990-91, Jesse H. Jones Sr. High Sch., Houston, 1992—. Adj. tutoring David Livingston and Assoc., Houston, 1960-65; instr. Internat. Hispanic U., Houston, 1971-74, Houston C.C., 1984—, Internat. Ednl. Comm. Ctr., High Point, N.C., 1990, Houston C.C. Sys., 1991; invited judge Kiev, Ukraine Math. and Sci. Competitions, 1989; facilitator Tex. Coun. of Women Sch. Execs. Summer Conf., 1994—; active The Rice/HISD Sch. Writing Project; acad. sponsor secondary edn. svc. and sci. clubs. Pres. bd. dirs. Women for Justice, 1990-94; active Houston Photography Ctr., Mus. Fine Arts, Houston Health Objectives 2000, Children's Mus.; coord. study and enrichment tutoring program, 1994,

Recipient Tex. award for Excellence in Tchg. and Outstanding Svc. to the Cmty., 1994; scholar Precalculus Design Team, Dow Jones scholar Pa. State, Advance Placement scholar Tex. A&M, Woodrow Wilson; grantee NSF, Impact II. Mem. IEEE, Nat. Coun. Tchrs. Math., Nat. Coun. Tchrs. English, Am. Acoustic Soc., Assn. Calculating Machinery, Assn. for Early Childhood Edn. (internat. chairperson), Tex. Assn. Edn. Tech., Tex. Computers Educators Assn., N.Y. Acad. Sci., Internat. Coun. Computers in Edn., Phi Delta Kappa. Office: 7414 Saint Lo Rd Houston TX 77033-2732

ANDERSON, CONNIE, music educator; b. Spokane, Oct. 4, 1949; d. Edward Elias and Amy Alvira Clark; m. Lyle John Anderson, Aug. 28, 1971; children: Eric, Lori. BA, Cedarville Coll., 1973; MM, Wright State U., 1994. Tchr. piano, Spokane, 1962-68; sec. Ctrl. State U., Xenia, Ohio, 1971-73; tchr. piano Cedarville, Ohio, 1968—; prof. music Cedarville U., 1973—. Pianist Southgate Bapt. Ch., Springfield, Ohio, 1971—. Recipient Music award Cedarville Co., 1973. Mem. Am. Coll. Musicians, Nat. Fedn. Music Clubs, Nat. Cert. Bd. Adjudicator, Music Tchrs. Nat. Assn. Republican. Avocations: travel, reading, music, golf, skiing. Home: 136 Kyle Dr Cedarville OH 45314-9581 Office: Cedarville Ul 251 N Main St Cedarville OH 45314 E-mail: andersc@cedarville.edu.

ANDERSON, CYNTHIA BOOT, biological science educator; b. Salem, Mass., Mar. 22, 1957; d. Frank Edwin and Bernetta Cynthia Boot; m. Mark Gregory Anderson (div.). BS in Biology summa cum laude, Ariz. State U., 1979; MS in Biology, U. Ill., Urbana, 1981. Teacher Cert. Claremont Grad. Sch., 1985. Juice bench tech. Sunkist Growers Inc., Corona, Calif., 1981—82; microbiologist II Lake Alfred Rsch. Sta., Fla., 1982; quality control supr. Sunkist Growers Inc., Ontario, Calif., 1983—85; biology, chemistry tchr. Ganiesha H.S., Pomona, Calif., 1985; biology tchr. U. H.S., Irvine, 1985—86; prof. biological sci. Mt. San Antonio Coll., Walnut, Calif., 1986—. Microbiology rev. McGraw Hill Publishers, Hightstown, NJ, 2005—. Recipient award, Nat. Sch. Orch. Assn., 1975. Mem.: Am. Soc. Microbiology, Sierra Club, Nat. Wildlife Fedn. Avocations: gardening, walking, travel, sports, inline skating. Office: Mt San Antonio Coll 1100 N Grand Ave Walnut CA 91789

ANDERSON, DAWN MARIE, elementary school educator; b. Tampa, Fla., Nov. 24, 1963; d. James Edward and Mary Ann Kaphingst; m. Nicholas Slyvester Anderson, July 8, 2000. BS, U. South Fla., Tampa, 1986; MA, Nova Southeastern, Tampa, 1996. Nat. Bd. Cert. Tchr., 2005. Elem. art tchr. 74th St. Elem. Sch., St. Petersburg, Fla., 1987—. Office: 74th St Elem Sch 3801 74th St N Saint Petersburg FL 33709-4401 Office Phone: 727-893-2120.

ANDERSON, DAYNA, medical researcher; b. 1979; Rsch. specialist, Immunology Ariz. Respiratory Ctr. Mem. Prosoc philanthropy com. Mem. Susan G. Komen Breast Cancer Found., Catalina Coun. Boy Scouts Am. Spurs and Stars, Southern Ariz. Ctr. Against Sexual Assault. Named one of 40 Under 40, Tucson Bus. Edge, 2006. Achievements include published article in Jour. of Allergy and Clinical Immunology. Office: Arizona Respiratory Center PO Box 245030 1501 N Cambell Ave Ste 2349 Tucson AZ 85724-5030*

ANDERSON, DEBORAH LYNN, music educator; b. Pampa, Tex., Oct. 1, 1960; d. Richard Wayne Gattis and Roma Maxine Schaub; m. James Michael Gattis, May 21, 1983; children: Robert Cody, Lauren McKenzie. MusB in Edn., Tex. Tech U., Lubbock, 1982, West Tex. A&M U., Canyon, 1988. Cert. elem. classroom and music specialist K-8 Tex. Prodr.: (sch. CD) SOAR (Golden Apple award, 2003). Vol., chairperson Jr. League of Amarillo, Tex., 1997—99. Mem.: Tex. Music Educator's Assn. (life). Office: Liberty Elem Sch 4600 Quail Run Rd Flower Mound TX 75022 Office Phone: 972-350-5907. Business E-Mail: andersond@lisd.net.

ANDERSON, DENICE ANNA, editor; b. Detroit, Nov. 11, 1947; d. Carl Magnus and Geraldine Elizabeth (Willer) A. BA in Journalism, Mich. State U., 1970. Copy editor/reporter The State News, East Lansing, Mich., 1965—70; copy editor, entertainment editor The State Jour., Lansing, Mich., 1970—76; freelance writer State Jour., Lansing Mag., 1977—79; freelance corr. Collier's Year Book, NYC, 1977—79; copy editor, proofreader Booz, Allen & Hamilton, NYC, 1980—81, Rogers & Wells, NYC, 1981—83, Advanced Therapeutics Comm., NYC, 1983—84; freelance editor, 1984—, Santa Fe, 1984—, Clinton, Mich., 1984—; reporter, copy editor, photographer The Tecumseh Herald, Mich., 1999—2005. Contbr. articles to profl. jours. Bd. dirs., sec. March of Dimes, Lansing, 1972-76; vol., writer Polio Info. Ctr., NYC, 1984-88; vol. Vol. Involvement Svcs., Santa Fe, 1989. Mem. Editl. Freelancers Assn. Lutheran. Home: 210 E Church St Clinton MI 49236 Office Phone: 517-456-4990.

ANDERSON, DENISE LYNN, elementary school educator; b. Tex., July 26, 1958; d. Kirtland B. and Doreatha L. Watkins; m. Frederick Anderson, Mar. 16, 1985; 1 child, Samantha. BA, Mercer U., Macon, Ga., 1980, MEd, 1987. Tchr., coach Tift County Bd. Edn., Tifton, Ga., 1982—86; tchr. Houston County Bd. Edn., Perry, 1987—. Team leader Perry Mid. Sch., Ga., 1995—. Mem.: Profl. Assoc. Ga. Educators. Office: Perry Middle School 495 Perry Parkway Perry GA 31069 Office Phone: 478-988-6285.

ANDERSON, DENISE W., psychologist, writer, musician; b. Idaho Falls, Idaho, July 11, 1958; d. Lyle L. Ward, Ruby Haymore; m. Daniel J. Anderson; children: Grace, Dorothy, Camille, Teresa, Eliza, Rachel, Daniel, Jr. AA in Arts and Scis., Ricks Coll., 1978; BA in Univ. Studies, Valley City State U., 2001; Edn. Specialist in Sch. Psychology, Minot State U., 2006. Music performer, composer, recorder Anderson Music Studio, Ray, 1983—2003; newspaper columnist The Teller, Milnor, ND, 1998—2000, Ransom County Gazette, Lisbon, ND, 1998—2000; ind. writer, tchr. Ray, 1998—2003; sch. psychologist Rock Cmty. Scsh., Ft. Yates, ND. Parent educator The Parenting Coalition, Williston, ND, 1995—95; substitute tchr. Ray Pub. Sch., 2001—02. Columnist: The Voice of Experience, 2000—02. Vol. leader Williston Basin Food Co-op, 1983—87; mem., chmn. Piano Festival Thursday Musical Br., Nat. Fedn. Music Clubs, Williston, 1993—97; choir founder, dir. Gwinner Cmty. Choir, Gwinner, ND, 1998—98; foster parent Williams County Social Svcs., Williston, ND, 1994—96; tchr., lay leader LDS Ch., 1976—, dir. pub. affairs Wahpeton, ND, 1998—2000; mem., officer Piano Tchrs. Assn., Williston, 1983—87. Mem.: Nat. Assn. Sch. Psychologists, N.D. Assn. Sch. Psychologists, Am. Mother's Inc. (nat. bd., area III coord.), Ray Lions Club (mem. cmty. devel. com. 2001—02). Mem. Lds Ch. Avocations: creating with multi-media, music, writing, organization. Home: PO Box 325 Ray ND 58849 Office Phone: 701-770-1248. Personal E-mail: denisewa@mccray.com.

ANDERSON, DONNA KAY, musicologist, educator; b. Underwood, ND, Feb. 16, 1935; d. Freedolph E. and Olga (Mayer) A. PhD, Ind. U., 1966. Instr. piano MacPhail Sch. Music, 1956-59, Summit Sch., 1959-61; asst. prof. music history SUNY, Cortland, 1967-70, assoc. prof., 1970-78, prof., 1978—, chmn. dept. music, 1985-92, 95-97, faculty rsch. fellow, 1967-69, prof. emerita, 1997—. Spkr. in field. Author: Charles T. Griffes: Annotated Bibliography, Discography, 1977, The Works of Charles T. Griffes: A Descriptive Catalogue, 1983, Charles T. Griffes: A Life in Music, 1993; editor: Three Preludes for Piano, 1967, Four Impressions, 1970, Legend for Piano, 1972, De Profundis, 1978, Song of the Dagger, 1983, Seven English Songs, 1986, Rhapsody, 1992, The Pleasure Dome of Kubla Khan, 1993, The War-Song of the Vikings, 1995, Hampelas, 1995, Kinanti, 1995, Djakoan, 1995, Pieces for Children, 1995; editor, translator: Four German Songs, 1970, Nachtlied, 1983, Six German Songs, 1986, Three German Songs, 1995, A Winter Landscape, 1996, Belle Nuit, 2000, Three Japanese Melodies, 2000; contbr. Griffes biography to The Ency. of N.Y. State, 2005. Bd. dirs. YMCA, 1998—, bd. pres., 2006—; mem. Brooks outstanding tchrs. award com. SUNY, 1999—, chair Brooks outstanding tchrs. award com., 2001—. Recipient N.Y. State/United U. Professions Excellence award, 1991; summer grantee, 1972. Mem. Am. Musicol. Soc., Coll. Music Soc., Soc. Am. Music, Music Library Assn., Tri-M, Mu Phi Epsilon, Pi Kappa Lambda, Alpha Psi Omega, Phi Kappa Phi. Office: SUNY Performing Arts Cortland NY 13045 Business E-Mail: andersond@cortland.edu.

ANDERSON, DORIS EHLINGER, lawyer; b. Houston; d. Joseph Otto and Cornelia Louise (Pagel) Ehlinger; m. Wiley Anderson, Jr. (dec.); children: Wiley Newton III, Joe E. BA, Rice U., Houston, 1946; permanent high sch. tchr. cert., U. Houston, 1948; JD, U. Tex., 1950; MLS in Museology, U. Okla., Norman, 1985. Bar: Tex. 1950, U.S. Supreme Ct. Assoc. Ehlinger & Anderson, Houston, 1950-52, ptnr., 1965—; assoc. Price, Guinn, Wheat & Veltmann, Houston, 1952-55, Wheat, Dyche & Thornton, Houston, 1955-65; life mem. Rice Assocs., Houston, 1984—. Hist. lectr., Harvard Negotiation Seminar, 1992 Edn. for Ministry, U of South, 1999. Editor: Houston City of Destiny, 1980; contbr. articles to hist. pubs. and to Bayou Bend. Parliamentarian Harris County Flood Control Task Force, Houston, 1975-2003; dir. Houston Bapt. Mus Am. Architecture and Decorative Arts, 1980-90, curator costume, 1980; apptd. ambassador Inst. Texan Culture U. Tex, San Antonio; past pres. gen. San Jacinto Descendants; docent Bayou Bend Mus. Fine Arts, Houston. Recipient best interpretive exhibit award Tex. Hist. Commn., 1983, Outstanding Woman of Yr. award YWCA, Houston, 1983; named adm. Tex. Navy, 1980. Mem. ABA, UDC (pres. Jefferson Davis chpt.), Assn. Women Attys. Houston, Houston Bar Assn., Daus. Republic Tex. (parliamentarian gen.), Am. Mus. Soc., Harris County Heritage Soc., Kappa Beta Pi (pres. Lamda alumni). Episcopalian. Home: 5556 Cranbrook Rd Houston TX 77056-1600 Office: Ehlinger & Anderson 5556 Sturbridge Dr Houston TX 77056-1600

ANDERSON, DOROTHY FISHER, social worker, psychotherapist; b. Funchal, Madeira, May 31, 1924; d. Lewis Mann Anker and Edna (Gilbert) Fisher (adoptive father David Henry Fisher); m. Theodore W. Anderson, July 8, 1950; children: Robert Lewis, Janet Anderson Yang, Jeanne Elizabeth. BA, Queens Coll., 1945; AM, U. Chgo., 1947. Diplomate Am. Bd. Examiners in Clin. Social Work; lic. clin. social worker, Calif.; registered cert. social worker, N.Y. Intern Cook County (Ill.) Bur. Pub. Welfare, Chgo., 1945-46, Ill. Neuropsychiat. Inst., Chgo., 1946; clin. caseworker, Neurol. Inst. Presbyn. Hosp., N.Y.C., 1947; therapist, Mental Hygiene Clinic VA, N.Y.C., 1947-50; therapist, Child Guidance Clinic Pub. Elem. Sch. 42, N.Y.C., 1950-53; social worker, counselor Cedarhurst (N.Y.) Family Service Agy., 1954-55; psychotherapist, counselor Family Service of the Midpeninsula, Palo Alto, Calif., 1971-73, 79-86, George Hexter, M.D., Inc., 1972-83; clin. social worker Tavistock Clinic, London, 1974-75, El Camino Hosp., Mountain View, Calif., 1979; pvt. practice clin. social work, 1978-92; ret., 1992. Cons. Human Resource Services, Sunnyvale, Calif., 1981-86. Hannah G. Solomon scholar U. Chgo., 1945-46; Commonwealth fellow U. Chgo., 1946-47. Fellow Soc. Clin. Social Work (Continuing Edn. Recognition award 1980-83); mem. Nat. Assn. Social Workers (diplomate in clin. social work). Avocations: sculpture, tennis, travel, drawing, pastels.

ANDERSON, ELAINE JANET, science educator; b. Phila., Feb. 20, 1940; d. Lewis Clayton and Ellen McNeil (Stewart) Anderson. BS in Biology Edn., Bloomsburg U., 1962; MEd, Pa. State U., 1966, PhD in Secondary Edn., 1974. cert. biology, English instr., sci. supr., Pa. Biology educator numerous schs., 1962-71; dean of women, asst. prof. Schiller Coll., Bönnigheim, Fed. Republic of Germany, 1971-72; asst. scientist U. Wis., Madison, 1974-75; asst. prof. Pa. State U., University Pk., 1972-1978; div. dir. Pa. Dept. Health, Harrisburg, 1978-80; exec. dir. Nat. Diabetes Rsch. Interchange, Phila., 1980-83, Pa. Diabetes Acad., Harrisburg, 1983-86; owner, mgr.franchise Pip Printing, Mechanicsburg, Pa., 1986-91; asst. prof. Bloomsburg (Pa.) U., 1991-94; asst. prof. biology dept. Shippensburg (Pa.) U., 1994-98, assoc. prof., 1998—2003. Cons. Pa. Acad. for Profession of Teaching, Harrisburg. Author: A Single Person's Guide to Buying A Home: Why To Do It and How To Do It, 1993, Dragonfly, 2006. Co-chair Provincetown Conservation Commn.; chair Provincetown Cmty. Preservation Com.; del. Provincetown Dem. Convention, Mass., 2006. Mem. AAAS-Grad. Women in Sci. Affiliate (nominating com., pub. rels. com.), ASCD, Sch. Sci. and Math. Assn., Pa. Sci. Tchrs. Assn., Am. Ednl. Rsch. Assn., Assn. Pa. State Coll. and Univ. Faculties. Mem. Soc. Of Friends. Avocations: walking, travel, real estate, writing. Personal E-mail: ejande@verizon.net.

ANDERSON, ESTHER ELIZABETH, retired pediatrician, educator; b. Wabash, Ind., Aug. 6, 1924; d. William Earl Anderson and Marion Christine (Moore) Pelham. AB in Chemistry, Ind. U., Bloomington, 1945; MD, Ind. U. Sch. Medicine, Indpls., 1948. Cert. Am. Bd. Pediatrics, 1955. Intern Ind. U. Med. Ctr., Indpls., 1948—49, resident in pediat., 1949—51; fellow pediatric tchg. and rsch. La. State U. Sch. Medicine, New Orleans, 1951—53, mem. faculty dept. pediat., instr., asst. prof., assoc. prof., 1953—74; psychotherapist Primal Ctr., Denver, 1974—77; program mgmt. officer Indian Health Svc., Aberdeen, SD, 1979—96; ret., 1996. Dir. hematology and oncology rsch. La. State U. Sch. Medicine, 1954—74, dir. heritable disease clinic, 1968—74. Fellow: Am. Acad. Pediatrics; mem.: Am. Coll. Physician Execs., Brown County Med. Soc., Am. Med. Soc., Alpha Omega Alpha. Avocations: music, art, literature, travel, sports. Home: 2023 3d Ave Apt 108 Aberdeen SD 57401

ANDERSON, EVELYN LOUISE, elementary school educator; b. Abilene, Tex., Apr. 10, 1943; d. Dexter W. and Hattie M. Armstrong; m. E. Wade Anderson, Dec. 22, 1962; children: Cynthia Gail, Tresa Lynet. BA magna cum laude, Sul Ross State U., 1985. Kindergarten tchr. Socorro Ind. Sch. Dist., El Paso, Tex., 1985-86; tchr. kindergarten through 3d grade, resource rm. Ft. Stockton Ind. Sch. Dist., 1986-90; tchr. kindergarten Lydia Rippey Elem. Sch., Aztec, N.Mex., 1990—. Organizer Children's Libr., Ft. Stockton (Tex.) Pub. Libr., 1980-84, pre-school tchr. First Bapt. Ch., Ft. Stockton, Tex., 1979-84. Nominee Disney Tchr. awrd, 2000. Mem.: Coun. Exceptional Children, Kappa Delta Pi. Democrat. Avocations: writing, reading, travel, painting, crocheting. Home: 1709 Winter Ct Farmington NM 87401-2086

ANDERSON, FRANCILE MARY, secondary school educator; b. Poland, Ind., Nov. 10, 1926; d. Matthew Henry and Emma Alvina (Dettinger) Worthman; m. Robert Charles Anderson, Aug. 23, 1953; children: Sally Quick, Sue Wilkinson, Robert Charles, Russell. BA, U. Mich., 1948. Tchr. Pontiac (Mich.) Sch. Dist., 1948-54. Co-organizer Mich. Law Related Edn. Conf., Lansing, 1978; mem. exec. bd. North Ctrl. Assn. Commn. on Schs., Tempe, Ariz., 1996-99. Trustee North Oakland Med. Ctrs., Pontiac, 1994—; campaign chair United Way of Oakland County, 1995. Recipient Disting. Svc. award Mich. Assn. Secondary Sch. Prins., 1987; named to Mich. Edn. Hall of Fame, 1990. Mem. Oakland County Hosp. Assn. (pres.), Oakland County Bar Law Libr. Found., North Ctrl. Assn. Mich., North Oakland Med. Ctrs. Found. (pres.), Delta Kappa Gamma. Republican. Presbyterian. Home: 2570 Silverside Dr Waterford MI 48328-1760 Personal E-mail: franan1@earthlink.net.

ANDERSON, GAIL MARIE, retired librarian; b. St. Cloud, Minn., Apr. 26, 1945; d. George Elroy Carpenter and Blanche Doris (Flam) Carpenter Neel; m. Gordon Alexander Anderson, Aug. 24, 1971. B.S., St. Cloud State U., 1969. Cert. librarian, Minn.; cert. elem. tchr., Minn. Librarian, Cloquet Pub. Sch., Minn., 1969-70; jr. high media ctr. dir. Roseville Pub. Sch., Minn., 1970-78; asst. program dir., group dir. Afton Alps Ski Sch., 1973-82; library asst. U. Minn. Sch. Dentistry, Mpls., 1979-86; sch. librarian Desert Valley Sch., Bullhead City, Ariz., 1986—2006. Sec., Minn. Christian Youth Council, Mpls., 1960-63; mem. Minn. Ednl. Media Orgn. Methodist. Mem. Bullhead City Tchrs. Union (treas. 1987-2006), Jobs Daus. (guardian 1989-2002), Pheasants Forever. Avocations: outdoor sports, hunting, gardening, travel. Home: 9067 Deer Path Ln Breezy Point MN 56472

ANDERSON, GERALDINE LOUISE, medical researcher; d. George M. and Viola Julia-Mary (Abel) Havrilla; m. Henry Clifford Anderson, May 21, 1966; children: Bruce Henry, Julie Lynne. BS med. tech., U. Minn., 1959—63. Cert. med. technologist ASCP, clin. lab. sci. NCA. Med. technologist Swedish Hosp., Mpls., 1963-68; hematology supr. lab. Glenwood Hills Hosp., Golden Valley, Minn., 1968-70; assoc. scientist pediats. U. Minn. Hosps., Mpls., 1970-74; instr. health occupations, med. lab. asst. Suburban Hennepin County Area Vocat. Tech. Ctr., Brooklyn Park, Minn., 1974-81, 92-95, St. Paul Tech. Vocat. Inst., Brooklyn Park, 1978-81; rsch. med. technologist Miller Hosp., St. Paul, 1975-78; rsch. assoc. Children's and United Hosps., St. Paul, 1979-88; sr. lab. analyst Cascade Med. Inc., Eden Prairie, Minn., 1989-90; lab. mgr. VAMC, Mpls., 1990; tech. support scientist INCSTAR Corp., Stillwater, Minn., 1990-94; mem. network staff Clin. Design Group, Chgo., 1992-98; regulatory affairs product analysis coord. Medtronic Neurol., Mpls., 1995; quality assurance documentation coord. Lectec Corp., Minnetonka, Minn., 1995; clin. rsch. monitor Eli Lilly Rsch. Labs., Indpls., 1995-98; sr. clin. rsch. assoc. Covance, Inc., Princeton, NJ, 1998-99. Sr. clin. rsch. assoc. Parexel Internat., Inc., Chgo., 1999—2000; clin. rsch. assoc. AAI Internat., Boston, 2000—01; regional clin. rsch. assoc. Wyeth, Collegeville, Pa., 2001—02; health occupations adv. com. Hennepin Tech. Ctrs., 1975—90, chairperson, 1978—79; mem. hematology slide edn. rev. bd. Am. Soc. Hematology, 1977—96; mem. flow cytometry and clin. chemistry quality controll subcoms. Nat. Com. for Clin. Lab. Stds., 1988—92; cons. FCM Specialists, 1989—99, 2002—, Clin. Design Group, 1992—98; mem. rev. bd. Clin. Lab. Sci., 1990—91, The Learning Laboratorian Series, 1991; presenter in field. Contbr. articles to profl. jours. Charter orgns. rep. Viking Coun. troop 534 Boy Scouts Am., 1988—90; resource person lab. careers Robbinsdale (Minn.) Sch. Dist., 1970—79; active Women Scientists Spkrs. Bur., 1989—92, Helping Hands, 2002—, Med. Lab. Tech. Polit. Action Com., 1978—99; observer UN 4th World Conf. on Women, Beijing, 1995; del. Crest View Home Assn., 1981—; sci. and math. subcom. Minn. High Tech. Coun., 1983—88; bd. dirs. Big Pine Lake Property Owners, 1996—. Recipient Svc. awards and honors, Omicron Sigma. Mem.: NAFE, AAUW, AAAS, Grad. Women in Sci., Inc., Great Lakes Internat. Flow Cytometry Assn. (charter mem. 1992), Internat. Soc. Analytical Cytology, Am. Soc. Hematology, Minn. Med. Tech. Alumni, Assn. Clin. Rsch. Profls., World Future Soc., Assn. Women in Sci., Twin Cities Hosp. Assn. (spkrs. bur. 1968—70), Am. Soc. Clin. Lab. Sci. (del. to ann. meetings 1972—, chmn. hematology sci. assembly 1977—79, nomination com. 1979—81, bd. dirs. 1986—88), Am. Soc. Profl. and Exec. Women, Minn. Soc. Med. Tech. (sec. 1969—71), Minn. Emerging Med. Orgns., Nat. Assn. Women Cons., Inc., Soc. Tech. Comm., Assn. Clin. Rsch. Profls. (cert. clin. rsch. assoc.), Women in Comm., Inc., Am. Med. Writers Assn., Nat. Ch. Libr. Assn., Alpha Mu Tau, Sigma Delta Epsilon (corr. sec. XI chpt. 1980—82, pres. 1982—84, nat. membership com. 1990—92, nat. nominations chair 1991—92, nat. v.p. 1992—93, nat. pres.-elect 1993—94, nat. pres. 1994—95, bd. dirs. 1996—2001, chmn. bd. dirs. 2000—01). Personal E-mail: gerrylou@comcast.net.

ANDERSON, GILLIAN, actress; b. Chgo., Aug. 9, 1968; d. Edward and Rosemary A.; m. Errol Clyde Klotz, Jan. 1, 1994 (div. 1997); 1 child, Piper; m. Julian Ozanne, Dec. 29, 2004 (separated Apr., 2006) BFA, DePaul U., 1990; grad., Goodman Theatre Sch., Chgo. Appeared on TV series, X-Files, 1993-2002 (Emmy award for Outstanding Lead Actress in a Drama Series, 1997, Golden Globe award for Best Actress in a Drama Series, 1997); stage appearance in Absent Friends, Manhattan Theatre Club, 1991 (Theatre World award 1991), The Philanthropist, Along Wharf Theater, 1992, The Vagina Monologues, 1999, 2000, What the Night is For, 2002-03, The Sweetest Swing in Baseball, 2004; appeared in films Three at Once, 1986, A Matter of Choice, 1988, The Turning, 1992, X-Files the Movie, 1998, The Mighty, 1998, Playing By Heart, 1998, Hellcab, 1998, Princess Mononoke, 1999, The House of Mirth, 2000 (British Independent Film award for Best Actress, 2000); TV appearances Class of '96, 1993, Reboot, 1995, The Simpsons, 1997, Frasier, 1999, Harsh Realm, 1999.

ANDERSON, GINA MARIE, obstetrician, gynecologist; d. Ronald E. Anderson and Mary Roberts Scott. AB, Harvard U., Cambridge, Mass., 1987; MD, Med. Coll. Wis., Milw., 1996. Resident Parkland Meml. Hosp., Dallas, 1996—2000; asst. prof. ob-gyn. U. Tex. Southwestern Med. Ctr., Dallas, 2000—05, NJ Med. Sch., Newark, 2005—. Bd. mem. Jane's Due Process, Austin, Tex., 2001—03. Recipient Dr. Stanley Marinoff Vulvodynia Career Devel. award, Nat. Vulvodynia Assn., 2006; grantee, Assn. Profs. Ob-gyn., 2003. Fellow: Am. Coll. Ob-gyn.; mem.: Harvard Club NJ, Alpha Omega Alpha. Office: New Jersey Medical School Dept of OB/GY 185 S Orange Ave MSB E503 Newark NJ 07101 Office Phone: 973-972-5551.

ANDERSON, GLORIA LONG, chemistry professor; b. Altheimer, Ark., Nov. 5, 1938; d. Charley and Elsie Lee (Foggie) L.; 1 child, Gerald Leavell. BS, Ark. Agr. Mech. & Normal Coll., 1958; MS, Atlanta U., 1961; PhD, U. Chgo., 1968. Instr. S.C. State Coll., Orangeburg, 1961-62, Morehouse Coll., Altanta, 1962-64; teaching and rsch. asst. U. Chgo., 1964-68; assoc. prof., chmn. Morris Brown Coll., Atlanta, 1968-73, Callaway prof., chmn., 1973-84, acad. dean, 1984-89, United Negro Coll. Fund disting. scholar, 1989-90, Callaway prof. chemistry, 1990—, interim pres., 1992-93, Fuller E. Callaway prof. chemistry, 1993-99, 99—, dean sci. and tech., 1995-97, interim pres., 1998-99, Fuller E. Callaway prof. chemistry, 1999—. Contbr. articles to profl. jours. Bd. dirs. Corp. for Pub. Broadcasting, Washington, 1972-79, vice chmn. 1977-79; Pub. Broadcasting Atlanta, 1980—; mem. Pub. Telecommunications Task Force, Atlanta, 1980. Postdoctoral rsch. fellow NSF, 1969, faculty industry fellow, 1981, faculty rsch. fellow Southeastern Ctr. for Elec. Engring. Edn., 1984. Fellow Am. Inst. Chemists (cert. profl. chemist); mem. Nat. Sci. Tchrs. Assn., Am. Chem. Soc., Sigma Xi. Baptist. Home: 560 Lynn Valley Rd SW Atlanta GA 30311-2331 Office: Morris Brown Coll Dept Chemistry 643 ML King Jr Dr NW Atlanta GA 30314-4140

ANDERSON, GRETA MAE, health facility administrator, educator; b. Phila., June 8, 1939; d. Thomas Joseph McCabe and Martha Elizabeth (Christopherson) Warlaid; children: Cynthia Lee Gotten, Annette Louise Duest, Arthur John Schmidt. AS, Chippewa Valley Tech Coll., Eau Claire, 1975; BA Psychology magna cum laude, U. Wis., Eau Claire, 1994, MA Creative Writing, 1998. Mgr. clin. lab. Eau Claire Family Med. Clinic, 1976—2000; adj. instr. Chippewa Valley Tech. Coll., Eau Claire, 2001—05; tchg. missionary Grace Luth. Ch., Eau Claire, 2006—. Vol. Global Health Ministries, Mpls., 1989—. Home: 2810 113th St Chippewa Falls WI 54729

ANDERSON, GWYN C., computer company executive; b. LaCrosse, Wis., Aug. 8, 1966; d. Robert Bernard and Alice Helaine Anderson. Owner Enhanced Ideas, LaCrosse, 1996—; e-commerce webmaster www.enhanceideas.com. Avocations: rollerskating, camping, horseback riding, swimming, science fiction. Office: Enhanced Ideas PO Box 3602 La Crosse WI 54602-3602 Office Phone: 608-788-6156. E-mail: enhancedideas@earthlink.net.

ANDERSON, HOLLY GEIS, health facility administrator, educator, commentator; b. Waukesha, Wis., Oct. 23, 1946; d. Henry H. and Hulda S. Geis; m. Richard Kent Anderson, June 6, 1969. BA, Azusa Pacific U., 1970. CEO Oak Tree Antiques, San Gabriel, Calif., 1975-82; pres., founder, CEO Premenstrual Syndrome Med. Clinic, Arcadia, Calif., 1982—, Breast Healthcare Ctr., 1986-89, Hormonal Treatment Ctrs., Inc., Arcadia, 1992-94; with Thyroid Ctr., 2001—. On-air radio personality Women's Clinic with Holly Anderson, 1990—; lectr. in field. Author: (audio cassette) What Every Woman Needs to Know About PMS, 1987, PMS Talk, 1989; (video cassette)The PMS Treatment Program, 1989. Mem. NAFE, The Dalton Soc., Am. Hist. Soc. of Germans from Russia. Republican. Avocations: writing, genealogy, travel, hiking, boating. Office: PMS Treatment Clinic 150 N Santa Anita Ave Ste 755 Arcadia CA 91006-3148 Office Phone: 626-447-0679. Personal E-mail: hra3@earthlink.net.

ANDERSON, ILSE JANELL, clinical geneticist; b. Elmhurst, Ill., May 3, 1959; d. Lowell Leonard and Avis Janell Anderson; m. Nicholas Thomas Potter, June 24, 1989; children: Nils Andrew, Anders Matthew. BS in Biology, Lehigh U., 1981; MD, N.Y. Med. Coll., 1985. Diplomate Nat. Bd. Med. Examiners, Am. Bd. Pediatrics, Am. Bd. Med. Genetics. Resident pediatrics U. Conn., Farmington, 1985-88, fellow human genetics, 1988-91; clin. geneticist Med. Ctr. U. Tenn., Knoxville, 1991—. Mem. Phi Beta Kappa. Office: Univ Tenn Med Ctr 1930 Alcoa Hwy Ste 435 Knoxville TN 37920-1520

ANDERSON, IRIS ANITA, retired secondary school educator; b. Forks, Wash., Aug. 18, 1930; d. James Adolphus and Alma Elizabeth (Haase) Gilbreath; m. Donald Rene Anderson, 1951; children: Karen Christine, Susan Adele, Gayle Lynne, Brian Dale. BA in Teaching, U. Wash., 1969; MA in English, Seattle U., 1972. Cert. English teacher, adminr Calif. Tchr. Issaquah (Wash.) Sr. High Sch., 1969-77, L.A. Sr. High Sch., 1977-79. Nutrition vol Santa Monica Hosp Aux, Calif., Jules Stein Eye Inst, Los Angeles; mem Desert Beautirful, Palm Springs Panhellenic, Rancho Mirage Reps. Scholar W-Key Activities, Univ Wash. Mem.: LEV, AAUW (Anne Carpenter fellow 1998), DAR (1st vice regent Cahulla chpt), NEA, Women in Film, Assistance League of Palm Springs, World Affairs Coun., Calif. Ret. Tchrs. Assn., Coachella Valley Hist. Soc., Desert Music Guild, Palm Springs Press Women, Nat. Thespians, Wash. Speech Assn., Am. League Pen Women, Coachella Valley Panhellenic, Round Table West (3d pl. writing award 2003), Skeptics Soc., Bob Hope Cultural Ctr., Desert Celebrities, Living Desert Wildlife And Botanical Preserve, Nat. Women's Hist. Mus., Rancho Mirage Womens Club, CPA Wives Club, Palm Desert Womens Club.

ANDERSON, JANE A., scriptwriter; b. Calif., 1954; TV series include: The Facts of Life, 1984-86, Raising Miranda, 1988, The Wonder Years, 1989; TV movies include: The Positively True Adventures of the Alleged Texas Cheerleader-Murdering Mom, 1993 (Emmy award outstanding individual achievement in writing in a miniseries or special), The Baby Dance, 1998, If These Walls Could Talk 2, 2000, When Billie Beat Bobby, 2001, Normal, 2003; films: It Could Happen to You, 1994. How to Make an American Quilt, 1995, The Prize Winner of Defiance, Ohio, 2005; plays: The Baby Dance, Food and Shelter, Hotel Oubliette, Lynette at 3 A.M. Office: care Martin Gage The Gage Group 9255 W Sunset Blvd Ste 515 Los Angeles CA 90069-3301

ANDERSON, JANEIL EVA, mental health services professional; b. Big Timber, Mont., Dec. 5, 1978; d. Jerry and Cynthia Marie Riesinger; m. Douglas Ray Anderson, Oct. 15, 2004. BS in Biology, Mont. State U., Billings, 2002, postgrad., 2005—. Medication assistance program adv. St. Vincent Healthcare, Billings, 2004—06; mental health technician Cmty. Crisis Ctr., Billings, 2006—. Grad. student rep. U. Grad. Com., 2005—, Waterman, Wilson, McRae Grad. Scholarship Com., 2006; grad. student rep. steering com. NW Commn. on Colls. and Univs./Continuous Quality Improvement, 2006—. Mem.: ACA (life), Mont. Counseling Assn. (life), Grad. Student Assn. (assoc.; v.p. 2005—06). Roman Catholic. Avocations: running, reading, baking, cooking, scrapbooks. Home: 241 Uinta Park Dr Billings MT 59105 Office: Cmty Crisis Ctr 704 N 30th St Billings MT 59101 Office Phone: 406-259-8800. Business E-Mail: janderson@cccbillings.org.

ANDERSON, JEAN BLANCHE, fiction writer; b. St. Louis, Sept. 13, 1940; d. Clifford George and Blanche Jean (Pell) Schulze; m. Donald Wyckliffe Anderson; children: Thomas, Laura. AA, Harris Tchrs. Coll., 1960; student, U. Mo., 1965-66; BA, U. Alaska, 1977, MFA, 1980. Lectr. in English U. Alaska, Fairbanks, 1980-85, 88-89, vis. asst. prof., 1990-91; book reviewer Fairbanks Daily News-Miner, Heartland, Alaska, 1985-88. Resident fellow The Island Inst., Sitka, Alaska, 1996; faculty mem. Midnight Sun Writers' Conf., Fairbanks, 1990, 91, 92. Author: In Extremis and Other Alaskan Stories, 1989; co-editor Inroads: Alaska's Twenty-Seven Fellowship Writers, 1988; contbr. short stories, poems and essays to periodicals. Fellowship Alaska State Coun. on Arts, 1982; recipient PEN Syndicated Fiction award PEN Am. Ctr., 1985. Mem. Poets and Writers Inc. Home: 509 Aquila St Fairbanks AK 99712-1320 Personal E-mail: jeananderson509@yahoo.com.

ANDERSON, JENNIFER ANN, middle school educator; b. Tyler, Tex., Apr. 14, 1971; d. James Ralph Jr. and Judy Ann Ellis; children: Holly Ann, Connor Lee. BS, Stephen F. Austin U., Nacogdoches, Texas, 1995. Cert. tchr. Tex. 7-12 grade sci. tchr. New Summerfield Ind. Sch. Dist., Tex., 1995—97; integrated physics and chemistry tchr. Jacksonville Ind. Sch. Dist., Tex., 1997—98; 8th grade sci. tchr., chmn. dept. Whitehouse Ind. Sch. Dist., Tex., 1998—. Presenter workshops in field. Named Tchr. of Yr., Whitehouse Jr. High, 2004; TARGET grantee, Microsoft and Tex. Edn. Assn., 2003—06. Mem.: NSTA (licentiate), Sci. Tchrs. Assn. Tex. (licentiate). Baptist. Office Phone: 903-839-5590. Business E-Mail: andersonj@whitehouseisd.org.

ANDERSON, JEWELLE LUCILLE, musician, educator; b. Alexandria, La., Jan. 4, 1932; d. William Andrew and Ethel Dee (Hall) Anderson. Student, Springfield Coll., 1981-82; MusB, Boston U., 1984; postgrad., Harvard U., 1995-96. Cert. tchr. music and social studies Mass. Soloist Ch. of the Redeemer Episcopal Ch., Chestnut Hill, Mass., 1964-69, St. James Episcopal Ch., Cambridge, Mass., 1970-75; kindergarten tchr. and music dir. Trinity Episcopal Ch., Boston, 1984-86; chorus music dir. Spencer for Hire, Boston, 1986; music dir. Days in the Arts summer program Boston Symphony Orch., Tanglewood, Mass., summer 1991, 92; chorale dir. Boston Orch. Chorale, 1996-97; tchr. scholar Harvard Grad. Sch. of Edn., 1998-99. Founder Jewelle Anderson Found., Inc., Boston, 1996. Vol. ARC, Boston, 1994—; bd. dirs. Mattapan Cmty. Health Ctr., Boston, 1990—92; founder, pres. Dr. William and Ethel Hall Anderson Scholarship, 1989—. Recipient Am. Music award, Nat. Fedn. Music, 1970, Spl. Individual award, 1969, Outstanding Contbn. to Humanity award, Alexandria Civic Improvement Coun., 1967, Outstanding Achievement award, Boston Tchrs. Union, 2000, Cope Plaque for Outstanding Achievement, 2000, Action for Boston Cmty. Devel. award, 2003. Mem.: AAUW, Black Educators Alliance of Mass., Amnesty Internat., Women Svc. Club (head youth group 1989—, 1st v.p. 2002), Alpha Kappa Alpha. Democrat. Baptist. Avocations: walking, boating. Office: PO Box 124 Boston MA 02117-0124

ANDERSON, JOAN BALYEAT, theology studies educator, minister; b. Cin., Apr. 14, 1926; d. Hal Donal and Myrtle (Skinner) Hukill Balyeat; m. Jerry William Anderson, Jr., Sept. 13, 1947: children: Katheleen, Diane. AA, Stephens Coll., 1946. Ordained Christian minister Ohio, 1988. Christian ch. bible tchr., Cin., 1944—; Christian counselor, advisor, 1964—; founder, pres., dir., ruling elder, and pastor Loving God "Complete Bible" Christian Ministries and First Ch., Cin., 1988—. Christian Bible tchr., preacher, pastor daily and Sunday radio throughout the east and midwest, 1988—, world wide internet, 2006—. Mem. Am. Conservative Cause, 1998—2001, Capitol His. Soc., 2000—; legacy leader supporter George Washington's Mt. Vernon, 2001—; coord., collector Heart Fund, T.B., 1948—90; civic assn. officer, rep. edn. com. to all Madeira Schs., 1960—62; co-founder, officer Grassroots, Inc., Cin., 1962—65; mem. Cin. Art Mus., 1972—, Cin. Zoo, 1974—, Colonial Williamsburg Found., 1979—, Nat. Right to Life, 1980—, MADD, 1985—, Heritage Found., 1996—, Am. Conservative Union, 1998, Ronald Reagan Presdl. Found., 1998—, Parents TV Coun., 1998—2001, Am. Policy Ctr., 1998—2001, U.S. Justice Found., 1998—, Nat. Right to Work Legal Def. Found., 1998—, Nat. Security Ctr., 1998—, U.S. Intelligence Ctr., 1998—, Jud. Watch, 1999—, Young Ams. Found., 2000—; supporter The Liberty Com., 2001—; lifelong activist for preservation of U.S. Constn. and Bill of Rights; mem. U.S. Rep. Senatorial Adv. Com., Washington and Cin., 1987—88; mem. Rep. Senatorial Commn., Washington & Cin., 1996—2000; mem. Am. Prayer Network, 1998—. Master: Blue Book of Cin. Avocation: travel. Home: 7208 Sycamorehill Ln Cincinnati OH 45243-2101 Office: Loving God Complete Bible Christian Mins/1st Ch PO Box 43404 Cincinnati OH 45243-2101

ANDERSON, JOYCE LORRAINE, nurse; b. Newman Grove, Nebr., May 16, 1930; d. Fredrick Carl Stone and Hulda Caroline Nordgren; children: Bonita Lynne Peters, Richard Eugene. Student, Ctrl. C.C., Central City, Nebr., 1950. Rural tchrs. cert., cert. staff mem. Rural sch. tchr. Dist. 47 Platte County, St. Edward, Nebr., 1947—48, Dist. 40 Platte County, Lindsay, Nebr., 1948—51; nurse aid Hosp., Newman Grove, 1973—76; nurse aid, cert. staff mem. Newman Grove Mid Nebr. Luth. Home, 1977—2001. Active Newman Grove Civic Improvement Club, 1985—2001; vol. sing along leader Mid. Nebr. Luth. Home, Newman Grove, 1978—; life mem. Looking Glass United Meth. Ch., Newman Grove, 1930—; active United Meth. Women, 1950—; ch. pianist Looking Glass United Meth. Ch., Newman Grove, 1950—. Home: 53777 829 Rd Newman Grove NE 68758

ANDERSON, JUDITH ANN, artist, writer; b. Cin., May 14, 1940; d. Clair Henry and Jean (Akeman) Stagge; m. Rondal Ambrose Anderson, June 13, 1959 (dec.); children: Andrew, Christopher, Lynn. Celebrity tutor Am. Diabete's Auction Gala, Cin., 2002; tchr. Cin. Women's Club; tchr. workshops in field, 1997—. Closson's Art Gallery, Cin., 1998—2001, Cin. Art Mus., 2000, March of Dimes, Cin., 2001, full size horse for Lexington, Ky., wildcats for U. Ky., 2000—01, numerous acrylic on canvas paintings for pvt. collectors, Represented in permanent collections Cin. Music Hall; contbr. articles to profl. jours. Contbg. artist Wellness Cmty., 2003—. Mem.: Ky. Watercolor Soc., Cin. Art Club, Ohio Watercolor Soc., Tex. Watercolor Soc., Northwest Watercolor Soc., Nat. Watercolor Soc. Avocation: interior design. Home: 798 Kingsmeade Rd Westerville OH 43082

ANDERSON, JUDITH HELENA, English language educator; b. Worcester, Mass., Apr. 21, 1940; d. Oscar William and Beatrice Marguerite (Beaudry) A.; m. E. Talbot Donaldson, May 18, 1971 (dec. Apr. 1987). AB magna cum laude, Radcliffe Coll., 1961; MA, Yale U., 1962, PhD, 1965. Instr. English Cornell U., Ithaca, NY, 1964-66, asst. prof. English, 1966-72; vis. lectr. Coll. Seminar Program, Yale U., New Haven, 1973; vis. asst. prof. English U. Mich., Ann Arbor, 1973-74; assoc. prof. Ind. U., Bloomington, 1974-79, prof., 1979—, Chancellor's prof., 1999—, dir. grad. studies, 1986-90, 93, mem. governing bd. univ. Inst. for Advanced Study, 1983-85, 86-88. Morris W. Croll lectr. Gettysburg Coll., 1988, Kathleen Williams lectr., 89, 95; dir. Folger Inst. Sem., 1991; adv. bd. Textbase of Women Writers, Brown U., 1989—2000. Author: The Growth of a Personal Voice, 1976, Biographical Truth, 1984, Words that Matter, 1996, Translating Investments, 2005; editor: (with Elizabeth D. Kirk) Piers Plowman, 1990; (with Donald Cheney and David A. Richardson) Spenser's Life and the Subject of Biography, 1996; mem. editl. bd. Spenser Ency., 1979-90, Duquesne Studies in Lang. and Lit., 1976-2004, Spenser Studies, 1986—, Medieval and Renaissance Literary Studies, 2004—; contbr. articles to profl. jours. Rsch. grant Huntington Libr., 1978, 97; Woodrow Wilson fellow, 1961-64, NEH summer fellow and sr. rsch. fellow, 1979, 81-82, NEH fellow, 1985-86, Mayers Found. fellow, 1990-91, Dulin fellow Folger Libr., 1991, Nat. Humanities Ctr. fellow, 1995-96, Newberry-NEH fellow, 2002-03; recipient Outstanding Scholar award Office of Women's Affairs Ind. U., 1996 Mem. MLA (exec. com. Renaissance divsn. 1973-78, 86-90, del. to assembly 1991-93, publs. com. 1999-2002), AAUP, internat. Spenser Soc. (pres. 1980, 88, Lifetime Achievement award 2004), Renaissance Soc. Am. (rep. for English to coun. 1991-93), Milton Soc., Donne Soc. (exec. com. 2004—), Shakespeare Assn., Chaucer Soc., Phi Beta Kappa. Home: 2525 E 8th St Bloomington IN 47408-4214 Office: Ind U Dept English Bloomington IN 47405 Office Phone: 812-855-8224. Business E-Mail: anders@indiana.edu.

ANDERSON, KAREN JEAN, mayor, researcher, communications executive; d. Dana T. Schubert and Georgia D. Gewecke; m. Thomas Craig Anderson; children: Keith A., Audrey J., Timothy B. Student, U. Wis., 1960; BA in Comm., Met. State U., 1990. Devel., pub. rels. staff LWV Minn., St. Paul, 1980—86; coun. mem. large City of Minnetonka, 1986—93, mayor, 1994—2006. State and local sr. adv. com. homeland security adv. coun. The White Ho., Washington, 2002—03; chair leadership tng. coun. Nat. League Cities, 1999—99, strategic planning com., 1997—98; pres. League Minn. Cities, St. Paul, 1995—96; bd. trustees League Minn. Cities Ins. Trust, 1995—2001; gov. Ventura's met. coun. nominating com. The Gov.'s Office, 1999—99, gov. Carlson's met. coun. nominating com., 1992—98; commn. local and state govt. rels. Lt. Gov. Dyrstad's Office, 1991—93; adv. coun. state/local rels. Gov. Perpich's Office, 1989—91; pay equity adv. task force Minn. Dept. Employee Rels., 1991—92; founder, co-chair Minn. Regional Coun. Mayors, Mpls., 2004—06; mayor's regional housing task force Met. Coun., St. Paul, 2000—02, chair, livable cmtys. adv. com., 1995—99, livable communities adv. com., 1995—2001; commr. SW Suburban Cable Commn., Eden Prairie, 1986—2000; state and local sr. adv. com. U.S. Dept. Homeland Security, Washington, 2003—, state and local info. sharing task force, 2005—06, pvt. sector info. sharing task force, 2005, common culture task force, 06; pres. Nat. League Cities, 2001—02, adv. coun., 1997—99, officer, 2000—05; nat. homeland security consortium Nat. Emergency Mgmt. Assn., 2003—05. Adv. coun. Hubert H. Humprey Inst. Pub. Affairs, Mpls., 2004—06; mem., past pres. LWV Minnetonka, Eden Prairie, Hopkins Area, 1970—2006; v.p. Family Housing Fund, 1997—2006; bd. dirs., staff LWV Minn., St. Paul, 1975—92; adv. bd. Minn. Ctr. Women in Govt., Hamline U., 1988—99. Recipient Hope Washburn award, LWV Minn., 1979, C.C. Ludwig award, League Minn. Cities, 2002, Pres. award, Nat. League Cities, 2005, Founding Feminist award, Minn. Women's Polit. Caucus, 2005, Bravo! award, TwinWest C. of C., 2005, Maurice dorton Award, Sensible Land Use Coalition, 2005. Avocations: hiking, bicycling, travel. Home: 3311 Martha Ln Minnetonka MN 55345

ANDERSON, KAREN MAE, primary school educator; b. Portland, Oreg. d. Gordon and Rosa Flath; m. Frank W. Anderson, June 9, 1973; children: Katrina, Angeliea, Frank, Paul. BA in Music, Ariz. State U., Tempe, 1977; BA in Edn., Concordia U., Portland, Oreg., 1994; MS of Edn., Western Oreg. U., Monmouth, 2003. Mgr. of domestics Anderson Group, Washougal, Wash.; pre-sch. tchr. Woodburn, Oreg.; tchr. Woodburn Sch. Dist. Mem. CSR team Heritage Elem., Woodburn, 2004—06. Mem.: NEA, Oreg. Edn. Assn. Avocations: singing, studying wildlife, gardening. Office: Heritage Elem 440 Parr Rd Woodburn OR 97071

ANDERSON, KATHRYN M., history educator; BMus, Marietta Coll., Ohio, 1997; MEd, Ohio State U., Columbus, 1999. Lic. tchr. grades 1-8 State of Ohio Dept. Edn., 1997. 5th grade tchr. Dublin (Ohio) City Sch, 1999—2002; history tchr. Wiley Mid. Sch., University Heights, Ohio, 2003—06. Social studies dist. task force CH-UH Sch., University Heights, 2003—06. Women's History Projectn grant, Reaching Heights, 2005—06.

ANDERSON, KATHRYN PARKS, music educator; b. Trenton, Mo., Nov. 30, 1951; d. Carroll Lloyd and Viva Jean (Landes) Parks; m. Leander Albert Anderson, May 31, 1977; children: Lindsay Anderson Guerriere, Kirsten Joy. MusEdB in applied organ, Ctrl. Mo. State U., Warrensburg, 1972, MusM in applied organ, 1974. Cert. Mo. Life Tchg. Cert., Conn. Standard Tchg. Cert. Vocal, instrumental music tchr. Plainville Pub. Schs., Plainville, Conn., 1978—80; dir. music, organist Grace Bapt. Ch., Bristol, Conn., 1977—87; vocal, instrumental music tchr. Archdiocese of Hartford, Sacred Heart Sch., New Britain, Conn., 1986—2001; dir. music, organist Mill Plain Union Ch., Waterbury, Conn., 1987—92, First Bapt. Ch., Meriden, Conn., 1992—2001, Ch. of St. Mary, Newington, Conn., 2001—. Music cons. small Christian cmtys. Archdiocese of Hartford, Bloomfield, Conn., 2003—. Recorded choral and handbell music: various CD's. Mem.: Am. Guild of English Handbell Ringers, Nat. Assn. of Pastoral Musicians, Am. Guild of Organists (registrar Greater Hartford Conn. chpt. 1984—87), Phi Kappa Phi, Pi Kappa Lambda Honor Music Fraternity. Avocations: walking, fitness training, poetry. Home: 112 Butternut Ln Bristol CT 06010-8049 Office: Ch of St Mary 626 Willard Ave Newington CT 06111 Office Phone: 860-666-1858, 860-666-1591. Office Fax: 860-666-5720. E-mail: kathrynparksanderson@hotmail.com.

ANDERSON, KERRII B., food service executive; b. 1957; BS, Elon Coll., 1978; MBA, Duke U., 1987. CPA. With Peat, Marwick, Mitchell & Co., Greensboro, NC, 1978-84, RJ Reynolds Corp., Winston-Salem, NC, 1984-85, Key Co., Greensboro, NC, 1985-87; sec. M/I Schottenstein Homes Inc., Columbus, 1987—94, sr. v.p., CFO, chmn. bd., 1987—2000, asst. sec., 1994—2000; exec. v.p., CFO Wendy's Internat. Inc., Dublin, Ohio, 2000—, interim CEO, 2006—. Bd. dirs. The Lancaster Colony Corp., M/I Schottenstein Homes, Inc., Wendy's Internat. Inc. Mem. fin. com. The Columbus Found.; bd. mem. Grant-Riverside Hosp.; mem. dean's adv. com. Fisher Coll. Bus., Ohio State U. Office: Wendys Internat Inc One Dave Thomas Blvd Dublin OH 43017 also: 4288 W Dublin-Granville Rd Dublin OH 43017-0256*

ANDERSON, KRISTIE, construction company executive; b. Ringgold, Georgia, May 18, 1977; d. James Morris and Deborah Sue A. Student, Dalton State Coll. Sec., office mgr. Anderson Construction & Home Bldg., Rossville, Georgia, 1993-99; owner Kristie M. Anderson Home Bldg., Rossville, 1995—. Mem. Home Builder Assn. Republican. Avocations: art, reading. Home: 237 Meadowview Ln Ringgold GA 30736-2657 Office: Kristie Anderson Home Building 1355 Mack Smith Rd Rossville GA 30741-3749

ANDERSON, LASHAWN ECLEASHA, rehabilitation technician; b. Bklyn., Nov. 20, 1980; d. Louis and Ruth Emma Anderson; 1 child, Saniah. Pre-nursing cert., Trident Tech. Coll., 2002, AS, 2003. Cert. CPR; lic. CNA. Vol. Trident Med. Ctr., Charleston, SC, 2000—01; mem. support staff S.C. Sports Medicine, Charleston, 2000—04; CNA LifeCare Ctr. of Charleston, Charleston, 2001—05, rehab. technician, 2004—. Cons. Mary Kay, Suwanee, Ga., 2004—. Contbr. poetry to anthologies. Sec. Shammah Ministry, St. George, SC, 2004. Mem.: HERO (sec. 1997—98), Appian Am. Soc. Pentecostal. Avocations: poetry, reading, acting, modeling. Home: PO Box 1109 Holly Hill SC 29059

ANDERSON, LAURIE MONNES, state senator; b. Coronado, Calif., Dec. 31, 1945; 2 children. BA, Willamette U., 1968; MA, U. Colo., 1972; BSN, Radford U., 1982. Rsch. biologist, 1972—78; pub. health nurse, 1982—2000; state rep. Oreg., 2001—05. Sch. bd. Gresham-Barlow Sch. Dist., 1991—2001. Mem.: Oreg. Sch. Bd. Assn. (dir. 1996—). Democrat. Office: 900 Court St North East S 310 Salem OR 97301

ANDERSON, LEA E., lawyer; b. Clarksburg, W.Va., May 25, 1954; d. Jackson Lawler and Barbara Jean (Sanford) A.; m. Templeton Smith Jr., Aug. 2, 1980; children: Templeton Smith III, Suzanne Lea Smith. BA magna cum laude, W.Va. U., 1976, JD, 1979. Bar: W.Va. 1979, U.S. Dist. Ct. (so. dist.) W.Va. 1979, Pa. 1981, U.S. Supreme Ct. 1982. Assoc. Bowles, McDavid, Graff & Love, Charleston, W.Va., 1979-80, Goehring, Rutter & Boehm, Pitts., 1980-84, ptnr., 1984-89, mem., 1990—, sec., shareholder, 1993—. Mem. credit com. Alcobar Fed. Credit Union, 1985-87, mem. supervisory com., 1981; mem. vis. com. W.Va. Coll. Law, 1986-89, mem. W.Va. U. student affairs vis. com., 1996-99, chmn.; course planner and spkr. Estate Planning for Subsequent Marriages, 2002; spkr. Estate Planning in Divorce and Remarriage in Pa., 2001. Vol. March of Dimes, 1986, neighborhood coord., 1987-91; chmn. fundraising com. Southminster Nursery Sch., 1989; chmn. Windy Ridge, 1991-93; mem. Performing Arts for Children, South, 1991-94, v.p., membership com. 1993-94; mem. bd. deacons Southminster Presbyn. Ch., Mt. Lebanon, Pa., 1990-93, vice chmn. bd. deacons, 1993, session mem., elder, trustee, 1993-97, 2001—, v.p. trustees, 2002—, assoc. min. search com., 1997, dir. Christian edn. search com., 2002—; active Foster Sch. PTA, 1993-97, chmn. Univ. W. Va. Vis. Com. Mem. W.Va. Bar Assn., Pa. Bar Assn., Allegheny County Bar Assn. (chmn. edn. com. of young lawyers 1983-84, treas. 1984-85, mem. rules com. family law sect. 1993-94), Child Study Club of Mt. Lebanon (pres. 1989-91), Mt. Lebanon Aqua Club (treas. 1996-98, nominating com. 1997, 98, sec. 1999-2001), Phi Beta Kappa, Phi Kappa Phi, Phi Delta Phi. Republican. Office: Goehring Rutter & Boehm 1424 Frick Bldg 437 Grant St Ste 437 Pittsburgh PA 15219-6002 Office Fax: 412-281-2971. E-mail: landerson@grblaw.com.

ANDERSON, LESLIE ANN, secondary educator; b. Tulsa, Nov. 15, 1963; d. R. Doyle and Sylvia Ann (Flippin) P. BS, Okla. State U., 1986, MS, 1990. Cert. tchr. secondary bus. edn. Secondary and adult instr. Indian Meridian AVTS, Stillwater, Okla., 1988-94; profl. sec. instr. N.E. Tex. C.C., Mt. Pleasant, Tex., 1994—2002; assoc. faculty Collin County C.C. Dist., Plano, Tex., 2004—. Home: 1359 Hayward Dr Rockwall TX 75087-6615

ANDERSON, LESLIE J., lawyer; b. 1953; BA in English Lit. magna cum laude, Allegheny Coll., 1975; MA in English and Comparative Lit., Columbia Univ., 1976, MPhil, 1979; JD cum laude, Univ. Mich., 1983. Bar: Minn. 1983. Assoc. Dorsey & Whitney LLP, Mpls, 1984—91; ptnr., litig. group Dorsey & Whitney, Mpls., 1991, now ptnr., co-chair, employee benefits group. Staff mem. Mich.Yearbook of Internat. Legal Studies, 1981—82, editor-in-chief, 1982—83. Bd. dir. Greater Twin Cities Youth Symphonies, 2003—. Mem.: Minn. Women Lawyers, Minn. Advocates for Human Rights, Phi Beta Kappa. Office: Dorsey & Whitney LLP Ste 1500 50 S Sixth St Minneapolis MN 55402-1498 Office Phone: 612-343-7960. Office Fax: 612-340-2868. Business E-Mail: anderson.leslie@dorsey.com.

ANDERSON, LINDA JEAN, critical care nurse, psychiatric nurse practitioner; b. Louisville, Ky., Mar. 28, 1956; d. James Phillip and Ellabelle Jean (Crowder) Anderson; children: Bradley, Vanessa, Frances, Joseph; m. Donald W. Goodman. BSN, U. Louisville, 1989, MSN, 2000; postgrad. in health care adminstrn., Kennedy Western U., 2005—. ARNP, Ky., Ind. Staff nurse Audubon Regional Med. Ctr., Louisville, 1989-90; nurse clinician Vis. Nurses Assn. Louisville, 1990-95; staff nurse Southwest Hosp., Louisville, 1990-2000; rsch. coord. electrophysiology-cardiology U. Louisville, 1993-94; staff nurse Ctr. for Behavioral Health Bapt. East Hosp., 1996-2000; psychiat. clin. coord. U. Louisville Healthcare Univ. Hosp., 2000—02; pvt. practice Park View Psychiat. Svc., Jeffersonville, Ind., 2002—05, N.A. Saddiqui & Assocs., Louisville, 2005—, Frager Assocs., Louisville, 2005—. Mem. alumni bd. govs. U. Louisville Sch. Nursing, 1988-97. Mem. ANA, Internat. Soc. Psychiatric Nursing, Kentuckiann Coun. Psychiatric Nursing, Am. Psychiat. Nurses Assn., Sigma Theta Tau. Avocations: watercolor painting, charcoal & pencil sketching, poetry, flute. Office Phone: 502-394-0402.

ANDERSON, LISA, dean, political science professor, researcher; BA, Sarah Lawrence Coll.; MA in Law and Diplomacy, Tufts U.; PhD in Polit. Sci., Columbia U., certificate in Middle East Studies; LLD (hon.), Monmouth U., 2002. Asst. prof. govt. and social sci. Harvard U.; prof. Middle Eastern and North African studies Columbia U., NYC, 1986, dir. Middle East Inst., 1990—93, chair Polit. Sci. Dept., 1993—97, dean Sch. of Internat. and Pub. Affairs, 1997—, James T. Shotwell prof. internat. rels. Chair bd. dirs. Social Sci. Rsch. Coun.; bd. mem. Carnegie Coun. on Ethics in Internat. Affairs; mem. Coun. Fgn. Rels.; bd. mem. emeritus Human Rights Watch. Author: The State and Social Transformation in Tunisia and Libya, 1830-1980, 1986, Pursuing Truth, Exercising Power: Social Science and Public Policy in the Twenty-First Century, 2003; co-editor: The Origins of Arab Nationalism, 1991; editor: Transitions to Democracy, 1999; contbr. articles to profl. jours. Mem.: Am. Polit. Sci. Assn. (coun. mem. 2004—06), Middle East Studies Assn. (past pres.). Office: Columbia U Sch Internat & Pub Affairs Dean's Office 1414 Internat Affairs Bldg, MC 3328 New York NY 10027 Office Phone: 212-854-4604. Office Fax: 212-864-4847. E-mail: la8@columbia.edu.*

ANDERSON, LISA D., graphics designer, educator; d. Robert Boston Wilson and Fanny Ruth Dickey. Degree in Mech. Drafting, Mid-Florida Tech. Inst., 1982, Degree in Tech. Illustration, 1983; B in Graphic Design, U. Ctrl. Fla., 1986; MS in Edn., Nova Southeastern U., 1998; PhD, U. South Fla., 2000. Cert. web page design U. South Fla., 2003, web devel. U. South Fla., 2002, Train The Trainer Dvd Sonic, 2002. Mktg. graphic designer east coast Hansen Lind Meyer, Orlando; sr. graphic designer Harris Corp., Orlando, 1991—93; sr. illustrator Westinghouse, Orlando, 1992—95; sr. imager CGS, Tampa, 1995—98; chair advt. and computer graphics IADT, Tampa, 1998—2000, chair graphic design, 1998—2005, pres. interactive group, 2004—. Presenter, rschr. and cons. in field. Named Media Arts Employee Of The Yr., IADT, 2001; recipient Outstanding Contributions To Academic Excellence award, 2003. Mem.: ASCD (assoc.), Soc. For Instrnl. Tech. in Ed. and Tchr. Tng. (assoc.), Internat. Digital Media Assn. (assoc.), Am. Assn. for Computers in Edn. (assoc.), Easter Ednl. Rsch. Assn. (assoc.). Office: Ednl Interactive Group 31739 Hedgerow Dr Zephyrhills FL 33543

ANDERSON, LOUISE A., public health service officer; b. Aug. 24, 1948; d. Ambrose E. and Marie B. (Schroeder) Beckman; children: Christopher, Dawn. BSN, Ind. State U., 1970; MSN, Ind. U., 1988. RN, Ind. Staff nurse St. Joseph Hosp., Huntingburg, Ind., 1970-72; head nurse, charge, staff Union Hosp., Terre Haute, Ind., 1972-85; clin. instr. Ind. State U., Terre Haute, Ind., 1984-85, acting dir., 1985-86; dir. nursing Vigo County Health Dept., Terre Haute, Ind., 1988—; cons. Inst. State Dept. Health Indpls., 1989—. Hospice vol. nurse Hospice of the Wabash Valley, Terre Haute, 1980-83; fitness camp nurse YWCA, Terre Haute, 1979; exec. bd. mem. Am. Public Health Assn. (chair. com. on affiliates). Bd. edn. St. Patrick Ch. and Sch., Terre Haute, 1988-94; bd. dirs. Leadership Terre Haute, 1988-94, LWV, Terre Haute, 1995—; com. mem. Ind. LWV, Indpls., 1996—. Recipient Bd. Dirs. award Leadership Terre Haute; named Outstanding Alumni Ind. State U. Sch. Nursing, Star nominee Ind. State Dept. Health, 1996. Fellow Ill. Pub. Health Leadership Inst. (mentor 1996-97); mem. APHA, Am. Nurses Assn. (sec. 1982—, Ind. State Nurses Assn. (sec. 1982—), West Ctrl. Chpt. Environ. Health Assn. (Mem. of Yr., bd. mem., treas. 1996—), Ind. Pub. Health Assn., Assn. State & Territorial Dirs. Nursing (treas. exec. com. 1995—). Avocations: photography, writing. Office: Vigo County Health Dept 147 Oak St Terre Haute IN 47807

ANDERSON, M. JEAN, lawyer; b. Casper, Wyo., Sept. 27, 1943; Certificat, Universite de Paris, France, 1964; BA, Northwestern Univ., 1965; JD, Georgetown Univ., 1975. Bar: DC 1975, US Dist. Ct., DC 1976, US Ct. Appeals (DC cir. 1976, Fed. cir. 1995), US Ct. Internat. Trade 1987. Sr. trade adv. & spl. counsel to undersecretary for internat. trade U.S. Dept. Commerce, 1982—86, chief counsel internat. trade, 1986—88; ptnr, head internat. trade practice group Weil Gotshal & Manges LLP, Washington, 1989—. Adj. prof. Washington Coll. Law, Am. Univ., 1982—86, Georgetown Univ. Law Ctr., 1989—92. Editor (exec.): Georgetown Univ. Law Rev. Mem.: ABA (council mem. internat. law sect. 1995—, chair internat. trade com. 1992—93), DC Bar (chmn. internat. law sect. 1985—86). Office: Weilgotshallmanges 1300 I St NW Frnt 1 Washington DC 20005-3343 Office Phone: 202-682-7217. Office Fax: 202-857-0940. Business E-Mail: jean.anderson@weil.com.

ANDERSON, MARCIE, communications executive; BS in Bus. Mgmt., Bellevue Univ. Broadband installer Nortel Comm.; divsn. team leader Cox Comm., Ariz., project mgr., residential telephone svc. Atlanta, dir. data ops., v.p., bus. devel., 2002—. Fields instr. tech. U.S. Army, 1991. Mem.: Soc. Cable Telecom. Engrs. (Women in Tech. award 2003), Women in Cable TV. Office: Cox Comm 1400 Lake Hearn Dr Atlanta GA 30319*

ANDERSON, MARGARET ELLEN (MARGARET ELLEN ANDERSON), physiologist, educator; b. Omaha, June 17, 1941; d. Clarence Lloyd and Anita Emma (Kruse) A. BA, Augustana Coll., Sioux Falls, S.D., 1963; PhD, Stanford U., 1967. NIH postdoctoral fellow Harvard U., 1968—70; rsch. assoc. Lab. Neurobiology, U. P.R., 1970—71; vis. asst. prof. Clark U., 1972; asst. prof. Bennington (Vt.) Coll., 1973, Smith Coll., Northampton, Mass., 1973—79, assoc. prof. dept. biol. scis., 1979—85, prof., 1985—, dean sr. class, 1993—96, acting dir. Office Grad Study, 1997—98. Mem. Bingham award selection com. Transylvania U., Lexington, Ky., 1987-94, 97-98. Assoc. editor Advances in Physiology Edn., 1988-92; contbr. articles to sci. jours., including Tissue and Cell, Jour. Gen. Physiology. NSF predoctoral fellow Stanford U., 1967; rsch. grantee NIH, 1974-86, NSF, 1989-90. Mem. Am. Physiol. Soc., Soc. for Neurosci., Soc. Gen. Physiologists, Biophys. Soc. Office: Smith Coll Dept Biol Sci Northampton MA 01063-0001 Business E-Mail: manderso@smith.edu.

ANDERSON, MARGARET SUZANNE, elementary school educator, nurse; b. Belleville, Ill., Oct. 2, 1954; d. David Lloyd and Jimmie Aline Dillard; m. Ronald Nelson Anderson, Mar. 3, 1973; 1 child, Christopher; 1 child, Amy. ADN, Dalton Jr. Coll., Dalton, Ga., 1975; BS in Elem. Edn., Jacksonville State U., Jacksonville, Ala., 1986; MA in Elem. Edn., U. Ala., Gadsen, Ala., 1989. RN Ga., Ala. RN newborn nursery Hutcheson Meml., Ft. Oglethorpe, Ga., 1975—76; RN Sandmont Nursing Home, Trenton, Ga., 1976—77; RN post operative Bapt. Med. Dekalb, Ft. Payne, Ala., 1978—84; tchr. 6th grade Dekalb County Bd. Edn., Inder, Ala., 1986—. Avocations: travel, photography, reading, scrapbooks.

ANDERSON, MARION LEBLANC, history educator; b. Plaquemine, La., Dec. 2, 1949; d. Joseph LeBlanc, Jr. and Josephine Marion LeBlanc; 1 foster child, Marquis LeBlanc 1 child, DeShawn Renee. B Secondary Edn. History, So. U. and A&M Colls., Baton Rouge, 1973; M History, No. Ill. U., DeKalb, 1975. Tchr. History Dixon Pub. Schs., Ill., 1976—. Sec. Open Sesame Child Care, Dixon. Fellow, James Madison Found., 1995. Mem.: Ill. Edn. Assn. Region 20 (vice chair 2000), Dixon Edn. Assn. Home: 515 Madison Avenue Dixon IL 61021

ANDERSON, MARJO ELIZABETH, minister; b. Keyser, W.Va., Apr. 4, 1954; d. Donald David and Lorna Jo (Douglass) A.; m. Mark Roland Dollhopf, Aug. 14, 1977; children: Johann Roland Anderson-Dollhopf, Conrad Somers Anderson-Dollhopf. B of Music Edn., Wittenberg U., 1976; MDiv, Yale U., 1980. Ordained to ministry Luth. Ch. in Am., 1983. Dir. music St. James Luth. Ch., Southbury, Conn., 1977-80; pastoral assoc. St. Paul's Evang. Luth. Ch., Bridgeport, Conn., 1980-82; adminstrv. asst. Inst. Sacred Music Yale U., New Haven, 1983; asst. pastor Emmanuel Luth. Ch., Norwood, Mass., 1983-86; pastor St. John's Evang. Luth. Ch., New Britain, Conn., 1986-92. Mem. Bd. for Congregational Life, New Eng. Synod, Worcester, Mass., 1988—. Mem. New Eng. Synod Coun. Evang. Luth. Ch. in Am., 1988—; co-pastor Tabor Luth. Ch., Branford, 1993—. Democrat. Avocations: running, weightlifting, piano, organ, voice. Home: 507 Whitney Ave New Haven CT 06511-2306 Office: 45 Tabor Dr Branford CT 06405

ANDERSON, MARTHA JEAN, retired media specialist; b. Greenville, S.C., May 15, 1946; d. Benjamin Mason and Gladys (Harling) Anderson; m. Leroy A. Hamilton Sr., July 3, 2001 (div. Nov. 4, 2004). BS, Appalachian State U., Boone, N.C., 1968; M.Librarianship, Emory U., Atlanta, 1974, Diploma Advanced Study Librarianship, 1983. Libr. Arlington Schs., Atlanta, 1968-70, Archer Public High Sch., Atlanta, 1970-74; media specialist Woodmont High Sch. Greenville County Sch. Dist., Piedmont, S.C., 1974-76, media specialist Berea High Sch. Greenville, S.C., 1976-80, media specialist Hillcrest High Sch. Simpsonville, SC, 1980—2006. Chmn. Relay for Life in the Golden Strip Am. Cancer Soc., 2001, 2002, co-chmn., 2004, 2005. Recipient Citation award S.C. Occupational Info. Coord. Com., 1988. Mem. S.C. Assn. Sch. Librs., Reidville (S.C.) Hist. Soc. (charter mem., historian, pres. 2002-05), Rotary, Iota Alpha Delta Kappa (historian 1978-80, 88-90, 92-94, v.p. 1980-82, pres. 1982-84, 94-96, sgt.-at-arms 1990-92, chaplain 1998-2000) Methodist. Avocations: reading, gardening, needlecrafts. Office: Hillcrest High Sch 3665 S Industrial Dr Simpsonville SC 29681-3299 Office Phone: 842-355-3522.

ANDERSON, MARY ANN GRASSO, theater association executive; b. Rome, NY, Nov. 3, 1952; d. Vincent and Rose Mary (Pupa) Grasso; m. J. Wayne Anderson, Feb. 14, 2004. BA in Art History, U. Calif., Riverside, 1973; MLS, U. Oreg., 1974. Dir. Warner Rsch. Collection, Burbank, Calif., 1975-84; mgr. CBS TV/Docudrama, Hollywood, Calif., 1984-88; v.p., exec. dir. Nat. Assn. Theatre Owners, North Hollywood, Calif., 1988—. Instr. theatre arts UCLA, 1980-85, Am. Film Inst., L.A., 1985-88. Screen credits: The Scarlet O'Hara Wars, This Year's Blonde, The Silent Lovers, A Bunnies Tale, Embassy. Apptd. commr. Burbank Heritage Commn. Recipient Friend award, Tripod Sch., 1999, Stace award, Dolby, 2002, Intersoc. Ken Mason award, 2004. Mem.: Found. of the Motion Picture Pioneers, Acad. Motion Picture Arts and Scis., Retinitis Pigmentosa Internat. (The Vision award 1996), Bus. and Profl. Women's Assn. (Woman of Achievement award 1983), Phi Beta Kappa. Avocations: music, dance. Office: Nat Assn Theatre Owners 750 1st St NE Ste 1130 Washington DC 20002 Office Phone: 202-962-0054.

ANDERSON, MARY JANE, library director, consultant; b. Des Moines, Jan. 23, 1935; d. William Kenneth and Margaret Louise (Snider) McPherson; m. Charles Robert Anderson, Oct. 21, 1965 (div. Oct. 24, 1989); 1 child, Mary Margaret. BA in Edn., U. Fla., 1957; MLS, Fla. State U., 1963. Elem. sch. librarian Dade County Schs., Miami, Fla., 1957-61; children's/young adult librarian Santa Fe Regional Library, Gainesville, Fla., 1961-63; br. librarian Jacksonville (Fla.) Pub. Library, 1963-64, chief of children's services, 1964-66, head of circulation, 1966-67; pub. library cons. Fla. State Library, Tallahassee, 1967-70; dir. tech. processing St. Mary's Coll. of Md., St. Mary's City, 1970-72; coordinator children's services Balt. County Pub. Library, Towson, Md., 1972-73; exec. dir. young adult services div. ALA, Chgo., 1973-75, exec. dir. assn. for library service to children, 1973-82; pres. Answers Unltd., Inc., Deerfield, Ill., 1982-92; dir. Wilmington (Ill.) Pub. Libr., 1993-97; dir. media svcs. Newark (Ill.) County Sch. Dist., 1997-98; dir. Maud P. Palenske Pub. Libr., St. Joseph, Mich., 1998-2000; coord. Sr. Net Learning Ctr., Ariea IV Agy. Aging, St. Joseph, 2000—03; libr. cons., 2000—. Instr. and cons. in field; part-time faculty No. Ill. U., 1985-86, Nat. Coll. Edn., Evanston, Ill., 1989; head youth svcs. Waukegan (Ill.) Pub. Libr., 1988-93; mem. exec. com. U.S. sect. Internat. Bd. on Books for Young People, 1973-82; mem. adv. bd. Reading Rainbow, TV series, 1981-84; mem. sch. bd. Avoca Sch. Dist. 37, 1985-87; mem. ALSC Newbery Medal Com., 1991. Editor: Top of the News, 1971-73, Fla. State Library Newsletter, 1967-70, Nor'Easter (North Suburban Library System Newsletter), 1984-88; contbr. articles to profl. jours. Bd. dirs. Child Devel. Assocs. Consortium, 1975—83, Coalition for Children and Youth, 1978—80; downtown redevel. commn. City of Wilmington, 1996—98; coun. mem. Episcopal Diocese Chgo. Diocese, 1988—94, standing com., 1994—97, dep. to gen. conv., 1997, Bishop's search com., 1997—98, province V rep., 1998—99; mem. vestry St. Thomas' Episcopal Ch., Morris, Ill., 1996—98; active Episcopal Diocese West, Mich., Diocesan cons. team, 1999—, alt. dep. to gen. conv., 2003; deanery rep. St. Paul's Episc. Ch., St. Joseph, Mich., 2000—01, lay eucharistic min., 1999—, mem. vestry, 2003—05. Mem. ALA (coun. 1992-2000, com. on orgn. 1999-01), Rotary (sec.-treas. 1994-96, pres. 1996-97), Wilmington C. of C. (bd. dirs. 1996-97, sec. 1997), Caxton Club (Chgo.), Beta Phi Mu, Sigma Kappa. Episcopalian. E-mail: mjanderson@mich.com.

ANDERSON, MARY JANE, music educator; b. St. Louis, Oct. 9, 1954; d. William Edward and Katherine Ruth Anderson. Student, The Juilliard Sch., 1967—72; BFA Piano Performance, Stephens Coll., 1976; MusM Piano Performance, So. Ill. U., Edwardsville, 1991. Mem. piano faculty St. Louis Conservatory and Schs. for Arts, St. Louis, 1977—81, So. Ill. U., Edwardsville, 1984—; pvt. piano instr. St. Louis, 1975—. Adjudicator state and local piano competitions, Mo. and Ill.; soloist St. Louis Symphony, St. Louis Philharmonic; recitalist, orchestral soloist numerous performances throughout Midwest U.S., Pa, N.Y. Recipient 1st pl. Profl. Debut Recital, Artist Presentation Soc., 1975, 1st pl. Dimitri Mitropoulos Nat. Piano Competition, Stephens Coll., 1972; scholar, Dimitri Mitropoulos Piano Competition; Piano scholar, Am. Acad. Arts in Europe, 1975. Mem.: St. Louis Area Music Tchrs. Assn. (pres. 2002—06), Mo. Music Tchrs. Assn., Music Tchrs. Nat. Assn. Avocations: reading, fishing, crossword puzzles. Office: So Ill U Edwardsville Music Dept PO Box 1771 Edwardsville IL 62026-1771 Office Phone: 618-650-2022. Business E-Mail: manders@siue.edu.

ANDERSON, MELISSA ANN, science educator; b. Spearman, Tex., Oct. 2, 1972; d. Dallas Edward and Patsy Ann Haner; m. James Francis Anderson, July 15, 1995; children: Dallas, Jameson. BS in Biology, Pitts. State U., Kans., 1996; MS in Biology, West Tex. A&M U., Canyon, 2000. Instr. biology Amarillo (Tex.) Coll., 2000—. Author: (letter to the editor section) Amarillo Globe News, 2006—. Named Outstanding Young Ch. Woman, Christian Women United, 2002. Independent. Avocations: volleyball, pottery, scrapbooks, jewelry making, sprint triathlons. Business E-Mail: andersonma@actx.edu.

ANDERSON, MICHELLE J., dean, law educator; m. Gavin P. McCormick, Apr. 2006. BA with honors, U. Calif., Santa Cruz, 1989; JD, Yale U., 1994; LLM, Georgetown U., 1997. Bar: Calif. 1995. Law clerk to Hon. William A. Norris US Ct. of Appeals (9th cir.), 1994—95; supervising atty. Appellate Litig. Clinic Georgetown U. Law Ctr., 1995—97, vis. assoc. prof. Inst. for Pub. Representation, 1997; prof. Villanova U. Sch. Law, 1998—2006; dean CUNY Sch. Law, Flushing, NY, 2006—. Vis. prof. U. Pitts. Sch. Law, 2004; disting. scholar St. John's U. Sch. Law, 2005. Contbr. articles to law jours. Mem.: ABA, Soc. Am. Law Tchrs., Women in Transition, Pa. Coalition against Sexual Assault (bd. dirs.), Nat. Alliance to End Sexual Violence (bd. dirs., policy chair). Office: CUNY Law Sch 65-21 Main St Flushing NY 11367 Office Phone: 718-340-4370. E-mail: academicdeanoffice@mail.law.cuny.edu.

ANDERSON, MO, real estate company executive; m. Richard Anderson; 2 children. BS, U. Okla. Dist. v.p. Merrill Lynch Realty Nat., Okla. City; prin., owner office Century 21, Edmond, Okla., 1975; from owner and regional dir. Okla. Region to pres., CEO Keller Williams Realty Internat., Austin, Tex., 1992—95, pres., 1995—, CEO, 1995—. Avocation: piano. Office: Keller Williams Realty Inc 807 Las Cimas Pkwy Ste 200 Austin TX 78746

ANDERSON, MONICA LUFFMAN, school librarian, educator, real estate broker; b. Ramsgate, Kent, U.K., Sept. 28, 1914; arrived in U.S., 1952; d. Percy Victor Luffman and Rosalind Dismorr; m. Howard Richmond Anderson, Dec. 22, 1951 (dec.); children: Monica Jane, James Stewart. BA in English with honors, London U., 1936; MS in Libr. Sci., Simmons Coll., 1968; EdM in Ednl. Media, Boston U., 1970. Evacuation officer London Borough of Acton, 1940—41; dir. Coun. for Edn. in World Citizenship, London, 1941—47; from asst. to head of sect. with diplomatic status UNESCO, Paris, 1947—50; H.S. libr. Holliston, Mass., 1968—70; coord. libr. svcs. Lincoln-Sudbury (Mass.) Regional H.S., 1970—81; real estate broker Coldwell Banker Residential Brokerage, Wayland, Mass., 1982—. Author brochures. Troop leader Girl Scouts Am., Weston, Mass., 1963—65; tutor in English Laotian Refugees, Weston, Mass., 1981—82, Literacy Unltd., Framingham, Mass., 1998—. Democrat. Avocations: gardening, Boston Annual Walk for Hunger, reading.

ANDERSON, NANCI LOUISE, computer analyst; b. Lynchburg, Va., Sept. 21, 1944; d. Ashby Littleton and Louise Elvin (Kirby) Marsh; 1 child, Toni Lynn Nelson. AAS in Computer Sci., Ctrl. Tex. Coll., 1983, AAS in Microcomputer Tech., 1985, BA Computer Programming, 2001. Real estate salesperson Blake Isley Real Estate, Lynchburg, Va., 1974; sec. U.S. Army, Germany, 1975-80; office mgr. Am. Solar Energy Soc., Killeen, Tex., 1981-82; programmer BDM, West Fort Hood, Tex., 1982-87; analyst, programmer PRC, Inc., West Fort Hood, Tex., 1987—96; sys. mgr. Maden Tech Consulting, 1996—. Mem. Clipper User's Group. Avocations: reading, swimming, horseback riding, walking. Office: Maden Tech Cons USA OTC Network Ops Ctr Fort Hood TX 76544

ANDERSON, NANCY ODEGARD, medical/surgical nurse; b. Great Falls, Mont., Apr. 29, 1956; d. Hilton Emil and Delores Alvina (Guidice) Odegard; children: Jeremy, Scott. Student, Coll. of Great Falls, Mont., 1987; AS, No. Mont. Coll., 1988. Float nurse No. Mont. Hosp., Havre, Mont.; nurse Mont. Deaconess Med. Ctr., Great Falls, clin. nurse I med./surg. unit; clinic office nurse on call Spectrum Emergency Care, Inc., Malmstrom AFB, Mont.

ANDERSON, NORA, nurse; b. Oneida, N.Y., Mar. 28, 1949; d. George Henry and Agnes Mary (Kendrick) Wagner; m. John E. Pich, Oct. 31, 1970 (div. Nov. 1991); children: Thomas, John, Judith; m. G. Michael Anderson, Dec. 18, 1991. AAS in Nursing, Mohawk Valley C.C., 1992; BS, Utica Coll. Syracuse U., 1999. RN. Nurse N.Y. State Office Mental Health, Marcy, Utica, N.Y. Recipient 1st Pl. sculpture award Rome Art Assn.,1997, N.Y. State Fair, 1998, Utica Art Assn., 1997, 98, Di Spirito award for excellence in art. Mem. ANA (cert. mental health psychiat. nursing). Home: 313 Expense St Rome NY 13440-4030

ANDERSON, NORMA V., retired state legislator; b. Elyria, Ohio, July 6, 1932; Student, Denver U., Jones Real Estate Coll. Owner, operator KBJ Stables; office mgr. Capitol Solar; supr. Time, Inc.; mem. Colo. Ho. of Reps., Dist. 30, 1986-98, Fin. & State Affairs Coms., Legis. Coun., Colo. Senate, Dist. 22, Denver, 1998—2006, Judiciary, Appropriations Coms., Legis. Coun., State Compensation Bd., Colo. Uninsurable Health Ins. Bd.; majority leader, chair Legis. Audit, Edn., Trans. & Energy Coms.; vice-chair Health, Environ., Welfare & Inst. Com., Legis. Audit Com., Judiciary Com., Assembly on Fed. Issues; chair Minority Caucus, Bus. Affairs & Labor Com.; mem. labor dept. State Adv. Coun.; exec. com., chair Energy & Trans.; co-chair Social Security Task Force, DC. Mem. state adv. coun. labor dept.; bd. dir. state compensation, regional transp. dist., Foothills Found.; mem. West Chamber; mem. numerious senate coms. including most recently jud. com., appropriations com. Vice-chair Health Environ. Welfare Insts.; bd. dirs. Foothills Found.; mem. budget com. R-1 Sch. Dist; exec. com. Nat. Conf. State Legis.; vice-chair Arapahow House; adv. bd. Drug Control Systems Improvement, Com. Corrections; mem. Am. Cancer Soc., Bear Creek Jr. Sports Assn., Great Outdoors Colo. Republican. Office: State Capitol 200 E Colfax Ave Ste 274 Denver CO 80203-1716 Office Phone: 303-866-4859. E-mail: norma.anderson.senate@state.co.us.

ANDERSON, PAMELA DENISE, actress; b. Ladysmith, BC, Can., July 1, 1967; d. Barry and Carol Anderson; m. Tommy Lee, Feb. 19, 1995 (div. Feb. 28, 1998); children: Brandon Thomas Lee, Dylan Jagger Lee; m. Robert James "Kid Rock" Ritchie, July 29, 2006. Syndicated columnist Jane, 2002—, Marie Claire, 2002—, Can. Elle, 2002—; launched clothing line "The Pamela Collection", 2003—. Actor: (TV series) Home Improvement, 1991—93, Baywatch, 1992—97; actor, exec. prodr.: (TV series) V.I.P., 1998; actor(voice): Stripperella, 2003, Stacked, 2005—; (TV films) Baywatch: River of No Return, 1992, Come Die with Me: A Mickey Spillane Mike Hammer Mystery, 1994, Baywatch: Forbidden Paradise, 1995, Naked Souls, 1996, Baywatch: Hawaiian Wedding, 2003, (guest appearances): (TV series) Charles in Charge, 1990, Married.with Children, 1990, 1991, Top of the Heap, 1991, Days of Our Lives, 1992, The Nanny, 1997, Home Improvement, 1997, Just Shoot Me, 2001, Less Than Perfect, 2002, (guest appearances, voice) Futurama, 1999,: (films) Snapdragon, 1993, Raw Justice, 1994, Naked Souls, 1995, Barb Wire, 1996, Scary Movie 3, 2003, Borat, 2006, (music videos for) Aerosmith, Lit, Cinderella, Vince Neil, Bree Sharp, Methods of Mayhem, Jaz-Z, Kid Rock; author: (novels) Star, 2004. Activist PETA; participant Nat. Conf. Viral Hepatitis, Can. Liver Found.; founder Pamela Anderson Found.; grand marshall S.O.S. ride Am. Liver Found., 2002. Recipient Linda McCartney award for animal rights, 1999. Achievements include has appeared a record twelve times on the cover of Playboy. Office: William Morris Agy 151 El Camino Dr Beverly Hills CA 90212*

ANDERSON, PAMELA SUSAN, sports official, educator; d. Robert Lawrence Anderson and Barbara Lee Udstuen. BS cum laude, Mid. Tenn. State U., Murfreesboro, 1998; MS, Austin Peay State U., Clarksville, Tenn., 1999; PhD, Mid. Tenn. State U., Murfreesboro, 2006. Cardiopulmonary resuscitation ARC; volleyball ofcl. Nat. Collegiate Athletic Assn., coaching accreditation Program I and II U.S. Volleyball Assn., impact trainer U.S. Volleyball Assn. H.s. volleyball ofcl. Tenn. Secondary Sch. Athletic Assn., Nashville, 1994—; volleyball ofcl. PA of Volleyball Ofcls., Oxford, Kans., 1995—2006; exec. dir., head coach Music City Volleyball Club, U.S. Volleyball Assn., Nashville, 1999—2001; asst. prof. U. Tenn., Martin. Adj. instr. Mid. Tenn. State U., Murfreesboro; internat. mission worker Youth with a Mission, Amsterdam, Netherlands. Contbr. poster presentation, presentation. Coord., participant Habitat for Humanity, Nashville, 1992, builder La Paz, Bolivia; rescue worker Clarksville-Montgomery County Rescue Squad, Clarksville, 1997—98; ministry coord. I CARE Ministries, Franklin, Tenn., 1992—93, Missions Internat., Nashville, 1992; bd. dirs. So. Region Volleyball Assn., Birmingham, 1999—2004. Recipient All Am. Scholar award, 1998. Mem.: AAHPERD (assoc.). Office: U Tenn Dept Health and Human Performance 3017 Elan Ctr Martin TN 38238

ANDERSON, PATRICIA KAY, social work educator; b. Breckenridge, Tex., Nov. 29, 1939; d. Donald Raymon Anderson and Flora Estelle (Lane) Townsend. BA, Mary Hardin-Baylor Coll., 1963; MSW, Tulane U., 1967; postgrad., Tex. Woman's U., 1978-80. Lic. social worker, Tex. Caseworker S. Tex. Children's Home, Beeville, 1963-66; social worker Child Guidance Clinic, Ft. Worth, 1967-71; psychiat. social worker Mental Health/Mental Retardation, Sherman, Tex., 1971; chief social worker Lebe Hoch Hosp., Fredericksburg, Tex., 1972; adminstr. Kinsolving Inc., Belton, Tex., 1972-74; prof. U. Mary Hardin-Baylor, Belton, 1974—2005, Ellis prof., 1986. Editor mag. U. Mary Hardin-Baylor News, 1985-95. Mem.: ACSW, NASW, Pi Gamma Mu (chancellor 1984—90, v.p. 1990—96, pres. 1996—2002). Lutheran. Avocations: reading, creative writing. Home: 504 E 26th Ave Belton TX 76513-1616

ANDERSON, PAULETTE ELIZABETH, real estate developer, retired entrepreneur, retired elementary school educator; b. LA, 1942; d. John Paul and Frances Lillian Ross; m. Kenneth Jerome Anderson, Mar. 27, 1997; children: Melody Ann Helland, Edward Michael Helland. D of Ministry, Christian Internat. Grad., Pointe Washington, Fla., 1989—2001; BA Elem. Edn., Calif. State U. LA, Los Angeles, 1970; AA, Pasadena City Coll., Calif., 1960—63; MA in Elem. Edn., Ariz. State U., Tempe, 1975—76; DD, Christian Internat., Pointe Washington, Fla., 1977—88. Standard tchg. credential State of Calif., 1972, cert. standard elem. Ariz., 1977. Certification com. mem. Florence Mid. Sch., Florence, Ariz., 1978—79; advisor Wonderful Wonders, Phoenix, 1993—94; kindergarten & first grade Long Beach Hebrew Acad., Calif., 1969—70; fifth grade self contained Bullhead City Elem. Sch., Ariz., 1971—72; reading tchr. mid. sch. Florence Mid. Sch., Ariz., 1977—81; first grade tchr. Murphy Sch. Dist. -Sullivan, Phoenix, 1985—87; elem. tchr. grades 2, 5, 8 Roosevelt Sch. Dist.-Valley View, Phoenix, 1993—99, ret., 1999—; owner 42 unit apt. complexes. Curriculum guideline's com. mem. Roosevelt Sch. Dist., 1994—98; dist. scheduling com. mem. Rooselvelt Sch. Dist., 1997. Author: (non-fiction) Evidence of Holy Spirit GIven Glossolalia, (children's non-fiction) Polycarp, Martin Luther's Faith and Trust In Jesus. Organizer/pres. Nevitt Neighborhood Assn., Phoenix, 1987—99; organizer VCC Cares for food, 2001—, Rid Neighborhood of Graffiti project, Nevitt; developer Spanish ch. Valley Cmty. Ch., El Monte, Calif., 2004; elected precinct committeeman Rep. Party, Phoenix, 1988—99, chmn. dist. 23, 1994—96; chmn. Christian Coalition, Pasadena, 2000—01; v.p. God Provides Ministry, 2004—. Recipient Cert. of Appreciation, Nat. Rep. Senator Com., 1996, Lincoln Bust Award, Maricopa County Rep. Party, 1993, Vol. of the Yr., Dist. 23, 1998. Republican. Avocations: travel, archaeology. Office Phone: 423-894-6884. Personal E-mail: andersonpaulette@bellsouth.net. Business E-Mail: bebooks@highandliftedup.com.

ANDERSON, PEGGY REES, accountant; b. Casper, Wyo., Sept. 8, 1958; d. John William and Pauline Marie (Harris) Rees; m. Steven R. Anderson, May 26, 1984 (div. Sept. 1990). BS in Acctg. with honors, U. Wyo., 1980. CPA. Audit staff to sr. Price Waterhouse, Denver, 1980-84; asst. contr. to contr. Am. Investments, Denver, 1984-88; cons. ADI Residential, Denver, 1988-89; contr., treas. Plante Properties, Inc., Denver, 1989-92; acctg. mgr. Woodward-Clyde Group, Inc., Denver, 1992-96; internat. fin. mgr. USWest, Inc., Denver, 1996-98, Media One Group, Denver, 1998—2000; internat. fin. cons. Orica Inc., Denver, 2001—02; internat. acctg. coord. Newmont Mining Corp., Denver, 2003—04; assoc. mgr. Great-West Fin. Svcs., Denver, 2004—. Diving scholar U. Wyo., 1976-78. Mem. Colo. Soc. CPAs. Roman Catholic. Avocations: skiing, swimming, aerobics, needlepoint, golf.

ANDERSON, RACHAEL KELLER (RACHAEL KELLER), retired library director; b. NYC, Jan. 15, 1938; d. Harry and Sarah Keller; m. Howard D. Goldwyn; children: Rebecca Anderson, Michael Goldwyn, Bryan Goldwyn, David Goldwyn. AB, Barnard Coll., 1959; MS, Columbia U., 1960. Librarian CCNY, 1960-62; librarian Mt. Sinai Med. Ctr., N.Y.C., 1964-73, dir. library, 1973-79; dir. Health Scis Libr. Columbia U., N.Y.C., 1979-91, acting v.p., univ. libr., 1982; dir. Ariz. Health Scis. Libr., U. Ariz., Tucson, 1991-2001; assoc. dir. Ariz. Telemedicine Program, 1996—2001; ret., 2001. Bd. dirs. Med. Libr. Ctr. of N.Y., N.Y.C., 1983-91; mem. biomed. libr. rev. com. Nat. Libr. Medicine, Bethesda, Md., 1984-88, chmn., 1987-88; mem. bd. regents Nat. Libr. Medicine, 1990-94, chmn., 1993-94; pres. Ariz. Health Info. Network, 1995. Contbr. articles to profl. jours. Mem. Med. Libr. Assn. (pres.-elect 1996-97, pres. 1997-98, bd. dirs. 1983-86, 98-99), Assn. Acad. Health Scis. Libr. Dirs. (bd. dirs. 1983-86, 90-93, pres. 1991-92). E-mail: rachaela@ahsl.arizona.edu.

ANDERSON, REBECCA LYNN, music educator; d. Brian Lee and Sharon Lynn Lessman; m. John Wesley Anderson, July 2, 2004. BA in Music Edn., Mesa State Coll., Grand Junction, Colo., 2005. Choir tchr. West Mid. Sch., Grand Junction, Colo., 2005—; choir, music tchr. Quest Acad., Grand Junction, 2006—. Pvt. voice, piano tchr., Grand Junction, 2004—. Active Western Colo. Chorale, Grand Junction, 2005—; worship leader, team mem. Valley Bible Ch., Grand Junction, 2002—, bible sch. worship leader, 2006—. Avocations: crafts, hiking, exercise, piano.

ANDERSON, RHODA, language educator; b. Caney, Okla., Oct. 31, 1932; d. Sherman Thomas Miller and Eliza Doshie Wilson; m. Thomas Willie Anderson, Dec. 5, 1952; children: J. Wayne, Robert D. AAS, Blackfeet C.C., Browning, Montana, 1994. Cert. Appointed Missionary Assoc. Home Mission Bd. of So. Bapt. Conv., 1995, Conduct Literacy Missions Workshops N.Am. Mission Bd., 2000, Workshop Leader for Am. Indians Women's Missionary Union, MT., 1995; Choctaw Lang. Tchr. Choctaw Nation of Okla., 1999. Choctaw lang. tchr. Choctaw Nation of Okla., McAlester, Okla., 1999—; tchr. bi-lingual edn. Can. Pub. Sch., Canadian, Okla., 2000—05; tchr. Krebs Pub. Sch., Okla., 2005—. Choctaw dictionary rsch. com. mem. Choctaw Nation of Okla., Durant, Okla., 1999—. Author (writer): (create/write teaching aids/songs) in Choctaw Language. Tutor adults to read and write in English North Am. Mission Bd., McAlester, Okla., 2000—. Recipient Cert. of Achievement and Cert. of Excellence in Bus. Comm., Blackfet C.C., 2002. Fellow: N.Am. Mission Bd. (assoc.; adult reading and writing in english workshop leader 1999—2004, Pin/Recognition five); mem.: Chi-Ka-Sha Assn. (trainer). Baptist. Achievements include development of teaching curriculum in Choctaw Language. Avocations: i sew traditional choctaw clothing and beadwork, guitar, piano, singing.

ANDERSON, RITA MCKENZIE, psychologist; b. Boston, Nov. 25, 1972; d. Wallace Andrew and Angelina Rita (Bagnoli) McKenzie; m. Brien William Anderson, Oct. 22, 1994; 1 child, Liam Wallace. BA cumn laude, Framingham (Mass.) State U., 1974; MEd, Northeastern U., Boston, 1975; PhD, Temple U., 1983. Lic. psychologist, Mass. Psychologist F.S. Dubois Day Treatment Ctr., Stamford, Conn., 1982—86, in pvt. practice, Fairfield, Conn., 1984-86; psychologist, outpatient svcs. W.W. Johnson Life Ctr., Springfield, Mass., 1986-87, dir. outpatient svcs., 1987-88; self employed psychologist and ct. investigator, West Springfield, Mass., 1988—. Adj. psychology faculty Holyoke (Mass.) C.C., 1989-90, Springfield Tech. C.C., 1989-90. Contbr. articles to profl.jours. Mem. Agawam (Mass.) Dem. Com., 1992-94. Mem. APA, Mass. Psychol. Assn., Internat. Soc. for Study of Dissociation, Zonta Internat. (sec. 1990-98). Office: 380 Union St Ste 14 West Springfield MA 01089-4123 Office Phone: 413-731-1100. E-mail: blrgroup@yahoo.com.

ANDERSON, ROSE L. DYESS, elementary school educator, poet; b. Laurel, Miss., Dec. 24, 1941; d. James Lamar and Mildred Josephine (Moore) Dyess; m. Rushel Talmadge Anderson, May 13, 1965; 1 child, Joel Alan. BE, William Carey Coll., Hattiesburg, Miss., 1964; grad., Univ. So. Miss., Hattiesburg, Miss. Elem. tchr. Natchez-Adams Pub. Sch., Natchez, Miss., 1965—. Author: (poetry) Lifes Fleeting Days, 1996, The Winds of Change Keep on Blowing, 1997. Facilitator numerous workshops and conf. within dist., Miss. Early Childhood Conf, Summer Math and Sci. Conf., Miss. Univ. for Women; mentor tchr. for numerous student tchrs. Alcorn State Univ., Univ. So. Miss. Nominee Disney Tchr of the Yr., 1995; recipient Golden Apple award, Covington Rd. Ch. of Christ, Miss., 1996, Tchr. of the Yr., Frazier Primary Sch., Miss., 2002. Mem.: Miss. Edn. Assn., Nat. Libr. of Poetry, Alpha Delta Kappa (chaplin, treas., historian). Republican. Ch. Of Christ. Achievements include design of and edited a children's activity page for a religious newspaper, The Magnolia Messenger; motivational spkr. for ch. ladies day activites. Avocations: writing, painting, interior decorating, gardening, travel. Office: Frazier Primary Sch 1445 George F West Blvd Natchez MS 39120

ANDERSON, ROSE MARIE, insurance agent; b. Leonville, La., Aug. 10, 1945; d. Napoleon Badeaux and Marie Leonie Rivette; m. Earl William Anderson, Oct. 9, 1965; children: William Christopher, Charles Terrence. AS in Bus. adminstrn., T.H. Harris Tech. Coll., Opelousas, La., 1965. Claims clk. Dwight W. Andrus Ins. Agy., Lafayette, La., 1968-72; personal lines customer svc. rep. Trinity Universal Ins. Co., Lafayette, 1972-75; comml. lines underwriter CAR Ins. Agy., Alexandria, La., 1989-90; comml. lines CSR Jim Thomasee Ins. Agy., Alexandria, 1990-93; comml. underwriter B&S Underwriters, Inc., Alexandria, 1993-99. Bd. dirs. Horse Helping the Handicapped, Pineville, La., 1989-94. Mem. Nat. Assn. Ins. Women, Ctrl. La. Claims Assn., Lions (sec. Alexandria 1997-98, pres. 1989-99, zone chmn., Lion of Yr. award 1997). Home: 99 Ragan Dr Alexandria LA 71303-2264

ANDERSON, ROXANNA MARION, psychology professor; b. Detroit, Mar. 22, 1945; d. Carlynn Ellen and George Lawrence Anderson; children: Walter Clarence Blenman, Frederick Gerald Ford, Laverne Barbara Ford. BS, NYU, 1968—73, MA, 1973—75, PhD, 1990—97. Dir. support svcs. NYU, 1984—97; assoc. prof. psychology Bennett Coll., Greensboro, NC, 1997—2004, acting chair, 1998—99; asst. prof. N.C. A & T State U., Greensboro, 1998—2005; dean of students Ea. Music Festival, Greensboro, 1998—2000; assoc. prof. psychology Bennett Coll. for Women, Greensboro, 2004—05, William Penn U., Oskaloosa, Iowa, 2005—. Dir. On The Ground Smoking Cessation and Prevention Program, Greensboro, 2004—05; advocacy trainer Crisis Intervention Svcs., Oskaloosa, Iowa, 2005—06. Author: (abstract) APA Women's Health Conference, Psychosocial and Behavioral Factors in Women's Health: Research, Prevention, Treatment, and Service Delivery in Clinical and Community Settings; contbr. articles to profl. pubs. Co-chair Relection Com. for Alma Adams, Ho. of Rep., Greensboro, 2002; mem. Com. to Reelect Ho. Rep. Alma Adams, Greensboro, 2002—04; trainee Episcopal Diocese of N.C., Greensboro, 2004—05; mem. African Am. Atelier, Greensboro, 2002—03, chair, 2003—05. Recipient 2005 Faculty Tchg. Excellence award, Bennett Coll. for Women, 2005; grantee Bush-Hewlett Faculty Develop award, Bennett Coll., 2000. Mem.: APA, Southeastern Psychol. Assn., Assn. Black Psychologist (by-laws com. mem. 2004—06), Am. Psychol. Soc., Pi Gamma Mu. D-Liberal. Episcopal. Avocations: piano, quilting, travel. Home: 1001 N Market St Oskaloosa IA 52577 Office: William Penn Univ 201 Trueblood Ave Oskaloosa IA 52577 Office Phone: 641-673-1073. Office Fax: 641-673-1396. Personal E-mail: roxanna.anderson@gmail.com. Business E-Mail: andersonrm@wmpenn.edu.

ANDERSON, RUTH LIBERTY, retired special education educator; b. N.Y.C., Aug. 30, 1936; d. John Antonio and Ruth (Pedersen) Lopez; m. Peter Alan Anderson, Mar. 4, 1960; children: John Peter, James Thomas, Mark Harald. BSE, Wagner U., 1958; MSE, Nazareth U., 1981. Elem. tchr. Herricks Sch., Hyde Park, N.Y., 1958, Lincoln Sch., East Orange, N.J., 1958-60, Hillcrest Sch., Somerset, N.J., 1960-61; instr. Neighborhood Youth Corps, Utica, N.Y., 1964, 65; reading tchr. Cazenouia (N.Y.) Cen. Sch., 1968-70, spl. edn. tchr., 1970-72; tchr. Lewistown Porter Cen. Sch., Youngstown, N.Y., 1972-77; resource rm. tchr. Skaneateles (N.Y.) Mid. Sch., 1978—2001; ret. Cons. Schs. regarding adv. programs, N.Y., 1989—; presenter coun. exceptional children N.Y. State Middle Sch. conf. Mem. Coun. Exceptional Children, N.Y. State Tchrs. of Handicapped, Cen. N.Y. Tchrs. of Learning Disabled. Presbyterian. Avocations: music, reading, needlecrafts, crafts. Home: 3835 Sadler Rd Skaneateles NY 13152-8807 Office: Skaneateles Cen Sch 49 E Elizabeth St Skaneateles NY 13152-1337

ANDERSON, SARA SHUTTLEWORTH, artist, educator; b. Davenport, Iowa, Aug. 6, 1934; d. Thomas Henderson and Eloise Dorothy (Thompson) Shuttleworth; m. Theodore Charles Anderson June 21, 1955; children: Andrew, Dale, Eric, Tod. BA in Edn., Mills Coll., 1956; cert. in painting, Royal Acad. Fine Arts, Brussels, 1969; BA in Fine Arts, Calif. State U., Northridge, 1970. Cert. primary and elem. tchr. fine arts to jr. coll., life early childhood credential, Calif. Tchr. art Triton Mus. Art, Santa Clara, Calif., 1985-89; tchr. art, contract art cons., classroom facilitator Rose Avenue Sch., Oxnard, Calif., 1995—. Owner, coord. Ventura Harbor Village Art Gallery, 1992-95; vol., pres., cons. Art Docents Los Gatos, Calif., 1976-82. One-woman shows Leamington Coll., Eng., 1972, Western Instruments, 1993; 2-person show Doubletree Inn, 1994; exhibited in group shows Los Gatos Fellowship Gallery, 1983, Fremont Hub Shows, 1984, Santa Cruz Art League, 1984, San Jose, 1988, Los Gatos Art Assn., 1991, Triton Mus., 1992, Ventury Harbor Village Art Gallery, 1992-94, Ventura County Fair, 1993, City Hall, Ventura, Calif., 1995; author: (sketchbook) Seeing the Seaside, 1991; illustrator: Sword of the Teacher, 1996. Mem. Los Gatos Heritage Preservation Soc., 1978-90; pres. Los Gatos Friends of Arts, 1985-90. Named Arts Citizen of Yr., Town of Los Gatos, 1987; recipient awards for art, 1984—. Mem. Calif. Gold Coast Watercolor Soc. (signature mem.), Los Gatos Art Assn. Anglican. Avocations: grandchildren, husband, boating. Home: 607 Carpenteria Rd Aromas CA 95004-9718

ANDERSON, SHEILA K., mathematics professor; b. Dixon, Ill., Mar. 11, 1944; d. Chester Junior and Evelyne Maxine McFalls; m. Peter James Ulisse, May 20, 2006; children: James Scott, Cheri Lynn Capalbo. BS, U. Ill., Champagne, 1966; MS, Northeastern Ill. U., Chgo., 1984. Cert. tchr. Ill., Mo. Math. tchr. Hinsdale H.S., Ill., 1966—70; adj. faculty mem. Northeastern Ill. U., Chgo., 1984—91, Oakton C.C., DesPlaines, Ill., 1984—91, Sacred Heart U., Fairfield, Conn., 1991—93, So. Conn. U., New Haven, 1991—93; prof. math. Housatonic C.C., Bridgeport, Conn., 1993—, chmn. devel. studies, 1995—, acting academic dean, 2006—. Avocations: reading, travel, gardening, tennis. Office: Housatonic CC 900 Lafayette Blvd Bridgeport CT 06604 Office Phone: 203-332-5145. Office Fax: 203-332-5123. Business E-Mail: sanderson@hcc.commnet.edu.

ANDERSON, STACEY ANN, school psychologist; b. Crestline, Ohio, Mar. 4, 1964; d. James Edward Anderson, Sr. and Mary Jane (Vangeloff) Anderson. Postgrad., Walden U., 2004; MA in Psychology, U. W.Va. (now Marshall University), 1990; BS in Edn., Ashland Coll. (now Ashland U.), 1985. Cert. sch. psychologist Ariz., W.Va. Tchr. jr. h.s. sci. Crestview Local Schs., Ashland, Ohio, 1986—88; tutor Human Resource Bur., Mansfield, Ohio, 1987—88; substitute tchr. Kanawha & Jackson County Schs., Charleston, W.Va., 1988—90; counselor Sexual Assault Unit Family Svcs. Kanawha Valley, Charleston, W.Va., 1990; sch. psychologist Kanawha County Schs., Charleston, W.Va., 1990—91; sch. psychologist Yuma County Accommodation Sch. Dist. #99, Yuma, Ariz., 1995—2002; sch. psychologist Yuma Sch. Dist. 1, Yuma, Ariz., 1991—2002. Supr. interns Yuma Sch. Dist. 1, Yuma, 1994—2002. Mem. edn. com. Gila Mountain United Meth. Ch., Yuma, 2000—02; Bd. dirs. Learning Pad Presch., Yuma, 2000—02. Mem.: APA, Am. Psychol. Assn. Grad. Students, Nat. Assn. Sch. Psychologists, Psi Chi. Methodist. Avocations: travel, shopping, cars, biking, collecting. Office: Yuma Sch Dist 1 450 Sixth St Yuma AZ 85364

ANDERSON, STASIA ANN, medical researcher; children: Erica Ann, Helen Elise, Ian Andrew. BS, Drexel Univ., Phila., 1992; PhD, Pa. State U., Univ. Pk., 1992—97. Postdoctoral rschr. Wash. U., St. Louis, 1997—99, Pharmacia Corp., St. Louis, 1999—2001; staff scientist NIH, Nat. Inst. Neurol. Disorders and Strokes, Bethesda, Md., 2001—05; head Mouse Imaging Core NIH, Nat. Heart Lung and Blood Inst., Bethesda, Md., 2005—. Recipient Top Basic Sci. Abstract, Acad. Molecular Imaging, 2002. Mem.: Soc. for Molecular Imaging, Internat. Soc. for Magnetic Resonance in Medicine. Achievements include research in cellular magnetic resonance imaging of stem cells and immune cells in cancer and autoimmune disease. Office: NIH 10 Center Dr B1N256 Bethesda MD 20892 Office Phone: 301-402-0908.

ANDERSON, THERESA A., retail executive; With First Union Nat. Bank, Lowe's Co. Inc., Wilkesboro, NC, 1986—, mgr.divsnl. merchandising, 1996—98, v.p. merchandising, 1998—99, v.p. store support, 1999—2000, sr. v.p. ops. and merchandising support, 2000—01, sr. v.p. merchandising sales and svc., 2001—. Office: Lowes Co Inc 1605 Curtis Bridge Rd Wilkesboro NC 28697

ANDERSON, THERESA ANN, science educator; b. Phila., Aug. 30, 1972; d. Sarah Louise Anderson. B in Chemistry Edn., Fla. A&M U., Tallahassee, 1996; ThD, Z.E. Brown Bible Coll., Tallahassee, Fla., 2003. Cert. 6-12 chemistry tchr. Fla., 2003. Tchr. sci., head dept. sci. Fairview Mid. Sch., Tallahassee, 1998—. Office: Fairview Mid Sch 3415 Zillah Rd Tallahassee FL 32305 Office Phone: 850-488-6880. Personal E-mail: resetann@hotmail.com.

ANDERSON, VALERIE B., actress, writer; b. Boston, Jan. 4, 1961; d. Kittridge Anderson and Pamela Evelyn Booth; m. Remington Morris Patrick Murphy, Sept. 26, 1999. Cheerleader Phila. Eagles, 1980; model Reinhard Modelling Agy., Phila., 1980; comml. actress Sears, Phila., 1980; TV spokesperson Arpeggio's Restaurant, Phila., 1980. Subject of articles, radio program; spkr. in field; appearances on TV programs. Musician: (single) My Love Rolls Over, 1982, Dolly is a Swinger, 1984; author: (pen name Christina Alexandra) Five Lost Years: A Personal Exploration of Schizophrenia, 2000; author, illustrator: Reflections on the Word in Black and White, 2002, illustrator: book cover; exhibitions include Main Line Art Ctr., 2004—05. Flute scholar, Jenkintown Music Sch. Mem.: Nat. Alliance of Mentally Ill, Mensa, Am. Assn. People with Disabilities. Avocations: travel, piano. Home: PO Box 12 Abington PA 19001 Personal E-mail: rmurphy483@aol.com.

ANDERSON, VEANNE NIXON, psychology educator, researcher; b. Denver, Aug. 12, 1955; BSc, Colo. State U., 1977; PhD, McMaster U., Hamilton, Ont., Can., 1985. Postdoctoral researcher Erindale Coll.-U. Toronto, Missisauga, Ont., 1984-87; assoc. prof. psychology Ind. State U., Terre Haute, 1987—, coord. master's program dept. psychology, 1992—. Mem. APA (div. 35), Assn. Psychol. Sci., Nat. Women's Health Network, Midwestern Psychol. Assn., Phi Beta Kappa, Psi Chi. Office: Ind State U Dept Psychology Terre Haute IN 47809-0001 Business E-Mail: vanderson1@isugw.indstate.edu.

ANDERSON, VICKI, retired librarian; b. Hazleton, Pa., June 17, 1928; d. Steven and Edith Potochney; m. Richard Anderson. BA, San Diego State Coll., 1961; MLS, U. Calif., Berkeley, 1962; postgrad., U. Pa., 1985—86. Libr. San Diego City Pub. Libr., 1962—64, San Diego City Schs., 1965—90; ret., 1991. Mem. Calif. State Coun. Edn., San Francisco, 1968—71, San Diego Citizen Adv. Com., 1978; spkr. San Diego City Coll., 1965; instr. Grossmont (Calif.) Coll., 1975—80, San Diego State Coll., 1981. Author: Fiction Sequels For readers 10 to16, 1989, 2d edit., 1998, Fiction Index for Readers 10 to 16, 1992, Cultures Outside the Unted States in Fiction, 1994, Sequels in Children's Literature K-6, 1998, Immigrants in the United States in Fiction, 1994, Native Americans in Fiction, 1994; Dime Novel: Its History and Context in Children's Literature, 2005. Chmn. Public Employees Coord. Coun., San Diego, 1978—79; mem. N. Mt. Village Planning Com.; appointed mem. Ariz. State Sch. Redistricting Commn., 2006—07; committeeman North Mountain Precinct Dem. Party, Phoenix, 1995; state com. mem. Dem. Party State Com., Phoenix, 1995; active Legislative Dist. 18, Phoenix, 1994; mem. exec. com. Maricopa County Dem. Party, 2002; chmn. Legis. Dist. 6, 2002; mem. Legis. Dist. 10; pres. Kensington-Talmadge Cmty. Assn., San Diego, 1976—78; adv. coun. mem. Area Agy. on Aging, 2006—. Grantee, Dakota State Coll., 1970. Mem.: AAUW (v.p. fin.), Moon Hills Cmty. Group (chmn.), Ariz. Silver Haired Legislators (elected del.), Ariz. Writers Club. Democrat. Avocations: reading, sewing, weaving. Home: 12833 N Fifteenth Ave Phoenix AZ 85029 Personal E-mail: valjest@aol.com.

ANDERSON, VICKI SUSAN, legislative staff member, travel consultant; b. Seattle, Jan. 11, 1961; d. Vergil and VickiAnn Davis; m. Todd V. Anderson, Mar. 13, 1982 (div. May 1990); children: David V. Davis, Brandun C. Anderson. Grad., Northside H.S., Houston Voc. Ctr., Warner Robins, Ga., 1979. Computer operator The Boeing Co., Seattle, 1987; clerk, typist Wash. Dept. Licensing, Olympia, Wash., 1987-90; adminstrv. support Ho. of Reps., Olympia, Wash., 1987-90, supr., 1990—. Organizer food drive Farmers Market, Olympia. Mem. Am. Soc. Legis. Clks. and Secs. (site selection com., tech. and innovation com.). Southern Baptist. Avocations: charity fundraising, travel, family. Office: Ho of Reps PO Box 40600 Olympia WA 98504-0600 Home: 7447 Blockhouse Ln SW Rochester WA 98579-9272 E-mail: Anderson_VI@leg.wa.gov.

ANDERSON-BRUESS, JUDITH, social studies educator; b. Mexico City, Mexico, Jan. 9, 1967; d. Leopoldo and Juana Anderson; m. Doug Bruess, Aug. 30, 1997; 1 child, Athena Anderson Bruess. BA, U. Tex.- Pan Am., Edinburg, 1989—91. Cert. Tchr. Tex. Dept. Edn., 1991. Social studies tchr. Filemon Vela Mid. Sch., Brownsville, Tex., 1991—96, Thomas Jefferson HS, Dallas, 1996—97; social studies grade team leader Ruth Dowell Mid. Sch., McKinney, 1997—. We the people sponsor Ruth Dowell Mid. Sch., 2005—. Sponsor mock Congl. hearing Ruth Dowell Mid. Sch., 2005—06. Recipient Supreme Ct. Summer Inst., Law St., 2006. Democrat. Roman Catholic. Avocations: travel, politics. Home: 5657 /Fm1461 Mc Kinney TX 75071 Office: Ruth Dowell Mid Sch 5657 Fm 1461 Mc Kinney TX 75070 Office Phone: 469-742-6700. Home Fax: 469-742-6701; Office Fax: 469-742-6701. Business E-Mail: jbruess@mckinneyisd.net.

ANDERSON-FINTAK, HEATHER, lawyer; d. Landa and Don Anderson; m. Matthew Fintak, Dec. 27, 2001; 1 child, Aidan Fintak. BS in Bus., U. of Nev., Las Vegas, 1998; JD, Am. U., Washington, DC, 2002. Bar: Md. 2004, Nev. 2005. Project asst. ABA, Washington, 2001—02; staff atty. Legal Aid Bur., Inc., Hughesville, Md., 2002—05, Nev. Legal Services, Inc., Las Vegas, 2005—. Student atty. Internat. Human Rights Clinic, Washington, 2000—01. Intern, interviewer Lawyers Com. for Human Rights, Washington, 2002. Kenneth M. Devos scholarship, U. of Nev., Las Vegas, 1994—98, Coll. of Bus. Leadership grant, 1996—97, 1997—98. Mem.: Assoc. of Trial Lawyers of Am (assoc.). Liberal. Christian. Avocation: travel. Office: Nevada Legal Services Inc 530 S 6th St Las Vegas NV 89014 Office Phone: 702-386-0404. E-mail: hfintak@nlslaw.net.

ANDERSON-KOTTS, JUDITH ANNE, academic dean; b. Little Falls, Minn., June 23, 1943; d. Thomas Martin and Elda Rose Ethel (Klapel) McDonnell; m. Gene Wesley Anderson, Aug. 12, 1961 (div. 1993); children: Jeffery Thomas, Gregory Carl, Joel Michael, Julie Ann; m. Nick Kotts, Sept. 21, 1996. AA, Cambridge (Minn.) Anoka-Ramsey C.C., 1982; BA, Met. State U., St. Paul, 1987; MS, Cardinal Stritch Coll., Milw., 1990. Bookkeeper Peoples State Bank, Cambridge, 1971-77; bus. mgr. Cambridge Anoka-Ramsey C.C., 1979-90; ednl. coord. Barnes Bus. Coll., Denver, 1991-92, dir., 1994-96; acad. dean Parks Coll., Denver, 1995-96; assoc. dean edn., v.p. ops. Inst. Bus. & Med. Careers, Ft. Collins, Colo., 1996—2000; asst. dir. regulatory affairs Alta Colls. Inc., Westwood Coll. Schs., 2001—. Cons. for low-income families U. Minn. Extension Dept., Isanti County, 1987-90. Treas. Govt. Maple Ridge Twp., Isanti County, Minn., 1978-91; chmn. United Charities Dr., Maple Ridge Twp., 1980-85, Jefferson County Ext. Adv. Bd., 1994— Named State Vol. Gov. of Minn., 1987, 88, 89, 90. Mem. AAUW (Denver), Muskies Inc., Women for Fishing, Hunting and Wildlife, Lady Ducks, Nat. Outdoors Women, Phi Theta Kappa (Alpha Minn. chpt.), Rocky Mtn. Natural Colored Sheep Breeder's Assn. Republican. Mem. Covenant Ch. Avocations: horses, machine knitting, stuffed animal collecting, fishing, weaving. Home: 7180 Elm Street Enchanted Hls Longmont CO 80504-5433

ANDERSON-SPIVY, ALEXANDRA, news correspondent, editor, critic, writer, historian; b. Boston, Mass, May 14, 1942; d. Henry and Marion Ruth (Thompson) Fuller; m. Samuel O.J. Spivy; children: Lafcadio, Genevieve, Oscar. BA, Sarah Lawrence Coll., Bronxville, N.Y., 1961. Art editor Paris Rev., 1972-76, Village Voice, NYC, 1973-76; features assoc. Vogue mag., NYC, 1976-78; sr. editor Portfolio mag., NYC, 1979-83; editor-in-chief Arts and Antiques mag., NYC, 1983-85; exec. editor Am. Photographer, NYC, 1985-87; arts editor Smart mag., NYC, 1988-90; contbg. arts editor Esquire mag., NYC, 1990-94; NY editor The Argonaut, 1992-96; reviews editor The Art Jour., 1995-2000; editor-in-chief The Craftsman on CD-ROM, 1996—2002; projects editor Interactive Bur., 1996-99; editl. dir. Circle.com, 1999-2001; corr. Bloomberg.com, 2004—06. Chair bd. dirs. Franklin Furnace; bd. govs. Colby Coll. Art Mus.; profl. fellow Morgan Libr. Author: Anderson and Archer's SoHo: The Essential Guide to Art and Life in Lower Manhattan, 1979, Living With Art, 1988, Portraits of Olga, 1992, Keith Haring, Last Works, 1995, Gardens of Earthly Delight: The Art of Robert Kushner, 1997, Foliage: Photographs by Harold Feinstein, 2001; mem. adv. bd. Rev. Mag., 1998-2000. V.p. Mus. Modern Art, Contemporary Arts Coun.; pres., bd. dirs. Exhbns. Internat., 2000-06. Recipient Art Critics' award NEA, 1978; Travel grant Japan Found., 1976. Mem. Internat. Assn. Art Critics (pres. Am. sect. 1997-2001).

ANDERSSON, HELEN DEMITROUS, artist; b. Kotzebue, Alaska, Sept. 9, 1958; d. Thomas Wade Sr. and Rose (Koonook) Sours; children: Jason Ray, Gwendolyn Joyce Field. Student, U. Fairbanks, 1980, U. Hilo, Hawaii, 1981. Exhibited works in Anchorage Mus. History and Arts Show, Stephan Fine Arts, 1984. Recipient 1st pl. Alaska Silver Anniversary Juried Arts Show. Avocations: painting, drawings, carvings, sewing, beadwork.

ANDERT, DARLENE (DARLENE ANDERT-SCHMIDT), management consultant; BA in Bus. Mgmt. and Comm., Alverno Coll., Milw., 1983; MSA in Adminstrn., Ctrl. Mich. U., Mt. Pleasant, 1993; EdD, George Washington U., 2003. Cert.: Fla. Supreme Ct. (county ct. mediator); fin. mgr., mgmt. cons. Pres., owner Dance in Exercise, Inc., Milw., 1980-85; pres. Andert Governance Corp. (formerly Concepts in Mgmt., Inc.), Cape Coral, Fla., 1989—. Mem. bd. arbitrators NASD Regulation Inc., 2000. Author: Diversity at Work, 1995. Trustee Lee County Electric Coop., Inc., 1994—; past pres. Healthy Start Coalition of S.W. Fla., Inc. Mem.: ASTD, Nat. Assn. Bus. Women, Inst. Mgmt. Cons. Office: PO Box 100235 Cape Coral FL 33910 Office Phone: 239-549-7766. Business E-Mail: andert@andertgovernance.com.

ANDES, JOAN KEENEN, tax specialist; b. Clarksburg, W.Va., Apr. 23, 1930; 010d. Ree Martin and Mary Ruth (Pyle) Groghan; m. William Anderson Keenen, Oct. 15, 1949 (div. 1970); children: Paula Annette Keenen Skelton, William Ree; 1 foster child, Donald Monroe Dreyer; m. Ralph Paul Andes, Sept. 29, 1976. Pvt. sec. State Capitol, Charleston, W.Va., 1948-49; statis. typist various acctg. offices, Beaumont, Tex., 1949—60; owner Machine Acctg. and Computing, Beaumont, 1960-70, Automated Enterprises Keypunch Sch., Beaumont, 1962-72; pres. Applied Data Processing, Beaumont, 1970-83; owner Applied Info. Processing, Beaumont, 1983-90, APEX-Bookkeeping and Tax Svc., Beaumont, 1981—. Active Westgate Youth Group, 1984-90; vol. Mexican Mission Ch. of Christ, 1984—. Mem. Data Processing Mgmt. Assn. (pres. 1972-73, 80, awards chmn. 1985-86), Nat. Fedn. Ind. Bus. Women. Republican. Mem. Ch. of Christ. Avocations: counted cross stitch, collecting coke memorabilia, coin collecting/numismatics. Home: 1410 Marshall Place Dr Beaumont TX 77706-3221

ANDOLINA, NANCY JEAN, middle school educator, dancer, English and language arts educator; b. Dunkirk, NY, Feb. 11, 1949; d. Joseph H. Andolina and Frances Dolce. BA in Edn., SUNY, Fredonia, 1971, MA in English, 1977; postgrad., Ctr. Modern Dance, Las Vegas, 1974—83, Las Vegas Dance Theatre Studio, 1984—92. Reading and English tchr. Fredonia Cath. Sch., 1971—72; 1st grade tchr. Cuba (NY) Elem. Sch., 1974—74; 1st and 4th grade tchr. Lois Craig Elem. Sch., 1974—79; 4th grade tchr. John S. Park Elem. Sch., 1979—86; oral lang., study skills, drama tchr. Dell H. Robinson Jr. HS, 1986—91; English lang. arts tchr. Thurman White Mid. Sch., 1991—. Dancer Ronnie Greenblatt Modern Dance Theatre, 1980—83, Ecdysis Dance Theatre, 1983—84, co-dance dir. Allied Arts Coun., 1984—85. Tutor Juvenile Ct. Svcs., 1979; judge Las Vegas Search for Talent Contest, 1986—88; with Darwin R. Barker Libr. Summer Puppet Show Prodn., 1989; spkr. Parenting Conf., 1989—90. Recipient Above and Beyond award, 1988; Elective Dept. Art Festival grant, 1987. Mem.: NEA. Home: 4676 Limerick Ln Las Vegas NV 89121 Office: Thurman White Mid Sch 1661 Galleria Henderson NV 89014

ANDOLINO, ROSEMARIE S., airport terminal executive; b. 1967; BS in Mktg., DePaul Univ., Chgo. With City of Chgo., 1990—, with dept. planning and devel., 1999—, first dep. commr. planning devel. dept.; asst. to dir. Mayor of Chgo., 1995—99; exec. dir. O'Hare Modernization Program, 2005—. Named one of 40 Under Forty, Crain's Bus. Chgo., 2005. Office: O'Hare Modernization Project c/o Mayor's Office 121 N LaSalle St Chicago IL 60602*

ANDONUCCI-HILL, HEATHER L., psychologist; b. Rapid City, SD, Oct. 28, 1975; d. Robert Nebling and Christine T. Watters. BA in Psychology, St. Michael's Coll., 1998; MA, Calif. Sch. Profl. Psychology, 2004, student. Enhanced care coord. Child Guidance Greater Waterbury, Conn., 2004—. Instr. cardio kickboxing. Mem.: APA. Office: Child Guidance Clinic Greater Waterbury 70 Pine St Waterbury CT 06721 Office Phone: 203-756-7287.

ANDRADE, EDNA, artist, educator; b. Portsmouth, Va. d. Thomas Judson and Ruth (Porter) Wright; m. C. Preston Andrade, Jr., July 12, 1941 (div. 1960). BFA, Pa. Acad. Fine Arts/U. Pa., 1937. Supr. art elem. schs., Norfolk, Va., 1938-39; instr. drawing and painting Newcomb Art Sch., Tulane U., 1939-41; lectr. U. N.Mex., 1971; prof. Phila. Coll. Art, 1957—72, 1973—82, prof. emeritus, 1982—; prof. art Temple U., 1972-73. Adj. prof. art Ariz. State U., 1986—; critic Pa. Acad. Fine Arts, 1988—89. Artist, designer, OSS, 1942-44, free-lance designer, Washington, 1944-46, free-lance painter, designer, muralist, Phila. and, N.Y.C., 1946—, artist-in-residence, Hartford Sch. Art and Tamarind Inst., 1971, U. Sask., Can., 1977, U. Zulia, Maracaibo, Venezuela, 1980, Ariz. State U., Tempe, 1981, 83, Fabric Workshop, Phila., 1984, Hollins Coll., Va., 1985; vis. artist, Skidmore Coll., 1973, 74, one-woman shows, Phila. Art Alliance, 1954, Beaver Coll., 1963, East Hampton Gallery, N.Y.C., 1967, Peale Galleries Pa. Acad., 1967, Rutgers U., 1971, U. Hartford, 1977, Marian Locks Gallery, 1969, 1971,74, 77, 83, 1989, Phila., Hollins Coll., 1985; retrospective Pa. Acad. Fine Arts, 1993-94, Locks Gallery, Phila., 1993, 97, 99, 03, 06, Inst. Contemporary Art, Phila., 2003, Print Ctr., Phila., 2006; group shows include AAAL, In This Acad., Pa. Acad. Fine Arts, Phila., William Penn Meml. Mus., Harrisburg, Three Centuries Am. Art, Phila. Collects Art Since 1940, Phila. Mus. Art, Bklyn. Mus., Ft. Worth Art Ctr., Des Moines Art Ctr., Philbrook Art Ctr., Tulsa, Contemporary Phila. Artists, 1990, Phila. Mus. Art, Artists Choose Artists, Inst. of Contemporary Art, Phila., 1991, Klein Gallery, Univ. City Sci. Ctr., Phila., 1998, Phila. Mus. Art, 2000, others; represented in permanent collections, Phila. Mus. Art, Pa. Acad. Fine Arts, Print Club, Balt. Mus. Art, Addison Gallery Am. Art, McNay Art Inst., San Antonio, Montclair (N.J.) Art Mus., Nat. Collection Fine Arts, Libr. of Congress, USIA, Albright-Knox Art Gallery, Buffalo, Tamarind Collection, U. N.Mex. Mus., Woodmere Art Mus., Phila., Yale Art Gallery, Am. Tel. & Tel. Co., Bell of Pa., Phila., Fed. Res. Bank, Phila., Price-Waterhouse, Phila., Edwin A. Ulrich Mus. Wichita State U., Pepsi-Cola, Leeway Found., Phila., Please Touch Mus., Phila., Va. Mus. Fine Arts, Richmond, Dallas Mus. Art, Mus. Fine Arts, Houston, Del. Art Mus., Wilmington, Del. Mem. Mayor's Cultural Adv. Coun., Phila., 1984—85. Recipient 1st and 2d Cresson European Traveling scholarships Pa. Acad., 1936, 37, Eyre medal Phila. Water Color Club, 1968, Mary Smith prize Pa. Acad. Fine Arts, 1968, Childe Hassam Meml. purchases AAAL, 1967, 68, Hazlett Meml. award in arts, 1980, Honor award Women's Caucus for Art, 1983, Hunt award visual arts Phila. Women's Way, 1984, Roland Gallimore Meml. award Interior Design Coun., Phila. Mayor's Arts and Culture award, 1991, Founders award Samuel S. Fleisher Art Meml., 1993, Disting. Daughter Pa. award, 2002 Mem. Coll. Art Assn. (Disting. Tchr. of Art award 1996).

ANDRADE, MANUELA PESTANA, art educator; b. Funchal, Portugal, Oct. 10, 1937; d. Silvestre and Eulalia (Vieira Da Luz) Pestana; m. Manuel Cristao, Jan. 11, 1956 (dec. May 1970); 1 child, Maria Pestana Goldstein; m. Pedro Manuel Rapazote (div. Feb. 1977); 1 child, Antonio Pedro; m. Virgil Sousa Andrade, July 15, 1986. BA, U. Porto, Portugal, 1978, 82, MA, 1980, 84. Tchr. Externato liceal de Moncao, Portugal, 1971-74, Ministry Edn., Portugal, 1971-87; dept. head Prep. Sch. Ermezinde, Portugal, 1981-82, 83-84, master tchr., 1984-85, 86; tchr. Portuguese United Edn. Sch., 1987—, ednl. dir., 1988—. Author of poems; one-woman shows include Ctr. Internat. D'Art Contemporain, Paris, 1984, Funchal, Madeira, Portugal, 1984, Fall River (Mass.) Art Assn., 1988, Heritage Park, Fall River, 1988, Pilgrim Soc., Plymouth, Mass., 1989, Portuguese Am. Fedn. 25th Anniversary Festival, Bristol, R.I., 1990, Bentley Coll., Waltham, Mass., 1992, Portuguese Am. Women's Assn., Providence, 1998, Newport (R.I.) Art Mus., 1999; represented in permanent collections Nat. Kunsan U., South Korea, Calouste Gulbenkian Found., Portugal. Mem. Portuguese-Am. Bus. Assn., Portuguese-Am. Fedn., Nat. Soc. Fine Arts, Nat. Trust Historic Preservation, Casa da Madeira Norte, Portuguese Tchrs. Assn., Fall River Assn., Home: 27 Alfred St Fall River MA 02721-2620

ANDRAKE, NANCY CAROLYN, retired secondary school educator; b. Elmira, NY, Jan. 12, 1944; d. Stephen Francis Andrake and Theresa Ida Skoreski; m. Edward J. Jeziorski Jr., July 4, 1970 (div. Feb. 1984); children: Jennifer Granger, Carolyn Jeziorski, Edward Jeziorski, Patrick Jeziorski. BA cum laude, Coll. Misericordia, Dallas, 1965; MA, Fla. State U., 1967; postgrad., SUNY Stonybrook, Elmira Coll., SUNY Cortland, U. Del. Latin/English tchr. Hammondsport Sch. Dist., NY, 1966—70; Latin/Greek/English tchr. Horseheads Sch. Dist., NY, 1970—; English/study skills tchr. Elmira Summer Sch., NY, 1984—; ret. Horseheads Sch. Dist., 2005; English tchr. Taejon Christian Internat. Sch., Republic of Korea, 2005—; ret. Sales assoc. Kaufmann's Dept. Store, Horseheads, 1995—; cons. Latin Regents Exam NY State Dept. Edn., Albany, 1985—. Leader Girl Scouts Am., Hammondsport, 1965—70, Elmira, 1980—90; mem., pres. St. Casimir's Parish Coun., Elmira, 1984—90. Fellow Rockefeller Found., Am. Sch., Athens, 1989; grantee NEH, 1982; scholar Corning Sister Cities, to teach in Poland, 1999. Mem.: Nat. Jr. Classical League, NY State Jr. Classical League (co-chair 1986—96), Classical Assn. Empire State (bd. dirs. 1986—96), Am. Fedn. Tchrs., NY State United Tchrs., Horseheads Tchrs. Assn. (rep. 1985—90, 2002—), Lambda Iota Tau, Sigma Phi Sigma, Kappa Gamma Pi. Roman Catholic. Avocations: European travel, reading, music, taking students on trips. Home: 51 Ashland Ave Elmira NY 14903 Office: Horseheads High Sch 401 Fletcher St Horseheads NY 14845 E-mail: magistrahhds@yahoo.com.

ANDRAU, MAYA HEDDA, physical therapist; b. Digboi, Assam, India, Apr. 15, 1936; came to U.S., 1946; d. William Henry and Klara Irén Judit (Sima) Andrau; married, Sept. 1971 (div. July 1989); children: Francis Meher Traver, Darwin Meher Traver. BS Phys. Therapy, Columbia U., 1958; MA Social Anthropology, NYU, 1966. Lamaze cert. childbirth educator; lic. and registered phys. therapist. Phys. therapist Beekman-Downtown Hosp., N.Y.C., 1958—60; physiotherapist Stamford Hosp., Conn., 1963—64, Benedictine Hosp., Kingston, NY, 1966—69; pvt. practice in phys. therapy and lamaze Woodstock, NY, 1968—71; chief phys. therapist No. Duchess Hosp., Rhinebeck, NY, 1970—71; phys. therapist Waccamaw Pub. Health Dist. S.C. Dept. Health, Myrtle Beach, 1982—84; pain clinic specialist Pain Therapy Ctr. of Columbia, Richland Meml. Hosp., SC, 1986—87; phys. therapist Comprehensive Med. Rehab. Ctr., Conway, SC, 1988—92; phys. therapist, instr. conditioning program Pawleys Island Wellness Inst., SC, 1993; phys. therapist Total Care, Inc., North Myrtle Beach, SC, 1993—97. Instr. phys. conditioning and therapeutic exercise courses, 1980—97; instr. conditioning program Health Focus Brief for TV, 1990; pvt. phys. therapist and instr. Conditioning-Wellness Program UNCA (Coll. for Srs.), Asheville, NC, 1998, Asheville-Buncombe Tech. C.C., Asheville, 1999, Blue Ridge C.C., Flat Rock, NC, 1999—2000, Elderhostel, Montreat, NC, 1999, Montreat, 2001, Montreat, 2003—06, Crescent View Retirement Cmty., Arden, NC, 2001. Mem. Meher Spiritual Ctr., Inc., Alpha Kappa Delta. Follower of Avatar Meher Baba. Avocations: gardening, reading, walking, handwork, singing. Office Phone: 828-236-9196.

ANDRE, ANGELA RENEE, science educator; b. Vallejo, Calif., Nov. 1, 1977; d. John Peter and Gisela Nelson; m. Richard Thomas Andre, Apr. 7, 2001; children: Brynn N., Cannon N. AAS, Santa Rosa Jr. Coll., Calif., 1998; BS, Sonoma State U., Rohnert Park, Calif., 2000; credential tchg., Chapman U., Vacaville, Calif., 2001. Cert. athletic trainer Calif., 2000. Tchr. biology Rincon Valley Christian Sch., Santa Rosa, 2000—.

ANDRÉ, JOY LARAE, elementary school educator, adult education educator, language educator; b. L.A., Apr. 29, 1936; children: Scott, Brent. BA in Music and Edn., Pepperdine U., 1957, postgrad., 1958—75. Life tchg. credential Calif., cert. lang. devel. specialist Calif. Tchr. elem. and adult edn. L.A. Unified Sch. Dist., 1957—93; tchr. adult edn. Saddleback Valley Unified Sch. Dist., Mission Viejo, Calif., 1993—. Mentor tchr. selection com. L.A. Unified Sch. Dist., 1984, bilingual coord., 1985—91, master tchr., 1987—88, ESL coord., 1990—91. Recipient Govt. Studies Program award, Close Up Found., 1998; scholar, Pepperdine U., 1980; Coe fellow. Mem.: AAUW, United Tchrs. L.A., Calif. Ret. Tchrs. Assn., Orange County Natural History Assn., L.A. Conservancy, Laguna Niguel Women's Club (participant/vol. sec. 2002—03). Republican. Presbyterian. Avocations: photography, scrapbooks, collecting Indian art and miniature boxes, reading, travel. Home: 9 Killini Laguna Niguel CA 92677 E-mail: jandreln@hotmail.com.

ANDRE, PAMELA Q. J., library director; b. Lewiston, Maine, Sept. 29, 1942; d. Charles Custer and Wilma (Hall) Quimby; m. Ronald E. Jensen, Dec. 26, 1966 (div. 1971); children: Stacy, Jaylyn; m. James Roch Andre, Mar. 3, 1973; 1 child, Brett. BA, U. N.H., 1964; MLS, U. Md., 1969. Computer programm U.S. Navy Dept., Washington, 1964-66; computer systems analyst Libr. Congress, Washington, 1968-81, asst. chief MARC editorial div., 1981-84; assoc. dir. for automation Nat. Agrl. Libr., USDA, Beltsville, Md., 1984-94, dir., 1994—2000; pres. Internat. Assn. Agrl. Info. Specialists, 2003—. Cons. UN FAO Hdqrs., Rome, 1989, Egyptian Nat. Agrl. Libr., Cairo, 1990. Mem. editorial bd. Libr. Hi Tech, 1989—, Internet Rsch.: Electronic Networking Applications and Policy, 1991—, Microcomputers for Information Management, 1993—; contbr. articles to jours. in field. Recipient Superior Svc. award USDA, 1990; Svc. to the Profession Award, USAIN 2005. Mem. ALA, IAALD. Office: US Dept Agriculture Nat Agrl Libr 10301 Baltimore Ave Beltsville MD 20705-2326

ANDREASEN, NANCY COOVER, psychiatrist, educator, neuroscientist; d. John A. Sr. and Pauline G. Coover; children: Robin, Susan. BA summa cum laude, U. Nebr., 1958, PhD, 1963; MA, Radcliffe Coll., 1959; MD, U. Iowa, 1970. Instr. English Nebr. Wesleyan Coll., 1960—61, U. Nebr., Lincoln, 1962—63; asst. prof. English U. Iowa, Iowa City, 1963—66, resident, 1970—73, asst. prof. psychiatry, 1973—77, assoc. prof., 1977—81, prof. psychiatry, 1981—82, Andrew H. Woods prof. psychiatry, 1992—97, Andrew H. Woods chair psychiatry, 1997—. Sr. cons. Northwick Park Hosp., London, 1983; acad. visitor Maudsley Hosp., London, 1986; dir. Mental Health Clin. Rsch. Ctr., 1987—. Author: The Broken Brain, 1984, Introductory Psychiatry Testbook, 1991; editor: Can Schizophrenia be Localized to the Brain?, 1986, Brain Imaging: Applications in Psychiatry, 1988, Brave New Brain: Conquering Mental Illness in the Era of the Genome, 2001, The Creating Brain: The Neuroscience of Genius, 2005, Am. Jour. Psychiat., 1988—, 1989—93; editor-in-chief:, 1993—2005; contbr. articles to profl. jours. Recipient Rhonda and Bernard Sarnat award NAS, 1999, C. Charles Burlingame award, 1999, Arthur P. Noyes award in schizophrenia, 1999, Lieber prize Nat. Alliance for Rsch. on Schizophrenia and Depression, 2000, Pres.'s Nat. Medal Sci., 2000, Interbrew Baillet-Latour Health prize, 2003, William K. Warren award Internat. Schizophrenia Congress, 2005, Vanderbilt prize in Biomedical Sci., Vanderbilt U. Sch. Medicine, 2006; Woodrow Wilson fellow, 1958-59, Fulbright fellow Oxford U., London, 1959-60. Fellow Royal Coll. Physicians Surgeons Can. (hon.), Am. Psychiat. Assn. (Adolf Meyer award 1999, Disting. Svc. award 2004), Am. Coll. Neuropharmacologists, Royal Soc. Medicine; mem. Am. Acad. Arts and Scis., Am. Psychopathol. Assn. (pres. 1989-90), Inst. Medicine of NAS (coun. 1996—). Office: U Iowa Hosps and Clinics 200 Hawkins Dr Iowa City IA 52242-1057

ANDREASON, LEE (SHARON LEE ANDREASON), sculptor; b. Lebanon, Oreg., Mar. 20, 1937; d. LeRoy and Galdys Edwina (Wells) A.; m. Raymond Locke Eller, Aug. 30, 1957 (div. 1981); 1 child, Jordan Lee; m. Stoddard Pintard Johnston, Dec. 21, 1985 (div. 1998). Performing artist Screen Extras Guild, Hollywood, Calif., 1962-70, Santa Barbara, Calif., 1975, Pebble Beach, Calif., 1981—2002, Andalucia, Spain, 2000—. One-woman shows include Pacific Grove Art Ctr., 1984, Zantman Art Gallery, Carmel, 1989, Highlands Sculpture Gallery, Carmel, 1991, 92, 93, Galeria Brisamar, Marbella, Spain, 1993, Smith Cosby Gallery, Carmel, 1995, Silver Light Gallery, Carmel, 1996, 97, 98, 99, 2000, 2001, Marin-Price Galleries, 1997, Linnemann Gallery, Chgo., 1998, Galerie de Sculpture, Paris, 1999, Amsteleen Gallery, Amsterdam, 2000, Galeria Harpe, Marbella, Spain, 2000, Galeria Las Palomas, Gaucin, Spain, 2000, Gallery Chiromoyo, 2006; group exhbns. include Monterey County (Calif.) Mus. Art, 1984, Gallery Mack, Seattle, 1993, Am. Acad. Equine Art, Ky. Horse Park, Lexington, 1993, 94, 95, Galeria Serie, Madrid, 1993, Galeries Kriesler, Madrid, 1994-95, Galeria Brisamar, Marbella, 1995, Galeria Sculpture, Paris, 1995, 96, 98, 99, Signature Gallery, Del Mar, Calif., 1995, Signature Gallery, San Diego, 1995, Galeria Iris Ryman, Marbella, Spain, 1996, Nova Galeria De Arte, Malaga, Spain, 1996-2005, Gallery 444 Post St., San Francisco, 1999-2006, Ky. Derby Mus., Louisville, 1996, 97-99, Sommer Gallery, Puerto Banus, Spain, 2001-, Reflections Gallery, Sante Fe, 1999-, Horizon Gallery, Santa Fe, 2000-04, 06, David Lee Gallery, 1999-2003, Scottsdale, Ariz., Cody Gallery, Los Olivos, Calif., 2003-2005, Gallery Herbert Leidell, Munich, 2003, Nat. Sculpture Soc., N.Y.C., 2004, Caprichos, Sotogrande, Spain, 2004-05, Galeria el Chirimoyo Jimena de la Frontera, Spain, 2006-; most of her works are reproduced in bronze and sold for pvt. and pub. collections; represented in collections internationally. Founder, pres. Horse Power Internat., Inc., 1989-97, Horse Power Protection Projects, Inc., 1991-97; author horse protection legislation, Sacramento, 1993—. Recipient Gwendolyn May award for outstanding achievement for individual humane contbn. Monterey County SPCA, Monterey, Calif., 1994, recipient, Legion of St. Frances Awd., Internatl. Generic Horse Assn./Horse Aid, lifelong beneficience awd., 1999. Mem. Conv. on the Welfare and Protection of Animals in Transit (N.Am. Free Trade Agreement animal legis. group), Nat. Sculpture Soc. Avocations: sailing, horseback riding, travel to areas of ancient art and civilizations. Office Phone: 34-956-640-281. Business E-Mail: info@andreasonsculptures.com, lee@andreasonsculptures.com.

ANDREASSI, KIMBERLY THOMPSON, mathematics educator; d. William George and Betty Mae Thompson; m. Joseph John Andreassi, Dec. 3, 1959; children: Joseph John, Benjamin James. BA in Math., Conn. Coll., New London, 1984. Cert. tchr. math. Dept. Edn., 1993. Pension cons. New Eng. Life, Boston, 1985—91; tchr. math. Barnstable H.S., Hyannis, Mass., 1993—. Recipient Ruth Wells Sears Math. award, Conn. Coll., 1983. Mem.: NEA, Mass. Tchr. Assn. Liberal. Office Phone: 508-790-6445.

ANDREINI, ELIZABETH B., investment advisor, elementary school educator; b. Pitts., Aug. 7, 1949; d. Louis Ernest and Alice (McCoy) Braun; m. Alan John Andreini, Apr. 20, 1975 (div. July 1981); 1 chld, Alan John. AA, Centenary Coll. for Women, Hackettstown, N.J., 1969; student, U. Fla., 1969; BS, Youngstown (Ohio) State U., 1972. Cert. tchr., Calif.; registered rep. N.Y. Stock Exch. Asst. youth dir. YWCA, Portland, Maine, 1972-74; Oppenheimer & Co., N.Y.C., 1974-76; Paine Webber Jackson & Curtis, N.Y.C., 1976-77; Oppenheimer & Co., San Francisco, 1982-84; aide Reed Sch., Tiburon, Calif., 1985-87; K-1 tchr. Bright Beginnings Sch., Corte Madera, Calif., 1991-92; registered rep. Charles Schwab, Corte Madera, 1993—. Dir. Metrin Skincare bd. dirs. Pixley Arms Homeowners. Mem. task force New Corte Madera Recreation Ctr., 1995; mem. neighborhood emergency relief team Corte Madera Fire Dept., 1995. Mem. DAR, Mt. Tam Racquet Club, San Francisco Jr. League. Republican. Christian Scientist. Avocations: swimming, dance, running, golf, skiing. Office: Charles Schwab Corp 403 Corte Madera Town Ctr Corte Madera CA 94925-1215 Home: 825 Ketch Dr Apt 301 Naples FL 34103-4183

ANDREOLI, KATHLEEN GAINOR, nurse, educator, dean; b. Albany, NY, Sept. 22, 1935; d. John Edward and Edmunda Elizabeth (Ringlemann) Gainor; children: Paula Kathleen, Thomas Anthony, Karen Marie. BSN, Georgetown U., 1957; MSN, Vanderbilt U., 1959; DSN, U. Ala., Birmingham, 1979. Staff nurse Albany Hosp. Med. Ctr., 1957; instr. St. Thomas Hosp. Sch. Nursing, Nashville, 1958—59, Georgetown U. Sch. Nursing, 1959—60, Duke U. Sch. Nursing, 1960—61, Bon Secours Hosp. Sch. Nursing, Balt., 1962—64; ednl. coordinator, physician asst. program, instr. coronary care unit nursing inservice edn. Duke U. Med. Ctr., Durham, NC, 1965—70; ednl. dir. physician asst. program dept. medicine U. Ala. Med. Ctr., Birmingham, 1970—75, clin. assoc. prof. cardiovasc. nursing Sch. Nursing, 1970—77, asst. prof. nursing dept. medicine, 1971, assoc. prof., 1972—, assoc. prof. nursing Sch. Pub. and Allied Health, 1973—; assoc. dir. Family Nurse Practitioner Program, 1976, assoc. prof. cmty. health nursing Grad. Program, 1977—79, assoc. prof. dept. pub. health, 1978—79; prof. nursing, spl. asst. to pres. for ednl. affairs U. Tex. Health Sci. Ctr., Houston, 1979—82, acting dean Sch. Allied Health Scis., 1981, v.p. for ednl. svcs., interdisciplinary edn., internat. programs, 1983—87; v.p. nursing affairs Rush-Presbyn.-St. Lukes's Med. Ctr., Chgo., 1987—; dean Rush U. Coll. Nursing, 1987—2005, Kellogg emeritus dean, 2005—. Mem. nat. adv. nursing coun. VHA, 1992; adv. bd. Nursing Spectrum, midwest region, 1995—2005; cons. in field. Editor: Heart and Lung, Jour. of Total Care, 1971; editl. bd. Nursing Consult, Elsevier Publs., 2004—05; contbr. articles to profl. jours.; author, editor: Comprehensive Cardiac Care, 1983. Active Internat. Nursing Coalition for Mass Casualty Edn., 2002—; mem. adv. bd. Robert Wood Johnson Clin. Nurse Sch. Program; mem. vis. com. Vanderbilt U. Sch. Nursing; mem. Leadership Ill., 1991; mem. nat. nursing asdv. com. Voluntary Hosp. Am., 1991; mem. governing coun. Inst. for Hosp. Clin. Nursing Edn., Am. Hosp. Assn., 1993; bd. dirs. Ill. League for Nursing, 1994, Lyric Opera Chgo. Guild; bd. dirs., chair rsch. and edn. com. Rehab. Inst. Chgo., 2004—; adv. bd. Hospice Ptnrs. Recipient Founder's award, N.C. Heart Assn., 1970, Disting. Alumni award, Vanderbilt U. Sch. Nursing, 1985, Leadership Tex. award, 1985, Disting. Alumni award, U. Ala. Sch. Nursing, 1991, Henry Betts MD Employment Advocacy award, 2004, Sage Mentor award, Ill. Nursing Leadership Annual Conf., 2005. Fellow: Am. Acad. Nursing; mem.: ACNA, ANA, Internat. Nursing Coalition for Mass Casualty Edn., Inst. Medicine Chgo. (bd. govs. 2004—, sec. bd. 2005—), Nat. Nursing Adv. Coun. Hosps. Am., Am. Heart Assn. Coun. Cardiovasc. Nursing, Coun. Family Nurse Practitioners and Clinicians, Ala. Heart Assn., Nat. League Nursing, Inst. Medicine of NAS, Am. Assn. Colls. Nursing (dean emeritus 2005—), Rotary One Club Chgo., Phi Kappa Phi, Alpha Eta, Sigma Theta Tau (Dreher Outstanding Dean award 2003, Rehab. Inst. of Chgo. Henry Setts Disability Advocacy award 2004, U. Ill. Power Nursing Nursing Mentor award 2005, Sage Membership award Ill. Nursing Leadership Conf. 2005). Roman Catholic. Home: 1212 N Lake Shore Dr Apt 10AN Chicago IL 60610-2359 Office: 1212 N Lake Shore Dr Chicago IL 60610-2359 Office Phone: 312-266-8338. Business E-Mail: kathleen_g_andreoli@rush.edu.

ANDREW, DOLORES MOLCAN, retired art educator, artist; b. Corning, NY, July 11, 1928; d. Ferdinand Joseph and Evelyn May Molcan; m. R. Hugh Andrew, June 12, 1954; children: Julia, Douglas, Catherine. BFA in Painting, Syracuse U., 1951; postgrad., Towson State U., 1975-77; MFA in Art Edn., Md. Inst., 1982. Cert. tchr. embroidery, mixed media. Adult edn. tchr. Columbia (Md.) Assoc., 1971-72, Essex C.C., Balt., 1976-80, from asst. to assoc. prof. art, 1980—98; tchr. Rehoboth Art League, Rehoboth Beach, Del., 1985—, Goucher Coll., Towson, Md., 1990-95; supt. paintings & photography Md. State Fair, Timonium, 1987—2001, supt. fine arts, 2001—. Lectr. in field. Author: Italian Renaissance Textiles, 1986, Medieval Tapestry Designs, 1992, American Sampler Designs, 1996; designer copyrights for crewel designs; one woman shows include Gibson Island, Md., 1993, 98, 2005, Garrett C.C., McHenry, Md., 1994, Gibson Island, Md., 2005; others; contbr. illustrations to Balt. Sun, 1988-2000. Nat. dir. judging certification Nat. Acad. Needlearts, 1988-94, nat. pres., 1990-94, master judge Recipient Lifetime Achievement award, Nat. Acad. Needlearts, 2005. Em. NLAPW (pres. Carroll br. 1976-78, Md. state pres. 1992-94), Artists Equity Assn. (corr. sec. Md. chpt. 1987-92, recording sec. 1987-92), Md. Pastel Soc. (charter, pres. 1985-87), Embroiderers Guild Am. (charter). Democrat. Episcopalian. Avocations: reading, swimming, baking.

ANDREW, KATHRYN ANDERSON, elementary school educator; b. Carthage, S.D., Mar. 14, 1934; d. Alan Albert Anderson and Marie Victoria (Lee) McCaskey; m. Charles Alfred Andrew, June 28, 1959; children: Charles, Jennifer, Richard. BA in Elem. Edn., Colo. Coll., 1956. Tchr. Denver Pub. Schs., 1956-57, Coronado (Calif.) Pub. Schs., 1957-60, Lemoore (Calif.) Pub. Schs., 1965-66; tchr. at various schs. Arlington (Tex.) Indep. Sch. Dist., 1976-94, ret., 1994. Mem. campus planning com. Butler Elem. Sch., Arlington Tex., 1990-94. Pres. Nottingham Neighbors, Grand Prairie, Tex., 1974-75, mem., 1972-2006; mem. chancel choir First Presbyn. Ch., Arlington, 1973—. Named Newcomer Yr. City of Grand Prairie, 1973. Mem. NEA, Tex. State Tchrs. Assn., Arlington Choral Soc., Touch of Class Singers, Gamma Phi Beta. Republican. Presbyterian. Avocations: singing, travel. Home: 2410 Sir Guy Dr Grand Prairie TX 75050-2147

ANDREWS, DONNA L., professional golfer; b. Lynchburg, Va., Apr. 12, 1967; d. James Barclay and Helen Louise (Munsey) Andrews. BBA, U. N.C., 1989. Qualified golfer LPGA Tour, Fla., 1990; winner Ping-Cellular One Golf Tounament, Portland, Oreg., 1993, Ping-Welch's Golf Tournament, Tucson, Ariz., 1994, Dinah Shore Major Golf Tournament, Palm Springs, Calif., 1994, Longs Drugs Challenge, Lincoln, CA, 1998. Named to Lynchburg Area Sports Hall of Fame, 2001. Office: LPGA 100 International Golf Dr Daytona Beach FL 32124-1092

ANDREWS, ELIZABETH ANNE, human services and social work educator; b. Charlotte, N.C., June 21, 1947; d. Joshua and Barbara Wright. BA magna cum laude, Weber State U., Ogden, Utah, 1980; postgrad., Calif. State U., San Bernardino, 1984; MSW, Norfolk (Va.) State U., 1993. Asst. continuing edn. Weber State U., Ogden, 1976-80; tchr. Victor Valley Sch. Dist., Apple Valley, Calif., 1982-84, Hampton Roads Acad., Newport News, Va., 1984-86, Hampton (Va.) City Schs., 1986-88; CD program coord. Charter Colonial Inst., Newport News, 1989-91; dept. chair Roanoke-Chowan C.C., Ahoskie, N.C., 1993-96; ast. prof. Thomas Nelson C.C., Hampton, 1996—, asst. divsn. chair, 1997—. Va. state rep. So. Orgn. Human Svc. Edn., 1997—; bd. mem. Colonial Svcs. Bd., Williamsburg, Va., 1997—; cons., advisor Curriculum Improvement Project, N.C. C.C. Sys., Raleigh, 1995-97; suicide crisis team leader Hampton H.S., 1986-88. Author: (poetry) Faith at Work. Evening supr. H.E.L.P. House, Ahoshie, N.C., 1996; lay youth advisor Diocese So. Va. Episcopal Ch., Norfolk, Va., 1992-94; owner The Pickled Steamer Café, Avon, NC. Recipient 1st pl. award WSU Writing Contest, 1980. Mem. NASW, ACA (Va. rep. 1995-97), Nat. Orgn. Human Svc. Edn., Nat. Restaurant Assn., Phi Kappa Phi, Lambda Iota Tau. Office: Thomas Nelson CC PO Box 9470 Hampton VA 23607 Office Phone: 757-825-2782. Business E-Mail: andrewsa@tncc.edu.

ANDREWS, GAYLEN, public relations executive; Pres. Blitz Media-Direct, Middle Island, NY. Office: Blitz Media-Direct Communications Bldg PO Box 102 Middle Island NY 11953-0102 Office Phone: 631-924-8555. Business E-Mail: blitz4pr@att.net. E-mail: 2gandrews@optonline.net.

ANDREWS, JANE SILVEY, musician; b. Marshall, Tex., May 15, 1953; d. James Harold and Mary Louise Silvey; m. Robert Franklin Andrews, Nov. 22, 1980; children: Zane, Byron, Banning. BME, Centenary Coll. La., 1975; MM, S.W. Baptist Theological Sem., 1979, DMA, 1986. Prof. piano/theory So. Baptist Coll., Walnut Ridge, Ark., 1979-82; adj. prof. piano S.W. Baptist Theol. Sem., Ft. Worth, 1987—; staff accompanist Arlington Choral Soc., 1986—; keyboardist Tex. Wind Symphony, 2001—; pvt. piano tchr. Ft. Worth, 1986—; organist Overton Park United Meth. Ch., Ft. Worth, 1997—. Mem. Ft. Worth Piano Tchrs. Forum (pres. 1994-96), Ft. Worth Music Tchrs. Assn., Creative Motion Alliance (sec.) Baptist. Home: 7512 Meadow Creek Dr Fort Worth TX 76123-1002

ANDREWS, JANICE D., elementary school educator; b. Metropolis, Ill., Mar. 15, 1947; d. Leo Charles and Frieda Lavene (Lamb) Downey; m. Jerry D. Andrews, Jan. 8, 1972; 1 child, Jennifer Denise. BS, U. Tampa, 1969; MA, U. South Fla., 1977. Cert. elem. tchr., Fla., Cert. ESOL. Tchr. Pinellas County

Sch. Bd., St. Petersburgh, Fla., Hillsborogh County Sch. Bd., Tampa, Fla. Mem. NEA, Fla. Teaching Profession, Hillsborough Classroom Tchrs. Assn., Kappa Delta Pi, Phi Delta Kappa. Home: PO Box 10766 Tampa FL 33679

ANDREWS, DAME JULIE (JULIA ELIZABETH WELLS), actress, singer; b. Walton-on-Thames, Eng., Oct. 1, 1935; d. Edward C. and Barbara Wells; m. Tony Walton, May 10, 1959 (div.); 1 child, Emma Walton; m. Blake Edwards, 1969; adopted children: Amy Edwards, Joanna Edwards stepchildren: Jennifer Edwards, Geoffrey Edwards. Studied with pvt. tutors, studied voice with Mme. Stiles-Allen. Debut as singer, Hippodrome, London, 1947; appeared in pantomime Cinderella, London, 1953; appearances include (Broadway prodns.) The Boy Friend, NYC, 1954, (& Conn., 2005), My Fair Lady, 1956-60 (NY Drama Critics award 1956), Camelot, 1960-62, Putting It Together, 1993, Victor/Victoria, 1995 (Tony award nominee Best Actress in a Musical); films include Mary Poppins, 1964 (Acad. award for Best Actress 1964), The Americanization of Emily, 1964, Torn Curtain, 1966, The Sound of Music, 1966, Hawaii, 1966, Thoroughly Modern Millie, 1967, Star!, 1968, Darling Lili, 1970, The Tamarind Seed, 1973, 1979, Little Miss Marker, 1980, S.O.B, 1981, Victor/Victoria, 1982, The Man Who Loved Women, 1983, That's Life!, 1986, Duet For One, 1986, A Fine Romance, 1992, Relative Values, 2000, The Princess Diaries, 2001, Unconditional Love, 2002, Shrek 2 (voice), 2004, The Princess Diaries 2: The Royal Engagement, 2004; TV debut in High Tor, 1956; star TV series The Julie Andrews Hour, 1972-73 (Emmy award for Best Variety Series), Julie, 1992; also spls.; TV movies include Our Sons, 1991, One Special Night, 1999, Eloise at the Plaza, 2003; author: (as Julie Edwards): Mandy, 1971, The Last of the Really Great Whangdoodles, 1974; recs.: The King and I, 1992. Named World Film Favorite (female), 1967; named to 100 Great Britons, 2002; recipient Golden Globe award, Hollywood Fgn. Press Assn., 1964, 1965, Lifetime Achievement award, Kennedy Ctr., 2001. Achievements include knighted by Queen Elizabeth, 1999.

ANDREWS, MINERVA WILSON, retired lawyer; b. Rock Hill, S.C., Feb. 1, 1925; d. York Lowry and Minnie de Foix (Long) Wilson; m. Robert Taylor Andrews, Apr. 15, 1950 (dec. Aug. 2006); children: Susan Allison (Mrs. Robert N. Wiles), Stuart Davidson. AB, U. S.C., 1945; LLB, U. Va., 1948. Bar: Va. 1948. Trial atty. antitrust divsn. U.S. Dept. Justice, Washington, 1949—55; assoc. atty. Bauknight, Prichard, McCandlish & Williams, Fairfax, Va., 1963—72, Boothe, Prichard & Dudley, 1972—80; ptnr. Boothe, Prichard & Dudley, and McGuire, Woods, et al. (merged), McLean, Va., 1980—91; ret., 1992. Author: Carolina-Virginia Recollections, 1999, A Carolina-Virginia Genealogy, vol. 2, 2000. Pres. Nat. Soc. Arts & Letters, 1994—96; bd. dirs. Mclean Citizen Assn., 1968—2000, Fairfax/Falls Ch. United Way, Vienna, Va., 1988—2001; life elder Lewinsville Presbyn. Ch., McLean, 1980—2003; elder Westminster Presbyn. Ch., Charlottesville, Va., 2004—. Named Citizen of the Yr. Fairfax County Fedn. Citizen Assn. and Washington Post, 1997. Mem.: Nat. Soc. Arts and Letters (pres. Wash. chpt. 1973—74), Fairfax Bar Assn. (past chmn. real estate com.), Va. Bar Assn. (chmn. real property com. 1980—82, William B. Spong Jr. Professionalism award 2001), Va. State Bar (past chmn. real property sect.). Republican. Office: Court Square Bldg 310 4th St NE Ste 300 Charlottesville VA 22902-1288

ANDREWS, PAT R., political science professor; d. Richard and Frances Andrews; children: Lisa Taiz, Christopher Taiz. BA, San Jose State U., Calif., 1975; MA in Social Sci., Calif. State U, San Jose, 1983, MA in Polit. Sci., 1985. Cert. secondary edn. tchr. Calif., social sci. tchr. Calif. Chmn. polit. sci. dept. West Valley Coll., Saratoga, Calif., 1998—, chmn. social sci. divsn., 2002—. Author: (textbook) Government in Action, 1990, Voices of Diversity: Perspectives on American Ideals and Institutions, Voices of Diversity, Twentieth Century Perspectives on History and Government, Voices of Diversity Perspectives on American History, 1995, Voices of Diversity 20th Century Perspectives on History and Government, 2000. Recipient award for excellence, West Valley Coll., 2003; Dean's scholar, San Jose State U., 1975. Mem.: Assn. Cert. Educators (pres. 2004—06), Assn. Coll. Educators, Faculty Assn. Calif. Cmty. Colleges. Avocation: writing. Office Phone: 408-867-2200. Personal E-mail: pat_andrews@westvalley.edu.

ANDREWS, SALLY MAY, academic administrator; b. Westfield, Mass., Feb. 29, 1956; d. Roger N. and Dorothy M. (Goodhind) A. Student, U. Conn., Storrs, 1974-76; BA, Simmons Coll., Boston, 1978; MBA, Boston U., 1986. Payroll clk. Children's Hosp., Boston, 1978-79, asst. payroll supr., 1979-81, staff analyst dept. medicine, 1981-83, asst. adminstr. dept. medicine, 1983-86, adminstr. dept. medicine, 1986-97, vice chair adminstrn. and strategic planning dept. medicine, 1998-01; exec. dir. Osher Inst. and divsn. for rsch. and edn. in complementary and integrative med. therapies Harvard Med. Sch., Boston, 2002—. Mem. bd. overseers Lasell Coll., Newton, Mass., 1993-2001, trustee, 2001—. Mem. Adminstrs. Internal Medicine, Assn. Adminstrs. in Acad. Pediat. (pres. 1996-97). Congregationalist. Office: Osher Inst Harvard Med Sch Landmark Ctr Ste 22A 401 Park Dr Boston MA 02215 Business E-Mail: sally_andrews@hms.harvard.edu.

ANDREWS, SALLY S., lawyer; BA, Duke U.; MAT, Harvard U., U. N.C.; JD, U. Tex., 1984. Bar: Tex., U.S. Tax Ct., U.S. Dist. Ct. (so., no., ea. and we. dists.) Tex., U.S. Ct. Appeals (5th Cir.), U.S. Supreme Ct., 2003. With Rockefeller Bros. Fund; faculty assoc. Duke U. Med. Ctr., Tex. Med. Ctr. Sch. Pub. Health; pvt. practice Houston. Author: Elder Law Handbook Houston Bar, 1999, 2003, 2005; case editor: Tex. Internat. Law Jour., 1983—84. Adv. mem. tech. adv. com. Greater Houston YMCA, mem. endowment devel. com.; vol. Peace Corps, Ethiopia, mem. U.S. govt. selection and tng. staff; bd. dirs. Women's Bus. Support Network Found., 2003—, chair, 2006; dir. Women's Polit. Forum, 2004-. Recipient, 1996 Women on The Move award KHOU-TV, The Houston Chronicle, Star award Assn. Women Attys.; named Woman of Excellence, Houston Fedn. Profl. Women, 2005 Fellow: Houston Bar Found.; mem.: Women on the Move (judge 2004, chief judge 2005), Houston Bar (bd. mem. Houston Lawyer Referral Svcs. 2003—, treas. 2004—, chair fin. com. 2004—, v.p. 2006—, chair experience panel), State Bar Tex. (chair 1994—95), Houston Estate Fin. Forum, Houston Bus. and Estate Coun., Tex. Acad. Probate and Trust Lawyers, Coll. State Bar Tex., Christian Legal Soc., Tex. Exec. Women (past bd. mem.), Rotary (pres. Galleria area club 1995—96, asst. gov. 1996—98, 2001—02, Hall of Honor Rotarian of Yr., Multiple Paul Harris fellow, Internat. Svc. Citations 1999, 2004), Phi Beta Kappa, Phi Delta Phi, Phi Kappa Delta, Pi Sigma Alpha. Office: 2 Bering Pk 800 Bering Dr Ste 200 Houston TX 77057-2130 Office Phone: 713-787-6648. Personal E-mail: andrews_nelson@compuserve.com.

ANDREWS, THEODORA ANNE, retired librarian, educator; b. Carroll County, Ind., Oct. 14, 1921; d. Harry Floyd and Margaret Grace (Walter) Ulrey; m. Robert William Andrews, July 18, 1940 (div. 1946); 1 child, Martin Harry. BS with distinction, Purdue U., 1953; MS, U. Ill., 1955. Asst. reference libr. Purdue U., West Lafayette, Ind., 1955—56, pharmacy libr., 1956—79, instr. libr. sci., 1956—60, asst. prof., 1960—65, assoc. prof., 1965—71, prof., 1971—79, 1991—92, prof. libr. sci., pharmacy, nursing and health scis. libr., 1979—90, spl. bibliographer, 1991—92, prof. emeritus libr. sci., 1992—. Del. Ind. Gov.'s Conf. Librs. and Info. Svcs., 1978. Author: A Bibliography of the Socioeconomic Aspects of Medicine, 1975, A Bibliography of Drug Abuse Including Alcohol and Tobacco, 1977, A Bibliography of Drug Abuse, Supplement, 1977-80, 1981, Bibliography on Herbs, Herbal Remedies and Natural Foods, 1982, Substance Abuse Materials for School Libraries, An Annotated Bibliography, 1985, Guide to the Literature of Pharmacy and the Pharmaceutical Sciences, 1986; sect. editor Advances in Alcohol and Substance Abuse, 1981-92; contbr. articles to profl. jours. Mem. Purdue Women's Caucus, 1973—, v.p., 1975-76, pres., 1976-77, Internat. Women's Yr. Regional Planning Com., 1977. Grad. fellow, U. Ill., 1954—55. Mem. ALA, AAUP, Spl. Libr. Assn. (John H. Moriarty award Ind. chpt. 1972), Med. Libr. Assn., Am. Assn. Colls. Pharmacy, Kappa Delta Pi, Delta Rho Kappa. Baptist. Office: Purdue U Sch Pharmacy West Lafayette IN 47907

ANDREWS-MCCALL, MAXINE R., retired educational administration specialist; d. Emory Adolphus and Pasty L. Ramseur; m. Andrew Neal McCall, Oct. 16, 1999; children: Sabrina Molden, Gigi Slade, Thurman J. Andrews. BS, Fayetteville State U., N.C., 1956; MEd, NC Ctrl. U., Durham, 1963; EdS, East Carolina U., Greenville, 1975; EdD, U N.C., Greensboro, 1985. Tchr. Lewis Chapel Sch., Fayetteville, NC, 1956—66; sch. social worker Cumberland County Schs., Fayetteville, NC, 1966—69, curriculum supr., 1971—90; title III coord. Elizabeth State U., Elizabeth City, NC, 1969—71; asst. prin. Coll. Lakes Sch., Fayetteville, 1971—90; coord. ednl. leadership Fayetteville State U., 1990, master sch. adminstrn., 1990—2005. Mem. adv. bd. State Employees Credit Union, Fayetteville, 1996—99; mem. com. Crown Coliseum, Fayetteville, 1995—97. Recipient Nannie T. Goode award, Fayetteville State U., 1956. Mem.: NC Assn. Adminstrs., Assn. for Supervision and Curriculum Devel. (chpt. pres. 1975), Rotary, Phi Delta Kappa (chpt. pres. 1982), Delta Sigma Theta.

ANDREWS-MCCALL, MAXINE RAMSEUR, retired education educator; b. Cumberland County, N.C. d. Emory Adolphus and Patsy Lee (Evans) Ramseur; children: Sabrina, Gigi, Thurman James III. BS, Fayetteville State U., 1956; MEd, N.C. Cen. U., 1963; EdS, East Carolina U., Greenville, 1975; EdD, U. N.C., Greensboro, 1985. Tchr., social worker Cumberland County Schs., Fayetteville, 1956-69, elem. supr., 1971-84, secondary supr., 1984-90; asst. prof. edn. Fayetteville State U., NC, 1990—2005; dir. teaching fellows program Fayetteville State U.; coord. secondary edn. adminstrn. and supervision Fayetteville State U., ret., 2005. Coord. fed. programs Elizabeth City (N.C.) State U., 1969-71; chmn. various accreditation coms. Author handbook; contbr. articles to profl. jours. Mem. Assn. Supervision and Curriculum Devel. (chpt. pres. 1975, regional pres. 1987-89, state sec. 1988-91), NEA, Internat. Reading Assn., N.C. Assn. Educators (chpt. pres. 1979), Nat. Assn. Elem. Sch. Prins., N.C. Assn. Adminstrs., N.C. Coun. Social Studies, Jack and Jill Am., Phi Delta Kappa (pres. 1982), Delta Sigma Theta. Democrat.

ANDRIAN-CECIU, ROXANNE R., engineer, financial analyst; b. Bucarest, Romania, Dec. 2, 1960; came to the U.S., 1998; d. Alexandru and Adina Andrian; m. Aurel Mike Ceciu, Sept. 14, 1985; children: Sebastian, Stefan. Engring. diploma, Poly. Inst., Bucarest, 1984; MS, U. Paul Sabatier, Toulouse, France, 1992; PhD, U. Montreal, Can., 1999. Registered profl. engr., Can. Engr., supr. Machine Tool Enterprise, Bucarest, 1984-86; design engr. Machine Tool Inst., Bucarest, 1986-90; program coord. G. Soros Found. for An Open Soc., Bucarest, 1990-91; rsch./tchg. asst. U. Montreal, 1993-97; mfg. engr. Bombardier-Canadair, Montreal, 1998; design engr. GE, Erie, Pa., 1998-99; bus. analyst Six Sigma Black Belt, GE, Erie, 1999—. Cons., owner R. Andrian-Cons., Montreal, 1996-98. Mem. ASME (assoc., chmn. Erie chpt. 1999—), Soc. Mfg. Engrs., Soc. Automotive Engrs. (affiliate), Soc. Women Engrs. (sect. rep. Erie chpt. 1999—). Achievements include inventor of device for the tool-holders clamping, unlocking and rotation, tool magazine, device for tool transport.

ANDRUS, SHARON ARLENE, electrical engineer, researcher; d. Howard Guion Andrus and Helen Arlene Shindledecker; m. Daniel Trembley, May 5, 1998. AAS in Elec. Tech., Tompkins Cortland C.C., Dryden, N.Y., 1991; BA in Anthropology, SUNY, Cortland, 2006. Quality control insp. Deanco Inc., Ithaca, NY, 1993—95; tech. assoc. Diversifed T.E.S.T. Technologies, Groton, NY, 1995—98; engring. support and certification specialist Pathlight Tech. Inc., Ithaca, 1998—2001, Advanced Digital Info. Corp., Ithaca, 2001—04. Recipient Anthropology award for Outstanding Academic Achievement, SUNY Cortland Anthropology Dept., 2005. Mem.: Tau Sigma, Alpha Sigma Lambda, Phi Kappa Phi.

ANDRUS, TIFFANY SHANTEL, mathematics professor; b. Lake Charles, La., Apr. 7, 1983; d. Edward L. and Dianna L. Rose; m. Jason Andrus, Dec. 19, 2003. BS Math., McNeese State U., Lake Charles, La., 2004; MS Math. Scis., McNeese State U., 2005. Lab asst. remedial math. McNeese State U., Lake Charles, 2002—04, grad. asst., 2004—05, instr., 2005, instr. math., 2006—. Class leader vacation Bible sch. First United Pentecostal Ch., Lake Charles, 2003—06, musician, 2000—06. H.C. Brewer Scholarship, McNeese State U., 2005. Mem.: Math Assn. Am., Pi Mu Epsilon, Alpha Lambda Delta, Phi Kappa Phi (life). D-Conservative. Pentecostal. Achievements include research in A Class of Antiautomorphisms of Mendelsohn Triple Systems with Two Cycles. Avocations: reading, music, travel. Office: McNeese State University PO Box 92340 Lake Charles LA 70605-2340

ANDRZEJEWSKI, PAT **See BENATAR, PAT**

ANEJA, ALKA, child psychiatrist; b. New Delhi, Feb. 5, 1971; arrived in U.S., 1997; d. K.G. and Parkash Aneja; 1 child, Esha Grewal. B Medicine and Surgery, Maulana Azad Med. Coll., New Delhi, 1995; MA, Western Carolina U., 1999. Resident in adult psychiatry Drexel U., Phila., 2000—02, SUNY Upstate Med. U., Syracuse, NY, 2002—03, 2005—06; fellow in child psychiatry Johns Hopkins U., Balt., 2003—05. Rsch. asst. Western Carolina U., Cullowhee, NC, 1997—99; mem. staff Nat. Eating Disorders Screening Program, Cullowhee, 1998; presenter in field. Contbr. articles to profl. jours. Mem.: Am. Assn. Child and Adolescent Psychiatry, Am. Psychiat. Assn., Sigma Xi. Avocations: playing harmonium, music, art, cooking, meditation. Office: Kennedy Krieger Inst 3901 Greenspring Ave Baltimore MD 21211 Office Phone: 443-923-7620. Business E-Mail: aneja@kennedykrieger.org.

ANFINSEN, LIBBY ESTHER SHULMAN, social worker, clinical administrator; b. Jersey City, Dec. 20, 1937; d. Herman and Shirley Ann (Stiskin) Shulman; m. 2d, Christian Boehmer Anfinsen, Mar. 1, 1979; children: Mark H. Ely, Tobie R. Beckerman, Daniel J. Ely, David A. Ely. BA, Bklyn. Coll., 1954; MSW, NYU, 1956. Lic. cert. clin. social worker, Md.; diplomat in clin. social work; lic. clin. social worker. Clin. social worker NIH Clin. Ctr., Bethesda, Md., 1966-81; pvt. practice individual and group therapy Balt., Silver Spring, Md., 1980-95; dir. social svcs. Children's Hosp. and Ctr. for Reconstructive Surgery, Balt., 1983-85; social worker Balt. County Health Dept., Towson, Md., 1985-91. Devel. disabilities adminstr. Balt. County Health Dept., Balt. City Dept. Edn. Spl. Svcs. for Children with Learning Disorders, 1993-2001; interviewer child Devel. Rsch. Jerome Riker Found. for Persecution of Holocaust Children, Balt. and N.Y.C., 1983-95; mem. med. bd. NIH Clin. Ctr., Bethesda, Md.; organizer Israeli delegation Confs. of Nobel Prize Laureates, Lindau, 2003—. Contbr. articles to profl. publs. Comdr. USPHS, 1974-81. Mem. ACSW, NASW, Zionist Orgn. Am., Vols. for Israel, Israel Bond Prime Ministers Club, Israel Investment Club (Balt.). Jewish. Avocations: travel, reading, sailing, music, sports, writing. Home: 11205 Tildencrest Ct Potomac MD 20854-2770 also: 1740 Vineyard Trail Annapolis MD also: 11/3 Luppo St Jerusalem Israel Personal E-mail: lesa18@msn.com.

ANFINSON, DONNA MAE, retired elementary school educator, home economics educator; b. Williston, N.D., Nov. 24, 1944; m. Edward Anfinson, July 13, 1968; children: John, David. BS in Home Econs. Edn., N.D. State U., 1966; MA in Edn., Chapman Coll., 1970; BS in Elem. Edn., Minot State U., 1988. Cert. elem. tchr., N.D., Calif. Tchr. Dos Palos (Calif.) Joint Union High Sch., 1966-68, Grenora (N.D.) High Sch., 1968-69; substitute tchr. New Pub. Sch. Dist. 8, Williston, 1970-86, tchr. 1st and 2d grades, 1986—2004; ret., 2004. Tutor ESL, Zahl, N.D., 1980. Sunday sch. tchr. Zahl Luth. Parish, 1975-80, lay catechist, 1980-90; local leader 4-H Club, Zahl, 1989-92; advisor Williams County Jr. Leaders, 4-H, Williston, 1985-92. Mem. NEA, Nat. Coun. Tchrs. of Maths., N.D. Edn. Assn. (local pres. 1990-91). Avocations: photography, travel, children's activities. Home: 8231 138th Ave NW Zahl ND 58856

ANGEL, MARINA, law educator; b. NYC, July 21, 1944; BA, Barnard Coll., N.Y.C., 1965; JD magna cum laude, Columbia U., 1969; LLM, U. Pa., Phila., 1977. Bar: N.Y. 1969, Pa. 1971, U. S. Dist. Ct. (ea. dist.) Pa. 1971, U.S. Dist. Ct. (so. and ea. dists.) N.Y. 1973, U.S. Supreme Ct. 1974. Law clk. NAACP Legal Def. & Edn. Fund; atty. Phila. Voluntary Assn.; assoc. prof. Hofstra U. Law Sch., L.I., N.Y., 1971-78; assoc. Gordon & Shectman, PC, N.Y.C., 1973-75; prof. Temple U. Law Sch., Phila., 1979—, assoc. dean grad. legal studies, 1983-84, dir. summer sessions abroad Greece Athens, 1981-83, 85, 87, 89. Vis. prof. Queensland Inst. Tech.and Wollongong U., Australia, 1992, Tel Aviv Univ., 2001, Univ. Puerto Rico, 2002; Stoneman vis. prof. Albany Law Sch., 2006; gen. counsel Modern Greek Studies Assn., 1995—, Greek Am. Women's Network, 1995—; steering com. Temple U. Faculty Senate, 1996-1999. Author of numerous articles in profl. jours.; developed statistics for Pa. Bar Assn. Annual Report Card. Sec. bd. St. George Sr. Housing Corp., Phila., 1980-88; mem. exec. com. Community Legal Svcs., Phila., 1979-88. Named Most Outstanding Prof., Temple Law Sch., Phila., 1989. Mem. ABA (Margaret Brent Women Lawyers of Achievement award 2004), Penn. Bar Assn. (Anne X. Alpern award, 1998, Spl. Achievement award, 2003), Phila. Bar Assn. (Sandra Day O'Connor award 1996, mem Gender Bias Task Force), Assn. of Bar of City of N.Y., Assn. Am. Law Sch. (chair Women in Legal Edn. sect.). Office: Temple U Law Sch 1719 N Broad St Philadelphia PA 19122-6098

ANGELL, CARYE LOU, science educator; b. Crane, Tex. d. Will Young Benge III and Tommie Ethene Benge; m. Stephen Wayne Angell, Jan. 16, 1987; children: Lisa Farmer Coleman, Eric, Amanda, John. BS in Agr. Edn., Tarleton State U., Stephenville, Tex., 1978; MA in Edn., N.Mex. State U., Las Cruces, 1992. Cert. tchr. cert. N.Mex. Sci. tchr. Paint Rock Ind. Sch. Dist., Tex., 1978—81; tchr. San Vicente Ind. Sch. Dist., Big Bend National Park, Tex., 1981—85; sci. tchr. PR Leyva Jr. High, Carlsbad, N.Mex., 1985—, dist. sci. coord., 1989—. Mem.: Friends of Living Desert. Avocations: reading, fishing, horseback riding, boating. Home: 308 Coleman Rd Carlsbad NM 88220 Office: Carlsbad Sch PR Leyva 800 W Church Carlsbad NM 88220 Office Phone: 505-234-3318 ext. 260. Business E-Mail: caryelou.angell@carlsbad.k12.nm.us.

ANGELL, JEAN E., physical education educator, director; d. William and Emily Angell. BS, U. RI, Kingston, 1973. Cert. athletic adminstr. Nat. Interscholastic Athletic Administrators Assn. Head girls' basketball coach Scituate HS, North Scituate, RI, 1972—, phys. edn./health tchr., 1973—, dir. athletics, 1987—. Field hockey dir. RI Interscholastic League, Providence, 1994—, interscholastic volleyball ofcl., 2005—. Named Tchr. of the Yr., Scituate Sch. Dept., Basketball Coach of the Yr., RI HS Girls Basketball Coaches Assn.; named to Hall of Fame for Women, NE New Agenda. Mem.: RI Interscholastic Athletic Administrators Assn. (assoc.; exec. bd., pres. elect, pres. 1988—). Home: 507 Danielson Pike North Scituate RI 02857 Office: Scituate HS 94 Trimtown Rd North Scituate RI 02857 Office Phone: 401-647-7657. Personal E-mail: ja507@aol.com.

ANGELL, MARCIA, pathologist, editor-in-chief; b. Knoxville, Tenn., Apr. 20, 1939; BS, James Madison U., 1960; MD, Boston U., 1967. Resident in internal medicine Mt. Auburn Hosp., resident in pathology; resident in internal medicine Univ. Hosp.; resident in pathology New Eng. Deaconess Hosp.; with New Eng. Jour. Medicine, Boston, 1979—, exec. editor, 1988, interim editor-in-chief, 1999—. Lectr. Harvard U. Author: Science on Trial: The Clash of Medical Evidence and the Law in the Breast Implant Case; co-author: Basic Pathology. Named One of 25 Most Influential Ams. Time Mag., 1997. Mem. ACP, Inst. Medicine, Assn. Am. Physicians, Mass. Med. Soc. Office: New Eng Jour Medicine 10 Shattuck St Boston MA 02115-6011

ANGELL, MARY FAITH, federal magistrate judge; b. Buffalo, May 7, 1938; d. San S. and Marie B. (Caboni) A.; m. Kenneth F. Carobus, Oct. 27, 1973; children: Andrew M. Carobus, Alexander P. Carobus. AB, Mt. Holyoke Coll.; MSS, Bryn Mawr Coll.; JD, Temple U. Bar: Pa. 1971, U.S. Dist. Ct. (ea. dist) Pa. 1971, U.S. Ct. Appeals (3rd cir.) Pa. 1974, U.S. Supreme Ct. 1979; Acad. Cert. Social Workers. Dir. social work, vol. svcs. Wills Eye Hosp., Phila., 1961-64, 65-69; dir. soc. work dept. juvenile divsn. Defender Assoc., Phila., 1969-71; asst. dist. atty. City of Phila., 1971-72; asst. atty. gen. Commonwealth of Pa., Phila., 1972-74, deputy atty. gen., 1974-78; regional counsel ICC, Phila., 1978-80, regional dir., 1980-88; administrv. law judge Social Security Administrn., Phila., 1988-90; U.S. magistrate judge U.S. Dist. Ct. (ea. dist.) Pa., Phila., 1990—2004, chief U.S. magistrate judge, 2004—. Adj. prof. Temple U. Law Sch., Phila., 1976-94, clin. instr., 1973-76; co-chmn. Commn. on Gender, 3d Cir. Task Force on Equal Treatment in Cts., 1994—99; mem. com. on racial and gender bias in the justice sys. Supreme Ct. of Pa., 2000-02; bd. adv. Grad. Sch. Social Work and Social Rsch. Bryn Mawr Coll., 2004. Federal trustee Defender Assn. Phila., 1985-90; bd. dirs. Child Welfare Adv. Bd., Phila., 1984-90, Federal Cts. 200 Adv. Bd., Phila., 1987-88, Phila. Woman's Network, 1986-88. Recipient Sr. Exec. Svc. award U.S. Govt., 1980. Mem. NASW, FBA (chair exec. com., pres. 1990-92, recognition 1992), Nat. Assn. Women Judges, Fed. Magistrate Judges Assn. (dist. dir. 1994-98), Phila. Bar Assn. (chmn. com. 1976-77), Temple Am. Inn of Cts. (master 1993-98), Third Circuit Task Force on Equal Treatment in the Courts (co-chair Commn. on Gender 1994-97), Temple Law Alumni Exec. Bd. (Women's Law Caucus Honoree 1996). Office: US District Court 601 Market St 3030 US Courthouse Philadelphia PA 19106 Office Phone: 215-597-6079. Business E-Mail: chambers_of_chief_magistrate_judge_m_faith_angell@paed.uscourts.gov.

ANGELL, SAMANTHA, lawyer, educator; d. Cheri Santiago and Richard Parks; m. James Ryan Angell, May 10, 1973; children: Spencer James, Jackson Hugh. JD, Washburn Sch. Law, Topeka, 1999. Bar: Kans. 2000. Atty. Achterberg & Angell, Salina, Kans., 2000—. Adj. prof. Ft. Hays State U., Kans., 2005—. Mem. Salina Area United Way, 2004—06, Salina Cmty. Theatre, 2006; pres. Noon Network AMBUCS, Salina, 2005—06. Recipient Dist. AMBUC of Yr., AMBUCS Dist. 5D, 2004—05. Mem.: Kans. Women's Attorneys Assn. (dist. rep. 2005—06), Saline/Ottawa County Bar Assn., Kans. Bar Assn., Kans. Trial Lawyers Assn. R-Consevative. Office: Achterberg & Angell 118-B S 7th St Salina KS 67401 Office Phone: 785-820-9400.

ANGELO, BONNIE, journalist; b. Winston-Salem; d. Ernest J. and Ethel (Hudgins) A.; m. Harold R. Levy, Aug. 19, 1950; 1 child, Charles Christopher. BA, U. NC, 1944; LittD (hon.), Marist Coll., 1993. Reporter, women's editor Winston-Salem Jour. and Sentinel, 1944-53; women's editor Richmond Times-Dispatch, 1950; feature writer Newsday, 1953-55; Washington corr., 1955-63; syndicated columnist Newhouse Nat. New Svc., 1963-66; corr. WTTG-TV Panorama, 1966-77; Washington corr. Time mag., 1966-67; bur. chief London, 1978-85, New York, 1985-91; corr. at large, 1991-94; contbr., 1994—. Author: (non-fiction) First Mothers: The Women Who Shaped the President, 2000, First Families: The Impact of the White House on Their Lives, 2005. Mem. Women's Nat. Press Club, 1961-62. Recipient Disting. reporting in civil rights Paul Tobenkin Meml. Found., 1961; named to NC Journalism Hall of Fame. Office: Time and Life Bldg Rockefeller Plz New York NY 10020-2002 Mailing: Zachary Shuster Agy 160 Main St Northampton MA 01060

ANGELO, JULIE CRAWFORD, performing arts association administrator; b. Houston, Sept. 16, 1951; d. Priscilla and Clinton Althaus; m. Bill Angelo, Sept. 9, 1989. BA, U. North Tex., Denton, 1974. Exec. dir. Denton Cmty. Theatre, Tex., 1988—94, Am. Assn. of Cmty. Theatre, Lago Vista, Tex., 1994—. Bd. mem./treas. SW Theatre Assn., 1988—2000; bd. mem., v.p. planning and devel. Am. Assn. of Cmty. Theatre; bd. mem. Denton Cmty. Theatre, Tex., 1987—88; bd. mem., pres., treas. Lago Vista C. of C., Tex., 2002. Recipient Lifetime Achievement award, Denton Cmty. Theatre, 1994, Vol. of Yr. award, SW Theatre Assn., 1996, Disting. Svc. award, 1996; fellow, Am. Assn. of Cmty. Theatre, 1996, SW Theatre Assn., 1997. Mem.: Lago Vista Players (treas. 2006), Tex. Nonprofit Theatres. Office: Am Assn of Cmty Theatre 8402 BriarWood Cir Lago Vista TX 78645 Office Phone: 512-267-0711. Office Fax: 512-267-0712. Business E-Mail: angelo@aact.org.

ANGELOU, MAYA (MARGUERITE ANNIE JOHNSON), writer, actress; b. St. Louis, Apr. 4, 1928; d. Bailey and Vivian (Baxter) Johnson; m. Tosh Angelos, 1950, (div. 1952); m. Vusumzi Make, 1960 (div. 1963), m. Paul Du Feu, 1973 (div. 1981), 1 child Guy Johnson. Studied dance with, Pearl Primus, N.Y.C.; degrees (hon.), Smith Coll., 1975, Mills Coll., 1975, Lawrence U., 1976, Portland State U., 1973, Occidental Coll., 1979, Atlanta U., 1980, U. Ark., 1980, U. Minn., 1980, Austin Coll., 1980, Wheaton Coll., 1981, Kean Coll., 1982, Spelman Coll., 1983, Boston Coll., 1983, Winston-

Salem U, 1984, U. Brunesis, 1984, Howard U., 1985, Tufts U., 1985, Va. Commonwealth U., 1985, Northeastern U., 1992, Academy of Southern Arts & Letters, 1993, Brown U., 1994, U. Durham, UK, 1995, Hope Coll., 2001, Columbia U., 2003, Eastern Conn. U., 2003. Taught modern dance The Rome Opera House and Hambina Theatre, Tel Aviv; writer-in-residence U. Kans., Lawrence, 1970; disting. vis. prof. Wake Forest U., 1974-, Wichita State U., 1974, Calif. State U., Sacramento, 1974; apptd. mem. Am. Revolution Bicentennial Council by Pres. Ford, 1975-76; 1st Reynolds prof. Am. Studies, Wake Forest U. 1981-, a lifetime appointment. Author: I Know Why the Caged Bird Sings, 1970, Just Give Me A Cool Drink of Water 'Fore I Die, 1971, Georgia, Georgia, 1972, Gather Together in My Name, 1974, Oh Pray My Wings are Gonna Fit Me Well, 1975, Singin' and Swingin' and Gettin' Merry Like Christmas, 1976, And Still I Rise, 1978, The Heart of a Woman, 1981, Shaker, Why Don't You Sing?, 1983, All God's Children Need Traveling Shoes, 1986, Now Sheba Sings the Song, 1987, I Shall Not Be Moved, 1990, On the Pulse of Morning: The Inaugural Poem, 1993, Lessons in Living, 1993, Wouldn't Take Nothing for My Journey Now, 1993, My Painted House, My Friendly Chicken, and Me, 1994, The Complete Collected Poems of Maya Angelou, 1994, Phenomenal Women: Four Poems for Women, 1995, A Brave and Startling Truth, 1995, From a Black Woman to a Black Man, 1996, Kofi and His Magic, 1996, Extravagant Spirits, 1997, Making Magic in the World, 1998, Even the Stars Look Lonesome, 1997, A Song Flung Up To Heaven, 2002, Angelina of Italy, 2004, Amazing Peace, 2006 (winner of The Quill award for Poetry, 2006); (cookbooks) Hallelujah! The Welcome Table: A Lifetime of Memories with Recipes, 2004; (plays) Cabaret for Freedom, 1960, The Least of These, 1966, Gettin' Up Stayed On My Mind, 1967, Ajax, 1974, Moon On a Rainbow Shawl, 1988; (screenplays) Georgia, Georgia, 1972, All Day Long, 1974; author/prodr. Three Way Choice, Afro-American in the Arts (Golden Eagle award); wrote and presented Trying to Make it Home, 1988; writer for Oprah Winfrey's Harpo Prodns.; poetry writer for film Poetic Justice, 1993; appeared in plays: Porgy and Bess, 1954-55 (Europe), 1957 (U.S.), Calypso, 1957, The Blacks, 1960, Mother Courage, 1964, Medea, Look Away, 1973, Ajax, 1974, And Still I Rise, 1976, Moon on a Rainbow Shawl, 1988; (films) Porgy and Bess, 1959, Poetic Justice, 1993, How to Make an American Quilt, 1995, The Journey of August King, 1995, Madea's Family Reunion, 2006; dir. (films) Down in the Delta, 1998; (TV minseries) Roots, 1977 (Emmy Nom. best sup. actress), TV appearances include The Richard Pryor Special, Sister, Sisters, 1982, There Are No Children Here, 1993, Touched By An Angel, 1995, Moesha, 1999, Runaway, 2000; spoken word albums include The Poetry of Maya Angelou, 1969, Women in Business, 1981, Been Found, 1996; contbd. articles, short stories, poems to Black Scholar, Chgo. Daily News, Cosmopolitan, Harper's Bazaar, Life Mag., Redbook, Sunday N.Y. Times, Mademoiselle Mag., Essence, Ebony Mag., Calif. Living Mag, Ghanaian Times. Apptd. by Dr. Martin Luther King Jr. No. Coord., SCLC, 1959-60, apptd. by Pres. Ford to Bicentennal Commn., by Pres. Carter to Nat. Commn. on Observance of Internat. Women's Yr., ambassador, Unicef Internat., 1996. Chubb fellowship award Yale U., 1970, named Woman of Yr. in Comm., 1976; Ladies Home Jour. Top 100 Most Influential Women, 1983, The Matrix award, 1983, Living Legacy award, Women's Internat. Ctr., 1986, The North Carolina Award in Lit., 1987, Woman of the Yr. Essence Mag., 1992, Disting. Woman of N.C., 1992, Horatio Alger award, 1992, Grammy award best spoken word or non-traditional album, 1994 (for recording of "On the Pulse of the Morning"), Grammy award best spoken or non-traditional album, 1994 (for recording of "Phenomonal Woman"), NAACP Image Award for Outstanding Literary Work for "Even the Stars Look Lonesome", 1997, National Medal of Art, 2001; inducted into the Women's Hall of Fame, 1998; named one of Most Influential Black Americans, Ebony mag., 2006. Mem. AFTRA, Dirs. Guild Am., Equity, Harlem Writers Guild, Am. Film Inst. (trustee), Women's Prison Assn., Horatio Alger Assn. Dist. Americans, Nat. Soc. Prevention of Cruelty to Children (Maya Angelou Ctr. opened 1992), W.E.B. duBois Found., Nat. Soc. Collegiate Scholars, Nat. Soc. High School Scholars. Office: c/o Dave La Camera Lordly and Dame Inc 51 Church St Boston MA 02116-5417*

ANGIER, NATALIE MARIE, science journalist; b. NYC, Feb. 16, 1958; d. Keith and Adele Bernice (Rosenthal) A.; m. Richard Steven Weiss, July 27, 1991. Student, U. Mich., 1974-76; BA, Barnard Coll., 1978. Staff writer Discover Mag., NYC, 1980-83, Time Mag., NYC, 1984-86; editor Savvy Mag., NYC, 1983-84; journalism educator NYU, NYC, 1987-89; became reporter NY Times, NYC, 1990, now science correspondent Washington. Author: Natural Obsessions, 1988, The Beauty of the Beastly, 1995. Recipient Pulitzer Prize for beat reporting, 1991, Journalism award GM Ind. Bd., 1991, Lewis Thomas award Marine Biol. Labs., 1990, Journalism award AAAS, 1992, Disting. Alumna award Barnard Coll., 1993. Mem. Nat. Assn. Sci. Writers. Avocation: weightlifting. Office: NY Times Washington Bureau 1627 I St NW Fl 7 Washington DC 20006-4007*

ANGLIN, KAREN LOCHER, mathematics professor; b. Austin, Tex., Nov. 22, 1958; d. Benjamin Carter and Frances Greer Locher; m. Kevin Lynn Anglin, Jan. 5, 1980; children: Nathan, Nabil, Jasmine Anise, Austin. BS in Math., Tarleton State U., 1979; MS in Stats., Tex. A&M, 1980. Computer programmer Conoco, Midland, Tex., 1981—84; math. instr. Blinn Coll., Brenham, Tex., 1990—2005. Author: Cliffs Quick Review Math Word Problems, 2004. Leader Girl Scouts, Brenham, 1997—2005; mem. rabbit com. Washington County Fair, Brenham, 2001—. Recipient Outstanding Presenter, Conf. for Acad. Support Programs, 1998. Baha'I. Office: Blinn Coll 902 College Ave Brenham TX 77833

ANGSTADT, FRANCES VIRGINIA, language arts and theatre arts educator; b. Dover, Del., Oct. 11, 1953; d. T. Richard Sr. and Frances Virginia (Kohout) A. BA, Del. State U., 1976; MFA, Cath. U. Am., 1982; postgrad. in PhD program, Tex. U. Tech. Lighting designer, assoc. dir. écarté dance Theatre, Dover, 1981-93; alternative tchr. Lake Forest HS, Felton, Del., 1982-87; English tchr. Dover HS, 1987-89; lang. arts, theater tchr. Ctrl. Mid. Sch., Dover, 1989—2003; lighting designer Harrisburg (Pa.) Ballet, 1991-93; lang. arts, theater tchr. Ctrl. Mid. Sch., 2005—. Lighting designer, artistic advisor Act I Players, Dover, 1983-93, lighting designer Balt. Shakespeare Festival, 1994, Kimberly Mackin Dance Co., Balt., Axis Theatre, 1996-99, Women's Project at Theatre Project, Balt., 1997-2000; adj. faculty Del. State U., Dover, 1985-89, Wilmington Coll., Dover, 1996-2001, 2005-06, grad. asst. Tex. Tech. U., 2001-2005; tech. advisor 2d St. Players, Milford, Del., 1994-2001; dance leadership Visual and Performing Arts Commn., Dover, 1994-2000; English devel. com. state (testing) assessment team Dover Dept. of Edn., 1997-2000, ESL assessment team, 2000-2001, intern visual and performing arts, 2002-2003. Mem. Vietnam Vets. Meml. Com., Dover, 1985-87; sec., founding mem. Dover Arts Coun., 1988-93, tech. advisor, 1988-94; sec. Capital Educators Assn., Dover, 1993-2001; tech. advisor City of Dover First Night, 1997-2001; active Balt. Theatre Alliance; apptd. to adjudicator Del. Theatre Assn., 1986, 2004-05. Recipient Excellence in Lighting Design award Tex. Tech. U., 2003-04, Excellence in Lighting TETA Regional award Lighting Design ACTF Festival, Tex., 2005; All Am. Youth Honor Band scholar, 1972, Del. State U. scholar, Dover, 1974-76; Chancellor's guaranteed fellow Tex. Tech. U., 2001-05. Mem. ACLU, AAUW, Human Rights Commn., Nat. Gay & Lesbian Task Force, Nat. Coun. Tchrs. English, U.S. Inst. Tech. Theatre, Assn. Theatre Higher Edn., Theatre Communications Group, S.W. Theatre Assn., Tex. Educators Theatre Assn., Southwest Film and Theater Assn. Avocations: swimming, biking, voice, visual art, dance lighting. Home: 34 Pennwood Dr Dover DE 19901 Office Phone: 302-651-2700. Personal E-mail: gangsta53fva@aol.com.

ANGUIANO, LUPE, advocate; b. La Junta, Colo., June 12, 1929; d. Jose and Rosario (Gonzalez) A. Student, Ventural Jr. Coll., Calif., 1948, Victory Noll Jr. Coll., Huntington, Ind., 1949-52, Marymount Coll., Palos Verdes, Calif., 1958-59, Calif. State U., LA, 1965-67; MA, Antioch-Putney, Yellow Springs, Ohio, 1978. S.W. regional dir. NAACP Legal Def. and Ednl. Fund, L.A., 1965-69; civil rights specialist HEW, Washington, 1969-73; S.W. regional dir. Nat. Coun. Cath. Bishops, Region X, San Antonio, 1973-77; pres. Nat. Women's Employment and Edn. Inc., L.A., 1979-91; cons. Cisco Sys. Inc., 1998-99; pres., cons. Lupe Anguiano & Assocs., 1981—; dir. devel. La Jolla Inst., Van Nuys, Calif., West Valley Alliance; fund devel. dir. Girl Scouts of the San Fernando Valley, Chatsworth, Calif.; rep. Primerica, Valencia, Calif.; mktg. and fund devel. cons. self employed. Cons. Tex. Dept. Human Resources, Dept. Labor, Women's Bur., U.S. Office Pers. Mgmt., USCG, Washington, 1990-92; tech. cons. Cisco Sys. Inc.; developer regional networking acad., Oxnard Coll.; part-time faculty mem. Ventura (Calif.) Coll.; proposal reader U.S. Office Edn., Women's Equity Act; mem. Tex. Adv. Coun. on Tec.-Vocat. Edn., Calif. del. White House Conf. on Status of Mex.-Ams. in U.S., 1967; founding mem. policy coun. Nat. Women's Polit. Caucus, 1971—; Tex. and nat. del. Intrnat. Women's Yr., 1976-77; chmn. Nat. Women's Polit. Caucus Welfare Reform Task Force, 1977—; co-developer Cisco Networking Acad. in Ventura County high schs. Author (with others): U.S. Bilingual Edn. Act, 1967, Tex. AFDC Employment and Edn. Act, 1977; manuals for Women's Employoment and Edn. Model program. Co-chmn. Nat. Peace Acad. Campaign, 1977-81; founder, bd. dirs. Nat. Chicana Found. Inc., 1971-78; bd. dirs. Calif. Coun. Children and Youth, 1967, Rio Grande Fedn. Chicano Health Ctrs., S.W. rural states, 1974-76, Women's Lobby, Washington, 1974-77, Rural Am. Women, Washington, 1978—, Small Bus. Coun. Greater San Antonio; mem. Pres.'s Coun. on Pvt. Sector Initiatives, 1983. Recipient Cmty. award Coalition Mex.-Am. Orgns., 1967, Outstanding Svc. award Washington, 1968, Thanksgiving award Boys' Club, 1976, Outstanding Svc. award Tex. Women's Polit. Caucus, 1977, Liberty Bell award San Antonio Young Lawyers, 1981, Vista award for Exceptional Svc. to end poverty, 1980, Headliner award San Antonio Women in Comm., 1978, Woman of Yr. award Tex. Women's Polit. Caucus, 1978, Pres.'s Vol. Action award 1983, Leadership award Nat. Network Hispanic women, 1989; named Outstanding Woman of Yr., L.A. County, 1972, Woman of the 80's, Ms. Mag., 1980, Nat. Pres.'s award Nat. Image Inc., 1981, Wonder Woman Found. award, 1982, Pres.'s Vol. Action award, 1983, Adv. of Yr., San Antonio SBA, 1984; selected one of Am.'s 100 Most Important Women, Ladies Home Jour., 1988, 89; featured in CBS TV series An American Portrait, 1985, Leadership award Nat. Network Hispanic Women, 1989. Mem. Nat. Assn. Female Execs., Pres.'s Assn., Am. Mgmt. Assn. Roman Catholic. Office: Primerica 25060 Stanford Ave Valencia CA 91355-3411 Home: 1031 Kumquat Pl Oxnard CA 93036-1533 Office Phone: 805-983-8517. Personal E-mail: languiano@verizon.net.

ANGUS, GLORIA MICHELLE, elementary school educator; b. Porterville, Calif., May 7, 1976; d. Sharon Kay Angus. BA in Liberal Studies, Bethany Coll., Scotts Valley, Calif., 1997; MA In Edn., Nat. U., Fresno, Calif., 2001. Tchg. credential 1998. Tchr. Thomas Jefferson Mid. Sch., Madera, Calif., 1998—; presenter writing workshops, 2001—. Fellow, San Joaquin Valley Writing Project, 2001—. Mem.: Calif. Tchrs. Assn. Republican. Mem. Assemblies Of God. Avocations: reading, travel, decorating. Office: T Jefferson Mid Sch 1407 Sunset Ave Madera CA 93637

ANISIMOVA, TANYA, cellist, educator; b. Brozny, USSR, Feb. 15, 1966; came to U.S., 1990; d. Mikhail Alekseevich Anisimov and Zoya Hassanovna Islamova; m. Alexander Sergeevich Anufriev, Aug. 24, 1999. Diploma cum laude, Moscow State Conservatory, 1989; artist diploma, Boston U., 1992; M Musical Arts, Yale U., 1995. Cellist Moscow Conservatory String Quartet, 1987-89. Tchr. cello and chamber music; artistic dir. Mousetrap Concert Series, Washington Grove, Md., 1999; resident Va. Ctr. for Creative Arts, 1995, 96, 99. Composed, recorded CD Music from Mt. San Angelo, 1995. Recipient 1st prize Concertino Prague Internat. Competition, 1981, All-USSR String Quartets Competition, 1987, Laureate 1st Dmitri Shostakovich Chamber Music Competition, St. Petersburg, Russia, 1987, Min-On Internat. Chamber Music Competition, Tokyo, 1989; Meet a Composer Found. grantee, 1999. Mem. Nat. Music Tchrs. Assn., Kindler Cello Club. Avocations: painting, mushroom picking.

ANISTON, JENNIFER, actress; b. Sherman Oaks, Calif., Feb. 11, 1969; d. John and Nancy (Dow) Aniston; m. Brad Pitt, July 29, 2000 (div. Oct. 2, 2005). Attended, Fiorello La Guardia School of Music, Art & Performing Arts, N.Y.C. Actor: (TV series) Ferris Bueller, 1990, Molloy, 1990, The Edge, 1992, Muddling Through, 1994, Friends, 1994—2004 (Screen Actors Guild outstanding ensemble performance in comedy series, 1995, Emmy award best actress, 2002, Golden Globe award best actress, 2003, People's Choice award favorite female television performer, 2001, 2002, 2003, 2004), (guest appearances) Herman's Head, 1992—93, Quantum Leap, 1992, Burke's Law, 1994; host (TV Documentary) Growing Up Grizzly 2, 2004; actor: (TV films) Camp Cucamonga, 1990, Sunday Funnies, 1993; (films) Leprechaun, 1993, She's the One, 1996, Dream for an Insomniac, 1996, Til There Was You, 1997, Picture Perfect, 1997, The Thin Pink Line, 1998, The Object of My Affection, 1998, The Iron Giant (voice), 1999, Office Space, 1999, Rock Star, 2001, The Good Girl, 2002, Bruce Almighty, 2003, Along Came Polly, 2004, Derailed, 2005, Rumor Has It., 2005, Friends With Money, 2006, The Break-Up, 2006 (with Vince Vaughn Movies-Choice Chemistry, Teen Choice Awards, 2006), (off-broadway play) For Dear Life, Dancing on Checkers' Grave, (music videos) I'll Be There For You, 1995, Walls, 1996, I Want To Be In Love, 2001. Named Most Intriguing People, People Weekly, 1995; named one of Most Beautiful People in the World, People, 1999, 50 Most Beautiful People, 2002, 2003, 2004, 2005.*

ANJUM, UZMA, pre-school educator; b. Lahere, Punjab, Pakistan, July 14, 1967; arrived in U.S., 2000; d. Pervaiz Faruqi and Rukhsanda Iqbal; m. Sohail Anjum, Nov. 3, 1988; children: Sumayya, Humma, Muhammad. B in Psychology, Punjab U., Pakistan, 1986, M in Psychology, 1988. Certificate profl. studies Bradford U., U.K., 2000, cert. tchr. pre-sch., first aid, tchr. Mich. Tchr. Elixir Acad., Lahore, Pakistan, 1992—93, Greenhouse Sch., Salem, Mass., 1993—95, Beacon House Sch., Lahore, 1995—2000, Herlong Cathedral Sch., Detroit, 2001—04, IAGD Sch., Rochester Hills, Mich., 2005—. Coord. grade 5 Beacon House Sch., 1997—2000; dir. Program for Excellence Herlong Sch., 2002—04, dir. Challenger Program, 2002—04. Mem.: Nat. Assn. Ednl. Young Children, Mich. Tchrs. Assn., Nat. Assn. Scis. Avocations: reading, travel, shopping. Home: 2816 Charter Dr #210 Troy MI 48083 Office: IAGD Daycare Sch 879 W Auburn Rd Rochester Hills MI Personal E-mail: uzma.anjum@hotmail.com.

ANKNEY, RACHEL BLUE, language educator; d. Dean and Patricia Ann (Blue) Ankney. MFA, Old Dominion U., Norfolk, Va., 2002. Adj. prof. Old Dominion U., 2002; asst. prof. English Tidewater C.C., Va. Beach, 2003—. Adj. prof. Hampton U., Va., 2002. Editor: (student jour.) ChannelMarker. Faculty advisor The Write Thing-Student Group, Va. Beach, 2005—06. Mem.: Am. Writers and Writing Programs, MLA, VCCA. Office Phone: 757-822-7506.

ANNCHILD, CYNTHIA, educational consultant; b. Kilgore, Tex., Sept. 9, 1946; d. Walter Charles Hewitt and Blanche Ann Fraser; children: Lincoln McNulty, Anson McNulty. BA in Sociology, Wagner Coll., S.I., N.Y., 1968; postgrad., NYU, N.Y.C., 1968—69; Cert. Practitioner, Acad. Orton-Gillingham Educators, Amenia, N.Y., 1997. Tchr. U.S. Peace Corps, Abodeh, Iran, 1968—71, cross-cultural dir. Hamehdon, Iran, 1971—72; epidemiologist N.Y.C. Health Dept., 1972—73; owner The Bathhouse, Natural Toiletries, N.Y.C.; instr. ESL, King Abdul Azziz U. Women's Coll., Jeddah, Saudi Arabia, 1993—94; learning specialist Kildonian Sch., Amenia, NY, 1994—98, Ann Arbor Acad., Mich., 1998—2001, Emerson Sch., Mich., 2001—. Bd. dirs. Ann Arbor Acad., Mich.; program cons. Sch. Without Walls; spkr. in field. Founding mem. Artist Way Ann Arbor, Mich., 2000—06. Recipient Notable New Tchr. award, Kildonian Sch., 1994, Svc. Recognition award, Ann Arbor Acad., 2001. Mem.: Child and Adults with Attention Deficit Disorder and Hyperactivity Disorder, Internat. Dyslexia Assn., Learning Disabilities Assn. (bd. dirs. 1998). Avocations: creating multi-sensory learning games, travel, camping, hiking, sketching. Office: Emerson Sch 5425 Scio Church Rd Ann Arbor MI 48103 Office Phone: 734-665-9005 ext. 122. Office Fax: 734-665-8126. E-mail: cannchild@emerson-school.org.

ANNE, LOIS, artist, educator; b. Buffalo, Oct. 15, 1950; BFA, Alfred U., N.Y., 1972. Working and exhibiting artist, 1972—; coord. arts program Coastal Workshop, Camden, Maine, 1989—. Tchr. privately, pub. schs., galleries, museums and univs., 1968— Exhibited in shows at Albright-Knox Art Gallery, 1975, U. Maine at Augusta, 1977, 78, 86, 89, Wm. A. Farnsworth Art Mus., Rockland, Maine, 1980, Maine Coast Artists Gallery, Rockport, 1979, 81, 83, 90, 91, Portland (Maine) Sch. Art, 1981, 83, U. Maine at Orono, 1982, Fine Art Ctr., Taos, N.Mex., 1985, Waterville (Maine) Gallery Fine Arts, 1986, Ogunquit (Maine) Art Ctr., 1990, 94, Maine Crafts Assn., Deer Isle, 1990-94, Bensons Fibre & Wood, Camden, 1993, 94, White House, Washington, 1993, Colby Coll., Waterville, Maine, 1995 Mem. Maine Crafts Assn., Union of Maine Visual Artists (newsletter editor 1986-87), Mid Coast Graphic Artists Network Avocations: gardening, hiking, dance, travel, writing. Studio: 407 Main St Rockland ME 04841-3305

ANNIS, FRANCESCA, actress; b. London, May 14, 1944; d. Anthony and Mariquita Annis; 3 children. With RSC, 1975-78. Appeared in plays: The Tempest, The Passion Flower Hotel, Hamlet, Troilus and Cressida, Comedy of Errors, The Heretic, Mrs. Klein, Rosmersholm, Lady Windermere's Fan, Hamlet, (films) Cleopatra, 1963, Saturday Night Out, 1963, Murder Most Foul, 1964, The Pleasure Girls, 1965, Run With the Wind, 1966, The Sky Pirate, 1970, The Walking Stick, 1970, The Tragedy of Macbeth, 1971, Penny Gold, 1973, Krull, 1983, Dune, 1984, Under the Cherry Moon, 1986, El Rio de Oro, 1986, The Debt Collector, 1999, Milk, 1999, Onegin, 1999, Deceit, 2000, The Libertine, 2004, Revolver, 2005, (TV series) Great Expectations, 1967, Agatha Christie's Partners in Crime, 1983, Between the Lines, 1993, (TV films) Alexander Graham Bell, 1965, A Pin to See the Peepshow, 1973, Sign It Death, 1974, The Comedy of Errors, 1978, Why Didn't They Ask Evans?, 1980, The Secret Adversary, 1982, Coming Out of the Ice, 1982, The Maze, 1985, Onassis—The Richest Man in the World, 1988, Weep No More My Lady, 1992, Headhunters, 1994, Doomsday Gun, 1994, Deadly Summer, 1997, Reckless: The Movie, 1998, Deceit, 2000, Copenhagen, 2002.*

ANN-MARGRET, (ANN-MARGRET OLSSON), actress, performer; b. Stockholm, Apr. 28, 1941; came to U.S., naturalized, 1949; d. Gustav and Anna Olsson; m. Roger Smith, May 8, 1967. Student, Northwestern U. Performer radio shows, band tours; appeared with: George Burns, Las Vegas, 1961; headliner numerous appearances, Las Vegas, 1961—; made NYC debut Radio City Music Hall, 1991; actress numerous films including Pocketful of Miracles, 1961, State Fair, 1961, Bye Bye Birdie, 1962, Viva Las Vegas, 1963, The Pleasure Seekers, 1964, Kitten With a Whip, 1964, Bus Riley's Back in Town, 1964, Once A Thief, 1965, Cincinnati Kid, 1965, Stagecoach, 1966, Made in Paris, 1966, The Swinger, 1966, Murderers' Row, 1967, The Tiger and the Pussycat, 1967, R.P.M., 1970, C.C. & Company, 1971, Carnal Knowledge, 1971, Train Robbers, 1972, Outside Man, 1972, Tommy, 1975, Joseph Andrews, 1976, The Last Remake of Beau Geste, 1977, Magic, 1978, The Cheap Detective, 1978, Lookin' To Get Out, 1978, The Villain, 1979, Middle-Age Crazy, 1980, The Return of the Soldier, 1982, I Ought To Be in Pictures, 1982, Twice in a Lifetime, 1985, 52-Pick-up, 1987, A Tiger's Tale, 1988, A New Life, 1988, Something More, Newsies, 1992, Grumpy Old Men, 1993, Grumpier Old Men, 1995, Seduced by Madness, 1996, The Limey, 1999, Any Given Sunday, 1999, The Last Producer, 2000, Interstate 60, 2002, Taxi, 2004, Mem-o-re, 2005, Tales of the Rate Fink, 2006, The Break-Up, 2006, The Santa Clause 3: The Escape Clause, 2006; several TV spls., 1975-76; TV films Who Will Love My Children, 1983, A Streetcar Named Desire, 1984, Our Sons, 1991, Nobody's Children, 1994, Seduced by Madness: The Diane Borchardt Story, 1996, Blue Rodeo, 1996, Life of the Party: The Pamela Harriman Story, 1998, Happy Face, 1999, The 10th Kingdom, 2000, Perfect Murder, Perfect Town, 2000, A Woman's a Helluva Thing, 2001, A Place Called Home, 2004; mini-series The Two Mrs. Grenvilles, 1987, Alex Haley's Queen, 1993, Scarlett, 1994, Blonde, 2001; TV series Four Corners, 1998; author: (with Todd Gold) Ann-Margret: My Story, 1994. Recipient 2 Acad. award nominations, 4 Emmy nominations, 5 Golden Globes. Office: William Morris Agy 151 S El Camino Dr Beverly Hills CA 90212-2775*

ANNS, ARLENE EISERMAN, publishing company executive; b. Pearl River, NY; d. Frederick Joel and Anna (Behnke) Eiserman. Student, Fairleigh Dickinson U., 1946—48; BS, Utah State U., 1950; postgrad., Traphagen Sch. Design, 1957, NYU, 1958, Hunter Coll., 1959—60. Rsch. and promotion asst. Archtl. Record, N.Y.C., 1952-56; asst. rsch. dir. Esquire Mag., N.Y.C., 1956-62; rsch. mgr. Am. Machinist publ. McGraw-Hill, Inc., N.Y.C., 1962-67, mktg. svc. mgr., 1967-69, 69-71, sales mgr., 1976-77, dir. mktg., 1977-78; v.p. mktg. svcs. Morgan Gramplan, Inc., N.Y.C., 1971-72; mktg. dir. Family Health and Diversion mag., 1972-74; dist. sales mgr. Postgrad. Medicine, 1974-76; advt. sales mgr. Contempory Ob/Gyn, 1976-78, dir. profl. devel., 1978-80; pub. graduating engr., dir. mktg. Aviation Week Group, 1980-90; pub. World Aviation Directory; dir. comms. Aviation Week Group, 1990-92; v.p. Phase, Ltd., 1993—; owner, mgr. Barnahill Loblolly Tree Farm, 1993—. Mem. Am. Mktg. Assn., Pharm. Advt. Club, Advt. Women N.Y., Advt. Club N.Y., Sales Exec. Club, Employment Mgmt. Assn., Am. Soc. Pers. Adminstrs., Nat. Orgn. Disability (bd. dirs.), Internat. Platform Assn., Coll. Placement Coun., U. Va. Libr. Assoc. Bd., Svc. Corps Ret. Execs. (chair), Wings Club, Dir. Assn., Pi Sigma Alpha. Home: Barnahill Farm 6653 Celt Rd Stanardsville VA 22973-3638 Personal E-mail: theanns@earthink.net.

ANROMAN, GILDA MARIE, college program director, lecturer, educator; b. New Haven, Conn., July 19, 1959; d. Owen Francis Anroman and Edera (Vagnini) Felice. BA, Trinity Coll., Washington, 1983; M in Applied Anthropology, U. Md., 1994, grad. cert. in historic preservation, 1997, postgrad., 1994—. Cert. yoga instr. Clin. technologist Nat. Health Lab., Vienna, Va., 1983-85; dept. mgr., clin. technologist Anmed/Biosafe Inc., Rockville, Md., 1985-92; rsch. asst. U. Md., College Pk., 1992-94, instr. dept. anthropology, 1994-97, acad. advisor, 1996-99, asst. dir. College Park Scholars College Park, 1999—2000, asst. dir. undergrad. programs R.H. Smith Sch. Bus., 2000—03; program dir. Cath. U. of Am., Columbus Sch. Law, Washington, 2003—. Lectr. U. Md., 2003—. Rep. College Pk. Historic Dist. Commn., 1994-95. Scholar State of Conn., Hartford, 1977, Senatorial scholar, State of Md., Annpolis, 1995-99, Del. scholar, Annapolis, 1998-99; recipient Margaret Cook award for historic preservation Prince George's County, Md., 1997. Mem. AAUW, Am. Anthropol. Assn., Am. Hist. Assn., Am. Soc. Environ. History, Am. Studies Assn., Inst. of Early Am. History/Culture, Orgn. Am. Historians, Soc. for Hist. Archaeology, Nat. Trust for Historic Preservation, Nat. Coun. on Pub. History, Assn. for the History Medicine. Home: 34-D Ridge Rd Greenbelt MD 20770 Office: Cath Univ Am Columbus Sch Law Washington DC 20064 Business E-Mail: ganroman@eng.umd.edU.

ANSANELLI, ALEXANDRA, ballerina; b. Laurel Hollow, NY; Studied with Danny Holstein, Rosly, NY; student, Chautauqua Dance, Houston Ballet, Pacific N.W. Ballet Sch., Pa. Ballet Sch., San Francisco Ballet Sch., Sch. Am. Ballet, 1990. Apprentice N.Y.C. Ballet, 1996, mem. corps de ballet, 1996—98, soloist, 1998—. Dancer (ballets) Allegro Brillante, Danses Concertantes, A Midsummer Night's Dream, The Steadfast Tin Soldier, Tschaikovsky Pas de Deux, Walpurgisnacht Ballet, Fearful Symmetries, Suite from L'Histoire du Soldat, Afternoon of a Faun, The Four Seasons, Walton's Swan Lake, Polyphonia, Cheating, Lying, Stealing, many others. Named one of 20 Teens to Change the World, Teen People Mag., 1999; recipient Princess Grace award for emerging artists, Prince Albert of Monaco, 1997. Office: NYC Ballet NY State Theatre 20 Lincoln Ctr Plz New York NY 10023-5690

ANSARI, ANOUSHEH, digital home and multimedia management technology company executive, first female civilian space traveler; b. Tehran, Iran, 1966; emigrated to the US in 1984; m. Hamid Ansari, 1991. BSEE and Computer Sci., George Mason U., 1988; MSEE, George Washington U. Held engrng. positions MCI Telecommunications Corp., Comm. Satellite Corp. (COMSAT); co-founder, pres., CEO Telecom Technologies, Inc. (TTI) (acquired by Sonus Networks, Inc.), 1993—2000; co-founder, chmn. Prodea Systems, Inc., Plano, Tex., 2006—. US Delegate at ITU SG VII, SG XI and SG XVII; rep. Am. Nat. Standard Inst. T1S1 and T1X1. Contbr. to numerous technical papers. Mem., bd, trustee X-Prize Found. Vision Circle; past bd. dir. Make-a-Wish Found. (North Tex.), Collin County Children's Advocacy Ctr.; Ashoka Found. Named one of 40 Under 40, Fortune, 2001; recipient Ernst and Young Entrepreneur of Yr., Southwest Region, Tech. and Comm.

category, 1999, Nat. Entrepreneurial Excellence award, Working Women, 2000, George Mason U. Entrepreneurial Excellence award, George Mason Univ. Alumni Assn., 2001, George Washington U. Disting. Alumni Achievement award. Mem.: Nat. Soc. Profl. Engineers, IEEE, Eta Kappa Nu. Along with Amir Ansari (brother-in-law) made a multi-milion dollar contribution for the first non-governmental organization to launch a reusable manned spacecraft into space twice within two weeks to the X-Prise Foundation on May 5, 2004. To honor this donation the X-prize was renamed the Ansari X Prize; becoming the first Iranian in space and the first female civilian space tourist; will be the fourth space tourist part of the primary crew on the Soyuz TMA-9 mission in September, 2006, launching from Baikonur Cosmodrome in Kazakhstan; patents on Automated Operator Services and Wireless Service Node. Office: Prodea Systems Inc 6101 W Plano Pkwy Ste 210 Plano TX 75093*

ANSELM, CHERIE ANN, social sciences educator; b. Rochester, NY, July 24, 1978; BA in History and Edn., Niagara U., NY, 2000. Tchr. social studies Brockport Ctrl. Sch., NY, 2001—. Office: Brockport Central Schools 40 Allen St Brockport NY 14420

ANSELMI, ELVIRA, psychologist, researcher; d. Pasquale and Maria Arpino; m. Gregory D. Anselmi, Aug. 12, 1984; 1 child, Eustace J. PhD, Fairleigh Dickinson U., Teaneck, N.J., 1998; BA in Biology, NYU, 1983; MA in Psychology, Fairleigh Dickinson U., 1993. Lic. psychologist N.J. Clin. coord. traumatic brain injury model system Kessler Med. Rehab. Rsch. and Edn. Corp., West Orange, NJ, 1998—; pvt. practice in psychology, neuropsychology Parsippany, NJ, 2001—. Mem.: N.J. Assn. Cognitive Therapists, N.J. Psychol. Assn., APA. Achievements include research in the efficacy of psychological therapies in brain injury. Avocations: gardening, portrait drawing. Office: 239 New Rd Ste A-317 Parsippany NJ 07054 Office Phone: 973-233-0441. Business E-Mail: vanselmiphd@aol.com.

ANSETH, KRISTI S., tissue engineer, educator; b. ND; BS in Chem. Engring., Purdue U., 1992; PhD in Chem. Engring., U. Colo., 1994. Rsch. assoc. Purdue U., West Lafayette, Ind., 1995; rsch. fellow Mass. Inst. Tech., Cambridge, Mass., 1995—96; asst. prof. chem. engring. U. Colo., Boulder, Colo., 1996—98, Patten asst. prof. chem. engring., 1998—99, Patten assoc. prof. chem. engring., 1999—2002, asst. investigator Howard Hughes Med. Inst., 2000—; assoc. prof. surgery U. Colo. Health Sci. Ctr., Denver, 2000—; prof. chem. engring. U. Colo., Boulder, 2002—03, Tisone prof. chem. and biol. engring., 2003—, assoc. faculty dir. initiative in molecular biotech., 2003—, prof. (by courtesy), 2004—. Vis. rschr. Ecole Nationale Superieure de Chimie, Mulhouse, France, 1994. Recipient Career award, NSF, 1998—2002, First award, NIH, 1998—2003, Dow Outstanding New Faculty award, Am. Soc. Engring. Edn., 1999, Outstanding Young Investigator award, Materials Rsch. Soc., 2001, Curtis W. McGraw award, Am. Soc. Engring. Edn., 2003, Allan P. Colburn award, AIChE, 2003, Alan T. Waterman award, NSF, 2004, others; fellow, Am. Inst. Med. and Biol. Engring., 2001. Office: Dept Chem and Biol Engring ECCH 128 Univ Colo Boulder CO 80309-0424 Office Phone: 303-492-3147. Office Fax: 303-492-4341. E-mail: kristi.anseth@colorado.edu.*

ANSEVICS, NANCY LEAH, mental health services administrator; b. Bay City, Mich., Nov. 2, 1940; d. Arthur Truman and Ruby Leona (Cornelius) Repkie; children: Tamara D., Bradley J., Michael Aaron. BA in Psychology, Saginaw Valley State Coll., 1972; MA in Clin. Psychology, Cen. Mich. U., 1977; EdD in Ednl. Psychology and Counseling, U. S.D., 1986. Lic. profl. counselor; nat. bd. cert. counselor; bd. cert. forensic examiner; diplomate in forensic medicine. Dir. Cen. Clinic Alternative to Drug Abuse, Prevention and Treatment, Des Moines, 1975-77; assoc. psychologist Herbert S. Roth, PhD, Des Moines, 1977-79; doctoral intern Osawatomie State Hosp., State Kans. Psychology Dept., Topeka, 1980-83; psychologist II Youth Ctr. at Atchison, State Kans. Psychology Dept., Topeka, 1981-83; clin. psychologist Human Devel. Ctr., Duluth, Minn., 1984; psychologist I Fulton State Hosp., Jefferson City, 1985-86; psychologist II St. Joseph State Hosp., Jefferson City, 1986-88, program planning direct, 1989-90; exec. dir. pvt. practice Anstocks Forensic Mental Health Clinic, St. Joseph, Mo., 1990—; dir. mental health dept. corrections State of Mo., 1993-94. Grad. teaching asst. dept. clin. psychology Cen. Mich. U., 1974-75; guest lectr. grad. dept. social work Univ. Iowa, 1976; psychology instr. Grandview Coll., Des Moines, 1976-79; adj. prof. Mo. Western State Coll., 1991; presenter in field. Contbr. articles to profl. jours. Recipient Outstanding Sci. Achievement award Community Leaders of Am., 1984, Cert. Appreciation, U. S.D. Sch. of Law, 1985. Mem. APA, AAAS, Am. Assn. Advancement Psychology, Am. Assn. Sex Educators, Counselors and Therapists (cert. sex therapist), Assn. for Humanistic Psychology, Am. Correctional Assn., Phi Delta Kappa, Psi Chi. Jewish. Avocations: sculpture, skiing. Office Phone: 816-279-2481. Business E-Mail: afmhc@stjoelive.com.

ANSHAW, CAROL, writer; b. Grosse Pointe Shores, Mich., Mar. 22, 1946; d. Henry G. and Virginia (Anshaw) Stanley; m. Charles J. White III, Mar. 15, 1969. BA, Mich. State U., 1968. Book reviewer, Voice Literary Supplement, prof. Creative Writing Art Inst. Chgo. Author: They Do It All With Mirrors, 1978, Aquamarine, 1992, Seven Moves, 1996. Tutor Literacy Council of Chgo., 1989—. Recipient Nat. Book Critics Circle citation for excellence in reviewing, 1989. Mem. Nat. Book Critics Cir., Nat. Writers Union. Democrat. Achievements include Stories included in Best Am. Short Stories 1994, 1998. Avocation: swimming.

ANSLEY, JULIA E., retired elementary school educator, poet, writer; b. Malvern, Ark., Nov. 10, 1940; d. William Harold and Dorothy Mae (Hamm) Smith; m. Miles Ansley, Nov. 8, 1964 (div. June 1976); children: Felicia Dianne, Mark Damon. BA in Edn., Calif. State U., Long Beach, 1962; postgrad., UCLA Ext. Early childhood edn., life, gen. elem., kindergarten/primary, Miller-Unruh reading specialist credentials, Calif. Elem. tchr. L.A. Unified Sch. Dist., 1962—2003; ret., 2003. Coord. Proficiency in English Program, L.A., 1991-93, 98-2001; mem., advisor P.E.P. Instrnl. Tchrs. Network, 1993-2001, workshop presenter, staff devel. leader, and classroom demonstration tchr. in field; also poetry presentations, L.A., 1989—; owner Poetry Expressions, L.A.; self-markets own poetry posters; creator, presenter KIDCHESS integrated lang. arts program, 1987—. Author: (poetry vols.) Out of Heat Comes Light, From Dreams to Reality. Bd. dirs. New Frontier Dem. Club, L.A., 1990-93; mem. exec. bd. L.A. Panhellenic Coun., rec. sec., 1993-95; vol., cmty. orgns. Greater South L.A. Affirmative Action Project, 1995-96; elected tchr. rep. Ten Schs. Leadership Team, 1992-93; active local sch. leadership 6 schs. L.A. Unified Sch. Dist., elected mem. sch. site coun., local sch. leadership coun., shared-decision-making coun.; mem. Dem. Senatorial Campaign Com., Dem. Congl. Campaign Com., Cmty. Coalition, United Tchrs., LA, Action Grassroots Empowerment and Neighborhood Devel. Alternatives. Honored by Teacher mag., 1990; recipient Spirit of Edn. award Sta. KNBC-TV, L.A., 1990, Shiny Apple award L.A. Tchr. Ctr., 1992, Dedicated Tchr. award Proficiency in English Program, 1994; grantee L.A. Ednl. Partnership, 1985, 87, 89, 93. Mem. L.A. Alliance African-Am. Educators (exec. bd. 1991-94, parliamentarian 1992-94), Black Women's Forum, Black Am. Polit. Assn. (edn. co-chair 1993-95), Calif. Tchrs. Assn., So. Pverty Law Ctr., Sigma Gamma Rho. Mem. FAME Ch. Avocations: reading, listening to music, writing, playing chess (cert. chess instr. for grades K-3), political activist. Home: 3828 Sutro Ave Los Angeles CA 90008-1925 Office Phone: 323-964-2322.

ANSTAETT, JENNIFER GRIFFIN, lawyer; b. Sikeston, Mo., Dec. 14, 1975; m. Patrick Anstaett. BA in Eng., Ctr. Coll. Ky., 1998, BA in Hist., 1998; JD, Washington & Lee U. Sch. of Law, 2001. Bar: Ohio 2001, US Dist. Ct., Southern Dist. Ohio, US Supreme Ct. Assoc. Beckman Weil Shepardson LLC, Cin., 2004—. Planned giving com. Alzheimer's Assn., Ky., exec. com., Young Professionals, Ky.; bd. dir. Franciscan Haircuts from the Heart. Named one of Ohio's Rising Stars, Super Lawyers, 2005, 2006. Mem.: Assn. Professionals in Aging, Am. Health Lawyers Assn., Ohio Bar Assn., Cin. Bar Assn. (Basic Estate Planning Seminar Com.). Office: Beckman Weil Shepardson LLC American Book Bldg 300 Pike St Ste 400 Cincinnati OH 45202 Office Phone: 513-621-2100. Office Fax: 513-621-0106.*

ANTARAMIAN, JACQUELINE, actress; Actor: (TV series) The Siege, Law and Order; (Broadway plays) Julius Caesar, Wrong Mountain, (off-broadway plays) The Immigrant, The Wild Duck, The Rose Tattoo, Tartuffe, Desire Under the Elms, Arcadia, Twelfth Night, Blithe Spirit, The Three Sisters, Homebody/Kabul, The Imaginary Invalid, Candida, Miss Julie, Hedda Gabler; actor, actor: Nine Parts of Desire, (Barrymore Charlotte Cushman award Outstanding Lead Actress in a Play, 2006).*

ANTHONY, BARBARA COX, foundation administrator; b. Dec. 1922; m. Garner Anthony; children: Blair, James Cox Kennedy. Controller Cox Enterprises, Inc. Bd. dirs. Cox Enterprises, Atlanta; founder Barbara Cox Anthony Found., Hawaii; rancher, cattle breeder, Australia. Bd. trustee La Pietra: Hawaii Sch. for Girls, 1978—. Named one of World's Richest People, Forbes, 1999—, Forbes Richest Americans, 2006. heiress to James M. Cox founder of Cox Enterprises, Inc. Office: Cox Enterprises Inc 6205 Peachtree Dunwoody Rd Atlanta GA 30328 also: Barbara Cox Anthony Foundation PO Box 4316 Honolulu HI 96813 Office Phone: 678-645-0000. Office Fax: 678-645-1079.

ANTHONY, BERTHA M., minister; b. Osceola Mills, Pa., Dec. 28, 1928; d. Samuel Smith and Dovie C. Morgan; m. Ballard James Anthony, 1946 (dec. 1989); children: Eunice J. Thomas, Charles J.(dec.), Dovie Franquita Mason, Ida Marie Lanansha, Vanessa M. Lynch, Yette S. Cooksey, Vanteria L., Terrence E.(dec.). Ordained min. Ch. of God in Christ, 1987. Pastor Livingwater Ch. of God in Christ, Williamsport, Pa., 1987—. Judge of elections Blair County, Altoona, Pa., 2003—; mem. outreach ministry Ch. of Livingwaters, Williamsport, 1997—. Republican. Pentecostal. Home: PO Box 93 1111 17th Ave Altoona PA 16603

ANTHONY, CAROLYN ADDITON, librarian; b. Pitts., Nov. 27, 1949; d. Elwood Prince and Elizabeth Martha (Gruginskis) Additon; m. William W. Anthony, III, July 7, 1973; children: Margaret Susan, Lauren Elizabeth. AB, Colby Coll., 1971; MLS, U. R.I., 1973. Reference libr. Enoch Pratt Free Lib., Balt., 1973-75, head info. and referral svc., 1975-78; head info. svcs. Balt. County Pub. Libr., Towson, Md., 1978-80, head, info. and program svcs., 1980-85; dir. Skokie (Ill.) Pub. Libr., 1985—. Pres. Libr. Adminstr. Conf. No. Ill., 1988—89; chair adv. bd. Pub. Librs., 1986—89; bd. mem. Rush North Shore Med. Ctr., 2004—, pres. women's bd., 2004—06. Recipient Libr. of Yr., North Suburban Libr. Sys., 2004. Mem.: ALA (mem. coun. 1993—97), Ill. Libr. Assn. (pres. 1999—2000, award, Libr. of the Yr. 2003), Am. Libr. Trustee Assn. (bd. dirs.), Pub. Libr. Assn. (new stds. task force com. 1984—87, bd. dirs. 1987—89, 2005—), Met. Libr. Assn. (exec. com. 1990—93), Chgo. Libr. Club (pres. 1991—92), Rotary (pres. Skokie chpt. 1992—93). Democrat. Soc. Of Friends. Office: Skokie Pub Libr 5215 Oakton St Skokie IL 60077-3680 Office Phone: 847-673-7774. Business E-Mail: canthony@skokielibrary.info.

ANTHONY, KATHRYN HARRIET, architecture educator; b. NYC, N.Y., Sept. 11, 1955; d. Harry Antoniades and Anne (Skoufis) Anthony; m. Barry Daniel Riccio, May 24, 1980 (dec. Jan. 2001). AB in Psychology, U. Calif., Berkeley, 1976, PhD in Architecture, 1981. Rsch. promotion Kaplan/McLaughlin/Diaz Architects and Planners, San Francisco, 1980-81; vis. lectr. U. Calif., Berkeley, Calif., 1980-81, 82-83, San Francisco State U., Calif., 1981; assoc. prof. Calif. State Poly. U., Pomona, Calif., 1981-84; asst. prof. U. Ill., Urbana-Champaign, Ill., 1984-89, assoc. prof., 1989-96, chair bldg. rsch. coun., 1994-97, prof. architecture, 1996—, chair design faculty, 2002—. Guest lectr. numerous orgns., coll. and univ.; mem. numerous comm. Coll. of Fine and Applied Arts, Sch. Architecture, Housing Rsch. and Devel. Program, Dept. Landscape Architecture. Author: Design Juries on Trial: The Renaissance of the Design Studio, 1991, Designing for Diversity: Gender, Race, and Ethnicity in the Architectural Profession, 2001; co-author: Running for Our Lives: An Odyssey with Cancer, 2004; co-editor Jour. Archtl. Edn. 47:1, 1993; mem. editl. bd. Jour. Archtl. and Planning Rsch., 1989-92, Jour. Archtl. Edn., 1990-95, Environ. and Behavior Jour., 1991—; reviewer Landscape Jour., 1990; contbr. articles to profl. jours; co-designer, co-prodr. (exhibit) Shattering the Glass Ceiling: The Role of Gender and Race in the Archtl. Profession, Nat. Conv. AIA, 1996. Recipient Creative Achievement award, Assn. Collegiate Sch. Architecture, 1992, Collaborative Achievement award, AIA, 2003; fellow, Acad. Leadership Program Com. Instl. Coop., 1996—97; grantee summer, U. Calif., Berkeley, 1980, Calif. State U. and Coll., 1982, 1983, U. Ill., 1984, 1987, 1992, 1993, 1995, 1996, L.A. County Cmty. Devel. Commn., 1984, Nat. Endowment Arts, 1986—87, Decatur Housing Authority, 1988, Graham Found., 1989—91, 1993—96, 2005—06, US Army Constrn. Engring. Rsch. Lab., 1993. Mem. Environ. Design Rsch. Assn. (bd. dir. 1989-92, treas. 1990-92, co-editor Coming of Age: Proceedings of 21st Ann. Conf. 1990, Achievement award 2005), Chgo. Women in Architecture. Home: 309 W Pennsylvania Ave Urbana IL 61801-4918 Office: U Ill Sch Architecture 611 Taft Dr Champaign IL 61820-6922 E-mail: kanthony@uiuc.edu.

ANTHONY, MICHELE, former recording industry executive; b. 1956; BA with distinction, George Washington U.; JD, U. So. Calif. Bar: 1981. Ptnr. Manatt, Phelps, Rothenberg & Phillips; sr. v.p. Sony Music, NYC, 1990—93, exec. v.p., 1993-94, Sony BMG Music Entertainment, NYC, 1994—2006; COO Sony Music Label Group, US, NYC, 2004—06, pres., 2005—06. Bd. dirs. Recording Industry Assn. Am., Nat. Ctr. for Missing and Exploited Children; exec mem. bd. dirs. Rock and Roll Hall of Fame Found., Rock the Vote. Recipient Norma Zarky Entertainment Law award; named one of 100 Most Powerful Women in Entertainment, Hollywood Reporter, 2005. Mem. State Bar Calif., Beverly Hills Bar Assn., L.A. County Bar Assn., Order of Coif.*

ANTHONY, NAKIA LACQUERS, healthcare educator; b. Memphis, Dec. 16, 1974; d. Joselyn Ann Boatwright; m. Ellis O Anthony, Jan. 31, 1973; 1 child, Gavriel Baruch-Ellis. Master's Credits, Miss. Valley State U., Itta Bena, Miss., 2001—03. Respite care coord. Mercy Home Healthcare, Memphis, Tenn., 1999—; ednl. facilitator Dorsey-Ford Inst., Memphis, Tenn., 1998. Author: (children's literature) Meditations for God's Heritage. Pres. Bus. and Profl. Women's League, Memphis, 2003. Grantee, Tenn. Humanities Coun., 2001. Church Of God In Christ. Avocations: reading, motivational speaking. Office: Strong Tower Faith Ministry 2500 Mount Moriah Suite H232 Memphis TN 38115 E-mail: ntrememorial@yahoo.com.

ANTHONY, POLLY, broadcast executive; Sec. CBS Records, 1978; sr. v.p. promotion Epic Records, 1990—93, gen. mgr. 550 Music, 1993—94, pres. 550 Music, 1994, sr. v.p., 1994, pres., 1997—2003, Epic Records Group, 1999—2003; co-pres. Geffen Records, 2004, pres. Bd. dir. Recording Industry Assn. Am., M. Gray Music Acad. Mailing: Interscope Geffen A&M Records 2220 Colorado Blvd Santa Monica CA 90404*

ANTHONY, SHEILA FOSTER, government official; b. Hope, Ark., Nov. 8, 1940; m. Beryl F. Anthony; children: Alison, Lauren. BA, U. Ark., 1962; JD, Am. U., 1984. Bar: Ark. 1985, D.C. 1985, U.S. Ct. Appeals (D.C. cir.) 1987, U.S. Supreme Ct. 1992. Tchr. Ark. Pub. Schs., 1962-63, 74-76; with Dow, Lohnes & Albertson, Washington, 1985-93; asst. atty. gen. Dept. of Justice, Washington, 1993-95; commr. FTC, Washington, 1997—. Del. Dem. Nat. Conv., 1980; justice of the peace Union County, Ark., 1969; trustee South Ark. U., 1971-75. Democrat. Office: FTC 600 Pennsylvania Ave NW Washington DC 20580-0001

ANTHONY, SYLVIA, social welfare organization executive; b. Boston, Oct. 5, 1929; d. Charles and Josephine (Guastaferro) Caccamesi; children: Lyn Newbury, Edward Charles Souza Jr., Dean Souza. Student, Northeastern U., Boston, 1968-69, Lee Inst., 1966, 86-87. Lic. real estate broker, Mass. Founder, pres. Life for the Little Ones, Inc., Everett, Mass., 1987-94, Sylvia's Haven, Everett, 1994—2006, Devens, Mass., 1997—. Recipient Arthur L. Whitaker award Am. Bapt. Ch. of Mass., 1992, Recognition award Commonwealth of Mass. State Senate, Ho. of Reps., Gov. of Mass., 1997, 99, Mass. Gov.'s Hwy Safety Bur., 1998, Mayor Dean J. Mazzarella City of Leominster, 1999, named Hometown Hero WBZ TV, Boston, 2001; Daily Point of Light award Points of Light Found., 2002, Amb. for Peace award The Interreligious and Internat. Fedn. for World Peace, 2002; Commendation from Pres. George Bush, 2002. Address: PO Box 1166 Groton MA 01450 Office Phone: 978-772-0924.

ANTHONY, VIRGINIA QUINN BAUSCH, medical association executive; b. Odessa, Tex., June 9, 1945; d. William Francis and Florence Elizabeth (Decker) Quinn; m. E. James Anthony; 1 child, Justin. BA, Mt. Holyoke Coll., 1967. Exec. dir. Am. Acad. Child and Adolescent Psychiatry, Washington, 1973—. Recipient Spl. Presdl. citation Am. Psychiat. Assn., 1995, Exec. Achievement award AMA, 1999. Office: Am Acad Child & Adolescent Psychiatry 3615 Wisconsin Ave NW Washington DC 20016-3007 Business E-Mail: vqanthony@aacap.org.

ANTHONY, WILMA TYLINDA, retired customer service administrator; b. Friars Point, MIss., July 11, 1954; d. John Thomas and Ellen (Ward) Anthony. BS in Edn., Langston U., 1979; postgrad. in interdisciplinary studies, U. Oreg. Sales assoc. Meier & Frank, Eugene, Oreg., 1976—78; vault teller 1st Interstate Bank, Portland, Oreg., 1979—80; mapping analyst Portland GE Co., 1980—97; sales assoc. Nike, Beaverton, Oreg., 1998—99, cashier, 2000—06; ret., 2006. Profl. model, 1987—. Telethon divsn. chief Mt. Hood coun. Campfire, Inc., Gladstone, Oreg., 1982—; loaned exec. Columbia-Willamette United Way, 1982; in-house campaigner Portland GE Co., 1981; mem. planning adv. bd. City of Tualatin, Oreg.; vol. State Games of Oreg., 1987—88; line mem. Marshall for All Joining Hands, 1986; vol. mgr. hospitality U.S. Figure Skating Championship, 2005; active Nat. Fedn. Rep. women, Portland; sec. Multnomah Young Reps., 1986; elected com. person Precinct 7, Washington County, 1986, re-elected, 1988; sec. Washington Young Reps., 1988. Recipient Leadership in Cmty. Svcs. award, Portland GE, 1986, Hon. Mention Vol. of Yr. award, 1986, ACE award, 1998, 2000, Cmty. Involvement award, Nike, 2003. Mem.: Pumpkin Ridge, U.S. Women Open Golf Tournament (chartered mem.), Toastmasters (v.p. 1984, Competence cert. 1984), Kappa Delta Pi. Baptist.

ANTHONY-PEREZ, BOBBIE COTTON MURPHY, retired psychology professor; b. Macon, Ga., Nov. 15, 1923; d. Solomon Richard and Maude Alice (Lockett) Cotton; m. William Anthony, Aug. 22, 1959 (dec.); 1 child, Freida; m. Andrew Silviano Perez, June 20, 1979. BS, DePaul U., 1953, MS, 1954, MA, 1975; MS, U. Ill., 1959; PhD, U. Chgo., 1967. Tchr. Chgo. Pub. Schs., 1954-68; math. coord. U. Chgo., 1965; prof. Chgo. State U., 1968-95, coord. Black Studies Program, 1982-83, 90-94, prof. emeritus, 1995; with psychol. svcs. Chgo. Pub. Schs., 1971-72; rsch. coord. Urban Affairs Inst. Howard U., Washington, 1978; coord. higher edn., careers counseling, campus ministry Ingleside Whitfield Parish, 1978-84, comm. chmn., 1991-92, 95, comms. com., 2006. Contbr. numerous articles to profl. jours., chpts. to books. V.p. Cmty. Affairs Chatham Bus. Assn., 1981-85, asst. sec., 1985-86, sec., 1986-87, directory com., 1987, 88; bus. rels. chmn. Chatham Avalon Pk. Cmty. Coun., 1984—, newsletter editor, 1993-01; bd. dirs. United Meth. Found. at U. Chgo., 1980-84, Cmty. Mental Health Coun. Inc., 1979-83; pub. edn. chair Chatham Avalon unit Am. Cancer Soc., 1977-88, 90-97, pub. info. chair, 1988-94; pres. Aux. Chgo. chpt. Tuskegee Airmen, Inc., 1994-95, rec. sec., 1998-99, parliamentarian, 1991-95, newsletter feature writer, reporter, 1999—, historian, 2006. NSF fellow, 1957, 58, 59; recipient numerous awards religious, civic and ednl. instns. and assns. Mem. APA, Internat. Assn. Applied Psychology, Internat. Assn. Cross-Cultural Psychology, Internat. Assn. Ednl. and Vocat. Guidance, Assn. Black Psychologists (elder 1995—, pres. Chgo. chpt. 1995-96, past pres.), Chgo. Psychol. Assn., Nat. Coun. Tchrs. Math., Am. Ednl. Rsch. Assn., Midwest Ednl. Rsch. Assn., Am. Soc. Clin. Hypnosis, Midwestern Psychol. Assn., Chgo. Soc. Clin. Hypnosis. Methodist.

ANTICO-PIZZINAT, CONCETTA K., artist; b. Sydney, Australia, Aug. 15, 1960; arrived in U.S., 1985; d. Dominia Anthony Antico and Annette Elsie Denmeade; m. Jason Edward Pizzinat, June 7, 2003; children: Hunter Krustian Smith, Ava Mary Ann Pizzinat, Zen Jay Pizzinat. Diploma in edn., Sydney Inst. Advanced Edn., 1984. Analyst ICA Mortgage, San Diego, 1988—89; mgr., v.p. voice & drama Aetna Health Plans, 1989—92, analyst, 1995—97; pres. Art Tours, Inc., La Jolla, 1998—2002, Salon Art, Inc., 2002—06, Antico Fine Art, Inc., 2006—. Mem.: Calif. Art Club. Avocations: gardening, travel, painting. Office: Antico Fine Art Inc 5544 La Jolla La Jolla CA 92037

ANTIGNANE, DIANE PAQUIN, mathematics educator; m. John Antignane; children: Rebecca, Melissa, Tim. MEd, Ga. State U., Atlanta, 1985. Cert. tchr. mid. sch. Ga., 1985. Tchr. Lodi Pub. Schs., Lodi, NJ, 1971—76, DeKalb County Schs., Lithonia, Ga., 1980—91, Gwinnett County Schs., Snellville, Ga., 1991—92, Shelby County Schs., Bartlett, 1993—. Office Phone: 901-373-1410.

ANTIN, ELEANOR, artist; b. NYC, Feb. 27, 1935; d. Sol and Jeanette (Efron) Fineman; m. David Antin, Dec., 1961; 1 son, Blaise. BA, CCNY, 1958; student, Tamara Daykarhanova Sch. for Stage, N.Y.C., 1954-56. Prof. emeritus visual arts U. Calif., San Diego, prof. emeritus. Artist producer videotapes Representational Painting, 1971, King Tape, 1972, Caught in the Act, 1973, Little Match Girl Ballet, 1975, Adventures of a Nurse, 1976, The Nurse and the Hijackers, 1977, The Angel of Mercy, 1980, from the Archives of Modern Art, 1987; writer, dir. producer films Loves of a Ballerina, 1986, The Last Night of Rasputin, 1988, The Man Without a World, 1991, Vilna Nights, 1993, Minetta Lane, 1995; co-writer, dirs. film The Hunger Artist, 1997; one-woman exhbns. include Mus. Modern Art, N.Y.C., 1973, Whitney Mus., N.Y.C., 1978, 97, L.A. County Mus. Art, 1999, Ronald Feldman Gallery, N.Y.C., 1977, 79, 80, 83, 86, 95, 98, 2002, 05, Marella Arte Contemporanea, Milan, 2002, 05, LA Mus. Art, 1999; group shows include, São Paulo Biennal, Brazil, 1975, Hirschhorn Mus., Washington, 1979, 84, Mus. Modern Art, N.Y.C., 1990, 98, 2000, 02, Whitney Mus., N.Y.C., 1989, 99, 2005, Mus. Contemporary Art, L.A., 1995, 98, Biennale of Sydney, 2002, Kunsthalle Wein, Museumsplatz, Vienna, 2002; performances include Battle of the Bluffs, 1975-80, The Angel of Mercy, 1977-80, Before the Revolution, 1979, Recollections of My Life with Diaghilev, 1980-86, El Desdichado (The Unlucky One), 1983, Help! I'm in Seattle, 1986, 87, Who Cares About a Ballerina?, 1987, 88, The Last Night of Rasputin, 1988-2002; represented in permanent collections, Mus. Modern Art, N.Y.C., Whitney Mus., N.Y.C., San Francisco Mus. Modern Art, Wadsworth Atheneum, Hartford, Conn., Jewish Mus., N.Y., Art Inst. Chgo., L.A. County Mus. Art, Wash. U. Gallery Art, Witherspoon Art Mus., Walker Art Ctr.; artist performer at Venice Bienale, 1976, Mus. Contemporary Art, Chgo., 1978, Contemporary Arts Mus. Houston, 1978, 80, Kitchen Ctr. for Music, Video, Dance, N.Y., 1979, LACE, L.A., 1982, 86, Sydney Opera House, 2002; film festivals include Berlin, 1992, U.S.A., 1992, Women in Film, 1992, San Francisco Jewish, 1991, London Jewish, 1991; author: Being Antinova, 1983, Eleanora Antinova Plays, 1995, 100 Boots, 1999, (screenplay) The Man Without a World, 2002. Recipient Pushcart prize VI, Best of the Small Presses, 1981-82, Vesta award for performance LA, 1984, 16th Annual Crystal award Women in Film, 1992, Nat. Found. Jewish Culture Media Achievement award, 1998, Best Show awards Internat. Art Critics Assn., 1998-99, 2001-02; Nat. Endowment for Arts grantee, 1979; Guggenheim fellow, 1997.

ANTINONE, JO ANN ELLIOTT, music educator; b. Herford, Tex., May 30, 1973; d. Charles Franklin and Harriet Kinkler Elliott; m. Patrick Michael Antinone, June 3, 2003; children: Joshua Paul, John Philip, Sarah Christine. MusB, Southwestern U., Georgetown, Tex., 1995; MusM, Ithaca Coll., N.Y., 1997. Cert. tchr. Tex., 1995. Choir tchr. Mesquite Ind. Sch. Dist., Tex., 1998—2001; asst. choir dir. L.D. Bell H.S., Hurst, Tex., 2001—. Children's choir dir. Rush Creek Christian Ch., Arlington, Tex., 2005—06. Recipient Sweepstakes Choir awards, UIL Tex., 2002, 2003, 2004, 2005, 2006. Mem.: TMEA. Office Phone: 817-282-2551. Personal E-mail: elliottj@hebisd.edu.

ANTMAN, KAREN H., oncologist, educator, dean; b. N.J., July 26, 1948; MD, Columbia U. Coll. Physicians and Surgeons, 1974. Diplomate Am. Bd. Internal Medicine, Am. Bd. Med. Oncology. Intern Columbia Presbyn. Med. Ctr., N.Y.C., 1974—75, resident, 1975—77; fellow Dana Farber Cancer Inst., Boston, 1977—79; chief med. oncology Columbia U., N.Y.C.; attending physician N.Y. Presbyn. Hosp., 1993—; dir. Herbert Irving Cancer Ctr.; Wu prof. of medicine and prof. pharmacology Columbia U., N.Y.C., 1993—2004; dep. dir. translation and clinical services Nat. Cancer Inst.; provost, Med. Campus Boston U., 2005—, dean, Med. Sch., 2005—. Mem. editl. bd. New England Jour. of Medicine. Mem.: Am. Soc. for Blood and Marrow Transplantation (pres.), Am. Assn. for Cancer Rsch. (pres.), Am. Soc. Clinical Oncology (pres.). Office: Boston Univ Medical Sch 715 Albany St L-103 Boston MA 02118 Office Phone: 617-638-5300. Office Fax: 617-638-5258.

ANTOINE, ALISSA QUIANA, science educator; b. Alexandria, La., June 24, 1981; d. Lawrence and Katie Ruth Antoine. BS, So. U. and A&M Coll., Baton Rouge, La., 2003. Sci. tchr. Dekalb County Sch. Dist., Atlanta, 2003—. Mem.: NEA, Orgn. Dekalb Educators, Nat. Sci. Tchrs. Assn. Office: 922 Stephenson Rd Stone Mountain GA 30087 Office Phone: 678-676-4476. E-mail: alissa_q_antoine@fc.dekalb.k12.ga.us.

ANTOINE, JANET ANNE, social worker; b. Chgo., Nov. 1, 1945; d. Karl Frederick Abrath and Aniela Domitilda Chappas; m. Lawrence Verne Antoine Sr., Sept. 4, 1964 (dec.); children: Lawrence V. Jr., Dennis Patrick. BA, Loyola U., Chgo., 1969; MPS, Western Ky. U., 1977; MS in Social Work, U. Louisville, 1981. Social worker Cabinet for Human Resources, Brandenburg, Ky., 1977-79, Louisville, 1979-81, Cath. Charities, Louisville, 1981-82, dir. maternity svcs., 1982-84; social worker Cabinet for Human Resources, Louisville, 1984-86, Dept. of Vet. Affairs, U.S. Govt., Louisville, 1986—. Site supr. Sr. Companion program, Louisville, 1987—. Cmty. vol. Army Com Svc., Ft. Knox and Ft. Gordon, 1968-77, 2d St. Neighborhood Assn., 1979-96, Old Louisville Neighborhood Assn., 1982-92. Recipient VA Sec. Hand & Heart award, 1998-99. Mem. NASW, AAUW, NOW. Roman Catholic. Avocations: needlepoint, gardening, reading, painting, tennis. Home: 1840 Fleming Rd Louisville KY 40205-2420 Office: VA Med Ctr Louisville 800 Zorn Ave Louisville KY 40206-1433 Business E-Mail: Antoine.Janet@Louisville.Va.Gov.

ANTOLICK, LYNN ANN, music educator; b. Hazleton, Pa., Oct. 8, 1969; d. Kenneth A. and Jean L. Griffiths; m. William Michael Antolick, Oct. 14, 2000. BS Music Edn., Millersville U. Pa., 1991, MusM Edn., 2002; D Musical Arts, Shenandoah U., Winchester, Va., 2002. Cert. K-12 Instrumental/Vocal Music Educator Instrl. Levels 1 and 2 Pa., 2001. Dir. band, tchr. music Shenandoah Valley Sch. Dist., Pa., 1996—98; tchr. mid. sch. music, dir. strings Ctrl. Bucks Sch. Dist., Doylestown, Pa., 1998—99; tchr. k-5 vocal music, tchr. h.s. piano East Stroudsburg Area Sch. Dist., Pa., 1999—. Asst. dir. Hazleton Liberty Band, 2000—, sec., 2005—. Mem. ch. coun., choir, instrumental soloist Trinity Evang. Luth. Ch., Hazleton, 1987—2006. Mem.: Pa. State Edn. Assn., Pa. Music Educators Assn., Music Educators Nat. Conf.

ANTOLIK, ELENA ANNE, performing company executive, choreographer; b. Pitts., Pa., Nov. 6, 1973; d. Pietro and Teresa Porco; m. Jason Mark Antolik, Sept. 4, 2005. BA in Dance, Point Pk. U., Pitts., 1994, BS in Bus. Mgmt., 1995. Owner Elite Sch. Dance by Elena, North Huntingdon, Pa., 2001—. Recipient Choreography award, U.S. Tournament of Dance, 2005, 2004, Starpower Nat. Talent Competition, 2004, Applause Talent Presentations, 2005, Am. Artisitic awards, 2005. Mem.: Norwin C. of C. Avocations: reading, travel. Office: Elite Sch Dance by Elena 11639 Rte 30 Ste 4 North Huntingdon PA 15642 Office Phone: 724-978-0405. Office Fax: 724-978-0433. Business E-Mail: elite1173@choiceonemail.com.

ANTON, BARBARA, writer; b. Pocono Pines, Pa., Apr. 3, 1926; d. Walter B. and Emma Agnes (Hess) Miller; m. Albert Anton, June 23, 1949. Grad. Gemologist, Gemol. Inst. of Am., 1964. Fashion and design editor Nat. Jeweler Mag., N.Y.C., 1956-58; freelance writer novels/plays, 1956—; staff writer Writer's Guidelines and News Mag.; instr. sr. divsn. U. South Fla., 2000—. Writing instr. Sr. Acad./Elderhostel U. South Fla., 1999—. Contbr. articles to numerous nat. mags. including Cosmopolitan, Family Circle, Bride's Mag., Saturday Evening Post, Thera Lit. Mag.; author plays, (novels) Egrets to the Flames (Top Ten/Fla. Writers Festival, 1995), short stories, 13 plays produced off-Broadway, 1995—2003. Recipient First Prize Humor, Manatee Writers Contest, 2000—01, 1st prize, Father's Hall of Fame Contest, 2000—01, over 100 awards for various writings, 14 awards, Fla. Studio Theatre Shorts Contest. Mem. Dramatists Guild.

ANTON, CAROL J., small business owner, writer; b. Rice Lake, Wis., June 12, 1949; d. Edward Burton and Clementine Emma (Kuhrt) McManus; m. Jimmy Eugene Anton, Oct. 31, 1965; children: David E., Brandi J. Grad. high sch., Dora, N. Mex. Cert. marine mechanic; ceramics instr. Beauty councilor Vanda Beauty Councilors, Fla., 1967-69; owner Sunshine Ceramics, Elephant Butte, N. Mex., 1980-84; freelance writer, 1994—, Sierra County Sentinel, T-or-C, N. Mex., 1995—; co-owner, office mgr. Anton's Marine, Elephant Butte, 1969—. Cub scout leader, 1976; scout leader Rio Grande Girl Scout Coun., N. Mex., 1981-83; project chmn. children's grant T-or-C community theater, N. Mex., 1997, theater dir., 1991—, sec., treas.; pres. Truth or Consequence Cmty. Theatre, Inc., chmn. writers group; spl. chmn. Sierra Santas Inc. Recipient Hearts and Hands Acting Out award N.Mex. Arts Coun., 1997. Mem. Women of the Moose. Republican. Baptist. Avocations: reading, writing, crocheting, quilting, theater projects. Office: Anton's Marine PO Box 1063 Elephant Butte NM 87935-1063 Personal E-mail: sunnianton@zianet.com. Business E-Mail: jeanton@zianet.com.

ANTON, CHERYL L., sales executive; b. Toledo, Ohio, Nov. 3, 1953; d. Ralph Herbert Snyder and Coletta Marie Piekut Nickerson; 1 child, John Daniel. Student, U. Toledo, 1972-80. With Kroger Co., Toledo, 1972-80; dept. supr. merchandising, sales dir. Growth Unltd., Toledo, 1979-80; owner CJ's Bar, Toledo, 1980-82; sales rep. Armour Food Co., Orlando, Fla., 1983-85; dist. sales mgr. Jones Dairy Farm, 1985-87; regional sales mgr. Southland Corp., 1987-92; Southeast regional sales mgr. McLane Co., Orlando, 1995-97; mid-south regional sales mgr. Ty, Inc., 1999—. Mem. NAFE (network dir. 1979—), Nat. Assn. for Women. Democrat. Address: PO Box 3118 Bella Vista AR 72715-0118

ANTONACCI, LORI (LORETTA MARIE ANTONACCI), marketing executive, consultant; b. Riverton, Ill., Mar. 31, 1947; d. Antonio and Gena Marie A. BA, Bradley U., 1969. Broadcast copywriter Sta. WIRL-TV, Peoria, Ill., 1969; comms. specialist Walgreen Co., Chgo., 1970-72; creative supr. Nat. Assn. Realtors, Chgo., 1973-74; creative dir., prodr. Steve Sohmer, Inc., N.Y.C., 1975-79; promotion specialist Ziff-Davis Publs., 1979-80; promotion mgr. Psychology Today, 1980-81; mktg. svcs. dir. DIS Consulting, N.Y.C., 1982-84; promotion dir. Crain's N.Y. Bus., N.Y.C., 1984-85; pres. Antonacci & Assocs., 1985-99, mktg. dir., chief exec. group, 2000—. Advisor, instr. Gallatin Sch. NYU, 1986—. Co-founder, bd. dirs. Artists Talk on Art, Inc., 1974—; Artists Comm. Fed. Credit Union, 1986-89, N.Y. Women's Agenda, 1992, bd. dirs. 1992—, v.p. events 1993-95; bd. dirs. Women's City Club, N.Y.C., 1994—, v.p. devel. 1994-95; bd. dirs. Ctr. for Advancement of Youth, Family & Cmty. Svcs. 1997—. Recipient Golden Eagle award CINE, 1976; award U.S. Indsl. Film Festival, 1977; CEBA award, 1979; Bronze medal Internat. Film and TV Festival N.Y., 1979, Am. Graphic Design awards 1996-97. Mem. Advt. Women N.Y. (profl. devel. com. 1983-85, program com. 1986-90, chmn. speakers bur. 1988-90, chmn. pub. policy com. 1991-95, industry issues 1998—), Women in comm., Am. Women in Radio and TV. Address: 15 E 10th St New York NY 10003-5930

ANTONIUK, VERDA JOANNE, secondary school educator; b. Moline, Ill., Sept. 10, 1936; d. Joe Oscar and Verda Mathilde (Oakberg) Butts; m. Vladimir Antoniuk, Sept. 1, 1972; children: Daniel Sean, Stephen Dwight. Diploma in missions, Moody Bible Inst., 1957; BS in Edn., Ea. Ill. U., 1960; MA in Internat. Rels., Calif. State U. Stanlslaus, Turlock, 1981, cert. in ESL, 1989. Cert. tchr., ESL tchr., bilingual, crosscultural, lang. and acad. devel. cert., Calif. Tchr. Wheatridge (Colo.) H.S., 1960-61, Modesto (Calif.) City Schs., 1971-73, Modesto Jr. Coll., 1979-80, 84-89, Turlock Christian H.S., 1980-83, Turlock H.S., 1989—; part-time faculty edn. dept. Chapman U., 1995; missionary Oversease Missionary Fellowship, Littleton, Colo., 1961-69. Tchr. Turlock Adult Sch., 1969-79, 84-89, program dir. ESL, 1976-79, amnesty coord., 1986-89; cons. Britannica-ARC Project, Oakland, Calif. and Boston, 1993-94; ednl. cons. Valley Fresh, Turlock, 1987-88. Translator multi-media U.S. Constitution, Britannica, 1993; cons. to book on amnesty, 1987; contbt. to book Intervarsity Christian Fellowship, 1965. Sunday sch. supt. Evang. Free Ch., Turlock, 1979-82; cons. Spanish work Turlock Covenant Ch., 1990—; mem. Malaysian Youth Coun., Kuala Lumpur, 1967-68. Mem. Calif. Tchrs. English to Spkrs. of Other Langs., Nat. Assn. Bilingual Educators, Tchrs. of English to Spkrs. of Other Langs. Republican. Avocations: reading, macintosh computers, writing, collecting stamps and coins. Home: 553 South Ave Turlock CA 95380-5606

ANTOUN, ANNETTE AGNES, editor, publisher; b. Franklin, Pa., Mar. 7, 1927; d. Adrien Uriel and Charlotte Mary (McMullen) Adelman; m. Frederic George Antoun, July 19, 1947 (dec.); children: Frederic G., Gregory S., Lawrence J., Mark J. (dec.), Laureace A., Scott J., Jonathan M., Lisa A. Student, Allegheny Coll., Meadville, Pa. Founder, editor-pub. Paxton Herald, Harrisburg, Pa., 1960—; founder, owner Graphic Svcs., advt. and graphics, Harrisburg, 1972—; owner Comms. Sys. Design, 1978—; pres. Susquehanna Valley Assocs., Inc., 1978—. Co-editor French Creek Patriot, cmty. newspaper, Cochranton, Pa., 1972. Mem. comms. com. Tri-County United Fund, 1973, mem. com. children's svcs., 1975-79; bd. dirs. Pa. Am. Lung Assn., 1973-98, treas., 1976, sec., 1979-80, v.p., 1980-81, treas., 1996-98; counselor to bd. Am. Lung Assn., 1989-90; bd. dirs. Harris Commn., 1975-79, Cath. Social Svc. Harrisburg, 1972-76; mem. extension planning com. YMCA, 1975-79; mem. bd. govs. Camp Curtin YMCA, 1980-85; mem. exec. bd. Lower Paxton Coalition Cmty. Groups, 1973-93; mem. comms. bd. Cath. Diocese Harrisburg, 1971-80; co-chmn. Dauphin County Ethics Com., 1979-81; chmn. bldg. com. Juvenile Detention Home, 1976-80; chmn. fund raising com. Greater Harrisburg Arts Coun., 1977-79; mem. Dauphin County bd. com. children and youth, 1982-85; vice chmn. Dauphin County Election Voting Machine Com., 1982—; mem. Tri-County Solid Waste Mgmt. Com., 1983-87; bd. dirs. Salvation Army Rehab. Svcs., 1992—, Capitol Pavilion Rehab., 1992—; mem. exec. com. spl. events United Negro Coll. Fund, 1993-98; spl. events chmn. Ctrl. Pa. UNCF, 1993-94, bd. dirs. H. John Heinz Ctr., 1994—; vice chmn. Millenium commn. City of Harrisburg, 1999—. Recipient Advocate award Paxton Area Jaycees, 1969, 73, citation Am. Legion Pa., 1971, 74, CAP, 1972, medallion Am. Legion Pa., 1972; award Am. Cancer Soc., 1969-89, March of Dimes award, 1969-89, AARP award, 1988, MADD award Hist. Preservation award, All Am. City Participation award, Nat. award Am. Lung Assn., 1992, Am. Legion REgional award, 1994, Pioneer award John Heinz Ctr., 1996, Cmty. Svc. award VFW, 1996, award for historic rehab. City Harrisburg, 1992, Cit of Harrisburg award, 1998, Gettysburg Monument Preservation award, 1998; numerous others. Mem. Am. Lung Assn. Pa. (treas. 1995-98), Internat. Platform Assn. Home: 4910 Earl Dr Harrisburg PA 17112-2123 Office: 101 Lincoln St Harrisburg PA 17112-2543

ANTRIM, NANCY MAE, literature and language professor, consultant; b. Medford, Mass., Nov. 15, 1945; d. Harold Kenneth Wilkes and Mae Bunny; m. Douglas Antrim, Aug. 19, 1972; children: Heather Marie, Stephanie Mae, Megan Elizabeth, Kenneth Edward. BA, U. Tex., El Paso, 1968, MA, 1991, U. So. Calif., L.A., 1993, PhD, 1996. Cert. tchr. English and history with ESL endorsement Tex. Bd. Edn. Tchr., English & history Our Lady of the Valley, El Paso, 1972—73, Father Yermo HS, El Paso, 1973—75; tchr. ESL Riverside HS, El Paso, 1987—91; asst. lectr. U. So. Calif., 1991—95; asst. prof., linguistics U. Tex., El Paso; asst. prof., English & linguistics Sul Ross State U., Alpine, 2002—. Mentor prof. Hacienda Heights Elem. Sch., El Paso, 1998—2002; ESL cons. AMSCO Pub., 2004. Contbr. articles to profl. jours. Reader Huntington Libr.; bd. mem. Casa Hogar Inc., Alpine, 2004—. Grantee, U. Tex., El Paso, 2000, Sul Ross State U., 2003, 2006. Mem.: Linguistic Soc. Am., S.W. Tex. Popular Culture/Am. Culture Assn., Pilot Club, Phi Sigma Iota (regional v.p. 2001—). Avocations: reading, travel, lighthouses. Office: Sul Ross State Univ Box C-89 Alpine TX 79832

ANTUNES, MARILYN Z., mathematics educator; d. John Henry and Harriet Griesbach Zannie; m. Jose Charles Antunes, Aug. 17, 1968; 1 child, Mark. BA, Susquehanna U., 1967; MA, Miami U., 1969. Tchr. West End Christian Sch., Hopewell, Va., 1976—79; adj. instr. Chapman Coll., 1976—79, St. Leo Coll., 1979—96, U. Md., 1986—88, City Coll. Chgo., 1989—93; asst. prof. math. Richard Bland Coll., Petersburg, Va., 1996—; ops. rsch. analyst US Army Logistics Ctr., Fort Lee, Va., 1979—80; programmer Computer Scis. Corp., Prince George, Va., 1995—96. Dir. Gear Up Project Opportunity & Oasis Richard Bland Coll., 1996—; tutor Tri-City Literacy Coun., Petersburg, 1999—2004. Mem.: Va. Math. Assn. Tchrs., Math. Assn. Am. Lutheran. Avocations: piano, gourmet cooking, travel. Office: Richard Bland Coll 11301 Johnson Rd Petersburg VA 23805 Office Phone: 804-862-6159. Business E-Mail: mantunes@rbc.edu.

APEL, MARIE U., elementary school educator; m. John F. Apel; children: Chad, Nicholas, Brooke. Tchr. Cullman City Bd. Edn., Ala., 1982—. Recipient Outstanding Am. Tchrs. award, NHR, 2006. Mem.: Delta Kappa Gamma (assoc.).

APELBAUM, PHYLLIS L., delivery messenger service executive; 1 child, Mark. Instr. Am. United Cab Co., Chgo., 1957-65; gen. mgr. City Bonded Messenger Svc., Chgo., 1960-74; founder, pres. Arrow Messenger Svc., Inc., Chgo., 1974—. 1st chair Affirmative Action Adv. Bd. of Chgo., 1991-92; chair Variety Club Children's Carnival, Chgo., 1990-94; mem. bicycle com. City of Chgo., 1992-95, parking task force, 1993-95; gov. Ill. Coun. on Econ. Edn., Chgo., 1995—; mem. Lakefront SRO Adv. Bd., Chgo., 1989-94; mem. Chgo. Police bd., 1995—. Recipient Small Bus. Innovative Mgmt. award Bank of Am., 1994; named Entrepreneur of the Yr., Ernst & Young, 1992, Nat. Small Bus. Person of the Yr., Small Bus. Assn., 1990; named to Entrepreneurship Hall of Fame, U. Ill., Chgo., 1993. Mem. Messenger Courier Assn. of Am. (bd. dirs. 1989—), Messenger Svc. Assn. Ill. (co-founder, pres.), Nat. Assn. Women Bus. Owners, The Chgo. Network. Office: Arrow Messenger Svc Inc 1322 W Walton St Chicago IL 60622-5340

APEL-BRUEGGEMAN, MYRNA L., entrepreneur; b. Cleve., July 19, 1942; d. Melvin Arthur and Merle Ruth (Hoffman) Rehlender; children: Timothy, Kristen; m. Earl L. Brueggeman, May 7, 1994. BS in Edn., Kent State U., 1965, M. in Edn. Counseling, 1987. Cert. tchr., Ohio; lic. minister, Ohio. Owner, mgr. real estate investments, Kent, Ohio; owner, founder IHS Counseling Ctr., Ravenna, Ohio; owner, mgr., founder IHS Home Sweet Home, Ravenna, Ohio; owner IHS Bookstore; co-owner Chapel on the Lakes. Owner Stow Estates, LLC, Southington Estates, LLC, Orchard Estates, Orchard Plaza, LLC. Mem. NAFE, Ohio Manufactured Housing Assn. (bd. dirs., pres. We. Res. chpt.), Internat. Soc. Profl. Hypnotists, Sigma Epsilon, Chi Sigma Iota.

APLIN, GINA SUZETTE, secondary school educator, rancher; d. John Scott and Myrtie Adelia Beaver; m. Dustin John Aplin, Aug. 3, 2002. BS, Angelo State U., San Angelo, Tex., 2001. Cert. tchr. secondary sch. Tex., 2001. With sales Dell, Inc., Austin, Tex., 2002—03; tchr. theatre and speech Bangs (Tex.) H.S., 2004—. Dir.: UIL Theater (Tex. Regional Qualifier award, 2005). Mem.: Tex. Ednl. Theatre Assn. Bapt. Office Phone: 325-752-6822.

APODACA, CHRISTY MCCORMICK, exercise physiologist, athletic trainer; b. Colorado Springs, Colo., Dec. 27, 1971; d. Richard L. and Janice D. McCormick; m. Robert A. Apodaca, June 3, 2006. Degree in kinesiology, U. No. Colo., Greeley, 1994. Cert. prenatal fitness instr. Desert SW Fitness, athletic trainer Nat. Athletic Trainers Assn., health fitness instr. Am. Coll. Sports Medicine, peronal trainer Am. Coll. Sports Medicine. Athletic trainer Gt. Plains Phys. Therapy, Grand Forks, ND, 1995—96; exercise physiologist 319 Aeromed. Squadron, Grand Forks AFB, ND, 1996—99, 8 Med. Ops. Squadron, Kunsan Air Base, Republic of Korea, 1999—2001, 50th Space Wing, Schriever AFB, Colo., 2001—. Athletic trainer Armed Forces Athletic Trainers Soc., Colorado Springs, 2004—. Musician: New Century Big Band Jazz Group. Ch. vol. First Christian Ch., Colorado Springs, 2001—. Named champion, ND State Champion Body Bldg., 1998, 1999, So. Colo. Armed Forces Body Bldg., 2002. Mem.: Am. Coll. Sports Medicine (cert. health fitness instr., cert. personal trainer), Nat. Athletic Trainers Assn. (cert. athletic trainer). Mem. Christian Ch. (Disciples Of Christ). Avocations: fitness, saxophone, piano, weightlifting. Home: 6765 Magnum Ct Colorado Springs CO 80918 Personal E-mail: fitness_wolf@msn.com.

APOGI, EVELYN, retired anesthesiologist; b. Chgo., Ill., Feb. 19, 1915; d. Solomon and Rose Apogi; m. Hylan Arthur Bickerman, June 7, 1941 (dec.); children: Pamela, Peter. BA, Hunter Coll, 1935; MD, NY U., 1939. Intern Harlem Hosp., NY, 1939—41; resident Bellview Hosp., NY, 1941—43; dir., anesthesiology dept. Flushing Hosp., NY, 1944—89; ret. Mem. malpractice com. Queens County Med. Soc., 1960—65.

APPAREDDY, VIJAYA L., psychiatrist; b. India; came to US, 1983; d. Balakrishna Reddy; m. Ramesh Appareddy; 2 children. Grad., St. Francis Coll. for Women, Hyderabad, India; MD, Osmania U. Med. Sch., Hyderabad, India. Cert. General Psychiatry, Child and Adolescent Psychiatry. Fellow, child and adult psychiatry Mount Sinai Med. Sch., NYC; residency in adult psychiatry Elmhurst Gen. Hosp.; clinical asst. prof. Brown U. Med. Sch., RI; med. dir., residential unit Columbia Valley Hosp., Chattanoog, Tenn.; mem. President's Com. on Mental Retardation, 2003—. Bd. mem. HCA Valley Psychiatric Hosp., Chattanooga. Co-author: The Siblings of the Psychiatrically Disordered Child, Normal Sleep in Neonates and Children. Mem.: Chattanooga Psychiatric Network (sec., treasurer), Am. Med. Women's Assn. (pres. Chattanooga chapter), Am. Assn. of Physicians of Indian Origin (former vice chmn. & mem. bd. of trustees). Office: Admin Children and Families 370 L'Enfant Promenade SW Washington DC 20447

APPEL, CAROLE STEIN, writer, political organizer; b. Phila., Jan. 23, 1937; d. Joseph George and Charlotte Stein; m. Kenneth I. Appel, June 21, 1959; children: Andrew, Laurel, Peter. BS, Temple U., 1958; MA, U. Mich., 1959. From asst. editor to sr. editor, jours. mgr. U. Ill. Press, Urbana, 1969-93; cons. Writing Ctr., U. N.H., Durham, 1995—2001. Mem. com. on bias free lang. Assn. Am. Univ. Presses, N.Y.C., 1991-93. Author: (chpt.) University Press Editing and Publishing, 1994; editor (with Berkin and Pinch) Exploring Women's Studies: Looking Forward, Looking Back, 2005; contbr. articles to profl. jours. Bd. dirs. Champaign County chpt. ACLU, 1980-89; chair Strafford County Dem. Com., Dover, N.H., 1996—; sec. N.H. Dem. Party, 2003-2005; mem. allocations com. United Way Greater Seacoast, Portsmouth, N.H., 1999-2002. Woodrow Wilson Nat. Fellowship Found. fellow, 1958; recipient Horace W. Norton Meml. award ACLU, 1990, Jefferson-Jackson award N.H. Dem. Party, 2000, Dunfey-Kanteres award, NH Dem. Party, 2006. Mem. NOW (pres. Champaign County chpt. 1976). Democrat. Home: 16 Isaac Lucas Cir Dover NH 03820-4910

APPEL, GLORIA, advertising executive; BA in Eng. Lit., CCNY, MA in Edn. Exec. v.p. Grey Worldwide, N.Y.C., 1990—, mng. ptnr., 1990—. Office: Grey Worldwide 777 3rd Ave New York NY 10017-1401

APPEL, MINDY R., social worker; b. Monticello, NY, Mar. 25, 1957; d. Sy and Ruth (Minowitz) A. BA, Ithaca Coll., 1978; MSW, Tulane U., 1979. Cert. social worker, bd. cert. social worker Acad. Cert. Social Workers. Clin. social worker DePaul Hosp., New Orleans, 1980-86, New Orleans East Ctr. for Psychotherapy, Meth. Psychiat., 1986-88; dir. clin. svcs. CPC East Lake Hosp., New Orleans, 1990—96; pvt. practice New Orleans, 1996—2005; social worker The Orchid, Palm Springs, Fla. Mem. Nat. Assn. Social Workers. Address: 1745 Palm Cove Blvd #104 Delray Beach FL 33445 Office Phone: 561-926-7858.

APPEL, NINA SCHICK, law educator, dean, academic administrator; b. Feb. 17, 1936; d. Leo and Nora Schick; m. Alfred Appel Jr.; children: Karen Oshman, Richard. Student, Cornell U.; JD, Columbia U., 1959. Instr. Columbia Law Sch., 1959-60; adminstr. Stanford U., mem. faculty, prof. law, 1973—, assoc. dean, 1976-83; dean Sch. Law Loyola U., 1983—2004, dean emerita, prof. law, 2004—. Mem. Am. Bar Found., Ill. Bar Found., Chgo. Bar Found., Chgo. Legal Club, Chgo. Network. Jewish. Office: Loyola U Sch Law 25 E Pearson St Chicago IL 60611-2055 Office Phone: 312-915-7128. E-mail: nappel@luc.edu.

APPELBAUM, ANN HARRIET, lawyer; b. Decatur, Ill., 1948; d. Irving and Cecelia (Hecht) A.; m. Neal Borovitz, July 4, 1982; children: Abby, Jeremy. BA, Barnard Coll., 1970; JD, Boston U., 1973. Bar: N.Y. 1974, U.S. Dist. Ct. (so. dist.) N.Y. 1975, U.S. Ct. Appeals (2nd cir.) 1975, U.S. Supreme Ct. 1978. Assoc. Hart & Hume, N.Y.C., 1974-76, Warshaw, Burstein, N.Y.C., 1976-80; counsel Jewish Theol. Sem. & Jewish Mus., N.Y.C., 1980—. Mem. Nat. Assn. Coll. and Univ. Attys. Office: The Jewish Theological Seminary 3080 Broadway New York NY 10027-4650 Office Phone: 212-678-8804.

APPELBAUM, BERNARDINE, medical/surgical nurse; b. St. Louis, Nov. 8, 1936; d. John Stanislaus and Sophia Estelle Wojcicki; children: Robert John Jr., Stephen Joseph. Diploma in Nursing, St. John's Mercy Hosp., St. Louis, 1957. RN Ohio, CNOR. Nurse St. John's Mercy Hosp., St. Louis, 1957—60, 1963—64, Creve Couer Med. Ctr., Mo., 1960, St. Anthony's Hosp., St. Louis, 1962—63, St. Joseph Hosp, Kirkwood, Mo., 1964—66, Grandview Hosp., Dayton, Ohio, 1968—72, Good Samaritan Hosp., Dayton, 1972—2004, KMC/Sycamore Hosp., Miamisburg, Ohio, 2005—, Samaritan North Surgery Ctr., Dayton, 2006—. Tutor, reading vol. Centerville Sch. Dist./Normandy Sch., Centerville, Ohio, 2005—. Roman Catholic. Avocations: reading, travel. Home: 6880 Cedar Cove Dr Centerville OH 45459

APPELBAUM, DIANA KARTER, author; b. Ft. Belvoir, Va., Nov. 9, 1953; d. Peter and Elizabeth Carmen (Whitman) Karter; m. Paul Stuart Appelbaum, Mar. 31, 1974; children: Binyamin, Yonatan, Avigail. AB, Columbia U., 1975. Author: Thanksgiving, An American Holiday, 1984, The Glorious Fourth, 1989, Giants in the Land, 1993, Cocoa Ice, 1997, Reflections in Bullough's Pond: Economy and Ecosystem in New England, 2000. Recipient Booklist Mag. Top of the List prize, 1993. Mem. Author's Guild. Home: 39 Claremont Rd Apt 24 New York NY 10027 Office: care Houghton Mifflin Co 222 Berkeley St Boston MA 02116-3748

APPELBAUM, MARCI ANNE, theater director, educator; b. Oceanside, NY, Nov. 22, 1971; d. Richard and Adele Judith Appelbaum; life ptnr. Jeff Catanese. BA, Fla. State U., Tallahassee, 1992; diploma, Am. Musical and Dramatic Acad., NYC, 1994. Exec. dir. Attic Salt Theatre Co., Astoria, NY, 1998—, v.p., 1998—2006. Musician Erin Lee & Marci, NYC, 2004—; tchr. theater Trevor Day Sch., 1998—2006. Author: (educational book) Folktale Plays from Around the World, Read Aloud Plays: Colonial America; singer (composer): (children's music cd) Someone's Gotta Wanna Play (Children's Music Web award, 2005), Snowdance (ASCAPlus award, 2006); prodr.: (educational theater production) Newly Grown Tales; author (producer): (children's theatrical performance) The Sultan's Wife; prodr.: (children's theatrical performance) Feet Water. Mem.: Am. Fedn. TV and Radio Artists, Actor's Equity Assn., Children's Music Network, Mensa, Sigma Delta Tau. Liberal. Office Phone: 212-330-7100. E-mail: astc@atticsalt.org.

APPELL, LOUISE SOPHIA, retired consulting company executive; b. Northampton, Mass., Sept. 22, 1930; d. Romeo Edward and Phyllis Teresa (Szynal) Fortier; m. Melville Joseph Appell, July 26, 1953 (div. 1975); children: Melissande Foglio, David Maxcim; m. Clifford Harding Querolo, June 1, 1991 (dec. 1992). BA, Smith Coll., 1951; MA, U. Ky., 1966, PhD, 1972. Instr. U. Ky., 1966-68; dir. spl. edn. grad. program Catholic U. Am.,

Washington, 1969-76; assoc. dir. nat. com. Arts for the Handicapped, Washington, 1976-80; owner, pres. Louise Appell Cons. Svcs., Washington, 1980-82; assoc. Macro Systems, Inc., Silver Spring, Md., 1982-84, dir. edn. product devel., 1984-85, dir. ednl. product devel., 1985—, v.p., 1985—, ret., 1996. Personal E-mail: lsappell@verizon.net.

APPERSON, JEAN, psychologist; b. Durham, N.C., June 8, 1934; d. James Harry and Dorothy Elizabeth (Johnson) Apperson; m. Calvin Adams Pope, Mar. 23, 1956 (div. 1967); 1 child, Richard Allan. BA, U. S. Fla., 1966; MA, Mich. State U., 1970, PhD, 1973. Cert. in psychoanalysis Mich. Psychoanalytic Coun., 1990. Teaching asst. Mich. State U., E. Lansing, 1968-69; psychiatric technician St. Lawrence Community Mental Health Ctr., Lansing, Mich., 1968-69, psychology intern, 1969-71, Mich. State U. Counseling Ctr., 1971-73; clin. psychologist U. Mich. Counseling Ctr., Ann Arbor, 1973-81; pvt. practice psychology and psychoanalysis Ann Arbor, 1974—. Mem., chmn. Mich. Bd. Psychology, Lansing, 1984-91. Contbr. articles to profl. jours.; cons. editor Am. Psychol. Assn. Catalog of Selected Documents, 1975-80. USPHS grantee, 1969-70; NIMH grantee, 1970-71. Fellow Mich. Psychol. Assn. (chmn. women's issues com. 1981-83); mem. APA (com. on sci. and profl. ethics and conduct 1977-80), Mich. Soc. Psychoanalytic Psychology (treas. 1982-86), Mich. Psychoanalytic Coun. (tchg. and supervising analyst, mem. at large 1991-93, tng. com. 1992-2001, pres. 1995-97, v.p. for edn. and tng. 1998-2001), Assn. for Advancement of Psychology, Am. Women in Psychology, Mich. Women Psychologists. Democrat. Unitarian Universalist. Avocations: french language and culture, gardening, nature study, music. Home: 7224 Chelsea Manchester Rd Manchester MI 48158-9443 Office: Ste 23E 555 E William St Ann Arbor MI 48104-2428 Office Phone: 734-428-9110. E-mail: jeanatapp@aol.com.

APPLE, DAINA DRAVNIEKS, federal agency administrator; b. Kuldiga, Latvia, July 6, 1944; came to U.S., 1951; d. Albins Dravnieks and Alina A. (Bergs) Zelmenis; divorced; 1 child, Almira Moronne; m. Martin A. Apple, Sept. 2, 1986. BSc, U. Calif., Berkeley, 1977, MA, 1980. Economist Pacific S.W. Rsch. U.S. Forest Svc., Berkeley, 1976-85, mgr. regional land use appeals San Francisco, 1986-88, program analysis officer, engring., 1988-90, asst. regulatory officer, 1990-95, strategic planner nat. forest sys. resources program, 1995-98, policy analyst, 1998—2002; adminstr. workplace rels. Pacific Southwest Region, Vallejo, Calif., 2002—03, staff asst. to dep. chief programs and legislation, 2004—05, staff asst. to the dep. chief for R&D, 2005—. Author: Public Involvement in the Forest Service-Methodologies, 1977, Public Involvement, Selected Abstracts for Natural Resource Managers, 1979, The Management of Policy and Direction in the Forest Service, 1982, An Analysis of the Forest Service Human Resource Management Program, 1984, Organization Design-Abstracts for Natural Resources Users, 1986, Social and Legal Forces Changing the Management of National Forests, 1996, Water and the Forest Service, 2000, The Forest Service as a Learning Organization, 2000, Evolution of U.S. Water Policy, 2001; contbg. editor Jour. Women in Natural Resources, 1987—. Fellow Soc. Am. Foresters (chair Nat. Capital Soc. 2000), Phi Beta Kappa Soc.; mem. AAAS, ESA, Am. Assn. Biol. Scis., N.Y. Acad. Sci., Washington (D.C.) Acad. Scis., Am. Water Resources Assn., Forest History Soc., Am. Latvian Assn. (bd. dirs. 1995-97), Phi Beta Kappa Assocs. (nat. sec. 1985-88, pres. No. Calif. 1982-84), Commonwealth Club of Calif., Sigma Xi. Avocations: politics, ballroom dancing, tennis, films. Office: USDA Forest Svc R&D 1400 Independence Ave SW Washington DC 20250-1120 Office Phone: 202-205-1452. Business E-Mail: dapple@fs.fed.us.

APPLE, FIONA (FIONA APPLE MAGGART), singer, songwriter; b. NYC, Sept. 13, 1977; d. Diane McAfee and Brandon Maggart. Toured with Chris Isaak and The Counting Crows; host MTV 120 Minutes. Singer: (albums) Tidal, 1996, When the Pawn., 1999, Extraordinary Machine, 2005, (singles) Criminal, 1996 (Grammy award, Best Female Rock Vocal Performance, 1997, MTV Music Video award, Best Cinematography, 1998), Sleep to Dream, 1996 (MTV Music Video award, New Artist Video of the Year, 1997), Shadowboxer, 1996 (Top 10), Paper Bag, 1999, Parting Gift, 2005, O'Sailor, 2005; guest performer Saturday Night Live, 2005. Nominee Grammy award, Best New Artist, Best Rock Song, 1997, MTV Music Video award, Female Video of the Year, 1998, Grammy award, Best Female Rock Vocal Performance, Best Alternative Music Album, 2000, Grammy award, Best Country Collaboration with Vocals (with Johnny Cash), 2002. Address: 2100 Colorado Ave Santa Monica CA 90404-3504*

APPLE, JACKI (JACQUELINE B. APPLE), artist, educator, writer; b. NYC; Student, Syracuse U.; BFA, Parsons Sch. Design. Curator exhbns. and performance Franklin Furnace, N.Y.C., 1977—80; prodr., host Sta. KPFK-FM, North Hollywood, Calif., 1982—95; adj. prof. Art Ctr. Coll. Design, Pasadena, Calif., 1983—. Mem. faculty adv. com. Art Ctr. Coll. Design, Pasadena, 1993, Faculty Coun. rep., 2000-06; vis. faculty UCSD, LaJolla, 1995-99. Contbg. writer: L.A. Weekly, 1983-89; contbg. editor: Artweek, 1983-90, High Performance Mag., 1984-95; performance works include The Garden Planet Revisited, 1982, The Amazon, the Mekong, the Missouri and the Nile, 1985, Palisade, 1987, Fluctuations of the Field, 1989, (with J. Adler) A Stone's Throw., 2000, Kokoro No Mai, 2003, After the Fall.A Prophecy, 2004; writer, performer, dir., prodr.: (record) The Mexican Tapes, 1979-80, (performance/installation/audio work) Voices in the Dark, 1989-97, (radio art work) Swan Lake, 1989; artist, prodr.: (installations and audio work) The Culture of Disappearance, # 1-5, 1991-95; author, designer: (book, installation) Trunk Pieces, 1975-78, (cd) Thank You for Flying American, 1995, Ghost Dances/On the Event Horizon 1996; six part radio art series Redefining Democracy in America Parts, 1991-92; (site specific installation) Zeitghosts: Angels in the Architecture, 1996, Sanctuary, 1996, Hidden Desires, 1998, A Stone's Throw.The Last Witnesses, 2001; (photowork) ghost.dance series 1995—, (installation) Aviary of the Lost. 1994/2004, (photo/audio performance) You Don't Need a Weatherman, 1999; pub. art projects Aliso-Pico Cmty. Ctr., 1997-2000, Venice Oakwood Cmty. Ctr., 2000-03, Martin Luther King Rehab Ctr., 2000-03, Little Tokyo br. L.A. Pub. Libr., 2002-05; author: Doing It Right in L.A., 1990; prodr. EarJam Music Festival, 2000, 01, 02, 04. Recipient Vesta award Media Arts Women's Bldg., 1990, Faculty Enrichment grant Art Ctr. Coll. Design, 2001; NEA visual artists fellow, 1979, 81; InterArts program grantee NEA, 1984-85, 91-92; Calif. Arts Coun. Visual Arts/New Genres fellowship, 1996; grantee Durfee Foundation, 2003. Mem.: Internat. Art Critics Assn., Nat. Writers Union, Coll. Art Assn. (edn. com. 2005—), Am. Composers Forum. Home: 3532 Jasmine Ave Los Angeles CA 90034-4947 E-mail: jaworks@sprintmail.com.

APPLEBAUM, ANNE, journalist, writer; b. Washington, 1964; m. Radek Sikorski; children: Alexander, Tadeusz. Grad, Yale U., 1986. Correspondent The Independent, London, 1988—90; journalist Economist, London, 1988—92; fgn. editor Spectator Mag., London, 1993—94, deputy editor, 1994—; columnist The Daily Telegraph, London, 1994—; columnist, mem. editl. bd. Wash. Post, 2002—. Author: (book) Between East and West: Across the Borderlands of Europe, 1995, Gulag, A History, 2004 (Nat. Book award nominee, 2003, Pulitzer Prize for general nonfiction, 2004), several writings have appeared in The Wall St. Jour., the Fin. Times, The Internat. Herald Tribune, Fgn. Affairs, Boston Globe, The Ind., The Guardian, Commentaire, Suddeutsche Zeitung, Newsweek, The New Criterion, others. Recipient Charles Douglas Home Meml. Trust award, 1992; Marshall Scholar, London Sch. Economics, St. Antony's Coll., Oxford. Office: Washington Post 1150 15th St NW Washington DC 20071

APPLEBY, JOYCE OLDHAM, historian, educator; b. Omaha, Apr. 9, 1929; d. Junius G. and Edith (Cash) Oldham; children: Ann Lansburgh Caylor, Mark Lansburgh, Frank Bell Appleby. BA, Stanford U., 1950; MA, U. Calif., Santa Barbara, 1959; PhD, Claremont Grad. Sch., 1966. With Mademoiselle mag., 1950-52; asst. prof. history San Diego State U., 1967-70, asso. prof., 1970-73; prof. history, asso. dean Coll. Arts and Letters, 1973-75, prof., 1976-81. Vis. asso. prof. U. Calif., Irvine, 1975-76; vis. prof. UCLA, 1978-79, prof. history, 1981—; vis. fellow St. Catherine's Coll., U. Oxford, 1983; Harmsworth prof. Am. History, U. Oxford, 1990-91; Bd. fellows Claremont Grad. Sch. and U. Center, 1970-73 Author: Economic Thought and Ideology in Seventeenth-Century England, 1978, Capitalism and a New Social Order, 1983, Liberalism and Republicanism in the Historical Imagination, 1992; co-author: Telling the Truth about History, 1994; co-editor: Knowledge and Postmodernism in Historical Perspective, Inheriting the Revolution, 2000; mem. bd. editors Democracy, 1980-83, William and Mary Quar., 1980-83, 18th Century Studies, 1982-87, Ency. Am. Polit. History, Am. Hist. Rev., 1988—, Jour. Interdisciplinary History, 1989—, The Papers of Thomas Jefferson, 1988—, The Adams Papers, 1990—; contbr. articles to profl. jours.; mem. adv. bd. Am. Nat. Biography. Mem. Am. Acad. Arts and Scis., Am. Philos. Soc., Smithsonian Inst. (coun.), Am. Hist. Assn. (pres.), Orgn. Am. Historians (pres.), Inst. Early Am. History and Culture (coun. 1980-86, chmn. 1983-89). Home: 615 Westholme Ave Los Angeles CA 90024-3209 Office: UCLA Dept History Los Angeles CA 90024

APPLEFELD, FLORAINE B., cultural organization administrator; b. Balt., Aug. 25, 1936; m. Leroy S. Applefeld; children: Lynn Carol Henderson, Laurie Applefeld Segall. BA in Art History, Johns Hopkins U., Goucher Coll., Coll. Notre Dame, Md. Inst. Art. Art tchr. Balt. City Pub. Sch. Sys., 1965—75; educator Balt. Mus. Art, 1970—76; vol. dir. Balt. is Best program, 1976—88; radio moderator Sta. WCMB-Radio Profiles Interview program, 1984—87; vol. dir. Md. You Are Beautiful program, 1987—. Chairwoman Coalition for Appt. of Women to State Bds. and Commns., 1998—. Adv. bd. dirs. Md. Artists Equity Found., 1985—; founding bd. dirs., chair spl. events, mentoring chair Network 2000, 1993—; bd. dirs. Little People's Rsch. Fund, 1982—; Bd. dirs. Girl Scouts Cen. Md., 1995—; bd. dirs. 1st Night Annapolis, 1991—. Named one of Md.'s Top 100 Women, Daily Record; recipient Citation of Appreciation, Am. Bus. Women's Assn., Sta. WJZ-TV Hero award, J.C. Penny Co. Golden Rule award, Jimmie Swartz medallion, Disting. Woman award, Girl Scouts Cen. Md., Certs. Recognition, Soroptomist Internat. Balt., Miles W. Connor Disting. Svc. award, YWCA Cmty. Svc. award, Mayor William Donald Schaefer Unsung Heroine award. Mem.: Advt. Assn. Balt. (bd. dirs. 1975—87, 1991—92), Md. Commn. for Women. Office: 9th Fl 217 E Redwood St Baltimore MD 21202

APPLEGATE, CHRISTINA, actress; b. L.A., Calif., Nov. 25, 1971; d. Robert Applegate and Nancy Priddy; m. Johnathon Schaech, Oct. 20, 2001 (separated). Film appearances include: Jaws of Satan, 1980, Streets, 1990, Don't Tell Mom the Babysitter's Dead, 1991, Across the Moon, 1994, Vibrations, 1995, Wild Bill, 1995, Mars Attacks!, 1996, Nowhere, 1997, Claudine's Return, 1998, The Big Hit, 1998, Mafia!, 1998, The Giving Tree, 2000, Just Visiting, 2001, The Sweetest Thing, 2002, Heroes, 2003, View from the Top, 2003, Wonderland, 2003, Grand Theft Parsons, 2003, Employee of the Month, 2004, Anchorman: The Legend of Ron Burgundy, 2004, Surviving Christmas, 2004, Tilt-A-Whirl, 2005; TV appearances include: (series) Days of Our Lives, 1974, Washingtoon, 1985, Heart of the City, 1986, Married.With Children, 1987-97, All My Life, 1998, Jesse, 1998-2000, Friends, 2002, (TV movies) Grace Kelly, 1983, Dance 'til Dawn, 1988, Prince Charming, 2001, Suzanne's Diary for Nicholas, 2005. Off-broadway appearances include: Sweet Charity, 2005 (Theatre World award, 2005).*

APPLEHANS, CYNTHIA DIANE, art educator, artist; b. Denver, Feb. 9, 1961; d. Frank Henry and Frances Dora (Jansen) Cinquanta; m. Russ Alan Applehans, June 15, 1985; children: Rachel Anne, Brandon Ryan. BFA (hon.), U. Colo., Denver, 1987. Cert. art tchr. K-12 Colo., 1990. Graphic artist/designer Adolph Coors Co., Golden, Colo., 1982—83; graphic designer Schroader Design, Denver, 1983—85; art instr. City of Westminster, Colo., 1987—90; substitute art tchr. Jefferson County Pub. Schs., Denver, 1990—2000; tchr. art K-12 Jefferson County Hackberry Hill Elem. Sch., Arvada, Colo., 2000—. Mem. empty bowl fundraising dinner adv. bd. Arvada Soup Kitchen, Colo., 2003—; chairperson reflections art competition Jefferson County Pub. Schs., Denver, 1998—99, dir. judging panel reflections art competition, 1997—98. Exhibitions include Jefferson County Art Tchr. Exhbn., All About Eve Women in Art (Best in Show, 1999), one-woman shows include, children's book illustration. Facilitator and fundraiser art and dinner project Arvada Food Bank, 2003—06; artist Art for Aids, Denver, 1997—98. Recipient Colo. Scholars scholarship, U. Colo., 1986—87, 1989—90, Outstanding Achievement in the Sch. of Letters, Arts and Scs., 1989. Mem.: Soc. Children's Book Writers and Illustrators, Nat. Writers Assn., Nat. Art Edn. Assn. Avocations: tap dance, jazz dance, basketball. Office Phone: 303-982-0243.

APPOLD, CYNTHIA, visual arts educator; b. Huntington, N.Y., Oct. 15, 1955; d. John and Frances; children: Gabrielle, Joseph. AA in Gen. Studies with honors, Suffolk County C.C., 1976; BS in Art Edn. cum laude, SUNY, New Paltz, 1979; MA in Comm. Arts with distinction, N.Y. Inst. Tech., 1985. Permanent tchg. cert. N.Y. Mid./HS visual arts educator Rhinebeck (N.Y.) Pub. Schs., 1979-80; elem. visual arts educator Cobleskill (N.Y.) Pub. Schs., 1980-81; HS visual arts educator Glen Cove (N.Y.) Pub. Schs., 1982-84; Mid./HS visual arts educator Friend's Acad., Locust Valley, NY, 1984-85; HS visual arts educator Hicksville (N.Y.) Pub. Schs., 1985—. Computer graphics cons. Old Bethpage Schs., Bethpage, 1989—92; lectr., presenter, workshop coord. N.Y. State Computer and Tech. Educators, various locations, NY, 1990, N.Y. State Computer and Tech. Educators, various locations, 1991, 92, N.Y. State Computer and Tech. Educators, various locations, 1994, N.Y. State Tchrs. Assn., various locations, NY, 1988, NY, 89, NY, 91, NY, 92, NY, 95. Exhibited sculpture, paintings, photography Art Tchrs. Assn. Art Show, 1985, 86, 87, 89, 90, 91, 92, 94 (Award of Excellence 1987, Award of Merit 1994), Hicksville Cmty. Art Show, 1986, 87, 88, 2005. Leader Suffolk County Coun. Girl Scouts Am., Huntington, 1996—99; com. head N.Y. State Tchr. of Yr., Albany, NY, 1997, com. mem., 1998; mem., liaison Women on the Job Task Force, Mineola, NY, 1986—87; com. mem. L.I. Media Art Show, Dix Hills, NY, 1999—2001, N.Y. Inst. Tech. Alumni Adv. Com., 1998—2000. Recipient Art Educator Recognition award Pratt Inst., 1990; named 1996 Tchr. of Yr., N.Y. State Bd. Regents, 1995-96; Educators grantee R.I. Sch. Design, 1990. Mem.: AAUW, NOW (bd. dirs. Nassau chpt. 1986—89, sec. Nassau chpt. 1987—89), N.Y. State Art Tchrs. Assn. (presenter 1985—95, Recognition award 1995), L.I. Art Tchrs. Assn. (workshop presenter 1986—93, co-chair mems. exhibit 1992—94), Media Art Tchrs. Assn. (L.I. media art show com. 1999—2000), N.Y. State Computer and Tech. Educators (com. mem. 1990—92, student exhibit chair 1994, 1995 Outstanding Technologist), Nat. Mus. Women in Arts (charter mem.). Home: 26 Prairie Rd Huntington Station NY 11746-2721 Office: Hicksville H S 180 Division Ave Hicksville NY 11801-4899 Office Phone: 516-733-6621.

APSEL, ALYSSA, electrical engineer, computer engineer; BS Electrical Engineering, Swarthmore College, 1995; MS Electrical Engineering, California Institute of Technology, 1996; PhD Electrical Engineering, Johns Hopkins University, 2002. Undergraduate research fellow U. of Pa, SUNFEST, 1994; grad. research asst., electrical engineering Calf. Institute of Technology, 1995—97; grad. research asst., electrical and computer engineering Johns Hopkins U., 1998—; grad. research asst., army research lab Adelphi, 2000—. Teaching asst., engineering methodology Swarthmore College, 1993; teaching asst., integrated electronics Johns Hopkins U., 1998, teaching asst., lab asst., Advanced Integrated Circuits, 99. Fellow Caltech Institute Fellowship, California Institute of Technology, 1995—96, Abel Wolman Fellowship, Johns Hopkins University, 1997—98. Achievements include patents for Integrated electronic-optoelectronic devices and method of making the same, 2000; Low Power, Differential Optical Receiver in Silicon on Sapphire, 2001. Office: Johns Hopkins U Dept Computer & Electrical Engineering 3400 N Charles St Baltimore MD 21218

APT, JOAN FRANK, volunteer; b. Pitts., Sept. 4, 1926; d. Robert Frank and Cecelia Frank Moreell; m. Jerome Apt, Jr., Aug. 10, 1947; children: Jerome III, Judy Apt Nathenson(dec.). Student, Wheaton Coll., Norton, Mass. Co-founder Pitts. Pub. Theater, 1975—; bd. trustees, bd. dirs. Pitts. Symphony Orch., 1972—85, 1990—, Pitts. Symphony Assn., 1952—; former bd. trustees, bd. dirs. Depression, Awareness, Recognition, Treatment (DART), 1988, Pitts. Jazz Orch., 1987, Pa. Coun. on Arts, 1986—94; mem. prodn. com. Civic Light Opera, 1971—89; founder Pitts. chpt. Am. Israel Cultural Found., 1970—75; founding bd. Am. Wind Symphony, 1959—61; chmn. Benedum Ctr. Opening Night Gala Performance, 1987, Heinz Hall Opening Weekend, 1972. Named Woman of Spirit, Carlow Coll., 2002; recipient Golden Triangle award, City of Pitts., Mayor, 1959, Pitts. Woman of Yr. award in arts and music, Vectors/Pitts., 1988, Vita award in Arts, consolidated Natural Gas, 1990, Vita Vol. of Yr. award, Consolidated Natural Gas, 1991, Leadership award in arts and letters, YMCA, 1996, Disting. Dau. Pa.-Gov.'s award, 1997.

APTER, EMILY, language educator; BA in History and Lit., Harvard U., 1977; PhD in Comparative Lit., Princeton U., 1983. Prof. French NYU, N.Y.C. Recipient Guggenheim fellowship, 2003, Mellon fellowship, Rockefeller fellowship, ACLS fellowship, NEH fellowship, Coll. Art Assn. fellowship. Office: 19 University Pl 634 New York NY 10003

AQUADRO, JEANA LAUREN, graphic designer, educator; b. Key West, Fla., June 10, 1957; d. Charles Frasure and Geraldine Ferguson (Norton) A.; m. John A. Crawford; 1 dau., Lauren Olya Crawford. B Environ. Design magna cum laude, N.C. State U., 1979; MFA, Yale U., 1984. Graphic designer various projects for Cooper-Hewitt Nat. Mus. Design, Whitney Mus. Am. Art, Shearson Lehman Bros., Citicorp Investment Bank, Abbeville Press, UNICEF, others, N.Y.C., 1984-91; asst. dir. graphic design dept. Mus. Modern Art, 1988-89; design cons. Solomon R. Guggenheim Mus., 1989-91; prof. Savannah Coll., Savannah, Ga., 1991—2001; graphic design cons., 2001—. Bd. dirs. Wilderness S.E. Recipient The Am. Fedn. of Arts award of Excellence, 1988, Fed. design achievement award Nat. Endowment for Arts, 1992, Presidential award for design excellence Fed. Govt., 1994. Avocations: aquatic sports, travel, gardening. Studio: 3 Pinewood Ave Savannah GA 31406

AQUINO, MARY ANN, elementary school educator; b. Anacortes, Wash., Aug. 10, 1948; d. James Donald and Elnora Ann Larson; m. Victor Aquino Jr., Dec. 27, 1970; children: Flannery, Max. BA in Edn., Western Wash. U., Bellingham, 1970. 4th grade tchr. Blaine Elem. Sch., Wash., 1970—72; tchr. hearing impaired Albuquerque Pub. Schs., 1972—76; specialist in hearing impairment Ednl. Svc. Dist., Olympia, Wash., 1976—77; tchr. Rochester Pub. Schs., Wash., 1977—82; 8th grade tchr. Kent Pub. Schs., Wash., 1987—; head English dept. Mattson Mid. Sch., Kent, 2000—06. Vol. Natural Helpers, Mattson Mid. Sch., 2000—06; sponsor history contest Nat. History Days, Kent, 2000—06. Mem.: NEA, Kent Assn. Edn., Wash. Edn. Assn. Avocations: tennis, quilting, reading. Home: 28120 236th Ave SE Maple Valley WA 98038

ARABATZIS, CONSTANCE ELAINE, lawyer; b. Dania, Fla., Jan. 23, 1961; BS in Health Services Adminstrn., summa cum laude, CUNY, 1986; JD, NYU, 1989. Bar: Conn. 1990, NY 1991, DC 1991, US Dist. Ct. (so. dist.) NY 1992, Fla. 1993. Asst. dist. atty. King's County Dist. Atty. Office, Bklyn., 1989—92; assoc., comm. real estate litig. Finkelstein Borah Schwartz Altschuler & Golstein, 1992—94; in-house counsel Investments Ltd., Fla., 1994—95; sr. assoc. Stephens Lynn Klein & McNicholas, Fla., 1995—98; assoc. Baer Marks & Upham, 1998—2001; sr. assoc., Litig. & Dispute Resolution Group Dickstein Shapiro Morin & Oshinsky LLP, NYC, 2001—, diversity/pro bono coun. Mem.: Fla. Bar, DC Bar, Soc. Human Resource Mgrs., Phi Alpha Delta. Office: Dickstein Shapiro Morin & Oshinsky LLP 1177 Avenue of the Americas New York NY 10036-2714 Office Phone: 212-896-5430, 212-997-9880. Business E-Mail: arabatzise@dsmo.com.

ARAFAT-JOHNSON, DANYAH, secondary school educator, director; b. Ft. Worth, Jan. 10, 1969; d. Husam Rashed and Margaret Miller Arafat; m. Clinton Heath Johnson, May 18, 1955; children: Clay Elias, Brooks Husam. BA in English, Tex. A&M U., College Station, 1991, BA in Theatre Arts, 1991; MEd, U. North Tex., Denton, 2003. Cert. profl. educator Tex. Bd. Edn., 1993. Speech tchr. Cypress-Fairbanks Ind. Sch. Dist., Katy, Tex., 1993; speech/theatre arts dept. chair Humble (Tex.) Ind. Sch. Dist., 1996—97; theater arts dir., tchr. Keller (Tex.) Ind. Sch. Dist., 1997—2000; asst. dir. Huntington Learning Ctr., Watauga, Tex., 2001—02; theatre arts dir., tchr. Carroll Ind. Sch. Dist., Southlake, Tex., 2002—. Recipient Disting. Scholar award, Coll. Liberal Arts - Tex. A&M U., 1990; grantee Mid. Sch. Broadcast Journalism Unit, Keller Ind. Sch. Dist., 1999; Aggie Players Undergraduate Scholarship/Assistantship Award, Tex. A&M U., 1987—91. Mem.: United Educators Assn., Tex. Assn. for the Gifted and Talented (assoc.), Tex. Ednl. Theatre Assn. (assoc.; curriculum cons. 2005—06). Democrat. Office: George Dawson Middle School/Carroll ISD 400 South Kimball Ave Southlake TX 76092 Office Phone: 817-949-5556. Office Fax: 817-949-5555. Business E-Mail: arafatd@cisdmail.com.

ARAGNO, ANNA, psychoanalyst, author; b. Rome, Italy, Apr. 20, 1945; came to U.S., 1965; d. Riccardo and Anna-Rosa (Canitano) A.; m. Justino Edgardo Diaz, Oct. 3, 1967 (div. 1983); children: Natascia, Katya. BA, Empire State Coll., 1983; MA, New Sch. Social Rsch., N.Y., 1986; PhD, Union Inst., 1992. Lic. psychoanalyst, N.Y. Grad. staff Postgrad. Ctr. Washington Square Inst., N.Y.C., 1986—. Presenter, instr. at seminars in field. Author: Symbolization: Proposing a Developmental Pardigm for a New Psychoanalytic Theory of Mind, Forms of Knowledge: A Psychanalytic Study of Avian Intelligence.; contbr. scientific papers, articles to profl. jours. Fulbright scholar, 1965. Mem.: APA, Nat. Assn. Advancement of Psychoanalysis. Home: 140 W End Ave New York NY 10023-6131

ARAGON, LYNN D., retired physician; b. Alliance, Ohio, Nov. 19, 1935; d. Clifford Charles and Charlotte Ruth Daugherty; m. Pedro Juan Aragon, July 29, 1983; children: John C. Gillette, Karen G. Allen, Keith G. Gillette, Susan G. Meer. BS, Westminster Coll., New Wilmington, Pa., 1956; MD, U. Pitts., 1960. Lic. physician Pa., 1960, Ohio, 1985. Staff physician USPHS Indian Hosp., Pine Ridge, SD, 1961—63; emergency rm. physician Columbia Hosp., Wilkinsburg, Pa., 1963; gen. practice physician Gillette and Assocs., Pitts., 1963—85; same day ctr. physician HMO Health Ohio, Akron, 1985—97. Med. dir. of the med. assisting tech. program U. Akron, Ohio, 1989—95, mem. med. assisting adv. bd., 1989—95; vol. physician Open-M Free Clinic, Akron, 1998—2003. Vol. swim instr. ARC, Pitts., 1970—85. Recipient St. Luke award, Open-M Free Clinic, 2002. Mem.: AMA, Order Ea. Stars. Protestant. Avocations: travel, reading, computers, flying. Home: 9632 Skyway Dr Wadsworth OH 44281 Personal E-mail: laragon@neo.rr.com.

ARALDI, MARY-JANE SNYDER, nurse, educator; d. George Walter and Mary Elizabeth (Brennan) Snyder; m. Albert Araldi, Dec. 10, 1983; children: Gregory, Sarah, Meghan. Diploma in Nursing, Albany Med. Ctr. Sch. Nursing, NY, 1976; BS in Nursing, SUNY Coll. Tech., Utica, 1978; MSN in Nursing Adminstrn., U. Nev., Las Vegas, 1988; postgrad. certificate in Nursing Edn., Russell Sage Coll., Troy, NY, 1995. Staff educator Sacred Heart Nursing Home, Plattsburgh, NY, 1988—90, acting dir. nursing, 1990—91; staff nurse St. Peter's Hosp., Albany, NY, 1992—95; ednl. specialist Hudson Valley CC, Troy, NY, 1995—2001, temp. nursing faculty, 2002—03; adult edn. LPN faculty Wash.-Saratoga-Warren-Hamilton-Essex BOCES, Saratoga, NY, 2003—04; nursing faculty RN program Montgomery CC, Johnstown, NY, 2004—. Adj. nursing faculty Clinton CC, Plattsburgh, NY, 1989—92, Maria Coll., Albany, NY, 1993—95, Excelsior Coll., Albany, NY, 1994—; office nurse Upstate Neurology Cons., Albany, NY, 1994—; tchr. review course Kaplan Test Prep and Admissions, 2004—; tutor Clara Bacon Sch., Amsterdam, NY, 2005—; bd. dirs. Montgomery Transitional Svcs., Amsterdam, NY, 2006—. Reviewer: Prentice Hall, 2006. Safety instr. Am. Red Cross, Albany, 1994—; youth coun. coord. Town of Westerlo, NY, 1995—; mem. Hilltown Players, Berne, NY, 1998—. Recipient Achievement award, St. Peter's Hosp., 1993, 1994, Recognition award, Berne-Knox-Westerlo Bd. Edn., 1996. Mem.: PTA, Nat. League Nursing, NY State Nurse's Assn. (Dist. 10), Sigma Theta Tau. Protestant. Avocations: reading, skiing, crafts. Home: 194 Goodfellow Rd Westerlo NY 12193 Office: Fulton Montgomery CC 2805 State Hwy 67 Johnstown NY 12095 Business E-Mail: maraldi@fmcc.suny.edu.

ARANA, MARIE, editor, writer; b. Lima, Peru, Sept. 15, 1949; came to U.S., 1959; d. Jorge Enrique and Marie Elverine (Clapp) Arana; children: Hilary Walsh, Adam Williamson Ward; m. Wendell B. Ward Jr., Dec. 18, 1971 (d. Dec. 1998); m. Jonathan Yardley, Mar. 21, 1999. BA in Russian Lang. & Lit., Northwestern U., Evanston, Ill., 1971; MA in Linguistics, Brit. U. Hong Kong, 1977. Lectr. linguistics Brit. U. Hong Kong, 1978-79; sr. editor Harcourt Brace Jovanovich, Pubs., NYC and Washington, 1980—89; v.p., sr. editor Simon & Schuster Pubs., NYC and Washington, 1989—92; writer, editor Washington Post, 1992-99, Book World editor-in-chief, 1999—. Bd. dir. Ctr. Policy Rsch., Washington, 1994-99; Hoover Media fellow Stanford U., 1997, 2000. Author: Studies in Bilingualism, 1978, American Chica: Two Worlds, One Childhood, 2001, The Writing Life: Writers on How They Think and Work, 2003, (novels) Cellophane, 2006. Finalist National Book award, 2001, PEN Memoir award, 2001; recipient award for excellence in editing, ABA, 1985, Christopher award for excellence in editing, 1986, Books for a Better Life award, 2001. Mem. Nat. Assn. Hispanic Journalists (bd. dir. 1996-99), Nat. Book Critics Cir. (bd. dir. 1996-2000). Office: Washington Post 1150 15th St NW Washington DC 20071-0002

ARANDA, SANDRA LOUISE, speech pathology/audiology services professional; b. San Jose, Calif., Oct. 7, 1970; d. Peter Mora and Jerry Louise Aranda. BA in Speech-Lang. Pathology, San Jose State U., 1994, MA in Edn. Speech Pathology and Audiology, 1996; cert. in early childhood edn. infants and preschoolers with disabilities, 1996. Speech-lang. pathologist George Mayne Elem. Sch., Santa Clara, 1996—97, Mariano Castro Elem. Sch., Mountain View, 1996—97, Santa Clara Sch. Dist., 1997—98, Mountain View Sch. Dist., 1998—2000, Oak Grove Sch. Dist., San Jose, 2000—. Mem. support staff com. Santa Teresa Elem. Sch., 2000—. Mem.: AAUW, Calif. Speech Hearing Assn. (adv. bd. com. dist. 4 2001—02, Outstanding Achievement award 2003), Santa Clara Speech Hearing Assn. (co-social chair 1997—98, rec. sec. 1999—2000, v.p. 2000—01, pres. 2001—02, past pres. 2002—03), Am. Speech Hearing Assn. Roman Catholic. Avocations: reading, painting, cardio circuit training, animals, aqua aerobics. Home: PO Box 667 Morgan Hill CA 95038 E-mail: cccslplic@aol.com.

ARANGO, PENELOPE COREY, psychologist, consultant; b. San Francisco, Oct. 10, 1943; d. George Raymond Corey Jr. and Katherine Barnard; m. Jorge Arango, Aug. 18, 1976. Diploma de cultura Española, U. Madrid, 1962; cert. de langue et litterature Francais, Universite de Grenoble, 1964; BA in art, U. Miami, Fla., 1965; MA in psychology, U. No. Colo., 1977. Psychol. asst. dept. clin. psychology U. Fla., 1966—68; asst. psychologist - Spanish Dade County Pub. Schs., Miami, 1968—76; dir., healthcare divsn. Helmsley-Spear of Fla., Miami, 1986—91; dir., CQI, tng. & devel. CAC-United HealthCare of Fla., Miami, 1991—98; LAO continuing improvement facilitator Carrier Corp., Latin Am. Hdqs., 1998—2000; faculty mem. Bayer Inst. Healthcare Comms., West Haven, Conn., 1995—2005; v.p. Arango Group, Quality Mgmt. Cons., Miami, 2000—. Quality adv. bd. mem. Coral Gables C. of C., Coral Gables, Fla., 1992—93. Office: Arango Group 5153 SW 71st Pl Miami FL 33155 Office Phone: 305-665-3133.

ARANOFF, SHARA L., federal official; m. David Korn; 2 children. BA, Princeton U.; JD, Harvard U.; post grad., Institut Universitaire de Hautes Etudes Internationales, U. Geneva, 1984—85. Atty. Steptoe & Johnson LLP; atty. advisor Office Gen. Counsel U.S. Internat. Trade Commn., Washington, 1993—2001, sr. internat. trade counsel, 2001—05, commr., 2005—; mem. senate com. on fin. U.S. Senate, Washington, 2002—05. Office: US Internal Trade Commn 500 E St SW Rm 704 Washington DC 20436 Office Phone: 202-708-2880. Office Fax: 202-205-2798.

ARANOW, RUTH LEE HORWITZ, academic advisor, chemist, researcher; b. Bklyn., Aug. 25, 1929; d. David and Tillie Ethel (Wolf) Horwitz; m. George Aranow, Jr., June 25, 1950; children: David, Eric, Jeanne. BA, Bklyn. Coll., 1951; MA, Johns Hopkins U., 1952, PhD, 1957. Rsch. scientist Rsch. Inst. for Advanced Studies, Balt., 1957-69, Johns Hopkins U., Balt., 1970, NIH fellow, rsch. scientist, 1973, lectr. chemistry Sch. Continuing Studies, 1976-87, lectr. chemistry Sch. Arts and Scis., 1978-85, sr. acad. advisor, 1987—, fellow-by-courtesy dept. chemistry, 1974—. Rsch. advisor Feingold Assn. U.S., Arlington, Va., 1980—. Contbr. rsch. articles to sci. jours. Fulbright grantee, 1951; recipient Martin-Marietta rsch. award, Balt., 1963. Mem. AAAS (finalist congl. fellowship program 1977), Am. Phys. Soc., Sigma Xi. Avocations: photography, music, travel.

ARANT, PATRICIA, Slavic languages and literature educator; b. Mobile, Ala., Dec. 2, 1930; BA, Ala. Coll., 1952; A.M., Radcliffe Coll., 1957; PhD, Harvard U., 1963. Researcher U.S. Govt., Washington, 1952-56; asst. prof. Russian Vanderbilt U., Nashville, 1963-65; asst. prof., assoc. prof., prof. Slavic langs. and lits. Brown U., Providence, 1965-97, chmn. dept., 1989—96, assoc. dean Grad. Sch., 1981-88, prof. emerita Slavic langs. and lit., 1997—. Author: Russian for Reading, 1981, Compositional Techniques of the Russian Oral Epic, the Bylina, 1990. Grantee Am. Coun. Learned Socs.-Social Scis. Rsch. Coun., 1969, Internat. Rsch. and Exchs., 1973, 93, Kennan Inst., 1994. Mem. Am. Assn. Tchrs. Slavic and East European Langs., Am. Assn. Advancement Slavic Studies. Office: Brown U Box E Providence RI 02912 Home: 500 Angell St Apt 611 Providence RI 02906-4492 Office Phone: 401-863-2689. Business E-Mail: patricia_arant@brown.edu.

ARANYA, GWENDALIN QI, painter, priest, educator; b. Bklyn., July 25, 1967; d. Carroll Jean Yorgey and Donald Enix; children: Zarathustra Goertzel, Zebulon Goertzel, Scheherazade Goertzel. BA in linguistics, Temple U., 1988; MS in math., U. Nev., Las Vegas, 1992; MFA in painting, Howard U., Washington, DC, 2005. Ordained Zen priest Buddhist Order of the Hsu Yun. Exhibited in group shows at Vox Populi, Phila., 1988—89, Waikato Soc. Arts, New Zealand, 1995, New Century Artists, NYC, 2002—05, Howard U., Washington, DC, 2003—05, Artomatic, 2004—05, The Graham Collection Gallery, 2005—, DC Arts Ctr., Washington, 2006—, one-woman shows include Local Artist, Las Vegas, Internat. Art Gallery, Australia, 1996, Riverview Arts Ctr., NJ, 1999, Intro Art Gallery, 2001, Howard U., 2005, Cafe Nema, Washington, DC, 2006; designer Las Vegas Kardma, 1994, illustrator Linus Pauling: A Life in Science and Politics, 1995, The Evolving Mind, 1993. Mem.: Washington Project for the Arts Corcoran, Coll. Art Assn., Black Artists of DC, DC Arts Ctr., Nat. Conf. Artists, New Century Artists. Home: 4005 Delancy Dr Silver Spring MD 20906 Office Phone: 240-476-4445. Personal E-mail: garanya@yahoo.com.

ARATHUZIK, MARY DIANE, medical/surgical nurse; b. Jamaica Plain, Mass., Mar. 24, 1947; d. Paul P. and Anna K. (Johnson) A. BSN, Boston Coll., 1968, MS in Nursing, 1973; D of Nursing Sci., Cath. U. Am., 1986. Staff nurse, clinician Boston City Hosp., Boston, 1968-71; instr. nursing Boston Coll., Chestnut Hill, Mass., 1973-77; staff nurse, clinician Mass. Gen. Hosp., Boston, 1979-84; asst. dir. nursing St. Margaret's Hosp. for Women, Dorchester, Mass., 1986-88; asst. prof. coll. nursing U. Mass. at Boston, Dorchester, 1988—94, nursing grad. program dir., 1994-98, assoc. prof., 1995—2000, Emmanuel Coll., Boston, 2000—. Training grant program dir., U. Mass., Dorchester, 1998-01. Biomedical Rsch. Grantee, Fed. Training grant divsn. nursing. Mem. ANA, Nat. League for Nursing, Mass. League for Nursing, Oncology Nursing Soc. (Purdue Frederick Rsch. grantee), Sigma Theta Tau. Business E-Mail: arathuzi@emmanuel.edu.

ARAUJO, ILKA VASCONCELOS, musicologist, educator; arrived in U.S., 1997; d. Jose Mario and Maria Cleomar Vasconcelos Araujo; m. Aleksa Jovanovic, Sept. 18, 2004; 1 child, Isabella Araujo Jovanovic. Tech. Level, Conservatory Music Alberto Nepomuceno, Fortaleza, CE, Brazil, 1989; BMus in Piano Performance, State U. Ceara, Fortaleza, Brazil, 1995; MMus in Piano Performance and Pedagogy, U. Fla., Gainesville, 2001, PhD in Musicology, 2006. Piano and theory tchr. Juvenal de Carvalho H.S., Fortaleza, Brazil, 1993—94; piano tchr. Conservatory Music Alberto Nepomuceno, 1994—95, State U. Ceara, 1994—95; pianist and accompanist Maninha Mota Voice Sch., 1996—97; grad. tchg. asst. U. Fla., Gainesville, 1997—. Choir dir. Friends of Music Soc., Fortaleza, Brazil, 1992—93; co-director and co-founder Brazilian choir Brazilian Student Assn., Gainesville, Fla., 1997—2000; asst. mgr. Prague Internat. Piano Master Classes, Czech Republic, 1998—2001; pvt. instr. piano and accompanist, Gainesville, 1998—; co-organizer events, hostess and translator U. Fla. Sch. Music, 1998—, rep. grad. student coun., 2002—03. Composer: Instants, 2001— (3rd prize Fla. Juried Arts Exhbn., 2002); musician (pianist and lectr.): The Subjective Nationalitic Aspects in Liszt, Villa-Lobos and Ginastera, 2003, 20th Century Compositional Vocabulary featuring works by Villa-Lobos, Ginastera, and Ilka Araujo, 2004, Works of Schubert, Liszt, and Ginastera, 2004; musician: (pianist) Sonata No. 4 by Prokoviev, 2001, Works by Scriabin, Liszt, Villa-Lobos and Ilka Araujo, 2003, Vallee D'Obermann by Liszt, 2004, Works by Schubert, Liszt, Villa-Lobos, and Ginastera, 2004, Works by Villa-Lobos and Ginastera, 2004, Works by Liszt, Villa-Lobos, and Ginastera, 2004; musician: (master class presenter) Conservatory of Music and State Univ. Ceara, 2004—06, Music Acad.; performer: Programa Do Jo, 2004; contbr. scientific papers in musicology; performer: TV Verdes Mares, 2004; interviewed (various mags., TV programs, newspapers), 2005; performer: TV Ceara, 2006. Vol. pianist The Village, Gainesville, Fla., 1999—2000, The Atrium; pianist Lochloosa United Meth. Ch., Hawthorne United Meth. Ch., Hawthorne, Fla., 2000, Dunnellon Presbyn. Ch., 2003; pres. Brazilian Student Assn., Gainesville, Fla., 1998—99, v.p., 1999—2000. Named an Internat. Female Leader, Women's Leadership Conf., Gainesville, 2005; recipient First prize, Piano Competition Young Instrumentalists Festival, Brazil, 1994, Paurillo Barrozo Piano Competition, Brazil, 1995, Alec Courtelis Award, 2004, Presdl. award Outstanding Achievement and Contibn., U. Fla., 1999, 2000, Oustanding Student Recognition, U. Fla. Ctr. Internat. Studies, 1998, 2000, Student Academic award, U. Fla. Coll. Fine Arts, 1998, 2000; Grad. Tchg. assistantship, U. Fla., 1997—. Mem.: Nat. Guild Piano Teachers Assn., Soc. Composers Inc., Coll. Music Soc., Am. Music Soc., Phi Lambda Beta, Pi Kappa Lambda. Avocations: swimming, travel, reading. Business E-Mail: ilkarauj@ufl.edu.

ARBAN, DIANA MARIE, social sciences educator; m. Robert Anthony Arban, July 24, 1999; 1 child, Leah Marie. BA in Polit. Sci., U. Calif., San Diego, 1996; MA in Polit. Sci., San Diego State U., 2005. Tchr. social sci. Lewis Mid. Sch., San Diego, 1999—2003; tchr. social sci., English Temecula Valley Charter Sch., 2003—04; tchr. social sci. Gt. Oak H.S., 2004—. Head coach varsity girls soccer Gt. Oak H.S., 2004—. Avocation: soccer. Office: Great Oak HS 32555 Deer Hollow Way Temecula CA 92592 Office Phone: 951-294-6450 3206. E-mail: darban@tvusd.k12.ca.us.

ARBEITER, JOAN, artist, educator; b. N.Y.C., May 8, 1937; d. David and Winifred Arden (Lembke) Berman; m. Jay David Arbeiter, June 15, 1958 (div. May 1990); children: Lisa B., Gail Arbeiter Goldstein. BA, CUNY, 1959; MFA, Pratt Inst., 1982. Lic. art tchr. N.Y., N.J. Tchr. N.Y.C. Sch. Sys. Bd. Edn., 1959-63; dir. Joan Arbeiter Studio Sch., Metuchen, NJ, 1976-90; instr. art, coord. founds. Ducret Sch. Art, Plainfield, NJ, 1978—, instr. color and design, 1978—, instr. art history, 1981—2001; workshop instr. N.J. Teen Arts Festival, 1998—2003; artist in residence NJ Sch. Arts, 1995—2002; instr. art appreciation, 1983—. Juror various art orgns., NJ, 1981—; cons. Ednl. Testing Svc., Princeton, NJ, 1988; curator travelling art exhibit Age As a Work of Art, Plainfield, Boston, N.Y.C., 1985—86, Lives and Works, N.Y.C., 2000; presenter paper, slides Coll. Art Assn. Conf., San Antonio, 1995, N.Y.C., 2003; presenter, moderator Nat. Mus. Women in Arts, Wash., 1997, Artists Talk on Art, N.Y.C., 1997, 2000, 05. One-woman shows include Ceres Gallery, N.Y.C., 1987, 1989, 1993, 1997, 2000, 2001, Columbia U., 1986, Stony Brook-Millstone Watershead Assn. Gallery, Pennington, N.J., 1991, Wagner Coll., S.I., N.Y., 1992, Douglas Coll. Ctr., New Brunswick, N.J., 1992, 1996, Union County Coll., Cranford, N.J., 1999, Elizabeth Found., NYC, 2001, Cedar Crest Coll., Allentown, Pa., 2004, Du Cret Sch., Plainfield, NJ, 2006, exhibited in group shows at Ramapo Coll., Mahwah, 1980, Brookdale Coll., Lincroft, N.J., 1980, Westbeth Gallery, N.Y.C., 1980, Douglas Coll. Libr., New Brunswick, NJ, 1982, Ceres Gallery, 1983—, N.Y. Feminist Art Inst., N.Y.C., 1985—88, Ednl. Testing Svc., Princeton, NJ, 1986, Appalachian State U., Boone, NC, 1989, Soho 20 Gallery, N.Y.C., 1990, 1998, Noyes Mus., Oceanville, N.J., 1995, 1998, 2005, Krasdale Corp. Gallery, Bronx, N.Y., 1995, 2006, Monmouth Mus., Lincroft, 1996, Kingsbourgh CC, Bklyn., 1999, Kunstler Forum, Bonn, Germany, 1999, EPA, Washington, 2001—02, Solaris Gallery, Califon, N.J., 2004, Pratt Inst., Bklyn., 2006, Woman Made Gallery, Chgo., 2006, Represented in permanent collections Noyes Mus., Oceanville, Fairmount Chem., Newark, CSR Group Archs. and Builders-Leon Cohen, Nutley, N.J., JFK Med. Ctr., Edison, N.J., Muhlenberg Regional Med. Ctr., Plainfield, 1st Presbyn. Ch., Metuchen, N.J., MS Found., N.Y.C., pvt. collections; co-author: (book) Lives and Works: Talks with Women Artists, vol. 2, 1999. Recipient 1st pl. mixed media, Westfield Art Assn., 1978, 1st pl. all media award, Metuchen Cultural Arts Commn. Art Exhbn., 1988, Best in Show award, Middlesex County Mus., New Brunswick, N.J., 1989, AIA award, Hunterdon Arts Ctr. N.J., 1996, People's Choice award, Watchung Arts Ctr., N.J., 1998, Excellence award, Manhattan Arts Mag., 2000, Elan award for Mentoring Women's Studio Ctr., 2004; grantee, Vt. Studio Colony, 1987. Mem.: Varo Registry, Art Table, Women's Caucus Art, Coll. Art Assn., Women's Studio Ctr. (N.Y.C.) (hon.; bd. dirs.), Alpha Beta Kappa. Studio: 41 Victory Ct Metuchen NJ 08840-1430

ARBELBIDE, C(INDY) L(EA), librarian, historian, author; b. Stockton, Calif., Aug. 4, 1949; d. Garrett Walter and Fern Mable (Lea) A. AA in History, Santa Barbara City Coll., Calif., 1969; BS in Health & Phys. Edn., Oreg. State U., 1972; M in Libr. Sci., Emporia State U., 1980. Asst. dir. Child Youth Libr., Rappahannock County Libr., Washington, Va. Vis. author The White House, 1998, 99, 2000, 01; adv. com. Va. Libr. Youth Svc., 2006. Author: White House Easter Egg Roll, 1997; contbr. National Archives mag. prologue. Recipient Yellow Rose of Tex. Govt. award, 1992, Nat. Orgn. Vic. Asst. Achievement award, 1994, NPS Merit Letter, 1999, 2000, George Wash. Hon. medal, Freedoms Found., 2003. Mem. Am. Assn. State & Local History, Assn. Rural and Small librs., Va. Libr. Assn., Woman of Month Ladies Home Jour., US Women's Track & Field Team, Race Walking. Home and Office: 147 Dogwood Blossom Ln Front Royal VA 22630 Office: PO Box 55 Washington VA 22747

ARBOGAST, SALLY S., science educator; b. Camp Lejeune, N.C., Apr. 29, 1976; d. Craig S. and Sheila P. Statham; m. Sally Statham Statham, Mar. 9, 2002. MS, Longwood U., Farmville, Va., 1999. Environ. scientist Apex Environ., Richmond, Va., 1999—2002; tchr. sci. Hopewell Pub. Schs., Va., 2002—. Recipient Outstanding Performance award, Hopewell Pub. Schs., 2003. Office: 500 S Mesa Dr Hopewell VA 23860 Office Phone: 804-541-6402.

ARBUCKLE, PEGGY TRAWICK, special education educator, consultant; b. Newville, Ala., Apr. 18, 1939; d. Alex Trawick and Hattie Mae Humphrey; m. George H. Arbuckle (dec.); children: Gary Steven, Sandra. Undergrad., Ala. State U., 1955—57; BA, Kean U., 1976. Tchr. elem. edn. Roselle (N.J.) Bd. Edn., 1976—79; tchr. Ednl. Tng. Cons., East Orange, NJ, 1980—81, Essex County Svc. Commn., West Orange, NJ, 1981—. Dir. summer day camp Park Ave St. John's, East Orange, 1992—99. Lay spkr. United Meth. Ch. Mem.: N.J. Edn. Assn., Nat. Coun. Negro Women, Ala. State U. Alumni (treas. N.J. chpt. 1992—), Order Eastern Stars (grand matron Marth Grand chpt. 1996—). Home: 25 Porter Ave Newark NJ 07112

ARCHABAL, NINA M(ARCHETTI), historic site director; b. Long Branch, N.J., Apr. 11, 1940; d. John William and Santina Matilda (Giuffre) Marchetti; m. John William Archabal, Aug. 8, 1964; 1 child, John Fidel. BA in Music History cum laude, Radcliffe Coll., 1962; MAT in Music History, Harvard U., 1963; PhD in Music History, U. Minn., 1979. Asst. dir. humanities art mus. U. Minn., Mpls., 1975-77; asst. supr. edn. divsn. Minn. Hist. Soc., St. Paul, 1977-78, dep. dir. for program mgmt., 1978-86, acting dir., 1986-87, dir., 1987—. Bd. dirs. U.S. nat. com. Internat. Coun. Mus. V.p. Friends of St. Paul Pub. Libr., 1983-93; Minn. state hist. preservation officer, 1987—; chair State Hist. Records Adv. Bd., 1987—, St. Anthony Falls Heritage Bd., 1988—; trustee, bd. dirs. Am. Folklife Ctr., Libr. of Congress, 1989-98; bd. dirs. N.W. Area Found., 1989-98, St. Paul Acad. and Summit Sch., 1993-2002, St. Paul Riverfront Corp., 2000-03, Rsch. Librs. Group, 2004—; bd. regents St. John's U., Collegeville, Minn., 1997-2004; overseer Harvard Coll., Cambridge, Mass., 1997—; mem. bd. overseers Hill Mus. and Manuscript Libr., 2004—. NDEA fellow U. Minn., 1969-72, U. Minn. grad. fellow, 1974-75; recipient Nat. Humanities medal The White House, 1997. Mem. Am. Assn. State and Local History (sec. 1986-88), Am. Assn. Mus. (v.p. 1991-94, chair bd. dirs. 1994-96). Office: Minn Hist Soc 345 Kellogg Blvd W Saint Paul MN 55102-1906 Office Phone: 651-296-6126.

ARCHAMBAULT, NICOLE MARIE, speech pathology/audiology services professional, consultant; b. Anaheim, Calif., Nov. 24, 1973; d. Guy Rene and Donna Jean Archambault. BA in Speech and Hearing Scis., Wash. State U., 1996; MS in Speech and Hearing Scis., U. N.Mex, 1999. Cert. clin. competence speech-lang. pathology Am. Speech-Language Hearing Assn., 2000, lic. speech-lang. pathologist Calif. Speech-Language Pathology and Audiology Bd., 2000, Nev. Bd. of Examiners for Audiology and Speech Pathology, 1999, cert. Hanen Centre, 2002, interior decorator Decorator Tng. Inst., 2005, speech-lang. pathologist orofacial myofunctional therapist exec. Speech-language pathologist The Continuum, Reno, 1999—; pediatric speech-language pathologist Cedars Sinai Med. Ctr., L.A.; owner, dir. Talk For Tots, Santa Monica. Cons. Step By Step Early Childhood Devel. Ctr., Benjamin Links; sr. cons. Little Lima Bean Prodns.; co-owner Kids Places & Spaces Integrative Develop. Design Co., 2005—. Recipient ACE award, Am. Speech Lang. Hearing Assn., 2005; Maynard Lee Daggy scholar, Wash. State U., 1995, All-Am. scholar, U.S. Achievement Acad., 1996. Mem.: Internat. Assn. Orofacial Myology, Internat. Mind, Brain and Edn. Soc., Nat. Coalition Auditory Processing Disorders, Calif. Speech and Hearing Assn., Am. Speech-Lang. Hearing Assn. (Am. Continuing Edn. award 2003, 2005, 2006), Acad. Neurological Comm. Disorders and Sci. (assoc.), Soc. Children's Book Writers and Illustrators (assoc.), Golden Key Nat. Honor Soc. Office: Talk For Tots 1814 14th St Ste 210 Santa Monica CA 90404 Business E-Mail: talkfortots@msn.com.

ARCHBOLD, HEATHER D., personal trainer; d. William E. and Terri L. Fisher; m. Bryan A. Archbold, June 19. BS, Meth. Coll., N.C., 1998; M in athletic tng., Ind. State U., Terre Haute, 2000. Cert. athletic trainer. Clinical HS head athletic trainer Keystone Rehab. Sys., Middlefield, Ohio, 2000—03; clinical coll. athletic trainer Univ. Hosp. Health Sys., Cleve., 2003—. Home: 15755 Grove St Apt A4 Middlefield OH 44062-9284

ARCHBOLD, RONNA RAE, college administrator; b. Duluth, Minn., Sept. 22; d. Wilton Reuden and Georgia Adeline (Smith) A. BA, Walla Walla Coll., 1969; MEd, Worcester State Coll., 1981; postgrad. Boston Coll., 1983-86. Registrar Monterey Bay Acad., Watsonville, Calif., 1969-72; from asst. to assoc. dean women Walla Walla Coll., Coll. Place, Wash., 1972-76; from asst. to assoc. dir. admissions Atlantic Union Coll., South Lancaster, Mass., 1976-80, chief exec. officer pub. relations and recruitment, 1980-84, chief exec. officer fundraising and pub. relations, 1984-85, asst. to pres., 1985-86, asst. prof. speech comm. dept. English; pvt. practice salesperson, 1986—; electronic sales mgr. ea. region R.R. Bowker div. Reed Pub; sales mgr. Reed Pub, 1988-95, Ohio Tech., 1995-97, Ebsco Info. Svcs., 1997-2004, TDNET, 2004-, Atlantic Book Binders, 1986-88. Mem. Thayer Conservatory Orch., South Lancaster, 1981-83; organist, dir. choirs First Ch., Sterling, Mass., 1983—, St. Patrick's Ch., Rutland, Mass., 1977-83. Mem. Am. Guild Organists (bd. dirs.), Choisters Guild. Office Phone: 978-368-6338. Personal E-mail: rrarchbold@hotmail.com.

ARCHER, ANNE, actress; b. L.A., Aug. 25, 1947; d. John and Marjorie (Lord) A.; m. Terry Jastrow; children: Thomas, Jeffrey. Actor: (theatre) A Coupla White Chicks Sitting Around Talking, 1981, Les Liaisons Dangeruses, 1988, The Poison Tree, (films) The Honkers, 1972, Cancel My Reservation, 1972, The All-American Boy, 1973, Trackdown, 1976, Lifeguard, 1976, Paradise Valley, 1978, Good Guys Wear Black, 1978, Raise the Titanic, 1980, Hero At Large, 1980, Green Ice, 1981, Waltz Across Texas, 1983 (also writer), Too Scared to Scream, 1985, The Naked Face, 1985, The Check Is in the Mail, 1985, Fatal Attraction, 1987 (Golden Globe nominee 1987, Acad. award nominee 1988), Love at Large, 1990, Narrow Margin, 1990, Eminent Domain, 1991, Patroit Games, 1992, Body of Evidence, 1993, Short Cuts, 1993 (Golden Globe award Best Ensemble Cast 1994), Clear and Present Danger, 1994, Mojave Moon, 1996, Nico the Unicorn, 1998, Dark Summer, 1999, (voice) Whispers: An Elephant's Tale, 2000, Rules of Engagement, 2000, The Art of War, 2000, The Gray in Between, 2002, Uncle Nino, 2003, November, 2004, The Iris Effect, 2004, Man of the House, 2005; (TV series) Bob and Carol and Ted and Alice, 1973, The Family Tree, 1983, Falcon Crest, 1985, (TV movies) The Blue Knight, 1973, The Mark of Zorro, 1974, The Log of the Black Pearl, 1975, A Matter of Wife.and Death, 1976, The Dark Side of Innocence, 1976, Seventh Avenue, 1977, The Pirate, 1978, The Sky's No Limit, 1984, A Different Affair, 1987, A Leap of Faith, 1988, The Last of His Tribe, 1992, Nails, 1992, Jane's House, 1994, Because Mommy Works, 1994 (also co-prodr.), The Man in the Attic, 1995, Present Tenes, Past Perfect, 1995, Jake's Women, 1996, Almost Forever, 1996, Indiscretion of an American Wife, 1998, My Husband's Secret Life, 1998, Jane's House, 2000, Night of the Wolf, 2002, (voice) 2004: A light Knight's Odyssey, 2004; TV appearances include Storefront Lawyers, 1970, Hawaii Five-O, 1970, The FBI, 1971, The Mod Squad, 1971, Ironside, 1971, Alias Smith and Jones, 1971, Love American Style, 1971, Mannix, 1973, Harry O, 1974, 76, Little House on the Prairie, 1975, Switch, 1975, 76, McCloud, 1976, Petrocelli, 1975, 76, Beggars and Choosers, 2000, Boston Public, 2003, The L Word, 2004. Office: care Ilene Feldman Agency 8730 W Sunset Blvd Ste 490 Los Angeles CA 90069-2248

ARCHER, BARRIE W.S., art educator; b. East Liverpool, Ohio, Oct. 1, 1945; d. William L and Virginia P Smith; m. Thomas T Archer; children: Tristam Griffith, Alexis Dowding. BA, Mt. Union Coll., 1967; MA, Kent State U., 1993. Art tchr. Beaver Local H.S., Lisbon, Ohio, 1985—. Mentor Beaver Local Sch. Dist., Lisbon, Ohio, 2001—02, lead mentor, 2003—06; assessor State of Ohio, 2005—06. Rep. Dollars for Scholars, East Liverpool, 1996—2006. Mem.: East Ctrl. Ohio Art Edn. Assn. (regional dir. 1999—2001, pub. rels. chair 2002, 2d v.p. 2003—04, comml. exhibits mgr. 2005—06). Office: Beaver Local HS 13187 State Rte 7 Lisbon OH 44432

ARCHER, CRISTINA LOZEJ, meteorologist; b. Como, Italy, Apr. 21, 1970; d. Alessandra Bonfanti; m. Scott Mckinley Archer, Nov. 4, 2000; children: Eva Julia children: Emma Tiffany, Clara Maria. MS, Politecnico di Milano, Italy, 1995, San Jose State U., Calif., 1998; PhD, Stanford U., Calif., 2004. Post doctoral scholar Stanford U., 2004—05; atmospheric modeler Bay Area Air Quality Mgmt. Dist., San Francisco, 2005—. Cons. asst. prof. dept. civil and environ. engring. Stanford U., 2005—. Contbr. articles to profl. jours. Recipient Best thesis in environ. field award, Regione Lombardia, Milano, Italy, 1995. Mem.: Am. Meteorol. Soc. (assoc.). Roman Catholic. Achievements include research in first study on global wind power potential; discovery and study of an atmospheric vortex. Avocations: bicycling, beach, reading, knitting. Office: Bay Area Air Quality Dist 939 Ellis St San Francisco CA 94109 Office Phone: 415-749-5149. Personal E-mail: lozej@stanford.edu.

ARCHER, LILLIAN PATRICIA, academic administrator, dean; b. Lawrenceville, Va., Oct. 31, 1952; d. Wyatt and Marian Archer; m. James Leroy Drewery, July 7, 2000. BS, Morgan State U., 1976; MA, Coll. Notre Dame, 1990; EdD in Higher Edn., Morgan State U., 2002. Counselor CC Balt. County, 1992—99, interim dir. of human rels., 1998—99, dir. counseling, 1999—2001, sr. dir. student support svcs., 2001—02, sr. dir. counseling, acad. advisement and entry svcs., 2002—04, sr. dir. acad. and adminstrv. svcs., 2004—05, campus adminstr., 2005—06, campus dean, 2006—. Sys. appraiser Higher Learning Commn. of North Ctrl. Assn. of Colls. and Schs., Chgo., 2004—. Vol. Wigs for Kids, Cleve., 2004—04, South Balt. Emergency Relief (SOBER), Balt., 1999—2001; bd. dirs. Balt. Med. Sys.; mem. Balt. County Commn. on Women, 2006—. Fellow, Am. Coun. on Edn., 2003—04. Mem.: Am. Coll. Pers. Assn. (ACPA), Am. Assn. of Women in Cmty. Colleges (AAWCC). Avocations: reading, travel, writing. Office Phone: 410-455-4300. Personal E-mail: archerfellow@yahoo.com.

ARCHER, RUTH WALLACE, elementary school educator; b. Memphis, Sept. 29, 1950; m. Robert E. Archer, Aug. 22, 1970; children: Jon Taylor, Lauren Archer Peterson. MEd, U. Memphis, 1995. Cert. tchr. Tenn. Tchr. Memphis City Schs., 1976—. Phys. sci. network coord. Memphis City Schs., 2002—. Exec. dir. Tenn. Sci. Teachers Assn., Nashville, 2001—04. Mem.: Memphis Orgn. Sci. Tchrs. (pres. 2002—04). Office: Memphis City Schs 2009 Ridgeway Rd Memphis TN 38119 Office Phone: 901-416-8820. Business E-Mail: archerruthw@mcsk12.net.

ARCHER-SORG, KAREN S., secondary school educator; b. Ft. Wayne, Ind., Dec. 19, 1957; d. Paul Walter and Betty Irene (Harmon) Archer; m. Joseph Henry Sorg, Apr. 8, 1977; children: Joseph Henry II, Levi Paul. AA, Purdue U., 1987; BA, Ind. U., 1995. Cert. grantsmanship, Calif.; lic. mid. sch. social studies and sci. tchr., 2005. Rsch. asst. Ind. U., Ft. Wayne, 1987-89; coord. Gov.'s Commn. for a Drug-Free Ind., Ft. Wayne, 1989—2001; tchr. Jefferson Middle Sch. Staff Regional Adv. Bd., Ft. Wayne, 1989-97; mem. grants commn. Parks Bd., Ossian, Ind., 1990-97; mem. Stop Child Abuse and Neglect, Ft. Wayne, 1995-97. Past pres., co-founder No. Wells Soccer Club, Inc., Ossian, 1986-96; cons. Jr. Achievement, Ft. Wayne, 1994-1999; speaker Wells County Citizen's Against Drugs, Bluffton, 1993-96; vol. Smoke-Free Ind., Ft. Wayne, 1995—, schs. and town of Ossian, 1989-97; mem. Friends of Libr., 1999. Recipient Appreciation award Ossian Fire Dept., 1993, Norwell Comm., Ossian, 1994, Dept. of Mental Health, Indpls., 1997. Mem. Wells County Citizens Against Drug Abuse.

ARCHETTO, MARIA, music educator; BS in Music Edn., RI Coll., Providence, 1974; MA in Musicology, U. Rochester, NY, 1979, PhD in Musicology, 1991. Asst. prof. music history Syracuse U., NY, 1988—89; assoc. prof. music Oxford Coll., Emory U., Ga., 1992—. Adj. instr. musicology U. Rochester, Eastman Sch. Music, 1986—88. Editor: Francesco Portinaro, Il terzo libro di madrigali, Francesco Portinaro, Il quarto libro de madrigali; contbr. chapters to books. Chair bd. New Trinity Baroque, Atlanta; bd. mem. Emory Friends Music. Grantee, Fulbright-Hays Commn., 1982—84, Gladys Krieble Delmas Found., 1983—84, Porter Found., 2004—05; Ga. Governor's Tchg. fellow, State of Ga., 2003—. Mem.: Ga. Music Educators' Assn., Music Educators' Nat. Conf., Coll. Music Soc., Am. Musicological Soc., Pi Kappa Lambda. Office: Oxford College of Emory University 100 Hamill Street Oxford GA 30054 Office Phone: 770-784-4718.

ARCHEY, MARY FRANCES ELAINE (ONOFARO), academic administrator, educator; b. Elkins, W Va, Sept. 15, 1947; d. Ross and Carmela Gallo Onofaro; m. Rick Archey. BA in Social Sci. Edn., U. Pitts., 1968; MEd in Social Sci. Edn., Indiana U. of Pa., 1969; EdD in Higher Edn. Adminstrn. and Counseling, WVa. U., 1981; Profl. Cert. in Human Resource Devel., Pa. State U., 1996. Cert. nat. counselor 1984. Asst. prof. sociology West Liberty State Coll., Wheeling, W.Va., 1969—72; dean of students W. Va. Northern C.C., Wheeling, W.Va., 1972—85; asst. dean instrn. C.C. Allegheny County South Campus, West Mifflin, Pa., 1986—96; dean bus. and acctg. C.C. of Allegheny County, Pitts., 1996—99; dean arts and sci. C.C. of Allegheny County-South Campus, West Mifflin, Pa., 1999—2005, dean acad. affairs, 2005—. Adj. instr. bus. C.C. of Allegheny County-South Campus, West Mifflin, Pa., 1988—. Regional dir. U. Pitts. Alumni Assn., 2001—; past pres., current chair nominations com. U. Pitts. Alumnae Coun., 1998—; vol food packager Greater Pitts. Food Bank, Duquesne, 1995—; vol. tester, interviewer Greater Pitts. Literacy Coun., 1987—96. Fellow: The Ed. Policy and Leadership Ctr. (fellow 2002—03); mem.: ASTD, AAUW, Am. Coll. Personnel Assn., Am. Assn. Higher Edn. (life), Am. Counseling Assn., U. Pitts. Alumni Assn. (Vol. Excellence award 2005), St. Elizabeth's Women's Club, Phi Delta Gamma (v.p. 2000—), Beta Sigma Phi (svc. chairperson 1987—, Order of the Rose 1994), Delta Kappa Gamma-Alpha Phi Chpt. (past pres. 1996—, newsletter editor 1996—). Democrat. Roman Catholic. Avocations: reading, gardening. Home: 333 Old Clairton Rd Pittsburgh PA 15236 Office: CC of Allegheny -South Campus 1750 Clairton Rd West Mifflin PA 15122 Office Phone: 412-469-6304. Personal E-mail: marchey@ccac.edu.

ARCHIBALD, BRIGITTE EDITH, language educator; b. Kaiserslautern, Germany, Aug. 22, 1942; arrived in U.S., 1947; d. Ludwig and Alma (Schaefer) Zapp; m. John Duncan Archibald, Aug. 29, 1970; children: David Andrew, Elisabeth Anna. BA in Modern Lang., Kings Coll., 1964; MA in German, U. Mainz, Germany, 1966; PhD in Germanic Lang. & Lit., U. Tenn., 1975. Head libr. Thelma Dingus B. Libr., Wallace, NC, 1972—73; asst. prof. fgn. lang. NC A&T State U., Greensboro, 1976—82, assoc. prof. fgn. lang., 1982—95, prof. fgn. lang., 1995—. Oral proficiency assessor N.C. Dept. Pub. Instruction, 1994; presenter, cons. in field. Contbr. articles to profl. jours., local newspapers. Vol. neighbor to neighbor campaign Easter Seal Soc., 1992—94; vol. tchr. 4th grade German Caldwell Elem., 1984; judge Guilford County Elections, 1995—; vis. com. to McLeansville prison Trinity Ch., 1992—, mission com., 1990—, personnel com., 1992—97, Sunday sch. tchr., 1999—. Home: 1 Bayberry Ct Greensboro NC 27455 Office Phone: 336-334-7886. E-mail: editharchibald@juno.com.

ARCHIBALD, CHESTINA MITCHELL, minister; d. Thomas Mitchell and Rosa Lee Horne; m. Albert John Archibald II (dec. 1969); 1 child, Albert John III. BA, U. Dubuque, 1967; MDiv, Interdenominational Theol. Ctr., 1985; JD, Howard U., 1971. Dir. Wesley Found. Fisk U., Nashville, 1985—, univ. chaplain, 1987—97; pastor Key United Meth. Ch., Murfreesboro, Tenn., 2000—06. Freelance writer and motivational speaker. Editor: Say Amen, A.A. Book of Prayer, 1997; Secret of the Psalms; contbr. articles to profl. publs. Avocation: piano. Office: Wesley Found Fisk U 1034 17th Ave N Ste C Nashville TN 37208 Office Phone: 615-321-1134.

ARCHIBALD, CLAUDIA JANE, parapsychologist, counselor, consultant; b. Atlanta, Nov. 14, 1939; d. Claud Bernard and Doris Evelyn (Linch) A. B in Psychology, Georgia State U., 1962; BTh., Emory U., 1964; DD, Stanton Coll., 1969. Pvt. practice psycho-spiritual counselor, Atlanta, 1960-98; ret., 1998; minister Nat. Spiritualist Assn., Atlanta, 1969-72; parapsychologist Ctr. for Life, Atlanta, 1985-86, Inst. of Metaphysical Inquiry, Atlanta, 1980—, also bd. dirs., founder, 1980—. Motivational spkr., 1996—. Author: (book) Quantitative Symbolism, 1980, short stories; dir. Phoenix Dance Unltd., 1984-90; choregrapher (dance) Phoenix Rising, 1985. Vol. Aid Atlanta, 1987-89. Recipient City Grant award Bur. Cultural Affairs, Atlanta, 1985, 86. Mem. Am. Psychical Rsch. Assn., Soc. Metaphysicians (corr. Eng. chpt.), Am. Assn. Parapsychology, Nat. Assn. Alcoholism and Drug Abuse Counselors, Ga. Addiction Counselors' Assn., N.Am. Ballet Assn., Nat. Leather Assn., Echoes of the People, Native Am. Orgn., Sun Dancer, Regional Soc. Victorian Preservation (founder, dir. 1990—). Avocations: writing, painting. Home: 464 E Hightower Trl Social Circle GA 30025-3022

ARCHIBALD, JEANNE S., lawyer; b. Jan. 30, 1951; d. George R. Stokes and Eleanore (Moran) L.; m. Thomas P. Archibald, Aug. 19, 1972; children: Charles Edward. BA, SUNY, Stony Brook, 1973; JD, Georgetown U., 1977. D.C. bar: 1977. Staff asst. House Com. on Ways and Means, 1975-77, profl. staff mem., 1977-80; assoc. gen. counsel, chmn. sect. 301 com. U.S. Trade Rep., 1980-86; dep. asst. gen. counsel internat. affairs Dept. of Treasury, 1986-88, dep. gen. counsel, 1988-90, gen. counsel, 1990-93; mng. ptnr. Hogan & Hartson, Washington, 1993—, dir. internat. trade practice group. Office: Hogan & Hartson Columbia Sq 555 13th St NW Ste 800E Washington DC 20004-1161 Office Phone: 202-637-5740. Office Fax: 202-637-5910. Business E-Mail: JSArchibald@hhlaw.com.

ARCHULETA, RANDI LISA, psychologist; b. LA, Sept. 13, 1966; d. Robert Gurevitch and Susan Bea Westheimer; m. Anthony Gordon Archuleta, May 13, 1995; children: Anthony Jade, Emily Ann. BA, Pitzer Coll., 1988; PhD, Calif. Sch. Profl. Psychology, 1993. Lic. clin. psychologist. Staff psychologist Monsour Counseling Ctr., Claremont, Calif., 1994-99. Co-dir., founder Claremont Colls. Coalition on Disordered Eating (CODE), 1996-99, trainer oral licensure, 1997-99; peer edn. leader, 1999; adj. instr. U. N.Mex., Taos, 2002-. Sponsor Eating Disorder Awareness Week, 1997, 98. Mem. APA, AAUP (past pres. U.N.Mex. Taos branch). Office: 124 N Las Palmas Ave Los Angeles CA 90004-1048 Business E-Mail: randia@unm.edu.

ARCIERI, SANDY LEE, professional collector; b. Chgo., July 23, 1955; d. Adam Eugene and Marie Prudence (Worek) Prucznal; m. Dennis James Arcieri, July 22, 1979. BA in Math. and Edn., St. Xavier Coll., Chgo., 1977. Tchr. math. St. Peter and St. Paul Schs., Chgo., 1977-79; pvt. math. tutor, 1979-83; collector Jean Harlow personal effects, 1971—. Contbg. rschr. Life at the Marmont, 1987, Mayer and Thalberg: The Make-Believe Saints, 1988, Deadly Illusions, 1990, Bombshell, 1993, cable TV shows. Roman Catholic. Avocation: African art. Home: 9530 S Clifton Park Ave Evergreen Park IL 60805-2131

ARCURIO, JEAN CATHERINE, soprano, educator, director; d. Robert C. and Alice C. Walters; m. George Joseph Arcurio, III, June 14, 1975; 1 child, Joseph George. A in Music Performance, Mt. Aloysious Coll., Cresson, Pa., 1971; BS in Music Edn., Pa. State U., University Park, 1973. Cert. instr. II Pa. Vocal music dir. Conemaugh Valley Sch. Dist., Johnstown, Pa., 1984—. Pvt. and profl. vocal coach students, 1973—; soprano Johnstown (Pa.) Music League, 1976—; vocalist Johnstown Symphony Orch. Chorale, 2005—. Music dir., choreographer: Drama Club. Cantor and liturgy chairperson St. Patrick Ch., Johnstown, 1990—2006. Democrat. Roman Catholic. Office: Conemaugh Valley Sch Dist 1451 Frankstown Rd Johnstown PA 15902 Office Phone: 814-535-6970. Personal E-mail: jeanca@atlanticbb.net. Business E-Mail: jarcurio@mail.cv.k12.pa.us.

ARDEN, SHERRY W., publishing executive; b. NYC, Oct. 18, 1923; d. Abraham and Rose (Bellak) Waretnick; m. Hal Marc Arden (div. 1974); children: Doren, Cathy; m. George Bellak, Oct. 20, 1979. Student, Columbia U. Publicity dir. Coward-McCann, N.Y.C., 1965-67; producer Allan Foshko Assoc., ABC-TV, N.Y.C., 1967-68; sr. v.p., pub. William Morrow & Co., N.Y.C., 1968-85, pres., pub., 1985-89; owner Sherry W. Arden Lit. Agy., 1990—. Mem. Assn. Am. Pubs. (dir.) Clubs: Pubs. Lunch.

ARDIS, SUSAN BARBER, librarian, educator; b. Holly, Mich., Feb. 21, 1947; d. Raymond Walker and Joan Violet (Grove) Barber; m. Thomas John Ardis, Aug. 18, 1968; children: Jessica, Andrew. BA, U. Mich., 1968, AMLS, 1969. Head natural sci. libr. U. Mich., Ann Arbor, 1969-78; head reference Rosenberg Libr., Galveston, Tex., 1978-79; head Engring. Libr. U. Tex., Austin, 1979—. Author: An Introduction to Patent Searching, 1991, Electrical Electronic Engineering Information Sources, 1987, Toward the Electronic Library, 1994; contbr. articles to profl. jours. Mem. Spl. Librs. Assn., Am. Soc. Engring. Edn. Office: U Tex Austin Engring Libr Gen Librs ECJ 1 300 Austin TX 78713-7330

ARDISON, LINDA G., author, writing educator; b. Ft. Smith, Ark., Apr. 11, 1940; d. Bill Eugene and Mildred M. (Fry) Tanner; m. Gary Winship Ardison, June 10, 1962; children: Amy Roberts, Elizabeth Winship Senft, Matthew Tanner. AA, Stephens Coll., 1960; student, Middlebury Coll., 1960-61; postgrad., Bread Loaf Sch. of English, 1960; BA, U. Ark., 1962. Adminstrv. asst. Wachovia Nat. Bank, Winston-Salem, N.C., 1962-63; English tchr. Wiley Jr. High Sch., Winston-Salem, 1963-64; writing instr. York Coll. of Pa., 1984—2005. Vis. poet York Country Day Sch., 1986, instr. poetry workshop, 1993. Author: Essential Love: Poems About Mothers and Fathers, Daughters and Sons, 2000, (short story in anthology) Voices from the Couch, 2001; editor Standard lit. mag., 1959-60; asst. editor Keystone News, 1980-82; contbr. articles, poems, plays, short stories to jours. Bd. dirs. York County Med. Soc. Aux., York, 1978-80; mem. Jr. League of York, 1974-75; bd. dirs. Human Life Svcs., York, 1989-93. Recipient 3d place for fiction in annual coll. contest The Atlantic Monthly, 1960, First place fiction award New Millenium Writings, 1998; Bread Loaf scholar The Atlantic Monthly, 1960; Pa. Arts Coun. fellowship grantee, 1990-91. Republican. Avocations: reading, literary research. Home: 3015 Little Island Rd Virginia Beach VA 23456-4408 Personal E-mail: lgta@yahoo.com. Business E-Mail: lardison@ycp.edu.

AREEN, JUDITH CAROL, law educator, dean; b. Chgo., Aug. 2, 1944; d. Gordon Eric and Pauline Jeanette (Payberg) A.; m. Richard M. Cooper, Feb. 17, 1979; children: Benjamin Eric (dec.), Jonathan Gordon. AB, Cornell U., 1966; JD, Yale U., 1969. Bar: Mass. 1970, D.C. 1972. Program planner for higher edn. Mayor's Office City of N.Y., 1969-70; dir. edn. voucher study Ctr. for Study Pub. Policy, Cambridge, Mass., 1970-72; mem. faculty Georgetown U., Washington, 1972—, assoc. prof. law, 1972-76, prof., 1976—, prof. cmty. and family medicine, 1980-89, assoc. dean Law Ctr., 1984-87, dean, exec. v.p. for law affairs, 1989—2004, emeritus, 2004—, Paul Regis Dean prof. law, 2004—. Gen. counsel, project coord. Office Mgmt. and Budget, Washington, 1977—80; spl. counsel White House Task Force on Regulatory Reform, Washington, 1978—80; cons. NIH, 1984, NRC, 1985; bd. dirs. Equal Justice Works, Pro Bono Inst. Author: Youth Service Agencies, 1977, Cases and Materials on Family Law, 5th edit., 2006, Law, Science and Medicine, 1984, 3d edit., 2005. Mem. Def. Adv. Com. Women In Svcs., Washington, 1979-82; trustee Cornell Univ., 1997-01. Woodrow Wilson Internat. Ctr. Scholars fellow, 1988-89, Kennedy Inst. Ethics Sr. Rsch. fellow, Washington, 1982-98. Mem. ABA, DC Bar Assn., Am. Law Inst., Assn. Am. Law Schs. (pres. 2006). Business E-Mail: areen@law.georgetown.edu.

ARELLA, ANN MARIETTA, music educator, vocalist; b. Montclair, N.J., Jan. 29, 1951; d. Peter John and Evelyn Elizabeth (De Carlo) Arella; m. William John Wallace, Feb. 9, 1974 (dissolved May 1983); children: Ryan Wallace, Shannon Wallace. MusB, Ind. U., Bloomington, 1973; student, Manhattan Sch. Music, N.Y., 1975; grad. cert., William Patterson U., N., 1983; MA, New Jersey City Univ., N.J., 1991; postgrad., Shenanaoah Univ., Va., 2002—. Tchr. remedial reading & math Indep. Child Study Teams, Jersey City, 1983—86; tchr. choral music Lodi (N.J.) Bd. of Edn., 1986; singer Sacred Heart Ch., Suttern, NY, 1990—95, pianist, 1990—95; ch. music dir. Immaculate Conception, Mahwah, NJ, 1995—99; pvt. piano & voice tchr. Mahwah, NJ, 1998—2002. Ch. musician, 1974—99. Singer: Ridgewood Gilbert & Sullivan Opera Co., 1985—89; singer: (operatic soloist) Opera Festival di Roma, 2000; performer: Teotro Verdi, 1999. Fellow, Shenandoah Conservatory of Music, 2001. Mem.: NEA, Lodi Edn. Assn. (chmn. 1989—93, membership com. 1989—93, adj. rep. 1987—). Republican. Roman Catholic. Avocations: golf, weight training, decorating. Office: Lodi Bd Edn S Main & Hunter Sts Lodi NJ 07644 Home: 10 Winter St Mahwah NJ 07430-1331 E-mail: arella201@aol.com.

ARENA, KELLI, news correspondent; b. Bklyn., N.Y., Dec. 17, 1963; d. Melvin Mullins and Mary Ann (Scafa) Tracy. BFA, NYU, 1985. Prodr. various shows CNN, N.Y.C., 1985-89, prodr. spl. reports, 1988-89, line prodr., 1989-90, supervising prodr., 1990-92, exec. prodr. London, 1992, news editor N.Y.C., 1992-93, reporter, anchor, 1993—. Youth dir. St. George's Ch., N.Y.C., 1989-93. Recipient Peabody award U. Ga., 1987, Cable Ace award, 1987, Gold award Houston Internat. Film Festival, 1987, Nat. Headliner award Atlantic City Press Club, 2002, Emmy award for Sept. 11th coverage, CNN, 2002; named Top ten Fin. Journalist Jour. Fin. Reporting, 1989-92; named Best Corr. N.Y. Festivals, 2002. Mem. Soc. Am. Bus. Editors and Writers, Internat. Womens Media Found. Office: CNN 820 1st St NE Washington DC 20002-4243 E-mail: kelli.arena@turner.com.

ARENAL, JULIE (MRS. BARRY PRIMUS), choreographer; Tchr. Herbert Berghof Studio; asst. on tng. program Lincoln Center Repertory Theatre. Dancer with cos. of Anna Sokolow, Sophie Maslow, John Butler, Jack Cole, Jose Limon; choreographer: Marat/Sade for, Theatre Co. of Boston, Harvard U. Loeb Theatre, Municipal Theatre, Atlanta, Hair, on Broadway (Most Original Choreographer of Year award Sat. Rev. 1968), also London; dir., choreographer Hair, Stockholm (Best Dir.-Choreographer of Yr. award 1969); choreographer, dir. Isabel's a Jezebel; choreographer: Indians on Broadway, Fiesta for Ballet Hispanico, 1972, 20008 1/2, Boccaccio, 1975, A Private Circus, 1975, Free to Be You and Me, 1976, The Referee, 1976, El Arbito, 1978; choreographer for San Francisco Ballet, Nat. Ballet de Cuba, (film) King of the Gypsies, Great Expectations, Fur. Friends, 1980, Mistress, 1991, Once Upon a Time in America, Houston Grand Opera Co., Porgy and Bess, 1995, Great Expectations, 1997, (movie) The Good Shepherd, 2006; dir., choreographer (stage) Funny Girl, Tokyo, 1979-80; dir. N.Y. Express Hip Hop Dance Co., commd. by Spoleto Festival of the Two Worlds, N.C. and Italy; toured 7 cities in People's Republic of China. Grantee NEA, 1973, Oreg. Shakespeare Festival, 1997, Porgy and Bess City Opera, N.Y.C. Opera, 2000, Am. Family PBS TV Series, 2002, Hair Downtown Cabaret, Bridgeport, Conn., 2005; nominated Outstanding Dir. Choreographer Prodn. Ensemble award Conn. Critic Cir.; recipient Outstanding Dir. award 2005. E-mail: borbos@aol.com.

ARENDS, ANN M., elementary school educator, pianist; b. Fairbury, Ill., July 28, 1962; d. Leland George Wycoff and Barbara Jean Bauerle-Wycoff; m. Michael Alan Arends, June 20, 1987; children: Stephanie, Erica, Alyssa. BA, Carthage Coll., Kenosha, Wis., 1984. Cert. tchr. Ill. Elem. libr. Illini Ctrl., Mason City, Ill., 1989—90; accompanist Lincoln Coll., Lincoln, Ill., 1990—91; pvt. practice, 1984—99; music tchr. AFC Sch. Dist., Franklin Brow, Ill., 1996—2006, P.H. Miller Sch., Plano, Ill., 2006—. Pres. and corres. sec. Indian Creek Edn. Found., Ill., 1999—; pres., v.p. Waterman Elem. Parent Club; organist Waterman United Meth., Ill., 1995—, chair worship com., 2002—. Mem.: Music Educators Nat. Conf. Lutheran. Avocations: reading, piano. Home: 130 W Eisenhower St Waterman IL 60556

ARENS, CHRISTINE M., musician, educator, composer; b. Queens, N.Y., May 31, 1968; d. Hans and Claire M. Arens. BMusic, Belmont U., Nashville, 1989, M Music Edn., 1990. Profl. pianist self employed, Lake Wales, Fla., 1991—; owner Music by Christine, Lake Wales, 1992—; tchr. of piano self employed, Nashville and Lake Wales, 1989—; owner Chrisnote Pub., Lake Wales, 1999—. Pianist Marriott Hotels, Orlando, Fla., 1995—. Rec. artist, composer CD, With Quiet Intensity, 1999; author: (piano instrn. books) Bridge to Technique, 1997, Roundabout Etudes, 1997, The Adult's Music Odyssey at the Keyboard, 1996. Mem. Music Tchrs. Nat. Assn., Fla. State Music Tchrs. Assn., Ridge Music Tchrs. Assn. (sec. 1999—), Sigma Alpha Iota. Office: Music by Christine PO Box 7484 Winter Haven FL 33883-7484 E-mail: chrisnote2@aol.com.

AREVALO, CARMEN, government agency administrator; b. Tijuana, Mexico; U.S. Student, Montgomery Coll. With Nat. Weather Svc.; sec. to dir. Dryden Rsch. Ctr. NASA, Edwards AFB, Calif. Recipient Pride in NASA award. Office: NASA Dryden Flight Rsch Ctr PO Box 273 MS 2004 Edwards AFB CA 93523-0273 E-mail: carmen.arevalo@mail.dfrc.nasa.gov.

ARFSTEN, BETTY-JANE, nurse; b. N.Y.C., Sept. 28, 1946; d. William Paul and Jennie (Reyes) Brock; m. Oluf D. Arfsten, June 1, 1973 (dec.). BSN, Adelphi U., 1985; grad., Eastern Sch., 1966. RN, N.Y. Nurse clinician Meml. Sloan Kettering, N.Y.C., 1985-86; charge nurse Booth Meml. Med. Ctr., Flushing, N.Y., 1986-89; nurse coord. IVF Australia, Mineola, N.Y., 1990-93; occupl. health nurse Johnson Controls Inc., Tampa, Fla., 1994-99; triage nurse CIGNA Healthcare, Tampa, Fla., 2000—. After hours triage nurse CIGNA Health Care, Tampa, 2000—. Mem. AACN, NAACOG, Am. Assn. Occupl. Health Nurses, ADA, Am. Hosp. Assn., Am. Assn. Diabetes Educators, Am. Fertility Soc., Oncology Nurses Soc. Home: 18821 Tournament Trl Tampa FL 33647-2459

ARGERS, HELEN, writer, playwright; b. Valisburg, N.J. BA; graduate studies, Europe. Writer advt. copy. Workshop lectr. 6th Ann. Metro. Writers Conf. Seton Hall U., South Orange, N.J., 1996; lectr. hist. sociol. view of Am., 1876 N.J. Hist. Soc., 1998. Author: A Lady of Independence, 1982, Noblesse Oblige, 1994, (play) The Home Visit, 1986 (Winner Nat. One-Act-Play Competition 1986, Weisbrod award 1987), A Scandalous Lady, 1991, A Captain's Lady, 1991, An Unlikely Lady, 1992, The Gilded Lily, 1998, (short story) The Ozymandias Bush (Nelson Algren award finalist 1990), Repossession (Writer's Digest Short Story Competition award); author (under pseudonym Helen Archery) The Age of Elegance, 1992, The Season of Loving, 1992, Lady Adventuress, 1994, Duel of Heats, 1994; humor columnist Worrall Newspapers, 2003-06; classical and popular reviewer Arts and Entertainment for some 20 newspapers; contbr. articles to profl. jours. Recipient Resolution of Honor, State of N.J., 1994, 97.

ARGO, BETTY EARNEST, business owner; b. Jasper, Ala., Nov. 19, 1934; d. Curtis and Ola (Franklin) Sailors; m. John M. Earnest, Mar. 11, 1955 (dec. 1965); children: Brenda Earnest, Amy Earnest Freeman; m. Murry C. Argo. Student, Auburn (Ala.) U. Cert. realtor Realtor Inst. Ala., real estate masters designation Ala. Brakers Council. Freelance ins. agt., 1965-74, 80—; freelance in mktg. and mgmt., 1975-80; realtor Lawson Real Estate, Jasper. Mem. Nat. Underwriters Assn., Beta Sigma Phi. Avocations: art, music, travel. Home: 600 3rd Ave Jasper AL 35501-3723

ARGUEDAS, CRISTINA CLAYPOOLE, lawyer; b. 1953; BA, U. N.H.; JD summa cum laude, Rutgers U., 1979. Bar: Calif. Supreme Ct. 1979, U.S. Dist. Ct., No. Dist. Calif. 1979, So. Dist. Calif. 1983, Ctrl. Dist. Calif. 1982, Ea. Dist. Calif. 1982, Dist. Ariz. 1991, U.S. Ct. Appeals: Ninth Cir. 1980, Tenth Cir. 1985, U.S. Supreme Ct. 1983, U.S. Tax Ct. 1994. Dep. fed. defender U.S. Dist. Ct. (no. dist.) Calif.; ptnr. Arguedas, Cassman & Headley (formerly Cooper, Arguedas & Cassman), Emeryville, Calif., 1982—. Lawyer rep. U.S. Ct. Appeals (9th cir.) Jud. Conf.; adj. prof. Benjamin N. Cardozo Sch. Law, Yeshiva U., Boalt Hall Sch. Law. Named one of 50 Top Lawyers, Nat. Law Jour., 1998, Top Ten Lawyers in Bay Area, San Francisco Chronicle, 2003. Fellow: Am. Coll. Trial Lawyers; mem.: Am. Bd. Criminal Lawyers, Am. Inns of Ct. (master 1999—), Internat. Acad. Trial Lawyers, Calif. Attys. for Criminal Justice (past pres.). Office: Arguedas Cassman & Headley 803 Hearst Ave Berkeley CA 94710 Office Phone: 510-654-2000.*

ARIAS, ILEANA, psychiatrist, educator; AB, Bernard Coll., Columbia U.; MA, SUNY Stony Brook, PhD in Psychology. Rsch. assoc. SUNY, Stony Broko; asst. prof. U. Ga., 1985—2000, dir. clin. tng., clin. psychology prof.; chief etiology and surveillance br., divsn. violence prevention Centers for Disease Control, 2000—04, acting dir. Nat. Ctr. Injury Prevention and Control, 2004—. Contbr. articles to profl. jours.; mem. editl. bd. Jour. of Aggression, Maltreatment and Trauma, Rev. of Aggression and Violent Behavior, Violence and Victims. Office: Nat Ctr Injury Prevention and Control Vanderbilt Bldg Koger Ctr 2858 Woodcock Blvd Rm 1017B Atlanta GA 30333 Office Phone: 770-488-4696.*

ARIFI, FATANA BAKTASH, artist, educator; arrived in U.S., 2000; d. Mohammed Arif and Bibishreen Arifi. Diploma in Art, Women Orgn. Afghanistan, 1983; diploma in Painting, Maimanagi Art Inst., Kabul, Afghanistan, 1983; MFA, Kabul U., Afghanistan, 1987. Art instr. Kabul (Afghanistan) U., 1989—92; freelance artist, designer Afghan Internat. Orgn., 1994—99; dir. Maimanagi Fine Arts Ctr., Peshawar, Pakistan, 1995—99; art instr. Inst. of Fine Arts, Peshawar, 1996; founder, editor Art and Culture Jour., Peshawar, 1997—99; art instr. Hunarkada Acad. Visual and Performance Arts, Peshawar, 1998; sr. cert. framer Michael's Art and Crafts, Alexandria, Va., 2001—, instr. drawing and watercolor, 2005—; freelance artist, 2001—. Mem. selection com. Afghan Artistic Competitions, Peshawar, Pakistan; art dir. Afghan Musaic, 1999; artist mem. Gallery West, Alexandria, Va. Author: Drawing and Painting, 1988, Painting and it's Status in Afghanistan, 1998, Drawing Technical Metodes, 1999. Recipient award, Artist Festival, Japan, 1981, Nat. Painting award, Ministry of Culture, Afghanistan, 1983, 1985, 1987, award, Women Orgn., Afghanistan, 1983, Army Mus., Afghanistan, 1986, Nat. Assn. Artists of Afghanistan, 1986, Youth Orgn. Afghanistan, 1985. Mem.: Nat. Assn. Women Artists. Achievements include development of Handasism. Avocations: writing, poetry, cooking, music. Personal E-mail: fatana_ba@hotmail.com.

ARISON, MARILYN BARBARA (LIN ARISON), arts foundation executive; b. N.Y.C., May 10, 1937; d. Louis and Leona (Berger) Hersh; m. Bill Harvey, 1955 (div. 1964); 1 child, Michael; m. Ted Arison, Aug. 6, 1968;

children— Micky, Sharon. A.A., Miami Dade Community Coll., 1974; B.A., Skidmore Coll., 1976. Exec. sec. L.I. Water Co., N.Y., 1955-57; legal sec. Myers, Heiman & Kaplan, Miami, Fla., 1958-64; sec. Judge Lawrence King, Miami, 1965; freelance pub. relations, Miami, 1965-66; columnist Miami Rev., 1965-69; vice chmn., trustee Nat. Found. for Advancement in Arts, Miami, 1981. Contbr. travel articles to Miami Herald, Miami News. Mem. ARC Com., Miami, 1983—; mem. vis. com. U. Miami, 1984—; com. mem. Cultural Arts Found., Miami Beach, Fla., 1985—; trustee Am. Ballet Theatre, N.Y.C., 1984—, Gov.'s Mansion Found., Tallahassee, Fla., 1984. Mem. Lowe Art Mus. Friends of Art. Republican. Jewish. Office: Nat Found Advancement Arts 100 S Biscayne Blvd Ste 1800 Miami FL 33131-2021*

ARISON, SHARI, investment company executive; m. Ofer Glazer; 4 children. Grad., U. Fl. Chmn. Arison Holdings, 1999—, Arison Investments, 1999—; chmn., pres. Ted Arison Family Foundation, 1999—; controller Bank Ha'poalim, Israel. Named one of world's 100 richest people, Forbes Magazine, 2004. Achievements include Israel's wealthiest citizen, 1999-2004; shareholder, Carnival Cruise Lines. Office: c/o Carnival Corp 3655 NW 87th Ave Miami FL 33178

ARKING, LUCILLE MUSSER, nurse, epidemiologist; b. Centre County, Pa., Jan. 26, 1936; d. Boyd Albert and Marion Anna (Merryman) Musser; m. Robert Arking, May 8, 1958; children: Henry David, Jonathan Jacob. RN, Episcopal Sch. Nursing, 1958; BSN, U. Pa., 1968; MSN, Wayne State U., 1986, postgrad., 1991—96. Psychiat. rsch. nurse Boston City Hosp., 1958; hosp. supr. Phila. Psychiat. Ctr., 1959-61; pub. health nurse Cmty. Nursing Svc., Phila., 1961-64; DON Green Acres Nursing Ctr., Phila., 1966-67; head nurse U. Va., Charlottesville, 1967-68; asst. DON U. Ky., Lexington, 1968-70; asst. dir. nursing edn. Rio Hondo Hosp., Downey, Calif., 1973-75; DON Bellwood Hosp., Bellflower, Calif., 1974-75; nurse epidemiologist Henry Ford Hosp., Detroit, 1975-84, dir. hosp. epidemiology, 1984-89, sr. clin. epidemiologist, 1990-94; v.p. clin. svcs. Great Lakes Rehab. Hosp., Southfield, Mich., 1994-96; adminstr. Cadillac Nursing Ctr., Detroit, 1997-99; exec. dir. St. Anthony Nursing Care Ctr., Warren, Mich., 1999—2001; with office of internat. affairs Pusan (South Korea) Nat. U., 2001; with St. James Nursing Ctr., Detroit, 2002—03, Arking Cons. Assocs., 2003—. Lectr. drug abuse Fountain Valley, Calif., 1970-75; instr. Santa Ana Coll., 1971-73. Contbr. articles to profl. jours. Co-founder Parents and Friends Learning Disabilities Orgn., 1968-70; dean leader Cub Scouts, Fountain Valley, 1968-75; bd. dirs. Wellness Networks, Detroit, 1982-86; mem. Mich. Gov. AIDS Task Force, 1985-86, Mich. Med. Soc. AIDS Task Force, 1986. Women's Club of Centre County scholar, 1954-58; grantee Cmty. Nursing Svc. Ednl., 1963-64; USPHS nursing trainee, 1965. Mem. APHA (mem. epidemiology sect. 1975-99), ANA, Mich. Nurses's Assn. (AIDS task force 1987-89, HIV adv. com. 1989-90), Assn. Practitioners Infection Control, Sci. Rsch. Soc., Assn. Women in Sci., Sigma Xi. Office Phone: 248-689-5286. Personal E-mail: brkac@aol.com, arkinglm@aol.com.

ARKKELIN, CORA RINK, realtor; b. Custer City, Pa., Jan. 21, 1928; d. Frederick Henry Rink and Esther Harriet Rink-Reed; m. Wallace G. Arkkelin, Mar. 17, 1944 (dec. Apr. 1999); children: Wallace Jr. (dec.), Linda, Harold (dec.), Gerald, Daniel. Student, Kent State U., Lake Erie Coll. Machine operator Chanpion Hardware, Geneva, Ohio, 1950-57; office mgr., ins. agt. Miller Realty Ins., Geneva, Ohio, 1958-62; realtor, broker Miller Realty Co., Inc., Geneva, Ohio, 1962-88, Ara REalty, Geneva, Ohio, 1988-91, Coldwell Banker Hunter Realty, Geneva, Ohio, 1991—. Owner auto salvage yard; raced at Speedway 7, Conneaut, Ohio, 1970—94, Sharon Speedway, Hartford, Ohio, 1994—; racing at Painesville Speedway. Race car driver Powder Puff Derby, 1949-64, Men's Racing Divsn. Painesville Speedway, 1958-2004. Mem. Nat. Bd. Realtors, Ashtabula County Bd. Realtors (sec.-treas., Realtor of Yr. 1988), Tri County Racing Assn. (sec.-treas. 1963-64), Geneva Kiwanis. Avocation: auto racing. Home: 5434 W Maple Rd Geneva OH 44041-8127 Office: Coldwell Banker Hunter Realty 385 S Broadway Geneva OH 44041-1808 Office Phone: 440-466-9177. E-mail: hurricanecora50@yahoo.com.

ARLINGHAUS, SANDRA JUDITH LACH, mathematical geographer, educator; b. Elmira, N.Y., Apr. 18, 1943; d. Donald Frederick and Alma Elizabeth (Satorius) Lach; m. William Charles Arlinghaus, Sept. 3, 1966; 1 child, William Edward. AB in Math., Vassar Coll., 1964; postgrad., U. Chgo., 1964—66, U. Toronto, 1966—67, Wayne State U., 1968—70, MA in Geography, 1976; PhD in Geography, U. Mich., 1977. Vis. instr. math. U. Ill., Chgo., 1966; vis. asst. prof. geography Ohio State U., Columbus, 1977—78, lectr. math., 1978—79, Loyola U., Chgo., 1979—81, asst. prof. math., 1981—82; lectr. math. and geography U. Mich., Dearborn and Ann Arbor, 1982—83; founding dir. Inst. Math. Geography, Ann Arbor, 1985—; pres. Arlinghaus Enterprises LLP, Ann Arbor, 1998—. Guest lectr. U. Chgo., 1979, 87, 2000-01, U. Calif., 1979, Syracuse U., 1991, U. No. Iowa, 1991; guest lectr. U. Mich., Ann Arbor, 1983, 90-93, adj. prof. math. geography, population-environ. dynamics Sch. Natural Resources and Environ., 1994—, adj. prof. Coll. Architecture and Urban Planning, 1997, 2001-2004; cons. Transp. Rsch. Inst., Coll. Architecture, 1985-86, Coll. Edn., 1992, Cmty. Sys. Found., 1993—; prodr. Ann Arbor Cmty. Access TV, 1988-90; dir. spatial analysis divsn. Cmty. Sys. Found., 1996—, dir. fellowship tng. divsn., 1996; program chair AAG/TFI Learning Workshop, 2006; program chair Unleashing the Power of GIS/GPS, Taylor & Francis/Assn. Am. Geographers Workshop, Chgo. Author: Down the Mail Tubes: The Pressured Postal Era, 1853-1984, Essays on Mathematical Geography, 1986, Essays on Mathematical Geography-II, 1987, An Atlas of Steiner Networks, 1989, Essays on Mathematical Georgraphy-III, 1991, (eBook) Spatial Synthesis, 2005; co-author: Population-Environment Dynamics, Sectors in Transition, 1992 and later editions through 1998, Mathematical Geography and Global Art, 1986, Environmental Effects on Bus Durability, 1990, Fractals in Geography, 1993, (eBook) Graph Theory and Geography: An Interactive View, 2002, Spatial Synthesis Vol. I, Book I, 2005; editor, co-author: 3D Atlas of Ann Arbor, 2006; founder, editor, co-author Solstice, 1990—, Image Interactive Atlases, Image Game Series, Image Discussion Papers, Internat. Soc. Spatial Scis., 1995—; author, editor-in-chief Practical Handbook of Curve Fitting, 1994; co-author: (book chpt.) Handbook of Engineering, 2004; co-author, editor-in-chief Practical Handbook of Digital Mapping: Terms and Concepts, 1994; editor-in-chief Practical Handbook of Spatial Stats., 1995; editor internat. monograph series; reviewer Mathematical Reviews, 1992—; contbr. articles, book reviews to profl. jours. in field of geography, psychology, math., biology, history, philately. Mem. City of Ann Arbor Planning Commn., 1995-2003, sec., 1997-2002, chair, 2002-2003, vice-chmn., 2003; mem. City of Ann Arbor Environ. Commn., 2000-03; bd. dirs., chmn. Bromley Homeowners Assn., Ann Arbor, 1989-93, pres., 1990-93, 95-96; mem. ordinance revisions com. City of Ann Arbor, 1996-2003, mem. master planning com., 2002-03; donation GIS analysis City of Ann Arbor, 2003—, 3D virtual reality models downtown devel. task force, 2004, 3D Atlas of Ann Arbor, 2001—; bd. dirs. World Jr. Bridge Championships, Ann Arbor, 1990-91, Dolfins Inc., 1993-96; co-chair ACBL Compuware Spring North Am. Bridge Championships, Detroit, 2004; artist Math. Awareness Week, Lawrence Tech. U., 1988; trustee Cmty. Sys. Found., 1995-2001; co-vice chair citizens adv. com. NE Ann Arbor master plan revision, 1999-2000; adv. bd. City of Ann Arbor Police Dept. Neighborhood Watch, 2001—; mem. exec. com. Cmty. Sys. Found., 2003—, sec. bd. trustees, 2003—; donation GIS analysis Am. Contract Bridge League, 2005—. Finalist Pirelli Internat. award, 2002; recipient Cmty. Svc. award, City of Ann Arbor, 1999, Pres.'s Vol. Svc. award, Pres. Bush's Coun. Svc. and Civic Participation, 2003—, Pirelli Internat. award semifinalist, 2001, 2003. Fellow Am. Geog. Soc. (rep. search com. for curator of collection in Golda Meir Libr. U. Wis.-Milw. Libr. 1993-94); mem. AAAS, Am. Math. Soc., Math. Assn. Am., Assn. Am. Geographers, Internat. Soc. Spatial Scis. (founder), Regional Sci. Assn. Achievements include discovery of exact fractal characterization of the geometry of central place theory and its electronic interpretation; creator Spatial Synthesis; alignment of earth marking sculptures to solstices and equinoxes in Minnesota, Washington, Alaska, New Brunswick, Canada, and USSR; creator of one of world's first refereed electronic journals; creator of applications of chaos theory in geography and population environment dynamics, maps for major international projects for Syria and Pakistan; creator Google Earth models of 3D Ann Arbor, 2006. Office: U Mich Sch Natural Resources and Envrion Ann Arbor MI 48109 Business E-Mail: sarhaus@umich.edu.

ARLT, DEVON TAYLOR, small business owner; b. Weymouth, Dorset, Eng., Aug. 24, 1969; came to U.S., 1997; d. Charles Denison and Helen Joy Bate; m. Michael Trevor Webb, May 31, 1992 (div.); m. William Scott Landman, Aug. 30, 1997. Pers. adminstr. RAF, Uxbridge, 1987—92; pres. Bodytalk Fitness, Ltd., Haslemere, England, 1992—97, Elite Retail Leasing, Inc., Parkland, Fla., 1997—2005; owner Journey's End Farm (dressage facility), Global Bus. Funding Inc., Charlevoix, Mich., 2005—. Actress, model, TV presenter. Editor: (other) Flying Changes Publ.; prodr.: (workout video) Bodytalk Step Workout Video, 1992; contbr. articles on fitness to mags. Organizer charity events Starlight Found., 1995. Mem. Aerobics Orgn. Gt. Britain, Fitness Profls. U.K., Nat. Register Personal Trainers, IDEA Fitness Profls. Anglican. Avocations: exercise, horseback riding, dressage, travel, cycling. Home: 9108 Edenshire Cir Orlando FL 32836-6596 Office Phone: 877-866-3863. Office Fax: 231-487-0816. E-mail: devon@globalbusinesfunds.com.

ARMACOST, BARBARA ELLEN, law educator; b. Balt., 1954; BS, U. Va., 1976, JD, 1989; MTS, Regent Coll., U. BC, 1984. Bar: Va. 1989. Head nurse cardiovasc. unit U. Va. Hosp.; vol. mission hospital, La Pointe, Haiti; jud. clk. to Hon. J. Harvie Wilkinson III US Ct. Appeals 4th Cir., 1989—90; atty. adviser Office Legal Counsel US Dept. Justice, 1990—92; asst. prof. U. Va. Sch. Law, 1992—97, assoc. prof., 1997—98, prof., 1998—. Office: U Va Sch Law 580 Massie Rd Charlottesville VA 22903-1789 Office Phone: 434-924-3413. E-mail: bea4k@virginia.edu.

ARMACOST, MARY-LINDA SORBER MERRIAM, retired academic administrator; b. Jeannette, Pa., May 31, 1943; d. Everett Sylvester Calvin and Madeleine (Case) Sorber; m. E. William Merriam, Dec. 13, 1969 (div. 1975); m. Peter H. Armacost, July 10, 1993. Student, Grove City Coll., 1961-63; BA, Pa. State U., 1963-65, MA, 1965-67, PhD, 1967-70; HHD (hon.), Carroll Coll., 1991; LLD (hon.), Wilson Coll., 1994. Rsch. assoc. Pa. State U., University Park, 1970-72; asst. prof. speech Emerson Coll., Boston, 1972-79, dir. continuing edn., 1974-77, spl. asst. to pres., 1977-78, v.p. adminstrn., 1978-79; asst. to pres. Boston U., 1979-81; pres. Wilson Coll., Chambersburg, Pa., 1981-91, Moore Coll. Art and Design, Phila., 1991-93; sr. fellow Office of Women in Higher Edn. Am. Coun. on Edn., 1994—; interim pres. Moore Coll. Art and Design, Phila., 1998-99; pres. emerita, 2000. Cons. Govt. Edn. and Secondary Edn. Act Title III, Alameda County, Calif., 1968; adj. prof. U. Pa. Grad. Sch. Edn., 2003—. Bd. govs. New Eng. chpt. NATAS, 1980-81; bd. dir. Sta. WITF, Inc., Harrisburg, Pa., 1982-91, chmn. bd., 1988-91; bd. dir. Chambersburg Hosp., 1984-89, vice chmn. bd., 1987-89; bd. dir. Elderhostel, 1997-2002; vice-chmn., 2000-2002; trustee Monmouth U., N.J., 1994-99, Sta. WHYY-FM-TV, Phila., 1992-93, Boston Zool. Soc., 1980-81, Arts Boston, 1979-81, Scotland Sch. Vets. Children, Pa., 1984-90, Randolph-Macon Woman's Coll., Lynchburg, Va., 2001-02; bd. dir. Fla. Orch., 1993-97, co-chair edn. com., 1995-97, exec. com., 1995-97; exec. com. Found. for Ind. Colls., 1989-91, WEDU-TV, 1998-2002, chair planning com., exec. com., bd. dir., 1998-2002; pres. Chambersburg Area Coun. Arts, 1988-90; chmn. higher edn. com. Gen. Assembly Presbyn. Ch., 1987-90; elder Falling Spring Presbyn. Ch., 1988-90; fellow Am. Coun. Edn., 1977-78, commn. on govtl. rels., 1985-89, commn. on women, 1992-93; exec. com. Pa. Assn. Colls. and Univs., 1984-90, Assn. Presbyn. Colls. and Univs., 1983-88, pres., 1986-87; edn. adv. com. John S. and James L. Knight Found., 1998-2000; bd. dir., exec. com. Presbyn. Edn. Bd., Lahore, Pakistan 2003—. Recipient Disting. Alumna award Pa. State U., 1984, Disting. Dau. of Pa., 1986, Athena award Chambersburg C. of C., 1988, Outstanding Alumnae award Sch. Dist. Jeannette, 1991. Mem.: Phi Kappa Phi. E-mail: mlsma@cs.com.

ARMAND, MARGARET MITCHELL, mental health services professional; b. Port-au-Prince, Haiti, Nov. 14, 1950; arrived in U.S., 1968; d. Francois William Mitchell and Anne Marie Solages; m. Lucien J. M. Armand, June 30, 1970; children: Lucien George(dec.), Alain, Bernadette Francoise. BA in Counseling Psychology, U. Tex., 1978; MA in Counseling Psychology, 1982. Nat. bd. cert. in mental health, lic. in mental health. Spkr. and lectr. in field; presenter and panelist in field; adj. prof. Indian River C.C., 1988, U. Mass, 2000; adj. prof. Haiti Culture and Politics U. Mass., 2000. Contbr. articles to profl. and creative publs.; featured in: (documentary) Going Back to Our Roots, Benin, Africa; Miami Light Porject Immigration Documentary. Coordinator Haiti Nat. Office Popular Edn., 1987; mem. adv. bd. Mailman Segal Child Inst., Nova Southeastern U., 2000—. Nominee Universal Peace Ambassador, 2006; recipient award of excellence, Broward County Adult Vocational Edn., 1989, Haitian Women Political award, 1999, Haitian Woman Cmty. Involvement award, 2003. Mem.: ACA, Practioner Rsch. Scholars Inst., Broward County Mediators Assn., Nat. Fed. Vodouizant. Personal E-mail: margaretarmand@gmail.com.

ARMAN GELENBE, DENIZ, concert pianist; b. Ankara, Turkey, Oct. 8, 1944; came to U.S., 1962; d. Abdul Kerim and Ayse Mediha (Raif) A.; m. Erol Gelenbe, June 8, 1968; 1 child, Pamir Emre. Student, Eastman Sch. Music, 1962-64; MusB, Juilliard, 1967, MusM, 1968; postgrad., U. Mich., Ann Arbor, 1970-71. Founder, artistic dir., prof. piano Semaines Musicales de Rouen Paris U., 1985—93; founder, artistic dir. Arman Ensemble, NC, 1994—, Arman Ensemble, Arman Trio, Paris, 1994—. Dir. summer music program, Normandy, France, 1999—; vis. assoc. prof. piano U. Ctrl. Fla., Orlando, 1998—2003, artist in residence, assoc. prof. piano, 2001—03; sr. lectr., keyboard coord. for collaborative performance Trinity Coll. Music, London, 2003—; founder Schubertiad, Winter Park, Fla., 2000. Musician (recitals): Carnegie Weill Hall, Salle Gaveau, Nat. Gallery Art, Tonhalle, Wigmore Hall, 2003—05, Concerts de Midi; musician: (soloist) Ensemble Orchestral Paris, Dartington Internat. Summer Sch., 2006, New Japan Philharm., Ankara Presdl. Symphony Orch., Presdl. Symphony Orch., N.C. Symphony; musician: (CD) with Haydn Quartet, 1994, 2000, Arman Ensemble, 1996, Arman Trio, 2000, 2004;: Arman Trio, 2005, 2003;: Arman Trio, 2005, Wigmore Hall, 2006. Emerging Artist grantee, Durham, N.C., 1984. Mem. European Piano Tchrs. Assn., Chamber Music Am., Coll. Music Soc. Avocations: painting, reading, walking. Office: Trinity Coll Music King Charles Ct Old Royal Naval Coll, Greenwich London SE10 9JF England Home: Flat 813 St Johns 79 Marsham St Westminster London SW1 England Personal E-mail: dgelenbe@aol.com.

ARMANI, AIDA MARY, small business owner; b. Amman, Jordan, Apr. 13, 1952; came to U.S., 1956; d. Raji Naiem and Wardeh Elias (Kazanjian) Kawar; m. Steven Earl McBride, Apr. 7, 1973 (div. July 1983); children: Nathaniel Joseph, Aaron Keith. Beauty lic., Martin Anthony Beauty Sch., 1970; cert. in hypnotherapy, Sidona Inst. Hypnotherapy, 1995; cert. imagery therapist, Internat. Inst. Visualization, 1996. Stylist/colorist Jean-Madeline, Phila., 1970-74; colorist Hair Impulse, Media, Pa., 1975-80; colorist/stylist Talent, Bryn Mawr, 1980-83; colorist Salon 600, Bryn Mawr, Pa., 1983-86, James & Co., Wayne, Pa., 1986-87; colorist, cons., head dept., artistic dir. Raya-Haig Salon, Bala Cynwyd, Pa., 1987—; entrepreneur, owner Aida, Inc., West Chester, Pa., 1995—; animal imagery therapist, 2000—. Mem. artistic team Goldwell of Pa., 1995-96, educator, 1990-96; pvt. practice dream interpreter, hypnotherapy counselor, West Chester, Pa., 1995—. Inventor hair styling devices; appeared in opera Acad. of Music., Pa., 1996. Sunday sch. tchr. Ch. of the Savior, Wayne, Pa., 1981-86, leader divorced/singles group, 1987-92; mem. Internat. Inst. Visualization & Rsch., 1995-96. Mem. Internat. Beauty Soc., Art & Fashion, Intercoiffure Internat., Hair Color Exch. Avocations: needlepoint, dance, teaching sunday school, interior decorating. Home: 226 Chestnut St Newtown Square PA 19073-3306 Office: Raya-Haig Beauty Ctr 401 E City Line Ave Bala Cynwyd PA 19004-1122 also: Aida Armani Color Group 914 Lancaster Ave Bryn Mawr PA 19010

ARMANI, DONNA, science educator; BS, George Mason U., 1994, MEd, 1998. Sci. tchr. Loudoun County Pub. Schs., Ashburn, Va., 1996—; sci., math tchr. Briar Woods HS, Ashburn, Va., 2005—. Named Outstanding Sci. Tchr., Health Physics Soc., 2005; recipient Top Industry Practice award, Nuc. Energy Inst., 2005, Willowcroft award, Willowcroft Vineyards, 2000 and 2002. Mem.: NSTA, Va. Health Physics Soc., Va. Assn. Sci. Tchrs.

ARMATRADING, JOAN, singer, lyricist; b. St. Kitts, West Indian Islands, Dec. 9, 1950; BA with honors, U. London, 2001, MBE, 2001; Mus D, Birmingham U., 2002; DLitt, U. Liverpool, 2000, Aston U., 2006. Albums include Whatever's for Us, 1972, Back to the Night, 1974, Joan Armatrading, 1976, Show Some Emotion, 1977, To the Limit, 1978, Steppin' Out, 1979, Me Myself I, 1980, How Cruel, 1980, Walk Under Ladders, 1981, The Key, 1983, Track Record, 1983, Secret Secrets, 1985, Sleight of Hand, 1986, The Shouting Stage, 1988, Hearts & Flowers, 1990, The Very Best Of, 1991, Square The Circle, What's Inside, 1994, Lullabies, 1998, The Messenger, A Tribute Song to Nelson Mandela, 2000; CD: Lover's Speak, 2003; CD & DVD: Joan Armatrading: Live All the Way from America, 2004. Pres. Woman of the Yr. Lunch and Assemblyin the U.K., 2005—. Named Hon. fellow, Northampton U., 2003. Fax: 0181 992 6593. E-mail: admin@armatrading.com.

ARMEN, MARGARET MEIS, lawyer; d. Joseph John and Florence Catherine Meis. BA, Carlow Coll., 1969; JD, Cleveland State U., 1978. Bar: Ohio 1978, Washington, DC 1980. Tchr. Pitts. City Sch., 1969—70, Archdiocese of Washington, DC, 1970—73; pers. adminstr. Stouffer Foods Corp., Cleve., 1973—75, Hospitality Motor Inns, Inc., Cleve., 1976—78; atty. adv. US Govt. Accountability Office, Washington, 1978—, sr. atty., 1986—. Dir. Am. Assn. for Budget and Program Analysis, Washington, 1986—93, pres., 1993—94; dir. Pub. Fin. Pub., Inc., Washington, 1990—2002, pres., 2003—. Exec. editor: Cleve. State U. Law Rev., 1977—78; contbr. articles to profl. jours. Mem.: Exec. Women in Govt. (v.p. 2002—03), Internat. Alliance for Women (sec. 2004—05, counsel 2006—). Office: US Govt Accountability Office 441 G St NW Washington DC 20548 Business E-Mail: armenm@gao.gov.

ARMENDARIZ, ALMA DELIA, small business owner, researcher; b. Kansas City, Mo., Nov. 2, 1970; d. David Armendariz and Elena Leon Frankoviglia. Student, Washburn U., 1989-90, Fla. Keys C.C., 1993, Coll. of the Ozarks, 1990, Palm Beach C.C., 1998. Cert. capt. USCG. Rschr., first mate The Wild Dolphin Project, Grand Bahama Banks, The Bahamas, 1992; mem. search and recovery team Marine Mammal Stranding Network, Key West, Fla., 1992-94; rschr., first mate DolphinWatch, Key West, 1991-94; surveyor Grand Strand Bottlenose Dolphin Surveys, Myrtle Beach, S.C., 1995-96; mem. adv. bd., adminstr. Save-A-Pet of Fla., Palm Beach, 1998-2000; owner, operator, pres. DolphinWatch, Key West, Fla., 2000—03; co-owner, operator DolphinDream Charters, 2004—. Intern Ekotecture Internat. Environ. Architecture and Cmty. Planning, Palm Beach, 1991-93. Mem. Harbour Br. Oceanographic Inst., Fla. Keys Wild Dlphin Alliance, Dolphin Project; vol. Marine Mammal Conservancy Pilot Whale Rehab. and Release. Mem. World Wildlife Found., Women in the Arts, Surfrider Found., Ctr. for MarineConservation, Internat. Campaign for Tibet, Reef Relief, Harbour Br. Ocean. Inst., The Dolphin Project. Avocations: surfing, free diving, triathlon, travel. Home: 15A 12th Ave Key West FL 33040

ARMFIELD, DIANA MAXWELL, artist, educator; b. Ringwood, Eng., June 11, 1920; d. Joseph Harold Armfield and Gertrude Mary Uttley; m. Bernard Dunstan, 1949; 3 children. Student, Slade Sch. Art, Ctrl. Sch. Arts and Crafts. Tchr. Byam Shaw Sch. Art, 1959-89. Artist-in-residence, Perth, Australia, 1985, Jackson, Wyo., 89. One-woman shows include Browse & Darby, London, 1979-2003, 06, Royal Acad. Friends Rm. Gallery, 1995, 2004-05, Royal Cambrian Acad., 2001, Albany Gall, Cardiff, 2001, Albany Gallery, Cardiff, 2002, 05, 06, New Acad. Gallery, 2005; author: Mitchell Beazley Pocket Guide to Painting in Oils, Mitchell Beazley Pocket Guide to Drawing, The Art of Diana Armfield (Julian Halsby); represented in pub. collections at Yale Ctr. for Brit. Art, Govt. Eng., Faringdon, Mercury Asset Mgmt., Lancaster City, Victoria and Albert Mus. Textiles. Commr. HRH Prince of Wales, Reuters, Contemporary Art Soc. Wales, Natural Trust. Mem. Royal Acad. Art, New English Art Club (hon.), Royal Cambrian Acad. (hon. ret.), Pastel Soc. (hon.), Royal Watercolor Soc., Royal West of Eng. Acad. (hon. ret.). Avocations: music, gardening. Address: 10 High Park Rd Kew Richmond TW9 4BH England also: Llwynhir Parc Bala Gwynedd LL23 7YU Wales Office Phone: 0108-826-6633.

ARMFIELD, TERRI ELAINE, music educator, musician; b. Lincoln, Nebr., Sept. 29, 1955; d. Jesse Lee and Charlotte Irene Smith; m. Ted Duane Armfield, Dec. 18, 1976 (dec. May 12, 1995); children: Lisa Renee, Ben Jared. MusD in Oboe Performance, U. Ky., 2003; MusM, U. Northern Iowa, 2000; BFA in music edn., 1976. Adj. prof. oboe Asbury Coll., Wilmore, Ky., 2000—03; vis. instr., oboe and music theory Western Carolina U., Cullowhee, 2004—; 2d prin. oboist Asheville (NC) Symphony Orch. 2nd prin. oboist Asheville (N.C.) Symphony Orch., 2004—; freelance oboist. Mem.: Internat. Double Reed Soc. Avocations: travel, sewing, reading, exercise. Office: Western Carolina Univ 265 Coulter Cullowhee NC 28723 Home: PO Box 141 Cullowhee NC 28723-0141 Office Phone: 828-227-2471. E-mail: tarmfield@email.wcu.edu.

ARMINE, CINDY A., bank executive; Mgmt. positions with Citigroup Inc., NYC, 1981—, U.S. dir. compliance, corp. & investment banking & Smith Barney, mng. dir., chief compliance officer, global wealth mgmt., mem. mgmt. com., 2004—. Office: Citigroup Inc 399 Park Ave New York NY 10043*

ARMISTEAD, KATHERINE KELLY (MRS. THOMAS B. ARMISTEAD III), interior designer, travel consultant, civic worker; b. Apr. 14, 1926; d. Joseph Anthony and Katherine Arnold (Manning) Kelly; m. Thomas Boyd Armistead III, Nov. 29, 1952. Grad., Finch Jr. Coll., 1946. Cert. travel cons. Editor news Sta. WOR, N.Y.C., 1946—51; with Dumont TV, 1951—52; editor Social Svc. Rev., L.A., 1956—57; interior designer L.A., 1963—; travel cons. Gilner Internat. Travels, Beverly Hills, Calif., 1980—2006, Protravel, Beverly Hills, 2006—. Mem. editl. bd. Previews Mag., 1984—87. Pres. Jrs. Social Svc., L.A., 1962—64; nat. chpt. chmn. Assoc. Alumnae of Sacred Heart, 1960—66; pres. Las Floristas, 1967—68; coord. Jr. Mannequin Assisteens, Assistance League So. Calif., 1971—72; pres. docent coun. L.A. County Mus. Art, 1976—77, pres. decorative arts coun., 1977—80, chmn. Am. Antiques Conf., 1979—81, mem. costume coun., mem. past pres.' coun., 1981—, mem. capital gifts campaign com.; pres. L.A. Orphanage Guild, 1969—70, bd. dirs., 1970—. Recipient Eve award, Assistance League So. Calif. Mem.: Inst. Cert. Travel Agts., Am. Soc. Travel Agts., Lady Grand Cross Equestrian Order of the Holy Sepulchre of Jerusalem, Bel Air Garden Club, Birnam Wood Golf Club. Republican. Roman Catholic. Office Phone: 310-271-9566.

ARMITAGE, KAROLE, dancer; b. Madison, Wis., Mar. 3, 1954; Studied, N.C. Sch. of the Arts, with Bill Evans, U. Utah, 1971-72. Dancer Geneva (Switzerland) Opera Ballet, 1973-75, Merce Cunningham Dance Co., 1976-81; choreographer, artistic dir. The Armitage Ballet (formerly Armitage Dance Co.), N.Y.C., 1981—90; dir. MaggioDanza di Firenze, Florence, Italy, 1995—98; assoc. choreographer Centre Chorégraphique Nationale- Ballet de Lorraine, Nancy, France; dir. Venice Biennale of Contemporary Dance, 2004. Choreographer of ballets including: Ne, 1978, Do We Could 1979, Veritige, 1980, Drastic-Classicism, 1981, It Happened at Club Bombay Cinema, 1981, Slaughter on MacDougal Street, 1981, Paradise, version 1, 1981, The Last Gone Dance, 1983, Paradise, version 2, 1983, A Real Gone Dance, 1983, (with Rosella Hightower) The Nutcracker, 1983, Tasmanian Devil, 1984, GV-10, 1984, The Water Duets, 1985, The Mollino Room, 1985, The Elizabethan Phrasing of the Late Albert Ayler, 1986, The Tarnished Angels, 1987, Les Stances a Sophie, 1987, Duck Dances, 1988, Kammerdisco, 1988, GoGo Ballerina, 1988, Contempt, 1989, Forty Guns, 1990, Dancing Zappa, 1990, Jack and Betty, 1990, The Marmot Quickstep, 1991, Renegade Dance Wave, 1991, Overboard, 1991, Segunda Piel, 1992, Happy Birthday Rossini, 1992, Hucksters of the Soul, 1993, I Had A Dream. 1993, Hovering at the

Edge of Chaos, 1994, Tattoo and Tutu, 1994, The Dog Is Us, 1994, The Return of Rasputin, 1994, Apollo e Dafne, 1997, Time Is the Echo of an Axe Within a Wood, 2004; (dance for TV) Parafango, 1983, Ex-Romance, 1984; (arts program) The South Bank Show, 1985; (feature films) Without You, I'm Nothing, 1989, Chain of Desire, 1991, Search and Destroy, 1994; (videoclips) Love School for the Dyvinals, 1990, Vogue for Madonna, 1991, In The Closet for Michael Jackson, 1992; (world tours) Milli Vanilli, 1990, Madonna's Blonde Ambition, 1991, The Dyvinals, 1991; (videoclips for feature film) Kuffs, 1990; writer, dir., choreographer (feature film) Hall of Mirrors, 1992. Guggenheim fellow, 1986. Office: Armitage Found 9 N Moore St Ste 4 New York NY 10013-2414

ARMS, ANNELI (ANNA ELIZABETH ARMS), artist, educator; b. NYC, May 23, 1935; d. William Emil and Elizabeth Maria (Bodanzky) Muschenheim; m. John M. Arms, Sept. 1, 1956; 1 child, Thomas C. BA, U. Mich., 1958. Represented in permanent collections U.S. State Dept., NY Pub. Libr., Libr. of Congress, N.Y. Hist. Soc., Dana Libr., Rutgers U. Recipient Nora Mirmont award Heckscher Mus., 1984, Guild Hall Sculpture award, 1987; scholar Art Students League N.Y., 1958. Mem.: Fedn. Modern Painters and Sculptors (bd. dirs. 1988—, v.p. 1996—2005, pres. 2005—), Nat. Drawing Assn., Artists Equity N.Y., Artists Alliance East Hampton, Manhattan Graphics Ctr. (bd. dirs. 1995—, exhbns. dir. 2003—). Avocations: opera, movies, swimming, museums, reading. Studio: 113 Greene St New York NY 10012-3823 Personal E-mail: aarms2001@yahoo.com.

ARMSTRONG, ALEXANDRA, financial planner; b. Washington, Sept. 26, 1939; d. Rhoda Elizabeth (Forbes) Armstrong; m. Jerry J. McCoy, 1994. BA in History, Newton Coll. Sacred Heart, 1960. Cert. fin. planner, 1977. Exec. sec. Ferris & Co., Washington, 1961—66, registered rep., 1966—77; sr. v.p. Julia Walsh & Sons, Washington, 1977—83; pres. Alexandra Armstrong Advisors Inc., Washington, 1983—91; chmn. Armstrong, Welch & MacIntyre Inc., Washington, 1991—2000, Armstrong, MacIntyre & Severns, Inc., Washington, 2001—04, Armstrong, Fleming & Moore Inc., Washington, 2005—. Bd. experts Boardroom Reports, 1987—. Author: On Your Own: A Widow's Passage To Emotional and Financial Wellbeing, 1993, 3d edit., 2000. Vice chmn. Nat. Coun. Friends of Kennedy Ctr., Washington, 1987-91; pres. Nat. Capital coun. Boy Scouts Am., 1999-2000, chmn., 2000-01; mem. bd. visitors Sch. Bus. Georgetown U., 1988-91; v.p. programs Internat. Women's Forum, 1991-93, v.p. membership 1997-99, dir. IWF leadership found., 2001-04; bd. dirs. Reading is Fundamental, treas. 2000-04; chmn. Found. Fin. Planning, 1999-2000, bd. dirs. Named Bus. Woman of Yr. Washington Bus. and Profl. Women's Club, 1978; recipient award of excellence for commerce Boston Coll. Alumni Assn., 1985, Woman Who Makes a Difference award Internat. Women's Forum, 1992, Silver Beaver award Boy Scouts Am., 1991, Loren Dutton award, Internat. Assn. Registered Fin. Cons., 2003, Beta Gamma Sigma chpt. honoree Georgetown U., 1992. Mem. Fin. Planning Assn. (bd. dirs. 1980-87, chmn. emeritus, pres. 1986-87), Nat. Assn. Investment Clubs (columnist monthly mag. 1978—, Disting. Svc. award 1993), Nat. Assn. Securities Dealers (bus. conduct com. dist. 10 1986-89, vice chmn. 1988-89), Nat. Assn. Women Bus. Owners (pres. Capital Area chpt. 1980-81), D.C. Estate Planning Coun., Nat. Capital Area Coun., Econ. Club Washington, Cosmos Club Washington, Econ. Club N.Y.C., Fin. Planning Assn. (Lifetime Achievement award 2001) Republican. Roman Catholic. Home: 3560 Winfield Ln NW Washington DC 20007-2368 Office: 1850 M St NW Ste 250 Washington DC 20036 Office Phone: 202-887-8135.

ARMSTRONG, AMELIA LUCI, music educator; b. Wausau, Wis., July 20, 1982; d. James Dodd and Rosanne Christine Weber. B of Music Edn., Wartburg Coll., Waverly, Iowa, 2004. K-12 profl. music educator Iowa Bd. Edn., Wis. Bd. Edn. Pvt. voice tchr., Wausau, Wis., 2002—04; vocal music tchr. Platteville HS, Wis., 2004—. Mem. exec. bd. Music Boosters, Platteville, 2004—. Choir dir. St. Peter Church ELCA, Denver, Iowa, 2003—04, First English ELCA, Platteville, Wis., 2005—. Mem.: Music Educator's Nat. Conf., Am. Choral Dir.'s Assn. Lutheran. Avocations: cooking, reading, running. Office: Platteville HS 710 E Madison Platteville WI 53818 Office Phone: 608-342-4020 2233.

ARMSTRONG, ANNE LEGENDRE, retired ambassador; b. New Orleans, Dec. 27, 1927; d. Armant and Olive (Martindale) Legendre; m. Tobin Armstrong, Apr. 12, 1950 (dec. Oct. 7, 2005); children: John Barclay, Katharine, Sarita A. Hixon, Tobin and James L. (twins). BA in English, Vassar Coll., 1949. Co-chmn. Rep. Nat. Com., 1971-73; counsellor to U.S. Pres., 1973-74; U.S. amb. to Gt. Britain and No. Ireland London, 1976-77; chmn. adv. bd. Ctr. for Strategic and Internat. Studies (formerly affiliated with Georgetown U.), 1981-87, chmn. bd. trustees, 1987-99, chmn. exec. com., 1999—; chmn. Pres.'s Fgn. Intelligence Adv. Bd., 1981-90; dir. Promontory Interfinancial Network, LLC, 2003—. Commn. on Integrated Long Term Strategy, 1987; adv. coun. GM Corp., 1998. Bd. regents Smithsonian Instn., 1978-94, emeritus, 1994; bd. overseers Hoover Instn., 1978-97; co-chmn. Reagan-Bush Campaign, 1980; bd. regents Tex. A&M U., 1997-2003; U.S. Commn. on Nat. Security/21st Century, 1999-2001; mem. Gov.'s Coun. Sci. and Biotech. Devel., Gov.'s Task Force on Homeland Security; county commr. Kenedy County, 2005 Recipient Gold medal Nat. Inst. Social Scis., 1977, Rep. Woman of Yr. award, 1979, Texan of Yr. award, 1981, Presdl. Medal of Freedom award, 1987, Golden Plate award Am. Acad. Achievement, 1989; named to Tex. Women's Hall of Fame, 1986. Mem. English-Speaking Union (chmn. 1978-80), Coun. Fgn. Rels., Am. Assocs. of Royal Acad. Trust (trustee 1985-2005, vice-chmn. 1996), Alfalfa Club, Capitol Hill Club, Phi Beta Kappa. Republican.

ARMSTRONG, BRENDA ESTELLE, pediatrician, cardiologist; b. Rocky Mount, N.C., Jan. 19, 1949; d. Wiley Thurber and Marguerite (Carson) A.; 1 child, Bradlee Alexander Carson Armstrong. BA, Duke U., 1970; MD, St. Louis U., 1974. Diplomate Am. Bd. Pediatrics, Am. Bd. Pediatric Cardiology. Intern in pediatrics UCLA Med. Ctr., 1974-75; resident in pediatrics Duke U. Med. Ctr., Durham, N.C., 1975-76, fellow in pediatric cardiology, 1976-79, asst. prof. pediatrics, 1979-89, assoc. prof. pediatrics, 1987—, assoc. prof., 1989—, dir. admissions, 1996—. Chief clin. svcs. div. pediatric cardiology, Duke U., 1986—, chief fellowship tng., 1986—, chief of pediatric cardiac lab., 1984—; cons. to U.S. Army and USAF, 1982—. Mem. N.C. Environ. Mgmt. Commn., Raleigh, 1979-86; bd. dirs. Montessori Children's House of Durham, 1988—, Durham Striders Track and Field Club, 1984—. Recipient Golden Apple Teaching award Duke U. Med. Sch., 1981, Thomas Kinney Teaching award Duke U. Med. Sch., 1985; named YWCA Woman of Achievement, City of Durham YWCA, 1986. Mem. Assn. Black Cardiologists, Old North State Med. Soc. (Dr. of Yr. 1987), Nat. Med. Assn., N.C. Pediatric Soc., Am. Acad. Pediatrics., Links Inc. Democrat. Episcopalian. Avocations: music, reading, sports, knitting. Office: Duke U Div Pediatric Cardiology PO Box 3195 Durham NC 27715-3195

ARMSTRONG, DIANA ROSE, financial consultant; b. Alvada, Ohio, June 2, 1944; d. J. Joseph and Priscilla Rose Saltzman; m. Philip Bruce Armstrong; children: David Shannon, Laura Ann, Lisa Kay. BS in Edn., Bowling Green Sttae U., 1966, MS in Guidance and Counseling, 1969. CFP. Fin. planner Smith Barney, Morristown, N.J., 1994, sr. v.p. pres.'s coun., 1995—. Mem. AAUW. Republican. Avocations: reading, investing, cooking. Office: Smith Barney 10 Madison Ave Lbby 1 Morristown NJ 07960-7312 Home: 4 Trails End Ct Warren NJ 07059-6775

ARMSTRONG, DIANNE OWENS, language educator; d. James Hamilton Jones; m. David Seaton Armstrong, July 6, 1958 (div. June 0, 1967); children: Sydney Pollard, David Seaton Armstrong, Jr., Emily Hines, Malcolm Conger. BA, U. Ill., Champaign Urbana, 1957; MA, St. Johns U., Jamaica, N.Y., 1976; PhD, U. So. Calif., L.A., 1992. Instr. English UCLA, 1984—87; lectr. freshman writing program U. of So. Calif., L.A., 1988—93; adj. instr. English Santa Barbara City Coll., Calif., 1993—96; prof. English Ventura Coll., Calif., 1996—. Contbr. articles to profl. jours., ency. Vol. Faulding Hotel Ministry, Santa Barbara, 1999—2001. Named Instr. of the Yr., EOPS, Ventura Coll., 1996—97, Lectr. of the Yr., USC Writing Program, 1992. Democrat-Npl. Episcopal. Office: Ventura College 4667 Telegraph Rd Ventura CA 93003 Office Phone: 805-654-6400 2221. E-mail: darmstrong@vcccd.edu.

ARMSTRONG, L. C., artist; b. Humbolt, Tenn., Dec. 18, 1954; d. Arlie L. Clenney and Louray Armstrong; m. Philip Arthur Epstein, July 23, 1995; 1 child, Alexandra Armstrong Epstein. BFA, Art Ctr. Coll. of Design, Pasadena, 1982, San Francisco Art Inst., 1987. One-woman shows include Galerie Sophia Ungers Gallery, Cologne, Germany, 1991, 1992, Marsha Mateyka Gallery, Washington, DC, 1993, John Post Lee Gallery, N.Y., 1993, Bravin Post Lee Gallery, 1994, Angles Gallery, Santa Monica, 1994, 1999, Phillippe Rizzo Gallery, Paris, 1994, USF Contemporary Mus., Tampa, 1995, Marsha Mateyka Gallery, Washington, DC, 1997, Bravin Post Lee Gallery, N.Y., 1997, Hofstra Univ., Hempstead, N.Y., 1998, Marsha Mateyka Gallery, Washington, DC, 2000, 2003, Galerie Huebner, Frankfurt, Germany, 1998, 2000, Germany, 2005, Postmasters Gallery, N.Y., 1999, 2001, Corcoran Gallery of Art, Wash., DC, 1998, exhibited in group shows at Corcoran Gallery Art Biennial, Washington, 1991, Van Abbemuseum, Eindhoven, 2000, Laing Art Gallery, Eng., 2002, Bklyn. Mus., 2004, Blaffer Gallery, 2005, Marlborough Chelsea Gallery, NY, 2005. Pollack Krasner grantee, 1991. Home: 33 Harrison St New York NY 10013 Office: 55 Washington St #307 Brooklyn NY 11201 Office Phone: 718-852-4670.

ARMSTRONG, LILLIAN M., clinical counselor; b. Caguas, P.R., Mar. 27, 1946; d. Victor and Maria C. (Martinez) Soto; m. Daniel B. Armstrong, June 7, 1964; children: Daniel B. II, Ann Marie. AA, AS, Miami Dade Community Coll., Miami, Fla., 1981; BS, Fla. Internat. U., 1984; MS, Barry U., 1986. Cert. adult edn. tchr., Fla. Clin. counselor Metatherapy Inst., Homestead, Fla.; adult edn. tchr. Dade County Pub. Sch., Homestead, Fla.; chem. dependency therapist Archdioses of Miami, St. Luke's Ctr., Miami; pvt. practice clin. therapist Inst. of Psychology, Coral Gables, Fla.; counselor, interventionist with at risk students and family Circles of Care, Inc., Melbourne, Fla.; dir. social svcs. Hacienda Girls Ranch, Melbourne, Fla.; clin. case mgr. Children Psychiatric Hosp., Palm Bay, Fla.; adult edn. tchr. Brevard County Pub. Schs., Melbourne, Fla. Named NCO Wife of the Month. Mem. Fla. Internat. U. Alumni Assn., Barry U. Alumni Assn. Home: 1540 Palatka Rd SE Palm Bay FL 32909-5611

ARMSTRONG, MARCY LYNN, literature and language educator, special education educator; b. Galion, Ohio, Sept. 28, 1959; d. Larry Owen Armstrong and Marcia Lee Corbin. BS in Elem. Edn., Asbury Coll., Wilmore, Ky., 1982; MA in Sch. Guidance Counseling, Ea. Ky. U., Richmond, Ky., 1988. Cert. Rank 1 in Sch. Guidance Counseling Ea. Ky. U., 1993. Tchr. grade 3 Warner Elem. Sch. Jessamine County Bd. Edn., Nicholasville, Ky., 1982—84, tchr. grade 6, 1984—86, tchr. lang. arts grade 6, 1986—93; tchr. English grade 6 Jessamine Mid. Sch., 1993—95; tchr. English grade 7 and 8 West Jessamine Mid. Sch., 1995—2005, tchr. for students at risk grades 6 through 8, 2005—. Yearbook sponsor West Jessamine Mid. Sch., Nicholasville, Ky., 1987—; with extended sch. svcs. Jessamine County Bd. Edn., 1990—95; mem. Ky. tchg. internship program West Jessamine Mid. Sch., 1992—95; coach academic team future problem-solving Am. West Jessamine Mid. Sch., 1994—95; with extended sch. svcs. West Jessamine Mid. Sch., 1995—, tchr. rep. sch. site decision-making coun., 1996—98; sponsor Family Consumer Career Leaders of Am. West Jessamine Mid. Sch., 2000—. Summer intern open team Food for the Hungry Orgn., Romania, 2000, 2001; participant Relay for Life Am. Cancer Soc., Ky. and Ohio, 1999—2004; mem. global impact team Centenary United Meth. Ch., 2001—03; adv. bd. Sch. of Music Pianofest, Lexington, Ky., 1990—98. Nominee Outstanding Tchr. of Yr., Jessamine County Schs. Mem.: NEA, Nat. Mid. Sch. Assn., Jessamine County Edn. Assn., Ky. Edn. Assn. Republican. Avocations: reading, travel, needlecrafts, photography. Office: West Jessamine Mid Sch 1400 Wilmore Rd Nicholasville KY 40356-8932 Home: 109 Bass Pond Nicholasville KY 40356-1006 Office Phone: 859-885-2244.

ARMSTRONG, MARGARET, nursing administrator; b. Detroit, May 31, 1939; d. Walter and Adriana (Van Zorge) A. BSN, Wayne State U., Detroit, 1961; MSN, U. Calif., San Francisco, 1964; PhC, U. Wash., 1973. Instr. U. Iowa, Iowa City; asst. prof. nursing U. Rochester, NY; assoc. prof. nursing U. Utah, Salt Lake City; dep. dir. Navy Nurse Corps Res. Affairs USN, Washington; assoc. dir. nursing svc. Naval Med. Ctr., Portsmouth, Va.; dir., undergraduate program Sch. Nursing, Old Dominion U., Norfolk, Va., 1996—2001. Editor: McGraw Hill Handbook of Clin. Nursing; contbr. articles to profl. jours., chpts. to books; reviewer Science, 1981; co-editor Jour. Internat. Kirlian Rsch. Assn., 1976-80; editor Coll. Nursing/Integrated Academic Info. With USNR, 1961— Named Tchr. of the Yr., U. Iowa, 1968, Navy Leadership award, 1989; decorated Navy Commendation medal, Meritorious Svc. medal. Mem. ANA, Sigma Theta Tau. Home: 2308 Mossy Hollow Pl Virginia Beach VA 23454-2107 Personal E-mail: joelpeg@webtv.net.

ARMSTRONG, MARSHA SUSAN, elementary school educator; b. Jan. 13, 1950; d. Auda Junior Kirby and Phyllis Lou Nelson; m. Donald Lawrence Armstrong, Apr. 26, 1973; children: Shelia Renee, Tina R. Whalen, Eric; m. George David Day (div.); 1 child, Barbara Diane Day. AS, Conor State, Warner, Okla., 1977; BS, Univ. Tulsa, Tulsa, Okla., 1979; MEd, Northeastern St. Univ., Tahlequah, Okla., 1998. Elem. tchr. Alcott Elem., Tulsa, Okla., 1979—87, Wright Elem., Tulsa, Okla., 1987—92, 1996; reading tchr. 7th grade Haltom Mid. Sch., Haltom, Tex., 1992—94; gifted tchr. Burroughs Whitman, Tulsa, Okla., 1996—98; elem. tchr. Smith Elem., Owasso, Okla., 2000—01, Lindsey elem., Tulsa, Okla., 1998—2002; literacy coach Cooper Elem., Tulsa, Okla., 2005—. English tchr. Tulsa Cmty. Coll., Tulsa, Okla., 1995; profl. devel. chair Cooper Elem. Sch., Tulsa, Okla., 2001—05, reading suffiniecy chair, 2004—05. Mem.: Internat. Reading Assn., Tulsa Reading Coun., Okla. Edn. Assn., Tulsa Classroom Tchr. Assn., Alpha Delta Kappa, Kappa Kappa Iota (sec.). Republican. Bapt. Avocations: travel, writing, tennis, bowling. Fax: 918-746-9497. Personal E-mail: armstma@tulsa.schools.org.

ARMSTRONG, PATRICIA KAY, ecologist; b. Highland Park, Mich., Dec. 18, 1936; d. Elzine Munger and Vivian Beatrice (Thompson) Stoddard; m. Charles Willis Armstrong, Jan. 27, 1955; children: Jacqueline Joy Kline, Rebecca Raye Monroe. BA, North Ctrl. Coll., 1958; MS, U. Chgo., 1968. Biology tchr., sci. dept. head Washington Jr. HS, Naperville, Ill., 1960—70; asst. edn. prairie mgr. Morton Arboretum, Lisle, Ill., 1970—86; instr. field studies Coll. DuPage, Glen Ellyn, Ill., 1987—; ecological cons., owner Prairie Sun Cons., Naperville, 1985—. Founder Wild Ones Native Plants Nat. Soc., DuPage County, Ill., 1989—. Author (illustrator): Trilobites of the Chicago Region, 1962; author: (editor) (poetry) Summits of the Soul, 1978, Prairie Poetry, 1986, (botanical cookbook) Wild Plant Family Cookbook, 1997. Named Outstanding Part-Time Faculty, Coll. DuPage, 1998; recipient Landscape Design Naperville Prairie Yard, North Am. Prairie Conf., 1988, Willowbrook Wildlife Found., Ill., 2003, Ill. EPA, Chgo. Wilderness, 2003, Silver award, Ill. Landscape Contractors Assn., 2006. Mem.: Dupage County Environ. Comm., Ill. Native Plant Soc. (pres. 1981). Independent. Achievements include first woman instr. on Juneau ice field, Alaska 1968; climbed Mexico's 4 highest mountains solo, 1974. Avocations: mountain climbing, backpacking, camping, photography, writing. Home and Office: Prairie Sun Cons 612 Staunton Rd Naperville IL 60565 Personal E-mail: pat4nature@att.net.

ARMSTRONG, PEG JEAN, psychotherapist; b. Phila., Apr. 21, 1943; d. Robert Markle and Louise Oakley (Zulick) A. BA, Trinity U., 1964, MEd, 1968; cert. merit, U. Vienna, Austria, 1965. Lic. profl. counselor, Tex. Head resident counselor Trinity U., San Antonio, 1965-67, dir. residence, 1967-72, asst. dean students, 1972-83; pvt. practice in psychotherapy San Antonio, 1983—. Cons. specializing in grief and loss; facilitator Children's Transplant Assn., San Antonio, 1990—; mem. Adv. Coun. Legis. Affairs Tex. Senate; guest lectr. U. Tex. Health Sci. Ctr., San Antonio, 1991, Aerospace Med. Assn., Cin., 1991; tchr. San Antonio Coll., Incarnate Word Coll. Author: I-Openers, 1981; contbr. articles to profl. jours. Named Woman of Yr., Am. Bus. and PRofl. Women's Assn., 1972, Today's Woman, San Antonio Light Newspaper, 1983, 90. Mem. AACD, San Antonio Group for Psychoanalytic Studies, Internat. Acad. Med. Psychotherapy, Tex. Assn. for Counseling and Devel. Democrat. Avocation: travel.

ARMSTRONG, SANDRA ROGERS, secondary school educator, athletic trainer; b. San Diego, Sept. 21, 1971; d. Linda and Harry Heavner (Stepfather); m. Seth Armstrong, July 23, 2005. BA in Kinesiology and Phys. Edn., Calif. State U., Long Beach, 1997; MEd, Nat. U., Costa Mesa, Calif., 2001; postgrad., Cerritos Coll., Calif., 1996—98. Cert. tchr. Calif., 2001. Tchr., athletic trainer Cypress HS, Calif., 1998—. Mem.: Nat. Athletic Trainers Assn. Office: Cypress HS 9801 Valley View Cypress CA 90630 Office Phone: 714-220-4156.

ARMSTRONG, SHELLEY N., physical education educator, coach; b. Shawnee, Kans., Mar. 19, 1978; d. Steve and Jeanne Schneider; m. Bradley Scott Armstrong, Aug. 7, 2004. BS in Health and Exercise Sci., Centenary Coll. La., Shreveport, 2000, MA in Tchg., 2003; postgrad., Tex. Woman's U., Denton, 2004—. Cert. divsn. I coach NCAA, 2006, secondary health and phys. edn. tchr. La., 2003. Instr. health and exercise sci. Centenary Coll. La., 2004—, head coach men's and women's cross country, 2004—. Clin. rsch. assoc. Feist-Weiller Cancer Ctr. La. State U. Health Sciences Ctr., Shreveport, 2000—04. Dir. race Healthy Kids' Fun Run; mem. women's ministry team First United Meth. Ch., Shreveport. Grantee, Bd. Regents, 2006; Grad. Student scholar, Tex. Women's U., 2004—, Health Studies Departmental scholar, 2005—. Mem.: AAHPERD, Nat. Strength and Conditioning Assn., Am. Coaches Fedn., La. Assn. for Health, Phys. Edn., Recreation and Dance, Sunrise Triathlon Club, Red River Rd. Runners. Office: Centenary Coll La 2911 Centenary Blvd Shreveport LA 71134 Office Phone: 318-869-5277. Business E-Mail: sarmstro@centenary.edu.

ARMSTRONG SQUALL, PAULA ESTELLE, executive secretary; b. N.Y.C., Apr. 12, 1946; d. John Calvin and Irene (Shomo) A.; 1 child, Tonia Patricia Armstrong Fripp. Equivalency diploma, Malcolm King Coll., N.Y., 1988. Sec. Police Athletic League, N.Y.C., 1980-84, Harlem World Disco, N.Y.C., 1985-89, Nat. Black Theatre, N.Y.C., 1990-93, Manhattan Psychiat. Ctr., N.Y.C., 1994-95, Westside Bulletin Issues in Mental Health, 1996-97. Disc jockey (as Lady Pea). Avocations: art, poetry, ping pong/table tennis, music disc jockey, crochet.

ARNAUD, VELDA, finance educator; m. Carl Sakari; children: Charli Mae Sakari, Charles Max Sakari. BA, U. Oreg., Eugene, 1983, MA, 1991. Coord. delivery sys. U. Oreg., 1985—97; instr. Lane C.C., 1999—2002; assoc. program dir., gen. edn. Pioneer Pacific Coll., Springfield, 2002—04; instr. Lane C.C., 2004—. Leader Boy Scouts Am., Eugene/Springfield, 1998—2006; leader camp fire Wilani Coun., Eugene, 1995—97. Named Dist. Commr. Yr., Cascade Dist., Boy Scouts Am., 2006; recipient Dist. award Merit, 2002. Office: Lane Community College 4000 East 30th Avenue Eugene OR 97405 Office Phone: 541-463-5682. Office Fax: 541-463-3975. E-mail: arnaudv@lanecc.edu.

ARNDT, CARMEN GLORIA, secondary school educator; b. N.Y.C, Mar. 29, 1942; d. Charles Joseph and Pura Maria (Rios) A. BA in Spanish, Pace U., 1968; MA in Spanish, NYU, 1970; profl. diploma, Fordham U., 1975. Lic. asst. prin., prin. Simultaneous translator UN, N.Y.C., 1968; instr. Marymount Manhattan Coll., N.Y.C., 1968-70; tchr. Bd. Edn., N.Y.C., 1970—, dir. Bilingual Comprehensive H.S., 1975-78; chmn. sch. based mgmt./shared decision com. L.D. Brandeis H.S., N.Y.C., 1990—, asst. prin., 1984, interim acting asst. prin., 1994, coord. coop. tech./trades, 1993-96, ESL and fgn. lang. dept., 1994-96, bilingual grade advisor, 1998; ret. Chmn. restructuring com. Bd. Edn., N.Y.C., 1990—; bd. dirs. 1st N.Y.C. Comprehensive Bilingual Program, 1975-79; mem. adj. faculty Fordham U., N.Y.C., 1972-75, CCNY, 1985—; coord. ESL and fgn. lang. dept. Author: Conversational Spanish, 1975, Native Language Art K-8, 1975; contbr. articles to profl. jours.; featured in Dominicanos en New York (book). Electioneer, Dem. Party, N.Y.C. Mem. P.R. Edn. Assn. (chairperson-mentor 1988, del.), United Fedn. Tchr. (del. 1985-88), State Assn. Bilingual Edn., Am. Assn. Tchrs. of Spanish and Portuguese, Assn. Suprs. Curriculum Devel., Phi Beta Kappa. Roman Catholic. Avocations: crochet, reading, walking, writing. Home: Apt 3G 50 W 97th St New York NY 10025-6005

ARNDT, CYNTHIA, educational administrator; b. N.Y.C., Sept. 27, 1947; d. Charles Joseph and Pura Maria (Rios) A BA, Hunter Coll., 1971, MA, 1975; profl. diploma adminstrn., Fordham U., 1981. Adminstrv. asst. to asst. registrar Hunter Coll., N.Y.C., 1968—69; cataloguer asst. Finch Coll. Libr., N.Y.C., 1974; tchr. N.Y. Bd. Edn., N.Y.C., 1974—82; bilingual coord. Jr. H.S. 143, 1982—89; asst. prin. IS 164, 1989—93; project dir. Elem. Schs. in Restructuring Bilingual Sci., 1993—96; supr.-in-charge IS 136, 1996—97; asst. prin. Mott Hall, 1997—2004, prin., 2005—. Reviewer Booklist, 1981 Mem. ASCD, Am. Artist Soc., Hispanic Am. Hist. Soc., Nat. Coun. Social Studies, N.Y. State Assn. Curriculum Devel., Puerto Rican Edn. Assn., N.Y. State Assn. Bilingual Edn., Kappa Delta Pi, Phi Delta Kappa Democrat. Roman Catholic. Home: 110 W 90th St Apt 4C New York NY 10024-1209 Business E-Mail: carndt@nycboe.net.

ARNDT, DIANNE JOY, artist, photographer; b. Springfield, Mass., Dec. 20, 1939; d. Samuel Vincent and Carrie Lillian Annino; m. Joseph Vincent Bower, June 16, 1979 (dec.); 1 child by previous marriage, Christabelle Nita Arndt. Student, Art Students League, 1965-71; BFA with honors in Painting, Pratt Inst., 1974; postgrad., Columbia U., 1979-86; MFA, Hunter Coll., 1981. Photojournalist. Photo cons. to mags. and bus., N.Y.C., 1978—; artist, filmmaker, 1962—. One-woman shows include Modernage, N.Y., 1992, 96, 99-2000, 2002, others; group shows include Islip Art Mus., L.I., N.Y., 1999, White Walls Conceptual Art Jour., Chgo., 2000, numerous others; exhbns. include Am. Cultural Ctr., U.S., New Delhi and Bombay, 1987, Bathurst Arms Installation, Eng., 1987, Camden Arts, London, 1987, Nat. Inst. Archtl. Edn., 1988, Phillip Morris Traveling Photo Exhibit, 1988, Centennial Libr. Gallery, Isca Graphics, Edmonton, Alta., Can., 1988, Nat. Inst. Archtl. Edn., 1988, N.Y. Sci. & Tech. Gallery, N.Y., USSR, 1989, Mercer Gallery, 1989, Circolo Pickwick, Alessandria, Italy, 1989, Balt. Mus. Industry, 1992, Aaron Davis Hall, 1992, N.Y. City Coll., Alijira Gallery, Newark, 1994, UN, 1994, Phila. Art Alliance, Phila., 1995, Columbia U., 1995, Severoceske Mus., Liberec, Bohemia, 1996, Naproskovo Mus., Prague, 1996, Modern Age, N.Y.C., 1996, Lever House, N.Y.C., 1996, St. Marks/Bowery, N.Y.C., 1997, Eighth Floor Gallery, N.Y.C., 1997, Velan Gallery, Torino, Italy, 1998, Islip Art Mus., 1998, 99, Bound for Glory, N.Y., 1999-2000, In Frame, Chgo., 2000, St. Francis Coll., 2001; represented in permanent collections Archives Can. Postal Mus., Ottawa, Jean Brown Archives, Mass., Franklin Furnace, N.Y., Nat. Inst. Design and Lalit Kala Akademi, Ne WDelhi, Printed Masser, N.Y., Tate Gallery, London; films include Mullenium, N.Y., 1985, A.I.R., N.Y., 1978, Women's Interart Ctr., N.Y., 1976, Artists Space, N.Y., 1975. Mem. Am. Soc. Media Photographers, Am. Soc. Picture Profls., Artists Talk on Art (bd. dirs.), Profl. Women Photographers, Working Press Nation.

ARNDT, JANET S., former state legislator, educator; b. Providence, May 23, 1947; m. Kenneth G. Arndt; 4 children. AB, Gordon Coll., 1968; MEd, Boston U., 1970; student, U. Mass., 1998—, CAGS, 2002; EdD, U. Mass. Amherst, 2003; cert., Advanced Grad. Study. Specialist, counselor Early Childhood, 1987—2005; N.H. state rep. Dist. 27, Rockingham, 1992—2002; mem. children, youth and juvenile justice com. N.H. Ho. of Reps., mem. constn. and statutory rev. com., chmn. election law com., 1997—2002; prin. Perley Sch., Georgetown, Mass., 2005—. Asst. prof. Gordon Coll., 1995, N.H. Tech. Coll., 1997—2001, adj. prof., 2001—, chair early childhood, elem. and spl. edn. dept., 2002—. Mem. Friends of the Libr. of Windham, chmn., 1991-92; active Girl Scouts Am., publicity chairperson; scholarship chmn. Nat. Order of Women Legislators; exec. bd. Rockingham County; events chairperson Nesmith Libr.; mem. edn. task force ALEC, mem. ch. early childhood task force; mem. nat. coun. of state legislators Coun. of State Govt.; chair Rockingham County Register of Deeds, 1996-02; mem. early childhood mental health coun., 2003-; mem. bd. N.H. Kids Coll., 2003. Recipient M. Carter award for Outstanding Libr. Svc., 1995; named Leader of Yr. Windham Girl Scouts, 1995. Mem. N.H. Order Women Legislators, Gordon Coll. Alumni Coun. Address: 8 Crestwood Rd Windham NH 03087-1429 Office Phone: 978-867-4814. Business E-Mail: jarndt@gordon.edu.

ARNDT, LAURA BODEEN, mathematics educator; b. Memphis, Tenn., Feb. 13, 1952; d. Walter Guy and Laura Deming Lyons; m. Michael Charles Bodeen (div.); children: Matthew Wells Bodeen, Jeffrey Guy Bodeen, William Joseph Bodeen; m. J.T. Arndt, May 31, 2003. BS magna cum laude, Christian Bros. Univ., Memphis, Tenn., 1993. Cert. tchr. 7-12 math., computer sci. Tchr. Fayette County Sch., Somerville, Tenn., 1993—2005. Memphis Symphony advocate Memphis Symphony League, Memphis, 2003—; del. People to People Del. to China, 1999, 2006. Mem.: Nat. Edn. Assn., Tenn. Edn. Assn., Alpha Chi. Avocation: video games.

ARNETT, RITA ANN, business executive; b. Des Moines, Aug. 8, 1952; d. Roy Gardner and Rita Elizabeth A.; m. John Nick Allar, Aug. 5, 1990; children: Ebeneezer Shay, Hanii Shay, Eli Allar. BA cum laude, Ft. Lewis Coll., 1982. Editor Dolores Archael. Project, Colo., 1982-86; dir. Sunrise Youth Shelter Ute Mt. Ute Tribe, Towaoc, Colo., 1986-92; dep. dir. planning, devel. and compliance Aliviane NO-AD, Inc., El Paso, Tex., 1993—2002; owner Echelon Group, Inc., El Paso, Tex., 2001—; COO Echelon Group, El Paso, Tex., 2002—. Bd. dir. Rio Bravo Interfaith Pastoral Coun., El Paso; cons. St. Elizabeth's Hosp., Washington, 1999, Life Mgmt. Ctr., El Paso, 1996, West Care Found., Las Vegas, Nev., 2002-, Heritage Ranch Inst., Deming, N.Mex., 2002-, Quileute Tribe, LaPush Wa., 2005-, Verde Realty, El Paso, 2005-, Insight Mus. El Paso, 2006-. Grantee Ctr. for Substance Abuse Treatment, 1993, 96, 99, 2000-06, Ctrs. for Disease Control and Prevention, 1997-2000, Ctr. for Substance Abuse Prevention, 1999-2002, Health and Human Svc., 1987-93, 92-95, 94-97, Tex. Commn. Alcohol and Drug Abuse, 1993—, Tex. Dept. Health, 1993—, Tex. Dept. Protective and Regulatory Svcs., 1997—, Tex. Dept. Criminal Justice, 1995—, Tex. Workforce Commn., 2001-02, DeKalb County, Ga., 2003; U.S. fish & Wildlife Svc., 2003, Bur. Indian Affairs, 1991—, Gates Found., 1990, Colo. VOCA Bd., 1987, 88-93, 91-93, Colo. Divsn. Youth Svc., Dekalb County, Ga., U.S. Environ. Protection Agy., 2003-, Adminstrn. Native Am., 2005-, Calif. Dept. Corrections, 2005-. Democrat. Roman Catholic. Avocations: weight training, bicycling, gardening. Home: 4530 River Walk Las Cruces NM 88007

ARNEZ, NANCY LEVI, educational leadership educator; b. Balt., July 6, 1928; d. Milton Emerson Levi and Ida Barbour (Rusk) Levi Washington. AB, Morgan State Coll., 1949; MA, Columbia U., 1954, EdD, 1958. Tchr. English Druid Jr. H.S., Balt., 1949-52, Houston Jr. H.S., Balt., 1952-57; asst. to admissions officer Tchrs. Coll., Columbia U., N.Y.C., 1957-58, grad. asst., 1957; head dept. English Cherry Hill Jr. H.S., Balt., 1958-62; assoc. prof., dir. student teaching Morgan State Coll., Balt., 1962-66; co-founder Cultural Linguistic Early Childhood Follow Through Approach; prof., asst. dir./dir. Ctr. for Inner City Studies, Northeastern Ill. U., Chgo., 1966-74; prof., assoc. dean, acting dean Sch. Edn. Howard U., Washington, 1974-80, chmn. dept. ednl. leadership, 1980-86, prof., 1980-93, prof. emeriti, 1993—. Author: Partners in Urban Education: Teaching the Inner City Child, 1973, The Struggle for Equality of Educational Opportunity, 1975, Administrative Issues in the Implementation of the Response to Educational Needs Project, 1979, The Besieged School Superintendent, 1981, School Based Administrator Training, 1982; mem. editorial bd.: Phi Delta Kappan, 1975-80, Jour. Negro Edn., 1975-80, Black Child Jour., 1980—; contbr. articles to profl. jours. State treas., mem. exec. com. Md. State council UN Children's Fund, 1965; founder Operation Champ, Balt, 1965; mem. adv. bd. Better Boys Found., Chgo., 1966-74, Mus. African-Am. History, 1969; state chmn. Right to Read, Washington, 1973-80; treas. Com. to Elect Douglass Moore to City Council, 1982. Grantee, African Am. Inst., 1974, Spencer Found., 1976, AAUW, 1977. Mem. Am. Assn. Sch. Adminstrs. (editorial bd. 1982), Assn. for Study of Afro-Am. Life and History, African Am. Heritage Assn., African Am. Writers Guild, Nat. Alliance Black Sch. Educators, D.C. Alliance Black Sch. Educators (pres. 1986-88), Phi Delta Kappa. Presbyterian. Home: 3122 Cherry Rd NE Washington DC 20018-1612

ARNOLD, ALANNA S. WELLING, lawyer; b. Canton, Ohio, Jan. 13, 1951; d. Coen Edward and Clara M. Welling; m. Jack Mitchell Arnold, Aug. 28, 1971; children: Cassandra L., Shanna R. BA in Sociology magna cum laude, Kent State U., 1980, MA in Applied Sociology, 1981; JD, Loyola Law Sch., New Orleans, 1991. Instr. Phillips Jr. Coll., New Orleans, 1988-90; jud. extern U.S. Ct. (ea. dist.) La., New Orleans, 1990-91; ptnr. Milling, Benson, Woodward LLP, New Orleans, 1991—2000, John Brooks Cameron & Assocs., 2000—03; rsch. fellow Case Western Res. U., 2003—04. Pvt. practice, 2000—; legal aid atty. Cmty. Legal Aid, 2004—05; feature legal writer Take Charge! mag., 2005—. Contbr. articles to profl. jours.; mem. Loyola Law rev., 1989-91. Bd. dirs. Medina County YWCA, 2000-03, v.p., 2003; vol. Medina Rape Crisis Ctr., 2004, Medina Battered Women's Shelter, 2006, Guardianship Program;, 2005- coord. elect mediator's to pub. office project Cleve. Mediation Ctr., 2005—. Scholarship Gordon, Arrata McCullom, 1989-90, Outstanding scholarship Kent State U., 1980. Mem. Ohio Bar Assn., Medina County Bar Assn., Bar Applicants Admission, Com. Svc Commn. (chmn.), Zonta Club ABC (bd. dirs. 2005—, del. internat. conv. 2006, v.p., 2006—), Medina Women in Bus. (bd. dirs. 2004-, program chmn. 2003—). Democrat. Avocations: painting (watercolor), reading, movies, theater, travel. Office Phone: 330-315-5355. Business E-Mail: aarnoldesq@yahoo.com.

ARNOLD, ANN, artist, illustrator; b. Newcastle-upon-Tyne, 1936; d. Edmund Tefler; m. Graham Arnold, July 29, 1961. Illustrator (books) Fanny at Chez Panisse, 1992, Stop Smelling My Rose, 1997, The Children's Kitchen Garden: A Book of Gardening, Cooking, and Learning, 1997, illustrator, co-author Firehouse Max, 1997; co-author (with John Clare, Brian Patten and Eric Robinson): (books) Clare's Countryside, 1981; author: Gamblers & Gangsters: Fort Worth's Jacksboro Highway in the 1940s and 1950s, 1998, History of the Fort Worth Legal Community, 2000, History of the Fort Worth Medical Community, 2002, The Adventurous Chef: Alexis Soyer, 2002; Represented in permanent collections North Point Gallery, San Francisco, numerous exhibitions in London and the U.S. Mem.: Assn. Art Therapists (founding mem.). Address: c/o Pippin Properties Inc 155 E 38th St Ste 2H New York NY 10016

ARNOLD, BARBARA EILEEN, state legislator; b. North Adams, Mass., Aug. 3, 1924; d. Lester Flemming and Sarah (Van Hagen) Smith; m. William E. Arnold, Dec. 5, 1946; children: Wynn, Jeffrey, Gayle, Christopher. BA in Psychology, U. Mass.; postgrad., Keene State Coll. Spl. edn. tchr. Easter Seal Rehab. Ctr., Manchester, NH, 1967-74; state legislator NH, 1982-95; Rep. floor leader Ho. of Reps., 1989-95; mem. N.H. Coun. Vocat. Tech. Edn., 1986-95, State and Fed. Rels. Commn.; chmn. Manchester Rep. Del.; vice chmn. Ways and Means, 1992—95. Sec. N.E. State Coun. Vocat. Edn.; adv. bd. edn. N.H. Dept. Corrections; mem. adv. coun. adult rehab. Easter Seal Soc., NH, 1990—; state adv. com. Vocat. Child Care Programs, 1993—95; mem. com. for children, families, social svcs. Nat. Conf. of State Legislatures; bd. registration City of Manchester, 1999—; Manchester chmn. Dole for Pres. campaign, 1995, Gov. Judd Gregg for U.S. Senate, 1992, 2004; chair Manchester Rep. Com., 1993—95, George W. Bush for Pres., Manchester, 1999, 2004; chmn. Manchester Rep. Com., 1992—95; chmn. Manchester Senator John E. Sununu Campaign, 2002; past mem. vestry, registered lay leader, mem. diocesan commn., del. gen. conv. Episcopal Ch.; bd. dirs. ARC, 1975—96, chmn. bd. dirs., 1977—80. Mem. Nat. Order Women Legislators, Nat. Fedn. Rep. Women, Greater Manchester Federated Rep. Women's Club, N.H. Kappa Kappa Gamma Alumni Assn. (pres. 1990-91). Address: 374 Pickering St Manchester NH 03104-2744

ARNOLD, BEVERLY SUE, secondary school educator; b. Portland, Ind., July 1, 1949; d. Thomas Cartwright and Martha Helen (O'Brien) Brown; m. Steven Beard Arnold, Nov. 28, 1970; children: Eric Jason, Andrea Nichole, Abigail Leigh, Derek Ryan. BS, Ball State U., 1970, MA, 1974. Cert. tchr., Inc.; lic. secondary adminstr., 1995. Tchr., coach South Adams Schs., Berne, Ind., 1970-75, Jay Sch. Corp., Portland, Ind., 1975—. Coach Portland Summer Swim Team, 1965—; official Ind. High Sch. Athletic Assn., Indpls., 1973—. Bd. dirs. Jay County Girls Club, 1986-93, treas., 1986-89, v.p., 1992-93; elder 1st Presbyn. Ch., Portland, 1990-92, treas. women's assn., 1998—; escort runner Olympic Torch Relay, 1996. Mem. ASCD, AAUW, NEA, Ind. State Tchrs. Assn. Ctrl. Ofcls. Assn., Ind. Coaches of Girls Sports Assn. (gymnastics com. 1983-91, dist. Gymnastics Coach of Yr. 1985, 87, 88, 89, bd. dirs. 1991-, treas. 1993-97, State Swim Coach of Yr. 1990, 20-Yr. Coaching award 1993, Carmen Moreschini scholarship 1994, Swimming Sectional Coach of Yr. 1983, 85, 90, 91, Swimming Dist. Coach of Yr. 1999, Acad. All State chmn. 1997—, swimming com. 1996—, chmn. swimming com. 1998—, Ind. Swimming and Diving Hall of Fame Com., 30 Yr. Coaching award, 2003), Nat. HS Gymnastics Coaches Assn., Nat. Interscholastic Swim Coaches Assn., Am. Swim Coaches Assn., Ind. HS Swim Coaches Assn. (2nd runner-up Swimming State Coach of Yr. 1990), Jay Classroom Tchrs. Assn., Phi Delta Kappa. Republican. Avocations: swimming, dance theater, reading, water skiing, scuba diving. Office: Jay County High Sch 2072 W Hwy 67 Portland IN 47371-9802 Home: PO Box 808 Portland IN 47371-0808 Office Phone: 260-726-9306.

ARNOLD, CATHERINE ANDERSON, communications executive; d. William Columbus and Lillian Arnold; m. Joe Loyd Anderson, Aug. 30, 1997. BA, Morehead State U., 1969. Tchr., 1969—76; dir. Denver Classroom Tchrs. Assn., 1978—80; comm. and pub. affairs exec. Fla. Tchg. Profession/NEA, Tallahassee, 1978—80; prin. Comm. Art Specialists and Assoc., Tallahassee, 1984—89; pub. info. dir. Leon County Bd. County Commrs., Tallahassee, 1988—97; dir. comm. Fla. Dept. Environ. Protection, Tallahassee, 1997—2000, Fla. Dept. Juvenile Justice, Tallahassee, 2000—04; comm. and pub. affairs cons. C.A. Arnold Cons., Monticello, Fla., 2004—. Charter mem., chair Keep Tallahassee Leon County Beautiful, Inc., 1994—95; commn. com. United Way Big Bend, Tallahassee, 1995—96; bd. dirs. Fla. Pub. Rels. Assn., Tallahassee, 1980—86, Fla. Govt. Communicators Assn., Tallahassee, 1988—97; pres. Women In Comm., Inc., Tallahassee, 1992—93. Mem.: Altrusa, Rotary. Avocation: breeding and training horses.

ARNOLD, CHARLOTTE S., criminal justice agency executive, activist; b. Port Jervis, N.Y., Sept. 18, 1929; d. Abraham and Jennie Skolnick; m. John Arnold (dec.); children: Seth Ginsburg, Daniel Ginsburg, Deborah Marx. BA, SUNY, Albany, 1951. Vol., pres. Women in the Urban Crisis, Pitts., 1968—73; exec. dir. The Program for Female Offenders, Pitts., 1974—98. Mem. Pa. Gov.s Justice Commn., Harrisburg, 1975—90; mem. justice rev. bd. Pa. Bar Assn., Harrisburg, 1991—95. Author: (book) Get Out of Jail Free, 2005, Over These Prison Walls, 2006. Mem. bd. Urban League, Pitts., Better Bus. Bur.; mem. NAACP, NOW; bd. mem., sec. Palm Beach County Jail Bd., 2006—; mem. B'nai B'rith Women. Named Charlotte Arnold Day, Pitts. City Coun., 1997, Disting. Daughter of Pa., 1997; recipient Martin Luther King award, Hand-in-Hand, Inc., 1974, Person of Yr. award, Thomas Merton Ctr., 1974, Leadership award in Cmty. Svc., YWCA, Pitts., 1984, Human Svcs. award, Kaufmann's Program for Women in Bus., 1986, Liberty Bell award, Allegheny County Bar Assn., 1994. Achievements include first woman board member of the Better Business Bureau; featured in Savvy magazine article, 1985; CBS Morning News, 1985. Avocations: writing, reading, golf.

ARNOLD, DEBORAH J., lawyer; BA magna cum laude, U. Rochester, 1985; JD cum laude, George Washington U., 1988. Bar: DC, NJ. Of counsel Real Estate Dept. Venable LLP, Washington, DC. Office: Venable LLP 575 7th St NW Washington DC 20004 Office Phone: 202-344-4631. Office Fax: 202-344-8300. E-mail: djarnold@venable.com.

ARNOLD, FRANCES HAMILTON, chemistry educator; b. Pitts., July 25, 1956; d. William Howard and Josephine Inman (Routheau) A.; m. Andrew Evan Lange, Mar. 4, 1994; children: James Howard, William Andrew. BS magna cum laude, Princeton U., 1979; PhD in Chem. Engring., U. Calif., Berkeley, 1985. Asst. chem. engring. Calif. Inst. Tech., Pasadena, 1987-92, assoc. prof., 1992—, prof. chem. engring & biochemistry, Dick and Barbara Dickinson prof. chemical engring. and biochemistry. Vis. assoc. chemistry U. Calif., Berkeley, 1986—87; ann. lectr. Advanced Ctr. Biochemical Engring. Univ. Coll., London, 1994; William Rauscher Lectr. in Chemistry Rensselaer Polytechnic Inst., 1996; Purves Lectr. in Chemistry McGill U., 1998; Lindsay Disting. Lectr. Tex. A&M, 2003; Merck-Frosst Invited Lectr. Biochemistry U. Alberta, 2003; Sir Robert Price Lectr. CSIRO, Melbourne, 2003. Contbr. articles to profl. jours. Recipient Office Naval Rsch. Young Investigator award, 1988, NSF Presdl. Young Investigator award, 1989, Van Ness Award, Rensselaer Polytechnic Inst., 1994, Profl. Progress Award, AIChE, 2000; grantee David and Lucile Packard fellow, 1989. Mem.: NAE, AAAS (Sci. Innovation Topical Lectr.), Inst. Medicine, Santa Fe Inst. (Sci. Bd.), Am. Inst. Medical and Biological Engring., Am. Soc. Microbiology, Protein Soc., Am. Inst. Chem. Engrs., Am. Chem. Soc. (David Perlman Lectr. Award, ACS Biochemical Tech. 2003, Francis P. Garvan-John M. Olin medal 2005, Carothers award, ACS Del. divsn. 2003), Tau Beta Pi, Phi Beta Kappa. Office: Calif Inst Tech Div of Chem & Chem Engring 228B Spalding Pasadena CA 91125-0001 Office Phone: 626-395-4162. Office Fax: 626-568-8743. E-mail: frances@cheme.caltech.edu.*

ARNOLD, JANET NINA, health facility administrator, consultant; b. Poughkeepsie, N.Y., Apr. 23, 1933; d. Paul Dudley and Pauline Katherine (Board) Bartram; m. Robert William Arnold, Dec. 19, 1954; children: Paul Dudley, Janet Elizabeth. AB cum laude, Vassar Coll., 1955; postgrad. Sch. Med. Tech., Albany Med. Coll., 1955—56; MS Microbiology cum laude, Vassar Coll., 1963; MHSM, Webster Coll., 1981. Rsch. asst., med. technologist H. Aird Boswell, M.D., Troy, NY, 1956—59; tchg. supr., adminstrv. cons. Vassar Bros. Hosp., Poughkeepsie, 1959—69; asst. adminstr., lab. mgr. Boulder Meml. Hosp., Colo., 1975—80; cons. hosp. planning Mercy Med. Ctr., Denver, 1981—82; clin. lab. dir./adminstr. Humana, Denver, 1982—85, dir. MRI, 1985—. Cons. health care mgmt. Humana, Inc., 1982-96, Columbia/HCA Health Sys., 1992-96; pres. Arnold and Assocs., 1988—; acad./adminstrv. cons. U. Guam, Vassar Coll., Boulder Cmty. Hosp., Humana Int., 1990-97; adj. faculty Vassar Coll., adv. to med. lab., lectr. med. mycology, 1961-66, tchg. fellow 1961-63, chmn. unrestricted fund raising, 1989-96, co-chair major gifts, 2000-05; sec., bd. dirs. Sanitas Fed. Credit Union, 1977-78, pres., 1979-82 Assoc. editor Am. Jour. Med. Tech., 1980-88; contbr. articles to profl. jours Contbr. NMC, 1988-92 NSF rsch. fellow, 1960-62 Mem. Am. Acad. Microbiology, Soc. for Gen. Microbiology, Am. Soc. Med. Technologists, Colo. Pub. Health Assn., Soc. Women Environ. Profls., Med. Mycological Soc. Ams Republican. Episcopalian. Office Phone: 717-464-8536. E-mail: r-j-arnold-assoc@att.net.

ARNOLD, JEANNE FESSENDEN, retired physician; b. Bridgeport, Conn., Oct. 24, 1935; d. Alfred and Huldah F. (Vose) Arnold; m. Peter Faulkner Jeffries, Dec. 19, 1959; children: Walter, Joy, Jennifer, John, Charles, Robert, Arthur. AB, Colby Coll., Waterville, Maine, 1957; MD, Boston U. Med. Sch., 1961. Pvt. practice, Peterborough, NH, 1966—79; assoc. dir. Augusta Hosp., Maine, 1979—82, St. Elizabeth Hosp., Utica, NY, 1982—90; dir. Mercy Hosp., Jonesville, Wis., 1990—91, Malden Hosp., Mass., 1992—95. Mailing: PO Box 933 Walpole NH 03608

ARNOLD, KAREN DOROTHY, education educator; b. Long Branch, N.J., Sept. 19, 1957; m. Jeffrey R. Arnold, July 29, 1979. BA, Oberlin Coll., 1979; BMus, Oberlin Conservatory, 1979; MA, U. Ill., 1984, PhD, 1987. Assoc. dean of students Reed Coll., Portland, Oreg., 1987-88, acting v.p. student svcs., 1989-90; assoc. prof., dir. higher edn. program Boston Coll., Chestnut Hill, Mass., 1990—. Vis. scholar Radcliffe Murray Rsch. Ctr., Radcliffe Coll., Cambridge, Mass., 1994-95, Oxford Ctr. Higher Edn. Policy Studies, 2005. Author: Lives of Promise: What Becomes of High School Valedictorians, 1995; co-editor: Beyond Terman: Contemporary Longitudinal Studies of Giftedness and Talent, 1994; assoc. editor Rev. Higher Edn., 1996—; contbr. articles to profl. jours. John D. Corbally fellow U. Ill., 1986; Dept. of Edn. grantee North Ctrl. Regional Ednl. Lab., 1993-95, Spencer Found., Mellon Found., Hewlett Found., 2001-05. Mem. Nat. Assn. Student Pers. Adminstrs. (faculty liaison region I 1995—), Assn. Study of Higher Edn. Avocations: playing piano, hiking.

ARNOLD, KATHLEEN SPELTS, academic administrator; b. Miami, Fla., Oct. 25, 1941; d. John Keith and Mary Fay (Webber) Shay; m. Harold G. Arnold, Jan. 31, 1982; children from previous marriage: Melinda Kathleen Spelts, Meghan Shay Spelts, Richard John Spelts. BA, U. Colo., 1963. Tchr. Bear Creek HS, Jefferson County, Colo., 1963—64, 1965—67; asst. prodn. control mgr. Fordwerke, Cologne, Germany, 1964—65; state rep. Colo. Gen. Assembly, Denver, 1978—83; state senator Colo. State Senate, 1983—86, chmn. judiciary com., 1980—83, mem. state affairs com., 1985—86; del. Nat. Conf. State Legislators, 1980—83; candidate for Lt. Gov., 1986; regent U. Colo., 1989—, chmn. bd. regents. Chmn. Chatfield YMCA Fund Dr.; mem. curriculum coun. Jefferson County Schs.; sec. Littleton Fire Bd.; trustee Ind. Inst.; exec. dir. Colo. Reps.; chmn. Colo. Coun. Chs.; bd. dirs. U. Colo. Alumni Bd., Denver, 1987—90, United Bank, 1988—92, Child Health Policy Inst., Denver, 1992—. Mem.: S. Metro C. of C. Presbyterian. Home: 0303 Park Meadows Ln Carbondale CO 81623 also: 303 Park Meadows Ln Carbondale CO 81623-9130

ARNOLD, KATHRYN, artist, educator; b. Kansas City, Mo. Student, Kansas City Art Inst.; BFA in Painting and Drawing, U. Kans., 1991, MFA in Art, 1993. Represented by Duane Reed Gallery, St. Louis; Leedy-Voulkos Gallery, Kansas City; Ellen Paustcher Fine Art Cons., Chgo.; mem. faculty West Valley Coll., Saratoga, Calif., 2005—. Tchg. asst. U. Kans., Lawrence, 1993; adj. instr. Johnson County C.C., Overland Park, Kans., 1997; adj. asst. prof. Washburn U., Topeka, 1994-97; mem. faculty Kansas City Art Inst., 1995-97; resident Contemporary Artists Ctr., North Adams, Mass., 1995; lectr., panel participation David Levik Gallery, 1995, U. Minn., 1996, St. Cloud State (Minn.) U., 1996, U. Wis., Madison, 1997. One-woman shows include U. Kans., 1993, 94, Nat. Computer Tng. Ctr., Kansas City, 1994, Park Coll., Parkville, Mo., 1994, David Levik Gallery, Wesport, Kans., 194, 95, B.Z. Wagman Art Inc., St. Louis, 1994, Rockhurst Coll., 1996, U. Minn., 1996, Las Vegas Cultural Ctr., 1996, 97, Duane Reed Gallery, 1997, 90, Jan Casey & Assocs., San Francisco, 2005, 2006; group shows include Wichita Kans. Art Ctr., 1993, State of the Art Gallery, Ithaca, N.Y., 1993, David Levik Gallery, 1993-94, 95, Kansas City Artist's Coalition, 1994, 95, George Walter Vincent Smith Art Mus., Springfield, Mass., 1994, An Art Place, Inc., Chgo., 1994, 95, The Gallery Ctr., Indpls., 1994, New Harmony Gallery of Contemporary Art, 1994, Washburn U., Topeka, 1994, Contemporary Artists Ctr., North Adams, Mass., 1995, Tustin Renaissance, Calif., 1995, Roger Guffey Gallery, Kansa City, 1995, Art Inst. Chgo., 1996, Riverside Arts Ctr., Chgo., 1996, Korean Cultural Ctr., L.A., 1996, Johnson County C.C. Gallery of Art, 1996, Mulvane Art Mus., Topeka, 1996, 97, Ohio State U., 1996, Morgan Gallery, Kansas City, 1997, Leedy-Voulkos Gallery, Kansas City, 1997, Pelham (N.Y.) Art Ctr., 1997, U. Hawaii, Hilo, 1997, Lakelake Coll., Sheboygan, Wis., 1999, West Valley Coll., Scranton, Calif., 2005, Urbis Artium, San Francisco, 2006; permanent collections include Thompson & Mitchell Attys. at Law, Corp. Skills Internat., Sch. Fine Arts U. Kans., Bryan Cave Law Firm, Am. Kenpo Karate Acad. Kans., Topeka Pub. Libr., Ramada, McDonald-Douglas Corp., United Mo. Bank, U. Minn., Am. Legacy. Vol. Accessible Arts, Kansas City, 1997. NEA fellow, 1996; Kans. Arts Commn. Profl. Devel. grantee, 1993-94; recipient Recognition of Merit award Contemporary Artists Ctr., 1995, award Mass. Art League, 1994. Mem. Chgo. Artists Coaltion, Kansas City Artists Coalition, Coll. Art Assn., Phi Kappa Phi. Office: 301 8th St 245 San Francisco CA 94103 Office Phone: 415-863-8531.

ARNOLD, LAUREN, art historian, writer; b. Fox Lake, Ill., Dec. 27, 1949; d. Charles Harvey and Patricia Adelaide (Streeter) Arnold; m. Kenneth Pokorny (div. 1985); 1 child, Rachel Pokorny; m. Reay Stewart Dick, 1989; children: Ian Dick, Connor Dick, Caillie Dick. BA in History, U. Mich., Ann Arbor, 1979, MA in History of Art, 1981; cert. of mus. practice, U. Mich., 1983. Asst. to dir. U. Mich. Mus. Art, Ann Arbor, 1982—86; rsch. assoc. Ricci Inst. for Chinese-Western Cultural History/U. San Francisco, 1997—. Adj. lectr. U. San Francisco, 2002; presener, lectr. in field. Author: Princely Gifts and Papal Treasures: The Franciscan Mission to China and Its Influence on the Art of the West 1230-1350, 1999. Mem.: Coll. Art Assn. Episcopalian. Achievements include discovery of The Heavenly Horse painting, lost for 200 years in Forbidden City Beijing. Office: Ricci Inst for Chinese-Western Cultural History Univ San Francisco 2130 Fulton San Francisco CA 94117 Personal E-mail: laurenarnold@cs.com.

ARNOLD, LESLIE ANN, special education educator; b. St. Louis, Mo., Oct. 20, 1953; d. Eugene L. and Louisa French (Gale) A. BS, Central State U., 1975, MEd, 1981. Cert. spl. edn., learning disabilities, mental retardation tchr., Kans. Tchr. level III educable mentally handicapped Unified Sch. Dist. 345, Topeka, 1976-82; tchr., specialist mentally retarded and occupationally handicapped Sch. Dist. 619, Wellington, Kans., 1982-87; coord. vocat. options level IV educable mentally handicapped Wellington Unified Sch. Dist. 353, Wellington, Kans., 1987—; area adminstr. Sangamon Area Spl. Edn. Dist., Springfield, Ill., 2002—. Coord. spl. edn. Wellington Unified Sch. Dist., 1995-98, dir. spl. edn., 1998, dir. spl. svcs., Poplar Bluff, Mo., 2000-02; cons. in field. Grantee Vocat. Rehab., 1992-95, Kansas Transition Network, 1994-98, Charter Sch., 1997; Access to Gen. Edn. grantee Positive Behavioral Intervention Strategies,(PBIS), 2001, Sangamon Area Spl. Edn. Dist. (SASED), 2002-04.

ARNOLD, MARGARET MORELOCK, music educator, soprano; b. Craig AFB, Ala., May 12, 1959; d. William Daniel Morelock and Margaret Haynie Morelock Stapleton; m. Barry Raynor Arnold, Aug. 15, 1984. B of Music Edn., U. Montevallo, 1981; MEd in Music, U. South Ala., 1996. Cert. tchr. Fla., Ala. Tchr. music Staley Mid. Sch., Americus, Ga., 1981-82, Eastview Elem. Sch., Americus, Ga., 1982-84; tchr. music/mass prep. St. Thomas More Schs., Pensacola, Fla., 1984-85; tchr. music W.H. Rhodes Elem., Milton, Fla., 1985—; realtor Century 21, Richardson, Fla. Pvt. voice instr., Americus, 1981-84, Milton, 1989—; guest condr. Santa Rosa All-County Chorus, Milton, 1989, 95, Santa Rosa Celebrates the Arts, 1986-2003 Asst. dir.: arts festivals, 1993—; singer (soprano, soloist): Gulf Coast Chorale, Singfest, Inc., The Choral Soc. Pensacola, Change of Command, 2003; singer: (duet) with Jerry Hadley, 2005. Dir. elem. chorus performing for Santa Rosa Convalescent Ctr., Milton, 1985—, Whiting Field, 2003, Live at the Capital, Tallahassee, 1986, Santa Rosa Celebrates the Arts, 1986-, Ptnrs. in Edn.-K-Mart and City of Milton and WEAR-TV, 1990—. Computer Software grant Santa Rosa Ednl. Found., 1994; recipient Young Artist Competition S.E. Regional award Nat. Assn. Tchrs. Singing, S.E. region, 1993; winner State of Ala. Young Artist competition, 1993; named Tchr. of Yr., W.H. Rhodes Elem., 2002 Mem. NEA, Music Tchrs. Nat. Assn., Nat. Assn. Realtors, Fla. Assn. Realtors, Santa Rosa Profl. Educators, Music Educators Nat. Conf., Pensacola (Fla.) Music Tchrs. Assn., Delta Kappa Gamma (music chair 1988-94), Kappa Delta Pi, Phi Kappa Phi. Presbyterian. Avocations: walking, gardening, volunteer for nursing home. Home: 5820 Kirkland Dr Milton FL 32570-8251 Office: WH Rhodes Elem 5563 Byrom St Milton FL 32570-3822 Business E-Mail: arnoldm@santarosa.k12.fl.us.

ARNOLD, MARSHA DIANE, writer; b. Kingman, Kans., July 7, 1948; d. Eugene Willard Krehbiel and Elsie Irene (Lippincott) Raymond; m. Frederick Oak Arnold, Jan. 25, 1970; children: Amy Marie, Calvin Diedrich Oak. BA in English cum laude, Kans. State U., 1970. Cert. secondary English tchr., Kans., standard elem. tchr., Calif. Eligibility worker Dept. Social Svcs., San Mateo, Calif., 1970-71, San Rafael, Calif., 1971-79, Calif. Children Svcs., Dept. of Health, San Rafael, 1979-81; kindergym tchr. Calif. Parenting Inst., Petaluma, 1981; writer children's books, columnist Sebastopol, Calif., 1985—; tchr.'s aide Twin Hills Sch. Dist., Sebastopol, 1991-94. Spkr. in field. Author: Heart of a Tiger, 1995 (Jr. Lib. Guild selection 1995, 1997-98 Show Me Readers Award Master List, Internat. Reading Assn. Children's Disting. Book award 1996, Young Hoosier Book Award selection, Houston Chronicle Best Book of '95 Christmas Roundup), Quick, Quack, Quick, 1996, The

Bravest of Us All, 2000; contbr. columns, stories and articles to mags. Animal care vol. Boyd Mus. Sci., San Rafael, 1974-75, Calif. Marin Mammal Rehab. Ctr., Marin County, Calif., 1976; v.p. PTA, Sebastopol, 1985. Recipient Best Local Columnist award Calif. Newspaper Pubs. Assn., 1986, 87, 93, Marion Vannett Ridgway award for outstanding first published picture book for children by an author or illustrator, 1996. Mem. Soc. Childrens' Book Writers and Illustrators, Phi Kappa Phi, Kappa Delta Pi. Avocations: scuba diving, travel, nutrition. Home: 350 Mcgregor Ln Sebastopol CA 95472-5375

ARNOLD, MARY SPEARS, retired music educator; d. Robert Alva Spears and Frankie Mae Copeland. BS in Music Edn., Ala. State Coll.; MA in Music Edn., Ga. State U. Cert. music edn. Music tchr. Wedowee HS, Wedowee, Ala., 1956—57; music tchr., acting chair Carver Vocational HS, 1964—68; music tchr., chair Frederick Douglass HS, 1969—92. Adjudicator AA literary event, girls trios & boys quartet Ga. HS Assn., Ga., 1994—95. Mem. Evaluation Music Curriculum Westwood HS, 1988; mem. Atlanta Pub. Schs. Curriculum Com. Mem.: Music Educators Nat. Conf., Ga. Music Educators Assn.

ARNOLD, MARYGWEN SUELLA, language educator, medical/surgical nurse; d. Clarence Glen and Winifred Opal Arnold. AS in Nursing, Tyler Jr. Coll., Tex., 1974; diploma, Tex. Ea. Sch. Nursing, 1975; BS in Edn., U. Tex., Tyler, 1978, MEd in Reading, 1986, MA in English, 1989. Tchr. biology, life and earth sci. Troup High Sch., Tex., 1979—80; tchr. Spanish Chapel Hill Mid. Sch., 1983—84; tchr. biology, chemistry, Spanish and English Grace Cmty. High Sch., Tyler, 1980—85; instr. devel. writing, reading, English as 2d lang. Tyler Jr. Coll., 1989—2004, instr. English, 2004—. Mem.: Tex. Faculty Assn., Sigma Delta Pi, Alpha Chi. Avocations: piano, classical music.

ARNOLD, NANCY KAY, writer; b. Kalamazoo, May 9, 1951; d. Byron Lyle and Ada (Doorlag) A.; m. Louis Scott Hubert, May 5, 1989 (div. Jan. 29, 2002) BFA Painting, We. Mich. U., 1983, postgrad., 1985—86. Writer Advanced Sys. & Designs, Inc., Farmington Hills, Mich., 1987—89; pres., owner TechWrite, Kalamazoo, 1989—2002; writer Northrop Grumman IT, 2002—. Mandolinist Kalamazoo Mandolin and Guitar Orch., 2004—; music dir. Paw Paw Village Players Theatre, 2006. Author: (poetry) Tetragonal Pyramids, 1982; exhibited in group shows, Kalamazoo, 1983, We. Mich. U., 1982, 85, Kalamazoo Quar. Downtown Art Hop, 2004, 05, Pasta, Pasta Restaurant and Art Gallery, 2005, South Westridge Pilgram Park Ann. Exhibit, 2005. Mem. AAUW, NAFE, Kalamazoo County C. of C., Humane Farming Assn. Am Libertarian. Avocations: bicycling, skiing, reading, piano, singing, guitar, mandolin. Office: PO Box 481 Oshtemo MI 49077-0481 E-mail: nancya@kalnet.net.

ARNOLD, RUTH SOUTHGATE, librarian; b. Cin., Oct. 2, 1950; d. Roger Frederick Arnold and Harriet Hendershot Wolf Arnold; m. Louis Dolive; children: Caroline Elizabeth Dolive, William Arnold Dolive. BA, Eckerd Coll., 1972; MSLS, Simmons Coll., 1977. Cert. libr. Va. Info. specialist Warner-Eddison Assocs., Inc., Cambridge, Mass., 1977—79; asst. dir. Augusta County Libr., Fishersville, Va., 1979—81; tech. svcs. libr. Staunton (Va.) Pub. Libr., 1987—91, dir., 1991—. Mem. ednl. com. Woodrow Wilson Birthplace, Staunton, 1998—2002; v.p. Staunton (Va.) Downtown Devel. Assn., 2003—04, bd. mem., 2001—06. Named Woman of the Yr., Staunton Bus. & Profl. Women's Orgn., 1997; fellow Paul Harris, Rotary, 1995. Mem.: ALA, Va. Pub. Libr. Dirs. Assn. (sec., regional rep. 1997—2002), Va. Libr. Assn. (2d v.p. 2000—01, v.p./pres.-elect 2005, pres. 2006), Staunton Rotary Club (pres. 1998—99). Presbyterian. Avocations: choral singing, contra dancing. Office: Staunton Pub Libr 1 Churchville Ave Staunton VA 24401 Office Phone: (540) 332-3902. Office Fax: (540) 332-3906. Business E-Mail: arnoldrs@ci.staunton.va.us.

ARNOLD, SANDRA RUTH KOUNS, photographer; b. Cleburne, Tex., Jan. 20, 1941; d. Wyatt Allen and Ethel Louise (Gandillon) Kouns; m. William Patrick Arnold, Feb. 27, 1960; children: Allyson Arnold House, Lynn Ann Workman. Student, Hill Coll., 1975, student, 1978—79, Hill. Coll., 1995, Richland Coll., 1986, student, 1994, Sam Houton State U., 1996, Sam Houston State U., 1997, student, 2001; profl. cert., Tex. Sch. Profl. Photography. Lic. realtor Tex., cert. photographer Profl. Photographers Assn., Nat. Profl. Photographers Assn. Decorator, owner Baileys Home Improvements, Cleburne, 1971—77; realtor Red Carpet and Holliday Assocs., Cleburne, 1979—98; pub./patient rels. Meml. Hosp., Cleburne, 1982—86; mktg./patient rels. staff, asst. coord. Walls Regional Hosp., Cleburne, 1986; mgr. mktg. Harris Meth. Health Sys., Ft. Worth, 1986—88; dir. mktg./physician recruiting Kimbro Med. Ctr., Cleburne, 1988—92; profl. photographer, 1996—2004; owner antique shop My Favorite Things, 1995—98. Owner, v.p. A&A Plastic Co., 1969-2004; vocalist weddings, theaters, and chs., Cleburne, 1959—; mem. Harris Meth. Hosp. Chorale, Ft. Worth, 2004-05. Contbr. articles to profl. jours. Established Area Alzheimer Support Group, Cleburne, 1984, Cleburne Women's Tennis League; coord., cons. Adopt-A-Sch./Cleburne Schs., 1984—; mem., actress Carnegie Theater; active Johnson County Hist. Commn., PTA; vol. Johnson County Meml. Hosp., 1972—96; ARC; established crime watch neighborhood program, 1998; vol. mus. entertainment for hosp. patient; active St. Mark Meth. Ch., Cleburne. Named one of Outstanding Women of S.W., 1979. Mem.: Cleburne C. of C., Heritage Assembly (charter), Women's Forum, Beta Sigma Phi (pres., Woman of Yr. 1963, 1981). Avocations: music, genealogy, travel, antiques, yoga. Home and Office: PO Box 63 Cleburne TX 76033-0063

ARNOLD, SUSAN E., consumer products company executive; b. Pitts., Mar. 8, 1954; 2 children. BA, U. Pa., 1976; MBA, U. Pitts., 1980. Joined Procter & Gamble Co., Cin., 1980, brand asst., Dawn/Ivory Snow, 1980, sales tng. Phila., 1981, asst. brand mgr., Oxydol Cin., 1981—83, asst. brand mgr., Cascade, 1983—84, brand mgr., Gain/Spl. Assignment, 1984—85, brand mgr., Tide Sheets, 1985—86, brand mgr., Dawn, 1986—87, assoc. advertising mgr., PS& D Advertising, 1987, assoc. advertising mgr., laundry products, PS&D Divsn., 1987—88, assoc. advertising mgr., laundry specialty products, PS&D Divsn., 1988—89, advertising mgr., fabric softeners, BS&HCP Divsn., 1989—90, mgr., Noxell Products, Internat. Divsn. Canada, 1990—92, gen. mgr., deodorants/Old Spice (U.S.A.), 1993—96; v.p., gen. mgr., deodorants/Old Spice and Skin Products-US Procter & Gamble Co. N.Am., 1997—97, v.p., gen. mgr., laundry products-US, 1997—99; v.p., N.Am. Fabric Care Proctor & Gamble Co., Cin., 1999, pres., global skin care, 1999—2000, pres., global cosmetics & skin care, 2000, pres., personal beauty care, 2000—02, pres., global personal beauty care & global feminine care, 2002—04, vice chmn. global beauty care, 2004—, vice-chmn., beauty & health (oral care, personal health and pharm. businesses), 2006—, also bd. dirs. Bd. dir. Reflect.com, Cin. Zoo, Goodyear Tire & Rubber Co., 2003—05. Named Top Marketer and One of the 21 to Watch in the 21st Century, Advt. Age, Career Woman of Achievement, YWCA, 2000; named one of 50 Most Powerful Women in Bus., Fortune mag., 2002—, 50 Women to Watch, Wall Street Jour., 2004, 2005, 100 Most Powerful Women, Forbes Mag., 2006, 50 Most Powerful Women in Bus., Fortune mag., 2006; recipient Best Boss award, Cosmetic Exec. Women, 2003. Achievements include first women to reach a president-level position at Procter & Gamble Co; first women to be named to the vice chairman position at Procter & Gamble Co. Avocation: surfing. Office: Procter & Gamble Co 1 Procter & Gamble Plz Cincinnati OH 45202*

ARNOLD, VALERIE DOWNING, lawyer; b. Istanbul, Turkey, Jan. 6, 1967; BA in French, U. Minn., 1988; student, Universite de Savoir, Chambery, France, 1990; MA in French, U. Minn., 1992, JD, 1997. Bar: Minn. 1997, US Dist. Ct. (dist. Minn.) 2004. Shareholder Tuft & Arnold, P.L.L.C., Maplewood, Minn. Named a Rising Star, Minn. Super Lawyers mag., 2006. Mem.: Warren E. Burger Inn of Ct., Minn. Women Lawyers, Ramsey County Bar Assn., Minn. State Bar Assn. Office: Tuft & Arnold PLLC 2109 County Rd D East Ste A Saint Paul MN 55109 Office Phone: 651-771-0050. E-mail: val@tuftarnoldlaw.com.*

ARNOLD-OLSON, HELEN B., not-for-profit consultant; b. Cedar Rapids, Iowa, Sept. 22, 1948; d. Duane Arnold Sr. and Henrietta Dows; m. Edward R. Krieger Jr., May 23, 1970 (div. Aug. 1974); m. Reuben I. Olson, July 2, 1982; 1 child, Andrew R. Olson. B in Music cum laude, Cornell Coll., 1970. Office mgr. Irving R. Zimmerman Co., Chgo., 1973-75; loan officer comml. and residential Banco Mortgage Co., Chgo., 1975-77, 79-82; asst. v.p., mgr., mortgage lending Olympic Savings & Loan Assn., Berwyn, Ill., 1977-79; underwriter, cons. Fed. Housing Adminstrn., Chgo., 1976-83; co-owner, pres. and exec. chef Hawkeye Nut Co., Cedar Rapids, 1983-87; pres. Dows Farms, Inc., Cedar Rapids, 1987-96; dir. devel. YWCA of Cedar Rapids and Linn County, 1996—2000; pres. Green Light, LLC, Arnold-Olson Assocs., Hel's Kitchen, 2000—; nonprofit cons. Bd. dirs. The Dows Cos., Cedar Rapids, Cedar Rapids Airport Commn. Bd. dirs., co-chair capital campaign endorsement The History Ctr., Cedar Rapids, 1996—; v.p., bd. dirs. Friends of the Zoo, Cedar Rapids, 1997—; bd. dirs. Kingston Hill Home for Aged Women, Cedar Rapids, 1998—. Recipient Leadership for Five Seasons award Cedar Rapids Area C. of C., 1996. Mem. AAUW, Assn. Fund Raising Profls., Iowa Women's Found., Variety Club of Iowa (bd. dirs., past chair, Sunshine award 1999), Rotary. Presbyterian. Avocations: cooking, travel. Home and Office: Arnold-Olson Assocs 3840 Bever Ave SE Cedar Rapids IA 52403 E-mail: HBAO48@aol.com.

ARNOLD-ROGERS, JUDY, education educator, language educator, coach; b. Knoxville, Tenn., Sept. 15, 1949; d. James Elisha and Grace (Harrison) Arnold; m. Talbot Wentworth Rogers, Oct. 26, 1984; children: Jesse, Sarah. BA in English, Carson Newman Coll., 1970; MA in English, U. Tenn., 1972, EdD in Curriculum and Instrn., 1978, postdoct., 1985—. Cert. tchr. English grades 9-12 Tenn., supr. and adminstr. Tenn. Tchr. English, tennis coach Bearden Sr. High Sch., Knoxville, 1972—86; asst. prof. English Roane State C.C., Rockwood, Tenn., 1986—90; assoc. prof. edn. Tenn. Wesleyan Coll., Athens, Tenn., 1990—93, ednl. coord., women's tennis coach, 1990—91, 1992, chair edn. dept., 1991—93; prof. grad. edn. Lincoln Meml. U., Harrogate, Tenn., 1993—. Presenter in field. Contbr. articles to profl. jours. Mem.: NEA (del. rep. assembly, del. assemblies), AAUW (corr. sec. local br. 1999—2001, 2002—, br. pres. 2003—, chair membership, mem. ednl. equity com., 1st v.p. program chair Knoxville br., endowment winner leadership contributions), Tenn. Assn. Colls. Tchr. Educators, Tenn. Edn. Assn. (newsletter editor 1992, chair human rels. 1992—94, mem. higher edn. bd. dirs., PreK-Grad. bd. dirs.), Nat. Coun. Higher Edn., Nat. Coun. Tchrs. English (newsletter editor Assembly on Expanded Perspectives in Learning, mem. exec. bd.), Delta Kappa Gamma (pres 1996—98, Alpha Tau chpt., chair profl. devel.). Avocations: tennis, writing, music.

ARNONE, MARY GRACE, radiologic technologist; b. Bronx, N.Y., Dec. 28, 1961; d. Anthony Rocco and Mary Helen (Doring) A. AA, Acad. Health Sci., U.S. Army, 1982. Lic. radiologist NY, mammographer NY. Radiology technologist, 1982—, Our Lady of Mercy Hosp., Bronx, NY, 1988—. With U.S. Army, 1982-86. Democrat. Lutheran.

ARNOW, JODY L., accountant; b. Marshfield, Wis., Mar. 18, 1969; d. Robert Harold and Donetta Marie (Oertel) U.; m. Harley Hastings Thomas IV, July 23, 1994 (div. Aug. 1998); m. Charles Austin Arnow, Oct. 4, 2003. BS, Marquette U., 1991. Lic. massage therapist Ohio Med. Bd., 2005. Cost acct. Schwarz Pharm., Mequon, Wis., 1992-93, Wis. Dairies Coop., Baraboo, 1993-94, Acme Die Casting, Inc., Racine, Wis., 1994-97; sr. cost acct. Bosch Automation Tech., Racine, Wis., 1997-2001; gen. acctg. supr. Bosch Rexroth Corp., Racine, Wis., 2001; budget analysis mgr. Unifund, Cin., 2001—02, mgr. budgets and fin. analysis, 2002—03; cost analyst Kao Brands, Cin., 2004—; lic. massage therapist Kneading Tough Therapeutic Massage Ctr., West Chester, Ohio, 2005—. Mem. Inst. Mgmt. Accts., Kiwanis (bd. dirs. 1999, nominating com. 1999), An. Massage Therapy Assn. Republican. Avocations: volleyball, golf, skiing, piano/music, gardening. Home: 4869 Rialto Ridge West Chester OH 45069 Business E-Mail: jody@kneadingtouchtmc.com.

ARNS, LAURA, research scientist; PhD, Iowa State U., Ames, 2002. Rschr. Virtual Reality Applications Ctr., Iowa State U., Ames, 2002—03; assoc. dir., rsch. scientist Envision Ctr., Purdue U., West Lafayette, Ind., 2003—. Mem.: IEEE, Assn. Computing Machinery. Achievements include co-creator of open source software AGJuggler. Office: Envision Ctr Purdue Univ 128 Memorial Mall Stew B31 West Lafayette IN 47907

ARNTZ, BARBARA C., elementary school educator; b. Mauston, Wis., Aug. 30, 1932; d. Edwin and Oranda Ruth Lenore Kuska; m. Robert L. Arntz, Sept. 11, 1954 (dec. Dec. 1990). BE, Wis. State U., 1965. Cert. tchr. Wis. Tchr. Cherry Br. Sch., Woodford, Wis., 1951—52, Utica (Wis.) Grade Sch., 1952—53, Wayne Ctr. Sch., South Wayne, Wis., 1952—55, Brick Ch. Sch., Walworth, Wis., 1955—57, Walworth Grade Sch., Walworth, Wis., 1958—67, Westside Sch., Sun Prairie, Wis., 1967—90. Cons., presenter in field. Author: A Guide to Journal Writing, 1983, Student Guide to Olbrich Gardens, 1992. Vol. Ret. Sr. Vol. Program, Madison, Wis., 1994—; election ofcl. City Clk. Office, Madison, Wis., 1992—. Recipient Svc. award, State of Wis. DPI, 1990, Math Edn. award, Wis. Math. Coun., 1990. Mem.: Wis. State Hist. Soc. (docent 1998—). Avocations: painting, crocheting, poetry, sewing.

ARNTZENIUS, LINDA GALLIARD MCARDLE, writer; b. Glasgow, Scotland, May 19, 1953; d. Frank and Mary McArdle; m. Frank Willem Arntzenius, Apr. 26, 1986 (div. Nov. 2003); 1 child, Michael Robert. BA in Humanities with honors, Hatfield Poly., Eng., 1980; MSc in Logic and Sci. Method, London Sch. Econs., 1981; grad. cert., U. London, 1987; M in Profl. Writing, U. So. Calif., 1998. Editor, info. officer Assn. Commonwealth Univs., London, 1981—86; vis. rschr., tchg. asst. philosophy dept. Carnegie Mellon U., Pitts., 1987—88; editl. asst. Arundel Antiquarian Books, L.A., 1989—91; editor, writer U. So. Calif. News Svc., L.A., 1991—97; freelance writer Princeton, NJ, 1997—; adj. prof. Mercer County C.C., Trenton, NJ, 2001—02, The Coll. N.J., Trenton, 2002—. Pubs. officer Inst. Advanced Study, Princeton, NJ, 2003—. Contbg. editor: USC Trojan Family, 1992—98, KUSC Program Guide, 1996—98; editor: cmty. calendar USC Radio, KUSC, 1993—98; contbr. articles, poems, revs. to profl. and lit. publs.; staff writer Town Topics Newspaper, 2006—. Vol. editor newsletter Prototypes agy. for women at risk for AIDS, L.A., 1995—97; vol. caregiver Angel's Wing foster care, Trenton, NJ, 2000—. Recipient Hon. Mention, Allen Ginsberg Poetry Awards, 2000, Runner-up, N.J. Writers' Conf., 2001, Commendation, Allen Ginsberg Poetry Awards, 2001. Mem.: U.S. 1 Poets Coop., Scottish Poetry Libr., Amnesty Internat. Avocations: walking, travel. E-mail: larntzen@ias.edu.

ARNWINE, BARBARA RUTH, lawyer; b. 1951; BA, Scripps Coll.; JD, Duke Univ. Bar: NC 1977. Exec. dir. Lawyer's Com. for Civil Rights Under Law, Washington. Office: Lawyers Comt for Civil Rights Under Law Ste 400 1401 New York Ave NW Washington DC 20005 Office Phone: 202-662-8600. Office Fax: 202-638-0482. Business E-Mail: barnwine@lawyerscommittee.org.

ARON, EVE GLICKA SERENSON, personal care industry executive; b. NYC, Sept. 5, 1937; d. Max and Edith (Gitelson) Serenson; m. Joel Edward Aron, Dec. 13, 1964; children: Jennifer, Joshua, Eric. BS, CCNY, 1958; MS, Yeshiva U., 1960; MBA with honors, Iona Coll., 1985. Med. technician Albert Einstein Coll. Medicine, Bronx, NY, 1959-60; chemist Strasenburgh labs., Belleville, NJ, 1961-63, Roche Labs., Nutley, 1963-67; sr. chemist Pantene Labs. div. Roche, 1967-69; mgr. R&D Combe Inc., White Plains, NY, 1978-85, assoc. dir. R&D, 1985-95, dir. tech., 1995—2002; tech. cons. to personal care industry Ft. Myers, Fla., 2002—. Dir. website Vagisil Women's Health Ctr., 2000-02. Contbr. articles to profl. jours. Tutor Literacy Vols. of Am.; resident dir., bd. dirs. Sevilla Condo Assn., 2002-04; bd. dirs. Residents Alliance for a Quality Lifestyle. Mem.: Soc. Cosmetic Chemists (sec. Conn. chpt. 1989—90, chair 1992, chpt. advisor 1993, hospitality/membership chair 1994—96, program com. co-chair 1997, employment chair 1999—2002), Am. Chem. Soc. (legis. action network). Avocations: golf, tennis, walking, swimming. Home and Office: 10504 Sevilla Dr Apt 201 Fort Myers FL 33913 E-mail: eve.aron@earthlink.net.

ARON, NAN, lawyer, association executive; b. NYC, Jan. 4, 1948; d. Jerome I. and Joan B. A.; m. Bernard S. Arons, Dec. 28, 1969; children: Nicholas, Emma, Elena. BA, Oberlin (Ohio) Coll., 1970; LLB, Case Western Res. U., 1973. Lawyer EEOC, Washington, 1973-76, Nat. Prison Project, ACLU, Washington, 1976-79; exec. dir. Alliance for Justice, Washington, 1979—. Instr. George Washington U., Washington, 1977; adj. prof. law Georgetown U., 1979—. Author: Liberty and Justice for All-Public Interest Law in the 1980s and Beyond, 1988; contbr. articles to profl. publs. Bd. dirs. Oyster Sch. Community Coun., Washington, 1980—. Mem. Ams. for Dem. Action (bd. dirs. 1988—), Washington Coun. Lawyers (bd. dirs. 1979—). Jewish. Office: Alliance for Justice 11 Dupont Circle NW 2nd Fl Washington DC 20036*

ARONOFF, VERA, law librarian; b. Kiev, Ukraine, Sept. 17, 1934; arrived in U.S., 1981; d. Joseph and Khasya Davidovich; m. Leonard Aronoff, July 26, 1958; 1 child, Irene Aronoff-Kastanas. BA in Edn. with top honors, Pedagogical Inst., Nezhin, Ukraine, 1956; postgrad., Maywood Coll., 1984—86; MLS Syracuse U., 1989. Tchr. HS # 19, Kiev, 1956—61, Inst. Fgn. Langs., Kiev, 1961—79; asst. libr. Scranton (Pa.) Pub. Libr., 1981—85; rschr. Cornell U., Ithaca, NY, 1985—88; catalog libr. Loyola U. Law Sch., L.A., 1989—. Mem.: So. Calif. Assn. Law Librs., Am. Assn. Law Librs. Office: Loyola Law Sch PO Box 15019 919 S Albany St Los Angeles CA 90015-0019 Office Phone: 213-736-1419. Business E-Mail: vera.aronoff@lls.edu.

ARONOWICZ, ANNETTE, theology studies educator; b. Warsaw, Mar. 9, 1952; d. Yasha Aronowicz and Rose Arnold. PhD, UCLA, 1982. Instr. Stanford U., Palo Alto, Calif., 1982—85; prof. Franklin and Marshall Coll., Lancaster, Pa., 1985—, chair Judaic studies, 2000. Author: Nine Talmudic Readings by Emmanuel Levinas, Jews and Christians on Time and Eternity: Charles Peguy's Portrait of Bernard Lazare, Freedom from Ideology: Secrecy in Modern Expression. Recipient Dewey Teacher-Scholar award, Franklin and Marshall Coll.; fellow Jerusalem Fellow award, Jerusalem Fellows, 1996—97. Mem.: Am. Asssn. Religion, Assn. Jewish Studies, Am. Soc. for the Study of Religion (mem. exec. bd. 2005—). Office: Franklin & Marshall College College Ave Lancaster PA 17604-3003 Office Phone: 717-291-3875. Business E-Mail: annette.aronowicz@fandm.edu.

ARONSON, MARGARET RUPP, school psychologist; b. Lewistown, Pa., Dec. 12, 1921; d. Frederick Augustine and Claire S. (Schellenberg) Rupp; m. Morton Jerome Aronson, Oct. 31, 1948; children: Eris L. Aronson Renczenski, Frederick Rupp, Scott Charles, Eris L. Aronson Renczenski (dec. Oct. 2003) BA, Pa. State U., 1942, MS, 1943; JD, St. John's U., 1986. Nat. cert. sch. psychologist. Clin. psychologist Inst. Pa. Hosp., Phila., 1943-48, Georgetown Hosp., Washington, 1948-50; ind. cons. Patchogue (N.Y.) Pub. Schs., 1986-96, Luth. Ministries, Westchester, Queens and Nassau County, NY, 1996—. Editor Winter Olympics Pindar Press, 1980-82. Mem. Met. Golf Assn., Phi Beta Kappa, Phi Kappa Phi, Psi Chi. Avocation: golf. Home: Windsor Gate, Great Neck NY 11020

ARONSON, VIRGINIA L., lawyer; b. Bremerton, Wash., June 4, 1947; m. Simon Aronson. BA, U. Chgo., 1969, MA, 1973, JD, 1975. Bar: Ill. 1975. Ptnr. Sidley Austin LLP, Chgo. Staff mem. U. Chgo. Law Review, 1974—75; mem. exec. and mgmt. com. Sidley Austin LLP. Contbr. articles to profl. jours. Mem. leadership coun. Chgo. Pub. Edn. Fund; mem. bd. dirs. Chgo. Ctrl. Area Com. Mem. Am. Coll. Real Estate Lawyers, Chgo. Mortgage Attys. Assn., The Chgo. Network. Office: Sidley Austin LLP 1 South Dearborn St Chicago IL 60603 Office Phone: 312-853-7741. Office Fax: 312-853-7036. Business E-Mail: varonson@sidley.com.

ARORA, SHIRLEY LEASE, Spanish language educator; b. Youngstown, Ohio, June 3, 1930; d. Leland J. and Ruth (Brice) Lease; m. Harbans L. Arora; children: David, Alan. BA, Stanford U., 1950, MA, 1951; PhD, UCLA, 1962. Asst. prof. Spanish UCLA, 1962-70, assoc. prof., 1970-76, prof., 1976—, chmn. dept., 1981-91. Author: What Then, Raman, 1960 (Charles W. Follett award, Jane Addams award 1960), The Left-Handed Chank, 1966, Proverbial Comparisons in Ricardo Palma's Tradiciones peruanas, 1966, Proverbial Comparisons and Related Expressions in Spanish, 1977. Mem. MLA, Am. Folklore Soc., Calif. Folklore Soc. (v.p. 1983-85), Internat. Soc. for Folk Narrative Rsch., Internat. Soc. for Contemporary Legend Rsch., Asociacion Internacional de Hispanistas, Instituto Internacional de Literatura Iberoamericana. Office: UCLA Dept Spanish & Portuguese 5310 Rolfe Hl Los Angeles CA 90095-0001

ARP, ARLENE, elementary school educator; b. Detroit, Mich., Sept. 30, 1951; 1 child, Ila Arp-Spratt. BA in Religious Studies (hon.), Ind. U., 1993; cert. in Primary Edn., Montessori Tchr. Coll. Montessori Primary Education Teaching Certificate Montessori Tchr. Coll. NW, 1988. Primary montessori tchr. Nat. Ctr. for Montessori Edn., Seattle, 1987—92; early childhood tchr. Austin Ind. Sch. Dist., Tex., 1992—94, DeKalb County Sch. Dist., Atlanta, 1994—99, Pvt. Tutor, Atlanta, 1999—. Recipient Recognition for earning a Early Childhood.Generalist Nat. Bd. Certification for Profl. Tchg. Standards, DeKalb County Bd. of Edn., 1996. Mem.: Internat. Honor Soc. and Profl. Assn. in Edn. (hon.).

ARPS, CORABELL BENNETT, psychiatrist; b. Oklahoma City, Feb. 16, 1949; d. Phil Connell and Frances Corbin Bennett; m. Joseph Warren Arps, Jr., Jan. 8, 1974; children: Elizabeth Arps Seymour, Joseph Warren III. BS, Okla. State U., Stillwater, 1971; MD, U. Tex., Southwestern Med. Sch., Dallas, 1987. Diplomate Psychiatry 1993, Child & Adolescent Psychiatry 1994. Residency Timberlawn Psychiat. Hosp., Dallas, 1987—90, child psychiatry fellowship, 1990—92; psychiatrist, cons. Austin St. Homeless Shelter, Dallas, 1989—92; med. dir., adolescent inpatient svcs. The Acadia Hosp., Bangor, Maine, 1992—99, assoc. med. dir., 2000—03, med. dir., ambulatory svcs., 1999—2003, med. dir., child & adolescent partial hosp. programs, 2003; asst. clin. prof. Tufts U. Med. Sch., Bangor, Maine, Boston, 1998—. Mem. task force on homeless mentally ill Dallas County Mental Health Assn., 1990; bd. mem. Maine Coun. Adolescent Health, 2000—02. Mem. St. Mathew's Parish, Hampden, Maine. Recipient Faculty Tchg. Excellence award, Tufts U. Med. Sch., 1997, 1998, 1999. Mem.: Maine Psychiat. Assn., Am. Acad. Child and Adolescent Psychiatry, Am. Psychiat. Assn. (dist. br. exec. coun. 1989—92). Roman Catholic. Avocation: needlecrafts. Office: The Acadia Hosp 268 Stillwater Ave Bangor ME 04401

ARQUETTE, PATRICIA, actress; b. Chgo., Apr. 8, 1968; d. Lewis and Mardi Arquette; m. Nicholas Cage, Apr. 8, 1995 (div. May 18, 2001) m. Thomas Jane, June 25, 2006, 1 child, Harlow Olivia Calliope; 1 child (with Paul Rossi), Enzo Actress: (films) Pretty Smart, 1986, A Nightmare on Elm Street 3: Dream Warriors, 1987, Time Out, 1988, Far North, 1988, The Indian Runner, 1991, Prayer of the Rollerboys, 1991, Especially on Sunday, 1991, Inside Monkey Zetterland, 1992, Trouble Bound, 1993, Ethan Frome, 1993, True Romance, 1993, Holy Matrimony, 1994, Ed Wood, 1994, Beyond Rangoon, 1995, Flirting with Disaster, 1996, The Secret Agent, 1996, Infinity, 1996, Lost Highway, 1997, Nightwatch, 1997, Goodbye Lover, 1998, The Hi-Lo Country, 1998, Toby's Story, 1998, Stigmata, 1999, Bringing Out the Dead, 1999, Little Nicky, 2000, Human Nature, 2001, The Badge, 2002, Deeper Than Deep, 2003, Holes, 2003, Tiptoes, 2003, Fast Food Nation, 2006; (TV movies) Daddy, 1987, The Girl with the Crazy Brother, 1990, Dillinger, 1991, Wildflower, 1991 (CableACE award, 1991), Betrayed by Love, 1994; (TV series) Medium, 2005- (Emmy award for outstanding lead actress in a drama series, 2005); (TV appearances) thirtysomething, 1990, Tales From the Crypt, 1990. Spokesperson Lee Nat. Denim Day, 1999. Office: UTA 9560 Wilshire Blvd Fl 5 Beverly Hills CA 90212-2401*

ARQUIT, NORA HARRIS, retired music educator, writer; b. Brushton, N.Y., June 30, 1923; d. Samuel Elton George and Esther Cecelia (Gillen) Harris; m. Gordon James Arquit, Nov. 12, 1948; children: Christine Elaine Arquit, Kevin James Arquit, Candace Susan Arquit-Martel. BS in Music Edn., Ithaca Coll., 1945, MS, 1962; postgrad., St. Lawrence U., 1946-47, 74, Cornell U., 1970-71, N.Y. State Coll., Potsdam, 1973. Cert. aerospace edn. with techicians rating. Music dir., band dir., tchr. N.Y. and N.J. State Schs., 1945—80. Guest conductor U.S. Air Force Band, Washington, Dutch and Am. band students, Schiedam, Holland, opening Am.-Can. Seaway, Massena, N.Y., 1975; U.S. Navy Band, Washington, various massed bands in U.S.A., Canada, Europe; dir. bands Worlds Fair, 1964, 65; 1st woman guest conductor Tri-State Honors Band Phillips U., Enid, Okla.; dir., coord. St. Lawrence County ann. H.S. Band Day, 1973-2002; past supvr. coll. student practice tchrs., N.Y.; mem. Mid-States Commn. Secondary Schs. and Colls. Evaluations. Author: Before My Own Time and Since, 1978, From Hamlet to Cold Harbor, 1989, Our Lyon Line, 1993, The History of the New York State, Society of the National Society of the Daughters of the American Colonists, 1994. Past adjudicator h.s. and coll. band contests; past dir., coord. ann. St. Lawrence County Band Day; past capt. aux. USAF Civil Air Patrol; past John Philip Sousa bd. dirs. rep. to Hall of Fame enshrinement of Sousa NY. Named Dist. Band Master Am., First Chair Am.; recipient Letter of Commendation for People to People Diplomacy for work with student band groups, Embassy at the Hague, Europe, honored for 39 yrs. of svc. on Band Day, St. Lawrence County, 2002. Mem.: AAUW (past divsn. meeting rep.), DAR (life; hon. regent Cayuga chpt., past state com. chmn., genealogical chmn.), Women Band Dirs. Nat. Assn. (past nat. pres., Silver Baton), N.Y. State Ret. Tchrs. Assn., N.Am. Band Dirs. Coordinating Coun. (pres. 1978, past nat. v.p.), Am. School Band Dirs. Assn. (emeritus mem. 1980, N.Y. state chmn. 2003—, past chmn. internat. band com., past nat. and state ofcr., honored nat. covention 2003), Internat. Assn. U. Women, Colonial Daughters of the XVIIC (chpt. councillor 1988-91, past. mem. coms.), De Schilpen Mus. Soc. Netherlands, De Schilpen Soc. (Holland), Kings County Hist. Soc. Nova Scotia, Daughters of Union Vets., Denison Soc., Daughters Am. Colonists (N.Y. state regent 1991—94, hon. state regent, life 1994), Soc. Colonial Dames of Seventeenth Century (past state officer, past state pres, registrar), Colonial Daughters Seventeenth Century (Atlantic Coast chmn. 2000—, nat. com. chmn. 2000—, past pres.), Daus. Colonial Wars, Soc. New England Women, N.Y. Ct. Assts. of Nat. Soc. Women Descendents of Ancient and Honorable Artillery Co. (life; past state officer, corr. sec., com. chmn.), Soc. Magna Charta Dames and Barons, Plantagenet Soc., Colonial Order of The Crown (Charlemagne), Soc. Sons and Daus. of the Pilgrims, Soc. U.S. Daughters 1812 (past pres., past Onondaga chpt. pres., past state ofcr.), Soc. Daughters of Founders & Patriots of Am. (past pres., past state pres., registrar, life mem. Nat. Officers Club), Soc. Sons and Daughters of Colonial Wars, Soc. New England Women, Soverign Colonial Soc., Daughters of Am. Colonists (nat. com chmn. 1994—97, Atlantic sect.chmn genealogy 2003—), Summit N.J. Club (spl. panel), Nat. Fedn. Music Club (past editl.com.), N.Y. State Officers Club DAR, Ithaca Music Club (past pres.), Delta Omicron. Avocations: writing, photography, research. Home: 130 Christopher Cir Ithaca NY 14850-1702

ARRABAL, BERTA ISABEL, radio producer; d. Guido Arrabal and Berta Rodriguez de Arrabal; m. Tim Sutherland, Aug. 14, 2004; 1 child, Nicolas Hage-Arrabal. BA in Comm. Arts, Loyola Marymount U., 1984. Writer, prodr., editor Westwood One Radio Networks, Culver City, Calif., 1984—88; music editor, writer SALUDOS HISPANOS mag., Tarzana, Calif., 1988—99; writer, prodr., engr., Billboard Latin Hits countdown Spanish Internat. Mktg., L.A., 1989—90; radio prodr., writer, engr. Radio Marti, Miami, Fla., 1990—. Voice talent Radio Marti, Miami, Fla., 2002—04, radio divsn. supr. Take Your Sons and Daughters to Work Day, 2003—05. Soup kitchen asst. Salvation Army, Miami, Fla., 2002—02; home-building asst. Habitat For Humanity, Miami, Fla., 2004—04. Avocations: travel, music collecting, movies, church activities, Jr. NBA supporter (my son is on the team). Office: Office Of Cuba Broadcasting/Radio Marti 4201 NW 77th Ave Miami FL 33166 Office Phone: 305-437-7160. Personal E-mail: bertaarrabal@yahoo.com.

ARREDONDO, ADRIANNA LIZA, secondary school educator; d. Cruz and Elvira A. Arredondo. BA, U. Tex., San Antonio, 1987—90; BS, Tex. A&M, Kingsville, 1996—98. Cert. US history tchr. Tex., 1992, social studies tchr. Tex., 2004, in guidance & counseling Tex., 2005. Tchr. Harlandale ISD, Kingsborough Mid. Sch., San Antonio, 1992—2002, Harlandale ISD, Mc-Collum HS, San Antonio, 2002—. Social studies dept. chair. Recipient Tchr. of Yr., Kingsborough Mid. Sch., 2001—02. Mem.: Assn. Tchr. Profl. Educators (assoc.). Democrat.

ARREDONDO, PATRICIA, educational association administrator; D in Counseling Psychology, Boston U.; LHD (hon.), U. San Diego. Prof. U. N.H., Boston U.; adj. prof. Tufts U.; faculty mem., exec. training program, Bus. Sch. Columbia U.; assoc. prof., div. psychology in edn. Ariz. State U., Tempe. Spkr. in field. Contbr. Founder, pres. Empowerment Workshops, Inc., Boston, 1985—; adv. bd. Boston Mgmt. Consortium, Police Acad. Training Com., Boston Diversity Steering Com.; pres. bd. Parents & Children's Services; founding mem., co-chair Latino Profl. Network; bd. dir. Mass. Sch. Profl. Psychology, Freedom House, Sankaty Head Found. Recipient Disting. Profl. Svc. award, Assn. Counselor Edn. & Supervision, Mentor award. Fellow: Soc. for Psychol. Study of Ethnic Minority Issues, Div 45, APA (former pres.); mem.: Assn. for Multicultural Counseling and Devel. (former pres.), Nat. Psychol. Assn. (pres.), Chicana/o Faculty & Staff Assn. (Ariz. State U.) (pres.), Am. Counseling Assn. (pres., Kitty Cole Human Rights award). Fluent in Spanish. Mailing: Am Counseling Assn 5999 Stevenson Ave Alexandria VA 22304 Office: Ariz State Univ Coll of Edn Div of Psych & Edn Payne Hall Rm 446 PO Box 870611 Tempe AZ 85287-0611 Office Phone: 800-347-6647 ext. 232, 480-965-5909. Office Fax: 480-965-4400. E-mail: empow@aol.com, empower@asu.edu.

ARRIETA, DIANE MARIE, artist; b. Clearfield, Pa., Aug. 2, 1961; d. Henry Edward and Florence Marie (Bailor) Stricek; m. Leslie Harold Arrieta, Nov. 11, 1988. BA, Fla. Atlantic U., 1996. Artist, Tequesta, Fla., 1985—; adj. prof. Palm Beach C.C., Palm Beach Gardens, Fla., 1998—2000; grad. asst. Fla. Atlantic U., Boca Raton, 2000—01, sr. libr. tech. asst., 2001—. Lectr. in field. One-woman shows include Eissey Art Gallery, Palm Beach Gardens, Fla., 2003, Miami Art Exch., Delray Beach, Fla., 2004, Eissey Theatre, Palm Beach Gardens, Fla., 2004, Burrow-Student Union Gallery, Jupiter, Fla., 2004, SC Atrium Gallery, 2004, Indian River Ct. House, Vero Beach, Fla., 2005, John D. MacArthur Campus Libr., Jupiter, Fla., 2005, exhibited in group shows at Palm Beach C.C., Palm Beach Gardens, Fla., 1999, Period Gallery, Lincoln, Nebr., 2004, Ritz Carlton, Miami, Fla., 2004, Upstream People Gallery, Omaha, Nebr., 2005, North Water Gallery, Kent, Ohio, 2005, Brunei Gallery, London, 2005. Recipient McCoy Ceramic scholarship, Fla. Atlantic U., 1996, Grad. Asst. scholarship, 2000. Avocations: rollerblading, kayaking, boating, weight training, photography.

ARRIGO, JAN ELIZABETH, photographer, writer, artist; b. New Orleans, July 23, 1960; d. Joseph and Ruth Arrigo. BA, Loyola U., 1982; postgrad., CCNY, 1995—99. Italian Language Centro Fiorenza, Florence, Italy, 1994. Featured author New Orleans (La.) Jazz and Heritage Festival, 2005, New Orleans (La.) Book Fair, 2006. Author: New Orleans, 2003, Explore Jean Lafitte Nat. Hist. Pk. and Preserve, 2004, Cemeteries of New Orleans, A Journey through the Cities of the Dead, 2005; contbg. author: The Am. Art Book, 1999, The Ency. of Advt., 2003; photography, New Orleans Mus. of Art's Underexposed (2nd Pl. Photographer, 2003); prodr.(curator): (group show) Surreal N.Y., Soho Photo, (traveling exhbn.) The Sweet and Sour Animal Book Traveling Show; Exhibited in group shows at Duque Art Ctr., 2004, Arthur Roger Gallery, 2005, Grand Isle Juried Exhn., 2005, The Warehouse, Washington, 2006. Mentor Big Bros., Big Sisters, NYC, 2000—02; vol. Bellevue Hosp., New York, NY, 2001—02; docent The Internat. Ctr. of Photography, NYC, 1997—2000; panelist William Faulkner Words and Music Festival, 2002. Named a Voice of New Orleans, AFTRA. Mem.: Am. Soc. Media Photographers, Am. Soc. Journalists and Authors, New Orleans Press Club, Arts Coun. New Orleans. Office Phone: 504-699-0514. Personal E-mail: jea1900@yahoo.com.

ARRINGTON, CAROLYN RUTH, school system administrator, consultant; b. May 20, 1942; d. Robert Ray and Grace Dotson; m. Wayne Vernon Arrington; children: Kevin Ray, Kemp Gray, Korey shay, Wayne, Kimberly. AA, Ohio Valley Coll., 1962; BA, Fairmont State Coll., 1964; MA, W.Va. U., 1966, EdD, 1994. Cert. pub. sch. adminstr. Tchr. Greenbrier Bd. Edn., Lewisburg, W.Va., 1964-68; supr. Mason County Bd. Edn., Point Pleasant, W.Va., 1968-70; media specialist Kanawha County Bd. Edn., Charleston, W.Va., 1970-71; asst. dir., dir., asst. divsn. chief W.Va. Dept. Edn., Charleston, 1971-89, asst. state supt. schs., 1989-98; v.p. Arrington Assocs., Inc., 1998—2005; rsch. adv. Chio Valley U., 2005—. Adj. prof. Ohio Valley U., 2005—; cons., spkr. in field. Author: numerous poems, short stories. Bd. dirs. YWCA, Charleston, 1988—91. Recipient Merit medal Edn. Ohio Valley U.; SEA fellow US Dept. Edn., 1984 Mem. Assn. Ednl. Comm. and Tech. (pres. 1979-80, Edgar Dale award 1975, Spl. Svc. award 1982), Wva. Ednl. Media Assn. (pres. 1975-76). Office: Arrington Assocs Inc Charleston WV

ARRINGTON, ELISABETH CALVERT, elementary education educator, artist; b. Bethesda, Md., Mar. 17, 1956; d. Charles Breckinridge and Mary Mann (Nash) A.; m. Michael H. Walsh, Aug. 19, 1979 (div. Jan. 8, 1986); 1 child, Mary Taylor Walsh; m. Bryan J. Raymond, June 21, 1992; stepchildren: Alistair Raymond, Amory Raymond, Addison Raymond. BA in Art Technique, Mills Coll., 1978; BS in Edn. summa cum laude, U. So. Maine, 1988, postgrad. in Instrnl. Leadership, 1988—. Cert. elem. tchr., Maine. Dir. summer playgrounds, adult edn., tchr. pottery and art Brunswick (Maine) Recreation Dept., 1979-81; asst. tchr. M.S.A.D. 75, Topsham, Maine, 1979-81, tchr. adult edn. drawing/painting, 1981-83; tchr. crafts/weaving dept. spl. edn. Brunswick Sch., 1982-84; pvt. art lessons Art Studio, Brunswick, 1983-88; tchr. grad. 3 Woodside Elem./M.S.A.D. 75, 1988—. Presentor sci. workshops state sci. and math. confs., Maine, 1990-94; sci. co-chair curriculum com. M.S.A.D. 75, 1992-94. Artist numerous art exhbns. V.p. Big Bros./Big Sisters, Brunswick, 1981. Recipient Presdl. award for sci. and math. tchg. The White House, 1994. Mem. NSTA, Soc. Elem. Presdl. Awardees, Maine Tchrs. Assn., Coun. for Elem. Sci. Internat. Democrat. Avocations: poetry, reading, caring for iguana, framing art work. Office: Woodside Elem Sch 42 Barrows Dr Topsham ME 04086-1326

ARRINGTON, HARRIET ANN HORNE, historian, biographer, researcher, writer; b. Salt Lake City, June 22, 1924; d. Lyman Merrill and Myrtle (Swainston) Horne; m. Frederick C. Sorensen, Dec. 22, 1943 (div. Dec. 1954); children: Annette S. Rogers, Frederick Christian, Heidi S. Swinton; m. Gordon B. Moody, July 26, 1958 (div. Aug. 1963); 1 child, Stephen Horne; m. Leonard James Arrington, Nov. 19, 1983. BS in Edn., U. Utah, 1957. Cert. tchr., Utah, Ga. Supr. surg. secs. Latter-day Saints Hosp., Salt Lake City, 1954-58; tchr. Salt Lake City Schs., 1957-58, Glynn County Schs., Brunswick, Ga., 1958-59, 60—; from med. sec. to office mgr. Dr. Horne, Salt Lake City, 1962-83; tchr. Carden Sch., Salt Lake City, 1973-74, women's history rschr., biographer. Mem. Utah Women's Legis. Coun.; co-establisher, bd. dirs. Arrington Archives, Utah State U.; spkr. hist. and women's confs. Author: (essays) Heritage of Faith, 1988, Worth Their Salt, 1997, Nearly Everything Imaginable: The Everyday Life of Utah's Mormon Pioneers, 1999; contbg. author (biographies) Encyclopedia of Women in American History, 1999, Pioneer Women of Faith and Fortitude, 1999, Encyclopedia of Utah History, 1999, Turn of the Century Lineage Profiles, DAR, 1996. Dist. chmn. Utah Rep. Com., 1972-76; mem. art com. Salt Lake City Bd. Edn.; chmn. art exhibit Senator Orrin Hatch's ann. Utah Women's Conf., 1987; past pres. L.D.S. Women's Relief Soc., Twin Falls, cultural refinement and/or spiritual living tchr., Alaska, Ga., Utah, Idaho; chmn. Utah Women Artists' Exhbns., AAUW, Utah divsn., 1986-87, Springville Mus. of Art. Nominated Pres. Ronald Reagan's Vol. Action award Utah Women Artists' Exhbn., 1987; recipient resolution of appreciation Utah Arts Coun., 1989, Friends of the Humanities award Utah State U., 1995. Mem.: NSDAR (nat. vice chmn. Women in Am. History 2000—04, Heritage Club Lopaz level 2005), DAR (regent 1998—2000, Utah State DAR bd. historian 2000—02, Princess Timpanogos Utah Chpt., 1st vice-regent Princess Timpanogos, dir.), AAUW (Utah state cultural refinement chmn., cert. of appreciation 1988), Old Main Soc. Utah State U., Cannon-Hinckley History & Dinner Club, Classics Club (v.p. 2003—, program com. 2005—), Xi Alpha (past pres. alumni chpt.), Chi Omega. Avocations: art, writing, gourmet cooking, needlepoint. Home and Office: 2236 S 2200 E Salt Lake City UT 84109-1135 Personal E-mail: harrington@aol.com.

ARRINGTON, REBECCA CAROL, occupational health nurse; b. Longmont, Colo., Apr. 14, 1948; d. Theodore Victor Anderson and Lucinda Beth Panabaker; m. Charles Arthur Keeran, Aug. 2, 1968 (div. 1973); m. C. R. Arrington, Oct. 30, 1982. RN, St. Mark's Sch. Nursing, Salt Lake City, 1970; BS in Profl. Arts, St. Joseph's Coll., Standish, Maine, 1993. RN Okla. Recovery rm. nurse McArthur Pk. Med. Ctr., Irving, Tex., 1976-77; claims analyst Blue Cross/Blue Shield, Dallas, 1977-78, 78-79; staff RN Parkland Meml. Hosp., Dallas, 1978; occupl. health nurse City of Tulsa, 1979—, wellness coord., 1984—, mgr. occupl. health, 1997. Ind. assoc. Mannatech, 1998; privacy officer Health Ins. Portability & Acctg. Act, 2003. Mem.: ANA, Tulsa Area Assn. Occupl. Health Nurses (mem. nominating com. 1988—90, treas. 1990—93, pres. 1993—94), Okla. Nurses Assn., Am. Assn. Occupl. Health Nurses. Republican. Baptist. Avocations: sewing, crafts, fishing, camping. Office: City of Tulsa 1145 S Utica Ave Ste 453 Tulsa OK 74104-4041 Office Phone: 918-596-7083. E-mail: ambrosia@familynet.net, barrington@ci.tulsa.ok.us, stepstohealth@cimtel.net.

ARROTT, ELIZABETH, journalist; b. Detroit, Oct. 1, 1960; d. Anthony Schuyler and Patricia Graham Arrott; m. Rafael Alexeevich Ekimyan, Sept. 16, 1995; children: Alexei Rafaelevich Ekimyan, Elizabeth Rafaelevna Ekimyan, Catherine Rafaelevna Ekimyan. AB, Harvard U., 1983. Moscow corr. Voice of Am., Moscow, 1993-97; anchor NewsNow Voice of Am., Washington, 1998—. Mem. Ch. LDS. Home: 5026 Reno Rd NW Washington DC 20008-2951 Office: Voice of Am 330 Independence Ave SW Washington DC 20547-0003

ARROTT, PATRICIA GRAHAM, artist, educator; b. Pitts., July 27, 1931; d. George Patterson and Helen (Gilleland) Graham; m. Anthony Schuyler Arrott, June 6, 1953; children: Anthony Patterson, Helen Graham, Matthew Ramsey, Elizabeth. BFA in Painting and Design, Carnegie-Mellon Univ., 1954; postgrad., Nat. Acad. Design, N.Y.C., 1985-87, Art Students League, 1980-91. Cert. tchr. art, Pa. Instr. children's ceramics Handcraft House, Vancouver, B.C., Can., 1970-72; courtroom artist Vancouver, B.C., Can., 1972-73; pvt. portrait artist Vancouver, N.Y.C., 1975—; instr. Art Students League, N.Y.C., 1993-99. Group shows include Nat. Acad. Design, 1990, 92, 94, Cork Gallery, Lincoln Ctr., N.Y.C., 1991, Pen & Brush Club, N.Y.C., 1988-98, Silver Point Etc., 1992-93; represented by Eleanor Ettinger Gallery, N.Y.C., 1997—; exbhns include: Carnegie Mellon U. Fine Arts Alumni Regina Gouger Miller Gallery, Pitts., 2006. Recipient Helen M. Loggie Prize, 1990, and cert. of merit, 1994, Nat. Acad. Design; recipient Emily Nicholas Hatch award Pen & Brush Club, 1989-91, Elizabeth Morse Genius award, 1988, 90, 93, 95, others. Mem. Art Student's League (life; mem. bd. 1989-92, women's v.p. 1991-92), Am. Fine Arts Soc. (mem. bd. 1991-92), Mayflower Soc. (life), Kappa Kappa Gamma (life). United Presbyterian.

ARROWOOD, CATHARINE BIGGS, lawyer; b. Lumberton, N.C., Nov. 27, 1951; d. Isley Murchison and Janis (Bolton) Biggs; 1 child, Catharine Jeannette. BA cum laude, Wake Forest U., 1973, JD cum laude, 1976. Bar: N.C. 1973. Assoc. atty. gen. antitrust sect. Dept. Justice, Raleigh, N.C., 1976-77; ptnr., litig. Parker Poe Adams & Bernstein LLP, Raleigh, NC, 1977—, mem. mgmt. com., 1990—2001. Mem. panel of comml. arbitrators, Am. Arbitration Assn.; chair, Fed. Bar Adv. Council, 1995-96, Civil Justice Reform Act Com., ea. dist NC, 1997; mem. Gov.'s Adminstrv. Rules Review Commn., Raleigh, 1983-90; N.C. rep. Fourth Cir. Rules Com. Editor (assoc.): Wake Forest Law Rev. Chair bd. vis., Wake Forest Univ. Law Sch., 2001-02. Fellow Am. Coll. Trial Lawyers; mem. ABA, N.C. Bar Assn., Wake County Bar Assn. (pres. 2006—), Phi Beta Kappa. Democrat. Baptist. Office Phone: 919-890-4142. Office Fax: 919-834-4564. Business E-Mail: cbarrowood@parkerpoe.com.

ARROWOOD, LISA GAYLE, lawyer; b. Kansas City, Mo., Aug. 7, 1956; d. Paul Miller and Catherine Margaret (Alukas) A.; m. Philip D. O'Neill, June 25, 1983; children: Alexander Edwin O'Neill, Sean Matthew O'Neill, Madeleine Clarice O'Neill. AB, Brown U., 1978; JD, Harvard U., 1982. Bar: Mass. 1982, U.S. Dist. Ct. Mass., U.S. Ct. Appeals (1st cir.). Assoc. Hale and Dorr, Boston, 1982-88, jr. ptnr., 1988-92; ptnr. Todd & Weld, Boston, 1992—. Instr. Boston U. Sch. Law, 1984-85. Fellow Am. Coll. Trial Lawyers; mem. ABA, Mass. Bar Assn., Boston Bar Assn., Phi Beta Kappa. Office: Todd & Weld 28 State St 31st Fl Boston MA 02109 Office Phone: 617-720-2626. Business E-Mail: larrowood@toddweld.com.

ARROWSMITH, MARIAN CAMPBELL, secondary education educator; b. St. Louis, Nov. 12, 1943; d. William Rankin and Elizabeth (Mitchell) Arrowsmith; m. William Earl Schroyer, July 23, 1983; stepchildren: Carey Jo, Amy Lynn. BS, La. State U., 1961; MEd, Southeastern La. U., 1978. Lic. tchr., La.; cert. practicum supr. Inst. for Reality Therapy. Tchr. 1st grade McDonough #26, Jefferson Parish Sch. Bd., Gretna, La., 1966; 2nd grade tchr. Woodlawn High Sch., Baton Rouge, 1966-67; kindergarten tchr. Univ. Terrace Elem. Sch., Baton Rouge, summer 1967; 1st grade tchr. Westminster Elem. Sch., Baton Rouge, 1967-72, Elm Grove Elem. Sch., Harvey, La., 1972-73; kindergarden tchr. Westminster Elem. Sch., Baton Rouge, summers 1968, 69, 70, 71, Elm Grove Elem. Sch., summer 1973; 1st grade tchr. St. Andrews Episcopal Sch., New Orleans, 1973-74; kindergarten tchr. St. Tammany Parish Sch. Bd., Folsom, La., 1974-77; early childhood specialist St. Tammany Parish Sch. Bd., Covington, La., 1977-87; prin. Woodlake Elementary Sch., 1987-99, supr. of instrn., St. Tammany Parish, 1999-; off-campus coordinating asst. St. Tammany Parish for Dept. Continuing Edn., Southeastern La. U., 1985-87; condr. workshops in field; selected ofcl. pres. Sunbelt Region of Reality Therapists, 1983; regional dir. La. and Miss. Reality Therapists, Sunbelt Bd. of Reality Therapists, 1983. Author: Helping Your Child at Home, 1982-83; Handbook for Early Childhood Tutorial Program, 1983-84. Mem. Ctr. Learning Devel. and Learning, Regina Coedn. Child Devel. Ctr. (HeadStart), Jr. League. Mem. ASCD, La. Assn. Sch. Execs., Nat. Assn. Tchrs. Math., La. Assn. Tchrs. Math., Pontchartrain Yacht Club, Delta Kappa Gamma (v.p. 1986), Alpha Delta Kappa, Kappa Alpha Theta, Phi Delta Kappa. Democrat. Methodist. Avocations: horticulture, reading, fishing, dancing. Home: 1000 Montgomery St Mandeville LA 70448-5517 Office Phone: 985-892-2276. E-mail: marianarrowsmith@charter.net.

ARSHT, ADRIENNE, lawyer, broadcast executive, bank executive; b. Wilmington, Del., Feb. 4, 1942; d. Samuel and Roxana (Cannon) Arsht; m. Myer Feldman, Sept. 28, 1980. BA, Mt. Holyoke Coll., 1963; JD, Villanova U., 1966. Bar: Del. 1966. Assoc. Morris, Nichols, Arsht and Tunnell, Wilmington, 1966-69, Bregman, Abel and Kay, Washington, 1979-84; dir. govt. affairs TWA, N.Y.C., 1969-79; pres., chmn. bd. Land Title & Escrow Corp., Washington, 1981-86; v.p. Ardman Broadcasting Corp., Washington, 1984—, also bd. dirs.; chmn. bd. TotalBank Corp. Fla., Miami, 1986—; also bd. dirs. Totalbank Corp. Fla., Miami; chmn. Eve Stillman Corp., N.Y.C., 1989-99, also bd. dirs. Bd. dirs. Ardman, Inc., Washington, Capital Broadcasting, Inc., Kansas City, Mo., Trade Nat. Bank, Miami. Bd. dirs. Washington Opera Co., 1982-84, Am. Ballet Theatre, N.Y.C., 1984-90; founder, chmn. Van Guard Found., Washington, 1987-94, Fit and Fabulous, Washington, 1992-93; mem. exec. com. Lombardi Cancer Ctr., Washington, 1988-92; mem. Com. of 200, Coun. on Fgn. Rels.; chmn. bd. dirs. Kennedy Ctr. Prodns., inc., 1982—; U.S. adv. bd. women's internat. forum Dare to Dream Found.; exec. com., sec. Performing Arts Found., Miami. Named Woman of Yr., Am. Ballet Theatre, 1989. Mem. Del. Bar Assn., Women's Internat. Forum, Miami C. of C., Rana Soc. (founder). Office: Total Bank 2720 Coral Way Miami FL 33145-3271 Office Phone: 305-476-6258.

ARTERBERRY, PATRICIA, retired elementary school educator; b. Huntingburg, Ind., Apr. 11, 1947; d. Otis T. Barnett and Fanny Delores Wessel; m. Ronnie G. Arterberry, Oct. 15, 1994; children: Eric Alan, Randall Gene, Tony Gene. BS, U. Evansville (Ind.), 1970, MA, 1973. Tchr. grade 3 Tell City (Ind.) Troy Twp. Schs., tchr. primary grades; ret., 2005. Active Boy Scouts Am.; mem. United Meth. Ch. Recipient Dist. award of Merit, Boy Scouts Am., Coun. Silver Beaver award Mem. NEA, Ind. Tchrs. Assn., Tell City Troy Twp. Classroom Tchr. Assn., Order Ea. Star, Delta Kappa Gamma Home: 9575 Sweetwater Rd Tell City IN 47586-9707

ARTERIAN, HANNAH R., dean, law educator; b. 1949; BS, Elmira Coll., 1970; JD, U. Iowa, 1973. Bar: NY 1974. Assoc. Dewey, Ballantine, Bushby, Palmer & Wood, NYC, 1973—78; vis. assoc. prof. law U. Iowa, 1977, assoc. prof., 1978, Ariz. State U., 1979—82, prof., 1982—2002, assoc. dean, 1992—2001; dean, prof. law Syracuse U. Coll. Law, 2002—. Vis. prof. U. Houston, 1983—84. Mem.: Phi Beta Kappa, Order of the Coif. Office: Syracuse U Coll Law Ste 340 Syracuse NY 13244-1962 Office Phone: 315-443-2524. E-mail: arterian@law.syr.edu.

ARTERO, MARGARET T., academic administrator, military officer; d. Antonio C. and Josepha T. Artero; children: Jesika F., Keana L. PhD, U. Oreg., 1989. Chairwoman, counseling MA program U. Guam, Mangilao, 1989—; maj. Guam Army N.G., Barrigada, 1998—. Bd. mem. Inafa' Maolek, Agana, 2003—, mediator, 2002—; chairwoman Grad. Coun., U. Guam, Mangilao, Student Discipline and Appeals Com., Mangilao, Registration and Admissions Com., Mangilao, Grad. Curriculum Academic Com., Mangilao, U. Guam Commencement Com., Mangilao. Mem. Guam Health Coun., Agana; v.p. Guam Sch. Counseling Assn., Agana. Recipient Whittney Fellowship award, Whittney Fellowship Found. Mem.: Guam Psychol. Assn. (life), ACA (life), APA (life), Phi Delta Kappa (life). Achievements include research in suicide prevention. Avocations: travel, reading, music, multicultural interests, sports. Home: PO Box 2023 Hagatna GU 96932 Home and Office: Sch Education Univ Guam UOG Station Mangilao GU 96923 Office Phone: 671-735-2440. Home Fax: 671-653-2901; Office Fax: 671-734-3651. Business E-Mail: martero@uog9.uog.edu.

ARTERTON, JANET BOND, federal judge; b. Phila., Feb. 8, 1944; m. F. Christopher Arterton; two children. BA, Mt. Holyoke Coll., 1966; JD, Northeastern U., 1977. Law clk. to Hon. Herbert J. Stern U.S. Dist. Ct. N.J., 1977-78; ptnr. Garrison & Arterton, 1978-95; judge U.S. Dist. Ct. Conn., New Haven, 1995—. Fellow Am. Bar Found., Conn. Bar Found.; mem. ATLA, Nat. Employment Lawyers Assn., Conn. Employment Lawyers Assn., Conn. State Trial Lawyers Assn. (bd. govs. 1990-95), Conn. Bar Assn. (mem. adv. com. state ct. rules 1992, mem. fed. jud. selection com. 1991-93, mem. exec. com. women and the law sect. 1990-93, chairperson fed. practice sect. 1993-95. Office: US Dist Ct Conn 141 Church St New Haven CT 06510-2030

ARTHINGTON, CAROL ANN, elementary school educator; b. Duluth, Minn., Sept. 17, 1942; d. Harry Matthew Mleziva and Martha Suzannah Busse-Mleziva; m. Gary Lynn Arthington, Sept. 7, 1963; children: Michelle Lynn, Kurt Alan. BA, North Ctrl. Coll., 1964; MA with distinction, Calif. State U., Northridge, 1992; PhD, Union Inst. and U., 2001. Kindergarten tchr. Puffer Elem. Sch., Downers Grove, Ill., 1965—70; kindergarten/1st grade tchr. Bethlehem Christian Sch., Lake Oswego, Oreg., 1980—81; kindergarten tchr. Wilsonville (Oreg.) Elem. Sch., 1981—83; kindergarten art tchr. Hillcrest Christian Sch., Thousand Oaks, Calif., 1983—84; first grade tchr. Cornerstone Christian Sch., Camarillo, Calif., 1984—86; kindergarten tchr. Los Nogales Sch., Camarillo, 1986—87, Dos Caminos Sch., Camarillo, 1987—. Brain based learning presenter Jensen Learning, San Diego, 1997—98; after sch. art club tchr. Dos Caminos Scj., Camarillo, 1995—2006. Missions chair First Christian Ch. Newbury Park, Calif., 1992—2006. Recipient Hon. Svc. award, Dos Caminos PTA, 2006, Tchr. Excellence award, Amgen Corp., 1992. Home: 873 Tamlei Ave Thousand Oaks CA 91362 Office: Dos Caminos Elem Sch 3635 Appian Way Camarillo CA 93010 Office Phone: 805-482-9894. E-mail: carthington@hotmail.com.

ARTHUR, BEATRICE, actress; b. NYC, May 13, 1923; d. Philip and Rebecca Frankel; m. Gene Saks, May 28, 1950 (div. 1978); 2 children, Matthew, Daniel. Student, Blackstone Coll., also Franklin Inst. Sci. and Arts; student acting with, Erwin Piscator, Dramatic Workshop, New Sch. Social Research. Theatrical appearances include: Lysistrata, 1947, Dog Beneath the Skin, 1947, Gas, 1947, Yerma, 1947, No Exit, 1948, The Taming of the Shrew, 1948, Six Characters in Search of An Author, 1948, The Owl and the Pussycat, 1948, Le Bourgeois Gentilhomme, 1949, Yes Is for a Very Young Man, 1949, Creditors, 1949, Heartbreak House, 1949, Three Penny Opera, 1954, 55, Shoestring Revue, 1955, Seventh Heaven, 1955, The Ziegfield Follies, 1956, What's The Rush?, summer 1956, Mistress of the Inn, 1957, Nature's Way, 1957, Ulysses in Nightown, 1958, Chic, 1959, Gay Divorcee, 1960, A Matter of Position, 1962, Mame, 1966 (Tony award best supporting mus. actress), Fiddler on the Roof, 1964, Bermuda Avenue Triangle, 1996, For Better or Worse, 1996; one woman shows,.And Then There's Bea, San Francisco,2001, An Evening With Bea Arthur, L.A., 2001, Bea Arthur on Broadway: Just Between Friends, 2002; stock appearances with Fiddler on the Roof, Circle Theatre, Atlantic City, summer 1951, State Fair Music Hall, Dallas, 1953, Music Circus, Lambertville, NJ, 1953, resident commedienne, Tamiment (Pa.) Theatre, 1953; numerous TV and nightclub appearances, 1948-; motion picture appearances That Kind of Woman, 1959; Lovers and Other Strangers, 1970, Mame, 1974, History of the World Part I, 1981, Stranger Things, 1995; TV movie: My First Love, 1988; TV appearances include All in the Family, 1971, leading role in TV series Maude, 1972-78 (Emmy award for Best Actress in a Comedy Series 1977), The Golden Girls, 1985-92 (Emmy award for Best Actress in a Comedy Series 1988), The Beatrice Arthur Spl., TV series 30 Years of TV Comedy's Greatest Hits; TV guest appearance: Malcolm in the Middle, 2000, Futurama, 2001, Curb Your Enthusiasm, 2005. Vol. med. tech. USMC, WWII. Mem. Artists Equity Assn., SAG, AFTRA.

ARTHUR, MARGARET FERNE, nurse, insurance paramedic; b. Green Sulphur Springs, W.Va., Mar. 12, 1948; d. John Noel Ford and Violet Pansy Ayers; m. Dwight Ellis Harris, Dec. 31, 1967 (div.); children: Daniel Ellis, Naomi Ruth Okes, David Nathaniel; m. Rev. Harry Earle Arthur, Jr., Mar. 29, 1985. Student, Bluefield Coll., 1992, Concord Coll., 1993, W.Va. No. C.C., New Martinsville, 1998. LPN. LPN Raleigh Gen. Hosp., Beckley, W.Va., 1980-83, South Ga. Med. Ctr., Valdosta, 1983-84, Wythe County Cmty. Hosp., Wytheville, Va., 1984-86, St. Luke's Hosp., Bluefield, W.VA., 1984-89, Bluefield Regional Med. Ctr., 1986-97, Sistersville (W.Va.) Gen. Hosp., 1997, Reynolds Meml. Hosp., Glendale, W.Va., 1997—99. V.p. Dist. 22 LPN Assn. W.Va., 1977-79, pres., 1979-83, acting pres. Dist. 26, 1990-93; rev. panel mem. Nat. Coun. State Bds. Nursing, Chgo., 1998. Mem. Nat. Assn. for Practical Nurse Edn. and Svc. Methodist. Avocation: reading. Home: PO Box 5373 3910 Grand Central Ave Vienna WV 26105 E-mail: ncd00804@mail.wvnet.edu.

ARTHUR, ROSE ANN HORMAN, dean; b. Batchtown, Ill., June 13, 1931; d. John Henry and Trena Marie (Snyders) H.; m. Richard Laurence Arthur, May 1, 1971. BS in Religion and Edn. with honors, St. Louis U., 1962; MA in Religion and Edn., St. Mary's Grad. Sch. Theology, 1967; ThD in Theology and Edn., Grad. Theol. Union, 1979. Coord. women's studies Grad. Theol. Union, Berkeley, Calif., 1969-71; tchr. 6th grade Prince George County Schs., Beaver Heights, Md., 1971-72; dir. Ctr. Women Grad. Theol. Union, 1972-73; television tchr. grades 1-3 Govt. of Am. Samoa, 1973-79; rsch./resource assoc. Harvard U. Divinity Sch., Cambridge, Mass., 1979-80; exec. dir. Chgo. Cluster Theol. Schs., 1980-83; dean grad. & undergrad. Heritage Coll., Toppenish, Wash., 1983-88; dean Rivier Coll., Nashua, NH, 1988—96. Dir. distance learning grant Heritage Coll., 1986-88, dir. liberal arts edn. grant, dir. women's studies grant, 1987-88; dir. women's studies grant Rivier Coll./N.H. Humanities Coun., 1991-92; founder, dir. Rivier Inst. for Sr. Edn., 1997—. Author: The Wisdom Goddess: Feminine Motifs in the Nag Hammadi Documents, 1984. Mem. Alderwoman's Campaign, Chgo., 1981-82, Hyde Park Tenants' Assn., Chgo., 1980-82, Merrimack (N.H.) Dem. Orgn., 1993—; v.p. Merrimack Town Com., 1993-2004; mem. NH State Legislature, 1998-2000; candidate N.H. Senate, 2004. Recipient NH Older Worker of Yr. award, 2006—. Mem. Grad. Theol. Union Ctr. Women and Religion. Democrat. Avocations: reading, walking, canoeing, gardening. Home: 25 Island Dr Merrimack NH 03054-4159 Office: Rivier Coll 420 Main St Nashua NH 03060-5043 Office Phone: 603-897-8623. Business E-Mail: rarthur@rivier.edu.

ARTHUR, SUSAN HELENE, social studies educator; d. Ludwig Hedwig Roesler and Jeanna Sue Roesler-Nix; m. Art Arthur, Dec. 31, 1963; children: Heather Marie Arthur-Keener, Alicia-George. BS, South Ea. U., Durant, Okla., 1997. Cert. provisional elem. tchr. Tex. and Okla., 1997. Tchr. social studies grade 6 B. Mc Danile Mid. Sch., Denison, Tex., 1997—2005, chair dept. social studies dept. chair, tch. Am. History grade 8, cheerleader coach, 2003—. Tech. asst. B. Mc Daniel Mid. Sch., 2002—. Translator: (social studies curriculum) TARGET. Choir mem. Waples Meth. Ch., Denison, 1999—. Recipient Secondary Outstanding Tchr. of Yr., Denison Classroom Tchrs. Assn., 2004—05. Mem.: Delta Kappa Gamma Chi (assoc.; pres. & v.p. 2003—06). Independent. Methodist. Home: 3398 DesVoignes Rd Denison TX 75021 Office: B Mc Daniel Mid Sch 400 Lillis Lane Denison TX 75020 Office Phone: 903-462-7200. Office Fax: 903-462-7328. Personal E-mail: susan_arthur_art@yahoo.com. Business E-Mail: sarthur@denisonisd.net.

ARTHURS, MADELEINE HOPE, artist; b. Summit, N.J., July 4, 1966; d. Edward and Alberta (Bean) A. AB, Smith Coll., 1989; BFA with honors, Sch. of Visual Arts, N.Y.C., 1996, MFA, 1998. Intern Exit Art/The 1st World, N.Y.C., 1993-94; animation artist Magnet Pictures, Inc., N.Y.C., 1995; illustrator N.Y. Art Studios, Inc., N.Y.C., 1995; digital camera photographer Sonicnet, N.Y.C., 1995; digital programer Dia Ctr. for the Arts, N.Y.C., 1995-96; animation artist Curious Pictures, N.Y.C., 1995-96; animation Bill Plympton Studio, N.Y.C., 1996-97; archivist and studio asst. Alice Aycock/Fine Artist, N.Y.C., 1997—; animation cel painter MTV, N.Y.C., 1998-99. Painter Jeff Koons Studio, N.Y.C., 1999-00; guest artist Tchrs. and Writer PS76, Queens, N.Y., 1999, Project Read, 1999; asst. art tchr. Studio in a Sch., 2000; freelance illustrator Wall St. Jour., 2000—. One-woman shows include Smith Coll., 1988, 1st Ann. Premiere World Internat. Fine Arts Competition, 1998—99, Soho Photo Gallery, 2003, exhibited in group shows at Mus. Competition/Exhbn., Va., 1996, Soho Internat. Art Contest, N.Y.C., 1997, Sch. of Visual Arts Gallery, 1997, Exhbn./Chgo., 1997, Sch. of Visual Arts Gallery, 1998, Premiere World Internat. On-Line Fine Arts Competition, 1998, Competition/Exhbn./RSVP's Dream Competition, 1998, Catherine Lorillard Wolfe Art Club 102d ann. competition at Nat. Art Club, 1998, Best of Best Exhbn. SVA Visual Arts Mus., 2000, The Drawing Ctr. Slide Registry, 2000—, The Warehouse Exit Art/The 1st World Warehouse, 2000—, Momenta Art Gallery Benefit Exhbn., 2001, White Columns, 2002, Exit Art, N.Y.C., Represented in permanent collections Libr. of Congress, The Mag. Rack SVA Visual Arts Mus., exhibited in group shows at others, exhibitions include City Without Walls, NYC, 2003—05, Berger Mus., Paramus, NJ, 2006; contbg. photographer (book, nat. and internat. exhbns.) Here is New York: A Democracy of Photographs, 2001—02, photographer (photographs published) Sunday Telegraph Mag., 2002. Recipient Paula Rhodes Meml. award, 1998, Merit Scholarship award Sch. of Visual Arts, 1997-98, Steuben award, New Canaan, 1997, Rhodes Family award for Outstanding Achievement/Sch. Visual Arts, 1996, Gilbert Stone scholarship, 1995, Silas H. Rhodes scholarship, 1994-96, Martha Keilig prize for Best Still Life/Landscape in Oils, Smith Coll., Northampton, Mass., 1988,. Art Residency Hall Farm Ctr., Vt., 2001, others.

ARTL, KAREN ANN, business owner, author; b. Bainbridge, N.Y., July 4, 1950; d. Douglas Robert and Beverly Florence (Schofell) Moore; m. Robert Edward Gurney, June 15, 1969 (div. June 1981); children: Douglas Albert Gurney, Rebecca Susan Gurney; m. Jeffrey Joseph Artl, Nov. 8, 1986; 1 child, Grace Beverly. BA in Edn., SUNY Coll. at Oneonta, 1972; MA in Reading and Edn., Cleve. State U., 1981. Tchr. reading Independence (Ohio) Mid. Sch., 1979-81; sr. editor Am. Greetings Corp., Cleve., 1981-87; mem. adj. faculty Lorain Community Coll., Cleve., 1987-89; creative dir. Gibson Greetings, Inc., Cin., 1994-97; owner Cresta Creative, 1999—. Owner, pres. WordsWorth Studio, Inc.; conf. speaker, trainer, cons. Social Expression Industry. Author: You Can Write Greeting Cards, 1999, M. Washington, etc., 1991, (children's book) I'm Me and You're Not, 1991, How Noah Knew What to Do!, 1998, The Baby King, 1999, Babies of the Bible, 1999, The Animal Babies Easter, Ten Ways to Please God; inspirational plaque line for Christian market; editor CR Gibson/Gift Books, 1993, Gibson Greetings, 1993. Vol. Am. Cancer Soc., Cleve., 1991. Mem. AAUW, NAFE, Greeting Card Assn., Greeting Card Creative Network, Soc. Children's Book Writers. Lutheran. Avocations: writing inspirational materials, activities to combat illiteracy.

ARTS-MEYER, KATINA, interior designer; b. Chgo. d. Arthur C. Meyer and Constance Arts. BS, U. Mo., 1966; cert. honors in design and lit., U. Oslo, 1965; MA Cooper-Hewitt New Sch., N.Y.C., 1992. Journalist London Telegraph, Harpers Bazaar, London, 1970—75, Sunday Times London, 1975—82; pres., designer Katina Arts-Meyer, Ltd., Interior Design, N.Y.C., 1985—. Lectr. Parsons, NYU, Cooper-Hewitt Mus. Author/artist Parc Citroen, Vogue France, 1998; one-woman shows include "Wildflowers" and "Orchids", Jardin Gallery, 1985, 1988, Southampton Design Showcase, 1984, Kips Bay Design Showhouse, 1994, 1998; designer Kips Bay Design Showhouse, 2001, French Designer Showhouse, 1995, 2003; contbr. articles to mags. Bd. dirs. Hotel-des-Artistes, N.Y.C., 1994—98. Scholar Helena Rubenstein Found. for Design and Art, N.Y.C., 1985—87. Mem.: Nat. Heritage Soc., Decorative Arts Soc. Avocations: watercolor painting, biographies and histories, ballet, skiing, music. Office: Katina Arts-Meyer Ltd 71 E 77th St New York NY 10021 Office Phone: 212-744-8211.

ARTZ, CHERIE B., lawyer; b. Cin., Jan. 3, 1949; d. Joseph Meyer and Esther Epstein Fish; m. William Edward Artz, May 15, 1976; children: Rachel, Lindsey. BS, U. Cin., 1969; MA, George Washington U., 1973, JD with honors, 1985. Bar: Va. 1985, U.S. Ct. Appeals (fed. cir.) 1986, D.C. 1987, U.S. Supreme Ct. 1989, U.S. Ct. Appeals (4th cir.) 1990, U.S. Ct. Appeals (5th cir.) 1991, U.S. Ct. Appeals (6th cir.) 1992, Md. 1995. Tchr. Cin. Pub. Schs., 1969-71, Piscataway (N.J.) Pub. Schs., 1971-72; social worker Arlington (Va.) Juvenile Ct., 1973-82; law clk. U.S. Ct. Appeals Fed. Cir., Washington, 1985-86; lawyer Schnader Harrison Segal & Lewis, LLP, Washington, 1986—, ptnr., 1994—2001; v.p., gen. counsel Resource Cons., Inc., 2001—. Mem. George Washington U. Law Rev., 1984. Bd. dirs. Temple Rodef Shalom, Falls Church, Va., 1991—, pres., 1996-98; bd. dirs. Union Am. Hebrew Congregations, 2001—, Mid Atlantic Coun., Washington, 1998—; bd. overseers N.Y. Sch. Hebrew Union Coll., N.Y.C., 1999—; Fellow Am. Bar Found., 2001—. Home: 964 Saigon Rd Mc Lean VA 22102-2119 Office: Resource Cons Inc Ste 800 2650 Park Tower Dr Vienna VA 22180

ARTZ, ETHEL ANGELA CLEAVENGER, elementary school educator, consultant; b. Fort Belknap, Mont., Nov. 14, 1958; d. Kenneth James and Eliza Stanley C.; m. Jerome Daniel Artz, Aug. 15, 1998; 1 child, Reesa Eliza. BS in Elem. Edn., U. Mont., Billings, 1983; postgrad., U. Calif., Davis, 1996-98. Cert. pharmacy technician; cert. in conflict resolution and comm.; cert. in elem. edn. Aupair L.I. Governess, South Hampton, 1983; ednl. instr. Stockton (Calif.) Christian, 1983-86; ESL instr. Eikaiwa Gakuin Japanese Sch., Fukuoka, Japan, 1989-90, Cultural Homestay Internat., Granite Bay, Calif., 1990-91; ednl. field studies dir. Ednl. Tour Co., San Francisco, 1991-97; youth tng. specialist Indian Dispute Resolution Svcs., Sacramento, 1997-99; positive youth devel. character edn. specialist Sacramento City Unified Sch. Dist., 1999—. Participant Youth Travel Abroad work program, New Zealand, Australia, Europe, 1988; mem. Indian Edn., Havre, Mont., 1989—96; trainer, jr. dispute resolution svcs. cons. Indian Dispute Resolution Svcs., Inc.; with Sacramento County Office Edn., U.S. Dept. Housing and Urban Devel., Am. Indian Edn., Nat. Conf. Peacemaking and Conflict Resolution, George Mason U., Seminole Tribe Fla. Housing Dept. Office: Sacramento City Unified 520 Capitol Mall Fl 6 Sacramento CA 95814-4704 Home: 2019 Ceres Way Sacramento CA 95821

ARUTT, CHERYL, clinical and forensic psychologist, educator; b. Fort Knox, Ky., May 13, 1966; BA Women's Studies summa cum laude, UCLA, 1993; MA Clin. Psych., Calif. Sch. Prof. Psych., Los Angeles, 1995, PsyD, 1997. Lic. psychologist, Calif. Psychol. asst. Barbara Cort Counter, PhD, Beverly Hills, CA, 1995-99, forensic psychologist, 1999—; adj. asst. prof. Calif. Sch. Prof. Psychology, Los Angeles, 1999—; pvt. practice clin. psychologist Beverly Hills, CA, 1999—. Author: Healing Together: A Program for Couples, 1997 (named outstanding doctoral project CSPP, Los Angeles). Counselor, trainer, adv. Los Angeles Commn. on Assaults Against Women, 1991-97. Recipient George Heller Meml. scholarship Am. Fedn. TV and Radio Artists, 1991, John Dales Memorial Scholarship, SAG, Los Angeles, 1992. Mem. APA, Phi Beta Kappa. Office: 9735 Wilshire Blvd Ste 208 Beverly Hills CA 90212 Office Phone: 310-273-2755. E-mail: Dr_Arutt@hotmail.com.

ARUTYUNYAN, EMMA, radio broadcaster; b. Yerevan, Armenia, Aug. 14, 1946; arrived in U.S., 1988; d. Hambartsum and Vartanush (Babayan) A.; m. Sako Mkrtchyan, Feb. 17, 1971; 1 child, Aram. MS, State U. Yerevan, 1969. Radioastrophysicist, rsch. scientist Byurakan Astrophys. Obs., Armenia, 1969-78; mem. physics faculty Poly. Inst. Yerevan, 1978-87; internat. radio-broadcaster Voice of Am., Washington, 1992—2003; news editor Horizon TV, LA, 2003—. Pres. Ctrl. Com. Dosaaf USSR, Moscow, 1967. Contbr. sci. articles to profl. jours. Recipient award Ctrl. Com. Dosaaf USSR, Moscow, 1967. Mem. Smithsonian Instn. (nat. assoc.), Nat. Geog. Soc., Am. Mus. Natural History. Personal E-mail: earutyun@yahoo.com.

ARVANITAKIS, ZOE, neurologist, researcher; MD, U. Western Ontario, London, Can., 1994. Diplomate bd. cert. Resident in neurology U. Manitoba, Winnipeg, Canada, 1991; fellow in dementia Mayo Clinic, Jacksonville, Fla., 2001; asst. prof. Rush U. Med. Ctr., Chgo., 2001—. Rsch. mentor Rush U. Med. Ctr., Chgo., 2001—; med. jour. reviewer Neurology Archives of Neurology, 2004—; med. grant reviewer Alzheimer's Assn., Chgo., 2004—; med. course developer Am. Acad. Neurology, Rochester, Minn., 2005—; invited prof. Mayo Clinic, 2005—, Vanderbilt U., Nashville, 2005—; exec. mem. and sec. Women's Adv. Group to Dean Rush Med. Coll., Chgo., 2006—. Contbr. articles to profl. jours. Lobbying neurologist Alzheimer's Assn., Washington, 2006. Grantee, Mayo Clinic, 2000—01, Alzheimer's Assn., 2004—06, Nat. Inst. Aging, 2005—. Mem.: Am. Acad. Neurology (exec. mem. geriatric neurology sect. 2006—, councilor geriatric neurology sect. 2006—). Office: Alzheimers Disease Ctr Rush Univ Med Ctr Ste 8N 710 S Paulina Chicago IL 60612

ARVIA, ANNE L., bank executive; m. Jack Arvia; 2 children. BS in Acctg., Mich. State Univ. CPA. Acctg. mgr. Crowe, Chizekand Co. LLP; asst. controller ShoreBank Corp., Chgo., 1991—93, v.p., controller, 1993—96, sr. v.p., 1996—98, CFO, 1998—2001, pres., 2001—06, CEO, 2003—06, Nationwide Bank, Columbus, Ohio, 2006—. Bd. dir. Cmty. Investment Corp., Cmty. Initiatives Inc. Mem. Leadership Chgo. Named one of 100 Most Influential Women, Crain's Chgo. Bus., 2004, 25 Most Powerful Women in Banking, US Banker mag., 2005; named to 40 Under 40, Crain's Chgo. Bus., 2002. Mem.: Ill. CPA (Fin. Inst. Com.), Ill. Bankers Assn., Chgo. Fin. Exchange, Leadership Ill. Office: Nationwide Bank One Nationwide Plz Columbus OH 43215 Office Phone: 773-288-1000. Office Fax: 773-493-6609.*

ARVIN, ANN MARGARET, microbiology and immunology educator, researcher; BA, Brown U., 1966; MD, U. Pa., 1972. Resident U. Calif. San Francisco Med. Ctr., 1975; fellow Stanford (Calif.) Hosp. and Clinics, 1978; mem. faculty Stanford U. Sch. Medicine, 1978—, Lucille Packard Prof. Pediat., prof. microbiology and immunology, 1989—, assoc. dean rsch., 2001—. Cons. FDA Ctr. Biologics Evaluation & Rsch., 1994—; co-chair rsch. team investigating possible uses of flu virus in bio-terrorism Stanford U., 2003—; life sciences bd. NAS/NRC, 2004—. Trustee Am. Herpes Found.; mem. exec. com. VZV Rsch. Found. Recipient New Investigator award, Nat. Inst. Allergy & Infectious Diseases, 1981—84, Rsch. Career Devel. award, 1984—89, E. Mead Johnson award for rsch. in pediat., 1992, John F. Enders award, Infectious Diseases Soc. Am., 2002. Mem.: Assn. Am. Physicians, Inst. Medicine. Office: Stanford U Sch Medicine 300 Pasteur Dr Stanford CA 94305 Business E-Mail: aarvin@stanford.edu.*

ARVIN, LINDA LEE, counselor; b. York, Pa., May 12, 1952; d. Paul Henry and Mary Elizabeth (Stein) Honsermyer; m. Michael Eugene Arvin, Dec. 16, 1978 (div.); children: Melissa Elizabeth, Michael Alexis; m. Daniel A. Hitchcock October 14, 2002. BA, George Washington U., 1981; MS in Clin. Cmty. Counseling, 1999. Lic. Clin. Profl. Counselor Johns Hopkins U. Sr. staff Cmty. Ministry, Rockville, Md., 1989-92; sr. counselor Arlington Cmty. Residences, 1992-93; program dir. Montgomery County Coalition for the Homeless, Rockville, 1993-97; counselor ASG, Silver Spring, Md., 1998—2001; psychotherapist Threshold Svc., Silver Spring, Md., 2003—, Pvt. Practice, Kensington, Md., 2003—. Mem. ACA, AAUW, AMHCA Democrat. Avocations: ballroom dancing, music, travel. Home: 4202 E West Hwy Chevy Chase MD 20815-5911 Office: Threshold Svc 8818 Ga Ave Silver Spring MD also: 3720 Farragot Ave Ste 103 Kensington MD Office Phone: 240-281-5004. Personal E-mail: larvinlcpc@aol.com.

ARVISH, ELLEN MARIE, elementary school educator; b. Anaconda, Mont., May 26, 1951; d. Bernard Anthony and Mary Louise Arvish. BS Phys. Edn., Music, Great Falls Coll., Mont., 1973. Tchr. elem. phys. edn. and music St. Joseph Sch., Great Falls, 1973—74, Morisson Elem. Sch. Dist. #4, Troy, Mont., 1974—. Named to Who's Who Among Am. Tchrs. Home: 208 Mineral Ave Troy MT 59935 Office: Morisson Elem Dist 4 501 E Mospell Troy MT 59935

ARY, BONNITA ELLEN, registrar, federal official; b. Walden, Colo., July 26, 1932; d. Burney Grover and Maude Velisa (Bulis) Dowdell; m. Leo D. Ary, Aug. 16, 1950 (div.); children: Kristy L. Ary Ackerson, R. Craig. Cert. med. asst. Am. Assn. Med. Assts. Sec. Mountain Park REA, Walden, 1950—51; dep. treas. Jackson County, Walden, 1955—61; med. asst. Walden, 1961—66; bus. mgmt. asst. U.S. Forest Svc., Walden, 1967—84, support svcs. specialist, 1985—93; ret., 1993; registrar vital stats. State of Colo., Walden, 1961—. Bookkeeper for small bus., 1950—83. Mem. Walden Sch. Bd., 1971—79, registrar vital stats., 1961—2006; chmn. fin. bd. North Park Cmty. United Meth. Ch., 1980—84, chmn. bd. trustees, 1994—98; chmn. bd. dirs. North Park Med. Clinic, 1993—96. Office: 612 5th St Walden CO 80480

ARZOUMANIAN, LINDA LEE, school system administrator; b. Madison, Wis., Apr. 29, 1942; d. James Arthur Luck and Rosemary M. (Peacock) Engstrom; children: Stephan, Aaron. BS, Stout State U., Menomonie, Wis., 1964; MEd, Ohio U., Athens, 1969; EdD, Nova U., 1994. Cert. tchr. vocat., secondary, cmty. coll., Ariz. Residence hall asst. Ohio U., Athens, 1965-67; quality control supr. Advalloy, Inc., Palo Alto, Calif., 1967; tchr. adult edn. Eau Claire (Wis.) Pub. Sch., 1964-65; patient svc. dietitian Camden Clark Meml. Hosp., Parkersburg, W.Va., 1970; adminstr. pre-sch. Fishkill (N.Y.) Meth. Nursery Sch., 1976-84; substitute tchr. Tucson Unified Sch. Dist., 1987; tchr. pre-sch. Tanque Verde Luth. Presch., Tucson, 1988-89; cons., early childhood ednl. curriculum specialist Tucson Unified Sch. Dist., 1988-93; instr. Ctrl. Ariz. Coll., 1990-98, Prescott Coll., 1991-92; dist. moderator Sch. Cmty. Partnership Coun., Tucson, 1988-90; dir. child and family svcs. in prevention, early intervention and treatment in sys. managed care CODAC Behavioral Health Svcs., Tucson, 1990-99, dir. mgmt. info. sys., 1999, dir. cmty. svcs., 1999-2000; supt. of schs. Pima County, 2000—. Mem. supts. adv. cabinet Tucson Unified Sch. Dist., 1988-89, mem. curriculum and instrn. coun., 1989-90, spl. edn. pre-sch. adv. com., 1989-91, info. tech. bond rev. com., 1989—, sex edn. curriculum adv. com., core curriculum com., 1988-90, 2000 com., 1988-89, and various others; appt. Ariz. State Bd. Edn., 2002. Mem. Dutchess County Child Devel. Com., Poughkeepsie, N.Y., 1979-81; advancement chmn. troop 1968 Boy Scouts Am., Tucson, 1986, com. person troop 194, 1986-89; mem. joint com. on site based decision making Tucson Unified Sch. Dist./Tucson Edn. Assn., 1989-98; life mem. Ariz. PTA; mem. Early Childhood Edn. Coun. Consortium; mem. mgmt. com. Healthy Families of Pima County; commr. Met. Edn. Commn.; mem. Pima County Youth Coun., Greater Tucson Strategic Planning for Econ. Devel., mem. workforce investment bond. Mem.: AAUW, Ariz. Sch. Bds. Assn., Am. Assn. Edn. Svc. Agys. (Fed. Relations Repr. (Ariz.)), Tucson Assn. Edn. Young Children (past pres.), Nat. Assn. Edn. Young Children, Tucson Rep. Women, Pima County Supt. and Governing Bd. Collaborative, Tucson Hispanic C. of C., Tucson Met. C. of C., So. Ariz. Forums on Children and Families, Cath. Cmty. Svc. (bd. dirs.). Avocations: basketmaking, quilting, gardening, cooking. Home: 8230 E Ridgebrook Dr Tucson AZ 85750-2442 Office: 130 W Congress 4th Floor Tucson AZ 85701 Office Phone: 520-740-8451. Personal E-mail: lindaa1447@aol.com.

ASAAD, KOLLEEN JOYCE, special education educator; b. West Union, Iowa, July 13, 1941; d. Leonard Henry and Catherine Adelade (Bishop) Anfinson; children: Todd, Robin, Tara, Jason. BA in Elem. Edn., Upper Iowa U., 1961; MA in Spl. Edn. and Adminstrn., U. Cin., 1973. Elem. tchr. Fredericksburg (Iowa) Elem. Sch., 1961-62, Tyler Sch., Cedar Rapids, Iowa, 1962-64, Oasis Sch., 29 Palms, Calif., 1964-69, Longfellow Sch., Waterloo, Iowa, 1969-70; spl. edn. tchr. Fairview Sch., Cin., 1970-77; learning disabilities tchr. Lincoln Sch., Portsmouth, Ohio, 1977-78; dir. spl. edn. Vermilion Assn. for Spl. Edn., Danville, Ill., 1978-94; dir. edn. Swann Spl. Care Ctr., Champaign, Ill., 1994-97, ret., 1997. Mem. Vermilion County Mental Health Bd., 2006—; pres. Thrivent Cmty. Bd., 2006—; bd. mem. Crosspoints, Danville, Ill. Named Best Adminstr., Regional Supt. of Schs., 1991. Mem. Coun. for Exceptional Children, Coun. for Adminstrs. of Spl. Edn., Ill. Adminstrs. of Spl. Edn., Assn. Persons with Severe Handicaps, Ill. Ret. Tchrs. Assn. (state chair pub. rels.), Exec. Club. Lutheran. Avocations: reading, art. Home: 122 Mapleleaf Dr Catlin IL 61817-9646

ASADORIAN, DIANA C., electrical engineer, educator; b. Leninakan, Armenia, June 16, 1950; came to U.S., 1975; d. Eduard and Vartuhi (Seraidarian) Martirosyan; m. William R. Asadorian, July 22, 1978; 1 child, Ronald E. M in Electromech. Engring. Elec. Motors, Polytech. Inst., Odessa, USSR, 1972. Elect. engr. Odessa Cable Plant, 1972-75; draftsman Leviton Co., Bklyn., 1976-77; from engring. asst. to design engr. engring. and devel. CBS, N.Y.C., 1977-86, assoc. dir. engring. lab., 1986-89, dir. engring. lab. and drafting. engring. and devel., 1989-90, dir. tech. tng. and documentation engring., 1990—, assoc. dir. news engring. and document, 1994—. Mem. Soc. Motion Picture and TV Engring., Am. Soc. News Engring. and Documentation (assoc. dir.). Republican. Baptist. Avocation: concert pianist.

ASAI, SUSAN MIYO, music educator, consultant; b. N.Y.C., Apr. 11, 1952; d. Tiyo Doris and Ken William Asai; m. Thezeus Takis Sarris, July 9, 1991; 1 child, Ava Dongqun Asai-Sarris. B of Music Edn., Ithaca Coll., N.Y., 1974; MA in Music Edn., Columbia U., N.Y.C., N.Y., 1978; PhD, U. Calif., L.A., 1988. Japan program coord. 1986 Festival of Am. Folklife, Smithsonian Instn., Washington, 1985—86; Mass. touring coord. New Eng. Found. for the Arts, Cambridge, 1988—89; part-time faculty Wheelock Coll., Liberal Arts Divsn., Boston, 1991; prof. dept. music Northeastern U., Boston, 1991—. Prodn. asst. Japan Am. Theater, Japanese Am. Culture and Cmty. Ctr., L.A., 1984—85, prodn. coord. Osuwa Daiko concert, 1986. Musician: (performance) Japanese koto (13-string board zither); author: (book) Nomai Music and Dance of Northern Japan. Fulbright Grad. Rsch. grant, Japan-U.S. Ednl. Commn., 1983-1984. Mem.: Soc. for Ethnomusicology (assoc.; coun. mem. 2000—02), Soc. for Asian Music (assoc.; pres. 2001—06), Phi Beta Delta. Democrat. Lutheran. Avocations: tennis, playing piano, travel, reading fiction. Home: 55 Forest St Malden MA 02148 Office: Northeastern Univ Music Dept 360 Huntington Ave Boston MA 02115 Office Phone: 617-373-4709. Office Fax: 617-373-4129. Personal E-mail: smasai@verizon.net. E-mail: s.asai@neu.edu.

ASAKAWA, TAKAKO, dancer, educator, choreographer, director; b. Toyko, Feb. 23, 1939; came to U.S., 1962; d. Kamenosuke and Chiaki Asakawa. Student, Tokyo schs., 1962-91. Prin. dancer Martha Graham Dance Co., N.Y.C., 1962-76, 81—; dancer Alvin Ailey, 1968-69, Pearl Lang, 1967, Lar Lubovitch, 1974-80. Guest tchr. at numerous schs. and univs. throughout world, including Moscow Culture Exch. Program, Martha Graham Sch., Juilliard Sch.; co.-founder Asakawalker Dance Co.; dir. Paris Opera Ballet Co., Am. Ballet Theater, Het Nationale Ballet in Amsterdam and various univs. throughout world. Performed all major roles in GRaham reperatory throughout world, including Paris Opera House, Covent Garden; Broadway and TV performances include Eliza in The King and I, Bell Tel. Hour. Named Legendary Woman of Am., St. Vincent's Hosp. Mem. Am. Guild Musical Artists Home and Office: 20 W 64th St Apt 29-E/F New York NY 10023-7180

ASANBE, COMFORT BOLA, psychologist, educator; d. David Atte and Martha Abon Odeyemi; m. Joseph Adebola Asanbe, Feb. 27, 1982 (dec. Aug. 19, 1996); children: Olaniran Omoniyi, Opeyemi Ajike. BA, U. Ilorin, Nigeria, 1983; MA in Edn., Austin Peay State U., 1989; PhD, Tenn. State U., Nashville, 1996. Lic. psychologist/health svcs. provider Tenn. Bd. of Examiners in Psychology, 2003. Tchr. Ilorin Grammar Sch., Ilorin, Nigeria, 1980—83; instr. Austin Peay State U., Clarksville, Tenn., 1997—2001; psychologist Metro-Davidson County Sch. Sys., Nashville, 2001—02; asst. prof. Tenn. Technol. U., Cookeville, Tenn., 2002—. Psychology intern U. Tenn. Med. Ctr., Memphis, 2000—01; presenter in field. Workshop presenter Stephen's Ctr. for Child Abuse Prevention, Livingston, Tenn., 2003; exec. mem. Children Internat. Edn. Coun. (CIEC) Program, Clarksville, Tenn., 1992—98. Faculty Rsch. grantee, Tenn. Technol. U., 2004. Mem.: APA, Tenn. Psychol. Assn., Southeastern Psychol. Assn., Phi Kappa Phi, Psi Chi. Avocations: travel, cooking, sewing. Office: Tenn Technol U 1000 N Dixie Ave Cookeville TN 38505-001 Office Phone: 931-372-3217. Home Fax: 931-372-3400.

ASARCH, ELAINE, interior designer, anthropologist; b. Des Moines, Nov. 4, 1944; d. Morris and Rose (Sherman) Feintech; m. Richard Asarch, Aug. 17, 1965; children: Deborah, Chad, Jonathan, Adam, David. BA, U. Iowa, 1966; postgrad., U. Colo., 1992—. Tchr. spl. edn. Univ. Hosp. Schs., Iowa City, 1966-69; tchr. Raleigh Hill Elem. Sch., Portland, Oreg., 1969; learning therapist Psychol. & Guidance Ctr., Devner, 1974; interior designer Sipple/Asarch Design, Denver, 1981-83, Elaine Asarch Design Assocs., Englewood, Colo., 1983—. Dir., prodr. documentary on domestic violence; contbr. articles, photographs to Better Homes and Garden, 1980. Mktg. chmn. Jr. League of Denver, 1985-87; com. mem. Rose Found., Denver, 1997—; Pres., chmn. women's campaign Allied Jewish Fedn. of Denver, 1990-93; chmn. cmty. rels. com., 1994-96; steering com. Harvard Womens Studies in Religion, 1994-99; founder Cmty. Help and Abuse Info. Agy.; mayors transition team Parks and Recreation, 2004; pres. Civic Ctr. Conservancy, 2005. Recipient Ann. award, Yeshiva Toras Chaim, Denver, 1994, Tree of Life award, Herzl Day Sch., Denver, 1997, Golda Meir award, Allied Jewish Fedn. Colo., 2001. Mem. Am. Soc. Interior Designers (cert.). Achievements include research in relationship between environment and healing with relationship to medical practices. Home: 1000 E Tufts Ave Englewood CO 80110-5931 E-mail: elaine@efa1000.com.

ASBURY, CAROLYN, neuroscience researcher; Former dir. Pew Charitable Trusts' Health and Human Svcs. Program; formerly with Robert Wood Johnson Found.; now sr. fellow Leonard Davis Inst., Univ. Pa.; and sr. cons. Dana Found., NYC. Chair Nat. Orgn. Rare Disorders, Danbury, Conn., Treatment Rsch. Inst. Office: Dana Found Ste 900 745 Fifth Ave New York NY 10151 Business E-Mail: casbury@dana.org.

ASCENCAO, ERLETE MALVEIRA, psychologist, educator; b. Manaus, Brazil, Apr. 8, 1954; naturalized, U.S., 03; d. Alvaro de Azevedo and Adelia Malveira Ascencao. AA, Reinhardt Coll., 1978; BA, Berry Coll., 1980; MA, Emory U., 1982, BS in Mental Health Psychology, 1986, PhD, 1986, U. Tenn., 1995. Lic. psychologist. Psychotherapist Luron Mental Health Svcs., Nashville, 1995—97; psychol. examiner Tenn. Prison for Women, Nashville, 1996—97; assoc. prof. psychology Tenn. State U., Nashville, 1998—2004; clrin. psychologist Meharry Cmty. Wellness Ctr., Nashville, 2001—; dir. psychol. treatment svcs. and quality assistance Meharry Med. Coll., Nashville, 2004—, assoc. prof. psychiatry and behavioral sci., 2004—05; assoc. prof. dept. internal medicine Meharry Cmty. Wellness Ctr., 2005—, dir.dept. psychology and treatment svcs. Mem. share mothers project Vanderbilt U., Nashville, 2001; presenter in field. Contbr. articles to profl. publs. HIV outreach educator, pro bono clin. psychologist Meharry Med. Coll., 2001—. Recipient award for outstanding clin. work, Luton Mental Health Svcs., 1997; grantee, Meharry Med. Coll., Ctr. AIDS Rsch., 2004. Mem.: APA (regional trainer HIV/AIDS HOPE 1986—, expert in multicultural psychology, grantee), Tenn. Psychol. Assn. Democrat. Roman Catholic. Avocations: theater, music, literature. Home: 3410 Batavia St Nashville TN 37209 Office: Meharry Med Coll Dept Internal Medicine 1005 DB Todd Jr Blvd Nashville TN 37208

ASCH, SUSAN MCCLELLAN, pediatrician; b. Cleve., Dec. 31, 1945; d. William Alton and Alice Lonore (Heide) McClellan; m. Marc Asch, Sept. 10, 1966; children: Marc William, Sarah Susan, Rebecca Janney. AB, Oberlin (Ohio) Coll., 1967; MA, Mich. State U., 1968, PhD, 1975; MD, Case Western Res., 1977. Diplomate Nat. Bd. Med. Examiners, Am. Bd. Pediatrics, Am. Bd. Emergency Pediatrics. Instr. sociology Mich. State U., East Lansing, 1971-73; resident in pediatrics Children's Nat. Med. Ctr., Washington, 1977-80, chief resident in ambulatory and emergency pediatrics, 1979-80; asst. to dir. Office for Med. Applications of Rsch. NIH, Bethesda, 1980-81; pvt. practice in pediatrics Millinocket (Maine) Regional Hosp., 1981-84; assoc. dir. emergency Akron (Ohio) Children's Hosp., 1984-87; asst. prof. pediatrics Northeastern Ohio U. Coll. Medicine, 1984-87; dir. emergency St. Paul Children's Hosp., 1987-91; asst. prof. pediatrics U. Minn., 1987-93, clin. asst. prof., 1993—; pvt. practice pediatrics Stillwater, Minn., 1992—; sec. exec. com. med. staff Lakeview Meml. Hosp., 1999—2001, vice chief of staff, 2001—03, chief of staff, 2003—05, chair pediatrics, 2005—. Nat. faculty PALS Am. Heart Assn., Mpls., Dallas, 1987-94; mem. task force, sub-bd. emergency pediatrics Am. Bd. Pediatrics, 1987-91, mem. sub-bd. emergency pediat., 1991-93. Assoc. editor Pediatric Emergency Medicine, 1992, contbr., 1992, 96; author various publs., 1970—. State bd. dirs., nat. and affiliate faculty PALS Minn. affiliate Am. Heart Assn., 1988—; chmn. SIDS task force, Minn. Dept. Maternal and Child Health, St. Paul, 1990-92. Mem. Am. Acad. Pediatrics (nat. faculty advanced pediatric life support 1989—, exec. com. sect. on emergency pediatrics 1988-90, chair Minn. emergency pediatric com. 1989-91, nat. svc. commendation 1991), Minn. Med. Assn. (emergency svcs. com. 1990, ho. of dels. 1994), Alpha Omega Alpha. Democrat. Mem. Soc. Of Friends. Avocations: travel, cutting horses. Home: 34 N Oaks Rd North Oaks MN 55127-6325 Office: Stillwater Med Group 921 Greeley St S Stillwater MN 55082-5935 Office Phone: 651-439-1234. Business E-Mail: Susan@asch.org.

ASCHENBRENER, CAROL ANN, pathologist, educator; b. Dubuque, Iowa, Dec. 22, 1944; d. Lester Bernard and Marian Barbara (Wiehl) Kemp; m. Thomas D. Aschenbrener, June 10, 1968 (div. Oct. 1972); 1 child, Erin Jean. BA, Clarke Coll., 1966; MS in Anatomy, U. Iowa, 1968; MD, U. N.C., 1971. Diplomate Am. Bd. Pathology. Intern in pathology U. Iowa Hosps., 1971-72, resident in anatomic pathology, neuropathology, 1972-74; instr. pathology Coll. Medicine U. Iowa, Iowa City, 1974, asst. prof., 1974-79, assoc. prof., 1979-87, prof., 1987—, assoc. dean, 1983-88, sr. assoc. dean, 1988-90, exec. assoc. dean, 1990—. Bd. dirs. 1st Nat. Bank, Iowa City. Contbr. articles to profl. jours., chpts. to med. texts. Bd. dirs. alumni bd. Clarke Coll., Dubuque, 1983-87. Nat. Merit scholar, 1962-66; Am. Cancer Soc. fellow, 1972-73. Fellow Coll. Am. Pathologists, Am. Assn. Neuropathologists; mem. AMA (sect. del.), Assn. Am. Med. Colls. (chmn. student affairs nat. com. 1987-89), Iowa Med Soc. (sec., treas. bd. trustees 1985—), Liaison Com. on Med. Edn., Nat. Bd. of Med. Examiners, Nat. Cancer Inst. (edn. adv. com.), Alpha Omega Alpha. Democrat. Roman Catholic. Avocations: reading, travel, gardening, hot air ballooning. Home: 1603 16th St NW Apt 5 Washington DC 20009-3036

ASCHERL, AMY M., elementary school educator; b. Harlan, Iowa, June 14, 1978; d. Duane N. and Patty J. Assmann; m. Luke T. Ascherl, June 29, 1972. BA, U. No. Iowa, Cedar Falls, 2002. Tchr. Robert Blue Mid. Sch., Eagle Grove, Iowa, 2003—. Vis. scholar Mable M. Wright scholar, U. No. Iowa, 2000;, 1999, 2001. Mem.: NEA (corr.), AAHPERD (assoc.), Iowa Assn. Health, Phys. Edn., Recreation and Dance (assoc.). Office Phone: 515-448-4767.

ASCHHEIM, EVE MICHELE, artist, educator; b. N.Y.C., Aug. 30, 1958; d. Emil and Lydie Aschheim. BA, U. Calif., Berkeley, 1983; MFA, U. Calif., Davis, 1987. Asst. prof. Occidental Coll., L.A., 1990, Sarah Lawrence Coll., Bronxville, NY, 1994—97. Vis. critic Md. Inst. Coll. Art, Balt., 1998-2000; lectr. Princeton (N.J.) U., 1991, 93, 98, 2000, sr. lectr., 2001—, dir. visual arts program, 2003—. One-woman shows include Stefan Stux Gallery, 1997, Galerie Rainer Borgemeister, Berlin, 1999, 2001, Galleri Magnus Åklundh, Lund, Sweden, 1999, Galerie Benden and Klimczak, Cologne, Germany, 1999, U. Mass. Gallery, Amherst, 2003, Larry Becker Contemporary Art, Phila., 2004, Eve Aschheim Guy Coirriero, Patrick Verelst Gallery, Antwerp, 2004, Lori Bookstein Gallery, 2006; group exhbns. include Sackler Mus., Cambridge, Mass., 1997, Kunstmuseum Winterthur, Switzerland, 1998, Acad. der Künste, Berlin, 1998, Fonds régional d'art contemporain de Picardie and Mus. de Picardie Amiens, 1997, Parrish Mus., L.I., N.Y., 1999, Stark Gallery, N.Y.C., 1999, U. Calif., San Diego, 1999, Landesgalerie Oberosterreich, Linz, Austria, 1999, Pratt Gallery, N.Y.C., 1999, So. Meth. U., 2000, N.Y. Studio Sch., 2000, Hunter Coll. Leubsdorf Gallery, N.Y.C., 2000, Maier Mus., Lynchburg, Va., 2000, Tucson Art Mus., 2000, Mus. Contemporary Art, Miami, 2001, D.A.A.D. Galerie, Berlin, U. Art Mus. Calif. State U., Long Beach, 2001, Colby Coll., 2002, N.Y. Hist. Soc., 2002, O.S.P. Gallery, Boston, 2002, Black and White Gallery, Bklyn., 2003, U. Mass., Amherst, 2003, Bill Maynes Gallery, N.Y.C., 2003, Tang Mus., Saratoga, N.Y., 2004, Larry Becker Contemporary Art, Phila., 2004, Nat. Acad. Design, N.Y.C., 2004, Ins Licht Geruckt-Aus der Grafischen Sammlung, Kunstmuseum, Bonn, Germany, 2004, N.Y.-Hist. Soc., 2004, Lohin-Geduld Gallery, N.Y., 2005, The Am. Acad. Arts and Letters N.Y., Lori Bookstein Gallery, N.Y.C., 2005, Tang Mus., 2006, Pollak Gallery, Dallas; represented in permanent collections at Fogg Mus., Nat. Gallery, Washington, N.Y. Hist. Soc., Hamburger Bahnhof, Berlin, M.O.C.A., Miami, Met. Mus. Art, N.Y.C., Yale U. Art Gallery, Bonn Kunstmus., Mus. Modern Art, N.Y, Ark. Art Ctr., Pollock Gallery Meth. So. U., Dallas, Hood Mus. at Dartmouth Coll.; artist (catalogs) Eve Aschheim Paintings and Drawings, 1999, Eve Aschheim Drawings, 2003, Eve Aschheim Recent Work, 2005. Recipient Rosenthal award Am. Acad. Arts and Letters, 1997, Purchase prize, 2005; fellow NEA, 1989, Pollock-Krasner Found., 1990, 2001, N.Y. Found. for Arts, 1991; grantee Elizabeth Found., 1997. Mem. Am. Abstract Artists. E-mail: easchh@aol.com.

ASH, BARBARA LEE, education and human services educator; b. Boston, Sept. 2, 1940; d. Charles Edward and Helen Barbara (Elwell) Fox; m. Robert Irvin Ash, July 31, 1971 AS, Norwich U., 1960; BS, Boston U., 1962, MEd, 1966, EdD, 1982. Cert. bus. tchr., Mass. Tchr. Chatham (Mass.) Pub. Schs., 1962-63, Braintree (Mass.) Pub. Schs., 1963-66; asst. prof. Simmons Coll., Boston, 1966-73; prof., dept. chair Bunker Hill Community Coll., Charlestown, Mass., 1973-77; prof. Suffolk U., Boston, 1977—, dir. Human Resources Learning and Performance Grad. Programs, 1977—. Mem. adv. bd. Aquinas Coll., Newton, Mass., 1985—, Bunker Hill C.C., 1985—, LaSell Coll., Newton, 1985—, Mt. Ida Coll., 1985—; disting. lectr. Rider Coll., N.J., 1992. Contbr. articles to profl. jours. Recipient Suffolk U. Evening div. assoc. Outstanding Faculty Mem. award, 1991. Mem. Internat. Soc. Performance Improvement, Assn. Psychol. Type, Am. Soc. Tng. and Devel., Mass. Bus. Educators Assn. (pres. 1992-93, Tchr. of Yr. award 1990), Soc. Human Resource Mgmt., Orgnl. Devel. Network, Nat. Bus. Edn. Assn. (legis. advocacy com. 1993—), New Eng. Bus. Educators Assn. (sec. 1986, v.p. 1987, pres. 1988), Mass. Coalition Adult Edn. (bd. dirs.), N.Y. Assn. Contg. Cmty. Edn., N.E. Human Resources Assn., Phi Delta Kappa, Delta Pi Epsilon (corr. sec. Epsilon chpt. 1964, pres. 1966). Office: Suffolk U Beacon Hill Boston MA 02114

ASH, DOROTHY MATTHEWS, civic worker; b. Dresden, Germany, Nov. 10, 1918; came to U.S., 1924; d. Kurt Horst and Ana Matthesius; m. Harry A. Ash, Apr. 13, 1941 (dec. June 1981); children: Fredrick Curtis, Dorothea Ash Linklater. Dancer, 1933-40; treas. Inheritance Abstractors Inc., Chgo., 1949-70; reporter Miami (Fla.) Sun Post, 1983; reporter, columnist Social Mag., Miami, 1984—. Chmn. Miss Universe Pageant, 1983-85; cruise chmn. Miami U., 1984. Pres. Big Bros. and Big Sisters, 1982-83; founding mem. World Sch. of Arts, 1985—; founding Notable Douglas Gardens 1988: Pres.'s Club U. of Miami, 1989; founding and bd. mem. Cancer Link Rsch., 1990; mem. Bd. Animal Welfare; active Project: Newborn, Am. Cancer Soc., March of Dimes, chmn. quest for the best, 1988-92, winner celebrity gourmet gala, 1988; active Children's Resource, Erase Diabetes, founding and bd. mem. 1990, Cerebral Palsy Found., Theatre Arts League, Linda Ray Infant Ctr., Miami City Ballet, Am. Ballet; bd. dirs. Greater Miami Opera, 1975—; pub. rels. vol. Miami Heart Inst., 1988—; com. mem. Miami Beach (Fla.) Beautification Program, 1984; mem. bd. Miami Mayor's Ad Hoc Com., 1984; mem. com. Challenger Seven Meml., 1988; founding mem., bd. mem. Leading Ladies, Inc., 1998—; active Cousteau Soc.; numerous others. Named Woman of Yr., Big Bros. and Big Sisters, Miami, 1981, Best Dressed, Am. Cancer Soc., 1981, Outstanding Humanitarian and Civic Leader, Mayor City of Miami, 1985, Woman of the Yr., Project: New Born, 1985, Miss Charity, Biscayne Bay Hosp., 1986, Queen of Hearts, Miami Children's Hosp., 1988, Leading Lady, March of Dimes, 1998; recipient Shining Star award Bon Secours Hosp., 1993, Patron Recognition award Mia Heart Rsch. Inst., 1993, Goddess of Love award Villa Maria Hosp., 1995, Shining Angel, 2000, Star of the Century award Miami Heart Rsch. Inst., 2000, Miracle Maker award Big Bros./Big Sisters, 2001, Salute to Dorothy Ash, Mia Heart Inst., 2002, Hero of the Heart award Mia Heart Inst., 2003, Animal Welfare honoree Mia Heart Inst., 2003. Mem. Miami Internat. Press Club. Avocations: reading, writing, painting.

ASH, JENNIFER GERTRUDE, writer, editor; b. Jan. 16, 1963; d. Clarke and Agnes Ash; m. D.A. Joseph Rudick, Apr. 7, 1990; children: Clark Albert, Amelia, Eleanor. BA, Kenyon Coll., 1985; postgrad., New Sch. Social Rsch. Assoc. editor Women's Wear Daily, 1986-87; editor Town and Country, N.Y.C., 1992—95, writer, 1995—. Author: Private Palm Beach, 1992, The Expectant Father: Facts, Tips, and Advice for Dads-to-Be, 1995, revised edit., 2001. Fellow Frick Collection. Democrat. Roman Catholic.

ASH, KAREN ARTZ, lawyer; b. Bklyn., Dec. 23, 1955; d. Bernard and Helen Artz; m. David Charles Ash, June 11, 1977; 2 children. AB in Econs. with honors, Georgetown U., 1976; JD magna cum laude, N.Y. Law Sch., 1980. Bar: N.Y. 1981, U.S. Dist. Ct. (so. and ea. dists.) N.Y. 1981. Assoc. Kaye, Scholer, Fierman, Hays & Handler, NYC, 1980-83, Amster, Rothstein & Ebenstein, NYC, 1983-88, ptnr., 1988; ptnr., co-chair Intellectual Property Practice Katten Muchin Zavis Rosenman, NYC. Lectr. in field. Author: Grey Goods and What Does It Mean to You, Trademark Licensing Do's and Don'ts, Rule 60(b)(4) F.R.C.P.; research editor N.Y. Law Rev., 1980 (cert. of merit 1980); contbr. articles to profl. jours. Fundraiser Assn. for Help Retarded Children, N.Y.C., 1978—. Mem. ABA (chairperson trademark com. 1982—), Women's Bar Assn., N.Y. State Bar Assn., U.S. Trademark Assn., NOW, N.Y. Humane Soc. Democrat. Office: Katten Muchin Zavis Rosenman 575 Madison Ave New York NY 10022 Office Phone: 212-940-8554. Office Fax: 212-940-8776. E-mail: karen.ash@kmzr.com.

ASH, POLLY GAYENELLE, secondary school educator, minister; b. Cumberland, Va., Feb. 6, 1952; d. Morris T. and Edith Nash; m. Lionel Ash, June 18, 1972; children: Lionel, Terrin, Darius, Micah, Cycerli. BS in Edn., Adelphi U., N.Y., 1981; M in Edn., East Stroudsbourg U., Pa., 1987. Tchrs. aide Redfern Daycare, Far Rockaway, NY; tchr. Del. Valley Job Corps., Callicoon, NY, 1979—86, Sullivan Correctional Facility, Fallsburg, NY, 1986—97, Otisville Correctional Facility, NY, 1997—2003, Sullivan West HS, Lake Huntington, NY, 2003—. Adj. prof. Hunter Coll., N.Y.C., 1988—95, Marist Coll., Poughkeepie, NY, 1988—94; creative trainer. Recipient Tchr. of Yr., Correction Edn. Assn., 1991. Home: 4 Lazy J Rd Box 223 Beach Lake PA 18405

ASHANTI, (ASHANTI SHEQUOIYA DOUGLAS), vocalist; b. Glen Cove, N.Y., Oct. 13, 1980; Trained as dancer, Bernice Johnson Cultural Arts Ctr. Launched signature fragrance Precious Jewel by Ashanti, 2005. Singer with Ja Rule (songs) Always On Time, singer with Fat Joe What's Luv?, singer with the Notorious B.I.G. Unfoolish; singer: (albums) Ashanti, 2002 (Grammy award, 2002), Foolish/Unfoolish: Reflections on Love, 2002, Ashanti: The 7 Series, 2003 (nominated 2 Grammy awards, 2003), Chapter II, 2003, Ashanti's Christmas, 2003, Concrete Rose, 2004; actor: (films) Bride & Prejudice, 2004, Coach Carter, 2005, John Tucker Must Die, 2006; (TV films) The Muppets' Wonderful Wizard of Oz, 2005; dancer Polly; guest appearances include Sabrina, the Teenage Witch, 2002, American Dreams, 2002, Buffy the Vampire Slayer, 2003, Las Vegas, 2005. Office: Murder Inc 825 8th Ave 20th Floor New York NY 10019*

ASHBY, DENISE, medical/surgical nurse, director; b. Cleve., Sept. 13, 1954; d. Robert D. and Elaine M. (Kukla) Evans; m. Wayne T. Ashby, July 2, 1977; children: Bryan, Travis, Robert. BS in Nursing, U. Ky., 1977; MSN, U. Louisville, 1994. RN, Ky. Staff nurse Humana Hosp. Suburban, Louisville, 1977-85; staffing coord. Suburban Med. Ctr., Louisville, 1985-88, dir. med.-surg. unit, 1988-93, dir. urol. ctr., 1993-95, dir. med.-surg. nursing, 1995-98; v.p. patient svcs., chief nursing officer Flaget Meml. Hosp., Bardstown, Ky., 1998-2000; dir. Nolton Clin. Agy., 2000—. Recipient Nurse Excellence award, Humana Hosp. Suburban, 1982, Ky. Nurse Excellence award, 1995. Mem. ANA (cert. med./surg.), Sigma Theta Tau, Phi Kappa Phi. Home: 9105 Farnham Dr Louisville KY 40242-3430 Office Phone: 502-961-6886. Business E-Mail: denise.ashby@nortonhealthcare.org.

ASHDOWN, MARIE MATRANGA (MRS. CECIL SPANTON ASHDOWN JR.), writer, educator, cultural organization administrator; b. Mobile, Ala. d. Dominic and Ave (Mallon) Matranga; m. Cecil Spanton Ashdown Jr., Feb. 8, 1958; children: Cecil Spanton III, Charles Coster; children by previous marriage: John Stephen Gartman, Vivian Marie Gartman. Degree, Maryville Coll. Sacred Heart, Springhill Coll. Feature artist, women's program dir. daily program Sta. WALA, WALA-TV, Mobile; v.p., dir. Met. Opera Guild, NYC, opera instr. in-svc. program, 1970-80, Marymount Coll., NYC, 1979-85; exec. dir. Musicians Emergency Fund, Inc., NYC, 1985—. Internat. adv. coun. Van Cliburn Found., 1998—; cons. No. Ill. U. Coll. Visual and Performing Arts, 1985—; lectr. in field. Author: Opera Collectables, 1979, contbr. articles to profl. jours. Recipient Extraordinary Svc. award March of Dimes, Medal of Appreciation award Harvard Bus. Sch. Club NYC, Cert. Appreciation, Kiwanis Internat., Arts Excellence award NJ State Opera, Ciparío award, Albanese-Puccini award Lincoln Ctr., 2002. Mem. AAUW, Nat. Inst. Social Scis., Com. for U.S.-China Rels. Avocations: collecting art, antique porcelain, book binding. Home: 25 Sutton Pl S Apt 16K New York NY 10022-2456 Office: Musicians Emergency Fund Inc PO Box 1256 New York NY 10150-1256 Personal E-mail: dmat807@aol.com, mefndtn@aol.com. E-mail: meffndtn@aol.com.

ASHE, DIANE DAVIS, psychology professor, sport psychology consultant; d. Trenton Gene and Barbara Kathryn Davis; m. Alan Michael Ashe, Sept. 4, 1988; 1 child, Brandon Colin. BA, East Carolina U., 1983, MA, 1985; PhD, Fla. State U., 1993. Licensed Mental Health Counselor State of Fla., 1993, Sport Psychology Consultant Assn. for the Advancement of Applied Sport Psychology, 1994. Prof. of psychology Valencia Cmty. Coll., Orlando, Fla., 1993—; psychol. specialist Fla. Dept. of Corrections, 1989—91; psychotherapist self-employed, Orlando, Fla., 1993—2005; crisis counselor Apalachee Ctr. for Human Services, Tallahassee, 1988—89; asst. academic advisor for athletics Fla. State U., 1986—88; sport psychology cons. Fla. State Basketball, 1987—89; adj. prof. Stetson U., Celebration, Fla., 2001—03, Troy State U., Orlando, 1997—99. Reviewer N.Am. Jour. Psychology. Co-author (book) Celebrity Worshippers: Inside the Minds of Stargazers, 2004; contbr. articles to profl. jours., to jours. Parent vol. Celebration Sch. PTSA, Celebration, Fla., 2001—05; vol. Celebration Found., Celebration, Fla., 2002—04; mem. Celebration Women's Club, 2002—04, Celebration Booster Club, 2001—03; vol. Fla. Dem. Party, 2004, Cmty. Presbyn. Ch., Celebration, 2002—03; pres. of Fla. chpt. East Carolina U. Alumni Assn., 1995—2000; coach Youth Soccer, Celebration, Fla., 2001—02. Recipient Excellence in Tchg. award, Nat. Inst. for Staff and Orgn. Devel., 1997, Student Choice award, Valencia C.C., 2005. Mem.: APA, Assn. for the Advancement of Applied Sport Psychology, Am. Psychol. Soc. Home: 405 Celebration Ave Celebration FL 34747 Office: Valencia Community College 1800 S Kirkman Rd Orlando FL 32611 Office Phone: 407-582-1617. Personal E-mail: diane.ashe@celebration.fl.us. E-mail: dashe@valenciacc.edu.

ASHE, KATHY RAE, special education educator; b. Bismarck, N.D., Oct. 24, 1950; d. Raymond Charles and Virginia Ann (Mason) Lynch; m. Barth Eugene Olson, Aug. 11, 1973; 1 child, William Raymond; m. Fredrick A. Ashe, Aug. 5, 1994. BS, U. N.D., 1972, MS in Spl. Edn., 1987. Cert. elem. tchr. with spl. edn. credential, N.D. Instr. Grafton State Sch., N.D., 1972-74; tchr. spl. edn. Grand Forks Sch. Dist., N.D., 1974—. Bd. dirs. Agassiz Enterprises; mem. RAD com. Valley Jr. High; mem. transition governing bd., Region IV. Mem. spl. needs recreation program Grand Forks Park Bd., 1973—76; mem. Spl. Olympics Area Mgmt. Team, 1984—90; mem. region IV Low Incident Behavior Grant Com.; co-chair, vol. coord. Greater Grand Forks Soccer Club Tournament, 2000, 2001; bldg. rep. Grand Forks Edn. Assn., 2000—; bd. dirs. Assn. Retarded Citizens, Devel. Homes, Inc., N.D. Sch. Blind Found., pres., 1997—2003. Named N.D. Tchr. of Yr., Coun. Chief State Sch. Officers, 1981. Mem. AAUW (pres. 1998-2000, N.D. co-pres. 2004—), Delta Kappa Gamma (sec. 1984-86, pres. 1990-94), Alpha Phi (alumni pres. 1984-86, 90-91, alumni treas. 1995—), Phi Delta Kappa. Republican. Roman Catholic. Avocations: sporting events, civic work, cross stitch, bowling, golf. Home: 3208 Walnut St Grand Forks ND 58201-7665 E-mail: ashekathy@hotmail.com.

ASHENFELTER, HELEN LOUISE, elementary school educator; d. Stanley Maurice Jr. and Eleanor Louise Casteel; m. Howard King Ashenfelter, July 2, 1994. BS, W.Va. U., Morgantown, 1980, MS, 1982. Cert. K-12 spl. edn. W.Va. Tchr. Monongalia County Bd. Edn., Morgantown, 1980—. Rep. Math. Cadre Monongalia County, Morgantown, 2004—. Grantee, Menen Edn. Alliance, 1998—99. Mem.: Monongalia County Edn. Assn. Methodist. Avocations: stamping, crafts, reading, gardening, baking. Home: 508 Valley Rd Morgantown WV 26505 Office: Woodburn Sch Parson and Fortney St Morgantown WV 26505

ASHER, KATHLEEN MAY, communications educator; b. Vassar, Mich., Aug. 19, 1932; d. Thomas Henry and Jessie (Smith) Pierce; m. Donald William Asher, July 17, 1957; children: David Kevin, Diane Kerri. BS, Ctrl. Mich. U., 1956, MA, 1967. Cert. fundraiser Williamsburg Devel. Inst., cert. QTM trainer. Tchr. speech and theater Standish (Mich.) Pub. Schs., 1956-58, Vassar (Mich.) Pub. Schs., 1959-67; prof. speech, adminstr. Mott C.C., Flint, Mich., 1967-89; assoc. prof. speech Palm Beach C.C., Lake Worth, Fla., 1990—2001, fundraiser, 1991-95, 2003—, faculty polit. action chairperson, 1996-97, faculty emeritus, 2001, pres. elect, 2004. Cons. in speech, Flint, Mich., 1973—89; cons. quality total mgmt.; cons. in comms. and mgmt., Lake Worth, Fla., 2001—. Pres. Homeowner Assn., Lake Worth, 1993—95, 2003—, legal chair, 2003; mem. Vassar Zoning Bd.; officer City Coun.; chair Tuscola County Dem Com., 1975—85; del., whip Dem. Conv. and Rules Com., 1976; del. Fla. Dem. Conv., 1999. Mem. United Faculty Palm Beach C.C. (chpt. pres.), Fla. Tchg. Profession, NEA, Nat. Collegiate Hons. Coun. (collegiate 1991-95), Mich. Women's Studies Assn. (pres. 1974-75), C.C. Humanities Assn., Phi Theta Kappa (leadership prof.). Presbyterian. Avocations: percussion, reading, golf, bowling, biking. Home: 4713 Rainbow Dr Lake Worth FL 33463-3610 Office: Palm Beach CC 4200 Congress Ave Lake Worth FL 33461-4705 E-mail: profashl@directvinternet.com.

ASHER, SHOSHANA CHANA, mathematics professor; d. Lincoln Curtis and Laurel (Millsap) Rolling. MA in Math., U. Calif. Berkeley, 1978. Math. specialist Student Learning Ctr., U. Calif., Berkelely, 1978—80, lectr. math., 1979, readership in undergrad. math., 1979—81; math. tutor Math. Resource Ctr. Golden Gate U., San Francisco, 1996—, adj. lectr., math., 1996—; adj. faculty Menlo Coll. Profl. Studies Program, Atherton, Calif., 1998—2001, Menlo Coll., Atherton, 1998—2004. Rschr., applied math. Independent Rschr., San Francisco, 2004—. Chai circle mem. Chabad of Calif., West Coast, Los Angeles, 1996—; mitzvah mem. Jewish Family and Children's Svcs., 2001—; leadership circle mem. The Congregation Emanu-El, San Francisco, 2001—. Recipient Outstanding Tchg. award, Golden Gate U., Sch. of Tech., 2000. Mem.: Math. Assn. Am., Alumni Assn. U. Calif. Berkeley. Democrat. Jewish. Avocations: classical music, jazz, tennis, football, basketball. Office: Golden Gate U 536 Mission St San Francisco CA 94105 E-mail: sasher@europe.com.

ASHHURST, ANNA WAYNE, foreign language educator; b. Phila., Jan. 5, 1933; d. Astley Paston Cooper and Anne Pauline (Campbell) Ashhurst; m. Ronald G. Gerber, July 22, 1978. AB, Vassar Coll., 1954; MA, Middlebury Coll., 1956; PhD, U. Pitts., 1967. English tchr. Internat. Inst. Spain, Madrid, 1954-56; asst. prof. Juniata Coll., Huntingdon, Pa., 1961-63; asst. prof. Spanish dept. Franklin and Marshall Coll., Lancaster, Pa., 1968-74, acting chmn. Spanish dept., 1972, convenor, fgn. lang. council, 1972-74; assoc. prof. dept. modern fgn. langs. U. Mo., St. Louis, 1974-78. Author: La Literatura Hispano-Americana en la Crítica Española, 1980. Mem. Welcome Wagon, Lancaster, Pa., 1968—70, 1971—74; outreach vol. instr. Spanish, 2003—. Fulbright-Hays grantee, Colombia, S.Am., summer 1963; Ford Humanities fellow, summer 1970; Mellon fellow, 1970-71 Mem. AAUW (pres. Ferguson-Florissant br. 1989-91, 95-98, chmn. St. Louis area interbranch coun. 1992-94, chair environ. task force Mo. 1992-95, local arrangements chair for Mo. state conv. 1997, Woman of Distiction award 1998), Internat. Inst. in Spain, Instituto Internacional de Literatura Iberoamericana, Am. Assn. Tchrs. Spanish and Portuguese. Home: 2105 Barcelona Dr Florissant MO 63033-2805

ASHIMINE, TANYA, biology educator; b. Hawaii; d. Barbara and Al Wanamaker (Stepfather); m. Stanton Ashimine. BEd, MEd in Secondary Sci. Edn., U. Hawaii at Manoa, Honolulu, HI, 1988—92. Biology/zoology/physiology tchr. Kaiser HS, Honolulu, 1992—. Adv. - class of '97, 2001, star, labs Kaiser HS, 1993. Grantee Career Integration grant, Kamehameha Schs., 2004, Tech. grant, Best Buy Stores, 2006. Office Phone: 8083941246.

ASHISH-MISHRA, SONIA, psychiatrist; b. London, Eng., Apr. 3, 1969; arrived in US, 1996, permanent resident, 2005; d. Anil Kumar and Manjulika Sinha; m. Ashish Mishra; children: Deeksha Mishra, Mohana Mishra. BS, MB, Karnataka Inst. Med. Sci., India. Diplomate Am. Bd. Psychiatry and Neurology, lic. psychiatrist Miss. Intern Morehouse Sch. Medicine, Atlanta; resident in psychiatry Mercer Sch. Medicine, Macon, Ga.; psychiatrist Weems Cmty. Mental Health Ctr., Meridian, Miss., 2000—05; chief svc. MR unit Miss. State Hosp., Jackson, 2005—. Recipient Nat. Bravery award, Govt. India, New Delhi, 1981. Mem.: Am. Psychiat. Assn., Am. Assn. Physicians from India (life). Hindu. Avocations: reading, movies, travel.

ASHKIN, ROBERTA ELLEN, lawyer; b. NYC, July 1, 1953; d. Sidney and Beverly Ashkin. BA magna cum laude, Hofstra U., 1975; JD, St. John's U., N.Y.C., 1978. Bar: N.Y., 1979, U.S. Dist. Ct. (ea. and so. dists.), 1980, U.S. Dist. Ct. (no. and we. dists.) 2001. Program dir. Sta. WVHC-FM, N.Y.C., 1974-75; assoc. editor Matthew Bender, N.Y.C., 1975-79; assoc. Morris & Duffy, N.Y.C., 1979-81, Lipsig, Sullivan & Liapakis, N.Y.C., 1981-84, Julien & Schlesinger, P.C., N.Y.C., 1984-89; adminstrv. law judge N.Y.C. Dept. Transp., 1988-92; ptnr. Trolman & Glaser, P.C., N.Y.C., 1991-96, Baron & Budd, P.C., N.Y.C., 1996—2002; pvt. practice Ashklin Law Offices, N.Y.C., 2002—. Chmn. bd. Actor's Classical Troupe, 1987-89; bd. dirs. Daytop Village Found., 2002-03; sr. dir. women's policy Gephardt for Pres. 2004 Campaign. Mem.: ATLA, Trial Lawyers for Pub. Justice (bd. dirs.), N.Y. Trial Lawyers Assn. (dep. treas. 2001, sec. 2002, 2003, bd. dirs., sec. 2003), N.Y. State Bar Assn., Phi Beta Kappa. Office Phone: 212-965-0010. Personal E-mail: robertaashkin@aol.com.

ASHLEIGH, CAROLINE, art and antiques appraiser; BA, Worcester (Mass.) Coll., 1973; cert. in appraisal studies, NYU, 1994. Profl. lectr. on connoisseurship; appraiser Home and Garden TV Bloomfield Hills, Mich.; edn. dept. staff Cranbrook Art Mus., Bloomfield Hills, 1997—; columnist Detroit Monthly Mag., 1988—; edn. dept. staff Detroit Inst. Art, 1988—; regional rep. William Doyle Auctioneers, N.Y.C., 1997—2000; columnist Detroit Legal News, 1998—. Appraiser Chubbs Antique Roadshow, WGBH-TV, Boston, 1996—; cons. Sotheby's, CBS News "Inside Edition"; lectr. in field. Columnist: Antiques Roadshow Insider, Mich. Bar Jour., Detroit Monthly, 1995—96, Hour Detroit mag.; subject of feature presentations N.Y. Times, Art and Antiques, Detroit Free Press, Antique Trader Mag., others. Mem. Appraisers Assn. Am. (cert. sr. mem., Midwest regional rep.), Detroit Inst. Arts, Cranbrook Art Mus. Office Phone: 248-792-2929. E-mail: carolineashleigh@appraiseyourart.com.

ASHLEY, ELIZABETH, actress; b. Ocala, Fla., Aug. 30, 1941; d. Arthur Kingman and Lucille (Ayer) Cole; m. George Peppard (div.); 1 son, Christian Moore; m. James Michael McCarthy. Student ballet with, Tatiana Semenova; student, La. State U., 1957-58; grad., Neighborhood Playhouse, N.Y.C., 1961. Apptd. Pres.'s council 1st Nat. Council on the Arts, 1965-69; dir. Am. Film Inst., 1968-72 Appeared on Broadway in The Highest Tree, 1961, Take Her, She's Mine, 1962, Barefoot in the Park, 1963; motion pictures include The Carpet Baggers, 1963, Ship of Fools, 1964, The Third Day, 1965, Marriage of a Young Stockbroker, 1971, Paperback Hero, 1974, Golden Needles, 1974, Rancho Deluxe, 1975, 92 in the Shade, 1976, The Great Scout and Cathouse Thursday, 1976, Coma, 1978, Windows, 1980, Paternity, 1981, Lookin' to Get Out, 1982, Split Image, 1982, Dragnet, 1987, Dangerous Curves, 1987, A Man of Passion, 1988, Vampire's Kiss, 1989, Mallrats, 1995, Sleeping Together, 1997, Happiness, 1998, Just the Ticket, 1999, Home Sweet Hoboken, 2000, Hey Arnold! The Movie (voice), 2002; TV work includes (series) Evening Shade, CBS, 1990-94; TV movies include When Michael Calls, 1972, Second Chance, 1972, The Heist, 1972, Your Money or Your Wife, 1972, One of My Wives is Missing, 1976, The War Between the Tates, 1977, A Fire in the Sky, 1978, Svengali, 1983, Stage Coach, 1986, He's Fired, She's Hired, 1984, Warm Hearts, Cold Feet, 1987, The Two Mrs. Grenvilles, 1987, Orleans (series), The Rope, Blue Bayou, 1990, Reason for Living: The Jill Ireland Story, 1991, In the Best Interest of the Children, 1992, (mini series) The Buccaneers, 1995; stage appearances include The Enchanted, Washington, 1973, The Skin of Our Teeth, Washington, Broadway, 1975, Cat on a Hot Tin Roof, Stratford, Conn. and Broadway, 1974, Agnes of God; author: Postcards from the Road, 1978; TV guest appearances include Murder, She Wrote, Law & Order, The Larry Sanders Show, B.L. Stryker, Women ot the House, Burke's Law, others. Recipient Antoinette Perry award, 1962 Mem. Actors Equity, Screen Actors Guild, AFTRA. Office: Writers and Artists Agy 19 W 44th St Ste 1000 New York NY 10036-6095

ASHLEY, ELIZABETH, assistant dean, educator; b. Waycross, Ga., July 8, 1943; d. James Bryant and Henrietta (Hargreaves) Lewis; m. Rhett Ashley, Sept. 9, 1973 (div. July 1977); m. Stefan Mellin, June 21, 1978 (div. Feb. 1986). AA Stephens Coll., 1963; BA, U. Fla., 1965; MS, Fla. State U., 1969; MA, Ariz. State U., 1975. Cataloging libr. Columbia U., N.Y.C., 1967; circulation libr. Fla. State U., Tallahassee, 1968-69; acquisitions libr. Ariz. State U., Tempe, 1969-76, No. Ariz. U., Flagstaff, 1977-78; approval libr. Baker & Taylor Co., Somerville, N.J., 1979-80; dir. tech. svcs. Golden Gate Sem., Mill Valley, Calif., 1981-87; dir. tech. svcs. Windward C.C., Kaneohe, Hawaii, 1988-2004, prof. humanities, 1995—, acting asst. dean of instrn., 2004—. Author: A Midsummer Madness, 1979, Abraham Steele, 1981, The Skull, 1982, Getting Rich, 2003; actor (theatre) Mardi Gras Follies, 1999—, Dee Dee West in Follies, 2003. Founder, exec. dir. Friends of Trees Soc., 1983—; co-founder, chmn. Menehune Lane Co., 1989-2000. Mem. ALA, Hawaii Libr. Assn., Phi Theta Kappa, Phi Kappa Phi, Beta Phi Mu. Office: Windward Community Coll 45-720 Keaahala Rd Kaneohe HI 96744-3528 Business E-Mail: ashleyel@hawaii.edu.

ASHLEY, ELLA JANE (ELLA JANE RADER), medical technician; b. Dewitt, Ark., Mar. 6, 1941; d. Clayton Ervin and Emma Mae (Coleman) Funderburk; m. Albert Ashley, Sept. 27, 1957 (div. Nov. 1962); 1 child, Cynthia Gayle. Student, Westark Community Coll. Cert. clin. lab. technologist, clin. lab. scientist. Lab. asst. U. Ark. Med. Ctr., Little Rock, 1966-67; lab. technician II, rschr. in lithium carbonate Ark. State Hosp., Little Rock, 1967-68; staff technologist Cooper Clinic, Ft. Smith, Ark., 1969-71; asst. chief technologist Lab. of Am. (Labcorp), Ft. Smith, 1972—, ops. mgr., 1997—2003; ret. Lab. of America (Labcorp), 2003. Mem. profl. adv. panel Med. Lab. Observer, 1976—. Research in lithium carbonate. Mem.: Am. Soc. Med. Tech. Methodist. Avocations: travel, theater, concerts, painting. Home: 1310 S Houston St Fort Smith AR 72901-7271

ASHLEY, JANELLE COLEMAN, academic administrator; b. Malakoff, Tex., Mar. 29, 1941; d. Charlie Y. and Ellen (Ballow) Coleman; married; three children. BBA in Bus. Edn., Stephen F. Austin State U., 1962, MA in English, 1964; PhD in Mgmt., U. North Tex., 1972. Bus. tchr. Nacogdoches (Tex.) High Sch., 1963-65; instr. mgmt. Stephen F. Austin State U., Nacogdoches, 1965-73, prof. mgmt., 1976—. Dir. Small Bus. Inst., Stephen F. Austin U., 1976-78, acting chmn. dept. mgmt. and mktg., 1977-78, assoc. v.p. acad. affairs, 1978-81, dean sch. bus., 1981-92, v.p. acad. affairs, 1992—, mem. numerous coms.; personnel and mgmt. devel. cons. St. Regis Paper Co. Inc., Lufkin Telephone Exchange Inc., Conroe Telephone Co. Inc., Tex. Atty. Gen.'s Office, Nibco Inc., Lufkin Industries Inc., Moore Bus. Forms Inc., Henderson State U. Spl. adv. bd. Small Bus. Inst. Rev., 1983; contbr. numerous articles and cases to profl. jours. Pres. Nacogdoches County United Way, 1984, also bd. dirs., exec. bd., chmn. various coms.; chmn. compliance, monitoring and evaluation com. Deep East Tex. Pvt. Industry Council, 1984-85; bd. dirs. Nacogdoches Exposition Ctr., 1983-84, Health Facilities Devel. Corp., 1985-86, City Sesquicentennial Com., 1984-85; chmn. adminstrv. bd. First United Meth. Ch., 1984-85, mem. council on ministries, bldg., fin., other coms. Mem. Southwestern Bus. Adminstrn. Assn. (sec. 1984, v.p. programs and pres.-elect 1985, pres. 1986), Case Research Assn. (rev. bd.), Am. Assembly Collegiate Schs. Bus. (visitation com. 1983-86, continuing accreditation com. 1985-88, standars com. 1987-88, 90-92, nominating com. 1990-91, implementation com. 1991-92), Nacogdoches County C. of C. (pres. 1986-87, bd. dirs., v.p., various coms.), Kappa Delta Pi, Beta Gamma Sigma, Alpha Chi. Home: 4319 Mystic Ln Nacogdoches TX 75965-6520

ASHLEY, KATHLEEN LABONIS, music educator; d. Edward Francis and Modesta Bubnis Labonis; m. Richard Raymond Ashley, Nov. 24, 1984; children: Christopher, Lisa. B in music edn., Immaculata Coll., 1979; M in edn., Temple U., 1984. Cert. instrnl. II Pa. Secondary tchr. St. Basil Acad., Jenkintown, Pa., 1979—88; elem. tchr. St. Martin of Tours Dept. of Performing Arts, Phila., 1980—82; pre-sch. tchr. The Curiosity Shoppe, Doylestown, Pa., 1990—96; elem. tchr. Our Lady of Mt. Carmel, Doylestown, 1995—2000, St. Jude Sch., Chalfont, Pa., 1997—. Performing arts camp tchr. Brown Bag Arts Festival, Doylestown, Pa., 1991—96; ch. musician, performer St. Jude, Chalfont, Pa., 1997—. Composer: (songs) St. Jude School Song, 1997; arranger: instrumental music, 1979—; co-author: Pre-sch. and Elem. Sch. shows, 1990—2003. Steering com. for mid. states evaluation St. Basil Acad., Jenkintown, Pa., 1985; tchr. St. Jude Sch., Chalfont, Pa., 1994—. Scholar, Immaculata U., 1975—79. Mem.: Pa. Music Educators Assn., Nat. Cath. Educators Assn., Music Educators Nat. Conf. Avocations: drawing, painting, gardening, writing. Office: St Jude Sch 323 W Butler Ave Chalfont PA 18914 Office Phone: 215-822-9225.

ASHLEY, LOIS A., retired university reference librarian; b. Detroit, Aug. 1, 1942; d. S. Elbert and Gertrude B. Hobson; m. Melvin Allen Ashley, June 27, 1964 (dec. Nov. 1996); children: Scott E., Paul D., Craig R. AA, William Tyndale Coll., Farmington Hills, Mich., 1989, BA in Humanities, 1991; MS in LS, Wayne State U., 1993. Spl. corr. Mich. Blue Shield, Detroit, 1963-68; reservation agt. United Airlines, Dearborn, Mich., 1968-70; asst. Office of Records and Registration William Tyndale Coll., 1989-91; grad. rsch. asst. Wayne State U., Detroit, 1992-93; reference libr. U. Detroit Mercy, 1993-99; adj. Oakland C.C., 2000—. Organist Gracious Savior Luth. Ch., 2000—; mem. Friends of the Detroit Pub. Libr.; founding chair ret. mem. roundtable Mich. Libr. Assn., 2001. Recipient scholarships. Mem. ALA (Black Caucus), AAUW, Assn. Coll. and Rsch. Librs., Mich. Libr. Assn., Nat. Coun. Negro Women, Am. Guild Organists, Founders Soc. Detroit Inst. Arts, Women of the Evang. Luth. Ch. in Am., Beta Phi Mu, Delta Epsilon Chi. Mem. Evang. Luth. Ch. in Am. Home: 19934 Mark Twain St Detroit MI 48235-1607 Personal E-mail: lois.ashley@sbcglobal.net, lashleyma@aol.com.

ASHLEY, LYNN, social sciences educator, consultant; b. Rock Island, Ill., Nov. 18, 1920; d. Francis Ford and Cleo Marguerite (Monahan) Haynes; m. Edward Messenger Ashley, Aug. 16, 1946; children: Edward Jr., Ann Rice, Rebecca Pocisk, William. BS in Social Psychology, Union Inst., Cin., 1978; MEd., U. Cin., 1979, EdD, 1985. Clk. Lumberman's Mutual Casualty Co., Chgo., 1940-41; account asst. Quaker Oats Co., Chgo., 1941-43; riveter Douglas Aircraft Co., Chgo., 1943-44; organizer, dir. Forest Park Youth Ctr., Forest Park, Ohio, 1967-73; staffing coord. Presbytery of Cin., 1973-78; grad. teaching asst. U. Cin., 1978-84; pres. Nat. Corrective Tng. Inst., Cin., 1979—. Cons., trainer Hamilton County Probation Dept., Warren County Juvenile Ct., 1987—, Allen County Juvenile Ct., Worth Ctr., Allen County; adj. faculty Union Inst., 1986—, mem. undergrad. studies bd., mem. doctoral dissertation com. Spkr., adv. women vets. to schs. and orgns.; organizer cmty. rels. coun. City of Forest Park, 1983; mem. Cin.-Harare, Zimbabwe Sister Cities Assn., 1989—, Ohio Gov.'s Adv. Com. on Women Vets., 1993—99; field rep. Women in Mil. Svc. for Am. Found.; mem. ROTC oversight com. U. Cin., 2005—06; councilwoman City of Forest Park, 1981—85. With WAC, 1943—46. Recipient in Recognition award Forest Park City Coun., 1985, In Appreciation award Union Inst., 1987, Recognition award AMVETS, U. Cin., 1993, award Commonwealth of Ky., 1989; inducted into Ohio Vets. Hall of Fame, 1999. Mem. Am. Corrections Assn., Nat. Assn. Corrective Tng. Affiliates (pres. 1987), Women's Army Corp Vet. Assn. (selected rep. to dedication of Dole Inst. Politics, Internat. Conf. on WWII D-Day Mus., New Orleans), Assn. Family and Conciliatiion Cts., Am. Probation and Parole Assn. Avocations: photography, travel, computers, camping, fishing. Office: Nat Corrective Tng Inst 811 Hanson Dr Cincinnati OH 45240-1921 Office Phone: 513-825-9206.

ASHLEY, MARJORIE, retired secondary school educator; b. Schenectady, N.Y., Feb. 16, 1917; d. Richard J. and Margaret Middleton; m. John Edward Ashley, Aug. 20, 1940 (dec.); children: Richard M.(dec.), John E. Jr., Willard Bishop. BA cum laude, SUNY, Albany, 1955, MA, 1958; cert. in French, Goucher Coll., 1959. Tchr. Burnt Hills-Ballston Lake H.S., Burnt Hills, NY, 1956, Roger B. Taney Jr. High Sch., Camp Springs, Md., Oxon Hill (Md.) Sr. H.S. Contbr. commentaries Kerrville Times. Sec. AAUW, Kerrville, Tex., 1976—80, pres., 1980—82; chmn., patron Kerrville Performing Arts Soc., 1980—2001; active Point Theatre, Schreiner U. Recipient Lifetime Achievement award, Hill Country Arts Found., 2003. Mem.: LWV, Animal Welfare Soc. Kerr County, Hill Country Arts Found. Unitarian Universalist.

ASHLEY, MARJORIE LYNN, intravenous therapy nurse; b. Butler, Pa., Sept. 15, 1945; d. Arthur Lewis and Eleanor Jean (Oesterling) Grelling; m. Francis J. Ashley, Sept. 24, 1966; children: Deborah Lynne, Jeffery Michael. Diploma, Luth. Hosp. Sch. Nursing, 1966. RN, Mass.; cert. RN Intravenous. IV therapist Charlton Meml. Hosp., Fall River, Mass., 1973—. Mem. Infusion Nurses Soc., Assn. for Vascular Access. Home: 49 Mill St Lakeville MA 02347-2235 E-mail: mashleycrn@aol.com.

ASHLEY, RENEE, writer, creative writing educator, consultant; b. Palo Alto, Calif., Aug. 10, 1949; BA in English with honors, San Francisco State U., 1979, BA in French, 1979, BA in World and Comparative Lit., 1979, MA, 1981. Instr. creative writing West Milford (N.J.) Cmty. Sch., 1983-85; instr. creative writing, cons. artist residencies Rockland Ctr. for Arts, West Nyack, NY, 1985—; mem. MFA in Creative Writing faculty Fairleigh Dickinson U., 2001—. Author: Salt, 1991 (Brittingham prize in Poetry 1991), The Various Reasons of Light, 1998, The Revisionist's Dream, 2001, Someplace Like This, 2003; contbr. to anthologies including Touching Fire: Erotic Writings by Women, 1989, What's a Nice Girl Like You?, 1992, Breaking Up Is Hard to Do, 1994, Dog Music, 1996, (textbook) Writing Poems, 1995, The Breath of Parted Lips, Vol. II, 2004; contbr. to American Voice, Antioch Rev., Harvard Rev., Kenyon Rev., Poetry. Fellow N.J. State Coun. Arts, 1985, 89, 94, 2003, Yaddo, Saratoga Springs, N.Y., 1990, McDowell Colony, Peterborogh, N.H., 1993-94, NEA, 1997-98; grantee Poets and Writers, Inc., 1986, N.Y. State Coun. Arts, 1986; recipient Washington prize in poetry Word Works, Inc., 1986, Lit. Excellence award, Kenyon Review, 1990, 92, Pushcart prize, 2000. Mem. MLA, Acad. Am. Poets, Poetry Soc. Am. (Ruth Lake Meml. award 1987, Robert H. Winner award 1989). E-mail: reneea@verizion.net.

ASHLEY, SHARON ANITA, pediatric anesthesiologist; b. Goulds, Fla., Dec. 28, 1948; d. John H. Ashley and Johnnie Mae (Everett) Ashley-Mitchell; m. Clifford K. Sessions, Sept. 1977 (div. 1985); children: Cecili, Nicole, Erika. BA, Lincoln U., 1970; postgrad., Pomona Coll., 1971; MD, Hahnemann Med. Sch., Phila., 1976; M in Pub. Health, UCLA, 2000; M in bus. admin., Claremont Grad. U., 2003. Diplomate Am. Bd. Pain Mgmt., Am. Bd. Anesthesiologists. Intern pediatrics Martin Luther King Hosp., L.A., 1976-77, resident pediatrics, 1977-78, resident anesthesiology, 1978-81, mem. staff, 1981—; assoc. dean grad. med. edn. Charles Drew U. Medicine and Sci., 2002—. Named Outstanding Tchr. of Yr., King Drew Med. Ctr., Dept. Anesthesia, 1989, Outstanding Faculty of Yr., 1991. Mem. Am. Soc. Anesthesiologists, Calif. Med. Assn., L.A. County Med. Soc., Soc. Regional Anesthesia, Soc. Pediatric Anesthesia. Democrat. Baptist. Avocations: reading, crocheting, sailing. Business E-Mail: sashley@ladhs.org.

ASHLEY-IVERSON, MARY E., retired librarian; b. L.A., Oct. 30, 1947; d. Curtis Lee Gosey and Allie Mae Sheppard-Gosey; m. Billy G. Ashley Sr., Nov. 14, 1965 (dec. Apr. 17, 1995); children: Billy G. Ashley Jr., Dexter Arnett(dec.); m. Willis Iverson Sr., July 6, 1997. Grad., Centennial H.S., Compton, Calif., 1965. Libr. asst. Crenshaw H.S., L.A., 1982—84; libr. clk. Stuttgart (Ark.) Pub. Libr., 1992—99; ret., 1999. Chmn. Records Preservation Com., Stuttgart-DeWitt, 2000—; rec. sec. Stuttgart Civic League, Stuttgart, 1988—91; mem. Wall of Tolerance Nat. Com. for Tolerance, 2001; bd. dirs. There Is Hope, Humphrey, Ark., 1995—, Resource Ctr. Aging, Stuttgart, 2000—. Recipient Dedicated Cmty. Svc. award, Modern Woodman Am., 1993. Mem.: NAACP. Democrat. Baptist. Avocations: coins, antiques, crystal. Home: 301 W Taft Stuttgart AR 72160-2600

ASHMORE-HUDSON, ANNE, psychologist, writer, consultant; b. Atlanta; d. Clifford March and Mae (Walker) Ashmore; m. Alvin F. Poussaint, Nov. 4, 1973 (div. Oct. 1988); 1 child, Alan M., stepchildren Julia, Ayana; m. James La Garde Hudson, June 23, 1990. BA, Spelman Coll., 1963; MA in Social Work, Simmons Coll., 1965; PhD, U. Calif., Berkeley, 1979. Lic. clin. psychologist, qualified psychologist, Mass. Founder, pres. Urban Psychol. Svcs., Brookline, Mass., 1980-95; writer, cons., ind. rschr., Washington, 1995—. Bd. dirs. Mass. Sch. Profl. Psychology, 1991—95; designer, implementer workshops for industry and nonprofit orgns.; guest spkr. in field; cons. NBC, ABC, CBS affiliate stas., Newsweek, Boston Globe; pub. mem. sr. fgn. svc. selection bd. Dept. State; vis. scholar F. Franklin Frazier Inst., Howard U., Washington, 2000—03. Contbr. articles to profl. jours., newspaper and mags. Bd. dirs. United Way Mass., Boston, 1992-94, Sasha Bruce Youth Works, Washington, 1994—, Washington Ballet, 1999—; chmn. media images Links, Inc. Boston, 1995, chmn. Women in Transition from Welfare to Work, Washington, 1998, pres. Potomac chpt. The Links, 2002-06. Named Vol. of Yr., 1991-92, Cambridge (Mass.) YWCA; USPHS fellow U. Calif., 1970-78, fellow DuBois Inst., Harvard U., 1990-93, fellow writing program Johns Hopkins U. Mem. APA, Psi Chi. Avocations: photography, travel, growing orchids. Home and Office: 2200 20th St NW Washington DC 20009-5004 Fax: 202-234-0433. E-mail: annmachele@aol.com.

ASHTARI, MANZAR, neuroscientist; d. Hoshang Ashtari and Saidi Belghas; m. Ali Aravand, May 29, 1983; children: Pouneh Aravand, Puya Aravand. PhD, MIT, 1978—82. Cert. Am. Bd. Radiology Am. Coll. Radiology, 1992. Mr clin. physicist North Shore LIJ Health Sys., New Hyde Park, NY, 1984—2006. Cons. JFK Neuroscience Dept, Island, NJ, 2002—. Grantee, NIMH, 2004—06. Mem.: Internat. Soc. MRI in Medicine. Home: 268 Continental Dr New Hyde Park NY 11040 Office Phone: 718-470-7328. E-mail: ashtari@lij.edu.

ASHTON, BETSY FINLEY, broadcast journalist, author, lecturer; b. Wilkes-Barre, Pa., May 13, 1944; d. Charles Leonard Hancock Jones and Margaretta Betty (Hart) Jones Layton; m. Arthur Benner Ashton, Nov. 5, 1966 (div. 1972); m. Robert Clarke Freed, May 18, 1974 (div. 1981); m. Jacob B. Underhill III, Oct. 17, 1987. BA, Am. U., 1966; postgrad., Corcoran Sch. Art, 1968; postgrad. in fine arts, Am. U., 1969-71; student in painting, Corcoran Sch. Art, 1968. Tchr. art Fairfax County Pub. Schs., Va., 1967—70; reporter, anchor Sta. WWDC, Washington, 1972—73, Sta. WMAL-AM-FM, Washington, 1973—75; corr. Sta. WTTG-TV, Washington, 1975—76, Sta. WJLA-TV, Washington, 1976—82; consumer corr. CBS News and Sta. WCBS-TV, NYC, 1982—86; sr. corr. Today's Bus., 1986—87; contbr. personal fin. CBS Morning Program, 1967, Lifetime Cable TV, 1988—; anchor FNN Money Talk, 1989; exec. editor, producer Great Giving, 2000—. Bd. dirs. Lowell E. Mellett Fund Free Responsible Press, Washington, 1979-82; courtroom artist, Washington, 1978-81 Reporter TV news report Caffeine, 1981 (AAUW award 1982); reporter spot news 6 P.M. News, 1979 (Emmy award); author: Betsy Ashton's Guide to Living on Your Own, 1988. Concert master ceremonies Beethoven Soc., Washington, 1979-82. Recipient Laurel award Columbia Journalism Rev., 1984, Outstanding Alumna award Am. U., 1985, Outstanding Media award Am. U., 1986, Best Consumer Journalism citation Nat. Press Club, 1983. Mem. AFTRA, NATAS, Author's Guild, Newswomen's Club NY, Soc. Profl. Journalists (pres. NY chpt. 1994, 2000, Washington chpt. 1980-81, bd. dirs. NY chpt., co-chair 2004 nat. conv.), Friends of Thirteen (bd. dirs.), Kenyon Review (trustee, 2004-), Sigma Delta Chi Found. (bd. dirs., v.p. bd. 2004—), Alpha Chi Omega (v.p. chpt. 1964-66). Episcopalian. Avocations: painting, drawing, golf.

ASHTON, DAWNE BELINDA, retired secondary school educator; b. Chgo., Sept. 15, 1940; d. Arthur Elmer Albach and Ruth Evelyn Christensen Albach; m. Harold Edward Ashton (div.); children: Andrea Gabriela, Alexandra Kristi. BS, Brigham Young U., 1962; A of Interior Design, John F. Kennedy U., 1983. Cert. tchr. gen. secondary edn. Calif., in Spanish US Nat. Bd., 2003. Tchr. art, biology Pittsburg Sr. HS, Calif., 1962—63; vol. US Peace Corps, Santiago, Chile, 1963—65; tchr. art Sequoia Union HS Dist., Redwood City, Calif., 1966—68, tchr. art, Spanish, 1970—83, tchr. Spanish, 1985—2005; tchr. art San Dieguito Union HS Dist., Cardiff-by-the-Sea, 1969—70; ret., 2006. Site dir. Calif. Fgn. Lang. Project, Stanford, 1994—98; cons. tchr., peer assistance & rev. Sequoia Union High Sch. Dist., 2000—04; Fulbright-Hayes travel study leader, Chile, 2000. Author: (booklet) Mentor Teachers & Their Careers, 1993, Fulbrighters Abroad, 2000. Mem. steering com. Stanford (Calif.) U. Edn. Collaborative, 1992—96. Fellow, Rockefeller Found., Spain, 1986; grantee, Fulbright-Hayes, Argentina, Ecuador, 1988, NEH, Washington, 1994, Fulbright Tchr. Exchange, Chile, 1998—99. Mem.: Nat. Peace Corps Assn., Calif. Tchrs. Assn., Calif. Lang. Tchrs. Assn. Democrat. Latter-Day Saint. Home: 10343 N Morgan Blvd Cedar Hills UT 84062 Personal E-mail: dashton3@hotmail.com.

ASHTON, DORE, writer, educator; b. Newark; d. Ralph N. and Sylvia (Ashton) Shapiro; m. Adja Yunkers, July 8, 1952 (dec. 1983); children—Alexandra Louise, Marina Svietlana; m. Matti Megged, 1985 (dec. 2003). BA, U. Wis., 1949; MA, Harvard U., 1950; PhD (hon.), Moore Coll., 1975,

Hamline U., 1982, Minn. Coll. of Art, 2002. Asso. editor Art Digest, 1951-54; asso. critic N.Y. Times, 1955-60; lectr. Pratt Inst., 1962-63; head humanities dept. (Sch. Visual Arts), 1965-68; prof. Cooper Union, 1968—. Art critic, lectr., dir. exhbns. in arts; mem. Dedalus Found. Author: Abstract Art Before Columbus, 1957, Poets and the Past, 1959, Philip Guston, 1960, The Unknown Shore, 1962, Rauschenberg's Dante, 1964, Modern American Sculpture, 1968, Richard Lindner, 1969, A Reading of Modern Art, 1970, Pol Bury, 1971, Cultural Guide for New York, 1972, Picasso on Art, 1972, The New York School: A Cultural Reckoning, 1973, A Joseph Cornell Album, 1974, Yes, But, A Critical Biography of Philip Guston, 1976, A Fable of Modern Art, 1980, American Art Since 1945, 1982, About Rothko, 1983, Jacobo Borges, 1984, 20th Century Artists on Art, 1985, Out of the Whirlwind, 1987, Fragonard in the Universe of Painting, 1988, Terence La Noue, 1992, Noguchi East and West, 1992, Ursula van Rydingsvard, 1995, Gunther Gerzso, 1995, The Delicate Thread: Teshigahara's Life in Art, 1997, À Rebours: La Rebellión Informalista, 1999, The Black Rainbow: The Work of Fernando de Szyszlo, 2003, The Walls of the Heart: The Work of David Rankin, 2001, William Tucker, 2001, also monographs; co-author (with Denise Browne Hare): Rosa Bonheur, A Life and Legend, 1981; co-editor: Redon, Moreau, Bresdin, 1961; NY contbg. editor Studio Internat., 1961—74, Opus Internat., 1968—74, XXième Siècle, 1955—70, The Brooklyn Rail, 2004—, assoc. editor Arts, 1974—92, contbr. to Vision and Value series (Gyorgy Kepes) 1966, The New Art Anthology (Gregory Battcock), 1966. Adv. bd. Guggenheim Found. Recipient Mather award for art criticism Coll. Art Assn., 1963, Art Criticism prize St. Louis Art Mus., 1988; Guggenheim fellow, 1964; Graham fellow, 1963; Ford Found. fellow, 1960; Nat. Endowment for Humanities grantee, 1980 Mem. Internat. Assn. Art Critics, Phi Beta Kappa. Home: 217 E 11th St New York NY 10003-7302 Office: Cooper Union Advancement Sci and Art 41 Cooper Sq New York NY 10003-7136 Office Phone: 212-353-4273.

ASHTON, JEAN WILLOUGHBY, library director; b. Detroit, Mar. 1, 1938; d. Gerald Woodrow and Dorothy (McEwen) Willoughby; m. Robert William Ashton, Mar. 30, 1960; children: Katherine, Susanna, Emily, Isabel. BA, U. Mich., 1959; MA, Radcliffe Coll., 1961; PhD in Am. Lit., Columbia U., 1970; MLS in Libr. Sci., Rutgers U., 1985. Lectr. Fisk U., Nashville, 1962-64; asst. prof. English L.I. U., Bklyn., 1969-73; intern N.Y. Hist. Soc., 1984, reference libr. N.Y.C., 1984-87, assoc. libr. pub. svcs., 1987-89, acting libr., 1989-90, dir. libr., 1990-93, 2006—, v.p., 2006—; dir. rare books and manuscripts libr. Columbia U., N.Y.C., 1993—2006. Vis. lectr. N.Y. area Colls., 1976-80; lectr. N.Y. Coun. for the Humanities, 1988-92; coord. Comm. for Resources in N.Y. History, 1987-90. Author: (book) Harriet Beecher Stowe: A Reference Guide, 1976; co-author Emerging Voices: American Women Writers, 1650-1920, 1998; contbr. articles to N.Y. Times, Am. Lit. Realism, Prospects, Magill's Lit. Ann., New Bklyn., Imprint, Biblion, RQ. Vol. BAM Theater Co., Bklyn., 1980-81; mem. bd. govs. Rsch. Librs. Group, 1989-91.; mem. Metro Adminstrv. Svcs. Com., 1990-92; editl. bd. mem., Jour. of Rare Book and Manuscript Sect., Assn. Coll. Rsch. Librs.; adv. coun. (Am. Trust) British Libr.; trustees' libr. coun., NY Hist. Soc. Recipient Avery Hopwood Writing award U. Mich., 1959; Woodrow Wilson fellow Woodrow Wilson Found., 1959; faculty scholar Columbia U., 1966-67. Mem.: Archons of Colophon, Assn. Coll., Readership and Pub. Librs., Soc. History Authorship, Bibliog. Soc. Am., AM. Printing History Assn., ALA, The Grolier Club. Office: NY Historical Society 170 Central Park West New York NY 10024*

ASHTON, SISTER MARY MADONNA, health facility administrator; b. St. Paul; d. Avon B. and Ruth (Fehring) A. BA, Coll. St. Catherine, St. Paul, 1944; LHD (hon.), Coll. St. Catherine, 1996; MSW, St. Louis U., 1946; MHA, U. Minn., 1958; LHD (honorary), Hamline U., 1997. Joined Congregation Sisters of St. Joseph of Carondelet, Roman Cath. Ch., 1946. Dir. med. social service dept. St. Joseph's Hosp., St. Paul, 1949-56; dir. out-patient dept. St. Mary's Hosp., Mpls., 1958-59, asst. adminstr., 1959-62, adminstr., 1962-68, exec. v.p., 1968-72, pres., 1972-82; commr. health State of Minn., 1983-91; pres. Carondelet LifeCare Ministries, St. Paul, 1991-2000, ret., 2000. Dir. Client Security Bd. of Minn. Supreme Ct., 1993-98, St. Catherine's Coll., St. Paul; mem. bd. sci. counselors Nat. Cancer Inst. Recipient Sabra Hamilton award Program in Hosp. Adminstrn. U. Minn., 1958; Minn. Health Citizen of Yr. award, 1977, Gaylord Anderson Leadership award, 1988; Bush summer fellow Harvard Sch. Bus., 1976. Fellow Am. Coll. Healthcare Execs.; mem. Nat. Cath. Health Assn. (sec.). Home: 4401 Valley View Rd Apt 2 Minneapolis MN 55424-1805 E-mail: csj11@msn.com.

ASHWELL, RACHEL, entrepreneur, interior designer; b. Eng. children: Lily, Jake. Founder Shabby Chic by Rachel Ashwell Label, L.A., 1989—. Author: Shabby Chic, 1996, Rachel Ashwell's Shabby Chic Treasure Hunting and Decorating Guide, 1998, The Shabby Chic Home, 2000, The Shabby Chic Gift of Giving, 2001. Office: Rachel Ashwell Shabby Chic 6330 Arizona Cir Los Angeles CA 90045

ASHWORTH, BESSIE, benefits compensation analyst, writer; d. John Henry and Vivian Kennedy; m. Joe T. Ashworth, May 5, 1973; 1 child, Robert F. Kennedy. A in Bus. Adminstrn., Strayer U., 1992. Sr. adminstrv. asst. ANA, Washington, 1983—99; benefits asst. George Wash. U., Washington, 2005—. Founder, pres. Woman Thou Are Called Ministry, Washington, 2001—. Author: (book) Stagnated Christian, Special Special, Woman Thou Art Called. Supporter So. Poverty Law Ctr., Montgomery, Ala., 2005—06; elder Jericho City of Praise, 2004. Democrat. Avocations: swimming, travel, writing, sports. E-mail: bashworth1@verizon.net.

ASKEW, GLORIA YARBROUGH, dietician; d. Charlie Yarbrough and Maggie Yarbrough Dotson; m. Divorced; 1 child, None. BS, U. Memphis, 1970; MS, Rush U., 1980. Registered dietitian Commn. Dietetic Registration, 1975, cert. arobics instr. Am. Coun. Exercise, 1995, exercise leader Am. Coll. Sports Medicine, 1995. Therapeutic dietitian St. Mary Hosp., Gary, Ind., 1974—75; coord. clin. dietetics U. Chgo. Hosps., 1975—80; clin. nutrition mgr. Meth. Hosps., Memphis, 1981—86; nutrition svcs. cons. Hillhaven Corp., Memphis, 1986—90; clin. nutrition mgr. King Fahad Hosp., Al Baha, Saudi Arabia, 1991—92; dep. chief dietitian Riyadh Armed Forces Hosp., Saudi Arabia, 1992—95; nutrition cons. Martha Gregory & Assoc., Louisville, 1996—2000; dir. dietary svcs. Diversified Health Svcs., Memphis, 2000—02; dir. nutrition svcs. Graceland Nursing Ctr., Memphis, 2002—04; regional dir. of nutritional services Tara Cares, Orchard Park, NY, 2004—. Preceptor Dietary Managers Certification Course, Memphis, 1985—98. Mem.: Internat. Assn. Fitness Profls., Am. Dietetic Assn., River City Investors Investment Club (fin. ptnr. 2003—06). Home: 1835 Parkway Terr Memphis TN 38114 Office: Tara Cares 3690 Southwestern Blvd Orchard Park NY 14127 Office Fax: 901-278-0084. Business E-Mail: gaskew@tarahc.com.

ASKEW, KIM JUANITA, lawyer; b. Savannah, Ga., Nov. 14, 1957; BS summa cum laude, Knoxville Coll., 1979; JD, Georgetown U., 1983. Bar: U.S. Supreme Ct., DC 1983, Tex. 1984, U.S. Ct. Appeals (5th, 4th, and 8th cir.), U.S. Dist. Ct. (No. and ea. dist. Tex.). Law clk. U.S. Dist Ct. (No. Dist. Tex.); ptnr. Huges & Luce, LLP, Dallas. Contbr. articles to profl. pubs. Mem. bd. regents Georgetown U.; bd. dirs. Victims Outreach; dir., treas. Dallas Mus. Art; former dir. Greater Dallas C. of C.; former trustee Paul Quinn Coll.; former dir. Jr. League Dallas. Named Tex. SuperLawyer, Law & Politics Mag., 2003; named an Best Lawyers in Dallas, D Mag., 2005; named one of Best Lawyers in Am., Corporate Counsel, 2003; recipient Louise Raggio award, Dallas Women Lawyers Assn., 2003, Trailblazer award, J.L. Turner Legal Assn., 2003. Mem.: ABA (mem. com. commn. on women in profession 1993—97, mem. com. on meetings and travel 1997—2000, mem. continuing legal edn. com. 2000—03, sec. litigation sect. 2002—04, chair-elect litigation sect. 2005—, mem. ho. of dels., mem. membership com., mem. coun. fund for justice and edn.), Tex. Women Lawyers, Dallas Bar Assn. (former co-chair judiciary com.), State Bar Tex. (chair continuing legal edn. com. 1997—2000, chair litigation sect. 2001—02, chair bd. dirs. 2003—04, former chair evidentiary panel dist. 6A grievance com., bd. dirs., Presdl. Citation 2000, Gene Cavin award 1999), Am. Law Inst. (chair com. on size, fed. judiciary com.).

ASKEW, RILLA, author; b. Poteau, Okla., Jan. 26, 1951; d. Paul and Carmelita Askew; m. Paul Austin, Aug. 6, 1983. BFA, U. Tulsa, 1980; MFA, Bklyn. Coll., 1989. Author: Strange Business, 1992, The Mercy Seat, 1997, Fire in Beulah, 2001. Recipient Okla. Book award, Okla. Ctr. for the book, 1993, 1998, Western Heritage award, Cowboy Hall of Fame, 1998, O'Henry award, Soc. Arts and Scis., 1993, Am. Book award, Before Columbus Found., 2002, Myers Book award, Gustavas Myers Ctr., 2002. Mem.: PEN, Authors Guild, Assoc. Writing Programs.

ASKEY, THELMA J., federal agency administrator; b. Lakehurst, N.J. BA, Tenn. Tech. U., 1970; postgrad., George Washington U., Am. U. Press asst. Rep. John Duncan, 1972-74; editor Nat. Rsch. Coun. Marine Bd., 1974-76; asst. minority trade counsel Ho. Com. Ways and Means, 1976-79, minority trade counsel, 1979-94; staff dir. subcommittee trade Ho. Com. on Ways and Means, 1995-98; commr. U.S. Internat. Trade Commn., Washington, 1998—2000; dir. U.S. Trade and Devel. Agy., Arlington, Va., 2001—. Office: US Trade and Devel Agy Office Dir 1000 Wilson Blvd Ste 1600 Arlington VA 22209-3901 Office Phone: 703-875-4357.

ASKINE, RUTH PARSE, elementary school educator; b. Stuttgart, Ark., Aug. 27, 1936; d. John Edward and Mattie Lee (Scales) Parse; m. David James Askine, June 16, 1960; children: Rebecca Ellen Askine Brown, John Irvin Askine. BA, Rice U., 1958; MS, U. Houston-Clear Lake, 1981, MA, 1989. Cert. tchr., Tex. Elem. tchr. Bailey Elem. Sch., Pasadena, Tex., 1958-60; elem. tchr. Berkeley County Schs., Martinsburg, W.Va., 1967-69, Laurel (Del.) Middle Sch., 1970-77; elem. tchr. sci. Tex. Mil. Inst., San Antonio, 1977-78; elem. tchr. South Houston Elem., Pasadena, 1978-81, Young Elem., Pasadena, 1981-84; tchr. U.S. history Beverly Hills Intermediate Sch., Pasadena Ind. Sch. Dist., Houston, 1984-90; tchr. world history and econs. South Houston High Sch., 1990-92; tchr. honors econs., world geography Sam Rayburn High Sch., Pasadena, Tex., 1992—98. Pres. Southeast Coun. for Social Studies, Tex., 1989-90; coach acad. pentathlon team, grades 7, 8, Beverly Hills Intermediate Sch., Houston, 1988-99; coach acad. decathlon team, grades 11, 12, South Houston High Sch., 1990-92. Editor: Handbook for Teachers in Environmental Science, 1978, Confluent Economics Project, Levels 1-5, 1980. Elder First Presbyn. Ch., Pasadena, 1983-86, 98-2000. Mem. AAUW (sec. 1982-84, pres. 1999-2002), Pasadena Habitat for Humanity (bd. mem. 1999-2002), Pasadena Inerfaith Housing Found. (bd. mem. 2003—). E-mail: ruthaskine@earthlink.net.

ASKINS, JARI, lawyer, department chairman, state representative; b. Duncan, Okla., Apr. 27, 1953; d. Ollie M. and Jarita Askins. BA in Journalism, U. Okla., 1975, JD, 1980. Bar: Okla. V.p. closing office Stephens County Abstract Co., Duncan, Okla.; spl. dist. judge Stephens County, Okla., 1982—90; chmn. Okla. Pardon and Parole Bd., Okla. City, 1991—92; dep. gen. counsel Gov.'s Office, 1992—94; rep. Ho. of Reps., State of Okla., Okla. City, 1995—. Dep. majority fl. leader Okla. Ho. Reps., Okla. City, 2001—; mem. Okla. Judicial Conf., Okla. City. Mem Leadership Okla.; bd. trustees Cottey Jr. Coll., Nevada, Mo. Named to Okla. Woman's Hall of Fame, 2001. Mem.: ABA, Duncan C. of C. (Woman of Yr. 1995), Stephen's County Bar Assn., Okla. Bar Assn., Lions Club. Democrat. Office: 2300 N Lincoln Blvd Rm 301B Oklahoma City OK 73105 Home and Office: PO Box 391 Duncan OK 73534 E-mail: askinsja@lsb.state.ok.us.

ASKINS, NANCY ELLEN PAULSEN, training services executive; b. St. Paul, Nov. 2, 1948; d. Charles A. and Stasia (Sawicki) Paulsen; m. Arthur J. Askins, Apr. 28, 1979. BS in Home Econ., U. Cin., 1970, BS in Edn., 1971, MEd, 1972; postgrad., SUNY-Buffalo, 1974—76, Temple U., 1976, Walden U., 1988—92, Inst. Fin. Edn., 1982—85, Capella U., 2002. Cert. gaming supr. Edn. Inst. Am. Hotel and Motel Assn.; cert. strategic planning facilitator; cert. quality mgr. Asst. aquatic supr. Cin. Recreation Commn., 1969—72; adminstr. student affairs U. Cin., 1970—72; mem. faculty student affairs adminstrn. Tex. Luth. Coll., 1972—73; mem. faculty, student affairs adminstr. SUNY-Geneseo, 1974—76; student affairs adminstr. Temple U., Phila., 1976—78; tchr. drug awareness coord. Adams Sch. Harlandale Sch. Dist., San Antonio, 1973—74; career life ins. agt., fin. planning cons. Phoenix Mut. Life Ins. Co., Phila., 1978—81; registered rep., securities agt. Phoenix Equity Planning Corp., Phila., 1980—81; owner Paulsen-Askins Fin. Svcs., Somers Point, NJ, 1980—81; mem. women's task force Phoenix Cos., 1980—81; coord. tng. svcs. Collective Fed. Savs. & Loan Assn., Egg Harbor City, NJ, 1981—82, asst. v.p., tng. dir., 1982—84; mgr. tng. Shore Meml. Hosp., Somers Point, 1984—85, instr. wellness, 1984—88, dir. ednl. devel., 1986—89; dir edn. svcs. Holy Cross Hosp., Ft. Lauderdale, Fla., 1990—91, dir. cmty. and vol. svcs., 1991—94, part-time instr. wellness program, 1991—94; v.p. tng. and assoc. devel. Grand Casino, Biloxi, 1994—96; coord. tng. svcs. Gulf Coast Bus. Svcs., Gulfport, Miss., 1996—98; dir. quality Hollywood Casino Resort/Tunica, Robinsonville, Miss., 1998—2001; adj. prof. Webster U., Memphis, 2003. Adj. prof. bus. and social scis. Atlantic C.C. Coll., Mays Landing, N.J., 1986-89; facilitator Assertiveness Tng. Group, Interpersonal Comms. Group, orgnl. and leadership devel. seminars and cons.; owner, exec. corp. cons. Askins Tng. and Cons., 1981—; mem. bd. examiners Malcolm Baldrige Nat. Quality Award, 2001,02, 03, Pres.'s Quality Award, 2000, Tenn. Quality Award, 2000, Miss. Quality Award, 1999, 2000 (judge 2002); instr. Inst. Fin. Edn., 1982-85, Ednl. Inst., Am. Hotel ad Motel Assn., 1999-2001; nat. seminar leader, Fred Pryor / Career Track, 2000-; workshop presenter and spkr. in field; items writer Cert. Quality Improvement Assoc. Agy. chmn. United Way Campaign, Phila., 1979, 80; bd. dir. South Jersey Regional Theater, 1983-86, chmn., 1983-84; active ann. Muscular Dystrophy Telethon, Phila.; active Girl Scouts U.S., 1956-74, 84—; mem. Parish coun., parish enrichment com., 1984-88, cantor St. Joseph Roman Cath. Ch., Somers Point, 1979-89; mem., lector Christ the King Cath. Ch., Southaven, Miss., 1998-2003, St. Peter Cath. Ch., 2003—; chmn. com. Women's Club St. Luke's Cath. Ch., Coconut Creek, Fla., 1992-94, parish coun., 1993-94; bd. dir. Holly Shores Coun. Girl Scouts U.S., 1984-85; host fgn. exch. students Am. Scandinavian Student Exch. Program, 1985-87; mem. Somers Point Bd. Edn., 1986; mem. Libr. Adv. Bd. City of Margate, Fla., 1991-94, fundraising chmn., vice chmn., chmn. Recipient Brotherhood-Sisterhood Achievers award NCCJ, 1985, Rising Star award, 1997, Gold Dir. award, 1998 Carlson Learning Co., Inscape Publishing, Minn.; named Biloxi Career Woman Bus. Profl. Women/Lighthouse of Biloxi, 1995, Women of Achievement Woman of Yr. Bus. Profl. Women Clarksdale, Coahoma County, Miss., 1999. Mem. ASTD (treas. South Jersey chpt., nat. dir. savs. and lending industry group 1983-84, hosps. and healthcare industry group 1984-86, nat. conf. spkr. 1984-86, sec. Greater Broward/Ft. Lauderdale chpt. 1991, pres.-elect 1992, pres.1993, nat. dir.-elect 1990-91. dir. 1991-92, Interfaith Trainers Cons. Network), Internat. Cons. Assn., Am. Hotel & Motel Assn. (No. Miss. chpt. charter pres. 1999), Bus. and Profl. Women Buffalo (co-chair 2004-05), Women Robinsonville, Miss. (charter pres. 1999-2000), Bus. and Profl. Women Clarksdale (legis. com. chair, 1998-2000), Bus. and Profl. Women Lighthouse of Biloxi (v.p. membership, newsletter editor, chair 1997 Nat. Bus. Women's Week), Bus. and Profl. Women Miss. (state 2d v.p., state membership chair, 1996-97, state legis. chair, 1999-2000, nat. leadership chair, state pres.-elect 2002-03, state pres. 2003-04, nat. leadership chair 2004-05, individual devel. prgram co-chair Buffalo chpt., 2004-2005), Greater Camden Assn. Life Underwriters (state pres. 2003-04, chmn. Life Ins. Week for South Jersey 1978-79, bd. dir. 1979-81, pub. rels. chmn. 1979-81, chmn. state edn. 1981), Am. Soc. for Quality (features editor Competitive Advantage quality divsn. 2000-03), Am. Hosp. Assn., Am. Soc. Health Edn. and Tng., Am. Mgmt. Assn., Fla. Soc. Healthcare Edn. and Tng., Greater Mainland C. of C. (v.p., treas., membership coord. 1979-89, Pres. award 1983), Internat. Assn. Facilitators, U. Cin. Alumni of Greater Phila. Area (pres. 1980-89), Greater Ft. Lauderdale C. of C. (diplomat 1992-93, edn. com. 1993-94), Alliance/The Women's Network (bd. dir. 1983-84), Rotary Internat., Rotary of Gulfport, Rotary of Robinsonville, (sect. 1999, newsletter editor 1998-99, pres.-elect 1999-2000, pres. 2000-2001), Rotary (chairperson, long range planning com. 1999-2001, group study exch. com. 1999-2000, youth study exch. com. 1999-2000, chmn. matching grants com. 2001-2002). Democrat. Home: 444 Lockport St PO Box 428 Youngstown NY 14174-0428

ASKOV, EUNICE MAY, adult education educator; b. St. Louis, Nov. 20, 1940; d. David Hull and Marjorie Jane (Gutgsell) Nicholson; m. Warren Hopkins Askov, Jan. 22, 1967; children: David, Karen. BA in English, Denison U., 1962; MA in English, U. Wis., 1966, PhD in Curriculum and Instrn., 1969. English and reading tchr. Rich Twp. High Sch., Park Forest, Ill., 1962-64; reading svc. reading specialist U. Wis., Madison, 1965-66, project asst. Wis. R & D Ctr. for Cognitive Learning, 1966-67, rsch. assoc., 1969-72, lectr. dept. curriculum and instrn., 1968-69; coord. adult basic edn. programs U. Wis. Extension, 1966-67; remedial reading specialist Lincoln Jr. High Sch., Madison, 1966; adult basic edn. tchr. Madison Vocat., Tech. and Adult Schs., 1967-68; asst. prof. elem. edn. Minn. State U., Bemidji, 1972-74; assoc. prof. Pa. State U., University Park, 1974-79, prof. edn., 1980—2001, disting. prof., 2001—. Presenter seminars on adult edn., Germany, 1986, 93; cons., speaker in field; mem. editorial bd. Jour. Ednl. Rsch., Adult Edn. Quarterly, Adult Basic Edn., Am. Reading Forum Yearbook; mem. steering com. Adult Literacy and Tech.; mem. panel nat. work group on cancer and literacy Nat. Cancer Inst.; organizer, coord. Pa. State Coalition for Adult Literacy; mem. adv. coun. Nat. Coalition for Literacy. Contbr. articles to profl. publs. Fulbright sr. scholar, 1983; Literacy Leader fellow Nat. Inst. for Literacy, 1994-95; recipient Alumni Achievement award U. Wis.-Madison Sch. Edn., 1994, Career Achievement award Pa. State Coll. Edn.; Disting. fellow Flinders U. Inst. Internat. Edn., Australia, 1998; named to Reading Hall of Fame, 2005 Mem. Am. Assn. Adult and Continuing Edn. (chair, mem. various coms., bd. dir.),Commn. Profs. of Adult Edn., Am. Edn. Rsch. Assn., Am. Reading Forum, Internat. Reading Assn. (chair, mem. various coms.), Keystone State Reading Assn., Mid-State Literacy Coun. (bd. dir., pers. com., long range planning com.), Mid-State Reading Coun. (pres.), Pa. Assn. Adult and Continuing Edn., Phi Beta Kappa, Phi Delta Kappa. Democrat. Methodist. Avocations: travel, aerobics, hiking, reading. Office: Pa State U Inst for Study Adult Lit 200 Rackley Bldg University Park PA 16802-3202 Business E-Mail: ena1@psu.edu.

ASLAKSON, SARAH, artist; b. N.Y.C., Aug. 23, 1947; d. David A. and Edith (Silver) Wiesen; m. David Lee Aslakson, Sept. 1, 1968. BS, U. Wis., 1969, MSLS, 1970. Exhbns. include Bone and Joint Surgery Assn., Madison, Wis., 1982, Wustum Mus. Fine Arts, Racine, Wis., 1982, Fanny Garver Gallery, Madison, 1986-96, Katie Gingrass Gallery, Milw., 1986, 88-95, Art Resources, St. Paul, Minn., 1989, 92-94, Banaker Gallery, Walnut Creek, Calif., 1987,Edgewood Orchard Gallery, Fish Creek, Wis., 1992, West Bend (Wis.) Mus. Fine Arts, 1990, 92, Jan Cicero Gallery, Chgo., 1992-93, Kornbluth Gallery, Fairlawn, N.J., 1992-96, Cary Gallery, Rochester, Mich., Hadley Sch. Blind Invitational, Chgo., 1995, Wis. Acad. Arts and Scis., 1994, U. Wis., Platteville, 1995; permanent collections include: City of Milw., Swiss Colony, Minn. Dept. Revenue, Mpls., City of Milw. Visitors Ctr., Paine Art Ctr., Oshkosh, Wis., numerous others.

ASLAN, MADALYN, writer, educator; d. George Vincent Shea and Donna Marie Todd. BA with honors, U. London, 1984; BA, Cornell U., 1987; MFA, Sarah Lawrence Coll., 1991. Lectr. Coll. Psychic Studies, London, 2001—. Monthly astrologer AOL, 2006—. Author: What's Your Sign? A Cosmic Guide for Young Astrologers, 2002, Madalyn Aslan's Jupiter Signs, 2003; actor: (TV series) The Martian Chronicles, 1980; (films) D.H. Lawrence. Mem.: Nat. Coun. Geo-Cosmic Rsch., Nat. Campaign for Tolerance (life; founder), Am. Fedn. Astrologers (life). Home: 748 Page St San Francisco CA 94117 Office Phone: 212-631-5844. E-mail: madalyn@madalynaslan.com.

ASMAR, KATHLEEN, educational association administrator; b. Chgo., Dec. 30, 1952; d. Thomas Francis and Janice Elizabeth (Garrison) Martin; m. Mitchell Michael Asmar, Oct. 15, 1977; children: Michael, Elizabeth, Eric, John Philip. BA in Psychology, U. Houston, 1975; BS in Spl. Edn., U. So. Miss., 1996; MEd, William Carey Coll., 2004. Elem. adminstr. Immaculate Conception Sch., Laurel, Miss., 1996—. Alliance for cath. edn. leadership program U. Norte Dame, 2005. Roman Catholic. Office: Immaculate Conception Sch 835 W 6th St Laurel MS 39440-3436

ASNIEN, PHYLLIS ARLINE, humanities educator, writer; b. Cleve., June 23, 1937; d. Morris and Rebecca Berman Asnien; m. Michael Jay Tabor, Apr. 24, 1973 (div. Nov. 30, 1983); 1 child, Xanthe Rebecca Tabor. BS in Vocal Music Edn., Ohio State U., 1959; MA in Am. and English Lit., John Carroll U., 1967. Tchr. English lit., composition, dramatics Westlake (Ohio) Sr. H.S., 1964—68; adj. faculty remedial speech Cuyahoga C.C., Cleve., 1984; prof. humanities Lakeland C.C., Kirtland, Ohio, 1969—. Textbook revisionist Harper Collins Pubs., N.Y.C., 1990—97; spkr. in field. Author: (textbook) Humanities Considered, 1966; dramatist (plays) To the Sound of the Heartbeat, 1965, A Sudden Conviction, 1966. Bd. dirs. Carl Jung Soc., Cleve., 1993—95. Recipient scholarship, Citizens Exch. Corps., 1971, grant, NEH, 1984—85. Mem.: Ams. for the ARts Action Fund, Nat. Mus. Women in Arts (charter mem.), Delta Omicron. Achievements include development of year-long humanities inter-disciplinary program. Avocations: singing, swimming, Ikebana, yoga. Office: Lakeland CC 7700 Clocktower Dr Kirtland OH 44094 Office Phone: 440-525-7193. E-mail: phyllisa1973@earthlink.net.

ASP, JANNA C, healthcare educator; b. Elgin, Ill., Jan. 12, 1971; d. Charles H. and Janice K. Asp. M, Pk. U., Parkville, MO, 2006. Mo. Teacher Certificate - PC II Mo., 1998, Ill. Teacher Certificate - Standard Type 09 Ill., 1996. Health, phys. edn. Liberty Pub. Schools - Liberty Mid. Sch., Mo., 2000—; health, phys. edn. tchr. Hickman Mills Sch. Dist. - Ervin Mid. Sch., Kans. City, Mo., 1998—2000. Asst. 8th grade volleyball coach Liberty Jr. High Schools, Mo., 2000—; stuco advisor Liberty Mid. Sch., 2002—; asst. 8th grade track coach Ervin Mid. Sch., Kans. City, 2000, asst. 8th grade volleyball coach, 1999. Office: Liberty Pub Schools 1500 S Withers Rd Liberty MO 64068 Office Phone: 816-736-5410.

ASSAEL, ALYCE, artist; b. NYC, Dec. 12, 1938; d. Joseph and Betty (Abrams) Friedman; m. Henry Assael, Aug. 19, 1961; children: Shaun, Brenda. Grad., Parsons Sch. Design, 1960; BS, NYU, 1960, M in Am. Folk Art, 1985. Window designer Henri Bendel, N.Y.C., 1960; interior store designer Macy's, N.Y.C., 1960-62; interior showroom designer Glenn of Mich., N.Y.C., 1962-63; illustrator for fashion catalogs and promotion pieces, N.Y.C., 1962-63; fine artist paintings and photographs, N.Y.C., 1964-70. One-woman shows include U. Pa., Phila., 1975, Ann Harper Gallery, Amagansett, N.Y., 1995, exhibited in group shows at Louise Himmelfarb Gallery, Southampton, N.Y., 1980, M.J. Green Gallery, Bridgehampton, N.Y., 1980, Guild Hall Mus., East Hampton, N.Y., 1997, 1998, 1999, 2001, The Creative Merge Gallery, Southampton, N.Y., 2003, Stoa Gallery, Forest Hills, N.Y., 2004, 2005, 2006, Gone Local Gallery, Amagansett, 2006. Mem. Guild Hall Mus., Mus. Modern Art, Mus. Am. Folk Art, Queens Mus., Mus. of Women in the Arts. Avocations: photography, theater, films.

ASSELIN, HEATHER E., lawyer; BA, U. Calif., Fresno, 1993; JD, Creighton U. Sch. Law, 1996. Bar: Tex., lic.: US Dist. Cts. for So. and No. Dists. Tex. Dir. litigation and constrn./surety sects. Coats Rose. Named a Rising Star, Tex. Super Lawyers mag., 2006. Mem.: Assn. Gen. Contractors (Houston chpt.), Assn. Women Attys. (mem. jud. reception com.), Houston Bar Assn. (litigation and constrn. sects.) (mem. CLE com.). Office: Coats Rose Yale Ryman Lee 3 E Greenway Plz Ste 2000 Houston TX 77046 Office Phone: 713-653-7386. E-mail: hasselin@coatsrose.com.*

ASSENS, NATHALIE, construction executive; b. Versailles, Yvelines, France, Dec. 11, 1979; d. Bernard and Sophie Assens. Diplome d'Ingenieur Batiment, Ecole spéciale des Travaux publics, du Bâtiment et de l'Industrie, Paris, 2001; MS in Constrn. Mgmt., MIT, Cambridge, Mass., 2002. Cert. constrn. supr., Commonwealth of Mass., 2005; LEED accredited profl., US Green Bldg. Coun., 2005. Project mgr. Shawmut Design and Constrn., Boston, 2003—05, ZVI Constrn. Co, LLC, Brookline, Mass., 2005—. Fellow Civil and Environ. Engring. fellow, MIT, 2001—03. Mem.: Sigma Xi (assoc.). Office: ZVI Construction 131 Dummer St Brookline MA 02446 Office Phone: 857-221-7070. E-mail: nassens@zviconstruction.com.

ASSIE-LUMUMBA, N'DRI T., Africana studies educator; b. Potossou, Ivory Coast, 1952; d. Kouassi and Yaha (Kokora) Assie. Studnet, U. Abidjan, Ivory Coast, 1970-71; BA, U. Lyon, France, 1972; MA, U. Lyon, 1975; postgrad., U. Laval, Que., Can., 1976; PhD, U. Chgo., 1982. Rchr. U. Abidjan, 1975-76; postdoctoral fellow U. Houston, 1982-83; tchr., adminstr. U. Benin, CIRSSED, Lome, Togo, 1983-88; vis. Bard Coll., Annandale, NY, 1989, Vassar Coll., Poughkeepsie, NY, 1989-90; resident fellow Internat. Inst. for Ednl. Planning, Paris, 1990; dep. dir. Pan African Studies and Rsch. Ctr., Abidjan, 1996—; prof. Africana studies Cornell U., Ithaca, NY, 1991—. Cons. UNESCO, Paris, 1989, 94, UN Devel. Program, N.Y.C., 1997, 99, Forum for African Women, Nairobi, Kenya, 1997, Rockefeller Found., N.Y.C., 1999. Author: Les Africaine dans la politique, 1996; editor Jour. Comparative Edn., 1998—. Ford Found. fellow, 1991; Fulbright sr. rsch. felow, 1991-92; Rockefeller Found. grantee, 1996-97. Mem. AAUW, Assn. African Women for R&D (exec. com.), Comparative and Internat. Edn. Soc., Coun. for Devel. of Social Sci. Rsch. in Africa, Cornell Inst. for Social and Econ. Rsch., Pi Lambda Theta. Avocations: music (jazz, modern, african and classical), physical exercise, modern african dance, reading. Office: Cornell U Africana Studies 310 Triphammer Rd Ithaca NY 14850-2519

ASSINK, NELLIE GRACE, agricultural executive; b. Yakima, Wash., July 5, 1920; d. Martin Gilde and Grace Byl; m. George H. Assink, July 9, 1943 (dec. Nov. 1982); children: Macile Assink Zais, Jon Martin. BA, Whitman Coll./Conserv. Music, 1942, tchr.'s diploma in music and piano, 1942; postgrad., U. Wash. and Cen. Coll., 1944, 59. Gen. cert., Wash.; cert. supr. music. English tchr., libr. Mabton (Wash.) H.S., 1943-45; libr. Wide Hollow Sch., Yakima, 1948-49; English tchr., libr. Lower Naches (Wash.) Sch., 1960-80; pres. Assink Acres, Inc., Naches, 1982—. Ch. organist Meml. Bible Ch., Yakima, 1946-82; chmn. Christian Edn. Bd., 1981-82; bd. dirs., sec. Yakima County Farm Bur., 1985-99; libr. Meml. Bible Ch., Yakima, 1960—. Mem. Naches Union Irrigation Dist. (sec. 1993—), Yakima County Farm Bur. (past sec. 1997), Lower Naches Women's Club (pres. 1984-86, 2000-02), Yakima Music Club, Ch. Librs.-N.W. (past pres.). Republican. Avocations: genealogy, photography, classical piano. Home: 681 N Gleed Rd Naches WA 98937 Office: Assink Acres Inc 681 N Gleed Rd Naches WA 98937

ASTAIRE, CAROL ANNE TAYLOR, artist, educator; b. Long Beach, Calif., Aug. 26, 1947; d. John Clinton and Carolyn Sophie (Wright) Taylor; m. Frederic Astaire, Jr., Feb. 14, 1971; children: John Carroll, Johanna Carolyn. BFA, UCLA, 1969; grad. summer studies, Salzburg Summer Sch., Klessheim, Austria, 1969; cert. secondary sch. tchr., Calif. State U., Long Beach, 1971; postgrad., Calif. Polytechnic State U., San Luis Obispo, 1986-87. Cert. secondary sch. tchr. Calif. Tchr., tutor, cons. art edn. San Luis Coastal Unified Sch. Dist., San Luis Obispo, 1980-89. Author: (book) Left Handed Poetry from the Heart, 1983; Represented in permanent collections Yergeau Musée Interant. Art, Montreal, Can., Travis AFB Mus., Calif., Huntington Libr. Founder, trustee San Luis Coastal Unified Sch. Dist./Found. Arts Art Core, 1988—92; mem. adv. coun. Coastal Cmty. Edn. and Svc., San Luis Obispo, 1989—92; screening com. UCLA Alumni Scholarship, 1993—95; mem. archtl. needs assessment com. Art Ctr., San Luis Obispo. Recipient Nat. finalist, Kodak Internat. Newspaper Snapshot award, 1993, 1st pl. black and white photo award, Ann. Visions 99 Photography Group, 1st pl., B/W Visions, 2001. Mem.: Ctrl. Coast Photog. Soc. (two 1st place black-and-white photo awards), Oil Pastel Acrylic Group Brushstrokes (hon. mention 1994), San Luis Obispo Art Coun., Fine Arts Coun., San Luis Obispo Art Ctr., Nat. Mus. Women in Arts. Avocations: ballet, architecture, swimming, kayaking, reading. Office Phone: 805-541-5320.

ASTELL, CHRISTINE ANN, school guidance counselor; d. Robert Ernest and Reva Jane Housewright; children: Nicole Ann, Megan Corinne. MS in Counseling, Western Ill. U., Macomb, 2003. Elem. tchr. Corse Elem., Burlington, Iowa, 1998—2005; sch. guidance counselor Oak St. Mid. Sch., Burlington, Iowa, 2005—. Office Phone: 319-753-6773.

ASTER, RUTH MARIE RHYDDERCH, business owner; b. Cleve., Aug. 15, 1939; d. Roy William and Ruth Marie (Teckmeyer) Rhydderch; m. Ferdinand Aster, Nov. 23, 1963; children: Anneliese Ruth Aster Wilt, Christian Josef Roy Student, Cooper Sch. Art, Cleve., 1957; BS, Kent State U., Ohio, 1962. Tchr. art North Olmsted Jr. and Sr. H.S., Ohio, 1962—64; chmn. art dept. Andrews Sch. for Girls, Willoughby, Ohio, 1963—64; co-owner, treas. Aster Cabinet Shop, Chesterland, Ohio, 1963—; co-owner, v.p., treas. Ferdl Aster Ski Sch., Chesterland, 1964—; owner, v.p., sec., treas. Ferdl Aster Ski Shop, Chesterland, 1972—; owner, v.p., advt. designer, fashion buyer, tour advisor Ferdl Aster Sport Ctr., Chesterland, 1985—. Chmn. region IV U.S. Ski Assn., Colorado Springs, 1980—84, Alpine ofcl., 1983—88; ski racing coach U.S. Ski Coaches Assn., Park City, Utah, 1980—89; ski racing coach, Alpine ofcl. Fedn. Internat. Ski, Bern, Switzerland, Alpine ofcl.; adv. bd. First County Bank, Chesterland, 1992—2000; adv. coun. U.S. Postal Svc., Chesterland, 1993—2000; v.p., bd. mem. in charge zoning space Lake Cardinal Timbering Corp., 2002—. Exhibitions include Akron Mus. Art, 1959, Cleve. Gallery, 1962—64, Willoughby Fine Arts, 1963—65, Wagrain, Austria, 1979—, Fairmont Fine Arts, 1980—. Creator blind ski program Cleve. Sight Ctr., 1969; trustee Chesterland Hist. Found., 1985—, past pres., past v.p., past treas.; past chair, vice chair Chester Twp. Zoning Commr., 1987—; life friend Geauga West Libr., 1989—, bd. dirs., historian; dir. history ARC, Cleve., amb., 1999—; grad. Leadership Geauga, 1997; bd. dirs. Geauga County Libr. Found.; v.p. bd. dirs., mem. mktg. com. Geauga County Coun. for Arts and Culture, 2002—. Mem.: North Ea. Ohio Ski Retailers Assn. (bd. dirs.), Orchesis, Cmty. Improvement Corp. Geauga County (re-orgn. com., nominating com., trustee 1990—), Chesterland C. of C. (past pres., v.p., treas., trustee 1985—, sec. to exec. bd. 2001—, Bus. Person of Yr. 1993), Kent State U. Alumni Pvt. Sector Bus. Alliance, Internat. Platform Assn., Kent State U. Alumni Assn. (life), Chester Study Club (past v.p., pres. 1997—2003), Gamma Delta, Alpha Psi Omega, Chi Omega. Lutheran. Avocations: reading, hiking, hunting, collecting classic autos and historic homes. Office: Ferdl Aster Ski Shop 8330 Mayfield Rd Chesterland OH 44026-2520 Office Phone: 440-729-9472. E-mail: fasterskier@prodigy.net.

ASTERN, LAURIE, psychotherapist, physician assistant; b. NYC, Nov. 13, 1952; d. Seymour and Hilda (Weintraub) A. BA in Psychology, Fla. Atlantic U., 1983; MS in Counseling Psychology, Nova U., 1992; postgrad., Fielding Inst., 1996-98; AA Physician Asst., Maimi Dade CC, 2001. Diplomate Am. Bd. Med. Psychotherapists, lic. physician asst.; cert. MHC Fla., family mediator. Mem. crisis intervention and sexual assault staff Broward County, Ft. Lauderdale, Fla., 1984-86, victim advocate, 1986-88, substance abuse counselor, 1990-94; pvt. practice in psychotherapy Pompano, Fla., 1987—99; physician asst. Martin Army Cmty. Hosp., Ft. Benning, Ga., 1999—. Facilitator HIV AIDS support groups, Pompano, Fla., 1990—; founder PIC, Inc., Hollywood, Fla., 1980-85. Founder, dir. Ctr. for Victims of Crime, Pompano, 1987—. Recipient Innovation and Creativity award Broward County Bd. of Commrs., 1987. Mem. Nat. Assn. Drugs and Alcohol Counselors, Nova Southeastern U. Alumni Assn. Avocations: scuba diving, exploration third world countries. Office: Martin Army Cmty Hosp Fort Benning GA 31905

ASTEY, TRICIA ANNE, music educator; b. Garfield Heights, Ohio, Jan. 13, 1981; d. Timothy M. and Christina Pruchnicki; m. Scott Daniel Astey, Nov. 12, 1979. MusB in Edn., Baldwin-Wallace Coll., Berea, Ohio, 2003. Cert. music tchr. PK-12 Ohio. Pvt. lesson tchr., Cleve., 1997; music tchr. Bedford City Schs., Bedford Heights, Ohio, 2003—. Drama dir. Bedford City Schs., 2003—06; musical dir., accompanist. Recipient Musical Theater Devotion award, 2003; scholar, Baldwin-Wallace Coll., 1999—2003. Office Phone: 440-786-3322.

ASTLEY, AMY, editor-in-chief; married; 2 children. BA, Mich. State U., 1989. Editl. asst. House and Garden mag., asst. editor, assoc. editor; beauty assoc. Vogue mag., 1993—94, beauty dir., 1994—2005; editor-in-chief Teen Vogue, 2005—. Office: Teen Vogue 4 Times Sq New York NY 10036*

ASTLEY, SUZETTE LYNN, psychology educator, researcher; b. Des Moines, Apr. 12, 1951; d. John Charles and Lenore Barbara (DeCamp) A.; m. Richard Michael Stater, Oct. 13, 1990. BS, U. Iowa, 1973; MS, Kans. State U., 1978, PhD, 1984. Instr. Cornell Coll., Mt. Vernon, Iowa, 1982-84, asst. prof., 1984-88, assoc. prof. psychology, 1988—, chair dept. of psychology, 1985-89. Faculty fellow Associated Colls. of Midwest Urban Studies Program, Chgo., 1988. Contbr. articles to profl. publs. Recipient Rsch. Opportunity award NSF, 1986. Mem.: Psychonomic Soc., Midwestern Psychological Assn., Assn. for Psychological Sci. Home: RR 1 Box 51 692 Adams Ave Lisbon IA 52253-8510 Office: Cornell Coll 600 1st St SW Mount Vernon IA 52314-1098

ASTMAN, BARBARA ANN, artist, educator; b. Rochester, NY, July 12, 1950; d. George William and Bertha Dinah (Meisel) A.; m. Noel Robert Harding, Feb. 23, 1977 (div. 1983); m. Joseph Anthony Baker, Aug. 29, 1984; children: Amy Astman Baker, Laura Astman Baker. A degree, RIT, 1970; grad., Ont. Coll. Art, Toronto, 1973. Prof photography dept. Ont. Coll. Art and Design (formerly Ont. Coll. Art), Toronto, 1975—; faculty York U., Toronto, 1978-80, 86. Lectr. in field. One-woman shows include Baldwin St. Gallery Photography, Toronto, 1973, Ryerson Photo Gallery, Toronto, 1974, Nat. Film Bd. Can., Ottawa, 1975, S.A.W. Gallery Inc., 1976, Sable-Castelli Gallery Ltd., Toronto, 1977, 79-84, 86, 88, 90, Jean Marie Antone Gallery, Annapolis, Md., 1979, Whitewater Gallery, North Bay, Ont., Bruce Art Gallery, Canton, NY, 1980, Mendel Art Gallery, Saskatoon, Sask., 1981, So. Alta. Art Gallery, Edmonton, 1981, Art Gallery Peterborough, Ont., 1982, Galerie du Musee, Musee du Quebec, 1986, Ctr. d'Animation et de Diffusion de la Photographie, Quebec, 1986, Thunder Bay Art Gallery, Ont., 1992, Robert McLaughlin Gallery, Oshawa, Ont., 1993, McIntosh Gallery, London, Ont., 1994, Gallery Stratford, Ont., 1994, Art Gallery of Hamilton, 1995, Edmonton Art Gallery, Kamloops Art Gallery, B.C., 1996-2005, Jane Corkin Gallery (now Corkin Shopland Gallery), 1997, 99, 2001, 03, 05, Art Gallery of Windsor, 2004, Yukon Art Ctr., Whitehorse, Yukon, 2005, Koffler Art Gallery, Toronto, 2006; group exhbns. include Lamkin Camerawork Gallery, San Francisco, 1975, Art Gallery Ont., Toronto, 1975, 80, 84, 93, Rochester (NY) Meml. Art Gallery, Montreal Mus. Fine Arts, 1975, Harbourfront Art Gallery, Toronto, 1977, 80, Sable-Castelli Gallery Ltd., 77, 81, Anna Leonowens Gallery, Halifax, N.S., 1977, London (Ont.) Regional Art Gallery, 1978, 83, Edmonton (Ont.) Art Gallery, 1978, Winnipeg Art Gallery, 1979, Everson Mus., Syracuse, NY, 1979, Galerie Luca Polazzoli, Milan, 1979, H.F. Johnson Mus. Art, Ithaca, NY, 1979, George Eastman House, Rochester, 1979, Hamilton Art Gallery, La Galerie Powerhouse, Montreal, 1981, YYZ Gallery Toronto, 1982, Forum des Halles, Paris, 1985, Graves Art Gallery, Sheffield, U.K., 1985, San Diego Art Ctr., 1986, Hallwalls Gallery, Buffalo, 1986, La Galerie des Arts Lavalin, Montreal, 1988, Pro Mus. Contemporary Art, Finland, 1988, Kamloops Art Gallery, 1989, Koffler Gallery, Toronto, 1990, Art Gallery of Peterborough, Ont., 1992, Art Gallery of Hamilton, 1993, So. Alta. Art Gallery, Lethbridge, 1994; Art Gallery Hamilton, Gallerie Arts Tech., Montreal, Basel Art Fair, Switzerland, 1998-2005, Basel Art, Miami, 2002-05, Chgo. Art Fair, 1999, Nat. Gallery Can., Ottawa, 2000, Can. Mus. Contemporary Art, North York, Ont., 2000, Can. Mus. Contemporary Photography, Ottawa, 2000-01, Nat. Gallery Can., Ottawa, Art Gallery Hamilton, 2001, Kitchener-Waterloo Art Gallery, Ont., 2001, Art Basel, 2002-2005, Basel Art Fair, 2002-2005, Toronto Photgraphers Workshop, 2002, Confedn. Art Ctr. Art Gallery, Prince Edward Island, 2003, Art Gallery of Bishop's U., Que., 2003, McMichael Gallery, Kleinburg, Ont, 2004, Les Revenants Le Mois de la Photo Mai, Montreal Quebec, 2005, Art Gallery Peterborough, Ont., Can., 2006; public collections include Agnes Etherington Art Ctr., Kingston, Ont., Art Gallery Hamilton, Art Gallery Ont., Toronto, Bibliotheque Nationale, Paris, Gallery/Stratford, Nickle Arts Mus., Calgary, Alta., Robert McLaughlin Gallery, Oshawa, Winnipeg Art Gallery, Victoria and Albert Mus., London. Coord. Colour Xerox Artists' Program, Visual Arts Ont., Toronto, 1977-83; bd. dirs. Art Gallery at Harbourfront, Toronto, 1983-85; apptd. mem. City of Toronto Pub. Art Commn., 1986-89; mem. curatorial team WaterWorks Exhbn., Toronto, 1988; chmn. Toronto Arts Awards, Visual Arts Jury, 1988; bd. dirs. Arts Found. of Greater Toronto, 1989-92. Mem.: Royal Can. Acad. Arts. Office: 23 Alcina Ave Toronto ON Canada M6G 2E7 Address: Corkin/Shopland Gallery 55 Mill St Bldg 61 Toronto ON Canada M5A 3C4 E-mail: astmanba@aol.com.

ASTROTH, MARGO FOLTZ, mental health nurse, nurse psychotherapist; b. Washington, Feb. 17, 1945; d. Charles Tage Foltz and Margaret Edna Bell; m. Dennis J. Astroth, Sept. 16, 2000; m. W. David Wilson, June 24, 1967 (div. Sept. 9, 1987); children: Kimberly Margo Martin, Brett David Wilson, Colleen Jennifer Warthan. BSN, Wagner Coll., SI, NY, 1967; MS in Nursing, U. Calif., San Francisco, 1970. RN U. of State of N.Y. Edn. Dept., lic. clin. nurse specialist, adult psychiat. and mental health nursing, ANA, 1983, psychiat. mental health nurse, Calif. Bd. Mental Health Nursing, cert. clin. nurse specialist, Calif. Bd. Registered Nursing; group psychotherapist Nat. Registry Group Psychotherapists. Clin. nurse specialist inpatient mental health U.S. VA Hosp., Palo Alto, Calif., 1970—76; asst. prof. nursing baccalaureate program Point Loma Coll., San Diego, 1976—82; instr. nursing office of continuing edn. U. Calif. Sch. of Medicine, San Diego, 1976—78; clin. nurse specialist outpatient mental health U.S. VA Hosp., San Diego, 1983—84; pvt. practice nurse psychotherapist, cons. Garmisch-Partenkirchen, Bavaria, Germany, 1984—86; program dir. outpatient mental health svcs. Douglas Young Clinic, San Diego, 1986—89; instr. RN to BSN program U. Phoenix, San Diego, 1988—96; quality mgmt., program rev. and devel. San Diego County Mental Health Svcs., San Diego, 1989—95; pvt. practice nurse psychotherapist Encinitas, Calif., 1989—2005; psychosocial specialist emergency and ambulatory svcs. Sharp Grossmont Hosp., La Mesa, Calif., 1989—95; instr. RN to BSN/MSN/nurse practitioner program U. San Diego, 1994—2003; clinician psychiat. liaison team Scripps Health, Scripps Mercy Hosp., San Diego, 1996—2004, charge psychiat. liaison team, 2004—. Author: (book) Group Theory/Process for Nursing Practice, 1985, (vignettes) Touched by a Nurse; contbr. articles to profl. jours. Psychotherapist, critical incident stress debriefing Scripps Health, Response to Santana H.S. Shooting, Santee, Calif., 2001; bd. dirs. Western Inst. Found. for Mental Health, San Diego, 1989—90. Recipient Psychiat. Mental Health Nurse of the Yr., Advanced Practice/Expanded Role, Psychiat. Mental Health Clin. Nurse Specialists of San Diego, 2000. Mem.: Am. Psychiat. Nurses Assn., San Diego Group Psychotherapy Assn., Am. Group Psychotherapy Assn., Internat. Soc. of Psychiat. Mental Health Nurses, San Diego Soc. of Psychiat. Mental Health Nurses (chair 1996—97), Sigma Theta Tau (life). Lutheran. Avocations: travel, scrapbooking, hiking, jogging. Office: Scripps Health Scripps Mercy Hosp 4077 5th Ave San Diego CA 92103 Office Phone: 619-686-3763. E-mail: astroth.margo@scrippshealth.org.

ATAMIAN, SUSAN, nurse; b. Cambridge, Mass., Sept. 14, 1950; d. Raymond H. and Alice (Chakerian) A. BA, Simmons Coll., 1972, MS, 1995. RN, Mass.; cert. infection control. Staff nurse Mass. Gen. Hosp., Boston, 1972-74, pvt. duty nurse, 1975-76, staff nurse, 1976-77, Kimberly Nurses, Orange, Calif., 1982; rsch. study nurse Mass. Gen. Hosp., Boston, 1977-80, instr. nursing, 1982-84, sr. rsch. study nurse, 1984-87, dir. clin. rsch. nurse group, 1985-90, infection control nurse, 1988-90, infection control nurse clinician, 1990-92, coord., clin. rsch., vascular surg. div., 1992-99, individual assignments/spl. projects staff, 1999—2001, infection control practitioner, 2001—03, quality improvement nurse decision support unit, 2003—. Cons. nutrition and liver diseases, McGaw Labs., Santa Ana, Calif., 1980-81; chmn. faculty devel. libr. com. Shepard Gill Sch., Boston, 1983-84; mem. rsch. nurses forum, Mass. Gen. Hosp., 1992—. Class agt. 1972 Simmons Coll., 1972, 86-97, mem. com. alumnae fund, 1987-89, reunion com., 1990-2002, com. on classes, 1991-92, class of 1972 reunion fund chair, 1991-92, chmn. class of 1972 reunion fund 1996-97, v.p. Class of 1972, 1997—, mem. travel and edn. com., 2002—, nominating com., 2004—. Mem.: ANA, Coun. Armenian Am. Nurses (v.p. 2002—03, pres. 2003—), Assn. for Practitioners in Infection Control and Epidemiology, Rsch. Nurses Forum Mass. Gen. Hosp., Mass. Nurses Assn., Soc. for Vascular Nursing, Am. Nurses Found. Century Club, Simmons Coll. Alumnae Assn. (edn. and travel com. 2002—), Simmons Club Boston (bd. dirs. 1988—90, v.p. 1990—92, co-chmn. boutique 1992—94, mem. nominating com. 1994—95), Sigma Theta Tau, Simmons Coll. Nursing Honor Soc. Mem. Armenian Apostolic Ch. Avocations: travel, reading, knitting. Business E-Mail: satamian@partners.org.

ATCHLEY, NANCY FAYE, educator; d. Willie Maude Atchley. BS, Lee U., Cleve., TN, 1970; MEd, Mid. Tenn. State U., Murfreesboro, 1979. Tchr. Bradley County Bd. Ed., Cleve., Tenn., 1970—. Church Of God. Avocations: reading, motorcycling, travel. Office Phone: 423-476-0620. E-mail: bradleycountyschools.org.

ATCITTY, FANNIE L., elementary school educator, education educator; b. Shiprock, NM, Dec. 4, 1952; d. John and Betty Martin Lowe; m. Eugene Ronald Atcitty, Apr. 22, 1972 (dec. May 10, 2000); children: Antoinette, Ronald. BEd, Ea. N.Mex. U., 1978; M in Curriculum and Instrn., Doane Coll., 1997; M in Ednl. Leadership, Doane Coll., 2002. Elem. tchr. Central Consolidated Sch. Dist. 22, Shiprock, N.Mex., 1979—. Adj. instr. early childhood edn. program N.Mex. Highland U., Las Vegas, 1997—2002; adj. instr. edn. and tchr. prep. program Diné Coll., Shiprock, N.Mex., 1997—2002; profl. standards commn. mem. N.Mex. State Dept. Edn., Santa Fe, 2000—, tchr. assessment rev. panel, 1993—99, nat. coun. for accreditation of tchr. edn., 1997—. Contbr. poetry to lit. publs. Edn. chairperson Shiprock (N.Mex.) Cmty. Planning Commn., 1994—96; vice chair San Juan County Dem. Party, Farmington, 1998—2001; chairperson Cmty. Gov. Planning Bd., Shiprock, N.Mex., 1995—98; U.S Presdl. elector N.Mex., 1996. Recipient Golden Apple Found. award, Golden Apple Found. N.Mex., 2001. Mem.: Internat. Reading Assn., Am. Assn. Sch. Adminstrs., Las Amigas Women's Club. Democrat. Avocations: reading, walker, community events, gardening. Home: PO Box 3320 Shiprock NM 87420 Office: Mesa Elementary Sch PO Box 1803 Shiprock NM 87420

ATES, DELORIES, retired counseling administrator; 1 child, Mayla. BS, U. Cin., 1958, MEd, 1962. Home economics tchr. Cin. Bd. Edn., 1959—67, jr. high counselor, 1968—85, sr. high counselor, 1985—93, subs. tchr., 1993—. Mem.: Ohio Retired Tchrs. Assn., Cin. Fedn. Retired Tchrs., Greater Cin. Counselors Assn., Ohio Counselors Assn., Hamilton Co. Retired Tchrs. Assn., Alpha Kappa Alpha. Democrat. Protestant. Avocations: reading, cooking, gardening. Home: 718 Glensprings Dr Cincinnati OH 45246

ATHEY, SARAH ELIZABETH-MARKS, secondary school educator, social studies educator; b. Kalamazoo, Oct. 6, 1979; d. Brian Lyle and Kathleen Marie Marks; m. Nicholas Andrew Athey, July 31, 2004. BA in Edn., Mich. State U., East Lansing, 2003. Social studies tchr. South Lyon Cmty. Schs., Mich., 2004. Asst. varsity softball coach South Lyon H.S., 2004, sophomore class advisor, 2004. Mem.: Mich. Edn. Assn., Mich. Coun. for the Social Studies. Avocations: reading, ceramics, travel, athletics. Office: South Lyon High School 1000 N Lafayette South Lyon MI Personal E-mail: atheys@slcs.us.

ATKINS, CANDI, management consultant, small business owner; b. Chgo., Aug. 19, 1946; d. Norman R. and Catherine Kay (Coughlin) Wolfe; m. Peter J. Caswell, Jan. 29, 2005 (dec. June 9, 2006); children: James N., Amanda Kate. Assoc. in Edn., Thornton C.C., 1968. Chief exec. officer Candi Atkins & Assocs., Phoenix, 1992-95, Largo, Fla., 1995-97, Henderson, Nev., 1997—2004, San Francisco, 2004—, Eugene, Oreg., 2006—. Faculty Diablo Valley Community Coll., Pleasant Hill, Calif., 1982-85; nat. trainer HUD Occupancy Issues, 1984—. Author: Shopping for Big Wonderful Me, 1988, Management Forms for HUD Assisted Housing, 1991. Candi Atkins Day named in her honor Mayor of San Francisco, 1984; named to hon. Order Ky. Col. Mem. NAFE, Inst. Real Estate Mgmt. (exec. com. San Francisco chpt. 1980-84, instr. 1981-91, accredited resident mgr., cert. property mgr., Accredited Resident Mgmt. of Yr. 1980). Avocation: travel. Office Phone: 541-345-4010. Personal E-mail: caaconsulting@aol.com.

ATKINS, CINDY L., elementary school educator; d. Ronald C. and Pauline A. Smarch; m. Edward L. Atkins, May 18, 1985; children: Dominic S., Avery A. BA in Edn., U. Mich., Flint, 1990—92; MA in Art of Tchg., Marygrove Coll., Detroit, 1999—2000. Cert. Tchr. Mich. Dept. Edn. Tchr., grade 7 PHASD, Pt. Huron, Mich., 1998—. Office: Ft Gratiot Mid Sch 3985 Keewahdin Rd Fort Gratiot MI 48059 Office Phone: 810-984-6544.

ATKINS, EILEEN, actress; b. June 16, 1934; d. Arthur Thomas Atkins and Annie Ellen Elkins; m. Bill Shepherd. Student, Edmonton and Guildhall Sch. Appearances in plays, including Twelfth Night, Richard III, The Tempest, 1962, The Killing of Sister George, 1965 (Best Actress, Evening Std. Awards), The Cocktail Party, 1968, Vivat! Vivat Regina!, 1970 (Variety award), Suzanne Andler, As You Like It, 1973, St. Joan, 1977, Passion Play, 1981, Medea, 1986, The Winter's Tale, Cymbeline, 1988 (Olivier award), Mountain Language, 1988, A Room of One's Own, 1989, Exclusive, 1989, The Night of the Iguana, 1992, Vita and Virginia, 1993, Indiscretions, 1995 (Tony nom. best actress in a play, 1995), John Gabriel Borkman, 1996, The Retreat from Moscow, 2003-04 (Tony nom. best actress in a play, 2004), Doubt, 2006; films include Equus, 1974, The Dresser, 1984, Let Him Have It, 1990, Wolf, 1994; TV appearances include The Duchess of Malfi, Sons and Lovers, Smiley's People, Nelly's Version, The Burston Rebellion, Breaking Up, The Vision, In My Defence, 1990, A Room of One's Own, 1990, The Lost Language of Cranes, 1993, The Maitlands, 1993, Cold Comfort Farm, 1995; co-creator: Upstairs Downstairs, The House of Elliott. Recipient B.A.F.T.A. award, 1985. Address: care Jonathan Altaras Assoc 2 Goodwins Ct London WC2N 4LL England*

ATKINS, JANET NECETTE, science educator, department chairman; b. Greenville, Tex., Aug. 20, 1948; d. Bowman Guy and Jane Hurst Taylor; m. Jay Clark Atkins, Aug. 5, 1985; 1 child from previous marriage, Matthew H. Dellinger. BS in Edn., U. Miami, Coral Gables, Fla., 1971; MS in Sci., East Tex. State U., Commerce, Tex., 1984. Permit rehab. birds of prey Fish and Wildlife Svc. U.S. Dept. Interior, sci. permit rehab. birds of prey Tex. Dept. Parks and Wildlife. Tchr. sci. Bland Ind. Sch. Dist., Merit, Tex., 1982—83, Cmty. Ind. Sch. Dist., Nevada, Tex., 1983—85, Wylie Ind. Sch. Dist., 1985—89; tchr. and chair sci. dept. Royse City Ind. Sch. Dist., 1999—. Mem. Dist. Wide Ednl. Coun., Wylie, Tex., 1990—99; sec. Dist. Wide Ednl. Improvement Coun., 1995—99. Del. Rep. State Conv., San Antonio, 2004, Hunt County Rep. Conv., 2006; Sunday sch. tchr. Mem.: Tex. State Tchrs. Assn. (sec. 1996—99), Am. Fedn. Tchrs., Tex. Fedn. Tchrs., Nat. Sci. Tchrs. Assn. Republican. Baptist. Avocations: reading, interior decorating, travel, shopping. Home: 7568 FM 1565 Royse City TX 75189 Office Phone: 972-636-9991.

ATKINS, JOANNA PANG (JOANNA PANG), dancer, actress, choreographer, director; b. Berkeley, Calif., Feb. 09; d. Joseph H. Panganiban Sr. and Lynette Stevens DeFazio; m. Richard Atkins, 1982; 1 child, Davy Steven Atkins. Student, San Francisco State Coll., 1964-65. Child performer; dancer with ptnr. and brother Joey; with San Francisco Ballet and San Francisco Opera Co., 1952-63. Prin. dancer nat. and internat. tours Toy-Wing Oriental Dance Co., 1965—70; mem. faculty Ballet Arts, Oakland, 1963—64; instr., prin. performer Robicheau Ballet, Boston, 1969—72; cons., guest lectr., artist-in-residence N.J. State Coun. on Arts, 1994—2000; tchg. and performing artist Arts Coun. of the Morris Area, 1999—, Arts Horizons, 1999—; artist-in-residence for multi-cultural dance PS 152, Queens, NY, 1999—2000, PS 138, Bronx, NY, 1999—2002, Children's Cultural Art Ctr. at Montessori Children's House, Morristown, 2000—02; tchg. artist N.J. Wolf Trap program N.J. Performing Arts Ctr., 2001—; artist-in-residence PS63, N.Y.C., 2003, Wildwood Sch., Mt. Lakes, NJ, 2003, Glenwood Sch., Millburn, 2003—, Washington Sch., Summit, 2001—, Theodore Roosevelt Sch., Weehawken, 2002—05, Oak St. Sch., Basking Ridge, NJ, 2005—, Ctrl. Elem. Sch., East Hanover, NJ, 2006, Ctrl. Sch., Warren, NJ, 2006, Hillcrest Sch., Morristown, NJ, 2006. Appeared on The Ted Randall Dance Party, San Francisco, 1959-61, Dick Stewart Dance Party, San Francisco, 1961-62, Art Laboe Show, and Earl McDaniel Show, L.A., 1959, Lawrence Welk show, 1961, The Secrets of Isis, 1970; appeared with U.S. Govt. Mil. Shows, 1954-56, N.Y.C.

Ballet, 1955; appeared on stage in South Pacific, West Side Story, Music Man. Song of Norway, numerous others; appeared on TV shows Saturday Night Live, CBS Daytime 90, Edge of Night, The Doctors, All My Children; in films Voices, Once A Thief, Stardust Memories, others; appeared in TV commls.; dir., choreographer Getting to Know You, 1994, 97, In the Mirror, 1995, 98, Independence, 1996; dir., choreographer multicultural folk dance program St. Vincent Martyr Sch., Madison, N.J., 1995, Briarwood Sch., Florham Park, N.J., 1996—. Mem. SAG, AFTRA, Actors Equity Assn. Personal E-mail: PangAtkins@aol.com.

ATKINS, VERONICA, philanthropist; b. Russia; m. Robert C. Atkins (dec.). Profl. opera singer, 1963—76; mem. bd. dir. Atkins Nutrition, 2003, Robert Atkins Found., 1999—, chmn., 2005—. Co-author (with Robert Atkins): (cookbooks) Dr. Atkins' Quick and Easy New Cookbook, 1997. Named an 50 Most Generous Philanthropists, Fortune Mag., 2005. Office: Robert C Atkins Found 340 E 64th St New York NY 10021*

ATKINS, YVETTE, special education educator; d. Jacob Mintz and Frieda Levy; m. David Harris Atkins, Jan. 6, 1963; 1 child, Faith Lisa. BA summa cum laude with honors, Fairleigh Dickinson U., Teaneck/Hackensack, NJ, 1982; MA, Columbia U., NYC, 1985, MEd, 1987. Reading specialist State of NJ, 1983, special edn. tchr., 1983, sch. libr., 1988, media supr., 1990—. Advisor Virtual Classroom for Chronically Ill, Paramus, NJ, 2004—06, Buddy Club, Paramus, 1992—2006; learning therapist Westwood Learning Ctr., Ridgewood, NJ, 1988—2002. Developer: ednl. materials in field. Adviser, developer Cultural Connection youth exch., 1992—93; co-chmn. mid. sch. diversity Kean U., Union, NJ, 1994—; chmn. Blue Ribbon Sch. Walk program Am. Diabetes Assn., 2003—. Recipient Spl. Educator of Yr., Gov. of NJ, 1998, Tchr. of Yr. commendation, Bergen County, 1999, Best Practice award, NJ Intercultural Youth Exch., Citizenship award, Assn. Help Retarded Children, 1968. Mem.: Coun. Exceptional Children, Phi Omega Epsilon. Jewish. Avocations: gardening, music, boating, writing. Home: 253 Allen Rd Bayville NJ 08721 Office: Paramus Bd Edn West Brook Mid Sch 550 Roosevelt Blvd Paramus NJ 07652

ATKINSON, ALANNA BETH, music educator; b. Mobile, Ala., July 4, 1952; d. John Walter and Mildred Dalton Atkinson. BS in Music Edn., U. South Ala., 1974. Pvt. piano tchr., Mobile, 1973—; piano tchr. Indian Springs Elem. Sch., Mobile, 1975—2003, Morningside Elem. Sch., Mobile, 1987—2001, Kate Shepard Elem., 2003—, St. Mark Meth. Sch., 2003—. Organist Our Savior Luth., Mobile, 1973, Kingswood United Meth., Mobile, 1974—83, Forest Hill United Meth., Mobile, 1984—2002; vol. music leader Bible sch. Fulton Heights Meth., Mobile, 1998—; organist Westminster Presbyn., Mobile, 2002—; clarinetist Mobile Pops Band, 1995—; soprano Springhill Consort, 1992—97, Gloria Dei Chorale, 1999—2002; dulcimer player ch., cmty. and nursing home programs, Mobile, 1996—; tenor recorder West Minister Consort; mem. So. Ala. Presbyn. Cursillo, 2004, U. So. Ala. Guitar Ensemble, 2004. Recipient United Meth. Women Mission Pin, Kingswood Meth., 1983, Forest Hill Meth., 1985. Mem.: Mobile Music Tchrs. Assn. (2d v.p. 1978, 1982, treas. 1988—89, honors recital and social coms.), Am. Organist Guild (bd. dirs. 1984, 1990). Democrat. Presbyterian. Avocations: sewing, cats. Home: 1500 S Shan Dr Mobile AL 36693 Office Phone: 251-471-5451. E-mail: bethatkinson@mobis.com.

ATKINSON, BARBARA F., dean, medical educator, executive vice chancellor; b. Mpls., Oct. 19, 1942; MD, Jefferson Med. Coll., Thomas Jefferson Univ., 1974. Diplomate Am. Bd. Anatomic and Clin. Pathology, Am. Bd. Cytopathology. Intern Hosp. U. Pa., Phila., 1974—75, resident in pathology, 1975—78; mem. faculty U. Kans., Kansas City; dir. resident program U. Kans. Med. Ctr., Kansas City, exec. vice chancellor, dean Sch. Medicine. Assoc. scientist Wistar Inst. Anatomy and Biology, 1983—87; mem. staff dept. pathology Hosp. of U. Pa., 1978—87, dir. cytopathology, 1978—87, med. program dir. Sch. Cytotech., 1978—86; chmn. dept. pathology and lab. medicine Med. Coll. Pa., 1987—94; dir. Delaware Valley Regional Lab. Svcs., Med. Coll. Hosps. and St. Christopher's Hosp. for Children, 1991—96; chmn. dept. pathology and lab. medicine Med. Coll. Pa. and Hahnemann U., 1994—96; trustee Am. Bd. Pathology, 1992—95, pres., 1998—. Mem. editl. bd. Lab. Investigation, 1988—94, Modern Pathology, 1990—94, Human Pathology, 1992—94, manuscript reviewer Cancer, Diagnostic Cytopathology, Modern Pathology, 1988—94, abstract rev. bd. U.S. and Can. Acad. Pathology, 1989—92, rev. panel Am. Soc. Clin. Pathology Abstract, 1991—96; contbr. articles to profl. jours., chapters to books. Bd. dirs., treas. Laennec Soc. Phila., 1979—81; bd. dirs. Thyroid Soc. Phila., 1982—84; exec. com., bd. dirs. Med. Coll. Pa., 1994—96; bd. trustees Hahnemann U., 1994—96. Recipient Golden Apple Tchg. award for excellent sci. tchg., 1994; grantee, NIH, 1985—88, Takeda-Abbott R&D, 1989—94, NIA, 1991—94. Fellow: ASIM, Coll. Am. Pathologists; mem.: NAS (mem. Inst. Medicine), U.S. and Can. Acad. Pathology, Am. Soc. Clin. Pathology (Janet M. Glasgow Meml. scholarship 1974), Am. Soc. Cytopathology. Office: U Kans Med Ctr Mail Stop 2015 3901 Rainbow Blvd Kansas City KS 66160 Office Phone: 913-588-1440. Business E-Mail: batkinson@kumc.edu.

ATKINSON, BETH J., music educator; b. Detroit, Feb. 27, 1951; d. David Franklin and Winifred May Titmuss; m. Beth J. Titmuss, Aug. 9, 1975; children: Jamie Lynn Anderson, Scott Michael. MusB, U. Mich., Ann Arbor, 1974; MusB in Edn., U. Mich., Flint, 1989; MusM, Midwestern State U., Wichita Falls, Tex., 1977. Cert. tchr. Mich., 1989. Pvt. voice and piano tchr., Durand, Mich., 1974—91; dir. of youth and adult choirs United Meth. Ch., Durand, 1985—88; elem. music tchr. Howell Pub. Schs., Mich., 1991—. Singer: (perform full concert season annually) Carolyn Mawby Chorale. Mem.: NEA, Mich. Edn. Assn. Office Phone: 517-548-6283.

ATKINSON, HOLLY GAIL, physician, journalist, educator, human rights activist, writer; b. Detroit, Oct. 20, 1952; d. John S. and Patricia Atkinson; m. Galen Jay Guengerich, Nov. 18, 2000. BA in Biology magna cum laude, Colgate U., 1974; MD, U. Rochester, N.Y., 1978; MS in Journalism, Columbia U., N.Y.C., 1981. Diplomate Nat. Med. Bds. Intern in internal medicine Strong Meml. Hosp., Rochester, NY, 1978-79; rschr. Walter Cronkite's Universe show CBS News, N.Y.C., 1981-82; med. reporter CBS Morning News, N.Y.C., 1982-83; on-air co-host Bodywatch health show PBS, 1983-88; contbg. editor and health columnist New Woman mag., 1983-88; on-air corr., med. editor, sr. v.p. programming/med. affairs Lifetime Med. TV, 1985-93; assoc. editor Journal Watch, 1986-90; med. corr. Today Show NBC News, N.Y.C., 1991-94; editor HealthNews, 1994—2006; exec. v.p. Reuters Health, N.Y.C., 1994-98, pres., CEO, 1998-2000; CEO New Media Health Answers Inc., 2000; pres. allHealth.com (iVillage health), 2000—01; med. editor-in-chief Everydayhealth.com, 2006—. Lectr. dept. pub. health Cornell U. Med. Coll., 1997-2003, asst. prof., 2003—. Author: Women and Fatigue, 1986. Vol. nat. and local level Am. Heart Assn., 1984-91, bd. dirs., chmn. nat. comms. com. Am. Heart Assn., 1987-91; bd. dirs. Phys. Human Rights, 1994—, pres. 2002—, NOW Legal Def. and Edn. Fund, 1996-2006, Soc. Advancement Women's Health Rsch., 1997-99, Am. Lyme Disease Found, 1997-98. Recipient Young Achievers award Nat. Coun. Women, 1986, Achievement award Soc. Advancement Women's Health Rsch., 1995. Mem. Phi Beta Kappa.

ATKINSON, PAULA MARI, music educator; b. Flora, Ill., Apr. 17, 1951; d. Victor Paul and Marilyn Pauline Bonucchi; children: Katie Sue, Kristine Lynn. B of Music Edn., Ill. State U., Normal, 1973. Cert. elem., secondary tchr. Ill., 2006. Tchr. Oglesby Pub. Schs., Ill., 1973—. Clinician for Turn About Songs Maud Powell Festival, LaSalle, Ill., 2003—; elem. music festival accompanist Dist. 2 Ill. Music Educators Assn., Ill., 2004—; ch. organist St. Mary's Ch., Peru, Ill., St. Patrick's Ch., LaSalle. V.p. LaSalle Peru Twp. Band Parent Assn., Ill., 2003—05. Recipient Educators award, LaSalle County Regional Office of Edn., 1997, Band Booster award, Nat. Bands Assn., 2002-2006. Mem.: Nat. Assn. for Music Educators. Office Phone: 815-883-8932.

ATKINSON, SUSAN D., producing artistic director, theatrical consultant; b. Phila., May 23, 1944; d. Joseph A. and Josephine (Mierley) Davis; m. Robert Atkinson, 1971 (div. 1986). BA, Juniata Coll., 1966; postgrad., San Francisco State Coll., 1968-69, U. Calif., Berkeley, 1968-69. Dir. Am. Conservatory Theatre, San Francisco, 1967-72; guest dir. Berkeley Repertory Theatre Co., 1968-69; dir. Marin Shakespeare Festival, Marin County, Calif., 1968-69; producing artistic dir. Repertory Theatre Co. Bucks County, Doylestown, Pa., 1980-86, Bristol (Pa.) Riverside Theatre, 1986—; guest dir. Grove Shakespeare Festival, 1992. Bd. dirs. Pa. Coun. on the Arts, Harrisburg, Pa., 1989—. Mem. Soc. Stage Dirs. and Choreographers (cert.). Office: Bristol Riverside Theatre PO Box 1250 Bristol PA 19007-1250

ATKINSON, TRACEY BLAKE, artist, educator; b. Raleigh, NC, Jan. 16, 1976; d. Robert Claytor and Jane Barry Bishop Atkinson. MA in Art Edn., Teachers Coll., Columbia U., 2002—04; BFA in Illustration, Pratt Inst., 1995—99. Cert. tchr.in visual arts NY State, 2004. Catalogue prodn. artist Christie's, N.Y.C., 1999—2001; visual arts tchr. N.Y.C. Pub. Schools, Bklyn., 2004—. Freelance illustrator, Bklyn., 1999—. Illustration, Body Of Illustration Work (Cert. of Excellence award for Outstanding Merit in Illustration, 1999). Mem. LWV, Washington, 2003—05. Presdl. grant, Pratt Inst., 1997. Mem.: Nat. Art Edn. Assn., United Fedn. Tchrs. Avocations: painting, travel, reading.

ATLAS, LIANE WIENER, writer; b. N.Y.C. d. Louis and Frances (Ferne) Wiener; m. Martin Atlas, Mar. 5, 1944 (dec. Mar. 1997); children: Stephen Terry, Jeffrey L. AB, Vassar Coll., 1943; postgrad., Johns Hopkins U., 1953-55. Cert. fin. planner. Fgn. affairs officer Dept. State, Washington, 1962-68; sr. economist U.S. Commerce Dept., Washington, 1968-75, U.S. Treasury Dept., Washington, 1975-79, Riggs Nat. Bank, Washington, 1980-82; v.p. Fintapes Inc., Washington, 1984-87, pres., 1987-95; freelance writer Washington, 1995—. Mem. U.S. delegation UN Econ. Orgns., N.Y.C., Geneva, 1963, 64, 68, 79. Author: Middle East Financial Institutions, 1977, (audio cassettes) What Every Wife Should Know, 1986, rev., 1992, Financial Planning for Divorce, rev. edit. 1992; freelance writer Changing Times and other mags., 1982-87. Treas. Entertaining People/Washington Home, 1986—90, Smithsonian Craft Show, 1993—95, Smithsonian Women's Com., 1996—97; mem. Kennedy Ctr. Cirs. Bd., 1999—; info. specialist Nat. Gallery Art, 2004—; treas. NCC-OWL, 2005—06. Fellow in econs. Johns Hopkins U., Balt., 1954-55; recipient Cert. of Appreciation U.S. Treasury Dept., Washington, 1977. Mem.: OWL (treas. Nat. Capitol chpt. 2005—06), Washington Ind. Writers, Inst. CFPs, Smithsonian Women's Com., Washington Print Club, Vassar Club of Washington. Avocations: print collecting, travel. Home: 2254 48th St NW Washington DC 20007-1035

ATLAS, NANCY FRIEDMAN, judge; b. N.Y.C., May 20, 1949; BS, Tufts U., 1971; JD, NYU, 1974. Bar: N.Y. 1975, U.S. Dist. Ct. (so. and ea. dists.) N.Y. 1975, U.S. Ct. Appeals (2nd cir.) 1975, U.S. Dist. Ct. (so. dist.) Tex. 1982, U.S. Ct. Appeals (5th cir.) 1982, U.S. Dist. Ct. (no. dist.) Tex. 1989. Law clk. to Hon. Dudley B. Bonsal U.S. Dist Ct. (so. dist.) N.Y., 1974-76; assoc. Webster & Sheffield, 1977-78; asst. U.S. atty. So. Dist. N.Y., 1979-82; shareholder Sheinfeld, Maley & Kay, P.C., Houston, 1982-95, also bd. dirs.; judge U.S. Dist. Ct. Tex., Houston, 1995—. Lectr. numerous programs CLE. Mng. editor NYU Ann. Survey Am. Law, 1973-74; contbr. numerous articles to profl. jours. Chair Tex. Higher Edn. coord. Bd., 1992-95; mem. Tex. Coun. Workforce and Econ. Competitiveness, 1993-95. Fellow: ABA Found., Houston Bar Assn., State Bar Tex.; mem.: FBA, ABA (co-divsn. dir. litigation sect. 1996—98, co-chair ADR com. 1994—95, mem. coun. 1998—2001, bus. and litigation joint task force on bankruptcy practice 1994—98), Am. Law Inst., Houston Bar Found. (trustee), Phi Beta Kappa. Office: US Courthouse 515 Rusk St Ste 9015 Houston TX 77002-2605

ATLEE, DEBBIE GAYLE, sales consultant, medical educator; b. Oklahoma City, Jan. 8, 1955; d. Harold Phillip and Ella Ruth (Birks) A. BS in Nursing, U. Okla., 1977. RN, Okla.; cert. diabetes educator. Team leader ob-gyn Bapt. Med. Ctr. of Okla., Oklahoma City, 1977-80, asst. clin. supr. urology, 1980-81, nursing educator, diabetes educator, 1981-84; sales specialist Boehringer Mannheim Diagnostics, Inc., Indpls., 1984-99; diabetes educator Dept. Endocrinology U. Okla. Coll. Medicine, 1999-2000; bus. sales mgr. NovoNordisk Pharms., Inc., Princeton, NJ, 2000—02; diabetes case mgr. Ediba Diabetes Ctr. Excellence Integris Bapt. Med. Ctr., Okla. City, 2002—05; pres., CEO Debra Atlee Properties, 2005—. Mem. regional piloting adv. group Nat. Diabetes Adv. Bd., Oklahoma City, 1984-85. Named Outstanding Bus. Woman, Bus. and Profl. Women, Capitol Hill chpt., 1981, Salesperson of Yr. 1987; recipient Outstanding Sales Achievement award, 1985, 87, 90, 91. Mem. Am. Diabetes Assn. (exec. bd. Met. chpt. 1985—, pres. 1987), Am. Assn. Diabetes Educators, Western Okla. Diabetes Educators (pres. 1984, 2005, Outstanding Svc. and Dedication award 1984, chpt. svc. award 1985, chpt. edn. award 1984), Nat. Bd. Cert. Diabetes Educator, U.S. Power Squadron (bd. dirs. Oklahoma City 1984, 87), U. Okla. Alumni Assn. (life). Republican. Roman Catholic. Avocations: sailing, photography, gardening, music. Office Phone: 405-843-7417. E-mail: debbie.atlee@hotmail.com.

ATLER, VANESSA, gymnast; b. Valencia, Calif., Feb. 17, 1982; Mem. Sr. Pacific Alliance Team, 2000, U.S. Gymnastic Team. Recipient 5th pl. all around, 2d pl. vault, 4th pl. balance beam, 3d pl. floor exercise Catania Cup, 1995, 2d pl. uneven bars City of Pope Competition, 1996, 2d pl. all around, 2d pl. vault, 1st pl. uneven bars, 4th pl. balance beam, 3d pl. floor exercise Foxsport Challenge, 1997, 1st pl. all around, 2d pl. vault, 3d pl. uneven bars, 2d pl. balance beam, 1st pl. floor exercise Canberra Cup, 1997, 4th pl. all around, 1st pl. vault, 3d pl. uneven bars, 2d pl. balance beam, 1st pl. floor exercise Visa Am. Cup, 1998, 4th pl. vault, 2d pl. balance beam, 4th pl. floor exercise Internat. Team Championships, 1998, 1st team, 1st pl. vault, 1st pl. floor exercise Pacific Alliance Championships, 1998, 1st pl. vault, 1st pl. floor exercise Goodwill Games, 1998. Mem. Charter Oak Gliders. Avocations: reading, swimming, shopping.

ATNIP, LINDA, writer; b. Sewanee, Tenn., Feb. 9, 1949; d. Herman Louis and Frances Louise A. BS, Fla. State U., 1971. Actress Am. Internat. Pictures, Beverly Hills, Calif., 1973; mktg. svcs. mgr. Leisure Village, Camarillo, Calif., 1976-77; sales promotion mgr. Brentwood Pub., L.A., 1977-79; account exec. Performing Arts mag., Beverly Hills, 1979-80; coord. advt. and promotion NBC4-TV, Burbank, Calif., 1980-82; unit publicist Columbia Pictures TV, Burbank, 1982-85; publicist RAP Comms., L.A., 1985-88; entertainment editor New Orleans Mag., 1988-90; pub. Words of Light Prodns., L.A., 1990—. News reporter WPTV, Palm Beach, Fla., 1971-73. Author/performer: (poetry album) When the Heart Sings, 1990; author: (children's book) Miranda's Magic Garden, 1992; Conversations with Mr. Kiki, 2006; columnist (music review) Alternatives, New Orleans, 1989-2006; prodr./host: (TV show) When the Heart Sings, 1992-94. Performance grantee for one-woman show "The Dream Voyage," City of L.A. Cultural Affairs Dept., Barnsdall Art Park, Hollywood, Calif., 1992. Mem. Publicists Guild of Am., Screen Actors Guild, Fla. State U. Alumni Assn Avocations: painting, tai chi, jewelry designing. Office: Words of Light Prodns PO Box 39597 Los Angeles CA 90039-0597 Personal E-mail: lotara7@yahoo.com.

ATTAWAY, AMIE ELIZABETH, secondary school educator; b. Demopolis, Ala., Sept. 28, 1977; d. Huel Dale Attaway, Jr. EdB in Secondary Social Sci., Auburn U., Ala., 1999. Tchr. Demopolis H.S., 2000—. Cheerleader coach Demopolis H.S., 2004—. Mem.: Internat. Pilot Club (pres.-elect 2005—06). Republican. Episcopalian. Office: Demopolis High School 701 Hwy 80 West Demopolis AL 36732 Office Phone: 334-289-0294. Office Fax: 334-289-8777. Personal E-mail: amieattaway@yahoo.com.

ATTEE, JOYCE VALERIE JUNGCLAS, artist; b. Cin., Apr. 4, 1926; d. LeRoy Francis and Clara Marie (Becker) Jungclas; m. William Robert Attee III, Oct. 25, 1952; children: Robin Wilson, Wendy Ann. BA, Rollins Coll., Winter Park, Fla., 1948; postgrad., U. Cin., 1952, 54, Art Acad. Cin., 1962-64, Edgecliff Coll., Cin., 1967. One-man shows include Loring Andrews Rattermann Gallery, 1964, Town Club, 1966, 69, 72, 75, 78, 81-84, 90, 98, Jr. League Office, 1975, Court Gallery, 1969, Bissingers', 1970, 76, Cin. Nature Ctr., 1974, 78, Cin. Country Day Sch., 1974; group shows include Town Club Cin., 1984, Bissinger's, 1984, Cin. Art Mus., 1962, Zoo Arts Festival, 1961-62, 66, Town Club Cin., 1973-75, 77-85, Palm Beach (Fla.) Galleries, 1974, Showcase of Arts, 1976, Ursuline Ctr., 1976, Court Galleries, 1977, Indian Hill Artists, 1957-76, 82-83, 2002-03, Indian Hill, 2004, 05, 06, Kent Gallery, Galina, Md., 2006; regional and local shows Nat. League Am. Pen Women, 1977, 78, Nat. Bicentennial Show, Washington, 1976, James H. Barker Gallery, Palm Beach, Fla., 1979-82, Nantucket, 1982, Cin. Women's Club Show, 1979, Cin. Nature Ctr., 1983, Kimberton (Pa.) Gallery, 1988-89, Town Club, 1995, Indian Hill, 1996; author: Elbey Jay, 1964. Recipient 1st prize in still life or flowers Cin. Womans Art Club, 1965, 69; Marjorie Ewell Meml. award, 1975. Mem. Women's Art Club Cin. (past. v.p.), Jr. League Cin., Jr. League Garden Circle (pres. 1974-75, spkr. on flower paintings 1990), Univ. Club, Indian Hill Club, Cin. Woman's Club Episcopalian. Home: 8050 Indian Hill Rd Cincinnati OH 45243-3908

ATWATER, CYNTHIA D., English educator, secondary school educator; b. Weymouth, Mass. m. John Atwater, May 1985. MEd, Ea. Nazerene Coll., Quincy, Mass., 1989. HS English tchr. South Shore Christian Acad., Weymouth, 1994—. Sunday sch. tchr. Cmty. Bapt. Ch., Weymouth, 2002—06. Office: South Shore Christian Acad 45 Broad St Weymouth MA 02188

ATWATER, PHYLLIS Y., municipal official; b. Memphis, Nov. 4, 1947; d. Jeff D. and Thelda E. A.; m. John R. Ernst, Dec. 28, 1972. BA, Vassar Coll., 1968; MA, Boston U., 1970; postgrad., New Sch. Soc. Rsch., N.Y.C., 1974-82. Lectr. math. Tufts U., Medford, Mass., 1970-72; instr. math. higher edn. program Boston Model Cities Adminstrn., 1970-74, coord. program, 1971; instr. econs. SUNY, Old Westbury, 1977-82; dep. dir. adminstrn. and fin. Divsn. Solid Waste Mgmt., Commonwealth of Mass., 1984-88; pres. and chief operating officer Recoverable Resources/R2B2, Inc., Bronx, NY, 1989-91; dir. divsn. solid waste N.Y. State Dept. Environ. Conservation, 1992-93, regional dir. N.Y.C., 1993-95; pvt. practice computer svcs. cons., 1995-99; computer specialist N.Y.C. Dept. Employment, 1999—2002, assoc. commr. for info. tech. and adminstrn., 2002—03; admin. staff analyst N.Y.C. Dept. Small Bus. Svcs., 2003—. Assoc. Recycling Adv. Coun., EPA, Washington, 1990-93; vice chair Manhattan Solid Waste Adv. Bd., N.Y.C., 1991-92. Mem. founding bd. advisors N.Y. Feminist Art Inst., N.Y.C., 1979—81; bd. advisors The Labor Inst., N.Y.C., 1985—97, West Harlem Environ. Action Inc., N.Y.C., 1996—99; founder, pres., bd. dirs. Inst. for Labor and the Cmty., N.Y.C., 1997—; sec. bd. dirs. O.R.E., Inc., N.Y.C., 1998—; bd. dirs. Scenic Hudson, Inc., Poughkeepsie, NY, 2001—. Ford Found. fellow Nat. Fellowship Fund, 1975-78, Danforth Found., 1980-82.

ATWOOD, COLLEEN, costume designer; b. Ellensburg, Wash. Degree, Cornish Sch. Fine Arts, Seattle. Films include: Firstborn, 1984, (TV movie) Out of the Darkness, 1985, Bring on the Night, 1985, Manhunter, 1986, Critical Condition, 1987, Someone to Watch Over Me, 1987, The Pick-Up Artist, 1987, Torch Song Trilogy, 1988, Married to the Mob, 1988, Fresh Horses, 1988, For Keeps, 1988, Hider in the House, 1989, The Handmaid's Tale, 1989, Joe Versus the Volcano, 1990, Edward Scissorhands, 1990, Silence of the Lambs, 1991, Rush, 1991, Lorenzo's Oil, 1992, Love Field, 1992, Philadelphia, 1993, Born Yesterday, 1993, Cabin Boy, 1994, Wyatt Earp, 1994, Ed Wood, 1994, Little Women, 1994 (Acad. award nominee, best costume design 1994), Mars Attacks!, 1996, That Thing You Do, 1996, Beloved, 1998, Mumford, 1998, Sleepy Hollow, 1999, Golden Dreams, 2001, The Mexican, 2001, Planet of the Apes, 2001, The Tick, 2001, CinéMagique, 2002, Chicago, 2002 (Academy award, best costume design, 2003), Big Fish, 2003, Lemony Snicket's A Series of Unfortunate Events, 2004, Memoirs of a Geisha, 2005 (Costume Designer, British Acad. of Film and TV Arts, 2006, Achievement in Costume Design, Acad. Motion Picture Arts & Sciences, 2006)

ATWOOD, DEBRA SMITH, elementary school educator; b. Norfolk, Va., Jan. 14, 1965; d. Franklin Delenora and Dorothy Bateman Smith; m. Larry Archbell Atwood, Feb. 19, 1964; children: Olivia Michelle, Hayley Nichole, Elizabeth Ashley. B, Old Dominion U., Norfolk, Va., 1968. Tchr. Virginia Beach Pub. Sch. Sys., Va., 1987—. Dir. children's ministry Pky. Temple, Chesapeake, Va., 1999—2004. Recipient Tchr. Yr., Va. Beach Pub. Sch. Sys., 1993, 2006, Disting. Educator, 1989, 1992, 2005; grantee, Futures Founds., 2006. Mem.: NCTM.

ATWOOD, DONNA ELAINE, retired financial manager; b. Sewickley, Pa., Apr. 17, 1933; d. Donovan E. and Hazel Marie (Rush) Oelschlager; m. G. Richard Atwood, Oct. 22, 1955; children: Stephen Parker Atwood, Elaine Alden Atwood Henderson. BS in Commerce and Fin., Grove City Coll., 1955. Acctg. clk. 1st Nat. Bank, Coraopolis, Pa., 1949; asst. libr. Coraopolis Pub. Libr., 1949—51; acctg. asst. Aluminum Co. of Am., Pitts., 1951—55; sec. to dean Grad. Sch. Indsl. Adminstrn. Carnegie Mellon U., Pitts., 1955—56; fin. sec., acct. Third Presbyn. Ch., Pitts., 1956—65; fin. mgr., acct. Dominican Sisters of the Sick Poor, Ossining, NY, 1972—92; ret. Mother advisor Internat. Order Rainbow for Girls N.Y., 1980—83, state chmn., 1986—, mem. state adv. bd., 1987—, sec., 1997—, gen. chmn. Grand Assembly, 1987—94; pubs. chmn. Ossining Woman's Club, 1965—69, pres., 1969—71, house mgr., 1971—72; yearbook chmn. AAUW, Chappaqua, NY, 1964; treas. trustees Pleasantville United Meth. Ch., 1980—83, pastor parish rels. com., 1989—91, sec. United Meth. Women, 1993—96, auditor, 1988—2003, choir, 1980—2003. Mem.: PEO (guard 2006), DAR (chpt. libr. 1957, state page 1957—68), Women Descs. of Ancient and Honorable Arty. Co., Huguenot Soc., Daus. Am. Colonists (state page 1957—76, chpt. sec. 1961—64, nat. page 1968—79, state chmn. Golden Acorns and Pages 1970—73, nat. chmn. Golden Acorns and Pages 1973—79, state rec. sec. 1976—79, state chmn. pages 2000—03, state marshal 2003—06, state chair 2006—), Colonial Dames XVII Century, St. Officer's Club (pres. 2006—), Order Ea. Star (past matron 1962—63, grand Esther 1991, past matron 1996, chmn. com. 1997—2003, trustee 1997—2004). Personal E-mail: gratwood@aol.com.

ATWOOD, HOLLYE STOLZ, lawyer; b. St. Louis, Dec. 25, 1945; d. Robert George and Elise (Sauselle) Stolz; m. Frederick Howard Atwood III, Aug. 12, 1978 (div.); children: Katherine Stolz, Jonathan Robert. BA, Washington U., St. Louis, 1968; JD, Washington U., 1973. Bar: Mo. 1973. Jr. ptnr. Bryan Cave, St. Louis, 1973-82, ptnr., 1983—2001, mem. exec. com., 1995-2000, of counsel, 2002—. Bd. dirs. St. Louis coun. Girl Scouts U.S., 1976-86; trustee John Burroughs Sch., St. Louis, 1983-86. Mem. ABA, Met. St. Louis Bar Assn., Washington U. Law Sch. Alumni Assn. (pres. 1983-84), Noonday (St. Louis) (bd. govs. 1983-86). Office: Bryan Cave One Metropolitan Sq 211 N Broadway Saint Louis MO 63102-2733 E-mail: hsatwood@bryancave.com.

ATWOOD, MARGARET ELEANOR, writer; b. Ottawa, Ont., Can., Nov. 18, 1939; d. Carl Edmund and Margaret Dorothy (Killam) A. BA, U. Toronto, 1961; AM, Radcliffe Coll., 1962; postgrad., Harvard U., 1962-63, 65-67; LittD (hon.), Trent U., 1973, Concordia U., 1980, Smith Coll., Northampton, Mass., 1982, U. Toronto, 1983, U. Waterloo, 1985, U. Guelph, 1985, Mt. Holyoke Coll., 1985, Victoria Coll., 1987, Univ. de Montréal, 1991, McMaster U., 1996; LLD (hon.), Queen's U., 1974. Lectr. in English U. B.C., 1964-65, Sir George Williams U., 1967-68, U. Alta., 1969-70; asst. prof. English York U., Toronto, 1971-72; writer-in-residence U. Toronto, 1972-73, U. Ala., Tuscaloosa, 1985. Berg Chair NYU, 1986; writer-in-residence Macquarie U., Australia, 1987, Trinity U., San Antonio, 1989. Author: (poetry) Double Persephone, 1961, The Circle Game, 1967, The Animals in That Country, 1968, The Journals of Susanna Moodie, 1970, Procedures for Underground, 1970, Power Politics, 1973, Poems for Voices, 1970, You Are Happy, 1975, Selected Poems, 1976 (Am. edit. 1978), Selected Poems, 1966-84, 1990, Margaret Atwood Poems, 1965-75, 1991, Two-Headed Poems, 1978, True Stories, 1981, Interlunar, 1984, Selected Poems II: Poems Selected and New, 1976-1986, 1986, Morning in the Burned House, 1995; (novels) The Edible Woman, 1969 (Am. edit. 1970), Surfacing, 1972, (Am. edit. 1973), Lady Oracle, 1976, Life Before Man, 1979, Bodily Harm, 1981,

The Handmaid's Tale, 1985, Cat's Eye, 1988 (City Toronto Book award 1989, Coles Book of the Yr. 1989, Can. Booksellers Assn. Author of the Yr., 1989, Book of the Yr. award Found. for Advancement of Can. Letters, Periodical Marketers Can., 1989, Torgi Talking Book award 1989), The Robber Bride, 1993 (award for Fiction Can. Authors Assn., 1993, Trillium award for Excellence in Ont. Writing 1993, Regional Commonwealth Lit. award), Alias Grace, 1996 (Giller Prize 1996, Medal of Honor for Literature, Nat. Arts Club 1997), The Blind Assassin, 2000 (The Booker Prize 2000, nominee for Internat. IMPAC Dublin Literary award, Dashiell Hammett Prize, Internat. Assn. of Crime Writers, 2001), Oryx and Crake, 2003 (Booker prize shortlist, 2003), The Tent, 2006; (short stories) Dancing Girls, 1977, Bluebeard's Egg, 1983, Murder in the Dark, 1983, Wilderness Tips, 1991 (Trillium award 1992, Book of the Yr. award Periodical Marketers of Can., 1992), Good Bones, 1992; (juvenile) Up in the Tree, 1978, Anna'a Pet, 1980, For the Birds, 1990, Princess Prunella & the Purple Peanut, 1995; (non-fiction) Survival: A Thematic Guide to Canadian Literature, 1972, Second Words: Selected Critical Prose, 1982, Strange Things: The Malevolent North in Canadian Literature, 1995, Negotiating with the Dead, 2002, Writing With Intent: Essays, Reviews, Personal Prose: 1983-2005, 2005; Curious Pursuits, 2005. Recipient E.J. Pratt medal, 1961, Pres.'s medal U. Western Ont., 1965, YWCA Women of Distinction award, Gov. Gen.'s award, 1966, 1st pl. Centennial Commn. Poetry Competition, 1967, Union Poetry prize Chicago, 1969, Bess Hoskins prize of Poetry Chicago, 1974, City of Toronto Book award, 1977, Can. Booksellers Assn. award, 1977, award for short fiction Periodical Distbr. Can., 1977, St. Lawrence award for Fiction, 1978, Radcliffe Grad. medal, 1980, Molson award, 1981, Internat. Writer's prize Welsh Arts Council, 1982, Book of Yr. award Periodical Distbrs. of Can. and Found. for Advancement Can. Letters, 1983, Los Angeles Times Fiction award, 1986, Gov. Gen.'s Lit. award, 1986, Ida Nudel Humanitarian award, 1986, Toronto Arts award, 1986, Arthur C. Clarke award for Best Sci. Fiction, 1987, shortlisted for Ritz Hemingway prize, Paris, 1987, Commonwealth Lit. Prize regional award, 1987, 94, Silver medal for Best Article of Yr. Council for Advancement and Support of Edn., 1987, Nat. Mag. award 1st prize, 1988, Sunday Times award for literary excellence, YWCA Women of Distinction award 1988, Centennial medal Harvard U., 1990, John Hughes prize Welsh Devel. Bd., 1992, Commemorative medal 125th Anniversary of Can. Confedn., 1992, Trillium award for excellence in Ont. writing, 1995; Guggenheim fellow, 1981; decorated companion Order of Can., 1981, Order of Ont., 1990; named Woman of Yr. Ms. Mag., 1986, Humanist of Yr., 1987, Chevalier de l'Ordre des Arts et des Lettres, 1994. Fellow Royal Soc. of Can., Am. Acad. Arts and Scis. (fgn. hon. lit. mem. 1988). Achievements include invention of a remote-controlled pen, LongPen, that allows writers to sign books for fans from thousands of miles away. Office: c/o Carrol & Graf Avalon Publishing NY Divsn 245 W 17th St New York NY 10011-5300*

ATWOOD, MARY SANFORD, writer; b. Mt. Pleasant, Mich., Jan. 27, 1935; d. Burton Jay and Lillian Belle (Sampson) Sanford; m. John C. Atwood III, Mar. 23, 1957. Author: A Taste of India, 1969. Mem. San Francisco/North Peninsula Opera Action, Suicide Prevention and Crisis Ctr., DeYoung Art Mus., Internat. Hospitality Ctr., Peninsula Symphony. Mem.: AAUW, St. Francis Yacht Club. Republican. Office: 40 Knightwood Ln Hillsborough CA 94010-6132 Office Phone: 650-343-6524. E-mail: alasam40@mindspring.com.

ATWOOD, SONYA ELIZABETH, music educator; b. Mobile, Al., May 31, 1976; d. Benny Michael and Linda Simpson Atwood; 1 child, Hunter Wyatt Parker. AS, Faulkner State C.C., 1998; BS in Music Edn., U. Mobile, 2002. Cert. K-12 music educator Ala. Band dir. Wright Preparatory Sch., Mobile, 2002—05, Satsuma HS. Mem.: Ala. Bandmasters Assn., Music Educators Nat. Conf., Kappa Delta Pi. Avocations: piano, flute, martial arts.

AUBERGER, MARCIA A., lawyer; b. Rochester, NY, Nov. 8, 1963; BA, SUNY, Buffalo, 1985; JD, South Tex. Coll. of Law, 1989. Bar: Tex. 1989, DC 1998. Ptnr. Trademark Venable LLP, Washington, DC. Lectr. in field. Contbr. articles top profl. jours. Mem.: ABA (mem. Intellectual Property Sect.), Intellectual Property Owners Assn. (mem. US Trademark Law Com.), Women's Bar Assn. of DC, DC Bar (mem. Intellectual Property Sect.), Assn. for Protection of Intellectual Property, Am. Intellectual Property Law Assn., Internat. Trademark Assn., State Bar Tex. Office: Venable LLP 575 7th St NW Washington DC 20004 Office Phone: 202-344-4969. Office Fax: 202-344-8300. E-mail: maauberger@venable.com.

AUBIN, BARBARA JEAN, artist; b. Chgo., Jan. 12, 1928; d. Philip Theodore and Dorothy May (Chapman) A. BA, Carleton Coll., 1949; B Art Edn., Sch. Art Inst. Chgo., 1954, M Art Edn., 1955. Lectr. Centre D'Art & Haitian Am. Inst., Port-Au-Prince, Haiti, 1958-60; asst. prof. Sch. Art Inst. Chgo., 1960-67, Loyola U., 1968-71; lectr. Calumet Coll., Hammond, Ind., 1971-75; prof. art Chgo. State U., 1971-91; ret., 1991. Vis. prof., artist Wayne State U., Detroit, Mich., 1965; vis. artist St. Louis CC, Forest Park, Mo., 1980, 81, U. Wis., Green Bay, 1981; co-curator Art for the Next Millennium Kimo Theatre Gallery, Albuquerque, 1997; spkr. and exhibiting artist, Womens's Caucus For Art Regional Conf./Exhbn., 1999. One-woman shows include Countryside Arts Ctr., Arlington Heights, Ill., 1954, 87, Avant Arts Gallery, Chgo., 1954, Riccardo's Restaurant and Gallery, Chgo., 1956, Evanston Twp. HS, Ill., 1958, Centre d'Art, Port-au-Prince, Haiti, 1960, Chgo. Pub. Libr., 1960, Chgo. Acad. Fine Arts, 1965, Oxbow Summer Sch. Fine Arts, 1965, Lewis Towers Gallery, Loyola U., Chgo., 1970, Chgo. State U., 1971, 74, 85, North River Cmty. Gallery, Northeastern Ill. U., Chgo., 1974, Ill. Arts Coun., Chgo., Crossroads-Jr. Mus., Art Inst. Chgo., 1976, Fairweather Hardin Gallery, Chgo., 1978, 80, 85, 90, U. Wis., 1981, Illini Union Gallery, U. Ill., Urbana, 1986, Artemisia Gallery, Chgo., Katerina's, Chgo., 2002, Woman Made Gallery, Chgo., 2006; exhibited in group shows at Art Inst. Chgo., 1960, 78, 80, 85, 89, Vanderpoel Art Assn., Beverly Art Ctr., Chgo., 1992, Ancient Echoes, Chgo., 1992, Renaissance Ct., Chgo. Cultural Ctr., 1993, 2001, 2002, Artemisia Gallery, Chgo., 1994, Art Place Gallery, Chgo, 1994, Chgo. State U., 1994, Chgo. Women's Caucus for Art, 1994, 95, 98, 2000, Eastern Ill. U., Charleston, 1991, 1993-2001, ARC Gallery, Chgo., 1995, 97, 2004, 2005, N.Mex. Art League, Albuquerque, 1996, Mirage Gallery, Albuquerque, Barrington Arts Coun., 1997, Meridian Ctr., Washington, 1997, Chgo. Women's Caucus for Art, No. Ill. U., 1998, Peter Jones Gallery, 2000; Springfield Art Mus., Mo., 1999, (Patron Purchase award), Beacon St. Gallery, Chgo., 1999, DeKalb Area Women's Ctr., Ill., 1999, Mini-Millennium Women's Caucus For Art Nat. Gallery, 2000, Eastern Ill. U., Charleston, Ill., 2000, 01, Chgo. Cultural Ctr., 2001, 02, Arts Club Chgo., 2003, 2005, Oakton CC, 2004, 2005, Peter Jones Gallery, 2005, Women's Day Art Exhibits Oakton CC, 2005, 06, A.R.C. Gallery, Chgo., 2005, Art of the Book Plate Printworks Gallery, 2005, 2006; represented in permanent collections at Art Inst. Chgo., Ill. State Mus., Ball State Mus., Calumet Coll., Hammond, Ind., Shimer Coll., Waukegon, Ill., Kemper Group Collection, Long Grove, Ill., State of Ill. Bldg., Chgo., Seyfarth, Shaw, Fairweather & Geraldson, Washington, Ernst & Ernst, Chgo., Foote, Cone & Belding, Chgo., US League of Savs. and Loans, Chgo., Northside Industries, Chgo., Keck, Cushman, Mahin & Cate, Chgo., Gould, Inc., Rolling Meadows, Ill., First Nat. Bank Chgo., Internat. Mineral and Chem., Skokie, Ill., Wellesley Coll. Davis Mus., Mass.; reporter Women Artists News, 1977, 80, 83-86. V.p. Midwest region Womens Caucus Art, Chgo., 1982-88; founding mem. local chpt. Chgo. Women's Caucus Art, 1973, bd. dir., 2002-06; bd. dir. Chgo. Artists' Coalition, 1992-94 Recipient honorable mention Sr. Artist's Network South Shore Cutural Ctr., Chgo., 2006, George D. Brown Fgn. Travel fellow Sch. Art Inst. Chgo., 1955-56; Art grant Fulbright fellow, 1958-60, Huntington Hartford Fedn. grant, 1963, Project Completion grant Ill. Arts Coun., 1978-79, Chgo. Cultural Ctr., 2002, CAAPS grant, 2002. Mem. Arts Club Chgo., Chgo. Artists' Coalition, Chgo. Womens Caucus for Art. Home: The Hallmark 2960 N Lake Shore Dr #405 Chicago IL 60657-5645 E-mail: dittofeline@aol.com.

AUBRY, RENÉE L., secondary school educator; b. Scarsdale, N.Y., Mar. 7, 1963; d. Jules K. and Irma B. Aubry; m. Michael J. Rodrigues, June 27, 1992. BS in Geology, SUNY, Albany, 1985; student, U. Vt. Geology, Burlington, 1985—87; MS in Earth Sci. Edn., Queens Coll., N.Y.C., 1989. Cert. secondary sci. tchr. N.Y. State Bd. Edn. Jewelry tchr., LaCrosse coach, substitute tchr., chem. lab. asst. Edgemont HS, Scarsdale, NY, 1987—89; sci. tchr. East Ramapo Ctrl. Sch. Dist., Spring Valley, 1989—90; earth sci. tchr. Port Chester HS, 1990—. HS v.p. Port Chester Tchrs. Assn., 2000—06. Mem.: NSTA, Geol. Soc. Am. (N.Y. councilor), Nat. Assn. Geology Tchrs., Nat. Earth Sci. Tchrs. Assn., Sci. Tchrs. Assn. N.Y. State. Avocations: fossil & rock collecting, jewelry making. Office: Port Chester HS Port Chester NY 10573

AUCHTER, NORMA HOLMES, musician, music educator; b. Rochester, NY, Jan. 3, 1922; d. Robert Edgar and Ruby (Lyon) Holmes; m. Ervin Frank Auchter, June 4, 1955; children: Robert Holmes Auchter, Ceci Ann Albecker, Allan Neil Auchter. BMus with distinction, U. Rochester, 1942, MMus Theory, 1944, DMus Arts Performance and Lit., 1977; studied with Carl Friedberg, N.Y.C., 1950—54. Instr. U. Conn., Storrs, 1943-45, U. Tex., Austin, 1945-46; faculty Eastman Sch. Music, Rochester, 1946-50; piano instr. Middlebury (Vt.) Coll., 1956-61; lectr., accompanist, mus. dir. St. Michael's Coll., Winnoski, Vt., 1967-72; assoc. prof. Tex. Tech. U., Lubbock, 1972-75; piano instr. SUNY, Geneseo, 1976-78; piano/theory prof. U. NC, Pembroke, 1978—79; pvt. piano tchr. Houston, 1979—. Faculty Houston CC NW, 2003-04; piano instr. U. Vt., Burlington, 1960-72; co-owner Auchters House of Music, Burlington, 1956-72; debut recital, Town Hall, NYC, 1952; concert tours U.S., Can., 1950-57; entertainer, lectr. adjudicator, workshops, master classes, TV sch., U.S., Can., 1950—; performing mem. Tuesday Mus. Club, Houston, 1980—. Collaborating artist with Paul Alvarez violin concerts; books and recordings Cabaret Treasures for Violin and Piano, 1995, Salon Gems for Violin and Piano, 1997. Mu Phi Epsilon Postgrad. grant, 1974. Mem. Nat. Guild of Piano Tchrs. (adjudicator), Music Tchrs. Nat. Assn. Home: 2828 Hayes Rd # 2518 Houston TX 77082-6672 Office Phone: 713-598-8111. E-mail: nauchter@iqmail.net.

AUDIA, CHRISTINA, librarian; b. Carolina, W.Va., July 6, 1941; d. John and Roze (Horvath) A. BS in Edn., Wayne State U., 1967, MS in L.S., 1969. Cert. librarian, Mich. Chief libr. original cataloging dept. Detroit Pub. Libr., 1980-89, bibliographic database mgr., 1989—. Specialist for monograph cataloging Mich. Libr. Consortium, 1987-89; mem. Dalnet Database Standards Com., 1989—. Mem. ALA. Avocations: gardening, travel, metal detecting. Office: Detroit Pub Libr Database Mgmt Dept 5201 Woodward Ave Detroit MI 48202-4093

AUER, NANCY JANE, emergency physician, medical association administrator; b. Chattanooga, Dec. 6, 1943; MD, U. Tenn., 1975. Bd. cert. emergency medicine. Intern surgery City of Memphis Hosps., 1975—76; resident neurol. surgery U. Tenn. Hosp., Memphis, 1976—78; joined Swedish Med. Ctr., Seattle, 1989, asst. dir. dept. emergency svcs., chief of staff, v.p. med. affairs, 1999—. Med. dir. Seattle-King County Disaster Team; bd. mem. Washington Health Found.; mem. Boeing adv. com. on Leapfrog Initiative. Fellow: Internat. Fedn. for Emergency Medicine (hon.); mem.: King County Health Dept., Am. Heart Assn., Wash. State Med. Assn. (pres.), Am. Coll. Emergency Physicians (bd. dirs., pres. 1999, del. to AMA ho. dels., John G. Wiegenstein Leadership award 2001), Rainier Club, Bellevue Club. Office: Swedish Med Ctr Emergency Medicine 700 Minor Ave Seattle WA 98104

AUERBACH, ANITA L., psychologist; b. Flushing, N.Y., Dec. 23, 1946; d. Ben and Gussie (Zuckerman) Weiss; m. Steven Miles Auerbach, May 25, 1969. BA cum laude, SUNY, Buffalo, 1968, MA, 1970; PhD (N.Y. State Regents fellow 1970-72), George Washington U., 1977. Diplomate Am. Bd. Med. Psychotherapists, Internat. Acad. Behavioral Medicine. Chief rsch. Youth Crime Control Project D.C. Dept. Corrections, 1970-74; intern clin. psychology No. Va. Tng. Ctr., Fairfax, 1974-75, staff psychologist, then chief psychol. svcs., 1975-79; pvt. practice clin. psychology Commonwealth Psychol. Assocs. PLC, McLean, Va., 1979—; founder,dir. Commonwealth Psychol. Assocs., 1979—, pres., 1979—. Lectr. Washington Tech. Inst., 1972-74, George Mason U., 1978—82; asst. clin. prof. psychology George Washington U., 2003-2006; chair RXP Task Force Va. Acad. Clin. Psychologists, 2006-; cons. in field. Contbr. articles to profl. jours. Mem. adv. bd. World Children's Choir, 2000—02; mem. family edn. project Joseph P. Kennedy Jr. Found., 1977—79; mem. regional appeals bd. No. Va. Pub. Sch. Sys., 1977—79; mem. adv. bd. Value Options Behavioral Health, 2001—03. Recipient N.Y. State Scholar Incentive award, 1969. Mem. APA, Am. Soc. Clin. Hypnosis (approved cons.), Va. Acad. Clin. Psychologists, Va. Psychol. Assn., No. Va. Soc. Clin. Psychologists, Washington Soc. Study Clin. Hypnosis, Psi Chi, Alpha Lambda Delta. Office: 1479 Chain Bridge Rd Mc Lean VA 22101-5730 Office Phone: 703-734-0787.

AUERBACH, ETHEL LOUISE, healthcare facility administrator; BS in Edn. for the Exceptional Students, Barry U., 1960; M in Guidance and Counseling for the Exceptional Students, Barry U., 1966, Specialist Degree in Guidance and Counseling for the Exceptional Students, 1971; D in Edn./Adminstrn. and Leadership, Nova Southeastern U., 1981. Cert. adminstrn. and supervision Fla., guidance and counseling Fla., mental retardation Fla., sch. psychologist Fla., supervision in exceptional student edn. Fla., varying exceptionalities Fla. Counselor South Fla. Hosp., Thomas Jefferson Middle Sch.; tchr. Roosevelt Elem. Sch., Sunland Tng. Ctr., Ft. Myers, Fla., 1960—62; tchr. educable class Santa Clara Elem., 1962—65; tchr./counselor exceptional student program Riviera Middle Sch., 1966—70, counselor, chairperson exceptional student program, 1971—75, asst. prin. exceptional student program, 1975—76; asst. prin. Redland Middle Sch., 1976—77; asst. prin. exceptional student program Sylvania Heights Elem. Sch., 1977—80, Kensington Elem. Sch., 1980—88; asst. adminstr. Miami Cerebral Palsy Residential Svcs., Inc., 1989—92, adminstr., 1992—. Adj. instr. exceptional student edn. Barry U., Miami, 1991—93; mem. Coun. Exceptional Children. Named a Profl. Recognized Spl. Educator, Coun. for Exceptional Children; nominee Adminstr. of Yr., 1980; named to Barry U. Alumni Hall of Fame, 1994; recipient Esteemed Employees with Disabilities award, 1995. Mem.: CEC, Phi Gamma Sigma, Phi Delta Kappa, Kappa Delta Pi. Office: Miami Cerebral Palsy Residential Svcs 11750 SW 80 St Miami FL 33183 also: Miami Cerebral Palsy Residential Svcs 11801 SW 2nd St Miami FL 33183

AUERBACH, JUDITH DIANE, public health service officer; b. San Francisco, Aug. 14, 1956; d. Harold B. and Dorothy A. (Greenfeld) A. BA in Sociology, U. Calif., Berkeley, 1974, MA in Sociology, 1981, PhD in Sociology, 1986. Asst. prof. Widener U., Chester, Pa., 1986—87; Congl. sci. fellow Rep. Pat Schroeder's Office, Washington, 1988—89; dir. Inst. for Study Women and Men U. So. Calif., L.A., 1989—90; assoc. dir. govt. affairs Consortium Soc. Sci. Assocs., Washington, 1990—92; sr. program officer Inst. Medicine Nat. Acad. Sci., Washington, 1992—95; coord. chair behavioral and social scis. Office AIDS Rsch., NIH, Bethesda, Md., 1995; dir. behavioral and social sci. program and HIV prevention sci.; v.p. pub. policy Am. Found. for AIDS Rsch., Washington, 2003—. Vis. prof. UCLA, 1987-88; cons. in field; presenter in field Author: In the Business of Child Care, 1988; (with others) Family Day Care: Current Research, 1992, Children at Risk in America, 1993; co-editor: AIDS and Behavior: An Integrated Approach, 1994; contbr. articles to profl. jours. Recipient Best Policy Paper/Poster award Soc. Psychol. Study Soc. Issues, 1992; NEH fellow, 1987, Soc. Rsch. in Child Devel. fellow, 1988-89. Mem. Am. Sociol. Assn., Sociologists for Women in Soc., Assn. Pub. Policy Analysis and Mgmt. Democrat. Jewish. Office: AmFAR #802 1828 L St NW Washington DC 20036-5104

AUERBACHER, MARY JANE, church organist; b. Alhambra, Calif., Sept. 21, 1922; d. Alvah Jasper McConnel and Mamie Estelle Ruhe; children: Alice, Eleanore, Julia. BA, U. Redlands, 1944, MusB, 1947. Tchr. 1st grade Migratory Camp, Indio, Calif., 1944—45; founder Valley Pre. Sch. (accredited CAIS, WASC), Redlands, Calif., 1958; tchr. music Valley Prep. Sch., Redlands, 1960—76; organist, choir dir. several chs., San Bernadrino, 1976—. Dean Am. Guild Organists, Redlands, 1980; pres. Spinet, 1986. Author: Devotions, 1995. Bd. dirs. Valley Prep. Sch., 1976—; pres. Am. Bapt. Women, Redlands, 1981—83, 1990—92. Named Gifr Honor, AAUW, Redlands, 1984, Woman of Yr., City of Redlands, 1986; recipient Grail award, Knights of Round Table, 1988. Mem.: Redlands Cmty. Music Assn. Baptist. Avocations: birdwatching, hiking, reading. Home: 121 Sierra Vista Dr Redlands CA 92373 Office: Christ the King Luth Ch 1505 Ford St Redlands CA 92373 Personal E-mail: auere@juno.com.

AUGER, KIMBERLY ANN, elementary school educator; b. Everett, Mass., July 3, 1970; d. Robert Charles and Patricia Ann (Cahill) Auger. BA in Elem. Edn., Salem State Coll., 1992; EdM, Cambridge Coll., 2002. Tchr. Everett (Mass.) Pub. Sch., 1992—. Mem.: Mass. Tchrs. Assn. (bd. dirs. 2003—). Democrat. Roman Catholic. Avocations: bowling, skiing, travel. Home: 40 Woodward St Everett MA 02149 Office: Parlin Sch 587 Broadway Everett MA 02149

AUGER, TAMARA M., psychotherapist; b. Oshkosh, Wis. BA, U. N.Mex., 1987, MA, 1990. Lic. prof. clin. mental health counselor. Pvt. practice psychotherapy, Albuquerque, 1990—. Mem. Am. Counseling Assn., Am. Coll. Counselors, N.Mex. Counseling Assn. (ethics chair 1996-97, pres. elect 1997—), Lic. Profl. Counselors Assn. N.Mex. Avocations: woodworking, gardening. Office: 1400 Carlisle Blvd NE Ste D Albuquerque NM 87110-5667

AUGHENBAUGH, DEBORAH ANN, mayor, retired elementary school educator; b. Bklyn., Oct. 15, 1922; d. James R. and Alice Lillian (Walsh) Donecho; m. William Irving Hopwood, Mar. 31, 1946 (dec. July 1966); 1 child, William James; m. Kenneth Merle Aughenbaugh, Oct. 20, 1973 (dec. Sept. 1997). BS, Towson (Md.) State Coll., 1952; MS, Shippensburg (Pa.) U., 1967. Cert. elem. tchr., guidance counselor, Md. Tchr. Balt. City Pub. Schs., 1952-54, St. John's Cath. Ch., Frederick, Md., 1960-63, Frederick County Bd. Edn., Frederick, 1963-84; mem. city coun. City of Burkittsville, Md., 1971-74, 80-83, mayor Md., 1986-95; ret., 1995. Mem. Gov.'s Policy Com. on Edn., 1994-95, Frederick County Bd. Edn., 1995-2002, v.p., 2000-01; legis. com. Md. Assn. Bds. of Edn., 1995-97, 98-99. Chmn. Burkittsville Planning and Zoning Commn., 1969-79; mem. Frederick Recycling Com., 1989-91; mem. Frederick Solid Waste Adv. Bd., 1991-93; mem. Frederick County Bd. of Edn., 1995-2002, v.p., 2000-01; mem. Frederick County Park and Recreation Com.; mem. legis. com. Md. Assn. Bd. Edn., Nat. Bd. Edn., 1998—; mem. Frederick County Future Growth and Sch. Schedule Adv. Com. Mem. Frederick County Ret. Sch. Personnel (pres. 2004-), Md. Mcpl. League (pres. Frederick County chpt. 1992, state legis. com. 1985-95, chair 1992-93, bd. dirs. 1985-95), Nat. League Cities (human devel. com. 1991-95), Frederick County Public Sch. Employees (pres. elect 2002-03, pres. 2003-04, past pres 2005-06) Democrat. Avocations: reading, travel, crocheting. Home: 3940 Southview Ct Jefferson MD 21755

AUGUR, MARILYN HUSSMAN, distribution executive; b. Texarkana, Ark., Aug. 23, 1938; d. Walter E. and Betty (Palmer) H.; m. James M. Augur, Dec. 29, 1962; children: Margaret M. Hancock, Elizabeth H. Taylor, Ann Louise Hardaway. BA, U. N.C., 1960; MBA, So. Meth. U., 1989. Pres. North Tex. Mountain Valley Water, Dallas, 1989—. Bd. dirs. Camden News Pub. Co., Little Rock, Living Waters, Dallas, 2005—. Trustee Hussman Found., Little Rock, 1991—2005, Marilyn Augur Family Found., Dallas, 1991—, U. Tex. Southwestern Med. Found., 1993—, Nat. Jewish Hosp., 1993—2000; bd. dirs. Baylor Health Sys. Found., 1992—2001, chmn., 1995; mem. Tex. Bus. Hall Fame, 1992—98, exec. com., 1994—95; mem. Dallas Citizens Coun., 1994—2004; bd. dirs. Tate Lectr. Series, 1994—2000, Dallas County CC Dist. Found., 1995—, mem. exec. com., 2006—; bd. dirs. Dallas Helps, 1995—99; mem. adv. bd Salvation Army, 1996—; bd. dirs. Charter 100, 1998—, Baylor Oral Health Found. Bd., 1998—2001; mem. exec. bd. So. Meth. U. Dedman Law Sch., 1998—, Cox Bus. Sch., 1998—; chmn. William Booth Soc., 1999—2000; mem. vestry St. Michael and His Angels Ch., 2003—06; bd. dirs. Children's Health Care Sys. Found., 1998—. Mem. Dallas Country Club, Crescent Club, Dallas Women's Club, Beta Gamma Sigma. Episcopalian. Avocations: travel, skiing, trekking. Office: North Tex Mountain Valley Water 4209 McKinney Ave Ste 202B Dallas TX 75205-5439 Personal E-mail: ntmvw1@aol.com.

AUGUST-DEWILDE, KATHERINE, banker; b. Bridgeport, Conn., Feb. 13, 1948; d. Edward G. and Benita Ruth (Miller) Burstein; m. David deWilde, Dec. 30, 1984; children: Nicholas Alexander, Lucas Barrymore. AB, Goucher Coll., 1969; MBA, Stanford U., 1975. Cons. McKinsey & Co., San Francisco, 1975-78; dir. fin. Itel Corp., San Francisco, 1978-79; sr. v.p., CFO PMI Group, San Francisco, 1979-85, pres., CFO, 1988-91; CEO, pres. First Republic Thrift & Loan of San Diego, 1988-96; exec. v.p. First Republic Bank, San Francisco, 1987—, sr. v.p., chief fin. officer, 1985-87, COO, 1996—. Mem. policy adv. bd. Ctr. for Real Estate and Urban Econs., U. Calif., Berkeley, 1987—2000; bd. dirs. First Republic Bank, Trainer, Wortham & Co., Inc. Bd. dirs. San Francisco Zoöl. Soc., 1993-2001, vice-chair, 1995-2000; trustee Carnegie Found., 1999-2004, Town Sch. for Boys, San Francisco, 1999-2004, vice chmn., 2004-; mem. adv. coun. Stanford U. Grad. Sch. Bus., 2003-; trustee Mills Coll., 2004-. Mem. Women's Forum (bd. dirs.), Bankers Club, Belvedere Tennis Club, Villa Taverna. Home: 2650 Green St San Francisco CA 94123-4607 Office: First Republic Bank 111 Pine St San Francisco CA 94111-5602 Office Phone: 415-296-3707. Business E-Mail: kaugust@firstrepublic.com.

AUGUSTINE, JEAN MAGDALENE, Canadian government official, former member of parliament; b. St. George, Grenada, Sept. 9, 1937; BA, U. Toronto, Ont., 1972; MEd, U. Toronto, 1976, LLD (hon.), 1994. Elem. sch. prin. Met. Toronto Separate Sch. Bd., 1964; chair bd. dirs. Met. Toronto Housing Authority, 1964—88; mem. Can. Parliament for Etobicoke-Lakeshore, 1993—2006; parliamentary sec. to the Prime Min. of Can. Govt. of Can., 1993—96, min. state (multiculturalism) and (status of women), 2002—04. Vice chair ministerial task force on social security reform; mem. former chair standing com. on fgn. affairs and internat. trade, standing com. on citizenship and immigration; vice chair standing com. on human resources devel, mem. standing com. on human rights and status of persons with disabilities Ho. of Commons. Bd. dirs. Harbourfront, Cath. Children's Aid Soc., Can. Adv. Coun. on Status of Women, Ont. Jud. Coun., Urban Alliance on Race Rels., Grenada Assn., Metro Action Com. on Pub. Violence Against Women and Children, Etobicoke Social Devel. Coun.; mem. Toronto Mayor's Task Force on Drugs, Metro Toronto Drug Abuse Prevention Task Force, Toronto Crime Inquiry, 1991; former chair women's caucus Nat. Liberal Caucus, Ont. Caucus Comm. Com., Social Policy Sub-Com. on Housing. Recipient Vol. award and pin Govt. Ont., Caribana Achievement award, Bob Marley award, Kay Livingstone award, Women of Distinction award YWCA, Women on the Move award Toronto Sun, Can. Black Achievement award 1994. Mem. Can. Assn. for Parliamentarians on Population and Devel. (founder, chair), Nat. Sugar Caucus (chair, sec. state multiculturalism status of women, 2002-04). Office: Govt Can 1201-2067 Lakeshore Blvd W Toronto ON Canada M8V 4B8 Personal E-mail: jm_augustine@rogers.com.

AUGUSTINE-ASCHERL, JOAN MICHELLE, music educator; b. Mason City, Iowa, Aug. 2, 1964; d. Edgar Keyl and Treva Marie Augustine; m. Michael Raymond Ascherl, July 26, 1986; children: Jocelyn Michelle Ascherl, Madeline Frances-Marie Scherl. BA, Briar Cliff U., Sioux City, Iowa, 1986. Dir. choral music Akron-Westfeld Cmty. Schs., Akron, Iowa, 1986—87; dir. vocal music Newmon H.S., Mason City, 1987—97, Ft. Dodge Cmty. Schs., 1997—. Bd. dirs. Operative Concepts Childrens Threare, Ft. Dodge. Mem. Son Shine Singers, 2002—04, Mason City Cmty. Theatre, 1993—96; min. music Corpus Christi Ch., Ft. Dodge, 2000—06; bd. dirs. Operative Concepts Childrens Theatre, 2004—06. Mem.: Iowa Choral Dirs. Assn.

AUGUSTSON, EDITH, mental health clinician; b. Atlantic City, Dec. 3, 1975; d. Beth Augustson-Andt; 1 child, Nyasia. BA, Oswego State U., N.Y., 1997; MA, Towson State U., Md., 2001. Diplomate Am. Bd. Cert. Counselors, lic. clin. practicing counselor; addiction counselor, cert. Nat. Bd. Cert. Counselors. Pub. rels. coord. for Office of Diversity Resources Towson State U., Balt., 1999—2000; substitute sch. psychologist Balt. City Pub. Sch. Sys., 2000—01; clinician sch. based mental health program U. Md., Balt.,

2001—04; CEO House of Jude Childrens Homes, Inc., 2005—; sr. mental health therapist dept. psychiatry Johns Hopkins Bayview Med. Ctr., 2004—. Creator, developer girls mentoring program Beautiful Mindz inc., Balt., 2003—; clin. in-svc. adv. bd. mem. U. Md. and Balt. Mental Health Systems, 2003—; coord. summer mental health inst. partnership for homeless children U. Md., Balt., 2003—; sr. mental health therapist Johns Hopkins Bayview Med. Ctr., 2003—. Author: A New Home for Maurice, 2005. Recipient acad. recognition, United Fedn. Tchrs., 1993, Gov.'s Citation award, N.Y. State, 1993, Md. State Dels. award, Del. Nancy Hubers, 1999—2001, Womens Ctr. award, Towson State U. Women's Ctr., 2000; Senatorial scholar, Md. State Senators Office, 1999—2001. Mem.: APA (assoc.), Balt. Urban League (assoc.), Psi Chi (life), Alpha Kappa Alpha (life; various offices 1994—97). Avocation: walking. Office: JH BNC 1212 St Baltimore MD 21205 E-mail: edith@houseofjudechildrenshomes.org.

AUGUSTUS, SEIMONE, professional basketball player; b. Baton Rouge, La., Apr. 30, 1984; d. Seymore Augustus, Kim. BA, La. St. Univ., 2005. Guard Minn. Lynx, 2006—. Vol. Gus Young Ctr. Named Nat. Player Yr., Women's NCAA Basketball, 2005—06; recipient Cmty. Svc. award, NAACP, 2001. Achievements include being selected by Minn. Lynx with first overall pick in WNBA draft, 2006; three-time All-Am., 2004-2006, three-time All-SEC, three-time regional honors; four-time All-SEC Tournament, 2003-2006; mem. Kodak All-Am. Team, 2004-2006. Office: Minn Lynx 600 First Ave N Minneapolis MN 55403*

AUKOFER, CLARE ELIZABETH, newspaper editor; b. Milw., June 1, 1949; d. Herbert Anselm and Wanda Mary (Kaminski) A. BFA, U. Wis., Milw., 1972. Assoc. dir. comm. Ford's Theatre, Washington, 1973-74; assoc. editor Am. Rifleman mag., Washington, 1974-77; sr. comm. specialist GE, Rockville, Md., 1977-81, program mgr. comm. and edn. Charlottesville, Va., 1981-83; editor HELIX, dir. comm. U. Va. Health Scis. Ctr., Charlottesville, 1984-96; comms. cons., book editor U. Va. Ctr. for Study of Mind and Human Interaction, Charlottesville, 1996-98; pubs. dir. Cooper Ctr. Pub. Svc. U. Va., 1998-99; comms. dir. Prevent Cancer Found., Bristol, Va., 1999-2000; editor Special Sections Charlottesville Daily Progress, Va., 2000—. Adv. bd., adj. faculty U. Va. Continuing Edn. Pub. Program, 1994-96; theatre critic Charlottesville Daily Progress, 1981—. Chmn. arts com. 1st Night Va., Charlottesville, 1989-91; del. Charlottesville Dem. Caucus, 1991-99; mem. Charlottesville Dem. Com., 1998—; participant Leadership Charlottesville, 1992; vol. reading tutor Book Buddies. Inducted into Company of Good Cheer Pearson Internat. Can. Peacekeeping Ctr., N.S., 1998. Mem. Va. Assn. for Printing, Publs. and Pub. Rels. Profls. (pres. 1990-92, pres. emeritus 1992—). Avocations: theater, gardening, reading, ailurophile, equestrian activities. E-mail: caukofer@dailyprogress.com.

AULBUR, BETH ANNE, elementary school educator; b. Mexico, Mo., Jan. 23, 1955; d. Herman Adrian and Theresa Marie (Weins) A. BS in Edn., Ctrl. MEth. Coll., 1977; MEd, U. Mo., 1981. Tchr. 4th grade Northwestern R-I Sch., Mendon, Mo., 1977-90; tchr. chpt. 1 reading lab. Moberly (Mo.) Schs., 1990—. Mem. adv. bd. Moberly Chpt. 1, 1992—; mem. tchr. adminstr. bd. com. Moberly Pub. Schs., 1993-94. Mem. Mo. State Tchrs. Assn., Moberly Cmty. Tchrs. Assn. (co-pres. 1993-94), Beta Sigma Phi (pres. 1991-82, 84-85, 88-89, 95-96, 2005, v.p. 1986-87, rec. sec. 1979-80, 83-84, 93-94, 2003-05, corr. sec. 1991-92). Avocations: reading, walking, embroidery, music, travel. Office: Gratz Brown Elem 1320 Gratz Brown Rd Moberly MO 65270 Business E-Mail: rnanneman@cvalley.net.

AULL, SUSAN, physician; b. N.Y.C. d. Eugene and Ines Aull. BA, Vassar Coll., 1981; MD, N.Y. Med. Coll., 1986. Diplomate Am. Acad. Phys. Medicine and Rehab., Am. Acad. Pain Mgmt. Intern L.I. Coll. Hosp., Bklyn., 1986-87; phys. medicine and rehab. PGY II, III Westchester County Med. Ctr., Valhalla, NY, 1987-89; phys. medicine and rehab. PGY IV Lincoln Hosp., Bronx, NY, 1989-90, Ctrl. Fla. Physicians Rehab., Orlando, 1990-91; med. dir. dept. phys. medicine and rehab. Halifax Med. Ctr., Daytona Beach, Fla., 1992-99; med. dir. 21st Century Rehab. and Wound Mgmt. Ctr., Maitland, Fla., 1992; staff dept. internal medicine Winter Park (Fla.) Meml. Hosp., 1991-96; pvt. practice WWPM&R, Winter Park and Sarasota, 1991—2002; multi-specialty group practice, dir. phys. medicine and rehab. Ctrl. Fla. Physicians Rehab., Orlando, 1990-91; physician Advanced Sports Medicine Ctr., 2002—04, S. Aull MD PA, 2002—, IOM Svcs. Inc., 2004—. Electrodiagnostic cons. SEA Med. Svcs., PA, Goldenrod, Fla., 1990-96; adj. clin. prof. U. Ctrl. Fla., Orlando, 1991-96. Author: (with others) Strength Conditioning for Preventive Medicine, 1992, ISC Control Points - New Generation of Pressure Points, 1993. Recipient Leadership award Defensive Tactics Newsletter, 1993; grantee PPCT Mgmt. Systems, Inc., 1992. Fellow Am. Acad. Phys. Medicine and Rehab.; mem. AMA, Am. Acad. Pain Mgmt., Am. Coll. Sports Medicine. Office: 1921 Waldemere St Ste 609 Sarasota FL 34239 Office Phone: 941-917-6500.

AULT, ETHYL LORITA, special education educator, consultant; b. Bklyn., May 30, 1939; d. Albert Nichols Fadden and Marion Cecil (Corrigan) Snow; (div.); children: Debra Marie Ault Butenko, Milinda Lei Jones, Timothy Scott. BS, Ga. State U., MEd, 1976, cert. in spl. edn. 6th yr., 1984. Tchr. spl. edn. Butts County Sch. System, Jackson, Ga., 1972-73, Rockdale County Sch. System, Conyers, Ga., 1973-75, lead tchr., 1975-77; cons. spl. edn. Newton County Sch. System, Covington, Ga., 1977-79; curriculum specialist spl. edn. La Grange (Ga.) Sch. System, 1979-83, dir. spl. edn., 1983-94, dir. accredited studies curriculum, 1994—, dir. student svcs., 1995—; collaboration process trainer State of Ga., 1990—, dir. student svcs./spl. program, 1996-2000; fine arts cons. Troup County Schs., 2001—. Instr. La Grange Coll., 1984-97, assoc. prof., 1997—; mem. Tchr. Competency Testing Commn., Atlanta, 1988—, Task Force Documentation and Decision Making, Atlanta, 1988—. Contbg. editor: (manual) Mainstream Modification Handbook, 1989. Chairperson Jud. Adv. Panel, LaGrange, 1988; bd. dirs. Crawford Tng. Ctr. Adv. Panel, La Grange, 1985—; pres. West Ga. Youth Coun. Bd., La Grange, 1980—; mem. State Adv. Panel for Spl. Edn.; bd. dirs. Troup County Hist. Soc., 1999—; mem. State of Ga. Task Force on Alt. Edn., 1998—. Mem. Coun. Exceptional Children, Ga. Assn. Edn. Leaders, Ga. Assn. Curriculum and Instrn. Supervision, Ga. Coun. Adminstrs. Spl. Edn. (v.p. 1988—, pres.-elect 1989, pres. 1992—, Gifted State Task Force 1994—), La Grange Women's Club (v.p. 1989—), Profl. Assn. Ga. Spl. Educators (Adminstr. of Yr. 1993), Ga. Supporters of the Gifted, Nat. Assn. for Gifted Edn., Ga. Assn. for Gifted Students (pres.-elect 2000-2001), Kiwanis (pres.-elect LaGrange chpt. 1999-2000, pres. 2000-01, gov. elect 2004-2005, lt. gov. divsn. 12 Ga. 2005—), LaGrange Women's Club (pres. 2005—), Phi Delta Kappa (pres. 2000-2001), Lafayette Soc. Arts (bd. dirs., v.p., pres. 2005—). Democrat. Episcopalian. Avocations: swimming, fishing, walking, gardening. Home: 441 Gordon Cir Lagrange GA 30240-2621 Office: LaGrange Coll Board St Lagrange GA 30240 Business E-Mail: eault@lagrange.edu.

AUNE, ALISSA MARIE, music educator; b. Grass Valley, Calif., Oct. 18, 1978; d. Philip Sidney and Diane Victoria Aune. BA in Music, Calif. Poly. State U., San Luis Obispo, 2001. Music dir. Nipomo (Calif.) HS, 2002—. Dir.: Les Miserables Student Edition, (operetta) Pirates of Penzance. Named Tchr. of the Month, Nipomo HS, 2003. Office: Nipomo HS 525 N Thompson Rd Nipomo CA 93444 Office Phone: 805-474-3300. E-mail: aaune@lmusd.org.

AUNE, DEBRA BJURQUIST, lawyer; b. Rochester, Minn., June 13, 1956; d. Alton Herbert and Violet Lucille (Dutcher) Bjurquist; m. Gary ReMine, June 6, 1981 (div. June 1993); children: Jessica Bjurquist ReMine, Melissa Bjurquist ReMine; m. David Aune, Jan. 1, 1995. BA, Augsburg Coll., 1978; JD, Hamline U., 1981. Bar: Minn. 1981. Assoc. Hvistendahl & Moersch, Northfield, Minn., 1981-82; adjuster Federated Ins. Cos., Owatonna, 1982-84; advanced life markets advisor Federated Life Ins. Co., Owatonna, 1984-87; mktg. svcs. advisor Federated Ins. Cos., Owatonna, 1987-89, 2d v.p., corp. legal counsel, 1989-92, v.p. gen. counsel, 1992-95, 1st v.p., gen. counsel, 1996-99; ind. cons., 1999—. Mem. Hamline Law Rev., 1979-80. Pres. Owatonna Ins. Women, 1983-84; charter commr. City of Owatonna, 1992—. Mem. ABA, Minn. State Bar Assn., 5th Dist. Bar Assn., Steele County Bar Assn. (sec. 1986-87, v.p. 1987-88, pres. 1988-89), Assn. Life Ins. Counsel, Alliance Am. Insurers (legal com. 1989—). Lutheran. Office Phone: 952-250-9587. E-mail: db.aune@gmail.com.

AUNIO, IRENE M., artist; b. Finland; m. Ernesto Saasto, Dec. 9 (dec. June 2000); children: Laurel Esken, Ernest, Robert. Student, Arts Students League, N.Y.C., Bklyn. Mus. Tchr. art Adult Edn. Prokect, Bklyn.; tchr. painting Elder hostal Program, Conn.; artist-in-residence Johnson Studies Ctr., Vt., 2001—03, Vt., 2004. One-woman shows include Pen and Brush Club, N.Y., Bklyn. Mus., Panoras Gallery, Stony Brook Mus. Art, The Gallery Machias, Maine, Grist Mill Gallery, Chester, Vt., Jeanne Taylor Gallery, N.Y., Miriam Pearlman Gallery, Chgo., Belanthi Gallery, Bklyn., Brookhaven Gallery, Farmingdale, N.Y., Represented in permanent collections Evansville Mus. Fine Arts, Ind., Reading Mus. Fine Art, Pa., Norfolk Mus. Fine Art, Va., Va. State Coll., Seton Hall U., N.J., Art Students N.Y., The Nat. Bank Detroit, Ill., Std. Fed. Savings, Detroit, Detrout Edison, Ill., Macky Bell, Detroit, St. Joseph Mercy Hosp., Quaker Oats Co., Chgo., Dag Hammarskjord Plaza, N.Y., Pub. Svc. Elec. & Gas, N.J., Katz Comm., N.Y., Am. Hosp. Supply Corp., Chgo., Oakland Cmty. Hosp. Recipient Ranger Fund Purchase prize, Evansville Mus. Mem.: Nat. Assn. Women Artists, Allied Artists Am., Nat. League Am. Pen Women, Am. Watercolor Soc. Avocations: painting, swimming, dance. Office Phone: 631-423-3307.

AUR, MARINA V., choir conductor, music educator; b. Narva, Estonia, Russia, Jan. 4, 1963; came to the U.S., 1995; d. Victor Ivanovich and Zoja Dmitrievna Nikitin; m. Oleg Alfivich Aur, Oct. 14, 1988 (div. Feb. 1999). BA in Music, Coll. Music, Smolensk, Russia, 1982. Nat. cert. tchr. music in piano. Tchr. theory Sch. of Music, Narva, 1983-92; choir condr. Soc. of Finns, Narva, 1990-95, Day Star Christian Acad., Moses Lake, Wash., 1995—, Moses Lake Christian Sch., 1998—; pvt. piano tchr. Moses Lake, 1995—. Ch. pianist Ch. in Moses Lake, 1995—. Mem. Music Tchr. Nat. Assn. (audition chair Moses Lake chpt. 1999). Avocations: sewing, knitting, drawing, gardening, hiking. also: PO Box 1572 Moses Lake WA 98837-0245

AURELIAN, LAURE, medical sciences educator; b. Bucharest, Romania, June 17, 1939; came to U.S., 1963, naturalized, 1971; d. George I. and Stella (Ben-Joseph) A.; M.S., Tel-Aviv U., 1962; Ph.D., Johns Hopkins U., 1966; m. I.I. Kessler, Nov. 24, 1970; 1 dau., Amalia D. Asst. prof. dept. lab. animal medicine and microbiology Johns Hopkins U. Sch. Medicine, Balt., 1969-74, assoc. prof. dept. biophysics and biochemistry, 1975-82, assoc. prof. dept. comparative medicine and biophysics, 1974-82, prof. div. biophysics, 1982—; prof. dept. pharmacology U. Md., 1982—, dir. virology/immunology labs., 1984—; mem. NIH study sects. internat. teaching, 1973; mem. sci. adv. com. Internat. Biomed. Inst. UNESCO, 1987—. Recipient Hon. medal Disting. Contribution to Gynecol. Oncology U. Bologna, Italy, award Premio XXIV Casalli 90 ASS, Pro Loco Bronte Edizione Speciale Medicina, Catania, K. Vephvadze Meml. award Georgian Soc. Oncologists; ACS grantee, 1970-74; NIH grantee, 1969—; WHO grantee, 1980—; others; named Disting. Young Scientist, Md. Acad. Sci., 1970. Mem. David Boyes Soc. Gynecol. Oncology, Brit. Coll. Can. (hon.) Am. Soc. Microbiology, AAAS, Am. Assn. Immunologists, Soc. Exptl. Biology and Medicine, Md. Acad. Sci., N.Y. Acad. Sci., Am. Assn. Cancer Research, Reticuloendothelial Soc. Editor Jour. Soviet Oncology, 1980-86, European Jour. Gynecol. Oncology, 1982—, Internat. Jour. Oncology, 1993—, In Vivo, 1994-2004, Clin. and Diagnostic Lab. Immunology, 2000—, Frontiers in Biosci, 1997—, Genetics Vaccine and Therapy, 2003—, Cancer Therapy, 2003—; contbr. articles to profl. jours. Home: 3404 Bancroft Rd Baltimore MD 21215-3105 Office Phone: 410-706-3895. Business E-Mail: laurelia@umaryland.edu.

AUSENBAUM, HELEN EVELYN, social worker, psychologist; b. Chgo., May 16, 1911; d. Herbert Noel and Mayme Eva A. AB, U. Calif., Berkeley, 1938, MSW, 1956. Social worker Alameda Welfare Commn., Oakland, Calif., 1939-42; exec. dir. ARC, Richmond, Calif., 1943-51; tchr. fifth grade Castro Elem. Sch., El Cerrito, Calif., 1951-53; guidance cons. Oakland Pub. Schs., 1953-76; founder, dir. Orinda Counseling Ctr., 1959-95; program dir. Support Svcs., Walnut Creek, Calif., 1978-84. Chair Rossmoor Com. for Common Concern, 1994-96, Mental Health Task Force Contra Costa County, 1978-84; mem. Contra Costa County Adv. Coun. on Aging, 1984-97. Mem. chair nominating com. Rossmoor Dem. Club, 1996; mem. and co-chair Mental Health Profls. of Rossmoor. Mem. NASW, Rotary. Democrat. Presbyterian. Avocations: stamps, freighter travel, reading. Home: 1936 Tice Valley Blvd Walnut Creek CA 94595-2203

AUSLEY, GENEVA GARDNER, cosmetologist, foundation executive; b. Burksville, Ala., Nov. 4, 1933; d. Oscar and Clara (Davis) Gardner; m. Lee Ausley, Nov. 11, 1965; children: Crystal Judkins, Antoinette Judkins. Grad., Po-Roe Beauty Sch., Columbus, Ohio, 1959, Nat. Inst. Cosmetology, Washington, 1977. Lic. cosmetologist, N.J. Owner, operator Geneva's Beauty World, East Orange, NJ, 1959—; founder, dir. Nat. Sarcoidosis Family Aid and Rsch. Found., Inc., Newark, 1982—; asst. dir. House of Prayer Food Pantry. Recipient Outstanding Citizen cert. Mich. Ho. of Reps., 1972, Community Involvement award Concerned Black Nurses of Newark Inc., 1992. Mem. Modern Beautician Assn. N.J. (legis. agt. 1987—, Woman of Yr. award 1983, award 1992), Nat. Coun. Negro Women (past unit pres.). Democrat. Baptist. Office: Nat Sarcoidosis Family Aid 189 Renner Ave Newark NJ 07112-2111 Office Phone: 973-676-7900.

AUSTER, NANCY EILEEN ROSS, economics professor; b. NYC, Aug. 19, 1926; d. Norman L. and Edith Cornelia (Jacobson) Ross; m. Donald Auster, Aug. 18, 1946; children: Carol J., Ellen R. AB, Barnard Coll., 1948; MBA, Ind. U., 1954. Rsch. assoc. The Conf. Bd., NYC, 1948-51; editor publs. Bur. Bus. Rsch. Ind. U., Bloomington, 1954-56; lectr. St. Lawrence U., Canton, NY, 1962-66; from asst. prof. to prof. Canton Coll., SUNY, 1966-82, disting. svc. prof. econs., 1982-91, disting. svc. prof. econs. emeritus, 1991—. Pres. univ. faculty senate SUNY, 1973-75; mem. chancellor's adv. com. disting. tchg. prof. SUNY, 1983-86, chair, 1986-87. Author: (with Donald Auster) Men Who Enter Nursing: A Sociological Analysis, 1970; contbr. articles to profl. jours. Chair adv. coun. St. Lawrence County CETA, Canton, 1977-82. Recipient Professions Excellence award N.Y. State/United Univ. Professions, 1991; USPHS grantee, 1966-70. Unitarian-Universalist. Avocations: running, skiing, birding, quilting. Home: 21 Craig Dr Canton NY 13617-1211

AUSTIN, ANN SHEREE, lawyer; b. Tyler, Tex., Aug. 25, 1960; d. George Patrick and Mary Jean (Brookshire) A. BA cum laude, U. Houston, 1983; JD, South Tex. Coll., 1987. Bar: Tex. 1987, U.S. Dist. Ct. (no. dist.) Tex. 1988, U.S. Ct. Appeals (5th cir.) 1989, U.S. Dist. Ct. (we. dist.) Tex. 1990, U.S. Ct. Appeals (D.C. cir.) 1992, U.S. Supreme Ct. 1992, U.S. Dist. Ct. (ea. dist.) Tex. 1993. With First City Ops. Ctr., Houston, 1980-85; law clk. Lipstet, Singer, Hirsch & Wagner, Houston, 1985-86, Pizzitola, Hinton & Sussman, Houston, 1986-87; briefing atty. Hon. Hal M. Lattimore Ct. Appeals, 2d Jud. Dist., Ft. Worth, 1987-88; assoc. Cantey & Hanger, Ft. Worth and Dallas, 1988-93, Smith, Ralston & Russell, Dallas, 1993-94, Russell, Austin & Henschel, Dallas, 1994-95; pvt. practice Arlington, 1995-96; prin. Landau, Omahana & Kopka, Ltd., Dallas, 1996-97; asst. city atty. City of Dallas, 1997—2002; atty. Law Offices of W. Blake Hyde, 2002—. Tchr. Project Outreach State Bar of Tex., 1992. Author: Personnel Rules, Park & Recreation Department, City Dallas, 2000; co-author Annual Meeting of Invited Attorneys, Construction Law, 1992; chpt. editor: Cases and Materials on Civil Procedure, 1987. Mem. Ft. Worth Hist. Preservation Soc., com. mem., 1992; fundraiser Prevention of Child Abuse in Am., 1988—, Women's Haven. Mem. Tex. Young Lawyers Assn. (jud. rev. com. 1990, women in the profession com., profl. ethics and grievance awareness com. 1992-94), Dallas Bar Assn. (jud. com. 1992-94, ethics com. 1999-2001, cmty. involvement com., employment law sect. CLE com. 1999-2000), Dallas Assn. Young Lawyers, Dallas Women's Bar Assn., Ft. Worth Tarrant County Young Lawyers Assn. (treas. 1989-90, dir. 1989, co-chair Teen Ctr., co-chair Adopt-A-Sch. program, tchr. Constl. Rights, 5th grade class, chair CLE program), Tarrant County Women's Bar Assn., Am. Inns. of Ct., Garland Walker Inn; vol. Texas Mock Trial Competition. Methodist. Avocations: walking, reading, sky diving. Office: Law Offices of W Blake Hyde Ste 490/LB11 1301 E Collins Blvd Richardson TX 75081 Office Phone: 214-570-6296. E-mail: aaustin@stpaultravelers.com.

AUSTIN, BERIT SYNNOVE, retired small business owner, quality assurance professional; b. Oslo, July 22, 1938; came to U.S., 1957; d. Johan Andreas and Astrid (Bjerke) Irgens; m. William Paul Austin, Dec. 22, 1961 (div. 1978); children: Lisa Christine, Paul Erik, Ivar Jon; m. Eivind Funnemark, Feb. 20, 2000. AA, Saddleback Coll., 1984, AS, 1988. Accounts payable clk. Dynatech Corp., Santa Ana, Calif., 1976-78; accounts payable acct., jr. buyer/Kardex Brunswick Corp., Costa Mesa, Calif., 1978-81; fin. clk. Fluor Corp., Irvine, Calif., 1981-84; warehouse asst. Saddleback Coll., Mission Viejo, Calif., 1984—, instr. Norwegian lang. Mem. Sons of Norway Fraternal Internat. Soc. (historian 1972, publicity dir. 1973, asst. soc. dir. 1974, social dir. 1992, cultural dir. 1994, pres. 1996), Daus. Norway (pres. Turio Jespersen Lodge #44, Mission Viejo, Calif., 2005, 06). Republican. Lutheran. Avocations: gardening, bicycling, cross country skiing, travel. Home and Office: 33286 Baldwin Ave Lake Elsinore CA 92530 Personal E-mail: baustin7@yahoo.com.

AUSTIN, ELIZABETH RUTH, retired elementary school educator; b. Glendale, Calif., June 28, 1928; d. Lloyd Lewis Austin and Mary Elizabeth Berryman. BA, Scripps Coll., 1950; postgrad., Occidental Coll., 1950—51, UCLA, 1959, U. S.C., 1961, Orange State Coll., 1964, U. Calif., Santa Barbara, 1975. Admitting office clk. Hosp. Good Samaritan, L.A., 1976—93; elem. tchr. Alhambra, Calif., 1951—55, L.A., 1957—62, Newport Beach, Calif., 1962—65, San Marino, Calif., 1974—76; ret. Home: 1428 S Marengo Ave Alhambra CA 91803

AUSTIN, JEANNETTE HOLLAND, genealogist, writer; b. Atlanta, July 28, 1936; d. Laurel Benjamin Holland and Marguerite Elizabeth Evans; m. Jerry Franklin Austin, May 13, 1977 (dec. Mar. 1993); 1 child, Christopher Lewis (dec.); 1 child from previous marriage, Suzanne Teri Stucki. Legal sec. Smith, Field, Doremus & Ringel, Atlanta, 1954—63; profl. genealogist Atlanta, 1964—; owner www.genealoty-books.com, www.georgiapioneers.com. With Family History Ctr. Ch. LDS, Jonesboro, Ga., 1988—99. Author: The Georgians, 1984, Holland 1000-1988, 1988, Abstracts of Georgia Wills, DeKalb County Probate Records, etc., The Georgia Frontier, 3 vols., 2005. Recipient cert., Atlanta Ga. Temple, 2001. Republican. Mem. Lds Ch. Avocations: drawing, singing, painting, drama, biking. Home: 616 Waterford Pl Ne Atlanta GA 30342-2382 Personal E-mail: jha@georgiapioneers.com.

AUSTIN, JOAN KESSNER, mental health nurse; b. Tell City, Ind., Sept. 24, 1944; d. Edward E. and Dorothy A. (Ziegelgraber) Kessner; m. David Ross Austin, Dec. 18, 1965; 1 child, Janet Lynn. Diploma, Deaconess Hosp., Evansville, Ind., 1965; BS in Nursing, Tex. Woman's U., 1975; MS in Nursing, Ind. U., 1978, DNS, 1981. Clin. instr. Tex. Woman's U., Denton, Tex.; with Ind U. Sch. Nursing, Indpls., 1981—, dist. prof. dept. environ. health, 1999—, disting. prof. nursing, 1999—; dir. Ctr. for Enhancing the Quality of Life in Chronic Illness, Indpls., 2000—. Adj. prof. depts. psychiatry & neurology Ind. U. Sch. Medicine, Indpls.; adj. prof. psychology Ind. U. Purdue Sch. Sci.; pres. Am. Epilepsy Soc., 2005—; mem. rsch. commn. Internat. Bur. Epilepsy; profl. adv. bd. Epilepsy Found. Contbr. articles for profl. jours. Grantee Nat. Inst. Neurol. Disorders and Stroke., Distinguished Contribution to Nursing Research in the Midwest award, Midwest Nursing Rsch. Soc., 1993, Clin. Investigator award, Am. Epilepsy Soc., 1993, Spl. Recognition award, Epilepsy Found. Am., 1995, Social Accomplishment award, 1999, Jacob Javits Neurosci. award, NIH, 2000, Disting. Contbn. to Nursing Sci. award, Am. Nurses Found., 2004, Clemens award, Epilepsy Found. St. Louis, 2004. Fellow Am. Acad. Nursing, 1990; mem. Epilepsy Found. Am. (profl. adv. bd. 1987-95), Internat. League Against Epilepsy, Ind. State Nurses Assn., Inst. Medicine Home: 3040 N Ramble Rd W Bloomington IN 47408-1052 Office Phone: 317-274-8254. E-mail: joausti@iupui.edu.*

AUSTIN, KAREN, retail executive; b. Delphos, Ohio; BS in Computer Sci., Tri-State U. Various positions Kmart Corp., 1984—2002, sr. v.p., chief info. officer Troy, Mich., 2002—. Office: Kmart Corp 3100 W Big Beaver Rd Troy MI 48084

AUSTIN, LINDA LARUE, clergyperson; b. Bozeman, Mont., Apr. 26, 1945; d. William Harold and Edna May (Schenk) LaRue; m. Robert Earl Austin Jr., June 9, 1967. ThB, Northwest Christian Coll., 1967; MRE, Lexington Theol. Sem., 1970; student, Tarrant County Jr. Coll., Fort Worth, 1991. Ordained to ministry Disciples of Christ Ch., 1970. Student minister Orangeburg Christian Ch., Maysville, Ky., 1967-70; minister North Eaton Ch. of Christ, Grafton, Ohio, 1970-80, Bailey Rd. Christian Ch., Cuyahoga Falls, Ohio, 1980-82; office sec. Trinity Brazos Area of Christian Ch. in Southwest, Ft. Worth, 1983-90; instr. creative writing Tarrant County Coll., 1994—. Avocations: archaeology, sewing, gardening. Home: 2109 Jessie Pl Fort Worth TX 76134-2728 Office Phone: 817-320-0783. Business E-Mail: lindalarueaustin@jerson.com.

AUSTIN, LINDA S., psychiatrist; b. 1951; m. Marshall Austin (div.); children: Stephanie, Matt; m. John W. Hallett. At, Stanford U.; BA, Duke U., 1973; MD, Duke U. Sch. of Medicine, 1976. Resident in psychiatry Duke U.; clin. instr. psychiatry Georgetown U., Washington; pvt. practice Chevy Chase, Md.; staff Med. U. S.C., 1986—89, asst. prof. psychiatry, 1989—99, assoc. dean pub. edn., 1996, prof. psychiatry, 1999—2000; staff Ea. Maine Med. Ctr. Heritage Psychiat. Assn., Bangor, Maine, 2000—. Dir. Obsessive-Compulsive Disorder program Med. U. S.C., 1989, mem. Hurricane Hugo response team, 89; featured in Depression: The Storm Within Am. Psychiat. Soc., 1990; host What's on Your Mind Nat. Pub. Radio, 1990—; TV appearances. Author: (books) What's Holding You Back? Eight Critical Choices for Women's Success, 1999, Heart of the Matter: How to Find Love. How to Make it Work., 2003; editor: Responding to Disaster: A Mental Health Clinician's Guide, 1989. Fellow child psychiatry, Georgetown U. Address: Heritage Psychiat Assn Ea Maine Med Ctr 2016 Wappoo Dr Charleston SC 29412 Office Phone: 843-795-5858. Personal E-mail: lindaaustinmd@aol.com.

AUSTIN, LOLA HOUSTON, psychologist; b. San Antonio, Dec. 27, 1939; d. Albert and Sarah Leola Houston; m. Craig L. Austin, July 4, 1972; children: Madie Grabda, Polly Toro, Julia Austin Bingamon, Carrie Austin Young. BA in Edn., North Tex. State U., 1966; MA in Edn., U. Incarnate Word, 1973; PhD in Clin. Psychology, Fielding Inst., 1987; postgrad. study in neuropsychol. evaluation, Santa Barbara, Calif., 2000. Elem. sch. tchr. Edgewood Ind. Sch. Dist., San Antonio Ind. Sch. Dist., Northside Ind. Sch. Dist., San Antonio, 1960—75; reading specialist Northside Ind. Sch. Dist., San Antonio, 1971—76; owner, dir. D & R Reading Clinic, San Antonio, 1976; psychologist San Antonio, 1997; neuropsychol. evaluator Child Protective Svcs., San Antonio, 2000—. Co-chmn. fair King William Hist. Orgn., San Antonio, co-chair food booths. Mem.: APA, Nat. Acad. Neuropsychology, Delta Kappa Gamma (charter mem. Iota Beta chpt.). Office: McCullough Ctr for Mental Health Ste 101 2515 McCullough San Antonio TX 78212 Office Phone: 210-736-1762.

AUSTIN, LYNNE HUNZICKER, secondary school educator; b. East St. Louis, Ill., Apr. 22, 1940; d. Ashley Andrew and Marion Austin (Seward) Hunzicker; children: Kimberly L. Diehl, Jennifer L. Goers, Thomas Ashley Goers. AA, Stephens Coll., Columbia, Md., 1960; BS, U. Houston, Tex., 1963; MEd, George Mason U., Fairfax, Va., 1999. Rsch. asst. Forest Genetics Svc. Tex. A&M, Coll. Sta., Tex., 1963—64, rsch. asst. Dept. Oceanography, 1964—66; tchr. sci. Loudoun County Pub. Schs., Sterling, Va., 1980—. Office: Seneca Ridge Mid Sch 98 Senecca Ridge Dr Sterling VA 20164

AUSTIN, REGINA, law educator; BA, U. Rochester, 1970; JD cum laude, U. Pa., 1973. Law clk to Judge Edmund B. Spaeth Superior Ct of Pa., 1973—74; assoc. Schnader, Harrison, Segal & Lewis, Phila, 1974—77; asst.

prof. U. Pa. Law Sch., Phila, 1977—83, assoc. prof., 1983—90, prof., 1990—96, William A. Schnader prof., 1996—. Vis. prof. Stanford Law Sch., 1991, Brooklyn Law Sch., 1998, Columbia Law Sch., 2000; vis. assoc. prof. Harvard Law Sch., 1989—90. Contbr. articles to law jours. Office: U Pa Law Sch 3400 Chestnut St Philadelphia PA 19104 Office Phone: 215-898-5185. Office Fax: 215-573-2025. E-mail: raustin@law.upenn.edu.

AUSTIN, SANDRA IKENBERRY, nursing educator, consultant; b. Lexington, Va., Dec. 22, 1941; d. William Peters and June Virginia (Blackwell) Ikenberry; m. Joseph M. Austin, Apr. 10, 1965; children: Joseph M. Jr., Susan C., Christopher M. BSN, U. Va., 1963; MSN, U. Calif., L.A., 1967; EdD, U. Mass., 1997. RN, Mass. Pub. health nurse Dept. Health, Waynesboro, Va., 1963-64; instr. U. Va., Charlottesville, 1964-65; staff nurse Santa Monica (Calif.) Hosp., 1965-66; faculty nursing Boston U., 1968-69, Quinsigamond C.C., Worcester, Mass., 1969-70, Fitchburg (Mass.) State Coll., 1973-96; assoc. prof. nursing Framingham (Mass.) State Coll., 1997—; project dir., sr. health edn. cons. HealthCo Consulting Inc., Shrewsbury, Mass., 1996—. Mem. Shrewsbury Town Meeting, 1992—95; chair steering com. Framingham State Coll. Nursing Honor Soc., 1998, faculty counselor/advisor, 1999—, pres., 1999—; people to people ambassador program delegate China Healthcare Info., 2004. HBO and Co. Nurse scholar, 1995. Mem.: Assn. Critical Care Nurses, Nat. League Nursing (awards com. 1999—2001), Assn. Women's Health, Obstet. and Neonatal Nurses, Am. Ednl. Rsch. ASsn., Sigma Theta Tau (Epsilon Beta edn. chair 1993—95, Rho Phi chpt. pres. 2002—04, chpt. pres. 2005, faculty counselor 2000—, rsch. grant 1996), Pi Lambda Theta. Republican. Congregationalist. Avocations: computer multimedia production, reading, walking. Home: 100 Harrington Farms Way Shrewsbury MA 01545-4081 Office: Framingham State Coll Nursing Dept Framingham MA 01701 Office Phone: 508-626-4715.

AUSTIN, SANDRA J., small business owner; b. Clarkburg, W.Va., May 1, 1956; d. Mary Paden Austin Ford; adopted children: Michael Renwick, Reginald Renwick. Grad., Va. Learning Inst. Sch. of Massage, Falls Church, Va., 2000. Police cadet Met. Police D.C., Washington, 1974—77, police officer, 1977—91, drivers tng. instr., 1990—91, police detective, 1991—2000; ret.; massage therapist, owner Sanctus, Burke and Dumfries, Va., 2001—. Instr. percussion Boys and Girls Club, Washington, 1980—82; percussionist Met. Police D.C. Choir, 1980—82; founder Blue Angels Female Flag Football Team, 1996; percussionist gospel choir Howard U., 1974—77. Named Police Officer of Yr., Kiwanis, 1989, Policewoman of Yr., Women's Aux. Club, 1989, Uniformed Narcotic Officer of Yr., Coun. of God, 1989. Mem.: FOP (union rep. 1987—93). Avocations: softball, basketball, football, writing, crafts. Office: Sanctus 14806 Dixon Ct Woodbridge VA 22193-1940

AUSTIN, SUSANNAH LYN, music educator; d. Charles Max and Virginia Evelyn Stover; m. Mark David Austin, July 11, 1998; children: Sarah, David. MusB summa cum laude, U. Houston, 1997. Cert. music tchr. Tex., 1997. Orch. dir. Pasadena Ind. Sch. Dist., Tex., 1997—2000; tchr. gen. music Lamar Ind. Sch. Dist., Sugar Land, 2000—. Cellist The Woodlands Symphony, Tex., 1999—2001; pvt. instr. cello, Sugar Land, 1998—2005; substitute cellist Christ King Presbyn. Ch., Houston, 2000—; freelance cellist, 1998—. Grantee, LCISD, 2001; scholar, U. Houston, 1992—97; Deisenroth scholar, Augustana Coll., 1992. Mem.: Tex. Classroom Tchrs. Assn. (assoc.), Tex. Music Educators Assn. (assoc.).

AUSTIN, TERRI JO, state representative; b. Elwood, Ind., May 17, 1955; m. Michael Austin; 2 children. B in Elem. Edn., Ball State U., M in Spl. Edn.; degree in Ednl. Adminstrn. and Supervision, Butler U. Classroom tchr., dist. administr. Anderson Cmty. Sch. Corp., 1983—; nat. cons. U.S. Dept. Edn.; dir. Madison County Cmty. Alliances to Promote Edn.; state rep. dist. 36 Ind. Ho. of Reps., Indpls., 2002—, vice chair, commerce and econ. devel. com., mem. ways and means, pub. policy, ethics and vets. affairs, and tech. R & D coms. Asst. prof. Anderson U.; vice chair econ. trade and cultural affairs NCSL; pub. policy and vets. affairs RMM. Candidate Ind. Ho. of Reps., 2000; mem. alumni bd. Ball State Tchrs. Coll. Mem.: United Way of Madison County, AAUW, LWV, Anderson Area C. of C., Anderson Rotary Club. Democrat. Episcopalian. Office: Ind Ho of Reps 200 W Washington St Indianapolis IN 46204-2786 Office Phone: 800-382-9842. E-mail: h36@in.gov.

AUSTIN, WANDA MURRY, systems engineer; b. N.Y.C., Sept. 08; d. Murry Pompey and Helen Lewis; m. Wade Austin Jr.; children: Wade, Wendell. MS in Sys. Engring., U. Pitts., 1977; PhD in Sys. Engring., U. So. Calif., 1988. Engr. Rockwell Internat., Anaheim, Calif., 1977-79, Aerospace Corp., El Segundo, Calif., 1979—. Contbr. chpt. to book: Quantitative Simulation, 1991. Recipient Outstanding Achievement award Women in Aerospace, 1996, King Spirit of the Dream award Space and Missile Sys. Ctr., 1999. Fellow AIAA; mem. Soc. Women Engrs. (sr., award 1996). Office: Aerospace Corp 15049 Conference Ctr Dr Chantilly VA 20151

AUSTIN-STEPHENS, ANN-MARIE, retail executive; b. Sept. 13; Various marketing positions Proctor and Gamble Co.; dir. tech. and brand mktg. Frito-Lay Co., 1996—99; v.p. strategic planning Circuit City, 1999—2000, sr. v.p., 2000—. Mem.: Black Career Women's Execucircle. Office: Circuit City 9950 Mayland Dr Richmond VA 23233-1464

AUSTIN-THORN, CYNTHIA KAY, religious organization administrator, poet; b. Dallas, Feb. 24; d. Kenneth and Anita E. Fujii; m. George Austin, Dec. 20, 1978 (dec. July 1990); 1 child, Christopher; m. Kenneth Thorn, July 3, 1994 (dec. Aug. 1999). AAS, El Centro Coll., Dallas, 1987. Sr. accounts payable clk. Plymouth/Poco Shops, N.Y.C.; mgr. Funky Things, Huntington Beach, Calif.; with select inventory mgmt. office Joske's Dept. Store, Dallas; sec., receptionist George E. Austin Piano Tech., Dallas; owner, writer, design creator Son of Dust Creations, Dallas; active The Road to Damascus Ministries, Dallas. Contbg. poet: (anthologies) A Muse to Follow, 1996 (Editor's Choice award 1996), A Tapestry of Thoughts, 1996 (Editor's Choice award 1996), (cassettes) The Sound of Poetry, 1996, 97 (named 1 of 10 best poets 1996, 97), Searching for Soft Voices, 1997. Mem. choir 1st Family Ch., Dallas, 1996-97, 99, 2000, 2002. Recipient cert. of achievement 1st Family Ch., 1996, Editor's Choice award Internat. Libr. of Poets, 2006, Merit award Internat. Soc. Poets, 2006. Republican. Avocations: creative writing, song writing, singing in church plays, intercessory prayer, ministering to others. Home and Office: Apt B 10410 Lone Tree Ln Dallas TX 75218-3008 Personal E-mail: cynthiathorn@yahoo.com.

AUTRY, CAROLYN, artist, art history educator; b. Dubuque, Iowa, Dec. 12, 1940; d. William Tilden and Vela (Laseman) A.; m. Peter Elloian, May 27, 1966; 1 dau., Cybele Justine. BA, U. Iowa, 1963, MFA, 1965. Instr. art, art history Baldwin-Wallace Coll., Berea, Ohio, 1965-66; adj. assoc. prof. art history dept. art Ctr. for Visual Arts U. Toledo, 1966-2001. Artist-in-residence Sch. Arts in France, Lacoste, 1984, Lacoste, 87, adj. instr. in printmaking, 87. Exhbns. include San Francisco Mus. Art, 1973, Oakland Mus., 1975, Santa Barbara Mus., 1975, U. Mo., 1975, Ljubljana Internat. Biennial, 1975, 81, 87, Internationale Grafik Biennale, Frechen, W. Ger., 1976, Biella, Italy, 1976, Genoa, Italy, 1976, Leverkusen, Fed. Republic Germany, 1977, Phila. Mus. Art, 1980, 97, Visual Arts Ctr., Anchorage, Alaska, 1980, U. Louisville, 1981, U. Dallas, 1981, Grunwald Ctr. Graphic Arts, UCLA, 1981, Ohio State U., 1982, Belle Arts & Graphic Inc., Nyack, N.Y., 1982, Mus. Arts and Sci., Macon, Ga., 1983, U. Tenn., Knoxville, 1983, Pratt Graphics Ctr., NYC, 1983, Calif. State Coll. San Bernardino, 1983, Am. Embassy Cultural Ctr., Belgrade, Yugoslavia, 1983, Taipei Fine Arts Mus., 1983, 85, 87, 89, 91, 95, Museo Arte Contemporaneo, Ibiza, Spain, 1984, Drake U., 1985, Fla. State U., 1985, Irvine (Calif.) Fine Arts Ctr., 1986, Inter-graphic Internat., East Berlin, 1984, 87, Met. Mus. Art Ctr., Coral Gables, Fla., 1987, Fifth Internat. Graphic Exhbn., Catania, Italy, 1988, Korean Cultural Svc. Gallery, L.A., Walker Hill Gallery, Seoul, Korea, and Korean Embassy Cultural Ctr., Paris, 1989, Barbican Art Centre, London, Salford (Gt. Britain) Mus., Mead Gallery, U. Warwick, Coventry, Gt. Britain, Brighton and Poly. Gallery, Brighton, Gt. Britain, 1989, Internat. Exhbn. Prints, Kanagawa, Japan, 1989, 90, 95, 97, Gallery Fine Arts Ctr. Seoul, 1989, Nat. Exhbn. Prints, Ringling Sch. Art and Design, Sarasota, Fla., 1990, Internat. Impact Art Festival, Kyoto City Mus., Japan, 1990, 91, 92, 93, 94, Ohio Drawing and Printmaking Invitational, Upper Arlington, 1991, Fondation Mona Bismarck, Paris, 1991, Fine Arts Assn. Gallery, Hanoi, Republic of Vietnam, 1991, Prints Internat., 1992, Silvermine Guild Arts Ctr., New Caanan, Conn., 1993, Taejon (Korea) Expo Graphic Art, 1993, Soc. Am. Graphic Artists 65th Nat., N.Y.C., 1993, Architecture in Contemporary Printmaking, Boston Archtl. Ctr., 1994, Am. Inst. Architecture, Washington, 1994, U. N.H., 1995, Midwest Select, South Bend Regional Mus. of Art, Ind., 1994, Triton Mus., Santa Clara, Calif., 1995, Mansfield (Ohio) Art Ctr., 1995, 20th Harper Nat. Exhbn., Macomb, Ill., 1996, Hunterdon Art Ctr., Clinton, N.J., 1996, Soc. Am. Graphic Artists 66th Nat. Print Exhbn., Hanover, N.J., 1997, Internat. Print Triennial, Cracow, Poland, 1997, Fla. Printmakers Ann. Nat. Print Exhbn., Jacksonville, 1997, 00, Institut Franco-Américain, Rennes, France, 1997, Prized Impressions, Internat. Exhbn. of Prints, Phila. Mus. of Art, 1997, Nat. Print Exhbn., Calif. State Univ. Chico, 1997, 22d nat. Print Biennal Silvermine Guild Arts Ctr., Conn., 1998, Counterpoint Exhbn. Hill Country Arts Found., Tex., 1998, 99, 2000, Printmakers 98, Pittsburgh Ctr. for the Arts, Penn., 1998, U. Hawaii, Hilo, 2000, 13th Ann. McNeese Nat. Works on Paper Exhbn., McNeese State U., Lake Charles, La., Baton Rouge (La.) Gallery, 2000, Printwork 2K, 2000, The 7th Ann. Nat. Juried Exhbn., Barrett Art Ctr., Poughkeepsie, N.Y.C., 2000, 1st Biennial Nat. Print Competition, No. Ariz. U., Flagstaff, 2002, Internat. Print exhbn. invitational, Minsk, Belarus, 2002, Soc. Am. Graphic Artists 69th Nat. Exhbn. Arts Student League, NY, 2002, Interior/Exterior Landscapes, U. Wyo., Laramie and U. Dallas, Irving, Tex., 2002, 23d Nat. Print Exhbn., Art Link Contemporary Art Gallery, Ft. Wayne, Ind., 2003, L.S. Printmakers Soc. Juried Membership Exhbn., Brand Libr. Art Galleries, Glendale, Calif., 2003, Boston Printmakers Juried N.Am. Print Exhbn., 1971-81, 86-87, 2003, Soc. Am. Graphic Artists, Susan Teller Gallery, N.Y.C., 2004, Calif. State U., Chico, 2004, Calif. Soc. Printmakers 90th Ann. Exhbn., Works Gallery, San Jose, 2004, Artlink 24th Ann. Nat. Print Exhbn., Fort Wayne, Ind., 2004, 25th Ann. Nat. Print Exhbn., 2005, Calif. Soc. Printmakers 91st Ann. Exhbn., San Francisco Bay Model Visitor Ctr., Sausalito, 2005, Soc. Am. Graphic Artists, Art Students League of NY, 2005, Print Club Albany Artist Mem. Show, Cooperstown (NY) Art Assn. Gallery, 2005, Sidney Larsen Gallery, Columbia Coll., Mo., 2006, others; represented in permanent collections Libr. of Congress, Phila. Mus. Art, Worcester Art Mus., MountHolyoke Coll., U. Colo., Bradley U., Calif. State U., San Diego, Ga. State U., U. S.D., U.N.D., U. Louisville, St. Lawrence U., U.Dallas, Hunterdon Art Ctr., Clinton, N.J., Fitchburg (Mass.) Mus., Duxbury (Mass.) Art Complex, Elvehjem Mus. Art U. Wis.-Madison, Inst. per la Cultura E L'Arte, Catania, Italy, Lakeview Mus. Arts and Scis., Peoria, Ill., Nat. Mus. Fine Arts, Hanoi. Recipient Boston Printmakers N.Am. Print Exhbn. award 1971, 79, 80, 81, 87, Pennell award Libr. Congress, 1971, 75, Phila. Print Club awards, 1972, 75, 79, Wesleyan Coll. Internat. award of merit, 1980, Anne Steele Marsh award Hunterdon Art Ctr., Clinton, N.J., 1991, Bradley U. Nat. award, 1991, Friends of the Janet Turner Gallery Nat. Exhbn. award Chico State U., Calif., 1995, Exhbn. award 16th Nat. Print Exhbn., Artlink, 1996, Exhbn. award 17th Nat. Print Exhbn., 1997, Counterpoint, 2000, Nat. Exhbn. award The Hill Country Arts Found., 2000, Exhbn. award 5th Nat. Print Exhbn., Calif. State U., Chico, 2004; Ford Found. grantee, 1961-63, Ohio Arts Coun. grantee, 1979, 90, Yale-Norfolk Summer Sch. Art and Music scholar, 1962. Mem.: The Print Club of Albany (Ledyard Cogswell Jr. Meml. prize 1995), Coll. Art Assn. Am., Calif. Soc. Printmakers, Soc. Am. Graphic Artists (Jo Miller award 1985, Phillip Monteith award 1986, George Sherman Purchase prize 2005), LA Printmakers Soc., Boston Printmakers (Louis Black award 1971), Phi Beta Kappa. Address: 26114 W River Rd Perrysburg OH 43551-9128 Office Phone: 419-872-9558. Personal E-mail: autello@aol.com.

AUTRY, CHERYL RENEE, special education educator; b. Houston, Jan. 14, 1949; d. Joe and Susie Autry; children: Ajani Mazi, Kimani Khary. AA, Skyline Coll., 1978; BA, U. Calif.-Berkeley, 1981. Tchr. spl. edn. Spring Ind. Sch. Dist., Houston, 1996—. Author: (books) Harvest Time, Our World, short stories, poems. Founder, mem. Women History Mus., Washington, 1996, Friends of Pres. Clinton, Little Rock, 2004; leadership coun. So. Poverty Law Ctr., Montgomery, Ala., 2002. Mem.: Am. Fedn. Tchrs. Avocations: writing, gardening, walking. Home: 2238 Laurel Oaks Houston TX 77014

AUTTONBERRY, SHERI E., lawyer; BA, La. Tech U., 1996; JD, Vanderbilt U. Law Sch., 1999. Bar: Ohio 1999. Assoc. Katz, Teller, Brant & Hild, Cin., dir., Fine Arts Fund. Mem. Vol. Lawyers for the Poor. Named one of Ohio's Rising Stars, Super Lawyers, 2006. Mem.: Cin. Bar Assn. (legal adv.), Class X, Cin. Acad. Leadership for Lawyers. Avocations: reading, gardening, sports. Office: Katz Teller Brant & Hild 255 E 5th St Ste 2400 Cincinnati OH 45202-4724 Office Phone: 513-721-4532. Office Fax: 513-762-0012.*

AUWERS, LINDA S., lawyer; Grad., Stanford U.; PhD, Brandeis U.; JD, U. Houston Law Ctr. Prof. history Temple U.; atty. Schlanger, Cook, Cohn, Mills & Grossberg; v.p., asst. gen. counsel Compaq Computer Corp., Houston, 1995—99, v.p., assoc. gen. counsel, sec., 1999—2001, v.p., dep. gen. counsel, sec., 2001—02; sr. v.p., gen. counsel, sec. ABM Industries, San Francisco, 2003—. Mem.: Am. Corp. Counsel Assn. (mem. corp. & securities law com.), Am. Soc. of Corp. Secretaries (mem. public co. affairs com.). Office: ABM Industries 160 Pacific Ave Ste 222 San Francisco CA 94111

AUXER, CATHY JOAN, elementary school educator; b. Chambersburg, Pa., May 16, 1951; d. Pat and Joan Irene Wedo; m. Jeffrey Lynn Auxer, Aug. 21, 1971 (dec. Aug. 23, 1996); 1 child, Jeffrey Lynn Auxer Jr. BS in Edn., Shippensburg State U., 1974; MEd, Shippensburg U., 1978. Cert. tchr. Pa., Md. 1st grade tchr. Mooreland Elem. Sch., Carlisle, Pa., 1975—2000, Worcester Prep. Sch., Berlin, Md., 2000—. Cons. Apple Learning Interchange, Berlin, 2001—. Co-author: (pamphlet) Whole Language, 1981; author: (lessons online) Computer Learning Found., 2000—01. Recipient 2d pl. award for lesson plan, Computer Learning Found. Tchrs., 2001. Mem.: Internat. Reading Assn., Eastern Shore Reading Coun. Home: 18 Carriage Ln Berlin MD 21811 E-mail: occookiemd@aol.com.

AUYANG, GRACE CHAO, education educator, consultant; d. C.P. Chao and T.C. Chang; m. King Auyang, Aug. 4, 1974; children: Edward, Elizabeth. PhD, Temple U., Phila., 1978. Dept. chair U. Cin., 1994—2000, prof., 1999—. Cons. mgmt. and academic assessment U. Cin., 1994—. Editor: (textbook) Sociological Outlook (Diversity award, 1995); author: Writing, Editing, and Reviewing (Tchg. awards, 2005), articles to profl. jours. Mem. governing coun. Am. Women Studies Assn., Washington, 1995—97; bd. mem. Cin. Chinese Learning Assn., Cin., 1990—2000. Grantee, U. Cin., 1990, 1994, 1995, 1997, 2000, 2005, 2006. Mem.: AAUP, Am. Sociol. Assn. (sect. chair 1994—95), AAUW (assoc.). Protestant. Achievements include research in Global Culture and World Issues, Teaching Pedagogy, Science, Technology and Society, etc; Study Gender and Education Issues. Avocations: reading, writing, travel, painting, music. Office: Univ Cincinnati 9555 Plainfield Rd Cincinnati OH 45236 Office Phone: 513-745-5656. Business E-Mail: grace.auyang@uc.edu.

AVANT, PATRICIA KAY, nursing educator; b. Dallas, Aug. 15, 1941; d. Lem Barrett and Georgia Evelyn (Mullennix) Coalson; m. Gayle R. Avant, Sept. 6, 1963; children: Samantha Gay Foss, Celia Kay Drews. RN, Meth. Hosp., Dallas, 1962; BSN, Tex. Christian U., Ft. Worth, 1963; MSN, U. N.C., Chapel Hill, 1965; PhD, Tex. Woman's U., Denton, 1978. Chair family nursing U. Tex. Health Sci. Ctr., San Antonio, 2005—. Fellow Am. Acad. Nursing; mem. Royal Coll. Nursing (Australia), ANA (pres. Dist. 10 1983-84), Nat. League Nursing, (1st v.p. Tex. 1985-89), N.Am. Nursing Diagnosis Assn. (taxonomy chair 1994-98, pres. 2000-02). Democrat. Baptist. Home: 7601 Tallahassee Rd Waco TX 76712-3814 Office: U Tex Health Sci Ctr 7703 Floyd Curl Dr San Antonio TX 78229-3900 Office Phone: 210-567-5881. Business E-Mail: avantk@uthscsa.edu.

AVANTS, REBECCA MAXINE, biology educator; d. Robert Miller; m. James Avants; children: Desiree, Tarra. MS, Calif. State U., Fresno, 1999. Instr. biology and microbiology Fresno City Coll., 1989—; biology instr. Clovis West H.S., Fresno, Calif., 1999—. Grant adminstr. Clovis West H.S., Fresno, Calif., 2005—. Advisor parents assn. Calif. State U., Fresno, 2001—06. Recipient Crystal award Sci. Score Achievement, Clovis Unified Schs.; grantee Solar Project in Edn., Pacific Gas and Elec., A+ for Edn., BP, 2005—06. Mem.: Phi Kappa Phi. Home: 271 Omaha Clovis CA 93619 Office: Clovis West HS 1070 E Teague Fresno CA 93720 Office Phone: 559-327-2000.

AVEDON, MARCIA J., pharmaceutical executive; BA summa cum laude in Psychology, U. N.C., 1983; MS in Indsl. and Orgnl. Psychology, George Washington U., 1987, PhD with hons. in Indsl. and Orgnl. Psychology, 1989; MS in Exec. Program, Rutgers U. Intern U.S. Army Civilian Ctr., 1984; assoc. cons., sr. cons., cons. Booz-Allen & Hamilton, Inc., 1985—90; program mgr. Anheuser-Busch Cos., Inc., 1990—92, sr. cons., 1992—93, mgr. corp. succession planning, 1993—94, dir. mgmt. and orgn. devel. Campbell Taggart Inc., 1994—95; dir. orgn. and leadership devel. Honeywell Internat., 1995—97, v.p. human resources and comms. Performance Polymers, 1997—2000, v.p. human resources and comms. Performance Polymers and Chems., 2000—01, v.p. corp. human resources, 2001—02; v.p. talent mgmt. and orgn. effectiveness Merck & Co., Inc., Whitehouse Station, NJ, 2002, sr. v.p. human resources, 2003—. Adv. bd. Human ResourcesOfficer's Acad., mem. corp. leadership coun. Bd. dirs. Jersey Battered Women's Svcs., 2000—; mem. adv. bd. Masters in Human Resources U. S.C., 1998—; corp. sponsor Cornell Ctr. for Advanced Human Resource Studies, 2001—. Mem.: Pharm. Human Resources Assn., Healthcare Businesswomen's Assn., Am. Psychol. Assn., Human Resources Policy Assn. (mem. personnel roundtable), Soc. for Human Resources Mgmt., Soc. for Indsl. and Orgnl. Psychology. Office: Merck & Co Inc PO Box 100 1 Merck Dr Whitehouse Station NJ 08889-0100

AVENI, BEVERLY A., executive aide; b. Stamford, Conn., Sept. 2, 1959; d. Lucille F. (Ferretti) A.; m. Steven Munson. BA in Polit. Sci., U. Conn., 1981. Legal asst. Cummings and Lockwood, Stamford, 1981-86; family law paralegal Piazza, Melmed and Ackerly, P.C., Stamford, 1986-88; litigation paralegal Abate and Fox, Stamford, 1988-95; exec. aide to mayor City of Stamford, 1995—. Pres. Conn. Assn. Paralegals, 1989-91; mem. seminar faculty, co-author seminar skills book for paralegal Conn. Discovery Skills, 1995. Vol. counselor Rape and Sexual Abuse Crisis Ctr., Stamford, 1983-87; dist. rep. Dem. City Com., Stamford, 1992-96, sec., 1994-96; local coord. Sen. Christopher Dodd's 1992 Reelection Campaign, 1994-96; mem. congl. dist. adv. coun. Conn. Permanent Commn. on Status of Women, 1996; mem. commn. City of Stamford's XV Charter Revision Commn., 1994-95; mem. Mayor's cabinet; Mayor's rep. on various civic coms. and bds.; bd. dirs. Women's Bus. Devel. Ctr., 1999—. Avocation: exercise. Office: City of Stamford 888 Washington Blvd Stamford CT 06901-2902 Home: # B 71 Dora St Stamford CT 06902-5414 Office Phone: 203-977-4150.

AVENT, SHARON L. HOFFMAN, manufacturing company executive; b. St. Paul, Feb. 7, 1946; d. Ebba and Harold Hoffman; m. Terry Avent; 2 children. Student, Hamline U., St. Paul. With Smead Mfg. Co., Hastings, Minn., 1965—, pres., CEO, 1998—; acquired The Atlanta Group (now Smead-Europe), Hoogezand, Netherlands, 1998—. Bd. dirs. Hastings Public Sch. Found. Named Minn. World Trader of the Year, World Trade Week, Inc., 2002; recipient Spirit of Life honoree, City of Hope, 2003. Office: Smead Mfg Co 600 Smead Blvd Hastings MN 55033-2219

AVERHART, CELESTINE, surgical nurse; b. Beacon, N.Y., Oct. 16, 1960; d. Mayfield and Lela Mae (Glenn) A. BSN, Nazareth (Mich.) Coll., 1985. RN, Mich., Ga.; CNOR, Ga., 1990. Staff nurse Cmty. Hosp., Battle Creek, Mich., 1985, charge nurse, 1985—86; surg. nurse oper. rm. Battle Creek Health Svcs. Cmty.Hosp., 1986—91, Piedmont Hosp., Atlanta, 1991—2005, DeKalb Med. Ctr. at Hillandale, Lithonia, 2005—. Mem. Assn. Operating Rm. Nurses. Home: 2851 Bridle Creek Dr SW Conyers GA 30094-5695 E-mail: caverh7793@aol.com.

AVERILL, ELLEN CORBETT, retired secondary education science educator, administrator; b. Milledgeville, Ga. d. Felton Conrad and Vivian Iris (Brookins) Corbett; m. George Edmund Averill, July 31, 1971; 1 child, John Conrad BS, U. Ga., 1966, MS, 1971; tchg. cert., Columbus Coll., 1979, EdS, 1994. Cert. master gardener Ala., 2006, Ga., 2006. Grad. tchg. asst. U. Ga., Athens, 1966—68; tchr. sci. Decatur City Schs., Ga., 1971—72; tchr. sci., chair dept. Kendrick H.S., Columbus, Ga., 1980—2004; ret., 2004. Rsch. asst. Caretta Rsch. Project, Savannah (Ga.) Sci. Mus., 1985, NEWMAST, Kennedy Space Ctr., 1986; rsch. assoc. Inhalation Toxicology Rsch. Inst., Albuquerque, summer, 1990; instr. sci. Gov.'s Honor Program Valdosta State Coll., summer, 1991, Woodrow Wilson Biotech. Inst., Princeton, N.J., 1993 Contbr. articles to newspapers, jours.; inventor The Wrap-All, 1992 Vol. Hope Harbour, 2004—. Mem. NSTA (program com., regional conf. 1993), Nat. Assn. Biology Tchrs. (Outstanding Biology Tchr. 1990-91), Ga. Sci. Tchrs. Assn. (dist. VI rep. 1988-90, secondary rep. 1990-91, pres.-elect 1991-92, pres. 1992-93, conf. coord. ann. conf. 1992, Dist. VI Sci. Tchr. of Yr. 1995), Coalition for Excellence in Sci. Edn. (orgnl. com. 1992-93), Ga. Sci. Tchrs. Edn. Found. (chair 1994-98), Valley Area Sch. Tchrs. (charter, pres.-elect 1996-97, pres. 1997-98), Muscogee Area Literacy Assn. (treas. 1992-93), Phi Delta Kappa (Tchr. of Yr. 1992, v.p. 2002-), Delta Kappa Gamma (treas. 2006—). Unitarian-Universalist. Avocations: art, gardening, radio. Home: 126 Waterway Dr Cataula GA 31804-4407 Personal E-mail: eaverill@mchsi.com.

AVERSA, DOLORES SEJDA, educational administrator; b. Phila., Mar. 26, 1932; d. Martin Benjamin and Mary Elizabeth (Esposito) Sejda; m. Zefferino A. Aversa Jr., May 3, 1958; children: Dolores Elizabeth, Jeffray Martin, Linda Maria. BA, Chestnut Hill Coll., 1953. Owner Personal Rep. & Pub. Rels., Phila., 1965-68; ednl. cons. Franklin Sch. Sci. and Arts, Phila., 1968-72; pres., owner, dir. Martin Sch. Bus., Inc., Phila., 1972—. File reader, cons. for ct. reporting and travel tng. Southwestern Pub. Co., 1990; mem. ednl. planning com. Ravenhill Acad., Phila., 1975-76. Active Phila. Mus. ARt, Phila. Drama Guild; mem. Met. Opera Guild, 2002; sec. Rep. Exec. Com., Phila.; mem. 8th Ward Rep. Exec. Com. Mem.: Lower Bucks County C. of C., Am. Soc. Travel Agts. (PAC chmn. 1997—, sch. divsn., nat. educators com., sec. Del. chpt., edn. chmn.), Hist. Soc. Pa., World Affairs Coun. Phila., Phila. Hist. Soc., Pa. Sch. Counselors Assn., Am. Bus. Law Assn., Pa. Bus. Edn. Assn., Nat. Bus. Edn. Assn., Andrea Doria Survivor Assn., Chestnut Hill Coll. Alumnae Assn. (sec. class '53), Phila. Orch., Am.-Italy Soc., Met. Opera Guild, Stone Harbor Golf Club (Rep. exec. com. 8th ward Phila.). Roman Catholic. Home: 2111 Locust St Philadelphia PA 19103-4802 Office: 2417 Welsh Rd Philadelphia PA 19114-2213 Personal E-mail: msb-aversa@erols.com.

AVERY, CAROLYN ELIZABETH, artist; b. Hartford, Conn., Mar. 7, 1937; d. Russell Eugene and Frances Atwood Avery; m. Robert Franklin Mills, Oct. 11, 1975; stepchildren: Michelle Mills Garcia, Steven Robert; m. Clifton Messenger, Dec. 30, 1955 (dec. Feb. 1966); children: Stephen Lee, JoAnne Messenger Henderson, Gregory Clifton. One-woman shows include Springfield Libr. and Mus. Complex, Mass., Jasper Rand Mus., Westfield, Mass., Cottage Place Gallery, Ridgewood, N.J., Springfield Fine Arts Mus., 2006, exhibitions include Shore Rd. Gallery, Maine, Berkshire Art Gallery, Mass., Min. Theater of Chester Gallery, Mass., Woodwind Gallery, Maine, others, Green River Gallery, Millerton, N.Y., Gates St. Gallery, White River Junction, Vt., Arno Maris Gallery, Westfield (Mass.) State Coll., juried nat. group show: George Walter Vincent Smith Mus., two-person show, Burnett Gallery, Jones Libr., Amherst, Mass. Office Phone: 413-569-0384.

AVERY, MARY ELLEN, pediatrician, educator; b. Camden, NJ, May 6, 1927; d. William Clarence and Mary (Miller) Avery. AB, Wheaton Coll., Norton, Mass., 1948, DSc (hon.), 1974, Trinity Coll., 1976, U. Mich., 1975, Med. Coll. Pa., 1976, Albany Med. Coll., 1977, Med. Coll. Wis., 1978, Radcliffe Coll., 1978; DSc, U. So. Calif., 2003; DSc (hon.), Harvard U., 2005, MA (hon.), 1974; MD, Johns Hopkins U., 1952; LHD (hon.), Emmanuel Coll., 1979, Northeastern U., 1981, Russell Sage Coll., 1983, Meml. U.,

Newfoundland, 1993; DHL, Johns Hopkins U., 1999; LLD, Queen's U., Kingston, Ont., 2000, U. So. Calif., 2003; DSc (hon.), Harvard U., 2005. Intern Johns Hopkins Hosp., 1953—54, resident, 1954—57; rsch. fellow in pediat. Boston, 1957—59, Balt., 1959—69; assoc. prof. pediat. Johns Hopkins U., 1964—69; prof., chmn. dept. pediat. McGill U. Med. Sch., 1969—74; physician-in-chief Montreal Children's Hosp., 1969—74; Thomas Morgan Rotch prof. pediat. Harvard U. Med. Sch., Boston, 1974—97; physician-in-chief Children's Hosp. Med. Ctr., Boston, 1974—85; prof. emerita Harvard U. Med. Sch., Boston, 1997—. Mem. Med. Rsch. Coun. Can.; mem. study sect. NIH, 1968—71, 1984—88. Author: The Lung and Its Disorders in the Newborn Infant, 4th edit., 1981; author: (with A. Schaffer) Avery's Diseases of the Newborn, 8th edit., 2004; author: (with G. Litwack) Born Early, 1984, editor (with H.W. Taeusch and R. Ballard); author, editor: (with L. First) Pediatric Medicine, 1988, 2d edit., 1994, also articles:, mem. editl. bd.: Pediatrics, 1965—71, Am. Rev. Respitory Diseases, 1969—73, Am. Jour. Physiology, 1967—73, Jour. Pediatrics, 1974—84, Medicine, 1985, Johns Hopkins Med. Jour., 1978—82, Clin. and Investigative Critical Care Medicine, 1990—96, New Eng. Jour. Medicine, 1990—95. Trustee Wheaton (Mass.) Coll., 1965—85, Radcliffe Coll., Johns Hopkins U., 1982—88. Recipient Mead Johnson award in pediatric rsch., 1968, Trudeau medal, Am. Thoracic Soc., 1984, Nat. Medal of Sci., NSF, 1991, Marta Philipson award, Karolinska Inst., Stockholm, 1998; Markle scholar in med. scis., 1961—66. Fellow: NAS (mem. coun. 1997—), AAAS (dir. 1989, pres. 2004—05), Royal Coll. Physicians of Edinburgh, Am. Acad. Arts and Scis., Am. Acad. Pediat., Internat. Pediatric Assn. (standing com. 1986—89); mem.: Am. Pediatric Soc. (pres. 1990, John Howland award 2005), Royal Coll. Pediat. and Child Health (hon.), Inst. Medicine (coun. 1987, Walsh McDermott award 2000), Soc. Pediatric Rsch. (pres. 1972—73), Am. Physiol. Soc., Can. Pediatric Soc., Alpha Omega Alpha, Phi Beta Kappa. Office Phone: 617-355-8330. Business E-Mail: mary.avery@tch.harvard.edu.

AVILA, LIDIA D., principal; b. Phoenix; d. Pete A. and Elvira (Duarle) Avila. BA in Edn., Ariz. State U., MA in Counseling, 1968, EdD in Adminstrn. and Supr., 1981. Cert. elem. tchr., counselor, adminstr. Successively tchr., counselor, coord. Wilson Sch. Dist., Phoenix, 1958—73, prin., 1973—75, Glendale (Ariz.) Elem. Sch. Dist., 1976—88, Tucson, 1988—91, Phoenix, 1991—. Adult edn. tchr., Tempe, Ariz., 1966—68; fed. project reader cons., Phoenix, 1968—72; textbook cons. Active Robert A. Taft Inst. Govt., 1981; mem. steering con. 1st U.S.-China Ednl. Conf., Beijing, 1997; del. Inter-Club Coun. Women's Orgn. Greater Phoenix Area, Internat. Fed. U. Women Conf., Yokohama, Japan; mem. Ariz. Women's Town Hall, 1996; bd. dir. YWCA, 1968—70. Grantee Baylor U. Leadership/Mgmt. Inst., 1980, NDEA, UCLA Inst. Linguistics, Manila, Philippines, 1968. Mem.: AAUW (state pres., mem. edn. found. panel, reg. dir.), Nat. Assn. Elem. Sch. Prins. (participant nat. fellows program), Assn. Supervision and Curriculum Devel., Am. Bus. Women's Assn. (Woman of Yr. 1982), Alpha Delta (pres., Golden Gift award), Phi Delta Kappa, Delta Kappa Gamma. Office: 5810 N 49th Ave Glendale AZ 85301

AVILA, SUSAN ELIZABETH, elementary school educator; b. Phoenix, Mar. 18, 1974; d. Raul and Teresa Avila. BA, U. Notre Dame, Ind., 1998. Tchr. elem. reading and lang. arts Houston Ind. Sch. Dist., 2000—05, tchr. mid. sch. sci. and reading, 2005—. Coach pep squad Stevenson Mid. Sch., Houston, 2005—; asst. coach cheerleading Patterson Elem., 2003—05, coach drama, 2004—05, organizer interscholastic league, 2003—04. Recipient Poetic Achievement award, Patterson Elem., 2001—05. Avocations: travel, pottery, graphic design. Office: Stevenson Middle School 9595 Winkler Rd Houston TX 77017 Office Phone: 713-943-5700.

AVILES, ALICE ALERS, psychologist; b. N.Y.C; d. Jose Oscar and Pauline (Irizarry) Alers; m. Jose A. Aviles, Aug. 13, 1954 (div. Oct. 1981); children: Jeffrey (dec.), Brian, Gregory; m. Clifford M. Goldman, June 29, 1997. BS magna cum laude, SUNY, Oswego, 1955; MA, Queens Coll., 1978; PhD, Yeshiva U., 1984; postdoctoral diploma in psychoanalysis and psychotherapy, Adelphi U., 1991. Lic. psychologist, N.Y. Tchr. elem. schs., Spring Valley, NY, 1955, Erlangen Am. Sch., Germany, 1955—56, Uniondale, NY, 1956, Freeport, NY, 1957—58, Island Park, NY, 1973—75; psychology clk. Fifth Ave. Ctr. for Counseling and Psychotherapy, N.Y.C., 1978—80; psychology intern St. Vincent's Hosp. and Med. Ctr., N.Y.C., 1980—81; psychologist Kingsboro Psychiat. Ctr., Bklyn., 1981—84; psychologist to assoc. psychologist South Beach Psychiat. Ctr., Bklyn., 1984—86; pvt. practice Valley Stream, NY, 1985—. From staff psychologist to sr. psychologist Luth. Med. Ctr., Bklyn., 1986-95; cons. Beach Terrace Care Ctr., Long Beach, N.Y., 1995-97; mem. adv. com. Hispanic Counseling Ctr. of Family Svc. Assn. of Nassau County, Hempstead, N.Y., 1978-80; cons. Nassau County Extended Care Ctr., Hempstead, 1997-99, Resort Nursing Home, Far Rockaway, N.Y., 1998-2000, Woodmere (N.Y.) Rehab. and Health Care Ctr., 1999-2000. Ford found. grad. fellow, 1978-81. Mem. APA, N.Y. State Psychol. Assn., Nassau County Psychol. Assn. (mem. pvt. practice com. 1992-93), Adelphi Soc. Psychoanalysis and Psychotherapy. Office Phone: 516-791-8326.

AVINO-BARRACATO, KATHLEEN, construction executive, consultant; b. Bklyn., Nov. 30, 1956; d. Charles and Rosanna (Scarlota) A.; m. Joseph Moran Olague (div. Jan. 1986); m. Joseph Louis Barracato Jr., Aug. 23, 1986. B in Architecture, Pratt Inst., 1978; postgrad., U. Tex., 1984; cert. in constrn. mgmt., NYU, 1985—89. Draftsperson Michael Harris Spector and Assocs., Great Neck, NY, 1974—78; designer Brodsky & Adler, Architects and Engrs., NYC, 1978—79, Emery Roth and Son, Architects, NYC, 1979; borough design mgr., urban park designer NYC Dept. Parks and Recreation, Queens, 1979—81; project mgr. Lawrence D. White, Assocs., Austin, Tex., 1981; pvt. practice cons., educator Austin, 1981—85; head drafting dept. Durham Nixon-Clay Coll., Austin, 1982—84; asst. supt. constrn., constrn. mgr. NYC Dept. Social Svcs., 1985—87; project mgr. Racal-Chubb Security Systems, East Rutherford, NJ, 1987—88, Herbert Constrn. Co., NYC, 1988—89; instr. constrn. mgmt. Inst. Design & Constrn., Bklyn., 1989—; constrn. mgr. York/Hunter, Rutherford, 1989—91; dean acad. affairs Inst. Design and Constrn., Bklyn., 1992—; prin., indsl. edn. and tng., cons. KAB Cons., 1995—; v.p. Ritcher & Ratner Constrn., 2005—06; constrn. mgr. Perfect Renovation, NYC, 2006—. Mem. NAFE, Profl. Women in Constrn., Columbian Club. Republican. Avocations: photography, italian language. Home: 166 67th St Brooklyn NY 11220-4822 Office: Inst of Design and Constrn 121 Willoughby St Brooklyn NY 11201-5316 Office Phone: 516-225-8054. E-mail: barravino@netzero.net.

AVIV, DIANA L., public policy analyst, psychotherapist; b. Johannesburg, Nov. 17, 1951; came to U.S., 1975; d. Ervin Biderman and Miriam Weissman; m. Abraham Aviv (div.). BSW, Haifa U., 1972, U. Witwatersand, Johannesburg, 1974; M in Social Work, Columbia U., 1977. Psychotherapist S.E. Nassau Guidance Ctr., N.Y.C., 1977-79; exec. dir. Alternatives to Domestic Violence, N.J., 1979-81; dir. programs Nat. Coun. of Jewish Women, NYC, 1981-86; assoc. v.p. Jewish Coun. for Pub. Affairs, 1986-94; v.p. pub. policy United Jewish Communities, Washington, 1994—2003; pvt. practice in psychotherapy NJ, NY, Washington, 1979—; pres., CEO Ind. Sector, Washington, 2003—. Cons. Pub. Defenders Office, N.J., N.Y., 1980—. Steering com. Amos, 1999; bd. dirs. Coalition on Human Needs, 1999; v.p. Nat. Immigration Forum, 1999—. Recipient Profl. Excellence award N.Y. Assn. of New Am., 1999. Mem. NASW. Jewish. Avocations: hiking, exercising, reading, gardening, beadwork. Office: Ind Sector 1200 Eighteenth St NW Ste 200 Washington DC 20036*

AVOLIO, ANNETTE M., language educator; b. Montclair, N.J., Mar. 4, 1951; d. Americo P. and Phyllis M. Malanga; children from previous marriage: Louis R., Phylissa M. BA, William Paterson U., 1969; MA, Marygrove Coll., 2003. Cert. English tchr. N.J. Media specialist Immaculate Heart of Mary Sch., Wayne, NJ, 1988—96; tchr. basic skills West Paterson Bd. Edn., NJ, 1996—98; tchr. English Wayne Bd. Edn., 1998—. CCD tchr. Our Lady of Valley Ch., Wayne, 1990—98. Democrat. Roman Catholic. Home: 7 Falcon Pl Wayne NJ 07470 Office Phone: 973-389-2120. E-mail: NettieAMA@aol.com.

AVRECH, GLORIA MAY, psychotherapist; b. San Jose, Calif., Oct. 17, 1944; d. Benjamin and Lillian (Yudelowitz) A.; m. William Woodruff (dec. April 22, 2004). BA, U. Calif., Berkeley, 1966; MSW, U. Md., 1969; PhD, Inst. Clin. Social Work, Calif., 1987. Bd. cert. social worker; cert. Jungian analyst. Sch. social worker Balt. City Pub. Schs., 1969-70; psychiatric social worker Calif. Dept. Social Welfare Cmty. Svcs. Br., L.A., 1970-72; clin. social worker Pasadena (Calif.) Child Guidance Clinic, 1972-82; pvt. practice psychotherapist Pasadena, 1976—. Field instr. U. So. Calif. Sch. Social Work, L.A., 1978-82; dir. Hilde Kirsch Children's Ctr. Jung Inst. LA, 2005—. Contbr. book and movie revs., Jour. Psychological Perspectives, 1989-2003. VISTA fellow, Balt., 1967-68, Children's Bur. fellow, Balt., 1968-69. Mem. NASW, Soc. Clin. Social Work, Assn. Humanistic Psychology, Assn. Transpersonal Psychology, Analytical Psychology Club. Democrat. Avocations: shamanism, films, cats, cultural events. Office: 130 S Euclid Ave Ste 6 Pasadena CA 91101-2472

AVRETT, ROZ (ROSALIND CASE), writer; b. Upper Montclair, N.J., Apr. 19, 1933; d. William Lyon and Doris Edna (Clift) Case; m. William Thomas Reynolds, Feb. 20, 1960 (div. 1968); 1 child, Gerald William Thomas; m. John Glenn Avrett, Dec. 31, 1972. BA in Creative Writing, Chatham Coll., 1951-55. Copy trainee Young & Rubicam, Inc., N.Y.C., 1955-56; copy writer Hicks & Greist, Inc., N.Y.C., 1958-61; sr. copy writer Dancer-Fitzgerald-Sample, N.Y.C., 1961-63; creative supr. The Marschalk Co., N.Y.C., 1963-68; assoc. creative dir. BBDO Internat., N.Y.C., 1968-78; author N.Y.C., 1978—. Advt. lectr. Sch. of Visual Arts, 1970, 71. Author: My Turn, 1983, 72nd and Rodeo, 1983; author short stories. Patron Met. Opera. Recipient Leadership award Am. Biog. Inst., Raleigh, N.C. Mem. PEN, Author's Guild, People for Ethical Treatment of Animals, Met. Opera Club, River Club. Republican. Episcopalian. Avocation: opera.

AXELROD, LEAH JOY, tour company executive; b. Milw., Sept. 7, 1929; d. Harry J. and Helen Janet (Ackerman) Mandelker; m. Leslie Robert Axelrod, Mar. 10, 1951; children: David Jay, Craig Lewis, Harry Besser, Garrick Paul, Bradley Neal, Nell Anne. BS, U. Wis., 1951. Creative drama specialist Highland Park (Ill.) Parks and Recreation Dept., 1962-82; program specialist Pub. Libr., Highland Park, 1972-82; ednl. cons. Bd. Jewish Edn., Chgo., 1973-80; children's edn. specialist Jewish Cmty. Ctr., Chgo., 1975-82; tour cons. My Kind of Town Tours, Highland Park, 1975-79, pres., 1979—. Co-owner Tours at the Mart, 1992-95. Editor: Highland Park: All American City, 1976; co-author: Highland Park By Foot or By Frame, 1980, Highland Park: American Suburb, 1982; co-editor: Adventures in Highland Park, 2001. Founding mem., v.p. Highland Park Hist. Soc., pres., 1987—94, past pres., 1994—; bd. dirs. Ill. State Hist. Soc., 1989—, exec. bd. dirs., 1999—; founder, bd. dirs. Chgo. Jewish Hist. Soc., 1975—; bd. mem. Team Ill., 1999—, sec., 2001—03; exec. com., adv. bd. Apple Tree Theatre Co., assoc. bd. pres., 2001—03; active Highland Park Hist. Preservation Commn.; pres. B'nai Torah Sisterhood, 1982—84; Bd. dirs. Midwest Zionist Youth Commn.; bd. dirs. Highland Park Hist. Soc., 1996—, Friends Jens Jensen, 1995—99. Mem. Nat. Assn. Women Bus. Owners, Am. Theatre Assn., Ill. Theatre Assn. (dir. creative dramatics 1977-79), Hadassah Club (Highland Park chpt.), Chgo. Area Women's History Coun. Bd., Coun. for Ill. History. Home: 2100 Linden Ave Highland Park IL 60035-2516 Office Phone: 847-432-7003. Personal E-mail: tourtime@worldnet.att.net.

AXNER, CAROL CHRISTIE, elementary school educator; b. Altoona, Pa., Feb. 6, 1947; d. Robert Walter and Emilie Elizabeth (Boehling) Christie; m. Gerald Frederick Axner II, July 11, 1970. BS in Elem. Edn., Valparaiso U., 1969; MAT, Manhattanville Coll., 1973. Cert. tchr., N.Y. Tchr. St. John's Luth. Sch., Glendale, NY, 1969-70, Ossining Union Free Sch. Dist., NY, 1970—2005; ret. Asst. dir. No. Westchester-Putnam Tchr. Ctr., North Salem, N.Y., 1988-91; dir. Ossining Staff Devel. Ctr., 1992-2005; mem. N.Y. State Task Force on Tchr. Ctrs., Albany, 1992-2005. Mem. ASCD, Ossining Tchrs. Assn. (sec., 1st v.p.), N.Y. State United Tchrs. (del. 1982-2003), AFT (del. 1981-2002), Nat. Staff Devel. Coun. Avocations: travel, hiking, reading.

AXTHELM, NANCY, advertising executive; V.p./prodn. group head Grey Worldwide (formerly Grey Advt. Inc.), sr. v.p., dep. dir. broadcast prodn., 1990—92, sr. v.p., dir. broadcast prodn., 1992—93, exec. v.p., dir. broadcast prodn., 1993—. Office: Grey Worldwide 777 3rd Ave Fl 10 New York NY 10017-1302

AYARS, PATTI, human resources specialist, health products executive; B in Bus. Adminstrn. with highest distinction, U. Neb. Various internat. and domestic human resources positions Monsanto Corp./Pharmacia, 1981—2001; sr. v.p. human resources Roche Diagnostic Corp., Indpls., 2001—. Co-author: (book) Mastering Momentum: A Practical and Powerful Approach for Successful Change. Office: Roche Diagnostics Corp 9115 Hague Rd Indianapolis IN 46256-1025 Office Phone: 317-521-2000. Office Fax: 317-845-2221. Personal E-mail: payars01@aol.com.

AYDELOTTE, MYRTLE KITCHELL, retired nursing administrator; b. Van Meter, Iowa, May 31, 1917; d. John J. and Larava Josephine (Gutshall) Kitchell; m. William O. Aydelotte, June 22, 1956; children: Marie Elizabeth, Jeannette Farley. BS, U. Minn., 1939, MA, 1947, PhD, 1955; postgrad., Columbia U. Tchrs. Coll., 1948. Head nurse Charles T. Miller Hosp., St. Paul, 1939—41; surg. tchg. St. Mary's Hosp. Sch. Nursing, Mpls., 1941—42; instr. U. Minn., 1945—49; dir., dean State U. Iowa Coll. Nursing, 1949—57, prof., 1957—62; assoc. chief nurse VA Hosp. Rsch. for Nursing, Iowa City, 1963—64, chief nursing rsch., 1964—65; prof. U. Iowa Coll. Nursing, 1964—76, 1982—88; exec. dir. ANA, 1977—81; ret., 1988. Dir. nursing U. Iowa Hosps. and Clinics, 1968—76; mem. sci. adv. bd. Ctr. Health Rsch. Wayne State U., 1972—76, Inst. Medicine, 1973—; cons. U. Minn., 1970, 82, 90, U. Rochester, 1971, U. Mich., 1970, 73, U. Colo., 1970—71, U. Hawaii, 1972—73, Ariz. State U., 1972, U. Nebr., 1972—73. Mem. editl. bd.: Nursing Forum, 1969—72, Jour. Nursing Adminstrn., 1971; contbr. articles to profl. jours. Mem., v.p. Iowa City Libr. Bd., 1961—67; mem. Johnson County Bd. Health, 1967—70; mem. adv. com. family living courses Iowa City Bd. Edn., 1970—72. With Nurse Corps. U.S. Army, 1942—46. Mem.: ANA, Am. Acad. Nursing, Inst. Medicine, Sigma Theta Tau (rsch. com. 1968—72). Home: 1570 East Ave Apt 202 Rochester NY 14610

AYDT, MARY L, secondary school educator; b. Lake Forest, Ill., Oct. 10, 1944; d. Stanley Adam Wrona and Sophie Steplyk; m. James C. Aydt, June 29, 1968; children: Michael, Stephen, Peter. BS in Edn., No. Ill. U., 1966; MA in Edn., St. Xavier U., Chgo., 1997. Tchr. h.s. math. Mundelein Unit Dist., Ill., 1967—68, Sch. Dist. U-46, Elgin, Ill., 1968—74, h.s. math. tchr., 1985—. Sponsor Nat. Honor Soc. Sch. Dist. U-46, Elgin, coach geometry in math competition; tchr. math. local CC, Elgin, 1980—87; ESL tchr. YWCA, Elgin, 1980—87. Worker, local soup kitchen, Elgin, 1996—. Mem.: AAUW (corr. sec. 1998—), NEA, Elgin Tchr. Assn., Ill. Edn. Assn., Kappa Delta Pi. Roman Catholic. Avocations: sports, travel, needlecrafts. Home: 1500 Easy St Elgin IL 60123 Office: Elgin High Sch 1200 Maroon Dr Elgin IL 60120 Office Phone: 847-888-5100 ext. 8130.

AYERS, ANNE LOUISE, small business owner, consultant, counselor; b. Albuquerque, Oct. 22, 1948; d. F. Ernest and Gladys Marguerite (Miles) A. BA, Kans. U., 1970; MEd, Seattle Pacific U., 1971. Staff cons. in student devel. Cen. Wash. State U., Ellensburg, 1971-72; dir. Aerospace Def. Command Resident Edn. Ctrs. for N.D. and Mont. Chapman U., Orange, Calif., 1972-74; instr. psychology Hampton (Va.) U., 1973-75; edn. svc. specialist Gen. Ednl. Devel. Ctr., Fort Monroe, Va., 1975-77; edn. specialist U.S. Army Transp. Sch., Ft. Eustis, Va., 1977-79, Nat. Mine Health and Safety Acad., Beckley, W.Va., 1979-89; edn. svcs. specialist NASA Hdqrs., Washington, 1989-96; ret., 1996. Pres. Appalachian Love Arts, Martinsburg, W.Va., 1983—; tchr. undergrad. and grad. evening classes in psychology, 1972-74; program mgr. NASA Tchr. Resource Ctr. Network Program; sub. counselor Berkley County, W.Va. Inventor decorative pen/thermometer holder/corsage, psychedelic jewelry process. Mem. Nat. Soc. Inventors, Nat. Assn. Women Deans Adminstrn. and Counselors, Internat. Soc. Photographers, Alumnus of Growing Vision Century in Edn. (award), Mayflower Soc. Methodist. Avocations: travel, collecting gems and shells, coin collecting/numismatics, rock and fossil collecting, oboe and clarinet. Home and Office: 480 Tanbridge Dr Martinsburg WV 25401-4695

AYERS, DOLORES ELAINE, literature and language educator; d. Russell Nolan and Irene Frances Reeves; m. Johnny Lynn Ayers, Aug. 9, 1974; children: Ethan Ryan, Zane Hayden. B in English, Bethany Nazarene Coll., Okla., 1975; M in Adminstrn., Coll. SW, Hobbs, N.Mex., 2005. Tchr. Hobbs Mcpl. Sch., 1996—2006, head English dept. Owner Pro Sharp Sales and Svc., Hobbs, N.Mex., 2004—06. Former vol. Easter Seals, Hobbs, 2006. Mem.: ASCD, Hobbs Assn. Classroom Tchrs. (v.p. 2004—05), Phi Delta Kappa. Republican. Avocations: reading, cooking, antiques. Home: 815 Eagle Dr Hobbs NM 88240 Business E-Mail: ayersd@hobbsschools.net.

AYERS, JANET, technical college president; b. Bremen, Ga., Apr. 6, 1956; d. Etna Bentley; children: Jesset, Cole. BS in Edn., U. West Ga., Carrollton, 1977, MEd, 1981, EdS, 1986. Instr. Paulding County H.S., Dallas, Ga., 1977-78, Carroll Tech. Inst., 1977-81, chair bus. edn. divsn., 1981-88, v.p. student svcs., 1988-93, v.p. instructional and econ. devel., 1993-95, pres., 1995—. Bd. dirs. Ga. Edn. Advisement Coun., Carrollton. Mem. AAUW, West. Ga. LWV (pres. 1998-99), Ga. Assn. Supervision and Curriculum, Ga. Tech. Inst. Pres. Assn. (pres.), C. of C. of Carroll, Haralson, Douglas and Coweta Counties (bd. dirs.).

AYERS, JANICE R., social service administrator; b. Idaho Falls, Idaho, Jan. 23, 1930; 1 child, Thomas. MBA, U. So. Calif., 1952, MA, 1953. Gen. mgr. Tamasha Town and Pvt. Country Club, Anaheim, Calif.; asst. to dir. gen. svcs. Disneyland, Anaheim; state dir. Mental Retardation Assn., Las Vegas, Nev.; exec. dir., chief exec. officer 13-County Retired Sr. Vol. Program, Carson City, Nev. Cons. in field. Contbr. ariticles to profl. jours. Mem. Pub. Rels. Soc. Am., Nat. Assn. RSVP Dirs., Women in radio and TV, AAUW, Optimist Club, Las Vegas Club.

AYERS, KATHY VENITA MOORE, librarian; b. Amherst, Tex., Jan. 15, 1946; d. Charles Edward and Jean (Willman) Moore; children: Suzanne Flanary, Charles Flanary. BA, U. Ill., 1972, MLS, 1974. Cert. profl. libr., N.Mex.; cert. tchr., N.Mex. Dir. children's libr. Hayner Pub. Libr., Alton, Ill., 1974-76; dir. Ruidoso (N.Mex.) Pub. Libr., 1978-80; libr. media specialist Horgan Libr., N.Mex. Mil. Inst., Roswell, 1985-93; libr. N.Mex. Sch. Visually Handicapped, Alamogordo, 1993—, White Mt. Sch., 1999—2004. Workshop presenter Lewis & Clark Regional Libr. Systems, Ill., 1975; outreach programer Hayner Pub. Libr., 1974-76; del. Pre-White Ho. Conf., State of N.Mex., 1991. Contbr. articles to newspapers and profl. jours. Bd. dirs. Alton Symphony, 1975; mem. Altrusa, Ruidoso, 1979-84, Friend of Roswell Pub. Libr.; sec. Ruidoso Summer Festival, 1979; bd. dirs. Supts. Adv. Bd., Roswell, N.Mex., 1987-89; pres. Friends of Libr., Ruidoso, 1980-83, Parent Advocacy for Gifted Edn., 1990-92; v.p. Sunset PTA; bd. dirs. N.Mex. Libr. Found., 1992—; mem. State Task Force on Sch. Librs., 1999. Recipient Svc. award, Altrusa, 1979, Sunset PTA, 1989. Mem. N.Mex. Libr. Assn. (libr. devel. com., ednl. tech. roundtable vice chair 1991, chair elect 1992, co-chair state conv. local arrangements 1990-91, 2d v.p. 1993-94, 1st v.p. 1994-95, pres. 1995-96, Libr. Leadership award 2001), N.Mex. Acad. and Rsch. Librs. (vice chair 1992, pres. 1993), N.Mex. Taskforce for Sch. Librs., Kiwanis (bd. dirs. 1990-92). Avocations: travel, stained glass, music, hiking. Office: Bovina ISD PO Box 70 Bovina TX 79009

AYERS, KRIS, secondary school educator; d. Rolland and Mary Higgins. Bachelor's, Ft. Lervis, 1987; MA, U. N.C., 1993. Tchr. phys. edn./health Delta Middle Sch., Colo., 1988—90; tchr. spl. edn. Weld Dist. #6, Greeley, Colo., 1990—92, tchr. spl. edn. HS, 1992—96; tchr. phys. edn./health Thompson Valley HS, Loveland, Colo., 1996—. Mem.: AHPERD, COAHPERD. Office: Thompson HS 1669 Eagle Dr Loveland CO 80537 Business E-Mail: ayersk@thompson.k12.co.us.

AYERS, MARY ALICE, writer, English educator; b. N.Y.C. BA, Hunter Coll.; MEd, Ga. State U. Prof. English Fla. Internat. U., Miami. Author: (short story in anthology) The Infinite Dark (pub. reading Miami-Dade County Librs.); contbr. to numerous literary magazines including Paris Review, Partisan Review; featured on NPR's Sound of Writing, Cover to Cover: The Voice of Poetry. Grantee Ingram Merril Found.; fellow Millay Colony for the Arts, N.Y.; recipient PEN Syndicated Fiction award (2), Am. Short Fiction award; nominee Pushcart Prize. Phi Beta Kappa. Office: Florida Internat U Dm453 Univ Park Miami FL 33199-0001

AYLESWORTH, JULIE ANN, writer, personal care professional; b. Cin., Apr. 11, 1953; d. Robert Dean and Evelyn Jane (Francis) A. BA in Drama with honors, Vassar Coll., Poughkeepsie, N.Y., 1975. Adminstrv. asst. Gruber Realty Co., Cin., 1986-87, Gruber Design & Mktg., Cin., 1987-89. Radio broadcaster Radio Reading Svcs., Cin., 1980-81; job counselor Joy Ctr., Cin., 1980-81; consumer activist Marlowe House, Cin., 1984-86; dramatic coach Marlowe House, Cin., 1984-86; mem. Nightwriters, Highland Heights, Ky., 1986-88. Actress play Man of La Mancha, 1969; writer, dir. one-woman show Artist of the Woman as A Young Portrait, 1974; songwriter Color me Country, 2001, Land That I Love, 2002, Ain't No Place Like Cincinnati, 2001, There is a Light, 2002; contbr. articles to profl. jour. Telephone vol. Telecare, Cin., 1990; sch. crossing guard Cin. Police, 1978-80; founder, owner Jesus' Art House, 1986—; vol. Warmup America! Found. Recipient Recognition award Joy Ctr., Cin., 1981, Merit award Radio Reading Svcs., Cin., 1981, Golden Poet awards World of Poetry, Editors Choice Award, Internat., Soc. of Poets, 1990-2002, Mem. Willing, Enabled Consumers are Needed (pres. 1984-86), Acad. Am. Poets. Republican. Avocations: cello, horticulture, zoological, reading, investing. Home and Office: 1673 Cedar Ave #409 Cincinnati OH 45224

AYOTTE, KELLY A., state attorney general; b. Nashua, NH, 1968; BA in Polit. Sci. with honors, Pa. State U., 1990; JD, Villanova U., 1993. Bar: N.H., Maine. Law clerk for Hon. Sherman Horton, N.H. Supreme Ct., 1993—94; litigator McLane, Graf, Raulerson and Middleton, Nashua, NH, 1994—98; asst. atty. gen., homicide unit State of N.H., 1998—2000, sr. asst. atty. gen., chief, homicide unit, 2000—02, legal counsel to gov., 2003, dep. atty. gen., 2003—04, atty. gen., 2004—. Named among 11 Remarkable Women in NH, NH Mag.; recipient Kirby award, Bar Found., 2004. Republican. Office: Office of Atty General State House Annex 33 Capitol St Concord NH 03301-6397*

AYRES, GWYNETH CAROL, elementary school educator; d. Ralph Andrew and Freeda Rae Batson; children: James Allen, David Lee. AA, Seminole Jr. Coll., Okla., 1987; BS, Ctrl. State U., Edmond, Okla., 1989; MEd, U. Ctrl. Okla., Edmond, 1993. Cert. tchr. Okla. State Dept. Edn., 2004. Tchr. Gypsy Pub. Sch., Okla., 1989—92, Mason Pub. Schs., Okemah, Okla., 1992—94; libr. dir. Seminole Pub. Libr., Okla., 1995—2001; tchr./fed. programs coord. Schulter Pub. Schs., Okla., 2001—. Developer born to read program Seminole Pub. Libr., 1991—2001, developer of family literacy program, 1999—2001; mem. Summer Reading Program Com., Okemah, 2000—04; chairperson gifted and talented com. Schulter Pub. Schs., 2001—, chairperson Indian edn. com., 2001—, dist. coord. accelrated reader program, 2002—, chairperson, 2002—, mem. clep and curriculum com., 2004—, grant coord., 2004—05, mem. staff devel. com., 2004—; presenter edn. fair Okla. Edn. Assn., Tulsa, 2003; mem. Accelrated Reader Com. and Reading Sufficiency Com., Schulter, 2004—; master tchr. Okla. State Dept. Edn., Okla. City, 2005—06. Contbr. (curriculum devel.) Four Circles of Learning, Okla. State Dept. Edn.; contbr. curriculum materials. Spkr. local svc. orgns., Seminole, Okla., 1995—2001; presenter of over twenty-five tng. seminars on internet usage to both children and adults Seminole Pub. Libr., 1995—2001; developer vacation bible sch. curriculum United Pentecostal Ch., Okemah, Okla., 2000—03. Named Hon. mem., Schulter Pub. Schs. Thepian Soc., 2005; recipient Jr. Coll. Transfer Full-tuition scholarship, Ctrl. State U., 1987, Regent's Academic Full Tuition scholarship, 1987, UCO Student Tchg.

scholarship, 1989, Sinclair Maxwell Jr. Coll. scholarship, Seminole Jr. Coll., 1987, Edn. Fair award, Okla. Edn. Assn., 2004. Mem.: Okla. Edn. Assn. (assoc.). United Pentecostal Church. Avocations: camping, piano, travel, needlework. Office: Schulter Public Schs PO Box 203 Schulter OK 74460 Office Phone: 918-652-8200. Business E-Mail: gcayres@schulter.k12.ok.us.

AYRES, JANICE RUTH, social services administrator; b. Idaho Falls, Idaho, Jan. 23, 1930; d. Low Ray and Frances Mae (Salem) Mason; m. Thomas Woodrow Ayres, Nov. 27, 1953 (dec. 1966); 1 child, Thomas Woodrow Jr. (dec.). MBA, U. So. Calif., 1952, M in Mass Comms., 1953. Asst. mktg. dir. Disneyland, Inc., Anaheim, Calif., 1954-59; gen. mgr. Tamasha Town & Country Club, Anaheim, Calif., 1959-65; dir. mktg. Am. Heart Assn., Santa Ana, Calif., 1966-69; state exec. dir. Nev. Assn. Mental Health, Las Vegas, 1969-71; exec. dir. Clark Co. Easter Seal Treatment Ctr., Las Vegas, 1971-73; mktg. dir., fin devel. officer So. Nev. Drug Abuse Coun., Las Vegas, 1973-74; exec. dir. Nev. Assn. Retarded Citizens, Las Vegas, 1974-75; assoc., cons. Don Luke & Assocs., Phoenix, 1976-77; program dir. Inter-Tribal Coun. Nev., Reno, 1977-79; exec. dir. Ret. Sr. Vol. Program, Carson City, Nev., 1979—. Chair sr. citizen summit State of Nev., 1996; apptd. by Gov. Guinn, Nev. Commn. Aging, 2001; presenter in field; apptd. del. by Gov. of Nev. White House Conf. on Aging, 2005. Del. White Ho. Conf. on Aging, 2005; bd. suprs. Carson City, Nev., 1992—; obligation bond com., legis. chair; commr. Carson City Parks and Recreation, 1993—; bd. dirs. Nev. Dept. Transp., 1993; active No. Corp. for Nat. and Cmty. Svc. by Gov., 1994, V&TRR Commn., 1993, re-appointed by Gov., 2005—, chair, 1995, vice-chair, chair pub. rels. com., bd. dirs. Hist. V&TRR Bd.; chair PR Cmty./V&RR Commn. Nev. Home Health Assn.; appointed liaison Carson City Sr. Citizens Bd., 1995; chair summit Rural Nev. Sr. Citizens, Carson City; pres. No. Nev. R.R. Found., 1996—; chair Tri-Co-R.R. Commn., 1995, Gov.'s Nev. Commn. for Corp. in Nat. and Cmty. Svc., 1997—, pres., 1998, Carson City Pub. Transp. Commn., 1998—; Carson City Commn. for Clean Groundwater Act, 1998—; chairperson Celebrate Svc. Conf. Americore, 2000; appointed by Gov. of Nev. Commn. on Aging, 2001—; appointed by Nev. Gov. New Nev. Commn. to Restructure the Historic V&T R.R., 2002—; mem. Nev. Commn. on Aging, 2001—; apptd. rep. of gov. to Nev. Commn. Recruitment V&T RR, 2002; apptd. by Nev. Treas. Brian Krolicki Women's Commn. Fin., 2003—; re-appointed to commn. by Gov. Nev. Commn. for Nat. and Cmty. Svc., 2005—; apptd. del. to White House Conf. on Aging Nev. Gov., 2005. Named Woman of Distinction, Soroptimist Club, 1988, Outstanding Dir. of Excellence, Gov. State of Nev., 1989, Outstanding Nev. Women's Role Model, Nev. A.G., 1996, Woman of Distinction, Carson Valley Optimist, 2002, Nev.'s Outstanding Older Worker for Experience-Works, 2002, Oldest CEO in Nev., 2002, Outstanding Nev. Pvt. Citizen, Nev. Gov. Kenny Guinn, 2003, Outstanding Dir., Vol. Action Ctr., J.C. Penney Co., invitee to White Ho. for outstanding contbns. to Am.; named to White House Conf. on Aging as Gov. del., 2005; recipient Gold award, Western Fairs Assn., 2000, Woman of Distinction award, Soroptimist, 2003, Carson City Optimist, 2003, Nat. Optimist Conv., Reno, Nev., 2003, Outstanding Svc. to Seniors Blue Star award, Sanford Ctr. on Aging, 2004, Outstanding Contbn. to Success of Women in Bus., Carson Valley Sorpotomists. Mem.: AAUW, Nat. Assn. Ret. and Sr. Vol. Dirs., Inc. (pres. 2003, nat. pres. 2003—), Internat. Assn. Bus. Commentators, No. Nev. Railroad Found. (pres. 1996—, 2005—08), Am. Soc. Assn. Execs., Nev. Assn. Transit Svcs. (bd. dirs., legis. chmn.), Nev. Fair and Rodeo Assn. (pres.), Nat. Soc. Fund Raising Execs., Women in Radio and TV, Pub. Rels. Soc. Am. (chpt. pres., Outstanding 25 Yr. Svc. award 2004), Internat. Platform Assn., Am. Mktg. Assn. (bd. dirs. 1999—), Am. Mgmt. Assn. (bd. dirs.), Nat. Women's Polit. Caucus, Nev. Women's Polit. Caucus. Office: 444 E William St Ste 1 Carson City NV 89701 Office Phone: 775-687-4680 ext. 2. Business E-Mail: branded@rsvp.carson-city.nv.us.

AYRES, MARGARET M., lawyer; b. 1943; BA, Smith Coll., 1965; JD, Yale U., 1972. Assoc. Hogan & Hartson, Washington, 1972—77; chief counsel, Urban Mass Transp. Adminstrn. US Dept. Transp., Washington, 1977—81; ptnr. Davis Polk & Wardwell, Washington, 1982—89, counsel, Corp. Dept., 1989—. Office: Davis Polk & Wardwell 1300 Eye St NW Washington DC 20005 Office Phone: 202-962-7142. Office Fax: 212-450-6540. E-mail: margaret.ayres@dpw.com.

AYRES, MARY ELLEN, federal official; b. Spokane, Wash., June 23, 1924; d. Frank H. and Marion (Kellogg) A. Student, U. Wash., 1942-43; BA, Stanford U., 1946; postgrad., Am. U., 1960. With Henry von Morpurgo, Advt., 1946-47; reporter Wenatchee Daily World, Wash., 1947-50, Washington Post, 1951-52; with U.S. Fgn. Service, Dept. State, 1950-51; mem. editorial staff Changing Times, 1952-61; editor Family Guide, Kiplinger Washington Editors, 1958-61, Bur. Labor Stats., Manpower Adminstrn., U.S. Dept. Labor, 1962-67; pub. info. specialist Bur. Indian Affairs, U.S. Dept. Interior, 1967-75; writer-editor Bur. Labor Stats., 1975—. Tchr. newsletter class Dept. Agriculture Grad. Sch., 1975-89, editing style and technique class, 1987-89; past treas. Govt. Info. Orgn. Mem. publicity com. Nat. Capitol YWCA, 1982-83; dir. Wenatchee High Sch. Scholarship Found., 1988-95. Mem. Nat. Assn. Govt. Communicators (founding treas., dir. 1975-80, 89-91, chmn. Blue Pencil Contest 1987, nat. capital chpt. treas. 1989), Nat. Press Club (Washington), Washington Athletic Club (Seattle), Am. News Women's Club, Stanford U. Alumnae Assn., Kappa Kappa Gamma. Episcopalian. Home: 2400 Virginia Ave NW Apt C802 Washington DC 20037-2657 Office: Bur Labor Stats 2 Massachusetts Ave NE Washington DC 20212-0022 Office Phone: 202-691-5856. Office Fax: 202-691-7890. Business E-Mail: ayres_m@bls.gov.

AZAD, SUSAN STOTT, lawyer; BS, Oreg. State U., 1984; JD, UCLA, 1989. Bar: Calif. 1989. With Latham & Watkins, L.A., 1989—, ptnr., 1997—. Mem. assocs. com. Latham & Watkins, L.A., 1992—94, fin. com., 1995—97, ethics com., 2001—. Mem.: ABA, LA County Bar Assn. (litigation sect., former mem. jud. election evaluations com., former mem. Calif. and state bar ct. rules com.). Office: Latham and Watkins LLP 633 W Fifth St Ste 4000 Los Angeles CA 90071 Office Phone: 213-485-1234. Business E-Mail: susan.azad@lw.com.

AZARIAN, ANAIT, psychologist, researcher; b. Kadiaran, Armenia, Aug. 15, 1948; d. Gourgen Azarian and Shoushan Ovsepian; m. Vitali Skriptchenko, Mar. 3, 1973; children: Gary Grigorian, Sonia Grigorian. BS in Engrng., Polytech. Inst., Armenia, 1971; MA in Psychology, Moscow U., 1982, PhD in Psychology, 1989. Asst. prof. Coll. Edn., Kirovakan, Armenia, 1982—91; clin. psychologist Bradley Hosp., Providence, 1994—2004, pvt. practice, Providence, 2004—. Founder, dir. Child Psychotherapy Ctr., Armenia, 1989—91; vis. prof. Brown U., Providence, 1992—; cons. R.I. Family Ct., Providence, 1994—; witness expert in traumatic stress, R.I., N.J., 1994—. Editor: Psychological Treatment of Children and Adolescents, 1990. Grantee, Brown U., 1992—95. Mem.: Am. Acad. Experts in Traumatic Stress. Office: 1 Richmond Sq Ste 102K Providence RI 02906 Office Phone: 401-751-3281. E-mail: anait@cox.net.

AZARIAN, MARY, illustrator; b. Washington, D.C., Dec. 8, 1940; d. L. G. and Eleanor Schneider; m. Tomas Azarian, July 24, 1962; 3 children. BA, Smith Coll., 1963. Elementary sch. teacher, Walden, Vt., 1963—67; freelance printmaker and illustrator, 1967—; founder Farmhouse Press, 1969—. One-woman shows include Lyndon State Coll., U. Conn., Chandler Gallery, Northfield, Vt., Beaver Coll. in the Schlesinger Libr., Radcliffe Inst. Advanced Study, Harvard U., Brown U., Lyman Allyn Art Gallery, Conn., Brattleboro Mus., Vt., Helen Day Art Ctr., Snowflake Bentley, 1999 (Caldecott award, 1999), The Wild Flavor, 1973, The Art of Living and Other Stories, 1981, The Caprilands Kitchen Book, 1981, The Magic Dulcimer, 1983, The Man Who Lived Alone, 1984, The Wildman: A Short Fable, 1985, Country Kitchens Remembered, 1986, Stubbornness, 1986, Talk Less and Say More, 1986, Gridley Firing, 1987, Caring for Your Own Dead, 1987, As Sweet as Apple Cider, 1988, Sea Gifts, 1989, Not By Bread Alone, 1990, Salty Wisdom, 1990, Barley Break, 1992, Where the Deer Were, 1994, A Symphony for the Sheep, 1996, Barn Cat: A Counting Book, 1998, Faraway Summer, 1998, The Four Seasons of Mary Azerian, 2000, Visits with the Amish, 2000, The Race of the Birkebeiners: A True Story, 2001, When the Moon Is Full, 2001, Louisa May and Mr. Thoreau's Flute, 2002, From Dawn till Dusk, 2002, A Christmas Like Helen's, 2004; author, illustrator: Farmer's Alphabet, 1981, From Barley to Beer: A Traditional English Ballad, 1982 (Parent's Choice award for illustration, 1983), A Gardener's Alphabet, 2000.

AZARPAY, GUITTY, education educator; b. Teheran, Iran, Oct. 28, 1939; came to U.S., 1953; d. Rahim and Shekar (Dowlatshahi) A.; m. Ralph Werner Alexander, Dec. 18, 1963 (dec. 1998); 1 child, Vesa Alexander. PhD, U. Calif., Berkeley, 1964. Prof. U. Calif., Berkeley, 1963-94, U. Calif. Grad. Sch., Berkeley, 1994—. Author: Urartian Art & Artifacts, 1969, Sogdian Painting, 1981, Sasanian Sealstone: an Electronic Cataloging Project,2002; mem. editl. bd. Enclopaedia Iranica, 1994—. Mem. AIA, Am. Oriental Soc., Bulletin Asia Inst. Home: PO Box 908 Mill Valley CA 94942-0908 Office: Univ Calif Near Ea Studies Berkeley CA 94720-0001 E-mail: azarpay@comcast.net.

AZCUENAGA, MARY LAURIE, government official; b. Council, Idaho, July 25, 1945; AB, Stanford U., 1967; JD, U. Chgo., 1973. Bar: Dist. of Columbia, Calif., U.S. Supreme Ct. Atty. FTC, Washington, 1973-75, asst. to gen. counsel, 1975-76; staff atty. San Francisco regional office, 1977-80, asst. regional dir., 1980-81, asst. to exec. dir., 1981-82; litigation atty. Office of Gen. Counsel, 1982, asst. gen. counsel for legal counsel, 1983-84, commr. Washington, 1984-98; atty., shareholder Heller, Ehrman, White, & McAuliffe LLP, 1998—. Mem. Adminstrv. Conf. of the U.S., 1990-95. Trustee Food and Drug Law Inst., 1990-97, Advisory Bd. FDLI, 1997-98, Natl. Advertising Review Bd., 1998—, ERA Review Bd., 1998—. Office: 166 K St NW Ste 300 Washington DC 20006-1228

AZICRI, NICOLETTE MALY, art educator, artist; b. Erie, Pa., Dec. 10, 1950; d. Nicholas and Sophie Agnes (Maciulewicz) Maly; m. Max Azicri, Apr. 14, 1973; children: David, Danielle (twins). BS in Edn., Edinboro U., 1971, BFA in Ceramics, 1985, MA in Painting and Ceramics, 1988; MA in Counseling, Gannon U., 1976. Cert. elem. edn., spl. edn., elem. counseling. Tchr. spl. edn. and grades K-12 Sch. Dist. of City of Erie, 1972-95. Faculty Pa. State, Erie, Behrend, 1996. Exhibited in group shows at Three Rivers Art Festival, Pitts., 1990, 93, 95 (award), 2002, Westmoreland C.C., Youngwood, Pa., 1990, 93, 95, 97, 99, Carnegie Art Mus., Pitts., 1993, Am. Facism Nat. Exhbn., Artsquad Contemporary Gallery, Easton, Pa., 1993, Art Assn. Harrisburg, Pa., 1994, 98, 2004, Resurgam Nat. Exhbn., Resurgam Gallery, Balt., 1994, Nat. Art League's Art Exhbn., Douglaston-N.Y.C., 1994, Mari Galleries, N.Y.C., 1994, Nicolet Coll. Gallery, Rhineland, Wis., 1995 (award), Antiquarium Gallery, Omaha, 1995-96, Coastal Ctr. for the Arts, St. Simon Island, Ga., 1994, 96 (award), 98, Art Ctr. of No. N.J., New Milford, 1995, Greater Midwest Internat. Ctrl. Mo. State U. Art Ctr. Gallery, 1995 (award), An Art Place Inc. Gallery, Chgo., 1995, Impact Women's Gallery, Buffalo, 1996, State of Arts Gallery, Itchaca, N.Y., 1996, Navarro Coun. Arts, 1998 (award), Hoyt Inst. Fine Arts, 1997 (award), Dayspring Dance and Workshop Arts Ctr., L.I., N.Y., 1997, Warehouse Living Arts Ctr., Corsicana, Tex., 1997 (award), Swann Gallery, Detroit, 1997, The Art Network Gallery, Lndenhurst, N.Y., 1997, Tonowandas (N.Y.) Coun. on the Arts, 1997, Galex 37 Nat. Juried Exhibition Galesburg (Ill.) Civic Arts Ctr., 2003, 9th Annual Nat. Juried Show Prallville Mills, Artsbridge Gallery, Lambertsville, N.J., 2003, The Artful Women Nat. Juried Exhbn. Binney & Smith Gallery, Bethlehem, Pa., 2003, Prince St. Gallery, N.Y.C., 2004, NW Pa. Art Assn., 2004, Art of the State Juried Exhbn., Harrisburg, 2005, Wish you Were Here, AIR Gallery, 2005, others. Vol. Gertrude Barber Ctr., Erie, 1970, Hospitality House for Women, Erie, 1973-76, Spl. Olympics, Erie, 1973-76, 1st Night Erie Com., 1991-97, AAUW Holly Trail, Erie, 1994-96. Mem. AAUW, Erie Art Mus., Meadville Coun. of the Arts, Chautuaqua Art Assn., Nothwest Pa. Artists Assn. (sec. 1999-2006). Avocations: biking, reading, cooking. Home: 4000 Ridgewood Dr Erie PA 16506-4062 Office Phone: 814-835-3780. E-mail: nickieazicri@msn.com.

AZOCAR, FRANCISCA, clinical psychologist; b. Santiago, Chile, Jan. 24, 1962; d. Hernan Azocar and Lupe Jimeno; m. Fernando Diaz-Valdes, Oct. 28, 1983; children: Martin, Rodrigo, Gabriela. BA, U. Calif., Berkeley, 1985, MA, 1988, PhD, 1993. Clin. svcs. rsch. fellow U. Calif., San Francisco, 1993-95, asst. clin. prof., 1995-99; rsch. scientist United Behavioral Health, San Francisco, 1999—. Mem. APA, APHA. Avocation: skiing.

AZPEITIA, LYNNE MARIE, psychotherapist, educator, trainer, consultant; b. San Pedro, Calif., Mar. 10, 1951; d. Harlan Raymond and Virginia Grace (Dirocco) A.; m. Christopher Joseph Murphy, Mar. 24, 1979 (div. Sept. 1988); children: Jonathan Christopher, Matthew Joseph AA, Long Beach City Coll., 1971; BA, U. Calif., Santa Barbara, 1973; MA, Azusa Pacific Coll., 1978. Lic. marriage and family therapist, Calif. Grad. prof., clin. supr. and adminstr. Calif. Family Study Ctr., North Hollywood, Calif., 1979—94; grad. prof., adj. faculty Nat. U., L.A., 1994—96; pvt. practice psychotherapy, cons., coach, trainer Sherman Oaks, 1979—2002, Santa Monica, Calif., 2002—06. Bd. dirs. Va. Satir's Avanta Network, Palo Alto, Calif., 1986-89, 93-94, mem. faculty; bd. dirs. Va. Satir Family Camp, Big Sur, Calif., 1979-99, Morbrook Inst., 2005-; grad. prof., adj. faculty Phillips Grad. Inst., 1995-96, Pepperdine U., 2003 Mem. Am. Assn. Marriage and Family Therapy (approved supr.), Calif. Assn. Marriage and Family Therapists, Am. Family Therapy Assn., Calif. Entrepreneur Women, Calif. Women Bus. New Entrepreneurs Owners Democrat. Roman Catholic.

AZRACK, JOAN M., judge; b. NYC, Aug. 13, 1951; m. William G. Ballaine; two children. BS, Rutgers U., 1974; JD, NY Law Sch., 1979. Served in honors program, criminal div. U.S. Dept. of Justice, 1979-81; asst. U.S. atty. U.S. Attorney's Office (N.Y. ea. dist.), 1982-90; magistrate judge U.S. Dist. Ct. (N.Y. ea. dist.), 2nd circuit, Brooklyn, 1991—. Visiting instr. Nat. Inst. Trial Advocacy Harvard Law Sch. Office: US District Court 225 Cadman Plz E Rm 333 Brooklyn NY 11201-1818

AZRIELANT, AYA, jewelry manufacturing executive; b. Israel; Came to U.S. 1981. m. Ofer Azrielant; 3 children. BA in Fine Arts and Lit., Haifa U.; postgrad. in film-making, London. Designer, owner Aya Azrielant, N.Y.C. Avocation: collector of modern art. Office: Andin International Inc 609 Greenwich St New York NY 10014-3683 Fax: 212-886-6006.

AZUA, MARIA, computer company executive, computer engineer; b. Cuba; m. Ben Himmel. B magna cum laude, U. PR, 1982; MS in Computer Sci., U. Miami; MBA, Fla. Atlantic U. Cert. IT Architect IBM, Project Mgr. IBM. With Gould Electronics, Fla., Data Gen., NC; joined IBM, 1989, SWG fin. sector and industry standards architect mgr., disting. engr., 2004. Mem. La Red Familiar. Named to IBM Acad. Tech., 2002, WITI Hall of Fame, Women in Tech. Internat., 2006; recipient Technical Innovation award, Women of Color Tech. Conf., 2003. Achievements include over 30 patents. Office: IBM 1 New Orchard Rd Armonk NY 10504*

AZZARA, CANDICE, actress; b. Bklyn., May 18, 1945; d. Samuel and Josephine (Bravo) A. Studies with Gene Frankel, Hugh Whitfield, Lee Strasberg, David Craig, Neyneen Pires, Nora Dunfee, Dolores Bagley. Actor: (films) Hail, 1971, They Might Be Giants, 1971, Who is Harry Kellerman and Why Is He Saying Those Terrible Things About Me?, 1971, Made for Each Other, 1971, Hearts of the West, 1975, House Calls, 1978, Fatso, 1980, Easy Money, 1983, Don' Time on Planet Earth, 1988, Unstrung Heroes, 1995, Land of the Free, 1998, The Hungry Bachelors Club, 1999, Catch Me If You Can, 2002, Ocean's Twelve, 2004, In Her Shoes, 2005; (TV series) Soap, 1979, Who's the Boss, 1992, Caroline in the City, 1996—99; (TV films) Million Dollar Infield, 1982, Divorce Wars: A Love Story, 1982, Dance 'Til Dawn, 1988. Office: care The Gersh Agy 222 N Canon Dr Beverly Hills CA 90210-5302

AZZARONE, CAROL ANN, marketing executive; b. Jersey City, Aug. 1, 1946; d. Paul Buglione and Catherine (DellaFave) LiCalsi; m. Dominick L. Azzarone, May 13, 1967 (div. 1989); children: Anthony Paul, Kathryn Ann. AA, Bergen C.C., 1982; BA, Ramapo Coll., 1984. Editl. asst. McGraw-Hill, Inc., N.Y.C., 1964-69; real estate agt. Auburn Realty, Inc., Bergenfield, N.J., 1975-80, Weichert Realty, Morris Plains, N.J., 1975—; pub. rels. coord. Ridgefield (N.J.) Bd. Edn., 1982-84; mktg. dir. Spa Lady Corp., Fairfax, Va., 1984-86, Newson Fitness, Morristown, N.J., 1986-88; creative dir. Publ. Corp., Morristown, 1988-90; advt. dir. Ronton Advt., Union, N.J., 1990-98; mktg. v.p. Dynamic Tech. Group, Inc., Parsippany, N.J., 1998—. Adv. bd. N.J. Tech. Coun., 2001—03; cons. in field; spkr. in field. Editor (newsletters) Ridgefield Sch. News, 1982-84, Cliffside Park Sch. News, 1984-85, The Grapevine, 1985-86. Mem. adv. bd. N.J. Tech. Coun. N.J. Bell scholar N.J. Bell Corp., 1980, Bergen Community Coll. Alumni scholar, 1981. Mem. NOW, NAFE (First Place award of excellence 1996, Jersey award), Advt./Pub. Rels. Assn., NJ Advt. Club, Phi Theta Kappa. Democrat. Roman Catholic. Avocations: cross country skiing, horseback riding, biking, reading. Office: Dynamic Tech Group Inc 1055 Parsippany Blvd Parsippany NJ 07054-1230

AZZI, JENNIFER L., professional basketball player; b. Oak Ridge, Tenn., Aug. 31, 1968; d. James and Donna Azzi. Diploma, Stanford U., 1990. Basketball player Arvika Basket, Sweden, 1995—96, Viterbo, Italy, Orchies, France, San Jose Lasers, 1996—99, Salt Lake City Starzz, 1999—2002, San Antonio Stars, 2003—. Mem. Nat. Women's Basketball Team. Named Al-Pac 10 1st team, 1988, 1989, 1990, MVP, NCAA Final Four, 1990, NCAA West Region, 1990, Naismith Nat. Player Yr., 1990; recipient gold medal, Goodwill Games, 1994, World Championship Qualifying team, 1993, U.S. Olympic Festival West Team, 1987, 2 gold medals, World Championship and Goodwill Games, 1990, bronze medal, Pan Am. Games, 1991, World Championship team, 1994, Wade Trophy, 1990, Kodak All-Am. 1st team, 1989, 1990, gold medal, U.S. Olympic Team, 1996. Office: San Antonio Silver Stars One SBC Ctr San Antonio TX 78219

BAADH, VALERIE, choreographer, movement educator, theater producer, production designer; b. Burbank, Calif., Sept. 16, 1952; d. Uffe and Shirley (Goldberg) Baadh; m. Michael Earl Garrett, May 20, 1979; 1 child, John David Garrett; 1 child, Rose Kaiulani Garrett. BFA, Calif. Inst. Arts, 1973; MM, Spatial Dynamics Inst., 1996. Choreographer Pacific Ballet, 1975—77, Dancers' Group, San Francisco, 1981—83; ind. choreographer, 1984—. Dir. Kadeka Dances for Kids, San Francisco, 1982—84, Dancers Group/Footwork, 1983; faculty mem. San Francisco Waldorf Sch., 1990—; dir. San Francisco Movement Studio, 2005—; trustee Spatial Studies Inst., N.Y.C., 1994; internat. trainer OlymPeace Festivals, Olympia, Greece, 2001, Delphi, Greece, 03, Quito, Ecuador, 04. Choreographer Places, 1976, Half Past Eight, 1981, White Dance, 1982, Spy in the House of Love, 1983, Mother Goose Suite, 1984, Threefold Suite, 1993, Madeleine's Duet, 1995, Lambarena, 1996, with clarinetist Dov Goldberg Istanbul Late Night, San Francisco, 2003; prodr.: Bay Area Theatre Week, 1986, Event of the Year, 1986, Nina Watt Solos, 1986, Rosa Montoya Bailes Flamencos, 1987; prodn. designer: An Evening of Comedy and Dance with Robin Williams and Friends, 1985; author: The Autumn Adventure of Uffe the Gnome, 1998, The Valentines Adventure of Uffe the Gnome, 2000, Dance As Movement History, 2001. Home: 120 Solano St Brisbane CA 94005-1333 Office Phone: 415-431-2736. E-mail: vbaadh@earthlink.net.

BAARS, ELLA JANE, art educator; b. Paris, Tenn., Apr. 19, 1952; d. Elroy Vinson Griffin and Mattie Lou Futrell; m. Glenn George Baars, Aug. 14, 1971; children: Heather Rose, Amy Elizabeth. BA in Art, Maryville U., 1976; degree in elem. edn., Bethel U., 1994; M in Art Edn., Valdosta State U., 2002, degree in Ednl. Leadership, 2004. Nat. bd. cert. in art, cert. tchr. K-8 classroom, 9-12 math, preK-12 art Ga. Art instr. Henry County H.S., Paris, 1978—83; ednl. tng. specialist State of Tenn., Jackson, 1983—85; store owner Fashion Gallery, Paris, 1985—89; bus. mgr. Microtech, Paris, 1991—94; tchr. mid. grades Marion County Schs., Whitwell, Tenn., 1994—95; adult learning dir. Sequatchie County Schs., Dunlap, Tenn., 1995—96; art instr. Coffee County Schs., Douglas, Ga., 1996—. Cons., facilitator Tchr. Ctr., Kennesaw, Ga., 2001—; regional rep. Allstate Festival of Art and Design, 2002—; participant onlist profl. list Tchr. Leader Network, SC, 2003. Exhibitions include Ga. Art Edn. Assn., 1999, 2000, Wiregrass Exhibit, 2002, S.E. Ga. Regional Exhibit, 2002. Dir. Youth Art Camp, Douglas Pks. and Recreation, 1997—2002; mem. Page, Ga., 1999—; bd. dirs. Coffee Alliance for Arts, Douglas, 2000—. Mem.: Profl. Assn. Ga. Educators (facilitator 1999—), Wiregrass Art Assn. (orgnl. bd. 2002—), Ga. Art Edn. Assn. (state bd. mem. 2001—, treas., exec. bd., Youth Art Month 2002), Pi Lambda Theta. Baptist. Avocations: drawing, painting, crafts, camping, water sports. Office: Coffee H S 159 Trojan Way Douglas GA 31533 Business E-Mail: jbaars@coffeek12.ga.us.

BAAS, JACQUELYNN, museum director, art historian; b. Grand Rapids, Mich., Feb. 14, 1948; BA in History of Art, Mich. State U.; PhD in History of Art, U. Mich. Registrar U. Mich. Mus. Art, Ann Arbor, 1974-78, asst. dir., 1978-82; editor Bull. Museums of Art and Archaeology, U. Mich., 1976-82; chief curator Hood Mus. Art, Dartmouth Coll., Hanover, NH, 1982-84, dir., 1985-89, U. Calif. Berkeley Art Mus. and Pacific Film Archive, Calif., 1989-99, emeritus dir. Calif., 1999—; program dir. Awake: Art and Buddhism, 1999—2004. Collaborating curator 6th Gwangju Biennale, 2006; cons. in field; organizer exhbns.; ind. art historian; lectr. in field. Author: Smile of the Buddha: Eastern Philosophy and Western Art, 2005; co-editor: Buddha Mind in Contemporary Art, 2004; contbr. articles and essays to jours. and books. Mem. Coll. Art Assn. Am., Am. Assn. Mus. Address: PO Box 162 The Sea Ranch CA 95497-0162 Office Phone: 510-406-4455. Business E-Mail: jbaas@mcn.org.

BABA, MARIETTA LYNN, anthropologist, academic administrator; b. Flint, Mich., Nov. 9, 1949; d. David and Lillian (Joseph) Baba; m. David Smokler, Feb. 14, 1977 (div. 1982); 1 child, Alexia Nicole Baba Smokler. BA with highest distinction, Wayne State U., 1971, MA in Anthropology, 1973, PhD in Phys. Anthropology, 1975; MBA, Mich. State U., 1994. Asst. prof. sci. and tech. Wayne State U., Detroit, 1975-80, assoc. prof. anthropology, 1980-88, prof., 1988—, spl. asst. to pres., 1980-82, econ. devel. officer, 1982-83, asst. provost, 1983-85, assoc. provost, 1985-89, dir. internat. programs, interim assoc. dean Grad. Sch., 1988-89, assoc. dean Grad. Sch., 1989-90, acting chair dept. anthropology, 1990-92, chair dept. anthropology, 1996-2001; dean, prof. anthropology Mich. State U. Coll. Social Sci., East Lansing, 2001—. Program dir. transformations to quality orgns., dir. social, behav., and econ. scis. NSF, 1994—96; evolution rschr. Wayne State U., 1975—82; cons. GM Rsch. Labs., 1988—92, Electronic Data Sys., 1990—93, McKinsey Global Inst., 1991; rsch. contractor GM/EDS, 1990—94; vis. scholar IBM Almaden Svcs. Rsch. Inst., 2005; lectr. in field. Adv. for editor orgnl. anthropology: American Anthropologist, 1990-93; issued letters patent for method to map joint ventures and maps produced thereby; contbr. articles to profl. jours.; patentee in field. Mem. State Rsch. Fund Feasibility Rev. Panel, 1982—84; mem. adv. panel on tech. innovation and U.S. trade U.S. Congl. Office Tech. Assessment, 1990—91, mem. panel on electronic enterprise, 1993—94; active Leadership Detroit Class IV, 1982—83; dir. Mich. Tech. Coun. (S.E. divsn.), 1984—85. With USAF, 1992—94. Job Partnership Tng. Act grantee, 1981-90, NSF grantee, 1982, 84-85, 99-01. Fellow Am. Anthrop. Assn. (bd. dirs. 1986-88, exec. com. 1986-88, del. to Internat. Union Anthrop. and Ethnol. Sci. 1990-94, chair global commn. anthropology 1993-98), Nat. Assn. Practice Anthropology (pres. 1986-88), Soc. Applied Anthropology, Phi Beta Kappa, Sigma Xi (Morton Fried award 1991), Beta Gamma Sigma. Office Phone: 517-355-6675.

BABAO, DONNA MARIE, retired community health and psychiatric nurse, educator; b. St. Louis, May 6, 1945; d. Wilbert C. and Cecelia (Hogan) Bremer; widowed; 1 child, Tonya J. Diploma, Henry Ford Hosp. Sch. Nursing, Detroit, 1966; BSN, Calif. State U., Sacramento, 1978, MS in Nursing, 1990; MA in Edn., Calif. State U., Chico, 1985. Cert. pub. health nurse; master tchr. cert.; cert. clin. use of interactive guided imagery. Staff nurse U. Calif. Med. Ctr., San Francisco, 1968-72; staff and charge CCU nurse Children's Hosp. of San Francisco, 1972-78; pub. health nurse II Sutter-Yuba Health Dept., Yuba City, Calif., 1979-81; prof. nursing Yuba

Coll., Marysville, Calif., 1981-2000; psychiat. charge nurse Sunridge Hosp., Yuba City, 1994-96; RN case mgr. Home Health Care Mgmt. Inc., Chico, Calif., 2004—05; office nurse, case mgr. First Care Med. Clinic, Oregon House, 2005—. Mem. exam. item writing panel NCLEX-RN, 1998. Writer health column, 1986-90; chpt. to textbooks; reviewer nursing textbooks and jour. articles; contbr. articles to profl. jours. 1st lt. Nurse Corps, U.S. Army, 1966-68. Mem. Vietnam Vets. Am., Imagery Internat., Henry Ford Hosp. Alumni Assn. Nursing. Personal E-mail: dbabao@hotmail.com.

BABB, BARBARA A., lawyer, educator; BS with highest distinction, Pa. State Univ., 1973; MS, Cornell Univ., 1978, JD, 1981. Bar: N.Y., Md. Mng. atty. Legal Aid Bureau, Balt., 1986—89; assoc. prof. Univ. Balt., 1989—; dir. Ctr. for Families Children & the Courts, Univ. Balt. Vis. prof. George Washington Univ., 1999. Contbr. articles to prof. jour. Mem. Soros Grant Oversight Com.; mem. Chief Judge's ad hoc com. Family Divisions Md.; co-founder Domestic Law Pro Se Assistance Project, Md.; mem. bd. dir. People's Pro Bono Action Ctr., 1990—94; mem. editl. adv. bd. Family Ct. Rev., Md. Family Law Monthly. Recipient Regent's award, Univ. Sys. Md., Benjamin L. Cardin Disting. Svc. award, Md. Legal Svc. Corp. Mem.: Md. State Bar Assn., Assn. Am. Law Sch. (chair, Family & Juvenile Law sect.), ABA (mem. Adv. Council, standing com. substance abuse). Office: University of Baltimore School of Law 1420 N Charles St Baltimore MD 21201-5779

BABB, LISA MARIE, physical education educator; b. Abington, Pa., June 8, 1970; d. Janet Marie and Bruce James Lewis (Stepfather); 1 child, William Samuel. BS in Bible, Phila. Bible U., Langhorne, Pa., 1993; BS in Ednl., Phila. Bible U., 1999; MS in Edn., Wilkes U., Wilkes-Barre, Pa., 2005. Cert. Level II in edn. Pa., 2005. Tchr. Heartland Christian Sch., Sebring, Fla., 1993—94, Plumstead Christian Sch., Plumsteadville, Pa., 1994—98; head cross country coach CB East, Doylestown, Pa., 1995—99; health and phys. edn. tchr. Quakertown Cmty. Sch. Dist., Pa., 2003—. Youth leader First Bapt. Ch., Newtown, Pa., 1989—99. Recipient Randall C. Ostein award, PBU, 1993; scholar Leadership scholar, 1988—2003. Mem.: APHERD (assoc.), PSEA (assoc.). Democrat-Npl. Christian. Avocations: running, reading, photography, cooking. Office: Rishland Elementary School 500 Fariview Ave Quakertown PA 18951 Office Phone: 215-529-2492. Home Fax: 215-529-2451; Office Fax: 215-529-2451. Personal E-mail: lbabb@qcsd.org.

BABBITT, MARTHA E., science educator; d. Nelson Benjamin and Pearl Leone Betts; m. Donald W. Babbitt, July 8, 1995; children: Mary Ellen Crowley, William Christopher children: Kenneth Scott, Katharine Doreen Hubbard. MS in Edn., Western Conn. State U., Danbury, 1973; BS, N.Y. State U. Coll., Cortland, 1966. Tchr. Scotia-Glenville Ctrl. Schs., Scotia, NY, 1966—69, Newtown Mid. Sch., Conn., 1969—. Tchr. Amateur Radio Relay League Edn. and Tech. program, Newtown, Conn., 2003—. Sec. Northville Amateur Radio Assn., Candlewood Amateur Radio Assn.; mem. choir Salem Covenant Ch., Washington, Conn., 2001—, bldg. upkeep. Mem.: Candlewood Amateur Radio Assn. (sec.), Bridgewater Grange #153 (overseer 2001—). Home: P O Box 477 Bridgewater CT 06752 Office: Newtown Mid Sch 11 Queen St Newtown CT 06470 Office Phone: 203-426-7638. E-mail: babbittm@newtown.k12.ct.us.

BABBY, ELLEN REISMAN, educational association executive; b. Montreal, Que., Can., Oct. 21, 1950; came to U.S., 1973; d. Mark Reisman and Rose Gutwillig (Reisman); m. Lon Scott Babby, June 17, 1973; children—Kenneth Robert, Heather Lynn. Student, McGill U., 1968-70; BA, Beaver Coll., 1972; MA, Lehigh U., 1973, Yale U., 1976, M.Phil., 1977, PhD, 1980. Tchr. elem. schs. to coll. levels; instr. resident assoc. program Smithsonian Instn., Washington, 1980-82; exec. dir. Assn. for Can. Studies in U.S., Washington, 1982—91; with Nat. Fgn. Lang. Ctr. Johns Hopkins U., Washington, 1992-94; sr. dir. planning and devel. Nat. Assn. Fgn. Student Affairs Assn. Internat. Educators, Washington, 1995—97; v.p. Am. Coun. on Edn., Washington, 1997—. Author: Play of Language and Spectacle: A Structural Reading of Selected Texts by Gabrielle Roy, 1986. Contbr. articles on Quebec lit. to profl. jours. Mem. Am. Soc. Assn. Execs., Assn. Fund Raising Profls., Yale Alumni (del. 1989-92). Office: Am Coun On Edn One Dupont Cir #800 Washington DC 20036 Business E-Mail: ellen_babby@ace.nche.edu. E-mail: ellen@babby.com.

BABCOCK, BARBARA ALLEN, lawyer, educator; b. Washington, July 6, 1938; d. Henry Allen and Doris Lenore (Moses) Babcock; m. Thomas C. Grey, Aug. 19, 1979. BA, U. Pa., 1960; LLB, Yale U., 1963; LLD (hon.), U. San Diego, 1983, U Puget Sound, 1988. Bar: Md. 1963, DC 1964. Law clk. US Ct. Appeals, Washington, 1963; assoc. Edward Bennett Williams, 1964—66; staff atty. Legal Aid Agy., Washington, 1966—68; dir. Pub. Defender Svc. (formerly Legal Aid Agy.), 1968—72; asst. atty. gen. US Dept. Justice, 1977—79; assoc. prof. Stanford U., 1972—77, prof., 1977—, Ernest W. McFarland Prof. Law, 1986—97, Judge John Crown prof. law, 1997—2004, Judge John Crown prof. emerita, 2004—. Author (with others): Sex Discrimination and The Law: History, Theory and Practice, 1996; co-author (with Massaro): Civil Procedure: Problems and Cases, 2001; contbr. articles profl. jour. Recipient John Bingham Hurlbut Award for Excellence in Tchg., Stanford U., 1981, 1986, 1998, 2004, Margaret Brent Women Lawyers of Achievement Award, ABA, 1999. Democrat. Office: Stanford U Sch Law Stanford CA 94305

BABCOCK, CATHERINE EVANS, artist, educator; b. Rydal, Pa., Feb. 23, 1924; d. William Wayne and Marion (Waters) Babcock; m. Douglas Paul Torre, May 28, 1977; 2 stepchildren. Diploma, Sarah Lawrence Coll., Bronxville, N.Y., 1942; BFA, Temple U., Phila., 1944, MFA, 1948. Tchr. Rudolf Steiner Sch., 1949; tchr. jr. high sch. Stratford, Conn., 1959-63; tchr. elem. art Locust Valley Primary and Elem. Sch., 1963-68; instr. Darien Cmty. Ctr., 1975-81; art tchr. Rowayton Arts Ctr., Conn., 1979—, also bd. mem. Conn. Rec. sec. Portrait painter; artist to Sea Svc. (USCG and USN); equestrian artist Fairfield Hunt Club Show's Benefit Horse Show, 1993; watercolor tchr. Darien Cmty. Assn., 1993-94. Illustrator: Athenaeum, 1968 (Libr. award), Cutaneous Cryosurgery (Douglas Torre), 1978, rev., 1979; translator: Undertow (Finn Havrevold), 1968; painter, mural for Babcock Surg. Wards, Temple U. Hosp., Phila., 1944; designer display Cryosurgery of Skin Cancer, Dallas, 1979 (Gold award); art work appeared Carriage Barn Arts Ctr. Waveny Park, New Canaan, Conn., 2004; author: Biography in American References, 1989, Vikings Habitat, River of Dreams, 1994, Poetic Voices of America, 1995, Best Pastels, 1996, Chips and Chirps of Verses, 1998, Theatre of the Mind; exhbns. include internat. miniature shows Fine Arts Club, Washington, 1984, New Canaan Soc. for the Arts, 1988, 93, Grand Nat. Salmagundi Club, St. Petersburg Mus., Fla., Degas Pastel Soc., New Orleans, 1990-95, Mus. of Art, New Orleans, 1990, (portrait of husband) NY Hosp., Amb. Ernst Jaakson Mus. in Tallin, Estonia, 2001, Portrait of Sr. Ambassador of UN 1997, now in mus. in Estonia, 2001; Cert. of Excellence from Miniature Spc. of Washington for portrait of a firefighter, 2002; author numerous poems. Recipient awards including 10 USCG awards, Am. Acad. Dermatology Art Shows, 2 award, Rowayton Arts Ctr., 1993—94, Best Poems award, Nat. Libr. Poetry, 1996, Amherst Soc. award, Sparrowgrass Soc. award, cert. appreciation, USCG, 1971—82, Naval Sta. of N.Y., 1981, 1st prize, Rowayton Art Ctr., 2000, USCG award, Alexander Hamilton Custom House, 2000, Mdal of Honor, IBC Internat. Pro. Ctr., Cambridge, Eng., 2004, Internat. medal Honor, Cambridge, 2003, Albert Schweitzer Sci. and Peace medal, Spain, 2004. Mem. Internat. Soc. Poets (disting., life, Merit award 1997, medal 1997, 2 Silver cups 2003, 2004), Met. Portrait Inst., Conn. Pastel Soc., Pastel Soc. Am. (cert. of merit), USCG Art Program (ofcl. artist), COGAP Artist. Congregationalist. Home and Office: 122 Rowayton Ave Norwalk CT 06853-1409 Office Phone: 203-838-8082.

BABCOCK, HOPE SMITH, counselor, educator, program designer; b. Attleboro, Mass., July 3, 1941; d. Ezra Sheldon and Virginia (Fernandez) Smith; m. Robert C. Miner, June 20, 1959 (div. Oct. 1973); children: Eric, Robert, Jonathan, William, Garret; m. John A. Bucciarelli Jr., June 20, 1975 (dec. Aug. 1981); m. Richard B. Babcock, Nov. 8, 1997. AA, Brevard C.C., Cocoa, Fla.; BA, U. Ctrl. Fla., Orlando; MA, MHC, Webster U., Merritt Island, Fla. Cert. clin. hypnotherapist, pvt. practice forensic hypnotist; lic. real estate agt. Fla., domestic violence intervention specialist. Coord. suicide prevention jr./sr. high schs. Mental Health Assn., Rockledge, Fla., 1985-86; program designer, intervention arbitrator, instr. Juvenile Justice Ct. Alternatives, 1986-91; program designer, specialist, counselor, tchr. life skills Dept. Corrections-Probation/Parole Svcs., Cocoa, 1990—; counselor, tchr. Brevard County Jail, Sharpes, Fla., 1993-96; coord. parents, children, divorce Brevard County Ct. Sys., 1995-98; substance abuse counselor, life skills tchr. Alco-Rest Rehab. Ctr., Cocoa, 1997-2001. Cons., advisor Probationers Ednl. Growth Program, Cocoa, 1995—2001; bd. dirs. Turning Point Rehab. Ctr., Rockledge, 1996—98; domestic violence interventions svcs. facilitator Family Counseling Ctr., Rockledge, 2001. Program designer, implementer, arbitrator Juvenile Alternative Svcs. Program, 1985-91, Brevard County Mentoring Program, Merritt Island, 1999, Cmty. Crisis Response Team, 2002-. Named J.C. Penney's Cmty. Vol. of Yr., CCH Aux. Hosp., 1993; recipient numerous awards of recognition. Avocations: real estate investing, international travel, interior crafts and decorating. Home: 4560 Horse Shoe Bnd Merritt Island FL 32953-7900

BABCOCK, JANICE BEATRICE, health facility administrator; b. Milw., June 2, 1942; d. Delbert Martin and Constance Josephine (Dworschack) B. BS in Med. Tech., Marquette U., 1964; MA in Healthcare Mgmt. and Supervision, Cen. Mich. U., 1975. Registered med. technologist and microbiologist., clin. lab. scientist, epidemiologist; cert. bioanalytical lab. mgr. Intern St. Luke's Hosp., Milw., 1963-64; microbiologist St. Michael's Hosp., Milw., 1964-65; supr. clin. lab. svc. VA Regional Office, Milw., 1965-66; hosp. epidemiologist VA Ctr., Milw., 1966-74, supr. anaerobic microbiology and rsch. lab., 1974-78, adminstrv. officer, chief med. tech., 1978-83, quality assurance coord., 1983-86, asst. to chief of staff profl. svcs., 1986-92; coord. constrn. vet. affairs outpatient clinic VHA Med. Ctr., Milw., 1992-94; coord. Coop. Adminstrv. Support Unit (CASU) VHA Nat. Ctr. for Cost Containment, Milw., 1993-94; health sys. specialist managed care/primary care VHA Managed Care, Milw., 1994—. Lectr. Marquette U., 1966-86, U. Wis., 1966-86, Med. Coll. Wis., 1966-86. Contbr. numerous articles to profl. jours. Rec. sec. Wis. Svc. League, 1989-92, corr. sec., 1991. Recipient Wood VA Fed. Woman's award, 1975, Profl. Achievement award Lab. World jour., 1981, Disting. Alumni award Cen. Mich. U., 1986. Fellow Royal Soc. Health, Am. Acad. Med. Adminstrs. (Wis. state Dir. of the Yr. award 1989, Diplomate 1989, mem. editorial bd. Exec. jour. 1987—, editor 1994, regional dir. 1992—, mem. fed. exec. coun. 1994—); mem. Internat. Acad. Healthcare Mgmt., Internat. Soc. of Tech. Assessment in Health Care, Am. Soc. Microbiology, Am. Coll. Healthcare Execs., Am. Soc. Med. Tech. (Nat. Sci. Creativity award 1974, Nat. Microbiology Sci. Achievement award 1978, Mem. of the Yr. award 1979, Profl. Achievement Lectureship award 1981, French Lectureship award 1983), Assn. for Health Svcs. Rsch., Assn. Marquette U. Women (bd. dirs. 1987-93, v.p., sec.), Assn. Mil. Surgeons U.S. (lifetime), Nat. Assn. Med. Staff Svcs. (mem. editorial bd. Overview Jour. 1990-93), Wis. Assn. Med. Staff Svcs., Wis. Hosp. Assn., Fed. Execs. Assn. (Milw. 1983—), Alpha Mu Tau (pres. 1984-85), Alpha Delta Theta, Sigma Iota Epsilon, Alpha Delta Pi (Alumni Honor award 1979). Home: 6839 Blanchard St Milwaukee WI 53213-2853 Office: VHA Med Ctr 5000 W National Ave Milwaukee WI 53295-0001

BABCOCK, MARGUERITE LOCKWOOD, addictions treatment therapist, educator, writer; b. Jacksonville, Fla., Jan. 1, 1944; d. Allen Seaman and Emilie (Lockwood) B. BA in Art History, Am. U., 1965; M Counselor Edn., U. Pitts., 1982. Lic. profl. counselor, Pa.; cert. nat. cert. counselor, nat. cert. master's addiction counselor. Addictions therapist South Hills Health Sys., Pitts., 1979—81; addiction therapist, clin. supr., clin. dir. Alternatives Turtle Creek Mental Health/Mental Retardation/D&A Ctr., Pitts., 1981—86; addictions therapist, coord. Ligonier Valley Treatment Ctr., Stahlstown, Pa., 1986—88; addictions clin. supr., unit dir. Ctr. for Substance Abuse Mon-Yough, McKeesport, Pa., 1988—96; quality assurance Mon-Yough, McKeesport, 1996—97; clin. supr. Sojourner House, Pitts., 1997—2000; co-founder, addictions cons. consortium Outcomes Builders, 2000—. Adj. instr. in addictions courses Seton Hill Coll., Greensburg, Pa., 1989-91, C.C. Allegheny County, West Mifflin, Pa., 1989-91, Pa. State U., McKeesport, 1993-97; pvt. trainer, writer, Acme, Pa., 1985—; ind. info. profl. in addictions, 2003—. Co-author, co-editor: Challenging Codependency: Feminist Critiques, 1995; mem. editl. bd. Jour. Tchg. in Addictions, 2000—; contbr. articles to profl. jours. Fellow Andrew Mellon Found., 1966-68, NSF, 1967. Mem.: Alpha Lambda Delta, Phi Kappa Phi. Home and Office: 3533 Rt 130 Acme PA 15610-9712 Office Phone: 724-593-7139. E-mail: allele@lhtc.net.

BABCOCK-LUMISH, TERRY LYNNE, economic geographer; b. Miami, Fla., Mar. 30, 1976; d. Robert Malcolm and Saundra Ellen Lumish; m. Brian Christopher Babcock, June 20, 2001. BS, Carnegie Mellon U., Pitts., 1997; MPA, Ind. U., 1999; DPhil in Econ. Geography, U. Oxford, Eng., 2004. Lilly cmty. assistance fellow Gov. Frank O'Bannon's Children's Environ. Initiative, Inpls., 1997—99; presdl. mgmt. fellow Coun. of Econ. Advisers, US Dept. of Treasury, Washington, 1999—2001; rschr. To V.P. Al Gore, Alexandria, Va., 2001—02; assoc. fellow Rothermere Am. Inst., Oxford, 2002—; pres. Islay Consulting LLC, Tucson, 2005—; Wertheim fellow labor and work life program Harvard Law Sch. Bd. dir. Truman Scholars Assn., Washington, 2002—05, Renaissance House. Bd. dirs. Women's Found. So. Ariz., Women's Transition Project. Named one of 40 Under 40, Tucson Bus. Edge, 2006; recipient Sr. Leadership award, Carnegie Mellon U., 1997, Stephen Omer Lee award, 1996; Presdl. Mgmt. fellow, 1999—2001, Harry S Truman scholar, 1996, Clarendon scholar, U. Oxford/Oxford U. Press, 2002—05. Mem.: Ariz. List, Assn. Am. Geographers, Ariz. Town Hall, Nature Conservancy, Tucson Bus. Edge (named 40 under 40), Rotary Internat., Pi Alpha Alpha, Phi Kappa Phi, Phi Beta Kappa. Avocations: travel, hiking, gourmet cooking.

BABIN, SALLY WHEELER, secondary school educator, consultant; b. Charleston, W.Va., Apr. 8, 1934; d. Harold Winthrop and Fairy E. (Fuller) Wheeler; m. James L. Babin, Feb. 1, 1954; children: Harold Michael, Elizabeth Renee, Suzanne Louise, James Stuart, Anna Marie. BS in Applied Art, La. State U., 1956; cert. tchr. edn., McNeese State U., 1975. Cert. tchr., La. Rsch. asst. Levi Agr. Dept., Baton Rouge, 1956-57; substitute tchr. Calcasieu Parish Sch. Sys., Lake Charles, La., 1967-75, art specialist, 1976—, mem. staff devel. and insvc. tchr. tng. com., 1991—98; curriculum specialist Calcasieu Parish Sch., 1998—. Master tchr. Calcasieu Parish Art Camp, Lake Charles, 1981-92; computer cons., Lake Charles, 1991—; presenter spl. arts State Dept. Edn., Baton Rouge, 1977. Graphic artist environ. sci. text, 1985. Chairperson set, program design Calcasieu Cancer Soc., Lake Charles, 1987; art chairperson Lake Charles Meml. Hosp., 1988; mem. Nat. Mus. of Women in Arts, Washington, 1992—. Mem. Nat. Art Edn. Assn. (Regional Finalist Art Tchr. award 1991), La. Art Edn. Assn. (v.p. S.W. chpt. 1992—, Outstanding La. Art Tchr. award 1991), La. Computer Using Educators, Calcasieu Parish Bar Assn. (founding com. 1969—), Phi Delta Kappa. Democrat. Methodist. Avocations: swimming, gardening, drawing, writing. Office: Curriculum & Instrn 600 South Shatuck St Lake Charles LA 70601

BABINEAU, ANNE SERZAN, lawyer; b. Jersey City, Dec. 16, 1951; d. Joseph Edward and Mary (Golding) Serzan; m. Paul A. Babineau, Apr. 7, 1973; children: John Regis, Matthew Paul. BA, Coll. New Rochelle, 1973; JD, Seton Hall U., 1977. Bar: N.J. 1977, N.Y. 1983, U.S. Ct. Appeals (3d cir.) 1984. Staff atty. rate counsel div. N.J. Dept. Pub. Adv., Newark, 1977-78; assoc. Wilentz, Goldman & Spitzer, P.C., Woodbridge, NJ, 1979-85, ptnr., 1985—. Trustee N.J. Future. Mem. ABA, N.J. State Bar Assn. (former chair pub. utility sect.), The Counselors of Real Estate, Urban Land Inst. Roman Catholic. Office: Wilentz Goldman & Spitzer PO Box 10 90 Woodbridge Ctr Dr Ste 900 Woodbridge NJ 07095-1142 Office Phone: 732-855-6057. Business E-Mail: ababineau@wilentz.com.

BABITZKE, THERESA ANGELINE, health facility administrator; b. Madison, Ill., Dec. 19, 1925; d. Victor Joseph and Angela (Ziolkowski) Sobolewski; m. Douglas Christ Babitzke, May 2, 1953; children: Charlotte, Mary Ann, Rose Marie, Helen. Student, Quincy Coll., 1943; diploma, St. John's Sch. Nursing Edn., Springfield, Ill., 1949; student, U. Ill., Chgo., 1970; BA, St. Francis Coll., 1973; MA in Gerontology summa cum laude, Sangamon State U., 1982. Co-founder, admin. dir. Mayslake Village, Oakbrook, Ill., 1962, St. Paschal's Infirmary, Oakbrook, 1962; night supr. Godair Home, Hinsdale, Ill., 1958-72; DON King Bruwaert House, Hinsdale, 1973-76; head nurse Mt. Sinai Hosp., Chgo., 1976-82; DON Rosary Hill Home, Justice, Ill., 1989—. Election judge Rep. Com. DuPage County, 1953-98, 2003; adv. bd. Gower Grade Sch., 1973-76; adv. com. Burr Ridge Marriot Brighton Gardens Assisted Living, 1996— Named Ill. Nurse of Yr. of the Midwest, 1981, Catholic Woman of Yr. 1962, St. Mary's Ch., Joliet, Ill. Mem. Downers Grove and Suburban Nurses Club (pres. Downers Grove chpt.), U. of Ill. Gerontology, Forty and Eight, Premier Nurse Ill., Am. Legion Aux., Sigma Phi Omega (Eta chpt. U. Ill.). Roman Catholic. Avocations: travel, bicycling, doll collecting, reading.

BABLADELIS, GEORGIA, retired psychology educator; b. Manistique, Mich., Jan. 30, 1931; d. Alexander and Panayota Babladelis. BA, U. Mich., 1953; MA, U. Calif., Berkeley, 1957; PhD, U. Colo., 1960. Sr. clin. psychologist Guidance Clinic, Ala. County Probation Dept., 1960-63; prof. psychology Calif. State U., Hayward, 1963-94, prof. emerita, 1994—. Cons. Calif. Sch. Profl. Psychology, Berkeley, 1979—; U.S. dir. rsch. UNESCO, 1979; lectr. in field. Author: The Study of Personality, 1985; co-author: The Shaping of Personality, 1967; editor Psychology of Women Quar., 1974-82, Computer Users Newsletter, 1984-87; contbr. articles to profl. jours. Chosen One of 100 Outstanding Women in Psychology, Divsn. 35 APA, 1992; grantee USPHS, NIMH, NSF, others, 1969-79. Fellow APA, The Psychology of Women Soc. (divsn. 35), The Soc. for Study of Societal Issues (divsn. 9). Avocations: writing, reading.

BABROWSKI, CLAIRE HARBECK, retail executive; b. Ottawa, Ill., July 25, 1957; d. John Clayton Harbeck and Corrine Ann (Lavender) French; m. David Lee Babrowski, July 3, 1982; 2 stepdaughters. Student, U. Ill., 1975-77; MBA, U. NC, 1995. Dental asst., Ottawa, 1975-76; crew person McDonald's Corp., Ottawa, 1974-76, mem. restaurant mgmt. Champaign, Ill., 1976-80, ops. and tng. cons. St. Louis, 1980-84, ops. mgr., 1984-86, dir. nat. ops. Oak Brook, Ill., 1986-88, dir. ops. Phila., 1988-89, sr. regional mgr. Raleigh, NC, 1989—92, regional v.p., 1992—95, corp. v.p. ops., 1995—97, sr. v.p. ops., 1997—98, exec. v.p. U.S. Restaurant Sys., 1998—99, exec. v.p. Worldwide Restaurant Sys., 1999—2001, pres. McDonald's Asia/Pacific/the Middle East and Africa, 2001—03, chief restaurant ops. officer, 2003—04; exec. v.p., COO RadioShack Corp., Fort Worth, Tex., 2005—06, acting CEO, 2006. Chmn. NC Ronald McDonald's Children's Charities, Raleigh, 1989-95; relationship ptnr. Donatos Pizza, Pret A Manger, Chipotle Mexican Grill, chmn. bd. dirs.; mem. Com. of 200.; bd. dir. Delhaize Group, 2006-. Author: (manual) Training Consultants Development Program, 1987. Recipient Emerging Leader award, US Women's Svc. Forum. Mem. NC Restaurant Assn. (bd. dirs. 1992-95). Republican. Roman Catholic. Avocations: tennis, gardening. Office Phone: 817-415-3011. Office Fax: 817-415-2647.*

BABSON, JANE FRANCES, artist, writer; b. Leitchfield, Ky., Aug. 17, 1925; d. William Winstead McCall and Matilda Caroline Hahn; m. David Frederick Babson, Aug. 7, 1954; children: David Winstead, Leila Jane. BA, Mt. Holyoke Coll., 1947; MFA in Art and Art History, U. Ill., 1949. Registrar The Corcoran Gallery of Art, Washington, 1952—54, curator of prints, 1953—54. Author: The Epsteins: A Family Album, 1984, The Search for the Indian, 2001, (childrens books) The Nest on the Porch, 1988, Babson's Bestiary, 1990, A Story of Us, 2003, (DVD) Toward Freedom, (CDs) The Christmas Songs, Babson Singers; contbr. woodcut prints to collection of Nat. Air and Space Mus. Founder Stamford (Conn.) Art Assn., 1970. Named hon. citizen, City of Wakayama, Japan, 1984. Mem.: Nat. Trust for Historic Preservation, Am. Crafts Coun., Soc. Archtl. Historians, Greater N.Y. Ind. Pubs. Assn. (bd. dirs. 2002—). Avocations: swimming, travel, clothing design. Home and Office: The Winstead Press Ltd Diva Leila Prodns 202 Slice Dr Stamford CT 06907 Office Phone: 203-322-4941. Office Fax: 203-629-2545. Personal E-mail: winstead.press@verizon.net.

BACA, JOY, science educator; d. John and Linda Bearley; m. Rodger Baca, Sept. 7, 1992; children: Brandon, Brittany. BS in Biology, Tex. Woman's U., Denton, 1990—92. Tchr., sci. dept. head McKamy Mid. Sch., Flower Mound, Tex., 2000—. Finalist McKamy Teacher of Yr.

BACA, THERESA M., judge; b. Albuquerque, N.Mex., July 4, 1950; d. Patrick J. and Marie McDonald Baca; m. Eugene D. Sandoval (dec.); children: Marina, David. AB, St. John's Coll., Santa Fe, N.Mex., 1972; JD, U. Pa., Phila., 1975. Bar: N.Mex. Asst. dist. atty. 2d Jud. Dist. Atty., Albuquerque, 1980; staff atty. SBA, Albuquerque, 1980—84; met. ct. judge Met. Ct. Bernalillo County, Albuquerque, 1985—93; dist. ct. judge 2d Jud. Dist. Ct., Albuquerque, 1993—. Democrat. Roman Catholic. Avocations: reading, gardening. Office: 2d Jud Dist Ct PO Box 488 Albuquerque NM 87103

BACA, VERA JENNIE SCHULTE, art educator; b. Albuquerque, Mar. 2, 1950; d. Hugo Ross Schulte and Vera Loisa Pacheco-Schulte; m. Samuel Valdez Baca, Sept. 28, 1968; children: Jennifer Carisa, Paul Brian. Degree in interior decorating, Stratford Career Inst., Washington, 2002; cert. reiki pratcitioner, Miami Valley Reiki Ctr., Kettering, Ohio, 2002. Substitute tchr. Los Lunas Pub. Sch., N.Mex., 1979—88, St. Charles and St. Mary's, Belen and Albuquerque, N.Mex., 1983—88; teller, new accts. First Nat. Bank, Bosque Farms, N.Mex., 1988—90; art tchr. Resurection Cath. Sch., Lakeland, Fla., 1997—2000. Mem.: N.Mex. Art League. Republican. Roman Catholic. Avocations: stained glass, reading, tennis. Home: 5000 Cumbre Del Sur Ct NE Albuquerque NM 87111 Office Phone: 505-550-3442. Personal E-mail: finelinebyjennie@msn.com.

BACALL, LAUREN (BETTY JOAN PERSKE), actress; b. NYC, Sept. 16, 1924; m. Humphrey Bogart, May 21, 1945 (dec. Jan. 14, 1957); children: Stephen, Leslie; m. Jason Robards, July 4, 1961 (div. Sept. 10, 1969); 1 child, Sam. Student pub. schs., Am. Acad. Dramatic Art. Actress in Broadway plays Franklin Street, 1942, Goodbye Charlie, 1959, Cactus Flower, 1966-68, Applause, 1969-71 (Sarah Siddons award 1975); also road co., 1971-72, London co., 1972-73 (Tony award for best actress in a musical 1970), Woman of the Year, 1981 (Tony award for best actress in a musical 1981, Sarah Siddons award 1983), Sweet Bird of Youth, 1983 (London, 1985, Australia, 1986, L.A., 1987; (Films) To Have and Have Not, 1944, Confidential Agent, 1945, The Big Sleep, 1946, Dark Passage, 1947, Key Largo, 1948, Young Man With a Horn, 1949, Bright Leaf, 1950, How To Marry a Millionaire, 1953, Woman's World, 1954, The Cobweb, 1955, Blood Alley, 1955, Written on the Wind, 1956, Designing Woman, 1957, The Gift of Love, 1958, Flame Over India, 1959, Shock Treatment, 1964, Sex and the Single Girl, 1965, Harper, 1966, Murder on the Orient Express, 1974, The Shootist, 1976, Health, 1980, The Fan, 1981, Tree of Hands, 1987, Appointment With Death, 1987, Mr. North, 1988, Misery, 1990, A Star for Two, 1991, All I Want for Christmas, 1991, Ready to Wear (Prêt-à-Porter), 1994, My Fellow Americans, 1996, The Mirror Has Two Faces, 1996 (Golden Globe award, 1997, SAG award, 1997), The Line King: Al Hirschfield, 1996, Le Jour et la Nuit, 1997, Diamonds, 1999, Dogville, 2003, The Limit, 2003, Birth, 2004, (voice only) Howl's Moving Castle, 2004, Firedog, 2005, Manderlay, 2005, These Foolish Things, 2006; TV movies: The Paris Collections, 1968, Applause, 1973, A Commercial Break (Happy Endings), 1975, Perfect Gentlemen, 1978, Dinner at Eight, 1989, The Portrait, 1992, A Foreign Field, 1993, From the Mixed Up Files of Mrs. Basil E. Frankweiler, 1995, The Man Who Had Everything, 1998, Madeline: Lost in Paris, 1999 Too Rich: The Secret Life of Doris Duke, 1999; TV appearances include: "What's My Line?", 1953, 1965, The Rockford Files, 1979, Chicago Hope, 1998, So Graham Norton, 2000, The Sopranos, 2006; Author: Lauren Bacall: By Myself, 1978, Now, 1994, By Myself and Then Some, 2005 Recipient Am. Acad. Dramatic Arts award for achievement, 1963, Standard award London Evening, 1973, Nat. Book award, 1980; decorated comdr. Order of Arts and Letters (France), 1995; named 50 Most Beautiful People in the World, People, 1997. Office: care Johnnie Planco William Morris Agy 1325 Avenue of the Americas New York NY 10019-6026

BACARELLA, FLAVIA, artist, educator; b. Bklyn. d. Salvatore John and Angeline Mary B. MA, New Sch. for Social Rsch., N.Y.C., 1975; MFA, Bklyn. Coll./CUNY, 1983; student, N.Y. Studio Sch., 1980. Asst. prof. Herbert H. Lehman Coll., Bronx, 1995—. Grantee N.Y. Found. Arts, 1986. Mem. Coll. Art Assn. Office: Herbert H Lehman Coll Bedford Park Blvd W Bronx NY 10468 Office Phone: 718-960-8259. Business E-Mail: flavia.bacarella@lehman.cuny.edu.

BACARISSE, ANGELA, design educator, costume designer; b. Salem, Ill., Feb. 28, 1965; d. Glen David and Glenna Jo Seymour; m. Stephen Rene Bacarisse, Aug. 13, 2000; 1 child, Nicholas Rene Bacarrisse. BA, U. Del., Newark, 1987; MFA, U. Memphis, 1990. Staff lectr. James Madison U., Harrisonburg, Va., 1990—94; asst. prof. design Coll. Charleston, SC, 1994—95; cutter, draper Tex. Shakespeare Fest, Kilgore, 1996—2001; asst. prof. design U. NC, Asheville, 1995—2000; cutter, draper U. Houston, 2000—01; asst. prof. design Stephen F. Austin State U., Nacogdoches, 2001—. Costume designer Opera East Tex., Longview, 2003—, Summer Theatre at Mt. Holyoke, Mass., 1990—97, Pioneer Valley Summer Theatre, Mass., 2003. Mem.: Tex. Ednl. Theatre Assn., US Inst. Theatre Tech. Avocations: reading, needlecrafts, gardening, painting. Office: Stephen F Austin State U 1936 North St Nacogdoches TX 75962 Office Phone: 936-468-1126.

BACCUS, R. EILEEN TURNER, academic administrator; b. Oxford, N.C., Aug. 8, 1944; d. Nathaniel Benjamin and Gloria Constance (Davis) Turner; B.A., Fisk U., 1964; M.B.A., U. Conn., 1975, Ph.D., 1978; 1 son, Christopher Lloyd. Programmer, systems analyst IBM, N.Y., Mo., 1964-66; substitute tchr., Lakenheath AFB, Eng., 1967-69; asst. dir. fin. aid U. Conn., Storrs, 1970-74, asst. to dean Sch. Edn., 1974-77, dir. personnel services div., 1977-81; adminstr. treasury ops. Aetna Life & Casualty Co., Hartford, Conn., 1981-82, ops. mgr. discretionary asset mgmt., 1982-86; pres. Thames Valley State Tech. Coll., Norwich, Conn., 1986-92; pres. Northwestern Conn. Community Tech. Coll., Winsted, 1992-2004, ret.; cons. Ford Found., 1976, Tchr. Corps, 1977, Meriden (Conn.) Schs., 1979—; dir. Conn. Savs. & Loan Assn. Mem. planning com. Conn. Legis. Black Caucus, 1980; mem. mgmt. team Ujima, Inc., Hartford, 1978-80; co-chmn. bd. Hartford Scholarship Found., 1971-75; treas. bd. Cmty. Coun. Capitol Region, 1982-86; mem. community adv. bd. Jr. League Hartford, Inc., 1982—84. Mem. Am. Ednl. Rsch. Assn., Internat. Platform Assn., Links, Inc., Rotary Internat., Phi Delta Kappa, Pi Lambda Theta, Delta Sigma Theta. Democrat. Episcopalian. Home: 87 Woodland Ave Bloomfield CT 06002-1806

BACH, CYNTHIA, educational program director, writer; b. Oct. 28; BA in Art Edn., UCLA, 1955; MPA, U. So. Calif., 1978; LDS, Calif. Luth., 1993. Cert. gen. elem., spl. secondary art, and gen. jr. h.s. tchr. Staff asst. L.A. Unified Sch. Dist., 1976; rainbow tchr., gifted coord. Trinity Elem. Sch., L.A., 1978-81; field worker/in-svc. for parents and staff educator Hubbard Elem. Sch., Sylmar, Calif., 1981-90; student observer Liggett Elem. Sch., Panorama City, Calif., 1990-92; tng. tchr. Calif. State U. (Northridge)-Vena Sch., Arleta, Calif., 1992-93; pres. Comprehensive Learning Systems. Rsch. bd. advisors Am. Biograph. Inst., Inc. Author: Alternatives to Retail Marketing for Seniors (Bur. of Consumer Affairs); creator: (game) Mighty is the Word. Lectr. Sr. Citizens Bur. Consumer Affairs, City Hall; past pres. local PTA; del. Children's Def. Fund Conf., 1998; sch. bd. dirs. St. Martin-in-the-Fields Parish Sch.; mem. coun. bd. Amnesty Internat.; sponsor Christian Found. for Children and Aging; mem. Mus. of Tolerance, Alliance for Tolerance; co-founder scholarship fund for women ministers; ofcl. hostess rep. for vis. diplomats through the World Affairs Coun. City of Los Angeles; lay eucharistic min., 1998. Named 79 State Evaluation Mar Team-outstanding educator, Phi Alpha Alpha, Nat. Acad. Hon. Soc. Pub. Affairs Adminstrn., Order of Internat. Fellows Edn., on Wall of Tolerance, Montgomery, Ala., Internat. Woman of Yr., 2003; recipient Spl. Recognition award, 21st Century Award for Achievement, Pres.'s Award of Merit as outstanding citizen in field of edn.; scholar, Nat. Art, Chouinard Art Inst. Mem. NAFE, AAUW, 1st Century Soc. UCLA, Nat. Mus. Women in Arts (assoc.), Phi Alpha Alpha. Avocations: reading, theology, old movies, writing, gardening. Home: PO Box 127 Agoura Hills CA 91376-0127

BACH, MARY IRENE, music educator; b. Dallas, Nov. 25, 1944; d. Forrest Bedford McCord, Sr. and Mary Estelle McCord; m. Kelly Blake Glasco, Aug. 26, 1965 (div. Mar. 27, 1987); children: Kari Lynn Glasco, Kent McCord Glasco; m. Thomas Ray Bach, Sr., May 3, 1991 (div. Jan. 25, 2005). MusB in Edn., Sam Houston State U., Huntsville, Tex., 1967. Cert. tchr. Tex. Edn. Agy., 1967. Dallas Cowboys cheerleader, 1960—62; music tchr., choir dir. Conroe ISD - Elem. Pub. Schs., Tex., 1967—81; asst. dir. choir, accompanist Conroe ISD - McCullough H.S., The Woodlands, 1981—84; tchr. music, choir dir. Conroe ISD - Intermediate Sch., 1984—. Ch. organist, accompanist various schs., 1967—2005; accompanist civic choir Montgomery County Choral Soc., 1984—2000; ch. organist, accompanist First Presbyn. Ch., 2002—; Kodaly clinician Tex. schs., 1977—84; performer Studio One Singers, Conroe and The Woodlands, 1982—; music dir. little theatre Crighton Playhouse, Conroe, 1987—2006; singer Conroe Chorale - Civic Choir, 1998—2004. Recipient Tchr. Yr., Wilkerson Intermediate Sch. - ConroeISD, 1985, Reaves Intermediate Sch. - ConroeISD, 2000; scholar, Sam Houston State U., 1963—67, Dallas Rotary Club, 1963; Powell scholar, Sam Houston State U., Music Dept., 1966. Mem.: Orgn. Am. Kodaly Educators (assoc.), Gulf Coast Orff Assn. (assoc.), Tex. Choral Dirs. Assn. (assoc.; ways and means com. 2005—06), Orgn. Am. Kodaly Educators (assoc.), Kodaly Educators Tex. (assoc.), Assn. Tex. Profl. Educators (assoc.), Tex. Music Educators Assn. (assoc.), Delta Kappa Gamma (hon.; music dir. 1983—99). Methodist. Avocations: travel, scrapbooks, gardening, snorkeling.

BACHAND, ALICE JEANNE, school library media specialist; b. Sayre, Pa., Sept. 21, 1957; d. Charles Edward and Donna Jeanne (Osborne) Merrick; m. James Joseph Bachand, July 17, 1982; children: Janelle Alison, Jodi Nicole. Student, Paul Valéry U., Montpellier, France, 1977-78; BA, Wartburg Coll., 1979; MLS, Emporia State U., 1985. French tchr. Dunlap (Iowa) H.S., 1979, Clifton-Clyde H.S., Clyde, Kans., 1980-85; sch. libr. media specialist Hillcrest H.S., Cuba, Kans., 1984-86, Linn (Kans.) H.S., 1986-92, Clay Center (Kans.) Cmty. Middle Sch., 1992—. V.p. WELCA, Concordia, Kans., 1989-91; sec. of edn., ALCW, Concordia, 1982-84; brownie helper Girl Scouts of Am., Clyde, 1995-96; ch. librarian, Concordia Lutheran Ch., 1984—. Mem. NEA (Kans. chpt. pres. 1991-92), DAR, Kans. Reading Assn., Kans. Assn. Sch. Librarians (nominating com. 1992, Dist. IV coord. 2005-06), Thunderbird Reading Coun. Lutheran. Avocations: reading, sewing, crafts. Home: 1626 N 270 Rd Clyde KS 66938 Office: Clay Ctr Cmty Middle School 935 Prospect St Clay Center KS 67432-1849 Personal E-mail: alicebachand@hotmail.com.

BACHANT, JANET LEE, psychologist; b. N.Y.C., Mar. 30, 1944; d. Herbert and Muriel (Snyder) B.; m. Bo Rucker (div.); 1 child, Roddric; m. Roy Harvey Wallace, Oct. 12, 1980; 1 child, Miriam Bachant Wallace. BA, Lebanon Valley Coll., 1966; MA, New Sch. for Social Rsch., 1968, PhD, 1972. Lic. psychologist, N.Y.; registered psychoanalyst. Teaching and rsch. asst. New Sch. for Social Rsch., N.Y.C., 1966-71; faculty Inst. for Contemporary Psychotherapy, N.Y.C., 1984-89; faculty and supr. Postgrad. Ctr. for Mental Health, N.Y.C., 1988—; faculty Westchester Ctr. for Study of Psychoanalysis/Psychotherapy, White Plains, N.Y., 1988—. Mentor psychology Empire State Coll. SUNY, 2000—. Contbr. articles to profl. jours. Founder NY Disaster Counseling Coalition, chmn. bd. Fellow NDEA, 1966-68; scholar Lebanon Valley Coll. Alumni, Annville, Pa., 1965. Mem.: Pa. State Psychol. Assn. (Rsch. Competition 1st prize 1966, award 2006). Avocations: gardening, chopin, computers. Home and Office: 205 W 86th St New York NY 10024-3327

BACHELDER, BEVERLY BRANDT, secondary school educator, assistant principal, director; b. Fort Dodge, Iowa, June 24, 1954; d. Olaf Ottesen and Eleanor Berg Brandt; m. Robert Stephen Bachelder, Sept. 17, 1977; children: Stephen Edward, Elizabeth Margrethe. BA, Luther Coll., Decorah, Iowa, 1976; MusM, Yale U., New Haven, Conn., 1978; MA in Modern English Lit., U. Kent, Eng., 1979. Lic. asst. prin., secondary tchr., tchr. K-12 vocal music, 7-12 English Mass. Vocal music tchr. Douglas Sch. Sys., Mass., 1980—81; English lang. arts tchr. Douglas Jr., Sr. HS, 1982—2004; English dept. chair Douglas HS, 2003—04, acting asst. prin., 2004—05, asst. prin., 2005—06, dir. curriculum and instrn., 2006—; dir. music Zion Luth. Ch., Worcester, Mass., 1980—97, First Congl. Ch., Auburn, Mass., 1997—2000. Co-founder, advisor Nat. Jr. Honor Soc., Roberta Wagner Chpt., 1990—2003; organist, choir dir. Christ Episcopal Ch., Rochdale, Mass., 2000—; co-chair accreditation steering com. New Eng. Assn. Schs. and Colls., 2002—06. Mem. First Congl. Ch., Oxford, Mass., 1984. Finalist Mass. Tchr. of Yr. award, Mass. Dept. Edn., 1986; recipient Internat. Understanding award, Rotary Found., 1978-79, Douglas Tchr. of Yr. award, Douglas Jr./Sr. HS, 1986, Horace Mann Tchr. award, 1986-87. Mem.: ASCD, Nat. Assn. Secondary Sch. Prins., Am. Guild of Organists, Mass. Secondary Schs. Adminstrs.' Assn. Home: PO Box 67 North Oxford MA 01537 Office: Douglas HS 33 Davis St Douglas MA 01516 Office Phone: 508-476-3332. Personal E-mail: bjbach@charter.net.

BACHELOR, MALINDA MARY, elementary school educator; b. Detroit, Mich., Jan. 2, 1972; d. James Gerard and Karen Anne Cote; m. Bret Alan Bachelor, May 27, 2000; children: Orion Jareth Oettel, Bethany Dyana. BS, Fla. State U., Tallahassee, Fla., 1995. Cert. Elem. Edn. Fla., 2003. Demonstration tchr. Duval County Pub. Schs., Jacksonville, Fla., 2001—02, sch. design coach, 2002—03, dist. standards coach, 2003—. Curriculum writer Duval County Pub. Schs., 2004—; standards alignment Fla. Ednl. Tools, Inc., Jacksonville, 2002—03. Del. leader Student Ambs., Jacksonville, Fla., 2005—06. Office Phone: 904-348-5757. Personal E-mail: malindabachelor@hotmail.com.

BACHMAN, KATHARINE ELIZABETH, lawyer; b. Harrisburg, Pa., Oct. 28, 1953; d. Neal D. and Helen (Alexander) B. BA summa cum laude, Dickinson Coll., 1975; JD, NYU, 1978. Bar: Mass. 1978. Sr. ptnr., hiring ptnr. Hale & Dorr, Boston, 1978—2004; ptnr., vice chmn. Real Estate dept. Wilmer Cutler Pickering Hale & Dorr, Boston, 2004—. Bd. dirs. Greater Boston Legal Services. Editor (articles): Annual Survey of Am. Law. Mem. single family adv. com. Mass. Housing Fin. Agy., Boston, 1985—; trustee Dickinson Coll., Carlisle, Pa., 1987—; mem. New Eng. Adv. Com. Trust for Pub. Land; past chmn. Develop. & Fin. Task Force Boston 2000; mem. exec. com. Mass. chpt. Nat Assn. Indsl. & Office Properties. Named a Mass. Super Lawyer, Boston Mag., 2004; named one of Top 50 Female Mass. Lawyers, 2004; Root Tilden scholar. Mem. Am. Coll. Real Estate Lawyers, Mass. Bar Assn., Boston Bar Assn., New Eng. Women in Real Estate (past pres.), Phi Beta Kappa. Office: Wilmer Cutler Pickering Hale & Dorr 60 State St Boston MA 02109-1816 Office Phone: 617-526-6216. Office Fax: 617-526-5000. Business E-Mail: katherine.bachman@wilmerhale.com.

BACHMANN, GLORIA ANN, obstetrician, gynecologist, educator; b. Newark, Nov. 4, 1949; d. Paul Bachmann and Rose Detrolio; 1 child, Michael. BA, Rutgers U., 1970, MMS, 1972; MD, U. Pa., 1974. Diplomate Am. Bd. Ob-Gyn., Am. Bd. Med. Examiners. Resident in ob-gyn. Hosp. of the U. of Pa., 1974-78; instr. U. Medicine & Dentistry N.J./Robert Wood Johnson Med. Sch., New Brunswick, N.J., 1978-81; asst. prof. Robert Wood Johnson U. Hosp., New Brunswick, N.J., 1981-86, assoc. prof., 1986-92, prof., 1992—. Chief ob-gyn. Robert Wood Johnson U. Hosp., 1992—; dir. Women's Health Inst. Editl. bd. Maturitas, 1989—, Med. Crossfire, 1998, Managing Menopause, 1998—, Jour. of Reproductive Medicine, 1999—, Med. Aspects of Human Sexuality, 1989-92, OBG Mgmt., 1994—, Menopaul Mgmt., 1991-93, Obstetric Gynecology, 1990-94; contbr. chpts. to books and articles to profl. jours. Dir. Women's Wellness and Health Care Connection, New Brunswick, N.J., 1998—. Recipient Recognition award March of Dimes, 1982, 83, Planned Parenthood, 1987, 88, Award for Women's Health Edn. YMCA, 1984, Judge Advocate Gen. award Tri-State Metro, 1984, Lifetime Achievement award Middlesex County Comm. on the Status of Women, 1995, Women of Achievement award Del. Valley Girl Scouts, 1996. Fellow Am. Coll. Ob-Gyn. (Issue of the Yr. award 1988); mem. Am. Fertility Soc., Internat. Menopause Soc., Am. Med. Women's Assn. (Gender Equity Recognition 1994), N.J. Obs.-Gyn. Soc., N.Am. Menopause Soc., Acad. of Medicine of N.J., Phi Beta Kappa. Office: Robert Wood Johnson Med Sch Women's Health Inst 125 Paterson St Rm 2104 New Brunswick NJ 08901-1962 E-mail: gloria.bachmann@umdnj.edu.

BACHMANN, KAREN CHARLOTTE, artist, educator; b. Bronx, N.Y., Jan. 5, 1960; d. Emile Willie Bachmann and Charlotte Elise Seiter-Bachmann; m. Gregory Norman Gabel, Jan. 10, 2004; 1 child, Emilia Nina Gabel. BFA, Pratt Inst., Bklyn., 1982. Cert. continuous employment. Designer James Murphy Ltd., NYC, 1983—86; jeweler, goldsmith Elan Inc., NYC, 1989—92, Guillemin/Soulaine Inc., Greenwich, Conn., 1992—93; jeweler, modelmaker Tiffany & Co., N.Y.C., 1993—95; pres., owner and jewelry designer Karen Bachmann Designs, Bklyn., 1995—. Assoc. prof. Pratt Inst., Bklyn., 2000, Fashion Inst. Tech., N.Y.C., 2000—. Contbr. (book) 500 Bracelets; jewelry represented in numerous collections, including Mus. Arts & Design, NY, Electrum Gallery, London. Contbr., fundraiser Am. Cancer Soc., NYC, 2000—. Finalist Niche awards, 2001. Mem.: Soc. N.Am. Goldsmiths (assoc.), Am. Craft Coun. (assoc.), Mensa (life). Office: Karen Bachmann Designs 258 Ainslie St # 2 Brooklyn NY 11211-4914 Office Phone: 917-531-0012. Personal E-mail: karenbachmann@yahoo.com. E-mail: karen@karenbachmanndesigns.com.

BACHRACH, EVE ELIZABETH, lawyer; b. Oakland, Calif., July 4, 1951; d. Howard Lloyd and Shirley B. AB cum laude, Boston U., 1972; JD with honors, George Washington U., 1976. Bar: D.C. 1976, U.S. Dist. Ct. D.C. 1976, U.S. Ct. Appeals (D.C. cir.) 1976. Assoc. Stein, Mitchell & Mezines, Washington, 1976-79; assoc. gen. counsel Cosmetic, Toiletry, and Fragrance Assn., Washington, 1979-85; v.p., assoc. gen. counsel, corp. sec., 1985-95; v.p., deputy gen. counsel, corp. sec. Consumer Healthcare Products Assn., Washington, 1995-98, sr. v.p., gen. counsel, sec., 1998—. Guest lectr. Am. U., Washington, 1986—, George Washington Nat. Law Ctr., Washington, 1986—, Cath. U. Law Sch., 1988— Contbr. articles to profl. jours. Vol. lawyer Legal Counsel for the Elderly, Washington, 1978—. Mem.: ABA (food and drug com., antitrust sect., adminstrv. law sect.), Food Drug Law Inst. (chmn. writing awards com. 1982—88, vice chmn. 1987—89, chmn. 1990, adv. bd. 1998—2002, bd. dirs. 2002—, bd. dirs., editl. adv. bd. Update Mag. 2002—04, editl. adv. bd. Food Drug Law Jour., Disting. Svc. Leadership award 2005), Fed. Bar Assn. (chmn. food and drug com. 1986—90), D.C. Bar Assn. Avocation: classical pianist. Office: Consumer Healthcare Products Assn 900 19th St NW Washington DC 20006

BACHRACH, NANCY, retired advertising executive; b. Providence, Jan. 29, 1948; d. David and Maida Horovitz. BA magna cum laude, Conn. Coll. for Women, 1969; MA with honors, Brandeis U., 1973, PhD, 1975. Assoc. dir. Grey France, Paris, 1980—84; sr. v.p., account mgmt. Grey Advt., N.Y.C., 1985—91, exec. v.p., 1992—2001, chief mktg. officer, 2001. Author: The Irrefutability of Skepticism, 1975. Named one of 100 Best and Brightest Women, Advt. Age, 1988; named to Acad. Women Achievers, 1992. Office: Grey Advt Inc 777 3rd Ave New York NY 10017-1401

BACIGALUPO, SARAH ELIZABETH, literature and language educator; BA, Carroll Coll., Waukesha, Wis., 2000, MEd, 2004. Tchr. English tchr., dept. chair Howards Grove H.S., Wis., 2000—. Mem.: Nat. Coun. Tchrs. English. Office: Howards Grove Public Schools 401 Audubon Rd Howards Grove WI 53083 Office Phone: 920-565-4450. Business E-Mail: sbacigal@hgsd.k12.wi.us.

BACK, SHANNON LEE, music educator; b. Westminster, Calif., Aug. 3, 1975; adopted d. Billy and d. Cindy Scott; m. Robert R. Back, July 25, 1998; children: Hallie Back (deceased), Emma Ryan. Music Edn., Ga. So. U., Statesboro, 1993—98. Music tchr. Ebenezer Elem., Rincon, Ga., 1998—2006, Nevils Elem., 2006—. Recipient Tchr. of Yr., Ebenezer Elem., 2003—04. Mem.: Ga. Music Educators Assn., Sigma Alpha Iota (alumnae chpt.).

BACKES, RUTH EMERSON, counseling psychologist; b. Mt. Vernon, N.Y., Aug. 25, 1918; d. Robert Stewart and Harriett Elizabeth (Crofut) Emerson; m. Frederick Tregonning Backes (div. 1968, dec. 1981); children: Peter Frederick, Jill, Kim BS, NYU, 1939; MEd, U. Mass., 1978, EdD, 1985. Asst. dir. health edn. YWCA, Balt., 1939—41, New Haven, 1941—44; program dir. USO, Newfoundland, 1944—46; women's dir. YMCA, Wallingford, Conn., 1947—49; coord., vol. Mental Health Ctr., Meriden, Conn., 1964—66; coord. edn. and info. Conn. Mental Health Ctr., New Haven, 1966—74; pvt. practice Amherst, Mass., 1980—2000; ret., 2000. Faculty Antioch Grad. Sch., Keene, N.H., 1976-81; vis. rsch. scholar Ctr. for Rsch. on Women, Wellesley (Mass.) Coll., 1991-93; rsch. assoc. Five Coll. Women's Studies Rsch. Ctr., Mt. Holyoke Coll., South Hadley, Mass., 1993-94 Author: Bookstores of Amherst, 1989; contbr. articles to profl. jours.; mem. editl. bd. Workplace Democracy, Amherst, 1987-89, Mus. Insights, Amherst, 1989-90 Bd. dirs. Amherst Club, 1987-90, Hampshire Choral Soc., Northampton, Mass., 1984-87, Helen Mitchell House for Homeless Women and Children, Amherst, 1987-90; rep. Town Meeting, Amherst, 1986-93, 2004—; trustee 1st Congl. Ch., Amherst, 1992-95, chmn. bd. trustees, 1993-95 Mem. We. Mass. Assn. for Psychoanalytic Psychology, Nat. Assn. Ind. Scholars, Group for Psychoanalytic Studies Democrat. Avocations: gardening, theater, music. Home: 22 Lessey St Apt 612 Amherst MA 01002-2176

BACKSTEDT, ROSEANNE JOAN, artist; b. San Francisco, Dec. 15, 1941; d. Anthony and Tillie LaRocca; m. Lawrence Henry Backstedt, Aug. 9, 1964 (dec. May 2004); 1 child, Simone Rose. Student, San Francisco Art Inst., 1960-64, U. Oreg., 1966-68, Aesthetic Realism Found., 1976—. Mem. Ceres Gallery, N.Y.C., 1991—. One-woman shows include Sullivan County Mus., Hurleyville, NY, 1972, Hansen Gallery, NYC, 1973-77, The Viewing Rm., NYC, 1978, Noho Gallery, NYC, 1987, Ceres Gallery, NYC, 1991—; group shows include Elysian Art Gallery, San Francisco, 1962-64, Portland Art Mus., 1969, Terrain Gallery, NYC, 1979-85, 2000, 2005, Ligoa Duncan Gallery, NYC, 1980, Krasdale Food Corp., Bronx, 1989, 91, 94, Z Gallery, NYC, 1991-92, World Trade Ctr., NYC, 1991, Triplex Gallery, NYC, 1992, Snug Harbor Cultural Ctr., S.I., NY, 1992, Lincoln Ctr., NYC, 1994, Cedco Calendars, 1994-97, JCB Internat. Co., NYC, 1996, Univ. Luth Ch., Harvard Square, Mass., 1996, Mills Pond House, St. James, NYC, 1997, Artemisia Gallery, Chgo., 1997, Künstlerforum, Bonn, 1998, Orange County CC, Middletown, NY, 1998, Soho 20 Gallery, NYC, 1999, Kingsborough CC, Bklyn., 1999, Caelum Gallery, NYC, 2000-03, SUNY, Buffalo, 2000, Commerce Bank, NYC, 2004, Walter Wickiser Gallery, 2005, Noho Bid Blick Windows, 2005; presenter ART TALK, Aesthetic Realism Found., NYC, 1998-2001; author: Pathways, 2005; art reproduced in Marshall Cavendish, vol. 8, 2005. Office: Ceres Gallery 547 W 27th St 2d Floor New York NY 10001

BACKSTEIN, MICKI LYNN, social worker; b. Decatur, Apr. 15, 1979; d. Richard Eugene and Laura Cay Backstein. BA in Sociology/Psychology, DePaul U., Chgo., 2004. Mgmt. methods analyst U. Ill., Chgo., 2002—04; mem. screening assessment support svcs. crisis team Grand Prairie Behavioral Health Svcs., Flossmoor, Ill., 2004—, coord. individual care grand care, 2005—. Lutheran. Avocations: tennis, interior decorating, travel, jewelry making. Office: Grand Prairie Behavioral Health Services 19530 S Keazie Ave Flossmoor IL Home: 4235 S Langley Chicago IL 60653

BACKUS, MARCIA ELLEN, lawyer; b. Melrose, Mass., Sept. 8, 1954; d. Milo Morlan and Barbara (Cairns) B.; m. Robert M. Roach Jr., June 14, 1986. BA, U. Tex., 1976, JD, 1983. Bar: Tex. 1983. Assoc. Vinson & Elkins, Houston, 1983-90, ptnr., 1991—. Mem. ABA, State Bar Tex., Houston Bar Assn. Office: Vinson & Elkins 1101 Fannin St Ste 2300 Houston TX 77002-6910 E-mail: mbackus@velaw.com.

BACON, A. SMOKI, television host; b. Brookline, Mass., Jan. 29, 1928; d. Alfred Leon and Ruth Dorothy (Burns) Ginepra; m. Edwin Conant Bacon, May 11, 1957 (dec. July 1974); children: Brooks Conant, Hilary Conant Bacon Gabrieli; m. Richard Francis Concannon, Oct. 13, 1979. Student, Art Inst. Boston, 1947; grad., Jackson Von Ladau Sch. Design, 1951. Pub. rels. cons., Boston, 1968—; pres. Bacon-Concannon Assocs., Boston, 1979—95, ptnr.; dir. craftsmobiles Summerthing Program, Boston, 1966—73; dir. exhibits Citifair, Boston, 1974; dir. Victorian exhibits Bicentennial Boston 200, 1975, dir. spl. events, 1976; cons. spl. events. Inst. Contemporary Art, 1977—78; cons. spl. events Boston Tea Party Ship, 1976—79; fundraiser Mass. Assn. Mental Health, 1979; dir. promotions Met. Ctr., 1979; coord. grand finale celebration Boston Jubilee 350, 1979—80; coord. Elliot Norton Awards, 1983; pub. rels. Dyansen Gallery, Boston, 1987—88, French Speaking League, 1987; cons. spl. events Jordan Marsh, 1987; fundraiser, pub. rels. Boston Philharm., 1988; coord. 30th anniversary celebration Charles Playhouse, 1988; fundraiser Elliot Norton Awards, 1989; coord. benefit New Eng. Premiere of film Glory Afro-Am. Mus., 1990; pub. rels. cons. Boston Chamber Music Soc., 1990; pub. rels. Paul Sorota Gallery Fine Arts, 1990—91; fundraising cons. Internat. Inst., 1991; pub. rels., fundraiser Brookline H.S. Sesquicentennial Celebration, 1992—93; co-host radio show Celebrity Time, 1980—; co-host TV show On the Town, The Literati Scene. Guest lectr. Boston U. Sch. Pub. Rels., 1979, Mass Polit. Women's Conf., 1983, YMCA, 1986, ARC, 1987, Radcliffe Coll. 4 O'Clock Forums, 1989, Publicity Club Boston, 1990, Women's Italian Club, 1993, Brookline Rotary, 1995, Harvard Coll. Rotary Club, 1995, Ward 5 Dem. Com., 2004; contbg. editor Design Times Mag. Social calendar editor Boston Tab Newspaper, 1987-90; contbg. editor Design Times Mag.; columnist BeaconHill News, Beacon Hill Chronicle, The Tab, Commuter Mag. Candidate Dem. State Rep., Mass., 1980; Bastille Day chmn. French Libr. Boston, 1994—; local adv. com. Nat. Trust for Historic Preservation; bd. dirs. Boston Lit. Hour, Artvision; host parents com. Harvard Coll.; bd. dirs. Mugar Libr., Spl. Collections, 1994—; vis. com. Mus. Fine Arts, Egyptian Dept., 1994—; bd. trustees Boston Arts Festival, 1960-63; bd. dirs., treas. Samaritans, Boston, 1974-84; art auction chairperson WGBH-Pub. Radio-TV, Boston, 1969-70; bd. dirs. Urban League Ea. Mass., Boston, 1975-85, Elders Living at Home Program, Boston City Hosp. Kids Fund; former mem. numerous civic coms. Recipient Woman of Great Achievement award Cambridge Young Women's Assn., 1991, appreciation award The Samaritans, 1991, Leadership award Friends of Pub. Garden, 1975, Pub. Action for the Arts award, MUSE award Pub. Action for Arts, 2006; named one of Boston's 100 Female Leaders, Boston Mag., 1980, Boston Area Schs. Notable Grad. List Boston Globe, 1994; Honors on 70th birthday Gov. Argeo Paul Cellucci, Pres. of Senate Thomas Birmingham, Spkr. Ho. of Reps. Thomas Finnerman and Mayor of Boston Thomas Menino, 1998; Guest of Honor Womens' City Club Ann. Dinner Dance, 1979; honored Those Who Help Keep Boston's Non-Profit Agencies Alive Horizons for Youth, 1972, Charitable and Civic Endeavors Boston Italian Women's Club, 1995; donated personal ofcl. documents Women's Time Capsule Schlesinger Libr. Radcliffe Coll., 1981; honoree Gibon House Mus., 2003. Mem. AAUW, Harvard Club Boston, Women's City Club. Democrat. Avocation: artistics graphics. Home: 94 Beacon St Ste 1 Boston MA 02108-3329 Office: Bacon Concannon Assocs 94 Beacon St Boston MA 02108-3329 Office Phone: 617-523-1188. Office Fax: 617-523-1998. Personal E-mail: SmokiBacon@aol.com.

BACON, BARBARA MCNUTT, social worker; b. London, Nov. 6, 1946; came to U.S., 1952; d. Peter Joseph and Margaret (Stronge) O'Reilly; m. Michael McNutt, Nov. 15, 1969 (dec. 1977); m. John Lockhart Bacon, Apr. 29, 1978; children: Patricia, Ann Catherine BA, Ursuline Coll. for Women, 1968; postgrad., Harvard U., 1968-69; MEd, U. Ill., 1971; MSW, U. Iowa, 1981. Psychometrist Child Devel. Lab., Mass. Gen. Hosp. and Harvard Med. Sch., Boston, 1968-69; research assoc. Inst. Child Behavior and Devel., U. Ill., Champaign, 1969-78; clin. social worker Family and Children's Services, Davenport, Iowa, 1979-83; psychologist Gt. River Mental Health Ctr., Muscatine, Iowa, 1978-79; behavioral sci. coord. family practice residency program Mercy-St Luke's Hosp., Davenport, Iowa, 1979-82; family therapist Family Counseling Service, Albuquerque, 1984-88; pvt. practice Profl. Counseling Assocs., 1984-86; clin. dir. adolescent psychiatric program Charter Hosp., Albuquerque, 1987-89; psychotherapist Family Health Plan of Utah, 1990-95; with PSI Assocs., 1996—2000; sch. social worker Cleve.

Heights/University Heights Sch. Dist., 2000—. Cons. CIBA-Geigy Corp., Summit, N.J., 1975-77, Council for Children at Risk, Rock Island, Ill., 1981-83 Mem. Nat. Assn. Social Workers, Phi Beta Kappa Republican. Roman Catholic.

BACON, CAROLINE SHARFMAN, investor, consultant; b. Ann Arbor, Mich., Aug. 27, 1942; d. Mahlon Samuel and Mary Patricia (Potter) Sharp; m. William Lee Sharfman, Sept. 5, 1964 (div. 1985); m. James Edmund Bacon, Nov. 4, 1989. BA with distinction, U. Mich., 1964; MBA, Columbia U., 1975; MAR, Yale U., 2004. Assoc. Goldman, Sachs & Co., N.Y.C., 1975-80, v.p., 1980-83, Goldman Sachs Money Markets Inc., N.Y.C., 1983-90; sr. cons. investor rels. Burson-Marsteller, 1991; mng. dir. Johnnie D. Johnson & Co. Investor Rels., N.Y.C., 1992-95. Mem. Phi Beta Kappa, Phi Sigma Iota, Beta Gamma Sigma. Episcopalian.

BACON, JERI ANN, music educator; b. Phoenix, July 23, 1954; d. James Weldon and Jo Ann Hale; m. Francis Farquhar Bacon, Nov. 30, 1986; 1 child, Patricia Louise. MusB, Ariz. State U., 1977. Cert. music tchr. N.J., 2000, classroom tchr. N.J., 2002. Music tchr. Burlington Twp. (N.J.) Pub. Sch., 1999—2000, Tabernacle (N.J.) Pub. Schs., 2000—01, Bridgeton (N.J.) Pub. Schs., 2002—; elem. tchr., tutor Huntington Learning Ctr., Cherry Hill, NJ, 2002—; kindergarten tchr. Marlton (NJ) Christian Acad., 2003, Holmesburg Bapt. Christian Sch., 2004. Orch. dir. Cherry Hill Bapt. Ch., NJ, 1999—2004. Mem. Parent's T.V. Coun., LA, 2002—03. Mem.: Music Educators Nat. Conf., N.J. Music Educators Assn. Republican. Avocations: music, cross stitch. E-mail: jeriabacon@juno.com.

BACON, LISE, Canadian senator; b. Valleyfield, Canada, Aug. 25, 1934; Student, Coll. Marie de l'Incarnation, Academie Saint Louis de Gonzague, Institut Albert Thomas. Mgr. dept. Prudential Ins. Co. of Am., 1951—71; judge Can. citizenship ct., 1977—79; v.p. Can. Life and Health Ins. Assn. Inc., Quebec, 1979—81; mem. Nat. Assembly, Ottawa, ON, Canada, 1981—94; senator The Senate of Can., Ottawa, 1994—. Bd. dirs. Theatre du Rideau Vert, Montreal, Oxfam Quebec. Recipient Ordre du merite belgo-hispanique, Ordre de Saint Hubert, Dame Comdr. Merit, Sovereign Mil. Hospitaller Order of St. John of Jerusale, Rhodes and Malta. Office: 269-I Centre Block The Senate of Canada Ottawa ON Canada K1A 0A4

BACON, MARTHA BRANTLEY, small business owner; b. Wrightsville, Ga., Apr. 20, 1938; d. William Riley and Susie Mae (Colston) B.; m. Albert Sidney Bacon, Jr., Aug. 3, 1958 (dec.); children: Albert Sidney, III, Gregory Riley. BS, Ga. So., Statesboro, 1959; grad., Realtors Inst., 1959; Post Grad., U. Va., Charlottesville, 1978-80, Adrian Hall Interior Design, Savannah, Ga., 1984. Lic. real estate broker Ga., Va. Tchr. Chatham Bd. Edn., Savannah, Ga., 1961; co-owner mgr. Two Kentucky Fried Chicken Restaurants, Charlottesville, Va., 1967-80; real estate broker Real Estate III, Charlottesville, Va., 1978-83, Landmark Realty, Statesboro, Ga.; tree farmer Johnson Co., Ga., 1980—; mgr., co-owner Restaurant, 1987-92; co-owner Plunderosa Antiques and Collectibles, Statesboro, Ga., 1993—. V.p. Bd. Realtors Statesboro Ga. 1985; regional franchise agt., owner Ice Cream Churn of South Ga.; mem. adv. bd. Ga. So. U. Sch. Edn., 2002—. Chmn. Jaycettes Gov. Columbus, Ga., 1962; vol. First Bapt. Ch. Pers. Com., Charlottesville, 1978, U. Va. Hosp., 1980-83; com. mem. Athletic Hall of Fame Ga. So. U., adv. bd. Ga. So. U. Sch. Edn., 2002—; mem. Ga. Forestry Stewardship, 1991—. Recipient Outstanding Sales award Real Estate III Co. Charlottesville 1980; named Outstanding Jaycette 1961, Jaycettes Gov. Columbus, 1962. Mem. AAUW, Charlottesville Restaurant Assn., Westchester Garden Club, Ga. Restaurant Assn., Ga. So. Univ. Alumni Bd., Ga. So. Symphony Guild, Ga. So. Univ. Athletic Boosters Club, Pilot Club, Evergeen Garden Club, Ga. (v.p.), Optimist (Stateboro essay chmn.). Baptist. Avocations: bridge, auctions, theater. Home: 30 Golf Club Cir Statesboro GA 30458-9160

BACON, SHERRI LEAH, elementary school educator; b. Tipton, Mo., Jan. 24, 1968; d. Robert Lee and Sharon Regina (Schreck) Fulton. BS in Edn., Ctrl. Mo. State U., 1990; MS in Edn., Troy State U., 1996. 6-8th grade tchr. Moniteau R-V, Latham, Mo., 1990-92; 6th grade tchr. N.W. Middle Sch., Clarksville, Tenn., 1992-93; 1st grade tchr. Norman Smith Elem., 1993-94; early childhood ctr. tchr. Dawning Point, Enterprise, Ala., 1994-96; tchr. 3d grade Sacred Heart Sch., 1998-99, tchr. 1st grade Robbinsdale, Minn., 1999-2000; tchr. 3d grade Columbia Cath. Sch., Mo., 2000—. Mem. Gamma Sigma Sigma (pres., 1st v.p., sec., Outstanding Mem. award 1990), Kappa Delta Pi. Avocation: reading. Home: 11298 Campbell Bridge Dr Prairie Home MO 65068

BACON, SYLVIA, judge, law educator; b. Watertown, SD, July 9, 1931; d. Julius Franklin and Anne Rae (Hyde) B. AB, Vassar Coll., Poughkeepsie, NY, 1952; cert., London Sch. Econs., 1953; LLB, Harvard U. Law Sch., 1956; LLM, Georgetown Law Ctr., Washington, 1959. Bar: DC 1956, US Supreme Ct. 1963. Law clk. to fed. judge, 1956-57; asst. US Atty. Washington, 1957-65; assoc. dir. Pres. Commn. on Crime in DC, 1965-67; trial atty. spl. projects US Dept. Justice, 1967-69; exec. asst. US atty. Washington, 1969-70; judge DC Superior Ct., Washington, 1970-92; judge-in-residence Columbus Sch. Law Cath. U. Am., Washington, 1993-95, lectr., 1995—2002, disting. lectr., 2002—; adjudicator Office of Compliance, US Legis. Br., Washington, 1996—. Adj. prof. Georgetown Law Ctr., 1960-70, 72-74; faculty Nat. Inst. Trial Advocacy, 1973-75, 91—, participant, presenter fed. and local jud. confs., 1970-90; bd. dirs. Nat. Ctr. State Cts., 1975-79, Nat. Jud. Coll., 1980-87, DC Law Students in Ct., 2002-; lectr. Nat. Coll. Criminal Def., 1975-82; faculty Nat. Jud. Coll., 1974-79; lectr. Am. Acad. Jud. Edn., 1972-82. Recipient Lever award, DC Law Students In Ct., 2005. Mem. ABA (gov. 1988-91), AAUW, DC Bar Assn. (bd. dirs. 1965-67), DC Women's Bar Assn., Am. Inns of Ct., Exec. Women in Govt., Bus. and Profl. Women's Assn., Nat. Assn. Women Judges, Supreme Ct. Hist. Soc., Phi Beta Kappa. Home: 2500 Q St NW Washington DC 20007-4373 Office: Cath U Am Columbus Sch Law 3600 McCormack Dr NE Washington DC 20064-0001 Office Phone: 202-319-6618. Business E-Mail: bacon@law.edu.

BADDOUR, ANNE BRIDGE, pilot; b. Royal Oak, Mich. d. William George and Esther Rose (Pfiester) Bridge; m. Raymond F. Baddour, Sept. 25, 1954; children: Cynthia Anne, Frederick Raymond, Jean Bridge. Student, Detroit Bus. Sch., 1948—50; BA, Pine Manor Coll. Stewardess Ea. Airlines, Boston, 1952—54; instr. aero. Powers Sch., Boston, 1958; co-pilot, flight attendant Raytheon Co., Bedford, Mass., 1958—63; flight dispatcher, ferry Pilot Comerford Flight Sch., Bedford, 1974—76; adminstrv. asst., ferry pilot Jenney Beachcraft, Bedford, 1976; mgr., pilot Balt. Airways, Inc., Bedford, 1976—77; rsch. test pilot Lincoln Lab. Flight Test Facility MIT, Lexington, 1977—97. Aviation cons., corp. pilot Energy Resources, Inc., Cambridge, Mass., 1974-84; holder World Class speed records for single-engine aircraft; Boston to Goose Bay, Labrador, 1985, Boston to Reykjavik, Iceland, 1985, Portland, Maine to Goose Bay, 1985, Portland to Reykjavik, 1985, Goose Bay to Reykjavik, 1985; records for twin-engine aircraft: Sept Isles to Goose Bay, 1988, Mont Joll to Goose Bay, 1988, Presque Isle to Goose Bay, 1988, Millinocket to Goose Bay, 1988, Bedford to Goose Bay, 1988, Goose Bay to Narssassrag, Greenland, 1988, Narssassrag to Klevelevic, Iceland, 1988, Narssassrag to Reykjavik, 1988, Bedford to Narssassrag, 1988, Millinochet to Narssassrag, 1988, Presque Isle to Narssassrag, 1988, Bedford to St. John, 1991, Bedford to Charlottetown, 1991, Charlottetown to Kennebunk, 1991, Charlottetown to Portsmouth, 1991, Muncton to Bedford, 1991, St. John, to Kennebunk, 1991, St. John to Bedford, 1991, World Class Speed Records Single-Engine Aircraft, 1991, Bedford, Mass. to Sydney, Nova Scotia, Bedford, Mass. to Sydney, Nova Scotia to Bedford, Mass., Portsmouth, New Hampshire to Sydney Nova Scotia to Portsmouth, Brunswick to Sydney Nova Scotia to Brunswick. Mem. campaign coun. Mus. Transp., Boston; mem. coun. assocs. French Libr. in Boston; commr. Commonwealth of Mass., Mass. Aero. Commn., 1979—83; trustee bd. adminstrn. Amelia Earhart Birthplace Mus., 1992—93; trustee Daniel Webster Coll., Nashua, NH, 1995—; v.p., trustee Friends of the Libr. Spl. Collections Boston U., 1997—; trustee Viscaya Mus., 2002—; bd. dirs. Smithsonian Nat. Air and Space Mus., 1998—2005, Cambridge Opera, 1977—79, Miami-Dade Maritime Mus., 2004—. Named Pilot of Yr., New Eng. sect. Internat. Women Pilots Orgn./The Ninety-Nines Inc., 1992; named to Internat. Aviation Forest of Friendship, Atchison, Kans., 1991, Women in Aviation Internat. Pioneer Hall of Fame, 2005; recipient trophy, Phila. Transcontinental Air Race, 1954, New Eng. Air Race, 1957, Clifford B. Harmon trophy, Internat. Aviatrix, 1988, recipient Spl. Recognition award, FAA, 1990. Mem.: DAR, Women in Aviation Internat. (Pioneer Hall of Fame award 2005), Friends of Switzerland, Bostonian Soc., Nat. Pilots Assn., U.S. Sea Plane Pilots Assn., Assn. Women Transcontinental Air Race, Soc. Exptl. Test Pilots, Aircraft Owners Pilots Assn., Fedn. Aeronautique Internat., Nat. Aero. Assn., Ninety-Nines (New Eng. Safety trophy 1986), Beach Colony Club, Fairchild Tropical Garden Club, Harvard Travellers Club, Boston Women's Travel Club, Chilton Club, Belmont Hill Club, Aero Club New Eng. (v.p. 1978—80, dir. 1978—2002). Home: 96 Fletcher Rd Belmont MA 02478

BADE, MICHELLE L., music educator, director; b. Alliance, Ohio, Feb. 24, 1972; d. Michael Krita and Linda Pauli; m. Christopher Bade, July 22, 1995; children: Sarah, Michael, Ryan. MusB in Edn., Mount Union Coll., 1994; MusM in Edn., MusM, U. Okla., 1996. Cert. K-12 music in instrumental, vocal. Band dir. Okla. Christian Schs., Edmond, 1996—98; dir. music Grove Sch., Shawnee, Okla., 1998—2004; music tchr. Muncie Conservatory Schs., Ind., 2004—05; music dir. Daleville Elem., Ind., 2005—. Choir dir. Village United Meth. Ch., Oklahoma City, 1998; music leader G-Force Old Town Hill, Muncie, Ind., 2005—. Clarinet Kokomo Park Band, Kokomo, Ind., 2005—. Grantee Grant, Smart Music in the Classroom, 2003, Oceania Unit, 2006. Mem.: Ind. Educators Assn., Nat. Tchrs. Union. Avocations: running, softball, travel. Home: 2200 N Wicklow Muncie IN 47304

BADE, SANDRA LYNE, secondary school educator; d. Allan and L. Ruth Pearsall; m. James Albert Bade, June 10, 1972. BS in Edn., Ctrl. Mich. U., Mt. Pleasant, 1971. Cert. secondary edn. Mich., 1971. Educator Algonac H.S., Mich., 1971—. Class advisor Algonac H.S., 1971—83, sr. class advisor, 2002—, advisor Nat. Honor Soc., 2002—. Mem.: NEA, Algonac Edn. Assn., Mich. Edn. Assn. Office: Algonac High School 5200 Taft Rd Algonac MI 48001 Office Phone: 810-794-4911.

BADEL, JULIE, lawyer; b. Chgo., Sept. 14, 1946; d. Charles and Saima (Hrykas) Badel. Student, Knox Coll., 1963—65; BA, Columbia Coll., Chgo., 1967; JD, DePaul U., 1977. Bar: Ill. 1977, U.S. Dist. Ct. (no. dist.) Ill. 1977, U.S. Ct. Appeals (7th and D.C. cirs.) 1981, U.S. Supreme Ct. 1985, U.S. Dist. Ct. (ea. dist.) Mich. 1989, U.S. Dist. Ct. (no. dist.) Ind. 2002, U.S. Dist. Ct. (we. dist.) Mich. 2005. Hearings referee State of Ill., Chgo., 1974-78; assoc. Cohn, Lambert, Ryan & Schneider, Chgo., 1978-80, McDermott, Will & Emery, Chgo., 1980-84, ptnr., 1985-2001, Epstein, Becker & Green, PC, Chgo., 2001—. Legal counsel, mem. adv. bd. Health Evaluation Referral Svc. Chgo., 1980-89; mem. Finnish Coun. Finlandia U., 2006—. Author: Hospital Restructuring: Employment Law Pitfalls, 1985; editor DePaul U. Law Rev., 1976-77. Bd. dirs. Alternatives, Inc., 1990—2002, Chgo. chpt. Asthma and Allergy Found., 1993—94, Glenwood Sch.; bd. dirs. Finnish coun. Finlandia U.; mem. bus. adv. coun. Lake Forest Grad. Sch. Mgmt. Mem.: ABA, Finnish Am. Lawyers Assn., Chgo. Bar Assn., Labor and Employment and Animal Law (vice chair 2005—06, chair 2006—), Columbia Coll. Alumni Assn. (1st v.p., bd. dirs. 1981—86), Pi Gamma Mu. Office: Epstein Becker & Green 150 N Michigan Ave 35th Fl Chicago IL 60601-7553 Business E-Mail: jbadel@ebglaw.com.

BADEN, JOAN H., retired language educator; b. Kingston, N.Y., Dec. 31, 1926; d. Douglas Roy Alverson and Petronella Agnetta Bach; children: Barbara Fagan, Bruce. BA, SUNY, Albany, 1947, MA, 1948. Cert. tchr. N.Y. Tchr. Cornwall (N.Y.) H.S., 1947—51; instr. English SUNY, Albany, 1951—55, ret., 1955. Lectr. in field. Mem. arboretum adv. com. Town of Webster, NY, 1994—2004; docent Meml. Art Mus., Rochester, NY, 1981—2000. Named to Women's Hall of Fame, Webster, 1999. Mem.: Meml. Art Gallery, Am. Rose Soc. (judge horticulture design, Silver Honor medal 1999, Outstanding Judge 1996), Federated Garden Clubs (regional dir., past. pres.), Nat. Garden Club (regional dir. 1997—99, judge horticulture design, gardening cons., landscape design cons.). Presbyterian. Avocations: reading, travel, gardening. Home: 205 Curtice Pk Webster NY 14580

BADEN, SHERI LOUISE, primary school educator; b. Beamont, Tex., July 29, 1944; d. Charles Thomas and Elsie Louise (Stapleton) Barrett; m. Joseph R. Baden (dec.); children: Brandan Kyle, Derek Paul. BS in Elem. Edn., Lamar U., Beaumont, Tex., 1970. 3d grade tchr. French Elem. Sch., Beamont, 1968—69; 2d grade tchr. Longfellow Elem. Sch., Beamont, 1969—71; kindergarten tchr. All Sts. Sch., Beamont, 1973—. Named Nat. K Tchr. of Yr., Staff Devel. Educators, Tchr. of Yr., All Sts. Sch.; named to Hall of Fame for Educators, Lamar U., 2004. Mem.: SE Tex. Hike and Bike Coalition (bd. dirs.), Citizen's Police Acad. Alumni Assn., Order Ea. Star (Worthy Matron Beaumont chpt. 1984—85), Delta Kappa Gamma (program chmn. 2004—06, pres. 2006—). Episcopalian. Avocations: cycling, square dance, country and western dance. Office: All Sts Episcopal Sch 4108 Delaware Beaumont TX 77706

BADER, KATHLEEN M., chemicals executive; B in Liberal Arts, Notre Dame; MBA, U. Calif., Berkeley. Joined Dow Chem. Co., Chgo., 1973—2005, corp. v.p. Quality and Business Excellence, 1999, pres. bus. group styrenics and engineered products, corp. v.p., quality and bus. excellence Zurich, Switzerland, 2000—04; chmn., pres., CEO Dow Cargill, Minnetonka, Minn., 2004—05; pres., CEO NatureWorks LLC (formerly known as Cargill Dow LLC), Mpls., 2005—. Chair dept. pvt. sector sr. advisory com. Homeland Security; adv. coun. US Homeland Security, 2002—; bd. dirs. Textron Inc., Providence, 2004—. Internat. bd. dir. Habitat for Humanity; dean's coun. Harvard Sch. Govt. Named One of 50 Most Powerful Women in Internat. Bus., Fortune Mag., 2001—03; recipient Henry Laurence Gantt medal, ASME, 2005. Office: NatureWorks LLC PO Box 5830 Minneapolis MN 55440-5830 Office Phone: 877-423-7659.*

BADER, LORRAINE GREENBERG, textile stylist, designer, consultant, artist; b. Bklyn., Sept. 5, 1930; m. Martin Bader, June 24, 1950. Student, Parsons Sch. Design, 1948-49. Textile stylist, dir. design, fashion and spl. creative projects, color coord. Cortley Fabrics Corp., N.Y.C., 1950-64, Avon Fabrics, N.Y.C., 1964-67, R.S.L. Fabrics Corp., N.Y.C., 1967-71; textile stylist, fashion dir. Shirley Fabrics Corp., N.Y.C., 1971-76; interior designer, decorator Lorraine Bader Interiors, Lawrence, N.Y., 1976-79; textile stylist, dir. design, fashion, and spl. projects, color coord. Lida Inc., N.Y.C., 1979-81; textile designer Fresh Paint, N.Y.C., 1981-87; textile designer for women's wear, children's wear, fabrics, sweaters, scarves, dinnerware, tablecloths, placemats and bedding for home furnishings Lorraine Bader Designs, Hackensack, N.J., 1987-97, owner, designer Boynton Beach, Fla., 1998. Scholar Parsons Sch. Design, 1948. Mem.: Boca Raton Mus. of Art Guild (exhibiting mem.), Women in the Visual Arts, The Fashion Group. Avocations: antiques, interior decorating, faux decorative art, painting.

BADU, ERYKAH, singer, songwriter; b. Dallas, Feb. 26, 1971; children: Puma, Seven. Student, Dallas Sch. Arts. Singer, songwriter: single On and On, 1997 (Grammy award for best female vocal performance, 1998), Baduizm, 1997 (Grammy award for best R&B album, 1997), Live!, 1997, Mama's Gun, 2000, Worldwide Underground, 2003; actor: (films) Cider House Rules, 1999, Blues Brothers, 2000, House of D, 2004. Recipient Favorite New Soul/R&B Artist award, Am. Music Awards, 1998, Grammy award for Best Rap Performance by a duo or group for You Got Me, 1999.

BAE, SUE HYUN, psychologist, educator; b. Seoul, Kyung-Gee, Republic of Korea, Aug. 3, 1969; d. Jong Hoa Bae and Jeeyoung Kim. BA, U. Calif., Berkeley, 1991; MEd, MA, Columbia U., 1994; PhD, U. Chgo., 2001. Clin. adminstr. Heartland Alliance, Chgo., 1999—2001; asst. prof. Ill. Sch. Profl. Psychology Chgo., Argosy U., 2001—. Adj. faculty Ill. Inst. Art, Chgo., 2001; diversity tng. cons. Anixter Ctr., Chgo., 2003; child psychologist Anxiety Clinic M. Mark McKee, PsyD and Assocs., 2004—. Author: (book) The Psychotherapist's Perspective, 2003; contbr. articles to profl. jours. Recipient Faculty Rsch. award, Ill. Sch. Profl. Psychology, 2001. Mem.: APA, Soc. for Psychotherapy Rsch. Achievements include research in international psychology; cross-cultural studies, cross-cultural/multicultural psychotherapy; diversity training and teaching. Avocations: travel, golf, music. Office: Argosy U Ill Sch Profl Psychology 350 N Orleans Chicago IL 60605 Office Phone: 312-777-7680.

BAECKLER, VIRGINIA VAN WYNEN, librarian, writer; b. Englewood, N.J., June 18, 1942; d. Kenneth Gregg and Esther Grace (Thompson) Van Wynen; m. William W. Baeckler, Apr. 9, 1971; children— Gregg William, Sarah Angela. B.A., Cornell U., 1964, M.A., 1967; postgrad. Moscow State U. (USSR), 1967-69; M.L.S., Rutgers U., 1972. Head Slavic acquisitions Princeton U. Library, 1969-71; head Mercer County Library, Ewing, N.J., 1972-75; dir. Sources, Hopewell, N.J., 1975—; dir. Plainsboro (N.J.) Pub. Libr., 1991—. Author: Go, Pep and Pop!, 1976, PR for Pennies, 1978, Sparkle!, 1980, Storytime Science, 1986. Vol., tchr. YWCA of Princeton, N.J., 1979. Mem. Nat. Sci. Tchrs. Assn., Alliance for Arts and Edu.,ALA, Ednl. Media Assn. (lobbyist). Democrat. Home: 26 Hart Ave Hopewell NJ 08525-1425

BAEHMANN, SUSAN ELIZABETH, artist; b. Milw., May 16, 1945; d. Chester Reuben Smith and Dorothy Margaret (Meyer) Johnson; m. Dale Fredrick Baehmann, May 27, 1972; children: Edan Andrew, Hai Phan. BFA, U. Wis., 1978. Painting and drawing instr. U. N.C.-W., 1993-97; printmaking instr. St. John's Mus. Art, 1998-99. One-woman shows include Carroll Coll., Otteson Gallery, Waukesha, Wis., 1982-83, Bradley Galleries, Milw., 1982, 95, 91, The Fanny Garver Gallery, Madison, Wis., 1985, John Michael Kohler Art Ctr., Sheboygan, Wis., 1985, U. N.C., Wilmington, 1994; exhibited in group shows Artists of Southeastern N.C., St. John's Mus. Art, Wilmington, N.C., 1997, Cameron Mus. Art, 2004, Art du Monde, 16 Gallery tour of Japan, 1990-91, Milw. Art Mus., 1988-89, Art Inst. Chgo., 1985, 87, also numerous others; represented in 60 permanent corp., pub. and ednl. collections; represented in pvt. collections throughout 8 countries; work pub. in Women in Print: Prints from 3M by Contemporary Women Printmakers, 1995. Recipient Milw. Arts Commn. Purchase award, 1982, 87, Wis. Painters and Sculptors award, 1982, Catherine Lorillard Wolfe Cert. of Merit, Nat. Arts Club, 1983, Exceptional Achievement awrd UWM Alumni Assn. Art Show, 1987, Best of Show N.C. Art Assn. Spring Show, 1992, Exhibitors Choice award Spoleto, Charleston, S.C., 1995, Best of Show Arts Coun. Lower Cape Fear, 1995, 1st Pl. Drawing and Printmaking Summerfair, 1997, 2d pl. award Telfair Mus. Art, 1997, Best of Show Atalaya, 1999, Jurors award Airline Arts, 2003. Democrat. Avocation: horticulture. Home: 617 Goldeneye Ct Wilmington NC 28411 E-mail: artcatins@cs.com.

BAEHR, ELSA TELSER, clinical psychologist, neurotherapist; b. Chgo., June 5, 1929; d. Philip Stein and Mildred (Mayerson) Beck; m. Eugene Telser, Aug. 24, 1947 (div.); children: Joanne, Margaret, Elizabeth; m. Rufus Baehr, June 28, 1975. BA, Roosevelt U., Chgo., 1952; MA, Roosevelt U., 1954; PhD, Northwestern U., 1971. Lic. clin. psychologist, Ill.; cert. neurotherapist. Sr. psychologist Cook County Hosp., Chgo., 1974-78, adminstr. Outpatient Psychol. Clinic, 1976—78; pvt. practice psychotherapy Evanston, Ill., 1971—; clinical psychologist Baehr & Baehr, Ltd., Evanston, 1982—. Cons. Milw. Psychiatric Services, 1970-74; assoc. dept. psychiatry Northwestern U. Med. Sch., 1973—; clin assoc. U. Ill, Chgo., 1981-90; cons. dept. psychiatry Lakeside VA, Chgo., 1988-2003; adj. staff Charter-Barclay Hosp., Chgo., 1988-91. Fellow Internat. Soc. for Neuronal Regulation; mem. Am. Psychol. Assn., Ill. Psychol. Assn., Assn. for Clin. and Exptl. Hypnosis, Nat. Acad. Neuropsychology, Assn. Applied Psychophysiology Office: Concourse Office Plz 4711 Golf Rd Skokie IL 60076 Office Phone: 847-624-8060. Personal E-mail: ebaehr@hotmail.com.

BAENA, MARISA, professional golfer; b. Pereira, Colombia, June 1, 1977; Bachelor, Univ. Ariz. Achievements include Winner: HSBC Women's World Championship. Office: Ladies Professional Golf Assn 100 International Golf Drive Daytona Beach FL 32124-1092

BAER, DIANE DRAPER, artist; b. Balt., Nov. 4, 1945; d. Bernard Anthony and Mary Anna Draper; m. Robert Way Baer, Feb. 10, 1979; children: Kristin Michelle, Lauren Ashley. BA in Biology, McDaniel Coll., Westminster, Md., 1967. Electroencephalogram tech. U. Hosp., Balt., 1967—69; pers. counselor Snelling and Snelling, Balt., 1970—71; customer svc. rep. Md. Paper Box, Balt., 1971—73; dir. telephone sales and svc. Philips Roxane Lab., Balt., 1973—75; ednl. sales rep. Williams and Wilkins, Balt., 1976—79; pers. counselor Alan J. Blair, San Francisco, 1979—82. Sec., treas. Am. Heart Assn., Kirksville, 1992—96. Mem.: Kirksville Arts Assn. (adv. bd. 2000, bd. dirs. 2000—06, sec. 2000—06), Sr. Circle, Kirksville Women's Connection (hospitality chairperson 2004—06). Democrat.

BAER, KAREN FAUST, music educator, musician; b. Bklyn., Mar. 4, 1950; d. Morris Faust and Lillian Rosenberg; m. Paul Robert Baer, Aug. 27, 1972; children: Adam, Seth. MusB, Juilliard Sch., N.Y.C., 1971, MS, 1972; postgrad., Westminster Coll., 1984—86. Cert. music tchr. NY. Asst. prof. SUNY, Purchase, 1972—74; vocal music dir. Rockville Centre (NY) Schs., 1974—77, 1980—; profl. pianist, accompanist NY, Cin., Boston, Phila., Italy, 1980—, Baer-Nelson Duo, Profl. Piano Duo, Julliard Sch., Hofstra U., Kingsborough Coll., Heckscher Mus., L.I. Librs., 1994—. Presenter confs. in field; lectr., performer N.Y.C. schs.; mem. Auburn Collegium Chamber Music Group, 1984—86; accompanist Nassau Area All State Mixed Chorus, 1990—, NYSSMA All-State Conf. Concerts, 1994—2006, L.I. Masterworks, L.I. Philharm. Choruses, 2004; mem. theory faculty, pre-coll. divsn. The Juilliard Sch., 2005; chamber music recitals Princeton U., 2006. Performer: WQXR Radio, 1966—68, 2000, WNYC Radio, 6467, 1999; performer: (chamber music recitals) Tanglewood Music Ctr., 1971; performer: (concerts) Julliard Sch., Lincoln Ctr., Hofstra U. Town Hall, ALice Tully Hall; debut: Am. Symphony Orch., Carnegie Hall, 1968; internat. debut: Todi Music Festival, 1969; performer: Baer-Nelson Duo Premiere Multimedia Concert, Joslyn Mus., 2005. Bd. dirs. Met. Youth Orch., Manhasset, NY, 1997—2000. Fellow, Tanglewood Music Ctr., 1971, Juilliard Sch., 1972; grantee, Rockville Centre Edn. Found., 1996; scholar, Todi Music Festival, Italy, 1969. Mem.: United Fedn. Tchrs., Piano Tchrs. Build, Music Educators Nat. Conf., Nat. Music Educators Assn., NYSSMA. Jewish. Avocations: gardening, quilting. Home: 2755 Bellmore Ave Bellmore NY 11710 E-mail: kfbaer@hotmail.com.

BAER, MARIA RENÉE, hematologist, researcher; b. N.Y.C., Jan. 6, 1952; d. George Bernard and Evelyn Joan (Mandl) Schless; m. Alan Nathaniel Baer, June 4, 1978; children: Tamara, Nicholas. BA, Harvard U., 1973; MD, Johns Hopkins U., 1979. Prof. Roswell Park Cancer Inst., SUNY, Buffalo, assoc. prof. dept. pharmacology and therapeutics. Contbr. articles to profl. jours. Recipient Nat. Rsch. Svc. award, Divsn. Hematology Vanderbilt U., Nashville, 1984-86. Fellow ACP; mem. Am. Soc. Hematology, Am. Assn. Cancer Rsch., Am. Soc. Clin. Oncology, Cancer and Leukemia Group B, Divsn. Hematology Vanderbilt U., Nashville, 1982-84. Office: Roswell Park Cancer Inst Elm And Carlton St Buffalo NY 14263-0001 E-mail: maria.baer@roswellpark.org.

BAER, SUSAN M., airport executive; married; 1 child. BA in urban studies and anthropology, Barnard Coll.; MBA, NYU. Mgmt. analyst Port Authority of NY and NJ, mgr. pub. svcs. divsn. Tunnels, Bridges and Terminals Dept., mgr. Lincoln Tunnel, 1985—86, mgr. Port Authority Bus Terminal Manhattan N.Y.C., 1986—88, gen. mgr. Aviation Customer and Mktg. Svcs., 1988—94, gen. mgr. LaGuardia Airport Flushing, NY, 1994-98, gen. mgr. Newark Internat. Airport NJ, 1998—. Office: Newark Int & Teterboro Airports Conrad Rd, Bldg 1 Newark NJ 07114

BAERMANN, DONNA LEE ROTH, real estate property executive, retired insurance analyst; b. Carroll, Iowa, Apr. 28, 1939; d. Omer H. and Mae Lavina (Larson) Real; m. Edwin Ralph Baermann, Jr., July 8, 1961 (dec. Aug. 1997); children: Beth, Bryan, Cynthia. BS, Mt. Mercy Coll., Ames, 1973;

student, Iowa State U.-Ames, 1957-61. Cert. profl. ins. woman; fellow Life Mgmt. Inst. ins. agt. Luthern Mut. Ins. Co., Cedar Rapids, Iowa, 1973; home economist Iowa-Ill. Gas & Electric Co., Cedar Rapids, Iowa, 1973-77; supr. premium collection Life Investors Ins. Co. (now Aegon USA), Cedar Rapids, Iowa, 1978-83, methods and procedures analyst, 1987-94; pres., CEO Baermann Apts. Inc., 1992-94, owner, pres., 1992—. Mem. telecom. study group com. 1982-83, mem. productivity task force, 1984-94, TAB cert. facilitator, 2001—. Vol. Mercy Med. Ctr., Cedar Rapids, Iowa, 2002—; apptd. by Mayor and City Coun. Housing Bd. Appeals, Cedar Rapids, 2003. Mem. Internat. Platform Assn., Citizens Com. for Person with Disabilities, Nat. Assn. Ins. Women, Nat. Mgmt. Assn. (bd. dirs. Cedar Rapids chpt.), DAR, Knights of Malta (named Damsel of Ancient Order of St. John, N.Y.C.), Chi Omega. Republican. Presbyterian. Home: 361 Willshire Ct NE Cedar Rapids IA 52402-6922 Personal E-mail: dlrbaer@peoplepc.com.

BAESSLER, CHRISTINA A., medical/surgical nurse; b. Phila., Feb. 10, 1948; d. Harry and Mary (Moreken) B. Diploma, St. Agnes Sch. Nursing, 1968; student, Neumann Coll., 1977-81; BSN, LaSalle U., 1987, MSN, 1993. RN, Pa.; cert. CPR, BCLS. Project coord., asst. adminstr. Nat. Cardiovascular Rsch. Ctr., Haddonfield, N.J.; cardiac arrhythmia suppression trial project coord. Hahnemann U. Hosp., Phila.; grad. hosp. nurse researcher in cardiology Hahneman U. Hosp., Phila.; gallstone lithotripsy nurse clin. coord. Hahnemann U. Hosp., Phila., coord. electrophysiology rsch. and quality assurance, 1990—, antiarrhythmics verses implantable defibrillators rsch. coord., 1993—, allhat coord., 1994, affirm coord., 1995—, invest htn coord., 1998—, ramp coord., 1996—, defibrillator implant coord., 1996—. Contbr. articles to profl. publs. Recipient Vol. Recognition award S.E. Pa. chpt. Am. Heart Assn., 1982. Mem. AACN (life, pres. S.E. Pa. chpt. 1975-76), Am. Heart Assn. (nursing com. 1994—), Sigma Theta Tau (v.p. Kappa Delta chpt. 1989-94, rsch. award, 1995). Home: 848 Windermere Ave Drexel Hill PA 19026-1534 Office: MCP Hahnemann EPS/Cardiology MS-470 Broad & Vine Sts Philadelphia PA 19102

BAEZ, JOAN CHANDOS, vocalist; b. SI, NY, Jan. 9, 1941; d. Albert V. and Joan (Bridge) B.; m. David Victor Harris, Mar. 1968 (div. 1973); 1 son, Gabriel Earl. Appeared in coffeehouses, Gate of Horn, Chgo., 1958, Ballad Room, Club 47, 1958-68, Newport (R.I.) Folk Festival, 1959-69, 85, 87, 90, 92, 93, 95, extended tours to colls. and concert halls, 1960s, appeared Town Hall and Carnegie Hall, 1962, 67, 68, U.S. tours, 1970—, concert tours in Japan, 1966, 82, Europe, 1970-73, 80, 83-84, 87-90, 93—, Australia, 1985; rec. artist for Vanguard Records, 1960-72, A&M, 1973-76, Portrait Records, 1977-80, Gold Castle Records, 1986-89, Virgin Records, 1990-93, Grapevine Label Records (UK), 1995-97, Guardian Records, 1995-97, European record albums, 1981, 83, award 8 gold albums, 1 gold single; albums include Gone From Danger, 1997, Rare, Live & Classic (box set), 1993, Dark Chords on a Big Guitar, 2003, Bowery Songs, 2005; author: Joan Baez Songbook, 1964, (biography) Daybreak, 1968, (with David Harris) Coming Out, 1971, And a Voice to Sing With, 1987, (songbook) An Then I Wrote, 1979. Extensive TV appearances and speaking tours U.S. and Can. for anti-militarism, 1967-68; visit to Dem. Republic of Vietnam, 1972, visit to war torn Bosnia-Herzegovina, 1993; founder, v.p. Inst. for Study Nonviolence (now Resource Ctr. for Nonviolence, Santa Cruz, Calif.), Palo Alto, Calif., 1965; mem. nat. adv. coun. Amnesty Internat., 1974-92; founder, pres. Humanitas/Internat. Human Rights Com., 1979-92; condr. fact-finding mission to refugee camps, S.E. Asia, Oct. 1979; began refusing payment of war taxes, 1964; arrested for civil disobedience opposing draft, Oct., Dec., 1967. Office: Diamonds & Rust Prodns PO Box 1026 Menlo Park CA 94026-1026 Office Phone: 650-328-0266.

BAGBY, MARTHA L. GREEN, real estate holding company executive, writer, publishing executive; b. West Palm Beach, Fla., June 17, 1937; d. Hampton and Louise (Lambert) Green; m. Joseph R. Bagby, 1966; 1 child, Meredith E. AA, Palm Beach Jr. Coll., 1957; AB, U. Miami, 1959; MA, Pa. State U., 1964. Tchr. journalism, english Palm Beach County, 1959—62; instr. journalism Pa. State U., 1962—63; city editor, writer Palm Beach News and Life, 1963—64; editor Alfred Hitchcock Mag., Riviera Beach, Fla., 1964; editor, supr. editl. svc., pub. rels. employee newspaper Nat. Airlines, Inc., Miami, Fla., 1965—73; corp. sec., chmn. bd. Property Resources Co., Palm Beach, Fla., 1971—. Life dir. CareNet Global, 2002—; Ill. franchisee Burger King Corp.; founder Internat. Health Awareness Assn.; lectr. journalism Dade, Palm Beach counties; instr. Barry Coll., Miami; pub. The Bagbys Health Digest, 1985—. Author: Stranglehold, 1977, The Complete Real Estate Dictionary, 1992, The Real Estate Financing Deskbook, 1979-90; author: (with others) The Complete Real Estate Book. Mem. exec. bd. Childbirth and Parent Edn. Assn., Miami. Mem.: Internat. Assn. Corp. Real Estate Execs. (founder, trustee, exec. editor, dir. life), Women in Comm. (pres.), Air Transport Assn. Am., Airline Editors Conf. (chmn.), S. Fla. Indsl. Chmn. Internat. Council Indsl. Editors, Fla. Pub. Relations Assn. Office: 125 Brazilian Ave Palm Beach FL 33480-4221 Office Phone: 561-655-9510.

BAGGETT, KATHLEEN M., psychologist, research scientist; d. Sandra J. and Lonnie R. Clarkson; m. Ronald G. Baggett, Aug. 6, 1988. BA, MidAmerica Nazarene U., Kans., 1989; MS, U. Kans., Kans, 1997, PhD, 2000. Lic. Psychologist, Health Svc Provider Mo. State Com. of Psychologists, 2002. Asst. rsch. prof. Juniper Gardens Children's Project, Schiefelbusch Inst. Life Span Studies, Kansas City, 2003—; courtesy asst. prof. Dept. of Applied Behavioral Sci., U. of Kans., Lawrence, 2003—. Faculty Nat. Tng. Inst. on Effective Practices Supporting Soc. Emotional Devel. in Young Children, Tampa, 2003—; alt. mem. Human Subjects Com. U. of Kans. Instl. Rev. Bd., Lawrence, Kans., 1993—; editl. rev. bd. mem. Exceptional Children Jour. of the Coun. for Exceptional Children, 2003—; post-doctoral editl. rev. bd. mem. Child Maltreatment Jour. of the Am. Profl. Soc. on Abuse of Children, 2003—. Contbr. chapters to books. Post Doctoral fellow, U.S. Dept. of Spl. Edn., 2002-2003, Fed. rsch. grant, U.S. HHS- Head Start Bur., 2004-2007. Mem.: APA. Office: Juniper Garden's Children's Project 650 Minnesota Ave Kansas City KS 66101 Office Phone: 913-321-3143. Office Fax: 913-371-8522.

BAGGOTT, BRENDA JANE LAMB, elementary school educator; b. Augusta, Ga., Nov. 10, 1948; d. Morgan Barrett Jr. and Ollie Virginia (Toole) Lamb; m. John Carl Baggott, July 8, 1967 (div. Jan. 1998); children: Carla Baggott Walczak Becnel, John Carl Jr. Student, Truett McConnel Jr. Coll., 1966-67; BS in spl. Edn., Augusta Coll., 1974; postgrad., Southeastern La. U., 1976-77, U. New Orleans, 1977-78, U. Ctrl. Fla., 1987, 97—; MEd, Nova Southeastern U., 1997. Cert. spl. edn. tchr. in varying exceptionalities and mental handicaps, elem. tchr. ESOL, coaching for Spl. Olympics, Fla. Spl. Olympics tchr. Copeland Elem. Sch., Augusta, Ga., 1973-74; spl. edn. tchr. Percy Julian Spl. Sch., Marrero, La., 1974-78; Spl. edn. resource tchr. Rosemary Mid. Sch., Andrews, S.C., 1978; spl. edn. tchr. Bynum Elem. Sch., Gerogetown, S.C., 1979, Ridgewood Park Elem. Sch., Orlando, Fla., 1979-97; reading recovery tchr. Rock Lake Elem. Sch., Orlando, 1997—2002, corrective reading tchr., 2003—; lab tchr. Read 180, 2002—; instrnl. coach, 2004—. Curriculum coord. Percy Julian Spl. Sch., 1975-77; mem. state tchr. mentally handicapped exam validation team Inst. for Instnl. Rsch. and Practice, Fla. Dept. Edn., Tampa, 1990—. Coord. Orange County Spl. Olympics, Orlando, 1984-85, coach, 1974—. Mem. Coun. for Exceptional Children, Internat. Reading Assn., Orange County Reading Coun., Reading Recovery Coun. N.Am., Fla. Reading Assn. Democrat. Baptist. Avocations: directing children's choirs, coaching special olympics. Office: Rock Lake Elem Sch 408 N Tampa Ave Orlando FL 32805-1296

BAGHAEI-RAD, NANCY JANE BEBB, elementary school educator; b. Amsterdam, N.Y., Apr. 8, 1963; d. Warren D. Bebb and Joan Pipito (Ruck) B. BS, SUNY, Oswego, 1986; MEd, Lesley Coll., 1989; AAS, Cazenovia Coll., 1983; post grad., Columbia U. Cert. tchr., N.Y., N.J. Program dir. Adirondack Camp for Boys and Girls, Glenburnie, N.Y.; tchr. kindergarten Perth Cen. Sch., Amsterdam, N.Y.; tchr. St. Mary's Inst., Amsterdam; literacy evaluator Boston Plan for Excellence/Trotter Sch., Roxbury, Mass.; 1st grade tchr. Doane Stuart Sch., Albany, N.Y.; tchr. Mildred E. Strang Mid. Sch., Yorktown Heights, N.Y.; coord. gifted and talented, primary computer tchr. Highland Avenue Sch., Midland Park, N.J. Coord. elem. gifted and talented Scotia-Glenville Sch. Dist., NY; academic head Lower Sch. Brown Sch., Schenectady, NY. Named Tchr. of Yr. Gov. of N.J., 1994. Mem. ASCD. Business E-Mail: drad@nycap.rr.com.

BAGIN, KATHERINE, telecommunications industry executive; BS, Rutgers U., MS in Info. Sci.; exec. MBA, Harvard U. V.p., new svcs. devel. AT&T, NJ, NY, v.p., Internet Telephony divsn. NJ. Office: AT&T 175 E Houston San Antonio TX 78205-2233*

BAGINSKI, MAUREEN A., former federal agency administrator; b. Feb. 3, 1955; m. Michael Baginski. BA in Russian and Spanish, SUNY, Albany, MA in Slavic lang.; at, Moriz Torez Fgn. Lang. Inst., Moscow; LHD (hon.), U. Albany, 2005. Russian lang. instr. Nat. Security Agy./Ctrl. Security Svc., 1979, sr. ops. officer, nat. ops. ctr., signals intelligence nat. intelligence officer Russia, exec. asst. to the dir., dep. chief global access program, chief, directorate of ops., consumer products and svcs., asst. dep. dir. tech. and sys., chief, officer of the dir., dir. signals intelligence, 2001—03; exec. asst. dir. Office of Intelligence FBI, Washington, 2003—05; dir. intelligence sector BearingPoint, Inc., McLean, Va., 2005—06; pres., Nat. Security Systems Sector SPARTA, Inc., Arlington, Va., 2006—. Bd. dirs. SI Internat. Inc., 2006—, Argon ST, 2006—. Recipient Sustained Exec. Leadership award, Dir. Ctrl. Intelligence, Exceptional Civilian Svc award, Nat. Security Agy., Outstanding Leadership award, Dir. of Mil. Intelligence's Leadership award, Presdl. Rank award (2). Avocations: gardening, kayaking. Office: SPARTA Inc 1911 N Ft Myer Dr Ste 1100 Arlington VA 22209*

BAGLEY, CYNTHIA ELAINE, writer; b. Bella Coola, B.C., Can., Aug. 19, 1961; arrived in Germany, 1998, arrived in U.S., 2002; d. Dean Calvin and Coene Bagley; m. Edward D. Tune, Feb. 16, 1993. AA in Gen. Edn., U. Md., 1999, BA in English summa cum laude, 2001; postgrad., U. Okla. Customer svc. engr. Lockheed Martin, Quarry Heights, Panama, 1994—96; customer engr. Premier Office Sys., Las Vegas, Nev., 1997—98; with JayCo Svcs., Mannheim, Germany, 1998; program asst. Ramstein, Germany, 2002; ret., 2002. Author short stories, essays, revs. and poetry; contbr. articles to profl. jours. With USN, 1988—94. Mem.: MLA, Vasculits Found., Associated Writing Programs, Sigma Tau Delta, Phi Kappa Phi. Home: 710 Hotsprings Rd #207 Carson City NV 89706 E-mail: cynbagley@hotmail.com.

BAGLEY, EDYTHE SCOTT, theater educator; b. Marion, Ala. d. Obie and Bernice (McMurry) Scott; m. Arthur Moten Bagley, June 5, 1954; 1 child, Arturo Scott. BEd, Ohio State U., 1949; MA in English, Columbia U., 1954; MFA in Theater Arts, Boston U., 1965. Instr. Elizabeth City (N.C.) State Coll., 1953-56; asst. prof. Albany (Ga.) State Coll., 1956-57, A&T U., Greensboro, N.C., 1957-58, Norfolk (Va.) State Coll., 1963-65; assoc. prof. theater Cheyney (Pa.) U., 1971—96, chair dept. theater arts; ret. Cons. in black theater Mich. State U., East Lansing, 1969-71. Dir. coll. prodns., 1968-71. Spl. asst. to Coretta Scott King; charter mem. Kimmel Ctr. for Profl. Arts, Phila., Nat Constn. Ctr, Phila. Mem. NAACP, Nat. Coun. Negro Women, The Links Inc., Womens Internat. League for Peace and Freedom, The Phila. Martin Luther King Jr. Assn. for Nonviolence (bd. dirs.), The Martin Luther King Jr. Ctr. for Nonviolent Social Change (bd. dirs.). Baptist. Achievements include being featured in the book Sisters. Home: 2 Derry Dr Cheyney PA 19319 Office: Cheyney U Cheyney PA 19319

BAGLEY FREELS, NANCY VIRGINIA, secondary school educator; b. Luling, Tex., Jan. 17, 1945; d. Thomas Daniel and Carlene Virginia Bagley; m. Jim Earl Bagley Freels, Dec. 18, 1971; children: Bradley James Freels, Shelli Virginia Heard. BS in Home Econs., Tex. State U., San Marcos, 1967. Cert. OSHA and SERV safe Nat. Restaurant Assn., 2006. Dir. Learning Tree Schs., Humble and Atascocita, Tex., 1978—88; family and consumer scis. tchr. Hays Consol. Ind. Sch. Dist., Buda, Tex., 1988—. Dir., owner cmty. arts and crafts show Martindale (Tex.) Market Days, 2005—. Named Tchr. of Yr., Leo Club, 2000; recipient Starmaker award, Hays HS, 2003. Mem.: Family and Consumer Scis. Tchrs. Assn. Tex. Lutheran. Avocations: religion, fashion and interior design. Home: 193 Rector Kyle TX 78640 Office: Jack C Hays High School 4800 Jack C Hays Trail Buda TX 78610 Office Phone: 512-268-2911. Business E-Mail: freelsn@hayscisd.net.

BAGLIVO, MARY L., advertising executive; m. James Meguerian; children: John, Martha. Bachelors, Rutgers U.; M in Advt., Northwestern U. Account exec. Euro RSCG Tatham, Chgo., 1981-91, sr. ptnr., 1991-94, mng. ptnr., 1994-96, CEO, 1996-99; chief mktg. officer, exec. v.p., N.Am. J. Walker Thompson (unit of WPP Group), 1999-2000, COO, global bus. dir., N.Am., 2000—04; CEO, worldwide mktg. dir. Saatchi & Saatchi, NYC, 2004—. Bd. dir. Evanston Northwestern Healthcare, Advertising Week, 2005—. Mem.: The Advertising Club (bd. dirs. sr. v.p.), Phi Beta Kappa. Avocation: fashion. Office: Saatchi & Saatchi 375 Hudson St New York NY 10014-3620 Office Phone: 212-463-2000. Office Fax: 212-463-9855.*

BAGWELL, CAROL TESSIER, special education educator, consultant; b. Waterbury, Conn., Dec. 25, 1948; d. Armand Lester and Helen Marie (Shortt) Tessier; m. Mallory Mason Bagwell, 1976 (div. 1998); children: Nathan James, Matthew Philip. BS in Elem. Edn., Western Conn. State U., Danbury, 1971; MS in Spl. Edn., So. Conn. State U., New Haven, 1972; MS in 6th Yr. Ednl. Leadership, Ctrl. Conn. State U., New Britain, 2004. Cert. profl. educator pre-K to 12 Conn., ednl. adminstr. pres-K to 12 Conn. Spl. educator Bristol Pub. Schs., Conn., 1972—84, Region 1 Sch. Dist., Salisbury, Conn., 1990—2004; spl. edn. coord. Southington Pub. Schs., Conn., 2004—. Ednl. cons., Falls Village, Conn., 1998—; adv. bd. Spl. Edn. Parent Adv. Com., Falls Village, 2000—02; adminstrv. coun. Southington Pub. Schs., 2004—. Grantee Grad. fellow in spl. edn., So. Conn. State U., 1972. Mem.: ASCD, Learning Disabilities Assn. Am. Roman Catholic. Avocations: gardening, walking, reading, journal writing. Home: PO Box 242 Falls Village CT 06031 Office: Southington Bd of Education 49 Beecher St Southington CT 06489

BAHCALL, NETA ASSAF, astrophysicist; b. Israel, Dec. 16, 1942; d. Yehezkel Oscar and Gita (Zilberstein) Assaf; m. John Norris Bahcall, Mar. 21, 1966; children: Ron Assaf, Dan Ophir, Orli Gilat. BS, Hebrew U., Jerusalem, 1963; MS, Weizmann Inst. Sci., Israel, 1965; PhD, Tel Aviv U., 1970. Rsch. asst. astrophysics Calif. Inst. Tech., 1965-67; rsch. fellow Calif. Inst. Tech., 1970-71; rsch. assoc. at observatory Princeton U., 1971-74, rsch. staff mem. 1974-75, rsch. astronomer, 1975-79, sr. rsch. astronomer, 1979-83, chief gen. observer br., from 1983; with Space Telescope Sci. Inst., Balt.; prof. dept. astronomy Princeton (N.J.) U., 1990—, dir. coun. sci. and tech., 2000—. Contbr. articles to profl. jours. Mem. Am. Astron. Soc., Nat. Acad. Sci. Office: Princeton U Dept Astro-Physics Peyton Hall Princeton NJ 08544 E-mail: neta@astro.princeton.edu.

BAHL-MOORE, ELIZABETH ANN, artist, educator; b. Sayre, Pa., Dec. 29, 1978; d. John Anthony Bahl and Margaret Marie Hildebrandt; m. William Andrew Moore, June 13, 1998. BFA magna cum laude, Longwood U., Farmville, Va., 2002. Cert. tchr. Va. Instr. art Longwood Ctr. Visual Arts, Farmville, Va., 2003; tchr. art Culpeper (Va.) County Pub. Schs., 2003—. Instr. art summer enrichment Culpeper (Va.) County Pub. Schs., 2004; founder After Sch. Art Club Program Culpeper, 2004—05. One-woman shows include Artistic License, Culpeper, Va., 2005, Windmore Artist Mems. Show, Culpeper, 2005, Windmore Patron Art Show, 2006, exhibitions include Heart Va. Art and Craft Outdoor Festival, 2003—05, Windmere Artist Group Show, Colpeper, Va., 2005. Vol. Prince Edward Elem., Farmville, 2003; bd. dirs. Voices of Blue Ridge, Culpeper, 2004—. Mem.: NEA, Va. Edn. Assn., Nat. Art Edn. Assn., Va. Art Edn. Assn., Phi Kappa Phi. Office: Culpeper Middle Sch 14300 Achievement Dr Culpeper VA 22701

BAHNER, SUE (FLORENCE SUZANNA BAHNER), broadcast executive; d. William and Florence (Quinlivan) McElwee; m. David S. Bahner; children: Suzanna Elizabeth, Caryl Aileen. Grad., Columbia Bus. Coll., 1950. Various exec. sec. positions, 1954-74; office mgr. Sta. WYRD, Syracuse, N.Y., 1974, gen. mgr., 1974-80, Sta. WWWG-AM, Rochester, N.Y., 1980-93, WDCW, Syracuse, 1993-98; pres. The Cornerstone Group, 1986—90, Crossway Cons., 1997—. Bd. dirs. Rescue Mission, Syracuse, ENRB, 2005—; active Eastern Hills Bible Ch. Mem. Greater Syracuse Assn. Evangelicals (treas. 1993-97), N.Y. State Assn. Evangelicals (sec. 1998-2000), Nat. Religious Broadcasters (pres. ea. chpt. 1984-98, bd. dirs. 1983—, 2d v.p. 1998-2000, mem. exec. com. 1992—). Office: Natl Religious Broadcasters 7839 Ashton Ave Manassas VA 20109-2883

BAHR, ALICE HARRISON, librarian; b. N.Y.C., July 24, 1946; d. Arthur and Charlotte (Waterstradt) Harrison; m. Robert A. Bahr, Feb. 14, 1971; children: Aimee Marie Malone, Keith Lenert Bahr. BA, Temple U., 1968; MLS, Drexel U., 1972; MA, Lehigh U., 1975, PhD, 1980. Asst. reference libr. Lehigh U., Bethlehem, Pa., 1971-74, teaching asst., English Dept., 1974-80; instr. part-time Cedar Crest Coll., Allentown, Pa., 1980-82; project libr., govt. publs. Cedar Crest, Muhlenberg Coll. Librs., Allentown, 1980-84, project libr., online systems, 1985-88; dir. Spring Hill Coll. Libr., Mobile, Ala., 1988—. Author monographs on libr. subjects.; editor: Coll. and Undergraduate Librs., Future Teaching Roles for Academic Libr.; contbr. articles profl. jours. Recipient Lawrence Henry Gipson award for 18th Century Studies, Lehigh U., 1979. Mem. Am. Libr. Assn., Ala. Libr. Assn., Network Ala. Acad. Librs. (exec. coun., publications com., chmn.). Avocation: scuba diving. Office: Spring Hill Coll Libr 4000 Dauphin St Mobile AL 36608-1780

BAHR, CARMAN BLOEDOW, internist; b. Middletown, Ohio, Mar. 24, 1931; d. Edwin Louis and Berneice Mae (Bacon) Bloedow; m. Walter Julien Bahr, Aug. 28, 1968 (dec. Sept. 1971). BA cum laude, Miami U., Oxford, Ohio, 1952; MD, Ohio State U., 1956; MS, U. Okla., 1996. Cert. diabetes educator, 1986, 92. Intern St. Luke's Hosp., Chgo., 1956-57; resident U. Okla. Health Sci. Ctr., 1957-60; assoc. prof. medicine Okla. Health Sci. Ctr., 1971-93, prof. emeritus, 1993. Fellow: ACP (Joslin 50 Yr. medal 2001); mem.: AMA (Physician's Recognition award 1976, 1979, 1982, 1985, 1988, 1991, 1994, 1998), Okla. Med. Assn., Am. Med. Women's Assn., Western Okla. Diabetes Educators, Am. Assn. Diabetes Educators, Am. Diabetes Assn. (chpt. pres. 1989, Robert Endress award 1985), Phi Beta Kappa. Home: 5609 N Everest Ave Oklahoma City OK 73111-6729 Office: VA Med Ctr 921 NE 13th St Oklahoma City OK 73104-5007 Personal E-mail: cbb2@cox.net.

BAHR, CHRISTINE MARIE, special education educator; b. Rolla, Mo., July 4, 1958; m. Michael Welton Bahr, June 16, 1984. BA, Fontbonne Coll., 1980; MS, So. Ill. U., 1984; PhD, Ind. U., 1988. Project coord. Vanderbilt U., Nashville, 1986-88; assoc. prof. Western Mich. U., Kalamazoo, 1988—98; asst. acad. dean Saint Mary-of-the-Woods Coll., 1999—2006, interim chief academic officer, 2006—. Mem.: Coun. Exceptional Children. Office Phone: 812-535-5182. Business E-Mail: cbahr@smwc.edu.

BAHR, GAIL G., sportswriter; b. Albany, NY, Feb. 26, 1942; d. Henry Textor Kolb and Gertrude Louise Smith; m. Ronald Edwin Bahr, Oct. 23, 1959. BA, San Francisco State U., 1967. Self employed painter, 1960—; sports writer Inside Football, NJ, 1996—. Writer Amani.com, 2002—, wilhallen25.com, 2004—05. Avocations: travel, reading, sports, gardening.

BAHR, LAUREN S., publishing executive; b. New Brunswick, NJ, July 3, 1944; d. Simon A. and Rosalind J. Bahr. Student, U. Grenoble, France, 1964; BA (Branstrom scholar), MA, U. Mich., 1966. Asst. editor New Horizons Pubs., Inc., Chgo., 1967, Scholastic Mags., Inc., N.Y.C., 1968-71; supervising editor Houghton Mifflin Co., Boston, 1971; product devel. editor Appleton-Century-Crofts, N.Y.C., 1972-74; sponsoring editor McGraw-Hill, Inc., N.Y.C., 1974-75; editor Today's Sec. mag., 1975-77; sr. editor Media Systems Corp., N.Y.C., 1978; sr. editor coll. dept. CBS Coll. Pub., N.Y.C., 1978-82, mktg. mgr. fgn. langs., dir. mktg. adminstrn., 1982-83; from dir. devel. coll. divsn. to pub. cons. Harper & Row, N.Y.C., 1983-91; v.p., editl. dir. Atlas Edits., Inc., N.Y.C., 1991-98; dir. publs. Bank St. Coll. Edn., N.Y.C., 1999—2000; mng. editor Inkwell Pub., N.Y.C., 2000—02; editl. dir. 4 Lakes Colorgraphics, 2002—. Democrat. Jewish. Home: 444 E 82nd St #8A New York NY 10028-5903

BAHRYCH, SHARON, physician assistant; b. Tulsa, Okla., Aug. 4, 1954; d. Max Thomas and Glee Coffman Bahrych. BS, Baylor U., 1987; MPH, U. Tex., Houston, 1994. Nat. physician asst. cert. NCCPA, lic. physician asst. Colo. Physician asst. MD Anderson Cancer Ctr., Houston, 1988—90; physician asst., drug study coord. St. Luke's Episcopal Hosp., Houston, 1991—92; physician asst. Livingston (Tex.) Rural Health Clinic, 1993; physician asst., supr. dept. pediat. U. Tex. Sch. Medicine, Houston, 1994; physician asst. Med. Coll. Wis., Milw., 1995; asst. prof. So. Ill. U. Coll. Arts and Scis., Carbondale, Ill., 1997; freelance writer/spkr. Denver, 1998—; physician asst., clin. rschr., preceptor UCHSC/Denver Health Med. Ctr., Denver, 2000—. Presenter in field. Contbr. articles to profl. jours. Team leader Med. Svc. Internat., Denver, 1997; participant People to People Amb. Program, Tacoma, 2004. GI/Hepatology fellow, Schering-Plough Pharms., 2000. Mem.: Am. Assn. Physician Assts. (Runner-Up Inner City/Rural Health Physician Asst. award 2005), Colo. Author's League, Nat. Writer's Assn. (pres. 2000), Soc. Children's Book Writers and Illustrators. Avocations: hiking, swimming, skiing. Office: Denver Health Med Ctr MC 4000 660 Bannock St Denver CO 80204 E-mail: colorado-pa@verizon.net.

BAICA, MALVINA FLORICA, mathematician, educator, researcher; b. Oravita, Banat, Romania, Nov. 3, 1942; came to U.S., 1968, naturalized, 1973; d. Adam and Cornelia (Stefan) Bunghiu; m. Adrian Baica, Sept. 14, 1963. BS in Math. and Physics, U. Timisoara, Romania, 1964, MS in Math., 1965, Ill. Inst. Tech., 1974; PhD in Math., U. Houston, 1980. Asst. prof. Western Ill. U., Macomb, 1978-80, Marquette U., Milw., 1980-81, Marshall U., Huntington, W.Va., 1981-83, Valparaiso U., Ind., 1983-84, U. Wis., Whitewater, 1984—89, assoc. prof., 1989—92, prof., 1992—. Contbr. more than 50 articles to profl. jours. on algebraic number theory and number theory; author The Euler System for the Algebraic Number Theory and Mathematical Models in Pollution, 2000, The Algorithmic Solution of the Original Euclidean Fermat's Last Theorem, 2001, Several Star Problems in Analitic Number Theory, 2005. Recipient U. Wis. Excellence in Rsch. award, 1988, hon. diploma, Romanian ASTRA Assn., 2003. Mem. NY Acad. Scis., Pi Mu Epsilon. Achievements include development of an algorithm in a complex field which turned out to be the Generalized Euclidean Algorithm and The Euler System of the Algebraic Number Theory used to approach unsolved problems in algebraic number theory and number theory including Fermat's Last Theorem in Euclidean; discovery of Baica's trigonometric identities; research in algebraic number theory and number theory; contributor for the solution of Goldbach's problem and mathematical models for mechanical engineering applications. Office: U Wis Dept Math and Computer Sci Whitewater WI 53190 Home: 122 N Esterly Ave Whitewater WI 53190-1313 Office Phone: 262-472-1716. Business E-Mail: baicam@uww.edu.

BAICKER, KATHERINE (KATE BAICKER), federal official, economics professor; BA magna cum laude in Econ., Yale Univ., New Haven, Conn., 1993; PhD in Econ., Harvard Univ., Cambridge, Mass., 1998. Asst. prof. econs. then assoc. prof. Dartmouth Coll., NH, 1998—2005; rsch. faculty. Nat. Bur. Econ., 2001—; assoc. prof. pub. policy UCLA, 2005; mem. Coun. Econ. Advisers Exec. Office of the Pres., Washington, 2001—02, 2005—. Vis. prof. U. Chgo., 2003; spkr. in field. Contbr. articles to numerous profl. jours. Recipient William Masse award for outstanding record, Yale Univ., Tiffin Prize for outstanding academic record, Outstanding Tchr., Harvard Univ., 1998, Dissertation Prize Hon. Mention, Nat. Tax Assn., 1999, Dissertation Prize Winner, Nat. Academy of Soc. Ins., 1999; grantee John Heinz Meml. Fell., Yale Univ., Grad. Fell., Nat. Sci. Found., 1993—96, Health and Aging Fell., NBE/NIA, 1996—98. Office: Coun Econ Advisers 1800 G St NW 8th Fl Washington DC 20502*

BAIER, LUCINDA, corporate financial executive; BS in acctg., MS in acctg., Ill. State U. Self employed, 1984—87; experienced tax staff Arthur Andersen, 1987—89, experienced tax sr., 1989—90, tax mgr., 1990—93; corp. dir., taxes Gen. Dynamics, 1993—97; tax dir. ICI Americas, 1997, v.p.

taxation, 1998, v.p. fin., 1998—99; sr. v.p. fin., tax and treas. US Office Products, 1999, sr. v.p. merchandising, 1999—2000; v.p., taxes Sears, Roebuck and Co., 2000—01, v.p. fin. credit services and fin. products, 2001—03, sr. v.p., gen. mgr., credit and fin. products, 2003—. Mem.: Executives Club of Chgo.

BAIER, SUSAN LOVEJOY, music educator; b. Canandaigua, N.Y., Jan. 30, 1953; m. Michael Francis Baier, July 17, 1976; children: Michael Franklin, Kimberly Lovejoy. MusB magna cum laude, Grove City Coll., 1975; EdM, Converse Coll., 1994. Cert. tchr. S.C. String tchr. Akron (Ohio) Pub. Schs., 1975—76; Suzuki violin tchr. Jewish Cmty. Ctr., Pitts., 1976—78, Carnegie Mellon U. Pre-Coll., Pitts., 1976—78; string tchr. Spartanburg (S.C.) County Dist. 7, 1979—94, Spartanburg (S.C.) County Dist. 6, 1994—2002, dist. orch. coord., 2002—. Violinst Greater Spartanburg Philharm., 1995—; mem. string quintet, violin soloist Nazareth Presbyn. Ch., Moore, SC, 1995—. Named Outstanding Tchr., Tchg. Music mag., 2000. Mem.: S.C. Music Educators Assn. (orch. divsn., festival chmn., all-state chmn., treas., pres.-elect, pres.), Am. String Tchrs. with Nat. Sch. Orch. Assn., Music Educators Nat. Conf. Office: Dorman HS 1050 Cavalier Way Roebuck SC 29376 Office Phone: 864-342-8943. E-mail: baiersi@spart6.org.

BAIGIS, JUDITH ANN, nursing educator, academic administrator; b. Washington, Pa., July 26, 1941; d. Andrew J. and Mary Margaret (Mitchell) Baigis; m. Robert Wachbroit, June 26, 1989. Diploma, Geisinger Hosp. Sch. Nursing, Danville, Pa., 1962; BS, NYU, 1968, PhD, 1979. RN, Md., D.C. Instr. nursing NYU, N.Y.C., 1970-73, CUNY Lehman Coll., Bronx, N.Y., 1973-79; dir. community health nursing program U. Pa. Sch. Nursing, Phila., 1979-87; dir. long-term care Johns Hopkins U. Sch. Nursing, Balt., 1987-92; assoc. dean for rsch. Georgetown U. Sch. Nursing, Washington, 1992—, interim dean, 1998-99, prof., 1992—. Contbr. articles to nursing jours. Nat. Inst. Nursing Rsch. grantee, 1988-96. Mem. ANA, APHA, Am. Acad. Nursing, Assn. Community Health Nursing Educators. Office: Georgetown U Sch Nursing Box 571107 3700 Reservoir Rd NW Washington DC 20007-2111 Office Phone: 202-687-5127. Business E-Mail: baigisj@georgetown.edu.

BAIK-HAN, WON H., pediatrician, educator, consultant; b. Seoul, Jong Ro Gu, Republic of Korea, July 22, 1956; arrived in U.S., 1983; d. Hong In Baik and Ok Hee Chang; m. Muyol Han, Nov. 15, 1986; children: Jeffrey J. Han, Steven J. Han. MD, Ewha Woman's U., Seoul, 1981. Diplomate Am. Bd. Pediat. Intern Soon Chun Hyang U. Hosp., Seoul, Republic of Korea, 1981—82, resident in pediat., 1982—83; pediat. externship St. Elizabeth Hosp. Ctr., Youngstown, Ohio, 1983—84; vol. pediat. physician Flushing (N.Y.) Hosp. Med. Ctr., 1984—86, resident in pediat., 1986—89; fellow in allergy and clin. immunology St. Luke's/Roosevelt Hosp. Ctr., N.Y.C., 1989—91; clin. fellow in allergy & immunology and medicine Columbia U., N.Y.C., 1989—91; clin. pediat. allergy and immunology Flushing (N.Y.) Hosp. Med. Ctr., 1991—, dir. pediat. allergy and asthma clinic, 1991—, consulting physician medicine and pediat., 1991—, com. mem. pharmacy therapeutic com., 1999—. Dir. pediat. allergy Wyckoff Heights Med. Ctr., Bklyn., 1995—99; consulting physician pediat., allergy and immunology N.Y. Hosp. Queens, Flushing, 1997—2000; dir. pediat. allergy clinic Jamaica (N.Y.) Hosp. Med. Ctr., 2000—; asst. prof. pediat. Albert Einstein Coll. Medicine, Bronx, 1994—96, asst. clin. prof. pediat., 1999—; clin. asst. prof. pediat. Cornell U. Med. Coll., N.Y.C., 1997—99; regional spkr. allergy immunology Schering Plough Pharm. Co., NJ, 2001—. Author (with D.M. Rubin): Pediatric Emergency Medicine-Self Assessment and Review, 1994; author: (with A. Stock) Allergic & Immunologic Disease: Pediatric Emergency Medicine-Self Assessment and Review, 2nd edit., 1998. Consulting physician The Korean Am. Nail Assn. N.Y., Inc., Flushing, 1998—, The Korean Sr. Citizen Ctr., Corona, NY, 1999—. Recipient Presentation award for allergy and asthma, Soon Chun Hyang U. Hosp., Seoul, 1992, Physicians Recognition award, AMA, 1999—, Contbn. award for Korean Health Fair, Korean-Am. Nail Assn. N.Y., Inc., Flushing, 1999. Fellow: Am. Acad. Pediat.; mem.: Coalition for Asian Am. Children and Families (com. mem.), N.Y. Allergy, Asthma and Immunology Soc., Am. Acad. Allergy, Asthma and Immunology (Travel Grand award for rsch. project 1991), Hunter Coll. H.S. Korean-Am. Parents Assn. (pres. 2002—). Avocations: drawing and painting, playing pingpong and tennis, singing, collecting coins, stamps and collectibles, collecting antiques. Office: 1st Fl 143-20 Sanford Ave Flushing NY 11355 Office Phone: 718-460-3943.

BAILAR, BARBARA ANN, retired statistician; b. Monroe, Mich., Nov. 24, 1935; d. Malcolm Laurie and Clara Florence (Parent) Dezendorf; m. John Francis Powell (div. 1966); 1 child, Pamela; m. John Christian Bailar; 1 child, Melissa. BA, SUNY, 1956; MS, Va. Poly. Inst., 1965; PhD, Am. U., 1972. With Bur. of Census, Washington, 1958-88, chief Ctr. Rsch. Measurement Methods, 1973-79, assoc. dir. for statis. standards and methodology, 1979-88; exec. dir. Am. Statis. Assn., Alexandria, Va., 1988-95; sr. v.p. for survey rsch. Nat. Opinion Rsch. Ctr., Chgo., 1995—2001. Instr. George Washington U., 1984-85; head dept. math. and stats. USDA Grad. Sch., Washington, 1972-87. Contbr. articles, book chpts. to profl. publs. Pres. bd. dirs. Harbour Sq. Coop., Washington, 1988-89. Recipient Silver medal U.S. Dept. Commerce, 1980. Fellow Am. Statis. Assn. (pres. 1987); mem. AAAS (chair sect. stats. 1984-85), Internat. Assn. Survey Statisticians (pres. 1989-91), Internat. Statis. Inst. (Pres.'s invited speaker 1983, v.p. 1993-95), Cosmos Club. Personal E-mail: babailar@aol.com.

BAILEY, BEVERLY PARKER, secondary school educator; b. Ogden, Utah, Sept. 10, 1947; d. Henry Lisle Parker and Luella May Johnson; m. Jack Stephan Bailey (div.); children: Stephanie Wilcox, Valerie Hamaker, Shawn, Jeffrey, Natalie Cottle, Devan. BA in English and Spanish, Brigham Young U., 1969; MA in Linguistics, U. Utah, 2001. Cert. tchr. lang. Brigham Young U., 1964. Tchr. Murray City Sch. Dist., Murray, 1969—72, Davis County Sch. Dist., Farmington, Utah, 1989—. Tutor Davis Dist., Bountiful, Utah, 1987—89, textbook trainer, 2004—05. Youth leader LDS Ch. Named Tchr. of Yr., South Davis Jr. H.S., 2003; named to Davis Dist. Hall Fame, 2003; fellow, Fulbright Found., 2004; Spanish study abroad scholarship, Brigham Young U., 2002. Mem.: NEA, Utah Fgn. Lang. Assn., Delta Kappa Gamma. Mem. Lds Ch. Avocations: travel, gardening, reading, scrapbooks, photography. E-mail: bbailey@dsdmail.net.

BAILEY, CARLA LYNN, nursing administrator; b. Balt., June 4, 1957; d. Carlton L. and Helen P. (Wales) B. BSN, U. Md., Balt., 1979; MS in Health Sci., Towson (Md.) State U., 1987; PhD in Healthcare Mgmt., Century Brentwick U., 2000. Nurse clinician I, charge nurse, clin. nurse U. Md. Med. Systems, Balt., 1981—87; maternal transport coord. U. Md. Med. Systems Hosp., Balt., 1979—96; rsch. nurse Tokos Med. Corp., Balt., 1988—91; perinatal care coord. U. Md. Med. Systems/Hosp., 1993—99; perinatal programs dir. Md. Inst. Emergency Med. Svcs. Sys., 1999—. Mem. assoc. faculty U. Md. Sch. Nursing, 1993-95; mem. fetal and infant mortality rev. bd. Healthy Start; mem. State Commn. on Infant Mortality Prevention. Mem. Assn. Women's Health, Obstetric and Neonatal Nurses, Md. Nurse's Assn., Nat. Perinatal Assn. (bd. dirs.) Office Phone: 410-706-3931. E-mail: cbailey@miemss.org.

BAILEY, CATHERINE SUZANNE, psychologist; b. Dyess AFB, Tex., Jan. 2, 1958; d. Charles Stanley and Audrey Dorene (Hoy) B. BA, U. Minn., 1982; MA, U. Ariz., 1985, PhD, 1987. Vis. asst. prof. St. Mary's Coll., Notre Dame, Ind., 1987-88; postdoctoral fellow UCLA, 1988-90; psychol. asst. Psychol. Assessment Specialists, L.A., 1991—; pvt. practice clin. psychology Mission Viejo, Calif. Cons. in field, 1991-. Contbr. articles to profl. jours. NIMH grantee. Mem. Am. Psychol. Assn. Office Phone: 949-859-7166. Business E-Mail: dr.catherine.bailey@cox.net.

BAILEY, CATHERINE TODD, ambassador; b. Ind. m. Irving W. Bailey II. Former elementary sch. teacher; mem. & co-chmn. Rep. regents Rep. Nat. Com., 2000—04; chairperson Bush-Cheney re-election campaign, Ky.; US amb. to Latvia US Dept. State, Riga, 2005—. Co-founder Louisville Ronald McDonald House, 1984; founder, pres. Operation Open Arms, 2001—04; bd. dirs. McConnell Ctr. for Polit. Leadership & Excellence, U. Louisville, Kentucky Opera, Kentucky Arts and Crafts Found.; bd. dirs., presidential adv. com. Kennedy Ctr. Recipient S. Tilford Payne, Jr. award, 2002, Unsung Heroine award, 2003. Office: Am Embassy 4520 Riga Pl Washington DC 20521

BAILEY, DIANDREA MICHELLE, rehabilitation services professional; b. Petersburg, Va., Nov. 28, 1979; d. William Oscar and Gloria Turner Bailey. BA in english and speech pathology, Norfolk State U., 1997—99; MA, Norfolk State U., Norfolk, VA, 2000—02; MS degree in rehab counseling, Viriginia Commonwealth U., 2001—03; Post-Master's Cert. in Sch. Counseling, George Mason U., 2002—04; Post-Master's Cert. in Profl. Counseling, Va. Commonwealth U., 2003. Licensed Professional Counselor Va. Bd. of Counseling/Va., 2004, Certified Rehabilitation Counselor CRCC/ Nat., 2003, Certified Rehabilitation Provider Va. Bd. of Counseling, 2003. Vocat. rehab. counselor Va. Dept for the Blind and Vision Impaired, Richmond, Va., 2002—04, U.S. Dept. of Veterans Affairs, Harrisburg, Pa., 2004—. Mem.: Va. Rehab. Counselor Assn., Va. Counselor Assn., Nat. Rehab. Counselor Assn., Nat. Rehab. Assn., Chi Sigma Iota (life). Office: US Dept of Veterans Affairs 228 Walnut St Ste1150 Harrisburg PA 17108 Home: PO Box 266 Hopewell VA 23860-0266 Office Phone: 717-221-3750. Office Fax: 717-224-4570. Personal E-mail: diandrea151@cs.com. E-mail: vrcdbail@vba.va.gov.

BAILEY, DOROTHY JEAN, secondary school educator, consultant; b. Clarksdale, Miss., Jan. 24, 1948; d. A.D. and Nancy (Morbley) Bailey; 1 child, Miko Dawn Montgomery. AA Sociology, Compton Coll., 1969; BA Sociology, Cal State Univ. Long Beach, 1972; MA Pub. Adminstrn., Pepperdine Univ., 1977; MS Sch. Counseling, Univ. La Verne, 2001. Lic. real estate Calif., 1988, pupil personnel svcs. credential Calif., 2002. Social sci. analyst Libr. of Congress/Congressional Rsch. Svc., Washington, 1979—86; realtor Century 21 Sparrow, Long Beach, Calif., 1988—92; program coord. Martin Luther King Jr./Charles R. Drew Univ. of Medicine and Sci., L.A., Calif., 1989—90; case mgr./ early intervention network coord. Cal State Univ. Long Beach Found., Calif., 1992—94; cons. So. Calif. Alcohol & Drug Programs, Inc., Downey, Calif., 1994, Miller Children's Hosp. of Long Beach, Calif., 1994—95; program coord. Minority AIDS Program, L.A., Calif., 1995—97; tchr. advisor L.A. Unfied Sch. Dist/Harbor Occupl. Ctr., San Pedro, Calif., 1999—2001, tchr., 1997—. Mem.: Women Educators, Calif. Coun. for Adult Edn. (sec. 1999—2002, pres. 2002—03, State Excellence in Tchg. 2003). Avocations: collecting seashells, mentoring, reading, walking, art. Office: LA Unified Sch Dist/Harbor Occpul Ctr 740 N Pacific Ave San Pedro CA 90731

BAILEY, ELIZABETH ELLERY, economics professor; b. NYC, Nov. 26, 1938; d. Irving Woodworth and Henrietta Dana (Skinner) Raymond; children: James L., William E. BA magna cum laude, Radcliffe Coll., 1960; MS, Stevens Inst. Tech., 1966; PhD, Princeton U., 1972; LLD (hon.), De Paul U., 1988; Dr.Engring. (hon.), Stevens Inst. Tech., 2003. Successively sr. tech. aid, assoc. mem. tech. staff, mem. tech. staff, supr. econ. analysis group, rsch. head econs. rsch. dept. Bell Labs., 1960-77; commr. CAB, 1977-83, v.p., 1981-83; dean Grad. Sch. Indsl. Adminstrn. Carnegie-Mellon U., 1983-90;, 1990-91; John C. Hower prof. pub. policy and mgmt. Wharton Sch. U. Pa., Phila., 1991—. Vis. prof. Yale Sch. Ogn. and Mgmt., 1990-91; bd. dirs. Altria Group, CSX Corp., Tchrs. Ins. and Annuity Assn., Bancroft NeuroHealth; adj. asst., then assoc. prof. econs. NYU, 1973-77. Author: Economic Theory of Regulatory Constraint, 1973; editor: Selected Economics Papers of William J. Baumol, 1976; Deregulating the Airlines, 1985; bd. editors Am. Econ. Rev., 1977-79, Jour. Indsl. Econs., 1977-84. Founding mem., v.p. bd. trustees Harbor Sch. for Children with Learning Disabilities; trustee Princeton U., 1978-82, Presbyn. U. Hosp., 1984-91, Nat. Bureau Econ. Rsch., 1993—, Brookings Inst., 1988—, Bancroft Neuro Health, 1996-2004, Catalyst, 1988-90, Am. Assembly Collegiate Schs. of Bus., 1987-90, Nat. Bur. Econs. Rsch., 1993—; mem. exec. coun. Fedn. Orgns. for Profl. Women, 1980-82; chmn. Com. on Status of Women in Econs. Profession, 1979-82; mem. corp. vis. com. Sloan Sch. Mgmt., MIT, 1982-85; mem. adv. bd. Brookings Inst., 1987—, Ctr. Econ. Policy Rsch., Stanford U., 1983—, MIT econs. dept., 1989—, Princeton econs. dept., 1989—. Recipient Alumni Recognition award Radcliffe Coll., 1988, Dirs.' Choice award Nat. Women's Econ. Alliance Found., 1990; Program Design Trainee award Bell Labs; Bell Labs grantee Princeton U., 1972. Mem. Am. Econ. Assn. (exec. com. 1981-83, v.p. 1985), Am. Assn. Collegiate Schs. Bus. (bd. dirs. 1987—), Beta Gamma Sigma. Home: 253 Mountwell Ave Haddonfield NJ 08033-3859 Office: U Pa Wharton Sch Steinberg Hall—Dietrich Hall Philadelphia PA 19104-6372

BAILEY, EXINE MARGARET ANDERSON, soprano, educator; b. Cottonwood, Minn., Jan. 4, 1922; d. Joseph Leonard and Exine Pearl (Robertson) Anderson; m. Arthur Albert Bailey, May 5, 1956. BS, U. Minn., 1944; MA, Columbia U., 1945; profl. diploma, 1951. Instr. Columbia U., 1947-51; faculty U. Oreg., Eugene, 1951—, prof. voice, 1966-87, coordinator voice instrn., 1969-87, prof. emeritus, 1987—; faculty dir. Salzburg, Austria, summer 1968, Europe, summer 1976. Vis. prof., head vocal instrn. Columbia U., summers 1952, 59; condr. master classes for singers, developer summer program study for h.s. solo singers, U. Oreg. Sch. Music, 1988—, mem. planning com. 1998-99 MTNA Nat. Convention. Profl. singer, N.Y.C.; appearances with NBC, ABC symphonies; solo artist appearing with Portland and Eugene (Oreg.) Symphonies, other groups in Wash., Calif., Mont., Idaho, also in concert; contbr. articles, book revs. to various mags. Del. fine arts program to Ea. Europe, People to People Internat. Mission to Russia for 1990. Recipient Young Artist award N.Y.C. Singing Tchrs., 1945, Music Fedn. Club (N.Y.C.) hon. award, 1951; Kathryn Long scholar Met. Opera, 1945 Mem. Nat. Assn. Tchrs. Singing (lt. gov. 1968-72), Oreg. Music Tchrs. Assn (pres. 1974-76), Music Tchrs. Nat. Assn. (nat. voice chmn. high sch. activities 1970-74, nat. chmn. voice 1973-75, 81-85, NW chmn. collegiate activities and artists competition 1978-80, editorial com. Am. Music Tchr. jour. 1987-89), AAUP, Internat. Platform Assn., Kappa Delta Pi, Sigma Alpha Iota, Pi Kappa Lambda. Home: 17 Westbrook Way Eugene OR 97405-2074 Office: U Oreg Sch Music Eugene OR 97403

BAILEY, HELEN MCSHANE, historian, consultant; b. Gardner, Kans., Oct. 17, 1916; d. Harry Cramer and Maude Ethel (Kramer) McShane; m. James Edwin Bailey, Feb. 23, 1946; children: James Edwin, Barbara Ann Bailey Crawford. BA, Bethany Nazarene Coll., 1938. Adminstrv. asst. Office Chief of Staff, U.S. Army, Washington, 1941—48; historian U.S. Army ofcl. history of World War II, U.S. Army, Washington, 1948—58; rsch. asst. George C. Marshall Rsch. Found., Washington, 1958—59; historian Orgn. Joint Chiefs of Staff, Dept. Def., Pentagon, Washington, 1968—87; cons., 1987—. Mem.: Am. Hist. Assn., Soc. Historians Am. Fgn. Rels., World War Two Studies Assn., Soc. History in Fed. Govt. Republican. Lutheran. Home and Office: 9451 Lee Hwy Apt 415 Fairfax VA 22031-1812

BAILEY, JANET DEE, publishing executive; b. Newark, Aug. 23, 1946; d. Richard and Mary Louise (Dee) Shapiro; m. John Frederick Bailey, May 9, 1971; children: Jason David, Juliana Dee. BA, U. Del., 1968; MBA, Pace U., 1981. Prodn. editor Prentice-Hall, Inc., Englewood Cliffs, NJ, 1968-70; dir. publs. Spl. Libraries Assn., N.Y.C., 1970-76; dir. mktg. services Knowledge Industry Publs., White Plains, NY, 1978-81, v.p., 1984-85; dir. inventory and contracts Macmillan Book Clubs, N.Y.C., 1981-84; group pub. Elsevier Sci. Pub. Co., N.Y.C., 1985-95, v.p. global mktg., 1996-99; v.p. STM books and ref. John Wiley & Sons, 1999—. Mem. Assn. Am. Publishers (chmn. jours. com., PSP exec. coun., book award judge), Soc. for Scholarly Publishing.

BAILEY, JANNA, mathematics educator; b. Cin. d. Earl and Irene House; 1 child, Randi Brooke. BS/MA, Ea. Ky. U., Richmond, 1989. Cert. Secondary Tchr. Math. Ky. Bd. Edn., 1986. Tchr. South Laurel H.S., London, Ky., 1986—. Home: 1614 County Farm Road London KY 40741 Office: South Laurel High School 201 South Laurel Road London KY 40744

BAILEY, JOY HAFNER, counselor educator; b. Weehawkin, NJ, Aug. 15, 1928; d. Elmar William and Fern (Williams) Hafner; children: Kerry, Jan, Leslie, Liza, Annie Laurie, Kristin. BA, Austin Coll., 1974; MS, Tex. A&M U., 1975, EdD, 1977. Lic. marriage and family therapist, profl. counselor; nat. cert. counselor. Counselor, instr. Tex. A&M U., Commerce, 1976-80; dir. student support svcs. acad. and counseling program Ga. State U., Atlanta, 1980—2001, asst. prof. counseling and psychol. svcs., 1988—2001; ret., 2001; pvt. family practice and clin. supervision practice. Pvt. practice marriage and family therapy. Mem. APA, ACA, Am. Assn. Marriage and Family Therapists (approved supr.), Ga. Assn. Marriage and Family Therapists, Atlanta Mallet Club (v.p. 1989-92, pres. 1999-00), Psi Chi. Office Phone: 770-383-3094, 770-383-3094.

BAILEY, JOY Y., art educator; d. Nolan L. and Nancy L. Henry; m. Wayne O. Bailey, Jan. 12, 1980; children: Joshua N., Beau D. B History, William Jewell Coll., 1988, B Secondary Edn., 1988; M Art Edn., N.W. Mo. State U., 1995. Cert. tchr. Dept. Elem. and Secondary Edn., 1988, Nat. Bd. Edn., 2003. Tchr. art Lathrop Schs., Mo., 1988—94, Smithville RII Schs., Mo., 1994—. Chair dist. art dept. Smithville RII Schs., 1996—, tchr. adv. com., 1998—, mentor new tchrs., 1995—2004. Chair Smithville Arts Coun., 1996—99, mem., 1994, First Christian Ch., Smithville, 1985. Recipient Excellence Edn. award. Mem.: Cmty. Tchrs. Assn., Mo. State Tchrs. Assn., Nat. Art Edn. Assn., Mo. Art Edn. Assn. Avocations: art, pottery. E-mail: baileyj@smithville.k12.mo.us.

BAILEY, JUDITH IRENE, academic administrator, educator, consultant; b. Winston-Salem, N.C., Aug. 24, 1946; d. William Edward Hege Jr. and Julia (Hedrick) Hege; m. Brendon Stinson Bailey, Jr, June 8, 1968. BA, Coker Coll., 1968; MEd, Va. Tech., 1973, EdD, 1976; postgrad., Harvard U., 1994, 1994—95. Tchr. Chariho Regional H.S., Wood River Junction, RI, 1969—70, Prince William County Pub. Schs., Woodbridge, Va., 1968—72; asst. prin. Osbourn H.S., Manassas, Va., 1973; secondary sch. coord. Stafford (Va.) County Schs., 1973—74; middle sch. coord. Stafford County Schs., 1975—76; human rels. coord. Coop. Extension Svc. U. Md., College Park, 1976—79; dep. dir. Coop. Extension Svc. U. D.C., Washington, 1980-88; asst. v.p., dir. Coop. Extension U. Maine, Orono, 1988—92, interim v.p. for rsch. and pub. svc., 1992—93, v.p. rsch. and pub. svc., 1993—95, v.p. acad. affairs, provost, 1995—97; pres. No. Mich. U., Marquette, 1997—2003, Western Mich. U., Kalamazoo, 2003—06, prof. ednl. leadership, 2006—. Adj. prof. George Mason U., Fairfax, Va., 1978; grad. student adv. U. Md., 1979—80; spkr. and cons. in field; trustee Bronson Healthcare Group, Kalamazoo, 2003—; mem. steering com. Mich. Tri-Tech. Corridor, 2003—05; mem. governing bd. Bioscis. Rsch. and Commercialization Ctr., 2003—06; pres. Western Mich. U. Rsch. Found., 2006—06; mem. Mich. Strategic Econ. Investment and Commercialization Bd., 2006. Co-author: Contingency Planning for a Unitary School System; contbr. articles to profl. jours. Co-vice chmn. Lake Superior Cmty. Partnership, 1997—2003; bd. trustees Marquette (Mich.) Gen. Health Sys., 1998—2003; mem. Mich. Humanities Coun., 1999—2002, sec., treas., 2002; mem. adv. bd. Huntington Bank, 2003—; apptd. by gov. to Mich. Quarter Commn., 2004; mem. Am. Coun. Edn. Commn. on Women, 2004; trustee Southwest Mich. First; vice chmn. Greater Kalamazoo United Way, 2006; bd. dirs. Pine Tree State 4-H Found., 1988—97, Maine Toxicology Inst., 1992—95, Bangor (Maine) Symphony Orch, 1991—97, Shorebank, 1997—2003, Gilmore Keyboard Festival, 2003—. Recipient Disting. Alumni Achievement award, Coker Coll., 1998, Northwoods Woman Educator of Yr. award, 1999, Case V Chief Exec. Leadership award, 2002, Disting. Grad. Alumni Achievement award, Va. Tech., 2005; fellow Susan Coker Watson fellow, 1967. Mem.: AAUW, Grand Rapids Econ. Club, Econ. Club Marquette County (bd. dirs. 1997—2003), Rotary (Paul Harris fellow 2004), Epsilon Sigma Phi (sec. Mu chpt. 1987, v.p. 1988, State Disting. Svc. award), Phi Kappa Phi, Phi Delta Kappa. Republican. Avocations: cooking, hiking. Home: 1201 Short Rd Kalamazoo MI 49008 Office: Western Mich U Coll Edn 1903 W MIchigan Kalamazoo MI 49008-5202 Business E-Mail: judi.bailey@wmich.edu.

BAILEY, JUDY LONG, outreach and education specialist, social worker; d. John H. and Sibyl K. Long; m. Charles A. Bailey, Jan. 1, 2001. BA, West Ga. U., Carrollton, 1969. Social caseworker Coweta Dept. of Family Svcs., Newnan, Ga., 1971—72, Lexington (SC) Dept. of Family Svcs., 1972—74; social work supr. Prince William Dept. Social Svcs., Manassas, Va., 1974—76; program specialist U.S. Dept. Agr., Washington, 1976—80; program analyst U.S. EPA, Washington, 1980—. Vol. Animal Welfare League of Arlington, Va., 1979—97, Fairfax County Pk. Authority, Alexandria, Va., 1990—2000. Mem.: Nat. Audubon Soc., Best Friends Animal Soc., Nature Conservancy. Avocations: gardening, reading. Home: 5004 Grimm Drive Alexandria VA 22304 Office: US EPA 4502T 1200 Pennsylvania Ave NW Washington DC 20460

BAILEY, KEISHA AYANNA, mathematics educator; d. Edward Hampton and Jocelyn Elaine Bailey. BS in Math., Hampton U., Va., 1999, M in Tchg., 2000. Tchr. Lincoln Heights Elem., Charlotte, NC, 2000—01, math. tchr. James Martin Mid. Sch., Charlotte, 2001—. Office Phone: 980-343-5382.

BAILEY, KELLEY, foundation administrator; b. Houston, Mar. 17, 1962; d. Myron Edgar Bailey and Georgia Numsen (Reynolds) White BA Art History and Comm. cum laude, U. St. Thomas, 1993. Lic. FCC. Coord. sch. svcs., asst dir. vis. svcs. Houston Mus. Natural Sci., Edn. Sch. Svcs., Houston, 1991—94; coord. vol. svcs. and cmty. partnerships Hermann Hosp., Houston, 1996—98; adminstr. Vols. in Pub. Schs. Cmty. Partnerships Houston Ind. Sch. Dist., 1998—2001; prin. Cmty. Devel. Resources, Houston, 2001—04; dir. vol. svcs. and cmty. outreach Bering Omega Cmty. Svcs., Houston, 2002—04; dir. vol. svcs. Houston Symphony, 2005; pres., CEO Gulf Coast chpt. Lupus Found. Am., 2006—. Presenter Internat. Conf. on Vol. Adminstrn., Chgo., 1999—2003; instr. Vol. Mgmt. Acad. Houston C.C., 2001—04; cons. Susan G. Komen Breast Cancer Found., 2004; dir. Greater Houston Area Breast Health Summit, 2004—05; instr. Rice U., 2006. Mem. Jr. League of Houston, Inc., 1990-94; floor presenter Mus. Natural Sci., 1991-94; vol. Houston SPCA; mem. adv. bd. Houston Internat. Festival, 1992-93, chmn. curriculum guide com., 1992-93; bd. dirs. country selection com. Chrysalis Repertory Dance Co., 1995-97; bd. dirs., membership chair Houston Assn. Vol. Adminstrs., 1998-2000, bd. dirs. 2002-2004; mem. adv. coun. Ret. Srs. Vol. Program, Interfaith Ministries Greater Houston, 1999-2000; vol. team capt. Houston Mayor's Summit on Women, 1999; mem. com. Internat. Yr. of Vols., 2000-2003; mem. bd. advocates Planned Parenthood Houston and Southeast Tex., 2000-01; dir. vol. svcs. Houston Symphony Soc., 2005—Named Vol. of Yr. Jr. League Houston, 1991 Home: 4216 Purdue Houston TX 77005 Office: Lupus Founds Am 3720 Kirby Dr Ste 720 Houston TX 77098 Fax: 713-668-9576. Office Phone: 713-529-0126. Business E-Mail: kbailey@lupustexas.org.

BAILEY, LAURIE RUCKERT, music educator; b. Rochester, Pa., Feb. 8, 1960; d. Allen Lloyd and Martha Abigail Ruckert; m. Stephen Robert Bailey; children: Leslie Ruth, Stephanie Ann, Luke Robert. BS in Music Edn., King's Coll., Briarcliff Manor, NY, 1982. Cert. tchr. Del. Music tchr. Montrose Christian Sch., Md., 1982—84, Wilmington Christian Sch., Hockessin, Del., 1984—90, Red Lion Christian Acad., Bear, Del., 1995—99, Colonial Sch. Dist., New Castle, Del., 2004—; pvt. piano tchr. Wilmington, Del., 1988—99. Accompanist, 1980—; musical dir. Pine Creek Drama Camp, Newark, 2001—05. Contbr. articles to profl. jours. Worship leader New Life Alliance Ch., Newark, 1991—. Named Outstanding Musician, King's Coll., 1982; recipient Faculty Sr. award, 1982. Mem.: Music Educators Nat. Conf., Del. Music Edn. Assn. (sem. leader 2002), Am. Assn. Christian Schs. Internat. (sem. leader 2001, 2003). Avocations: reading, walking, baking. Office: Colonial Sch Dist 345 E Basin Rd New Castle DE 19720

BAILEY, MARGARET ELIZABETH, nurse, retired military officer; b. Selma, Ala., Dec. 25, 1915; d. Adam and Hattie Bailey. RN, Fraternal Hosp. Sch. Nursing, Montgomery, Ala., 1938; BA, San Francisco State Coll., 1959. RN, N.Y., Ala. Enlisted U.S. Army Nurse Corps, 1944, advanced through grades to col., 1970; staff nurse, oper. rm. nurse Mercy Hosp., St. Petersburg,

Fla., 1938-40; staff nurse, asst. head nurse Seaview Hosp., Staten Island, N.Y., 1940-44; supr. surg. svcs. Sta. Hosp., Camp Beale, Calif., 1945-46; supr. psychiat. & neurol. svc. Second Gen. Hosp., Laundstuhl, Fed. Republic Germany, 1956-57; evening, night supr. Letterman Gen. Hosp., San Francisco, 1958-59; asst. chief dept. nursing U.S. Army Hosp., Zama, Japan, 1960-61; supr. psychiat. and neurology svc. Fitzsimons Gen. Hosp., Denver, 1963-65; chief dept. nursing 130th Gen. Hosp. Chinon, France, 1965-66, 33rd Field Hosp., Wurzburg, Germany, 1966-67, U.S. Army Hosp., Ft. Devens, Mass., 1967-69; health manpower tng. specialist Job Corps Health Office, Office Econ. Opportunity, Washington, 1969-71; ret. U.S. Army Nurse Corps, 1971. Past con. Surgeon Gen. of the Army; past chmn. adv. com. Fed. City Coll. Nursing, Washington; mem. bd. dirs. Greater S.E. Community Ctr. for Aging, Washington, 1990—. Author: The Challenge, 1999, Autobiography of Colonel Margaret E. Barley, 1999; mng. editor: The Rockett, 1982-84; contbr. articles to profl. jours. Treas. pastor's aid club, asst. fin. sec. helping hand club, deaconess Nineteenth St. Bapt. Ch., Washington; past historian The Army Officer's Wives Club, Ft. Myers, Va. Decorated Legion of Merit; named Outstanding Women of Yr., Mass. Profl. Woman's Club, 1967, Black Nurse of Yr., Black Nurses Assn. Greater Washington Area, 1990 Rock of Yr., ROCKS, 1991; recipient Women's Honors in Pub. Svc. award Minority Fellowship Program and Cabinet of Human Rights, ANA, 1988. Mem. ANA, Nat. League for Nurses, D.C. Nurses Assn. (past chmn. membership com.), D.C. League for Nursing (past mem. bd.), Assn. Mil. Surgeons, Ret. Officers Assn. (past 2nd v.p., past 1st v.p., past pres., bd. dirs. Montgomery County chpt.), Sigma Theta Tau, Chi Eta Phi (past pres. Alpha chpt., past corr. sec., past chmn. speaker's bur., others, past chaplain, chmn. Africare spl. project, asst. N.E. regional dir., chmn. programs and projects com.). Baptist. Avocations: reading, golf, theater, bowling.

BAILEY, MARY BEATRICE, retired health science association administrator; b. Pitts., Dec. 24, 1933; d. Harry Chantler and Beatrice Iseli (Koenig) B. Diploma in Nursing, Allegheny Gen. Hosp., Pitts., 1956; BSNE, Chatham Coll., Pitts., 1956; MSN, Duke U., Durham, 1967. Cert. nursing adminstr., advanced. Staff nurse, head nurse, nursing supr. Allegheny Gen. Hosp., Pittsburgh, 1956-60; nursing instr. pediatrics Duke U. Sch. Nursing, Durham, N.C., 1960-61; nursing instr. med. surg Rex Hosp. Sch. Nursing, Raleigh, N.C., 1962-63; nursing supr. Rex Hosp., Raleigh, 1964-71, patient care coord., 1972-86, clin. dir., 1987, dir. nursing info. system, 1987-95. Author: The Role of the Mother with her Hospitalized Child, 1966. Vol. Rn open door clinic, Raleigh, 1987-88, Meals on Wheels, Wake Co., 1996—, Raleigh Little Theatre, 1993—; mem. N.C. Coalition for Choice; elected N.C. Bd. of Nursing, 1991-93, 94-96. Named to The Great 100 N.C. Nurses, 1992. Mem. NOW, N.C. Coun. Women's Orgns., N.C. League for Nursing, N.C. Nurses Assn. (life, treas. 1977-79), Great 100 (charter treas. 1989), Zonta Club of Raleigh (charter treas.). Democrat. Episcopalian. Avocations: reading, theater, music, sports. Home: 311 Furches St Raleigh NC 27607-4015

BAILEY, PATRICIA PRICE, lawyer, former government official; b. Ft. Smith, Ark., June 20, 1937; m. Douglas L. Bailey; 2 children. BA in History cum laude, Lindenwood Coll., 1959; MA in Internat. Affairs, Tufts U., 1960; JD summa cum laude, Am. U., 1976. Bar: D.C., U.S. Ct. Appeals (D.C. cir.), U.S. Ct. Appeals (8th cir.), U.S. Supreme Ct. Editor, rsch. analyst Bur. of Intelligence and Rsch., U.S. Dept. State, 1960—61; exec. asst. Bur. for Latin Am., then asst. to dep. coord. Alliance for Progress, AID, 1961—66; advisor fgn. affairs Rep. F. Bradford Morse, 1967—68; legal asst. Office of Counsel to Pres. in White House, 1976; spl. asst. to asst. atty. gen. U.S. Dept. Justice, 1977—79; exec. asst. to gen. counsel U.S. Merit systems Protection Bd., 1979; commr. FTC, Washington, 1979—88; ptnr Squire, Sanders & Dempsey, Washington, 1989—. Bd. dirs. Arbella Mut. Ins. Co.; bd. dirs., trustee Avdel PLC; mem. adv. com. Impact of Women in Pub. Office Rutgers U. Eagleton Inst. Politics. Contbr. articles to profl. jours. Mem. Dean's Adv. Coun. Washington Coll. Law of Am. U., Spl. Commn. to Rev. Honor System and Honor Code at West Point, 1988; bd. dirs. The Washington Ctr., 1987—89, Women's Legal Def. Fund, 1982—83, Found. for Women's Resources, Lindenwood Coll. Recipient Spl. Recognition award, Nat. Assn. Attys. Gen., 1987, Philip Hart Pub. Svc. award, Consumer Fedn. Am., 1985. Mem.: Women's Bar Assn. of D.C. (bd. dirs. 1981—83, bd. dirs. Women's Bar Assn. Found. 1981—85, named Woman Lawyer of Yr. 1988). Office: Squire Sanders & Dempsey PO Box 407 1201 Pennsylvania Ave NW Washington DC 20044

BAILEY, RITA MARIA, investment advisor, psychologist; b. Germany; d. Ludwig and Getrude Fleischmann; m. William W. Bailey; children: Anne Christine, Cynthia Patricia. BS in Psychology, Austin Peay U., 1975, MA in Psychology, 1977, postgrad., 1977—79. Cert. counselor Tenn. Editor U.S. Army Spl. Warfare Inst., Ft. Bragg, NC, 1970—74, edn. officer, 1979-82, Augsburg (Germany) Cmty. Ctr., 1982-85; pvt. practice counseling Leavenworth, Kans., 1985-90; pvt. practice investments, 1990—. Author: Extroversion and Introversion, 1978, Special Warfare Training Plan, 1981; author, editor: tng. manual Foreign Small Arms, 1982. Dir. Energy Conservation Campaign, Clarksville, 1976; founder, dir. Women's Support Ctr., Leavenworth, 1986. Mem.: Nat. Assn. Investors, Alpha Mu Gamma. Roman Catholic. Avocations: long distance swimming, gardening, German poetry.

BAILEY, SANDRA, secondary school educator, department chairman; d. Robert Jordan and Florence Husby; m. Tom Bailey, June 22, 1974. Student, U. Uppsala, Sweden, 1965—66; BA in Social Sci., San Diego State U., 1967; MA in Internat. Rels., U. Wash., Seattle, 1970. Cert. K-12 tchr. Wash., secondary tchr. Calif. English tchr. Skiffgarden Hosp., Uppsala, 1965—66; tutor Urban League, San Diego, 1967—68; spl. edn. tchr. reading, math, English, biology Shasta Union H.S. Dist., Redding, Calif., 1968—69; tchr., advisor, chmn. dept. Edmonds Sch. Dist., Wash., 1970—2000; tchr., chmn. dept. Shoreline Sch. Dist., Wash., 2000—. Leader/tchr. Internat. Baccalaureate, Edmonds, 1993—2000; adj. prof. learning styles Seattle Pacific U., 1994. Contbr. articles to profl. publs. Commr., supporter, rep. to Japan Edmonds Sister City Commn., 1988—95; v.p. guild, chmn. various jobs Olympic Ballet, Edmonds, 1984—2003; coun. leader, tchr., youth leader, mem. Russian com. First Luth. Ch., Shoreline, 1978—2006. Recipient Fulbright-Hays scholar to China, US Govt., 1999, Excellent tchg. award, Shorewood HS, 2001, award, Edmonds Sch. Dist., 1985—88, 1991, 1995—98, Civic Svc. award, Edmonds City Coun., 1995, Angel award, Olympic Ballet, 1999; grantee, NSF, 1963; Howard I Neff scholar, Parent Orgn., 1963—64, U. Uppsala scholar, King of Sweden, 1965—66. Mem.: NEA (assoc.), Alpha Lambda Delta. Democrat. Avocations: writing, painting, travel. Home: 18355 Ridgefield Rd NW Shoreline WA 98177 Office: Shoreline School Dist 18560 1st Ave NE Shoreline WA 98155

BAILEY, SHANNON D., elementary school educator; d. J. W. and Jean Bailey. BS, Francis Marion U., Florence, 2003. Ins. agt. asst. Coleman Ins. Agy., Dillon, SC, 1999—2003; scientist IRIX Pharms., Florence, 2003; tchr. mid. sch. sci. JV Martin Jr. H.S., Dillon, 2003—. Coach jr. varsity cheerleading Dillon H.S., 2005—; coach b-team cheerleading JV Martin Jr. H.S., 2004—05; dir. recreational cheerleading Dillon County Parks and Recreation, 2002—03. Mem. Jr. Charity League, Dillon, 2002—05, Booster Club, 2003; bd. mem. MacArthur Ave. Players, 2000—03. Scholar, Francis Marion U., 1999—2003; Life scholar, 1999—2003. Office Phone: 843-774-1212. Personal E-mail: shander99@aol.com.

BAILEY, SHARON L., history educator, literature and language educator; b. Roswell, N.Mex., Jan. 11, 1967; d. Kenneth Scott and Rita Jean Bailey. BS, Ea. N.Mex. U., 1990. Lic. Level II Profl. Grades 7-12 N.Mex. Tchr., hist., English Roswell Ind. Sch. Dist., N.Mex., 1991—. Lead tchr., dept. chair Univ. High Sch., Roswell, 1999—; mentor, tchr. Roswell Ind. Sch. Dist., 2003—, supt. adv. bd., 1998; presenter in field. Mem., donor So. Povert Law Ctr., 2004. Recipient Tchr. Yr., Roswell Ind. Sch. Dist., 1995—96, Laureote award, 1997. Mem.: NEA. Democrat. Baptist. Avocations: dog training, history, reading, antiques, decorating. Office: Univ High Sch Roswell Ind Sch Dist 25 Martin St Roswell NM 88203

BAILEY, STEPHANIE B.C., city health department administrator; married; 3 children. BS, Clark U., Worchester, Mass.; MS in health svcs. adminstrn., Coll. of St. Francis; MD, Meharry Med. Coll., Nashville. Dir., health Metro Pub. Health Dept. of Nashville/Davidson Co., 1995—. Bd. dirs. Centerstone Cmty. Health Ctrs. Inc., 2002—. Mem. Nat. Adv. Com. on Rural Health, Nat. Adv. Com. for Elimination of Tuberculosis, Nat. Adv. Com. to CDC Dir. Recipient Excellence in Pub. Health award, ASTHO, 1999, Milton and Ruth Roemer Prize for Creative Local Public Health Work, Am. Public Health Assn., 2004, Dr. Nathan Davis award for Outstanding Govt. Service, AMA, 2005. Mem.: Nat. Assn. of County and City Health Officials (bd. mem.). Office: Metro Pub Health Dept 311 23rd Ave N Nashville TN 37203

BAILEY, SUSAN MCGEE, educational administrator, researcher, educator; b. Boston, June 10, 1941; d. Hugh Paul and Florence Anna (Brockett) McGee; m. Jerald Elliott Bailey, June 25, 1966 (div. Mar. 1976); 1 child, Amy. BA, Wellesley Coll., 1963; postgrad., Boston U., 1965; MA, U. Mich., 1969, PhD, 1971; LittD (hon.), Pine Manor Coll., 1993, Merrimack Coll., 1998. Tchr. elem. and mid. sch., Mich., Taiwan, Dominican Republic, 1963-67; tchg. fellow U. Mich. and Mich. State U., 1968-70; postdoctoral fellow Johns Hopkins U., Balt., 1972-73, 1972-73; bur. chief Conn. State Dept. Edn., Hartford, 1974-78; dir. Policy Rsch. Office Harvard U., Cambridge, Mass., 1978-80; dir. Resource Ctr. Ednl. Equity, Washington, 1980-85; exec. dir. Ctr. for Rsch. on Women Wellesley (Mass.) Coll., 1985—, exec. dir. Wellesley Ctrs. for Women, 1995—. Adj. prof. Cen. Conn. State U., New Britain, 1976-78; prof. women's studies and edn. Wellesley Coll., 1996—; presenter in field. Author: How Schools Shortchange Girls, 1992; editor: Girls in School, 1992; co-author: Policies for the Future, 1982; mem. cons. bd. Jour. Ednl. Equity and Leadership, 1980-86; contbr. articles to profl. jours. Vol. tchr. YMCA, Bethesda, Md., 1980-93: bd. dir. PATH, Natick, Mass., 1988-92, Elem. Extended Day, Bethesda, Md., 1984-86, Conn. Pub. TV, 1977-78; bd. dir. Nat. Coun. Rsch. on Women, 1988-94, pres. bd., 1992-94; founding bd. dir. N.E. Coalition Ednl. Leaders, 1977-78; bd. trustees Regis Coll., Weston, Mass., 1995-2000. Recipient Abigail Adams award Mass. Women's Polit. Caucus, 1992; state policy fellow Inst. for Ednl. Leadership-George Washington U., 1978-79, Social Sci. Ednl. Rsch. fellow U. Fellowship-U. Mich., 1968-70. Mem. Am. Ednl. Rsch. Assn. (chair spl. interest group rsch. on women in edn. 1986-87, Willystine Goodsell award 1989, Activist/Policy award 1992), Phi Lambda Theta, Phi Delta Kappa. Avocations: walking, bicycling, gardening. Office: Wellesley Coll Wellesley Ctrs for Women 106 Central St Wellesley MA 02481-8268

BAILEY, SUSAN RUDD, physician; BS, Tex. A&M U., 1979, MD, 1981; postgrad., Mayo Grad. Sch. Medicine, 1981-84, 84-86. Diplomate Am. Bd. Pediatrics, Am. Bd. Allergy and Immunology; lic. Tex. Assoc. cons. dept. pediatrics Mayo Clinic, Rochester, Minn., 1987; pvt. practice, allergy and clin. immunology Fort Worth (Tex.) Allergy and Asthma Assocs., 1988—. Instr. in pediatrics Mayo Med. Sch., 1986-87; bd. dirs. Accreditation Coun. on Continuing Med. Edn., 2004—; presenter in field. Mem. editl. bd. Annals Allergy, Asthma and Immunology, 1997—2003; contbr. articles to profl. jours. Bd. visitors Scott and White Clinic, 1994—; adv. bd. M.D. Anderson Physicians, 1992-94; bd. regents Tex. A&M U. Sys., 1999-2005; mem. AMA Coun. Med. Edn. Exec. Com., 2005- Recipient Residents' award Northwest Pediatric Soc., 1984, Leon Unger award Am. Coll. Allergists, 1985, Geigy fellow, 1987, travel grantsee, dist. fellow Am. Coll. Allergy, Asthma & Immunology, 1998. Mem. AMA (chmn. med. student sect. 1980-81, chmn. com. on women in medicine 1987-89, com. med. edn. 2004—, chair Tex. del. 2006), Mayo Assn. Fellows (treas. 1984-85), Mayo Alumni Assn. (exec. com. 1983-87, 95-02), Cojoint Com. Continuing Med. Edn., The Mayo Alumnus (adv. bd. 1983-87), Tarrant County Med. Soc. (bd. dirs. 1990—, v.p. 1994-95, pres.-elect 1995-96, pres. 1996-97, trustee 1998-01), Minn. Med. Assn. (trustee 1984-85), Tex. Med. Assn. (vice spkr. 1997-01, spkr. 2001-05, various coms.), Am. Acad. Pediats., Am. Coll. Allergy and Immunology (bd. regents 1994-97, chair publs. com. 2003-), Am. Assn. Cert. Allergists, Alpha Omega Alpha, Alpha Zeta, others. Office: 5929 Lovell Ave Fort Worth TX 76107-5029 Office Phone: 817-315-2550. E-mail: susanruddbailey@yahoo.com.

BAILEY, VICKY A., lobbyist; b. Indpls. BS, Purdue U.; postgrad., Ind. U., Indpls. Promotions dir. Glass Container divsn. Owens-Ill., Inc., Alton; asst. admissions officer Ind. U. Sch. Medicine; commr. Fed. Energy Regulatory Commn., 1993—2000; pres. PSI Energy, Inc., Ind., 2000—01; asst. secy. int. affairs and domestic policy U.S. Dept. Energy, Washington, 2001—04; ptnr. Johnston & Associates, LLC, Washington. Rep. to bd. trustees N.AM. Electric Reliability Coun.; mem. exec. com. Gt. Lakes conv. Mid-Am. Regulatory Commrs. Conf.; mem. Keystone Ctr. Energy Bd.; mem. Harvard Electricity Policy Group. Mem. Ind. Coun. for Econ. Edn.; active Boys and Girls Club of Indpls.; past pres. Indpls. Pub. Schs. Edn. Found., Ind. Humanities Coun., Nat. Coalition of 100 Black Women. Recipient Ind. Sagamore of the Wabash award. Mem. Nat. Assn. Regulatory Utility Commrs. (exec. and electricity coms.). Republican.

BAILEY-DAY, KAY LYNN, psychotherapist; b. Knoxville, Nov. 1, 1956; d. Guy Vernie and Weyburn Reid Bailey; children: Lydia April Austin, Jennifer Brooke Austin. BA in Psychology and Edn., Lenoir-Rhyne Coll., Hickory, N.C., 1991; MA in Agy./Cmty. Counseling, Lenoir-Rhyne Coll., 1998. Lic. profl. counselor NC. Evening coll. transfer counselor Lenoir-Rhyne Coll., Hickory, 1997—98; ednl. talent search facilitator Western Piedmont CC, Morganton, NC, 1998—99; pub. sch. liaison Caldwell CC, Hudson, NC, 1999—2000; counseling therapist Seasons of Hope, Hickory, 2000—04; domestic violence group facilitator Family Guidance, Hickory, 2004—; mental health mgr. CNC/Access Inc., Hickory, 2000—05; geriatric mental health mgr. Adult Life Program, Hickory, 2005—06; therapist Universal Mental Health, 2006—. Group facilitator psychiat. after care group Women's Resource Ctr., Hickory, 2001—02, vol. Rape Crisis Ctr., 1992—93. Mem.: Am. Counseling Assn. Avocations: gardening, reading, dance, travel, exercise. Office: Universal Mental Health Morganton NC 28613 Office Phone: 828-438-0006.

BAILEY-WELLS, DEBORAH, lawyer; BA with honors, Mills Coll., 1980; JD, Univ. San Francisco, 1984. Bar: Calif. 1984, US Dist. Ct. (no., ctrl., so. & ea. Calif.), US Ct. Appeals (9th & Fed. cir.), US Supreme Ct. Adminstrv. ptnr. & mem. mgmt. com. Kirkpatrick & Lockhart Nicholson Graham LLP, San Francisco. Contbr. articles to profl. jours. Mem.: ABA, Am. Intellectual Property Bar Assn., Internat. Trademark Assn., San Francisco Intellectual Property Law Assn., Silicon Valley Intellectual Property Assn. Office: Kirkpatrick & Lockhart Nicholson Graham LLP 10th Fl 4 Embarcadero Ctr San Francisco CA 94111-4121 Office Phone: 415-249-1065. Office Fax: 415-249-1001. Business E-Mail: dbaileywells@klng.com.

BAILLIE, MIRANDA LEE, secondary school educator; b. Sandusky, Ohio, Apr. 2, 1982; d. Gary Dean and Toni Jean Borchardt; m. Christopher Heim Borchardt, May 29, 2004. BA, Wilmington Coll., Ohio, 2004. Cert. tchr. Md. Math. tchr. Glen Burnie (Md.) HS, 2004—, jr. varsity girls basketball coach, 2005—, track and field asst. coach, 2006—. Nominating com. Nat. Youth Leadership Forum, Washington, 2005—, Congl. Youth Leadership Coun., Washington, 2005—. Home: 608 Sprite Way Glen Burnie MD 21061 Office: Glen Burnie High Sch 7550 Baltimore Annapolis Blvd Glen Burnie MD 21060 Office Phone: 410-761-8950. Personal E-mail: mbaillie@aacps.org.

BAILLOS, MARIANNE TKACH, secondary school educator; b. Cleve., Aug. 8, 1938; d. Michael Tkach and Mary Bugosh; children: Paul Michael, Peter Emanuel, Philip Andrew. BS, Mich. State U., 1960. Cert. tchr., Mich., Iowa, Va. Tchr. Singer Sewing Machine Co., Cleve., 1954; English tchr. Greece, 1960-61; tchr. Baldwin (Mich.) Pub. Schs., 1961-62, Waverly Pub. Schs., Lansing, Mich., 1962-67; mgr. real estate property Mason City, Iowa, 1978-88; area dir. Am. Cancer Soc., Mason City, 1987-89; tchr. Orange H.S., Orange County Schs., Orange, Va., 1991-92, Bassett H.S., Henry County Schs., Bassett, Va., 1992-95, Lancaster H.S., Lancaster County, Va., 1995-97, Dublin Mid. Sch., Pulaski County Schs., Pulaski, Va., 1997—. Del. Third Conf. Women's Issues, Beijing, China, 2002. Mem.: AAUW (v.p. programs Va. 1999—2001, pres. Mason City 1980—82). Eastern Orthodox. E-mail: mbaillos@verizon.net.

BAILYN, LOTTE, psychologist, educator; b. Vienna, July 17, 1930; came to U.S., 1937; d. Paul Felix Lazarsfeld and Marie (Jahoda) Albu; m. Bernard Bailyn, June 18, 1952; children: Charles, John. BA in Math. with high honors, Swarthmore Coll., 1951; MA in Social Psychology, Harvard U., 1953, PhD in Social Psychology, 1956; PhD (hon.), U. Piraeus, Greece, 2000. Rsch. assoc. Grad. Sch. Edn., Harvard U., Cambridge, Mass., 1956-57, rsch. assoc. dept. social rels., 1958-64, lectr., 1963-67; instr. dept. econs. and social sci. MIT, Cambridge, 1957-58, rsch. assoc. Sloan Sch. Mgmt., 1969-70, lectr., 1970-71, from sr. lectr. to prof., 1971-91, T Wilson prof. mgmt., 1991—2005, prof. mgmt., 2005—, chair MIT faculty, 1997-99; acad. visitor Imperial Coll. Sci., Tech. and Medicine, London, 1991, 1995, 2000; disting. vis. prof. Radcliffe Coll., 1995-97. Trustee Cambridge Savs. Bank, 1975-98; mem. adv. coun. Suffolk U. Mgmt. Sch., Boston, 1983-86; mem. sr. coun. Leadership Devel. Inst., Rutgers U., 1986-89; panel mem. NAS, NRC, Washington, 1988-90; mem. task force in career devel. and maintenance IEEE, Washington, 1982-90; vis. scholar Imperial Coll. Sci. and Tech., London, 1982, New Hall, Cambridge (Eng.) U., 1986-87; scholar-in-residence Rockefeller Found. Study and Conf. Ctr., Bellagio, Italy, 1983; vis. fellow U. Auckland, N.Z., 1984. Author: Mass Media and Children, 1959, Living with Technology, 1980, Breaking the Mold: Women, Men, and Time in the New Corporate World, 1993, Breaking the Mold: Redesigning Work for Satisfying Lives, 2006; co-author: Working with Careers, 1984, Relinking Life and Work: Toward a Better Future, 1996, Beyond Work-Family Balance: Advancing Gender Equity and Workplace Performance, 2002; mem. editl. bd. Jour. Engrng. and Tech. Mgmt., Cmty., Work and Family, Human Rels.; contbr. chpts. to books and articles to profl. jours. Trustee Radcliffe Coll., 1974-79, Cambridge Fin. Group, Inc., 1998-2005; bd. dirs. Families and Work Inst., 1995—, Cambridge Savings Bank, 1998-2005; adv. group, Creating Options: Models for Flexible Faculty Career Pathways, Office of Women in Higher Edn., Am. Coun. Edn., 2003-; com. Women in Sci. and Engring., Nat. Acad. Sci., 2004—, Women in Acad. Sci. and Engring., Nat. Acads., 2005-2006. Recipient Grad. Soc. medal Radcliffe Coll., 1998, Everett Cherrington Hughes award for careers scholarship Acad. of Mgmt., 2003, Work Life Legacy award, Families and Work Inst., 2005. Fellow APA; mem. Acad. Mgmt., Am. Sociol. Assn. Home: 170 Clifton St Belmont MA 02478-2604 Office: MIT Sloan Sch Mgmt 50 Memorial Dr Cambridge MA 02142-1347 Business E-Mail: lbailyn@mit.edu.

BAIMA, JULIE MARTIN, special education educator; b. Lincolnton, N.C., July 26, 1969; d. Thomas Luther Martin and Grace Turbyfill Caudle; m. Charles Joseph Baima, Nov. 21, 1992; children: Madison Lyndsey, Ronald Thomas. BS, Ga. Coll., 1991, EdM, 1996; specialist in edn., Ga. Coll. and State U., 2000. Cert. early childhood edn. tchr., specific learning disabilities tchr., mental retardation specialist. Spl. edn. tchr. Washington County Bd. Edn., Sandersville, Ga., 1992—93, Bibb County Bd. Edn., Macon, Ga., 1993—2002, Monroe County Bd. Edn., Forsyth, Ga., 2002—. Mem.: NEA, Ga. Edn. Assn., Macon Jr. Woman's Club (1st v.p. 2000—02, pres. 2002—). Republican. Episcopalian. Avocations: walking, reading, scrapbooks. Home: 230 Northridge Dr Macon GA 31220

BAIMAN, GAIL, real estate broker; b. Bklyn., June 4, 1938; d. Joseph and Anita (Devon) Yalow; children: Steven, Susan, Barbara. Student, Bklyn. Coll., 1955-57. Lic. real estate broker, N.Y., Pa., Fla.; hypnotherapist, stress mgmt. cons.; firewalk instr. Pers.-pub. rels. dir. I.M.C., Inc., N.Y.C., 1970-72; pres., broker Gayle Baiman Assocs., Inc., N.Y.C., 1972-74; v.p., broker Tuit Mktg. Corp., Mt. Pocono, Pa., 1974-83; pres., broker Timeshare Sales, Inc., St. Petersburg/Orlando, Fla., 1983-98; founder, CEO Universal Rembrance U. Inc., 1998—. Author: Vacation Timesharing, A Real Estate, 1992. Mem. Am. Resort Developers Assn., Better Bus. Arbitration Assn., Internat. Resale Brokers Assn. (co-founder), Chmns. League, Better Bus. Bur. Arbitrators. Office Phone: 727-430-2415. E-mail: GBaiman@aol.com.

BAIN, MARISSA, social worker; b. Providence, Sept. 30, 1977; d. Bruce Alan and Laurie Eleanor Bain. BA, U. R.I., 1999; MSW, R.I. Coll., 2000. Cert. cmty. support prof. R.I. Social worker NRI Cmty. Svcs., Woonsocket, 1999—, program mgr., 2003—06, coord. trauma svcs., 2006—. Vol. adv. Sexual Assault and Trauma Resource Ctr., Providence, 1997—99. Mem.: NASW, NOW (R.I. chpt.), Planned Parenthood Fedn. Am. Democrat. Home: 2 Fera St Apt 107 North Providence RI 02904-4163 Personal E-mail: mbain5@cox.net.

BAINBRIDGE, DONA BARDELLI, marketing professional; b. Irvington, NJ, Feb. 27, 1953; d. Alfred and Dona Ellen (Self) Bardelli; m. Harry M. Bainbridge, May 23, 1981 (dec.); 1 child, Harry Michael. Cert. de Langue, Sorbonne U., France, 1974; BA, U. Ky., 1975; MA in Internat. Studies, Am. U., 1978; MSc in Econs. and Social Planning in Devel. Countries, London Sch. Econs.; cert. London Art Course, Christie's Edn., England, 2005. Rsch. assoc. Woodrow Wilson Internat. Ctr. for Vis. Scholars, Washington, 1976—77, World Bank, Washington, 1977—79; legis. asst. to Congressman Marc Lincoln Marks Washington, 1979—80; itnernat. trade analyst Internat. Trade Adminstrn. U.S. Dept. Commerce, Washington, 1980—82; internat. mgmt. cons. Coopers and Lybrand, 1982—86; v.p. Bankers Trust Co. Internat. Pvt. Banking, 1986—88; sr. mktg. dir. internat. svcs. BDO Seidman, N.Y.C., 1988—90; founder, pres. D.H. Bainbridge Assocs., 1990—. Chmn. mem. com., mem. mktg. com., bd. dirs., vice chair Camp Sloane YMCA, 2000; trustee, co-chair capital campaign The Washington Episcopal Sch., Bethesda, Md., 1996—98; trustee The Town Hill Sch., Lakeville, 1999—2004, N.W. Ctr. for Family Svcs., Lakeville, 2002—04; mem. adv. bd., chmn. White Plains Salvation Army, 1992—93; mem. adv. bd. pediat. dept. Georgetown U. Hosp., 2005—; bd. mem. Camp Sloane YMCA, Lakeville, Conn., 1990—2004; chair nat. membership Am. Friends of London Sch. Econs., 1981—83, nat. bd. dirs., 1982—84, 1994—96; chair Washington Com. Women's Studies in Religion program Divinity Sch. Harvard U., 1996—98. Mem.: Soc. Internat. Devel. (D.C. chpt.), Bus. and Profl. Women's Clubs Am. (acad. scholar 1971), Fin. Women's Assn. NY, Nat. Press Club, Kiwanis. Democrat. Lutheran.

BAINS, LESLIE ELIZABETH, banker; b. Glen Ridge, N.J., July 28, 1943; d. Pliny Otto and Dorothy Ethel (Keeley) Tawney; m. Harrison Mackellar Bains Jr.; Harrison III, Tawney Elizabeth. BA, Am. U., 1965. Asst. treas. Citicorp, N.Y.C., 1965-73; v.p. Mfrs. Hanover, N.Y.C., 1973-80; v.p., divsn. exec. Chase Manhattan Bank, N.Y.C., 1980-86, v.p., group exec., 1986-87, sr. v.p. group exec., 1987-91; mng. dir. Global Pvt. Banking Group Citibank, N.Y.C., 1991-93; exec. v.p. Republic Nat. Bank, N.Y.C., 1993-2000; sr. exec. v.p. HSBC Bank USA, N.Y.C., 2000—, mem. sr. mgmt. com. Bd. dirs., chair fin. com. Interplast, 1991. Chmn. Ednl. Cable Consortium, Summit, NJ, 1987—91; bd. dirs., chair fin. com. Interplast Found.; bd. dirs. Junior Achievement of N.Y.; mem. exec. com., bd. dirs., chair devel. com. Roundabout Theater; bd. trustees Am. U., 1994—, vice chair bd. trustees, 2001—; bd. dirs. Jr. Achievement, N.Y.C., 1996—, chair investment com.; bd. visitors Terry Sanford Inst. Pub. Policy Duke U., Duke U. Med. Sch. Named Achiever of Yr. YWCA, 1985, One of Top 100 Women in Corp. Am., Bus. Month., 1989. Fellow Fgn. Policy Assn; mem. Am. Bankers Assn. (bd. dirs. pvt. banking coun.), Fin. Women Internat. (vice chmn. Edn. Found. 1980-81, treas. 1981-83, v.p. 1983-84, pres. 1984-85), Fin. Women's Assn., Women and Founds., Coun. Fgn. Rels., The Econ. Club of N.Y. Office: HSBC Bank USA 452 5th Ave New York NY 10018-2706

BAINTON, DOROTHY FORD, pathologist, educator; b. Magnolia, Miss., June 18, 1933; d. Aubrey Ratcliff and Leta (Brumfield) Ford; m. Cedric R. Bainton, Nov. 28, 1959; children: Roland J., Bruce G., James H. BS, Millsaps Coll., 1955; MD, Tulane U. Sch. of Medicine, 1958; MS, U. Calif., San Francisco, 1966. Postdoctoral rsch. fellow U. Calif., San Francisco, 1963-66, postdoctoral rsch. pathologist, 1966-69, asst. prof. pathology, 1969-75, assoc. prof., 1975-81, prof. pathology, 1981—, chair pathology, 1987-94, vice chancellor acad. affairs, 1994—2004; ret. Mem. Inst. of Medicine, NAS, 1990—. Grantee, NIH, 1968—98. Fellow AAAS, Am. Acad. Arts & Scis.; mem. FASEB (bd. dirs.), Am. Soc. for Cell Biology, Am. Soc. Hematology, Am. Soc. Histochemists and Cytochemists, Am. Assn. of Pathologists. Democrat. Address: 50 Ventura Ave San Francisco CA 94116 E-mail: dbainton@mac.com.

BAIR, DEBORAH LYNN, primary school educator; b. St. Paul, Minn. d. Darrold Herman and Mary Louise Niederkorn. BA in Elem. Edn., Metro State Coll., Denver, Colo., 1975; MA in Reading, U. Colo., Denver, 1981. Tchr., grades 2-3 Warder Elem., Arvada, 1975—97, tchr., kindergarden, 1997—2005. Vol. Alterra Sterling House, Arvada, 1998—2005; bd. mem., spiritual dir. Beginning Experience, Ft. Collins, 1986—90; staff mem. Ann. Christian Renewal Conf., Denver, 1984—2000. Recipient Tchr. of Yr. Hon. Mention, Denver, 1984, Value award - Exemplary Performance, Jeffco Schs., Arvada, 2004. Mem.: Colo. Orgn. Kindergarten Tchrs., Arvada Hist. Soc., Colo. Hist. Soc. Avocations: hiking, stamp collecting/philately, gardening, history, card making. Home: 10820 W 63rd Av #A Arvada CO 80004

BAIR, SHEILA COLLEEN, federal agency administrator, former education educator; b. Wichita, Kans., Apr. 3, 1954; d. Albert E. and Clara F. (Brenneman) B.; m. Scott P. Cooper; children, Preston, Colleen. BA in Philosophy, U. Kans., 1975, JD, 1978. Bar: Kans. 1979. Teaching fellow U. Ark. Sch. Law, Fayetteville, 1978-79; atty.-advisor HEW, Kansas City, Mo., 1979-81; legal and policy advisor to Senator Bob Dole US Senate, Washington, 1981-86; of counsel Kutak, Rock & Campbell, Washington, 1986-87; dir. rsch. Bob Dole for Pres., Kans., 1987-88; legis. counsel NY Stock Exch., Washington, 1988-91, sr. v.p. govt. rels., 1995—2000; commr. Commodity Futures Trading Commn., Washington, 1991—95, acting chmn., 1993; asst. sec. for fin. institutions US Dept Treasury, Washington, 2001—02; Dean's prof. fin. regulatory policy U. Mass., Amherst, 2002—06; mem. FDIC, Washington, 2006—, chmn., 2006—. Author: Rock, Brock, and the Savings Shock, 2006. Recipient Treasury medal, 2002, Disting. Achievement award, Assn. Edn. Publishers, 2005. Mem.: Soc. Children's Book Writers & Illustrators, Exchequer Club, ABA, Women's Campaign Fund, Mass. Savings Makes Cents, NASD Ahead-of-the-Curve Adv. Com., Women in Housing & Fin. Ctr. for Responsible Lending, Ins. Marketplace Standards Assn. Office: FDIC 550 17th St NW Washington DC 20429

BAIRD, ALICE KNAR, retired education educator; b. Sivas, Turkey, Nov. 11, 1918; arrived in U.S., 1920; d. Harry and Marguerite Seradarian Shamlian; m. James Abington Baird, Dec. 2, 2000; m. Lloyd William Barter (div.); 1 child, Andrea Marguerite Kopp. BA, Eastern Mich. U., 1939; MA, U.Mich., 1944; PhD, U. Mich., 1957. Tchr. Mich. Pub. Sch., 1939—55; asst. prof. edn. U. Detroit, 1957—60; asst. to assoc. prof. of English and edn. Miami U., Oxford, Ohio, 1960—67; English prof. Chgo. State U., 1967—89. Chmn. Dept. English and Speech, 1980—83; vis. prof. Nanjing U., Nanjing, China, 1986. Author: Spelling by Sound and Sequence: A Phonemic Speller, 1975, Tools: A Guide to Basic Grammar and Writing, 1987, Saroyan's Armenians: An Anthology, 1992, Theaters of the Heart and Mind, 1998; contbr. articles to profl. jours. Avocation: sculpting. Home: 85Nottingham Cross Bowling Green OH 43402

BAIRD, ALISON ELIZABETH, neurologist; b. Melbourne, Victoria, Australia, July 5, 1961; came to U.S., 1996; d. Cameron William Baird and Lorna Isabel Murfitt. MBBS, U. Melbourne, 1985, PhD, 1996; MPH, Harvard U., 1999. Intern Austin Hosp., Melbourne, 1986, resident med. officer, 1988-89, med. registrar, 1990-91, neurology registrar, 1994-95; neurology fellow Beth Israel Deaconess Med. Ctr., Boston, 1996-98, instr. neurology, 1998—. Lectr. in field. Reviewer: (jours.) Stroke, Jour. Cerebral Blood Flow and Metabolism; contbr. articles to profl. jours. Recipient Doris Duke Clin. Scientist award, 1998-01, Young Investigator award Australian Brain Found., 1992; Nat. Health and Med. Rsch. Coun. of Australia scholar, 1992-94, tuition scholar Harvard U. Sch. Pub. Health, 1998-00; Neil Hamilton Fairley fellow Nat. Health and Med. Rsch. Coun. Australia, 1996-99. Fellow Royal Australasian Coll. Physicians (Bushell Traveling fellow in medicine or allied scis. 1996); mem. Am. Acad. Neurology (corr. assoc., Michael S. Pessin Stroke Leadership prize 1999), Australian Assn. Neurologists (Young Investigator award 1994), Stroke Soc. Australasia, European Stroke Coun. E-mail: abaird@caregroup.harvard.edu.

BAIRD, CAROL LOWRY, elementary school educator; d. Thomas G. and Anna L. Lowry; m. Billy N. Baird, Aug. 13, 1966; children: Bryan Neal, Colin Lane. AA in Liberal Arts, Wood Jr. Coll., 1964; BA in Elem. Edn., Millsaps Coll., 1966; MEd in Elem. Edn., Miss. Coll., 1968. Cert. AAA in elem. edn., nat. bd. cert. tchr. Tchr. 1st and 2d grades Jackson Pub. Schs., Miss., 1966—77; tchr. 1st grade Clinton Pub. Schs., Miss., 1977—78, Jackson Pub. Schs., Miss., 1978—. Presenter in field; after-sch. tutor John Hopkins Elem. Sch. Bible sch. tchr. 1st United Meth. Ch.; neighborhood vol. Diabetes Assn., Am. Lung Assn., March of Dimes; monthly vol. Nature Nuts series Clinton Nature Ctr. Named Project NEED Tchr. of Yr., 2005, Outstanding Educator, Parents for Pub. Schs., 2002, PTA Vol. of Yr., 2000; recipient Presdl. award for excellence in sci. tchg., 2004, Disneyland Tchr. award, 2005, grants in field, Lysol/Nat. Sci. Tchrs. Assn. Sci. and Your Health Challenge award, 2003. Mem.: Soc. Elem. Presdl. Awardees, Miss. Profl. Educators Assn., Jackson Area Reading Coun., Internat. Reading Assn., Nat. Coun. Tchrs. Math., Nat. Sci. Tchrs. Assn., Miss. Sci. Tchrs. Assn. (Tchr. of Yr. 2004—05). Methodist. Home: 1008 Old Vicksburg Rd Clinton MS 39056 Office: John Hopkins Elem 170 John Hopkins Rd Jackson MS 39209

BAIRD, CHRISTINE MARY, secondary school educator; b. Ft. Dodge, Iowa, Jan. 1, 1965; d. Walter Henry and Virginia Dorothy Wiemers; m. Chris Lyndon Baird, Aug. 8, 1992. BA, Buena Vista Coll., Storm Lake, Iowa, 1987. Lic. Tchr. Iowa Bd. Edn., 1987. English tchr. Twin Rivers Cmty. Sch., Bode, Iowa, 1987—92, Nishna Valley Cmty. Sch., Hastings, 1992—. Adv. to yearbook staff, 1987—96; facilitator Young Writer's Conf., 1990; coach Nishna Valley Individual Speech Team, Hastings, 1992—; com. mem. Homecoming Com., Hastings, 1995—; mem. selection com. Nat. Honor Soc., Hastings, 2001—. Recipient Gov.'s Scholar Favorite Tchr. award, Office of Gov., Iowa, Des Moines, 2004, 2006. Mem.: NEA (local chpt. treas. 1990—92), Beta Sigma Phi (local chpt. pres. 1997, local chpt. sec. 2003, scholarship com. 2004). Roman Catholic. Avocations: reading, gardening, music, sports, photography. Office: Nishna Valley Cmty Sch 58962 380th St Hastings IA 51540

BAIRD, LAUREL COHEN, clinical nurse; b. Chgo., Dec. 1, 1943; d. Carl Eugene and Joan Adele (Arenz) Patterson; m. Sidney Henry Cohen, June 29, 1968 (div. Nov. 1981); children: Elizabeth Ann Cohen, David Arthur Patterson, Douglas Edward (dec. 2003), Deborah Sue; m. Frederick Joseph Foti, Jan. 19, 1985 (div. June 1994) m. Jack W. Baird, Nov. 10, 2001. Diploma in nursing, Swedish Covenant, 1967; BS, Moody Bible Inst., 1976. RN, N.J., Md. Staff nurse Overlook Hosp., Summit, N.J., 1980-82; pub. health nurse Patient Care Svc., West Orange, N.J., 1982-83; hospice nurse The Hospice, Inc., Montclair, N.J., 1984-92; fin. svc. rep. Primerica Fin. Svcs., Duluth, Ga., 1985-89; coord. home care Vis. Nurse Assn. Essex Valley, East Orange, N.J., 1993-96; Medicare case mgr. Aetna US Healthcare Cmty. Outreach, Fairfield, NJ, 1996-99; on-site nurse Johns Hopkins Cmty. Physicians, 1999—2001, Sun Plus Home Care, Pleasant Hill, Calif., 2001; hospice nurse care mgr. Sutter VNA and Hospice, Concord, 2002—; benefit analyst Genworth Fin. Assurance, 2004—. State coord. La Leche League, N.J., 1976-78; hospice vol. The Hospice, Inc., 1992-98; mem. MADD, Rep. Presdl. Task Force, 1989. Lt. (j.g.) USNR, 1967-69. Mem. Adoptees Liberty Movement Assn. (spokesman 1977-83), DAR. Republican. Presbyterian. Avocations: orchid culture, gardening, marathoning, speed walking, piano. Home: 303 Eastgate Lane Martinez CA 94553-

BAIRD, LISA P., marketing executive; m. Robert Baird; 2 children. Grad., Pa. State U. Brand mgr. General Motors; with Proctor & Gamble, Bristol-Myers Squibb, Warner Lambert; v.p., worldwide advertising IBM, 2000—03, v.p., worldwide integrated marketing communications, 2003—05; sr. v.p., marketing NFL, 2005—. Office: c/o NFL 280 Park Ave New York NY 10017*

BAIRD, PATRICIA ANN, physician, educator; b. Rochdale, Eng. arrived in Can., 1955; d. Harold and Winifred (Cainen) Holt; m. Robert Merrifield Baird, Feb. 22, 1964; children: Jennifer Ellen, Brian Merrifield, Bruce Andrew BSc in Biol. Sci. with honors, McGill U., 1959, MD, CM, 1963; DSc (hon.), McMaster U., 1991; D (hon.), U. Ottawa, 1991; LLD (hon.), Wilfrid Laurier U., 2000. Intern Royal Victoria Hosp., Montreal, Que., Canada, 1963-64; resident, fellow in pediat. Vancouver Gen. Hosp., B.C., Canada, 1964-67; instr. pediat. U. B.C., Vancouver, 1968-72, from asst. prof. to prof., 1972-94, Univ. Killam Disting. prof., 1994—; head dept. med. genetics Grace Hosp., Vancouver, 1981-89, Children's Hosp., Vancouver, 1981-89, Health Scis. Centre Hosp., 1986-89. Med. cons. B.C. Health Surveillance Registry, 1977-90; chmn. genetics grants com. Med. Rsch. Coun., Ottawa, Ont., Can., 1982-87, mem. coun., 1987-90; mem. Nat. Adv. Bd. on Sci. and Tech. to Fed. Govt., 1987-91; mem. genetic predisposition study steering com. Sci. Coun. Can., 1987-90; chair Royal Commn. on New Reproductive Technologies, 1989-93, Premier's Coun. on Aging Sr. Issues, 2005—; co-chair Nat. Forum Sci. and Tech. Couns., 1991; v.p. Can. Inst. for Advanced Rsch., 1991-2002, vice chmn. bd., 2002—; bd. dirs. Biomed. Rsch. Centre, 1986-89; bd. govs. U. B.C., 1984-90; temporary cons. WHO, 1999, 2000, 01, mem. human genetics ELSI planning group, 2000-02, mem. expert adv. panel on human genetics, 2002—03. Contbr. articles to med. jours. Decorated officer Order of Can., 2000, Order of B.C., 1992; recipient Commemorative medal for Confedn. of Can., 1992, Queen's Golden Jubilee medal, 2002. Fellow RCP Can., Royal Soc. Can., Can. Coll. Med. Geneticists (v.p. 1984-86); mem. Am. Soc. Human Genetics (chair nominating com. 1987-89), B.C. Med. Assn., Can. Med. Assn., Genetics Soc. Can., Genetic Epidemiology (adv. bd. 1991-94), Internat. Fedn. of Gyn. and Obs. (mem. ethics com. 1997-99). Avocations: skiing, bicycling, music. Office: U BC Dept Med Genetics Vancouver BC Canada V6T 1Z3 Business E-Mail: pbaird@interchange.ubc.ca.

BAIRD, PENNY DRUE, interior designer; b. N.Y.C., July 19, 1951; d. Philip Robert and Terri Baird; m. Fred Deutsch, Dec. 31, 1991; children: Alexander Baird Deutsch, Benjamin Baird Deutsch, Philip Baird Deutsch; 1 child, Adam Baird Alpert. BA, U. Rochester, 1973; PsychD, Yeshiva U., 1991; attended, NY School of Interior Design. Pres. Dessins LLC, N.Y.C., 1982—. Archtl. Digest, 1997, 1998, 2000. Pres. City Meals on Wheels, N.Y.C., 1985—90; mem. women's com. N.Y. Hosp., N.Y.C., 1994—; mem. women's bd. Albert Einstein Coll. Medicine, N.Y.C., 1990—. Mem.: Phi Beta Kappa. Office: Dessins LLC 787 Madison Ave New York NY 10021

BAIRD, ZOË, lawyer; b. Bklyn., June 20, 1952; d. Ralph Louis and Naomi (Allen) B.; 2 children. AB, U. Calif., Berkeley, 1974, JD, 1977. Bar: Washington, 1979, Calif. 1977, Conn. 1989. Law clk. Hon. Albert Wollenberg, San Francisco, 1977-78; atty., advisor Office Legal Counsel U.S. Dept. Justice, Washington, 1979-80; assoc. counsel to Pres., The White House, Washington, 1980-81; assoc., then ptnr. O'Melveny & Myers, Washington, 1981-86; counsellor, staff exec. GE, Fairfield, Conn., 1986-90; v.p., gen. counsel Aetna Life & Casualty, Hartford, 1990-93, sr. v.p., gen. counsel, 1993-96; pres. Markle Found., N.Y.C., 1998—. Bd. dirs. Chubb Corp., Boston Properties. Bd. dirs. Lawyers for Children Am., Brookings Inst. Mem. Am. Law Inst., Coun. on Fgn. Rels., Convergys Corp. Office: Markle Found 10 Rockefeller Plaza 16th Fl New York NY 10020-1903 Business E-Mail: info@markle.org.

BAIRRINGTON, RUTH ELLEN, retired secondary school educator, retired education educator; b. Denver, Nov. 5, 1927; d. Guy Lewis Hall and Winifred Lucille Stanbrough; m. Noble Bairrington, Feb. 22, 1948 (dec.); children: Linda Carol, Philip Kevin. BA, Baylor U., Waco, Tex., 1960, MA, 1963; MEd, Colo. Coll., Colorado Springs, 1990. Cert. tchr. Colo. Instr. Baylor U., 1960—62, Colo. Coll., 1963—65; sr. English tchr. Cheyenne HS, Colorado Springs, 1965—67, Hanover Sch., Colorado Springs, 1967—68; English instr. U. Colo., Colorado Springs, 1969—73. Drama and poetry tchr. Elder Hostel, Colorado Springs, 1989, drama and poetry tchr., Greek and Shakespeare, 92. Author: History of Campfire Girls in Colorado Springs, 1985, The Outsider, 1988. Leader, guardian Camp Fire Girls Inc., Waco, 1955—63, leader, guardian, officer Colorado Springs, 1971—77; historian North State Symphony League, 1966—; Sunday sch. tchr. 1st Bapt. Ch., Waco, 1955—63, 1st Christian Ch., Colorado Springs, 1983—95. Grantee, Baylor U., 1960—62. Mem.: Delta Kappa Gamma. Avocations: sewing, writing, piano, reading. Home: 1606 Hominy Way Redding CA 96003

BAIRSTOW, FRANCES KANEVSKY, arbitrator, mediator, educator; b. Racine, Wis., Feb. 19, 1920; d. William and Minnie (DuBow) Kanevsky; m. Irving P. Kaufman, Nov. 14, 1942 (div. 1949); m. David Steele Bairstow, Dec. 17, 1954; children: Dale Owen, David Anthony. Student, U. Wis., 1937-42; BS, U. Louisville, 1949; student, Oxford U., England, 1953-54; postgrad., McGill U., Montreal, Que., Can., 1958-59. Rsch. economist U.S. Senate Labor-Mgmt. Subcom., Washington, 1950-51; labor edn. specialist U. P.R., San Juan, 1951-52; chief wage data unit WSB, Washington, 1952-53; labor rsch. economist Can. Pacific Ry. Co., Montreal, Que., Canada, 1956-58; asst. dir. indsl. rels. ctr. McGill U., 1960-66, assoc. dir., 1966-71, dir., 1971-85, lectr., indsl. rels. dept. econs., 1960-72, from asst. prof. to assoc. prof. faculty mgmt., 1972—83, prof., 1983-85; lectr. Stetson Law Sch., Fla.; spl. master Fla. Pub. Employees Rels. Commn., 1985-97. Cons. Nat. Film Bd. Can., 1965—69; arbitrator Que. Consultative Coun. Panel Arbitrators, 1968—83, Ministry Labour and Manpower, 1971—83, United Air Lines and Assn. Flight Attendants, 1990—95, Am. Airlines and Transport Workers Union, 1997—98, State U. Sys. Fla., 1990—2003, FDA, 1996—98, Social Security Adminstrn., 1996—2003, Am. Airlines, 1997—, Tampa Gen. Hosp., 1996—, Cargo Internat. Airlines, 2001, Govt. of Fla. and Fla. State Police, 2002—, Bell South and Comm. Workers Am., 2003—, USAF at Warner Robins and AFGE, 2003—; mediator Can. Pub. Svc. Staff Rels. Bd., 1973—85, So. Bell Tel., 1985—, AT&T and Comm. Workers Am., 1986—; cons. on collective bargaining arbitration OECD, Paris, 1979. Contbg. columnist: Montreal Star, 1971—85. Chmn. Nat. Inquiry Commn. Wider-Based Collective Bargaining, 1978; dep. commr. essential svcs. Province of Que., 1976—81. Recipient Sefton award, U. Toronto, 2005; Fulbright fellow, 1953—54. Mem.: Ctrl. Fla. Indsl. Rels. Rsch. Assn. (pres. 1999), Nat. Acad. Arbitrators (bd. govs. 1977—80, program chmn. 1982—83, v.p. 1986—88, nat. coord. 1987—90), Indsl. Rels. Rsch. Assn. Am. (mem. exec. bd. 1965—68, chmn. nominating com. 1977), Can. Indsl. Rels. Rsch. Inst. (mem. exec. bd. 1965—68). Home and Office: 4650 54th Ave S # 511 Saint Petersburg FL 33711

BAIUL, OKSANA, former figure skater, clothing designer; b. Dnepropetrovsk, Ukraine, Nov. 16, 1977; d. Marina Baiul. Clothing designer Oksana Baiul Collection. Skating tours include Champions on Ice, 1993, 94, 95, 96, 97, 98, The Great Skate II: Charity Event, 1995, Great Skate III, 1997, Nutcracker on Ice, 1995, CBS Spl.: Too Hot to Skate, 1995, 96, Sergei Grinkov: Celebration of a Life, 1996, CBS Spl.: Wizard of Oz on Ice, 1996, An Evening with Champions: Charity Benefit, 1997, 98, Fire on Ice: Charity Event, 1998, 75 Yrs. of Disney Magic, 1998, FTD Champions on Ice, 1999. Recipient 2d Pl. award women's figure skating European Championships, 1993, 1st Pl. award women's figure skating World Figure Skating Championships, 1993, Gold medal women's figure skating Olympic Games, 1994, 2d Pl. Nikon Championship, 1994, 4th Pl. Am. Skating Invitational, 1994, 2d Pl. Ice Wars Overall Team Results, 1995, 98, 2d Pl. Gold Championships, 1995, 2d Pl. Rock'n' Roll Championships, 1996, 1st Pl. Ice Wars Overall Team Results, 1997, 3d Pl. Skate TV Championships, 1998, among others. Office: Oksana Baiul Collection GO Enterprises 177 Main Street 395 Fort Lee NJ 07024

BAJCSY, RUZENA KUCEROVA, computer science educator; b. Bratislava, Czechoslovakia, May 28, 1933; came to U.S., 1968; d. Felix and Marguita (Weisz) Kucerova; m. Sherman Frankel. PhD in Elec. Engrin., Slovak Tech. U., Bratislava, 1967; PhD in Computer Sci., Stanford U., 1972. Asst. prof. elect. engrin. Slovak Tech. U., 1967-68; rsch. scientist artificial intelligence lab. Stanford (Calif.) U., 1968-72; prof. computer science U. Pa., Phila., 1972—2001, chair computer and info. sci. dept., 1985-90, dir. Grasp Lab., 1985—2001; dir. Nat. Sci. Found., asst. dir. comp. sci. Washington, 1998—2001; dir. Ctr. Info. Tech. Rsch. in Interest of Soc. U. Calif., Berkeley, 2001—. Vis. scientist INRIA, France, 1979; vis. prof. U. Copenhagen, Denmark, 1984, 1988, U. Pisa, Italy, 1988; Forsythe lectr. Stanford U., 1989; cons. in field. Editor periodicals including Computer Vision. Fellow IEEE, Assn. Computing Machinery; mem. NAE, Inst. Medicine NAS. Office: 284 Hearst Meml Mining Bldg Berkeley CA 94720-1764

BAJICH, MILENA TATIC, psychologist; b. Bosanski Novi, Bosnia-Herzegovina, Mar. 3, 1964; arrived in U.S., 1971; d. Stevo and Ljubica Tatic; m. Stojan Bajich, Oct. 23, 1994; 1 child, Stevan. BS, Loyola U., Chgo., 1986; PsyD, Chgo. Sch. Profl. Psychology, 1994. Lic. clin. psychologist Ill. Asst. tng. dir., program coord. Miwest Mental Health Care Providers, Chgo., 1992—97; clin. psychologist Albany Care/Greenwood Care Rehab. Homes for Severe Psychopathology, Evanston, Ill., 1996—2001, Milena Tatic Bajich, PsyD, Chgo., 1996—, Paladin, LLC, Chgo., 1997—2004, Fabian Carbonell, M.D., S.C., Chgo., 2000—; allied profl. staff St. Joseph Hosp./Resurrection Healthcare, Chgo., 2003—. Mem. ethics com. Adm. at The Lake, Chgo., 2005—; adj. faculty Ill. Sch. Profl. Psychology, Chgo., 1996—2000. Exhibitions include paintings and drawings, invited, Commemmorative 911 Exhibit, Samuel Akainyah, 2002. Choir pres. Stevan St. Mokranjac Choir, Chgo., 2003; mem. Serbian Nat. Fedn., Pitts., 1994. Named Ea. Europe-Poland, Chekoslovakia invitee, Global Initiatives, 2004; recipient Recognition in Behavioral Scis. award, 1998; scholar, Chgo. Sch. of Profl. Psychology, 1987, 1990. Mem.: APA, (assoc.), Psi Chi. Serbian Orthodox. Avocation: travel. Office: # 408 2800 N Sheridan Chicago IL 60657 Office Phone: 773-561-5524. Office Fax: 773-561-5524. E-mail: mbajich@aol.com.

BAJOR, RENEE ALLYSON, special education educator; b. L.A., Calif., Feb. 26, 1964; d. Andrew Donald Bajor and Sandra Lee Ladd. AA, L.A. Pierce Coll., Woodland Hills, California, 1985; BA in Deaf Studies cum laude, Calif. State U., Northridge, 1991; MBA, Internat. U. Japan, Niigata, 2001. Interpreter for deaf L.A. Pierce Coll., 1985, profl. clear multiple subject tchg. credential State of Calif. Commn. Tchr. Credentialling, 1993, clear crosscultural, lang. and academic devel. State of Calif. Commn. Tchr. Credentialling, 2002, cert. gifted and talented edn. U. Calif., Riverside, 2006. Sign lang. interpreter Calif. State U., Northridge, 1984—93, San Bernardino Valley Coll., 1993—2005; math. tchr. Landmark Mid. Sch., Moreno Valley, 1996—2004; fourth grade tchr. Creekside Elem. Sch., Moreno Valley, 2004—. Home and hosp. tchr. Moreno Valley Unified Sch. Dist., Calif., 1996—; tech. advisor Creekside Elem. Sch., 2004—, English lang. devel. specialist, 2006. Troop leader Girl Scouts USA, Van Nuys, Calif., 1985—93, San Bernardino, 1996—97; vol. L.A. Marathon, 2005; altar server Christ the Redeemer Cath. Ch., Grand Terrace, 1993—99. Recipient Gold award, Girl Scouts USA, 1982, Gold and Silver Leadership awards, 1982, Tchr. of Yr., Landmark Mid. Sch., 1998. Mem.: Moreno Valley Educators' Assn., Calif. PTA (auditor 2006), Girl Scouts USA (life). Roman Catholic. Avocations: travel, quilting, reading, cooking, languages. Office: Moreno Valley Unified Sch Dist 13563 Heacock St Moreno Valley CA 92553 Office Phone: 951-571-4560. Office Fax: 951-571-4565. E-mail: rbajor@mvusd.k12.ca.us.

BAJURA, RITA A., research scientist; B in Chem., Mercyhurst Coll., Erie, Pa.; M in Engring., West Va. Univ. With Dept. of Energy, 1980—, dir., Nat. Energy Tech. Lab., 1996—. Appointed to West Va. State's Energy Task Force, 2001. Named to Acad. of Disting. Alumni of Mech. Engring and Mech., West Va. Univ., 2000; recipient Achievement award for contributions to coal industry, Washington Coal Club, 2001, Pitt award, annual award for innovation in coal conversion, Univ. Pitts. Sch. Engring., 2002.

BAKELY, LISA MENG, elementary school educator; b. Kansas City, Mo., Oct. 9, 1963; d. Douglas Donald and Lenore Rue Meng; m. Peter Jon Bakely, May 28, 1984; children: Andrew Peter, Matthew Christian. BA, Pk. Coll., Parkville, Mo., 1995. Cert. tchr. Mo., 1999. Swimming instr. Kansas City Chpt. ARC, 1985—95; tchr. Kansas City Mo. Sch. Dist., 1996—. Democrat. Methodist. Avocations: reading, swimming, needlecrafts. Office: Swinney Elementary 1106 W 47th St Kansas City MO 64112-1215 Office Phone: 816-418-6387. Office Fax: 816-418-6280. Business E-Mail: lbakely@kcmsd.net.

BAKER, ADRIENNE MARIE, lawyer; b. Bklyn., Sept. 29, 1959; d. Pat Adrian and Marie Frances (Patti) Catanese. SB in Physics, MIT, 1981; JD magna cum laude, Boston U., 1985, LLM in Taxation, 1991. Bar: Mass. 1985, U.S. Ct. Claims 1986, U.S. Patent and Trademark Office 1986, N.Y. 1988, U.S. Dist. Ct. Mass. 1990. Assoc. Gaston & Snow, Boston, 1985-87, Coudert Bros., N.Y.C., 1987-88, Dechert Price & Rhoads, Boston, 1988-93; ptnr. Dechert LLP (Dechert Price & Rhoads), Boston, 1993—. Contbr. articles to profl. jours. Justinian Law Soc. scholar, 1985. Mem. ABA, Boston Bar Assn. Roman Catholic. Avocations: cooking, tennis, squash, sailing, travel. Office: Dechert LLP 200 Clarendon St 27th Fl Boston MA 02116 E-mail: adrienne.baker@dechert.com.

BAKER, ALDEN, artist; b. Manhattan, N.Y., Jan. 10, 1928; d. Samuel Burtis Baker and Grace Whalley Higgins; m. Robert Oppenheim, Aug. 21, 1963 (dec. June 1986); 1 child, Jessica Oppenheim. Cert., Berkeley Secretarial Sch., 1948; student, Cape Sch. Art, summer 1957-63, Art Students League, N.Y.C., 1965-66. Reporter, ch. and sch. editor Montclair (N.J.) Times, 1951-53; publicity dir. Newark Mus., 1953-56; editor, pub. rels. dir. Assn. Jr. Leagues Am., N.Y.C., 1956-64. Pastel demonstrator, Xian, China, 1997. Exhbns. include Manhattan's Lincoln Ctr., LEver House, Salmagundi Club, Pen and Brush Club, Nat. Arts Club, Allied Artists Am., Catherine Lorillard Wolfe Art Club, Pastel Soc. Am., Hudson Valley Art Assn., The Queens, Bergen and Hammond Mus., Copley Gallery, Boston; curator: The Best of Pastel II, 1999; featured in Am. Artist Mag., 1995, The Pastel Jour., 2001. Mem. Pastel Soc. Am. (bd. dirs. 1994-2005, master pastelist, signature, critiques chmn., bd. dirs., Mr. and Mrs. Andrew Giffuni award 1999), Pen and Brush, Inc. (chmn. pastel sect. 1997-2000, 2 solo exhbns. awards), Hudson Valley Art Assn. (Dianne Bernhard Silver Medal award), Am. Artist Profl. League (various awards), Art Ctr. N.J. (pres., newsletter editor, exhbn. chair), Salmagundi Club (Dianne Bernhard Gold medal 2000) Unitarian Universalist. Home: 49 Druid Hill Rd Summit NJ 07901

BAKER, AMY ELAINE, assistant principal; b. Washington, June 12, 1975; d. Ann and Doug Graybeal (Stepfather). BS in elem. edn., U. of Ctrl. Fla., 1993—97; M in ednl. leadership, U. of South Fla., 2002—03. Florida Educational Leadership Dept. of Edn./Fla., 2003, Elementary Education Dept. of Edn./Fla., 1997. Tchr. Chickasaw Elem., Orlando, 1998—99, Venice Elem., 1999—2003; curriculum coord./instrnl. tech. facilitator Garden Elem., Venice, Fla., 2003—04; asst. prin. Glenallen Elem., North Port, Fla., 2004—. Chmn. Sch. Adv. Coun. - Garden Elem., Venice, 2003—04, Sch. Adv. Coun. - Venice Elem., 2002—03. Mem. Jr. League of Sarasota, Fla., 2002, Young Professionals Group - C. of C., Sarasota, Fla., 2005. Nominee Sally Mae First Tchr. award Nominee, Chickasaw Elem., 1999; recipient Tchr. of the Yr., Venice Elem. Sch., 2002—03, PALS Outstanding Cmty. Svc. Project Recipient, Sarasota County Schools, 2002—03; Edge of Excellence, Safe and Orderly Schools grant, Sarasota County Schools/Edn. Found., 2001—02, 2002—03, 2003—04. Mem.: Sch. Based Administrators, Alpha Delta Pi (mem. edn. v.p., social chmn. 1995—97, Sister of the Yr. 1996). Avocations: exercise, travel. Office Phone: 941-426-9517.

BAKER, ANDREA J., sociologist, educator; d. James and Beatrice Plotkin. PhD, Case Western Res. U., Cleve., 1979. Assoc. prof. sociology Ohio U., Lancaster, 1979—; field rsch. assoc. URSA Inst., San Francisco. Author: Double Click: Romance and Commitment of Online Couples; co-editor: Online Matchmaking. Distance Edn. grantee, Ohio U., 2000.

BAKER, ANN LONG, language educator; b. Shelbyville, Ind., Sept. 2, 1954; d. Martin Meredith Cherry and Lois Jayne Slaton; m. Scott Elliott Baker, Aug. 23, 1975; children: Kyle Martin, Holly Alison. BA with distinction in Spanish Edn., Purdue U., 1976; MA Edn., U. Evansville, 1982. Lectr. in Spanish U. Evansville, Ind., 1984—2000, asst. prof. Spanish, 2000—, 2005—, chair dept. fgn. langs., 2003—05. Interpreter Pan Am. Games, Indpls., 1987. Active Castle H.S. PTO, Castle H.S. Band Boosters Orgn. Mem.: MLA, Ind. Fgn. Lang. Tchrs. Assn., Soc. Hispanic Am. (past pres., treas.), Am. Coun. Tchg. of Fgn. Langs., Am. Assn. Tchrs. of Spanish and Portuguese, Kappa Delta Pi, Alpha Lambda Delta, Phi Sigma Iota, Sigma Delta Pi, Phi Beta Kappa, Phi Kappa Phi. Home: 7277 Nottingham Dr Newburgh IN 47630 Office: U Evansville 1800 Lincoln Ave Evansville IN 47722 Office Phone: 812-488-2196. Business E-Mail: ab39@evansville.edu.

BAKER, BARBARA JEAN, pediatrician, psychiatrist; b. San Francisco, Oct. 13, 1944; d. Edgar Eugene Baker and Marian Reed Logan; children: Tamar Joanne Rose, Jaqueline Ruth Baum, Gabrielle Sharon Baum. BA, U. Calif., Berkeley, 1966; MD, Boston U., Boston, Mass., 1970. Cert. Bd. Cert. Peidat. 1978, Bd. Cert. Gen. Pyschiatry 1993, Bd. Cert. Child Psychiatry 1993. Pediat. residency U. Colo. Med. Ctr., Denver, 1971—73; child psychiatry fellowship Northwestern U. Med. Ctr., Chgo., 1987—91; pediat. staff physician William Beaumont Army Hosp., El Paso, Tex., 1973—74; med. dir. Infant Welfare Soc. Chgo., Chgo., 1974—87; attending physician Lutheran Gen. Hosp., Pk. Ridge, Ill., 1991—93; med. dir. Parry Resident Treatment Ctr., Portland, Oreg., 1993—2000, Waverly Children's Home, Portland, Oreg., 1993—2000; pyschiatric cons. Morrison Child and Family Ctr., Portland, Oreg., 1998—, Christie Sch., Maryhurt, Oreg., 2002—. Mem.: Am. Acad. Psychiatry, Am. Acad. Child and Adolescent Psychiatry. Protestant. Avocations: genealogy, travel. Home: 9023 NW Benson St Portland OR 97229 Office: Morrision Child and Family Svcs 3355 SE Powell Blvd Portland OR 97202

BAKER, BONNIE MARIE, real estate broker; b. Seattle, July 1, 1955; d. Richard Harold and Jeannette Dell Pingrey; m. Ryan H. Baker (div.); children: Misha L., Malia M., Monet A. Grad. in Liberal Studies, Edn., U. Calif., Sonoma, 1977; MA in Early Childhood Edn., U. Calif., San Jose, 1988. Tchr. Challenger Schs., Orem, Utah, 1979—81; tchr., dir., owner Leader Day Care and Sch., San Jose, Calif., 1982—93; owner, pub. Family Fanfare Mag., San Jose, Calif., 1981—83; tchr. state math., sci. Va. State Math./Sci. Ctr., Richmond, Va., 1994—95; dir. Day Schs., Tulsa, Okla., 1995—96; realtor assoc. John Hausam Realtors, Broken Arrow, Okla., 1996—98; broker assoc., tng. dir. Coldwell Banker Radergroup, Tulsa/Broken Arrow, Okla., 1998—. Personal performance coach Accelerated Performance Coaching, San Diego, 1999—2002; tng. dir. Coldwell Banker Radergroup, Tulsa, Okla., 2001—05. Pres., v.p. Broken Arrow Bus. Women's Assn., Okla., 1998—2005; grad. alumni Leadership Broken Arrow, Okla., 2003; bd. dirs. Margaret Hudson Program, Tulsa, Okla., 1999—2001. Recipient Vol. of Yr. award, State of Va. PTA, 1995. Mem.: Residential Sales Coun., Womens Coun. Realtors, Greater Tulsa Assn. Realtors (edn. com. 2005). Avocations: home decorating, gardening, antiques, public speaking. Office: 501 S Aspen Ave Broken Arrow OK 74012 Office Phone: 918-251-4142.

BAKER, BRINDA ELIZABETH GARRISON, community health nurse; b. Groveland, Ga., May 9, 1946; d. Archie and Nora Lee (Haynes) Garrison; m. Jerome Baker, Feb. 1970 (div. 1972); children: Katrina Lenyse Adams, Kelbert Lenard Adams. Student, Savannah (Ga.) State Coll., 1964-68; LPN, Savannah Tech. Sch., 1968; ADN, Armstrong State Coll., 1984, BSN, 1990; postgrad., Armstrong Atlantic State U. RN, Ga.; cert. provider BLS, Am. Heart Assn. LPN Candler Gen. Hosp., Savannah, 1968-72, staff nurse Cross Country Traveling Corps, 1990; LPN Ga. Regional Hosp., Savannah, 1972-74, sr. staff nurse, 1989-92; LPN St. Joseph Hosp., Savannah, 1974-84, staff nurse, 1984-90; sr. nurse, clinic supr. Chatham County Health Ctr., Savannah, 1992-95, clinic supr., 1995—. Part-time clin. instr. Armstrong State Coll., Savannah, 1991—. Mem. ANA, Ga. Nurses Assn., Assn. Nurses in AIDS Care. Democrat. Roman Catholic. Avocations: bowling, reading, gardening, music, sports. Home: 1307 E 71st St Savannah GA 31404-5735 Office: Chatham County Health Dept 2 Wheeler St Savannah GA 31405

BAKER, CARLENE POFF, real estate agent, reporter; b. Blytheville, Ark., Sept. 29, 1934; d. Carl Allen and Albie Elizabeth (Ryan) Poff; m. William T. Baker, July 7, 1956 (dec. Oct. 11, 1992); 1 child, Lisa Kay. Student, Miss. County C.C., 2003—. Legal sec. Reid & Roy, Attys., Blytheville, 1951—60; co-owner Baker Printing, Blytheville, 1961—82; real estate sales assoc. Logan Real Estate, Blytheville, 1982—; hearing reporter Social Security Adminstrn. Office Hearings and Appeals, Little Rock, 1982—. Author: Papa, 1979, The Quiet Man, 1991, Albie's Story, 2002; contbr. articles to mags., columns in newspapers. Mem.: Ark. Realtors Assn., Nat. Realtors Assn., Miss. County Writers Guild (pres. 1981—). Republican. Baptist. Avocations: writing, travel, music. Home: PO Box 945 Blytheville AR 72316 Office: 520 Chickasawba Blytheville AR 72315 Office Phone: 870-762-2033.

BAKER, CAROLYN SIMMONS, library director, consultant, researcher; AAS in Libr. Sci., LCC, Kinston, NC, 1979; MLS, NC Ctrl. U., 1998; BSBA, NC Wesleyan Coll., 1985. Instr. Wake Tech. CC, Raleigh, NC, 1988—98; libr. III NC A&T, Greensboro, 1997—98; Greensboro libr. dir., 1998—99; dir. archives Shaw U., Raleigh, 1999—. Mem.: Order Ea. Star.

BAKER, CONSTANCE H., lawyer; b. Washington, Sept. 2, 1948; AB summa cum laude, Vassar Coll., 1969; JD, Cath. U. Am., 1975. Bar: Md. 1975, DC 1998. Asst. atty gen., prosecutor Md. Physicians State Md., 1979-81; ptnr. Health Care Group Venable LLP, Balt. Guest lectr. managed care liability Johns Hopkins U. Sch. Medicine and Sch. Profl. Studies and Bus. Edn., 1997—. Editl. bd. mem. Physician Orgns. and Med. Staff, 1997; contbr. articles to profl. jours. Bd. dirs. HopeWell Cancer Support. Mem. ABA (sect. on healthcare law), AMA (mem. Doctors Adv. Svc. 1993-), Md. State Bar Assn. (sect. on health care law), Am. Health Lawyers Assn. (bd. dirs. 1977-88), Wranglers Law Club. Office: Venable LLP 1800 Mercantile Bank & Trust Bldg 2 Hopkins Plz Ste 1800 Baltimore MD 21201-2982 also: 575 7th St NW Washington DC 20004 Office Phone: 410-244-7535. Office Fax: 410-244-7742. Business E-Mail: chbaker@venable.com.

BAKER, CORNELIA DRAVES, artist; b. Woodbury, N.J., Mar. 2, 1929; d. Carl Zeno and Cornelia (Powell) Draves.; m. Philip Douglas Baker, July 16, 1955; children: Brinton, Todd, Claudia, Samuel. Student, Ohio Wesleyan U., 1947-50, Goethe U., Frankfurt, Germany, 1950-52. Travel dir. Am. Youth Hostels, Inc., N.Y.C., 1953-57. Artist Cornelia Gallery, Kumamoto, Japan, 1990—; gallery dir. Presbyn. Ch., Franklin Lakes, N.J., 1988-97, Marcella Geltman Gallery, New Milford, N.J., 1993-96; bd. dirs. Bergen Mus. Art and Sci., N.J., 1996-2000, corr. sec., mem. exec. com., 1999-2000. One-woman shows include Ramapo Coll., 1986, Shimada Mus., Kumamoto, 1990, Sekaikan Gallery, Tokyo, 1990, Am. Ctr., Fukuoka, 1990, Bergen Mus. Art and Sci., 1993, L'Atelier Inc. Gallery, 1994, N.Y. Theol. Sem., N.Y.C., 1996, The Gallery, Franklin Lakes, 1997, 2003, Office Congressman S.R. Rothman, Hackensack, N.J., 1997, Lee Hecht Harrison, Paramus, N.J., 1998, Willows Cafe, Ramsey, N.J., 2000, The Gallery, Franklin Lakes, 2003; represented in permanent collections Bergen Mus. Art and Sci., Paramus, Beekley Internat. Skiing Fine Art and Graphics. Chair social problems com. Borough of Franklin Lakes Coun., 1973-76. Recipient Best of Show award Ringwood Manor Assn. of the Arts, 1987, Bergen Mus. Art and Sci., 1989, Emeriti award for excellence N.J. Ctr. for Visual Arts, 1989, Excellence cert. Internat. Art Competition, 1988, Women Making History in Arts award Bergen County, N.J., 1993, Crabbie award Art Calendar, 1994, Gold prize RISO Edn. Found., Japan, 1997, Artist Showcase award Manhattan Art Internat., 2000, merit award Salute to Women in Arts. 2000. Mem. Nat. Assn. Women Artists (printmaking jury chmn. 1992-94), Salute to Women in the Arts (pres. 1988-90), Mastodon Artists Soc. (life), Altrusa Club of Bergen County, N.J. Republican. Presbyterian. Avocation: travel. Home: 293 Green Ridge Rd Franklin Lakes NJ 07417-2011 Personal E-mail: cdbaker@optonline.net.

BAKER, DEBORAH, editor, writer; b. Charlottesville, Va., Mar. 28, 1959; d. Jeffrey John Wheeler and Barbara Ann Baker; m. Amitav Ghosh, Feb. 15, 1990; children: Lila, Nayan. Affiliated degree, Cambridge (Eng.) U., 1980; BA, U. Va., 1981. Editl. dir. Overlook, N.Y.C., 1986-88; assoc. pub. Sheep Meadow, The Bronx, 1993-95; exec. editor Kodansha, N.Y.C., 1995-99; sr. editor Little Brown, N.Y.C., 2000—. Author: In Extremis: The Life of Laura Riding, 1993 (finalist for Pulitzer prize), Making a Farm: The Life of Robert Bly, 1982. Office: 40 McCormick Williams 6th Fl 27 W 20th St New York NY 10011

BAKER, DEBORAH, medical educator; BA in Spanish and Geology, U. Tex., Austin, 1982; postgrad. in Astronomy, Ocean Geology, Biology, U. Tex., San Antonio, 1989; postgrad. in Rocket Sci., U. Ala., Huntsville, 1991; postgrad. in Marine Biology, Tex. A&M U., Galveston, 1992; postgrad. in Neurology and Environ. Sci., MD Anderson Cancer Ctr., Austin, 2003—06. Tchr. health, anatomy and physiology SACS, San Antonio; tchr. biology, life sci., dept. head Cornerstone, San Antonio; tchr. pre-chemistry, life sci., computer St. Mary's Hall, San Antonio; tchr. ESL U. Novgorod, Russia; head dept. geology Anson Jones Mid. Sch., San Antonio; tchr. Spanish I and II, life sci., biology Castle Hills H.S., San Antonio. Docent Friedrich Wilderness Park, San Antonio; CPR instr. Am. Red Cross; leader and mentor Nat. Youth Leadership Conf., Washington. Author: (poetry collections) New Wings, YHWH, Thirsting, 1985—92; various media, 1999—. Sponsor knitting club Warm Up Am., Texas, Mont., 2005—06; team mem. Konnarock, UEW, Appalachian Tr., Va., Gospel of John, Chisinau, Moldova, 1995—98. Recipient Thanks to Tchrs. Excellence, KENS 5, 1992, Yuri Gagarin Cosmonaut award, Star City Cosmonaut Training, Russia, 1994, Outstanding Coll. Student of Am., OCSA, 1989. Mem.: Assn. Christian Schs. Internat., Assn. Pilots, Alpha Sigma Alpha. Avocations: hiking, swimming, crafts, music.

BAKER, DIANE R.H., dermatologist; b. Toledo, Nov. 17, 1945; BS, Ohio State U., 1967, MD cum laude, 1971. Diplomate Am. Bd. Dermatology. Intern U. Wis. Hosp., Madison, 1971-72, resident in dermatology, 1972-74, Oreg. Health Sci. Ctr., Portland, 1974-76; pvt. practce, Portland, 1976—. Clin. prof. dermatology Oreg. Health Sci. U., 1986—; mem. med. staff Meridian Park Hosp., Tualatin, Oreg., 1981—; dir. Am. Bd. Dermatology, 1995—, v.p., 2001. Mem.: AMA (del. 1995—), Oreg. Dermatol. Soc., Am. Dermatol. Assn. (v.p. 2001), Am. Acad. Dermatology (v.p. 1990), Alpha Omega Alpha. Office: 1706 NW Glisan St Ste 2 Portland OR 97209-2225

BAKER, DINA GUSTIN, artist; b. Phila., Nov. 07; d. Albert Isadore Kevles and Rose Schwartz; m. John Calvin Gustin (dec. July 4, 1964); m. William Baker, Jan. 5, 1968. Student, Phila. Coll. Fine Arts, 1940, Barnes Found, 1942—46, Templer Tyler Sch. Fine Arts, 1943, Art Students League, 1945, Hayter Atelier 17, N.Y.C., 1945. One-woman shows include Roko Gallery, NYC, 1963, Angeleski Gallery, 1965, Regensburg (Germany) Mus., 1974, Amerika House, Munich, 1974, Hamburg, Germany, 1974, Ingber Gallery, NYC, 1976, 1978, 1980, 1982, Brigham Young U., Provo, Utah, 1983, Utah State U., Logan, 1983, Gracie Lawrence Gallery, Delray Beach, Fla., 1999, 2000, Ora Sorensen Gallery, Delray Beach, 2000—02, Represented in permanent collections Bergen Mus. Arts and Scis., Paramus, NJ, Rutgers U., Nelson Hall, Piscataway, NJ, NYU, Gannet Found., Columbia U., NYC, Boca Raton Mus., Fla., exhibited in group shows at Guild Hall, East Hampton, NY, 1954, Art USA, NYC, 1955, Acad Fine Arts, Phila., 1963, Nat. Acad. Design, NYC, 1968, Lehigh U., Bethlehem, Pa., 1977, Montclair Art Mus., NJ, 1978, Parrish Mus., Southampton, NY, 1981, Ingber Gallery, NYC, 1984, Bergen Mus. Arts and Scis., Paramus, NJ, 1984, Adlena Adlung Gallery, NYC, 1991, Rutgers U., 1996, Gracie Lawrence Gallery, 1996, 1999, 2000, Ora Sorensen Gallery, 2000, 2002, 2003, 2005, Ezair Gallery, NYC, 2006. Scholar, Phila. Coll. Fine Arts, 1940, Art Students League, 1945, Barnes Found., 1942—45. Mem.: Women in the Arts. Home: Bay Hill estates 11820 Blackwoods Ln West Palm Beach FL 33412 Office Phone: 15612140305.

BAKER, DONNA DOUGAN, elementary school educator; m. Thomas E. Baker, Dec. 31, 1983; m. Thomas Greene Dougan (div.); children: Thomas Arthur Dougan, Christina Louise Dougan. Student, Iowa State U., Ames, 1961—63, Ohio State U., Columbus, 1965—66; BS, Castleton State Coll., Vt., 1969, MA with great distinction, 1975. Cert. continuing profl. Vt., tchr. permanent N.Y. Vol. Peace Corps, Colombia, 1963—65; tchr. pre-1st and 1st grade Argyle Ctrl. Sch., Argyle, NY, 1967—70; tchr. 6th grade Rutland Southwest Supervisory Dist., Poultney, Vt., 1976—95, tchr. 5th grade, 1995—. Student tchr. supr. Green Mountain Coll., Poultney, Vt., 1985—, Castleton State Coll., Castleton, 1985—. Named Outstanding Vt. Tchr., RSWSU, 1994. Mem.: NEA, Vt. Edn. Assn. Avocations: reading, writing, skiing, gardening, quilting. Home: 10 Woodell Rd Granville NY 12832

BAKER, ELLEN SHULMAN, astronaut, physician; b. Fayetteville, N.C., Apr. 27, 1953; d. Melvin Shulman; m. Kenneth J. Baker; 2 daughters. BA in Geology, SUNY, Buffalo, 1974; MD, Cornell U., 1978; grad. Air Force Aerospace Medicine Course, Brooks AFB, San Antonio, Tex., 1981; MS in Public Health, U. Tex., 1994. Diplomate Am. Bd. Internal Medicine. Resident U. Tex. Health Sci. Ctr., San Antonio; med. officer NASA Lyndon B. Johnson Space Ctr., Houston, 1981-84, astronaut candidate, 1984-85, astronaut, 1985—, mission specialist Shuttle Orbiter Atlantis flight STS-34, 1989, mission specialist Shuttle Columbia flight STS-50, 1992, mission specialist Shuttle Atlantis flight STS-71, 1995, lead astronaut for med. issues; astronaut rep. Edn. Working Group at Johnson Space Ctr. Achievements include having logged more than 686 hours in space. Avocations: skiing, swimming, running, movies, music, reading. Address: NASA Johnson Space Ctr Astronaut Ofc 2101 NASA Parkway Houston TX 77058

BAKER, FAITH MERO, retired elementary education educator; b. Pitts., May 9, 1941; d. Vincent G. and Georgetta (Rothwell) Mero; m. Gerald A. Baker, Dec. 22, 1968; children: Jeremy D., Kara L. BA, Carlow Coll., 1963; MEd, U. Pitts., 1965, postgrad., 1966—68. Cert. elem. and spl. edn. tchr. Tchr. sci. Pitts. Pub. Schs., 1963—64, tchr. spl. edn., 1968—87, tchr., primary sci. specialist, 1987—98; ret., 1998. Leader instrnl. team Fulton Acad., Pitts., 1988—; facilitator, tchr. Project Wild and project Aquatic Wild, Project Learning Tree, Pitts., 1988—; mem. leadership team Fulton Acad. for New Am. Schs.-area Sch. to Career. Leader Girl Scouts U.S.A., Monroeville, Pa., 1979-86; mem. Supts. Roundtable Gateway Schs., Monroeville, Pa., 1987-89. Mem.: AAUW (chair scholarship com Monroeville br. 1996—), Pa. Bus. and Profl. Women's Assn. (polit. action com., pres. Monroeville 1987—88, 1992—93, bd. dirs. dist.3), Pitts. Fedn. Tchrs. (bldg. steward 1968—98), U. Pitts. Alumni Assn. (asst. v.p. 1987—88, sec. 1989—91, alumnae coun. recording sec. 1998—2000), Delta Kappa Gamma, Alpha Delta Kappa (treas. 1992—99), Phi Delta Gamma (pres. 1982—84, regional coord. 1984—86, sec. Kappa chpt. 1986—90, nat. v.p. 1992—94, nat. pres. 1994—96, nat. treas. 1998—2000, chpt. 2d v.p. 1999—2000, 1st v.p. 2000—02, pres. 2003—, class rep. Carlow U. alumnae bd.). Democrat. Roman Catholic. Avocations: sewing, gourmet cooking, writing, short stories and poetry. Home: 102 Penn Lear Dr Monroeville PA 15146-4734 E-mail: fayze@adelphia.net.

BAKER, GLORIA MARIE, artist; b. Petersburg, Ind. m. James Daniel Baker; children: David, Christopher. Pvt. practice, Evansville, Ind., 1976—. Painting tchr. Ivy Tech. C.C., Evansville, Ind. One-woman shows include Mus. Arts and Sci., Evansville, 2003, Aztec Village, 1994 (Grumbacher Gold Medallion and The Excellence Gold award, 1994), The Dedicated, 1991 (Brown and Williamson Tobacco Corp. award, 1991, Dr. Martin Hydrus award Ga. Watercolor Soc., 03), The Domes, 1997 (2d pl.), Ascent to the Cathedral, 1998 (St. Cuthbert's Mill award, 1998, Grumbacner Bronze award), Double Ascent, 1999 (Winsor & Newton award, Document Framing Svc. award, 1999, 1st pl. Evansville Art Guild, Peabody Coal Co. award), Past, Present & Future, 1997, The Ascent (Houston B. Adams award, Evansville Mus. Arts & Sci.), Cathedral of Light, 2000 (2d pl., Dir.'s Choice award, 2000), The Dedicated, 1993, Best of Watercolor, Best of Watercolor 2, Landscape Inspirations, The Complete Best of Watercolor, Vol.s 1 & 2, Chgo. Art Rev., 4th edit., Evansville Mus. of Arts and Sci. GiftShop, 2003. Chmn. Celia Sprue Assn., Evansville, 1995—. Nominee Internat. Visual Artist of the Yr., Internat. Biog. Ctr./Cambridge, England, 2004. Mem.: Niagara Frontier Watercolor Soc., Watercolor Soc. Ala. (signature mem.), Ga. Watercolor Soc. (winner Nat. Exhibit 2003, Dr. Martin Hydrus award 2003), Pa. Watercolor Soc., Ky. Watercolor Soc., Petroleum Wives Club (v.p. 2003). Avocations: golf, gardening, reading, ballroom dancing. Home: 2711 Knob Hill Dr Evansville IN 47711 Personal E-mail: james_18510@msn.com.

BAKER, HARRIET KUGLEY, elementary school educator; b. Charleston, SC, June 10, 1943; d. Henry Asbury and Helen Halsall Kugley; m. Douglas Neil Baker, Mar. 30, 1968 (dec.); 1 child, David Nelson. BA, Furman U., 1965. 3d grade tchr. Aragona Elem. Sch., Virginia Beach, Va., 1965—67, Monaview Elem. Sch., Greenville, SC, 1967—70; 4th grade tchr. Armstrong Elem. Sch., Greenville, 1989—94, 5th grade tchr., 1994—. Mem. supt.'s cabinet, mem. dist. steering com. Greenville County Schs., 1991—93. Numerous leadership roles Berea First Bapt. Ch., Greenville, 1968—2006. Named Tchr. of Yr., Alliance for Quality Edn., 1992—93, Educator of Yr., Berea Lions Club, 2006; recipient Bus. Edn. Partnership Pro award, 1991, Exemplary Sci. Tchr. award, Alliance for Quality Edn., 1992; grantee, 1991—95, 2004, 2006. Avocations: travel, piano, writing poetry. Home: 320 Westcliffe Way Greenville SC 29611 Office: Armstrong Elem Sch 8601 White Horse Rd Greenville SC 29611

BAKER, HELEN DOYLE PEIL, realtor, contractor; b. LA, June 26, 1943; d. James Cyril and Jacqueline (White) Doyle; m. Gary Edward Peil, Aug. 5, 1967 (dec. May 6, 1969); children: Andrea Christine Peil, Kevin Doyle Peil; m. Nathaniel W. Baker, Jr., Jan. 1, 1971 (div. July 23, 1983). AA, Santa Monica Coll., 1963; postgrad., U. Wash., 1963-64. Lic. real estate agt., cert. domestic violence counselor. Sales, mgmt. trainee Saks Fifth Ave., Beverly Hills, Calif., 1958-63; flight attendant Am. Airlines, Los Angeles, 1964-67; realtor, assoc. Stapleton Assocs., Honolulu, 1978-80; realtor Dolman Assocs. Inc., Kailua, Hawaii, 1980-87; loan rep. Honolulu Mortgage Co., Kailua, 1986-87; pres., owner, realtor Helen Baker Properties, Inc., Honolulu, 1987-93; v.p. Internat. Property Investment, Inc., Honolulu, 1993-94; owner Property Investment Internat., Honolulu, 1994—; loan officer Western Pacific Mortgage, Inc., 1999—2003; sr. mortgage cons., sales mgr. The Lender, LLC, 2003. Pres. Global Listing Svc. Hawaii Inc., 1990—96. Dir. Kailua Cmty. Coun., 1987—91; pres., v.p., sec. Aikahi Cmty. Assn., Kailua, 1980—85; vol. Am. Cancer Soc., Heart Assn. Schs., Kailua, 1971—86; adv. spouse abuse shelter, 1995—98; mem. Windward Spouse Abuse Coalition. Mem.: Mil. Officers Assn. Am. (sec. Hawaii chpt. 2005—), C. of C., Rotary. Avocations: tennis, exercise, reading, travel, music. Office: Property Investment Internat PO Box 37066 Honolulu HI 96837-0066 Office Phone: 808-753-7793. Personal E-mail: propinvst@hawaii.rr.com.

BAKER, HOLLIE L., lawyer; b. 1953; BA, Baylor Univ., 1975; JD, Univ. Denver, 1982. Bar: Colo. 1982, DC 1987, Mass. 1997, US Ct. Appeals (Fed cir.), US Patent & Trademark Office. Ptnr., vice chmn. Intellectual Property dept. Wilmer Cutler Pickering Hale & Dorr, Boston. Contbr. articles to profl. jours. Mem.: ABA (council mem., Intellectual Property Law sect.), Am. Intellectual Property Law Assn., Boston Patent Law Assoc., Licensing Exec. Soc., Patent & Trademark Office Soc. Office: Wilmer Cutler Pickering Hale & Dorr 60 State St Boston MA 02109 Office Phone: 617-526-6110. Office Fax: 617-526-5000. Business E-Mail: hollie.baker@wilmerhale.com.

BAKER, JACQUELINE MADDEN, special education educator; b. Ft. Hood, Tex., Oct. 3, 1949; d. Jack Jr. and Darseyphene (Moak) Madden; m. Vaughn Willard Baker, June 29, 1985; 1 child, Amanda Courtney. BS in Elem. Edn., U. Tex., 1974, MEd in Curriculum and Instrn., 1981. Cert. elem. and spl. edn. tchr., Tex. Tchr. spl. edn. Austin (Tex.) Ind. Sch. Dist., 1974-87, Arlington (Tex.) Ind. Sch. Dist., 1987-90, Eastland (Tex.) Ind. Sch. Dist., 1990-94; tchr. Weatherford (Tex.) Ind. Sch. Dist., 1994—. Staff devel. presenter, Austin, 1977-87; staff devel. presenter on Stevenson Lang. Skills Program, Arlington, 1987-90. Treas. Harris Elem. Sch. PTA, Austin, 1984-85. Mem. Phi Kappa Phi. Methodist. Home: 158 Canyon Creek Ct Weatherford TX 76087-4035

BAKER, JAN E., music educator; d. Roy and Ruth Baker. BS in Elem. Edn., East Tex. State U., Commerce, 1983, MEd, 1987. Cert. Orff Schulwerk Memphis State U. Music tchr. Univ. Pk. Elem., Dallas, 2019—. Dir.: (musical) Snow Day, 2006. Pres. Tree Top III HOA, Irving, 1997—2001. Named Tchr. of Yr., Univ. Pk. Elem. Sch., 2005. Mem.: Am. Orff-Schulwerk Assoc. (v.p. Tex. chpt. 2006—), Tex. Music Educator's Assoc. Avocations: camping, cycling, Jazzercise. Office: Univ Park Elem 3505 Amherst Dallas TX 75225

BAKER, JANE E., secondary school educator; b. Birmingham, Ala., Sept. 13, 1956; d. John R. and Betty (Cockrell) B. BS, Auburn U., 1978; MA, U. Montevello, 1991. Tchr. Minor Jr. High Sch., Edgewater Jr. High Sch., Birmingham; instr. spl. studies U. Ala., Birmingham; tchr. Warrior (Ala.) Middle Sch.; second mile tchr. Jefco Bd. Edn., Birmingham, 1990; tchr. Bottenfield Jr. High Sch.; asst. prin. Shades Valley high Sch./Jefferson County Internat. Baccalaureate Sch.; prin. Minor Jr. High Sch., Gresham Mid. Sch., Shades Valley High Sch. Mem. Am. Heart Assn., Middle Sch. Study, Am. Cancer Soc., Nat. Mid. Sch. Assn., Nat. Assn. Secondary Sch. Prins., Ala. Assn. Secondary Sch. Prins.

BAKER, JANEL FAITH, music educator; b. Greenville, Ohio, Mar. 6, 1971; d. Eugene Merle and Dorothy Mae Cloyd; m. Mark Allen Baker; 1 child, Seth Nathaniel. BA in Music Edn., Taylor U., Upland, Ind., 1989—93; MA in Music Edn., Ball State U., Muncie, Ind., 1995—2000. Music tchr. Rossville Consolidated Schs., Ind., 1993—. Mem. Morning Star Ch., 1995—. Mem.: Ind. Choral Dirs. Assn., Music Educators Nat. Conf., Ind. Music Educators Assn. (Ind. Music Educator of Yr. 2003). Avocations: music, piano. Home: 4216 Coventry Dr Kokomo IN 46902 Business E-Mail: jbaker@rossville.k12.in.us.

BAKER, JEAN HARVEY, history professor; b. Balt., Feb. 9, 1933; d. F. Barton and Rose (Lindsay) Hopkins Harvey; m. R. Robinson Baker, Sept. 12, 1953; children— Susan Dixon, Robinson Scott, Robert W., Jean Harvey. AB, Goucher Coll., Towson, Md., 1961; MA, Johns Hopkins U., Balt., 1965, PhD, 1971. Lectr., instr. history Notre Dame Coll., Balt., 1967-69; instr. history Goucher Coll., Balt., 1969, asst. prof. history, 1969-75, assoc. prof. history, 1975-78, prof. history, 1979-82, Elizabeth Todd prof. history, 1981—. Author: The Politics of Continuity, 1973, Ambivalent Americans, 1976, Affairs of Party, 1983, Maryland: A History, Mary Todd Lincoln: A Biography, 1986, The Stevensons: A Family Biography, 1995, Sisters: The Lives of American Suffragists, 2005; co-author: Civil War and Reconstruction, 2002; editor: Md. Hist. Mag., 1979, Votes for Women: The Suffrage Battle Revisited, 2001, James Buchanan, 2004, Sisters: The Lives of the Suffragists, 2005. Am. Coun. Learned Socs. fellow, 1976, NEH fellow, 1982, Newberry Libr. fellow, 1991, Rockefeller Found. fellow, 1998; recipient Faculty Teaching prize Goucher Coll., 1979, Willie Lee Rose prize in Southern history, 1989. Mem.: Am. Hist. Assn., Orgn. Am. Historians, Berkshire Conf. Women Historians, Phi Beta Kappa. Democrat. Office: Goucher Coll History Dept 1021 Dulaney Valley Towson MD 21204 Office Phone: 410-337-6267. Business E-Mail: jbaker@goucher.edu.

BAKER, JOY DOREEN, art educator, artist; d. Herman D. and Sylvia Newfield Bragin; children: Amy Beth Baker-Bridge, Lawrence Adam. Assoc., Fashion Inst. Tech., 1957; Cert. in Graphic Design and Textile Design, Sch. Visual Arts, NYC, 1980; student, Trotta Sch. Fine Arts, Queens. Asst. buyer active sportswear Lord & Taylor, NYC, 1956; showroom sales rep. Brooks &

Co., 1956—57; owner, designer, ptnr. Studio J, Inc., Washington, 1968—78; pub. rels., direct mail campaign Abbeville Press, Inc., NYC, 1978—85; mktg. rschr. EJ Rhodes Assocs., NYC, 1985—90; owner, designer, adminstr. Joy Designs, Inc.; mem. faculty Fine Arts Sch., Ednl. Alliance, NYC, 1992—96; instr. dept. fashion Acad. Art Univ., San Francisco, 2002—. Mem. exec. com. Washington Fashion Group. Exhibitions include Fla., Washington, N.Y.C., San Francisco. Mem. Internat. Women's Mus., San Francisco, Nat. Mus. Women in Arts, Washington; active Sunday youth and family program Congregation Emanu-El. Avocations: museums, theater, travel, reading, learning Italian. Office: Acad Art Univ Fashion Dept Fl 7 180 New Montgomery St San Francisco CA 94105 Office Phone: 415-752-7596.

BAKER, JOYCE MILDRED, medical/surgical nurse, volunteer; b. Racine, Wis., Oct. 19, 1927; d. Roy Ross Kelly and Ruth Alice Guy Kelly; children: James, Thomas, William, Donald, Frank(dec.). RN, Mt. Sinai Hosp., Chgo., 1948. RN Wis., cert. CPR, recovery rm. specialist, pediat., geriatrics, Wis. Pediat. RN St. Luke's Hosp., Racine, 1948—54; recovery rm. RN St. Mary's Hosp., Racine, 1955—62; supr. RN Lincoln Luth., Racine, 1962—73; charge RN Ridgewood Healthcare, Racine, 1973—94; acute care nurse So. Wis. Ctr., Racine, 1973—94. Vol. ARC Nat. Disaster Team, 1994—2000, Luth. Thrift Shop, Racine, 1998—, Baby Books for New Mothers, St. Luke's Hosp., Racine, 2000—03, Our Saviour Food Pantry, Racine, 2002—, Racine Emergency Shelter Task Force, 1995—, Christmas Lights at the Zoo, 2000—, United Way, 2004—; vol. tutor San Juan Diego Sch., 2004—; vol. Homeless Assistance Leadership Orgn., 2005—; mem. Racine Downtown Parish Assn., 2000—, Downtown Parish Com., 2001—; vol. Homeless Assistance Leadership Orgn., 2005—; vol. and mem. Olympia Brown Unitarian Ch., Racine, 1995—2003; bd. mem. Cerebral Palsy, 2002—03; adv. bd. task force Racine Emergency Shelter, 2004—. Mem.: Kiwanis (pres. 2001—05). Avocations: writing, cooking, baking. Home: Apt 406 3608 Douglas Ave Racine WI 53402

BAKER, JUDITH ANN, retired computer technician; b. Junction City, Kans., Mar. 2, 1947; d. David Daniel and Mildred Elaine Bates; m. Jimmy Ray Baker, Oct. 8, 1972; 1 child, Jimmy Ray Jr. Student, East Ctrl. U., 1993—98. Cert. travel and tourism Draughon Coll., 1988. ADA support group leader, newsletter editor Multiple Sclerosis Assn. Am., Okla., 1995—. Leader support group Multiple Sclerosis Soc. Am., Ada, Okla., 2003—. Recipient Best Support Group Leader award S.E. region and 10 state area, Multiple Sclerosis Soc. Am., 2005. Mem.: Ada Writing Club. Avocations: writing, painting, crafts, decorating. Home: 3816 US Hwy 377 Ada OK 74820 Office Phone: 580-310-0181. E-mail: paradise@adacomp.net.

BAKER, KATHERINE JUNE, elementary school educator, minister, artist; b. Dallas, Feb. 3, 1932; d. Kirk Moses and Katherine Faye (Turner) Sherrill; m. George William Baker, Jan. 30, 1955; children: Kirk Garner, Kathleen Kay. BS, BA, Tex. Women's U., 1953, MEd, 1979; cert. in religious edn., Meadville Theol. U., 1970; postgrad., North Tex. State U., 1987—; DD (hon.), Am. Fellowship Ch., 1981. Cert. elem. and secondary tchr., adminstr., Tex.; lic. and ordained min. Kingsway Internat. Ministries, 1991. Mgr. prodn. Woolf Bros., Dallas, 1953-55; display mgr. J.M. Dyer and Co., Corsicana, Tex., 1954; advt. artist Fair Dept. Store, Ft. Worth, 1954-56; artist, instr. Dutch Art Gallery, Dallas, 1960-65; dir. religious edn. 1st Unitarian Ch., Dallas, 1967-69; edn. dir. day care, tchr. Richardson (Tex.) Unitarian Ch., 1971-73; dir. camp Tres Rios YWCA, Glen Rose, Tex., 1975-76; dir. program of extended sch. instrn. Hamilton Park Elem. Sch. Richardson Ind. Sch. Dist., 1975-78, tchr. Dover Elem. Sch., 1979—80, tchr. Jess Harben Elem. Sch., 1980—92; founder ednl., editorial and arts/evang. assn. Submitted Ministries, Richardson, 1992—. Dir. Flame Fellowship Internat., 1987—94, state rep., 1994—99, asst. state overseer (Tex.), 1999—2001, chaplain, 2002—; mem. Extended Sch. Day Program Employee Manual, Extended Sch. Day Courses, Day+ Extended Day Newsletter, RISD Magnet Sch., 1975—79. Contbr. articles to ch. newspaper, 1967-69, newsletters; editor Metro Dallas Chpt. Newsletter, 1992—; exhibited in group show at Tex. Art Assn., 1966; one-woman show Dutch Art Gallery - Northlake Ctr., Dallas, 1965. Advocate day care Unitarian Universalist Women's Fedn., Boston, 1975—76, mem. nominating com., 1976—77; cert. instr. aquatics program Arthritis Found. YMCA AFYAP, Plano Rehab. Hosp., 1997—99, Aquatics Inst. Oak Point Ctr., Plano, 1999—, Aquatics Inst. Fun Fit Crew, 2001—04; overseer Mosries singles group First Family Ch., 2004—. Mem. NEA, ASCD, Nat. Coun. Social Studies, Tex. State Tchrs. Assn. (treas. Richardson chpt. 1984-85), Tex. Ret. Tchrs. Assn., Richardson Ret. Tchrs. Assn., Women's Ctr. Dallas, Sokol Athletic Ctr., Smithsonian Assn., Dallas Mus. Assn., Alpha Chi, Delta Phi Delta (pres. 1952-53), Phi Delta Kappa. Avocations: gospel and folk singing, guitar, volleyball, camping. Office Phone: 972-235-1178. Personal E-mail: baker3963@sbcglobal.net.

BAKER, KATHY WHITTON, actress; b. Midland, Tex., June 8, 1950; m. Donald Camillieri, 1985 (div. 1999); 2 children; m. Steven Robman, June 2003. Appearances include (theatre) Fool for Love, 1983 (Obie award 1983, Theatre World award 1984), Desire Under the Elms, 1984, Aunt Dan and Lemon, 1986, (films) The Right Stuff, 1983, Street Smart, 1987 (Nat. Soc. Film Critics Best Supporting Actress award 1987), Permanent Record, 1988, A Killing Affair, 1988, Clean and Sober, 1988, Jacknife, 1989, Dad, 1989, Mr. Frost, 1989, Edward Scissorhands, 1990, Article 99, 1992, Jennifer 8, 1992, Mad Dog and Glory, 1993, To Gillian on Her 37th Birthday, 1996, Inventing the Abbotts, 1997, The Cider House Rules, 1999, Things You Can Tell Just By Looking at Her, 2000, The Glass House, 2001, Ten Tiny Love Stories, 2001, Assassination Tango, 2002, Cold Mountain, 2003, 13 Going on 30, 2004, Nine Lives, 2005, All the Kings Men, 2006, (TV films) Nobody's Child, 1986, The Image, 1990, One Special Victory, 1991, Weapons of Mass Distraction, 1997, Oklahoma City: A Survivor's Story, 1998, Lush Life, 1993, Not in This Town, 1997, ATF, 1998, A Season of Miracles, 1999, Sanctuary, 2001, Door to Door, 2002, Too Young to Be a Dad, 2002, Picking Up and Dropping Off, 2003, Sucker Free City, 2004, Spring Break Shark Attack, 2005, Father and Sons, 2005, (TV series) Picket Fences, 1992-1996 (Emmy award Outstanding Lead Actress in a Drama Series, 1993, 1995, Golden Globe award, Best Actress in a TV Drama Series, 1994), Boston Public, 2001-2002, Murphy's Dozen, 2003.*

BAKER, KRISTI ANN, music educator, composer; b. Topeka, Dec. 10, 1957; d. J. Roland and Lila Ann (Kern) Williams; m. Charles Burton Baker; children: Barbara Lynn, Elizabeth Catherine. BS, Kans. State U., 1979, MusM, 1984. Cert. k-12 music tchr. Kans., 1979. Pvt. piano instr., Topeka, 1972—75; grad. tchg. asst. Kans. State U. Dept. Music, Manhattan, 1979—81; band, choral dir. Wakefield (Kans.) Pub. Schs., 1981—84; elem. music tchr. Ware Elem. Sch., Ft. Riley, Kans., 1984—88; choral dir. Junction City Mid. Sch., Junction City, Kans., 1988—2003, Abilene H.S., 2003—05, Osawatomie HS and Mid. Sch., Osawatomie, 2005—. Private piano, voice instr., Junction City, Abilene and Osawatomie, Kans., 1981—; ch. organist, choir master various chs., Manhattan, Junction City, Abilene, Kans., 1988—; mem. commn. on music, liturgy Episc. Diocese of Kans., 2001—; adj. instr. applied piano Ottawa U., Kans., 2006—. Composer: (sacred choral work) A Song for Advent, 1988, The Magic of Your Dreams, 2000, St. John's Mass, 2006, performer 6 European tours. Named Winner youth talent auditions, Topeka Symphony Orch., 1974; recipient Superior Plus ratings, Nat. Piano Tchrs. Guild, 1968—75. Mem.: Music Educators' Nat. Conf., Kans. Music Educators Assn. (chair north ctrl. dist. middle level honor choir program 1995—96, 2002—03, chair Kans. state middle level honor choir program 2004—05), Music Tchrs. Nat. Assn., Music Tchrs. Nat. Assn., Am. Choral Dirs. Assn., Order of the Eastern Star (Worthy Matron Melita chpt. no. 116 2005—06), Job's Daughters of Kans. (grand dir. music 2000—01, guardian sec. Bethel #7 2000—01, dir. music Bethel #1 2003—05, Bethel guardian Bethel 2005—, grand dir. music 2006, 2006—). Republican. Episcopalian. Avocations: needlepoint, sewing, water sports. Home: 1211 Parker Ave Osawatomie KS 66064-1601 Office: Osawatomie HS 1200 Trojan Dr Osawatomie KS 66064-1696 Office Phone: 785-263-1260 119, 913-755-2191 233. E-mail: kabaker@cebrridge.net.

BAKER, LAURA KAY, art gallery owner, writer; b. Urbana, Ill., July 25, 1951; d. Warren Henry and Christie Ann Schuetz; m. Thomas Hall Baker, Mar. 19, 1972; children: Nicholas Warren, Allison Whitney. Student, St. Andrews U., Scotland, 1969, Ill. State U., Normal, 1969—71, Ga. State U., 1980—82; Assoc., Parkland Coll., Champaign, Ill., 1972. Owner Silver Shaman, Albuquerque, 1974—80, Tanner Chaney Gallery, Albuquerque, 1987—; novelist Albuquerque, 1993—. Nat. workshop coord. Romance Writers Am., Dallas, 1996—96; sec., treas. Land of Enchantment Romance Authors, Albuquerque, 1993—96. Author: (novels) Stargazer, 1998 (Daphne du Maurier, 1999, Nat. Readers Choice Nominee, 1998, Golden Quill nominee, 1999, Aspen Gold best single title, 1998), Legend, 1998 (Daphne du Maurier, 1999, RITA nominee, 1999), Broken In Two, 1999 (Daphne du Maurier, 2000), Raven, 2001 (Daphne du Maurier, 2002); contbr. articles to profl. jours. Seminar tchr. numerous orgns.; writing judge numerous writers orgns.; pres. PTA Manzano H.S., Albuquerque, 2001—04. Recipient Svc. award, YMCA, 1996, Romance Writers Am., 1998. Mem.: Novelists, Inc. (conf. coord. 2002, 2004). Independent. Avocations: embroidery, piano. Office: Tanner Chaney Gallery 323 Romero NW #4 Albuquerque NM 87104 Office Phone: 505-247-2242. Personal E-mail: lbaker10@aol.com.

BAKER, LESLIEGH, bank executive, lawyer; b. El Paso, Tex., June 10, 1960; d. Gilbert and Ferne Schrier. BA, U. Calif., Irvine, 1983; JD, Western State U., 1990. Bar: Calif. 1990. Intern, law clk. Legal Aid Soc. Orange County, Santa Ana, Calif., 1989-90; assoc. Konapalsky & Baker, Newport Beach, Calif., 1990-92, Law Offices of Richard L. Grant, Tustin, Calif., 1992-94; pvt. practice Costa Mesa, Calif., 1994-97; v.p. Bank of Yorba Linda, a divsn. of BYL Bank Group, Mission Viejo, Calif., 1997—. Mem. Dedicated Animal Welfare Group, Mission Viejo, 1999; vol. Pediat. Cancer Rsch. Found., Orange, 1995, 96. Mem. State Bar Calif., Fin. Women Internat. Avocations: boating, fishing, camping, crafts.

BAKER, LORI LEE, medical/surgical nurse; b. Manitowoc, Wis., Nov. 9, 1964; d. Clarence Zeman and Virginia Clara (Gollata) Kelmm; m. Kenneth G. Baker, Oct. 19, 1985; children: Danielle Michelle, Adrienne Lee. AA, Nat. U., San Diego, 1987; ADN magna cum laude, Forest Park Community Coll., St. Louis, 1990; BSN, U. Mo., St. Louis, 1991; postgrad., U. Wis., Oshkosh, 1993-95. RN, Mo., Wis. Staff nurse Deaconess Hosp., St. Louis, Holy Family Meml. Hosp., Manitowoc, Wis.; mem. nursing faculty Lincoln Meml. U., 1996-99. Family nurse practitioner Team Health; with Profession Edn. Sys., 1998—. With USMC, 1983-90. Home: 180 Laura Ln London KY 40744-7863

BAKER, LUCINDA, writer; b. Atlanta, Ill., July 10, 1916; d. Hazle Howard and Adah Rebecca (Mason) B.; m. Willard Alan Greiner, June 27, 1946. Student, Ariz. State Coll., 1934-38. Author: Place of Devils, 1976, Walk the Night Unseen, 1977, Memoirs of First Baroness, 1978, The Painted Lady, 1998; contbr. short stories to mags. Mem. Author's Guild, Mystery Writers Am., Romance Writers Am.

BAKER, LYNNE RUDDER, philosophy educator; b. Atlanta, Feb. 14, 1944; d. James Maclin and Virginia (Bennett) Rudder; m. Thomas B. Baker III, Feb. 1, 1969. BA, Vanderbilt U., 1966, MA, 1971, PhD, 1972; student, Johns Hopkins U., 1967-68. Asst. prof. philosophy Mary Baldwin Coll., Staunton, Va., 1972-76, Middlebury (Vt.) Coll., 1976-79, assoc. prof., 1979-84, prof., 1984-94, acting dean arts and humanities, 1982, chairperson humanities divsn., 1982-85, acting chairperson philosophy, 1986-87; prof. U. Mass., Amherst, 1989—, dir. philosophy grad. program, 1994—. Mem. panel to select summer seminars NEH, Washington, 1982, mem. panel to select fellows, 1989—90; Gifford lectr. U. Glasgow, Scotland, 2001. Author: Saving Belief: A Critique of Physicalism, 1988, Explaining Attitudes: A Practical Approach to the Mind, 1995, Persons and Bodies: A Constitution View, 2000; contbr. scholarly articles to profl. jours. Trustee Vanderbilt U., Nashville, 1969-70, mem. alumni bd. dirs., 1985-89. Mellon fellow, 1974, NEH fellow, 1983-84, Nat. Humanities Ctr. fellow, 1982-83, Woodrow Wilson Internat. Ctr. for Scholars fellow, 1988-89. Mem. Am. Philos. Assn. (program com. 1983, exec. com. 1992-95), Soc. for Philosophy and Psychology, Soc. Christian Philosophers (exec. com. 1992-95), Soc. Women in Philosophy, Phi Beta Kappa. Democrat. Episcopalian. Office: U Mass Dept Philosophy Amherst MA 01003

BAKER, MARSHALYN ELAINE, elementary school educator; b. Lewiston, Maine, Dec. 13, 1951; d. Marshall Everett and Florence Maybelle (Billings) Wing; m. Richard Paul Baker, Aug. 24, 1974; children: Ryan Paul, Randen Paul. BEd, U. Maine, 1973, MEd, 1977. Cert. K-8 gen. elem. edn., K-12 literary specialist, K-8 exceptional edn., 7-12 exceptional edn. Tchr. SAD #47, Belgrade, Maine, 1973-74, 75-93, Oakland, Maine, 1993—, Old Town (Maine) Sch. Dept., 1974-75. Author: Math Textbook, 1994. Chairperson Don C. Stevens Trust Fund, Belgrade, 1983-91, 94—. Recipient Presdl. Award for Excellence in Sci. and Math. Teaching, NSF, State of Maine, 1994, New Mast appointee NASA, 1995. Mem. Nat. Coun. Tchrs. Math., Assn. Tchrs. of Math. in Maine (exec. bd. 1995—). Republican. Methodist. Avocation: reading. Home: RR 1 Box 392 Belgrade ME 04917-9760 Office: Williams Jr High Sch 19 Pleasant St Oakland ME 04963-5034

BAKER, MARSHINA, physical education educator; b. Shelby, N.C., May 6, 1957; d. James Winifred and Selma Patricia Baker; 1 child, Antwon Mendes. BS, St. Augustine's Coll., Raleigh, N.C., 1980; MS, N.C. Ctrl. U., Durham, 1984. Phys. fitness specialist Washington Srs. Wellness Ctr., 1985—90; program assoc. Am. Heart Assn., Washington, 1990—91; tchr. D.C. Pub. Sch., Washington, 1994—97; lectr. Bowie State U., Md., 1994—; tchr. Prince George's Pub. Sch., Upper Marlboro, Md., 1997—2000; lectr. No. Va. C.C., Alexandria, 1999—, Prince George's C.C., Largo, Md., 1999—. Author: Foundations of a Health Lifestyle, 2003. Mem.: ASCD, AAHPERD, Nat. Assn. for Sport and Phys. Edn., Am. Assn. for Health Edn. Democrat. Baptist. Avocations: travel, reading, exercise, gardening, music. Office: Bowie State Univ 14000 Jericho Park Rd Bowie MD 20715 Office Phone: 301-860-3780. Office Fax: 301-736-1236. Personal E-mail: marshina5503@aol.com.

BAKER, MARY ALICE, communications educator, consultant; b. Stuart, Okla., Sept. 9, 1937; d. James Roy and Emma M. (Bird) B. BS, U. Okla., 1959, MA in Speech, 1966; PhD in Comm., Purdue U., 1983. Speech and debate tchr. SE High Sch., Oklahoma City, 1959-65; instr. Ea. Ill. U., Charleston, 1966-69; prof. Lamar U., Beaumont, Tex., 1966-75, 78—, 1978—2005, apptd. univ. prof., 2005—, dir. forensics, 1969-75, Regents' Merit prof., 1984, pres. faculty senate, 1986-88, prof., 2005—. Contbr. articles to profl. jours. Trustee Edn. Com. for Nat. Coun. for Tchr. Retirement Sys., 2003—05; mem. R & D com. Nat. Coun. Tchr. Retirement Sys., 2003; trustee Tchrs. Retirement Sys. Tex., 1999—2006, chair ethcis com., vice chmn. bd., 2003—05. David Ross fellow, 1977; named Univ. Prof. of Yr. Lamar U., 2005 Mem. Tex. Speech Comm. Assn. (regional rep. 1978-88), Nat. Comm. Assn. Am., Tex. Assn. Coll. Tchrs. (regional v.p. 1985-88, pres.-elect 1988-89, state pres. 1989-90, state bd. legis. liason 1997-99), Tex. Forensics Assn. (pres. 1974), Internat. Comm. Assn., Zeta Phi Eta, Alpha Delta Pi. Democrat. Episcopalian. Avocations: reading, politics, travel. Office: Lamar U Dept Communication Beaumont TX 77710

BAKER, MARY ELIZABETH, elementary school educator; M Edn., U. Mo., Columbia, 1982. Cert. Tchr. Nat. Bd., 2004. Tchr. Fairview, Sydney, NSW, Australia, 1974—77, Francis Howell Sch. Dist., St. Charles, Mo., 1982—. Office: Francis Howell Sch Dist 2445 Hackmann Saint Charles MO 63302

BAKER, MARY JANE, social worker; b. Watertown, Mass., Oct. 21, 1917; d. Lenox Stanley and Mary Angela (Rue) Karner; m. David Curtis Baker, Aug. 28, 1942; children: Peter Rue, Nancy Jewell Baker Aucella. AB, Tufts U., 1939; MSS, Simmons Coll., Boston, 1944. Cert. Acad. Cert. Social Workers. Caseworker Family Welfare, Fairfield, Conn., 1940-42; social worker ARC Army Hosp., 1943-44; psychiat. social worker N.H. Program Alcohol and Drug Abuse, Berlin, North Conway, 1966-76; pvt. practice North Conway, 1976—. Avocations: gardening, piano. Mailing: Rt 16 Box 15 Jackson NH 03846

BAKER, MITCHELL, computer software development foundation administrator; AB in Asian Studies, U. Calif., Berkeley, JD. Former assoc. gen. counsel Netscape Comm. Corp.; joined mozilla.org, 1998, gen. mgr., 1999—; pres. Mozilla Found., 2003—. Bd. dirs. Open Source Applications Found.; adv. bd. SpikeSource. Named one of 100 Most Influential People of 2005, Time mag. Office: Mozilla Corp 1981K Landings Dr Mountain View CA 94043-0801

BAKER, NANCY L., university librarian, educator; BA with honors, U. Conn., Storrs, 1972; MLS, U. Mich., Ann Arbor, 1973; MA in English Lit., SUNY, Binghamton, 1978. Asst. reference libr. SUNY, Binghamton, 1973—76; sr. reference libr. Middlebury Coll., Vt., 1976—78; head reference dept. U. Ky., Lexington, 1978—81; head gen. reference dept. U. Utah, Salt Lake City, 1981—84; asst. dir. librs. for undergrad. svcs. U. Wash., Seattle, 1984, assoc. dir. librs. pub. svcs., 1984—91; dir. librs. Wash. State U., Pullman, 1991—2000; univ. libr. U. Iowa, Iowa City, 2000—. Instr. libr. sci. Coll. Libr. Sci., U. Ky., 1978—81, Grad. Sch. Libr. and Info. Sci., U. Wash., 1990, Sch. Libr. and Info. Sci., U. Iowa, 2002—04, adv. com., 2000—. Contbr. articles to profl. jours. Recipient Scholarship Award, Conn. Libr. Assn., 1972. Mem.: ALA, Iowa Libr. Assn., Assn. Rsch. Librs. (bd. dirs. 2000—03). Office: U Iowa Librs 100 Main Library Iowa City IA 52242-1420 Home: 30 Alder Court Iowa City IA 52246 Office Phone: 319-335-5897. Office Fax: 319-335-5900. E-mail: nancy-l-baker@uiowa.edu.*

BAKER, P. JEAN, lawyer, mediator; b. June 28, 1948; BS summa cum laude, Wright State U., Dayton, Ohio, 1973; MBA, Northeastern U., Boston, 1989; JD, Calif. Western U., San Diego, 1993. Bar: Calif. 1993; cert. mediator. With GenRad Inc., Boston, 1974-82; mktg./sales staff GE Co., Boston, 1982-84; major accounts mgr. Fluke Mfg. Co., Boston, 1984-89; pub. rels. mgr. Racal Dana, Irvine, Calif., 1989-90; legal intern Pub. Defenders Dependancy, San Diego, 1992; law clk. Civil divsn. U.S. Atty., San Diego, 1992; personal injury atty. L.H. Parker, Long Beach, Calif., 1993; mediator/atty. Baker & Assocs., San Diego, 1993-94; dir. Orange County region Am. Arbitration Assn., Irvine, 1994-97, v.p. Washington, 1997—. Mediator San Diego Mediation Ctr., 1993-97; trainer mediation skills Am. Arbitration Assn., 1994-97; adj. prof. Western State U., Irvine, 1995-96; MCLE presenter San Diego County Bar, 1994, State Bar of Calif., 1996, ABA, 1997-2003; mediator Superior Ct., San Diego, 1994-97, U.S. Bankruptcy Ct. (cen. dist.) Calif., 1995-97; adj. prof. Columbus Sch. of Law, Washington, 1997-2001, Georgetown Law Sch., 2005-; coach Georgetown Law Sch. Mediation Advocacy Team, 2003 Bd. dirs. Legal Aid Soc., San Diego, 1994, T. Homann Law Assn., San Diego, 1994, Counsel for Ct. Excellence, 2003-04. Recipient Am. Jurisprudence awards, 1992. Mem. ABA, D.C. Bar Assn., State Bar of Calif., Energy Bar Assn., Va. Bar Assn., Md. Bar Assn., Women's Bar Assn. Avocations: tennis, golf. Office: American Arbitration Assn 1776 Eye St NW Ste 850 Washington DC 20006 Office Phone: 202-223-7093. E-mail: BakerJ@adr.org.

BAKER, PAMELA, lawyer; b. Detroit, Apr. 6, 1951; d. William D. and Lois (Tukey) Baker; m. Jay R. Franke, June 10, 1972; children: Baker Eugene, Alexandra Britell. AB, Smith Coll., 1972; JD, U. Wis. Madison, 1976. Bar: Ill. 1976, Wis. 1976. Ptnr. Sonnenschein, Nath & Rosenthal, Chgo., also co-mng. ptnr. Chgo. office, chair nat. employee benefits and exec. compensation practice group. Contbr. articles to profl. jour. Fellow Am. Coll. Employee Benefits Counsel (charter), Am. Bar Found.; mem. ABA (mem. employee benefits com. 1984—, chair-elect 1998-99, chair 1999-2000, mem. plan mergers and acquisitions com. 1985— mem. fed. regulation of securities com. 1989—, chair 1989-95), Ill. State Bar Assn. (sec. employee benefits sect. coun. 1989-90, vice chair 1990-91, chair 1991-92), Chgo. Bar Assn. (employee benefits com. 1978—, sec. 1984-85, vice chair 1985-86, chair 1986-87, fed. taxation com. 1980—, exec. coun. 1982-85). Office: Sonnenschein Nath & Rosenthal Sears Tower 233 S Wacker Dr Ste 8000 Chicago IL 60606-6491

BAKER, PAMELA HUDSON, special education educator; b. Fredericksburg, Va., Dec. 27, 1961; d. Spencer Hampton and Jeanette Tolson Hudson; m. Robert Eugene Baker, May 16, 1987. BS, Coll. William and Mary, Williamsburg, Va., 1984; MEd, Coll. William and Mary, 1987; EdD, Bowling Green State U., Ohio, 2002. Cert. tchr. spl. edn. and math. Va., 1987. Program coord. Newport Acad., Newport News, Va., 1995—97; instr. Ashland U., Ohio, 1997—2002, asst. prof., 2002—03, 2004—05, U. N.C., Greensboro, 2003—04, George Mason U., 2005—. Contbr. articles to profl. jours. Mem.: Coun. for Children with Behavior Disorders, Coun. for Exceptional Children, Kappa Delta Pi, Phi Kappa Phi. Office Phone: 703-993-1787. Business E-Mail: pbaker5@gmu.edu.

BAKER, PATRICIA, health foundation administrator; BS, Wayne State U.; MS, U. Wis. Dir. Conn. govt. program Oxford Health Plans; exec. dir. The Women's Ctr., Waukesha, Wis., 1978-85; assoc. editor, dir. Planned Parenthood, Wis., 1985—87; exec. dir. Planned Parenthood Conn.; nat. program dir. March of Dimes Birth Defects Found., until 1999; exec. dir. Conn. Health Found., Farmington, 1999—.

BAKER, PAULA BOOKER, secondary school educator; d. Paulette Love; m. Ronald Baker, II; 1 child, Ronald III. Bachelor's degree, Tuskegee U.; Master's degree, Troy State U., Dothan, Ala.; Doctorate, Ga. So. U., Statesboro. Cert. tchr. Ga., Ala., P-12 ednl. leadership Ga. Title I coord.; tchr. Ednl. rschr., 2002—; presenter Ga. Edn. Rsch. Assn. Contbr. articles to profl. jours. Named Tchr. of the Yr., 2001; recipient, 2005. Mem.: Am. Edn. Rsch. Assn. (presenter), Alpha Kappa Alpha. Office Phone: 770-254-2840. Personal E-mail: pmbb27aka@hotmail.com. Business E-Mail: paula.baker@cowetaschoos.net.

BAKER, PEGGY NELL, retired secondary school educator; b. Hackleburg, Ala., Jan. 8, 1940; d. Bill Baker and Stella Pearl Williams; m. Norman Howard Fennell, Jan. 23, 1988; children from previous marriage: Roger Arley Davis, Byron Roger Davis. BS, U. North Ala., Florence, Ala., 1962; MEd in Math., U. Ga., Athens, 1970, ednl. specialist degree, 1971. Cert. tchr. Ga., Ala. Tchr. Phil Campbell HS, 1931—63, 1964—65, 1984—86, Tarrant HS, Tarrant, 1965—67, Kennedy HS, 1967—69, Burney Harris HS, Athens, Ga., 1971—72, Haleyville HS, Ala., 1972—84, Lurlene Wallace Jr. Coll., 1986—93, Thompson HS, Alabaster, Ala., 1993—2000, Jefferson State Coll., 2000—05, Bessemer State Coll., 2000—05. Part-time tchr. Bevil CC, NW CC. Fellow, U. Ga., 1970—71; grantee, NSF, 1969—70. Mem.: Franklin County Tschrs. Assn. (pres. 2006—), Nat. Edn. Assn. Democrat. Bapt.

BAKER, PROVIDENCE, judge; d. Procopio and Olivia Impastato; m. Gary McLouth, June 25, 1988; children: Deborah McKain, Jacqueline Pierce, Jeffrey Stefanko. BA cum laude, Russell Sage Coll., Troy, NY, 1979; JD, Western New Eng. Sch. Law, Springfield, Mass., 1982. Bar: NY 1983, U.S. Dist. Ct. (no dist.) NY 1983, U.S. Supreme Ct. 1996. Asst. atty. gen. NY State Office Atty. Gen., Dept. Law, Albany, 1983—99; asst. commr. dep. counsel NY State Divsn. Housing, 1999—2005; adminstrv. law judge NY State Liquor Authority, 2006—. Trainer Nat. Inst. Trial Advocacy; negotiator Rensellaer County Settlement Week; arbitrator 3rd Judicial Dist., 2006, atty./client fee dispute resolution program character and fitness com., 1998—. V.p. Hist. Pastures Homeowners Assn., bd. dirs., Homeless and Travelers Aid Soc. Capital Dist., pres. bd. dirs. Recipient Pro Bono award, NY State Women's Bar Assn., Albany chpt. Mem.: Italian Am. Bar Assn., Albany County Bar Assn., Rensselaer County Bar Assn., Capital Dist. Trial Lawyers Assn., NY State Bar Assn. (govt. atty. com. 2006), Phi Kappa Phi. Republican. Roman Catholic. Avocations: gardening, golf, travel, reading. Home: 11 Empire Cir Slingerlands NY 12159

BAKER, REBECCA LOUISE, musician, music educator, consultant; b. Covina, Calif., Apr. 12, 1951; d. Allan Herman and Hazel Margaret (Maki) Flaten; m. Jerry Wayne Baker, Dec. 22, 1972; children: Jared Wesley, Rachelle LaDawn, Shannon Faith. Grad. high sch., Park River, N.D.; student, Trinity Bible Inst., 1968-69. Sec. Agrl. Stblzn. & Conservation Svc. Office, Park River, ND, 1969; pianist, singer Paul Clark Singers & Vic Coburn Evangelistic Assn., Portland, Oreg., 1969-72; musician, singer Restoration Ministries Evangelistic Assn., Richland, Wash., 1972-80; musician, pvt. instr. Calvary Temple Ch., Shawnee, Okla., 1980-81; organist, choirmaster St. Francis Episcopal Ch., Tyler, 1984-87; co-founder, owner Psalmist Sch. of Music & Recording Studio, Whitehouse, 1983—; pianist/entertainer Willowbrook Country Club, Tyler, Tex., 1991—; pianist, vocalist Mario's Italian Restaurant, Tyler, 1994—. Pianist Garner Ted Armstrong, Tyler, 1986—; pianist, dir. Children's Choir, Calvary Bapt. Ch., Tyler, 1987—; pianist, entertainer Ramada Hotel, Tyler, 1988-90; pianist Whitehouse (Tex.) Sch. Dist. choirs, 1988—; accompanist Tyler Area Children's Chorale, 1988-90, Univ. Interscholastic League; pvt. instr. keyboard and vocal. Composer: Religious Songs (12 on albums), 1979; pianist, arranger, prodr., rec. artist 6 albums; editor, arranger: Texas Women's Aglow Songbook, 1987; editor Shekinah Glory mag., 1989—; developer improvisational piano course; star, prodr. weekly, nationally syndicated mus. religious programs for TV, 1995, 96, Proclaim His Glory, 1997—; played for receptions honoring Gov. George Bush, Tex. Senator Phil Gramm and Congressman John Bryant. Performer, spkr. many charitable, civic and religious orgns., Tex. and U.S. including AAUW, Kiwanis Clubs; co-founder Psalmist Mins. Internat., 1988—; founder, pres. Christian Music Tchr.'s Assn., 1991; worship leader Mayor's Prayer Breakfast, Tyler, 1994. Mem. Women's Aglow Fellowship (music dir., spkr., performer at retreats and tng. seminars). Republican. Full Gospel. Avocations: travel, reading, interior decorating, collecting. Home and Office: Psalmist Music & Recording PO Box 4126 Tyler TX 75712 Office Phone: 903-581-5461. E-mail: sweetpsalmisi@netzero.com.

BAKER, ROSALYN HESTER, state senator; b. El Campo, Tex., Sept. 20, 1946; BA, Southwest Tex. State U., 1968; grad., U. Southwestern La., 1969. Lobbyist, asst. dir. Govt. Rels. Nat. Edn. Assn., Washington, 1969-80; owner, retail sporting goods store Maui, Hawaii, 1980-87; legis. aide to Hon. Karen Horita Hawaii Ho. of Reps., Honolulu, 1987, mem., 1989-93, house majority leader, 1993, state senator Hawaii, 1993-98, majority leader, 1995-96; dir. office econ. devel. County of Maui, Hawaii, 1999—2002, chair senate health com. Hawaii, 2003—, asst. majority floor leader. Co-chair ways and means com., 1998, rules com. Hawaii State Dem. Conv., 1990, resolutions com. 1994; mem. energy environ. com., trans., mil. affairs, govt. ops. com.; vice chmn. consumer protection and housing com; former unit pres. Am. Cancer Soc. Del.-at-large Dem. Nat. Conv., 1984, 92, 96; mem. exec. com. Maui County Dem. Com., 1986-88; mem. Maui Workforce Investment Bd., Lahaina Town Action Com.; former vice chmn. Maui Svc. Area Bd. om Mental Health and Substance Abuse; former unit pres. Am. Cancer Soc., bd. dir., Hawaii-Pacific, Inc., Maui Econ. Devel. Bd.; mem. sub-com. pediat. emergency svcs. Inst. Medicine, 2004-06. Mem.: Maalaea Cmty. Assn., Kihei Cmty. Assn., West Maui Taxpayers Assn., Rotary Club Lahaina Sunrise. Democrat. Home: PO Box 10394 Lahaina HI 96761-0394 Office: State Capitol Rm 220 Honolulu HI 96813 Office Phone: 808-586-6070. Business E-Mail: senbaker@capitol.hawaii.gov.

BAKER, RUTH MARY, psychotherapist; b. Providence, R.I., Sept. 16, 1946; d. James Joseph Hogan and Rose Marie (Murray) Bancroft; m. Ronald Raymond Baker, Dec. 12, 1965; children: Bonnie Jean O'Donnell, Sara Jane, Jessica Marie Fleetner, Vanessa Jo. AS in Drug and Alcohol Counseling, Norwalk (Conn.) C.C., 1990; BS in Human Resources, Charter Oak Coll., Farmington, Conn., 1993; M in Psychotherapy and Counselling, City U., London, 1995. Asst. dir. religious edn. St. Mary's Ch., Ridgefield, Conn., 1986-87; drug and alcohol counselor intern Arms Acres Hosp., Carmel, N.Y., 1988, Norwalk Hosp., 1989; vol. counselor Family Recovery Ctr., Wilton, Conn., 1989, New Canaan (Conn.) Cares, 1990-92; gen. counselor for various doctors Orpington, Eng., 1996-97; pvt. practice psychotherapist Oxted, Eng., 1994-97; grief min. Holy Family Parish, Pasadena, Calif., 1999—. Spritual dir. Francisican Renewal Ctr., Scottsdale, Ariz. Vol. St. Joseph's Christian Life Ctr., Cleve., 1977-85; active vol. Holy Family, South Pasadena, Calif.; women's program dir. Kenosha (Wis.) Youth Found., 1974-75, YMCA, Wausau, Wis., 1972-74; jr. varsity tennis coach Mayfield Sr. H.S. Mem.: AAUW, British Assn. Counseling, Soc. Existential Analysis, Spiritual Dirs. Internat. Roman Catholic. Avocations: tennis, golf, skiing, hiking, needle-crafts. Home: PO Box 333 Crested Butte CO 81224-0333 Home (Winter): 7448 E Thorntree Dr Scottsdale AZ 85262

BAKER, SHARLYNN RUTH, livery and limousine service owner; b. York, Nebr., May 9, 1969; d. Curtis Dail and Carolyn Jean (Klinsky) Baker. BA with emphasis on edn., Park Coll., Parkville, Mo., 1996; attended, Chgo. State Univ., 1992—93, Kans. City Art Inst., 1997; AA, Kans. City Kans. Cmty. Coll. Pres. Five Star Livery Svc., Inc., Kans. City, Mo., 1993—. Mem. Greater Kans. City C. of C., Mo., 2002—. Author: numerous poems; one-woman shows include Nine Ten Penn Penthouse, 1996, Park Coll. Acad. Support Ctr., 1996, Pi Kappa Cino Coffee House, 1997, Kans. City Clay Guild, 1999. Active Mo. Dem. Party, Kans. City, 2001—; jr. mem. Nelson Atkins Mus. Art: Young Friends Art, Kans. City, 1997—. Mem.: Am. Bus. Women's Assn. Democrat. Avocations: drawing, music, movies. Office: Five Star Livery Svc Inc PO Box 411042 Kansas City MO 64141 Office Phone: 816-531-2700. Business E-Mail: fivstarliv@aol.com.

BAKER, SHIRLEY KISTLER, academic administrator; b. Lehighton, Pa., Mar. 16, 1943; d. Harvey Daniel and Miriam Grace (Osenbach) Kistler; m. Richard Christopher Baker, Oct. 22, 1966; children: Nicholas Christopher, India Jane. BA, Muhlenberg Coll., 1965; MA, MALS, U. Chgo., 1974. Undergrad. libr. Northwestern U., Evanston, Ill., 1974-76; access libr. Johns Hopkins U., Balt., 1976-82; assoc. dir. librs. MIT, Cambridge, 1982-89; dean univ. librs. Washington U., St. Louis, 1989-95, vice chancellor for info. tech., dean univ. librs., 1995—. Contbr. articles to profl. jours. Mem. ALA, Nat. Info. Standards Orgn. (bd. dirs. 1990-94), Assn. Rsch. Librs. (bd. dirs. 1996-2002, pres. 2000-01), Coalition for Networked Info. (steering com. 1999—), Mo. Libr. Network Corp. (bd. dirs. 1990-00). Democrat. Avocations: reading, travel. Home: 6310 Alexander Dr Saint Louis MO 63105-2223 Office: Washington U Campus Box 1061 1 Brookings Dr Saint Louis MO 63130-4899 E-mail: baker@wustl.edu.*

BAKER, SUSAN CHILTON, health facility administrator, consultant; b. Englewood, N.J., Mar. 11, 1956; d. Robert Carter and Elizabeth Dean Chilton; children: Abigail Grace, Robert Austin. BA, Colby Coll., 1978; MBA, U. N.H., 1993. Cust. support/product mgr. IDX Corp., Boston, 1981—87; med. bus. cons., 1987-93; v.p. profl. affairs Porter Med. Ctr., Middlebury, Vt., 1993-94; dir. ops., cmty. practices Dartmouth-Hitchcock Clinic, Dartmouth-Hitchcock Alliance, Lebanon, NH, 1994—; ed. bus. cons., 987-93. Cubmaster Boy Scouts Am., Grantham, N.H., 1996-99. Mem. Med. Group Mgmt. Assn., Healthcare Fin. Mgmt. Assn. Democrat. Presbyterian. Office: Dartmouth-Hitchcock 1 Medical Center Dr Lebanon NH 03756-0002 Home: 34 Lakeview Ter Ashland MA 01721-2218

BAKER, SUSAN HIMBER, school psychologist; b. N.Y.C., Dec. 28, 1943; d. Louis L. and Charlotte T. (Brenner) Himber; m. William M. Baker, June 8, 1963 (div. 1981); children: Laura Baker Pinkley, Robin Baker Howse. BA, Oberlin Coll., 1964; MAT, Duke U., 1965; MEd, Converse Coll., 1982; EdS, U. S.C., 1990. Nationally cert. sch. psychologist and counselor. Tchr. Orange County Jr. High Sch., Hillsboro, N.C., 1964-65; ednl. evaluator Behavior Evaluation Ctrs., Spartanburg, S.C., 1977-79; sch. psychologist Spartanburg Sch. Dist. 3, 1979—2004. Co-chmn. Youth Suicide Task Force, 1990. Player Spartanburg Philharm. Orch., 1974—, pres. 1989-91; mem. Spartanburg Symphony Guild, 1989—; dir. contemporary choir St. Paul the Apostle Cath. Ch., Spartanburg, 1974-90, mem., 1990—. Mem. Nat. Assn. Sch. Psychologists, S.C. Assn. Sch. Psychologists, Piedmont Assn. Sch. Psychologists (treas. 1989-90, sec. 1990-), Spartanburg Philharm. Music Club (treas.). Democrat. Avocations: reading, music, flute. Home: 148 Henson St Spartanburg SC 29307-3047

BAKER, SUSAN MARIE VICTORIA, writer, artist, musician; b. Phila., Pa., Aug. 30, 1961; d. John Joseph and Dorothy Phyllis Erdlen. BA in Liberal Arts/Comm., Rowan U., 1983; postgrad., U. of Arts, Phila. Ordained priestess. Prin., owner Star Limo Trans. and Tourism Co., Sedona, Ariz. Art critic and healing artist. Author 3 books; songwriter (performed and published under name Chelsea Mann); art editor Avant mag., 1981; contbr. poetry to various publs.; composer numerous songs. Active animal rights and environ. activities; mem. Newport Cultural Arts Alliance, Sedona Arts Ctr. and Ascension Group. Recipient awards for poetry, creative writing.

BAKER, SUSAN P., public health educator; b. Atlanta, May 31, 1930; d. Charles Laban and Susan (Lowell) Pardee; m. Timothy Danforth Baker, June 23, 1951; children— Timothy D., David C., Susan L. AB, Cornell U., 1951; MPH, Johns Hopkins U., 1968; ScD (hon.), U. N.C., 1998. Rsch. assoc. Office of Chief Med. Examiner, Balt., 1968-81; rsch. assoc. Sch. Hygiene and Pub. Health, Johns Hopkins U., Balt., 1968-71, asst. prof., 1971-74, assoc. prof., 1974-83, prof. health policy and mgmt., 1983—, assoc. chmn. dept. health policy and mgmt., 1997-99, joint appointment in environ. health scis., 1975—, joint appointment in pediatrics, 1983—, dir. Injury Prevention Ctr., 1987-88, co-dir., 1988—94, acting head div. pub. health, 1988-90, joint appointment emergency medicine Sch. Medicine, 1991—. Vis. prof. U. Minn. Sch. Pub. Health, 1975-87; chmn. nat. rev. panel for nat. accident sampling sys. Dept. Transp., Washington, 1976-81; vice chmn. com. on trauma rsch. Nat. Rsch. Coun., Washington, 1984-85; mem. adv. com. on injury control CDC, 1989-95; mem. Armed Forces Epidemiol. Bd., 1996-2000, 04—; commr. West Latir Ditch Assn., N.Mex., 1990—; vis. lectr. in injury prevention Harvard Sch. Pub. Health, 1984-87; John T. Law meml. lectr. U. Calgary, Alta., 1984; expert panel Age 60 rule FAA, 1991-93; cons. and lectr. in field. Author: (monograph) Fatally Injured Drivers, 1970 (Prince Bernhard medal 1974), The Injury Fact Book, 1984, 2d edit., 1992, Saving Children: A Guide to Injury Prevention, 1991, Injury Prevention: An International Perspective, 1998; contbr. articles to books and articles to profl. jours. Recipient Charles A. Dana award for pioneering achievements in health, 1989, Johns Hopkins U. Disting. Alumnus award, 1996, APHA Excellence award, 1999, Stebbins award Johns Hopkins Bloomberg Sch. Pub. Health, 2006; named to Md. Women Hall of Fame, 2006. Fellow Am. Assn. Automotive Medicine (bd. dirs. 1971-76, pres. 1974-75, award of merit 1985, Abe Mirkin Svc. award 2002), Aerospace Med. Assn. (editl. bd. 1994—, John Stapp award 2005); mem. APHA (governing coun. 1975-77, jour. bd. 1983-87, award for excellence 1999), Am. Trauma Soc. (bd. dirs., Disting. Achievement award 1981, Stone lectr. 1985), Am. Assn. for Surgery of Trauma (hon., Fitts oration award 1996), Phi Beta Kappa, Delta Omega. Office: Johns Hopkins U Bloomberg Sch Pub Health 624 N Broadway Baltimore MD 21205-1900 E-mail: sbaker@jhsph.edu.

BAKER, TANIA ANN, biology professor, researcher; BS in Biochemistry (with distinction), U. Wisconsin, 1983; PhD, Stanford U. Med. Sch., 1988. Postdoctoral fellow, dept. biochemistry Stanford U. Med. Sch., 1988—89; postdoctoral fellow, Nat. Inst. Diabetes and Digestive and Kidney Disease NIH, 1989—92; asst. prof. biology MIT, 1992—97; asst. investigator Howard Hughes Medical Inst., 1994—97, assoc. investigator, 1997—2002, investigator, 2002—; assoc. prof. biology MIT, 1997—2002, prof. biology, 1999—2002, E.C. Whitehead prof. biology, 2002—. Asst. molecular biologist Mass. Gen. Hospital, Boston. Contbr. articles to profl. jours. Recipient Sundra Found. Rsch. award for support of rsch. of jr. faculty in life sciences, 1992—93, Robert A. Swanson Career Develop. Professorship in the Life Sciences, 1992—94, Young Investigator award, NSF, 1993, Harold E. Edgerton award, Eli Lilly award, Am. Soc. of Microbiology; Undergraduate Rsch. Fellowship to Cold Springs Harbor Lab., 1982, Mary Shine Peterson Fellowship for Undergraduate Rsch., 1982—83, Helen Hay Whitney Found. Fellowship for Postdoctoral Rsch., 1989—92. Fellow: Am. Soc. for Microbiology (Eli Lilly and Co. Rsch award 2001), Am. Acad. Arts & Sciences; mem.: Am. Soc. for Biochemistry & Molecular Biology (Schering-Plough Scientific Achievement award 1998). Office: MIT Biology Dept 77 Massachusetts Ave Room 68-523 Cambridge MA 02139 also: Howard Hughes Medical Inst 400 Jones Bridge Rd Chevy Chase MD 20815-6789 Office Phone: 617-253-3594. Office Fax: 617-252-1852, 617-253-8267 (lab). Business E-Mail: tabaker@mit.edu.*

BAKER, VERONICA ANN, secondary school educator, writer; arrived in US, 1949; d. Ray Warren and Geraldine Mary (Delany) Amos; m. Charles William Baker, Sept. 4, 1960 (dec.); 1 child, Stephen William. AS in Engring., Pa. State U., State College, 1958; BA in Secondary Edn., We. Mich. U., Kalamazoo, 1977; MA, Mich. State U., Lansing, 1982. Tchr. St. Joseph Pub. Schs., Mich., 1979—83, 1990—96; tech. writer Cook Nuc. Power Plant, Bridgman, Mich., 1985—89. Mem. sch. bd. Lakeshore Pub. Schs., Stevensville, Mich., 1976—80, 1982—86, pres. sch. bd.; pres., mem. Lakeshore Jr. Women's Club, Stevensville, 1973—78; pres., founder Centennial Com., Stevensville, 1976; vol. Casa dela Luz Hospice, Tucson, 2005—; sec. Oro Valley Friends of Libr., 2003. With U.S. Army, 1958—60. Recipient Disting. Tchg. Achievement, Nat. Coun. Geographic Edn., 1995. Mem.: Sassy Single Club Newcomers (pres. 2004), Newcomers Club Tucson (various positions 1999—). Republican. Roman Cath. Avocations: photography, reading, hiking, travel. Home: 10456 N Buck Ridge Dr Oro Valley AZ 85737

BAKER, VICKI L., science educator; children: Marin Beth, Cameron. BA, U. Calif., Berkeley, 1980. Tchr. mid. sch. sci. Alvarado Mid. Sch., Union City, Calif., 1992—; nat. bd. support provider Stanford U., Palo Alto, 2002—. Case writer WestEd, San Francisco, 2004—06. Scholar, Carnegie Found., 2003—04. Mem.: Calif. Sci. Tchrs. Assn. Home: 326 W Broadmoor Blvd San Leandro CA 94577 Office: Alvarado Middle School 36104 Alvarado Blvd Union City CA 94577 Office Phone: 510-489-0700. Personal E-mail: vicki_baker@nhusd.k12.ca.us.

BAKER, YVONNE BELL, elementary school educator; d. Sylvia Collins and Victor Bell; 1 child, Otis McDowell Baker, Jr. BS, So. U., Baton Rouge, La., 1970, MEd, 1977. Reading Specialist La. Dept. of Edn., 1981, Supr. Student Tchg. La. Dept. of Edn., 1981, Elem. Grades La. Dept. of Edn., 1977, Art La. Dept. of Edn., 1970, English La. Dept. of Edn., 1970. Tchr. Assumption Parish Sch. Bd., Napoleonville, La., 1970—72, St. Francis Xavier Cath. Sch., Baton Rouge, 1973—74, Ascension Parish Sch. Bd., Donaldsonville, 1974—. Mem.: NEA (assoc.). Home: 13313 ALBA Dr Baker LA 70714 Office Phone: 225-621-2470. Business E-Mail: bakerbrown@apsb.org.

BAKER-BOWENS, HELEN L., administrative assistant, genealogy researcher; b. Bronx, N.Y., Mar. 7, 1948; d. Kenneth L. and Ruth Jane (Watson) Baker; children: Clinton, George, Alphonso, Belynda, Marc. BA, St. Peter's Coll., Jersey City, 1984. Adie to city councilman Cit of Jersey City, 1982-84, exec. asst. to coun. pres., 1984-87; shelter mgr. Spouse Abuse Shelter, Clearwater, Fla., 1987-89; ch. sec. Lighthouse Bapt. Ch., Jersey City, 1979—85, Mt. Olive AME Ch., Clearwater, Fla., 1996—. Vice chair bd. Corp. of Employment and Tng., Jersey City, 1983-87. Author: (genealogy) Mt. Olive AME State Historical Designation, 1999, Nat. Designation, 2000. Mem. N.J. State Dem. Com., 1984. Recipient Mary McLeod Bethune award Women's Coalition, Jersey City, 1985. Mem. African Meth. Episcopal Ch. Avocations: genealogy, reading, fishing. Office: Mt Olive AME Ch 600 Jones St Clearwater FL 33755-4136

BAKER-GARDNER, JEWELLE, interior designer, business consultant; b. Ayden, NC, May 23, 1925; d. Roland Ray and Helen Wingate (Jackson) Cannon; m. Paul Thomas Baker, July 25, 1956 (dec. 1963); children: Paula Jewelle Baker Bryan, Paul Thomas Jr.; 1 stepchild, Blanche Baker Miller; m. Fred Calvin Gardner, Apr. 19, 1969 (dec. May 1983); 1 stepchild, Angela Gardner Jones Hollowell. Student, Woods Bus. Sch., New Bern, N.C., 1942-45; BA, Am. Sch. Design, N.Y.C., 1948; BFA, U. N.C., Greensboro, 1950. Dept. head Navy Supply, Cherry Point, N.C., 1941-45; ptnr. Cannons Paint & Wallpaper Co., Ayden, 1945-70; exec. v.p. Baker Furniture Co., Kinston, N.C., 1950-63, pres., treas., 1963-69; operator Cannon Farms, Ayden, 1956—; with consumer program Drexel Co., 1965-66; owner Jewelle Baker Cons., Kinston, 1969—; v.p. Gardner Homes, Elizabeth City, N.C., 1972-81, CEO, 1982—; bus. cons. Gardner Constrn. Co., Kinston, 1975-81, chmn. bd. dirs., CEO, 1982—; bus. cons. Lenoir Plumbing & Heating Co., Kinston, 1975-81, chmn. bd. dirs., CEO, 1982—; owner, moderator GenealogyPITT Co. N.C. Friends in Rsch., 1998—. Cons. Carolina Power & Light, 1963-65, N.C. Solar Energy Assn., 1977-79, Nutritional Therapy, Durham, N.C., 1979-81; lectr., 1950-63; del. U.S.-China Joint Session on Industry, Trade and Econ. Devel., Beijing, 1988. Columnist Ayden Dispatch and Greenville News Leader, 1940-56; prodr. Performer Baker's Commls., 1960-69. Mem. Devel. Auth. of Neuse River Coun. of Govts., 1984-85. Mem. C. of C. Kinston (bd. dirs., v.p., chmn. retail mchts. divsn.), So. Retail Furniture Assn., Nat. Retail Furniture Assn., N.C. Mchts. Assn., N.C. Farm Assn., Assn. Gen. Contractors Am., Cmty. Coun. for the Arts, Internat. Platform Assn., N.C. Zool. Assn., N.C. Art Soc., Kinston Country Club, Coral Bay Club, Pineknoll Golf and Country Club, Sea Water Marina Club. Democrat. Mem. Ch. Disciples Of Christ. Home: 1708 Elizabeth Dr Kinston NC 28504-3416 Office: Gardner Constrn Co PO Box 856 Kinston NC 28502-0856 E-mail: jewelle@coastalnet.com, jewellebaker@cox.net.

BAKER KNOLL, CATHERINE, lieutenant governor; b. Pitts. d. Nicholas James and Theresa Mary (May) Baker; m. Charles A. Knoll Sr. (dec.); children: Charles A. Jr., Mina B., Albert B., Kim Eric. BS in Edn., Duquesne U., 1952, MS in Edn., 1973. Dir. western Pa. region Safety Adminstrn. Dept. Transp., Pitts., 1971-79; exec. dir. community svc. Dept. of Adminstrn., Allegheny County, Pa., 1980-88; treas. Pa. Treasury Dept., Harrisburg, 1988—2003; lt. gov State of Pa., 2003—. Owner, operator pvt. bus. firm, Pitts., 1952-70. Mem. Pa. Dem. State Com., Pa. Fedn. Dem. Women, YMCA Bd., Pitts., Harrisburg, Duquesne U. Alumni Bd., Mom's House, Zontas Inc. Bd. Mem. Nat. Assn. State Treas., Women Execs. in State Gov., Coun. State Gov. (exec. com. ea. region). Democrat. Roman Catholic. Office: Office Lt Governor 200 Main Capitol Bldg Harrisburg PA 17120 Office Phone: 717-787-3300. Office Fax: 717-783-0150.*

BAKER-MORRIS, KAY, special education educator; b. Tulsa, Nov. 25, 1952; d. Charles Fred and Virginia L. Robinson; m. Don Baker (div.); children: Chandler Baker, Kyle Baker; m. Ron Morris. BEd, Northeastern State U., 1975, MEd, 1978. Cert. spl. edn. tchr. Okla. Spl. edn. tchr. Nowata (Okla.) Pub. Sch., 1975—78, Copan (Okla.) Pub. Sch., 1978—86, Bartlesville (Okla.) Pub. Schs., 1986—, dist. contact for individual edn. program for computers, 2004—, tchr. summer testing program, 1995—. Assessor Nat. Bd. Tchr. Cert., Tulsa, 2002; cons. Coun. Exceptional Children, 2000; presenter in field. Author: Case Study of Exceptional Child, Exceptional Children in Group Home Setting, 1975; contbr. Past pres., v.p., sec. Bartlesville Fraternal Order of Police; active State Bd. Fraternal Order of Police, Ladies Aux. Named Tchr. of Yr., Copen Pub. Schs., 1985, Outstanding Educator, Coun. for Exceptional Children, 1995. Mem.: NEA (rep.), Okla. Edn. Assn., Bartlesville Edn. Assn. (v.p. 1995—2004). Democrat. Baptist. Office: Bartlesville Pub Schs 1100 SE Jennings Bartlesville OK 74003 Home: 801 SE 13th Bartlesville OK 74006

BAKER-ROELOFS, MINA MARIE, retired home economist, educator; b. Holland, Mich., Mar. 1, 1920; d. Thomas and Fannie (DeBoer) Baker; m. Harold Eugene Roelofs, Aug. 16, 1985; children: Howard, Donald, Ann. BS, Iowa State U., 1942, MS, 1946; postgrad., Ariz. State U., 1965, Ind. State U., 1968, 76. Dietitian Annville (Ky.) Inst., 1942-45; chmn., tchr. family and consumer scis. Cen. Coll., Pella, Iowa, 1946-85, ret., 1985. Mem. dean's grad. adv. coun. Iowa State U., Ames, 1955-56, coord. coop. plan, 1967-85. Editor: Dandy Dutch Recipes, 1991; co-editor: Pella Collectors Cookbook, 1982, A Taste of the World, 1992; author: Mina's Memories of Dutch Family Life, 2004. Mem. com. Pell Hist. Soc. Recipient Career award Iowa State U. Coll. Family Consumer Sci., 2003; grantee Govt. Cross-Cultural, 1974, NEH, 1980. Mem. AAUW, Am. Assn. Family and Consumer Sci. (life), Iowa Assn. Family and Consumer Sci. (pres. 1953-55, sec. 1979-81, Disting. Svc. award 1985, Hall of Fame award 2005), Iowa Elder Hostel Tchr. Ctrl. Coll. Aux., PEO Sisterhood, Women's Social and Literary Club (pres. 1990-92). Republican. Mem. Reformed Ch. Avocations: photography, reading, crafts. Home: 229 Main St Pella IA 50219-2024

BAKHSHI, NANDITA, bank executive; Various mktg., product mgmt. and sales mgmt. positions Bank One Corp.; dir. alternative delivery Home Savings of Am.; dir. self-svc./ATM banking FleetBoston Fin. Group, sr. v.p. Office: FleetBoston Fin Corp 100 Federal St 10034F Boston MA 02110

BAKKE, HOLLY C., bank commission official; m. Mark Mattia; 1 child, Christian. BA, Drew U., 1973; grad. fellow, Inst. Court Mgmt. of Nat. Ctr. St. Courts, 1978; JD, Seton Hall U., 1982. Spcl. dep. commr. ins. litigation practices NJ Dept. Ins.; exec. dir. NJ Surplus Lines Ins. Guaranty Fund, 1989—2002, NJ Property-Liability Ins. Guaranty Assn., 1989—2002, NJ Med. Malpractice Reinsurance Assn., 1989—2002; commr. NJ Dept. Banking and Ins., 2002—. Mem.: NJ State Bar Assn. Office: PO Box 325 Trenton NJ 08625 E-mail: hbakke@dobi.state.nj.us.

BAKKE, LUANNE KAYE, music educator; b. Rochester, Ind., Apr. 3, 1937; d. Lyman Dean and Anna Lorraine (Bull) Burkett; m. Ronald Roark (div. 1981); m. Jacques Roland Bakke, Feb. 24, 1988; 1 child, Kathleen Anne. BA, Calif. St. U., Northridge, 1977; MusM, Calif. State U., Fullerton, 1981. Instr. Calif. State U., Fullerton, 1979—81, City Coll. Chgo., Karlsruhe, Germany, 1985—86, Gadsden City Coll., Gadsden, Ala., 1986—87; pvt. practice piano & voice Lander, Wyo., 1995—. Music dir. Wood'N Ship Prodn., L.A., Calif., 1978—80; prodr. & dir. Off the Track Singers, L.A., 1975—77. Contbr. The Anniston Star Newspaper, 1982—91; composer: (plays) The Adventure of Doraleen, 1981. Pres. Pomona Valley Music Tchrs. Assn., 1969; music dir. Anniston Cmty. Theater, Anniston, Ala., 1987—89; cmty. choir dir. Harmonic Jam, Granite Falls, Minn., 1992—95; creator Performing Arts in Miniature, 1997—. Recipient Frank Jones award for leadership in the arts, City of Anniston, 1986. Mem.: Music Tchrs. Nat. Assn., Pi Kappa Lambda. Republican. Avocations: scuba diving, hiking, care of animals. Home and Office: PO Box 514 Lander WY 82520 E-mail: jbakke@wyoming.com.

BAKOWSKI, NANCY, chemist; BS in Chem., Oswego Univ. Laboratory sci. US Fed. Govt., Sterling Drug; dir., corp. training BioReliance, dir., mktg., dir., sales; dir., worldwide corp. strategic mktg. Team Bus. Mem.: Assn. Women in Sci. (exec. dir. 2006—). Office: Assn Women in Sci Ste 650 1200 NY Ave NW Washington DC 20005 Office Fax: 202-326-8960.*

BAKSH, BRENDA J., communications educator; d. Charles R. and Pearl Morgan Thompson; children: Ellen A. Thompson, Rick L. Thompson. MA, W.Va. U., Morgantown, W.Va., 1966. Asst. prof. Tri-State Coll., Angola, Ind., 1967—72; dir. Logan (W.Va.) County Head Start Program, 1978—90; prof. So. W.Va. Comm. and Tech. Coll., Logan, 1986—. Office: Southern WV Comm and Tech College Logan WV 25601 Office Phone: 304-792-7098. Business E-Mail: brendab@southern.wvnet.edu.

BALA, MADELEINE JEANETTE, music educator; b. Reading, Pa., Oct. 20, 1981; d. Stanley Peter and Rochelle Judith Bala. MusB Edn., Pa. State U., University Park, 2003. Cert. tchr. music comprehensive K-12 Commonwealth Pa., Dept. Edn. Del. Tchr. gen. music Cape Henlopen Sch. Dist., Lewes, Del., 2003—. Pvt. saxophone instr., Lewes, Del., 2001—; tchr. after sch. tutoring program Milton Elem. Sch., Milton, Del., 2003—; coach Odyssey Mind Henlopen Sch. Dist., Milton, Del., 2004—. Masterclass scholar, Faenza Internat. Saxophone Festival, Italy, 2002, Performance scholar, Theodore Presser Found., 2002. Mem.: Del. State Educators Assn., Del. Music

Educators Assn., Music Educators Nat. Conf. Avocations: reading, movies, running, beach, rollerblading. Home: Unit 1206 17054 N Brandt St Lewes DE 19958 Personal E-mail: mjb382@psualum.com.

BALASKI, BELINDA L., actress, educator, artist; d. Lester Anthony Balaski and Norma Jean Jahn; 1 adopted child, Sharisse M. Bray. Actress, owner, tchr., creator BB's Kids Acting Sch., LA, 1986—. Author: (plays) The T-Files, 1999; star The Howling, Are You My Mother, Bobby Jo and the Outlaws, The Runaway, others. Recipient Best Supporting Actress, LA Drama Critics Cir., 1972, Robbie award for Best Supporting Actress, 1973, Robbie award for Best Actress, 1974. Office: BB's Kids Acting Sch PO Box 461011 Los Angeles CA 90046 Office Phone: 323-650-5437.

BALAS-WHITFIELD, SUSAN, artist; b. NJ; m. Marshall Whitfield. B.A., Rutgers U., Newark, 1964, N.Y. U., N.Y., 1961—64, Douglass Coll., New Brunswick, 1960—61. Tchr. WM. R. Satz. Sch., Holmdel, NJ, 1976—89; artist, 1976—. Author: (novels) Into The Triangle, A Teacher's Trot, 1989. Pres. Ranch Property Owners Assoc., Durango, Colo., 2000—03. Recipient Artist of the Yr., Durango Co. C. of C., 2003. Mem.: Pastel Soc. of Am. (signature, award for Excellence 2004), Salmagundi Club. Avocations: motorcycling, skiing, running, hiking. Home: 308 CottonWood Creek Rd Durango CO 81301 Studio: 22521 E Rowland Dr Aurora CO 80016 Office Phone: 970-259-0774. E-mail: susan@balasart.com.

BALBACH, LISA JEAN, information scientist, educator; d. Lester J. and Kathryn J. Beernink; m. Daniel Joseph Balbach, Oct. 25, 1991; children: Danielle J., Dylan T. BBA, U. Minn., 1985; MA in Bus. Edn., U. Minn., Mpls., 1990. Cert. group fitness instr. Am. Coun. on Exercise, 1990. Programmer, analyst West Pub. Co., St. Paul, 1985—89; rsch. asst. U. Minn., St. Paul, 1990; adminstrv. mgmt. instr. North Hennepin C.C., Brooklyn Park, Minn., 1990—91; computer info. sys. instr. Kirtland C.C., Roscommon, Mich., 1991—, cmty. edn. instr., 1991—95. Coach Odyssey of the Mind, Prudenville, Mich., 1998—2000, AYSO Soccer, Prudenville, 1999—2004; den leader Cub Scouts, Prudenville, 2002—05. Mem.: Internat. Web Master Assn. Democrat. Roman Catholic. Avocations: jogging, aerobics, golf, photography, weightlifting. Office: Kirtland Community College 10775 N St Helen Rd Roscommon MI 48653 Office Phone: 989-275-5000 414.

BALCOMB, MARY NELSON, small business owner; b. Mich., Apr. 29, 1928; d. Andrew and Selma (Martin) Nelson; m. Robert S. Balcomb, July 3, 1948; children: Stuart V., Amis. AA, Am. Acad. Art, 1948; BFA cum laude, U. N.Mex., 1968; MFA, U. Wash., 1971. Advt. mgr. Broome Furniture Co., Albuquerque, 1949-55; designer Custom Interiors, Albuquerque, 1956-66; art tchr. Sandia Girls' Sch., Albuquerque, 1966-68; co-owner Woolcot, Inc., Bellevue, Wash., 1975-80; owner Balcomb Design Studio, Silverdale, Wash., 1981—. Author: Nicolai Fechin, Russian-American Artist, 1975 (Rounce and Coffin award), Les Perhacs, Sculptor, 1975, William F. Reese, American Artist, 1984 (Rounce and Coffin award), Robin-Robin/A Journal, 1995, Sergei Bongart, Russian-American Artist, 2002; contbr. articles to periodic jours. Creator Children's Art Ctr. Found., Seattle, 1972, bd. dirs., 1972-80. Recipient Painting award Frye Art Mus., 1994, Honorarium Prix de West Nat. Cowboy Hall of Fame and We. Heritage Mus., 1995. Mem. Author's Guild, Phi Kappa Phi, Lambda Rho. Home: PO Box 1922 Silverdale WA 98383-1922

BALD, DIANA, broadcast executive; Sta. mgr. Univision 65/Telefutura 28, Phila., gen. mgr., 2004—. Adv. bd. Philly Creative Guide. Bd. dirs. Multi-cultural Affairs Congress, Phila., Police Athletic League, Phila. Recipient 40 Under 40 award, Phila. Bus. Jour., 2006. Mem.: Phila. Advt. Club (pres. 2005—06, chmn. 2006—). Office: WUVP Channel 65 Univision 1700 Market St Philadelphia PA 19103 Office Phone: 215-568-2800, 215-568-0984.*

BALDASSANO, CORINNE LESLIE, radio executive; b. NYC, May 16, 1950; BA cum laude, Queens Coll., CUNY, 1970; MA in Theatre, Hunter Coll., CUNY, 1975; MBA in Fin., NYU, 1986. Various local and nat. radio programming positions, 1970—89; v.p. programming ABC Radio Networks, 1990-94, Unistar Radio Networks, L.A., 1994, SW Networks, N.Y.C., 1994-95, sr. v.p. programming, 1995—97; gen. mgr. radio divsn. AP, 1997-99; v.p. broadcast programming soundsbig.com, 1999—2000; v.p. Content LMiV, 2000; owner Translucent Media, 2001—05; sr. v.p. programming and mktg. Take on the Day LLC, 2005—. Vice chair L.A. Regional Alumni, Stern Sch. Bus., NYU, 2004—. Named one of 20 Most Influential Women in Radio, Radio Ink Mag., 1999. Mem.: NYU Bus. Forum (bd. dirs. 1988—91, v.p., treas. 1990—91). Avocations: travel, theater, dance, music, films.

BALDERSTON, JEAN MERRILL, marriage and family therapist, poet, writer; b. Providence, Aug. 29, 1936; d. Frederick Augustus and Helen May (Cleveland) Merrill; m. David Chase Balderston, June 1, 1957. BA, U. Conn., 1957; MA, Columbia U., 1965, EdD, 1968. Pvt. practice psychotherapist, N.Y.C., 1968—. Adj. faculty Douglas Coll. for Women, New Brunswick, N.J., Rutgers U., New Brunswick, Montclair State Coll., Upper Montclair, N.J., CUNY (Hunter Coll. & Queens Coll.), Columbia U., N.Y., Mt. St. Vincent U., Can., 1965-70; editorial bd. N.Y. Quarterly, N.Y.C., 1971-76. Poems have appeared in various lit. mags., and anthologies. Co-recipient The Writer Mag. Emily Dickinson award, Poetry Soc. Am., 2000. Mem. APA, Am. Assn. Marital and Family Therapy, Poetry Soc. Am., Acad. Am. Poets, Emily Dickinson Internat. Soc., Friends of Poets and Writers, Poets Ho., Am. Scandinavian Found. Avocations: travel, languages. Home and Office: 1225 Park Ave # 8C New York NY 10128-1758 Office Phone: 212-876-4111.

BALDNER, KAREN A., artist, art educator; b. Baton Rouge, Nov. 9, 1952; d. Thomas and Gabriella Baldner. Student, Acad. Bildedenen Kunste, Munich, 1974-76; BFA in Printmaking, Ind. U., 1981, MFA in Printmaking with honors, 1986. Vis. asst. prof. U. Ark., Fayetteville, 1987-88, Ind. U. Hope Sch. Art, Bloomington, 1990-91, St. Mary's Coll. Md., St. Mary's City, 1992-93; asst. prof. Bucknell U., Lewisburg, Pa., 1988-90; assoc. prof. Herron Sch. Art, Indpls., 1998—. Pvt. tchr. paper and bookmaking, 1983—; condr. workshops in hand papermaking and book binding Coe Coll., Cedar Rapids, Iowa, 1986, Miami U., Oxford, Ohio, 1992, 94, Columbus (Ga.) State U., 1995, 2000, IAPMA Conf., Chgo., 2002, N.W. Ark. Sch. Sys., 1995-98; resident Ill. State U., Normal, 1997; artist-in-resident Ark. Arts Coun., 1995-96, 97-98; conf. presenter, lectr. in field. One-woman shows include Paper Press Gallery, Chgo., 1992, Artemesia Gallery, Chgo., 1992, 97, St. Mary's Coll., 1993, Soho 20 Gallery, N.Y.C., 1993, 94, 95, Northcutt Steele Gallery, Billings, Mont., 1996, Anne Kitrell Gallery, U. Ark., Fayetteville, 1997, Matrix Gallery, Sacramento, 1997, Mendelsohn Gallery, Bloomington, Ind., 1999, New Harmony Ind.Gallery, 2000, Indpls. Art Ctr., 2002, Olin Gallery, Roanoke Coll., 2003, Jewish Comty. Ctr., Indpls., 2004, DAI, Heidelberg, Germany, 2004; exhibited in group shows, 1991—, including Papermaking Mus., Düren, Germany, 1991, Gallery 451, Rockford, Ill., 1992, Spaces Gallery, Cleve., 1991, Gemeente Bibliothek, Rotterdam, The Netherlands, 1993, Lite Rail Gallery, Sacramento, 1993, Massillon (Ohio) Mus., 1994, Haggin Mus., Stockton, Calif., 1994, Soho 20 Gallery, 1994, 96, 97, 99, 2000, 01, 02, Evansville (Ind.) Mus. Arts and Scis., 1994, Columbia (Mo.) Coll., 1995, Matrix Gallery, 1995 (Best in Show award), Woman Made Gallery, Chgo., 1995, 96, 98, 2000, Fine Arts Ctr. Gallery, U. Ark., 1996, Katherine Nash Gallery, U. Minn., Mpls., 1996, Edna Carlsten Gallery, U. Wis., Stevens Point, 1997, Columbia Coll., Chgo., 1998, DePauw U., Greencastle, Ind., 1999, Mc Neese State U., Lake Charles, La., 2001, Ind. U., Kokomo, 2002, The Ctr. for Book Arts, Ellipse Art Ctr., Arlington, 2003, Ind. State Mus., 2005; represented in collections at Ind. U., Sch. Fine Arts Libr., Bloomington, Ind. U. Sch. Fine Arts, Artists Books Collection, Kinsey Inst., Ind. U. Fine Arts Collection, Bookarts Collection, Ark. Arts Ctr., Ctr. for Drawing; work reviewed in various publs. Recipient Best of Show award No. German Photography Competition, 1987, merit award 50th Quad State Exhbn., Quincy (Ill.) Art Ctr., 2000; Kiel U. exch. scholar Ind. U., 1986-87; Fulbright travel grantee, Germany, 1986-87, faculty devel. grantee Bucknell U., 1989, grantee Ludwig Vogelstein Found., 1991-92, Nat. Endowment Arts grantee Mid Am. Arts Alliance, 1996, grantee Ind. Arts Commn., 2000; fellow Ark. Arts Coun. for Works on Paper, 1998; Creative Renewal Arts fellow, Indpls. Arts Coun., 2003; Individual Artist grantee Ind. Arts Commn., 2004. Mem.: The Ctr. for Book Arts, Internat. Assn. Papermakers, Mid.-Am. Coll. Arts Assn., Coll. Arts Coun., Friends of Dard Hunter, Soho 20 Gallery. Home: 629 N College Ave Bloomington IN 47404 Business E-Mail: kbaldner@iupui.edu.

BALDRIDGE, JANE L., graphic and fine artist; b. Stevens Point, Wis., Feb. 23, 1959; d. Ralph Bayard and Elizabeth (McIntosh) Baldridge; m. Mark Harrington Brown, Oct. 11, 1978 (div. 1982); 1 child, Jason David Cook. Student, Calif. Inst. Arts, Valencia, 1977-78, Alfred Glassel Sch. Art, Houston, 1978-81. Artist, Tex., Calif., Mich., N.C., 1972—; owner The Village Gallery, Brooklyn, Mich.; salesperson, framer Fidler's Gallery, Wilmington, N.C.; asst. pub. Cape Fear Real Estate Directory, Wrightsville Beach, N.C.; owner, designer Artspeaks, Wilmington. Curator Arts Coun. Lower Cape Fear, Wilmington; tchr., lectr. in schs., Wilmington; advt. agy. cons. Exhibited in shows at Art Gallery Originals, Winston-Salem, N.C., Sea Pines Gallery, Hilton Head, S.C., Feast of the Pirates Art Show, Wilmington, N.C., St. John Mus., Wilmington, N.C., New Elements Gallery, Wilmington, New Eng. Art Inst., Boston, Women's Ctr. 10th Ann. Art Show, Chapel Hill, N.C., Piney Woods Art Festival, Wilmington, Fayetteville (N.C.) Mus. Art, Arts Festival, Dalton, Ga., Creative Resource Gallery, Wilmington, Art Mus., Mytrle Beach, S.C., Lincoln Ctr., N.Y.C., World Festival Paper, Kranj, Slovenia, Louise Cameron Mus. Art, numerous others; represented in collections at Merrill Lynch, Dean Witter Reynolds Inc., Landmark Homes, Inc., Libr. of Congress Print Collection, others. Pres. NJ ROTC Booster Club, 2004—. Recipient Gold medal for Adams Cup (sailing, 1976, Gold medal for Art, Scholastic awards, 1974, Pres.'s award Calif. Inst. of the Arts, 1978, numerous awards for art; regional artist grantee, 1994, 2000. Mem. St. Louise Cameron Mus. Art, N.C. Coastal Fedn., Citizens Protecting Resources. Office: Artspeaks 8947 Shipwatch Dr Wilmington NC 28412-3537

BALDRIDGE, KIM, science educator; BS in math., Minot State U., ND, 1982; MA in math., ND State U., 1985, PhD in theoretical chemistry, 1988. Joined San Diego Supercomputer Ctr., 1989, dir. integrative computational scis., 2002—; adj. prof. chemistry U. Calif., San Diego, 1997—. Hon. guest prof. U. Basel. Recipient award, Fulbright Found., 1997, Agnes Fay Morgan rsch. award, Iota Sigma Pi, 2000. Fellow: AAAS, Am. Phys. Soc. Office: San Diego Super Computer Ctr Dept Chemistry 9500 Gilman Dr La Jolla CA 92093-0505

BALDRIGE, LETITIA, writer, management consultant; b. Miami Beach, Fla. d. Howard Malcolm and Regina (Connell) B.; m. Robert Hollensteiner; children: Clare, Malcolm. BA, Vassar Coll., 1946; postgrad., U. Geneva, 1946-48; DHL (hon.), Creighton U., 1979, Mt. St. Mary's Coll., 1980, Bryant Coll., 1987, Kenyon Coll., 1990. Personal-social sec. to amb. Am. Embassy, Paris, 1948-51; intelligence officer Washington, 1951-53; asst. to amb. Am. Embassy, Rome, 1953-56; dir. pub. rels. Tiffany & Co., 1956-60; social sec. The White House, 1961-63; pres. Letitia Baldrige Enterprises, Chgo., 1964-69; dir. consumer affairs Burlington Industries, 1969-71; pres. Letitia Baldrige Enterprises, Inc., Washington, 1972—. Author: Roman Candle, 1956, Tiffany Table Settings, 1958, Of Diamonds and Diplomats, 1968, Home, 1972, Juggling, 1976, Amy Vanderbilt's Complete Book of Etiquette, 1978, Amy Vanderbilt's Everyday Etiquette, 1979, The Entertainers, 1981, Letitia Baldrige's Complete Guide to Executive Manners, 1985, Letitia Baldrige's Complete Guide to a Great Social Life, 1987, Complete Guide to the New Manners for the '90s, 1990, New Complete Guide to Executive Manners, 1993, (novel) Public Affairs Private Relations, 1990, More Than Manners! Raising Today's Kids to Have Kind Manners and Good Hearts, 1997, In the Kennedy Style, 1998, Legendary Brides, 2000, A Lady, First, 2001, New Manners fr New Times, 2003. Mem. adv. bd. Woodrow Wilson House, Washington, Malcolm Baldrige Nat. Quality Awards, Woodrow Wilson Nat. Fellowship Found. Republican. Personal E-mail: lbaldrige@aol.com.

BALDVINS, LYNN ANN, medical/surgical nurse, army officer; b. Keene, N.H., Sept. 24, 1954; d. Jon Otto and Nancy Edith (Low) B. BSN, U. N.H., 1976; MSN, U. Tex., El Paso, 1985. Commd. officer AUS, 1976, advanced through grades to lt. col., 1992; chief nursing edn. and staff devel. svc. Evans Army Community Hosp., Ft. Carson, Colo., Germany; clin. mgr. neurosurgery staff devel. Evans U.S. Army Community Hosp., Ft. Carson, Colo., 1989—92; retired AUS, 1997; mgr. infection prevention Meml. Hosp., Colorado Springs, Colo., 1997—. Decorated Meritorious Svc. medal. Mem. ANA, Assn. Practitioners in Infection Control and Epidemiology, Sigma Theta Tau. Home: 7550 Colby Ct Colorado Springs CO 80919-3927 Office: Meml Hosp 1400 E Boulder St Colorado Springs CO 80909-5599

BALDWIN, BILLIE SUE, principal; b. Roanoake, Va., Jan. 30, 1945; d. William S. Board and Jacqueline T. Carmack; m. Robert Nelson Baldwin, June 17, 1967; children: Christopher Brent, Stephanie Herndon. B in Music Edn., Longwood U., 1966. Music tchr. Woodrow Wilson Jr., Roanoke, Va., 1966—67; music cons. Henrico County Sch., Richmond, Va., 1967—70; tchr. St. Catherine's Sch., Richmond, 1982—98, prin., 1998—. Spkr. in field. Pres. Bon Air Jr. Women's Club, Richmond. Mem.: ASCD, Nat. Mid. Sch. Assn., Va. Assn. Ind. Schools, Nat. Assn. Ind. Schools. Avocations: piano, music. Home: 11610 Bondurant Dr Richmond VA 23236 Office: St Catherines Sch 6001 Grove Ave Richmond VA 23226

BALDWIN, BONNIE, physician; b. Dallas, Dec. 18, 1954; d. Eugene and Mary Ellen Jericho; m. Robert Talbot Baldwin, May 28, 1985; children: Robert, Ryan. AB, Duke U., Durham, N.C., 1977; MD, Baylor Coll. Medicine, 1985. Gen. surgery resident U. Tex.-Houston, 1985-88; plastic surgery resident Baylor Coll. Medicine, Houston, 1988-91; asst. prof. M.D. Anderson Cancer Ctr., Houston, 1991-97; physician pvt. practice, Houston, 1997—. Med. advisor Reach for Recovery, Houston, 1999, cons. M.D. Anderson, 1998—. Contbr. articles to profl. jours. Named Best Scientific Exhibit Am. Soc. Aesthetic Plastic Surgery, 1997. Fellow ACS; mem. Am. Soc. Plastic Surgery, Soc. Surg. Oncology. Office: Cons in Plastic Surgery 7737 Southwest Fwy Ste 201 Houston TX 77074-1865 Office Phone: 713-791-1975. Business E-Mail: bjb@bonniebaldwinmd.com.

BALDWIN, CARLITA ROSE, minister; d. Carl Lamont and Alexinia Young Baldwin. AA, Russell Sage Coll., Troy, N.Y., 1980; BA, U. Albany, Albany, N.Y., 1989; MDiv., Howard U., Washington, DC, 2002. Itinerant Elder AME Ch. - Wash. Ann. Conf., 2002. Russian linguist and strategic debriefer USAF, Washington, 1980—2000; educator - mid. sch. (lang. arts) Anne Arundel County Pub. Sch., Millersville, Md., 2001—03; doctoral student U. Conn., Storrs, Conn., 2003—. Assoc. min./youth min. AME Ch., Md., 1997—2005. Tech. sgt. USAF, 1980—2000, various locations. Decorated Joint Svc. Commendation Medals Def. Intelligence Agy. and Nat. Security Agy., Joint Svc. Commendation Medal, Joint Svc. Achievement Medals US Air Force and Nat. Security Agy.; recipient Nat. Dean's Honor List, 2000, Disting. Honor Grad. and Outstanding Speech Award, USAF - NCO Leadership Sch., 1989; scholar Trustee Honor Scholarship, Howard U., 1998 - 2000; Multicultural Honors Fellowship, U. Conn., 2003 - present, Grad. Assistantship, 2003 - present. Mem.: World Coun. for Gifted and Talented (assoc.), Nat. Assn. for Gifted Children (assoc.), Human Resources Mgmt. Assn. (assoc.), Altrusa Internat., Inc. (life), Women in Mil. Svc. (life), DAV (life), Am. Legion (life), Pi Lambda Theta Internat. Honor Soc. and PA in Edn. (life), Delta Sigma Theta Sorority, Inc. (life). Democrat-Npl. African Meth. Episcopal. Avocations: water sports, reading, puzzles. Office: Univ Conn 2131 Hillside Rd Unit 3007 Storrs Mansfield CT 06269-3007 Office Phone: 860-486-1790. Office Fax: 860-486-2900. Business E-Mail: carlita.baldwin@uconn.edu.

BALDWIN, DOROTHY LEILA, secondary school educator; b. Irvington, N.J., Feb. 28, 1948; d. Daniel Thomas and Lillian Frances (Wainright) B. BA, Kean Coll., Union, N.J., 1969, MA in Edn. and Humanities, 1971; EdD in Adminstrn. and Supervision, Seton Hall U., 1987, cert. reading specialist, 1979, cert. bus. adminstr., 1985. Tchr., reading coord. St. Paul Apostle Sch. Irvington, 1969-74; tchr. Summit (N.J.) Jr. High Sch., 1975-79; social studies coord. K-9, chmn. dept. 7-9 Summit Pub. schs., 1979-87; social studies supr. Livingston (N.J.) Pub. Schs., 1987; prin. Point Road Sch, Little Silver, NJ, 1987-89; dir. gifted edn. K-12 Clifton, NJ, 1989-90; prin. Sch. Two, Clifton, NJ, 1989-90, Deerfield Sch., Mountainside, 1990-92, Eisenhower Sch., Bridgewater-Raritan, NJ, 1992—2003; prof. Fairleigh Dickinson U., Teaneck, NJ, 2003—. Adj. prof. Montclair (N.J.) U., Passaic County C.C., Morris County C.C.; tchr. adult and cmty. schs.; workshop coord.; cons. in field. Author books; contbr. articles to profl. jours. PTA scholar, 1965. Mem. ASCD, Nat. Assn. Elem. Sch. Prins., Nat. Coun. Social Studies, Am. Assn. Sch. Adminstrs., N.J. Assn. Elem. Sch. Prins., N.J. Prins. Ctr., Somerset County Assn. Elem. Sch. Prins., Phi Delta Kappa, Kappa Delta Pi. Home: 737 River Rd Chatham NJ 07928-1136 Office: Fairleigh Dickinson U 1000 River Rd Teaneck NJ 07666 Office Phone: 201-692-2863. Business E-Mail: dbaldwin@fdu.edu.

BALDWIN, IRENE S., hotel executive, real estate developer; b. Dodge City, Kans., Sept. 8, 1939; d. Albert A. McMichael and Eleanor L. (Johnson) McMichael McGrath; m. Miles Edward Baldwin, June 30, 1961. BS, Friends U., 1961. Dress designer, Wichita, 1959-61; social worker Sedgwick County, Kans., 1963-65; owner motel chair Kans., 1965—. Comml. and agrl. real estate investor, 1971—; corp. sec.-treas. Baldwin, Inc., Kans., 1970—, fin. advisor, 1970—; pvt. practice fin. cons., Colby, Kans., 1975—; founder, advisor Charitable Found., Kans., 1980—; fundraiser various charitable orgns., 1982—; pvt. placement of homeless animals, Kans. and Nebr., 1965—; helped develop 1st artificial front leg for canines, 1985. Contbr. articles to profl. jours.; author: (short stories) My Pal Chopper, 2002. Fundraiser various charitable orgns., 1982—; pvt. placement of homeless animals, Kans. and Nebr., 1965—. Avocations: horseback riding, hiking, travel, sewing, drawing. Address: 2320 S Range Ave Colby KS 67701-9056

BALDWIN, JANET SUE, library media specialist; b. McPherson, Kans., Feb. 15, 1951; d. Gerald William and Eleanor Elizabeth (Markham) Jackson; m. Gregory Lee Baldwin, Aug. 11, 1972; children: Ryan Gregory, Chase Jackson. BS in Edn., U. Kans., 1973. Cert. elem. edn. educator, libr. sci. Tchr. Eskridge (Kans.) Grade Sch., 1973-76; elem. tchr. Dover (Kans.) Grade Sch., 1976-81, libr., 1981-89; libr. media specialist Hudson Elem. & Belvoir Elem. Sch., Topeka, 1989-92, Crestview Elem. Sch., Topeka, 1992-96, New Meadows Elem. Sch., Topeka, 1996—. Chpt. 1 storyteller Chase Mid. Sch., Topeka, summer 1992; computer instr. to tchrs. Summer Acad., Topeka, 1993; tchr. computers Bishop Elem. Sch., Topeka, summers 1994, 95. Mem. NEA, Kans. Reading Assn. (hospitality conf. co-chair 1992, membership com. chair 1995-96, Outstanding Kans. Reading Educator Topeka nominee 1994), Kans. Nat. Edn. Assn., Kans. Assn. Sch. Librs. Home: 551 NE Edgewood Dr Topeka KS 66617-1534

BALDWIN, JANICE MURPHY, lawyer; b. Bridgeport, Conn., July 16, 1926; d. William Henry and Josephine Gertrude (McKenna) Murphy; m. Robert Edward Baldwin, July 31, 1954; children: Jean Baldwin Grossman, Robert William, Richard Edward, Nancy Baldwin Kitsos. AB, U. Conn., 1948; MA, Mt. Holyoke Coll., 1950; postgrad., U. Manchester, Eng., 1950—51; MA, Tufts U., 1952; JD, U. Wis., 1971. Bar: Wis. 1971, U.S. Dist. Ct. (we. dist.) Wis. 1971. Staff atty. legis. coun. State of Wis., Madison, 1971-74, sr. staff atty., 1975-94; pvt. practice Madison, 1994—. Atty. adviser HUD, Washington, 1974—75, Washington, 1978—79. Fulbright fellow, 1950—51. Mem. AAUW, NOW, LWV (sec. 1996-99, v.p., 1999-2001, bd. dirs. Dane County 1996-2003, exec. com. 1997-2003, nominating com. 2002-04, unit leader 2004—), U.S. and Wis. Women's Polit. Caucus, Legal Assn. for Women (chmn. Marygold Meili award com. 1997-99), Wis. Bar Assn. (pres. govt. lawyers divsn. 1985-87, bd. govs. 1985-89, treas. 1987-89, participation of women in bar com. 1987-98, professionalism com. 1990-97, bd. bar examiners rev. 1990-94, law-related edn. com. 1992-95, govt. lawyers divsn. 1981—), Dane County Bar Assn. (legis. com. 1980-81, long range planning com. 1990-97, law for pub. com. 1993-94), Wis. Women's Network, U. Wis. Univ. League, Older Women's League, Fulbright Assn., Internat. Crane Found., Coalition of Wis. Aging Groups, Nat. Women's History Mus. Home and Office: 125 Nautilus Dr Madison WI 53705-4329 Personal E-mail: jbaldwin125@charter.net.

BALDWIN, LEAH ZAVIN, minister, writer, interior designer, educator; b. Portland, Oreg., June 21, 1945; d. William Herman and Gail Grebe Zavin; m. Gerald Lee Baldwin, Feb. 25, 1989; children: Gina Marie, Tasha Noelle, Krista Nicole. BA cum laude, Colo. Womens Coll., 1967; student, Portland State U., 1987, Rhema Bible Coll., 1992. Cert. in tchg. Lewis & Clark Coll., 1970. Tchr., Vienna, 1967—68, Beaverton (Oreg.) Sch. Dist., 1970—74; asst. chaplain Good Samaritan Hosp., Portland, 1982—85, Meridian Pk. Hosp., Portland, 1985—89; tchr. elem. sch. Tigard, Tualatin (Oreg.) Sch. Dist., 1992—95; pvt. practice minister, cons. Portland, 1995—. Min., patient adv. Tigard Care Ctr., 1982—86, Emanuel Children's Hosp., Portland, 1982—, Portland Good Samaritan Hosp., 1982—85, Tualatin Meridian Pk. Hosp., 1985—89, Dorenbecher Children's Hosp. Contbr. articles to newspapers. Vol. hospice, Cannon Beach, Oreg., 1996—2005; patient advocate, 2004—06, Providence, 2004—05; vol. hospice Portland, 1996—2005. Avocations: walking, guitar, singing, interior decorating, writing.

BALDWIN, MARIE HUNSUCKER, retired secondary school educator; b. Dallas, Dec. 22, 1923; d. Clyde Augustus and Charlotte (Moore) Hunsucker; m. Brewster Baldwin, Aug. 20, 1946 (dec. July 1992); children: Jean Baldwin McLevedge, David, Stephen, Christopher. BS in Edn., Tex. Tech. U., 1944; MFA in Writing, Norwich U., 1988. Tchr. Pub. Sch., Corpus Christi, Tex., 1944-45, Presbyn. Day Sch., Corpus Christi, 1945-46, Pub. Sch., Moriah, NY, 1964-66; field dir. Vt. Girl Scout Coun., Burlington, 1966-78; ret. Vice chair Vt. State Dem. Com., Montpelier, 1976-80; apptd. mem. Gov.'s Adult Edn. Coun., 1985-89; founder, pres. Vt. Caths. for Free Choice, 1989—; elected Justice of the Peace, Middlebury, Vt., 1989—. Mem. ACLU (bd. 1984-90), AAUW, LWV (founder, pres. 1952-56), Cath. Daus. Am., Bus. and Profl. Women. Avocations: creative writing, walking, reading.

BALDWIN, PATRICIA ANN, lawyer; b. Detroit, May 3, 1955; d. Frank Thomas and Margaret Elyne Mathews; m. Jeffrey Kenton Baldwin, Aug. 23, 1975; children: Matthew, Katherine, Timothy, Philip. BA summa cum laude, Ball State U., 1976; JD, Ind. U., 1979. Bar: Ind. 1979, U.S. Dist. Ct. (so. dist.) Ind. 1979. Ptnr. Baldwin & Baldwin, Danville, Ind., 1979-94; dep. pros. atty. Hendricks County, Danville, 1980-90, pros. atty., 1995—; dep. pros. atty. Boone County, Ind., 1990-94. Sec.-treas., dir. T.F.W., Inc., Danville, 1983—90. Active Girl Scouts U.S., 1964—2000; vol. Boy Scouts Am., 1986—; mem. Hendricks County Rep. Women, 1976—, pres., 2001—03; mem. parish coun. Mary Queen of Peace Cath. Ch., 1976—80, 1981—83; bd. dirs. Cath. Social Svcs., Archdiocese of Indpls., sec. bd. dirs., 1986—92; bd. dirs. Cummins Mental Health Ctr., 1982—86, Youth as Resources Hendricks County, 1995—2001. Mem.: Hendricks County Bar Assn., Ind. Pros. Attys. Assn., Nat. Dist. Attys. Assn., Danville Conservation Club. Office: One Courthouse Sq #105 Danville IN 46122 Office Phone: 317-745-9283.

BALDWIN, SUSAN OLIN, commissioner, management consultant; b. Battle Creek, Mich., Sept. 1, 1954; d. Thomas Franklin and Gloria Joan (Skidmore) Olin; m. James Patrick Baldwin, Sept. 15, 1979; children: Christopher Mark, David James. BA, Miami U., Ohio, 1976; JD, U. Cin., 1979. Bar: Ohio 1979, Mich. 1984. Assoc. editor Am. Legal Pub. Co., Cin., 1979—80; corp. atty. Hosp. Care Corp., Cin., 1980—84; legal counsel Peak Health Plan, Cin., 1984; assoc. Cook & Goetz, P.C., Bloomfield Hills, Mich., 1984—91, Pringle & Assocs., P.C., Farmington Hills, Mich., 1991—94; exec. dir. Calhoun County Econ. Devel. Forum, Battle Creek, 1994—2003; owner Am. Computer Svcs., Battle Creek, 2002—; commr. Battle Creek City, 2003—, mem. Mich. mcpl. league transp. and infrastructure com., 2005—.

Mem. steering com. Ctr. Workforce Excellence, 1994—96, Barriers to Employment, 1996—2003; bd. dirs. BC, Cal, Kal Inland Port Devel. Corp., 1996—, Forum Greater Kalamazoo, 1995—2001, Calhoun County Health Improvement Program, 1998—99; mem. Battle Creek Cmty. Leadership Acad., 1996—97, Battle Creek Area C. of C., 1998—2003, mem. adv. bd., 1998—, S.W. Mich. Healthplan Purchasing Alliance, 1998—2000; adv. bd. Starr Commonwealth Battle Creek Child Guidance Ctr., 1998—; mem. Cmty. Devel. Block Grant Coun., 1996—99, Mich. Women in Mcpl. Govt., 2005—, sec., 2006—. Contbr. articles to profl. jours. Pres. Hunter's Green Homeowner's Assn., Independence, Ky., 1982—83; chairwoman Safety Town Cmty. Project, 1993—95; v.p. fin. Jr. League Battle Creek, 1996—98; key communicator Minges Brook PTA, 1993—2001, treas., 1994—96, 1998—99; bd. dirs. Vol. Ctr. Battle Creek, 1999—, sec., 2003—; bd. dirs. Battle Creek Cmty. Found. Philanthropic Devel. Com., 1998—, Lakeview Sch. Dist. Com. Continuous Improvement, 1999—2002; chair S. Ctrl. Mich. Jr. Achievement Campaign, 1999, Calhoun County Crossroads Initiative, 1999—2002; bd. dirs. Habitat for Humanity, 2003—; mem. Mayor's Commr. Compensation Commn., 1997—2003; mem. capital campaign com.-making BC Green Leila Arboretum, 1999—2000; mem. exec. bd. Battle Creek Unltd., 2003—; bd. dirs. Binder Park Zoo, 2004—. Mem.: ABA, Am. Businesswomen's Assn. (v.p. 1980—81, editor 1980), Ohio State Bar, State Bar Mich., Battle Creek Area C. of C. (bd. dirs. 1998—), Birmingham Evening Newcomers Club (treas. 1986—87, pres. 1988), Phi Alpha Delta, Alpha Lambda Delta. Office: 164 W Hamilton Ln Battle Creek MI 49015-4030 Office Phone: 269-963-8124. Personal E-mail: sbaldwin4bc@aol.com.

BALDWIN, TAMMY, congresswoman, lawyer; b. Madison, Wis., Feb. 11, 1962; life ptnr. Lauren Azar. AB in Govt. and Math., Smith Coll., Northampton, Mass., 1984; JD, U. Wis., Madison, 1989. Mem. City Coun., Madison, Wis., 1986; supr. Dane County Bd. Suprs., 1986-1994; atty. pvt. practice, 1989-92; mem. Wis. State Assembly from 78th Dist., 1993-99, US Congress from 2nd Wis. dist., 1999—, mem. energy and commerce com. Mem.: Nat. Women's Polit. Caucus, Wis. State Bar Assn., Internat. Network Lesbian and Gay Officials, ACLU, NOW. Democrat. First woman to serve in the US House of Representatives. from Wis.; first openly gay person to be elected to Congress as a non-incumbent. Office: US Ho Reps 1022 Longworth Ho Office Bldg Washington DC 20515 Office Phone: 202-225-2906.*

BALE, JUDITH R., health science association administrator; Dir., bd. on Global Health Inst. Medicine, Washington, 1998—. Office: Global Health IOM 2101 Constitution Ave NW Washington DC 20418-0007

BALER, BLANCHE KIMOTO, retired child psychiatrist; b. Ceres, Calif., Nov. 30, 1924; d. Kusutaro Kimoto and Toku Kanazawa; m. Lenin Allen Baler (dec.); children: Laura, Claudia Baler Mellen, Carleton. PhD in Psychology, Boston U., 1951, MD, 1954. Staff psychiatrist Hawthorn Ctr., Northville, Mich., 1976—94; ret. Recipient asst. fellowship in psychology, Boston U., 1946—50; scholar, Dakota Wesleyan U., 1943, 1944, 1945, Boston U. Sch. Medicine, 1953. Mem.: Am. Psychiat. Assn. Avocations: gardening, interior decorating, international travel. Home: 1144 Aberdeen Dr Ann Arbor MI 48104

BALES, MARY CATHERINE, gifted and talented educator; b. Lake City, Fla., Nov. 15, 1954; d. Gregory Winston Methvin and Juanelle Combs Bennett; children: John Wesley, Jessica Amanda. M of Edn., U. North Fla., 1983, postgrad., 1987—88. Tchr. of emotionally handicapped Westside Elem., Glen St. Mary, Fla., 1979—86; tchr. of gifted Baker County Schs., Fla., 1986—. Acad. team coach Baker County H.S. Hi-Q Team, Glen St. Mary, 1986—88, 1993—; club sponsor Baker County H.S. Rideing Club, 1990—; future problem solving team coach Baker County Schs., 1996—2004; rsch facillitator U. North Fla., 1987—88; facillitator U. South Fla. Inst. for Edn., 1986—87. Swim team coach Baker County Bullets, 1988—89. Recipient Fla. Master Tchr. award, State Fla., 1985. Mem.: Baker County Horsemen's Assn., Fla. Assn. for Gifted, Union County Riding Club. Home: 7809 Cahone Ct Macclenny FL 32063 Office: Baker County High Sch One Wildcat Dr Glen Saint Mary FL 32040

BALES, VIRGINIA SHANKLE, health science association administrator; BA in Chemistry, Emory U., Atlanta, 1971, MPH, 1977. Dep. dir. Nat. Ctr. Chronic Disease Prevention and Health Promotion Ctrs. for Disease Control and Prevention, 1988—98, dep. dir. program mgmt., 1998—2002, dir. adult and cmty. health divsn. Nat. Ctr. for Chronic Disease Prevention and Health Promotion, 2002—. Office: CDC DHHS Mailstop D14 1600 Clifton Rd NE Atlanta GA 30329-4018

BALEY, JOAN MARIE, elementary school educator; d. Alfred J. and Angeline Beitler; m. Frank T. Baley, Mar. 24, 1984. BA in Edn., St. Xavier U., 1976; postgrad., Chapman U., Loyola U. Tchr. 3d grade Archdiocese of Chgo., St. Christina Sch., 1976, Archdiocese of Chgo., St. Thomas More Sch., 1976—98; tchr. 6th grade Archdiocese of Chgo., St. Christina Sch., 1998—2002, tchr. grades 7-8, dir. sci., 2002—. Facilitator Rainbow program St. Thomas More Sch., 1976—98, coord. grade level., 1976—98, St. Christina Sch., 1998—, chair sci., 1998—, mem. liturgy team, 1998—, peer mediator facilitator, 1998—. Nominee Golden Apple award, 1990; recipient, 1991, Disney award, 2000. Mem.: Nat. Sci. Tchrs. Assn. Avocations: golf, interior decorating, crafts. Office: St Christina Sch 3333 W 110th St Chicago IL 60655

BALFOUR, ANA MARIA, office manager; b. Buenos Aires, Dec. 16, 1942; came to the U.S., 1962; d. Alfredo Hector and Luisa (Zagnoni) Malaccorto; m. Guillermo Aylmer Balfour, July 10, 1964; children: Michele, Valeria, Alexandra. Student, U. Buenos Aires, 1961-62; BA, Am. U., 1964. Tchr. Ft. Rucker (Ala.) Middle Sch., 1964-65; med. asst. F.R. Leyva & G.A. Balfour, M.D., P.C., Washington, 1968-73, office mgr., 1973-88, adminstr., 1988—. Contbr. articles to profl. jours. Fundraiser Operation Smile, Stone Ridge Country Day Sch.-Sacred Heart; docent The Kreeger Mus., Washington, 1996— Mem. Comisión Esperanza Damas Argentinas, So Others May Eat, Ivy Found. (bd. dirs.), Com. Hispanic Designers, Com. Am.'s Film Festival. Roman Catholic. Avocations: gardening, latin american art, reading. Office: Foxhall Pediat 3301 New Mexico Ave NW Washington DC 20016-3622

BALIS, JANET, Internet company executive; BA, Columbia Coll.; MBA, Harvard Univ. Bus. Sch. Former radio prodr. Newsweek Mag.; mgmt. cons. AT Kearney; with media and entertainment banking investment group Goldman Sachs; co-founder The Mascot Network; former pres. sales, mktg. Time, Inc.; currently sr. v.p., sales mktg. AOL Media Networks. Named one of 40 Under 40, Crain's NY Bus. Mag., 2006. Office: AOL Media Networks 22000 AOL Way Dulles VA 20166*

BALIS, JENNIFER LYNN, academic administrator, computer scientist, educator; b. Hamlin, W.Va., Nov. 23, 1946; 1 child, Ted Berndt. AA, Del Mar Coll., 1987; BA, U. Tex., 1989; BS, So. Ill. U., 1992. Peer counselor U. Tex., Edinburg, 1989—90; tchr. Mission Ind. Sch. Dist., Tex., 1990; instr. San Diego Job Corps, 1992—95; instr. computer tech. Kaskaskia Coll., Centralia, Ill., 1997—2002. Coord. Kaskaskia Coll. Vandalia Ctr., Ill., 1999—2001. Website designer A 2/7 CAV, 2005—. Chmn., sec. Mulberry Grove Zoning Bd. Appeals, Ill., 1999—2002; vol. advocate S.A.F.E., 2003—; founder, coord. arthritis edn. and care group Salem Twp. Hosp., Ill., 2004—; computer tutor for sr. citizens, 2002—; Tai Chi health instr. Salem Cmty. Ctr., 2003—; ombudsman Ill. Dept. Aging, 2004—; healthy living adv., educator, 2004—; tax-aide, site coord. AARP, Salem, 2006—; chmn. Healthy Living, World Tai Chi Festival, 2004. With USNR, 1984—2004. Mem. Am. League Poets, Psi Chi (pres. 1989-90) Republican. Roman Catholic. Avocations: natural healing, folk medicine, mineral collector, archery, tai chi. Personal E-mail: jennibalis@yahoo.com.

BALKOWIEC, AGNIESZKA ZOFIA, science educator, researcher; b. Sokolow Podlaski, Poland, Sept. 30, 1968; d. Anna and Jerzy Michal Balkowiec. MD, Med. U. Warsaw, Poland, 1993, PhD, 1995. Instr. physiology Med. U. Warsaw, 1993—95, asst. prof., 1995—99; rsch. assoc. Case Western Res. U., Cleve., 1997—2001, instr. neuroscis., 2001—02; asst. prof. Oreg. Health & Sci. U., Portland, 2002—. Reviewer profl. jours. Contbr. articles to profl. jours. Recipient Sci. award, Polish Min. Health and Social Welfare, 1994, 1996, Prime Min. of Poland, 1996; fellow, Found. Polish Sci., 1995; grantee, Am. Heart Assn., 2002—, NIH, 2004—, Nat. Heart, Lung and Blood Inst., 2004—. Mem.: Am. Dental Edn. Assn., Am. Heart Assn. (basic cardiovas. scis. coun. 2002, grantee 2002—), Soc. Neurosci. Achievements include discovery of the role of activity of nerve cells in regulation of growth factors; invention of setup for immunodetection of growth factors released from neurons following electrical stimulation. Avocations: travel, gourmet cooking, classical music, photography. Office: Oregon Health & Sci U 611 SW Campus Dr Portland OR 97239 Office Phone: 503-418-0190. Business E-Mail: balkowie@ohsu.edu.

BALL, AMY CATHERINE, education program manager; b. Abingdon, Va., Aug. 24, 1975; d. Willis and Darlene Crabtree Ball. BA in sci., Va. Tech. U., 1996; M, Hollins U., 1998. Sales mktg. Farm Success, Abingdon, 1996—98, Kirklands, Roanoke, Va., 1998; mktg. dir. CFC Inc., Culpeper, Va., 1999—2000; educator The Crisis Ctr., Bristol, Va., 2000—02; edn. program dir. Washington County Schs., Abingdon, 2002—. Mem. adv. bd. CAUSE, Emory, Va., 2000—, Teen Dating Violence Coalition, Charlottesville, Va., 2001—02. Chmn. Bristol Coalition, 2002. Va. Exposition grantee, 1994. Mem.: Internat. Boer Goat Assoc., Va. Forage Coun., Am. Angus Assn. Democrat. Home: 26912 Denton Valley Rd Abingdon VA 24211 Office: Damascus Neighborhood Academy 21308 Monroe Rd Abingdon VA 24236

BALL, ARDELLA PATRICIA, librarian, educator; b. Nashville, Dec. 15, 1932; d. Otis Hugh and Mary Ellen Boatright; m. Wesley James Ball, June 15, 1931; children: Wesley James, Roderic Lynn, Weselyn Lynette, Patrick Wayne. AB, Fisk U., Nashville, 1953; MSLS, Atlanta U., 1956; ScD, Nova U., 1991. Tchr., libr. Fayetteville (Tenn.) H.S., 1954-57; children's libr. N.Y. Pub. Libr., summer 1957; cataloger Ala. A&M U., Huntsville, 1957-59; sr. cataloger St. Louis U., 1960-65; cataloger G.E.L. Regional Libr., Savannah, Ga., 1965-68, Armstrong Atlantic State U., Savannah, 1968-74, instrnl. devel. libr., 1974-77, libr. media educator, 1977—. Author course manuals for core media courses. Mem. Ga. Libr. Assn., Ga. Media Assn. Democrat. Mem. Ch. of Christ. Home: 67 Amanda Dr Savannah GA 31406 Office: Armstrong Atlantic State U 11935 Abercorn St Savannah GA 31419-1909 Office Phone: 912-927-5332. E-mail: ballarde@mail.armstrong.edu.

BALL, ARNETHA, education educator; BA in Edn., U. Mich., 1971, MA in Speech Pathology, 1972; PhD in Lang., Literacy and Culture, Stanford U., 1991. Ethnic studies resource specialist, speech pathologist, classroom tchr. Richmond (Calif.) Unified Sch. Dist., 1972—73; adminstrv. dir., classroom tchr. Children's Creative Workshop, Richmond, 1974—80; classroom tchr. Aurora (Ill.) Elem. Sch., 1984—86; speech pathologist Audiology Assocs. of Dayton, Ohio, 1986—87; external program evaluator L.A. Unified Sch. Dist., 1991—92; postdoctoral fellow U. Mich., 1991—92, asst. prof. edn., 1992—98, assoc. prof. edn., coord. literacy, lang. and culture program, 1998—99; assoc. prof. edn. Stanford (Calif.) U., 1999—. Mem. exec. com. Conf. on Coll. Composition and Comm., 1996—; mem. Standing Com. on Rsch., 1995. Contbr. articles to profl. jours.; mem. editl. bd.: Urban Education, 1996—, Assessing WRiting, 1995. Mem.: Nat. Coun. Tchrs. of English Found. (trustee 1996—), Am. Ednl. Rsch. Assn. (chair divsn. G nominating com. 1998—). Achievements include research in linking sociocultural and linguistic theory with educational practices; linguistic resources; linguistic practices among culturally and linguistically diverse populations. Office: Stanford U Sch Edn 485 Lasuen Mall Stanford CA 94305-309

BALL, BETTY JEWEL, retired social worker, consultant; b. Sherman, Tex., Aug. 9, 1933; d. Emmett Jesse and Ethel Viola (Chesnut) B. BS, Okla. Bapt. U., Shawnee, 1954; M.Religious Edn., Carver Sch., Louisville, 1958; MSW, Smith Coll., Northampton, Mass., 1964. Cert. and lic. clin. social workers, Ill. Psychiat. social worker Inst. for Juvenile Rsch., Chgo., 1964-66; dir. child devel. ctr. Infant Welfare Soc. Chgo., 1966-71; dir. day hosp. for children Madden Mental Health Ctr., Chgo., 1971-78; child and adolescent coord. Ill. Dept. Mental Health, Chgo., 1978-83; pvt. practice social work cons. Hoffman Estates, Ill., 1983-93. Home and Office: 1225 Via Rafael San Marcos CA 92069-7102

BALL, BRENDA JOYCE SIVILS, retired secondary school educator; Tchr., English, AP lit. and writing Pine Bluff High Sch., Ark. Contbr. Named Ark. State English Tchr. of Yr., 1992.

BALL, CAROL J., elementary school educator; b. Baudette, Minn., Sept. 4, 1958; d. Jerome J. and Marian (Horntvedt) Pirkl; m. Harold R. Ball, Jan. 15, 1977; children: Shawn, Lisa. BS magna cum laude, Black Hills State Coll., 1986; MA, St. Scholastica Coll., 2000. Tchr. elem. sch. South Pk. Elem. Sch., SD, 1988—. Mem. NEA, S.D. Edn. Assn. Avocations: reading, travel, gardening. Office: South Pk Elem Sch 207 Flormann St Rapid City SD 57701

BALL, CHAR LEE FRANCES, retired special education educator; b. Seattle, July 13, 1942; d. Charles Herman and Margaret Alice (Cornett) Packer; m. Bobby B. Ball, July 1, 1961; children: Craig Allen, Robert James. Student, Umpqua Community Coll., Roseburg, Oreg., 1970-90, U. Oreg. Finishing sch. tchr. Montgomery Wards, 1960—65; cosmetologist Fairhaven Salon of Beauty, Roseburg, 1960-66, Zee's Beauty Shop, Roseburg, 1966-69; instructional asst. Riverside Sch., Roseburg, 1972-75; instructional asst. Chpt. I Firgrove Elem. Sch., Roseburg, 1975-77, Eastwood Elem. Sch., Roseburg, 1978-86, instructional assistant for emotionally disturbed, 1986—99; ret., 1999. Douglas County chmn. Easter Seals, Roseburg, 1982-87; adult leader Douglas Fir dist. Boy Scouts Am., 1972-80; pres. PTO Riverside Sch., Roseburg, 1974. Mem. Oreg. Sch. Employees Assn., Order Eastern Star (worthy matron 1969-70, 87-88, 96-97, 99-2000, 2000-01, 04-05, 05-06, grand com. mem. 1987, grand rep. to Wyo. 1991-93, grand marshal 1999-2000, Grand Page capt. 2002-03, mem. revision of bylaws com. 2005-), Internat. Grand Rep. Orgn., Epsilon Sigma Alpha (chpt. pres. 1986-87, dist. pres. 1986-87, Woman of Yr. 1983). Democrat. Presbyterian. Avocations: fishing, hunting, arts and crafts, dance, reading. Home: 1560 NE Morris St Roseburg OR 97470-1530

BALL, DEBORAH LOEWENBERG, dean, education educator; BA, Mich. State U., 1976, MA, 1982, postgrad., 1981—83, PhD, 1988. Elementary classroom teacher, 1975—88; mem. faculty Mich. State U., East Lansing, 1988—96; Arthur F. Thurnau prof. U. Mich. Sch. Edn., Ann Arbor, 2000—03, William H. Payne collegiate prof. math., 2003—, interim dean, 2005—. Lead author Stds. for Tchg. sect. Profl. Stds. for Tchg. Math., Nat. Coun. Tchrs. Math., 1989—91; mem. adv. bd. Investigations in Number, Data, Space, 1991—96; mem. Commn. on Behavioral and Social Sci. Edn. Nat. Rsch. Coun., NAS, 1996—99, mem. math. learning study, 1999—2000; chair math. study panel RAND Project: Improving the Quality of Educational Research and Devel., 1999—2000; mem. commn. on undergrad. experience U. Mich., 2000—01; co-chair tchr. edn. study Internat. Commn. on Math. Instrn., 2002—; bd. trustees Math. Scis. Rsch. Inst. U. Calif., Berkeley, 2003—. Contbr. articles to profl. jours.; mem. editl. bd.: Am. Ednl. Rsch. Jour., 1999—, Jour. Ednl. Rsch., 1990—93, Elem. Sch. Jour., 1991—. Recipient Raymond B. Cattell Early Career award for programmatic rsch., Am. Ednl. Rsch. Assn., 1997, Award for outstanding Scholarship on Tchr. Edn., Assn. Colls. and Schs. of Edn. in State Univs. and Land Grant Colls. and Affiliated Pvt. Univs., 1990. Office: U Mich 1110 Sch Edn Bldg 610 E University Ann Arbor MI 48109-1259

BALL, HEATHER L., special education educator, consultant; d. Stephen James and Cheryl Ann George; m. Meredyth James Ball, Aug. 12, 2000. BA, RI Coll., 1994; MS in Edn., Duquesne U., 1998; cert. of advanced study, U. Maine, 2003. Cert. ednl. specialist Maine, tchr. students with disabilities Maine, tchr. Maine. Faculty U. Phoenix, 2002—; lectr. U. Maine, Machias, 2002—, spl. edn. program coord., 2005—. Ednl. cons. Garrity Andrews LLC, Hampden, Maine, 2004—; info. specialist Autism Soc. of Maine, Winthrop, 2004—. Mem.: ASCD (assoc.), Maine Administrators of Svcs. for Children with Disabilities (assoc.), Coun. for Exceptional Children (assoc.), Pi Lambda Theta (assoc.). Office: Univ Maine 9 O'Brien Ave Machias ME Office Phone: 207-255-1381. Business E-Mail: hball@maine.edu.

BALL, JOYCE, retired university librarian and dean; b. N.J., Oct. 31, 1932; d. Frank Geza and Elizabeth Martha (Hopper) Csaposs; m. Robert S. Ball, Sept. 10, 1955; children: Stephanie, Valerie, Steven Robert; m. Stefan B. Moses, Mar. 30, 1980. AB, Rutgers U., 1954; MA, Ind. U., 1959; MBA, Golden Gate U., San Francisco, 1979. Fgn. documents librarian Stanford U., 1955-66; head documents librarian, then head reference div. U. Nev., Reno, 1966-75, head public services, 1975-80; univ. librarian Calif. State U., Sacramento, 1980-87. Mem. Nev. Gov's Adv. Council on Libraries, 1974-78; mem. panel judges Am. Book Awards, 1980; mem. adv. bd. U.S. Dept. Edn. project Libraries and The Learning Soc., 1983-84. Editorial bd.: Coll. and Research Libraries, 1975-80; Contbr. articles to profl. jours. Recipient Louise Maxwell award Sch. Library and Info. Sci. Alumni of Ind. U., 1984. Mem. Assn. Coll. and Research Libraries (dir., pres. 1983-84), ALA. Democrat.

BALL, KATHLEEN M., mathematics educator; b. Cambridge, Mass., Apr. 25, 1951; d. Charles and Louise Delima Ball; children: Shawn M Dumas, Jonathan M Dumas, Jennifer R Dumas. MS in Tech., Lesley U., Cambridge, Mass., 2001. Cert. tchr. math. Fla., 2006. Math. tchr. Cathedral H.S., Springfield, Mass., 1988—98, West Springfield H.S., Mass., 1998—2002, Gulf Coast H.S., Naples, Fla., 2002—04, Palmetto Ridge H.S., Naples, 2004—. Union rep. CCEA, Naples, 2004—06. Home: 18214 Heather Rd Fort Myers FL 33912 Office: Palmetto Ridge High School 1655 Victory Ln Naples FL 34120 E-mail: ballka@collier.k12.fl.us.

BALL, MARION JOKL, academic administrator; b. South Africa; d. Ernst and Erica Jokl. Student, Northwestern U., 1957-58; BA in Math. with distinction, U. Ky., 1961, MA in Math., 1965; EdD, Temple U., 1978. Math tchr. Bryan Station High Sch., Lexington, Ky., 1961-62; programmer, instr. dept. behavioral sci., and computer sci. U. Ky. Med. Ctr., Lexington, 1965-68; asst. dir., med. computer activity, asst. prof. Temple U., Phila., 1968-72; dir. computer systems and mgmt. group, assoc. prof. Temple U. Health Scis. Ctr., Phila., 1972-85; dir. acad. computing U. Md., Baltimore, 1985-87, assoc. v.p. info. resources, prof., 1985-91; v.p. Info. Svcs. U. Maryland, 1991—; adj. prof. sch. nursing Johns Hopkins U., Baltimore; v.p. clin. solutions divsn. Healthlink Inc., Houston, 2001—. Bd. dirs. Intellimed, CliniCom, Inc., 1986-88; panel mem. Nat. Libr. Medicine, 1985-86, 1988—; adv. bd. Systems Dimensions Ltd., 1974-75, Nat. Assn. Hosp. Admitting Mgrs., 1983-85, Sperry Corp., 1984—, MEAD Co., 1985, Office Tech. Assessment, 1987, Educom Consulting Group, 1988-89; chmn. Am. Med. Informatics Assn. Transition Task Force on Membership, 1989; chmn. Am. Med. Informatics Assn. internat. affairs com.; U.S. rep. MEDINFO, 1983—, MEDINFO scientific program com., 1989—; rsch. devel. com. Am. Med. Record Assn., 1978-83; mem. tech. subcom. com. on improving patient records, Inst. Medicine, co chair, 1989-91; cons. in field. Author: Selecting a Computer System for the Clinical Laboratory, 1971, What is AComputer?, 1972, How to Select a Computerized Hospital Information System, 1973; author: (with S Charp) Be a Computer Lieterate!, 1978, author: (with K. Hannah)Using Computers in Nursing (nursing book yr. award 1985), 1984; author: (with others) Healthcare Information Management Systems: A Practical Guide, 1990, New Hospital Information Systems, 1988, Nursing Informatics: Where Caring and Technology Meet, 1988, Cancer Informatics: Essential Technologies for Clinical Trials, 2002. Fellow NSF, Phila. Coll. Physicians. Mem. Am. Med. Informatics Assn. (Morris F. Collen Award, 2002), Am. Assn. for Med. Systems and Informatics, Am. Hosp. Assn., Am. Med. Records Assn., Internat. Med. Informatics Assn. (pres. 1992—), Assn. for Computing Machinery, Healthcare Information and Mgmt. Systems Soc. (bd. dirs. 1989-92), Montessori Soc., Network of Women in Computer Tech., Phila. Coll. Physicians, Inst. Medicine (tech. subcom. and bd. dirs. on improving the patient record 1989—, Mortarboard Sr. Woman's Honor Soc., Delta Phi Alpha, Kappa Delta Pi, Phi Mu Eplison; fellow Am. Coll. Med. Informatics, 1984-. Home: Roland Pk N 5706 Coley Ct Baltimore MD 21210-1344 Office: U of Md Info Svcs 100 N Greene St Baltimore MD 21201-1563

BALL, PATRICIA ANN, physician; b. Lockport, N.Y., Mar. 30, 1941; d. John Joseph and Katherine Elizabeth Ball; m. Robert E. Lee, May 18, 1973 (div. 2004); children: Heather Lee, Samantha Lee. BS, U. Mich., 1963; MD, Wayne State U., 1969. Diplomate Am. Bd. Internal Medicine, Am. Bd. Hematology, Am. bd. Med. Oncology. Intern, resident Detroit Gen. Hosp., 1969-71; resident Jackson Meml. Hosp., Miami, Fla., 1971-72; fellow Henry Ford Hosp., Detroit, 1972-74; staff physician VA Hosp., Allen Park, Mich., 1974-77; pvt. practice in hematology and oncology Bloomfield Hills, Mich., 1977—. Faculty dept. medicine Wayne State U. Sch. Medicine, Detroit, 1974—. Mem.: AMA, ACP, Mich. Soc. Hematology and Oncology, Oakland County Med. Soc., Mich. Med. Soc., Detroit Inst. Arts, Founders Soc., Alpha Omega Alpha. Avocations: photography, skiing. Office: 44038 Woodward Ave Ste 101 Bloomfield Hills MI 48302-5036 Office Phone: 248-360-8244. E-mail: pball@dmc.org.

BALL, TERESA SUSAN, secondary school educator; b. Knoxville, Tenn., Aug. 9, 1977; d. Roger Alford and Carol Susan Ball. BA, Emory U., Atlanta, 1998; MEd, Ga. State U., Atlanta, 2001. Tchr. Gwinnett County Pub. Schs., Lawrenceville, Ga., 2001—. Family selection com. mem. Atlanta Habitat for Humanity, 2005—06; ga. to ga. humanitarian missions Peachtree Rd. United Meth. Ch., Atlanta, 2004—06. Mem.: NEA.

BALL, VALDESHA LECHANTE', physician; b. Atlanta, Ga., July 16, 1977; d. Ann English and Theo Warren Ball. BS, Xavier U. La., New Orleans, 1999; MD, Meharry Med. Coll., Nashville, Tenn., 2005. Pres. Meharry Med. Coll. Psychiat. Soc., Nashville, 2000—02; mem. resident program Menninger dept. psychiatry and behavioral scis., psychiatry residency program Baylor Coll. Medicine, 2005—. Coord. Depression Screening - Meharry Med. Coll. Cmty. Day, Nasvhille, Tenn., 2002—03. Vol. Habitat for Humanity, New Orleans, 1996—99, Hands on Nashville Cmty. Svc. Orgn., 2002—03, Mt. Zion Bapt. Ch. Ann. Health Fair, Nashville, 2004. Recipient Rafael Hernandez M.D. award, Dept. of Psychiatry and Behavioral Sciences of Meharry Med. Coll., 2005, Howard Hughes scholar, Xavier U. of LA, 1995—99; Partnership for Sight scholarship, Allergan/Tom Joyner Found., 2003, Atlanta Med. Assn. scholarship, Atlanta Med. Assn., 2001. Mem.: Mary Susan Moore Med. Soc., Nat. Med. Assn., Tex. Soc. Psychiat. Physicians, Am. Med. Student Assn., Student Nat. Med. Assn., Delta Sigma Theta. Home: 8181 Fannin St #2024 Houston TX 77054

BALLANCE, ANN ELIZABETH, elementary school educator, consultant; b. Evanston, Ill., Nov. 8, 1949; d. Lewis Charles Ballance and Mildred Luella Herkner; m. Mark Eugene Crouch (dec.); children: Matthew Paul Crouch, Elizabeth Lynn Crouch; m. Neil Edward DeMarco (div.). BA in English, U. Mich., 1971; MA in Tchg., Northwestern U., 1972. Classroom tchr. Ill., Philippines, Kans., Mo. and Colo. schs., 1971—94; rsch. assoc. Vanderblit U., Nashville, 1994—2000; ednl. cons. Plato Learning, Bloomington, Minn., 2001—03; west regional trainer Leap Frog Sch. House, Emeryville, Calif., 2003—05; nat. literacy cons. Pearsen Achievement Solutions, Glenview, Ill., 2005—. Named Trainer of Yr., Plato Learning, 2001, Leap Frog Sch. House, 2002, 2003. Mem.: ASCD, Nat. Staff Devel. Coun., Internat. Reading Assn. Avocations: reading, theater, gourmet cooking. Office: 8336 Cabin Peak St Las Vegas NV 89123

BALLANTINE, MORLEY COWLES (MRS. ARTHUR ATWOOD BALLANTINE), editor; b. Des Moines, May 21, 1925; d. John and Elizabeth (Bates) Cowles; m. Arthur Atwood Ballantine, July 26, 1947 (dec. 1975); children— Richard, Elizabeth Ballantine Leavitt, William, Helen Ballantine Healy. AB, Ft. Lewis Coll., 1975; LHD (hon.), Simpson Coll., Indianola, Iowa, 1980, U. Denver, 2002. Pub. Durango (Colo.) Herald, 1952-83, editor, pub., 1975-83, editor, chmn. bd., 1983—; dir. 1st Nat. Bank, Durango,

1976—2002, Des Moines Register & Tribune, 1977-85, Cowles Media Co., 1982-86. Mem. Colo. Land Use Commn., 1975-81, Supreme Ct. Nominating Commn., 1984-90; mem. Colo. Forum, 1985—; trustee Choate/Rosemary Hall, Wallingford, Conn., 1973-81, Simpson Coll., Indianola, Iowa, 1981-2002, U. Denver, 1984-2002, Fountain Valley Sch., Colorado Springs, 1976-89, trustee emerita, 1993—; mem. exec. com. Ft. Lewis Coll. Found., 1991—. Recipient 1st place for editl. writing Nat. Fedn. Press Women, 1955, Outstanding Alumna award Rosemary Hall, Greenwich, Conn., 1969, Outstanding Journalism award U. Colo. Sch. Journalism, 1967, Disting. Svc. award Ft. Lewis Coll., Durango, 1970, Athena award Female Cmty. Leader, 1997; named to Colo. Cmty. Journalism Hall of Fame, 1987, Colo. Bus. Hall of Fame, 2002; named Citizen of Yr., Durango Area Chamber Resort Assn., 1990, Colo. Philanthropist of Yr. Colo. Assn. Found./Assn. Fundraising Profls., 2000, Bonfils-Stanton Found. award, 2002. Mem. Nat. Soc. Colonial Dames, Colo. Press Assn. (bd. dirs. 1978-79), Colo. AP Assn. (chmn. 1966-67), Federated Women's Club Durango, Mill Reef Club (Antigua, W.I.) (bd. govs. 1985-91). Episcopalian. Address: care Durango Herald PO Drawer A Durango CO 81302

BALLANTYNE, MAREE ANNE CANINE, artist; b. Sydney, NSW, Australia, Oct. 22, 1945; came to U.S., 1946; d. Charles Venice and Yvonne Mavis (McSpeerin) Canine; m. Kent McFarlane Ballantyne, Apr. 22, 1967; children: Christopher Kent, Joel Sokson. AA, Del Mar Coll., 1966; BA in English, U. Tex., 1971; postgrad., U. South Ala., 1974, U. Houston, 1981, Sonoma State U., 1982, 84, 85. Exhibited paintings in Mass., Tex., Ala.; creator logo for Gulf Coast Area Childbirth Edn. Assn., 1972, logo for Calif. Health Resources, 1985; contbr. articles to profl. jours. Charter mem. Gulf Coast Area Childbirth Edn. Assn., Mobile, Ala., 1971-76; mem. Mus. Guild, Corpus Christi, 1978-80, Art Mus., Mobile, 1972-76, Nat. Trust for Hist. Preservation, 1977-80. Recipient Cert. Appreciation, USCG, 1993, Letter of Appreciation USCG, 1993. Mem. Nat. Mus. Women in Arts (charter). Avocations: reading about poet and artist william blake, women artists and literature, raising tropical plants, creating hand-painted greeting cards. Home: 1920 SW 56th Ave Plantation FL 33317-5938

BALLARD, ERNESTA, lumber company executive; BA, U. Pa.; MA, MBA, Harvard U. Regional adminstr. Pacific NW EPA, 1983—86; CEO Cape Fox Corp., 1989-94; founder, prin. Ballard & Assocs., Ketchikan, Alaska, 1994-97; commr., Dept. Environ. Conservation State of AK, Juneau, 2002—04; sr. v.p. corp. affairs Weyerhaeuser Co., Federal Way, Wash., 2004—. Mem. bd. govs. U.S. Postal Svc., Washington, 1997—2005. Bd. dirs. Alaska Forest Assn., S.E. Alaska Regional Aquaculture Assn., Ketchikan Gen. Hosp., LifeCenter NW. Office: Weyerhaeuser Co PO Box 9777 Federal Way WA 98063-9777

BALLARD, KAYE, actress; b. Cleve. d. Vincent James Balotta. Actress (broadway shows) Carnival, Molly, Pirates of Pennzance, Golden Apple, Over the River and Through the Woods!, (road shows) Three to Make Ready, Wonderful Town, Gypsy, (with Sandy Dennis) Odd Couple, (movies) Ritz, House is Not a Home, Eternity, Which Way the Front, Modern Love, Tiger Warsaw, Falling in Love Again, Freaky Friday, The Girl Most Likely, Baby Genius, (TV shows) Mothers-in-Law, Doris Day Show, (plays) Over the River and Through the Woods, 1999, Arci's Place, 2000; 150 appearances and many guest appearances on different shows; recording (with Jaye P. Morgan) Jaye & Kaye, Long Time Friends; appeared at White House, 2 command performances in Eng. (Steven Sondheim record with all-star cast) Follies, Unsung Sondheim; (CD) The Ladies Who Wrote the Lyrics (with Arthur Siegel). Office: PO Box 922 Rancho Mirage CA 92270-0922

BALLARD, LAURA CLAY, small business owner; b. Biloxi, Miss., June 29, 1951; d. Elbert Homer Jr. and Jacqueline May (Giblin) Clay; m. Steven Anthony Register (div. Apr. 1982); 1 child, Steven Scott; m. Frank James Butscher, Aug. 20, 1982 (div. Nov. 2000); m. Raymond Michael Ballard, Oct. 7, 2001. AS in Bus. Adminstrn., Jefferson State Jr. Coll., 1986; BS Social and Behavioral Sci. cum laude, U. Ala., 1987. Teletype operator Blue Cross Blue Shield, Columbus, Ga., 1971-72, asst. supr. data control, 1972-77; mgr. data processing So. Foods, Inc., Columbus, 1977-80, Zurn Industries, Birmingham, Ala., 1980-85; pres. Maid for All Seasons, Inc., Birmingham, 1989-92; owner ViZual Studio, Trussville, Ala., 1993—, Columbus, Ohio, 1993—; realtor Century 21 and Realty South, Trussville, 1997-99; customer rels. mgr. Jay Toyota, 2000—02; dir. customer rels. The Maids, Birmingham, 2002; adminstr. customer rels. L. Kianoff & Assocs., Birmingham, 2002—04. Avocations: gardening, photography, golf, birdwatching, computers. Home: 6275 Brookstone Blvd Columbus GA 31904-2962 Personal E-mail: laura@lauraclayballard.com.

BALLARD, LINDA CHRISTINE, financial aid director; b. Houston, Aug. 19, 1959; d. Roosevelt Larue Sr. and Helen Ruth B.; 1 child, Alexandria Nickole Ballard-Demming. BBA, U. Houston, 1982; MBA, U. Phoenix, 2006. Data control supr. U. Houston, 1982-85, data entry supr., 1985-87, fin. aid. counselor, 1987-92, U. St. Thomas, Houston, 1992-93, dir. fin. aid, 1993—2000; dir. fin. aid and vet. affairs U. Houston at Clear Lake, Tex., 2000—01; dir. fin. aid Tex. So. U., Houston, 2001—. Chair sexual harassment com. U. Houston, 1991-93; mem. staff devel. com. U. St. Thomas, 1993-96, mem. data mgrs. com., 1995-97, 99, mem. scholar com., 1994-99, mem. enrollment mgmt. com., 1998-2000; mem. early awareness com. Tex. Assn. Fin. Aid Adminstrn., 2000—; presenter in field. Dir. youth dept. Greater True Vine Ch.; deacon New Hope Cmty. Ch. Mem. Nat. Assn. Fin. Aid Adminstrs., Tex. Assn. Fin. Aid Adminstrs. (early awareness com. 2000—), Nat. Coalition Builders Inst. (train the trainer). Avocations: high school awareness programs, travel, financial aid compliance issues, workshops in field. Home: 5326 Linden Chase Ln Houston TX 77066-3218 Office: Texas Southern University 3100 Cleburne Houston TX 77004

BALLARD, MARY MELINDA, corporate communications specialist, consumer products company executive; b. Sikeston, Mo., Apr. 21, 1958; d. Claude M. and Mary (Birnbach) B.; m. Emil Pena, Jan. 1, 1989 (div. July 1990); m. Ronald C. Allison, Oct. 1994; 1 child, Reese Colton Allison. BA, Monmouth U., 1976; MBA, NYU, 1980; postgrad., Columbia U. V.p. corp. comm. United Brands Co., N.Y.C., 1976—79; v.p. mktg. Oscar de la Renta Ltd., 1979—81; pres., CEO Ficom Internat., Inc., N.Y.C., 1981—89; exec. v.p. Ruder Finn Inc., N.Y.C., 1989—; dir., CEO MBP Interests Inc., 1989—; ptnr. Affinity Ins. Advisors, 2003—, Kamero Ptnrs., 1994—; pres. Policyholders of Am., 2002—; officer, dir. Tex. Interlock Corp., 1995—96; exec. v.p., CFO Millenium Tech. Transfer, Inc., 1996—; dir. Capital Bank, 1994—, officer, 1997—; ptnr. Affinity Ins. Advisors, LLP, 2004—. Bd. dirs. Reese Colton Enterprises, Inc., Millenium Tech. Transfer, Inc., Nat. Coun. Real Estate Investment Fiduciaries, Capital Bancshares; pres. Policyholders of Am., 2002—; mem. adv. bd. Tex. Tech U., 2002—; cons., ins. adviser. Contbr. articles to profl. jours. Trustee Ballard Family Found., Children's Aid Soc.; exec. mem. Tex. Dem. Roundtable, 1994—. Recipient CLIO Ann. Report award Fin. World, 1984, 86. Mem. Internat. Assn. Bus. Communicators (Golden Quill 1984), Pub. Investor Relsa. Inst. Methodist. Avocations: collecting art, thoroughbred race horses, ranching. Home and Office: 15 Orange St Charleston SC 29401 Personal E-mail: mballardal@aol.com.

BALLARD, ROBERTA A., pediatrician, educator; AB in Chemistry, Earlham Coll., 1061; MD, U. Chgo., 1965. Diplomate Am. Bd. Pediat., Am. Bd. Neonatal Medicine, Am. Bd. Neonatal and Perinatal Medicine (chmn. 1992-95). Intern, then resident in pediat. U. Chgo. Hosps., 1965-67; resident in pediat. Stanford (Calif.) U., 1967-68; fellow in neonatology George Washington U. Hosp., Washington, 1968-69; fellow Cardiovasc. Rsch. Inst., 1970-72; acting dir. newborn svcs., instr. pediat. George Washington U. Hosp., Washington, 1969-70; dir. newborn svcs. Mt. Zion Med. Ctr.-U. Calif., San Francisco, 1972-90, chief dept. pediat., 1975-90, asst. clin. prof. pediat., 1973-75, adj. asst. prof., 1975-87, adj. assoc. prof., 1985-88, prof., 1988-91; chief div. neonatology dept. pediat. Children's Hosp. Phila., 2004; dir. neonatology and newborn svcs. Hosp. of U. Pa., Phila., 1994—2004; prof. pediat.-ob-gyn., dir. neonatology fellowship progrram U. Pa. Sch. Medicine, 1991—2004. Mem. panel for consensus devel. infantile apnea and home monitoring NIH, 1986-87; mem. adv. bd. neonatal network Nat. Inst. Child Health and Human Devel., 1991—. Editor: Pediatric Care of the ICN Graduate, 1988, (with W. Taeusch) Schaffer and Avery's Diseases of the Newborn, 6th edit., 1991, 8th edit., 2004; reviewer Pediat., Jour. Pediat., Jour. Perinatology, Pediat. Pulmonology, Pediat. Rsch., New Eng. Jour. Medicine, Am. Jour. Ob-gyn., Archives Pediat. and Adolescent Medicine; mem. editl. bd. Contemporary Pediat.; contbr. articles to profl. jours. Grantee, NIH, 1993—. Mem. Am. Acad. Pediat., Soc. for Pediat. Rsch., Am. Pediatric Soc. Achievements include research on prevention and treatment of respiratory diseases in the newborn, antenatal steroids, chronic lung disease, inhaled nitric oxide to prevent chronic lung disease. Office: Childrens Hosp Phila 3535 Market Ste 1584 Philadelphia PA 19104-4399 E-mail: ballard@email.chop.edu.

BALLARD, SUSAN DOYON, library director; d. Alfred O. and Mary M. Doyon; m. Roger P. Ballard, June 28, 1985. BA in English Lit., U. NH, 1974; MS in Libr. and Info. Sci., Simmons Coll., 1975. Media Supervisor Dept. of Edn., NH, 1978, Computer Technology Educator Dept. of Edn., NH, 2000. Dist. libr. Londonderry (NH) Sch. Dist., 1975—78, media coord., 1978—85, dir., libr. and media svcs., 1985—95, dir., libr. media and tech. svcs., 1995—; instr. Fitchburg (Mass.) State Coll., 1984, Plymouth (NH) State Coll., 1989; adj. faculty Rivier Coll., Nashua, NH, 2003—. Editor: (book) The Count on Reading Handbook. Mem. Thomson Gale Adv. Bd., 2004—, H.W. Wilson Libr. Adv. Panel, 2004—. Named to Hall of Fame, Londonderry H.S., 1987; recipient NH Excellence in Edn. award for Ednl. Media, NH Dept. of Edn., 1994, Commitment to Excellence in Edn., Greater Manchester Chamber of Commerce, 2001. Mem.: ASCD, NH Ednl. Media Assn. (pres. 1992—93, Outstanding Svc. award 1994, Pres.'s award 1997), NH. Libr. Assn., New Eng. Ednl. Media Assn. (pres. 1994—95), Internat. Soc. for Tech. in Edn., Assn. for Ednl. Comm. and Tech., Am. Assn. of Sch. Librarians (sec. 1993—96, Nat. Sch. Libr. Media Program of Yr. 2000), NH Soc. for Tech. in Edn., Gamma Delta Epsilon, Alpha Xi Delta. Office: Londonderry Sch Dist 268 Mammoth Rd Londonderry NH 03053 Office Phone: 603-432-6920 ext. 108. Business E-Mail: sballard@londonderry.org.

BALLARIAN, ANNA NEVARTE, retired art educator; b. Rochester, NY, Aug. 15, 1910; d. Aram M. and Adelina (Essayan) B. Design Diploma, Rochester Athenaeum (now RIT), 1930; BS in Art Edn., NYU, 1935; MA in Fine Arts, Alfred U., 1941; MA in Fine Art, Columbia U., 1949; postgrad., Alfred U. Art supr. and tchr. Rochester Pub. Schs.; art and craft prof. Columbia U., N.Y.C., 1946-47; artist, tchr. in residence Art Ctr., Cannon Beach, Oreg., 1967-68; asst. prof. U. Idaho, 1948; vis. prof. U. B.C., Can., 1964, Calif. State U., Hayward, 1970; prof. art, dir. SUNY, Plattsburgh, 1948-57; prof. art Calif. State U., San Jose, 1957-77; adv. for artist residency program Villa Montalvo, Saratoga, Calif., 1977-99. Author book on fabric collage; contbr. articles to mags.; exhibited works at N.Y. Craft Mus., 1973, San Francisco Mus. Art, Rochester Meml. Art Gallery, and in pvt. shows. Mem. Nat. League Am. Pen Women Inc. (dir. fine arts), Phi Kappa Phi, Delta Kppa Gamma (treas.). Christian. Avocations: painting, crafts, calligraphy, piano music, sports (skiing, tennis, hiking).

BALLENTINE, ROSALIE SIMMONDS, former attorney general; Atty. gen., St. Thomas, V.I.

BALLESTEROS, PAULA MITCHELL, nurse; b. Jonesport, Maine, Oct. 18, 1950; d. Paul Frederick and Janice Madeline (Beal) Mitchell; m. Ernesto Gascon Ballesteros, Apr. 4, 1981; children: Christopher, Jonathan. BS in Profl. Arts, St. Joseph's Coll., 1984; BSN, Husson/Ea. Me. Med. Ctr. Baccalaureate Sch. Nursing, 1994; MS in Bus., Husson Coll., 2004. Cert. Nursing Adminstrn. Patient care mgr. Eastern Maine Med. Ctr., Bangor, 1974—, trustee, 1993-95. Chairperson adv. bd. Ea. Maine Tech. Coll., Bangor, Me., 1993-94; pres. Me. Coun. Nurse Mgrs., 1991-93, Ea. Me. Med. Ctr. auxiliary, Bangor, Me., 1993-95. Contbr. articles to profl. jours. Mem. St. Joseph Hosp. Auxiliary. Mem. Am. Orgn. Nurse Execs., Penobscot Med. Soc. Auxiliary, Me. Assn. Hosp. Auxiliaries (pres. 1994—). Democrat. Protestant. Avocations: skiing, tennis, reading. Home: 78 Packard Dr Bangor ME 04401-2531 Office: Ea Maine Med Ctr 489 State St Bangor ME 04401-6616 Office Phone: 207-973-7371. Business E-Mail: pballesteros@emh.org.

BALLEW, KATHY I., controller; b. Sterling, Colo., Mar. 31, 1958; d. Arthur LeRoy Nelson and Dixie Irene Mann; m. Mark Ballew, Dec. 12, 1975 (div. Sept. 23, 1999); children: Mark Douglas, Amanda Jo. Revenue audit Red Lion Casino, Elko, Nev., 1988, accounts payable, 1988, accounts receivable, 1988—89, office mgr., 1990—95, contr. Winnemucca Properties, 1995—99, contr. McClaskey Properties, 1999—. Avocations: fishing, camping, crafts. Home: 1910 Ruby View Dr Elko NV 89801

BALLEW, LAURIE K., psychiatrist; b. Magnolia, Miss. d. J.E. and Elsie W. Ballew. BS, MS, Murray State U., 1972; EdD, Vanderbilt U., 1983; DO, Univ. Osteopathic Med., Des Moines, 1994. Speech pathologist Pennyroyal MH-MR Ctr., Hopkinsville, Ky., 1972-73, JAMP Spl. Edn., Olmstead, Ill., 1973-80; program devel. assoc. Murray State U., Murray, Ky., 1980-81; pvt. practice speech pathology Paducah, Ky., 1981-90; intern Broadlawns Med. Ctr., Des Moines, 1994-95; resident U. Louisville, 1995-98; psychiatrist Communicare, Inc., Leitchfield, Ky., 1998-2000; asst. prof. U. Louisville, 2000—. Co-dir. GERO psychiatry, dir. adult ADHD svcs. U. Louisville Hosp. Mem. Am. Psych. Assn., AMA, Ky. Med. Psychiat. Assn. (pres. 2003-04), Ky. Psychiat. Assn., Jefferson County Med. Soc. Avocations: reading, music, gardening, old movies. Office: 5 East Psychiatry 530 S Jackson St Louisville KY 40202-1675 also: 5 East Psychiatry 530 S Jackson St Louisville KY 40202-1675

BALLIF-SPANVILL, BONNIE, psychologist, educator; BS with honors, Brigham Young U., 1962, PhD with distinction, 1966. Asst. rschr. R&D Ctr. U. Hawaii, Honolulu, 1966—68; with Fordham U. Grad. Sch. at Lincoln Ctr., N.Y.C., 1968—93, dir. Ctr. for Applied Motivation Rsch., 1975—84, coord. ednl. psychology and rsch. programs, 1979—83, 1985—87, chair divsn. psychology and edn. svcs., 1987—90; prof. psychology Brigham Young U., Provo, Utah, 1994—, dir. Women's Rsch. Inst., 1994—, mem. various univ. coms., 1994—. Cons. U.S. Govt., 1965—72, The Delphi Rsch. Group, N.Y.C., 1976—89; presenter in field. Contbr. articles to profl. jours. Recipient Bene Merenti award, 1988. Fellow: APA, Am. Psychol. Soc.; mem.: AAUW, Consortium on Peace, Rsch., Edn. and Devel., Nat. Women's Studies Assn., Assn. for Women in Devel., Internat. Peace Rsch. Assn., Phi Kappa Phi. Office: Brigham Young Univ 1063 JFSB Provo UT 84602

BALLMAN, PATRICIA KLING, lawyer; b. Cin., May 1, 1946; d. John Joseph and Margaret Elizabeth (Stacy) Kling; children: Andrew J., Cara E. BS with honors, St. Louis U., 1967; JD with honors, Marquette U., 1977. Bar: Wis. 1977, U.S. Dist. Ct. (ea. and we. dist Wis.) 1980, U.S. Ct. Appeals (7th Cir.) 1983, U.S. Ct. Appeals (8th Cir.) 1986, U.S. Supreme Ct. 1986. Ptnr. Quarles & Brady, Milw., 1977—. Officer lawyer regulation Dist. II Com. Mem. fin. divsn., chair pers. subcom. United Way, 2000—02; past chair Shorewood Bd. of Rev.; mem. Gov.'s Task Force on Ethics Reform in Govt., 2002; bd. dirs. The Benedict Ctr., 2004—, Wis. Law Found. Master: Fairchild Inns of Ct.; mem.: ABA, Am. Acad. Matrimonial Lawyers (pres. Wis. chpt. 2002—04), Wis. Bar Assn. (pres. 2002—03), Milw. Bar Assn. (pres. 1995—96). Office: Quarles & Brady 411 E Wisconsin Ave #2040 Milwaukee WI 53202-4461 Office Phone: 414-277-5000. E-mail: pkb@quarles.com.

BALLONE, EILEEN MARIE, music educator, musician, organist; b. Hackensack, N.J., May 6, 1946; d. Frank Albert and Marie Lillian (Mancini) Caiazzo; m. Henry Frederick Ballone, May 4, 1968; children: Brian James, Marie Elena. BA in Elem. Edn., Caldwell Coll., 1986; MS in Elem. Edn., Marywood Coll., 1992; student, Fairleigh Dickinson U., 1965—66, Bergen C.C., Paramus, N.J., 1979—81. Liturgically cert. musician Archdiocese Newark; cert. elem. edn. tchr., nursery sch. tchr. N.J. Pvt. organ tchr., 1963—; with N.J. Bell Tel. Co., 1967—68, Am. Book-Stratford Press, INc., Saddle Brook, NJ, 1968—70; music tchr. Sacred Heart Sch., Rochelle Park, NJ, 1979—84, Annunciation Sch., Paramus, NJ, 1981—83, St. Anne's Sch., Fair Lawn, NJ, 1983—85, St. Philip the Apostle Sch., Saddle Brook, 1984—86; music tchr. grades K-8 St. Francis Assisi Elem. Sch., Ridgefield Park, NJ, 1986—; music tchr., chair music dept. Paramus Cath. Girls Regional H.S., 1986—90; music tchr. grades K-8 St. Leo's Elem. Sch., Elmwood Park, NJ, 1990—91, St. Philip the Apostle Elem. Sch., Saddle Brook, 1999—2000. Organist, choir dir. St. Michael's Ch., Palisades Park, NJ, 1967—77; asst. organist St. Margaret Cortona Ch., Little Ferry, NJ, 1978—84, St. Philip the Apostle Ch., Saddle Brook, 1978—84, head organist, 1984—86; dir. music, organist, choir dir. Our Lady Queen of Peace Ch., Maywood, NJ, 1987—99; dir., organist children's choir St. Francis Assisi Ch., Ridgefield Park, 1999—2003, dir. children's bell choir, 2000, dir., organist, choir dir., 2000—02; dir. music, organist, choir dir. St. Margaret Cortona Roman Cath. Ch., Little Ferry, 2002—. Den mother Cub Scouts Pack 222 St. Philip the Apostle Parish, Saddle Brook; com. mem. Brownie Troop 772 St. Philip the Apostle Parish, Saddle Brook; v.p. St. Philip the Apostle Home-Sch. Assn., Saddle Brook, 1977—79, pres., 1979—83. Mem.: Nat. Pastoral Musicians Assn. (pres. 2004—), Am. Fedn. Musicians, Nat. Assn. Pastoral Musicians (pres. music edn. divsn. 2004—, chpt. mem., dirs. music ministry divsn.), Choristers Guild, N.J. Music Edn. Assn., Music Educators Nat. Conf., Nat. Cath. Edn. Assn. Roman Catholic. Home: 23 Rochelle Pkwy Saddle Brook NJ 07663-4616 Office Phone: 201-641-9159. Personal E-mail: musicmomemb@yahoo.com.

BALLOU-PORTZ, CYNTHIA CELENE, music educator; b. Mpls., Oct. 12, 1947; d. William Houghtaling and Bernice Leola (Briggs) Ballou; 1 child, Frederick William Portz. BS in Music, Mankato State Coll., Minn., 1970; BS in Edn., Mankato State U., 1973. Vocal music tchr. K-12 Tiskilwa (Ill.) Pub. Schs., 1970—71; vocal music tchr. K-6 Rockford Sch. Dist., 1973—75, Pipestone Area Schs., Pipestone, Minn., 1975—. Music adjudicator Minn. State H.S., Pipestone County, 2001—; chairperson staff devel. Ind. Sch. Dist. 2689, Pipestone, 2000—04; mem. Nat. Staff Devel. Coun., Marshall, Minn., 1997—99. Choir dir. First Luth. Ch., Pipestone, 1995—; asst. dir., mem. Al Opland Singers, Pipestone, 1978—89; bd. dirs. Hiawatha Manor, Inc., Pipestone; bd. dirs. and dir. Pipestone Children's Theater, 1990. Mem.: Minn. Music Educators Conf., Edn. Minn., Music Educators Nat. Conf. Avocations: historical re-enactment, camping, travel, reading, gardening. Home: 712 S Hiawatha Ave Pipestone MN 56164 Office: Pipestone Area Schools 1401 7th St SW Pipestone MN 56164 Office Phone: 507-825-6763.

BALLS, TEDRA MERRILL, secondary school educator; b. Logan, Idaho, Mar. 18, 1948; d. Lyman Wood and Norma Murdock Merrill; m. Mack Wayne Balls, Mar. 18, 1968; children: Heidi Gae Luker, Nicholas Lyman, Katie Jill. BA, Idaho State U., Pocatello, 1985. Cert. tchr. Idaho. Mid. sch. English tchr. Sch. Dist. 25, Pocatello, 1985—99, ap English, journalism tchr., adv., 1999—. Office: Century High Sch 7801 Diamondback Dr Pocatello ID 83204 Office Phone: 208-478-6863. Personal E-mail: ballste@d25.k12.id.us.

BALL-SARET, JAYNE ADAMS, small business owner; b. East St. Louis, Ill., Apr. 10, 1956; d. H. Jay and Faye M. (Adams) Ball; m. Mitchell I. Saret. BA, Ea. Ill. U., 1977, MA, 1983. Interior designer Carter's Furniture, Charleston, Ill., 1977-85; from customer svc. advisor to dir. client svc. Consol. Comm., Mattoon and Charleston, 1985—94; owner, designer Grand Ball Costumes, 1985—. Pres., dir. Charleston Cmty. Theatre, 1983—85. Mem.: Phi Alpha Eta. Republican. Avocations: singing, directing, acting, sewing. Office: Grand Ball Costumes 609 6th St Charleston IL 61920-2018 Office Phone: 217-345-2617.

BALMASEDA, LIZ, columnist; b. Puerto Padre, Cuba, Jan. 17, 1959; AA, Miami-Dade (Fla.) C.C., 1979; BS Comm., Fla. Internat. U., 1981. Intern Miami Herald, Fla., 1980, with Spanish lang. publ. Fla., 1981, gen. assignment reporter Fla., feature writer Fla., 1987, with Sunday Mag. tropic Fla., 1990, columnist Fla., 1991—; ctrl. Am. bur. chief Newsweek, El Salvador, 1985; freelance columnist NBC News, Honduras. Appeared on NBC Today Show, Oprah show. Recipient 2d place Ernie Pyle award Scripps Howard Found, 1984, 3d place feature writing Fla. Soc. Newspaper Editors, 1st prize Guillermo Martinez-Marquez contest Nat. Assn. Hispanic Journalists., 1989, Pulitzer Prize for commentary, 1993, 1st prize commentary Fla. Soc. Newspaper editors. Office: The Miami Herald One Herald Plaza Miami FL 33132

BALM-DEMMEL, DARLINE DAWN, retired minister; b. Marshall, Minn., Dec. 16, 1933; d. Russell Neil and Laura Esther (Seiler) Miller; m. Thomas Ree Balm, Apr. 15, 1954 (div. Dec. 1981); children: Stephen Paul, Jonathon Mark, Brian Scott, Michelle Dawn; m. Gary Harold Demmel, June 28, 1987; stepchildren: Matthew, Tanya. BA, Westmar Coll., 1954; MA, U. No. Iowa, Cedar Falls, 1968; postgrad., State U. Iowa, 1977—79; MDiv, U. Dubuque Theol. Sem., 1987. Cert. secondary tchr., Iowa; ordained to ministry United Meth. Ch. as deacon, 1987, as elder, 1990. Tchr. elem. Lisle Pub. Sch., Ill., 1954—55, substitute tchr., 1956—61; tchr. English, coach speech and drama, libr. Kee H.S., Lansing, Iowa, 1961—63; tchr. Dysart, Iowa, 1964—69; instr. English Westmar Coll., LeMars, Iowa, 1970—76, recruiter, 1976—77; rsch. asst. U. Iowa, Iowa City, 1978; receptionist, sec. Wesley Found., Iowa City, 1978—79; promotion adminstr. Ctrl.-0-Fax Corp., Waterloo, Iowa, 1980—81, coord. mktg. promotion, 1981—86; sec. dist. supt. Dubuque Dist. United Meth. Ch., Iowa, 1985—86; pastor United Meth. Ch., Sherrill, Iowa and East Dubuque, Ill., 1986—94; dist. supt. Sioux City Dist. United Meth. Ch., Iowa, 1994—2001; asst. to bishop Iowa United Meth. Ch., 2001—04; ret., 2004; supt. Mason City dist. United Meth. Ch., 2006—. Bd. dirs. Morningside Coll., Sioux City, 1994—2000, Shesler Hall, Sioux City, 1994—2001, Okiboji United Meth. Camp, Iowa, 1994—2001; vice chmn. Dist. Coun. Ministries, United Meth. Ch., Waterloo, 1984—86; cons. Home Interiors and Gifts, LeMars, 1972—76. Mem.: LWV (pres. Blackhawk-Bremer counties chpt. 1983—85, pres. Dubuque County chpt. 1992—94, fin. chmn., pres. LeMars chpt., publicity chmn., 2d v.p.), AAUW. Democrat. Avocations: reading, piano, travel, theater, walking. Home: 603 W 9th St Cedar Falls IA 50613 E-mail: dargar@cfu.net.

BALMORI, DIANA, landscape designer; b. Gijon, Spain, June 4, 1936; d. Clemente and Dorothy (Ling) Hernando-Balmori. Diploma in architecture, U. Tucuman, Argentina, 1960; BA in Urban History, UCLA, 1968, PhD, 1973; student in Landscaping, Radcliffe U., 1989. Asst. prof. SUNY, Oswego, 1974-78, assoc. prof., 1978-79; assoc. Cesar Pelli & Assocs., New Haven, 1977-81, prin. for landscape and urban design, 1981-90; prin. Balmori Assocs., New Haven, 1990—; critic Yale U. Sch. Architecture, 1990—; lectr. Yale U. Sch. Forestry and Environ. Studies, 1990—; Davenport Chair of Archtl. Design Yale Sch. of Architecture, 2004. Apptd. mem. Commn. Fine Arts, 2003. Author: Beatrix Farrand, Beatrix Jones Ferrand (1872-1959) Fifty Years Of American Landscape Architecture, 1982, Beatrix Farrand's American Landscapes, 1985, Transitory Gardens, Uprooted Lives, 1993, Redesigning the American Lawn, 1993, Saarinen House and Garden: A Total Work of Art, 1995; contbr. Beatrix Farrand At Dumbarton Oaks: The Design Process of a Garden; co-author: The Land and Natural Development (LAND) Code: Guidelines for Environmentally Sustainable Land Development. Chmn. civic alliance World Trade Ctr. Meml. Com., N.Y.C.; mem. program com. N.Y. New Visions; bd. dirs. Minetta Brook Com. for Comprehensive Design Landscape Plan for White Ho. Recipient Pub. Space award Conn. chpts. AIA/Am. Soc. Landscape Architects, 1990, Judges award Harry Chapin Media Aawards, 1995; grantee Ossabaw Found., 1980, N.Y. State Coun Arts, 1987, Carolyn Found., 1990, Nat. Endowment for the Arts, 1990, 92; rsch. fellow NYU, 1982. Mem. Am. Soc. Landscape Architects, Catalog of Landscape Records (bd. dirs.), Van Alen Inst. (mem. exec. com.), Am. Hist. Assn. Office: Balmori Assocs 820 Greenwich St Fl 3 New York NY 10014-5137 E-mail: diana.balmori@yale.edu.

BALOGA, LUCILLE WUJCIK, psychologist; b. Plymouth, Pa., May 2, 1953; d. Stanley C. and Irene Wujcik; B.A., King's Coll., 1975; M.Ed., Pa. State U., 1976; M.S., Marywood Coll., 1984; m. John Louis Baloga, June 26, 1976. Employment counselor Pa. Bur. Employment Security, 1976; counselor Wyoming Valley West Sch. Dist., Kingston, Pa., 1976-77; counselor Tunkhannock (Pa.) Area Sch. Dist., 1977-85; counselor psychologist, Hanover Area Schs., 1985—. Wyoming County coordinator Pa. Spl. Olympics, 1978—; mem. elem. edn. adv.com. Wilkes Coll., 1980—; Girl Scout leader, 1982—; bd. dirs. Wyoming County Assn. Retarded Citizens, Wyoming Valley chpt.; Robter J. Ell Outstanding Svc. Alumni award, King's Coll., 2005. Diabetes Assn. Mem. Am. Personnel and Guidance Assn., Pa. Personnel and Guidance Assn., Am. Sch. Counselors Assn., Luzerne County Counselors Assn., NEA, Pa. State Edn. Assn., Tunkhannock Area Edn. Assn. (dir.), Am. Bus. Women's Assn. (Women of Yr. Wyoming Valley chpt. 1985), Mensa, Psi Chi. Democrat. Roman Catholic. Office: 1600 Sans Souci Pkwy Wilkes Barre PA 18706-6030

BALOGH, ANNE MARCELINE, personnel consultant; b. New Haven, Conn., Aug. 25, 1932; d. Mario and Rose Marie (Onofrio) Iannotti; m. Dominic Vincent Balogh, June 6, 1955 (dec. Aug. 1996); children: Rosanne, Dominic Jr., Christopher, Stephanie. AS, Quinnipiac Coll., 1952. Cert. personnel cons. Mgr. Fuller Brush Co., Conn., 1971-75; co-onwer Baloghs Restaurant, Hamden, Conn., 1975-80; with Rita Personnel, Hamden, Conn., 1980-91, Cheney Assocs., Hamden, Conn., 1991—. Mem. bus. adv. bd. Easter Seals, New Haven; mem. divsn. I athletic exec. bd. Quinnipiac U. Mem. Human Resource Assn. Greater New Haven, Quinnipiac Coll. Alumnni Assn. (nat. alumni bd. govs.). Republican. Roman Catholic. Avocations: travel, art, volunteerism. Home: 731 Still Hill Rd Hamden CT 06518-1104 Office: Cheney Divsn Headway Tech Resources 2321Whitney Ave Hamden CT 06518-2340

BALOGH, MARY, writer; b. 1944; BA in English lang. and lit. with honors, U. Wales, 1965, diploma of edn., 1967. English tchr. Kipling HS, Saskatchewan, Canada, 1967—82, Windthorst HS, Saskatchewan, 1982—88, prin., 1982—88. Author: numerous books including most recently, A Masked Deception, 1985, The Trysting Place, 1986, Secrets of the Heart, 1988, A Gift of Daisies, 1989, A Promise of Spring, 1990, Devil's Web, 1990, Snow Angel, 1991, Christmas Beau, 1991, A Christmas Promise, 1992, Courting Julia, 1993, Tempting Harriet, 1994, Lord Carew's Bride, 1995, The Temporary Wife, 1997, The Last Waltz, 1998, One Night for Love, 1999, More Than a Mistress, 2000, No Man's Mistress, 2001, A Summer to Remember, 2002, Slightly Married, 2003, Slightly Wicked, 2003, Slightly Scandalous, 2003, Slightly Tempted, 2004, Slightly Sinful, 2004, Slightly Dangerous, 2004. Home: Box 571 Kipling SK Canada S0G 2S0 Office: c/o Random House 1745 Broadway New York NY 10019 E-mail: author@marybalogh.com.

BALSAMELLO, MELISSA (MARLEY), elementary school educator; b. Red Bank, N.J., Aug. 5, 1975; d. Lucille (Perillo) M.; m. Jason R. Balsamello, Feb. 26, 2002 BA in Psychology Douglass Coll., Rutgers U., 1997, EdM in Spl. Edn., 1998, postgrad., 1998—2001. Cert. early childhood edn., elem. edn., spl. edn., supr., psychology, dance/vocat. arts. Religious edn. tchr. St. Leo and Great, Lincroft, N.J., 1991-93; respite care provider, counselor ARC of Somerset, Manville, N.J., 1995; group leader, tchr. Happy Campers Ecology Camp, New Brunswick, 1996; tchg. asst., subsitute tchr. Douglass Child Study Ctr., New Brunswick, 1996-98; tchg. asst., field worker Douglass Devel. Disability Ctr., New Brunswick, 1995-96; store mgr. Pyramid Books, Highland Park, N.J., 1997-98; tchr., camp group leader Douglass Girl's Camp, New Brunswick, 1997-98; adminstrv. asst. to pres. United Bolt & Besel, 1998; tchr. 1st grade Franklin Park Sch., Somerset, NJ, 1998—2002, dance ensemble advisor, choreographer, 2000—02; 1st grade tchr., PTO tchr. rep., lunch supr., mentor, tutor Woodrow Wilson Sch., Westfield, NJ, 2002—05; pre-K autism tchr. Jefferson Sch., 2005—06; labor asst., 2005—06; 1st grade mentor, 2005—06. Mem. selection com. Douglass Alumni Soc., 1995-97; program facilitator Coll. Orientation and Recruitment Svcs., 1995-96; house chairwoman Coll. Residence Life, 1995-98; mentor Douglass Coll. Emerging Leaders Program, 1995-98; divsn. leader, specialist Daisy Recreation, East Brunswick, 1997-99; counselor Friday Night Live, East Brunswick, 1999-2000; divsn. leader/specialist Daisy Recreation Ctr., East Brunswick, 1997-98; honors rev., tutor 2-8th, Edison, N.J., 1999-2003. Singer: (band) Hola Diablo, 2005—. Pres. Am. Assn. Mental Retardation, Rutgers chpt., 1995-96; vol., asst. coach N.J. Spl. Olympics, 1996-97; mem. music ministry Zarapath Christian Ch., 2000—, mem. marriage ministry, women's ministry, 2006—. Recipient Presdl. Cmty. Svc. award, Ocean Twp., Washington, 1992, scholarship North Monmouth AAUW, 1996-97. Mem. ASCD, N.J. Edn. Assn., Am. Ednl. Rsch. Assn., Franklin Twp. Edn. Assn., Am. Assn. Mental Retardation (pres. chpt. 1995-97), N.J. Assn. Edn. Young Children, Rutgers U. Student Edn. Assn., Assn. Labor Assts. and Childbirth Educators, Doulas N.Am., Am. Shoppers Panel, Chi Sigma (pres. 1995). Avocations: dance, singing. Home: 24 Briar Cir Green Brook NJ 08812 Office Phone: 732-424-8436. Personal E-mail: mrandmrsb@verizon.net.

BALSTAD, ROBERTA, social scientist; b. Mpls., June 25, 1940; d. Gerhard Oliver and Laverne K. (Anderson) Balstad; m. Gary David Lange, Nov. 26, 1959 (div. 1968); m. Floyd John Miller, June 15, 1969 (div. 2004); 1 child, Aaron Gerhard. BA, U. Minn., 1964, MA, 1970, PhD, 1973. Rsch. assoc. AIA, Washington, 1974; staff assoc. Social Sci. Rsch. Coun., Washington, 1975-81; exec. dir. Consortium Social Sci. Assns., Washington, 1981-84; divsn. dir. NSF, Washington, 1984-93; pres., CEO Consortium Internat. Earth Sci. Info. Network (CIESIN), University Center, Mich., 1993-98; adj. prof. natural resources policy behavior U. Mich., 1993-97; sr. rsch. scientist, sr. fellow, dir. CIESIN Columbia U., NYC, 1998—. Guest scholar Woodrow Wilson Internat. Ctr. Scholars, 1994; sr. assoc. mem. St. Anthony's Coll., U. Oxford, England, 1991—92; mem. chmn. NATO adv. panel on Advanced Sci. Insts./Advanced Rsch. Workshops, Brussels, 1988—91; chmn. steering com. space applications and commercialization Nat. Rsch. Coun., 1999—2002, mem. exec. com. Space Studies Bd., 1995—2000, mem. climate rsch. com., 1997—99, mem. com. on global change rsch., 1999—2002; chmn. U.S. Nat. Com. on Sci. and Tech. Data, 2003—; mem. U.S. Nat. Com. IIASA, 1995—; chmn. adv. bd. Luxembourg Income Survey, 1987—91. Author: City and Hinterland, 1979; editor (with Harriet Zuckerman) Science Indicators: Implications for Research and Policy, 1979; contbr. articles to profl. jours.; translator poetry of Jorge Luis Borges, 1989-91, N.P. von Wyk Louw, 1998 Bd. trustees Newport Schs., Kensington, Md., 1986-91, St. Anthony's Coll. Trust, U. Oxford, 1994—, sec., 1997-2000, chair, 2000—, bd. dirs. Open Geospatial Consortium 2003—; adv. trustee Environ. Rsch. Inst. Mich., 1995-98. Recipient NSF Meritorious Svc. award, 1993. Fellow: AAAS (com. mem., chmn. 1987—93), NY Acad. Scis.; mem.: Coun. Fgn. Rels., Am. Lt. Translators Assn., Internat. Social Sci. Coun. (com. 1991—95, v.p. 1992—94), US Man Biosphere Program (com., chmn. 1989—91), Cosmos Club. Lutheran. Office: CIESIN Columbia U PO Box 1000 Palisades NY 10964-8000 Office Phone: 845-365-8988. Business E-Mail: roberta@ciesin.columbia.edu.

BALTER, BERNICE, religious organization administrator; Exec. dir. Women's League for Conservative Judaism, N.Y.C., 1978. Nat. adv. bd. MAZON. Mailing: Women's League for Conservative Judaism 475 Riverside Dr New York NY 10115 Office Phone: 212-870-1260 ext. 7157. Office Fax: 212-870-1261. E-mail: bbalter@wlcj.org.

BALTER, FRANCES SUNSTEIN, civic worker; b. Pitts. d. Elias and Gertrude Susntein; m. James Stone Balter, May 15, 1948; children: Katherine (Mrs. Ross Anthony) (dec.), Julia Frances, Constance Cantor, Daniel Elias. Student, Sarah Lawrence Coll., 1939-41, New Sch. Social Rsch., 1941-43; cert. Inst. Arts Adminstrn., Harvard U., 1973. Adminstrv. asst., assoc. prodr. Ednl. TV Sta. WQED-TV, Pitts., 1963-67; prodr., mng. dir. Freedom Readers, 1964-67; co-founder, incorporator, sec. bd. dirs. Pitts. Coun. Arts, 1967-70; cultural cons. Mayor's Office Dir. Office Cultural Affairs, Pitts., 1968. Initiator Three Rivers Arts Festival 1960; co-dir. Ohio and Miss. River Valley Art Festival, 1961-62; mem. Pa. Coun. Arts, 1972-78; co-founder Pioneer Crafts Coun., Mill Run, Pa., 1972; exec. dir. Poetry on the Buses, 1974—. Author of poems. Bd. dirs. Coun. for Arts MIT, 1985-93, Palm Beach Festival, 1987-89. Named Woman of Yr. Art Post-Gazette, 1969. Mem. Nat. Soc. Arts and Letters (Pitts. chpt.).

BALTES, SARA JAYNE, reading educator, elementary school educator; b. Burlington, Iowa, Apr. 22, 1965; d. Henry Charles and Helena Louise Savage; m. Damian John Baltes, Aug. 6, 1988; children: Brianna Marie, Bryant John. BA in Elem. Edn., Wartburg, Waverly, Iowa, 1997. 1st grade tchr. Hampton Cmty. Sch., Iowa, 1987—90; 2d grade tchr. New Hampton Cmty. Sch., 1990—93, at-risk coord., 1993—95, Title 1 reading and reading recovery tchr., 1995—. Reading tchr. New Hampton Sch., 1995—, mem. extended learning program com., 2000—; org. Read Across Am., 2004—05. Mem. youth com. Trinity Luth. Ch., New Hampton, 2003—06, mem. gospel choir, 2003—06. Mem.: Internat. Reading Assn., Reading Recovery Coun.of North Am., Kappa Delta Pi (v.p. 1986—87). Avocations: reading, crafts, golf, baking. Home: 2367 190th St New Hampton IA 50659 Office: New Hampton Elementary New Hampton IA 50659

BALTIMORE, PAMELA A. GRAYSON, social worker, consultant; b. Camden, N.J., Aug. 16, 1961; d. Edward Daniel III and Janice Diane Grayson; m. Roderick Taylor Baltimore, Sept. 23, 1989; 1 child, Sebastian. B in Social Work, Rutgers U., 1987, M in Social Work, 1992. Lic. clin. social worker, N.J.; N.J. state cert. sch. social worker. Juvenile investigator State of N.J. Office of Pub. Defender, Camden, 1982-87; residential counselor Steinenger Ctr., Camden, 1989-90; family svc. specialist III State of N.J. Divsn. Youth and Family Svc., Camden, 1988-92; program supr., therapist Family Counseling Svc., Camden, 1992-99; cons. Pennsauken, N.J., 1999—. Pres. Rutgers U. EOF Adv. Bd., Camden, 1999—; deaconness Rock Ch. Family Worship Ctr., Phila., 1996—; mem. PTA, Roosevelt Sch., Pennsauken, 1998—. Mem. NASW, Delta Sigma Theta. Democrat. Avocations: reading, music, arts and crafts, cooking.

BALTIMORE, RUTH BETTY, social worker; b. Wilkes-Barre, Pa., Feb. 27, 1926; d. Samuel Jr. and Theresa (Bergsmann) Bloch; m. Martin Joseph Baltimore, Feb. 6, 1949; children: Francie, Sandy. BA in Psychology, Skidmore Coll., 1948; postgrad., U. Scranton, 1965, 70. Social worker Wyoming Valley West Sch. Dist., Kingston, Pa., 1966-89; ret. Cons. in field. Co-author: (booklet) Guide for Teachers on Reporting Child Abuse, 1970. Bd. dirs. Youth Svcs. Commn., Wilkes-Barre, 1986-87, Victims Resource Ctr., Wilkes-Barre, 1990—; bd. dirs. Luz County Adv. Bd. Children and Youth, Wilkes-Barre, 1988—, vice-chair, 1991, chair, 1992-96. Recipient Connie Coun. Svc. award Nat. Coun. Jewish Women, Wilkes-Barre, 1959. Mem. Valley Tennis and Swim Club (pres.-elect 1994, pres. 1995-96). Avocations: tennis, golf, reading. Home: 630 Newberry Estate Dallas PA 18612

BALTZ, PATRICIA ANN (PANN BALTZ), retired elementary school educator; b. Dallas, June 20, 1949; d. Richard Parks and Ruth Eileen (Hartschuh) Langford; m. William Monroe Baltz, Sept. 6, 1969; 1 child: Kenneth Chandler. Student, U. Redlands, 1967-68; BA in English Lit. cum laude, UCLA, 1971. Cert. tchr. K-8, Calif. Tchr. 4th grade Arcadia (Calif.) Unified Sch. Dist., 1972-74, 92—, substitute tchr., 1983-85, tchr. 3dr grade, 1985-87, tchr. 6th grade, 1987-90, tchr. 4th and 5th grade multiage, 1990—2005, ret., 2005. Sci. mentor tchr. Arcadia Unified Sch. Dist., 1991-94; mentor Tech. Ctr. Silicon Valley, San Jose, Calif., 1991. Tchr. rep. PTA, Arcadia, 1980-93; mem. choir, children's sermon team, elder Arcadia Presbyn. Ch., 1980-93; chaperone, vol. Pasadena (Calif.) Youth Symphony Orch., 1988-90; vol. Am. Heart Assn., 1990-92. Recipient Outstanding Gen. Elem. Tchr. award, Outstanding Tchr. of the Yr. award Disney's Am. Tchr. Awards, 1993, Calif. Tchr. of Yr. award Calif. State Dept. Edn., 1993, Georgie award Girl Scouts of Am., 1993, The Self Esteem Task Force award L.A. County Task Force to Promote Self-Esteem & Personal & Social Responsibility, 1993, Profl. Achievement award UCLA Alumni Assn.; apptd. to Nat. Edn. Rsch. Policies & Priorities Bd., U.S. Sec. Edn. Richard Riley; Pann Baltz Mission Possible Scholar named in her honor. Mem. NEA, Nat. Sci. Tchrs. Assn., Calif. Tchr. Assn., Arcadia Tchrs. Assn. Avocations: reading, singing, calligraphy, book-making, computers. Home: 1215 S 3rd Ave Arcadia CA 91006-4205

BALTZER, REBECCA A., musicologist, researcher, consultant; b. Memphis, June 17, 1940; d. Ralph Neal and Sherard Rawles Baltzer; m. Charles Edward McCarthy, Mar. 17, 1984. AB in English magna cum laude, Randolph-Macon Woman's Coll., 1962; MA in Musicology, Boston U., 1964, PhD in Musicology, 1974. Part-time instr., lectr. in music Boston U., 1964—67; prof. musicology Sch. Music U. Tex., Austin, 1967—, assoc. dean Grad. Sch., 1982—86. Cons. Nat. Endowment for Humanities, Washington, 1979—80, Ednl. Testing Svc., Princeton, NJ, 1986—88; vis. prof. music Princeton U., 1996. Editor, transcriber: Le Magnus liber organi de Notre-Dame de Paris, 1995, co-editor, contbr.: book of essays The Divine Office in the Latin Middle Ages, 2000 (Hon. Mention in Philosophy & Religion, from the Profl. and Scholarly Pub. (PSP) br. of the Assn. of Am. Publishers, 2001); co-editor: The Union of Words and Music in Medieval Poetry, 1991; editor of the music: edition & translation of medieval poetry Guillaume de Machaut: Remede de Fortune, 1988; contbr. articles to profl. jours. Dissertation fellow, AAUW, 1966—67. Mem.: Soc. for Am. Music, Early Music Am., Coll. Music Soc., Medieval Acad. Am. (local arrangements chair ann. meeting 2000), Am. Musicological Soc. (bd. dirs. 1980—82, v.p. 1988—90, treas., mem. exec. com. 1993—2000, Alfred Einstein award 1973), Pi Kappa Lambda, Phi Beta Kappa. Episcopalian. Avocations: reading, photography, travel. Home: 68 Sundown Parkway Austin TX 78746-5258 Home Fax: 512-471-7836.

BALTZLEY, PATRICIA CREEL, mathematics educator; b. Ft. Benning, Ga., Dec. 14, 1952; d. Buckner Miller and Mary Madeleine (O'Neill) Creel; m. Kevin Gerard Robinson, Nov. 15, 1975 (div. Dec. 21, 1981); children: Kevin G. Jr., Timothy Eugene; m. Jeffrey Lynn Baltzley, July 23, 1988 (dec. Dec. 1996); m. Joseph Leroy Deveny, May 28, 2006. Student, St. Joseph's Coll., 1971-72; BA in Math., Coll. Notre Dame, 1975; MS in Math., Shippensburg State U., 1986. Cert. advanced profl., Md.; cert. in adminstn. and supervision. Acct. trainee Md. Nat. Bank, Balt., 1975-76; math. tchr. Notre Dame Preparatory Sch., Towson, Md., 1976-78, Carroll County Bd. Edn., Westminster, Md., 1978-91; math. program developer Ctr. for Social Orgn. of Schs. Johns Hopkins U., Balt., 1991—95; K-12 math. specialist Baltimore County Pub. Schs., 1995—98, 6-12 math. supr., 1998—2004, dir. Pre K-12 math., 2004—. Adj. prof. Coll. Notre Dame, Balt., 1992-2005, Johns Hopkins U., 1995-97, Western Md. Coll., 1997-2003, Loyola Coll., 2000-03; cons. Ctr. for Social Orgn., Johns Hopkins U., Learning Inst.; ind. cons. in field. Pres. Seton Ctr., Emmitsburg, Md., 1982-86; vol. Seton Shrine Ctr., Emmitsburg, 1986—95. Recipient Presdl. Award for Excellence in Teaching Math. NSF, 1989; named Md. Math. Educator of Yr., 1997. Mem. ASCD, NEA, Md. Coun. Tchrs. Math. (pres. 1991-93), Nat. Coun. Tchrs. Math., Coun. Presdl. Awardees in Math., Md. Coun. Suprs. Math. (pres. 2000—05), Coun. Adminstrs. and Suprs. in Edn. Democrat. Roman Catholic. Avocations: reading, basketball, walking. Home: 830 Glendale Rd York PA 17403-4130 Office: Baltimore County Pub Schs 9611 Pulaski Park Dr Ste 305 Baltimore MD 21220 Office Phone: 410-887-4052. E-mail: pbaltzley@bcps.org.

BALZER, DONNA CAROL, retired secondary school educator; b. Des Moines, Iowa, June 20, 1935; d. Carroll William and Dorothy Margaret Balzer. BA, Simpson Coll., 1959; MS, Mich. State U., 1964. Cert. tchr. Iowa. Tchr. phys. edn. Thomas Jefferson HS, Council Bluffs, Iowa, 1959—70, Hoover Middle Sch., Sioux City, 1971—91. Recipient Vol. award, Animal Lifeline Iowa-No Kill Shelter, Des Moines Botanical Ctr., Crosslake C. of C. Mem.: Am. Assn. Phys. Edn. Health Recreation Dance, Sierra Club (del. Iowa chpt. 2004—05, v.p. ctrl. Iowa chpt. 2004—), Eastern Star, Alpha Delta Kappa (chair to state pres. 1990, pres. Tau chpt. 2004—06). Avocations: golf, photography, ceramics, boating, hiking.

BAMBERGER, PHYLIS SKLOOT, lawyer, educator, retired judge; b. N.Y.C., May 2, 1939; d. George Joseph and Martha (Wechselblatt) S.; m. Michael A. Bamberger, Dec. 19, 1965; children: Kenneth, Richard. BA, Bklyn. Coll., 1960; LLB, NYU, 1963. Bar: N.Y. 1963, U.S. Supreme Ct. 1967, U.S. Ct. Appeals (2d cir.) 1965, U.S. Dist. Ct. (so. dist.) N.Y. 1966, U.S. Dist. Ct. (ea. dist.) N.Y. 1979. Assoc. Legal Aid Soc., N.Y.C., 1963-67; assoc.-in-charge criminal appeals Bur. Legal Aid Soc., N.Y.C., 1967-72; atty.-in-charge, fed. def. svcs. unit/appeal Legal Aid Soc., N.Y.C., 1972-88; judge N.Y. State Ct. Claims designated to sit in the N.Y. State Supreme Ct., Bronx County, 1988—2005. Instr. N.Y. State Judicial Inst. and other venues, 1990—; mem. N.Y. State Chief Judge's Jury Project, 1993—94; mem. com. on alternatives to incarceration Office of Ct. Adminstrn., 1994—96, mem. criminal law and procedure adv. com., 1994—98, co-chair, 1998—; mem. N.Y. State Chief Judge's Commn. on the Jury, 2003—, mem. com. the Future of Indigent Def. Svcs., 2004—06, mem. probation task force, 2006—. Author: Criminal Appeals Handbook, 1984; editor, contbr. Practice Under the Federal Sentencing Guidelines, 1988, 90, 93, 2000 (also supplements); author, compiler Recent Developments in State Constitutional Law, 1985; contbr. numerous articles to publs. Mem. ABA, N.Y. State Bar assn. (co-chair presdl. com. on problems in criminal justice sys. 1986-88, mem. com. on the future of the profession), Assn. of Bar of City of N.Y. (mem. coun. on criminal justice 2004—, chair com. on provision of legal svcs. to persons of moderate means 1995-98, 21st century com. 1992-95, chair com. on probation 1993-94), Phi Beta Kappa.

BAMBERGER, SHEILA LISTER, retired secondary school educator; b. N.Y.C., Sept. 23, 1935; d. Louis and Rebecca (Levitan) Lister; m. Henry Bamberger, June 21, 1959; children: Judith, Miriam BS, SUNY, Albany, 1957; postgrad., CUNY, 1957—60, SUNY, New Paltz, 1966—68, Syracuse U., 1989—91; MST, U. N.H., 1996. Cert. secondary math. tchr., N.Y. Tchr. Malverne Pub. Schs., NY, 1957—61; bookkeeper Leitman, Siegel & Payne, P.A., Birmingham, Ala., 1977—79; tchr. Ctrl. Dauphin Sch. Dist., Harrisburg, Pa., 1980—82, Utica City Sch. Dist., NY, 1982—88; tchr. math. Clinton Ctrl. Sch., NY, 1988—99; facilitator Mohawk Valley Inst. of Learning in Retirement, 1999; treas. Clinton Ctrl. Sch., 1999—2001. Co-exec., v.p. Nat. Assn. of Ret. Reform Rabbi's, 2005—. Bd. dir., officer Vassar Hosp. Assn., Poughkeepsie, N.Y., 1972-75; bd. dir. A Better Chance, Clinton, 1990-2001, chmn. acad. com. 1991-98, treas, 1999-2001; bd. mem. Charles T. Sitrin Home, Players of Utica, treas 2005—; mem. nat. women's com. Brandeis U., regional pres., 1976-78; donor treas. Hadassah, 1987— Recipient Outstanding Educator award Rotary Internat., Utica, 1985, 87, 91, Svc. award Hadassah, 1989, 90 Mem. Nat. Coun. Tchrs. Math., Assn. Math. Tchrs. N.Y. State (county chmn. 1987—, chmn. publs. 1990-93, chmn. hospitality com. 1992, chmn. registration com. 1993, v.p. 2001), Assn. Math. Tchrs. Oneida County (organizer, compiler Mathletics 1983), SUNY-Albany Alumni Assn. (treas. 1989-92, Svc. award 1977, 87), Delta Kappa Gamma (v.p. 1988-92, pres. 1992-94) Avocations: tennis, bridge, gardening, sewing. Home: 122 Proctor Blvd Utica NY 13501-6119

BAMMEL-LEE, SHARLYN D'ANN, elementary school educator, consultant; b. San Antonio, Tex., Mar. 17, 1954; d. Noel Milton and Jacqueline Bobbie Smith; m. Jerry Bob Lee, May 28, 2005; children from previous marriage: Brian Howard Bammel, Kevin Noel Bammel, David Lewis Bammel, Laura D'Ann Bammel. BA in Psychology, Baylor U., Waco, Tex., 1976. Cert. tchr. Hardin-Simmons U., 1996. Instr. human rels. and math. Tex. State Tech. Inst., Waco, 1976—77; instr. quilting and sewing Sew Spl., Boerne, 1982—84, 1986—89; spl. projects and records specialist Hardin-Simmons U., Abilene, 1992—94; tchr. 5th grade Abilene Ind. Sch. Dist., 1996—2003, elem. math and sci. specialist, 2003—04; instrnl. coord. Lee Elem. Abilene Ind. Sch. Dist., 2004—05; elem. instrnl. coord. math. and sci. Abilene Ind. Sch. Dist., 2004—. Self-employed piano tchr., Hanover, NH, 1989—92, Abilene, Tex., 1992—; math. cons. Sharon Wells Consulting, Lubbock and Abilene, 2005—. Vol. sci. tchr. Young Astronauts, West Lebanon, NH, 1989—92; youth leader grades 7-8 Abilene Bible Ch., Tex., 1993—98. Named Parent Vol. of Yr., Lincoln Mid. Sch., 1995—96, Outstanding Grad., W.B. Irvin Sch. Edn., 1996; recipient PTA Life award, 1999, Tchr. Tribute award, Abilene Reporter News, 1999, Spotlight on Tchrs. award, Bonham Elem. Sch., 2000. Mem.: Nat. Sci. Tchrs. Am., Nat. Coun. Tchrs. Math., Assn. Tchrs. Prin. Educators. Avocations: piano, quilting, cross stitch, reading, tutoring students. Home: 5450 Hwy 277 S Abilene TX 79606 Office: Abilene ISD Adminstrn Bldg 241 Pine PO Box 981 Abilene TX 79604 Office Phone: 325-677-1444.

BANAS, C(HRISTINE) LESLIE, lawyer; b. Swindon, Wiltshire, Eng., Oct. 29, 1951; arrived in U.S., 1957; d. Stanley M. and Helena Ann (Boryn) Banas; m. Dale J. Buras, May 1, 1976; children: Eric Buras, Andrea Buras. BA magna cum laude, U. Detroit, 1973; JD cum laude, Wayne State U., 1975. Bar: Mich. 1976, U.S. Supreme Ct. 1980. Atty. Hyman & Rice, Southfield, Mich., 1976-77, Hyman, Gurwin, Nachman, Friedman & Winkelman, Southfield, 1977-82, ptnr., 1982-87, Honigman Miller Schwartz and Cohn LLP, Bloomfield Hills, Mich., 1987—. Contbr. articles to profl. jours. Bd. mem. Inforum Ctr. Leadership; bd. visitors Law Sch. Wayne State U., bd. visitors Coll. Nursing; mem. Mich. Land Title Stds. Mem.: ABA, Urban Land Inst., Fed. Bar Assn., State Bar Mich. (bd. dirs. real property law sect. coun., coun. vice chair), Detroit Athletic Club, Inforum (past pres.). Roman Catholic. Avocations: gardening, photography, skiing. Office: Honigman Miller Schwartz and Cohn LLP Ste 100 38500 Woodward Ave Bloomfield Hills MI 48304-5048 Office Phone: 248-566-8406. Business E-Mail: lbanas@honigman.com.

BANAS, SUZANNE, middle school educator; b. Miami, Fla., Mar. 28, 1959; d. Frank and Norma (Eliscu) B. BA in Sci., U. Miami, 1981, MS, 1986; PhD, Union Inst., 1994. Cert. tchr. sci. gifted LD & EH, Fla.; Nat. Bd. Cert. Tchr. early adolescence generalist Nat. Bd. Profl. Tchg. Stds. Lead tchr. Dade County Pub. Schs., Miami, 1988—; curriculum writer Gender Equity Network, Miami, 1993—97, Arise Found., Miami, 1995—97; tchr., chairperson dept. sci., team leader Cutler Ridge Mid. Sch., Miami, 1990—; adj. prof. Fla. Internat. U., Miami, 1996—. Advisor Acad. for Instrnl. Leadership, Miami, 1994-96, Annenberg Challenge Grant, Miami, 1995-96; cons. Urban Sys. Initiative, 1995-98; Internet tchr. trainer/mentor, 1998—. Recipient Fla. Explores! award Fla. State U./TDRA, 1993, Tchr. of Yr. award Cutler Ridge Mid. Sch., 1996, Sharing success award dept. of environ. edn., 2000. Mem. Miami Dade County Sci. Tchrs. Assn. (pres. 1994—), Fla. Assn. Sci. Tchrs. (bd. dirs. 1998—), Nat. Sci. Tchrs. Assn. Office: Richmond Heights Mid Sch Sci Zoo Magnet 15015 SW103 Ave Miami FL 33176

BANASZYNSKI, CAROL JEAN, secondary school educator; b. Hawkins, Wis., Jan. 3, 1951; BS in Biology, U. Wis., LaCrosse, 1973; MS in Profl. Devel., U. Wis., Whitewater, 1987; MS in Ednl. Leadership, Cardinal Stritch U., 2002. Tchr. Deerfield Cmty. Schs., 1973—. Coach Youth T-ball/softball; co-chairperson Adopt-A-Highway; group leader 4-H Club; counselor Boy Scout Environtl. Merit Badge program Recipient Wis. H.S. Tchr. of Yr., 1997-98, Wis. Tchr. of Yr. 1998, Award of Excellence Wis. Assn. of Sch. Bds., 1997, Wis. Dept. of Instrn., 1997, Wis. Edn. Assn. Coun., 1997, Wis. Legis. Citation for Tchg. Excellence, 1997-98; named Educator of Yr. Nat. H.S. Assn., 1998, Outstanding Tchr. Radioshack/Tandy, 1999; Kohl fellowship, 1997, Monsanto fellowship, 2000. Mem. ASCD, Nat. Biology Tchrs. Assn., Nat. Sci. Tchrs. Assn., Wis. Secondary Sci. Tchrs. (state conf. presenter), BioNet, DEA (scholarship com. chairperson), Wis. Edn. Assn. Coun.

BANBURY, DEMBY BOWMAN, director; b. Richmond, Va., Nov. 10, 1961; d. Warren Bowman and Mary Lou Helwig; m. John Archie Banbury, Aug. 15, 1997; 1 child, Pierce. BS in Biology, 1983; MS in Edn., James Madison U., Harrisonburg, Va., 1985. Lic. biology and GT Biology tchr. Va., 2007. Biology tchr. McLean H.S., Va., 1985—2004, asst. dir. student activities, 2004—. Varsity coach McLean H.S., 1985—, dir. field hockey camp, 1998—2003, sci. dept. chair, 2000—04; awards chairperson Fairfax County Pub. Schools Women and Sports Program, 1995—2006; youth field hockey dir. McLean Youth Assn., 1998—. Chairperson 50th anniversary celebration Mclean H.S.; classroom parent vol. St.James Sch., Falls Church, Va., 2006—06. Named All- Met Co-Coach of Yr. for Field Hockey, Wash. Post Sports Dept., 1986, Gt. Falls Dist. Coach of Yr., Gt. Falls Dist. Tennis Coaches, 1992, Budget Rent A Car Coach of Yr., Nat. Found. for Women In Sports, 1994, McLean Youth Citizen of Yr., Coach of Yr., Women's Sports Found., Liberty Dist. Lacrosse Coach of Yr. Mem.: Va. Interscholastic

Athletic Adminstrs. Assn., Nat. Fedn. State H.S. Assns., Nat. Field Hockey Coaches Assn., Nat. Assn. Biology Tchrs. (Outstanding Biology Teacher Va. award). Avocations: reading, gardening, tennis, exercise. Office Phone: 703-714-5863.

BANCEL, MARILYN, fund raising management consultant; b. Glen Ridge, NJ, June 15, 1947; d. Paul and Joan Marie (Spangler) B.; m. Rik Myslewski, Nov. 20, 1983; children: Carey, Roxanne. BA in English with distinction, Ind. U., 1969. Cert. fund raising exec. Ptnr. The Sultan's Shirt Tail, Gemlik, Turkey, 1969-72; prodn. mgr. High Country Co., San Francisco, 1973-74; exec. dir. East Bay Performance, Inc., 1976—79; pub. Bay Arts Rev., Berkeley, Calif., 1976-79; dir. devel. Oakland (Calif.) Symphony Orch., 1979-81; assoc. dir. devel. Exploratorium, San Francisco, 1981-86, dir. devel., 1986-91; prin. Fund Devel. Counsel, San Francisco, 1991-93; v.p. The Oram Group, Inc., San Francisco, 1993—. Co-chmn. capital campaign com. Synergy Sch., San Francisco, 1995-2000; adj. prof. U. San Francisco, 1993-2002. Author: Preparing Your Capital Campaign, 2000. Mem. adv. bd. Mus. City of San Francisco, 1995—, San Francisco Bot. Gardens, 1998-99; mentor Assn. Fundraising Profl. Mentor Program, 1994-. Fellow U. Strasbourg, France, 1968. Mem. Assn. Fundraising Profls. (bd. Golden Gate chpt. 1996-98, chmn. National Philanthropy Day, 2000, Outstanding Fundraising Exec. award 2002), Giving Inst., Devel. Execs. Roundtable, Phi Beta Kappa. Democrat. Avocation: gardening. Office: 328 Duncan St San Francisco CA 94131-2022

BANCROFT, ANN E., polar explorer; b. Mendota Heights, Minn., 1955; d. Dick and Debbie Bancroft Former tchr., coach, wilderness instr., St. Paul, Minn. Mem. Steger Internat. Polar Expedition, 1986 (first woman to reach the North Pole by dogsled); leader Am. Women's Antarctic Expedition, 1993 (first women's team to reach the South Pole on skis); mem. The Bancroft Arnesen Expdn. (first all women's crossing of Antarctica), 2000; founder (with Liv Anderson) yourexpedition internat. motivation co. Subject (corp. video) Vision of Teams, 1998, (documentary) Poles Apart, 1999; featured in Remarkable Women of the 20th Century, 1998. Founder Ann Bancroft Found; spokesperson Learning Disabilities Assn., Wilderness Inquiry (co-chair capital campaign), Girl Scouts U.S.A; bd. dirs. Youth Frontiers; judge Nuclear-Free awards, Nat. Women's Hall of Fame inductions. Named Ms. Mag. Woman of Yr., 1987 Glamour Mag. Woman of Yr., 2001; inductee Girls and Women in Sport Hall of Fame, 1992, Nat. Women's Hall of Fame, 1995; recipient Women First award YWCA, 1993; first woman in world to travel across the ice to North and South poles; (with Liv Anderson) first women in history to sail and ski across Antartica's landmass. Mem.: Melpomene Inst. and Medica (adv. bd.). Office: Your Expedition 1920 Oliver Pl S Minneapolis MN 55405-2420 Fax: 612-333-1325. E-mail: susan@yourexpedition.com.

BANCROFT, BARBEE N., nursing educator; b. Springfield, Mo., Nov. 1, 1950; d. Beauford Almon and Carol Jean Bancroft. BSN, East Carolina U., Greenville, N.C., 1972; MSN, PNP, U. Va., Charlottesville, 1978. RN Va., registered PNP, Va. Nurse Joseph Ladd Sch., Newport, RI, 1972—73, Georgetown U. Hosp., Washington, 1973—76; instr. to asst. prof. U. Va., Charlottesville, 1978—80; pres. CPP Assoc., Chgo., 1983—; vis. prof. U. Ark., Little Rock, 1990—96. Author: Medical Minutiae, 1991, ABCs of Diet and Disease, 2001, Live a Little, Laugh a Lot, 2004; editor: bimonthly newsletter for health care profls., 1985—. Recipient Entrepreneurial Leadership award, U. Va.-Charlottesville, 2001, Disting. Svc. award, Nat. Assn. Biology Tchrs., 2004. Mem.: ILSPAN. Democrat. Avocations: tennis, bicycling, reading. Office: CPP Associates Inc 3100 N Sheridan Rd #1C Chicago IL 60657

BANCROFT, MARGARET ARMSTRONG, lawyer; b. Mpls., May 9, 1938; d. Wallace David and Mary Elizabeth (Garland) Armstrong; m. Alexander Clerihew Bancroft, Mar. 14, 1964; 1 child, Elizabeth Armstrong. BA magna cum laude, Radcliffe Coll.-Harvard U., 1960; JD cum laude, NYU, 1969. Bar: NY 1971. Reporter Mpls. Star and Tribune, 1960-61, UPI, NY, 1961-66, NJ, 1961—66; of counsel Law Firm of Dechert LLP. Adj. prof. law NYU Sch. Law; vis. prof. Debrecen U. Faculty Law, Hungary, 2006. Bd. dirs., exec. com. Vis. Nurse Svc. NY; chair. Vis. Nurse Svc. NY Home Care, Inc. Mem. ABA (bus. law sect.), N.Y. State Bar Assn. (securities regulation com.), Assn Bar City N.Y. (com. on investment mngmt. regulation), Am. Law Inst. Office: Law Firm of Dechert LLP 30 Rockefeller Plz Fl 22 New York NY 10112-2200 Office Phone: 212-698-5590. Business E-mail: margaret.bancroft@dechert.com.

BANCROFT, RENA MERRITT, retired academic administrator; b. Clinton, NC, Sept. 14, 1931; d. William Edward and Sadie Blanche (Herring) Merritt; m. Richard G. Bancroft Sr. (dec.). BS, Syracuse U., 1952, MS, 1953; PhD, U. Calif., Berkeley, 1986. Cert. tchr., adminstr. Calif. Tchr. Black River-Evans Mills (NY) Sch. Sys., 1953—55, North Syracuse (NY) Ctrl. Sch. Dist., 1955—57, Oakland (Calif.) Unified Sch. Dist., 1958—65; tchr., adminstr. San Mateo (Calif.) Union HS Dist., 1966—85; pres. San Francisco CC Dist., 1985—90, dean adult/continuing edn., 1990—92; cons. in edn. Calif. State Dept. Edn., Sacramento, 1992—95. Mem. Mayor's Cmty. Devel. Com., San Francisco, 1990—95; bd. dirs. Korean Cmty. Ctr., San Francisco; mem. San Francisco Abidjan, Ivory Coast Sister City Com., 1992—, edn. chmn., 1992—; mem. com. Mus. African Diaspora; mem. Rockefeller Found. Spl. Adminstrs. Insts., NYC, 1986—88. Mem.: AARP, Calif. Assn. Ret. Tchrs., Delta Sigma Theta (chmn. edn. com.). Dfl. Methodist. Avocations: reading, writing. Home: 66 Cleary Ct 705 San Francisco CA 94109

BANDEKA, FAUN ANN, elementary school educator; b. Price, Utah, Aug. 19, 1947; d. Harold Burdean and Verena A. (Anderson) Nielson; m. Daryl G. Bandeka, Oct. 19, 1974; children: Trisha Lynn, Philip Aaron. BS, U. Utah, 1973. 2nd grade tchr. Gallup-McKinnley County Sch., Gallup, N.Mex., 1973-74; tchr. third and first grades Gallup-McKinnley County Schs., 1975-77; third grade tchr. San Juan County Schs., Monticello, Utah, 1974-75; tchr. first and second grade Granite Sch. Dist., Salt Lake City, 1987—. Nat. dir. Pledge of Allegiance Centennial, Salt Lake City, 1991-92, Utah state dir., 1991-92; dir. Cmty./Sch. Centennial Celebration, Salt Lake City, 1995-96. Author: (textbook) Preparing Children for School, 1985, Utah: A Centennial Portrait, 1995; composer musical selections. Sec. Kearns Town Coun., Kearns, Utah, 1997-99; mem. Kearns Coalition, Kearns, 1997—; vol. editor/creator: Kearns Chronicle, 1998—; chairperson Miss Kearns Teen Scholarship Pageant, 1997-99. Recipient New Constellation award, Nat. Flag. Found., Washington, 1992, Tchr.'s medal of honor, Freedoms Foun. at Valley Forge, 1993, Centennial Book place, Utah State Archives, Salt Lake City, 1996, Unsung Hero award, Valley View Meml. Estates/West Valley City, 1999, Excel Outstanding Educator finalist, Granite Sch. Dist., 2000, Fulbright Meml. Fund Master Tchr., 2001, Internat. Soc. Poets award, 2002, Internal. Educator of the Yr., 2003, 2004; grantee Fulbright Tchrs. grant, Internat. Inst. Edn. and Japanese/U.S. Edn. Commn., Japanese Govt., 1997. Mem. Salt Lake Composers Guild, NEA, Fulbright Meml. Fund (alumni), Internat. Poets Soc., Swedish Heritage Soc. Republican. Mem. Lds Ch. Avocations: reading, hiking, writing, scrap books. Office: Hillside Elem Sch 4283 South 6000 West West Valley City UT 84128 Office Phone: 801-964-7595.

BANDES, SUSAN JANE, museum director, educator; b. NYC, Oct. 18, 1951; d. Ralph and Bessie (Gordon) Bandes. BA, NYU, 1971; MA, Bryn Mawr Coll., 1973, PhD, 1978; postgrad., Mus. Mgmt. Inst., Berkeley, Calif., 1990. Asst. prof. Sweet Briar Coll., Va., 1978-83; project dir. Am. Assn. Mus., Washington, 1983-84; program officer J. Paul Getty Trust Grant Program, L.A., 1984-86; prof., dir. Kresge Art Mus. Mich. State U., East Lansing, 1986—. Author, editor: Caring for Collections, 1984, Affordable Dreams: The Goetsch-Winckler House and Frank Lloyd Wright, 1991; author: Abraham Rattner, The Tampa Museum of Art Collection, 1997, Pursuits and Pleasures: Baroque Paintings from the Detroit Institute of Arts, 2003; editor: The Prints of John S. de Martelly, 1903-1979; author, curator: Pursuits and Pleasures: Baroque Painting from the Detroit Institute of Arts, 2003. Recipient award Am. Philos. Soc., 1981, Publ. award AIA, 1990; Samuel H. Kress fellow, 1972-73, 75-76, Whiting fellow, 1976-77; Fulbright-Hayes grant, 1974-75. Mem. Nat. Inst. for Conservation (treas. 1986-90), Mich. Alliance for Conservation (treas. 1994-95, sec. 1996-97, treas. 1997-98, pres. 1998-2000), Mich. Mus. Assn. (bd. dirs. 1987-92), Mich. Coun. for Humanities (coun. 1988-92), Midwest Art History Soc. (bd. dirs. 1997-2000). Avocation: collecting oriental rugs. Office: Mich State U Kresge Art Mus East Lansing MI 48824 Office Phone: 517-353-9834. Business E-Mail: bandes@msu.edu.

BANDO, PATRICIA ALICE, academic administrator; b. Detroit, Apr. 4, 1953; d. Hiro Walter and Fumi Patricia (Takemoto) B. BS in Dietetics, Mich. State U., 1975; MA in Food Svc. Adminstrn., NYU, 1985. Registered dietitian. Dietetic intern The N.Y. Hosp., N.Y.C., 1975-76, clin. dietitian, sr. dietitian/adminstrv., 1981-86; food and beverage mgr. Trump Palace Hotel, Atlantic City, N.J., 1986; gen. mgr., dining dept. Cornell U., Ithaca, N.Y., 1986-89, asst. dir., dining dept., 1989-92, dir., dining dept., 1992-95; dir. dining dept. Boston Coll., Chestnut Hill, Mass., 1995—2004, assoc. v.p. aux. svcs., 2004—. Mem. ADA, Mass. Dietetic Assn., Nat. Assn. Coll. and Univ. Food svcs. (conf. edn. chair 1996-97), Soc. Foodsvc. Mgmt., Nat. Restaurant Assn., Mass. Restaurant Assn. (bd. dirs. 2003—, Employer Choice award 2003, IFMA Silver Plate award 2004, R&I Ivy award 2006), New Seabury Country Club, Omicron Nu. Episcopalian. Home: 14 Holly Way Framingham MA 01701-4857 Office: Boston Coll Aux Svcs 140 Commonwealth Ave Chestnut Hill MA 02467-3843

BANE, ALMA LYNN, computer scientist, educator, director; b. Galveston, Tex., Oct. 3, 1947; d. Clinton LaVon and Betty Jane Lynn; m. Charles William Bane, Feb. 3, 1973; children: Greta Kay Hecker, Deborah Elizabeth Farnsworth, Cynthia Ann Coats. AAS, Alvin C.C., Tex., 1971; BS, Tex. A&M U., Commerce, 1975, MS, 1976. Cert. data processing Inst. for Certification Computer Profls., 1982; vocat. office edn. tchr. Tex. Edn. Agy., 1973. Spl. clk. Tex. Instruments, Dallas, 1966—70; VOE instr. Aldine Ind. Sch. Dist. - McArthur H.S., Tex., 1971—74; computer sci. grad. asst. Tex. A&M U., Commerce, 1975—76; computer sci. tech. instr. Tex. State Tech. Coll., Waco, 1978—80; bus. application programmer analyst So. Farm Bur. Ins. Co., Waco, 1980—89, data security supr., 1989—98, corp. bus. resumption coord., 1999—2000; computer info. systems instr. Tarleton State U. - COBA, Stephenville, Tex., 2000—; data rsch. adminstr. Tarleton State U. - OPEIR, Stephenville, Tex., 2004—. Vice chmn. Tex. Cardinals, Inc., San Antonio, 2003—, Tex. Pot of Gold Found., Dallas, 2004—; worthy grand matron Grand Chpt. Tex., Arlington, 1998—99. Mem.: Assn. Info. Tech. Profls (student assn. com. 2003—05, pres. Heart of Tex. chpt. 1983—84, Individual Performance Bronze and Silver awards 1982, 1985), Order Ea. Star (worthy matron Waco 7 1982—83, worthy matron Stephenville chpt. #801 2004—06, vision quest coord. for Tex. Gen. Grand chpt. 2006—). Avocations: travel, reading, photography. Office: Tarleton State University Box T-0505 Stephenville TX 76402 Office Phone: 254-968-9416. Business E-Mail: abane@tarleton.edu.

BANE, GLENICE GAIL, music educator; b. San Diego, Apr. 20, 1948; d. Glenn Lorraine and Florence Gertrude DeWald; m. James Wallace Bane, Feb. 16, 1974; children: Shannon Marie, Jamie Suzanne. BS in Edn., Kent State U., Ohio, 1971; MEd, Ind. Wesleyan U., Independence, Ohio, 2006. Cert. tchr. Ohio, 1971. Tchr. music Cuyahoga Heights Sch. Dist., Ohio, 1971—73, Mayfield City Sch. Dist., Ohio, 1973—76, Solon City Sch. Dist., Ohio, 1985—. Choral condr. All- Am. Youth Honor Choir, Miami, Fla., 1972—75. Dir.(founder Our Gang Players): (mus. dir.) Children's Musical Theater. Recipient Outstanding Profl. award, Ind. Wesleyan U., 2006. Mem.: Music Educators Nat. Conf. (assoc.), Ohio Music Edn. Assn. (assoc.), Chautauqua Lit. and Sci. Cir. (life). Avocations: writing, travel, photography. Home: 7521 Canal Rd Valley View OH 44125-5730 Office: Solon City Sch Dist 6795 Solon Blvd Solon OH 44139-4198 Office Phone: 440-349-6220. Home Fax: 216-328-2200; Office Fax: 440-349-8048. Personal E-mail: banegg@adelphia.net. E-mail: gbane@solonboe.org.

BANE, MARY JO, dean, political science professor; b. Princeville, Ill., Feb. 24, 1942; d. Fred W. and Helen (Callery) B.; m. Kenneth Winston, May 31, 1975. BS in Internat. Rels., Georgetown U., 1963; MAT, Harvard U., 1966, DEd, 1972. Tchr. English U.S. Peace Corps, Liberia, 1963-65; tchr. social studies Arlington Pub. Schs., Mass., 1966-67; tchr. English and social studies Brookline Pub. Schs., Mass., 1968-71; rsch. assoc. Ctr. Ednl. Policy Rsch. and Huron Inst. Harvard U., Cambridge, Mass., 1971-72, project co-dir. Ctr. Study of Pub. Policy, 1972-75, assoc. prof. edn., lectr. in sociology, 1977-80, assoc. prof. pub. policy, 1981-86, dir. Malcolm Wiener Ctr. for Social Policy, 1987-92, prof. pub. policy, 1986-90; Malcolm Wiener Prof. of Social Policy Kennedy Sch. of Govt., Harvard U., Cambridge, Mass., 1990-92, prof. pub. policy, 1997—98, Thornton Bradshaw prof. pub. policy and mgmt., 1998—, chair mgmt. and leadership, academic dean, 2006—; lectr. in Sociology U. Mass., Boston, 1972-75; assoc. dir. Ctr. Rsch. on Women, asst. prof. edn., lectr. in sociology Wellesley Coll., 1975-77; dep. asst. sec. for program planning and budget analyst Office Planning and Budget U.S. Dept. Edn., Washington, 1980-81; exec. dep. commr. N.Y. State Dept. Social Svcs., 1984-86, commr., 1992-93; asst. sec. Adminstrn. for Children and Families Dept. Health and Human Svcs., Washington, 1993-96. Ida Bean vis. prof. U. Iowa, 1980; chair bd. overseers panel study income dynamics Inst. Rsch. U. Mich., 1982-86; regents lectr. U. Calif., Berkeley, 1987; mem. adv. com. urban poverty NAS, 1986-90, chair com. child devel. rsch. and pub. policy, 1987-90; mem. pres. adv. coun. Columbia U. Tchrs. Coll., N.Y.C., 1988-92; mem. grants adv. coun. Smith Richardson Found., 1989-92; bd. dirs. Manpower Demonstration Rsch. Coun., 1989-92, 97—; active William T. Grant Found. Commn. on Work, Family and Citizenship, 1987-88. Author: (with others) Inequality: A Reassessment of the Effects of Family and Schooling in America, 1972, Here to Stay: American Families in the Twentieth Century, 1974, Japanese translation, 1981, (with George Masnick) The Nation's Families 1960-90, 1980, Welfare Realities: From Rhetoric to Reform, 1994, Lifting Up the Poor: A Dialogue on Religion, Poverty and Wledare Reform, 2003; editor: (with Donald Levine) The Inequality Controversy, 1975, (with Manuel Carballo) The State and the Poor in the 1980s, 1984, (with Kenneth I. Winston) Gender and Public Policy: Cases and Comments, 1993, Who Will Provide? The Changing Role of Religion in American Social Welfare, 2000, Taking Faith Seriously, 2005; contbr. articles to profl. jours. Fellow Nat. Acad. Pub. Adminstrn.; mem. Am. Sociol. Assn., Population Assn. Asm., Assn. Pub. Policy Analysis and Mgmt. Avocations: hiking, reading, gardening. Office: Harvard Univ Kennedy Sch Govt 79 John F Kennedy St Cambridge MA 02138-5801 Office Phone: 617-496-9703. Office Fax: 617-496-9053. E-mail: mary_jo_bane@harvard.edu.*

BANERJEE, MARIA NEMCOVA, Russian language and literature educator; b. Prague, Czechoslovakia, Nov. 22, 1937; naturalized citizen, 1966; d. Joseph and Marie (Karlikova) Nemec; m. Dibyendu Kumar Banerjee, Nov. 18, 1961. BA, Coll. Marie de France, Montreal, Que., Can., 1955; MA, U. Montreal, 1957; PhD, Harvard U., 1962. Tchr. fellow Harvard U., Cambridge, Mass., 1958-62, vis. mem. Russian Rsch. Ctr., 1983—; asst. prof. Brown U., Providence, 1962-64; asst. prof. Russian, Smith Coll., Northampton, Mass., 1966-71, assoc. prof., 1971-81, prof., 1981—, chmn. dept., 1994—. Author: Terminal Paradox, 1990, 3d edit., 1992, Paradoxes Terminaux, 1993, A Lime Tree in Prague, 1997, Dostoevsky: The Scandal of Reason, 2006; contbr. articles to profl. jours. Mem. Mass. Dem. Com. Mem. Am. Assn. for Advancement Slavic Studies, Czechoslovak Acad. Arts and Scis. Roman Catholic. Avocations: gardening, tennis, travel. Office: Smith Coll Dept Russian Northampton MA 01063-0001 E-mail: mbanerje@smith.edu.

BANEY, LORI A., medical technician, educator; b. Burke, S.D., Dec. 2, 1962; d. George E. and Lois L. Baney. AAS in Vet. Tech., Colby C.C., Kans., 1983; AAS in Histology, Presentation Coll., S.D., 1987; BS in Human Resources, Friends U., Wichita, 1994. Histology technician St. Luke's Hosp., Aberdeen, SD, 1986—87; history/serology technician S.D. State U. Diagnostic Lab., Brookings, 1987—89; instr. Colby C.C., 1989—. Mem.: AAUW, Kans. Vet. Technicians Assn. (pres. and nat. assn. liaison 1989—), Nat. Assn. Vet. Technicians Am. Personal E-mail: lori@colbycc.org.

BANG, MICHELE ALENE, protective services official; d. Billy Bang Jr. and Deborah Mae Mangen; m. Darcy Rae Burns, June 1, 1991. BS, U. Nebr., Lincoln, 1991; MBA, U. Nebr., Omaha, 2001. Tchr. Millard Pub. Schs., Omaha, 1992—93; police officer Omaha Police Dept., 1993—2002, police sgt., 2002—. Small bus. owner Mojo's Coffeehouse, 1997—2002. With USNR, 1987—92. Mem.: Law Enforcement Against Discrimination (v.p. 2004—06), Nebr. Assn. Women Police (v.p., pres. 1999—2006). Democrat. Lutheran. Avocations: reading, gardening, walking, politics, home projects. Office: Omaha Police Dept 505 S 15th St Omaha NE 68102

BANGERT, COLETTE STUEBE, artist; b. Columbus, Ohio, July 7, 1934; d. Alfred Carl and Frances H. Stuebe; m. Charles Jeffries Bangert, June 9, 1959. BFA, John Herron Arts Inst., 1957; MFA, Boston U., 1958. Art instr. Ferry Hall Sch. for Girls, Lake Forest, Ill., 1958—59; artist, reader's adv. Topeka Pub. Libr., Kans., 1962—69; instr., art dept. Avila Coll., Kansas City, Mo., 1969—72; tchg. assoc., art dept. U. Mo., Kansas City, 1972—74; pvt. art practice, 1974—. Adv. bd. U. Kans., Emily Taylor Women's Resource Ctr., 1982—99, pres., 1995—98. One-woman shows include Krasner Gallery, NYC, 1963, 1980, Lawrence Gallery, Kansas City, 1979, 1980, 1982, 1983, North Dakota Mus. Art, Grand Forks, 1984, Lawrence Art Ctr., 2002, Fields Gallery, Lawrence, Kans., 2006, Represented in permanent collections Mus. Modern Art, NYC, Hallmark Collection, Kans. City, Mo., Mulvane Art Mus., Topeka,Kans., Sheldon Meml., Lincoln, Nebr., Springfield Art Mus., Mo., Victoria and Albert Mus., London, Spencer Art Mus., Lawrence, Kans., U. Okla. Mus. Art; contbr. articles to profl. jours. Mem.: Kansas City Artists Coalition (founder, past pres.). Home: 721 Tennessee Lawrence KS 66044

BANGERTER, RENEE TANNER, literature educator; b. Fullerton, Calif., Nov. 15, 1972; d. Marvin and Jolene Swensen; m. Ryan Bangerter, May 20, 1995; children: Ethan, Alyse, Hannah. BA in English, Brigham Young U., Provo, Utah, 1996, MA in English, 1998. ESL tchr. La Sierra H.S., Fullerton, 1998—2000; adj. English instr. Fullerton Coll., 1999—2001, asst. prof. English, 2001—. Lectr. Calif. State U., Fullerton, Calif., 2000—01. Women's instr. LDS Ch., Fullerton, 2005—06. Office: Fullerton College 321 E Chapman Ave Fullerton CA 92831 Office Phone: 714-992-7453. Business E-Mail: rbangerter@fullcoll.edu.

BANGS, MARY CONSTANCE (C BANGS), artist, curator; b. Elmira, NY, Oct. 19, 1946; d. Orval Ernest Bangs and Mary Isabelle Engle; m. Victor Louis Zeringo, June 29, 1969 (div. June 1978); m. Gregory Lee Matloff, Aug. 8, 1986. BFA, Phila. Coll. of Art, 1970; MFA, Pratt Inst., 1975. Curator discoveries dept. parks and recreation City of New York, 1980—90; curator discoveries Elders Share the Arts, Bklyn., 1991—96; instr. Empire State Corp. Coll. SUNY, Bklyn., 1993—2005; with spl. projects Art Resource Transfer, Inc., N.Y.C., 2000—01. Instr. Tchrs. Coll., Columbia U., N.Y.C., 1985; adv. bd. Space Activity Soc., Internat. Astron. Fedn., Paris, 1995—2004; curator Messages From Earth, N.Y.C., 2000—; artist cons. Marshall Space Flight Ctr., Huntsville, Ala., 2001, Huntsville, 02, Huntsville, 03, Huntsville, 04, NASA faculty fellow, 2002—04. Curator (exhibitions) Discoveries: Exhbns. of the City's Underknown Older Artists, 1980—90; holographic space billboards, 2001, Represented in permanent collections Libr. of Congress, Chrysler Mus., Norfolk, Va., Mint Mus., Charlotte, N.C., Pratt Inst., Bklyn., Accademia dei Fisiocritici, Siena, Italy, Pantcra Contrade Mus., Dipartimento di Fisica, Universita Degli Studi do Siena, Italy, Pace U., Civic Ctr. Campus, N.Y.C., Annabel Taylor Hall, Cornell U., Ithaca, N.Y., one-woman shows include Tompkins County Ctr. for Culture and Performing Arts, Ithaca, 1979, Pace U. Art Gallery, 1985, Ten Brooks Gallery, 1991, Belanthi Gallery, 1992, Accademia dei Fisiocritici, Siena, 1994, Art Resources Transfer, Inc., 1997, Audart, N.Y.C., 1998, Art Resources Transfers, Inc., 1999, 2001, Corridor Gallery, 2002, 2003, 2004, Gallery 718, Bklyn., 2003, Sonya, 2002, 2003, 2004, Boro Hall, 2005, Bklyn. Borough Hall, numerous group shows including most recently, exhibited in group shows at Taipei Gallery, NYC, 2001—02, Las Vegas Mus. of Art, 2002, 2005, Forms of Divinity, Brave Destiny, Williamsburg Hist. Ctr., Bklyn., N.Y., 2003—05, Corridor Gallery, Bklyn., 2003, 2005, West Bath Gallery, N.Y.C., 2003, Williamsburg Art and Hist. Ctr., Bklyn., 2003—04, Galerie Lelong, N.Y.C., 2003, P.M.S., Bklyn., 2004, Bklyn. (N.Y.) Borough Hall Pratt Inst., 2005. Recipient Pub. award, United Press, 1981; grantee, NASA, 2001; scholar Jerome Found., Bob Blackton Printmaking Workshop, N.Y.C., 1982. Mem.: Artist's Equity (bd. adv. 1996—98). Home: 417 Greene Ave Brooklyn NY 11216 Office Phone: 718-638-7586. Personal E-mail: gregmat0@aol.com.

BANK, BARBARA J., sociology educator; b. Chgo., Dec. 13, 1939; d. Julius Charles and Anna Catherine (Damm) Bank; m. Bruce Jesse Biddle, June 19, 1976. BS in Edn., Ill. State U., Normal, 1961; MA, U. Iowa, 1968, PhD in Sociology, 1974. Tchr. Rich Twp. H.S., Park Forest, Ill., 1961-63; from instr. to prof. emerita U. Mo., Columbia, 1969—, dir. grad. studies dept. sociology, 1978-82, chair dept. sociology, 1981-84. Vis. fellow Australian Nat. U., Canberra, 1984-85, 88, 93. Author: Contradictions in Women's Education, 2003; co-editor: Gender, Equity, and Schooling: Policy and Practice, 1997; assoc. editor Social Psychology of Edn., 1994-2000; contbr. articles to profl. jours.; presenter in field. Recipient Purple Chalk Tchg. award Coll. Arts and Scis., U. Mo., 1998; Fulbright sr. scholar, 1985; William T. Kemper fellow Excellence in Teaching, 2000. Mem. profl. orgns. Avocations: travel, reading. Home: 924 Yale Columbia MO 65203-1874 Office: U Mo Dept Sociology Columbia MO 65211-0001 Office Phone: 573-882-9174. Business E-Mail: bankb@missouri.edu.

BANK, MELISSA S., writer; BA in Am. studies, Hobart & William Smith Colleges, 1982; MFA in fiction, Cornell U., 1988. Editl. asst. Putnam Pub. Group, NYC; copywriter McCann Erickson, NYC. Author: The Girls' Guide to Hunting and Fishing, 1999, The Wonder Spot, 2005; Stories have appeared in Chgo. Tribune, Zoetrope, The North American Rev., Other Voices, Ascent. Office: Penguin Group 375 Hudson St New York NY 10014 Address: c/o Molly Friedrich Aaron Priest Literary Agy 708 Third Ave New York NY 10017

BANKE, KATHY M., lawyer; b. Glendale, Calif., Mar. 1, 1953; married; 2 children. BA, Calif. State U., Sacramento, 1973; JD, U. Colo., Boulder, 1979. Bar: Calif. 1979, US Dist. Ct. Ea. Dist. Calif. 1979, US Dist. Ct. No. Dist. Calif. 1982, US Dist. Ct. Ctrl. Dist. Calif. 1983, US Ct. Appeals 9th Cir. 1983, US Supreme Ct. 2000, US Ct. Appeals 3rd Cir. 2004. With Crosby Heafey Roach & May (combined with Reed Smith in 2003), 1982—2003; ptnr. Reed Smith LLP, Oakland, Calif., 2003—, also practice group leader appellate group. Adj. asst. prof. law in civil appellate advocacy Hastings Coll. Law, 1990—93; practitioner-advisor in civil appellate advocacy Boalt Hall Sch. Law, 1994—98. Mem.: Calif. Acad. Appellate Lawyers, Am. Acad. Appellate Lawyers. Office: Reed Smith LLP 1999 Harrison St Ste 2400 Oakland CA 94612-3572 Office Phone: 510-466-6765. Office Fax: 510-273-8832. Business E-Mail: kbanke@reedsmith.com.

BANKHEAD, SHERRY L., lawyer; b. Gatesville, Tex., Feb. 12, 1971; BA, U. Tex., Austin, 1994; JD, South Tex. Coll. Law, Houston, 1998. Bar: Tex. 1998. Assoc. atty. Johnson, Spalding, Doyle, West & Trent LLP, Houston. Named a Rising Star, Tex. Super Lawyers mag., 2006. Mem.: ABA, Houston Young Lawyers Assn., Houston Bar Assn. Office: Johnson Spalding Doyle West & Trent LLP 919 Milam St Ste 1700 Houston TX 77002 Office Phone: 713-222-2323. E-mail: sbankhead@js-llp.com.*

BANKO, RUTH CAROLINE, retired library director; b. Phillipsburg, NJ, Mar. 28, 1931; d. Arthur William and Virginia Miller (Wilson) Osborn; m. Marvin Kenneth Banko (dec.); children: David, Sallie, Susan, Joseph, Elisabeth. Cert. libr. tech. asst., Northampton AreaC.C. Salesman Stanley Home Products, 1958-95; dir. Riegelsville (Pa.) Pub. Libr., 1974-97. Social ambudsman County Agy. on Aging, Doylestown, Pa.; asst. dir. Pearl Buck Found., Dublin, Pa.; mem. Riegelsville Fire Aux., 1992—; councilman, Planning Commn., Riegelsville Borough Coun., 1972-89; mem. States Legis. Com., 1972-88; mayor Borough of Riegelsville, 1990-97; disaster chmn., blood chmn., bd. mem. ARC, Doylestown, 1966-86; pres. jr. high and area coun. PTA, Easton, 1966-74; pres. Boro Coun., 1980-81; v.p., trustee Riegelsville Pub. Libr. Recipient Svc. award ARC, Doylestown, Bucks County Libr. Dist., Life Membership award PTA, 1972; named children's rm. in her honor Ragelsville Pub. Libr., 2005 Mem. Pa. Boroughs Assn. (legis. com. 1972-97), Pa. Mayors Assn., Easton Area Coun. PTAs (life). Democrat. Lutheran. Home: 449 Easton Rd Riegelsville PA 18077-0223

BANKS, CAROLYN DUTY, retired history educator; b. Rogers, Ark., May 11, 1932; d. Jeff Davis and Lois White Duty; m. Warren Eugene Banks (dec.); children: Karen Marie, Keith Randolph(dec.). BA, U. Ark., 1960, postgrad., 1961—63. Cert. tchr. Ark. Tchr. Washington (Ark.) secondary schs., 1961—80; mem. fine arts staff U. Ark., 1967—69; self employed rschr., editor Ark., 1987—97; staff writer Hist. Soc. Jour., Fayetteville, Ark., 2000—. Rschr., editor: geneal. book In the Line of Duty, 1997; contbr. articles to profl. jours. Mem. Dem. Women's Club Washington County, Ark.; bd. dirs. U. Ark. Retirement Assn., Fayetteville, 1996—2000. Mem.: DAR, NWA Scottish Soc., Washington County Hist. Soc., Third Order of St. Francis, 20th Century Club (pres. 1992), Scottish Knights Templar (dame 2004), Phi Beta Kappa, Delta Delta Delta. Episcopalian. Avocations: historical research and writing, raising skye terriers, gardening, exercise.

BANKS, DEIRDRE MARGARET, retired church organization administrator; b. Melbourne, Australia, May 9, 1934; came to U.S., 1975; d. Haldane Stuart and Vera Avice (Fisher) B. MA, Simpson Coll., 1980. Missionary nurse Leprosy Mission, Kathmandu, Nepal, 1960-69; dean of women Melbourne Bible Inst., 1970-75; asst. to dir. Bible Study Fellowship, Oakland, Calif., 1975-79; dir. adult ministries First Covenant Ch., Oakland, 1980-87, assoc. pastor for adults, St. Paul, 1987-89; exec. dir. Covenant Women Ministries, Chgo., 1989-99; interim pastor Bowie Ch. of the Redeemer Covenant, Md., 2005; ret. Spkr. in field. Chair ch. edn. bd. Pacific S.W. Conf. Evang. Ch., 1985-87, Gilead Group, Oakland, 1985-87; bd. dirs., chair Gilead Group Housing for Abused and Homeless Women and Children; bd. chmn. Barnabas Project for Abused and Homeless Women and Children, 1990-93; mem. bd. world mission Evang. Covenant Ch., 1986-89; bd. Covenant Enabling Residences Inc. for Developmentally Disabled Adults, pres., 1996-98; pastor Mission Covenant Ch., Orange, Mass., 2000-04. Mem. Evangel. Covenant Ch. Personal E-mail: dmbanks7@aol.com.

BANKS, DONNA JO, food products executive; b. Ft. McClellan, Ala., Sept. 6, 1956; d. Walter Dow and Joanne (Phelps) Cox; m. Bobby Dennis Banks, Dec. 27, 1983; children: Cynthia Marie, Elizabeth Anne, Sarah Diane. BS, U. Tenn., 1979, MS, 1980; PhD, Mich. State U., 1984. Assoc. statistician Kellogg Co., Battle Creek, Mich., 1983-84, mgr. product evaluation and stats., 1984-87, dir. cereal product devel., 1987-91, v.p. rsch. and devel., 1991-97, sr. v.p. rsch. and devel., 1997—99, sr. v.p. global innovation, 1999—2000, sr. v.p. rsch., quality and tech., 2000—04, sr. v.p., worldwide innovation and operations, 2004—. Bd. mem. Mich. Life Scis. Corridor. Bd. mem. Mich. State U. Found. Named Disting. Alumni, Mich. State U. Coll. Agr. and Natural Resources, 2000; named one of 25 Masters of Innovation, BusinessWeek, 2006; named to Acad. Women Achievers, YWCA N.Y.C., 1998. Mem.: Product Devel. Mgmt. Assn., Am. Assn. Cereal Chemists, Internat. Food Techs., Am. Statis. Assn., Sigma Xi. Democrat. Baptist. Avocations: racquetball, tennis, needlecrafts, sewing. Office: Kellogg Co 1 Kellogg Sq Battle Creek MI 49016-3599*

BANKS, RELA, sculptor; b. Yaroslav, Poland, Oct. 8, 1933; came to U.S., 1947; d. Jacob and Frieda (Weintraub) Heuberg; m. Stanley Frederic Banks, Aug. 9, 1953; children: Andrew Howard, J. Monica, Gary Mitchell. Student, Mus. Modern Art, 1957, Art Students League, NYC, 1958-61, Summit Art Ctr., NJ, 1966-75. Chmn. nat. juried exhibit Summit Art Ctr., 1976, mem. adminstrv. com., 1977-79, chmn. standing com. spl. events, trustee; mem. exec. com. Phoenix Gallery, N.Y.C., 1983; chmn. membership com. Stone Sculpture Soc. N.Y., 1980-82. One-woman shows include Robins Art Gallery, South Orange, N.J., 1973, Montclair (N.J.) Coll., 1974, Caldwell (N.J.) Coll., 1974, 83, Summit Art Ctr., 1976, Newark Acad., Livingston, N.J., 1976, Douglas Coll., New Brunswick, N.J., 1978, First Women's Bank, N.Y.C., 1979, Phoenix Gallery, 1979, 81, 83, Morris Mus. Arts and Scis., Morristown, N.J., 1983, Ann Leonard Gallery, Woodstock, 1983, NECCA Mus., Bklyn., Conn., 1985, Schiller-Wapner Galleries, N.Y.C., 1985, 87, Ann Norton Sculpture Galleries, West Palm Beach, Fla., 1987, David Gary Ltd, Millburn, N.J., 1988; exhibited in group shows at Phoenix Gallery, 1979, 83, Morris Mus. Art, 1979, 83, Invitational Woodstock Artists Assn., 1980, 84, Eilaine Benson Gallery, Bridgehampton, N.Y., 1980, Searles Art Ctr., Great Barrington, Mass., 1980, Nabisco Art Gallery, 1981, Summit Art Ctr., 1981, First Womens Bank, 1981, Fairleigh Dickinson U., Madison, N.J., 1983, NYU Grad. Sch. Bus., 1983, AT&T Gallery, Basking Ridge, N.J., 1984, Shering Plough Gallery, N.J., 1984, New Orleans Mus. Art, 1986, Gallery Contemporary Art at U. Colorado Springs, Colo., 1986, Schiller-Wapner Galleries, 1986, Lever House, N.Y.C., 1986, Aldrich Mus. Contemporary Art, Ridgefield, Conn., 1986, Okla. Art Ctr., Oklahoma City, 1987, "After Henry Moore", Emily Lowe Mus., Hofstra U., Hempstead, N.Y., 1988, group exhibition, Poland; represented in permanent collections New Orleans Mus. Art, Everson Mus., Syracuse, N.Y., Morris Mus. Sci. and Art, Okla. Art Ctr., Vassar Coll. Gallery, Poughkeepsie, N.Y., Millburn (N.J.) Pub. Library, Minn. Mus. Art, Mpls., Woodstock Hist. Soc., Fordham U., Lincoln Ctr., N.Y.C., Aldrich Mus. Contemporary Art, Warsaw Mus., Poland, various pvt. and corp. collections. Mem. Woodstock Artists Assn. Office: Rela Banks Studio 272 Yerry Hill Rd Woodstock NY 12498 Office Phone: 845-679-2798.

BANKS, SANDRA C., retired elementary school educator; b. Carthage, Mo., Oct. 30, 1952; d. Robert and Geneice Peavie; m. George Banks, Sept. 28, 1974; children: Jermaine, Erin. BS in Elem. Edn., Jackson State U., 1974; M in Elem. Edn., Maryville U., 1992; reading cert., Harris Stowe Coll., 1991. Reading specialist Normandy Sch. Dist., St. Louis, tchr. Recipient Employee of Yr., Bel Ridge Elem. Sch., 1990, Alumnus of Yr., Jackson State U., 1999. Mem.: MNEA.

BANKS, TYRA (TYRA LYNNE BANKS), retired model, television personality; b. LA, Dec. 4, 1973; d. Don Banks and Carolyn London. CEO, TYInc.; founder Tyra Banks Scholarship, 1992, T-Zone summer camp for girls, 2000-; lectr. at UCLA, Johns Hopkins, Georgetown U., others. Appeared on covers of Elle, Essence, Sports Illustrated, GQ Mag., Cosmopolitan, Shape, Harper's Bazaar, Esquire, Arena, Vogue, Victoria's Secret Catalog (contract with mag.). Featured in comml. for Cover Girl, Coors, McDonald's, Nike, Pepsi, Nat. Milk Processor Promotion bd.; writer (book) Tyra's Beauty Inside and Out, 1997; Actor: (films) Higher Learning, 1995, A Woman Like That, 1997, Love Stinks, 1999, Love & Basketball, 2000, Coyote Ugly, 2000, Halloween: Resurrection, 2002, (voice) Eight Crazy Nights, 2002, Larceny, 2004; (TV films) Inferno, 1992, The Apartment Complex, 1999, Life-Size, 2000; (TV series) Fresh Prince of Bel-Air, 1993-94; Creator, writer, prodr., host, judge (TV series) America's Next Top Model, 2003-, host, exec. prodr. The Tyra Banks Show, 2005-; (guest appearances) (TV series) include New York Undercover, 1997, The Oprah Winfrey Show (several appearances), Just Shoot Me, 1999, Mad TV, 2000, 2004, Felicity, 2000, Who Wants to Be a Millionaire, 2000, Soul Food, 2001, American Dreams, 2004 and several others. Named one of 50 Most Beautiful People in the World, People, 1994, 1996, 100 Most Influential People, Time Mag., 2006. Achievements include being the first African American Woman on the cover of Sports Illustrated Swimsuit Issue. Office: Handprint Entertainment c/o Benny Medina 1100 Glendon Ave Ste 1000 Los Angeles CA 90024*

BANKSON, MARJORY ZOET, former religious association administrator; m. Peter Bankson. BA in Govt. and Econs., Radcliffe Coll., 1961; M in Am. History, U. Alaska, 1961; postgrad., Va. Episcopal Sem., 1985; LLD, Va. Theol. Sem., 1999. H.S. history and English tchr.; counselor Dartmouth Coll., 1969-70; profl. potter, 1970-80; pres. Faith at Work, Falls Church, Va., 1985-2001. Editor, contbr. Faith@Work mag.; has written for Living Pulpit, Response, The Seminary Journal. Author: Braided Streams: Esther and a Woman's Way of Growing, Seasons of Friendship: Naomi and Ruth as a Pattern, This Is My Body: Creativity, Clay, and Change, The Call of the Soul: Six Stages of Spiritual Development, 1999 (videos) The Potter and Clay, With Tongues of Fire: Five Women from the Book of Acts. Mem. Ch. of the Savior, 1976—, Seekers Ch., Washington, DC, preacher, teacher Sch. Christian Living. Office: 106-B East Broad St Falls Church VA 22046-4501 E-mail: faithatwork@aol.com.

BANKSTON, SHERRI RENEE, secondary school educator, director; b. Lewisville, Tex., Sept. 10, 1980; d. Gerald R. and Susan J. Untz; m. Andrew Charles Bankston, June 10, 2006. B in Music Edn., Baylor U., Waco, Tex., 2004. Cert. tchr. Tex. Musician (clarinetist): Ft. Worth Cmty. Band. Martha Barkema, McCracken, & Glennis Goodrich McCrary scholar, Baylor U., 1999—2004, Ednl. grant, Music & Tech., 2005—06. Mem.: Tex. Music Educators Assn. (All-State Band award 1999), Mu Phi Epsilon. Personal E-mail: overture99@aol.com.

BANNER-GRAY, MARION G., secondary school educator; Tchr. biology Naugatuck (Conn.) H.S., 1996—. Office: Naugatuck High School 543 Rubber Ave Naugatuck CT 06770 Office Phone: 203-720-5298. Business E-Mail: graym@naugy.net.

BANNING, DONNA ROSE, art educator; b. Belle Fourche, SD, July 2, 1934; d. Anzley Meltiah and Rose Helen (Kapsa) Walker; m. Robert Orval Banning (dec.); children: Bruce, Connie, Bernie, Callie. AA, Fullerton Coll., Calif., 1967; BA, Calif. State U., Fullerton, 1969; MA, Calif. State U., Long Beach, 1976. Cert. tchr. Calif., tchr. art K-12 Calif., state adminstr. K-12 Calif. Instr. visual arts El Modena H.S., Orange, Calif., 1970—2003; dist. dept. chair fine arts Orange (Calif.) Unified Sch. Dist., 1974—78, 1982—92; crafts instr. Rancho Santiago Coll., Santa Ana, Calif., 1971—75, ceramics instr., 1974—92; visual arts instr. Calif. State U., Long Beach, 1977—78, 2004; ret., 2003. Instr. art edn. Chapman Coll., Orange; cons. Calif. sch. dists., Orange County, 1991—; mem. Calif. State Framework and Criteria Com., 1994—2002, Legis. Action Com. Arts Edn., 1991—2002, Calif. Arts Assessment Networkcc, 1991—; lectr. art edn. Calif. State U., Long Beach, 2004—; presenter in field. Contbr. Named Tchr. of Yr., Calif. Gifted and Talented Assn., 1998, Disneyland Creativity Tchr. of Yr., Disneyland, 1998. Mem.: Orange County Arts Adminstrs. (Secondary Arts Tchr. of Yr. 2002), So. Calif. Ceramic Design Assn., Calif. Art Edn. Assn. (past pres., Tchr. of Yr. 2000), Nat. Art Edn. Assn. (v.p. 2004—, Pacific Region Tchr. of Yr. 2001), Calif. Alliance Arts Edn. Avocations: painting, pottery. Home: 2391 N Waterberry St Orange CA 92865-2851 Office Phone: 714-637-3244.

BANNON, DESIREE, mathematics educator; d. F. Jude and Jean M. Schappert; m. Brian M. Bannon, June 1, 2002. BA in Math. and Psychology, King's Coll., Wilkes-Barre, Pa., 2001; MEd, Wilkes U., Wilkes-Barre, Pa., 2005. Cert. instrnl. II, tchr. math. grades 7-12 Pa., 2005. Tchr. math. HS Hanover Area Sch. Dist., Pa., 2002—. Asst. coach varsity girls' volleyball Hanover Area Sch. Dist., 1999—. Mem.: Pa. State Edn. Assn., Luzerne County Coun. Tchrs. of Math. Office: Hanover Area Sch Dist 1600 Sans Souci Pkwy Hanover Township PA 18706

BANSAL, PREETA D., lawyer; b. Roorkee, India; d. M.K. and Prem Lata Bansal. AB magna cum laude, Harvard-Radcliffe Coll., 1986; JD magna cum laude, Harvard Law Sch., 1989. Law clerk to Chief Judge James L. Oakes US Ct. of Appeals, Second Circuit, 1989—90; law clerk to Justice John Paul Stevens US Supreme Ct., 1990—91; counsel Arnold & Porter, Washington; counselor to asst. atty. gen. Joel Klein US Dept. of Justice, Washington, 1993—96; special counsel Office of the White House Counsel, Washington, 1996; counsel Gibson, Dunn & Crutcher, NYC, 1996—99; solicitor gen. State of NY, 1999—2001; vis. prof. of constitutional law U. Nebr. Coll. of Law, 2002; counsel Skadden, Arps, Slate, Meagher & Flom, 2003—. Commentator on legal issues CNN, CSPAN & PBS news programs; vis. fellow John F. Kennedy Sch. of Govt., Harvard U., 2003; commr. & chair US Commn. Internat. Religious Freedom, 2003—; commr. NYC Mayor Bloomberg's Election Modernization Task Force, 2005—. Author: (numerous articles) Harvard Law Review, Yale Law Journal, Fordham Intellectual Property, Media & Entertainment Law Journal, Villanova Law Review. Office: Skadden, Arps, Slate, Meagher & Flom Four Times Square New York NY 10036 Office Phone: 212-735-2198. Office Fax: 212-777-2198. E-mail: pbansal@skadden.com.

BANTA, VICKI K., mathematics educator; d. Vilas Kenneth and Helen Marie Fortney; m. Thomas F. Miller, June 2, 1978 (div. May 1991); m. Geoffrey M. Banta, July 17, 1993. BS in Edn., U. Wis., Whitewater, 1971, MEd, 1980. Math. tchr. Oconomowoc HS, Wis., 1972—93, K-12 math. coord., 1990—91, math. dept. chair, 1990—93; math. tchr. Viroqua HS, 1993—, math. team leader, 1994—. Sec. Milw. Area Math. Coun., 1991—93; co-chair math. steering com. Viroqua HS, 1997—99, excellence in edn. com. mem., 1998—, sr. class adv., 1999—2004. Mem. Vernon County Rep. Party, Wis., 1994—; ch. coun. Immanuel Luth. Ch., Viroqua, 1999—2003, edn. com. mem., 1999—2003. Recipient Staff Recognition award, Oconomowoc HS, 1991, I Made a Difference award, Viroqua HS, 2000, Presdl. award for Excellence in Math. & Sci. Tchg., Wis. Dept. Pub. Instrn. & Nat. Com., Washington, D.C., 2001, Tchr. Who Made a Difference award, Carleton Coll., 2004. Mem.: NEA, Nat. Coun. Tchrs. Math., Wis. Edn. Assn., Coulee Region United Educators, Viroqua Edn. Assn. (bldg. rep. 1998—2000, exec. bd. 1998—2000, scholarship com. 2000—02), Viroqua Performing Arts Booster Club, Viroqua Booster Club, Whitewater Country Club, Am. Legion Aux., Eagles Aux., VFW Aux., Phi Kappa Phi. Avocations: reading, golf, exercise. Office: Viroqua HS 100 Blackhawk Dr Viroqua WI 54665 Business E-Mail: banvic@viroqua.k12.wi.us.

BANTA, VIVIAN L., insurance company executive; b. Lebanon, July 1950; arrived in US, 1968; m. Robert Field; 2 stepchildren. B in psychology, U. of Pacific, Stockton, Calif., 1972. With Bank of Am., 1972—87, Chase Manhattan Corp., 1987—97, sr. v.p. global securities svcs., 1991—93, exec. v.p. global securities svcs., 1993—95, exec. v.p. global investor svcs. (Chase Manhattan Corp. merged with Chemical Banking Corp.), 1995—97; sr. v.p., chief adminstrv. officer individual fin. svcs. Prudential Fin., 1998—2000, exec. v.p., CEO US Consumer Group, 2000—02, vice chmn. ins. divsn., 2002—. Named one of the 50 Most Powerful Women in Bus., Fortune, 2001, 2002, 2003, 2004, 2005, 100 Most Powerful Women, Forbes mag., 2005—06, 10 Most Powerful Women in NJ Bus., Star-Ledger, 2006. Office: Prudential Fin Inc 751 Broad St Newark NJ 07102-3777*

BANTZ, JODY LENORE, psychologist; b. Waukesha, Wis., July 2, 1975; d. Leonard Jerome and Dolores Ethel Bantz. BA, U. Wis., Whitewater, 1997; MA, Calif. Sch. Profl. Psychology, 1999, PhD in Psychology, 2003. Lic. clin. psychologist 2005. Psychology intern Springall Acad., San Diego, 1998—99, The Ctr., San Diego, 1999—2000, Jewish Family Svcs., San Diego, 2000—01; residential counselor Vista Balboa Crisis Ctr., San Diego, 1999—2000; rehabilitation therapist Telecare San Diego Choices, San Diego, 2000—01; multidisciplinary clinician Desert Regional Med. Ctr., Palm Springs, 2002—03; clinician, lic. clin. psychologist Sharper Future, Palm Desert, 2002—. Mem. Calif. Coalition on Sexual Offending, 2003—. Recipient Acad. Achievement award, U. Wis., 1997. Mem.: APA, Assn. Treatment Sexual Abusers. Libertarian. Protestant. Avocations: running, reading, hiking, theater. Office: 73255 El Paseo 18 Palm Desert CA 92260 also: 901 E Tahquitz B 201 Palm Springs CA 92262 Office Phone: 760-488-5054.

BAO, KATHERINE SUNG, pediatric cardiologist; b. Soochou, Kiangsu, China, Sept. 7, 1920; came to U.S., 1953; d. Yung H. Bao and Ming King; m. William S. Ting, May 2, 1948; children: Gordon K., Albert C. MD, Nat. Ctrl. Univ. Med. Coll., Nanking, China, 1944. Diplomate Am. Bd. Pediatrics. Intern Mercer Hosp., Trenton, NJ, 1953; resident in pediats. and cardiology Children's Meml. Hosp. Northwestern U., Chgo., 1954-57; fellow in pediatric cardiology Children's Hosp. L.A., Calif., 1957-59, attending cardiologist Calif., 1960—; chief pediatric cardiology City of Hope Med. Ctr., Duarte, Calif., 1965-68; chief heart bd. L.A. Unified Sch. Dist. and PTA Splty. Health Clinics, L.A., 1968—90; attending pediatrician, cardiologist Hollywood Presbyn. Med. Ctr., L.A., 1970—, UCLA, L.A., 1973—. Vis. pediatric cardiologist to univs. in Taipei Nat. Sci. Coun., Republic of China, 1983; U.S. pres.'s appointee Pres.'s Com. on Nat. Medal of Sci., 1983-85; adv. com. on health and med. care svcs. Dept. Health Svcs., Calif., 1988-90; pres. Chinese Physicians Soc. of So. Calif., 1969; speaker in field. Active Rep. Eagle, Rep. Presdl. Task Force, Rep. Presdl. Round Table. Rsch. Fellow Cardiologist, NIH, 1960-63; recipient Physician of Yr., Hon. Svc. award Calif. Congress of PTA, Inc., 1984, U.S. Rep. Senatorial Medal of Freedom, 1994; named Internat. Scientist of Yr., IBC, Cambridge, Eng., 2001, Woman of the Yr., ABI, 2002. Fellow Am. Acad. Pediatrics; mem. AMA, AAAS, World Med. Assn., Calif. Med. Assn., L.A. County Med. Assn., Am. Heart Assn., Internat. Cir. of L.A. World Affairs Coun., N.Y. Acad. Scis., Hollywood Acad. Medicine (pres. 1995), Scripps Clinic La Jolla (coun.). Achievements include pioneered research in cardiac arrhythmia in infants and children; research in congenital heart disease in adults. Office: PO Box 10456 Beverly Hills CA 90213-3456

BAPOOJI RYAN, ANITA B., lawyer; BA with distinction, Queen's U., 1994; LLB, U. Toronto, 1997. Bar: Mass., Ontario, US Dist. Ct. (Dist. Mass.), US Ct. Appeals (1st Cir.). Spl. asst. dist. atty. Middlesex County, Mass., 2003; assoc. Litig. Practice Group Testa, Hurwitz & Thibeault, Boston, mem. securities litig. group, mem. ins. risk mgmt. team; assoc. Litig. Dept. Goodwin Procter LLP, Boston, 2005—. Mem.: Boston Bar Assn. (co-chair bus. litig. sect. 2003—05), Boston Lawyers Group (assoc. adv. com.). Office: Goodwin Procter LLP Exchange Place 53 State St Boston MA 02109 Office Phone: 617-570-1998. E-mail: abapooji@goodwinprocter.com.*

BAQUERO, MARIA JOAQUINA, elementary school educator; b. Arroyo, P.R., May 26, 1956; d. Bienvenido and Gloria (Soliván) B.; m. Eduardo Santos De Choudens, July 14, 1978; children: Eduardo José Santos, Verónica Maria Santos, Juan Manuel Santos. BA in Natural Scis., U. Coll. of Cayey, P.R., 1978; AA in Computer Programming, San Juan (P.R.) City Coll., 1986; MEd, U. Phoenix, Guaynabo, P.R., 1991. Tchr., sci. head dept. Colegio Nuestra Senora del Pilar, Cupey, P.R., 1978-81; testing adminstr. Learn Aid, Co., Cupey, 1981-83; elem. sch. tchr. Am. Mil. Acad., Guaynabo, 1983—. Sci. club adviser Colegio Nuestra Sra. Pilar, Cupey, 1978-81; sci. fair coord. Am. Mil. Acad., Guaynabo, 1988—. Boys/girls scout adviser Am. Mil. Acad., Guaynabo, 1986—. Recipient Presdl. award for excellence in sci. and math. tchg. Pres. of the U.S., Washington, 1994. Mem. Nat. Coun. Tchrs. Math., Nat. Coun. Suprs. Math., Math. Assn. Am., Planetarium Assn. Roman Catholic. Avocations: gardening, reading, horseback riding. Office: American Military Academy Guaynabo PR 00970

BAR, ROSELYN R., legal association administrator, lawyer, executive secretary; b. 1958; BA, U. Rochester; JD, Bklyn. Law Sch. Bar: NY 1984, Fla. 1984, Calif. 1990. Atty. Skadden, Arps, Slate, Meagher, and Flom, NYC, L.A.; corp. counsel Sun Am. Inc.; asst. gen. counsel, asst. corp. sec. Martin Marietta Materials, Raleigh, NC, 1994—2001, v.p., gen. counsel, sec., 2001—, sr. v.p., gen. counsel, sec., 2005—. Mem.: Fla. Bar Assn., Calif. Bar Assn., NY Bar Assn. Office: Martin Marietta Materials Inc 2710 Wycliff Rd PO Box 30013 Raleigh NC 27622 Office Phone: 919-783-4603. E-mail: roselyn.bar@martinmarietta.com.

BARAB, PATSY LEE, nutritionist, realtor; b. Indpls., Sept. 24, 1934; 1 child, Gregory (dec.); m. John D. Barab Jr., Apr. 8, 1995. BS, Mich. State U., 1956, MA, 1970. Asst. prof. Med. Coll. Ga., Augusta, 1972-82; nutrition cons., 1982—. Assoc. Meybohm Realty, Inc., Augusta, 1987—. Docent Morris Mus. Art, 1992—; mem. program com. Gertrude Herbert Art Inst., 1992—94; mem. promotion com. Imperial Theater, bd. dirs., 2001—03. Mem.: AARP, CRS, GRI, Nutritionists in Nursing Edn. (nat. chmn. 1983—84), Nutrition Today Soc. (charter), Soc. Nutrition Edn., Ga. Dietetic Assn., Am. Dietetic Assn., Million Dollar Club (life), Pi Beta Phi, Omicron Nu. Home and Office: 3051 Walton Way Augusta GA 30909 Personal E-mail: patsypink3@aol.com.

BARACK, ROBIN SHEFFMAN, psychologist; b. St. John's, Nfld., Can., Jan. 20, 1946; d. Samuel B. and Alice (Serlin) Sheffman; m. Joseph P. Barack, June 14, 1966 (div. 1988); children: Shawn Beth, Ryan David; m. Philip Litwak, April 25, 1999. BA, U. Miami, 1966; MEd, U. Pitts., 1968, PhD, 1984. Lic. psychologist, cert. sch. psychologist, Pa. Tchr. Shaler Area Sch. Dist., Pitts., 1966-67, Allegheny County Intermediate U., Pitts., 1969; psychoednl. diagnostician Pitts. Child Guidance Ctr., 1969-81; sch. liaison, prin. Western Psychiat. Inst., Pitts., 1982-85, dir. psychoednl. assessment, 1985-86; clin. instr. dept. psychiatry U. Pitts., 1974—; pvt. practice Pitts., 1984—. Consulting psychologist K.D. Tillotson Sch., Pitts., 1984-89, Temple Emanuel Nursery Sch., Mt. Lebanon, Pa., 1984-97; bd. dirs. Chartiers Mental Health/Retardation, Bridgeville, Pa., 1985-90. Contbr. articles to profl. publs. Bd. dirs. Temple Emanuel of the Hills, Mt. Lebanon, 1984-89. Mem. Am. Psychol. Assn., Am. Orthopsychiat. Assn., Assn. Children with Learning Disabilities (adv. bd. 1980-91), Pa. Psychol. Assn., Pitts. Psychol. Assn. (edn. com. 1986-1999). Avocations: reading, walking. Office: 401 Shady Ave Ste C-107 Pittsburgh PA 15206-4409

BARAD, JILL ELIKANN, former family products company executive; b. NYC, May 23, 1951; d. Lawrence Stanley and Corinne Elikann; m. Thomas Kenneth Barad, Jan. 28, 1979; children: Alexander David, Justin Harris. BA in English and Psychology, Queens Coll., 1973. Asst. prod. mgr. mktg. Coty Cosmetics, NYC, 1976-77, product mgr. mktg., 1977; account exec. Wells Rich Greene Advt. Agy., LA, 1978-79; product mgr. mktg. Mattel Toys, Inc., LA, 1981-82, dir. mktg., 1982-83, v.p. mktg., 1983-85, sr. v.p. mktg., 1985-86, sr. v.p. product devel., 1986, exec. v.p. product design and devel., exec. v.p. mktg. and worldwide product devel., 1988-89; pres. girls and activity toys divsn. Mattel Toys, Inc. (name now Mattel, Inc.), LA, 1989-90; pres. Mattel USA, LA, 1990-92; pres., COO Mattel, Inc., LA, 1992-97, pres., CEO, 1997, chmn., CEO, 1997-2000. Trustee emeritus Queens Coll. Found.; chair exec. adv. bd. Children Affected by AIDS Found.; mem. bd. advisors The For All Kids Found., Inc.; mem. exec. bd. med. scis. UCLA.

BARADZI, AMELIA, stained glass artist, restorationist; b. Bay Shore, New York, Mar. 26, 1947; d. Stephen A. and Frances (De Palma) Baradzi. BA, La. Tech. U., 1970. Cert. K-6 tchr., La. Tchr. St. John's Elem. Sch., Central Islip, NY, 1971—72; pres. Stained Glass Creations Ltd., Bay Shore, NY, 1972—91; sec., treas. Baradzi Glass Inc., Bay Shore, NY, 1991—92; owner, mgr. Amelia Baradzi Studio, Bay Shore, NY, 1993—, L.I. Stained Glass Restoration and Conservation Studio, Bay Shore, NY, 1995—, Stained Glass Restoration Co., Bay Shore, NY, 1998. Designer, mfr., commissions art glass Poinsettia, 1985-87, Story of Creation, 1987, Peacock, 1989; designer, mfg. leaded glass Edwardian flowercases and sconces, 1994; restoration of St. Andrews Ch. Saltaire, Fire Island, NY., 2003, Bay Shore Jewish Ctr., N.Y., 2006. Mem. Bus. Improvement Dist., Bay Shore, N.Y. 1994-95. Roman Catholic. Avocations: fishing, gardening, painting, reading. Home and Office: Amelia Baradzi Studio 50 Bay Ave Bay Shore NY 11706-8753 Office Phone: 631-665-5011. E-mail: abarad@optonline.net.

BARAJAS, NANCY HELEN, assistant principal; d. Gene and Doris Jean Dees; m. Don Anthony Barajas, June 7, 1986; children: Gene Anthony, Nicholas Samuel, Alexis Gabrielle. AA, Clayton State Coll., Morrow, Ga., 1989; BA, Ga. State U., Atlanta, 1991; MEd, Ga. Coll., Milledgeville, 2002. Cert. tchr. Ga. Bd. Edn., Tex. Bd. Edn. K-5 Spanish tchr., Houston, Tex., 1991—92; 9-12 Spanish tchr. Henry County Pub. Schs., McDonough, Ga., 1992—95; 9-12 Spanish tchr. Clayton County Pub. Schs., Jonesboro, 1995—97; k-5 Spanish lead tchr. Atlanta Pub. Schs., 1997—98; asst. prin. Houston Ind. Sch. Dist., Tex., 2005—. Mem.: ASCD. Office: Houston Ind Sch Dist Deady Mid Sch 2500 Broadway Houston TX 77012

BARAN, CHRISTINE, systems analyst; b. Rochester, N.Y., Apr. 21, 1958; d. Wolodymyr and Olha (Zyrak) B. AS, Rochester Inst. Tech., 1978, BS, 1980. Computer programmer Infodata Sys., Rochester, N.Y., 1980-83; sys. analyst Acumenics, Bethesda, Md., 1983-85; staff cons. Martin Marietta, Greenbelt, Md., 1985-88; sys. analyst, computer specialist Smithsonian Inst., Washington, 1988—. Cons. USAID, Washington, 1983-90 Recipient Discovering Undeveloped Engrng. Scientific Talent, Eastman Kodak Co., 1975—80. Mem. NAFE, LWV. Republican. Mem. Ukrainian Catholic. Home: 8607 Chase Glen Cir Fairfax Station VA 22039-3308 Office: Smithsonian Instn Comptr Office 955 Lenfant Plz SW Washington DC 20024-2119

BARAN, SHIRLEY WALTERS, artist, sculptor; m. Helko Eli Baran; 3 children. Student, Corcoran Mus. Sch. Art, 1943-45, U. Ark., 1945-48, Pratt Inst., 1945-48. Co-owner, illustrator Baran-Walters Advt., Tulsa, Okla., 1949-65; free lance illustrator, painter, sculptor Greenville, S.C., 1966-81; art coord. Her Majesty Industries, Greenville, S.C., 1966-81; illustrator, layout artist Millbrae Sun, Calif., Boutique Villager, Burlingame, Foster City Progress, Millbrae Leader, San Carlos Inquirer, Belmont Courier Bull., 1982-93. Freelance designer Clay Art Co., San Francisco, 1987—; doll designer Friends Forever, Windsor, Calif., 1987—. Recipient Merit award S.C. Watercolor Soc., 1978, Best in Category Original Sculpture Doll award Doll Artisan Guild, 1987, 89, Internat. Doll Expo, 1995. Office: Watercolors & Porcelain Figures PO Box 21313 Reno NV 89515 Personal E-mail: westlady@775.net.

BARAN, XIAOLEI YU, physician, psychiatry professor; d. Tian Shou and Ai Fu (Yang) Yu; m. Mark Richard Baran, Dec. 21, 2002. MD, Shanghai Second Med. Coll., 1983. Med. resident Shanghai Med. Coll., 1983—85, NY Med. Coll., Valhalla, 1991—92; rsch. fellow Am. Health Found., Valhalla, 1990—91; psychiat. resident NY Hosp.-Cornell Med. Ctr., White Plains, 1992—95; psychiat. fellow Cornell Med. Coll., 1995—96, instr. in psychiatry, 1995—98; asst. prof. psychiatry Weill Cornell Med. Coll., NYC, 1998—2005, asst. prof. clin. psychiatry, 2005—; attending psychiatrist NY Presbyn. Hosp., White Plains, 2006—. Mem.: Am. Psychiat. Assn. (gen. mem. 1992). Office: NY Presbyn Hosp 21 Bloomingdale Rd White Plains NY 10605 Office Fax: 914-682-6907. Business E-Mail: xyu@med.cornell.edu.

BARANOWSKI, MARY LOU, elementary school educator; b. Wausau, Wis., Apr. 5, 1958; d. Audrey Emily Moser. BS, U. Wis., La Crosse, 1981; MA, San Diego State U., 1991. Cert. phys. edn. tchr. Calif., 1986, tchr. Nat. Bd. for Profl. Tchg., 2001. Cross country/track coach Waukesha (Wis.) Pub. Schs., Wis., 1981—85; grad. tchg. asst., asst. women's cross country coach U. Wis., La Crosse, 1985—86; phys. edn. tchr. Francis Parker Elem., San Diego, 1987—88; phys. edn./drug and alcohol edn. tchr. Rancho Pk. Hosp. and Residential Treatment Facility, El Cajon, Calif., 1988—89; phys. edn. tchr. San Diego Unified Sch. Dist., Lindbergh Schweitzer Elem., 1989—. Curriculum writer Sports, Phys. Activity and Recreation for Kids, San Diego, 2004. Author: (children's book) The Adventures of Petey. Cons. Spl. Olympics So Get Into It, 2000—06. Named Grad. Student of Yr., San Diego State U., 1991, Tchr. of Yr., Lindbergh Schweitzer Elem. Sch., 1996, 1998, 1999, 2000; recipient Hon. Svc. award, Lindbergh Schweitzer Parent Tchr. Assn., 2001, Leadership in Coordinated School Health award, Am. Cancer Soc., 2004. Mem.: Calif. Assn. for Health, Phys. Edn., Recreation, and Dance (assoc. Outstanding Svc. award 2005), Am. Assn. for Health, Phys. Edn., Recreation and Dance (assoc.). Avocations: dance, writing. Office Phone: 858-496-8400. Business E-Mail: mbaranowski@sandi.net.

BARANSKI, CHRISTINE, actress; b. Buffalo, May 2, 1952; d. Lucien and Virginia (Mazerowski) B.; m. Matthew Cowles, Oct. 15, 1983; children Lily & Isabelle. BA, Juilliard Sch., 1974. Participant, Voices of the Arts Kennedy Ctr. for Performing Arts, Washington, 2006. Actress: (plays) include 'Tis a Pity She's a Whore, The Real Thing (Antoinette Perry award 1984, Tony award, best actress, 1984), Cat on a Hot Tin Roof, She Stoops to Conquer, Angel City, Blithe Spirit, Coming Attractions, The Undefeated Rumba Champ, Otherwise Engaged, A Midsummer Night's Dream (Obie award 1983), Rumors (Antoinette Perry award 1989, Tony award, best actress, 1989), Nick and Nora, 1991, Lips Together Teeth Apart, 1992; (films) Soup for One, 1982, Lovesick, 1983, Crackers, 1984, 9 1/2 Weeks, 1986, Legal Eagles, 1986, The Pick-up Artist, 1987, Reversal of Fortune, 1990, The Night We Never Met, 1993, Life with Mikey, 1993, Addams Family Values, 1993, The War, 1994, The Ref, 1994, Getting In, 1994, New Jersey Drive, 1995, Jeffrey, 1995, The Birdcage, 1996, The Odd Couple II, 1998, Bulworth, 1998, Cruel Inventions, 1999, Bowfinger, 1999, How the Grinch Stole Christmas, 2000, The Guru, 2002, Chicago, 2002, Marci X, 2003, Welcome to Mooseport, 2004; (TV series) Another World, 1983, All My Children, 1984, Cybill, 1995-98 (Emmy award for best supporting actress in a comedy series, 1995, Am. Comedy Award for funniest supporting female performer in a TV series, 1996), Happy Family, 2003; (TV films) Playing for Time, 1980, A Midsummer Night's Dream, 1982, Big Shots in America, 1985, The House of Blue Leaves, 1987, To Dance with the White Dog, 1993, Eloise at the Plaza, 2003, Eloise at Christmastime, 2003, Welcome to Moosetown, 2004. Actress, exec. prodr.: (TV series) Welcome to New York, 2000-01.*

BARASH, SUSAN SHAPIRO, writer, humanities educator; b. N.Y.C. d. Herbert Lester and Selma (Meyerson) Shapiro; m. Richard J. Ripps (div.); 3 children; m. Gary A. Barash, Nov. 8, 1997. BA, Sarah Lawrence Coll.; M in English and Creative Writing, NYU, 1987. Prof. critical thinking, gender studies Marymount Manhattan Coll., N.Y.C., 1997—. Mem. adv. bd. Collegiate Press, San Diego; lit. panelist NY State Coun. on Arts; judge Internat. Emmys. Author: (book) A Passion for More: Wives Reveal the Affairs that Make or Break Their Marriages, Sisters: Devoted or Divided, The Men Out There: A Woman's Little Black Book, Second Wives: The Pitfalls and Rewards of Marrying Widowers and Divorced Men, Mothers In Law and Daughters In Law: Love, Hate, Rivalry, and Reconciliation, Reclaiming Ourselves: How Women Dispel a Legacy of Bad Choices, Inventing Savannah, Women of Divorce: Mothers, Daughters, Stepmothers - The New Triangle, The New Wife: The Evolving Role of the American Wife, (book) Tripping the Prom Queen: The Truth about Women and Rivalry. Mem.: Authors Guild, Writers Guild of Am. East. Avocations: films, swimming, travel. Office: Marymount Manhattan Coll 221 E 71st St New York NY 10021

BARAZZONE, ESTHER LYNN, academic administrator, educator; b. Charleston, W.Va., Mar. 7, 1946; d. Vincent and Alma Gladys (Wilson) B.; m. Jay Reise, Aug. 25, 1977 (div. 2004); children: Matthew, Nicholas. BA, New Coll., 1967; MA, Columbia U., 1969, PhD, 1982; cert. bus. adminstrn., U. Pa., 1981; D (hon.), Doshisha Women's Coll., 1999, Seoul Women's U., 2000. Mem. faculty Hamilton and Kirkland Coll., Clinton, NY, 1974-81; assoc. dir. corp. and found. rels. U. Pa., Phila., 1982-83; assoc. provost, dir. corp. and found. rels. Swarthmore (Pa.) Coll., 1983-87; v.p., acad. affairs, dean Phila. Coll. Textiles, 1987-92; pres. Chatham Coll., Pitts., 1992—. Bd. dirs. Dollar Bank. Author (with others): To Beijing and Beyond, 1998; contbg. author Succes Stories' Presidential Essays, 2000., 2000. Bd. dirs. Benedum Found., 2003, Coun. Internat. Exchange of Scholars, The Carnegie, Pitts., 1993, Hist. Soc. Western Pa., 1993, World Affairs Coun., Pitts., 1994, Allegheny Conf., 1998, Duquesne Club, 2001; mem. adv. bd. Pitts. Symphony Orch., 1993. Grantee Am. Coun. Edn.-Nat. Identification Program Forum, 1992, YWCA, 1996; fellow Columbia U., 1968-72; Fulbright scholar Fulbright Internat. Scholar Exch., 1967-68; named Woman of Yr. Edn., Vectors of Pitts., 1999, Disting. Daughter of Pa., 2001; recipient Susan B. Anthony award, 1999, Pres.' medal Fatima Jinnah Women's U., Pakistan, 2001. Mem. Internat. Women's Forum (founding mem.), Coun. Ind. Colls. (bd. dirs., exec. com.), Duquesne Club, Longue Vue Club, Pitts. Golf Club. Office: Chatham Coll Woodland Rd Pittsburgh PA 15232 E-mail: barazzone@chatham.edu.

BARBAREE, DOROTHY A., secondary school educator; b. Barnesville, Ga., Aug. 18, 1933; d. James Reginald and Annie Laurie (Butler) Askin; m. James Arthur Barbaree, Aug. 30, 1953 (div. Jan. 1999); children: Anne Shelley Barbaree Taylor, James Arthur., Jr. BS in Edn., U. Ga., 1954. Tchr. Griffin-Spalding County H.S., Griffin, Ga., 1955-57; libr. Regional Libr., Waycross, Ga., 1961; antiques dealer Cellar Door Antiques, Rock Hill, S.C., 1982—. Mem. societal concerns com. United Meth. Ch.; area coord. Equal Rights Coalition, S.C., 1978; mem. Ga. Status of Women Commn., 1969; chmn. March of Dimes, 1965, area coord. State of Ga., 1967; pres. Newcomers club, 1966, Jr. Women's Club, 1966, local chpt. LWV, 1973; with Waycross (Ga.) Svc. League, 1959—. Recipient State of Ga. Good Citizen award Ga. Fedn. Women's Clubs, 1966; named to Outstanding Young Women of Am., 1964, Personalities of the South, 1971. Mem. AAUW (state chair pub. policy 1977, Named Scholarship award 1994), LWV. Avocations: taking college classes, volunteering in congressman's office, tutor ing. Home: 3008 Harlinsdale Dr Rock Hill SC 29732-0214

BARBE, BETTY CATHERINE, marketing professional, retired financial analyst; b. Chgo., Dec. 24, 1930; d. Norbert Lambert and Helen Weishaar; m. Edward William, Aug. 8, 1953; children: Leonard Walter, Roger Andrew. Student, U. Toledo, 1970, 85. Acct. Gorr Printing, Allstate Ins., Muntz TV, Chgo., 1947-53; hostess Welcome Wagon Internat., Maumee, Ohio, 1965-70; v.p. sec., cost acctg. Craftmaster, Toledo, 1970-72; sec., estimator Grinnell Fire Protection, Toledo, 1972-73; exec. sec., payroll Crow, Inc. Aviation, 1973-77; asst. city clk., payroll City of Perrysburg, 1977-83, tax adminstr., 1983-98, ret., 1998; mktg. exec. Melaleuca, Inc. The Wellness Co., 2003—. Sec., vice chair Ohio Women's Policy and Rsch. Commn.; mem. adv. coun. Ohio Bicentennial Commn.; reading coach Evening St. Sch., Park Elem. Sch., Bluffsview Elem. Sch., 2001; active Big Sisters of Toledo, 1979, YWCA; vol. New Albany LPGA Golf Classic, Jamie Farr LPGA Golf Classic, Worthington Rep. Women's Club, 1999, Ptnrs. for Citizenship and Character; tutor Ohio Reads. Paul Harris fellow Dublin-Worthington Rotary, Rookie Rotarian of Yr., 1999-00; honoree Maumee Valley coun. Girl Scouts U.S., 1990; named Woman of Yr., Bus. and Profl. Women Black Swamp Region II. Mem. Internat. Inst., Nat. Notary Assn., Nat. Fedn. Bds. and Profl. Women, Key to the Sea Bus. and Profl. Womens Orgn. (pres. 1982-84), Maumee Bus. and Profl. Women (pres. 1995-97), Maumee Valley Toastmasters (pres. 1989—, area gov.), Toledo Opera Soc. Assn., Two Toledos (sec., 1st v.p.), Christ Child Soc., Maumee C. of C. (sec.), Samagama Club, Zonta II (treas.), Maumee Valley Historical Soc., Rotary (sec. Dublin-Worthington chpt.). Republican. Roman Catholic. Avocations: football, reading, sewing, crafts, travel. Home: 806 Drummond Ct Columbus OH 43214 Office: Melaleuca Inc Wellness Co 3910 So Yellowstone Hwy Idaho Falls ID 83402-6003 Personal E-mail: babybarby4@aol.com.

BARBEAU, ADRIENNE, actress; b. Sacramento; m. Billy Van Zandt, Jan. 1, 1993; three children. Student, Foothill Coll., Los Altos, Calif. Actress: (Broadway debut) Fiddler on the Roof, (Broadway) Grease, 1971-72 (Theatre World award 1971-72), (Off-Broadway) The Property Known as Garland, 2006, (feature films) The Fog, 1980, Escape from New York, 1981, Cannonball Run, 1981, Swamp Thing, 1982, Creepshow, 1982, The Next One, 1984, Back To School, 1985, Two Evil Eyes, 1989, Fatherhood, 1992, A Wake in Providence, 1999, The Convent, 2000, Across the Line, 2000, No Place Like Home, 2000, The Unholy, 2005, (TV movies) Having Babies, 1976, Red Alert, 1977, Crash, the True Story of Flight 401, 1978, Someone's Watching Me!, 1978, Tourist, 1980, Seduced, 1985, Bridge Across Time, 1985, Double Crossed, 1991, Burden of Proof, 1993; regular (TV series) Maude, 1972-78, Drew Carey, 1998-00, Carnivale, 2003-05; performer (music CD) Adrienne Barbeau Nationwide Concert Performances; author: (non-fiction) There Are Worse Things I Could Do, 2006. Hon. chairperson Entertainment Industry Com. for Safety Belts, Concern II.

BARBEN, SHERRY L., music educator, choir director; d. James F. Seiple and Frances G. Stadel; m. Edward R. Barben, June 16, 1979; children: Edward J., Benjamin R. MusB, Susquehanna U., Selinsgrove, Pa., 1978; MEd, Pa. State U., University Park, 1982. Profl. tchg. cert. Pa. Music tchr. Tulpehocken Area Sch. Dist., Bernville, Pa., 1978—79; pvt. piano tchr. Selinsgrove, 1978—84; elem. music tchr. Selinsgrove Area Sch. Dist., 1979—87; youth choir dir. St. Paul's United Ch. of Christ, Selinsgrove, 1980—84; pvt. piano tchr. New Cumberland, Pa., 1988—90; nursery sch. dir. Camp Hill Presbyn. Ch., Pa., 1990—96; mid. sch. music tchr. Selinsgrove Area Sch. Dist., 1997—; choir dir. Sharon Luth. Ch., Selinsgrove, 1997—. Youth musical dir. Camp Hill Presbyn. Ch., 1994—96, Sharon Luth. Ch., 2000—; coord./tchr. world music drumming partnership Susquehanna U. and Selinsgrove Area Sch. Dist., 2001—; musical dir. h.s. musical Selinsgrove Area Sch. Dist., 2002—05; mid. sch. music camp counselor Ctrl. Oak Heights, Milton, Pa.; presenter in field. Chmn. White Christmas Com., Selinsgrove, 1982, Camp Hill Presbyn. Ch. Nursery Sch., 1989—91; chmn. worship and music Sharon Luth. Ch., 2000—02. Mem.: Pa. Music Educators Assn., Am. Choral Dirs. Assn., Music Educators Nat. Conf., Phi Delta Kappa, Sigma Alpha Iota (life). Republican. Lutheran. Avocations: reading, antiques. Home: 36 Kingswood Dr Selinsgrove PA 17870 Office: Selinsgrove Area Sch Dist 401 N 18th St Selinsgrove PA 17870 Office Phone: 570-372-2267. Personal E-mail: erbarben@ptd.net.

BARBER, EDDICE BELLE, retired education educator; b. Mo., Oct. 26, 1920; d. Alonzo A. and Hattie Eunice Barber. BS, NW Mo. State Tchrs. Coll., Maryville, 1942; MA, U. Colo., Boulder, 1948; PhD, U. Minn., Mpls., 1972. Sch. tchr., Rural, Mo., 1939—41; tchr. Pub. HS, Braddyville, Iowa, 1941—43, Massena, Iowa, 1943—47, Pub. Jr. Coll., Parsons, Kans., 1947—56; prof. Minn. State U., Mankato, 1956—84; ret., 1984. Co-founder Minn. State U. for Srs., Mankato, 1995. Recipient Vol. of Yr. award, Minn. State U., 2005. Mem.: AAUW (past pres., Kans. state officer, Minn. state officer), Delta Kappa Gamma (past pres.). Avocations: theater, classical music. Home: 313 Davis St Mankato MN 56001

BARBER, ELAINE T. See FUDA, SIRI NARAYAN K.K.

BARBER, ELIZABETH JEAN, vocalist, educator, artist; b. Bakersfield, Calif., Aug. 17, 1936; d. Robert Scott Davidson and Helen Lenore Ingledue-Davidson; m. Charles Walter Barber, May 12, 1979; m. Serge Katzen (dec.); 1 child, Dena Katzen Seidel. BA, Occidental Coll., 1958; MA, Howard U., 1984; DMA, U. Md., 1991; cert., Hochschule fur Musik, Munich, 1962; cert. in Opera Repertoire, UCLA Opera Workshop, 1960. Artist Marietta Mus., Glendale, Md.; pvt. music tchr. Annapolis, 1974—79, Bowie, 1979—84, Hyattsville, Md., 1984—91; prof. Papua New Guinea U., Port Moresby, 1993—96. Soloist: L.A. Philharmonic Orch., 1958—59, Heidelberg Opera Ho., 1963—64, Prince Georges County Opera Co.; author: Complete Works of Hayne von Ghizeghem, 1991, A Piano Course, 2002. Vol. Bethesda Cares, Md., 1992, G Swat, Greenbelt, 2004; book drive participant Christian Sci. Ch., Hyattsville. Fulbright scholar, 1959. Mem.: Bowie Music Tchrs. Assn., Annapolis Music Tchrs. Assn. (treas.), Mortar Bd., Sigma Alpha Iota (past pres.). Democrat. Christian Scientist. Avocations: dog walking, hiking, photography, writing, theater.

BARBER, JOAN MARIE, artist; b. Portland, Oreg., Mar. 11, 1941; d. Wesley John and Borghild (Hovde) Wachtman; m. Willson Benn Barber, Dec. 31, 1965; children: Katherine Rose, Olive Mae. Grad., Portland Mus. Art Sch., 1963. Exhibitions include Hoorn-Ashby Gallery, N.Y.C., Nantucket, Mass., 1996—, Ute Stebich Gallery, Lenox, Mass., 1996—, Erlich Gallery, Marblehead, Mass., 2002, 2003, 2004, Ferrin Gallery, Lenox, Mass., 2004, 2005, Gallery Camino Real, Boca Raton, 2005—06, Ferrin Gallery, Lenox, Mass., 2006, Gallery Camino Real, Boca Raton, Fla., 2005, 2006, Flomenhaft Gallery, N.Y.C., 2006, Lascano Gallery, Gt. Barrington, Mass., 2006, one-woman shows include Hanna Gallery, Stockbridge, Mass., 1993, 1994, 1995, Ute Stebich Gallery, 1997, 1998, 2001, 2003, Deloney-Newkirk Gallery, Santa Fe, N. Mex., 1999, 2000, 2001, 2004, Selby Fleetwood Gallery, Santa Fe, 2005, 2006, numerous group shows including most recently, exhibited in group shows at Flomenhaft Gallery, N.Y.C., 2006, exhibitions include two-person show, 2006. Democrat.

BARBER, MARGARET MCADOW, education educator; b. Mexico, Mo., June 25, 1942; d. Lewis Harlowe and Ruth Todd McAdow; m. David Lindsay Barber, Jan. 5, 1985; m. Janos Jozsef Lazar, June 14, 1969 (div.); children: Anna Elizabeth Lazar, Margaret Ellen Lazar, Kathryn Janis Lazar. BA, Tex. Christian U., Ft. Worth, 1964; MA, Tex. Christian U., 1966, PhD, 1977. Lectr. U. of So. Colo., Pueblo, Colo., 1991—95, asst. prof. english, 1995—2001; assoc. prof. english Colo. State U., 2001—. Editor: Computers and Composition: Special Issue on Diversity; author: The Longman Guide to Columbia Online Style, Argument Now: A Brief Rhetoric, 2005, Instructor's Guide To Argument Now, 2005; contbr. chapters to books, articles; author: Argument Now, 2005. Pres. Citizens for Clean Air and Water in Pueblo, Colo., 2000—06; mem. Better Pueblo, 2003—06, Human Rights Campaign, Pueblo, Citizen's Project, Colo. Springs, 1995—2006; social justice chair Christ Congl. Ch., Pueblo. Named Outstanding Woman of Pueblo, Pueblo Women's History Week, 2001; recipient Friend of the EPA, EPA, 2004, Award for Excellence in Tchg., Provost, U. of So. Colo., 1999; Hazardous Waste Mapping Project, EPA/Rocky Mountain Steel Mill, 2004—06, grant, U. of So. Colo., 2002—03, EPA, 2004. Mem.: ACLU, AAUP, Sigma Tau Delta, Philanthropic Ednl. Orgn. D-Liberal. Protestant. Avocations: gardening, hiking, travel, music. Office: Colo State U 2200 Bonforte Blvd Pueblo CO 81001 Office Phone: 719-549-2651. E-mail: margaret.barber@colostate-pueblo.edu.

BARBER, MARTHA GAYLE, lawyer; b. High Point, NC, Oct. 7, 1953; BA, Duke Univ., 1975; JD, Wake Forest Univ., 1981. Bar: NC 1982. Ptnr., chair, intellectual property-trademark, copyright group Alston & Bird LLP, Charlotte, NC. Frequent author, spkr. on trademark issues. Mem.: Internat. Trademark Assn. (bd. dir. 2000—03). Office: Alston & Bird LLP Ste 4000 Bank of Am Plz 101 S Tryon St Charlotte NC 28280-4000 Office Phone: 704-444-1018. Office Fax: 704-444-1111. Business E-Mail: mbarber@alston.com.

BARBER, PATRICIA LOUISE, clinical specialist; b. St. Paul, Jan. 11, 1953; d. James Bernard and Margaret Mary (Neagle) B. BSN, U. Minn., 1975; cert. nurse practitioner, U. Ill., 1978. RN, Colo., Ill., Minn. Staff nurse U. Minn., Mpls., 1974-75; transplant coord. U. Ill., Chgo., 1978-90; nurse practitioner emergency rm. Denver Presbyn., 1990-93; nurse practitioner in-patient svc. cardiovascular Denver Presbyn. St. Luke's Med. Ctr., 1993-95, nurse practitioner nephrology, 1995-96, nurse practitioner in-patient svc., 1996-99; assoc. prof. of nursing Health Edn. Ctr. C.C. Denver, 1999—2005, assoc. prof. nursing, 2004—06, acting chair nursing, bd. dirs., 2006; nurse practitioner cardiovasc. Cardiovasc. Assocs., Denver, 2003—. Cons. in field, Chgo., 1983—. Editor: Resource Manual for Transplant Coordinators, 1982. Co-chmn. S/A Patient Svcs. Com., 1983-90. Mem. N.Am. Transplant Coords. Orgn. (co-chmn. 1979-90, Honors 1983), Am. Diabetes Assn. (speakers bur. 1982—), Nat. Kidney Found. (bd. dirs. 1983-90). Avocations: fundraiser, volunteering, pet therapy. Office: C C Denver Health Edn Ctr 1070 Yosemite Cir Denver CO 80230-6921 Office Phone: 303-365-8372. Business E-Mail: trisha.barber@ccd.edu.

BARBER, VICTORIA, school system administrator, consultant; b. Iron, Ill., May 9, 1951; d. Willis C. and Leota D. Ruff; m. Louis Sherman Barber, Feb. 6, 1982; children: Sherri Palmer, Scott. BA in Govt. and Journalism, Calif. State U., Sacramento; MA in Govt., Calif. State U., Calif. State U., 1974; MA in Spl. Edn., Chapman Coll., 1977; EdD in Ednl. Psychology, U. Pacific, Stockton, 1982. Secondary tchg. credential Calif., learning handicapped specialist credential, gen. adminstrn. credential, cert. credential to perform sch. psychol. svcs., credential to supervise pupil personnel svc. Tchr., diagnostician and resource specialist Melvin-Smith Sch., 1971—74; cons. Calif. Assembly, 1974—75; coord. ednl. cons. Learning Time and Ednl. Rsch. Cons., 1975—79; cons. ednl. and sch. fin. svcs., 1979—; dir. spl. svcs. El Dorado County Supt. Schs. Office, 1983—84, asst. supt. bus. svcs., 1984—90, dept. supt. adminstrv. svcs., 1990—94. Spl. cons. Supt. Pub. Instrn., 1973; lect. Calif. State U., Sacramento, 1974, Sacramento, 86, Sacramento, 93. Author: numerous papers and articles in field. Mem. El Dorado County First 5 Commn., 1999—, exec. com., 2000; mem. bd. Marshall Hosp., 1991—2001, v.p. fin. affairs, 1998—2001; mem. bd. El Dorado Forum, 1991—, pres., 2003—04; bd. dirs. Valley Vision, 1996—, v.p., 1997—2000; mem. bd. Western Slope Boys & Girls Club, 1997—, chair bd. devel. com., 2002—; mem. bd. El Dorado Cmty. Found., 2003—; bd. chairperson El Dorado County JOB ONE, 1997—99, bd. dirs. exec. coun., 1997—; bd. dirs. Am. Heart Assn., 1992—96; mem. El Dorado C. of C., 1992—, chair edn. coun., 1994—, bd. dirs., 2001—, pres., 2005; bd. dirs. Fin. Crisis and Mgmt. Assistance Team, 1996—; mem. interagy. coordinating bd. El Dorado County Children & Families Network, 1994—2002; mem. bd. Econ. Devel. Corp., 1990—94; bd. dirs. Mother Lode Rehab. Enterprises, 2005; mem. gov's adv. com. on charter schs., 2004—; mem. adv. com. Calif. Sch. Bds. Assn. Supts., 1999—; mem. superintendency com. Assn. Calif. Sch. Adminstrs., 1999—2001, pres. El Dorado County charter, 1999—2001; mem. adv. com. State Supt. Pub. Instrn. Pub. Schs. Accountability Act, 1999—, co-chair alternative accountability task force, 2000—; mem. Horace Mann League, 2000—; mem. adv. com. Chapman Univ., 1996—; mem. State Supt.'s Task Force on Sch. Effectiveness, 1988—92; sub-com. chairperson and mem. gov's task force on spl. edn. fin. State Dept. Edn., 1986—88; mem. Nat. Univ. credentials adv. com., 1987—89; legis. chairperson Spl. Edn. Local Plan Area Adminstrs., 1984—94, fin. chairperson, 1985—94; mem. adv. com. Consumnes River Coll., 1987—89, mem. found. adv. com., 2000—; co-chairperon sponsorship com. Women's Ctr., 1994—2000, 2002—; chair edn. sub-com. Econ. Providers Network, 1994—97; mem. El Dorado County Round Table on Human Rights, 1993—. Named Superintendent of Yr., Small Sch. Districts Assn., 2006; named one of Women Who Mean Bus., Sacramento Bus. Jour., 2004, Woman of Distinction, Cameron Park Soroptimist Club, 2001; named to Early Childhood Hall of Fame, El Dorado Assn. for Edn. of Young Children, 2002; recipient recognition for leadership and contbns. to spl. edn. field, 9th Internat. Conf. Learning Disabilities, 1987, Exec. Leadership award, Calif. County Supts. Ednl. Svcs. Assn., 1999, Perpetual award, 2000, Outstanding Cmty. Svc. award, El Dorado County C. of C., 1999, Sugarloaf Cmty. Recognition award, Sugarloaf Found., 2006; fellow, Am. Leadership Forum, 2001. Mem.: Bus. and Profl. Women's Orgn. (v.p. 1989—90, pres. 1991—92), Am. Assn. U. Women, Calif. County Supts. Ednl. Svcs. Assn. (bd. dirs. 1997—, pres. 1998), Mother Lode Rehab. Enterprises (bd. dir. 2005—), LWV, Kiwanis, Delta Kappa Gamma Soc. Office: El Dorado County Office Edn 6767 Green Valley Rd Placerville CA 95667 Business E-Mail: vlbarber@edcoe.k12.ca.us.

BARBER-FOSS, KIM DANEEN, athletic trainer; b. Regina, Sask., Canada, Apr. 29, 1970; d. Colin Campbell and Dorothy Barber; m. Edward Allen Foss, Oct. 10, 1998; children: Allen Campbell Foss, Sydney Elizabeth Foss. BS in Athletic Tng., N.D. State U., Fargo, 1992; BS in Sociology, N.D. State U., 1992; MS in Sports Medicine, U. Oreg., Eugene, 1994, MS in Biomechanics, 1994. Cert. athletic trainer Nat. Athletic Trainers Assn., 1992. Athletic trainer Valley Phys. Therapy, Middletown, Conn., 1994—95; project coord. Med Sports Systems, Iowa City, 1995—98; asst. athletic trainer Linn-Mar Cmty. Sch. Dist., Marion, Iowa, 1999—2000, head athletic trainer/dir. of sports medicine, 2000—05; athletic trainer/rschr. Cin. Children's Hosp. Sports Medicine Biodynamics Ctr., 2005—. Women in athletic tng. Ohio rep. GLATA Dist. 4, Cin., 2005—, NATA Dist. 4, Cedar Rapids, 2004—05. Contbr. articles to profl. jours. Recipient U.S. Achievement Acad. All Am. scholar, Achievement Acad., Curriculum scholar, Nat. Athletic Trainers Assn., 1992. Mem.: Ohio Athletic Trainers Assn., Nat. Athletic Trainers Assn., Phi Eta Sigma, Phi Kappa Phi. Home: 3970 Lovell Ave Cincinnati OH 45211 Office: Cincinnati Children's Hospital 2800 Winslow Ave Cincinnati OH 45206 E-mail: kim.foss@cchmc.org.

BARBER-FREEMAN, PAMELA TELIA, mathematician, educator, researcher; d. Lewis Eugene and Lucille Evans Barber; children: Leonardo Eugene Freeman, Lance Esonn Freeman, Lucyll Elizabeth Freeman. PhD, U. of Okla., Norman, 1993. Math tchr. Millwood Pub. Schools, Okla. City, 1972—85; counselor/dir. Rose State Coll., Midwest City, Okla., 1985—88; assoc. prof. Miss. State U., 1993—2000, Prairie View A&M U., Tex., 2000—. Editor: (jour.) Jour. of Rsch. Assn. of Minority Professors; contbr. articles to profl. jours. Del. Dem. Party, Okla., 1985, chairperson precinct 240, precinct chair, 1984—88, chairperson for ho. dist. 101, del. Okla. City, 1985; tchr. and facilitator Brookhollow Bapt. Ch., Houston, 2001—03, disciple Ch. Without Walls, 2001—03. Nominee HL Bd. of Trustees Black History Month Program, Miss. State U., 1996—97; named Oustanding African Am. Faculty, Miss. State U. African Am. Student Body, 1998; named to Order of Endowed Scholars, Miss. State U., 1997; recipient Tchr. Edn. Equity Project Ctr. for Advanced Study in Edn., CUNY - NSF, 1994; fellow Acad. of Excellence, Tex. A&M U., Tex. A&M U. Sys. Regents' Initiative, 2004; grantee Office of Rsch., Miss. State U., 1994, Miss. Insts. of Higher Learning, 1996—99, Miss. State U., 1997, Prairie View A&M BioMedical and Behavorial Scis. Rsch. Program, 2003. Fellow: Tex. A&M U. Sys. Acad. for Educator Devel. (assoc.). Achievements include research in MATH-PLACE resource ctr. funded through Dwight D. Eisenhower grant; tchr. networking, tng. and design (TR3); African Am. parental support (BAIT); multicultural evaluation (MERGES). Avocations: pencil art, piano. Office: Assoc Prof PO Box 4349 Prairie View TX 77446 E-mail: pamela_freeman@pvamu.edu.

BARBERIE, JILLIAN, newscaster, meteorologist; b. Ontario, Can., Sept. 26, 1966; m. Bret Barberie (div.). BA in broadcast journalism, Mohawk Coll. of Applied Arts & Tech. Weathercaster The Weather Network, Canada, 1990—92, WSVN, Miami, 1992—93, KTTV Fox 11 10 O'clock news, Los Angeles, 1993—95; co-anchor, weathercaster Morning News and Good Day LA, KTTV Fox 11, 1995—; weathercaster Fox NFL Sunday, 2006—. Newscaster NFL on Fox, 2000—. Actress: (TV series) V.I.P., 1999—2002; guest apperances Clueless, 1996; Live! with Regis and Kathy Lee, 2000; Fastlane, 2002. Office: Fox Broadcasting 10201 Pico Blvd Los Angeles CA 90035*

BARBEY, ADÉLAÏDE, publisher; b. Vallorcine, France, Aug. 21, 1948; 1 child, Alice Gissinger-Barbey. Attachée de direction Inst. Etudes Politiques, Paris, 1971-74; chargée de mission French Ministry Culture, Paris, 1974-79; exec. editor Hatier, Paris, 1979-82; pub. Hachette Littérature Générale, Paris, 1982-95, mng. dir. TF1 Édits., 1996; cons. World Bank, NYC, 2002—. Cons. in field.

BARBIE, CATHY THERESE, middle school educator; b. Ottumwa, Iowa, Apr. 29, 1955; d. Willard Eugene and Andree Marie (Joseph) Watts; m. Billy Joe Barbie, July 26, 1986; children: Bryan Michael Joseph (dec.), Joshua Ryan. BA, U. No. Iowa, Cedar Falls, 1977. Cert. tchr. English, speech, theatre, social studies, U.S. history. Tchr. Alburnett (Iowa) H.S., 1978-79, Salmon (Idaho) H.S., 1980-82, Shishmaref (AK) H.S., 1982-84, Emmonak (AK) H.S., 1984-86, Rocky Boy (Mont.) Tribal Sch., 1986-87; instr. English Big Sandy (Mont.) Schs., 1987-89; mid. sch. instr. social studies Eagle Valley Mid. Sch., Carson City, Nev., 1989—, head dept. social studies. Avocation: professional crafter/designer. Home: 5300 Goni Rd Carson City NV 89706-0352

BARBO, DOROTHY MARIE, obstetrician, gynecologist, educator; b. River Falls, Wis., May 28, 1932; d. George William and Marie Lillian (Stelsel) B. BA, Asbury Coll., 1954, DSc (hon.), 1981; MD, U. Wis., 1958. Diplomate Am. Bd. Ob-Gyn. Resident Luth. Hosp. Milw., 1958-62; instr. Sch. Medicine Marquette U., Milw., 1962-66, asst. prof., 1966-67; assoc. prof. Christian Med. Coll. Punjab U., Ludhiana, India, 1968-72; assoc. prof. Med. Coll. Pa., Phila., 1972-87, prof., 1988-91, U. N.Mex., Albuquerque, 1991-99, prof. emerita, 1999—; med. dir. Women's Health Ctr., Albuquerque, 1991-99. Acting dept. chair Christian Med. Coll., Punjab U., 1970; dir. Ctr. for Mature Woman Med. Coll. Pa., 1983-91; examiner Am. Bd. Ob-Gyn, 1984-97; bd. dirs. Ludhiana Christian Med. Coll. Bd., choir mem., 2005—; bd. dirs. Colorado Springs., Colo., chair, 2005, Svc. Master Co. Ltd., Downers Grove, Ill., 1982-91; bd. trustees Asbury Coll., 1996—, vice chair bd. trustees, chair acad. com. Co-author: Care of Post Menopausal Patient, 1985; editor: Medical Clinics of N.A., vol. 71, 1987; assoc. editor, contbg. author: Textbook of Women's Health, 1998; contbr. chpt. to book. Student chpt. sponsor Christian Med. and Dental Soc., Phila., 1973-93, trustee, 1991-95, pres., chair bd. trustees, 1997-99, chair com. for continuing med. and dental edn.; tchr., elder Leverington Presbyn. Ch., Phila., 1988-91; interviewer Readers Digest Internat. fellowships, Brunswick, Ga., 1982—; bd. dirs. Phila. chpt. Am. Cancer Soc., 1980-86, vol., 1984. Named sr. clin. trainee USPHS, HEW, 1963-65, one of Best Woman Drs. in Am. Harper Bazaar, 1985. Fellow ACS (sec. Phila. chpt. 1990), ACOG, Am. Fertility Soc.; mem. Obstet. Soc. Phila. (pres. 1989-90), Phila. Colposcopy Soc. (pres. 1982-84), Philadelphia County Med. Soc. (com. chmn. 1989-90), Alpha Omega Alpha. Avocations: gardening, travel, collecting antiques.

BARBOSA, SHAMEKA BROWN, copywriter; b. Far Rockaway, N.Y., Oct. 4, 1975; d. Jimmy Royce and Willene Brown; m. Michael Barbosa, Nov. 2, 2002. BA, Syracuse U., 1996; MS, Va. Commonwealth U., 1999. Jr. copywriter Newbridge Comm., N.Y.C., 1996—97; v.p./sr. copywriter Foote, Cone & Belding, N.Y.C., 1999—. Recipient Silver EFFIE award, N.Y. Am. Mktg. Assn., 2002, Gold World medal, N.Y. Festivals, 2002; Roaring 20s-Spl. Report, Advt. Age, 2003. Mem.: Adv. Women N.Y., African Ams. in Advt. (bd. dirs., co-chair corp. membership 2002—03), Am. Assn. Advt. Agys. (bd. dirs. Multicultural Advt. Intern Program Alumni Assn. 2002—03), Advt. Club of N.Y., One Line Club. Office: Foote Cone & Belding 100 W 33d St New York NY 10001 E-mail: shamekabrown@hotmail.com.

BARBOSA, TANYA MARIE, athletic trainer; b. Providence, Feb. 9, 1982; d. Manuel Rebelo and Zelia Maria Barbosa. BS in Athletic Tng., Lasell Coll., Newton, Mass., 2004—04. Cert. profl. rescuer BOC ATC, 2005. Resident athletic trainer Bryant U., Smithfield, RI, 2004—05; athletic trainer MIT, Cambridge, Mass., 2005—. Athletic trainer region 1 girls soccer camps Olympic Devel. Program, RI, 2001—; athletic trainer boys soccer Nat. U-14, Mass., 2001—. Mem.: Nat. Athletic Trainers Assn. Home: 39 Ridgecrest Terr # 10 West Roxbury MA 02132

BARBOUR, CAROL GOODWIN, psychologist; b. Morganton, N.C., Sept. 15, 1946; d. Jesse Otho and Edith Adele (Goodwin) B.; m. Sidney Gilman. A.B., Duke U., 1967; Ph.D., U. Mich., 1981, grad. Mich. Psychoanalytic Inst., 2000. Research analyst State of Ill., Chgo., 1968-69; psychologist Med. Student Mental Health Service U. Mich., Ann Arbor, 1977-80, postdoctoral fellow in clin. psychology, adolescent inpatient psychiatry, 1980-82, adj. supr. Psychol. Clinic, 1982-83; pvt. practice psychoanalysis and psychotherapy, Ann Arbor, 1980—; dir. psychiat. services Lakewood Clinic, Novi, Mich., 1982-85, clin. supr., staff psychologist, 1985-88; cons. psychologist Mercywood Hosp., 1986-89; clin. supr. psychiatry U. Mich., Ann Arbor, 1988—; faculty Mich. Psychoanalytic Inst., 2000—. Fulbright grantee, U.S. Ednl. Found. in India, 1967-68. Mem. Am. Psychoanalytic Assn., Am. Psychol. Assn., Phi Beta Kappa. Home: 3411 Geddes Rd Ann Arbor MI 48105-2518 Office: 555 E William St Ste 23L Ann Arbor MI 48104-2428 Office Phone: 734-665-4374. E-mail: barbour@umich.edu.

BARBOUR, CATHERINE JEAN, actress, set designer, director, mime; b. Dover, Del., Nov. 8, 1932; d. Peter Joseph Callovini and Lydia Clara Shane; m. Alan Gregory Barbour, June 18, 1960. Cert., Am. Acad. Dramatic Arts, 1960; BA magna cum laude, Marymount Manhattan Coll., 1987; MFA, NYU, 1991. Tchr., dir. Am. Acad. Dramatic Arts, N.Y.C., 1963-71; asst. dir., performer, tchr., dir. The Am. Mime Theatre, N.Y.C., 1965—. Adminstrv. asst. Internat. Mimes and Pantomimists, N.Y.C., 1973-74; tchr. Am. mime class San Deigo Sch. Creative and Performing Arts, 2006. Set piece design for Music Box; performances with The Am. Mime Theatre include Dreams, Evolution, Sludge, Six, Couplings, Abstraction, Peepshow, Unitaur, Pageant; appeared in Captain Celluloid vs. The Film Pirates (film), 1968; appeared on The Today Show, 1975, TV Tokyo-Asayan, 1999; exhibits include Nat. Arts Club, NYC, 2001-06, Sauander-O'Reilly Galleries, NYC, 2001. Recipient Jehlinger award Am. Acad. Dramatic Arts, NYC, 1960, Merit award, Art Students League NY, 2004. Mem. Am. Watercolor Soc. (assoc.), Rehoboth Art League, Inc., Art Students League N.Y. (Merit award 2004—), 1100 Watercolor Soc., Sons of the Desert, Nat. Movement Theater Assn., Drama League of N.Y. Avocations: art, sculpture, writing, set designing. Office: The American Mime Theatre 61 4th Ave New York NY 10003-5204 Office Phone: 212-777-1710. E-mail: AmMime@aol.com, Mimestar@aol.com.

BARBOUR, CHARLENE, management firm executive; b. Smithfield, N.C., Aug. 23, 1949; d. Charles Ray and Charlotte June (Langdon) B.; m. Phil Barbour, Apr. 14, 1968; 1 child, Phillip Shaun. AA in Bus., Hardbarger Jr. Coll., 1968. Adminstrv. asst. N.C. Dept. Human Resources, Raleigh, 1970-80; account exec. Olson Mgmt. Group, Raleigh, 1980-86; pres., CEO Mgmt. Concepts, Inc., Garner, N.C., 1986—. Founder, ptnr. Wall St. Mortgage Corp., 1996. Pres. Garner chpt. ABWA, 2001—02; chmn. adv. bd. North State Bank Garner, 2000—03. Mem. Assn. Execs. N.C. (CEO conf. chmn. 1992-93, program com. 1992-93, trade show com. 1992-93), Garner C. of C. (comm. chmn. 1989, bd. dirs. 1995-98, vice chmn. membership and comm. 1989-92, chair pub. rels. 1996-97, vice chairwoman 1997-98, chairwoman 1998-99), Buena Vista Hospitality Group (coun. advisors 1992), Nat. Assn. of RV Parks and Campgrounds (mem. 2020 vision com. 1999-00, Exec. Dir. of Yr. award 1994), Campground Assn. Mgmt. Profls. (founder), Cardinal Club (founder), Rotary (founding mem. Garner Mid-day club 2000). Democrat. Baptist. Avocations: boating, golf, water activities. Home: 2320 Amelia Rd Clayton NC 27520-8307 Office: Mgmt Concepts Inc 605 Poole Dr Garner NC 27529-2597 Office Phone: 919-779-7516. E-mail: cbarbour@mgmt4u.com.

BARBOUR, CLAUDE MARIE, minister, educator; b. Brussels, Oct. 2, 1935; came to U.S., 1969; Diploma d'État d'Infirmières, École d'Infirmières, Paris, 1956; diploma d'Études Religieuses, Faculté Libre de Théolog, Paris, 1958; MST, N.Y. Theol. Sem., 1970; DST, Garrett Evang. Theol. Sem., 1973. Ordained to ministry Presbyn. Ch., 1974. Youth counselor Young Women's Christian Assn., Geneva, 1959-61, Edinburgh, 1965-67; missionary Paris Evang. Missionary Soc., So. Africa, 1962-64; deaconess Ch. of Scotland, Edinburgh, 1967-69; from asst. to assoc. pastor First United Presbyn. Ch., Gary, Ind., 1974-80; from asst. to assoc. prof. Cath. Theol. Union, Chgo., 1976-86, prof., 1986—, McCormick Theol. Sem., Chgo., 1990-96. Founder, dir. Shalom Ministries and Community, Chgo., 1975—; parish assoc. First Presbyn. Ch., Evanston, Ill., 1983—. World Coun. Chs. scholar, Geneva, 1969, United Presbyn. Ch. Commn. on Ecumenical Mission and Rels., N.Y., 1972; recipient Laskey award United Meth. Ch. Womens Div. the Bd. Global Ministries, N.Y., 1972, Civic award Ind. Women's Coun., 1976, Challenge of Peace award Chgo. Ctr. for Peace Studies, 1991, Martin P. Wolf O.F.M. award Justice, Peace and Integrity of Creation Coun. of the English-Speaking Conf. of the Order of Friars Minor, 1996, Blessed are the Peacemakers award World Coun. Chs., 2005. Mem. AAUW, Internat. Assn. for Mission Studies, Nat. Assn. Presbyn. Clergywomen, Am. Soc. Missiology, Assn. Prof. Mission, Midwest Fellowship Prof. Mission, Assn. Presbyn. in Cross-Cultural Mission. Home: 1649 E 50th St Apt 21A Chicago IL 60615-6110 Office: Catholic Theological Union 5401 S Cornell Ave Chicago IL 60615-5664 Business E-Mail: barbour@ctu.edu.

BARBOUR, KELLI D., assistant principal, secondary school educator; d. Patricia Ann and Robert Charles Jackson; m. Robert Todd Barbour, June 24, 1995; children: Brandon Robert, Collin Jackson. BA in Social Sci., McKendree Coll., Lebanon, Ill., 1991; M in Ednl. Adminstrn., So. Ill. U., Edwardsville, 1998. Cert. Ill., 1992, edn. adminstrn. Ill., 2001. Tchr. Triad H.S., Troy, Ill., 1994—, asst. prin., 2004—, student coun. advisor, 2003—, model UN advisor, 2003—. League v.p. St. Jacob (Ill.) Baseball/Softball Assn., 2002—06. D-Liberal. Methodist. Avocation: travel. Office Phone: 618-667-8851 ext. 7141.

BARCA, KATHLEEN, marketing executive; b. Burbank, Calif., July 26, 1946; d. Frank Allan and Blanch Irene (Griffith) Barnes; m. Gerald Albino Barca, Dec. 8, 1967 (dec. May 1993); children: Patrick Gerald, Stacia Kathleen. Student, Pierce Coll., 1964; B in Bus., Hancock Coll., 1984. Teller Security Pacific Bank, Pasadena, Calif., 1968-69, Bank Am., Santa Maria, Calif., 1972-74; operator Gen. Tel. Co., Santa Maria, 1974-83, supr. operator, 1983-84; account exec. Radio Sta. KRQK/KLLB, Lompoc, Calif., 1985—87; owner Advt. Unlimited, Orcutt, Calif., 1986-88; regional mgr. A.L. Williams Mktg. Co., Los Alamos, Calif., 1988-89; supr. Matol Botanical Internat., 1989-91; account exec. Santa Maria Times, 1989-95; owner a-garagesale.com, 2000—03, Network Mgmt., 2003—. Author numerous local TV and radio commercials, print advt. Activist Citizens Against Dumps in Residential Environments, Polit. Action Com., Orcutt and Santa Maria; chmn. Community Action Com., Santa Maria, Workshop EPA, Calif. Div., Dept. Health Svcs. State of Calif.; vice coord. Toughlove, Santa Maria, 1988-89; parent coord., mem. steering com. ASAP and Friends, 1988-89; mem. Sloco Access, 1997-99; mem. Friends San Luis Obispo Bot. Gardens, 1997-99; v.p. Seneca Hosp. Aux., 1998-2000; active Fire Svcs., 1998-2000. Mem. NAFE, Womens Network-Santa Maria, Ctrl. Coast Ad (recipient numerous awards), Santa Maria C. of C. (amb. representing Santa Maria Times 1990-94, asst. chief amb. 1993-94), Chester Piecemakers Quilt Club, Lake Almaner Womens Club. Democrat. Avocations: raising exotic birds, writing childrens books.

BARCLAY, ELLEN S., not-for-profit developer; b. Rochester, N.Y., Aug. 30, 1957; d. Harley J. and Virginia J. Barclay. BA, Coll. Wooster, 1979; MA, U. Fla., 1982. Coord. Conf. Coun. for Advancement and Support of Edn., Washington, 1983—86; dir. Profl. Edn. Svcs. Coun. Advancement and Support of Edn., Washington, 1988—94; dir. Conf. Svcs. and Procurement Coun. for Advancement and Support of Edn., Washington, 1994—98; coord. Conference and Spl. Events Nat. Parks and Conservation Assn., Washington, 1986—88; exec. dir. Am. String Tchrs. Assn., Fairfax, Va., 1998—2001; dep. exec. dir. Coun. Internat. Exch. of Scholars, Washington, 2001—05; pres. Forum Regional Assn. Grantmakers, Washington, 2005—. Grantee Grant, Fund for the Improvement of Postsecondary Edn., 2000. Mem.: Am. Soc. Assn. Execs. Avocations: travel, gardening. Office: Forum Regioal Assn Grantmakers 1111 19th St NW Ste 650 Washington DC 20015 Home: 5347 Nevada Ave Nw Washington DC 20015-1771

BARCLAY, KATHLEEN S., automotive executive; b. Milw. B in Bus., Mich. State U., 1978; MBA, MIT, 1991. With GM, Detroit, 1978—81; retail mgr. Southland Corp., Reno, Chgo.; human resource compensation mgr. Allen-Bradley Co., Milw.; with GM, Warren, Mich., 1985—, mgr. salaried personnel corp. staffs, 1987—88; mgr. labor rels. Chevrolet-Pontiac-GM Can., 1988—91, mgr. exec. compensation, 1991; dir. compensation GM, 1992—95, dir. human resources vehicle sales svc., 1995, gen. dir. human resources mgmt. N.Am. ops., 1996—98, v.p. global human resources, 1998—. Bd. dirs. Cowdrick Group, Mich. Virtual Univ. Bd. govs. MIT; alumni bd. dirs. Mich. State U. Sloan fellow, MIT, 1991. Fellow: Nat. Acad. Human Resources (bd. dirs.); mem.: Detroit Women's Econ. Club. Office: GM Corp 300 Renaissance Ctr Detroit MI 48265-3000 Office Phone: 313-556-5000, 313-556-1988. Fax: 248-696-7300.

BARCLAY, MARTHA JANE, science educator, research scientist; b. Warren County, Ill., July 5, 1948; d. George Leonard and Edna Virginia Ault; children: Brad children: Austin. BS, U. Ill., 1970; MS, Ind. U., 1972; PhD, U. Tenn., 1979. Registered dietitian. Asst. prof. U. Iowa, Iowa City, 1979—86; prof. Western Ill. U., Macomb, 1986—. Rschr. Coun. Food and Agrl. Rsch., Champaign/Urbana, 1997—2003, McDonough County Extension Coun. Treas. McDonough County Teen Ct. Bd., Macomb, 2000—02. Named Hospitality Educator of Yr., Illinois Hotel and Lodging Assn., 2001-2002. Mem.: Ill. Assn. Family and Consumer Scis., Am. Assn. Family and Consumer Scis., Ill. Dietetic Assn., Am. Dietetic Assn., Midwest CHRIE (pres. 1990—91), Internat. CHRIE. Office: Western Ill U 1 University Cir Macomb IL 61455 Office Phone: 309-298-1775. Business E-Mail: MJ-Barclay@wiu.edu.

BARCROFT, JUDITH, artist, actress; b. Washington, July 06; d. James Lawrence and Jean McCardell Williams; m. Wisner McCamey Washam, June 15, 1969; children: Ian Miller Washam, Amy Lawrence Washam Masterson. AA, Stephens Coll., Columbia, Mo., 1962; BS in Speech, Northwestern U., 1964; student, Borghese Gallery, Rome, 1958, N.Y. Art Students League. Co-founder Christian Arts Guild, N.Y.C.; art therapist, one step program Phoenix House, N.Y.C., 1991—93. Actress: (Broadway plays) Betrayal; Elephant Man; Play's the Thing; Mating Dance; All God's Chillun Got Wings; Shimada; Dinner at Eight; (plays, off-Broadway) Motherbird; Tennessee Waltz; Solitaire; Double Solitaire; Monsieur Amilcar; Spiel; Cloud Nine; Bishop Street; Myself Alma Mahler; Breaking the Prairie Wolfe Code; Shoe Palace Murray, 2005; Cool Wet Dark Low; (numerous roles in regional theatre); (TV) All My Children, 1971—79; Another World, 1965—71; Ryan's Hope; Edge of Night; One Life to Live; As the World Turns; Nurse; Spencer for Hire; actress (films) Yours Always Sam, 2005, The Red State Project; Mississippi, My Tie, 2006; exhibitions include Fair Harbor Art Show, Fire Island, N.Y., 1985—93, Saltaire Music and Art Festival, Fire Island, 1985—92, Art Students League Concourse, N.Y.C., 1985—87, Art on the Drive, Riverside Pk., N.Y.C., 1986—88, Point O'Woods Casino Gallery, Fire Island, 1987—93, Chuck Levitan Galler, Metro Art Auction for UNICEF, 1987, Garrison Arts Ctr., Garrison, N.Y., 1987, Cork Gallery, Lincoln Ctr., N.Y.C., 1987, Nat. Arts Club, N.Y.C., 1987, Ledo Gallery, N.Y.C., 1987, Steve Bush Gallery, N.Y.C., 1986, 1987, Union League Club, N.Y.C., 1986, 1987, Art Lovers Gallery, N.Y.C., 1987, 1988, Open Studios, West Side Arts Coalition, N.Y.C., 1987, 1988, Hell's Kitchen Art Show, N.Y.C., 1988, Schneyer & Shen Gallery, N.Y.C., 1987, 1988, Morin-Miller Galleries, N.Y.C., 1988, Pleiades Gallery, N.Y.C., 1988, Stockwell Gallery, N.Y.C., 1988, Pen & Brush Club, N.Y.C., 1989, Phase III Gallery, Tulsa, Okla., 1990, Nat. Cathedral Sch., Washington, D.C., 1991, Lever House, N.Y.C., 1991, Clinton Preservation Show, N.Y.C., 1993, Vortex Lobby & Stage, Sanford Meisner Theatre, N.Y.C., 1993, Art Open End, Broadway Mall Gallery, N.Y.C., 1994, Andre Zarre Gallery, N.Y.C., 1994, Broadway Mall, N.Y.C., 1987—94, 2006, WSAC, A Rich Fabric of Art Summer Salon, Fire Island Lighthouse art show, Salmaqundi Club, 2006. Lay min. Ch. of Heavenly Rest, N.Y.C.; lector Stephens Minister Order of St. Luke's, Ch. Heavenly Rest; lector, vestry, chalice bearer, Bible study ldr. St. Andrew's By-The-Sea, Saltaire, Fire Island, NY. Recipient Best Actress award, Acad. Theatre Artists & Friends, 1989; Art Merit scholarship, N.Y.C. Art Students League, 1987. Mem.: Artists Equity, Leger de Main Galleries, Westside Arts Coalition, Artists Fellowship, Art Students League (bd. control 1987—90), Allied Artists (assoc.). Avocations: cooking, dance, writing, bible study.

BARCUS, MARY EVELYN, primary school educator; b. Peru, Ind., Apr. 3, 1938; d. Arthur Gibson and Mildred (Neher) Shull; m. Robert Gene Barcus, Aug. 9, 1959; children: Jennifer Sue, Debra Lynn. BS, Manchester Coll., 1960; MA, Ball State U., 1964. Kindergarten tchr. Miami Elem. Sch., Wabash, Ind., 1960-64; elem. tchr. Crooked Creek Sch., Indpls., 1964-72; preschool tchr. Second Presbyn. Preschool, Indpls., 1980-85, Speedway Coop., Indpls., 1985-86; tchr. asst. St. Monica Cath. Sch., Indpls., 1990; preschool tchr., fun club tchr. Arthur Jordan YMCA, Indpls.; preschool tchr. Indpls. (Ind.) Children's Mus., 1979—. Docent sch. tours Children's Mus., Indpls., 1987—; interpreter at Indpls. children's mus.; facilitator Systematic Tng. Effective Parenting, Indpls. Writer: (children's songs) Piggback Songs for Infants and Toddlers, 1985, Piggyback Songs in Praise of God, 1986; editor elem. sch. newspaper; producer (with others) weekly show for cable TV. Profl. vol., libr. helper in local sch. systems; office helper North Cen. High Sch.; served on PTOs in various capacities; mem. Crossroads Guild, Parents Day Out of St. Luke's Meth. Ch., past mem. ch. bd., Two's Tchr. Early Childhood Ctr.; Sun. sch./vacation ch. sch. tchr.; bd. dirs. Manchester Coll. Parents Assn. Mem. AAUW (charter, sec.), NEA (life), Ind. Assn. Edn. Young Children (state conf. com.), Pi Lambda Theta. Democrat. Mem. Church of Brethren. Home: 2230 Brewster Rd Indianapolis IN 46260-1521

BARD, ELLEN MARIE, former state legislator, retired small business owner; b. Mpls., Jan. 11, 1949; d. James Donald and Elaine (Frank) B.; m. Robert George Stiratelli, 1973; 1 child, Allison. BA, Pomona Coll., 1971; MS, Boston U., 1972, MIT, 1980. Rsch. analyst Mass. Parole Bd., Boston, 1972-78; dir. market rsch. Bay Banks, Inc., Boston, 1978-79; rsch. assoc. Internat. Coal Refining Co., 1980-82; owner, founder Techlink Corp., Jenkintown, Pa., 1982—2000; mem. Pa. Ho. of Reps., Harrisburg, 1994—2004; ret., 2004. Writer, spkr., TV prodr., host Bard Means Business. Twp. commr., Abington, Pa., 1990-94; bd. dirs. Montgomery County Lands Trust, 1993—; founder, bd. dirs. Earth Right, 1990—; founder Abington Trails Adv. Com., 1995—; mem. coun. of pres.'s assocs. Manor Jr. Coll., 1995—; mem. adv. bd. Abington Coll., Pa. State U., 1998—. Named Legislator of Yr., Pa. Tax Collectors Assn., 1996, Policymaker Yr., Penn Future, 2002, Legislator of Yr., Pa. Ortho. Soc., 2002; recipient Cmty. Svc. award Willow Grove C. of C., 1996, Friend of Edn. award Abington Sch. Dist. Republican.

BARDACH, JOAN LUCILE, clinical psychologist; b. Albany, N.Y., Oct. 3, 1919; d. Monroe Lederer and Lucile May (Lowenberg) B. BA, Cornell U., 1940; AM in Psychology, NYU, 1951; PhD in Clin. Psychology, 1957; cert. in psychoanalysis and psychotherapy, NYU, 1970. Supr. clin. psychologist NYU Rusk Inst. Rehab. Medicine, 1959-61; asst. chief and acting chief psychologist Rusk Inst. Rehab. Medicine, 1962-65, dir. psychol. services, 1965-82; research psychologist, mem. faculty N.Y. Med. Coll., 1961-62, clin. prof. rehab. medicine (psychology), 1976—; supr. postdoctoral program psychoanalysis and psychotherapy NYU, 1978—; pvt. practice clin. psychology and psychoanalysis N.Y.C., 1957—. Non-govtl. orgn. rep. to UN Internat. Ctr. Sociol., Penal and Penitentiary Rsch. and Studies, Messina, Italy, 1985—; prin. investigator NIMH, 1976-81; mem. adv. bd. Coalition Sexuality and Disability, Planned Parenthood, 1983-89; cons. in field. Contbr. articles to profl. jours., chpt. to books. Recipient 3 awards for ednl. film, Choices: In Sexuality With Physical Disability, Internat. Film Festivals, Pioneer award for Sexual Attitude Reassessment Workshops The Coalition on Sexuality and Disability, 1989; NIMH fellow Inst. Sex Rsch., U. Ind., 1976. Fellow Am. Orthopsychiat. Assn.; mem. APA, Am. Congress Rehab. Medicine, Sex Info. and Edn. Council U.S., Nat. Register Health Service Providers in Psychology, Eastern Psychol. Assn., N.Y. State Psychol. Assn. Home and Office: 50 E 10th St New York NY 10003-6223 Office Phone: 212-673-2436.

BARDEN, LAURA MARIE, science educator; b. Rochester, N.Y. d. Eldred McKenna Barden and Theresa Mary (Manda) Brandstetter. BA, U. Tex., Dallas, 1982, MAT, 1985; PhD, U. Md., 1991. Tchr. Garland Ind. Sch. Dist., Tex., 1982-88; asst. prof. sci. edn. Western Ill. U., Knoxville, 1991—95, asst. prof., 1998—2004, prof., 2004—. Office: Western Ill U Dept Biol Sci 1 Univ Cir Macomb IL 61455

BARDEN, SHIRLEY RAMSEY, credit union executive; b. Santa Cruz, Calif., Oct. 26, 1935; d. Alfred Benjamin and Margaret (Wood) Ramsey; m. Stephen Otis Barden, June 29, 1957; children: Susanne Eleonore, Deborah Anne, Cynthia Louise. Student, U. Calif.-Berkeley, 1954—57. Mgr. DPST Fed. Credit Union, City of Industry, Calif., 1973—76, Paper Mill Employees Fed. Credit Union, Pomona, Calif., 1976—79; pres., asst. treas. Riverside Schs. Credit Union, Calif., 1979—. Active Contra Costa County Planned Parenthood, 1960—72; sec. Claremont United Ch. of Christ Congregational, Women's Fellowship, 2004—05. Mem.: Rancho Cucamonga Hist. Soc. (editor ECO del CASA 1998—2004, chmn. Las Guias), Mountain View Homeowners Assn. (sec. 2005—), Credit Union Adv. Coun. to Security Pacific Nat. Bank (organizing chmn., chmn.-elect), Credit Union Exec. Soc. (Golden Mirror award 1983), Calif. Credit Union League (pres. Mt. Baldy chpt. state com. 1976, state stblzn. com. 1979, Project Tomorrow com. 1979, chmn. Palm Tree Conf. state com. 1979, legis. rep. Tri County chpt. 1983—84). Democrat. Home: 1320 San Bernardino Rd SP 66 Upland CA 91786

BARDIN, MARY BETH, telecommunications company executive; m. Keith Bardin; 3 children. B in Journalism, Ohio U., 1977. Reporter AP; with pub. rels. Fidelity Investments, Dallas; joined GTE, Stamford, Conn., 1988, mgr. customer comms., dir. employee comms., asst. v.p. internal comms., v.p. pub. affairs GTE telephone ops., 1994-97, v.p. pub. affairs nat. ops., 1997, sr. v.p. pub. affairs and comms., 1998—2000; (GTE and Bell Atlantic merged to form

Verizon Comm., 2000); exec. v.p. pub affairs and comm. Verizon Comm. Inc., N.Y.C., 2000—. Adv. Bd. Coll. Comm. Ohio U. Office: Verizon Comm Inc 1095 Ave of the Americas New York NY 10036

BARDOLE, BETTY JEAN, elementary school educator; b. Lake City, Iowa, Apr. 6, 1932; d. Byron C. and Velma May (Freetly) McMeekin; m. Duane I. Bardole, Dec. 22, 1951 (dec. 1985); children: Barbara Jo, Alan E. BA, Buena Vista Coll., 1967. Cert. elem. tchr., Iowa. Tchr. Garfield Sch., Rockwell City, Iowa, 1951-52; book-keeper, office mgr. visual aids prodn. Iowa State U., Ames, 1952-53, film editor visual aids prodn., 1953-54; supt. sec. Lytton Cmty. Sch., Iowa, 1958-64; tchr. Rockwell City Cmty. Sch., Iowa, 1967-94; ret., 1994; bookkeeper, editor Lytton Town Crier, 2000—. Evaluator NSF, Washington, 1986; trainer tchrs. health class Arrowhead Area Edn. Agy., Ft. Dodge, Iowa, 1988, '91, '92. Recipient Vol. award Gov. of Iowa, 1989. Mem. NEA, Iowa Edn. Agy., Sci. Acad. Iowa, Iowa Hist. Soc., Iowa Wildlife Fedn., Sac County Hist. Soc., Social Studies Soc. Republican. Presbyterian. Avocations: reading, walking, knitting, travel.

BARDWICK, JUDITH MARCIA, management consultant; b. NYC, Jan. 16, 1933; d. Abraham and Ethel (Krinsky) Hardis; m. John Bardwick, III, Dec. 18, 1954 (div.); children: Jennifer, Peter, Deborah; m. Allen Armstrong, Feb. 10, 1984. BS, Purdue U., 1954; MS, Cornell U., 1955; PhD, U. Mich., 1964. Lectr. U. Mich., Ann Arbor, 1964-67, asst. prof. psychology, 1967-71, assoc. prof., 1971-75, prof., 1975-83, assoc. dean, 1977-83; clin. prof. psychiatry U. Calif., San Diego, 1984—; pres. In Transition, Inc. (name changed to Judith M. Bardwick, PhD, Inc., 1991), La Jolla, Calif., 1983—. Mem. population rsch. study group NIH, 1971—75. Co-author: (book) Feminine Personality and Conflict, 1970; author: Psychology of Women, 1971, In Transition, 1979, The Plateauing Trap, 1986, Danger in the Comfort Zone, 1991, In Praise of Good Business, 1998, Seeking the Calm in the Storm, 2002; mem. editl. bd. Women's Studies, 1973—, Psychology Women Quar., 1975—; contbr. articles to profl. jours. Mem. social sci. adv. com. Planned Parenthood Am., 1973. Fellow: APA; mem.: Am. Psychosomatic Soc., N.Y. Acad. Scis., Midwest Psychol. Assn., Phi Beta Kappa. Home and Office: 1389 Caminito Halago La Jolla CA 92037-7165 Office Phone: 858-456-1443. Personal E-mail: jmbwick@san.rr.com.

BARDYGUINE, PATRICIA WILDE, dancer, performing company executive; b. Ottawa, Ont., Can., July 16, 1928; came to U.S., 1943; d. John Herbert and Eileen Lucy (Simpson) White; m. George Bardyguine, Dec. 14, 1953; children: Anya, Youri. Student, Profl. Children's Sch., N.Y.C. Dancer Am. Concert Ballet, N.Y.C., 1943-44, Marquis De Queras Ballet Internat., N.Y.C., 1944-45, Ballet Russe De Monte Carlo, tours nationwide, 1945-49; guest artist Roland Petit Ballet De Paris, 1949; prin. ballerina Met. Ballet, touring throughout Europe, 1950, N.Y.C. Ballet, 1950-65; dir. Harkness House, N.Y.C., 1965-67; ballet mistress Am. Ballet Theater, N.Y.C., 1969-82; ret. artistic dir. Pitts. Ballet Theatre, 1997—, advisor, tchr., 1997—. Dir. Am. Ballet Theater Sch., 1979-82; dance panelist Nat. Endowment for Arts, N.Y. State Coun. for the Arts; judge Lausanne Internat. Competition; guest tchr., coach N.Y.C. Ballet, Joffrey Ballet, Dance Theater of Harlem, The Royal Ballet of Stockholm, Internat. Summer Seminar, Cologne, Germany, Heinz Bosl Found., Munich, St. Moritz, Japan, Australia, Republic of Korea. Soloist six European tours, also tour of Orient; numerous TV appearances; commd. by N.Y. Philharm. to choreograph ballets Festival, 1964, At the Ball, 1965, Viennese Evening, 1966, Petite Suite, 1967. Adminstr. scholar fund Sch. A. Ballet Group; mem. Nat. Bd. Regional Ballet; Fulbright panelist. Recipient YWCA award for Leadership in Arts and Letters, 1990, Cultural award for Extraordinary Contbns. to Cultural Life in Region, Pitts. Ctr. for Arts, 1997, Cultural award for outstanding contbns. to cultural climate of the region Pitts. Ctr. for Arts, 1997; named Pitts. Woman of Yr. in Arts and Music, 1994. Mem. Am. Guild Mus. Artists, AFTRA, Dance/USA (bd. dirs.). Office: Pitts Ballet Theatre 2900 Liberty Ave Pittsburgh PA 15201-1511

BAREFOOT, ANNE FARLEY, secondary education educator, consultant; b. Hallsboro, N.C., Mar. 9, 1934; d. Chester Arthur and Mildred Collier (Norment) Farley; m. Joe Blake Barefoot, Aug. 29, 1952; children: Jo Anne Barefoot Biser, Fredrick Arthur. BSS, East Carolina U., 1956, MA, 1960; EdS, U. S.C., 1985. Tchr. sci. Columbus County Schs., Delco, N.C., 1955-64, Whiteville (N.C.) H.S., 1964-93; nat. sci. cons. Glencoe Publs., 1993—2005. Author: Science Connections, 1989, Science Interactions, 1991. Recipient Presdl. award NSF, 1983, N.C. Bus. Sci. Teaching award Region IV, 1983, 87, Austin Bond award East Carolina U., 1984, Outstanding Alumni award, 1986. Mem. NSTA (life, bd. dirs. dist. IV), NEA, Am. Assn. Physics Tchrs., Am. Chem. Soc., N.C. Sci. Tchrs. Assn., Assn. Presdl. Awardees in Sci. Teaching (past pres.), Sigma Xi. Democrat. Methodist. Avocation: reading. Office: 1221 Dismal Rd Hallsboro NC 28442-9407

BARETTA, MARSHA MOTYL, elementary school physical education educator; b. Hartford, Conn., July 14, 1950; d. Michael Samuel and Regina McAdoo Motyl; m. John Dominic Baretta, Feb. 17, 1973 (div. June 20, 1984); children: Jason Michael, Kimberly Mary. BS, So. Conn. State U., 1972; MS, Ctrl. Conn. State U., 1979; MEd, Springfield Coll., Mass., 1991. Cert. CPR, first aid Am. Heart Assoc, 1990; profl. educator State of Conn. Dept. Edn., 1972. Phys. edn. tchr. South Windsor Bd. Edn., Conn., 1972—. Test devel. cons. Ednl. Testing Svcs., Princeton, NJ, 1990—94; portfolio scorer Conn. State Dept. Edn., 2000—03; sec. Conn. Governor's Com. on Phys. Fitness, 2002—. Head coach Spl. Olympics Conn., Wethersfield, Conn., 1992—2003, Spl. Olympics Conn. Ea. Regional Mgmt. Team, Wethersfield, 2000—03; bd. dirs. Greater Hartford Jaycees, 1986—89; exec., mgmt. com. Canon Greater Hartford Open, 1988—90; bd. dirs. Tri-Town YMCA, Wethersfield, 2000—04. Recipient Governor's Civic Leadership award, Greater Hartford Jaycees, 1983—90, Cmty. Svc. award, Sec. of State, Conn., 2003. Mem.: South Windsor Edn., Conn. (assoc.), Conn. Assn. Health, Phys. Edn., Recreation & Dance (assoc.; exec. officer 1986—88, Profl. Svc. award 1993), Am. Alliance Health, Phys. Edn. Recreation & Dance (assoc.), Amateur Ski Instructor's Assn. (licentiate; cert. instr.), Mt. Laurel Skiers (assoc.). Democrat-Npl. Roman Catholic. Avocations: skiing, bicycling, golf. Office: Wapping Elem Sch 91 Ayers Rd South Windsor CT 06074 Office Phone: 860-648-5010. Office Fax: 860-684-5802. E-mail: mbaretta@swindsor.k12.ct.us.

BARFOOT, JOAN, writer; b. Owen Sound, Can., May 17, 1946; BA, U. We. Ont. Reporter Windsor Star, 1967-69; feature and news writer Mirror Publs., Toronto, Can., 1969-73, Toronto Sunday Sun, 1973-75; with London Free Press, 1976-79, 80-94. Can. del. First Internat. Feminist Book Fair and Festival, U.K., 1983; judge Gov.-Gen.'s award for English Lang. Can. Fiction, 1995, Trillium Lit. award, 1996, 2000. Author: Abra, 1978, Dancing in the Dark, 1982, Duet for Three, 1985, Family News, 1989, Plain Jane, 1992, Charlotte and Claudia Keeping in Touch, 1994, Some Things About Flying, 1997, Getting Over Edgar, 1999, Critical Injuries, 2001, Luck, 2005. Recipient First Novel award Books in Can., 1978, Marian Engel award, 1992. Mem. Writer's Union of Can., PEN Can. Address: 286 Cheapside St London ON Canada N6A 2A2

BARGAGLIOTTI, LILLIAN ANTOINETTE, nursing educator; b. Millington, Tenn., Dec. 29, 1949; d. Benard Wood and Georgeanne (Lowe) McIllwain; m. Ronald M. Prentice, Apr. 24, 1970 (div. 1975); m. bill L. Bargagliotti, July 8, 1978; 1 child, William Benard. RN, Tacoma Gen. Hosp., 1971; BSN, U. Tenn., 1976; MS, U. Calif., San Francisco, 1978; D in Nursing Sci., U. Calif., 1984. Staff nurse Tacoma (Wash.) Gen. Hosp., 1971, St. Joseph's Hosp., Tacoma, 1971-75, City of Memphis Hosp., 1975-76; instr. N.W. Miss. Jr. Coll., Senatobia, 1976-78; inservice coord. Eden Hosp., Castro Valley, Calif., 1978-79; instr. Ohlone Coll., Fremont, Calif., 1979-84; assoc. prof. nursing San Francisco State U., 1984-85; assoc. dean, prof. nursing U. San Francisco, 1985-89, interim dean, prof. nursing, 1989-91; assoc. DON Davies Med. Ctr., 1992; dean, prof. nursing Loewenberg Sch. Nursing, U. Memphis, 1992—2005, prof., 2005—. Clin. evaluator SUNY Western Performance Assessment Ctr., Long Beach and Palo Alto, Calif., 1982-85; program evaluator Collegiate Commn. for Nursing Edn. Contbr. articles to profl. jours. Capt. USAR, 1976-78. Mem. ANA, Tenn. Nurses Assn., Assn. Oper. Rm. Nurses (mem. jour. editl. bd. 1987-90), Nat. League for Nursing (program evaluator, pres.-elect 2003-05, pres., 2005-, bd. govs., trustee found. bd.), Tenn. Assn. Deans/Dirs. Nursing (pres. 1997-99, 99-2001), Sigma Theta Tau. Republican. Mem. Ch. of Christ. Home: 7423 Wood Rail Cv Memphis TN 38119-9007 Office: U Memphis 102 Newport Hall Memphis TN 38152-3740 Business E-Mail: tbargagl@memphis.edu.

BARGER, BARBARA ELAINE, medical and surgical nurse, nursing educator; b. Franklin, Pa., Oct. 11, 1952; d. Clarence Burton and Shirley Louise (Ream) Haylett; m. James Clair Barger, Oct. 25, 1986; 1 child, Jenny Lynn. AD, Clarion U.-Venango Campus, Oil City, Pa.; BA, Eastern Nazarene Coll., Wollaston, Mass. Instr. Palm Beach County Schs., Belle Glade, Fla.; charge nurse Franklin Regional Med. Ctr.; instr., PN coord. CCAVTS, Shippenville, Pa.; charge nurse Sugar Creek (Pa.) Rest; with operating rm. Brookville Hosp. Mem. Nat. League Nursing, Pa. Nurses Assn.

BARGER, LINDA KALE, choral director; b. Charlotte, N.C., Apr. 14, 1948; d. Jack and Alma Kale; children: William Jackson, Chastity Lynn Barger Page. MusB, U. N.C., Greensboro, 1972; postgrad., U. N.C., 1988; postgrad., Belmont Abbey U., 1994—95; degree computer applications with windows, Gaston Coll., 1999; degree music comp. and theory, N.C. Sch. Sci. and Math, 2001. Band dir. Highland Jr. High, Gastonia, NC, 1974—76; music specialist Ashley Jr. H.S., Gastonia, NC, 1976—81, Highland Jr. H.S., Gastonia, NC, 1978—81; dir. choral William C. Friday Jr. H.S., Dallas, 1981—91; Cherryville HS choral dir. Gaston County Schs., Cherryville, 1991—2002. Choir dir. First Presbyn. Ch., Cherryville, NC, 1977—79; chmn. All-County Choral Festival, Gaston County, NC, 1981—82; interim music dir. First Bapt. Ch., Cherryville, NC, 1981; choral dir. William C. Friday Jr. H.S., Dallas, 1981—91; mem. bd. dirs. Lincoln Arts Guild Cmty. Concerts, Lincolnton, NC, 1981; interim choir dir. Dallas Bapt. Ch., Dallas, 1984, New Hope Bapt. Ch., Gastonia, NC, 1985—87; choir dir. First United Meth. Ch., Cherryville, NC, 1987—95; chs cheerleading coach of the award-winning chs cheerleaders Cherryville H.S., Cherryville, NC, 1992—97; state bd. dirs. N.C. Music Educators Assn., NC, 1994—2002; pres. Dist. 2 NC Music Educators, Gaston, Lincoln, Cleve., Polk, Rutherford, McDowell Counties, NC, 1994—2002; theater arts tchr. Cherryville H.S., Cherryville, NC, 1999—2002; mem. barbara bair scholarship com. NC Music Educators Assn., NC, 2000—02; Gaston County music textbook adoption com. Gaston County Schs., Gastonia, NC. Musician (accompanist): (first all-county choral festival) Gaston County Choral Festival, 1977; dir.(choral director): (musical) All-County Junior High Choral Festival, 1978, (state choral contests) William C. Friday chorus, Various performances, 1986. Mem. team Relay for Life Cancer Orgn., Cherryville, NC, 2001—02. Mem.: NEA, Assn. of Classroom Tchrs., Gaston County Theater Arts Tchrs. Assn., Gaston County Choral Dirs. Assn., Am. Choral Dirs. Assn., N.C. Assn. Educators, Cherryville Music Club (past pres. 1981—83). Office: Cherryville HS 313 Ridge Ave Cherryville NC 28021 Business E-Mail: bargerl@gaston.gcs.k12.nc.us.

BARGER-MARCUSIU, EVA, cardiovascular nurse; b. Berwyn, Ill., Apr. 4, 1957; d. James Malcolm and Wretha (Chester) Catlin; children: Tyler Raymond, Gwendolyn Marie, Ian Hunter, Alex James. Assoc. Life Sci., Parkland Jr. Coll., 1977, Assoc. Nursing, 1982; BS, U. Ill., Urbana, 1988; MS in Nursing, U. Ill., Peoria, 1990. Critical care RN; cert. ACLS. Staff nurse oncology Carle Found. Hosp., Urbana, 1982-84, asst. mgr. colon/rectal, 1984-85, staff nurse critical care, 1985—, hemodialysis nurse, 1988—; cardiovascular clin. specialist Carle Clinic, Urbana, 1988—; clin. instr. nursing Parkland Jr. Coll., Champaign, Ill., 1990—. Mem. AACCN, NAFE. Home: 801 W Main Mahomet IL 61853 E-mail: emarcusiu@carle.com.

BARGMANN, CORNELIA I., neuroscientist, science educator; b. Va. B in biochemistry, U. Ga., 1981; PhD, MIT, 1987. Postdoctoral rschr. MIT; named asst. prof. U. Calif., San Francisco, 1991, investigator Howard Hughes Med. Inst., 1995—, prof., 1998—, vice chair dept. anatomy, 1999—. Recipient Lucille P. Markey award, Takasago prize, W. Alden Spencer award, Charles Judson Herrick award, 2000; Searle scholar, 1992. Mem.: NAS, AAAS. Office: UCSF Dept Anatomy 513 Parnassus Ave PO Box 0452 San Francisco CA 94143-0452

BARHAM, K. DAWN, music educator, lyricist; d. Paul and Janice Barham. MusB in Edn., U. So. Miss., 1986—86, MusM in Edn., 1998. Orff Schulwerk Certification Miss. State U., 1990, Student Teacher Advisor Miss. State Dept. of Edn., 1991. Music educator Lowndes County Sch.s, Columbus, Miss., 1989—93; performing arts dir. Miss. Sch. Math & Sci., 1993—. Singer (composer): (sound recording) Dodging Shadows; singer: Broken Promises. Fundraiser ARC, Columbus, Miss., 2000—00, LaBonheur's Children's Hosp., Memphis, 2001—01, Salvation Army, Columbus, 2002—05, Free Mammogram Program, Bay St. Louis, 2001—03; pres. Lowndes County Fedn. Dem. Women, 2004—05; youth choir dir. St. Paul's Episcopal Ch., 2000—01; bd. mem. Miss. Boy Choir, Columbus, 2000—04. Named Star Tchr., 2005—06; recipient Best Scenic Design, Miss. Theater Assn., 1996, 1998, Best Direction, 1996, Winner, 1996, Superior Ratings, 1996, 1997, 1998, Overall Merit, 1997; scholar, Miss. Institutions Higher Learning, 1996, 1997. Mem.: Miss. Music Educator's Assn., Miss. Music Educator's Nat. Conf., Miss. Music Educator's Assn. Episcopalian. Office: Miss Sch Math and Sci 1100 College St W 1627 Columbus MS 39701 Office Phone: 662-329-8531. Home Fax: 662-329-8531; Office Fax: 662-329-8531.

BARIL, NANCY ANN, gerontological nurse practitioner, consultant; b. Paterson, N.J., May 10, 1952; d. Kenneth Gerald and Jeanette Elenore (Girodet) Keiser; m. Joel Mark Baril, Apr. 15, 1984; children: Jason Kenneth, Jennifer Jean. AA, Gulf Coast C.C., Panama City, Fla., 1976; BSN, Fla. State U., Tallahassee, 1978; MSN, UCLA, 1983. Registered pub. health nurse, Calif.; ANA cert. gerontol. nurse practitioner. Charge nurse, nurse preceptor Cedar Sinai Med. Ctr., L.A., 1979-83; nurse Nursing Svcs. Inc., Sherman Oaks, Calif., 1980-83; nurse practitioner Santa Monica (Calif.) Peer Counseling Ctr., 1983; nurse cons., gerontol. nurse practitioner Summit Health Ltd., Burbank, Calif., 1983-85; nurse cons. Geriatric Assocs., Granada Hills, Calif., 1983-85; nurse cons., gerontol. nurse practitioner ARA Living Ctrs., Glendale, Calif., 1986-87; DON, gerontol. nurse practitioner Astoria Convalescent Hosp. Sign of the Dove, Sylmar, Calif., 1988-91; gerontol. nurse practitioner Balboa Plz. Med. Group, 1991-98, Absolute Health Care, Mission Hills, Calif., 1998-2000, Ctr. Sr. Health, Akron, Ohio, 2000—01, Health Strata, Nashville, 2001—03, Dr. Martin Freimer, East Stroudsburg, Pa., 2003—. Mem. PTA, Granada Hills, 1985. Mem. ANA, Calif. Coalition Nurse Practitioners, Calif. Nursing Assn., Gerontol. Soc., Sigma Theta Tau (rec. sec. 1983-85). Democrat. Episcopalian. Home: 115 Ledgeview Dr Hawley PA 18428 Office: 100 Plz Ct East Stroudsburg PA 18301 Office Phone: 570-424-6763. Personal E-mail: nannynp@aol.com.

BARKAN-CLARKE, JACQUELINE MIA, artist, educator, art therapist, jewelry designer; d. Stanley Howard and Beverly Adrian Barkan; m. Steven Jay Clarke, Nov. 19, 2000; 1 child, Natasha Rose Clarke. BFA, AAS, Fashion Inst. of Tech., NYC, 1992; MA, Hofstra U., Hempstead, NY, 2000. Asst. art dir. Cross-Cultural Comm., Merrick, NY, 1990—; asst. curator Stage Gallery, Merrick, 1999—2002; art therapist United Cerebral Palsy Ctr./The Children's Learning Ctr., Roosevelt, NY, 2000; creative arts therapist Brunswick Hosp. Ctr., Amityville, NY, 2000—02, Bellmore and Hudson Valley, NY, 2000—; supervising activities therapist Elmhurst Hosp. Ctr./Intermediate.Sch. 145, Jackson Heights, NY, 2002—03; supervising art therapist South Oaks Hosp. Ctr., Amityville, 2003—04; instr. Molloy Coll., Rockville Centre, NY, 2004—. Guest instr. art therapy Touro Coll., NYC, 2002; workshop instr. SUNY, Farmingdale, 2003; substitute grad. instr. art therapy Hofstra U., 2004; art therapist, expressive weaving workshop instr. Creative Ctr. for Women with Cancer, NYC, 2004; juror Beacon Artists Union, NY, 2006. Author: My Sacred Circle Mandala Journal; poet: The New Scribes, Vol VI, No I, The New Scribes, Vol V, No I & II, Waterways-Poetry in the Mainstream, Paumanok: Poetry & Pictures of Long Island, Women Poets (Cross-Cultural Monthly), Paterson Literary Rev.; Exhibited in group shows at The Paterson (NJ) Mus., Howland Cultural Ctr., Beacon, NY, Stage Gallery, Merrick; poet and illustrator An ABC of Fruits & Vegetables, illustrator Medicinal Purposes, Vol I, No VII; (cover art for poetry chapbook), Then & Now, (cover and text art for poetry book), This Pot Has Pepper. Mem.: Beacon Arts Cmty. Assn. (assoc.), Am. Assn. Museums (assoc.), Clin. Art Therapists of LI (assoc.), NY Coalition Creative Arts Therapists (assoc.), NY Art Therapy Assn. (assoc.), Am. Art Therapy Assn. (assoc.), Handweavers Guild Am. (assoc.). Office: Molloy Coll Art Dept PO Box 5002 Rockville Centre NY 11571-5002 Office Phone: 516-678-5000. Personal E-mail: miaart@aol.com.

BARKEMEIJER DE WIT, JEANNE SANDRA, graphic artist, illustrator, writer, multimedia consultant; b. Santa Ana, Calif., July 6, 1955; d. Hendrik Pieter and Nelly Maria Barkemeijer de Wit; m. Johnne J. Johnson, Sept. 6, 1996. Student, Am. Coll. Paramed. Arts Scis., Santa Ana, 1977-78, Computer Learning Ctr., Anaheim, Calif., 1985-86, Regional Occupational Program, Buena Park, Calif., 1986, Cen. Counties Regional Occupational Program, Santa Ana, 1986-87, 90-94, Rancho Santiago Coll., 1990-94. Cert. respiratory therapy tech. Freelance artist, writer, photographer, Santa Ana, 1972—; respiratory therapist Good Samaritan Hosp., Anaheim, 1978-79, Tustin (Calif.) Community Hosp., 1979-81, United Western Med. Ctrs., Santa Ana, Anaheim, 1981-86; office mgr., dir. spl. accounts D-Link Systems, Inc., Irvine, Calif., 1986-90; graphic artist, illustrator, contbg. writer West 17th mag., Santa Ana, 1990-94, also editor-in-chief, 1991; art dir. John Henry Found., Garden Grove, Calif., 1996—2000; bookkeeper and office mgr. Progeny Properties, Anaheim, Calif., 2002—. Graphic artist Santa Ana Unified Schs., 1974. Exhibited in group shows including Torrana Art League, 1970-72, Buzza Gibson Gallery, 1970, various galleries in Japan, Amsterdam, and N.Y., 1970, Very Spl. Arts Gallery, 1999-2002; illustrator: Sexual Positions for Chronic Lung and Cardiac Patients, 1984; author, designer numerous storyboard diskettes, 1988—; illustrations exhibited, The Very Special Arts Gallery, 1999-2002; contbg. photographer Smashing Books!, 2000; recs. include (CD's) Fragments, Dance With Me; webmaster for numerous sites. Vol. lab. technician Health Fair Expo 1992; vol. therapist Cancer Assn. Great Am. Smoke-Out, Costa Mesa, 1979-86, Lung Assn. Scamp Camp for Asthmatic Children, Santa Ana, 1986; vol. artist Heart Assn., L.A., 1986; vocalist, guitarist Easter Seal Telethon Orange County, 1978. Recipient Cert. Thanks Heart Assn., 1985, Cert. Appreciation Health Fair Expo Nat. Health Laboratories, 1992, Columbia medalist Front Page Graphics, 1990, Pacemaker award, 1991, 2d Pl. for layout and design, 2nd Pl., 1993, 1st, 2d and 4th pl., 3d Hon. Mention award JACC State Competition for mag. illustration, 1992. Democrat. Avocations: volunteering, music, theater. Home: 1551 W Chateau Ave Anaheim CA 92802-1315

BARKER, BARBARA ANN, ophthalmologist; b. Paterson, NJ, Nov. 10, 1943; d. Earle Louis and Dorothy Louise (Williamson) Barker; m. Joel Ira Papernik, July 28, 1972; children: Deborah Papernik, Ilana Papernik. BA magna cum laude, Conn. Coll., 1965; BS, Yale U., 1967; MA, Rutgers U., 1974; MD, Mt. Sinai Sch. Medicine, 1976. Diplomate Am. Bd. Ophthalmology. Intern Beth Israel Med. Ctr., 1977; resident Mt. Sinai Sch. Medicine/Beth Israel Med. Ctr., 1980, fellow in glaucoma, 1980-81, fellow cornea, refractive surgery, 1981-82; pvt. practice medicine specializing in ophthalmology, N.Y.C., 1983—. Rsch. technician The Rockefeller U., N.Y.C., 1965—66; tchr. Riverdale Country Sch., N.Y.C., 1967—68; rsch. asst. Sloan Kettering Inst., N.Y.C., 1969—72; asst. clin. prof. Mt. Sinai Sch. Medicine, N.Y.C., 1982—; mem. staff N.Y. Eye and Ear Hosp., Beth Israel/St. Luke's/Roosevelt Hosp. Recipient Resident Best Paper award, Beth Israel Med. Ctr., 1989, Honor award, Am. Acad. Ophthalmology, 1955; grantee Beth Israel Rsch. grant, 1983, NSF, 1966. Fellow: ACS, N.Y. Acad. Medicine; mem.: AMA, N.Y. County Med. Assn., Women's Med. Soc. NYC, Am. Med. Women's Assn., Phi Beta Kappa. Home: 11 E 86th St New York NY 10028-0501 Office: 70 E 96th St New York NY 10028 Office Phone: 212-289-2244. Personal E-mail: bbarkermd@aol.com.

BARKER, CELESTE ARLETTE, computer scientist; b. Redding, Calif., Apr. 19, 1947; d. Edwin Walter Squires and Rachel (Kinkead) Layton; m. Julius Jeep Chernak, Sept. 13, 1970, (div. 1980); children: Sean Matthew, Bret Allen; m. Jackson Lynn Barker, Oct. 8, 1988. BA in Art, San Francisco State U., 1970; AA in Engring. Tech., Coll. Marin, 1980; MBA in Mgmt., Golden Gate U., 1988. Cert. netware engr. Art tchr. San Rafael (Calif.) Schs., 1971—75; owner, photographer Julius Chernak Photography, Novato, Calif., 1970—76; draftsman Donald Foster Drafting, San Rafael, 1975—76; surveyor Parks Dept. State Calif., Inverness, 1976; electric draftsman Pacific Gas & Electric, San Rafael, 1976—78, electric engring. estimator, 1978—79, mktg. rep. Santa Rosa, 1980—85, valuation analyst San Francisco, 1985—86, budget analyst, 1986—88, budget system project mgr., 1988—89, fin. asset mgr. Vallejo, Calif., 1989—90; ops. mgr. San Francisco Mus. Modern Art, 1990—91; cons. CB Cons., Atlanta, 1991—93; computer local area network mgr. Ga. Inst. Tech., Atlanta, 1993—94; systems integrator Bank South, Atlanta, 1994—95; mgmt. info. sys. mgr. Dinwiddie Constr., San Francisco, 1995—96; process, project mgr. Sybase, Inc., Emeryville, Calif., 1996—98; Wintel delivery mgr. Fair-Isaac Cos., San Rafael, Calif., 1998—2000; dir. support Kabira Techs., San Rafael, Calif., 2000—01; dir. profl. svcs. and tech. support Guardian Edge Tech., San Francisco, 2002—. Dir. Mariner Green Townhomes Assn., treas. 1987-88. Mem. Sierra Club. Avocations: photography, painting, backpacking. Home: 29 Woodside Way San Rafael CA 94901-1439 Business E-Mail: cbarker@guardianedge.com.

BARKER, JANICE MARIE, elementary school educator; b. Freeport, Ill., June 1, 1958; d. John Graydon and Jeneane Mae Trevethan; m. Michael Robert Barker, June 20, 1981; children: Lucas, Jose, Jack. BA in Sci. and Phys. Edn., Ctrl. Coll., Pella, Iowa, 1980. Spl. edn. tchr. Warren Jr./Sr. HS and Apple River Mid. Sch., Warren, Ill., 1980—85; tchr. phys. edn. and strength tng. Warren Jr./Sr. HS, 1995—, volleyball coach jr. HS athletics, 1985—97, jr. HS student coun., 1999—2003. Cub scout den leader Boy Scouts Am. Recipient Spirit award, Warren Endowment Com., 2003. Mem.: NSCA, Ill. Assn. Health, Phys. Edn., Recreation and Dance. Home: 303 Platt St Warren IL 61087

BARKER, JULIE A., school system administrator; b. Rochester, N.Y., July 30, 1968; d. Philip Noto and Angela Terrell; m. Scott M. Barker; children: Brandon, Colby. BA in History and Secondary Social Studies, SUNY, Cortland, 1990, MA in History, 1995. Cert. tchr. secondary social studies N.Y. State Edn. Dept. Secondary social studies tchr. Maine-Endwell (N.Y.) Ctrl. Sch. Dist., 1991—95, Pittsford (N.Y.) Ctrl. Sch. Dist., 1995—2000, curriculum coord. - social studies, 2000—. Facilitator Franklin Covey Co., Salt Lake City, 2000—; instrnl. coach Pittsford Ctrl. Sch. Dist., 1999—. Bd. dirs. Pittsford Youth Svcs., 1998—2001; dir. vacation Bible sch. Ch. of the Transfiguration, Pittsford, 2003—. Mem.: ASCD, N.Y. State Coun. Social Studies. Office: Pittsford Ctrl Sch Dist 10 Grove St Pittsford NY 14534 Office Phone: 585-218-1782. Office Fax: 585-218-1721. E-mail: julie_barker@pittsford.monroe.edu.

BARKER, NANCY LEPARD, university official; b. Owosso, Mich., Jan. 22, 1936; d. Cecil L. and Mary Elizabeth (Stuart) Lepard; m. J. Daniel Cline, June 6, 1960 (div. 1971); m. R. William Barker, Nov. 18, 1972; children: Mary Georgia Harker, Mark L. Cline, Richard E., Daniel P., Melissa B. Van Arsdel, John C. Cline MD, Helen Grace Garrett, Wiley D., James G. BSc, U. Mich., Ann Arbor, 1957; DHum (hon.), Northwood U., 2001. Spl. edn. instr. Univ. Hosp. U. Mich., Ann Arbor, 1958-61; v.p. Med. Educator, Chgo., 1967-69; asst. to chmn., dir. careers for women Northwood U., Midland, Mich., 1970-77, asst. prof., chmn. dept. fashion mktg. and merchandising, 1972-77, dir. arts programs and external affairs, 1972-77, v.p. univ. rels., 1978-2001, office of the pres., 2001—. Bd. dirs. Alden B. Dow Creativity Ctr., Midland; cons., lectr. in field. Co-author: (children's books) Wendy Well Series, 1970-72; contbr. chpts. to books, articles to profl. jours. Advisor Mich. Child Study Assn., 1972—; chmn. Matrix: Midland Festival, 1978; bd. dirs. Nat. Coun. of Women, 1971—, pres., 1983-85, chmn. centennial com., 1988; mem. exec. bd. Mich. ACE Network for Women Leaders in Higher Edn., 2001—; bd. dirs. ArtServe, Mich., 2003—, Family and Children's Svcs., Internat. Coun. Women, Paris. Nominee, (3) Mich. Women's Hall of Fame; named 1st ann. Disting. Educator of Yr., Am. Coun. on Edn./MI Network, 2001; named one of Outstanding Young Women in U.S. and Mich., 1974;

recipient Hon. award, Ukrainian Nat. Women's League, 1983, Disting. Woman award, Northwood U., 1970, Outstanding Young Woman award, Jr. C. of C., 1974. Mem. Internat. Coun. Women (bd. dirs. Paris 1991—), The Fashion Group, Internat. Furnishings and Design Assn. (pres. Mich. chpt. 1974-77), Mich. Women's Studies Assn. (founding mem.), Arts Midland Coun. (pres. 2 terms, 25th Anniversary award), Internat. Women's Forum, Mich. Women's Forum, Contemporary Rev. Club, Midland County Lawyers' Wives, Zonta, Phi Beta Kappa, Phi Kappa Phi, Alpha Lambda Delta, Phi Lambda Theta, Phi Gamma Nu, Delta Delta Delta. Office: Northwood Univ 209 Revere Midland MI 48640-4255 Office Phone: 989-631-9864. E-mail: barkermid@aol.com.

BARKER, SARAH EVANS, judge; b. Mishawaka, Ind., June 10, 1943; d. James McCall and Sarah (Yarbrough) Evans; m. Kenneth R. Barker, Nov. 25, 1972; 3 children. BS, Ind. U., 1965, LLD (hon.), 1999; JD, Am. U., 1969; LLD (hon.), U. Indpls., 1984; D in Pub. Svc. (hon.), Butler U., 1987; LLD (hon.), Marian Coll., 1991; LHD, U. Evansville, 1993; LLD (hon.), Wabash Coll., 1999, Hanover Coll., 2001; D of Civil Law (hon.), 2003. Bar: Ind. 1969, U.S. Dist. Ct. (so. dist.) Ind., 1969, U.S. Ct. Appeals (7th cir.) 1973, U.S. Supreme Ct., 1978. Legal asst. to senator U.S. Senate, 1969-71; spl. counsel to minority, govt. ops. com. permanent investigations subcom., 1971-72; dir. rsch. scheduling and advance Senator Percy Re-election Campaign, 1972; asst. U.S. atty. So. Dist. Ind., 1972-76, 1st asst. U.S. atty., 1976-77, U.S. atty., 1981-84; judge U.S. Dist. Ct. (so. dist.) Ind., 1984—, chief judge, 1994—2000. Assoc., then ptnr. Bose, McKinney & Evans, Indpls., 1977-81; mem. long range planning com. Jud. Conf. U.S., 1991-96, exec. com., 1989-91, standing com. fed. rules of practice and procedure, 1987-91, dist. judge rep., 1988-91; mem. jud. coun. 7th cir. Ct. Appeals, 1988-2000, jud. fellows commn. U.S. Supreme Ct., 1993-98; jud. adv. com., sentencing commn., 1995-97, bd. advisors, Ind. U., Purdue U., Indpls., 1989—; mem. pres.'s cabinet Ind. U., 1995—; bd. visitors Ind. U. Sch. of Law, Bloomington, 1984—; bd. dirs. Clarian Health Ptnrs., 1996—, Christian Theol. Sem., 1999-2001; bd. dirs. Einstein Inst. for Sci., Health and the Cts., 2001— Recipient Peck award Wabash Coll., 1989, Touchstone award Girls Club of Greater Indpls., 1989, Leach Centennial 1st Woman award Valparaiso Law Sch., 1993, Most Influential Women award Indpls. Bus. Jour., 1996, Paul Buchanan award of excellence Indpls. Bar Found., 1998, Thomas J. Hennessy award Ind. U., 1995, Disting. Citizen fellow Ind. U., 1999-2001; named Ind. Woman of Yr., Women in Comm., 1986, Ind. Univ. Disting. Alumni, 1996, Disting. Citizen fellow Ind. U., 1999-2001, Singing Hoosiers Disting. Alumni award Ind. U., 2000, Man for All Seasons award St. Thomas More Soc., 2000. Mem. ABA, Ind. Bar Assn., Indpls. Bar Assn. (Antoinette Dakin Leach award 1993), Fed. Judges Assn. (exec. com., bd. dirs. 2001—), Com. on Budget (judicial conf. 2001-), Einstein Inst. Sci., Health and Cts. (bd. dirs. 2001-), U.S. Judicial Conf. (spl. redaction rev. panel 2000-), Christian Theol. Sem. (bd. trustees 1999-), Lawyers Club, Kiwanis. Republican. Methodist. Office: US Dist Ct 210 US Courthouse 46 E Ohio St Indianapolis IN 46204-1903

BARKER, SHEILA, chemist, educator; BS in Geology, West. Tex. State U., Canyon, 1984; MS in Biology, Wayland Bapt. U., Plainview, Tex., 1990. Tchr. Bays Ranch Ind. Sch. Dist., Tex., 1984—88, Amarillo Ind. Sch. Dist., 1989—. Mem. curriculum com. Amarillo Ind. Sch. Dist., 2003—06. Mem.: Chemistry Assn. Soc.Tex., Nat. Sci. Tchrs. Assn. Baptist. Office: Amarillo Ind Sch Dist 4225 Danbury Amarillo TX 79109

BARKER, SYLVIA MARGARET, nurse; b. Glens Falls, NY, Sept. 11, 1914; d. Victor Howell and Julia Helen (Lansing) B. Student, Green Mountain Coll., 1933; diploma, Mt. Sinai Hosp. Sch. Nursing, 1936; BS, Columbia U., 1947, MA, 1951. RN, N.Y. Staff nurse Mt. Sinai Hosp., N.Y.C., 1936-37, gynecology head nurse, 1937-40, nursing arts asst. instr., 1940-41, nursing of children instr., 1941-45, nursing arts instr.-in-charge, 1945-48; instr. in charge nursing arts Michael Reese Hosp., Chgo., 1948-50; nursing of children supr. Mt. Sinai Hosp., N.Y.C., 1951-66, asst. dir. insvc. edn., 1966-72, assoc. dir. nursing, 1972-77, acting dir. nursing, assoc. dir. nursing, 1972, assoc. dir. nursing affairs, 1977-86, cons. nursing adminstrn., 1986-94. Hon. clin. assoc. faculty CUNY, 1984-87, 89-91; presenter SUNY, Downstate, 1982, N.Y. State Nurses Assn., 1982, Mt. Sinai Hosp., N.Y.C., 1983, 91, 92, United Hosp. Fund and Office of Profl. Discipline, N.Y.C., 1983, Cornell Med. Ctr., 1984, CCNY, 1984-91, Charleston W.Va. Eye, Ear, Nose and Throat Clinic, 1986, Hunter-Bellevue Sch. Nursing, 1987-91. Author: SMB-A Memoir, 2001, SMB-A Memoir Vol. 2 "As I Was Saying", 2003, SMB-A Memoir Vol. 3, 2004; co-author: The Sinai Nurse; contbr. articles to profl. jours. Bd. dirs. Nurses House, 1991—95, 2001—04, sec., 1995—97, pres., 1997—2001. Recipient Alumni Achievement award Nursing Edn. Alumni Assn. Tchrs. Coll., 1994, Leadership in Profl. and Allied Orgns. Achievement award, 1999; writings and papers in Archives of Found. N.Y. State Nurses Assn., 1993; Guggenheim scholar Mt. Sinai Hosp. Sch. Nursing, 1936. Mem.: ANA (Coun. Nursing Adminstrn. Membership award 1998, Disting. Membership award 1998), N.Y. Counties RNs Assn. (bd. dirs. 1983—85, chair bylaws com. dist. 13 1983—91, exec. dir. 1993—94, search com., Recognition 50 Yr. Membership award 1989, Jane Delano Disting. Svc. award 1982), N.Y. State Nurses Assn. (bylaws com. 1982—85, nurses house inc. bd. dirs. 1991—95, nominating com. 1995, sec. 1995—97, pres. 1997—2001, bd. mem. 2001—04, Nursing Svc. Adminstrn. award 1984, Recognition 50 Yr. Membership award 1986, Hon. Recognition award 1992), So. N.Y. League for Nursing, Nat. League for Nursing, Alumni Assn. of Mt. Sinai Hosp. Sch. Nursing (bd. dirs. 1981—84, pres. 1987—91, treas. 1991—95, sec. 1995—2002, bd. dirs. 2002—05, sec. 2005—), Sigma Theta Tau. Avocations: ballet, philharmonic orchestra, reading, writing, collecting owls. Home and Office: 788 Columbus Ave Apt 6K New York NY 10025-5942

BARKER, VIRGINIA LEE, nursing educator; Diploma, Ind. U. Sch. Nursing, 1952, BS, 1955, MS, 1961, EdD, 1969. Dean sch. nursing, prof. Alfred (N.Y.) U., 1969-78; prof., dean nursing U. Louisville, 1978-81; dean Mary Black Sch. Nursing, prof. U. S.C., Spartanburg, 1981-90; dean profl. studies, prof. nursing SUNY, Plattsburg, 1990-98, prof. nursing Plattsburgh, 1990—. Cons. nursing program NY Regents Coll., 1972—91; dir. federally funded telenursing project rural upstate NY, 1993—2005; dir. project to develop virtual reality simulations edn. physicians, nurses, allied health pers. SUNY, Plattsburgh, 1995—; advisor to students in RN-BSN program over no. NY, 2000—. Contbr. articles to profl. jours., papers nat. and internat. confs. Mem. ARC. Grantee Disting. Practitioner, N.Y. State Nurses Assn. Mem.: AAUW, ANA, Internat. Coun. of Nurses, S.C. Deans and Dirs. Nursing Fedn. (chmn. 1989), Am. Assn. Higher Edn., S.C. League Nursing, Nat. League Nurses (com. mem. 1976—77), N.Y. State Nurses Assn. (pres. 1976—77), Ind. U. Sch. Nursing Alumni Assn. (pres. 1960), Kappa Delta Pi, Phi Kappa Phi, Sigma Theta Tau. Business E-Mail: virginia.barker@plattsburgh.edu.

BARKETT, ROSEMARY, federal judge; b. Ciudad Victoria, Tamaulipas, Mex., Aug. 29, 1939; arrived in U.S., 1946, naturalized, 1958; BS summa cum laude, Spring Hill Coll., 1967; JD, U. Fla., 1970; LLD (hon.), Stetson U., St. Petersburg, Fla., 1987; LHD (hon.), Fla. Internat. U., Miami, 1987; LLD (hon.), John Marshall Law Sch., Chgo., 1990; LHD (hon.), U. So. Fla., Tampa, 1990; DCL (hon.), Spring Hill Coll., Mobile, Ala., 1990; LLD (hon.), Rollins Coll., Orlando, Fla., 1992, Nova U., Ft. Lauderdale, Fla., 1992. Bar: Fla., U.S. Dist. Ct. (so. dist.) Fla., U.S. Ct. Appeals (5th cir.), U.S. Supreme Ct. Pvt. practice, West Palm Beach, Fla., 1971—79; judge 15th Jud. Cir. Ct., Palm Beach County, Fla., 1979—82, administrative judge civil divsn., 1982—83, chief judge, 1983—84; appellate judge 4th Dist. Ct. Appeal, West Palm Beach, Fla., 1984—85; justice Supreme Ct. Fla., Tallahassee, 1985—92, chief justice, 1992—94; cir. judge U.S. Ct. Appeals (11th cir.), Miami, 1994—. Bd. dirs. Lawyers for Children, U.S. Assn. Constl. Law; faculty U. Nev., Reno, Nat. Jud. Coll., Fla. Jud. Coll., Appellate Judges Seminar, Inst. Jud. Adminstrn., NYU; lectr. in field; vis. com. Miami U. Law Sch.; bd. visitors St. Thomas U. Mem. editl. bd.: The Florida Judges Manual. Named Women of Distinction, Crohn's & Colitis Found., 1997; named to Fla. Women's Hall of Fame, 1986, Miami Centennial Hall of Fame, 1996; recipient Woman of Achievement award, Palm Beach County Commn. on Status of Women, 1985, Hannah G. Solomon award, Nat. Coun. Jewish Women, 1991, Lifetime Achievement award, Latin Bus. Profl. Women, 1992, Breaking the Glass Ceiling award, Fla. Fedn. Bus. Profl. Women's Clubs, Inc., 1993, Disting. Jurist award, Miss. State U., 1995, Margaret Brent Women Lawyers of Achievement award, ABA Commn. Women in Profession, 1996, Harriette Glasner Freedom award, ACLU, 1999. Fellow: ABA (Minority Justice Honoree 1992); mem.: Fla. Commn. on Status of Women, Dade Marine Inst., Fed. Judges Assn., Am. Law Inst., Assn. Trial Lawyers Am. (Achievement award 1986), Acad. Fla. Trial Lawyers (Achievement award 1988, Rosemary Barkett award named in her honor 1992), Palm Beach Marine Inst., Nat. Assn. Women Judges (Honoree of Year 1999), Fla. Assn. Women Lawyers (Judge Mattie Belle Davis award 1991, Rosemary Barkett Outstanding Achievement award named in her honor 1999), Am. Acad. Matrimonial Lawyers (award 1984), Palm Beach County Bar Assn., Fla. Bar Assn. Office: US Ct of Appeals (11th cir) Fla 99 NE 4th St Rm 1223 Miami FL 33132-2140*

BARKEY, DEBRA LYNN, music educator; b. Iowa City, Oct. 11, 1951; d. Harry Laverne and Phyllis Lucille Baker; m. Gary Ronald Barkey, Dec. 29, 1973; children: Jill Elaine, Amanda Kate. MusB, U. Iowa, Iowa City, 1973; MA in Music Edn., Tex. Woman's U., Denton, 2004. Choir dir. West Branch Ind. Sch. Dist., Iowa, 1973—75; jingle singer Tanner Studios, Memphis, 1978—80; adminstrv. asst. Tandy Corp., Ft. Worth, 1981—89; choir dir. Azle Ind. Sch. Dist., 1991—98, Hurst & Southlake Ind. Sch. Dist., 1998—2004, Bowie High Sch., Arlington, 2004—. Free-lance accompanist, Iowa, Tex., 1969—; dir. ch. choir Ctrl. Christian Ch., Ft. Worth, 1983—90. Mem.: Tex. Music Condrs. Assn., Music Educators Nat. Conf., Tex. Choral Dirs. Assn. Methodist. Avocations: reading, golf. Home: 429 Fieldwood Terr Hurst TX 76053 Office: Arlington Ind Sch Dist 2101 Highbank Dr Arlington TX 76018

BARKIN, ELAINE RADOFF, composer; b. NYC, Dec. 15, 1932; m. George J. Barkin, Nov. 28, 1957; 3 children. BA in Music, Queens Coll., 1954, MFA in Composition, 1956; PhD in Composition and Theory, Brandeis U., 1971; Cert. in Composition and Piano, Berlin Hochschule Musik, 1957; studied with Karol Rathaus, Irving Fine, Boris Blacher, Arthur Berger. Lectr. in music Queens Coll., 1964-70, Sarah Lawrence, 1969-70; from asst. to assoc. prof. music theory U. Mich., 1970-74; from asst. prof. to prof. composition and theory U. Calif., L.A., 1974-97. Vis. asst. prof. Princeton (N.J.) U., 1974; lectr. in field. Asst. to co-editor: Perspectives of New Music, 1963-85; composer String Quartet, 1969, Sound Play for violin, 1974, String Trio, 1976, Plein Chant, alto flute, 1977, Ebb Tide, 2 vibraphones, 1977,.the Supple Suitor.for soprano and five players, 1978, (chamber mini opera) De Amore, 1980, Impromptu for violin, cello, piano, 1981, (theatre piece) Media Speak, 1981, At the Piano, piano, 1982, For String Quartet, 1982, Quilt Piece graphic score for 7 instruments, 1984, On The Way To Becoming for 4-track Tape Collage, 1985, Demeter and Persephone for violin, tape, chamber ensemble, dancers, 1986, 3 Rhapsodies, flutes and clarinet, 1986, Encore for Javanese Gamelan Ensemble, 1986, Out of the Air for Basset Horn and Tape, 188, To Whom It May Concern 4 track tape collage, reader and 4 players, 1989, Legong Dreams, oboe, 1990, Gamélange for harp and mixed gamelan band, 1992, Five Tape Collages, Open Space CD #3, 1993, "for my friends' pleasure," soprano and harp, 1994, numerous improvised group and duo sessions on tape; produced cassette and video: New Music in Bali, 1994; "touching all bases" for electronic bass, electronic percussion, and Balinese gamelan, 1996, e: an anthology (music, texts and graphics) 1975-95, "poem" for wind ensemble, 1999, (Chamber Music and Improvisations) Open Space, 2000, (CDs) Song for Sarah for Violin, 2001, Ballade for Violoncello, 2002, Tambellan, 2004, Open Space, 2004, Colors for mixed gamelan, 2004, Four Midi Pieces, 2005. Recipient Fulbright award, 1957, awards NEA, 1975, 79, awards Rockefeller Found., 1980, Meet the Composer award, 1994. Home: 12533 Killion St Valley Village CA 91607-1533

BARLAND, SARAH ELIZABETH, secondary school educator; b. College Station, Tex., May 19, 1976; d. David Kenneth Barland and Mary Sue Carter. BA in Exercise Sports Sci., SW Tex. State U., San Marcos, 2001. Std. tchg. cert. SBEC/Tex., 2001. Tchr. Mesquite Ind. Sch. Dist., Tex., 2001—03, Carrollton-Farmers Br. Ind. Sch. Dist., Tex., 2003—. Dance tchr. Am. Dance and Drill Team, Salado, Tex., 2001—. Mem.: Drill Team Dirs. Am. Democrat. Roman Catholic. Avocations: dance, running, travel. Home: 6909 Windhaven Pkwy #35 The Colony TX 75056 Office: R L Turner High School 1600 S Josey Lane Carrollton TX 75006 Office Phone: 972-968-5485. Personal E-mail: sbarland@hotmail.com. Business E-Mail: barlands@hotmail.com.

BARLOW, ANNE LOUISE, pediatrician, medical researcher; b. Skipton-in-Craven, Eng., Jan. 28, 1925; came to U.S., 1951, naturalized, 1954; m. Howard Cadwell, May 19, 1951; children: Barbara Anne, John James Stewart; m. Alastair Ramsay, Dec. 19, 1969. MB BS, London Sch. Medicine for Women, U. London, 1948; diploma in child health, Royal Colls. Eng., 1950; MPH with honors, Yale U., 1952. House physician North Lonsdale Hosp., Barrow-in-Furness, Lancashire, Eng., 1948-49; house surgeon Royal Infirmary (Glasgow), Scotland, 1949; resident to profl. unit of child health Royal Hosp. for Sick Children, Glasgow, 1949-50; jr. hosp. med. officer Knightswood Infectious Diseases Hosp., Glasgow, 1950; Rotary Found. Internat. fellow U. Toronto Med. Sch., Ont., Canada, 1950-51; research asst. Yale U. Sch. Pub. Health, New Haven, 1952-53; clinic physician in cancer prevention Arlington, Va., part-time 1953-54; resident, staff physician William H. Maybury Tb Sanatorium, Northville, Mich., 1954-56; research dir. Detroit Feeding Study with the Detroit City Health Dept., 1954-56; research asst., instr. sch. health U. Pitts. Grad. Sch. Pub. Health, 1957-62; pvt. practice medicine specializing in pediatrics Pitts., 1959-62; mem. courtesy staff St. Margaret Hosp., Pitts., 1959-62; research assoc. Tice Lab for Tb research, Cook County Hosp., Chgo., 1962; med. writer product info. Abbott Labs., North Chicago, Ill., 1963-66, med. specialist antibiotic medicine, 1966-68; mgr. clin. devel. pharm. products div. Abbott Lab., North Chicago, Ill., 1968-71, asst. med. dir., 1971-72, mgr. parenteral nutrition hosp. products div., 1972-73, med. dir., 1973-80, v.p. med. affairs hosp. products div., 1980-84; pres. Albamed, Inc., 1985—2005; asst. clin. prof. Med.Coll. Pa., 1988. Cons. maternal, child and sch. health, dir. well baby clinic Lake County (Ill.) Health Dept., 1963-76; pres. Tb Sanatorium Bd. Lake County Health Dept., Ill., 1976-79; dir., pres. Lake County Bd. Health, 1979-82; health officer Village of North Barrington, Ill., 1964-67; physician-adviser Head Start Lake County Community Action Project, 1970-84; chmn. profl. adv. com. Lake County Health Dept., 1972-84; preceptor Pediatric Nurse Assoc. Program; chmn. bd. Sutton Place Behavioral Health Inc., 2000-05. Contbr. articles on maternal and infant care, pediatrics and nutrition; patentee high calorie solution of low molecular weight glucose polymer mixtures useful for intravenouse adminstrn. Bd. dirs. Heart Assn. of Lake County, 1979-84, chmn. nutrition com. 1980-82, v.p. 1982-83, pres., 1983-84; mem. sch. bd. Grant Twp. Cmty. H.S. (Ill. Dist. 124), 1973-79; sec. to governing bd. Spl. Edn. Dist. of Lake County, 1977-79; assoc. Nat. Coll. Edn., Evanston, Ill., 1976-84; chmn. Am. Women's Hosp. Svc., 1986-95, 2004-; vol. Guardian ad Litem, 1989-2004. Recipient award of merit for outstanding contbns. to pub. health, Ill. Pub. Health Assn., 1975, award of merit for outstanding cmty. svc., Lake County Cmty. Action Project, 1976, award for outstanding and dedicated svc. as pres., Lake County TB Sanatorium Bd., 1979, TWIN award, YWCA, 1983, Charlotte Danstrom award for excellence, Women in Mgmt., 1984, award for volunteering in medicine, AMA Found., 2006. Mem. AAAS, NOW, LWV, AMA (chair sr. physician gov. com. 1996-2005), Am. Med. Women's Assn. (councilor for orgn. and mgmt. 1977-79, treas. 1980, 1st v.p. 1981, pres. 1983, chair found. 1992-95, Elizabeth Blackwell medal 1992), Fla. Med. Assn. (vice chair Internat. Med. Grad. sect. 1998-2004, coun. on pub. health 2000-05), Med. Women's Internat. Assn. (v.p. N. Am. 1993-95), Pan-Am. Med. Women's Alliance (pres. 2000), Nassau County Med. Soc. (pres. 2002-03). Home and Office: 20 S 19th St Fernandina Beach FL 32034-2767 Personal E-mail: czardaska@bellsouth.net.

BARLOW, BARBARA ANN, surgeon; b. Lancaster, Pa., June 20, 1938; d. William Barlow and Esther Stoll Barlow Lowry; m. Andre Zmurek. BA in psychology, Vassar Coll.; MA in psychology, Columbia U.; MD, Albert Einstein Coll. Medicine, 1967. Diplomte Am. Bd. Surgery. Intern Bronx (N.Y.) Mcpl. Hosp., 1967-68, resident in surgery, 1968-73; resident in pediatric surgery Columbia-Presbyn. Med.-Babies Hosp., N.Y.C., 1973-75; chief pediatric surgery Harlem Hosp., N.Y.C., 1975—2000, chief of surgery, 2000—; prof. surgery and epidemiology Columbia U. and Mailman Sch. Pub. Health, N.Y.C.; founder, exec. dir. Injury Free Coalition for Kids, 1988—. Recipient Safe Cmty. Award, US Dept. Transp., 1996, David E. Rogers award, Assn. Am. Med. Colleges, 2001, Disting. Career Award, Injury Ctrl. and Health Svcs. Sect., APHA, 2001, Pub. Svc. Award, Alfred P. Sloan Found., 2003. Mem. ACS, Am. Acad. Pediatrics (Injury and Poison Prevention Fellow Achievement Award, 1997), Am. Assn. for Surgery of Trauma, Am. Pediatric Surg. Assn., N.Y. Surgery Soc. Achievements include Featured in the Nat. Libr. Medicine exhibit "Changing the Face of Medicine" honoring women physicians, 2003. Office: Columbia U Mailman Sch Pub Health 722 W 168th St Rm 1709 New York NY 10032

BARLOW, JEAN, art educator, painter; b. L.A., Calif., Dec. 13, 1940; d. Sydney R. and Rose (Ballen) Barlow; m. Gordon M. Nunes, Sept. 21, 1973 (dec. Dec. 1991). BA cum laude, UCLA, 1963, MA, 1965, MFA, 1968. Tchg. assoc. UCLA, 1964-68; instr. Univ. Adult Sch., L.A., 1966-70; lectr. Calif. State U., Long beach, 1967-69; instr. Beverly Hills (Calif.) Adult Edn., 1969; East L.A. Jr. Coll., 1969-70; lectr. UCLA, 1986, instr. ext. divsn., 1969-96; instr. Santa Monica (Calif.) City Coll., 1969—. Mentor program mem. Santa Monica City Coll., 1989—90; pvt. art tchr., LA, 1970—96; cons. in field. One woman shows include Jenet Gallery, L.A., 1965, Santa Monica City Coll., 1974; new works on view at home, invitation only, 2001-05; exhibited in group shows at So. Calif., 1965, Orlando Gallery, L.A., 1967, 68, Santa Monica City Coll., 1974, 78, 80, 87, 88, 91, 94, 95, Living Room Gallery, 1997, Bergemot Station T2, 1999, Brentwood Park Group Art Exhibit, Plaza de la Raza Art Gallery, 2003, Mt. Saint Mary's Coll., 2005; invitational pastel drawing Scripps Coll., So. Calif., 1965. Avocations: drawing and painting, photography, home landscape and decoration, creative cooking, writing.

BARLOW, JO, psychotherapist; b. Johnson City, N.Y., Jan. 18, 1953; d. Mason and Charlotte A. (Laughlin) Barlow; m. Roland B. Newton, Jr., Dec. 15, 1973 (dec. Feb. 1987); children: Matthew T. Newton, Casey R. Newton; m. Michael A. Morrongiello, Oct. 11, 1997. AA, Broome C.C., Binghamton, N.Y., 1980; BA, SUNY, Binghamton, 1991; MSW, Marywood Coll., Scranton, Pa., 1993. LCSW N.Y. Trust officer, asst. v.p. Chase Lincoln First Bank, N.A., Binghamton, 1972-89; clin. social worker Family and Children's Soc., Binghamton, 1993-95; sch. social worker Bd. of Coop. Ednl. Svcs., 1995—97, Greater So. Tier Bd. Cooperative Ednl. Svcs., 1997—. Pvt. practice psychotherapy and cons., Vestal, N.Y., 1995-97; co-facilitator Grief and Loss Support Group, Binghamton, 1991-92. Environ. activist Citizen Action of N.Y., Binghamton, 1986-92; founding trustee, sec. Binghamton Boys and Girls Club Found., 1988-89. Mem. NASW. Avocations: gardening, reading, cooking, drawing, painting. Home: 166 E 2nd St Corning NY 14830-2802 Office: BOCES 459 Philo Rd Elmira NY 14903

BARLOW, MARGARET, editor, writer; b. Far Rockaway, NY, Dec. 12, 1943; d. Jeanne S. and Irvin Guttmann; children: John D., Johanna B. Divine. BA, Pa. State U., State College, 1965; MA, Pa. State U., 1967. Assoc. editor Woman's Art Jour., 1979—2005, co-editor, 2005—. Author: (book) Women Artists, Our Florida Legacy: Land, Legend, Leadership. Home: 2017 Ted Hines Drive Tallahassee FL 32308 Personal E-mail: mbarlow37@comcast.net.

BARLOW, NADINE GAIL, planetary geoscientist; b. La Jolla, Calif., Nov. 9, 1958; d. Nathan Dale and Marcella Isabel (Menken) Barlow. BS, U. Ariz., 1980, PhD, 1987. Instr., planetarium lectr. Palomar Coll., San Marcos, Calif., 1982; grad. rsch. asst. U. Ariz., Tucson, 1982-87; postdoctoral fellow Lunar and Planetary Inst., Houston, 1987-89; NRC assoc. NASA/Johnson Space Ctr., Houston, 1989-91, vis. scientist, 1991-92, support scientist exploration programs office, 1992; vis. scientist Lunar and Planetary Inst., Houston, 1992-95; assoc. prof. U. Houston, Clear Lake, 1991-95; pres. Minerva Rsch. Enterprises, 1995-99; asst. prof. astronomy, dir. Robinson Obs. U. Ctrl. Fla., Orlando, 1996—2002; asst. prof. dept. physics and astronomy No. Ariz. U., Flagstaff, 2002—06, assoc. prof., 2006—. Co-dir. intern program Lunar and Planetary Inst., 1988—89. Editor: A Guide to Martian Impact Craters, 1988; assoc. editor: Encyclopedia of Earth Sciences, 1996; contbr. articles to profl. jours. Named among Outstanding Women and Ethnic Minorities Engaged in Sci. and Engring., Lawrence Livermore Nat. Lab., 1991, Alumna of the Yr., Palomar Coll., 2003; recipient Asteroid named in Her Honor. Mem.: AAUW (v.p. interbranch coun. 1990—91, chmn. Tex. task force women and girls in sci. and math. 1991—92, pres. Clear Lake chpt. 1991—93, dir. state pub. policy 1991—94, program v.p. 1993—95, mem. pub. policy com. 1994—95, chmn. steering com. Tex. edn. equity 1994—95, Tex. Woman of the Yr. 1992), Geol. Soc. Am. (mem. planetary geology divsn. nominating com. 1996—97), Am. Geophys. Union, Meteoritical Soc., Am. Astron. Soc. (pres. officer divsn. planetary scis. 1993—99, mem. status women in astronomy com. 1987—90, 1995—98, mem. exec. com. divsn. planetary scis. 1999—2002, treas. divsn. planetary scis. 2004—). Achievements include identification of possible source craters for Martian meteorites; research in compilation primary data source on impact craters on Mars. Office: No Arizona Univ Dept Physics and Astronomy NAU Box 6010 Flagstaff AZ 86011-6010 E-mail: nadine.barlow@nau.edu.

BARNA, LILLIAN CARATTINI, school system administrator; b. NYC, Jan. 18, 1929; d. Juan Carattini and Dolores Elsie Nieves (Alicea); m. Eugene Andrew Barna, July 1, 1951; children: Craig Andrew, Keith Andrew. AB, Hunter Coll., 1950; MA, San Jose State U., 1970. Tchr. N.Y.C. Sch. Dist., 1950—52, Whittier (Calif.) Sch. Dist., 1952—54, tchr. HS, 1954—56; tchr. presch. Long Beach and Los Gatos, Calif., 1958—67; supr. early childhood edn. San Jose (Calif.) Unified Sch. Dist., 1967—72, sch. adminstr., 1972—80, supt. schs., 1980—84, Albuquerque Pub. Schs., 1984—88, Tacoma Sch. Dist. 10, 1988—93; cons. in field; exec. dir. Large City Schs. Supts., 1993—. Named Outstanding Sch. Dist. Supt., Wash. State; named to Hunter Coll. Hall of Fame; recipient Sorptomist Internat. Woman of Yr. award, 1980, Western Region Puertorican Council Achievement award, 1980, Calif. State U. Outstanding Achievement in Edn. award, 1982, Woman of Achievement award, Santa Clara County Commn. on Status of Women/San Jose Mercury News, Disting. Alumni award, San Jose State U., Shero award, Am. Assn. Sch. Adminstrn., 2005. Mem.: LWV, Am. Assn. Sch. Adminstrs. (Disting. Leadership award, Shero award 2006), Assn. Calif. Sch. Adminstrs., Women Leaders in Edn., Pan Am. Round Table, Rotary Club Saratoga, Delta Zeta, Phi Kappa Phi. Office: Large City Schs Supt PO Box 2096 Saratoga CA 95070 Office Phone: 408-867-4190. E-mail: lcbels@aol.com.

BARNARD, DEBORAH E., lawyer; b. Boston, Apr. 8, 1962; BA cum laude, Smith Coll., 1984; JD magna cum laude, Boston U., 1987. Bar: Mass. 1987, Ill. 1991. Ptnr. Holland & Knight LLP, Boston, mem. dir. com., nat. chair, Women's Initiative. Instructor, first year rsch. and writing program Boston U. Sch. Law. Contbr. articles to profl. jours. Participated in LeadBoston Nat. Conf. for Cmty. and Justice; bd. dir. The City Sch.; class agent Milton Acad. Class of 1980. Mem.: ABA. Office: Holland & Knight LLP 10 St James Ave 11th Fl Boston MA 02116 Office Phone: 617-619-9240. Business E-Mail: dbarnard@hklaw.com.

BARNARD, KATHRYN ELAINE, nursing educator, researcher; b. Omaha, Apr. 16, 1938; d. Paul and Elsa Elizabeth (Anderson) B. BS in Nursing, U. Nebr., Omaha, 1960; MS in Nursing, Boston U., 1962; PhD, U. Wash., Seattle, 1972; DSc (hon.), U. Nebr., 1990. Acting instr. U. Nebr., Omaha, 1960-61, U. Wash., Seattle, 1963-65, asst. prof., 1965-69, prof. nursing, 1972—, assoc. dean, 1987-92, founding dir. Ctr. on Infant Mental Health and Devel., 2001—, Charles and Gerda Spence Endowed Prof. in Nursing, 2002—. Bd. dirs. Nat. Ctr. for Clin. Infant Programs, Washington, 1980-Chmn. rsch. com. Bur. of Community Health Svcs., MCH, 1987-89. Recipient Lucille Petry award Nat. League for Nursing, 1968, Martha Mae Eliot award Am. Assn. Pub. Health, 1983, Professorship award U. Wash., 1985 Fellow Am. Acad. Nursing (bd. dirs. 1980-82); mem. Inst. Medicine (Gustav O. Leinhard Award, 2002); mem. Am. Nurses Assn. (chmn. com. 1980-82, Jessie Scott award 1982, Nurse of Yr. award 1984), Soc. Research in Child Devel. (bd. dirs. 1981-87), Sigma Theta Tau (founders award in research 1987, Episteme Award, 2003). Democrat. Presbyterian. Home: 11508 Durland Ave NE Seattle WA 98125-5904 Office: University of Washington Family & Child Nursing Box 357920 Seattle WA 98195-7920

BARNARD, PATRICIA A., human resources specialist; b. Dayton, Ohio, Mar. 24, 1949; BS in Sci., Elem. Edn. and English, U. Dayton, 1971; MS in Human Resources Adminstrn. and Orgnl. Effectiveness, Ctrl. Mich. U., 1996. With audit dept. Fla. Power and Light, Miami, Fla., 1972; fin. analyst, pers. adminstrn., asst. to CEO Mead Corp., Dayton, 1972—82, and 401(k) ops., 1982—85, mgr. coll. recruiting and rels., exempt ops. supr., retirement plans and 401(k), 1985—87; dir. compensation, benefits, staffing and EEO Zellerbach, Dayton, 1987—94; dir. spl. projects Georgia-Pacific Corp., Atlanta, 1994, dir. human resources, comm. papers, 1994—95, group dir. human resources, paper, 1995—97, group dir. human resources, paper and chemicals, 1997—98, v.p. compensation and benefits, 1998—99, sr. v.p. human resources, 1999—2001, exec. v.p. human resources, 2001—. Mem., mentor Ga. 100; mem. HR Leadership Forum, HR Roundtable, Ga. State U.; bd. dirs. Metro Atlanta Recovery Residences, Inc., Big Bros. and Big Sisters, N.W. Ga. Girl Scout Coun., Inc., Leukemia and Lymphoma Soc., Salvation Army. Mem.: Soc. for Human Resources Mgmt. (chmn. bd. Atlanta chpt.), Exec. Mgmt. Assn. Office: Georgia Pacific Corp 133 Peachtree St NE Atlanta GA 30303

BARNER, SHARON R., lawyer; BS cum laude, Syracuse U., 1979; JD, U. Mich., 1982. Bar: OH, Ill. Ptnr. Foley & Lardner LLP, Chgo., mem. mng. com., chairperson intellectual property litig. practice group. Contbr. articles to profl. jours. Mem.: ABA, Fed. Bar Assn., Nat. Bar Assn., Ill. State Bar Assn., Grateful Hand Found. (bd. dirs.). Office: Foley & Lardner LLP 321 N Clark St Ste 2800 Chicago IL 60610-4764 Office Phone: 312-832-4569. Business E-Mail: sbarner@foley.com.

BARNES, ADRIENNE, public information officer; b. Balt., June 17, 1962; d. Glen McKoy and Carolyn B. Dunn. BA, U. Md., 1985. Asst. mayor's rep. Mayor's Office, Balt., 1988-90, mayor's rep., 1990-93; HUB dir. Housing and Cmty. Devel., Balt., 1993-95; asst. chief info. svc. Dept. Pub. Works, Balt., 1995-97, chief cmty. affairs, 1997—. Active Big Sisters Club, Balt., 1989—, 43/44 Dem. Club, Balt., 1989—; chair Environ. Control Bd., Balt., 1998—. Mem. Nat. Orgn. Black Pub. Adminstrs. Avocations: reading, travel, working with youths. Office: Dept Pub Works 200 Holliday St Baltimore MD 21202-3618 also: Pub Works Dept 600 Abel Wolman Mcpl Bldg Baltimore MD 21202

BARNES, ANDRÉA RENEÉ, lawyer; d. Holiness Barnes, Jr. and Betty Jean Barnes; 1 child, Holiness Jamal. BA, Tougaloo Coll., Miss., 1994—98; MBA, Jackson State U., Miss., 2000; JD, Thurgood Marshall Sch. Law, 2004. Bar: Miss. 2004. Law clerk Hinds County Cir. Ct., Jackson, Miss., 2004—. Adj. prof. Hinds Cmty. Coll., Jackson, Miss., 2006. Mem.: Metro Black Women Lawyers Assn., Am. Trial Lawyers, Miss. Bar Assn. Avocation: singing. Office: Hinds County Cir Ct PO Box 327 Jackson MS 39205

BARNES, BETTY JEAN, educational administrator; b. Aug. 11, 1948; BS, Miss. State U., Starkville, 1971, MEd, 1978; postgrad., U. Miss., Oxford, 1987. Tchr. Burnsville (Miss.) Sch., 1972-84; dir. exceptional children Tishomingo County Schs., Iuka, Miss., 1984—. Vol. Am. Cancer Soc., 8 yrs., Tishomingo Manor Nursing Home, 9 yrs. Mem.: Miss. Profl. Educators, Coun. Adminstrs. in Spl. Edn., Miss. Spl. Edn. Coop, Delta Kappa Gamma. Office: Tishomingo County Schs 1620 Paul Edmondson Dr Iuka MS 38852-1212

BARNES, BRENDA C., food products executive; m. Randall C. Barnes; 3 children. BA in econ., Augustana Coll., 1975, LHD (hon.), 1997; MBA, Loyola U., 1978. With PepsiCo, 1975—98, v.p. mktg. Frito-Lay, bus. mgr. Wilson Spring Sporting Goods; pres. Pepsi-Cola S., 1992; COO Pepsi-Cola N. Am., 1994—96, pres., CEO, 1996—98; interim pres., COO Starwood Hotels & Resorts Worldwide Inc., 1999—2000; COO Sara Lee Corp., Chgo., 2004—05, pres., 2004—05, chmn., CEO, 2005—. Adj. prof. Kellogg Grad. Sch. Mgmt., 2002, N. Central Coll., 2002; bd. dirs. Sara Lee Corp., 2004—, Avon Products Inc., NY Times Co., Sears Roebuck & Co., Staples Inc., Lucas Film, LTD, PepsiAmericas, Inc., Grocery Manufactures Assn. Chair bd. trustees Augustana Coll.; mem. steering com. Kellogg Ctr. for Exec. Women, Northwestern U. Named one of Most Powerful Women, Forbes mag., 2005—06, 50 Women to Watch, Wall Street Journal, 2005, 50 Most Powerful Women in Bus., Fortune mag., 2006. Mem.: Grocery Mfr. Assn. (bd. dir.). Office: Sara Lee Corp 3 First Nat Plz Chicago IL 60602 Office Phone: 312-726-2600.*

BARNES, CHARLOTTE ELIZABETH, retired elementary school educator; d. Cecil Ray and Elizabeth Lorene Coe; m. Charles Winfred Barnes, June 15, 1958; children: Kelly Elizabeth Barnes-Abeyta, Elizabeth Dawn-Barnes Reid, Amy Elizabeth Barnes Adams, Charlotte Susan Elizabeth. BS in Elem. Edn., U. Idaho, 1961; MS in Elem. Edn., No. Ariz. U., 1999. Cert. elem. edn. Ariz., ESL Ariz. 4th grade tchr. Moscow (Idaho) Unified Sch. Dist., 1961—62; 5th grade tchr. Madison (Wis.) Unified Sch. Dist., 1962—64; 2d grade tchr. Flagstaff (Ariz.) Unified Sch. Dist., 1991—92, 5th grade tchr., 1992—2004. Ticket sales chairperson Flagstaff Symphony Orch., 1972—74. Mem.: La Leche League (Flagstaff Ariz. founding mother 1972—92), Phi Delta Kappa. Democrat. Methodist. Avocations: exercise, travel, nutrition, learning, mentoring. Home: 250 N Circle Dr Flagstaff AZ 86001-4716

BARNES, CYNTHIA LEPRE, university administrator; b. Newark, June 20, 1950; d. Robert Louis and Ann Frances (Fonzino) Lepre; m. John David Barnes, Sept. 7, 1985. BA, Montclair State Coll., Upper Montclair, N.J., 1972; postgrad., Montclair State Coll., 1995—, Harvard U., 1995. Dir. Arts Internat. Gallery, Woodbridge, N.J., 1973-74; pub. rels. coord. Essex County Heart Assn., East Orange, N.J., 1974-76; chpt. devel. dir. The Arthritis Found., Westfield, N.J., 1976-79; dir. alumni rels. Montclair State Coll., Upper Montclair, 1979-85, asst. to pres., 1985-90, adminstr. Montclair State U. Found., 1992—, exec. asst. to v.p. for instl. advancement, 1990-97, dir. devel., 1997—2005, asst. v.p. u. advancement, 2005—. Bd. dirs. Coun. for Advancement and Support Edn., Mid-Atlantic region, 1982-83; cons. Nat. Liver Found., Cedar Grove, N.J., 1978-79. Editor Montclair State Coll. Alumni Life, 1979-85, Vision, 1988-90, Arthritis Found. News, 1976-79. Dir. S. Orange Maplewood Edn. Found., 1991-93; com. mem. March of Dimes Campaign for Healthier Babies, 1990-94; nominating com. Girl Scout Coun. Greater Essex County, pres., 2005-, bd. dirs., 1995—, mktg. com., 1996—, strategic planning com., 1997—. Named One of 30 Women to Know YWCA, Montclair, 1992. Democrat. Roman Catholic. Avocation: travel. Home: 14 Lancaster Ave Maplewood NJ 07040-1702 Office: Montclair State U Office Instl Advancement Montclair NJ 07043

BARNES, CYNTHIA LOU, retired gifted and talented educator; b. Yale, Okla., Jan. 14, 1934; d. Ira and Billie (Reed) Canfield; m. Edward M. Barnes, Jr., June 1, 1954; children: Edis, Barbara, Warren, Adrienne. BS, U. Tulsa, 1970; MS, Okla. State U., 1981. Substitute tchr. Tulsa Pub. Schs., 1970-73, kindergarten tchr., 1981-94, gifted edn. tchr., 1994-97, cons. Guide for Tchg. Gifted in the Regular Classroom, 1996, substitute tchr., 1997—2002, 2nd semester gifted edn. tchr. Carver Mid. Sch., 1998; pre-sch. tchr. Meml. Drive Meth., Tulsa, 1976-81; ret., 1997. Curriculum coord. Barnard Elem. Sch., Tulsa, 1992—97, site-base co-chmn., 1992—93; bd. dirs. Gt. Expectations Educators, Inc., Tulsa; cons. kindergarten guide Tulsa Pub. Schs., 1985; presenter Elem. Educators Conf., 1994, 97. Author: (curriculum guide) Special Connections, 1996. Confirmation class coord. 1st Meth. Ch., Broken Arrow, Okla., 1999—2002, Collinsville (Okla.) Story Hour Reader, 2001—02. Grantee, Tulsa Edn. Fund, 1994, 1996. Mem.: Okla. Assn. Gifted, Creative, Talented, Tulsa Classroom Tchrs. Math. (conf. presider 1994), Tulsa County Reading Coun. Home: 7824 E 22nd Pl Tulsa OK 74129-2416

BARNES, FRANCES JOHNSON, retired secondary school educator; b. Culpepper, Va., July 6, 1920; d. John Henry Johnson and Sadie Stewart; children: Sylvia-Lynn Barnes Craig, Lora Barnes Turner. BA, Howard U., Washington, 1941; MA, Columbia U., NYC, 1943, profl. diploma, 1959, EdD, 1969. Instr. Howard U., 1945—46; tchr. pvt. nursery schs., NYC, 1951—53, Washington Pub. High Schs., 1954—58, NYC Pub. Secondary Schs., 1959—60; tchr., head program for visually handicapped Montgomery County Pub. Schs., Rockville, Md., 1959—60; tchr. asst. Tchrs. Coll. Columbia U., 1960; ednl. cons., 1968—95; ret., 1995. Author: Handbook for School Personnel Serving the Visually Handicapped Child, 1964; editor: (poetry anthology) LOVE from Black Women to Black Men, 2d edit., 1977; contbr. poetry to lit. publs. Founder Barnes-Draine Endowed Scholarship Fund, Howard U., Washington, 1985—, Teach Love Fund, Poise Found., Pitts., 1997—; mem. Pa. State Real Estate Commn., Harrisburg, 1980—81; dir., dist. v.p. Nat. Assn. Real Estate Lic. Law Ofcls., 1984—86; arbitrator, nat. consumer Coun. BBBs, Inc., Pitts., 1985—90; mem. Mayor's Task Force on Women in Renaissance II, Pitts., 1986, Cmty. Housing Resource Bd., Pitts., 1986—92; mem., vol. Fair Housing Partnership Greater Pitts., 1992—; mem. Pitts. Commn. Human Rels., 1993—2004; bd. dirs., v.p. United Way Allegheny County, 1983—; ptnr. Habitat for Humanity, 1990—; mem. adv. bd. Women's Polit. Caucus Allegheny County, Pitts., 1982; bd. dirs. Funeral Consumers Alliance Western Pa., 1985—. Recipient Outstanding Accomplishment in Letters award, Delta Sigma Theta, 1977, Literary award, Nat. Assn. Negro Bus. and Profl. Women, 1977, Fair Housing award, US Dept. HUD, Office Fair Housing and Equal Opportunity, 1987, Proclamation, Dr. Frances Johnson Barnes Day, Mayor of Pitts., 1987, Golden Rule award, J.C. Penney, 1992, Kupenta award, Kunto Writers Workshop, U. Pitts., 2002, Greater Pitts. Racial Justice award, YWCA, Pitts., 2005. Mem.: LWV, NAACP, Women's Assn. Pitts. (pres.), Assn. Edn. and Rehab. of Blind and Visually Impaired (life), Coun. for Exceptional Children (life), Nat. League Am. Pen Women, Vintage, Women's Assn. U. Pitts. (hon.), UN Assn. Pitts., Urban League Pitts., World Clown Assn., Internat. Poetry Forum (assoc.; mem. adv. coun. 1975—), Century Club, Kappa Delta Pi (life), Pi Lambda Theta (life), Kappa Mu (life). Unitarian Universalist. Achievements include research in visual impairment in fiscal urban primary schools of Quito, Ecuador. Avocations: painting, poetry, yoga, writing.

BARNES, INA JEAN, retired elementary educator; b. Albuquerque, Mar. 18, 1947; d. Frederick Joseph and Mary Jo (Jones) Ponzer; m. William Anderson Barnes, June 8, 1968; 1 child, William Joseph. BS, U. N.Mex., 1969, MA, 1975. Elem. sch. tchr. Grants/Cibola County Schs., Grants, N.Mex., 1969-94, ret., 1994. Recipient Literacy award Internat. Reading Assn., 1995. Mem. AAUW (Woman of Yr. 1994-95), Retired Tchrs. Assn., Magna Charta Dames, Delta Kappa Gamma (pres. Psi chpt. 1980-82, 94-96, 2d v.p. 1995-97). Democrat. United Methodist. Avocations: reading, travel, crafts, gardening, collecting antiques. Home: 209 Washington Ave Grants NM 87020-2735

BARNES, JANET LYNN, artist; b. Balt., Mar. 9, 1959; d. Edwin Lee and Mary Magdeline B. BA in Visual and Performing Arts, U. Md., 1979. Prin., owner Crop Cir. Ceilings, Balt. Author: Brunch with Beethoven, 2002; one-woman shows include City Hall, Balt., 1998, John Hopkins Space Telescope, 1998, book cover, Poe's Last Supper, 1998. Hon. bus. chmn. adv. coun. Nat. Rep. Congl. Com., 2003. Recipient Nat. Leadership award, Nat. Rep. Congl. Com., 2003. Mem.: Nat. and World Wildlife, Artists Equity NY, Md. Hist. Soc., Nat. Trust Hist. Preservation, Wash. Soc. Jungian Psychology, Md. Hang Glider Assn., Catherine Lorillard Wolfe Art Club, Salmagundi Club, Delta Pi Alpha. Republican. Avocations: hang-gliding, reading, writing, house renovation, African grey parrot. Home: 236 S Castle St Baltimore MD 21231

BARNES, JENNIFER J., lawyer; BA, Miami U., 1976; MS, Ohio State U., 1979; JD, U. San Diego Law Sch., 1988. Trial atty. Immigration and Naturalization Svc., Atty. Gen. Honor Law Program, US Dept. Justice, 1988—90; asst. gen. counsel Office Gen. Council, Immigration and Naturalization Svc., assoc. gen. counsel, Gen. Law divsn.; appelate counsel Immigration and Naturalization Svc. and Exec. Office Immigration Review, 1994—95; assoc. gen. counsel Office Gen. Counsel, Exec. Office Immigration Review, US Dept. Justice, 1995—. Mem.: DC Bar Assn., Calif. Bar Assn. Office: US Dept Justice Exec Office Immigration Review Office Dir 5107 Leesburg Pike Ste 2600 Falls Church VA 22041

BARNES, JHANE ELIZABETH, fashion design company executive, designer; b. Balt., Mar. 4, 1954; d. Richard Amos and Muriel Florence (Chase) B.; m. Howard Ralph Feinberg, Dec. 12, 1981 (div.); m. 2d, Katsuhiko Kawasaki, Feb. 12, 1988. A.S., Fashion Inst. Tech., 1975. Pres., designer Jhane Barnes for ME, N.Y.C., 1976-78; pres., designer, owner Jhane Barnes Inc., N.Y.C., 1978—; owner Jhane Barnes Textiles, LLC, 1998—. Recipient Coty award Menswear Am. Fashion Critics, 1980, 1984, Contract Textile award Am. Soc. Interior Designers, 1983, 84, Product Design awards Inst. Bus. Designers and Contract Mag., 1983-86, 94, Outstanding Am. Menswear Designer award Woolmark, 1990, Dalmore, 1990, Good Design award 1997, 98, 99, Best of Neo Con award. I.D. 40, 1996, 97, 98, 99, 2000; named Most Promising Designer Cutty Sark, 1980, Outstanding Designer, 1982, Outstanding Menswear Designer, Coun. of Fashion Designers Am., 1982, Design Resources Coun., 1989, 94, Designer of Yr., Neckwear Assn. Am., 1997. Office: Jhane Barnes Inc 119 W 40th St Fl 20 New York NY 10018-2500 Fax: 212-575-2506.

BARNES, JO ANNE, investment advisor; b. Berwyn, Ill., Feb. 1, 1947; d. Robert Marshall and Margaret Hickman Barnes; children: Katherine Dorothy Schock, Alice Margaret Schock. BA in English, U. Minn., 1969; MAT in English, Northwestern U., 1972. CFP. Tchr., adviser New Trier H.S., Winnetka, Ill., 1972-75; editl. proofreader Arthur Andersen & Co., St. Charles, Ill., 1980-82; registered rep., v.p. investments Howe Barnes Investments, Chgo., 1983-91; exec. v.p., dir. mktg. Podesta & Co., Chgo., 1992; pres., chief investment officer Barnes Alliance, Inc., Chgo., 1993-96; portfolio mgr. Vestor Capital Corp., Chgo., 1997; sr. investment mgr. Vanguard Group, Valley Forge, Pa., 1997—. Host, prodr., writer (TV show) On Your Side, 1985-86; co-author, editor Investor's Workshop, 1994-96. Chmn. Planning Commn., Hampshire, Ill., 1978-80; dir. Builders Skills, Niles, Ill., 1988-90; pres., trustee Salem United Meth. Ch., Barrington, Ill., 1991-93; dir., treas. Women's Opportunity Fund, Oakbrook, Ill., 1995-98. Mem.: Religious Soc. of Friends (Pa.), Nature Conservancy, Audubon Soc. Avocations: poetry, hiking, music, writing. Home: 2025 Greene's Way Cir Collegeville PA 19426

BARNES, JOY VERVENE, retired literature and language educator; b. Clovis, N.Mex., June 13, 1940; d. Byron B. and Stella C. Barnes. BA in Edn., Ariz. State U., Tempe, 1962; MA in Edn., Calif. State U., Dominguez, 1980. Cert. tchr. Tchr. LA Unified Sch. Dist., 1963, 1964—2002, dean of students Perry Jr. HS Gardena, Calif., 1976—2000; tchr. Benson Unified Sch. Dist., Ariz., 1963—64; ret., 2002. Spkr., presenter in field. Co-chmn. Sch. Based Mgmt., Gardena, 1984—2002; mem. Measure Oversite Com., Napa, Calif., Dem. Com. Mem.: United Tchrs. LA (chmn. 1984—2002). Home: 114 Alston Ln Napa CA 94558-2665

BARNES, JUDITH ANN, real estate company executive; b. Milw., Mar. 10, 1949; d. Einar and Eleanor Svea (Russell) B.; divorced; children: Krista Svea, Erik Leif. BA, Gustavus Adolphus Coll., 1970; grad., Wis. Sch. Real Estate, Milw., 1979; postgrad., Carroll Coll., 1980, U. Wis., 1978—80, postgrad., 1992. Tchr. Oak Grove Mid. Sch., Bloomington, Minn., 1970—71, Mukwonago H.S., Wis., 1971—72; sales mgr. Lincoln Park Homes, West Allis, Wis., 1972—73, v.p., 1973—74, pres., 1974—97, Palm Coast, Fla., 1997—2000; assoc. Coldwell Banker Comml. (Nicholson-Williams), 2000—01; with Hammock Dunes Real Estate Co., 2001—. Chmn. Mfrd. Housing Subdivision S.E. Wisc., Madison, 1978-80; sec. Southeastern Wis. Housing, Milw., 1981-82, treas., 1982-84. Bd. dirs. Waukesha YMCA, 1985-87, v.p. 1987-89; bd. dirs. YMCA Heritage Found., 1994-97, Waukesha County United Way, 1984-87, Hammock Dune Homeowners Assn., 2004-06; coun. pres. Stetson U., 1996-2000; mem. alumni bd. Gustavus Adulphus Coll., St. Peter, Minn., 1974-80; trustee The Cooper Inst., Naples, Fla., 1987-93, mem. adv. bd., 1993—. Recipient Dedicated Svc. award Wis. Mfrd. Housing, 1975-84, 88, Vol. of Yr. award Univ. Lake Sch., 1995. Mem. Wis. Mfrd. Housing Assn. (bd. dirs. 1975-80), Ind. Bus. Assn. Wis. (trustee U. Lake 1991-96), Merrill Hills Country Club (chair golf 1991), Milw. Women's Dist. Golf Assn. (bd. dirs. 1993, v.p. 1994, pres. 1995-96), Vasa Lodge, Hammock Dunes Country Club (adv. bd.). Republican. Lutheran. Avocations: golf, photography. Home: 3 Anastasia Ct Palm Coast FL 32137-2273 Office Phone: 386-446-6319. Personal E-mail: jbhd@bellsouth.net.

BARNES, KAREN KAY, lawyer; b. June 22, 1950; d. Walter William and Vashti (Greenlee) Sessler; m. James Alan Barnes, Feb. 12, 1972; children: Timothy Matthew, Christopher Michael. BA, Valparaiso U., 1971; JD, DePaul U., 1978, LLM in Taxation, 1980. Bar: Ill. 1978, U.S. Dist. Ct. (no. dist.) Ill. 1978. Ptnr. McDermott, Will & Emory, Chgo., 1978-88; prin. William M. Mercer, Inc. and predecessor firm, Chgo., 1989-93; staff dir. legal dept. McDonald's Corp., Oak Brook, Ill., 1993-95, home office dir. legal dept., 1995-97, mng. counsel, 1998—. Instr. John Marshall Grad. Sch. Law, Chgo., 1986-87; mem. adv. bd. John Marshall Sch. Law, 1996-2004; bd. dirs. Flutes Unlimited; mem. adv. bd. dirs. Plan Sponsor Mag., 2000-; mem. defined contbn. adv. bd. Internat. Bus. Forum, Inc., 2004-. Contbr. case note to DePaul Law Rev., 1976, note and comment editor DePaul Law Rev., 1976-77, editor Taxation For Lawyers, 1986-88; mem. editl. adv. bd. Thompson Pub. Co. retirement plan comms., 2005—. Mem. Am. Coll. Employee Benefit Counsel (bd. dirs. 2006-), Chgo. Bar Assn. (chair employee benefits com. 1991-92, co-chair symphony orch. 1999-2001), Midwest Pension Conf. (name changed to Midwest Benefits Coun.), WEB (pres. Chgo. chpt. 1986-88, v.p. nat. bd. 1988, pres. 1989-90, mem. adv. bd. 2001—), Profit Sharing Coun. Am. (legal and legis. com. 1994—, bd. dirs. 1997-2004, 06-, 2d vice chair 1997-98, 1st vice chair 1998-2000, chair 2000-02). Lutheran. Home: 586 Crescent Blvd # 402 Glen Ellyn IL 60137 Office: McDonald's Corp 2915 Jorie Blvd Oak Brook IL 60523 Business E-Mail: karen.barnes@us.mcd.com.

BARNES, KAY, mayor; b. Mar. 30, 1938; BS in Secondary Edn., U. Kans.; MS in Secondary Edn. and Pub. Adminstrn., U. Mo., Kansas City. Staff mem. Westport area Cross-Lines Coop. Coun.; pres. Kay Waldo, Inc., human resources devel. co., Kansas City, Mo.; mayor City of Kansas City, Mo., 1999—. Condr. over 400 pub. seminars Nat. Seminars, Inc.; cons., keynote spkr. 14 regional confs. through U.S., Am. Bus. Women's Assn.; former co-host, prodr. cable TV show Let's Talk; former instr. U. Mo., Kansas City, U. Kans., Ctrl. Mich. U. Author: About Time! A Woman's Guide to Time Management. Co-founder Ctrl. Exch.; vol. Cross-Lines Coop. Coun.; a founder women's resource svc. U. Mo., Kansas City; developer multicultural women's speaking panels through western U.S.; mem. Jackson County (Mo.) Legislature, from 1974; mem. Kansas City City Coun., from 1979; chmn. Tax Increment Financing Commn., 1993-97; pres. bd. dirs. Women's Employment Network; mem. or dir. numerous other orgns., including Women's Found. Greater Kansas City, Greater Kansas City Sports Commn.; mem. chancellor's adv. bd. of Women's Ctr., U. Mo., Kansas City; co-chair of the US Conf. of Mayors Small Business/Partner America Task Force, mem. of the Conference's Community Development and Housing Standing Com.; serves Nat. Adv. Coun. of Fannie Mae. Named One of 7 Outstanding Women in Kansas City, 1977. Mem. Greater Kansas City C. of C. (com.). Office: Mayor's Office City Hall 29th Fl 414 E 12th St Ste 2902 Kansas City MO 64106-2778 Office Fax: 816-513-3518. Business E-Mail: mayor@kcmo.org.*

BARNES, LILI DARNELLE, music educator, director; b. Cleve., Sept. 5, 1956; d. Johnes Green and Dorothy Mae Bradford; m. Robert Timothy Barnes, Nov. 28, 1998; 1 child, Garrett Paul Bradford. MusB, Heidelberg Coll., 1978; MEd, Trenton State U., 1993; postgrad., Boston U., 2004—. Cert. tchg. Ohio, 1993. Music tchr. Wickliffe Elem., Ohio, 1978—87, vocal music dir., 1987—91, Wickliffe Mid. Sch., 1993—2000; music dept. chair Wickliffe City Schs., 1997—2004; musical dir. Wickliffe HS & Mid. Sch., 1988—91, 1993—; vocal music dir. Wickliffe HS, 2003—, Dhahran Sch., Saudi Arabia, 1991—93, musical dir., 1992. Conf. presenter Ohio Mid. Sch. Assn., Toledo, 1994—95, Cleve., 1994—95. Recipient The Golden Apple Achiever award, Ashland U., 1998; grantee SMARTKids grant, SMARTBoard, 2003. Mem.: Wickliffe Edn. Assn. (pres. 2003—, v.p. 2000—03), Rotary Internat., Wickliffe Chpt. Baptist. Avocations: horseback riding, swimming, computers, poetry, music composition. Home: 1733 E 298th St Wickliffe OH 44092 Office: Wickliffe HS 2255 Rockefeller Rd Wickliffe OH 44092 Office Phone: 440-944-0800.

BARNES, MADGE LOU, physician; b. Clayton, NC, Nov. 30, 1958; BA in Biology & Premed, East Carolina U., Greenville, SC, 1981, MD, 1987. Diplomate Am. Bd. Family Medicine, 2004. Cert. CDL examiner CONCENTRA, Dallas, 2004—; med. dir. Concentra Occupl. Health, Ft. Worth, 2004—05; med. dir. pub. health divsn. Environ. & Health Svcs., Dallas, 2006—. Bd. pres. Celebrating Life Found., Dallas, 1999—2002; mentor, spkr. debutante program Potter's Ho. Ch., 2001—; mentor, spkr. Tng. for Excellence, 2003. Recipient Mentor Yr. award, Core Debutante Program, 2005. Fellow: Am. Acad. Family Physicians; mem.: Am. Acad. Family, Tex. Med. Assn., Dallas County Med. Soc., Tex. Acad. Family Physicians, Childhood Obesity Coalition, Am. Heart Assn., African Am. and Hispanic Coalitions. Nondenominational. Avocations: travel, sports, reading, history. Office: 2922 Mlk Blvd B Bldg Ste 301 Dallas TX 75215 Business E-Mail: madge.barnes@dallascityhall.com.

BARNES, MAGGIE LUE SHIFFLETT (MRS. LAWRENCE BARNES), nurse; b. Redmond, Tex., Mar. 29, 1931; d. Howard Eldridge and Sadie Adilene (Dunlap) Shifflett; m. T.C. Fagan, Jan. 1950 (Dec. Feb. 1952); 1 child, Lawayne; m. Lawrence Barnes, Sept. 2, 1960. Student, Cogdell Sch. Nursing, 1959—60, Western Tex. Coll., 1972—76; postgrad., Meth. Hosp. Sch. Nursing, Lubbock, Tex., 1975; BSN, West Tex. State U., Canyon, 1977; cert. legal nurse cons., Kaplan Coll., 2001. RN Tex., cert. gerontol. nurse. Floor nurse D.M. Cogdell Meml. Hosp., Snyder, Tex., 1960-64, medication nurse, 1964-76, asst. evening supr., 1976-78, charge nurse, after 1978, evening nursing supr., 1980; nursing supr. for 5 counties West Ctrl. Home Health Agy., Snyder, 1983—89; emergency rm. evening supr. Mitchell County Hosp., 1983-89; dir. nurses Snyder Oak Care Ctr., 1989-91, Mountain View Lodge, Big Spring, Tex., 1991-92, Med. Arts Hosp. Home Health, Lamesa, 1992—93, Metplex Home Health Svcs., Snyder, 1993-94, ret., 1994; weekend RN Snyder Oaks Care Ctr. CNA Sch. instr.; leader Bible study, 1997—; vol. Helping Children Read Sch., Bible study at nursing homes; regional coord. home health svcs. Beverly Enterprises, 1983; legal nurse cons. Grad. Kaplan Coll., Boca Raton, Fla., 2001. Den leader Boy Scouts Am., Holliday, Tex., 1960-61; active PTA, Snyder, 1960-69; adviser Sr. Citizens Assn.; mem Tri-Region Health Sys. Agy., 1979—; adv. bd. Scurry County Diabetes Assn., 1982—; vol. reading program; ch. sec.-treas. Apostolic Faith Ch., 1956-58 Mem.: DAR, Emergency Dept. Nursing Assn., Vocat. Nurses Assn. Tex. (bd. dirs. 1963—65, divsn. pres. 1967—69), Rock and Roll Quilting Club (coord.). Avocation: bible study with nursing home residents. Home: 249 County Rd 349-B Snyder TX 79549 Office Phone: 325-573-1214.

BARNES, MARGARET ANDERSON, minister, statistician; b. Johnston County, N.C. m. Benjamin Barnes, Dec. 26, 1959. BS, N.C. Ctrl. U., 1958; MA, U. Md., 1975; PhD, Columbia Pacific U., 1986. Lic. ins. agt., Md.; ordained Christian min. and elder in World Evangelism, 1992. Math. tchr. Tarboro (N.C.) Sch. Sys., 1959-61; math. statistician Bur. of Census, Suitland, Md., 1962-67, 69-70, Govt. of D.C., 1967-68; cons. NIH, Bethesda, Md., 1970-72, chief of data stds., 1972-73; with exec. clearance office HEW, Rockville, Md., 1973-77; founder, pres. MABarnes Cons. Assoc., Lanham, Md., 1978-95. Commr. State of Md. Accident Fund, Balt., 1979-89; mem. adv. bd. Universal Bank, Lanham, 1980-83, Interstate Gen. Corp., St. Charles, Md., 1981-83; founder Christian Ministries, 1983—, Christ Centered Ministries Esprit, 1995—, Mleecole Pub., 1997—; profiled for First Record: "Women of Achievement in Prince George's County History", 1994. Author: But I Love You, How You Can Know God, 1998, The Last One, A Bible for Dummies, vol 1, 2004. Chairwoman Glenwood Park Civic Assn., Lanham, 1967-80. Democrat. Avocations: piano, sewing, reading, song, prose and poetry writing, artistic designing. Home: PO Box 586 Lanham Seabrook MD

20703-0586 Office: Christ Centered Ministries Esprit PO Box 802 Lanham Seabrook MD 20703-0802 Office Phone: 301-459-4990. Personal E-mail: mpub95@aol.com. Business E-Mail: mbarnes@movingchurch.com.

BARNES, SANDRA HENLEY, retired publishing company executive; b. Seymour, Ind., Jan. 15, 1943; d. Ray C. and Barbara Henley; m. Ronald D. Barnes, Sept. 3, 1961; children: Laura, Barrett and Garrett (twins). Student, Ind. State U., 1962-63. Asst. sales mgr. Marquis Who's Who, Indpls., 1973-79, sales, svc. mgr., 1979-82, mktg. ops. mgr., 1982-84, mktg. mgr. Chgo., 1984-86, dir. mktg. Wilmette, Ill., 1986-87; v.p. mktg. Macmillan Directory Div., Wilmette, 1987-88; group v.p. product mgmt. Marquis Who's Who, Wilmette, 1988-89, pres., 1989-92; v.p. Reed Reference Pub., New Providence, N.J., 1992-96; v.p., fulfillment Reed Elsevier-New Providence, 1996-97, LEXIS-NEXIS, Dayton, Ohio, 1997-98, Lexis Law Pub., Charlottesville, Va., 1997-98, Congrl. Info. Svc., Bethesda, Md., 1997-98; sr. v.p. Ednl. Comms., Inc., Lake Forest, Ill., 1998—2001; gen. mgr. Marquis Who's Who, New Providence, NJ, 2002. Republican. Avocation: reading. Office: 121 Chanlon Road New Providence NJ 07974 Home: 2452 N White Pine Dr Flagstaff AZ 86004-7179

BARNES, SHARON D., director, music educator; b. Roanoke, Va., Apr. 16, 1958; d. Kermit Wayne and Doris Grisso Dudley; m. Kenneth Lane Barnes, June 16, 1978; 1 child, Derrick Cameron. BA cum laude, Hollins Coll., 1979, MA in Liberal Studies, 1985. Classical music dir. WVTF-FM Radio, Roanoke, Va., 1978-81; piano and voice instr. Roanoke Music Ctr., 1979-80; ind. piano and voice instr. Roanoke, 1979-92; piano instr. The Bandroom, Roanoke, 1980-91; acad. advisor Mary Baldwin Coll., Roanoke, 1997—. Choir dir. Westhampton Christian Ch., Roanoke, 1981-84; faculty Mary Baldwin Coll., Roanoke Ctr., Staunton, Va., 1986—, Va. We. C.C., Roanoke, 1991-98; instr. online course Introduction to Listening, 1999; presenter in field. Vocal soloist area chs., Roanoke, 1975-99; youth choir dir., accompanist Westhampton Christian Ch., Roanoke, 1997-99; PTA mem. Back Creek Elem., Roanoke, 1996-99; com. mem. Bd. Edn. Westhampton Christian, Roanoke, 1999—. Presser scholar Hollins (Va.) Coll., 1978. Mem. Internat. Alliance Women in Music, Music Tchrs. Nat. Assn., Va. Music Tchrs. Assn., Assn. of Continuing Higher Edn., Roanoke Valley Soc. for Prevention of Cruelty to Animals, Nat. Wildlife Assn., Phi Theta Kappa. Avocations: hiking, swimming, reading. Home: 6423 Ran Lynn Dr Roanoke VA 24018-5403 Office: Mary Baldwin Coll/Roanoke Ctr 108 N Jefferson St Ste 816 Roanoke VA 24016-1922 Office Phone: 540-767-6172. E-mail: sbarnes@mbc.edu.

BARNES, SHIRLEY MOORE, retired psychiatric social worker, genealogist; b. Bedminster, N.J., Jan. 13, 1931; d. George and Marian (Van Nuys) Moore; m. William E. Barnes, Sept. 13, 1952; children: John Leighton, Ellen Leigh, Kimberley Jean. Student, Tusculum Coll., Greeneville, Tenn., 1948-50; BA, Rutgers U., 1952; MSW, U. Pa., 1954. Lic. clin. social worker, Vt. Caseworker Children's Aid Soc., Phila., 1952-55; psychiat. social worker West Jersey Hosp. and Psychiat. Clinic, Camden, N.J., 1960-61, VA Hosp., Brockton, Mass., 1972, Mental Health Svcs. Vt., Springfield, 1973-77, adminstr., coord. aftercare and rehab., 1977-82, psychiat. social worker, supr., 1982-96, developer psycho-rehab. for retarded and mentally ill Proctorsville, 1980-82, founder Beekman House, 1979; ret., 1996. Author: Thomas Edward Currin, Sr., Margaret Jane Cubbon, 1993, The Kindred Venturers, 1994, (with G. Moore) A Special Union, 1998The Lineage and History of the Four Van Nuys Sisters, 2002, The History & Lineage of Alexander Baird and His Descendants in Somerset County, N.J., 2002, The Pioneers of Billerica, 1654-1660, 2005; contbr. articles to various publs. Bd. dirs. J.F. Tatum Sch. PTA, Haddonfield, N.J., 1966-68, High Rock Sch. PTA, Needham, Mass., 1971-72. Recipient 1d place for best all around work in art dept. N.J. Federated Women's Clubs, 1966. Mem. NASW, Acad. Cert. Social Workers, Nat. Geneal. Soc., New Eng. Hist. and Geneal. Soc. Avocations: genealogy, art, embroidery. Home: 13 Blossom Dr Billerica MA 01821-3114

BARNES, SUZANNE MARTIN, speech pathology/audiology services professional; d. Villard Jr. and Gertrude Herndon Martin; m. Reginald Davis Barnes Jr., Feb. 24, 1968; children: Curtis Martin, Laura Julie. BA in Speech and Lang. Pathology, U. Okla., Norman, 1966; MA, Columbia U. Cert. hypnotherapist. Lang. and speech pathologist Lenox Hill Hosp., NYC, 1968—70, Meth. Hosp., Arcadia, Calif., 1976—77; dir. Suzanne Barnes & Assocs., Sierra Madre, Calif., 1977—. Participating group therapist UCLA; guest lectr. Grad. Sch. Orthodontics; cons. in field. Author: (book and video) Taming the Tongue Thrust, The Stuttering Kit. Vol. Jr. League, Pasadena, Calif., 2006. Named Bus. Leader with Outstanding Partnership with Edn., City of Pasadena; Vet. Rehab. scholar, Columbia U. Mem.: Internat. Assn. Onofacial Myology (cert.), Calif. Speech Lang. Hearing Assn. (Outstanding Achievement award), Am. Speech Lang Hearing Assn., San Gabriel Valley Assn. Speech-Lang. Pathologists (founder). Avocations: yoga, tennis, travel, knitting. Office Phone: 626-355-3882. Fax: 626-355-3882. E-mail: suzspeech@mindspring.com.

BARNES, SYLVIA, family practice physician; b. Dayton, S.C., Dec. 6, 1948; d. Arthur and Lucile B.; children: Paul, Lynette, Kathryn. BS, Baldwin Wallace U., 1983; MD, Northeastern Ohio U., 1990. Physician Rapid Response, Akron, Ohio, 1992-93, Summerville (S.C.) Family Practice, 1993-96, Carolina Med. Ctr., Summerville, 1996-98, Unifour Family Practice, Hickory, N.C., 1998—. Educator in field; guest lectr. dept. biology Baldwin Wallace U., 1984; sign lang. and liturgial mime commencement spkr. Cayahoga C.C., 1983. Recipient Better Homes and Garden cooking award. Mem. AMA (Physician Recognition award 1997), Am. Acad. Family Practice (cert., physician recognition award), Am. Soc. Clin. Pathologists (med. technologist), N.C. Family Practice, S.C. Acad. Family Practice, Christian Med. Soc., S.C. Med. Disaster Team, Med. Mission Team. Avocation: nature photography. Office: Unifour Family Practice 2712 Hwy 1275 Hickory NC 28602

BARNES-KEMPTON, ISABEL JANET, retired microbiologist, dean; b. Union City, N.J., Sept. 22, 1936; d. Carl Robert and Isabel Sarah (Cappelletti) B.; m. John D. Bowman, June 15, 1978 (dec. Nov. 1986); m. Arnold J. Kempton, Feb. 5, 2000. BS, Pa. State U., 1958; MS, Cornell U., 1960; PhD, Hahnemann Med. Coll., 1969; postgrad., Inst. Ednl. Mgmt. Harvard U., 1991. Asst. prof. microbiology Hershey Med. Ctr., Pa. State U., 1968-73; asst. prof., then assoc. prof. Sangamon State U., Springfield, Ill., 1973-76; assoc. prof. med. tech. U. Wis., Madison, 1976-85; interim dean Sch. Allied Health Professions, 1981-84; prof. med. tech. Ferris State U., Big Rapids, Mich., 1985-2000; dean Coll. Allied Health Scis., 1985-2000, acting v.p. Acad. Affairs, 1992-93. Mem. Mich. Bd. Podiatric Medicine and Surgery, 1995—2002. Bd. dirs. Mecosta County Gen. Hosp., 1988-99, sec. 1991-94, pres., 1996-97, v.p. 1997-99, Alliance for Health, 1993-2002, Mich. Hemophilia Found., 1989-95, 97—2005, sec. 1991-94; active Mecosta Health Svcs., 1998-2002, Mecosta County Cmty. Found., 2000—, pres, 2005—; coord. St. Andrews Manna Food Pantry, 2002—; mem. Tamarack Dist. Libr. Bd., 2003—; pres. bd. Tamarack Dist. Libr., 2003—. Fellow Assn. of Schs. of Allied Health Professions (bd. dirs. 1989-91); mem. Coll. Health Deans (pres. 1988-90).

BARNETT, AMY DUBOIS, editor-in-chief; m. Nathan Grant. BA, Brown U.; MFA, Columbia U. Mng. editor Fashion Almanac Mag., 1996—98; editor-in-chief Inside NY, 1999; mng. editor Fashion Planet Website; columnist, features editor Total NY Website; editor Essence Mag., 1999—2000; editor-in-chief Honey Mag., 2000—03; mng. editor Teen People, 2003—. Bd. dir. Lions' Reach. Recipient ALDO award for fashion journalism, 1997. Office: Teen People/Time Inc 1271 Ave of the Americas New York NY 10020-1393 Office Fax: 212-467-4633. E-mail: amy.barnett@teenpeople.com.*

BARNETT, BERTHA L. STRICKLAND, elementary school educator; b. Levelland, Tex., May 22, 1941; d. Marshall Howard and Juanita O. (Hogan) Strickland; m. Kenneth W. Barnett, May 27, 1961; children: Keith, Karol, Kyle, Kelly, Kelvin, Kenric. Student, Draughon's Bus. Coll., Lubbock, Tex., 1960; BA, U. Tex., Arlington, 1980; MA, North Tex. State U., 1987. Cert. English, elem. tchr., Tex. Legal sec. Allison, Mann and Allison, Levelland, 1960-61, 64-65, Saunders, Scott, Brian and Humphrey, Amarillo, Tex., 1961-62; sec. C. of C., Amarillo, 1964; legal sec. Cullen, Morgan, Britain and White, Amarillo, 1966-67, Allison, Davis and Allison, Levelland, 1969; 1st grade tchr. J.L. Boren Elem. Sch., Mansfield, Tex., 1980—2001, Imogene Gideon Elem., 2001—03; ret., 2004. Tutor Mansfield Ind. Sch. Dist., 2004—. Mem. United Educator's Assn., Kappa Delta Pi. Home: 2606 Hardwood Trl Mansfield TX 76063-7582

BARNETT, BONNIE ALLYN, lawyer; b. Phila., 1958; BA summa cum laude, Temple Univ., 1979, JD summa cum laude, 1982. Bar: Pa. 1982, NJ 1996. Law clerk, Hon. James T. Giles US Dist. Ct. (ea. dist), Pa., 1982—84; joined Drinker Biddle & Reath LLP, Phila., 1984, ptnr., chair, environ. practice group. Articles editor Temple Law Rev., lectr. in field. Named a Pa. Super Lawyer, 2004; recipient, 2005. Office: Drinker Biddle & Reath LLP One Logan Sq 18th & Cherry Sts Philadelphia PA 19103-6996 Office Phone: 215-988-2916. Office Fax: 215-988-2757. Business E-Mail: bonnie.barnett@dbr.com.

BARNETT, CHERYL JIVIDEN, elementary school educator; b. So. Charleston, W.Va., Oct. 8, 1957; d. Irvin Merrill and Patricia Hammack Jividen; m. Roderick Eldon Barnett, July 5, 1975; 1 child, Andrew Jividen. BS in Music Edn., Asbury Coll., 1979; MA in Music Edn., Marshall U., 1981. Cert. music tchr. grades K-12 W.Va. Music tchr. Winfield (W.Va.) H.S., 1980—99; 'music tchr. Eastbrook Elem. Sch., Winfield, 1980—99, Winfield Middle Sch., 1999—. Mem.: NEA, Music Educators Nat. Conf. Avocations: genealogy, scrapbooks, reading. Office: Winfield Middle Sch 3280 Winfield Rd Winfield WV 25213

BARNETT, EMILY, artist; b. Bklyn., Oct. 23, 1947; d. Murray and Marion (Cohen) B.; m. Alan Sbarsky, Dec. 9, 1975; 1 child, Jessica. BA, CUNY, 1969; MFA, La. State U., 1976. Instr. Nassau County Mus. of Art, Roslyn Harbor, NY, 1987—2001; faculty Parsons Sch. of Design, N.Y.C., 1980—. Adj. asst. prof. Suffolk C.C., N.Y., 1992-2000, Hofstra U., N.Y., 2000—; adj. asst. prof. Adelphi U., 2005—; artist-in-residence Platte Clove, 2003. One-woman shows include Custer Inst. Observatoryu Gallery, 2002, Adelphi U., 2004, Heckscher Mus. Satellite Gallery, L.I., 1997, Fairleigh Dickinson U., 1995, Suffolk C.C., 1991, Noho Gallery, N.Y., 1983, 85, 88, 91, Nassau C.C./Firehouse Gallery, L.I., 2000, Jamaica Bay Wildlife Refuge, 2001, Islip Art Mus. Store, 2002, NC Mus. Nat. Sci., 2006; group shows include Parrish Art Mus., 1999, NY Soc. Etchers, 2002, 2003, Watermark Gallery, 2002, Jane Voorhees Zimmerli Art Mus., 2002, African Am. Mus., L.I., 1997, 98, 2000, Fine Art Mus. of L.I., 1995, Gwenda Joy Gallery, Chgo., 1995, The Hutchins Gallery/L.I. U., 1996, Wave Hill, Bronx, N.Y., 1997, Elaine Benson Gallery, L.I., 2000, Islip Art Mus., 2000, others; permanent collections include Adelphi U., N.Y., City of Seattle Portable Works, Siena Coll., N.Y., Zimmerli Art Mus., N.J., Nassau C.C., West Pub. Co. Recipient West Pub. Co. purchase award, 1995, Fine Arts Mus. of L.I., 1993, 95, Heckscher Mus., L.I./Pall Corp. award, 1992, Thomas B. Clarke award Nat. Acad. Design Ann. Juried Exhibit, 1990, 1st prize Contemporary Portraiture from the N.E., 1987, Purchase award Nassau C.C. 15th Open Print, Drawing and Watercolor Competition, 1985, Elizabeth Stanton Blake Meml. award Nat. Assn. Women Artists, 1985, Richardson-Vicks award Silvermine Ctr. for the Arts, N.Y., 1982, Irwin Zlowe award Nat. Assn. Women Artists, Print Purchase award City of Seattle, 2003, NY Found. For the Arts S.O.S., 2003, Platte Clove Artists-in-Residence, 2003, numerous others; artist-resident grantee Millay Colony, 1998. Home: 222 Carle Rd Carle Place NY 11514-1729 E-mail: emilybarnett@msn.com.

BARNETT, HELAINE M., lawyer; b. N.Y.C., Nov. 13, 1939; d. Harry and Helen (Chafets) Meresman; m. Victor Jules Barnett, June 28, 1959; children— Craig Edward, Roger Lawrence. Bars: N.Y. 1964, U.S. Dist. Ct. (so. dist.) N.Y. 1970, U.S. Dist. Ct. (ea. dist.) N.Y. 1970, U.S. Ct. Appeals (2d cir.) 1972, U.S. Supreme Ct. 1967. B.A., Barnard Coll., 1960; LL.B., NYU, 1964. Assoc. appellate counsel Criminal Appeals Bur., Legal Aid Soc., N.Y.C., 1966-71, Civil Appeals Bur., 1971-74, asst.-atty.-in-charge civil divsn., 1974—94, atty.-in-charge, 1994-2003; adj. prof. law, Benjamin N. Cardozo Sch. Law, 1980-82, 84-85; pres. Legal Services Corp., 2004-. Mem. N.Y. Gov.'s Adv. Com. to Establish Criminal Justice Inst., 1983; bd. dir. Nat. Equal Just. Lib., Am. Univ., 2004-; co-chair N.Y. State Commn. to Promote Public Confidence in Jud. Elections, 2004-. Recipient Am. Jurisprudence prize NYU Law Sch., 1962. Mem. N.Y. State Bar Assn. (chmn. com. pub. interest law 1984—), Assn. Bar City N.Y. (treas., mem. exec. comm.), ABA (mem. com. profession, standing com. ethics and profl. responsibility, bd. gov. ho. del., governance commn.), Am. Law Inst. Contbr. articles to profl. jours. Office: Legal Services Corp 23rd Fl 3333 K St NW Washington DC 20007-3522

BARNETT, JESSICA VINCENT, lawyer; BA in French and Polit. Sci., McGill U., 1996; JD cum laude, NYU, 2001. Bar: RI 2001, Mass. 2002, US Ct. Appeals (1st Cir.), US Dist. Ct. (Dist. Mass.). Law clk. Hon. Victoria Lederberg RI Supreme Ct., 2001—02; atty. Foley Hoag LLP, Boston. Mem.: Mass. Lesbian & Gay Bar Assn., Boston Bar Assn., ABA, RI Bar Assn. Office: Foley Hoag LLP Seaport World Trade Ctr West 155 Seaport Blvd Boston MA 02210-2600 Office Phone: 617-832-3029. Office Fax: 617-832-7000. E-mail: jbarnett@foleyhoag.com.*

BARNETT, MARILYN, advertising executive; b. Detroit; d. Henry and Kate (Boesky) Schiff; children: Rhona, Ken. BA, Wayne State U. Founder, part-owner, pres. Mars Advt. Co., Southfield, Mich. Bd. dirs. Mich. Strategic Fund; apptd. to Mich. bi-lateral trade team with Germany. Named Outstanding Retail Woman of Yr., Outstanding Retail Mktg. Exec., Oakland U., Entrepreneur of Yr., Oakland Exec. of Yr.; named to Mich.'s Top 25 Women Bus. Owners List. Mem. AFTRA (dir.), SAG, Exec. Women Am., Am. Women in Radio & TV (Top Agy. Mgmt. award, Outstanding Woman of Yr.), Internat. Women Forum, Com. of 200, Women's Econ. Club (Ad Woman of Yr.), Adcraft. Office: Mars Advt 25200 Telegraph Rd Southfield MI 48034-7496 Office Phone: 248-936-2234. Business E-Mail: barnettm@marsosa.com.

BARNETT, MARTHA WALTERS, lawyer; b. Dade City, Fla., June 1, 1947; d. William Haywood and Helen (Hancock) Walters; m. Richard Rawls Barnett, Jan. 4, 1969; children: Richard Rawls, Sarah Walters. BA cum laude, Tulane U., 1969; JD cum laude, U. Fla. Coll. Law, 1973; LLD (hon.), Flagler Coll., 1995, Stetson U., 2000, Nova Southwestern U., 2000; LHD (hon.), DePaul U., 2001; LLD (hon.), Wake Forest U., 2003. Bar: Fla. 1973, U.S. Dist. Ct. (mid. and so. dists.) Fla. 1973, U.S. Ct. Appeals (3d, 4th and 11th cirs.) 1975, DC 1989. Assoc. Holland & Knight LLP, Tallahassee, 1973—78, ptnr., 1979—, chair, dirs. com., past chair. pub. law dept. Bd. dirs., v.p. Fla. Lawyers Prepaid Legal Svc. Corp., 1978—80, pres., 1980—82, legis. com., 1983—84, mem. commn. on access to justice, 1984—86, exec. coun. tax sect., 1987—88, exec. coun. pub. interest. sect., 1989—91; active Fla. Commn. Ethics, 1984—87, chairperson, 1986—87, Fla. Taxation and Budget Reform Commn., 1989—; legal adv. bd. Martindale-Hubbell/Lexis-Nexis, 1990—; chair Ho. of Dels., 1994—96; spkr., lectr. in field. Governor's appointee to the Fla. Commn. on Ethics State Fla., 1984—88, chair, Fla. Commn. on Ethics, 1986—87, mem. Governor's Select Com. on Workforce 2000, 1988—89, Governor's appointee to Constitutional Taxation & Budget Reform Commn., 1990—94, Governor's appointee to Constitution Revision Commn., 1997—98; mem. exec. com. Fla. Tax Watch, 2002; bd. dirs. Lawyers Com. Civil Rights Under Law; bd. adminstrs. Tulane Ednl. Fund; mem. Fla. Commn. on Human Rels., 1977—79; bd. trustee Fla. Tax Watch, 1983—; trustee U. Fla. Coll. Law, 1996—; mem. adv. coun. U. Fla. Law Ctr.; mem. Fla. Blue Key; founding mem., bd. dir. Fla. Women's Alliance; founding mem., past pres. Capital Women's Network, 1977—79; vice-chair Fla. Sales Tax on Svcs. Study Commn., 1986—87; mem. Fla. Coun. Econ. Edn., 1989—96, Fla. Edn. Found., 1991—96, Fla. Supreme Ct. Historical Soc.; bd. govs. Fla. Chamber, 2001. Named Nat. Women of Distinction, Girl Scouts U.S.A., 2002; named one of The 50 Most Influential Women Lawyers in Am., Nat. Law Jour., 1998; recipient Arabella Babb Mansfield award, Nat. Assn. Women Lawyers, 1996, Hillary Clinton Glass Cutter award, 1996, Alumnae of Distinction, U. Fla., 1997, Nat. Assn. Pub. Interest Law award, 1998, Newcomb Coll. Outstanding Alumna, 1999, Kate Stoneman award, Albany Law Sch., 1999, Nat. Legal Aid and Defender Assn. award, 2000, Disting. Alumna award, Tulane U., 2001, Medal of Honor award, Fla. Bar. Found., 2002, Rosemary Barkett award, Fla. Assn. Women Lawyers. Fellow: Am. Bar Found. (life); mem.: ABA (exec. coun. sect. on individual rights and responsibility 1974—86, chair, sect. individual rights and responsibilities 1984—85, task force on minorities in profession 1984—86, House of Delegates 1984—, mem. FJE Resources Com. 1985—89, commn. on legal problems of the elderly 1986—88, bd. govs. 1986—89, 1986—89, consortium on legal svcs and the pub. 1987—89, commn. on women in profession 1987—90, chair bd. govs. fin. com. 1988—89, chair, bd. govs. fin. com. 1988—89, long range planning com. 1988—91, chair commn. on pub. understanding about the law 1990—93, chair, commn. on pub. understanding about the law 1990—93, bd. editors ABA Jour. 1990—94, exec. coun. sect. legal edn. and admission to bar 1990—94, bd. editors, ABA Jour. 1990—96, chair, assembly resolutions com. 1991—94, ex-officio, Am. Bar Endowment 1994—96, ex-officio, Am. Bar Found. 1994—96, bd. govs. 1994—96, chair, Consortium on Legal Services and the Public 1996, exec. coun. sect. legal edn. and admission to bar 1996—99, mem. FJE Coun. 1996—99, Ctrl. European and Eurasian Law Initiative (CEELI) Exec. Bd. 1997—, pres.-elect 1999—2000, bd. govs. 1999—2001, bd. editors ABA Jour. 1999—2001, pres. 2000—01, mem. standing com. on legal aid to indigent defendents, mem. standing com. on prepaid legal svcs.), Tallahassee Women Lawyers Assn., Nat. Assn. Women Lawyers, Am. Judicature Soc. (bd. dir. 1986—89), Bar DC, Tallahassee Bar Assn., Fla. Bar Assn. (exec. coun. pub. interest law sect. 1989—91, mem. legis. com., mem. commn. on access to justice, exec. coun. of the tax sect.), Am. Law Inst., Nat. Inst. Dispute Resolution (sec.-treas. 1988—94, bd. dirs. 1988—94, Gov. appt. Fla. Constitution revision Commn. 1997—98), Phi Delta Phi, Phi Kappa Phi. Office: Holland & Knight LLP 315 S Calhoun St Ste 600 Tallahassee FL 32301 Office Phone: 850-425-5620. Business E-Mail: martha.barnett@hklaw.com.

BARNETT, MARY LORENE, real estate manager; b. Saline County, Mo., Nov. 29, 1927; d. Grover Cleveland Renno and Emma Zue Rennison; m. Eugene Earl Boone, Aug. 24, 1946 (div. Aug. 1961); 1 child, Priscilla Sue Boone; m. Charles Owen Barnett, Nov. 11, 1961; 1 child, Robert E. BA in Psychology magna cum laude, Washburn U., 1979. Asst. contr. 1st State Savs., Sedalia, Mo., 1960-61; bookkeeper New Empire Ins., Sedalia, 1961-63; office mgr. Klassic Mfg., Sedalia, 1963-66; real estate mgr. Topeka, Kans., 1970—. Author: Charles Renno Family Record, 1996, Charles Renno Family, 1997. Bd. dirs. Shawnee County Coun. on Aging, Topeka. Recipient cert. of appreciation Bd. of County Commrs., Topeka, 1995. Mem. DAR, AAUW, LWV, Topeka Women's Club (1st v.p.), Ea. Star, Phi Kappa Phi, Psi Chi. Republican. Avocations: genealogy, poetry. Home: 3819 SW Lincolnshire Rd Topeka KS 66610-1360

BARNETT, MARY LOUISE, elementary school educator; b. Exeter, Calif., May 1, 1941; d. Raymond Edgar Noble and Nena Lavere (Huckaby) Hope; m. Gary Allen Barnett, Aug. 9, 1969; children: Alice Marie, Virginia Lynn. BA, U. of Pacific, 1963; postgrad., U. Mont., 1979-82, U. Idaho, 1984—. Cert. life elem. tchr., Calif.; standard elem. credential, Idaho; elem. tchr., Mont. Tchr. Colegio Americano de Torrean, Torreon, Coahuila, Mexico, 1962-63, Summer Sch. Primary Grades South San Francisco, 1963-66, Visalia (Calif.) Unified Sch. Dist., 1966-69, Sch. Dist. # 1, Missoula, Mont., 1969-73, Fort Shaw-Simms Sch. Dist., Fort Shaw, Mont., 1976-83, Sch. Dist. #25, Pocatello, Idaho, 1983-93, Greenacres Elem., Pocatello, 1993-94; tchr. 2d grade Bonneville Elem., Pocatello, 1994-95; tchr. Windsong Presch., Missoula, Mont., 1995-98, Headstart of Missoula, 1998-99; dir. Mary's Munchkins Presch., Missoula, 1999—. Beauty cons. Mary Kay; adv. coun. Missoula Aging Svcs., 2006—. Foster mom Ednl. Found. Fgn. Students, Pocatello, Idaho, 1986-89; vol. Am. Heart Assn., Am. Cancer Soc., Pocatello, 1986-88, Bannock March of Dimes, Pocatello, 1988, Pocatello Laubach Lit. Tutoring, 1989; state v.p. membership, del. to P.W. Australian Mission Study; vice moderator Kendall Presbyn. Women, moderator, 1991—; moderator Kendall P.W. 1990-92; deacon, dean, treas. Presbyn. Ch., 1997—. Recipient scholarship Mont. Delta Kappa Gamma Edn. Soc., Great Falls, Mont., 1976, Great Falls AAUW, 1980, Great Falls Scottish Rite, 1981, Five Valleys Reading Assn., Missoula, Mont., 1982. Mem. AAUW (v.p. 2002—, mem. com. Idaho divsn. 1990-92, book chair 1995—, pres. Missoula chpt. 1998-2003, v.p. membership Missoula chpt. 2002—), ASCD, NEA, Nat. Coun. Tchrs. English, Internat. Reading Assn., Assn. Childhood Edn. Internat., Mont. Assn. Early Childhood Edn. (pres. Missoula chpt. 2004-06, moderator 2006—), Laubach Literacy Tutors (sec. 1993—), Bus. and Profl. Women Pocatello (sec. 1993—, contact advisor Missoula After 5 1999—), Mortar Bd., Alpha Lambda Delta, Delta Kappa Gamma (state fellowship chmn., corr. sec. Pocatello chpt. 1986-88, 2d v.p. 1994-96, chmn. Western expansion, 200-03), Moose (musician 1981-82), Order Eastern Star (musician 1984-85), Gamma Phi Beta (sec. Laubach Tutors 1993-95), Delta Kappa Gamma (2d v.p. chpt. 1996—, pres. 2000—). Democrat. Presbyn. Avocations: music, aquacise, aerobics, crafts, cross stitch. Home: 103 E Crestline Dr Missoula MT 59803-2412 Office: Lewis and Clark Sch 2901 Park Missoula MT 59801 Office Phone: 406-542-4035. Personal E-mail: Gabmarybarnett@peoplepc.com.

BARNETT, OLA WILMA, psychology educator; b. L.A., Jan. 26, 1940; d. William and Ruth Carol (Phillips) King; m. Donald Joseph Barnett, Nov. 27, 1941; children: Darlene Ola Blake, Donna Shirley Johnson. BA, UCLA, 1962, MA, 1965, PhD, 1971. Research asst. UCLA, 1961-67; asst. prof. psychology Calif. State Poly. U., San Luis Obispo, 1967-70; asso. prof. psychology Pepperdine U., Malibu, Calif., 1970-79, prof. psychology, 1979—. Sponsor Camp David Gonzales Tutorial Program, 1974-77; researcher on spouse abuse. Contbr. articles to profl. jours. Recipient Vol. Service award Atascadero State Hosp., 1970; Action grantee, 1972-73, Robert Ellis Simm grantee. Mem. Am. Psychol. Assn., Nat. Council Crime and Delinquency, Am. Psychology-Law Soc., Coalition Against Domestic Violence, Am. Soc. Criminology, Acad. Criminal Justice Scis., Psi Chi. Mem. Ch. of Christ. Achievements include rsch. on spouse abuse. Home: 24301 Sylvan Glen Rd Calabasas CA 91302-2362 Office: Pepperdine U Social Sci Dv Malibu CA 90265

BARNETT, PATRICIA ANN, development professional; b. Culver City, Calif., Jan. 25; d. Howard Taft and Sarah (Ross) B. BJ, U. Tex., 1978; MLA, So. Meth. U., 2002. Program specialist Dallas C. of C., 1978-79, comm. specialist, 1979-81; mgr. pub. rels. Trailways Corp., Dallas, 1981-82, dir. pub. rels., 1982-85; sr. account exec. Keller-Crescent Co., Dallas, 1985-87; dir. comm. Office of Pvt. Sector Initiatives The White House, Washington, 1987-89; dir. pub. affairs United Way Am., Alexandria, Va., 1989-91; dir. pub. rels. Dally Advt., Ft. Worth, 1992-94; dir. corp. and found. rels. So. Meth. U., Dallas, 1994-96, dir. major gifts, 1996—2001; dir. devel. Dedman Coll., 2001—. Mem.: Jr. League Dallas. Republican. Avocations: history, travel, literature, folk art, bookbinding. Office: So Meth U PO Box 750402 Dallas TX 75275-0402 Office Phone: 214-768-2691. E-mail: tbarnett@smu.edu.

BARNETT, REBECCA LYNN, communications executive; b. Atlanta, May 7, 1957; d. Robert Joe and Maude (Dickerson) B. BS in Edn., Auburn U., 1980; MBA, Emory U., 1982; postgrad., Duke U., 1991, U. Mich., 1993. Resident dir. Emory U.; camp dir. NW Ga. Girl Scout Coun., Atlanta, 1982; account exec. So. Bell, Atlanta, 1982-83; sales mgr. So. Bell Advanced Systems, Atlanta, 1983-84; asst. product mgr. Bell South Services, Atlanta, 1984-85, product mgr., cons., 1985-94; project mgr., cons. A&A Cons. Svcs., 1995-96; sr. product mgr., webmaster Telemate Software, Atlanta, 1996-97; pres. Dot-Dot.Com, 1997—. Treas., sec. Videotex Industry Assn., Washington, 1985—; dir., sec., v.p. Baker Design Group, Atlanta, 1985—; chair Product Team, Atlanta, 1985-92; v.p. Worldwide Videotex, 1990-95. Coauthor: All You Need is an Idea, Gateway 2000, Local Government Opportunities in Videotex. Trainer instr. NW Ga. coun. Girl Scouts U.S., Atlanta, 1981-92; mem. Nat. Dem. Com., Washington, 1985-87; dir. instrs.

outdoor living skills Am. Camping Assn., Bradford Woods, Ill., 1986-90. Recipient Eagle award, Appreciation award Girl Scout. Mem. NOW, Info. Industry Assn., Am. Mktg. Assn., Internat. Interactive Comm. Soc., Interactive Svcs. Assn. (treas., bd. dirs. 1991-95), Atlanta Interactive Mktg. Assn., Sierra Club. Home: 884 Derrydown Way Decatur GA 30030-4161 Office: Dot Dot Com LLC Ste 468 2107 N Decatur Rd Decatur GA 30033

BARNETT, ROCHELLE, accountant; Grad., Queens Coll.; M in Acctg., C.W. Post Coll., LI Univ. CPA N.Y., Fla., Conn. Sr. cons. Mark Paneth & Shron LLP, Woodbury, NY, ptnr., 1991, 1979—2000, mng. ptnr., 2000—04; ret. Adv. bd. Touro Law Sch. Named Woman of Distinction, March of Dimes, 1995, NY Accountant Advocate of Yr., U.S. Small Bus. Assn., 1998; named one of LI Top 50 Women Profl., 2001. Mem.: AICPA, Nat. Assn. Women Bus. Owners (former exec. v.p., former treas. Long Island chpt., founder, chairperson com. of 100), Long Island Assn. (Women In Bus. Advocate of Yr. 1995), N.Y. State Soc. CPA (former chair coop. with bankers & other credit grantors com., former bd. dirs.), N.Y. Oil Heat Assn., Oil Heat Inst. Long Island. Office: Marks Paneth & Shron LLP 88 Froehlich Farm Blvd Woodbury NY 11797-2921 Office Phone: 516-992-5901. Office Fax: 516-992-5902. E-mail: sbarnett@markspaneth.com.

BARNETT, SUE, nurse; b. Waukegan, Ill., Apr. 8, 1956; d. Jackie Laverne and Catherine Mary (LaMarche) B. AAS in Nursing, Elgin (Ill.) C.C., 1977. RN, Ill.; ANCC cert. in psychiat. and mental health nurse. Home health nurse Adv. Health Care, Oak Brook, Ill., 1977-97; staff nurse Fox Valley Nursing Home, South Elgin, Ill., 1978-79, Elgin Mental Health Ctr., 1979—. Music min., vol. St. John Neumann Ch., St. Charles, Ill., 1977—; vol. Labarus House Shelter, St. Charles, 1997—. Mem. Ill. Nurses Assn. (local unit sec. 1981-84, local unit grievance rep. 1984-96, local unit vice chair 1984-94, conv. rep. 1990-92). Roman Catholic. Avocations: reading, singing, volunteer work. Office: Elgin Mental Health Ctr-Gahagan Unit 750 S State St Elgin IL 60123-7692

BARNETT, VIVIAN ENDICOTT, curator; b. Putnam, Conn., July 8, 1944; d. George and Vivian (Wood) Endicott; m. Peter Herbert Barnett, July 1, 1967; children: Sarah, Alexander. AB magna cum laude, Vassar Coll., Poughkeepsie, N.Y., 1965; MA, NYU, 1971; postgrad., CUNY, 1979—81. Research asst. Solomon R. Guggenheim Mus., N.Y.C., 1973-77, curatorial assoc., 1978-79, assoc. curator, 1980-81, rsch. curator, 1981-82, curator, 1982-91; dir. Roethel Benjamin Archive at Guggenheim Mus., N.Y.C., 1991—. Author: (book) The Guggenheim Museum: Justin K. Thannhauser Collection, 1978, The Guggenheim Museum Collection 1900-1980, Kandinsky at the Guggenheim, 1983, 100 Works by Modern Masters from the Guggenheim Museum, 1984, Kandinsky and Sweden, 1989, Kandinsky in Major Collections in the West, 1989, Kandinsky Watercolours: Catalogue Raisonnè, vol I 1900-1921, 1992, Kandinsky Watercolours: Catalogue Raisonnè, vol II 1922-1944, 1994, Kleine Freuden, 1992, Das bunte Leben: Kandinsky in Lenbachhaus, 1995, The Blue Four: Feininger, Jawlensky, Kandinsky, Klee in the New World, 1997, The Blue Four Collection at the Norton Simon Museum, 2002, Kandinsky Drawings: Catalogue Raisonne, vol. I, 2006; contbg. author: Kandinsky in Paris: 1934-44, 1985, Exiles and Emigres: 1933-1945, 1997, The Joy of Color: The Merzbacher Collection, 1998, Mies in America, 2001, Die Brucke in Dresden, 2001, Art of Tomorrow: Hilla Rebay and Solomon Guggenheim, 2005, Klee and America, 2006. Fellow John Simon Guggenheim, 1990, Inst. Advanced Study, Princeton, 2003—04. Mem.: Coll. Art Assn. Am., Internat. Coun. Museums, Soc. Kandinsky (sec. 1992—2001). Office: Solomon R Guggenheim Mus 1071 5th Ave New York NY 10128-0112 Office Phone: 212-423-3612. Personal E-mail: vbarnett@att.net.

BARNETTE, NELLIE MARIE, elementary school educator; b. Norton, Va., Apr. 7, 1951; d. Floyd J. Stidham and Hester O. Wampler; 1 child, Michael Ryan. BA in Elem. & Mid. Sch. Edn. magna cum laude, U. Va., Wise, 1984. Tchr. Wise County, Pound, Va. Co-chair SACS JW Adams, Pound, 1990—2004; mem. rev. team Floyd County, 2002. Recipient Excellence Energy Edn. award, Va. Mining Assn., Norton, 2005. Mem.: Nat. Sci. Tchrs. Assn., WCEA, Va. Edn. Assn. Democrat. Baptist. Avocations: hiking, reading, travel. Home: 10139 Sportsman Dr Wise VA 24293 Office: JWAC 10824 Orb y Cantrell Hwy Pound VA 24279

BARNETT-EVANSON, FILA, artist, executive recruiter; BA, Keane U., Union, N.J., 1967; student, N.Y. Sch. Interior Design, N.Y.C., 1967-68. Interior/visual designer, N.Y.C., 1968-79; pub. Resources, San Diego, 1980-82; video producer San Diego, 1982-85; yoga/stress mgmt. Stress Break, Inc., San Diego, 1985-90; artist Laguna Beach, 1990—, Carmel, 1990—; western dir. mktg. Cancer Treatment Ctrs. Am., Brea, Calif., 1991-93; pres. Exec. Search Profls., Inc., Carmel, 1998, Laguna Beach, Calif., 1998—. Mem. docent coun. Orange County Mus. Art. Mem. The Inside Edge.

BARNEWALL, MARILYN MACGRUDER, retired banker; b. Indpls. d. Robert Danforth MacGruder and Hester Bruce Wooden Brown; m. Gordon Gouverneur Barnewall, Aug. 1970 (div. Jan. 1973); children: John Clyde, Katherine Barnewall Coomer. Graduate degree, Colo. U., 1978. Reporter Wyoming Eagle, Cheyenne, 1956—57; mgr. Combined Ins. Co., Denver, 1961—65; dir. public relations Nat. Camera, 1966—68; mag. editor, asst. to pub. Bell Publs., 1968—70; v.p. mgr. United Bank, Denver, 1972—79; pres., CEO MacGruder Agy. Inc., Denver, 1979—89, Cin., 1989—; editorialist Grand Junction (Colo.) Free Press, 2003—06, Bus. Reform, 2004—06, World Net Daily, 2004—06. Expert witness for equal credit for women Colo. State Legis., 1977. Author: A Banker's Pragmatic Approach to the Upscale, 1982, Profitable Private Banking: The Complete Blueprint, 1986, National Private Banking Profitability Survey, 1987, Warren, Gorham & LaMont National Private Banking Profitability Survey, 1987, Profitable Private Banking: The Complete Blueprint, 1989. Bd. mem. Camp Fire Girls, Colo. State U. Family Action Ctr., Am. for Effective Law Enforcement, United Negro Coll. Fund, Metro Denver Urban Coalition, Big Brothers. Mem.: Leukemia Soc. of Am. (chair, fundraiser 1976). Avocations: writing, photography, genealogy, travel, cooking. Home: 679 Brentwood Dr Palisade CO 81526 Personal E-mail: marilynmacg@gmail.com.

BARNEY, CAROL ROSS, architect; b. Chgo., Apr. 12, 1949; d. Chester Albert and Dorothy Valeria (Dusiewicz) Ross; m. Alan Fredrick Barney, Mar. 22, 1970; children: Ross Fredrick, Adam Shafer, John Ross. BArch, U. Ill., 1971. Registered architect, Ill. Assoc. architect Holabird & Root, Chgo., 1972-79; prin. architect Orput Assoc., Inc., Wilmette, Ill., 1979-81; prin. architect, pres. Ross Barney Arch., Chgo., 1981—, also bd. dirs. Studio prof. Ill. Inst. Tech., Chgo., 1993-94; asst. prof. U. Ill., Chgo., 1976-78. Prin. works include Glendale Heights Post Office, Ill., Little Village Acad. Pub. Sch., Fed. Bldg., Oklahoma City, Swenson Sci. Bldg., U. Md. Plan commr. Village of Wilmette, 1986-88, mem. Econ. Devel. Commn., 1988-90, chmn. Appearance Rev. Commn., 1990-2000; trustee Children's Home and Aid Soc. Ill., Chgo., 1986—; mem. adv. bd. Small Bus. Ctr. for Women, Chgo., 1985—. Recipient Fed. Design Achievement award, 1992; Francis J. Plym travelling fellow, 1983. Fellow AIA (bd. dirs. Chgo. chpt. 1978-80, v.p. 1981-82, Disting. Svc. award Chgo. chpt. 1978, Ill. Coun. 1978, Firm award 1995, Honor award 1991, 94, 99, 2002, Thomas Jefferson award for pub. architecture 2005); mem. Nat. Coun. Archtl. Registration Bds. (cert.), Chgo. Women in Architecture (founding pres. 1978-79), Chgo. Network, Cliff Dwellers Club (bd. dirs. 1995). Home: 601 Linden Ave Wilmette IL 60091-2819 Office: Ross Barney Arch 10 W Hubbard St Chicago IL 60610 Office Phone: 312-832-0600 ext. 221. Business E-Mail: crb@r-barc.com.

BARNEY, CHRISTINE J., artist; b. Bath, NY, Sept. 9, 1952; d. Willis H. and Elsa P. (Heney) Barney. BA, Goddard Coll., 1975; MA, NYU, 1988. Proprietor, designer, craftsperson Laurel Mountain Glass, Bosswell, Pa., 1975-83; tchg./tech. asst. Alfred (N.Y.) U., 1983-85; freelance designer Seguso Arte Vetro, Murano, Venice, Italy, 1985-87; studio artist, 1989—. Artist-in-residence Golden Glass Studio and Sch., Cin., 1991—92; guest artist Artpark, Lewiston, NY, 1992, Lewiston, 94; vis. artist Ohio State U., 1992, Tyler Sch. Art, Phila., 1993; lectr. in field. One-woman shows include Kavesh Gallery, Sun Valley, Kethun, Idaho, 1991, Christy/Taylor Gallery, Boca Raton, Fla., 1990—92, Vespermann Gallery, Atlanta, 1994, Portia Gallery, Chgo., 1997, 1997, Glass Gallery, Bethesda, Md., 2000, Bethesday, Md., 2001, Art Elements Gallery, Milw., 2001, Oxford Gallery, Rochester, N.Y., 2004, exhibited in group shows at Traver-Sutton Gallery, Seattle, 1982, So. Alleghenies Mus. Art, Loretto, Pa., 1983, Querini Stampaglia Gallery, Venice, 1984, U. di Architettura de Venezia, 1985, 80 Washington Sq. East Galleries, N.Y.C., 1988, Spaso Ho., Am. Embassy, Moscow, 1988—89, Grohe Gallery, Boston, 1989, 1995, Newark Mus., 1989, Sotheby's, N.Y.C., 1990, N.J. Ctr. Visual Arts, 1990, Morris Mus., Morristown, N.J., 1991, 1997, Mus. Am. Glass, Millville, N.J., 1993, Gallery at Wheaton Village, Millville, 1994, S. Shore Art Ctr., Cohasset, Mass., 1996, Holsten Gallery, Stockbridge, Mass., 1999—2001, Morgan Glass Gallery, Pitts., 2001, Yates County Arts Ctr., NY, 2002, Oxford Gallery, Rochester, 2002, Eleven Eleven Sculpture Space, Washington, 2003, Kane Marie Gallery, Virginia Beach, Va., 2003, Ariana Gallery, Royal Oak, Mich., 2004, Represented in permanent collections Corning Mus. Glass, Mus. Am. Glass, Millville, Tropicana Products, Inc., Bradenton, Fla., Centeon Pharm., King of Prussia, Pa., Merck & Co., Rahway, N.J.; contbr. articles to profl. jours. Creator Arts in Achievement awards Middlesex County Cultural and Heritage Commn., 1990—94; creator Artpark award, 1993. Recipient Carnegie Inst. prize, 1981; Creative Glass Ctr. Am. fellow, 1988, 1996, N.J. State Coun. Arts fellow, 1989—90. Avocation: dance. Home: 432 Monmouth St Jersey City NJ 07302-2326 Personal E-mail: sculptureglass@aol.com.

BARNHART, CYNTHIA, engineering educator, researcher; BS in Civil Engring., U. Vt., 1981; MS in Transp., Mass. Inst. Tech., 1985, PhD in Transp. and Civil Engring., 1988. With Mass. Inst. Tech., 1992—, co-dir. ctr. transp. and logistics, leader engring. systems group, asst. prof. to prof. civil and environ. engring. Founder Large-Scale Optimization Group Mass. Inst. Tech., 1997; bd. dirs. Inst. Ops. Research Mgmt. Scis. (INFORMS); spkr. in field. Assoc. editor: Operations, Research, and Transportation Science; contbr. articles to profl. jours. Recipient Jr. Faculty Career award, Gen. Electric Found., Presdl. Young Investigator award, NSF. Achievements include research in models and algorithms to improve carrier operations (focusing on airlines). Office: Mass Inst Tech 77 Massachusetts Ave Bldg 1-229/E40-149A Cambridge MA 02139 Office Phone: 617-253-3815. Business E-Mail: cbarnhar@mit.edu.

BARNHART, CYNTHIA ROGERS, editor, writer; b. Bronxville, N.Y., Aug. 29, 1934; d. Arthur Howard and Doris Helen (Kraeger) Rogers; m. Robert Knox Barnhart, Sept. 16, 1955; children: Michael G., John R., David F., Katherine E., Rebecca L. BA, Bryn Mawr Coll., 1957; guest sr., Barnard Coll., 1956-57. From gen. editor. to asst. mng. editor Clarence L. Barnhart, Inc., Bronxville, 1976-92; asst. mng. editor Rogers Knox & Barnhart, Inc., Garrison, NY, 1992—; sr. editor Cambridge Dictionary Am. English Cambridge U. Press, N.Y.C., 1998—2003, sr. devel. editor ESL/EFL reference, 1998—2003, mng. editor Cambridge Dictionary of Am. Idioms, 2001—03; freelance author, editor, 2003—04. Co-author: Let's Read, 1970, author revised edit., 1996; editor: World Book Dictionary, Barnhart Abbreviations Dictionary, Chambers Dictionary of Etymology (formerly Barnhart Dictionary of Etymology), Barnhart Dictionary of New English, 1, 2, 3, Barnhart Concise Dictionary of Etymology, Am. Heritage Dictionary of Science. Dir. Girl Scouts Am., Briarcliff Manor, N.Y., 1969-70; pres. Bryn Mawr Club Westchester, N.Y., 1972-74; sec. S.E. Dem. Com., 1995-97; mem. Putnam County Dem. Party, exec. com. 1996-98; mem. steering com. Barnard Project Continuum, 2003—; established Homehill Farm Breeding Shetland Sheep and Wool, 2004. Democrat. Avocations: breeding border terriers, making teddy bears and toys, gardening. E-mail: barnbuks@westnet.com.

BARNHART, DOROTHY MAY KOHRS, small business owner; b. Des Moines, Apr. 27, 1933; d. Oliver John and Lily Mabel (Smith) Kohrs; children: Jacqueline, Dwaine Jr., Kelly stepchildren: Billy Jo, Jack, Cindy. Attended, Internat. Acctg. Soc., Chgo., Drake U., 1956, Area II C.C., 1987—88. Bookkeeper Iowa Credit Union League, 1954—69, Grand Printing Art-O-Type, 1970—72; office mgr. Am. Bus. Forms & Sys., Inc., 1972—76; forms dept. mgr. Action Forms/Action Printers Co., 1976—77; office mgr. Elliott Beechcraft Flying Svc., 1977—81; tel. selling rep. Coca Cola Co., 1983—84; adminstrv. asst. Coalition for Family and Children's Svc. in Iowa, Des Moines, 1984—97; pres. and owner Wellness Games, Ltd., 1985—. Coord. ann. statewide conf. Coalition Family and Children's Svc. in Iowa, 1987—97; inventor Wellness Game, 1982; coord. Chronic Pain Outreach of Ctrl. Iowa, 1984—, Midwest regional dir., 1985—87; conf. coord. Mercy Hosp., 1982—84; coord. fundraisers, Wellness Game marathons; writer TV show featuring Wellness board game, 2001—04. Mem. choir Growth Group at Powell III; mem. Iowa Women's Polit. Caucus; mem. choir Grace United Meth. Ch.; mem. disability action com. Des Moines Area Urban Mission Coun. Fellow: Internat. Biographical Ctr. (adv. coun., humanitarian svc. award); mem.: NAFE, Women's C. of C. of Des Moines. Democrat. Home: #15 2525 County Line Rd Des Moines IA 50321

BARNHART, JO ANNE B., federal agency administrator; b. Memphis, Aug. 26, 1950; d. Nelson Alexander and Betty Jane (Fitzpatrick) Bryant; m. David Lee Ross, Feb. 14, 1976 (div. June 1983); m. David Ray Barnhart, May 24, 1986. Student, U. Tenn., 1968—70; BA, U. Del., 1975. Space and time buyer DeMartin-Marona & Assocs., Wilmington, Del., 1970—73; adminstrv. asst. Mental Health Assn., Wilmington, 1973—75; dir. SERVE nutrition program Wilmington Sr. Ctr., 1975—77; legis. asst. to Sen. William V. Roth, Jr., Washington, 1977—81; dep. assoc. commr. Office Family Assistance, HHS, Washington, 1981—83, assoc. commr., 1983—86; rep. staff dir. U.S. Senate Govt. Affairs Com., 1987—90; asst. sec. family support HHS, Washington, 1990—91, asst. sec. for children and families, 1991—92; staff U.S. Sen. William V. Roth, 1993—; comnr. Social Security Admin., Baltimore, Md., 2001—. Mem. adv. bd. on welfare indicators U.S. Dept. HHS, 1996—. Campaign mgr. U. S. Sen. William V. Roth, 1988, 1994; polit. dir. Nat. Rep. Senatorial Com., 1995—97, polit. and pub. policy cons., 1997—2001; mem. Social Security adv. bd., 1997—2001; commr. Social Security, 2001—. Republican. Methodist. Office: Social Security Admin Office of Commr Altmeyer Bldg 6401 Security Blvd Baltimore MD 21235-6401

BARNHART, NIKKI LYNN CLARK, elementary school educator; b. Terre Haute, Ind., Mar. 14, 1940; d. Wilbur Ellis and Margaret Jane (Cork) Clark; m. James Walter Barnhart; children: Tracey Lynn, Kelly Jean, Darby Jane, Holly Anne. BEd, Shippensburg U., 1961, MEd, 1964; cert. reading specialist, Western Md. U., 1979; EdD, U. Md., 1984. Cert. elem. tchr., English tchr., guidance counselor, Pa.; cert. Reading Recovery. Tchr. Chambersburg (Pa.) Schs., 1961-62, Spring Grove (Pa.) Area Schs., 1963-66, Hanover (Pa.) Pub. Schs., 1967-2000. Presenter profl. conf. and convs. Author: Hanover through History, 1976. Mem. Hanover Borough Coun., 1993—; consistory mem. Emmanuel Ch., Hanover, 1984-92. Chpt. I parent mini-grantee Pa. Dept. Edn., 1996; recipient Outstanding Elem. Educator award Phi Delta Theta, 1999. Mem. Internat. Reading Assn. (exemplary program award for bldg. 1997), South Ctrl. Reading Coun. (various offices, Celebrate Literacy award 1996), Delta Kappa Gamma (Eta chpt., Alpha Alpha State Golden Anniversary award 1980, Alpha Alpha State Founder's award 1982). Republican. Mem. United Ch. of Christ. Avocations: reading, cooking. Office: Clearview Sch 100 W Clearview Rd Hanover PA 17331-1615

BARNHILL, JANE COOK, commissioner; m. John W. Barnhill Jr. Owner bed and breakfast James Walker Homestead, Allcorn House; commr. Tex. Hist. Commn., Austin, 1995—, vice chair. Mem. Washington County Hist. Commn., Brenham Heritage Mus.; bd. dirs., ethics com. Trinity Med. Ctr.; bd. dirs. Friends of the Gov.'s Mansion. Recipient Clara Driscoll Award, Preservation Tex., 2001. Mem.: Heritage Soc. Washington County (pres.), Brenham Maifest Assn. Office: PO Box 12276 Austin TX 78711-2276

BARNHILL, MURIEL, retired nurse; b. Corbin, Ky., Nov. 3, 1947; d. Henry Carl and Nannie Catherine (Cotton) Hinkle; m. William Lewis Barnhill, Jan. 23, 1965; children: Susan, Alicia, Brian. Assoc. in Nursing, Cumberland Coll., 1978. RN. Med.-surg. charge nurse Southeastern Ky. Bapt. Hosp., Corbin; dir. nursing Hillcrest Nursing Home, Corbin; community home health nurse Whitley County Home Health Agency, Williamsburg, Ky. Church clerk, chmn. missions outreach.

BARNICK, HELEN, retired judicial clerk; b. Max, N.D., Mar. 24, 1925; d. John K. and Stacy (Kankovsky) Barnick. BS in Music cum laude, Minot State Coll., 1954; postgrad., Am. Conservatory of Music, Chgo., 1975-76. With Epton, Bohling & Druth, Chgo., 1968-69; sec. Wildman, Harrold, Allen & Dixon, Chgo., 1969-75; part-time assignments for temporary agy. Chgo., 1975-77; sec. Friedman & Koven, Chgo., 1977-78; with Lawrence, Lawrence, Kamin & Saunders, Chgo., 1978-81; sec. Hinshaw, Culbertson et al., Chgo., 1982; sec. to magistrate judge U.S. Dist. Ct. (we. dist.) Wis., Madison, 1985-91; dep. clk., case adminstr. U.S. Bankruptcy Ct. (we. dist.) Wis., Madison, 1992-94; ret., 1994. Chancel choir 1st Bapt. Ch., Mpls., Fourth Presbyn. Ch., Chgo., Covenant Presbyn. Ch., Madison, Wis.; choir, dir. sr. high choir Moody Ch., Chgo.; dir. chancel choir 1st Bapt. Ch., Minot, ND; mem. Festival Choir, Madison; bd. dirs., sec.-treas. Peppertree at Tamarack Owners Assn., Inc., Wisconsin Dells. Mem.: Bus. and Profl. Women Assn., Christian Bus. and Profl. Women (chmn.), Madison Civics Club, Symphony Orch. League, Sigma Sigma Sigma. Home: 7364 Old Sauk Rd Madison WI 53717-1213

BARNICLE, MARY ANNE, music educator, piano accompanist; b. Bridgeport, Conn., Nov. 28, 1946; d. Edward Joseph and Anna Marie (Kolesar) Petrovick; m. Stephan Patrick Barnicle, Aug. 23, 1969; children: Michael, Patricia, Daniel, Kevin. MusB in Music Edn., U. Hartford, 1969, MusB in Piano Pedagogy, 1969; MEd in Fine Arts, Fitchburg State Coll., 1991. Cert. dir. fine arts 1989, music dept. chair Conn., 1994. Vocal music tchr. Avon Middle Sch., Conn., 1969—70; vocal/gen. music tchr. Canton Pub. Schs., Conn., 1981—94, head music tchr., 1989—94, music dept. chair, 1994—2004; vocal music tchr. Canton Jr. HS, HS, 1994—97; vocal music, music theory & tech. Canton HS, 1994—2004. Pvt. piano tchr. Hartt Sch. Studio, Conn., 1970—2004, Simsbury Home, Conn., 1970—2004, home studio, Fayetteville, NC, 2004—. Mem. Canton Creative Arts Coun., Conn., 1982—2002; bd. mem., pres. Simsbury Summer Theater for Youth, Conn., 1985—95; accompanist, orchestra mem. Theater Guild Simsbury, Conn., 1988—94; mem. profl. devel. consortium Farmington Valley Schs., Farmington Valley, Conn., 1989—91; mem., music dept. rep. Canton Parents for Music, Conn., 1990—2004; music dir., accompanist Canton Benefits Productions, Conn., 1993—94; mem. edn. adv. bd. Hartford Symphony Orchestra, Conn., 1990—92; curriculum revision com. mem. Canton Pub. Schs., 1992—2004; organist, accompanist, soloist various chs., Conn., 1970—2004; organ scholar participant Music Ministry of St. Patrick Ch., Fayetteville, NC, 2005—06. Recipient Educator of Yr., Canton C. of C., 1999; grantee Paul Harris fellow, Avon/Canton Rotary Club Internat., 2003. Mem.: NEA, Am. Choral Dirs. Assn., Nat. Assn. Music Edn. Democrat. Avocation: singing. Home: 214 Viking Dr Fayetteville NC 28303 Personal E-mail: mabarnicle@nc.rr.com.

BARNUM, BARBARA STEVENS, retired nursing educator, writer; b. Johnstown, Pa., Sept. 2, 1937; d. William C. and Freda Inzes (Claycomb) Burkett; m. H. James Barnum (dec.); children: Lauren, Elizabeth, Catherine, Anne (dec.), Shauna, Sallee, David. AA in Nursing, St. Petersburg Jr. Coll., 1958; BPh, Northwestern U., 1967; MA, DePaul U., 1971; PhD, U. Chgo., 1976. RN, Ill., N.Y. Dir. nursing svcs. Augustana Hosp. and Health Care Ctr., Chgo., 1970-71; dir. staff edn. U. Chgo. Hosps. and Clinics, 1971-73; prof. U. Ill., Chgo., 1973-79; dir. div. health svcs., sci. and edn. Columbia U. Tchrs. Coll., N.Y.C., 1979-87; editor Nursing & Health Care Nat. League for Nursing, N.Y.C., 1989-91; editor div. nursing Columbia-Presbyn. Med. Ctr., Columbia U., N.Y.C., 1991-95; prof. Sch. Nursing Columbia U., N.Y.C., 1995-98; ret., 1998. Chmn. bd. Barnum & Souza, N.Y.C., 1989-92; civilian cons. to surgeon gen. USAF, 1980-87. Author: Nursing Theory, Analysis, Application and Evaluation, 4th edit., 1994, Writing for Publication: A Primer for Nurses, 1995; author: (with K. Kerfoot) The Nurse as Executive, 4th edit., 1995; author: Spirituality and Nursing: From Traditional to New Age, 1996, 2d edit., 2003, Teaching Nursing in the Era of Managed Care, 1999, The New Healers: Minds and Hands in Complementary Medicine, 2002, (fiction) The Haunting of Lisa Tilden, 1999; editor: Nursing Leadership Forum, 1994—98. Mem. governing bd. Nurses House, 1979-86, Nat. Health Coun., 1981-90, others. Fellow Am. Acad. Nursing (governing bd. 1982-84); mem. Sigma Theta Tau (Founders' award 1979). Home: 80 Park Ave Apt 15G New York NY 10016-2547 Personal E-mail: barbbarnum@aol.com.

BARNUM, MARY ANN MOOK, information management manager; b. Arlington, Va., Apr. 3, 1946; d. Conrad Payne and Barbara Heer (Held) Mook; m. William Douglas Barnum, Aug. 10, 1968. BS in Math., Radford U., 1967. Cert. tchr., Va., N.J., N.Mex. Math. tchr. Prince William County Schs., Woodbridge, Va., 1967-68; mathematician RCA Svc. Co., Andros Island, Bahamas, 1968-70; math. tchr. Cinnaminson (N.J.) Schs., 1970-73, Alamagordo (N.Mex.) Sch. System, 1973-74; data svcs. supr. A.M. Best Co., Oldwick, N.J., 1975-78; assoc. mgr. AT&T Communications, Piscataway, N.J., 1978-86; mgr. AT&T Info. Mgmt. Svcs., Piscataway, N.J., 1986-90, AT&T Bus. Comm. Svcs., Somerset, N.J., 1990-91; mem. tech. staff AT&T Network Systems, Berkeley Heights, N.J., 1991-95, Lucent Techs., Warren, N.J., 1995-96; mgr. AT&T, Morristown, NJ, 1996—98; retired. Sec. Cherry Hill (N.J.) Jaycettes, 1972-73; trustee Friends of Clarence Dillon Libr., Bedminster, N.J., sec., 1989-90, pres., 1990-92, mem., 1986-2000; mem. Far Hills Environ. Commn., 1990-92, chmn., 1992-94; mem. Far Hills Planning Bd., 1994-2000, Wildewood Women's Club, 2000-, Computer Group, 2001-, Wildewood Garden Club, 2000-; mem. Symphony League, Columbia, SC, 2001-. Mem. IEEE, DAR (2d v.p. Columbia chpt. 2006—), Descendants of Washington's Army at Valley Forge (capt. of the guard 1988-90, dep. adjutant gen. 1990-92, adjutant gen. 1992-96), Kappa Delta Pi. Presbyterian. Home: PO Box 23329 Columbia SC 29224

BARNWELL, ADRIENNE KNOX, pediatric psychologist; b. Elkhart, Ind., Jan. 31, 1938; d. Everett K. and Arlyne F. (Miller) Knox; m. Franklin H. Barnwell, June 13, 1959; 1 child, Elizabeth B. BS, Northwestern U., 1959, MA, 1962, PhD, 1965. Lic. psychologist, Minn. Vis. prof. Northwestern U., Evanston, Ill., 1967-70, Hamline U., St. Paul, 1971-73; dir. pediatric psychology dept. pediatrics St. Paul Ramsey Med. Ctr., 1971-88; dir. child and family svcs. Gillette Children's Hosp., St. Paul, 1987—2003, lead psychologist, 2003—. Cons. St. Paul Rehab. Ctr., 1974-82, East Communities Family Svcs., Maplewood, Minn., 1983-92, Alpha Phase Program, 1992-97; rsch. assoc. pediatrics and psychiatry U. Minn., 1976—, clin. asst. prof. psychology, 1976-2003. Mem. APA, N.Y. Acad. Sci., Soc. Pediatric Psychology, Am. Soc. Clin. Hypnosis. Home: 2015 Kenwood Pky Minneapolis MN 55405-2304 Office: Gillette Children's Hosp 200 University Ave E Saint Paul MN 55101-2598 Business E-Mail: abarnwel@gillettechildrens.com.

BAROLINI, TEODOLINDA, literary critic; b. Syracuse, NY, Dec. 19, 1951; d. Antonio and Helen (Mollica) B.; m. Douglas Gardner Caverly, June 21, 1980 (dec. Nov. 1993); 1 child: William Douglas; m. James J. Valentini, Feb. 10, 2001. BA, Sarah Lawrence Coll., Bronxville, N.Y., 1972; MA, Columbia U., N.Y.C., 1973, PhD, 1978. Asst. prof. Italian U. Calif., Berkeley, 1978-83; assoc. prof. Italian NYU, 1983-89; prof., 1989-92; chmn. dept. Italian Columbia U., N.Y.C., 1992—2004, Lorenzo Da Ponte prof. Italian, 1999—. Author: Dante's Poets, 1984, transl. into Italian as Il miglior fabbro 1993, (Howard R. Marraro prize MLA 1986, John Nicholas Brown prize Medieval Acad. Am. 1988), The Undivine Comedy, 1992, transl. into Italian as La commedia senza Dio, 2003, Dante and the Origins of Italian Literary Culture, 2006; co-editor: (with H.W. Storey) Dante for the New Millennium, 2003; editor: Medieval Constructions in Gender and Identity, 2005; contbr. articles to profl. jours. AAUW fellow, 1977, ACLS fellow, 1981, NEH fellow, 1986, Guggenheim fellow, 1998. Fellow Medieval Acad. Am., Am. Acad.

Arts and Scis., Am. Philos. Soc.; mem. MLA, Dante Soc. Am. (v.p. 1983-86, 91-94, 95-97, pres. 1997-2003), Renaissance Soc. Am. Office: Columbia U Dept Italian 510 Hamilton Hall New York NY 10027 Business E-Mail: tb27@columbia.edu.

BARON, IRENE JO, secondary school educator, artist, aerial photographer; b. Cleve., Oct. 6, 1938; d. Herbert Herman and Lois Marie (Moore); m. Jacques A. Baron, Feb. 28, 1968 (div. 1981); 1 child, Dominique Michelle. BA, Hiram Coll., 1960; MEd, Ohio U., 1990; postgrad., Tex. A&M U., 1964, Coll. of LaVerne, 1980. Cert. tchr., Ohio. Tchr., Los Angeles and Newark, Ohio, 1960-66; info. specialist Battelle Meml. Inst., Bangkok, 1966-70; tchr., dept. chmn. Office Sec. of Def., Kaiserslautern, Fed. Republic Germany, 1970-72; tchr. various pub. schs., Minn., 1979-81, Zanesville, Ohio, 1981—. Instr. ARC swimming, canoeing, sailing, first aid, Zanesville and Bangkok, 1955-70, dir. water safety, Muskingum County, 1964-66; mem. Nat. Ski Patrol, 1964-66; owner Aerial View Pictures. Author: Close Proximity of Rainbows, 1987; artist numerous paintings, 1950—. Trustee West Muskingum Acad. Fund, Zanesville, 1982-87. Recipient Ednl. award Rogge Meml. Found., 1984; named one of Outstanding Young Women of Am., 1971. Mem. NEA, Nat. Sci. Tchrs. Assn., Ohio Edn. Assn., West Muskingum Edn. Assn., Sci. Edn. Coun. Ohio, Ohio Acad. Sci., Hiram Coll. Alumni Assn. (Outstanding Achievement award 1988), Authors Club, Profl. Aerial Photographers Assn. Internat., Phi Delta Kappa. Achievements include Nat. award winning aerial photographer through Smithsonian Mag. Avocations: author, white water rafting, pilot. Home: 705 Overland Ave Wilmington DE 19804

BARON, SHERI, advertising agency executive; b. Bklyn., Sept. 3, 1955; d. Irwin Murray Glaser and Rosalind (Mendelson) Krasik; m. Peter T. Colonel, Sept. 20, 1981 (dec.); m. Alan R. Baron, Dec. 14, 1996. BA in Psychology, SUNY, Courtland, 1977. Account exec. Ted Bates Co., N.Y.C., 1978-80, SSC&B Advt. (name now Lowe), N.Y.C., 1980-82, v.p. acct. supr., 1983-84, sr. v.p. mgmt. supr., 1984-88, exec. v.p., 1988-94, bd. dirs., 1990-94; pres., COO, chief strategic officer Gotham Inc., 1994—. Named to Am. Advt. Fedn. Hall of Achievement, 1993, 40 Under 40 List, Crain's N.Y. bus., 1994. Mem. Advt. Women N.Y., Cosmetic Exec. Women, Fashion Group Internat. Office: Gotham Inc 100 5th Ave Fl 16 New York NY 10011-6996 Home: 4 Glendcare Rd Upper Saddle River NJ 07458 Business E-Mail: sherib@gothaminc.com.

BARON, SUSAN, publishing executive; BA, Carnegie Mellon Univ. Sr. leadership positions Reader's Digest, Pleasantville, NY, Family Circle, NYC, McCalls Mag.; sr. leadership positions, Integrated Mktg., Am. Baby Group, Hispanic Ventures Meredith Corp., 2002—06, pub., Parents Mag., 2006—. Office: Parents Mag Meredith Corp 125 Park Ave New York NY 10017-5529*

BARONE, ANGELA MARIA, artist, researcher; b. Concesio, Brescia, Italy, June 29, 1957; arrived in U.S., 1983; d. Giuseppe and Adelmina (D'Ercole) Barone. Laurea cum laude in geol. scis., U. Bologna, Italy, 1981; PhD in Marine Geology, Columbia U., 1989; cert. in profl. photography, N.Y. Inst. Photography, 1992; cert. in fine art painting and drawing, N. Light Art Sch., Cin., 1993. Collaborative asst. Marine Geology Inst., Bologna, 1981-83, Inst. Geology and Paleontology, Florence, Italy, 1982-83, Sta. de Geodynamique, Villefranche, France, 1982; grad. rsch. asst. Lamont-Doherty Geol. Obs., Palisades, NY, 1983-89, postdoctoral rsch. asst., 1989; postgrad. rschr. Scripps Instn. of Oceanography, La Jolla, Calif., 1990-92; artist San Diego, 1993—. Contbr. articles to profl. jours. Mem.: Am. Geophys. Union (co-pres. meeting session 1990), Nat. Mus. Women Arts (assoc.). Office Phone: 858-453-6417.

BARONE, JESSICA LYNN, geology educator; BA in Geol. Scis., SUNY, Geneseo, 1997; MS in Geology, Ball State U., Muncie, Ind., 2000. Undergrad. tchg. asst. SUNY Geneseo, 1996—97; grad. tchg. asst. Ball State U., 1997—99; geologic field technician Lee & Ryan Environ. Consulting, Muncie, 1999—2000; adj. prof. Ball State U., 2000—01; asst. prof. geology Monroe C.C., Rochester, NY, 2001—. Undergrad. rsch. grantee, SUNY Geneseo, 1996, grad. rsch. grantee, Am. Assn. Petroleum Geologists, 1999, Ky. Geol. Survey, 1999. Achievements include petrological and geochemical analysis of mine spoil to determine the source of high-MG groundwater, Star Fire Mine, Kentucky. Home: 19 Portsmouth Ter # 7 Rochester NY 14607 Office: Monroe CC 1000 E Henrietta Rd Rochester NY 14623 Office Phone: 585-292-2448.

BARONE, KRISTEN THERESE, elementary school educator; b. Reading, Pa., Aug. 28, 1982; d. Deborah Ann and John Anthony Barone. BS, Lebanon Valley Coll., Annville, Pa., 2004. Elem. music tchr. Frederick County Pub. Sch. Dist., Frederick, Md., 2004—. Choir dir. Frederick (Md.) County Pub. Sch. Dist., 2004—; piano instr. Keyboard World, Hagerstown, Md., 2005—. Grantee, Frederick Cmty. Found., 2005—06. Mem.: Orff Schulwerk. Roman Catholic. Avocations: tennis, running, travel, singing. Home: 1018 Queen Anne's Ct Hagerstown MD 21740 Office: Parkway Elem 300 Carroll Pkwy Frederick MD 21701 Office Phone: 240-236-2627.

BARONE, ROSE MARIE PACE, writer, retired educator; b. Buffalo, Apr. 26, 1920; d. Dominic and Jennie (Zagara) Pace; m. John Barone, Aug. 23, 1947 BA, U. Buffalo, 1943; MS, U. So. Cal., 1950; cert. advanced study, Fairfield U., Conn., 1963. Tchr. Angola (N.Y.) High Sch., 1943-46, Puente (Calif.) High Sch., 1946-47, Jefferson High Sch., Lafayette, Ind., 1947-50; dir. Warren Inst., Bridgeport, Conn., 1951-53; instr. U. Bridgeport, 1953-54; tchr. bus. subjects Bassick H.S., Bridgeport, 1954-74, Harding H.S., Bridgeport, 1974-80; instr. Fairfield U., Conn., 1969; freelance writer, 1980—. Chair State Poetry Festival, 1987. Founder Pet Rescue; chmn. comty. affairs com. Area Coun. Cath. Women, 1988-90, sec., 1990-91, chmn. family affairs com., 1991, v.p., 1992-93; chmn. comty. affairs Ch. Women United, 1992—, state area chmn., 1995-97, sec., 2003, state UN chair, 1997—. Pace-Barone Minority yearly scholarship Fairfield U., Auerbach Found. scholar, 1956; recipient Playwriting prize Conn. Federated Women's Clubs, 1955, 1st prize for poetry, 1985, Short Story award Federated Women Conn., 1987, 88, 90, Citizen award Bridgeport Dental Assn., 1982, State/Town Hero award, 1986, Anniversary medal and marble statuette Fairfield U., Cmty. Care Successful Aging award, 1992, Salute to Women award YWCA, 1993, Woman of Substance award, 1994, State Commission Arts award, 2000, RSVP award, 2001. Mem. NEA, AAUW (treas. 1957-58, named gift grant 1989, cultural and poetry chair 1992—, rec. sec. 1992-93, internat. rels. 1993-94, v.p. program 1995-97, contest chair 1995—, Conf. of Women award 1997, Fairfield Citizen, Vol. Extraordinaire, 2001), Am. Assn. Ret. People (v.p. 1987-88, pres. 1988-89, 94-95, instr. 55 Alive, cmty. affairs chair 1990—), Owl (sec. 1987-89, pres. 1989-90), Nat. League Am. PEN Women (Bridgeport historian 1966-84, state historian 1983—, treas. br. 1985-88, state pres. 1986-88, state lit. chair 1988-95, br. membership chair 1990, Nat. Historian award 1976, 88), Fairfield Area Poets (founder, pres. 1990—, editor 5 vols. Conn. poets), UN Assn. USA (pres. Bridgeport 1964-66, 68-70, v.p. 1988—, chmn. area UN Days 1960—, pres. Conn. 1971—, state chmn. UNICEF to 1984, area UNICEF Ctr. 1984—, state historian 1984—, chair Internat. Kite Fly), Conn. Bus. Tchrs., Bridgeport Edn. Assn. (sec. 1966-68), VFW (aux. 1989—), Am. Legion (aux. contest chair 1989—, historian 1993-95, Aux. Nat. Cmty. Svc. award 1993), Fairfield Arts Coun., Fairfield Philatelic Soc. (sec. 1971-78, founder advisor Philatelic Jrs. 1972-80), Fairfield U. Women's Club (founder, pres. 1950, 74—, v.p. 1973-74), Southport Women's Club (garden dept. sec. 1981-85, chmn. 1985-87), John & Rose Marie Barone Resource Ctr. St. Vincent's Coll., Pi Omega Pi. Home: 1283 Round Hill Rd Fairfield CT 06430-7329

BARONE, SHERRY JOY, test engineer; b. Phila., June 23, 1960; d. Leonard and Linda Gwen (Berger) B. BS, U. Md., 1982; MBA summa cum laude, Nat. U., 1985. Registered profl. engr. Computer programmer Office Instl. Studies, U. Md., College Park, 1982; lead software engr. RCA Astro-Electronics, Princeton, N.J., 1982-83; sr. test engr. ITT Gilfillan, Van Nuys, Calif., 1983-87; sr. project engr. Hughes Aircraft/Raytheon, L.A., 1987—. Cons. AMJ Acctg. Firm, L.A., 1984-85, IBM, L.A., 1985—. Author: (with others) Children and Computer, 1982. Mem. IEEE, Am. Computing Machinery Club, Soc. Women Engrs., Soc. Test Engrs., Gilfillan Mgmt. Assn., ITT Ski Club (Van Nuys). Democrat. Jewish. Avocations: east asian history, art, sports. Office: PO Box 92426 Los Angeles CA 90009-2426 Office Phone: 310-446-7407. E-mail: sjbarone@raytheon.com, seasidecon@aol.com.

BARON-MALKIN, PHYLLIS, artist, educator; b. Newark, Apr. 15, 1927; d. Jack and Sadie Green; m. Milton Malkin (div.); m. Murray Baron; children: Kim, Robin, Jacki, Dara. Student, Culinary Sch. N.Y., 1947, Nat. Acad. Design, N.Y.C., 1970—76, Sch. Interior Design, Miami, Fla., 1978. Owner, designer Kirojada Sugar Creations, 1960—70; prin., owner Dade County Taxi, 1961—78, Jewelers, Ft. Lauderdale, Fla. Judge numerous art shows; ran outdoor art shows. Exhibited in group shows at Internat. Fine Arts Exhibit, Calif., Nat. Acad. Design, 1970—76, Newark Pub. Libr., Lever House, N.Y., Bernardsville State Show, Salmagundi Club, Nat. Arts Club, Miniature Show N.J., Catherine Larriland Wolfe Club, N.Y., Coun. Jewish Women, Teaneck, N.J., Greenwich Village, N.J. State Show, East Orange, Audonbon Show, Newark Mus., Jersey City Mus., one-woman shows include South Orange Gallery, N.J., Originique Gallery, Korby Gallery, Bloomfield Gallery, Delaney Gallery, Ft. Lauderdale, Tattum Gallery, represented in numerous pvt. collections. Apptd. Broward County Art Coun.; mem. arts counsel Broward County, 1974. With Air Svc. Command, 1945—46. Mem.: Nat. Pastel Soc. (selected to form organization). Democrat. Achievements include paintings being hung in galleries and private collections in Europe and nationwide in the U.S. Home: 7042 Golf Pointe Cir Tamarac FL 33321

BARR, ANN HELEN, director; d. John Roger and Hester Ann (Davis) Barr. B in Music Edn., Coll. Wooster, 1964; MA in Music Edn., UCLA, 1972. Tchr. music Huber Heights (Ohio) Schs., 1964—67; reconciliation specialist Merrill Lynch Pierce, Fenner & Smith, LA, 1968—72; tchr. Dayton (Ohio) Pub. Sch., 1978—98; flight dir. Challenger Learning Ctr., Dayton, 1998—2000, lead flight dir., 2000—. Hunger fund chair Westminster Presbyn. Ch., Dayton, 1984—; mem. Westminster Choir. Named Aerospace Tchr. of Yr. in Ohio, AFA, 2004; recipient 1000 mission award, Challenger Ctr., 2004; Kettering Found. grantee, 1983, Electronic Data Sys. grantee, 1999. Mem.: Civil Air Patrol, White Shrine of Jerusalem (worthy high priestess 1984). Avocations: gardening, travel, quilting, bridge, softball. Office: Challenger Learning Ctr 1401 Leo St Dayton OH 45404 Office Phone: 937-542-6196. Personal E-mail: ahbarr@juno.com. Business E-Mail: abarr@dps.k12.oh.us.

BARR, EMILY L., broadcast executive; BA in Film Studies, Carleton Coll., 1980; MBA in Mktg., George Washington U., 1986. News editor KSTP-TV, St. Paul, Minn., 1980-81, news promotion specialist, 1981-82; writer, prodr. WJLA-TV, Washington, 1983-85; advtg. & promotion mgr. KHOU-TV, Houston, 1985-87, dir. creative svcs., 1987-88; dir. broadcast ops. WMAR-TV, Balt., 1988-93, acting gen. mgr., 1993, asst. gen. mgr., 1993-94; pres., gen. mgr. Sta. WTVD, Raleigh, N.C., 1994-97, Sta. WLS-TV, Chgo., 1997—. Grad. leadership program Greater Balt. Com., 1990; active NAPTE, 1988—, BPME, 1983-93, CBS Promotion Caucus, 1987-88. Vol. Mus. Broadcast Comms.; bd. dirs. United Cerebral Palsy-Chgo., Children's Meml. Hosp. Found.; commr. Chgo. State St. Commn. Recipient Dante award Joint Civic com. for Italian Americans, 1998. Mem. Ill. Broadcast Assn., Chgo./Midwest TV Acad., Chgo. C. of C. (bd. dirs.), Chgo. Cen. Area Com. (bd. dirs.). Office: 190 N State St Chicago IL 60601-3302

BARR, GINGER, business owner, former state legislator; b. Kansas City, Mo., Dec. 4, 1947; d. W.M. and Ann (Armstrong) Barr; m. Edwin P. Carpenter, Jan. 2, 1984. BS, Baker U., Baldwin, Kans., 1969. Tchr. secondary edn., 1969-71; cemetery mgmt. Topeka Cemetery, Kans., 1971-76, Maplewood/Meml. Lawn Cemeteries, 1973-80, v.p., Graceland/Fairlawn Cemeteries, Decatur, Ill., 1976-94, pres., 1994—. Rep. Kans. State Legislature, 1983-91, vice chmn. fed. and state affairs com., 1987-89, chmn., 1989-91; pres. Crifter Care Co., 1987—; bd. dirs. World Topeka Famous Zoo, 1986-91, Humane Soc., Topeka, 1983-87, Shawnee County Mainstream Coalition, edn. chmn, 1995—; mem. Jr. League, Topeka, 1985; trustee Baker U., 1986-90; v.p. Topeka Blood Bank, 1991-93, pres., 1992, 93; active Auburn Community Action Project, 1993. Mem. Am. Cemetery Assn. (dir. 1980-82, sec. 1980-83), Kans. Cemetery Assn. (pres. 1979-80), Kans. Young Reps. (chmn. 1977-79), Ill. Cemetery Assn. (bd. dirs. 1994-95, v.p. 1995, pres. 1996). Republican. Home: 9421 SW Hoch Rd Auburn KS 66402-9664

BARR, JOYCE A., ambassador; BA magna cum laude, Pacific Lutheran U.; MPA, Harvard U.; MS in Nat.l Resource Strategy, Industrial Coll. of Armed Forces. Joined Fgn. Svc., US Dept. State, 1979, assigned to Stockholm, 1980, Budapest, 1982, 1985, Khartoum, Sudan, 1989, Ashgabat, Turkmenistan, 1998, counselor for mgmt. affairs Kuala Lumpur, Malaysia, sr. watch officer, US amb. to Republic of Namibia, 2004—. Legis. asst. to Senator Daniel Patrick Moynihan and Congressman Bennie G. Thompson. US Congress; post mgmt. officer Bur. of East Asia and Pacific Affairs; recruitment officer Bur. of Personnel; human rights officer Middle East and South Asia, Bur. of Human Rights and Humanitarian Affairs; desk officer US Industrial Develop. Orgn. and the World Tourism Orgn. Office: US Embassy in Namibia 2540 Windhoek Washington DC 20521-2540

BARR, LOIS FAYE, public relations executive, freelance/self-employed writer; b. Seward, Alaska, July 24, 1941; d. James Clyde and Martha Henrietta (Hanson) Barr. BJ, U. Mo., 1963. With Salt Lake Tribune, 1963—66; state desk reporter Bay City Times, Mich., 1966—67; copywriter Sta. KTLN, Denver, 1967; reporter Denver Post, 1967—73; dir. pub. rels. Keystone Resort div. Ralston Purina Co., Keystone, Colo., 1975—80; publicist MGM Grand Hotel, Reno, 1981—82; dir. pub. rels. The Westin Hotel, Vail, Colo., 1982—83; pub. rels. cons. Kinzley-Hughes, Inc., 1985—86; owner Barr None Enterprises, 1986—. Home: 1818 Marion St # 701 Denver CO 80218 Office Phone: 720-305-1652. Personal E-mail: sm0054@yahoo.com.

BARR, MARILYN G., school system administrator; b. Potsdam, NY; d. Merrill Blount and Gertrude Evelyn (Rutherford) Dollinger; m. Donald H. Barr, Sept. 20, 1975; children: Matthew, Jeffrey. AAS in Bus., SUNY, Canton, 1973; BA in History, SUNY, Brockport, 1986, EdM, 1988; CAS in Sch. Adminstrn., SUNY, Oswego, 2001. Tchr. history Rush Henrietta Ctrl. Sch., Henrietta, NY, 1987—2000, dir. curriculum, 2000—05; asst. supt. instrn Clyde Savannah Ctrl. Sch., Clyde, 2005—06, supt., 2006—. Office: Clyde Savannah Ctrl Sch 215 Glasgow St Clyde NY 14433-1299

BARR, MARLENE JOY, volunteer; b. Grosse Pointe Farms, Mich., Feb. 25, 1935; d. Max John and Viola Christina (Funke) Bielenberg; m. John Monte Barr, Dec. 17, 1954; children: John Monte Jr., Karl Alexander, Elizabeth Marie Letter. Student, Mexico City Coll., 1955; BA, Mich. State U., 1956; MA, Ea. Mich. U., 1959. Cert. elem. tchr. Tchr. A.G. Erickson Sch., Ypsilanti, Mich., 1956-66; chair 5th grade tchrs., sec. curriculum coun. Ypsilanti Pub. Schs., 1961-66; receptionist Barr, Anhut, and Assoc., P.C., Ann Arbor, Mich., 1989-95; vol. Thrift Shop Assn. of Ypsilanti, 1969—; block coord. Ypsilanti Recycling, 1990—. Adv. coun. Fletcher Sch., 1980—81; v.p. Thrift Shop Assn., Ypsilanti, 1979—81, pres., 1981—83, 2002, scheduling chmn., 1993—96, chmn. nominating com., 1998—99; asst. leader Girl Scouts U.S., 1978—81; sec. troop 290 Boy Scouts Am., 1989—95, treas., 2000—; rm. mother Fletcher Elem. Sch., Ypsilanti, 1982—83; chancel choir Emmanuel Luth. Ch., 1980—96, 1998—, youth coord., sec. youth standing com., 1983—89, ch. coun., 1986—90, sec. endowment com., 1995—96, chmn. ch. nominating com., 1999—2000; bd. dirs. Ypsilanti Cmty. Choir, 1984—; active High/Scope Ednl. Rsch. Fedn. Endowment Bd., 1993—96. Mem.: AAUW (life; chmn. gourmet arts study group 1968—), U.S. Power Squadron (Ann Arbor chpt.), Geneal. Soc. Wash. County, Law Wives of Washtenaw County (editor 1970—72), P.E.O. (chaplain 1991—93, chpt. pres. 1997—99, chmn. program com. 2000—01, treas. 2001—03, chmn. program com. 2004—05, v.p. 2005), Depot Town Assn., Ypsilanti Hist. Soc. (life), Marquette County Hist. Soc. (life), Friends of the Ypsilanti Dist. Libr., Ann Arbor Bike Touring Soc. (co-chair One Hell of a Ride 1995), Chandler Birthday Club (treas. 1990), Ladies Lit. Club (corr. sec. 1976—78, sec. bd. trustees 1982—86, v.p. 1986—90, pres. 1990—92, treas. bd. trustees 1992—97), Ann Arbor Women's City Club (life; chmn. ways and means com. 1995—97, chmn. Home Tour 1996—97, asst. mem. chmn. 1998—99, chmn. mem. com. 1999—2000, nominating com. 2000, chmn. Home Tour 2001, chmn. mem. com. 2001—02, nominating com. 2002), Alpha Delta Kappa (pres. Beta Zeta chpt. 1965—68, pres. Area X Pres. Coun. Mich. chpt. 1966—68, historian 1986—88, chmn. ways and means com. 1994—96, co-historian 2002—04, chmn. altruistic com. 2004—06, chmn. 40th anniversary celebration, chmn. geneology). Lutheran. Avocations: skiing, bicycling, hiking, boating, genealogy.

BARR, MARY JEANETTE, art educator; b. Chgo., Dec. 30, 1928; d. George Leonard and Leonore Loretto (Marsicano) Tompkins; m. David Harper Barr, Aug. 28, 1954; children: Michael, Nadine, Thomas, Ellen. BS, Ill. State U., 1971, MS, 1981, EdD, 1988. Art specialist teaching cert. K-12, Ill. Art specialist K-8 Chester-East Lincoln Sch. Dist. #61, Lincoln, Ill., 1971-74, Lincoln Elem. Sch. Dist. #27, 1974-80; instr. art edn. Ill. State U., Normal, 1980-85; prin. Carroll Elem. Sch., Lincoln, 1985-87; prof. art edn. Wichita (Kans.) State U., 1988-90, U. of West Ga., Carrollton, 1990—. Art tchr. Lincoln Recreation Dept., summers, 1975-79, Carrollton Cultural Arts Ctr., summers, 2000-05; writer grant Arts in Gen. Edn. program Lincoln Elem. Sch. Dist. 27, 1979-80; presenter tchr. inst. workshops Ill. State Bd. Edn., 1980-83; mem. Ill. Curriculum Coun., Ill. State Bd. Edn., 1982-88, sec., 1987; panelist gen. meeting Ill. Assn. Art Educators State Conf., Peoria, 1984; workshop participant Getty Ctr. Edn. in the Arts, Cin., 1993; judge numerous profl. and amateur art shows. Author: (with Michael Youngblood) Illinois Art Education Association Position Paper on Art Education, 1987; The Illinois Curriculum Council: Visions and Directions, 1988; contbr.: Art Activities for the Handicapped, 1982. Float designer/parade Jr. Women's Club, Lincoln, 1974-80; chmn. mural C. of C., Lincoln, 1980; festival presenter Carrollton Elem. Schs., 1993, 94; judge H.S. art show U.S. Rep. Darden, Carrollton, 1993, Dallas, Ga., 1994, Gov.'s Honors Art Show, Carrollton, 2002. Recipient Ada Bell Clark Welsh Scholarship Ill. State U., 1984, Exemplary Svc. award Ill. State U. Student Elem. Edn. Bd., Ill. State U., 1985. Mem. ASCD, AAUP, Nat. Art Edn. Assn. (Tchr. of Yr. 1984), Assn. Tchr. Educators, Found. Internat. Cooperation (chpt. chair 1963—), Ga. Art Edn. Assn. (bd. mem. ret. tchrs. 1998-2005, Higher Edn. Tchr. of Yr. 1994). Roman Catholic. Avocations: watercolor painting, walking, travel. Home: 110 Frances Pl Carrollton GA 30117-4332 Office: State Univ West Ga 1600 Maple St Carrollton GA 30118-0002

BARR, M.E. See BIGELOW, MARGARET

BARRAGÃN, CELIA SILGUERO, elementary school educator; b. Corcoran, Calif., Feb. 4, 1955; d. Frutoso Silguero and Olinda Gonzalez S.; m. Mario Barragãn Jr., Nov. 12, 1977; children: Maricela Aimē, Mario Armando. BS, S.W. Tex. State U., 1976, MA, 1977. 3rd grade tchr. Crockett Elem. Sch., San Marcos, Tex., 1977—78, Bowie Elem. Sch., San Marcos, 1978—84; 5th grade tchr. Travis Elem. Sch., San Marcos, 1984—94, Hernandez Intermediate Sch., San Marcos, 1994—99; asst. prin., bilingual coord. Bonham Elem. Sch., San Marcos, 1985—86, title I reading tchr., trainer, cons., 1995—99; coord., tchr. AVID Miller Jr. H.S., San Marcos, Tex., 1999—2000; ESL/Dyslexia tchr. Miller Jr. High, 2000—01; ESL/dyslexia tchr. Goodnight Jr. H.S., 2001—04; 4th grade bilingual tchr. Comal Intermediate Sch., New Braunfels, Tex., 2004—, 5th/6th grade bilingual/ESL tchr., 2005—06; 5th grade bilingual tchr. Frazier Elem., 2006—. Winter High ability program tchr. S.W. Tex. State U.; project math trainer, migrant tchr., Princeville, Ill.; mem. Tomas Rivera Mex. Am. Children's Book award com. Tex. State U., San Marcos; cons., nat. trainer Lang. Cir. Project Read, Minn. Recipient Latino award for cmty. recognition S.W. Tex. State U.; named Tchr. of Yr., Canyon Intermediate Sch., 2005 Mem. Internat. Reading Assn., Tex. Reading Assn., Tex. State Tchrs. Assn., Tex. Assn. Bilingual Edn., Tex. Classroom Tchrs. Assn., San Marcos (Tex.) Assn. Bilingual Edn. (v.p. 1990-91, 94—, pres. 1995—, Bilingual Tchr. of Yr. 1991, Travis Elem. Tchr. of Yr. 1993, Hernandez Intermediate Tchr. of Yr. 1995, Secondary Tchr. of Yr. 1995, Canyon Intermediate Tchr. of Yr. 2005, KENS 5 ExCel Tchr. of Yr. nominee, 2005), Orton Dyslexia Soc., Nat. Coun. Tchrs. Math., Nat. Assn. Bilingual Educators, Ill. Migrant Edn. Assn., Tex. Assn. Gifted and Talented, N.J. Writing Project, Assn. Comprehensive Edn. in Tex. Roman Catholic. Home: 1763 Loma Verde Dr New Braunfels TX 78130-1297 Office: Frazier Elem New Braunfels TX 78130 Office Phone: 830-221-2275. Business E-Mail: celia.barragan@comalisd.org.

BARRAGAN, LINDA DIANE, religious organization administrator; b. Oct. 14, 1950; BA summa cum laude, Bklyn. Coll., 1974. Ordained to ministry Ch. of Scientology, 1980. Pub. rels. dir. Ch. of Scientology N.Y., N.Y.C., 1974-82, pres., 1980-87, corp. dir., 1980-88, dir. spl. affairs, 1982—91; v.p. RC & A Inc., 1992—95, sr. v.p., 1995, RC & A Group, Inc., 1995—; deputy COO In Touch Media Group, Inc., 2005—. Dir. Task Force on Mental Retardation, N.Y. chpt., N.Y.C., 1974-76; vol. Narconon, N.Y.C., 1977; dir. Am. Citizens for Honesty in Govt., N.Y.C. chpt., 1979-82, Nat. Commn. on Law Enforcement and Social Justice, N.Y.C. chpt., 1976-79. Mem. Internat. Assn. Scientologists. Avocations: walking, reading, cooking, biking, movies.

BARRANGER, MILLY SLATER, theater educator, writer; b. Birmingham, Ala., Feb. 12, 1937; d. C. C. Slater and Mildred (Hilliard) Hinson; m. G. K. Barranger, 1961 (div. 1984); 1 child, Heather Dalton Barranger Case. BA, U. Montevallo, 1958; MA, Tulane U., 1959, PhD, 1964. Lectr. La. State U., New Orleans, 1964-69; asst. to assoc. prof. Tulane U., New Orleans, 1969-82, chmn. dept. theatre, 1971-82, Alumni disting. prof., 1997—2003, Alumni disting. prof. emerita, 2003—; prof. U. N.C., Chapel Hill, 1982—2003, chmn. dramatic art, 1982-99; producing dir. PlayMakers Repertory Co., Chapel Hill, 1982-99. Pres. Am. Theatre Assn., 1978-79; disting. vis. assoc. prof. U. Tulsa, 1981; vis. young prof. in humanities U. Tenn., Knoxville, 1981-82; scholar-in-residence Yale Sch. Drama, New Haven, Conn., 1982. Author: Theatre: A Way of Seeing, 1980, 1986, 1991, 1995, 2002, 2006, Theatre: Past and Present, 1984, rev. edit., 2001, Understanding Plays, 1990, 1994, 2004, Jessica Tandy, 1991, Margaret Webster, 1994, Margaret Webster: A Life in the Theater, 2004; co-editor: Generations: An Introduction to Drama, 1971, Notable Women in American Theatre, 1989; contbr. articles to profl. jours. Trustee The Paul Green Found., 1982—. Recipient New Orleans Bicentennial award for achievement in the arts, 1976, award for profl. achievement S.W. Theatre Conf., 1978, Pres.'s award U. Montevallo, 1979. Mem. Coll. of Fellows of the Am. Theatre (bd. dirs. 1998-2001); Nat. Theatre Conf. (pres. 1991-93), League Profl. Theatre Women. Avocations: films, travel.

BARRAZA, LUPE, retail executive; Dist. mcht. Brand Ctrl.; store mgr. Whittier Stores; with Sears, 1983—; v.p., in-store ops. Sears, Roebuck & Co. Chain and dept. store mgr. The Ed Hardy Team. Office: Sears Roebuck & Co 3333 Beverly Rd Hoffman Estates IL 60179 Office Phone: 847-286-2500. Office Fax: 847-286-7829.

BARRÉ, LAURA, finance company executive; b. 1973; With Smith Barney Unit Citigroup Inc., 1999; analyst Bank One Corp., 2000; CFO, private client svcs. J.P. Morgan Chase & Co., Chgo. Bd. dirs. Arts of Life, 2004—. Named one of 40 Under Foty, Crain's Bus. Chgo., 2005. Office: Bank One Private Client Svcs IL-0291 300 S Riverside Plz Chicago IL 60606*

BARREDO, RITA M., auditor; b. Torrington, Conn., June 24, 1953; d. Avelino and Josephine (DiNoia) B. BA, U. Conn., 1975; BS, Post Coll., 1981; MS in Acctg., U. Hartford, 1984, MBA, 1990. CPA Conn.; cert. info. sys. auditor; internal auditor, mgmt. acct., govt. auditing profl., cert. in homeland security, cert. info. tech. profl., diplomate Am. Bd. Forensic Accts., Am. Bd. Forensic Examiners. Timekeeper Timex Corp., Waterbury, Conn., 1976-85; auditor Def. Contract Audit Agy., Lowell, Mass., 1985—. Mem. AICPA, Am. Coll. Forensic Examiners, Am. Womens Soc. CPAs, Conn. Soc. CPA (continuing profl. edn. com. 1989-95, 97— social and recreation com.

1996-97), Inst. Mgmt. Accts. (sec. Waterbury chpt. 1994—), Inst. Internal Auditors, Info. Sys. Audit and Control Assn. Home: 130 Dawes Ave Torrington CT 06790-3627 Office: Def Contract Audit Agy 400 Main St East Hartford CT 06108-0968 Personal E-mail: rbarredo01@snet.net.

BARREIRO, VALERIE, choreographer, educator; b. San Juan, PR, Mar. 11, 1977; d. Jorge L. Barreiro and Irene Winchester. AA, Miami Dade Cmty. Coll., Fla.; BFA, New World Sch. of Arts, Miami. Dance tchr., choreographer DanceWorks, Miami, Fla., 1999—2006; dancer Univsion Prodns., Miami, 1998—2006; dance dir. SouthMiami Sr. Magnet Dance Program, Miami, 1999—2006; dancer Miami Heat Dancers, 2005—06; dance tchr. Dance Town Studios, 2006. Office: South Miami Sr High 6856 SW 53d St Miami FL 33155

BARRERA, ELVIRA PUIG, retired counselor, academic administrator; b. Alice, Tex., Dec. 11, 1943; d. Carlos Rogers and Delia Rebecca (Puig) B.; 1 child, Dennis Lee Jr BA, Incarnate Word Coll., 1971; M Counseling and Guidance, St. Mary's U., San Antonio, 1978; specialist degree marriage and family therapy, St. Mary's U., 1989. Lic. profl. counselor, marriage & family therapist, lic. chem. dependency counselor. Tchr. Edgewood Ind. Sch. Dist., San Antonio, 1965—74, Dallas Ind. Sch. Dist., 1971—72, Northside Ind. Sch. Dist., San Antonio, 1974; ednl. cons. Region 20-Edn. Svc. Ctr., San Antonio, 1974—79; coord. career edn. San Antonio Ind. Sch. Dist., 1979—84, counselor, 1984—91, vice prin., 1998—2005; ret., 2005. Cons. SBA, 1981, U.S. Office Edn., Washington, 1981-82, Tex. Edn. Agy., Austin, 1979-80; cons., writer San Antonio Ind. Sch. Dist. and Tex. Edn. Agy., 1985; cons. various edn. publs.; family coord. CATCH project U. Tex. Health Sci. Ctr., Houston, 1991-94; counselor Austin Ind. Sch. Dist., 1994-97, dist. transition counselor, 1997-98 Chairperson career awareness exploring divsn. Boy Scouts Am., 1982-87 Named Disting. Alumna, Incarnate Word Coll., 1983, Hall of Fame Internat. Profl. and Bus. Women, 1995; recipient Spurgeon award Boy Scouts Am., 1985, Merit award, 1986, Growth award, 1986 Mem. Am. Assn. Marriage and Family Therapy, San Antonio Hash House Harriers (treas. 1990-91), Incarnate Word Coll. Alumni Assn. (adv. bd. 1990—), St. Mary's U. Alumni Assn. (v.p. Austin alumni chpt. 2003—), The Harp and Shamrock Soc. Tex., Delta Kappa Gamma (Kappa Beta chpt. 2d v.p. 1982-84, 1st v.p. 1986-88, sec. 2005-06, pres. 2006-) Roman Catholic. Avocation: running. Home: 907 Aurora Cir Austin TX 78757-3415

BARRETT, BARBARA MCCONNELL, ranch owner, lawyer; b. Indiana County, Pa., Dec. 26, 1950; d. Robert Harvey and Betty (Dornheim) McC.; m. Craig R. Barrett, Jan. 19, 1985. BS, Ariz. State U., 1972, MPA, 1975, JD, 1978, LHD (hon.), 2000. Bar: Ariz. 1978, U.S. Dist. Ct. Ariz. 1979, U.S. Supreme Ct. Ariz. 1979. Atty. The Dial Corp., Phoenix, 1976-80; assoc. gen. counsel, asst. sec. Southwest Forest Industries, Inc., Phoenix, 1980-82; vice chmn. CAB, Washington, 1982-83, mem., 1983-84, vice chmn., 1984-85; ptnr. Evans, Kitchel & Jenckes, P.C., Phoenix, 1985-88, 1989; dep. adminstr. FAA, Washington, 1988-89; pvt. practice internat. bus. and aviation law Paradise Valley, Ariz., 1989—; pres., CEO American Mngmt. Assn., N.Y.C., 1997-98, Triple Creek Ranch, Mont., 1993—; fellow Inst. Politics, Kennedy Sch. Harvard U., 1999. Chmn. bd. dirs. Valley Bank Ariz., 1997-03; chmn. nominating com. The Lovelace Inst., 1995-99, U.S.-Afghan Women's Coun., 2003—, mem., chmn., US Adv. Commn. Pub. Diplomacy, 2003—, past mem. Adv. Com. on Women in the Svcs., nominated as Sec. USAF, 2003; treas. Asia-Pacific Econ. Cooperation Edn. Found., 1995-99; mem. exec. com., vice chairperson career opportunities subcom. US Dept. Def., 1989-93; mem. adv. com. Gov.'s Regional Airport, Pres.'s Adv. Com. on Trade Negotiations; mem. Adminstrv. Coun. US, 1982-85; chmn. US Sec. of Commerce Export Leaders Conf., 1988, Transp. Cluster Gov.'s Strategic Partnership for Econ. Devel., 1992-94; mem. Ariz. Disease Control Rsch. Commn., 1991-93, Bus. Coun., UN, 1997-98, Nat. Ctr. Polit. Analysis, 1997-98, Dean's Coun. of 100, Ariz. State U., 1998-, nat. campaign cabinet mem., Campaign for Leadership, 1999-2002, Def. Bus. Bd., 2003-; v.p. East Valley Partnership, 1992-94; v.p. Internat. Women's Forum, 1991-99, pres., 1999-01, mem. coun. fgn. rels., 1994—; mem. Phoenix Coun. Fgn. Rels., 1981; mem. steering com. Thunderbird Internat. Symposium, 1992-99; mem. global dispute resolution Global Ctr. Dispute Resolution, 1999—; mem. adv. bd. China Mist Tea Co., 1998-99, Harvard Leadership Bd., 1999-02; mem. corp. adv. bd., Pacific Coun. Internat. Policy, 1999-2001; bd. trustees, Irish Cultural and Learning Found., 2002-; mem. exec. com., heritage Found. Pres.'s Club, 2004-; bd. dirs. Samaritan Health Sys./Samaritan Charitable Trust, 1992-1998, Exponent, Inc., 1997-, Ctr. Internat. Pvt. Enterprise, 1998-, Nat. Legal Ctr. Pub. Interest, Ariz. Cmty. Found., 1999-2002, Ratheon, 1999-, Horatio Alger Assn., 2000-, Freedom House, 2001-, Nat. Constn. Ctr., 2001. Chmn. Ariz. Dist. Export Coun., 1985-92, Ronald W. Reagan Scholarship Program, mentor, 1984-86, Airshow Can. Symposium, 1989, 91; chmn. World Trade Ctr. Ariz., 1992-94, chmn. emerita; dir. class 11 program, 1979, United Way Valley of Sun, charter participant, 1979-80, alumni bd. dirs., bd. dirs. Bronze Soc., cabinet mem., co-chmn., 1990-93; bd. dirs. Samaritan Med. Found., 1981-83, grants and contracts com. chmn., 1985-98; bd. dirs. Nat. Air and Space Mus. Smithsonian Inst., 1988-89, Palms Clinic and Hosp. Corp., 1987-2000, Goldwater Inst., 1991-02; trustee, devel. com., chairperson Thunderbird Garvin Sch. Internat. Mgmt., Glendale, Ariz.; trustee, nominating and devel. com. Embry-Riddle Aeronaut. U., Prescott, Ariz., Daytona Beach, Fla., 1989-97; pres. World Affairs Ariz., 1987-88; vice chmn. Kid's Voting USA, 1991-98; dir., nominating com. chmn dir., ARC, 1993-98, past nominating com. chmn., 1994-96, past pub. support vice-chmn., 1996-98; candidate Gov. Ariz., 1994; trustee Lovelace Inst., 1995-99; vice regent, trustee George Washington's Fredericksburg Found., 1997—; pres. bd. Maricopa Colls. Found., 1997-98; adv. coun. mem., St. Mary's Food Bank, 1997-98; mem. Gov.'s Task Force Canamex Corridor, 1998-01; sr. adv. com. Inst. Politics, Harvard, 1999—; emeritus bd. mem., Maricopa Cmty. CC's Found., 2002-; adv. bd. mem., Boys Hope Girls Hope, 1999-, Our Mil. Kids, Inc., 2005-; global coun. mem., Internat. Mus. Women, 2004-. Named Woman of Yr., Ariz. State U., 1971, named to Hall of Fame, Coll. Pub. Programs, 1989, Coll. Liberal Arts, 1997; recipient Disting. Achievement award Ariz. State U., 1987, Coll. Bus., 1994, Woman Who Made a Difference award Internat. Women's Forum, 1988, Dick Cheney citation U.S. Sec. of Def., 1992, FAA Adminstr.'s award, 1989, Woman of the Yr. Network of Women in Hospitality, 1998, Horatio Alger award, 1999, Beta Gamma Nationwide Achievement award, 2000, Girl Scouts Today and Tomorrow award, 2000, Homeroom Hero award Teach for Am., 2002, Disting. Women's award Northwood U., 2001, Medal of Hon. DAR, 2003; named to Internat. Forest Friendship Hall of Fame, 2003; named one of 100 Women Who Made A Difference in Aviation, 2003; Dubois scholar, 1977. Mem. Am. Mgmt. Assn. (truste, chmn. exec. com., pres. N.Y.C. 1997-98, Lifetime Achievement award, 2002), Nat. Assn. Corp. Dirs. (faculty 1999, bd. dirs. 2000-02), Ariz. State U. Law Soc. (bd. govs. 1990-93), Ariz. State U. Found. (bd. dirs., program chair 1996—), Ariz. Women in Internat. Trade (bd. dirs., exec. com. 1987-93), Phoenix C. of C. (bd. dirs. 1987-93), Reagan Alumni Assn., Nat. Policy Forum, mem., Internat. Women's Forum (pres. 1982-), Nat. Assn. Women Judges (resource bd. mem. 2000-), Ariz. Women's Forum, Charter 100, Circumnavigators, Lewis and Clark Trail Heritage Found., Ariz. Acad., Ariz. State U. Alumni Assn., Network exec. Women in Hospitality, Women in Aviation, Internat., Women's Fgn. Policy Group, Women in Mil. Aviation, Econ. Club of Phoenix (past pres. 1990—).

BARRETT, CATHERINE L., state representative; b. Cin., June 14, 1941; married; 3 children. BA in Bus. Adminstrn., Union Inst., Cin.; grad., Ctr. Policy Alternatives Flemming Fellows Inst.; fellow, Coun. State Govts. Bowhay Inst. Legis. Leadership Devel. Former mayor, Forest Park, Ohio; state rep. dist. 32 Ohio Ho. of Reps., Columbus, 1998—, ranking minority mem., human svcs. subcom., edn. mem., health, and ins. coms. Past councilwoman Forest Park City Coun. Recipient Ohio Hunger Heroine award, Ohio Assn. 2d Harvest; Harvard JFK Sch. Govt. Sr. Execs. in State and Local Govt. fellow, Eleanor Roosevelt Global Leadership Inst. fellow. Mem.: LWV, Negro Women Coun., Ohio, Ky. and Ind. Regional Coun. Govts., Forest Park Bus. Assn., Cin. Woman's Polit. Caucus, Cin. C. of C., Forest Park Women's Club, Delta Sigma Theta. Democrat. Office: 77 S High St 10th fl Columbus OH 63215-6111

BARRETT, COLLEEN CROTTY, air transportation executive; b. Bellows Falls, Vt., Sept. 14, 1944; AA with highest honors, Becker Jr. Coll., 1964. Legal sec. Oppenheimer Rosenberg Kelleher & Wheatley, San Antonio, 1968—72, adminstrv. asst., paralegal, 1972—78; corp. sec. Southwest Airlines, Dallas, 1978—, exec. asst. to pres. and chmn., 1980—85, v.p. adminstrn., 1985—90, exec. v.p. customs, 1990—2001, pres., 2001—, COO, 2001—04. Bd. dirs. JC Penney Co., Southwest Airlines. Named one of Most Powerful Women, Forbes mag., 2005; recipient Horachio Alger award, 2004. Mem.: Leadership Tex. Roman Catholic. Office: SW Airlines Co PO Box 36611 Dallas TX 75235-1611 Office Phone: 214-792-4112. Business E-Mail: vickie.shuler@wnco.com.

BARRETT, ELIZABETH ANN MANHART, psychotherapist, consultant, nursing educator; b. Hume, Ill., July 11, 1934; d. Francis J. and Grace C. (Manhart) Fridy; children: Joseph B., Jeffrey F., Paula G. Brown, Pamela M. Temple, Scott D. BSN summa cum laude, U. Evansville, 1970, MA, 1973, MSN, 1976; grad., Gestalt Assocs. Psychotherapy, 1982; PhD in Nursing, NYU, 1983; grad., Am. Inst. for Mental Imagery, 1995. From instr. to asst. prof. nursing U. Evansville, Ind., 1970-76; staff nurse Welborn Bapt. Hosp., Evansville, 1975-76, Bellevue Psychiat. Hosp., N.Y.C., 1976-79; clin. tchr. CUNY, 1977-82; asst. prof. Adelphi U., 1979-80; group practice Nurse Healers, 1979-82; pvt. practice psychotherapy, 1980—. Nurse rschr. Mt. Sinai Med. Ctr., N.Y.C., 1982-86, asst. dir. nursing, 1983-86; assoc. prof. Hunter Coll., N.Y.C., 1986-89, prof., 1994-2001, prof. emerita, 2001—, dir. grad. studies, 1989-92, coord. Ctr. for Nursing Rsch., 1993-2001; cons. Internat. Soc. Univ. Nurses; co-chair adv. com. Martha E. Rogers Ctr. for Study of Nursing Svc., 1994-96; sec., treas. Am. Inst. for Mental Imagery, 2002—; com. mem. Regional Health Planning Coun., Evansville, 1974-77. Mem. editl. bd. Alt. Therapies in Health and Medicine, 1995—. Recipient Disting. Nursing Alumnus award NYU, 1994, Disting. Nurse Rschr. award Found. N.Y. State Nurses Assn., 1995. Fellow Am. Acad. Nursing; mem. ANA (cert. psychiat.-mental health), NOW, Nat. League Nursing, Ea. Nursing Rsch. Assn. (charter), Ea. Nursing Rsch. Soc., Soc. Rogerian Scholars (co-founder, 1st pres. 1988-90), Phi Kappa Phi, Sigma Theta Tau (Upsilon chpt. pres. 1986-88), Alpha Tau Delta, Sigma Xi. Home: 415 E 85th St Apt 9E New York NY 10028-6358 Office: 16 E 96th St Ste 1 A New York NY 10128 Office Phone: 917-371-7269. E-mail: eambarrett@nyc.rr.com.

BARRETT, JANE HAYES, lawyer; b. Dayton, Ohio, Dec. 13, 1947; d. Walter J. and Jane H. Barrett BA, Calif. State U.-Long Beach, 1969; JD, U. So. Calif., 1972. Bar: Calif. 1972, US Dist. Ct. (cen. dist.) Calif. 1972, US Ct. Appeals (9th cir.) 1982, US Supreme Ct. Assoc. Lawler, Felix & Hall, LA, 1972—84; ptnr. Arter & Hadden, 1984—94, DLA Piper, 2002, Morrison Foerster, 2006—; mng. ptnr. Preston, Gates & Ellis, 1994—2002. Lectr. bus. law Calif. State U., 1973-75. Mem. adv. bd. Harriet Buhai Legal Aid Ctr., 1991-96, mem. bd. pub. counsel, 1996-98; pres. Pilgrim Parents Orgn. 1990-91; chmn. fin. Our Mother Good Counsel Sch.; bd. regents Loyola, HS, 2000—; mem. adv. coun. Ctr. on Ethnic and Racial Diversity. Named Outstanding Grad. Calif. State U., Long Beach, 1988, Outstanding Alumnae Polit. Sci., 1993, So. Calif. Super Lawyer, LA Mag., 2003, 04, Best Lawyer in Am., 2006. Fellow Am. Bar Found.; mem. ABA (bd. govs. 1980-84, chmn. young lawyers divsn. 1980-81, com. on delivery of legal svcs. 1985-89, exec. coun. legal edn. and admissions sects. 1985-89, fin. sec. torts and ins. practice 1982-83, adv. mem. fed. judiciary com. 9th circuit rep. 2000-05, mem. minority and ethnic diversity bd., v.p. 1997—, Am. Bar Endowment 1999, bd. dirs. 1990—, sec. 1993-95, v.p. 1998-99, pres., 1999-00, bd. fellows young lawyers divsn. 1992—, del 9th cir. jud. conf., atty. del. US Dist. Ct. ctrl. dist. Calif. Atty. Conf. 2002-05, US Dist. Ct. Ctrl. Dist. Calif. (discipline com. 2004—, chair sect. com., admissions com. 2005—), 9th Cir. Atty. Conf. (del. 2005), Calif. State Bar (com. adminstrn. of justice, editl. bd. Calif. Lawyers 1981-84), Legion Lex (bd. dirs. 1990-93), Los Feliz Homeowners Assn. (bd. dirs.). Democrat. Office: Morrison Foerster 555 W 5th St Los Angeles CA 90013 Business E-Mail: jbarrett@mofo.com.

BARRETT, JANET TIDD, academic administrator; b. Crystal City, Mo., Nov. 29, 1939; d. Lewis Samuel and Mamie Lou (Hulvey) Tidd; m. David Clark Barrett, June 3, 1961; children: Barbara, Pam. Diploma in nursing, St. Lukes Hosp. Sch. Nursing, 1960; BSN with honors, Washington U., St. Louis, 1964, MSN, 1979; PhD, St. Louis U., 1987. Assoc. prof. Maryville Coll., St. Louis, 1979-89; acad. dean Barnes Coll., St. Louis, 1989-91; dir. BSN program Deaconess Coll. Nursing, St. Louis, 1991-2000, acad. dean, 2000—02; nursing cons., 2002—. Contbg. author to Beare and Meyers: Principles of Medical-Surgical Nursing; dancer with St. Louis Strutters, 2003-. St. Lukes Hosp. scholar; recipient Sister Agnita Claire Day Rsch. award St. Louis U.; named Ms. Mo. Sr. Am., 2005. Mem.: Mo. League Nursing, Nat. League Nursing, St. Luke's Alumni Assn., Pi Lambda Theta, Sigma Theta Tau. Personal E-mail: barretjan@hotmail.com, jtbarrett02@charter.net.

BARRETT, JESSICA (DONNA ANN NIPERT), psychotherapist; b. Paterson, NJ, July 25, 1952; d. Donald Alfred and Gloria Emma (Lustica) Nipert; m. John David Barrett, Sept. 9, 1977 (div. June 1982); 1 child, Ashley Elizabeth. BA, UCLA, 1975; MA, Azusa Pacific U., 1981. Lic. marriage, family, child therapist; cert. hypnosis profl. With employee relations Engrs. and Architects Exec. Assn., L.A., 1975-79; practicing psychotherapy Toluca Lake and Burbank, Calif., 1983—; instr., supr. Phillips Grad. Inst., Encino, Calif., 1986-2000; psychotherapist Pasadena (Calif.) Outpatient Eating Disorders Program, 1987-88. Cons. Texaco Employee Assistance Program, Studio City, 1985—86, NBC Employee Assistance Program, Burbank, 1986—87, Burbank, 1993—; spl. therapist United Behavioral Health, Managed Health Networks, Cigna Behavioral Health, 1989—, Value Options Provider, 1986—, Health Mgmt. Resource Svcs., 1985—99; assessment and referral liaison Nat. Resource Cons., San Diego, 1983—93, Employee Support Sys. Corp., Orange, Calif., 1985—, Health and Human Resource Ctr., 1984—92, Blue Cross Preferred Provider and EAP Network, 1995—, U.S. Behavioral Health, 1998—. Mem. Employee Assistance Profls. Assn. (bd. dirs. 1983-86), Am. Assn. Marriage and Family Therapists (clin. 1983—), Phillips Grad. Inst. Alumni Assn. (sec.-treas. 1987-88, v.p. programs 1988-89), Eye Movement Desensitization Reprocessing Internat. Assn. (charter, cert therapist). Avocations: theater, improvisational comedy, piano, literature, travel. Office Phone: 818-841-1159. E-mail: jestbareit@adelphia.net.

BARRETT, JUDITH ANN, salon owner; b. N.Y.C., Dec. 15, 1940; d. William Patrick and Eleanor Margaret (McClaurey) B. Grad., Aquinas H.S., 1958. Sec. Avon Products, N.Y.C., 1960-73; owner The Girl's Beauty Shop, Port Richey, Fla., 1974—2002. CEO, founder Enraged People Against Rape, Pasco, Fla., 1990-93; mem. adv. bd. Sexual Assault Victims Examination, Pasco County, 2003—; bd. dirs. Pasco County WAVES Unit, 2004—; vol. Hospice, 1999-2005. With USNR, 1969-72. Recipient Outstanding Contbrn. and Dedication to Fla Residents, U.S. Congress M. Bilirakis, Washington, 1992, Cmty. Svc. Pres. award Cmty. Svc. Coun. of W. Pasco, 1992, Humanitarian award Pasco County Sheriffs Dept., 1991-92, J.C. Penney Golden Rule award, 1996, Cmty. Hero award Pasco County, 1997; resolutions for outstanding contbn. to people of Pasco, Bd. Pasco County Commrs., 1999. Mem.: Waves Nat., 2d Amendment Rep. Club, West Pasco Rep. Club, Am. Legion. Republican. Roman Catholic. Avocations: tennis, writing, poetry.

BARRETT, KRISTA E., psychotherapist, educator; b. Chgo., July 19, 1967; d. Jack Arthur and Barbara Ann Barrett. BA in Psychology cum laude, U. Tex., Austin, 1988; MSW, Columbia U., 1991. Family and group therapist Ctr. for Family Counseling, Oakland, Calif., 1991—93; program therapist Heights Hosp., Albuquerque, 1993—95; program coord. children's unit Meml. Hosp., Albuquerque, 1995—98; pre-sch. social worker Albuquerque Pub. Schs., 1998—2003. Field instr. Highlands U. N. Mex., Albuquerque, 1995; psychotherapist, pvt. practice, Albuquerque, 1997—. Named Nat. Merit Scholar, 1998. Mem.: Harwood Art Ctr., Sand Tray Tng. Inst. N. Mex., Nat. Assn. Social Workers, N. Mex. Assn. for Play Therapy (charter bd., treas. 2000—02), Nat. Assn. for Play Therapy, Psi Chi. Avocations: printmaking, tai chi, yoga, Jungian analysis, digital video. Office Phone: 505-888-1121. Personal E-mail: kbeez1234@yahoo.com.

BARRETT, LIDA KITTRELL, mathematics professor; b. Houston, May 21, 1927; d. Pleasant Williams and Maidel (Baker) Kittrell; m. John Herbert Barrett, June 2, 1950 (dec. Jan. 1969); children: John Kittrell, Maidel Horn, Mary Louise. BA, Rice U., 1946; MA, U. Tex., Austin, 1949; PhD, U. Pa., 1954. Instr. math. U. Conn., Waterbury, 1955-56; vis. appointment U. Wis., Madison, 1959-60; lectr. U. Utah, Salt Lake City, 1956-61; assoc. prof. U. Tenn., Knoxville, 1961-70, prof., 1970-80, head math. dept., 1973-80; assoc. provost No. Ill. U., DeKalb, 1980-87; dean, arts and scis. Miss. State U., Mississippi State, 1987-91; sr. assoc. Edn. and Human Resources Directorate NSF, Washington, 1991-95; prof. math. U.S. Mil. Acad., West Point, NY, 1995-98; adj. prof. U. Tenn., 1998—2001. Math. and math. edn. cons., Knoxville, Tenn., 1964-80, 98—. Contbr. articles on topology, applied math. and math. edn. to profl. jours. Mem. Math. Assn. Am. (pres. 1989, 90), Am. Math. Soc., Soc. Indsl. and Applied Math., Nat. Coun. Tchrs. Math., Am. Assn. Higher Edn., Phi Kappa Phi, Sigma Xi. Episcopalian.

BARRETT, LINDA L., real estate consultant; b. Hudson, Mich., Aug. 16, 1948; d. David John and Georgia Elizabeth (Spengler) B.; m. Carl Gugino; 1 dau., Toni. Student, U. Mich., 1970—73. Cert. residential brokerage mgr. Sales mgr. Collins Real Estate, Hudson, Mich., 1973-79; owner, broker Homeland Real Estate, Lake Leann, Mich., 1979-82; mgr. broker Mid-Mich. Real Estate, Jackson, Mich., 1982-85; exec. v.p. Michael Saunders & Co., Sarasota, Fla., 1986-95, cons., 1995—. Adv. bd. Sotheby's Internat. Mem. Econ. Devel. Coun., Com. of 100; bd. dirs. Emerald Pointe. Mem. AAUW, NAFE, Internat. Real Estate Fedn., Nat. Mktg. Inst., Nat. Assn. Realtors, Fla. Assn. Realtors, Sarasota C. of C., Global Travel Internat. Network, 2000 Notable Am. Women, Econ. Devel. Coun., CRB, Holistic Options, Profl.'s Network Investment Orgn., Field Club, The Oaks, Longboat Key Club. Avocations: gardening, golf, yoga, travel, tai chi.

BARRETT, LOIS YVONNE, minister; b. Enid, Okla., Nov. 9, 1947; d. Hugh Preston and Audrey Lucille (Wilson) B.; m. Thomas Bruce Mierau, June 26, 1977; children: Barbara, Susanna, John. BA, U. Okla., 1969; MDiv, Mennonite Bibl. Sem., 1983; PhD, Union Grad. Sch., 1992. Ordained to Christian ministry, 1985. Assoc. editor The Mennonite, Newton, Kans., 1971-77; editor The House Ch. newsletter, Wichita, Kans., 1978-80, 83-85; instr. Great Plains Sem. Edn. Prog., North Newton, Kans., 1985, 90, 92; co-pastor Mennonite Ch. of the Servant, Wichita, Kans., 1983-92; exec. sec. Commn. Home Ministries Gen. Conf. Mennonite Ch., Newton, 1992—. Mem. exec. coun. Inst. Mennonite Studies, Elkhart, Ind., 1983—; mem. ecumenical peace theology working group Mennonite Cen. Com., Akron, Pa., 1988-92; writer Inter-Mennonite Confession of Faith com., 1988-95; editorial com. Mennonite Ency. V, 1985-87. Author: The Vision and the Reality, 1983, Building the House Church, 1986, The Way God Fights, 1987, Doing What is Right, 1989. Convener Chs. United for Peacemaking, Wichita, 1986, 88-89, bd. dirs., 1983-90; pres. Midtown Citizens Assn., 1977-78; mem. Citizens Participation Orgn., 1977-80. Recipient Am. Bible Soc. award, 1983. Mem. Am. Acad. Religion, Am. Soc. Ch. History, Phi Beta Kappa. Home: 1508 Fairview St Wichita KS 67203-2634 Office: Gen Conf Mennonite Ch Commn Home Ministries 722 N Main St Newton KS 67114-1819

BARRETT, LORA MCNEECE, art educator, artist; BA, Elms Coll., 1972; MEd, U. Mass., 1987, EdD, 1993. Lic. profl. tchr. Mass. Art tchr. Holyoke (Mass.) Pub. Schs., 1972—84, tchr. support team, 1984—89, dir. parent involvement, 1989—91, arts resource tchr., 1991—, art dept. head, 1996—. Asst. prof. U. Mass., Amherst, 1996—; signature mem. Cape Cod Plein Air Painters. Contbr. book Flower Teachers: Stories for a New Generation, 2002. Nominee Disting. Tchg. award, U. Mass., Amherst; named Mass. Visual Arts Educator of the Yr., Mass. Alliance for Arts in Edn., 2001. Mem.: NEA, Mass. Art Edn. Assn. (Mass. Mid. Sch. Art Tchr. of the Yr. 2002), Mass. Tchrs. Assn., Nat. Art Edn. Assn., Pastel Painters Soc. Cape Cod. Democrat. Avocation: pastel and oil painting. Office: FAC 438 Univ Mass Amherst MA

BARRETT, NANCY SMITH, academic administrator; b. Balt., Sept. 12, 1942; d. James Brady and Katherine (Pollard) Smith; children: Clark, Christopher. BA, Goucher Coll., 1963; MA, Harvard U., 1965, PhD, PhD, Harvard U., 1968. Dep. asst. dir. Congl. Budget Office, Washington, 1975-76; sr. staff Council of Econ. Advisors, Washington, 1977; prin. research assoc. The Urban Inst., Washington, 1977-79; dep. asst. sec. U.S. Dept. Labor, Washington, 1979-81; instr. Am. U., Washington, 1966-67, asst. prof. econs., 1967-70, assoc. prof., 1970-74, prof., 1974-89; dean Coll. of Bus. Adminstrn. Fairleigh Dickinson U., Teaneck, NJ, 1989-91; provost, v.p. acad. affairs Western Mich. U., Kalamazoo, 1991-96, U. Ala., Tuscaloosa, 1996—2003, Wayne State U., Detroit, 2003—. Author: Theory of Macroeconomic Policy, 1972, 2d rev. edit., 1975, Theory of Microeconomic Policy, 1974, (with G. Gerardi and T. Hart) Prices and Wages in U.S., 1974; contbr. articles on econs. to profl. jours. Woodrow Wilson fellow, 1963-64; Fulbright scholar, 1973. Mem.: Am. Econs. Assn., Phi Beta Kappa. Office: Wayne State Univ 4092 Faculty Adminstrn Bldg Detroit MI 48202 Home: 2033 Shorepointe Grosse Pointe Woods MI 48236 Office Phone: 313-577-2200. E-mail: nancy.barrett@wayne.edu.

BARRETT, PAULETTE SINGER, public relations executive; b. Paris, Dec. 20, 1937; came to U.S., 1947; d. Andrew M. and Agatha (Kinsbrunner) Singer; m. Laurence I. Barrett, Mar. 9, 1957 (div. 1983); children: Paul Meyer, David Allen, Adam Singer. BA, NYU, 1957; MS in Journalism, Columbia U., 1958. News dir. Yardney Electric Corp., N.Y.C., 1958-61; freelance writer newspapers and pub. relations orgns., N.Y.C. and Washington, 1961-73; assoc. dir. pub. info. Columbia U., N.Y.C., 1973-77; from account exec. to v.p., then sr. v.p. Edelman Pub. Rels. Worldwide, N.Y.C., 1977-80, sr. v.p. and gen. mgr., 1980, exec. v.p., gen. mgr., 1986-88, exec. v.p., dir. corp. affairs div., 1988-89; exec. v.p. Rowland Co., N.Y.C., 1980-82; exec. dir. communications UJA-Fedn./N.Y., N.Y.C., 1982-86; sr. v.p., mng. dir. Hill and Knowlton, Chgo., 1989-90; pres. Barrett Comm., Chgo. and N.Y.C., 1990—. Established The Barrett Workshops, tng. svcs., 1999—; comm. counsel The Barrett Group, 2002—. Pres. Found. of Women Execs. in Pub. Rels., 2003—. E-mail: paulettebarrett@earthlink.net.

BARRETT, SUSAN IRIS, actor, educator; b. Bklyn., Aug. 16, 1960; d. Albert and Martha Barshatzky. BA, Wagner Coll., Staten Is., NY, 1982; MA, U. Leeds, UK, 1986. Actor Playmakers Repertory Co., Chapel Hill, NC, 2005, 29th St. Repetoire, NYC, 1997—, various tv programs, 2003—04, Women's Theatre of NJ, 2003—05. Mem. Polaris North, NYC, 2003—. Vol. reader and prin. SAG Book, NYC, 2000—. Jewish. Avocations: painting, yoga, writing. Home: 312 West 48th ST #24 New York NY 10036

BARRETT, TINA, professional golfer; b. Balt., June 5, 1966; d. Barbara Smith; m. Dan Friedman, Nov. 27, 1993. BA cum laude, Longwood Coll., 1988. Winner Eastern Amateur, 1987, Md. State Amateur, 1988; golfer Ladies Pro Golf Assn., 1988—. Avocation: Baltimore Orioles and Pheonix Suns fan. Office: c/o LPGA 100 International Golf Dr Ste B Daytona Beach FL 32124-1082

BARRETT-CONNER, ELIZABETH, physician, medical educator; Grad., Mt. Holyoke Coll. Postdoctoral fellow in clin. medicine of the tropics London Sch. Hygiene and Tropical Medicine; mem. staff U. Minn., Johns Hopkins U., Balt.; chair dept. cmty. and family medicine U. Calif., San Diego. Office: U Calif San Diego 9500 Gilman Dr La Jolla CA 92093-5004

BARRETT-CONNOR, ELIZABETH LOUISE, epidemiologist, educator; b. Evanston, Ill., Apr. 8, 1935; m. James D. Connor; 3 children. BA in Zoology, Mt. Holyoke Coll., 1956; MD, Cornell U., 1960; DCMT in clin. medicine of tropics, London Sch. Hygiene and Tropical Medicine, 1965; DSc (hon.), Mt. Holyoke Coll., 1985; PhD (hon.), U. Utrecht, The Netherlands, 1996, U. Bergen, Norway, 1996, U. Helsinki, Finland, 2000. Diplomate Am. Bd. Internal Medicine, 1968, Nat. Bd. Med. Examiners, lic. Fla., 1965, Calif., 1970, cert. advanced epidemiology U. Minn., 1967, genetics Johns Hopkins U., 1968. Intern Parkland Meml. Hosp., Dallas, 1960—61, resident, 1961—63; resident infectious disease Jackson Meml. Hosp., Miami, Fla.,

1963—64; instr. medicine U. Miami, Fla., 1965-68, asst. prof. medicine Fla., 1968-70; asst. prof. community and family medicine U. Calif., San Diego, 1970-74, assoc. prof. community and family medicine, 1974-81, prof. community and family medicine, 1981—, acting chair dept. community and family medicine, 1981-82, chmn. dept. family and preventative medicine, 1982-97. Mem. hosp. infection control com. VA Med. Ctr., San Diego, 1971-81; Kelly West Meml. lectr. Am. Diabetes Assn., Indpls. 1987; vis. prof.Royal Soc. Medicine, London, 1989; John Rankin lectr. U. Wis., 1989; Don McLeod Meml. lectr., Halifax, N.S., Can., 1990; Elizabeth Blackwell lectr., Rochester, Minn., 1991; Lila Wallace vis. prof. N.Y. Hosp.-Cornell Med. Ctr., N.Y.C., 1992; Donald P. Shiley vis. lectr. Scripps Clinic and Rsch. Found., La Jolla, Calif., 1993; Leonard M. Schuman lectr. U. Mich., 1993; disting. vis. U. Western Australia, 1997; disting. lectr. geriatrics Duke U. Med. Ctr., Durham, N.C., 1998; Heath Clark lectr.,London, 1989, Pickering lectr., Cambridge, England, 2000. Contbr. articles to profl. jours. Recipient Frederick Murgatroyd prize, 1965, Kaiser award for excellence in tchg., 1982, Dr. of Yr. award San Diego Health Care Assn., 1987, merit award Nat. Inst. Aging, 1987, Making a Difference for Women's Health award Soroptimists, La Jolla, 9195, clin. svc. award Soc. for Advancement Women's Health Rsch., 1997, health award NIH, 1999, Stokes award Am. Soc. Preventative Cardiology, 2003; grantee NIH 1970—. Master: ACP (pubs. com. 1988—90, James D. Bruce Meml. award 1994); fellow: Am. Coll. Preventive Medicine (Katharine Boucot Sturgis lectr. 1986), Royal Soc. Medicine, Am. Coll. Nutrition, Am. Coll. Epidemiology (hon.), Royal Soc. Health, Am. Heart Assn. (chmn. budget com. coun. on epidemiology 1987—88, chmn. coun. on epidemiology 1989, Ancel Keys lectr. 1995, Elizabeth Barrett-Connor rsch. award 1995, Merit award 1998); mem.: APHA (chmn. epidemiology sect. 1989—90, Wade Hampton Frost lectr. 1993), Am. Soc. Preventive Medicine, N.Y. Acad. Scis., Internat. Bone and Mineral Soc., Am. Geriat. Soc., Am. Diabetes Assn., Western Assn. Physicians, Calif. Acad. of Preventative Medicine, Assn. Practitioners in Infection Control, Am. Soc. Tropical Medicine and Hygiene (emeritus), Internat. Epidemiol. Assn., Infectious Disease Soc. Am., Am. Fedn. Clin. Rsch., Am. Venereal Disease Assn. (v.p. 1977—78), Soc. Epidemiol. Rsch. (pres. 1983, Cassell Meml. lectr. 1997), Inst. Medicine, Assn. Tchrs. Preventive Medicine (bd. dir. 1987—99, Outstanding Educator award 1992), Sigma Xi, Phi Beta Kappa. Office: U Calif San Diego Family and Preventive Medicine 9500 Gilman Dr # Mc0607 La Jolla CA 92093-0607

BARRETTE-MOZES, SUSAN JEAN, counselor, psychotherapist; b. Tucson, Oct. 20, 1966; d. Thomas Marvin and Kathleen Marie Barrette; 1 child from previous marriage, Hannah Mozes. BA cum laude, U. Ariz., Tucson, 1989; MA in Anthropology, Carleton U., Ottawa, Can., 1993; MA in Mental Health Counseling with distinction, Webster U., Merritt Island, Fla., 2000. Nat. bd. cert. counselor, lic. assoc. counselor Ariz. Bd. Behavioral Health Examiners; cert. guidance counselor Ariz. Dept. Edn. Rschr. Dept. Nat. Def. Hdqs., Ottawa, 1993—98; program dir. Mil. Family Response Ctr. Def. Hdqs. Can., 1995—98; registered mental health therapist Brevard Counseling Ctr., Dept. Disability Determinations Social Security, Devereux Mental Health Agy., 2000—01; profl. counselor Sunnyside Unified Sch. Dist., Tucson, 2001—. Mem. Animal Cruelty Task Force Pima County, Tucson, 2005—06, Animal Welfare Alliance So. Ariz., 2005—06, Tucson Zool. Soc. Mem.: Am. Counseling Assn., Soc. Applied Anthropology, So. Poverty Law Ctr. Avocations: ballet, jazz, tap, modern dance. Home: 7257 E Montecito Dr Tucson AZ 85710 Office: Sunnyside Unified Sch Dist # 12 5093 S Liberty Ave Tucson AZ 85706 E-mail: suzyjeanb@cs.com.

BARRICK, MARLA CARYN, music educator; b. Henderson, Tex., Dec. 1, 1966; d. Jerry Don and Toni Peterson Hale; m. Stephen Carl Barrick, Dec. 23, 1989; children: Christopher Weldon, Kaitlyn Nicole. EdM, U. of Tex., Austin, Tex., 1993—96; MusB edn., Baylor U., Waco, Tex., 1987—90; AA, Kilgore Jr. Coll., Kilgore, Tex., 1985—87. Cert. All-Level Music Edn. Tex., 1990, All Level Special Edn. Tex., Elem. Comprehensive Educ. Tex., ED/Autism Endorsement Tex. Music educ. specialist Temple ISD, Temple, Tex., 1990—94; music edn. specialist Copperas Cove ISD, Copperas Cove, Tex., 1994—2003, target reading tchr., 2003—. Children's choir dir. First Bapt. Ch., Copperas Cove, Tex., 1999—. Contbr. clinician Time Mgmt. for Music Educators/Tex. Music Educators Assn. Com. chair First Bapt. Ch., Copperas Cove, Tex., 2001—03. Recipient Semi-Finalist, Excellence in Tchg., HEB, 2003, Tchr. of the Week, Toyota, 2003, Excellence in Tchg., Killeen Daily Herald, Tchr. of the Month, Applebees. Mem.: Growing Minds Club, Assn. of Tex. Prof. Educators (campus rep. 1994—2003), Music Educators Nat. Conf., Tex. Music Educators Assn. Home: 2501 Dennis St Copperas Cove TX 76522 Office Phone: 254-547-2235. Personal E-mail: barrick@vvm.com. E-mail: marla@ccisd.com.

BARRIENTOS, JANE ELLEN, art educator; b. Agawam, Mass., July 20, 1953; d. John Carleton and Madeline (Ploof) Bitgood; m. Moises Jonas Barrientos, June 25, 1973. BA in Econs., Westfield State Coll., 1978; cert., Paier Coll. Fine Art, 1995. Owner Agawam Arts & Crafts Shop, 1973-85; instr. art Am. Decorative Arts Studio, West Springfield, Mass., 1985—. Represented by Lenox (Mass.) Gallery, 2004—. Author: The Art of Deception Vol. I, 1997, Vol. II, 1998, Vol. III, 1999; contbr. articles to profl. jours. Mem. Acad. Artists Assn., Holyoke Art League, Friends West Springfield Libr., PTA. Avocations: sailing, travel, hiking. Office: Am Decorative Arts Studio 33 Cooper St West Springfield MA 01089-2807 Office Phone: 413-736-8882. E-mail: janetrompe@comcast.net.

BARRILE, JUDITH, science educator, consultant; b. Hannibal, Mo., Dec. 13, 1946; d. William Homer and Josephine S. Cloninger; m. Anthony C. Barrile, Jr., July 14, 1968; children: Anthony III, John. BS, Pa. State U., University Park, 1967, MS, 1969. Cert. tchr. biology Va., tchr. chemistry Va. Rsch. tech. Pa. State U., University Park, 1968—70; instr. to lectr. Gloucester County Coll., Sewell, NJ, 1970—78; tchr. Fairfax County Pub. Schs., Springfield, Va., 1992—. Mailing: 9420 Goldfield Ln Burke VA 22015-4212

BARRINGER, JOAN MARIE, counselor, educator, artist, writer; b. Washington, Sept. 30, 1955; d. John Thomas and Maria Reginia Barringer. BA in Latin Am. Studies, George Mason U., 1981; grad. in Creating and Selling Short Stories, Inst. Childrens Lit., 1995; MA in Edn. and Counseling, George Mason U., 1999. Translator and receptionist Brazilian Embassy, Cultural Inst., Washington, 1975—83; dir. and founder day care Rainbow City Army-Navy Country Club, Arlington, Va., 1983—87; visitors svcs. Nat. Gallery Art, Washington, 1991—94; workshop and leadership conf. asst. Women's Ctr., Vienna, Va., 1996—2000; career counselor Dept. Rehab. Svcs., Alexandria, Va., 1998—99, Ind. Art. Bus. Studio of Nat. Arts, 2002—. Author: (book of poems) Metronome, 1979; contbr. poetry: Great Contemporary Poetry, 1978; designer CD cover, singer Gift of Love; Fairfax (Va.) Jour., 1992, Montgomery (Va.) Jour., 1992, exhibitions include Graffiti Gallery, 2002, Greenbelt Cmty. Ctr., 2003, Joanne Rose Gallery, 2003, Rehoboth Art League, 2004, Angel Eyes, 2004, Mimi's American Bistro, 2004—05, Represented in permanent collections Inova Hosp., one woman show, Vienna Arts Soc., 2006. Pres. Hampton Roadrunners, 2004—; leader Internat. Essential Tremor Found. support group Georgetown Hosp., Washington; election officer U.S. Govt., Va., 2001; fundraiser Unity Ch. Recipient award, Vienna Photo Show, 2004, 2005. Mem.: Vienna Photog. Soc., Assn. Rsch. and Enlightenment (wayshower 2001—), Women's Caucus for Art (editor, lay out designer, writer, photographer newsletter 1999—2001), Sigma Pi Alpha. Avocations: genealogy, travel, interior decorating, yoga, photography, Oceanography. Home: 11107 Hampton Rd Fairfax Station VA 22039 Personal E-mail: joanmarie5@aol.com.

BARRINO, FANTASIA MONIQUE See FANTASIA

BARRISH, CAROL LAMPERT, psychologist; b. N.Y.C., Oct. 6, 1945; d. J. William and Sally (Bobrick) Lampert; m. Michael Louis Barrish, June 30, 1974; children: Jordan Seth, Jessica Lynne. BA, Queens Coll., 1967; MA, Columbia U., 1972; PhD, NYU, 1993. Licensed psychologist; cert. learning disabilities cons.; lic., cert. spl. edn. tchr.; cert. reading specialist; cert. tchr. Tchr., team leader elem. sch. Englewood (N.J.) Bd. Edn., 1969-72, reading cons., 1973-74; curriculum coord. Adams Town House, N.Y.C., 1974-75; ednl., learning disabilities cons. N.Y.C., 1974—; reading/learning disabilities specialist, 1975—; clin. psychology intern Risk Inst., NYU Hosp., N.Y.C., 1990-91; psychologist com. for spl. edn. N.Y.C. Bd. Edn., 1992—; spkr. for tchr. trainer groups, project coord. dist. 4, lecturer, 1998—. Pvt. clin. practice for cognitive psychology, sch., N.Y.C. Author: (with others) Assessment of Social Skills Problems with Learning Disabled Adolescents, 1993. Mem. APA, N.Y. State Psychol. Assn., Orton Dyslexia Soc., Children and Adults with Attention Deficit Disorder, Nat. Assn. Sch. Psychologists, Kappa Delta Pi. Avocations: tennis, skiing. Office: 305 E 86th St Apt 4G West New York NY 10028-4702

BARRITT, EVELYN RUTH BERRYMAN, nurse, educator, dean; b. Detroit, Sept. 4, 1929; d. George C. and Ruby (Mathews) Berryman; m. Ward LeRoy Barritt, Oct. 28, 1951; 1 dau., Kelli Jo. AA, Graceland Coll., 1949; diploma, Independence Sanitarium and Hosp. Sch. Nursing, Mo., 1952; BSN., Ohio State U., 1956, MA, 1962, PhD, 1971. Asst. instr. nursing Atlantic City Hosp., 1952-53; staff nurse Shore Meml. Hosp., Somers Point, NJ, 1953-54, Ohio State U. Hosp., Columbus, 1954-55; instr. White Cross Hosp., Columbus, 1955-57; asso. dir. nursing service Riverside Meth. Hosp., Columbus, 1957-64; asst. exec. dir. Ohio Nurses Assn., Columbus, 1964-65; dean Capital U. Sch. Nursing, Columbus, 1965-72, Coll. Nursing, U. Iowa, Iowa City, 1972-79, prof. nursing, 1972-80; prof. Sch. Nursing U. Miami, Fla., 1980—, dean Fla., 1980-85. Bd. dirs. Health Coun. South Fla., 1988—, pres., 1990-92; bd. dirs. So. Fla. Perinatal Network, Inc., 1980-89, pres., 1984-86; mem. Fla. Bd. Ind. and Pvt. Colls. and Univs., 1980; co-chmn. Dade County Indigent Care Task Force, 1991-93. Author: Florence Nightingale: Her Wit and Wisdom, 1975; author, editor: Thoughts on CareGiving, 1998; contbr. articles to profl. jours. Mem. ANA, Ohio Nurses Assn. (pres. dist. 1966-68), Iowa Nurses Assn., Fla. Nurses Assn., Graceland Univ. Alumni Assn., Am. Assn. Higher Edn., Am. Assn. Colls. Nursing (pres. 1976-78). Home: 416 Park Blvd N Venice FL 34285-1332

BARRON, BRIGID, education educator; BS in Psychology, U. Calif., Santa Cruz, 1984; MA in Psychology, Vanderbilt U., 1989, PhD in Clin. Developmental Psychology, 1992. Intern in child clin. psychology U. Wash., 1991—92; instr. Peabody Coll., Vanderbilt U., 1992—93; sr. rsch. assoc. Learning Tech. Ctr., Vanderbilt U., 1992—95; asst. prof. edn. Stanford (Calif.) U., 1996—. Mem. adv. bd. tech. task force SPEAK-UP! Leadership Program for Girls; cons. Plugged-In Tech. Access Ctr., Cmty. Kids Children's Program. Office: Stanford U Sch Edn 485 Lasuen Mall Stanford CA 94305-3096

BARRON, CAROL ANN, painter; b. Houston, Nov. 25, 1941; d. Dean Smith and Norma Christine Shuttleworth; m. Richard Adolphus Barron, June 21, 1969; children: Dean Brent, Laura Ann. BFA, Miss. U. Women, Columbus, 1963. Coord. Gaddis Group Studio, Jackson, Miss., 1992—. Pvt. watercolor instr., Jackson, Miss., 1997—2000. Illustrations, Maggie's Golden Moment, 2005, appeared in, Watercolor Magic mag., 2004, exhibitions include Magnolia Fine Arts Competition, 1993 (2d pl.), Miss. Watercolor Soc. Membership Show (hon. mention, 1993, 3d pl., 1994, 1st pl., 1997, 1998, hon. mention, 2000, Best in Show, 2001, 2d pl., 2003, hon. mention, 2004), Miss. Watercolor Soc. Grand Nat. Show (2d pl., 1994, Gaddis award, 1996, Patron's award, 2000, Simmons Assoc. award, 2001, Art Appreciation award, 2003, Friends award, 2004). Bd. mem. Covenant Sch. Arts, Jackson, Miss., 2000—03. Mem.: Miss. Watercolor Soc. (signature mem.), Am. Watercolor Soc. (signature mem.), Nat. Watercolor Soc. (signature mem.), Art Study Club (pres. 2006). Presbyterian. Home: 4020 NE Dr Jackson MS 39211

BARRON, ILONA ELEANOR, secondary school educator, consultant; b. Sept. 19, 1929; m. George Barron; 1 child, Fred. Cert. elem. tchg., No. Mich. U., 1951; BS in Elem. Edn., Ctrl. Mich. U., 1961; MA in Edn., U. Mich., 1966; postgrad., Mich. State U. Cert. reading specialist. Tchr. Elem. Schs., 1952—67; dir. Title I reading Saginaw Twp. Cmty. Schs., Mich., 1967—68, reading cons., 1971—. Cons. elem. intern Mich. State U., East Lansing, 1968—71; cons. elem. reading Saginaw Twp. Pub. Schs., 1972—. Mem.: NEA, Saginaw Area Reading Coun., Saginaw Twp. Edn. Assn., Mich. Edn. Assn. Achievements include development of methods of teaching developmental reading skills and enrichment. Home (Winter): 35702 Clubber Ct Zephyrhills FL 33541 Home (Summer): 25366 W State Hwy M 64 Ontonagon MI 49953

BARRON, MARLENE, education educator; b. Balt., May 14, 1939; d. Alexander and Lillian Ray (Sklar) Bass; m. Joseph Lackey Barron (div.); children: Leslie Rachel, Charles Jeffrey, Joshua Simon. BA in Psychology, Barnard Coll., 1965; Montessori Tchr. Edn., Fairleigh Dickinson U., 1966-67; MS in Edn., Wagner Coll., Staten Island, N.Y., 1966-68; postgrad., Richmond Coll., Staten Island, 1968-70; PhD in Curriculum and Instrn., NYU, 1995. Cert. tchr., N.Y.; cert. tchr. and cons. Montessori Accreditation Coun. Tchr. Edn., 2005. Founding head of sch. S.I. Montessori Sch., 1965-79; head of sch. West Side Montessori Sch., N.Y.C., 1979—, co-dir. tchr. edn. program, 1992—; prof. NYU, N.Y.C., 1982—. Commr. Montessori Accreditation Coun. for Tchrs., 2005—; cons. in field; workshop facilitator in field; presenter in field. Author: Sensorial Ideas, 1984, I Learn to Read and Write the Way I Learn to Talk, 1991, Ready, Set, Count, 1995, Ready Set, Read and Write, 1995, Ready, Set, Cooperate, 1996, Ready, Set, Explore, 1996, others; contbr. numerous articles to profl. jours. Bd. dirs. Early Childhood Resource and Info. Ctr., 1986—91, NY Pub. Libr., 1986—96. Mem.: Montessori Accreditation Coun. for Tchr. Edn. (commr. 2005—), Internat. Assn. for Montessori Edn. (sec.-treas. 1997—2000), Ind. Sch. Admissions Assn. Greater N.Y. (bd. dirs. 1989—, treas. 1994—), Am. Montessori Soc. (bd. dirs. 1984—87, pres. 1987—89, treas.). Office: West Side Montessori Sch 309 W 92d St New York NY 10025-7213 Business E-Mail: marlene.barron@nyu.edu.

BARRON, MYRA HYMOVICH, lawyer; b. July 5, 1938; d. Leo and Lillian Estelle (Berman) Hymovich; m. Jerome Aure Barron, June 18, 1961; children: Jonathan Nathaniel, David Jeremiah, Jennifer Leah. AB cum laude, Smith Coll., 1959; student, L'Institut des Hautes Etudes, Geneva, 1957—58; MA, Johns Hopkins U., 1961; JD, Georgetown U., 1970. Bar: Va. 70, DC 72, NY. Instr. econs. U. ND, Grand Forks, 1962—64; econ. rsch. asst. U. N.Mex., Albuquerque, 1964—65; legal aid staff atty. Fairfax County, Va., 1971—72, asst. county atty. Va., 1974—81; assoc. Melvin & Melvin, Syracuse, NY, 1973; counsel Fairfax County Redevel. and Housing Authority, Fairfax, Va., 1981—88; ptnr. Sprenger & Lang (formerly Weissbrodt, Swiss & Mc Grew), 1989—98, Weinberg & Jacobs, Rockville, Md., 1998—2000, of counsel, 2001—04. Dep. gen. counsel Housing and Devel. Law Inst., 1988—94, of counsel, 1994—2000. Editor: Jour. Affordable Housing and Cmty. Devel. Law, ABA, 1993—99; contbr. articles to housing jours.; mem.: Georgetown Law Jour., 1967—68. Recipient Samuel Bowles award, Smith Coll., 1959. Mem.: LWV (local chmn. nat. events 1962—64), ABA (mem. governing com. 1994—99, co-chmn. profit practice group 2000—03, mem. forum on affordable housing and cmty. devel. law). Home: 3231 Ellicott St NW Washington DC 20008-2061 Personal E-mail: mhbarron@earthlink.net.

BARRON, ROS, artist; b. Boston, July 4, 1933; d. Louis and Ida (Titel) Myers; m. Harris Barron, Apr. 19, 1953; children: Matt Lewis, Nina Rebecca. B.F.A., Mass. Coll. Art, 1954. Fellow Bunting Inst., Harvard U., 1966-68; co-dir. Zone Visual Theater Co., 1970; assoc. prof. art U. Mass.-Harbor Campus, Boston, 1974—. Vis. artist U. Colo., Boulder, 1983; presenter Arts at the Bunting, 1997. Producer numerous video performance tapes.; one-woman shows include North Hall Gallery, Mass. Coll. Art, Boston, 1988, Watson Gallery, Wheaton Coll., Norton, Mass., 1989, Harbor Gallery U. Mass., Boston, 1990, Mobius, Boston, 1993, Brick Bottom Gallery, Boston, 1996; exhbns. include Whitney Mus. Am. Art, 1967-68, Helen Shlien Gallery, Boston, 1979, 82, Mus. Modern Art, NYC, 1980, 84, Le Nouveau Musee, Lyon, France, 1979, Montevideo Gallery, Amsterdam, Holland, 1979, World Wide Video Festival, Kijkhuis, Holland, 1984, Hirschhorn Mus., Washington, 1984, North Hall Gallery; travelling group exhbns. include Project Rembrandt Biennial, 1991-92, Women's Caucus for Art, 1992; represented in permanent collections Mus. Fine Arts, Boston, Harvard U., Smith Coll. Collection, Worcester Art Mus., Addison Gallery Am. Art., Inst. Contemporary Art, Boston, Samuel P. Harn Mus. Art, U. Fla., Gainesville, Mus. Modern Art, NYC; performance Art: (with Harris Barron) Mr. & Mrs. Zone: Art Life Art, Mobius Theatre, Boston, 1987, Performance Art: (with Harris Barron) Mr. & Mrs. Zone Again, Mobius Theatre, Boston, 1997, Eartheart and other video works, Mobius Theatre, Boston, 1999, Eagle Air, The Life and Work of Harris Barron, 2001. Bd. dirs. Boston Performance Artists. Recipient Design award HUD, 1968; N.Y. Found. for Arts grantee, 1972; Guggenheim Found. grantee, 1972; Nat. Endowment Arts grantee, 1975; Rockefeller Found. grantee, 1978-80; Mass. Council Arts grantee, 1981-82, 83 Address: 30 Webster Pl Brookline MA 02445-7937 Office Phone: 617-232-9544.

BARRON, SHERRY, music educator; b. Chattanooga, Tenn., July 23, 1962; d. Darryl Woolery. B of Music Edn., La. State U., Baton Rouge. Cert. music tchr. La., 1997. Tchr. music Baton Rouge Symphony Orch., 2005. Piano tchr., Baton Rouge. Recipient Tchr. of Yr. award, Baton Rouge Symphony Orch., 2005. Home: 9676 Wesson St Baton Rouge LA 70809

BARRON, (MARY LOU) SLATER, artist, retired educator; b. East Orange, NJ, July 2, 1930; d. Louis and Williamina Fullerton Slater; m. Thurston B. Barron, July 7, 1950 (div. 1976); children: Janet, J. Scott, Jennifer, Maribeth. BA in Sociology and Psychology, Susquehanna U., 1951; postgrad., Orange Coast Coll., 1972—74; BA in Studio Art, U. Calif., Irvine, 1975; MFA in Drawing and Painting, Calif. State U., Long Beach, 1978. Lifetime C.C. credential Calif. Instr. design Brooks Coll., Long Beach, 1978—2000; instr. art Calif. State U., Long Beach, 1978, 1984; instr. design Fashion Inst. Design and Merchandising, L.A., Interior Design Inst., Irvine, Calif., U. Calif., Irvine. Pres. artists' coun. Long Beach Mus. Art, 1993; mem. adv. bd. for pub. art Pub. Corp. Arts, Long Beach, 1995—98. One-woman shows include Four Wall Studio, Santa Ana, Calif., 1974, The Floating Wall, Santa Ana, 1975, Orange Coast Coll., Costa Mesa, Calif., 1976, Calif. State U., Long Beach, 1978, Stage One Gallery, Orange, Calif., 1981, Fiberworks Gallery, Berkeley, Calif., 1981, Loyola Marymount U., L.A., 1983, Long Beach City Coll., 1984, Mus. Ariz. State U., Tempe, 1986, Mendenhall Gallery, Whittier (Calif.) Coll., 1988, Guggenheim Gallery, Chapman Coll., Orange, 1992, Watkins Gallery, Queens Coll., Charlotte, N.C., 1992, Pacific Place, San Pedro, Calif., 1998, Chez Shaw Gallery, Long Beach, Calif., 2005, Utopia, Long Beach, 2005, exhibited in group shows at El Camino Coll. Gallery, Torrance, Calif., 1997, Orange County Ctr. for Contemporary Art, Santa Ana, 1998, Commune di Orzinuovia, Brescia, Italy, 1999, Main Libr., Long Beach, 1999, Eleven Seven Gallery, 1999, Long Beach Mus. Art, 2000, Long Beach City Coll., 2001, Furlong Art Gallery, U. Wis., Stout, 2001—02, many others, Represented in permanent collections Long Beach Mus. Art, Laguna Beach Mus. Art, L.A. County Mus. Art, Smithsonian White House Collection, Ripley's Believe It or Not!, many others. Lt. (j.g.) USN, 1953—55. Named Visual Artist of Yr., Pub. Corp. Arts, 1987—88. Home: 2299 Oregon Ave Long Beach CA 90806 Office Phone: 562-426-3801.

BARRON, STEPHANIE, curator; AB, Barnard Coll., Columbia U., 1972; student, Harvard Inst. Arts Adminstrn., 1973; MA, Columbia U., 1974; postgrad., CUNY, 1975-76. Intern, curatorial asst. Solomon R. Guggenheim Mus., 1971-72; Nat. Endowment Arts intern in edn. Toledo Mus. Art, 1973-74; exhbn. coord. Jewish Mus., N.Y.C., 1975-76; assoc. curator modern art L.A. County Mus. Art, 1976-80, curator Twentieth Century art, 1980-94, coord. curatorial affairs, 1993-96, sr. curator Twentieth Century art, 1995—, v.p. edn. and pub. programs, 1996—2003; chief curator Modern and Contemporary Art, 2002—. Lectr., panelist in field. Contbr. articles to profl. jours. Mem. art adv. panel IRS, 1996—; advisor U.S. Holocaust Mus., 1996—; trustee Scripps Coll., 1996—; mem. steering com. Villa Aurora, 1994—; mem. bd. Stiftung Mortizburg, Halle, Germany, 2005-, Magritte Assn., 2005-. Decorated comdr.'s cross Fed. Republic of Germany, Order of Merit (Germany); recipient George L. Wittenborn award ARLIS, 1991, award for best Am. exhbn. of yr. Assn. Internat. Critics Art, 1991, 97, Theo Wormland Kunstpreis, 1992, George L. Wittenborn award, 1992, Alfred H. Barr Jr. award Coll. Art Assn., 1992, E.L. Kirchner prize, Switzerland, 1997, First Pl. award Am. Assn. Art Mus., 1998, Hon. Mention, ARLIS, 1998; named Woman of Yr., Bus. and Profl. Women of UJA, Jewish Fedn., 1991, Friends of Tel Hashomer, 1991; Nat. Endowment of Arts fellow, 1986-87; John J. McCloy fellow in art, 1981. Fellow Am. Acad. Arts and Scis.; mem. Am. Assn. Mus., Internat. Mus. Modern Art (internat. com. mus.), Internat. Coun. Mus., Internat. Com. for Mus. and Collections of Modern Art, Art Table. Office: LA County Mus Art 5905 Wilshire Blvd Los Angeles CA 90036-4597 Business E-Mail: sbarron@lacma.org.

BARROS, COLLEEN, federal agency administrator; BS, U. Md.; MPA, Am. U. With NIH, 1979—, budget analyst, 1979, sr. adminstrv. officer Office of Dir.; assoc. dir. adminstrn. Nat. Inst. Aging, 1995—2004; acting dep. dir. mgmt. NIH, 2004, dep. dir. mgmt., CFO, 2004—. Recipient PHS Superior Svc. Award, 1995, Presdl. Rank Award, 2003, 4 NIH Dir.'s Awards. Office: NIH 9000 Rockville Pike Bethesda MD 20892

BARROW, DINDRIA COZETTE, elementary school educator, special education educator; b. Aurora, Colo., Jan. 1, 1974; d. Stephen Lance Barrow and Deborah Kay Wetzel; life ptnr. Michael John Grochowicz, Oct. 23, 1997. BEd, Pacific Luth. U., 1995; postgrad., Pacific Oaks Coll., 2005—. Cert. in elem. edn., spl. edn., early childhood edn. and spl. edn., biculturalism and ESL, Wash. Tchr. asst. North Tacoma Montessori Ctr., Tacoma, 1992—95; tchr., camp leader Erly Childhood Edn. Acad., Puyallup, Wash., 1996—98; spl. edn. tchr. McIlvaigh Mid. Sch., Tacoma, 1998—99, title 1 tchr., 1999—2002, humanities tchr., 2002—04, lang. arts elective tchr., 2004—05. Contbr. poetry to anthologies; author: (poetry) Of Diamonds & Rust, 1991, Thoughts and Dreams Remembered, 1998. Youth organizer, participant MetroParks Cmty. Hearing, Tacoma, 2000; vol. adult English tutor Tacoma Cmty. House, 2000—01; vol. Girls Club, 2000—01; neighborhood dir. East Side Neighborhood Adv. Coun., 2000—01. Mem.: Wash. State Assn. Multicultural Edn., Nat. Assn. Multicultural Edn., Centrum Arts & Scis. Socialist Workers Party. Avocations: writing, singing, travel, cooking. Personal E-mail: dindria@comcast.net.

BARROW, TAWANA WALKER, psychiatrist, consultant; b. Bklyn., Mar. 23, 1972; d. Ronald Lee and Irene (James) Walker; m. Clay L. Barrow, Sept. 2, 1995; 1 child, Maia Grace. BA with honors, U. NC, Chapel Hill, 1993; MD, Emory U., 1997. Resident in psychiatry Emory U., Atlanta, 1997—2001; sr. psychiatrist Santee-Wateree Dept. Mental Health, Sumter, SC, 2001—; psychiatrist Healthy Mind, LLC, Sumter, 2003—. Mem.: SC Psychiat. Assn., Am. Psychiat. Assn. Avocation: gardening. Office: Santee-Wateree Dept Mental Health 215 N Magnolia St Sumter SC 29150

BARROWMAN, CONNIE L., investment advisor; b. Champaign, Ill., Feb. 17, 1952; d. John E. And Maryellen Childs; m. Robert A. Barrowman, Aug. 29, 1970; children: Stephanie, Todd. BA, Eastern Ill. U., 1986; MS in Health Svcs. Adminstrn., Coll. of St. Francis, 1991; MBA, St. Francis U., 1999. Mgr. Park Cir. Lab. Callahan, Lord, King, Ltd., Champaign, 1974-80; cardiovasc. technologist Carle Clinic Assn., Urbana, Ill., 1980-81, ECG supr., 1981-84, mgr. cardiovasc. svcs., 1984-88, asst. dir. patient care, 1988-91, dir. Carle Heart Ctr., 1991—2003; investment rep. Edward Jones Investments, 2003—. Vol. Am. Heart Assn., Champaign, 1992—. Mem. Am. Acad. Cardiovasc. Adminstrn., Exec. Club (Champaign). Office: Edward Jones Investments 2506 Galen Champaign IL 61821 Office Phone: 217-355-1499. Personal E-mail: clbarrowman@aol.com.

BARROWS, ROXANE RENEE, dean, mathematics professor; b. Glen Allen, Alaska, Feb. 26, 1966; d. Edward George and Sheryl Margaret Threm; m. Steven Barrows, Aug. 31, 1991; 1 child, Bailey Jo. BS in Info. Systems, Ohio State U., Columbus, 1988; MS in Math., Ohio U., Athens, 1991, post grad. in Higher Edn. Math instr. Ohio U., Athens, 1991—93, Hocking Coll., Nelsonville, Ohio, 1993—97, math coord., 1997—2001, assoc. dean, 2001—. Adv. bd. mem. Computes Sci. HC, Nelsonville, 2000—; adv. bd. mem., assoc.

dean Learning Ctr., Nelsonville, 2002—; adv. bd. mem. Tri-County Vocat. Sch., Nelsonville, 2003—04; presenter in field. Author: several textbooks; contbr. articles to profl. jours.; presenter in field. Instr. Girl Scouts, Nelsonville, 2003. Nominee Excellence in Instrn. award, Hocking Coll., 2003; recipient Cert. Achievement Sch. Arts and Scis., 2002, Cert. Achievement for Recognition of Integration of Success Skills into Math. Classes, 2003, Pinnacle award, Phi Theta Kappa, 2002. Mem.: Nat. Coun. Instrnl. Adminstr., Am. Math. Assn. (nom. Disting. Svc. award 2002, nom. Outstanding Devel. Educator 2004), South Ea. Ohio Ctr. Excellence in Math. and Sci. (team mem. task force for retention and recruitment), Math. Assn. Am., Ohio Math Assn., Ohio Assn. Devel. Edn. (vol. proposal reader, Outstanding Rsch. and Pub. award 2002, nom. Outstanding Devel. Educator 2004). Avocations: scrapbooks, ice skating, antiques, stamping. Home: 6 Stratmore Blvd Athens OH 45701 Office: Hocking Coll 3301 Hocking Pwy Nelsonville OH 45764 Office Phone: 740-753-6162. Business E-Mail: barrows_r@hocking.edu.

BARRY, JOYCE ALICE, dietician, consultant; b. Chgo., Apr. 27, 1932; d. Walter Stephen and Ethel Myrtle (Paetow) B. Student, Iowa State Coll., 1950—52, Loyola U., 1952—58; BS, Mundelein Coll., 1955; postgrad., Simmons Coll., 1963—64, U. Ga., 1979, Calif. We. U., 1980. Registered dietitian. Prodn. supr. Marshall Field & Co., Chgo., 1955-59; dir. food svcs. Women's Ednl. and Indsl. Union, Boston, 1959-62, Wellesley Pub. Schs., Mass., 1962-70; regional dietitian Canteen Corp., Chgo., 1970-83; gen. mgr. bus. devel. Plantation-Sysco, Orlando, Fla., 1983-87; dir. product devel., corp. quality assurance, procurement Marriott Internat. Hdqrs., Washington, 1987-95; owner food svc. cons. svc., 1995—. Cons. Stokes Food Svcs., Newton, Mass., 1960-70; vis. lectr. Affiliate Produce for Better Health Found. Mem.: AAUW, Nutrition in Complementary Care, Nat. Assn. Female Execs., Nat. Hist. Trust, Sch. Nutrition Svcs., Am. Dietetics Assn. (career adv. cons.), Food and Culinary Profls., Dietitians in Bus. and Comm., Smithsonian Instn. (assoc.), Washington Opera Guild, Met. Opera Guild. Republican. Roman Catholic. Home and Office: 1009 Pearce Dr Apt 102 Clearwater FL 33764-1107 Office Phone: 727-669-6454. Personal E-mail: joyce4374@yahoo.com.

BARRY, MARY H., college official; BS in Speech and Drama, Bowling Green State U.; M Mgmt., Northwestern U.; JD, Western State U. V.p. 1st Nat. Bank, Chgo.; dir. Citibank, S.D.; sr. v.p. Marquette Banks, until 1990; dir. Nat. Coll., 1990-91; dir. acad. affairs, adminstrn. and Calif. Ctr. Profl. Edn., U. Phoenix, 1992-98; v.p. edn. Corinthian Colls., Inc., postsecondary edn. co., Santa Ana, Calif., 1998—. Maj. USMC, 1971—79. Office: Corinthian Colls 6 Hutton Centre Dr Ste 400 Santa Ana CA 92707-5764

BARRY, MARYANNE TRUMP, federal judge; b. NYC, Apr. 5, 1937; d. Fred C. and Mary Trump; m. John J. Barry, Dec. 26, 1982; 1 child, David W. Desmond. BA, Mt. Holyoke Coll., 1958; MA, Columbia U., 1962; JD, Hofstra U., 1974, LLD (hon.), Seton Hall U.; LLD (hon.), Caldwell Coll.; LLD (hon.), Kean Coll. Bar: N.J. 1974, N.Y. 1975, U.S. Ct. Appeals (3d cir.), U.S. Supreme Ct. Asst. U.S. Atty., 1974-75; dep. chief appeals div., 1976-77; chief appeals div., 1977-82; exec. asst. U.S. Atty., 1981-82; 1st asst., 1981-83; judge U.S. Dist. Ct., N.J., 1983-99, U.S. Ct. Appeals (3d cir.), Newark, 1999—. Chmn. Com. on Criminal Law Jud. Conf. of U.S., 1994-96. Recipient Sandra Day O'Connor Medal of Honor, 2004. Fellow Am. Bar Found.; mem. ABA, N.J. Bar Assn., Am. Judicature Soc. (bd. dirs.), Assn. Fed. Bar of NJ (pres. 1982-83); mem. NY Bar Assn. Office: US Ct Appeals PO Box 999 Newark NJ 07101

BARRY, MILDRED CASTILLE, artist; b. Sunset, La., Feb. 23, 1924; d. Joseph Hippomene and Beatrice Victoria (Tinney) Castille; m. Francis Xavier Barry, Aug. 16, 1947; children: Christopher, Kevin, Maureen, Robin, Shane, Kim. BA in Edn., Sam Houston U., 1958. Cert. tchr., Tex. Tchr. Sacred Heart Elem., Conroe, Tex., 1959-67, Conroe Sam Houston Elem., 1967-68, Houston Ind. Sch. Dist. Elem., 1968-69. Tchr., stuent of Ernest Gaines, author-in-residence U. So. La., Lafayette, 1985-87. Exhibited in group shows Opelonsas, La., 1973 (1st pl.). With WAC, 1944-45. Recipient 1st pl. award, Miss. Festival of Arts, 1958. Mem. Writers Guild. Roman Catholic. Avocations: reading, writing, painting, sewing, travel. Home: 309 Beverly Dr Lafayette LA 70503-3109 Personal E-mail: mimsyfan@yahoo.com.

BARRY, NADA DAVIES, retail business owner; b. London, Dec. 2, 1930; d. Ernest Albert J. and Natalie Emma (Rossin) Davies; m. Jacob J. Ebeling-Koning, Aug. 1952 (div. 1962); m. Robert I Barry, 1963 (div. 1976); children: Natasha E.-K. Sigmund, Derek B. Ebeling-Koning, Gwen E.-K. Waddington, Trebor C. Barry. Student, Mills Coll., 1948-50; BA, Barnard Coll., 1952. Owner The Wharf Shop, Sag Harbor, N.Y., 1968—. Founder Sag Harbor Youth Com. Bd. dirs. The Hampton Day Sch., Bridgehampton, N.Y., 1966-74, Youth Advocacy Resource Devel., 1997-01; active Noyac Civic Coun., LWV of The Hamptons; founder Sag Harbor Youth Com. Mem. AAUW, Sag Harbor C. of C. (bd. dirs.), Nat. Trust Historic Preservation, Nature Conservancy, So. Poverty Law Ctr., Sag Harbor Hist. Soc., Sag Harbor Whaling Museum, Mills Coll. Club (N.Y. chpt.), Williams Coll. Club. Avocations: gardening, photography, travel, shelling, theater. Office: The Wharf Shop PO Box 922 Sag Harbor NY 11963-0025

BARRY, NANCY MARIE, bank executive; b. Kansas City, Kans., Aug. 2, 1949; d. John Joseph and Lorna Marie Barry. BA in Econs., Stanford U., 1971; MBA, Harvard U., 1975. Divsn. chief pub. sector mgmt. World Bank, Washington, 1986-87, divsn. chief indsl. devel., 1987-90; pres. Women's World Banking, NYC, 1990—2006. Founding mem. World Bank Consultative Group to Assist the Poorest-Policy Advisory Group, Washington; adv. com. Harvard Social Enterprise, Mass. Named Woman of the Yr., Fin. Women's Assn., 2006; named one of 100 Most Powerful Women in World, Forbes mag., 2005. Mem. Harvard Club. Office: Women's World Banking 8 W 40th St Fl 9 New York NY 10018-3993 Office Fax: 212-768-8519. E-mail: nmbarry@swwb.org.*

BARRY, PATRICIA DOWLING, psychotherapist, consultant; b. St. Albans, Vt., Oct. 3, 1941; d. James Edward and Anita Lina (Wiegand) Dowling; m. Richard J. Barry, May 4, 1963 (div. July 1982); children: Michelle, Catherine, Elizabeth. BS, Cen. Conn. State U., 1976; MSN, Yale U., 1979; PhD, Union Inst., 1991. Asst. prof. U. Hartford, Conn., 1979-80; psychiatric liaison nurse cons. St. Francis Hosp., Hartford, 1980-85; pvt. practice specializing in psychotherapy Hartford, 1985-93; lectr. Yale U. Sch. Nursing, 1989—; assoc. prof. U. Conn. Sch. Nursing, 1989—. Staff Dept. of Psychiatry Hartford Hosp. Author: Psychosocial Nursing Assessment and Intervention, 1984, 3d edit., 1996, Mental Health and Mental Illness, 1985, 6th edit., 1998. Bd. dirs. LWV, West Hartford, 1976-78; chmn. bd. dirs. Blue Hills Hosp., Hartford, 1982-86. Recipient Disting. Alumna award Yale U., 1989, rsch. award Nat. Psychiat. Consultation-Liaison Nursing Conf., 1993. Mem. Conn. Nurses Assn. (sec. 1987-88, bd. dirs. 1986-92, Vera Keane Dist. Svc. award 1992), Conn. United for Rsch. Excellence (bd. dirs. 1991-94), Hartford Golf Club, Hartford Club (pres. Bus. Group), Sigma Theta Tau. Roman Catholic. Home and Office: 60 Linnard Rd West Hartford CT 06107-1234 Office Phone: 860-231-8717.

BARRY, SANDRA, school system administrator; Degree, Neb.-Wesleyan U., Calif. State U., Fullerton. Educator and adminstr. Buena Pk. Sch. Dist., 1968—97; supt. Anaheim (Calif.) City Sch. Dist., 2000—. Office: Anaheim City Sch Dist 1001 South East St Anaheim CA 92805 Office Phone: 714-517-7510.

BARRYMORE, DREW, actress; b. Culver City, Calif., Feb. 22, 1975; d. John and Jaid Barrymore; m. Jeremy Thomas, Mar. 20, 1994 (div. Feb. 1995); m. Tom Green, July 7, 2001 (div. Oct. 15, 2002). Co-owner Flower Films, 1995—. Appearances include (films) Altered States, 1980, E.T.: The Extra-Terrestrial, 1982, Irreconcilable Differences, 1984, Firestarter, 1984, Cat's Eye, 1985, Poison Ivy, 1992, Bad Girls, 1994, Boys on the Side, 1995, Batman Forever, 1995, Mad Love, 1995, Wishful Thinking, 1996, Scream, 1996, Like a Lady, 1996, Everyone Says I Love You, 1996, All She Wanted, 1997, Best Men, 1997, Never Been Kissed, 1998 (also prodr.), Home Fries, 1998, The Wedding Singer, 1998, Ever After: A Cinderella Story, 1998, Never Been Kissed (also exec. prodr.), 1999, Olive, the Other Reindeer, 1999 (voice & exec. prodr.), Titan A.E., 2000 (voice), Charlie's Angels, 2000 (also prodr.), Donnie Darko (also exec. prodr.), 2001, Riding in Cars With Boys, 2001, Confessions of a Dangerous Mind, 2002, Charlie's Angels: Full Throttle (also prodr.), 2003, Duplex, 2003 (also prodr.), 50 First Dates, 2004, Fever Pitch (also prodr.), 2005, Curious George, 2006 (voice), Lucky You, 2006; (TV episodes) Amazing Stories, 1985, Con Sawyer and Hucklemary Finn, 1985, 2000 Malibu Road, 1992; (host) Hansel and Gretel, 1986; (TV movies) Suddenly Love, 1978, Bogie, 1980, The Screaming Woman, 1986, Babes in Toyland, 1986, Conspiracy of Love, 1987, Beyond Control: The Amy Fisher Story, 1993; (TV spls.) Screen Actors Guild 50th Anniversary, 1984, Night of 100 Stars II, 1985, Happy Birthday, Hollywood, 1987, Disney's 30th Anniversary, 1987; co-auther (book) Little Girl Lost. Named one of 50 Most Powerful People in Hollywood, Premiere mag., 2004—05; recipient Star, Hollywood's Walk of Fame, 2004. Office: Creative Artist Agency 9830 Wilshire Blvd Beverly Hills CA 90212*

BARSHEFSKY, CHARLENE, lawyer, former diplomat; b. Aug. 11, 1950; BA with honors, U. Wis., 1972; JD, Catholic U., 1975. Ptnr. Steptoe & Johnson, Washington, 1975-93; dep. U.S. trade rep. Exec. Office of the Pres. of the U.S., Washington, 1993-96, U.S. trade rep., 1996—2001; pub. policy scholar Woodrow Wilson Internat. Ctr., Washington, 2001; sr. internat. ptnr. Wilmer, Cutler, & Pickering, Washington, 2001—. Mem.: bd. dirs., Intel Corp., 2004-. Office: Wilmer Cutler & Pickering 2445 M St Washington DC 20037-1420 Office Phone: 202-663-6130. Office Fax: 202-663-6363.

BART, MURIEL, library educator; b. N.Y.C., May 9, 1926; d. Harry and Sarah Deborah (Israelite) Singer; m. Leonard Eugene Bart, Feb. 15, 1953; children— Andrew Harrison, Jonathan James. BA U. Conn., 1947, MA, 1948; MLS, Queen's U., SUNY, 1966. Cert. sch. adminstr., NY Tchr. social studies N.Y.C. Bd. Edn., 1949-54, libr. tchr., 1964-67, libr.-in-charge, 1967-87; dir. N.Y.C. Sch. Libr. Sys., 1987-89, ednl. cons., 1989—; mem. editl. adv. bd. High Points, 1970—, asst. to bd. examiners, 1980-87; lectr. in field; workshop leader. Author The First of Her Kind, 2004; contbr. articles, book revs. to profl. jours. NDEA/ESEA grantee, 1972. Mem. ALA (chmn. vocat. tech. panel 1983-85), N.Y.C. Sch. Librs. Assn. (chmn. edn. com. 1974-76), NY Libr. Club (sec. 1978-80, pres. 1985-86), Women's City Club. Personal E-mail: Murlen4@aol.com.

BART, POLLY TURNER, construction executive; b. Peterborough, N.H., Feb. 28, 1944; 1 child, Greta Rose Zagarino. BAcl, Radcliffe Coll., 1965; PhD in City Planning, U. Calif., Berkeley, 1979. Contbr. President's Nat. Urban Policy Report to Congress, Washington, 1980; asst. prof. housing U. Md., College Park, 1980—88; salesperson Coldwell Banker Comml. Real Estate Svcs., 1984—87; pres. Investment Properties Brokerage, Inc., Balt., 1988—2003, Greenbuilders, Inc., 2003—. Co-founder Comml. Real Estate Women Balt. Home and Office: 4033 Osborne Rd Reisterstown MD 21136 Office Phone: 410-833-4814. E-mail: ptbptb@aol.com.

BART, SUSAN THERESE, lawyer; b. Chgo., June 6, 1961; BA, Grinnell Coll., 1982; JD, U. Mich., 1985. Bar: Ill. 1985, U.S. Ct. Appeals (7th cir.) 1985. Law clk. to Hon. Richard D. Cudahy, Fed. Ct. Appeals (7th cir.), 1985—86; with Hopkins & Sutter, 1986—94, ptnr., 1992—94, Sidley Austin LLP, 1994—. Articles editor U. Mich. Law Review, Ann Arbor, 1984-85. Author: Education Planning and Gifts to Minors, 2004; co-author: Illinois Estate Planning: Forms and Commentary, 1997 (Outstanding Achievement award Assn. for Continuing Legal Edn., 1998), rev., 2005; editor: ACTEC Jour. Mem. bd. dirs., exec. com. Ill. Inst. Continuing Legal Edn.; sec., bd. dirs. The Next Theatre; mem. bd. trustees Roosevelt U.; mem. bd. dirs. Domestic Violence Legal Clinic. Mem. Phi Beta Kappa, Order of the Coif. Avocations: classics, literature, theater. Office: Sidley Austin LLP One S Dearborn St Chicago IL 60603

BARTEET, BARBARA BOYTER, retired social worker; b. Vivian, La., Oct. 19, 1935; d. Boyce Oliver and Agnes Pauline Boyter; m. James Bernard Barteet; children: Lindsey, Lezlie, Tracy, Jeffrey. AA, Yuba Jr. Coll., Marysville, Calif., 1968; BA, La. State U., Baton Rouge, 1971, MSN in Libr. Sci., 1972, MSN in Social Work, 1984; student music, Ann Arundel C.C., Md., 1996—. LCSW Calif., 1988, Md., 1995. Social Worker La. State Penitentiary, Angola, 1984—86; social worker Jerry Pettis VA Meml. Hosp., Loma Linda, Calif., 1986—89, U.S. Army, Germany, 1989—94. Civilian Ambassador United States, Beijeng, Nanking, Shanghai, China, 1996, India, Nepal, New Delhi, Agra, Jaipur, Katmandu, 1997. Mem.: AAUW, Nat. Assn. Gold Star Wives. Presbyterian. Avocations: reading, piano, singing, travel. Home: 514 West Ct Glen Burnie MD 21061-4778 Personal E-mail: bbarteet1803@msn.com.

BARTEL, JEANINE M., actor; b. Glenclove, N.Y., Aug. 27, 1976; d. John and Roseanne Theresa Bartel; m. Alex Fry, Sept. 28, 2003. BFA, Tex. Christian U., 1998. Actor numerous films. Actor: (films) Bklyn. Lobster, Nail Polish, Exit Reality, The Goddaughter; (TV series) Law & Order, All My Children, Guiding Light, (numerous commercials). Self esteem youth speaker Cath. Sch. and continuing edn. programs, 2002—05. Mem.: SAG, Actors Equity Assn. Avocations: writing, dance, weightlifting. Personal E-mail: Jeaninebartel2@verizion.net.

BARTEL, LAVON LEE, academic administrator, food scientist; b. Salem, Oreg., Nov. 12, 1951; d. Harvey C. Bartel and Jeanne Marie (Siddall) Bartel Shelton; m. David George Struck, Sept. 14, 1974. BS with honors, Oreg. State U., 1973, MS, 1975; PhD, U. Wis., 1979. Registered dietitian. Teaching asst. Oreg. State U., Corvallis, 1973-75; rsch. asst. U. Wis., Madison, 1975-79; asst. prof. Whittier (Calif.) Coll., 1979-82, U. Vt., Burlington, 1982-87, extension specialist extension svc., 1987-89, assoc. dean, 1989-96, assoc. dir. div. agr./life scis., ext. and natural resources, 1989-96; dean, dir. U. Maine Coop. Ext., Orono, 1996—. Cons. Vt. food industry, 1982-89; bd. dirs. Earth's Best, Middlebury, Vt., 1984-88; bd. dirs. Maine Rural Devel. Coun, 1996-98, Maine Food and Agr. Com. N.E. Regional Ctr. for Rural Devel., 1996-2000, Nat. 4H Coun., 1998-03; bd. dirs., mem. exec. com. N.E. Regonal Aquaculture Ctr., 2000-03; mem. partnership task force Coop. State Rsch. Edn. and Ext. Svc., 2002-04; chair governing com. Nat. eXtension, 2004-05. Contbr. articles to profl. jours. Mem. APHA, Vt. Dietetic Assn. (pres. 1989-90, chair coun. of practice 1987-88, chair 1993-94, hunger and malnutrition practice group 1994-97), Maine Dietetic Assn. (hunger and environ. nutrition 2000-), Vt. Home Econs. Assn. (sec.-treas. 1987-89), Inst. Food Tech. (profl. mem.), Assn. Women in Sci., Ext. Coun. on Orgn. and Policy (budget com. 1993-94, program leadership com. 1995, co-chair strategic planning coun. 1996-97, ext. bd. chair 2004-05, budget and legis. com. 2005—), Phi Kappa Phi. Avocations: sea kayaking, canoeing, gardening, camping, computers. Office: U Maine Coop Ext Sys 5741 Libby Hall Orono ME 04469-5741 Office Phone: 207-581-2811. Business E-Mail: lbartel@umext.maine.edu.

BARTELS, JEAN ELLEN, nursing educator; b. Two Rivers, Wis., July 15, 1949; m. Terry D. Bartels, Aug. 14, 1971; children: Justin Dean, Ashlee Jill. Diploma, Columbia Hosp. Sch. Nursing, 1970; BSN with honors, Alverno Coll., Milw., 1981; MSN, Marquette U., Milw., 1983; PhD in Nursing, U. Wis., Milw., 1990. Staff nurse ICU Columbia Hosp., Milw., 1970-76; prof. nursing Alverno Coll., Milw., 1983-99, dean nursing, 1990-99; chair Sch. Nursing Ga. So. U., Statesboro, 1999—. Asst. edn. editor Jour. Profl. Nursing; contbr. articles to profl. jours. Mem.: AACN (past pres.), ANA, Am. Assn. Higher Edn., Am. Ednl. Rsch. Assn., Am. Assn. Colls. Nursing, Internat. Soc. for Sci. Study Subjectivity, Mu Kappa, Sigma Theta Tau. Home: 912 Brittany Ln Statesboro GA 30461-4499 Office: Ga So U PO Box 8158 Statesboro GA 30460-1000 Office Phone: 912-681-5455. E-mail: jbartels@georgiasouthern.edu.

BARTELS, MARILYNN RAE, education educator; b. Dubuque, Iowa, Nov. 12, 1973; d. Roger and Catherine Bartels; m. Ryan Less, Sept. 22, 2001. BS, Iowa State U., 1992—96; MS, Oreg. State U., 1997—2000. Asst. to the exec. dir. River Action, Davenport, Iowa, 2000—02; adj. biology instr. Scott C.C., Bettendorf, Iowa, 2000—02; biology instr. Black Hawk Coll., Moline, Ill., 2002—06, asst. prof. of biology, 2006—. Edn. adv. com. mem. River Action, Davenport, Iowa, 2005—06; solid waste program adv. com. mem. City of Davenport, Davenport, Iowa, 2005; planning com. mem. XStream Cleanup, Davenport, Iowa. Student Rsch. grant, NW Sci. Assn., 1999, Portland Garden Club, 1999. Mem.: Iowa Native Plant Soc., Ill. Native Plant Soc., Am. Inst. of Biol. Sciences, Ecol. Soc. of Am. Office Phone: 309-796-5235.

BARTELS, URSULA BRENNAN, lawyer; b. Abington, Pa., Aug. 22, 1957; life ptnr. Laura Zucker; children: Benjamin, Julia. AB, Bryn Mawr Coll., 1979; JD, U. Va., 1983. Bar: Pa. 1983, Conn. 2002. Assoc. Stradley, Ronon, Stevens & Young, Phila., 1983-88; assoc. gen. counsel, v.p. SmithKline Beecham, Phila., 1988-99; v.p., gen. counsel, sec. Boehringer Ingelheim Corp., Ridgefield, Conn., 1999—2004; v.p., gen. counsel Chiron Corp., Emeryville, Calif., 2004—. Bd. trustees Food & Drug Law Inst., Washington, 1996-99, mem. fin. & audit com. Mem.: ABA, Pa. Bar Assn., Phila. Bar Assn. Office: Chiron Corp 4560 Horton St Emeryville CA 94608

BARTELSTONE, RONA SUE, gerontologist; b. Bklyn, Jan. 10, 1951; d. Herbert and Hazel (Mittman) Canarick; m. Alan Joel Markowitz. BS in Social Welfare, SUNY, Buffalo, 1972; MSW, Ind. U., 1974. Lic. clin. social worker Fla., diplomate in social work, cert. care mgr., advanced social work case mgr. Social worker YM-YWHA of Greater Ny, NY, 1974-75; dist. supr. NYC Housing Authority, Bklyn., 1975-77; field instr. Barry U. Sch. Social Work, 1980-81; project dir. United Family & Children's Svc., 1977-81; faculty Miami Dade Cmty. Coll., 1981-82; adult educator Sch. Bd. Dade County, 1981-82; med. social worker Mederi Home Health Agy., 1979-82; mem. adj. faculty Nova U., 1986-88; pvt. practice Rona Bartelstone Assocs., Inc., Ft. Lauderdale, Fla., 1981—; team leader curriculum devel., cert. in geriatric care mgmt. U. Fla., 2002. Adj. faculty Fla. Internat. U. S.E. Ctr. on Aging, 1996; conf. co-chair, Vancouver, BC, Canada, 2001; co-chair Internat. Care Mgmt. Conf., 2003; adv. bd. Caregivers Marketplace, 2003; coalition ptnr. And Thou Shalt Honor Care Mgmt. Conf., 2003; cons. and trainer in field. Contbr. articles to various mags., chapters to books. Mem. funding panel Area Agy. on Aging, Miami, 1985—89; active Friends of the Family Counseling Svcs., Miami, 1983—88; adv. bd., chair internship subcom. Lynn U., 1993—97; exec. bd. Fla. Geriatric Care Mgrs., 1993—2000, pres.-elect, 1998—2000; chair tng. com., exec. v.p. Alzheimer's Assn., Miami, 1994—97, bd. dirs., 1999, v.p., 1999—2002; co-chair Nat. Acad. Cert. Care Mgrs., 1994—97, v.p., 1997—; trustee Fla. Coun. on Aging, 1996—2002; team leader curriculum devel. U. Fla. Dept. Continuing Edn.; bd. dirs. Jewish Vocat. Svcs., Miami, 1985—92. Recipient Dade County Citizen of the Yr. award, 1982, NASW Social Worker of the Yr. award, 1982-83, Trail Blazer award, 1984, Up & Comers award in health care Price Waterhouse and So. Fla. Bus. Jour., 1990. Mem.: NICLC, NASW (treas. 1987—89), Internat. Care Mgmt. Conf. (co-chair 2003), Fla. Coun. on Aging (trustee 1996—2002), Fla. Geriatric Care Mgr. Assn. (exec. bd 1993—2000, pres.-elect 1998—2000, Broward County care mgmt. licensing com. 2001—), Nat. Acad. Cert. Care Mgrs. (co-chmn. 1994—97, v.p. 1997—2005), Assn. Profl. Geriatric Care Mgrs. (pres. 1988—94, chmn. credential com. 1993—), Nat. Coun. on Aging, Am. Soc. on Aging (bd. dirs. 2003—06), Gerontology Soc. Am., Caregivers Market Place (adv. bd. 2003—04). Democrat. Jewish. Home: 5342 SW 33rd Way Fort Lauderdale FL 33312-5574 Office: 2699 Stirling Rd Ste C304 Fort Lauderdale FL 33312-6592 Office Phone: 954-967-8999. E-mail: rbartelstone@rbacare.com.

BARTENSTEIN, JEULI, federal agency administrator; b. Chgo., Dec. 27, 1950; d. Eugene and Sylvia (Myers) B.; m. Michael William Carleton, Mar. 23, 1991. BA with highest honors, U. Ill., 1972; postgrad., U. Calif., Berkeley, 1973-75; MPA, SUNY, Albany, 1980. Aide to maj. leader N.Y. State Assembly, Albany, 1979-80; budget examiner U.S. Dept. Health and Human Svcs., Washington, 1980-85; program analyst solid waste USEPA, Washington, 1985-89, program mgr. environ. edn., 1989-90, dep. dir. EPA Inst., 1990-97, sr. policy analyst, 1998—; dep. dir. The Center Peace Corps, Washington, 1997-98. Internat. trainer USEPA, USAID, UN, Argentina, Hungary, India, Slovakia, Mex., 1993—; mgmt. cons. Creative Cons., Washington, 1996—; seminar leader Fed. Women's Program, Albany, 1980; owner, designer greeting card co. Hat Chat, 1988-91. Author: poem; contbr. article to profl. jour. Pres., v.p., fin. chair, mem. com. chair bd. dirs. Reading Is Fundamental, No. Va., 1987—; mentor, advisor The Women's Ctr., Vienna, pub. spkr., 1990—; tutor DC Pub. Schs., 1980-87. Recipient Leadership in Info Tech. Tng. award Industry Adv. Coun., 1997, Hammer award for reinvention Vice Pres. Gore, 1996. Mem. Am. Soc. Pub. Adminstrn., NOW, Nat. Women's Mus., Presdl. Mgmt. Alumni Group. Avocations: bowling, travel, basketry, charitable fundraising, needlecrafts.

BARTER, MARY F., academic administrator; BA, U. Minn., 1964; MS, U. Wis., Milw., 1969, PhD, 1975. Supt. Three Village Cen. Sch. Dist., L.I., NY, 1992—99, Durango (Colo.) Sch. Dist. 9-R, 1999—. Recipient Disting. Supt. and Outstanding Supt. awards, Suffolk County and N.Y. Coun. Sch. Supts. Mem.: Horace Mann League, N.Y. Assn. for Women in Adminstrn. (bd. dirs.), Wis. Elem. Kindergarten Nursery Educators (pres.), N.Y. Coun. Sch. Supts. (pres.), Am. Assn. Sch. Adminstrs. (exec. com., women adminstrs. adv. com., fed. policy and legis. com., exec. dir.'s adv. com., del. assembly). Office: Durango Sch Dist 9-R 201 E 12th St Durango CO 81301

BARTH, CARIN MARCY, former federal agency administrator; BS summa cum laude, Ala.U.; MBA, Vanderbilt U., 1986. Mem. bd. dir. Southwest Bank Tex., Houston; founder, pres. LB Capital Inc., Houston, 1987; CFO US Dept. Housing & Urban Devel., Washington, 2004—06. Mem. investment com. City Houston; mem. bd. Texas Tech Univ.; chmn. bd. dir. Ronald McDonald House, Houston; chmn. bd. gov. Houston Forum.

BARTH, FRANCES, artist; b. N.Y.C., July 31, 1946; BFA, Hunter Coll., 1968, MA, 1970. Instr. Princeton U., 1975—79, Sarah Lawrence Coll., Bronxville, NY, 1979—85; prof. Yale U., New Haven, 1986—2004; dir. Mt. Royal Sch. of Art, Md. Inst. Coll. of Art, 2004—. One-woman shows include, N.Y.C., 1974—, Jan Cicero Gallery, Chgo., 1981, 1985, U. Mass. Amherst, 1994, E.M. Donahue Gallery, N.Y.C., 1994, 1997, 2000, Millersville Coll., Pa., 1995, Marcia Wood Gallery, Atlanta, 1998, 2001, 2002, Moravian Coll., Pa., 1999, Donahue Sosinski, N.Y.C., 2000, Dartmouth Coll., N.H., 2005, NY Studio Sch., NYC, 2006, exhibited in group shows at Moore Coll. Art, 1970, Whitney Mus. Am. Art, N.Y.C., 1972—73, Houston Mus. Contemporary Art, 1972, Corcoran Gallery Art, Washington, Bard Coll., Annandale-on-Hudson, N.Y.C., 1973, Trenton State Coll., 1974, Princeton U. Art Mus., 1975, High Mus. Art, Atlanta, 1976, Bennington Coll., 1976, San Francisco Art Inst., 1978, U. Pa., 1978, MIT, 1978, Jan Cicero, CHI, 1995, Moravia Coll., Pa., 1999, William Patterson Coll., Wayne, N.J., 1979, NYU, 1979, Va. Commonwealth U., Richmond, 1980, Sarah Lawrence Coll., 1981, Mus. Modern Art, 1981, Cleve. Mus. Art, 1983, Indpls. Mus., 1984, 1985, Princeton U., 1985, Hunter Coll., 1986, Yale U., 1987, Bennington Coll., 1991, Am. Acad. Arts and Letters, 1988 (Purchase award, 2004), Met. Mus. Art, 1990, Andre Emmerich Gallery, 1991, La Viglie, Nimes, France, 1995, Charles Cowles Gallery, N.Y.C., 1996, Am. Acad. Arts and Letters, 1999, 2004, Tucson Mus. Art, 2003, Am. Acad. Arts and Letters, 2004, Represented in permanent collections New 20th Century Wing, Met. Mus. Art, N.Y.C., Mus. Modern Art, Akron Art Inst., Albright-Knox Gallery, Am. Can Co., Greenwich, Conn., Amerada Hess Corp., N.Y.C., Chase Manhattan Bank, Cornell U., IBM Corp., N.Y.C., Mobil Oil Corp., Prudential Inst. Co., N.J., Whitney Mus. Am. Art, Lehman Bros., N.Y.C. and Chgo., Isham, Lincoln & Beale, Chgo., Security Pacific Nat. Bank, L.A., Swiss Bank Corp., N.Y.C., Cameron Iron Works, Houston, Mus. Modern Art, N.Y.C., Paul Haim Found., Paris, Humana, Inc., Louisville, Coudert Bros., N.Y.C., Dallas Mus. Art, Tucson (Ariz.) Art Mus. Grantee Creative Artists Pub. Svc., 1973, NEA, 1974, 82, N.J. State Coun. on Arts, 1987, Adolph and Esther Gottlieb Ind. Support, 1993; John Guggenheim fellow, 1977; recipient Joan Mitchell Found. award, 1995.

BARTH, JESSICA L., mathematics educator; d. Diana M. and Everett A. DeGraaf; m. Carl A. Barth, Dec. 31, 2001; children: Zavier M., Caleigh M. BA, Western Mich. U., Kalamazoo, 2000—03. Cert. Tchr. Mich. Dept. Edn., 2003. Math. educator Comstock HS, Kalamazoo, 2003—, volleyball coach, 2003—04. Sophomore class adv. Comstock HS, 2005—; educator D.A.L.T., Kalamazoo, 2005—. Grantee Full Volleyball scholarship, Marshall U., 1996—2000. Office: Comstock HS 2701 N 26th St Kalamazoo MI 49088 Office Phone: 269-388-9400.

BARTH, M. JANE, secondary school educator; b. Hutchinson, Minn., Mar. 23, 1950; d. Albert Leo and Margaret Janice (Ditmore) B. BS, Winona State U., 1972; BA, Humboldt State U., 1981; MA, George Mason U., 1989. Lic. postgrad. profl., Va. State Bd. Edn. Tchr. English and history Greene Vocat. H.S., Xenia, Ohio, 1983; tchr. adult edn. Prince William County Schs., Independent Hill, Va., 1983-84; tchr. lang. arts Woodbridge (Va.) Mid. Sch., 1984-89; tchr. English and history Stonewall Jackson H.S., Manassas, Va., 1989—2001; tchr. lang. arts South Jr. H.S., St. Cloud, Minn., 2002—. Mem. adv. bd. Oak Cares, Burke, Va., 1996. Lt. (j.g.) USNR, 1975-79 NEH fellow, Sarah Lawrence Coll., 1995. Mem. AAUW, Nat. Coun. Tchrs. of English, Orgn. Am. Historians. Unitarian Universalist. Avocations: writing, painting, hiking, swimming, bicycling. Office: South Jr HS 1120 15th Ave S Saint Cloud MN 56301 Home: 118 6th Ave SE Saint Joseph MN 56374-9517

BARTH, UTA, artist, educator; b. Berlin, Jan. 29, 1958; BA, U. Calif., Davis, 1982; MFA, UCLA, 1985. From asst. prof. to assoc. prof. art dept. U. Calif., Riverside, 1990—. One-woman shows include Galleria by the Water, L.A., 1985, Frederick S. Wight Gallery, L.A., 1985, Addison Gallery of Am. Art, Andover, Mass., 1990, Howard Yezersky Gallery, Boston, 1990, Rochester (N.Y.) Inst. Tech., 1993, Calif. Mus. Photography, Riverside, 1993, Wooster Gardens, N.Y.C., 1994, Mus. Contemporary Art, L.A., 1995, ACME, Santa Monica, Calif., 1995, 98, Tanya Bonakdar Gallery, N.Y.C., 1996, London Projects, London, 1996, 98, S.L. Simpson Gallery, Toronto, Ont., Can., 1996, Mus. Contemporary Art, Chgo., 1997, Andrehn-Schiptjenko, Stockholm, 1997, 99, Tanya Bonakdar Gallery, N.Y., 1998, Lawing, Houston, 1998, Rio Hondo Coll. Art Gallery, Whittier, Cailf., 1998, Bonakdar Jancou Gallery, N.Y., 1998, 99, Rena Branston Gallery, San Francisco, 1999, ACME, L.A., 1999, Galerie Camargo Vilaça, São Paulo, 1999, Lannan Found., Santa Fe, N. Mex., 1999, Henry Art Gallery, Seattle, Washington, 2000, Kunstmuseum Wolfsburg, Germany, 2000; group shows include 56th Ann. Crocker Kingsly Exhbn., Crocker Art Mus., Sacramento, Cailf., 1982, Five Photographers, Joseph Dee Mus. of Photography, San Francisco, Calif., 1982, Proof and Perjury, L.A. Inst. Contemporary Art, 1986, Artist Exhbn., Beverly Hills, 1987, Thick and Thin-Photgraphically Inspired Painting, Fahey/Klein Gallery, L.A., 1989, Spirit of Our Time, Contemporary Arts Forum, Santa Barbara, Calif., 1990, Abstraction in the 90's, Jan Kesner Gallery, L.A., 1992, Tom Solomon's Garage, L.A., 1994, Long Beach (Calif.) Mus. Art, 1994, Mus. De Beyard, Netherlands, 1994, L.A. County Mus. Art, 1994, San Bernardino County Mus., 1994, The New Mus., N.Y.C., 1995, Mus. Modern Art, N.Y.C., 1995, Rooseum-Ctr. for Contemporary Art, Malmo, Sweden, 1996, Magasin 3 Stockholm Konsthall, 1996, Wexner Ctr. for Art, Columbus, Ohio, 1997, Mus. Contemporary Art, Miami, 1997, Whitney Mus. Art, N.Y.C., 1997, 98, Mus. Contemporary Art, L.A., 1998, Matthew Marks Gallery, N.Y.C., 1997, Parco Gallery, 1997, De Appel Found., Amsterdam, The Netherlands, 1997, IKON Gallery, Birmingham, Eng., 1998., Mus. Fine Arts, Houston, 1998, Worcester (Mass.) Art Mus., 1999, Laband Art Gallery, L.A., 1999, Conceptual Art as Neurobiological Praxis, Thread Waxing Space, N.Y., 1999, Photography: An Expanded View, Recent Acquisitions, Guggenheim Mus., N.Y., 1999, Shift, ACME, L.A., 1999, Kerlin Gallery, Dublin, Ireland, 1999, Apposites Opposites, Mus. Contemporary Art, Chgo., 1999; featured in Photography at Princeton, TimeOut, Flash Art, Arforum, Art in Am., Art Monthly, Art & Text, The Birmingham Post, Jour. of Contemporary Art, L.A. Times, Paper Mag., others. Grantee NEA, 1990-91, 94-95, Art Matters Inc., 1992-93, 95; Fellow Nat. Arts Assn., 1983-84, Nat. Endowment for the Arts, 1990-91, 1994-95, Guggenheim Meml. Found., 2004. Home and Office: 3411 Colbert Ave Los Angeles CA 90066-1234

BARTHEL, SARAH ANN MORAN, secondary school educator; b. Van Nuys, Calif., June 2, 1978; d. Geoffrey Hunter and Ruth Ann Moran; m. Paul Ernest Barthel, July 21, 2001. BS, Bethany Coll., W.Va., 1999; MA in Edn., Chapman U., Orange, Calif., 2002. Cert. tchr. Calif. Resident asst. Bethany Coll., 1996—98, shop foreman coll. theater, 1998—99; math. and drama tchr., drama dir. Lompoc HS, Calif., 2000—. Pvt. tutor HS and coll. math., Pismo Beach, Calif., 1999—2000. Home: 515 W College Ave Lompoc CA 93436-4401

BARTHLOW, MICHELLE JONES, political science educator; d. Carey E. and Myrtle Jones; m. Steven D. Barthlow, June 21, 2003; children: Wesley Phelps, Derrick A. Phelps. BS in sci. edn., U. Fla., 1984, MA in edn., 1985. Cert. edn. specialist Piedmont Coll., Ga., 2005, sci. tchr. 7-12, math. 7-12 Ga., advanced placement nat. chemistry tchr. Ga. Math. tchr. Newberry HS, Fla., 1985—90, Gainesville HS, Fla., 1990—93; sci. dept. chair Wayne County HS, Jesup, Ga., 1999—2003; instrnl. lead sci. tchr. Etowah HS, Woodstock, Ga., 2003—. Vol. Ga. Bapt. Children's Home, Baxley, Ga., 1996; com. mem. Anna Keith Meml. Scholarship, Jesup, Ga., 1998—2003; vol. City of Refuge Urban Homeland Outreach, Atlanta, 2004, Faith Luth. Sch. Fundraiser, Marietta, Ga., 2006. Mem.: Nat. Sci. Tchrs. Assn. Avocations: walking, travel, reading, sports. Home: 1679 Morningside Trace Marietta GA 30062 Office: Etowah HS 6565 Putnam Ford Rd Woodstock GA 30189 Personal E-mail: michelle.barthlow@cherokee.k12.ga.us.

BARTHOLET, ELIZABETH, law educator; b. NYC, Sept. 9, 1940; d. Paul and Elizabeth (Ives) Bartholet; divorced; children: Derek DuBois, Christopher, Michael. BA in English Lit., cum laude, Radcliffe Coll., 1962; JD magna cum laude, Harvard U., 1965. Bar: US Supreme Ct. 1969, Mass. 1978. Staff counsel Pres.'s Commn. on Law Enforcement and Adminstrn. of Justice, Washington, 1966—67; staff atty. NAACP Legal Def. & Ednl. Fund, Inc., NYC, 1968-72; counsel VERA Inst. of Justice, NYC, 1972-73; pres., dir. Legal Action Ctr., NYC, 1973-77; asst. prof. law Harvard Law Sch., Cambridge, Mass., 1977-83, prof., 1983—, Morris Wasserstein pub. interest prof. law, 1996—, faculty dir. child advocacy program, 2004—. Civil Rights Reviewing Authority US Dept. Edn., 1979—81; adv com. on intercountry adoption US Dept. State, 1990—2000. Author: Family Bonds: Adoption and the Politics of Parenting, 1993, pub. in 1999 as Family Bonds: Adoption, Infertility, and the New World of Child Production; contbr. articles to profl. journals. Mem. overseers com. to visit Harvard Law Sch., 1971-77; bd. overseers Harvard Coll., 1973-77; mem. assisted reproductive tech. ethics com. Brigham and Women's Hosp., 1990—; mem. IVF ethics com. Boston Fertility & Gynecology Assn., 1991—; mem. adv. com. Internat. Concerns Com. for Children, 1993-; mem New Eng. com. NAACP Legal Def. & Ednl. Fund, Inc., 1994-98; mem. adv. coun. Appleseed Found., 1996-; bd. dirs. Legal Action Ctr., 1977—, vice chair bd., 1998-. Recipient Friends of Adoption Award for Adoption Lit., Adoptive Parents Com., 1993, Media Achievement Award, Cath. Adoptive Parents Assn., 1994, Friends of Adoption Award, Open Door Soc., 1994, Alumnae Recognition Award, Radcliffe Coll., 1997, Award for Advocacy on Behalf of Foster Children, Mass. Appleseed Ctr., 1998. Mem. Assn. Bar City of NY (exec. com. 1973-77), Am. Arbitration Assn. (labor panel 1980-, comml. panel 1995-), Soc. Am. Law Teachers (bd. dirs. 1977-89), Fed. Mediation and Conciliation Svc. Roster Arbitrators, Am. Acad. Adoption Attorneys (hon.), Harvard Club. Democrat. Office: Harvard Law Sch 1563 Massachusetts Ave Cambridge MA 02138 Office Phone: 617-495-3128. Office Fax: 617-496-4947. Business E-Mail: ebarthol@law.harvard.edu.

BARTHOLOMEW, SHIRLEY KATHLEEN, municipal official; b. Marysville, Wash., Jan. 26, 1924; d. Clarence E. and Mary (Hall) B. Grad. high sch., Marysville, 1943. Sec. Everett (Wash.) Broadcasting Corp. Inc., 1960-77, 1st Pacific Broadcasting, Everett, 1977-80. News dir. Sta. KRKO, Everett, 1943-80. Mem. coun. COunty of Snohomish, Everett, 1980-89, chmn., 1987-88; mem. Marysville City Coun., 1994-2001. Named to Edward R. Morrow Broadcast Hall of Fame, 1980; recipient Mng. Editors Citation AP, 1958-73. Republican. Avocations: opera, symphony.

BARTHWELL, ANDREA GRUBB, health care consultant, former federal official; b. June 1954; BS in Psychology, Wesleyan U.; MD, U. Mich. Pres. Encounter Med. Group; pres., CEO BRASS Found., Chgo.; exec. v.p. Human Resources Devel. Group; dep. dir. for demand reduction Office Nat. Drug Control Policy, Washington, 2002—04; founder, CEO EMGlobal LLC, 2004—. Mem. nat. adv. bd. Ctr. for Substance Abuse Treatment; mem. drug abuse adv. com. FDA; mem. AIDS com. Ill. Dept. Alcoholism and Substance Abuse; mem. Nat. Black Alcoholism and Addictions Coun. Recipient Betty Ford award, Assn. Med. Edn. & Rsch. in Substance Abuse, 2003. Mem.: Am. Methadone Treatment Assn., Soc. Addiction Medicine (pres. bd. dirs.).

BARTIZAL, DENISE, psychologist; b. Naperville, Ill., Oct. 14, 1963; d. H. J. and Dolores Underwood Bartizal; m. Jeff Ellis, Oct. 5, 2002. BA, Tulane U., 1984; MS, NOVA Southeastern U., 1993; PsyD, Caribbean Ctr. Advanced Studies, 1998. Nat. bd. cert. behavior analyst. Mental health technician NOVA Geriatric Inst., Lauderhill, Fla., 1992—93; behavior analyst Dept. Children and Families, Ft. Lauderdale, Fla., 1993—97; psychologist intern Fed. Correctional Instn., Petersburg, Va., 1997—98; sr. psychologist Ctrl. State Hosp., Petersburg, 1998—2001, Southside Va. Tng. Ctr., Petersburg, 2000—01; dir. dept. psychology Catawba State Hosp., Va., 2001—. Spkr. in field. Mem.: APA, Aerobics and Fitness Assn. Am., Assn. Behavior Analysis. Republican. Episcopalian. Avocations: travel, classic fiction, exercise. Office: Catawba State Hosp PO Box 200 Catawba VA 24070

BARTLETT, ALICE BRAND, psychoanalyst, educator, researcher; b. Carrollton, Mo., Oct. 27, 1950; d. Daniel Arthur and Nellie May (Farmer) Brand; m. Thomas Sidney Bartlett, Aug. 12, 1989. BA, U. Mo., 1972, MLS, 1973; postgrad., Topeka Inst. Psychoanalysis, 1979-96. Dir. libr. Mo. Inst. Psychiatry, St. Louis, 1973-74; chief libr. Menninger Clinic, Topeka, 1975—2001, psychotherapist, 1984—, assoc. dean info./media Karl Menninger Sch. Psychiatry, 1988—2001, E. Greenwood prof., 1990—2001, prin. investigator Child and Family Ctr., 1995—2001; pvt. practice tng. supr., psychoanalyst Greater Kans. City Psychoanalytic Inst., 2001—. Cons. C.F. Menninger Meml. Hosp., Topeka, 1987-2001; bd. dirs., Psychoanalytic Rsch. Consortium, N.Y.C. and Topeka, 1989-95; bd. dirs. Psychoanalytic Electronic Pub. Contbr. articles to profl. publs. Interfuture scholar, 1971-72. Mem. Am. Psychoanalytic Assn. (chair libr. com. 1991—, Liddle grantee 1985), Topeka Psychoanalytic Soc. (recorder 1983-86, program chair 1993-97, pres. 2000-04), Greater Kansas City & Topeka Psychoanalytic Ctr. (pres. 2006—). Office: Carriage House on Holliday Park 1213 SW Western Topeka KS 66604 Office Phone: 785-234-3873. E-mail: abartlett1@mindspring.com.

BARTLETT, CHERYL ANN, public health service administrator; b. Norwich, Conn., June 28, 1954; d. William Jr. and Frances (Fredette) B.; m. Rogers Washburn Cabot Jr., June 5, 1982 (div. July 1995); m. Bruce Templin Miller, Sept. 10, 1995. ASN, Quinnipiac Coll., 1979; student healthcare adminstrn., Stonehill Coll. Cert. Infection Control, dialysis nursing, HIV/AIDS nursing. Nursing supr. Nantucket (Mass.) Cottage Hosp., 1981-95, dir. nursing, 1995, dir. clin. svcs., 1995-97; public health officer Public Health Assocs. of Nantucket, Southeastern, Mass., 1989—; exec. dir. Nantucket AIDS Network, 1989—. Spkr. in field. Bd. dirs. Nantucket Housing Authority Properties Inc., Nantucket, 1997—; apptd. pres. Cmty. Action Com., Cape Cod and Islands, 1993—; selectman Town of Nantucket, 1993-96, county commr., 1993-96, chmn. Nantucket Bd. Health, 1992-94; mem. Coun. for Health and Human Svcs., 1990-93, chmn., 96—, chmn., 1998-99; pres. bd. dirs. Family and Children's Svc. Recipient Cmty. Recognition award AIDS Action Com. of Mass., 1996, Outstanding Cmty. Health Program, U.S. Dept. of Health and Human Svcs., 1993, Outstanding Citizens award Nantucket Rotary Club, 1992, Recognition for Dedication and Commitment for the Care of AIDS Patients, Mass. State Senate, 1991, Mass. House of Reps., 1991. Mem. ANA, Assn. of Nurses in AIDS Care (govt. rels. com. 1997, chmn. govt. rels. com. 1999), Assn. of Infection Control Practitioners (nominating com. 1991-92, bd. dirs.), Mass. Nurses Assn., Alpha Sigma Lambda. Avocations: reading, gourmet cooking, 3rd world travel, public health volunteer work. Office: Nantucket AIDS Network 35 Old South Rd Nantucket MA 02554-2895 E-mail: cbartlett@nanet.org.

BARTLETT, D. JANE, retired psychology educator; b. Dewey, Okla., July 23, 1937; d. Adolphus Carroll and Clarice Iva (Berryhill) Redwine; m. Bruce Loren Bartlett Sr., Sept. 11, 1955; children: Carroll James (Buddy) (dec.), Bruce Loren Jr., Melanie Ann Gill. BSE Cum Laude in English, Ctrl. Mo. State U., 1969, MSE in Guidance and Counseling, 1976. Counselor Trenton (Mo.) Jr. Coll., 1981-82, Mo. Valley Coll., Marshall, 1985-99, assoc. prof. psychology, 1985-99; ret., 1999. Lay min. Christian and Presbyn. Chs., 1976—; counselor, grant cons., seminar and workshop presenter; co-founder Mary Montgomery Hospice. Pres., treas. Mental Health Assn. Saline County; bd. mem. Bi-County Svc. Inc.; adv. bd. Foster Grandparents; mem. Heart to Heart, Saline County Youth Com. Recipient Mo. Gov.'s awrd for excellence in tchg., Jefferson City, 1990. Mem. APA, Tchrs. of Psychology, Inspiritice Soc., Pi Gamma Mu. Home: 204 Rothrock Ave Richmond MO 64085-1232 Personal E-mail: djb_bartlett@sbcglobal.net.

BARTLETT, DEDE THOMPSON, association executive; m. James Wesley Bartlett; children: Katherine, John. BA, Vassar Coll.; MA, NYU. V.p., corp. sec. Philip Morris Cos. Inc., 1991-94, v.p. corp. affairs programs, 1995—2002; comms. cons., 2002—. Chair adv. bd. Nat. Domestic Violence Hotline; mem. adv. coun. Woodrow Wilson Nat. Fellowship Found.; bd. dirs. Corp. Alliance to Edn Ptnr. Violence, Am. U. Ctr. Asia. Recipient honors, YWCA, N.Y.C., Nat. Ctr. for Victims of Crime, Plays for Living, Nat. Coun. Jewish Women, Ctr. Against Domestic Violence, Lifetime TV. Mem.: Women in Mgmt., Internat. Women's Forum.

BARTLETT, DENISE MARGARET, science educator; b. Fort Knox, Ky., May 21, 1960; d. Guy Walter and Mary Jane Bartlett. BS, North Tex. State U., Denton, 1982. Cert. tchr. Tex., 1982. Tchr. Carrollton-Farmers Br. Ind. Sch. Dist., Tex., 1982—. Grant, Carrollton-Farmers Br. Ednl. Found. Mem.: Tex. State Tchrs. Assn. (assoc.), Nat. Coun. Tchrs. of Math. (assoc.), Phi Delta Kappan (assoc.). Office Phone: 972-968-5000.

BARTLETT, DIANE SUE, counselor; b. Laconia, N.H., Dec. 6, 1947; d. Fred Elmer and Dorothy Pearl (Wakefield) Davis; m. Josiah Henry Bartlett, Aug. 23, 1980; 1 stepchild, Juliet; 1 child from previous marriage, Fred Louis Hacker. AA, Plymouth State Coll., 1982, MEd, 1988; B in Gen. Studies summa cum laude, U. N.H., 1984. Lic. clin. mental health counselor. Mental health counselor, Ossipee, NH, 1995—; police comm. specialist Divsn. Motor Vehicles, Concord, NH, 1970-76, br. office mgr., 1976-83, coord. motor vehicle registrations, 1983-84; tax collector City of Dover, NH, 1984; intern Lakes Region Mental Health Divsn., Laconia, NH, 1985; counselor Latchkey Pastoral Counseling, Laconia, 1984-87; family therapist Children's Best Interest, Laconia, 1988—. Mental health counselor Carroll County Mental Health Svcs., Wolfeboro, NH, 1988—95; participant N.H. Ann. Conf. Status and Role Women, Concord, 1985—87. Mem. Moultonboro (N.H.) Sch. Feasibility Study Commn., 1978, Carroll County Domestic Violence Coun., 1997—, Friends of Families Carroll County, 1995—; mem. adminstrv. bd. dirs., chmn. pastor-parish rels. com. United Meth. Ch., Moultonboro, 1983—94, mem. adminstrv. bd. dirs. N.H. ann. conf., 1986—88. Grantee, N.H. Charitable Found., 1985. Mem.: ACA, Am. Mental Health Counselors Assn. Avocations: skiing, swimming, reading, writing. Home: PO Box 14 Moultonborough NH 03254-0014 Office: Mountainside Bus Ctr 127 Route 28 Ossipee NH 03864-7300 Office Phone: 603-539-3333.

BARTLETT, ELIZABETH LOUISE, psychiatrist; b. Boston, Mass., Aug. 21, 1960; d. Richard Atherton and Ruth Avis Bartlett; children: Sara Carolyn Brer, Matthew Thomas Brer. BA in English, Smith Coll., Northampton, Mass., 1981; BS, U. Mass., 1983; MD, NY Med. Coll., 1988. Lic. Maine, NY. Cons. psychiatrist Ctrl. Maine Med. Ctr., Lewiston, Maine, 1992—94; psyhiatrist St. Mary's Hosp., Lewiston, 1992—94; psychiatrist Andress Psychiatric Assoc., Lewiston, 1992—2001; psychiatrist Jackson Brooke Hosp., Augusta, Maine, 1995—98; counselor Ahes Counseling, Lewiston, 2006—. Bd. dirs. Little Blessings Childcare, Lewiston, 1997—99; mentor Maine Music Soc., Lewiston, 1997—. Mem.: APA. Independent. Unitarian. Avocations: singing, piano, writing, quilting. Home: 27 6th St Auburn ME 04210

BARTLETT, ELIZABETH SUSAN, audio-visual specialist; b. Bloomington, Ind., Sept. 11, 1927; d. Cecil Vernon and Nell (Helfrich) Bartlett; m. Frederick E. Sherman, July 8, 1955 (div. 1978). Student, Ind. U., 1946—48. Traffic-continuity dir. WTTS-Radio, Bloomington, Ind., 1947—48; traffic continuity dir. WTTV-TV, Indpls., 1949—57, program dir., 1958—59; creative dir. Venus Advt. Agy., Indpls., 1960—68; prodn. mgr. Nat. TV News, Detroit, 1968—71; owner, prodr. Susan Sherman Prodns., Greenwich, Conn., 1971—73; audiovisual officer NSF, Arlington, 1973—2001. Cons. NSF, 2001—; lectr. in field. Concept writer/prodr. film: The Observatories, 1981; prodr.: Science: Woman's Work, 1982, Keyhole of Eternity, 1975, What About Tomorrow?, 1978, The American Island, 1970, The New Engineers, 1986, Discover Science, 1988, A Brain, Books and a Curiosity, 1992, Radio Astronomy: Observing the Invisible Universe, 1999, Breaking the Code: The Arabidopsis Genome, 2000, others. Recipient Silver award Internat. Film and TV Festival of N.Y., 1970, 74, 2001, Gold medal Nat. Ednl. Film Festival, 1982, 89, Chris Bronze plaque Columbus Film Festival, 1982, Bronze award Internat. Film & TV Festival of N.Y., 1982, Gold award 1976, Gold Camera award U.S. Indsl. Film Festival, 1982, Silver Cindy award, Info. Film Prodrs. Assn., 1982, award for creative excellence U.S. Indsl. Film Festival, 1975, Techfilm Festival award, 1979, 80, 88, Gold award Houston Internat. Film Festival, 1987, Art Direction Mag. Creativity award, 1988, Videographer award of Distinction, 2001, Silver award, 2001, Aurora Festival Gold award, 2001; named Outstanding Woman for Contbn. in Arts, Federally Employed Women, 1984. Mem.: Am. Women in Radio and TV (chpt. pres. 1953—56, 1969—70), Coun. on Internat. Non-Theatrical Events (adv. bd., Golden Eagle award 1970, 1974, 1976—79, 1982, 1987, 1999), Washington Film and Video Coun. (pres. 1978—79). Home: 809 S Columbus St Alexandria VA 22314-4206 Office Phone: 703-292-7726.

BARTLETT, JANET SANFORD (JANET WALZ), school nurse practitioner; b. Bryn Mawr, Pa., Aug. 13, 1930; d. Edward Joseph Walz and Anna Downing (Little) Walz Tomlin; m. Joseph Richard Bartlett, May 6, 1952 (div. April 1972); children: Cheryl, Elaine, Karen, Lee, Patrick, Michael. Diploma nursing, Meml. Mission Sch. Nursing, 1953; EMT-I cert., El Paso C.C., 1983. RN, N.C., Tex. Office nurse William F. Hillier, M.D., Asheville, N.C., 1953-55; school nurse Ysleta Ind. Sch. Dist., El Paso, 1973-93. Author: (manual) Sch. Nurse Manual, 1979, Volunteer's Handbook, 1979, (cookbook) Bartlett Heritage Cookbook; editor: (newsletter) Nurses Notes Newsletter, 1983-88; co-creator, copyright, D.K. Buster, 1989. Mem. El Paso Health Issues Forum, 1985—88; co-chair El Paso Oral Health Commn., 1987—; life mem. PTA; pres. El Paso coun., bd. dirs. Campfire Girls, Inc., 1971—74, leader Blue Birds, Camp Fire guardian; active Boy Scouts Am., Girl Scouts Am.; com. chair El Paso chpt. Am. Cancer Soc.; co-chair Ysleta Sch. Dist. Employee Wellness, 1989—90, compiler manual; sec. Unite El Paso Birth Packet Com., 1993—96, chmn., 1996—; founder, chmn. Health Connection, 1996—; apptd. oral health svcs. adv. com. Tex. Bd. Health, 1995—2003, vice chmn., 1999—2001; mentor Sageland Elem. Sch., 1994—97; mem. adv. com. Tex. Oral Health Coalition, 2004—; mem. vestry St. Alban's Anglo Cath. Ch., 1996—99, 2006—, sr. warden, 1997—99. Recipient Outstanding Staff Support award Ysleta Vol. Svcs., 1988-89, Stand Up for El Paso award KDBC TV, 1991, REACH award YWCA/El Paso Healthcare System, 1992, Pub. Health Partnership award El Paso City-County Health and Environ. Dist., 1998, Older El Pasoans Hall of Fame award Mayor's Adv. Bd. on Aging, 1999, Access award ADA Coun. on Access, Prevention and Interprofl. Rels., 2003, E. Bud Tarrson Access to Oral Health Care award ADA Found., 2003, certificate of merit, Tex. Dental Assn., 2005; named Woman of Yr. El Paso Parks and Recreation, 1995; named to Ysleta Ret. Sch. Employees Assn. Hall of Fame, 2000, El Paso Women's Hall of Fame, El Paso Women's Commn., 2002. Mem. Nat. Assn. Sch. Nurses, Tex. Sch. Nurse Assn. (Pres.'s award 1990, Tex. Sch. Nurse of Yr. 1991), Tex. Assn. Sch. Nurses Region 19 (v.p. 1982, 83, historian 1996—, Sch. Nurse of Yr. 1990), Ysleta Sch. Nurses Assn. (pres. 1988, Sch. Nurse of Yr. 1987, World Healer award 1995), Assistance League of El Paso (yearbook chmn. 1994, 95, Sch. Bell. com. 1994-2004). Avocations: swimming, knitting, cooking, travel. Home: 10249 Bayo Ave El Paso TX 79925-4347 Personal E-mail: jbartlett@elp.rr.com.

BARTLETT, JENNIFER LOSCH, artist; b. Long Beach, Calif., Mar. 14, 1941; BA, Mills Coll., 1963; B.F.A., Yale U., 1964, M.F.A., 1965; studied with Jack Tworkvov, James Rosenquist, Al Held, Jim Dire. Instr. Sch. Visual Arts, N.Y.C. One-woman shows include Mills Coll., Oakland, Calif., 1963, Reese Paley Gallery, N.Y.C., 1972, Paula Cooper Gallery, N.Y.C., 1974, 76, 77, 79, 81, 82, 83, 85, 87, 88, 90, 91, 92, 94, Saman Gallery, Genoa, Italy, 1974, 78, John Doyle Gallery, Chgo., 1975, Contemporary Art Ctr., Cin., 1975, Dartmouth Coll., 1975, Wadsworth Atheneum, Hartford, Conn., 1977, San Francisco Mus. Modern Art, 1978, U. Calif., Irvine, 1978, Hansen-Fuller Gallery, San Francisco, 1978, Balt. Art Mus., 1978, Art Mus. South Tex., Corpus Christi, 1978, Margo Leavin Gallery, Los Angeles, 1979, 81, 83, U. Akron, 1979, Carleton Coll., 1979, Heath Gallery, Atlanta, 1979, 83, Galerie Mukai, Tokyo, 1980, Akron Art Inst., 1980, 89, 92, Albright-Knox Art Gallery, Buffalo, 1980, Joslyn Art Mus., Omaha, 1982, Tate Gallery, London, 1982, McIntosh/Drysdale Gallery, Houston, 1982, Gloria Luria Gallery, Bay Harbor Islands, Fla., 1983, Rose Art Mus., Brandeis U., Waltham, Mass., 1984, Long Beach Mus. Art., Calif., 1984, Univ. Art Mus., U. Calif.-Berkeley, 1984, Knight Gallery, Charlotte, N.C., 1985, Walker Arts Ctr., Mpls., 1985, Nelson-Atkins Mus. of Art, Kansas City, Mo., 1985, Bklyn. Mus., 1985, La Jolla Mus. Coll. Art, Calif., 1986, Mus. of Art, Carnegie Inst., Pitts., 1986, Whitechapel Art Gallery, London, 1986, Cleve. Mus. Art, 1986, Greg Kucera Gallery, Seattle, 1986, 92, Harvard U. Grad. Sch. of Design, Cambridge, Mass., 1987, Milw. Art Mus., 1988, John Berggruen Gallery, San Francisco, 1988, 90, 93, Knoedler Gallery, London, 1989, 90, Richard Gray Gallery, Chgo., 1991, 93, 96, Maier Mus. Randolph-Macon Women's Coll., Lynchburg, Va., 1992, Nancy Drysdale Gallery, Washington, 1992, Santa Fe Inst. Fine Arts, 1993, Gallery Camino Real, Boca Raton, Fla., 1994, Orlando (Fla.) Mus. Art, 1994, Locks Gallery, Phila., 1995, Gagosian Gallery, Beverly Hills, Calif., 1996, 97, others; group exhbns. include Mus. Modern Art, N.Y.C., 1971, 77, 78, 79, 80, 81, 83, 85, Whitney Mus. Am. Art, N.Y.C., 1972, 73, 77, 78, 79, 81, 82, 83, 86, 89, 91, Walker Art Ctr., Mpls., 1972, Kunsthaus, Hamburg, Fed. Republic Germany, 1972, Paula Cooper Gallery, N.Y.C., 1972, 73, 74, 76, 77, 78, 81, 83, 84, 85, 86, 87, 88, 90, 93, Corcoran Gallery Art, Washington, 1975, Art Inst. Chgo., 1975, 76, 86, Kunstmuseum, Dusseldorf, Fed. Republic Germany, 1976, Kassel, Fed. Republic Germany, 1977, Contemporary Arts Mus., Houston, 1980, Am. Acad. Arts and Letters, N.Y.C., 1981, 83, 85, 92, Sarah Lawrence Art Gallery, Bronxville, N.Y., 1984, Archer M. Hunting Art Gallery, U. Tex.-Austin, 1984, Hudson River Mus., Yonkers, N.Y., 1984, Tucson Mus. Art, 1984, Leo Castelli Gallery, N.Y.C., 1984, Gerald Peters Gallery, Dallas, 1994, Numark Gallery, Washington, 1995, others; represented in permanent collections, Mus. Modern Art, N.Y.C., Met. Mus. Art, N.Y.C., Whitney Mus. Am. Art, N.Y.C., Phila. Mus. Art, Walker Art Ctr., Mpls., Yale U. Art Gallery, New Haven, Art Mus. S.Tex., Corpus Christi, R.I. Sch. Design, Providence, Art Gallery S. Australia, Adelaide, Goucher Coll., Balt., Amerada Hess, Woodbridge, N.J., Dallas Mus. Fine Arts, Modern Art Mus. Fort Worth, Tex., Richard B. Russell Fed. Bldg. and U.S. Courthouse, Atlanta, others. Recipient Harris prize Art Inst. Chgo., 1976, 86; recipient Creative Arts award Brandeis U., 1983, award Am. Acad. Arts and Letters, 1983, AIA award, 1986; Creative Artists Public Services fellow, 1974; Lucas vis. lectr. award Carleton Coll., 1979 Address: 134 Charles St # 114 New York NY 10014-2538 also: Paula Cooper Inc 534 W 21st St New York NY 10011-2812 also: c/o Gagosian Gallery 456 N Camden Dr Beverly Hills CA 90210

BARTLETT, KATHARINE TIFFANY, dean, law educator; b. New Haven, Feb. 16, 1947; d. Edgar Parmelee and Elizabeth (Clark) B.; m. Christopher H. Schroeder, Aug. 13, 1975; children: Emily, Ted, Elizabeth. BA, Wheaton Coll., 1968; MA, Harvard U., 1969; JD, U. Calif., Berkeley, 1975. Bar: Calif. 1975, N.C. 1980, U.S. Dist. Ct. (no. dist.) Calif. 1975, U.S. Dist. Ct. (mid. dist.) N.C. Law clk. to presiding justice Calif. Supreme Ct., San Francisco, 1975-76; atty. Legal Aid Soc. of Alameda County, Oakland, Calif., 1976-79; A. Kenneth Pye prof. of law Duke U., Durham, NC, 1979—; dean, 2000—. Vis. prof. UCLA, 1985-86, Boston U., 1990. Grad. prize fellow Harvard U., 1968-69, fellow Nat. Humanities Ctr., 1992-93. Mem. Am. Law Inst., Soc. Am. Law Tchrs., N.C. Women Attys., Am. Law Inst. (reporter for principles of family dissolution), Phi Beta Kappa. Democrat. Office: Duke Univ Law Sch Sci Dr and Towerview Rd Box 90362 Durham NC 27708-0362 Office Phone: 919-613-7001. E-mail: bartlett@law.duke.edu.

BARTLETT, NORMA THYRA, retired administrative assistant; b. Raymond, SD, June 7, 1922; d. Wilhelm Emil and Olga Sophie (Mailand) Claussen; m. Fred Otis Metcalf, Mar. 29, 1941 (dec. Apr. 1963); children: Linda E. Lepak, Barry Otis (dec. Feb. 2000); m. Francis Grindal Bartlett, Dec. 27, 1963 (dec. Jan. 2004). BA, U. Wash., Seattle, 1969; Diploma, Inst. of Children's Lit., 1997. Cert. profl. sec. Office mgr. Fed. Old Line Ins. Co., Everett, Wash., 1949-55; supr. office svc. Scott Paper Co., Everett, Wash., 1958-63; tchr. bus. edn. Canyon Park Jr. H.S., Seattle, 1969, Bellevue (Wash.) C.C., 1969; exec. asst. Peoples Bank, Starkville, Miss., 1970-76; prin. Satellite Steno Svc., Starkville, Miss., 1976-77; office mgr. Donald Wiley & Assocs., Sydney, Australia, 1977-80. Bd. dirs. United Cmty. Fund Snohomish County, Everett, Wash., 1961-62; pres. Scott Paper Co. Fellowship Fund, Everett, 1961, TLRC Helping Hands, 2005-. Hon. life mem. United Luth. Ch. Women, Everett, Wash., 1958—; organizer, charter pres. Starkville Bus. and Profl. Women, 1972-74; pres. Welcome Wagon Club, Ocean Springs, Miss., 1982-83, Tacoma Luth. Retirement Cmty. Helping Hands, 2005—; tutor Jackson County Literacy, Ocean Springs, 1985-88; organizer Discourse, Ocean Springs, 1985-86. Norma T. Bartlett scholarship named in her honor Starkville Area Bus. and Profl. Women, 1978. Mem.: AAUW (Gig Harbor br. media rep. 1997—99), Intertel, Mensa (local sec. 1989—91, editor newsletter 1987—89), U. Wash. Alumni Assn. Democrat. Lutheran. Avocations: needlecrafts, reading, writing, travel, organist. Home: 1305 N Highlands Pkwy Apt C1 Tacoma WA 98406-2171 E-mail: fgbart@comcast.net.

BARTLETT, RHONDA WOODWARD, library manager; d. Richard Jordan and E. Jolene Woodward; m. J. David Bartlett, July 2, 1978; 1 child, Julianne Woodward. BBA in Mgmt., Ga. State U., 1980. Unit mgr. Kroger Co., Smyrna, Ga., 1977—2001; libr. mgr. Elizabeth Harris Libr. Lake Blackshear Regional Libr. Sys., Unadilla, Ga., 2001—. Ptnrs. in edn. mem. Brown Elem. Sch., Smyrna, Ga., 1995—2001, Norton Pk. Elem. Sch., Smyrna, Ga., 1995—2001. Sec., treas. Downtown Devel. Authority, Unadilla, Ga., 2005; mem. Citizens Adv. Bd., Smyrna, 1995—2001; zone fundraising coord. Scottish Rite Children's Hosp., Smyrna, 1993. Avocations: walking, reading. Office: Elizabeth Harris Libr 312 Harman St PO Box 930 Unadilla GA 31091 Office Phone: 478-627-9303. Office Fax: 478-627-9303. E-mail: rwbartlett@lbrls.org.

BARTLETT, SHIRLEY ANNE, accountant; b. Gladwin, Mich., Mar. 28, 1933; d. Dewey J. and Ruth Elizabeth (Wright) Frye; m. Charles Duane Bartlett, Aug. 16, 1952 (div. Sept. 1982); children: Jeanne, Michelle, John, Yvonne. Student, Mich. State U., 1952-53, Rutgers U., 1972-74. Auditor State of Mich., Lansing, 1951-66; cost acct. Templar Co., South River, NJ, 1968-75; staff acct. Franco Mfg. Co., Metuchen, NJ, 1975-78; controller Thomas Creative Apparel, New London, Ohio, 1978-80; mgr. gen. acctg. Ideal Electric Co., Mansfield, Ohio, 1980-85; staff acct. Logangate Homes, Inc., Girard, Ohio, 1985-88; pvt. practice acctg. Youngstown, 1985—; acct. Universal Devel. Enterprises, Liberty Twp., Ohio, 1987-88. V.p. Lang Industries, Inc., Youngstown, 1984-93. Author: (play) Our Bicentennial-A Celebration, 1976. Mem. various orchs., Mich., Va., Ohio, soloist, Mich., Va.; mem. Human Rels. Commn., Franklin Township, 1971-77, Friends of Am. Art; treas. Heritage Found., New Brunswick, N.J., 1973-74, New London Proceeds Corp., 1979-83; commr. Huron Park Commn., Ohio, 1979-83; elected Dem. com. mem., N.J., Ohio, 1970-82; vol. IRS for small bus., 1988-94, Children's Mus., 2005—; mem. planning com. Youngstown State U. Tax Insts., 1990-95, presenter, 1990-98; bd. dirs., treas. Discovery Place, Inc., 1991-95; mem. planning com. for Children's Miracle Network Telethon, Tod's Children's Hosp., Youngstown, 1985-2001; mem. citizens adv. bd. Mahoning County Juvenile Ct., 2004—; bd. dirs., treas. Youngstown Arts and Entertainment Dist. Assn., 2003—; bd. dirs. First Night Youngstown, 2006; founder Youngstown Farmer's Market, 2003—; mem. Mahoning Valley Children's Mus., 2004—. Mem.: NOW (treas. Youngstown chpt. 1986—93), NAFE, Am. Soc. Notaries, Am. Soc. Women Accts. (bd. dirs. 1986—88, v.p. 1988—89, pres. 1989—91, scholarship com. 1991—2001, chair chpt. devel. 1995—96, bd. dirs. 1996—2001, 1996—, chair program com. 1997—2001), First Nigh Youngstown (bd. mem.), Youngstown Arts & Entertainment Dist. Assn., Youngstown Opera Guild, Internat. Platform Assn., Women's Jour. Network, Nat. Women's Polit. Caucus, Bus. and Profl. Women (v.p. 1980—2001), Citizen's League Greater Youngstown, Friends of Am. Art, Chataqua Lit. and Sci. Cir., Sci. Cir. Club (pres. 1979—), Chataqua Lit. Club, Franklin JFK Club (treas. 1970—72, v.p. 1973—78), Investment Club (pres. 1997—99, treas. 1999—2001). Democrat. Unitarian Universalist. Avocations: music, knitting, needlecrafts. Office Phone: 330-398-5347. Personal E-mail: sbartlett328@hotmail.com.

BARTLEY, LINDA L., musician, music educator; b. Amarillo, Tex., 1948; MusB in Edn., Mich. State U., MusM, D of Musical Arts. Asst. prof. clarinet SUNY, Fredonia, NY, 1974—75, Ark. Tech U., Russellville, 1981—83; assoc. prof. clarinet Ctrl. Mich. U., Mt. Pleasant, 1987—92; prof. clarinet U. Wis., Madison, 1992—. Vis. prof. clarinet U. Western Ont., London, 1975—81; prin. clarinet London Symphony Orch., 1975—81, Madison Symphony Orch.; clarinetist Grand Teton Music Festival, Jackson Hole, Wyo., 1989—2001, Powers Woodwind Quintet, Mt. Pleasant, 1987—92, Wingra Woodwind Quintet, Madison, 1992—. Musician (soloist/recitalist): Internat. Clarinet Assn.; contbr. articles to profl. jours. Mem.: Chamber Music Am., Coll. Music Soc., Internat. Clarinet Assn. (state chair, grants com. mem., young artist competition judge). Office: School of Music University of Wisconsin 455 N Park St Madison WI 53706-1483 Office Phone: 608-263-1910. Business E-Mail: lbartley@wisc.edu.

BARTLING, PHYLLIS MCGINNESS, oil company executive; b. Chillicothe, Ohio, Jan. 3, 1927; d. Francis A. McGinness and Gladys A. (Henkelman) Bane; m. Theodore Charles Bartling; children: Pamela, Theodore, Eric C. Student, Ohio State U., 1944-47. Bookkeeper, Bartling & Assocs., Bartling Oil Co., Houston 1974-80; sec.-treas., dir. both cos., 1980. Co-chmn. ticket sales Tulsa Opera, 1956-61; bd. dirs. Tex. Speech and Hearing Ctr., Houston, 1967-70. Republican. Episcopalian. Avocations: gardening, bicycling, cooking, golf. Home and Office: 11 Inwood Oaks Dr Houston TX 77024-6803

BARTLING, SARA, language educator; d. Carlos Fernando de la Garza and Sara Nelida Rocha, Russell Morris (Stepfather); m. James Bartling, Aug. 8, 1998; children: Sara Garriga, Brandis Sauer. MBA, Tex. A & M Internat., Laredo, 1993; MA in Edn., U. Phoenix, 2004. Cert. reading specialist Ariz., 2005, sch. guidance counselor Ariz. Dept. Edn., 2004. Tchr. Gililland Mid. Sch., Tempe, Ariz., 2002—05; lang. arts coach Arredondo Elem. Sch., Tempe, 2005—. Grantee, Lewisville Edn. Found., 2001, ASSET, 2006. Office: Arredondo Elem Sch 1330 E Carson Dr Tempe AZ 85282 Office Phone: 480-897-2744. Business E-Mail: sbartling@tempeschools.org.

BARTNOFF, JUDITH, judge; b. Boston, Apr. 14, 1949; d. Shepard and Irene F. (Tennenbaum) B.; m. Eugene F. Sofer, Sept. 10, 1978; 1 child, Nelson Bartnoff Sofer. BA magna cum laude, Radcliffe Coll., 1971; JD (Harlan Fiske Stone scholar), Columbia U., 1974; LLM, Georgetown U., 1975. Bar: DC 1975, US Dist. Ct. DC 1975, US Ct. Appeals (DC cir.) 1980, US Ct. Appeals (fed. cir.) 1985, US Ct. Appeals (11th cir.) 1988, US Ct. Appeals (3d cir.) 1989, US Claims Ct. 1991. Fellow Inst. Pub. Interest Representation Georgetown Law Ctr., Washington, 1974—75; staff atty. Coun. Pub. Interest Law, Washington, 1975—77; spl. asst. to asst. atty. gen. criminal divsn. Dept. Justice, Washington, 1977—78, assoc. dep. atty. gen., 1978—80; spl. asst. U.S. atty. Office of US Attys., Washington, 1980—81, asst. U.S. atty., 1982—85; assoc. Patton, Boggs & Blow, 1987—87, ptnr., 1988—94, assoc. ind. counsel, 1993—94; assoc. judge Superior Ct. of DC, Washington, 1994—, presiding judge domestic violence unit, 2006—. Mediator US Dist. Ct. DC, 1991-94; mem. com. on pro se litig. US Dist. Ct., 1991-94. Mem. D.C. Bar Task Force on Children at Risk, 1997—98, D.C. Child Support Guidelines Commn., 2003—. Fellow Am. Bar Found.; mem. Nat. Assn. Women Judges, DC Bar, Women's Bar Assn. Office: 500 Indiana Ave NW Washington DC 20001-2131 Office Phone: 202-879-1988. Business E-Mail: bartnofj@dcsc.gov.

BARTO, DEBORAH ANN, physician; b. West Chester, Pa., July 27, 1948; d. Charles Guy and Jeannette Victoria (Golder) B. BA, Oberlin Coll., 1970; MD, Hahnemann U., 1974; Reiki III, N.W. Sch. Healing, 2003. Cert. Reiki master. Intern, resident Kaiser Permanente Hosp., San Francisco, 1974-77; dir. med. oncology Evergreen Hosp., Kirkland, Wash., 1980-85, head oncology quality assurance, 1992-94; med. dir. Cmty. Home Health Care Hospice, Seattle, 1981-84. Hosp. ethics com. Evergreen Hosp., 1995-98, integrative care com., 1996-2001. Mem. Evergreen Women's Physicians, Reiki III. Democrat. Buddhist. Avocation: horseback riding. Office: Evergreen Profl Plz 12911 120th Ave NE Ste E60 Kirkland WA 98034-3047

BARTO, REBECCA LYNN, systems analyst; b. Tokyo, Aug. 9, 1962; came to U.S., 1968; d. Jackie Don Baize and Hisako (Ogawa) Ishimoto; children: Tanya Lynn, Andrew James. Student, U. Pitts., 1982-87, U. Tex., 1980-82. Coordinator data mgmt. and outreach, liaison to Ctr. Continuing Edn. Health Scis. U. Pitts., 1983-87; cons. TRW-Fla. Ops. Def. Systems Group, Cape Canaveral Air Force Sta., 1987-90, bus. analyst, 1987-90; self-employed bus. analyst Pt. Saint John, Fla., 1990-97; nurse emergency dept. and case mgr., 1997—2003; emergency dept. sys. integration coord., clin. info. sys. analyst, 2003—. Democrat. Roman Catholic. E-mail: hlfbreed@earthlink.net.

BARTO, SUSAN CAROL, writer; b. Bklyn., June 21, 1941; d. William O. and Eda (Birra) Forcellon; m. Harry W. Barto, Mar. 11, 1960; 1 child, William M. Cert., Katherine Gibbs, 1960; student, Union Coll., 1979-82. Sec. dean of students Montclair (N.J.) State Coll., 1960; sec. Presbyn. Synod of N.J., East Orange, N.J., 1961-62; exec. sec. Union County Rep. Com., Westfield, N.J., 1971-79; legis. aide State Senator James Vreeland-Morris County, N.J., 1977-79. Author of short stories. County com. woman Union County Rep. Com., Westfield, 1970-82; active New Providence (N.J.) Libr. Bd., 1979-86. Recipient plaque of appreciation New Providence (N.J.) Libr. Bd., 1986. Mem. Friends of the Hunterdon Mus. of Art (pres. 1996-99). Presbyterian. Home and Office: 1 Fisher Ct Lebanon NJ 08833-2107

BARTOLACCI, PAULETTE MARIE, elementary school educator, aerobics instructor; b. Phillipsburg, Pa., Aug. 19, 1969; d. Anthony Thomas and Pauline Virginia (Leh) B. BS in Elem. Edn., St. Joseph U., Phila., 1991; MS in Bilingual, Bicultural Studies, Lehigh U., 1997. 6th grade tchr. Our Lady of Perpetual Help, Bethlehem, Pa., 1992-93; 1-4th grade lang. arts tchr. for ESOL children Allentown (Pa.) Sch. Dist., 1993-97, interim asst. to dir. instrl. support svcs., 1998, 6th grade lang. arts tchr., 1997—, insvc. steering com. mem. Fellow Pa. State Nat. Writing Project, Fogelsville, Pa., 1993—, outreach mem., 1995—; cheerleading coach S. Mountain Middle Sch., Allentown, 1998-99, mem. leadership team for stds.-based edn., support tchr. for student tchrs., peer mentor for peer edn., also mem. sch. coun. Grantee Nat. Writing Project, Pa. State U., 1995-99. Mem. ASCD, Pa. Edn. Assn., Allentown Edn. Assn., Nat. Coun. Tchrs. of English, Aerobics and Fitness Assn. Am. (cert., instr. summer 1998) Republican. Roman Catholic. Avocations: aerobics, singing, jazz dancing, guitar. Home: 524 City View Dr Nazareth PA 18064-1244

BARTOLI, CATHERINE P., legal assistant; b. Holdrege, Nebr., Jan. 16, 1951; d. Myrom L. and Catherine Trenchard Potter; 1 child, Genevieve Haggard. B Music Edn., U. Nebr., Lincoln, 1973. Music tchr. Wilbur-Clatonia Ind. Sch. Dist., Wilbur, Nebr., 1973—74, Grand Island Ind. Sch. Dist., Nebr., 1974—76; legal sec. U. Tex. Law Sch., Austin, 1982—92; exec. asst. Supreme Ct. Tex., Austin, 1992—. Choir dir. various Presbyn. chs., 1974—2005. Mem.: Tex. Choral Dirs. Assn., Am. Choral Dirs. Assn., Presbyn. Assn. Musicians, Sigma Alpha Iota (pres. Austin alumnae chpt. 1986—88, 2000—02, Sword of Honor 1987, Rose of Honor 2002, alumnae grantee 2004). Avocations: singing, reading. Office: Supreme Ct Tex 201 W 14th St Austin TX 78701

BARTOLI, CECILIA, soprano; b. Italy, 1967; d. Pietro Angelo and Silvana B. Attended, Academia de Santa Cecilia. Recording artist Decca/London, 1986—. Stage debut, Verona, 1987; appearances include La Scala, Met. Opera, Opéra Bastille, Carnegie Hall, Berlin, Nantes, Warsaw, Naples, Zürich, Orch. Hall, Chgo.; albums: include Rossini Recital, 1990, Mozart Arias, 1991, Rossini Heroines, 1992, Arie Antiche, 1992, The Impatient Lover: Italian Songs by Beethoven, Schubert, Mozart, Haydn, 1993 (Grammy award for best classical vocal performance, 1994), Mozart Portraits, 1995, An Italian Songbook, 1997 (Grammy award for best classical vocal performance, 1997), Vivaldi album, 1999 (Grammy award for best classical vocal performance, 2000), Gluck Italian Arias, 2001 (Grammy award for best classical vocal performance, 2001), The Salieri Album, 2003, Opera proibita, 2006. Named Musical America's Vocalist of Yr., 1993, recipient Culture award, NY Mag., 2006. Mem.: Royal Acad. of Music, London (hon.).*

BARTON, ALICE, physician, educator; b. West Long Branch, N.J., Sept. 29, 1953; d. David Knox and Ruth B. Barton; children: Lara, Seth, Peter. BA, Harvard U., 1975; MD, N.Y. Med. Coll., 1992. Diplomate Am. Bd. Internal Medicine. Tchr. art history Westover Sch., Middlebury, Conn., 1975-78; gen. surgery intern N.Y. Med. Coll., N.Y.C., 1992-93, resident in neurol. surgery, 1993-95; resident in internal medicine Stamford (Conn.) Hosp., 1995-97; attending physician ER Horton Hosp., Middletown, N.Y., 1997-98; attending physician HIV Ctr. St. Luke's-Roosevelt Hosp., N.Y.C., 1998-99; attending physician, asst. prof. medicine Ctr. Spl. Studies Cornell U. Med. Sch., N.Y.C., 1999—2003; attending physician, asst. clin. prof. medicine Brown U. Sch. Medicine, Providence, 2003—. Contbr. essays, articles to profl. jours. Recipient Janet M. Glasgow Meml. Achievement award, Am. Med. Women's Assn., Samuel Spiegel, MD Meml. award, N.Y. Med. Coll., 1992. Mem.: Phi Beta Kappa, Alpha Omega Alpha. Home: 3 Hidden St Providence RI 02906-1418 Office: Brown Univ Sch Medicine 1075 Smith St Providence RI 02908 Office Phone: 401-421-4400.

BARTON, BETTY LOUISE, school system administrator; b. Shawnee Mission, Kans., Jan. 12, 1931; d. David and Dora Elizabeth (Grother) Schulteis; m. William Clayton Barton, Aug. 11, 1951; children: Linda Ann, Sharon Elaine. BA, Washburn U., 1951; MS in Curriculum and Instrn., Kans. U., 1976, EdD, 1983. Cert. ednl. adminstrn., curriculum and instrn., Kans. Classroom tchr. Topeka Pub. Schs., 1951-52; music tchr. Shawnee Mission Schs., 1959-62, classroom tchr., 1962-65, 69-72, asst. prin., 1976-83, prin., 1983—96; elem. adminstr. DeSoto (Kans.) Schs., 2001—. Bd. dirs. Headstart, Shawnee Mission, 1991—, Child Abuse Coalition, Shawnee Mission, 1984-94, Parents as Tchrs., Shawnee Mission, 1989-93, Srs. Serving Schs., Shawnee Mission. Bd. dirs. Multidisciplinary Team, Johnson County, Kans., 1992-94; mem. early childhood adv. com. Johnson County C.C., 1988-93. Named Adminstr. of Yr., Shawnee Mission Schs., 1996; recipient award for outstanding dissertation, Internat. Reading Assn., 1984. Mem. ASCD, Shawnee Mission Adminstrs. Assn. (pres., Adminstr. of Yr. 1990), Phi Delta Kappa. Lutheran. Avocations: music, writing, gardening, reading. Home: 9301 High Dr Leawood KS 66206-1918 Office: Cherokee Elem Sch 8714 Antioch Rd Shawnee Mission KS 66212-3698

BARTON, JANICE SWEENY, chemistry professor; b. Trenton, N.J., Mar. 22, 1939; d. Laurence U. and Lillian Mae (Fletcher) S.; m. Keith M. Barton, Dec. 20, 1967. BS, Butler U., 1962; PhD, Fla. State U., 1970. Postdoctoral fellow Johns Hopkins U., Balt., 1970-72; asst. prof. chemistry East Tex. State U., Commerce, 1972-78, Tex. Woman's U., Denton, 1978-81; assoc. prof. Washburn U., Topeka, 1982-88, prof., 1988—, chair chemistry dept., 1992—. Mem. undergrad. faculty enhancement panel NSF, Washington, 1990; mem. NSF instr. lab. improvement panel, 1992, 96, 99; mem. NSF-AIRE site visit team, 2000; WUKBRIN (NIH grant) coord., 2001—. Contbr. articles to profl. jours. Active Household Hazardous Waste Collection, Topeka, 1991, Solid Waste Task Force, Shawnee County, Kans., 1990; mem. vol. com. YWCA, Topeka, 1984-87; bd. dir. Helping Hand Humane Soc., 2002—; grant coord. Kans. Biomedical Rsch Infrastructure Network, 2002—. Rsch. grantee Petroleum Rsch. Fund, Topeka, 1984-86, NIH, Topeka, 1985-88; instrument grantee NSF, Topeka, 1986, 95. Mem. Am. Chem. Soc. (sec. Dallas-Ft. Worth sect. 1981-82), Kans. Acad. Sci. (pres.-elect 1991, pres. 1992, treas. 1995—), Biophys. Soc., Sigma Xi (pres. TWU club 1980-81), Iota Sigma Pi (mem.-at-large coord. 1987-93). Home: 3401 SW Oak Pky Topeka KS 66614-3218 Office: Washburn U Dept Chemistry Topeka KS 66621 E-mail: janice.barton@washburn.edu.

BARTON, KATIE, music educator; b. Redlands, Calif., Sept. 3, 1960; d. Galilee and James Glanville; m. Robert Barton, July 21, 1984; children: James, Emily, Lauren. BA in Music Edn., UCLA, 1983; cert. in tchg., U. Redlands, Calif., 1984. Instrumental music tchr. Redlands Unified Sch. Dist., 2003—. Leader Girl Scouts of Am., Redlands, 1995—2006. Recipient Hon. Svc. award, Calif. PTA, 2000, 2006. Mem.: So. Calif. Sch. Band and Orch. Assn.

BARTON, MISCHA, actress; b. London, Eng., Jan. 24, 1986; Actor: (films) Polio Water, 1995, Lawn Dogs, 1997, Pups, 1999, Notting Hill, 1999, The Sixth Sense, 1999, Paranoid, 2000, Skipped Parts, 2000, Lost and Delirious, 2001, Julie Johnson, 2001, Tart, 2001, Octane, 2003, The OH in Ohio, 2006; (TV films) New York Crossing, 1996, Fankie & Hazel, 2000, A Ring of Endless Light, 2002; (TV series) Kablam, 1996, All My Children, 1996, The O.C., 2003—06 (TV Choice Actress, Teen Choice Awards, 2006), (TV appearances) Once and Again, 2001, Fastlane, 2003. Office: William Morris Agency 151 El Camino Dr Beverly Hills CA 90212*

BARTON, NOREEN DUFFY, secondary school educator; b. Phila., June 7, 1926; d. John Joseph and Mary Josephine (McDonough) Brett; m. Thomas Francis Duffy, Feb. 22, 1960 (div. June 1971); children: Thomas B., John F., Joseph D.; m. Patrick Joseph Barton, Nov. 11, 1995. BA, Montclair (N.J.) State Coll., 1948; MEd, U. Va., 1966. Cert. secondary math., bus. and acctg. tchr., N.J. Tchr. math. and bus. Egg Harbor (N.J.) City High Sch., 1948-55, coach girls basketball, 1948-51; instr. math. North Adams (Mass.) Coll., 1964-65, Frostburg (Md.) State Coll., 1969-70; tchr. math. So. Regional High Sch., Manahawkin, NJ, 1964-65, 75—, chmn. dept., 1958-60; chess coach, 1979—. Tchr. confrat. Christian doctrine Star of Sea Sch., Atlantic City, 1958-60, Holy Spirit High Sch., Absecon, N.J., 1975-86; tchr., prin. Assumption Sch., Ponoma, N.J., 1971-75. Scholar NSF, 1959-60. Mem. NEA, Nat. Coun. Tchrs. Math., N.J. Math. Assn., N.J. Edn. Assn., So. Regional Tchrs. Assn. (assoc. rep. 1988—). Roman Catholic. Avocations: chess, watching baseball, basketball and football. Home: 739 Bayview Dr Absecon NJ 08201-1208 Office: So Regional High Sch RR 9 Manahawkin NJ 08050

BARTON, RUTH, language educator; b. Sweetwater, Tex., July 7, 1934; d. John William and Ruby Catherine (Templeton) Pendergrass; m. Tom K. Barton, Apr. 21, 1957 (dec. July 1997); children: Belle Barton Rosing (dec.), Elliott Marshall. BJ, U. Tex., 1955; MS, U. Wis., 1961, PhD, 1969. Reporter Ft. Worth (Tex.) Press, 1955-57; claims rep. Social Security, Detroit, 1958-59; prof. English Colo. Coll., Colorado Springs, 1964—2003; ret. Advisor Cutler Pubs., Inc., Colo. Coll., Colorado Springs, 1970—, dir. writing program, 1983-99; presenter in field, 1978-2001. Author: (with others) Power, Gender, Values, 1987, Biographical Dictionary of Contemporary Catholic American Writing, 1989. Ruth Barton award named in her honor, Cutler Publs., Inc., 1996, Gresham, Riley award, 1998. Mem. Soc. Literature and Sci., Children's Lit. Assn. (newsletter layout editor 1992-98). Avocations: making pottery, travel, watching wildlife. Home: 1210 Custer Ave Colorado Springs CO 80903-2611 Office: The Colo Coll 14 E Cache La Poudre St Colorado Springs CO 80903-3298 Fax: (719) 389-6837. Business E-Mail: rbarton@colorado.college.edu.

BARTON/STRICKLAND, TAMMY KAY, elementary school educator, coach; d. Larry Don and Gena K. Barton (Stepmother), Janet K. and Phil Welch (Stepfather); m. Christopher M. Strickland, Mar. 18, 2006. BEd, Northeastern State U., Tahlequah, Okla., 1998. Cert. tchr. Okla. State Dept. Edn., 1998. Nat. events coord. All Star Sports Complex, Tulsa, 1997—; tchr./coach Haskell Mid. Sch., Broken Arrow, Okla., 1998—. Mem.: Broken Arrow Edn. Assn. Christian. Home: 212 E Austin St Broken Arrow OK 74011 Office: Haskell Mid Sch 412 S 9th St Broken Arrow OK 74012 Office Phone: 918-259-4360. Business E-Mail: tbarton@ba.k12.ok.us.

BARTON-COLLINGS, NELDA ANN, political organization worker, bank executive; b. Providence, Ky., May 12, 1929; m. Harold Bryan Barton, May 11, 1951 (dec. Nov. 1977); children: William Grant (dec.), Barbara Lynn, Harold Bryan, Stephen Lambert, Suzanne; m. Jack C. Collings, Mar. 28, 1992 (dec. Feb. 2000). Student, Western Ky. U., 1947-49; grad., Norton Meml. Infirmary Sch. Med. Tech., 1950; student, Cumberland Coll., 1978, LLD (hon.), 1991. Lic. nursing home adminstr.; registered med. technician. Pres. Barton & Assocs. Inc., Corbin, Ky., 1977—2002; past pres., now chmn. Hazard Nursing Home Inc., Ky., 1977—2002, Health Sys. Inc., Corbin, Ky., 1978—2002, Corbin Nursing Home Inc., 1978—2002, Williamsburg Nursing Home, Inc., 1978—2002; pres. Key Distbg. Inc., 1980—, pres., chmn. bd., 1981-97; past pres., now chmn. The Whitley Whiz Inc., Williamsburg, 1983—2002; chmn. bd. dirs., now dir. Tri-County Nat. Bank., 1985-97; bd. dirs., now chmn. Harlan Nursing Home, Inc., 1986—2002; chmn. bd. dirs. Knott Co. Nursing Home, Inc., 1986; pres. Tri-County Bancorp, Inc., 1987—2002; chmn. bd. Instl. Pharmacy, Corbin, Ky., 1990—2002; past pres., now chmn. bd. Wolfe County Health Care Ctr., 1990—2002; pres. Bretors, LLC, 2004—; chmn. Tri-County Cineplex, LLC, 2004—. Mem. exec. com. Corbin Deposit Bank, 1982-84; bd. dirs. Greensburg (Ky.) Deposit Bank, Williamsburg (Ky.) Nat. Bank, Campbellsville Nat. Bank, McCreary Nat. Bank, Tri County Nat. Bank, Somerset Nat. Bank, Laurel Nat. Bank; chmn., organizer, dir. Green County Bancorp Inc., 1987—2002; organizer, dir. Laurel Nat. Bank, 1996—2002; mem. nat. adv. com. SBA, 1990-92; active Nat. Policy Forum, 1994—96. Mem. Fedn. Coun. on Aging, 1982-87; bd. dirs. Leadership Ky., 1984-88, adv. com., 1987—92; bd. dirs. Cumberland Coll. Found., 1995, mem. devel. bd., 1981—; v.p. Southeastern Ky. Rehab. Com., 1981-93; mem. Fair Housing Task Force, Corbin, 1981-84, Ky. Mansions Preservation Found. Inc., 1970-2004, Corbin Cmty. Devel. Com., 1970-83; cub scout den mother, 1965-67; pres. Corbin Cen. Elem PTA, 1963-65; vice chmn. 9th dist. PTA, 1958-59; Rep. nat. committeewoman for Ky., 1968-96, sec., 1993-96; del. Rep. Nat. Conv., 1976, 88, 96, 2000, 04; vice-chmn. Rep. Nat. Com., 1984-93; sec.-treas. Nat. Rep. Inst. Internat. Affairs, 1984-86; bd. mem. Ky. Econ. Devel. Fin. Auth., 2000-03, Ky. Econ. Devel. Partnership Bd., 2003-; active numerous other polit. orgns. Recipient Ky. Woman of Achievement award Ky. Bus. and Profl. Women, 1983, Recognition award Joint Rep. Leadership, U.S. Congress, Dwight David Eisenhower award, 1970, John Sherman Cooper Disting. Svc. award Ky. Young Reps. Fedn., 1987, Outstanding Layperson award Ky. Med. Assn., 1992, Nelda Barton Comty. Svc. award Ky. Assn. Health Care Facilities, 1992, 5th Dist. Rep. Party Recognition award, 1996, Tribute to Nelda Barton-Collings Rep. Party of Ky. and 5th Dist. Lincoln Club, 1997, Disting. Recognition award Ky. State Senate, 2002, Hon. Lifetime award Ky. Mansion Preservation Found., 2004; Nelda Barton Collings Rep. internship award established by Rep. Party of Ky., 1997, Jefferson County Ky. Office for Women Hall of Fame, 1999, Ky. State Senate Cert. for Outstanding Women in Bus. and Leadership, 1999; named Ky. Col., 1968, Ky. Rep. Woman of Yr., Ky. Fedn. Rep. Women, 1969; named to 5th Dist. Lincoln Club Hall of Fame, 1996; Nelda Barton Day proclaimed by Mayor of Corbin, 1973; Western Ky. U. Acad. scholar, 1947-49. Mem. Am. Coll. Nursing Home Adminstrs., Ky. Assn. Health Care Facilities (legis. com. 1980-97, Ira O. Wallace award 2002), Ky. Assn. Nursing Home Adminstrs. (bd. dirs., polit. action com. 1979—), Ky. Med. Aux. (chmn. health edn. com. 1975-77), Ky. Commn. on Women, Women's Aux. So. Med. Assn. (Ky. counselor), Whitley County Med. Aux. (pres. 1959-60), Aux. Ky. Med. Assn., Ky. Mothers Assn. (parliamentarian 1970—, hon. Mother of Ky. award 1983), Ky. C. of C. (bd. dirs. 1983—, v.p. Region 5 1985—, 1st vice chmn. 1989, chmn. 1990-91). Avocations: fishing, painting. Home: 1311 7th Street Rd Corbin KY 40701-2207

BARTOSHUK, LINDA M., otolaryngologist, educator; BA in Psychology, minors in Astronomy and Math., Carleton Coll., 1960; MS in Psychology, Brown U., 1963, PhD in Psychology, 1965; DSc (hon.), Carleton Coll., 2001. Pre-doctoral fellow PHS, 1960—64, NSF, 1960—64; lectr. Brown U., 1966—68; affiliate asst. prof. Clark U., 1966—69; rsch. psychologist Natick Labs, 1966—70; asst. John B. Pierce Found., 1970—73, assoc., 1974—85, fellow, 1985—89; asst. prof. dept. epidemiology and pub. health Yale U., 1971—76, assoc. prof. depts. epidemiology and pub. health and psychology, 1976—85, prof. depts. epidemiology and pub. health and psychology, 1985—88, prof. sect. otolaryngology dept. surgery and prof. dept. psychology, 1989—. Chair Gordon Conf. on Chem. Senses, 1978; mem. various coms. NIH, NRC. Editor: Chem. Senses, 1982—84; cons. editor: Perception and Psychophysics, 1972—86, Sensory Processes, 1976—79; contbr. articles to profl. jours. Recipient Pepper Neuroscience Investigator award, 1984—92, Manheimer award, Monell Chem. Senses Inst., 1990, Kreshover award, Nat. Inst. Dental Rsch., 1990, Disting. Contbn. award, New Eng. Psychol. Assn., 2000. Fellow: AAAS; mem.: APA (mem. at large exec. com. div. 6 1984—87, mem. NSF working group for com. on rsch. support 1985—87, program chair div. 6 1987, pres. div. 6 1988—89, pres. elect div. 1 2001, fellow div. 6 comparative and physiol. psychology, Neal Miller Lectr. 2000), NAS, Am. Assn. Dental Schs. (mem. women's affairs adv. com.), Soc. Exptl. Psychologists, Soc. for Study of Ingestive Behavior (bd. govs. 1987—89, 2000—03), Psychonomic Soc. (mem. publ. com. 1987—92), Ea. Psychol. Assn. (mem. program com. 1983—86, bd. govs. 1987—90, pres. 1990—91), Assn. Chemoreception Scis. (exec. chair 1980—81, Award for Outstanding Achievement in chem. senses 1998), Am. Psychol. Soc. (bd. dirs. 2001—03), Phi Beta Kappa, Sigma Xi. Office: Dept Surgery Yale Univ 333 Cedar St PO Box 208041 New Haven CT 06520-8041 Office Phone: 203-785-2587. Fax: 203-737-3290. E-mail: linda.bartoshuk@yale.edu.*

BARTOW, BARBARA JENÉ, university program administrator; b. Buffalo, June 26, 1950; d. Nicholas Michael Bojack and Lillian Lenore Bennett; m. Michael Hartzell Bartow; children: Barbara Simmons, Edward Michael Hagen. AA in Journalism, Miami Dade Jr. Coll., 1970; M. in Non-fiction Writing, USAF Air U., 1975, M. Adminstrn. Auto. mechanic Amoco, Miami, Fla., 1969-70; cargo dispatcher McKinley Transport Worldwide, Ont., Can., 1970-72; office adminstr. Modernage Furniture, Miami, 1972-74. Social svc. rep. Vets. Adminstrn. and DAV and Am. Legion, 1976—; commdr. DAV and Am. Legion, 1985-86; deputy chief of staff DAV, 1986. Contbr. poetry to World of Poetry, Internat. Soc. Poets, Internat. Libr. of Poetry, Libr. of Congress, 1990—. Active crisis intervention CASA, Fla., 1984-86; foster parent DCFS, Ill.; Dem. polit. activist, Ill., Fla., N.Y., Pa., 1976—. Sgt USAF, 1974-80. Recipient citation of merit DAV, Fla., 1985. Roman Catholic. Avocations: writing, social work, wheelchair racing. Home: 1515 Lantern Ln Joliet IL 60433-2910

BARTOW, DIANE GRACE, marketing professional, sales executive; b. Maspeth, NY, Apr. 20, 1948; d. Alfred Otto and Charlotte Florence (Bronnenkant) Bruggeman; m. Eugene A. Bartow, aug. 29, 1992; children: Jason, Trudi. AAS, Queensborough C.C., 1967; BS, Nova Southeastern U., 1979. Jr. acct. Exxon, N.Y.C., 1967-69; acct. BRM Assocs., N.Y.C., 1969, Texaco, N.Y.C., 1969-74; supr. Eutectic, Flushing, N.Y., 1974-76; regional industry dir. Am. Express, N.Y.C., 1976-83; v.p. Eastern Exclusives, Boston, 1983-85; pres. The Mktg. Dept., 1985-86; sr. v.p., gen. mgr. Rogers Merchandising Inc., 1986-92; exec. v.p., COO Bartow Ins. Agy., Inc., 1992—. Seminars Marketing to Win. Author tng. manual, travel newsletter, 1982, Ins. Update, 1992. Trustee, v.p. Murray Hill Neighborhood Assn., 1982, pres., 1997—; trustee 7 E 35th Corp., 1983; chmn. judging Promotion and Advt. awards, 1990, awards chair, 2001-02. Mem. Nat. Assn. Advt. and Promotional Allowances (judging chair 1996-00), Am. Soc. Travel Agts. (tour rels. com. 1983), Am. Hotel and Motel Mgmt. Assn., Am. Film Assn., Am. Mgmt. Assn., Life Underwriters, Sigma Mu Omega (pres. Bayside (N.Y.) 1966-67). Home: 7 E 35th St New York NY 10016-3810 Office Phone: 800-570-8225, 631-242-4745.

BARTOW, NICOLE A., secondary school educator; b. Lincoln, Nebr., Feb. 2, 1970; d. Douglas William and Judith Dian Bartow. BA English Lit., George Mason U., 1991; JD, Santa Clara U., 1994; MEd, Marymount U., 1998. Bar: Calif. 1994; cert. secondary social studies tchr. 1997. Law clk. Joyce Kitchens, Atlanta, 1994; tchr. social studies Loudoun County Pub. Schs., Sterling, Va., 1997—. Editor: Santa Clara Law Rev., 1993—94. Mem. ACLU, Va., 2002—. Mem.: Loudoun Edn. Assn., Calif. Bar Assn. Avocations: travel, reading, football. Office: Park View High Sch 400 W Laurel Ave Sterling VA 20164 Personal E-mail: nabartow@hotmail.com. Business E-Mail: nbartow@loudoun.gov.

BARTZ, CAROL A., computer software company executive; b. Winona, Minn., Aug. 29, 1948; m. William (Bill) Marr; children: Bill, Meredith, Layne BS in Computer Sci. with honors, U. Wis., 1971; DSc (hon.), Worcester Poly. Inst.; LittD (hon.), William Woods U.; LittD, NJ Inst. Tech. With sales mgmt. dept. 3M Corp., Digital Equipment Corp., 1976-83; mgr. customer mktg. Sun Microsys., 1983-84, v.p. mktg., 1984-87, v.p. customer svc., 1987-90, v.p. worldwide field ops., exec. officer, 1990-92; chmn., pres., CEO Autodesk, Inc., San Rafael, Calif., 1992—2006, exec. chmn., 2006—. Pres. Sun Fed., from 1987; bd. dirs. AirTouch Comm., Bea Sys., Cadence Design Sys., Cisco Sys., Inc., 1994-, Network Appliance; mem. President's Export Coun., 1994, President's Coun. Advisors on Sci. and Tech.; adv. coun. bus. sch. Stanford U. Bd. dirs. U. Wis. Sch. Bus., Nat. Breast Cancer Rsch. Found., Found. for Nat. Medals Sci. and Tech.; mem. adv. coun. Stanford U. Bus. Sch.; mem. Com. of 200; adv. for women's health issues; former mem. Ark. of Gov.'s Econ. Summit, Little Rock; mem. Sec. of Edn.'s Commn. on Future of Edn., 2005. Recipient Donald C. Burnham Mfg. Mgmt. award Soc. Mfg. Engrs., 1994, Horatio Alger Award, 2000, named one of 100 Most Influential Women in Business, San Francisco Bus. Times, 2004, 100 Most Powerful Women in World, Forbes mag., 2005, World's 30 Most Respected CEOs, Barron's mag., 2005. Mem. Calif. C. of C. (bd. dirs.). Avocations: gardening, tennis. Office: Autodesk Inc 111 McInnis Pkwy San Rafael CA 94903-2700*

BARTZ, DEBRA ANN, retired military officer, pilot; b. Chgo., Jan. 19, 1960; d. Robert Herman and Yvonne Anita (Schwarz) B. BS, U.S. Air Force Acad., 1982; MS in Human Resources Mgmt., Golden Gate U., 1989; diploma in fitness and nutrition, 1999. Commd. 2d lt. USAF, 1982, advanced through grades to maj., 1986, copilot Beale AFB, Calif., 1983-86, pilot, 1986-89, air ops. officer, 1989-90; liaison officer USAF Acad., 1992—2002; ret. USAF, 2002; capt. 737 United Airlines, San Francisco, 1998—2005, capt. 767, 2005—. Pilot Milw. Air Nat. Guard, 1990-97. Democrat. Avocations: bike riding, running, swimming, weight training. Office Phone: 925-673-8527. Personal E-mail: flyingk9s@aol.com.

BAR-YAM, MIRIAM, psychologist, consultant, researcher; b. Jerusalem, Feb. 6, 1929; came to U.S., 1954; d. Joseph Nahum Mark and Nechama Hochberg; m. Zvi Bar-Yam, Oct. 30, 1951; children: Aureet, Yaneer, Sageet. BA summa cum laude, U. Pitts., 1957; MEd, Harvard U., 1963, EdD, 1969. Lic. psychologist Mass. Asst. prof. Boston U., 1969-76, assoc. prof., 1977-84; vis. prof. Hebrew Coll., Boston, 1985-86, 89, Northeastern U., Boston, 1986-87; dir. Inst. for Multidimensional Psycholog. Assessment Counseling & Tng., Brookline, Mass., 1984—. Dir. Project for Improving Tchg., Technion, Haifa, Israel, 1971-72, Project for Gifted Children, 1971-72; prin. Israeli Cooperative Sch., Boston, 1973-76, Exptl. Sch., Haifa, Israel, 1976-77; dir. State adj. prof. Lesley Coll., Cambridge, Mass., 1987—. Editor: Aureet, 1993; contbr. articles to profl. jours. Chmn. Women Profl. Devel. at Boston U., 1977-84; bd. mem. Internat. Maritime Ctr., Boston, 1986-90, Trustees of the Israel Cultural Ctr., Boston, 1985—; program com. mem. Technion Soc., Boston, 1986—. Mem. APA, Am. Ednl. Rsch. Assn., Internat. Soc. for Study Behavioral Devel., Internat. Coun. Psychologists (distinction 1987, 91, 92), Jewish. Avocations: gymnastics, travel, gardening, music, hiking. Home: 12 Lake Ter Newton MA 02459-2145 Office: Lesley Univ 14 Wendell St Cambridge MA 02138-1817 E-mail: miriam@necsi.org.

BARZDA, SUSAN MARIE, special education educator, art educator; d. John Anthony and Verona Jewel (Brickner) Barzda. MusB, Heidelberg Coll., 1974; postgrad., Muskingum Coll., 2003—. Lic. tchr. music k-12 Ohio Dept. Edn., 1974, Qualified Mental Retardation Professional (QMRP) Ohio Dept. of Mental Retardation, Devel. Disability, 1980. Instr. instrumental and vocal music Rolling Hills Local Sch. Dist., Byesville, Ohio, 1974—76; tchr. music, supr. Cambridge Devel. Ctr., 1976—87; dir. high sch. band, tchr. music appreciation Bishop Rosecrans Cath. High Sch., Zanesville, 1981—85; adminstrv. asst. II Cambridge Devel. Ctr., 1987—93, 1989—93, qualified mental retardation profl., 1993—. Dir., instr. majorettes, drill team, and fife and drum corps Rolling Hills Local Sch. Dist., Byesville, Ohio, 1974—76, instr. Meadowbrook unit Guernsey county bicentennial fife and drum corps, 1975—76; dir. YMCA Y-ettes Baton Twirling Corps, 1978—81; coord. Spl. Olympics Cambridge Devel. Ctr., 1981—84, mem. devel. centers mini-team improve quality of svcs. individuals with mental retardation, 1977—79, mem. Ohio's mini-teams devel. centers, 1977—79, adult basic edn. grant coord., 1986—90. Play selection com. chair Cambridge Pertorming Arts Ctr., 1986—2003; sec. Cambridge City Band, 1980—81, Zanesville Meml. Concert Band, Zanesville, 2002—03; S.E.Ohio regional rep. Ohio Cmty. Theatre Assn., Columbus, 1999—2002, bd. mem.-at-large, 2002—, sec., 2004; clarinettist Dominic Greco Concert Band, Dover, 2002—03; tenor saxophone player Dick Simcox Big Band, Cambridge, 1981—85; clarinetist Southeastern Ohio Symphony, New Concord, 1982—84; mem., pit orch. mem., actress, dancer, choreographer, prodr., dir., musical dir., Cambridge Performing Arts Centre, 1977—2003; clarinettist Zanesville Meml. Concert Band, 1982—2003, Coshocton Cmty. Band, 2002—03. Recipient Jean Lisle Meml. award, Alliance Music Study Club, 1970, Dick Beal Outstanding Regional Rep. award, Ohio Cmty. Theatre Assn., 2002; scholar, Quota Club Alliance, Ohio, 1970; Rhodes-King scholar, Heidelberg Coll., 1970—71. Mem.: Philalethean Women's Soc. Alumni (life). Independent. Avocations: clarinet, acting, genealogy, travel. Office: Cambridge Developmental Ctr 66737 Old 21 Rd Cambridge OH 43725 Personal E-mail: subar@cambridgeoh.com.

BARZILAY, JUDITH MORGENSTERN, federal judge; b. Russell, Kans., Jan. 3, 1944; d. Arthur and Hilda Morgenstern; m. Sal (Doron) Barzilay, Aug. 19, 1973; children: Ilan, Michael. Student, Stern Coll., 1961—62; Bachelors, Wichita State U., 1965; MLS, Rutgers U., 1971, JD, 1981. Bar: N.J. 1981. Tchr. English Wichita (Kans.) H.S., 1965-67; editor Carter Wallace Pharms., Cranbury, N.J., 1967-68; tchr. English Hamilton Sch., Hamilton Twp., N.J., 1968-69; ref. libr. Suffolk County Coll., Selden, N.J., 1971-74, Somerset Coll., Somerville, N.J., 1975-76, East Brunswick (N.J.) Libr., 1977-78; law clk. to Hon. Robert Tarleton N.J. Superior Ct., Jersey City, 1982-83; atty. Williams, Caliri, Miller & Otley, Wayne, N.J., 1982-83, US Dept. Justice, N.Y.C., 1983-86, Siegel, Mandell & Davidson, N.Y.C., 1986-88; sr. atty. Sony Electronics, Park Ridge, NJ, 1988—89, v.p. import-export ops., 1989—95, v.p. govt. affairs, 1996—98; judge U.S. Ct. Internat. Trade, N.Y.C., 1998—. Mem. Treasury Sec.'s Com. on Comml. Ops. of U.S. Customs Svc., Washington, 1996-98. Bd. trustees Ramapo Coll., Mahwah, N.J., 1996-98. Recipient Tribute to Women and Industry award YWCA of Bergen County, N.J., 1993, Disting. Alumna award Wichita State U., 1996. Mem. Am. Assn. Exporters and Importers (exec. bd. dirs. 1992-98). Jewish. Office: US Ct Internat Trade One Federal Plz New York NY 10278 Fax: 212-264-5487.

BASA, ENIKÖ MOLNÁR, retired librarian; b. Huszt, Hungary, Sept. 7, 1939; came to the U.S., 1950; d. Julius Valentine and Terézia (Fejér) Molnár; m. Péter Basa, Nov. 19, 1966. BA, Trinity Coll., 1962; MA, U. N.C., 1965, PhD, 1972. Instr. U. Md., College Park, 1965-69; asst. prof. Dunbarton Coll., Washington, 1970-72; lectr. Am. U., Washington, 1972-75, Hood Coll., Frederick, Md., 1975-76; editor, serials cataloger Libr. of Congress, Washington, 1977—2003; ret., 2004. Mem. symposium Libr. Congress, 1996; lectr. U. Debrecen, Hungary, 2004, vis. lectr. U. Szeged, 2004 Author: Sandor Petőfi, 1980; editor: Twayne World Authors, 1974—, Hungarian Literature, 1993; translator: (play) Screenplay from Örkény, 1983; assoc. editor The Comparatist, 1976-82, editorial bd., 1992—; jour. rev. editor: Hungarian Studies Newsletter, 1975-82; guest editor: Rev. Nat. Lits., 1992; contbr. chpts. to books and articles and book revs. to profl. jours. Recipient Gold medal Pres. of Republic of Hungary, 1997; Kluge Staff fellow Libr. of Congress, 2002-03. Mem. MLA (Hungarian sect. chair 1982, 90), So. Comparative Lit. Assn. (founding v.p. 1977-79, 89—, sec.-treas. 1985-89, pres. 1992-94), Am. Hungarian Educators Assn. (pres. 1974-80, 88-92, exec. dir. 1980—), Internat. Assn. Hungarian Studies, Libr. Congress Profl. Assn. (v.p. 1991, pres. 1996). Avocations: reading, travel, needlecrafts. Home: 4515 Willard Ave Apt 2210 Chevy Chase MD 20815-3685 E-mail: eniko.basa@verizon.net.

BASCOM, RUTH F., retired mayor; b. Ames, Iowa, Feb. 4, 1926; d. Frederick Charles and Doris Hays Fenton; m. John U. Bascom, June 14, 1950; children: Lucinda, Rebecca, Ellen, Thomas, Paul, Mary. BS, Kans. State U., Manhattan, 1946; MA, Cornell U., 1949. Tchr. Dickinson County Cmty. H.S., Kans., 1946-48, Nat. Coll. Edn., Chgo., 1949-51. Co-chair Cascadia High Speed Rail, 1995-98. Chair City and State Bicycle Com., 1971-83; chair Met. Park Bd., Eugene, 1972-82; bd. pres. Youth Symphony, 1962-68; city councilor City of Eugene, Oreg., 1984-92, coun. v.p., pres., 1988-90, mayor, 1993-97; v.p., pres. LWV, Eugene, 1967-69; chair Oreg. Passenger Rail Com., 2000-05; state bd. 1000 Friends of Oreg., 1999-05. Recipient Gold Leaf award Internat. Soc. Arboriculture, 1993; dedicated Ruth Bascom Riverbank Trail Sys., 2003. Democrat. Congregationalist. Avocations: music, tree farm, bicycling. Home: 2114 University St Eugene OR 97403-1542 E-mail: jbascomr@pacinfo.com.

BASDEN, CAMERON, ballet mistress, dancer; b. Dallas; Scholarship student, The Joffrey Ballet Sch., 1976-77. Dancer Dallas Ballet, 1975-76, Joffrey II Dancers, N.Y.C., 1977-79, The Joffrey Ballet, N.Y.C., 1979—, asst. ballet mistress, 1990-93, ballet mistress N.Y.C., Chgo., 1993—. Prof. dance Manhattanville Coll. Actor: (films) The Company, 2003. Office: Joffrey Ballet 70 E Lake St Fl 1300 Chicago IL 60601-5917

BASHAM, MONNIE, retired mental health services professional; b. Wilmar, Ark., Aug. 16, 1922; d. Jesse Madison and Tommie (Bond) Barber; children: Kay Sharon Basham Walker, Richard. Attended, Edmonds CC, Wash., 1978—79; BA in Counseling, Antioch U., Seattle, 1981, MA in Psychology, 1983. Counselor, therapist, Seattle, Minden, La., Hot Springs, Ark.; ret. Contbr. articles to profl. publs. Vol. counselor East Side Cmty., Belleview, Wash.; mem. adv. bd. Courage Ho., Hot Springs, Independenced Ho., Hot Springs; fundraiser Homes for Abused Women, Hot Springs; Sunday sch. tchr., grief counselor First United Meth. Ch., Hot Springs. Mem.: AAUW, La. Assn. Lic. Counselors, Am. Assn. Lic. Counselors. Democrat. Avocations: travel, reading, sewing, gardening, hiking.

BASIL, MICHELLE L., lawyer; BA with honors, U. Calif., Berkeley, 1994; JD, U. Calif., 1997. Bar: Mass. 1997. Ptnr. Bus. Dept. Nutter, McClennen & Fish LLP, Boston. Mem.: Boston Bar Assn. Office: Nutter McClennen & Fish LLP World Trade Ctr West 155 Seaport Blvd Boston MA 02210 Office Phone: 617-439-2477. Office Fax: 617-310-9477. E-mail: mbasil@nutter.com.*

BASILE, SHEILA, secondary school educator, consultant; b. Hendersonville, N.C., Sept. 6, 1952; d. John Leroy and Mildred Irene (Burrell) Brevard; m. Anthony John Basile, June 7, 1951; children: Laurel, Cheryl, Anthony John. BA, Western Carolina U., Cullowhee, N.C., 1975; MA, Columbia U., 1979. Cert. in English and reading edn. K-12, N.Y. Cons. self employed, New Rochelle, 1981—. Cons. leadership assessment and feedback Ctr. for Creative Leadership, Greensboro, N.C., 1995-97; mgmt. tng. cons. Nestle, Pitney Bowes, HBO, 1990-95. Recipient Chmn.'s awrd Nynex-Bell Atlantic, White Plains, N.Y., 1993, Corp. Quality award, 1993. Mem. Internat. Assn. Career Mgmt. Profls., Nat. Coun. Tchrs. English, N.Y. State English Coun., Orphan Train Heritage Soc. Am., Hauppauge Indsl. Assn., Advancement for Commerce, Industry & Tech., Inc., Rotary Club (mem. event steering com. 1999), Orienta Beach Club (Mamaroneck, N.Y.; mem. entertainment com. 1999). Avocations: running, special community events planning, writing, public speaking. Office: Lee Hecht Harrison 225 Broadhollow Rd Melville NY 11747 E-mail: Teddybell@aol.com.

BASINGER, KAREN LYNN, renal dietitian; b. Mechanicsville, Md., July 4, 1955; d. Leonard Marcus and Mary Jane (Harding) Brookbank; m. Joseph Andrew Basinger, Nov. 17, 1984; 1 child, James Marcus. BS, U. Md., 1977; MS, Hood Coll., 1987. Lic. nutritionist. Libr. technician Bowie (Md.) State Coll., 1973-79; instr. St. Mary's County Adult Edn., Leonardtown, Md., 1979-80; home economist Zamoiski Co., Balt., 1977-83; nutritionist/WIC coord. South County Health Plan, Prince Frederick, Md., 1979-80; nutritionist Walter Reed Army Med. Ctr., Washington, 1980-82; renal dietitian Mid Atlantic/BMA, Camp Springs, Md., 1982-87, Kidney Care Ctr., Landover, Md., 1987-99; instr. dietary intern program Andrews AFB, 1988-91; renal dietitian Silver Spring (Md.) Artificial Kindey Ctr., 1998—; outpatient dietitian Holy Cross Hosp., Silver Spring, 1999-2000; renal dietitian DaVita-Wheaton, Md., 1999—. Cons. Leisure World Med. Ctr., 2002—; adj. prof. Montgomery Coll., Rockville, 2004—; lectr. in field. Profl. adv. bd. Nat. Kidney Found./NCA, 1989-94; chair coun. on renal nutrition Nat. Kidney Found., 1993-94, program chair, 1990-92. Recipient Spl. Recognition Nat. Kidney Found./NCA, 1990, 92, Recognized Renal Dietitian/NCA, 1991, 94. Mem.: Washington Met. Coun. on Renal Nutrition (chair 1986—94, nutrition symposium chair 1989, chair 1986—94, 2001—02), Am. Dietetic Assn. (legis. chair renal practice group 2003—), Md. Home Econs. Assn. (bylaws chair 1982—94), Am. Home Econs. Assn., Am. Nutritionists Assn., U. Md. Aumni Assn. Democrat. Lutheran. Avocation: cross-stitch.

BASINGER, KIM (KIMILA ANN BASINGER), actress; b. Athens, Ga., Dec. 8, 1953; d. Don Basinger; m. Ron Snyder-Britton, Oct. 1980 (div. Dec. 1988); m. Alec Baldwin, August 19, 1993 (div. Feb. 2002), child, Ireland. Student, Neighborhood Playhouse, N.Y.C. Model Eileen Ford Agy., N.Y.C., 1972-77; ind. actress, 1977—. (feature films) Hard Country, 1981, Mother Lode, 1982, Never Say Never Again, 1983, The Man Who Loved Women, 1983, The Natural, 1984, Fool for Love, 1985, 9 1/2 Weeks, 1986, No Mercy, 1986, Blind Date, 1987, Nadine, 1987, My Stepmother Is an Alien, 1988, Batman, 1989, The Marrying Man, 1991, Final Analysis, 1992, Cool World, 1992, The Real McCoy, 1993, Wayne's World 2, 1993, The Getaway, 1994, Ready to Wear (Prêt-à-Porter), 1994, L.A. Confidential (Golden Globe award for best supporting actress, 1998) (Academy Award for best supporting actress, 1998), 1997, I Dreamed of Africa, 2000, Bless the Child, 2000, 8 Mile, 2002, People I Know, 2002, The Door in the Floor, 2004, Elvis Has Left the Building, 2004, Cellular, 2004, The Sentinel, 2006, Even Money, 2006; (TV series) Dog and Cat, 1977; TV films include Katie-Portrait of a Centerfold, 1978, The Ghost of Flight 401, 1978, Killjoy, 1981, The Mermaid Chair, 2006; (TV miniseries) From Here to Eternity, 1980; (TV appearances) Gemini Man, 1976, Charlie's Angels, 1976, The Six Million Dollar Man, 1977, McMillan and Wife, 1977, Vega$, 1978, The Simpsons (voice only), 1998, 2002. Office: c/o Ron Meyer CAA 11288 Ventura Blvd #414 Studio City CA 91604*

BASKERVILLE, ELIZABETH BONHAM, pediatrician; b. Los Angeles, Calif., May 1, 1942; d. Harry Herbert Baskerville and Elizabeth Trumbo Baskervile; children: Matthew Dalton, David John Everett. BA, Stanford U., Palo Alto, Calif., 1964; MD, U. So. Calif., 1968. Pediatrician Self-Employed, Ontario, Oreg., 1972—77, Santa Cruz, Calif., 1977—83, Capitola, Calif., 1983—2001, Capitola Pediat., Calif., 2001—. Advocate for children Sexual Molest/Assault Evaluation, Ontario, Oreg., 1972—77; advocate and developer Sexual Assault Programs, 1978—89. Author: (book) Baby Basics, 2000, David's Kiss, 2000. Fellow: Am. Acad. Pediatrics; mem.: AMA. Avocations: photography, needlecrafts, writing. Office: Capitola Pediat 4145 Clare St Ste A Capitola CA 95010 Office Phone: 831-476-1933. Personal E-mail: ebaskerv@skyhighway.com.

BASKERVILLE, LEZLI, educational association administrator; BA, Douglass Coll.; JD, Howard U. Law Sch. Law clk. DC Ct. Appeals; staffer US Congress; mem. appellate team Lawyers Com. Civil Rights Under Law; exec. dir. Nat. Black Leadership Roundtable; nat. legis. counsel NAACP; adminstrv. appeals judge employee appeals Washington; founding mem. The Baskerville Group; v.p. govt. relations The Coll. Bd., 2000—03; outside counsel Nat. Assn. for Equal Opportunity in Higher Edn., program dir.; mem. brief writing team in Bakke, Weber and Fullilove cases; legal rsch. assoc. for prof. Herbert O. Reid, Sr. Nat. Assn. for Equal Opportunity in Higher Edn., Silver Spring, Md., interim pres., 2004, pres., CEO, 2004—. Named one of nation's top 10 black women in higher edn., AOL Black Voices, 100 Most Influential Black Americans, Ebony mag., 2006. Achievements include being first female pres. of Nat. Assn. for Equal Opportunity in Higher Edn. Office: Nat Assn Equal Opportunity in Higher Edn 8701 Georgia Ave Ste 200 Silver Spring MD 20910*

BASKERVILLE, VIOLA OSBORNE, state government official; b. Richmond, Va., Oct. 29, 1951; d. Clifton Cleveland and Josephine (Braxton) Osborne; m. Archer Lewis Baskerville, Jan. 24, 1975; children: Timothy Ryan, Sean Alexandre. BA, Coll. William & Mary, 1973; JD, U. Iowa, 1979. City coun. mem. City Richmond, 1994-96, vice mayor, 1996-97; del. Gen. Assembly Va., Richmond, 1998—2006, sec. of adminstrn., 2006—. Mem. City Planning Commn., Richmond, 1994-96. Bd. visitors Longwood Coll., Farmville, Va., 1989-97; mem. Ginter Park Resident's Assn. Recipient Disting. Svc. award United Order Tents, 1997, Outstanding Woman Govt./Politics award, YWCA, 1998; Fulbright scholar U. Bonn, Germany, 1973-74; Flemmings fellow, 1999. Mem. Richmond Renaissance (bd. dirs.). Democrat. Episcopalian. Avocation: genealogy. Home: 3223 Hawthorne Ave Richmond VA 23222-2518 Office: Patrick Henry Bldg Richmond VA 23219 Office Phone: 804-786-1201. E-mail: vbaskerville@comcast.net.

BASKIN, BARBARA HOLLAND, retired education educator, researcher; b. Detroit, Aug. 27, 1929; d. Carl Floyd and Ruth Holland (Herman) Harriman; m. Alex Baskin, Aug. 15, 1954 (div. Nov. 1984); children: Julie S. Baskin Gamlin, Amy Shael Baskin. BA, Wayne State U., 1951, EdD, 1968; MA, U. Mich., 1957. Ednl. cons. Krell Software, Inc., Stony Brook, N.Y., 1982-83, dir. ednl. software devel., 1984-85; dir. program in spl. edn. and devel. disabilities SUNY, Stony Brook, 1981-85, assoc. prof. social sci. interdisciplinary program, 1981—96; ret. Dir. cons. Bd. Cooperative Ednl. Svcs. Inst. for Gifted and Talented, Suffolk County, N.Y., 1981-83; dir. gifted youth program Saturday Sci. & More, Stony Brook, 1977-84. Co-author: Notes from a Different Drummer, Vol. 1, 1977 (ALA award 1977, Pres.'s Com. on the Employment of the Handicapped award 1978), Books for the Gifted Child, 1980 (Outstanding Reference Book of the Yr. ALA 1980), More Notes from a Different Drummer, Vol. 2, 1984; co-creator: (software) Plato's Cave, 1985 (Cert. of Honor 1986). Bd. govs. Canine Companions Internat., Farmingdale, N.Y., 1990; com. mem. N.Y. State Citizen's Task Force on Child Abuse and Neglect, Albany, 1989-91; bd. dirs. Suffolk County Coalition for Children and Families, Centerreach, N.Y., 1989-91; co-chmn. campus chpt. NOW, 1989-91; v.p. Mother Child Home Program, 1981-93, pres. 1994-2002; dir. child and family studies program SUNY, Stony Brook, 1993—; bd. mem. Greater Port Jefferson Arts Coun., 1997—. Recipient Conversation in the Disciplines award N.Y. State, 1988; named Woman of Yr. in Edn., Three Villages Times, 1980. Mem. Univ. Assn., Coun. for Exceptional Children, Nat. Assn. for Gifted Children. Avocations: reading, bridge, travel, puzzles.

BASKIN, ROBERTA, television correspondent; b. Atlanta, Jan. 16, 1952; d. Alan Baskin and Suzanne Pallister; m. James Albert Trengrove, Sept. 19, 1987; children: Chelsea, Vanessa. Student, Elmira Coll., 1969-70. Dir. Consumer Affairs Office, Syracuse, N.Y., 1974-77; consumer reporter Sta. WMAQ-TV, Chgo., 1977-79; investigative reporter Sta. WLS-TV, Chgo., 1979-84; consumer editor Sta. WJLA-TV, Washington, 1984-91; corr. CBS News, Washington, N.Y.C.; exec. dir. Ctr. for Pub. Integrity, Washington, 2005—. Bd. mem. Fund for Investigative Journalism, Washington, 1992-94. Telethon host Sta. WETA-TV, Washington, 1987-94. Recipient Peabody awards U. Ga., 1982, 86, Edward R. Murrow award Radio-TV News Dirs. Assn., 1983, 90, duPont-Columbia awards Columbia U. Sch. of Journalism, 1987, 90, Ohio State awards. Mem. NATAS (16 local Emmy awards Chgo., Washington chpts.), Am. Fedn. TV and Radio Artists (bd. dirs. 1993-94). Avocation: scuba diving. Office: Ctr for Pub Integrity 910 17th St NW Ste 700 Washington DC 20006

BASKIN, VICTORIA, child and adolescent psychiatrist; b. Kaliningrad, Russia, Aug. 31, 1952; arrived in US, 1993; d. Mark Monin and Bertha Umantseva; m. Simon Baskin, Apr. 23, 1971; 1 child, Anna. MD with honors, Dnepropetrovskaja Medicinskaja Academija, Ukraine, 1975. Intern Children's Hosp. #3, Dnepropetrovsk, Ukraine, 1975—76; pediatrician Children's Hosp. #2, Dnepropetrovsk, Ukraine, 1976—87, child and adolescent psychiatrist, 1987—93; adult psychiatrist Wayne State U., Detroit, 2001—04, child and adolescent psychiatrist, 2004—. Clin. dir. Children's Hosp. #2, Dnepropetrovsk, 1982—87. Family edn. and counseling group Univ. Psychiat. Ctr., Livonia, Mich., 2004—05. Mem.: AMA, Am. Acad. Child and Adolescent Psychiatry (resident award 2004), Am. Psychiat. Assn. Avocations: reading, travel, exercise, cooking. Home: 29557 Sierra Pointe Cir Farmington Hills MI 48331 Office: Univ Psychiat Ctr-Livonia 16836 Newburgh Rd Livonia MI 48154 Office Phone: 734-464-7660 ext. 107. Office Fax: 734-464-5885. E-mail: victoriabaskin@hotmail.com.

BASKINGER, WILMA, elementary school educator; b. Passaic, N.J., Apr. 30, 1945; d. Richard Donkersloot and Cornelia Butyn; m. George Joseph Baskinger Sr., Aug. 2, 1974; children: Samuel Richard, George Joseph Jr., Rebecca Ann. BA, Paterson State Coll., 1967; MA, Jersey City (N.J.) State Coll., 1993. Cert. elem. tchr. N.J.; cert. handicapped tchr. English, N.J. Jr. h.s. tchr. Clifton (N.J.) Bd. Edn., 1968-79; presch. tchr. Sunshine Sch., Butler, N.J., 1990-93; spl. edn. tchr., elem. tchr. Butler (N.J.) Bd. Edn., 1993—. Mem. adv. bd. lit. mag. Clifton Bd. Edn., 1970-72, advisor newspaper, 1973-79. Mem. Pompton Plains Reformed Bible Ch.; leader On Eagles' Wings Support Group. Mem.: Phi Delta Kappa. Office: Aaron Decker Sch 98 Decker Rd Butler NJ 07405-1598

BASKINS, ANN O., lawyer, former computer company executive; b. Red Bluff, Calif., Aug. 5, 1955; m. Thomas C. DeFilipps. AB in Hist., Stanford U., 1977; JD, UCLA, 1980. Bar: Calif. 1980. Assoc. Crosby, Heafey, Roach & May, 1980—81; atty. Hewlett-Packard Co., Palo Alto, Calif., 1982—85, sr. atty., 1985—86, asst. sec., 1985—99, corp. counsel, 1986—99, corp. sec., 1999—2006, sr. v.p., gen. counsel, 2000—06. Mem.: ABA, Assn. Gen. Counsel, Am. Soc. Corp. Secs., Am. Corp. Counsel Assn.*

BASKOVITZ, DIANA, retired elementary school educator; d. Nathan and Esther Baskovitz. BA, U. Chgo., 1956, MA, 1966. Stenographer Railroad Retirement Bd., Chgo., 1944—47; steno & circulation dir. Am. Trade Mag., Chgo., 1948—53; elem. tchr. Chgo. Bd. Edn., 1958—85; ret., 1985. Contbr. articles to profl. jours. Mem.: Chgo. Lyric Opera, Chgo. Symphony Orchestra, Spertus Mus., Chgo. Hist. Soc., Field Mus. Chgo., Art Inst. Chgo., Hadassah, Mu Phi Epsilon Internat. Music. Avocations: travel, theater, reading.

BASLAW-FINGER, ANNETTE, education educator, consultant; b. Paris, Oct. 11, 1929; arrived in U.S., 1943; d. David and Shulamit Notik Szer; m. Seymour Maxwell Finger, June 12, 1988 (dec. July 2005); m. Alfred A. Baslaw, Feb. 11, 1951 (dec. July 6, 1978); children: Robin, Michele Friedman, David. BA, Bklyn. Coll., 1951; MA, Hofstra U., N.Y., 1965; PhD (with distinction), NYU, 1969. Exec. sec. L.R. Dooley, Inc., N.Y.C., 1951—52; French copywriter Morse Internat., N.Y.C., 1952—54; French tchr. Glen Cove (N.Y.) HS, 1958—65, Roslyn (N.Y.) HS, 1969; dir. French edn. Columbia Tchrs. Coll., N.Y.C., NY, 1969—73; chairperson fgn. lang. and internat. edn. NYU, 1973—77, dir. fgn. lang. and bilingual edn., 1977—94; ret., 1994. Contbr. articles to profl. jours. Ann. spkr. Long Island and N.J. Schs., 1995—2003, Temple Sholom, Pompano Beach, Fla., 1998—2006. Decorated Order Palmes Academiques France; Danforth fellow, 1965—69. Mem.: MLA (bd. dirs.), N.Y. State Assn. Fgn. Lang. Tchrs. (bd. dirs.), Am. Assn. Tchrs. of French (pres. LI chpt.), Mus. Jewish Heritage, Inst. on Mediterranean Affairs at UN (dep. to pres.), Pi Delta Phi, Kappa Delta Pi (pres.), Phi Beta Kappa, Pi Lambda Theta (pres. Rho chpt.). Avocations: travel, ballet, theater, art, books. Home: 50 Sutton Pl S New York NY 10022 also: 133 N Pompano Beach Blvd Pompano Beach FL 33062

BASLER, LINDA GERBER, retired elementary school educator; b. Harrisburg, Pa., Oct. 10, 1942; d. Boyd Bushey and Evelyn Romaine (Coulson) Gerber; m. Lawrence Edward Basler, Aug. 14, 1965; children: Elizabeth Wilson, Anne Marie. BS, Shippensburg U., 1964, MS. Tchr. Shippensburg Area Schs., 1964—99. Sch. bd. mem. (facilities, athletic, transp., budget, student rels. coms.) Shippensburg Area Schs., 2001—05, after sch. program, 2004—06; bd. mem. Shippensburg Pub. Libr., 2001—06; 1964 reunion com. mem. Shippensburg U., alumni bd. mem., 2006—; lectr. and greeter Meml. Luth. Ch., Shippensburg, 1969—2005, building com. Mem.: PSERS, Shippensburg Area Edn. Assn., Pa. State Edn. Assn., NEA, Red Hat Soc. Republican. Lutheran. Avocations: reading, travel. Home: 11 Wooded Dr Shippensburg PA 17257 Personal E-mail: lelgb@supernet.com.

BASQUIN, MARY SMYTH (KIT BASQUIN), museum administrator; b. NYC, July 3, 1941; d. Joseph Percy and Virginia Sandford (Gibbs) Smyth; m. Maurice Hanson Basquin, Feb. 4, 1967 (div. Feb. 1984); children: Susan, Peter Lee, William. BA, Goucher Coll., Balt., 1963; MA, Ind. U., 1970; postgrad., Union Inst. and U., Cin., 2003—. Asst. dir. pub. rels. Indpls. Mus. Art, 1971-72; dir. Washington Gallery, Frankfort, Ind., 1972-79, Indpls., 1977-79, Kit Basquin Gallery, Milw., 1981-83; curator edn. Haggerty Mus. Marquette U., Milw., 1988-95; dir. outreach Milw. Wis. Humanities Coun., 1995-98; curator Marvin Lowe Retrospective, Ind. U. Art Mus., 1998; mktg. William Doyle Galleries, NYC, 1999, exhbn. mgr., 2000; rsch. assoc. Bklyn. Mus. Art, 2000; asst. print study rm. Met. Mus. Art, NYC, 2000—. Instr. art history Concordia U., Mequon, Wis., 1991, instr. Marquette U., Gaza, 1996; pres. contemporary art soc. Milw. Art Mus., 1986-87, prints and drawings subcom., 1991-99, pres. Print Forum, 1996-97; mem. program com. Midwest Mus. conf., Milw., 1992. Wis. editor: New Art Examiner, 1980—81; mem. St. Barts Singers, 1999—; contbr. articles to profl. jours. Trustee Ten Chimneys Found., Genesee Depot, Wis., 1997-99; mem. adv. bd. Ten Chimneys Found., 2000-01; mem. alumnae bd. The Spence Sch., N.Y., 2005—. Mem. Univ. Club NY, Univ. Club Milw., Coll. Art Assn, James Joyce Soc. Episcopalian. Avocations: singing, fashion, theater, swimming. Home: 1675 York Ave Apt 19A New York NY 10128-6756

BASS, EVELYN ELIZABETH, elementary school educator; b. Magnolia, Ark., Sept. 28, 1948; d. Marvin and Catherine (Grissom) Scott; m. Burlin Lee Hughes, July 17, 1971 (div. Aug. 1984); children: Tionna Latrice, Lee Otis Williams Jr.; m. John W. Bass Sr., July 23, 2000, (dec.) BA, Ark. Bapt. Coll., 1971; MS in Edn., Ouachita Bapt. Coll., Arkadelphia, Ark., 1988; degree, U. Little Rock, 2000—02. Tchr. Pulaski County Spl. Sch. Dist., Little Rock, 1971-97; exec. dir. Lenea's Children's Cottage, Little Rock, 1997—; advisor Choice Care Inc., Little Rock, 1998—; owner, pres. Evelyn's Tutoring Svc., Little Rock, 1998—; presch. tchr. Graceland Kids' Educare Ctr., 2000—. Child devel. assoc. instr., advisor Grace Holiness Christian Acad., 1999—, head instr., prin., 2004—; cons. in field; vocalist of praise/hymn. Author, composer: (poetry and songs) The Printed Word, 1993; (CDs) The Printed Word, 2003, (sound track and children's music book) Never Say Never, 2003; author: The Printed Word/Woman of God, 1995, (poetry) Listen! The Lord is Speaking, 2004. Traffic judge Willard Proctor, Jr. Campaign, 1996, cir. ct. judge, 2000. Democrat. Apostolic. Avocations: singing, songwriting, writing. Home: 5505 Western Ln Little Rock AR 72209 Office Phone: 501-312-1038. E-mail: evelynbass@sbcglobal.net.

BASS, HILARIE, lawyer; b. NYC, Nov. 22, 1954; BA magna cum laude, George Washington Univ., 1972; JD summa cum laude, Univ. Miami, 1981. Bar: Fla. 1981, US Dist. Ct. (so., middle districts) Fla., US Ct. Appeals (11th cir.), US Supreme Ct. Shareholder, chair nat. litig. practice group Greenberg Traurig LLP, Miami, Fla. Adj. prof. litig. Univ. Miami. Mem., exec. com. United Way, Dade County, 1995—, chair, bd. dir., 1997—99; bd. trustees Univ. Miami, 2003—. Named Bus. Woman of Yr., So. Fla. Bus. Jour., 2001; named one of So. Florida's Top Lawyers, So. Fla. Legal Guide, 2001—05, Best of the Best Rainmakers, Coral Gables Living Mag., 2003, Legal Elite, Fla. Trend Mag., 2004; recipient Dorothy Shula award for volunteerism, United Way of Miami-Dade, 2000. Mem.: ABA (bd. gov. 1990—93, chair, coun. for fund for justice and edn. 2000—02, mem., ho. of del. 1988—95, 2000—), Fla. Bar Found. (bd. dir. 1988—93, pres.). Office: Greenberg Traurig LLP 1221 Brickell Ave Miami FL 33131 Office Phone: 305-579-0745. Office Fax: 305-579-0717. Business E-Mail: bassh@gtlaw.com.

BASS, LYNDA D., retired medical/surgical nurse, nursing educator; b. Suffolk, Va., d. H.M. and Katie Lea Bass. BSN, NC Agrl. and Tech. State U., Greensboro, 1968; MSN, Cath. U. Am., Washington, 1974. Med.-surg. nurse Kenner Army Hosp., Ft. Lee, Va., 1968—71, Walter Reed Army Med. Ctr., Washington, 1968—71; staff nurse Providence Hosp., Washington, 1971—73, clin. educator, 1988—94; gen. surgery clin. specialist George Washington U. Hosp., Washington, 1974—77; clin. nurse specialist Walter Reed Army Hosp., Washington, 1977—78; coord. clin. staff devel. Mt. Vernon Hosp., Alexandria, Va., 1978—79; clin. nurse preceptor Greater SE Cmty. Hosp., Washington, 1979—81; instr. clin. nursing edn. Suburban Hosp., Bethesda, Md., 1980—83; edn./tng. quality assurance coord. Howard U. Hosp., Washington, 1983—88; edn. specialist Vets. Affairs Md. Healthcare Sys., Balt., 1995—2002. Adj. faculty Cath. U. Am., 1975—76. Active Women in Mil. Svc. for Am. Meml. Found. Capt. USAR, 1967—71, Vietnam. Mem.: Nat. Nursing Staff Devel. Assn., Vietnam Vets. Am., Chi Eta Phi.

BASSETT, ANGELA, actress; b. N.Y.C., Aug. 16, 1958; m. Courtney Vance, 1997; 2 children. BA in African-Am. studies, Yale U., 1980; MFA, Yale Sch. of Drama, 1983. Appeared in (plays) Colored People's Time, 1982, The Mystery Plays, 1984-85, The Painful Adventures of Pericles, Prince of Tyre, 1986-87, Joe Turner's Come and Gone, 1986-87, (Broadway) Ma Rainey's Black Bottom, Fences, 2006, (Broadway) Joe Turner's Come and Gone, 1988, King Henry IV Part I, 1987; (TV movies) Line of Fire: The Morris Dees Story, 1991, The Jacksons: An American Dream, 1992, A Century of Women, 1994, Ruby's Bucket of Blood, 2001 (also producer), The Rosa Parks Story, 2002 (also exec. producer); guest appearances (TV Series) The Cosby Show, 1985, 1988, Spenser: For Hire, 1985, A Man Called Hawk, 1989, Tour of Duty, 1989, 227, 1989, thirtysomething, 1989, Alien Nation, 1990, The Flash, 1991, Nightmare Café, 1992, The Bernie Mac Show, 2003; (films) F/X, 1986, Kindergarten Cop, 1990, Boyz N the Hood, 1991, City of Hope, 1991, Innocent Blood, 1992, Malcolm X, 1992, Passion Fish, 1992, What's Love Got to Do with It, 1993 (Acad. award nominee for best actress 1993, Golden Globe award best actress in a musical or comedy 1994), Strange Days, 1995, Panther, 1995, Waiting to Exhale, 1995, A Vampire in Brooklyn, 1995, Contact, 1997, How Stella Got Her Groove Back, 1998, Wings Against the Wind, 1999, Cosm, 1999, 50 Violins, 1999, Music of the Heart, 1999, Supernova, 2000, Whispers: An Elephant's Tale, 2000 (voice), Boesman and Lena, 2000, The Score, 2001, Sunshine State, 2002, Masked and Anonymous, 2003, The Lazarus Child, 2004, Mr. 3000, 2004, Akeelah and the Bee, 2006; exec. prodr. Our America, 2002. Home: 9000 W Sunset Blvd Ste 711 West Hollywood CA 90069-5807*

BASSETT, CAROL ANN, journalism educator, writer; b. Langley AFB, Va., Mar. 2, 1953; d. William Brainard and Genevieve (Rivaldo) B. BA summa cum laude in Humanities, Ariz. State U., 1977; MA in Journalism, U. Ariz., 1982. Ptnr. Desert West News, Tucson, 1985-90; freelance writer Tucson, 1980-95; freelance writer for mags. Missoula, Mont., 1995-98; mem. faculty Sch. Journalism U. Mont., Missoula, 1996-98; mem. faculty Sch. Journalism and Comm. U. Oreg., Eugene, 1998—. Author: Essays in American Nature Writing, 2000, American Nature Writing, 2001, A Gathering of Stones: Journeys to the Edges of a Changing World, 2002 (finalist Oreg. Book award 2003), Organ Pipe: Life on the Edge, 2004; editor Tucson Weekly, 1989-90; contbr. numerous articles to nat. and internat. mags. including N.Y. Times. Recipient 2d Place Gen. Reporting award Ariz. Press Club, 1987, Gold medal for best environ. documentary Houston Internat. Film Festival, 1990, 1st Place Gen. Reporting award Ariz. Press Club, 1992, Silver Medal for Energy Issues documentary, Houston Internat. Film Festival, 1992; co-recipient Alfred I. duPont Columbia award, 1984-85, First Place award Investigative Reporting, 1986, 1st Place Polit. Reporting, 1989, First Amendment Journalism award, 1986; grantee Fund for Investigative Journalism, 1985, 87, Corp. for Pub. Broadcasting, 1988, Oxfam Am., 1991. Address: Sch Journalism Univ Oreg Eugene OR 97403 Office Phone: 541-346-2033. Business E-Mail: cbassett@uoregon.edu.

BASSETT, DEBRA LYN, lawyer, educator; d. James Arthur and Shirley Ann Bassett. BA, U. Vt., 1977; MS, San Diego State U., 1982; JD, U. Calif., Davis, 1987. Bar: Calif. 1987, DC 1990, U.S. Dist. Ct. (no. and ea. dists.) Calif. 1988, U.S. Ct. Appeals (9th cir.) 1988, U.S. Supreme Ct. 1991. Guidance counselor Addison Cen. Supr. Union, Middlebury, Vt., 1982-83, Milton (Vt.) Elem. Sch., 1983-84; assoc. Morrison & Foerster, San Francisco, 1986; jud. clk. U.S. Ct. Appeals (9th cir.), Phoenix, 1987-88; assoc. Morrison & Foerster, San Francisco and Walnut Creek, Calif., 1988-92; sr. atty. Calif. Ct. Appeal (3d appellate dist.), Sacramento, 1992-99; assoc. prof. Mich. State U., East Lansing, 2002—04, Fla. State U. Coll. Law, Tallahassee, 2004—, Loula Fuller and Dan Myers prof. law, 2004—; vis. prof. law U. Calif., Davis, 2005—06. Tutor civil procedure, rsch. asst. U. Calif., Davis, 1985—87, instr., 1998, lectr., 1998—2002; adj. prof. McGeorge Sch. Law, 1998—99, dir. legal process, 1999—2000, vis. prof., 2000—01. Editor: U. Calif. Law Rev., 1985—86; sr. articles editor:, 1986—87. Mem.: ABA (vice chmn. ethics com. young lawyers divsn. 1989—91, exec. com. labor and employment law com. 1989—90), APA (assoc.), Am. Law Inst., Order of the Coif. Democrat. Avocations: music, tennis, travel, hiking. Office: Fla State U Coll Law 425 W Jefferson St Tallahassee FL 32306 Home: 801 Middlebrooks Cir Tallahassee FL 32312 Office Phone: 850-644-4248.

BASSETT, ELIZABETH EWING (LIBBY BASSETT), writer, editor, consultant; b. Cleve., July 22, 1937; d. Ben and Eileen Grace (Ewing) B.; m. Robert Richter, Feb. 20, 1994. AA, Bradford Jr. Coll., Mass., 1957. Girl Friday Time-Life, animated film cos., others, 1957-63; asst. producer, stage mgr. N.Y. State Pavilion at N.Y. World's Fair, 1963-64; writer, reporter, editor AP, N.Y.C., 1965-72; free-lance corr. AP, Newsweek, Voice of America, UNICEF, ABC Radio, Africa, 1972-74; resident corr. ABC News, Cairo, 1974-77; dir. publs. and comm. World Environment Ctr., N.Y.C., 1978-85; cons. writer, editor, editorial designer Women's Environ. and Devel. Orgn., 1989—98, UN orgns. and others, 1985—2000; co-organizer Project on Religion and Human Rights, 1994-95. Guest lectr. Am. U. Cairo, Rutgers U., Columbia U., L.I. U., Hunter Coll., CUNY; press officer Global Survival Conf., Oxford, Eng., 1988; press coord. Global Forum on Environ. and Devel., Moscow, 1990, Parliamentary Earth Summit, Rio de Janeiro, 1992; info. officer Internat. Green Cross/Global Forum, Kyoto, Japan, 1993; comm. coord. World Women's Congress for a Healthy Planet, Miami, 1991; press. coord. WEDO Web, NGO Forum on Women, China, 1995. Author: The Growth of Environment in the World Bank, World Environment Center, 1982, UNEP N.Am. News, 1986-91, Shared Vision, 1988-92, The Global Forum Decade, 1995, Earth and Faith: A Book of Reflection for Action, 2000, also others; editor, designer: Women in African Economies--From Burning Sun to Boardroom, 2000, Liberian Women Peacemakers, 2004; assoc. editor, designer: The Bella Abzug Reader, 2003; cons. writer, editor Inst. for Pvt. Investors, 1999—. Mem.: Soc. Profl. Journalists, Soc. Environ. Journalists.

BASSETT, JEAN WILLIAMS, elementary school educator; b. Washington, Dec. 31, 1926; d. James John and Bertha J. (Friedli) W.; m. Robert Louis Bassett, Nov. 6, 1948 (dec., 1998); children: Carole Bassett Rainey, Robert Louis Jr., Scott James. BA in French and Spanish, U. Md., 1948; MA in Edn., Cen. Conn. State U., 1968. Cert. tchr., Conn. Head tchr. 1st Congl. Ch. Nursery Sch., Bloomfield, Conn., 1960-67; elem. tchr. Metacomet Sch., Bloomfield, 1967-71, unit leader, 1971-81; elem. tchr., unit leader Laurel Sch., Bloomfield, 1981-92, ret., 1992. Curriculum developr Bloomfield Bd. Edn., 1969-92; mem. supt.'s adv. bd., 1972-76., mem. profl. devel. bd., 1987-92, workshop presenter, 1975-80; workshop presenter U. Hartford (Conn.), 1975-80; master tchr. Capitol Region Edn. Coun., Windsor, Conn., 1986-92. Mem. diaconate 1st Congl. Ch., 1982-88, mem. coun., 1988-90; mem. Community Awareness Task Force, Bloomfield, 1987-91; mem. bell ringing choir; vol. Meals on Wheels; vol. buyer for shop at sr. housing complex; mem. Warrenton United Meth. Ch., organizer churchwide bazaar, 1999; vol. Fanquier Hosp. Recipient Tchr. of Yr. award Bloomfield Bd. Edn., 1981, career incentive grantee, 1988; Fed. Govt. grantee, 1975. Mem. Wintonbury Hist. Soc., South Wales Women's Group, Duplicate Bridge Club, Bridge Club, Delta Kappa Gamma. Republican. Avocations: gardening, aerobics, bridge. Office: Bloomfield Bd Edn Park Ave Bloomfield CT 06002-3233 Home: 6696 Club House Ln Unit 111 Warrenton VA 20187

BASSETT, TINA, communications executive; b. Detroit; m. Leland Kinsey Bassett; children: Joshua, Robert. Student, U. Mich., 1974, 76-78, 81, Wayne State U., 1979-80. Advt. dir. Greenfield's Restaurant, Mich. and Ohio, 1972-73; dir. advt. and pub. rels. Kresco, Inc., Detroit, 1973-74; pub's. rep. The Detroiter mag., 1974-75; pub. rels. dir. Detroit Bicentennial Commn., 1975-77; prin. Leland K. Bassett & Assocs., Detroit, 1976-86; intermediate job devel. specialist Detroit Coun. of the Arts, 1977; project dir. Detroit image campaign dept. pub. info. City of Detroit, 1975, spl. events dir., 1978, dep. dir. dept. pub. info., 1978-83, dir. dept. pub. info., 1983-86; pres., prin. Bassett & Bassett, Inc., Detroit, 1986—. Publicity chmn. Under the Stars IV, V, VI, VII, VIII, IX and X, Benefit Balls, Detroit Inst. of Arts Founders Soc., 1983-88, Mich. Opera Theater, Opera Ball, 1987, Grand Prix Ball, 1989; co-chair, prodr. Mus. Hall Ctr. for Performing Arts, pub. chmn., 1996; bd. dirs. Weizman Inst. Sci., 1996-97, Detroit Inst. Arts, 2006—; mem. Cinema Arts Coun., 1996—. Named Outstanding Woman in Agy. Top Mgmt., Detroit chpt. Am. Women in Radio and TV, 1989, one of Most Powerful Women in Mich., CORP Mag., 2002. Mem. AIA (hon., pub. dir. 1990-91, bd. dirs., Richard Upjohn fellowship 1991), Detroit Hist. Soc., Internat. Women's Forum, Music Hall Assn., Pub. Rels. Soc. Am. (Advt. Woman of Yr. 1989), Woman's Advt. Club Detroit. Home: 30751 Cedar Creek Dr Farmington Hills MI 48336-4989 Office: Bassett & Bassett Inc 1400 First National Bldg 660 Woodward Av Detroit MI 48226-3581 Office Phone: 313-965-3010. Office Fax: 313-965-3016.

BASSI, SUZANNE HOWARD, retired secondary school educator, volunteer; b. Santa Ana, Calif., Feb. 26, 1945; d. David Gould and Marian (Matthews) H.; Roger Joseph Bassi, Aug. 25, 1973; children: Carrie, Steven, Gregory. BA, Rosary Coll., River Forest, Ill., 1966; MA in Teaching, U. Ill., Champaign, 1973. Tchr. Resurrection HS, Chgo., 1966-67, Proviso Twp. HS, Hillside, Ill., 1967-76; home day care operator Palatine, Ill., 1980-84; mem. bd. Palatine Elem. Sch. Dist. # 15, 1987-95. Rep. candidate for state rep. dist. 54, Ill., 1996, 98, state rep., 54th Dist., 1998—; vice chmn. Ed-Red, Park Ridge, Ill., 1993, chmn., 1994-96; legis. chmn. Ill. Assn. of Sch. Bds., North Cook divsn., Lombard, Ill., 1994-96. Named Those Who Excel, Ill. State Bd. Edn., 1992. Mem. LWV (former bd. dirs., legis. chair), Palatine Rep. Women's Orgn. Republican. Roman Catholic. Home: 2509 Honeysuckle Ln Rolling Meadows IL 60008

BASSIL, JANICE, lawyer; b. Brookline, Mass., Apr. 16, 1954; BA cum laude, Brandeis U., 1975; JD, Boston U., 1978. Bar: Mass. 1978, U.S. Dist. Ct. Dist. Mass. 1978, U.S. Ct. Appeals First Cir. 1978. Atty. Mass. Defender's Com., 1978—84, White Inker & Aronson, 1984—88; ptnr. Carney & Bassil, Boston, 1989—. Adj. prof. Boston U. Sch. Law. Contbr. chapters to books. Named one of top Boston lawyers, Boston Mag., 2004; recipient Award Zealous Advocacy of Poor, Edward J. Duggan Private Counsel, 1997, Award of Excellence, Frank J. Murray Inns Ct., 1998. Fellow: Am. Coll. Trial Lawyers, Am. Acad. Matrimonial Lawyers; mem.: Mass. Continuing Legal Edn. (bd. trustees, former pres.), Friends of Spl. Libraries at Boston U. (bd. trustees). Office: Carney And Bassil 20 Park Plz Ste 1405 Boston MA 02116-4311 Business E-Mail: jbassil@CarneyBassil.com.

BASSUK, ELLEN LINDA, psychiatrist; b. NYC, Feb. 8, 1945; d. Irving and Molly (Pakarow) B.; children: Daniel, Sarah. BA, Brandeis U., 1964; MD, Tufts U., 1968; Dr.P.S. (hon.), Northeastern U., 1993. Diplomate Am. Bd. Psychiatry. Intern Mt. Auburn Hosp., Cambridge, Mass., 1968-69; resident psychiatry Univ. Hosp., Boston, 1969-70, Boston State Hosp., Boston, 1970-71, Beth Israel Hosp., Boston, 1971-73, dir. psychiat. emergency svcs., 1974-82; fellow Bunting Inst., Cambridge, Mass., 1982-84; assoc. prof. psychiatry Harvard Med. Sch., Boston, 1983—. Founder, pres. Nat. Ctr. on Family Homelessness, Newton, Mass., 1988—; mem. Com. on Health Care of Homeless Persons Inst. of Medicine, Washington, 1986-88. Editor: The Practitioners Guide to Psychoactive Drugs, 1977, 83, 91, 97; editor-in-chief Am. Jour. Orthopsychiatry, 1994-98; contbr. numerous articles to profl. jours. Fellow Am. Psychiat. Assn.; mem. Mass. Psychiat. Soc. Office: Nat Ctr Family Homelessness 181 Wells Ave Newton MA 02459-3332 Home: 70 Montvale Rd Newton MA 02459 Office Phone: 617-964-3834 14. E-mail: ellen.bassuk@familyhomelessness.org.

BAST, KAROLYN ANNE (KAY BAST), dance educator, choreographer; b. Tulsa, Mar. 12, 1940; d. Lowell R. and Dorothy J. Butterfield; m. A. Daniel Bast, Aug. 17, 1963; children: Terri Lynn, Robin Kay, Steven Christopher. AA, Citrus Jr. Coll., Azusa-Glendora, Calif., 1970; BS, Calif. Polytech. U., Pomona, 1972, MS, 1981. Dance dir. The Show Stoppers, Chino, Calif., 1978-87; Europe dance dir. The Dance Masters, Alta Loma, Calif., 1992—. Dir. internat. dance tours; founder Internat. Performing Arts Competition, Anaheim, Calif., 1985-89. Author: Tap: The Dance of Sound, 1982. Mem. cultural planning com. Chino, Calif., 1982—, city parade dir., 1980-82; pres. Assistance League of Pomona Valley, 1991-92. Recipient numerous dance title awards. Republican. Lutheran. Avocations: needlepoint, crafts, interior decorating, travel. Home: PO Box 1594 Upland CA 91785-1594

BASTIANICH, LIDIA MATTICCHIO, chef, food service executive; b. Italy, 1947; Owner Buonavia Restaurant, Forest Hills, NY, 1972—81, Villa Secondo, Fresh Meadows, NY, 1979—81, Felidia Restaurant, NY, 1981—; co-owner Becco Restaurant, NY, 1993—, Lidia's Restaurant, Kansas City, Mo., 1998—; founder, pres. Esperienze Italiane Travel, 1996—. Founder, owner Lidia's Flavors of Italy, 1988—; host, chef Lidia's Italian Table, 1998—2001, Lidia's Italian Am. Kitchen, 2001—, Lidia's Family Table, PBS Series. Author: (montly syndicated column) on Italian food, (cookbooks) La Cucina di Lidia, 1990, Lidia's Italian Table, 1998, Lidia's Italian American Kitchen (and host of PBS series of same name), 2001, Lidia's Family Table, 2004. Established Lidia Matticchio Bastianich Found., 1999. Office: Felidia Restaurant 243 E 58th St New York NY 10022 Office Phone: 212-758-1479. Business E-Mail: info@lidiasitaly.com.*

BATAILLE, GRETCHEN, academic administrator; B of English, Calif. Polytech. State U., M of English Edn.; DA, Drake U. Chair dept. English Ariz. State U., assoc. dean acad. personnel, until 1994; provost U. Calif., Santa Barbara, 1994-97; provost, acad. v.p. Wash. State U., Pullman, 1997-2000; sr. v.p., v.p. acad. affairs U. NC Sys., Chapel Hill, 2000—06; interim chancellor NC Sch. Arts, Winston-Salem, 2005—06; pres. U. No. Tex., Denton, 2006—. Author: Living the Dream in Arizona: The Legacy of Martin Luther King, Jr., 1992, Native American Women: A Biographical Dictionary, 1994, Ethnic Studies in the United States, 1998, others. Office: U N Tex PO Box 311277 Denton TX 76203-1277 Office Phone: 919-962-4614. Business E-Mail: bataille@northcarolina.edu.*

BATCHELDER, ALICE M., federal judge; b. Wilmington, Del., Aug. 15, 1944; m. William G. Batchelder III; children: William G. IV, Elisabeth. BA, Ohio Wesleyan U., 1964; JD, Akron U., 1971; LLM, U. Va., 1988; LHD (hon.), Lake Erie Coll., 1993; LLD (hon.), U. Akron Sch. of Law, 2001. Tchr. Plain Local Sch. Dist., Franklin County, Ohio, 1965—66, Jones Jr. High Sch., 1966-67, Buckeye High Sch., Medina County, 1967-68; assoc. Williams & Batchelder, Medina, Ohio, 1971-83; judge U.S. Bankruptcy Ct., Ohio, 1983-85, U.S. Dist. Ct. (no. dist.) Ohio, Cleve., 1985-91, U.S. Ct. of Appeals (6th cir.), Cleveland, 1991—. Mem. Com. on Bankruptcy Edn., Fed. Jud. Ctr., 1988—91, Jud. Conf. Adv. Com. on Bankruptcy Rules, 1993—96, Jud. Conf. on US Com. on Automation and Tech., 2000—03. Editor-in-chief Univ. Akron Law Rev., 1971. Recipient Outstanding Alumni award, U. Akron Sch. of Law, 1993, Hon. award, 1996, Women of Distinction award, Medina County YWCA, 1997. Mem. Fed. Judge's Assn., Fed. Bar Assn., Medina County Bar Assn.*

BATCHELDER, ANNE STUART, retired publishing executive, political organization worker; b. Lake Forest, Ill., Jan. 11, 1920; d. Robert Douglas and Harriet (McClure) Stuart; m. Clifton Brooks Batchelder, May 26, 1945; children: Edward, Anne Stuart, Mary Clifton, Lucia Brooks Student Lake Forest Coll., 1941-43. Clubmobile driver ARC, Eng., Belgium, France, Holland and Germany, 1943-45; pub., editor Douglas County Gazette, 1970-75, 79-90. Bd. dirs. Firstier Bank Omaha; dir., treas. U.S. Checkbook Com. Mem. Rep. Ctrl. Com. Nebr., 1955-62, 70-83, vice chmn. Ctrl. Com., 1959-64, chmn., 1975-79, mem. fin. com., 1957-64; chmn. women's sect. Douglas County Rep. Fin. Com., 1995, vice chmn. com., 1958-60; v.p. Omaha Woman's Rep. Club, 1957-58, pres., 1959-60; alt. del. Nat. Conv., 1956, 72, del., 1980, 84, 88; mem. Rep. Nat. Com. for Nebr., 1964-70; asst. chmn. Douglas County Rep. Ctrl. Com., 1971-74; 1st v.p. Nebr. Fedn. Rep. Women, 1971-72, pres., 1972-74; chmn. Nebr. Rep. Com., 1975-79; vice-chmn. Bldg. Fedn. Rep. Women, 1998—; mem. Nebr. State Bldg. Commn., 1979-83; Rep. candidate for lt. gov., 1974. Sr. v.p. Nebr. Founders Day, 1958; trustee Hastings Coll., 1977—; bd. dirs. YWCA, 1983-89, Omaha Libr. Found., 1991-2000, Libr. Found., 2000—; past trustee Brownell Hall, Vis. Nurse Assn.; past pres. Nebr. chpt. Freedoms Found. at Valley Forge; chmn. fin. George Bush for Pres., Nebr., 1987-88; apptd. Kennedy Ctr. Performing Arts, 1989, 94, Pres.' Adv. Com. on the Arts, 1990-92, Nat. Com. for the Performing Arts, 1992—; mem. Nebr. Rep. State Fin. Com., 1990, Nat. Fin. Com. Bush-Quayle, 1992; active Omaha Meth. Hosp. Found., Brownell-Talbot Sch. Found.; mem. Uta Halee Home for Girls, 1980—. Elected to Nebr. Rep. Hall of Fame, 1984; named Citizen of the Yr. Midlands Coun. Boy Scouts Am., 1997; recipient Silver Beaver, Boy Scouts Am., Spirit award Uta Halee Home for Girls, 1999. Mem. Mayflower Soc., Colonial Dames, P.E.O., Nat. League Pen Women Omaha Country, Omaha, Halee Spirit of Youth. Presbyterian. Home: 6875 State St Omaha NE 68152-1633

BATCHELOR, KAREN SUE, music educator; b. Lake Charles, La., Sept. 22, 1961; d. James W. and Maxyne Harris Batchelor. MusB in Piano Pedagogy, McNeese State U., Lake Charles, La., 1985. Cert. elem. tchr. La. Choir dir., organist Westminister Presbyn. Ch., Lake Charles, 1984—92, Wesley United Meth. Ch., Lake Charles, 1992—93; classroom tchr. First Meth. Sch., Lake Charles, 1988—97; organist St. Luke-Simpson United Meth. Ch., Lake Charles, 1993—2001; music tchr. D.A. Combre Elem. Sch., Lake Charles, 1997—2000, Ralph Wilson Elem. Sch., Lake Charles, 2000—01, J.D.Clifton Elem. Sch., Lake Charles, 1997—2004, A.A. Nelson Elem. Sch., Lake Charles, La., 2004—; music dir. Sweetlake United Meth. Ch., La., 2002—. Recipient KPLC Class Act award, KPLC TV, 2004. Mem.: Vocal Music Tchrs. Orgn. (HS honor choir accompanist 2001—), Sigma Alpha Iota (chpt. treas. 1998—2002, chpt. pres. 2002—). Office: A A Nelson Elem Sch 1001 Country Club Rd Lake Charles LA 70605 Office Phone: 337-477-1775.

BATCHVAROVA, MADLEN TODOROVA, music educator, conductor; d. Todor Bachvarov and Stefka Bachvarova. MusB, Acad. for Music and Dance Art, Bulgaria, 1991; MusM in Choral Conducting, Ga. state U., 1997; Mus D, U. of Ala., 2000. Condr. Plovdiv Choral Soc., Bulgaria, 1992—94; piano accompanist Secondary Music Sch., Plovdiv, Bulgaria, 1992—94; grad. tchg. asst. U. of Ala., Tuscaloosa, 1997—2000; asst. prof. music Columbus State U., Ga., 2000—01; asst. prof. music, dir. choral programs Hanover Coll., Ind., 2001—. Mem. internat. jury Internat. Choral Festival, Preveza, Greece, 2002. Singer: (CD recording) John Adams (GRAMMY for Best Choral Performance, 1997); singer: (chorus) (music performance at carnegie hall) Brahms, Requiem. Mem.: Am. Choral Dirs. Assn., NARAS, Pi Kappa Lambda. Office: Hanover Coll POBox 890 Hanover IN 47243 E-mail: batchvarova@hanover.edu.

BATE, MARILYN ANNE, psychologist; b. Dillonvale, Ohio, May 23, 1939; d. Louis Edward and Veronica (Koval) Dezera; m. Brian Richard Bate, Sept. 7, 1968 (div. Apr. 1976); children: Jennifer, Julia. BSc, Ohio State U., 1961; MA, Case Western Res. U., Cleve., 1965, PhD, 1974. Lic. psychologist. Elem. tchr., sch. psychologist Cleve. City Schs., 1961-67; sch. psychologist, spl. edn. coord. Cleveland Heights (Ohio), U. Heights, Ohio City Schs., 1967-70; sch. psychologist Mayfield (Ohio) City Schs., 1970-71, Cleve. City Schs., 1971-79, North Olmsted (Ohio) Schs., 1979-82; instr. Cuyahoga Community Coll., Cleve., 1967-82; pvt. practice Cleve., 1967-82; psychologist Dept. Def. Dependent Schs., Aviano, Italy, 1982-86; pvt. practice Columbus, Ohio, 1986—2000; ct. psychologist Franklin County Ct. Common Pleas, Columbus, 1987—2000; sch. psychologist Montgomery County Pub. Schools, Silver Spring, Md., 2000—. Mem. adv. bd. Eastpark Elem. Sch., Middleburg Heights, Ohio, 1985; vol. Son of Heaven, Columbus, 1989. Mem. APA, Am. Correctional Assn., Nat. Sch. Psychology Assn. (charter mem.), Ohio Psychol. Assn. (mem. ethics com. 1986-92, exec. bd. 1992—), Ctrl. Ohio Psychol. Assn. (exec. bd. 1986—, treas. 1990-92, pres. 1993), European Sch. Psychology Assn. (treas. 1985), Ohio Sch. Psychology Assn. (co-chmn. ethics com. 1976-86, exec. bd. 1992-2000), Cleve. Sch. Psychology Assn. (pres. 1969-71), Md. Sch. Psycology Assn. Avocations: skiing, gardening, crafts. Home: 8706 Ramsey Ave Silver Spring MD 20910-3469 Office: Spring Mill Field Office 11721 Kemp Mill Rd Silver Spring MD 20902 Office Phone: 301-649-8003. E-mail: marilyn_a_bate@mcpsmd.org.

BATEMAN, ANDREA R., insurance agent; b. Park Ridge, Ill., Oct. 17, 1975; BS, Roosevelt U., 2000. Cert. Lic. Ins. Agent Ill. Ins. agent/owner Dave Rundblad, Inc./Allstate, Park Ridge, Ill., 1996—. Home: 545 N Rose Ave Park Ridge IL 60068 Office: Allstate Ins 1580 N Northwest hwy #15 Park Ridge IL 60068

BATEMAN, ANGELA ANDERSON, anesthetist; b. Raleigh, N.C., Nov. 14, 1952; d. Samuel Garland and Joy Brown Anderson; m. Ronald Bruce Bateman, Apr. 27, 1986. BSN, Atlantic Christian Coll., 1974; student, Southwestern Sem., 2004—. Staff nurse Wake Med. Ctr., Raleigh, 1974—75, Durham Regional Sch. Anesthesia, 1975—77; cert. registered nurse anesthetist Alamance County Hosp., Burlington, NC, 1977—85, Iredell County Meml. Hosp., Statesville, NC, 1986—87, Critical Health Sys., Raleigh, 1987—. Instr. clin. anesthesia Raleigh Sch. Nurse Anesthesia, NC, 1995—. Named Outstanding Clin. Educator, Critical Health Sys., 2003. Mem.: Am. Assn. Nurse Anesthetists. Avocations: camping, needlepoint, beading. Office: Critical Health Sys Raleigh NC Personal E-mail: abateman@earthlink.net.

BATEMAN, CAROL VAUGHAN, pharmacist; b. Richmond, Va., Dec. 23, 1941; d. Harold Benjamin and Verna Pearl (Vaughan) B. Student, Vanderbilt U., 1960-61; BS in Chemistry, U. Richmond, 1964; BS in Pharmacy, U. S.C., 1970. Registered pharmacist, S.C., Hawaii. Pharmacist Camden (S.C.) Walgreen Agy., 1970-74; pharmacist, IV supr. Providence Hosp., Columbia, S.C., 1974-81; asst. pharmacy dir. Hilton Head Hosp., Hilton Head Island, 1981-87, interim pharmacy dir., 1987-88; asst. pharmacy mgr. Revco, 1988-90; pharmacist Self Meml. Hosp., Greenwood, S.C., 1990-93, kinetics pharmacist, 1993—. Vice chmn. S.C. Bd. Pharmacy, 1996-97, chmn. 1997-98; clin. instr. U. S.C. Coll. Pharmacy, 1984—. Editor: Prescriptions for the Kitchen, 1987. Mem. S.C. Heart Assn. Task Force on Hypertension, 1975-81; bd. dirs. Planned Parenthood of Hilton Head, 1986-88; vol. Greenwood Free Clinic, 1997—, Vols. in Med. Missions, 1993—; bd. dirs. Abbeville County Hist. Soc., 1993-96, v.p. 1997-98, pres., 1999—; mem. Rockcreek Homeowners Assn., 1991—; co-founder S.C. Recovery and Intervention Pharmacist Team, 1988-89. Mem. S.C. Pharm. Assn. (chmn. continuing edn. com. 1974-78, v.p. 1978-79, mem. awards com. 1982-84, chmn. conv. com. 1984-85, pres. 1988-89, S.C. Pharmacist of Yr. award 1976), Am. Pharm. Assn., S.C. Soc. Health-Sys. Pharmacists (ann. award 1975), 8th Dist. Pharm. Assn. (v.p. 1991-92), Nat. Assn. Bds. of Pharmacy (mem. task force on stds. for enteral and parenteral care 1994-95, co-chmn. dist. III convention 1998), Am. Soc. Health-Sys. Pharmacists, Faculty House U. S.C., U. S.C. Alumni Assn., Phi Lambda Sigma. Republican. Methodist. Avocations: gardening, travel, collecting orientalia and pharmacy antiques, walking. Home: 401 Rock Creek Blvd Greenwood SC 29649-8918 Office: Self Meml Hosp 1325 Spring St Greenwood SC 29646-3875

BATEMAN, MAUREEN SCANNELL, lawyer; b. NYC, July 27, 1943; d. Daniel Thomas and Gertrude Rose (Lally) Scannell; m. Frank Coffroth Bateman, June 26, 1971; 1 child: Daniel Frank. AB, Manhattanville Coll., 1964; JD, Fordham U., 1968. Bar: N.Y. 1969, Mass. 1998. Assoc. attorney Willkie Farr & Gallagher, N.Y.C., 1968-69, Davis Polk & Wardwell, N.Y.C., 1969-78; asst. resident counsel Morgan Guaranty Trust Co., N.Y.C., 1978-80; v.p., counsel Bankers Trust Co., N.Y.C., 1980-90; mng. dir., gen. counsel U.S. Trust Corp. N.Y., N.Y.C., 1990-97; exec. v.p., gen. counsel State St. Bank & Trust Co., Boston, 1997—2003; ptnr. Holland & Knight, NYC, 2004—. Office: Holland & Knight 195 Broadway 24th Fl New York NY 10007 Business E-Mail: maureen.bateman@hklaw.com.

BATEMAN, SHARON LOUISE, public relations executive; b. St. Louis, Oct. 18, 1949; d. Frank Hamilton and Charlotte Elizabeth (Hogan) Bateman. Student, Drury Coll., 1967-69; BJ, U. Mo., 1971. Asst. dir. pub. rels. Cardinal Glennon Hosp. Children, St. Louis, 1971-76; staff asst. pub. rels. Ozark Air Lines, St. Louis, 1976-80; mgr. corp. rels. Kellwood Co., St. Louis, 1980-83; mgr. corp. comm. May Dept. Stores Co., St. Louis, 1983-86, dir. corp. comm., 1986-94, v.p. corp. comms., 2000—06; mgr. comm. Arthur Andersen, St. Louis, 1995-96; mgr. editl. and adminstrv. svcs. Falk Design Group, St. Louis, 1996—2000; oper. v.p. corp. comms. and corp. giving Federated Dept. Stores, Inc., Cin., 2006—. Bd. dirs. St. Michael's Houses, 1996—97, Gateway Greening, 1999—2001, The Wellness Cmty., 2004—06. Recipient Best Regional Airline Employee Publ. award, Editor's Assn. Am. Transp. Assn., 1978. Mem.: Pub. Rels. Soc. Am. (sec.St. Louis chpt. 1983, bd. dirs. 1988—90, v.p. 1991), Internat. Assn. Bus. Comms. (pres. St. Louis chpt. 1977). Office: Federated Dept Stores Inc 7 W Seventh St Cincinnati OH 45202

BATEMAN, VEDA MAE, industrial psychologist, management consultant; b. Winnipeg, Man., Can., Aug. 8, 1921; came to U.S., 1930; d. Norman Silver and Veda Moncrieff (Maxwell) B. ME, Vanderbilt U., 1944; BA, U. Tenn., 1951, MA, 1953, PhD, 1959. Lic. psychologist, Tenn.; cert. indsl. psychologist and cons. Adminstrv. asst. to pres. Nashville (Tenn.) Bridge Co., 1940-45; program dir. Am. Red Cross, Germany, France, Korea, 1945-47; exec. dir. Children's Home, Knoxville, Tenn., 1947-55; corp. dir. of personnel and loss prevention Millers, Inc., Knoxville, 1955-65; corp. dir. rsch. and devel., safety and systems analyst Allied Stores, Millers Inc., Knoxville, 1965-87; mgmt. cons. Bateman Cons., Knoxville, 1987—. Mem., officer Knox Children's Found., Knoxville, 1955—, Vols. of Am., Knoxville, 1965—, ARC, Knoxville, 1980-83, Overlook Mental Health Ctr., Knoxville, 1983-87; vol. counselor Sr. Corps of Ret. Execs., 1988—; vol. tax counselor Tax Counseling for the Elderly, 1988—; treas. Strong Found., Knoxville, 1992—, Sr. Citizens' Awareness Network (SCAN), 1996—. Mem. APA, Tenn. Psychol. Assn., Green Meadow Country Club. Methodist. Home and Office: 3608 Blow Dr Knoxville TN 37920-2877

BATEN, AMANDA ZOE, psychologist; b. NYC, Jan. 4, 1967; d. Marvin and Susan Jill Baten. BA, U. Wis., Madison, 1990; MSc, San Francisco State U., 1994; PhD in Clin. Psychology, Wright Inst., 1999. Cert. Holistic Health and Nutrition Counselor. Staff psychologist Woodhill Hosp., Bklyn., 1999—2001; assoc. prof. City U. NY, NYC, 2001—02, Montefiore Med. Ctr., Bronx, NY, 2002—03; psychologist, cons. Pvt. Practice, NYC, 2001—. Nutritional psychologist cons. Remede Naturopathics, NYC, 2005—06. Bd. mem. Fresh Art, 2002—05. Mem.: Assn. for the Advancement of Behavior Theraphy, NY Psychol. Assn. Avocations: yoga, hiking, cooking, guitar. Office: Remede Naturopathics 214 Sullivan St #3B New York NY 10012

BATES, BARBARA J. NEUNER, retired municipal official; b. Mt. Vernon, NY, Apr. 8, 1927; d. John Joseph William and Elsie May (Flint) Neuner; m. Herman Martin Bates, Jr., Mar. 25, 1950; children: Roberta Jean Bates Jamin, Herman Martin III, Jon Neuner. BA, Barnard Coll., 1947. Confidential clk. to supr. Town of Ossining, N.Y., 1960-63, receiver of taxes N.Y., 1971-90; ret.; pres. BNB Assocs., Briarcliff Manor, N.Y., 1963-83, Upper Nyack Realty Co., Inc., Briarcliff Manor, 1966-71. V.p. Ossining (N.Y.) Young Rep. Club, 1958; pres. Young Womens Rep. Club Westchester County (N.Y.), 1959-61; regional committeewoman N.Y. State Assn. Young Rep. Clubs, 1960-62; mem. Westchester County Rep. Com., 1963-95; mem. Ossining Women's Rep. Club, 1960-92, pres., 1984-85; mem. Westchester County Women's Rep. Club, 1957-92. Mem. DAR, Jr. League Westchester-on-Hudson, Receivers Taxes Assn. Westchester County (legis. liaison, v.p., pres. 1984-85), Hackley Sch. Mothers Assn. (pres. 1968), R.I. Hist. Soc., Ossining Hist. Soc., Westchester County Hist. Soc., Landmark Preservation Soc. S.E., Ossining Woman's Club, Brewster/Carmel Garden Club. Home: 23 Bloomer Rd Brewster NY 10509-1026 also: 663 Reynolds Rd Chepachet RI 02814-1629 E-mail: cmajvkb@yahoo.com.

BATES, BEVERLY JO-ANNE, artist, educator; b. Pitts., Jan. 29, 1938; d. Joseph Whitfield and Thelma Alease (McMullen) Loftin; divorced; children: Roy F. Jr., Brian Whitfield, Stephen Jeffrey. BS in Art Edn., W.Va. State Coll., 1959; MEd in Art Edn., U. Pitts., 1973, postgrad., 1985-88, Temple U., 1963-64, RISD, 1984. Art tchr. Pitts. Pub. Sch. System, 1959, 70-75, print tchr. Brashear High Sch., 1975-78, coord. art dept., printmaking tchr. Pitts. High Sch., 1970—; art tchr. N.J. Pub. Schs., Camden, N.J., 1961; print instr. Selma Burke Art Ctr., Pitts., 1971, Pitts. Arts and Crafts Ctr., 1972; panel mem. visual arts Pa. Coun. on Arts, Harrisburg, 1979—. Com. mem. Links Inc. Nat. Art Com., Washington, 1992—; mem. adv. bd. Manchester Craftsman's Guild, Pitts., 1985—, Visions, 1990—. Author: (catalogues) Black American Art, 1977 (Meade award 1977), 1978 (W. Pa. Prize 1978); one-person shows include Westmoreland Mus., 1991, Visual Arts Gallery, C.C. of Allegheny County, 1991, Kipp Gallery, Indiana U. Pa., 1991, Westminster Coll. Art Gallery, 1991, others; exhibited in group shows at Pitts. Ctr. for Arts, 1982, 83, 84, 85, 87, 88, 90, 91, 92, Carnegie Mus., 1982, 86, 90, 92, S.G. Galleries, 1992, LaTeste, France, 1992, U. Pitts. Kimbo Gallery, 1990, 91, 92, Carson St. Gallery, 1991, others. Bd. trustees Pitts. Ctr. for Arts, 1989—; bd. dirs. Soc. Contemporary, Pitts., 1990—, Soc. Arts and Crafts. Honors fellow R.I. Sch., Providence, 1984; recipient Frick Fellowship award Pitts. Bd. Edn., 1975, Outstanding Art Edn. award Pitts. Bd. Edn., 1984, Youth Arts award Pa. Art Edn. Assn., Pitts., 1988, Outstanding Art Edn. award Pratt Inst., Bklyn., 1989, Jurors award Pitts. Print Group, 1991, Images show U. Pitts., 1992. Mem. The Links Inc. (bd. mem. nat. arts com.), Nat. Art Edn. Assn., Pa. Art Edn. Assn., Pa. Coun. on Arts (past panel mem.), Pitts. Print Group (past bd. mem.), Associated Artists Pitts. (past bd. mem.), Nat. Conf. Artists, Pa. Alliance for Art Edn. (bd. mem.). Avocations: art, printmaking, reading, travel. Home: 6922 Meade St Pittsburgh PA 15208-2402 Office: Pitts High Sch 925 Brushton Ave Pittsburgh PA 15208-1613 Personal E-mail: jbates6220@aol.com.

BATES, CAROL GARRISON, secondary school educator; b. Oxford, Ga., June 11, 1940; d. Webb Black and Mary Elizabeth (Thomson) Garrison; m. Sturgis Goodwin Gates, Aug. 19, 1963 (div. 1996); children: Cynthia Diane, Mary Elizabeth, Carol Patricia, Meredith Anne. AB, Emory U., 1962; MEd, Ga. State U., 1985; postgrad., Emory U., 1985-86, U. Va., 1985. Cert. social studies tchr., Ga. Tchr. social studies Fulton County Sch. Sys., Atlanta, 1982—. Mem. Master Tchrs. of Econ. Edn., 1985—; social studies tchr. Ga. Gov.'s Honors Program (instr. 1994, 1995), social studies dept. chair, McClarin HS. Author: U.S. History Resource Guide, 1991; co-author: Anthropology Resource Guide, 1991; editor: Political Science Resource Guide, 1992. Named Tchr. of the Yr., McClarin HS, 1991, 2006; RJR Nabisco fellow, 1987. Mem. Ga. Coun. for Social Studies, Nat. Coun. Social Studies, Ga. Assn. Econ. Educators, Profl. Assn. Ga. Educators, Kappa Delta Pi, Kappa Kappa Gamma. Democrat. Methodist. Office: McClarin High Sch 3605 Main St College Park GA 30337-2614 Business E-Mail: batescg@fulton.k12.ga.us.

BATES, CHERYL A, music educator; b. Oklahoma City, Okla., Nov. 20, 1959; adopted d. Charles S and Marguerite H Miller; m. Don R Bates, Oct. 16, 1982; 1 child, Colin T. MusM, U. of Houston, Houston, TX, 1984—88; MusB, U. of Okla., Norman, OK, 1978—82. Texas Teacher Certification Tex. Edn. Agy., 1987. Music specialist Epps Island Elem., Houston, Tex., 1988—92; choir dir. Bammel Mid. Sch., Houston, 1992—98; adj. prof. Houston CC, Houston, Tex., 1991—92; tchg. fellow U. of Houston, Houston, Tex., 1986—87, 1998—2000; assoc. prof. Tomball Coll., Houston, Tex., 2000—. Bd. of directors The Regional Arts Coun., Tomball, Tex., 2000—02; clinician Tex. Music Educators Assn., San Antonio, 2001, San Antonio, 02. Dir.: (choral conducting) UIL Competitions (Four UIL Sweepstakes Awards for Outstanding Concert and Sightreading Performance, 97-8), American Classics Music Festivals (Two Outstanding Performance and Best in Class Awards, 97-8), Splashtown Choral Festivals (Two Best in Class Awards, 97-8); singer: (concert) Andre Bocelli in Concert at the Compaq Center, John Rutter conducts Brahm's German Requiem. V.p. North Houston Gamma Phi Beta Alumni, Houston, Tex., 1992—94. Fellow, U. of Houston Sch. of Music, 1986-87 and 1998-2000; grantee Innovative Project Grant, Tomball Coll., 2002; scholar Piano Scholarship, U. of Okla., 1978-1982. Mem.: Music Educators Nat. Conf., Am. Choral Directors Assn., Tex. Choral Directors Assn., Coll. Music Educators, Tex. Music Educators Assn., Mu Phi Epsilon, Gamma Phi Beta. Home: 11902 Quail Creek Houston TX 77070 Office: Tomball College 30555 Tomball Parkway Tomball TX 77375 E-mail: cheryl.a.bates@nhmccd.edu.

BATES, DAWNA JOYCE, retired secondary school educator, department chairman; b. Latrobe, Pa., Mar. 1948; d. Thomas Alvin and Velma Mae Richards; m. Craig Robert Bates, Aug. 15, 1970; 1 child, Jody Lyn Bertoli. M, Slippery Rock U., Pa., 1976. Cert. tchr. Pa. Tchr. Greater Latrobe Sch. Dist., 1970—, dept. head health and phys. edn. K-12, 1990—. Basketball coach Greater Latrobe Sch. Dist., 1982—. Trustee, choir dir., tchr., youth fellowship dir. Bethany United Meth. Ch., Latrobe, 1948—; asst. dir. 4th of July Religious Svc., Latrobe, 1996—; trainer, disaster vol., bd. dirs. Chestnut Ridge Red Cross, Latrobe; trustee Am. Heart Assn., Latrobe, 1990—, bd. dirs. Recipient Claira Barton award, ARC, 1992, Children's Empowerment award, Latrobe Chamber-Westland Clinic, 2003, Cmty. Champions Jefferson award, Pitts. Post Gazette-United Way, 2003. Mem.: AAHPERD (assoc.), Pa. Soc. Health, Phys. Edn., Recreation and Dance. Methodist. Home: 125 Armel Rd Latrobe PA 15650 Office: Greater Latrobe Sch Dist Latrobe Elem Sch 1501 Ligonier Latrobe PA 15650 Office Phone: 724-539-9777. E-mail: dbates@wiu.k12.pa.us.

BATES, GWEN LEE, health facility administrator, consultant; d. Marion Luther and Jennie V. Purcell; children: Ruth Denice Decker, Timothy James. Cert. tech. Sr. ops. tech. Stauffer Chem., Baytown, Tex.; supr. safety & environ. Waste Control Svcs., Channelview, Tex.; tech. writer, tng. specialist Myers Tng. Svc., Galena Park, Tex.; cons., tech. writer, editor Enron Global Asset Ops., Houston; compliance trainer Compliance Solutions Occupations, Denver; mgr. quality HS&E Spar Tec, Inc., Houston; mgr. corp. HS&E J. Ray McDermott, S.A., Houston. Mem. Greater Houston Partnership Clean Air, Clean Water & Wetlands Coms. Mem.: Nat. Fire Protection Assn. Avocations: gardening, bowling, drawing, poetry. Office: J Ray McDermott SA 757 N Eldridge Pky Houston TX

BATES, KATHY, actress; b. Memphis, June 28, 1948; d. Langdon Doyle and Bertye Kathleen (Talbot) Bates; m. Anthony Campisi, 1991 (div. 1997). BFA, So. Meth. U., 1969. Actor: (plays) Vanities, 1976, Semmelweiss, Crimes of the Heart, The Art of Dining, Goodbye Fidel, 1980, Chocolate Cake and Final Placement, 1981, 5th of July, 'night, Mother, 1983 (Tony nomination, Outer Critics Circle award), Two Masters: The Rain of Terror, 1985, Curse of the Starving Class, Frankie and Johnny in the Clair de Lune (OBIE award 1988), The Road to Mecca; (films) Taking Off, 1971, Straight Time, Come Back to the Five and Dime, Jimmy Dean, Jimmy Dean, Summer Heat, Arthur 2: On the Rocks, Signs of Life, High Stakes, Men Don't Leave, Dick Tracy, White Palace, Misery, 1990 (Acad. award for Best Actress 1990, Golden Globe award), At Play in the Fields of the Lord, 1991, Fried Green Tomatoes, 1991 (Golden Globe nomination, BAFTA nomination), The Road to Mecca, 1992, Prelude to a Kiss, 1992, Used People, 1992, A Home of Our Own, 1993, North, 1994, Curse of the Starving Class, 1994, Dolores Claiborne, 1994, Angus, 1995, Diabolique, 1996, The War at Home, 1996, Primary Colors, 1998, Swept from the Sea, 1998, Titanic, 1998, The Waterboy, 1998, Baby Steps, 1999, Dash and Lilly, 1999, My Life as a Dog, 1999, Bruno, 2000, Rat Race, 2001, American Outlaws, 2001, About Schmidt, 2002, Love Liza, 2002, Dragonfly, 2002, Around the World in 80 Days, 2004, The Bridge of San Luis Rey, 2004, 3 & 3, 2005, Rumor Has It, 2005, Failure to Launch, 2006; (TV series) The Doctors, 1977, All My Children, 1984; (TV films) Johnny Bull, 1986, Murder Ordained, 1987, Roe vs. Wade, 1989, No Place Like Home, 1989, Hostages, 1993, Talking with, 1995, The West Side Waltz, 1995, The Late Shift, 1996, Annie, 1999, My Sister's Keeper, 2002, Warm Springs, 2005; dir. (TV films) Fargo, 2003, actor, dir. Ambulance Girl, 2005; actor, exec. prodr. The Ingrate, 2004; TV guest appearances include The Love Boat, 1978, St. Elsewhere, 1986, 87, China Beach, 1989, LA Law, 1989, 3rd Rock from the Sun, 1999, (voice) King of the Hill, 2001, Six Feet Under, 2003-05. Office: Susan Smith & Assocs 121 N San Vicente Blvd Beverly Hills CA 90211-2303*

BATES, LURA WHEELER, retired trade association executive; b. Inboden, Ark., Aug. 28, 1932; d. Carl Clifton and Hester Ray (Pace) Wheeler; m. Allen Carl Bates, Sept. 12, 1954; 1 child, Carla Allene. BSBA, U. Ark., 1954. Cert. constrn. assoc. Sec.-bookkeeper, then office mgr. Assoc. Gen. Contractors Miss., Inc., Jackson, 1958—77, dir. adminstrv. svcs., 1977—98, asst. exec. dir., 1980—98; owner Ditty Bay Supply Co., 1987—98; ret., 1998. Adminstr. Miss. Constrn. Found., 1977-98; sec. AIA-Assoc. Gen. Contractors Liaisonship Coms., 1977-98; sec. Carpenters Joint Apprenticeship Coms., Jackson and Vicksburg, 1977-98. Editor NAWIC Image, 1968-69, Procedures Manual, 1965-66, Public Relations Handbook, 1967-68, Profl. Edn. Guide, 1972-73, Guidelines & Procedures Handbook, 1987-88; author digests in field. Sec. Marshall Elem. Sch. PTA, Jackson, 1962-64, v.p., 1965; sec.-treas. Inter-Club Coun. Jackson, 1963-64; tchr. adult Sunday sch. dept. Hillcrest Bapt. Ch., JAckson, 1975-82; dir. Bapt. Women WMU, 1987—, sec., 1992—; tchr. adult Sunday sch. dept. 1st Bapt. Ch., Crystal Springs, Miss., 1989-98; mem. exec. com. Jackson Christian Bus. and Profl. Women's Coun., 1976-80, sec., 1978-79, pres., 1979-80. Named Outstanding Woman in Constrn. Miss., 1962-63, 74, 75, 85, 86, 95, 96 Fellow Internat. Platform Assn.; mem. AAUW, NAFE, Nat. Assn. Women in Constrn. (life, chpt. pres. 1963-64, 76-77, 92-93, 2003-04, nat. v.p. 1965-66, 77-78, nat. dir. Region 5 1967-68, nat. sec. 1970-71, 71-72, pres. 1980-81, coord. cert. constrn. assoc. program 1973-78, 83-84, guardian-contr. Edn. Found. 1981-82, chmn. nat. bylaws com.1974-75, 82-83, 85-86, 95-96, nat. parliamentarian 1983-92, Named Outstanding Mem., 1964, 74-84, 85-86, 95-96, Miss Hospitality 2002-03), Nat. Assn. Parliamentarians, U. Ark. Alumni Assn. (life, pres. ctrl. Miss. chpt. 1992-95), Floral Club, Delta Delta Delta (50 Yr. Golden Cir. 2002). Home: 1007 Lee Ave Crystal Springs MS 39059-2546

BATES, MARCIA JEANNE, information scientist educator; b. Terre Haute, Ind., July 30, 1942; d. Robert Joseph and Martha Jane B. BA, Pomona Coll., 1963; MLS, U. Calif., Berkeley, 1967; PhD, U. Calif., 1972. Peace corps vol., Saraburi, Thailand, 1963-64, Nongkhai, Thailand, 1964-65; jr. specialist Inst. Libr. Rsch., U. Calif., Berkeley, 1968; acting instr. U. Calif., Berkeley, 1969-70; asst. prof. U. Md., College Park, 1972-76, U. Wash., Seattle,

1976-80, assoc. prof., 1980-81, U. Calif., Los Angeles, 1981-91, prof., 1991—, prof. and dept. chmn. libr. and info. sci., 1993—95. Cons. U.S. Libr. Congress, Washington, 1986, 91, 2002-03, Getty Art Hist. Info. Program, Santa Monica, Calif., 1988-91, Info. Access Co., Foster City, Calif., 1992-95; mem. editl. bd. Jour. of Asis &T, 1989—, Libr. Quar., 1993-2001. Co-author: For Information Specialists, 1992; contbr. articles to profl. jours. Recipient Distinguished Lectureship award N.J. Am. Soc. for Info. Sci., New Brunswick, 1991. Fellow AAAS (sect. T electorate nominating com. 1980-84, chmn. 1983-84, sect. T com. mem.-at-large, 2001-04), mem. ALA (Frederick G. Kilgour award, 2001), Am. Soc. Info. Sci. and Tech. (bd. dirs. 1973-74, Best Jour. Article Yr. award, 1980, 99, Rsch. award 1998), Assn. Records Mgrs. Adminstrs., Calif. Libr. Assn. (mem. task force on future of Libr. profession, 1993-95), Phi Beta Kappa. Achievements include design of information systems and interfaces for search and subject access in information retrieval systems. Office: Grad Sch Edn & Info Studies UCLA 405 Hilgard Ave Los Angeles CA 90095-1520

BATES, MARGARET P., historian; BA, Barnard Coll.; MA, Wash. U., St. Louis. Dir. Coun. Basic Edn., Washington. Internat. bd. advisors Monterey Inst. Internat. Studies; bd. trustees York Sch., Carmel/Monterey, Calif.; mem. pres.'s coun. Calif. State U. Monterey Bay; former trustee Barnard Coll.; former mem. Calif. State Bd. Edn.

BATES, MARTHA COPENHAVER, elementary school educator; b. Abilene, Tex., Dec. 22, 1933; d. Robert Madison Copenhaver and Mildred Ailene Manton; m. Charles Benjamin Bates, Apr. 9, 1960; children: Benjamin Madison, Lelia Ann, William Andrew. BS in Psychology, Coll. William and Mary, 1956; MEd in guidance and counseling, Loyola Coll. of Balt., 1974. 1st grade tchr. Montgomery(Md.) County Pub. Schs., 1956—57; mem. staff subscriber svc. and enrollment dept. Group Hospitalization, Inc., Wash., DC, 1957—59; 1st grade tchr. Balt. County Pub. Schs., 1958—61, 2d & 3d grade tchr., 1962—64, elem. sch. guidance counselor, 1973—96; ret., 1996. Chmn., bd. dirs. Noah's Ark Preschool, Upper Falls, Md., 2001—. Methodist. Home: 202 Frazier Ct Joppa MD 21085-4434

BATES, YASMIN T., bank executive; BS in Bus. Adminstrn., Univ. Ill. Comml. banking trainee Harris Trust and Savings Bank, Chgo., 1976—79, bank officer, team leader, cash mgmt. sales and consulting staff, 1979—81, asst. v.p., section mgr. sales and consulting, 1981—91, v.p., divsn. adminstr., met. banking divsn., 1991—94; pres. Harris Chgo. Cmty. Bank, Chgo., 1994—98; pres., city region Harris Bank, Chgo., 1998—2003, exec. v.p., Chicagoland banking, south divsn., 2003—. Nat. adv. bd. Fannie Mae; spl. allocations com. United Way, Chgo.; bd. dir. Glenwood Sch. for Boys. Named one of Chicago's 100 Most Influential Women, Crain's Chicago Business mag., 2004. Mem.: Univ. Chgo. vis. forum, Urban Bankers Forum of Chgo., Am. Bankers Assn. (cmty. devel. com.), Univ. Ill. bus. adv. coun. Office: Harris Trust and Savings Bank 111 W Monroe St Chicago IL 60603

BATES APPLETON, SHIRLEY GRAVES, music educator; b. Lawrenceburg, Tenn., Sept. 8, 1945; d. Olnie Clyde and Charlotte (Smith) Graves; children: Charlotte Bates Lynn, Caroline Bates Scudder, Camille Bates Mickle. BA, Belmont U., Nashville, 1964—67; MA, Mid. Tenn. State U., 2000; postgrad., Cumberland U., 2003. Orff Schulwerk Music Memphis State U., cert. tchr. Tenn. Fifth grade tchr. Gleneyrie Sch., Shelbyville, Ky., 1967—68; music tchr. Lakeside Elem. Sch., Chattanooga, Crossroads Elem. Sch., Lebanon, Tenn., 1977—79, Ramona Elem. Sch., Jacksonville, Fla., 1981—82; Orff music specialist Buena Vista Mid. Sch., Nashville, 1983—90, Glendale Mid. Sch., Nashville, 1990—2002; adj. faculty Motlow State C.C., Nashville, 2001—01; Orff music specialist Stanford Montessori Elem. Sch., Nashville, 2002—. Advocate for at-risk children, organizer tutoring classes ho. devels.; coord. mission effort at-risk children Christ Ch. Named Tchr. of the Yr., Nashville Mid. Sch. Assn., 1991, Tchr. of Yr., Metro Nashville Pub. Schools, 2003; recipient Brotherhood Sisterhood Award, Nat. Coun. of Christians And Jews, 1993-95, 1997, 2002, SE Regional choral competition, Prodn. Co. of Broadway-based Joseph and the Amazing Technicolor Dreamcoat, 1995, 1997; grantee, Frist Found., 1997, Frist Found., 2003, Metro Nashville Dept. of Edn., 1999; Tchr. Study grant, HCA Project Pencil, 1993. Mem.: Music Educators Nat. Conf. (assoc.). Pentecostal. Avocation: sewing.

BATESON, MARY CATHERINE, retired anthropology educator; b. N.Y.C., Dec. 8, 1939; d. Gregory and Margaret (Mead) B.; m. J. Barkev Kassarjian, June 4, 1960; 1 child, Sevanne Margaret. BA, Radcliffe Coll., 1960; PhD, Harvard U., 1963; DHL (hon.), Fordham U., 1994, U. Redlands, 1996, DePaul U., 1998, Marygrove Coll., 1999, Mills Coll., 2000. Instr. Arabic Harvard U., 1963-66; assoc. prof. anthropology Ateneo de Manila U., 1966-68; sr. rsch. fellow psychology and philosophy Brandeis U., 1968-69; assoc. prof. anthropology Northeastern U., Boston, 1969-71; rschr. U. Tehran, 1972-74; vis. prof. Northeastern U., 1974-75; prof. anthropology, dean grad. studies Damavand Coll., 1975-77; prof. anthropology, dean social sci. and humanities U. No. Iran, 1977-79; vis. scholar Harvard U., 1979-80; dean faculty, prof. anthropology Amherst Coll., 1980-87; Clarence J. Robinson prof. anthropology and English George Mason U., 1987—2002, prof. emerita, 2002—. Pres. Inst. Intercultural Studies, 1979—; vis. prof. Spelman Coll., 1996; scholar in residence, Radcliffe Inst. Advanced Studies, Harvard U., 2000-01; Harvard Grad. Sch. Edn., 2001-04. Author: Arabic Language Handbook, 1967, 2d edit., 2003, Structural Continuity in Poetry: A Linguistic Study of Five Early Arabic Odes, 1970, Our Own Metaphor: A Personal Account of a Conference on Consciousness and Human Adaption, 1972, 3d edit., 2004, With a Daughter's Eye: A Memoir of Margaret Mead and Gregory Bateson, 1984, 3d edit., 2001, Composing a Life, 1989, 3d edit., 2001, Peripheral Visions: Learning Along the Way, 1994, Full Circles, Overlapping Lives: Culture and Generation in Transition, 2000, Willing to Learn: Passages of Personal Discovery, 2004; co-author: Angels Fear: Towards an Epistemology of the Sacred, 1987, 2d edit., 2005, Thinking AIDS, 1988; co-editor: Approaches to Semiotics: Anthropology, Education, Linquistics, Psychiatry and Psychology, 1964. Mem. adv. bd. Cities at Peace Nat. Fellow Ford Found., 1961-63, NSF, 1968-69, Wenner-Gren Found., 1972, Bunting Inst., 1983-84, Guggenheim Found., 1987-88. Mem. Am. Anthrop. Assn., Lindisfarne Assn., Nat. Ctrs. Atmospheric Rsch. (adv. bd.), Phi Beta Kappa. E-mail: mcatb@attglobal.net.

BATES-ROMEO, DELORES ALVENIA, music educator, consultant; b. L.A., June 9, 1928; d. Albert and Athaliah Lydia (Crone) Bates; m. Nick Romeo, Dec. 4, 1986. BS, Emporia State U., 1956; cert., Empire Sch. Piano Tuning, 1960. Tchr. music Emporia Pub. Schs., Kans., 1950—55; supr. music Junction City Pub. Schs., Kans., 1955—59; tchr. music, 4th grade, organist Episcopal Ch., LaMesa, Calif., 1959—60; dir. music, tchr. classroom Lakeside Pub. Schs., Calif., 1960—86; owner, tchr. Bates Music Studios, LaMesa, Spring Valley, El Cajon, San Diego, Calif., 1962—; instr. music U.S. Sch. Music, N.Y.C., 1963—; music dir., coord. pvt. schs. La Mesa, 1970—72. Organist, choir dir. various chs.; cons. elem. tchrs. Junction City Pub. Sch., 1955—59; counselor tchr., students and future tchrs. various pub. and pvt. schs. Mem.: NEA (life), Music Educators Nat. Conf. (life). Avocations: art, reading, herbs, exercise, cooking. Office: Bates Romeo Music and Arts Ctr 3295 Greyling DR #B San Diego CA 92123-2229 Office Phone: 858-277-4442.

BATES STOKLOSA, EVELYNNE (EVE BATES STOKLOSA), educational consultant, educator; b. Camden, N.J., Mar. 13, 1946; d. Linwood T. and Eve Mary (Widzenas) Bates; m. Leslie E. Stoklosa, Apr. 15, 1968; children: Phillip J., Kristine L. BS in Home Econs. Edn., Buffalo State U. Coll., 1968, MS in Home Econs. Edn., 1971, Cert. Advanced Studies, 1994. Cert. sch. dist. adminstr. Tchr. Parkside Elem. Sch., Kenmore, N.Y., 1968-69, Kenmore West High Sch., 1968-71, 73-75, Kenmore Jr. High Sch., 1977-80, Ken-Ton Continuing Edn., Kenmore, 1980-87, Kenmore Mid. Sch., 1981—2001. Owner, pres. EBS Decors, Tonawanda, N.Y.; edn. cons. Villa Maria Coll., Buffalo, 1980-2000; adv. bd. interior design dept.; facilitator student of the month award program Kenmore Mid. Sch., 1982—, active mem. sch. planning team, 1984—, facilitator design team, 1990—; participant Buffalo Summits, 1994; ind. fashion cons. Editor parent informational pamphlet, 1992, faculty informational newsletter, 1992-94. Vol. Frankl Loyd Wright Found. of the Martin House Restoration Corp., 1999-, Sawgrass Ponte Verde Practice Range, PGA, Fla., 2001-, Nationwide Golf Tour 18th Green, 2001-; vol. various charitable functions and events in and around Buffalo; mem. Amateur Chamber Music Players, 2000—, Buffalo Philharmonic Orch. Women's Com. Found., 2000—. Erie County Nutrition Assn. grantee. Mem. AAUW (bd. dirs. 1992-94), ASCD, DAR (life), Family and Consumer Scientists Am. (life), Am. Vocat. Assn., Am. Fedn. Tchrs., N.Y. State Home Econs. Tchrs. Assn. (Tchr. of Yr. 1992-93, Most Outstanding Leadership and Creativity award 1987), N.Y. State Assn. Family and Consumer Sci. Educators (life), N.Y. State United Tchrs., Western N.Y. Women in Adminstrn., Kenmore Tchrs. Assn. (bldg. rep.), Opera Buffs Western N.Y. (life), Amatuer Chamber Mus Soc., Chautaqua Lit. and Sci. Cir. (life), Phi Delta Kappa, Phi Upsilon Omicron. Avocations: travel, singing, swimming, golf, piano.

BATHAEE, SOUSSAN, engineering technician; b. Tehran, Iran, Jan. 23, 1953; arrived in U.S., 1983; d. Mohammad Bathaee and Farokhlagha Hassanpour. BSCE, Calif. State U., Fullerton, 2002; postgrad., 2004—. Overseas supr. Atomic Energy Orgn., Tehran, Iran, 1972—80; overseas drafts person London, 1980—83; drafts person Earl Walls Assocs., San Diego, 1984—85; job capt. Rsch. Facilities Design, San Diego, 1985—90; engrng. svc. technician County of San Bernardino, Calif., 1991—2002, ret., 2002; freelance engr. LDIC, San Jose, Calif., 2002—. Mem.: AIA, ASCE, Archtl. Engrng. Inst., Great Riverside C. of C. Moslem. Home: 42045 Kaffirboom Ct Temecula CA 92591

BATORY, JOAN ANNE, solid waste and environmental administrator; b. Phila., Sept. 2, 1944; d. Joseph John and Beatrice Elizabeth Thomas Trybala; m. Joseph Patrick Batory, Dec. 26, 1967. BA, Immaculata Coll., 1966; MA, Rowan U., 1972. Cert. secondary tchr., Pa. Tchr. Camden (N.J.) Pub. Schs., 1966-71; pres. Natural Resource Studies, Inc., Cherry Hill, Pa., 1973-74, Environ. Analysis Inc., Pennsauken, N.J., 1974-75; dir. Camden County Environ. Agy., 1975-85; project mgr. U.S. Dept. Interior, Nat. Pk. Svc., Phila., 1985-88; solid waste coord. Chester County, West Chester, Pa., 1988-98; recycling coord. City of Phila., 1998-2000; environ. cons. Phila., 2000—. Commr. N.J. Pinelands Commn., Pemberton, 1979-85; bd. dirs. Pa. Resources Coun., pres., 1997-98; bd. dirs. Newtown Square; stakeholder adv. com. Commonwealth of Pa. Waste Mgmt., 1996-97; founder Camden County Eco-Ctr., Cherry Hill, 1972-73. Contbr. numerous waste mgmt. plans. Bd. dirs. Girl Scouts of Am., Camden County, 1973-74; officer Newton Creek Conservancy, Collingswood, N.J., 1976-84. Recipient St. Catherine's medal Kappa Gamma Pi, 1965, Pollution Prevention award U.S. EPA, 1991, Outstanding Mcpl. Recycling award Pa. Resources Coun., 1996. Mem. Nature Conservancy, Pinelands Preservation Alliance, Rotary (West Chester bd. dirs. 1989-93, Phila. bd. dirs. 2000-02, v.p. 2002-04, pres. 2004-). Avocations: hiking, birding, gardening. E-mail: jbatory@verizon.net.

BATSHAW, MARILYN SEIDNER, education administrator; b. East Orange, N.J., Aug. 19, 1946; d. Gerald and Sylvia (Weinstein) Seidner; 1 child, Andrew Curt. BA, Newark State Coll., Union, N.J., 1968; MA, Kean Coll., Union, 1972, prin. cert., 1984. Cert. hearing aid dispenser, audiologist, elem. and deaf and hearing impaired tchr., supr., prin., N.J. Tchr. of deaf N.J. Dept. Edn., Trenton, 1972-74, audiologist, 1974-82, cons. in spl. edn., 1982-86; prin., dir. edn. Lakeview Sch., Cerebral Palsy Assn. Middlesex County, Edison, NJ, 1986-94; prin. ARC Essex Sch., Livingston, NJ, 1994-96; billing and eligibility case mgr. Prudential Health Care Group, Cranbury, NJ, 1997-99; dir. ESC Sch. West Amwell Campus Hunterdon County Ednl. Scvs. Commn., Lambertville, NJ, 1999; supr. Bright Beginnings Learning Ctr. Middlesex County Ednl. Svcs. Commn., Piscataway, NJ, 1999—2001; supr. special edn. North Arlington Bd. Edn., NJ, 2001—. Officer Parents for Deaf Awareness. Mem. ASCD, N.J. ASCD, Ednl. Audiology Assn., Am. Speech-Lang. and Hearing Assn. (cert. clin. competence in audiology), N.J. Speech-Lang. and Hearing Assn., A.G. Bell Assn., Am. Auditory Soc., Am. Acad. Audiology, N.J. Acad. Audiology, Coun. Exceptional Children, N.J. Coun. Exceptional Children, Nat. Assn. Edn. Young Children. Home: 3305 Avery Ct Somerset NJ 08873 Office: North Arlington HS Child Study Team 222 Ridge Rd North Arlington NJ 07031 Office Phone: 201-991-6800 2102. E-mail: mbatshaw@aol.com.

BATSON, DAWN KIRSTEN, music educator, cultural consultant; b. Port-of-Spain, Trinidad and Tobago, Oct. 7, 1959; d. Henry Arthur Batson and Esther Stephanita Kafiluddi-Batson. BSc in Music Edn., Hofstra U., 1981; Diploma in Radio and TV Prodn., Announcer Tng. Studios, N.Y.C., 1982; MusM in Music Industry, U. Miami, Coral Gables, Fla., 1993, PhD, 1995. Announcer, prodr. Trinidad and Tobago Radio and TV, Port-of-Spain, 1982—; music tchr. Trinity Coll., Maraval, Trinidad and Tobago, 1983—91; conf. coordination staff U. Miami Office of Confs., Coral Gables, 1992—93; dir. steelband ensemble U. Miami, Coral Gables, 1991—96; assoc. prof. music, dir. steelband Fla. Meml. Coll., Miami, 1996—; chmn., bd. dirs. Trinidad and Tobago Nat. Steel Orch., Port-of-Spain, 2000—03; assoc. prof. music, bus. Ind. State U., 2004—06; assoc. prof. Fla. Meml. U., 2006—. Musical dir. Pamberi Steel Orch., San Juan, Trinidad and Tobago, 1986—98, Woodtrin Steel Orch., Maraval, Trinidad and Tobago, 1983—90; cultural cons. Consulate Gen. Trinidad and Tobago et. al., 1998—2002. Composer: works for steel orch. Fulbright-Hayes fellow, North Africa, 2000, Inter-Am. Found. fellow, 1994. Mem.: Fla. Steelband Assn. (pub. rels. officer 2001—). Avocations: dance, hiking, reading, travel. Home: 8611 NW 29th St Sunrise FL 33322 Office: Fla Meml Coll 15800 NW 42d Ave Miami FL 33054

BATSTONE, JOANNA LOUISE, physicist; BSc in Chem. Physics, U. Bristol, 1982, PhD in Physics, 1985. Computer scientist IBM Thomas J. Watson Rsch. Ctr., Hawthorne, NY, 1989—2000, sr. tech. staff mem., sr. mgr., 2000—05, sr. tech. staff mem., software group, 2005—06; dir. distributed computing IBM Rsch., 2006—. Mem. adv. bd. Bio IT Coalition, 2005. Recipient Robert Lansing Hardy Gold Medal award Minerals, Metals & Materials Soc., 1991, Cosslett award Microbeam Analysis Soc., 1989, Burton award Microscopy Soc. Am., 1995. Mem.: NY Acad. Scis. Womens Investigators Network. Office: IBM TJ Watson Rsch Ctr 30 Saw Mill River Rd Hawthorne NY 10532 Business E-Mail: batstone@us.ibm.com.

BATT, ALYSE SCHWARTZ, application developer; b. Bronx, NY, Aug. 8, 1960; d. Irwin Aaron and Beryl (Leff) Schwartz; m. David Charles Batt, Feb. 14, 1993; children: Shannon Paige, Megan Brooke. AAS in Data Processing, SUNY, Farmingdale, 1980; BBA in Bus. Computers, Hofstra U., 1987; MS in Mgmt. Engrng., L.I. U., 1995. Programmer trainee State Ins. Fund, N.Y.C., 1980; programmer analyst cons. Bradford Nat. Corp., N.Y.C., 1981-83; programmer E.F. Hutton, N.Y.C., 1983; programmer analyst Chase Manhattan Bank, N.Y.C., 1983-87; sr. systems analyst Met. Life Ins. Co., N.Y.C., 1987-89; sr. programmer analyst Orion Pictures Corp., N.Y.C., 1989-91, JPMorgan Chase, N.Y.C., 1991—. Leader Jr. Girl Scouts. Mem.: Ladies Aux. Massapequa Fire Dept. (pres., v.p., treas.), Greater L.I. Road Runners Club, N.Y. Road Runners Club, Massapequa Road Runners Club, Commack Skating Club, Bayshore Skating Club. Republican. Jewish. Avocations: roller skating, running. Home: 153 Massachusetts Ave Massapequa NY 11758-4111

BATTAGLIA, LYNNE ANN, judge; b. Buffalo, 1946; BA in Internat. Relations, Am. U., 1967, MA, 1968; JD, U. Md., 1974; JD (hon.), U. Baltimore Sch. of Law, 2001. Asst. US atty. Dist. Md., 1978—82; sr. trial atty. special litigation US Dept. of Justice, 1984—88; chief criminal investigations div. Office of Atty. Gen., 1988—91; chief of staff Office of U.S. Sen. Barbara A. Mikulski, 1991—93; US atty. Dist. Md., 1993-2001; judge Md. Ct. Appeals, 2001—. Adjunct prof. U. Md. Sch. of Law, 1981—; mem. Task Force on Sentencing & Intermediate Sanctions, 1995—96, Md. Alternative Dispute Resolution Commn., 1998—2000; chair Jud. Commn. Professionalism, 2004—. Author: Obeisance to the Separation of Powers, and Protection of Individuals' Rights and Liberties: The Honorable John C. Eldridge's Approach to Constitutional Analysis in the Court of Appeals of Maryland, 2003. Co-chair Women's Health Promotion Council, 1999—2001; mem. Safe Schools Interagency Steering Com., 1999—2001; vice-chair Md. Commn. for Women, 2000—01. Named one of Maryland's Top 100 Women, Daily Record, 1996, 1999, 2001; recipient Dorothy Beatty Memorial award, Women's Law Ctr. of Md., 1994, Margaret Brent-Juanita Jackson Mitchell award, 2002—03, Md. Leadership in Law award, Daily Record, 2003, Professional Legal Excellence award, Md. Bar Foundation, 2004, Lifetime Achievement award, U. Balt., 2006. Mem.: James MacGill Am. Inns of Ct., Howard County Bar Assn., Baltimore City Bar Assn. (chair gender issues subcom., former chair jud. administration com.), Md. State Bar Assn. (chair jud. administration council 2006—, mem. gender equality com., mem. civility task force). Office: Robert C Murphy Ct Appeals Bldg 361 Rowe Blvd Annapolis MD 21401 Office Phone: 410-260-1565.

BATTEN-BISHOP, ANN LOUISE, theater educator; d. Newton Robert and Marjorie Sorensen Batten; m. Glenn Thomas Bishop, Dec. 19, 1987; children: Stephanie Ann Bishop, William Robert Bishop. BA, U. North Tex., Denton, 1974. Cert. tchr. Tex., 1974. Theatre arts dir. Spring Oaks Jr. H.S., Houston, 1974—80; theatre arts tchr. Westchester Jr. H.S., Houston, 1980—86, Spring Br. Mid. Sch., Houston, 1986—91, Spring Oaks Mid. Sch., Houston, 1991—2001, Garland McMeans Jr. H.S., Katy, Tex., 2001—. Mem. missions com. Bear Creek United Meth. Ch., Houston, 1999—; exec. bd. dirs. Theatre Under the Stars, Houston, 1981—87; state and local workshop presenter Tex. Ednl. Theatre Assn., Houston, 1985—, sec., 1995—2005; trainer theatre educators and pers. Ctr. Ednl. Devel., Austin, Tex., 2000—; mem. state com. to write and evaluate standards for the Tex. exams of educator standards for the theatre cert. test Tex. Edn. Agy. and Ednl. Testing Svc. and Oak Hill Tech., Inc., Austin, 2003—. Recipient Tex. Theatre Educator of Yr., Tex. Ednl. Theatre Assn., 2000—01, award, PTA, 2000. Mem.: Tex. Ednl. Theatre Assn. (life). Conservative. Christian- Methodist. Avocations: travel, volunteering, reading, cooking. Office: Garland McMeans Jr HS 21000 Westheimer Pkwy Katy TX 77450 Office Phone: 281-237-8119. Business E-Mail: annbattenbishop@katyisd.org.

BATTERSBY, KATHERINE SUE, elementary school educator; b. Middletown, NY, Nov. 17, 1960; d. George William and Joanne Marie (Endrich) Blaha; m. Jeffery Aaron Battersby, Sept. 18, 1988; children: Kristin Sierra, Joanna Reye, Colon Muir. BS cum laude, SUNY, Potsdam, 1983; MEd, SUNY, New Paltz, 1992. Coord. internat. sch., Spanish instr. Christian Min., Reynosa, Mexico, 1983—85; receptionist Chase NBW Bank, White Plains, N.Y., 1985-86; adminstr. NYNEX Bus. Ctr., White Plains, N.Y., 1986-87; admin. asst. Rsch. Inst. Am., N.Y., 1987-88; tchr. Haldane Elem. Sch., Cold Spring, N.Y., 1989—. Singer: Crane Chorus, 1978—82, Lake Placid Winter Olympics, 1980. Mem. PTA, Am. Fedn. Tchrs., N.Y. State United Tchrs., N.Y. State Tchrs. Retirement Sys. Avocations: reading, hiking, photography, travel, spanish. Office: Haldane Elem Sch Craigside Dr Cold Spring NY 10516 Personal E-mail: kathy@reyespoint.com.

BATTIN, PATRICIA MEYER, librarian; b. Gettysburg, Pa., June 2, 1929; d. Emanuel Albert and Josephine (Lehman) Meyer; m. William Thomas Battin, June 16, 1951 (div. 1975); children: Laura, Joanna, Thomas BA, Swarthmore Coll., 1951; MS in LS, Syracuse U., 1967. Asst. libr. SUNY-Binghamton, 1967-69, asst. dir. for reader svcs., 1969-74; dir. libr. svcs. Columbia U., N.Y.C., 1974-78, v.p., univ. libr., 1978-87; interim pres. Research Libraries Group, Palo Alto, Calif., 1982, also dir., 1974-87; pres. Commn. on Preservation and Access, Washington, 1987-94. Trustee Coun. on Libr. Resources, Washington, 1984-94, EDUCOM, Princeton, N.J., 1982-88, Lehigh U., 1989-98, CAUSE, Boulder, Colo., 1993-96; mem. adv. com. on coun. on libr. and info. resources Frye Leadership Inst. Contbr. articles to profl. jours., Co-author: The Mirage of Continuity: Reconfiguring Academic Information Resources for the 21st Century, 1998. Recipient Nat. Medal for the Humanities, 1999. Mem. ALA, Assn. Rsch. Librs. (trustee 1982-85), Phi Beta Kappa, Beta Phi Mu.

BATTISTA, BOBBIE, public relations executive, former television news anchorperson; BS in Radio, TV and Film Prodn., Northwestern U. With WAKS Radio, Raleigh, NC; prodr., anchor morning news report and spl. programs Sta. WRAL-TV, Raleigh, NC, 1976-77, anchorperson evening news, 1977; with CNN Headline News, 1981-88; joined CNN, 1988, former anchor various newscasts, former co-anchor CNN Today, former co-anchor World News, Prime News, Newsday, former co-anchor CNN Satuday Morning, CNN Sunday Morning; former anchor CNN Saturday; host Talk-Back Live CNN, 1999—2001; principal Atamira Comm., Atlanta, 2001—. Guest lectr. univs., orgns., convs. worldwide; mem. Ga. Exec. Women's Network, Bd. of Dirs. Network; bd. adv. So. Inst. for Bus. and Professional Ethics. Writer, asst. prodr. (documentary) Fed up with Fear, 1981 (George Foster Peabody award). Named Outstanding News Personality, 1984, Best Newscaster, 1986; recipient George Foster Peabody award, 1981. Mem. Women in Comms., Sigma Delta Chi. Office: Atamira Comm 3400 Peachtree Rd Ste 300 Atlanta GA 30326

BATTISTA, DIANE RUSSO, elementary school educator, music educator, personal trainer; b. Utica, NY, Oct. 31, 1954; d. Salvatore A. and Mary S. Russo; m. Arthur J. Battista, Aug. 22, 1986. MusB, Crane Sch. of Music, S.U.C, Potsdam, N.Y., 1976; MEd, S.U.C., Cortland, N.Y., 1986. Cert. Group Fitness Instr. Aerobics and Fitness Assn. of Am./Calif., 1988, Permanent Music/Elem. Ed. Tchg., Grades N-12 N.Y., 1980, Spinning Instr. Mad Dogg Athletics Assn., 1998, CPR Am. Red Cross/N.Y., 1976. Vocal and instrumental music tchr. grades k-8 Utica City Sch. Dist., Utica, NY, 1976—80; vocal, gen., choral music tchr. Our Lady of Lourdes Sch., Utica, NY, 1982—85; aerobics instr. New Hartford Adult Edn., 1990—2000; group fitness instr., personal trainer, nautilus instr., guest clinician, new staff trainer YWCA, Utica, NY, 1980—90; group fitness instr., personal trainer, spinning instr., guest clinician, new staff mentor Lady of Am. Fitness Clubs, New Hartford, NY, 1999—2003; pvt. instrumental tchr. Self-employed, Utica, NY, 1976—; vocal, gen., choral and instrumental music tchr./grades k-9 New Hartford Sch. Dist., New Hartford, NY, 1981—. Mem., chair Model Schs. Music Tech. Com., 1990—2000; staff mentor New Hartford Schs., 2002—. Contbr. articles to profl. jours. Nominee Tchr. of the Yr., Oneida County, 2004; grantee Music Tech. Grant, N.Y. State Model Sch., Music Educators Nat. Conf.; scholar Gertrude Curran Music Scholarship, Gertrude Curran Found., 1972-1976. Mem.: AAUW (assoc.), Mad Dogg Athletics (assoc.), NY State United Tchrs. (assoc.), Internat. Dance Educators Assn. (assoc.), Aerobics and Fitness Assn. of Am. (assoc.), Oneida County Music Educators Assn. (assoc.). Avocations: reading, dance, entertaining, calligraphy, photography. Office: Myles Elementary School 100 Clinton Road New Hartford NY 13413

BATTLE, WILLA LEE GRANT, clergywoman, educational administrator; b. Webb, Miss., Sept. 30, 1924; d. James Carlton and Aslean (Young) Grant; m. Walter Leroy Battle, July 4, 1941. Diploma, Northwestern Coll., Mpls., 1956; B.A. cum laude, U. Minn., 1975, M.A., 1979; Ph.D. summa cum laude, Trinity Sem., 1982. Ordained to ministry, 1959. Founder, pastor Grace Temple Del. Ctr., Mpls., 1958—; founder, pres., Willa Grant Battle Ctr., Mpls., 1980—; founder House of Refuge Mission, Haiti, W.I., 1957—; adminstr., dir. Kiddie Haven Pre-Sch., Mpls., 1982. Mem. Interdenominational Ministerial Alliance (sec. 1986—), Mpls. Ministerial Assn., AAUW, AAUP, U. Minn. Alumni Assn. (life), NAACP, Nat. Council Negro Women, Christian Educators, Nat. Assn. Female Execs. Home: 220 E 42nd St Minneapolis MN 55409-1634 Office: Willa Grant Battle Ctr 1816 4th Ave S Minneapolis MN 55404-1844

BATTLES, ROXY EDITH, novelist, consultant, educator; b. Spokane, Wash., Mar. 29, 1921; d. Rosco Jirah and Lucile Zilpha (Jacques) Baker; m. Willis Ralph Dawe Battles, May 2, 1941 (dec. 2000); children: Margaret Battles Holmes, Ralph, Lara. AA, Bakersfield (Calif.) Coll., 1940; BA, Calif. State U., Long Beach, 1959; MA, Pepperdine U., 1976. Cert. tchr. English, adult basic edn. and elem. edn., Calif. Freelance writer 50 nat. and regional mags., 1940—; tchr. elem. Torrance (Calif.) Unified Schs., 1959-85; tchr. adult edn. Pepperdine U., Torrance, 1969-79, 88-89; freelance children's author, 1966—; mystery novelist Pinnacle Publs., NYC, 1980; with Tex. A&M U., 1988. Instr. Mary Mount Coll., Harbor Coll., 1995; author-in-residence Young Authors Festival, Am. Sch. Madrid, 1991; participant First Educators to Japan Exch., 1973; lectr. in field. Author: Over the Rickety

Fence, 1967, The Terrible Trick or Treat, 1970, 501 Balloons Sail East, 1971, The Terrible Terrier, 1972, One to Teeter-Totter, 1973, 2d edit., 1975, Eddie Couldn't Find the Elephants, 1974, reprints, 1982, 84, 88, What Does the Rooster Say, Yoshio?, 1978, reprinted in Swedish, German, French, 1980, The Secret of Castle Drai, 1980, The Witch in Room 6, 1987, 3d edit., 1989, The Chemistry of Whispering Caves, 1988, rev. edit., 1997, Computer Encryptions in Whispering Caves, 1997; playwright: Roxy, 1995, The Lavender Castle, 1996, mus. version, 1997, Sacred Submarine, 2000, Embarking on Rebellion, 2001. Active So. Calif. Coun. on Lit. for Children and Young People, 1973-80, 87—. Recipient Commendation UN, 1979. Mem. S.W. Manuscripters (founder), Surfwriters. Home: 560 S Helberta Ave Redondo Beach CA 90277-4353 Office Phone: 310-540-2331. Personal E-mail: groxy@aol.com.

BATTRELL, ANN, dental hygienist, educator, dental association administrator; 2 children. BS in Dental Hygiene, Northwestern Univ., Chgo.; postgrad. work, Univ. Mo., Kansas City. Dental hygienist, 1979—; strategic planning cons. Am. Dental Hygienists' Assn., Chgo., mgr. edn. to dir. edn., 2000—04, asst. exec. dir. strategic planning, 2004—05, exec. dir., 2005—. Dental hygiene faculty Northwestern Univ. Dental Sch., Palm Beach (Fla.) Cmty. Coll. Mem.: Am. Dental Hygientists' Assn. (pres. 1996—97). Office: ADHA Ste 3400 444 N Michigan Ave Chicago IL 60611 Office Phone: 312-440-8900.

BATTS, ALICIA J., lawyer; AB, Harvard Coll., 1987; JD, Columbia U. Law Sch., 1990. Bar: NY 1991, DC 1993. Assoc. Howrey Simon Arnold & White LLP, Skadden, Arps, Slate, Meagher & Flom LLP; atty.-advisor to Fed. Trade Commr. Mozelle W. Thompson, 1998—2000; ptnr. Foley & Lardner, 2000—04, Dickstein Shapiro Morin & Oshinsky LLP, Washington, 2004—. Contbr. articles to law jour.; editl. bd. Antitrust Law Jour.; co-editor: Clayton Act Com. Newsletter. Bd. dirs. Appleseed Found. Named one of Am. Top Black Attys., Black Enterprise, 2003. Mem.: ABA, DC Bar, Nat. Black Bar Assn. (regular panelist), Minority Corp. Counsel Assn. (regular panelist). Office: Dickstein Shapiro Morin & Oshinsky LLP 2101 L St NW Washington DC 20037-1526 Office Phone: 202-777-4411. Business E-Mail: BattsA@dsmo.com.

BATTS, BARBARA JEAN, academic administrator, director; b. Bloomsburg, Pa., Nov. 18, 1962; d. Kenneth Philip abd Mary Barbara (Sock) Wiest; m. Pierre Louis Batts, Feb. 26, 1988; children: Pierre Louis II, Patrick Rian, Camille Mari, Keira Lynaé. Diploma, Nat. Corr. Schs., Scranton, Pa., 1984; BS in Edn., Bloomsburg U., 1984; MEd in Ednl. Leadership, Tchg., and Learning, Millersville U., 2002. Cert. elem. prin., elem. supr., elem., nursery and kindergarten tchr. Pa. Substitute tchr. various sch. dists., Lancaster, Pa., 1984-86; resident advisor Community Svcs., Mountville, Pa., 1985-86, residential program supr., 1986-87; tchr. Millersville (Pa.) U., 1986; program dir. Provident Enterprises, Hellam, Pa., 1987; behavior specialist Community Found., Sellersville, Pa., 1987; presch. supr., tchr. Learning Ladder, Lancaster, 1988-89; sales assoc. Lane Bryant, Lancaster, 1990-90, co-mgr., 1990—; classroom facilitator Lancaster City Sch. Dist., 1996—2002; instrnl. facilitator Harrisburg City Sch. Dist., 2002—05, coord. math., sci. and tech. curriculum, 2005—. Recipient various pub. speaking awards Collegiate Forensic Assn., 1981-84. Mem. ASCD. Non Denominational. Home: 810 N Duke St Lancaster PA 17602-2022 Office: 2101 N Front St Bldg #2 Harrisburg PA 17110 Office Phone: 717-703-4046. Business E-Mail: bbatts@hbgsd.k12.pa.us.

BATTS, DEBORAH A., federal judge; b. Phila., Apr. 13, 1947; d. James A., Jr. and Ruth Violet (Silas) Batts; 2 children. BA, Radcliffe Coll., 1969; JD, Harvard U., 1972. Summer atty. Foley, Hoag & Eliot, Boston, Mass., 1970, Kaye, Scholer, Fierman, Hays & Handler, N.Y.C., 1971; law clerk to Hon. Lawrence W. Pierce U.S. Dist. Ct. (so. dist.) N.Y., N.Y.C., 1972-73; assoc. atty. Cravath, Swaine & Moore, N.Y.C., 1973-79; asst. U.S. atty. criminal divsn. U.S. Dist. Ct. (so. dist.) N.Y., N.Y.C., 1979-84; assoc. prof. law Fordham U., 1984-94, adj. prof. law, 1994—; spl. assoc. counsel dept. investigation N.Y.C., 1990-91; commr. law revision com. State of N.Y., 1990-94; judge U.S. Dist. Ct. (so. dist.) N.Y., N.Y.C., 1994—. Bd. trustees Cathedral Sch., N.Y.C., 1990-96; mem. faculty Corp. Counsel Trial Advocacy Program, 1988-94. Contbr. articles to legal jours. Trustee Spence Sch., 1987-95. Mem. ABA, Second Cir. Fed. Bar Coun., Assn. Bar. City N.Y., Lesbian and Gay Law Assn. Greater N.Y., Met. Black Bar Assn. Office: US Courthouse 500 Pearl St Rm 2510 New York NY 10007-1316

BATTS, DOROTHY MARIE, clergywoman, educator, writer; b. Elm, NC, Dec. 22, 1942; d. Randolph Hall and Mattie Gear; m. Jesse Lee Batts Jr., Oct. 14, 1961; children: Terrance Christopher, Timothy Connell, Tonnetta Caressia, Tabitha Cynthia, Travis Carlos; adopted children: Renee, Aja, Tamatha, LeDell, Alice. A in Bibl. Studies, Bethel Bible Coll. and Sem., B in Bibl. Studies, 1999, MA in Theology, PhD in Theology, Bethel Bible Coll. and Sem., 2001. Ordained minister Sprit-fill Christian Ch., 1977; cert. chaplain, Hawaii; cert. counselor Armed Forces; CNA. Christian minister, travelling counselor, South Africa, 1968—; Red Cross vol. Womack Army Hosp., Ft. Bragg, NC, 1981; nurses asst. Fayetteville, NC, 1982; pastor Revivals for Jesus Ch., Southern Pines, NC, 1980-88, Fayetteville, NC, 1981-89; pastor, tchr. Outreach for Jesus Ch., Hope Mills, 1989—; founder., pres. Outreach for Jesus Ch. and Christian Edn. Ctr., Inc.; Christian minister, traveling Christian Word of God counselor Korea, Europe, Hawaii, throughout the US. Spkr. in field. Author Christian books, 1987-93, Bible college study guides, 1987-93, The Book of Exodus, 2000, Between the Old and New Testament, Mathew Study Guide, 2001, The Book of Acts (Power of Holy Spirit), 2001, The Christians Consitutes (The Book of Romans, 1st and 2nd Corinthians, 2002, Doctrin of the Tabernacle, 2002, Developing Into His Image in Difficult Times, 1990, Galatian, 2001, Women in Leadership and Ministry Fan the Flames, 2002, (children and youth book) Prayers for Personal Conflict, 2006, Daily Bread of Poratic Encouragement and Enlightment, 2006. Drug abuse support counselor Cape Fear Med. Ctr., Fayetteville, 1984, support and prayer counselor mentally disturbed, 1984; prayer support counselor, visitor VA Hosp., Fayetteville, 1993; vol. ct. counselor Fayetteville Ct. System, 1974-75, prison telephone counselor. Recipient Soldiers for Christ award US Mil., 2d Mile award Revivals for Jesus, Asheboro, 1984, awards WIDU Radio Sta., 1989. Avocations: writing, travel, bowling, reading, playing scrabble. Home: 404 Old Farm Rd Fayetteville NC 28314-1315 Office: Outreach for Jesus Ch PO Box 65088 Fayetteville NC 28306-1088 Office Phone: 910-423-2999.

BAUER, BARBARA, information technology executive; V.p. software engrng. and devel. Sun Microsystems Inc. Pres. Girl's Count. Named to Hall of Fame, Women In Tech. Internat., 2005.*

BAUER, BARBARA A., financial consultant; Student, Syracuse U., 1973—75, Wilma Boyd Airline Travel Sch., 1975. Script editor various networks, L.A., 1976—88; v.p. You, Inc., Palos Verdes Estates, Calif., 1980—83; cons. Pub. Broadcasting Sys., L.A., 1981—89; fin. cons., pres. Fin. Diversified Mgmt., Laguna Niguel, Calif., 1989—. Founder, Bauer Living Fulfillment Found., 1992—, sr. health homecare and estate cons., 1993—, sr. health and rehab. cons. svcs., 1994—. Fashion model at charitable events, 2000—; mem. Adv. Commn. Human Rights and Protection, 2003—; advocate Disabled Am. Vets., 2003—. Mem. ACLU, NAFE, DAV (adv.), Orange County Bus. Women, Entrepreneurs of Am., Delta Delta Delta. Office: Fin Diversified Mgmt 28241 Crown Valley Pkwy Suite F-600 Laguna Niguel CA 92677-4441

BAUER, BARBARA ANN, marketing consultant; b. Fairfield, Ohio, Dec. 4, 1944; d. Charles P. and Grace J. (Peteka) B.; m. Joseph J. Strojnowski. AA, So. Sem. Jr. Coll., Buena Vista, Va., 1964; BA, Am. U., 1966. Pub. relations, advt. specialist Sta. WOR-AM-FM-TV, N.Y.C., 1966-67; pub. relations mgr. Continental Corp., N.Y.C., 1967-68; dir. corp. communications Am. Internat. Group, N.Y.C., 1968-80; dir. mktg. mgmt. infos. CIGNA Corp., Phila., N.Y.C., 1980-83; asst. v.p. Citicorp Credit Services Inc., N.Y.C., 1983-87; v.p., dir. mktg. Skandia Am. Group, N.Y.C., 1987-88, v.p. corp. communications, 1988-89; pres. Bauer Mktg. and Communications, Goshen, NY, 1989—. Mem. Reinsurance Cons. Network. Lifetime mem. Girl Scouts U.S. Mem.: Ins. Media Assn. (adv. bd.), Assn. Profl. Ins. Women (chair pub. rels., advisor bd. dirs.), Pub. Rels. Soc. Am. (accredited, counselors' acad.). Office Phone: 845-294-3550. E-mail: barbarabauer@pioneeris.net.

BAUER, CYNTHIA RENAE, nurse; b. Sacramento, Sept. 13, 1958; d. James Russell and Lois Ann Lawson; 1 child, Richard Gregory. BS in Nursing cum laude, U. San Francisco, 1980; MSN, Sacramento State U., 2005. Cert. pub. health nurse, U. San Francisco, 1980, RN Calif., 1980, health svcs. credential, Sacramento State U., 2004. Nurse Woodland (Calif.) Meml. Hosp., 1980—85; charge nurse hemodialysis Bapt. Hosp., Pensacola, Fla., 1986—88, U. West Fla., Milton, 1988—91, St. Vincent Medical Ctr., Jacksonville, Fla., 1991—94, DePaul Medical Ctr., Norfolk, Va., 1994—96, Vacaville Dialysis, Calif., 1998—99; sch. nurse Yolo County Office Edn., Woodland, Calif., 1999—. Den leader Cubscouts, Woodland, 1998—2001; sponsor African child Christian Children, 2003—; mem. com. Spl. Edn. Adv. Com., 2005. Recipient Nurse of Distinction award, DePaul Medical Ctr., 1995, award, Spl. Edn. Adv. Com., 2005. Mem.: Nat. Assn. Sch. Nurses, Calif. Sch. Nurse Orgn. (vice-chair spl. edn. 2004—), Sigma Theta Tau. Avocations: reading, travel. Home: 6 Darby Ct Woodland CA 95776 Office: Yolo County Office Edn Greengate Sch 285 W Beamer St Woodland CA 95695 Office Phone: 530-668-3852.

BAUER, IRENE SUSAN, elementary school educator; b. Elyria, Ohio; m. Robert D. Bauer; 1 child, Jacquelyn I. BS in Edn., Ohio U., 1973. Tchr. OBerlin Pub. Schs., Ohio; owner Puti's, Amherst; tchr. Country Day Sch., Charles Town, W.Va., head.

BAUER, JEAN MARIE, accountant; b. Morristown, NJ, Sept. 10, 1958; d. Earl F. and Patricia A. (O'Brien) W.; m. Ronald F. Bauer, Sr. AA in Acctg., County Coll. of Morris, 1978; BSBA, Coll. of St. Elizabeth, Convent Station, N.J., 1986. Sec. to payroll supr. Monroe Calculator, Morris Plains, N.J., 1979-80; clk. typist Stewart Title, Morris Plains, 1980-81; with BASF Corp., Florham Pk., NJ, 1981—, credit rep. chems. div. Parsippany, NJ, 1986-88, property acct. III Mount Olive, N.J., 1988—. Co-leader folk group Sacred Heart Ch. of Dover, N.J., 1981, adult leader youth group, 1982, eucharistic minister, 1993—, vol. religious edn. chr. St. Jude Ch., Budd Lake, N.J., 1993; spl. dep. registrar boro Mountain Lakes, N.J., 1976. Named one of Outstanding Young Women in Am., U.S. Jaycees, 1985. Mem. Cath. Daughters Am. (treas. Dover chpt. 1987-89, regent 1989-91). Republican. Avocations: needlepoint, cooking, travel, gardening. Home: HC 1 Box 1896 Tafton PA 18464-9718 Office: BASF Corp Property Acctg 100 Campus Dr Florham Park NJ 07932

BAUER, JENNIFER ELIZABETH, performing company executive; b. Lake Forest, Ill., Sept. 6, 1974; BA in Theatre and English, Ripon Coll., Wis., 1996; MFA in Theatre, U. Memphis, 2006. Chpt. coord. Lyric Opera Chgo., 1996—99; project mgr. Chgo. Symphony Orch., 1999—2001; exec., artistic dir. Waco (Tex.) Civic Theatre, 2001—03; dir. artistic programming WPAA, Waco, 2004; sr. dir. Shakespeare Theatre N.J., 2005. Dir.: (children's opera) Aesop's Fables; asst. dir. Of Mice and Men, prodn. stage manager (opera) The Promise, asst. dir. Corps of Discovery. Mem. Chgo. Coun. Fgn. Rels., 1998—2001; bd. dirs. St. Francis de Sales, Lake Zurich, 1997—98; cert. religious edn. tchr. Cath. Ch., Chgo., 1992—2005; conv. com. Am. Assn. Cmty. Theatres, Irving, Tex., 2001—03; artistic dir. ACT, Lake Zurich, Ill., 1996—99; alumni bd. dirs. Ripon Coll., 1997—2000, class agt., 1996—; adv. Alpha Delta Pi, Atlanta, 1996—. Mem.: Soc. Stage Dirs. Choreographers (assoc.), Phi Kappa Phi (life), Alpha Delta Pi (life). Liberal. Roman Catholic.

BAUER, JUDY MARIE, minister; b. South Bend, Ind., Aug. 24, 1947; d. Ernest Camiel and Marjorie Ann (Williams) Derho; m. Gary Dwane Bauer, Apr. 28, 1966; children: Christine Ann, Steven Dwane. Ordained to ministry Christian Ch., 1979. Sec., adminstrv. asst. Bethel Christian Ctr., Riverside, Calif., 1975—79; founder, pres. Kingdom Advancement Ministry, San Diego, 1979—; co-pastor Bethel Christian Ctr., Rancho Bernardo, Calif., 1991—2004; coll. funding advisor, 2002—03. Trainer, mgr., cons. Tex., Ariz., Calif., Oreg., Wash., Alaska, Okla., Idaho, Rep. South Africa, Guam, Egypt, The Philippines, Australia, Can., Mozambique, Malawi, Mex., Zimbabwe, Poland, Guatemala, Israel, Scotland, Ireland, Japan, Singapre, others, 1979—; pres. Witty Outerwear Distbrs. Internat., Inc., 1993—96; mktg. exec. Melalueca, 1999—2002; founder, co-pastor Bernardo Christian Ctr., San Diego, 1981—91; adult tchr. Bethel Christian Ctr., 1973—81, undershepherd minister, 1975—79, evangelism dir., 1978—81; chaplain La Mesa Fed. Penitentiary, Tijuana, Mexico, 1998—2001; bd. dirs. Strong Tower Rehab. Ministry, San Diego; pres., founder Bethel Christian Ctr., Ranco Bernardo, Calif., 1991—2004; condr. leadership tng. clinics, internat. spkr., lectr. in field. Author; Fishers of Men 101, Spiritual Gifts 201, Discipleship, 301, also syllabus, booklet, tng. material packets. Pres. Bernardo Christian Ctr., San Diego, 1981-91. Mem. Internat. Conv. Faith Ministries, Inc. (area bd. dirs. 1983-88). Address: Kingdom Advancement Min 40335 Winchester Rd E283 Temecula CA 92591 Personal E-mail: jbauer2@ix.netcom.com. Business E-Mail: kam@kingdomadvancementministries.org.

BAUER, JULIE A., lawyer; b. Elmhurst, Ill., Mar. 26, 1960; BA with distinction, U. Va., 1982; JD magna cum laude, U. Ill., 1985. Bar: Ill. 1985, U.S. Dist. Ct. Ill. (no. dist.) 1987, U.S. Dist. Ct. Ill. (ctrl. dist.) 1993, U.S. Ct. Appeals (7th cir.) 1993, U.S. Dist. Ct. Ill. (so. dist.) 2003. Law clk. U.S. Dist. Ct. Ill. (no. dist.), 1985—87; assoc. to ptnr. Winston & Strawn LLP, Chgo., 1987—, chair hiring com., mem. diversity initiative, mem. audit com. Pres. Pro Bono Advocates, 1997—99; mem. bd. visitors U. Ill. Coll. Law, 2001—04. Fellow: Am. Bar Found.; mem.: Alliance for Women (exec. com. mem. 1999—, co-vice chair 2001—02, co-chair 2002—03), Seventh Cir. Bar Assn. (mem. bd. govs. 2004—06, sec. 2006—), Chgo. Bar Assn. (bd. mgrs. 2004—06), Order of Coif. Office: Winston & Strawn LLP 35 W Wacker Dr Chicago IL 60601-9703 Office Phone: 312-558-5973. Office Fax: 312-558-5700. E-mail: jbauer@winston.com.

BAUER, LORAIN, art educator; b. St. Louis, May 3, 1933; d. William Henry and Mattie Nannie Perkins; m. Wiley Howard, Jr., 1984 (dec.); children: Keith Richard, Sheila Maria, Wanda Kathleen, Wiley Howard III; m. Frank Bauer, June 17, 1990. AA, Sherter Coll., 1953; BA, Occidental Coll., 1955; student, Washington U., 1981, Stowe Tchrs. Coll., 1982. Sec. Bus Adminstrv. Harps, St. Louis, 1985—87; nutritionist Sutler County, St. Louis 1978—83; makeup artist Lamar Harps, St. Louis, 1977—87; tchr. St. Louis Pub. Schs., 1980—89, One Stroke Painter, Clermont, Fla., 1998—2005, Home Art Tng., Clermont, 2003—; substitute tchr. Dist. 214, Arlington Heights, Ill., 1999. Sr. tchr. Palatine (Ill.) Sr. Ctr.; tchr. art Hobby Lobby Stores, Palatine, Michael Stores, Chgo. Sr. adv. Betty Hill Found., L.A.; judge St. Louis (Mo.) Voter Registration. Recipient Yes I Can award, St. Louis (Mo.) Argus, 1981, Best Tchr. award, Dist. 204, 1991. Mem.: March of Dimes, Nat. Coun. Negro Women. Home: 2109 Grouse Ln Rolling Meadows IL 60008

BAUER, MARGARET DONOVAN, literature and language professor, editor; b. Franklin, La., Feb. 24, 1963; d. Carl W. Bauer and Janie Colvin Desonier. BA, La. State U., Baton Rouge, 1985; MA, U. La., Lafayette, 1989; PhD, U. Tenn., Knoxville, 1993. Vis. asst. prof. Tex. A&M U., College Station, 1993—95, Wabash Coll., Crawfordsville, Ind., 1995—96; prof. East Carolina U., Greenville, NC, 1996—, asst. prof., 1996—2000, assoc. prof., 2000—. Author: William Faulkner's Legacy, The Fiction of Ellen Gilchrist; editor NC Lit. Rev (Best Jour. Design, Coun. Editors of Learned Jours., 1999). Named Rives Chair of So. Lit., East Carolina U. Dept. English, 2004—; recipient Scholar-Tchr. award, East Carolina U., 2004. Mem.: NC Lit. and Hist. Assn. (exec. bd. 1997—2006), Soc. for Study of So. Lit. Democrat. Office: East Carolina U English Dept 2201 Bate Greenville NC 27858-4353 Office Phone: 252-328-1537. E-mail: bauerm@ecu.edu.

BAUER, MARIA CASANOVA, computer engineer; b. Cienfuegos, Las Villas, Cuba, Jan. 1, 1954; came to U.S., 1979; d. Manuel José and Loida Eugenia (Ojeda) Casanova; m. Lawrence D. Bauer, Feb. 14, 1997; 1 child, Ingrid. BSEE cum laude, U. Miami, 1985; MS, U. Cen. Fla., 2000. Software engr. Martin Marietta Corp., Orlando, Fla., 1986-89; computer engr., mgr. software acquisition, Tng. Sys. divsn. Naval Air Warfare Ctr., Orlando, 1989-97; project dir. U.S. Army Simulation, Tng. and Instrumentation Command, Orlando, 1000—. Software arch. U.S. Army Simulation, Tng. and Instrumentation Command, Orlando, 1997-2000. Mem. IEEE, Golden Key, Sigma Xi, Tau Beta Pi, Eta Kappa Nu, Phi Kappa Phi. Achievements include co-development of weapons system for Desert Storm. Home: 3212 Lake George Cove Dr Orlando FL 32812-6844 E-mail: maria_bauer@stricom.army.mil.

BAUER, MARION DANE, writer; b. Oglesby, Ill., Nov. 20, 1938; d. Chester and Elsie (Hempstead) Dane; m. Ronald C. Bauer, June 25, 1959 (div. Dec. 1988); children: Peter Dane, Elisabeth Alison. AA, LaSalle-Peru-Oglesby Jr. Coll., 1958; student, U. Mo., 1958—59; BA in Lang. Arts, U. Okla., 1961, postgrad., 1961—62. Author: Shelter from the Wind, 1976 (Notable Children's Book ALA, 1976), Foster Child (Golden Kite Honor Book award Soc. Children's Book Writers, 1977), Tangled Butterfly, 1980, Rain of Fire, 1983 (Tchrs.' Choices award Nat. Coun. Tchrs. of English, 1984, Revs. Choice award ALA Booklist, 1983, Children's Book award Jane Addams Peace Assn., 1984), Like Mother, Like Daughter, 1985, On My Honor, 1986 (Newbery Honor Book, 1987, Notable Children's Book ALA, 1986, Best Books of 1986 Sch. Libr. Jour., Editors' Choice Booklist, 1986, Pub.'s Weekly Choice the Yrs.'s Best Books, 1986, Flicker Tale Children's Book award, N.D., 1989, Golden Archer award, Wis., 1989, William Allen White Children's Book award, Kans., 1989, BBY, IRA selection for Janusc Korczak Lit. Competition Poland, 1990), Touch the Moon, 1987, A Dream of Queens and Castles, 1990, (drama) God's Tears: A Woman's Journey, Face to Face, 1991 (Children's Book of Distinction, Hungry Mind Rev., 1992), What's Your Story? A Young Person's Guide to Writing Fiction, 1992 (Notable Children's Book ALA, 1992), Ghost Eye, 1992, A Taste of Smoke, 1993, A Question of Trust, 1994; editor: Am I Blue? Coming Out from the Silence, 1994, When I Go Camping With Grandma, 1995, A Writer's Story, From Life to Fiction, 1995, Alison's Wings, 1996, Our Stories, A Fiction Workshop for Young Authors, 1996, Alison's Puppy, 1997, If You Were Born a Kitten, 1997, Turtle Dreams, 1997, Alison's Fierce and Ugly Halloween, 1997, Bear's Hiccups, 1998, Christmas in the Forest, 1998, An Early Winter, 1999, Sleep, Little One, Sleep, 1999, Jason's Bears, 2000, Grandmother's Song, 2000, My Mother is Mine, 2001, If You Had a Nose Like an Elephant's Trunk, 2001, Frog's Best Friend, 2002, Love Song for a Baby, 2003, Runt, 2002, Land of the Buffalo Bones, 2003, Toes, Ears and Nose, 2003, Why Do Kittens Purr, 2003, Wind, 2003, Snow, 2003, Rain, 2004, Clouds, 2004, The Double-Digit Club, 2004 (CBC Best Books award, 2004), The Very Best Daddy of All, 2004, A Recipe for Valentine's Day, 2004, Easter is Coming, 2005, The Blue Ghost, 2005, A Bear Named Trouble, 2005, If Frogs Made Weather, 2005, Waiting for Christmas, 2005, Niagara Falls, 2005, The Mississippi River, 2005, Baby Bear Discovers the World, 2006, The Grand Canyon, 2006, A Mama for Owen, 2006, Killing Miss Kitty and Other Sins, 2006; contbr. short stories to mags. and books in field. Mem.: Soc. Children's Book Writers and Illustrators, Authors League Am., Authors Guild. Democrat. Home: 8861 Basswood Rd Eden Prairie MN 55344-7407 Office: Clarion 215 Park Ave S New York NY 10003-1603 Office Phone: 952-941-3102. Personal E-mail: mdanebauer@aol.com.

BAUER, MARY JANE, lyricist; b. Scottsbluff, Nebr., May 11, 1955; d. Henry and Martha (Thompson) B.; m. Rodney Ray Pace, Sept. 11, 1997 (div.); children: John Ray Stauffer, Crystal Dawn Stauffer, Martha Jane Stauffer, David Andrew Stauffer. Grad. H.S., Bridgeport, Nebr. Songwriter, lyricist: Is It True? and Our Beacon In The Night?; Album: The Songs of Praise, 1997, A Gift of Love, 1998. Mem. Nat. Environ. Soc., Nat. Childrens Cancer Fund, Disabled Am. Vets., Nat. Arbor Day Found., Colonial Williamsburg Found., Eagles. Avocations: singing, writing, fishing, art, beadwork.

BAUER, SARAH L., literature and language educator, coach; b. Pittsfield, Ill., May 26, 1976; d. John Walter and Marilyn Joyce Bauer. BA in English, Western Ill. U., Macomb, 1999. Cert. tchr. Ill., 1999. English tchr. Pikeland Sch. Dist., Pittsfield, Ill., 1999—2003, West Pike Sch. Dist., Kinderhook, 2003—05, Brown County H.S., Mt. Sterling, 2005—. Head volleyball coach Pikeland Sch. Dist., Pittsfield, Ill., 1999—2003, West Pike Sch. Dist., Kinderhook, 2003—05, Brown County HS, Mt. Sterling, 2005—06. Mem.: Nat. Coun. Tchrs. English (assoc.). Office: Brown County HS 500 Main St Mount Sterling IL 62353 Office Phone: 217-773-3345. E-mail: sbauer@bcsd1.net.

BAUER, VIRGINIA S., state agency administrator; b. May 4, 1956; m. W. David Bauer, 1980 (dec. Sept. 11, 2001); children: David, Stephen, Jackie. BA in Psychology, Rosemount Coll. With Merrill Lynch, Red Bank and Westfield, NJ; dir. NJ Lottery, 2003—04; CEO, sec. NJ Commerce, Econmic Growth and Tourism Commn., Trenton, NJ, 2004—. Bd. dirs. Family and Children's Services, Monmouth County, NJ; advocate for 9/11 victims. Office: NJ Commerce Economic Growth & Tourism Commn 20 W State St PO Box 820 Trenton NJ 08625 Office Phone: 609-777-0885. Office Fax: 609-777-4097.

BAUGH, CYNTHIA, elementary school educator; b. Jamaica, WI, June 3, 1944; d. Samuel Theophylas and Louise Agatha Palmer; m. Hector Adolph Baugh, July 31, 1965; children: Ann Marie, Wayne. BS in Edn. cum laude, Fla. Internat. U., 1998; MS in Edn., U. Miami, 2003. Tchr. Fruitful Vale All Age Sch., Portland, Jamaica, 1964—72, New Day All Age Sch., Kingston, Jamaica, 1972—78, Amron's Acad., NYC, 1977—88, Cammpbell Dr. Elem. Sch., Leisure City, Fla., 1998—99, Dante B. Fascell Elem. Sch., Miami, Fla., 1999—; sec., technician South Miami Hosp., Miami, Fla., 1988—98. Mem.: Coun. Exceptional Children, Golden Key Honor Soc. Avocations: reading, gardening, drawing. Home: 16230 SW 107 Pl Miami FL 33157

BAUGH, LISA SAUNDERS (LISA SAUNDERS BOFFA), chemist, researcher; b. Houston, Aug. 27, 1969; d. James Robert Saunders Jr. and Diane Hussey Young; m. Alexander Bowman Boffa, June 7, 1991 (div. Oct. 2000); m. Simon David Peter Baugh, Sept. 15, 2001. BS in Chemistry with high honors, U. Tex., 1991; PhD in Chemistry, U. Calif., Berkeley, 1996. Vis. scholar polymer sci. and engrng. dept. U. Mass., Amherst, 1994-96; sr. rsch. chemist Air Products and Chems., Allentown, Pa., 1996-97; sr. chemist ExxonMobil Rsch. and Engrng., Annandale, NJ, 1997—2005, rsch. assoc., 2005—. Lectr. in field; owner The Copy Chemist Sci. Editl. Svc., 2005—. Editor: Transition Metal Catalysis in Macromolecular Design, 2000, Late Transition Metal Polymerization Catalysis, 2003; contbr. articles to profl. jours. and textbooks, features to texbooks. Violinist/violist Ctrl. Jersey Symphony Orch.; prin. violist Hunterdon (N.J.) Symphony. Named Dean's Honored Grad., 1991, grad. fellow NSF, U. Calif.-Berkeley, 1991-94, Nat. Merit scholar U. Tex., 1987-91. Mem.: Nat. Assn. Sci. Writers, Am. Chem. Soc. (sec. gen., program chair catalysis and surface sci. secretariat 2001, assoc. women chemists com. 2002—04, mem. editl. adv. bd. Chemistry Mag. 2003—, membership chmn. polymer materials sci. and engrng. divsn. 2004—05, mem.-at-large polymer materials sci. and engrng. divsn. 2000—), Alpha Chi Sigma, Phi Beta Kappa. Achievements include patents in field. Office: ExxonMobil Rsch & Engrng Route 22 East LC124 Annandale NJ 08801 Business E-Mail: Lisa.S.Baugh@ExxonMobil.com.

BAUGH, TERRY, marketing professional; b. Logan, Utah, May 6, 1949; d. Howard Carlos and Ruth Lundahl Baugh. BA, Utah State U, 1971. Tchr. San Juan Sch. Dist., Blanding, Utah, 1971—72, Granite Sch. Dist., Salt Lake City, 1972—74; editl. asst. Univ. Svc., Salt Lake City, 1974; press aide U.S. Senate, Washington, 1975—77; assoc. v.p. Porter Novelli & Assocs., Washington, 1977—83; sr. v.p., gen. mgr. Needham Porter Novelli, N.Y.C., 1983—84, sr. v.p. Washington, 1984—85; pres. T.Baugh & Co., Ind., Washington, 1985—. Mem.: Am. Mktg. Assn., Nat. Press.

BAUGHMAN, JANINE KAY, music educator; b. Greenville, Ohio, June 8, 1961; d. Ellis Gene and Shirley Ilene (Amburn) Fourman; m. Randy Ivor Baughman, June 21, 1986; 1 child, William. BA in Music Edn., Bowling Green State U., Ohio, 1983. Tchr. music Otsego Elem. and Mid. Sch., Grand Rapids, Ohio, 1983—85, Otsego HS and Mid. Sch., Tontogany, Ohio, 1985—. Mem. choir First United Meth. Ch., Bowling Green, Ohio, 1989—. Mem.: NEA, Music Educators Nat. Conf., Ohio Educators Assn., Ohio Music Educators Assn. (contrast selection com. 1992, 1993, mem. adv. bd. triad 2005—, lead vocal affairs 1995). Democrat. Meth. Avocations: sports, theater, crafts, movies. Office: Otsego Local Schs Box 290 Tontogany Rd Tontogany OH 43565 Business E-Mail: ots_aca-jb@nwoca.org.

BAUGHMAN, LEONORA KNOBLOCK, lawyer; b. Bad Axe, Mich., Mar. 21, 1956; d. Lewie L. and Jannette A. (Krajenka) K.; m. Jene W. Baughman, Dec. 5, 1981; children: Wesley J. and Adrianne J. Student, Cen. Mich. U., 1973-75; AB, U. Mich., 1977; JD, U. Notre Dame, 1981. Bar: Mich. 1981, U.S. Dist. Ct. (ea. dist.) Mich. 1982. Assoc. Foster, Swift, Collins & Coey, P.C., Lansing, Mich., 1981-86; staff atty. Chrysler Fin. Corp., Troy, Mich., 1987-97; v.p. gen. mgr. sales and underwriting U.S. East Chyrsler Ins. Co., Southfield, Mich., 1997—. Mem. ABA, Mich. Bar Assn., Nat. Assn. Women Lawyers, Am. Bankruptcy Inst., State Bar Mich. (sec. bus. law sect., speaker 4th ann. comml. law seminar). Office: Chrysler Financial 27777 Inkster Rd Farmington Hills MI 48334-5326

BAUM, CYNTHIA GAIL, psychologist, educator, association administrator; b. Balt., July 27, 1957; d. Paul Arthur and Marjorie Joan (Hinkle) B.; m. Steven Joseph Choquette, Aug. 10, 1985; 1 child, Emily Michelle BS, Denison U., 1978; MS, U. Ga., 1980, PhD, 1982. Lic. psychologist, Md., Va., D.C. Intern Med. U. S.C., Charleston, 1980—81; asst. prof. psychology Va. Polytechnic Inst. and State U., Blacksburg, 1982—86; asst. prof. Cath. U. Am., Washington, 1986—89; dir. spl. projects APA, Washington, 1989, dir. edn. programs, 1990—92, asst. exec. dir. edn., 1993—94; dean, prof. Am. Sch. Profl. Psychology, Arlington, Va., 1994—2000; regional v.p., campus pres. Argosy U., Chgo., 2000—02, v.p. nat. partnerships and clin. edn., 2005—; campus pres. Art Inst. Washington, 2003—05. Cons. Hollins Coll., Roanoke, Va., 1983-86, Counseling Assocs. S.W. Va., 1986, Gaithersburg (Md.) Guidance and Evaluation Svcs., 1989-94; dir. undergrad. psychology program Va. Polytechnic Inst. and State U., 1985-86; adj. assoc. prof. Cath. U., Washington, 1990-94; invited spkr. Georgetown U. Hosp., Washington, 1990; spkr., vol. Summit Hall Elem. Sch., Gaithersburg, 1989-90; vol. Thurgood Marshall Elem. Sch., Gaithersburg, 1997—; mem. adv. bd./on-air host Distance Learning Network, 1997-98; mem. adv. coun. Petworth Assembly, Nat. Cmty. Devel. Orgn. Author: (with others) Handbook of Child Psychopathology, 1989; prodr.: (videotape) Career Encounters in Psychology, 1991; editor: Graduate Study in Psychology, 1990-94; assoc. editor: The Behavior Therapist; contbr. articles to profl. jours Grantee Nat. Inst. Drug Abuse, 1992, Johnson Found., 1991, Profl. Exam. Svc., 1993, Phi Beta Kappa, Phi Kappa Phi; named alumni scholar Denison U., 1993, Advocate award Assn. Advancement Psychology, 2000 Fellow APA (co-chair task force on scholarly work 1992), Nat. Coun. Schs. and Programs in Profl. Psychology (chair adv. com. 1996-98, chair program com. 1998—, pres. exec. com. 2001-04), Assn. Advancement of Behavior Therapy (coord. conv. edn. 1993-96, chair specialties and proficiencies com.), Md. Psychol. Assn.; mem. D.C. Psychol. Assn., Va. Psychol. Assn., Am. Assn. Higher Edn., Sigma Xi Avocation: aerobics. Home: 16923 Horn Point Dr Gaithersburg MD 20878-2085 Office: Argosy Univ 20 S Clark St Ste 2800 Chicago IL 60603 Office Phone: 301-740-2126. E-mail: cbaum@argosyu.edu.

BAUM, ELEANOR, electrical engineering educator; b. Poland, Feb. 10, 1940; came to U.S., 1942; d. Sol and Anna (Berkman) Kushel; m. Paul Martin Baum, Sept. 2, 1962; children: Elizabeth, Jennifer. BSE.E., CUNY, 1959; M.E.E., Poly Inst. N.Y., 1961, PhD, 1964; DS (hon.), Union Coll., 1993, Notre Dame, 1995. Engr. Sperry Gyrosoope Co., N.Y.C., 1960-61; instr. Poly. Inst. N.Y., N.Y.C., 1961-64; asst. prof. elec. engring. Pratt Inst., N.Y.C., 1964-67, assoc. prof., 1967-71, prof., chmn. dept. elec. engring., 1971-84, dean Sch. Engring., 1984-87; dean Sch. Engring., Cooper Union for Advancement Sci. and Art, N.Y.C., 1987—; exec. dir. Cooper Union Rsch. Found., N.Y.C., 1987—. Cons. engring. to various corps.; accreditation visitor Accreditation Bd. Engring. and Tech., 1983—, bd. dirs., fellow, 1994; organizer career confs. for careers in engring., careers for women, N.Y.C., 1970—; chair bd. examiners Grad. Record Exam., 1984-90; bd. dirs. Alleghany Powers Systems, U.S. Trust Co., Avnet, Inc.; commr. Engring. Workforce Commn., 1990—; mem. engring. adv. bd. NSF, 1989-94; mem. adv. bd. Duke U., Rice U., U.S. Mcht. Marine Acad., 1992—; mem. U.S./Japan Engring. Edn. Task Force, 1994—. Contbr. tech. articles and articles on engring. careers and edn. to profl. jours. Recipient Disting. Alumnus award Poly. Inst. N.Y., 1986, Alumni Achievement award CCNY, 1986, Emily Warren Roebling award Womens' Hall of Fame, 1988, Achievement award Mich. State U., 1992, Outstanding Woman Scientist award, 1992 Assn. Women Sci. Fellow IEEE (Steinmetz award 1990), Soc. Women Engrs. (Upward Mobility award 1990, Achievement award engrs. joint com. L.I. 1995); mem. Am. Soc. Engring. Edn. (bd. dirs. 1989—, v.p. 1992-93, pres. 1995—, various nat. task forces), Nat. Engring. Deans Coun. (bd. dirs. 1987—, chair 1990-93), N.Y. Met. Deans Assn. (chmn. 1985-90), N.Y. Acad. Scis. (bd. govs. 1994—), Order of Engr. (bd. govs. 1985-92, competitiveness policy coun. subcom. critical techs. 1992—, nat. rsch. coun. bd. engring. edn. 1991-95), Eta Kappa Nu, Tau Beta Pi (Achievement award Mich. Tech. U. 1995).

BAUM, INGEBORG RUTH, librarian; b. Berlin, Sept. 20; d. Ella Koch; Oberlyceum (scholar), Kassel, Germany, 1926-33; postgrad. Georgetown U., 1963-70; m. Albert Baum, Feb. 16, 1938 (div. 1960); children: Harro Siegward, Helma Sigrun (Mrs. George Meadows). Came to U.S., 1951, naturalized, 1957. Export corr. Bitter-Polar, Germany, 1933-35, Henschel Locs, Germany, 1936; exec. sec. Fieseler Airplane Mfrs., Germany, 1936-38; interpreter, sec. UNRRA, Germany, 1946-48; payroll supr., civilian dept. U.S. Army, Wetzlar PX, Germany, 1948-51; asst. librarian Supreme Council, Ancient and Accepted Scottish Rite, Washington, 1951-70, librarian and museums curator, 1970-93, ret., 1993; appraiser rare books and documents; v.p. Merical Elec. Contractors, Inc., Forestville, Md., 1974-83. Mem. Am. Soc. Appraisers, Calligraphers Guild. Mem. Ch. Jesus Christ of Latter-day Saints. Free-lance contbr. to Pabelverlag, Rastatt, Germany, Harle, Ofcl. Publs., Inc., Soc. for Contemporary Am. Lit. in German, others. Avocations: travel, art. Office: 1733 16th St NW Washington DC 20009-3103

BAUM, JEANNE ANN, psychotherapist; b. Bklyn., Sept. 24, 1937; d. Joseph and Elizabeth (Bengelsdorf) Masch; m. Stanley Baum, June 29, 1958; children: Richard Arthur, Laura Diane, Carol Lisa. BA, Bklyn. Coll., 1958; postgrad., Temple U., 1967, 69-71; JD, Suffolk U., 1973; MS in Edn., U. Pa., 1991. Bar: Mass., 1973, Pa. 1976, U.S. Dist. Ct. (ea. dist.) Pa. 1982, U.S. Ct. Appeals (3d cir.) 1982); cert. family therapist. Social case worker State Bd. Child Welfare, Camden, N.J., 1959, Camden County Welfare Bd., 1960; trial atty. Nat. Labor Rels. Bd., Phila. and Boston, 1973-75; assoc. Blank, Rome, Claus & Comisky, Phila., 1976-78; atty. Interstate Commerce Commn., Phila., 1979-82; pvt. practice Phila., 1985-90; fellow Ctr. for Cognitive Therapy U. Pa., 1994—. Adj. instr. St. Joseph's U., Phila., 1979. Columnist, Newton (Mass.) Times, 1973. Bd. govs. Lawyers Alliance for Nuclear Arms Control, Phila., 1983-1990, sec. exec. bd., 1984-88; bd. dirs. Citizens Com. on Pub. Edn. in Phila., 1992-1997, sec., 1993-1995; bd. dirs. Ctr. in Park for Older Adults, Phila., 1984-89, Eagleville (Pa.) Hosp., 1986-2004, Social Action Com. Reconstrn. Coll., Phila., 1984-85. Recipient Am. Jurisprudence prize, Temple U. Sch. Law, Phila., 1971. Mem. Phila. Bar Assn. Avocations: travel, music, reading, gardening, camping.

BAUMAN, SUSAN, communications executive; BA, U. Mich. With J. Walter Thompson, Jack Tinker and Ptnrs., Telpac; founder, pres. Broadcast Traffic and Residuals (merged with Talent Ptnrs. in 2002), NYC, 1973—2002; with Talent Ptnrs., NYC, 2002—. Recipient Women Mean Bus. award, Chase Bank. Office: Talent Ptnrs 123 W 18th St New York NY 10001

BAUMAN, SUSAN JOAN MAYER, mayor, lawyer, commissioner; b. NYC, Mar. 2, 1945; d. Curt H. J. and Carola (Rosenau) Mayer; m. Ellis A. Bauman, Dec. 29, 1968. BS, U. Wis., 1965, JD, MS, 1981; MS, U. Chgo., 1966. Bar: Wis. 1981, U.S. Dist. Ct. (we. dist.) Wis. 1981, U.S. Ct. Appeals (7th cir.) 1983, U.S. Dist. Ct. (ea. dist.) Wis. 1985. Tchr. Madison (Wis.) Pub. Sch., 1970-78; research asst. U. Wis. Law Sch., Madison, 1981; ptnr. Thomas, Parsons, Schaefer & Bauman, Madison, 1981-84; sole practice Madison, 1984-85; ptnr. Bauman & Massing, Madison, 1985-87; pvt. practice, Madison, 1987-97; mayor City of Madison, 1997—2003; mem. Wis. Employment Rels. Commn., 2003—. Alderman Madison Common Coun., 1985-97, coun. pres., 1989-90; commr. equal opportunities com. City of Madison, 1985-89; mem. Econ. Devel. Commn., 1986-87, chmn. human resources com., 1987-90, mem. affirmative action com., 1988-93; mem. Cmty. Action Commn., 1988-97, pres., 1991-96; mem. Pub. Health Commn., 1991-97, Monona Terr. Conv. and Cmty. Ctr. Bd., 1993-97; pres. South Madison Health and Family Ctr., Inc., 1993-97; bd. visitors U. Wis. Coll. Letters and Scis., Madison, 1997—2003; mem. exec. com. Wis. Alliance Cities, 1996-2003; mem. adv. bd. U.S. Conf. Mayors, 1999—2003; dir. Safe Cmtys. Coalition Madison County. Mem. Wis. Bar Assn., Dane County Bar Assn., Wis. Indsl. Rels. Alumni Assn. (pres. 1985-86), Madison Civics Club. Democrat. Avocations: knitting, reading, backpacking, cross country skiing. Home: 125 N Hamilton St 407 Madison WI 53703 Office: Wis Employment Rels Commn 18 S Thornton Ave Madison WI 53707-7870 Office Phone: 608-266-3297. Personal E-mail: sjmbauman@aol.com.

BAUMAN-ANTONIELLO, ALLISON, special education educator; b. Manhasset, N.Y., July 26, 1975; d. Mark and Sara Bauman; m. Richard Antoniello, Nov. 11, 2005. BS, Dowling Coll., Oakdale, N.Y., MS, 2001. Spl. edn. tchr. asst. Southampton (N.Y.) Elem. Sch., 1997—98; spl. edn. tchr. Mattlin Mid. Sch., Plainview, NY, 1998—.

BAUMANN, BARBARA JEAN, elementary school educator; d. Harry William and Jenny Mae Zeiters; m. James Frank Baumann, June 26, 1976; children: Daniel, Jonathan, Michael. BA, U. Ill., Champaign, 1974; MS, Ill. State U., Normal, 1992. Tchr. Fieldcrest South Elem., Minonk, Ill., 1974—. Adv. com. Regional Office Edn., Washburn, Ill., 1998—2006. Pres. MADD, Woodford County, Minonk, Ill., 1999—2005. Recipient Art award, Sun Found./Ill. Arts Coun., 2006; grantee, McDonald's Charities, 2004, 2006, Nat. Bank, Peoria, Ill., 2006. Mem.: Internat. Reading Coun., ASCD, Delta Kappa Gamma (Alpha Beta chpt.). Avocations: reading, gardening, crafting, quilting. Office: Fieldcrest South Elem 523 Johnson St Minonk IL 61760 Office Phone: 309-432-2838. Office Fax: 309-432-2192. E-mail: baumann@fieldcrest.k12.il.us.

BAUMANN, CAROL EDLER, retired political scientist; b. Plymouth, Wis., Aug. 11, 1932; d. Clarence Henry and Beulah Hanetta (Weinhold) E.; m. Richard Joseph Baumann, Feb. 28, 1959; children: Dawn Carol, Wendy Katherine. BA in Internat. Rels., U. Wis., Madison, 1954; PhD in Internat. Rels., London Sch. Econs./Polit. Sci., 1957. Chmn. internat. rels. major U. Wis., Milw., 1962-79; dep. asst. sec. Bur. of Intelligence and Rsch./Dept. of State, Washington, 1979-81; prof. U. Wis., Milw., 1972-95, dir. internat. studies and programs, 1982-88, prof. emeritus, 1995—; dir. Inst. of World Affairs, Milw., 1964-97, dir. emeritus, 1997—. Internat. edn. adv. coun. U. Wis. Milw., 2000—. Author: Program Planning About World Affairs, 1991, The Diplomatic Kidnappings, 1973; editor: Europe in NATO: Deterrence, Defense, and Arms Control, 1987, Western Europe: What Path to Integration?, 1967. Mem. Gov.'s Commn. on the UN, 1964-79, 82-89, 2004—; Dem. candidate 9th Congl. Dist., 1968; mem. World Affairs Coun. of Milw., 1964-75; bd. dirs. Wis. World Trade Ctr., 1987-2001, Wis. Dist. Export Coun., 1987-2003, Ea. Shores Libr. Sys., 1999—, Inst. World Affairs, U. Wis., Milw., 2000—. Recipient Pub. Svc. Achievement award Common Cause, Wis., 1991, World Citizen of Yr. award Internat. Inst. Wis, 2004; Marshall scholar, 1954-57. Mem. Fgn. Policy Assn. (bd. dirs. 1990—, editl. adv. com. 1977-79, 82-88), Nat. Coun. World Affairs Orgns. (pres. 1977-79, bd. dirs. 1992-96), UN Assn. of USA (bd. dirs. 1977-79, 82-89), Soc. for Citizen Edn. in world Affairs (pres. 1977-79), Phi Kappa Phi, Phi Beta Kappa. Democrat. Lutheran. Avocations: walking, swimming, reading, travel, creative writing. Home: W6248 Lake Ellen Dr Cascade WI 53011-1322 Personal E-mail: rbaumann4@wi.rr.com.

BAUMANN, LINDA ADRIENE, lawyer; d. Richard Baumann and Frances Madeline Rosen; children: Gregory Faron, Douglas Faron, Daniel Faron. BA magna cum laude, Brown U., Providence, R.I., 1972; JD, Columbia U. Law Sch., N.Y.C., 1975, Parker cert. in internat., fgn. law with honors, 1975. Bar: Washington 1975, NJ 1997, U.S. Dist Ct., N.J. 1997. Atty.-advisor US Dept. Health Edn. and Welfare, Rockville, Md., 1975—76; fgn. svc. officer US Dept. State, Washington, 1976—77, atty-advisor Legal Adviser's Office, 1977—81; assoc. (part-time) Swidler & Berlin, 1984—87, Fox, Weinberg & Bennett, 1988—93; adj. faculty Princeton U., 1994—96; of counsel Reed Smith LLP, Princeton, Wash. DC, 1997—2002, ptnr., 2003—06; mem. Arent Fox PLLC, Washington, 2006—. Editor: (law rev.) Columbia U. Law Sch., 1974—75; editor-in-chief Health Care Fraud & Abuse: Practical Perspectives, 2002, mem. adv. bd. The Health Lawyer, 2000—02, Rehab Report, 2002—, Physician Practice Compliance Alert, 2003—. Mem. Princeton U. Standing Com. Status Women, 1994—96; mem. bd. McCarter Theatre Assoc. Bd., Princeton, 1995—99, Princeton U. Friends Internat. Ctr., 1995—99, Appleseed Found, Pub. Interest Law Ctr. NJ, 1998—. Named 1 of 12 Outstanding Fraud and Compliance Lawyers Nationwide, Nightingale's Healthcare News, 2004—; Internat. fellow, Columbia U., NYC, 1974—75, Harlan Fiske Stone scholar, Columbia U. Law Sch., 1973—75. Mem.: ABA (vice chair health law sect. pub. 2001—02, vice-chair program 2002—03, co-chair Washington Healthcare Summit 2003—05, gov. coun. health law sect. 2003—, liaison to commn. women in profession 2005—, co-chair breast cancer task force 2006—), Am. Health Lawyers Assn. Office: Arent Fox PLLC 1050 ConnAve NW Washington DC 20036 Office Phone: 202-857-6239. Business E-Mail: baumann.linda@arentfox.com.

BAUMANN, PATRICIA APRIL, orthopedic surgery fellow; b. Bethpage, N.Y., Dec. 1, 1965; d. Walter C. Sr. and Marilyn Adell (Potavin) B.; m. Douglas Timothy Dolan, Apr. 27, 1996. BS, Cornell U., 1987; MS in Edn., U. Miami, 1990; DO, Nova Southeastern U., 1994. Lic., Fla., Ill.; diplomate Am. Bd. Orthop. Surgery, 2004. Marine biologist U. Miami, Coral Gables, Fla., 1988-90; intern Doctors Hosp., Columbus, Ohio, 1994-95; resident in orthop. surgery Frankford Hosp., Bucks County, Pa., 1995-99; fellow U. Chgo., 1999-00. Clin. asst. prof. Ohio State U., 2005—, Nebr. State U., 2006—. Author: (with others) Field Guide to Exuma Cays Land and Sea Park, 1989, Heterotopic Ossification, 1994; editor: Labs in Marine Biology, 1990; contbr. articles to profl. jours. Recipient All Ivy Honorable Mention award Ivy League Women's Ice Hockey, 1986-87; named Most Valuable Player, Cornell Women's Ice Hockey, Cornell Athletics, 1986-87. Fellow Am. Osteopathic Acad. Orthopedics.; mem. Am. Osteopathic Assn. Avocation: ice hockey. Home: 305 River Island St Merritt Island FL 32953 Office: Premier Orthopedics 7075 N US Hwy 1 Ste 100 Port Saint John FL 32927

BAUMER, BEVERLY BELLE, journalist; b. Hays, Kans., Sept. 23, 1926; d. Charles Arthur and Maryme Mae (Lord) Baumer. BS, U. Kans., 1948. Summer intern reporter Hutchison (Kans.) News, 1946—47; continuity writer, women's program dir. Sta. KWBW, Hutchison, 1948—49; dist. editor Salina (Kans.) Jours., 1950—57; commd. writer State of Kans. Centennial Yr., 1961; contbg. writer Ford Times, Kansas City Star, Wichita (Kans.) Eagle, Ojibway Publs., Billboard, Modern Jeweler, Floor Covering Weekly, other bus. mags., 1962—69; owner, mgr. apts. Hutchison, 1970—; broadcaster Reading Radio Rm., Sta. KHCC-FM, Hutchison, 1982—; columnist Hutchison Record, 1983—86. Author: book of poems, 1941; editor: A Simple Bedside Book for People Who are Kinda, Sorta Interested in Genealogy, 1983. Participant People to People Citizen Amb. Program, China, 1988; mem. Rep. Presdl. Task Force. Info. officer, maj. Kans. Wing Hdqurs. CAP, 1969—72. Recipient News Photo award, AP, 1952, Human Interest Photo award, Nat. Press Women, 1956. Mem.: Nat. Geneal. Soc., Am. Film Inst., Am. Soc. Profl. and Exec. Women, Kans. Press Women, Nat. Fedn. Press Women, Suffolk County Hist. Soc., Fellows Menninger Found., U. Kans. Alumni Assn., Internat. Platform Soc., Daus. Am. Colonists (organizeing regent Dr. Thomas Lord chpt., state chmn. insignia com.), Plantagenet Soc., Colonial Dames 17th Century (chaplain, charter mem. Henry Woodhouse chpt.), Order Descs. Colonial Physicians and Chirugiens, Daus. Colonial Wars, Ben Franklin Soc. (nat. adv. bd.), DAR, Nat. Soc. Sons and Daus. Pilgrims (elder Kans. br.), Kans. Soc. Daus. Am. Colonists, Nat. Soc. Daus. Am. Colonists, Nat. Soc. Daus. Founder and Patriots Am., Nat. Soc. Magna Charta Dames. Home and Office: 122 Downing Rd Hutchinson KS 67502-4453

BAUMGARTEN, DIANA VIRGINIA, gerontological nurse; b. Bklyn., May 24, 1943; d. Francis and Leah (Cuoghi) DeMarco; married; children: Elizabeth Salonia, Matthew, Edward. AS, Broward C.C., 1991. RN, Fla. Pediats. staff nurse North Broward Med. Ctr., Pompano Beach, Fla., 1991; staff nurse Tamarac (Fla.) Convalescent Ctr., 1992, nursing supr. Ft. Lauderdale, Fla., 1992-93; corp. nurse cons. HBA Health Mgmt. Corp., Ft. Lauderdale, Fla., 1993-94; acting DON Broward Convalescent Home, Ft. Lauderdale, 1994; acting asst. DON Springtree Walk Nursing Ctr., Sunrise, Fla., 1994; resident assessment coord., infection control officer Broward Convalescent Home, Ft. Lauderdale, 1994-95; asst. dir. nursing Adon Hillhaven Convalescent Ctr., Fla., 1995-97; dir. nursing Menorah House, 1997-98; legal nurse cons., case mgr. J.R. Health Mgmt., 1998-99; nurse specialist State of Fla., Agy. for Health Care Adminstrn., 1999—2001; geriatric care mgr. Eldercare Mgmt. Inst., 2001—; Q1 specialist Hospice and Home Care by the Sea, 2001—. Mem. ANA, Nat. Gerontol. Nurses Assn., Fla. Nurses' Assn., Phi Theta Kappa. Avocations: flute, classical music. Home: 11417 Little Bear Dr Boca Raton FL 33428-2609

BAUMRIND, DIANA, research psychologist; b. NYC, Aug. 23, 1927; AB, Hunter Coll., 1948; MA, U. Calif., Berkeley, 1951, PhD, 1955. Cert. and lic. psychologist, Calif. Project dir. psychology dept. U. Calif., Berkeley, 1955-58; project dir. Inst. of Human Devel., 1960—, also rsch. psychologist and prin. investigator family socialization and devel. competence project. Lectr. and cons. in field; referee for rsch. proposals Grant Found., NIH, 1970—, NSF, 1970—. Contbr. numerous articles to profl. jours. and books; author 2 monographs; mem. editorial bd. Devel. Psychology, 1986-90, Parenting: Science and Practice, 2000—. Recipient Rsch. Scientist award, NIMH; grantee NIMH, 1955-58, 60-66, Nat. Inst. Child Health and Human Devel., 1967-74, MacArthur Found., Grant Found., 1967—. Fellow Am. Psychol. Assn., Am. Psychol. Soc. (G. Stanley Hall award 1988), Soc. Research in Child Devel. Office: U Calif Inst of Human Devel 1217 Tolman Hall Berkeley CA 94720-1691 Office Phone: 510-642-3603.

BAUMRIND, LYDIA, psychologist; b. Bklyn., May 5, 1954; d. Seymour Harvey and Rosalyn Muriel (Greenwald) B.; m. Gerry Oster; children: Michael, Samara. BA, Brandeis U., 1975; EdD, Boston U., 1983. Counselor Durg Rehab. Clinic, Mass. Gen. Hosp., Boston, 1975-77; therapist Project Turnabout, Weymouth, Mass., 1976-77, Mass. Gen. Hosp.-Boston Clinic, 1977-78; trainee, intern Greater Lawrence (Mass.) Mental Health Ctr., 1977-78; prof. Mass. Bay Community Coll., Wellseley, 1978-79; psychotherapist Ctr. for Human Behavior, Taunton, Mass., 1978-91; psychologist Brookline (Mass.) Ctr. for Adolescent and Adult Counseling, 1985—, also bd. dirs. Active sch. groups, Brookline, 1989—. Boston U. scholar, 1978. Mem. APA, Mass. Psychol. Assn., Nat. Register Health Providers in Psychology. Avocations: reading, art, dance, skiing, hiking. Office: 1415 Beacon St Ste 124 Brookline MA 02446-4898

BAUMRIND, ROSALYN MURIEL GREENWALD, psychologist; b. N.Y.C., Aug. 03; d. Samuel Howard and Rose (Halpern) Greenwald; m. Seymour Harvey Baumrind, Dec. 31, 1949 (dec.); children: Martin Mark, Lydia, Sandra. BA magna cum laude, Bklyn. Coll., 1950, MA, 1954; PhD, Adelphi U., 1967. Cert. clin. psychologist, N.Y. High sch. tchr. N.Y.C. Bd. Edn., 1950-62, Hebrew Inst. L.I., 1957-62; psychologist, phys. medicine and rehab. Elmhurst Gen. Hosp., Queens, N.Y., 1964; asst. psychologist VA Hosp. Ft. Hamilton, Bklyn., 1965-67; asst. prof. sch. edn. Bklyn. Coll., CUNY, 1967-85; pvt. practice, supervision of psychotherapists N.Y.C., 1967—. Cons. in field. Contbr. articles to profl. publs.; author TV tapes. Recipient award NIMH, 1963-65. Mem. Am. Acad Psychotherapists (exec. coun. 1984-90), Am. Psychol. Assn., Am. Group Psychol. Assn., Phi Beta Kappa. Avocations: music, piano, sculpture, reading, body training. Home and Office: 141 E 37th St New York NY 10016-3117

BAUNER, RUTH ELIZABETH, library director; b. Quincy, Ill. d. John Carl and M. Irene (Nutt) B. BS in Edn., Western Ill. U., 1950; MS, U. Ill., 1956; postgrad., So. Ill. U., 1974, PhD, 1978. Asst. res. libr. Western Ill. U., Macomb, 1950; tchr., libr. Sandwich (Ill.) Twp. High Sch., 1950-54; circulation dept. asst. U. Ill. Libr., Urbana, 1955; asst. edn. libr. So. Ill. U., Carbondale, 1956-63, acting edn. libr., 1963-64, edn. and psychology libr., 1965-93, assoc. prof. curriculum and instrn. dept., 1971-93; coord. freshman yr. experience program, vis. assoc. prof. Coll. of Liberal Arts, Carbondale, 1994-96. Dir. Grad. Residence Ctr. Librs., So. Ill. U., 1973-79; subject matter expert Learning Resources Svc. Interactive Video, Carbondale, 1990-91, also scriptwriter; faculty emeritus So. Ill. U., 2004—. Co-author: The Teacher's Library, 1966; contbr. articles to profl. jours. Pres. alumni constituency bd. Coll. Edn., Carbondale, 1988—89; mem. Carbondale Bd. Ethics, 1989—2001; tchr. I Can Read Program, 2001—03; mem. Carbondale Citizens Adv. Commn., 1999—2001; bd. dirs. So. Ill. U. chpt. UN, 1985—86, 1994—97; mem. faculty bd. So. Ill. Learning in Retirement, So. Ill. U. Emeritus Assn.; bd. dirs. Jackson County AARP, 1997—99, 2001—03, 2006—, So. Ill. U. Emeritus Faculty Assn., 2004—; mem. friends bd. Mcleod Playhouse, 2005—. Recipient Luck Has Nothing To Do With It award, Oryx Press, 1993. Mem.: AAUW (univ. rep. Carbondale br. 1988—89), ALA, Ill. Libr. Assn., Assn. Coll. and Rsch. Librs. (chmn. edn. and behavioral scis. sect. 1976—77, Most Active Mem. award 1968—93), AAUP (v.p. So. Ill. U. chpt. 1972—73), Delta Kappa Gamma, Phi Kappa Phi, Phi Delta Kappa (Women of Distinction award 1999). Office: 1206 W Freeman St Carbondale IL 62901-2351

BAUROTH, NANCY ANN, journalist, former marketing executive; b. Phila., Oct. 12, 1949; d. Harry William and Mary Octavia (Coffman) B. Dir. advt. and pub. rels. Doubleday & Co., N.Y.C., 1974-80; dir. product advt. Merrill Lynch & Co., N.Y.C., 1989-82, dir. mktg. comm. and cash mgmt., 1982-84; v.p., dir. mktg. direct access electronic banking Citibank, 1984-86; op-ed columnist Charlotte (N.C.) Observer, 1998—. Lectr. advt. writing CUNY, 1978, 79. Honoree Boston Soc. Fin. Analysts, 1982, creative workshop honoree Advt. Age, 1983. Mem. Fin. Comm. Soc. (honoree 1982), Pubs. Advt. Club (v.p. 1976-80). Republican. Presbyterian. Home: 10305 Threatt Woods Dr Charlotte NC 28277-2428 Personal E-mail: nbauroth@carolina.rr.com.

BAUSER, NANCY, social worker, counselor; BS in Edn., U. Mich., 1973; MS in Social Work, U. Wis., 1976. Diplomate Am. Acad. Experts Traumatic Stress Specialists; bd. cert. disability trauma, bd. cert. expert in traumatic stress. Social worker 2 alcohol treatment programs; disability peer counselor dual-diagnosis treatment program, 1995—2002. Social worker, peer counselor; presenter BIA's 14th Ann. Symposium, 1995, Second World Congress Brain Injury, Seville, Spain, 1997. Author: Acceptance Groups for Head Injured Survivors, 1991, Acceptance Groups for Disability Survivors, 1993, Acceptance Groups for Survivors, A Guide for Facilitators, 2001; contbr. articles to profl. jours. Mem.: NASW, Am. Bd. Cert. Disability Trauma (BCETS, BCDT 2004), Acad. Cert. Social Workers (ACSW 1984), Am. Acad. Cert. Social Workers, Am. Acad. Experts Traumatic Stress Specialists (diplomate), Assn. Traumatic Stress Specialists. Home: 4260 Wabeek Lake Dr Bloomfield Hills MI 48302 Office Phone: 248-737-9939. E-mail: nancy@survivoracceptance.com.

BAUTISTA, LINA JUDITH, psychiatrist; b. Quezon City, The Philippines; came to U.S., 1982; d. David Guzman and Pacita Sadang (Carpio) B.; m. Lahsen Joe Mahi, May 3, 1991; children: Leilani Jolina, Lucas Jamil. MD, U. Santo Tomas, Manila, 1982. Counselor Hale Nani Nursing Home, Honolulu, 1983-84; counselor adv. King County Rape Relief, Seattle, 1984-85; intern in medicine and neurology U. Utah, 1985-86, gen. resident psychiatry Salt Lake City, 1986-88, 90-91, child and adolescent psychiatry fellow, 1988-90; staff physician Charter North Hosp., Anchorage, 1992—, Alaska Regional Hosp., Anchorage, 1997—. Med. dir. residential unit Charter North Hosp., Anchorage, 1992-94, med. dir. childrens unit, 1993-97, med. dir. youth svcs., 1997—, med. exec. com., 1992—, credentials com., 1993—, pres. med. staff, 1993-94, 97—; assoc. affiliate prof. U. Alaska, Anchorage, 1994-96; clin. instr. WAMI program for med. students U. Wash., 1994-96; rschr. in field. Mem. AMA, Am. Psychiat. Assn., Acad. Child and Adolescent Psychiatry, Alaska Med. Assn., Alaska Psychiat. Assn., Utah Psychiat. Assn. Avocations: skiing, crafts, writing, family activities, travel. Office: Charter North Hosp 2530 Debarr Rd Anchorage AK 99508-2996

BAUWIN, ROBERTA ELIZABETH, counselor, director; b. Ashtabula, Ohio, Aug. 4, 1960; d. Robert Anthony and Marie Louise (Kastner) B. BA, Bluffton Coll., 1982; postgrad., Mont. State U., 1986-87; MA, No. Ariz. U., 1989. Human resources coord. TW Svcs., Yellowstone Nat. Park, Wyo., 1982-86; resident dir. Mont. State U., Bozeman, 1986-87; residence hall dir. No. Ariz. U., Flagstaff, 1987-89, Ohio State U., Columbus, 1989-90; asst. coord. student pers. SUNY, Binghamton, 1990-92; child and family counselor Fla. Dept. Health and Rehab. Svcs., St. Petersburg, 1992-93; res. supr. Youth and Family Connection, St. Petersburg, 1993—; mgr. Cmty. and Partnership Devel. United Way Tampa Bay, Tampa, Fla., 2006—. Consulting trainer Women's Ctr., Binghamton, 1990; cons. Corning (N.Y.) Community Coll., 1991, Lourdes Wellness Ctr., Binghamton, 1992; bd. dirs. Save Your Own Lives, Binghamton, 1992—. Co-author workbook in Breaking Co-Dependency series. Vol. YWCA, Binghamton, 1991-92, Mental Health Assn., Binghamton, 1992. Mem. ACA, Am. Coll. Pers. Assn. (directorate), Am. Mental Health Counseling Assn., Am. Multicultural Counseling Assn., Nat. Coun. Self-Esteem. Avocations: hiking, photography, reading, mountain biking, antiques. Home: 1740 Ashton Abbey Rd Clearwater FL 33755-1306 Office: United Way Tampa Bay 1000 N Ashley Dr Ste 800 Tampa FL 33602

BAVARIA, JOAN, finance company executive; b. 1944; Student, Mass. Coll. Art, U. Mass., CFA Program. Investment officer Bank of Boston, 1967—75; co-founder, pres. Social Investment Forum, 1981—86; founder, pres., CEO Trillium Asset Mgmt., 1982—. Chair Coalition Environmentally Responsible Econs. (CERES), 1989—2001; mem. bd. Earth Justice Legal Def. Fund, Ctr. Environ. Leadership, LightHawk, Social Investment Forum, 1981—89; spkr., writer in field. Chair Nat. Adv. Com. Policy and Tech. Com. (advisors to EPA); mem. dean's com. internat. devel., John F. Kennedy Sch. Govt. Harvard U.; mem. adv. bd. Greening of Industry Network; mem. adv. bd. Corp. Environ. Mgmt. Program U. Mich.; mem. bd., sec. Green Seal, 1991—99; mem. bd. Coun. Econ. Priorities, Indsl. Cooperative Assn. Loan Fund. Named Woman Yr., New Eng. Women Bus. Owners, 1994, Hero for Planet, Time Mag., 1999, Sci. Am. 50, Sci. Am. mag., 2002; recipient 2 Regional awards, Working Women mag., 1999, Entrepreneurial Excellence award, 1999, Millennium award corp. environ. leadership, Global Green and Green Cross Internat., Pres. Mikhail Gorbachev, 2000. Achievements include encouraging major companies to endorse the Coalition Environmentally Responsible Econs. principles for environmental management such as GM, BankAmerica, IT&T, Sun Company, Polaroid and Ben & Jerry's. Office: Trillium Asset Mgmt Corp 711 Atlantic Ave Boston MA 02111-2809 Office Fax: 617-482-6179.

BAW, CINDY A., literature and language professor; b. Little Rock, Ark. d. Walter James and Ruth Ellen Aldridge; m. John Dennis Baw; children: Stacy, Marcy. BA, U. Tex., Arlington; M, U. North Tex., Denton; post grad. in Counseling and Psychology, Dallas Bapt. U. Tchr. English Smithfield Mid. Sch., Ft. Worth, Tarrant County Coll., Hurst. Tchr. Future Outstanding Coll. and Univ. Students, Hurst, Tex.; mem. faculty Cornerstone honors program Tarrant County Coll., planner at-risk curriculum, faculty mentor and first contact; spkr. Greater Southwest Women's Conf. Author: Children of the Bible, poetry; developer: workbooks. Inservice curriculum designer Tex. Assn. Christian Schs., Hurst, Tex.; svc. learning projects Alliance Children, Tarrant County Women's Shelter; spkr. Gt. Hills Retreat Min. Named Outstanding Christian Lay Person; recipient Chancellor's Exemplary Tchg. award, Tarrant County Coll., Golden Apple award, Northeast Tarrant C. of C. Mem.: Tex. Assn. Gifted and Talented, Tex. Academic Skills Coun., C.C. Humanities Assn., Nat. Campaign Tolerance, Christianity and Lit., Alpha Chi (chaplain). Avocations: reading, exercise. Office: Tarrant County Coll NE 828 W Harwood Rd Hurst TX 76054-3219 Home: 8317 Thornbird Dr North Richland Hills TX 76180

BAWA, AVANTIKA, artist, educator; b. Ootacamund, Tamil Nadu, India, Sept. 16, 1973; d. Parambir Singh and Shashi Bawa. MFA, Sch. Art Inst. Chgo., 1998. Prof. Ill. Inst. Art, Chgo., 1998—99, Savannah Coll. Art and Design, Ga., 1999—. Dir. Aquaspace Gallery, Savannah, 1999—2005. Installations, Navigating Spaces. Presdl. Fellowship, Savannah Coll. Art And Design, 2003. Home: 1600 Peachtree St Atlanta GA 30303 Home Fax: 912-525-5200. Business E-Mail: abawa@scad.edu.

BAWDEN, NINA (MARY BAWDEN), author; b. Eng., 1925; Author: Who Calls the Tune (in U.S. as Eyes of Green), 1953, The Odd Flamingo, 1954, Change Here for Babylon, 1955, The Solitary Child, 1956, Devil by the Sea, 1957, Just Like a Lady (in U.S. as Glass Slippers Always Pinch), 1960, In Honour Bound, 1961, Tortoise by Candlelight, 1963, The Secret Passage (in U.S. as The House of Secrets), 1963, On the Run (in U.S. as Three on the Run), 1964, Under the Skin, 1964, A Little Love, A Little Learning, 1966, The White Horse Gang, 1966, The Witch's Daughter, 1966, A Handful of Thieves, 1967, A Woman of My Age, 1967, The Grain of Truth, 1968, The Runaway Summer, 1969, The Birds on the Trees, 1970, Squib, 1971, Anna Apparent, 1972, Carrie's War, George Beneath a Paper Moon, 1974, The Peppermint Pig, 1975, Afternoon of a Good Woman, 1976, Rebel on a Rock, 1978, Familiar Passions, 1979, Walking Naked, 1981, Kept in the Dark, 1982, The Ice House, 1983, The Finding, 1985, Finding, 1985, Circles of Deceit, 1987, Keeping Henry, 1988, The Outside Child, 1989, Family Money, 1991, Humbug, 1992, The Real Plato Jones, 1993, In My Own Time, 1994, A Nice Change, 1997, Off the Road, 1998, Ruffian on the Stair, 2001, Dear Austen, 2005. Recipient S.T. DuPont Golden Pen award for alifetime's svc. to lit., 2004. Address: care Curtis Brown Ltd 10 Astor Pl New York NY 10003-6935 also: 22 Noel Rd London NI 8HA England also: 19 Kapodistriou Nauplion 21100 Greece E-mail: ninakrak@btinternet.com.

BAXENDALE, SONIA A., diversified financial services company executive; Grad., U. Toronto. Various positions American Express Canada, Saatchi & Saatchi; joined Canadian Imperial Bank of Commerce, Toronto, 1992—, former mng. dir., former exec. v.p., asset mgmt., card products and collections, former exec. v.p., global private banking and investment mgmt., 2000—02, sr. exec. v.p., wealth mgmt., 2002—05, sr. exec. v.p., retail markets, 2005—. Bd. chmn. CIBC Securities Inc., CIBC Trust Corp., TAL Private Mgmt. Ltd., CIBC Asset Mgmt. Inc.; bd. dirs. CIBC Trust Co. Bahamas Ltd., CIBC Bank & Trust Co. Cayman Ltd., CIBC Investor Services Inc., TAL Global Asset Mgmt. Inc. Named one of Canada's Top 40 Under 40, 2000, 25 Women to Watch, US Banker mag., 2005. Office: Canadian Imperial Bank of Commerce 5650 Yonge St Toronto ON M2M 4G3 Canada*

BAXI, LAXMI V., obstetrician, gynecologist, medical educator; b. India; came to the U.S., 1976; d. Ishwardas Bhatia; m. Vibhakar K. Baxi, 1969. MBBS, Seth G. S. Med. Coll., Bombay U., 1962; MD, King Edward Meml. Hosp., Bombay, 1966. Diplomate Am. Bd. Ob-Gyn and maternal fetal medicine sub-specialty, 1998-04. Rotating intern, resident ob/gyn King Edward Meml. Hosp., Nowrosjee Wadia Maternity Hosp., Bombay, 1962-69; sr. registrar ob-gyn. King Edward Meml. Hosp., Bombay, 1969-72; asst. prof. ob-gyn. Lokmanya Tilak Med. Coll., Bombay, 1972-76; chief resident ob-gyn. C.M.D.N.J., Rutgers Med. Sch., St. Peter's Med. Ctr., N.J., 1976-77; fellow in maternal fetal medicine Coll. Physicians and Surgeons Columbia U., 1977-79; asst. prof. clin. ob-gyn. Columbia U. Coll. Physicians & Surgeons, N.Y.C., 1979-80, asst. prof. ob-gyn., 1980-87, assoc. prof. ob-gyn., 1987-91, prof. clin. ob-gyn., 1992—, assoc. chair ob-gyn., 1997, vice chair ob-gyn., 1998—2003. Asst. attending ob-gyn. Sloane Hosp. for Women, Presbyn. Hosp., N.Y.C., 1979-87, assoc. attending, 1987-91; vis. prof. dept. ob-gyn. King Edward Meml. Hosp., Bombay, 1986; co-dir. obstet. svc. Sloane Hosp. for Women, Columbia Presbyn. Med. Ctr., N.Y.C., 1991-92, dir., 1992-96, attending ob-gyn., 1992—, assoc. chair ob/gyn, 1997, vice chair ob-gyn., 1998-2003, acting dir. maternal-fetal medicine & maternal-fetal medicine fellowship program, 1995-96, 98-99; mem. N.Y. State Bd. Profl. Conduct Dept.; senator Columbia U., 2005—; presenter in field. Reviewer: Obstetrics and Gynecology, Jour. Maternal Fetal Medicine, Jour. Perinatal Medicine, Am. Jour. Ob-Gyn., Soc. for Perinatal Obstetricians; co-editor: Jour. Assn. Med. Women in India, 1974-75; cons. internat. bd. editors: Jour. Ob-Gyn. India; contbr. articles to profl. jours Mem. fin. com. City NY Dept. Health, Bur. Maternity Svcs. and Family Planning; Health; diplomate Am. Bd. ob-gyn amd Maternal-Fetal Medicine, 1981, 1987, 1995. Grantee Diabetic Found., 1990-91, Newborn Lung Ctr., 1979, 80, 81. Fellow Coll. Physicians and Surgeons; mem. Soc. for Gynecol. Investigation, Am. Coll. Ob-Gyn., N.Y. Obstet. Soc., N.Y. Acad. Medicine (sec. divsn. ob-gyn. 1985-86, chairperson divsn. ob-gyn. 1986-87), Indian Coll. Ob-Gyn. (founding mem.), Soc. Perinatal Obstetricians, Assn. Med. Women India (life), Assn. Profs. Ob-Gyn., Am. Diabetes Assn., Jacob's Inst. Women's Health (founding mem.), Sloane Alumni Assn. (pres. 1992-93). Avocation: indian classical music and dancing. Office Phone: 212-305-5899. Business E-Mail: lvb1@columbia.edu.

BAXLEY, LUCY, lieutenant governor; b. Ala. m. Jim Smith (div.); children: Becky Nichols, Louis. Licensed realtor; Treas. State of Ala., 1994—2002, lt. gov., 2002—. Former spokesperson Senior Promise; Women's Philanthropy Bd. Auburn U. Recipient Senior Citizens' Golden Eagle Statesman of Yr., Outstanding Woman Leader, Am. Assn. of U. Women. Mem.: Nat. Assn. Lt. Govs., Ala. Fedn. of Dem. Women (chair adv. coun.), U. Ala. XXXI. Democrat. Methodist. Office: Ste 725 11 S Union St Montgomery AL 36130 Office Phone: 334-242-7900. Business E-Mail: lucybaxley@ltgov.alabama.gov.*

BAXLEY, PAMEL W, secondary school educator; b. Spartanburg, SC, Oct. 1, 1952; d. William Edward and Betty Sue Hartsell Willis; m. William W. Baxley, May 10, 1974 (dec. Aug. 1, 2001); children: William Joshua, Sarah Elizabeth, Joseph Edward. BA, Clemson U., 1974; M in Edn., U. SC, 1980; Edn. Specialist, Valdosta State U., 1992. National Board Professional Teaching Certificate Nat. Bd. of Profession Tchg. Standards, 2000, South Carolina Teaching Certificate SC. Dept. of Edn., 1974. Spl. edn. tchr. SC. Pub. Schools, 1974—80; assistantship U. SC, Columbia, 1980; spl. edn. tchr. Lexington Sch. Dist. #2, West Columbia, SC, 1980—83; 6th grade math tchr. Denmark Olar Elem. Sch., SC, 1983—84; 5th grade tchr. Barnwell Elem. Sch., SC, 1984—85; 2nd grade tchr. Spalding Dr. Elem. Sch., Atlanta, 1985—86; kindergarten tchr. Garrison Pilcher Elem. Sch., Thomasville, Ga., 1986—92; elem. sch. tchr. Alma Elem. Sch., Gaffney, SC, 1992—96; sci. tchr., spl. tchr. Spartanburg Sch. Dist. #4, Woodruff, SC, 1996—. Superivsised interns and practice tchr. Horry County Sch., Conway, SC, 1975—78; spl. edn. tchr. Lexington Sch. Dist. #2, West Columbia, SC, 1980—83; 6th grade tchr. Denmark-Olar Elem. Sch., SC, 1983—84; grant writing Barnwell Elem. Sch., SC, 1984—85; 2nd grade tchr. Spalding Dr. Elem. Sch., Atlanta, 1985—86; 5th grade tchr. Barnwell Elem. Sch., SC, 1985—86; kindergarten tchr. Garrison-Pilcher Elem. Sch., Thomasville, Ga., 1986—92; sci. tchr., spl. tchr., Spartanburg Sch. Dist. 4, Woodruff, SC, 1996—; cons. for math sci. in the state wide systemic initiative Piedmont Upstate Hub, Spartanburg, SC, 1995—2000; conf. presenter Internat. Reading Assn., Hilton Head Island, SC, 1995—2003; work with literacy groups, children and adults interested in literacy events Spartanburg Dist. 4, Woodruff, SC, 1996—; grant writing-educational improvment act funds Spartanburg Dist. #4, Woodruff, SC, 1997—; tchr. specialist, cons. State Dept. of Edn., Coulmbia, SC, 2001—03, grant writer, Columbia, SC, 2001—02. Mem. First Bapt. Ch., Woodruff, SC, 1996. Recipient Disting. Tchr. of Reading Alma Elem., Cherokee County Reading Coun., 1995; grant, SC. Dept. of Edn., 2002, 2002. Mem.: ASCD, South Caroling Sci. Teachers, SC. Edn. Assocation, Internat. Reading Assosiation (state corr. sec. 2004—06). Achievements include development of curriculum guides and pacing guides for math and science for schools while a teacher specialist; initiated and implemented literacy and math assessment program to assist teachers at the beginnig of the year while a teacher specialist; assisted in designing kit training programs that helped train hundreds of teachers in the ESTEEM science program. Office: Woodruff Primary Sch Lucy P Edwards Rd Woodruff SC 29388 Office Phone: 864-476-3174. Business E-Mail: pbaxley@spartanburg4.org.

BAXLEY, YVETTE, secondary school educator; b. Mass., Jan. 11, 1973; d. Peter and Marie Morris. BS in Biol. Sci., Miss. State U., Starkville, 1997, BS in Secondary Edn., 1997. Cert. tchr. Nat. Bd. for Profl. Tchrs., 2002. H.S. tchr. Clinton (Miss.) Pub. Schs., 1997—2002; tchr. Clark Middle Sch., Anchorage Sch. Dist., 2002—04, Bartlett H.S., Anchorage, 2004—. Instr. U. Anchorage, 2003—. Office: Bartlett High School 1101 N Muldoon Rd Anchorage AK 99506 Office Phone: 907-742-1800. Business E-Mail: baxley_yvette@asdk12.org.

BAXTER, BARBARA MORGAN, Internet service provider executive, educator; b. Cleve., Apr. 14, 1939; d. James Clifford and Mildred Elizabeth (Button) Baxter; m. David S. Unkefer, Dec. 28, 1956 (div.); children: Rachel, Clifford David, Elizabeth, Monica, Todd James. BSBA in MIS, Bowling Green State U., 1977, MBA, 1979, postgrad. in psychology, 1984, Wright State U., 1984-85. Clk. J.C. Baxter Co., Minerva, Ohio, 1962-66; v.p., co-founder Sherwood Plastics, Inc., Fostoria, Ohio, 1966-75, pres., CEO, 1975-89, Compututor Inc/Internet of Sandhills, Southern Pines, N.C. Mem. adj. faculty Tiffin (Ohio) U., 1984-90; MIS cons. to small bus., 1984-90; adj. continuing edn. faculty Sandhills C.C., Pinehurst, N.C., 1992-93; adj. faculty St. Andrews Coll., Lauringburg, N.C., 1993; CEO, co-founder CompuTutor, Inc., Southern Pines, N.C., 1994—, Internet of the Sandhills ISP, 1996—. V.p. Carroll County Young Reps., 1960-61; mem. Carroll County Rep. Cen. and Exec. Com., 1961-65, Wood County Rep. Com., 1967-70; troop leader, troop organizer, badge cons. Girl Scouts U.S., 1967-81; vestrywoman, sr. warden Trinity Episcopal Ch., Fostoria, 1972-75; therapist Community Hospice Care Seneca County, Tiffin, 1987-89, also Carroll, Wood, Fostoria Counties; del. U.S.-China Trade Talks People to People, Spokane, Wash., 1988; adv. bd. Tiffin U. Students in Free Enterprise, 1986-87; tchr. applied econs. Jr. Achievement, 1988-89. Mem. Ladies Oriental Shrine N.Am., DAR, Alpha Lambda Delta. Avocation: classical music.

BAXTER, BETTY CARPENTER, academic administrator; b. Sherman, Tex., Oct. 10, 1937; d. Granville E. and Elizabeth (Caston) Carpenter; m. Cash Baxter; children: Stephen Barrington, Catherine Elaine. AA in Music, Christian Coll., Columbia, Mo., 1957; MusB in Voice and Piano, So. Meth. U., Dallas, 1959; MA in Early Childhood Edn., Tchrs. Coll., Columbia, 1972, MEd, 1979, EdD, 1988. Cert. life coach, cons. Baxter Coaching & Consulting, 2005. Tchr. Riverside Ch. Day Sch., N.Y.C., 1966—71; head mistress Episcopal Sch., N.Y.C., 1972—87, head mistress, emeritus, 1987—; founding head Presbyn. Sch., Houston, 1988—94; dir. Chadwick Village Sch., Palos Verdes Peninsula, Calif., 1995—; head sch. St. Margaret's Episcopal Sch., Palm Desert, 2001—02; cert. life coach Baxter Coaching and Consulting, 2004—. Author: The Relationship of Early Tested Intelligence on the WPPSI to Later Tested Aptitude on the SAT. Mem.: ACA, ASCD, Nat. Notary Assn., Internat. Coach Fedn., L.A. Assn. Sch. Heads, Nat. Assn. Edn. Young Children, Ind. Sch. Assn. Admissions Greater N.Y. (former exec. bd.), Nat. Assn. Elem. Sch. Prins., Nat. Assn. Episcopal Ch. (former gov. bd., editor Network publ.), Delta Kappa Gamma, Kappa Delta Pi. Republican. Episcopalian. Office: 72-828 Joshua Tree St Palm Desert CA 92260 Office Phone: 310-291-7489. E-mail: bettybaxtercoach@earthlink.net.

BAXTER, BEVERLEY VELORIS, economic association administrator, educator; b. Eugene, Oreg., July 5, 1943; d. J. Clifford Baxter and O. Veloris Crenshaw; m. Doyle R. Dobbins, July 7, 1962; children: Kendall Reé Baxter Dobbins, Kalen Dobbins, Konlee Baxter Dobbins. Certificate, Graduate Sch. Ecumenical Studies, Bossey, Switzerland, 1965, William Temple Coll., Rugby, Eng., 1965; BS, Phillips U., 1966, MEd, 1967; MA, U. Del., 1971, PhD, 1976. Tchg. asst. U. Del., Newark, 1971—76; asst. prof. dept. English Temple U., Phila., 1977—79; real estate investor Wilmington, Del., 1979—83; dir. edn. programs First Unitarian Ch., Wilmington, 1983; exec. asst. to county exec. New Castle County, Wilmington, 1983—84; v.p. Blue Ball Properties, Wilmington, 1985—93; exec. dir. The Com. of 100, Wilmington, 1993—. Dir. Del. Bus. Pub. Edn. Coun., Wilmington, 1988—2003, Wilmington Area Planning Coun. Wilmington Initiatives Steering Com., 1995—; mem. Gov.'s State Planning Citizens Adv. Coun., Del., 1995—, Del. State C. of C. Small Bus. Alliance Legis. Com., 1997—; mem. working group De. Dept. Transportation; mem. Del. Dept. Natural Resources & Environ. Control Regulatory Adv. com.; bd. dirs., treas. Wiley Coll., Marshall, Tex. Author: Diaries and Journals of Americans Held Prisoner During the Revolutionary War, 1976; editor: For Your Info., 1995. Pres. bd. dir. Montessori Cmty. Sch., Wilmington, 1996—2000; mem. Task Force on Early Childhood Edn., 2004—; bd. dir. Unitarian Universalist Svc. Com., Cambridge, Mass., 1985—91; pres. First Unitarian Ch., Wilmington, 1979—82, bd. dir., 1979—82, Friends of Rockwood Mus., Wilmington, 1986—88. Recipient Disting. Svc. award, Unitarian Universalist Svc. Com., 1991, Economic Turnaround Cert. of Appreciation, Wilmington 2000, 1995, Liveable Cmty. award, Wilmington Area Planning Coun., 1998. Mem.: The Associates, The Bus. Group, New Castle County C. of C. (state affairs coun., county govt. coun.). Unitarian Universalist. Avocations: music, reading, gardening, skiing. Office: The Com of 100 704 King St Ste 5/2 Wilmington DE 19801

BAXTER, JOAN ANNA PATTEN, technical writer; b. Phila., July 5, 1933; d. Frank Perc and Anna Calvert Patten; divorced; children: Stephen Paul, William Jeffrey, Timothy David. AA, Pa. State U., Lima, 1983; Cert. in Mgmt., Widener U., Chester, Pa., 1984; BS, West Chester (Pa.) U., 1987; MA Communications, West Chester U., 2004. Coord. purchases, installation Scott Paper Co., Phila., 1988-91; tech. writer McGraw Hill Pub., Delran, N.J., 1994-95; cons. PC trainer Archdiocese of Phila., 1996; quality assurance tester Bell Atlantic Graphics, Audubon, Pa., 1996-97; writer product devel. Franklin Pub. Inc., Burlington, N.J., 1997-98; tech. writer, processes Telespectrum, Phila., 1998—; coord. Y2K project Simon & Schuster, Wayne, Pa., 1998—99; system analyst Bd. Edn., Phila., 2000; tech. writer Independence Blue Cross, 2000; tech. writer processes, procedures and svc. descriptions Agere Sys., Inc., Allentown, Pa., 2002; tech. writer IKON Office Solutions, Malvern, Pa., 2003; documentation specialist Centocor Johnson & Johnson, Horsham, Pa., 2005. Devel. editor Boyd & Fraser, Boston, 1992; implementor, supr. Temple U. Sch. Dentistry, Phila., 1980-84; adminstrv. asst. Brandywine Conservancy, Chadds Ford, Pa., 1976-80, Roy F. Weston Inc., West Chester; propr. Baxter Enterprises, 1994-96. Recipient Chapel of Four Chaplains award, 1982. Mem. AAUW (pub. policy com. 1991-99), U.S. Power Squadron, Delaware Blue Hen Coun. (dir. 1996-99). Republican. Christian Scientist. Avocations: tennis, music, art. Home: 926 Tyson Dr West Chester PA 19382-7571 E-mail: jpbaxter_19103@yahoo.com.

BAXTER, JUDITH A., medical nurse; b. Trenton, Mo., May 17, 1953; d. William Samuel and Garnet Alma (Sharp) Klinginsmith; m. Richard K. Baxter, Sept. 9, 1977; children: Katrinka, Randi, Colt, Courtney, Charlie. Student, U. Mo., 1972; AS with honors, Trenton Jr. Coll., 1977. Lic. Practical Nurse, Mo. Charge-med. nurse Sunnyview Nursing Home, Trenton, 1977-78; staff nurse Excelsior Springs (Mo.) County Hosp., 1982; TX-med. nurse Woodland Manor Nursing Home, Arnold, Mo., 1986-90; staff nurse St. Anthony's Med. Ctr. Rehab., St. Louis, 1990—. Home: 2845 Frisco Hill Rd Imperial MO 63052-2043

BAXTER, KATHLEEN BYRNE, academic administrator; b. Rockville Center, Jan. 31, 1976; d. Anthony Campbell and Margaret Regan Baxter. BA in English, Villanova U., 1997; MA in Higher Edn. and Student Pers. Adminstrn., Teachers Coll., Columbia U., 2000. Asst. dir. event planning Teachers Coll., Columbia U., N.Y.C., 1998—2000; asst. dir. programs MIT, Cambridge, 2000—02; dir. leadership and first yr. programs Simmons Coll., Boston, 2002—03; assoc. dir. Ctr. for Career Edn., Columbia U., N.Y.C., 2003—. Mem. Franciscan Children's Hosp. Young Profl. Coun., Brighton, Mass., 2000—03. Mem.: Assn. Coll. Pers. Adminstrs., Nat. Assn. Pers. Adminstrs., Kappa Delta Pi, Delta Delta Delta. R-Liberal. Catholic. Avocations: travel, running, reading.

BAXTER, MEREDITH, actress; b. Los Angeles, June 21, 1947; d. Tom and Whitney (Blake) Baxter; m. Bob Bush, June 23, 1966 (div. 1969), children: Ted, Eva; m. David Birney, Apr. 10, 1974 (div. 1989), children: Kate, Peter and Mollie (twins), m. Michael Blodgett, Oct 21, 1995 (div. 2000). Student, Interlochen Arts Acad., Mich. Prin., Meredith Baxter Skin Care Products Actress (films) including Ben, 1972, Stand Up and Be Counted, 1972, Bittersweet Love, 1976, All the President's Men, 1976, The November Plan, 1976, (TV movies) The Cat Creature, 1973, The Stranger Who Looks Like Me, 1974, The Imposter, 1975, The Night That Panicked America, 1975, Target Risk, 1975, Little Women, 1978, The Family Man, 1979, Beulah Land, 1980, The Two Lives of Carol Letner, 1981, Take Your Best Shot, 1982, Family Ties Vacation, 1985, The Rape of Richard Beck, 1985, Kate's Secret, 1986, The Long Journey Home, 1987, Winnie, 1988, She Knows Too Much, 1989, Jezebel's Kiss, 1990, The Kissing Place, 1990, Burning Bridges, 1990, A Bump in the Night, 1991, A Mother's Justice, 1991, A Woman Scorned: The Betty Broderick Story, 1992, The Betty Broderick Story: Part 2, 1992, (also exec. prodr.) Darkness Before Dawn, 1993, My Breast, 1994, One More Mountain, 1994, For the Love of Aaron, 1994, Betrayed: A Story of Three Women, 1995, After Jimmy, 1996, Inheritance, 1997, Miracle in the Woods, 1997, Let Me Call You Sweetheart, 1997, Holy Joe, 1999, Down Will Come Baby, 1999, Miracle on the 17th Green, 1999, The Wednesday Woman, 2000, A Mother's Fight for Justice, 2001, Aftermath, 2001, Murder on the Orient Express, 2001, A Christmas Visitor, 2002, Angel in the Family, 2004, On the Rocks, 2005; (plays) Guys and Dolls, Talley's Folley, Butterflies are Free, Varieties; star (TV series) Bridget Loves Bernie, 1972-73, Family, 1976-80, Family Ties, 1982-89, The Faculty, 1996; (TV spls.) Vanities, 1981, Missing.Have You Seen This Person?, 1985, Diabetes Update, 1986, Other Mothers, 1993, TV's Funniest Families, 1994; other TV appearances include The Interns, Police Woman, Medical Story, City of Angels, McMillan and Wife, The Streets of San Francisco. Mem. Am. Diabetes Assn. Mailing: c/o Constance Freiberg Envision Entertainment Ste 300 9255 Sunset Blvd West Hollywood CA 90069

BAXTER, MYRTLE MAE (BOBBI BAXTER), artist; b. Weableau, Mo., Nov. 10, 1928; d. Maxwell and Maude Bell Dorrel; m. Clarence Edgar Baxter, Dec. 31, 1945; children: Kenneth Wayne, Gary Dee, Joyce Evelyn. Profl. cert., Nevada (Mo.) Beauty Sch., 1970; degree in art, Am. Art Sch., 1987. Hair stylist Beauty Box, Butler, Nev., 1993-96; tchr. art to children Baxter Art Gallery, Butler, 1993-95. Exhibited in group shows Roscoe (Mo.) Mus. Soc., 1978-79 (1st place best of show award), Iola (Kans.) Guild, 1985-86, 1st award), Cottey Coll., Nevada, 1985-86, Royal Arts Coun., Versailles, Mo., 1985-86, (1st, 2d, 3d. awards, Best of Show), Table Rock (Mo.) Art Assn., 1996-97 (Best of Show award), Stover (Mo.) Art Assn., 1990-91, Warrensburg Coll. Art Gallery, 1995, Image Art Gallery, Carthage, Mo., 1997, Lamar (Mo.) Art League, 1996-97 (1st, 2d and 3d awards), Royals Arts Coun. Art Show, 1997 (Best of Show award), Harrisonville, Mo. (Best of Show Fine Arts award, 1997) Bates Five County Art Show, 2005; author: Memories, 2005; contbr. poetry On the Wing of Poetry. Leader, v.p. Summit 4-H Club, Butler, 1975-80; pres. Ladies Aid Club, Butler, 1985-86; in charge festival Roscoe (Mo.) Art Festival, 1996-97. Recipient 5 awards, Orlando Art Conv., 2003, Crystal award, Black Internat. Soc. Poets, 2006. Mem. Butler Art Club (pres. 1973-74), Tri-County Art Assn. (v.p., show chmn. 1980-81, bd. dirs. 1980, sec. 1980-81), Bates County Art League (mem. 1980-81, 89, show chmn. 1978-79), Harrisonville Art Assn. (v.p. 1995-96, program organizer),

Mo. Coun. Arts (program organizer 1995), Warrensburg Art Assn., Greater Kansas City Art Assn., Nat. Mus., Women in the Arts, Bates County Art League. Democrat. Methodist. Avocations: painting on location, hiking, bicycling, exercising, attending art meetings. Home: RR 5 Butler 52 E Box 65 Butler MO 64730-1852

BAXTER, NANCY, medical writer; b. Grand Rapids, Mich., Oct. 3, 1950; d. Robert Emerson and Mary (Knoblauch) B. BA in Journalism, Am. U., 1972. Asst. dir. publs. Am. Speech, Lang. & Hearing Assn., Washington, 1973-77; mng. editor Biomedia, Inc., Princeton, N.J., 1977-79, Continuing Profl. Edn. Ctr., Inc., Princeton, 1981-82; editor A.M. Best Co., Oldwick, N.J., 1979-81; med. writer, editor Biomed Info. Corp., N.Y.C., 1982-83; pres. Baxter Med. Comms. Co., Warren, N.J., 1983—. Mem.: Am. Med. Writers Assn. Home and Office: 18 Stiles Rd Warren NJ 07059-5413 Office Phone: 908-755-4589. Personal E-mail: baxmedcomm@aol.com.

BAXTER, RUTH HOWELL, educational administrator, psychologist; b. Washington; d. Robert R. and Georgie (Murray) Lassiter; m. Edward A. Howell; children: Robert, Astrid, Mova, Mava, Josephine. BS, D.C. Tchrs. Coll.; MA in Edn., George Washington U.; cert. (N.Am. Com. of Oslo scholar), Oslo U.; grad. Adminstr.'s Acad. Class, D.C. Public Schs. Founder, dir., propr. Jewels of Ann. Pvt. Day Sch., Washington, 1970—; tchr. Newlands Infant, Southampton, Eng.; instr. math. demonstration lessons dept. edn. Howard U. Dir. early childhood edn. workshop Brent Elem. Sch., Washington; tchr. adult edn. Bel Air Sch., Woodbridge, Va.; founder, cons. Ask Dr. Ruth Rdnl. Cons. Group; mem. Ednl. Instn. Licensure Commn. Task Forces; mem. Mayor's Pre-White House Conf. on Libraries and Info. Services; exec. high sch. internship program D.C. Public Schs. Author: A Norwegian Birthday Party; contbr. children's stories to various publs. Mem. planning com. Eastern region Jr. Red Cross, Washington; cons. coll. youth motivation task force program Nat. Alliance for Bus.; bd. dirs. Ctr. Ednl. Change D.C. Pub. Schs. Fulbright scholar; North Atlantic scholar; named Outstanding Tchr. of Yr., Future Tchrs. Am.; recipient Outstanding Contbn. award Nat. Assn. Negro Women, Commemorative Medal of Honor. Mem. APA, EVa. Psychol. Assn., English Speaking Union, Columbia Women (sec.), Zeta Phi Beta (life), Phi Delta Kappa. Home: 13349 Delaney Rd Dale City VA 22193

BAXTER, SANDRA L., government agency administrator; BA in English, Howard U.; M in Education, Loyola Coll.; EdD in Social Policy, Harvard Grad. Sch. of Education, 1995. Sr. evaluator US Gen. Acctg. Office; exec. dir. Nat. Inst. Literacy, 2001—. Office: Nat Inst for Literacy 1775 I Street NW Ste 730 Washington DC 20006 Office Phone: 202-233-2025.

BAXTER, SHEILA R., career military officer; b. Franklin, Va., Apr. 4, 1955; B in Health and Phys. Edn., Va. State Coll., 1977; disting. mil. grad., Reserve Officer's Training Corps; M in Health Svcs. Mgmt., Webster U. Med. svcs. offficer U.S. Army, 1978, advanced through grades to brigadier gen., 2004, asst. surgeon gen., dep. chief of staff for force sustainment med. command US Army Med. Services Corp. Ft. Sam Houston, Tex., 2004—05; comdr. Madigan Army Med. Ctr., Tacoma, 2005—. Evangelist Ch. of God and Christ. Decorated Legion of Merit, Bronze Star, Meritorious Svc. Medal with four oak leaf clusters, Army Commendation Medal with two oak leaf clusters, Army Achievement Medal with two oak leaf clusters, Kuwait Liberation Medal, Expert Field Med. Badge, others; recipient Hon. Silver award for excellence in cmty svc., Lord Mayor of Pirmasens, Germany. Office: Madigan Army Med Ctr Bldg 9040 Fitzsimmons Dr Tacoma WA 98431

BAXTER-KEGLER, DEMETRA M., principal; d. Andrew Dan Hanes and Cynthia Ann Lathan; 1 child, Clinten A. Kegler. BS, SFASU, Nacogdoches, Tex., 1995, MEd, 1998. LMS/ABU tchr. Jasper (Tex.) Ind. Sch. Dist., 1995—98; asst. prin. West Orange-Cove County Ind. Sch. Dist., Orange, Tex., 1998—2002; prin. Theodore Roosevelt Sch., Ft. Apache, Ariz., 2002—03, Mary V. Riley Sch., Whiteriver, Ariz., 2003—04, Lexington (Tex.) Ind. Sch. Dist., 2004—06. Trainer IANICI-NVCPI, Lexington, 2000—. Recipient T.P. and Jenny Lou White award, SFASU, 2000. Mem.: ASCD, Tex. Alliance Black Sch. Educators, Tex. Elem. Prin. and Supt. Assn., Delta Sigma Theta. Office: Lexington Ind Sch Dist 222 5th St Lexington TX 78947 Office Phone: 979-773-2525. Office Fax: 979-773-4455. Business E-Mail: kegler@lexington.isd.tenet.edu.

BAXTER-LOWE, LEE ANN, science educator; b. Oshkosh, Wis., June 28, 1950; d. James Paul and Jane G. Matejowec; m. Kenneth N. Lowe, Nov. 12, 1983; children: Ashley, Lindsay. BS, U. Wis., 1972, PhD, 1976. Lab. investigator Blood Rsch. Inst., Milw., 1987-94; dir. DNA diagnostics Blood Ctr. Southeast Wis., Milw., 1987-94; dir. molecular genetics program Richland Meml. Hosp., Columbia, S.C., 1994-98; prof. U. Calif., San Francisco, 1998—. Cons., reviewer NIH, Bethesda, Md., 1990—. Contbr. articles to profl. jours.; inventor/patentee in field. Rsch. grantee NIH, 1988—. Mem. AAAS, Am. Soc. Immunologists, Am. Soc. Histocompatibility & Immunologenetics, Am. Soc. Hematology, Transplantation Soc. Office: UCSF Box 0508 San Francisco CA 94143-0508 Home: 907 Alturas Way Mill Valley CA 94941

BAY, WILLOW, news anchor; b. NYC, Dec. 28, 1963; m. Robert Iger, Oct. 7, 1995; children: Max, William. BS in Lit. cum laude, U. Pa.; MBA, NYU. Corr. NBC Today Show, Live: With Regis & Kathie Lee; co-host NBA weekly mag. show NBA Inside Stuff, 1991—98; co-anchor Good Morning Am./Sunday, 1994—97; former corr. ABC World News Saturday, World News Sunday; co-anchor (with Judd Rose) CNNewsstand: Entertainment Weekly and CNN & Fortune, 1998-99; co-anchor Moneyline, 1999—2004; anchor MSNBC Live, 2004—. Office: MSNBC 1 MSNBC Plz Secaucus NJ 07094

BAYARD, SUSAN SHAPIRO, adult education educator, small business owner; b. Boston, Dec. 26, 1942; d. Morris Arnold and Hester Muriel (Blatt) Shapiro; m. Edward Quint Bayard, Jan. 4, 1969; children: Jeffrey David, Lucy Quint. BA, Syracuse U., 1964; MA, U. Calif., Berkeley, 1966; cert. in advanced grad. study, Boston U., 1984. Rsch. chemist Harvard Med. Sch., Boston, 1966; asst. scientist Polaroid Corp., Cambridge, Mass., 1966—67; instr. Boston U., 1968—70, Wheelock Coll., Boston, 1978—81; chmn. sci. dept. Tower Sch., Marblehead, Mass., 1981—85; dir., owner Bayard Learning Ctr., Marblehead, 1985—94; vis. lectr. Salem State Coll., Mass., 1994—2000, coord. Instrnl. Design Lab., 1995—2000, coord. PALMS presvc. program, 1998—2000; dir. Ctr. Tchg., Learning and Assessment North Shore C.C., Danvers, Mass., 2003—. Ednl. cons., workshop facilitator Swampscott (Mass.) Pub. Schs., Lynn (Mass.) Pub. Schs., Marblehead, Mass., 1986—96; instr., cons. N.E. Consortium, North Andover, Mass., 1986—94. Mem. Curriculum Evaluation Com., Swampscott, 1978—80, Mass. Ednl. TV Program Selection Com., 1979—87, Supt. Screening Com., Swampscott, 1987, Town Meeting, Swampscott, 1988—, Sch. Improvement Coun., Swampscott, 1988—89. Named Outstanding Woman Grad. Student, Boston U. Women's Guild, 1977; grantee, NSF, Syracuse U., 1962, 1964. Mem.: Nat. Sci. Tchrs. Assn., Pi Lambda Theta. Jewish. Avocations: tennis, reading, computers, piano.

BAYEN, UTE JOHANNA, psychology professor, researcher; b. Krefeld, Germany, Oct. 21, 1964; d. Franz-Joseph Martin-Bayen and Hannelore Anna Bayen; children: Daniel Klaus Martin, Michael Joseph. MS in Psychology, Albert-Ludwigs U., Freiburg, Germany, 1990; PhD in Human Devel. and Family Studies, Pa. State U., State College, 1994. Asst. prof. psychology U. Memphis, 1995—96; asst. prof. U. NC, Chapel Hill, 1996—2003, assoc. prof., 2003—. Mem. cognition and perception study sect. NIH, Ctr. Sci. Rev., 2004—. Assoc. editor: Exptl. Psychology Jour, 2006—, cons. editor: Jour. Exptl. Psychology: Learning, Memory, and Cognition, 2002—, Aging, Neuropsychology, and Cognition, 2005—. Recipient Postdoctoral award, APA, 1995, Gordon H. DeFriese Career Devel. Aging Rsch. award, Inst. Aging, U. NC, Chapel Hill, 2002; fellow, German Nat. Fellowship Found., 1985—94, AARP, 1993—94, Alexander von Humboldt Found., 2004—05; grantee, Nat. Inst. Aging, 2000—, Alexander von Humboldt Found., 2001—04. Mem.: Women Cognitive Sci., German Soc. Psychology, The Psychonomic Soc. Office: Univ of North Carolina at Chapel Hill Cb# 3270 Chapel Hill NC 27599 Business E-Mail: ubayen@unc.edu.

BAYES, BEVERLEY JOAN, retired pediatrician; b. Regina, Can., Nov. 1, 1937; came to U.S., 1988; d. Frederick Charles and Sylvia Mae (Hickling) B.; m. Edgar Gibson Merson, May 25, 1988; children: Jennifer Alice Merson Hersberg, Andrew Charles Merson, Keith Graham Merson. MD, U. Toronto, 1961. Diplomate Am. Bd. Pediat. Intern Toronto (Can.) Gen., 1961-63; resident Hosp. for Sick Children, Toronto, 1963-64, 65-68, Royal Hosp. for Sick Children, Glasgow, Scotland, 1964-65, Children's Hosp. Nat. Med. Ctr., Washington, 1968-69; pediat. Fairfax County (Va.) Health Dept., 1972-82, North Va. Pediat. Assoc., Falls Church, 1982-99, ret., 1999. Family life edn. com. Fairfax County Coun. PTAs, 1982-84. Fellow ACP, Am. Acad. Pediat. (program chair Va. chpt. 1992-93). Presbyterian. Avocations: music, gardening, reading, travel, painting.

BAYLES, JENNIFER LUCENE, museum program director, educator; b. Tokyo, May 26, 1953; d. Lewis Allen Bayles and Rosemary (Beuhler) Fraser; m. Robert Steinfeld, July 4, 1992; children: Noah Isaac Steinfeld, Ezra Milton Steinfeld. BA in Art History with honors, Ind. U., Bloomington, 1976; MA in Art History, U. Mich., 1984, cert. in mus. practice, 1984. Curatorial apprentice Indpls. Mus. Art, 1976; mus. apprentice Portland (Oreg.) Art Mus., 1976-78, asst. curator edn., 1978-81; asst. curator photographic collection dept. art history U. Mich., Ann Arbor, 1981-83, rsch. and editl. asst. Mus. Art, 1982-83; intern dept. mus. edn. Art Inst. Chgo., 1983-84; curator edn. Albright-Knox Art Gallery, Buffalo, 1984—2001, educator spl. projects, 2001—. Horace H. Rackman Grad. scholar, 1981—83, Acad. scholar, U. Mich., 1982. Mem.: Am. Assn. Mus. (regional rep. edn. com. 1979—81). Office: Albright-Knox Art Gallery 1285 Elmwood Ave Buffalo NY 14222-1096 Office Phone: 716-270-8252. E-mail: jbayles@albrightknox.org.

BAYLESS, ALICE PAIGE, psychologist; m. Nathan Wayne Bayless, Aug. 7, 1976; children: Katharine Everett, Andrew Thomas. BA, U. Tex., Austin, 1971; M, SW Tex. State U., San Marcos, 1980; Specialist in Sch. Psychology, Winthrop U., Rock Hill, SC, 1997. School Psychologist II SC Dept. of Edn., 1993, Nationally Certified School Psychologist NASP, 1989, Associate School Psychologist Tex. Edn. Agy., 1980, Special Education Teacher Tex. Edn. Agy., 1976. Sch. psychologist Austin Ind. Sch. Dist., Tex., 1980—93, Richland Sch. Dist. One, Columbia, SC, 1994—98, Lexington/Richland Sch. Dist. 5, Columbia, SC, 1998—. Mem.: NASP. Office: Lexington/Richland Sch Dist 5 Box 938 Ballentine SC 29002 Office Phone: 803-732-8100. Personal E-mail: apbay@bellsouth.net. E-mail: abayless@lex5.k12.sc.us.

BAYLESS, BETSEY, state official; b. Phoenix; BA in Latin Am. Studies and Spanish, U. Ariz., 1966; MPA, Ariz. State U., 1974; DHL (hon.), U. Ariz., 2001. V.p. pub. fin. Peacock, Hislop, Staley & Given, Inc., Phoenix; asst. dir. Ariz. Bd. Regents; acting dir. dept. revenue State of Ariz., dir. dept. adminstrn., sec. of state, 1997—2003; dir. Ariz. Dept. Adminstrn., 2003—. Bd. suprs. Maricopa County, 1989-97, chmn. bd., 1992, 94, vice chair, 1997; mem. Ariz. Bd. Investment, 2003—; bd. dirs. Child Help Ariz.; mem. Nat.bd. dirs. U. Ariz. Coll. of Bus. and Pub. Adminstrn.; adv. bd. Ariz. State U. West. Bd. dirs. Xavier Coll. Preparatory Found., Charter 100, Valley Leadership Class VI, Ariz. Rep. Caucus, Ariz. Women's Forum, 4-H Found., Ariz. Cmty. Found.; mem. leadership bd. U. Ariz. Health Svcs.-Phoenix Campus. Named to Hall of Fame, Ariz. State U. Coll. Pub. Programs; recipient Disting. Citizen award U. Ariz. Alumni Assn., Woman of Yr. award Capitol chpt. Bus. and Profl. Women, Disting. Achievement award NEH Fellowship, Achievement award Nat. Assn. Counties, 1993, Citizen award Bur. Reclamation, 1993, Woman of Achievement award Xavier Coll. Preparatory, 1995. Mem. Phi Beta Kappa (Freeman medal 1966). Republican.

BAYLEY, SUZANNE LUDEY, civic volunteer; b. Vienna, W.Va., Apr. 14, 1920; d. Charles Addison and Patty (Spence) Ludey; m. Thomas Way Bayley, Feb. 7, 1942 (dec.); children: Patty Ruth Bayley Dhondt, Thomas Way Bayley III, Charlotte Ann Bayley Schindelholz. Attended, Rollins Studio of Acting, 1938-1939; BA, Finch Coll., 1940. Founder Children's Theatre Bur., Parkersburg, W.Va., 1946—48; actress, dir., adminstr. Actors Guild of Parkersburg, 1956—57; pres. Actors Guild At Theatre Group, 1962, play reading chair, 1963—65, bldg. chair, 1975—76; mem. founding com. Artsbridge Fine Arts Coun., Parkersburg, 1977. Prodr. Eden on the River, Blennerhassett Drama Assn., 1987. Mem. Jr. League, Parkersburg, 1942-62; v.p. Friends of Blennerhassett, 1975; commr. Blennerhassett Island project, 1988-91, docent, 1988-95. Recipient Lifetime Achievement award Altrusa Club and YWCA, 1992, Lifetime Achievement award for arts Finch Coll., 1996; Cmty. Svc. award named in her honor Actors Guild, 1976. Mem.: Nat. Soc. Arts and Letters, Serra Club Internat. Republican. Roman Catholic.

BAYLOR, LAURIE CAROL, emergency nurse practitioner; b. Waterloo, N.Y., Aug. 25, 1970; d. Laurence Calvin and Nancy Carol (Westmiller) B. LPN, Finger Lakes Area Voc. Ctr., 1989; AAS, Cayuga County Community Coll., 1991. RN, N.Y. LPN Auburn Meml. Hosp., N.Y., nurse, 1991—; LPN Seneca Nursing Home, Waterloo, N.Y. Rep. United Way. Recipient Reubens award. Mem. Nurses Svc. Orgn. Office Phone: 315-255-7211.

BAYM, NINA (NINA BAYM STILLINGER), literature educator, researcher; b. Princeton, N.J., June 14, 1936; d. Leo and Frances (Levinson) Zippin; m. Gordon Baym, June 1, 1958; children— Nancy, Geoffrey; m. Jack Stillinger, May 21, 1971 BA, Cornell U., 1957; MA, Harvard U., 1958, PhD, 1963. Asst. U. Calif.-Berkeley, 1962-63; instr. U. Ill., Urbana, 1963-67, asst. prof. English, 1967-69, assoc. prof., 1969-72, prof., 1972—, Jubilee prof. liberal arts and scis., 1989—, dir. Sch. Humanities Urbana, 1976-87, sr. Univ. scholar, 1985, assoc. Ctr. Advanced Study, 1989-90, permanent prof. Ctr. Advanced Study, 1997—2004, Swanlund Endowed chair, 1997—2004. Author: The Shape of Hawthorne's Career, 1976, Woman's Fiction: A Guide to Novels By and About Women in America, 1978, 2d rev. edit., 1993, Novels, Readers and Reviewers: Responses to Fiction in Antebellum America, 1984, The Scarlet Letter: A Reading, 1986, Feminism and American Literary History, 1992, American Women Writers and the Work of History, 1790-1860, 1995, American Women of Letters and the 19th Century Sciences, 2002; gen. editor: Norton Anthology of American Literature; sr. editor Am. Nat. Biography; also author essays, edits., revs.; mem. editl. bd. Am. Quar., New Eng. Quar., Legacy, A Jour. of 19th Century Am. Women Writers, Jour. Aesthetic Edn. Am. Lit., Tulsa Studies in Women's Lit., Am. Studies, Studies Am. Fiction, Am. Periodicals, Hemingway Rev., Resources for Am. Lit. Study, Am. Lit. History, Cambridge U.P. Studies in Am. Lit. and Culture; mem. editl. adv. bd. PMLA. Guggenheim fellow, 1975-76, AAUW hon. fellow, 1975-76, NEH fellow, 1982-83; rec pient Arnold O. Beckman award U. Ill., 1992-93, Hubbell Lifetime Achievement medal, Am. Let. Sect., 2000. Mem. MLA (exec. com. 19th century Am. Lit. divsn., chmn. 1984, chmn. Am. Lit. sect. 1984, Hubbell Lifetime Achievement medal 2000), Am. Studies Assn. (exec. com. 1982-84, nominating com. 1991-93), Am. Lit. Assn., Am. Antiquarian Soc., Mass. Hist. Soc., Nathaniel Hawthorne Soc. (adv. bd.), Western Lit. Assn., Mortar Bd., Phi Kappa Phi, Phi Beta Kappa. Office Phone: 217-244-7328, 217-333-2391. Business E-Mail: baymnina@uiuc.edu.

BAYMILLER, LYNDA DOERN, social worker; b. Milw., July 6, 1943; d. Ronald Oliver and Marian Elizabeth (Doern) Baymiller. Student, U. Hawaii, 1962, Mich. State U., 1965; BA, U. Wis., 1965, MSW, 1969. Vol. Peace Corps, Chile, 1965—67; social worker Luth. Social Svcs. Wis. and Upper Mich., Milw., 1969—77, contract social worker, 1978—79; dist. supr. Childrens Svc. Soc. Wis., Kenosha, 1977—78; supr. social work Sauk County Dept. Human Svcs., Baraboo, Wis., 1979—90; mgr. sales and relief -trainee Wal-Mart, 1992—93, cashier, 1993—. Author: (with Clara Amelia Hess) Now-Won, A Collection of Feeling Poetry, 1973. Bd. dirs. Sauk County Mental Health Assn., 1979-84; mem. Harmony chpt. Sweet Adelines, West Allis, Wis., 1970-75, pres. chpt., 1971; pres. bd. dirs. Growing Place Day Care Ctr., Kenosha, 1977-78; mem. Baraboo Centennial Com., 1982; pres. bd. dirs. Laubach Lit. Coun., Baraboo, 1986-88; mem. Sauk County Humane Soc., 1987—2006, sec., 1988-90. Mem. NASW, Acad. Cert. Social Workers, AAUW (br. sec. 1982-84), U. Wis. Alumni Assn. (life), Am. Legion Aux., DAR, Nat. Soc. Magna Carta Dames, Eddy Family Assn. (life), Nat. Soc. Ancient and Hon. Arty. Co. Mass. (life), Wis. Soc. Daus. of 1812 (rec. sec. 1994-96), Sauk County Hist. Soc., Internat. Crane Found. (patron), Daus. Colonial Wars, Daus. Am. Colonists, Zool. Soc. Milwaukee County (life, bd. dirs. Zoo Pride 1975-77), Am. Bus. Women's Assn., Order Ea. Star (grad. rep. Miss. in Wis. 1988-90), Order White Shrine of Jerusalem, Cameo Club, Baraboo Citizens, Police and Fire Acad. Alumni Assn., Alpha Xi Delta.

BAYNE, KATHRYN ANN, elementary school educator; b. Berlin, NH, Nov. 16, 1971; d. Earl Lester and Marion Rebecca Hanson; m. John Stuart Bayne, Apr. 30, 1994; children: Hailey Lynn, Caroline Paige. BS in Crops, Soil and Environ. Scis., Va. Tech. U., Blacksburg, 1993. Tchr. Victoria Elem. Sch., Va., 1994—. Mem. adv. bd. Southside Va. CC, Keysville, Va., 2003—. Mem.: Nat. Sci. Tchr. Assn., Va. Assn. Sci. Tchrs. Avocations: gardening, cooking, travel. Home: 622 Courthouse Rd Chase City VA 23924 Office: Victoria Elem Sch 1521 8th St Victoria VA 23974

BAYS, JUNE MARIE, counselor, social worker; b. LaSalle, Ill., Feb. 16, 1941; d. John Frederick and Esther Marie Nielsen; m. James Philip Bays, June 29, 1963; children: Timothy James, Daniel Mark. Diploma in Nursing, Evanston Hosp. Sch. Nursing, 1962; BS, Western Mich. U., 1983, MSW, 1986. Lic. clin. social worker, Ind. Med. surg. nurse Evanston Hosp., 1962-63; psychiat. staff nurse U. Hosp., Madison, Wis., 1963-65, Madison Gen. Hosp., 1965-66; therapist Madison Ctr., South Bend, Ind., 1986-90; social work clin. specialist U. N.C. Hosp., Chapel Hill, 1990-91; therapist Samaritan Counseling Ctr., South Bend, Ind., 1991-95, Bethel Coll. Counseling Ctr., Mishawaka, Ind., 1995—. Mem. NASW, Am. Assn. Christian Counselors. Avocations: reading, sewing, travel, art. Office: Bethel Coll Counseling Ctr 1001 W Mckinley Ave Mishawaka IN 46545-5509

BAYS, LOUISE MARIE, elementary school educator; b. Reading, Pa., June 13, 1945; d. Leo and Marie Louise Disend; children: Colleen Michelle Merays, Ryan Michael. BS, West Chester State U., Pa., 1967; MEd, Duke U., Durham, N.C., 1968. Tchr. Barron Elem. Sch., Hampton, Va., 1968—70, Lafayette and Keller Elem. Sch., San Diego, 1970—76; substitute tchr. Nassau County Sch., Nassau County, NY, 1982—84; tchr. sci., social studies and religion Diocese of Bklyn., Cambria Heights, NY, 1984—. CCD tchr. Cath. Ch., Roosevelt, NY, 1986—89, Cambria Hts., 1995—2002. Mem.: Nat. Sci. Tchrs. Assn., N.Y. State Tchrs. Assn. Roman Catholic. Avocations: reading, gardening, travel. Office Phone: 718-527-0123.

BAYSINGER, KARA, lawyer; b. St. Cloud, Minn., Aug. 26, 1966; BA in Polit. Sci., U. Mich., 1988; JD, Loyola U., 1994. Bar: Ill. 1994, Calif. 1999. Asst. to gen. counsel Provident Ins. Co., Waukegan, Ill., 1988—90; compliance analyst Benefit Trust Life Ins. Co., Lake Forest, Ill.; asst. v.p. legal and regulatory affairs Celtic Life Ins. Co.; dir.-counsel product approval & compliance Bankers Life and Casualty Co., 1994—97; spl. counsel ins. regulatory practice group Long & Levit LLP, 1997; ptnr. Sonnenschein Nath & Rosenthal LLP, San Francisco, vice chair Ins. Practice Group. Co-chair Calif. adv. bd. BizWorld. Mem.: Calif. Bar Assn., Ill. Bar Assn. Office: Sonnenschein Nath & Rosenthal LLP 685 Market St, 6th Fl San Francisco CA 94105 Office Phone: 415-882-2475. Office Fax: 415-543-5472. Business E-Mail: kbaysinger@sonnenschein.com.

BAZAN, ANGELA LYNN, social studies educator; b. Madison, Wis., Apr. 6, 1973; d. Edward Max Bazan; 1 child, Avery Lynn. BSc in Edn., U. Wis., Whitewater, 1998. Tchr. Deerfield H.S., Wis., 1998—. V.p., bd. dirs. Muscular Dystrophy Assn., Madison, Wis., 1999. Grantee, U. Wis. Whitewater/State Hist. Soc. of Wis., 2003—. Mem.: Orgn. Am. Historians (licentiate). Liberal. Catholic. Office: Deerfield Cmty Schs 300 Simonson Blvd Deerfield WI 53558 Office Phone: 608-764-5431. Office Fax: 608-764-5433. Business E-Mail: bazana@deerfield.k12.wi.us.

BAZEMORE, TRUDY MCCONNELL, librarian; d. Charlie Arthur and Elizabeth Bruns McConnell; m. John Everett Bazemore, Jr., Nov. 5, 1983. BA in Interdisciplinary studies magna cum laude, Coastal Carolina U., Conway, S.C., 2001. Libr., tech. svcs. Georgetown Pub. Libr., SC, 1978—89, libr., reference svcs., 1989—93, head, pub. svcs., 1993—2001, asst. dir., 2001—. Mem.: Nat. Geneal. Soc., Founding Families of S.C., S.C. Hist. Soc., Interagency Coun., Am. Libr. Assn., Ribbon Club of Georgetown, Phi Theta Kappa, Alpha Sigma Lambda, Phi Sigma Tau. Methodist. Avocations: genealogy, gemology, photography, travel, art. Office: Georgetown County Pub Libr 405 Cleland St Georgetown SC 29440

BAZIK, EDNA FRANCES, mathematician, educator; b. Streator, Ill., Dec. 26, 1946; d. Andrew and Anna Frances (Vagasky) B.; BSEd, Ill. State U, 1969; postgrad. Hamilton Coll., summer 1971, Ill. State U., 1972, Augustana Coll., summer 1973; MEd, U. Ill., 1972; PhD, So. Ill. U., 1976, gen. adminstrv. cert., 1980. Tchr. math. Northlawn Jr. High Sch., Streator, 1969-74; instr. math. edn. So. Ill. U., 1974-76; asst. prof. math. Concordia U., 1976-78; asst. prof. math. Ill. State U., Normal, 1978-85; assoc. prof. math. Eastern Ill. U., 1985-88; math. specialist, coord. Oak Park (Ill.) Pub. Schs., 1988-89; math coord. Hinsdale Sch. Dist. 181, 19892005; assoc. prof. math. edn. Nat. Louis U., Lisle, Ill., 2005—; coord. inservice presentations, workshops for tchrs.; cons. to sch. dists. NSF grantee, 1980—. Presdl. award NSF, 1990. Mem. AAUP, Ill. State Bd. Edn. (mem. assessment team math. 1998—), Assn. Tchr. Educators, Ill. Assn. Tchr. Educators, Nat. Coun. Tchrs. Math. (chair elections com. 1990-91, Ill. Coun. Tchrs. Math. (mem. governing bd.,chmn. 2004-05, dir. coll. and univ. level), Math. Assn. Am., Nat. Coun. Suprs. Math., NEA, Ill. Edn. Assn., Sch. Sci. and Math. Assn., U.S. Metric Assn., Am. Ednl. Rsch. Assn., Assn. Supervision and Curriculum Devel., Ill. Assn. Supervision and Curriculum Devel., Ill. Standards Achievement Test Math Validation Com., Ill. State Bd. Edn. Math. Assessment Com., Assn. Childhood Edn. Internat., Coun. Exceptional Children, Ill. Curriculum Coun., Rsch. Coun. Diagnostic and Prescriptive Math., Kappa Delta Pi, Phi Delta Kappa (pres. Ill. State U. chpt. 1982-83), Pi Mu Epsilon, Delta Kappa Gamma, Phi Kappa Phi. Republican. Lutheran. Co-author: Elementary Mathematical Methods, 1978, Mind Over Math, 1980, Teaching Mathematics to Children with Special Needs, 1983, Step-by-Step: Addition, 1984, Step-by-Step: Subtraction, 1984, Step-by-Step: Multiplication, 1984, Step-by-Step: Division, 1984, Problem-Solving Sourcebook, 1985, Step-by-Step: Fractions, 1987, Step-by-Step: Decimals, 1988. Home: 1501 Darien Lake Dr Darien IL 60561-5069 Office: Nat-Louis Univ Math Edn Program Coord 850 Warrenville Rd Lisle IL 60532 Office Phone: 630-874-4350. Business E-Mail: edna.bazik@nl.edu.

BAZZONE, THERESA (TERRY) A., sales executive; Student, Bentley Coll. Sales mgr. Corp. Software, Inc., 1987—92; dir. software product mktg. div. Tech Data Corp., Clearwater, Fla., 1992—96, v.p., gen. mgr. strategic bus. dev. unit, 1996—2002, sr. v.p. US sales, 2002—. Office: Tech Data Corp 5350 Tech Data Rd Clearwater FL 33760-3122

BEACH, JEAN MRHA, food products executive; BA, Wellesley Coll.; MA in Fin. and Acctg., U. Chgo. V.p. Enron Upstream Products; sr. v.p. commodity and trading risk mgmt. Tyson Foods, Inc., Springdale, Ark., 2002—. Office: Tyson Foods Inc 2210 W Oaklawn Dr Springdale AR 72762-6999

BEACH, LISA FORSTER (ELIZABETH FORSTER BEACH), artist, educator; b. Ypsilanti, Mich., Feb. 3, 1937; d. Ralph Dale and Mildred E. Bruce; m. Donald M. Forster, Apr. 19, 1962 (div. June 1988); children: Alan, Kenneth, Susan; m. David E. Beach, Feb. 14, 1989. BS in Art Edn., Edinboro U. of Pa., 1959; MFA, Rochester Inst. Tech., 1987. Art instr. Mercer (Pa.) Sch. Sys., 1959-60, Irondequoit (N.Y.) Pub. Schs., 1961-62; painting instr. Meml. Art Gallery of U. of Rochester, Rochester, N.Y., 1983-85; tchg. asst. Edgar Whitney Painting Tours, 1983-84; art instr., dir. Topnotch Resport and Spa, Stowe, Vt., 1989-95; painting instr. Stowe Hollow Studio, 1989—; drawing and painting instr. Vt. Inst. Life Long Learning Elder Hostel, Stowe, 1992—; painting instr. C.C. Vt., 1997—. Ski instr. Stowe Mt. Resort, 1990—; mem. visual arts com. Helen Day Art Ctr., Stowe, 1988—; membership campaign chmn. Meml. Art Gallery of U. of Rochester, Rochester, 1971; chmn. art divsn. PBS Channel 21 Auction, Rochester, 1972. Mem. Nat. Watercolor Soc. (signature mem.), No. Vt. Artists, Profl. Ski Instrs. Am. (cert. level II). Avocations: skiing, hiking, tennis, reading, windsurfing. Office: Stowe Hollow Studio 288 Upper Pinnacle Rd Stowe VT 05672-4529

BEACH, MARGARET SMITH, retired language educator; b. Decaturville, Tenn., Dec. 9, 1937; d. Luther Grant and Eva Irene Mallard; m. James Edward Smith (dec. 1960); children: James Edward III(dec.), John Fitzgerald; m. John D. Beach, July 26, 1975; stepchildren: John D. Jr., Michael Jerome. BA in English, Agrl. and Indsl. State U., Tenn., 1961; MS in Psychology, Tenn. State U., 1982. English and French tchr. Townsend HS, Winchester, Tenn., 1959—61, Nashville Christian Inst., 1961—63; part-time English tchr. Burt HS, Clarksville, Tenn., 1963—64; tchr. Cobb Elem. Sch., Clarksville, Tenn., 1963—69; English and French tchr. Wharton HS, Nashville, 1969—70, Neely's Bend Jr. HS, Madison, Tenn., 1970—91; ret., 1991. Chairperson English dept. Neely's Bend Jr. Mid. Sch., Madison, Tenn., 1974—76; cheerleader co-sponsor Neely's Bend Jr. HS, Madison, Tenn., 1975—76; English accreditation chairperson Neely's Bend Mid. Sch., Madison, Tenn., 1978—79, sch. newspaper sponsor, 1980—81; faculty rep. Tchrs. Union, Nashville, 1978—80; writer proficiency test items Metro. Nashville Schs., 1984—85. Author: (book) Creative Poems, 1974, Ethnic Poetry for All, 1998, Religious Poems of Faith, 2001; poet Our World's Best Loved Poems, 1983. Recipient Cert. of Appreciation, Met. Bd. of Edn., 1991, Award of Appreciation, Alumni Assn., 1992, 1996, 2002, Award of Dedication, 1996, Cert. of Appreciation, Nat. Coun. of Tchrs. of English, 1998, Cert. of Merit, Tenn. Ret. Tchrs. Assn., 2000—01. Mem.: Ret. Tchrs. Assn. Avocations: writing, reading, storytelling, poetry, performing. Office: Agape Pearl Publ PO Box 280653 Nashville TN 37228 Office Phone: 615-242-2307. E-mail: mrgrtmlmsb@aol.com.

BEACH, NANCY ANN HELEN, special education educator; b. Kansas City, Kans., Nov. 10, 1944; d. Charles Andrew and Victoria Virginia (Handzel) Nugent; divorced; children: Cathe, Denise, Michelle. AA, East Los Angeles Coll., 1964; BS, Calif. State U., L.A., 1966; postgrad., UCLA, 1966-70. Cert. English teaching credential (life). Tchr. Calif. Pub. Schs., San Gabriel Valley, 1966-77; recreation therapist State of Calif., Pomona, 1966-67; recreation supr. City of Baldwin Park (Calif.), 1967-70; restaurant owner Baldwin Park, 1977; instr. English So. Bay Coll., Baldwin Park, 1984-89; instr. English and success skills Eldorado Coll., West Covina, Calif., 1989-90; tchr. blind and retarded spl. edn. Los Angeles County Schs., 1990—. Author: Reading Skills, 1971. Bd. dirs. pub. rels. com. CAP, El Monte, Calif., 1960-64. Democrat. Avocation: race car driving.

BEACH, REGINA LEE, librarian; b. Georgetown, Ohio, Dec. 22, 1963; d. H. LeRoy and R. Jean (Wardlow) B. BSBA, BA, Ohio No. U., 1987; MLS, Kent State U., 1990; MS in Bus. Adminstrn., Miss. State U., 1999. Serials cataloger, libr. U. Mich., Ann Arbor, 1990-92; libr. Allen Correctional Inst., Lima, Ohio, 1993-94; serials cataloger, libr. Miss. State U., Mississippi State, 1994-99; head info. tech., libr. U. Ark., Little Rock, 1999—2001; head tech. svcs. and systems Tex. A&M U., Kingsville, 2001—. Mem. ALA, ASIS, Southeastern Libr. Assn., Ark. Libr. Assn. Avocations: walking, running, swimming, aerobics, camping. Office: MSC 197 Jernigan Libr Tex A&M U Kingsville TX 78363

BEACHAM, JANIS SCHLUETER, educational consultant; b. St. Louis, Oct. 15, 1952; d. Elmer John and Alice Grace Schlueter; m. Ralph Howard Beacham, Aug. 11, 1979; children: Wendy Beacham Seaba, Melissa Beacham Smith, Tristan Micheal. BS in Edn., Ctrl. Mo. State U., Warrensburg, 1974, MS in Adult Edn., 1979; PhD, U. Mo., Kansas City, 1987. Cert. adult basic edn. tchr. Mo. Dept. of Elem. and Secondary Edn., 1979, career and tech. edn. dir. Mo. Dept. of Elem. and Secondary Edn., 1986. Tchr. jr. and sr. high math. Sherwood Jr./Sr. H.S., Creighton, Mo., 1974—76; comm. and computational skills ctr. coord./instr. Cass County Area Vocat./Tech. Sch., Harrisonville, Mo., 1976—79; instr. adult basic edn. Raytown Adult Learning Ctr., Harrisonville, Mo., 1977—81; rsch. assoc. U. Mo., Kansas City, 1979—81; industry tng. specialist GM High Tech Tng. Ctr., Wentzville, Mo., 1982—84; adminstrv. asst. II-vocat. edn. St. Louis Pub. Schs., 1984—87; asst. to v.p. acad. affairs Lewis & Clark C.C., Godfrey, Ill., 1987—89; corp. dir. of edn. Nat. Tng. Ctr., St. Louis, 1989—90; industry tng. and devel. specialist Beacham & Assocs., St. Louis, 1990—97; constrn. tng. tech prep consortium coord. Associated Gen. Contractors, St. Louis, 1997—99; edn. cons. Beacham & Assocs., St. Louis, 1999—. Spl. needs divsn. publs. com. mem. Am. Career, 1976—2000; evaluator career edn. infusion project Kansas City, Mo. Pub. Schs., 1980—81; coord. study tour: exemplary programs for serving the handicapped and disadvantaged Nat. Ctr. for Rsch. in Vocat. Edn., Ohio State U., 1984; com. chairperson to develop vocat. supplemental tchr. position description Mo. Dept. of Vocat. and Tech. Edn., 1986—87; exec. bd. mem. Mo. Vocat. Assn., 1981—82; pres. Mo. Vocat. Spl. Needs Assn., 1982—83; evaluation team mem. Mo. Dept. of Vocat. and Tech. Edn., 1986—87; extemporaneous speaking contest edn. chairperson SkillsUSA, Kansas City, Mo., 1994—2003; ann. conf. presenter Nat. Tech Prep Network, Kansas City, Mo., 1998; Mo. sch. improvement evaluation team Mo. Dept. of Elem. and Secondary Edn., 1999—2003; extemporaneous speaking contest tech. chairperson SkillsUSA, Kansas City, Mo., 1999—2003; bd. dirs. Ill. Coun. of Vocat. Adminstrs. Mem. So. Poverty Law Ctr., Montgomery, Ala., 2004—06, Amnesty Internat.; family ptnr. Habitat for Humanity, Kansas City, Kans., 2002—05; den leader Boy Scouts of Am., Olathe, Kans., 2002—06; bd. dirs. Unidos En Cristo (Hispanic Ministry), Olathe, Kans., 2003—06. Recipient Example That Works award, St. Louis Sch.-To-Careers Inc., 1999, 10 Years of Svc. award, Skills USA, 2003; grantee, U.S. Dept. of Edn., 1976-1979, Nat. Ctr. for Rsch. in Vocat. Edn., Ohio State U., 1984-1987; David and Vera Mace grant, U. Mo.-Kansas City Women's Coun., 1981. Mem.: ASCD, AAUW, NAFE, Phi Delta Kappa. Achievements include development and implementation of National Exemplary Program for Disadvantaged and Handicapped, National Center for Research in Vocational Education, Ohio State University. Avocations: travel, sailing, reading. Office: Beacham & Assocs Olathe KS 66061 Personal E-mail: tbeachargh@aol.com.

BEAIRD, DIAN SANDERS, middle school educator; b. Murchison, Tex., Dec. 18, 1946; d. Jessie Jackson and Lola Mae (Burton) Sanders; m. Richard Lewis Cox, May 24, 1969 (div. Nov. 1993); 1 child, Stuart Scott; m. Charles A. Beaird, Dec. 1994. AA, Kilgore Jr. Coll., 1967; BA, Stephen F. Austin State U., 1969, MEd, 1983. Cert. provisional gen. elem. edn., provisional h.s. history, govt. and polit. sci. Tchr. 8th grade Am. history and 7th grade Tex. history Chapel Hill Ind. Sch. Dist., Tyler, Tex., 1970-79; tchr. 6th-7th grade regular, advanced, remedial reading Sabine Ind. Sch. Dist., Gladewater, Tex., 1981—. Mem., tutor East Tex. Literacy Coun., Longview, 1992—; sec. Sabine Jr. High PTO, Gladewater, 1990-91; faculty sponsor cheerleaders Chapel Hill Ind. Sch. Dist., Tyler, 1970-73, rep. curriculum com., 1976, historian PTO, 1974; mem. anthology com. N.J. Writing Project in Tex., Kilgore, 1991; selected hostess Internat. Reading Conf., Tucson, 1992. Presenter: The Toothpaste Millionaire, 1992; contbr.: (short story) Vocies from the Heart, 1991. Leader Girl Scouts Am., Tyler, 1973; counselor Camp Natowa-Campfire Girls, Big Sandy, Tex., 1970; dir. Bible Sch., 1st Meth. Ch., Overton, Tex., 1980; sec. Young Dems., Kilgore, 1965-67, Gregg County Dems, 2004-; actress Gallery Theater, Jefferson, Tex.; mem. Opera House Theater and Galley Theater, 1992—, bd. dirs., 1996—; bd. dirs. Opera House, 1996. Named Outstanding Tchr. in Tex., Macmillan/McGraw Hill, 1991, Tchr. of Month Kilgore Rotary Club, 2005, Globe Tchr. of Yr., 2004-2005; Free Enterprise Forum scholar East Tex. Bapt. U., 1991. Mem. Internat. Reading Assn. (presenter 1992), Tex. Mid. Sch. Assn., Piney Woods Reading Coun., Tex. State Tchrs. Assn. (campus rep. 1990—, sec. Chapel Hill Ind. Sch. Dist. 1971-72), Laubach Literacy Action, Delta Kappa Gamma. Avocations: reading, travel, camping, acting. Home: PO Box 1146 Hallsville TX 75650-1146 Office: Sabine Jr H S RR 1 Box 189 Gladewater TX 75647-9723

BEAL, CAROL ANN, lawyer; b. N.Y.C., Aug. 8, 1962; d. Harry Steven and Margot Sanders; m. Kenneth I. Beal, Dc. 4, 1988; children: Zachary, Eric. BA in Psychology, SUNY, Binghamton, 1983; JD, St. John's U., 1986. Bar: N.Y. 1987, U.S. Dist. Ct. (ea. dist.) Conn. Sr. assoc. A.F. Pennisi, Forest Hills, N.Y., 1986-88, jr. ptnr., 1988-90; ptnr. C.A. Beal, Forest Hills, 1990-93, Beal & Beal, Jericho, N.Y., 1993—. Lectr. on landlord-tenant law, co-operatives and condominiums, wills, trusts and estates, 1986—. Named Bus. Woman of Yr., N.Y. State Bus. Adv. Counsel, 2003; recipient Recognition cert., 2003, 2005. Mem. Queens Bar Assn., Landlord Tenant Assn., Nassau Bar Assn., Syosset Tennis Acad. Avocations: tennis, skiing. Office: Beal & Beal 34 Birchwood Park Cres Jericho NY 11753-2343 E-mail: carolabeal@aol.com.

BEAL, DEBORAH L., environmental scientist, educator; b. Flint, Mich. d. Lillia Leibig; m. Kent Elwood, June 14, 1998; children: Megan Elwood-Madden, David Elwood, Lauren. PhD, U. Mo., Columbia, 1991. Asst. prof. Western Ill. U., Macomb, Ill., 1990—91, Ill. Coll., Jacksonville, Ill., 1991—96, prof. and chair environ. studies, 2003—. Author web based education modules. Recipient Alumni Achievement award, Frank Excellence in Tchg. award; grantee, NSF, 2000—01. Achievements include research in bioacoustics in the southern flying squirrel. Office: Ill Col 1101 W Coll Jacksonville IL 62650 Office Phone: 217-245-3463.

BEAL, SHANNON, nursing educator; d. Terry and Kay Roper; children from previous marriage: Rocky, Randy. MSN, U. Phoenix, 2002. RN N.Mex Bd. Nursing, 1994. Staff nurse Carlsbad Med. Ctr., N.Mex., 1993—2006; field nurse Lakeview Christian Home Health, 1997—2006; asst. prof. nursing N. Mex. State U., 2006—. Office: N Mex State Univ Carlsbad 1500 Univ Dr Carlsbad NM 88220 Office Phone: 505-234-9300.

BEALE, JUDITH ANN, music educator; b. Natrona Hghts., Pa., Apr. 11, 1950; d. William Ray and Theoris Elaine Plants; m. Philip Albion Beale (div.); children: Philip Albion Jr.(dec.), David Morgan. BS, Geneva Coll., Beaver Falls, Pa., 1972; MMus. Edn., Ga. State U., Atlanta, 1977. Cert. Orff Tchr. Tng. Am. Orff Schulwerk Assn., Cleve. Music tchr. Beulah Elem. Sch., Douglasville, Ga., 1972—77, Arbor Sta. Elem. Sch., Douglasville, Ga., 1977—87, Mt. Carmel Elem. Sch., Douglasville, Ga., 1984—88, Murdock Elem. Sch., Marietta, Ga., 1990—96, Ford Elem. Sch., Acworth, Ga., 1996—; Orff Level I Movement instr. U. Memphis, Tenn., 2004, U. Ga., Athens, 2005—; Orff Level I and II Movement instr. Cobb County Schs., Marietta, 2005—. Clinician for coll. workshops GMEA, Atlanta AOSA. Mem. chorus and ensemble sect. leader Ga. Festival Chorus, Marietta, 1999—; orch. clarinetist Mt. Parah N. Ch. of God, Marietta, 1996—. Named Tchr. of Year, Arbor Sta. Elem. Sch., Douglasville, Ga., 1983, Murdock Elem. Sch., 1996, Lifetime Mem., PTA, 1995. Mem.: Profl. Assn. Ga. Educators, Ga. Music Educators Assn. (state elem. chair 1999—2001), Atlanta Am. Orff Schulwerk Assn. (asst. treas. 1999—, scholarship award), Alpha Kappa of Alpha Delta Kappa. Republican. Avocations: drawing, fabric painting, sewing, swimming. Home: 1659 Heyford Cir Kennesaw GA 30152 Office: Ford Elem Sch 1345 Mars Hill Rd Acworth GA 30101

BEALL, CYNTHIA, anthropologist, educator; b. Urbana, Ill., Aug. 21, 1949; d. John Wood and J. Alene (Beachler) Beall. BA in Biology, U. Pa., 1970; MA in Anthropology, Pa. State U., 1972, PhD in Anthropology, 1976. Asst. prof. Case Western Res. U., Cleve., 1976—82, assoc. prof. of anthropology, 1982—87, prof. anthropology, 1987—. Co-editor: Jour. of Cross-Cultural Gerontology, 1986—95; contbr. articles to profl. jours. Active Internat. Rsch. Exch. Program, 1990, 1991. Fellow Nat. Program for Advanced Study and Rsch. in China, NAS, 1986—87, 1997; Rsch. grantee, NSF, 1981, 1983, 1986—87, 1993—95, 1997, 2000, 2002, 2005, Am. Fedn. for Aging Rsch., 1983, 1986, Nat. Geog. Soc., 1983, 1986—87, 1993, 1995. Fellow: AAAS; mem.: NAS (coun. 2002—05), Internat. Coun. Sci. (exec. bd. 2005—), Assn. Anthropology and Gerontology, Soc. Study Human Biology, Human Biology Coun. (exec. com. 1989—92, pres. 1992—94), Am. Assn. Phys. Anthropology (exec. com. 1989—92), Am. Anthrop. Assn., Am. Philo. Soc. Achievements include research in human adaptation to high altitude. Office: Case Western Res U Dept Anthropology 238 Mather Meml Bldg Cleveland OH 44106-7125 Business E-Mail: cmb2@case.edu.

BEALL, GRACE CARTER, business educator; b. Birmingham, Ala., Sept. 12, 1928; d. Edgar T. and Kate (Eubank) Carter; m. Vernon D. Beall, Aug. 27, 1948; children: Robert, Timothy. BS, La. Coll., 1949; MEd, La. State U., 1955; postgrad., U. Wis., East Tex. State U., Temple U., Southwestern Bapt. Theol. Sem., U. Ga. Tchr., asst. prin. Franklin Parish Sch. Bd., Crowville, La., 1949-54; tchr. Grant Parish Sch. Bd., Dry Prong, La., 1954-55; tchr., coord. Rapides Parish Sch. Bd., Pineville, La., 1955-73; assoc. prof. La. Coll., Pineville, 1974-93, past vice chair of faculty, prof. emeritus, 1993—. Cons. in field; sec.-treas. Gulf Coast Athletic Conf., 1983—, Nat. Assn. Intercollegiate Athletics Dist. 30, 1983—. Vice chair Civil Svc. Bd., Pineville, La., 1975—; vol. chaplain assoc. Rapides Regional Med. Ctr., Alexandria, La., 1993—. Recipient Outstanding Svc. award La. Vocat. Assn., 1971, Outstanding Secondary Educators Am., 1973. Mem. AAUP (past sec.), La. Bapt. Hist. Assn. (pres., bd. dirs.), La. Coll. Ret. Faculty Assn. (pres. 1998—), Phi Delta Kappa (historian), Delta Kappa Gamma (past pres.), Kappa Kappa Iota, Omicron Delta Kappa, Delta Mu Delta. Republican. Baptist. Avocations: reading, travel, volunteer work. Home: 3232 Crestview Dr Pineville LA 71360-5804

BEALL, PAMELA HONN, psychologist, consultant; b. Mattoon, Ill., Mar. 24, 1955; d. Kenneth Franklin and Dorothy Marie (Linder) Honn; m. Thomas Allen Beall IV, June 23, 1985; children: Christopher Allen, Brittany Alane. BS in Psychology, Evangel Coll., Springfield, Mo., 1976; MS in Edn., Ea. Ill. U., Charleston, 1979. Nat. cert. counselor; lic. clin. profl. counselor. Community care coord. East Ctrl. Ill. Area Agy. on Aging, Bloomington, 1979-80; outpatient therapist Iroquois Mental Health Ctr., Watseka, Ill., 1981-86, 90-91, cons., part-time outpatient therapist, 1987-89, 91-93; program psychologist Paxaton (Ill.) Community Hosp., 1986-87; coord. good beginnings program Ctr. for Children's Svcs., Danville, Ill., 1987-88; psychol. cons., Milford, Ill., 1993—. Instr. psychology Kankakee (Ill.) C.C., 1981-84, 89, Danville Area C.C., 1983-86; cons. evaluator Dept. Rehab. Svcs., Danville, 1981-85; mem. exec. bd. Tgn. and Edn. Coordinating Com., Champaign, Ill., 1985-93. Vol. reading programs sch. sys. Milford; tchr. religion Milford Christian Ch., 1992—2002, vocal soloist, music and drama ministry, 1992—2002. Mem. ACA, Ill. Assn. Mental Health Counselors, Evangel Coll. Alumni Assn. Avocations: hiking, playwriting, costume design, set construction, mentoring. Home: RR 3 Box 52D Milford IL 60953-9431

BEALS, BETSY JONES, elementary school educator; b. Durham, N.C., Mar. 6, 1946; d. Robert Monroe and Pauline Mae (Lawrence) Jones; m. Allen Mason Beals Jr., June 19, 1966; 1 child, Aric. Student, Elon Coll., 1964-66, N.C. State U., 1966-67; BA in Edn., U. N.C., 1969. Cert. mentor tchr., Nat. Bd. Cert. EMC/PE 2001. Coord. elem. phys. edn. Chapel Hill Pub. Schs., NC, 1968-69; instr. phys. edn. Ravenscroft Sch., Raleigh, NC, 1970—82; dir. Camp Adventure, Raleigh, 1976-78, Ravenscroft Camp, Raleigh, 1978-82; elem. phys. edn. specialist Lincoln Heights Gifted and Talented Magnet Sch., Fuquay-Varina, N.C., 1982-83, Northwoods Elem. Sch., Cary, N.C., 1983—; mentor Wake County Pub. Sch., Raleigh, 1985—. Workshop cons., Cary, 1977—; historian Phys. Edn. Leadership Tng., Reidsville, N.C., 1985—, bd. dirs. and fall inspirational leader, 1988—. Author: Simple Soccer, 1989, Fabulous Fitness Fun, 1990; editor (newspaper) N.C. Pepi-gram, 1989-91. Sec. Reedy Creek Community, Cary, 1985-89; vice-chmn. Cedar Fork Twp., Morrisville, N.C.; chair com. Cary Clean Keep Am. Beautiful, 1986-89; dir. events Wake County Spl. Olympics; vol. Sr. Games. Recipient Tchr. of Yr. awards Lincoln Heights Elem., 1982, Northwood Elem., 1983 and 1987, N.C. Gov.'s Fitness award, 1989, 91, Tchr. of the Yr., Wake County Physical Edn., 2003, Tchr. of the Yr., Southern Dist.-NASPE Elem. Physical Edn., 2005 Mem. ASCD, AAHPERD (Elem. Tchr. of the Yr. 2004, Honor award, 2005), N.C. Alliance Health, Phys. Edn., Recreation and Dance (coord. PEPI, sec. 1987-89, 91-92), Raleigh Boychoir (chair com. 1985-88). Republican. Mem. United Ch. of Christ. Avocations: travel, photography, golf, skiing, dance. Home: 2335 Old Reedy Creek Rd Cary NC 27513-2113 Office: Northwoods Elem Sch 8850 Old Chapel Hill Rd Cary NC 27513-3705

BEALS, JENNIFER, actress; b. Chgo., Dec. 19, 1963; m. Alexandre Rockwell, 1986 (div. 1996); m. Ken L. Dixon, 1998; 1 child. Grad. in Am. Lit., Yale U. Actress: (films) My Bodyguard, 1980, Flashdance, 1983, The Bride, 1985, Split Decisions, 1988, La Partita, 1988, Sons, 1989, Vampire's Kiss, 1989, Dr. M, 1990, Blood and Concrete, 1991, Day of Atonement, 1992, In the Soup, 1992, Dear Diary, 1994, Dead on Sight, 1994, Mrs. Parker and the Vicious Circle, 1994, Devil in a Blue Dress, 1995, Let it Be Me, 1995, Four Rooms, 1995, Arabian Knight, 1995, Wishful Thinking, 1996, The Search for One-eye Jimmy, 1996, The Prophecy II, 1998, Body and Soul, 1998, The Last Days of Disco, 1998, Fear of Flying, 1999, Something More, 1999, Without Malice, 2000, Militia, 2000, Out of Line, 2001, The Anniversary Party, 2001, 13 Moons, 2002, Roger Dodger, 2002, Runaway Jury, 2003, Catch That Kid, 2004, Break a Leg, 2005, Desolation Sound, 2005, The Grudge 2, 2006; (TV movies) La Madonne et le dragon, 1990, Terror Stalks the Class Reunion, 1992, Indecency, 1992, Night Owl, 1993, The Picture of Dorian Grey, The Twilight of the Golds, 1998, The Spree, 1998, A House Divided, 2000, The Big House, 2001, After the Storm, 2001, They Shoot Divas, Don't They?, 2002; (TV spl.) Cinderella, Faerietale Theatre, 1985; (TV series) 2000 Malibu Road, 1992, Nothing Sacred, 1997, The L Word, 2004; (TV mini-series) Feast of All Saints, 2001; TV guest appearance The Outer Limits, 1995. Mailing: L Word Season III Productions Inc 8275 Manitoba St Vancouver BC V5X 4L8 Canada*

BEALS, KAREN MARIE DOWNEY, pastor; b. Phila., Dec. 9, 1948; d. Garner Harris and Mae Frances (Thacker) Downey; m. Edward Roy Beals Jr., Feb. 2, 1970 (dec. Apr. 2001); 1 child, Katie Adrianne Downey. AA, Peace Coll., 1969; BA in Fine Arts, U. Colo., 1971, MA in Spl. Edn., 1977; MDiv, San Francisco Theol. Sem., 1994, student, 2003—. Ordained Min. of Word and Sacrament Presbytery of Kiskimentas, Yatesboro, PA, 1994; cert. Tchr. Colo., 1972, Calif., 1989. With life, health, and disability ins. sales Mut. Omaha and Pacific Mut. Life Ins. Cos., 1972—75; remedial reading tchr. Pikes Peack Bd. Coop. Svcs., Widefield, Colo., 1975—78; with customer rels., customer svc., claims Pacific Mut. Small Group Ins., Newport Beach, Calif., 1979—81; owner, operator, sales, lectr., ednl. cons. Beals on Wheels, Dana Point, Calif., 1983—86; dir. Children and Family Ministry South Laguna Beach United Meth. Ch., Calif., 1987—90; chaplain Sharp Hosps., Murrieta Hot Springs, San Diego, Calif., 1993—94; intern in ministry St. Mark Presbyn. Ch., Newport Beach, 1993—94, Geneva Presbyn. Ch., Laguna Hills, Calif., 1993—94; pastor Elk County Presbyn. Parish, Ridgway, Wilcox, Dagus Mines, Pa., 1994—99, Olivet Neighborhood Mission, Cedar Rapids, Iowa, 1999—2004, Olivet Presbyn. Ch., Cedar Rapids, 1999—2004, Springville Presbyn. Ch., Iowa, 2004—, Linn Grove Presbyn. Ch. and Retreat Ctr., Mt. Vernon, Iowa, 2004—. Trainee, workshop attendee in field; chair, church growth and evangelism com. Presbytery of Kiskimentas, Yatesboro, Pa., mem. presbytery coun.; chair evangelism confs. Synod of Trinity, Ligonier, Pa.; co-leader New Day, New Ch. Workshop; ministry com., peacemaking com., commn. lay pastor com., ch. redevelopment and revitalization groups Presbytery of East Iowa, Iowa City, discernamentarian, mem.; co-leader, cons. Cultivating Passionate Spirituality Retreats; 215th gen. assembly commr., apptd. mem. peacemaking com., Denver; environ. task force Ecumenical Ministries of Iowa, Des Moines. Bd. dirs Springville Area Neighborhood Svc. and Info., Iowa, 2005—. Ch. Leadership Devel. Fund grant, Synod of Trinity. Presbyterian. Avocations: reading, knitting, walking, contemplative prayer, wine tasting. Office: 165 Broadway PO Box 18 Springville IA 52336

BEALS, NANCY FARWELL, former state legislator; b. El Paso, July 21, 1938; d. Fred Whitcomb and Katharine Doane (Pier) Farwell; m. Richard William Beals, June 30, 1962; children: Katharine, Robert, Susannah. BA in Polit. Sci., Bryn Mawr Coll., 1960; MA in Teaching, Harvard U., 1961. Group leader Exptl. Internat. Living, Putney, Vt.; jr. high sch. tchr. Wincehster (Mass.) Pub. Schs., 1961-62; high sch. tchr. Hamden (Conn.) Pub. Schs., 1962-64; state rep. Conn. Gen. Assembly, Hartford, 1993—2003; mem. adv. bd. Parenting Support Program Yale-New Haven (Conn.) Hosp., 2003—, chairperson adv. bd. Parenting Support Programs, 2005—. Mem. state adv. coun. on spl. edn., 2000-02. Mem. various local and regional offices PTA, Chgo. and Hamden, 1970-83; local pres., state bd. dirs. LWV, Conn., 1979-92; mem., sec., chmn. Hamden Bd. Edn., 1983-92; mem. citizen's adv. bd. High Meadows Residential Treatment Facility, 1993—; treas. Spring Glen Civic Assn., 2003—; bd. dirs. Hamden Edn. Found., 2001-04. Recipient Citizenship award for Conn. Philip Morris Corp., 1992, Hamden Notable award Friends of Hamden Libr., 1986, Children's Hero award Children's Trust Fund, 1995, Disting. Legislator award Conn. Assn. Bds. of Edn., 1998, Master Builder award Habitat for Humanity of Greater New Haven, 2002; named Legislator of Yr. Conn. Libr. Assn., 1994, Caucus of Conn. Dems., 1997, Conn. Coalition on Aging, 2002; Flemming fellow Ctr. for Policy Alternatives, 1995. Democrat.

BEALS, NANCY LUNSFORD, photographer; b. Cin., Jan. 9, 1937; d. Carlton A. and Lucille P. Lunsford; m. Kamilo R. Biscevic, Aug. 3, 1963 (div. 1981); children: Carlton, Richard, John, Camilla; m. Lincoln Henry Beals, Sept. 7, 2002. BAA, U. Cin., 1958. Illustrator GE Co., Cin., 1958-65; tech. illustrator ATE Assocs. Inc., Alameda, Calif., 1981-82, data dept. mgr., 1982-88; desktop publ. supr. Fed. Res. Bank of San Francisco, 1988-89, office adminstr., 1989-95; owner NancyB.Cards, Vacaville, Calif., 1995—. Organist, choir dir. St. Margaret Mary's Ch., Oakland, Calif., 1977-87. Recipient awards Alameda Photographic Soc., No. Calif. Camera Club Coun., Photographers Forum. Mem. Alameda Photographic Soc., Delta Delta Delta (pres. alumnae chpt. 1961-63). Avocations: photography, walking, piano, drawing. Office: PO Box 483 Vacaville CA 95696-0483 Office Phone: 707-421-2224. Office Fax: 707-421-2226.

BEAM, DEBORAH ANN, science educator; b. Islip, N.Y., July 14, 1967; d. Horst John and Winifred Louise Vogel; m. Terrence Scott Beam, Jan. 14, 1995; children: Sarah, Rachel, Matthew. BS in Secondary Edn., Biology Sci., SUNY, Cortland, 1989; MS in Sci. Edn., Chem. Physics, SD State, Brookings, 1996. Cert. adolescent sci. tchr. Nat. Bd. Sci. tchr. Ely H.S., Pompano Beach, Fla., 1989—91, Scarsdale H.S., NY, 1991—96, Arlington H.S., LaGrangeville, 1996—2001, Red Hook H.S., 2001—. Biology mentor N.Y. State; jr. varsity field hockey coach Scarsdale H.S., 1991—95; jr. varsity and varsity field hockey coach Arlington H.S., LaGrangeville, 1996—2001; instr. profl. devel. sci. tchrs. Dutchess County, 2000—; environ. club adv. Red Hook H.S., 2001—. Troop leader Girls Scouts of U.S., Pine Plains, NY, 2005—06. Named Outstanding Sci. Tchr., NY Sci. Tchrs. Assn., 2001; grantee, Cmty. Found., 1998, 1999, 2001, Mid Hudson Tchr. Ctr., 2000, TIPA, 2005. Mem.: ASCD, Sci. Tchrs. Assn. N.Y., Nat. Sci. Tchrs. Assn., Nat. Assn. Biology Tchrs. Avocations: camping, hiking, hunting, collecting. Home: 180 Willow Glen Rd Red Hook NY 12571 Office: Red Hook HS 103 W Mkt St Red Hook NY 12571 Office Phone: 845-758-2241 ext. 3122. Personal E-mail: beamsci@peoplepc.com.

BEAM, SUSAN PUTNAM, elementary school educator; b. Rutherfordton, N.C., May 4, 1958; d. Hugh Deaver and Jacquolia Sullivan Putnam; m. James Steven Beam, Mar. 28, 1981; children: Dustin Perry, Daniel Sullivan. BA in Elem. Edn., Clemson U., S.C., 1980. Tchr. elem. edn. Grover Elem., NC, 1980—93, Washington Elem., Shelby, NC, 1993—. Coord. Earth Day Washington Elem., Shelby, 1996—2006. Edn. chairperson 1st United Meth. Ch., Cherryville, NC, 1998—2003. Named Woman of Yr., 1st United Meth. Ch., 2001, Cleveland County Schs. Tchr. of Yr., 2005—06, Washington Elem. Tchr. of Yr., 2005—06, Grover Elem. Tchr. of Yr., 1988—89. Mem.: NEA, N.C. Assn. Educators. Democrat. Methodist. Avocations: reading, sewing, swimming. Home: 138 Harbor Point Dr Cherryville NC 28021

BEAM, TERESA ANN, biology professor; b. Huntington, Ind., June 10, 1968; d. Thomas Eugene Elick and Cynthia Louise Stuck; m. Jon Gerard Beam, Dec. 7, 1968; children: Isaac J., Martina T. BS, U. St. Francis, Ft.

Wayne, Ind., 1991; PhD, U. Notre Dame, Ind., 1996. Concurrent asst. prof. U. Notre Dame, 1996—97; vis. asst. prof. Valparaiso (Ind.) U., 1997—98; assoc. prof. U. St. Francis, 1998—. Vis. scholar U. Notre Dame, 2005—; adj. assoc. prof. Ind. U. Sch. Medicine, Ft. Wayne, 2006—; chair instnl. rev. bd. U. St. Francis, 2000, sec. academic coun., chair dept. biology, 2006—; dir. Three Rivers Sci. Symposium, Ft. Wayne, 2000—06. Patentee in field. Recipient Tchg. Excellence and Leadership award, U. St. Francis, 2003. Mem.: Assn. Coll. and Univ. Biology Educators, Ind. Acad. Sci., Ind. Coll. Biology Tchrs. Assn. Roman Catholic. Avocations: water-skiing, bicycling. Office: U St Francis 2701 Spring St Fort Wayne IN 46808 Office Phone: 260-434-3245. Office Fax: 260-434-7580. E-mail: tbeam@sf.edu.

BEAMAN, COLLEEN K., education educator, choreographer; b. Teaneck, N.J., June 18, 1952; d. Fredric Norbert and Dorothy (Greenawalt) Kelly; m. James Russell Beaman, July 31, 1976; children: Brian James, Michael Henry, Kimberly Diane, Patrick Kelly. BFA, U. Ariz., 1974, MEd, 1982, student, 1993—. Tchr. Pace U., N.Y.C., 1969—71; tchr. ESL Casa Grande Union H.S., Casa Grande, 1974—75; head theatre dept. Palo Verde Theatre Tucson Unified Sch. Dist., Tucson, 1975—78; prof. Ctrl. Ariz. Coll., Gila River Reservation, Ariz., 1975; prof. musical theater U. Ariz.; choreographer Tucson Ballet Co.; tchr. math. & sci. Tucson Unified Sch. Dist., 1997—; tchr. of tchrs. U. Ariz., Tucson, 2000—. 2nd v.p. Fred Kelly Dance Studio, Inc., Oradell, NJ, 1970—81; choreographer Miss Am. Pagent, Pima County, Ariz., 1978; co-dir./choreographer So. Ariz. Lighthouse Corp., Tucson, 1984; adj. prof. Pima C.C., Tucson, 1998—; entertainer Scott's Oquange Lake, NY, 1985. Master of ceremonies: Nat. Tap Dance Day awards show, 2000. Founder Fred Kelly Found., 2000—; mem. U. Ariz. Theatre Arts Bd., 1995—. Recipient Ariz. Career Educator award, Ariz. Edn. Assn., 1975, Nat. Best Prodn. award, Intenrat. Thespian Soc., 1977. Mem.: Am. Fedn. Garden Indian Ridge (treas. 1976—), Pima County Bar Aux. (treas. 1976—), Disabled Am. Vets. Aux. (life), Pima County Rep. Club. Republican. Roman Catholic. Home: 3540 N Camino de Vista Tucson AZ 85745-9798

BEAMAN, JOYCE PROCTOR, retired secondary and elementary school educator, writer; b. Wilson, N.C., Apr. 27, 1931; d. Jesse David and Martha Pauline (Owens) Proctor; m. Robert Hines Beaman; 1 child, Robert David. BS, East Carolina Coll., 1951, MA, 1952. English and French tchr. Stantonsburg (N.C.) H.S., 1952-53, Snow Hill (N.C.) H.S., 1953-60, Saratoga (N.C.) Ctrl., 1960—78, libr., 1972-78, Elm City (N.C.) Mid. Sch., 1978-82, Spaulding Elem. Sch., Spring Hope, N.C., 1987-92. Mem. Competency Test Commn. N.C., Raleigh, 1983-84. Author: Broken Acres, 1971, All for the Love of Cassie, 1973, Bloom Where You Are Planted, 1975, You Are Beautiful: You Really Are, 1981, Teaching: Pure and Simple, 1998, A View from the Pew: A Tribute to Pastors, 2006. Recipient Terry Sanford Creativity and Innovation in Edn. state award, 1977. Mem. Kappa Delta Pi, Delta Kappa Gamma (state chmn. 1978-80). Home: 8427 Piney Grove Church Rd Walstonburg NC 27888-9626

BEAMER, LAURA, women's health and genetic health nurse; b. Chgo., Jan. 26, 1956; d. Frederick Richard and Bernice Elaine (Linklater) Curr; children: David, Amy, James, Daniel. ADN, Purdue U., 1983, BSN, 1988, MSN, 1990; postgrad., Rush U., 1996—. RN, Ind., Ill.; cert. high risk perinatal nurse, family nurse practitioner. Instr. prenatal Porter Meml. Hosp., Valparaiso, Ind., staff nurse; staff nurse, staff educator Northwestern Meml. Hosp., Chgo.; lectr. Ind. U., Gary. Mem. ANA, AWHONN, Internat. Soc. Nurses in Genetics, Ind. State Nurses Assn., Sigma Theta Tau. Office: Ind U Northwest 3400 Broadway Gary IN 46408-1101

BEAMER, YVONNE MARIE, psychotherapist, counselor; b. Cumberland, Md., Jan. 6, 1947; d. William Walter and Ruthella Louise (Smith) Barr; m. Charles Wesley Beamer, Jan. 5, 1974; children: Marie Lynn, Ann Christine. BA, W.Va. U., 1969. Cert. nat. chem. dependency counselor; lice. ind. chem. dependency counselor. Tchr. English and lang. arts Ft. Ashby (W. Va.) High Sch., 1969-70; field advisor, field dir. Shawnee G.S. Coun., Cumberland, Md., 1970-73; job counselor Md. Correctional Tng. Ctr., Hagerstown, Md., 1973-74; home tchr. Frederick (Md.) County Bd. of Edn., 1984-86; addictions counselor Frederick County Substance Abuse Program, 1986-88; intake admissions counselor Laurelwood Hosp., Willoughby, Ohio, 1988-92; intake/admissions counselor Glenbeigh Hosp., 1992; addictions counselor Cmty. Action Against Addiction, 1993-99; intake assessment counselor, primary counselor East Side Cath. Ctr. & Shelter, Cleve., 1999—. Intake coord. East Side Cath. Ctr. and Shelter/Iwo San programs, 1999—. Ch. organist All Souls Episc. Ch., Balt., 1976-82, St. James Episc. Ch., Mt. Airy, Md. 1982-88; mem. choir St. Andrew's Episcopal Ch., 1998—; choir mem. Bethany Assembly God Ch., 2004—. Mem. Buckeye Squares, Phi Beta Kappa, Sigma Phi Omega. Avocations: dance, piano, organ, singing, swimming, reading. Home: 3920 Spokane Ave Cleveland OH 44109-3834 Office: East Side Cath Ctr and Shelter/Iwo San Programs 11811 Shaker Blvd Cleveland OH 44120-1927

BEAN, CALANDRA LESHUN, mathematics educator; b. Memphis, June 22, 1973; d. Larry Gene and Deborah Kay Dumas; children: Keandria LeShun, Kelan DeUnte'. BS, LeMoyne Owen Coll., Memphis, 1995; MA, U. Phoenix, 2005. Legislative sys. analyst I State of Tenn. Comptr. of Treasury, Nashville, 1995—96; math tchr. East HS, Memphis, 1996—98, Mt. Juliet (Tenn.) HS, 1998—98, Antioch (Tenn.) HS, 1999—2003, Riverdale (Riverdale) HS, 2003—; programmer/analyst Healthcare Mgmt. Sys., Nashville, 1999—99. Named Tchr. of the Yr., Antioch HS, 1999. Mem.: CCEA, NEA. Office: Riverdale HS 160 Roberts Dr Riverdale GA 30274 Office Phone: 770-473-2905. Personal E-mail: calandrabean@bellsouth.net. Business E-Mail: cbean@clayton.k12.ga.us.

BEAN, JOAN NONA, merchant, consultant; b. Chgo., Aug. 9, 1929; d. Joseph John and Otylia Jeanette (Lokanski) Nowicki; m. Alfred E. Brock, Feb., 1950 (div. 1953); m. Harry Raymond Bean, July 22, 1954 (dec. Mar. 1973); children: Harry R. II, Elise Josan, James Nathaniel. Student, N.W. Bus. Coll., 1947, Columbia Coll., 1951. Model Patricia Vance Agy., Chgo., 1944-48, Conover Agy., N.Y.C., 1949-50; owner Judy Bean, Inc., St. Louis, 1966-88. Sec. Fashion Group St. Louis, 1978—. Active Mo. Botanical Gardens, St. Louis, Friends of St. Louis Art Mus., St. Louis Zoo Friends. Home: 4466 W Pine #18C Saint Louis MO 63108

BEAN, LORI J., chemistry professor; b. Ogdensburg, May 15, 1962; m. Paul E. Bean. BS, St. Lawrence U., Canton, N.Y., 1984; MS, U. Conn., Storrs, 1986; MBA, U. Toledo, Ohio, 1994. Rsch. asst. Med. Coll. Ohio, Toledo, 1986—91; adj. faculty Owens CC, Perrysburg, Ohio, 1993—94; assoc. prof. Monroe County CC, Mich., 1996—. Instrnl. staff devel. com. Monroe County CC, 1996—; co-founder Math and Sci. Society, Monroe County CC, 1999, co-adv., 1999—; instrnl. tech. com. Monroe County CC, 2002—, curriculum com., 2005—. Mem. & chair, various theatrical committees Perrysburg Schs., 2004—; sci. odyssey after sch. mentoring Lincoln Elem. Sch., Monroe, Mich., 2004—. Grantee Found. grant, Monroe County CC, 2004—06. Mem.: Am. Chem. Soc. Avocation: visiting national parks. Office: Monroe County CC 1555 S Raisinville Rd Monroe MI 48161

BEAN, MANYA, psychotherapist, educator; b. Athens, Greece, Mar. 18, 1937; arrived in U.S., 1959; d. Charilaos and Bebe Coulentianos; children: Justin, Marina, Adrian. Student, U. Athens, U. Tenn.; BA, U. Pitts., 1961; MA, U. Md., 1963; PhD in Psychoanalysis and Psychology, Union Inst., 1989. Pvt. practice psychoanalysis, Phila. and NJ, 1982—; psychoanalyst Affiliates in Psychotherapy, Northfield, NJ, 2003—. Leader support groups for cancer patients Gilda's Club, Atlantic City, 2003—; instr. Atlantic County New Sch., Pleasantville, NJ, 1973—79, Stockton State Coll., Pomona, NJ, 1979—83, Atlantic CC, Mays Landing, NJ, 1979—82, Mays Landing, 2002, Phila. Sch. Psychoanalysis, 1989—, So. NJ Psychoanalytic Inst., Brigantine, 2004—; adj. prof. Union Inst. and U., Cin., 1992—; presenter infield. Author: To Shy to Surrender: Poems by Manya Coulentianos Bean, 1993, Rape, Incest, Battery!, 2000; translator: The Haiki Handbook, 1985, Wind in the Long Grass, 1991; contbr. articles to profl. publs. Bd. dirs. So. NJ Psychoanalytic Inst., 2005—. Mem.: ACA, Inst. Noetic Sci., Am. Psychotherapy Assn., NJ Mental Health Counselors Assn., Nat. Assn. Advancement Psychoanalysis. Home: 16 N Curran Dr Absecon NJ 08201-1308

BEAN, MELISSA, congresswoman; b. Chgo., Jan. 22, 1962; m. Alan Bean; children: Victoria, Michelle. AA in Bus., Oakton Cmty. Coll., 1982; BA in Polit. Sci., Roosevelt U., 2002. Dist. sales mgr. DJC Corp., 1982—85; br. mgr. MTI Systems Inc. Arrow Electronics, 1985—89; dist. mgr. UDS Motorola, 1989—91; area mgr. SynOptics Comm. Inc., 1991—94; v.p. sales Dataflex Corp., 1994—95; pres. Sales Resources Inc., 1995—2004; mem. US Congress from Ill. Dist. 8, 2005—; mem. Fin. Svcs. com., Small Bus. com. Mem. Palatine C. of C.; past pres. Deer Lake Homeowners Assn. Mem.: Nat. Assn Women Bus. Owners, Barrington Area Profl. Women. Democrat. Serbian Orthodox. Office: 512 Cannon House Office Bldg Washington DC 20005 Office Phone: 202-225-3711. Office Fax: 202-225-7830.

BEAN, VIRGINIA ANN (GINNY BEAN), marketing executive; b. Grand Rapids, Mich., June 23, 1952; d. John Theunis and Muriel MacNaughton (Reeves) B.; m. Ronald Eugene Daley, Nov. 7, 1986; children: Jackson Phillip Wesley Daley, Bryan Augustin Daley, Geoffrey Eugene Daley. BA in Theater, Hiram Coll., 1974; MBA, NYU, 1987. Dir. fiscal ops. Cultural Coun. for Arts, N.Y.C., 1980-86; v.p. creative mktg. devel. Swiss Colony, Monroe, Wis., 1987—; pres. Ginny's, Monroe, 1995—; v.p. creative mktg. rsch. Swiss Colony, Wis. Creator: Ginny's Catalog, 1992—, Colors Catalog, 2005. Bd. dirs. Rainbow Day Care, Monroe, 1989-92. Avocations: theater, sewing, parenting. Office: Ginny's 1112 7th Ave Monroe WI 53566-1364

BEANE, JUDITH MAE, retired psychologist; b. Durham, N.C., Mar. 28, 1944; d. Joseph William Sr. and Antoinette Gwathmey (Dew) B. BA, Campbell U., 1967; MRE, Golden Gate Bapt. Theol. Sem., 1972; PhD, Profl. Sch. of Psychology, San Francisco, 1988. Lic. psychologist, Calif. Home missionary So. Bapt. Home Mission Bd., Atlanta, 1967—69; loan officer Coop Credit Union, Corte Madera, Calif., 1969—70; emergency svcs. specialist Cmty. Action Marin, San Rafael, Calif., 1976—78; coord. program Marin Treatment Ctr., San Rafael, 1980—85; sec. St. Paul's Episcopal Ch., San Rafael, 1979—81; psychol. intern Raleigh Hills Hosp., Redwood City, Calif., 1984; psychol. asst. Lic. Psychologists, San Anselmo, Calif., 1985—92; psychologist Mill Valley, Calif., 1992—93; mng. dir. Ch. Resource Svcs. Inc., Lancaster, Va., 1997—2001; social worker Lancaster Dept. Social Svcs., 2004; ret., 2004. Cons. Ross (Calif.) Hosp., 1991; guest spkr. Turn on Marin, San Rafael, Calif., 1985; coord. rural domestic violence project MP-NN CSB, 2001—02; outreach therapist Youth and Family Svcs., 2002, mental health therapist II, 2002—04, No. Neck-Mid. Peninsula Cmty. Svcs. Bd., 1995—97. Bd. dirs. Open Door Ministries, Inc., Sausalito, Calif., 1971—; deacon Kilmarnock Bapt. Ch., Lancaster, 1996—99. Recipient award Marin County People Speaking, 1985. Mem. APA (assoc.), ACA, Calif. State Psychol. Assn., Am. Assn. Christian Counselors. Baptist. Avocations: handcrafts, reading. Home: PO Box 172 Lancaster VA 22503-0172 Personal E-mail: jbeane@oonl.com.

BEANE, MARJORIE NOTERMAN, academic administrator; b. Adams, Minn., Oct. 3, 1946; d. Matthias Hubert and Anna Helen (Boegeman) Noterman. BA, Marillac Coll., St. Louis, 1969; MEd, U. Ariz., 1979; PhD, Loyola U., Chgo., 1988. Tchr. St. Alphonsus Sch., Prospect Heights, Ill., 1969-73; tchr., asst. prin. St. Raphael Sch., Chgo., 1973-75; prin. St. Theresa Sch., Palatine, Ill., 1975-84; pres. Mallinckrodt Coll. of the North Shore, Wilmette, Ill., 1986-90; sr. v.p. for adminstn. Loyola U., Chgo., 1991—. Trustee Mallinckrodt Coll. of the North Shore, 1980-90; cons. Jospehinum High Sch., Chgo., 1976, St. Viator High Sch., Arlington Heights, Ill., 1986. Mem. History of Women Religious, Fedn. Ind. Ill. Colls. and Univs. (exec. com. 1989), Wilmette C. of C., Sisters of Christian Charity (councilor 1980-88). Rotary. Roman Catholic. Avocations: sewing, bicycling, swimming, travel. Office: Loyola U 820 N Michigan Ave Fl 1 Chicago IL 60611-2196

BEAR, DINAH, lawyer; b. Lynnwood, Calif., Oct. 22, 1951; d. Henry Louis and Betty Jean (Isenhart) B. BJ, U. Mo., 1974; JD, McGeorge Sch. Law, 1977. Bar: Calif. 1978, D.C. 1981, U.S. Supreme Ct. 1982. Dep. gen. counsel Council on Environ. Quality, Washington, 1981-83, gen. counsel, 1983—. Contbr. articles to profl. publs. Recipient Disting. Svc. award Sierra Club, 1993, Chmn.'s award Natural Resources Coun. of Am., 1993. Mem. ABA (chmn. standing com. on environ. law), D.C. Bar Assn. Jewish. Avocation: gardening. Office: Coun Environ Quality 722 Jackson Pl NW Washington DC 20503-0002

BEARCE, JEANA DALE, artist, educator; b. St. Louis; d. Clarence Russell and Maria Emily Dale; m. Lawrence F. Rakovan, June 7, 1969; children: Barbara Emily, Luke, Francesca. B.F.A., Washington U., St. Louis, 1951; MA, N.Mex. Highlands U., 1954. Vis. artist, various lectureships, India, Pakistan, 1961-62, 93; founder art dept. U. Maine, Portland, 1965, chmn. and dept. rep., 1965-70, asst. prof. art, 1967-70, assoc. prof., 1970-81, prof., 1982—. Reflections South India sabbatical, 1992—93. Exhibited one-woman shows, Portland Mus. Art, Maine, 1958, U. Maine, Orono, 1958, 65, 69, 77, 80, Madras Govt. Mus., India, 1962, Gallery 65, Paris, 1964, Bristol Mus. Art, R.I., 1965, Center Gallery, N.Y.C., 1974, Benbow Gallery, Newport, R.I., 1979, Ctr. for the Arts, Chocolate Ch., Bath, Maine, 1988, USM Gallery, 1991, Main Gallery U. So. Maine, 1991, others, group show, Boston Mus. Art, Library of Congress, Phila. Print Club, Springfield Mus., Mo., Birmingham Mus. Art, Ala., others; represented permanent collection, St. Louis Art Mus., U.S. Edn. Found. in India, New Delhi, U. Maine, Orono and Portland, Bklyn. Mus. Art, Cornell U. Mus. Art, Calif. Coll. Arts and Crafts, Sarasota Art Assn., Fla., Bowdoin Coll., Brunswick, Maine; executed murals, N.Mex. Highlands U., Bowdoin Longfellow-Hawthorn Library, Brunswick, sculpture reliefs, St. Bartholomew, Cape Elizabeth, Maine, St. Charles Ch. Brunswick; retrospective, Maine Ctr. for the Arts, 1988. Mem. artist's com. Maine Art Gallery, 1957—75, 1980—87; mem. Maine com. Skowhegan Sch. Painting and Sculpture, 1972—. Recipient various awards; recipient Fannie Cook award People's Competition, 1958, 59; sabbaticals to India: Return to India-Creative Paintings and Printmaking, 1987, South India-Painting and Printmaking, 1993, The Maine to India Series USM Environ. Studies Ctr., 1996, Tibet The Maine Art Gallery, Wiscasset, 1999, Summer Invitational, Ctr. for Maine Contemporary Art, 2002, Maine Coast Artists, Rockport, 2002. Mem.: Bowdoin Coll. Mus. Assocs. Home: 327 Maine St Brunswick ME 04011-3310 Office: U So Maine College Ave Gorham ME 04038-1004

BEARD, AMANDA, swimmer, Olympic athlete; b. Irvine, Calif., Oct. 29, 1981; Student, U. Ariz., Tucson. Mem. Pan Pac Team, 1995; swimmer U.S. Olympic Team, Atlanta, 1996, Sydney, 2000, Athens, 2004. Holder Am. record for 100 meter breastroke, 1996. Achievements include winning gold medal in 4x100m medley, silver medal in 100m, 200m breast, Atlanta Olympic games, 1996; being the second youngest gold medalist in USA swimming history, Atlanta Olympic games, 1996; winning bronze medal in 200m breast, Sydney Olympic games, 2000; winning gold medal in 100m, 200m breast, Pan Pacific games, 2002; winning gold medal, 200m breast, World Championships, 2003; winning gold medal in 100m, 200m breast, 200m IM, US National Championships, 2004, 200m IM, 2003; winning gold medal in 200m breast, silver medal in 200m IM, 4x100m medley relay, Athens Olympic games, 2004. Office: US Swimming Inc One Olympic Plz Colorado Springs CO 80909

BEARD, ANN SOUTHARD, diplomat, oil industry executive; b. Denver, Jan. 13, 1948; d. William Harvey and Cora Alice Cornelia (Caldwell) Southard; m. Terrill Leon Beard, Dec. 20, 1970 (div. Oct. 1980); 1 son, Jeffery Leon; m. Rainer G. Froehlich, Feb. 12, 1988 (div. 1992). BA, Willamette U., 1970; postgrad., U. Calif., San Diego, 1981-82. Exec. asst. Kidder Peabody & Co., San Francisco, 1970-72; adminstrv. aide Arthur Anderson & Co., Portland, Oreg., 1972-73; owner, mgr. Beard's Frame Shoppes, Inc., Portland, 1973-80; dir. mktg. Multnomah County Fair, Portland, 1979; owner, CEO Ann Beard Spl. Events, San Diego, 1980-82, Frame Affair, Inc., San Diego, 1982-86; pres. Jack Oil Co., Inc., Greeley, 1982—; chancellor, v.p. programs Consular Corps. Coll., Phila., 2002—05. Mem. Pres.'s Small Bus. Adv. Coun.; co-owner, v.p. Froehlich Internat. Travel, La Jolla, Calif., 1987-92; chief of protocol Mayor Susan Golding's Office, City of San Diego, 1993-2001; pres., CEO, Diplomacy & Internat. Protocol, San Diego, 2001—; chmn. 1st Nat. Protocol Officers Assn. conf. U.S. Dept. State, Washington; chmn. 1st Internat. Protocol Conf., Ottawa, Can.; pres. 146 Co., Inc., Greeley, 1970-88; mem. San Diego Consular Corps; cons. SBA, San Diego, 1980-85; prof. San Diego State U., 2002—, Palomar Coll., 2004-05, SAIC U., 2004-05, Smithsonian Inst. Assocs. Program, 2004—; internat protocol advisor Molecular Pictures.com.; VIP ceremonies Presdl. Inauguration, 2005; lectr., presenter in field Bd. dirs. San Diego Master Chorale, 1981-92, La Jolla Rep. Women Fedn., 1992-96; mem. state bd. Miss. Calif. Pageant/Miss. Am., 1982-87; citizens adv. bd. Drug Abuse Task Force/Crime Prevention Task Force, San Diego, 1983-87; campaign coord. Bill Mitchell for City Coun., 1985; candidate for Congress; staff aide to dep. mayor, 1987; active Lead San Diego Alumni, 1988, Scripps Hosp. Aux., 1992—, Internat. Vis. Coun., 1993-2003, San Diego County Comm. on the Status of Women, 1993-96; active Internat. Affairs Bd., San Diego, 1993-2001; chancellor, Consular Corps Coll., Phila., 2001-05; founder, nat. chmn. Nat. Protocol Resource Bd., USA, 2002—, founder, internat. pres. Protocol and Diplomacy Internat., U.S., 2002-04. Mem. Am. Mktg. Assn., World Affairs Coun., San Diego C. of C., Save Our Heritage Orgn., Charter 100 San Diego, San Diego 1970 Alumna Willamette U., 1909 Univ. Club (bd. dirs. 1992-2003, pres. 1996-98), Univ. Club San Diego (mktg., devel. and social dir. 1987-88), Pres., Protocol and Diplomacy Internat., Delta Gamma. Office Phone: 858-481-5661. Personal E-mail: bearddiplomacy@yahoo.com.

BEARD, BERNICE TALBOTT, writer, publisher; b. New Windsor, Md., Sept. 1, 1927; d. Edwin Warfield and Henrietta Alice (Snader) Talbott; m. Paul William Beard, Oct. 9, 1948; 1 child, Jeffrey Paul. BA cum laude, Western Md. Coll., 1974, MA, 1981. Stenographer, sec. Balt. Gas. and Elec. Co., 1944-51; feature writer Carroll County Times, Westminster, Md., 1956-57; asst. dir. admissions, counselor Western Md. Coll., Westminster, 1963-72, exec. asst. to pres. and elected sec. bd. trustees, 1972-89; freelance writer Westminster, 1989—. Campus rep. Am. Coun. Edn. Advancement of Women in Higher Edn., Western Md. Coll., 1979-85, sec. coll. corp., 1985-89. Author: At Your Own Pace: Travel Your Way in Your Motorhome, 1997, 2d edit., 2003, Alaska at Your Own Pace: Traveling by RV Caravan, 1998, Colorado at Your Own Pace: Travelling by Motorhome with Friends, 1999, 301 Ways to Make RV Travel Safer, Easier, and More Fun, 2001; contbr. articles to mags. and newspapers. Mem. Nat. Mus. Women in Arts (charter mem.). Republican. Mem. Ch. of Brethren. Avocations: travel, photography. Business E-Mail: arborhousepublishing@verizon.net.

BEARD, DEBORAH A., therapist, educator; b. Lincoln, Ill., Aug. 15, 1951; d. Everett D. and Lola J. Thompson; m. Charles W. Beard, May 22, 1971; children: Rachel A., Miriam Kamalana R. BS in Human Resources, Friends U., Wichita, 1992, MS in Family Therapy, 1996. Human resources mgr. Parsons Precision Products, Inc., Kans., 1989-98, Power Flame Inc., Parsons, 1998-99; prof. psychology Labette County Coll., Parsons, 1999; tchr. The Learning Ctr. at Middle Sch., USO 503, Parsons, 1999; prof. psychology Platte Valley Bible Coll., Scottsbluff, Nebr., 2000—03; therapist Panhandle Mental Health Ctr., Scottsbluff, 2003—. Guest spkr. in field. Republican. Christian. Avocations: music, movies. Office: Thompson-Beard Panhandle Mental Health Ctr 4110 ave D Scottsbluff NE 69361 Office Phone: 308-635-3171. Personal E-mail: debthompsonbeard@hotmail.com. E-mail: dbeard@pmhc.net.

BEARD, ELIZABETH LETITIA, physiologist, educator; b. New Orleans, Apr. 2, 1932; d. Howard Horace and Irene (Handley) Beard. BA in Biology, Tex. Christian U., 1952, BS in Med. Tech., 1953, MS in Med. Tech., 1955; postgrad., Smith Coll., 1953-54, Vanderbilt U., 1954-55; PhD in Animal Physiology, Tulane U., 1961. Instr. dept. biol. scis. Loyola U., New Orleans, 1955-58, asst. prof., 1958-62, assoc. prof., 1962-68, prof., 1969—, chmn. premed. com., 1978—; rsch. assoc. dept. physiology Sch. Medicine Tulane U., New Orleans, 1960-63, prof. biology med. reinforcement and enrichment program, 1968-94. Vis. prof. dept. physiology and biophysics Med. Sch. Harvard U., 1983-84, dept. neuropharmacology Scripps Rsch. Inst., La Jolla, Calif., spring 2001; vis. scientist Am. Indian Rsch. Opportunities Programs at Mont. State U., 1994. Contbr. articles on rsch. in physiology to profl. publs. Project rev. com. New Orleans Health Planning Coun., 1974-77, bd. dirs., 1975-78; soprano soloist Holy Name of Jesus Ch., 1978—, pres. sch. bd., 1976-79; grad. rsch. com. La. chpt. Am. Heart Assn., 1970-72, 81-83, undergrad. rsch. com., 1978-81, 89-93; active Met. Mus. Art, New Orleans Mus. Art. NIH grantee, 1962-64, 67-69, La. Heart Assn. grantee, 1966-67, Edward Schleider Found. grantee, 1974-77, New Orleans Cancer Assn. grantee, 1962-63; Libby Rsch. fellow Sch. Medicine Tulane U., 1961. Mem. AAUP, AAAS, Am. Physiol. Soc., Soc. Exptl. Biology and Medicine, Christian Med. and Dental Soc. (participant internat. med. missions 1993—), Sigma Xi. Office: 6363 St Charles Ave New Orleans LA 70118-6143 Home: # 22 6363 Saint Charles Ave New Orleans LA 70118-6143 Office Phone: 504-865-2768. Business E-Mail: Beard@Loyno.edu.

BEARD, JANET MARIE, health facility administrator; b. Olean, N.Y., Feb. 18, 1930; d. Paul Claude and Virginia Marie (Mahaney) B. Grad. in nursing, St. Catherine's Hosp., 1951; BS in Clin. Nursing, St. John's U., 1959, MS in Nursing Adminstrn., 1961; MS in Adminstrv. Medicine, Columbia U., 1968. RN, N.Y.; lic. nursing home adminstr. Adminstrv. supr. Mary Immaculate Hosp., Jamaica, N.Y., 1957-66; asst. adminstr. Cath. Med. Ctr. Bklyn. and Queens, Jamaica, 1968-70; asst. dir. Yale-New Haven Med. Ctr., 1971-72, St. Barnabas Hosp., Bronx, N.Y., 1972-78, v.p., 1978-83; chief exec. officer Bethel Nursing and Rehab. Ctr., Croton on Hudson, N.Y., 1983—. Contbr. articles to profl. jours. Active Bronx Cmty. Bd. 6, 1977-83; active Fedn. Protestant Welfare Agys., N.Y.C., 1978-88; planning com. Div. on Aging, N.Y.C., 1978-88; adv. com. Aging in Am., Bronx, 1978-87; treas. Ft. Schuyler House, Bronx, 1977-83; pres.-elect alumni assn. Columbia U. Sch. Pub. Health, 1987-88, pres., 1988-89; mem. longterm planning com. Hudson Valley Health Systems Agy., 1989—; mem. planning coun., task force on AIDS Westchester County Health Dept., 1987-89, Westchester Health Planning Coun., 1992—; exec. adv. bd. health care mgmt. Iona Coll., 1987-92. Fellow Am. Coll. Health Care Execs.; mem. Am. Coll. Health Care Adminstrs., N.Y. State Pub. Health Assn. (Lower Hudson Valley chpt.), N.Y. Assn. Homes and Svcs. for the Aging (housing com. 1985-87), Ossining C. of C. (bd. dirs. 1987-92), Rotary (pres. Croton-on-Hudson 1992-93, Paul Harris fellow 1994), Princeton Club. Office: The Bethel Homes 19 Narragansett Ave Ossining NY 10562-2899 also: Bethel Nursing and Rehab Ctr 67 Springvale Rd Croton On Hudson NY 10520-1343

BEARD, LILLIAN B. MCLEAN, pediatrician, consultant; b. N.Y. d. Johnie Wilson and Woodie (Durden) McLean; m. Delawrence Beard. BS, Howard U., 1965, MD, 1970. MD, 1970. Pvt. practice pediat. Lillian M. Beard, Washington, 1973—; assoc. prof. pediat. George Washington U., 1983—; asst. prof. cmty. medicine Howard U., 1983—; contbg. editor Good Housekeeping Mag., N.Y.C., 1989-95; health adv. WUSA-TV, Washington, 1993-95; health and med. contbr. ABC-TV, Washington, 2000—04. Comm. cons. to industry including: Nestle Nutritional Products; mem. bd. dirs. Nat. Women's Econ. Alliance, 1993-2000, Children's Hosp., 1993-2002. Recipient Disting. Leadership award Nat. Assn. Equal Opportunity in Higher Edn., 1993, Disting. Svc. award Nat. Med. Assn., 1990, Hall of Fame in Medicine award, 1994, Healthy Babies Project "Making a Difference" award, 1995, Howard U. Alumni Achievement award, 1996. Fellow Am. Acad. Pediat.; mem. Nat. Med. Assn., Am. Acad. Pediat. (physician recognition awards 1993—). Home: 10517 Alloway Dr Potomac MD 20854-1662 Office: 10801 Lockwood Dr Ste 260 Silver Spring MD 20901

BEARD, LYDIA JEAN, research scientist, educator; b. Lima, Ohio, Oct. 30, 1967; d. Jerry and Mary Kate Worford; children: Abigail Marie, Jonathan Matthew. MS, Bowling Green State U., Ohio, 1995. Adj. faculty Lakeland C.C., Cleve., 2003—; rsch. asst. Markowitz Lab. Case Western Res. U.,

Cleve., 2005—. Home: 2543 E 127th St Downstairs Cleveland OH 44120 Office: Markowitz Lab 3101 Wolstein Bldg 2103 Cornell Rd Cleveland OH 44106 Office Phone: 216-368-5233. Personal E-mail: lydia29@sbcglobal.net. Business E-Mail: ljb8@case.edu.

BEARDEN, AMY JEAN, social studies educator, department chairman; b. Nashviille, Ark., Dec. 30, 1963; d. Wilda Sue Kilkler; m. Brian Scott McFarland, Aug. 17, 1985; children: Jesse Tyler, Cameron Scott. BS in Edn., Henderson State U., Arkadelphia, Ark., 1986. Social studies tchr., chairperson Nashville (Ark.) H.S., 1990—. Democrat. Mem. Church Of Christ. Avocations: travel, reading, walking. Office Phone: 871-845-3261. Business E-Mail: beardea@nps.dmsc.k12.ar.us.

BEARE, MURIEL ANITA NIKKI, public relations executive, author; b. Detroit, Mar. 7, 1928; d. Elbert Stanley and Dorothy Margaret (Welch) Brink; m. Richard Austin Beare, June 15, 1946; 1 child, Sandra Lee. AA, Miami Dade C.C., 1974; BA, Skidmore coll., 1979. Writer Key West (Fla.) Citizen, 1959; Miami News, 1967; field dir. Fla. Project HOPE, 1967-68; southeastern area dir., 1968-69; asst. v.p. pub. rels. I/D Assocs., Inc., Miami, 1969-70; pres. Nikki Beare & Assocs., Miami, 1971—; v.p. South Fla. office Cherenson, Carroll & Holzer, Livingston, NJ, 1973; sr. v.p. D.J. Edelman, Inc., 1981-83. Co-owner South Miami Travel Svc., 1976-78; pres. Gov.'s Sq. Travel, Inc., Tallahassee, 1979-85, Travel Is Fun, Miami, 1985-90; owner Silver Beare Travel, Inc., 1995-99; bd. dirs. corp. sec. Imperial Bank; reporter Tallahassee Dem., Focus Gadsden, Bus. Matters Mag. Author: Pirates, Pineapples and People: Tales and Legends of the Florida Keys, 1961, From Turtle Soup to Coconuts, 1964, Bottle Bonanza, A Handbook for Antique Bottle Collectors, 1965; prodr. cable TV program Traveler's Digest, 1986-92; moderator, prodr. Women's Powerline, Sta. WIOD, Miami, 1972-77; reporter Tallahassee Dem., 2005—, Tortoise, 2005—, Bus. Matters, 2005—. Chmn. adv. bd. Met. Dade County Libr., 1964; active Greater Miami Host Com., Met. Dade County Com. Status Women, 1971-76; former chmn. City of Miami Commn. Status Women, 1985-92; active Met. Gen. Land Use Master Planning Com. Employment Handicapped, 1970-72; chmn. Met. Dade Fair Housing and Employment Appeals Bd., 1975-78; active Miami YWCA's; chmn. Handicapped and Elderly subcom. Met. Dade Transit Devel. Com.; mem. Fla. Ins. Commn. Task force, 1975, Dade County Dem. Exec. Com., 1972-76, South Fla. Health Planning coun., 1972-74; founding mem. Nat. Women's Polit. Caucus, 1971—; pres. Capitol Women's Polit. Caucus; v.p. Fla. Women's Polit. Caucus, NWPC, Fla.; v.p. Herstory, 1971—; candidate Fla. Senate, 1974, Fla. Ho. of Reps., 1976; past pres. adv. bd. Inst. for Women, Fla. Internat. U.; pres. Fla. Feminist Credit Union, 1975-78; bd. dirs. Cmty. Health Inst., South Dade County, 1975-77; mem. Jobs for Miami, 1980-88; chmn. Fla. Gov.'s Small Bus. Adv. Coun., 1981-83, Greater Miami Tourism Coalition, 1983-85; del. White House Conf. on Small Bus., 1980, 86; chmn. publicity com. Asta World Congress, 1989,chmn. com. travel persons with disabilities; co-chmn. Fla. Internat. U. Sch. Journalism and Mass Comms. adv. bd., 1984-92; v.p. Havana Learning Ctr., Inc., 1995—; mem. consumer svcs. bd. Fla. Dept. Agr., 1998—. Recipient Silver Image award Pub. Rels. Assn., 1967-68; named to Fla. Women's Hall of Fame, 1994. Mem. AAUW, LWV, NOW, Hist. Assn. So. Fla., Friends of Everglades, Women's C. of C. So. Fla., Am. Soc. Travel Agts., Women in Comms., Nat. Assn. Women Bus. Owners, Pub. Rels. Soc. Am., Fla. Pub. Rels. Assn., Her Story of Fla., Inc., Women's Inst. Freedom of the Press, Antique Bottle Collectors Assn. Fla., Caribbean Tourism Orgn., South by Southeast Profl. Women In Travel, Vet. Feminists Am. Democrat. Office: Nikki Beare & Assocs Inc 7858 Havana Hwy Havana FL 32333-9594 E-mail: nikkibeare@aol.com.

BEARE-ROGERS, JOYCE LOUISE, retired research and development executive; b. nr. Pickering, Ont., Can., Sept. 8, 1927; d. Frederick John and Sarah May (Michell) Beare; m. Charles Graham Rogers, Dec. 30, 1961; 1 child, Anne Catherine. BA, U. Toronto, Ont., 1951, MA, 1952; PhD, Carleton U., Ottawa, Ont., 1966; DSc (hon.), U. Man., Winnipeg, Can., 1985, U. Guelph, Ont., 1993. Rsch. assoc. U. Toronto, 1952-54; instr. Vassar Coll., Poughkeepsie, 1954-56; chemist Food, Drug Directorate, Ottawa, 1956-65; rsch. scientist Health Can., Ottawa, 1965-75; rsch. mgr. Bur. Nutritional Scis., Ottawa, 1975-91. Adj. prof. U. Ottawa, 1980-92; cons. Food and Agrl. Orgn. UN, 1992-94; Hilditch lectr. U.K., 1994; trustee Nat. Inst. Nutrition (Can.), 1997-99. Editor: Methods for Nutritional Assessment of Fats, 1985, Fat Requirements for Development and Health, 1988; contbr. articles on dietary fats to profl. jours. Decorated Order of Can.; recipient Queen's Jubilee medal Govt. of Can., 1977, Medaille Chevreul award Inst. Corps Gras, 1984, Crompton award McGill U., 1986, Normann medal German Assn. for Fat Rsch., 1987, Commemorative medal for 125th Anniversary of Fedn. of Can., 1992, Queen's Golden Jubilee medal 2002. Fellow: Am. Inst. Nutrition, Royal Soc. Can. (panelist on food biotechnology 2000—01, hon. treas. 2000—04, chair com. awards and medals 2004—); mem.: Can. Biochem. Soc., Can. Soc. for Nutrition Scis. (pres. 1984—85, Bordon award 1971, McHenry award 1993), Internat. Soc. Fat Rsch. (pres. 1991—92), Am. Oil Chemists Soc. (pres. 1985—86, Lifetime Achievement award Can. sect. 1995). Avocations: hiking, canoeing, cross country skiing, reading. Home: 41 Okanagan Dr Ottawa ON Canada K2H 7E9 E-mail: jbrogers@sympatico.ca.

BEARMAN, TONI CARBO See **CARBO, TONI**

BEA ROBERTS, BARBARA ANN, legal secretary; b. Richmond, Va., Nov. 26, 1957; d. Arthur and Edith (Thompson) B.; m. Alan Roberts; 1 child, Michael T. Sec. IEEE, Washington, 1981-83, Greenhoot, Inc., Washington, 1983-85; legal sec. Friedlander, Misler, Friedlander, Sloan & Herz, Washington, 1985-88, Arnold & Porter, Washington, 1988-97, Dickstein, Shapiro, Morin & Olshinsky, Washington, 1997-99, Hale and Dorr, Washington, 1999-00, Littler, Mendelson PC, 2000—01, KMZ Rosenman, 2001—. Democrat. Mem. Seventh-Day Adventist Ch. Office: KMZ Rosenman 1025 Thomas Jefferson St NW # 700E Washington DC 20007

BEASLEY, BARBARA STARIN, sales executive, marketing professional; b. Nashville, Dec. 31, 1955; d. Donald Francis and Martha Murry (Bridges) S.; m. Johnny Mark Beasley, Oct. 22, 1983; children: John Thomas, Cara Nicole. BFA, So. Meth. U., 1976. Cert. strategic mktg. mgmt., Harvard Bus. Sch. Producer Bill Stokes Assn., Dallas, 1976-80; Mary Kay Cosmetics, Inc., Dallas, 1980-93; sr. v.p. mktg., 1987-89; exec. v.p. sales, 1990-93; sr. v.p. mktg. Nest Entertainment, Dallas, 1994-99, sr. v.p. sales and mktg., 1999-2000; freelance writer, 2000—. Mem. Leadership Tex., 1986. Avocation: birdwatching.

BEASLEY, MARY CATHERINE, retired secondary school educator, retired administrator; b. Portersville, Ala., Nov. 29, 1922; d. Albert Otis and Beulah Green (Killian) Reed; m. Percy Wells Beasley, Dec. 15, 1956 (dec. Dec. 1958). BS in Home Econs., Bob Jones U., 1944; MS, Pa. State U., State College, 1954, EdD, 1968. Tchr. Geraldine and Collinsville (Ala.) High Sch., 1944-45; vocat. home econs. tchr. Glencoe (Ala.) High Sch., 1945-48, Washington County High Sch., Chatom, Ala., 1948-51; home econs. tchr. Homewood Jr. High Sch., Birmingham, Ala., 1958-60; asst. supr. and subject matter specialist Ala. Dept. Edn., Montgomery, 1951-57; asst. prof. Samford U., Birmingham, 1960-62; instr. U. Ala., Tuscaloosa, 1951, asst. prof. then assoc. prof., 1962-68, dir. continuing edn. in home econs., 1968-84, prof., 1984-88, prof. emeritus consumer sci. Coll. Human Environ. Sci., 1988—. Author: (with others) Human Ecological Studies, 1986. Pres. Joint Legis. Coun. of Ala., 1973-75; dir. On Your Own Program, 1970-80; v.p. bd. dirs. Collinsville Cemetery Assn., 2000-02, pres., 2002—. Recipient Creative Programming award Nat. U. Extension Assn., 1979, Women of Achievement award, 2000; named N.E. Ala Woman of Distinction, Girl Scouts North Ala., Inc., 2002. Mem. Am. Home Econs. Assn. (chmn. rehab. com. 1973, 75, leader 1986), Southeastern Coun. on Family Rels. (pres. 1982-84, Disting. Svc. award 1988), Ala. Home Econs. Assn. (pres. 1961-63, leader 1985), Ala. Coun. on Family Rels. (pres. 1981-83, Disting. Svc. award 1987), Altrusa Club of Tuscaloosa (pres. 1988-89, exec. bd. Ft. Payne/DeKalb 1989-93, corr. sec. 1995-96), Collinsville Study Club (v.p. 1992-94, pres. 1996-98, 2002--, reporter 1998-2000, parliamentarian 2000-2002), Ala. Federated Womens Clubs (dir. dist. II 1999-00), Alpha Delta Kappa (treas. Tuscaloosa chpt. 1973-75), Phi Upsilon Omicron, Kappa Omicron Nu. Republican. Baptist. Home: PO Box 680596 Fort Payne AL 35968-1606

BEASLEY, MAURINE HOFFMAN, journalism educator, historian; b. Jan. 28, 1936; d. Dimmitt Heard and Maurine (Hieronymus) Hoffman; m. William C. McLaughlin, May 20, 1966 (div. 1969); m. Henry R. Beasley, Dec. 24, 1970; 1 child, Susan Sook BA History, U. Mo., 1958; MS Journalism, Columbia U., 1963; PhD Am. Civilization, George Washington U., 1974. Edn. editor Kansas City Star, Mo., 1959—62; staff writer Washington Post, 1963—73; from asst. prof journalism to prof. U. Md., College Park, 1975—87, prof., 1987—, grad. dir. Coll. Journalism, 2000—02; sr. lectr. Fulbright Jinan U., Guangzhou, China, 2000. Author: Eleanor Roosevelt and the Media: A Public Quest for Self-Fulfillment, 1987, First Ladies and the Press: The Unfinished Partnership of the Media Age, 2005; author: (with others) Women in Media, 1977, The New Majority, 1988, Taking Their Place! Documentary History of Women and Journalism, rev., 2002 (Outstanding Acad. Books Choice, 1994, award Text and Academic Authors Assn., 2004); editor: White House Press Conferences of Eleanor Roosevelt, 1983; co-editor: Voices of Change: Southern Pulitzer Winners, 1978, One Third of a Nation, 1981 (hon. mention Washington Monthly Book award, 1982), Eleanor Roosevelt Encyclopedia, 2000 (Editor's Choice award Booklist, 2001); mem. adv. bd. Am. Journalism, 1983—, Jour. Mass Media Ethics, 1981—, Journalism and Comm. Monographs, 2002—; corr. editor: Journalism History, 1995—; contbr. articles to profl. jours. Violinist Washington Conservatory Orch., 2001—; pres. Little Falls Swimming Club, Inc. 1988-89; bd. dirs. Sino-Am. Ctr. for Media Tech. and Tng. Gannett Tchg. Fellowship Program fellow, 1977, Pulitzer Traveling fellow Columbia U., 1963; Eleanor Roosevelt studies grantee Eleanor Roosevelt Inst., 1979-80, Arthur Schlesinger rsch. fellow and grantee Roosevelt Inst., 1998; named One of Nation's Outstanding Tchrs. of Writing and Editing Modern Media Inst. (Poynter) and Am. Soc. Newspaper Editors, 1981, Most Outstanding Woman U. Md. College Park, Pres. Commn. on Women's Affairs, 1993; recipient Haiman award Speech Comm. Assn., 1995, Founders Disting. Sr. Scholar award AAUW Ednl. Found., 1999, Columbia U. Sch. Journalism Alumni award, 2000, Smith-Cotton H.S. Hall Fame award, Sedalia, Mo., 2000, Alumni award U. Mo., 2004 Mem.: AAUW (v.p. Coll. Pk. br. 2002—04), Women in Comm., Am. Journalism Historians Assn. (pres.-elect 1988—89, pres. 1989—90, Kobre award for lifetime achievement 1997, Rsch. Paper award named in her honor 1998), Internat. Assn. Mass. Comm. Rsch., Soc. Profl. Journalists (chair nat. hist. site com. 1986—87, bd. dirs. Washington chpt. 1988—90, pres. 1990—91, dir. region 2, nat. bd. dirs. 1991—92, Disting. Local Svc. award 1994, First Amendment award (with others) 1998), Assn. Edn. in Journalism and Mass Comm. (sec. history divsn. 1986—87, vice-head 1987—88, head history divsn. 1988—89, chair profl. freedom and responsibility 1990—91, exec. com. 1990—91, nat. pres. elect 1992, pres. 1993—94, leader People-to-People delegation to China and Hong Kong 1994, exec. com. 1994—95, Outstanding Contbn. to Journalism Edn. award 1994, Disting. Leadership award 2001), Nat. Press Club, Am. News Women's Club (bd. govs. 2001—03), Am. Hist. Assn., Orgn. Am. Historians, Omicron Delta Kappa, Phi Beta Kappa (v.p. Gamma chpt. 2005—). Democrat. Unitarian Universalist. Home: 4920 Flint Dr Bethesda MD 20816-1746 Office: U Md Coll Journalism College Park MD 20742-7111 Office Phone: 301-405-2413. Business E-Mail: mbeasley@jmail.umd.edu.

BEASLEY-MARTIN, MONICA RACHAEL, minister, director; d. Mildred Louise and Edward Marcel Beasley; m. Thomas Booker Martin, Apr. 25, 1984; 1 child, Brandon Martin. BA, Ohio State U., 1979; ThM, Vision Christian U., 1993. Itinerant Elder North Ohio Ann. Conf. of the A.M.E. Ch., 1993. Gospel music d.j., program dir. W.G.F.T. Radio Sta., Youngstown, 1985—88; founder, dir. Feed My Sheep Ministries, Youngstown, Ohio, 1992—; pastor St. James A.M.E Ch., Youngstown, 1993—97; substitute tchr. Youngstown Bd. Edn., Youngstown, 1998—; program dir. Boys & Girls Club, Youngstown, 1996—97; dir. Parent Ctr.,Toy Libr., Youngstown, 1997—98; co-founder Rainbow Players Performance Arts Co., Youngstown, 2004—; pastor Sheridan African Meth. Episcopal Ch., 2005—. Youth program drama tchr. Youngstown Playhouse, 2005—06; ind. bus. agt. Primerica, 2006. Actor: (play) Hansel & Gretel (Youth Theater, Best Performance Adult Female, 2003), Carousel (Youngstown Area Cmty. Theater Award for Featured Actress Musical, 2004), Raisin (Youngstown Area Cmty. Theater Award for Character Performance/ Musical, 2004), Taming of the Shrew (Youngstown Area Cmty. Theater Award Cameo Performance, 2003), Idora Forever (Arthur Award, 2002). Com. mem. Dream Team, Grass Roots Com., Youngstown, 2004—06; vice chair Human Rels. Commn., Youngstown, 1995—98; bd. dirs. Youngstown Playhouse, 2004—06. Mem.: Youngstown Area Cmty. Theater Alliance (nominating com. 2004—06). Avocations: reading, acting. Home: 223 Richards Dr Youngstown OH 44505 Office Phone: 330-386-4055. Personal E-mail: sistapray@yahoo.com.

BEATO, CRISTINA V., government agency administrator; b. Cuba, 1958; BS, U. N.Mex., MD, 1984. Diplomate Am. Bd. Family Practice. Assoc. dean clin. affairs, chief med. officer U. N.Mex. Health Sci. Ctr., 1999—2001; med. dir. Youth Diagnostic and Devel. Ctr., 1999—2001; dep. asst. sec. health office pub. health and sci. U.S. Dept. Health and Human Svcs., 2001—02, prin. dep. sec. health, 2002—03, acting asst. sec. health, 2003—. Rear adm. USPHS. Office: US Dept Health and Human Svcs 200 Independence Ave SW Washington DC 20201 Office Phone: 202-690-7694. Business E-Mail: cheato@usphs.dhhs.gov.

BEATON, MEREDITH, enterostomal therapy clinical nurse specialist; b. Danvers, Mass., Oct. 5, 1941; d. Allan Cameron and Arlene Margaret (Jerue) Beaton; m. William Paul Hollingsworth, Nov. 19, 1983 (div.); 1 stepchild, Brendon R. Diploma, R.I. Hosp. Sch. Nursing, Providence, 1968; BS in Nursing, U. Ariz., 1976; MS in Human Resource Mgmt., Golden Gate U., 1984; postgrad., U. Tex., 1988; EdD, U. N.Mex., 1995; MS in Nursing, U. Phoenix, 1998. Cert. enterostomal therapy nurse, health edn. specialist. Commd. ensign USN, 1968, advanced through grades to lt. comdr., 1979, charge nurse USA, PTO, 1968-88; command ostomy nurse, head ostomy clinic Naval Hosp. Portsmouth, Va., 1985-88; pres., CEO Enterostomal Therapy Nursing Edn. and Tng. Cons. (ETNetc), Rio Rancho, N.Mex., 1989-99; mgr. clin. svcs. western area Support Systems Internat., Inc., Charleston, S.C., 1990-92; pres., CEO, Paumer Assocs. Internat., Inc., Rio Rancho, N.Mex., 1992—2001; sr. cons. enterostomal therapy nursing, edn., & tng. cons.; dir./provost N.Mex. Sch. Enterostomal Nursing, Rio Rancho, 1996-2000; enterostomal therapy nurse, clin. nurse specialist, educator Presbyn. Health Care Svcs., Albuquerque, 1992-95; sr. cons. Enterostomal Therapy Nursing Edn. & Tng. Cons. A Divsn. of Paumer Assocs., Rio Rancho, N.Mex., 1995—2001. Dir./provost N.Mex. Sch. ET Nursing, Rio Rancho, 1995—2000; clin. svcs. mgr. Paper Pak Products Inc., 2000—02; sch. nurse Colinas del Norte Elem. Sch., Rio Rancho Pub. Schs. Sys., N.Mex., 2002—06; lectr. in field. Reviewer: RN Mag. Mem. adminstrv. bd. Baylake United Meth. Ch., Virginia Beach, 1980-83; chmn. bd. deacons St. Paul's United Ch., Rio Rancho, moderator, 2001-02, also vice moderator; active Am. Cancer Soc.; mem. adv. bd. Keep Rio Rancho Beautiful, 1998-2003; bd. dirs. N.Mex. Mus. Mil. History. Mem. Wound, Ostomy and Continence Nurses Soc. (nat. govt. affairs com., govt. affairs com. Rocky Mountain region, newsletter editor, pub. rels. com., regional pres. 1989-93, nat. sec. 1994-95), United Ostomy Assn., World Coun. Enterostomal Therapists (mem. editl. bd. 2003-), N.Mex. Health Care Assn., N.Mex. Assn. for Home Care, N.Mex. Assn. Sch. Nurses, N.Mex. Assn. for Continuity of Care, Assn. Advanced Wound Care (bd. dirs.), Women Vets. N.Mex. (bd. dirs.). Republican. Avocations: hot air ballooning, gourmet cooking, flower arranging, interior design.

BEATTIE, ANN, writer, educator; b. Washington, Sept. 8, 1947; d. James and Charlotte (Crosby) B.; m. Lincoln Perry. BA, Am. U., 1969; MA, U. Conn., 1970; L.H.D. (hon.), Am. U., 1983. Vis. asst. prof. U. Va., Charlottesville, 1976-77, vis. writer, 1980, Edgar Allan Poe prof., 2001—; Briggs Copeland lectr. English Harvard U., Cambridge, Mass., 1977. Author: Chilly Scenes of Winter, 1976, Distortions, 1976, Secrets and Surprises, 1979, Falling In Place, 1980, Jacklighting, 1981, The Burning House, 1982, Love Always, 1985, Where You'll Find Me, 1986, Alex Katz, 1987, Picturing Will, 1990, What Was Mine, 1991, My Life, Starring Dara Falcon, 1997, Park City: New & Selected Stories, 1998, Perfect Recall, 2000, The Doctor's House, 2002, Follies: And New Stories, 2005. Recipient Disting. Alumnae award Am. U., 1980, award in lit. Am. Acad. and Inst. Arts and Letters, 1980, PEN/Malamud award for excellence in short fiction, 2000; Guggenheim fellow, 1977. Mem. PEN, Am. Acad. Arts and Letters (v.p. lit., 1989-99), Am. Acad. Arts and Scis., Authors Guild. Office: care Janklow and Nesbit 445 Park Ave New York NY 10022-2606

BEATTIE, DIANA SCOTT, biochemistry professor; b. Cranston, R.I., Aug. 11, 1934; d. Kenneth Allen and Lillian Francis (Barton) Scott; m. Benjamin Howard Beattie, June 30, 1956 (div. 1975); children: Elizabeth, Sara, Rachel, Ruth; m. Robert Nathan Stuchell, Feb. 6, 1976 (div. 1991). BA, Swarthmore Coll., 1956; MS, U. Pitts., 1958, PhD, 1961. Research assoc. U. Pitts., 1961-67, VA Hosp., Pitts., 1967-68; faculty Mt. Sinai Sch. Medicine, N.Y.C., 1968-85, prof. biochemistry, 1976-85; prof., chmn. dept. biochemistry W.Va. U. Sch. Medicine, Morgantown, 1985-2001, chmn. dept. biochemistry and molecular pharmacology, 2001—06; dean undergrad. campus Oman Med. Coll. Mem. grad. faculty biomed. sci. CUNY, 1968-86, biochemistry, 1971-85, biology, 1974-85; mem. grad. faculty biochemistry W.Va. U. Sch. Medicine, Morgantown, 1985-2006; vis. prof. U. Louvain, Belgium, 1982, U. Nairobi, Kenya, 1993, Shandong U., China, 2000, Oman Med. Coll., 2005, 2006; mem. ad hoc biochemistry study sect. NIH, 1976-77, 79-81, mem. phys. biochemistry study sect., 1981-85, 1993-97; chmn. phys. biochemistry study sect., 1983-85, 1995-97; mem. metabolic biology panel NSF, 1986-89; mem. basic sci. merit rev. panel VA, 1989-92. Contbr. articles to profl. jours.; mem. editorial bd. Archives of Biochemistry and Biophysics, 1975-78, 85-2000, Jour. Bioenergetics, 1975—. Recipient award Met. N.Y. chpt. Assn. for Women in Sci., 1979; grantee NSF, 1970-92, 97—2001, NIH, 1966-2004; Fogarty internat. fellow, 1982, Fulbright fellow, 1993. Mem. Am. Soc. Biol. Chemists (membership com. 1987-89), Am. Soc. Cell Biology, Biophysics Soc., Assn. Med. Sch. Depts. Biochemistry (exec. com. 1989-92, pres.-elect 1995, pres. 1996), Am. Assn. Med. Schs. (coun. acad. socs. 1989-2001, adminstrv. bd. 1994-99, chair 1998), Nat. Bd. Med. Examiners (biochemistry test com. 1991-93, chair 1994-95, cell biology test com. 1998-2001, mem. adv. com. for med. sch. programs 2003-06), Nat. Caucus Basic Biomed. Chairs (vice chair 1991-2006). Home: 324 Dream Catcher Cir Morgantown WV 26508-9473 Office: WVa U Sch Medicine Dept Biochemistry Morgantown WV 26506 E-mail: dbeattie@hsc.wvu.edu.

BEATTIE, STEPHANIE SHANNON, human resources specialist; b. Greenville, S.C., Aug. 19, 1968; d. Jerry Nelson and Judith Farley Beattie. BS, Presbyn. Coll., Clinton, S.C., 1990; MA in Counseling, Webster U., 1997, MA in Human Resources and Devel., 2003. Residential counselor Luth. Family Svcs., Pelzer, SC, 1990—92; drug/alcohol counselor Methodone Clinic, Greenville, 1992—94; social worker Dept. Social Svcs., Greenville, 1994—2004; mgr. employee/vol. rels. The Blood Connection, Greenville, SC, 2004—. Mem. consumer adv. bd. Greenville Mental Health, 1999. Roman Catholic. Avocations: golf, skiing, landscaping. Office: The Blood Connection Greenville SC 29605 Office Phone: 864-255-5005 1078.

BEATTS, ANNE PATRICIA, writer; b. Buffalo, Feb. 25, 1947; d. Patrick Murray Threipland and Sheila Elizabeth Jean (Sherriff Scott) B. BA with honors, McGill U., Montreal, Que., Can., 1966. Contbg. editor National Lampoon mag., N.Y.C., 1970-74; writer Saturday Night Live NBC, N.Y.C., 1975-80; creator, prodr. Square Pegs CBS, Los Angeles, 1982-83; co-exec. prodr. A Different World NBC, Los Angeles, 1987-88; exec. prodr. The Stephanie Miller Show, 1994-95. Writer, creative cons. Saturday Night Live 25th Ann. Spl., 1999; exec. story cons. (WETV) Committed, 2000-01; head writer WGA Awards, 2004; co-exec. prodr., co-dir. John Waters Presents Movies That Will Corrupt You, Here! TV, 2006; adj. prof. writing divsn. Sch. Cinema-TV, U. So. Calif., 2003-06. Co-editor: (humorous books) Titters, 1976, Saturday Night, 1977; co-author: (humorous books) Titters 101, 1984, The Mom Book, 1986; author book for Broadway mus. Leader of the Pack, 1985; humor columnist L.A. Times, 1997-98. Mem. AFTRA, SAG, Writers Guild Am. (award 1976, 77, 2000), Dirs. Guild Am., Women in Film, Dramatists Guild, NATAS (2 Emmy awards, 6 Emmy award nominations 1975-80, 2000). Office Phone: 310-550-4525. Personal E-mail: beattsclass@aol.com.

BEATTY, FRANCES, civic worker; b. Chgo., Apr. 17, 1940; d. Pasquale and Rose (Brunetti) Calomeni; m. Robert Alfred Beatty, Aug. 24, 1963; children: Bradford, Roxanna Beatty Goebel. BA, Northwestern U., l96l; MA, U. Chgo., 1967. Tchr. math. Proviso West High Sch., Hillside, Ill., 1961-66. Active Oak Brook Dist. 53 Sch. Bd., 1979-85; women's bd. Field Mus. Natural History, Chgo., 1985—, founders coun., 1988—, treas. women's bd., 1991-93; governing bd. Chgo. Symphony, 1985-92; trustee Chgo. Symphony Orch., 1992-96, life trustee, 2005—; women's bd. Ravinia Festival, Highland Park, Ill., 1987—, Northwestern U., Evanston, Ill., sec. women's bd., 1999-2001, libr. bd., 1990-95; women's bd. U. Chgo.; mem. coun. Wellness House, Hinsdale, Ill., 1994; com. mem. Chgo. Humanities Festival, 1999-2003; treas. 626 Landmark Found., 2005—. Mem.: 626 Found. (sec., treas. 2005—), Merit Sch. Music, Alumnae of Northwestern U. (pres. 1996—98), The Antiquarian Soc. Art Inst. Chgo., John Evans Club, Woman's Athletic Club Chgo. (3d v.p. 1985—87, 1st v.p. 1992—94, pres. 1994—96).

BEATTY, MARIA LOIS, elementary school educator; b. Milw., Mar. 9, 1961; d. Keith Albert and Barbara Ann McQuillan; m. Patrick Michael Beatty, June 17, 1985; children: Sarah Marie, John Michael. EdM, U. Cin., 1985. Cert. profl. educator Ohio, 1985. Phys. educator Crosby Elem. Sch., Harrison, Ohio, 1986—. Named Tchr. of Yr., Crosby Elem. Sch., 1999, PTA Educator of Yr., Crosby Elem. PTA Bd., 2000; grantee, SW Schs., 1988, 1994, 1995, 1996, 1999, 2000, 2001. Mem.: NEA (assoc.), AAHPERD (assoc.). Home: 4346 Stone Trace Ln Hamilton OH 45011 Office: Crosby Elementary School 8382 New Haven Rd Harrison OH 45030 Office Phone: 513-738-1717. Office Fax: 513-738-1718. Personal E-mail: mariabeatty@southwestschools.org.

BEATY, BARBARA A., secondary school educator; b. Dallas, Tex., Mar. 20, 1948; d. Cecil Lamoine and Hilda Mae Johnson; m. Dennis Wade Beaty, Feb. 17, 1968; children: Christopher Wade, Diana Lynn. BA, U. Tex., 1971. Tchr. Nichols Jr. H.S. Arlington (Tex.) Ind. Sch. Dist., 1971—75; tchr. Lakeside H.S., Hot Springs, Ark., 1982—83; tchr. Young Jr. H.S. Arlington Ind. Sch. Dist., 1983—97, tchr. Martin H.S., 1997—. Mem.: Kiwanis Internat. (George Hixson award 2003—04), Kappa Alpha Theta. Home: 5725 Trails Edge Ct Arlington TX 76017 Office: 4501 Pleasant Ridge Rd Arlington TX 76017

BEATY-GUNTER, SHARON E., music educator; b. Marietta, Ga., Aug. 3, 1953; d. James Webster and Reba Jo (Marshall) Earley; m. Marcus Eugene Gunter, May 28, 1993; 1 child by previous marriage, John Kevin Beaty. Degree in Vocal Performance, Ga. State U., Atlanta; PhD in Music Edn., U. Wexford. Sr. ct. clk. Fulton County, Atlanta, 1971-74; adminstrv. sec. Northside Hosp., Atlanta, 1975-77; auto analyst Cigna Ins., Atlanta, 1977-82; office trainer Travelers Ins., Atlanta, 1992-95; dir., owner Strings & Keys, Inc., Cumming, 1976—. Office mgr., pers. dir. Main Source Germany, Cumming, 1995-96; music dir. Bethelview Meth. Ch., Cumming, 1982; youth choir dir. North Lanier Bapt. Ch., Cumming, 1989-91. Author, creator vocal instrn. video Share the Song in Your Heart, 1997; composer sacred inspirational music. Entertainment assoc. March of Dimes, Cumming, 1999, Am. Cancer Soc., Cumming, 1997-99, City of Cumming Meml. Day Svcs., 1996-98, City of Cumming Vietnam Moving Wall, 1998. Recipient award Literary Competition, Ga. Bd. Edn., 1971, Outstanding Choral award City of Cumming, 1998. Mem. Nat. Assn. Music Makers, Nat. Piano Tchrs. Guild, Music Tchrs. Nat. Assn., Ga. Music Tchrs. Assn. Office: Gunter Music Studio Inc 2210 Goldmine Dr Cumming GA 30040-4322

BEAUBIEN, ANNE KATHLEEN, librarian; b. Detroit, Sept. 15, 1947; d. Richard Parker and Edith Mildred Beaubien; m. Philip Conway Berry, Feb. 7, 2004. Student, Western Mich. U., 1965-67; BA, Mich. State U., 1969; MLS, U. Mich., 1970. Reference libr., bibliographic instr. U. Mich. Libr., Ann Arbor, 1971-80, dir. MITS, 1980-85, dir. coop. access svc., 1985—, head bus. and fin. office, 1995—2000, grants officer, 2000—. Author: Psychology Bibliography, 1980; co-author: Learning the Library, 1982; contbg. articles to profl. jour., editor, conf. proc., 1987. Mem. vestry St. Clare's Episcopal Ch., Ann Arbor, 1986—89, 2002—03; pres. Ann Arbor Ski Club, 1978—79. Recipient Woman of Yr. Award, Ann Arbor Bus. and Profl. Women's Club, 1982; Disting. Alumnus Award; Sch. Info. and Libr. Studies, U. Mich., 1987. Mem. ALA, Assn. Coll. and Rsch. Librs. (pres. 1991-92). Avocations: skiing, bicycling, ballroom dancing. Office: U Mich Libr 106 Hatcher Grad Libr Ann Arbor MI 48109 Office Phone: 734-936-2322. Business E-Mail: beaubien@umich.edu.

BEAUCHAMP, FRANCIS DRAKE, real estate agent; b. Wellington, Tex., Feb. 7, 1940; d. Lemuel Clyde and Nora Cooke Drake; m. John R. Beauchamp, Aug. 24, 1963; children: Robert Drake, John Stuart. BA cum laude, U. Tex., 1962. Med. typist Baylor Hosp., Dallas, 1962—63, St. Paul's Hosp., Dallas, 1963—64; sci. tchr. Dallas Pub. Sch. Sys., 1964—66; real estate agt. Kuper Realty (now Kuper Sotheby's Internat. Realty), San Antonio, 1986—91, v.p., mktg. dir., relocation dir., 1995—, v.p. relocation dirs., 2001—. Mktg. dir. Casas, Haciendas and Ranchos mag. Bd. dirs. Jr. League, San Antonio, 1976—80; pres. Alamo Heights PTO, San Antonio, 1978—79; historian Bexar County Med. Wives, San Antonio, 1974. Mem.: San Antonio Area Relocation Orgn., Employees Relocation Coun. (cert. relocation profl.), Tex. Assn. Realtors, Relocation Dirs. Coun. Republican. Episcopalian. Avocations: bridge, fishing, gardening. Office: Kuper Sotheby's Internat Realty 6606 N New Brunfels San Antonio TX 78209 Office Phone: 210-477-9325.

BEAUCHAMP, VALDIVIA VÂNIA SIQUEIRA, translator; b. Recife, Brazil, June 17, 1944; d. Francisco Targino and Angelica (Lucas) De Siqueira; m. Jimmie Willis Beauchamp (div. 1970); 1 child, Angélica R. BS in Journalism, U. Centro Unifica De Brasilia, 1978; MA in Portuguese and Spanish Lit., NYU, 1992. Registered profl. journalist. Social comm. sec. Office of Brazilian Presidency, Brasilia, Brazil, 1984-90; Portuguese translator Family Court, N.Y.C., 1993; translator, broker asst. Josephthal Lion & Ross, N.Y.C., 1995, U.S. Securities and Futures, N.Y.C., 1999—. Reporter, corr., founder, tchr. Lang. Sch. Multilinguas, Brazil, 1984-; tchr. Portuguese and Spanish, Sigma Delta Pi, Purdue U., Ind., 1982-84, NYU, 1990-92. Author: Stigma, Saga for a New World, 2004. Founder literary hour NYU; liberal artist Lafayette Art Mus., 1982-84. Mem. NYU Alumni, C. of C. of the Rockways (exec. dir. 1998). Avocations: painting, piano, horseback riding, fishing, golf. Personal E-mail: vbeauchamp@nyc.rr.com.

BEAUDET-FRANCÈS, PATRICIA SUZANNE, photography editor; b. Chgo., Aug. 6, 1951; d. André Marcel and Helen Gertrude (Joiner) B.; m. Gérard Jean-Pierre Frances, June 27, 1997. Sr. photography editor Playboy Enterprises Inc., Chgo., 1970—. Contbg. photographer Rolling Stone Illustrated History of Rock and Roll, 1992; rschr., photo editor Playboy (photographs pub. 50 yrs.): The Playboy Book: Forty Years, 1994, Playboy: 50 Years The Photographs Featured; prodr. CD Instrumental Journey, 2002. Democrat. Roman Catholic. Avocations: photography, travel, cinema, workouts, reading. Home: PO Box 31351 Chicago IL 60631-0351 Office Phone: 312-373-2715. E-mail: pattyb@playboy.com.

BEAUDRY, DIANE FAY, medical quality management executive; b. Manitowoc, Wis., Mar. 6, 1947; d. Ruben William and Gertrude Katherine (Novak) Puta. BSN, Alverno Coll., 1971; MS in Ednl. Adminstrn., U. Wis., Milw., 1979, PhD in Urban Edn., 1991. Staff nurse St. Mary's Hosp., Milw., 1971-72, St. Anthony's Hosp., Milw., 1972-74; nurse coord. Pvt. Initiative in PSRO, Wis., 1974-75; insvc. instr. Deaconess Hosp., Milw., 1975-77, insvc. coord., 1977-81; dir. nursing staff devel./quality assurance Good Samaritan Med. Ctr., Milw., 1981-84, dir. quality assurance, 1984-85, dir. utilization mgmt., 1985-88; mgr. quality mgmt. Sinai Samaritan Med. Ctr., Milw., 1988-89, dir. med. staff svcs. and quality mgmt., 1989-97, dir. quality mgmt., 1997—2002, Aurora St. Luke's Med. Ctr., 1997—. Author: (with others) Interdisciplinary QA: Issues in Collaboration, 1991 Mem. Nat. Assn. for Healthcare Quality, Alverno Coll. Alumnae Assn., U. Wis. Alumni Assn., Delta Epsilon Sigma, Kappa Gamma Pi. Avocations: ballroom dancing, motorcycle riding. Home: 11047 N Riverland Ct # 36W Mequon WI 53092-4900 Office: Aurora St Luke's Med Ctr PO Box 2901 Milwaukee WI 53201-2901 Office Phone: 414-649-7138. Business E-Mail: diane.beaudry@aurora.org.

BEAUDRY, ROBIN SHARKEY, secondary school educator; b. Toms River, NJ, Mar. 22, 1970; d. Robert and Elizabeth Sharkey; m. Chris Beaudry, Oct. 8, 2000; children: CJ Sharkey, Erin Eileen. BS, West Chester U., Pa., 1992. Cert. health and phys. edn. NJ, 1992, drivers edn. instr. NJ, 2002, project adventure phase 1 NJ, 2000. Tchr. Manchester H.S., NJ, 1993, Raritan H.S., Hazlet, NJ, 1993—. Coach basketball team Raritan H.S., Hazlet, 1994—2001, coach varsity soccer team, 1998—2003, coach dance team, 2003—. Mem.: MCEA (assoc.), NEA (assoc.), UFHS (assoc.). Office: Raritan HS 419 Middle Rd Hazlet NJ 07730 Office Phone: 732-264-8411. Business E-Mail: rbeaudry@mail.hazlet.org.

BEAUFORD, SANDRA, nurse, data processing executive; b. N.Y.C., Feb. 7, 1950; d. Ethel Beauford; children: Gary, Michael, David Sumerlin-Beauford. A.S, Manhattan C.C., 1974; BSN, Herbert H. Lehman Coll., 1976. CCRN, cert. parish nurse. Critical care mgr. Botsford Hosp., Farmington, Mich., 1990—92; asst. mgr. Henry Ford Hosp., Detroit, 1992—96; clin. mgr. Taylor Ambulance, Detroit, 1996—98; o.r. quality coord. Oakwood Hosp., Dearborn, Mich., 1999—; parish nurse Oakwood Hosp. Greater Grace Temple, Dearborn, Mich., 2000—01. Author: On The Road to Your New Beginning, 2000 (Bravo award, 2001, 2002). Facilitator customer svc. enhancement program Oakwood Hosp., 2002—. Lt. USAF, 1974—78, Mclaughin Air Force Base. Mem.: Am. Heart Assn. (logistic com.), American Coll. Cardiology, Soc. Thoracic Surgeons. Pentecostal. Avocations: basketball, photography, reading. Office: 18101 Oakwood Blvd Dearborn MI 48124-4089

BEAUMONTE, PHYLLIS ILENE, retired secondary school educator; b. Seattle, Dec. 15; d. Albert Hendrix and Bessie Dorothy (Buford) Ratcliff; m. Pierre Marshall Beaumonte, Mar. 12, 1962 (div. Aug. 1974). BA in Polit. Sci., U. Wash., 1973, BA in Editl. Journalism, 1973, MPA, 1975; postgrad., N.W. Theol. Union, Seattle, 1990-92; M in Pastoral Studies/Theology, Seattle U., 2001. Cert. tchr. K-12 Wash. Adminstrv. intern Office of the City Coun., Seattle, 1974; guest lectr. Pacific Luth. U., Tacoma, 1975; tchr. Hebrew Acad., Seattle, 1979; instr./tchr. Seattle Ctrl. C.C., 1988; tchr. Seattle Pub. Schs., 1980—2000; coord. hs Bus. Ptnrs. in Pub. Edn., Seattle, 1989-92; social studies chairperson Rainier Beach HS, Seattle, 1992—2000; ret., 2000. Cons. RA Beau Enterprises, Seattle, 1987—; participant Ctr. R&D in Law-Related Edn. Wake Forest U., Winston-Salem, NC, 1994; adv. com. Wash. State Commn. Student Learning, Social Studies Acad. Learning Requirements, 1994—; part-time faculty South C.C., Seattle, 1998—99. Author: (poetry) Satyagraha; author, editor: Roses and Thorns, 1994, writer, pub.: Parent Guardian Handbook: A Guide to Understanding Public Education and Standardized Testing, 2002. Mem. King County Women's Polit. Caucus, Seattle, 1993—; v.p. Ch. Women United, Wash. and Idaho, 1976—78, pres., 2002—, Seattle Ch. Women United, 2001—02; mem. candidate evaluation com. Seattle Mcpl. League, 1972—74; Seattle edn. sch. rep. Seattle Tchrs. Union, 1983—85; alumni advisor Grad. Sch. Pub. Affairs U. Wash., 1994—; pres. Black Heritage Soc. Wash. Scholar Minority Journalism, U. Wash., 1972. Mem.: NAACP (mem. exec. bd., v.p. state conf. Wash., v.p. state conf. Oreg., v.p. state conf. Alaska, state chair edn., Daisy Bates Adv. award), Edn. Social and Pub. Svcs. Assn. (pres.), Nat. Coun. Social Studies, Nat. Coun. History Edn. (cert. of appreciation 1993), Internat. Soc. Poets (life Internat. Poet of Merit award 1993), Mus. History and Industry, Sigma Gamma Rho. Baptist. Avocations: singing, writing, reading, teaching. Home: 10012 61st Ave S Seattle WA 98178-2333

BEAUPAIN, ELAINE SHAPIRO, psychiatric social worker; b. Boston, Nov. 1, 1949; d. Abraham and Anna Marilyn (Gass) S.; m. Dean A. Beaupain, Feb. 14, 1987; 1 child, Andrew. BA, McGill U., Montreal, Que., Can., 1971, MSW, 1974. Ind. clin. social worker, Mass.; cert. social worker, Maine; cert. social worker with ind. practice lic., Maine; lic. ind. clin. social worker, Mass. Psychiat. social worker Bangor (Maine) Mental Health Inst., 1974-75; outpatient therapist The Counseling Ctr., Bangor, 1975-76, Millinocket, Maine, 1979-86; asst. core group leader adolescent unit Jackson Brook Inst., Portland, Maine, 1986-87; area dir. Cmty. Health and Counseling Svcs., 1981-86; pvt. practice social work, 1987—. Psychotherapy with individuals, couples and families Millinocket and Bangor, 1987—. Mem. AAUW, NASW, Acad. Cert. Social Workers (diplomate 1992). Democrat. Office: 122 Pine St Bangor ME 04401-5216

BEAUSOLEIL, DORIS MAE, retired federal agency housing specialist; b. Chelmsford, Mass., Jan. 9, 1932; d. Joseph Honorious and Beatrice Pearl (Smith) Beausoleil. Student, State Tchrs. Coll., Lowell, Mass., 1949-51; BA in Sociology and Psychology, Goddard Coll., Plainfield, Vt., 1954; MA in Human Rels., NYU, 1957; postgrad., CUNY, N.Y.C., 1988-97. With divsn. human rights State of NY, NYC, 1960-69, housing dir., 1966-68; housing cons. Nat. Com. Against Discrimination Housing, NYC, 1969—70, Edwin Gould Found., NYC, 1970—71; human resources cons. interfaith housing strategy com., housing cons. Fedn. Prot. Welfare Agys., Inc., NYC, 1971—72; housing cons., 1972—74; equal opportunity compliance specialist NY/NJ Dept. Housing and Urban Devel., NYC, 1975—2000, fed. women's program coord., 1975—79, br. chief Title VI sect. 109 compliance divsn. fair housing and equal opportunity region II, 1979—84, coord. sect. III, 1998—2006, pub. trust specialist, 2000—06. Mem. adv. panel Housing Mag., 1979. Founding mem. N.Y. State HUD Com.; cons., examiner N.Y. State Civil Svc. Commn., 1970—93; bd. dirs. Nat. Assn. Human Rights Workers, 1974—77. Mem.: Citizens Housing and Planning Coun., Goddard Coll. Alumni Assn. (sec. 1988—90), Rep. Bus. Women's Club (pres. 1985—88, bd. dirs. 1989—91). Unitarian Universalist. Avocations: painting, animal rights activism. Home: 392 Central Park W Apt 14N New York NY 10025-5868 Personal E-mail: d_beausoleil@verizon.net.

BEAVER, BARBARA LEANN, elementary school educator, writer; b. Dallas, Dec. 1, 1963; d. Ronald A. Williams and Barbara L. Vines, Marta Williams (Stepmother); m. Franklin D. Beaver, May 30, 1997; 1 child, Amber M.; m. Raymond P. Mullen, June 29, 1984 (div.); children: Joshua D. Mullen, Jacqueline A. Mullen. BS, Tex. A&M, Commerce, 1989; M of Liberal Arts, So. Meth. U., Dallas, 2001. Cert. tchr. Tex., 1989. Math tchr. Waxahachie Jr. H.S., Tex., 1989—91; elem. tchr. Jefferson Davis Elem. Sch., Dallas, 1991—93; math and sci. tchr. A. C. New Mid. Sch., Balch Springs, 1993—97; advanced placement tchr. Met. Christian Sch., Dallas, 1997—2000; info. tech. lead tchr. Ed Vanston Mid. Sch., Mesquite, 2001—. Mentor tchr. Ed Vanston Mid. Sch., Mesquite, Tex., 2001—. Author: (magazine and newsletter articles) A Love and Logic Funny Moment. Victim responder Victim Relief Ministries, Dallas. Recipient Mesquite Apple Corps award, Vanston Mid. Sch., 2006. Mem.: Alpha Delta Kappa (assoc.). Mem. Evang. Ch. Avocations: writing, photography, soccer. Office Phone: 972-882-5801.

BEAVER, BONNIE VERYLE, veterinarian, educator; b. Mpls., Oct. 26, 1944; d. Crawford F. and Gladys I. Gustafson; m. Larry J. Beaver, Nov. 25, 1972 (dec. Nov. 1995). BS, U. Minn., 1966, DVM, 1968; MS, Tex. A&M U., 1972. Instr. vet. surgery and radiology U. Minn., 1968-69; instr. vet. anatomy Tex. A&M U., College Station, 1969-72, asst. prof., 1972-76, assoc. prof., 1976-82; prof. Tex A&M U., College Station, 1982-86, prof. vet. small animal medicine and surgery, 1986—, chief medicine, 1990-99. Mem. vet. medicine adv. com. HEW, 1972-74, nat. adv. food and drug com., HEW, 1975, com. on animal models and genetic stocks NAS, 1984-86, 87-89, panel on microlivestock NRC, 1986-87, task force on animal use study Inst. Lab. Animal Resources, 1986, adv. com. for Pew Nat. Vet. Edn. Program, Pew Charitable Trusts, 1987-92, 10th symposium on Vet. Med. Edn. Com., 1988-89; Frank K. Ramsey lects. Iowa State U., 2004; T.S. Williams lectr. Tuskegee U., 2006. Mem. editl. bd. Applied Animal Ethology, 1981-82, 83-84, VM/SAC, 1982-85, Applied Animal Behavior Sci., 1982-84, 84-86, 86-88, 88-2000, Bull. on Vet. Clin. Ethology, 1994-1999, Jour. Am. Animal Hosp. Assn., 1995—, Jour. Vet. Behavior: Clin. Applications and Rsch., 2005—; contbr. articles to profl. jours. V.p. Brazos Valley Regional Sci. and Engring. Fair, 1974—83, dir., 1983—85; bd. dirs. Brazos Valley unit Am. Cancer Soc., 1976—83, v.p., 1976—83. Named Citizen of Week, The Press, 1981, Outstanding Woman Vet. of 1982, Disting. Practitioner, Nat. Acads. Practice; recipient Friskies PetCare award Am. Animal Hosp. Assn., 2001, Bustad Human-Animal Bond award, 2001, Elanco Disting. Lectr. award, 2002, Frank K. Ramsey Lectr. award, 2004. Mem.: AVMA (exec. bd. 1997—2006, chair exec. bd. 2001—02, pres.-elect 2003—04, pres. 2004—05, Animal Welfare award 1996), AAAS, Am. Soc. Lab. Animal Practitioners, Am. Assn. Human-Animal Bond Veterinarians, Am. Assn. Food Hygiene Veterinarians, Am. Horse Coun., Ark. Med. Vet. Assn., Am. Quarter Horse Assn., Tex. Palomino Exhibitors Assn., Palomino Horse Breeders Am. (v.p. 1983—88, treas. 1984—85, pres.-elect 1988—89, pres. 1989—90), Nat. Acad. Practice, Am. Coll. Vet. Behaviorists (chair organizing com. 1976—91, pres. 1991—96, charter diplomate 1993—, exec. dir. 1996—), Animal Behavior Soc., Am. Assn. Bovine Practitioners, Am. Assn. Equine Practitioners, La. Vet. Med. Assn., Am. Vet. Soc. Animal Behavior (pres. 1975—80), Am. Animal Hosp. Assn., Brazos Valley Vet. Med. Assn., Tex. Vet. Med. Assn. (3d v.p. 1990, 2d v.p. 1991, 1st v.p. 1992, pres.-elect 1993, pres. 1994, Legacy of Svc. award 2005), Phi Delta Gamma (pres. 1974—75), Phi Zeta (nat. pres. 1979—81), Sigma Epsilon Sigma, Phi Sigma, Delta Soc. Office: Tex A&M Univ Coll Vet Medicine Vet Small Animal Medicine & Surgery College Station TX 77843-4474

BEBIS, CONCHITA JUBAN, mathematics educator; b. Cebu, Philippines, Aug. 19, 1959; d. Ignacia Molejon and Prudencio Duran Juban; children: Anna Celeste Juban, Ralphy Ramonito Juban. BS in Secondary Edn., Bukidnon State Coll., Malaybalay City, Philippines, 1978—82, MA in Edn., 1984—85; Cert. in Biology, Ctrl. Mindanao U., Musuan, Bukidnon, Philippines, 1985—86. Cert. Tchr. Tex. Dept. Edn., 2003. Secondary math tchr. San Agustin Inst. Tech., Valencia, Philippines; sch. tchr. San Isidro Coll. HS Dept., Malaybalay; master tchr. 1 Bukidnon Nat. HS, Malaybalay, Philippines, 1989—2000; math tchr. Lee HS, Houston, 2000—. Math inservice facilitator PA_PROBE Divsn. of Bukidnon, Malaybalay, 1998—2000; dept. math coord. San Isidro Coll., HS Dept, Malaybalay; chmn., scholarship com. Bukidnon Nat. HS, Malaybalay, 1996—98, sr. curriculum adviser, 1996—98, math olympiad coach, 1996—98. Recipient Valedictorian, San Isidro HS, Kadingilan, Bukidnon, Philippines, 1978, Gold medalist, Regional Leader Sch. Region X, 1990; fellow Study grant, PA-PROBE (Philippines-Australia Project in Basic Edn.), 1998; grantee scholarship, BSC-DECS, Philippines, 1978—82. Mem.: Houston Fedn. Tchrs. Home: 11770 Westheimer #2605 Houston TX 77077 Office: Lee HS 6529 Beverly Hill Ln Houston TX 77077 Office Phone: 713-787-1700. Home Fax: 713-787-1723; Office Fax: 713-787-1723. Business E-Mail: cbebis@houstonisd.org.

BEBOUT, JENNIFER LUCILLE, science educator; b. Buffalo, Dec. 2, 1977; d. George A. and Jane E. Bebout. BS in Biol. Scis., Wright State U., 2000, MEd, 2002. Cert. tchr. Ohio. Sci. tchr. West Carrollton HS, Ohio, 2002—. Nat. honor soc. co-advisor West Carrollton H.S., Ohio, 2003—06, S.A.D.D. co-advisor, 2005—, homecoming dance co-advisor, 2005—. Recipient Significant Educator award, West Carrollton Edn. Recognition Assn., 2003, 2004, 2005, 2006; grant, Wright State U. Honor's Program, 1999, Wright State U., 2001. Avocations: hiking, reading, listening to music. Office: West Carrollton HS 5833 Student St West Carrollton OH 45449 Office Phone: 937-859-5121 8844. Personal E-mail: dancingdaphnia@hotmail.com. E-mail: jbebout@wcsd.k12.oh.us.

BECA, MONIQUE, psychologist; arrived in U.S., 1991; d. Henryk Geca and Zofia Geca-Wiraszka. BA, Multnomah Bible Coll., Portland, Oreg., 1994; MA in Marriage and Family, George Fox U., Newberg, Oreg., 1996, MA in Clin. Psychology, 2001, D in Psychology, 2003. Histopathology tech. Jewish Hosp./Oncology, Lublin, Poland, 1987—89; mental health therapist Woodland Park Hosp., Portland, Oreg., 1995; family therapist Pacific Gateway Hosp., Portland, Oreg., 1995—96; mental health therapist Juvenile Dept. Donald E. Long, 1996—98; mental health cons. Multnomah, Portland, Oreg., 1998—2002; psychologist Patton State Hosp., Calif., 2002—04, Napa State Hosp., Calif., 2004—. Cons. in field. Student counselor Camp, Canada, 1990—91; translator Vienna, 1989—90; vol. Vols. of Am., Portland, Oreg., 1991—94. Mem.: APA. Avocations: photography, hiking, jogging, reading, classical music. Office Phone: 707-253-5071.

BECHTEL, KRISTEN KING, chemistry educator; b. York, Pa., Apr. 18, 1969; d. Max Russell and Margaret Candler King; m. William John Bechtel, Oct. 21, 1995; children: Max Elliot, Evan Sebastian, Avery William. BS in Chemistry, Shippensburg U., Pa., 1991; MA in Chemistry, Bucknell U., Lewisburg, Pa., 1997. Cert. tchr. level 1 Commonwealth of Pa., 1991, tchr. level 2 Commonwealth of Pa., 1996. Tutor chemistry Shippensburg U., 1989—90; tchr. sci. York City Sch. Dist., Pa., 1991—92; tchr. chemistry Selinsgrove Area Sch. Dist., Pa., 1992—96, Gettysburg Area Sch. Dist., Pa., 1996—. Sci. tech. engring. and math. club advisor Gettysburg Area Sch. Dist., Gettysburg, Pa., 2005—; prof. chemistry Harrisburg Area C.C., Gettysburg, 2003—. Mem.: NEA, Pa. State Edn. Assn. Lutheran. Avocations: travel, hiking, rock climbing, sewing. Home: 1195 Myerstown Rd Gardners PA 17324 Office: Gettysburg Area High School 1130 Old Harrisburg Rd Gettysburg PA 17325 Office Phone: 717-334-6254 ext 6184. Personal E-mail: bechtel5@comcast.net. Business E-Mail: kbechtel@gettysburg.k12.pa.us.

BECHTEL, SHERRELL JEAN, psychotherapist; b. Birmingham, Ala., Sept. 23, 1961; d. Lewis Eugene and Sarah Rozelle (Sherrell) B. BS in Social Work, U. Ala., Birmingham, 1989; MSW, U. Ala., Tuscaloosa, 1990; DD, World Christianship Ministries, Fresno, Calif., 1997. Cert. addiction specialist; cert. group psychotherapist; lic. clin. social worker, Tenn., Ga.; ordained minister. Vol. counselor Planned Parenthood, Birmingham, 1986-88; intern Bradford Adult Chem. Dependency, Birmingham, 1989; rsch. staff asst. U. Ala., Tuscaloosa, 1989-90; intern counselor Bradford Adolescent Chem. Dependency, Birmingham, 1990; primary counselor The Crossroads, Chattanooga, 1990-92; owner S. J. Bechtel LCSW, CAS, Chattanooga, 1991—, PowerandVictoryLiving.com. Rschr. Ala. Commn. Youth, Montgomery, 1989-90; trainer Legal and Jud. Aspects Child Welfare, Decatur, Ala., 1989; presenter Ala. Victim Compensation, Mobile, 1990; speaker Limestone Correctional Facility, Huntsville, 1990; lectr. Grad. Sch. Social Wk., Tuscaloosa, 1990, U. Tenn., Chattanooga. Author: Power and Victory Living Bible Study, 2005. Spkr. Victims of Crime and Leniency, Tuscaloosa, 1990; vol. ARC Disaster Mental Health/Direct Svcs.; broadcaster Power and Victory Ministry, 2000—; subcom. mem. Atty. Gen. Alliance Against Drug Abuse, Birmingham, 1989; mem. Tenn. Coun. on Children and Youth-Legis./Policy; planning com. Holistic Health Retreat, Birmingham, 1988. Mem. NASW (pres. student orgn. 1986-89), Tenn. Alcohol Drug Assn., Jewish Community Ctr., Phi Kappa Phi. Avocations: tennis, woodworking, softball, bowling, water sports. Office: 109A Jordan Dr Chattanooga TN 37421-6732 E-mail: sb4jc1@aol.com.

BECK, ARIADNE PLUMIS, psychologist, psychotherapist, management consultant; b. Orange, N.J., Jan. 24, 1933; d. George Nicholas and Panagiota Beatrice (Drevas) Plumis; m. Robert Nason Beck, Feb. 16, 1958. AAS, Fashion Inst. Tech., N.Y.C., 1952; BS, Cornell U., 1954; MA, U. Chgo., 1969. Lic. clin. psychologist, Ill.; cert. group psychotherapist, Nat. Registry Cert. Group Psychotherapists, 1996. Teaching asst., rsch. asst. U. Chgo., 1955-60; staff counselor Counseling and Psychotherapy Rsch. Ctr., U. Chgo., 1959-66; dir. instruction in programs of counseling the disadvantaged Extension div., U. Chgo., 1960-71; dir. Counseling Ctr., Ill. Inst. Tech., Chgo., 1971-77; pvt. practice Oak Brook, Chgo., Des Plaines, Ill., 1972—; mgmt. cons. SAGE Cons., 1987—. Coord. Chgo. Group Devel. Rsch. Team, Indian Head Park, 1980—; lectr., workshop leader various mental health, ednl. and bus. instns., 1961—. Co-editor (with Carol M. Lewis) The Process of Group Psychotherapy: Systems for Analyzing Change, 2000; contbr. chpts. to books; contbr. articles to profl. jours. Inspired Ariadne P. Beck scholarship Ill. Sch. Profl. Psychology, Chgo., 1989. Fellow Am. Group Psychotherapy Assn. (chmn. rsch. com. 1986-88), mem. APA, ACA, Soc. for Psychotherapy Rsch., Ill. Group Psychotherapy Assn. (pres. 1977, Disting. Svc. award 1986, Ariadne P. Beck scholarship named in her honor 1994). Avocations: botanical art, gardening, sewing, photography, ceramics. Home and Office: 6357 Blackhawk Trl Indian Head Park IL 60525-4315

BECK, CHRISTINA SUE, music educator; b. Carlyle, Ill., Dec. 12, 1981; d. Randy Lappe and Pamela McNelly; m. Ryan Beck, June 19, 2004. BA in Music summa cum laude, Ill. Coll., Jacksonville, 2004. Cert. K-12 music educator Mo., 2005. Elem. music tchr. Faith Christian Acad., Kansas City, Mo., 2004—05, Neely Elem., St. Joseph, Mo., 2005—. Youth group vol. McCarthy Bapt. Ch., St. Joseph, Mo., 2005—06. Mem.: Mo. State Tchrs. Assn., Phi Beta Kappa. Southern Baptist. Avocations: music, reading, scrapbooks. Office: Neely Elementary School 1909 South 12th St Saint Joseph MO 64506 Office Phone: 816-671-4280.

BECK, DENISE GAIL, secondary school educator; b. Tipton, Ind., July 16, 1955; d. Harold William and Wilda Jean (Orr) Unger; m. Eric Byron Beck, June 24, 1978 (dec. May 2005); children: Jason Tyler, Vanessa Janean. BS, Butler U., 1977, MS, 1981; postgrad., Purdue U., 1982; student, Ind. U., 1986. English tchr. Western Boone Jr.-Sr. High Sch., Thorntown, Ind., 1977—. Mem. Nat. Coun. Tchrs. English, Ind. Tchrs. Writing. Office: 403 Glenldale Dr Lebanon IN 46052-1917

BECK, ELAINE KUSHNER, elementary and secondary school educator; b. Phila., May 31, 1942; d. Joseph and Emma Kushner; m. Stuart Edwin Beck, June 20, 1964; children: Adam, Barry, Caroline. BS, Drexel U., 1963; Masters equivalent, Temple U., Pa. State U., West Chester U., 1984. Cert. tchr., Pa. Tchr. grades 4, 5, 6 Upper Darby (Pa.) Sch. Dist., 1963-64; tchr. high sch. Francis Hammond-Alexandria (Va.) Sch. Dist., 1964-65; tchr. adult edn. YMCA, Alexandria, 1966-67; tchr. mid. sch. Haverford Sch. Dist., Havertown, Pa., 1980—2004; ret., 2004. Bus. owner Lady Elaine Creations, Havertown, 1976-80. Contbg. editor: Passoverama, 1979-80; author (teaching program) The Equipment Scavenger Hunt, 1989. Mem. strategic plan com. Haverford Sch. Dist., Havertown, 1995-96; organizer sr. citizen dances, Havertown, 1992, 93, 94; pres., v.p., mem. adv. bds. sisterhood Temple Beth Hillel/Beth El, 1980-81. Recipient Dominick Recchiuti Humanitarian award, 1992; named one of Top 5 Home Econs. Tchrs. in U.S., Home Baking Assn., 1994; Ptnr. in Edn. grantee Sun Oil Co., 1989. Mem.: NEA, Nat. Audubon Soc., Pa. Edn. Assn., Hadassah, Sierra Club, Nature Conservancy, World Wildlife Fund, Phi Sigma Sigma (honored Drexel U. chpt. 1998), Omicron Nu, Key and Triangle. Avocations: exotic bird training, wild bird watching, sailing, environmentalism, biking. Home: 624 Greythorne Rd Wynnewood PA 19096-2509

BECK, IRENE CLARE, educational consultant, writer; b. N.Y.C., Dec. 18, 1944; d. James E. and Helen (Carroll) Clare; m. William J. Beck, Aug. 9, 1986; children: Daniel, James Chesire. BA, St. Mary's Coll., 1966; MA, Fairfield U., 1977; EdD, U. Rochester, 1982; Grad. Cert. Women's Studies, DePaul U., 1998. Cert. tchr., N.Y. Tchr. Elem. Sch., N.Y.C., 1966-68, Montessori Acad. N.Y., Bklyn., 1968-73; faculty Housatonic Community Coll., Bridgeport, Conn., 1975-77, Nazareth Coll., Rochester, NY, 1977-83; faculty dir. Sheppard Pratt Nat. Ctr. Human Devel., Balt., 1983-91; exec. dir. William & Irene Beck Found., 1987—. Cons. Headstart Programs, Rochester, 1980-83, Family Day Care Tng., Rochester, 1980-83; mem. women's studies faculty program DePaul U., 1999—; presenter workshops and seminars. Author: Expect Respect, Let Me Tell You (manuals), (No Hang Ups (telephone audiotape), 1987, In Tune With Teens (booklet), 1990; weekly news col. Parents and Teens, 1987-90; freelance writer, 1986—; contbr. articles to profl. jours.; sr. editor What's Working for Girls in Illinois, 1996-99. Mem. AAUW, Assn. Childhood Edn. Internat. Avocations: hiking, swimming, biking.

BECK, JANE, dance educator, choreographer; b. Newark, May 18, 1959; d. David and Beatrice G. Beck; m. Frederick B. Meltzer, Aug. 18, 1991 (div. May 28, 1998); 1 child, Brea Beck Meltzer. BFA, Boston Conservatory, 1981; MEd, Temple U., Phila., 1988. Cert. tchr. Pa., Temple U., 1988, Fla., 2000. Actress, choreographer Green Mt. Guild Summer Stock, White River Junction, Mt. Snow, Stowe and Killington, Vt., 1981; dance dir. Pine Crest Sch., Boca Raton, Fla., 1990—92; actress local and nat. TV commls. and infommercials West Palm Beach, Fla., 1992—95; co-host entertainment TV program Palm Beach County Channel 20, West Palm Beach, 1994—95; performing arts dir. Poinciana Day Sch., West Palm Beach, 1998—2000; dance dir. U.B. Kinsey/Palmview Elem. Sch. Arts, West Palm Beach, 2000—. Asst. to prodr., choreographer: (Off Broadway) Hello, I'm Not In Right Now, 1983; prodr., choreographer: Jane Beck Presents, Inner City Rhythm, Kravis Ctr. for Performing Arts, 2005. Office Phone: 561-802-2145.

BECK, JEAN MARIE See WIK, JEAN

BECK, JILL, academic administrator, dance educator; b. Worcester, Mass., Aug. 10, 1949; d. John Jacob and Helen Bernadette (Provost) Lindberg; m. Robert Joel Beck, Apr. 21, 1973. BA, Clark U., 1970; MA, McGill U., 1976; PhD, CUNY, 1985. Cert. tchr. and profl. reconstructor in Labanotation. Dir. edn. Dance Notation Bur., NYC, 1980-83; sr. lectr. S. Australian Coll. Advanced Edn., Adelaide, 1983-85; guest faculty U. Mich., 1985, U. Colo, 1986, Denison U., 1987; faculty Am. Dance Festival, Durham, N.C., 1985, The Juilliard Sch., NYC, 1985, asst. dir. dance div., 1988-89; chmn. theatre and dance dept., CUNY, 1985-87, dir. grad. studies dept. dance, 1987; faculty, cons. Hartford Ballet, Conn., 1983, chmn. dance dept. Southern Meth. U., CUNY, dean, Sch. of Arts, U. Calif. Irvine, 1995-03, pres. Lawrence U., Wis., 2004-. Project dir. Ct. Coun. on the Humanities and Arts, 1989-90; cons. Universal Ballet Co. of Korea, 1988-89; project dir. Fund for Improvement Post-Secondary Edn., Washington, 1982-85, NEH, 1983-85, CUNY Research Found., 1981-82; dance dir., cons. Dance Notation Bur., NYC, 1983, mem. profl. adv. com., 1982-84, 85-88; mem. Internat. Conf. Kinetography Laban, 1982—; mem. exec. com. Internat. Movement Notators Alliance, 1984-85; co-chmn. Soc. Dance History Scholars Conf., NYC, 1985-86; dir. program in advanced studies Am. Dance Festival, 1986; stage dir. Lincoln Ctr. student programs, 1987; Dir. dance revivals Doris Humphrey choregraphy, 1981—, Anna Sokolow choreography, 1982—, founder and dir. ArtsBridge Am., 1996, daVinci Ctr. Learning through Arts, 2001. Editor Dance Notation Jour., 1983-85; author several monographs, dance textbooks, and instructional videotapes. Recipient Exhibit award CUNY, 1982, Jack Linquist award, Clara Barton award, Learning for Life award. Democrat. Avocations: travel, art collecting. Office: Off of Pres Lawrence Univ PO Box 599 Appleton WI 54912*

BECK, LOIS GRANT, anthropologist, educator, author; b. Bogota, Colombia, Nov. 5, 1944; d. Martin Lawrence and Dorothy (Sweet) Grant; m. Henry Huang; 1 dau., Julia Huang. BA, Portland State U., 1967; MA, U. Chgo., 1969, PhD, 1977. Asst. prof. Amherst (Mass.) Coll., 1973-76, Univ. Utah, Salt Lake City, 1976-80; from asst. to assoc. prof. Washington U., St. Louis, 1980-92, prof., 1992—. Author: Qashqa'i of Iran, 1986, Nomad, 1991; co-editor Women in the Muslim World, 1978, Women in Iran from the Rise of Islam to 1800, 2003, Women in Iran from 1800 to the Islamic Republic, 2004. Grantee Social Sci. Rsch. Coun., 1990, NEH, 1990-92, 98, Am. Philos. Soc., 1998. Mem. Mid. East Studies Assn. (bd. dirs. 1981-84), Soc. Iranian Studies (exec. sec. 1979-82, edit. bd. 1982-91, coun. 1996-98). Office: Washington U Dept Anthropology CB1114 1 Brookings Dr Saint Louis MO 63130-4899 Office Phone: 314-935-5252. Business E-Mail: lbeck@artsci.wustl.edu.

BECK, MARILYN MOHR, columnist; b. Chgo., Dec. 17, 1928; d. Max and Rose (Lieberman) Mohr; m. Roger Beck, Jan. 8, 1949 (div. 1974); children: Mark Elliott, Andrea; m. Arthur Levine, Oct. 12, 1980. AA, U. So. Calif., 1950. Freelance writer nat. mag. and newspapers, Hollywood, Calif., 1959-63; Hollywood columnist Valley Times and Citizen News, Hollywood, Calif., 1963-65; West Coast editor Sterling Mag., Hollywood, Calif., 1963-74; free-lance entertainment writer LA Times, Calif., 1965-67; Hollywood columnist Bell-McClure Syndicate, 1967-72; chief Bell-McClure Syndicate (West Coast bur.), 1967-72; Hollywood columnist NANA Syndicate, 1967-72; syndicated Hollywood columnist NY Times Spl. Features, 1972-78, NY Times Spl. Features (United Feature Syndicate), 1978-80, United Press abroad, 1978-80, Internat. Editors News and Features, Chgo. Tribune/NY Daily News Syndicate, 1980-97; columnist TV Guide, 1989—92, Creators Syndicate, 1997—. Creator, host Marilyn Beck's Hollywood Outtakes spls. NBC, 1977, 78; host Marilyn Beck's Hollywood Hotline, Sta. KFI, LA, 1975-77; Hollywood reporter Eyewitness News, Sta. KABC-TV, LA, 1981, (TV program) PM Mag., 1983-88; on-air corr. E! TV, 1993-99, CompuServe Entertainment Authority, 1994-96, eDrive Internet Authority, 1996-97, e!online Internet Hollywood Authority, 1997-2000, Compuserve, 2000—, aeNTV-.com, 2001-02; author: (non-fiction) Marilyn Beck's Hollywood, 1973, (novel) Only Make Believe, 1988; co-author: Unfinished Lives, What If.?, 1996. Recipient Citation of Merit LA City Coun., 1973, Press award Pub. Guild Am., 1974, Bronze Halo award So. Calif. Motion Picture Coun., 1982. Address: 4926 Delos way Oceanside CA 92056

BECK, MARTHA ANN, curator, director; BA in English Lit., Vassar Coll., 1960; postgrad., NYU, 1963-67. Editor, writer, rschr. The Frick Collection, 1962-64; curatorial asst. drawings dept. The Mus. Modern Art, 1968-75; founder, dir. The Drawing Ctr., 1975-90, The Ctr. for Internat. Exhbns., 1992—. Served on numerous juries and panels including Nat. Endowment for the Arts, SUNY Thayer Family Fellowships, The Westchester Coun. on the Arts and the Jerome Found. Fellowships; lectr. in field. Author: (screenplays) Ashenden's Adventures as British Agent During World War I, 2005—06. Recipient NYU scholarship, 1964-65. Home: 9 Gramercy Park S New York NY 10003-1742 Office Phone: 212-473-4918.

BECK, MARTHA CATHERINE, philosophy educator; b. Mpla., Apr. 3, 1953; d. Kenneth and Catherine Beck; children: Rachel Phillips, Carl Phillips, Erica Phillips. BA, Hamline U., St. Paul, 1975; MA, Bryn Mawr Coll., Pa., 1978, PhD, 1993. Humanities prof. Anoka-Ramsey C.C., Anoka, Minn., 1982—84; adj. prof. philosophy U. St. Thomas, St. Paul, 1984—91; asst. prof. philosophy Coll. St. Catherine, St. Paul, 1991—96; assoc. prof. philosophy Lyon Coll., Batesville, Ark., 1996—. Resident scholar Inst. for Cultural and Ecumenical Rsch., Collegeville, Minn., 2003—03; vis. scholar Coll. St. Benedict, St. Joseph, Minn., NEH summer seminar Duke U., Durham, NC, 1994, NEH summer seminar, San Diego, 2002—02, Coun. Internat. Ednl. Exch., Ankara, Turkey, 2006—06. Bd. dirs. Ark. Coalition Peace and Justice, Little Rock, 2006, Interfaith Com. on Peacemaking, Little Rock, 2005—06. Studium scholar, Coll. St. Benedict, 1998—2005. Mem.: Am. Philos. Assn., Phi Beta Kappa (hon.). Methodist. Avocations: flute, hiking, photography, symphony, accordion. Home: 990 East Main St # 4 Batesville AR 72501 Office: Lyon Coll 2300 Highland Ave Batesville AR 72501 Office Phone: 870-793-1774. Personal E-mail: mbeck@lyon.edu.

BECK, NEVA ANN, retired special education educator; b. Anderson, Ind., Sept. 23, 1941; d. Russell Earl and Audrey Eunice (Rogers) McCord; m. John Bernard Beck, Feb. 12, 1966; 1 child, Reanna Lynn. BS, Ball State U., 1964, MA, 1966. Cert. elem. and spl. edn. tchr., Ind. Tchr. 1st grade Anderson (Ind.) Community schs., 1964-72, tchr. spl. edn., 1981-84; tchr. learning disability Carmel (Ind.) Clay Co-op., 1984—2005, rep., 1989—; ret., 2005. Mem. AAUW (pres. study group 1989-90, bd. dirs. Anderson br., pres. creative arts 1991-92, pres. Antiques study group, 1992-93, 96-97, pres. creative arts study group 1997—), Beta Sigma Phi. Republican. Avocations: antiques, music, arts. Home: 5001 Woodrose Ln Anderson IN 46011-8761 Office: Frankton Elem 405 Sigler St Frankton IN 46044

BECK, PAMELA L., realtor; b. Emporia, Va., June 6, 1974; d. Lemuel Gary and Betty Lou Langley; 1 child, Tanah. AA, AAS, Enterprise State Jr. Coll., Enterprise, Ala., 1998. Realtor David Kahn & Co., Montgomery, Ala., 2000—01; relocation dir. Century 21 Profl. Svc., Montgomery, Ala., 2001—04, broker, 2005—. Amb. C. of C., Montgomery, Ala., 2004. Mem.: Montgomery Assn. of Realtors, Nat. Assn. of Realtors, Ala. Assoc. of realtors. Office Phone: 334-462-9989.

BECK, PHYLLIS WHITMAN, lawyer, retired judge; b. N.Y.C. d. Irving and Dora (Sugar) Whitman; m. Aaron T. Beck; children: Roy, Judith, Daniel, Alice. AB magna cum laude, Brown U.; JD, Temple U., 1967, degree (hon.), 1997. Bar: Pa. 1967. Pvt. practice law, Phila., 1967-74; assoc. prof. Temple U. Law Ctr., Phila., 1974-76; vice dean U. Pa. Law Sch., Phila., 1976-81; judge Pa. Superior Ct., 1981—97, sr. judge, 1997—2005; of counsel Pepper Hamilton LLP, Phila., 2006—. Chmn. Pa. Gov.'s Commn. on Jud. Reform, 1987—88; Phi Beta Kappa lectr. Brown U., Providence; Lindbach lectr. Bryn Mawr Coll.; bd. dirs. Mann Ctr. for Performing Arts. Contbr. articles to profl. jours. Pres. Found. Cognitive Therapy, 1974—; chair bd. Independence Found.; bd.dirs. Temple Law Sch., Free Libr. of Phila., Acad. Vocal Arats, Jewish-Am. History Mus.; mem. Joint State Govt. Commn. on Domestic Rels. Law, 1995—; mem. Pennsylvanians for Modern Cts.; mem. bd. consultors Villanova Law Sch.; mem. bd. overseers U. Pa. Sch. Nursing. Named a Disting. Dau. of Pa.; recipient Leadership award, Med. Coll. Pa., Phila., William Brennan award, Phila. Bar Assn., 1997, Sandra Day O'Connor award, 2005. Mem. Am. Law Inst., Am. Bar Found., Am. Judicature Soc. (bd. dirs., Herbert Harley award 1995), Pa. Bar Assn. (Jud. award 1990, Anne Alperin award 1997, Sandra Day O'Connor award, 2005), Women in the Profession, Nat. Assn. Women Judges (Murray award 1998), Disting. Dau. of Pa. 2000. Office: Pepper Hamilton LLP 3000 Two Logan Sq 18th & Arch St Philadelphia PA 19103 Office Phone: 215-981-4447. E-mail: beckp@pepperlaw.com.

BECK, RHONDA JOANN, paramedic, educator, writer; b. Hawkinsville, Ga., Apr. 20, 1965; d. Franklin Lamar and Ida (Scarborough) Woodard; m. Gary Wendell Bramlett, Apr. 9, 1983 (div. May 1995); 1 child, Gary Michael Bramlett; m. Kenneth Steve Beck, June 8, 1997. Gen. Banking Degree, Am. Inst. Banking; A of Healthcare, Ctrl. Ga. Tech. Coll., Macon, 2004. Cert. BTLS, CPR, PHTLS, ACLS, BLS instr. trainer, emergency med. technician-paramedic, instr. Collateral clk. Bank South, N.A., Perry, Ga., 1986-94; emergency med. technician Taylor Regional Hosp., Hawkinsville, 1993-94; paramedic Med. Ctr. Ctrl. Ga., Macon, 1994-99; emergency med. technician instr., paramedic instr. Ctrl. Ga. Tech. Coll., Macon, 1997—; paramedic Houston Med. Ctr., Warner Robins, Ga., 1997—. Instr. ACLS, Pediat. Life Support, PreHosp. Trauma Life Support, Basic Trauma Life Support, Am. Heart Assn.; reviewer Delmar Thomson, 1999—, Jones & Bartlett, 2000-, GEMS Faculty, 2003-present, Am. Geriatric Soc.; Brady, 2001—. Author: Emergency Care and Transportation of the Sick and Injured, student workbook, AAOS, 8th edit., 2001; pub. author, reviewer: Jones & Bartlett; author: Emergency Care of the Sick and Injured-EMT Intermediate, 2004. Vol. firefighter Houston County Vol. Fire Dept., Hayneville, Ga., 1986-95. Recipient Heartsaver award Laerdal Med. Corp., 1994, Vol. Svc. award Am. Lung Assn. Ga., 1995. Democrat. Baptist. Avocations: reading, swimming, exercise, writing, coin collecting/numismatics. Office: Houston County EMS Warner Robins GA 31093 E-mail: takai_sensei@yahoo.com.

BECK, SUSAN REBECCA, voice educator, consultant; d. Henry Sanford and Kathleen (Underwood) Beck; m. Alan Joseph Milton, May 25, 1975; children: Alan Joseph Milton, Suzanne Kathleen Milton. BS in Music Edn., Ga. So. U., 1971; MusM Edn., Syracuse U., 1982. Cert. tchr. Ga. State Bd. Edn., 1971. Choral dir. Toombs County HS, Lyons, Ga., 1971—72; dir. choral activities Tift County Sch. Sys., Tifton, Ga., 1972—81; grad. asst. Sch. Music Syracuse U., 1981—82; choral dir., vocal and piano coach Tiftarea Acad., Chula, Ga., 1983—85; choral dir. Tift County Bd. Edn., 1986—99; dir. choral activities Crisp County Bd. Edn., Cordele, Ga., 1999—. Condr. summer music camp Abraham Baldwin Coll., Tifton, 1972—74; approved adjudicator for all-state and choral festival Ga. Music Educators Assn., Atlanta, 1974—; instr. music faculty staff devel. Chatham County, Savannah, 1975; music dir. anad cons. summer choral program Valdosta State U., Ga., 1975; clinician choral techniques and sight reading Fitzgerald HS, Ga., 1975—80; clincian choral techniques and sight reading Early County Sch. Sys., Blakely, Ga., 1975—88; dist. 2 choral chair Ga. Music Educator's Assn., Atlanta, 1975—2000; instr. music edn. staff develpoment Dougherty County Sch. Sys., Albany, Ga., 1976; honor choir condr. DeKalb County Sch. Sys., Marietta, Ga., 1976; clinician for sightreading techniques Donaldsonville Sch. Sys., Donaldsonville, Ga., 1976—86; choral seminar condr. for choral dirs. Ga. State U. Sch. Music, 1977; sight reading instr. Woodward Acad., Atlanta, 1977—78; clinician choral techniques and sight reading Americus HS, Ga., 1978; sight reading Griffin HS, Ga., 1978; instr. for staff devel. Dougherty Sch. Sys., Albany, 1985; honor choir condr. Bufford Sch. Sys., Ga., 1988; sight reading clinician Conyers HS, Ga., 1989; condr. honor choir Fayette County Sch. Sys., Ga., 1990; founding co-dir. Tifton Choral Soc., 1991—94; guest condr. Dalton Sch. Sys., Ga., 1994; all state regional chair Ga. Music Educator's Assn., Atlanta, 1999—; guest condr. for winter season Albany Chorale, 1995; adj. prof. Ga. SouthWestern U., Americus, 2003—04; guest condr. for honor choir Gwinnett County Sch. Sys., Athens, Ga., 2004; honor choir condr. Dougherty County Sch. Sys., Albany, 2005. Author: (article) Ga. Music News Jour.; dir.: (performance) Tift County Women's Chorus Choral Music (Cert. of excellence, 1979); contbr.: performance Tift County HS Vocal Jazz, 1979 (Cert. of Excellence, 1979); dir.: (performancce) Vocal Jazz Ensemble for Am. Choral Dirs. Assn., (performance tour) European Tour as Georgia Youth Chorale, (performance) Choral Tour of Bahamas, Nat. Peanut Festival Competition; musician: (choral performance) State Conf. Ga. Music Educator's Conf.; contbr.: performance Polovetsian Dances with Atlanta Symphony Orch.; musician: (concert of varied classical choral music) Ga. Music State Conf.; dir.: (peformance of women's choral music) Ga. Music State Conf.; musician: (performance of vocal jazz music) Ga. Music State Conf. (Peformamce choir for Kirby Shaw, nationally recognized composer and arranger, 1979); composer: (sight reading text book) Let's Take Note; dir.: (performance) Carl Weber's Mass in G Major (Cert. of Excellence, 1975), (choral performance) varied styles and periods. Fund drive chair United Way, Tifton, 1982—83, v.p., 1983—94, pres., 1984—85. Recipient Star Tchr., Kiwanis Club, 1974—80, Outstanding Young Women of Am., Outstanding Inc. Mem.: NEA, Ga. Music Educator's Assn. (assoc.; state awards and recognition chair 2002, v.p. 1996—98), Am. Choral Dirs. Assn. (life; vocal jazz chair 1980—82). Office Phone: 12293763430.

BECK, TIFFANY, secondary school educator; BA, Ouachita Bapt. U., Arkadelphia, Ark., 2001. Lic. tchr. Ark. Theater/dance tchr. Arkansas HS, Texarkana, Ark., 2002—. Redline drill team dir. Ark. HS, 2002—; movement instr. TexRep, Inc., Texarkana, Tex., 2002—. Prodr.: 2007 Miss Texarkana Scholarship Pageant. Com. chair Ark. Mcpl. Auditorium Commn., Texarkana, 2005—06. Mem.: Delta Kappa Gamma. Office: Arkansas HS 1500 Jefferson Ave Texarkana AR 71854 Office Phone: 870-774-7641 ext 119.

BECK, URSULA, art educator, artist; Founding exec. dir. Taos Inst. Arts, N.Mex., Taos Art Sch. Office: Taos Art Sch PO Box 2588 Taos NM 87571 Office Phone: 505-758-0350. Office Fax: 505-758-4880. Business E-Mail: tas@laplaza.org.

BECKER, AMY SALMINEN, librarian; b. Marquette, Mich., May 1, 1977; d. Jack Edwin and Doris Marie Salminen; m. Brian James Becker, June 26, 1999; 1 child, Samuel Jacob. EdB, Concordia U., 1999; M in Libr. and Info. Sci., Dominican U., River Forest, Ill., 2002. Libr.'s profl. cert. Ill. Math./religion/computer sci. tchr. Luther HS N., Chgo., 1999—2000; libr. page Austin-Irving br. Chgo. Pub. Libr., 2001; evening reference asst. Concordia U., River Forest, 2001—02; tech. svcs. libr., cataloger Peter White Pub. Libr., Marquette, 2002—. Reviewer Superiorland Preview Ctr., Marquette, 2004—; honors soc. advisor Luther HS N., Chgo., 1999—2000. Sec. No. Ill. dist., zone 10 Luth. Women's Missionary League, 2000—02; treas. Redeemer Women's League Redeemer Luth. Ch., Marquette, 2003—05, Sunday sch. tchr., 2004—06. Mem.: Mich. Libr. Assn., Beta Phi Mu. Lutheran. Avocations: drawing, quilting, reading, running. Home: 417 E Magnetic St Marquette MI 49855 Office: Peter White Pub Libr 217 N Front St Marquette MI 49855 Office Phone: 906-226-4316. Office Fax: 906-226-1783. Personal E-mail: amysalminenbecker@yahoo.com. Business E-Mail: abecker@uproc.lib.mi.us.

BECKER, BARBARA LYNN, lawyer; b. Nov. 27, 1963; BA, Wesleyan U., 1985; JD, NYU, 1988. Bar: N.Y. 1989. Formerly ptnr. Chadbourne & Parke LLP; now ptnr. Gibson, Dunn & Crutcher LLP, N.Y.C. Mng. editor Rev. of Law and Social Change, 1984-85. Bd. dirs. Urban Pathways, N.Y.C. Mem. Phi Beta Kappa. Office: Gibson Dunn & Crutcher LLP 200 Park Ave New York NY 10166

BECKER, BEVERLY JUNE, educator; b. Paterson, N.J., July 28, 1930; d. George Lawrence and Adelaide (Hulse) B. AB, Wellesley (Mass.) Coll., 1951; MEd, U. N.C., Greensboro, 1954; PhD, U. Oreg., Eugene, 1967. Instr. U. Nebr., Lincoln, 1954-56, Mt. Holyoke Coll., S. Hadley, Mass., 1956-59; prof. edn. Skidmore Coll., Saratoga Springs, N.Y., 1959-93. Vis. prof. U.S. Mil. Acad., 1984-85. Recipient Merit award, Ea. Assn. for Phys. Edn. of Coll. Women, 1977, Outstanding Civilian Svc. Medal, Dept. of the Army, 1985. Fellow Am. Coll. Sports Medicine; mem. Nat. Assn. for Phys. Edn. in Higher Edn. (pres. 1986-88, Past Pres.'s award 1991, Disting. Svc. award 1994), Ea. Assn. for Phys. Edn. of Coll. Women (pres. 1974), AAPHERD, Nat. Assn. for Kinesiology and Physical Edn. in Higher Edn.

BECKER, DOREEN DORIS, medical/surgical nurse; b. Elgin, N.D., May 22, 1944; d. Carl Ruff and Dorothy Buttmann; m. Glenn Alan Watson, Jan. 19, 2002; m. Roy Ernest Becker, June 5, 1964 (dec. Sept. 6, 1993); 1 child, Allen Roy. Degree in Nursing, U. Chgo., 1963. Nurse Columbia Hosp., Grand Forks, ND, 1976—77, surg. nurse, 1977—90; surg. nurse supr. Columbia HCA, Plano, Tex., 1990—92, med. records coder, 1993—2001, Baylor Hosp., Richardson, Tex., 2001—02, Med. City, Dallas, 2002—05, Med. Ctr., Rowlett, Tex., 2005—. Instr. HCA Med. Ctr., Plano, 1990—92. Instr. Red Cross, Braddock, ND, 1966. Recipient Medicorp award, Mott HS, 1962. Methodist. Avocations: marathon running, bicycling, fishing, fossils, rocks. Home: 616 Buffalo Bend Plano TX 75023

BECKER, DOROTHY LORETTA, education educator, librarian; b. Long Beach, Calif., May 27, 1933; d. Francis Ryan and Constance Marie Wolff; m. Paul Hermann Karl Heinz Peter Becker, Feb. 14, 1964 (div. Nov. 1971). BS, U. Calif., L.A., 1954; MLS, San Jose State U., 1981. Tchr. Monterey (Calif.) Peninsula Unified Sch. Dist., 1956—91, reading specialist, cons., 1966-78, sch. libr., 1978-81; supr. student tchrs. Chapman U., Monterey, 1991-99; reference libr. Monterey County Free Librs., Seaside, Calif., 1996—2003. Mem. Ikebana Internat., Friends of Monterey Symphony; vol. Carmel Bach Festival; elder, Stephen min., leader First Presbyn. Ch., Monterey. Mem. Calif. Ret. Tchrs. Assn., Total Reading Assn. (cons. 1966—), Delta Kappa Gamma Soc. Internat. (Calif. corr. sec. 1993-95, Calif. state exec. sec. 1995-97, Chi state strategic plan ad hoc com. 1995-99, chmn. Chi state bylaws 1999-2001), Chi State Learning Is For Everyone Found. (pres. bd. dirs. 1999-2002, bd. dirs. 1999-2005). Democrat. Avocations: travel, reading, literacy advocate, flower arranging.

BECKER, GAIL ROSELYN, museum director; b. Long Branch, N.J., Oct. 22, 1942; d. Joseph and Adele (Michelsohn) B. BA, Vassar Coll., 1964. Exhibit project officer U.S. Info. Agy., Washington, 1967-87, chief devel. and prodn. exhibits, 1987-91; exec. dir. Louisville Sci. Ctr. (formerly Mus. History and Sci.), 1991—. Bd. dirs. Louisville Advanced Tech. Coun., 1993-2000, Louisville Com. Fgn. Rels., Main St. Assn., 1998—, Arts and Cultural Attractions Coun., 1999—; active Leadership Louisville. Recipient Presdl. Design awards Nat. Endowment for the Arts, Washington, 1984, 88, 92, Special Achievement award U.S. Info. Agy., Washington, 1988. Mem. Am. Assn. Mus. (bd. dirs. 1994-97), Assn. Sci.-Tech. Ctrs. (bd. dirs. 1992—2003, pres. 1999-2001), Vassar Coll. Alumnae Assn., Rotary. Office: Louisville Sci Ctr 727 W Main St Louisville KY 40202-2681

BECKER, HELANE RENÉE, financial analyst, finance company executive; b. NYC, May 7, 1957; d. Arnold and Ella Florence (Feldman) Becker; m. George Paul Roukas, Sept. 6, 1980 (div.); children: Samuel Matthew Roukas, Hannah Beth Roukas. BA, Montclair State U., 1979; MBA in Fin., NYU, 1984. Options coord. Donaldson Lufkin & Jenrette, N.Y.C., 1979-81; mktg. coord. E.F. Hutton & Co., N.Y.C., 1981-82; securities analyst Prudential-Bache Securities, N.Y.C., 1982-86; v.p., analyst Drexel Burnham Lambert, N.Y.C., 1986-87; mng. dir., analyst Lehman Bros., N.Y.C., 1987-94, Smith Barney, N.Y.C., 1995-98; sr. v.p., prin. Buckingham Rsch. Group, N.Y.C., 1998—2003; prin., mng. dir. Benchmark Co., N.Y.C., 2003—. Spkr. in field. Contbr. Corp. Travel Mag., 1990. Mem. Senate Commn. on Civil Tilt Rotor. Named to Investor All-Am. Rsch. Team, 1985-94, 5 Star Mine Analyst, Best Analyst, Wall St. Jour., 2000, 01. Mem. Soc. Airline Analysts (pres. 1996-98), Profl. Women in Bus., Wings Club, NYU Alumni Assn. NJ, Wyoming Club, Friends of Fencing (pres.). Avocations: skiing, tennis, swimming, golf. Office: Benchmark Co 40 Fulton St New York NY 10038 Office Phone: 212-312-6764. Personal E-mail: hbecker@benchmarkcap.com, helane_b@yahoo.com.

BECKER, JILL, newscaster; married; children: Gregory, Matthew. BA in Mass Comm., U. South Fla. With Sta. WTLV-TV, Jacksonville, Fla., 1978, Sta. KTHV-TV, Little Rock, 1980, Sta. WSB-TV, Atlanta, 1981; co-anchor Sta. WXIA-TV, Atlanta, 1988—. Recipient Best News Anchor Emmy award, NATAS, 1999. Office: Sta WXIA-TV 1611 W Peachtree St Atlanta GA 30309

BECKER, JOANN ELIZABETH, retired insurance company executive; b. Chester, Pa., Oct. 29, 1948; d. James Thomas and Elizabeth Theresa (Barnett) Clark; m. David Norbert Becker, June 7, 1969. BA, Washington U., St. Louis, 1970, MA, 1971. CLU, ChFC, FLMI/M, CFA. Tchr. Kirkwood (Mo.) Sch. Dist., 1971-73; devel. and sr. devel. analyst Lincoln Nat. Life Ins. Co., Ft. Wayne, Ind., 1973-77, systems programming specialist, 1977-79, sr. project mgr., 1979-81, asst. v.p., 1981-85, 2d v.p., 1985-88, v.p., 1988-91; pres., CEO The Richard Leahy Corp., Ft. Wayne, 1991-93; pres. Lincoln Nat. Corp. Equity Sales Corp, Ft. Wayne, 1993-94; v.p. portfolio mgmt. group Lincoln Nat. Investment Mgmt. Co., Ft. Wayne, 1994-97, dir. investment mgmt., sr. v.p., 1997—2000, ret., 2000. Contbr. articles to profl. jours. Bd. dirs. Ind. Humanities Coun., Indpls., 1991-96, treas., exec. com., 1994-95, devel. com., 1995-96; bd. dirs. Auburn Cord Duesenberg Mus., Ind., 1995-2000, devel. and exec. com., 1997-2000; bd. dirs. Priest Lake Mus., 2005—; pres. Priest Lake Mus. Assn., 2006—. Named Women of Achievement, YWCA, Ft. Wayne, 1986, Sagamore of Wabash, Gov. State of Ind., 1990. Fellow Life Mgmt. Inst. Soc. Ft. Wayne (pres. 1983-84, honors designation 1980); mem. Life Ins. Mktg. Rsch. Assn. (Leadership Inst. fellow, exec. com. 1993-94, fin. svcs. com. 1993-94), Am. Mgmt. Assn., So. Ariz. Watercolor Guild (chair fundraising com. 2006—), Ft. Wayne C. of C. (chmn. audit-fin. com. 1989-2000).

BECKER, KARLA LYNN, information technology manager, consultant; b. West Point, NY, Nov. 3, 1956; d. Fred D. and Margaret Erika (Buckmann) Spinks; m. Eric Louis Becker; children: Erika Margaret Augusta Ashmore, Eric Robert. BA, Ind. U.-Purdue U. at Indpls., 1982; MS, Ind. U., 1986. Cert. software quality engr.; Hatha and Kundalini yoga tchr., registered yoga alliance tchr. Mgr. Eastside Chiropractic Clinic, Indpls., 1978-80; English tutor univ. div. Ind. U.-Purdue U. at Indpls., 1980-82, composition instr. English dept., 1982-83, tech. writer computing services, 1983-84; tech. writer Ind. U. Adminstrv. Computing, 1984-87; mgmt. info. svcs. cons., writer, support adminstr. Simon Property Group, Indpls., 1987-97; sys. cons. KFORCE.COM, Indpls., 1997-99; assoc. info. cons. Eli Lilly & Co., Indpls.,

1999—. Author: Composing Technical Documents, 2000; editor: Lit. Jour., Genesis, All-Am. Mag., Am. Collegiate Press Assn., 1983; author numerous poems; contbr. articles to profl. jours. Mem. Am. Soc. Quality, Soc. Tech. Communication (Cert. of Achievement 1985), Sigma Delta Chi, Pi Lambda Theta. Democrat. Roman Catholic. Avocations: singing, yoga. Personal E-mail: karla11@hotmail.com.

BECKER, KATHY GAIL, medical/surgical nurse; b. Lebanon, Mo., July 12, 1957; d. Cecil Julius and Mary Eveline (Walters) Newell; m. Randy Lee Waterman, Oct. 15, 1976 (div. 1991); 1 child, Brandon Lee Waterman; m. Michael Lee Becker, Mar. 6, 1992. Lic. LPN, Vo Tech. Sch., Waynesville, Mo., 1980; ADN, State Fair C.C., Sedalia, Mo., 1995. LPN charge nurse Lebanon Care Ctr., Lebanon, Mo., 1980-90; LPN staff nurse Cox Med. Ctr., Springfield, Mo., 1990-91, Citizens Meml., Bolivar, Mo., 1991-92, Lake Ozark Gen. Hosp., Osage Beach, Mo., 1992-96; RN supr. St. John's Breech Regional Med. Ctr., Lebanon, Mo., 1996—. Author (poems) The Day My Savior Died, 1989 (Golden Poet award 1989), Forgive Me, 1990, Yesterday, 1994 (Editor's Choice award 1994), A Tear Stained Face. Recipient Lake Ozark Gen. Hosp. scholar, 1994. Avocations: collecting cameos, poetry.

BECKER, KYRA J., neurologist, educator; Student, St. Mary's Coll. Md.; BS in Biology summa cum laude, Va. Tech.; MD, Duke U. Diplomate Am. Bd. Neurology and Psychiatry, 1995. Intern internal medicine Johns Hopkins Hosp., Balt., resident neurology, clin. fellow critical care neurology; rsch. fellow Stroke Br. NIH, NINDS, Bethesda, Md.; attending neurologist Greenbelt (Md.) Neurol. Assocs., 1995—96; asst. prof. neurology and neurol. surgery Sch. Medicine U. Wash., Seattle, 1996—2001, assoc. prof. neurology Sch. Medicine, 2002—, co-dir. Stroke Ctr., 1996—. Mem. critical care adv. com. Harborview Hosp., 1996—, med. dir. stroke unit, 1998—; mem. neurol. devices panel, med. devices adv. com. Ctr. for Devices and Radiol. Health FDA, 2000—. Ad hoc reviewer: Glia, Stroke, Neurology, Annals of Neurology, Critical Care Medicine, Jour. Neuroimaging, Jour. Neuroimmunology, Am. Jour. Physiology, Jour. Neurol. Scis., Jour. Lab. and Clin. Medicine, Jour. AMA, Jour. Cerebral Blood Flow and Metabolism, Inst. for Lab. Animal Rsch. Jour., mem. editl. bd.: Stroke, 2002—, Neurocritical Care, 2002—; contbr. chapters to books, articles to profl. jours. Recipient Eleanor Naylor Dana award, Am. Health Found. Mem.: Hazel K. Goddess for Stroke Rsch. in Women (mem. med. adv. bd. 2000—), Am. Assn. Immunologists, Cardiovasc. Collaborative Clin. Leadership Group, Pugest Sound Stroke Interest Group (pres. 1999—), Am. Stroke Assn. (mem. stroke coun. 1997—, mem. exec. com. affiliate liaison coun. 1999—2001, abstract grader internat. stroke conf. 2000—, mem. stroke coun. membership com. 2001—, chair profl. edn. com. Operation Stroke 2000—), Internat. Soc. Cerebral Blood Flow and Metabolism, Am. Acad. Neurology (critical care and emergency neurology sect. 1997—, course dir. neurology of critical illness 1998—2001, stroke sect. 1999—, exec. com. 2002—, course lectr. hematologic causes of stroke 2002—), Alpha Omega Alpha, Phi Kappa Phi, Phi Beta Kappa. Achievements include patents for increased resistance to stroke by developing immunologic tolerance to Myelin or components thereof.

BECKER, LINDSEY A., art educator; b. Brunswick, Maine, Feb. 9, 1955; d. Arthur Milliken and Rose Koharian Pletts; m. Harvey David Becker, Apr. 17, 1981; children: Ashley Rose, Kendra Starr. BS, U. So. Maine, Portland, 1978; MA, Coll. Notre Dame, Belmont, Calif., 1988. Art tchr. Great Salt Bay Cmty. Sch., Damariscotta, Maine, 1978—80, Sequoia H.S., Redwood City, Calif., 1990—. Avocations: reading, theater. Home: 1144 Virginia Ave Redwood City CA 94061 Office: Sequoia High Sch Brewster AVe Redwood City CA 94061 Office Phone: 650-367-9780 ext. 6021. Business E-Mail: lbecker@sequoia.org.

BECKER, MARY LOUISE, political scientist; b. St. Louis; d. W. R. and Evelyn (Thompson) Becker; divorced; children: James, John. BS, Washington U., St. Louis, 1949, MA, 1951; PhD, Radcliffe Coll., Cambridge, Mass., 1957; postgrad., U. Karachi, Pakistan, 1953-54. Intelligence rsch. analyst Dept. State, Washington, 1957—59; internat. rels. officer AID, Washington, 1959—64, cmty. rels. officer, 1964—66, sci. rsch. officer, 1966—71, UN rels. officer, 1971—91; pres. Internat. Devel. Enterprises, Washington, 1992—. Adviser U.S. dels. 19th, 21st, 23d, 24th, 26th, 28th, 30th, 32d, 34th Governing Coun. sessions UN Devel. Program; adv. U.S. del. 3d prep. com. meeting World Conf. UN Decade for Women; adviser U.S. dels. UNICEF exec. bd. sessions, 1987—91; mem. U.S. Com. for UN Fund for Women; lectr. internat. rels. civic orgns., student groups, 1954—. Author: Muhammed Iqbal, 1965; contbg. editor: Concise Ency. of Mid. East, 1973; contbr. articles to profl. jours. Mem. adv. bd. chmn. internat. student placement Washington Citizenship Seminar Nat. YMCA-YWCA, Washington, 1961—71. Blewett fellow, Washington U., 1951, resident fellow, Radcliffe Coll., 1952—56, Fulbright scholar, U. Karachi, 1953—54. Mem.: AAUW, Nat. Press Club, Mo. Soc. Washington (sec. 1959—60), S. Asian Muslim Studies Assn. (v.p. 1992—), UN Assn. (bd. dirs. Nat. Capital area 1991—), Mid. East Inst., Asia Soc., Assn. Asian Studies, Soc. Internat. Devel., Am. Polit. Sci. Assn., Harvard Club (Washington), Chimes, Mortar Bd., Pi Sigma Alpha, Eta Mu Phi, Beta Gamma Sigma, Alpha Lambda Delta. Presbyterian. Home: 2301 E St NW Washington DC 20037-2829 Office: North Bldg Ste 700 601 Pennsylvania Ave NW Washington DC 20004-2601

BECKER, NANCY ANNE, state supreme court justice; b. Las Vegas, May 23, 1955; d. Arthur William and Margaret Mary (McLoughlin) Becker. BA, U.S. Internat. U., 1976; JD, George Washington U., 1979. Bar: Nev. 1979, D.C. 1980, Md. 1982, U.S. Dist. Ct. Nev. 1987, U.S. Ct. Appeals (9th cir.) 1987. Legis. cons. D.C. Office on Aging, Washington, 1979—83; assoc. Goldstein & Ahalt, College Park, Md., 1980—82; pvt. practice Washington, 1982—87; dep. city atty., prosecutor criminal div. City of Las Vegas, 1983; judge Las Vegas Mcpl. Ct., 1987—89, Clark County Dist. Ct., Las Vegas, 1989—99, chief judge, 1993—94; assoc. justice Nev. Supreme Ct., 1999—. Cons. MADD, Las Vegas, 1983—87. Contbr. articles to profl. jours. Pres. Clark County Pro Bono Project, Las Vegas, 1984—95. Mem.: NCCJ, Am. Businesswomen's Assn. (treas. Las Vegas chpt. 1985—86), Southern Nev. Assn. Women Attys. (past officer), Soroptimist Internat., Vietnam Vets. Am., Las Vegas and Latin C. of C. Office: Nevada Supreme Ct 200 Lewis Ave 17th Fl Las Vegas NV 89101*

BECKER, NANCY JANE, information science educator; b. Irvington, N.J., June 3, 1948; d. George Henry and Vida Jacqueline (Collins) B.; m. James Edward Weissinger, Sept. 4, 1971 (div. Aug. 1989); children: Jeffrey Michael, Erica Kathleen. BA, Seton Hall U., 1972; MLS with honors, Columbia U., 1992, EdD, 1999. Reference dept. intern Columbia U., N.Y.C., 1991-92, reference libr. Tchr. Coll., 1992-93, electronic info. resources libr., 1993-96; instr. info. sci. St. Johns U., Jamaica, N.Y., 1996-99, asst. prof., 1999—. Presenter in field. Contbr. articles to profl. jours. Mem. ALA, AAUP, Assn. Coll. and Rsch. Librs. (com. chair 1995-96, 98-99, sect. chair 1997-98), Am. Ednl. Rsch. Assn., Assn. Libr. and Info. Sci. Edn., Am. Soc. for Info. Sci. and Tech., (chair 2002-), Beta Phi Mu. Dem. Roman Cath. Avocations: hiking, reading. Office: St Johns Univ 8000 Utopia Pkwy Jamaica NY 11432-1343 Home: 415 Claremont Ave Apt 1B Montclair NJ 07042-1815 E-mail: beckern@stjohns.edu.

BECKER, NANCY MAY, nursing educator; b. Reading, Pa., July 28, 1949; d. Theodore R. and Minerva M. (Deiseroth) B. Diploma, Reading Hosp. Sch. Nursing, 1970; BS, Albright Coll., 1979; MS, U. Del., 1981. RN Pa., Del. Nurse mgr. Cmty. Gen. Hosp., Reading, 1974-76; nurse educator Albright Coll., Reading, 1980-87; clin. nurse specialist Polyclinic Med. Ctr., Harrisburg, Pa., 1987-89; asst. prof. Lehigh Carbon C.C., Schnecksville, Pa., 1989-95, dir. nursing programs, 1995-97, dean allied health/dir. nursing, 1998—2001, dean profl. accreditation and curriculum, dir. nursing, 2001—06, interim v.p. acad. and student affairs, 2001—02, v.p. academic and student affairs, DON, 2006—. Mem. ANA, Nat. League Nursing, Sigma Theta Tau.

BECKER, PHYLLIS, systems analyst; b. Plainfield, N.J., Nov. 9, 1963; d. Stephen and Jean Mae Potasky; m. Andrew D. Becker, Feb. 14, 1993; 1 child, Samuel. BS in Computer Sci., Kean U., 1986; MS, Stevens Inst., 1998. Programmer ITT Def. Comms., Nutley, N.J.; sys. analyst AT&T, Somerset, N.J., CSC, Somerset. Republican. Jewish. Avocations: cat and dog care, sewing, needlecrafts. Office: CSC 500 Atrium Dr Somerset NJ 08873 Personal E-mail: pbecker@csc.com.

BECKER, RACHEL J., biology educator; d. Eugene B. and Ruth A. Becker. BS in Biology, Grove City Coll., Pa., 1997; MEd, Slippery Rock U., Pa., 1998. Biology tchr. Highlands Sch. Dist., Natrona Hts., Pa., 1999—. Master tchr. Oceanic Sci. Inst., Pitts., 2002—. Recipient Integrating Tech. award, Hewlett Packard, 2004—05. Mem.: Pa. Sci. Tchrs. Assn., Nat. Sci. Tchrs. Assn. Office: Highlands High School 1500 Pacific Ave Natrona Heights PA 15065

BECKER, SANDRA NEIMAN HAMMER, lawyer; b. N.Y.C., June 17, 1947; d. Melvin and Bernice (Lebowitz) N.; m. Otto R. Hammer, Aug. 25, 1969 (div.); m. Brandon Becker, May 20, 1978; children: Elliott M.N., Gabriel W. BA, CCNY, 1969; JD, U. San Diego, 1978; LLM, NYU, 1981. Bar: Calif. 1978, U.S. Dist. Ct. (so. dist.) Calif. 1979, U.S. Ct. Appeals (9th cir.) 1979. Adminstrv. analyst Consumer Affairs Unit, Syracuse, N.Y., 1973-75; atty. food and drug advt. FTC, Washington, 1978-79, atty. advt. practices div., 1984-88; with Office Gen. Counsel, Electric Rates Fed. Energy Regulatory Commn., Dept. Energy, Washington, 1988-92; regulatory counsel Ctr. for Food Safety and Applied Nutrition, FDA, 2002—03. Mng. editor Food Drug Cosmetic Law Jour., Washington, 1981-85. Food and Drug fellow Food and Drug Law Inst., 1978-80. Home: 713 Lamberton Dr Silver Spring MD 20902-3036 E-mail: srnb@aol.com.

BECKER, SUSAN KAPLAN, management and marketing communication consultant, educator; b. Newark, Jan. 4, 1948; d. Charles and Janet Kaplan; m. William Paul Becker, 1969 (div. 1977). BA in English cum laude, with distinction, U. Pa., 1968, MA, 1969, PhD, 1973, MBA in Fin., 1979. Instr. English Bryn Mawr (Pa.) Coll., 1972-74; assoc. editor U. Pa., Phila., 1975, asst. dir., lectr. urban studies, 1975-77; fin. analyst Phila. Nat. Bank, 1979-82; asst. v.p. Chem. Bank, N.Y.C., 1982-84; v.p. Bankers Trust Co., N.Y.C., 1984-85; prin. Becker Cons. Svcs., N.Y.C., 1985—; adj. assoc. prof. mgmt. comm. Stern Sch. Bus. N.Y.U., 1990—2005. Cons./evaluator Pa. Humanities Council, Phila., 1977-78; mem. editorial bd. Mgmt. Comm. Quar., 1993-97. Author: How to Develop Profitable Financial Products for the Institutional Marketplace, 1988; contbr. articles and revs. to profl. jours. Vol. N.Y. Cares, 1989-92, N.Y.C. affiliate Am. Heart Assn., 1995-97. U. Pa. fellow, 1968-72; E.I. DuPont de Nemours fellow, 1979, N.Y. Regents Coll. Teaching fellow, 1968-70. Mem. Internat. Comm. Assn. (reviewer tech. and comm. divsn. 1991), Fin. Women's Assn. N.Y. (profl. devel. com. 1995-2006, grad. scholarship com. 2006—), The Wharton Club N.Y. (career devel. com. 2003—) Democrat. Avocations: painting and drawing, swimming. Office: 155 E 29th St New York NY 10016-8173 Office Phone: 212-689-1659. Business E-Mail: skbecker@beckerconsultingsvcs.com.

BECKERMAN, ALYSSA, gymnast; b. Long Branch, N.J., Jan. 23, 1981; d. Howard and Melanie Beckerman. Mem. UCLA Gymnastics Team, 2000—03; former mem. Cin. Gymnastics Team. Recipient 9th pl. all around U.S. Classic, 1997, 10th pl. all around Am. Classic, 1998, 4th pl. all around, 4th pl. uneven bars, 5th pl. balance beam U.S. Classic, 1998. Mem. Cin. Gymnastics Acad. Avocations: rollerblading, shopping, internet, music. Office: UCLA Women's Gymnastics PO Box 24044 Los Angeles CA 90024

BECKERMAN, ELLEN, theater director; d. Barry and Nancy Greyson Beckerman. AB, Princeton U., NJ, 1991. Founder, dir. LightBox Theater, Bklyn. Instr. theater Princeton (N.J.) U., NJ, La. State U., Syracuse (N.Y.) U. Named Artist in Residence, HERE Art Ctr., 2000—02; fellow, The Drama League, 2001, NEA, 2003—05; grantee, Soho Rep, 2005. Mem.: ACLU, Network Ensemble Theatres, Lincoln Ctr. Dirs. Lab., Assn. Performing Arts Presenters, Lit. Mgrs. and Dramaturgs Am., Soc. Stage Dirs. and Choreographers (assoc.), Amnesty Internat. Avocations: writing, travel, photography, yoga, meditation. Home Fax: 917-940-4963. Business E-Mail: company@lightboxtheatre.org.

BECKETT, FAYE TRUMBO, school psychologist; b. Baton Rouge, La., Apr. 29, 1943; d. Leslie Orval and Thelma May Trumbo; m. Robert Earl Beckett, Nov. 19, 1994; children: Denisea Lynn Ray, Douglas Tracey Ray, Heather Dean Ray. BS, U. Memphis, 1981, MS, 1983. Cert. sch. psychologist. Sch. psychologist Memphis City Schs., 1983—87, Tipton & Lauderdale Counties, 1987—2004, Tipton County, 1989—. Various ch. positions, 1963—2005. Recipient Key Man Cert., Parkway Village Jaycettes, 1970, Rosetta I. Miller award, Memphis State U., 1982. Mem.: Tenn. Assn. Psychol. Examiners, Tenn. Assn. Sch. Psychologists, Nat. Assn. Sch. Psychologists.

BECKETT, VICTORIA LING, physician; m. Peter G.S. Beckett, 1954 (dec. 1974); 1 child, Paul T. (dec.); m. Joseph C. Sharp, 1996. BA, Mt. Holyoke Coll., 1945; MD, U. Mich., 1949; MA, St. Mary's U., 1995. Intern Mpls. Gen. Hosp., 1949-50; fellow Mayo Grad. Sch., 1951-55; clin. instr. Wayne State U. Sch. Medicine, Detroit, 1956-67; staff cons. internal medicine oncology svc. Henry Ford Hosp., Detroit, 1957-60; rsch. physician Darling Meml. Ctr., Detroit, 1965-69; rsch. assoc. rheumatology Trinity Coll. Dublin U., 1970-72, postgrad. tutor, 1972-73, dir., 1973-76; cons. physician in rheumatology Federated Dublin Vol. Hosps., 1973-76; staff cons. rheumatology Mayo Clinic, 1976-90, emeritus staff, 1990—; asst. prof. medicine Mayo Med. Sch., 1976-90; med. dir. Rochester Health Care Ctr., Minn., 1985—90. Author: Living Medicine: Memoir Snap Shots, 2004. Fellow: ACP; mem.: Mayo Med. Alumni Assn., Am. Coll. Rheumatology (ret. mem.), Minn. State Med. Assn., Zumbro Valley Med. Soc., Phi Beta Kappa, Sigma Xi. Methodist. Avocation: teaching exercise class. Office Phone: 507-284-2691.

BECK-HALLENBECK, DEBRA KAY, music educator, musician; d. Ralph Dwight and Dorah Mae Hendricks; m. Steven Mark Hallenbeck, Nov. 17, 2004; children: Jessica Kay Beck, Elizabeth Marie Beck, Kathryn Emmalee Beck. MusB cum laude, Christopher Newport U., 2001. Lic. tchg. with endorsement in instrumental edn. Va., 2001. Dir. bands Oscar Smith Mid. Sch., Chesapeake, Va., 2001—05, Deep Creek H.S., Chesapeake, 2005—. Freelance musician, Hampton Roads, Va., 1994—. Musician (clarinetist): Tidewater Winds Profl. Concert Band, 1999—2005. Dir. music, organist Cradock Bapt. Ch., Portsmouth, Va., 2000—05; bd. of directors Bay Youth Orchestras of Va., Norfolk, Va., 2004—05. Mem.: Music Educators Nat. Conf. (licentiate). Office: Deep Creek High Sch 2900 Margaret Booker Dr Chesapeake VA 23323 Office Phone: 757-487-0859. Office Fax: 757-558-5305. Business E-Mail: beckdka@cps.k12.va.us.

BECKINGHAM, KATHLEEN MARY, education educator, researcher; b. Sheffield, Yorkshire, Eng., May 8, 1946; arrived in U.S., 1976; d. Philip and Mary Ellen (Flint) B.; m. Alan Edward Smith, Oct. 7, 1967 (div. Oct. 1978); m. Robert Bruce Weisman, July 25, 1986; 1 child, Caroline Mary Weisman. BA, U. Cambridge, Eng., 1967, MA, 1968, PhD, 1972. Grad. student Strangeways Rsch. Lab., Cambridge, 1967-70; postdoctoral Inst. Molecular Biology, Aarhus, Denmark, 1970-72; rsch. assoc. Nat. Inst. Med. Rsch., London, 1972-76; rsch. assoc., instr. U. Mass. Med. Sch., Worcester, 1976-80; asst. prof. Rice U., Houston, 1980-85, assoc. prof. biochemistry, cell biology, molecular biology, 1985-92, prof., 1992—. Recipient award, Camille and Henry Dreyfus Found., 1979. Office: Rice U Dept Biochemistry and Cell Biology PO Box 1892 Ms-140 Houston TX 77251-1892

BECKLES, INGRID, mortgage banker; b. Washington, May 27, 1961; d. Frank Neville Beckles and Maria Beckles Jenkins; m. David Alan Fountain, July 3, 1981 (div. Jan. 1987); children: Kaiesha Nicole. BS, U. Md., 1988. Asst. br. mgr. Chevy Chase (Md.) Savs. Bank/B.F. Saul Mortgage Co., 1983-84, staff auditor, 1984-87, v.p., mgr. policies and procedures dept., 1989-91, v.p., mgr. ctrl. processing divsn., 1991, v.p. mgr., quality control dept., 1986-91; asst. v.p., regional ops. mgr. S.E. region PNC Mortgage Corp. Am., Vernon Hills, Ill., 1991-93, 2d v.p., underwriting mgr. Nat. Mortgage Ctr., 1993-96, mem. corp. fair lending initiatives staff, 1993—, v.p., chief underwriter, 1996-98, v.p., customer focused intiatives, 1998-99, v.p. credit policy and quality assurance, 1999—. Spkr. HUD and Joint Ctr. for Housing Studies, 1994, HUD Working Group for Underwrirring and Bus. Practices, 1994—, Nat. Assn. Real Estate Brokers, 1995, Fannie Mae Nat. and Regional Risk Adv. Coun., 1995-96, VA Working Group on Underwriting and Bus. Practices, 1996—, Mortgage Bankers Assn., Nat. Underwriting Conf., 1997, Freddie Mac-Nat. Mgr.'s Meeting, 1998. Bd. dirs. Robert Taylor Boys and Girls Club, Chgo., 1998—. Mem. NAFE, Mortgage Bankers Assn. Am., Women in the Arts. Episcopalian. Avocations: horseback riding, piano, tennis, bicycling.

BECKMAN, BRENDA MARSHALL, educational consultant; b. New Malden, Surrey, Eng., May 8, 1934; came to U.S., 1960; d. Norris Bishop and Edith Rosamund (Clappé) Marshall; m. Erik Beckman, Oct. 23, 1959 (div. 1975); children: Monika Rotunno, Kristina Beckman-Brito, Diana Duperre. AA, Macomb County Community Coll., 1972; BA in Polit. Sci., Oakland U., 1973; MA in Polit. Sci., Cen. Mich. U., 1974. Instr. polit. sci. Delta Coll., University Center, Mich., 1974-75, Affirmative Action officer, 1977-78, assoc. dean instrn., 1978-83, dean acad. affairs, 1983-85; lectr. polit. sci. Saginaw Valley State Coll., University Center, 1975-76; instr. polit. sci. Oakland U., Rochester, Mich., 1977-78; exec. dean East campus Pima CC, Tucson, 1985-86, v.p. acad. affairs, 1987, exec. dean, v.p. East campus, 1987-89, acting pres., 1989-90, sr. v.p., 1990; assoc. dir. League for Innovation in the CC, 1990—96, sr. league cons. Phoenix, 1998—; search cons./retreat facilitator Assn. CC Trustees, 1996—2003; interm pres. Aims CC, Greeley, Colo., 2001—03; coach Achieveing the Dream initiative U. Tex., Austin, 2006—. Cons. in field. Co-author: Community College Programs for Older Adults: A Resource Directory of Guildlines Comprehensive Programming Models and Selected Programs, 1992, Energizing and Focusing the Movement: National Organizations Impacting Community, Technical, and Junior Colleges, 1992; contbg. author: Preparing Professional Women for the Future, 1985 (collection of papers) Adjunct Faculty, 1988; contbr. articles to profl. jours. Trustee El Dorado Hosp., Tucson, 1986-90; bd. dir. Pima County Econ. Devel. Coun., 1989-90, Tucson Econ. Devel. Corp., 1989-90. Recipient Governance award AAUP, 1982, Leadership award Leadership Alumni Tucson C. of C., 1991, Outstanding Adminstr. award Pima Community Coll. Found.; named Woman on the Move YWCA, 1989; U. Mich. Ctr. for Higher Edn. fellow, 1984-85. Episcopalian. Avocations: swimming, reading, music. Office: League for Innovation CC 4505 E Chandler Blvd Phoenix AZ 85048-7690

BECKMAN, ERICKA, artist, filmmaker; b. Hempstead, N.Y., July 7, 1951; d. Robert Beckman and Ellen (Kathrine) Von Hofen. BFA, Wash. U.; MFA, Calif. Inst. of Arts, L.A. Prof. dept. media and performing arts Mass. Coll. Art, 1983—. One-woman shows include The Kitchen, NYC, 1986, Walker Art Ctr., Mpls., 1986, 2005, Milw. Art Mus., 1987, Hirshhorn Mus., 1987, Whitney Mus., NYC, 1987, 1991, PS-1 Ctr. for Contemporary Art, 1999, MOMA, NY, 2003, exhibited in group shows at Palais Des Beaux Arts, Brussels, 1986, L.A. Mus. Contemporary Art, 1989, ICA-Boston, 1991, ICA-London, 1992, Koln (Germany) Kunstverin, 1992, Galerie Nat. du Jeu de Paume, Paris, 1992, Ctr. Pour L'Arte Contemporaine, Geneva, 2000, Whitney Mus. Art, NYC, 2000, NY Film Festival, 2002, Shanghai Duolun Mus. Modern Art, 2004, Musee D'Orsay, Paris, 2005, Met. Mus., NYC, 2005. NEH grantee, 1982, 1994, NY State Coun. on the Arts grantee, 1983, 1990, The Jerome Found. grantee, 1983, NY Found. for the Arts grantee, 1989, Mass. Coun. on the Arts grantee, 1989, Lef Found. grantee, 2004, ArtsLink Collaborative Projects grantee, 1999. Home: 358 Broadway New York NY 10013-3922 Office Phone: 617-879-7474. E-mail: ebeckfilm@earthlink.net.

BECKMAN, JUDITH, art educator; b. Amityville, N.Y., Mar. 12, 1951; d. Charles Frederick and Helen Marie (Colville) B. Student, U. Miss., 1969-71, George Washington U., 1971, U. Guadalajara, Mex., 1972, City Coll. City U. N.Y., 1978, Columbia U., 1979; BFA, Colo. U., 1973; MFA, Ohio U., 1975; postgrad., Ohio State U., 1980-88. Teaching assoc. Ohio U., Athens, 1974-75; silkscreen artist Chromacomp, Inc., N.Y.C., 1976; vis. artist Coll. Misericordia, Dallas, Pa., 1977; instr. Spanish Am. Inst., N.Y.C., 1978-79; prodn. coordinator Chromacomp, Inc., N.Y.C., 1978; instr. Coll. Misericordia, Dallas, Pa., 1978, Malcolm-King Coll., N.Y.C., 1979-80; bilingual instr. Lincoln Sch., Orange, N.J., 1979-80; teaching assoc. Ohio State U., Columbus, 1980-88; gallery dir. Kenyon Coll., Gambier, Ohio, 1988-89, Franklin U., Columbus, 1989-93. Mem. curriculum com. dept. art history Ohio State U., Columbus, 1984-85; vis. lectr. Ohio State U., Mansfield, 1988; vis. instr. Oberlin (Ohio) Coll., 1988, Kenyon Coll., 1989; art instr. Columbus Torah Acad., 1989-90; instr. Brigham Young U., 1990-91, Ohio U. Chillicothe, 1994—; lectr. Pontifical Coll. Josephinum, Columbus, 1992—; instr. Columbus State Cmty. Coll., 1995—. Exhibited in group shows at Community Gallery, N.Y.C., 1978, The Massillon (Ohio) Mus., 1978, Western Ill. U., Macomb, Ill., 1979, Springfield Art Mus., 1980, Zaner Gallery, Rochester, N.Y., 1981, Frick Art Mus., Wooster, Ohio, 1983, Spark Gallery, 1984, Ohio State U. Gallery, 1985, El Paso Mus. of Art, 1987, Artreach Gallery, Columbus, 1987, Artreach Gallery, Columbus, 1987, 88, Columbia Coll., Mo., 1988, Columbus Art League, 1988-89, North Coast Coll. Soc., Cleve., 1990; presentations include Case Western Res. U., 1982, Ohio State U., 1984, 85, Newcomb Coll./Tulane U., New Orleans, 1985; contbr. articles to profl. jours. Instr. Rape Prevention program Ohio State U., 1980-90; mem. adv. bd. Thompson Recreation Ctr., Columbus, 1986-89. Ohio State grantee, 1986, Com. for the Visual Arts Exhbn. grantee, 1978, Bklyn. Arts and Culture Assn. grantee, 1979, Women's Rsch. grantee Brigham Young U., 1990; Women Scholars fellow Ohio State U., 1992. Mem. Coll. Art Assn., Women's Caucus for Art (pres., co-founder Ohio chpt., nat. bd. dirs. 1992-95), Nat. Mus. Women in Arts, Columbus Art League, Artreach Inc., Ohio State U. Grad. Student Assn. (pres. 1983-84), Zeta Tau Alpha, Alpha Lambda Delta. Avocation: Tae Kwon Do. Home: 5635 Thompson Rd Ashville OH 43103-9579

BECKMAN, JUDITH KALB, financial counselor and planner, educator, writer; b. Bklyn., June 27, 1940; d. Harry and Frances (Cohen) Kalb; m. Richard Martin Beckman, Dec. 16, 1961; children: Barry Andrew, David Mark. BA, Hofstra U., 1962; MA, Adelphi U., 1973, cert., 1984. CFP; registered investment adviser, stockbroker. English tchr. Long Beach H.S., 1962-65; Promotion coordination pub. rels. Mandel Sch. for Med. Assts., Hempstead, N.Y., 1973-74; exec. dir. Nassau Easter Seals, Albertson, N.Y., 1974-76; dir. pub. info. Long Beach (N.Y.) Meml. Hosp., Long Beach, 1976-77; account rep. First Investors, Hicksville, N.Y., 1977-78; from sales asst. to acct. exec. Josephthal & Co. Inc., Great Neck, N.Y., 1978-81; v.p., fin. planner Arthur Gould Inc., Great Neck, N.Y., 1981-88; pres. Fin. Solutions (affiliated with Seco West Ltd., Goldner Siegfried Assocs. Inc.), Westbury, NY, 1988—2002; with Am. Portfolio Fin. Svcs., 2002—. Adj. instr. Adelphi U., Garden City N.Y., 1981-83, Molloy Coll., Rockville Ctr., N.Y., 1982-84; lectr. SUNY, Farmingdale, 1984-85; creater, presenter seminars, workshops on fin., investing, 1981—; adv. bd. L.I. Devel. Corp., 1993—; advisor investment clubs, 1996—. Fin. columnist The Women's Record, 1985-93; writer quar. newspaper The Reporter, 1987. Coord. meat boycott, L.I., 1973; mentor SUNY Old Westbury, 1989-93; co-founder, chair L.I. del. High Profile Men and Women, Colonie Hill, Hauppauque, N.Y., 1985; treas. L.I. Alzheimer's Found., 1989-93, trustee, 1993-95; apptd. to Nassau County Women's Adv. Coun. by County Exec., 1990; chief adv. coun. Ctr. for Family Resources, 1996-98; bd. dirs. L.I. Small Bus. Assistance Corp., 2003—, sec., 2003—; bd. dirs. For Our Children and Us, Inc., 2002—; adviser to 2 investment clubs. Recipient citation for leadership Town of Hempstead, N.Y., 1986, 89, L.I. Press Club award, 1987, 92, Mentor award SBA, 1989, Fin. Svcs. award SBA, 1991, L.I. Assn. Fin. Svc. Advocate award, 1991, Woman of Distinction in Bus. award Women on the Job, 1989, Bus. Leadership citation Nassau County, N.Y., 1989, Supr. award Town of Hempstead, 1989, Pathfinder Bus. award, 1997, Bus. Adv. of Yr. N.Y. Dist. award U.S. SBA, 1998, Women's Bus. Advocate award, 1998, NAWBO LI Small Bus. Entrepreneur of the Yr. award, 1998; named one of 50 Leading Bus. Women,

L.I. Bus. News, 2002, 2003, one of 90 Women in 90 Yrs. Making a Difference, Girls Scouts Nassau County, 2002. Mem. Nat. Assn. Women Bus. Owners L.I. (bd. dirs. 1987-89, membership chair 1996, v.p. membership 1996-98, v.p. edn. 1998-99, v.p. R&D 2002-03), Women's Econ. Developers of L.I. (bd. dirs. 1985-92), Internat. Assn. Fin. Planners, Inst. Cert. Fin. Planners, Fin. Planning Assn. L.I., L.I. Ctr. Bus. and Profl. Women (adv. coun. 1996-98, pres. 1984-86, Pres.' award 1992, Hall of Fame Achiever inductee 2001, steering com., co-founder L.I. Women's Agenda 1998, exec. v.p. Women's Agenda 1998-2000), Art League L.I. (bd. dirs. 2002—, chair investment and fin. com.), Kiwanis (bd. dirs. 1994-97, chair fund raising 1994, chair cmty. svcs. 1995-97, v.p. membership 1996), Am. Portfolio Fin. Svcs. Inc. (adv. bd. mem., 2006). Republican. Jewish. Avocations: theater, classical music, opera, reading. Home: 2084 Beverly Way Merrick NY 11566-5418 Office: Fin Solutions Fin Planning Office 2084 Beverly Way Merrick NY 11566-5418 also: 400 Post Ave Ste 200 Westbury NY 11590-2226 Office Phone: 516-333-1370. E-mail: jbeck0627@aol.com.

BECKMANN, KATHLEEN ANN, music educator; b. Binghamton, N.Y., Apr. 10, 1954; d. Eugene Stickle and Mary Catherine Baxter; m. Allan Graham, Jr. Beckmann, Aug. 16, 1975; children: Allan, Carolyn, Melinda. MusB, State U. Coll. Potsdam, N.Y., 1975; MusM, SUNY, Fredonia, 2003. Music tchr. Monticello Ctrl. Sch., NY, 1975—78, Wappingers Ctrl. Sch., Wappingers Falls, NY, 1978—81, Hyde Park Ctrl. Sch., NY, 1990—. Condr. No. Dutchess Symphony Orch., 2006. Editor: Orchestrations, 1994—98. Recipient Crane Merit award, SUNY-Potsdam, 1975. Mem.: N.Y. State Sch. Music Assn. (string adjudicator), Nat. Sch. Orch. Assn. (exec. bd. 1994—98), Nat. Condrs. Guild, Am. String Tchrs. Assn., Music Educators Nat. Conf., Sigma Alpha Iota (parliamentarian). Avocations: tennis, travel, biking. Home: 3 Robin Ln Wappingers Falls NY 12590 Office: F D Roosevelt High Sch S Cross Rd PO Box 2032 Hyde Park NY 12538 Office Phone: 845-229-4021 x 1238.

BECKMANN, LAURA R., healthcare educator; b. St. Louis, Mo., Dec. 29, 1962; d. Larry D. and Doris L. Hampton; m. Dennis M. Beckmann, Apr. 16, 1988; children: Kristi L., Brett M., Garrett G. BA, SW Mo. State U., 1985; MA, St. Mary's U., Overland Park, Kans., 2006. Profl. waterskier/instr. Lake of the Ozarks Water Show, Ft. Osage, 1979—87; phys. edn., health tchr. Ferguson-Florissant Sch. Dist. - Cross Keys Mid. Sch., 1986—98, Ferguson-Florissant Sch. Dist. - McCluer H.S., 1998—2001; curriculum coord. Ferguson-Florissant Sch. Dist., 2001—, local wellness policy coord. Tech prep coord. Ferguson-Florissant Sch. Dist., Mo.; phys. edn., health program rev. com. U. Mo., Florissant; local wellness policy coord. Ferguson-Florissant Sch. Dist., adminstration ctr. emergency response team leader, 21st century mid. sch. after sch. sports/elem. track meet coord., elem. swimming program coord., cross keys mid. sch. intramurals dir., coach-volleyball, track, north county sch. bus. partnership rep., coordinated sch. health adv. coun. chmn., co-chair of practical arts adv. coun., st. louis moahperd summer workshops facilitator, cpr certification coord./instr.; phys. edn., health grade level expectations writing com. Dept. of Elem. and Secondary Phys. Edn., Jefferson City, Mo. Waterski performer, instr. Lake St. Louis Water Ski Team. Recipient Exemplary Gold Phys. Edn. Program Award Winner, Mo. Assn. for Health, Phys. Edn., Recreation, and Dance, 1996, 1998; grant, Cable Tec Commn., 2004—06, DHSS, 2004—, Mo. Found. For Health, 2005—. Mem.: SMCAA, Mo. NEA, Mo. Assn. for Health, Phys. Edn., Recreation, and Dance, Am. Alliance for Health, Phys. Edn., Recreation, and Dance, Lake St. Louis Ski Team. Catholic. Achievements include design of FFSD Web-based Fitness Data Analysis Program (K-12); FFSD School Health Index. Avocations: volleyball, travel, water-skiing. Office: Ferguson-Florissant Sch Dist 1005 Waterford Dr Florissant MO 63033 Office Phone: 314-506-9052. Office Fax: 314-506-9978. Personal E-mail: lbeckmann@centurytel.net. E-mail: lbeckmann@fergflor.k12.mo.us.

BECKMANN, M. PATRICIA, biochemist; BA, Evergreen State Coll.; PhD, Univ. Ariz.; postgraduate Fulbright Scholar, Uppsala Univ., Sweden. Vis. scientist Nat. Cancer Inst., Bethesda, Md.; rsch scientist & mgmt. positions Immunex Corp. (now Amgen Corp.), 1988—2002; mem. biotech. venture capital team Vulcan Capital, Seattle, 2002—05; chief sci. officer Homestead Clinical Corp., Seattle, 2005—. Bd. mem. Oregon Biotechnology Assn.; mem. sci. adv. bd. Nura Inc. Contbr. articles to profl. jours. Named Nat. Inventor of the Yr., Intellectual Property Owners Assn., 2001. Mem.: Wash. Biotechnology & Biomedical Assn. Achievements include holding over 30 U.S. patents; discovering TNF receptor molecules, marketed as Enbrel, for patients with rheumatoid arthritis. Office: Homestead Clinical Corp 1616 Eastlake Ave E Seattle WA 98102*

BECKSTRAND, KARIN, music educator; b. Hutchinson, Minn., Dec. 19, 1966; d. Wallace and Helen Beckstrand. MusB Edn., U. Wis., River Falls, 1990; M in Music Edn., U. Nebr., Lincoln, 1997. Music educator Round Lake Schs., Minn., 1990—93, Somerset Area Schs., Wis., 1993—95, Stillwater Area Schs., Minn., 1995—96; grad. tchg. asst. U. Nebr., Lincoln, 1996—97; music educator Fridley H.S., Minn., 1997—2002, Hayes Elem. Sch., 2002—. Music rep. Minn. State H.S. League, Mpls., 1998—2002; team leader Bands of Am., Indpls., 1991—. Presentor and presider (music conventions) Teaching the Small Marching Band. Recipient Chancellor's award, U. Wis. River Falls, 1990. Mem.: Music Educator's Nat. Conf. (corr.), Minn. Music Educator's Assn. (life). Avocations: running, triathalons, music. Office Phone: 763-502-5246.

BECKWITH, BARBARA JEAN, journalist; b. Chgo., Dec. 11, 1948; d. Charles Barnes (dec.) and Elizabeth Ann (Nolan) Beckwith. BA in Journalism, Marquette U., 1970. News editor Lake Geneva (Wis.) Regional News, 1972-74; asst. editor St. Anthony Messenger, Cin., 1974-82, mng. editor, 1982—. Mem. Cath. Conf. Comm. Com., 1990—92. Mem.: Internat. Cath. Union of the Press (1st v.p. 2005—), Cath. Union of the Press, Cath. Journalism Scholarship Fund (bd. dirs. 1993—, v.p. 1995—96, pres. 1996—99, 2001—), Nat. Cath. Assn. for Broadcasters and Communicators (bd. dirs. 1989—96, 1997—98), Fedn. Ch. Press Assns. of Internat. Cath. Union of the Press (3d v.p. 1989—92, pres. 1992—2004, 3d v.p. 2004—), Cath. Press Assn. (bd. dirs. 1986—96, v.p. 1988—90, pres. 1990—92, best interview 1982, best photo story 1985, St. Francis de Sales award for outstanding contbn. to Cath. journalism 1994, best poetry 1997). Office: St Anthony Messenger 28 W Liberty St Cincinnati OH 45202-6498 Office Phone: 513-241-5615 x 170.

BECKWITH, MARY ANN, art educator; b. Phila., May 17, 1945; d. Raymond Leonard Liss, Leona Mary Liss; m. John Phillip Beckwith, Dec. 28, 1966; children: Susan Lynn Allen, Carl. BA, Marygrove Coll., 1967. With Mich. Bell Telephone, 1967—73; prof. art Mich. Tech U., Houghton, 1973—. Author: (bBook) Creative Water: A Step-by Step Guide and Showcase, 1997 (Signature Membership: National Watercolor Society, 2000). Mem.: Soc. Layeriest Multimedia, Transparent Watercolor Soc. Am. (assoc.; pres. 1993—95). Office: 1400 Townsend Dr Houghton MI 49931-1200 Home Fax: 906-487-1841. Business E-Mail: mabeckwi@mtu.edu.

BECKWITH, SANDRA SHANK, federal judge; b. Norfolk, Va., Dec. 4, 1943; BA, U. Cin., 1965, JD, 1968. Bar: Ohio 1969, Ind. 1976, Fla. 1979, U.S. Dist. Ct. (so. dist.) Ohio 1971, U.S. Dist. Ct. Ind. 1976, U.S. Supreme Ct. 1977. Pvt. practice, Harrison, Ohio, 1969—77, 1979—81; judge Hamilton County Mcpl. Ct., Cin., 1977—79, 1981—86, commr., 1989—91; judge Ct. Common Pleas, Hamilton County Divsn. Domestic Rels., 1987—89; assoc. Graydon, Head and Ritchey, 1989—91; judge U.S. Dist. Ct. (so. dist.) Ohio, 1992—2004, chief judge, 2004—. Mem. Ohio Chief Justice's Code of Profl. Responsibility Commn., 1984, Ohio Gov.'s Com. on Prison Crowding, 1984-90, State Fed. Com. on Death Penalty Habeas Corpus, 1995—; pres. 6th Cir. Dist. Judges Assn., 1998-99; chair So. Dist. Ohio Automation Com., 1997—. Mem. advisory bd. Tender Mercies. Mem. Fed. Judges Assn., Fed. Bar Assn. (exec. com.), Judicial Conf. of U.S. (mem. com. on defender svcs.) Office: Potter Stewart US Courthouse Ste 810 Cincinnati OH 45202 Office Phone: 513-564-7610. Business E-Mail: sandra_beckwith@ohsd.uscourts.gov.

BEDELIA, BONNIE, actress; b. N.Y.C., Mar. 25, 1948; d. Philip and Marian (Wagner) Culkin; m. Kenneth Luber, Apr. 15, 1969; children: Yuri, Jonah. Student, Hunter Coll., N.Y.C.; studied with Uta Hager, Herbert Berghof studios; studied with Lee Strasberg, Actors Studio. Stage appearances include The Glass Menagerie, 1970, The Sea Gull, 1970, As You Like It, 1970, Midsummer Night's Dream, 1970, (T.V. series) The Division, 2001-04; Broadway appearances include Isle of Children, 1960, Enter Laughing, 1963, The Playroom, 1965, Happily Never After, 1966, My Sweet Charlie, 1967 (Theatre World award 1967); film appearances include Gypsy Moths, 1969, They Shoot Horses, Don't They?, 1969, Lovers and Other Strangers, 1970, Rosalie, 1972, Between Friends, 1973, The Big Fix, 1978, Heart Like a Wheel, 1983, Death of an Angel, 1986, The Boy Who Could Fly, 1986, Violets are Blue, 1986, The Stranger, 1987, Die Hard, 1988, Prince of Pennsylvania, 1988, Fat Man & Little Boy, 1989, Presumed Innocent, 1990, Die Hard II, 1990, Needful Things, 1993, Speechless, 1994, Judicial Consent, 1994, Homecoming, 1996, Any Mother's Son, 1997 (Cable Ace award), Bad Manners, 1998, Gloria, 1999, Anywhere But Here, 1999, Sordid Lives, 2000, Manhood, 2003, Berkley, 2004; TV series Love of Life, 1961-67, The New Land, 1974, mini-series Salem's Lot, 1979, A Season in Purgatory, 1996, Flowers for Algernon, 2000; TV films Then Came Bronson, 1969, Sandcastles, 1972, Hawkins on Murder, 1973, A Message to My Daughter, 1973, A Time for Love, 1973, Heatwave, 1974, A Question of Love, 1978, Walking Through the Fire, 1979, Fighting Back, 1980, Million Dollar Infield, 1982, Memorial Day, 1983, The Lady from Yesterday, 1985, Alex, The Life of a Child, 1986, When the Time Comes, 1987, Somebody Has to Shoot the Picture, 1990, Switched At Birth, 1991, A Mother's Right: The Elizabeth Morgan Story, 1993, The Fire Next Time, 1993, Fallen Angels (The Quiet Room), 1993 (Emmy nomination, Guest Actress - Drama, 1994), The Gift, 1994, Shadow of a Doubt, 1995, Legacy of Sin: The William Coit Story, 1995, Her Costly Affair, 1996, To Live Again, 1998, Locked in Silence, 1999, Picnic, 2000. Recipient Golden Globe award, 1983.

BEDELL, BARBARA LEE, journalist; b. Annapolis, Md., July 10, 1936; d. Royal Lee and Kathryn Rosalee (Alton) Sweeney; m. Raymond Lester Bedell, July 1, 1955 (div. 1979); children: Patricia Bedell Pulito, Barbara Ann Bedell Porrini, Raymond, Robert. DHL (hon.), Mt. St. Mary Coll., 2000. Dir. woman's programming, host daily talk show Sta. KLME, Laramie, Wyo., 1962-68, Sta. WKIP, Poughkeepsie, NY, 1968-70; asst. soc. editor, feature writer Poughkeepsie Jour., 1968-70; dir. comm. and publs. Spackenkill Sch. Dist., Poughkeepsie, 1970-73; columnist, reporter Times Herald-Record Newspaper, Middletown, NY, 1973—. Bd. dirs. Middletown Day Nursery, 1988—; mem. steering com. Dr. Martin Luther King Jr. Cmty. Wide Celebration, 1992—; lectr. on various topics to civic, polit., religious, social orgns., 1961—. Mem. 75th Anniversary Com., Cheyenne, Wyo., 1965; mem. Rep. Precinct Com., 1961-68, Albany County Bd. Electors, 1966-68; mem. com. history and heritage collection Orange County C.C., Middletown, 1984; mem. 100th Anniversary Com., Middletown, 1983-88; bd. dirs. divsn. marshal 1988 Parade; apptd. del. Gov. Mario Cuomo's N.Y. State Conf. on Librs., 1981; campaign chair United Way, 1996; bd. dirs. Literacy Vols. of Am.; kettle chmn. Salvation Army, 1999. Recipient 1st in N.Y. feature writing award Am. Cancer Soc., 1973, Disting. Svc. award NAACP, 1980, 96, Hadassah Myrtle Wreath award, 1979, Cmty. Svc. award Boy Scouts Am., 1990, Humanitarian award Human Rights Commn., 1997, Orange County Agr. Soc. award, Svc. awards from numerous svc. clubs and lodges, chs., assns., Spirit of Caring award Hospice Orange and Sullivan Counties, 2005, Coop. Ext. Friend of Ext. award Cornell U., 2005; named Mrs. Wyo., Mrs. Am. Pageant, 1967, N.Y. State All-Am. Family, 1972, Lions Knight of the Blind award, 1999, Pinnacle award U.S. Harness Racing Hall of Fame, 2002, Masonic DeWitt Clinton award, 2002. Mem. Nat. Fedn. Press Women (8 awards for feature writing 1967-70, top Wyo. state award for radio script writing 1966), Elks (Mother of Yr. award 1989), SAR (Woman of Yr. award 1991), US Harness Writers' Assn. (Good Gal award 2005), Kiwanis, Lions, Rotary. Home: PO Box 458 Walker Valley NY 12588-0458 Office: Times Herald-Record PO Box 2046 Middletown NY 10940-0558 E-mail: bbedell@th-record.com.

BEDELL, ELIZABETH SNYDER (BETTY BEDELL), editor-in-chief, marketing professional; b. Jacksonville, Fla., Mar. 26, 1940; d. Ralph Edward and Elizabeth Follin Snyder; m. David Thorpe Bedell, June 16, 1961 (div. Aug. 1974); children: Charles, Elizabeth Bedell Coyle, George. Student, Hollins U.; BA, U. North Fla. Founding editor Kalliope, A Jour. of Women's Lit. and Art, 1978—81; tchr. Stanton Coll. Prep., Venetia Elem., 1981—84; freelance writer, editor, 1984—93, 1997—; program developer St. Vincent's Found., Inc., 1993—98; editor Betty Snyder Bedell Editl. Svcs., Jacksonville, 1999—. Chmn. garden and grounds Ximenez-Fatio Mus. House, St. Augustine, Fla.; bd. dirs. Jr. League, Jacksonville. Mem.: Colonial Dames, Fla. Yacht Club Jacksonville. Home and Office: 4242 Ortega Blvd # 21 Jacksonville FL 32210 E-mail: ebedell@bellsouth.net.

BEDENBAUGH, ANGELA LEA OWEN, chemistry educator, researcher; b. Seguin, Tex., Oct. 6, 1939; d. Wintford Henry and Nelia Melanie (Fischer) Owen; m. John Holcombe Bedenbaugh, Dec. 27, 1961; 1 child, Melanie Celeste. BS cum laude, U. Tex., 1961; PhD in Organic Chemistry, U. S.C., 1967. Instr. chemistry lab. U. Tex., Austin, 1960—61; rsch. assoc. chemistry U. So. Miss., Hattiesburg, 1966—80, rsch. assoc. prof. chemistry and biochemistry, 1980—, bd. mem. women's studies program, 1996—97. Co-prin. investigator Bell South Found. grant, 1998; dir. website NASA grant, 1999-00; project dir. math. and sci. ptnr. program U.S. Dept. Edn., 2004-06; mem Nat. Def. Coun. Author: Nomenplayture, 1998; co-author: (with John H. Bedenbaugh) Handbook for High School Chemistry Teachers, 1985, Teaching First Year Chemistry, 4th edit., 1993, Teaching Physical Science, Vols. 1 and 2, 2003; patentee in field. Adminstrv. bd. Parkway Heights United Meth. Ch., 1974-75, women's unit leader, 1973-75, women's unit treas., 1977, Wesleyan Svc. Guild v.p., 1970, Sunday Sch. tchr., 1973-74; bd. dirs. Forrest Stone Area Opportunity Inc., 1970-72, bd. dirs. exec. com., 1972, com. to rewrite pers. policies and procedures, 1971, Headstart monitoring com., 1971-72, pers. screening com., 1971; nat. Women's Polit. Caucus, 1976—; mem. Toastmasters Internat., 1986—, club. pres., 1993, area gov., 1994; adminstr., dir. Tchr. Mentoring Initiative through Bell South Found. Grant, 1998-2000; Miss. state coord. Bldg. a Presence for Sci., 2002-; mem. Gov.'s Edn. Summit, 2004; mem. U.S. Dept. Edn. Math. and Sci. Partnership, 2004-2006; active Arthritis Found., Arbor Day Found. Recipient John and Angela Bedenbaugh award Coastal Miss. Assn. H.S. Chemistry Tchrs., 1996—; rsch. grantee U.S. Dept. Energy, U. So. Miss., 1979-80, NSF, U. So. Miss., 1985, Adminstrv. Dir. Rsch. grant, 1988-91, 1993-96, 2001-04, NSF, 2000-05, grantee Miss.-NASA Space Consortium, 1999-2000, 2000-01 Mem. NSTA (nat. resource rev. panel for rev. of instrnl. materials), LWV, AAUW, Am. Chem. Soc. (chmn. 1984-85, program chmn. 1983-84, exec. bd. 1983—, grantee 2002, Chemist of Yr. award 1991, Johnnie Marie Whitfield Svc. award 2004), Miss. Sci. Tchrs. Assn. (exec. bd. 1994—, pres.-elect 1998-2000, pres. 2000-02, state bldg. a presence for sci. coord. 2002—, rep., coord. continuing edn. credit units, Disting. Sci. Tchr. award 1994), Nat. Wildlife Fedn., Wilderness Soc., Union of Concerned Scientists, Nat. Resources Def. Coun., Delta Kappa Gamma (pres. Miss. br. 1989-91, chmn. internat. rsch. com. 1980-82, chmn. internat. computer share fair at internat. conv. 1994, editor U.S. Forum Connection 2000-), Nat. Audubon Soc., Sierra Club, Commonwealth Club, Sigma Xi (charter, sec.-treas. 1967-69, treas. 1970, pres. 1973-74, program chmn. 1972-73), Nature Conservancy, Smithsonian Instn., Nat. Parks Conservation Assn., Humane Soc. U.S., MADD, ASPCA, The Wings. Democrat. Methodist. Home: 63 Suggs Rd Hattiesburg MS 39402-3639 Office: Univ So Miss 118 College Dr 8466 Hattiesburg MS 39406-1000 Business E-Mail: angela.bedenbaugh@usm.edu.

BEDFORD, AMY ALDRICH, public relations executive; b. Pendleton, Oreg., July 13, 1912; d. Edwin Burton and Elsie (Conklin) Aldrich; m. J.M. Bedford (wid.); 1 child, Jacqueline Bedford Brown. BS, Oreg. State U., 1933. Mgr. comml. dept. East Oregonian, Pendleton, 1950-75, mgr. pub. rels., 1975—; corp. sec. East Oregonian Pub. Co., Pendleton, 1950-2000. Bd. dirs. Oreg. Status of Women Com., 1972-75, Oreg. Law Enforcement Commn., 1975-82; active Arts Coun. Pendleton. Recipient Pendleton First Citizen award C. of C., 1962, Gov.'s award for the Arts, 1988, Woman of Achievement award Oreg. Commn. for Women, 1998, Paul Harris award Rotary, 1993. Mem. Women in Communications, Oreg. Press Women, AAUW (pres. 1956-58, grantee 1965), LWV, Pendleton River Parkway Found., World Affairs Coun. Oreg., Altrusa. Avocations: reading, travel, music, theater. Home: PO Box 1456 Pendleton OR 97801-0360 Office: East Oregonian Pub Co PO Box 1089 Pendleton OR 97801-1089 Office Phone: 541-276-2211. Business E-Mail: jacbrown@eastoregonian.com.

BEDIGUIAN, MARIAMIG JINX, operating room nurse; b. Neptune, N.J., July 13, 1956; d. Haig Leon and Mary (Durna) B. BSN, George Mason U., 1979. RN, Va., N.J.; cert. nurse operating room, 1983. Operating room staff nurse Jersey Shore Med. Ctr., Neptune, 1979—, clinical nurse III, svc. leader gynecology and laser, 1992-94, svc. leader gen., gynecology and genitourinary endoscopy, 1994-98; operating rm. staff nurse Monmouth Med. Ctr., Long Branch, N.J., 1994-96. Focus panel mem., oper. rm. cons. Ansell Med. Corp., Eatontown, N.J., 1993; oper. rm. cons. Armenian Gen. Benevolent Union, Saddle Brook, N.J., Plastic and Reconstructive Surgery Ctr., Yerevan, Armenia, 1992. Recipient Chief Residents award Jersey Shore Med. Ctr. Obs.-Gyn. Residency Program, 1993, Florence Nightingale award, Jersey Shore Med. Ctr., 2001, United Surgical Ptnrs., Inc. Nursing Clin. Excellence award, 2004. Mem. Assn. Oper. Rm. Nurses (product fair co-chair 1987-90, 93, chair seminar com. 1985, chair program com. 1985-88, 99-2002, v.p. 1983-85, bd. dirs. 1985-89, 95-97, audit com. 1987-88, Congress del. 1984, alt. del. 1987), Nat. Assn. Orthopaedic Nurses (bd. dirs. 1994—, chair program com. 1998—), Am. Nurse Assn., N.J. State Nurses Assn., Va. State Nurse Assn., George Mason U. Coll. Nursing Alumni Assn., George Mason U. Alumni Assn., Mary Washington Coll. Alumni Assn., Armenian Students Assn., Phi Mu (rec. sec. 1977-78), Sigma Theta Tau Hon. Nursing Soc. Avocations: music, languages, travel, dance. Home: 12 Inlet Ter Belmar NJ 07719-2142 Office: Operating Rm Jersey Shore Med Ctr 1945 Corlies Ave Neptune NJ 07753-4896

BEDNAR, SUSAN GAIL, social worker, consultant, social sciences educator; b. Chgo., Ill., May 28, 1949; d. Charles and Evelyn Bednar; m. Bruce Kevin Barnard, Nov. 15, 1988. BA in Sociology, U. Ill., 1973, MSW, 1996. LCSW Ill., cert. Domestic Violence Counselor III Nat. Assn. Forensic Counselors. Addictions therapist Prairie Ctr. Health Systems, Danville, Ill., 1997—98; clin. dir. DeWitt County Human Resource Ctr., Clinton, Ill., 1998—99; program coord. Shelby County Cmty. Svcs., Shelbyville, Ill.; clin. assoc. Dovetail Consulting, Crystal Lake, Ill., 2000—01; rsch. asst. Ind. U., Indpls., 2000—02; cons. Champaign, Ill., 2001—; clin. social worker in pvt. practice, 2003—. Dir. Mental Health Assn., Champaign, Ill., 1996—97. Contbr. Counseling Female Offenders and Victims, articles to profl. jours. Mem.: NASW, Assn. Family and Conciliation Cts., Ill. Soc. Clin. Social Work, Am. Sociol. Assn., Assn. for Conflict Resolution, Nat. Assn. of Forensic Counselors. Avocation: horse owner. Office: Susan G Bednar LCSW 6 Dunlap Ct Savoy IL 61874 Office Phone: 217-352-8502. Business E-Mail: sgbednar@advancenet.net.

BEDNAR-STANLEY, MONICA MARY, science educator, educational consultant; b. Tarzana, Calif., May 3, 1963; d. Allen Frank and Noreen Janice Bednar; m. David Warren Stanley, Aug. 25, 1991; children: Nathan Ray Stanley, Savanna Rose Stanley. BSc in Mech. and Aeronautical Engring., U. Calif., Davis, 1985; MA in Ednl. Adminstrn., Nat. Univ., Sherman Oaks, Calif., 1993. Mech. engr. Hughes Aircraft Co., el Segundo, Calif., 1990—91; bilingual tchr. L.A. Unified Sch. Dist., 1991—97, bilingual coord., 1996—98; sci. tchr. Ventura Unified Sch. Dist., Ventura, Calif., 1999—. Pres. PTA; v.p. cmty. track club. Grantee, Earthwatch, 2004. Mem.: Astronomy Soc. Ventura. Avocations: track and field, wake boarding, kayaking, bicycling, hiking.

BEDNASH, GERALDINE POLLY, educational association administrator; b. San Antonio, May 6, 1943; d. David Anthony and Bernice (Brewer) Parrott; m. Thomas Francis Bednash, June 24, 1967; children: Thomas F. Jr., Joseph Andrew. B of Nursing, Tex. Women's U., 1965; M of Nursing, Cath. U. Am., 1977; PhD, U. Md., 1989. Cert. nurse practitioner. Nurse Binghamton (N.Y.) Gen. Hosp., 1967-69; instr. Broome County Community Coll., Binghamton, 1967-71; asst. prof. No. Va. Community Coll., Annandale, 1977-78, George Mason U., Fairfax, Va., 1978-86; dir. govt. rels. Am. Assn. Coll. Nursing, Washington, 1986-89, exec. dir., 1989—. Co-chmn. Nat. Com. Nursing Implementation Project, Washington, 1990-91; cons. in field. Contbr. articles to profl. jours. Polit. action chmn. Va. Nurses Assn., 1979-83; nurse clinician So Others Might Eat, Washington, 1981-83. Capt. U.S. Army, 1963-67. Primary Care fellow Robert Wood Johnson Found., U. Md., 1981-82, Nat. Rsch. Svc. fellow, Washington, 1983-87. Fellow Am. Acad. Nursing; mem. ANA, Sigma Theta Tau. Roman Catholic. Avocations: skiing, horticulture. Office: Am Assn Coll Nursing 1 Dupont Cir NW Ste 530 Washington DC 20036-1135

BEDRICK, BERNICE, retired principal, science educator; b. Jersey City, Sept. 29, 1916; d. Abraham Lewis and Esther (Cowan) Grodjesk; m. Emanuel Arthur Bedrick, Dec. 25, 1938 (dec. 1967); children: Allen Paul, Jane Bedrick Abels; m. Samuel Milberger, Sept. 23, 1984 (dec. 1984); stepchildren: Susan Milberger Rafael, Stanford. BS, U. Md., 1938; MA, NYU, 1952. Cert. tchr., N.J. Tchr. Linden (N.J.) Pub. Sch. System, 1950-69, supr. sci. curriculum, 1969-79, sch. prin., 1979-87; ret., 1987. Co-author: A Universe to Explore, 1969; developer program of safety and survival N.J. Dept. Edn., 1975. Founder, mem., bd. dirs., v.p. edn. Temple Mekor Chayim, Linden; pres. bd. trustees Linden Pub. Libr., 1989-90, v.p., 1991; pres. Friends of Linden Libr., 1987-92, 95-97, coord. used books sales, 1990—, founder, 1987; bd. trustees Temple Beth-El Mekor Chayim, Cranford, N.J., 1999—, bd. edn., 1999—. Recipient Cmty. Vol. Svc. award B'Nai B'Rith, 1993, Outstanding Sr. Citizen of Yr., City of Linden, 1996; honored with Bernice Bedrick rm. at Sunnyside br. Linden Pub. Libr., 2001. Mem.: NEA (life), Nat. Sci. Tchrs. Assn., N.J. Sci. Tchrs. Assn., N.J. Prins. and Suprs. Assn., N.Y. Acad. Scis., Linden Edn. Found. (bd. dirs.), Am. Fedn. Sch. Adminstrs. (chpt. pres. 1984—86), Nat. Coun. Jewish Women (life), N.J. PTA (life), N.J. Edn. Assn. (life), Linden Ceramics Club (life; sec. 1991—92, 1995—99, pres. 2000—), Hadassah (life), Phi Kappa Phi, Alpha Lambda Delta, Alumni Assn. U. Md. (life). Home: 2016 Orchard Ter Linden NJ 07036-3719

BEDROSSIAN, URSULA KAY KENNEDY, editor; b. Austin, Tex., Dec. 8, 1948; d. Richard Arch and Ursula Marie (Jones) Kennedy; m. Carlos Wanes Bedrossian, Aug. 8, 1970; children: Vanessa, Richard, Robert. BS, Jacksonville U., 1972; MEd, Vanderbilt U., 1984; PhD, St. Louis U., 1991. Registered med. technologist and cytotechnologist Am. Soc. Clin. Pathologists. Med. technologist Del Oro Med. Lab., Houston, 1977-78; edn. coord., lab. supr. dept. family practice U. Tex. Med. Sch., Houston, 1978-81; rsch. asst. VA Med. Ctr., Nashville, 1981-84; clin. instr. dept. pathology St. Louis U., 1985-89; dir. edn. and quality I DMC Univ. Labs., Detroit, 1991-97. Mng. editor Wiley-Liss, N.Y.C., 1989—. Mng. editor Diagnostic Cytopathology, 1984—; asst. editor The Prostate, 1992-95; contbr. articles to sci. jours. Dir. med. relief Armenian Gen. Benevolent Union, 1993-97. Recipient commendation U.S. Army 101st Workhorse Bn., Badhersfeld, Germany, 1985. Mem. Clin. Lab. Mgmt. Assn., Am. Soc. Cytotech. (liaison to Papunivolaou Soc. Cytopathology 1993—, scientist mem. Am. Soc. Cytopathology), Armenian Am. Bus. Coun., Brazilian Cultural Club. Avocations: geology, natural sciencies, travel, speaking spanish and portuguese. Office: Biomed Comm Oak Park IL 60302

BEE, ANNA COWDEN, dance educator; b. Feb. 17, 1922; d. Porter Guthrie and Marion Irene (McCurry) Cowden; m. Alon Wilton Bee, Oct. 21, 1942; children: Anna Margaret Bee Foote, Alon Wilton. AB, Samford U., 1944; student, Chalif Sch. Dance, N.Y.C., 1950-54. Mem. faculty Byram H.S., JAckson, 1945-52, Hinds Jr. Coll., Raymond, Miss., 1952—. Dir. Hi-Steppers, girls' precision dance group; chaperone Miss Mississippi to Miss Am. Pageant; condr. charm clinics for teenagers; judge beauty pageants. Prodr. half-time shows for Gator Bowl, 1958, 64, 81, Sugar Bowl, 1960, Hall of Fame Bowl, 1977-79, Mid-Am. Bowl, 1988, Sr. Bowl, 1988. Bd. dirs. Multiple Sclerosis Soc., Jackson, 1966-72; state chmn. Miss. Easter Seals

Soc. campaign, 1966, 79; chmn. women's divsn. United Way, Jackson, 1973; commencement spkr. Hinds C.C., 1999. Recipient Hinds C.C. Svc. award, 1993, Miss Miss. Vol. of Yr. award, 1995, Miss Am. Vol. of Yr. award, 1995, Dance Tchrs. Unlimited Lifetime Achievement award, 1996, Dance Tchrs. United Achievement award in dance, 1996; named Woman of Achievement, Jackson Bus. and Profl. Women's Club, 1967-78, Outstanding Vol. Goodwill Industry Miss., 1997, Golden Isles Bowl Classic, 1997; Miss. Legislature commendation for contbn. to youth, 1981; Anna Cowden Bee Hall named in her honor Hinds C of C., bd. trustees, 1993; named Ageless Hero, Blue Cross/Blue Shield, 2001, Hometown Hero, WJTV, 2000; honored Legis., 2003, Hinds CC Higher Edn. Appreciation Day-Working Acad. Excellence (HEADWAE). Mem. Nat. Faculty Dance Educators Am., Dance Masters Am., Miss. Edn. Assn., Miss. Assn. Health and Phys. Edn., Beta Sigma Omicron. Baptist. Home: 256 Azalea Ct Brandon MS 39047-7264 Office: Hinds Cmty Coll Box 10415 Raymond MS 39154 Office Phone: 601-857-3346.

BEEBE, GRACE ANN, retired special education educator; b. Wyandotte, Mich., Feb. 16, 1945; d. Cecil Vern and Elizabeth Lucille (Tamblyn) B. BA, Ea. Mich. U., 1967; MEd, Wayne State U., 1970; postgrad., U. Mich., 1973-78; MDiv, Meth. Theol. Sch., Ohio, 2004. Cert. spl. edn. tchr., Mich. Tchr. POHI 1st grade Grand Rapids (Mich.) Pub. Schs., 1967-69; tchr. title VI Taylor (Mich.) Pub. Schs., 1970-73, tchr. Physically or Otherwise Health Impaired pre-kindergarten, 1973-79, tchr. POHI 1st-3rd grades, 1979-81, tchr. POHI pre-kindergarten, 1981-84, tchr., cons. POHI, 1984-2000; ret., 2000. Probationary deacon United Meth. Ch., 2004. Area coord. Indian Trails Camp, Grand Rapids, 1979-97; Brownie troop leader Girl Scouts U.S., 1997-98. Recipient Recognition award 4-H Wayne County Handicapped Riding, 1986, Indian Trails Camp, 1990; Ronald McDonald Children's Charities grantee, 1990; State of Mich. Spl. Edn. scholar, 1966-67, Vocat. Rehab. scholar, 1969-70, Alford Seminary scholar, 2001-04. Mem. SCADS (alt. rep.), N.Am. Riding for the Handicapped Assn., Mich. Fedn. Tchrs., Physically Impaired Assn. Mich., Taylor Fedn. Tchrs. (ancillary v.p. 1990-92), Taylor Handicapped Assn., Allen Park Assn. for Handicapped, Trenton Hist. Soc. (exec. bd. 1988-97), Coun. for Exceptional Children, Phi Delta Kappa, Alpha Delta Kappa. Democrat. United Methodist. Avocations: gardening, walking, reading. Home: 2225 Emeline St Trenton MI 48183-3653 Personal E-mail: Beebega@aol.com.

BEEBE, MARY LIVINGSTONE, curator; b. Portland, Oreg., Nov. 5, 1940; d. Robert and Alice Beebe; m. Charles J. Reilly. BA, Bryn Mawr Coll., Pa., 1962; postgrad., Sorbonne, U. Paris, 1962—63. Apprentice Portland Art Mus., 1962—64, Boston Mus. Art, 1964—66; curatorial asst. dept. drawing Fogg Art Mus., Harvard U., Cambridge, Mass., 1966-68; prodr. Am. Theatre Co., Portland State U., Oreg., 1969—72; exec. dir. Portland Ctr. for Visual Arts, 1972—81; dir. Stuart Collection U. Calif., San Diego, 1981—. Cons. in field; lectr. in field; mem. art steering com. Portland Devel. Commn., 1977-80, New Denver Internat. Airport, 1990-97; bd. dirs. Henry Gallery, U. Wash., Seattle, 1977-80; project cons. Nat. Rsch. Ctr. for Arts, N.Y.C., 1978-79; bd. dirs. Western Assn. Art Museums, Art Mus. Assn. San Francisco, 1978-84; bd. dirs., trustee Art Matters Inc., N.Y.C., 1984-, Balboa Art Conservation Ctr., San Diego, 2001-; trustee Russell Found., 1982-94, bd. dirs., 1983-85; hon. mem. bd. dirs. Portland Ctr. for Visual Arts, 1981-88; mem. arts adv. bd. Centre City Devel. Corp., San Diego, 1982-94, U. Calif. San Francisco Mission Bay, 1999—, Indpls. Mus. Art, Art and Nature Pk. adv. bd., 2003-05, nat. adv. bd. Headlands Ctr. for the Arts, San Francisco; panel mem., cons. Nat. Endowment Arts; mem. adv. com. Port of San Diego, 1983-88, San Diego Design Ctr., 1987-88, ART/LA, 1987-94, Pearl Art Found., Portland, 1998-2000, inSITE94, inSITE97, inSITE00, inSITE03 and 05, San Diego, 1993-, Friends of Art and Preservation in Embassies Profl. Sculpture adv. com., Wash., 2003-; mem. pub. art adv. com. Harvard and Radcliffe, 1989-93, U. Wash., Seattle, 1989-96, Commn. for Arts and Culture, San Diego, 2003-; juror numerous art exhbns. Nat. Endowment Arts fellow, 1979. Author: Landmarks: Sculpture Commissions for the Stuart Collection at the University of California, San Diego, 2001; contbr. articles to profl. jours. Recipient Allied Professions award AIA, 1992, Nat. Honors award, 1994. Achievements include having the Stuart Collection featured on CBS Sunday Morning with Charles Kuralt, 1993. Office: U Calif San Diego Stuart Collection 9500 Gilman Dr La Jolla CA 92093-0010 Office Phone: 858-534-2117. Business E-Mail: mbeebe@ucsd.edu.

BEEBE, SANDRA E., retired language educator, artist, writer; b. March AFB, Calif., Nov. 10, 1934; d. Eugene H. and Margaret (Fox) B.; m. Donald C. Thompson. AB in English and Speech, UCLA, 1956; MA in Secondary Edn., Calif. State U., Long Beach, 1957. Tchr. English, Garden Grove (Calif.) High Sch., 1957-93, attendance supr., 1976-83, ret., 1993. Tchr. watercolor courses, Asilomar, Calif., 1997; jury chmn. N.W.S., 1997. Contbr. articles to English Jour., chpts. to books; watercolor artist; exhbns. include AWS, NWS, Okla. Watercolor Soc., Watercolor West, Midwest Watercolor Soc., Butler Inst. Am. Art, Youngstown, Ohio, Kings Art Ctr., Audubon Artists N.Y.; cover artist Exploring Painting, 1990, title page Understanding Watercolor, American Artist, 1991. Mem. faculty Asilomar, 1997; chmn. of jurors N.W.S. Open, 1997. Named one of the Top Ten Watercolorists The Artists Mag., 1994; recipient Best Watercolors award Rockport Press, 1995; chosen for Design Poster selection, 1995, 97. Mem. Am. Watercolor Soc. (dir. 1999—), Nat. Watercolor Soc., Midwest Watercolor Soc., Watercolor West, Allied Artists N.Y., Knickerbocker Artists N.Y., Audubon Artists N.Y., West Coast Watercolor Soc., Rocky Mountain Nat. Watermedia Honor Soc., Jr. League Long Beach, Kappa Kappa Gamma. Republican. Home: 239 Mira Mar Ave Long Beach CA 90803-3899 E-mail: sebeebeaws@aol.com.

BEECH, SHELLY CHRISTINE, dancer, educator, small business owner; d. Douglas Clayton Beech and Karen Kay Case; m. Kenneth Louis Wehmeyer; 1 child, Hayden Louis Wehmeyer. BFA in Oil Painting, Okla. State U., Stillwater, Okla., 1988. Cert. jazz instr. Tex. Assn. Tchrs. Dance Inc., 1997, Chgo. (Ill.) Natiional Assn. Dance Masters, 1999, jazz examiner Tex. Assn. Tchrs. Dance Inc., 2001. Instr. ballet YWCA, Salina, Kans., 1979—80, Della's Sch. Dance, Salina, 1980—82, Elizabeth Shelley Williams Sch. Dance, Enid, Okla., 1982; prin., owner Art of Motion Dance Studio, Bartlesville, Okla., 1989—. Del. Nat. Dance Week, Tulsa, Okla., 2000—05; dance instr. fine arts program West Side Cmty. Ctr., Bartlesville, 1991; judge Okla. Kids, Okla., 1993; instr. tap Positions Dance Studio, Babylon, NY, 1989—91; printer Universal Ltd. Art Editions, West Islip, NY, 1989—91. Choreographer Bartlesville (Okla.) Jr. Miss Pageant, 1991—96. Named Bartlesville's Best Art Adv., Examiner's Readers Choice, 2005; recipient Sr. Jazz Group Divsn. 1st Pl. award, Chgo. (Ill.) Nat. Assn. Dance Masters, 1999, Phys. Fittness Dance award, Pres. U.S., 2003, Bartlesville's Best Dance Instrn. award, Examiner's Readers Choice, 2004, 2005, 20th Anniversary award, Art of Motion Dance Studio, 2006; scholar, Okla. U., 1982, Okla. U. Art Dept., 1982, Bill Goldson and Okla. State U. Art Dept., 1988. Mem.: Tex. Assn. Tchrs. Dance Inc. (2nd v.p. 2005), Okla. Dance Masters Assn. (parliamentarian 1996—97), Internat. Tap Assn. Roman Cathlic. Avocation: painting. Office: Art of Motion Dance Studio 5801 SE Adams Blvd Bartlesville OK 74006 Office Phone: 918-333-3412.

BEECHEM, KATHLEEN, bank executive; m. Pete Beechem. BA in English, Thomas More Coll.; MA, Indiana Univ. Exec. v.p. US Bank, Cincinnati, Ohio. Co-chmn. Women's Leadership Initiative United Way, Cincinnati; pres. bd. Jobs for Cincinnati Grads. Bd. dir. Cincinnati Youth Collaborative; exec. com. YWCA. Named one of 50 Most Powerful Women, Fortune Mag., 2004. Office: US Bancorp 800 Nicollet Mall Minneapolis MN 55402

BEECHER, MARGUERITE ANN, elementary school educator; d. Jack and Marguerite Eva Causey; m. Jack Beecher, Oct. 7, 1967; children: Michael Brennan, Richard Quin, Jack Stanton. BS, Miss. U. for Women, Columbus, 1964. Cert. tchr. Ga. Tchr. 4th grade Dekalb County Bd. Edn., Decatur, Ga., 1964—65, Seminole County Bd. Edn., Sanford, Fla., 1965—66, Mt. Healthy City Schs., Cin., 1967—68; tchr. 3d grade Jefferson Parish Sch. Bd., Metairie, La., 1971—74; tchr. 4-6th grade St. Tammany Sch. Bd., Covington, La., 1982—89; tchr. ESOL, 4th grade Manatee County Sch. Bd., Bradenton, Fla., 1989—95; tchr. 3d and 4th grade Dekalb County Bd. Edn., Decatur, Ga., 1995—. Mem. leadership team Chesnut Charter Sch., 2000—03, guidance adv. coun., 2004—06, assessment action team, 2004—. Mem. DAR, 1979—, MUW Alumni Assn., 1965—, Jr. League. Mem.: AAUW, Profl. Assn. of Ga. Educators, Nat. Assn. Educators. Avocations: reading, cooking, running, travel, Hummel collector. E-mail: jbeecher@bellsouth.net.

BEECHINOR, DIANE BLANCHE, education educator; b. Gettysburg, Pa., Oct. 23, 1960; d. Robert Michael and Blanche Mattsson Beechinor. BS in Wildlife Biology, SW Tex. State U., San Marcos, 1982, MS in Biology, 1986. Cert. tchr. Tex. Asst. instr. SW Tex. State U., San Marcos, 1986—87; biology tchr. Edna HS, Tex., 1987—88; sci. tchr., dept. chair Tex. Mil. Inst., San Antonio, 1988—91; assoc. prof. Palo Alto Coll., San Antonio, 1991—2006; dept. chair, assoc. prof. Northeast Lakeview Coll., 2006—. Co-owner Beechscenes Photos. Scholarship chair Exec. Women's Golf Assn., San Antonio, 2003—05. Mem.: Tex. CC Tchrs. Assn. Avocations: photography, travel, golf. Office: Northeast Lakeview Coll 8300 Pat Brooker Rd San Antonio TX 78223

BEEDLE, DAWN DANENE, marketing professional; b. Mexico, Mo., July 16, 1968; d. Ronald Wayne and Delores Kay (Eastin) B. BA, William Woods Coll., 1990. Retail mgr. Kirlins Hallmark, Columbia, Mo., 1991-94, dist. mgr. Chgo./Milw., 1994, St. Louis, 1994-96, corp. tng. mgr. Quincy, Ill., 1996-2000, dir. recruiting and tng., 2000—04; mktg. specialist Mo. Grape and Wine Program, Columbia, 2004—. Republican. Avocations: gardening, exercise, cooking, travel. Home: 12 Broadway Village Dr Apt C Columbia MO 65201

BEEHLER, TOBI LORRAINE, elementary school educator, education educator; b. Montebello, Calif., Nov. 1, 1950; d. Robert Thomas and Helen Gore; m. Patrick Alan Beehler, Jan. 21, 1995; children: Courtney Helaine Klems, Tyler James. BS in Phys. Edn., Calif. State U., Fullerton, 1972, MS in Ednl. Adminstrn., 1980. Continuing tchg. cert. Wash. Elem. tchr. Yakima (Wash.) Sch. Dist., 1989—. Stakeholder Wash. State U. CO-TEACH Grant, Pullman, 1999—2005; state-wide sci. assessment revision developer Ednl. Svc. Dist. 105, Yakima, 2000; mem. strategic planning com., outcomes subcom. Yakima Sch. Dist., 1994; adj. prof. Heritage U., Toppenish, Wash., 1991—94, Ctrl. Wash. U., Ellensburg, 2001—, mem. profl. edn. adv. bd., 2002—. Mem. Yakima Schs. Found., 2001—03. Nominee, KCTS Golden Apple award, 1993; named Best Supporting Actress, Warehouse Theatre, Yakima; recipient cert. of appreciation, Yakima Sch. Dist., 1989, 1994; grantee, Yakima Ret. Tchrs. Assn., 2006. Mem.: NEA, Nat. Sci. Tchrs. Assn., Yakima Edn. Assn., Wash. Edn. Assn. Avocations: singing, flower arranging, gardening. Office: Yakima Sch Dist 104 N 4th Ave Yakima WA 98902

BEEKLEY, CYNTHIA XANTHOPOULOS, school system administrator; b. Pottstown, Pa., Aug. 29, 1940; d. George E. and Mary E. (Anthony) Xanthopoulos; m. David C. Beekley, June 16, 1962; children: Matthew, Alec. BA, Pa. State U., 1961; MS, Kans. State U., 1965; Edn. Specialist, U. Toledo, 1984; EdD, U. Mich., 1994. Cert. supt., Ohio. Tchr. Lower Dauphin H.S., Hummelstown, Pa., 1961-62; English tchr. Maumee (Ohio) H.S., 1962-68, Springfield High Sch., Holland, Ohio, 1977-84; from asst. prin. to prin. Springfield H.S., Holland, Ohio, 1984-95; asst. prof. ednl. adminstrn. and supervision Bowling Green (Ohio) State U., 1995-97; asst. supt. Springfield Local Schs., Holland, 1997—99, supt., 1999—. Mem. Phi Delta Kappa, Phi Kappa Phi. Home: 642 Ann Wesley Ct Holland OH 43528-8338 Office: Springfield Local Schs 6900 Hall St Holland OH 43528 Office Phone: 419-867-5605. E-mail: sp_cxb@nwoca.org.

BEEKS, CHERYL ELAINE, elementary school educator; b. Concord, NC, Aug. 28, 1946; d. Ray Edward and Maxine (Peterson) Barringer; m. Raymond Neil Beeks, July 12, 1971; 1 child, Alison Elaine Rios. B in Music Edn., So. Meth. U., Dallas, 1968. Tchr. Lamesa (Tex.) Ind. Sch. Dist., 1968—69, 1970—73, Loraine (Tex.) Ind. Sch. Dist., 1976—77, Highland Ind. Sch. Dist., Roscoe, Tex., 1980—. Coach 5th grade events Univ. Interscholastic League, Roscoe, 1980—, elem. poetry judge, 1995—. Pianist, organist Hermleigh (Tex.) United Meth. Ch., 1990—, treas., 1995—98; lay delegate United Meth. Northwest Conf., Lubbock, Tex., 1999—. Mem.: Tex. Assn. Cmty. Schs., Tex. Music Edn. Assn., Nat. Assn. Music Edn. Home: 206 Lowe Hermleigh TX 79526 Office: Highland Ind Sch Dist 6625 FM608 Roscoe TX 79545 Personal E-mail: cheeks5@yahoo.com. Business E-Mail: cbeeks@highland.esc14.net.

BEELER, BULAH RAY, retired medical/surgical nurse; b. San Saba, Apr. 8, 1929; d. Noah Bassett and Cora Estelle (Lawrence) Gillentine; m. Waddie O.J. Beeler, June 1, 1948; 1 child, Hubert Dale Diploma, Lubbock Vocat. Sch. Nursing, 1972. Lic. vocat. nurse, Tex.; cert. in CPR. Staff nurse Crosbyton Clinic Hosp., Tex., 1957—2005, dept. mgr. pharmacy, 1992—97; ret., 1997. Named Lic. Vocat. Nurse of Yr. Lubbock divsn., 1987 Home: 610 W 8th St Apt 15 Idalou TX 79329-9108

BEELER, CHARLOTTE JEAN, oil and supply company executive, interior design business executive; b. Normal, Ill., Dec. 9, 1928; d. John William and Viola Maude (Walters) Geske: m. Charles Gilbert Beeler, Feb. 12, 1949; children: Judy Ann Kjellander, Mark Geske, David William. Student, Ill. Wesleyan U., 1946-48, Ill. State U., 1962, 75; degree in interior design, Ray Coll. of Design, Chgo., 1991. Lic. interior designer Ill. Gift buyer Dixie Truckers, McLean, Ill., 1967-78, gift buyer, mgr. Tuscola, Ill., 1978-80; adminstrv. mgr. travel stores Dixie Truckers Home, dba Shirley Oil and Supply Co., McLean and Tuscola, 1983-91; sec. bd. dirs. Dixie Truckers, McLean and Tuscola, 1985—. Owner, designer Creative Interiors, 1987—. Rep. precinct committeewoman, McLean, 1960-76; mem. bd. visitors Ill. Wesleyan U., 1980; trustee Wesley United Meth., Bloomington, 1986—, vice chmn., 1989; bd. dirs. YWCA, 1980-85, treas. bd. dirs., 1983-85; bd. dirs. Centrillio coun. Girl Scouts U.S.A., 1990-91, Route 66 Assn., 1994—, mem., 1990—, mem. Hall of Fame com., 1991—; mem. McLean County Greenways Adv. Com., 1999. Mem.: PEO, Am. Soc. Interior Designers, Sigma Kappa, Ill. Wesleyan U. Alumni Assn. Avocations: reading, bridge, sculpture. Home: Creative Interiors 124 Hawthorne Lake Rd Bloomington IL 61704-8530 also: 3500 Gulf Of Mexico Dr # 102 Longboat Key FL 34228-2828 Personal E-mail: cj.beeler@verizon.net.

BEELER, SANDRA GILLESPIE, realtor; b. Knoxville, Jan. 27, 1946; d. Robert Burl and Dorothy Aileen Warren; m. William Gene Beeler, Aug. 19; m. James Stephen, Sr. Gillespie (div.); 1 child, James Stephen Gillespie Jr. Lic. realtor Tenn., 1987. Collections supr. General Motors Accept Corp., Knoxville, 1966—82; mgr., buyer MS Apropos, Knoxville, 1983—86; realtor Re/max Preferred Properties, Knoxville, 1987—. Chair numerous coms. Knoxville Area Assn. Realtors, Knoxville, 1995—2003, pres., 2000, State Chpt. of Cert. Residential Specialists, Tenn., 2000. Recipient Realtor of Yr., Knoxville Area Assn. of Realtors, 2001, Hall of Fame award, Knoxville, 2003, Hall of Fame, Re/max Internat., 1998, Lifetime Achievement award, 2004. Mem.: CRS of Tenn. (state pres. 2000, CRS of Yr. 2001), Women's Council of Realtors, SRES, REBAC. Avocations: travel, entertaining. Office: Re/max Preferred Properties 117 Center Park Dr Knoxville TN 37922

BEELER, SHERRI, secondary school educator; d. John J. and Patricia J. Beeler. BA, Northwestern Coll., Orange City, Iowa, 1989; MA, Calif. Luth. U., Thousand Oaks, 1994. Cert. tchr. Oreg. Lit. and theater tchr. Cascade Christian HS, Jacksonville, Oreg., 1990—93, 1994—. Office: Cascade Christian HS 525 E St Jacksonville OR 97530-9005

BEEMER, MARGARET (PEGGY), history educator; b. L.A. d. Paul Henry and Patricia Loretta Rohe Beemer; children: Pedro Iñaki De Sasia Beemer, Xabier Lautaro De Sasia Beemer. BA in Religion, Santa Clara U., Calif., 1974; MA in Religion, U. Calif., Santa Barbara, 1977; MA in History, U. Calif., L.A., 1980, PhD in History, 1986. Instr. Calif. State U., Northridge, 1984—2000; tchr. history Windward Sch., L.A., 1995—2000; tchr. history, chmn. dept. St. Margaret of Scotland Episcopal Sch., San Juan Capistrano, Calif., 2000—. Founding mem. Movimiento Pro-Emancipacion de la Mujer Chilena, North Hollywood, Calif. Mem.: ASCD, World History Assn., Nat. Social Studies Suprs. Assn., Nat. Coun. for History Edn., Calif. Coun. for History Edn. Office: St Margaret of Scotland Episcopal Sch 31641 La Novia San Juan Capistrano CA 92675 Office Phone: 949-661-0108. Personal E-mail: pegbeemer@aol.com. E-mail: peg.beemer@smes.org.

BEEN, VICKI LYNN, law educator; b. 1956; BS, Colo. State U., 1978; JD, NYU, 1983. Bar: NY 1984. Law clk. to Judge Edward Weinfeld US Dist. Ct. So. Dist. NY, NYC, 1983—84; law clk. to Justice Harry Blackmun US Supreme Ct., 1984—85; assoc. Debevoise & Plimpton, NYC, 1986—87; assoc. counsel Office of Independent Counsel for Iran/Contra Matters, Washington, 1987—88; assoc. prof. Rutgers Sch. Law, Newark, 1988—90, NYU Sch. Law, 1990—95, prof., 1995—, Elihu Root prof. law, faculty dir. Root-Tilden-Kern scholarship program, dir. Furman Ctr. Real Estate & Urban Policy. Vis. prof. law Harvard Law Sch., 1995—96. Office: NYU Sch Law Vanderbilt Hall Rm 314H 40 Washington Sq S New York NY 10012-1099 Office Phone: 212-998-6223. Office Fax: 212-995-4590. E-mail: vicki.been@nyu.edu.

BEER, CLARA LOUISE JOHNSON, retired electronics executive; b. Bisbee, Ariz., Jan. 14, 1918; d. Franklin Fayette and Marie (Sturm) Johnson; m. Philip James McElmurry, May 15, 1937 (div. July 1944); children—Leonard Franklin, Philip James Jr.; m. William Sigvard Beer, July 15, 1945 (dec. Aug. 1977); 1 son, Douglas Lee; m. Kenneth Christy Huntwork, May 1, 1982 (dec. Jan. 2003). Student, Merritt Bus. Sch., Oakland, Calif., 1935, Bus. Instrn. Sch., Palo Alto, Calif., 1955. Sec., artist M.R. Fisher Studios, Oakland, 1936-40; piano, organ instr. Anna May Studios, Palo Alto, 1948-50; pvt. piano, organ instr. Palo Alto, 1949-56; sec. Stanford Electronics Labs., Stanford U., 1955-58; corporate sec. and exec. sec. to chmn. bd. Watkins-Johnson Co., Palo Alto, 1958-88. Dir., sec. Watkins-Johnson Internat., 1968-88, Watkins-Johnson Ltd., 1971-88, Watkins-Johnson Assocs., 1977-88. Mem. Nat. Secs. Assn., Christian Bus. and Profl. Women's Coun. (sec. 1966-67, adviser 1968) Home: 24157 Hillview Rd Los Altos CA 94024-5222

BEERBOWER, CYNTHIA GIBSON, lawyer; b. Dayton, Ohio, June 25, 1949; d. Charles Augustus and Sarah (Rittenhouse) Gibson; m. John Edwin Beerbower, Aug. 28, 1971; children: John Eliot, Sarah Rittenhouse. BA, Mt. Holyoke Coll., 1971; JD, Boston U., 1974; LLB, Cambridge U., Eng., 1976. Bar: N.Y. 1975. Assoc. Cadwalader, Wickersham & Taft, N.Y.C., 1975-76, Simpson, Thacher & Bartlett, N.Y.C., 1977-81, ptnr., 1981-93; internat. tax counsel, dept. asst. sec. Dept. Treasury, Washington, 1993-96; chmn., CEO Reeve Ct. Ins. Ltd., 1997—2001; prin. Quellos Group, 2001—04; mng. dir. XE Capital, 2004—05, Paget LLC, 2005. Mem. ABA, Assn. Bar City N.Y., N.Y. State Bar Assn. (com. co-chmn. 1987-93). Presbyterian. Home: 720 Park Ave New York NY 10021-4954

BEERITS, JANET PENROSE ROBINSON, sculptor; b. Abington, Pa., Apr. 24, 1917; d. Otho Ernest Cox Robinson and Florence Gillingham Willard; m. Henry Christopher Beerits, Aug. 14, 1943; children: Christopher John, Susan Willard, Peter Cox. BA, Wellesley Coll., Mass., 1938, MA, 1940; student in Sculpture, Pa. Acad. Fine Arts, Phila., 1962—66; MFA in Sculpture, U. Pa., Phila., 1971. Tchr. Dept. Art Wellesley (Mass.) Coll., 1938—42. Recipient Stimson prize, award, Pa. Acad. Fine Arts, 1964; Durant scholar, Phi Beta Kappa Wellesley (Mass.) Coll., 1938. Mem.: Maine Women in Fine and Performing Arts (pres. 1980—82), Deer Isle Artsts Assn. (exhibn. chmn. 1975—78, v.p., pres.). Democrat. Mem. Soc. Friends. Avocation: gardening. Home: 108 Sheepscot Rd Alna ME 04535

BEERMAN, MIRIAM, artist, educator; b. Providence; d. William and Rose (Nochemsohn) Beerman; m. Julian F. Jaffe (dec. 1973); 1 child, William Jaffe. Student, Atelier 17, Paris, 1953; BFA, R.I. Sch. Design, 1945; postgrad., Art Students League, N.Y.C., 1945-46, New Sch. for Social Rsch., NYU. Prof. painting and drawing Queensborough C.C., CUNY, 1972—95; instr. Jersey City State Coll., 1973—75, Montclair (N.J.) Art Mus. Art Sch., 1974—90, Montclair State Coll., 1980—89. Artist-in-residence MacDowell Colony, 1959, Ossibaw Island, Ga., 1974, Va. Ctr. for Creative Arts, Sweet Briar, 1985-87, 89-96, 98, 2000-02, Leighton Artist's Colony, Banff Ctr., Alta., Can., 1986-87, Millay Colony, Austerlitz, NY, 1992, Blue Mountain Ctr., Blue Mountain Lake, NY, 1994, 96, 98, Camargo Found., 1980, Mid-Atlantic Arts Found., 2000, Women's Studio Workshop, 2000; vis. artist Burston Graphic Ctr., Jerusalem, 1980. One-woman shows include LI U., Bklyn., 1965, Chelsea Gallery, NYC, 1969, Benton and Bowles, NYC, 1970, Bklyn. Mus., 1971, Graham Gallery, NYC, 1972, 77, Montclair Art Mus., 1974, 87, Mus. St. John the Divine, NYC, 1977, Gallery One, Montclair State U., 1978, Camargo Found., Cassis, France, 1980, Va. Ctr. for Creative Arts, Sweetbriar, 1986, Millersville (Pa.) U., 1986, Pratt Inst., NYC, 1989, NJ State Mus., Trenton, 1991, Klarfeld Perry Gallery, NYC, 1993, Suffolk C.C., Selden, NY, 1993, Bergen (NJ) Mus., 1996, Jersey City Mus., 1997-98, Baird Ctr., South Orange, NJ, 2001, Tomasulo Gallery, NJ, 2001, U. Wis., 2002, Chautauqua Ctr. for Visual Arts, NY, 2004; exhibited in group shows at Robeson Ctr. Gallery, Newark, 1986, Contemporary Arts Ctr., New Orleans, 1986, Stadtiche Galerie, Regensburg, Germany, Monmouth Mus., 1987-88, Hunterdon Art Ctr., Clinton, NJ, 1989, Holman Hall Art Gallery, Trenton, 1989, Women's Caucus for Art, NYC, 1990, Studio Mus., NYC, 1990, Morris Mus., Morristown, NJ, 1991, Rutgers U., New Brunswick, NJ, 1991, Chgo. Art Expo, 1993, Corcoran Gallery Art, Washington, 1994, 2004, Jersey City (NJ) Mus., 1995, Newark Pub. Libr. Artist Book Collection, 1995, Ctr. for Book Arts, NYC, 1996, 98, 2002, Rutgers Ctr. for Innovative Printmaking, New Brunswick, NJ, 1997, Montclair Art Mus., 1997, Mus. Modern Art, Dominicana, Santa Domingo, 1998, Nat. Mus. Women in the Arts, Washington, 1999, NJ State Mus., Trenton, 1999, Conn. Coll., 1999, Bristol Meyers-Squibb Gallery, Lawrenceville, NJ, 2000, Sterling Art Libr., Yale U., 2000, Gallery 241, Montclair, 2001, Pacifico Fine Arts, NYC, 2002, William Paterson U., Wayne, NJ, 2004, William Paterson U. Artist Book Collection, 2005, Everson Mus., Syracuse, NY, others; represented in permanent collections U. Del., Nat. Mus. Women in Arts, Washington, Israel Mus., Jerusalem, Israel, U. Oreg., Newark Mus., Whitney Mus., Am. Art, Bklyn. Mus., Montclair Art Mus., Arnot Art Mus., Morris Mus., Met. Mus. Art, NY, Mus. Art, RISD, Providence, Queens Mus., NY, Jersey City Mus., Jewish Mus., NYC, Women's Studio Workshop, Rosendale, NY, Allen Meml. Art Mus., Oberlin, Ohio, Skirball Mus., LA, Spertus Mus., Chgo., Neuberger Mus., Purchase, NY, Bass Mus., Miami (Fla.) Beach, Kresge Mus., Lansing, Mich., Corcoran Gallery of Art, Everson Art Mus., Syracuse, Sterling Art Libr. Yale U., NJ State Mus., Trenton, 1949-1990, Smithsonian Archives of Am. Art, 1979-2005, Abraham Lincoln Ofcl. Libr. and Mus., Springfield, Ill, 2005 Recipient Childe Hassam Purchase award Am. Acad. Arts and Letters, 1977, prize 11th R.I. Arts Festival, 1969, Ives prize RISD, Disting. Artist award NJ State Coun. on Arts, 1987, Grand prize Am. Impressions Ben Shahn Galleries William Patterson U., 2003, Abraham Lincoln Presdl. Libr., Springfield, Ill.; grantee NY State Coun. on Arts, 1971, NJ State Coun. on Arts, 1978, 83, 87, Womens Rsch. and Devel. Fund, CUNY, 1986, Rutgers Ctr. for Innovative Printmaking, 1987, 97, Rutgers Ctr. for Innovative Printmaking, 1989, 98, Joan Mitchell Found., 1994, Mid Atlantic NEA, 1996, Dodge Found. artist residency, 1998, 2000, 02, Womens Studio Workshop, Rosendale, NY, 1999-2000, Pollock-Krasner Found., 2000, Midatlantic Arts Found., 2000, E.D. Found.; Fulbright fellow, Paris, 1953-55, Ossibaw Island Residency, Ga., 1975, Forest fellow Millay Colony, 1992, San Diego Art Mus., others.

BEERS, SYDNEY (SYDNEY DAVOLOS), theater producer; b. 1961; m. Steven B. BFA in Theater. Subscription sales assoc. Roundabout Theater, prodn. mgr., gen. mgr. Gen. mgr.: numerous theatrical performances; actor: (plays). Office: Roundabout Theater Co Ste 1200 231 W 39th St New York NY 10018 Office Phone: 212-719-9393.

BEERY, AMY SUZANNE, music educator; b. Millersburg, Ohio, Jan. 4, 1964; d. Gordon Ralph and Reva Jane Gamertsfelder; m. Max Ralph Talmadge Beery, Aug. 10, 1985; children: Steven Ralph, David Talmadge, Sarah Suzanne. BA in Music Edn., Mt. Vernon Nazarene U., Mt. Vernon, Ohio, 1986; MusM, U. Akron, Ohio, 2000. Cert. elem. tchr. Ohio, 1991. Music specialist K-8 Lucas Local Schs., Ohio, 1987—89, St. Mary's Ctrl.

Sch., Martins Ferry, Ohio, 1991—92; migrant tutor Old Ft. Schs., Ohio, 1994—96; licensing field rep. Ohio Dept. Edn., divsn. Early Childhood Edn., Northwest & Northeast Regions, Ohio, 1995—97; music specialist preK-5 Lakewood City Schs., Ohio, 1997—98; music specialist K-12 Barberton City Schs., Ohio, 1998—. Choir dir. children-adult Rocky River United Meth. Ch., Ohio, 1996—98; pvt. music instr. voice and piano, Akron, Ohio, 1998—; tng. level dir. Summit Choral Soc. Children's Choir, Akron, 1999—2003. Mem.: Voices of Canton, Inc. (assoc.), NEA (assoc.), North Coast Kodaly Assn. (assoc.; sec. 2000—04), Orgn. Am. Kodaly Educators (assoc.), Nat. Assn. for Music Edn. (assoc.), Ohio Music Edn. Assn. (assoc.). Home: 177 N Firestone Blvd Akron OH 44301 Office Phone: 330-848-4232.

BEERY-POLGLASE, PENELOPE (PIXIE), education educator; d. Jack and Margaret Beery-Polglase; m. Jack Beery, Sept. 6, 1987; children: Rhea Beery-Fox, Kaya Winter Beery. BA in Edn., Art, and Social Sci., Western Mich. U., Kalamazoo, 1965; MS, Pepperdine U., Malibu, Calif., 1985; postgrad., Nova Southeastern U., Ft. Lauderdale, Fla., 2003—. Landscape arch. cert. of completion, UCLA; sch. adminstrn. clear credential Calif. Commn. for Tchr. Credentialing, gen. tchg. life credential Calif. Commn. for Tchr. Credentialing, profl. devel. cert. L.A. Unified Sch. Dist., profl. devel. collaborative L.A. Unified Sch. Dist., UCLA sci. project, English lang. devel. and specially designed acad. instrn. in English Senate Bill 1969, State of Calif. Tchr. women's health initiatives UCLA, 1953—2003; tchr. Chgo. Pub. Schs., 1965—69, L.A. Unified Sch. Dist., L.A., asst. prin. Victoria Ave. Elem. Sch. South Gate, Calif., 2003—05, coord. yearround programs L.A., 1982—86, coord. categorical programs, 1986—87, tchr. Birdielee V. Bright Elem. Sch., Ten Schs. Program, 1987—98; asst. prin. Independence Elem. Sch., South Gate, Calif., 2005—; enrichment tchr. Will Rogers Learning Comty. Santa Monica (Calif.) Malibu Unified Sch. Dist., 1994—95; instr. English as 2d Lang., Comty. Adult Programs Santa Monica City Coll., 1995—96; instr. Tchr. Tng. Acad. L.A. Unified Sch. Dist., 1996—98, instr. new tchr. orientation, 1996—98, tchr. early childhood edn. programs, 1997—99, adviser dist. intern program, 1998—2000; trainer of trainers CA Formative and Support Sys. for Tchrs. Calif. Commn. on Tchr. Credentialing, L.A., 2000—; specialist tchr. coaches dist. J L.A. Unified Sch. Dist., 2000—03, literacy trainer, 2000—03; trainer of trainers Towards Equity Calif. Commn. on Tchr. Credentialing, L.A., 2000—; external evaluator Calif. State Dept. Edn., Sacramento, 2001—02; instr. Beyond the Bell Intervention program L.A. Unified Sch. Dist., L.A., 2003—. Adj. prof. Nova Southeastern U., L.A., 2002—03, Loyola Marymount U., L.A., 2002—; adj. instr. Pepperdine U.; presenter in field; student tchr. supr. U. So. Calif. Commr. for sex equity L.A. Unified Sch. Dist., 1987—90; leader Girl Scout Troop 181, Westchester, Calif.; beautification chair Will Rogers Learning Cmty., Santa Monica, 1994—99. Recipient Math Innovation grant, L.A. Edn. Partnership, 1997, 1998, Cmty. Gardening Program grant, U.S. EPA, 1998, First Pl. award in landscape archtl. design, UCLA Ext., 1989; grantee, Gardening Angeles Partnership, 1995—98, Gardens for Kids, 1996—98, Nat. Youth Gardens, 1997—98. Mem.: Women in Ednl. Leadership (membership chair 2002—04, treas. 2004—06, pres.-elect 2006, pres. 2006—). Home: PO Box 9416 Venice CA 90295 Personal E-mail: w-e-l2006@hotmail.com.

BEESON, ANN, lawyer; MA in Anthropology, U. Tex.; JD, Emory U. School Law, 1993. Attorney Human Rights Watch; assoc. legal dir. ACLU, 1995—. Named one of America's top 50 Women Litigators, Nat. Law Journal. Avocations: amateur pilot, singing. Office: c/o ACLU 125 Broad St 18th Floor New York NY 10004

BEESON, MARY, internist, endocrinologist, researcher; b. Seattle, Oct. 5, 1952; d. Robert and Sophie Beeson; m. John Lewis Holcomb, Oct. 22, 1975; 1 child, James Holcomb 1 stepchild, John Lewis Holcomb Jr. BS cum laude, U. San Francisco, 1989; MD, Tulane Med. Sch., New Orleans, 1994. Cert. Am. Bd. Internal Medicine, 2002, Am. Bd. Holistic Medicine, 2002. Rsch. asst. Salk Inst., La Jolla, Calif., 1972—75; athletic dir. Centro Salute, Stresa, Italy, 1984—86; personal trainer and excise instr., 1980—93; intern internal medicine Alameda County Hosp., Tampa, 1994—2001; resident internal medicine U. South Fla, 1995—97, fellow in endocrinology, 1997—99, rsch. fellow endocrinology, 1999—2001; pvt. practice Gulf Coast Endocrine and Diabetes Ctr., Clearwater, 2001—. Owner and dir. Bilancia Med. Spa, Tampa, 2002—. Author: Through the Eyes of an Angel, 2002; contbr. articles to profl. jours. Vol. tutor New Orleans City In Sch. Vol. Tutorial Program, 1991—92; student interviewer Tulane Admissions Com., 1993—94; mem. Hillsborough Assn. Retarded Citizens, Tampa, Fla., 1998. Grantee, NIH, 1999—2002; scholar, Tulane Med. Sch., 1993—94, Nat. Health Svc. Corps, 1993—94. Mem.: Am. Coll. Advancement of Medicine, Am. Soc. Laser Medicine and Surgery, Am. Bd. Holistic Medicine. Roman Catholic. Avocations: running, bicycling, skiing, triathalons, photography. Home: 701 Seddon Cove Way Tampa FL 33602-5702 Office: Gulf Coast Endocrine and Diabetes 417 Corbett Clearwater FL 33756 Office Phone: 727-443-2307. Personal E-mail: mbh@tampabay.rr.com.

BEESON, MONTEL EILEEN, human services administrator, gerontologist; b. El Dorado, Ark., Dec. 22, 1939; d. Waymon Willett and Myrtle May (Roach) B. BS Recreation, Calif. State U., Hayward, 1963; MA Edn. and Human Devel., Holy Names Coll., Oakland, Calif., 1979. Lic. nursing home adminstr.; cert. cmty. coll. instr.; cert. in gerontology. Dist. exec. Ariz. Cactus-Pine coun. Girl Scouts U.S.A., Phoenix, 1963—66, dist. exec. San Francisco Bay coun. Oakland, Calif., 1966—68, bus. mgr., 1968—71, exec. dir. Shabonee coun. Moline, Ill., 1971—73, exec. dir. Tongass-Alaska coun. Ketchikan, 1973—74, exec. dir. Muir Trail coun. Modesto, Calif., 1974—78; asst. adminstr. Beulah Home, Inc., Oakland, 1980—86; exec. dir. Cmty. Adult Day Health Svcs., Oakland, 1987—88, Greenhills Retirement Ctr., Millbrae, Calif., 1988—89; elder care cons., 1986—. Mem. Am. Coll. Health Care Adminstrs., Am. Soc. on Aging. Avocations: cross country skiing, history, travel, reading, music. Home: 3393 Kiwanis St Oakland CA 94602-4005

BEETLE, KATE, artist, illustrator; b. East Orange, N.J., Mar. 6, 1951; d. Garrii LeClair and Lorraine Frances Ebert. BS in Geology, Richard Stockton Coll., Pomona, N.J., 1979. Exhibitions include Sunapee Crafts Fair, 1986—88, Sharon Arts Annual, 1989, 1994, League of N.H. Craftsmen Annual, 1993, Handed Down, Rivier Coll., 1994, ABC-The Letter Arts, 1996, WCA-NH Innaugural, 1996, juried exhibits, Sharon Arts Ann., 1989, 1994, League N.H. Craftsmen Ann., 1993, ABC-The Letter Arts, 1996, Handed Down, River Coll., 1994, WCA-N.H. Inaugural, 1996, Sunapee Crafts Fair, 1986—88. Vol. Manadnock Humane Soc. Recipient 2 Louie awards Internat. Greeting Card Assn., 1997. Mem. Granite Scribes (archivist), Sharon Arts Ctr., Nat. Mus. Women in the Arts. Democrat. Unitarian Universalist. Avocations: gardening, baking, piano, tatting. Office: 33 Longacre Ln Alstead NH 03602

BEEZLEY, SARA SUE, lawyer; b. Nov. 1955; BA, So. Meth. U.; JD, Duke U. Bar: Kans. 1979. Atty., Girard, Kans. Mem.: Kans. Bar Assn. (pres. 2002—03). Office: 126 S Ozark Girard KS 66743

BEEZY, MIRIAM CLAIRE, lawyer; BA, UCLA, 1977; JD, Southwestern U., 1986. Bar: Calif. 1988, U.S. Dist. Ct., Ctrl. Dist. Calif. 1988, U.S. Dist. Ct., No. Dist. Fla. 1988, U.S. Dist. Ct., Dist. Nev. 1989, U.S. Dist. Ct., No. Dist. Tex. 1989, U.S. Dist. Ct., Ea. Dist. Calif. 1990, U.S. Dist. Ct., So. Dist. Calif. 1992. Ptnr. Foley & Lardner LLP, L.A., chairperson trademark & copyright practice group. Co-author: Incorrect Use of Marks Can Become Costly for Owners, 2003, Co-Branding, Done Correctly, Makes Great Marketing, 2003. Mem.: Nat. Inst. Entertainment & Media Law, Southwestern U. Sch. Law (bd. dirs.), L.A. World Affairs Counsel, L.A. Intellectual Property Law Assn. (mem. 1988—), Internat. Trademark Assn. (industy adv. coun. 1997—2000, external affairs com., treaty promotion sub-com. 2000—02), Calif. Women Lawyers, State Bar Calif. (intellectual property sect. 1988—), L.A. Bar Assn. (intellectual property & unfair competition sect. 1988—), Beverly Hills Bar Assn. (intellectual property liaison legis. com. 1989—91, patents, trademarks & copyrigths sect., chairperson 1990—91, bd. gov. 1992—95). Office: Foley & Lardner LLP 2029 Century Park E 35th Floor Los Angeles CA 90067-3021 Office Phone: 310-975-7966. Office Fax: 310-557-8475. Business E-Mail: mbeezy@foley.com.

BEFFORT, SUE WILSON, state legislator; b. Albuquerque; BA, So. Meth. U. Mem. N.Mex. Senate, Dist. 19, Santa Fe, 1996—; mem. fin. com. N.Mex. Senate. Republican. Home: 67 Raindance Rd Sandia Park NM 87047

BEGLEY, CHARLENE, electronics executive; b. Oct. 30, 1966; married; 3 children. BS in Bus. Adminstrn. magna cum laude, U. Vt., 1988. With transp. sys. GE, 1988—90, corp. audit staff, 1990—94, v.p. ops. capital mortgage svc., 1994—97, CFO transp., 1997, dir. fin. plastics, 1998—99, v.p. corp. audit staff, 1999—2001, pres., CEO transp. sys., 2001, CEO, pres. plastics, 2004—. Named one of 50 Most Powerful Women in Business, Fortune mag., 2006, 50 Most Powerful Women in Bus., 2006. Office: GE Plastics 1 Plastics Ave Pittsfield MA 01201 Office Phone: 413-448-7110.*

BEGLEY, HEIDI MARIE, nurse, entrepreneur; d. Donald Joseph Stubblefield and Shirley Ann Miller, adopted d. Henry Miller; m. Paul Wyatt Begley, Aug. 21, 1982; children: Brock Paul, Bart Charles, Paul Andrew. ASN, Purdue U. North Ctrl., Westville, Ind, 1989. RN Ind., Ky. Dir. nursing Tioga Pines, Monticello, Ind., 1991—95; asst. dir. nursing Our Lady of Holy Cross, San Pierre, Ind., 1995—98, 2006—; charge nurse pediat. psychology Caritas Peace, Lousiville, 2000—03; staff nurse Bapt. Hosp. East, Louisville, 2003—05. Legal nurse cons. Begley Exec. Svcs. and Tng., Shelbyville, Ky., 2005—. Mem. Orissa Project Inc., Kokomo, Ind., 1997—2006. Mem.: Am. Mensa (assoc.; editor newsletter Kentuckiana group), Alpha Lambda Delta. Baptist. Avocations: writing, missions, travel. Home: 509 S Main St Wanatah IN 46390 Office: Our Lady of Holy Cross 7520 S Hwy 421 San Pierre IN 46374 Office Phone: 219-828-4111. Personal E-mail: heidibegley@aol.com.

BEGLEY, RENEE, history educator; d. Thomas J. and LaVerne Thole; m. Robbie Begley, Aug. 9, 2003. BS in Adolescent Edn., Miami U., Oxford, Ohio, 2002; MS in Curriculum and Tchr. Leadership, Miami U., 2005. Am. history tchr. Mason City Schs., Ohio, 2002—, student coun. advisor.

BEGONIA, MARIA, biology professor; arrived in U.S., 1978; m. Gregorio Begonia; children: Michael, Mark. BS, U. of the Philippines, 1975; MS, Miss. State U., Starkville, 1981; PhD, U. Mo., Columbia, 1989. Rsch. asst. U. Philippines, 1975—78, rschr., project leader, 1982—89; grad. rsch. asst. Miss. State U., Starkville, 1978—81, rsch. asst., 1989—92; grad. rsch./tchg. asst. U. Mo., Columbia, 1986—89; vis. asst. prof. Jackson State U., Miss., 1993—99, asst. prof., 1999—2003, assoc. prof., 2003—. Review panelist NSF, Washington, 2003, Washington, 04, Washington, 05. Assoc. editor: Jour. Miss. Acad. Sci., 2002—; contbr. articles to profl. jours. Mem.: Miss. Acad. Scis. (dir. 2003—06, assoc. editor jour. 2002—), Nast. Sci. Tchrs. Assn., Am. Soc. for Microbiology, Philippine Soc. for Microbiology (life), St. Pauls Women's Guild, Filipino-Am. Assn. MIss. Avocations: reading, dance, gardening. Office: Jackson State U Dept Biology PO Box 18540 1400 JR Lynch St Jackson MS 39217

BEGUHN, SANDRA E., poet, writer; b. Kirksville, Mo., Nov. 3, 1942; d. Charles Elwin and Loeta Elaine (Payton) Funk; m. Lynn L. Beguhn, June 29, 1963; children: Kelly Lyn Beguhn Simpson, John Christopher. Student, MaryCrest Coll., Davenport, Iowa, 1962-63. Contbr. poetry to Capper's Weekly, Lyrical Iowa, Nat. Libr. of Poetry, Creative Arts and Enterprises. Mem.: Poetry Guild, Durango Colo. Poetry Gathering, Famous Poets Soc., Sparrowgrass Poetry Forum, Illiad Press, Mu Chi Sigma Soc. (pres.). Methodist. Avocations: travel, photography, writing. Home: 2115 W 34th St Davenport IA 52806-5301 E-mail: xalthim@mchsi.com.

BEGUM, MOMOTAZ, medical researcher, consultant, medical educator; b. Dhaka, Bangladesh, Oct. 7, 1960; arrived in U.S., 1994; d. Mohammad and Begum Ali; m. Hashib Dean Faruque, June 24, 1984; 1 child, Munim Hasib Deen Faruque. MB, BChir in Med. Scis., U. London, Dhaka, Bangladesh, 1984; MPH in Health Edn. and Promotion, U. Okla., 1997. Lic. physician Bangladesh. Med. officer Rushmono Gen. Hosp., Dhaka, 1985-88, Iran, 1988-91; resident med. officer Dhaka Med. Coll. Hosp., 1993-94; sr. med. officer, counselor maternal and child health and family planning New Al-Rajhi Hosp., Dhaka, 1994; staff physician, physician mgr. Internat. Ctr. Diarrhoeal Diseases Rsch., Dhaka, 1994; grad. rsch. asst. dept health promotion scis. U. Okla. Med. Ctr., Oklahoma City, 1995-96, grad. rsch asst. urinary incontinence project col. pub. health, 1996, grad. rsch asst. Ctr. Prevention Rsch. Native Ams., 1996-97, rsch asst. II Ctr. Am. Indian Health Rsch., 1997-98. Cons. Johnson & Johnson, 1996, Worksite Health Screening Programs, Oklahoma City, 1996—97; pub. health instr., prodn. editor newsletter Okla. State Dept. Health, Oklahoma City, 1998—99, edn. rsch. specialist material and infant health family planning divsn., 1997; extern Birth and Beyond Okla. State Med. Assn., Oklahoma City, 1999; rschr., cons. Ctr. Am. Indian Health Rsch., 2000—. Contbr. articles to profl. jours. Organizer Multicultural Social, Internat. Students Spring Activity Day, Grad. Student Orientation, Internat. Student Awareness Day, Multicultrual Award Banquet; rep., pres. Internat. Student Assn., Coll. Pub. Health, U. Okla. Med. Ctr., Oklahoma City, 1995—97, mistress ceremony, 1996; v.p. Internat. Student Orgn., 1995—97; alumni rep. Faculty-Student Task Force Recreation Self-Study Coll. Pub. Health, 1998—99. Recipient All-Am. Scholar Collegiate award, U.S. Achievement Acad., 1997, Outstanding Health Edn. Student award, Okla. Pub. Health Assn., 1996. Mem.: Bangladesh Med. Assn., Internat. Student Assn. U. Okla. Med. Ctr. (pres., Outstanding Internat. Student award 1996—97), Dhaka Med. Coll. Student Orgn. (Patient Welfare Soc. and Blood Donation chpt.), Alpha Epsilon Lambda. Avocations: organizing activites, travel, music, cooking.

BEHAN, KATHLEEN A. (KITTY BEHAN), lawyer; b. Milw., July 28, 1963; BA magna cum laude, Yale U., 1985; JD, Columbia U., 1989. Bar: Md. 1989, DC 1991. Staff counsel Nat. Security Project ACLU, 1989—90; assoc. Arnold & Porter LLP, Washington, 1990—96, ptnr., 1996—, co-chair pro bono com. Bd. dirs. probono.net, So. Ctr. for Human Rights, Atlanta, Am. Assn. People with Disabilities; bd. trustees Metrostage, Alexandria, Va.; bd. advisors Tahirih Justice Ctr., Falls Church, Va. Named one of Washington's Top 40 Lawyer's Under 40, Washingtonian Mag., 1998, The Top 50 Women Litigators, Nat. Law Jour., 2001, The Top 40 Litigators Under 40. Mem.: Women's Bar Assn. DC (bd. dirs.). Office: Arnold & Porter LLP 555 12th St NW Washington DC 20004-1206 Office Phone: 202-942-5533. Office Fax: 202-942-5999.

BEHAN, PAMELA S., sociology professor; b. Stafford, Kans., Apr. 20, 1948; d. Nathan P. Budd and Helen E. Raikes; m. Edward M. Behan, Mar. 19, 1983; 1 child, Nathan J. PhD in Sociology, U. Colo., Boulder, 2000. RN Boulder Meml. Hosp., 1971—72, 1976—79, Boston Children's Hosp., 1972—75; ops. mgr. Boulder Sch. of Massage Therapy, 1979—81; RN Boulder Hospice, 1983—84; news analyst U. Colo. Office of Pub. Rels., Boulder; asst. prof. sociology U. Houston Downtown, 2000—. Author: (monograph) Solving the Health Care Problem: How Other Nations Succeeded and Why the United States Has Not. Mem. Gold Hill (Colo.) Town Coun., 1984—85; vol. Gold Hill Fire Dept., 1975—80, 1983—87; mem. Gold Hill Hist. Zoning Com., 1986—87; vol. Columbine Elem. Sch., Boulder, 1988—91, Colo. Sch. Mediation Project, Boulder, 1991—92. Grantee, Houston Health SVcs. Rsch. Collaborative, 2006—. Mem.: AAUW, Am. Sociol. Assn. Achievements include research in the role of financial considerations in health care utilization decisions. Office: U Houston Downtown 1 Main St Houston TX 77002 Office Phone: 713-221-8536. E-mail: behanp@uhd.edu.

BEHAN, SANDRA HOLLOWAY, science educator; b. Bridgeport, Conn. d. Delmo Pennington Holloway and Martha Olivia Bridges; m. Richard Lewis Behan, Sept. 15, 1962; children: Janet Sandra Abbott, Brenda Margaret DiFilippo. BA in Ecology and Biology, Goddard Coll., Plainfield, Vt., 1976, MA in Ecology and Biology, 1978; MSW, U. Conn., West Hartford, 2006. Tchr. Samoana H.S., Pago Pago, Am. Somoa, 1970—73, 1976—80, Am. Internat. Sch., Dusseldorf, Germany, 1973—76, Am. Samoa C.C., Pago Pago, 1980—82, The Canterbury Sch., New Milford, Conn., 1982—. Cons. in field. Author: Ecology of American Samoa, 1976. Mem.: NASW, Nat. Sci. Tchrs. Assn. Democrat. Avocations: jewelry design, hiking, gardening, travel, stained glass. Home: 36 Luzi Dr Bantam CT 06750 Office: Canterbury Sch 101 Aspetuck Ave New Milford CT 06776

BEHAR, JOY, television personality; b. Brooklyn, N.Y., Oct. 7, 1943; m. Joe Behar, 1965 (div. 1981); 1 child; m. Steven Janowitz, 1982. BS in Sociology, Queens Coll.; MA in English, SUNY, Stony Brook. Teacher Lindenhurst H.S., Long Island, NY. Corrs. Comedy Cen.; host call-in radio show on WABC. Profl. actress: (tv series) Baby Boom, (tv pilot) The Rock, (guest appearances) Dr. Katze (CableACE award), (discussion panel) Politically Incorrect; (movies) Cookie, 1989, This is My Life, 1992, Manhattan Murder Mystery, 1993, Love Is All There Is, 1996, M Word, 1996; Broadway appearances include The Food Chain, The Vagina Monologues, Comedy Tonight; author Joy Shtick or What Is the Existential Vacuum and Does It Come with Attachments?, 1999; co-host The View, 1997-. Office: 320 W 66th St New York NY 10023-6304

BEHARRY, AVALAURA GAITHER, healer; b. Middletown, Conn., Mar. 17, 1976; d. Alfreda G. and Arthur L. Gaither; m. Anthony R. Beharry, June 7, 2002. BS in Psychology, Howard U., Washington, DC, 1998, MSW, 2002. LCSW Washington, 2004; cert. Reiki master tchr. Internat. Assn. of Reiki Profls., hypnotherapist Nat. Guild of Hypnotists, Inc., holistic aromatherapist N.W. Coll. for Herbal and Aromatic Studies. Statistician/demographer U.S. Bur. of the Census, Suitland, Md., 1998—2000; pres. Beharry Investments, Inc., Lanham, Md., 2002—; chief devel. officer LINKS, Inc., Greenbelt, Md., 2004—05; holistic healer/educator Avalaura's Healing Ctr., College Park, Md., 2005—. Recipient Trustee scholarship, Howard U.- Coll. of Arts and Sci., 1995-1998, scholarship, Hope Inc., 2000, Grad. assistantship, Howard U., 2000-2002; Dwight Eisenhower Transp. fellowship, Dept. of Transp., 1997-1998. Mem.: NASW, Internat. Natural Healers Assn., Assn. for Comprehensive Energy Psychology, Internat. Assn. of Reiki Profls., Nat. Guild of Hypnotists, Inc. Office: Avalaura's Healing Ctr College Park MD 20740 Office Phone: 301-675-8723. Home Fax: 301-345-5830; Office Fax: 301-345-5830. Personal E-mail: avalaura@avalaura.com.

BEHBEHANIAN, MAHIN FAZELI, surgeon; b. Kermanshah region, Iran; arrived in U.S., 1959; d. M Jaafar and Ozra (A.) B.; m. Abolfath H. Fazeli, Sept, 4, 1969; children: Pouneh, Pontea. BS, Wilmington (Ohio) Coll., 1961; MD, Med. Coll. Pa., Phila., 1965. Diplomate Am. Bd. Surgery. Gen. surgeon Lankenan Hosp., Phila., 1970; chief surgery, pres. med. staff Imperial Ct. Hosp., Teheran, Iran, 1971-79; gen. surgery Riddle Meml. Hosp., Media, Pa., 1980—; pvt. practice Phila., Chester, Media, Pa., 1984—. Chief subdivsn. gen. surgery Riddle Meml. Hosp., Media, 1998—. Editor-in-chief Behkoosh Jour. of Medicine, Teheran, 1976-79. Recipient Gilson Colby Engel award, 1966. Fellow ACS; mem. Am. Women Surg. Soc., Am. Soc. Breast Surgeons, Am. Herenia Assn., Pa. Med. Soc., Del. County Med. Soc. Office: Riddle Meml Health Care Ctr 1088 W Baltimore Pike Media PA 19063-5136 also: Lankenau Med Bldg Ste 414 Wynnewood PA 19096 Office Phone: 610-565-6625. E-mail: mahinmd@aol.com.

BEHLER, DIANA IPSEN, Germanic and comparative literature educator; b. N.Y.C. d. Walter and Marie (Kroger) Ipsen; m. Ernst Behler, Nov. 24, 1967; children: Sophia, Caroline. BA, U. Wash., 1965, MA, 1966, PhD, 1970. Asst. prof. Germanics Germanics U. Wash., Seattle, 1971-74; assoc. prof. Germanics and comparative lit. U. Wash., Seattle, 1974-81, prof., 1981—, chmn. dept Germanics, 1978-88, 1990. Author: The Theory of the Novel in Early German Romanticism, 1978; translations: Hegel, Jacobi, Fichte; author essays on Romanticism, Henry Crabb Robinson, Friedrich Nietzsche, Thomas Mann, Heinrich Heine; contbr. articles to profl. jours. NEH fellow, 1972-73. Home: 5525 NE Penrith Rd Seattle WA 98105-2844 Office: U Wash Dept Germanics PO Box 353130 Seattle WA 98195-3130

BEHLMAR, CINDY LEE, medical association administrator, management consultant; b. Smyrna, Tenn., July 4, 1959; d. James Wallace and Barbara Ann (Behlmar) Gribble. BBA, Coll. William and Mary, 1981; MBA, Old Dominion U., 1995. Cert. mgmt. acct.; gen. mediator. Adminstrv. extern Hampton Gen. Hosp., Va., 1981-82; from mktg. rep. to supr. mktg. svcs. PruCare of Richmond, Va., 1983-85; exec. dir. PhysicianCare, Inc., Newport News, Va., 1986-89; provider rels. cons. Va. Health Network, Richmond, 1989-91; ind. cons. Tidewater Health Care, Virginia Beach, Va., 1991-92; COO Tidewater Phys. Therapy, Inc., Newport News, 1993-95; ind. cons. Yorktown, Va., 1996-97; contract mgr. Sentara Health Mgmt., Virginia Beach, 1998-99; state mgr. managed care Va. Oncology Assocs., 1999—2004; adminstr. Peninsula Emergency Physicians, Inc., 2004—. Sec., bd. dirs. Greater Peninsula Area Med.-Bus. Coalition, Newport News, 1987-89; symposium faculty mem. Am. Hosp. Assn., Orlando, Fla., 1987, Washington, 1988; profl. spkr. in field. Mem. ch. coun. St. Mark Luth. Ch., Yorktown, Va., 1988-91. Fin. Exec. Inst. scholar, 1993. Mem. Inst. Mgmt. Accts., Toastmasters Internat. (club pres. 1997-98, area gov. 1998-99, Club Toastmaster of Yr. 1997-98, Dist. Spirit Success award 1998, Dist. Area Gov. of Yr. 1998-99, Disting. Toastmaster 1999), Phi Kappa Phi, Beta Gamma Sigma. Avocations: reading, art, fashion, music, piano. Home: 922 Hanson Dr Newport News VA 23602-8910 Office: Peninsula Emergency Physicians Inc Ste E 11828 Canon Blvd Newport News VA 23606-4250 Office Phone: 757-599-4922. E-mail: CiLeBe@aol.com.

BEHNKE, DOLEEN, computer and environmental specialist, consultant; b. Alameda, Calif., Sept. 23, 1950; d. Charles Joseph Ziegler and Dola Faye (Cushing) Peterson; m. Glen A. Pellett, June 26, 1971 (div. 1986); children: Mark Dolan Pellett, Michael Jay Pellett; m. Danny L. Carr, Dec. 29, 1986 (div. 1996); m. Jon T. Behnke, June 28, 1996. BA, U. Wis., Madison, 1973. Notary pub. Mich. Budget analyst Ednl. Testing Svc., Princeton, N.J., 1979-80; tech. recruiter Uniforce Svcs., Inc., Rock Hill, S.C., 1983-84; mgr. tng. and documentation Electronic Data Systems Corp., Troy, Mich., 1985-87; tech. writer, trainer, analyst cons. CES, Inc., Troy, 1989-92; pres. D'Carr Co., Inc., Roseville, Mich., 1988-93; tech. writer, trainer, cons. Eaton Corp., Southfield, Mich., 1988-93; pres., CEO Carr-Ben Tech Ltd., Lake Orion, Mich., 1996—97, bd. dirs.; pres. Bent Key Enterprises, Inc., 2004—. Cons. Hazardous Materials Info. Exch., Washington, 1989—; installer, instr. Gt. Plains Acctg., Fargo, ND, 1990—; cons., tech. writer Saturn Corp., 1991—92, Blue Cross Blue Shield, Southfield, Mich., 1992—93, Southfield, 1995—96; tech. writer FANUC Robotics, N.A., Inc., Auburn Hills, Mich., 1993—95. Co-author: CIW-Weld Monitor, 1990, 1993. Elected trustee for charter township, Oxford, Mich., 2004—. Mem.: NAFE, AAUP, Charter Township of Oxford (trustee 2004—), Great Oaks Civitan, Key Club (dist. chair 2002—03, mktg. dist. chair 2002—, dist. adminstr. 2003—), Oxford-Orion Kiwanis, Kiwanis Internat. (internat. com. K-Kids 2001—), Roseville Kiwanis (pres. 1995, lt. gov. elect 1996—97, lt. gov. 2001—02, cert. Kiwanis instr. 2002—). Republican. Roman Catholic. Avocations: piano, swimming, computers, politics. Personal E-mail: dfb876@charter.net.

BEHNKE, MARYLOU, pediatrician, educator; b. Orlando, Fla., Sept. 1, 1950; d. Ernest Edmund and Elizabeth (Kolb) Behnke. BS in Chemistry, U. Fla., 1972, MD, 1976. Diplomate Am. Bd. Pediatrics, Am. Bd. Neonatology-Perinatology. Intern dept. pediat. Coll. Medicine U. Fla., Gainesville, 1976-77, resident, 1977-79, chief resident, 1979-80, fellow in neonatology, 1981-83, asst. prof., 1979-81, 83-89, assoc. prof., 1989-99, prof., 1999—, adj. asst. prof. Coll. Nursing, 1988-89, adj. assoc. prof., 1989-99, mem. senate-at-large, 1984-89, 2004—07, mem. grad. studies faculty, 1988-2000. Presenter nat. and internat. meetings, 1981—; med. dir. ICU Shands Hosp., Gainesville, 1983—89, neonatal devel. follow-up program, 1989—; ad hoc mem. spl. rev. com. human devel. rsch. NIH, 1991—96, chair, 1993, 94, mem. human devel. and aging-3 study sect., 1998—99; mem. BBBP-6 study sect., 1999—2002. Mem. editl. bd.: Death Studies, 1983—94; contbr. articles to profl. jours., chapters to books. Grantee, NIH, 1984—87, 1991—, Nat. Inst. Drug Abuse, 1991—, Ctr. Substance Abuse Treatment, 1993—95. Fellow: Am. Acad. Pediat. (sect. perinatal pediat. com. substance abuse); mem.: Am.

Pediatric Soc., Fla. Soc. Neonatal Perinatologists, Fla. Interagency Coord. Coun. Infants and Toddlers, Soc. Pediatric Rsch., Nat. Perinatal Assn., Soc. Pediat. Rsch., Alachua County Med. Soc., Fla. Med. Assn. Republican. Mem. Ch. Of Christ. Avocation: reading. Home: 426 SW 40th St Gainesville FL 32607-2749 Office: J Hillis Miller Health Ctr Dept Pediatrics PO Box 100296 Gainesville FL 32610-0296 Office Phone: 352-392-4193. Business E-Mail: behnkem@peds.ufl.edu.

BEHNKE, MICHELLE A., lawyer; b. 1961; BA, JD, U. Wis. Bar: Wis. 1988. Pvt. practice. Spkr. in field; mem. bd. attys. profl. responsibility, dist. 9 com., 1994—2002; mem. bd. visitors Wis. Law Alumni Assn., 1995—; treas. Equal Justice Coalition, 1997—98. Contbr. articles to profl. jours. Mem.: ABA, Legal Assn. Women, Dane County Bar Assn., State Bar Wis. (co-chair diversity outreach com. 1994—99, bd. dirs. practice mgmt. sect. 1998—2000, pres.-elect 2003—04, pres. 2004—05, past pres. 2005—), Madison Breakfast Rotary Chpt., Rotary Internat. Office: 222 N Midvale Blvd Ste 17 Madison WI 53705 Office Phone: 608-233-9024.

BEHR, MARION RAY, artist; b. Rochester, NY, Sept. 12, 1939; d. Justin Max and Sophie Gusta (Koffler) Rosenfeld. B.Art Edn., Syracuse U., 1961, M.F.A., 1962; m. Omri Marc Behr, June 24, 1962; children: Dawn Marcy Yael, Darrin Justin Mason, Dana Marisa Jana. Curator, contbr. Internat. Electrotech Print Show World of Electrotech: N.J. Print Coun. Contbr. publs. for stories, crafts, mag. covers and toy designs to nat. mags. including McCall's, Good Housekeeping, Lady's Circle, 1962-77; one-woman shows include Douglas Coll., 1983, Pargot Gallery, 1989, Eldorado Gallery, 1992, Beamsderfer Gallery, 1992, Hunterdon Art Gallery, 1993; Hunterdon Mus. Art, 1998; Inst. Cultural Peruano Norteamericano, 1999, Johnson Gallery, 2002, Discover Jersy Arts (artist of the month 2005); exhibited in group shows at Contemporary Am. Artists, Scarsdale, N.Y., 1964, Douglass Coll., 1977, John Szoke Gallery, 1989, Kanagawa Prefectual Gallery, Yokohama, Japan, 1989, 80 Washington Sq. East Gallery, N.Y.C., 1990, Juniper Gallery, Napa, Calif., 1991, Eldorado Gallery, Colorado Springs, Colo., 1992, B. Beamsderfer Gallery, Highland Park, N.J., 1992, Artsquad Gallery, Easton, 1993, Lever House, 1995, Audubon Artists, 1995, 97, 99, Cork Gallery, 1996, Cheltenham Ctr. for Arts, 1996, Krasdale Gallery, 1998, Nat. Acad. Mus., 1998, Stark & Stark, 1998, Grounds for Sculpture, 2001, Zimmerli Art Mus., Rutgers U., New Brunswick, 80th Fifth Ave Gallery, 2004, German Archtl. Ctr., Berlin, 2004, Hunteron Mus., 2005, Redbrick Gallery, Beverly, Mass., 2006, Ortho Gallery, Raritan, NJ, 2006; permanent print collection Smithsonian Instn. Nat. Mus. Art History, 1995, Jane Voorhees Zimmerli Art Mus., 1993, 96, 2002, 04, 05, Piero Gallery, 2004, Thai Royal Art Collection, Bangkok, 1995, Inst. Cultural Peruano Norteamericano, Peru, 1999, Bethanien Gallery, Berlin, 2004, World of Electrotech, N.J. Print Coun., 2005, Ben Shahn Gallery, 2006, Redbrick Gallery, Beverly, Mass., 2006, Ben Shshn Gallery, 2006, Newark Pub. Libr., 2006; creator survey Women Working Home-the Invisible Workforce, 1978; pres. Women Working Home, Inc., Edison, N.J., 1980—; condr. workshops; author: (with others) Women Working Home: The Homebased Business Guide and Directory, 1981, 2nd edit., 1983; contbr. articles to popular mags., 1988-89, popular art jours., 1991-98, numerous articles to profl. jours.; illustrator Jewish Holiday Book, 1977; inventor (with Omri Behr) acid free, environmentally safe graphic etching process; installed Electrotech processor and taught first non toxic intaglio etching class at Stanford U., 1999; installed electroetch and established non-toxic etching in the Inuit Artists Holman Eskimo Co-op Art Center, Holman Island, NWT, Canada, 1999, U. Al Moutamid IBN Abbad, Asilah, Morocco, 2000, Howard U., Washington, Syracuse U., N.Y., 2001, U. Alaska, Juneau, U. Alaska, Fairbanks, 2001, Druckwerkstatt Bethanien, Berlin, 2001, Christchurch Poly. and UCOL, Wanganui, New Zealand, 2004; extensive radio and TV appearances rep. Nat. Alliance Homebased Businesswomen. Mem. Kean for Gov. campaign, 1981; mem. White House Conf. on Free Enterprise Zones, 1982, Nat. Assn. of Women Artists, 1992, Soc. Am. Graphic Artists, So. Graphics Coun., 1992, Print Coun. N.J., 1993; trustee Women's Bus. Ownership Ednl. Conf., Inc., N.J., 1985; apptd. to N.J. Devel. Authority for Small, Minority and Women's Bus. Commn., 1986; Presdl. del. White House Conf. on Small Bus., 1986. Recipient N.J. Women in Bus. Advocate of the Yr. award SBA, 1984, Merit award Am. Artist Profl. League, Woman of Yr. in Bus. and Industry award, 1985, Audubon Artists Merit award, 1995, Purchase award Am. Impressions Ben Shahn Gallery, William Patterson U., 2006; named Artist of Month (August) Discover Jersey Arts, 2005; Syracuse U. alumni grantee, 1957; Arts and Humanities grantee Charles E. Lindbergh Fund, 1993-94. Mem. Nat. Alliance Homebased Businesswomen (pres. 1980-82, legis. chair 1982-85; originator, founder), Women's Caucus for Art, Audoban Artists. Jewish. E-mail: electroetch@prodigy.net.

BEHREND, KRISTEL NICOLE, music educator; b. Beavercreek, Ohio, Aug. 14, 1973; d. Neil David and Patricia Alice Ferguson; m. Michael James Behrend, June 17, 2000; children: Isabella Shea, Francesca Lucille. MusB Edn. and Voice Performance summa cum laude, U. Akron, Ohio, 1996. Cert. music tchr. K-12 Ohio. Tchr. music k-4 Black River Local Schs., Homerville, Ohio, 1996—2001; tchr. toddler music Gymboree, Medina, Ohio, 2001—04; tchr. music grades 1-2 Lodi Primary Sch., Ohio, 2004—. Pvt. voice tchr., Wadsworth, Wooster, Ohio, 2001—04; dir. youth choir First Christian Ch., Wadsworth, 1996—; owner 3-D Design.Daisies, Dragons, and Divas. Singer: Lyric Theater Ensemble. Recipient Honors scholar, U. Akron, 1994, Outstanding Undergrad. Music Edn. award, 1996; grantee, Walmart, 2005; Voice scholar, U. Akron, 1994. Mem.: Music Educators Nat. Conf., Ohio Music Educators Assn. (assoc.). Democrat. Avocations: painting, beading, sewing, travel, reading. Office: Lodi Primary School 301 Mill St Lodi OH 44254 Personal E-mail: kbehrend@hotmail.com.

BEHRENS, ALISA D., dancer, educator, performing company executive; b. Oklahoma, Mar. 12, 1976; d. Alan David and Sally Ann Behrens. BBA, U. Okla., Norman, 1998; MEd, Tex. Christian U., Ft. Worth, 2002. Cert. tchr. Tex. Market rschr. Marvin F. Paer & Co., Dallas, 1998—99; corp. liaison Dallas Bapt. U., 2000; dance instr. Tarrant County Coll., Ft. Worth, 2000—01; dance dir. Ft. Worth Acad. Fine Arts, 2001—06. Camp counselor Kanakuk Camps, Branson, Mo., 1996—98, Sky Ranch Camp, Tyler, Tex., 2000. Home: 5412 Bryce Canyon Dr Fort Worth TX 76137-3706

BEHRENS, BEREL LYN, physician, academic administrator, health facility administrator; b. New South Wales, Australia, 1940; MB, BS, Sydney U., Australia, 1964. Diplomate Am. Bd. Pediatrics, Am. Bd. Allergy and Immunology. Intern Royal Prince Alfred Hosp., Australia, 1964; resident Loma Linda (Calif.) U. Med. Ctr., 1966-68, Henrietta Egleston Hosp. for Children, Atlanta, 1968—69, T.C. Thompson Children's Hosp., Chattanooga, 1969—70; faculty pediatrics Loma Linda U., 1970-72, with dept. pediatrics, 1972—, dean Sch. Medicine, 1986-91, pres., 1990—, Loma Linda U. Med. Ctr., 1999—; pres., CEO Loma Linda U. Adventist Health Scis. Ctr., 1997—. Office: 11175 Campus St Loma Linda CA 92354 E-mail: myhanna@ahs.llumc.edu.

BEHRENS, ELLEN ELIZABETH COX, writer, counselor, educator; b. Fremont, Ohio, July 25, 1957; d. William Luther and Dorothy Cox. BA in English, Denison U., 1979; MFA in Creative Writing, Bowling Green State U., 1990. Writer in residence Ohio Arts Coun., 1991-94; ednl. devel. counselor Sch. Social Work Delphi Chassis Sys. facility U. Mich., Sandusky, Ohio and Flint, Mich., 1994-2000; mgr. instrnl. design and project mgr. Novations Learning Technologies, Lansing, Mich., 2000—04; dir. edn. Nat. Assn. Coll. U. Food Svcs., 2004—. Adj. faculty Firelands Coll., Terra Tech. Coll., 1988-94; cons. Bowling Green State U., 1991-94. Author: None But the Dead and Dying, 1996; asst. editor: Mid-American Review, 1988-90, fiction editor, 1990-94, advisory editor, 1994—; contbr. short stories to anthologies, Wastelands Rev., Descant, Fiction, Echoes, Paragraph, other literary mags. Individual Artist fellow Ohio Arts Coun., 1992. Mem. ASTD, Bowling Green State U. Creative Writing Alumni Assn. (bd. dir. 1990—), Ohioana Libr. Assn. Office: NACUFS Ste 280 2525 Jolly Rd Okemos MI 48864-3680 Office Phone: 517-332-2494. Business E-Mail: ebehrens@nacufs.org.

BEHRENS, JUNE ADELLE, writer; b. Maricopa, Calif., Apr. 25, 1925; d. Mark H. and Mattie Aline (Stafford) York; m. Henry William Behrens, Aug. 23, 1948; children: Terry Lynne, Denise Noel BA, U. Calif., Santa Barbara, 1947; MA Edn. Adminstrn., U. So. Calif., L.A., 1961; postgrad., UCLA, 1964—65, postgrad., 1973—74. Tchr. Hermosa Beach City Schs., Calif., 1947—48, Torrance Schs., Calif., 1950—54, 1956—58, Am. Dep. Schs., France, Germany, 1954—56; tchr., adminstr., reading specialist L.A. City Schs., 1958—80; reading specialsit Carson Sch., Calif., 1968—74; with Park We. Pl. Sch., San Pedro, Calif., 1974—80; writer, 1962—. Author: Soo Ling Finds A Way, 1965, Who Am I?, 1968, Walk in Neighborhood, 1968, Earth is Home, 1971, Farm, 1971, Desert, 1973, Feast of Thanksgiving, 1974, Death Valley, 1980, The Manners Book, 1980, Whalewatch!, 1980, (biography) Ronald Reagon, 1981, Gung Hay Fat Choy, 1982, Hanukkah, 1983, Powwow, 1983, (biography) Sally Ride, 1984, I Can Be An Astronaut, 1984, I Can Be A Truck Driver, 1985, I Can Be A Pilot, 1985, Miss Liberty, First Lady, 1986, Samoans!, 1986, I Can Be A Nurse, 1986, Whales of the World, 1987, Passover, 1987, (biography) Juliette Low, 1988, (biography) George Bush, 1989, Dolphins!, 1989, Sharks!, 1989, (biography) Barbara Bush, 1990, Spanish California and the Mission Trail, 1993 Docent Mus. Natural History Named Disting. Alumni of Yr., U. Calif. Santa Barbara, 1979 Mem. Internat. Reading Assn., So. Calif. Coun. on Lit.-Children & Young People, Soc. Children's Book Writers, Delta Kappa Gamma Democrat. Avocations: tennis, theater, travel. Home: 829 Mission Canyon Rd Santa Barbara CA 93105-2171

BEHRENSMEYER, ANNA K., curator, research scientist; m. Bill Behrensmeyer; children: Kristina, Sarah. BA in Geology, Washington U., St. Louis, 1967; MA in Geology, Harvard U., 1969, PhD in Geology and Vertebrate Paleontology, 1973. Miller rsch. fellow U. Calif., Berkeley, 1973—75, lectr. earth sci. dept. Santa Cruz, 1976—77; postdoc. fellow depts. geology and anthropology Yale U., New Haven, 1978—81; rsch. paleobiologist dept. paleobiology Nat. Mus. Natural History Smithsonian Instn., Washington, 1981—; co-dir. evolution of terrestrial ecosystems program Nat. Mus. Natural History Smithsonian Inst., 1988—, acting assoc. dir. sci., 1993—96. Adj. prof. dept. geosci. U. Ariz., 1987—; adj. prof. dept. geology U. Pa., Phila., 1991—. Assoc. editor: Paleobiology, 1979, 1982, 1985, Palaios, 1989—, Paleoclimatology, 1989—, bd. assoc. editors: Jour. Human Evolution, 1985—87; contbr. articles, chapters to books. Grantee SI Women's Com. Grant, 2000—02, grant (2), NSF, 2002—. Mem.: Geol. Soc. Am., Paleontological Soc., Soc. Vertebrate Paleontology, Soc. Econ.Paleontologists and Mineralogists, Internat. Assn. Sedimentologists. Avocations: hiking, camping, reading, storytelling, drawing. Office: Nat Mus Natural History Dept Paleontology Smithsonian Institute Washington DC 20560-0534

BEHRMANN, JOAN GAIL, editor; b. NYC; d. Jerome and Jeanette (Siberman) Metzner; m. Larry Jinks, Oct. 2, 1960 (div. 1970); children: Laura Jinks Kastigar, Daniel Cariton Jinks; m. Nicolas Lee Behrmann, Dec. 21, 1972. BA, Queens Coll., 1956; MS, Columbia U., 1958. Reporter Charlotte Observer, NC, 1958-60, Miami Herald, Fla., 1960-64, Miami News, 1965-66; asst. prof. Miami Dade CC, 1968-72; assoc. prof. Boston U., 1975-78; Sunday editor The Saratogian, Saratoga Springs, NY, 1979-80; editor Gannett Westchester, Westchester County, NY, 1981-83; page one editor, entertainment editor USA Today, Rosslyn, Va., 1983-87; exec. editor Desert Sun, Palm Springs, Calif., 1987-95; arts editor Detroit News, 1996-2000; ret., 2000; freelance writer Trash or Treasure column, theater revs. Detroit News, 2001—05. Co-author: Questioning Media Ethics, 1978. Founder Every Women's Coun., Glen Falls, NY, 1978—80; bd. dirs. Coll. of Desert Found., Palm Desert, 1993—95, Jewish Family Svcs., Palm Springs, 1994—95, Palm Springs Opera Guild, 1989—91, Adult Well-Being Svcs., Detroit, 1997—2000, Mich. Opera Theatre, 2000—05, Santa Fe Opera Guild, 2005—. Recipient Athena award, Palm Springs C. of C., 1991. Mem.: Am. Soc. Newspaper Editors, Assn. Press Mng. Editors Orgn. (bd. dirs. 1991—96, com. chair 1996—97). Avocations: travel, reading. Personal E-mail: jbehrmann@aol.com.

BEHROUZ, ELIZABETH JEAN, service director; b. New London, Conn., May 6, 1957; d. Dale and Jane (Senne) Daggett; m. Homayoun Behrouz, Jan. 1983; twins: Darmaan, Shaheen. BS in English, Mt. Scenario Coll., Ladysmith, Wis., 1982. Exec. asst. to dean grad. studies Lincoln U., Jefferson City, Mo., 1983-85, prison ednl. program coord., 1983-85; exec. asst. to sales tax divsn. mgr. Mo. Dept. Revenue, Jefferson City, 1985-87; staff asst. Office of Senator Christopher S. Bond, Jefferson City, 1989-91, dir. Office Constituent Svcs., 1992—.

BEICKEL, SHARON LYNNE, psychologist; b. Hanford, Calif., Mar. 1, 1943; d. William Wayne and Kathleen (Haun) B.; m. Wilbur Oran Hutton, Aug. 8, 1964 (div. Aug. 1974); m. Roland G. Bomstad Jr., Sept. 1, 1991. BS, Ea. Oreg. State U., 1965; MS, U. Oreg., 1970, PhD, 1977. Lic. psychologist, Oreg., Ariz. With U. Oreg., Eugene, 1966-78, dir. Debusk counseling ctr., 1975-76, intern in psychology, 1976-77; psychologist Ariz. State U., Tempe, 1978-84; pvt. practice Tempe, 1978-84; psychologist Beickel and Assocs., Eugene, 1984—; clin. dir. Aslan House Counseling Ctr., Eugene, 1985-86. Cons. Vocat. Rehab., Eugene, 1986—. Mem. APA, Oreg. Psychol. Assn. (bd. dirs. 1986-88, chair profl. affairs com. 1989-90, peer support com. 1994—), Lane County Psychol. Assn. (sec., treas. 1986-87, bd. dirs. 1986-90, pres.-elect 1993-94, pres. 1994-95, past pres. 1995-96). Home: 1678 Orchard St Eugene OR 97403-2034 Office: 1678 Orchard St Eugene OR 97401 Office Phone: 541-344-6789.

BEIDER, MARLYS ANNA, hotel executive, writer; b. Hannover, Germany, Feb. 7, 1945; d. Walter Schroeder and Elfriede (Ellen) Pallenberg-Schroeder; m. Harold Beider, Apr. 21, 1971 (dec.); children: Jacqueline Lee Shear, Kenneth Harry, Kelly Tema Rubin, Daniel Ayal. Bus., Buhmann Fachschule, 1960—63. V.p. Mid Am. Hotel Corp., Chgo., 1975—90, pres., 1990—. Author: (novels) Fateful Parallels, Continuum. Woman's bd. mem. North Shore Country Day Sch., Winnetka, Ill., 1981—91; adv. bd. The Theatre Sch. DePaul U., Chgo.; v.p. To Protect Our Heritage PAC, Chgo., 1985—90. Mem.: Royal Melbourne. Avocations: writing, opera, golf, hiking.

BEIDLER, MARSHA WOLF, lawyer; b. Bridgeton, NJ, Feb. 29, 1948; d. Benjamin and Esther (Lourie) Wolf; m. John Nathan Beidler, Aug. 18, 1974; children: Dora E., Evan A. BA, Dickinson Coll., Carlisle, Pa., 1969; JD, Rutgers U., Camden, N.J., 1972; LLM in Taxation, NYU, 1979. Bar: Pa. 1972, Fla. 1973, N.J. 1975; Fla. bar bd. cert. tax lawyer. Estate and gift tax atty. IRS, Phila., 1972-74, Trenton, NJ, 1974-76; atty. McCarthy & Hicks, Princeton, NJ, 1976-81; ptnr. Pinto & Beidler, Princeton, 1981-83; prin. Smith, Lambert, Hicks & Miller, Princeton, 1983-88; ptnr. Drinker, Biddle & Reath, Princeton, 1988—2005, of counsel, 2006—. Sec. Mercer County Estate Planning Council, 1977-86; prof. paralegal studies Rider Coll., Trenton, 1982; lectr. estate planning various corps. and univs. Bd. dirs. Birth Alternatives, Princeton, 1980; bd. dirs. Mercer Council on Alcoholism, Trenton, 1985-86. Fellow Am. Coll. Trusts and Estate Counsel; mem. ABA (taxation sect., real property, probate and trust sect.), Fla. Bar Assn., N.J. Bar Assn. (taxation sect.). Office: Drinker Biddle & Reath 105 College Rd E PO Box 627 Princeton NJ 08542-0627 Office Phone: 609-716-6515. Business E-Mail: marsha.beidler@dbr.com.

BEIER, ANITA P., air transportation executive; BS in Bus. Adminstrn., U. Md., MBA. Economist Fed. Railroad Adminstrn., 1979—81; various fin. positions in econ. and fin. analysis, budgeting and acctg. CSX Corp., 1981—96, v.p. fin. planning, 1998; CFO Am. Comml. Lines, 1997—98; v.p., contr. US Airways Group, Inc., US Airways, Inc., Arlington, Va., 1999—2004, sr. v.p., contr., 2004—. Office: US Airways 2345 Crystal Dr Arlington VA 22227

BEIER, CAROL ANN, state supreme court justice; b. Kansas City, Kans., Sept. 27, 1958; Student, Benedictine Coll., 1976-77, The Poynter Inst., 1979; BS, U. Kans., 1981, JD, 1982-85; ML in Judicial Process, U. Va. Sch. Law, 2004. Bar: Kans., 1985, D.C., 1988; U.S. Dist. Kans., 1985; U.S. Ct. Appeals (10th cir.) 1986. With Balloun & Bodinson, Olathe, Kans., 1983; jud. clk. U.S. Ct. Appeals (10th cir.), Olathe, 1985-86; staff atty. Nat. Women's Law Ctr., Washington, 1986-87; assoc. Arent, Fox, Kintner, Plotkin & Kahn, Washington, 1987-88, Foulston & Siefkin, Wichita, Kans., 1988-93, ptnr., 1993—2000; judge Kansas Ct. of Appeals, 2000—03; justice Kans. Supreme Ct., 2003—. Dir. Kans. Defender Project, Lawrence, 1989-90, Kans. Appellate Clinic, Lawrence, 1989-90; vis. asst. prof. U. Kans. Sch. of Law, Lawrence, 1989-90, lectr. Wichita State U., 1994; fellow Georgetown Women's Law and Pub. Policy Program, Washington, 1986-87. Articles editor U. Kans. Law Rev., 1984-85. Pres. Wichita Women Atty.'s Assn., 1993-94; bd. dirs. Kans. Civil Liberties Union, Wichita, 1990-94. Recipient Bernard Kilgore award, Soc. Profl. Jours., U. Kans., 1980, Louise Mattox Atty. of Achievement award Wichita Women's Attys. Assn., 2003. Fellow Kans. Bar Found., ABA, Sam A. Crow Inn of Ct. (master); mem. ABA, Kans. Bar Assn., D.C. Bar, Wichita Bar Assn., Women's Atty. Assn. Topeka, Order of the Coif. Office: Kansas Supreme Ct 301 W 10th Topeka KS 66612

BEILER, ANNE F., food company executive; m. Jonas Beiler; 2 children. Mgr. concession stand Md. Farmers Mkt., 1987; owner concession stand Farmers Mkt., Downingtown, Pa.; owner, chair, CEO Auntie Anne's, Gap, Pa., 1988—. Recipient Entrepreneur of Yr. award Inc. Mag., 1992, 94, Spirit of Achievement award Jr. Achievement Orgn. Ctrl. Pa., 1998; named one of 50 Pa.'s Best 50 Women in Bus., 1998. Office: Auntie Anne's Inc 160A Route 41 Gap PA 17527-9410

BEILER, HOLLY ANNE, education educator; d. George W. and Marilyn T. Beiler; 1 child, Kayla C. Hale. Adminstrv. Licensure, N.Mex Highlands U., Rio Rancho, N. Mex., 2004; M in Secondary Edn., U. N.Mex, Albuquerque, N. Mex., 2002; B of Bus. Edn., Ea. N.Mex U., Portales, N. Mex., 1994. Tech. resource tchr. Albuquerque Pub. Sch., Albuquerque, 1999—2003, tchr., 1995—99, grant project mgr., 2003—. Examiner Quality N.Mex, Albuquerque, 2004; ind. cons., Albuquerque, 2000—04. Contbr. profl. devel. curriculum; presenter Nat. Sch. Bd. Assn., Milken Educator's Conf., New Mex. State Tech. Conf. Grantee Sliver Quality Edn. for All, N.Mex Pub. Edn. Dept., 2004-2005, Enhancing Edn. Through Tech., 2004-2005, IDEA and Tech. Mem.: ASCD (assoc.). Office: Albuquerque Pub Sch 6400 Uptown Blvd NE Ste 220E Albuquerque NM 87110 Office Phone: 505-830-8096. Personal E-mail: holly_beiler@yahoo.com. Business E-Mail: beiler@aps.edu.

BEIMERS, GERTRUDE HII, writer; b. Kanowit, Sarawak, East Malaysia, Dec. 13, 1955; came to U.S., 1986; d. James Mee-chiong and Angela Mee Ing (Yong) Hii; m. George Jacob Beimers, Apr. 5, 1986. Grad. secondary sch., Sibu, East Malaysia, 1972. Nun Discalced Carmelite, Kuching, East Malaysia, 1972-84. Author: Out of the Mouth of a Chinese Dragon, 1995, When Chinese Dragons Dance, 1996. Democrat. Roman Catholic. Avocations: book collecting, baking, chinese cooking. Home: PO Box 2667 Port Aransas TX 78373-2667

BEINECKE, CANDACE KRUGMAN, lawyer; b. Paterson, N.J., Nov. 26, 1946; d. Martin and Sylvia (Altshuler) Krugman; m. Frederick W. Beinecke II, Oct. 2, 1976; children: Jacob Sperry, Benjamin Barrett. BA, NYU, 1967; JD, Rutgers U., 1970. Bar: N.Y. 1971. Assoc., then ptnr. Hughes, Hubbard & Reed, N.Y.C., 1970—, chair, 1999—. Bd. dirs. First Eagle Funds, N.Y.C., 1996—, chair bd. dirs., 2004—; bd. dirs. ASTROM, 2001—. Bd. dirs. Merce Cunningham Found., N.Y.C., Jacob's Pillow Dance Festival, Lee, Mass., The N.Y.C. Partnership; mem. vis. com. Met. Mus. Art Watson Libr. Mem. ABA, Assn. Bar City of N.Y., River Club, Women's Forum. Office: Hughes Hubbard & Reed One Battery Park Plaza New York NY 10004-1466

BEINECKE, FRANCES G., environmentalist; MS, Yale U. With Natural Resources Def. Coun. (NRDC), NYC, 1973—, exec. dir., 1998—2006, pres., 2006—. Bd. dirs. World Resources Inst.; co-founder NY League of Conservation Voters; lectr. in field. Office: Natural Resources Def Coun 40 W 20th St New York NY 10011 Office Phone: 212-727-2700. Office Fax: 212-727-1773.

BEINFELD, MARGERY COHEN, neurobiology educator; b. Washington, Oct. 21, 1945; d. Robert Abraham and Mabel (Blake) Cohen; m. Solon Beinfeld, June 1970; children: Benjamin Ezra, Molly Toba. BA, Washington U., St. Louis, 1968, PhD, 1973. Postdoctoral fellow St. Louis U., 1973-75, Washington U., St. Louis, 1975-79; staff fellow NIAMDD, NIH, Bethesda, Md., 1979-81; asst. prof. St. Louis U. Med. Sch., 1981-85, assoc. prof., 1985-88, prof., 1988-95, Tufts U. Sch. Medicine, 1995—. Contbr. chpts. to books, articles to profl. jours, rschr. in field. NIH grantee, 1976-79, 81—. Recipient Am. Inst. Chemists award, 1989, Robert J. Boucek, M.D. Research Award, 1997. Democrat. Jewish. Avocations: gardening, skiing, hiking, bicycling. Office: Tufts U Sch Med 136 Harrison Ave Boston MA 02111-1817

BEIRO FARABOW, SARA, lawyer; b. Alexandria, Va., Dec. 29, 1963; d. Alexander Aloysius and Jean Ann (O'Connell) B. BS in Fin., Va. Tech., 1986; JD, Coll. William & Mary, 1990; LLM, Georgetown U., 1997. Bar: Va. 1990, U.S. Ct. Appeals (4th cir.) 1990, U.S. Dist. Ct. (ea. dist.) Va. 1992, D.C. 1993, U.S. Dist. Ct. D.C. 1993, U.S. Ct. Appeals (fed. cir.) 1993. Atty. Seyfarth Shaw LLP, Washington, 1990—. Pro bono atty. Alexandria Battered Women's Shelter, No. Va. Legal Aid, 1991-95; law mentor Coll. William & Mary Law Sch., 1992—. Mem. ABA, Va. Bar Assn., Alexandria Bar Assn., Am. Soc. Internat. Law, Women in Internat. Law Interest Group (co-chair 1998-2002). Roman Catholic. Avocation: jogging. Office: Seyfarth Shaw LLP 815 Connecticut Ave NW Ste 500 Washington DC 20006-4042

BEISWINGER, VIRGINIA GRAVES, secondary school educator; b. Algood, Tenn., July 9, 1928; d. James Wallace and Anna Virginia (Swackhammer) Graves; m. George Lawrence Beiswinger, Dec. 24, 1950; children: Gail Anne Beiswinger Stone, George William. BS, U. Mo., 1950; MA, Washington U., St. Louis, 1954; postgrad., Immaculata (Pa.) Coll., 1982. Tchr. John Burroughs Sch., Clayton, Mo., 1950, Maplewood (Mo.)-Richmond Heights Schs., 1950-52, St. Louis Pub. Schs., 1952-59, Birmingham (Mich.) Pub. Schs., 1966-67; tchr. chemistry Conestoga Sr. High Sch., Berwyn, Pa., 1967-93; ret., 1993. Mem. adv. bd. Tredyffrin-Easttown Tchrs. Ctr., 1990-93. Republican. Episcopalian.

BEITING, SARAH LOUISE, library director; b. Highland Park, Mich., Jan. 17, 1962; d. William H. and Elsie Holmes Peck (Stepmother); m. Christopher Joseph Beiting, Oct. 25, 1986; children: Magdalen Ann, Kateri Rose, Elizabeth Marie, Anton Joseph. BA, Kalamazoo Coll., 1984; MLIS, Wayne State U., 2002. Database and info. officer Health Edn. Authority, Oxford, England, 1994—97; rare book salesperson John King Used and Rare Books, Detroit, 1998—2000; libr. dir. Ave Maria Coll., Ypsilanti, Mich., 1999—. Co-author: (directory) Health Promotion in Primary Care. a Sample from the National Database. Mem. Secular Franciscan Order, Mich., 1987—. Mem.: ALA, Fellowship of Cath. Scholars, Mich. Libr. Assn. Roman And Byzantine Catholic. Avocations: rare books, concerts, internet surfing, lectures and debate. Office: Ave Maria College 300 W Forest Ave Ypsilanti MI 48197 Office Phone: 734-337-4222. Office Fax: 734-337-4187. Personal E-mail: spbeiting@aol.com. E-mail: sbeiting@avemaria.edu.

BEITLER, KAREN ANN, biology professor, technologist; d. Eugene and Eleanor LaFavci; m. Donald L. Beitler, July 19, 1983; children: Carrieann Dulaney, Andrea Pearson, Amber, Ryan, Luis Arroyo. AS in Early Childhood Edn., Mattatuck CC, Conn., 1978; BS in gen. sci., Calumet Coll. of St. Joseph., Ind., 1983; BS in med. tech., St. Mary Sch. Med. Tech., Conn., 1989. Med. technologist Am. Soc. Clin. Psychologists, Waterbury, Conn., 1989—, Clin. Lab. Sci., Nat. Credentialing Agy., Waterbury, Conn., 1989—; sci. tchr. State of Conn., New Haven, 2003—. Home: S Meriden Rd Cheshire CT 06410

BEKAVAC, NANCY YAVOR, academic administrator, lawyer; b. Pitts., Aug. 28, 1947; d. Anthony Joseph and ELvira (Yavor) Bekavac. BA, Swarthmore Coll., 1969; JD, Yale U., 1973. Bar: Calif. 1974, U.S. Dist. Ct. (cen. dist.) Calif. 1974, U.S. Dist. Ct. (no. dist.) Calif. 1975, U.S. Ct. Appeals

(9th cir.) 1975, U.S. Dist. Ct. (so. dist.) Calif. 1976, U.S. Surpeme Ct. 1979, U.S. Ct. Appeals (8th cir.) 1981. Law clk. at large U.S. Ct. Appeals (D.C. cir.), Washington, 1973-74; assoc. Munger, Tolles & Rickershauser, L.A., 1974-79, ptnr., 1980-85; exec. dir. Thomas J. Watson Found., Providence, 1985-87, cons., 1987-88; counselor to pres. Dartmouth Coll., Hanover, N.H., 1988-90; pres. Scripps Coll., Claremont, Calif., 1990—. Adj. prof. law UCLA Law Sch., 1982—83; mem. Calif. Higher Edn. Roundtable, 1996—; trustee Am. Coun. Edn., 1994—97; bd. dir. Electro Rent Corp. Author: (books) Imagining the Real Future, 1996. Bd. mgrs. Swathmore Coll., 1984—; trustee Wenner-Gren Found. Anthrop. Rsch., 1987—94; bd. trustees Am. Coun. Edn., 1994—97; chair Assn. Ind. Colls. and Univs., 1996—97. Recipient Human Rights award, LA County Commn. Civil Rights, 1984; fellow Woodrow Wilson fellow, Thomas J. Watson fellow, 1969. Mem.: WestEd. (bd. dir.), Women's Coll. Coalition, Am. Assn. Ind. Calif. Colls. and Univs. (chair 1996), Commn. on White House Fellowships (chmn., selection com. 1993—94), Seaver Found. (bd. dir.), Sierra Club. Avocations: hiking, reading, travel. Office: Scripps Coll Office of Pres 1030 Columbia Ave Claremont CA 91711-3986 Office Phone: 909-621-8148. E-mail: president@scrippscollege.edu.*

BELAG, ANDREA SUSAN, artist; b. NYC, Nov. 21, 1951; d. Julius Belag and Harriet (Goldberg) Belag-Lange; m. James Cole Bowness, Apr. 20, 1980 (div. Aug. 1989). Student, N.Y. Studio Sch., 1971-74. Lectr. visual arts program Princeton (N.J.) U., 1995; instr. Sch. Visual Arts, 1995—, SUNY., Purchase, 1992, Md. Inst. Coll. of Art, Baltimore, 1993; resident Bellagio Study Ctr. Curator Eight Painters, Jersey City Mus., 1980, 1981 Invitational, Selected Drawings, 1983, Ralph Hilton 1946-84, 1985, Mystery Show, 1985, The Mirror in Which Two Are Seen as One, 1989, Drawn Out, Kansas City (Mo.) Art Inst., 1987.; vis. artist N.Y. Studio Sch., 1983, Bard Coll., 1984, N.J. Coun. of Arts (fellowship juror), 1985, Kansas City Art Inst., 1987, N.Y. Feminist Art Inst., 1989, RISD, Providence, 1993, Hampshire Coll., 1999, Concordia U., Montreal, Que., Can., 1999. One-person shows include Jersey City Mus., 1979, N.J. State Mus., Trenton, 1984, John Davis Gallery, Akron, 1985, N.Y.C., 1987, 88, David Beitzel Gallery, N.Y.C., 1991, (monotypes), Richard Anderson Fine Arts, N.Y.C., 1992, 93, 94, Rutgers U., New Brunswick, N.J., 1995, Littlejohn Contemporary Art, N.Y.C., 1996, Bill Maynes Gallery, N.Y.C., 1998, 2000, 02, Galerie Heinz Holtmann, Cologne, Germany, 1998, 2000, 02, Bill Maynes Gallery, N.Y.C., N.Y., 2003; numerous group shows include Westport Arts Ctr., Conn., Mead Art Mus. & U. Gallery, U. Mass., Amherst, Warren Robbins Gallery, The U. Mich. Sch. Art & Design, Ann Arbor, Pratt Inst., NY, Rhona Hoffman Gallery, Chgo., Newhouse Ctr. Contemporary Art, Snug Harbor Cultural Ctr., Staten Island, NY, Graham Modern Gallery, NY, Tibor de Nagy Gallery, NY, Newark Museum; represented in mus. collections including Newark Mus., N.J. State Mus., Moriss Mus. of Arts and Scis.; work represented in numerous publs. Fellow N.J. Coun. for Arts, 1984, Nat. Endowment for Arts, 1987, Mariposa Found. fellow Corp. of YADDO, 1994; grantee Blue Mountain Ctr., 1993; Guggenheim fellow, 1999, Bellagio Study Ctr. fellow Rockefeller Found., 2003. Studio: 137 W Broadway New York NY 10013 Personal E-mail: abelag@earthlink.net.

BELAGA, DEBRA S., lawyer; b. Fairborn, Ohio, 1954; AB magna cum laude, Brown U., 1975; JD, Stanford U., 1978. Bar: Calif. 1978, US Ct. Appeals (9th Cir.), US Dist. Ct. (No., Ea. So., and Central Districts of Calif.), US Claims Ct. Head litigation dept. O'Melveny & Myers LLP, San Francisco, mem. class action practice group, firmwide head, environmental class action practice group, mem. policy com. Faculty mem., deposition skills tng. program Practicing Law Inst., 1986, 87, 88; evaluator, early neutral evaluation program US State Dist. Ct. (No. Dist. Calif.). Sr. editor Stanford Jour. of Internat. Law, 1977—78. Mem.: Am. Arbitration Assn. (arbitrator), San Francisco Bar Assn., ABA (mem., sect. on litigation, mem., sect. tort and insurance), Phi Beta Kappa. Office: O'Melveny & Myers LLP Embarcadero Ctr West 275 Battery St San Francisco CA 94111-3305 Office Phone: 415-984-8750. Office Fax: 415-984-8701. Business E-Mail: dbelaga@omm.com.

BELANGER, LAURA HEWLETTE, environmental scientist, consultant; b. Columbia, SC, Jan. 1, 1977; d. Earl Durant and Sue Swartout Hewlette; m. Matthew David Belanger, Apr. 23, 2005. Student, Evergreen State Coll., 1996; BS in Recreation Mgmt. summa cum laude, Appalachian State U., 1998; MA in Energy and Environ. Analysis, Boston U., 2004. Program dir. Camp Ton-A-Wandah, Hendersonville, NC, 1998—2000, Adventure Treks, Inc., Hendersonville, 2000—03; environ. scientist CR Environ., Falmouth, Mass., 2004; americorps program dir. Carolina Mountain Land Conservancy, Hendersonville, 2004; project mgr. Environ. Permitting Cons., Inc., Greenville, SC, 2005—. Mem. recreation mgmt. adv. coun. Appalachian State U., Boone, NC, 1999—2001. Eric DeGrott scholar, Appalachian State U., 1998. Mem.: Soc. Wetland Scientists, Mensa (life), Alpha Chi (life). Achievements include research in determinants of OPEC production: implications for OPEC behavior. Avocations: travel, photography. Home: 662 Holiday Dr Hendersonville NC 28739 Office: Environmental Permitting Consultants In 125 W Stone Ave Greenville SC 29609 Office Phone: 864-271-3040. Personal E-mail: laurabelanger@gmail.com. Business E-Mail: laura@envirpermit.com.

BELANGER, SHARON AMLING, special education educator; b. Berkley, Calif., Apr. 28, 1961; d. Harold Warner and Martha Elizabeth Amling; m. Gregory James Belanger, June 15, 1983; children: Joshua James, Jason Alexander, Joel Gregory, Justin Michael. BA, Calif. State U., 1983; MEd, U. Minn., 2001. Cert. computer, ednl. tech. U. Minn.; lic. emotional behavioral disorders tchng. U. Minn., specific learning disabilities tchng. U. Minn., cert. multiple subjects tchr. Calif. State U. Eighth grade tchr. Fond du Lac Ojibwe Sch., Cloquet, Minn., 1994—95, mid. sch. sci. tchr., 1995—96, spl. edn. tchr., 1996—2002, spl. edn. coord., 2002—. Spl. edn. adv. coun. State Dept. Edn., Minn., 1998—2002; bd. dirs. Minn. Coun. Exceptional Children, 2000—02; adj. prof. U. Minn., 2001—02; adv. bd. exceptional children Bur. Indian Affairs, 2005—; adj. prof. Fond du Lac Tribal, C.C., 2005—06. Mem.: Coun. Exceptional Children. Office: Fond du Lac Ojibwe Sch 49 U Rd Cloquet MN 55720 Office Phone: 218-878-7551. Business E-Mail: sharonbelanger@fdlrez.com.

BELCHER, ANGELA, engineering educator; Attended, Santa Barbara City Coll., 1986—88; BA in Creative Studies, U. Calif. Santa Barbara, 1991, PhD in Chemistry, 1997. Intern in gravitational and space biology NASA Kennedy Space Ctr., 1988; undergraduate researcher, Plant Biochemistry Lab., UCLA, 1988—89, undergraduate researcher, Ctr. for Evolution and Origin of Life, 1988—89; undergraduate researcher, plant molecular biology lab U. Calif. Santa Barbara, 1989—91, summer field rsch., 1989—90, postdoctoral fellow, 1997—99; faculty, dept. chem. and biochemistry U. Tex., Austin, Tex., 1999—2002; John Chipman Career Devel. assoc. prof. materials sci. and engring. MIT, Cambridge, Mass., 2002—05, Germehausen prof. material science and engring. and biol. engring., 2005—. Spkr. in field. Author: numerous rsch. articles, including in Science and Nature; research mentioned in Forbes Mag., 2001, Technology Insider, MIT Report, & Technology Review, NY Times, 2004. Named one of PopSci Brilliant 10, Popular Science Mag.; recipient Army Young Investigator award, 1999, Du Pont Young Investigators award, 1999, Beckman Young Investigator award, 2000, IBM Faculty Partnership award, 2000, Presdl. Early Career award in Sci. and Engring., 2000, Harvard U. Wilson Prize in Chemistry, 2001, World Technology award, 2004; Alfred P. Sloan Rsch. Fellow, 2001, Harrington Faculty Fellow, 2001, MacArthur Fellowship, 2004. Office: Biological Engring 16-244 MIT 77 Mass Ave Cambridge MA 02139-4307 Office Phone: 617-252-1163. Business E-Mail: belcher@mit.edu.*

BELCHER, LA JEUNE, automotive executive; b. Chgo., Nov. 16, 1960; d. Lewis Albert and Dorthy (Brandon) B. BA, Northwestern U., 1982; postgrad., Am. Inst. of Banking, 1983-84; cert. paralegal, Roosevelt U., 1998; MS in Mgmt. and Orgnl. Behavior, Benedictine U., 2005. Notary pub.; securities lic.; ins. lic., Ill. Securities processor Am. Nat. Bank, Chgo., 1983, divisional asst., 1983-84; mgmt. trainee Toyota Motor Distbrs., Carol Stream, Ill., 1984-85, dist. parts mgr., 1985-90, sr. customer rels. adminstr., 1990-99; fin. rep. Waddell and Reed, 1992; from wholesale specialist, parts cons. to retail ops. cons. Toyota Motor Distbr., Aurora, Ill., 1998—2001, signature process mgr., 2002—04, signature ops. mgr., 2004. Rep. to Japan-U.S. Toyota Dealer Meeting, Tokyo, 1985; owner Crystal Clear Concepts. Author: (booklet) The Cutting Edge: 127 Tips to Improve Your Professional Image. Mem. alumni admissions coun. Northwestern U., Evanston, Ill.; bd. dirs. Boys and Girls Club; comty. docent Art Inst. Chgo. Mem. NAFE, NAACP, Northwestern Club Chgo., Toastmasters (edn. v.p. 1988, 94, 95, advt. v.p. 1989, pres. 1990-93), Delta Sigma Theta. Office: Toyota Motor Distbrs 2350 Sequoia Dr Aurora IL 60506-6211 Office Phone: 630-907-6450.

BELCHER, LISA ROOP, social studies educator; d. David Bryant Roop and Sheila Ann Beasley; m. Stephen Ray Belcher, July 26, 2003. BA in Social Scis., Gardner-Webb U., Boiling Springs, NC, 1999. Tchr. social scis. Patrick County High Sch., Stuart, Va., 1999—. Mem.: Delta Kappa Gamma. Office: Patrick County High School 215 Cougar Lane Stuart VA 24171 Office Phone: 276-694-7137. Office Fax: 276-694-6997. E-mail: hs-soc-4@patrickcounty.org.

BELCK, NANCY GARRISON, dean, educator; b. Montgomery, Ala., Aug. 1, 1943; d. Lester Moffett and Stella Mae (Whaley) Garrison; m. Jack Belck, May 27, 1976; 1 child, Scott Brian. BS, La. Tech. U., 1964; MS, U. Tenn., 1965; PhD, Mich. State U., 1972. Cert. tchr., La. State textile specialist coop. extension svc. U. Ga., Athens, 1965-67, chair, dir. Tucson, 1976-79; asst. prof./instr. Mich. State U., East Lansing, 1967-73; family econ. researcher USDA Agrl. Res. Svcs., Hyatsville, Md., 1973-75, nat. extension evaluation coord. Washington, 1978-79; dean, prof. Coll. Human Ecology U. Tenn., Knoxville, 1979-87; dean, prof. Coll. Edn. Cen. Mich. U., Mt. Pleasant, 1987—91, interim provost, v.p. acad. affairs, 1988-89; provost, vice chancellor academic affairs La. State U., 1991—93; chancellor So. Ill. U., Edwardsville, 1994—97, U. Neb., Omaha, 1997—. Author: Development of Egyptian Universities Linkages, 1985, Mid-Career Administrators, 1986, Textiles for Consumers, 1990. Mem. exec. com. Mich. Milescular Inst., Midland, strategic planning team Pub. Schs., Mt. Pleasant, 1989—; chair Women's Networking Group, Mt. Pleasant, 1990—. Mem. Am. Home Econs. Assn., Am. Assn. for Higher Edn., Am. Assn. for Colls. Tchr. Edn., Am. Home Econs. Assn., Rotary, Sigma Iota Epsilon, Omicron Nu, Phi Delta, Kappa, Omicron Delta Kappa, Phi Kappa Phi. Avocations: gardening, walking, travel, international food tasting. Office: U of Nebraska at Omaha Office of the Chancellor Omaha NE 68182

BELFORD, ROZ, real estate broker; b. Romania; came to U.S., 1950; d. Aaron and Marsha (Sax) Roth; m. Melvin Belford, Sept. 14, 1951 (dec. Nov. 1997); 1 child, Marsha. Baccalaureate, Heidelberg U., Germany, 1949; student, Sorbonne U., Paris, 1949-50. Pvt. practice real estate and mortgage broker, Singer Island, Fla., 1984—. Mem. AAUW, Internat. Real Estate Inst., Am. Hotel and Motel Assn., Am. Technion Soc. (v.p. Palm Beach chpt.), Women's Am. ORT (v.p. chpt.). Jewish.

BEL GEDDES, JOAN, writer; b. L.A. d. Norman and Helen (Sneider) Bel G.; m. Barry Ulanov, Dec. 16, 1939 (div. 1968); children: Anne, Nicholas, Katherine. BA, Barnard Coll. Columbia U., 1937. Researcher and theatrical asst. to Norman Bel Geddes, Inc., N.Y.C., 1937-41; publicity dir. Compton Advt., Inc., N.Y.C., 1942, new program mgr., 1943-47; pub. info. officer UNICEF, N.Y.C., 1970-76, chief editl. and publs. svcs., 1976-79, cons. devel. edn., promoter Universal Children's Day (over 100 countries), 1979-85, editor Almanac World's Children, 1985-90; editor Pate Inst. Bull., 1988-94. Tchr. drama Birch Wathen Sch., N.Y.C., 1950; mem. faculty Inst. Man and Sci., Rensellaerville, N.Y., 1969. Interviewer-hostess: weekly radio program Religion and the Arts, NBC, 1968; author: Small World: A History of Baby Care from the Stone Age to the Spock Age, 1964, How to Parent Alone: A Guide for Single Parents, 1974, To Barbara With Love--Prayers and Reflections by a Believer for a Skeptic (Catholic Press Assn. award 1974), Are You Listening, God?, 1994, Childhood and Children, a Compendium of Customs, Superstitions, Theories, Profiles, and Facts, 1998, Children Praying, Why and How to Pray with Your Children, 1999, (with others) Art, Obscenity and Your Children, 1969, American Catholics and Vietnam, 1970, The Future of the Family, 1971, Holiness and Mental Health, 1972, The Children's Rights Movement, 1977, And You, Who Do You Say I Am?, 1981; translator: (with Barry Ulanov) Last Essays of Georges Bernanos, 1955; editor: Magic Motorways (Norman B. Geddes), 1940, Earth: Our Crowded Spaceship (Isaac Asimov), 1974; editor in chief: My Baby mag, 1954-56, Congratulations mag, 1954-56. Rep. Balkan-Ji-Bar Internat. Orgn. for Child and Youth Welfare of the World, UN. Mem. Authors League Am., Assn. Former Internat. Civil Servants, The Coffee House, Teilard de Chardin Assn., Mcpl. Arts Soc. N.Y., Internat. Inst. Rural Reconstrn. (mem. internat. coun.), Thomas More Soc. (pres. 1966), Barnard Coll. Alumnae Assn. (class v.p. 1972-76, 92—, pres. 1976-82), N.Y. City Mission Soc., Guilford Friends of Music, Pate Inst. Human Survival (bd. dirs. 1989-95, editor bi-monthly bull. 1990-93), The Charles A. and Anne Morrow Lindbergh Fund, Citizens Against Govt. Waste. Roman Catholic.

BELGIOVENE, MELANIE C., science educator; b. NYC, Nov. 27, 1977; d. Ronald Kenneth Kram and Noel Ann Krom; m. Michael Belgiovene, July 20, 2003. BS in Chemistry, SUNY, Oneonta, 1999; MS in Edn., NY Inst. Tech., Old Westbury, 2005. Chemist Bell Flavors & Fragrances, Middletown, NY, 1999—2000; tchr. sci. Monticello Sch., 2000—01, Valley Ctrl. Sch., Montgomery, 2001—. Avocations: walking, reading, gardening. Office: Valley Ctrl Sch Dist 1189 Rte 17K Montgomery NY 12549

BELICH, KAY S., music educator; d. Robert W. and Lorna O. Schoenfeld; m. Sam M. Belich, Aug. 16, 1975; children: Aaron F., Eva A. MusB, U. Wis., Madison, 1974; MusM, The Juilliard Sch., N.Y.C., 1977. Lic. tchr. Wis., 1991. Singer NYC Opera Co., 1977—90; elem. sch. music tchr. Kenosha Unified Pub. Sch. Dist., Wis., 1991—96, West Allis/West Milw. Pub. Sch. Dist., 1996—; studio vocal and instrumental tchr. freelance, N.Y. and Milw., 1968—, opera and concert singer N.Y. and Milw., 1972—; u. instr. Cardinal Stritch U., Milw., 1999—. Apprentice singer Ctrl. City Opera Co., Colo., 1975; union del. NYC Opera Touring Co., 1990; cooperating tchr. for student tchr. Carthage Coll., Kenosha, Wis., 1993—94; mentor West Allis/West Milw. Pub. Sch. Dist., 2001—02; cooperating tchr. for student tchr. Cardinal Stritch U., Milw., 2002—03. Singer performances include Cami Hall recital. Ch. coun. mem. Grace and St. Paul's Luth. Ch., NYC, 1980—81; various positions Mt. Hope Luth. Ch., West Allis, Wis., 1991—. Recipient First Pl. award, Wis. Fedn. of Music Clubs, 1974; U. Wis. scholar, 1970—74, regional finalist, Met. Opera, 1978. Mem.: Milw. Civic Music Assn., Wis. Sch. Music Assn., Music Educators' Nat. Conf., Take Off Pounds Sensibly (treas. 1998—). Lutheran. Achievements include Solo Debuts: with New York City Opera, 1982; with Music Under the Stars, 1991; with Skylight Opera Theatre, 1993; with Racine Symphony, 1996; with Waukesha Symphony, 1997. Avocation: organic gardening. Home: 2141 South 105 St West Allis WI 53227-1211 Office: Hoover School 12705 West Euclid Ave New Berlin WI 53151-4611 also: Cardinal Stritch Univ 6801 North Yates Rd Milwaukee WI 53217-3985

BELINSKY, ILENE BETH, lawyer; b. Boston, Jan. 30, 1956; d. Harry Lewis and Ann Natalie (Rubin) B. B.A., Simmons Coll., 1977; J.D. cum laude, New Eng. Sch. Law, Boston, 1980. Bar: Mass. 1980, U.S. Dist. Ct. Mass. 1981, U.S. Ct. Appeals (1st cir.) 1981, U.S. Supreme Ct. 1984. Reservitz, Steinberg & Belinsky P.C., Brockton, Mass., 1980-85; ptnr., 1985—; bd. dirs. Southeastern Mass. Legal Assistance Corp., New Bedford, 1982-86. Bd. dirs. Brockton unit Am. Cancer Soc., 1983, 84. Mem. Mass. Bar Assn. (dir. young lawyers div. 1984-86), Mass. Women's Bar Assn., ABA, Plymouth County Bar Assn., Assn. Trial Lawyers Am., Mass. Acad. Trial Lawyers. Republican. Jewish. Office: 528 Pleasant St Brockton MA 02301-2515

BELISSARY, KAREN, interior designer; b. Columbia, S.C., May 20, 1959; d. James Charles and Linda Gail (Bouknight) B. BFA in Design, N.Y. Sch. Interior Design, 1989; grad., Nat. Ctr. Paralegal Studies, Atlanta, 1991; postgrad. in bus. internat. studies, LaSalle U. Pvt. practice interior design, Florence, S.C., 1989—; owner New Generations Adult Day Ctr., New Generations Home Care. Dir. Pee Dee region Am. Intercultural Exch., Florence, 1989—. Sec. Soc. for Autistic Children, Florence, 1983; v.p. Florence County Dem. Com., 1985; group leader Friends Florence Mus., 1986; bd. dirs. Heart Fund, Florence, 1987, Internat. Women's Club Florence, 1988-89, Florence Area Arts Coun., 1986-87; mem. Friends of Libr., Florence; mem. Florence County Dem. Party; bd. dirs. Symphony Guild, Sr.Citizens Ctr., Alzheimer's Assn. Mental Health. Named Outstanding Mem., Soc. for Autistic Children, 1983; grantee Young Adult League, 1987. Mem. NOW, LWVAm. Soc. Interior Designers, Amnesty Internat., Florence (S.C.) Bus. Women Network, Greenpeace, The Door (pres.), Area Arts Coun. (hon.), Quinby Garden Club (sec., pres. Tea and Topic), Colonial Heights Garden Club Greek Orthodox. Avocations: tennis, swimming, bicycling, writing, reading. Home: 3719 Gentry Dr Florence SC 29501-7717 Office: Am Intercultural Exch 1521 S Irby St Florence SC 29505 Office Phone: 843-629-0103.

BELK, JOAN PARDUE, language and literature educator; b. Lancaster, SC, Oct. 4, 1933; d. William Hazel and Alfleda Steele Pardue; m. Joe Harvey Belk, Sr.; children: Joe Harvey Jr., Jennifer Elizabeth. Degree, Winthrop U., 1954; BA summa cum laude, U. Houston, 1957. Cert. tchr. Tex. Asst. to dir. librs. U. Houston, Houston, 1957—61; tchr. English Galena Park H.S., Galena Park, Tex., 1961—62; tchr. English (advanced placement) Meml. H.S., Houston, 1962—96; instr. English Houston C.C., 1996—2002; copy editor Kaplan Profl. Schs., Houston, 2006—. Musician, piano accompanist, piano tchr. Editor articles for profl. pubs. Mem. Happy Hide-a-Way Civic Assn., Crosby, 1972—, Royal Spring Civic Assn, Houston, 1989—, newsletter editor, 2002—; mem. Cancer Fighters Houston, Inc., 1998—, bd. dirs., 2003—, 2006—, Woman's Club Houston, 2004—, v.p. comm., 2006—; chmn. evaluations com. Expanding Your Horizons (conf. jr. HS girls), Houston, 1997—2003; active Chancel Choir; accompanist children's choir, elder Spring Branch Presbyn. Ch., Houston. Recipient Excellence in Tchg. award, So. Meth. U., 1992, Mrs. James P. Houstoun Found. award, 1957, Phi Mu Alumnae award, 1957; Friedheim Found. scholar, Winthrop U., 1954. Mem.: AAUW (com. chair 1997—2003), NEA, Nat. Coun. Tchrs. English, Spring Br. Edn. Assn., Tex. State Tchrs. Assn., Spring Branch Ind. Sch. Dist. Minority Lit. Reading and Discussion Group (discussion leader 1990—96), U. Houston Reading and Discussion Group (sec. 1990—), Tex. Coun. Tchrs. English, Spring Br. Coun. Tchrs. English, Outstanding Lit. Book Club, Les Belles Lettres Club (pres. 1967—68), Shadow Oaks Garden Club (v.p. 1958—60, pres. 1960—61), En Amie Book Rev. Club, Kappa Delta Pi (award 1957), Phi Kappa Phi (treas. 1958—60, award 1957), Delta Kappa Gamma (rsch. com. chair 1998—2002, yearbook com. chair 2004—05). Presbyterian. Avocations: piano, bridge, travel, crocheting. Home: 2014 Southwick Dr Houston TX 77080 Personal E-mail: joebelksr@aol.com.

BELKNAP, JODI PARRY, graphics designer, writer, small business owner; b. New Canaan, Conn., June 4, 1939; d. Corliss Lloyd and Joan (Pike) Parry; m. William Belknap III, Feb. 20, 1970 (div. Nov. 1982). AB in English and Writing, Barnard Coll., 1962; MA in Drama and Theater, U. Hawaii at Manoa, Honolulu, 1988. Cert. elem. tchr. Calif. Tchr. grade 6 Ruth Fyfe Sch., Las Vegas, Nev., 1963-64; tchr. grades. 2,3 Schilling Sch., Hayward, Calif., 1964-69; master tchr. U. Calif., Hayward, 1967-69; editor Island Heritage Ltd., Honolulu, 1970-73; Pacific bur. chief OAG Publs. (Dun and Bradstreet), Honolulu, 1972-82; freelance writer, columnist various mags. and publs., 1976-88; owner Belknap Pub. and Design, Honolulu, 1987—. Author: Majesty, The Exceptional Trees of Hawaii, 1982, Kaanapali, 1981, Halekulani, 1982, (children's book) Felisa and the Magic Tikling Bird, 1973; book prod., publ.: How the B-52 Cockroach Learned to Fly, 1995, Hula Is Life, 1998, Ko Olina, Place of Joy, 2002, Washington Place, A First Lady's Story, 2004; prin. design projects for Sheraton Hotels in Hawaii, 1988—, others; prodr., pub. Paper Dying for Collage and Crafts, 2004, Dancing and Romancing with Pele, 2005, others. Bd. dirs. Hawaii Vocal Arts Ensemble. Recipient Gold award Hospitality Mktg. Assn. Internat., 1995, award Hawaii chpt. Pub. Rels. Soc. Am., 1993, 94, Ilima award of excellence Internat. Assn. Bus. Communicators, 1989, 90. Mem. Soc. Children's Book Writers, Nat. League Am. Pen Women. Avocations: swimming, hiking, family trips. Address: Belknap Pub PO Box 22387 Honolulu HI 96823-2387 Personal E-mail: jodibelknap@hawaii.rr.com.

BELKOV, MEREDITH ANN, landmark administrator; b. Chgo., Sept. 26, 1939; d. Louis and Sylvia (Charak) B. Student, U. Md. Recreation dir. Dept. Pks. and Recreation, Washington, 1960-69; outdoor recreation specialist Nat. Pk. Svc., Washington, 1971-73; chief disvn. recreation Golden Gate Nat. Recreation Area, San Francisco, 1973-75; chief interpretation and visitor svcs. Nat. Visitor Ctr., Washington, 1975-78, Dept. Interior Mgmt., Washington, 1978-79; supt. Chickamauga (Ga.) and Chattanooga (Tenn.) Nat. Mil. Park, 1979-87, Jean Lafitte Nat. Hist. Pk. and Preserve, New Orleans, 1987-90, Statue of Liberty, Ellis Island, N.Y.C., 1990—. Bd. dirs. N.Y. Conv. and Visitors Bur., Greater New Orleans Tourist and Conv. Commn., Inc., New Orleans Jazz and Heritage Found. V.p. Chattanooga Symphony and Opera, U. Tenn. Roundtable, Chattanooga Audubon Soc. Fellow NCCJ; recipient Freedom Found. award. Mem. Nat. Pk. and Recreation Assn., Hist. Soc., Mus. Coun. N.Y. Jewish.

BELL, ANGELA, music educator; b. St. Louis, Feb. 1, 1932; d. John Simonds Bell, Jr. and Florence Sippy Bell. MusB, Oberlin Conservatory, Ohio, 1954; MusM, American Conservatory, 1972; studied with Cecile de Horvath, Chgo., 1954—62; student, Great Russian Sch. Piano Playing. Pvt. piano tchr., Chgo., 1955—87, St. Louis, 1987—2006. Mem.: Mo. State Music Tchrs. Assn. Home: 4483 Lindell Blvd Saint Louis MO 63108 Office Phone: 314-533-0725.

BELL, ANNE MARIE, music educator; d. David and Anne Jenkins; m. Eric D Bell; children: Ryan, Dylan. B in Gen. Studies, U. New Orleans, 1996; MMus, Norfolk State U., Va., 1998; postgrad., Shenandoah U., Winchester, Va., 2004. Cert. tchr. Va., 2002. Proofreader and copyist, Portsmouth, Va., 1996—2004; H.S. orch. dir. and elem. strings tchr. Va. Beach City Pub. Sch. Sys., 1999—2006; orch. dir. Blair Mid. Sch., Norfolk, Va., 2006—. Sr. regional orch. chair Southeastern Region, Va. Beach, 2003; guest condr. Va. Beach All City Area Orch., 2005. Web designer and maintainer (website) Anne Bell's Clarinet Website Index: ABC Index, www.anne-bell.woodwind.org (Informative Music Site Award, 1999). Parent rep. Port Norfolk Sch. Improvement Com., Portsmouth, Va., 2001—02. ML2 USN, 1987—93, USS McKee. Decorated Navy Achievement medal US Navy, SW Asia Svc. medal with 2 stars and Nat. Def. Svc. Medal; recipient I make a difference award, Bayside H.S. and Old Donation Ctr. Elem., 2002, 2004; Bldg. Futures grantee, Va. Beach Edn. Assn., 2002. Mem.: Am. Fedn. of Musicians, The Nat. Assn. for Music Edn., Golden Key (life). D-Liberal. Avocations: early music, crafts, reading, do it yourself projects. Personal E-mail: bell@whro.net.

BELL, CARRIE ANN, science educator, consultant; d. Ollie Lee Bell and Alberta Common Bell Williams. BS in Biology, Delta State U., Miss., 1979, BS in Edn., 1982, MS in Natural Sci., 1984, Edn. Specialist, 1991. Nat. bd. cert. tchr. Miss. Tchr. jr. high/H.S., Benoit Sch. Dist., Miss., 1984—85; tchr. chemistry/advanced biology Rosedale H.S., Miss., 1985—91; tchr. 7th grade sci. Solomon Jr. H.S., Greenville, Miss., 1991—92; tchr. chemistry Cleve. H.S., Miss., 1992—2003; tchr. 6th grade sci. West Bolivar Mid. Sch., Rosedale, Miss., 2003—. Chair dept. sci. West Bolivar MId. Sch., Rosedale, Miss. Key leader Building a Presence for Sci., Miss.; mentor World Class Tchg. Program, Delta State, Cleve., Miss., 2001—03; adopt-a-sch. rep. Baxter/Cleve. H.S., Miss., 1999—2003. Finalist Presdl. award for excellence in math and sci., State of Miss., 2003; recipient Star Tchr. award, Rosedale H.S., 1990, Above and Beyond Tchr. of Yr. award, Cleve. H.S., 1999, Tchr. of Yr. award, Am. Chemistry Soc., 2000. Mem.: NSTA, ASCD, Delta Sci.

Tchrs.' Assn., Miss. Profl. Educator's Assn., Miss. Sci. Tchrs. Assn. (bd. dirs. 1998—, Outstanding H.S. Tchr. of Yr. 2003). Democrat. Baptist. Avocations: writing, gardening. Home: PO Box 51 625 Magnolia Ave Pace MS 38764-0051 Office: West Bolivar Sch Dist PO Box 189 Hwy 1 S Rosedale MS 38769 Office Phone: 662-759-3743. Office Fax: 662-759-3743.

BELL, CHRISTINE MARIE, secondary school educator; b. Bluefield, W.Va., Nov. 5, 1961; d. Robert Warren and Therese (Wolinski) Stroh; m. Harlin Lindel Bell, Aug. 3, 1991; children: Shelby Katherine. BA, Mary Washington Coll., Fredericksburg, Va., 1983; MEd, U. Va., 1986. Cert. history and social studies tchr., Va. Adminstrv. asst. U. Va. Hosp., Charlottesville, 1984-85; tchr., counselor Oakland (Va.) Residential Sch., 1986-87; tchr. social studies Hopewell (Va.) High Sch., 1987—, coord. computers for edn. program, 1991-93. (workshops) Va. Gov. Best Practice Ctr., 2001; (documentaries) Dept. of Edn. Hour, 2001. Advisor model exec. br. YMCA, Richmond, Va., 1991-92, advisor model gen. assembly, 1991—. Recipient YMCA service to youth award, YMCA, 1996, Resolution of Appreciation, Va. Dept. of Edn. Sch. Bd., 2001, Tchr. of the Yr., Hopewell City Sch., 2001. Mem. APA (affiliate), ASCD, Nat. Coun. for Social Studies, Va. Geog. Soc., New Va. Dept. of Edn. Database ofexemplary educators, Avocations: politics, reading, travel, swimming, jogging. Home: 96 Sand Hill Rd Williamsburg VA 23188-6600 Office: Lafayette High Sch Williamsburg VA 23188

BELL, CLARE LOUISE, writer, engineer; b. Hitchin, Hertfordshire, U.K., June 19, 1952; came to U.S., 1957; d. Ronald Lancelot Bell and Edna Kathleen (Wheldon) Steward. BA, U. Calif., Santa Cruz, 1975; postgrad., U. Calif., Davis, 1978; MSME, Stanford U., 1983. Field asst. U.S. Geol. Survey, Menlo Park, Calif., 1976-78; test equipment engr. IBM, San Jose, Calif., 1978-89; freelance writer San Jose, 1989—. Author: Ratha's Creature, 1983 (co-recipient Children's Choice award Internat. Reading Assn. 1983, Best Book for Young People award ALA 1983), Clan Ground, 1984 (ALA Best Book for Young People 1984), Tomorrow's Sphinx, 1986, People of the Sky, 1989, Ratha and Thistle-chaser, 1990 (ALA Best Book for Young People award 1990), Jaguar Princess, 1993; (with M. Coleman Easton) Daughter of the Reef, 1992, Sister of the Sun, 1993; also short stories. Mem. San Jose Peace Ctr., 1989—, Green Party, 1990—; supporter Stas. KQED, KTEH, Pacifica Radio Sta. KPFA. Mem. ACLU, Nat. Writers Union, Sci. Fiction Writers Am., Electric Vehicle Assn. Avocations: electric cars, music, hiking, bicycling, swimming. Home and Office: 544 Summit Dr Santa Cruz CA 95060-9666

BELL, CONSTANCE CONKLIN, child care association administrator; b. Columbus, Ohio, June 2, 1934; d. John Brevoort and Josephine (Suttles) Conklin; m. Robert Kilborne Hudnut, Sept. 12, 1957 (div. June 1975); children: Heidi A., Robert K. Jr., Heather E., Matthew C.; m. Gerald Duane Bell, June 25, 1977. BA, Ohio Wesleyan U., 1956; postgrad., Union Theol. Sem., 1956-57. Tchr. Cen. Presbyn. Ch. Nursery Sch., N.Y.C., 1956-59; ctr. coordinator Greater Mpls. Day Care Assn., 1973—, asst. dir., 1977, assoc. dir., 1982, exec. dir., 1991—95. Minn. Licensing Com., 1985—, Minn. Child Care LIcensing Com., 1986-87. Author: How to Start A Child Care Center, 1977, rev. edit., 1983, Sick Child Care, A Problem for Working Parents and Employers, 1983; (with others) Business and Childcare Handbook, 1981. Mem. social ministries com. Greater Mpls. Coun. of Chs., 1983-88, bd. dirs., 1988-92, strategic planning comm. 1993—, Mpls. Community Bus. Employment Alliance, 1984-85, Project Self-Sufficiency, Mpls., 1984—; mem. priorities com. United Way Mpls. Area, 1984-88, mem. mgmt. United Way Com. Success by Six, 1988—2002; elder St. Luke's Presbyn. Ch., 1978-81. Recipient special recognition award, City of Minn., 1995, Ruth Hathaway Jewson Disting. Service to families award, Coun. of family relations, 1995, Resolution of Commedation, Hennepin County commr., 1995. Mem. Minn. Assn. for Edn. of Young Children (area award 1987), Mn assn. for educ of young children (pres. 1990-93), Minn. Children's Lobby, Child Care Works Steering Com., Parents in the Workplace (co-dir. 1983—), Kappa Alpha Theta (pres. Delaware, Ohio chpt. 1955-56); bd. congregations concerned for children, 1990—. Democrat. Office: Greater Mpls Day Care Assn 1628 Elliot Ave Minneapolis MN 55404-1620

BELL, DAWN MARIE, pharmacist, educator; b. Morgan City, La., Aug. 1, 1966; d. Joe Franklin Bell and Diane Marie White; m. Riley Anderson Vann, May 28, 1995. D Pharmacy, U. Fla., 1992. Cert. pharmacotherapy specialist. Resident U. Ill., Chgo., 1992-93; fellow in cardiovascular medicine U. Fla., Gainesville, 1993-95; asst. prof. clin. pharmacy W.Va. U., Morgantown, 1995—. Mem. adv. bd. Cor/Key Pharms.; spkr. in field. Mem. edtl. adv. bd. Medscape Pharmacotherapy; contbr. articles to profl. jours., chpt. to book. Chair med. product safety workgroup W.Va. Health People 2010, 1999—; co-advisor Med. Explorer Post, Boy Scouts Am., 1997-99/—. Mem. Am. Coll. Clin. Pharmacy (chair clin. practice affairs com. 1999-2001—, chair-eect. women's health practice and rsch. network 1998-99, chair com. on added qualifications in cardiology 1998-99, Genentech cardiovasc.r fellow 1994-95), PPine Country Club, Phi Lambda Sigma. Avocation: triathlons. Office: W Va U PO Box 9520 Morgantown WV 26506-9520 E-mail: dbell@hsc.wvu.edu.

BELL, DELORIS WILEY, physician; b. Solomon, Kans., Sept. 30, 1942; d. Harry A. and Mildren H. (Watt) Wiley; children: Leslie, John. BA, Kans. Wesleyan U., 1964; MD, U. Kans., 1968. Diplomate Am. Bd. Ophthalmology. Intern St. Luke's Hosp., Kansas City, Mo., 1968-69; resident U. Kans. Med. Ctr., Kansas City, 1969-72; practice medicine specializing in ophthalmology Overland Park, Kans., 1973—. Mem. AMA, Kans. Med. Soc. (pres. sect. ophthalmology 1985-86, spkr. house 1994-97), Am. Acad. Ophthalmology (councillor 1988-93, chmn. state govtl. affairs 1993-97, bd. trustees 2000-03), Kans. Soc. Ophthalmology (pres. 1985-86), Kansas City Soc. Ophthalmology and Otolaryngology (sec. 1984-86, pres.-elect 1988, pres. 1989). Avocations: photography, travel. Office: 7000 W 121st St Ste 100 Shawnee Mission KS 66209-2010 Office Phone: 913-498-2015. Personal E-mail: cd2cdb@gmail.com.

BELL, ELVA GLENN, retired secondary school educator, retired counseling administrator, interpreter; b. Phila., Sept. 3, 1922; d. Arthur Edward Glenn, Ruth Ann Marie Demby Glenn; m. Howard Wesley Bell, Sr.; children: Howard Bell, Jr., Linda Bell-Powell. BS in Edn., Cheyney State Coll., 1945; MS in Edn., Temple U., 1970. Case worker Dept. Pub. Assistance, Phila., 1945—51; tchr., guidance counselor Phila. Sch. Dist., 1956—71; guidance counselor Abington (Pa.) Sch. Dist., Pa., 1971—82; interpreter at Clivden - Hist. Mansion Nat. Trust Property, Germantown, Pa., 1987—. Sch./cmty. rep. human rels. adv. coun. Abington Sch. Dist., 1974—. Mem., chairperson ways and means com. United Neighbors, Willow Grove, 1975—; mem. Abington Coalition of Civics - Abington Township, 1996—; bd. mem., Unity Day chairperson, life mem. NAACP - Willow Grove, 1939—; Congl. sr. intern CLOSE-UP, Washington, 1997—. Recipient Cmty. Svc. and Leadership award, Citizens for Progress, 1976, Trailblazer award, Willow Grove NAACP, 1985, Cmty. Svc. and Leadership award, Optimist Club Lower Montgomery County, 1986, Ho. of Reps. citation, Pa., 1987, 1999, Martin Luther King award, Abington Twp., 1988, Svc. award, Willow Grove NAACP, 2001, Cmty. Svc. award, Pa. Human Rels. Commn., Montgomery County Adv. Coun., 2005. Mem.: AAUW, Black Women's Ednl. Alliance (treas., fin. sec. 1980—86, newsletter editor, Svc. award 1986, Cmty. Svc. and Leadership award 1986), Zeta Phi Beta Sorority - Beta Delta Zeta Chpt. (vol.). Lutheran. Avocations: travel, church activities, community activist.

BELL, FELICIA RENEE, elementary school educator; b. Augusta, Ga., June 7, 1978; d. Franklin Roosevelt and Byrdyne Wood Bell. BS, Albany State U., 2000; MEd, Ga. State U., 2005. Legal asst. UPS Capital, Atlanta; tchr. Atlanta Pub. Schs., chmn. sci. dept., grade level chmn. Harper Archer Mid. Sch. Mem.: Nat. Sci. Tchr. Assn., Kappa Delta Pi. Avocations: travel, reading, sewing.

BELL, FRANCES LOUISE, medical technologist; b. Milton, Pa., Apr. 28, 1926; d. George Earl and Kathryn Robbins (Fairchild) Reichard; m. Edwin Lewis Bell II, Dec. 27, 1950; children: Ernest Michael, Stephen Thomas, Eric Leslie BS Biology cum laude, Bucknell U., Lewisburg, Pa., 1948; med. technologist, Geisinger Meml. Hosp., 1949. Registered med. technologist. Med. technologist Burlington County Hosp., Mt. Holly, NJ, 1948—50, Robert Packer Hosp., Sayre, Pa., 1950, Carle Hosp./Clinic, Urbana, Ill., 1951—52, St. Joseph Hosp., Reading, Pa., 1972—83. Vol. Crime Watch, City Hall, Reading, 1985-90, Am. Heart Assn., Reading, 1956-2000, March of Dimes, Reading, 1956-72, Am. Cancer Soc., Reading, 1956-71, Multiple Sclerosis, Reading, 1956-72, Reading Musical Found., 1985-90, Hist. Soc. Berks County; corr. sec. women's aux., 1986-90; fin. sec. aux. Albright Coll., 1988-95; hospitality co-chmn. women's com. Reading Symphony Orch., 1989-90, editor yearbook women's com., 1992-96; editor yearbook Reading Symphony Orch. League, 1996-2003; chmn. hospitality Reading-Berks Pub. Librs., 1988-91; mem. Friends Reading Mus., Berks County Conservancy Mem. AAUW (hon. life, assoc. editor bull. 1961-63, cultural interests rep. 1967-68), Woman's Club Reading (treas. 1986-88, fin. sec. 1991-2004), United Meth. Women, World Affairs Coun. Berks County, Libr. Soc. Albright Coll., Phi Beta Kappa Republican. Methodist. Avocations: music, photography, art. Home: 1454 Oak Ln Reading PA 19604-1865

BELL, GENEVIEVE, anthropologist; Grad., Bryn Mawr Coll., Pa.; PhD in Anthropology, Stanford U. Tchr., anthropology, Native Am. Studies Stanford U.; anthropologist, people and practices rsch. group Intel, Santa Clara, Calif., 1998—. Contbr. articles to profl. jours. Mem.: Nat. Assn. for the Practice of Anthropology. Office: Intel 2200 Mission College Blvd Santa Clara CA 95052 Office Phone: 503-264-7510. Office Fax: 503-264-2225.*

BELL, GLORIA JEAN, academic administrator, literature educator, dean; b. Greensboro, N.C., Oct. 10, 1939; d. John T. and Mary Ellen (Gray) Bell. BA, So. Wesleyan U., 1961; MA, U. N.C., 1963; PhD, U. Colo., 1982. English tchr. N.W. Guilford HS, Greensboro, 1962-63; tchr. Partlow State Sch., Tuscaloosa, Ala., 1963-64; English and reading tchr. Tuscaloosa HS, 1964-65; English instr. U. Ala., Birmingham, 1965-70; asst. prof. English Presbyn. Coll., Clinton, SC, 1974-77; faculty mem. So. Wesleyan U., Central, SC, 1977—, English prof., 1981—, chair divsn. humanities, 1981-93, acad. v.p., dean, 1993—. Mem. transfer adv. bd. Tri-County Coll., Pendleton, SC, 1993—98, chair, 1996—97. Contbr. articles to profl. jours. Ad hoc com. mem. Wesleyan Ch., 1997—; S.E. regional steering com. Conf. Christianity and Lit., 1985—88, 1994—96; mem. Clemson Area Leadership Program, 1995; judge Lt. Gov.'s Award for Composition, Pickens County, 1981. Recipient Govs. Disting. prof., Susan B. McWhorter Outstanding Woman Profl., 1998. Fellow: Coun. Christian Colls. & Univs. (exec. leadership inst.); mem.: S.C. Women Higher Edn. (conf. steering com. 1983—84, 1996—97), Phi Delta Kappa. Avocations: travel, needlepoint, gardening, reading. Office: Southern Wesleyan U PO Box 1020 907 Wesleyan Dr Central SC 29630-9748

BELL, HELEN LAVIN, artist; b. Allentown, Pa. d. Thomas Joseph and Anna Helen Lavin; m. Paul Edward Bell, June 10, 1950; children: Celine Butler, Sharon Neiman, Paul Jr., Christine Schlacter. Student, Western Md. Coll., 1945-47, Md. Inst. Art, 1947-48, Telfair Acad. Arts, 1958-59, U. Calif., Riverside, 1970-71, 80-81. Asst. art dir. Davison's, Atlanta, 1950—. One-woman shows include Riverside (Calif.) Art Mus., 1980, 2003-04, Rizzoli Internat., Costa Mesa, Calif., 1987, Zola Fine Art, Beverly Hills, Calif., 1990, EOS Gallery, Redlands, Calif., 2003, Mission San Juan Capistrano, Calif., 2005, Sandstone Gallery, Laguna Beach, Calif., 2005, others; group shows include City of Riverside, Calif., 1975, Riverside County Mus., Beaumont, Calif., 1976, 90, Calif. Poly. U., Pomona, 1987, Corp. Rental program L.A. County Mus. Art, 1989-95, Calif. Small Works, Santa Rosa, 1992, 93, Carte Blanche, 1996, Made in Calif., Brea, 1997, 2006, Echoes and Visions II, V, 2002, Laguna Niguel, Calif., 1998, Millard Sheets Small Works Gallery, 2001, EOS Gallery, Redlands, Calif., 2003, Riverside Art Museum, Riverside, Calif., 2003, J. Wayne Stark Gallery, Tex. A&M U. Coll. Station, 2004. Event chair Nat. Charity League, Riverside, Calif., 1979-83; trustee Riverside Art Mus., 1979-82. Merit scholar Telfair Acad. Arts and Scis., Savannah, Ga., 1958. Mem. Redlands Art Assn. (trustee 1985-87, 91-95, 2005), Art Alliance (pres. 1979-80, com. chairs 1978, 81, 82, 2000), Nat. Assn. Women Artists, Inc., Calif. Art Club (painting patron), So. Calif. Plein Air Painters Assn. Republican. Roman Catholic. Avocations: swimming, travel. Studio: 6359 Dulcet Pl Riverside CA 92506 Office Phone: 951-682-9289. Personal E-mail: sabrplt@msn.com.

BELL, JANICE LEE, finance educator; b. Laredo, Tex., Oct. 2, 1964; d. Billy R. Casas and Gloria L. (Butler) Casas; m. Doyle B. Bell, Jan. 28, 1984; children: Dee Wade, Martha Faye. BS in Edn., Northeastern State U., 1997, MEd in Sch. Adminstrn, 2005. Cert. Bus. Edn. Okla. State Dept. Edn., Vocational Edn. Okla. Dept. Career, Tech. Bus. edn., humanities tchr. Watts (Okla.) Pub. Sch., 1999—. Bus. edn. dept. chair Watts Pub. Sch., 1999—, humanities dept. chair, 2004—. Democrat-Npl. Bapt. Office: Watts Public Sch Rt 2 Box 1 Watts OK 74964 Office Phone: 918-422-5132. E-mail: jlbell@sstelco.com.

BELL, JOANN, nurse; b. Newport News, Va., Dec. 18, 1931; d. Odell Henry and Shearell Virginia (Roark) Padgett; children: Greta Miller, Jack Bell Jr., Margaret Pancake, Terry Bell. Diploma in gen. edn., Logan, W.Va., 1977; cert. emergency med. tech., Logan, 1978. Cert. Nat. Crisis Prevention Inst., adult CPR and standard first aid ARC, CPR Am. Heart Assn. LPN Holden (W.Va.) Hosp., 1979-88, Logan Health Village, 1989; pvt. duty nurse Chapmanville (W.Va.) Residence, 1989-90; LPN VOCA Corp., Man, W.Va., 1990, 1991—2000; pvt. duty nurse Holden Residence, 1991; LPN Logan Mingo Mental Health Ctr., 1991. Mem. AFL-CIO. Democrat. Avocations: reading, writing children's stories, family activities. Home: 74 Mallory Ave Monaville WV 25636-9748

BELL, JULIE MARIE, health facility administrator, consultant; b. Mt. Clemens, Mich., Aug. 21, 1974; d. John and Helen Mary Bell. BA in Psychology and Bus., Siena Hts. U., Adrian, Mich., 1997; MS in Psychology, U. Detroit Mercy, 2000; PhD in Psychology. Cert. Baldridge examiner, green belt Six Sigma, master change agt. Constrn. asst. Triangle Elec., Madison Hts., Mich., 1996—98; human resource cons. Aero Svcs., Internat., Troy, Mich., 1998—2000; sr. orgnl. cons. St. John Health, Warren, Mich., 2000—; sr. mgr. orgnl. devel. DaimlerChrysler, internal cons. Auburn Hills, Mich. Cons. in field; mem. adv. bd. U. Detroit-Mercy, 2001—. Girl's athletic coach St. Anne Cath. Sch., Warren, 2004—; care ptnr. Providence Hosp., Southfield, Mich., 2004—; Shoes for Children vol. Little Rock Bapt. Ch., 2003—. Scholar McCracken scholar, McCracken Basketball Camps, Ind., 1999. Democrat. Roman Catholic. Avocations: reading, travel, home decorating, pets. Office: Saint John Health 28000 Dequindre Rd Warren MI Business E-Mail: jmb179@dcx.com.

BELL, KAREN A., dean; BA in sociol., SUNY Potsdam; MFA in dance, Sarah Lawrence Coll. Prof. SUNY Potsdam, Elmira Coll., Wells Coll.; visiting asst. prof. Cornell U.; prof. Ohio State U., 1980—; chairperson Dept. Dance, Ohio State U., 1995—; assoc. dean Coll. Arts. Ohio State U., 1995—2001, interim dean, 2001—02, dean, 2002—. Individual Artist Fellowship, Ohio Arts Coun., Academic Leadership Fellow, Com. Instl. Cooperation, 1991—92. Mem.: Nat. Assn. Sch. Dance (commn. accreditation, evaluator), Am. Coll. Dance Festival Assn. (bd. dirs., northeast regional rep.). Office: Office of Dean OSU Coll Arts 152 Hopkins Hall 128 North Oval Mall Columbus OH 43210 Office Phone: 614-292-5171. Office Fax: 614-292-5218. E-mail: bell.1@osu.edu.

BELL, KASEY ANN, elementary school educator; d. Marilyn and Glenn Bell. BA, U. Tex., Austin, 2000. Cert.: Tex. (Paralegal) 1997; Tchr. Tex., 2005. Asst. buyer Foley's, Houston, 2000—01; tchr. lang. arts Park Crest Mid. Sch., Pflugerville, Tex., 2003—. Coach cheerleading Park Crest Mid. Sch., 2003—; mem. lang. arts curriculum com. Pflugerville Ind. Sch. Dist., 2005—. Recipient Cert. of Recognition, Am. Heart Assn., 2003—04.

BELL, KATHY DAWN, medical/surgical nurse; b. Camden, N.J., Apr. 15, 1967; d. Ernest and Carol (Henson) B. AS, Camden (N.J.) County Coll., 1993. LPN, N.J. Dietary aide Copper River Convalescent Home, Pennsauken, N.J., 1982-84; nurses aide Praza Med. Ctr., Camden, 1985-87; LPN Greenbriar Nursing Home, Woodbury, N.J., 1990-92, St. Mary's Cath. Home, Cherry Hill, N.J., 1992-94. Recipient George Miller award Preston Gunning, Camden, 1986. Mem. NAFE (adv. 1993—), Nat. League for Nursing (adv. 1990—). Baptist.

BELL, LAURA DENISE, music educator; b. Dallas, Jan. 4, 1979; d. Donna and Steve Bradford; m. Terry Bell, May 20, 2000. BA in Sociology, U. N.Tex., Denton, 1998; MusB in Music Edn., U. N.Tex., Denton, 2001. Cert. tchr. Tex., 2001. Band dir. Carrollton Farmers Br. Ind. Sch. Dist., Tex., 2001—. Mem.: Tex. Music Educators Assn. Office: CFBISD-Ted Polk Mid Sch 2001 Kelly Blvd Carrollton TX 75006 Office Phone: 972-968-4637.

BELL, LEE PHILLIP, television personality, television producer; b. Chgo. d. James A. and Helen (Novak) P.; m. William Joseph Bell, Oct. 23, 1954; children: William J., Bradley, Lauralee. BS in Microbiology, Northwestern U., Evanston, Ill., 1950. With CBS-TV, Chgo., 1952-86; pres. Bell-Phillip TV Prodns., 1985—. Bd. dirs. William Wrigley, Jr. Co., Chgo. Bank Commerce, Phillips Flowers Inc. TV and radio shows include Lee Phillip Show, Chgo., from 1952, Lady and Tiger Show WBBM Radio, from 1962, WBBM TV from 1964; hostess Noon Break, numerous TV Spls. including Forgotten Children, The Rape of Paulette (nat. Emmy award, duPont Columbia award); Children and Divorce (Chgo. Emmmy award) co-creator: (with William Bell) The Young and the Restless CBS-TV daytime drama, 1973 (Emmy award); co-creator, exec. producer The Bold and the Beautiful, 1987—. Bd. dirs. United Cerebral Palsy, Chgo. Unlimited, Northwestern U. Hosp., Chgo. Heart Assn., Nat. Com. Prevention of Child Abuse, Mental Health Assn., Children's Home and Aid Soc., Salvation Army, Chgo., Family Focus; mem. Chgo. Maternity Ctr.; life mem. Northwestern U. Bd. Trustees. Recipient 16 Chgo. Emmys; Top Favorite Female award TV Guide mag., 1956, Outstanding Woman of Radio and TV award McCall's mag., 1957-58, 65, bd. govs. award Chgo. chpt. Nat. Acad. TV Arts and Scis., 1977, William Booth award for community svc. Salvation Army, 1990; named Person of Yr. Broadcast Advt. Club, Chgo., 1980. Mem. Am. Women Radio and TV (Golden Mike award 1968, Broadcaster of Yr. 1993), Acad. TV Arts and Scis. (bd. dirs.), Chgo. chpt. Acad. TV Arts and Scis., Women's Athletic Club of Chgo., Comml. Club, Delta Delta Delta. Home: 9955 Beverly Dr Beverly Hills CA 90210 Office: CBS c/o Bold and Beautiful 7800 Beverly Blvd Los Angeles CA 90036-2188 Office Phone: 323-575-2812. Business E-Mail: markpinciotti@boldandbeautiful.tv.

BELL, LINDA GREEN, psychology educator, therapist; b. Austin, Tex., July 12, 1944; d. Leslie Mason and Anna Violet Weber Green; m. David Chalres Bell, Dec. 27, 1965; children: Michael James, Eric Matthew, Claire Toshiko Ishikawa. BA, Oberlin (Ohio) Coll., 1967; MA, U. Tex., 1968; PhD, Duke U., 1973. Postdoctoral rsch. fellow U. Chgo., 1974-76; rsch. asst. Scientific Methods Inc., Austin, 1964-67; vis. rschr. Nat. Inst. of Mental Health, Ichikawa, Chiba, Japan, 1985-87; prof. psychology and family therapy U. Houston-Clear Lake, 1976—. Rchr. in field; presenter and workshops in family rsch. and family therapy. Contbr. articles to profl. publs. Vol. Peace Corps, Senegal, Liberia, 1968-70. Grantee, NIMH, 1976—77, 1977—83, Hogg Found. for Mental Health, 1978—82, Tex. Coord. Bd. for Higher Edn., 1998—2002. Fellow: APA, Nat. Coun. on Family Rels., Am. Family Therapy Acad., Am. Assn. for Marriage and Family Therapy. Democrat. Mem. Soc. Of Friends. Avocation: music.

BELL, LINDA J., broadcast executive; b. Ramer, Ala., June 25, 1959; d. Charlie E. and Ethel L. Bell. BS in Broadcast Journalism, Troy U., Troy, Ala., 1981. Comml. ops. asst. WXIA-TV, Atlanta, 1989—91; comml. ops. supr. Turner Broadcasting System, Atlanta, 1991—96; prodr., prodn. coord. Creflo Dollar Ministries, Atlanta, 1996—99; comml. traffic/prodn. asst. The Weather Channel, Atlanta, 1999—2002; prodn. asst. WAKA-TV, Montgomery, Ala., 2003—04; instant replay dir. Montgomery Biscuits Baseball, 2004—; prodr., pub. affairs dir. Trinity Broadcasting Network, Montgomery, 2003—. Co-author: Of Poetry and Praise, 2005. Mem. So. Poverty Law Ctr., Montgomery, 2003—; switcher Mt. Paran Ch. of God, Atlanta, 1999—2001; Sunday sch. tchr. A.M.E. Zion Ch., Ramer, Ala., 2002—04. Capt. USAR, 1982—2000. Mem.: Delta Sigma Theta. Methodist. Avocations: writing, tennis, baking, decorating, football.

BELL, LINDA R., writer, photographer; b. Columbia, Tenn., Nov. 13, 1949; d. William Fleming Jr. and Dorothy Virginia (Cecil) Rainey; m. Dennis L. Bell, Sept. 11, 1971 (div. Dec. 1980); m. Talmadge Martin Warren, Dec. 17, 1983. BSChemE cum laude, U. Tenn., 1971, MS in Engring. magna cum laude, 1972. Process engr. E.I. du Pont de Nemours, Inc., Chattanooga, 1972-75; design engr. Olin Corp., Charleston, Tenn., 1975-78; environ. engr. TVA, Knoxville, 1978-85; instr. writing U. Tenn., Knoxville, 1985-88. Freelance writer and photographer, Knoxville, 1982—; speaker Presdl. Mgmt. Interns, Knoxville, 1980; featured guest poet Espirit & Espirit Seminars, Nashville, 1982. One-woman shows include Thompson Photo Products, Knoxville, 1986, 1990, 1991, Farragut Arts Coun., Tenn., 2003, 2004, Meadow View Garden Ctr., Lenoir City, Tenn., 2006, numerous group shows; author: Environmental Development Plan Ammonia from Coal Project, 1979, vol. of poems Love Puzzles, 1982, January Summers, 1982, Heartprints, 1989, (non-fiction) The Red Butterfly, 1983, What I Remember, 2004; contbr. numerous articles and poems to lit. jours. and nat. mags., numerous photographs to regional and nat. mags. and calendars. Vol. Girl Scouts US, 1966-69; swim instr. ARC, 1970-71. Finalist Nat. Wildlife photography competition, 2004; nominee Pushcart prize, 1985; named one of Outstanding Young Women of Am., 1985; recipient 1st pl. award, Knoxville Zoo Photo Contest, 1983, Winner of the Week Cat Calendar award, Workman Pub. Co., 1989, Stray of the Month Cat Calendar award, 1991, 1993, 1994, 1999, Best Photography Annual, 1992, Ann. Writing Competition award, Writer's Digest, 1992, 1993, Poetry award, Now & Then Appalachian Poetry Competition, 2002. Mem.: NAFE, Knoxville Writers Guild, Tenn. Writers Alliance, Humane Soc. Tennessee Valley, Nat. Wildlife Fedn. (life; Backyard Habitat award 1986), Lupus Found. Am. (bd. dirs. East Tenn. chpt. 1985—2003), Knoxville Recycling Coalition, Tau Beta Pi (life). Presbyterian. Avocations: swimming, gardening, reading, travel. Office: 10211 Julie Ln Knoxville TN 37932-1620 Office Phone: 865-705-4624.

BELL, M. JOY MILLER, financial planner, real estate agent; b. Enid, Okla., Dec. 29, 1934; d. H. Lee and M.E. Madge (Hatfield) Miller; m. Richard L.D. Berlemann, July 21, 1957 (div. Nov. 1974); children: Richard Louis, Randolph Lee; m. Donald R. Bell, Aug. 17, 1996; children: Jeri, Johnna, Nolan, Charles, Mary. BSBA, N.Mex. State U., 1956. CFP; grad. Realtors Inst.; fellow Life Underwriting Tng. Coun. Tchr. bus. and math. Alamogordo (N.Mex.), Las Cruces (N. Mex.) and Omaha Pub. Schs., 1956-63; tchr., dir. Evelyn Wood Reading Dynamics So. N.Mex. Inst., 1967-68; registered rep. Westamerica Fin. Corp., Denver, 1968-76; gen. agt. Security Benefit Life, Topeka, 1969—2001, Delta Life & Annuity, Topeka, 1969—2001; registered rep. AGF Sponsors, Inc., Denver, 1976—; pres., broker Fin. Design Corp. R.E. (name changed to Bell, Inc. 1997), Las Cruces, 1977—; with Allianz L.I. Co. N.Am., 2000—. Mrs. U.S. Savings Bonds ofcl. goodwill amb. U.S. Treasury, U.S. Savs. Bond Divsn., Washington, 1968-70. Contbr. articles to profl. jours. V.p. programs Dona Ana County Fedn. Rep. Women. Recipient Top Sales Person award Investment Trust and Assurance, 1976-77; named Outstanding Young Woman of N.Mex., 1970, Outstanding Young Women of Am., 1970. Mem. Nat. Assn. Realtors, Nat. Assn. Ins. and Fin. Advisors, Nat. Assn. Ret. Fed. Employees (v.p. programs local chpt.), Internat. Assn. Registered Fin. Planners, Fin. Planners Assn., S.W. N.Mex. Assn. of Ins. and Fin. Advisors (treas. 1990-91, pres.-elect 1991-92, pres. 1992-93), Las Cruces Assn. Realtors (bd. dirs.), Multiple Listing and Info.Svcs., Inc. (treas. 2002, pres.-elect 2004, pres. 2005), Las Cruces City Alumnae Panhellenic, Altrusa, Order Ea. Star, Delta Zeta. Presbyterian. Home: 4633 Lamar Rd Las Cruces NM 88005-3558 Office: Bell Inc PO Box 577 Las Cruces NM 88004-0577 Office Phone: 505-526-9166. E-mail: joybell@bellinc.com.

BELL, MAXINE TOOLSON, state legislator, librarian; b. Logan, Utah, Aug. 6, 1931; d. John Max and Norma (Watson) Toolson; m. H. Jack Bell, Oct. 26, 1949; children: Randy J. (dec.), Jeff M., Scott Alan (dec.). Assocs. in Libr. Sci., Coll. So. Idaho; CSI, Idaho State U., 1975. Librarian Sch. Dist. 261, Jerome, Idaho, 1975-88; mem. Idaho Ho. of Reps., 1988—. Bd. dirs. Idaho Farm Bur., 1976-77; rep. western states Am. Farm Bur. Women, 1990-93, vice chmn., 1993—; vice chmn. Am. Farm Bur., 1993-2005, chmn. appropriations com., 1999—; mem. Jerome County Rep. Precinct Com., 1980-88. Recipient Pres. medallion award, Idaho State U., 2005. Home: 194 S 300 E Jerome ID 83338-6532 Personal E-mail: mbell@magielink.com.

BELL, PATRICIA WRIGHT, music educator; b. Balt., Mar. 4, 1955; d. Henry Leroy and Mary Ann Wright; children: Mary Catherine, Joseph Christopher. Assocs. Degree, Anne Arundel C.C., Arnold, Md., 1977; BS in Music Edn., Towson State U., 1982; Master's Equivalency, Western Md. Coll., 1992. Advanced profl. cert. Anne Arundel County Pub. Schs. Music tchr. Old Mill Mid. Sch. South, Millersville, Md., 1984—94, Chesapeake Bay Mid. Sch., Pasadena, Md., 1994—. Chairperson Mid. Sch. All County Chorus for Anne Arundel County, 2000—. Mem.: Music Educators Nat. Conf., Mid. Sch. Choral Dirs. Anne Arundel County (spokesperson 2000—). Avocations: music, tennis, golf, boating, singing. Office: Chesapeake Bay Mid Sch 4804 Mountain Rd Pasadena MD 21122

BELL, ROBINETTE N., psychiatrist, educator; d. Laurence A. Nixon and Virginia Morris; m. M. Neil Redford, July 16, 1971; children: Suzanne, Donald, Dana. AB, Smith Coll., Northampton, Mass., 1951; MD, Albert Einstein Coll. Medicine, Bronx, 1959. Editl. staff Look Mag., NYC, 1951—58; instr. psychiatry Columbia U., 1971—81, asst. clin. prof., 1981—95, assoc. clin. prof., 1995—2004, U. Colo., Denver, 2004—. Psychiatrist pvt. practice, NYC, 1967—2003, Denver, 2004—. Mem.: Am. Psychiat. Assn. Avocations: reading, travel, dog breeding.

BELL, SANDRA ELIZABETH, corporate financial executive; b. Toronto, Ont., Can., Apr. 23, 1957; came to U.S., 1961; d. Alexander James Bell and Marion Ann (Scaysbrook) Robinson. BA in Econs., Ohio State U., 1979; MBA, Harvard U., 1983. Mgmt. trainee, systems analyst First Nat. Bank of Cin., 1979-81; asst. v.p. E.F. Hutton & Co., N.Y.C., 1983-87; v.p. The Deerpath Group, Lake Forest, Ill., 1988-91; mng. dir. Deutsche Bank Securities Inc., N.Y.C., 1991—2004; exec. v.p., CFO Fed. Home Loan Bank of Cin., 2004—. Mem. Phi Beta Kappa. Avocations: skiing, tennis, reading. Office: Fed Home Loan Bank 221 E 4th St Fl 10 Cincinnati OH 45202 Office Phone: 513-852-7524. E-mail: bellse@fhlbcin.com.

BELL, SUSAN JANE, nurse; b. Columbus, Ohio, July 24, 1946; d. Donald Richard Bell and Martha Jane (McDowell) Nichols; m. Robert Earlin Ward, Oct. 24, 1964 (div. 1984); children: Duane Allen Ward, Melissa Jane Ward, Bryan Thomas Ward. Degree in nursing, Columbus Sch. Practical Nursing, 1986; ADRN, Columbus State C.C., 1989; student, Franklin U., 1993, Edn. Direct Nutrition and Fitness; diploma in nutrition and fitness, Penn Foster Coll. RN Ohio; cert. CPR. Nurse's asst. Riverside Meth. Hosp., Columbus, 1970-80, Norworth Convalescent Ctr., Columbus, 1980-86; nurse, charge nurse Heartland Thurber Care Ctr., Columbus, 1986-89; staff nurse Am. Nursing Care, Columbus, 1989—; medicare home visitation, staffing and pvt. duty nurse Telemed, Columbus, 1989—; asst. head nurse Northland Terr., Columbus, 1989; supr. Elmington Manor, Columbus, 1989; staff nurse cardiac step down unit Grant Hosp., Columbus, 1989-92; nurse med. ICU, CCU and pediatric ICU, 1992-93; charge nurse critical-skilled unit First Cmty. Village Health Care Ctr., Columbus, 1992-95; supr., charge nurse St. Rita's Home; charge nurse Mother Angeline McCrory Manor, 2005—. Pvt. duty ALS ventilator patients Med. Pers. Poole. Sponsor Childreach. Mem. NAFE, ASPCA, World Wildlife Found., Nature Conservancy, Ohio Hist. Found. (archives/libr. divsn.), Nat. Audubon Soc., Environ. Def. Fund, Nat. Wildlife Fedn., Humane Soc. U.S., Am. Coun. on Exercise, Columbus Met. Mus. Art (supporting), Internat. Assn. Global Execs., Nat. Notary Assn., Nat. Mus. of Women in the Arts, Ohio Hist. Soc.-Archives Libr., Omtermat/ Exec. Guild, Rotary, Sierra Club. Avocations: bodybuilding, power lifting, swimming, music, crocheting. Personal E-mail: bellcanine@aol.com.

BELLAMY, CAROL, international organization administrator; b. Plainfield, NJ, Jan. 14, 1942; BA in Psychology, Gettysburg Coll., 1963; JD, NYU, 1968. Asst. commr. Dept. Mental Health and Mental Health Retardation Svc., NYC; with Peace Corps., Guatemala, 1963—65; assoc. Cravath, Swaine & Moore, NYC, 1968—71; mem. NY State Senate, 1973—77; pres. NYC Coun., 1978—85; prin. Morgan Stanley & Co., NYC, 1986—90; mng. dir. Bear Stearns, NYC, 1990—93; dir. Peace Corps., Washington, 1993-95; exec. dir. UNICEF, 1995—2005; pres., CEO World Learning, Brattleboro, Vt., 2005—, pres. Sch. Internat. Training, 2005—. Former trustee, NYC Pension Sys., mem., NY Met. Transit Authority, First v.p. Nat. League of Cities. Fellow, Harvard U. Kennedy Sch. Govt. Mem.: Phi Alpha Alpha. Avocation: Mets baseball fan. Office: World Learning PO Box 676 Kipling Rd Brattleboro VT 05302-0676

BELLAMY, GAIL ANNE GHETIA, magazine editor, author, speaker; b. Lakewood, Ohio, Dec. 19, 1949; f. George and Janice Arlene (Fleming) Ghetia; m. Stephen Paul Bellamy, Nov. 17, 1990. BA, Ohio U., 1971; postgrad., Case Western Res. U., 1971; PhD, The Union Inst. and Univ., 2000. Mng. editor Restaurant Hospitality mag., Cleve., 1980—. Contbg. columnist Cleve. Free Times newspaper, 1992-98; workshop presenter Dept. Cmty. Svcs., Cleve., 1993—, Lakeland CC, Mentor, Ohio, 1993-2000; online dining columnist Am. Online, 1995-98; nat. adv. bd. Culinary Arts Inst., Miss. U. for Women; contbg. editor Tableware Today mag., Bloomfield, N.J., 1997—; adj. prof. Ursuline Coll., 2000-; tutor Empire State Coll./SUNY, 2002, 03; faculty mem. PWLGC Literary Ctr., Cleveland, 2002-. Author: Design Spirits, 1995, Victual Reality, 2000, Cleveland Food Memories, 2003; contbr. chapters to books; co-editor: Ohio Writer mag., 2001—03; contbr. articles to profl. jours.; food host Supper and the Silver Screen. Vol. lectr. Write-on Cleve!, 1993—; vol. examiner Am. Radio Relay League, 1994—; bd. dirs. Ursuline Sophia Ctr., Cleve., 1999—2005. Recipient Communicators award/Merit cert. Women in Comm., 1993. Mem.: Internat. Assn. Culinary Profls., Les Dames D'Escoffier, Press Club of Cleve., Soc. Profl. Journalists, Internat. Foodsvc. Editl. Coun. (bd. dirs. 1994—95, pres. 1996, bd. dirs. 1997, 1999, sec. 2004, bd. dirs. 2004—, Betty Bastion Outstanding Svc. award 2005), Am. Soc. Bus. Press Editors (1st pl./Editl. Ctrl. Region Competition award 1994), The Poets' and Writers' League of Greater Cleve. (pres. bd. trustees 2000—06), Am. Radio Relay League, Acad. Am. Poets. Avocations: violin, viola, mentor writing programs. Office: 1300 E 9th St Cleveland OH 44114

BELLAMY, IVORY, elementary school educator, consultant; b. Tuscaloosa, Ala., Feb. 21, 1952; d. Iverson Gandy Sr. and Betty Belle Gand; children: Cinnamon Nicole Jones, Cecily Dawn Jones. BA, Stillman Coll., Tuscaloosa, Ala., 1974. Cert. Tchr. Ala. Asst. dir. admissions U. Miami, Coral Gables, Fla., 1984—88; tchr. Fayette County Schs., Fayetteville, Ga., 1990—93, Clayton County Schs., Jonesboro, Ga., 1998—. Author (Book of Poetry): Life Is a Million Good-byes, 2005. Achievements include Founder, CEO Sisters Inc. Avocations: crafts, poetry, writing. Office: Martin Luther King Jr Elem 5745 W Lee and Mill Atlanta GA 30349 E-mail: ivorybellamy@bellsouth.net.

BELLAMY, JOAN ELIZABETH, psychologist, consultant; b. Hutchinson, Kans., Jan. 20, 1935; d. Portel Arthur and Elizabeth S. (Linscheid) Guyer; m. Bruce M. Bellamy, 1957; children: Portel, Ruth E., Jennifer, John J. BS, Kans. State U., 1957; MS, U. Kans., 1971; EdS in Marriage and Family Therapy, Wichita State U., 1981; PhD, Massey U., Palmerston North, New Zealand, 1990. Cert. marriage and family therapist. Tchr. U.S. Dept. Edn. Group, Croix Chapeau, France, 1959-62; counselor human rels. pub. schs. Arlington, Va., 1967-76; psychologist Mental Health Ctr., Hutchinson, 1977-81, Taranaki Base Hosp., New Plymouth, New Zealand, 1982-85, Taranaki Psychology, New Plymouth, 1984-87; assoc. prof. Laredo (Tex.) State U., 1987-89; psychologist Horizons Mental Health Ctr., Hutchinson, 1989-90, Alder Psychology, Hutchinson, 1989—; coord. peer counseling USD 308, Hutchinson, 1990—; owner Wildlife Canyon Mental Health Clinic, Garden Valley, Idaho, 2001—; marriage and family therapist Garden Valley, Idaho, 2001—. Exec. dir. Skylights Drug and Alcohol Treatment Facility, Hutchinson, 1993-94; presenter S.W. Psychol. Conf., Austin, 1992. Author: Stress in Families, 1989; mem. editorial staff Crisis Intervention pamphlet, 1990. Pres. bd. dirs. Unitarian Ch. Group, Hutchinson, 1989-92; bd. dirs. Heritage Festival, Hutchinson, 1990; pres. parents inc. Twin Oaks Boys Home, Hutchinson, 1991-92; sponsor Octagon Club of Hutchinson High Sch., 1991-92; mem. AIDS Task Force of Reno County. Kans. State Div. Drug and Alcohol grantee, 1990, United Meth. Health Min. grantee, 1992; recipient Mental Health Contbn. award State Mental Health Assn., 1991. Mem. APA, Am. Assn. Marriage and Family Therapists, Nat. Peer Helpers Assn., Kans. Peer Helpers Assn. (pres. 1991-92), Optimist Club of Hutchinson, Phi Delta Kappa, Delta Kappa Gamma. Mem. Unitarian Ch. Avocations: painting, swimming, antiques, travel. Home: 1 Happy Hollow Dr Garden Valley ID 83622-5187

BELLAMY, KRISTI MICHELLE, prosecutor; b. Wilmington, NC, Oct. 15, 1975; d. Verida Bellamy Sarratt. BA, U. NC, Chapel Hill; JD, U. Iowa. Bar: NC 2001, Ga. 2001, U.S. Supreme Ct. 2006, Ct. Appeals 4th Circuit 2004, Ea. Dist. NC 2004. Magistrate judge Brunswick County Ct. Ho., Boliva, NC, 2000; judicial clk. NC Ct. Appeals, Raleigh, 2001—05; legal specialist NC Indsl. Commn., Raleigh, 2005—. Student mentor MicroMash Bar Rev., Chgo., 2002—. Bd. mem. Fair Housing Hearing Bd., Raleigh, 2006—, NC Assn. Black Lawyers. Mem.: Wake County Bar Assn., N.C. Assn. Black Lawyers (mem. bd. 2006—), Order of the Eastern Star, Phi Alpha Delta Legal Fraternity. Democrat. So. Bapt. Avocations: reading, baking, interior decorating. Home: 7205 Lake Vista Dr Apt 103 Raleigh NC 27613 Office: NC Indsl Commn 4340 Mail Service Ctr Raleigh NC 27699-340 Office Phone: 919-827-2542. Personal E-mail: kristibellamy@hotmail.com.

BELLAMY, RENEE ADELE, secondary school educator; b. Queens, NY, Feb. 3, 1966; d. Lloyd and Annie Mae Bellamy; 1 child, Chauncey Payne Jr. BS, Howard U., 1988; MS, Queens Coll., 1994; postgrad., Columbia U., 1996—98; advanced cert. in edn., Hunter Coll., 2003. Cert. tchr. NY, sch. adminstr., supr. NY, CPR/Automated Elec. Defibrilator, first aid. Libr. aide Howard U., Washington, 1984—87; tour guide Washington Nat. Zoo, 1985—87; HS tchr. NY Dept. Edn., Bronx, 1988—91, middle sch. tchr. Queens, 1991—, asst. prin., 2001—03. Basketball and cheerleading coach Middle Sch. 72, Queens, 1993—2001, sch. health coord., 1997—2000; coach adaptive phys. edn. NYC Dept. Edn., 2000; coach sports and fitness league Champs Mid. Sch., 2004—; coach girls crew team Middle Sch. 210, Queens, 2006—; sch. health educator facilitator, 2005—06. Cubmaster Boy Scouts Am., Queens, 1998—2001; ptnr. fundraising Spl. Olympics, NY, 2000—05; v.p. St. Peter Claver Parents Assn., Queens, 2001—02. Recipient Cert. Appreciation, Spl. Olympics, 2005. Mem.: ASCD, Am. Fedn. Tchr., Wildlife Conservation Soc., Eastern Star, Phi Delta Kappa. Achievements include creaton of Bellamy Drill and Bellamy Beat fitness routines. Avocations: gardening, dance, interior decorating, reading, coaching. Office: Middle Sch 210 93-11 101 Ave Ozone Park NY 11416

BELLANTONI, MAUREEN BLANCHFIELD, manufacturing and retail executive; b. Warren, Pa., Mar. 18, 1949; d. John Joseph and Patricia Anne (Southard) Blanchfield; m. Michael Charles Bellantoni, Aug. 12, 1972; children: Mark Christopher, Melissa Catherine. BS in Fin., U. Bridgeport, 1976; MBA, U. Conn., Stamford, 1979. Fin. analyst Dictaphone Corp., Rye, N.Y., 1970-73, Gen. Telephone & Electronics, Stamford, 1973-74, Smith Kline Ultrasonic Products, now Branson, Danbury, Conn., 1974-77; fin. mgr. Gen. Foods, White Plains, N.Y., 1977-80; contr. Branson Ultrasonics Corp. div. Emerson Electric, Danbury, Conn., 1980-88, v.p. fin., 1988-90; v.p. fin., CFO Automatic Switch Co. divsn. Emerson Electric, Florham Park, NJ, 1990-93, PYA/Monarch, Inc. divsn. Sara Lee Corp., Greenville, SC, 1993-94; v.p. fin. CFO Meat Group Sara Lee Corp., Cordova, Tenn., 1994-97; pres., COO BilMar Foods divsn. Sara Lee Corp., 1997-98; exec. v.p., CFO Rohn Industries Inc., Peoria, Ill., 1999-2000; CFO divsn. Diageo Burger King Corp., Miami, Fla., 2000—01, sr. v.p. fin., 2001—02; sr. v.p., CFO CP Kelco, Chgo., 2003—04; exec. v.p., CFO Intega Life Scis. Holding, Plainsboro, NJ, 2006—. Vice chair Nat. Legacy Campaign Cancer Fund, Franciscan Sister of Poor Found. Mem. Fin. Execs. Inst., S.C. C. of C., Danbury C. of C. (leadership program 1989), Beta Gamma Sigma. Avocations: golf, tennis, racquetball. Office Phone: 609-936-6822. Personal E-mail: maureenbellantoni@comcast.net. Business E-Mail: maureen.bellatoni@integra-ls.com.

BELLER, LUANNE EVELYN, retired accountant; b. Ft. Dodge, Iowa, Feb. 5, 1950; d. Gerald L. and Evelyn E. (Liston) Heyl; m. Stephen M. Beller, June 28, 1970; children: Clancy Dee, Corby Lu. BA, Oreg. State U., 1977; MBA, Rochester Inst. Tech., 1981. CPA, Ill. Plant acct. DuBois Plastic Products, Avon, N.Y., 1977-79; coll. acct. SUNY, Geneseo, 1979-81; gen. acctg. supr. MasterFoods, USA (formerly M&M/Mars, Inc.), Cleveland, Tenn., 1981—83, Hackettstown, NJ, 1983—84, sales rep. Jacksonville, Ill., 1984—86, terr. sales supr., 1986—88; gen. acctg. coord. MasterFoods USA (formerly Kal Kan Foods, Inc.), Columbus, Ohio, 1988-90, fin. info. coord., 1990-92, gen. acctg. supr., 1992-97, site svc. and fin. mgr., 1997—2004; ret., 2004. Vol. Girl Scouts U.S.A., Jacksonville, 1985—88, Bexley, Ohio, 1988—2004; mem. sound control com. Bexley United Meth. Ch., 1989—2001, chair edn. com., 1998—2001, mem. edn. com., 1996—2004, LOGOS vol., 1996—2002, mem. diversity team, 2001—02; com. mem. Meth. Theol. Sch. Ohio Partnership, 2001—02; vol. children's programs St. John's United Meth. Ch., Corpus Christi, 2005—. Mem. Phi Kappa Phi, Beta Gamma Sigma, Beta Alpha Psi. Democrat. Avocation: reading.

BELLI, REBECCA SUE, elementary school educator, music educator; b. Sikeston, Mo., Mar. 20, 1954; d. William Charles and Marguerite Miller Tope; m. Mark Charles Belli, Dec. 22, 1979; children: NIcholas Charles, Marguerite Elizabeth, Christopher Michael. MusB in Edn., S.E. Mo. State U., Cape Girardeau, Mo., 1976. Lic. tchr. music Mo., 1976, Ind., 1976, music specialist N.C., 1985, tchr. N.C., 1993. Dir., choral music Carroll Co. Schs., Flora, Ind., 1976—78; music specialist New Madrid (Mo.) County Schs., 1978—79, Davenport (Iowa) Diocese Cath. Schs., 1980—84; tchr. vocal music and theatre arts Currituck Co. Schs., Barco, NC, 1985—89; music specialist Gaston Co. Schs., Gastonia, NC, 1990—91, tchr. elem. sch., 1993—95, music specialist elem. sch., 1995—. Dir. afterschool summer camp Christ United Meth. Ch., Gastonia, 2002. Lay leader Christ United Methl. Ch., Gastonia, 1996—98, chmn. worship, 2000—03, leader youth, 1999—2003. Grantee, Gaston County Edn. Found., 2000, 2002, 2006. Mem.: NEA, N.C. Assn. Educators, United Meth. Women (sec. 2003—05), Sigma Alpha Iota (life; chaplain 1974—76, Sword of Honor 1976). Republican. Meth. Avocations: reading, sewing, jewelry making, swimming, hiking. Office: Belmont Central Elementary School 310 Eagle Rd Belmont NC 28012

BELLINO-STRICKLAND, ROSEANNA, secondary school educator; b. NYC, Feb. 21, 1949; d. John Joseph and Sophie Frances Bellino; children: Jessika, Laura. BS, Bklyn. Coll., 1969; MS, Queens Coll., NY, 1972, U. Colo., Boulder, 1979. Cert. tchr. NY, Colo., aquatics instr. Elem. sch. tchr. Huntington Schs., Mellville, NY, 1969—76; health tchr. Adamsiz Schs., Thornton, Colo., 1979—85, 1996—. Home: 3575 W 111th Dr Unit B Westminster CO 80031-6866

BELLIS-JONES, CYNTHIA AXFORD, science educator; b. Berea, Ohio, Jan. 30, 1953; d. Norman Edgar and Jane Guest Axford; m. Hugh William Bellis-Jones, Apr. 25, 1980; children: Hugh Hunter, Christopher Ailwyn, Heather Jane. AA, Sullins Coll., 1972; BA in Edn., U. Ky., 1974, MEd, 1989. Cert. tchr. Ky. Vet. asst. Fayette Vet. Clinic, Lexington, Ky., 1974—79; instr. Ky. Equine Edn. Program, Lexington, 1979—81; broodmare/farm mgr. Tree Haven Farm, Lexington, 1981—87; sci. tchr. Harrison County Bd. Edn., Cynthiana, Ky., 1988—. Leader Scott County 4H, Georgetown, Ky., 1997—. Mem.: NEA, Ky. Edn. Assn., Pinto Orgn. Ly., Midsouth Combined Tng. and Dressage Assn. Republican. Avocations: equine hunting, jumping and eventing, showing dogs. Home: 1145 Hill Rd Paris KY 40361 Office: Harrison County Mid Sch 269 Education Dr Cynthiana KY 41031 Office Phone: 859-234-7123. E-mail: FoxrunFarmKy@aol.com.

BELLISSIMO, MARY E., art educator; b. Ellwood City, Pa., Oct. 26, 1955; d. James J. and Inese Bellissimo. BSEd Art Edn., Indiana U. of Pa., 1977; MSEd Classroom Tech., Wilkes U., 2004. Long range planner and tchr. of gifted Laurel Sch. Dist., Pa., 1978—79; art tchr. Easton Area Sch. Dist., 1979—. Mem.: Lehigh Valley Arts Coun., Easton Edn. Assn., NEA, St. Jane Frances de Chantal Ch., Pa. State Edn. Assn. Avocations: gardening, travel, social orgns. Home: 2529 Madison Ave Bethlehem PA 18017-3872 Office: Easton Area Sr High Sch 2601 William Penn Hwy Easton PA 18045

BELLIVEAU, KATHRIN PAGONIS, lawyer; b. Fall River, Mass., Aug. 25, 1968; d. Constantine Peter and Betty (Jamoulis) Pagonis; m. James Joseph Belliveau, June 20, 1998. BA magna cum laude, Wellesley Coll., 1990; JD, Boston Coll., 1993. Bar: R.I. 1993, U.S. Dist. Ct. R.I. 1994. Assoc. Tillinghast Collins & Graham, Providence, 1993-96, Adler Pollock & Sheehan, Providence, 1996-97; mng. atty. Hasbro, Inc., Pawtucket, RI, 1997—. Bd. dirs. Children's Mus., Providence, 1998—, Caritas House, Pawtucket, 1997—. Mem. ABA, Wellesley Club of R.I. (bd. dirs. 1996—), Phi Beta Kappa. Greek Orthodox. Avocations: tennis, golf, skiing, cooking. Office: Hasbro Inc 1027 Newport Ave Pawtucket RI 02861-2500

BELLM, JOAN, civic worker; b. Alton, Ill., June 20, 1934; d. Harvey Jacob and Alma Lorene (Roberts) Goldsby; m. Earl David Bellm, Oct. 1, 1955; children: David, Lori, Michael. Bd. dirs. Drug Watch Internat., 1991-02, lifetime hon. dir., 1998—; exec. dir. Ctr. for Drug Info., 1998—. Editor Best of IDEA newsletter, 1991-96, Drug Watch World News, 1996-02; chmn. Drug Watch Internat. editl. rev. com., 1996-02; columnist weekly newspaper, 1998—. Organist, dir. jr. choir St. Mary's Cath. Ch., 1958-78; mem. adv. bd. Carlinville (Ill.) Area Hosp., 1981-86; trustee Blackburn Coll., Carlinville, 1983-86; bd. dirs. Cath. Children's Home, Diocese of Springfield, Ill., 1986—; founder, bd. dirs., state networker Ill. Drug Edn. Alliance, 1982-86, pres., 1987-89; bd. dirs., nat. networker Nat. Fedn. Parents for Drug-Free Youth, Washington, 1984-86; mem. Ill. Gov.'s Adv. Coun. on Alcoholism and Substance Abuse, 1989-93; dir. Ctr. for Drug Info., 1998—; founder Drug Watch Internat., 1991, Internat. Drug Strategy Inst., 1993, invited participant Internat. Private Sector Conf. on Drugs, Seville, 1993, advisor U.N. Internat. Drug Ctrl. Program, 1994; numerous others. Recipient letter of endorsement Pres. of U.S., 1981, citation of recognition Ill. Dept., Am. Legion, 1981, Meritorious Svc. award, 1982, award Ill. Drug Edn. Alliance award, 1984, Southwestern Ill. Law Enforcement Commn., 1984, Carlinville Sch. Bd., 1985, Outstanding Svc. award Nat. Fedn. Parents, 1986, award Ill. Alcohol and Drug Dependence Assn., 1986, Optimist Internat., 1987, Ill. Drug Edn. Alliance, 1988, Outstanding Citizen award Blackburn U., 1989, Citizen of Yr. award, Carlinville, 1990; Leadership award Drug Watch Internat., 2001. Home: PO Box 227 Carlinville IL 62626-0227

BELLO, JUDITH HIPPLER, lawyer, trade association administrator; b. Alexandria, Va., May 31, 1949; BA in history summa cum laude, U. NC, 1971; JD, Yale Law Sch., 1975. Bar: D.C. 1975. Office legal adviser Dept. State, Washington, 1977-82; from dep. to gen. counsel, US trade rep. Sec. Commerce for Import Adminstrn., Washington, 1982—89; ptnr. Sidley & Austin, Washington, 1989-96; joined Pharm. Rsch. and Mfrs. Am. (PhRMA), 1996—, exec. v.p. policy and strategic affairs Washington, 1996—2001. Mem. Pres. Commn. on Federal Ethics Law Reform; policy official and atty. Dept. Commerce and State; editl. adv. bd. Am. Jour. Internat. Law, Georgetown Law and Policy in Internat. Bus., George Wash. Jour. Internat. Law and Econ.; adv. bd. and com. US Export-Import Bank, Syracuse U. Maxwell Sch. Citizenship and Pub. Affairs, Atlantic Coun., Brookings Instn. Coun. on Pub. Policy Edn.; vis. lectr. in field. Author: (with Alan F. Holmer) The Antidumping and Countervailing Duty Laws: Key Legal and Policy Issues, 1987, Guide to US-Can. Free-Trade Agreement, 1990; editor: North American Free Trade Agreement, 1994; contbr. numerous articles to profl. jours. Recipient Overall Excellence award DC Bar Com., 1985, Meritorious Pub. Svc. award USCG, 1978; named one of 100 Most Powerful Women in Wash., Washingtonian mag., 2001. Mem. ABA (internat. sect. co-chmn. trade com. 1986-90, couns. 1987-90), DC Bar (internat. sect., chmn. steering com. 1987-88; co-chmn. trade com. 1983-86), Am. Soc. Internat. Law (editl. adv. bd. 1982-89, coun. 1994-96, bd. dirs. 1995-2000), Coun. on Fgn. Rels., Aspen (Colo.) Strategy Group, Phi Beta Kappa. Office: PhRMA 100 15th St NW Washington DC 20005 E-mail: jbello@phrma.org.

BELLO, MARIA ELANA, actress; b. Norristown, Pa., Apr. 18, 1967; 1 child, Jackson Blue McDermott. BS in Polit. Sci., Villanova U. Co-founder Harlem's Dream Yard Drama Project, 1992. Actress: (off-Broadway plays) include The Killer Inside Me, Small Town Gals With Big Problems, Urban Planning; film appearances include Maintenance, 1992, Permanent Midnight, 1998, Payback, 1999, Coyote Ugly, 2000, Duets, 2000, Sam the Man, 2000, China: The Panda Adventure, 2001, Auto Focus, 2002, 100 Mile Rule, 2002, The Cooler, 2003, Nobody's Perfect, 2004, Secret Window, 2004, Silver City, 2004, Assault on Precinct 13, 2005, A History of Violence, 2005, The Sisters, 2005, The Dark, 2005, Thank You for Smoking, 2006, World Trade Center, 2006, Flicka, 2006; (TV films) The Commish: In the Shadow of the Gallows, 1995, Born in Brooklyn, 2001; (TV series) Mr. & Mrs. Smith, 1996, ER, 1997-98 (Screen Actors Guild award for outstanding performance by an ensemble in a drama series, 1997). Co-founder Dream Yard Drama Project for Kids, Harlem, NYC. Office: Creative Artists Agy 9830 Wilshire Blvd Beverly Hills CA 90212*

BELLO, MARY, physician; b. Paterson, N.J., Dec. 27, 1954; d. John Vincent and Rose (Piccirilli) B.; m. Michael Mutter, June 3, 1984; children: Michael Mutter, Jonathan Mutter. BA, Rutgers U., 1977; BS, LI U., 1980; MD, Ross U., 1984. Diplomate Am. Bd. Family Practice. Intern St. Joseph's Hosp., Paterson, NJ, resident; family physician pvt. practice, 1985—; clin. asst. prof. family medicine UMDNJ. Fellow Am. Acad. Family Physicians. Republican. Roman Catholic. Avocation: antique doll collecting. Office: 400 Franklin Tpke Ste 106 Mahwah NJ 07430-3517 Office Phone: 201-327-3333.

BELLON, VENETIA ROCHELLE, retired financial consultant; b. Beaufort West, Cape, South Africa, July 24, 1941; arrived in U.S., 1965; d. Michael and Roslyn (Sklaar) Bellon; m. Barry Fenroy Bass, Jan. 17, 1963 (div. Aug. 15, 1977); children: Tracey Bass Shilling-Hysjulien, Dayana Sebo; m. Andrew Jackson Ponton, III, Oct. 2004. Cert. Cert., U. Capetown, South Africa, 1960; BA in History, U. Tex., 1981, MA, LBJ, U. Tex., 1984. Tchr. Ellerton Jr. Sch., Capetown, 1961—63, Girls' HS, Pietermaritzburg, South Africa, 1964; mktg. mgr. Austin Mag., 1978; officer corp. Bank Am., Va., 1987—91; mortgage cons. Penn Nat. Bancshares, McLean, Va., 1993—95, Access Nat. Mortgage, Reston, 1995—99, Countrywide Home Loans, Alexandria, Va., 2001—06; ret., 2006. Conf. coord. Third World Militarization, 1984; mem. Amnesty Internat.; mem. task force Gov. State of Tex., 1984. Mem.: NAFE, AAUW, Ptnrs. of Conscience, So. Poverty Law Ctr., Tex. Execs., Amnesty Internat., Nat. Yiddish Book Ctr. Democrat. Jewish. Avocations: abstract expressionism, travel, crossword puzzles.

BELLOSPIRITO, ROBYN SUZANNE, artist, writer; b. Glen Cove, NY, Sept. 11, 1964; BA, L.I. U., 1986. Asst. Slide Libr. The Met. Mus. Art, N.Y.C., 1987-88, The Frick Art Reference Libr., N.Y.C., 1988-89; pub., editor The Exhibitioner Art Mag., Old Brookville, N.Y., 1993—, curator exhbns., 1994—. Exhbns. include Crystal Art Gallery, N.Y.C., 1988, Hutchins Gallery, Greenvale, N.Y., 1990, 91, Nassau County Mus. Art, Roslyn, N.Y., 1990, Sakura Gallery, Kennedy Airport, N.Y.C., 1992, PAAS Gallery, N.Y.C., 1992, Ward-Nasse Gallery, N.Y.C., 1992, 94, Outrlimits Art Gallery, Franklin Square, N.Y., 1993, Sea Cliff (N.Y.) Gallery, 1993, 94, Prince St. Gallery, N.Y.C., 1994, Foster Freeman Gallery, San Antonio, 1994, UN 4th Conf. on Women, Beijing, 1995, Ticknor Gallery/Harvard U., 1996, Fine Arts Mus. L.I., Hempstead, 1996, Islip (N.Y.) Art Mus., 1996, Galerie Observatoire 4, Montreal, 1996, Hillwood Art Mus., Brookville, N.Y., 1997, Fitton Ctr. for

Creative Arts, Hamilton, ohio, 1997, Ghost Fleet Gallery, Nags Head, N.C., 1997, Watchung (N.J.) Arts Ctr., 1997, Barnes & Noble, N.Y.C., 1998, Soc. Illustrators, N.Y.C, 2001, IMAC, Huntington, NY, 2002, Oyster Bay Hist. Soc., N.Y., 2003-2004, Michael Peter Hayes Salon, East Norwich, NY, 2005, others; permanent collections include Nat. Mus. Women in Arts, 1-800-Flowers, Inc., and pvt. homes. Grantee Puffin Found., 1997. Personal E-mail: bellspirit@aol.com.

BELLOVARY, CATHY, social services administrator, volunteer; b. Milw., Feb. 18, 1947; d. John Randolph and Florence Agnes Melster; m. Frank David Bellovary, Apr. 24, 1971; children: Anthony, Nicholas. BS, Purdue U., 1969; postgrad., Dominican Coll., U. Wis., Milw. Speech and lang. clinician Racine (Wis.) Unified Sch. Dist., 1969-74; dir. speech and lang. svcs. Racine Unified Schs., 1974-77; facilitator support groups Waukesha County Tech. Coll., Pewaukee, Wis., 1983-93, Family Svc. Waukesha, Wis., 1993-98; exec. dir. Waukesha County Food Pantry, Waukesha, 1990-97; dir. aging svcs. Waukesha County, 1997—. Mem. Women's Health Svcs., Waukesha, 1991—; exec. bd. mem. United Way-Waukesha County, 1996—; aging svcs. rep. Waukesha County Health Coun., Waukesha, 1997—; mem. sr. health ctr. adv. com. Waukesha Meml. Hosp.; chmn. Waukesha County Nutrition Coalition, Waukesha, 1998—; mem. County Execs. Cabinet, 1998—; spkr. in field. Contbr. articles to newsletters. Fundraiser, mem., com. chair Jr. League, Racine, Milw., 1973-83; past pres., v.p., sec., treas., com. chair Waukesha Svc. Club, 1981—; past pres., v.p Friends of the Libr., Waukesha, 1989-96; past pres., v.p., sec., treas. Waukesha Tng. Ctr., 1991-98. Named Woman of Achievement, Altrusa Club, Waukesha County, 1991, Woman of Distinction, YWCA Waukesha County, 1993, Most Powerful Woman in Waukesha County, Waukesha Freeman, 1993. Mem. Wis. Aging Dirs., Waukesha County Mental Health Assn., Southeastern Wis. Area Agy. on Aging (Waukesha County dir.), Westwood Health Club, Antique Comb Collector's Club, Purdue Alumni Assn. Republican. Episcopalian. Avocations: volunteering, antique collecting, reading, travel. Home: S28w29541 Pamela Cir Waukesha WI 53188-9519 Office: Waukesha County Dept Aging Svcs 1320 Pewaukee Rd Ste 130 Waukesha WI 53188-3878

BELLOWS, LAUREL GORDON, business lawyer; m. Joel J. Bellows. BA, U. Pa., 1969; JD, Loyola U., Chgo., 1974. Bar: Ill. 1974, Fla. 1975, U.S. Dist. Ct. (no. dist.) Ill. 1975, U.S. Dist. Ct. (no. dist.) Ga. 1980, Calif. 1981, U.S. Dist. Ct. (cen. dist.) Calif. 1980. Ptnr. Bellows and Bellows, Chgo., 1975—. Editor Loyola U. Law Rev., 1973-74; co-author: Trial Techniques in Business and Commercial Cases, 1988-2000. Past pres. women's bd. Traveller's Aid Soc., Chgo.; past chmn. Chgo. Network, 1992—; mentor Woman of Destiny program, 1990-91. Mem. ABA (bd. govs. 2001—, sec.-treas. 1991-92, past chmn. commn. on women 1993-95, mem. fed. jud. com. 1999—), Ill. Bar Assn., Chgo. Bar Assn. (bd. mgrs. 1983-85, sec. 1987-89, pres. 1991-92), Women's Bar Assn. Ill., Women's Bar Assn. Ill. Found. (bd. dirs. 1988—), Am. Arbitration Assn. (arbitrator 1976—, award 1990). Office: Bellows and Bellows PC 209 S LaSalle St Ste 800 Chicago IL 60604 Office Phone: 312-332-3340. Business E-Mail: lbellows@bellowspc.com.

BELL-ROSE, STEPHANIE, foundation administrator; b. Bklyn. m. Christopher Rose; 3 children. AB with honors, Harvard U., JD; MPA, John F. Kennedy Sch. Govt. Counsel, program officer for pub. affairs Andrew W. Mellon Found.; founding pres. Goldman Sachs Found., NYC, 1991—. Advisor Hauser Ctr. for Non-Profit Orgns., Harvard U.; mem. chmn.'s adv. coun. Coun. on Fgn. Rels.; mem. Exec. Leadership Coun., Contributions Coun., Bus. Higher Edn. Forum. Contbr. articles to profl. jours. Trustee, bd. v.p. Barnes Found.; trustee Am. Mus. Natural History. Recipient Fay Prize, Radcliffe Coll., Leadership Award, Westchester Children's Assn., Links of NYC, Nat. Coun. of Negro Women; grantee Rockefeller Fellowship. Mem.: Harvard Alumni Assn., Nat. Urban League.*

BELLVILLE, MARGARET (MAGGIE BELLVILLE), communications executive; B in Social Scis., SUNY, Binghamton; grad. advanced mgmt. program, Harvard U. With GTE Wireless/Contel Cellular, Inc., 1986—93; sr. v.p. Century Comm., L.A., 1993—95; from v.p. ops. to exec. v.p. ops. Cox Comm., Inc., 1995—2001; pres., CEO Incanta, Atlanta, 2001—02; exec. v.p. ops. Charter Comm., Inc., St. Louis, 2002—03, exec. v.p., COO, 2003—04. Mem. exec. vom., bd. dirs. Calif. Cable TV Assn.; bd. dirs. Cable Positive, Women in Cable and Telecomm. Found.; advisor Nat. Cable and Telecomm. Assn. Task Force on Diversity. Named Woman of Yr., Women in Cable, Calif. chpt., Woman to Watch, Women in Cable, Atlanta chpt., Woman of Yr., Women in Cable nat.; named one of Top 10 Women in Bus. in Atlanta. Office: Charter Comm Inc 12405 Powerscourt Dr Saint Louis MO 63131

BELL WILSON, CARLOTTA A., state official, consultant; b. Detroit, Dec. 7, 1944; d. Albert Powell (dec.) and Elfrieda (Bertram) Bell; divorced; children: Lizette C. Wilson, SaMia M. Wilson, Shira M. Ingram. AA, Wayne County C.C., Detroit, 1975; BS, Wayne State U., 1979; MEd, Bowling Green State U., 1983. Dental asst. Fred Colvard, DDS, Detroit, 1968-73; edn. coord. Merrill Palmer Inst., Detroit, 1979-81; head start evaluator Cmty. Devel. Inst., Wayne County, 1981; grad. asst. Bowling Green (Ohio) State U., 1981-83; child care worker Meth. Children's Village, Detroit, 1984-85; tchr. New Calvary Head Start, Detroit, 1985; child welfare specialist Mich. Dept. Social Svcs., Detroit, 1985-93; resource program analyst teen parent program Family Independence Agy., Lansing, Mich., 1993—2002. Conf. presenter U. Mich., Ann Arbor, 1995, Mich. Assn. Cmty. and Adult Edn., Bellaire, 1995, Baker Coll., Flint, Mich., 1996. Mem. Mich. Profl. Soc. on Abuse of Children, Internat. Assoc. Infant Massage (cert. infant massage instr.). Roman Catholic. Avocations: gardening, pottery, cultural activities, travel. Home: 2110 Chene Detroit MI 48207

BELOFF, ZOE, filmmaker, educator, photographer; b. Edinburgh, Scotland; arrived in N.Y.C., 1980; Student, Edingburgh (Scotland) U.; MFA in Film, Columbia U., 1983. Tchr. digital media Pratt Inst.; adj. prof. City Coll. N.Y., 1989—, Coll. SI. Prodr.: (CD-ROM) include The Vanishing Machine of Miss Natalija A., Illusions, Where There There There Where, Beyond (First prize Apple QuickTime VR Competition, 1998); (film performances) include Claire and Don in Slumberland, A Mechanical Medium, Lost, Life Underwater; (films) include Echo, A Trip to the Land of Knowledge, Shadow land or light from the other side, Lost, Wonderland USA, Nightmare Angel. Work has been exhibited at MoMA, N.Y. Film Festival, Rotterdam Film Festival, Pacific Film Archives, Pompidou Ctr., others. Recipient Finishing Funds Award, Experimental TV Ctr., 1996, 2000, 2002, Found. Contemporary Performance Arts Fellowship, N.Y. Found. for the Arts, 1997; grantee, Art Matters Inc., 1986, 1989, 1997, The Jerome Foundations Inc., Apparatus Prodns., 1992, Nat. Endowment for the Arts, 1993, Individual Artist Grant, N.Y. State Coun. for the Arts, 1996, 2001, Guggenheim Found., 2003.

BELOK, CAROL JEAN, nurse, alcohol/drug abuse services professional; b. Chgo., Feb. 13, 1934; d. Eugene Archibold and Lorraine Edwards; m. Chester Arthur Wiskowski, Aug. 14, 1953 (div. 1975); children: Lance Edward Wiskowski, Dane Andrew Wiskowski, Tara Lynn Wiskowski; m. Stephen Shepherd Belok, June 7, 1996. AAS in Nursing, Fayetteville Tech. Inst., NC, 1968—70; BS with honors, Fla. State U., Tallahassee, 1978—89; MEd, U. Okla., Norman, 1992—96. Cert. alcohol & drug abuse prevention and control Dept. Army, Acad. Health Scis., 1990, addiction profl. Fla. Cert. Bd., 1997; RN State Bd. NC, 1970, State Bd. Fla, 1970; cert. tchr. Sch. Bd. Fla., 2002. RN Panama Canal Govt., Ancon, 1970—90; drug & alcohol abuse counselor Alcohol & Drug Abuse Prevention and Control Program, Corozal, Panama, 1990—96. Adult basic edn. instr. Sarasota County Sch. Bd., Fla., 2002—03. Vol. Sr. Friendship Ctr., Venice, Fla., 2000—06; Stephen min. United Ch. Christ, Venice, 2001—06. Recipient Sustained Superior Performance award, US Army, 1986, Exceptional Performance Rating award, 1990—96. Mem.: NY Acad. Sci. (life). Independent. Protestant. Avocations: reading, travel, tennis, bridge, swimming. Home: 404 Huntridge Dr Venice FL 34292

BELOTSERKOVSKAYA, YANINA, internist; b. Kishinev, Moldova, Russia, May 30, 1950; came to U.S., 1990; d. Yefim and Etel Belotserkovsky; m. Mikhail Furman, Mar. 3, 1973; children: Vitaly, Zina. MD, Kishinev State Med. Sch., 1973. Diplomate Am. Bd. Internal Medicine. Physician Mcpl. Hosp., Kishinev, 1974—90; resident in internal medicine Interfaith Med. Ctr., Bklyn., 1993—96; physician S.I. U. Hosp., 1996—. Mem. AMA (assoc.), ACP (assoc.). Avocations: travel, reading. Office: S Levit Med Ctr 1220 Avenue P Brooklyn NY 11229-1009 Office Phone: 718-376-1004. E-mail: mikefurm@email.com.

BELSON, ABBY AVIN, writer; b. Bklyn., Apr. 1, 1935; d. Raphael and Molly Avin; m. Joel Jay Belson, June 17, 1956; children: Gabrielle Belson Rattner, Nicole Belson Goluboff. BA, Barnard Coll., N.Y.C., 1956; MA, Columbia U., N.Y.C., 1959. Tchr. N.Y.C. Sch. Sys., 1956—59; adj. lectr. Queens Coll., CUNY, 1961—64; freelance writer, 1970—83; editor med. pubs. Mount Sinai Med. Ctr., N.Y.C., 1983—94; freelance writer, 1994—. Bd. dirs. Conservative Synagogue of Jamaica Estates, Jamaica, NY, 1993—96. Recipient MacEachern award, Pub. Rels. Soc. Am., 1989, Med. Journalism award 1st prize, Sandoz Pharms., 1989, Med. Journalism award, 1991. Mem.: Nat. Assn. Sci. Writers. Avocations: gardening, swimming. Personal E-mail: ajbelson@yahoo.com.

BELT, JEAN RAINER, art gallery owner; b. Selma, Ala., Sept. 12, 1942; d. Sterling Price and Saidee (Crook) Rainer; m. Kemplin C. Belt, Aug. 31, 1963; children: Keven Curtis, Kelly B. Jones. BS in Math., U. Ala., 1964. Founder, ptnr. Corp. Art Source, Montgomery, Ala., 1983-92, owner, 1992—, CAS Gallery & Frames, Montgomery, Ala., 1994. Juror Jubilee Galleria Art Show, Montgomery, 1987, Riofest, Harlingen, Tex., 1989-90, BCA on My Own Time, Montgomery, 1990; guest lectr. Riofest, 1990; dir. Armory Gallery Arts Coun. Montgomery, 1989-91; advisor Montgomery Bus. Com. Arts, 1990-94, 97— (Bus. in Arts award 1989); curator Armory Gallery, Montgomery, 1989. Bd. dirs Arts Coun. Montgomery, 1980-94, 97—, pres., 1985-87, 92-93; mem. adv. bd. Montgomery Symphony Assn., 1993—; pres. Jr. League Montgomery, 1984, treas., 1981; Stephen min. 1st United Meth. Ch., Montgomery, 1992-94, mem. adminstv. bd., 2000—; bd. dirs. Vol. Info. Ctr., 1997—, mem. exec. bd., sec., 1998-2000, v.p. 2000-02, pres. bd. dirs., 2002—; bd. dirs. Arts Coun. of Montgomery. Named Vol. Action Ctr. Vol. of Yr., 1989; recipient Bus. in the Arts award Montgomery Bus. Com. for the Arts, 1989, Disting. Vol. in the Arts award Art Coun. Montgomery, 1996. Mem. Am. Soc. Appraisers (v.p. Ala. chpt. 2001—), Montgomery C. of C., U. Ala. Alumni Assn. Avocations: tennis, painting, gardening. Office: Corp Art Source 2960 Zelda Rd # F Montgomery AL 36106-2649

BELTON, BETTY KEPKA, retired art educator, artist; b. Wilson, Kans., Mar. 11, 1934; d. Frank and Rose Betty (Kepka) Hochman; m. Glen S. Belton, 1969 (div. 1974); 1 child, Risa-Marie. BS in Art Edn., Emporia State U., 1956; MS in Art Edn., Ft. Hays State U., 1966. Cert. art tchr., Kans. Jewelry apprentice Ursula Letovsky, Omaha, 1957-60; designer Hallmark Cards, Kansas City, Mo., 1960-62; art tchr. Linn (Kans.) Unified Sch. Dist. 223, 1966-69; murals, design Parsons (Kans.) Jr. High Sch., 1974-75; freelance writer, designer, artist Better Homes and Gardens, Creative Crafts, Woman's Day, Popular Crafts, Eng., 1975-77; inspector El Kan, Ellsworth, Kans., 1977-79; dist. coord., art tchr. Unified Sch. Dist. 328, Wilson, Kans., 1979-98, ret., 1998. Adv. bd. Wilson C. of C., 1980-84, Kans. Scholastic Art Awards, 1991-94; mem. Inst. for Improving Visual Arts in Edn., The Getty Ctr., Cin. Art Mus.; participant, cultural contbr. Smithsonian Instn., Nat. Park Svc., Washington, 1976; workshop leader Kans. State U., Manhattan, 1983; nat. folk art contbr. Kans. Future Homemakers, Reston, Va., 1988; panelist Southwest Regional Rural Arts Conf., Garden City, Kans., 1989, Arts in Edn., Kans. Arts Commn., Salina, 1991; cons. DeCordova Mus. Art, Lincoln, Mass., 1990; instr. MIdland Ctr. For Arts, Mich. Author: Egg Lap Studio and Batiking Method for Making Czechoslovakian Kraslice, 1984; contbr. Crafts in America, 1988, American Folk Masters, 1992; prepresented in collection Internat. Mus. Folk Arts, Santa Fe; atentee lap studio for Czech Kraslice, 1984. Recipient Nat. Heritage fellowship Nat. Endowment Arts, Washington, 1988, Gov.'s award Kans. Gov. Joan Finney, Topeka, 1992, Master Folk Artist Apprenticeship Program, Kans. State Hist. Soc., 1985-86, 87-88, 91-92, Disting. Alumni award Emporia State U., 2002 Mem. NEA, Kans. Art Edn. Assn. (Art Enhancer award 1985), Czech Soc. Arts and Scis., Ellsworth Area Arts Coun. (v.p. 1992-94, adv. bd.), Midland Artist Guild (Best of Show Drawing award, 2005), Midland Artist Guild (Best Group Show Drawing award, 2005). Avocations: czech folklore, history, giving workshops, public speaking, prairie grasses. Home: PO Box 1214 Midland MI 48641 Office Phone: 989-687-6861.

BELTZ, SHERREE LYNNE, music educator; b. Washington, Pa., Sept. 13, 1972; d. Walter A. and Wilma J. Piechnick; m. Jeffrey Pierce Beltz, Mar. 13, 1975. MusB in Music Edn., Mercyhurst Coll., Erie, Pa., 1994. Cert. tchr. Pa. Dept. of Edn., 1994. Office adminstr. Camp Dresser & McKee, Inc., Pitts., 1996—99; choral/theater dir. Cambridge Springs H.S., Pa., 1999—. Mus. theater dir. Penncrest Sch. Dist., Saegertown, Pa., 2000—; singer St Jude's Ch., Erie, Pa., 2000—; vocalist First Presbyn. Ch., Pitts., 1997—98, East Liberty Presbyn., Pitts. Singer (performer): (dinner theater performances) A Canterbury Feast, Medieval Dinner Theater, Riverside Inn Christmas, (theater performances) Pittsburgh Savoyards; singer: (soprano soloist) Carl Orff's Carmina Burana with West Liberty College/Community Choir at Capitol Music Hall, Wheeling, WV. Bd. trustees Pitts. Savoyards, 1998—99. Mem.: Pa. Music Educators Assn., Music Educators Nat. Conf. Avocations: travel, camping, swimming, arts/crafts. Office: Cambridge Springs High School 698 Venango Ave Cambridge Springs PA 16403 Office Phone: 814-398-4631.

BELTZNER, GAIL ANN, music educator; b. Palmerton, Pa., July 20, 1950; d. Conon Nelson and Lorraine Ann (Carey) Beltzner. BS in Music Edn. summa cum laude, West Chester State U., 1972; postgrad., Kean State Coll., 1972, Temple U., 1972, Westminster Choir Coll., 1972, Lehigh U., 1978. Tchr. music Drexel Hill Jr. H.S., 1972-73; music specialist Allentown (Pa.) Sch. Dist., 1973—; tchr. Corps Sch. and Cmty. Devel. Lab., 1978-80, Corps Cmty. Resource Festival, 1979-81, Corps Cultural Fair, 1980, 81. Mem. bd. assocs. Lehigh Valley Hosp. and Health Network. Mem. Mus. Fine Arts, Boston, aux. Allentown Art Mus., aux. Allentown Hosp.; mem. woman's com. Allentown Symphony, The Lyric Soc. of the Allentown Orch.; mem. Allentown 2nd and 9th Civilian Police Acads.; bd. dirs. Allentown Area Ecumenical Food Bank, Allentown Arts Commn; mem. Growing with Sci. partnership—Air Products and Chems., Inc. and Allentown Sch. Dist., Good Shepherd Home Aux. Decorated Dame Comdr., Ordre Souverain et Militaire de la Milice du St. Sepulcre; recipient Cert. of Appreciation, Lehigh Valley Sertoma Club; Excellence in the Classroom grantee Rider-Pool Found., 1988, 91-92. Mem. AAUW, NAFE, ASCD, Am. String Tchrs. Assn., Am. Viola Soc., Internat. Reading Assn., Internat. Platform Assn., Allentown Edn. Assn., Music Educators Nat. Conf., Pa. Music Educators Assn., Am. Orff-Schulwerk Assn., Orgn. Am. Kodaly Educators, Am. Recorder Soc., Phila. Area Orff-Schulwerk Assn., Soc. Gen. Music, Am. Assn. Music Therapy, Internat. Soc. Music Edn., Internat. Tech. Edn. Assn., Assn. for Tech. in Music Instrn., Civil War Roundtable Ea. Pa., Choristers Guild, Lenni Lenape Hist. Soc., Lehigh Valley Arts Coun., Allentown Symphony Assn., Midi Users Group, Pa.-Del. String Tchrs. Assn., Nat. Sch. Orch. Assn., Lehigh County Hist. Soc., Confedn. Chivalry (life mem. of merit, grand coun.), Maison Internat. des Intellectuels Akademie, Order White Cross Internat. (apptd. dist. comdr. for Pa./U.S.A. dist., nobless of humanity), Airedale Terrier Club of Greater Phila., Kappa Delta Pi, Phi Delta Kappa, Alpha Lambda. Republican. Lutheran. Home: PO Box 4427 Allentown PA 18105-4427

BELUE, JANIE A., music educator; b. Sheffield, Ala., Aug. 25, 1952; d. Alver Kendrick and Lucille Counce Belue. AA, N.E. Miss. C.C., Booneville, 1974; MusB in Edn., Miss. State U., Starkville, 1974, cert. in gifted edn. and adult edn., 1980. Cert. music edn. Nat. Bd., N.C. Adminstrv. dir. Camp Crestridge for Girls, Ridgecrest, NC, 1985—; chorus tchr. Alcorn Cen. H.S., Glen, Miss., 1978—84; tchr. gifted edn. Burnsville (Miss.) Elem. Sch., 1984—91; dir. Montreat (N.C.) Morning Sch., 1991—92; music tchr. Emma and Pisgah Elem. Schs., Asheville, NC, 1992—. Contbr.: (video) The Gift of Flight (Creative Tchr. of Yr. in N.C., 1995). Asst. min. music 1st Bapt. Ch., Black Mountain, NC, 1991—2005. Mem.: Music Educators N.C. Home: 10 E Keesler Ave Apt F Black Mountain NC 28711-3294 Personal E-mail: jabelue@aol.com.

BELUSO, KAREN MAE, performing company executive, music educator; b. Covina, Calif., Apr. 20, 1967; d. Paul Bellosillo and Fenicula Pandan Beluso; m. Antonio Juan Elizalde, Sept. 9, 1995; children: Paul Elizalde, Patrick Elizalde. MusB, Juilliard Sch., NYC, 1985, MusM, 1991. Head dept. performing arts Portledge Sch., Locust Valley, NY, 1996—2006; asst. exec. dir. Children's Orch. Soc., Manhasset, NY, 2006—. Recipient Alumni award, Profl. Children's Sch., 1998. Roman Catholic.

BELVAL, JOSEPHINE ANTANETTE, retired elementary school educator; b. Newton, Mass., Dec. 1, 1937; d. Natale and Geraldine (Rizzo) Scarcella; m. Peter C. Belval, July 8, 1961; children: Linda, Peter, Scott. BS in Bus. Adminstrn., Boston U., 1959, MEd, 1960. Cert. elem. tchr., Mass. Tchr. Natick (Mass.) Sch. System, 1959-61, Needham (Mass.) Sch. System, 1973—96; ret., 1996. Mem. various coms. Needham Sch. System, 1974—. Bd. dirs. St. Bartholomew Guild, Needham, 1975—; mem. Broadmeadow PTC, Needham, 1973—, Greater Boston Coun. of Reading, 1991—. Recipient Supt.'s Svc. award for Disting. Achievement, Needham Sch. System, 1990-91. Fellow Mass. Tchrs. Assn., Needham Edn. Assn.; mem. Boston U. Women's Grad. Club (sec.), Needham Jr. Women's Club (chmn. activities 1978-83).

BELYEU, MISTY LYNN, elementary school educator; b. Opelika, Ala., June 30, 1981; d. Randall Lynn and Susan Floyd Belyeu. BS in Edn., Troy State U., Ala., 2003. 5th grade tchr. Auburn City Schs., 2003—, summer sch. tchr., 2004—05. Colonial Williamsburg curriculum writer, Va., 2006; tchr. Camp Invention, Auburn, 2006. Grantee, Auburn FACES, 2005, Colonial Williamsburg grant, Hal Thomoson/ALSOE, 2005. Mem. Lds Ch.

BELZBERG, EDET, filmmaker; BA, U. Colo., Boulder, 1991; MA, Columbia U. Sch. Internat. and Pub. Affairs, 1997. Tchr., Tisch Sch. Arts NYU, 2001; frequent lectr., Sch. Journalism Columbia U. Assoc. prodr. (documentaries) Anthem, 1997, dir. & prodr. A Master Violinist, 1997 (John M. Patterson Enterprise award, Columbia U. Sch. Journalism, 1997), Children Underground, 2001 (Spl. Jury prize, Sundance Film Festival, 2001, Best Documentary Film award, Internat. Documentary Assn., 2001), The AMC Project: Lookalikes, 2003, Gymnast, 2005. MacArthur Fellow, John D. and Catherine T. MacArthur Found., 2005.

BELZER, ELLEN J., negotiations and communications trainer, consultant; b. Kansas City, Mo., May 22, 1951; d. Meyer Simmon and Fay (Weinstein) B. Student, U. Okla., 1969-70, U. Ibero-Americana, Mexico City, 1971; BA, Northwestern U., 1973; MPA, U. Mo., Kansas City, 1976. Rsch. asst. dept. polit. sci. Northwestern U., Evanston, Ill., 1970-73; adminstrv. asst. Ctrs. for Regional Progress Midwest Rsch. Inst., Kansas City, 1974; various positions to dir. socioecons. div. Am. Acad. Family Physicians, Kansas City, 1974-86; pres. Belzer Seminars and Cons., Kansas City, 1986—, Healthcare Collaborator, Inc., Kansas City, 2000—03. Instr. communication Avila Coll., Kansas City, 1987-92, dept. continuing edn. U. Kans., Lawrence, 1989-92; instr. dispute resolution Johnson County C.C., Overland Park, Kans., 2005—; spkr. on negotiation strategies, conflict resolution techniques, communication skills, 1986—; mediator for hosps., physician groups, state health depts., cmty. health ctrs., others. Contbr. articles to profl. publs. and mags. including Working Woman, Hospital Practice, and Family Practice Management, also monographs. Campaign vol. for local candidate, Kansas City, 1970, 82, 99. Democrat. Home and Office: 21 W Bannister Rd Kansas City MO 64114-4009 Personal E-mail: belzersc@juno.com.

BEMIS, MARY FERGUSON, magazine editor; b. NYC, Dec. 28, 1961; d. Edmund Augustus and Anne Adoian (Nalbandian) Bemis. BFA in Writing, Johnson State Coll., 1983. Co-editor, co-pub. Ave. Literary Rev. Ave. Publs. Inc., Burlington, Vt., 1983-85; editor Unique Hair and Beauty Mag., 1994; editor Lady's Circle Mag. Lopez Publs., N.Y.C., 1987-94, editor, 1989-94; freelance editor, writer Mus. Sci., Boston, 1991-93; freelance editor Woman's Day Spl. Interest Publs., 1996—98; sr. editor Am. Salon and Am. Spa Mags., 1988—98; editor-in-chief Am. Spa Mag., 1998—2003; bd. dirs. Internat. Spa Assn., 2003; spa reporter, founder Founder Insider's Guide to Spas, 2004—; contbg. editor Skin Inc. mag., 2004—. Spa adviser Shape mag., 2004. Co-editor: The Green Mountain Rev., 1982—83, Nature Through Her Eyes: Art and Literature by Women, 1994, Journey Into the Wilderness, 1994; sr. editor Am. Salon Mag., 1996—98, editor-in-chief Am. Spa Mag., 1998—2003; contbg. editor: Luxury Spa Finder mag., 2004. Mem.: Am. Soc. of Mag. Editors. Democrat. Unitarian Universalist. Mailing: Allured Publishing 362 S Schmale Rd Carol Stream IL 60188-2787 E-mail: MFBEMIS@aol.com.

BEN-AMI, DORIT AMALIA, psychiatrist; b. Jerusalem, Nov. 11, 1962; d. Robert Shalom and Daisy Nedjma Avital; children: Yochanan Oz, Ilan Shalom, Noga Shachar Shoshana. BSc, Hadassah Med. Sch. Hebrew U., Jerusalem, 1986; MD, Hebrew U., Jerusalem, 1989. Diplomate Psychiatry Israel Bd. Psychiatry, Neurology. Med. intern Bikkur Holim Hosp., Jerusalem, 1990—91; psychiatry resident Eitanim-Kfar Shaul Mental Health Ctr., Jerusalem, 1992—97; rsch. coord. U. Mich., Ann Arbor, 2000—02, psychiatry resident, 2002—. Post grad. student Western Pa. Family Ctr., Pitts., 1998—2000. Mem., counselor Israel Scouts Movement, Jerusalem, 1972—78; mentor, big sister P.E.R.A.C.H., Hebrew U., 1983—85; chief resident, rep. Israel Psychiat. Assn., Jerusalem, 1993—96; mem. Young Israel Southfield Synagogue, Mich., 2000. With Israel Def. Force, 1980—82. Recipient Faculty prize for Disting. Clin. Work, Hebrew U., Haddasah Med. Sch., 1993, You're Super! Patient-Nominated award for Disting. Clin. Care, U. Mich., 2005. Mem.: Israel Med. Assn., Israeli Psychiat. Assn. (assoc.), Am. Psychiat. Assn. (assoc.). Home: 21405 Constitution Southfield MI 48076 Office Phone: 248-855-5541.

BEN-AMI, LEORA, lawyer; BS, SUNY, Stony Brook; JD cum laude, SUNY, Buffalo. Law clk. to Sr. Circuit Judge Philip Nichols, Jr., US Ct. Appeals Fed. Circuit, 1984—85; ptnr. Clifford Chance, chair Am. Intellectual Property Group; ptnr. Kaye Scholer LLP, 2003—. Spkr. on patent law at conferences and seminars. Contbr. articles in field. Named one of 45 under 45, Am. Lawyer Media, 2003. Mem.: Am. Intellectual Property Law Assn., NY Patent, Trademark and Copyright Law Assn., Fed. Circuit Bar Assn., NY State Bar Assn. Office: 425 Park Ave New York NY 10022-3598 Office Phone: 212-836-8000. Office Fax: 212-836-8689. Business E-Mail: lbenami@kayscholer.com.

BENATAR, PAT (PAT ANDRZEJEWSKI), rock singer; b. Bklyn., Jan. 10, 1953; m. Neil Geraldo; 1 child, Haley. Albums include: In the Heat of the Night, 1979, Crimes of Passion, 1980, Precious Time, 1981, Get Nervous, 1982, Live From Earth, 1983, Tropico, 1984, Seven the Hard Way, 1985, Wide Awake in Dreamland, 1988, Best Shots, 1989, True Love, 1991, Gravity's Rainbow, 1993, All Fired Up: The Very Best of Pat Benatar, 1994, Heartbreaker: 16 Classic Performances, 1996, Innamorata, 1997, 8-15-80, 1998, Synchronistic Wanderings: Recorded Anthology 1979-99, 1999, Live at Electric Ladyland, 2002, Greatest Hits Live, 2003, Go, 2003, The Best of Pat Benatar Vols. I & II, 2004, Greatest Hits, 2005; popular recs. include Treat Me Right, Hit Me With Your Best Shot, Love is a Battlefield, Hell is for Children. Recipient Grammy award for best female rock vocal performance, 1981, 82, 83, 84 also: Gold Mountain Mgmt care Danny Goldberg 2575 Cahuenga Blvd W # 470 Los Angeles CA 90068-2102 E-mail: info@benatar.com.

BENAVIDES, DEBORAH ANN, academic advisor; d. Willie A. and Theresa L. Benavides. BA in Theatre, Incarnate Word Coll., 1983; MA in Edn., U. Tex., San Antonio, 2002. Bldg. supr. univ. ctr. ops. office U. Tex., San Antonio, 1988—96, internat. student program coord. office multicultural programs, 1996—99, academic advisor Coll. Liberal and Fine Arts,

1999—2002, academic advisor Sch. Arch., 2002—. Vol. Esperanza Peace and Justice Ctr., San Antonio, 1995—2001. Mem.: Tex. Academic Advisors Network. Avocations: music, reading, art, photography. Office: U Tex 501 W Durango Blvd San Antonio TX 78207 Office Phone: 210-458-3010. E-mail: dabenavides@utsa.edu.

BENAVIDES, GRETA LOUISE, elementary school educator, entrepreneur; b. Denver, July 28, 1956; adopted d. Edwin M. and Mariam Jayne Randall; m. Francisco Vega Benavides, July 3, 1994; children: Dane David Fredericksen children: Robyn G. Fredericksen, Masi Brede Fredericksen. BA in Fine Arts with honors, Calif. State U., Fullerton, 1996; MA in Edn., Biola U., 2000. Cert. tchr. Calif. 2d grade tchr. South Whittier (Calif.) Sch. Dist., 1997—; supr. Herbalife, L.A., 2003—. Supr. Home Sch., Buena Park, Calif., 1984—, young adult fine art instr., 1994—2003; tutor disabled students South Whittier Sch. Dist., 1999—2003. Exhibitions include Santa Ana Coll., 1984, Irvine Fine Arts Ctr., 1986; prodr.: (compact disc) Sing the Wondrous Story, 2003. Union rep. Calif. Tchrs. Assn., Whittier, 1997—2003; mem. chorus St. Linus Ch., 2000—03. Recipient Best in Show award, 1984; advanced classroom instrn. grantee, Whittier Credit Union, 2002. Democrat. Roman Catholic. Achievements include original research in the effects of reading comprehension on colored paper for persons with scotopic sensitivity. Avocations: painting, photography, promoting healthy nutrition, promoting public awareness of important political issues. Office: Los Altos Sch 12001 Bona Vista Ln Whittier CA 90605 Office Phone: 562-941-3711. Personal E-mail: teacher174@hotmail.com, gretafrancisco@adelphia.net.

BENBOW, CAMILLA PERSSON, dean, psychology professor; b. Lund, Sweden, Dec. 3, 1956; came to U.S., 1965, naturalized, 1985; m. David Lubinski; children: Wystan R., Bronwen G., Trefor A., Evan M., Lovisa D., G. Byron, Lena C. BA in Psychology with honors, Johns Hopkins U., 1977, MA in Psychology, 1978, MS in Edn. of the Gifted, 1980, EdD with distinction in Edn. of Gifted, 1981. Dir. Office of Precollegiate Programs for Talented & Gifted Iowa State U., 1987-98, Johns Hopkins U., Balt., 1977-79, asst. dir. Study of Mathematically Precocious Youth, 1979-81, assoc. dir., 1981-85, co-dir., 1985-86, dir., 1986—, assoc. rsch. scientist dept. psychology, 1981-86, asst. prof. sociology, part-time, 1983-86; assoc. prof. psychology Iowa State U., Ames, 1985-90, prof. psychology, 1990-95, chair dept. psychology, 1992-98, disting. prof., 1995-98, interim dean coll. edn., 1996-98; dean Peabody Coll. of Edn. and Human Devel., Vanderbilt U., Nashville, 1998—. Sr. editor: Academic Precocity: Aspects of Its Development, 1983, Intellectual Talent: Psychometric and Social Issues, 1996; contbr. articles to profl. jours. Recipient John Curtis Gowan prize Nat. Assn. Gifted Children, 1980, 81; Rsch. award Am. Ednl. Rsch. Assn., 1982; Spencer fellow, alt., 1984, 85, 86, Rsch. paper award Mensa, 1985, 86, 89, 94, 95 Mensa Lifetime Achievement award, 2004; Early Scholar award Nat. Assn. Gifted Children, 1985, Disting. Scholar award 1992, George A. Miller award APA, 1999. Mem. Johns Hopkins Soc. Scholars, Phi Beta Kappa, Sigma Xi. Office: Vanderbilt Univ Peabody Coll Edn/Human Devel Deans Office Box 329 Peabody Sta Nashville TN 37203 Office Phone: 615-322-8407. Business E-Mail: camilla.benbow@vanderbilt.edu.

BENCINI, SARA HALTIWANGER, concert pianist; b. Winston Salem, N.C., Sept. 2, 1926; d. Robert Sydney and Janie Love (Couch) Haltiwanger; m. Robert Emery Bencini, June 26, 1954; children: Robert Emery, III, Constance Bencini Waller, John McGregor. Mus. B., Salem Coll., 1947; postgrad. grad. Juilliard Sch. Music, 1948-50; M.A., Smith Coll., 1951; D In Mus. Arts, U. N.C., Greensboro, 1989. Head piano dept. Mary Burnham Sch. for Girls, Northampton, Mass., 1949-51; pianist, composer dance and drama dept. Smith Coll., 1951-52; head music dept. Walnut Hill Sch. for Girls, Natick, Mass., 1952-54; pvt. piano tchr., High Point, N.C., 1954-66; concert pianist appearing in Am. and Europe, 1948—; duo-piano performances with PBS-TV, Columbia, S.C., 1967, Winston Salem Symphony, N.C., 1964-68, Ea. Mus. Festival, Greensboro, N.C., 1969. Mem. DAR. Democrat. Presbyterian.

BENCIVENGA, ALISON R., elementary school educator; b. NYC, Mar. 25, 1951; d. Stan and I. Pearl Karr; m. John J. Bencivenga, July 26, 1975; children: Michael F., Catherine A., Margaret J.E. MS, LI U., Sparkill, NY, 1992. Cert. tchr. Tex. Tchr. Georgetown (Tex.) Ind. Sch. Dist., 1994—. Mediation coord., trainer Benold Mid. Sch., Georgetown, 2000—, social studies dept. chair, 2005—. Named Tchr. of the Yr., Benold Mid. Sch., 2000—01, Secondary Tchr. of the Yr., Georgetown ISD, 2000—01; recipient Excellence in Tchg. award/Rising Star Secondary Edn., HEB, 2004; scholar, Japan Fulbright Meml. Fund, 2004. Mem.: Delta Kappa Gamma. Office: Benold Mid Sch 3407 Northwest Blvd Georgetown TX 78628 Office Phone: 512-943-5090. Personal E-mail: bencivengaa@georgetown.txed.net.

BENCIVENGO, CATHY ANN, lawyer; BA, Rutgers U., 1980, MA, 1981; JD magna cum laude, U. Mich., 1988. Bar: Calif. 1988, US Dist. Ct. (no., ea., so. Calif. dist.), US Ct. Appeals (9th, Fed. cir.), US Supreme Ct. Ptnr., co-chmn. Patent Litigation practice group DLA Piper Rudnick Gray Cary, San Diego. Adj. faculty Univ. San Diego Law Sch., 1999; judge pro tem San Diego County Small Claims Ct.; dir. San Diego Mediation Ctr., 1999—2000. Eagleton Inst. of Politics Fellow. Mem.: San Diego Bar Found. (dir.), ABA, Fed. Bar Assn., Fed. Cir. Bar Assn., San Diego County Bar Assn. (co-chmn. Intellectual Property sect. 1993—94, dir. 1996—98, treas. 1997, v.p. 1998, chmn., lawyer referral & info. svc.), Order of the Coif.

BENDELIUS, BONNIE SUE, elementary school educator; b. Westwood, N.J., Oct. 28, 1961; d. Arthur George and Virginia Brown Bendelius; m. Brian Vincient Harr, Sept. 22, 1998. BA in Early Childhood Edn., Clemson U., S.C., 1983; MA in Early Childhood Edn., Oglethorpe U., Atlanta, 1992. Tchr. The Village Sch., Cheyenne, Wyo., 1983—86, R.D. Head Elem. Sch., Lilburn, Ga., 1987—91, Norcross Elem. Sch., Ga., 1991—98, Knight Elem. Sch., Lilburn, Ga., 1998—2002, Pharr Elem. Sch., Snellville, Ga., 2002—. Costumer, actor: Kaliedoscope Children's Theater; Abracadabra! Children's Theater. Mem.: Red Hat Soc., Tucker Quarterback Club, Phi Delta Kappa. Avocations: theater, sewing, football. Home: 5202 Addison Tr Lilburn GA 30047 Personal E-mail: b2tigers@yahoo.com.

BENDER, BETTY BARBEE, food service professional; b. Lexington, Ky., Apr. 29, 1932; d. Richard Carroll and Sarah Elizabeth (Rodes) Barbee; m. David H. Bender, Dec. 14, 1957; children: Bruce, Carroll. BA in Home Econs., Mont. State U., 1954; MS in Food Service Mgmt., Miami U., Oxford, Ohio, 1980. Adminstrv. dietitian Mass. Gen. Hosp., Boston, 1955—56; asst. chief dietitian Meth. Hosp., Indpls., 1957—61; chief dietitian Cmty. Hosp., Indpls., 1961—63; supervising dietitian Chgo. area ARA, 1963—67; asst. supr. food svc. Dayton Bd. Edn., Ohio, 1969, mgr. food svc., 1969—98. Cons. Nat. Frozen Food Assn., Washington, 1983, Crescent Metal Products Co., Cleve., 1985; nat. food svc. mgr. Meat Inst., 1998-2003; clin. nutritionist Jessamine County Health Dept., 2003—. Contbr. articles to profl. jours. Recipient 26th Ann. Foodsvc. Facilities Design award Instrs. Mag. for Commissary Design, 1972, Silver and Gold Plate awards Internat. Foodsvc. Mfrs. Assn., 1985, Pres.'s award Ohio Sch. Food Svc. Assn., 1987, FAME Golden Star award, 1992; recognized for outstanding contbns. to child nutrition program Ohio Ho. of Reps., 1972, 84. Mem. Am. Sch. Food Svc. Assn. (nat. pres. 1983, chmn. 1978-80, maj. city sect.), Ohio Sch. Food Svc. (pres. 1977), Dayton Sch. Adminstr. Assn., Dayton Sch. Mgmt. Assn. (pres. 1993-94), Am. Dietetic Assn. (cert., chair dietary practice group 1990-91, award for Excellence in Mgmt. Practice 1992, Food Svc. Dir. Yr. 1994), Ohio Dietetic Assn., Dayton Dietetic Assn., Soc. Nutrition Edn. (panel 1983). Democrat. Avocations: bridge, golf, swimming. Home: 1953 E Hickman Rd Nicholasville KY 40356-8838 E-mail: bbender831@aol.com.

BENDER, BETTY WION, librarian; b. Mt. Ayer, Iowa, Feb. 26, 1925; d. John F. and Sadie A. (Guess) Wion; m. Robert F. Bender, Aug. 24, 1946. BS, N.Tex. State U., Denton, 1946; MA, U. Denver, 1957. Asst. cataloger N. Tex. State U. Library, 1946-49; from cataloger to head acquisitions So. Meth. U., Dallas, 1949-56; reference asst. Ind. State Library, Indpls., 1951-52; librarian Ark. State Coll., 1958-59, Eastern Wash. Hist. Soc., Spokane, 1960-67; reference librarian, then head circulation dept. Spokane (Wash.) Public Library, 1968-73, library dir., 1973-88. Vis. instr. U. Denver, summers 1957-60, 63, fall 1959; instr. Whitworth Coll., Spokane, 1962-64; mem. Gov. Wash. Regional Conf. Libraries, 1968, Wash. Statewide Library Devel. Council, 1970-71 Bd. dirs. N.W. Regional Found., 1973-75, Inland Empire Goodwill Industries, 1975-77, Wash. State Library Commn., 1979-87, Future Spokane, 1983-88, vice chmn., 1986-87, pres., 1987-88. Recipient YWCA Outstanding Achievement award in Govt., 1985 Mem. ALA (mem. library adminstrn. and mgmt. assn. com. on orgn. 1982-83, chmn. nominating com. 1983-85, v.p./pres.-elect. 1985-86, pres. 1986-87), Pacific N.W. Library Assn. (chmn. circulation div. 1972-75, conv. chmn. 1977), Wash. Library Assn. (v.p./pres.-elect 1975-77, pres. 1977-78), AAUW (pres. Spokane br. 1969-71, rec. sec. Wash. br. 1971-73, fellowship named in honor 1972), Spokane and Inland Empire Librarians (dir. 1967-68), Am. Soc. Pub. Adminstrn. Clubs: Zonta (pres. Spokane chpt. 1976-77, dist. conf. treas. 1972). Republican. Lutheran. Home: 221 E Rockwood Blvd Apt 504 Spokane WA 99202-1274

BENDER, JANET PINES, artist; d. Nathan and Hana (Leff) Pines; m. Irwin Robert Bender, Feb. 25, 1966. BS, U. Wis., 1955; MA, Northwestern U., Evanston, Ill., 1956; postgrad., U. Ill./Loyola U., Chgo., 1955-56, Tyler Sch. Fine Arts, Phila., 1957. Tchg. arts North Orange Cmty. Coll., 2005—. Docent Long Beach Mus. Art, Mus. of Latin Am. One-woman shows include One Ill. Ctr., Chgo., 1979, 87, Olive Hyde Gallery, Fremont, Calif., 1980, 81, N.A.M.E. Gallery, Chgo., 1982, W.A.R.M. Gallery, Mpls., 1984, A.R.C. Gallery, Chgo., 1985, 87, 89, 94, 96, 98-2000, 2002, R.H. Love Galleries, Chgo., 1989, 92, 98, Soho 20 Gallery, N.Y.C., 1990, Galerie Thea Fischer-Reinhardt, Berlin, Germany, 1990, 98, catalog, exhib. travels to Munich & Antwerp, R.H. Love Contemporary Gallery, Chgo., 1992, 97, Unitarian Ch. Evanston, Ill., 2000; exhibited in group shows at ARC 30th Ann. Atelier Gym, Tokyo, 2000, 2001, Amos Eno Gallery, N.Y., 2001, Red Head Gallery, Toronto, Canada, 2001, Creative Art Workshop, New Haven, CT, 2000, Sydney Coll. of Art, Australia, 1999-2000, Mus. Sci. and Industry, Cho., 1995, 96, 98, Atelierhof, Bremen, Atelier, Gedok Gallery, Hamburg, Germany, 1999, Creative Art Workshop, New Haven, 2000, Artimesia Gallery, Chgo., 1996, Gallery 750, Sacramento, 1996, Women's Nat. Art Gallery, Washington, 1995, Rockford (Ill.) Art Mus., 1994, U. Wis. Art Gallery, Madison, Amos Enos Gallery, N.Y.C., 1993, Tonali Gallery, Mexico City, 1992, Renaissance Soc., Chgo., 1986, Ill. State Mus., 1983, 72nd Newport (R.I.) Nat. Exhbn., 1983, Chauttaqua Nat. Exhbn., 1981, Zolla Leiberman Gallery, Chgo., 1980, Holter Mus., Helena, Mont., 1997, Swan Gallery, Sydney (Australia) Coll. Art Gallery, 1998, Atelierhof Kunsthandwerkev, Bremen, Germany, 1999; represented in permanent collections at Mus. Sci. and Industry, Chgo., Young & Rubicam, Chgo., Brown-Forman Corp., Louisville, Nugent Wenckus Corp., Chgo., Louis Zahn Drug Co., Melrose Park, Ill, Fuller Comml. Brokerage Co., Chgo., Dynamark Inc., Chgo., Aabott Distbn., Miami, Art Beasley Inc., San Diego, Siegel, Denberg, Vanasco, Shivkovsky, Moses and Shoenstadt, Chgo., Altschuler, Melvoin & Glassner, Chgo., Shafer, Meltzer & Lewis Assocs., Wilmette, Ill., Schiff, Hardin & Waite, Chgo, art res. Byrdcliff Art Colony, 1998, Haguro-Machi, Japan. Bd. dirs. Art Residents Chgo. Gallery, Chgo., 1984—; juror Ill. Assn. Fine Arts Awards, 1993. Recipient Ill. Arts Coun. Project Completion grants, 1979, 81-82, Visual Arts Fellowship grant Ill. Arts Coun., 1983; fellow Northwestern U., 1955-56. Mem. NAFE, Women's Caucus for Art, Nat. Woman's Mus., Mus. Contemporary Art, Art Inst. Chgo., Chgo. Artist Coalition, Ill. Arts Alliance, Met. Mus. Art (N.Y.), Coll. Art Assn., Peace Mus., Ill. State Gallery, Com. fr Artist Rights (organizing com. 1988), Siam House, Pi Lambda. Avocations: reading, tennis, swimming, travel, theater. Personal E-mail: jpb614@verizon.net.

BENDER, JUDITH, journalist, editor; d. Samuel and Edith Bender. BA, U. Mich., 1954; MS, Columbia U., 1964. Reporter Passaic Herald News, Clifton, NJ, 1964—65, Knickerbocker News, Albany, NY, 1965—69; reporter, editor Newsday, Melville, NY, 1969—2000; freelance writer, 2000—; consulting editor Columbia Journalism Rev., N.Y.C., 2002—. Recipient award for Washington corr., Soc. for Profl. Journalists, 1982, Pub. Svc. award, N.Y. State Pubs. Assn., 1974. Mem.: Alumni Assn. Grad. Sch. Journalism Columbia U. (v.p. 2005—06). Office: Columbia Journalism Rev Grad Sch Journalism 2950 Broadway New York NY 10027

BENDER, VIRGINIA BEST, computer scientist, educator; b. Rockford, Ill., Feb. 10, 1945; d. Oscar Sheldon and Genevieve Best; m. Robert Keith Bender, July 19, 1969; children: Victoria Ruth, Christopher Keith. BS in Chemistry, Math., No. Ill. U., 1967; postgrad., U. Ill., 1967—69; MBA, Loyola U., Chgo., 1973. Cert. computer profl. Sr. sys. rep. Burroughs Corp., Chgo., 1969-73; sys. analyst Marshall Field & Co., Chgo., 1973-74; project leader Fed. Home Loan Bank, Chgo., 1974-76; sr. sys. analyst United Air Lines, Elk Grove Village, Ill., 1976-78; supr. Kemper Group, Long Grove, Ill., 1978-82; prof. computer info. sys., coord. computer info. sys. William Rainey Harper Coll., Palatine, Ill., 1982—2002, prof. emeritus, 2002—. Spkr. Midwest Computer Conf., DeKalb, Ill., 1988, moderator, 91; exch. prof. Maricopa CC, Mesa, Ariz., 1990, rsch. sabbatical, 93, 98; spkr. conf. info. tech. League for Innovation, Kansas City, Mo., 1995; steering com. Midwest Computer Conf., 1995—99; facilitator ToolBook User's Conf., Colorado Springs, Colo., 2000, presenter, Colo. Springs, 2001—03; adj. prof. SUNY/Westchester C.C., Valhalla, 2003—. Nat. chief mother-dau. group Indian Maidens YMCA, Des Plaines, 1982—83; mem. Vols. Pks. Environ. Edn. Westchester County Dept. Pks., Recreation and Conservation, NY, 2002—; mem. Master Singers of Westchester, 2005—; choir Kingswood United Meth. Ch., Buffalo Grove, Ill., 1982—2002, asst. organist, 1982—89; choir 1st Congl. Ch., Chappaqua, NY, 2002—, bell choir, 2003—, substitute organist, 2003—; bd. dirs. Consumer's Energy Coop., Inc., 2003—06, webmaster, 2004—. Named Tchr. of the Month, Burroughs Corp., Chgo., 1972. Mem.: No. Ill. Computer Soc., Ill. Assn. Data Processing Instrs., Inst. Cert. Computer Profls. (life), Am. Guild Organists (webmaster 2006—, dir. 2006—), No. Ill. Alumni Assn. (life), Mortar Bd., Sigma Zeta, Phi Theta Kappa. Avocations: swimming, needlecrafts, playing piano, organ, and marimba. Personal E-mail: vbender@hotmail.com.

BENDIG, JUDITH JOAN, information systems specialist, computer company executive; b. Erie, PA, Oct. 28, 1955; d. Richard W. and Rhea Agnes (Hain) B. BS magna cum laude in music edn., Edinboro State Coll., 1977. Tech. cons. Inco, Inc., Washington, 1982; sr. systems analyst Devel. Sci. Services, Inc., Arlington, 1982-85; dir. computer systems ADEENA Corp., Arlington, Va., 1985-86; prin. cons. Pricewaterhouse Coopers, Fairfax, Va., 1995—; prin. systems cons., integration mgr. WANG Labs., Inc., Bethesda, Md., 1986-95; v.p. F&B Computer Assocs., Bethesda, Md., 1986-95; prin. cons. Price Waterhouse Coopers, Fairfax, Va., 1995—. With USN, 1978-82, served to Capt., USNR, 1978—; mem. Arlington Community Band, 1986—. Mem. NAFE Assn. Computing Machinery, IEEE (assoc.), Naval Res. Assn. Republican. Roman Catholic. Home: 7733 Vinewood Ct Gainesville VA 20155-2852

BENDIX, HELEN IRENE, lawyer; b. NYC, July 24, 1952; d. Gerhard Max and Eva Gabriela (Sternberger) B.; m. John A. Kronstadt, Nov. 29, 1974. BA, Cornell U., 1973; JD, Yale U., 1976. Bar: Calif. 1976, D.C. 1978, U.S. Dist. Ct. D.C. 1980, U.S. Dist. Ct. (ctrl. dist.) Calif. 1986, U.S. Ct. Appeals (D.C. cir.) 1981, U.S. Ct. Appeals (9th cir.) 1987, U.S. Dist. Ct. (so. dist.) Calif. 1990. Law clk. to Hon. Shirley M. Hufstedler U.S. Ct. Appeals (9th cir.), L.A., 1976-77; assoc. Wilmer Cultler & Pickering, Washington, 1977-79; asst. prof. law UCLA, 1979-80; from assoc. to ptnr. Leva Hawes Symington Martin & Oppenheimer, Washington, 1980-85; of counsel Gibson Dunn & Crutcher, L.A., 1986-89; ptnr. Heller Ehrman White & McAuliffe, L.A., 1989-96; sr. v.p., gen. counsel KCET Cmty. TV of So. Calif., 1996—; judge Mcpl. Ct. L.A. Jud. Dist., 1997-2000, Superior Ct. L.A., 2000—. Vis. prof. law UCLA, 1985-86; chair ADR com. L.A. Superior Ct., 2004. Co-author: Moore's Federal Practice, Vols. X and XI, 1976, Vols. XII and XIII, 1979; contbr. articles to profl. jours. Violinist Palisades Symphony, Pacific Palisades, Calif., 1989—. Mem. European Union Ctr. of Calif., (mem. exec. adv. bd. 2003-05), Am. Law Inst., DC Bar Assn., Calif. State Bar Assn. (chair internat. law sect. 1990-91), Calif. Judges Assn., L.A. County Bar Assn. (past pres. dispute resolution svcs.), Jud. Coun. Calif. (mem. ad hoc com. on canon 6D 1998, working group on mediator ethics 2000, mem. access and fairness adv. com.), Chancery Club, Phi Beta Kappa. Office: Dept 18 111 N Hill St Los Angeles CA 90012-3014

BENDIX, JANE, artist, writer, illustrator; b. Lansing, Mich., Oct. 20, 1920; d. Helmer and Violet Walstrum; m. Reinhard Bendix, July 5, 1940 (dec. Feb. 1991); children: Karen, Erik, John. BA, U. Chgo., 1941; postgrad., Art Inst. Chgo., 1941-43. Freelance artist, 1941—. Author: Mi'ca, 1987 (Kinderbuch prize 1987), Mi'ca, Buffalo Hunter, 1992, Türkishöhle, 1990, Chaco. The Anasazi Mystery, 1997, The Secret Map, 2000; exhbns. San Francisco, 1988, Oakland, Calif., 1979, Goldern, Switzerland, 1965, Oxford, Eng., 1966, Washington, 1975, Berlin, Germany, 1990. Mem. Calif. Watercolor Assn. Home: 3 Orchard Ln Berkeley CA 94704-1821

BEN-DOR, GISSELLE, conductor, musician; b. Montevideo, Uruguay; came to U.S., 1982; m. Eli Ben-Dor; children: Roy, Gabriel. Student, Acad. of Music, Tel Aviv; artist diploma, Rubin Acad. Music, Tel Aviv; M, Yale Sch. of Music, 1982. Music dir. Annapolis Symphony, Md., Pro Arte Chamber Orch. of Boston; condr. Norwalk (Conn.) Youth Symphony; conducting fellow L.A. Philharm. Inst., 1984, Tanglewood Music Ctr., 1985; resident condr. Houston Symphony, 1991; music dir. Santa Barbara Symphony, Calif., 1994—. Resident condr. Houston Symphony; condr. variety conducting activities including prestigious summer festivals, competitions, 1983-87, Hungarian Nat. Symphony, Budapest Philharm., others; guest condr. orchs. in Uruguay, Ea. Europe, Israel and U.S. including Barvarian Radio Orch., Boston POPS, New World Symphony, Women's Philharm, San Francisco, Minn. Orch. in Summerfest Festival, 1986, N.Y. Philharm., 1993, 95, Orquestra del Teatro Nacional, Brazil, Ulster Orch., Israel Philharm., 1991, Carnegie Hall, 1991, others; past music dir. Houston Youth Symphony; past acting orch. dir. Shepherd Sch. Music Rice U.; music dir. Boston ProArte Chamber Orch., Annapolis Symphony. Condr. Israel Philharm. Orch. (play) The Rite of Spring; recs. with London Symphony, Israel Chamber Orch., (CD) London Symphony Orch., Sofia Soloists, Boston ProArte Chamber Orch.; numerous TV appearances. Am.-Israel Cultural Fund scholar, Frances Wickes scholar; Leonard Bernstein fellow; recipient Bartók prize Hungarian TV Internat. Condrs. Competition, 1986. Office: Santa Barbara Symphony Orch Arlington Theatre 1900 State St Ste G Santa Barbara CA 93101-8424 also: Del Rosenfield Assoc 714 Ladd Rd Bronx NY 10471-1204 E-mail: delrosdra@aol.com.

BENEDEK, MELINDA, television executive; BA, Oxford U., 1972; JD, Columbia U., 1977; French Law Degree, 1974. Owner High Wire Ltd., 1981—84; ptnr. Pollock, Bloom & Dekom; exec. v.p. Imagine Films; exec. v.p. bus. affairs Twentieth Century Fox, L.A.; exec. v.p. bus. affairs and prodn. Showtime Networks, L.A. Office: ShowtimeNetworks 1633 Broadway Fl 37 New York NY 10019-6708 also: Showtime Networks 14610 Washington Dr Fontana CA 92335-6262 Fax: 310-234-5397.

BENEDICT, GAIL CLEVELAND, music educator; b. Rockville Ctr., N.Y., Dec. 15, 1942; d. Walter Charles and Louise Cleveland; m. Donald Alexander Davis, July 4, 1967 (div. Apr. 14, 1980); 1 child, Scott Paul Davis; m. Robert Lorin Benedict, July 6, 1983. BS in Music Edn., SUNY, Fredonia, 1964; MS in Adminstrn. and Supervision, Nova U., 1980; EdD, U. Sarasota, Fla., 1982. Cert. tchr. Fla., N.Y. Music tchr., dept. chair North Country Elem. Sch., Stony Brook, NY, 1964—66; music tchr., chorus dir. Narimasu Elem. Sch., Tokyo, 1966—67; vocal music tchr. Mineral Wells (Tex.) H.S., 1967—68; music tchr., chorus dir. Park Ave. Elem. Sch., Amityville, NY, 1968—70; music tchr., resource tchr. Magruder Elem. Sch., Newport News, Va., 1970—72; music specialist Skyview Elem. Sch., Pinellas Park, Fla., 1979—; adj. instr. Nova Southea. U., Tampa, Fla., 1991—. Gen. mgr. V.I. Properties, St. Petersburg, Fla., 1989—. Author: (book) Cruzan Child, 2002. Grantee, Pinellas County Arts Coun., 2001. Mem.: Pinellas Co. Music Educators Assn. (vocal chair 1980—83), Fla. Elem. Music Educators Assn. (chair Dist. III 1979—84), Music Educators Nat. Conf. Avocations: travel, reading, history, writing. Home: 6712 Cardinal Dr S Saint Petersburg FL 33707 Office: Skyview Elem Sch 8601 60th St N Pinellas Park FL 33782 E-mail: drmommusic@aol.com.

BENEDICT, HELEN ELIZABETH, psychologist, university administrator; b. South Charleston, W.Va., Dec. 14, 1946; d. Donald Banks and Winifrede (Thornhill) B.; m. Andrew William Kovacs Jr., Aug. 11, 1979; stepchildren: William, Nancy Kovacs Westfall. BA, Conn. Coll., 1968; PhD, Yale U., 1976. Lic. psychologist, Tex.; registered play therapist/supr. Internat. Bd. of Examiners of Cert. Play Therapist-Supr./Profl. Asst. prof. dept. psychology Mich. State U., East Lansing, 1975-81; asst. prof. dept psychology Baylor U., Waco, Tex., 1981-83, assoc. prof., dir. clin. tng., 1983-85, assoc. prof., dept. chair, 1986-90, prof., dept. chair, 1990-92, prof., dir. clin. tng., 1992—. Psychol. cons. Mich. State U. Day Care Ctr., East Lansing, 1977-81, Lonnie McLennan Head Start Ctr., Waco, 1981-98, Waco VA Hosp., Waco, 1983—, Olin Teaque VA Hosp., Temple, Tex., 1983—, Corsicana Head Start, 1985—. Contr. articles to profl. jours. Mem. Policy Coun. for EOAC Headstart, Waco, 1984-89; elder People's Ch., East Lansing, 1978-80, First Presbyn. Ch., Waco, 1991-94, deacon, 1983-85. NIMH postdoctoral fellow, 1970-72. Mem. Am. Psychol. Assn., Soc. for Research in Child Devel., Tex. Psychol. Assn., Phi Beta Kappa. Presbyterian. Avocation: birding. Office: Baylor U Dept Psychology Waco TX 76798

BENEDICT, STEPHANIE MICHELLE, purchasing agent, sales consultant; b. North Kansas City, Mo., Aug. 28, 1980; d. Stephen Richard and Hope Marvel Benedict. MusB in Edn., Ctrl. Mo. State U., Warrensburg, 2003. Purchasing agt. Polymeric Imaging, Inc., North Kansas City, 2003—; sales cons. Lemongrass Spa Products, LLC, Bailey, Colo., 2004—. Clarinetist North Star Cmty. Band, Kansas City, 2003—06; vol. State Rep. Silvey Campaign, Kansas City, 2004—05. Scholar, Dept. Music Ctrl. Mo. State U., 2001, 2002; Regents scholar, Ctrl. Mo. State U., 1998—2000, Glenn Bixby Music scholar, Dept. Music Ctrl. Mo. State U., 2001, Merville Meverden Edn. scholar, 2002, Edith Brooks Music scholar, 2002. Mem.: Music Educators Nat. Conf. (assoc.), Collegiate Music Educators Nat. Conf. (assoc.), Mo. State Tchr.'s Assn. (assoc.), Kappa Delta Pi (assoc.), Rho Lambda (assoc.), Alpha Phi (assoc.; v.p. program devel. 1999—2000, chaplain 2000—01, marshall 2000—01, v.p. program devel. 2001—02, founding mem., treas. Kansas City Met. Alumnae chpt. 2003—05). R-Consevative. Disciples Of Christ. Avocations: musical ensembles, travel, photography, crafts, walking. Office: Polymeric Imaging Inc 117 E 14th Ave Kansas City MO 64116 Business E-Mail: stephanie@polymericimaging.com.

BENEDICT, THERESA MARIE, retired mathematics educator; b. East Rutherford, N.J., Feb. 6, 1939; d. Michael and Rosaria Trivigno; m. Willliam F. Benedict, Oct. 3, 1964' children: Gerard Michael, Willliam Francis. BS in Edn., Seton Hall U., 1978; MA in Adminstrn., Jersey City State Coll., 1989. Math tchr. Wayne (N.J.) Hills High Sch., 1978-79, Ramsey (N.J.) High Sch., 1980, Lakeland Regional High Sch., Wanaque, N.J, 1980—2000, ret., 2000. Advisor Vol. in Edn., Passaic County, N.J., 1986-89, Student Asst. Team, Lakeland High Sch., Wanaque, N.J., 1990-2000; coord. student/tchr. lunch program for at-risk students, 1991-2000. Leader 4-H Clubs, Wayne, N.J., 1975-88; advisor Parish Ch. Coun., Wayne, N.J., 1989-95, 2001-05; church eucharistic minister, 1986—; vol. Ch. Outreach Program; vol. with sick and poor, 2003—. Dame, Order of Malta. Roman Catholic. Avocations: horticulture, cooking, hiking. Home: 45 Brandywine Rd Wayne NJ 07470-3201

BENEFIELD, JANIS WILSON, school librarian, media specialist; b. San Angelo, Tex., Apr. 17, 1947; d. Woodrow and Madolynne Bradley Wilson; m. Harry Clayton Reno, Sept. 21, 1968 (dec. Nov. 10, 1968); m. Lester Benefield; 1 child, Bradley Lynn. BA, U. Houston, 1968; MLS, North Tex. State U., 1974. Lic. tchr. secondary english State Bd. Educator Certification, Tex., 1969, tchr. secondary french State Bd. Educator Certification, Tex., 1969, cert. profl. all-level learning resources specialist State Bd. Educator

Certification, Tex., 1977. Tchr. Gabbs (Nev.) Sch., 1969—71, Mary S. Black Intermediate Sch., Battle Mountain, Nev., 1971—73; dist. libr. Dolores County Schs., Dove Creek, Colo., 1973—74; children's and young adult libr. Moore Meml. Pub. Libr., Texas City, Tex., 1974; libr. media specialist Westchester Jr. H.S., Houston, 1975—85; libr. resources and media specialist Nottingham Elem. Sch., Houston, 1985—. Freelance storyteller, Houston, 2001—. Tutor Spring Br. Ind. Sch. Dist., Houston, 2000—05; leader Tallowood Bapt. Ch., Houston, 1983—88. Named Tchr. of Yr., Nottingham Elem. Sch., 2002; grantee, Apache Corp., 2003; J. Landon Short Mini grant, Partnerships and Vol. Programs Dept., 1990, 1991, 2003, 2005. Mem.: Tex. Computer Edn. Assn., Tex. Assn. for Gifted and Talented, Tex. Libr. Assn., Pi Delta Phi (sec. 1967—68, award French Cultural Svcs. Houston 1968), Beta Phi Mu. Conservative. Southern Baptist. Avocations: travel, reading, ballet, flute, walking. Home: 14800 Memorial Drive 274 Houston TX 77079 Office: Nottingham Elementary School 570 Nottingham Oaks Trail Houston TX 77079 Office Phone: 281-560-7460.

BENERIA, LOURDES, economist, educator; b. Boi, Lleida, Spain, Oct. 8, 1939; came to U.S., 1964; d. Agusti Beneria and Josepa Farre; children: Jordi, Marc. Licenciatura, U. Barcelona, Spain, 1961; MPhil, Columbia U., 1974, PhD in Econs., 1975. Coord. program on rural women ILO, Geneva, 1977-79; asst. prof. Rutgers U., New Brunswick, N.J., 1975-81, assoc. prof., 1981-86; prof. city and regional planning and women's studies Cornell U., Ithaca, NY, 1987—, dir. program on gender and global change, 1987—92, 2000—03, dir. Latin Am. studies program, 1993—97, dir. internat. studies in planning, 2003—; pres. Internat. Assn. for Feminist Econs., 2003—. Recipient Narcis Monturiol award for rsch. in the social scis., Barcelona. Office: Cornell Univ CRP W Sibley Hall Ithaca NY 14853-2148

BENFIELD, ANN KOLB, retired lawyer; b. Reading, Pa., May 1, 1946; d. Curtis Kepler and Stella (Kolb) B. BA, George Washington U., 1969, MA, 1974; JD, U. Ky., 1983. Ky. 1983, U.S. Ct. Appeals (6th cir.) 1985, U.S. Supreme Ct. 1987; cert. mental health consumer cons./educator; cert. trained mediator. Probation officer Superior Ct. of D.C., Washington, 1973-78; jud. law clk. to chief judge U.S. Dist. Ct. (we. dist.) Ky., Louisville, 1983-86, jud. atty. to fed. sr. judge, 1989-95; trial atty. Ogden, Welsh and Newell (formerly Ogden & Robertson), Louisville, 1986-89; pvt. practice Louisville, 1995—2001; ret., 2002; pro bono practice, 2002—. Adj. prof. U. Louisville Sch. Law, 1993, pro bono legal svcs., 2001-. Mem. exec. com., bd. dirs. Ky. chpt. ACLU, 1988-89, 91—2005, nat. bd. dirs., 1992-94, sec., 1995-96, treas., 1996-98, mem. legal panel, 1988—; mem. Reproductive Freedom Adv. Com., 1994-2001; mem. steering com. Fellowship Reconciliation, Louisville, 1997-2002; mem. governing coun. U. Louisville Women's Ctr., 1998-2001; rape crisis advocate Ctr. for Women and Families, 1997—2005, domestic violence advocate, 1998-2005; bd. dirs., gen. counsel Depressed Self-Help Svcs., Inc., 1998-2000. Fellow: Ky. Bar Found. (bd. dirs. 1994—96, charter mem.); mem.: Louisville Bar Assn., Ky. Alliance Against Racism and Polit. Repression (life), Ky. Bar Assn. (Donated Legal Svcs. Recognition award 2000, 2001, 2003), Ky. Paso Fino Horse Assn. (sec. 2000—01), Amicus Club of ACLU (founder Ky. chpt. 2004), Phi Beta Kappa, Order of Coif.

BENFIELD, KIMBERLY JOYCE MCFALL, media specialist; d. Kenneth C. and Joyce L. McFall; m. Willard E. Benfield, May 29, 2003. BA, Ark. Tech U., Russellville, 1996. Lifetime tchg. cert. Tex., Class A tchg. cert. NC. Band dir. Channelview Ind. Sch. Dist., Tex., 1996—97; asst. band dir. Spring Br. Ind. Sch. Dist., Houston, 1997—99; dir. of bands Alexander County Schs., Taylorsville, NC, 2000—06; media specialist Charlotte Mecklenburg Schs., NC, 2006—. V.p. Alexander County Internat. Reading Assn., Taylorsville, NC, 2004—06. Louise M. Plybon scholar, Appalachian State U., 2006. Mem.: NC Sch. Libr. Media Specialists, NC Music Educators Assn., Internat. Reading Assn. (v.p. 2004—06), Sigma Phi Alpha, Tau Beta Sigma. Republican. Baptist. Avocations: travel, reading, gardening, camping, outdoor activities. Office: Winget Park Elem Sch 12235 Winget Rd Charlotte NC 28278 Office Phone: 980-343-1063. Business E-Mail: kimberly.benfield@cms.k12.nc.us.

BENFIELD, LINDA E., lawyer; b. Denver, Colo., Feb. 23, 1960; BA magna cum laude, Colo. U., 1981; JD with honors, U. Chgo., 1985. Bar: Wis. 1985, D.C., Colo. Ptnr. Foley & Lardner LLP, Milw., chairperson environ. regulation practice group. Mem.: State Bar Wis., Colo. Bar Assn., D.C. Bar, Milw. Ballet (chairperson bd. 2003—, gen. counsel & bd. mem. 1996—2003), Racine Lead Adv. Bd. (mem. 1993—96), United Performing Arts Fund (cabinet 2003), Wildspace Dance Co. (bd. pres. 2001—03, bd. mem. 1995—2003). Office: Foley & Lardner LLP 777 E Wisconsin Ave Milwaukee WI 53202-5306 Office Phone: 414-297-5825. Office Fax: 414-297-4900. Business E-Mail: lbenfield@foley.com.

BENFORD, CATHERINE S., music educator; d. Peter Sydney and Takiko Benford. Student, SW Tex. State U., San Marcos, 1991—99. Cert. elem. educator Tex. State Bd. for Educator Cert., 1999, secondary music educator Tex. State Bd. for Educator Cert., 2003. Music specialist Robertson Elem., Round Rock, Tex., 2000—04; asst. band dir. Stony Point H.S., Round Rock, 2004—. V.p. Revolution Performing Arts Assn., San Antonio, 2003—04. Named M-Powered Educator, M-Audio, 2005—. Mem.: Austin Stars Performing Arts Assn. (sec. bd. dirs. 2005—), Tau Beta Sigma (life; v.p. 1997—98). Office: Stony Point High School Bowman Round Rock TX 78664 Office Phone: 512-428-7185. Business E-Mail: cathy_benford@roundrockisd.org.

BENGLIS, LYNDA, artist, sculptor, educator; b. Lake Charles, La., Oct. 25, 1941; d. Michael A. and Leah Margaret (Blackwelder) B. BFA, Sophie Newcomb Coll., 1964; Doctorate (hon.), Kans. Art Inst., 2000. Asst. prof. sculpture U. Rochester, 1970-72; vis. artist Yale-Norfolk, summer 1972; prof. Hunter Coll., 1972-73; vis. artist Calif. Inst. Arts, 1974, 76, Kent State U., 1977, Skowhegan Sch. Painting Sculpture, 1979, 99; vis. prof. Princeton, 1975; prof. Hunter Coll., 1980—, U. Ariz., Tucson, 1981, Sch. Visual Arts fine arts workshop, 1985-90, 2006—; Avery prof. Bard Coll., 1987; master artist Atlanta Ctr. Arts, New Symerna, Fla., 1989; prof. Quinnipiac Coll., 1998-99. One-woman shows include U. R.I., 1969, Paula Cooper Gallery, N.Y.C., 1970-71, 74-78, 80, 82, 84, 87, 90, 94, Hayden Gallery, Cambridge, Mass., 1971, Kans. State U., 1971, Fuller-Gross Gallery, 1972-74, 77, 79, 82, 86, 88-89, Portland Center Visual Arts, 1972, The Clocktower, N.Y.C., 1972, Tex. Gallery, Houston, 1974-75, 77, 79-81, 84, 89, Margo Leavin Gallery, LA, 1977, 80, 83, 85, 87, 89, 91, Dart Gallery, Chgo., 1979, 81-83, 85, Real Art Ways, New Haven, 1979, Ga. State U., Atlanta, 1979, Galerie Albert Baronian, Belgium, 1979, 81, U. South Fla., Tampa, 1980, Lowe Art Mus., Miami, 1980, Atlanta Ctr. Arts, New Symerna, Fla., 1989, David Heath Gallery, Atlanta, 1980, 85, 92, Chatham Coll., Pitts., 1980, Susanne Hilberry Gallery, Birmingham, Mich., 1980, 83, 85, U. Ariz., 1981, Tilden-Foley Gallery, New Orleans, 1984, 86, 89, Landfall East, NYC, 1987, Cumberland Art Gallery, Nashville, 1988, Tilden Foley, New Orleans, 1989, Richard Gray Gallery, Chgo., 1990, 93, High Mus. Art, Atlanta, 1991, Galerie Six Friedrich, Munich, 1998, Charim Klocker Gallery, Vienna, 1998, Kappatos Gallery, Athens, 1998, Cheim & Read Gallery, NY, 1998-99, Galerie Simmone Sterne, New Orleans, 1999, Opulent, Cheim & Read Gallery, 1999-2000, Guild Hall Mus., 1999, Weatherspoon Art Gallery, 2000, Meadows Mus., 2000, Liquid Properties, Cheim & Read Gallery, 2000-01, Simple Marks, Cheim & Read Gallery, 2002-03, Sculpture 1969 to 2004, Cheim & Read Gallery, 2003-04, Graces, Cheim & Read Gallery, 2005, Suzanne Hilberry Gallery, Detroit, 2005; exhibited in group shows Queens Mus. Art, 1999, Bellas Artes, Sante Fe, 1991, Illeme Biennale de Sculpture, Monte Carlo, Monaco, 1991, Am. Acad. and Inst. Arts and Letters, 1991, 94, 2000, CU Art Galleries, U. Colo., Boulder, A. B. Galeries, Paris, 1992, Morris Mus., Morristown, NJ, 1993, Okla. Mus. Fine Art, 1993, Fine Arts Mus. South, Mobile, Ala.,1993, Rhone Hoffman Gallery, 1992, Juilan Pretto, NYC, 1992, Brooke Alexander Editions, NYC, 1993, Penine Hart Gallery, NYC., 1993, Hunter Coll. Art Gallery, NYC, 1993, Auckland (N.Z.) City Art Ctr., 1993, Bykert Gallery, NYC, 1969, Detroit Inst. Arts, 1969, Milw. Art Ctr., 1971, Walker Art Ctr., Mpls., 1971, 81, Balt. Mus. Art, 1975, Mus. Contemporary Art, Chgo., 1977, 80, Stedelijk Mus., Amsterdam, 1978, Mus. Modern Art, NYC, 1979, 86-87, Palazzo Reale, Milan Italy, 1979, Guggenheim Mus., NYC, 1979, 87, Contemporary Arts Mus., Houston, 1980, San Diego Mus. Art, 1980, Whitney Mus., NYC, 1981; Between the Geometry and the Gesture, N.Am. Sculpture 1965-75 by minister of culture Valesquez Palace, Madrid, 1986, Wadsworth Atheneum, Hartford, 1987, Albright Knox Art Gallery, Buffalo, 1987, The New Sculpture, 1965-67: Between Geometry and the Gesture, Whitney Mus., 1990, Albright Knox Gallery, Cin., 2005, others; represented in permanent collections Mus. Modern Art, NYC, Guggenheim Mus., Whitney Mus., Walker Art Ctr.; Olympic Com. artist, 1983, High Mus. Art, Atlanta, Balt. Mus. Art, Canberra, Nat. Gallery Australia, Mus. Fine Arts, Houston, New Orleans Mus. Art, Phila. Mus. Art, Burroughs-Wellcome Corp., Research Triangle Park, NC, Hokkaido Mus. Modern Art, Sapporo, Japan, American Sculptors, NY, LA, Kamakura Gallery, Tokyo, Nat. Mus. Am. Art, Washington; subject of mag. and jour. articles and books; juror, participant nat. competitive exhbn. co-sponsored by South Bend Regional Mus. art, Ind. Women's Caucus for Art, 1992. Recipient Australian Art Coun. award 1976, Distinction award Nat. Coun. Art Adminstr., 1989; Yale-Norfolk scholar, 1963, Max Beckman scholar, 1965; Guggenheim fellow, 1975, Avery fellow, Bard Coll., 1987; grantee Artpark, 1976, Nat. Endowmnt for Arts, 1979, 90. Address: c/o VAGA 350 Fifth Ave Ste 2820 New York NY 10118 Office Phone: 212-226-7979. Personal E-mail: lbenglis@earthlink.net.

BENHAM, HELEN, music educator; b. NYC, Dec. 4, 1941; d. Charles Mead and Dorothea Wheaton Benham; m. Samuel S. Kim, June 12, 1965; 1 child, Sonya Wheaton Guardo. MusB, Oberlin Conservatory Music, 1962; BA, Oberlin Coll., 1963; MS, The Juilliard Sch., 1965; PhD, Rutgers U., 2001. Music faculty Diller-Quaile Sch. Music, N.Y.C., 1964—75, Mannes Coll. Music, N.Y.C., 1966—82, Monmouth Conservatory Music, Red Bank, NJ, 1967—; prof. music Brookdale C.C., Lincroft, NJ, 1973—. Concert artist, piano and harpsichord. Author: Piano for the Adult Beginner Books I and II, 1977. Trustee, sec. A. Louis Scarmolin Trust. Named Outstanding Young Women of Am., 1978. Mem. Music Tchrs. Nat. Assn., Nat. Guild Piano Tchrs., Am. Musicological Soc., Shore Music Educators Assn. Avocations: swimming, walking. Home: 960 Elberon Ave Long Branch NJ 07740-4709 Office: Brookdale CC Music Dept 765 Newman Springs Rd Lincroft NJ 07738-1597 Office Phone: 732-224-2065.

BENING, ANNETTE, actress; b. Topeka, May 29, 1958; m. J. Steven White, 1984 (div. 1991); m. Warren Beatty, March 12, 1992; children: Kathlyn Bening Beatty, Benjamin Beatty, Isabel Ashley Ira Beatty, Ella Corinne Beatty. Student, Mesa Coll.; theatre degree, San Francisco State U.; studied at, Am. Conservatory Theatre. Films include The Great Outdoors, 1988, Valmont, 1989, The Grifters, 1990 (Acad. award nomination best supporting actress 1990), Postcards from the Edge, 1990, Guilty by Suspicion, 1991, Regarding Henry, 1991, Bugsy, 1991, Love Affair, 1994, Richard III, 1995, The American President, 1995, Mars Attacks!, 1996, The Siege, 1998, American Beauty, 1999 (Acad. award nom. best actress), In Dreams, 1999, What Planet Are You From, 2000, Open Range, 2003, Being Julia, 2004 (Named Best Actress Nat. Bd. Rev. Motion Pictures 2004, Golden Globe for Best Actress, 2005), Running with Scissors, 2006; stage appearances Coastal Disturbances, 1986, (Tony award nomination 1986, Clarence Derwin award 1987, Theatre World award 1987), Spoils of War, 1988, Hedda Gabler, 1999; TV movies: Manhunt for Claude Dallas, 1986, Hostage, 1988; TV series: Liberty's Kids (voice only); TV appearances: Sesame Street, 1969, Miami Vice, 1987, Wiseguy, 1987, The Sopranos, 2004. Avocation: scuba diving. Office: Creative Artists Agy c/o Kevin Huvane 9830 Wilshire Blvd Beverly Hills CA 90212-1804*

BENITEZ, BRIGIDA, lawyer; b. Nov. 11, 1968; BS with high honors, U. Fla., 1990; JD cum laude, Boston Coll., 1993. Bar: Mass. 1993, DC 2002, U.S. Supreme Ct., U.S. Dist. Ct., DC and U.S. Ct. Appeals (4th, 6th, 7th, 8th and DC cir.). Ptnr., litig. dept., internat. arbitration dept. Wilmer, Cutler, Pickering, Hale & Dorr, LLP, Washington. Spkr. in field; mem. advisory com. Minority Corp. Counsel Assn. Contbr. articles to profl. jours.; editor (in chief): Boston Coll. Law Rev. Recipient Excellence in Legal Profession award, Mex. Am. Legal Def. and Ednl. Fund, 2004, Woman of the Year, Hispanic Bus. Mag., 2005; Nat. Hispanic Scholar. Mem.: ABA (standing com. election, law advisory commn.), Barristers, Women's Bar Assn. DC (former co-chair litigation forum), Hispanic Bar Assn. DC (pres.), Hispanic Nat. Bar Assn. (former v.p. external affairs), DC Bar (pro bono com.). Office: Wilmer Cutler Pickering Hale & Dorr LLP 1801 Pennsylvania Ave Washington DC 20006 Office Phone: 202-663-6678. Office Fax: 202-663-6363. E-mail: brigida.benitez@wilmerhale.com.

BENJAMIN, ADELAIDE WISDOM, retired lawyer, community volunteer and activist; b. New Orleans, Aug. 23, 1932; d. William Bell and Mary (Freeman) Wisdom; m. Edward Bernard Benjamin Jr., May 11, 1957; children: Edward Wisdom, Mary Dabney, Ann Leith, Stuart Minor. Student, Hollins Coll., 1950-52; BA in English, Newcomb Coll., 1954; JD, Tulane U., 1956; student, Loyola U., New Orleans, 1980-81; grad. extension program Sewanee Theol. Sch., U. South, 1982. Assoc. Wisdom, Stone, Pigman and Benjamin, New Orleans, 1956-58; tchr. ext. courses Sewanee Theol. Sem., 1984-88; ret., 1959. Spkr., panelist on sch. issues various local and nat. groups. Mem. Tulane Law Rev., 1954—56, compiler, editor, pub. Trinity Ch. supplemental songbook, 1980. Trustee Mary Freeman Wisdom Charitable Found., sec., 1987—92, pres., 1990—94, treas., 1994—, pres., 2000—; sec. bd. dir. YWCA, New Orleans, 1967—68, 1st v.p., 1968—69; bd. dir. Kingsley House, New Orleans, 1971—77; trustee Metairie Pk. Country Day Sch., 1971—79, sec., 1976—79; mem. adv. bd. Tulane Summer Lyric Theatre, Tulane U., 1972—, pres. adv. bd., 1977—79; bd. dir. Children's Hosp., New Orleans, 1976—79; mem. adv. bd. Pub. Radio Sta. WWNO, 1980—; bd. dir. Parenting Ctr., 1981—; pres. E&A Charitable Found., New Orleans, 1983—; pres. bd. New Orleans Symphony, 1984—89; mem. Loving Cup selection com. New Orleans Times Picayune, 1985; bd. dir. La. Mus. Found., New Orleans, 1989—, S.E. La. coun. Girl Scouts US, New Orleans, 1989—97, Loyola U., New Orleans, 1989—99, mem. exec. com., 1996—99, hon. bd. mem., 2003—; bd. dir. Louise S. McGehee Sch., New Orleans, 1990—, v.p., 1991—97, hon. bd. dir., 1991; pres. New Orleans Mus. Art Fellows Forum, 1991—; mem. exec. com. La. Mus. Found., New Orleans, 1991—; bd. dir. Newcomb Children's Ctr., New Orleans, 1991—94; mem. adv. bd. dept. psychiatry La. State U. Med. Ctr., 1992—; mem. exec. bd. La. Philharm. Orch., 1992—; mem. Newcomb Dean's Coun., 1997—, pres., 2002—; bd. dir. Nat. D-Day Mus., New Orleans, 1998—2002; bd. trustees Rosa Mary Charitable Found.; sec. parish coun. Trinity Episc. Ch., New Orleans, 1973—75, sec. vestry, 1975—79, active, leader Trinity Quartet, 1979—84. Recipient Weiss Brotherhood award Nat. Conf. Christians and Jews, 1986, Outstanding Philanthropist, Nat. Soc. Fundraising Exec., 1986, Volunteer Activist Award, St. Elizabeth Guild, 1986, Jr. League Sustainer award, 1987, Disting. Alumna award McGehee Sch., 1987, George Washington Honor Medal for Individual Achievement, Freedom Found. at Valley Forge, 1988, Living and Giving award Juvenile Diabetes Found. 1991, Outstanding Citizen New Orleans award La. Colonials, 1994, Jacques Yenni award Outstanding Cmty. Svc. Sch. Bus. Adminstrn. Loyola Univ., 1994, Integritas Vitae award for outstanding cmty. svc. Loyola U., 1994, Classical Arts Patron award Tribute to the Classical Arts, 1998, Big Bros./Big Sisters award for cmty. svc., New Orleans, 2004; named Goodwill Ambassador for Louisiana Gov.'s Commn. Internat. Trade, Industry and Tourism, 1987, Sweet Art, Contemporary Arts Ctr., 1988, Significant Role Model, Young Leadership Coun., 1988, Woman of Distinction S.E. La. Girl Scout Coun., 1992; named among Outstanding Alumni Class of 1954, Tulane U., 2004. Mem. ABA, LWV, La. Bar Assn., New Orleans Bar Assn., Jr. League New Orleans (exec. com. 1971-72, bd. dir. 1967-72), Ind. Women's Orgn., Com. 21, Am. Symphony Orch. League, Quarante Club (2d v.p. 1978-79), Debutante Club, Le Debut des Jeunes Filles Club, New Orleans Town Gardners (pres. 1979-80), Thomas Wolfe Soc. (life mem.). Home: 1837 Palmer Ave New Orleans LA 70118-6215

BENJAMIN, ANGELA M., art educator; b. Upland, Pa., June 13, 1950; d. Robert Joseph and Marie Elizabeth (Haebel) Benjamin; m. John W. Hodges, Mar. 12, 1977; children: Kathryn Anne Hodges, Matthew Aaron Hodges, Robert Dustin Hodges. BA in Art Edn., Mansfield U., 1973; post grad., Temple U. and Pa. State U., 1979; postgrad., U. Arts, 1989—. M equivalency cert. State of Pa., 1995. Art instr. Elwyn Inst., Media, Pa., 1974—78; art tchr. Avon Grove Sch. Dist., West Grove, Pa., 1988—. Part time art tchr. Chester County Art Assn., West Chester, Pa., 1984—. Mem. coms. Soc. of Friends. Grantee, Violette de Mazia Trust, Wayne, Pa., 2003—. Mem.: Turtle Dove Folk Club (bd. dirs. 2003—). Avocations: gardening, painting, printmaking. Home: Po Box 198 Unionville PA 19375

BENJAMIN, JENNIFER, health educator; b. Aurora, Colo., Jan. 30, 1980; d. Gregory and Kristin Benjamin; m. Jennifer Benjamin, July 7, 2007. MEd, U. Nev., Las Vegas, 2006. Cert. athletic trainer Nat. Athletic Trainers Assn. Tchr., head athletic trainer Denver Pub. Schs., 2002—04; grad. asst. U. Nev., Las Vegas, 2004—06; wellness coach Wellness Coaches USA, Las Vegas, 2006—. Recipient U. Nev.-Las Vegas GPSA grant, U. Nev. Bd. Regents, 2005. Home: 1226 Pagentry Dr North Las Vegas NV 89031 Office: Wellness Coaches USA 400 Stewart Ave Las Vegas NV 89101

BENJAMIN, LORNA SMITH, psychologist; d. Lloyd Albert and Esther Smith; children: Laureen, Linda. AB, Oberlin Coll., 1955; PhD, U. Wis., 1960. NIMH fellow dept. psychiatry U. Wis., 1958-62, clin. psychology intern, 1960-64, asst. prof., 1966-71, assoc. prof., 1971-77, prof. psychiatry, 1977-88; prof. psychology U. Utah, 1988—. Adj. prof. psychiatry U. Utah, 1988-; rsch. assoc. Wis. Psychol. Inst., Madison, 1962-66. Contbr. articles to profl. jours. Mem.: APA, Soc. Psychotherapy Rsch., Phi Beta Kappa. Office: Univ Utah Dept Psychology 380 S 1530 E Salt Lake City UT 84112-8934 Office Phone: 801-581-4463. E-mail: lsb_3@msn.com.

BENJAMIN, M. SUSAN, special education educator; d. Nicholas A. and Mary B. Caspero; m. Paul W. Benjamin; children: Michael P., John D. BS, James Madison U., 1976; MEd., George Mason U. Cert. prin. Ariz., tchg. Ariz., supr. Ariz. Spl. ed tchr. emotionally disabled Arlington (Va.) County Schs., 1977—79, Phoenix (Ariz.) Union HS Dist., 1979—80, Paradise Valley Unified Sch. Dist., 1986—93, dept. chair, 1993—95, prin., 1995—2001, asst. dir. spl. edn., 2001—. Pres. Homeowners Assn., Phoenix, 1984—85; mem. PV Planning Com., Phoenix. Mem.: State Ariz., Positive Behavior Supports Schools Com., Phi Delta Kappa. Office: Paradise Valley Unified Sch Dist 15002 N 32nd St Phoenix AZ 85032 Office Phone: 602-787-5012.

BENJAMIN, REGINA MARCIA, physician, administrator; b. Mobile, Ala., 1956; B in chemistry, Xavier U., New Orleans, 1979; MD, U. Ala., Birmingham, 1984; MBA, Tulane U., 1991. Internship and residency Med. Ctr. of Ctrl. Ga., Macon; med. dir. nursing homes, 1990—95; founder, adminstr. Bayou La Batre (Ala.) Rural Health Clinic, Inc., 1990—; assoc. dean rural health U. South Ala. Coll. Medicine. Med. mission, Honduras, 1993. Recipient Nelson Mandela Award for Health and Human Rights, Kaiser Family Found., 1997, Nat. Caring Award, Caring Inst., 2000, President's Award, U. Ala. Birmingham, 2001. Fellow: Am. Acad. Family Physicians; mem.: Med. Assn. State of Ala. (pres. 2002—03), NAS, AMA (Women in Medicine Panel 1986—87, pres. Edn. and Rsch. Found. 1997—98). Achievements include First African Am. woman to become pres. of a state med. soc. in the US, 2002; featured in Nat. Libr. Medicine exhibit Changing the Face of Medicine honoring women physicians, 2003. Office: 318 Patrician Dr Spanish Fort AL 36527-9461

BENN, CANDACE MARILEA, elementary school educator; b. L.I., N.Y., Apr. 2, 1980; d. Mervin Leroy and Antoinette Patricia Foster; m. Jason Edward Benn, July 12, 2003; 1 child, Lanai Taylor. BS, Va. State U., Petersburg, 2002. Daycare counselor Chester Child Devel., Chester, Va., 1999—2002; Head Start tchr. Woodlawn Learning Ctr., Dinwiddie, Va., 2003—. Mem.: Am. Counselors Assn., Nat. Urban League, Va. Counseling Assn., Pi Lambda Theta. Home: 4408 Widgeon Ct Petersburg VA 23803

BENNER, MARY WRIGHT, freelance/self-employed conference director; b. Chgo., Aug. 4, 1956; d. Robert V.L. and Sara Helen (Beeler) W.; m. Thomas G. Benner, Aug. 8, 1987; children: Sara Eleanor, Robert Fox. BA, Conn. Coll., 1979; MBA, Columbia U., 1983. Rsch. assoc. Acad. for Contemporary Problems, Washington, 1979-81; rating specialist Standard & Poor's, N.Y.C., 1983-84; asst. adminstr. Twp. of Princeton, NJ, 1984-86; v.p. Fin. Guaranty Ins. Co., N.Y.C., 1986-99, mgr. dept. govt. affairs, 1997-99; pres. Wright Benner Assocs., 1999—; program dir. The Conf. Bd., 2002—. Bd. dirs. Nat. Com. for Pub./Pvt. Partnerships, 1997-99; mem. sponsor adv. com. Women Exec. in State Gov., 1998-99; mem. steering com. Rebuild Am. Coalition, 1997-99; co-chair Uniting Citizens for Housing Affordability in Newton, 2000-04; chair out reach commn. Eliot Ch. of Newton, 2001—. Mem. Pub. Works Forum (bd. dirs. 1986-88), Assn. for Govtl. Leasing and Fin. (bd. dirs. 1991-95, treas. 1994-95), Assn. Fin. Guaranty Insurers (chmn. com. govt. affairs 1997-99), Rebuild Am. Coalition (exec. bd. dirs. 1998-88), Cape Cod Chamber Mus. Festival, (v.p., bd. dirs. 2000-03), Can-Do (bd. dirs. 2005-). Avocations: cooking, tennis. Home and Office: 136 Washington St Newton MA 02458-2250 Personal E-mail: mwbenner@rcn.com.

BENNER, PATRICIA ANN, retired literacy educator; b. San Francisco, Sept. 27, 1934; d. Reed M. and Myrtle L. Clarke; m. Norman L. Benner (div.); children: Laurie Ann, David Clarke; m. Alex McKeon; children: Michael McKeon, Kerry Leglu McKeon. BA in English, San Francisco State U., Calif., 1956; MA in Reading, San Jose State U., Calif., 1980. Cert. gen. secondary credential San Francisco State U., life credential gen. secondary Calif., basic edn. credential Calif., reading specialist credential Calif. Reading tchr. Continuation HS, San Francisco, 1957—59; reading, English tchr. San Jose HS, 1959—64, Metro. Adult Edn. Program, Calif., 1960—69, tchr., 1969—78; reading tchr. West Valley C.C., Calif., 1968—69; lang. arts tchr. Lincoln HS, San Jose, 1978—78; reading tchr. Evergreen Valley Coll., 1980—94; reading cons. statewide, Calif., 1970—; literacy trainer McQuire Facility for Men, Calif., 1993—, Women's Correctional Ctr., San Mateo County, Calif., 1993—. Avocations: reading, gardening, travel, tutoring. Home: 23405 Deerfield Rd Los Gatos CA 95033 Office Phone: 408-353-1058. Personal E-mail: patbenner1@earthlink.net.

BENNER, PAULA ROXANNE, academic administrator, educator; b. St. Joseph, Mich., July 26, 1954; d. Richard Newton Benner and Elsa Patricia Stolpe Benner Soden. BA, NYU, 1978; MS in Edn., U. Pa., 1988. Cert. reading specialist, Pa. Ednl. specialist Summit Lighthouse Study Group of Phila., 1975—; park aide Statue of Liberty Nat. Monument, Liberty Island, N.Y., 1979; tutor Coll. Bound, Broomall, Pa., 1991-92; ednl. cons. World Book Ednl. Products, Chgo. and Phila., 1991-92, 95; grad. asst. U. Pa., Phila., 1995-96; adminstr. Wyeth Nutritionals Inc. Internat., St. Davids, Pa., 1995-99; coord. Penn-West Phila. sch. partnership program U. Pa., Phila., 1999; tchr. reading Sch. Dist. Phila., 1999—. Title I reading specialist Girard Coll., 2000. Author curriculum materials I Can Be A Hero Like Hercules!, 1997, Benjamin Franklin's Art of Virtue Journal, 2006; prodr., actress in drama The Vision of General Washington, 1987 (cert. of appreciation). Sec., officer, trustee Summit Lighthouse Study Group, 1979-81, 89, 92-95, 99—; rep. Grad. Sch. Edn. Student Assn., U. Pa., 1986-87; vol. United Way, Phila., 1998; electioneer Chgo. Bd. Election Commrs., 1991. Mem. Character Edn. Partnership, Patchwork—A Storytelling Guild (storyteller), Assn. Uniting Art and Religion, Ch. Universal and Triumphant, Chi Sigma Chi (treas. 1992). Avocations: art, music, literature, drama, spirituality. Home: 43 Ann Rd Broomall PA 19008-1302

BENNETT, ALISON MERCEDES, human resources specialist; b. Jackson, Mich., June 25, 1980; d. Kerry Robert and Marsha Alison Klinger; m. Todd Jeffrey Bennett, Aug. 10, 2000. Masters in Bus. Indsl. Mgmt. Counseling, Wright State U.; BA in Psychology, Wilmington Coll. Corp. trainer Warner Healthcare, Inc., Cin., 2003—04; human resources generalist Berkeley Premium Nutraceuticals, Cin., 2004—06, regulatory compliance mgr., 2006—. Mem.: Am. Mensa. Home: 3858 Springboro Rd Lebanon OH 45036 Personal E-mail: aklinger35@hotmail.com.

BENNETT, AMANDA, editor; m. Terence B. Foley; 2 children. Grad. cum laude, Harvard U., 1975. Auto industry reporter Wall St. Jour., Pentagon & State Dept. reporter, Beijing corr., mgmt. editor/reporter, nat. economics corr., chief Atlanta bur.; mng. editor projects The Oregonian, 1998—2001; editor, v.p. Lexington Herald-Leader, Ky., 2001—03; editor, exec. v.p. Phila. Inquirer, 2003—. Mem. Pulitzer Prize Bd., 2002—. Author: Death of the Organization Man, 1991; co-author (with Sidney Rittenberg): The Man Who Stayed Behind, 1993; co-author: (with Terence B. Foley) In Memoriam, 1998. Co-recipient Pulitzer Prize for nat. reporting, 1997. Office: Philadelphia Inquirer PO Box 8263 400 N Broad St Philadelphia PA 19101 Business E-Mail: abennett@phillynews.com.*

BENNETT, ARLIE JOYCE, clinical social worker; b. Central Lake, Mich., Nov. 22, 1921; d. Charles Herbert and Bernice Evelyn (Miller) B. Student, Alma (Mich.) Coll., 1946-48; BA, U. Mich., 1950, MSW, 1955. Bd. cert. diplomate emerita Am. Bd. Examiners in Clin. Social Work. Social worker Ypsilanti (Mich.) State Hosp., 1950-54; staff social worker Kalamazoo Child Guidance Clinic, 1955-67, chief social worker, 1967-71; clin. social worker State Tech. Inst. Rehab. Ctr., Plainwell, Mich., 1971-90; pvt. practice, Kalamazoo, 1991-92. Field instr. Mich. State U., 1959-76, Western Mich. U. Sch. Social Work, Kalanazoo, 1971-90, U. Mich., 1967-71. Author: Pie Is in the Eye of the Beholder, 1980, War and Memory, 1991; editor newsletter Late Show Connection, 1993—; also articles, reports in field Vol. record reviewer Cath. Family Svcs. Agys., Kalamazoo; bd. dirs. Youth Opportunities Unltd., Kalamazoo, 1968—1980. Tech. sgt. WAC, AUS, 1944-46, ETO. Mem. NASW (past chmn. and officer), AAUW (legis. chmn. Kalamazoo br. 1985-89, 93-95, pres. 1991-93, pub. policy chmn. 1999-2002), Mensa (local coord. 1990—), Loners Am. (pres. Mich. chpt. 1990-92, 97-98), U. Mich. Alumnae Club (past pres. and officer), Phi Kapa Phi. Avocations: poetry, writing, camping, seat weaving. Home: 1110 W Maple St Kalamazoo MI 49008-1846 Office Phone: 269-349-6293.

BENNETT, BROOKE, Olympic athlete; b. Tampa, Fla., May 6, 1980; Grad., Durant HS, Plant City, Fla., 1998. Swimmer; winner gold and silver medals Pan-Am Games, 1995; winner gold medal Pan Pacific Games, 1995, 97; gold medalist 800m freestyle Olympic Summer Games, 1996; sponsor swim team Brower Aquatic Suns, Davie, Fla.; gold medalist 400m freestyle, Sydney, 2000, 800m freestyle, Sydney, 2000. Recipient Spring Nationals Kiphuth award, 1996, Spring Nationals Phillips Performance award, 1996, USOC Sports Woman of the Yr. for swimming, 1995. Avocation: horseback riding. Office: c/o USA Swimming 1 Olympic Plz Colorado Springs CO 80909-5746

BENNETT, CAROL(INE) ELISE, retired reporter, actress; b. New Orleans, Dec. 27, 1938; d. Gerald Clifford Graham and Edna Doris (Toennies) Kerr; m. Ralph Decker Bennett, Jr., Feb. 27, 1966; children: Ralph Decker III, Katherine Elise. BA, U. B.C., Vancouver, Can., 1960; BLS, McGill U., Montreal, Que., Can., 1962. Libr. various locations, 1962-76; reporter TV/radio Washington-Ala. News Report, Washington, 1981-2001; ret., 2001. Actor: (plays) Girl in My Soup, 1978; (films) Kennedy, 1983, Prime Risk, 1984; host (TV series) Modern Maturity, 1986—88; author (with Terese Loeb Kreuzer): How to Move to Canada, A Primer for Americans, 2006. Vol. reader Rec. for Blind, Washington, 1985—. Mem.: AAUW, AFTRA, SAG, Nat. Press Club, Soc. Profl. Journalists. Avocation: tennis. Home: 115 Southwood Ave Silver Spring MD 20901-1918

BENNETT, CATHERINE MARGARET, music educator; b. Antwerp, Belgium, Jan. 23, 1970; d. George William and Betty Louisa Eberling; m. Chad Baylus Bennett, May 20, 2000; children: Caelyn Mckenna children: Chase Baylus George. B, S.W. Tex. State U., 1993. Asst. band dir. Crowley (Tex.) HS, 1993—94, Pflugerville HS, 1994—98; assoc. dir. bands James Bowie HS, Austin, Tex., 1998—. Chair fine arts dept. Bowie HS, 2004—. Recipient Citation of Excellence, John Phillip Sousa Found., 2003. Mem.: World Assn. Symphonic Bands and Ensembles (assoc.), Nat. Assn. Music Edn. (assoc.), Tex. Music Educators Assn. (assoc.), Tau Beta Sigma (assoc.). Home: 9245 Vigen Cir Austin TX 78748 Office: James Bowie HS 4103 W Slaughter Ln Austin TX 78749 Personal E-mail: cb52000@flash.net. E-mail: ceberlin@austin.isd.tenet.edu.

BENNETT, SISTER ELSA MARY, retired secondary school educator; b. Muskegon, Mich., Dec. 13, 1930; d. Thomas B. and Elsa (Koelbel) B. BS, Our Lady of Lake Coll., San Antonio, 1955, MEd, 1971. Registered massage therapist, Tex.; Reiki master. Tchr. phys. edn. parochial schs., Abilene, Tex., Tulsa, San Antonio, Houston, Ennis, Tex., Alexandria, La., 1954, tchr., coach San Antonio, 1969—74, 1986—87, pub. schs., Mich., 1974—78; tchr. St. Augustine Sch., Laredo, Tex., 1978—79; adminstr., coach Our Lady of Lake U., 1979—86; phys. therapy aide Warm Springs Rehab., San Antonio, 1989—90; tchr. San Antonio Ind. Sch. Dist., 1990—2000; ret., 2000. With pub. rels. dept. San Antonio City Parks and Recreation Dept., 1987-89; masseuse, Reiki and water aerobics instr. Retirement Ctr. at Our Lady of the Lake Convent, San Antonio, 2000—. Instr. ARC, San Antonio, 1952. Mem. AAHPER and Dance, Tex. Assn. Health, Phys. Edn., Recreation and Dance. Avocations: golf, swimming, sailing, bowling, travel. Home: 2318 Town Grove Dr San Antonio TX 78238-5023

BENNETT, HELEN, psychotherapist; b. Antwerp, Belgium, Sept. 7, 1937; came to U.S., 1946; d. Emil and Maria (Klein) Fruchter; m. Ronald Sanford Bennett, 1956 (div. 1976); children: Denice, Miriam (dec. 1996), Sharon, Ruth. BA, Wayne State U., 1978, MSW, 1980. Lic. clin. social worker, Mich. Therapist Pontiac Mental Hosp., Mich., 1978—79; social worker Cath. Social Svcs., Mich., 1979-80; head of mental health Fathers for Equal Rights of Am., Southfield, Mich., 1980—. Cons. Sid Young's Retailers, Jackson, Mich., 1990—; divorce therapist, mediator, 1980—. Editor Father's Jour. Mem. NASW, World Fedn. Mental Health, Women's Freedom Network. Avocations: oil painting on canvas, sculpture, composer, poetry, voice. Home and Office: 25440 Lois Lane Dr Southfield MI 48075-6160 Office Phone: 248-353-5354.

BENNETT, JANIS M., elementary school educator; b. West Covina, Calif., June 26, 1978; d. Ron E. Mitchell; m. Michael D. Bennett; children: Julia Anderson, Mallory. Degree in Hist. Studies, U. Tex., Richardson, 2003. Lic. tchr. State Bd. Edn., 2004. Dept. head Burnett Jr. High, Wylie, Tex., 2003—, mentor, tchr., 2005—06. Target am. history grant recipient Region 10, Richardson, 2005—. With USAF, 1996—2000. Scholar, Dallas Bapt. U., 2006. Mem.: ATPE. Office Phone: 972-429-0987.

BENNETT, JEAN LOUISE MCPHERSON, physicist, research scientist; b. Kensington, Md., May 9, 1930; d. Archibald Turner and Margaret Fitch (Willcox) McPherson; m. Harold Earl Bennett, Aug. 17, 1952 (div. Nov. 1984). BA summa cum laude, Mt. Holyoke Coll., 1951, DSc (hon.), 1992; MS, Pa. State U., 1953, PhD in Physics, 1955. Physicist Wright Air Devel. Ctr., Dayton, Ohio, 1955—56, Naval Ordnance Test Sta. (now Naval Air Warfare Ctr. Weapons Divsn.), China Lake, Calif., 1956—85; sr. rsch. scientist Naval Air Warfare Ctr. Weapons Divsn., China Lake, 1987—93, 1995; vis. prof. U. Ala., Huntsville, 1986—87, Mt. Holyoke Coll., South Hadley, Mass., 1994—95; ret., 1996. Mem. NRC Evaluation Panel Nat. Bur. Stds., Ctr. for Radiation Rsch., 1979-85, Nat. Inst. Stds. and Tech. Mfg. Enging. Lab., 1988-94, U.S. Nat. Com. for Internat. Commn. for Optics, 1984-85, 88-95; vis. scientist Inst. Optical Rsch., Royal Inst. Tech., Stockholm, Mar.-Sept., 1988, 98, 99, 2000, 01. Author: (with Lars Mattsson) Introduction to Surface Roughness and Scattering, 1989, rev., 1999; author: Surface Finish and Its Measurement, 1992; contbr. sci. articles to profl. jours.; patentee in field. Recipient Tech. Achievement award Soc. Photo-Optical Instrumentation Engrs., 1983, L.T.E. Thompson award Naval Weapons Ctr., 1988, Women in Sci. and Enging. Lifetime Achievement award, 1993, Outstanding Sci. Alumni award Pa. State U., 1999; named sr. fellow Naval Weapons Ctr., 1989, Disting. Fellow, 1994. Fellow Optical Soc. Am. (v.p. 1984, pres.-elect 1985, pres. 1986, past pres. 1987, chmn. book publ. com. 1991-94, David Richardson medal 1990); mem. Am. Inst. Physics (subcom. on books 1990-94), Phi Beta Kappa, Sigma Xi, Sigma Delta Epsilon, Iota Sigma Pi, Pi Mu Epsilon, Sigma Pi Sigma. Achievements include being the first woman to receive PhD in Physics at Pa. State U., 1955; first woman pres. Optical Soc. of Am. Office: Code 4T41A0D Michelson Lab Naval Air Warfare Ctr Stop 6302 1900N Knox Rd China Lake CA 93555 E-mail: jbennett@ridgenet.net.

BENNETT, JODI LYNN, music educator; b. Mankato, Minn., Mar. 18, 1974; d. Harold Edwin and Ruth Ann Jacobson; m. Jason Michael Bennett, June 12, 1999; children: Bryan Harrison, Ashlyn Delany. BS in Tchg., Minn. State U., 1997. Music tchr. New Ulm (Minn.) Pub. Schools, 1998—2000; vocal and classroom music tchr. Waterville (Minn.) -Elysian-Morristown Pub. Schs., 2000—. Mem., alto sect. leader Magnum Chorum, St. Louis Park, Minn., 2005—. Reserve mem. Riverbend Hand Bell Choir, Mankato, Minn., 2002—06. Mem.: Am. Choral Dirs. Assoc. (assoc. Minn. Young Condr. Dianloue grantee 1999). Dfl. Lutheran. Avocations: reading, scrapbooks, knitting, jewelry, stamping. Office: WEM Pub Schs 500 E Paquin St Waterville MN 56096 Office Phone: 507-362-4431.

BENNETT, JUDITH MACKENZIE, historian; b. Neptune, N.J., Jan. 12, 1951; d. John Charles and Jean MacKenzie Bennett; life ptnr. Cynthia B. Brilliant. AB, Mt. Holyoke Coll., South Hadley, Mass., 1973; MA, U. Toronto, 1974; Licentiate, Pontifical Inst. Mediaeval Studies, Toronto, Can., 1978; PhD, U. Toronto, 1981. Asst. to chaired prof. history U. N.C., Chapel Hill, 1981—2005; prof. history U. So. Calif., L.A., 2005—. Author: (book) Women in the Medieval English Countryside: Gender and Household in Brigstock before the Plague, 1987, Beer, and Brewsters in England: Women's Work in a Changing World, 1300 to 1600, 1996 (Otto Grundler Prize), A Medieval Life: Cecilia Penifader of Brigstock, 1998, Medieval Women in Modern Perspective, 2000, History Matters: Patriarchy and the Challenge of Feminism, 2006, Medieval Europe: A Short History, 2005; editor: Sisters and Workers in The Middle Ages, 1989, Singlewomen in the European Past, 1250-1800, 1999. Recipient Walter D. Love Prize, North Am. Conf. Brit. Studies, 1992; fellow, Am. Coun. Learned Socs., 1984, 2005—06, John Simon Guggenheim Meml. Found., 1989-90, Nat. Humanities Ctr., 1993—94, NEH, 2005—06. Fellow: Royal Hist. Soc., Medieval Acad. Am.; mem.: Am. Hist. Assn., North Am. Conf. Brit. Studies, Berkshire Conf. Women Historians (trustee 1995—98), Coordinating Coun. for Women in History (co-pres. 1994—97). Office: Dept History Univ So Calif Los Angeles CA 90089-0034 Office Phone: 213-821-2544.

BENNETT, JUDY A., music educator; b. Madison, S.D., Apr. 10, 1952; d. George Raymond and Berthein Cary Gannon; m. Jeffrey A. Bennett, June 15, 1974; children: Don Dean, Christopher Lee, Alexander Jeffrey. BS, Dakota State U., 1978. Vocal/gen. music tchr. Uinta County Sch. Dist. #1, Evanston, Wyo., 1978—92, Sch. Dist. La Crosse, Wis., 1992—96, Galena (Ill.) Pub. Schs., 1996—98, Albany (Wis.) Pub. Schs., 1998—2001; H.S. vocal music tchr. Sch. Dist. Monroe, Wis., 2001—05. Composer songs. Dir. Cmty. Choir, Evanston, 1978—86, Hazel Green, Wis., 1998; bd. dirs. Monroe Theatre Guild, 2000. Mem.: NEA, Wis. Choral Dirs. Assn. (5 Star award 2005), Monroe Edn. Assn., Wyo. Edn. Assn., Music Educators Nat. Conf. Home: 1706 23rd Ave Monroe WI 53566 Office: Monroe High School 1600 26th St Monroe WI 53566 Personal E-mail: j_bennett@charter.net. E-mail: judy.bennett@monroe.k12.wi.us.

BENNETT, KATHLEEN MAVOURNEEN, elementary school educator; b. Harlingen, Tex., Jan. 26, 1943; d. Owen James Bennett and Betty Margaret Bell. BS, No. Mich. U., 1966. Cert. elem. edn. Mich. Tchr. Head Start, Iron Mountain, Mich., 1966, Iron Mountain Pub. Schs., 1966, Gladstone (Mich.) Area Schs., 1967. Chair Sch. Improvement Team, Gladstone, Mich., 1988—90; dir. musicals various elem. schs. Actor: Area Children's Theatre. Active Recreation Adv. Bd., Escanaba, Mich., 1980—82; dir. children's musicals; actor children's theater. Named Disting. Alumni, No. Mich. U., 1988. Mem.: AAUW (pres., Outstanding Educator Escanaba br. 1980), Mich. Edn. Assn. (sec. 1977—79, Outstanding Person in Edn. award 2003). Democrat. Episcopalian. Avocations: reading, walking, movies, interior decorating, travel. Home: 321 S 6th St Escanaba MI 49829

BENNETT, MARGARET ETHEL BOOKER, psychotherapist; b. Spartanburg, S.C., June 15, 1923; d. Paschal and Ovie (Grey) Booker. BS, N.C. AT&T State U., 1944; MSW, U. Mich., 1947; PhD, Wayne State U., 1980. Diplomate Cert. Bd. Social Workers; cert. marriage counselor, cert. social worker, Mich. Caseworker, field instr. Family Svcs. Soc. Met., Detroit, 1947-52; caseworker, field instr., casework supr. Wayne County Cons. Center, 1952-60, Psychiat. Social Svcs., Wayne County Gen. Hosp., 1960-62; psychotherapist, field instr., asst. dir. Wayne County Mental Health Clinic, 1962-76; asst. dir. psychiat. social svc. Wayne County Psychiat. Hosp., 1976-77; dir. med. social svc. Wayne County Gen. Hosp., 1977-78; treatment cons. Project Paradigm, 1978-83; pvt. practice psychotherapy Detroit, 1965—; psychotherapist, pres. Booker Bennett & Assocs., 1980—. Founder Consultation Center of Ecorse, Mich., 1961; lectr. U. Mich., 1969-76. Co-author: The Handbook of Psychodynamic Therapy; contbr. articles to profl. jours. Bd. dirs. Crossroads, 1980-86; exec. coun. Episcopal Diocese of Mich., 1974-77, 80-83, exec. com., 1982-85, lic. lay reader, 1983—, healing min.; governing bd. Cathedral Ch. of St. Paul, Detroit, 1971-74, 76-77, 79-82, v.p. governing bd., 1977, sub-deacon, 1985—; bd. dirs. Cathedral Terr., 1981-87, U. Mich. Women, 1982-88, v.p., 1988-90, pres., 1990-92, Wayne State U. Sch. Social Work Alumni Assn., 1981-86; lic. Lay reader Episcopal Diocese Mich., 1983—, sub deacon Cathedral Ch. St. Paul, Detroit, Mich., 1985—; trustee bishop Page Found., 1986—; head verger Cathedral Ch. St. Paul, Detroit, 1988—, lay eucharistic min. Episc. Diocese Mich., 1989—, chalice bearer, 1989—, healing min., 1995—, Dean's cross for Disting. Svc., 1993; active Verger's Guild Episc. Ch.; eucharistic minister, St. John's, Detriot, 2004—, lay reader, 2004—. Fellow Am. Orthopsychiat. Assn.; mem. Mich. Assn. Marriage and Family Therapy, Nat. Assn. Equal Opportunity in Higher Edn. (Disting. Alumni award), Am. Assn. Marriage and Family Therapy, Acad. Cert. Social Workers (cert.), Mich. Assn. Clin. Social Workers, Nat. Assn. Social Workers, Nat. Coalition 100 Black Women, Assn. Advancement Psychoanalysis, Phi Delta Kappa, Alpha Kappa Alpha. Democrat. Episcopalian. Home: 1971 Glynn Ct Detroit MI 48206-1742 Office: 11000 W Mcnichols Rd Detroit MI 48221-2357 E-mail: mbb10265@aol.com.

BENNETT, MARIA BETH, literature and language educator; d. Linzy Norris and Mary Edna Slaydon; m. Timothy P. Bennett, July 25, 1998. BA, Lyon Coll., Batesville, Ark, 1994; MA, Ark. State U., Jonesboro, 2000. Instr. English Ark. State U., Jonesboro, 1998—2003, U. Ark. C.C. at Batesville, Batesville, Ark., 2003—. Dir. U. Ark. C.C. at Batesville Ensemble, 2003—; creator and faculty dir. U. Ark. C.C. at Batesville Talent Showcase, 2003—; v.p. faculty senate U. Ark. C.C. at Batesville, 2004—05, pres. faculty senate, 2005—06; creator and dir. fair U. Ark. C.C. at Batesville Renaissance Days, 2005—. Mem.: Sigma Tau Delta. Republican. Mem. Full Gospel Ch. Avocations: reading, sewing, volleyball, swimming, travel. Office: U Ark CC at Batesville PO Box 3350 Batesville AR 72503-3350 Fax: 870-793-4988.

BENNETT, NANCY EVANS, secondary school educator; b. Rochester, N.Y., May 14, 1944; d. Fank Clinton, Jr. and Roberta (Evans) Bennett; children: Karen, Lindsay. BS, Davis & Elkins Coll., 1966; MS, U. So. Calif., Brussels, 1976. Cert. tchr. N.J., Pa. Tchr. Bald Eagle (Pa.) Schs., 1966-68, John Hill Sch., Boonton, NJ, 1969, Antwerp Internat. Sch., Ekeren, Belgium, 1976, Meml. Jr. Sch., Whippany, NJ, 1976-84, Bernardsville (N.J.) Schs., 1985-93; tchr., supr. K-8 sci. Summit (N.J.) Pub. Schs., 1993-95; supr. math/sci. Hackettstown (N.J.) Pub. Schs., 1995-98; tchr. math/sci. Unity Charter Sch., NJ, 1998-99; tchr. sci. Mendham (N.J.) Boro Schs., 1999—. Presenter in field. Active East Hanover (N.J.) Sch. Bd., 1987—89. Mem.: ASCD, NSTA, NEA, N.J. Edn. Assn., N.J. Sci. Tchrs. Assn. (trustee), Am. Chem. Soc., Jr. League, Embroiderers Guild Am. (pres.). Home: 5 Cypress Cir Morristown NJ 07960-6786 Office: Mendham Boro Schs 100 Dean Rd Mendham NJ 07945

BENNETT, OLGA SALOWICH, civic worker, graphic arts researcher, consultant; b. Detroit, June 30, 1925; d. Nicholas Stefanovich and Maria Elarionovna (Mikuliak) Salowich; m. Robert William Bennett, Dec. 20, 1947 (dec. Aug. 2003); 1 child, Susan Roberta. Student, U. Mich., 1943-45, Parsons Sch. Design, 1948, U. Md., Nagoya, Japan, 1959; BA, NYU, 1975. Graphic artist Silver & Co., N.Y.C., 1948-50; editor, pub. Bull., organizer radio series LWV, Pitts., 1950-55; instr. Nanzan U., Nagoya, 1959; aide, cons. to U.S. hon. consul, Safi, Casablanca, Morocco, 1962-65; chmn. internat. affairs LWV, Montclair, N.J., 1966-73; conf. coord. UN Assn., Madison, N.J., 1974; weekly broadcaster LWV, San Juan, P.R., 1979-81; lectr. color theory Cunard, Ltd., London, Miami, Fla., 1985-88. Bd. dirs., docent Ctr. Fine Arts, Miami, 1990-92; docent Bass Mus. Art, Miami Beach, Fla., 1990-92, Vizcaya Mus. Art, Miami, 1983—; cons. on corp. overseas placement. Author artist brochures, edn1. pamphlets; translator Russian-Am. Conf., Miami, 1990. Mem. panel theater award com. New Theater, Miami, 1991; mem. Nat. Mus. of Women in the Arts; bd. dirs. Kings Creek South Condominium Assn., 1996-99. Mem. AAUW, LWV (life), UN Assn., NYU Alumni Assn., New Sch. Alumni Assn., Fgn. Policy Assn., Great Decisions Program (discussion leader), World Affairs Coun. Houston, League of Women Voters of Houston (life). Democrat. Russian Orthodox. Home: 3811 Audley St Apt 24107 Houston TX 77098-2913

BENNETT, PEGGY ELIZABETH, librarian, library director, educator; b. Columbus, Ga., Aug. 22, 1935; d. William Osborne and Ola Lee (McMahan) B. BA in Chemistry, So. Coll., 1956; cert. med. technologist, Glendale Sch. Med. Tech., Glendale, 1957; MS in Libr. Sci., Fla. State U., 1971. Med. technologist Glendale (Calif.) Hosp., 1957-59, Columbus (Ga.) Med. Ctr., 1960-61; sec. Seventh-Day Adventists Ch. Orgns., various, 1961-67; med. technologists Warm Springs (Ga.) Found., 1967-69, Thrash Labs., Columbus, Ga., 1969-70; libr. So. Coll. Seventh-Day Adventist, Collegedale, Tenn., 1971—; dir. librs. So. Coll. of Seventh-Day Adventist, Collegedale, 1986—. Presenter in field, 1979-87; developer Processing Ctr. for Southeastern Adventist Sch. Librs., 1981; cons. Adventist Network of Gen. Ednl. Librs., Collegedale, 1981—, Girl's Preparatory Sch., Chattanooga, 1984-85; mem. Sirs Mandarain Adv. Bd. Author: Library Pathfinder for MIT, 1972; contbr. articles to profl. jours. Mem. ALA, Assn. of Seventh-Day Adventists Librs. (v.p. 1981-82, pres. 1982-83), Southeastern Libr. Assn., Chattanooga Area Libr. Assn., Solinet Lambda Users' Group (exec. com. 1984, steering com.), Beta Phi Mu. Seventh Day Adventist. Avocations: tennis, aerobic walking, crafts. Office: So Adventist U Industrial Dr Collegedale TN 37315

BENNETT, TANYA LONG, language educator, writer; b. Big Spring, Tex., May 17, 1964; d. Donna Gay Campbell and Philip Mitchell Long; m. Charles Alan Bennett, May 7, 1993; children: Zachary Dean, Lucas Patton, Tyler Grace. BA English, Angelo State U., San Angelo, TX, 1986; MA English, Tex. A&M U., College Station, 1989; PhD English, U. Tenn., Knoxville, 1996. Cert. Secondary Tchr. Tex., 1986. Instr. English U. Tenn., Knoxville, 1996—2001; prof. English North Ga. Coll. and State U., Dahlonega, 2001—. Contbr. articles on lit. work of Lee Smith, on lit. work of Ana Castillo. Mem. sch. bd. Hall County Pub. Schs., Gainesville, Ga., 2006. Fellow, Carr Found., 1986; scholar, 1982—86; Hodges Better English Fellowship, U. Tenn. English Faculty, 1989—90, Emperor Fellowship, 1995. Mem.: Soc. Study of So. Lit. (corr.), Multi-Ethnic Lit. U.S. (corr.). Avocations: travel, writing, birdwatching, gardening. Office: North Ga Coll and State Univ 82 College Circle Dahlonega GA 30597

BENNETT, TINA, literary agent; b. Berkeley, Calif., 1967; BA, Stanford U., Palo Alto, Calif.; MPhil, Oxford U., Eng.; grad. study, Yale U., New Haven, Conn. Lit. agt. Janklow & Nesbit Assoc., NYC, 1994—. Grantee Marshall Scholarship. Office: Janklow & Nesbit Assoc 445 Park Ave New York NY 10022 Office Phone: 212-421-1700. Office Fax: 212-980-3671.*

BENNETT, TONI ZIMMER, special education educator; b. Rochester, N.Y., Feb. 25, 1945; d. Joseph Austin and Gladys Lucille (Wood) Zimmer; m. cArlton Neil Bennett, Dec. 14, 1963; children: Shannon Dale, Neil Lee. BA, Northwestern U., 1966, MEd, 1971, EdS, 1984. Cert. elem. educator, spl. educator, adminstr., supr., assessor. Asst. adminstr. Natchitoches Head Start, L.A., 1966; spl. edn. tchr. Northwestern State U., Natchitoches, 1972-79, adj. faculty, 1972—, project dir., inclusive edn. tchr. tng. grant Natchitocles, 1993-94; pupil appraisal supr. La. Dept. Edn., Baton Rouge, 1979-82; spl. edn. tchr. Parish Sch. Sys., Natchitoches, 1966-72, pupil appraisal coord., 1982-88, prin., 1988-90, ednl. assessment diagnostician Sabine, 1992-93; spl. edn. coord. La. Dept. Edn., Baton Rouge, 1990—; personnel evaluation/prof. accountability regional coord. L.A. Dept Edn., Baton Rouge, 1994-96; site liaison La. Dept. Edn., 2003—; dir. Reg. Svc. Ctr. VI La. Dept Edn./Northwestern State U., 1996—2000; pres. Edn. Cons. Firm O.A.S.I.S. (Options for All Students in Sch.), 2000—. Cons. in field. Author: Programming Basic Curriculum Skills, 1987, Content Standards Strategies Guide for La., Curriculum Based Assessment Tool for La. Content Standards, STRANDS: A Standards-Based Resource; field test cons. (test) Inventory of BAsic Arthmetic Skills, 1983, Individual Evaluation Procedures in Reading, 1983. Mem. Gov.'s Blue Ribbon Com. to Restructure Pre-Service Edn. Named Edn. Assessment Pilot Program Participant, La. Dept. Edn., 1979, La. Ednl. Assessment Tchr. of Yr., 1992. Mem. Natchitoches Assn. Retarded Citizens (bd. dirs. 1986-90, v.p. 1987-88, pres. 1988-90), La. Ednl. Diagnosticians (state treas. 1983-90), La. Coun. for Mental Retardation (state treas. 1982-84), La. Ednl. Assessment Tchrs., Coun. for Exceptional Children (La. Fedn. chair Yes I Can), Phi Delta Kappa. Baptist. Home: 528 Stephens Ave Natchitoches LA 71457-6033 Office: LA Dept Edn Baton Rouge LA 70804

BENNETT, VELMA JEAN, elementary school educator; b. Jacksonville, Fla., Sept. 29, 1942; d. William Bud Baily, Daniel (stepfather) and Dessie Mae (Coleman) Ray; m. Warren Carlton Bennett, May 2, 1958 (div. Apr. 1968); children: Arlene, Beverly, Carla, Doreen Bennett-Samuel, Eric, Rodney. Student, Boston State Coll., U. Mass., Boston, 1976-82, Am. Inst. for Fgn. Study, Kenya, 1980; MEd, Cambridge Coll., 1983; postgrad., Emmanuel Coll., Mass., 1995, Harvard U., 1995-96; MA of Edn. in Sch. Adminstrn., Emmanuel Coll., 2004. Tchr. middle grades St. James Ednl. Ctr., Boston, 1971-76; student tchr. William Monroe Trotter Sch., Boston, 1981; tchr. Crispus Attucks Children's Ctr., Roxbury, Mass., 1981-83; head tchr. Ellen Jackson Children's Ctr., Boston, 1983-84; tchr. grade 1 Franklin Delano Roosevelt Sch., Hyde Park, Mass., 1984-85; tchr. Henry Grew Sch., Hyde Park, 1985-87; tchr. grade 1 Ralph Waldo Emerson Sch., Roxbury, 1987-88; tchr. Hamilton Elem. Sch., Brighton, Mass., 1988-93. Chairperson, mem. parent involvement Boston Pub. Schs., 1993-97, sch. based union rep., 1994-95, sec. healthy kids program, 1994-96, faculty senate acting sec., 1996-97. Author of poetry. Active Shaklee, Roxbury, Mass., 1989-96, Peoples Bapt. Ch., Boston, 1990. Mem. Internat. Women's Writing Guild, Acad. Am. Poets, Internat. Soc. Poetry. Democrat. Baptist. Avocations: sign making, decorating, writing. Office Phone: 617-522-1856. Personal E-mail: vjbaneba@netscape.net.

BENNETT, VIRGINIA COOK, music educator, consultant; d. Leland LeRoy and Janet Roberts Cook; m. Edward James Bennett, Jan. 30, 1965; children: Susan Elizabeth, Edward James. MusB in Edn., Drake U., 1965, MusM. in Edn., 1978; PhD, U. Iowa, 1991. Instr. music and choirs Cedar Rapids (Iowa) Schs., 1965—66; instr. Newton (Iowa) Cmty. Schs., 1967—68, instr. elem. music, 1974—79; lectr. music edn. Drake U., Des Moines, 1979—80; chair music dept. and choir dir. Des Moines Area C.C., Ankeny, Iowa, 1984—97; assoc. prof. and chair, music edn. area Drake U., Des Moines, 1997—. Cons., curriculum and assessment various sch. dists., Iowa, 1998—; clinician Nebr. Music Educators State Conf., Lincoln, 2000, Ohio Music Educators State Conf., Cinn., 2000, Wis. Music Educators State Conf., Madison, 2001, N.D. Music Educators State Conf., Fargo, 2001, Minn. Music Educators State Conf., Mpls., 2001, Mich. Music Educators Ann. Conf., Ann Arbor, 2002, S.D. Music Educators Ann. Conf., Brookings, 2002, National Assn. For Music Edn. Nat. Conf., Nashville, 2002—, Mountain Lake (Va.) Symposiam on Tchg. Music Methods, Mountain Lake, Va., 2003. Contbr. articles to profl. jours. Mem. Governors Adv. Com. on Intergovernmental Affairs, Iowa, 1985—87; founding bd. mem. Newton Cmty. Edn. Found.,

Iowa, 1986—91; co-chair c.c. campaign United Way, Ankeny, Iowa, 1993—97; v.p. Newton Cmty. Schools Bd. Edn., Iowa, 1984, mem., 1984—91, pres., 1985—86. Mem.: Music Educators Nat. Conf., Iowa Alliance Arts Edn., Iowa Choral Dirs. Assn., Am. Choral Dirs. Assn., Iowa Music Educators Assn. (pres. 1996—98, Disting. Svc. Award 2001), Nat. Assn. Music Edn. (north ctrl. divsn. pres., nat. exec. bd. mem. 2000—02), Pi Kappa Lambda, Kappa Alpha Theta, Mu Phi Epsilon. Methodist. Avocations: reading, travel. Office: Drake University 25th and University Des Moines IA 50311 Home: 2325 N Wayne Ave Chicago IL 60614-3118 Office Phone: 515-271-2823. Personal E-mail: vandjbenn@aol.com. E-mail: virginia.bennett@drake.edu.

BENNETT-GREENLEAF, LINDA FAY, special education educator; d. Millard and Doretha Bennett; m. Oscar Charles Greenleaf, June 8, 1976; children: Patricia A. Greenleaf, Oscar Charles Greenleaf III. BS, Prairie View A&M U., Tex., 1975, MEd. Asst. prin. Houston Ind. Sch. Dist., 1985—2003; tchr. spl. edn. Jasper Ind. Sch. Dist., 2003—. Mem. Ho. of Faith, Houston, 2004—06. Home: 12051 Circle Dr E Houston TX 77071 Office: Jasper Ind Sch Dist Jasper TX 75951 Office Phone: 409-382-1182. Home Fax: 713-778-1673.

BENNETT-HAMMERBERG, JANIE MARIE, small business owner, writer, consultant, administrative assistant; b. Chgo., Oct. 25, 1945; d. John Raymond Harvey and Violet Cleora (Yancey) Bennett-Harvey; m. Richard Arndt Hammerberg, May 9, 1964; children: Susan Jean, Richard John. Student, Joliet (Ill.) Jr. Coll., 1972-73, Lewis U. Sec. Valley View Sch. Dist., Romeoville, Ill., 1972—83; sec., adminstrv. asst. Babson Bros. Chem. Divsn., Romeoville, 1987-90; owner, operator real estate Hammer-Smith Mgmt., Romeoville, 1986—, St. Charles Pastoral Ctr., Romeoville, 1997—2001. Adminstrv. asst. Lewis U., 1995-; freelance cons. Contbg. author numerous poetry anthologies; freelance writer. Vol. numerous charitable founds., including AIDS Found., Chgo., 1983—, Muscular Dystrophy Assn., Chgo., 1983—. March of Dimes, Chgo., 1983—. Walk for Babies, Chgo., 1983—, Am. Cancer Soc., Chgo., 1983—, AHA Soc., Chgo., 1983—, Parkinson's Disease, Chgo., Avon Breast Cancer 60 Mile Walk, Chgo., 1983-, Officer friendly programs UIC, Chgo., Neighbor Newspaper Reporter, Plainfield, 2000-; hon. heart and sole vol. Muscular Sclerosis Found., Chgo., 1983-95; officer friendly programs U. Ill. Hosp., 1982-90; mem. bd. Homeowners Assn. Recipient several employee, Hon. Mention and Pres.'s awards, Editor's Choice awards Nat. Libr. of Poetry, Owings Mills, Md., Dickinson award The Amherst Soc., Balt., 1991, Golden Poet awards, Dickinson Recognition award, Best & Outstanding Poem awards, 1995, 96, 97, 98, Poet of yr., !SP, 2000-2002, Pres.'s award Lit. Excellence NAR, Illiad Press, 2002, Twentieth Century award Achievement, Life fellow award, 21st Century award Achievement, Noble prize United Cultural Conv.; named Outstanding Poets Best Poems of 90's Selected Works World's Best Poets, 1994-98, Intellectuals of the 20th Century, Leading Intellectuals of World, Internat. Women of the Millenium, Woman of the Yr., 2000, Internat. Amb.; honored laureate Verses Mag. Summer Prose, 1999, Wall of Tolerance Nat. Campaign Tolerance, 2001; named to Ill. and Nat. Poetry Soc., Internat. Poetry Hall of Fame, Am. Biog. Inst.'s Hall of Fame; nominated Outstanding People of the 20th Century, 2000, Outstanding Women of the 20th Century, 2000. Mem. Ill. State Poetry Soc., ABWA, Internat. Poetry Hall of Fame, Am. Poetry Soc., Internat. Soc. of Poets (charter, life), Nat. Authors Registry, Acad. Am. Poets, Nat. Multiple Sclerosis Soc., Fedn. State Poetry Soc., Am. Bus. Womens Assn., others. Avocations: walking, running, exercise, crafts, music. Home: 21307 Silktree Cir Plainfield IL 60544-9360

BENNINGFIELD, CAROL ANN, lawyer; b. San Antonio, Dec. 8, 1952; d. Gordon Lane Benningfield and Ann Benningfield McCraw. BA in Polit. Sci., S.W. Tex. State U., 1975; JD, U. Tex., 1979. Bar: Tex. 1979, U.S. Dist. Ct. (so. dist.) Tex. 1995. Staff atty. Tex. Dept. Labor and Stds., Austin, 1979; staff counsel Tex. Chem. Coun., Austin, 1979-80; assoc. Wiley, Garwood, San Antonio, 1981-83; account exec. Dean-Witter Reynolds, San Antonio, 1983-89; pvt. practice, Rockport, Tex., 1990—. Gala com. San Antonio Stock Show and Rodeo, 1981-83; mem. Target 90 Goals for San Antonio, 1984-85; deacon First Presbyn. Ch., Rockport, 1992-95, choir, 1990-96; active Rockport Art Assn., 1990—; trustee Aransas County Ind. Sch. Dist., Rockport, 1993-96, sec., 1993-96. Fellow Tex. Bar Found. Tex.; mem. San Antonio Young Lawyers (membership chmn. 1982), Rockport Fulton C. of C. (dir. 1992-94, awards com. chmn., v.p. 1993), Rotary.

BENOIT, JO, psychologist, consultant; 1 child. PsyD, Rutgers U., George Washington U., U. Mich. Psychologist St. Elizabeth Hosp., Washington, 1978—82; psychologist, therapist Receiving Home Children and Young Adults, Washington, 1979—82; CEO J. Benoit Profl. Svcs., Inc., Washington, Tex., 1988—97; pvt. practice Pa., 1997—, NJ, Del. Cons. JFK Co., Phila.; jury cons. Mem.: APA, AMA, Phila. Soc. Clinical Psychologists.

BENOIT, LEILANI, computer scientist, educator; BA, N.Mex. State U., Las Cruces, 1996, MA, 1998. Cert. tchr. N.Mex. Dept. of Edn., 1998. Tchr. Las Cruces Pub. Schs., N.Mex., 1998—2003; instr. computer tech. DACC, Las Cruces, 2000—. Advisor Tech. Student Assn., Las Cruces, 2000—03. Editor: (video) Tech Club Promo (Nat. TSA - Top Ten, 2003). Instr. Disibility Group, Las Cruces, 2005, Kids Computer Camp, Las Cruces, 2004—06. Mem.: Tech. Student Assn. (assoc.; advisor 2002—03, Top 10 Video Editing award 2003). Office Phone: 505-528-7281.

BENOIT, LILLIAN RIQUELMY, science educator, mathematics educator; b. Jennings, La., Feb. 23, 1950; d. Herbert A. and Lilly May Riquelmy; m. Carl P. Benoit, Jan. 30, 1971; children: Alan, Michael, Amy, Brian. BS in Edn., McNeese State U., 1971. Fifth grade tchr. St. Margaret's Cath. Sch., Lake Charles, La., 1971; second grade tchr. St. Tammany Pub. Sch., Slidell, La., 1973—74; science tchr. Our Lady Immaculate Sch., Jennings, La., 1980—84; fifth grade tchr. Jefferson Davis Parish, Jennings, 1985—. Workshop presenter Jefferson Davis Parish, Jennings, La. Mem.: Nat. Sci. Tchrs. Assn., La. Sci. Tchrs. Org., Cath. Daughters of the Am., Pink Ladies. Avocations: reading, painting, piano. Home: 214 13th St Jennings LA 70546

BENOIT, LOIS ELAINE, director, retired music educator; b. St Anna, Calif., July 19, 1952; d. Philip and Elaine Mae Garippa; m. Michael Thomas Benoit, July 26, 1975; children: Alisha Lois, Michal Margaret, Nathan Michael. M, Coll. St Rose, Albany, N.Y., 1995. Music tchr. Hoosick Falls Ctrl. Sch., NY, 1990—2006; childcare exec. dir. Morning Star Childcare Ctr., 1985—. Youth dir. liaison Hoosick Area Partnership Parents and Youth, Hoosick Falls, NY, 2005—. Recipient Masons Cmty. award, 2004; grantee, Cmty. Bus. Sponsors, 2006. Mem.: N.Y. State Music Assn. (life), N.Y. State Edn. Early Childhood (life), Music Educators Nat. Conf. (life), N.Y. Teachers Assn. (life). Independent. Achievements include development of community programs for youth. Avocations: travel, crafts, raising golden retrievers, gardening. Home: 623 Johnson Hill Rd Hoosick Falls NY 12090 Office: 22022 NY 22 Hoosick Falls NY 12090 Office Phone: 518-686-7408.

BENOIT, MARILYN B., psychiatrist, consultant; b. Trinidad & Tobago, 1943; MD, Georgetown U., 1973; M in Health Svcs. Adminstrn., George Washington U., 1993. Diplomate Am. Bd. Psychiatry and Neurology with subspecialty in child and adolescent psychiatry. Resident in psychiatry Georgetown U., Washington, 1973—75, resident in child psychiatry, fellow in child psychiatry, 1975—77, clin. assoc. prof. psychiatry; med. dir., exec. dir. Devereux Children's Ctr., 1993—98; pvt. practice, cons. Washington, 1998—. Pvt. practice psychiatry. Fellow: Am. Acad. Child and Adolescent Psychiatry (past pres. 2001—03); mem.: AMA, Am. Psychiat. Assn. Office: 1015 33d St NW 115 Washington DC 20007 Office Phone: 202-607-3032. E-mail: bartolom@aol.com.

BENOWITZ, JUNE MELBY, historian, educator; b. Portland, Oreg., Mar. 8, 1949; d. Harold Eugene and Peggy Terry Melby; m. Elliot Benowitz, Sept. 29, 1979. AS in History, Portland C.C., 1979; BA in History, Portland State U., 1981, MA in History, 1988; PhD in History, U. Tex., Austin, 1996. Adj. history instr. Portland State U., 1991—93, Portland C.C., 1994—95, Keiser Coll., Sarasota, Fla., 1997—2002, Manatee C.C., Bradenton, Fla., 2001—02; asst. prof. history U. South Fla., Sarasota/Manatee, 2002—. Faculty adv. Coll. Democrats, Sarasota-Manatee History Club, U. South Fla. Author: Days of Discontent, 2002, Encyclopedia of American Women and Religion, 1998 (Choice Mag. award, 1999); contbr. chapters to books. Mem.: Am. Hist. Assn., Orgn. Am. Historians, Phi Alpha Theta, Phi Kappa Phi. Evangelical Lutheran. Avocations: hiking, swimming, bird study and care, reading, theater. Office: Univ South Florida 8350 N Tamiami Trail Sarasota FL 34243-2049

BENSHOOF, JANET LEE, lawyer, association executive; b. Detroit Lakes, Minn., May 10, 1947; m. Richard Klein; children: David, Eli. BA in Polit. Sci. & Sociology, summa cum laude, U. Minn., 1969; JD, Harvard U., 1972. Dir. law reform South Bklyn. Legal Svcs., 1972-77; dir. reproductive freedom project ACLU, NYC, 1977-92; founder, pres. Ctr. Reproductive Law & Policy, NYC, 1992—2002, pres. emeritus. Guest lectr. Yale U., Columbia U., Rutgers U., Case Western Reserve U., Lectr. on Law, reproductive rights, Harvard U. Law Sch., 2005. Contbr. articles to profl. jours. Recipient Margaret Sanger award, 1986, Christopher Tietze Humanitarian award Nat. Abortion Fedn., 1988, Gloria Steinem award Ms. Found. Women, N.Y.C., 1989, 10 for 10 award Ctr. Population Optiums, 1990, Civil Liberties Heroine, Freedom From Religion Found., 1992; named one of 100 Most Influential Lawyers in Am. Nat. Law Jour., 1991, 94; MacArthur Found. Fellowship grant, 1992. Mem. ABA, Am. Pub. Health Assn., N.Y.C. Bar Assn. E-mail: jbenshoof@law.harvard.edu.

BENSON, BARBARA ELLEN, state agency administrator; b. Rockford, Ill., June 5, 1943; d. Olander Anton and Eleanor Margaret (Lydon) B. BA, Beloit Coll., 1965; MA, Ind. U., 1969, PhD, 1976. Editor Eleutherian Mills-Hagley Found., Wilmington, Del., 1973-80; dir. libr. Hist. Soc. Del., Wilmington, 1980-90, exec. dir., 1990—. Adj. assoc. prof. history U. Del., 1990—. Author: Logs and Lumber, 1989, (with Michael Biggs) Wilmington: the City and Beyond, 1990; contbr. articles to jours., chpts. to books. Vice chairperson Del. Humanities Forum, 1987-92, chairperson, 1992-94; bd. dirs. Sister Cities, Wilmington, 1985-89, ofcl. visitor to Kalmar, Sweden, 1985; bd. dirs. State Records Commn. Del., 1987-; mem. rev. bd. Del. Hist. Preservation, 1990-96; bd. dirs. Hist. Red Clay Valley, 1994-96, Wilmington Rotary, 1997-99, Del. African-Am. Mus., 1996-; chair, Rockwood Mansion and Park Adv. Com., 2000-; mem. New Castle County Human Resources Adv. Bd.; mem. adv. com. Del Hist. Records, 1987-. Mem.: Mid Atlantic Regional Archivists (bd. dirs. 1983—87), Am. Assn. State and Local History (state awards chmn. 1987—94, state membership com. 1996—), Am. Assn. Museums, Old Swedes Found. Office: Hist Soc Delaware 505 N Market St Wilmington DE 19801-3004

BENSON, BELINDA LOU, school system administrator; d. Douglas J. and Goldie E. Blanton; m. Robert D. Benson, May 25, 1991; 1 child, Michael Lee Kraft, Jr. AAS, Richland Coll., Dallas, 1997; Bachelor's, Amberton U., Garland, Tex., 2003. Cert. Caribbean Destination Specialist Inst. Cert. Travel Agents, Wellesley, Mass., 1997, meeting profl. Conv. Industry Coun., Wash. D.C., 2006. Meeting profl. Richland Coll., 1998—, adj. faculty travel, expn. & meeting mgmt., 2005. Mem. music com. Calvary Bapt. Ch., Garland, 1999—2002; mem. steering com. DCCCD Renewal Week, Dallas, 2003—06. Recipient Employee of Month, Dallas Heart Group, 1993, Outstanding Employee of Month (Sept.), Richland Coll., 2000. Mem.: DCCCD Profl. Support Staff Assn. (assoc.), Soc. Govt. Meeting Profls. (assoc.), Meeting Profls. Internat. (assoc.). Baptist. Avocations: travel, cooking, gardening, embroidery, history. Office: Richland Coll 12800 Abrams Rd Dallas TX 75243 E-mail: bbenson@dcccd.edu.

BENSON, BEVERLY J., lawyer; BA in Polit. Sci. magna cum laude, Augsburg Coll., Mpls., 1981; JD, William Mitchell Coll. Law, St. Paul, Minn., 1985. Bar: Minn. 1985, US Dist. Ct. 1986, US Supreme Ct. 1990. Asst. atty. Stearns County Atty's Office, St. Cloud, Minn., 1986—89, Hennepin County Atty's Office, Mpls., 1989—. Adj. instr. William Mitchell Coll. Law, St. Paul, 1999; spkr., presenter and cons. in field of criminal law. Editor: Hennepin County Resourse Manual for Effectively Prosecuting Drug Cases, 7 vols., 1992. Recipient Outstanding Cmty. Svc. award Hennepin County, Minn. State Bar Assn., 1990—92, Vol. Svc. award, Minn. Indian Women Resource Ctr., 1997, Grace Norris award, LWV, 1999—2000, Appreciation cert., Minn. State Coll. and U., 2002; scholar, Office Violence Against Women, 2005. Office: Hennepin County Attys Office C-2100 HCGC 300 S Sixth St Minneapolis MN 55487 E-mail: bev.benson@co.hennepin.mn.us.

BENSON, ELIZABETH POLK, art specialist; b. Washington, May 13, 1924; d. Theodore Booton and Rebecca Dean (Albin) Benson. BA, Wellesley Coll., 1945; MA, Cath. U. Am., 1956. Mus. aide, curator Nat. Gallery of Art, Washington, 1946-60; curator Pre-Columbian Collection Dumbarton Oaks, Washington, 1962-79, dir. Ctr. for Pre-Columbian Studies, 1971-79; rsch. assoc. Inst. Andean Studies, Berkeley, Calif., 1980—. Lectr. Cath. U. Am., Washington, 1968—69; adj. prof. Columbia U., N.Y.C., 1973; sr. lectr. U. Tex., Austin, 1985; Andrew S. Keck disting. vis. prof. Am. U., Washington, 1987; cons. Montreal Mus. Fine Arts, 1980—84, 1990—92; mem. adv. bd. L.Am. Indian Lits. Jour., Pitts., 1989—; co-curator traveling exhbn. Birds and Beasts of Ancient L.Am., 1995—98; mem. exec. com. Peruvian Am. Rsch. Found., 2004—; mem. adv. bd. Found. for the Advancement of Mesoam. Studies, 1994—2000. Author: The Maya World, 1967, 1972, 1977, The Mochica, 1972, Birds and Beasts of Ancient Latin America, 1997; co-editor: Olmec Art of Ancient Mexico, 1996, Ritual Sacrifice in Ancient Peru, 2001. Mem.: Coll. Art Assn., L.Am. Indian Lits. Assn. (v.p. 1989—), The Lit. Soc., Soc. Women Geographers (mus. com. 1994—2006). Home and Office: 8314 Old Seven Locks Rd Bethesda MD 20817-2005

BENSON, IRENE M., nurse; b. Chgo. BSN, Loyola U., 1980; MS, Saint Xavier U., 1993. RN Ill., cert. critical care nurse, emergency room nurse, trauma nurse specialist, med. surg. nurse, clin. nurse specialist. Staff nurse hematology/oncology unit Michael Reese Hosp. and Med. Ctr., Chgo., 1980-86, operating rm. nurse, 1980—86; staff nurse trauma ICU Loyola U., Maywood, Ill., 1986-87; staff nurse telemetry U. Ill., Chgo., 1987-88; staff nurse emergency room Cook County Hosp., Chgo., 1988—90, tour supr. emergency rm., 1990—91; clin. nurse specialist med.-surg. nursing John H Stroger Jr Hosp Cook County (formerly Cook County Hosp.), 1993—; staff nurse emergency rm. St. Francis Hosp., Blue Island, Ill., 1991-94, U. Ill., Chgo., 1992—98; clin. instr. Triton Coll., River Grove, Ill., 1998—, clin. cons. trainer, 2000—. Trauma nurse instr. USAF, 1990—. Lt. col. USAF Res., 1982—. Mem.: Ill. Soc. for Advanced Practice Nursing, Am. Assn. Critical Care Nurses, Nat. Assn. Clin. Nurse Specialists, Internat. Assn. of Forensic Nurses, Ill. Nurses Assn., Acad. of Med.-Surg. Nurses, Emergency Nurses Assn., Res. Officers Assn. (life), Sigma Theta Tau Internat. Roman Catholic. Avocations: reading, sky diving, travel. Office: John H Stroger Jr Hosp Cook County 1901 W Harrison St Chicago IL 60612-3785

BENSON, JADE, science educator; b. Holdenville, Okla., Oct. 2, 1978; d. Jackie Gene and Jan Sue Brown; m. Kelley Lynn Benson, May 22, 1999. BS, East Ctrl. U., Ada, Okla., 2002. Tchr. sci. Byng Pub. Sch., Ada, Okla., 2002—; summer tchr. and resident advisor Upward Bound Math/Sci., 2002—. Avocations: running, scrapbooks, softball. Office: Byng Pub Sch 500 S New Bethel Blvd Ada OK 74820-1177 Home: 730E 22nd Ada OK 74820

BENSON, JEANNE P., music educator; b. Taylorville, Ill., July 21, 1948; d. George A. Pranske and Rosetta S. Strohl; m. Wayne A. Benson, Nov. 29, 1969; 1 child, Jennifer Leigh. BS Edn., Eastern Ill. U., 1970. Vocal dir. Cissna Park Sch., Ill., 1970—72; vocal, piano instr. Kankakee Sch. Dist., Ill., 1982—. Vocal dir. New Park Singers, Kankakee, 1988—; vocal dir., mgr. Kankakee Orch. Chorus, 1986—; vocal dir. Kankakee Valley Theatre, 1978—. Mem.: Ill. Music Educators, Music Educators Nat. Conf. Office Phone: 815-933-0709.

BENSON, JOAN, musician, educator; b. St. Paul; d. John Raymond and Frances (Ostergren) B. MusM, U. Ill., 1952; performer's cert., Ind. U., 1953; pvt. studies with Edwin Fischer, Switzerland, 1953-57; pvt. studies with Fritz Neumeyer, Fed. Republic Germany, 1958-59; pvt. studies with Santiago Kastner, Portugal, 1960. Concert musician, worldwide, 1962—; lectr. early keyboard Stanford U., Palo Alto, Calif., 1970-76; asst. prof. U. Oreg., Eugene, 1976-82. Mem. artist faculty Aston Magna Acad., Mass., 1980, 82; adj. prof. U. Oreg., 1982—; artistic advisor Boston Clavichord Soc., 1996—. Albums: Repertoire, 1962, Music of C. P. E. Bach for Piano and Clavichord, 1972, Pasquini and Haydn on Clavichords of the Boston Museum of Fine Arts, 1982, Kuhnau and C.P.E. Bach on Clavichord, 1988; contbr. music notes to Titanic and Focus record labels; contbr. articles to internat. profl. jours. Recipient Kate Nell Kinley award. Mem. Am. Musicol. Soc. Home: 2795 Central Blvd Eugene OR 97403-2528 Business E-Mail: joanb@uoregon.edu.

BENSON, JOANNE E., retired lieutenant governor; b. Jan. 4, 1943; m. Robert Benson; 2 children. BS, St. Cloud State U. Mem. Minn. Senate, St. Paul, 1991-94; lt. gov. State of Minn., St. Paul, 1994-98; CEO, Minn. Bus. Acad., St. Paul, 1999—2005.

BENSON, KATHERINE ALICE, psychology educator; b. Mpls., June 12, 1949; d. Gerald Philip and Gladys Irene (Berg) B.; m. James Lyman Staebler, Aug. 8, 1981 (div. Sept. 1986); 1 child, David James. B.A. summa cum laude, U. Minn., 1972; M.S., U. Mass.-Amherst, 1976, Ph.D., 1979. Instr. psychology U. Mass., Amherst, 1977-78; asst. prof. U. Minn., Morris, 1978. Precinct chmn. Ward 1 Stevens County Democratic-Farmer-Labor Party, 1982-85, dir., 1986—. Grantee Council on Liberal Edn., 1980, U. Minn. Grad. Sch., 1981-83; U. Minn. Grad. Sch. fellow, 1983; Bush Found. sabbatical fellow, 1985-86. Mem. Minn. Commn. on Martin Luther King, Jr., Holiday. Mem. Minn. Women Psychologists, AAAS, Am. Psychol. Assn., Soc. Research in Child Devel., Nat. Women's Studies Assn., NOW (Minn. chpt. adv. bd. 1983-84), Bus. & Profl. Women. Unitarian-Universalist. Contbr. articles to profl. jours. Office: U Minn Div Social Sci Morris MN 56267

BENSON, KATHLEEN SEVIER KAVANAGH, retired counselor; b. Chattanooga, Tenn., Mar. 1, 1934; d. Gerald Rodgers Kavanagh and Adelaide Lenoir Burdette; m. Gregory King Benson, Jr. (div.); children: Gregory III, Mabry Bond, Avery Lenoir(dec.). BA, U. Tenn., 1954. Head wine divsn. Knoxville (Tenn.) Beverage Co., 1973—74; acct. exec. WETE AM and FM Radio, Knoxville, 1974—76; sales rep. Carrier Heating and Air Conditioning, Knoxville, 1976—77; mem. staff Tenn. Second Congl. Dist., Knoxville, Tenn., 1979—83; counselor Tenn. Dept. Human Svcs., Knoxville, 1983—94, ret., 1994. Precinct chmn. Knox County Rep., Knoxville, 1964—74; pres. Episc. Churchwomen; sr. warden St. Michael and All Angels; bd. dirs. Lenoir City (Tenn.) Mus., 1998—2000; bd. edn. Knox County Sch. Bd., 1966—86. Named Hon. Tenn. Col., Gov. Lamar Alexander, 1979. Mem.: Col. David Henley Assn. (bd. dir.), First Families Tenn., United Daus. Confederacy (bd. dir. 2001—03), Nat.Soc. DAR (regent 2003—05), Mensa (local sec.), Chi Omega Fraternity Alumni Assn. (pres.). Republican. Episc. Avocations: writing, gardening, antiques. Home: 3063 Kingston Pike Knoxville TN 37919

BENSON, LUCY WILSON, historian, consultant; b. NYC, Aug. 25, 1927; d. Willard Oliver and Helen (Peters) Wilson; m. Bruce Buzzell Benson, Mar. 30, 1950 (dec. Mar. 1990). BA, Smith Coll., 1949, MA, 1955; LHD (hon.), Wheaton Coll., 1965; LLD (hon.), U. Mass., 1969; LHD (hon.), Bucknell U., 1972; LLD (hon.), U. Md., 1972; LHD (hon.), Carleton Coll., 1973; LLD (hon.), Amherst Coll., 1974, Clark U., 1975; HHD (hon.), Springfield Coll., 1981; LHD (hon.), Bates Coll., 1982; LLD (hon.), Lafayette Coll., 1999. Mem. jr. exec. tng. program Bloomingdale's, N.Y.C., 1949-50; asst. dir. pub. rels. Smith Coll., 1950-53; rsch. asst. dept. Am. studies Amherst Coll., 1956-57; pres. Amherst LWV, Mass., 1957-61, pres. Mass., 1961-65, nat. pres., 1968-74; mem. Gov.'s cabinet and sec. human svcs. Commonwealth of Mass., 1975; mem. spl. commn. on adminstrv. rev. U.S. Ho. of Reps., Washington, 1976-77; under sec. State Security Assistance, Sci. and Tech. U.S. Dept. State, Washington, 1977-80; cons. U.S. Dept. State and SRI Internat., Washington, 1980-81; pres. Benson and Assocs., Amherst, 1981—. Vice-chair Citizen Network Fgn. Affairs; bd. dirs. Dreyfus Fund, others, Internat. Exec. Svc. Corps., Amherst Cinema Arts Ctr., 2006—. Pub. adv. com. U.S. Trade Policy, 1968; mem. town meeting Amherst, 1957—74, 2000; mem. fin. com., 1960—66; mem. Gov. Mass. Spl. Com. Rev. Sunday Closing Laws, 1961, Mass. Adv. Bd. Higher Ednl. Policy, 1962—65, Gov. Mass. Com. Rev. Salaries State Employees, 1963; adv. com. racial imbalance and edn. Mass. Bd. Edn., 1964—65; Mass. adv. com. U.S. Commn. Civil Rights, 1964—73; vice-chair Mass. Adv. Coun. Edn., 1965—68; Mass. Com. Children and Youth Com. to Study Report by U.S. Children's Bur. Mass. Youth Svc. Divsn., 1967; steering com. Urban Coalition, 1968, exec. com., 1970—75, 1980—84, co-chair, 1973—75; vis. com. John F. Kennedy Sch. Govt., Trilateral commn. Coun. Fgn. Rels.; former bd. govs. Am. Nat. Red Cross, Common Cause, Women's Action Alliance; bd. govs. Internat. Ctr. Election Law and Adminstrn., 1985—87; spl. commn. Mass. Legislature Study Budgetary Powers Trustee U. Mass., 1961—62; trustee Edn. Devel. Ctr., Newton, Mass., 1967—72, Nat. Urban League, 1974—77, Brookings Instn., 1974—77, Smith Coll., 1975—80, Alfred P. Sloan Found., 1975—77, 1981—2000, Bur. Social Sci. Rsch., Inc., 1985—87; bd. dirs. Catalyst, 1972—90, Atlantic Coun. U.S., 1988—, vice-chair, 1993—2000; trustee Lafayette Coll., 1985—2000, vice-chair, 1990—2000, trustee emeritus, 2000—. Recipient Achievement award, Bur. Govt. Rsch. U. Mass., 1963, Disting. Svc. award, Boston Coll., 1965, Northfield Mt. Hermon Sch., 1976, Disting. Civil Leadership award, Tufts U., 1965, medal, Smith Coll., 1969; fellow, Radcliffe Inst., 1965—67. Mem.: ACLU, NAACP, Coun. On Fgn. Rels., Internat. Inst. Strategic Studies, Nat. Acad. Pub. Adminstrn., Jersey Wildlife Preservation Trust Channel Islands, E African Wildlife Soc., Assn. Am. Indian Affairs, Urban League, UN Assn. Home and Office: 46 Sunset Ave Amherst MA 01002-2097 Office Phone: 413-549-5007.

BENSON, MARIE CHAPMAN, insurance agent; b. Geneva, Ala., June 1, 1909; d. Charles Daniel and Lollie (Pilley) Chapman; m. Wilfred Tyner Benson, June 28, 1933 (wid. Mar. 1984); children: Laurie Lynn Benson Morris, Beverly Ree Benson, Joseph Daniel Benson; 1 foster child: Juan Manuel Hernandez. BS in Piano, Huntingdon Coll., 1930, Cert. in Pub. Sch. Music, 1930; postgrad., U. Va. Lic. ins. agt.; cert. music instr., Ala. Instr. of piano, Geneva, 1930-32; organizer/instr. music Geneva Elem. Sch., 1930-32; attendance officer Geneva County Schs., 1932-33; v.p. Benson Wholesale Co., Geneva, 1956-74, v.p. of leasing co., 1964-74; v.p., dir. Dixieland Foodstores, Geneva, 1956-74, Brundidge (Ala.) Mfg. Co., 1961; ins. agt. Security Ins., Geneva, 1963—. Pianist/organist Meth. Ch., Geneva, 1919-79; ptnr. C.D. Chapman Co., Geneva, 1930—. Vice-pres. PTA, Geneva, 1947-48, pres. Geneva Garden Club, 1954-56; bd. dirs. Geneva Recreation Ctr.; pres. United Meth. Women, Dothan (Ala.) Dist., 1956-60, organizer dist. prayer groups; sec. Christian Personhood/Ala.-W. Flor. Meth. Conf., Montgomery, 1962-64; mem. Rep. Presdl. Club, Washington; endowed chmn. Christian faith and philosophy Huntingdon Coll., Montgomery, 1991; elected del. to 4th Assembly, Dothan Dist. Soc. Christian Svc., Milw., 1960; others. Hon. Mother of Yr., Am. Mothers Com., State of Ala., Birmingham, 1971; Paul Harris fellow Geneva Rotary Club, 1979. Mem. Athenaeum Federated Club (pres. 1955-57, pres. 1968-70, Merit Mother award 1968), 6th Dist. Federated Club of ALA (treas.). Avocations: growing roses, gardening, reading, travel, writing. Address: PO Box 1382 Dothan AL 36302

BENSON, NEALA LAWRENCE, volunteer; b. Ottumwa, Iowa, June 30, 1937; d. Matt Lancaster and Edna Caldwell Lawrence; m. Charles L. Benson, Oct. 24, 1959; children: Jeffrey Lawrence, Jennifer Benson Litchman, Christopher Marvin. BS in Journalism, Iowa State U., Ames, 1959. Family page editor Ottumwa Daily Courier, Ottumwa, Iowa, 1959; asst. spl. events and fashion coord. Boston Store, Milw., 1959—61; owner Civic Newcomer Welcoming Svc., Ames, Iowa, 1982—85; cmty. vol., 1962—. Past pres. Red Friars Dance Club, Beta Tau Delta, Ames Internat. Festival Orchestra Assn., Festival Guild, Mary Greeley Med. Ctr. Aux., Mary Greeley Med. Ctr. Found.n, Ames Jayceetes, Ames H.S. Quarterback Club; past interior design coord. Mary Greeley Med. Ctr.; past chair Mary Greeley Med. Ctr. Benefit

Ball; past co-chair Mary Greeley Med. Ctr. Fantasy of Trees; docent Univ. Museums; past pres. Story County Rep. Women; past bd. mem. Story County Planning and Zoning Commn.; past com. mem. Vision Ames; past pres. First United Meth. Women, Ames, Iowa; past bd. mem. First United Meth. Ch. Found., past treas.; past bd. mem. Octagon Ctr. Arts, Iowa State U. Meml. Union, Mary Greeley Med. Ctr. Found., Mary Greeley Med. Ctr. Aux., Northcrest Retirement Cmty., Ames Cmty. Arts Coun., Ames City-Wide PTA; past treas. and chair Mary Greeley Med. Ctr. Art Com.; past cmty. rep. Ames Triribune Editl. Bd.; past mem. fund raising com. Israel Family Hospice Ho., past chair art com.; past bd. mem. Northcrest Retirement Cmty., past mem. admission com., past mem. pers. com., past mem. nominating com. Recipient Outstanding Svc. award, Mary Greeley Med. Ctr. Aux., 1988, Outstanding Sorority Alumna award, Iowa State U. Greek Sys., 1995, Unsung Hero award, Rotary Club and Ames Tribune, 2000, Order of Omega, Nat. Honor Soc. Mem.: Am. Heart Assn. (pub. rels. chair Go Red Luncheon), Ames C. of C. (Cmty. Involvement award 1990), Ames Found. (v.p., past bd. mem.), Youth and Shelter Svcs. Found. (bd. mem., past mem. bldg. fund raising com.), Ames Alumni Panhellenic Assn. (past pres.), Cynthia O. Duff Questors (past pres.), Kiwanis (past pres., past bd. mem.), PEO Internat. (chpt. LN, past pres.), Gamma Gamma, Order of the Knoll, Keystone Soc., Delta Delta Delta (alumnae chpt., past pres., Grigsby award 1994). Republican. Avocations: travel, reading, gardening, cooking, walking. Home: 614 Hodge Ave Ames IA 50010-5616

BENSTEIN, BARBARA DUBRAY, cytotechnologist, educator; b. Detroit, Nov. 23, 1955; d. Robert James and Shirley Loretta DuBray; m. David Carl Benstein, Sept. 7, 1991. BS in Biology, U. Tenn., Martin, 1977; BS in Cytotech., U. Tenn., Memphis, 1978; MS in Biology, Memphis State U., 1986; PhD in Biology, U. Memphis, 2003. Cytotechnologist U. Tenn., Memphis, 1978-91, instr., 1978-84, asst. prof., 1984-93, assoc. prof., 1993-99, prof., 1999—. Chmn. cytotechnology exam. com. Am. Soc. Clin. Pathology Bd. Registry, 1993-95. Edtl. adv. bd. Cancer Cytopathology Jour., 1996—; author, Atlas of Cytopathology videodisc, 1987. Recipient Excellence in Tchg. award Student Govt. Assn. U. Tenn., 1992, 95, Pub. Svc. award U. Tenn. Nat. Alumni Assn., 1999; named to Imhotep Leadership Soc. U. Tenn., 1994; Cytotechnology Tng. grantee Am. Cancer Soc. 1995-96. Mem. Am. Soc. Cytopathology (chair programs rev. com. 2000-2001, mem. exec. bd. 2002-2005, Cytotechnologist award for Outstanding Achievement 1996, Excellence in Edn. award 1999), Am. Soc. Clin. Pathology (bd. registrars, bd. govs. 2002—), So. Assn. Cytotechnologists (pres. 1994), Am. Soc. Cytotechnologists, Internat. Acad. Cytology, Phi Kappa Phi. Office: Univ Tenn Memphis Ste 674 930 Madison Ave Memphis TN 38163-0001 Office Phone: 901-448-8559. E-mail: BBenstein@utmem.edu.

BENSUR, BARBARA JEAN, art educator, researcher; b. Erie, Pa., Feb. 11, 1950; d. Jean Elizabeth and Durker William Braggins; children: Adele, Rebecca. BA, Mercyhurst Coll., 1972; MA, U. Md., 1992, PhD, 1995. Cert. art tchr. grades K-12, adminstrv. endorsement. Art tchr. St. Mary's County Pub. Schs., Leonardtown, Md., 1989—98; instr. Frostburg (Md.) State U., 1996—98; asst. prof. Millersville (Pa.) U., 1998—. Exhibitions include Delaware County C.C., 2001 (Purchase award, 2001), 30th Ann. Spring Arts Festival, 2001, Lancaster Open Award Exhibit, 2001, Millersville Faculty Art Show, 2001; contbr. articles to profl. jours. Cons. Demuth Found., Lancaster, 2000—01. Mem.: Am. Edn. Rsch. Assn., Pa. Art Edn. Assn., Nat. Art Edn. Assn. Roman Catholic. Avocation: jogging. Home: 743 Steeplechase Rd Landisville PA 17538 Office: Millersville Univ Art Dept PO Box 1002 Millersville PA 17551 Home Fax: (717) 871-2004; Office Fax: (717) 871-2004. Business E-Mail: barbara.bensur@millersville.edu.

BENTAS, LILY HASEOTES, retail executive; Chmn, pres. Cumberland Farms, Canton, Mass., 1989, pres., CEO, 1991—. Office: Cumberland Farms Inc 777 Dedham St Canton MA 02021-1484*

BENTLEY, CAROL LIGON, retired library and information scientist; b. Brownsville, Tenn., Mar. 8, 1927; d. Gavin and Ethel Ligon; m. Harry Bentley, Jan. 11, 1962; children: Patrice, Harry Dion. BE, Chgo. State U., 1969, MS in Edn., 1973, No. Ill. U., Dekalb, 1979, EdS, 1989. Tchr. elem. sch. Oliver Wendell Holmes Sch., Chgo.; libr., tchr. Richard Crane H.S., Chgo.; from instr. to prof. Chgo. State U., prof. Vol. Am. Diabetes Assn., Chgo., 2003—06, Am. Heart Assn., Chgo., 2006. Mem.: Nat. Hook-Up Black Women, Assn. Black Women in Higher Edn. (Leadership award 2000), Schamburg Ctr. Rsch. in Black Culture, Chgo. State U. Alumni Assn. (bd. dirs.), Phi Delta Kappa (dir. Chgo. chpt.). Home: 9211 S Halsted St Chicago IL 60620

BENTLEY, CHARMAINE CLARK O'FALLON, secondary school educator; b. Austin, Tex., Dec. 15, 1954; d. Harold Roy and Maria Rafaela Bentley; m. Charles Oliver Mixon, May 4, 1980; 1 child, Charlotte Farrar Mixon. BA in Anthropology, U. Tex., 1977, BS in Geol. Sci., 1977, M in Tech., 2006; BS in Computer Sci., SW Okla. State U., 1984, MEd in Math., 1988. DATA engr. Dresser Industries, Magcobar DATA, Oklahoma City, 1972-82; tchr. Dallas Ind. Sch. Dist., 1988—, tchr., technologist F.D. Roosevelt H.S., 1992—2003, chmn. computer sci. curriculum com., 1997-98, 2003—04. Presenter in field. Asst. troop leader Girl Scout U.S., Farmers Branch, Tex., 1992-95, Sunshine Literacy Project Coord., 1989-91; v.p. IB Parent Booster com. Clark H.S., Plano, Tex., 1995-96, sec., 1996-97; troop chmn. Boy Scout Am., Elk City, Okla., 1986-87; mem. F.D. Roosevelt H.S. Site Based Decision Com., 1998-2005, sec., 1998-2001, sec. student support team, 2005—. Recipient Award of Appreciation, City of Farmers Branch, 1990; scholar F.D. Roosevelt HS, 1991, 94. Mem. IEEE, Am. Assn. Petroleum Geologists, Nat. Coun. Tchrs. Math., Internat. Soc. Tech. Edn. (computer sci. spl. interest group), Tex. Computer Edn. Assn., Assn. Tex. Profl. Educators, Tex. Computer Edn. Assn. Computer Sci. (computer sci. spl. interest group, area 5 rep. 2000-02, sec./treas. 2002—), Assn. Computing Machinery, Computer Sci. Tchrs. Assn. (steering com. 2003-04, bd. dirs. 2005—, chmn. membership com. 2005—). Episcopalian. Avocations: reading, woodworking, photography, gardening. Office Phone: 972-925-6800. Personal E-mail: charmainebentley@csta.acm.org.

BENTLEY, DIANNE H. GLOVER, minister, consultant; BA, Drew U., Madison, N.J., 1976; MDiv, Drew Theol. Sch., 1997. LCSW HIV prevention counselor Pa. Dept. Health, 2003. Cons., trainer L.E.A.D., 2004; pastor First United Meth. Ch. of Sayre, 1997—. Dir. Ministry Resource Libr., Madison, NJ, 1994—97; pres. Bridge of Penn-York Valley Churches, Sayre, 1999—2002; chair Poverty Task Group, 2000—05, Teen Pregnancy Prevention Task Force, 2002—. Mentor Prudential Youth Leadership Inst., Wyo. Ann. Conf. United Meth. Ch.; mem. Com. Status and Role Women, Pa.; pres. Valley Clergy Assn., 2006—. Recipient Edwin A. Lewis Theology award, Drew Theol. Sch., 1997, GFWC Short Story award, 1991. Mem.: Binghamton Dist. Pastors' Assn., Lambda Iota Tau. Methodist. Office: PO Box 222 Sayre PA 18840

BENTLEY, DONNA GALE, school librarian; d. Baffrey Leon and Melba Jean Bentley. MLS, UCLA, 1979—81. Arts and sciences libr. U. La Verne, Calif., 1992—. Mem.: ALA. Office: Univ La Verne 2040 Third St La Verne CA 91750 Office Phone: 909-593-3511 4312. Office Fax: 909-392-2733.

BENTLEY, DORIS BROUSSARD, retired educator, consultant; b. Loreauville, La., July 8, 1919; d. Jean Edmond and Martha Anna (Camos) Broussard; m. George F. Bentley, July 7, 1945 (dec. Mar. 1953); children: George F. Jr., Edmond B., Suzanne M., Richard C., William C. BS, La. State U., 1938, MEd, 1956, PhD, 1971. Adminstrv. sec. McNeese State U., Lake Charles, La., 1939-43; sec., clk. U.S. Army, New Orleans, 1943-44; tchr. Iberia Parish Schs., New Iberia, La., 1953-59; prof. U. La., Lafayette, 1959—86; cons., vol. Lafayette, 1986—. Treas. Bayou Coun. Girl Scouts USA, Lafayette, 1985-96; region I, alt. regional mgr., coord. Women Bus. Ownership Svc. Corps of Retired Execs., Lafayette, 1987-2005; mem. Mcpl. Civil Svc. Bd., Lafayette, 1985-94. Mem. NEA, AAUW (state pres. 1980-82), La. Retired Tchrs. Assn., Cath. Daughters of Am. Avocations: music, art, crafts, writing.

BENTLEY, EDITH LOUISE, secondary school educator; b. Eustis, Fla., Sept. 19, 1966; d. William Olin and Claudia Lucile Bradshaw; m. Christopher James Bentley. B Music Edn., Stetson U., 1988; MEd, U. Ctrl. Fla., 1991. Band dir. Trinity Christian Sch., Apopka, Fla., 1988—. Sponsor Trinity Christian Sch. Jr. Beta Club, Apopka, Fla., 1991—; mid. sch. lead tchr. Trinity Christian Sch., Apopka, Fla., 2002—. Mem.: Music Educators Nat. Conf., Fla. Bandmasters Assn., Kappa Delta Pi. Office: Trinity Christian Sch 1022 S Orange Blossom Trail Apopka FL 32703 Office Phone: 407-886-0212. Personal E-mail: EBentley00@aol.com. Business E-Mail: bentley110@tcsapopka.org.

BENTLEY, JOYCE ELAINE, customer service officer; b. Bartow, Fla., Dec. 25, 1955; d. Charlie and Nola Mae (Brown) Turner. BSBA, Fla. Meml. Coll., 1978; postgrad., Webster U., 1998—. Purchasing clk. Polk County Sheriff's Office, Bartow, 1978; acct. I Heartland Pvt. Industry Co., Bartow, 1978-80, internal auditor, 1980-83, sr. acct. exec. Lakeland, Fla., 1983-88, sr. auditor, 1988-89; mgr. Heartland Pvt. Industry Coun., 1989-91, dir. career specialist, 1991-94, human resource dir., 1994-96; customer svc. officer Polk County Work Force Devel. Bd., 1996—. Co-woenr, social affairs cons. JoyLynn's Memories, Bartow, 1986—. Chair Agy. Coun. for Emplyment and Tng., Lakeland, 1986-88, U.S. Census, Polk County, 1989—; bd. dirs. The Econ. Devel. Bd.; adv. bd. Women in the Workforce, 1992—; grad. leadership Bartow; mem. quality improvement coun. Floral Ave. Elem. Sch.; chair audit com., mem. budget com., mem. choir Burkett Chapel Primitive Bapt. Ch. Recipient Oustanding Citizen award of the Polk County Opportunity Coun., 1991, Angel awrd Early Childhood Resources, Extra Ordinary Cmty. Svc. award Polk County chpt. FAMU Alumni, 1998. Mem. NAACP (exec. bd. dirs., treas., Freedom Fund banquet chair), Bartow C. of C. (Can Do award), Am. Bus. Women's Assn., Internat. Assn. Pers. for Employment Security, Toastmasters, Fla. Meml. Alumni (treas. 1986-91, pres. 1991—), Order Eastern Star, Delta Sigma Theta (project chair 1988—). Democrat. Avocations: bike riding, horseback riding, cooking, shopping, travel. Home: PO Box 923 Bartow FL 33831-0923

BENTLEY, KAREN GAIL, elementary school educator; b. Salina, Kans., Oct. 21, 1956; d. John Kennedy and Merle Lynn Blundon; m. Rodney Ray Bentley, Feb. 17, 1984 (dec. Sept. 1996). MusB cum laude, U. Mo., 1978; MusM, So. Ill. U., 1981. Grad. asst. So. Ill. U., Edwardsville, 1980—81; dir. music Ind. Congrl. Ch., St. Louis, 1978—81; tchr. elem. music Western Hghts. Schs., Oklahoma City, 1981—. Bd. dirs. Civic Music, 1985—, Orch. League, 1994—; bd. rep. PTA, 1992—; cantor Christ the King Cath. Ch., 1985—95. Republican. Episcopalian. Avocations: theater, raising Great Danes. Home: 11117 Quail Creek Rd Oklahoma City OK 73120 Office: John Glenn Elem Sch 6500 S Land Oklahoma City OK 73159

BENTLEY, LINDA DIANE, application developer, artist; d. Eddie M. Purdy and Marcella M. (Boyer) Vickers; m. James L. Bentley, Dec. 31, 1976; children: Jason James, Shannon Marie. Student, Concord Coll., Athens, W.Va., 1973-75, N.W. Tech. Coll., Wausau, Wis., 1989; AA in Computer Info. Sys., North Ctrl. Tech. Coll., 2005. Caregiver Human Svcs./CHR, Medford, Wis., 1985-95; bank teller Taylor Credit Union, Medford, 1990-91; mgr. Homz Mgmt. Corp., Madison, Wis., 1990-96; freelance proofreader, Stetsonville, Wis., 1994-98; owner, mgr. Cobalt Blue Arts and Crafts, Stetsonville, 1995—; Microsoft AAPD intern Fed. Hwy. Adminstrn., 2004—. Vol. Am. Heart Assn., 1993, ARC, 1997—, March of Dimes, 1997. Avocations: camping, boating, photography. Office: Blue Tamarak Computing LLC PO Box 156 Conrath WI 54731

BENTLEY, LISSA FRANCES, elementary school educator; b. N.Y.C., June 30, 1963; d. George Albert III and Nancy Ann (McNamara) B.; m. Matthew Levy, July 27, 2002; 1 child, Greer Davis Bentley Levy. AB, Smith Coll., 1985; MA, Columbia U., 1988, MEd, 1997. Legal asst. Davis Polk & Wardwell, N.Y.C., 1985-87; presch. tchr. Episcopal Sch., N.Y.C., 1988-89; elem. tchr. Greenwich (Conn.) Pub. Schs., 1989—. Lector, eucharistic min. St. Mary Ch., Greenwich, 1991—. Mem. Greenwich Edn. Assn. (rep. profl. rights and responsibilities com. 1994-97), Greenwich-Stamford Smith Club (alumnae admissions coord. 1989-99), Kappa Delta Pi. Avocations: reading, biking, bird watching. Office: North Street Sch 381 North St Greenwich CT 06830-3999 Office Phone: 203-869-6756.

BENTLEY, MARGARET ANN, librarian; b. Tawas City, Mich., June 13, 1956; d. Rupert A. and Joy A. (Bills) B. AB in English, Gordon Coll., 1978; MA in Libr. Sci., U. Mich., 1979. Cert. libr. Mich. Adult svcs. libr., asst. dir. Shiawassee Dist. Libr. (formerly Owosso Pub. Libr.), Owosso, Mich., 1979—. Mem.: AAUW (treas. 1984—2006), Mich. Libr. Assn., Phi Alpha Chi, Lambda Iota Tau, Beta Phi Mu. Avocations: reading, crafts, camping. Office: Shiawassee Dist Libr 502 W Main St Owosso MI 48867-2607 E-mail: margaret61356@yahoo.com.

BENTON, GERALDINE ANN, preschool owner, director; b. Plymouth, N.H., Apr. 25, 1960; d. Alton G. and Geraldine (Holecek) B. BS, Plymouth State Coll., 1984; MA in Curriculum and Tech., U. Phoenix, 2005. Cert. bus driver, N.H. Pvt. practice tutor; bus driver Robertson Transit, Campton, N.H., 1986-96; owner, dir. Mad River Learning Ctr. and Daycare, Thornton, N.H., 1996—; sub. tchr., 1982-96. Mem. Interested Citizens in Town Govt. Mem. Nat. Head Injury Found., Nat. Arbor Day Found., Nat. Audubon Soc., Nat. Wildlife Found. Home: PO Box 25 Campton NH 03223-0025 Office Phone: 603-726-3883.

BENTON, MARJORIE CRAIG, federal agency administrator; m. Charles William Benton, three children. LHD, Nat. Coll. Edn., 1981, Lincoln Coll., 1982, Columbia Coll., 1983, Northwestern U., 1983; LLD (hon.), John Marshall Law Sch., 1984; D of Pub. Svc. (hon.), St. Xavier Coll., Chgo., 1987; PhD (hon.), Mundelein Coll., 1988. Pub. del. U.S. Mission to UN, 1977, del. spl. session on disarmament, 1978; mem. commn. UN Assn., 1978-79; spl. adv. UN Disarmament Commn., 1979; U.S. rep. UNICEF, 1980-83; mem. Commn. on White House Fellowships, Washington, 1993, chmn. bd. dirs., 1994—. Vice chair Pub. Media, Inc., Chgo.; bd. dirs. Royal Packaging Industries, Van Leer, The Netherlands; co-chair Am. for Strategic Arms Limitation Talks, 1977-79; U.S. Commr. Internat. Yr. of Child; mem. adv. com. Agy. Internat. Devel. Private Voluntary Orgns., 1981-82; co-chair Symphony for Survival, Chgo., 1982. Co-founder The Peace Mus., Chgo., Chgo. Found. for Women, Women's Issues Network, Chgo.; hon. chair Save the Children Fedn., N.Y.; pres. Chapin Hall Ctr. for Children U. Chgo.; chair bd. dirs. Coun. on Founds., Washington, 1994-96; mem. com. on univ. resources Harvard U., Cambridge, Mass., Internat. Humn Rights Law Inst. DePaul Coll. of Law, Chgo., Inst. Social & Econ. Policy in the Middle East, Harvard U., Middle East Policy Coun., Washington; mem. Bernard Van Leer Foundation, The Netherlands, The Van Leer Group Foundation, The Netherlands; trustee Benton Foundation, Washington, DC; del. Dem. Nat. Conv., 1972, 76, 82, 88, 92; commn. del. selection Dem. Nat. Com., 1973, 88; del. Dem. Mid-Term Conv., 1974, 78, 83; mem. procedures com. Dem. Nat. Conv., 1978; mem. Ill. Dem. Platform com., 1975; Ill. co-chair Inaugural Com., 1977; mem. rules com. Dem. Nat. Conv., 1980, 87; mem. affirmative action com. Ill. Dems., 1984; del.-at-large Dem. Nat. Conv., 1984. Recipient Oustanding Pub. Svc. award UNICEF, 1978, Alumni Svc. award Nat. Coll. Edn., 1979, Woman of Achievement award, Cleve. City Women's Club, 1980, Adlai Stevenson award, 1981, Outstanding Achievement in Cmty. Leadership award YMCA, 1982, Better Govt. Assn. award, 1983, Lincoln award Ill. Citizenx for Handgun Control, Louis Lerner Disting. Svc. award Ill. Pub. Action Coun., Leadership award Chgo. Chpt. Nat. Assn. Fundraising Execs., Woman of Achievement award, Girl Scouts of Am., Chgo., Jane Addams Internat. Women's Leadership award, 1991, Full Circle award, 1993; Co-recipient Disting. Grantmaker Award, Coun. on Founds., 2004; Midwest Women's Ctr. 10th Anniversary Honoree, 1986. Mem. Chgo. Pediat. Soc. (hon.), Am. Orthopsychiatric Assn., Arts Club Chgo., Econ. Club Chgo., River Club N.Y.

BENTON, SUZANNE, sculptor, mask ritualist, printmaker, painter; b. N.Y.C., Jan. 21, 1936; d. Alex and Florence (Matkoff) Elkins; children: Daniel, Janet. BA in Fine Arts, Queens Coll., 1956. Creator Mask Ritual Theatre, over 220 mask ritual performances throughout U.S. and world; performance at Woudschoten, Ziest, Holland, 1982; presentation at Geilsdorfer Gallery, Cologne, Germany, 1982; 3-day workshop in maskmaking and storytelling, London, 1982; artist-in-residence Oberlin Coll., Ohio, 1983; affiliate Image Theatre N.Y.C.; guide Art and Mythology tour of Greece, 1985, Weir Farm Nat. Historic Site, Wilton, Conn., 1999, Artist Studio, Asilah, Morocco, 2000, Byrdcliffe Artist Colony, Woodstock, N.Y., 2001, Custom House Studios, Wespont County Mayo, Ireland, 2003, Helene Wurlitzer Found., Taos, N.Mex., 2006; lectr. numerous workshops and seminars; one-woman shows of sculpture include Wadsworth Atheneum, Hartford, Conn., 1975, Internat. Christian Coll., Tokyo, 1976, Chemould Gallery, Bombay, 1977, Hellenic Am. Union, Athens, 1977, Internat. House, New Orleans, 1978, BITEF Internat. Theatre Festival, Belgrade, Yugoslavia, 1978, Condon Gallery, N.Y.C., 1981, Korean Cultural Svc. Galleries, N.Y.C., 1982, Gallerie Fuchs, Dusseldorf, 1983, Amerika Haus, Koln, W.Ger., 1984, Kent Sch., Conn., 1984, Union Am. Hebrew Congregation Bldg, 1984, Amerika Haus, Stuttgart, 1986, 88, 89, Fairfield Libr., Conn., 1986, Asia Soc., N.Y.C., 1986, Image Theatre, N.Y.C., 1988, C.G. Jung Ctr., N.Y.C., 1988, Ctrl. Conn. State U., New Britain, 1989, Spectrum Ctr., London, 1987, Silo, New Milford, Conn., 1987; one-woman shows of sculpture and printmaking Interchurch Ctr., N.Y.C., 1988, 89, Gutman Libr., Harvard U., 2001, Stamford, 2002; retrospective exhbn. sculpture, painting and printmaking Silvermine Guild Arts Ctr., New Canaan, Conn., 2003, Queens Coll. Art Ctr., CUNY, Queens, 2005, Eckerd Coll., St Petersburg, Fla., 2006; group shows include USIS, Eastern Europe, 1971-75, Stamford Mus., Conn., 1976, Expo '74, Seattle, Nat. Sculpture Conf., Kans. U., 1974, Joods Hist. Mus., Amsterdam, 1986, Women's Studio Workshop, 1988, Hunterdon Art Ctr., Clinton, N.J., 1988, San Francisco Craft and Folk Art Mus., 1988, On the Wall, Est Village, N.Y.C., 1988, 89, author: The Art of Welded Sculpture, 1975. Nat. coord. NOW Women in the Arts, 1973—76; convenor Conn. Feminists in the Arts, 1970—72; artistic and mng. dir. Positive Power, Women's Caucus of Art, Conn., 2000—02; co-chair Salute to Feminists in the Arts, Vet. Feminists of Am., 2003. Grantee Conn. Commn. on Arts, 1973, 74, United Meth. World and Women's Divsn., 1976, United Presbyn. Program Agy., 1976, United Ch. Bd. Homeland Ministries, 1976, USIS, Tunisia, 1983, Istanbul, 1986, Helene Wurlitzer Found., 2006; recipient Pioneer Feminist award, Vet. Feminists Am., 1996. Mem.: Silvermine Guild of Art, Nat. Assn. Women Artists (Amelia Peabody award 1979), Nat. Korean Women's Sculpture Assn. (hon.), Adams Ho., Harvard U. (hon. assoc.). Home: 22 Donnelly Dr Ridgefield CT 06877-5611 Personal E-mail: suzanne@suzannemasks.com.

BENTON-BORGHI, BEATRICE HOPE, secondary school educator, consultant, writer; b. San Antonio; d. Donald F. and Beatrice H. Benton; m. Peter T. Borghi; children: Kathryn B. Borghi, Sarah B. Borghi. BA in Chemistry, Mass. State Coll. (now Mass. Coll. Liberal Arts), North Adams; MEd, Boston U.; MA, Ohio State U., Columbus; PhD, Ohio State U. Tchr. chemistry Cathedral H.S., Springfield, Mass.; tchr. chemistry and history Munich (W.Ger.) Am. H.S.; tchr. English, Tokyo; tchr. chemistry and sci. Marlborough (Mass.) H.S.; project dir., adminstr. ESEA, Marlborough Pub. Schs.; CEO, pres., chmn. bd. dirs. Open Minds, Inc. Project dir., proposal writer Title III, Title IX, U.S. Dept. Edn.; evaluation teams New Engl. Assn. Schs. and Colls.; organizer symposium Am. Assn. Colls. Tchr. Edn., Washington, 2005; mem. regional dept. edn. com.; vis. prof. Ohio Dominican U. Coll. Edn.; presenter, cons., lectr. in field. Author: Project ABC (Access By Computer), Kathryn Borghi Digital Libr., Alternative Funding/Recycling Project, Down the Aisle, Best Friends, A Thousand Lights, Whoa, Nellie!, Best Friend Jour., Down the Aisle Jour., Whoa, Nellie! Jour., A Thousand Lights Jour., Best Friend: Teacher and Parent Guide, Whoa Nellie! Teacher and Parent Guide, Down the Aisle: Teacher and Parent Guide, Subtle Inclusion Through Literature, Kathryn Borghi Digital Library with Accessible Technology Center Model, 2001, others; contbr. articles to profl. jours. Energy conservation rep. Marlborough's Overall Econ. Devel. Com., 1976; mem. strategic planning subcom. Upper Arlington Sch., Ohio, 1994, Ohio, 1999, 2005, tech. Ohio, 1999, mem. testing com., 1994, mem. tech. com., 2005; chmn. Marlborough's Energy Conservation Task Force, 1975; dir. Walk for Mankind, 1972; sec. Group Action for Marlborough Environment, 1975—76; pres. Sisters, Inc., dba Open Minds Inc.; Project Digital Jones Mid. Sch., Upper Arlington, Ohio, 2001—03; bd. dirs. Girls Club, Marlborough, 1979. Mem. AAUW, ASCD, AERA, Coun. Exceptional Children, Nat. Women's Health Network. Home: 2449 Edington Rd Columbus OH 43221-3047 Office: Ohio Domimican U Columbus OH 43221

BENYSHEK, DENITA MAREE, psychotherapist, educator, artist; b. Belleville, Kans., Nov. 24, 1955; d. Eldon Ray and Marian Frances (Filipi) Benyshek; 1 child, Hans. BFA magna cum laude, Wichita State U., Kans., 1979; student, Pilchuck Glass Sch., Washington, 1994; MFA in Painting, U. Wash., Seattle, 1995; Marriage and Family Therapy MA in Psychology, Saybrook Grad. Sch., 2004. Lectr. U. Alaska, Fairbanks, 1984-88; art instr. Pratt Fine Arts Ctr., Seattle, 1989-97; adj. prof. North Seattle C.C., 1995-97; intern Federal Way Youth and Family Svcs., Wash., 2003—04; pvt. practice. Performance artist "Farewell Rose", U. North Iowa, 1982, "Deerfield", McPherson Coll., 1983; artist-in-residence Young & Assocs., Alaskan bush, 1983-96; vis. artist Coll. Folk Arts and Culture, Pskov, Russia, 1993; grant panel juror King County Arts Commn., Seattle, 1991, Seattle Arts Commn., 1991, 96; program dir. Artists Unltd., Seattle, 1989-90; mem. adv. bd. Works of Heart, Wichita, Kans., 2005. Artist over 50 nat., juried exhibits including: Redefining Visionary Art, N.Y.C., 1989, Paint and Glass, Tucson, 1995, Whatcom Mus. History and Art, Bellingham, Wash., 1996, Bellevue Art Mus., 1996; 18 solo exhibits including: Anderson Glover Gallery, Kirkland, Wash., 1997; permanent collections include Glasmuseet, Ebeltoft, Denmark, Culture Heritage Collection Harborview Med. Ctr., Seattle, Wash., King County Arts Commn., Wash., PUb. Arts Commn., Olympia, Wash., U. Wash. Med. Ctr., Seattle; author: Season of Dead Water, 1990. Dir. N.W. Women Artists Lecture Series, Seattle, 1991; mem. curatorial com. Ulrich Mus. Arts, Wichita, 1975-79; bd. dirs. Women in the Arts, Wichita, 1983-85. Kans. Bd. Regents scholar, 1973-78, Miller Art scholar, 1975-79, scholar Pilchuck Glass Sch., Washington, 1994; Binney & Smith, Inc. grantee, 1994, 95, Ucross Found., Wyo., 1984; U. Wash. W.W. Stout fellow, 1994-95; tuition assistance grantee Saybrook Grad. Sch., 2005; recipient Alfred G. and Elma M. Milotte Art Scholarship, Seclef-Hoetzel Scholars Merit award, CHE scholarship program for students of Czech descent. Mem. APA, Am. Assn. Marriage and Family Therapists, Artist Trust, moveon.org, Found. for Shamanic Studies, Soc. for Psychology of Aesthetics, Creativity and the Arts. Avocations: gardening, hiking, ecopsychology, birdwatching, camping. Address: PO Box 2118 North Bend WA 98045 Office Phone: 425-214-6485. Personal E-mail: creativity@centurytel.net.

BENYUS, JANINE M., writer; Grad. in Natural Resource Mgmt. and English Lit., Rutgers U., NJ. Mem. Biomimicry Guild; lectr. U. Mont. Author: Field Guide to Wildlife Habitats of the Western US, Field Guide to Wildlife Habitats of the Ea. US, 1989, Northwoods Wildlife: A Watcher's Guide to Habitats, 1989, Biomimicry: Innovation Inspired by Nature, 1997; co-author: Beastly Behaviors: A Zoo Lover's Companion, 1993, Secret Language & Remarkable Behavior of Animals, 1998. Recipient Earth award, Wings WorldQuest Women of Discovery Awards, 2006. Office: Biomimicry Guild PO Box 575 Helena MT 59624*

BENZ, NANCY ANN, music educator; b. Buffalo, June 9, 1960; d. Alfred Anthony and Edna Irene Ulrich; m. James Edward Benz, Aug. 20, 1988; children: Elizabeth, Alexander. MusB, Ithaca Coll., N.Y., 1982; MFA Music Performance, SUNY Buffalo, 1988. Tchr. strings Lancaster Ctrl. Sch. Dist.,

NY, 1983—84, 1987—89, Williamsville Ctrl. Sch. Dist., NY, 1989—90, Clarence Ctrl. Sch. Dist., NY, 1990—. Adj. tchr. Suzuki music Buffalo Suzuki Strings, 1983—; mem. Amherst Symphony Orch. W. Grant Egbert scholarship, Ithaca Coll., 1978—82. Mem.: Erie County Music Edn. Assn., NY State Sch. Music Assn., Musicians Union, Local 92, Suzuki Assn. Am. Avocations: travel, gardening, sewing, orchids. Home: 323 Sereca Pl Lancaster NY 14086 Office: Clarence Mid Sch 10150 Greiner Rd Clarence NY 14031

BENZIES, BONNIE JEANNE, clinical and addictions psychologist; b. Chgo., May 3, 1943; d. Roy Benzies and Margaret Lucille (Hernly) Benzies-Sorensen. BS, MacMurray Coll., 1965; MS, Ill. Inst. Tech., 1971, PhD, 1980; cert. in substance abuse counseling, Loop Coll., 1986. Lic. clin. psychologist. Statistician, psychologist State of Ill., Chgo., 1966-73, psychologist Manteno, 1976—82, Ingalls Meml. Hosp., Harvey, 1982—84, Cook County Juvenile Ct., Chgo., 1987—88; pvt. practice Chgo., Hanover Park, Palatine, Glen Ellyn and Wheaton, 1984—; pub. svc. adminstr. State of Ill., Elgin, 1988—, dir. cmty. psychology, 2002—. Grad. tchg. asst. Ill. Inst. Tech., Chgo., 1973-74; mem. Mentally Ill Substance Abuser Cert. Com. State of Ill., 1996-97; bd. mem. Joint Commn. Accreditation Hosp. Orgns., Nat. Task Force on Depressive Disorders, 1991-94; mem. Ill. Coun. on Problem and Compulsive Gambling, 2002-, sec., 2005-06. Co-author Time Questionnaire, 1979; contr. scientific papers. Mem. Statewide Subcom. on Mentally Ill Substance Abusers, 1991-93. MacMurray scholar, 1961-65, Am. Legion scholar, 1963-64. Mem. Christian Assn. Psychol. Studies. Avocations: tennis, horseback riding, travel, church and community service. Home: 23W155 Foxcroft Dr Glen Ellyn IL 60137-6928 Office Phone: 847-742-1040 ext. 3354.

BERANEK, CARLA TIPTON, music educator; b. Aberdeen, Md., Nov. 8, 1964; d. B.G. Carl William and Shirley Ann (Sanders) Tipton; m. John Fred Beranek, Mar. 23, 1996. B in Music Edn., James Madison U., 1986; MusM, U. Tex., 1988. Provisional cert. prin. K-12, Ky., tchg. instrumental music K-12, Ky., tchg. vocal music K-12, Ky., tchg. all-level music, Tex., tchg. elem. self-contained 1-8, Tex., cert. temporary mid-mgmt. adminstr., Tex. Tchr. gen. music, choir Temple (Tex.) Ind. Sch. Dist., 1989-92, Ft. Worth Ind. Sch. Dist., 1992-96; tchr. band, orch., keyboard Fayette County Pub. Schs., Lexington, Ky., 1996; gifted/talented facilitator Sch. for the Creative & Performing Arts, 1998—. Presenter in field. Del. leader student exchange Ft. Worth Sister Cities Internat., 1994. Mem. ASCD, Ky. Music Educators Assn., Music Educators Nat. Conf., Ky. Edn. Assn., Fayette County Edn. Assn., U. Tex. Ex-Student Assn. (life), Kappa Kappa Psi (chpt. sec. 1985-86, s.w. dist. pres. 1987-88), Phi Delta Kappa. Democrat. Methodist. Home: 359 Avawam Dr Richmond KY 40475-9193 Office Phone: 859-381-3338. E-mail: cberanek@fayette.k12.ky.us.

BERANEK, KIM MARIE, music educator; b. Racine, Wisc., Mar. 13, 1962; d. Donald L. Frosland and Naomi B. Larrabee Frosland; m. David John Beranek, Dec. 20, 1985; children: Jonathan, Timothy, Samuel, Daniel. BA in Music Edn., Northwest Nazarene U., 1985; MA in Music Edn., U. Oreg., 1992. Lic. tchr. Oreg., Idaho. Music tchr. Medford (Oreg.) Sch. Dist., 1985—90, Eugene (Oreg.) Sch. Dist., 1990—91, Salem-Keizer Sch. Dist., Salem, Oreg., 1991—. Accompanist Rogue Valley Choral, 1985—90, S-KHONOR Choir, 1990—94; specialist Weather's Music Corp., Salem, 1994—; cons. Oregon Dept. Educators Music Educators, Salem, 1985—2005; coord. North by Northeast Homeschoolers, Salem, 1996—. Mentor Music Specialists, Oreg., 1985—; mem. A.C. Gilbert House and Discovery Ctr., Salem, 1991—, Oreg. Mus. Sci. and Industry; cert. mem. Harmony Road and Music in Me, 1995—2006; mem. music com. South Salem Nazarene Ch., 1991—, choir dir., 2002—03; vol. Women of Faith, 2000—05. Mem.: Friends of Music (chmn. Mary Eyre educator and hon. 2005), Oreg. Music Educators Assn., U. Oreg. Alumni Assn., Northwest Nazarene U. Alumni Assn., Nazarene Mission Soc., Ft. Clatsop Hist. Assn., Phi Delta Lamba Hon. Soc. Republican. Nazarene. Avocations: reading, travel, homeschooling, piano, teaching. Home: 2770 Foxhaven Dr SE Salem OR 97306-2519 Office Phone: 503-399-3311. Personal E-mail: kimberanek@comcast.com.

BERCH, REBECCA WHITE, state supreme court justice, lawyer; b. Phoenix, June 29, 1955; d. Robert Eugene and Janet Kay (Zimmerman) White; m. Michael Allen Berch, Mar. 9, 1981; 1 child, Jessica. BS summa cum laude, Ariz. State U., 1976, JD, 1979, MA, 1990. Bar: Ariz. 1979, U.S. Dist. Ct. Ariz., U.S. Ct. Appeals (9th cir.), U.S. Supreme Ct. Assoc., ptnr. McGroder, Tryon, Heller, Rayes & Berch, Phoenix, 1979-85; dir. legal rsch. and writing program Ariz. State U. Coll. Law, Tempe, 1986-91, 94-95; solicitor gen. State of Arizona, Phoenix, 1991-94, 1st asst. atty. gen., 1996—98; judge Ariz. Ct. Appeals, 1998—2002; justice Ariz. Supreme Ct., Phoenix, 2002—, vice chief justice, 2005—. Mem. Judicial Ethics Advisory Com., Bd. Certified Ct. Reporters, Arizona Supreme Ct. Com. on Examinations, Arizona Judicial Coll. Bd.; co-chair Arizona Appellate Practice Inst. Co-author: (Book) Introduction to Legal Method and Process, 1985, 2002, Teacher's Manual for Introduction to Legal Method and Process, 1992, 2002, Handling Complex Litigation, 1986; Bd. editors Jour. Legal Writing Inst., 1993—2002; contbr. articles to profl. jours. and newspapers. Bd. dirs. Tempe-Mesa chpt. ACLU, 1984—86, Homeless Legal Assistance Project, Phoenix, 1990—98. Recipient Outstanding Service award, Arizona Atty. General's Office, 1992, 1994, Outstanding Alumnus award, Ariz. State U. Coll. Law, 1999. Mem. Ariz. Women Lawyer's Assn. (Profl. Achievement award 2002), Ariz. State Bar Assn. Republican. Methodist. Avocations: reading, travel. Office: Ariz Supreme Ct 1501 W Washington St Phoenix AZ 85009-3831 Office Phone: 602-542-4535. Business E-Mail: Rberch@Azbar.org.*

BERCI, MARGARET ELIZABETH, education educator; b. Budapest, Hungary, Jan. 24, 1947; arrived in U.S., 200e; d. Bela and Margaret (Kiss) Berci; children: Jason Cory Hidegh, Joseph Christopher Hidegh. BEd in Social Studies, U. Calgary, Can., 1971, MA in Curriculum and Instrn., 1997, PhD in Ednl. Context, 2001. Classroom tchr. Calgary Roman Cath. Schs., 1969—75, instr., 1980—92; bus. mgr. Pro-Dent Lab. Ltd., 1975—90; instr. Chinook Coll., 1992—2002; field advisor U. Calgary, 1996—97, instr., 1998—2000, sessional instr., 2001; assoc. prof. edn. Coll. S.I., CUNY, 2002—. Presenter in field; peer reviewer Can. Jour. Edn.; mem. adv. and editl. bd. jour. Educating the Creative Mavericks. Contbr. articles, revs. to profl. publs. Social studies curriculum liaison Chinook Coll., 1999—2002; tchr. rep. to leadership team Calgary Bd. Edn., 1994—96, social studies rep. to learning and tchg. com., 1997—98, social studies curriculum leader, 1998—99; team mgr. Team Alta. to Western Can. Summer Games, 1990, Calgary Patriots Swim Club, 1988—89, pres., 1989—91. Recipient award of merit, Alta. Tchrs.' Assn., 2001, Exec. Svc. award, 2002; grantee, Com. on Excellence in Learning Tech., 2003—05, CUNY, 2004; Edn. grantee, Calgary Roman Cath. Schs., 1968—69, grad. rsch. scholar, U. Calgary, 1997—99. Mem.: Soc. Profs. Edn., Rsch. Social Studies Edn., Philosophy of Edn. Soc., Nat. Coun. Social Studies, Can. Philosophy Edn. Soc., Can. Assn. Curriculum Studies, Can. Assn. Founds. of Edn., Can. Soc. Study of Edn., Am. Hungarian Educators' Assn., Am. Ednl. Rsch. Assn., Kappa Delta Pi (pres. 2000—01, v.p. 1999—2000, historian 1999—2000). Office: CUNY Coll SI Dept Edn 3S-208 2800 Victory Blvd Staten Island NY 10314 Office Phone: 718-982-4133. Business E-Mail: berci@mail.csi.cuny.edu.

BERDICH, ALLA, psychiatrist; b. Kiev, Ukraine, Oct. 4, 1940; came to U.S., 1979; d. Boris and Hava Tsipershteyn; 1 child, Irene Krepak. MD, Kiev Med. Sch., 1963. Diplomate Am. Bd. Psychiatry and Neurology. Intern/residency Michael Reese Hosp., Chgo., 1982—86; staff psychiatrist Humana Health Care Plan, Chgo., 1982—2006, Kiev Psychiat. Hosp., 1963-79; pvt. practice Fla., 2006—. Mem. Am. Psychiat. Assn. Office: 4700 Sheridan St Hollywood FL 33021

BERDINE, LINDA, information technology executive; Sr. tech. mgr. McDonnell Douglas Corp.; div. dir. Planning Rsch. Corp.; v.p. telecommunications Network Strategies; v.p. Cincinnati Bell; CIO U.S. Ho. Rep., Washington; founder & pres. Berdine & Associates; sr. v.p. info. tech. & CIO Soza & Co.; founder, pres. G&B Solutions Inc., McLean, Va., 2001—. Mem. Congressional delegation to Hungary, Poland & Czech Republic; chmn. legis. branch telecommunications standards com.; bd. dir. Fed. Data Ctr. Directors, Govt. Interagency Council for Info. Resource Mgmt.; U.S. rep. Internat. Council Info. Tech.; bd. mem. Govt. Info. Tech. Exec. Council; pres. Bethesda chapter AFCEA. Named a Heroine in Tech., March of Dimes & Women in Tech., 2005. Office: G&B Solutions Ste 120 1749 Old Meadow Rd Mc Lean VA 22102*

BERENBAUM, MAY ROBERTA, entomology educator; b. Trenton, N.J., July 22, 1953; BS, Yale U., 1975; PhD, Cornell U., 1980. Asst. prof. entomology U. Ill., Urbana-Champaign, 1980-85, assoc. prof. entomology, 1985-90, prof. entomology, 1990-95, head dept., 1992—, Swanlund prof. entomology, 1996—. Assoc. editor Am. Midland Naturalist, 1982-85; mem. editl. bd. Jour. Chem. Ecology, Chemoecology, Proceedings of the Nat. Acad. Scis. USA. Recipient Presdl. Young Investigator award NSF, 1984, Founder's award Entomol. Soc. Am., 1994. Fellow AAAS, Am. Assn. Arts and Sciences, Encol. Soc. Am. (George Mercer award, Robert MacArthur award); mem. NAS (council mem.), Am. Philos. Soc., Entomol. Soc. Am. (fellow 2002; Founder's award), Phytochem Soc. Am., Internat. Soc. Chem. Ecology, Sigma Xi. Achievements include research in chemical aspects of insect-plant interaction, evolutionary ecology of insects, phototoxicity of plant products, host-plant resistance. Office: U Ill Dept Entomology 286 Morrill Hall 505 S Goodwin Ave Urbana IL 61801-3707 E-mail: maybe@uiuc.edu.*

BERENSON, ABBEY BELINA, gynecologist, educator; b. Nashville, Aug. 19, 1958; d. Leon and Florence (Keiles) B.; m. Steven Mitchell Kornblau, Nov. 24, 1983; children: Ilyse Samantha, Jake Alexander. BA summa cum laude, U. Tex., 1980; MD, Baylor U., 1984. Lic. gynecologist, Tex. Resident in ob-gyn. Baylor Coll. Medicine, Houston, 1984-88; fellow in pediat. gynecology Queen Charlotte's and Chelsea Hosp., London, 1991; asst. prof. U. Tex. Med. Br., Galveston, 1989-93, assoc. prof., chief divsn. pediat. and adolescent gynecology, 1993-98, prof., chief divsn. pediat. and adolescent gynecology, 1998—. Reviewer: Jour. Adolescent Health, Pediats., Obstetrics and Gynecology, Archives of Pediats. and Adolescent Medicine, Jour. Reproductive Medicine; contbr. numerous articles to profl. publs. including Jour. Adolescent Health, Adolescent Pediat. Gynecology, Pediats., Am. Jour. Ob-Gyn. James and Minnie Edmonds scholar. Fellow ACOG (bd. cert.), Ctrl. Assn. Obstetricians and Gynecologists (pres. 2004), Soc. Adolescent Medicine; mem. Internat. Fedn. Gynecologists Obstetricians (expert adv. panel 1997-2000), Soc. Gynecologic Investigation, N.Am. Soc. Pediat. and Adolescent Gynecology (abstract rev. com. 1992-93, com. position statements 1996). Achievements include research on appearance of external genitalia in prepubertal girls; physical abuse in pregnancy; contraceptive compliance in adolescents; drug abuse in pregnancy.

BERENTSON, JANE, editor; Editor Am. Lawyer; sr. editor Worth Mag., NYC, exec. editor, 1995—2002; and editor Equity Mag., NYC, 1995—2002; exec. editor Real Simple Mag., NYC, 2004—05, Inc. Mag., NYC, 2002—04, editor, 2005—. Editor: (books) Dressing for Dinner in the Naked City: And Other Tales from the Wall Street Journal's Middle Column, 1994. Office: Editor Inc Mag 375 Lexington Ave New York NY 10017 Office Phone: 212-389-5300.

BERES, MARY ELIZABETH, religious organization administrator; b. Birmingham, Ala., Jan. 19, 1942; d. John Charles and Ethel (Belenyesi) Beres. BS, Siena Heights Coll., Adrian, Mich., 1969; PhD, Northwestern U., 1976. Joined Dominican Sisters, 1960. Tchr. St. Francis Xavier Sch., Medina, Ohio, 1962-64, St. Edward Sch., Detroit, 1964-67, Our Lady of Mt. Carmel Sch., Temperance, Mich., 1967-69, asst. prin., 1968-69; tchr. math. St. Ambrose H.S., Detroit, 1969-70; vis. instr. Cornell U., 1973-74; assoc. prof. orgn. behavior Temple U., Phila., 1974-84; assoc. prof. mgmt. Mercer U., Atlanta, 1984-91; founder, sr. assoc. Leadership Sys., Atlanta, 1988—, Mid-Atlantic chpt. Prioress Dominican Sisters of Adrian, Atlanta, 2004—. Mem. World Pilgrims, 2002—; bd. dir. Aquinas Ctr. Theology, 2001—; organizer of symposia in corp. leadership, orgn. change and cross-cultural comm. Contbr. chapters to books. Bd. dir. Ctr. for Ethics and Social Policy, Phila., 1980—84, Assn. Global Bus., 1989—91; program planning com. of interdepartmental group in bus. adminstrn. U. Ctr. in Ga., 1987—91, chair, 1988—90; trustee Adrian Dominican Ind. Sch. Sys., Adrian, Mich., 1971—79; pres. bd. dirs. New Ventures Network, 1998—2001; active Atlanta Clergy and Laity Concerned, 1986—95; econ. pastoral imlementation com. Archdiocese of Atlanta, 1988—89, Atlanta Archdiocesan Planning and Devel. Coun., 1991—93; episcopal moderator women Religious Archdiocese of Atlanta, 1993—97, Atlanta Conf. Sisters, 1984—, pres., 1993—97, 2001—06; vicar Consecrated Life Archdiocese of Atlanta, 2001—06. Recipient Legion of Honor membership Chapel of the Four Chaplains, Phila., 1982, Disting. Tchg. award Lindback Found., 1982, Cert. for Humanity Mercer U, 1985. Mem. Acad. Mgmt., Dominican Sisters drian, Mich. (strategic planning com. 2000-01), Faith Alliance Met. Atlanta, 2004-. Democrat. Roman Catholic. Office: Mid-Atlantic Mission Chpt PO Box 76453 Atlanta GA 30358 Personal E-mail: mbberes@bellsouth.net.

BERETS, EILEEN TOLKOWSKY, artist; b. Antwerp, Belgium, July 15, 1930; arrived in U.S., 1940; d. Marcel and Marthe Germaine (Kleinberg) Tolkowsky; m. Donald J. Berets, June 24, 1956 (dec. Feb. 2002); children: James Carl, Susan Lee. BA Economics, Wellesley Coll., 1952; student, Art Student's League, N.Y.C., 1953—56; studied, with Ethel Todd George, Stamford, Conn., 1983, with Ethel Todd George, 1984, with Diane Faxon, Stamford, 1984—92; student, Silvermine Guild, 1984—87. Cons. Stone Studio, Stamford, Our World Gallery, 1991—. One-Woman and duo shows include U. Conn., Stamford, 1984, Stamford Art Assn. Landmark Tower, 1986, New Canaan (Conn.) Art Assn. Waveny Carriage Barn, 1988, Greenwich (Conn.) Art Soc. Marsh & McLennan, 1989, Conn. Commn. Arts Legis. Bldg., Hartford, 1990, Our World Gallery, Stamford, 1991, Darien (Conn.) Libr., 1992, Art in the Garden, 1995, Conn. Ballet Ctr., 1997-98; exhibited in group shows at Nat. Arts Club, N.Y.C., 1984, Stamford Art Assn., 1984-98 (2d prize 1991, 1st prize 1997), Art Soc. Old Greenwich, 1984-93, Conn. Art Ann. Competition Stamford Mus., 1985, 88, 91, 97, Greenwich Art Soc., 1985-2004 (Best Watercolor award 1989, Allan Bernard award 1996), New Canaan Soc. Arts, 1992-2004 (2d pl. prize watercolor 1998), AAUW Salute to Conn. Artists Invitational, 1983-88, Stamford Cmty. Arts Coun. Eight Watercolorists, 1985, Conn. Pub. TV Preview Exhbn., Hartford, New Haven, Stamford, 1990-91, Hartford Architecture Conservancy, 1991, Wellesley Coll., 1992, 97, Stamford Art Assn. Lucas Industries, 1992-93, Arts in the Garden, 1995, Faber Birren Nat. Color Award Show, 1996, 2006, Arthur Ross Gallery, 1996, Caron Gallery, Chester, Conn., 2001-03; represented in permanent collections Stamford Art in Pub. Places Program, 1990-95, Lending Art Collection Greenwich Pub. Libr., 2005, Pres.'s Office Turner Entertainment Co., L.A., Pres.'s Office Conservation Mgmt. Inc., Washington; commissions include Fellowship for Jewish Learning, Conservation Mgmt., Inc., Washington Dir., v.p., pres. LWV, Stamford; sec., dir. Family and Children's Svcs.; Stamford rep. South We. Regional Planning Agy.; chair task force mass transp. Stamford Area Commerce and Industry Assn.; dir. Stamford Art Assn., 1994—, pres., 1999-2000 Mem.: Nat. League Am. Pen Women. Home: 47 E Ridge Rd Stamford CT 06903-4337

BERG, AMIE G., lawyer; b. Houston, Feb. 11, 1964; BBA magna cum laude in Fin., U. Houston Honors Coll., 1996; JD, U. Houston Law Ctr., 1999. Bar: US Dist. Ct. (so. dist. Tex.) 1999, US Dist. Ct. (ea. dist. Tex.) 2000, US Dist. Ct. (no. dist. Tex.) 2000, US Dist. Ct. (we. dist. Tex.) 2000, US Supreme Ct. 2003, US Ct. Internat. Trade 2003. Risk mgmt. analyst Hines Interests Ltd. Partnership; intern Staff of US Magistrate Judge Marcia Crone; assoc. atty. litigation sect. Baker Hostetler, Houston, 1999—. Named a Rising Star, Tex. Super Lawyers mag., 2006. Mem.: Risk and Ins. Mgmt. Soc. (Houston chpt.), Tex. Bar Assn., Houston Bar Assn., Woodlands Fit Marathon Tng. Team. Office: Baker Hostetler 1000 Louisiana Ste 2000 Houston TX 77002-5009 Office Phone: 713-646-1361. Office Fax: 713-751-1717. E-mail: aberg@bakerlaw.com.*

BERG, BARBARA KIRSNER, health education specialist; b. Cin., Dec. 6, 1954; d. Robert and Mildred Dorothy (Warshofsky) Kirsner; m. Howard Keith Berg, Apr. 8, 1984; children: Arielle, Allison, Stacy. BA, Brandeis U., 1976; MEd, U. Cin., 1977. Cert. health edn. specialist Nat. Commn. for Health Edn. Credentialing, Inc., Mass. Health educator S.W. Ohio Lung Assn., Cin., 1977-79; coord. adminstrv. edn. N.E. Regional Med. Edn. Ctr., Northport, N.Y., 1979-81; patient health edn. coord. VA Med. Ctr., Buffalo, 1981-87; clin. asst. prof. SUNY, Buffalo, 1982-87; dir. comty. health edn. N.W. Hosp. Ctr., Balt., 1987-89; coord. law and health care program U. Md. Sch. Law, Balt., 1989-90; med. mgmt. cons. Dr. Howard K. Berg, Owings Mills, Md., 1990—; health edn. coord. Balt. Hadassah, 2005—. Cons. health edn. Edward Bartlett, Assoc., Rockville, Md., 1987-88; mem. adult edn. com. Chizuk Amuno Congregation, Balt., 1993-99, mem. bd. dir., 1996-98, chair cultural arts com., 1996-98. Bd. dir., mem. Am. Lung Assn. Western N.Y., Buffalo, 1983-86, Pumpkin Theater, Balt., 1990-91; chair domestic concerns com. Balt. Jewish Coun., 1994-96, chair govt. rels. com., 1996-98, sec., bd. dir., 1996-98, 2d v.p. 1998-2000; sec. women's dept. Associated Jewish Charities, Balt., 1994-97; mem. sch. bd. nominating cov. Baltimore County, 1995-99; pres. Pikesville Mid. Sch. PTA, 1998-2001, Owings Mill H.S. Parent Tchr. Student Assn., 2004-2005, v.p. leadership, 2002-2004. Recipient Vol. of Yr. award, Pikesville C. of C., 2005. Mem.: APHA, Soc. Pub. Health Edn., Balt. Brandeis Alumni Assn. (pres.), Am. Jewish Com. (treas. 2005), Phi Delta Kappa. Jewish. Avocations: reading, travel. Home and Office: 12116 Heneson Garth Owings Mills MD 21117-1629

BERG, DARLA GAYE, writer; b. Wenatchee, Wash., Oct. 17, 1952; d. Edward Jay and Elsie Louise (Jackson) Jones; m. Mark Allen Kerr, June 12, 1970 (div. May 1972); m. Thomas Wayne Berg, May 19, 1978; 1 child, Mackenzie Marie. Student, Regents Coll. Mail room, service rep., personnel Pacific N.W. Bell, Seattle, 1970—80, Americorps, 1993—94; dir., creator after sch. program St. Barnabas Ch., Bainbridge Island, Wash., 1994—96; grant writer, 1993—. Promoter Parenting Classes, Bainbrige Island. Coauthor: Architectural Doc. Production, 1991; editor: The Technical Advisor. Personnel com. St Barnabas Day Sch., 1996-97; bd. v.p. St. Barnabas After Sch. Program, 1993-97; instr. Episcopal Ch., 1993-97; staff mem. St. Barnabas Ch., asst. pastoral care, tchr., 1991-97. Recipient numerous grants. Episcopalian. Avocation: writing for adolescents. E-mail: bengtdm@earthlink.net.

BERG, ELIZABETH ANN, writer; b. St. Paul, Minn., Dec. 2, 1948; d. Arthur Peter and Marion Jeanne (Loney) Hoff; m. Howard Jonathan Berg, Mar. 30, 1974; children: Julie Marin, Jennifer Sarene. A in applied sci., St. Mary's Coll., 1974; student, Univ. Minn., 1966-69. Author: Durable Goods, 1993, Talk Before Sleep, 1994, Range of Motion, 1995, The Pull of the Moon, 1996, Open House, 2000, True to Form, 2002, Say When, 2003, The Art of Mending, 2004, The Year of Pleasures, 2005, We Are All Welcome Here, 2006. Avocations: quilting, cooking. Address: Author Mail Random House 1745 Broadway New York NY 10019 Mailing: care Lisa Bankoff ICM 40 W 57th St New York NY 10019*

BERG, GRACIA M., lawyer; b. Apr. 26, 1945; BA, Augsburg Coll., 1961; JD, Univ. Notre Dame, 1980; diploma, Inst. Internationale des Droits de L'Homme, Strasbourg, France. Bar: DC 1980. Dep. gen. counsel to asst. gen. counsel, Antidumping and Countervailing Duty Investigations Internat. Trade Commn.; atty. Steptoe & Johnson, 1987; counsel, internat. trade Gibson Dunn & Crutcher LLP, Washington. Mem.: ABA. Office: Gibson Dunn Crutcher 1050 Connecticut Ave NW Washington DC 20036 Office Phone: 202-887-3644. Office Fax: 202-530-9652. Business E-Mail: GBerg@gibsondunn.com.

BERG, JANICE CAROL, elementary school educator; b. Painesville, Ohio, Feb. 18, 1953; d. Kenneth White Edds and Audrey Helen Nelson; children: Peter James, Steven Alan. BS in Elem. Edn., Slippery Rock State Coll., 1975; MEd, Slippery Rock U., 1987, cert. in early childhood edn., 1995; cert. reading specialist, Clarion U., 1994. Cert. elem. tchr. Pa. 3d grade tchr. Brookville (Pa.) Area Sch. Dist., 1975—76; 5th grade tchr. Seoul (Rep. of Korea) Fgn. Sch. Dist., 1977—78, 1st grade tchr., 1978—79; reading specialist Punxsutawney (Pa.) Area Sch. Dist., 1994, Allegheny-Clarion Valley Sch. Dist., Foxburg, Pa., 1996—. Sub. tchr. Derry Twp. Sch. Dist., Hershey, Pa., 1990; pvt. tutor, Brookville, Pa., 93. Room mother PTO, Elizabethtown, Pa., 1985; den leader, chmn. com. Boy Scouts Am., Elizabethtown, 1987—94; vacation bible sch. dir., tchr., Sunday sch. tchr., chmn. Christian edn. com. Mem.: Pa. State Edn. Assn., Seneca Reading Coun. (pres., corr. sec. 2001—02), Allegheny-Clarion Valley Edn. Assn., Keystone State Reading Assn. (mem. conf. membership com. 2002), Butler Outdoor Club (sec. 2004—05). Avocations: swimming, hiking, bicycling, reading, table tennis. Home: 404 Walnut St Emlenton PA 16373

BERG, KAREN LYNN ANDERSON, elementary school educator; b. Oak Park, Ill., Oct. 29, 1956; d. Ralph Lewis and Barbara Ann (Caspers) Brown; m. Timothy William Anderson, June 7, 1980 (dec. Nov. 1990); m. Terence Michael Berg, June 23, 2001. BA, U. No. Colo., 1978, MA, 1985; adminstrn. cert., Denver U., 2001. Intern Cherry Creek Schs., Walnut Hills Elem. Sch., Englewood, Colo., 1978-79; customer svc. rep. United Bank Am., Denver, 1979-80; substitute tchr. Cherry Creek Schs., Aurora (Colo.) Pub. Schs., 1980-82; advisor of Master's prog. in Whole Learning Regis U., Denver, 1991—98; tchr. Independence Elem. Sch., Aurora, 1982—85, Indian Ridge Elem. Sch., Aurora, Colo., 1985—. Dir. steering com. Regis U. Literacy Inst., 1985-94; steering com., Regis U. Early Childhood Inst., 1990-93; staff devel. liaison Cherry Creek Schs., 1991—; mem. Literacy Planning for Cherry Creek Schs., 1995-2004; chair Young Life Com., 2006—. Deacon Cherry Creek Presbyn. Ch., 1997—2000. Recipient Cherry Creek Schools Tchr. of Yr., 1988, Tchr. Who Makes a Difference award Channel 4, 1989. Mem. ASCD, Internat. Reading Assn., Young Life (com. chair 1990-96, vol. leader 1990-96, com. mem. 1998—). Republican. Presbyterian. Avocations: skiing, hiking, reading, tennis, entertaining. Home: 5558 S Telluride St Centennial CO 80015-2643 Office: Indian Ridge Elem 16501 E Progress Dr Aurora CO 80015-4135 Office Phone: 720-886-8411.

BERG, LILLIAN DOUGLAS, chemistry professor; b. Birmingham, Ala., July 9, 1925; d. Gilbert Franklin and Mary Rachel (Griffin) Douglas; m. Joseph Wilbur Berg, Jr., June 26, 1950 (dec. Nov. 1997); children: Anne Berg Jenkins, Joseph Wilbur III, Frederick Douglas. BS in Chemistry, Birmingham So. Coll., 1946; MS in Chemistry, Emory U., 1948; AA in Music, No. Va. C.C., Annandale, 2002. Instr. chemistry Armstrong Jr. Coll., Savannah, Ga., 1948-50; rsch. asst. chemistry Pa. State U., University Park, 1950-54; instr. chemistry U. Utah, Salt Lake City, 1955-56; prof. chemistry No. Va. C.C., 1974-96, 98—. Adj. prof. No. Va. C.C., 1998—. Mem. Am. Chem. Soc., Am. Women in Sci., Am. Guild Organists, Mortar Bd. Soc., Iota Sigma Pi, Sigma Delta Epsilon, Phi Beta Kappa. Avocation: liturgical organist/conductor. Home: 124 Villa Dr Poquoson VA 23662 Office Phone: 757-868-8005.

BERG, LORINE MCCOMIS, retired guidance counselor; b. Ashland, Ky., Mar. 28, 1919; d. Oliver Botner and Emma Elizabeth (Eastham) McComis; m. Leslie Thomas Berg, Apr. 27, 1946; children: James Michael, Leslie Jane. BA in Edn., U. Ky., 1965; MA, Xavier U., 1969. Tchr. A.D. Owens Elem. Sch., Newport, Ky., 1963-64, 6th dist. Elementary Schs., Covington, Ky., 1965-69; guidance counselor Twenhofel Jr. H.S., Independence, Ky., 1969-78, Scott H.S., Taylor Mill, Ky., 1978-84. Bd. dirs. Mental Health Assn., Covington, Ky, 1970-76, v.p., 1973 (valuable svc. award 1973); mem. Lakeside Christian Ch., Ft. Mitchell, Ky. Named to Honorable Order of Ky. Colonels, Hon. Admissions Counselor U.S. Naval Acad.; cited by USN Recruiting Command for Valuable Assistance to USN, 1981. Mem. Am. Assn. of Univ. Women, Covington Art Club, Retired Tchrs. Assn., Kappa Delta Pi, Delta Kappa Gamma, Phi Delta Kappa. Democrat. Avocations: painting, dance, reading, arts and crafts. Home: 11 Idaho Ave Covington KY 41017-2925

BERG, MADELAINE R., lawyer; b. Bklyn., Aug. 13, 1951; d. Gerald and Lorraine (Nodkin) B. BA, Bklyn. Coll., 1973, MFA, 1975; JD, Bklyn. Law Sch., 1980. Bar: N.Y. 1981, U.S. Dist. Ct. (so. dist.) N.Y. 1981, Pa. 1992, U.S.

Dist. Ct. (ea. dist.) Pa. 1992. Spl. counsel, environ. law practice area Stroock & Stroock & Lavan LLP, N.Y.C., 1980—. Contbr. articles to profl. jours. Office: Stroock & Stroock & Lavan LLP 180 Maiden Ln New York NY 10038-4982 Office Phone: 212-806-5823. Office Fax: 212-806-6006. Business E-Mail: mberg@stroock.com.

BERG, NANCY S., science association director; BS, Univ. Mich. Staff mgr. robotics internat. SME, 1982—84, product devel., Expositions Divsn., 1984, also strategic, fin. planning, mgmt., coord., exec. dir., 2005—. Mem. bd. Greenfield Coalition, Nat. Sci. Found. Mem.: Assn. Exposition Mgmt., Am. Soc. Assn. Execs. Achievements include only woman heading a major engrng./tech. soc. Office: SME One SME Dr Dearborn MI 48121*

BERG, PATRICIA ELENE, molecular biologist; b. Dubuque, Iowa, Sept. 17, 1943; d. Clifford Jay and Dorothy Ruth (McKibben) Emerson; 1 child, Bridget K. Mora; m. Robert S. Weiner. SB in Math., U. Chgo., 1965; PhD in Microbiology, Ill. Inst. Tech., 1973. Postdoctoral fellow U. Chgo., 1973-78; dir. genetic engrng. Bethesda Rsch. Labs., Rockville, Md., 1978-80; expert NIH, Bethesda, 1980-82, sr. staff fellow, 1982-85, Nat. Inst. Digestive Diseases and Kidney, 1985-91; assoc. prof. divsn. of pediatric hematology/oncology Sch. Medicine U. Md., Balt., 1991-98; assoc. prof. dept. biochem. and molecular biology George Washington U. Med. Sch., Washington, 1999—. Contbr. articles to profl. jours. and to NY Times, Washington Post, L.A. Times, AP, Reuters; reported on CNN, Fox, CBS, 160 TV stas., U. Chgo. scholar, 1961—65. Mem. AAAS, Am. Soc. Microbiology, Am. Soc. Hematology, Am. Assn. Cancer Rsch., Sigma Xi. Achievements include discovery of BP1, gene expressed in over 80 percent of breast cancer patients. Office: George Washington U Med Sch Dept Biochem/Molecular Biol 2300 Eye St NW Washington DC 20037-2336 Business E-Mail: bcmpeb@gwumc.edu.

BERG, TERESA G., elementary school educator; b. Morton, Wash., Sept. 24, 1975; d. Clyde and Sandra Ramsey; m. Darryl L. Berg, July 6, 2002; children: Alicia, Kalee. AA, AS, Lower Columbia Coll., 1995; BA in Human Devel., Wash. State U., 1998, BA in Elem. Edn., 2002. Tchr.'s asst. Cmty. Child Care Ctr., Pullman, Wash., 1995—98; tchr. Lewis County Head Start, Centralia, Wash., 1998—2000, Adna (Wash.) Elem. Sch., 2003—. Asst. mgr. dep. program Cmty. Child Care Ctr., 1998. Co-author: Quick Quotes Instant Journaling, Moments Idea Book, Quick Quotes Instant Journaling, Life Stories Idea Book. Faciliatator project ARC, Chehalis, Wash., 2005. Mem.: Internat. Reading Assn. Avocations: scrapbooks, travel. Office Phone: 360-748-7029.

BERGÉ, CAROL, writer; b. NYC, 1928; d. Albert and Molly Peppis; m. Jack Bergé, June 1955; 1 child, Peter. Asst. to pres. Pendray Public Relations, N.Y.C., 1955; disting. prof. lit. Thomas Jefferson Coll., Allendale, Mich., 1975-76; instr. adult degree program Goddard Coll., 1976; tchr. fiction and poetry U. Calif. Extension Program, Berkeley, 1976-77; assoc. prof. U. So. Miss., Hattiesburg, 1977-78; vis. prof. Honors Ctr. and English dept. U. N.Mex., 1978-79, 87; vis. lectr. Wright State U., 1979, SUNY, Albany, 1980-81; tchr. Poets and Writers, Poets in the Schs. (N.Y. State Council on Arts), 1970-72, Poets in the Schs. (Conn. Commn. Arts). Summer writing confs. Squaw Valley, Ind. U., U. Calif., Santa Cruz, 1975-1980; propr. Blue Gate Gallery of Art and Antiques, 1988-2003. Author: (fiction) The Unfolding, 1969, A Couple Called Moebius, 1972, Acts of Love: An American Novel, 1973 (N.Y. State Coun. on Arts CAPS award 1974), Timepieces, 1977, The Doppler Effect, 1979, Fierce Metronome, 1981, Secrets, Gossip & Slander, 1984, Zebras, or, Contour Lines, 1991; (poetry) The Vulnerable Island, 1964, Lumina, 1965, Poems Made of Skin, 1968, The Chambers, 1969, Circles, as in the Eye, 1969, An American Romance, 1969, From a Soft Angle: Poems About Women, 1972, The Unexpected, 1976, Rituals and Gargoyles, 1976, A Song, A Chant, 1978, Alba Genesis, 1979, Alba Nemesis, 1979, (reportage) The Vancouver Report, 1965; editor Center Mag., 1970-84, pub., 1991—; editor Miss. Rev., 1977-78, Subterraneans, 1975-76, Paper Branches, 1987, Light Years: The N.Y.C. Coffeehouse Writers and Multimedia Artists of the 1960s, 2005; contbg. editor Woodstock Rev., 1977-81, Shearsman mag., 1980-82, S.W. Profile, 1981, Caprice, 2000-05; editor, pub. Center Press, 1970-93; pub.: Medicine Journeys (Carl Ginsburg), Coastal Lives (Miriam Sagan), 1991; co-pub.: Zebras (Carol Berge). Nat. Endowment Arts fellow, 1979-80 Mem. Authors' League, Poets and Writers, MacDowell Fellows Assn., Nat. Press Women Home: 2070 Calle Contento Santa Fe NM 87505-5406 E-mail: carolberge@earthlink.net.

BERGEN, CANDICE, actress, writer, photojournalist; b. Beverly Hills, Calif., May 9, 1946; d. Edgar and Frances (Westerman) B.; m. Louis Malle, Sept. 27, 1980 (dec. 1995); 1 child, Chloe; m. Marshall Rose, June 15, 2000. Student, U. Pa. Model during coll. Actor (films) The Group, The Sand Pebbles, 1966, The Day the Fish Came Out, Live for Life, 1967, The Magus, 1968, Soldier Blue, The Executioner, The Adventurers, Getting Straight, 1970, The Hunting Party, 1970, Carnal Knowledge, 1970, 19 T.R. Baskin, 1971, 11 Harrowhouse, 1974, Bite the Bullet, The Wind and the Lion, 1975, The Domino Principle, The End of the World in Our Usual Bed in a Night Full of Rain, Oliver's Story, 1978, Starting Over, 1979, Rich and Famous, 1981, Gandhi, 1982, Stick, 1985, Miss Congeniality, 2000, Sweet Home Alabama, 2002, View from the Top, 2003, The In-Laws, 2003; (TV films) Arthur the King, 1985, Murder by Reason of Insanity, 1985, Mayflower Madam, 1987, Shelley Duvall's Bedtime Stories, Vol. 7, 1993, Mary and Tim, 1996 (TV appearances) What's My Line, 1965, Coronet Blue, 1967, The Muppet Show, 1976, The Way They Were, 1981, 2010 (voice), 1984, Trying Times, 1987, Seinfeld, 1990, Images of Life: Photographs that have Changed the World, 1996, The Human Face (miniseries), 2001, Murphy Brown: TV Tales, 2002, Sex and the City, 2002; (TV series) Murphy Brown, 1988-98 (Emmy award, Leading Actress in a Comedy Series, 1989, 90, 92, 94, 95), Boston Legal, 2004-; (TV miniseries) Hollywood Wives, 1985, Trying Times, Moving Day; author Knockwood; photojournalist credits include articles for Life, Playboy; dramatist: (play) The Freezer (included in Best Short Plays of 1968).

BERGEN, JEANNINE EVELYN, psychologist; b. New Hyde Park, NY, July 13, 1972; d. Virginie Elise and Joseph Bergen; m. Jon James Cerabone, Aug. 12, 2000. MS, cert. advanced study, SUNY, Albany, 1996, PsyD, 1999. Lic. School Psychologist NY, 2000. Sch. psychologist Questar III, Rensselaer, NY, 1997, Brittonkill Sch. Dist., Troy, 1997—98, H. Frank Carey H.S., Franklin Sq., NY, 1999—, Kidz Therapy Svcs., Garden City, NY, 2003—. Sch. psychologist Rothman Therapeutic Services, Plainview, NY, 2002—. Grant, Sewanhaka Ctrl. H.S. Dist., 2002—03. Mem.: APA, NASP. Avocations: music, travel, theater. Office: H Frank Carey H S 230 Poppy Ave Franklin Square NY 11010 Office Phone: 516-539-9463.

BERGEN, POLLY, actress; b. Bluegrass, Tenn. d. William and Lucy (Lawhorn) Burgin; m. Freddie Fields, Feb. 13, 1956 (div. 1976); children: Kathy, Pamela, Peter. Pres. Polly Bergen Cosmetics, Polly Bergen Jewelry, Polly Bergen Shoes. Author: Fashion and Charm, 1960, Polly's Principles, 1974, I'd Love To, But What'll I Wear, 1977; author, producer for TV: Leave of Absence, 1994; Broadway plays include Champagne Complex, John Murray Andersons' Almanac, First Impression, Plaza Suite, Love Letters, Follies (Best Supporting Actress Tony and Drama Desk nominee), The Vagina Monologues, Cabaret; films include Cape Fear, Move Over Darling, Kisses for My President, At War with the Army, The Stooge, That's My Boy, The Caretakers, A Guide for the Married Man, Making Mr. Right, Cry-Baby, 1990, Dr. Jekyll and Ms. Hyde, When We Were Colored, 1994; performed in one woman shows in Las Vegas, Nev., and Reno; albums: Bergen Sings Morgan, The Party's Over, All Alone By the Telephone, Polly and Her Pop, The Four Seasons of Love, Annie Get Your Gun and Do Re Mi, My Heart Sings, Act One Sing Too; numerous TV appearances including star of The Polly Bergen Show, NBC-TV; other TV appearances include The Helen Morgan Story, 1957 (Emmy award as best actress), To Tell the Truth, The Lightning Field, The Surrogate, For Hope; miniseries include The Winds of War (Emmy nomination), 79 Park Ave, War and Remembrance, 1988 (Emmy nomination); writer, prodr. NBC movie Leave of Absence, 1994. Bd. dirs. Martha Graham Dance Ctr., The Singer Co., Soc. Singers, Calif. Abortion and Reproductive Rights Action League, Show Coalition; hon. canister campaign chairperson Cancer Care, Inc., Nat. Cancer Found.; founder Nat. Bus. Coun. for ERA; mem. Planned Parenthood Fedn., Am. Bd. Advs.; mem. nat. adv. com. NARAL, Hollywood Women's Polit. Com. Recipient Fame award Top Ten in TV, 1957-58, Troupers award Sterling Publs., 1957, Editors and Critics award Radio and TV Daily, 1958, Outstanding Working Woman award Downtown St. Louis, Inc., Golden Plate award Am. Acad. Achievement, 1969, Outstanding Mother's award Nat. Mothers' Day Com., 1984, Best Achievement in New Jewelry Design award, 1986, Cancer Care award, 1989, Woman of Achievement award LWV, 1990, Extraordinary Achievement award Nat. Women's Law Ctr., 1991, Freedom of Choice award Calif. Abortion and Reproductive Rights Action League, 1992; Polly Bergen Cardio-Pulmonary Rsch. Lab., Children's Rsch. Inst. and Hosp., Denver dedicated, 1970. Mem. AFTRA, AGVA, SAG, Actors Equity. Office: 1746 S Britain Rd Southbury CT 06488-3200 E-mail: zimzack@msn.com.

BERGENFELD, JENNIFER REBEKAH LYNN, lawyer; d. Edward Irwin and Ann Ruth Frankel; m. Bergenfeld David, Nov. 28, 1999. BA in Internat. Affairs, George Wash. U., 1990; MA, NYU, 1992; JD, Yeshiva U., 1997; MBA, NYU, 2002. Bar: N.Y. 2000. Asst. v.p., asst. dir. compliance KBW Asset Mgmt. Keefe Bruyette & Woods, N.Y., 1997—2002; counsel, v.p. AllianceBernstein LP, N.Y., 2002—. Editor: Legal And Regulatory Climate For Investment In South Africa, 1994—97 (Best Note award Yeshiva U., 1997), Jour. Internat. and Comparative Law. Mem.: Assn. of the Bar of the City of NY, Fin. Women's Assn. Office Phone: 2129692291. Personal E-mail: jenniferbergenfeld@gmail.com.

BERGER, AUDREY MARILYN, psychologist; b. Bklyn., Nov. 2, 1955; d. Alexander and Elaine (Kosloff) B.; children: Michelle Caitlin, Rachael Lynn. BA with highest honors, SUNY, Binghamton, 1976; MA, U. Iowa, 1978, PhD, 1981. Lic. clin. psychologist, N.Y. Staff psychologist Rochester (N.Y.) Psychiat. Ctr., 1981-83, Rochester Regional Forensic Unit, 1984-85; asst. dir. counseling ctr. Rochester Ints. Tech., 1985-87; pvt. practice, Rochester, 1987—. Contbr. chpt. to Handbook of Family Psychology and Therapy, 1985; contbr. articles to profl. jours. Named one of Outstanding Young Women of Am., 1983. Mem. APA, N.Y. State Psychol. Assn., Genesee Valley Psychol. Assn., Phi Beta Kappa. Office: 300 White Spruce Blvd Rochester NY 14623-1608 Office Phone: 585-292-0095. E-mail: shrinkrap4u2@yahoo.com.

BERGER, BARBARA, special education educator, educational consultant; b. Bklyn. d. Salvatore and Jean Pisano; m. Charles R. Berger; children: Allison, Rachel. AAS in Merchandising, Fashion Inst. Tech., N.Y.C., 1963; BS in Elem. Edn., Empire State Coll. SUNY, Old Westbury, 1988; MS in Edn., Hofstra U., Hemstead, N.Y., 1992. Rep. GEICO Ins. Co., Hempstead, NY, 1963—69; tchg. asst. No. Pky. Sch., Uniondale, 1981—89; spl. edn. tchr. Syosset Home Tutoring, 1998—99; tchr. asst. Garden City H.S., Garden City, 1989—2001; pres. Exceptional Student Learning Svcs., 2001—. Mem.: Coun. Exceptional Children, Garden City Ret. Tchrs. Assn.

BERGER, BARBARA PAULL, social worker, marriage and family therapist; b. St. Louis, June 18, 1955; d. Ted and Florence Ann (Vines) Paull; m. Allan Berger, Dec. 27, 1980 (dec.); children: Melissa Dawn, Tammi Alyse, Jessica Lauren. BS, U. Tex., Austin, 1977; MSSW, U. Wis., Madison, 1978. Diplomate Am. Bd. Clin. Social Work; lic. social worker, Tex., Ky., Ind., Fla.; lic. marriage and family therapist. Clin. social worker Child and Family Svcs., Buffalo, 1980-81, United Cerebral Palsy Assn., St. Louis, 1982-83; clin. social worker/coord. Jewish Family Life Edn. Jewish Family Svc., Dallas, 1984-85, 88-90; instr. Miss. Delta C. C., Greenville, 1991; child and adolescent therapist United Behavioral Sys., Louisville, 1993-94; therapist Inpsych, Louisville, 1994-98, Beacon Behavioral Health Group, Louisville, 1998-2000, Louisville Behavioral Health Sys., 2000—05, pvt. practice, Coral Springs, Fla., 2005—. Mem. NASW, Acad. Cert. Social Workers, Am. Assn. Marriage and Family Therapy, Phi Kappa Phi, Pi Lambda Theta, Omicron Nu. Home: 4747 SW 13th Pl Deerfield Beach FL 33442-8231 Office Phone: 954-755-8247. Business E-Mail: barbarabergerlcsw@comcast.net.

BERGER, CAROLYN, state supreme court justice; BA, U. Rochester, 1969; MA in Elementary Education, Boston U., 1971; JD, Boston U. Sch. of Law, 1976; LLD (hon.), Widener U. Sch. of Law, 1996. Bar: Del. 1976. Dep. atty. gen. Del. Dept. of Justice, 1976—79; assoc. Prickett, Ward, Burt & Sanders, Wilmington, Del., 1979, Skadden, Arps, Slate, Meagher & Flom, Wilmington, Del., 1979—84; vice chancellor Del. Ct. of Chancery, Wilmington, Del., 1984—94; justice Del. Supreme Ct., 1994—. Assoc. mem. Bd. of Bar Examiners. V.p. then pres. Milton & Hattie Kutz Home; mem. Wilmington Community Advisory Council, Junior League of Wilmington; bd. mem. Jewish Federation, Del. Region Nat. Conference of Christians & Jews. Mem.: Del. Bar Assn., Am. Bar Assn., Rodney Inn of Court, Am. Law Inst., Am. Bar Foundation. Office: Del Supreme Ct Carvel State Office Bldg 820 N French St Fl 11 Wilmington DE 19801-3509*

BERGER, DIANNE GWYNNE, family life educator, consultant; b. NYC, Mar. 10, 1950; d. Harold and Mary Bell (Mott) Gwynne; m. Robert Milton Berger, Aug. 25, 1974 (dec. Nov. 2001); children: Matthew Robert, Daniel Alan Gwynne. BS, Cornell U., 1971; MS, Drexel U., 1974; PhD, U. Pa., 1992. Cert. home econs. tchr., sexuality educator, family and consumer sci. educator and family life educator, Pa.; cert. supervision, curriculum and instrn. Tchr. family and consumer scis., health, sexuality Wallingford-Swarthmore (Pa.) Sch. Dist., 1972—. Cons., Swarthmore, 1986—, Swarthmore Presbyn. Ch., 1995, Elwyn Insts., Media, Pa., 1989-91, Phila. Task Force on Sex Edn., 1991-93. Cons. Trinity Coop. Day Nursery, Swarthmore, 1980-93, Renaissance Edn. Assn., Valley Forge, Pa., 1987-94, A Better Chance, Inc., Swarthmore, 1990-91; bd. mem. Adolescent Wellness and Reproductive Edn. Found. Grantee Impact, Inc., 1990, Am. Cancer Soc., 2001. Mem. NEA, Am. Assn. Family and Consumer Scis. (presenter), Soc. for Sci. Study of Sex (sec. ea. region presenter), Nat. Coun. on Family Rels., Am. Assn. Sex Educators, Counselors and Therapists (chmn. Delaware Valley sect. 1996-98). Home: 304 Dickinson Ave Swarthmore PA 19081-2001 Office Phone: 610-892-3470. E-mail: DBerger@wssd.org, bergerdg@gmail.net.

BERGER, ELLEN TESSMAN, psychologist; b. Berlin, Feb. 3, 1922; came to U.S., 1938; d. Arthur and Regina (Schainthal) Philipsborn; m. Jack Robert Tessman, June 20, 1951 (div. 1961); m. Arthur Victor Berger, Dec. 8, 1967. BA, U. Calif., Berkeley, 1944; PhD, Pa. State U., 1955. Lic. psychologist, Mass. Pre-doctoral intern U. Calif. Psychiat. Inst., San Francisco, 1947-48; postdoctoral intern Judge Baker Child Ctr., Boston, 1956-57, staff psychologist, 1957-93, cons., 1993—; instr. Med. Sch. Harvard U., Boston, 1969—; NIMH postdoctoral rsch. fellow Harvard U. Sch. Edn., Cambridge, 1970-71. Assoc. The Tavistock Clinic, London, 1975-76. Contbr. articles to profl. jours. Fellow Mass. Psychol. Assn.; mem. APA, N.Y. Acad. Sci., Sigma Xi. Avocations: visual arts, art collector. Home: 9 Sparks St Cambridge MA 02138-4711 Office: Judge Baker Childrens Center 53 Parker Hill Ave Roxbury Crossing MA 02120-3225

BERGER, GISELA PORSCH, psychotherapist; b. Milw., Mar. 3, 1962; d. Kurt Wilhelm Bernhardt and Gudrun Margarete (Wolf) Berger; m. Phillip James Townsend, May 20, 1984 (div. June 1993); m. John Patrick Molinard, Apr. 2005; children: Patrick Bernhardt and Margarethe Josephine. BA, Purdue U., 1984; MEd, The Citadel, Charleston, S.C., 1992; PhD, U. Md., 2005. Lic. profl. counselor, S.C., 1996, Va., 2004, Master Addictions Counselor, 1996, Nat. Cert. Counselor, 1996. Clin. counselor Berkeley County Commn. Alcohol and Drug Abuse, Moncks Corner, S.C., 1993-94, Cmty. Control Ctr., Charleston, 1995-96; program dir. Voca Corp., Washington, 1997-98; grad. asst. U. Md., College Park, 1997—2000; clin. counselor No. Va. Family Svcs., Falls Church, 2001—03. Pres. Company Grade Officers' Coun., Charleston AFB, 1986-87; adj. faculty Marymount U., Arlington, Va., 1999-2004. Capt. USAF, 1984-90. Mem. ACA, Nat. Assn. Alcoholism and Drug Addiction, Mensa (program chair 1995-96), Alpha Tau Chi (pres. 1991-93). Presbyterian. Avocations: reading, crossword puzzles, walking.

BERGER, JOYCE MURIEL, foundation administrator, writer, editor; b. N.Y.C., Oct. 20, 1924; d. Samuel and Daisy (Lichtenstein) Zeitlin; m. Arthur Seymour Berger, Feb. 11, 1946. BA magna cum laude, NYU, 1944, MA, 1946. Editor Theta Psychical Rsch. Found., Durham, NC, 1978-80; sec.-treas., libr. Survival Rsch. Found., adminstr. Internat. Inst. for Study of Death, Miami, Fla., 1980—. Convener confs. Internat. Inst. Study of Death, Miami, 1985, 87, Survival Rsch. Found., Miami, 1986. Co-author: Reincarnation Fact or Fable, 1991, Encyclopedia of Parapsychology, 1991, Fear of the Unknown, 1995; co-editor: To Die or Not to Die, 1990, Perspectives on Death and Dying, 1989; lectr. and seminar coord. in field. Right to Die conf. grantee Fla. Endowment of the Humanities, Tampa, 1987. Mem. Am. Soc. for Psychical Rsch., Soc. for Psychical Rsch., The Book Group of South Fla., Phi Beta Kappa. Avocations: bridge, tennis, travel, recording for the blind.

BERGER, KAY JACKSON, psychiatric social worker; b. Kansas City, Mo., Apr. 14, 1937; d. Lowell Cleve and Ruth LeOla (Riggins) Jackson; m. Roger Wayne Berger; children: Angela, Randall, Dustin (dec.). BSW, Iowa State U., 1978; MSW, U. Iowa, 1985. Lic. social worker. Med. social worker Mary Greeley Med. Ctr., Ames, Iowa., 1978-82; psychiat. social worker McFarland Clinic, Ames, 1986—98; ret., 1998. Mem. NASW. Avocations: ballroom dancing, aerobics, writing, sewing. Home: 4121 Dawes Dr Ames IA 50010-4118

BERGER, LAURA ANN, dance studio owner; b. Westland, Mich., Mar. 29, 1979; d. Ann and Randall Stepp (Stepfather). Owner LA Dance, Lake Orion, Mich., 1998—. Nat. competition judge Kids Artistic Revue, South Gate, Calif., 2003—, Halle of Fame, West Bloomfield, Mich., 2006—. Named Top Secondary Studio, Kids Artistic Revue, 2002, Top Prodn., 2002; named one of Top 50 Studios Across the Country, Dance Tchr. and Dance Spirit Mags., 2005; recipient Studio Spirit award, Kids Artistic Revue, 2002, World Fast Dance champion, 2003, Mid-West Invitational Hustle champion, 2003, Best Choreography award, Nexstar, 2005, Hall of Fame, 2006. Office: LA Dance 2651 S Lapeer Rd Lake Orion MI 48360 Office Phone: 248-393-1339. E-mail: ladance329@yahoo.com.

BERGER, LAURA PATRICIA, psychologist; b. Lansing, Mich., Oct. 16, 1949; d. Richard Anthony and Donna Rose (Munson) Berger. BA, Tex. Tech. U., 1975; MA, Western Mich. U., 1981; postgrad. in substance abuse, 1990. Lic. masters social worker Mich., 1988; alcohol and drug counselor Nev., 2003. Therapist Delano Clinic, Borgess Med. Ctr., Kalamazoo, 1986—91; therapist substance abuse clinic Western Mich. U., 1991—94; therapist Psychiat. Mgmt. Resources, Tucson, 1995—96; co-owner MicroAge, Advanced Sys. Group, Tucson, 1995—98; rschr. U. Ariz., Tucson, 1998; tchr. substance abuse Washoe County Sch. Dist., Reno, 2002—06. Staff asst. Cmty. Info. Sys. Hyman Svcs., Western Mich. U., 1979—81; career counselor Women's Svcs., 1981; supr. clinical interns Univ. Substance Abuse Clinic, We. Mich. U., Kalamazoo, 1991—94; pvt. practice Berger & Assoc., Reno, 2004—06; tchr. psychology Truckee Meadows C.C., Reno, 2005—06. Vol. counselor Women's Program YWCA, Tuscon, 1995—98. Fellow: APA; mem.: Assn. Behavioral Analysis (assoc.). Roman Cath. Avocations: tennis, sailing, travel, hiking. Home: 1216 Conway Lane Reno NV 89503 Office: Berger and Assocs 5365 Mae Anne Ave Reno NV 89523 Office Phone: 775-224-4686. Business E-Mail: lberger@tmcc.edu.

BERGER, LEE HOLLINGSWORTH, secondary school educator; b. Rocky Mount, NC, May 25, 1949; d. Harry D. and Norma (Large) Hollingsworth; m. Frederick A. Berger, Dec. 26, 1971; children: Jennifer Michelle, Amy Caroline, Stephanie Paige. AB in Edn., U. N.C., 1971; MA, Western Carolina U. Tchr. 6th grade St. Louis (Mo.) City Schs., 1971-72; adminstrv. asst. U. Fla., Gainesville, 1972-74; tchr. mid. sch. Macon County Schs., Franklin, N.C., 1984-85; social worker adolescent pregnancy prevention program Macon County Health Dept., Franklin, 1985—86; tchr. English and Journalism Macon County Schs., Franklin, 1986—. Mem. N.C. Assn. Educators, Beta Sigma Phi, Kappa Delta Pi. Episcopalian. Home: 805 Hemlock Hills Dr Franklin NC 28734-0228 Office: Macon Early Coll PO Box 1029 Franklin NC 28744 Office Phone: 828-332-0306. Business E-Mail: lee.berger@mcsk-12.org.

BERGER, LINDA FAY, writer; b. Ft. Worth, Mar. 12, 1943; d. Walter Bob and Bertha Fay (Christensen) B. AA, Tarrant County Jr. Coll., Ft. Worth, 1976; BBA, U. Tex., Arlington, 1981; MBA, North Tex. U., 1987. Cert. profl. sec. Profl. Sec. Assn. Internat. With Tex. Refinery Corp., Ft. Worth, 1961-91, file clk., telex operator, departmental sec., exec. sec., asst. pers. dir., pers. dir. Co-author: A Joyful Journey, 1995. Mem. Profl. Secs. Internat. (sec. 1969-79), Tex. Assn. Bus. (sec. 1990), Order Ea. Star (Riverside chpt. 834). Mem. Unity Ch. Avocations: travel, yoga, reading, cooking. E-mail: linda@dns-tx.com.

BERGER, MARGARET ADLERSBERG, law educator; b. Vienna, July 13, 1932; d. David and Gisela (Magasanik) Berger; m. Mark H. Berger, Jan. 31, 1954; children: Joshua M., David A. BA, Radcliffe Coll., 1953; JD, Columbia U., 1956. Bar: NY 1956, US Supreme Ct. 1960. Assoc. Nordlinger, Riegelman, Benetar & Charney, NYC, 1956—58; ptnr. Berger & Berger, NYC, 1958—62; rsch. assoc. Columbia U., NYC, 1962—67; law clk. US Dist. Ct. (ea. dist.), Bklyn., 1967—68; Suzanne J. & Norman Miles Prof. Law Bklyn. Law Sch., 1973—. Author: Weinstein's Evidence, 1975; co-author: Litig. on Behalf of Women, 1980, Cases and Materials on Evidence, 1983; co-author: (with Weinsten, Mansfield and Abrams) (textbook) Evidence: Cases and Materials, 1997. Reporter, Working Group on Post-Conviction Issues Nat. Commn. Future of DNA Evidence; reporter to adv. com. Fed. Rules of Evidence; cons. Ford Found. Carnegie Commn. Sci., Tech. and Govt. Mem.: Nat. Acad. Sci. (panel on sci., tech. and law), Assn. Bar City of NY(reporter adv. com. evidence rules), ABA. Office: Bklyn Law Sch 250 Joralemon St Rm 911 Brooklyn NY 11201-3700 Office Phone: 718-780-7941. E-mail: margaret.berger@brooklaw.edu.

BERGER, MIRIAM ROSKIN, dance therapist, educator; b. NYC, Dec. 9, 1934; d. Israel and Florence Roskin; m. Meir Berger, July 16, 1967; 1 child, Jonathan Israel. Student, Barnard Coll., N.Y.C., 1952—53; BA, Bard Coll., Annandale-on-Hudson, N.Y., 1956; postgrad., CCNY, 1956—58; D Arts, NYU, 1998. Dir. alumni Bard Coll., Annandale-on-Hudson, NY, 1958—59, bd. govs., 2000—; dance therapist Manhattan Psychiat. Ctr., N.Y.C., 1959—60; performer, educator Jean Erdman Theater of Dance, N.Y.C., 1959—62; dir. adult program Hebrew Arts Sch., N.Y.C., 1981; mem. faculty Dance Notation Bur., N.Y.C., 1974—75, 1977; asst. prof. dance therapy program NYU, 1975—, acting dir. dance therapy program, 1991, dir. dance edn. program, 1993—2002; dir. creative arts therapies Bronx Psychiat. Ctr., N.Y.C., 1970—90; mem. faculty Pratt Inst., 2004—05, Harkness Dance Ctr. 92d St. Y, 2005—. Workshop leader in field; tchr., Sweden, 1981—2004, Netherlands, 1991—2002, Germany, 1993—99, Czech Republic, 1997—2005, Poland, 2000, Republic of Korea, 02, Greece, 2004—, Israel, 2004—, Spain, 2005; keynote spkr. Israel Dance Conf., 2004. Prodr. off-Broadway The Coach with the Six Insides, 1962-63; author, prodr. Non-Verbal Group Process, 1978; co-editor Am. Jour. Dance Therapy, 1991-94; led dance therapy session Senate hearing on Aging, 1992; contbr. articles to profl. jours.; editl. bd. Arts in Psychotherapy, Jour. Dance Edn., Amer. Jour. Dance Therapy. Chair Nat. Coalition of Creative Arts Therapies Assns., 2002—; bd. dirs. Theater Open Eye, 1978—82, v.p. bd. trustees, 1982—89, pres., 1989—94. Recipient NYU scholarship, 1981, Best Paper award Med Art World Congress on Arts and Medicine, 1992 Mem.: Acad. Registered Dance Therapists, Am. Dance Therapy Assn. (founder, bd. dirs. 1967—76, v.p. 1974—76, credential com. 1976, 1982, keynote speaker at nat. conf. 1991, v.p. 1992, pres. 1994—98, chmn. internat. panel 1995—, Marian Chace award 2002), Dance Libr. Israel (v.p. 1999—, Hall of Fame inductee 2005). Business E-Mail: miriam.berger@nyu.edu.

BERGER, NANCY, lawyer; b. Newark, N.J., Oct. 31, 1953; d. Lawrence and Betsy Greenberg Berger. BA, U. Nebr., 1971—73; JD, U. Chgo. Law Sch., 1973—76. Bar: Ill. 1976, Nebr. 1980, Fla. 1995. Clin. prof. of law IIT/Chgo.-Kent Coll. of Law, Chgo., 1976—77; law firm assoc. Jacobs,

Burns, Sugarman & Orlove, Chgo., 1977—79; staff atty. Fla. Health & Rehabilitative Svcs., Fort Lauderdale, Fla., 1995—96; supervising staff atty. Glantz & Glantz, P.A., Plantation, 1996—. Recipient Haskell award, U. Nebr., 1972. Office: Glantz & Glantz PA 7951 SW Sixth St Plantation FL 33324 Office Phone: 954-424-1200.

BERGER, PAT(RICIA EVE), artist, educator; b. N.Y.C., Mar. 17, 1929; d. Marion Sigmund and Florence (Hyman) Gardner; m. Jack Berger, Jan. 8, 1948 (div. 1971); children: Kenneth Steven, Russell Howard; m. Merlin Clarence Czoschke, Apr. 30, 1978. Student, Art Ctr. Sch. Design, L.A., 1947-48, UCLA, 1955-59, 63-66, student, 1974-76. Art unltd. chmn. Downey (Calif.) Mus. Art; muralist Millard Sheets, 1975-77; artist-in-residence Brandeis Inst., Simi Valley, Calif., 1961-65, 70; painting/drawing instr. L.A. Unified Sch. Dist., 1971-2003; permanent collections include Skirball Mus., L.A., Long Beach Mus. Art, U. Minn. Law Sch., Karpeles Manuscript Libr. Mus., Buffalo, N.Y., Julia and David White Artists' Colony, Ciudad Colon, Costa Rica, San Diego Mus. Art, Springfield (Mo.) Art Mus., Polk County Bank, Mo., Palm Springs Desert Mus., Sodertalje Konstall, Sweden, City of La Mirada Collection, Calif., Hallmark Cards, many others. One woman shows at Mendenhall Gallery, Whittier Coll., 1982, Riverside Art Ctr. and Mus., 1983, Moosart Gallery, Miami, 1985, Bridge Gallery, L.A., 1986, Jewish Fedn. Galleries, L.A., 1988, West L.A. City Hall Gallery, 1990, La Artcore Ctr., L.A., 1998, 2002, 2004, Karpeles Manuscript Libr. Mus., Calif., 2000-01, U. Judaism, 1991, 2000, others; group shows include Valerie Miller Gallery, Palm Desert, 1988-93, Jewish Mus., 1989, 91, 93, Square House Mus., Tex., 1990, Long Beach Mus. Rental Gallery, 1990, Finegood Art Gallery, Calif., 1990, 2005, West '93 and the Law travelling exhibit, 1983, 84, 91, Biblical Art Ctr., Dallas, 1993, Fukuoka Prefectural Mus., Japan, 2001, Kitakyushu Mcpl. Mus., Japan, 2001, 2005, Costello Childs Contemporary, Phoenix, 2004—, West Valley Art Mus., Surprise, Ariz., 2006, Metro GAllery, BAkersfield, Calif., others. Mem. fine arts coun. U. Judaism. Mem. Jewish Initiative of So. Calif., L.A. Artcore (bd. mem. fine arts coun. U. Judaism), Nat. Watercolor Soc. (past pres.), Watercolor USA Honor Soc. (past bd. dirs.). Avocations: photography, painting, mask making and collecting. Home: 2648 Anchor Ave Los Angeles CA 90064-4602 Office Phone: 310-838-8346. Personal E-mail: bergerartist@aol.com.

BERGER, PATRICIA WILSON, retired librarian; b. Washington, May 1, 1926; d. Thomas Decatur Wood and Nina Hughes; m. George Hamilton Combs Berger, May 20, 1970. BA, George Washington U., 1965; MSLS, Cath. U. Am., 1974. Asst. libr., ops. rsch. office Johns Hopkins U., Chevy Chase, Md., 1949-51, asst. ops. rsch. analyst, 1951-54; head libr. CEIR, Washington, 1954-55; chief, tech. info. and libr. svcs. Human Rels. Area Files Yale U., Washington, 1955-57; tech. info. officer, chief libr. Inst. for Def. Analyses, Washington, Arlington, Va., 1957-67; dir. tech. info. and security programs Lambda Corp., Arlington, 1967-71; chief libr. U.S. Commn. on Govt. Procurement, Washington, 1971-72; head gen. ref. br., later dep. chief libr. U.S. Patent and Trademark Office, Arlington, 1972-76; chief libr. divsn. U.S. Nat. Bur. Stds., Gaithersburg, Md., 1976-78; dir. info. resources and svcs. U.S. EPA, Washington, 1978-79; chief libr. and info. svcs. U.S. Nat. Bur. Stds., Washington, 1979-83, dir. Office Info. Svcs., 1990-92; chief info. resources and svcs. Nat. Inst. Stds. and Tech., 1983-91; ret., 1992. Cons. libr., info. and security matters, 1965-95; del. 1st White House Conf. on Librs. and Info. Svc., 1979; bd. dirs. Universal Serial and Book Exch., 1983-84; chmn. Nat. Info. Std. Orgn., Am. Nat. Std. Inst., 1981-83, elected Nat. Info. Std. Orgn. fellow, 1989. Mem. editl. bd. Sci. and Tech. Librs., 1979—92; contbr. articles to profl. jours. Apptd. by Govs. of Va. to Libr. of Va. Bd., 1986-90, 90-95, vice chair, 1992-93, chair, 1993-94; bd. dirs. Va. Commn. for Reenactment of Battle First Bull Run, 1960-61; bd. dirs. Freedom to Read Found., 1988-90, 92-94; apptd. U.S. Postmaster Gen's. Commn. Lit., 1990-92. Recipient Internat. Women's Yr. award Dept. Commerce, 1976, Bronze medal, 1980, Silver medal, 1984, Outstanding Adminstrv. Mgr. award, 1985, H.W. Wilson Pub. Co. award, 1980, Disting. Svc. award U. Richmond Librs., 1989, Cert. of Recognition, Gov. State of Va., 1989, Resolution of Esteem, Va. State Libr. Bd., 1988, award Coun. Libr. and Media Technicians, 1989; named Outstanding Alumnus in Libr. and Info. Sci., Cath. U. Am., 1988, 20th Century Nat. Libr. Adv., Am. Libr. Assn./Am. Libr. Trustees Assn. Nat. Adv. Honor Roll, 2000, Outstanding Scientists, Engrs. and Adminstrs. Nat. Inst. Stds. and Tech./Nat. Bur. Stds., 2006; Cert. of appreciation Martin Luther King Jr. Fed. Holiday Commission, 1996. Mem AAAS (elected assn. fellow 1992), Spl. Librs. Assn. (exec. bd. Washington chpt. 1970-71, pres. Washington chpt. 1977, elected assn. fellow 1987), ALA (coun. 1984-88, exec. bd. 1986-90, v.p./pres.-elect 1988-89, pres. 1989-90), D.C. Libr. Assn. (Ainsworth Rand Spofford Pres.'s award 2001), Fed. Librs. Roundtable (pres. 1982-83, Achievement award 1985, portrait to be hung in the Nat.Galleryof the US Bur. Stds., 2006), Cosmos Club, Chi Omega, Beta Phi Mu. Episcopalian. Home: 105 Queen St Alexandria VA 22314-2610 Personal E-mail: pberger@his.com.

BERGER, PEARL, library director; b. NYC, Nov. 30, 1943; d. Baruch Mayer and Tova (Brandwein) Rabinowitz; m. David Berger, June 14, 1965; children: Miriam Esther, Yitzhak, Gedalyah Aaron. B in Religious Edn., Yeshiva U.; BA, Bklyn. Coll., 1965; MLS, Columbia U., 1974. Diploma tchr. Hebrew. Tchr. Hebrew & Jewish studies Yeshiva of Crown Heights, Bklyn., 1963-65; asst. libr. YIVO Inst. Jewish Rsch., NYC, 1976-80; head tech. svcs. Librs. Yeshiva U., NYC, 1980-81, head libr. Pollack Libr., 1981-83, head libr. main ctr. librs., 1983-85, dean librs., 1985—. V.p. Coun. Archives and Rsch. Librs. in Jewish Studies, 1984-86, pres. 1986-89. Assoc. editor: Jour. Judaica Librarianship, 1983-2004, mem. editl. bd. 2004-; first v.p. Met. Reference and Rsch. Libr. Orgn., 1996-99; contbr. articles to profl. jours.; compiler catalog Guide to Yiddish Classics on Microfiche, 1980. Recipient Benjamin Gottesman Libr. Chair Yeshiva U. Mem. ALA, Metro. Ref. Rsch. Libr. Agy. (trustee 1991—2002, sec. 1993-99, 1st v.p. 1996-99), Assn. Jewish Librs. (rsch., spl. librs. divsn., v.p. 1982-84, pres. 1984-86, voting rep. Nat. Info. Stds. Orgn. 1995-2000, v.p., pres.-elect 2000-01, pres. 2002-04). Office: Yeshiva U Dean of Libraries 500 W 185th St New York NY 10033-3299*

BERGER-GRANET, NANCY SUE, nursing researcher; b. N.Y.C., Apr. 22, 1957; d. Morris H. and Marilyn (Resnick) B.; 1 child. BSN, U. Colo., 1988. RN 1977. Staff nurse intensive care Hosp. U. Pa., Phila., 1981-84; clin. rsch. nurse U. Colo. Health Sci. Ctr., Denver, 1985-90, VA Med. Ctr., Denver, 1989-90; dir. clin. rsch. U. Colo. Health Sci. Ctr., 1990-94; clin. rsch. assoc. Bayer Corp., Berkeley, Calif., 1994-97; clin. rsch. mgr. Cygnus, Inc., Redwood City, Calif., 1997—98, Roche Palo Alto, Calif., 1998—. Contbr. articles to profl. jours. Mem. Am. Assn. Urological Assocs., Assocs. Clin. Pharm., Sigma Theta Tau. Democrat. Jewish. Avocations: hiking, reading, cooking. Office: Roche Palo Alto 3431 Hillview Ave Palo Alto CA 94063

BERGERON, EARLEEN FOURNET, actress; b. New Orleans, Aug. 7, 1938; d. Earl Joseph Fournet and Lucia (Cuccia) Wadsworth; m. James Ronald Bergeron Sr., June 17, 1961; children: Blanche Theresa, Michele Yvette, James Ronald Jr. B in Social Sci. in Theatre and Speech, Loyola U., 1960. Actor: (plays) The Secret Affairs of Mildred Wilde, 1977, The Boyfriend, 1977, The Shadow Box, 1979, California Suite, 1980, Hay Fever, 1985, Brighton Beach, 1986, Beyond Therapy, 1987, Steel Magnolias, 1988, 1989, Nunsense, 1990, Broadway Bound, 1991, The Women, 1993, Nunsense II, 1995, Stomping Grounds, 1995, 1996, Angels in America, Part I: Millenium Approaches, Part II: Perestroika, 1997, Spareribs, 1998, Come Back Little Sheba, 1999, The Cripple of Inishmann, 2001, Ancestral Voices, 2002, Our Town, 2002, Morning's At Seven, 2004, The Aristocats, 2005, (comml.) Goodwill, 1988, Schumpert Medical Center, 1991, Cunningham and McDonald, Plastic Surgeons, 1991, JB Cable Ads, 1995, Pierre Bossier Mall, 1996; (films) Man in the Moon, 1990; (TV series) Rescue 911, 1991. Bd. dirs. Port Players, Shreveport, La.; assoc. mem. Co. Repertory Theatre, Inc., Project Shakespeare in Schs.; active Shreveport Med. Aux., 1968—97, mem. exec. bd., 1976—78; mem. Shreveport Opera Guild, 1972—97; area leader fund dr. Am. Cancer Soc., Shreveport, 1985—89. Named one of Outstanding Team Capts., United Way Fund, 1969. Mem.: Shreveport Little Theatre Guild (bd. dirs. 1985—86), Strand Theatre, Majorie Lyons Playhouse, Shreveport Little Theatre. Roman Catholic.

BERGERON, PATRICIA ANN, retired education educator, consultant; b. Bklyn., Oct. 7, 1940; d. Louis Vincent and Viola Helen Fryzell; children: Michael Leo Boulé, Ann Patricia Boulé(dec.). BS in Edn., Castleton State Coll., Vermont, 1962; MEd, Lesley Coll., 1986; cert. in Human Devel., Harvard U., 1987. Cert. tchr. Mass. State Dept. Edn., 1995. Ednl. tech. specialist Boston Pub. Schs., 1987—88; pvt. practice ednl. tech. cons. Burlington, Vt., 1988—89; ednl. tech. specialist IBM Ednl. Sys., Burlington, 1989—90; dir. acad. computing Champlain Coll., Burlington, 1990—94; coord. ednl. tech. Canton Pub. Schs., 1994—98, Belmont Pub. Schs., 1998—99; mgr. Sch. Tech. Svcs. Family Edn. Network, Boston, 1999—2000; mgr. Tech. Evaluation Svcs. Edn. Alliance Brown U., Providence, 2000—01; grants officer Lesley U., Cambridge, Mass., 2002; pvt. edn. cons. Weymouth, Mass., 2003; part-time mus. guide Plymouth Antiquarian Soc., Mass., 2004—06; ret., 2005. Edn. cons. Coll. for Lifelong Learning U. Sys. N.H., Gorham, 1987—90; part-time tech. plan reviewer Mass. State Dept. Edn., Melrose, Mass., 1996—99. Judge JFK Profiles in Courage Essay Contest, 2006. Personal E-mail: pberge@juno.com.

BERGESON, DONNA POTTIS, lawyer; b. Warwick, N.Y., Aug. 21, 1960; BA magna cum laude, U. S.C., 1981, JD, 1984. Bar: Ga. 1984. Ptnr., group leader, health care regulatory group Alston & Bird LLP, Atlanta. Mem. ABA, Atlanta Bar Assn., Gwinnett County Bar Assn., State Bar of Ga., Ga. Acad. Hosp. Attys., Phi Beta Kapa, Phi Eta Sigma. Office: Alston & Bird LLP 1 Atlantic Ctr 1201 W Peachtree St NW Atlanta GA 30309-3424 Office Phone: 404-881-7278. Office Fax: 404-881-7777. Business E-Mail: dbergeson@alston.com.

BERGESON, TERESA, school system administrator; b. Mass. BA in English, Emmanuel Coll., Boston, 1964; M in Counseling and Guidance, Western Mich. U., 1969; PhD in Edn., U. Wash. Tchr., sch. guidance counselor, Mass., Alaska, Wash.; exec. dir. Ctrl. Kitsap Sch. Dist., 1989-92, Wash. State Commn. on Learning, 1993-95; state supt. pub. instrn. Olympia, Wash., 1997—. V.p. Wash. Edn. Assn., 1981, pres., 1985—89. Mem.: Wash. Edn. Assn. (v.p. 1981—85, pres. 1985—89). Office: Old Capital Bldg PO Box 47200 Olympia WA 98504-7200 Office Fax: 360-753-6712. E-mail: bergeson@ospi.wednet.edu.

BERGFORS, CONSTANCE MARIE, artist, educator; b. Quincy, Mass., Feb. 8, 1931; d. Fred Eric Bergfors and H. Margaret Sandberg; m. Andrew E. Rice, Dec. 2, 1972; children: Stefan Andrej, Brandt Eric. BA, Smith Coll., 1952; postgrad., Concoran Coll. Art, Washington, D.C., 1956, postgrad., 1957, postgrad., 1981, postgrad., 1982, Acad. di Belle Arte, Palermo, Naples, and Rome, Italy, 1957—60. Dir. Cabin John Visual Studies Workshop, Cabin John, Md., 1970—75; founding mem. Gallery 10, Washington, 1974—78; tchr. sculpture dept. Corcoran Sch. Art, Washington, 1991—95. Judge art scholarships for h.s. srs., 1981—2001. One-woman shows include Peabody, Rivlin, Gore, Caldouhos and Lambert Law Firm, Washington, 1970, Gallery Modern Art, Fredericksburg, Va., 1974, Gallery 10, Washington, 1974, 1976, U.S. Govt., 1978, Langley, Va., 1985, Galleria Editalia, Rome, 1980, Strathmore Hall Arts Ctr., Rockville, Md., 1984, Capital Ctr. Gallery, Landover, Md., 1984, Plum Gallery, Kensington, Md., 1986, 1988, 1991, Cmty. Gallery Lancaster, Pa., 1988, South Shore Art Ctr., Cohasset, Mass., 1988, Urban Inst., Washington, 1996, Workshop Gallery, Cabin John, Md., 1997, Temple Sinai Commn., Washington, 1998, Renwick Alliance visits the Workshop Gallery, 2000, Arts Coun. of Montgomery County, 2000, exhibited in group shows at 14 Sculptors Gallery, N.Y.C., 1977, Art Barn, Washington, 1983, Georgetown Ct. Artists' Space, 1984, Arlington Arts Ctr., Va., 1984, 1985, Three Rivers Arts Festival, Pitts., 1984, Sculpture 84 Washington Square, Washington, 1984, Washington Women's Art Ctr., 1985, Audubon Naturalist Soc. Sculpture Show, Washington, 1985, Brandeis Coll. Art Exhibit, Rockville, Md., 1986, D.C. Sculpture Now Show Summer Sch. Mus., Washington, 1989, Bldg. Mus., 1989—90, Montgomery County Art Exhibit, Rockville, Md., 1990, Internat. Sculpture 90 Montgomery Coll., 1990, Washington Sculpture Group Show Summer Sch., Washington, 1990, Mus. Nat. de Belas Artes, Rio de Janeiro, 1991—92, Oxon Hill Manor Found., Oxon Hill, Md., 1992, Fairfax County Coun. Arts Northern Va. C.C., Annandale, Va., 1992, Washington Sculptors Group Exhbn., Bethesda, Md., 1992, Fairfax County Coun. Arts Northern Va. C.C., 1993, The Cutting Edge: 20 Years at Gallery 10, Washington, 1994, Corcoran Sch. Art Washington Square, 1994, Washington Sculptors Group Show Washington Square, 1995, Arts 901, 1996, Bldg. Mus., 1999—2000, Represented in permanent collections. Recipient Mary Lay Thom award for Outstanding Achievement in Sculpture, Washington, 1983, Montgomery County Purchase prize, Exec. Office Bldg, Rockville, Md., 1987, 3rd prize, Montgomery County Art Exhibit, Strathmore Hall, Rockville, Md., 1990. Avocations: travel, architecture, archaeology. Home: 6517 80th St Cabin John MD 20818-1208

BERGGREN-MOILANEN, BONNIE LEE, education educator; b. L'Anse, Mich., June 2, 1940; d. Alvin Carl and Emma Leola (Wandell) Lydman; m. Grant Lorns Berggren, Jr., Aug. 22, 1959 (dec.); children: Grant Victor Berggren, Rex Alvin Berggren, Konnie Kay Berggren-Schneider; m. Glenn Moilanen, 2003. BA, U. Hawaii, 1961; MA, Ea. Mich. U., 1988; MA in Ednl. Adminstrn., No. Mich. U., 1991. Tchr. home econs. Baraga (Mich.) Twp. Schs., 1960-61, L'Anse Twp. Schs., 1963-65, Spencerport (N.Y.) Cen. Schs., 1979-84; presch. tchr. NCA Sch., Cmty. Action Agy., Hermansville, Mich., 1971-73; circulation supr. Spring Arbor (Mich.) Coll. Libr., 1985-87; adj. prof., supr. student tchrs. No. Mich. U., Marquette, 1989—96; co-owner, co-mgr. Menominee (Mich.) Floral, 1993-96; curriculum and tng. coord./spl. project coord. Campus Crusade for Christ, Children of The World Dept., San Clemente, Calif., 1997-2000; sr. staff Internat. Student Resources Campus Crusade for Christ, Madison, Wis., 2000—06; affiliate staff mem. Bridges Internat., Upper Great Lakes Region, Mich., 2006—. Tchr. trainer Negaunee Pub. Schs., Negaunee, Mich., 1988—90; leader workshop Republic-Michigamme Schs., Republic, Mich., 1989—90; mem. evaluation team Marquette Pub. Schs., 1991; mem. tchr. edn. adv. coun. No. Mich. U., Marquette, 1991—96, mem. Hoppes award com., 1990—92, mem. pers. com., 1992; spkr. in field. Illustrator: Grandmother Wandell's Rainbow Book of Poems, 1977. Libr. bd. Republic-Michigamme Schs., 1988—91; spkr. Christian Women's Club, 1989—90; bd. regents Liberty U., 1990—91; active Operation Carelift to Russia, 1997, Operation Sunrise to Africa, 2002. Fellow: Roberts Wesleyan Coll.; mem.: AAUW, DAV Aux. (life; Mich. historian 1975), AAUP, Concerned Women Am., U. Hawaii Alumni Assn., Ea. Mich U. Alumni Assn., Univ. Women No. Mich. U., Phi Delta Kappa, Phi Kappa Phi. Baptist. Avocations: reading, travel, writing, crafts. Home: HC 2 Box 772A Lanse MI 49946-9517 Personal E-mail: gamoilan@up.net.

BERGMAN, ANNE NEWBERRY, civic leader; b. Weatherford, Tex., Mar. 12, 1925; d. William Douglas and Mary (Hunter) Newberry; m. Robert David Bergman, Aug. 17, 1947; children: Elizabeth Anne Bozzell, John David, William Robert. BA, Trinity U., San Antonio, 1945; postgrad., UCLA, 1946-47. Councilperson City of Weatherford, 1986-91, mayor pro tem, 1990-91; pres. Weatherford Libr. Found., 1987-97, bd. dirs., 1987—. Heritage gallery com. Weatherford Pub. Libr. (Mary Martin collection), 1993-98. Founder Hist. Home Tour, Weatherford, 1972; co-chair Spring Festival Bd., 1976, Weatherford Planning and Zoning Commn., 1980—85; fundraising chair Weatherford Libr. Found., 1985—86; chair Tex. State Rev. Com. Cmty. Devel. Block Grants, 1987—91; pres. Tex. Fedn. Rep. Women, 1975—77; del. Nat. Rep. Conv., 1988; pres. Episcopal Churchwomen's Cabinet, Diocese of Ft. Worth, 1999—2001; del. Episcopal Ch. Women Triennial, Episcopal Ch. U.S.A., 1997, 2000. Named Outstanding Rep. Woman, Tex. Fedn. Rep. Women, 1981. Mem. Parker County Rep. Women, DAR (Weatherford chpt.), Weatherford C. of C. (Outstanding Citizen of the Yr. 1988), Friends of Weatherford Pub. Libr. (life, charter pres. 1959-61, pres. 1973-74). Avocations: sailing, bridge. Home: 609 W Josephine St Weatherford TX 76086-4055

BERGMAN, ARLENE, lawyer; b. NYC; BS, Adelphi U., 1974, MS, 1975; RN, CUNY, 1984; JD, Yeshiva U., 1990. Bar: NY 1991, US Dist. Ct. So. Dist. NY, US Dist. Ct. Ea. Dist. NY. Tchr. learning disabled; pvt. duty nurse; staff nurse Meml. Sloan Kettering Cancer Ctr.; joined Wilson, Elser, Moskowitz, Edelman & Dicker LLP, NYC, 1997, now ptnr. Office: Wilson Elser Moskowitz Edelman & Dicker LLP 23rd Fl 150 E 42nd St New York NY 10017-5639 Office Phone: 212-490-3000 ext. 2542. Office Fax: 212-490-3038. Business E-Mail: bergmana@wemed.com.

BERGMAN, JANET EISENSTEIN, food industry executive; b. N.Y., Jan. 28, 1959; d. T. Donald and Ellen (Roob) Eisenstein; m. David J. Bergman, July 14, 1985; 1 child, Jennifer Sarah. BA, Yale U., New Haven, Conn., 1981; MBA, Harvard U., Boston, 1985. Analyst asst. v.p. Putman Mgmt. Co., Boston, 1985-88; corp. v.p. Sara Lee Corp., Chgo., 1989—93, exec. dir., 1988—89, v.p., investor relations and corp. affairs, 1993—2001, sr. v.p., investor relations and corp. affairs Chgo., 2001—. Mem. Charted Finl. Analyst., Econ. Club (Chgo.). Avocations: reading, cooking.

BERGMAN, MARILYN KEITH, lyricist, writer; b. Bklyn. d. Albert A. and Edith (Arkin) Katz; m. Alan Bergman, Feb. 9, 1958; 1 child, Julie Rachel. BA, NYU; MusD (hon.), Berklee Coll. Music, 1995, Trinity Coll., 1997. Lyricist, collaborator (with Alan Bergman) (numerous pop, theatrical and film score songs, TV themes) Bracken's World, 1969—70, The Sandy Duncan Show, 1972, Maude, 1972—78, Good Times, 1974—79, The Nancy Walker Show, 1976, The Dumplings, 1976, Alice, 1976—82, In the Heat of the Night, 1988—94, Brooklyn Bridge, 1991—93, The Powers That Be, 1993, TV film lyrics The Hands of Time (from Brian's Song), 1971, Queen of the Stardust Ballroom, 1975 (Emmy award for best dramatic underscore and best musical material, 1975, score only), Sybil, 1976 (Emmy award for best dramatic underscore 1976, 1976), Too Many Springs (from Hollow Image), 1979, theatrical scores Something More, 1964, Ballroom, 1978 (Grammy award nominee for best cast show album, 1979), The Lady and the Clarinet, 1980, feature film songs The Marriage Go-Round, from The Marriage Go-Round, 1960, Any Wednesday, from Any Wednesday, 1966, Make Me Rainbows, from Fitzwilly, 1967, (score) In the Heat of the Night, 1967, The Windmills of Your Mind, from the Thomas Crown Affair, 1968 (Acad. award for best song, 1968, Golden Globe award best original song, 1969), His Eyes, Her Eyes, from The Thomas Crown Affair, 1968, You Must Believe in Spring, from Young Girls of Rochefort, 1968, Maybe Tomorrow, from John and Mary, 1969, Tomorrow Is My Friend, from Gaily, Gaily, 1969, There's Enough to Go Around, 1969, A Smile, A Mem'ry and an Extra Shirt, from A Man Called Gannon, 1969, Sugar in the Rain, from Stiletto, 1969, What Are You Doing the Rest of You Life?, from The Happy Ending, 1969 (Acad. award nominee for best song, 1969), I Was Born in Love With You, from Wuthering Heights, 1970, Sweet Gingerbread Man, from The Magic Garden of Stanley Sweetheart, 1970, Nobody Knows, 1970, Move, from Move, 1970, Pieces of Dreams (Little Boy Lost), from Pieces of Dreams, 1970 (Academy award nominee for best song, 1970), The Costume Ball, from Doctors' Wives, 1971, All His Children, from Sometimes a Great Notion, 1971 (Acad. award nominee for best song, 1971), Rain Falls Anywhere It Wants To, from the African Elephant, 1971, The Summer Knows, from Summer of '42, 1971 (Grammy award nominee for song of the year 1972, 1972), A Face in the Crowd, from Le Mans, 1971, Marmalade, Molasses and Honey, from The Life and Times of Judge Roy Bean, 1972 (Acad. award nominee for best song, 1972), Love's the Only Game in Town, from Pete and Tillie, 1972, Molly and Lawless John, 1972, The Way We Were, from The Way We Were, 1973 (Grammy award for song of the year, 1973, Acad. award for best song, 1973, Golden Globe award for best original song, 1974, Grammy award for best original score, 1974), Breezy's Song, from Breezy, 1973, In Every Corner of the World, from Forty Carats, 1973, Summer Wishes, Winter Dreams, from Summer Wishes, Winter Dreams, 1973, Easy Baby, from 99 and 44/100%, 1974, There'll Be Time, from Ode to Billy Joe, 1975, Evening Sun, Morning Moon, from The Yakuza, 1975, I Believe in Love, from A Star is Born, 1976 (Grammy award nomination best original score, 1977), I'm Harry, I'm Walter, from Harry and Walter Go to New York, 1976, Hello and Goodbye, from Noon to Three, 1976, Bobby Deerfield, from Bobby Deerfield, 1977, The Last Time I Felt Like This, from Same Time Next Year, 1978 (Acad. award nominee for best song, 1978), The One and Only, from The One and Only, 1978, There's Something Funny Goin' On, from.And Justice For All, 1979, I'll Never Say Goodbye, from The Promise, 1979 (Acad. award nominee for best song, 1979), Where Do You Catch the Bus for Tomorrow, from A Change of Seasons, 1980, Ask Me No Questions, from Back Roads, 1981, How Do You Keep the Music Playing?, from Best Friends, 1982 (Acad. award nominee for best song, 1982), Think About Love, 1982, Comin' Home to You, from Author! Author!, 1982, Tootsie, from Tootsie, 1982, It Might Be You, 1982 (Acad. award nominee for best song, 1982, Grammy award nominee for best original score, 1983), If We Were in Love, from Yes, Giorgio, 1982 (Acad. award nominee for best song, 1982), Never Say Never Again, from Never Say Never again, 1983, Papa, Can You Hear Me?, from Yentl, 1983 (Academy award nomination best song, 1983), The Way He Makes Me Feel, 1983 (Acad. award nominee for best song, 1983), Will Someone Ever Look at Me That Way?, 1983 (Acad. award best original score and Grammy award nomination for best original score, 1984, Acad. award nominee for best original song, 1983), Yentl, 1983 (Acad. award for best original score, 1983), Little Boys, from The Man Who Loved Women, 1983, Something New in My Life, from Mickey and Maude, 1984, The Music of Goodbye, from Out of Africa, 1985, I Know the Feeling, from The January Man, 1989, The Girl Who Used to Be Me, from Shirley Valentine, 1989 (Acad. award nominee for best song, 1989, Golden Globe nominee for best original song, 1990, Grammy award nominee, 1990), Welcome Home, from Welcome Home, 1989, Most of All You, from Major League, 1989, Dreamland, from For the Boys, 1991, Places That Belong to You, from The Prince of Tides, 1991, It's All There, from Switch, 1991, Moonlight, from Sabrina, 1995 (Acad. award nominee for best original song, 1996, Golden Globe nominee, Grammy nominee), The Best of Friends, from Bogus, 1996, Love is Where You Are, from At First Sight, pop songs You Don't Bring Me Flowers, 1978 (Grammy award nominee for song of the year, 1978), In the Heat of the Night, The Summer Knows, Nice 'N' Easy (Grammy award nominee for song of the year, 1960), Someone in the Dark, L.A. Is My Lady, After the Rain, I Was Born in Love With You, That Face, Look Around, I Love to Dance Like They Used to Dance, What Matters Most, One Day, A Child Is Born, Sleep Warm, Sentimental Baby, Live It Up, If I Close My Eyes, Yellow Bird, Like a Lover, Where Do You Start?, On My Way to You, Ordinary Miracles (Cable Ace award and Emmy award for best original song), A Ticket to Dream (Emmy Awd. for best song), albums Never Be Afraid for Bing Crosby, The Ballad of the Blues for Jo Stafford, 1999, Barbra Streisand: The Concert (Ace nominee for writing of a spl.). Named to songwriters hall of Fame, 1980; recipient singers salute to songwriter award, Clooney Found., 1986, Aggie award, Songwriter's Guild, 1987; grantee Am. Film Inst., 1976. Mem.: ASCAP (pres., chmn. bd. dirs. 1994—). Office: ASCAP 7920 Sunset Blvd Ste 300 Los Angeles CA 90046

BERGMAN, MICHELLE D., lawyer; b. Berlin; m. Jeffrey Bergman. Diploma, Ouachita Baptist U., 1989; MBA, Tulane U., JD, 1994. Intern Philip Morris, NY, Thacher, Proffitt & Wood; with Latham & Watkins, Donaldson, Lufkin & Jenrette; asst. gen. counsel AEA Investors; v.p., gen. counsel, corp. sec. Duane Reade, Inc., NYC, 2002—. Mem.: Order of Coif. Avocation: reading. Office: Duane Reade Inc 440 Ninth Ave New York NY 10001*

BERGMAN, NANCY PALM, real estate investment company executive; b. McKeesport, Pa., Dec. 3, 1938; d. Walter Vaughn and Nellie (Sullivan) Leech; m. Donald Bergman; 1 child, Tiffany Palm Taylor. Student, Mt. San Antonio Coll., 1970, UCLA, 1989—93. Corporate sec. U.S. Filter Corp., Newport Beach, Calif., 1965—. Pres. Jaguar Research Corp., L.A. and Atlanta, 1971-; owner Environ. Designs, L.A., 1976—; pres. Prosher Corp., L.A., 1978-83; now pres., dir. Futura Investments, L.A.; CEO Rescor, Inc. Author: Resident Managers Handbook. Elder Beverly Hills Presbyn. Ch., 2006. Home: 1255 Benedict Canyon Dr Beverly Hills CA 90210 also: 23540 Tapatia Rd Homeland CA 92548 Office: PO Box 15246 Beverly Hills CA 90209

BERGMAN, NOMI, communications executive; m. Neal Bergman; 3 children. Grad., Betsy Magnes Leadership Inst.; BA in Econ., Stats., Univ. Rochester, NY. Computer programmer, cons. mgmt. info. divsn. Arthur Andersen & Co., Advanced Pub. Systems; with cable ops. Newhouse Pub.;

v.p., gen. mgr. high speed data devel. Time Warner Cable; exec. v.p., strategy and devel. Advance/Newhouse Comm., 2002—. Involved with Women in Cable Telecom., CableLabs, NCTA, SCTE, CTAM. Recipient Women in Tech. award, Soc. Cable Telecom. Engrs., CableTec Expo., 2004. Office: Women in Cable Telecom Ste 250 14555 Avion Pkwy Chantilly VA 20151*

BERGMANN, BARBARA ROSE, economics professor; b. N.Y.C., July 20, 1927; d. Martin and Nellie Berman; m. Fred H. Bergmann, July 16, 1965; children: Sarah Nellie, David Martin. BA, Cornell U., 1948; MA, Harvard U., 1955, PhD, 1959; PhD (hon.), De Montford U., 1996, Muhlenberg Coll., 2000. Economist U.S. Bur. Labor Stats., N.Y.C., 1949-53; sr. staff ecomomist, cons. Council Econ. Advisors, Washington, 1961-62; sr. staff Brookings Inst., Washington, 1963-65; sr. econ. advisor AID, Washington, 1966-67; assoc. prof. U. Md., College Park, 1965-71, prof. econs., 1971-88; disting. prof. econs. Am. U., Washington, 1988-97, prof. emeritus, 1997—. Author: (with Chinitz and Hoover) Projection of a Metropolis, 1961; (with George W. Wilson) Impact of Highway Investment on Development, 1966; (with David E. Kaun) Structural Unemployment in the U.S., 1967; (with Robert Bennett) A Microsimulated Transactions Model of the United States Economy, 1985, Saving Our Children from Poverty: What the United States Can Learn from France, 1996, In Defense of Affirmative Action, 1996, Is Social Security Broke? A Cartoon Guide to the Issues, 1999, (with Suzanne W. Helburn) America's Child Care Problem: The Way Out, 2002, The Economic Emergence of Women, 2d edit., 2005; mem. editl. bd. Am. Econ. Rev., 1970-73, Challenge, 1978—, Signs, 1978-85; columnist econ. affairs N.Y. Times, 1981-82. Mem. Economists for McGovern, 1977; mem. panel econ. advisors Congl. Budget Office, Washington, 1977-87; mem. price adv. com. U.S. council on Wage and Price Stability, 1979-80. Fellow Am. Acad. Polit. and Social Sci.; mem. AAUP (coun. 1980-83, pres. 1990-92), Am. Econ. Assn. (v.p. 1976, adv. com. to U.S. Census Bur. 1977-82), Ea. Econ. Assn. (pres. 1974), Internat. Assn. for Feminist Econs. (pres. 1999), Soc. for Advancement of Socio-Econs. (pres. 1995-96). Democrat. Home: 5430 41st Pl NW Washington DC 20015-2911 E-mail: bbergman@umd.edu, bberg@american.edu.

BERGMANN, RENEE F., lawyer; b. Honesdale, Pa., May 26, 1967; d. Robert Emerson Howell and Mae Margaret Rowe; m. Steven C. Bergmann, Nov. 18, 1987; 1 child, Danielle M. BS, Thomas Edison State Coll., 1997; JD, Rutgers U., 2000. Bar: Pa., N.J. Assoc. Weira Demtres, Phila., 2000—03, Nixon Peabody, Phila., 2003—. Named a Rising Star-Pa. Super Lawyers, Phila. Mag., 2005. Mem.: Pa. Bar Assn. (treas. 2006—, co-chair comm. com. 2005—06, mem. exec. coun. 2005—), ABA. Catholic. Office: Nixon Peabody LLP 1818 Market St 11th Fl Philadelphia PA 19103 Business E-Mail: rbergmann@nixonpeabody.com.

BERGNER, JANE COHEN, lawyer; d. Louis and Selma (Breslaw) Cohen; m. Alfred P. Bergner, May 30, 1968 (dec. Sept. 24, 2002); children: Lauren, Justin. AB, Vassar Coll., 1964; LLB, Columbia U., 1967. Bar: DC 1968, U.S. Dist. Ct. DC 1968, U.S. Ct. Appeals (DC cir.) 1968, U.S. Ct. Fed. Claims 1969, U.S. Ct. Appeals (fed. cir.) 1969, U.S. Tax Ct. 1979, U.S. Supreme Ct. 1992. Trial atty. tax divsn. U.S. Dept. Justice, Washington, 1967-74; assoc. Arnold & Porter, Washington, 1974-76, Rogovin, Huge & Lenzner, Washington, 1976-83; of counsel Arter & Hadden, 1983-86; ptnr. Spriggs & Hollingsworth, 1986-89, Feith & Zell, P.C., 1989-93; pvt. practice Washington, 1993—. Mem. jud. confs. U.S. Ct. Fed. Claims, U.S. Tax Ct. Author: Tax Court Practice and Court of Federal Claims Practice, West's Federal Forms, 2006, Mertens Law of Federal Income Taxation, Chpt. 50, U.S. Tax Court; contbr. articles to profl. jours. Bd. dirs. Jewish Social Svc. Agy., Washington; former mem. cmty. adv. bd. Sta. WAMU-FM, Washington. Fellow Am. Coll. Tax Counsel; mem. ABA (sect. taxation, govt. rels. com., ct. procedure com., civil and criminal penalties com., chmn. subcom. important devels. 1991-93, chmn. regional liaison meetings com. 1993-95, sect. litig.); Vassar Coll. Class Alumnae (chair spl. gifts com. 25th reunion), DC Bar (chair taxation sect. 1985-90, chair tax audits and litig. com. 1990-93, Outstanding Sect. award 1986, Cmty. Outreach award 1993), Fed. Bar Assn., Women's Bar Assn. DC, Washington Estate Planning Coun., Women's Tax Luncheon Group, Columbia U. Law Sch. Alumni Assn., Svc. Guild Washington, Vassar Club. Office: Ste 650 1615 L St NW Washington DC 20036 Office Phone: 202-626-8215. Business E-Mail: jbergnerlaw@abanet.org.

BERGNER, JOHN F., lawyer; b. Pratt, Kans., Mar. 27, 1957; BBA in Fin., WAshburn U., 1979, JD, 1982; ML in Taxation, Georgetown U, 1985. Bar: Kans. 1982, Mo. 1982, Tex. 1985, U.S. Dist. Ct. Kans. 1982, U.S. Ct. Appeals (D.C. cir.) 1983, U.S. Tax Ct. 1983. Tax advisor Touche Ross & Co., Kansas City, Mo., 1982-83; tax law clk. Steptoe and Johnson, Washington, 1984; atty. advisor to Damiel J. Dinan U.S. Tax Ct., Washington, 1984-85; atty. Winstead, McGuire, Sechrest & Minick, Dallas, 1985—. Mem. Nat. Com. Planned Giving; adv. coun. Tex. Cmty. Found., Children's Med. Ctr. Found., Tex.; bd. dir. Bryan's House, Dallas; mem. Estate Planning Coun. S.W. Med. Found., Tex.; bd. gov. Dallas Estate Planning Coun., 1998—2000. Named Schultz Scholar, Washburn U. Sch. Bus., 1977—79; named one of the Best Lawyers in Dallas, D Mag., 2001, 2003, 2005. Fellow: Am. Coll. Trust and Estate Counsel; mem.: Tex. Bd. Legal Specialization (bd. cert. Estate Planning & Probate Law), Mo. Bar Assn., DC Bar Assn., Kans. Bar Assn., Tex. Bar Assn., Dallas Bar Assn. (past chmn.), ABA (vice chmn. Estate Gift & Taxes Com., past chmn. Cmty. Property Sub-Com.), Shriners, Masons. Republican. Methodist. Avocation: numismatist specializing in early Am. copper coinage. Office: Winstead McGuire Sechrest & Minick 5400 Renaissance Tower 1201 Elm St Dallas TX 75270 Office Fax: 214-745-5390. E-mail: jbergner@winstead.com.

BERGQUIST, SANDRA LEE, medical and legal consultant, nurse; b. Carlton, Minn., Oct. 13, 1944; d. Arthur Vincent and Avis Lorene Portz; m. David Edward Bergquist, June 11, 1966; children: Rion Eric, Taun Erin. BSN, Barry U., 1966; MA in Mgmt., Central Mich. U., 1975; student U. So. Calif., 1980-82. RN, advanced RN practitioner; cert. physician asst. Commd. 2d lt. USAF, 1968, advanced through grades to lt. col., 1985; staff and charge nurse USAF, 1968-76, primary care nurse practitioner, McConnell AFB, Kans., 1976-79, officer in charge Wheeler Med. Facility, Wheeler AFB, Hawaii, 1979-83, supr. ambulatory care services, Elgin AFB, Fla., 1983-84; med.-legal cons., Pensacola, Fla., 1985—; risk mgr., quality assurance coordinator HCA-Twin Cities Hosp., Niceville, 1986-88. Bd. dirs. Elder Svcs. Okaloosa County, Fla., 1984-2003; adv. bd. Gentiva Home Health, 1990—; chair Niceville/Valparaiso Task Force on Child Abuse Prevention, Fla., 1985-88; chair home and family life com. Twin Cities Women's Club, Niceville, 1985-88; chair advancement com. Gulf Coast coun. Boy Scouts Am., 1985-87; instr. advanced and basic cardiac life support Hawaii Heart Assn. and Tripler Army Med. Ctr., 1981-83. Decorated Commendation medal with 1 oak leaf cluster, USAF Meritorious Svc. medal, Air Force Commendation medal. Mem. AACN, Am. Assn. Physician Assts., Assn. Mil. Surgeons U.S., Soc. Ret. Air Force Nurses, Soc. Air Force Physician Assts., Twin Cities Women's Club. Lutheran. Avocations: computer programming, reading, handicrafts.

BERGSTROM, BETTY HOWARD, consulting executive, foundation administrator; b. Chgo., Mar. 15, 1931; d. Seward Haise and Agnes Eleanor (Uek) Guinter; m. Robert William Bergstrom, Apr. 21, 1979; children: Bryan Scott, Cheryl Lee, Jeffrey Alan, Mark Robert, Philip Alan. BS in Speech, Northwestern U., Evanston, Ill., 1952, postgrad., 1983, U. Nev., Reno, 1974. Dir. sales promotion and pub. rels. Sta. WLS-AM, Chgo., 1952; account exec. E.H. Brown Advt. Agy., Chgo., 1956—59; v.p. Richard Crabb Assocs., Chgo., 1959—61; pres., owner Howard Assocs., Calif. and Chgo., 1961—76; v.p. Chgo. Hort. Soc., 1976—90; pres. Bergstrom Assocs., Chgo., 1990—; exec. dir. Ariz. Found. for Women, 1996—98. Mem. editl. bd. Garden mag., 1977-84, Glenview Cmty. Ch., 1977-89, Fourth Presbyn. Ch., 1990—, trustee, 1994-97, elder, 2005—; editor Garden Talk, 1976-86; contbr. articles on fund devel., horticulture, edn. advt. and agr. to profl. jours.; editor Ill. AAUW Jour., 1966-67. Del. Ill. Constl. Conv., 1969-70, mem. com. legis. reform, 1973-74, cts. and justice com., 1971-74; apptd. mem. Ill. Hist. Libr. Bd., 1970, Ill. Bd. Edn., 1971-74; bd. dirs., v.p. Chgo. Lights, 2006-. AAUW fellowship grant named in her honor; recipient Communicator of Yr. award Women in Comm., 1983; named Outstanding Fundraising Exec., 1997. Mem.: LWV (state v.p. Ariz. 1999), AAUW (Pres.'s award 1988), Assn. Fund Raising Profls. (bd. dirs. 1983—92, sec. 1986, v.p. 1990—92, nat. bd. dirs. 1990—92, bd. dirs. 1996—, pres.-elect 1997, nat. del. assembly 1997—99, pres. 1999, internat. bd. dirs. 2000—06, vice chmn. 2002—03, cert. fund raising exec., Outstanding Fund Raising Exec.-Ariz. 1997), U. So. Calif. Alumni Assn., Am. Assn. Bot. Garden and Arboreta, Ariz. Women's Coun. (pres. 1999), Nat. Women's History Mus. (chmn. nat. bd. dirs. 2000—02, nat. adv. coun.), Charter 100, Am. Assn. Museums, Garden Writers Am., Northwestern U. Alumni, Fortnightly Club (bd. dirs. 1994—96). Office: Ste 49C 111 E Chestnut St Chicago IL 60611-6020 Office Phone: 312-280-1248. Personal E-mail: bhbergstrom@sbcglobal.net.

BERGSTROM, JOAN MARGOSIAN, education educator; b. Boston, July 20, 1940; d. Sally (Chooljian) Walden; m. Gary Leonard Bergstrom, Sept. 3, 1966; 1 child, Craig. BS in Edn., Tufts U., 1962; MS in Ednl. Psychology, U. Mich., 1963; PhD in Edn., U. Mass., 1972; postgrad., Northwestern U., 1979. Tchr. lab sch. U. Mich., Ann Arbor, 1962-63; instr. U. R.I., Kingston, 1963-64; asst. prof. Cornell U., Ithaca, N.Y., 1964-66; prof. grad. sch. Wheelock Coll., Boston, 1972—, dir. Ctr. for Internat. Edn. and Leadership/Innovation, 1992—, coord. Master's and Bachelor's Degree and Diploma programs in Singapore, Bermuda, Bahamas Boston, 1991—. Founder, pres. Activities Club, 1988—2003, Children's Out-of-Sch. Time Inc., 1988—; co-founder Workplace Connections, 1996—99. Author: The Best Summer Ever: A Parent's Guide, 1995, School's Out--Help Your Child Have a Fun and Fabulous Summer, 1986, School's Out--Now What? Help Your Child Have a Fabulous Summer!, 1988, School's Out--Now What? Choices For Your Child's Time--Afternoons, Weekends, Vacations, 1984, 2d edit., 1990, School's Out! It's Summer, 1992, (with C. Bergstrom) All the Best Contests for Kids, 1988, 5th edit., 1995 (Parents' Choice award in Doing and Learning 1990), (with R. Margosian) Teaching Young Children: Basic Concepts and Resources, 1976, (with L. Joy) Going to Work? Choosing Care for Infants and Toddlers, 1981, (with R. Margosian, F. Olson) Enhancement of Growth and Learning in Early Childhood, 1976, (with J. Gold) Checking Out Child Care: A Parent Guide, 1975, transl. Spanish, 1976, transl. Chinese, 1977, Swedish Day Nurseries: Focus on Programs for Infants and Toddlers, 1974, (with G. Morgan) Issues in the Design of a Delivery System for Preventative Services to Children and Their Families, 1975; contbr. chpts. to books, articles to jours. Overseer Boys and Girls Club, 1985—2003; trustee Tufts U., 1996—; bd. overseers Gerald J. and Dorothy R. Friedman Sch. of Nutrition, Sci. and Policy, 1999—, chairperson, 2002—; trustee Mus. Sci., Boston, 2003—; Bd. dirs. Prospect Hill Parents' and Children's Ctr., 1983—95; bd. mem. Child Health Inst. NJ at UMDNJ-The Robert Wood Johnson Med. Sch., 2001—. Recipient Outstanging Young Women of Mass., 1971, Outstanding Young Women of Am., 1966, 1971. Mem. Activities Club (pres. 1987-2003). Home: 220 Boylston St Apt 1516 Boston MA 02116-3951

BERGUM, LAUREN JEAN, art educator; b. West Allis, Wis., Jan. 8, 1981; d. Steven John and Pamela Perlick Bergum. BA in Studio Art, U. Iowa, 2003. K-12 tchg. cert. U. Iowa, 2003. Student tchr. Reepham H.S., England, 2003; substitute tchr. Pub. Schs., Longmont & Arvada, Colo., 2004; lead tchr. day care Children's World, Boulder, 2004; k-6 art educator Lincoln Acad., Arvada, 2004—05. Mem. PTA Lincoln Acad. Mktg. asst. & dancer, dance marathon for children with cancer, Iowa City, Iowa, 2002—03; art tchr. Vols. for Peace, Siennica, Poland, 2005; builder Habitat for Humanity, Longmont, Colo., Poland, 2005—. Avocations: soccer, snowboarding, skiing, whitewater kayaking, drawing. Home: 1429 North St Boulder CO 80304

BERGVIG, CHYRL RAE, counselor; b. Lincoln, Nebr., Sept. 11, 1949; d. Raymond E. and Leona M. (Willcoxon) B. AA, Iowa Cen. Community Coll., 1969; BS, Parsons Coll., 1971; MS, Iowa State U., 1978. Cert. elem. tchr., physical edn., guidance, counseling. Counselor, physical edn., guidance Graettinger (Iowa) Community Sch., 1977-85; counselor West Sioux Cmty. Sch., Hawarden, Iowa, 1985—92; asst. prin., counselor Clear Lake (Iowa) Cmty. Sch., 1992—. Emergency contact person ARC, Hawarden, 1988-91. Mem. Am. Assn. Counseling Devel., Iowa Sch. Counselors Assn. (pres. elect 1990-91, pres. 1991-92). Avocations: travel, golf. Home: 601 S 14th St Clear Lake IA 50428-2641

BERKA, MARIANNE GUTHRIE, health and physical education educator; b. Queens, N.Y., Dec. 25, 1944; d. Frank Joseph and Mary (DePaul) Guthrie; m. Jerry George Berka, June 1, 1968; children: Katie, Keri. BS, Ithaca Coll., 1966, MS, 1968; EdD, NYU, 1990. Tchr. Northport H.S., 1966—67; prof. Health, Phys. Edn. and Recreation Nassau C.C., Garden City, NY, 1968—. Adj. assoc. prof. Hofstra U., Hempstead, NY, 1998—. Mem.: AAHPER, AAHPERD, Am. Coll. Sports Medicine (cert. health/fitness instr.), Am. Assn. Sex Educators, Counselors and Therapists (cert. sex educator), N.Y. State Assn. Health, Phys. Edn., Recreation and Dance (J.B. Nash scholarship com. 1983—2000, Nassau Zone Disting. Svc. award 1988, Nassau Zone Higher Edn. Tchr. of Yr. 2003), Assn. Women Phys. Educators N.Y. State (chpt. chmn. 1973—74, chpt. treas. 1980—84). Roman Catholic. Office: P226 HPER Nassau Community Coll Garden City NY 11530 Home: Brightwaters NY 11718 Office Phone: 516-572-8147. Business E-Mail: berkam@ncc.edu.

BERKELMAN, MARY HOBBIE, retired elementary school educator, adult education educator; b. Sodus, NY, July 16, 1935; d. Thomas Charlton and Elizabeth Morgan Hobbie; m. Karl Berkelman, Oct. 10, 1959; children: Thomas, James, Peter. BSc, Cornell U., 1957; MA, Elmira Coll., 1995. Cert. Tchr. (kindergarten through sixth grade) N.Y., 1957. Elem. tchr. Ithaca City Sch. Dist., NY, 1957—60; substitute tchr. Am. Sch. Rome, 1960—61; adult basic edn., GED tchr. Tompkins County Jail, Ithaca, 1979—86; substitute tchr. Tompkins County Schs., NY, 1986—88; elem. tchr. Dryden Ctrl. Sch., NY, 1988—2000, mem. ungraded classroom task force, 1991—92. Com. mem. Jail Program Adv. Com., Ithaca, 1979—86, Elem. Sch. Site Based Teams, Dryden, Freeville, NY, 1995—97. V.p. Ithaca PTA Coun., 1975—77; sec. Hist. Ithaca Bd., 1979—81. Mem.: LWV Tompkins County (v.p. 2001—03, pres. 2003—05), Cornell U. Campus Club, Friends of Libr. (book sale fine sorter 1975—2005, bd. mem. 1984—86), Cayuga Chamber Orch. Bd. (bd. mem. 2003—05, sec. 2005—). Avocations: music, birdwatching, photography, travel, gourmet cooking. Home: 380 Pky Ithaca NY 14850 Personal E-mail: mberkelman@netscape.net.

BERKELMAN, RUTH, medical educator; AB, Princeton U., 1973; MD, Harvard U. Med. Sch., 1977. Epidemic intelligence svc. officer CDC, 1980—82, med. epidemiologist, Epidemiology Program Office, 1982—83, chief, epidemiologic studies branch, Epidemiology Program Office, 1983—86, dir., divsn. surveillance & epidemiologic studies, Epidemiology Program Office, 1986—88, chief, surveillance br., Divsn. HIV/AIDS, 1988—92, dep. dir., Nat. Ctr. Infectious Diseases, 1992—97, sr. advisor to Dir., 1998—2000; cons. Nuclear Threat Initiative, 2001; Rollins prof. Emory U., Rollins Sch. Pub. Health, 2002—, dir. Ctr. Pub. Health Preparedness & Rsch., 2002—. Chmn. Pub. and Sci. Affairs Bd. Am. Soc. Microbiology, 2004—. Trustee Princeton U., 2000—04. Recipient Sec.'s award for Disting. Svc., CDC, 1997, Certificate of Recognition, Coun. State & Territorial Epidemiologists, 1995; John Maclean Fellow, Princeton U., 1995. Mem.: Inst. Medicine. Office: Rollins Sch Pub Health 1518 Clifton Rd Mailstop 1518-002-1AA Atlanta GA 30322 Office Phone: 404-727-5409. Office Fax: 404-712-8345. E-mail: rberkel@sph.emory.edu.

BERKENES, JOYCE MARIE POORE, social worker, director; b. Des Moines, Aug. 29, 1953; d. Donald Roy and Thelma Beatrice (Hart) Poore; m. Robert Elliott Berkenes, Jan. 3, 1976; children: Tiffany Noelle, Cory Matthew. BA in Social Work and Biology, Simpson Coll., Indianola, Iowa., 1975. Cons. in field, 1975—76; resident counselor and group home mgr. Chaddock Boys Home, Quincy, Ill., 1976-78; social service dir. North Adams Nursing Home, Mendon, Ill., 1978; home tchr. Head Start, Camp Point, Ill., 1978-79, home tchr. supr./edn. and parent involvement coordinator, 1979-82; family counselor Iowa Children's and Family Services, Des Moines, 1982-85; family counselor and vol. coordinator Luth. Social Services, Des Moines, 1985-89; coordinator/educator/social worker Parent-Infant Nurturing Ctr., Meth. Med. Ctr., Des Moines, 1989-95; social worker The Homestead, 1995-97; state program mgr. Healthy Families Iowa Projects of Home Care Iowa, Des Moines, 1997-01, Healthy Families Am. Trainer, 1998—; program dir. HOPES/ Healthy Families Iowa Prevent Child Abuse Iowa, 2001—03; rep. State Domestic Violence Response Tng. Team Iowa Dept. Pub. Health, 2003—04; program mgr. for home care Generations Inc., 2004—05; med. social worker oncology Iowa Meth. Med. Ctr., 2005—. Mem. Greater Des Moines Child Abuse and Neglect Coun. Bd. Mem. Prevent Child Abuse Iowa, Prevent Child Abuse Am. Mem. Internat. Assn. Infant Massage, Abbie Gardner Questers. Democrat. United Ch. Christ. Avocations: collecting antiques, reading, piano, ballet. Home: 2901 NE 80th St Altoona IA 50009-9423

BERKERY, ROSEMARY T., lawyer, investment company executive; b. 1953; BA magna cum laude in English, Coll. Mt. St. Vincent; JD, St. John's U. Sch. Law, Jamaica, NY. Bar: N.Y. 1980. Corp. and securities lawyer Shearman & Sterling, NYC, 1978—83; atty. Merrill Lynch & Co., Inc., NYC, 1983—95, sr. v.p., assoc. gen. counsel, 1995—97, co-dir. global securities rsch. and econs. grp., 1997—2000, sr. v.p., dir. US pvt. client mktg. and investments, 2000—01, exec. v.p., gen. counsel, 2001—. Editor: St. John's Law Rev. Office: Merrill Lynch and Co Inc 4 World Fin Ctr 250 Vesey St New York NY 10080

BERKLEY, EMILY CAROLAN, lawyer; b. Richmond, Va., Mar. 2, 1950; d. Charles Garvice and Edna Gray (Berkley) Broom; m. Richard E. Bird, Sept. 6, 1969 (div. Mar. 1988); children: Jessica A. Bird, Martel J. Bird. Student, Coll. of William and Mary, 1968—70; BS in Psychology cum laude, Tufts U., 1972; JD magna cum laude, Temple U., 1977. Ptnr. Ballard Spahr Andrews & Ingersoll LLP, Phila., 1977—. Seminar panelist Pa. Bar Inst., 1992, 1998—2003, 2005, Practicing Law Inst., 1993—2005, Phila. Compliance Roundtable, 2004—05. Long range planning com. Performing Arts for Tredyffrin-Easttown Sch. Dist., Berwyn, Pa., 1989, chair subcom. on creativity, futures com., 1990; active United Way, 1989-91; bd. dir. Devon-Strafford Little League, 1992-95. Fellow: Am. Bar Found. (life); mem.: ABA (bus. law sect. chair task force on exporation of Uniform Comml. Code 1995—97, vice chair internat. comml. law subcom. 1997—99, bus. law sect. liaison U.S. Sec. of State's adv. com. on pvt. internat 1997—99, chair legal opinion com. 2004—, mem. uniform comml. code com., fed. regulation securities com., corp. compliance com.), N.Y. TriBar Opinion Com., Phila. Bar Assn., Pa. Bar Assn. (officer 2003—, bus. law sect., chair legal opinion com., chair article 9 task force, secured trans.), Am. Law Inst., Am. Coll. Comml. Fin. Lawyers (bd. regents 1993—2001, pres. 2000). Office: Ballard Spahr Andrews et al 1735 Market St Ste 5100 Philadelphia PA 19103-7599 Office Phone: 215-864-8611. Business E-Mail: berkley@ballardspahr.com.

BERKLEY, MARY CORNER, neurologist; b. Balt., Apr. 6, 1926; d. Henry Evans and Eleanor (Diggs) Corner; m. Kelly McKenzie Berkley, Sept. 3, 1955 (dec. Oct. 1984); children: Henry Evans, Robert Bruce; m. Warren Frederick Gorman, May 31, 1986 (dec. Mar. 2000). AB, Bryn Mawr Coll., 1946; MD, Johns Hopkins U., 1950. Diplomate Am. Bd. Psychiatry and Neurology. Intern, resident Cin. Gen. Hosp., 1950-52; resident in medicine Strong Meml. Hosp., Rochester, N.Y., 1952-53, fellow in neurology, 1953-56; pvt. practice Rochester, 1956-58, Janesville, Wis., 1958-60; resident in neurology U. Mich. Med. Ctr., Ann Arbor, 1960-64; sr. instr. Hahnemann Med. Coll., Phila., 1965-68; pvt. practice neurology Gallipolis, Ohio, 1968-70, Mt. Vernon, Ill., 1970-76; staff neurologist VA Med. Ctr., Phoenix, 1976-95, ret., 1995. Fellow Am. Acad. Neurology; mem. Alpha Omega Alpha.

BERKLEY, SHELLEY (ROCHELLE LEVINE BERKLEY), congresswoman, lawyer; b. NYC, Jan. 20, 1951; m. Lawrence Lehrner; 2 children. BA in Polit. Sci., U. Nev., Las Vegas, 1972; JD, U. San Diego Sch. Law, 1976. Counsel S.W. Gas Corp.; dep. dir. Nev. Commerce Dept.; mem. Nev. State Assembly, 1982—84; vice chair bd. regents Nev. Univ. and Cmty. Coll. Sys., 1990—98; v.p. govt. and legal affairs Sands Hotel, 1996—98; mem. US Congress from 1st Nev. dist., 1999—, mem. transp. and infrastructure com., internat. rels. com., vets. affairs com. Bd. chair Nev. Hotel and Motel Assn.; nat. dir. Am. Hotel-Motel Assn.; del. White House Conf. on Tourism. Bd. trustees Sunrise-Columbia Hosp. and Med. Ctr., Las Vegas. Recipient Clark County Mother of Yr., 1994, Humane Legislator of Yr. award, Am. Humane Assn., 2000, Medal of Merit, Jewish War Vets. of the U.S.A., 2003, Outstanding Dem. of Yr., Paradise Democratic Club. Mem.: Women's Democratic Club Clark County, Clark County Bar Assn., US Bar Assn., So. Nev. Assn. Women Attys., Nev. State Bar Assn. Democrat. Jewish. Office: US Ho Reps 439 Cannon Ho Office Bldg Washington DC 20515-2801 Office Phone: 202-225-5965. E-mail: shelley.berkley@mail.house.gov.*

BERKMAN, CLAIRE FLEET, psychologist; b. New Orleans, Dec. 5, 1942; d. Joel and Margaret Grace (Fishler) Fleet; m. Arnold Stephen Berkman, Apr. 27, 1975; children: Janna Samantha, Micah Seth Siegel. BA, Boston U., 1964; EdM, Harvard U., 1966; EdD, Boston U., 1970. Asst. prof. Counseling Ctr. Mich. State U., East Lansing, 1971-75, assoc. prof., 1975-78, assoc. prof. dept. psychiatry, 1975-82, clin. assoc. prof., 1986-87; pvt. clin. practice, 1975—. Cons. Cath. Family Social Service, Lansing, 1979-83; mem. adv. bd. Cir. Ct. Family Counseling Program, 1982-88. V.p. Kehillat Israel Synagogue, 1975-76, pres., 1992-94; bd. dirs. Jewish Welfare Fedn., Lansing, 1974-75, 84-87; mem. children's task force State Bar Mich., 1993-95. NDEA fellow, 1968-70. Mem. APA, Mich. Psychol. Assn., Mich. Soc. Forensic Psychologists, Nat. Soc. Arts and Letters (pres. Mid-Mich. chpt. 2000-02). Office: 4084 Okemos Rd Okemos MI 48864-3258 Office Phone: 517-349-8388.

BERKMAN, LISA F., public health educator; PhD, U. Calif., Berkeley, 1977. Thomas D. Cabot prof. pub. policy Harvard Sch. Pub. Health, Boston, chair Dept. of Soc., Human Develop., and Health. Contbr. articles to profl. jours. Mem.: Inst. of Medicine of NAS. Achievements include research in on psychosocial influences on health outcomes. Office: Harvard Univ Kresge Bldg Rm 709 677 Huntington Ave Boston MA 02115

BERKOWITZ, BOBBIE, medical educator; BS in Nursing, U. Wash., M of Nursing; PhD in Nursing Sci., Case We. Res. U. Chief nursing svcs. Seattle-King County Dept. Pub. Health, 1986—93; dep. sec. Wash. State Dept. Health, 1993—97; dir. Turning Point Nat. Program Office Robert Wood Johnson Found.; mem. faculty U. Wash. Sch. Nursing, Seattle, 1996—, prof. and chair dept. psychosocial and cmty. health Sch. Nursing, 1998—2004, alumni endowed prof. nursing, 2004—, dir. Ctr. for the Advancement of Health Disparities Rsch. Adj. prof. dept. health svcs. U. Wash. Sch. Pub. Health & Cmty. Medicine, Seattle; mem. Wash. State Bd. Health, 1988—93; apptd. by gov. Wash. Health Care Commn., 1990—92; bd. dirs. Hanford Environ. Health Found.; vice-chair, bd. dirs. QualisHealth; vice-chair The Pub. Health Found. Bd.; bd. trustees Group Health Cooperative, 2004—. Mem. editl. bd.: jour. Pub. Health Nursing, Am. Jour. Pub. Health, sr. assoc. editor: jour. Policy, Politics, & Nursing Practice, assoc. editor: jour. Nursing Outlook. Recipient Sch. Nursing Disting. Alumni award, U. Wash.; scholar, Ctrs. for Disease Control and Prevention's Pub. Health Leadership Inst., 1993—94. Fellow: Am. Acad. Nursing; mem.: NAS, Inst. Medicine (co-chair com. on pub. health performance monitoring). Office: U Wash Psychosocial and Cmty Health Box 357263 Seattle WA 98195-7263*

BERKRAM, PATRICIA CLARKE, religious studies educator; b. Jersey City, N.J., Dec. 27, 1937; d. Thomas Joseph Clarke and Florence Fay Pallander; m. Joseph Bergalowski (div.); children: Donna Gordon Bergalowski, Peggy Corbitt Bergalowski, Joseph Bergalowski, Bernadette Sloyer Bergalowski; m. Elmer Magus Berkram, Oct. 24, 1974; stepchildren: Gail Kent, Bruce, Steven, Darrol. AS in Nursing, Felician Coll., 1971; BA in Bible & Theology magna cum laude, Berean Coll., 1993; MDiv, Assembly of God Theol. Seminary, 1997; DMin, Fuller Theol. Seminary, 2000. Ordained min. Assemblies of God, 1997. RN Bayonne Hosp., NJ, 1971—73; staff nurse Indian Health, Browning, Mont., 1973—74, RN, 1973—85; bible tchr. Cut

Bank Assembly God, Mont., 1987—96; prof., bible & theology Ctrl. Indian Bible Coll., Monridge, SD, 1996—98, Black Hills Indian Bible Coll., Rapid City, SD, 1999—2000, Asia Theol. Ctr. for Evangelism & Missions, Singapore, 2000—. Contbr. articles to profl. jours.; author: Shame Shame Go Away, 2004. Mem.: Am. Assn. Christian Counselors. Independent. Avocations: piano, puzzles, reading, walking. Home: 666 E Sweetgrass Rd Cut Bank MT 59427 Office: Asia Theol Ctr for Evangelism & Missions 20 Tampines Ste 43 Singapore Singapore

BERKWITS, GLORIA KOZIN, psychiatrist; d. Aaron Leib and Adele Kozin; m. Edward Berkwits, June 24, 1952; children: Leland, Jeffrey, Michael. BA, Wayne State U., 1947; MD, U. Mich., 1951. Diplomate Am. Bd. Neurology and Psychiatry. Resident VA Hosp., Downey, Ill., 1952—55; fellow in child psychiatry Inst. Juvenile Rsch., Chgo., 1955—57, supr. therapy, 1957—58; pvt. practice Chgo., 1959—. Interdepartmental com. Ill. Commn. Children, 1966—68; cons. psychiatrist Cook County Pediat. Neurology, Chgo., 1968—74; clin. asst. prof. psychiatry Northwestern U., Evanston, Ill., 1986—. Contbr. articles and presentations in field. Vol. cons. Beard Sch., Chgo., 2001—; vol. Field Mus., Chgo., 2003—. Fellow: Am. Psychiat. Assn.; mem.: Ill. Coun. Child and Adolescent Psychiatry.

BERLAND, GRETCHEN K., medical educator, filmmaker; BA, Pomona Coll., 1986; MD, Oreg. Health and Sci. U., 1996. Internship and residency Wash. Univ. Med. Ctr. in St. Louis Barnes Hosp., 1996—99; fellowship UCLA Robert Wood Johnson Clin. Scholars program, 1999—2001; asst. prof., internal med. Yale U. Sch. of Med., New Haven, 2001—. Contbr. articles to profl. jours.; contbr. WGBH TV for PBS Primetime-Condition Critical, MacNeil/Lehrer for PBS & NBC-Hard Choices and A Time For Change, GBH TV for the NOVA Series. Named a MacArthur Fellow, 2004. Office: Yale Univ Med Sch-Internal Med 333 Cedar St PO Box 208033 LMP 87 New Haven CT 06520 Office Phone: 203-737-5157. Office Fax: 203-737-5358. Business E-Mail: gretchen.berland@yale.edu.*

BERLENBACH-COBURN, SUSAN L., elementary school educator; b. Bay Shore, NY, Sept. 25, 1960; d. Frederick J. Berlenbach and Lois C. Walters; m. Michael E. Coburn, July 20, 1985; children: Tristan F. Coburn, Jillian S. Coburn. MusB, SUNY, Potsdam, 1982; MEd, Keene State Coll., NH, 1988; cert. in fine arts adminstrn., Fitchburg State Coll., 1988. Cert. tchr. NH. Tchr. Kearsarge Regional Mid. Sch., New London, NH, 1983—. Mem.: NEA, NH Music Educators Assn. (gen. music chair 2006), Am. Choral Dirs. Assn. Democrat. Avocations: camping, photography, travel. Office: Kearsarge Regional Mid Sch 114 Cougar Ct New London NH 03257 Office Phone: 603-526-6415. Business E-Mail: scoburn@kearsarge.k12.nh.us.

BERLIN, BEATRICE WINN, artist, printmaker; b. Phila., May 27, 1922; d. Benjamin and Pauline (Neubauer) Winn; m. Herbert Edward Berlin, Oct. 21, 1945; m. Warren Joseph Sturmer, Aug. 21, 1971; children: Arlene (dec.), Janice. Attended, Moore Coll. Art, Phila. Coll. Art; student, Samuel Maitin, Hitoshi Nakazato, Kenjilo Nanao. Lectr. Phila. Print Club, 1964—68; instr. Intaglio techniques Long Beach Island Ctr. Arts and Sci., N.J., 1970; freelance artist Pa., 1963—76, Calif., 1976—. Pub. collections, Phila. Mus. Art, Bklyn. Art Mus., N.Y. Pub. Libr., Phila. Main Libr., De Cordova Mus., Mass., U. So. Calif., N.J. State Mus., Temple U., Phila., U. Pa., Lebanon Valley Coll., Pa., Ocean City Cultural Ctr., N.J., San Francisco Art Mus., Achenback Coll., among others. Recipient Phila. Water Color Club drawing prize, 1976, 82, best in show prize, Ocean City, N.J. Boardwalk, 1973, purchase prize, Lebanon Valley Coll., 1973, Hazelton Art League, 1972, first prize Cheltenham Art Ctr. Nat. Print Exhbn., 1970. Mem.: Artists Equity Assn., Calif. Soc. Printmakers.

BERLIN, DORIS ADA, psychiatrist; b. Newark, May 23, 1919; d. Samuel and Fanny (Lippman) B.; m. Saul R. Kelson (div.); children: Joel, Tamar; m. Lewis H. Acker. BS in Pharmacy, Columbia U., 1940; MD, Med. Coll. Va., 1948; MPH in Community Mental Health, U. Mich., 1966. Cert. Am. Bd. Psychiatry and Neurology; lic. psychiatrist N.Y., Va., Ohio, Mich., Tex., Calif. Intern Beth Israel Hosp., N.Y.C., 1948-49; resident in psychiatry Bellevue Hosp., N.Y.C., 1949-52; pvt. practice N.Y.C., 1952-57, Toledo, 1957-66, Fishkill and Poughkeepsie, N.Y., 1984—. Clin. asst. in psychiatry NYU Coll. Medicine, 1952-57; asst. in psychiatry U. Hosp., N.Y., 1952-53; clin. asst. vis. neuropsychiatrist Bellevue Hosp., N.Y., 1954-57; lectr. mental health Sch. Pub. Health U. Mich., 1966-68; dir. profl. edn. Toledo State Hosp., 1969-70; clin. assoc. prof. N.Y. Sch. Psychiatry, 1970-81; dir. residency program Hudson River Psychiat. Ctr., Poughkeepsie, 1970-83, others. Mem. citizens adv. bd. Lucas County (Ohio) Welfare Dept., 1963-67, chair, 1965-66; bd. dirs. Jewish Family Svc., Toledo, 1969-70; mem. policy coun., rehab. com. Toledo Area Program on Drug Abuse, 1970; bd. dirs. Dutchess County Assn. for Sr. Citizens, 1993-96. Grantee NEH, 1979. Fellow Am. Psychiat. Assn. (chair editl. bd. Hosp. and Cmty. Psychiatric Jour., 1979-80, task force on cmty. mental health ctrs., 1983-88, com. on advertisers and exhibitors 1989-92, vice-chair lifers caucus, 1990-91, chair lifers orgn. 1992), Am. Coll. Psychiatrists (Laughlin fellowship com. 1976-79); mem. Am. Acad. Psychoanalysis (com. on psychoanalysis and cmty. mental health 1967-68), Dutchess County Med. Soc. (psychiatrists' rep. to coun. 1985-95, treas. 1987).

BERLINER, BARBARA, retired librarian, consultant; b. Bklyn., July 14, 1947; d. Robert and Mildred M. (Sklar) Morris; 1 child, Stefanie Lauren. BA in Anthropology, NYU, 1969; MLS, Columbia U., 1970. Libr. N.Y. Pub. Libr., N.Y.C., 1970-81, sr. libr., telephone reference, 1981-86, supervising libr., tele. reference, 1986-92, head libr., Mid-Manhattan sci. and bus., 1992-93; coord. NYPL Express, N.Y.C., 1993—2002. Cons. John Wright, N.Y.C., 1991; bibliographer Collier's Encyclopedia. Author: The Book of Answers, 1990. Mem. ALA, Planetary Soc. Avocations: sports, astronomy. Home: 235 Portside Dr Edgewater NJ 07020

BERLINER, RUTH SHIRLEY, real estate company executive; b. N.Y.C., June 20, 1928; d. Irving William and Florence (Tomback) Blum; m. Arthur Ivan Berliner, Sept. 23, 1948; children: Daniel Scott, Michael Robert, Eric Lance. BA, Empire State Coll., Westbury, N.Y., 1974; diploma, Wilsey Sch. Interior Design, Hempstead, N.Y., 1975; MBA, Adelphi U., 1980. Lic. real estate broker, N.Y. Sec. to dir. librs. NYU, N.Y.C., 1948-50; sec. Paragon Mut. Syndicates Inc., N.Y.C., 1958-72; v.p. Paragon Mut. Investors Svcs., N.Y.C., 1972-78; pres. Ruth S. Berliner, Inc., N.Y.C., 1978—. Pres. Irmed Corp., 1983—; cons. E. 59th St. Assocs., N.Y.C., 1962-70, Amrep Corp., N.Y.C., 1968-75, FKBA Assocs., N.Y.C., 1974-78; mem. stores com. Real Estate Bd. N.Y., 1984-96. V.p. NYU Dental Sch. Parents Assn., 1974-76; bd. dirs. Hadassah, Hewlett, N.Y., 1978-87; advisor Citizens for Charter Change, N.Y.C., 1987—. Mem. Nat. Assn. Realtors, Real Estate Bd. N.Y. (store com. 1984-98, econ. devel. com. 1994-99), Inwood Club, Nat. Realty Club, Williams Club, N.Y. Athletic Club. Avocations: tennis, swimming, dance, painting. Office Phone: 212-757-0063.

BERLINER, WENDY ALISSA, lawyer; b. 1973; married; 1 child. BA cum laude, Brandeis U., 1995; JD, Yeshiva U., 1998. Bar: Conn. 1999, Mass. 1999, NY 1999, US Ct. Appeals (1st Cir.) 2001, US Dist. Ct. (Dist. Mass.) 2002. Tchr. rsch. and writing Boston U. Sch. Law; law clk. Conn. Superior Ct.; law clk. to Hon. Hugh H. Bownes US Ct. Appeals (1st Cir.); assoc. Kirkpatrick & Lockhart Nicholson Graham LLP, Boston, Demeo & Assoc. PC, Boston, 2006—. Office: Demeo & Assoc PC One Lewis Wharf Boston MA 02110 Office Phone: 617-263-2600. Office Fax: 617-263-2300. E-mail: wberliner@jdemeo.com.*

BERLOWITZ, LESLIE, cultural organization administrator; BA in English with honors, NYU, 165; MA in English, Columbia U., 1967. Mem. dept. English NYU, N.Y.C., 1967-96, asst. dean U. Coll. Arts and Scis., Washington Square Coll. Arts and Scis., 1969-73, dir. acad. program devel., 1973-81, asst. v.p. acad. affairs, 1981-84, assoc. v.p. acad. affairs, 1984-88, dep. v.p. acad. affairs, 1988-91, v.p. instnl. advancement, 1991-96; exec. officer Am. Acad. Arts and Scis., Cambridge, Mass., 1996—. Founder, dir. The Humanities Coun., 1977-96, Faculty Resource Network, 1985-96; nat. dir. Americorps, Project SafetyNet, 1995-96. Editor: (with Denis Donoghue and Louis Menand) America in Theory, 1988, Greenwich Village: Culture and Counterculture, 1990. Bd. dirs. Mass. Inst. Psychoanalysis; panelist Boston Jewish Film Festival; exec. bd. Corp. Yaddo; active Fund for Artists' Colonies, Inc., Coun. Internat. Edn. Exch., Urban Rsch. Ctr., Am. Jewish Congress, Fedn. Jewish Philanthropies, Joseph S. Gruss Found.; panelist NEH. Recipient Pacesetter award Tougaloo Coll., 1993. Fellow N.Y. Inst. Humanities, Am. Acad. Arts & Scis. 2004; mem. MLA, Century Assn. (N.Y.). Office: Am Acad Arts and Scis Norton's Woods 136 Irving St Cambridge MA 02138-1929 Fax: (617) 576-5055.

BERMAN, ARIANE R., artist; b. Danzig, Mar. 27, 1937; m. Mario La Rossa, 1965. B.F.A., Hunter Coll., N.Y.C., 1959; M.F.A., Yale, 1962; AAUW and Found. des Etats-Unis fellow, U. Paris, 1962-63. Juror nat. screening com. Fulbright grants, 1976-77, chmn. screening com., 1977-78. One man shows at Center Gallery, Conn., 1963, Harry Salpeter Gallery, N.Y.C., 1966, Brentano's Art Gallery, N.Y.C., 1973, Graphic Art Gallery, Tel Aviv, 1973, Galleria San Sebastianello, Rome, 1973, Eileen Kuhlik Gallery, N.Y.C., 1971, 73, Pub. Mus., Oshkosh, Wis., 1974, Wustum Mus. Fine Arts, Racine, Wis., 1974, Fontana Gallery, Pa., 1963, 71, 74, Galleria d'Arte Helioart, Rome, 1974, Munson Gallery, Conn., 1975, Ward-Nasse Gallery, N.Y.C., 1975, 77, 80, Phila. Art Alliance, 1980, Silvermine Guild Artists, Conn., 1976, Kornblee Gallery, N.Y.C., 1982, Babson Coll., Mass., 1983, Northwood Inst., Mich., 1983, Westenhook Gallery, Mass., 1984, Phoenix Gallery, N.Y.C., 1985, 87, Concordia Coll., Bronxville, N.Y., 1989, Gallery 84 Inc., N.Y.C., 1992, L'Artisanat, Mass., 1992, others; exhibited in group shows at Galerie Atrium Artis, Geneva, Switzerland, 1975, F 15 Gallery, Norway, 1974, Galeries Raymond Duncan, Paris, 1964, Asso. Am. Artists, N.Y.C., 1971, Circle Galleries Ltd., N.Y.C., 1974, Margo Feiden Galleries, N.Y.C., 1972, Gallery 500, Pa., 1973, Van Straaten Gallery, Chgo., 1974, Genesis Gallery, N.Y.C., 1978, Marymount Coll., N.Y.C., 1983, NYU, 1982, Fairleigh Dickenson U., 1982, Allentown Art Mus., Pa., 1982, numerous others; represented in permanent collections at Am. Petroleum Inst., Israel Ministry of Tourism, USIA, McGregor-Doniger, Inc., Shipley Sch., Bryn Mawr, Pa., Readers Digest, N.J. Bd. Edn., Athena Gallery, New Haven, Charles E. Ellis Coll., Newton Square, Pa., Hearst Corp., Met. Mus. Art, Phila. Mus. Art, Phila. Art Alliance, Ms. mag., Seventeen, Redbook, Feminist Press, Duke U., Newspaper Advt. Bur., Purdue U., Phila. Child Guidance Ctr., others. Recipient Yale Painting prize, 1960, Purchase award Purdue U., 1964, Stella Drabkin Meml. award, ACPS Purchase prize, 1973, Catherine Lorillard Wolfe Arts Club Gold medal, 1973, Hon. mention Hudson River Mus., 1974, Artists Equity award, 1985. Mem. Am. Color Print Soc., Nat. Assn. Women Artists, Yonkers Art Assn., Women's Caucus for Art, Met. Painters and Sculptors, Pen and Brush, League of Present Day Artists, Sheffield Art League, Silvermine Guild of Artists, Soc. Women Artists (past corr. sec.), Hunter Coll. Alumni Assn. (Hall of Fame 1974) Home: 161 W 54th St New York NY 10019-5322 Office Phone: 212-765-2030.

BERMAN, BARBARA, educational consultant; b. N.Y.C., Oct. 15, 1938; d. Nathan and Regina (Pasternak) Kopp; children: Adrienne, David. BS, Bklyn. Coll., 1959, MS, 1961; adminstrv./supervision cert., Coll. S.I., 1971; EdD, Rutgers U., 1981. Tchr. N.Y.C. Pub. Schs., 1959-70; project coord., dir. fed. projects Rutgers U., New Brunswick, NJ, 1976—80; math. cons. B&F Cons., S.I., NY, 1978—2003, BB Consulting, S.I., NY, 2003—; dir. fed. math. project Ednl. Support Systems, Inc., S.I., 1981-94; dir. Foresight Sch., S.I., 1985—, Great Beginnings Infant and Toddler Ctr., 1989—. Cons. to sch. dists. for restructuring/sch. reform and math. staff devel. Co-author of many books and articles on teaching mathematics for elem. and jr. h.s. tchrs. Mem. Nat. Coun. Tchrs. Math., Nat. Staff Devel. Coun., N.Y. Acad. Scis., Nat. Coun. Suprs. Math. Avocations: reading, travel, theater. Office: BB Consulting 446 Travis Ave Staten Island NY 10314-6149 Office Phone: 718-698-3636. Business E-Mail: bbconsultants@earthlink.net.

BERMAN, CAROL, retired commissioner; b. Bklyn., Sept. 21, 1923; d. Hyman and Sarah (Levy) B.; m. Seymour Jerome Berman, May 19, 1944; children: Elizabeth, Charles. BA, U. Mich., 1943. Trustee Bd. Edn., Lawrence, NY, 1973-77; senator State of N.Y., Albany, 1978-84; spl. rep. State Divsn. for Housing, Hempstead, NY, 1985-86; commr. N.Y. State Commn. on Lobbying, Albany, 1988-92, N.Y. State Commn. of Elections, Albany, 1992—2005; ret., 2005. NY co-chair Nat. Jewish Dem. Coun., 1988-05, Met. Airport Noise Mitigation Rev. Commn., 1992; vice-chair Nassau Dem. County Com., Mineola, NY, 1970-72. Mem. Phi Beta Kappa, Phi Kappa Phi. Jewish. Avocation: golf. Home: 42 Lord Ave Lawrence NY 11559-1324

BERMAN, CAROL WENDY, psychiatrist; b. N.Y.C., Sept. 14, 1951; d. Irving and Dora (Adler) B.; m. Martin Farber, Feb. 5, 1994. BA, U. Calif., Berkeley, 1972; MD, NYU, 1981. Diplomate Am. Bd. Psychiatry and Neurology. Intern, resident in psychiatry St. Lukes-Roosevelt Hosp., N.Y.C., 1982-85; rsch. fellow in psychiatry NYU Med. Ctr., N.Y.C., 1986-87, mem. attending staff, 1987—; pvt. practice, N.Y.C., 1988—. Author: (book) 100 Questions and Answers About Panic Disorder, 2005, (plays) Under the Dragon, Sunshine Sally; contbr. numerous articles to med. jours.; patentee device to prevent drunk driving. Active legal problems of mentally ill, Bar Assn. City N.Y., 1993-95. Recipient writing prize Psychiat. Annals, 1987. Mem. Am. Psychiat. Assn. Office: 866 U N Plz Rm 473 New York NY 10017-1822

BERMAN, CHERYL R., advertising company executive; b. Chgo. BA in Journalism, U. Ill., Urbana. Copywriter, various positions Leo Burnett Co., Chgo., 1974-99, chief creative officer, chmn. U.S. bd. dirs., 1999—. Composer advt. music for McDonald's, Hallmark, Kraft, Walt Disney World, Chgo. Bulls; songwriter/composer Remember the Magic, Celebrate the Future Hand in Hand. Named Ad Woman of Yr. Women's Advt. Club Chgo., 1997.

BERMAN, DEBBIE L., lawyer; b. 1966; AB in Economics, summa cum laude, Brandeis U., 1987; JD cum laude, Harvard Law Sch., 1990. Bar: Ill., US Ct. (No. Dist. Ill.), US Tax Ct. Ptnr., co-chmn. trade secrets and unfair competition practice Jenner & Block LLP. Mem. alum. admissions coun. Brandeis Univ., 1990—; comm. mem. EZRA Multi-Service Ctr., 1996—; mem. bd. dir. Jewish Cmty. Ctr. Chgo., 1998—2003, Jewish United Fund/ Jewish Fedn. Chgo., 2003—; v.p., mem. bd. trustees Temple Anshe Sholom, Chgo., 2001—. Named Ill. Super Lawyer in 1st Amendment and media, 2005, Super Lawyer in bus. litigation, 2006; named one of 40 Under Forty, Crain's Bus. Chgo., 2005, New Stars, New Worlds, Lawdragon mag., 2006; recipient Chambers USA award for media and entertainment, 2006, Davis, Gidwitz & Glasser award, Jewish Union Fund/Jewish Fedn. Met. Chgo., 2005. Mem.: Chgo. Bar Assn., Ill. Bar Assn., ABA, Intellectual Property Law Assn. Chgo., Am. Intellectual Property Law Assn., Brandeis Univ. Nat. Alum. Assn., Phi Beta Kappa. Office: Jenner & Block LLP One IBM Plz Chicago IL 60611-7603 Office Phone: 312-923-2764. Office Fax: 312-840-7764. E-mail: dberman@jenner.com.

BERMAN, ELEANOR, writer; b. Birmingham, Ala., May 7, 1934; d. Abraham and Bertha (Sirote) Greenwald; children: Thomas, Eric, Terry Ellen. BA, Smith Coll., Northampton, Mass., 1955. Author: The Cooperating Family, 1977, Re-entering, 1980, The Palm-Aire Spa 7-Day Plan, 1987, Entertaining for Business, 1990, Grandparenting ABC's, 1999, Away for the Weekend travel guides, 1982—2003, Traveling Solo, 1997, 1999, 2001—03, 2005, Recommended Bed and Breakfast Inns: New England, 1998, 2000, 2002, 2006, New York Neighborhoods, 1999, 2001, 2004, New York Top 10, 2002; contbr. Eyewitness Guide to New York, 1994 (Thomas Cook award, best travel guide of yr), articles to publs. Mem.: N.Y. Travel Writers (pres. 1995—96), Soc. Am. Travel Writers.

BERMAN, ELLEN SUE, energy and telecommunications executive, theatre producer; Student, U. N.C., Greensboro, 1960-62, U. N.C., Chapel Hill, summer 1961, U. Calif., Berkeley, summer 1962; BA in Russian, Barnard Coll., 1964. Legis. asst. Senator Joseph Tydings, 1965-66; rsch. assoc. Washington Poverty Program United Planning Orgn., 1966-70; pres. Consumer Energy Coun. Am. Rsch. Found., Washington, 1973—. Mem. Office Tech. Assessment Residential Energy Conservation Adv. Com., 1976-77, Magnetic Fusion Adv. Com., 1986-87, Aspen Inst. Energy Policy Forum; mem. coun. for the Arts MIT, 1995—; mem. Com. on Energy and Econ. Devel. NAACP; mem. German Marshall Fund Adv. Com. on Energy Efficiency in Swedish Bldgs. Co-author: A Decade of Despair, A Compendium of Utility-Sponsored Appliance Rebate Programs, Transportation, Energy and Environment: Balancing Goals and Identifying Policies, 1995, Restructuring the Electric Utility Industry: A Consumer Perspective, 1998; author: Equity and Energy: Rising Energy Prices and the Living Standards of Lower Income Americans, 1983, Oil, Gas or ? A Guide to Saving Heating Dollars, The Consumer and Energy Impacts of Oil Exports, Operating Costs of Refrigerators/Freezers and Room Air Conditioners, If You Want to Lower Your Heating Bill, It's Time to Raise the Roof, A Comparative Analysis of Utility and Non-Utility Based Energy Services Companies, A State by State Compendium of Energy Efficiency Programs Using Oil Overchange Funds; (reports) The Consumer and Energy Impacts of Oil Exports, 1984, A Comprehensive Analysis of a Crude Oil Import Fee: Dismantling a Trojan Horse, 1982, A Comparison of Crude Oil Decontrol and Natural Gas Deregulation: An Analysis of the Impract of Immediate Decontrol of Crude Oil and Related Products on End Use Consumers, Natural Gas Deregulation: A Case of Trickle Up Economics, 1982; pub. The Quad Report, 1993—. Bd. dirs. Barnard in Washington, 1994—; bd. trustees Wider Opportunities for Women; bd. mgrs. Adas Israel Congregation, 1996—; chmn. bldgs. and gounds com. Woodley Park Towers condominium. Named Woman of the Eighties, Ladies Home Jour., 1979; grantee German Marshall Fund. Mem. Barnard Coll. Washington Alumnae Assn. (bd. dirs.), Cosmos Club (admissions com., mem. coun. arts, named one of Key Women 2004). Home: 2737 Devonshire Pl NW Washington DC 20008-3479 Office: Consumer Energy Coun Am 2000 L St NW Ste 802 Washington DC 20036-4913 Office Phone: 202-659-0404.

BERMAN, GAIL, film company executive; b. Aug. 17, 1956; m. Bill Masters, 1980; 2 children. B in Theater, U. Md., 1978. Former exec. prodr. Comedy Channel, HBO; from v.p. TV to pres. and CEO Sandollar Prodns., 1991—97, advisor, 1997—98; founding pres. Regency TV, 1998—2000; pres. entertainment Fox Broadcasting Co., 2000—05; pres. Paramount Pictures, Hollywood, Calif., 2005—. Named one of 100 Most Powerful Women in Entertainment, Hollywood Reporter, 2003, 2004, 2005, 50 Most Powerful Women in Am Bus., Fortune Mag., 2003, 100 Most Powerful Women, Forbes mag., 2005—06; recipient Lucy award, Women in Film, 2003. Office: Paramount Pictures Corp 5555 Melrose Ave Los Angeles CA 90038 Office Phone: 310-369-1000.*

BERMAN, JENNIFER R., urologist; BA in Spanish and psychology, Hollins Coll., 1986; MS in human anatomy and physiology, U. Md. Sch. Medicine, 1988; MD, Boston U. Sch. Medicine, 1992. Resident in gen. surgery U. Md., 1994, resident in urology, 1998; fellow in urology/pelvic floor reconstructive surgery David Geffen Sch. Medicine, LA, 2001; former co-dir. (with sister Laura) Network Excellence in Women's Sexual Health, 1998—2004; co-dir. women's sexual health clinic Boston U. Sch. Medicine, masters med. sci. thesis advisor, 1998, instr. urology, 2000—01; dir. female sexual medicine ctr. UCLA, 2001—; asst. prof. urology UCLA Med. Ctr., 2001—; co-host (with sister Laura) Berman & Berman, Discovery Health Channel, 2004—. Vis. prof. U. Kan. Med. Ctr., 2002, Emory U., Atlanta, 2003; lectr. in field; mem. editl. bd. Healthgate Inc., Sexual Health Capsule and Comment; mem. sci. adv. bd. Quanlilife Pharm., Cellegy Pharm., Auxillum. Co-author (with sister Laura): For Women Only: A Revolutionary Guide to Overcoming Sexual Dysfunction and Reclaiming Your Sex Life, 2001, Secrets of the Sexually Satisfied Woman, 2005; contbr. articles to profl. jour. Named Women's Health Adv. Yr., Calif. Gov. Conf. Women, 2001; recipient Rising Star Yr., Nat. Assn. Women Bus. Owners, 2002, Women of Action award, Israel Cancer Rsch. Fund, 2002, Women Who Make a Difference award, LA Bus. Jour., 2002, Outstanding Programming award, Cable Positive /TV Guide, 2003. Mem.: AMA, Am. Urological Assn., Soc. Study Impotence, Sexual Medicine Soc. N. Am., Internat. Soc. Study Women's Sexual Health.

BERMAN, LAURA, journalist, writer; b. Detroit, Dec. 8, 1953; d. Seymour Donald and Rose (Mendelson) B. AB, U. Mich., 1975. Writer, reporter Detroit Free Press, 1976-86; columnist The Detroit News, 1986-93; freelance writer, 1994—; sr. writer The Detroit News, 1995-98; columnist Detroit News, 1998—. Spkr. in field, vis. prof. Univ. Mich., Dearborn, 2005 Mem. Soc. Profl. Journalists. Office: The Detroit News 999 Haynes St Ste 260 Birmingham MI 48009 E-mail: lberman@detnews.com.

BERMAN, LAURA, sex therapist; BA in anthropology, U. Vt., 1990; MA in health edn., NYU Sch. Edn., 1992; MSW, NYU, 1994, PhD in philosophy, 1997. Fellow in human sexual therapy NYU Med. Ctr., 1997; former co-dir. (with sister Jennifer) Women's Sexual Health Clinic, Boston U. Med. Ctr.; co-dir. (with sister Jennifer) Network Excellence Women's Sexual Health; clinical asst. prof. ob-gyn. and psychiatry Feinberg Sch. Medicine Northwestern U.; dir. Berman Ctr., Chgo., 2004—; co-host (with sister Jennifer) Berman & Berman: For Women Only, Discovery Health Channel, 2004—. Co-author (with sister Jennifer): For Women Only: A Revolutionary Guide to Overcoming Sexual Dysfunction and Reclaiming Your Sex Life, 2001, Secrets of the Sexually Satisfied Woman, 2005; actor: (TV series) Sexual Healing, 2006. Found. bd. mem. Soc. Sci. Study Sexuality (SSSS). Named one of 40 Under 40, Crains' Chicago Business, 2005; recipient Rising Star Yr., Nat. Assn. Women Bus. Owners, LA, 2002, Women Action award, Israel Cancer Rsch. Fund, 2002. Mem.: Am. Assn. Sex Educators, Counselors, and Therapists, Internat. Soc. Study Women's Sexual Health, Am. Assn. Social Workers. Office: Berman Ctr LLC 211 E Ontario Ste 800 Chicago IL 60611 Office Phone: 800-709-4709, 312-255-8088. Office Fax: 312-255-8007.*

BERMAN, LORI BETH, lawyer; b. N.Y.C., June 27, 1958; d. George Gilbert and Sara Ann (Abrams) B.; m. Jeffrey Ganeles, Nov. 26, 1983; children: Caryn Elissa, Steven Aaron. BA magna cum laude, Tufts U., 1980; JD, George Washington U., 1983; LLM, U. Miami, 2002. Assoc. Margolies, Edelstein & Scherlis, Phila., 1983-84, White and Williams, Phila., 1984-87, Brownstein Zeidman & Schomer, Washington, 1987-89; v.p. legal & compliance Pointe Savs. Bank, Boca Raton, Fla., 1990-95; dist. rep. Congressman Robert Wexler, Boca Raton, 1997-99; assoc. Belson & Lewis, Boca Raton, Fla., 2002—. Mem., Jour. Internat. Law and Econs. Mem. exec. coun. United Jewish Appeal Fedn., Washington, 1987-89, Boca Raton, 1990—, Leadership Boca, 1992. Mem. ABA, D.C. Bar Assn., Fla. Bar Assn., Boca Raton C. of C. Democrat. Jewish. Office Phone: 561-750-7600.

BERMAN, LOUISE MARGUERITE, education educator, writer; b. Hartford, Conn., July 6, 1928; d. Jacob and Anna Bertha (Woike) B. AB, Wheaton Coll., 1950; MA, Columbia U., 1953, EdD, 1960. Instr. Central Conn. State Coll., New Britain, 1954-58; asst. prof., then assoc. prof. curriculum U. Wis., Milw., 1960-65; assoc. sec. Assn. for Supervision and Curriculum Devel., Washington, 1965-67; prof. edn. U. Md., College Park, 1967-93, prof. emerita, 1993—, dir. U. Center for Young Children, 1967-75, prof. dept. ednl. policy, planning and adminstrn., 1967-93, interim chmn. dept., 1978-81, assoc. dean Coll. Edn., 1979-81. Vis. prof. U. P.R., 1969, U. B.C., 1977, 78; mem. U.S. Nat. Com. for Early Childhood Edn., 1969- Author: From Thinking to Behaving, 1967, New Priorities in the Curriculum, 1968, Supervision, Staff Development and Leadership, 1971, Beyond Confrontation: An Analysis of Power, 1973, (with Jessie A. Roderick) Curriculum: Teaching the What, How and Why of Living, 1977; editor: (with Jessie Roderick) Feeling, Valuing, and the Art of Growing: Perspectives on the Affective, 1977, (with Alice Miel) Educating for World Cooperation, 1983; (with others) Toward Curriculum for Being: Voices of Educators, 1991, Being Called to Care, 1994; mem. editl. bd. Teaching Education, Jour. of Curriculum and Supervision, Ednl. Forum. Trustee McCormick Theol. Sem., 1994-2003; headmaster's adv. coun. St. Patrick's Episcopal Day Sch., 1996-2003, curriculum cons., 1997-98; elder NY Ave. Presbyn. Ch. Mem. ASCD (bd. dirs., pres. Md. unit 1978-79), Am. Ednl. Rsch. Assn. (disting. contbr. to curriculum award divsn. B), World Coun. on Curriculum and Instrn. (exec. com. 1971-74, 82-83, pres. 1979-81, pres. adv. coun. 1999—), Common Cause, World Future Soc., Profs. Curriculum, Cosmos Club, Pi Lambda Theta, Kappa Delta Pi (laureate, counsellor 1992-96), Phi Delta Kappa. Presbyterian. Home: 4000 Cathedral Ave NW Apt 243B Washington DC 20016-5278

BERMAN, MIRA, advertising agency executive; b. Danzig, June 1, 1928; d. Max and Riva (Gutman) B.; m. Richard D. Freedman, Jan. 23, 1972. Student, Profl. Children's Sch., Berkshire Music Sch. and Festival, Juilliard Sch. Music, David Mannes Coll. Music, NYU, Columbia U. Chief copywriter Girl Scouts U.S., 1948-50; sr. copywriter Bamberger's, 1950-52; advt. dir., head women fashions Bond Stores, 1952-55; copy dir. Robert Hall, 1955-56; advt. copy dir. Gimbel's, N.Y.C., 1956-57; dir. pub. rels., fashion Snellenburg's, 1957-59; sr. v.p. pub. rels. and advt. Lavenson Bur. Advt., 1959-66; pres. Allerton, Berman & Dean, 1966-76; chairperson, chief exec. officer Gemini Images, Inc., 1976-86; pres. The Bradford Group, 1986—. Mem. faculty master's degree program in tourism and travel adminstrn. New Sch. for Social Research, N.Y.C.; Co-chmn. 1st ann. Internat. Symposium Travel and Tourism, Am. Mgmt. Assn.; co-chmn. 1st ann. Marketing Through Retailers Symposium, 1966-67, staff lectr., 1967-70; condr. Modern Bank Practices Seminars; Am. Assn. Advt. Agencies rep. to Nat. Advt. Rev. Bd. Author: Marketing Through Retailers, 1967, also Spanish and Japanese edits; Travel editor: Woman's Life Mag. Exec. dir. Am. Friends of Ezrath Nashim Hosp., Jerusalem Geriatric and Mental Health Ctr., 1986-91, The Africa Travel Assn., 1990—, Assembly of Nat. Tourist Office Reps., 1991—, Nat. Coun. of Women U.S.A., 1988-90, Am. Israel Opera Found., 1986-89; dir. devel. PROMESA Found., Inc. Recipient Israel Ministry Tourism award; Fashion Gold medal; Carl V. Cesery award Tile Contractors Assn. Am.; silver award; bronze award; AMITA Sister award; winner Gold medal Internat. Film and TV Festival N.Y., Grand award. Mem. Am. Advt. Fedn. (named one of Ten Top Women in Advt.), Fin. Publicist Assn. Am., The Fashion Group, Pub. Rels. Soc. Am. (bd. govs.), Phila. Pub. Rels. Assn., Am. Soc. Travel Agts., Soc. Advancement Travel for Handicapped (dir. travellers with disabilities awareness week), International Tourism Assn., Nat. Coun. Women, Women Execs. Internat. (exec. dir.) Home: 116 Central Park S New York NY 10019-1559 Office: The Bradford Group 347 5th Ave Ste 610 New York NY 10016-5010 Office Phone: 212-447-0027. Office Fax: 212-725-8253. Business E-Mail: bradfordmktg@aol.com.

BERMAN, MIRIAM NAOMI, librarian; b. Phila., May 27, 1929; d. Max Isaac and Sonia Leona (Brown) Mosevitzky; m. Aaron Arthur Berman, July 4, 1955; children: David Hirsh, Raphael Judah, Michael Jonah. BA, CUNY, 1950, MA, 1952; MLS, Pratt Inst., 1975. Lic. profl. librarian, N.Y.; lic. elem and secondary tchr., N.Y. Tchr. Crown Heights Yeshiva, Bklyn., 1950-52, Pub. Sch. 26/N.Y.C. Bd. Edn., Bklyn., 1952-64; exec. Aaron Berman Gallery, N.Y.C., 1976-77; librarian Bklyn. Pub. Library, 1977-79, Aviation High Sch., L.I., N.Y., 1979-89, Sheepshead Bay High Sch., Bklyn., 1989-96; ret., 1996. Juror Art Auction Com., N.Y.C., 1972-77. Mem. N.Y.C. Library Assn. (treas. 1985-87). Avocations: music, art, theater, ballet.

BERMAN, PATRICIA KARATSIS, art director; b. San Francisco, Oct. 2, 1953; d. George Emanuel and Hermoine Linda (Foster) Karatsis; m. William Issachar Berman, May 15, 1979; children: Ian, Melissa, Benjamin. BS, Duke U., 1975; MA, NYU, 1977. Dir. Vorpal Gallery, N.Y.C., 1976-83; visual arts coord. East End Arts Coun., Riverhead, N.Y., 1983-89, program dir., 1989-94, exec. dir., 1994-97; dir. mem. svcs. Alliance on N.Y. State Orgns., 1997—2005, assoc. dir., 1999—2005. Cons. N. State Coun. on Arts, NYC, 1985—, Suffolk Assn. Jewish Schs., Huntington, NY, 1985; adj. lectr. dept. anthropology Bklyn. Coll., 1976-77, Drew U., 1977; adj. tech. asst. dept. instrn. Suffolk County CC, 1992-93; bd. dirs. Riverhead Bus. Improvement Dist., chair; panelist NJ State Coun. on Arts, 2005 Contbr. articles to East End Arts News; host cable arts show, 1986-87. Adminstr. L.I. Baroque Ensemble, 1996—; panelist N.J. State Coun. on the Arts, 2005—; Trustee Commack (N.Y.) Jewish Ctr., 1984—86. Mem. Duke U. Alumni (AAAC chair Suffolk County 1998-2004). Home: 22 Daisy Ln Commack NY 11725-4106 E-mail: pkbarts@aol.com.

BERMAN, RACHEL, dancer; b. Berkeley, Calif., Nov. 14, 1963; d. Ronald Berman and Judith Ellen Harding; m. Eric Charles Benz, Nov. 20, 1988. BFA, SUNY, Purchase, 1985. Dancer Ballet Hispanico of N.Y., N.Y.C., 1985-87, Joyce Trisler Danscompany, N.Y.C., 1987-89, May O'Donnel Concert Dance Co., N.Y.C., 1988, Paul Taylor Dance Co., N.Y.C., 1989—; dir. Tau Dance Studio, Honolulu, 2002—. Dancer benefit for Paul Newman's Hole in Wall Gang Camp for Children, 1995, Paul Taylor: Speaking in Tongues, PBS Dance in Am. TV program, 1991, Paul Taylor: The Wrecker's Ball, PBS Dance in Am. TV program, 1996; profiled in Vanity Fair mag., 1993, cover story in Dance mag., 1997. Active Dancers Responding to AIDS, 2003-. Avocations: scuba diving, travel, swimming, sewing. Office: Paul Taylor Dance Co 552 Broadway Fl 2D New York NY 10012-3947

BERMAN, RENEE CAGGIANO, lawyer; b. Malden, Mass., June 27, 1977; d. Benjamin J. and Deborah C. Caggiano; m. David Jason Berman, Sept. 14, 2003; 1 child, Ethan J. JD, Suffolk U. Law Sch., Boston, MA, 2000—03. Bar: Conn. 2003, U.S. Dist. Ct., Conn. 2004. Asst. fin. dir. Clapprood for Congress, Boston, 1998; legislative/media cons. Pub. Strategies, Inc., New Haven, 1999—2000; assoc. Nuzzo & Roberts, Chesire, Conn., 2003—04, Law Offices of Frank J. Riccio LLC, Bridgeport, Conn., 2004—; legislative advisor Connsensus Govtl. Consulting, Hartford, Conn., 2002—03. Pro bono atty. Law Works, Conn., 2004—. Vol. for read aloud day in new haven pub. schools New Haven County Bar Assn., New Haven, Conn., 2006; del. Mass. Dem. Conv., Springfield, Mass., 2001—01. Recipient Scholar award, Sigma Delta Tau, 1996—97. Mem.: Greater Bridgeport County Bar Assn., New Haven County Bar Assn. (assoc.). Democrat-Npl. Avocation: reading. Office: Law Offices of Frank J Riccio 923 East Main St Bridgeport CT 06608 Office Phone: 203-333-6135.

BERMAN, SANDRA RITA, retired personnel director; b. Washington, June 21, 1938; d. Max and Ethel (Gerber) Fulton; m. Malcolm C. Berman, Mar. 3, 1957; children: Steven, Gary, Richard. Student, Towson U., Villa Julie Coll. Lic. real estate agt., Md. Dir. pers. Fairfax Savs. Assn., Balt., 1983-94, ret., 1994. Former den mother, organizer Boy Scouts Am.; past pres. Mothers Club, Homewood Sch., former pres. Ft. Garrison Elem. Sch. PTA; 1st v.p. Beth El Sisterhood, Balt., 1982-84, pres., 1984-86; del. Women's League for Conservative Judaism, Balt., 1984; trustee Beth El Congregation, 1984-95, also chmn. various coms.; mem. Congregation B'nai Torah, Boca Raton, Fla.; bd. dirs. Md. Bd. Barber Examiners, 1987-94. Mem. Hadassah (life), Order Ea. Star. Democrat. Avocations: boating, travel, reading, music, tennis.

BERMAN, SHARI SPRINGER, film director, scriptwriter; b. NYC, July 1964; m. Robert Pulcini. BA, Wesleyan U., 1985; MFA in Film, Columbia U., 1985. Author: (screenplays) Am. Splendor, 2003 (Grand Jury prize Sundance Film Festival, 2003, Critics award Cannes Film Festival, 2003, Open Palm award IFP, 2003, New Dir.'s award Edinburgh (Scotland) Internat. Film Festival, 2003, Best Film, Montreal's (Can.) Comedia Festival, 2003, Critics award Deauville Film Festival, 2003, nominated Best Adapted Screenplay Acad. Awards, 2003, Best Adapted Screenplay, Writers Guild, 2003, Best Film and Best Screenplay, Nat. Soc. Film Critics and LA Film Critics Assn., 2003, Best First Feature, NY Film Critics Cir., Chgo. Film Critics, Toronto Film Critics and Fla. Film Critics, 2003); co-dir.: (films) Off The Menu: The Last Days of Chasen's, 1997 (One of Ten Best Movies of 1998, USA Today and CNN, 1998, Best Documentary Grand Jury award Hamptons Internat. Film Festival, Spl. Jury award Locarno Internat. Film Festival, Spl. Jury award Newport Film Festival), The Young and the Dead, 2000, Hello, He Lied, 2002.

BERMAN ROBINSON, SHERRY H., science educator, consultant; b. Bkyln., Apr. 2, 1951; d. Arthur and Zelda Bowen; 1 child, Rachel Berman. BS in Chemistry and Math., SUNY, Buffalo, 1971; MS in Chemistry, U. Ill., Chgo., 1972; Tyre 75 in Gen. adminstr., Loyola U., Chgo., 1991. Sci. tchr. Homewood Flossmoor HS, Ill., 1972—76, Homeward Flossmoor HS, Ill., 1979—81; sci. and math. instr. Syracuse U. & Onadga CC, Syracuse, NY, 1976—79; chemistry tchr. Consolidated HSD 230, Orland Park, Ill., 1981—2006. Presenter in field. Recipient Excellence in Chemistry Tchg. award, Chem. Industries Coun., 1986, 1998, Nat. Catalyst award winner, Chemical Manufacturing Assn., 1988, Tandy Tech. award. Mem.: NSTA, Am. Chemical Soc., ISTA (Semi Finalist Shell Sci. Tchr. award 1992, 1993), IEA, NEA, Phi Beta Kappa. Democrat. Jewish. Avocations: piano, chemistry, baseball, swimming. Personal E-mail: sbr51@hotmail.com.

BERMUDEZ, EUGENIA M. See DIGNAC, GENY

BERN, DORRIT J., apparel executive; b. Apr. 28, 1950; 3 children. BSc in Bus., U. Wash., 1972. Various positions The Bon Marche, Joske's; v.p. women's apparel Sears, Roebuck & Co., 1987—92, group v.p. women's apparel & home furnishings, 1993—95; pres., CEO Charming Shoppes, Inc., Bensalem, Pa., 1995—, vice chmn., 1995—97, chmn., 1997—. Bd. dirs. So. Co. Atlanta, Charming Shoppes, Inc., 1995—, Office Max Inc., 2006—. Mem. Active Keeping Kids Warm, Bensalem, Pa. Recipient Pa. Best 50 Women in Bus. award, 1997, Women of Distinction award, The Phila. Bus. Jour., Nat. Assn. Women's Bus. Owners, Forum Exec. Women, 1998, Entrepreneur of the Yr., Ernst & Young, 2001, Visionary Woman award, Moore Coll. Art & Design, 2004, H.U.G. award, Intimate Apparel Sq. Club, 2005, Paradigm award, Greater Phila. C. of C., 2006. Mem.: Women Bus. Leaders, Com. of 200, Fashion Group Internat., Atlanta C. of C. (bd. dirs.). Office: Charming Shoppes Inc 450 Winks Ln Bensalem PA 19020-5993*

BERNABEI, LYNNE ANN, lawyer; b. Highland Park, Ill., Apr. 11, 1950; d. Guy and Anna (Tamarri) Bernabei. BA, Harvard U., 1972, JD, 1977. Bar: DC 1997, admitted to practice: US Dist. Ct. (DC) 1977, US Ct. Appeals (DC Cir.) 1979, US Ct. Appeals (3rd Cir.) 1985, US Ct. Appeals (Fed. Cir.) 1988, US Supreme Ct. 1988, US Ct. Appeals (4th Cir.) 1992, US Ct. Appeals (6th Cir.). Clk. US Dist. Ct. Judge William Bryant, Washington, 1977-78; assoc. Tigar & Buffone, Washington, 1978-80; clin. instr. Georgetown U., Washington, 1980-81; gen. counsel Govt. Accountability Project, Washington, 1981-85; ptnr. Newman, Sobol, Trister & Owens, Washington, 1985-87, Bernabei & Katz, Washington, 1987—2006, Bernabei Law Firm PLLC, Washington, 2006—. Co-author: The High Citadel: On the Influence of Harvard Law School, 1978; contbr. articles to profl. jours. and revs. Named one of 75 Best Lawyers in Washington, Washingtonian mag., 2002. Fellow: Coll. Labor and Employment Lawyers; mem.: ATLA, ABA, Nat. Lawyers Guild, Trial Lawyers for Pub. Justice. Office: Bernabei Law Firm PLLC 1775 T St NW Washington DC 20009-7124 Office Phone: 202-745-1942. Business E-Mail: bernabei@bernabeipllc.com. E-mail: lbernabei@aol.com.

BERNAL, HARRIET JEAN DANIELS, real estate agent; b. Cin., Sept. 28, 1931; d. Ernest Richard and Amy Lillian (Jeffries) Daniels; m. Gil Bernal, July 9, 1950; children: Gil Jr., Lisa, Nicholas, Colette, Michelle. AA in Theatre Arts, Los Angeles City Coll., 1949-62; student, Kimballs Real Estate Sch., Burbank, Calif., 1974; AA in Humanities, Glendale Coll., 1982; BA in Polit. Sci. Pre-Law, Calif. State U., Los Angeles, 1987. Lic. real estate agt. Dancer, entertainer Greek Theatre, Los Angeles, 1949-50; travel, reservation agt. Iver's Dept. Store, Los Angeles, 1970-73, editor, dept. store news letters, 1972-73; sec. to area supt. and social chmn. Los Angeles Bd. Edn., 1973-74; exec. sec. CBS-TV City, Los Angeles, 1974; real estate salesperson, relocation mgr. Century 21 Realty, Los Angeles, Pasadena, Calif., San Marino, Calif., 1974-86; real estate salesperson Coldwell Banker Residential, Pasadena, Cailf., 1986-89, Glendale, Cailf., 1989-91, John Douglas Co., Pasadena, Calif., 1991-93; real estate sales, leasing agt., loan cons. Bill Davis & Assoc., South Pasadena, Calif., 1993—. Contbr. articles on sch. sci. ctrs., schs. in Russia, and schs. for the handicapped for local sch. paper, Ann. awards. Pres. San Pascual Elem. Sch. PTA, L.A., 1969-70, hon. life mem., 1970—; first soprano Consortium Angeli, 1991-92; fundraiser various groups to elect Mayor Tom Bradley, L.A.; wedding hostess Pasadena (Calif.) Ch. of Angels, 1980-88, also lic. lay minister. Mem. Pasadena Bd. Realtors (local govt. com., polit. affairs com.), Met. Player Guild. Democrat. Episcopalian. Avocations: acting, singing, writing, jewelry making, painting. Home: 1075 Rutland Ave Los Angeles CA 90042-1536 Office: Dilbeck Betters Home & Gardens Realtors 1499 Huntington Dr South Pasadena CA 91030-4552

BERNARD, APRIL, poet, literature educator; BA, Harvard U. Former sr. editor Premiere, GQ, Vanity Fair; instr. Amherst Coll., Yale U.; prof. lit., MFA core faculty Bennington Coll., 1998—2003, assoc. dean acad. affairs Vt., 2003—. Author: (novels) Pirate Jenny, (poetry) Blackbird Bye Bye (Walt Whitman prize, Acad. Am. Poets), Psalms: Poems, 1993, Swan Electric: Poems, 2002; contbr. poems, literary essays, and articles to various publs. Guggenheim fellow, 2003. Office: Bennington Coll One College Dr Bennington VT 05201 Office Phone: 802-442-5401. E-mail: aprilbernard@earthlink.net.

BERNARD, BETSY J., former telecommunications industry executive; b. May 1955; BS, St. Lawrence U.; MBA, Fairleigh Dickinson U.; MS, Stanford U.; LLD (hon.), Pepperdine U., 2003. Various positions in sales, mktg., opers. AT&T; pres., CEO Pacific Telesis Group Pacific Bell Comms., 1995-97; CEO AVIRNEX Comms. Group, 1997-98; pres. U S West Long Distance US West, Inc., 1998, exec. v.p. retail markets Denver, 1998—2000; exec. v.p., nat. mass markets Qwest Comm. Internat., 2000—01; pres., CEO AT&T Consumer unit, 2001—02; pres. AT&T Bus. unit, 2002—03, AT&T Corp., Bedminster, NJ, 2002—03. Bd. dir. Prin. Fin. Group, 2001—, Zantaz.com, United Technologies, 2003—, URS, 2004—, BearingPoint, Inc., 2004—. Featured in Eleven Commandments of Wildly Successful Women. V.p. comms. Internat. Women's Forum; bd. dirs. Mile High United Way; active Denver Cmty. Named Most Influential Bus. Woman, San Francisco, 1996. Mem.: Wise Women's Coun.*

BERNARD, CAROLINE A., lawyer; b. Frankfurt, Germany, Jan. 22, 1973; d. John van Valzah and Mary Anne Marie Bernard. BS Internat. Trade and Fin., La. State U., Baton Rouge, 1995; JD Admiralty cert., Tulane U., New Orleans, 1999. Bar: La. 1999, S.C. 2003. Asst. dist. atty. Orleans Parish Dist. Attys. Office, New Orleans, 1999—2003; asst. solicitor 9th Jud. Cir. Solicitor Office, Charleston, SC, 2003—04; assoc. Motley Rice LLC, Mt. Pleasant, SC, 2004—. Active Jr. League Charleston, 2005—. Mem.: ATLA, WLA, S.C. Trial Lawyers Assn. Avocations: tennis, swimming, reading. Office: Motley Rice LLC 28 Bridgeside Dr Mount Pleasant SC 29464

BERNARD, CATHY S., management corporation executive; b. Bronx, N.Y., Nov. 13, 1949; d Burton and Norma (Ebb) B. BBA, George Washington U., 1971, M of Pub. Adminstrn., 1978; MA, U. Miami, 1972. Cert. property mgr. Staff asst. HEW, Washington, 1970-74; evaluation specialist OEO, Washington, 1974; tchr. St. Patrick's Acad., Washington, 1975; asst. prof. No. Va. C.C., Woodbridge, 1976-78; adj. prof. Prince George's CC, 2002; staff dir. Dem. Nat. Conv., N.Y.C., 1976; pres., chief exec. officer CSB Assocs. Mgmt. Corp., Riverdale, Md., 1977—. Mem. Housing Opportunities Commn., Kensington, Md., 1979-93, chmn., 1988, vice chair, 1980, 87, chair pro tem, 1986, chair housing honor roll, 1985-88, Moderate Priced Dwelling Unit Commn.; mem. exec. coun. Inst. Real Estate Mgmt., Washington, 1982-87, cert. property mgr.; adj. prof. bus. Prince Georges C.C., 2002. Adv. coun. Suburban Hosp., Bethesda, Md., 1984-89; bd. dirs. Ivymount Sch. for Handicapped, Potomac, Md., 1984—, chmn. bd. dirs., 2003, chair property com., chair bldg. expansion project, 1999-2002; treas. Jewish Coun. on Aging, 1988; bd. dirs., chair property com. Jewish Found. for Group Homes, Rockville, Md., 1989-91; bd. dirs. Roundhouse Theatre, Wheaton, Md., 1994—, treas., 1995—; bd. dirs. McLean Sch. Md., 2001, trustee 2001—04, vice chmn., sec., site com. chair, 2002; bd. dirs. Bethesda's Imagination State, 2003—; trustee Temple Emanuel, Kensington, Md., 1994-97; candidate Md. State Legislature, 1986; pres. Cmty. Housing Res. Bd., 1985. Recipient Hughes award for property mgmt., 1980, Jewish Coun. award, 1989. Mem. Montgomery County C. of C. (bd. dirs., v.p. housing com. 1981-82), Apt. and Office Bldg. Assn. (bd. dirs., chmn. affordable housing com. 1990-99). Office: CSB Assocs Mgmt Corp PO Box 647 Riverdale MD 20738-0647

BERNARD, MARCELLE THOMASINE, physician; b. N.Y.C., Aug. 11, 1920; d. Rene Jules and Antoinette (Byrnes) Bernard. AB Magna cum laude, Coll. of St. Elizabeth, 1941; MD, N.Y. Med. Coll., 1944. Diplomate Nat. Bd. Med. Examiners. Intern Flower and Fifth Ave. Hosps., 1944—45; gen. practice medicine N.Y.C., 1947—75; attending phys. St. Francis Hosp., Bronx, NY, 1950—57, Union Hosp., N.Y.C., 1957—75; attending staff Frances Schervier Home and Hosp., N.Y.C., 1952—75; pres. med. bd., 1959—60; sec., 1962; attending staff St. Patrick's Home, N.Y.C., 1954—75; pres. med. bd., 1962. Mem. exec. com. Bronx Tb and Health Assn., 1956—60; hon. surgeon Life Sav. Svc., N.Y.C., 1959—62; v.p. Bronxboro Commn. on Aging, 1961—62. Mem. Ladies of Charity. Lt. USMC, lt. Women's Res. USN, 1945—47. Fellow: Am. Geriatrics Soc., Am. Acad. Family Practice.

BERNARD, PAMELA JENKS, lawyer; b. Montgomery, Ala., Nov. 27, 1955; d. Harford Perry and Mable (Sawyer) Jenks; m. Geoffrey Pedrick Bernard, Sept. 19, 1981. BA, U. Fla., 1976, JD, 1981. Bar: Fla. 1982, U.S. Dist. Ct. (mid. dist.) Fla. 1983, U.S. Ct. Appeals (11th cir.) 1983. Asst. atty. U. Fla., Gainesville, 1982-83, assoc. gen. counsel, 1983-87, gen. counsel, 1987—2006; v.p., gen. counsel Duke U., Durham, NC, 2006—. Pvt. investment trustee, Gainesville, 1976-83. Mem. Nat. Assn. Coll. and Univ. Attys. (former pres.). Office: Duke U Office of Univ Counsel Box 3024 Med Ctr Durham NC 27710 Office Phone: 919-684-3955. E-mail: pam.bernard@duke.edu.*

BERNAY, BETTI, artist; d. David Michael and Anna Gaynia (Bernay) Woolin; children: Manette Deitsch, Karen Lynn. Grad. costume design, Pratt Inst.; student, Nat. Acad. Design, N.Y.C., Art Students League. Exhibited one man shows at Galerie Raymond Duncan, Paris, France, Salas Municipales, San Sebastian, Spain, Circulo de Bellas Artes, Madrid, Spain, Bacardi Gallery, Miami, Fla., Columbia (S.C.) Mus., Columbus (Ga.) Mus., Galerie Andre Weil, Paris, Galerie Hermitage, Monte Carlo, Monaco, Casino de San Remo, Italy, Galerie de Arte de la Caja de Ahorros de Ronda, Malaga, Spain, Centro Artistico, Granada, Spain, Circulo de la Amistad, Cordoba, Spain, Studio H Gallery, N.Y.C., Walter Wallace Gallery, Palm Beach, Fla., Mus. Bellas Artes, Malaga, Harbor House Gallery, Crystal House Gallery, Internat. Gallery, Jordan Marsh, Fontainebleau Gallery, Miami Beach, Carriage House Gallery, Galerie 99, Pageant Gallery, Miami Beach, Rosenbaum Galleries, Palm Beach; exhibited group shows at Painters and Sculptors Soc., Jersey City Mus., Salon de Invierno, Mus. Malaga, Salon des Beaux Arts, Cannes, France, Guggenheim Gallery, Nat. Acad. Gallery, Salmagundi Club, Lever House, Lord & Taylor Art Gallery, Nat. Arts Gallery, Knickerbocker Artists, N.Y.C., Salon des Artistes Independants, Salon des Artistes Francais, Salon Populiste, Paris, Salon de Otono, Nat. Assn. Painters and Sculptors Spain, Madrid, Phipps Gallery, Palm Beach, Artists Equity, Hollywood (Fla.) Mus., Gault Gallery Cheltenham, Phila., Springfield (Mass.) Mus., Met. Mus. and Art Center, Miami, Fla., Planet Ocean Mus., Charter Club, Trade Fair Ams.; represented in permanent collections including Jockey Club Art Gallery, Miami, Mus. Malaga, Circulo de la Amistad, I.O.S. Found., Geneva, Switzerland, others. Bd. dirs. Men's Opera Guild, Project Newborn Neonatal unit Jackson Meml. Hosp.; mem. adv. bd. Jackson Meml. Hosp. Project Newborn; mem. women's com. Bascom Palmer Eye Inst., mem. adv. coun.; mem. working com. Greater Miami Heart Assn., Am. Heart Assn., Am. Cancer Soc., Alzheimer Grand Notable, 2d Generation Miami Heart Inst., Sunrisers Mentally Retarded, Orchid Ball Com., Newborn Neonatal Intensive Care Unit, U. Miami, Jackson Meml. Hosp.; founder Mt. Sinai Hosp., Miami; benefactor Miami Heart Rsch. Inst.; grand benefactor Neonatal Project Newborn, Jackson Meml. Hosp., Miami Opera, Am. Cancer Soc., Am. Heart Assn., Alzheimers Notable Care Unit, Greater Miami Opera Guild, March of Dimes, CancerLink, Sylvester Cancer Unit; adv. coun. Bascom Palmer Eye Inst.; founder Mt. Sinai Hosp. Recipient medal City N.Y., medal Sch. Art Leagues, N.Y.C., Prix de Paris Raymond Duncan, others. Mem. Nat. Assn. Painters and Sculptors Spain, Nat. Assn. Women Artists, Société des Artistes Français, Société des Artistes Independants, Fedn. Francais des Sociétés d'Art Graphique et Plastique, Artists Equity, Am. Artists Profl. League, Am. Fedn. Art, Nat. Soc. Lit. and Arts, Met. Mus. and Arts Center Miami, Pres.'s Club U. Miami, Palm Bay Club, Jockey Club, Turnberry Club, Club of Clubs Internat. Address: 10155 Collins Ave Apt 1705 Bal Harbour FL 33154-1629

BERNDT, ELLEN GERMAN, lawyer; b. Schenectady, N.Y., 1953; BS, Denison U., 1975; JD, Capital U., 1984. Bar: Ohio 1984. Legal asst. Borden Chem. Inc., Columbus, Ohio, 1978-84, corp. atty., 1984-90, asst. sec., corp. atty., 1990-96; corp. sec., asst. gen. counsel Hexion Specialty Chem., Inc. (formerly known as Borden Chem. Inc.), 1996—. Mem.: Ctrl. Ohio Corp. Counsel Assn. (pres. 1997), Soc. Corp. Sec. and Goverance Profls., Assn. Corp. Coun. Office: Hexion Specialty Chemicals Inc 180 E Broad St Columbus OH 43215-3799

BERNE, PATRICIA HIGGINS, psychologist, writer, educator; b. Indpls., Feb. 21, 1934; d. Edward Robert and Esther Josephine (Maschino) Higgins; m. John Henry Berne, June 19, 1957 (div. May 1979); children: Suzanne, Eve, Serena; m. Louis M. Savary, Oct. 11, 1992. Student, Am. U., 1970-72, George Washington U., 1974; MA, Goddard Coll., 1976; PhD, Union Inst., Cin., 1978. Lic. clin. psychologist, Washington. Counselor Campus Ministry Georgetown U., 1978-80; dir. Counseling Ctr. Trinity Coll., Washington, 1979-81; pvt. practice Washington, 1982—; pvt. practice, therapist The Life Ctr., Tampa, Fla., 1992—. Co-dir. Inner Devel. Assocs., Washington, 1990—, adj. prof., 1981—; adj. faculty at several colls. and univs., 1978—; lectr. at confs. internationally, 1980—; cons. DMA, Salem, Mass., 1984-89. Co-author: Prayerways, 1980, Building Self-Esteem in Children, 1981, Dreams and Spiritual Growth, 1984, Kything, 1988, Dream Symbol Work, 1991. Mem. APA,, EMDRIA, EMDR, Assn. for Transpersonal Psychology, Inst. for Noetic Sci., DC Psychol. Assn., Am. Soc. Clin. Hypnosis, Am. Counseling Assn., Am. Psychol. Assn. Roman Catholic. Avocations: travel, theater, mentoring, kayaking. Office: Inner Devel Assocs 3404 Ellenwood Ln Tampa FL 33618-3425 Office Phone: 813-961-8046. Personal E-mail: lousavary@yahoo.com.

BERNE, SUZANNE, writer, educator; b. Washington, 1961; married; children: Avery, Louisa. BA, Wesleyan Univ., Conn., 1982; grad., Iowa Writers' Workshop. Reporter New Haven Advocate; lectr., English, Am. History Harvard Univ. Author: (novels) A Crime in the Neighborhood, 1997 (Orange prize for fiction, Great Britain, 1999), A Perfect Arrangement, 2001, The Ghost at the Table, 2006. Recipient Nat. Endowment for Arts fellowship. Mailing: c/o Algonquin Books of Chapel Hill PO Box 2225 Chapel Hill NC 27515-2225*

BERNER, JUDITH, mental health nurse; b. Tamaqua, Pa., June 19, 1938; d. Ralph Edgar and Ethel Mary (Williams) B. Diploma in nursing, Temple U. Hosp., 1959; AS, Coll. of Ganado, 1975, MS in Cmty. Health, D of Med. Adminstrn. (hon.); BA, Stephens Coll., 1977; MEd, U. Ariz., 1980; LD (hon.), U. Iceland. RN, N.Mex. Nursing adminstr. Project HOPE Internat. Office & Hosp. Ship, Washington, 1970-72; assoc. adminstr. Navajo Nation Health Found., Ganado, Ariz., 1972-79; clin. instr. psychiat. nursing Mo. So. State Coll., Joplin, 1986; nurse/therapist Presbyn. Kaseman Hosp., Albuquerque, 1986-93; emergency svcs. clinician for mental health svcs. Presbyn. Healthcare Sys., 1994-95, Heights Psychiat. Hosp., 1994-95, Charter Heights Behavioral Health Sys., Albuquerque, 1995-2000; regional clin. coord. Mental Health Svcs., Inc., 1995-97; psychiat. cons.-liaison nurse U. N.Mex. Health Scis. Ctr., 1996—2003, Medication Monitoring, Pathways, Inc., 2000—. Mem. ANA (cert. in psychiat. and mental health nursing), AACD, Internat. Acad. Behavioral Medicine, Counseling and Psychotherapy, Inc.

BERNER, MARY, publisher; Publisher, v.p. Glamour Mag., to 1999; pres., CEO Fairchild Publs., NYC, 1999—2005; pres. Fairchild Divsn., Conde Nast Publications, NYC, 2005—. Office: Conde Nast Fairchild Divsn 4 Times Square New York NY 10036-8191

BERNER HARRIS, CYNTHIA KAY, librarian; b. Concordia, Kans., Aug. 31, 1958; d. William Clifford and Donna Darlene (Brown) B.; m. Dwight Harris, May 1, 1999. AA, Cottey Coll., 1978; BA, U. Kans., 1980; MALS, U. Denver, 1981. System cons. Panhandle Libr. Network, Scottsbluff, Nebr., 1981-82; dir. Winfield (Kans.) Pub. Libr., 1982-84; from Westlink br. mgr. to coord. ext. svcs. Wichita (Kans.) Pub. Libr., 1984-95, coord. adminstrv. svcs., 1995—2000, dir. of librs., 2000—. Editor Propeller mag., 1995-96 (Jr. League Wichita); editor (newsletter) LWV, Wichita Met., 1993. Pres. PEO Sisterhood (chpt. IM), Wichita, 1989—90; active Jr. League Wichita; project chair STARBASE, 1997—98, dir. cmty. rels., 1998—99; trustee at large Bibliog. Ctr. for Rsch., 2001—05, exec. com., 2002—04; tech. adv. bd. City of Wichita, 2000—; fin. chair Nat. Conf. for Cmty. and Justice Walk, 2003; chmn.affiliates bd. Kans. Ctr. for Book, 2005—. Mem.: ALA, Kans. Libr. Assn. (chair pub. libr. sect. 1988—89, legis. com. 1997—2001, nominating com. 1998—99, legis. com. 2002—05, govt. affairs com. 2005—, chair govt. affairs com. 2006—), Mountain Plains Libr. Assn. (chair profl. devel. grants com. 1983—84, 1986—87, chair pub. libr. sect. 1988—89, chair intellectual freedom com. 1988—90, sec. 1996—97, nominating com. 1998—2000), Pub. Libr. Assn. (dir. pub. libr. sys. sect. 1995—98, dir. pub. libr. sys. com. 1998—2001). Presbyterian. Home: 6418 Oneil St Wichita KS 67212-6327 Office: Wichita Pub Libr 223 Main St Wichita KS 67202 E-mail: ictbooks@yahoo.com.

BERNHARD, LISA, news correspondent; Intern Rolling Stone mag.; asst. editor Us mag.; correspondent E!, Romance Classics, Total TV, The Cable Guide; dep. editor TV Guide; entertainment correspondent Fox News Channel, 2003—; interviewed numerous celebrities including Michael, Jackson, Ellen DeGeneres, and Paul McCartney. Guest appearances include: Today Show, The View, Access Hollywood, CBS Early Show. Office: Fox News Network LLC 1211 Avenue of the Americas New York NY 10036

BERNHARD, SANDRA, actress, comedienne, singer; b. Flint, Mich., June 6, 1955; d. Jerome and Jeanette B., 1 child. Stand-up comedienne nightclubs, Beverly Hills, Calif., 1974-78; films include Cheech and Chong's Nice Dreams, 1981, The King of Comedy, 1983 (Nat. Soc. Film Critics award), Sesame Street Presents: Follow That Bird, 1985, Track 29, 1988, Without You I'm Nothing, 1990, Hudson Hawk, 1991, Truth or Dare, 1991, Inside Monkey Zetterland, 1993, Dallas Doll, 1994, Unzipped, 1995, Catwalk, 1995, Plump Fiction, 1996, Somewhere in the City, 1997, Lover Girl, 1997, The Apocalypse, 1997, An Alan Smithee Film: Burn Hollywood Burn, 1997, I Woke Up Early the Day I Died, 1998, Exposé, 1998, Wrongfully Accused, 1998, Dinner Rush, 2000, Playing Mona Lisa, 2000, The Third Date, 2003; also appears in Heavy Petting, 1988, Perfect, 1985, The Whoopee Boys, 1986, Casual Sex?, 1988; stage appearances (solo) Without You I'm Nothing, 1988, Giving Till It Hurts, 1992, I'm Still Here.Damn It, 1998-99, Sandra Bernhard: Everything Bad and Beautiful, 2006; TV appearances (host) Living in America, 1990; regular guest The Richard Pryor Show, Late Night with David Letterman; TV series Instant Comedy with the Groundlings, The Hitchhiker, The Full Wax, Tales from the Crypt, Roseanne, Space Ghost Coast to Coast, The Larry Sanders Show, Clueless, Chicago Hope, Highlander, Comedy Central's The A-List, 1992-1993, Superman (voice), Ally McBeal, Hercules (voice), 1999, The Sandra Bernhard Experience (host), 2001-2002; (TV movies) Freaky Friday, 1995, The Late Shift, 1996; albums (co-author 8 songs) I'm Your Woman, 1985, Without You I'm Nothing, 1988, Excuses for Bad Behavior, Part I, 1994; books include Confessions of a Pretty Lady, 1988, Love Love Love, 1993, May I Kiss You On The Lips, Miss Sandra?, 1998.*

BERNHARDT, MARCIA BRENDA, mental health counselor; b. Jersey, N.J., Aug. 22, 1938; d. Jerome and Mitzie (Cohen) B. BA, Fairleigh Dickinson U., 1960; MA, Columbia U., 1960-63, postgrad., 1968-70, Hunter Coll., 1973-74. Nat. cert. counselor. Rsch. asst. Tchrs. Coll., Columbia U., N.Y.C., 1963-64; counselor JOIN, N.Y.C., 1965-66; project assoc. Bd. Higher Edn. N.Y., N.Y.C., 1966-68, Tchrs. Coll, Columbia U., N.Y.C., 1968-70; counselor Nassau Community Coll., Garden City, N.Y., 1970-72; rsch. scientist Div. for Youth, N.Y.C., 1972-73; rsch. assoc. Family Svc. Assn., N.Y.C., 1974-76; counselor Div. Blind Svcs., West Palm Beach, Fla., 1984-96. Sec., chairperson adv. bd. com. Lighthouse for the Blind, West Palm Beach, 1984-90. Mem. AAUW, Am. Mental Health Counselors Assn., Am. Soc. for Handicapped Children in Israel, Hadassah. Democrat. Jewish. Avocations: theater, ballet, opera, art, swimming. Home: 40 Chatham B West Palm Beach FL 33417-1807 Personal E-mail: marciabrend@aol.com.

BERNHARDT, VICTORIA L., director, researcher; d. Richard L. and Marilyn M. Bernhardt; m. James E. Richmond, June 10, 1990. BS, Iowa State U., Ames, 1974, MS, 1977; PhD, U. Oreg., Eugene, 1981. Rsch./evaluation N.W. Regional Ednl. Lab., Portland, Oreg., 1976—79; rsch. cons. Calif. Dept. of Edn., Sacramento, 1980—81; evaluation cons. Calif. Commn. on Tchr. Credentialing, Sacramento, 1981—86; dir., inst. for advanced studies Calif. State U., Chico, 1986—91, exec. dir. Edn. for the Future, 1991—. Author: (book) Using Data to Improve Student Learning in Elementary Schools, The School Portfolio Toolkit: A Planning, Implementation, and Evaluation Guide for Continuous School Improvement, Designing and Using Databases for Sch. Improvement, The Sch. Portfolio: A Comprehensive Framework for Sch. Improvement, First and Second Edition, Data Analysis for Comprehensive Schoolwide Improvement, 1st and 2d edits., Using Data to Improve Student Learning in Middle Schools, Using Data to Improve Student Learning in High Schools, Using Data to Improve Student Learning in School Districts; co-author: The Example School Portfolio, A Companion to the School Portfolio: A Comprehensive Framework for School Improvement. Achievements include development of school portfolio for continuous school improvement; data analysis for school improvement. Office: Edn for the Future 400 W First St Chico CA 95929-0230 Office Phone: 530-898-4482.

BERNI, ROSEMARIAN RAUCH, rehabilitation and oncology nurse; b. Portland, Oreg., Sept. 30, 1925; d. George Laverne and Mabel (Rose) Rauch; m. Albert Hawthorne Berni, Oct. 25, 1947; children: George, Michael, William, Albert. Student, Oreg. State Coll., 1943-44; BS in Nursing, Univ. Oreg., 1947; M in Nursing, U. Wash., 1973. RN Wash., Oreg. Clin. nursing instr. Univ. Oreg. Sch. of Nursing, Portland; spl. duty nurse Doernbecher Hosp., Portland, Oreg., 1948; night supr. Halcyon Psychiat. Hosp., Seattle, Wash., 1962; staff nurse psychiat. nursing unit U. Wash. Hosp., Seattle, 1963, head nurse phys. medicine and rehab. nursing unit, 1964-66, asst. dir. nursing, 1966-67; dir. rehab. med. intermittent catheter team U. Hosp. and Harborview Med. Ctr., Seattle, 1973-82; rehab. clin. nurse specialist U. Wash. Med. Ctr., Seattle, 1973—. Clin. instr. U. Wash. Sch. Nursing, 1967-76, instr. dept. rehab. medicine, 1967-73; dir. nursing svc. Rehab. Nursing Unit, Dept. Rehab. Medicine, U. Wash., Seattle, 1967—; asst. prof. dept. rehab. medicine, U. Wash., 1973-78, assoc. prof. emeritus, 1981, mem. grad. sch. faculty, 1975—; dir. Rehab. Nursing Pathways in Depth, 1967—; chmn. rehab. nursing ctr., ARN 1981; presenter World Rehab. Fund, Cyprus; active on numerous hosp. and univ. coms., presenter many seminars and workshops in Wash. and nationwide. Author: (with Fordyce, Wilbert E.) Behavior Modification and the Nursing Process, 1973, 2nd edit., 1977; contbr. articles to profl. jours. and chpts. to books; producer films, audio and video presentations and course curricula. Vol. RN, Whidbey Island, Wash., 1981-2000; tutor pub. schs. Recipient Svc. award, Wash. State Health Facilities Assn., 1974, Wash. State Heart Assn., 1976, Leadership award, Rehab. Nursing Inst., 1981. Mem. ANA (coun. clin. nurse specialists), Nat. League of Nursing, Assn. of Rehab. Nurses (founding pres. Wash. chpt., nat. pres. 1980, Leadership award 1980), Assn. Women in Sci., N.Y. Acad. Sci., N.W. Neurological Rehab., Nat. Stroke Assn., Wash. State Head Injury Found., Univ. Wash. Alumni Assn., Sigma Theta Tau, Alpha Lambda Delta, Alpha Tau Delta. Home: PO Box 868 Freeland WA 98249-0868 Office: Stroke Support Group Whidbey Gen Hosp Dept Rehab Medicine Seattle WA 98195-0001

BERNICK, CAROL LAVIN, consumer products company executive; m. Howard Bernick; three children. BA, Tulane U., 1974. Dir., v.p. Alberto-Culver Co., 1984, exec. v.p. worldwide mktg., 1990, chmn. bd., 2004—; pres. Alberto-Culver USA, 1994, Alberto-Culver N.Am., 1998, vice chmn., 1998; pres. Alberto Culver Consumer Products Worldwide, 2002. Founder Friends of Prentice; mem. women's bd. Boys and Girls Clubs, Chgo.; regent Lincoln Acad. Ill.; mem. exec. com. of adv. bd. Kellogg Sch., Northwestern U.; mem. Tulane U. Bd.; bd. dirs. Northwestern Meml. Healthcare. Recipient Leadership in Bus. award YWCA Met. Chgo., 1992, award for philanthropy Harvard Club of Chgo., Disting. Alumni award Tulane U., 2003. Mem. World Pres. Orgn., Econ. Club Chgo., Exec. Club Chgo., Com. 200 Chgo. Network. Office: Alberto-Culver Co 2525 Armitage Ave Melrose Park IL 60160-1163 Office Phone: 708-450-3000. Personal E-mail: cbernick@alberto.com.

BERNMÚDEZ, CARMEN, trust company executive; b. Costa Rica, 1944; m. Thomas J. Feeney, 1986. Attended, Colegio Superior de Señprotas, Santa Monica City Coll. Bull fighter, Costa Rica, Mex. City, 1962—67; various positions TWA, 1967—85; chmn., treas. Marathon Asset Mgmt. Co., 1985—94; founder, chmn., CEO Mission Mgmt. & Trust Co., 1994—. Apptd. hon. consul of Costa Rica to US by Pres. of Costa Rica. Worked with Central Am. Free Trade Agreement (CAFTA). Recipient Woman of Enterprise, Avon, 2001, Leading Woman Entrepreneur, STAR Group (sponsored by IBM and Chase Manhattan Banking), 2001. Mem.: US Hispanic C. of C., Nat. Minority Supplier Devel. Coun., Nat. Law Ctr. for InterAmerica Free Trade. Achievements include first woman to run a Fiduciary Trust co. in US. Office: La Paloma Corp Ctr 3567 E Sunrise Dr Ste 235 Tucson AZ 85718-3203 Office Phone: 520-557-5559.

BERNOT, JANE CATHERINE, retired education educator; b. Washington, June 18, 1923; d. Cleveland Hensel and Jeffie Washington (Abel) Stauffer; m. Joseph John Bernot, June 18, 1951; children: Joseph Michael, John Cleveland. AA, George Washington UNiv., Washington, 1944; BS in Physical Edn., George Washington Univ., Washington, 1945; MA in Health Edn., N.Y. U., N.Y., 1950; PhD, The Fielding Inst., Santa Barbara, 1980. Cert. sex eductaor Am. Assn. of Sex Educators Counselours and Therapists, 1978, sex counselor Am. Assn. of Sex Educators Counselours and Therapists, 1989, First Aid, Safety Edn. Am. Red Cross. Tchr. ballroom, tap, ballet Franklin B. Walker Dance Studios, Washington, 1940—41; exercise tchr., mgr. Emile Health Club, Washington, 1942—45; physical edn. tchr. Paul Jr. H.S., Washington, 1945—46; health and physical edn. tchr. Pub. Sr. H.S., Washington, 1946—57, Bethesda Chevy Chase H.S., Chevy Chase, Md., 1957—60; prof. natural sci. Monotgomery Coll., Takoma Pk., Md., 1960—92, coach women's volleyball, 1980. Editor: (jour.) AAHPRED, 1986; contbr. articles pub. to profl. jour. Islands in crisis project Virgin Islands Assn. for Health, 1988—89. Mem.: Nat. Dance Assn., GWU Women's P.E. Alumnae Assn. (pres. 1955—65), Am. Assn. of Heath Physical Edn. (life; pres. 1973—74), Am. Alliance of Health Physical Edn. Recreation and Dance (life; pres. 1963—64). Achievements include During my 50 yr. career I have devel., produced, and presented over 100 ednl. sessions at profl. meetings conventions and conf. and served on chaired on com; development of taught first water exercise credited coll. course. Avocations: jewelry making and design, writing, psychic phenomena, water exercising.

BERNS, BEVERLY J., language educator; d. Gerald and Mary Carr; m. John Berns, June 14, 2003. BA in English, U. No. Iowa, Cedar Falls, 2000. Tchr. Nashua (Iowa)-Plainfield Cmty. Schs., 2001—. Mem.: Nat. Coun. Tchrs. English.

BERNS, PAMELA KARI, artist, publisher; b. Sturgeon Bay, Wis., Sept. 4, 1947; d. Robert Matthew and Judith B. BA, Lawrence U., 1969; MFA, U. Wis., Madison, 1971. Owner, mgr. Sta. Gallery, Ephraim, Wis., 1968—79; pub., editor Chgo. Life Mag., 1984—. One-woman shows include Francis Hardy Gallery, Ephraim, Wis., 1976; group shows include New Horizons, Chgo., 1975, Watercolor Soc., Racine, 1972-82 (2d prize 1976, 82); represented in permanent collections State of Ill. Ctr., Bergstrom-Mahler Art Ctr.; poster design Peninsula Arts Assn., Fish Creek, Wis., 1980 Mem. adv. bd. Chgo. Media Watch. Recipient V.I.P. in her Cmty. award NOW, 1977. Mem. Chgo. Artists Coalition (art dir. 1980-85). Avocations: piano, painting.

BERNSON, MARCELLA S., psychiatrist; b. N.Y.C., Aug. 24, 1952; d. Maxwell Isaac and Priscilla Edith (Zuckerman) Bernson; m. Robert A. Foster, Aug. 7, 2001. BA in Biology summa cum laude, Hofstra U., 1973; MD, Albert Einstein Coll. Medicine, 1976. Diplomate Am. Bd. Psychiatry and Neurology. Resident in psychiatry Bronx (N.Y.) Mcpl. Hosp. Ctr., 1976—79; assoc. dir. med. student edn. in psychiatry U. Medicine and Dentistry N.J.-N.J. Med. Sch., Newark, 1979—81; pvt. practice psychiatry Westfield, NJ, 1981—86; cons. psychiatrist Healthwise EAP, Elizabeth, NJ, 1985—86; staff psychiatrist Elizabeth Gen. Med. Ctr., 1985—88, 1992—95, med. chief adult ambulatory svcs. dept. psychiatry, 1986—87, asst. dir. dept. psychiatry, 1987—88; dir. tng. psychiat. svc. VA Med. Ctr., East Orange, NJ, 1988—89; med. dir. partial care Occupl. Ctr. Union County, Roselle, NJ, 1989—92; cons. psychiatrist Union County Ednl. Svcs. Commn., Westfield, 1992—95; med. dir. Richard Hall CMHC, Bridgewater, NJ, 1995—99, staff psychiatrist, 2003—; with devel. disabilities ctr. Morristown (N.J.) Meml. Hosp., 1999—2003. Instr. U. Medicine and Dentistry N.J.-N.J. Med. Sch., Newark, 1979—81, asst. prof. clin. psychiatry, 1988—89; mem. human rights com. Divsn. Devel. Disabilities, State of N.J. Mem.: N.J. Psychiat. Assn. (Union County rep. 1989—90, Morris County rep. 2000—02), Am. Psychiat. Assn. Avocation: short fiction. Office: Richard Hall CMHC 500 N Bridge St Bridgewater NJ 08807

BERNSTEIN, BONNIE, sportscaster; b. Howell, N.J., Aug. 16, 1970; BS magna cum laude in Broadcast Journalism, U. Md. Sports and news dir. Sta. WXJN Radio, Lewes, Del., 1992-93; weekend news anchor Sta. WMDT-TV, Salisbury, Md., 1993; weekday sports anchor Sta. KRNV-TV and Sta. KRNV Radio, Reno, 1993-95; Chgo.-based corr. SportsCenter ESPN, 1995-98; sportscaster CBS, 1998—, NFL Sidelines Reporter, 2001—. Acad. All-Am. gymnast U. Md. Recipient Thomas M. Fields Academic and Athletic Excellence award. Office: CBS Sports 51 W 52nd St 25th Fl New York NY 10019 E-mail: Bbernstein@cbs.com.

BERNSTEIN, CAROL, molecular biologist; b. Paterson, N.J., Mar. 20, 1941; d. Benjamin and Mina (Regenbogen) Adelberg; m. Harris Bernstein, June 7, 1962; children: Beryl, Golda, Benjamin. BS in Physics, U. Chgo., 1961; MS in Biophysics, Yale U., 1964; PhD in Genetics, U. Calif.-Davis, 1967. NIH fellow zoology dept. U. Calif.-Davis, 1967—68; rsch. assoc. Dept. Microbiology to rsch. assoc. prof. U. Ariz., Tucson, 1968—2004, rsch. assoc. prof. cell biology and anatomy Coll. Medicine, 2004—. Proposal reviewer NSF, 1978—87, VA, 1983, Wellcome Trust, 2001—03, Michael Smith Found. for Health Rsch., Canada, 2003, Associazone Italiana Per La Ricerca Sul Cancro, 2003. Author (with Harris Bernstein): Aging, Sex and DNA Repair, 1991; mem. editl. bd.: Electronic Jour. Biotech.; contbr. articles to profl. jours. and encys. Panel mem. grad fellow rev. NSF, 1984—86, NAS, 1991—94, NSF, 1998, 1999, 2004. Grantee NSF, 1975—77, 1977—79, NIH, 1979—81, 1982—87, 1997—, Ariz. Disease Control, 1986—89, 1991—, Nat. Found., 1975—76. Mem. AAUP (pres. Ariz. state conf. 1983-86, 90-2004, Ariz. chpt. 1983, del. nat. coun. 1986-89, treas. nat. assembly state conf. 1990-92, designated lobbyist 1990—), Am. Soc. Microbiology (invited spkr. 1982), Am. Assn. Cancer Rsch. (platform spkr. 1994), Genetics Soc. Am. Democrat. Home: 2639 E 4th St Tucson AZ 85716-4417 Office: U Ariz Coll Med Dept Cell Biology and Anatomy Tucson AZ 85724-5044 Office Phone: 520-626-6069. Personal E-mail: bernstein3@earthlink.net. Business E-Mail: bernstei@u.arizona.edu.

BERNSTEIN, DEBORAH, psychiatrist; b. Long Beach, N.Y., May 25, 1965; d. Leo and Paula Bernstein; m. David Kleinman, June 26, 1988. BA summa cum laude, Stern Coll., N.Y.C., 1987; MD, Albert Einstein Coll. Medicine, Bronx, N.Y., 1991. Pvt. practice, Phila., 1997—. Author: Secrets of Fat-Free Kosher Cooking. Mem.: Am. Psychiatric Assn., Am. Neuropsychiatric Assn. Office: Ste 404 210 W Rittenhouse Sq Philadelphia PA 19103-5771 Office Phone: 215-732-3485.

BERNSTEIN, DIANE, psychotherapist; b. Jacksonville, Fla., Aug. 30, 1957; d. Arthur Harold and Barbara (Ettinger) B. BS in Human Devel., U. Calif., Davis, 1980; MSW, U. So. Calif., 1982. Lic. clin. social worker. Chmn. social work dept. Beverly Palms Rehab. Hosp., Los Angeles, 1982-83; asst. program dir. A Touch of Care, West Los Angeles, Calif., 1983-85; asst. dir. of residential program San Fernando Valley Child Guidance Clinic, Northridge, Calif., 1985-87; head psychosocial svcs. Immune Suppressed Unit Hollywood (Calif.) Community Hosp., 1987—89; psychotherapist Midway Hosp. AIDS Unit, LA, 1989—97; pvt. practice, 1997—. Vol. NOW, Los Angeles, 1980—. Mem. Nat. Assn. Social Workers, Omicron Nu. Democrat. Jewish. Avocations: reading, travel, kayaking. Home: 5392 Janisann Ave Culver City CA 90230-5305

BERNSTEIN, ELLEN, business owner; b. Lansberg, Germany, Oct. 14, 1946; arrived in U.S., 1949; d. Harry and Betty (Lokensky) Dru; m. Alan Mark Bernstein, Nov. 7, 1971; children: Gary Drew, Randy Scott. Student, Fashion Inst. of Tech., 1964-65, Heffley Queensboro Coll., 1965. master advt. specialist. With Handmacher-Vogel, N.Y.C., 1965-68; sales exec., office mgr. Lee Mar Blouses, N.Y.C., 1968-84; sales exec. Rhoda Lee Blouses, N.Y.C., 1984-85, All-Types Advt., Pomona, N.Y., 1985-87; pres., owner Accent on Promotions, Inc., Pomona, N.Y., 1987—. Mem. com. Comm. Profls. of Rockland, Children's Mus.; vol. Venture Assn.; vice chair fundraising SAAGNY Found., 2006—. Mem. Westchester Women in Comm., Rockland Bus and Women's Network (bd. dir. publicity com. 1985—, pres. 1991-93), Specialty Advt. Assn. Greater N.Y. (edn. com. 1990-92, bd. dir. 1999—, pres. 2003-04), Rockland Bus. Assn. Women's Forum (co-chair Women's Forum). Avocations: art, volleyball, horseback riding, reading. Office Phone: 845-362-0994. E-mail: accenton@yahoo.com.

BERNSTEIN, GERDA MEYER, artist; Student, Art Inst. Chgo., MFA, 1978. Founder Artists, Residents of Chgo., 1973. One woman shows include Angeleski Gallery, N.Y.C., 1960, Artists, Residents of Chgo. Gallery, 1974, 75, 78, Elmhurst (Ill.) Coll., 1979, Karl Ernst Osthaus Mus., Hagen, West Germany, 1982, A.I.R. Gallery, N.Y.C., 1985, 89, Neuer Berliner Kunstverein, 1987, Bochum (Germany) Mus., 1987, Badischer Kunstverein, Karlsruhe, Germany, 1987, Rockford (Ill.) Coll., 1991, Beacon St. Gallery, Chgo., 1993, Fassbender Gallery, Chgo., 1994, 97, Robert F. DeCaprio Art Gallery, Moraine Valley Coll., Palos Hills, Ill., 1994, Alt. Mus., N.Y.C., 1995, Alternative Mus., N.Y.C., 1995, Ellis Island Immigration Mus., N.Y.C., 1996, Fassbender Gallery, Chgo., 1997, 2000, Reicher Gallery, Lake Forest, 2001, Fassbender-Stevens Gallery, Chgo., 2003, Kuusthaus Potsdam, Germany, 2003, Indian U. N.W., Gary, Ind., 2006; exhibited in group shows at Art Inst. Chgo., 1954, 55, 56, 77, 82, 89, 92, 94, Isaac Delgado Mus., New Orleans, 1954, San Francisco Mus. Art, 1955, U. Chgo., 1961, U. Wis., Madison, 1962, 93, Whitney Mus. Am. Art, N.Y.C., 1973, Carleton Coll., Northfield, Minn., 1974, Sangamon State U., Springfield, Ill., 1974, Ill. State Mus. Art, Springfield, 1976, A.I.R. Gallery, 1977, 84, 88, 1134 Gallery, Chgo., 1977, U. Mo., St. Louis, 1977, U. Ill., Urbana and Chgo., 1977, Cultural Ctr., Chgo., 1978, 81, 89, Rutgers U., New Brunswick, N.J., 1979, Columbia Coll., Chgo., 1981, Print Club Phila., 1981, Midwest Mus. Am. Art, Elkhart, Ind., 1981, Purdue (Ind.) U., 1981, Mus. Contemporary Art, Chgo., 1984, No. Ill. U., DeKalb, 1984, 90, Neuer Berliner Kunstverein, 1984, Women's Interart Ctr., N.Y.C., 1985, U.N. Conf. Women, Nairobi, Kenya, 1985, Ministerio de Cultura, Madrid, 1986, Chgo. Office Fine Arts, 1989, Franklin Furnace Gallery, N.Y.C., 1991, Peace Mus., Chgo., 1993, Spertus Mus., Chgo., 1994, Minn. Mus. Am. Art, St. Paul, 1995, Southeastern Ctr. Contemporary Art, Winston-Salem, N.C., 1995-96, Ellis Island, N.Y., 1996, U. Wis. Art Mus., Milw., 1993, Spertus Mus., Chgo., 1994, Fassbender Gallery, Chgo., 1995, S.E. Ctr. Contemporary Art. Cleve., 1996, Glaffer Gallery, U. Houston Art Mus., 1997, Suburban Fine Arts Ctr., Highland Pk., Ill., 1997, Tampa Bay Holocaust Mu., Tampa Bay, Fla., 1998, Knoxville Mus. Art, Tenn., 1998, Telfair Mus. Art, Savannah, Ga., 1999, NJ. State Mus., 1999, Tucscon Mus. Art, Huntsville, Ala., 2000, DeCirdiva Art Mus., Lincoln, Mass., 2000, South Bend Mus. Art, Ind., 2001, Frye Mus., Seattle, 2002, Internat. Artists Mus., Lodz, Poland, 2004-2005. Active Feminist Majority, Planned Parenthood, So. Poverty Law Ctr., Amnesty Internat., Holocaust Mus. Mem. NOW. Democrat. Avocations: reading, walking, music. Home: 1728 N North Park Ave Chicago IL 60614-5710 Studio: 1060 W Adams Chicago IL 60607

BERNSTEIN, JEAN NEWMAN, retired public health information officer; b. Cin., Aug. 19, 1923; d. Emil Carr Newman and Henrietta Cohn; m. Sanford Bernstein (div.); children: Marc Laurence, Jolie Amanda; children: Leyna Francesca, Shari Amidavida. Attended, U. Calif., LA, 1940—42. Asst. to dir. pub. info. Cedars Lebanon Hosp., Hollywood, Calif., 1947—49; dir. program in pub. edn. and cmty. rels. Manteno State Hosp., Ill., 1949—52; ret. Pres. Alliance for Survival, Santa Ana, Calif., 1979—2000; mem. emeritus South Laguna Civic Assn., Laguna Beach, Calif., bd. dirs., 1995—, Laguna Canyon Conservancy, Laguna Beach, 1993—. Recipient Paul Delp Peace award, Interfaith Peace Ministry, Orange, Calif., 2002, Laguna Treasure award, Laguna Beach Environ. Com., 2002, Lifetime Achievement award, South Laguna Civic Assn., 2003. Mem.: Women for Orange County (bd. dirs. 1990—2000). Home: 30832 Driftwood Dr Laguna Beach CA 92651

BERNSTEIN, LESLIE, academic administrator, biostatistician, epidemiologist; BA, U. Calif., 1965; MS, U. So. Calif., 1978, PhD, 1981. Rsch. assoc. dept. preventive medicine U. So. Calif., LA, 1981-82, asst. prof. biostats./epidemiology, 1982-88, assoc. prof. biostats./epidemiology, 1988-91, prof. biostats./epidemiology, 1991—, sr. assoc. dean faculty affairs, 1996—2003, AFLAC Inc. chair in cancer rsch., 1997—, vice provost med. affairs, 2003—05. Sci. dir. U. So. Calif. Cancer Surveillance program, 1988—; mem. bd. sci. counselors Nat. Cancer Inst., 2001-06; mem. sci. adv. panel Calif. Gov., 1989-92; mem. sci. com. Internat. Soc. Study Esophageal Diseases, 1994—; chair adv. com. L.I. Breast Cancer Cancer Study, Columbia U., 1994-2000; chair external adv. com. Nurse's Health Study Harvard U., 1995—; sci. adv. com. Registry for Rsch. on Transplacental Carcinogenesis, U. Chgo., 1997—; external adv. com. No. Calif. Cancer Ctr., Hawaii Cancer Ctr., 1997—. Contbr. over 350 articles to profl. jours. Office: U So Calif/Norris Cancer Ctr Keck Sch Medicine 1441 Eastlake Ave 4449 Los Angeles CA 90033-0804 Business E-Mail: lbern@usc.edu.

BERNSTEIN, LISA E., law educator; b. 1964; BA in Economics, U. Chgo., 1986; JD cum laude, Harvard U., 1990. Bar: NY 1994. Law clk. US Dist. Ct. Dist. Mass., Boston, 1990—91; assoc. prof. law Boston U. Sch. Law, 1991—95, Georgetown U. Law Ctr., 1995—96, prof., 1996—98, U. Chgo. Law Sch., 1998—. Vis. rsch. fellow in law & economics Harvard Law Sch., 1991; vis. assoc. prof. law U. Pa. Sch. Law, 1995, Georgetown U. Law Ctr., 1994; vis. prof. U. Chgo. Law Sch., 1997, Columbia U. Sch. Law, 1998. Mem.: Am. Law & Economics Assn. (bd. mem. 1999—). Office: U Chgo Law Sch 1111 E 60th St Chicago IL 60637 Office Phone: 773-834-2881. E-mail: lbernst621@aol.com.

BERNSTEIN, MAUREEN ANN, theater educator, director; b. Modesto, Calif., Aug. 24, 1953; d. Francis Paul and Ann Bernice Abell; m. Lawrence A. Bernstein, Nov. 17, 1983; 1 child, Frankie Jonathan. BA in Theatre, U. Nev., 1976, MEd in Curriculum and Instrn., 1998, postgrad., 2005—. Cert. tchr. Nev., 1994. Student tchr. Eldorado H.S., Las Vegas, 1994—94; theatre dir. Valley H.S., 1994—97; grad. asst., urban tchg. partnership & instr. with nat. youth sports program as part of master's thesis project U. Nev., 1997—98; theatre dir. chair dept. performing and visual arts Desert Pines H.S., 1999—. Mentor Student Theatrical Adjudicated Rev. Shows, Las Vegas, 2001—, bd. dirs.; mentor Student/Tchr. Mentorship Program, Desert Pines H.S., 2002—. Author: (plays) Hip Hop Goes the Shakespeare; dir.: (plays) Hip Hop Goes the Shakespeare (State Adjudicated Show: Nev. State Thespians, 2002), Playwright's Connection, Les Miserables; (plays) Scapin, The Tempest, Stand and Deliver, The Hobbit, Special Delivery New on

Broadway, The Grinch Who Stole Christmas, Scrooge, Pippin, Evita, Peter Pan, Babes in Arms, Story Theatre, Alice in Wonderland, Dreamgirls, Romeo and Juliet, Grease, Fame, The Tales of Narnia, The Lion, Witch and the Wardrobe. Sponsor, dir. Thespian Troupe 6125, 2004—05; conf. dir., coach students Nev. State Thespians, bd. dirs., 2005—. Recipient Supporting Actress award, Am. Coll. Theatre Festival, 1974; Devos Talent scholar, U. Nev., Las Vegas Theatre Dept., 1972—76. Mem.: NEA, Actors Fund, Broadway Cares, Theatre Comm. Guild, Ednl. Theatre Assn., Nev. State Thespian Bd. Tchr. Profls., Clark County Edn. Assn., Clark County Assn. Theatre Teachers (v.p. 2002). Liberal. Avocations: music, antiques. Office: Desert Pines High School 3800 E Harris Ave Las Vegas NV 89110 Office Phone: 702-799-2196 ext 4051. Personal E-mail: bthespian@aol.com. E-mail: maureen_bernstein@interact.ccsd.net.

BERNSTEIN, NADIA JACQUELINE, lawyer; b. Salford, Lancashire, Eng., Feb. 26, 1945; arrived in U.S., 1948; d. David Colin and Rose (Bolton) Cohen; m. David J. Adler, Mar. 1977 (div. 1992); m. Robert Bernstein, May 1997. BA, CCNY, 1966; JD, NYU, 1973. Bar: NY 1974, US Dist. Ct. (so. and ea. dists.) NY 1974, US Ct. Appeals (2d cir.) 1975, US Supreme Ct. 1983. Assoc. Rosenman Colin Freund Lewis & Cohen and predecessor firms, NYC, 1973-82; ptnr. Rosenman & Colin, NYC, 1983-87; v.p., gen. counsel Montefiore Med. Ctr., NYC, 1987-89, sr. v.p., gen. counsel, 1989-98; v.p., gen. counsel, corp. sec. C.R. Bard, Inc., Murray Hill, NJ, 1999—2004; prin. The NJ Bernstein Law Firm, 2004—. Mem. legal affairs com. Greater NY Hosp. Assn., NYC, 1987—99; mem. conf. bd. Coun. Chief Legal Officers, 1999—2004; mem. NJ Gen. Counsel's Group, 1999—2004; instl. rev. bd. Montefiore Med. Ctr., 2005—. Mem. bioethics task force, mem. commn. women's equality Am. Jewish Congress, NYC, 1989—94; mem. bd. ethics Village Briarcliff Manor, NY, 1997—2006; bd. dirs. Berkeley-in-Scarsdale Assn., NY, 1989—91. Mem.: ABA (forum on health care, law practice mgmt. com. antitrust law sect., corp. practices com. bus. law sect.), Am. Corp. Coun. Assn. (law mgmt. com. 2000—04), Advanced Med. Tech. Assn. (legal com. 2002—04), Women Bus. Leaders US Health Care Industry, Exec. Women NJ (honoree 2000), NY State Bar Assn. (exec. com. health law sect. 1996—99), Am. Health Lawyers Assn., Assn. Bar City of NY. Democrat. Office: 1 Sunnyside Ct Briarcliff Manor NY 10510

BERNSTEIN, PENNY L., biologist, educator; b. Newark, Mar. 30, 1947; d. Arthur and Grace E. Bernstein; m. Lowell Thomas Lambert; 1 child, Christopher Lambert. BA, U. Pa., 1969, PhD, 1978. NIMH postdoctoral fellow Inst. of Animal Behavior, Rutgers U., Newark, 1978—80; rsch. assoc. Rutgers U., New Brunswick, NJ, 1984—85, Wetlands Inst., Stone Harbor, NJ, 1983—84; asst. prof. Kent State U., Canton, Ohio, 1994—2000, assoc. prof., 2000—. Vis. rschr. Smithsonian Inst., Washington, 1981, Cornell U., 2002. Mem. editl. bd.: Anthrozoos, 2000—06; assoc. editor Anthrozoos, 2006—. Mem. Supt.'s Adv. Com., Canal Fulton, 1989—. Recipient Distinguished Teaching Award, 2000; grantee, NSF, 1995—98, Am. Philos. Soc., 1979, Edn. Conf. Grant, Martha Holden Jennings Found., 1998. Mem.: Internat. Soc. Anthrozoology (asst. newsletter editor 1999—2001, sec. 2001—), Soc. for Integrative and Comparative Biology, Am. Ornithol. Union, AAAS, Animal Behavior Soc. (chair edn. com. 2000—). Office: Kent State U Stark 6000 Frank Ave Canton OH 44720

BERNSTEIN, PHYLISS LOUISE, psychologist; b. Balt., Nov. 27, 1940; d. Samuel Wilfred and Helen Dorothy (Gerson) Wilke; m. Robert Bernstein, June 7, 1964; children: Steve, Susan, David. BA in Psychology summa cum laude, Avila Coll., 1980, MS in Psychology summa cum laude, 1981; PhD in Couseling Psychology with high honors, U. Mo., Kansas City, 1986. Lic. psychologist Mo. Psychotherapist Community Counseling Ctr., Kansas City, Mo., 1983-85; assoc. psychologist Counseling and Human Devel. Svcs., Kansas City, Mo., 1985-86; psychologist in pvt. practice Kansas City, Mo., 1996—. Staff privileges Bapt. Med. Ctr., Menorah Med. Ctr.; dir. Jewish Vocat. Svcs., Kansas City, 1988—91, U. Mo. Edn. Dept., Kansas City, Jewish Family and Children Svcs., Jewish Cmty. Found. Contbr. Life mem. Nat. Coun. Jewish Women, Kansas City; bd. dirs. Avila Coll.; adv. bd. mem. Friendship Ho., 2001—. Mem.: APA, Greater Kansas City Psychol. Assn., Psi Chi, Pi Lambda Theta, Phi Kappa Phi. Avocations: scuba diving, bungy jumping, skiing, horseback riding.

BERNSTEIN, PHYLLIS J., financial consultant; b. N.Y.C., Oct. 10, 1955; d. Stanley and Esther Bernstein; m. Robert Kuchner, Dec. 10, 1978. BBA, Hofstra U., 1977. CPA NY. Staff auditor promoted to sr. Pantasote, Greenwich, Conn., 1977—79; sr. promoted to mgr., corp. auditing RCA (now GE), N.Y.C., 1979—85; tech. mgr., personal fin. planning AICPA, N.Y.C., 1985—88, sr. tech. mgr., personal fin. planning, 1988—91, dir., personal fin. planning, 1991—2001; pres. Phyllis Bernstein Consulting, Inc, N.Y.C., 2001—. Editl. adv. bd. mem. Jour. of Accountancy, Jersey City, 2002—; editl. adv. bd. The Tax Advisor, Jersey City, 2002—; adv. bd. mem. Personal Fin. Planning Monthly, Denver, 2002—, Fee-only Client Newsletters, Jericho, NY, 1998—; founder AICPA Ctr. for Investment Adv. Services, 1998—2000; creator and dir. AICPA Personal Fin. Specialist Designation Program, New York, NY, 1985—2001, AICPA Personal Fin. Planning Membership Sect., New York, NY, 1985—2001. Author: (trade book) Financial Planning for CPAs, 2000, Investment Advisory Relationships: Managing Client Expectations in an Uncertain Market, 2002; contributor and editor: book Guide to Registering as an Investment Advisor, 1997; editor: (newsletter) The Planner, 1985—. Sec. and concours chair Jaguar Touring Club, Monclair, NJ, 1995—98; mem. Young Leadersip Cabinet United Jewish Appeal, N.Y.C., 1994—2000; bd. dirs. Jewish Fedn. of Ctrl. NJ Endowment Found., Scotch Plains, 1998—2002; chair investment com. Jewish Fedn. Ctrl. N.J., 2002. Named Top 100 Most Influential Persons in Acctg., Acctg. Today, 1997—2001, Top 10 Names to Know in PFP, 1999—2002, One of four movers, shakers and decision makers, Fin. Planning mag. Mem.: AICPA (legis. and regulation task force pers. fin. planning sect. 2001—02), NY State Soc. of CPAs (fin. planning com. 2002), Fin. Planning Orgn., All-Star Fin. Group (v.p. 2002), Jaguar Touring Club (sec. and concours chair 2000). Democrat. Avocations: skiing, travel, shopping, dining, restoring Jaguars, gardening. Office: Phyllis Bernstein Consulting Inc 7 Penn Plaza Ste 1600 New York NY 10001 Business E-Mail: phyllis@pbconsults.com.

BERNSTEIN, SYLVIA, artist; b. Bklyn. d. Charles and Anna (Finkelman) Schwartz; m. Michael C. Bernstein, Mar. 5, 1934; children: Davida, Holly, Deborah. Student, NAD, N.Y.C. Exhibited one-woman shows, Ruth White Gallery, Silvermine Guild Artists, Conn., Galeria Irla Kert, Montreal, Columbia Mus. Art, S.C., New Britain Mus. Am. Art, Conn., Hove Mus., Eng., group shows, Met. Mus. Art, N.Y.C., 1967, Whitney Mus. Am. Art, N.Y.C., Bklyn. Mus., Portland Mus., Maine, Pa. Acad. Fine Arts, AAAL, Wadsworth Atheneum, Hartford, Conn.; represented permanent collections, Whitney Mus. Am. Art, Bklyn. Mus., Corcoran Gallery, Washington, Denver Art Mus., Norfolk Mus. Arts. and Scis., Va., Hudson River Mus., N.Y., Parrish Mus., Southampton, Columbia Mus., S.C., Wadsworth Atheneum, Hartford, Conn., Springfield Art Mus., Represented, Okla. Mus. Art, represented, New Britain Mus. Am. Art., Va. Mus. Fine Arts, Richmond, Nat. Mus. Women in the Arts, Washington, Adlai E. Stevenson Meml. Collection, IBM, NYNEX, also pvt. collections. Recipient Medal of Honor, Grumbacher award and Roy W. Johnson award Nat. Assn. Women Artists, Alfred Khouri Meml. award Brockton Art Assn., Lesser award Audubon Artists, 1989.

BERON, GAIL LASKEY, real estate analyst, real estate appraiser, consultant; b. Detroit, Nov. 13, 1943; d. Charles Jack Laskey and Florence B. (Rosenthal) Eisenberg; divorced; children: Monty Charles, Bryan David. Cert. real estate analyst, Mich. Chief/staff appraiser Ft. Wayne Mortgage Co., Birmingham, Mich., 1973-75; pvt. practice fee appraiser S.C., Iowa, Mich., 1976-80; pres. The Beron Co., Southfield, Mich., 1980—. Cons. ptnr. Real Estate Counseling Group Conn., Storrs, 1983—, Real Estate Counseling Group Am., prin., 1984—; lectr. real estate confs. Recipient M. William Donnally award Mortgage Bankers Assn. Am., 1975. Mem. Appraisal Inst. (nat. faculty 1991-97), Soc. Real Estate Appraisers (bd. dirs. Detroit chpt. 1980-82, nat. faculty 1983-91), Am. Inst. Real Estate Appraisers (bd. dirs. Detroit chpt. 1982-86, nat. faculty 1984-91), Nat. Assn. Realtors, Detroit Bd. Realtors, Southfield Bd. Realtors, Women Brokers Assn. (treas. Southfield chpt. 1981-83), Young Mortgage Bankers (bd. dirs. 1974-75). Avocations: art, music, piano, reading. Office: Beron Co 7008 Bridge Way West Bloomfield MI 48322-3527

BERQUIST, KATHERINE PAULINE, lawyer; d. Edward Paul and Robin Kaye Biciolis; m. Michael Jon Berquist, Sept. 4, 2004. BA in History, St. Vincent Coll., Latrobe, Pa., 1999; JD, Duquesne U., Pitts., Pa., 2004. Intern Superior Ct. Pa., Pitts., 2000; law clk. Margolis Edelstein, Pitts., 2000—02; intern Fed. Dist. Ct., Pitts., 2002; law clk. Israel, Wood & Grimm, Pitts., 2003; intern Allegheny County Ct. of Common Pleas, Pitts., 2004; jud. law clk. Superior Ct. Pa., Pitts., 2005—06; staff atty. Southwestern Pa. Legal Svcs., 2006—.

BERRESFORD, SUSAN VAIL, foundation administrator; b. NYC, Jan. 8, 1943; d. Richard Case and Katherine Vail (Marsters) Besserford Hurd; m. David F. Stein (div.); 1 child, Jeremy Vail Stein. Student, Vassar Coll., 1961-63; BA cum laude in Am. History, Radcliffe Coll., 1965. Vol. UN Vol. Services, NYC, summer 1962; sec. to Theodore H. White, summer 1964; program officer Neighborhood Youth Corps, NYC, 1965-67; program specialist Manpower Career Devel. Agy., NYC, 1967, human resources adminstrn. specialist, 1968; freelance cons., writer Europe & US, 1968-70; project asst. Nat. Affairs Div. Ford Found., NYC, 1970—72, program officer, 1972—80, officer in charge women's programs, 1980—81, v.p. US and Internat. Affairs program, 1981-95, v.p. Worldwide Programming Div., 1989, exec. v.p., COO, 1995-96, pres., 1996—. Bd. mem. Coun. on Founds.; mem. Trilateral Commn., Coun. Fgn. Rels. Chair bd. dirs. United States Artists (USA) Bd.; adv. bd. mem. Trinidad Trust Fund, Calif.; mem. European Found. Centre's Governing Coun. Named one of 100 Most Powerful Women in World, Forbes mag., 2005—06. Mem.: Am. Acad. Arts and Scis. Office: Ford Foundation 320 East 43rd St New York NY 10017*

BERRIEN, JACQUELINE A., lawyer; b. 1961; BA in govt. and English, Oberlin Coll.; JD, Harvard U. Bar: NY 1987. Atty. Am. Civil Liberties Union, NY, Voting Rights Project, Lawyers' Com. Civil Rights, Wash., DC; asst. counsel NAACP Legal Def. Fund, 1994—2001, assoc. dir.-counsel, 2004—; program officer Peace & Social Justice Program, Ford Found., 2001—04. Adj. prof. NY Law Sch. Contbr. articles to prof. legal jour. Office: NAACP Legal Def Fund Ste 1600 99 Hudson St New York NY 10013 Office Phone: 212-965-2200.

BERRIGAN, HELEN GINGER, federal judge; b. New Rochelle, Apr. 15, 1948; m. Joseph E. Berrigan Jr. BA, U. Wis., 1969; MA, Am. U., 1971; JD, La. State U., 1977. Staff rschr. Senator Harold E. Hughes, 1971-72; legis. aide Senator Joseph E. Biden, 1972-73; asst. to mayor City of Fayette, Miss., 1973-74; law clk. La. Dept. Corrections, 1975-77; staff atty. Gov. Pardon, Parole and Rehab. Commn., 1977-78; prin. Gravel Brady & Berrigan, New Orleans, 1978-94, Berrigan, Litchfield, Schonekas, Mann & Clement, New Orleans, 1984-94; judge U.S. Dist. Ct. (ea. dist.) La., New Orleans, 1994—. Active La. Sentencing Commn., 1987. Active Com. of 21, 1989, pres., 1990-92, ACLU of La., 1989-94, Forum for Equality, 1990-94, Amistad Rsch. Ctr. Tulane U., 1990-95. Mem.: New Orleans Assn. Women Attys., La. Assn. Criminal Def. Lawyers, La. State Bar Assn. Office: US Dist Courthouse 500 Poydras St Rm C556 New Orleans LA 70130-3313

BERRONG, CHRISTINE R., music educator, voice educator; b. Raritan, N.J., Oct. 8, 1968; d. Gerald J. and Sandra R. Berrong. BA, Augustana Coll., Rock Island, Ill., 1990; MA in Tchg., Nat.Louis U., Evanston, Ill., 1993. Cert. elem. tchr. Ill., 1993. Tchr. Diamond Lake Sch. Dist. #76, Mundelein, Ill., 1993—; musician/vocalist Chgo., 1990—. Webmaster Diamond Lake Sch. Dist. #76, 2002—. Musician (vocalist): (opera) The Patriots. Mem.: Nat. Coun. for Social Studies (assoc.), ASCD (assoc.). Office: West Oak Middle Sch 500 Acorn Lane Mundelein IL 60060 Office Phone: 847-566-9220. Personal E-mail: cberrong33@hotmail.com. Business E-Mail: cberrong@d76.lake.k12.il.us.

BERRY, ALICE ALLEN, retired music educator; b. Bowling Green, Ky., June 23, 1946; d. Oscar Ainsworth and Dorothy (Maddox) Allen; m. Thomas Kay Berry, June 18, 1967; 1 child, Carl Thomas. B in Music Edn. cum laude, Murray State U., 1968. Cert. tchr. Ky., tchr., supr. spl. K-14 Ill. Choral music tchr. McCracken County Pub. Schs., Lone Oak, Ky., 1968—69, Cmty. Unit Sch. Dist. #186, Murphysboro, Ill., 1969—2002. Guest festival choral dir. Jefferson County Music Tchrs. Assn., Ina, Ill., 1993; guest dir. Murphysboro Voices United, 1993; adjudicator music contests Ill. Grade Sch. Music Assn., 1996—, Ill. HS Assn., 1980—; guest choral dir. So. Ill. Grade Sch. Vocal Music Festival, 1998, 2000, 02; guest festival choral dir. Miss. Valley Conf., Belleville, Ill., 2005; guest pianist Walnut St. Bapt. Ch., Carbondale, Ill., 2003. Performer (singer): (guest soloist) Quad State Festival Chorus, 1965, All State Chorus, 1964. Vol. Meals on Wheels, Jackson County Sr. Citizens, Murphysboro, 2002—, So. Ill. U. Choral Union, Carbondale, 2003—; vol. music dir. Cmty. Ecumenical Vacation Bible Sch., Lebanon, Ill., 2003—; choral dir. 1st Bapt. Ch., Murphysboro, 1974—78, 1981—2001; choir dir. United Meth. Ch., Murphysboro, 1969—70; guest choral dir. Cantata United Meth. Ch., Murphysboro, 2002. Named Unsung Hero, Sta. WSIL-TV, 1996, Class Act, 2002. Mem.: NEA (life), Jackson County retired Tchrs. Assn., Am. Choral Dirs. Assn., Ill. Music Edn. Assn. (adjudicator 1983, choral chmn. dist. 6 1988—, 25-Yr. Recognition award 1995), Music Educators Nat. Conf., Ill. Ret. Tchrs. Assn., Sigma Alpha Iota. Home: 2019 Commercial Ave Murphysboro IL 62966 Personal E-mail: atberry@midwest.net.

BERRY, BECKY, music educator; b. Ohio; m. Kim Berry; 1 child, Allison. BFA, Fla. Atlantic U., Boca Raton, 1976. Cert. tchr. Fla. Music/performing arts tchr. A.C.Perry Elem. Sch., Miramar, Fla., 1977—85, Nova Eisenhower Elem. Sch., Davie, Fla., 1985—91, Griffin Elem. Sch., Cooper City, Fla., 1991—98, Everglades Elem. Sch., Weston, Fla., 1998—. Music coord., youth choir dir. Pky. Christian Ch., Plantation, Fla., 1979—94. Dir.: (over 100 mus. prodns.). Finalist Arts Tchr. of Yr., Broward County Cultural Divsn., 2005; named Tchr. of Yr., Everglades Elem. Sch., 2005, Nova Eisenhower Elem. Sch.; recipient, A.C. Perry Elem. Sch. Mem.: Broward Music Educators Assn., Fla. Elem. Music Educator's Assn., Music Educator's Nat. Conf., Fla. Music Educators Assn. Avocations: singing, directing children's musicals. Office: Everglades Elem Sch 2900 Bonaventure Blvd Weston FL 33331 E-mail: becky.berry@browardschools.com.

BERRY, CAROL ANN, insurance company executive; b. Walla Walla, Wash., Sept. 8, 1950; d. Alan R. and Elizabeth A. Berry; m. Mark Brooks. BA, Wash. State U. Cert. compliance profl. Asst. mgr. L.A. reg. claims CIGNA, Santa Monica, Calif., 1981—83; reg. adminstr. Equicor, Sherman Oaks, Calif., 1983—89; dir. sys. for managed care Blue Cross of Calif., Woodland Hills, 1989—90; dir. field account svcs. Managed Health Network, L.A., 1990—93; pres. VertiHealth Adminstrs., Chatsworth, Calif., 1993—2000; cons., expert witness, 2000—01; sr. v.p. Claim Recoveries Unlimited, 2001—04, HealthLogic Sys. Corp., 2004—06; pres. PCG Software Inc., Malibu, 2006—. Lectr. in field. Mem. Pres.'s Commn. Status of Women. Mem.: NAFE, Healthcare Execs., Health Care Adminstrs. Assn. (past pres. bd. dirs.), Health Fin. Mgmt. Assn., Wash. State U. Alumni Assn. Home: 6155 Lockhurst Dr Woodland Hills CA 91367-1203 Office Phone: 877-789-1291 ext. 205. E-mail: cberry8@sbcglobal.net.

BERRY, CHARLENE HELEN, librarian, musician; b. Highland Pk., Mich., Jan. 4, 1947; d. Harold Terry and Mattie Lou (Colvin) B. BSE, Wayne U., 1964-68, MA, 1969-70, MLS, 1971-74; postgrad., Howard Sch. Broadcast Arts, 1992, Irene's Myomassology Inst., 1997; DMin, U. Sem. Ch., 1997. Ordained music minister. Libr. asst. Wayne State U., Detroit, 1970-74; libr. serials cataloger SUNY, Stony Brook, 1975-79; cataloger Madonna U., Livonia, Mich., 1980—. Organist various area chs., Detroit, 1981—, 1st Ch. of Christ, Wyandotte, Mich., 1986—; music min. Gospel Light House Ministries, Detroit, 1991—; scholar, performer, tchr. hammer dulcimer, 1986—; libr. cons. Superior Twp. (Mich.) Libr. Bd., 1989-91; host Charlene Berry's Dulcimer World, Sta. WCAR, Garden City, Mich., WALE, Providence, R.I., WLLZ 560 AM, Southfield, Mich., 1997—, Sta. WPON AM 1460, Southfield, Mich., 1997—. Composer: Dulcimer Delights, 1991, marches, waltzes, free compositions and solo symphony, 1993, Dulcimer Praise, 1993, Fruits of the Spirit, 1993; solo recs.: Traditional Dulcimer, 1989, Christmas Dulcimer, 1989, Sacred Dulcimer, 1990, Dulcimer Fun, 1991, Dulcimer Praise, 1993, Fruits of the Spirit, 1993, Dulcimer Americana, 1994; (video) Hammering the Hammer Dulcimer, 1994, Music of Light/Light and Life, 1995, Under der Linden, 1996, Joy, Peace, Healing, 1998, Hymms of Prayer and Praise, 1999. Pres. Libr. Staff Assn., SUNY, 1978-79; ch. libr. Ch. Bds. Coms., Long Island, Detroit, 1975—; bd. dirs. Livonia Symphony Soc.; performing artist Mich. Touring Arts Agy., 1994—. Recipient Performance award Silver Springs Dulciner Soc., 1988, 89, 90, Interat. Order of Merit, ASCAP; named Internat. Woman of Yr., 1992-93, Most Admired Woman of Decade. Fellow Internat. Biographical Assn. (life). Am. Biographical Inst. (Woman of Yr. 1993); mem. AAUW, ALA, NAFE, Am. Biographical Rsch. Assn. (hon. dep. gov.), Bus. and Profl. Women, Am. Soc. of Notaries, Am. Fedn. Musicians, Am. Guild Organists (bd. dirs. 1985-88), Plymouth C. of C., Luth. Ch. Musicians Guild, Order Ea. Star, Kappa Delta Pi. Home and Office: Dulcimer Evente 49616 Oak Dr Lot 67 Plymouth MI 48170-2353

BERRY, DALE M., physical education specialist; b. Jackson, Mich., Sept. 25, 1950; d. Elwyn Darrold and Dorothy May Berry. BS, Mich. State U., East Lansing, 1972; MA in Physical Edn., Ball State U., Muncie, Ind., 1975; postgrad., Ind. U. Purdue U., Ft. Wayne, 1982; MA, Western Ky. U., Bowling Green, 1992. Lic. tchr. grades K-12 phys. edn./health, grades 7-12 social studies. Phys. edn. specialist, coach Richmond H.S., Ind., 1973—75, Mississinew Jr. High, Gas City, Ind., 1975—79, Pierceton Middle Sch., Ind., 1979—81; phys. edn. specialist grades K-5 Bloomfield Elem., Bardstown, Ky., 1991—93, Floyds Knobs Elem., New Albany, Ind., 1994—. Cross country, track, jump rope team, ski club coach Floyds Knobs Elem., 1994—; presenter in field. Author: Great Activities, 1997. Active ARC, Louisville; capt. Relay for Life team Am. Cancer Soc., New Albany; active S.E. Christian Ch., 1995, choir mem., 2005. Recipient PE Tchr, of Year, Ind. Elem., 1998, Ky. Excel award, WHAS-TV Channell 11, 2000. Mem.: AAHPERD, IAHPERD (Elem. Phys. Edn. Tchr. of Yr. 1998), ISTA, NEA, Miss. State U. Alumni Assn. Baptist. Avocations: reading, skiing, swimming, travel, softball. Home: 120 Lochwood Ct New Albany IN 47150 Office: Floyds Knobs Elem 4484 Scottsville Rd Floyds Knobs IN 47119

BERRY, ESTER LORÉE, vocational nurse; b. St. Joseph, La., Sept. 19, 1945; d. Sim and Ruby Jordan; (div.); children: Roderick Bryant, Pamela Elaine. A in nursing and art, Calif. State U., 1996; diploma in poetry and writing, Internat. BIB Ctr. Lic. vocat. nurse. Ward clk. Santa Fe Hosp., Compton, Calif., 1969-72; supr. J.C. Penney's, Carson, Calif., 1973-80; asst. mgr. Std. Comm., Carson, 1981-84; lic. vocat. nurse, nurse King Drew Med., L.A., 1984-94; medicine nurse Martin Luther Jr. Hosp., 1996-99; poet Nobles Theatre of the Mind, Paris, London, N.Y.C., 2004—. Author numerous poems. Named hon. mem., Vets. Am., 1999—2001, Best Poet of Yr., 2001; named to Wall of Tolerance, Ala., 2004, Comdrs. Club, DAV, 2002—03; recipient Editors Choice award, 1999—2001, Bronze Leader award, Comdr. Club, DAV, 2001, Silver Internat. Poet of Merit, Bronze Commemorative medallion, Best Poet award, 2002—03, Best Poet of Yr. award, Internat. Libr. Poetry, 2004, certificate, Profl. Women's Adv. Bd., Wall of Tolerance award, So. Poverty Law Ctr., 2004, Editor's Choice award for outstanding achievement in poetry, Internat. Libr. Poetry, 2006, Laureate award, 2006. Mem.: Am. Libr. Inst. (mem. profl. women's adv. bd. 2004). Avocations: fishing, sewing, photography, crocheting, outdoor camping. Home: Apt P230 27-700 Landau B Cathedral City CA 92234

BERRY, GAIL W., psychiatrist, educator; b. Kalamazoo, Mich., Nov. 7, 1939; BA, Kalamazoo Coll., 1960; MD, NYU, 1964; cert. in psychoanalysis, N.Y. Med. Coll., 1976. Lic. Am. Bd. Psychiatry and Neurology. Clin. instr. psychiatry Mt. Sinai Sch. Medicine, N.Y.C., 1969—76, asst. clin. prof. psychiatry, 1976—; tng. and supervising psychoanalyst Psychoanalytic Inst. N.Y. Med. Coll., Valhalla, NY, 1980—; assoc. attending psychiatrist Mt. Sinai Hosp., N.Y.C., 1981—. Adj. prof. psychiatry N.Y. Med. Coll., Valhalla, 1984—. Fellow: Am. Psychiat. Assn. (life; disting.); mem.: Am. Acad. Psychoanalysis (asst. editor jour. 1984—2002), Am. Acad. Psychoanalysis and Dynamic Psychiatry (consulting editor jour. 2002—).

BERRY, HALLE MARIA, actress; b. Cleve., Aug. 14, 1966; d. Jerome and Judith (Hawkins) B.; m. David Christopher Justice, Dec. 31, 1992 (div. 1996); m. Eric Benet, Jan. 24, 2001 (div. Jan. 3, 2005). BA, Cuyahoga C.C., Cleveland, 1986. Spokeswoman, Revlon cosmetics, 1996-. Actress in films Jungle Fever, 1991, The Last Boy Scout, 1991, Strictly Business, 1991, Boomerang, 1992 (Image award nom. 1992), Father Hood, 1993, The Program, 1993, The Flintstones, 1994, Losing Isaiah, 1995, The Rich Man's Wife, 1996, Executive Decision, 1996, Race The Sun, 1996, Girl 6, 1996, B*A*P*S, 1997, Bulworth, 1998, Why Do Fools Fall in Love, 1998, Victims of Fashion, 1999, Ringside, 1999, X-Men, 2000, Swordfish, 2001, Monsters Ball, 2001 (Acad. award best actress 2002), Die Another Day, 2002, X2: X-Men United, 2003, Gothika, 2003, Catwoman, 2004, (voice) Robots, 2005, X-Men: The Last Stand, 2006; (TV movies) Solomon & Sheba, 1995, The Wedding, 1998, Oprah Winfrey Presents: Their Eyes Were Watching God, 2005; actress, exec. prodr., (TV films) Introducing Dorothy Dandridge, 1999 (Emmy award best actress 2000, Golden Globe award best actress 2000, Image award, SAG award and three NAACP Image awards 2000), exec. prodr. Lackawanna Blues, 2005; TV mini-series Queen, 1992; TV series include Living Dolls, 1989, Knots Landing, 1992; (TV appearances) Amen, 1991, A Different World, 1991 They Came From Outer Space, 1991, Martin, 1996, Frasier (voice only), 1998, The Bernie Mac Show, 2002. Named Miss Teen All-Am., 1985, Miss USA first-runner up, 1986, Miss U.S.A., 1987. First African Am. actress to win Academy award for best actress for the film Monsters Ball, 2002. Mailing: Vincent Cirrincione Assoc Ltd Ste 205 8721 Sunset Blvd West Hollywood CA 90069*

BERRY, IRIS ELIZABETH, academic administrator; b. Columbus, Ga., Sept. 1, 1951; d. Billie Collins Berry and Vera Ruth Drane. BS in Phys. Edn., U. NC, Greensboro, 1973; AS in Phys. Therapy, North Shore CC, Beverly, Mass., 1989; postgrad., Salem State Coll., Mass., 1991—92. Lic. massage therapist, phys. therapist asst., cert. Sutton dance notation instr. Adminstrv. asst. Zipporah Films, Inc., Boston, 1974—79; sec. No. Textile Assn., Boston, 1981—82, EMCO Transducers & Instrumentation, Inc., Marblehead, Mass., 1985—89; phys. therapist asst. Orthop. and Sports Medicine Specialist, North Andover, Mass., 1989—91, North Shore Phys. Therapy, Marblehead, 1991—95; instr. Marblehead Sch. Ballet, 1978—88, 1993—99; guest lectr., clin. supr. Salem State Coll., Mass.; athletic trainer Marblehead HS, 1991—2003; massage therapist, athletic trainer, phys. therapy asst. Berry Muscular Therapy, Swampscott, Mass., 1995—; instr. Spa Tech. Inst., Ipswich, Mass., 1995—, head anatomy and physiology dept., 1995—2006, site and edn. dir., 2003—. Guest lectr. Salem State Coll., 1993—, clin. supr., 1991—2003. Author: Anatomy and Physiology Workbooks and Teacher Guides, 1998, 2006; editor: Hot Rock Massage, 2006. Mem. North Shore Civic Ballet Co., 1974—88. Mem.: Athletic Trainers Mass., Assn. Massage and Bodywork Profls., Nat. Athletic Trainer Assn. (examiner, cert.), Alpha Lambda Kappa. Avocations: dance, reading, crafts, cooking. Office: Spa Tech Inst 126 High St Ipswich MA 01938 Business E-Mail: iberry@spatech.edu.

BERRY, JANET CLAIRE, librarian; b. Jonesboro, Ark., Dec. 1, 1948; d. Troy Berry and Olivia Rosetta (Irwin) Thompson; m. Julius Jerome Mitcham, Mar. 27, 1970 (div. 1981); m. Gary Neville Hays, Nov. 10, 1987 (div. 1989); m. Norman M. Floyd, Nov. 21, 2003 BSE, U. Cen. Ark., 1970; MLS, Vanderbilt/Peabody U., 1981. Libr./tchr. Greenbrier (Ark.) High Sch., 1970-72; employment counselor Dixie Employment Agy., Little Rock, 1973-76; sr. libr. asst. U. Ark. for Med. Sci., Little Rock, 1976-85; coord. cataloging svc. Ark. State Libr., Little Rock, 1985—. Instr. U. Ark., Little Rock, 1986-88. Editor La Docere for Am. Bus. Women's Assn. newsletter (regional top 5 award 1991, 92), The Voter, 2002—. Mem. West Baseline Neighborhood Assn., sec., 1997—2005; mem. Leion Hut Neighborhood Assn., sec.,

1997—2005, Southwest Little Rock United for Progress, 1998-2005, v.p., 1999, pres., 2000—05; mem. environ. task force City of Little Rock, 1999-2003; bd. dirs. Friends of Ctrl. Ark. Libr. Sys., 1999—2003. Mem. ALA, Ark. Libr. Assn. (pres. 1983-84), Ark. Region Sports Car Club of Am. (editor 1988-98, 2006—), Am. Bus. Women's Assn. (La Petite Roche chpt., editor 1990-92, 1992 Woman of Yr.), LWV (Pulaski county chpt.). Methodist. Avocations: road rallies, working sports car races, bird watching, caring for cats, civic meetings. Office: Ark State Libr One Capitol Mall Little Rock AR 72201 Office Phone: 501-682-2303. E-mail: jberry@asl.lib.ar.us.

BERRY, KAREN S., music educator; m. Dirk Berry; children: David, Jason. B Music Edn., Grace Coll., Winona Lake, Ind., 1978. Music tchr. Mansfield Christian Sch., Ohio, 1978—80, St. Patrick Sch., Carlisle, Pa., 1999—. Office: St Patrick Sch 87 Marsh Dr Carlisle PA 17013-9101

BERRY, KATHRYN-GRACE, geriatrics nurse; b. Linden, Tex., Sept. 28, 1929; d. Wright Allen and Gladys Bowden; m. Wayman Byron Berry, Jan. 6, 1947; children: Ron, James Byron, Celia Elizabeth Froehlig. Diploma in nursing, Univ. Ala., 1969. Cert. nursing Ala. Nurse, Huntsville, 1970—80; charge nurse various nursing homes, Pulaski, Tenn., 1980—85, Andmore, Ala., 1987—90; tchr. GED program Huntsville, 1990—97. Active Christians Helping Others, Ardmore, 1985—95; mem. Friends Ardmore Libr., 1990—95; pres. United Meth. Women, 1985. Avocations: oragami, reading, boating, fishing, crafts, painting. Home: 809 Stuart Ln Brentwood TN 37027-5824

BERRY, KEYSHA ROSHAWN, science educator; d. Herman and Glenda Patten Frazier; m. Roland Berry, May 22, 1993; children: Roland Jr., Rhian. BS, Prairie View A&M U., Tex., 1992. Sci. educator Foster Mid. Sch., Longview, Tex., 1196—. Mem.: Assn. Tex. Pub. Educators (assoc.), Delta Sigma Theta (life). Office: Foster Middle School 410 S Green St Longview TX 75601 Office Phone: 903-753-1692. Office Fax: 903-758-1571. E-mail: kberry@lisd.org.

BERRY, LORRAINE LEDEE, state senator; b. St. Thomas, V.I., Nov. 15, 1949; d. Joseph and Emelda Ledee; m. Richard Berry; children: Roxanne, Kurt. Student, U. V.I. Mem. V.I. Legis., 1982—, pres., 1997-99, 2005—. Mem. econ. devel., agr., consumer protection, health, govt. and operation coms.; chair fin. com. Office: Capitol Bldg PO Box 1690 St Thomas VI 00804-1690 Office Phone: 340-693-3507. E-mail: LBerry19@hotmail.com, lberry@senate.gov.vi.

BERRY, MARY FRANCES, history professor, former federal agency administrator; b. Nashville, Feb. 17, 1938; d. George Ford and Frances Southall (Wiggins) B. BA, Howard U., 1961, MA, 1962; PhD, U. Mich., 1966, JD, 1970; degree (hon.), Cen. Mich. U., Howard U., U. Akron, 1977, Benedict Coll., U. Md., Grambling State U., 1979, Bethune-Cookman Coll., Clark Coll., Del. State Coll., 1980, Oberlin Coll., Langston U., 1983, Marian Coll., Haverfod Coll., 1984, Colby Coll., CUNY, 1986, DePaul U., 1987. Bar: D.C. 1972. Asst. prof. history Central Mich. U., Mt. Pleasant, 1966-68; asst. prof. Eastern Mich. U., Ypsilanti, 1968-69, assoc. prof., 1969-70, U. Md., College Park, 1969-76; acting dir. Afro-Am. studies, 1970-72, dir., 1972-74, acting chmn. div. behavioral and social scis., 1973-74, provost div. behavioral and social scis., 1973-76; prof. history, prof. law U Colo. at Boulder, 1976-80, chancellor, 1976-77; prof. history and law Howard U., Washington, 1980—87; Geraldine R. Segal prof. Am. Social Thought U. Pa., Philadelphia, 1987—; asst. sec. for edn. US Dept. Health Edn. & Welfare, Washington, 1977-80; vice chairperson U.S. Commn. on Civil Rights, Washington, 1980—82; chaiperson U.S. Commn. on Civil Rights, Washington, 1993—2004. Adj. assoc. prof. U. Mich., 1970-71; mem. com. visitors U. Mich. Law Sch., 1976-80; mem. nat. adv. panel on minority concerns Coll. Bd., 1980-84; mem. adv. bd. Feminist Press, 1980—; mem. research adv. com. Joint Ctr. for Polit. Studies, 1981—; mem. editorial adv. com. Marcus Garvey Papers, 1981—; mem. adv. bd. Inst. for Higher Edn. Law and Governance, U. Houston, 1983—. Author: Black Resistance/White Law, 1971 (rev. 1994), Military Necessity and Civil Rights Policy, 1977, Stability, Security and Continuity, Mr. Justice Burton and Decision-Making in the Supreme Court, 1945-58, 1978, (with John Blassingame) Long Memory: The Black Experience in America, 1982; Why ERA Failed, 1986, Politics of Parenthood: Child Care, Women's Rights, and the Myth of the Good Mother, 1993, The Pig Farmer's Daughter and Other Tales of American Justice, 1999, Health Care Challenge: Acknowledging Disparity, Confronting Discrimination, And Ensuring Equality, 1999, My Face Is Black Is True: Callie House and the Struggle for Ex-Slave Reparations, 2005; assoc. editor Jour. Negro History, 1974-78; contbr. articles, revs. to profl. jours. Bd. dirs. ARC, Washington, 1980—; trustee Tuskegee U., 1980—; mem. adv. bd. Project '87, 1978—; mem. council UN U., 1986— Recipient Athena (disting. alumni) award U. Mich., 1977, Roy Wilkins Civil Rights award NAACP, 1983, Image award, 1983, Allard Lowenstein award, 1984, President's award Congl. Black Caucus Found., 1985, Woman of Yr. award Nat. Capital Area YWCA, 1985, Hubert H. Humphrey Civil Rights award Leadership Conf. on Civil Rights, 1986, Rosa Parks award SCLC, Black Achievement award Ebony Mag., Woman of Yr. award Ms. Mag., 1986. Mem. ABA, Nat. Bar Assn., D.C. Bar Assn., Nat. Acad. Public Administrn., Orgn. Am. Historians (exec. bd. 1974-77), Assn. Study of Afro-Am. Life and History (exec. bd. 1973-76), Am. Hist. Assn. (v.p. for profession 1980-83), Am. Soc. Legal History, Coalition 100 Black Women (hon.), Delta Sigma Theta (hon.) Independent. Office: U Pa 208 College Hall Rm 216E Philadelphia PA 19104 E-mail: mfberry@sas.upenn.edu.

BERRY, MARYANN PARADISO, minister; d. Joseph and Mary Mainolfi Paradiso; m. Wayne Robert Berry, Jan. 4, 1975; children: Maria, John. BS in Bus. Adminstrn. cum laude, Marist Coll., 1975; cert. of studies, Faith Fellowship World, Sayreville, N.J., 1985, Sch. Bibl. Studies, Poughkeepsie, N.Y., 1996. Ordained min. Christian Faith Ctr., Bloomfield, NJ, 1990, Covenant Ministries, Sayreville, 1992. Co-owner Mid-Hudson Alarm Co., Poughkeepsie, 1975—80; children's music dir., elder, tchr. Bible Coll. Faith Fellowship Ministries, Sayreville, 1982—88; min. Christian Faith Ctr., Bloomfield, NJ, 1988—91; pastor, dean Sch. Bibl. Studies John 3:16 Christian Ctr., Unionvale, NY, 1991—. Co-host Christian radio broadcast Faith for Today, 2005—. Author: Answered Prayer, 1984. Vol. father's day parade Dutchess County Health Families, 2003—. Mem.: Covenant Ministries Internat., Assn. Faith Chs. and Ministries. Avocations: reading, hiking, piano, guitar. Office: John 3:16 Christian Ctr 3112 Rt 82 Unionvale NY 12585 Office Phone: 845-677-0625. Personal E-mail: mab3331@verizon.net.

BERRY, PAMELA C., secondary school educator; b. Oct. 24, 1941; d. Joseph Charles and Elenor (Kucharski) B.; 1 child, Katie Julia. BA, Western Mich. U., 1965; MA, U. Mich., 1975; Edn. Specialist, Wayne State U., 1985, postgrad. Lic. profl. tchr. Tchr. East Prairie Jr. H.S., Vicksburg, Mich., 1965-66, Allen Park (Mich.) H.S., 1966—, English dept. chair, 1969-81, tchr. English, 1993—. Rsch. asst. U. Mich., Ann Arbor, 1973-75, Wayne State U., Detroit, 1981-82, dir. politics in edn., 1981-82; spl. projects dir. Allen Park Pub. Schs., 1981-92; cons. Humanistic Mgmt. Sys., Columbus, Ohio, 1981-82; mem. Internat. Yr. of the Child, Wayne State U., Detroit, 1981-82; mem. std. setting com., (task force ensuring excellent educators, 2001) Mich. Dept. Edn., Lansing, 1998, content adv. com., 1998—, mem. task force State Bd. Edn., 2002; tech. liaison Allen Park Pub. Schs.; trainer Trainers County Mentoring Program. Pres. Young Dems., 1978-82; precinct dir. Dem. Party, del., 1985—. Nominee Phoebe Apperson award, Nat. PTA, 1985, Disney Tribute to Tchrs.; recipient Disting. Tchr. of Writing, Northwood U., 2001. Mem. Nat. Coun. Tchrs. English, Mich, (nominee Disney Tribute to tchr., Mich. Tchr. Yr.), Coun. Tchrs. English, Mich. Reading Assn., Phi Delta Kappa. Avocations: golf, reading, travel, theater, writing.

BERRY, REBECCA DIANE, artist, educator; b. Mexico, Mo., June 23, 1952; d. Paul Gilmore and Joanna Clayton Sappington; m. Dennis Gale Berry, Dec. 1, 1973; children: Jessica Laraine, Ginger Renee. AA, Columbia Coll., 1972; BA, William Woods U., 1992, MA, 1996. With Mexico Ledger, Mo., 1972—73; clk. Lacrosse Lumber, Mexico, 1973—79; tchr. Van-Far H.S., Vandalia, Mo., 1993—. Free-lance artist. V.p. PTA, 1989—90; leader 4-H, 1989—; team leader Jr. Team, 2000; active Drug & Violence Free Task Force; vol. Becky Erdel State Rep. campaign, 1998; Sunday sch. tchr. Mexico, 1986—; trustee United Meth. Ch., 2002—03. Named to Est. Leaders Honor Roll, U. Mo., 2002; recipient Tchr. of Yr. award, Van-Far Sch. Dist., 2002, Oustst anding Tchr. award, 2006. Mem. Nat. Art Edn. Assn. (Cmty. 2000 mem.), Mo. Art Edn. Assn., Fulton Art Guild, Mex. Art Guild, Sigma Delta Phi. Methodist. Avocations: painting, horseback riding, drawing, volunteering. Home: 27360 ACR 808 Mexico MO 65265 Office: Van Far High Sch 2200 W Highway 54 Vandalia MO 63382-1199 Office Phone: 573-594-6442. Business E-Mail: rberry@vf.k12.mo.us.

BERRY, SHARON ELAINE, interior designer; b. Kansas City, Mo., May 27, 1945; d. Ralph Epping Hohmann and Ruth Justine (Sturm) Hohmann Gibson; m. Max Allen Berry, Apr. 8, 1984. Grad. high sch., Kansas City; grad, Pierce Sch. Interior Design, 1972. Designer Danie Dunn Interiors, Kansas City, 1972-76, 80-83; co-owner, operator Clift-Willard Interiors, Leawood, Kans., 1976-80; head decorating dept. Carpets by Johnson and Johnson, Overland Park, Kans., 1983-84; owner, operator Nouveau Interiors, Shawnee Mission, Kans., 1984-92; coord. Met. Orgn. To Counter Sexual Assault, Kansas City, 1994-96, mem. adv. bd. adult survivor program, 1996—; pres. Recovery Records, 1996-98; dir. funding and devel. Cypress Recovery, Inc., Olathe, Kans., 1999-2000, bd. dirs., 1998; dir. fund devel. Rick's Place Found., 2000—01; owner Wild Berry Interior Design, 2002—. Vol. Design Excellence Awards Com., Kansas City, 1982-88; designer Designers Showhouse, Kansas City, Mo., 1975-90; participant Design '81 Congress, Helsinki, 1981, Gourmet March of Dimes, 1988, 90; writer City Limits, entertainment mag., Family News mag. Editor newsletter Survivors United Reading Empowerment (S.U.R.E.); contbr. to anthology The Bridge Is Out But I Can Fly; co-writer, co-prodr. CD Who Will Save the Children; editor, writer, newsletter Cypress Recovery. Vol. exec. dir. Recovery Is For Everyone Found., Olathe, 1996; vol. dir. pub. rels. Women's Resource Network, Shawnee Mission, 2000-02; v.p. internat. tng. in comm. JoCo Club. Recipient 2 Telly awards, gold award Houston Internat. Film Festival, 2d place Kans. Film Festival, cert. of merit Internat. Film and Video competition for video Who Will Save the Children, 1995. Avocations: writing, painting, sewing, gardening. E-mail: wildberry@prodigy.net.

BERRYMAN, JOAN EILEEN, elementary school educator; d. Glen Elmo and Marian Eileen Berryman. BS in botany, Colo. State U., Ft. Collins, 1976, MEd, 1987. Sci. tchr. Montrose County Schs., Colo., 1980—. Musician: Montrose Cmty. Band, 2004—. Vol. Montrose Hist. Mus., 1996—2004. Mem.: Colo. Assn. Sci. Tchrs., Nat. Edn. Assn., Nat. Sci. Tchrs. Assn., Colo. Edn. Assn. (bd. dirs. 2002—, award 1997). Democrat. Home: 636 S Junction Ave Montrose CO 81401 Office: Columbine Mid Sch PO Box 10,000 Montrose CO 81402

BERRYMAN, MARY ANNE PIERCE, elementary school educator; b. Morrilton, Ark., June 4, 1937; d. Homer Rowland and Margaret (Oldham) Pierce; m. James Cleo Berryman, Aug. 5, 1961; children: James Andrew, Cathryn Anne. BA in Interior Design, U. Okla., 1959; MS in Religious Edn., Southwestern Seminary, Ft. Worth, 1961; tchr.'s cert., Ouachita Bapt. U., Aradelphia, Ark., 1970. Salesperson Ellison's Furnishings, Ft. Worth, 1961-62; interior designer J.C. Penny Co., Ft. Worth, 1962-63; tchr. Arkadelphia Pub. Schs., 1970—2003; ret., 2003. Chmn. Arkadelphia Drive for Arthritis Found., 1977. Named Tchr. Yr., Arkadelphia C. of C., 1984-85, State of Ark. Exemplary Tchr. of Econs., 1991-92. Mem. AAUW (local pres. 1976-77, chmn. Ark. state edn. found. 1977-78, lt. gov. 1985-86, gov. Ozark Dist. 1998-99, named. Disting. Gov., 2000), S.W. Reading Coun. (pres. 1978-79), Civitan (lt. gov. Ozark dist. 1989-90), Civitan (local v.p., sec., pres.), Delta Kappa Gamma, Kappa Kappa Iota (pres. 1986-88, 94-96, state bd. pos. 2), Civitan Club (local v.p., pres. 1988-89).

BERSCHEID, ELLEN S., psychology professor, writer, researcher; b. Colfax, Wis., Oct. 11, 1936; d. Sylvan L. and Alvilde (Running) Saumer; m. Dewey Mathias Berscheid, Nov. 21, 1959. BA, U. Nev., 1959, MA, 1960; PhD, U. Minn., 1965. Market rsch. analyst Pillsbury Co., Mpls., 1960-62; asst. prof. psychology and mktg. U. Minn., Mpls., 1965-66, asst. prof. psychology, 1967-68, assoc. prof., 1969-71, prof., 1971-88, Regents' prof. psychology, 1988—. Mem. NRC Assembly Behavioral and Social Scis., 1973-77. Co-author: Interpersonal Attraction, 1969, 78, Equity: Theory and Research, 1978, Close Relationships, 1983, Psychology of Interpersonal Relationships, 2005, also numerous articles; mem. numerous edit. bds., past editorships. Recipient Disting. Scientist award Soc. Exptl. Social Psychology, 1993. Fellow APA (Donald T. Campbell award 1984, editor Contemporary Psychology Jour. 1985-91, Disting. Sci. Contbn. award 1997, Presdl. Citation 2003), Soc. Personality and Social Psychology (pres. 1985), Soc. for Psychol. Study Social Issues, Am. Acad. Arts and Scis.; mem. Internat. Soc. for the Study Personal Relationships (pres. 1990-92), Soc. Exptl. Social Psychology (exec. bd. 1971-74, 77-80, 85-89, Disting. Scientist award 1993). Lutheran. Avocation: interior design. Home: 329 Park Cir Menomonie WI 54751 Office: U Minn Dept Psychology N309 Elliott Hall Minneapolis MN 55455 Business E-Mail: bersc001@umn.edu.

BERSI, ANN, lawyer; b. San Jose; BA, MA, San Diego State U.; JD, Calif. Western Sch. of Law; PhD in Higher Edn. Adminstrn., U. Conn. Bar: Calif. Past mem. law firms Morris, Brignone & Pickering, Lionel, Sawyer & Collins, Las Vegas; dir. employee rels. State of Nev., 1981-83; exec. dir. State Bar Nev., 1983-89; dep. dist. atty. civil divsn. Clark County Dist. Atty.'s Office, Las Vegas, 1995—2005. Past instr. pub. adminstrn. Pace U., N.Y.; legal counsel Clark County Sch. Dist. Bd. Trustees, Clark County Bd. Equalization, 1995-2005; mem. State Jud. Selection Commn., 2000—, Nev. Tax Commn., 2005— Mem. State Bar Nev. (pres. bd. govs. 1999-2000). Office: 5216 Painted Lakes Way Las Vegas NV 89149

BERSIN, MOLLIE KLAPPER, physician; b. Pitts., June 10, 1917; d. Abraham Louis Klapper and Anna Davidovitch; m. Herbert Bersin, Dec. 7, 1950 (dec. 1993); children: David, Anne. B Edn., Wayne U., Detroit, 1941; MD, Hahneman Med. Coll., Phila., 1950. Tchr. handicapped Elizabeth Schs., NJ, 1941—46; gen. practitioner Ross-Loos Med. Group, L.A., 1951—53; sch. physician L.A. City Schs., 1953—60, examining physician Employee Health Office, 1960—70, supervising physician Employee Health Office, 1970—73, dir. Employee Med. Svcs., 1973—82. Avocations: quilting, piano, reading.

BERSIN, SUSAN JOYCE-HEATHER (REIGNBEAUX JOYCE-HEATHER BERSIN), critical care nurse, police officer; b. Reservation, MD, July 11, 1945; d. Richard George Sr. and Ireene Rose (Brenner) Bersin; m. Robert Joseph Okragley, Dec. 23, 1972 (div. Apr. 1993); 1 child, MaryRose Reignbeaux. BS in Zoology, Kent State U., 1975, BSN, 1976, BS in Chemistry, 1976; MS in Med.-Surg Nursing, Case Western Res. U., 1979. RN, Ohio; cert. critical care nurse. Driver Waite Transport, Akron, Ohio, 1967-68, Cleve. Transit System, 1968-70; CEO, chief technician Corvair Repair & Mobile Svc., Cleve., 1970—; critical care nurse Deaconess Hosp., Cleve., 1976-79, St. Luke's Hosp., Cleve., 1979-81, St. John Hosp., Cleve., 1981—; police officer Cleve. Police Dept., 1971—. Served with USN, 1963-67, Viet Nam. Mem. Sigma Theta Tau (charter mem. Delta Xi chpt.). Roman Catholic. Avocations: reading, ice figure skating, aeronautics and sky-diving. Home: 1285 W 117th #4 Cleveland OH 44107-3036

BERSON, BELLA ZEVITOVSKY, librarian; b. Bklyn., Aug. 15, 1925; d. Nathan and Enda (Vieman) Zevitovsky; m. Jerome Abraham Berson, June 30, 1946; children— Ruth, David, Jonathan BA, NYU, 1945; MA in L.S., U. Wis., 1969. Staff devel. officer Yale U. Library, New Haven, 1975, asst. librarian for personnel, 1976-82, assoc. univ. librarian, 1982—90, assoc. univ. librarian, dir. med. library, 1984—90. Fellow Branford Coll. Mem. Phi Beta Kappa, Beta Phi Mu

BERT, CAROL LOIS, retired educational assistant; b. Bakersfield, Calif., Oct. 15, 1938; d. Edwin Vernon and Shirely Helen (Craig) Phelps; m. John Davison Bert, Sept. 26, 1964; children: Mary Ellen, John Edwin, Craig Eric, Douglas Ethan. BSN, U. Colo., 1960. Med. surg. nurse U.S. Army, Washington, 1960-62, Ascom City, Korea, 1962-63, San Antonio, 1963, Albuquerque, 1964-65; ednl. asst. Jefferson County Schs., Arvada, Colo., 1979-2000, ret. Sec. Parent Tchr. Student Assn. Arvada West H.S., 1987-88. Mem. Colo. Quilting Coun. (1st v.p. 1988, 89, Hall of Fame 1992). Avocations: quilting, reading, camping, fishing, tennis. Home: 5844 Oak St Arvada CO 80004-4739

BERT, CLARA VIRGINIA, retired secondary school educator, retired school system administrator; b. Quincy, Fla., Jan. 29, 1929; d. Harold C. and Ella J. (McDavid) Bert. BS, Fla. State U., 1950, MS, 1963, PhD, 1967. Cert. tchr. Fla., home economist, pub. mgr. Tchr. Union County High Sch., Lake Butler, Fla., 1950-53, Havana High Sch., Fla., 1953-65; cons. rsch. and devel. Fla. Dept. Edn., Tallahassee, 1967-75, sect. dir. rsch. and devel., 1975-85, program dir. home econs. edn., 1985-92, program specialist resource devel., 1992-96, program specialist, spl. projects, 1996-99, program dir. grants mgmt., 1999-2000; ret., 2000. Field reader US Dept. Edn., 1974—75; cons. Nat. Ctr. Rsch. Vocation Edn., Ohio State U., 1978. Author, editor: booklets. Mem. devel. bd., mem. adv. bd. Fla. State U. Coll. Human Scis. Family Inst., 1994—; mem. nat. com. for the capital campaign Fla. State U. Found., 2002—. Named Disting. Alumna, Coll. Human Scis., Fla. State U., 1994; recipient Dean's award, 1995; US Office Edn. grantee, 1976, 1977, 1978. Mem.: Am. Ednl. Rsch. Assn., Nat. Coun. Family Rels., Am. Vocat. Edn. Rsch. Assn. (nat. treas. 1970—71), Fla. Vocat. Home Econs. Assn., Fla. Vocat. Assn., Am. Vocat. Assn., Am. Home Econs. Assn. (state treas. 1969—71), Fla. State U. Alumni Assn. (bd. dirs. home econs. sect. 1976—81, pres.-elect 1978—79, 1979—80), Fla. State U. Ctr. Club, Havana Golf and Country Club, Phi Delta Kappa, Sigma Kappa (pres. corp. bd. 1985—91), Delta Kappa Gamma (pres. 1974—76), Kappa Omicron Nu (chpt. pres. 1965—66), Kappa Delta Pi.

BERTA, MELISSA ROSE, mathematics professor; b. Van Nuys, Calif., Apr. 29, 1966; d. Alexander Rocco and Patricia Ann Yguado; m. Brad Braden Berta, July 12, 1986; children: Joseph Brandon, Lisa Marie. AS in Math. and Sci., Coll. Canyons, 1989; BS in Math., Calif. State U., 1993; MS in Math., U. Nebr., 1996. Fellow Calif. State U., Northridge, 1992—93; tchg. asst. U. Nebr., Lincoln, 1994—96; adminstrn. asst. Berta Engering., Laguna Hills, Calif., 1996—98; instr. math. Santiago Coll., Orange, Calif., 1998—2001, Orange Coast Coll., Costa Mesa, Calif., 1998—, Saddleback Coll., Mission Viejo, Calif., 1998—2005. Leader Girl Scouts Am., Rancho Santa Margarita. With U.S. Army, 1984—87. Larson Minority Grad. fellow, U. Nebr., 1994—95. Mem.: Faculty Assn. Calif. CC. Home: 17 Calle Espolon Rancho Santa Margarita CA 92688

BERTAGNOLLI, LESLIE A., lawyer; b. Bloomington, Ill., Nov. 11, 1948; BA, Ill. State U., 1970, MA, 1971; PhD, U. Ill., 1975, JD, 1979. Bar: Ill. 1979. Ptnr. Baker & McKenzie, Chgo. Office: Baker & McKenzie 130 E Randolph Dr Ste 3700 Chicago IL 60601-6342

BERTELSEN, KARYN, school system administrator, principal; b. Standardville, Utah, Nov. 20, 1944; d. John and Edith Piccioni; m. Bruce Bertelsen; children: Kristy Lee, Kelly Ann. AS, Coll. Eastern Utah Price, Utah, 1965; BS, Utah State Univ., Logan, Utah, 1967; MEd, Brigham Young Univ., Provo, Utah, 1983; EdD, Univ. Utah, Salt Lake City, 2002—. Family & consumer sci. tchr. Allessandro Jr. High, Moreno Valley, 1967—68; FACS/P.E. tchr. Helper Jr. High, Helper, Utah, 1969—83; adult roles Davis Sch. Dist., Farmington, Utah, 1983—88, nutrition coord., 1988—89, asst. prin., 1990—96, prin., 1994—. Accreditation team facilitator Ut. State office of Edn.; accreditation team Univ. Phoenix; team jr. high rep. Gov. Leavitt's H.S. Requirements. Founder Teen Help-Line, 1995; rep. Bountiful City Improvement Com., 2000—. Recipient Utah Mid. Sch. Prin. of the Yr., UASSP, 2001, Davis County's Women of the Yr., 2002, Utah Vocat. Tchr. of the Yr., 1990. Mem.: Davis C. of C., Nation Assn. of Sec. Prin., Utah Middle Sch. Assn., League of Women Voters, Phi Delta Kappa. Avocations: reading, helping others. Home: 1827 Maple Lane Bountiful UT 84010 E-mail: kbertselsen@dsdmail.net.

BERTERMANN, LAURA LYNN, secondary school educator; d. James Howard and Paula Gene Cogar; m. Daniel Edward Bertermann, Aug. 9, 1992; children: Madeline Tyler, Payton Lynn. BS in Biol., Ill. State U., 1991; MEd in Curriculum and Instrn., Nat. Louis U., Ill., 1996; MA in Ednl. Leadership, Northeastern Ill. U., Chgo., 2005. Sci. tchr. Woodland Jr. High, Gages Lake, Ill., 1991—92, Vernon Hills HS, Ill., 1992—. Home: 1425 Mayfair Ln Grayslake IL 60030 Office: Dist 128 Vernon Hills HS 145 N Lakeview Pkwy Vernon Hills IL 60061 Office Phone: 847-932-2000 8553.

BERTERO, KAREN E., lawyer; b. Mar. 16, 1957; AB, Univ. Calif., Berkeley, 1978; JD, UCLA, 1981. Ptnr. corp. transactions and securities Gibson Dunn & Crutcher LLP, LA. Mem. exec. com. and diversity com. Gibson Dunn & Crutcher. Mem.: ABA, State Bar Calif., Order of Coif, Phi Beta Kappa. Office: Gibson Dunn & Crutcher LLP 333 S Grand Ave Los Angeles CA 90071-3197 Office Phone: 213-229-7360. Office Fax: 213-229-6360. Business E-Mail: kbertero@gibsondunn.com.

BERTINE, DOROTHY WILMUTH, artist, educator, accountant, genealogist, poet, writer; b. Madill, Okla., Sept. 28, 1916; d. Oliver Olen Wilkerson and Nina Keortinka Bennett; m. George Franklin Bertine II (dec. 1995). BS, Okla. State U., 1942; MA, Tex. Woman's U., Denton, 1975; advanced studies with many famous art tchrs. in painting workshops worldwide as, Dong Kingman, Mildred Sheets, Milford Zornes, Frances Skinner, Clara Ely, Edgar Whitney. CPA Tex., 1944. Acct., CPA, Dallas, 1943—45, Houston, 1945—68, Brownsville, Tex., 1963—68; instr., life mem. Brownsville Art League, 1959—70; student to Frances Skinner Houston Museum Art Sch., Houston, 1956—63; tchr. Tex. Women's U., Denton, Tex., 1973—75; tchr., head art dept. Denton Parks and Recreation, 1976—85; instr. in continuing edn. U. North Tex., 1982—83; lectr. workshops local painting groups Okla., Tex., Colo., 1976—96; acct., CPA Austin, Tex., 1944—. Bd. mem. Southwestern Watercolor Soc., Dallas, 1983—84; bd. mem., founding mem. Denton Hist. Landmark Commn., 1983—85; bd. mem., genealogist Denton Hist. Commn., 1976—85; regent, geneologist Daughters of Am. Revolution, 1999—2001. Author, illustrator Design Elements Used in High Victorian Houses, 1975, Principles and Elements of Design:, 1989, Pierre Bertine 1686 and Allied Families, 1994, Ancestors and Descendants of Lucy Ann and George E.C. Bennett, 1989, DeHaven Ancestry Book, 1994; over 20 solo art exhibits and over 40 group exhibits; contbr. artistic works to profl publs.; Represented in permanent collections Brownsville Art League, Laredo Art Ctr, Tex., Heard Mus. Sci., McKinny, Tex., State Mus. NJ, Trenton, Citizens Nat. Bank, Tex., over 40 more permanent collections throughout the US; contbg. artist (book) The Collected Best of Watercolor America, 2002, International Dictionary Encyclopedia of Modern and Contemporary Art, 2004 (cert. merit and medal, 2004), 2005 (cert. merit and medal, 2005), La Mer. Regards de Pientres et d'ecrivains, 2005, International Dictionary Encyclopedia of Modern and Contemporary Art, 2006 (cert. merit and medal, 2006), Art, Peintres et Sculpteurs du XV au XXI Siecle, 2006. Asst. precinct chmn. Rep. Party, Houston, 1953—63; artist in residence Tex. and Denton Hist. Commn., Denton, 1980—83; tchr. adult bible classes Ch. of Christ, Houston, 1960—, Brownsville, 1960—, Denton, 1975—; pres. co-founder Nat. Registry for DeHaven Family 1698. Named Best of Watercolor painting light and shadow, 1997; recipient Grumbacher Art award, Southwestern Watercolor Soc., Dallas, Tex, 1982, Best of Show Pres. award, Soc. Watercolor Artists, Ft. Worth, Tex., 1986, Tex. Fine Arts Regional citation, Tex., 1967, 1st Place Graphics, Nacogdoches Ann., 1973, Dist. Svc. award, Tex. Hist. Commn., 1980—81, Acad. Knight of Verbano, 2004—05; Ann. Scholarship award, Delta Psi Delta Nat. Hon. Art Orgn., Denton, Tex., 1974—75. Mem.: Soc. Watercolor Artists (signature mem. 1986), So. Watercolor Soc. (exhibiting mem. 1982), Associated Creative Artists (signature mem. 1984—), Southwestern Watercolor Soc. (signature mem., bd. mem. 1982—), Laredo Art Ctr.

(life), La. Watercolor Soc. (life; academical mem. 1980—2006), Brownsville Art League (life; instr., bd. mem. 1959—). Republican. Ch. Of Christ. Avocations: poetry, genealogy. Office: studio d'Bertine PO Box 2965 Denton TX 76202 Office Phone: 940-387-9993.

BERTINI, CATHERINE ANN, former international organization official; b. Syracuse, NY, Mar. 30, 1950; d. Fulvio and Ann (Vino) B.; m. Thomas Haskell, 1988. BA, SUNY, 1971; DHL (hon.), SUNY, Cortland, 1999; DSc (hon.), McGill U., Montreal, Can., 1997; DSc, Pine Manor Coll., 2000; DHL (hon.), Am. U. Rome, 2001; D in Pub. Svc. (hon.), John Cabot U., Rome, 2001; PhD (hon.), Slovak Agrl. U., Nitra, Slovak Republic, 2001; DHL (hon.), Loyola U., 2002, U. S.C., 2003, Dakota Wesleyan U., 2003, Colgate U., 2004. Youth dir. N.Y. Rep. State Com., 1971-74; with Rep. Nat. Com., 1975-76; mgr. pub. policy Container Corp. Am., 1977-87; dir. Office Family Assistance, U.S. Dept. Health and Human Svcs., 1987-89; acting asst. sec. U.S. Dept. HHS., 1989; asst. sec. USDA, 1989-92; UN panel mem. sec. gen.'s High Level Personalities on African Devel., UN, 1992-95; exec. dir. UN World Food Programme, Rome, 1992—2002; personal humanitarian envoy UN Sec. Gen., 2002; policy maker in residence Gerald Ford Sch. Pub. Policy U. Mich., 2002; chmn. U.N. Sys. Standing Com. on Nutrition, 2002—; under-sec. gen. mgmt. U.N., 2002—05. Bd. dirs. Tupperware Corp., Orlando, 2005—. Mem. Ill. State Scholarship Comm., 1979-84; mem. Ill. Human Rights Comm., 1985-87; spl. envoy of Sec. Gen. to the Horn of Africa, 2000. Recipient Leadership in Human Svcs. award Am. Pub. Welfare Assn., 1990, Pub. Svc. award Am. Acad. Pediatrics, 1991, Leadership award Nat. Assn. WIC Dirs., 1992, Internat. Girl Guides and Girl Scouts, 2002, Chgo. Coun. Fgn. Rels., 2004, Quality of Life award Auburn U., 1994, Disting. Alumni award Nelson A. Rockefeller Coll. Pub. Affairs and Policy, 1997, Award for Excellence Assn. African Journalists, 2002, World Food Prize Laureate, 2003, Global Leadership award, 2004. Fellow Harvard U., 1986.

BERTINO, PATRICIA NOLAN, science educator; b. Ellenville, N.Y., Nov. 28, 1950; d. Arthur J. and E. Doris Nolan; m. Anthony (Bud) Bertino, Aug. 9, 2001. BA in Biology, SUNY-Oneonta, 1972; MSc in Tchg., Union Coll., 1976. Tchr. biology Scotia-Glenville HS, NY, 1968—2006. Advisor ski club Scotia-Glenville HS, 1982—86; cons. Bertino Consultants, Scotia, 2001—; presenter in field. Mem.: Cornell Inst. Biology Tchrs., Biology and Life Sci. Assn., Sci. Tchr. Assn. N.Y., Nat. Assn. Biology Tchrs.

BERTOLET, CAROLINE LYNNE GEORGEANNE, special education educator, labor union administrator; b. Phila., Oct. 16, 1948; d. George Clayton and Caroline E. Werner; m. William B. Bertolet, II, June 6, 1980; 1 child, Leslie Lynne Hollingsworth. BS, Indiana U. Pa., 1970; MA in Psychology, West Chester U., Pa., 1974; cert. in spl. edn. supervisory, Pa. State U., 1983, cert. elem. and secondary prin., 1996. Tchr. Marple Newtown Sch. Dist., Newtown Square, Pa., 1970—, chairperson student assistance program, 1998—2004, mem. negotiating team, 2005—06. Chairperson registration SPCA Walk for Paws, Chester County, Pa.; treas. SPCA Aux., Chester County, Pa. Mem.: Pa. State Edn. Assn. (profl. rights and responsibilities commr. 2002—), Marple Newtown Edn. Assn. (pres. 2002—, grievance chair 1988—), Pi Lambda Theta. Avocations: gardening, reading, knitting, swimming, aerobics. Home: 1181 Fielding Dr West Chester PA 19382 Office: Marple Newtown Sch Dist 120 Media Line Rd Newtown Square PA 19073

BERTOLINO, JENNIFER ANN, elementary school educator; b. Riverside, Calif., Oct. 15, 1970; d. Thomas Wilson and Jay Todd, Colleen Wilson (Stepmother) and Kenneth Todd (Stepfather); m. John Bertolino, Sept. 6, 1997; children: John, Charles, Macy. MS in Environ. Sci., U. Houston, 2001. Cert. tchr. Tex. Environ. investigator Galveston County Health Dist., La Marque, Tex., 2001—04; mid. sch. sci. tchr., sci. coord. Odyssey Acad., Galveston, Tex., 2004—. Mem. Galveston Police Meml. Found., 1997—2005; treas. John Bertolino Campaign, Santa Fe, Tex., 2005—06. Named Tchr. of Yr., Odyssey Acad., 2004—05. Mem.: NSTA, Tex. Sci. Edn. Leadership Assn. Avocations: hiking, running, baseball. Office: Odyssey Acad 901 13th St Galveston TX 77550 Office Phone: 409-750-9289. Personal E-mail: jenbertolino@yahoo.com. Business E-Mail: jbertolino@odyssey-academy.com.

BERTONCIN, GERALDINE JOHNNIE, elementary school educator; b. Washington, Jan. 31, 1951; d. John Boyd and Leone Marthe King; m. David Vincent Glide, July 26, 1970 (div. June 1993); children: Derek Justin Glide, Lisa Christine Glide; m. Richard Bertoncin, Mar. 29, 1997. BA, Georgian Ct. Coll., Lakewood, N.J., 1987; postgrad., Shenandoah U., Winchester, Va., 2000. Cert. tchr., elem. edn., English N.J. Dept. Edn. 1st grade tchr. Emma Havens Young Elem. Sch., Brick, NJ, 1989—90; 7th grade English/social studies tchr. Vets. Meml. Mid. Sch., Brick, 1990—. Gen. equivalency diploma English tchr. Point Pleasant HS, 1991—93; spl. edn. tchr. Camp Beadelston, Brick Meml. HS, 2001. V.p. PTO, Brick, 1978—85; mem. PTA, Brick, 1989—; active AHA, Brick, 2000—04. Recipient Gov.'s Tchr. of Yr. award, N.J. Dept. Edn., 2004. Mem.: Brick Town Edn. Assn., N.J. Edn. Assn. Democrat. Roman Catholic. Avocations: walking, boating, theater, bicycling, travel. Office: Veteran's Meml Mid Sch 115 Hendrickson Ave Brick NJ 08724

BERTRAM, CHRISTINE G., artist, painter, graphics designer; b. New Bedford, Mass., Dec. 28, 1952; d. Samuel David Doran and Marjorie Ruth (Dore) B.; children: Christian Allan, Michael Doran. BFA in Painting, Swain Sch. Design, 1974; MFA, Bklyn. Coll., 1976; BFA in Design/Typography magna cum laude, U. Mass., Dartmouth, 1995. Freelance scrimshaw artist, Mattapoisett, Mass., 1980-87; graphic designer New Bedford Std. Times, 1997—2002. Designer visual prevention program State of Mass. Lead Paint Prevention Program, 1995; designer Beth Soll Dance Inc., Boston, 1994-95; project mgr., rschr. Office of Hist. Preservation, New Bedford, 1978-80. Author: Palmers Light House, 1978; co-author: History of North Bedford, 1979; designer numerous posters, books, invitations, pamphlets, logos; exhibited in various art exhbns., 1974—. Vol. Tchrs. Ctr. Sch., Mattapoisett, 1989—2001, Boy Scouts Am., Mattapoisett, 1986—; Sunday sch. tchr. Congl. Ch., Mattapoisett, 1984—2002. U.S. govt. grantee for rsch. involved in New Bedford becoming a Nat. Park. Avocations: antique restoration, braided and hooked rugs, sewing, painting, gardening. Home: 124 Acushnet Rd Mattapoisett MA 02739-1221 E-mail: christieb43@aol.com.

BERTRAM, CONNIE N., lawyer; b. Yorktown, Va., Sept. 19, 1965; BBA, Coll. William and Mary, 1987; JD with honors, George Washington U., 1990. Bar: Va. 1990, US Dist. Ct. Va. (ea. dist.) 1990, DC 1992, Md. 1999, US Dist. Ct. DC 1999, US Ct. Appeals (fourth cir.) 1999, DC Ct. Appeals, Va. Supreme Ct. Ptnr. Labor and Employment Depts. Venable LLP, Washington. Spkr. in field; instr. deposition program Nat. Inst. Trial Advocacy, 1996—, instr. trial skills program, 2001—; adj. prof. legal rsch. and writing George Washington U., 1995—96. Editor: George Washington Jour. Internat. Law and Economics, 1989—90; contbr. articles to profl. jours. Named Leading Lawyer labor and employment field, Legal Times, 2004; recipient Best Lawyers in employment, Washingtonian mag., 2004. Mem.: ABA (mem. labor and employment sect.), Fairfax Bar Assn. (mem. labor employment sect.), DC Bar Assn. (co-chair steering com. labor and employment sect. 2000—03, program chair), Va. State Bar Assn., Phi Delta Phi (v.p. 1988—89), Omicron Delta Kappa. Office: Venable LLP 575 7th St NW Washington DC 20004 also: 8010 Towers Crescent Dr Vienna VA 22182 Office Phone: 202-344-4835, 703-760-1647. Office Fax: 202-344-8300, 703-821-8949. E-mail: cnbertram@venable.com.

BERTRAM, JEAN DESALES, writer; b. Burlington, Iowa, Sept. 28; d. Val Randall and Ruth Cecilia Bertram; 1 child, Larkin Bertram-Cox Montgomery. BA, U. N.C., Greensboro, 1942; MA, U. Minn., 1951; PhD, Stanford U., 1963. Reporter Greensboro News Record, 1942-43; founder dept. pub. rels. Burlington Industries, Greensboro, 1943-49; asst. to dean edn. U. N.C., Greensboro, 1949-50; instr. U. Minn., Mpls., 1950-51; dir. radio performance Mpls. Vocat. High Sch., 1951-52; dir. Children's Theatre Touring Co., Jr. League Mpls., 1951-52; prof. theatre arts San Francisco State U., 1952-88. Cons. Wadsworth Pub. Co., Belmont, Calif., 1966; dir. Readers' Repertory, San Francisco State U., 1967-72; dir. Jean De Sales Bertram Players, San Francisco, 1971-74; founder, developer storytelling program San Francisco State U., 1971-88; cons. Scott-Foresman, Chgo., 1983; senator acad. senate San Francisco State U., 1983-84, dir. com. for lectures, arts and spl. programs, 1985-87; tax preparer, 1994. Author: (textbooks) The Oral Experience of Literature, 1967, The Actor Speaks, 4 edits., 1981-87, Tell Me a Story!, 5 edits., 1982-88; author, dir. Girl Scout Nat. Convention pageant Finding Your Own Adventure, 1955; prodr., dir., adapter, editor: (religious plays) A Symphonetic Easter Drama, 1954, The Awakening, 1954, The Vision of Isaiah, 1970, The Cherry Tree, 1971; author, dir.: (plays) American Cameos, 1976, Jeremiah The Prophet, 1999; author: (poem) Cosmorama, 1971; actress one-woman show numerous women from Shakespeare's plays, 1971-88; author: (short story) The Giraffe and the Canary, 1999; contbr. articles to profl. jours. Stanford-Wilson fellow Stanford U., 1962-63. Mem. Acad. Am. Poets, Phi Beta Kappa (sec. Omicron of Calif. chpt. 1977-79, 83-88, pres. 1979-81, v.p. 1981-83, ofcl. del. Triennial coun. 1979, 82). Avocations: sculpturing in clay, poetry writing, photography.

BERTRAND, BETTY HARLEEN, nurse; b. Little Rock, Ark., July 17, 1960; d. Harley Walter and Joyce Elaine (Bryant) Baker; m. Robert K. Bertrand, June 13, 1980; children: Mary, Jessie, Alyssa, Jared. AA, Cerro Coso C.C., 1981; ADN, Texarkana Coll., 1989; BSN, U. Ark. Med. Sch., 1994. RN, Tex.; lic. vocat. nurse; cert. low risk neonatal care. Nurse asst. Ridgecrest (Calif.) Cmty. Hosp., 1982-85; lic. vocat. nurse Wadley Regional Med. Ctr., Texarkana, Tex., 1986-89, RN, 1989-92; field supervising nurse HealthCor Home Health, Texarkana, 1992-93; nurse Blankenship Dialysis Ctr., Texarkana, 1993-95; clin. instr. Texarkana Coll., 1995-97, instr. vocat. nursing program, 1997—; nurse St. Michael Health Care Ctr., 1995—. Baptist. Avocations: reading, cross stitching, crochet, parenting, piano. Home: 102 Pine Valley Rd Texarkana TX 75501-9320 E-mail: dadmomb@msn.com, bbertran@texarkanacollege.edu.

BERTRAND, TINA LOUISE, political science professor; d. James E. Bertrand and Evelyn Mae Busbee-Bertrand. PhD in Polit. Sci., Emory U., Atlanta, 1999. Dir., model UN acad. program McMurry U., Abilene, Tex., 1999—. Mem., dir. mentorship program Nat. Collegiate Conf. Assn., NYC, 2004—06. Grantee, KIVA Exec. Bd., McMurry U., 2000, 2006; Sam Taylor fellow, Gen. Bd. Higher Edn. and Ministry, United Meth. Ch., 2003, 2006. Mem.: Acad. Coun. UN Sys. Achievements include research in UN Scandals and their Impact on US Public Opinion. Office: McMurry U McM Station 998 Abilene TX 79697 Office Phone: 325-793-4616. Office Fax: 325-793-4770.

BERTSCH, KELLY FRANCES, mathematics educator; b. Wharton, Tex., Sept. 27, 1964; d. Sandra Horn Smith; m. Michael Anthony Bertsch, May 18, 1985. BS in Math. cum laude, U. Houston, Tex., 1996. Sys. analyst Dow Chem., Freeport, Tex., 1988—92; tchr. math. Sweeny Ind. Sch. Dist., Tex., 1996. Cons. various schs. and svc. ctrs., Tex., 1998. Treas. Sweeny Lions Club - Ednl. Br., Tex., 2000. Recipient Outstanding H.S. Tchr. award, U. Tex., 2005. Mem.: Delta Kappa Gamma (corr.; 2d v.p. 2002). Office Phone: 979-491-8100.

BERTSCH, PATRICIA ANN, nature center director; b. Orange, NJ, Jan. 14, 1969; d. Margaret Mary and John Patrick Murray; m. Leon James Bertsch, Oct. 19, 1997. BS in Marine Biology, Richard Stockton Coll., 1991. Instr. Marine Sci. Consortium, Wallops Island, Va., 1992—93, Barrier Island Environ. Edn. Ctr., John's Island, SC, 1993—94; ednl. coord. Jenkinson's Aquarium, Point Pleasant, NJ, 1995—95; pk. naturalist Trailside Nature & Sci. Ctr., Mountainside, NJ, 1995—98, asst. dir., 1998—2002, dir., 2002—. Intern Kewalo Basin Marine Mammal Lab., Honolulu, 1995—96; vol. Earthwatch, Mass., 1999; exec. dir. Trailside Mus. Assn., Mountainside, 2002—; mem. Cranford Environ. Commn., 2004—. Mem.: Alliance N.J. Environ. Edn. (assoc.). Avocations: birdwatching, camping, hiking, kayaking, travel. Home: 110 Kenilworth Blvd Cranford NJ 07016 Office: Trailside Nature & Sci Ctr 452 New Providence Rd Mountainside NJ 07092 Office Fax: 908-789-3270. E-mail: pbertsch@ucnj.org.

BERZON, FAYE CLARK, retired nursing educator; b. New Britain, Conn., Sept. 26, 1926; d. Bernard Francis and Elizabeth Tillie (Gross) Clark; m. Harry Berzon, June 18, 1961. Diploma, Beth Israel Hosp., 1947; BSN, Boston U., 1957, MSN, 1959; cert. advanced grad. studies, U. Mass., 1987, cert. in gerontology, 1993, adv. cert. in gerontology, 1994. Staff, head nurse, instr. Beth Israel Hosp., Boston, 1948-58; instr. nursing Simmons Coll., Boston, 1958-62, Cath. Labore Sch. Nursing, Dorchester, Mass., 1962-67; asst. prof. nursing Boston U. Sch. Nursing, 1967-70; div. chmn. human svcs. Massasoit CC, Brockton, Mass., 1973-79, prof. nursing, 1970-92, chair nursing dept., 1988-91. Mem. acad. adv. com. to Mass. Bd. Higher Edn., 1975-76; ombudsman in nursing home South Shore Elder Svcs., 1993—. Author: (with Govoni, Berzon, Fall) Drugs and Nursing Implications, 1965, Nursing Outlook, 1970. Vol. Milton Meals on Wheels, Mass., 1978—90; scholarship com. New Eng. Sinai Hosp., 1992—, bd. advisors, 1996—; bd. dirs. Temple Israel-Saaron, 2000—, coun. aging, 2004—; adv. com. Respiratory Therapy Dept. Massasua C.C., 1976—. Mem. ANA, Nat. League Nursing (scholar 1963-79, accreditation visitor 1976-86), Nursing Archives, Mass. Assn. Older Ams., Mass. Gerontology Assn., Beth Israel Hosp. Nurses Alumnae Assn. (co-pres.), Hadassah-Landy-Kaplan Nurses Coun. (life), Sigma Theta Tau. Jewish. Home: 52 Harold St Sharon MA 02067-2544

BERZON, MARSHA S., federal judge; b. Cin., Apr. 17, 1945; BA, Radcliffe Coll., 1966; JD, Boalt Hall Sch. Law, 1973. Bar: Calif. 1973, D.C. 1975. Clerk Judge James Browning, 9th Cir., 1973—74, Justice William Brennan, 1974—75; atty. Woll & Mayer, Washington, 1975—77, Altshuler, Berzon, Nussbaum, Berzon & Rubin, San Francisco, 1978—2000; judge U.S. Ct. Appeals 9th Cir., 2000—; assoc. gen. counsel AFL-CIO, 1987—99. Lectr. U. Calif. Sch. Social Welfare, Berkeley, Calif., 1992, La. State U. Sch. of Law, 2003; practitioner-in-residence Cornell Sch. of Law, NY, 1994, Ind. U. Law Sch., 1998. Mem.: Fed. Bar Assn., State Bar of Calif., DC Bar Assn., Am. Law Inst., Am. Bar Found. Office: US Ct Appeals 9th Cir 95 7th St San Francisco CA 94103-1526 Office Phone: 415-556-7800. Office Fax: 415-556-9491.

BESCH, LORRAINE W., special education educator; b. Orange, N.J., June 27, 1948; d. Robert Woodruff and Minnie (Wrightson) B.; m. William Lee Gibson, July 10, 1982. AA in Liberal Arts, Mt. Vernon Coll., 1968; BA in Sociology, U. Colo., 1970; MA in Spl. Edn., U. Denver, 1973. Cert. handicapped thcr., N.J. Elem. resource rm. tchr. Beeville (Tex.) Ind. Sch. Dist., 1973-75; trainable mentally retarded tchr. Kings County Supt. Schs., Hanford, Calif., 1975-78; h.s. resource rm. tchr. Summit (N.J.) Bd. Edn., 1980-81, Westfield (N.J.) Bd. Edn., 1981-99, head coach field hockey, 1981-83, mem. crisis mgmt. team, 1982-87, in class support tchr. English, 1993-99. Named to Women's Inner Circle Achievement, 1996; recipient Internat. Sash of Academia, ABI, 1997. Mem. AAUW, Smithsonian Nat. Mus. Am. Indian (charter), Sky Meadows Cir. Nat. Mus. Women in Arts, CEC (learning disabilities divsn.), Westfield Edn. Assn. (del. 1983-90, tech. com. 1993-94, conf. funds com. 1994-99), Hartford Family Found. (v.p., sec. 1991-97, trustee 1997—), Wrightson-Besch Found. (sec.-treas. 1994-99, pres. 1999—), Archaeology Conservancy (life), 1892 Founders Soc., Morristown Meml. Health Found., Col. Williamsburg Burgesses, Nat. Trust Historic Preservation, N.J. Hist. Society. Avocations: travel, reading, gardening, cooking, tennis. Home: 8 Lone Oak Rd Basking Ridge NJ 07920-1613

BESCH, NANCY ADAMS, county official; b. Lancaster, Pa., Nov. 12, 1926; AB in Psychology, Wilson Coll., 1948, LHD, DHL (hon.), 1989. Commr., vice chair Cumberland County, 1992-95, commr., chair, 1995—. Bd. dirs., publ. info. tng. com. chair County Commrs.' Assn. of Pa.; Capital Region Chamber of Commerce "Envision" Task Force; v. chmn. So. Ctrl. Assembly for Effective Governance; Capital Region Econ. Devel. Corp. Bd. Coun. mem. Camp Hill Borough, 1984-91; bd. dirs. Camp Hill Sch., 1975-81; commr. liaison Cumberland County Libr. Sys. Bd.; mem. exec. bd. Cumberland-Perry Mental Health/Mental Retardation; comm. mem. cmty. adv. bd. Harrisburg Acad. 1998-2001; mem. Capital Region Funders Collaborative, Cmty. Connections, Keystone Area Coun. Boy Scouts (exec. com., mem. Bd. of NE Coun. Boy Scouts of Am.), Fund Devel. Com. Hemlock Girl Scout Coun., Inc. 1980-99, Cmty. Devel. Block Grant Adv. Com. of Pa. Dept. of Cmty. and Econ. Devel., Cumberland County Children and Youth Svcs. Adv. Com., DUI Task Force, Domestic Violence Svcs. Cumberland and Perry Counties; polity com. Presbytery of Carlisle; personnel sub-com. Synod of The Trinity Presbyn. Church, USA. Recipient Outstanding Publ. Ofcl. award, Pa. Assn. County Human Svcs., 1998, Pa.'s Mem. of Yr. award County Commr.'s Assn., 1997, Dist. Daughters of Pa. award, awarded by Govnr. Ridge, 1997, Catalyst award Capital Region Econ. Devel. Corp. for Leadership in Support of Devel. in Harrisburg Region, 1994, Elected Ofcls. award Pa. Libr. Assn., 1993, Trustee award Dist. Svc. Wilson Coll., 1988, Dist. Alum. award, Wilson Coll. 1989, Hemlock award for Svc. Hemlock Girl Scout Coun., Ketchum, Inc. award for Leadership in Am. Philanthropy, "Thanks" Badge Girl Scouts of Am., hon. membership prog. agy. Presbyn. Church U.S.A.; fellow Am. Assn. State Psychology Bds., 1991, Silver Beaver award Keystone Area Coun. Boy Scouts Am., 1999; named to "Movers and Shakers in Central Pa." List Ctrl. Pa. Bus. Jour., 1998. Mem. Susquehanna Alliance, West Shore Chamber of Commerce, Cumberland Cty. Hist. Soc., Cumberland Cty. Transp. Authority. Home: 209 Willow Ave Camp Hill PA 17011-3653

BESEDA, AMY JO, special education educator; b. Waco, Tex., Jan. 19, 1978; d. Norbert and Cheryl Kaska; m. Paul Beseda, Jan. 18, 2003; 1 child, Abbey. BS in Edn., Baylor U., 2001; Master's, Tex. Women's U., 2004. Cert. ednl. diagnostician. Spl. edn. tchr. Grapevine-Colleyville Sch. Dist., Tex., 2001—06; ednl. diagnostician, 2006—. Office Phone: 817-237-7833. Personal E-mail: amybeseda@yahoo.com.

BESHAR, CHRISTINE, lawyer; b. Paetzig, Germany, Nov. 6, 1929; came to US, 1952, naturalized, 1957; d. Hans and Ruth (vonKleist-Retzow) von Wedemeyer; m. Robert P. Beshar, Dec. 20, 1953; children: Cornelia, Jacqueline, Frederica, Peter. Student, U. Hamburg, 1950-51, U. Tuebingen, 1951-52; BA, Smith Coll., 1953. Bar: NY 1960, US Supreme Ct. 1971. Assoc. Cravath, Swaine & Moore, NYC, 1964-70, ptnr., 1971—. Bd. dirs. Catalyst for Women Inc., 1977-94; trustee Colgate U., 1978-84, Smith Coll., 1987-97; mem. state bd. Nature Conservancy, NY, 1993-96. Inst. Internat. Edn. fellow, 1952-53; recipient Disting. Alumnae medal Smith Coll., 1974. Fellow: Am. Coll. Probate Counsel; mem.: Fgn. Policy Assn. (bd. dirs. 1978—87), UN Assn. (bd. dirs. 1975—89), NY Bar Found. (bd. dirs. 1977—2001), NY State Bar Assn. (ho. of dels. 1971—80, v.p. 1979—80), Assn. Bar City NY (exec. com. 1973—75, v.p. 1985—86), Am. Bar Found., Gipsy Trail Club, Cosmopolitan Club. Office: Cravath Swaine & Moore 825 8th Ave 43d Fl New York NY 10019-7475 also: Stone House Farm PO Box 533 Somers NY 10589-0533 Office Phone: 212-474-1698. Business E-Mail: cbeshar@cravath.com.

BESHAR, SARAH E., lawyer; b. Perth, Australia, Feb. 16, 1959; came to US, 1986; d. Ronald Ernest and Gweneth (June) Jones; m. Peter Justus Beshar, Jan. 5, 1991; children: Isabel Emma, Henry Frederick. BJ, U. Western Australia, 1980, LLB, 1981; BCL, Magdalen Coll., Oxford U., 1984. Bar: New South Wales 1983, Western Australia 1984, NY 1986. Assoc. Allen, Allen & Hemsley, Sydney, Australia, 1981-82, Freshfields, London, 1984-85, Davis Polk & Wardwell, NYC, 1986—94, ptnr., 1994—. Menzies Scholar in Law Brit./Australian Menzies Assn., 1982, Commonwealth Scholar Govt. of Australia, 1983. Episcopalian. Office: Davis Polk & Wardwell 450 Lexington Ave New York NY 10017 Office Phone: 212-450-4131. Office Fax: 212-450-3131. E-mail: sarah.beshar@dpw.com.

BESHUR, JACQUELINE E., animal trainer, farmer, writer; b. Portland, Oreg., May 8, 1948; d. Charles Daniel and Mildred (Domreis) Beshears. BA, UCLA, 1970; MBA, Claremont Grad. Sch., 1980; postgrad., City U., Seattle, 1989-90. Dir. and founder L.A. Ctr. for Photog. Studies, 1972-76; precious gem distbr. Douglas Group Holdings, Australia, 1976-78; small bus. owner BeSure Cleaning, 1981-90; animal trainer, exotic livestock farmer, writer, 1990-2000. Dir. County Citizens Against Incineration, 1987—, Ames Lake Protection Com., 1989—. Mem. Bridges for Peace, Nature Conservancy, Wash. Wilderness Coalition, Issaquah Alps Club. Republican. Office: BeSure Tng PO Box 225 Carnation WA 98014-0225

BESS, AIMEE LYNN, performing arts educator; d. Pamela J Parisi. BS, Ctrl. Conn. State U., 2002. Cert. tchr. spl. edn. Conn., 2002, dance tchr. Conn., 2006. Tchr. Waterbury Arts Magnet Sch., Conn., 2004—, Eastbury Sch., Glastonbury, Conn., 2002—04. (choreography) Various, dancer (performer) New England Sea Wolves Dance Team and Christopher Lee Prodns., Walt Disney World, (dance) Boogie Woogie Bugle Boy (America's Natinal Talent Winner, 1995), Eastbury Dance Club Show, WAMS Spring Dance Concert, Cotton Eyed Joe (Over All Highest Score, IDC, 2006). Office Phone: 203-573-6300.

BESSANT, CATHY (CATHERINE POMBIER BESSANT), bank executive, marketing professional; b. Jackson, Mich. m. John E. Clay; 2 children. BBA in Fin., Mktg. and Eng. Lit., U. Mich. Joined NationsBank, 1982; pres., cmty. devel. bank Bank Am. Corp. (formerly NationsBank), 1998—2000; pres., mortgage lending ops. Bank Am. Corp., pres., consumer real estate banking, 1999—2000, pres., Fla. ops., 2000—01, chief mktg. exec., 2001—06, pres. global treasury services, 2006—. Trustee Enterprise Found. Bd. dirs. Children's Theatre Charlotte, Blue Cross Blue Shield Fla., Inc. Named one of Most Powerful Women in Banking, US Banker Mag., 2003. Office: Bank Am Corp 100 N Tryon St Charlotte NC 28255*

BESSER, SANDRA HERMAN, school nurse practitioner; b. Phila., Aug. 20, 1956; d. Solomon and Phyllis June Herman; m. Bruce Michael Besser, Oct. 9, 1955; children: Rebecca Leigh, Aaron Joel. BS, Widener U., 1978; MS, U. Md., 1981. RN Md. Charge nurse, clin. nurse Johns Hopkins U., Balt., 1978—79; unit nurse coord. Levindale Hebrew Home and Hosp., 1979—80, 1984—86; faculty Union Meml. Hosp. Sch. Nursing, 1981—84, Johns Hopkins Hosp. Sch. Nursing, 1983—84; staff nurse Balt. County Hosp., 1987—91; patient educator and staff nurse Carroll County Gen. Hosp., 1991—95; faculty Howard County C.C., 1992, Frederick C.C., 1993; nurse Balt. County Pub. Schs., 1993—. Presenter in field. Contbr. articles to profl. jours. Mem.: Nat. Assn. Sch. Nurses (assoc. Sch. Nurse of Yr. 1996). Home: 3907 Long Lake Dr Owings Mills MD 21117 Office: Balt County Sch-Glyndon Elem 445 Glyndon Dr Reisterstown MD 21136 Office Phone: 410-887-1130. Personal E-mail: sklnurse@msn.com. Business E-Mail: sbesser@bcps.org.

BESSEY, CAROLINE A., education educator; d. Robert and Elizabeth Hobson; m. Bob Bessey, Mar. 19, 1972; children: Heather, Amber. BA, Grinnell Coll., Iowa, 1970; MA, U. Wash., Seattle, 1971. Instr. Rogue C.C., Medford, Oreg., 1989—. Mem.: OCTM. Office: Rogue CC 202 S Riverside Ave Medford OR 97501 Office Phone: 541-245-7790.

BEST, AMY L., education educator; d. Gary and Natalie Best; m. J. Christopher McCauley, 1998; 1 child, Elizabeth. BA in Sociology, Ithaca Coll., NY, 1992; MA in Sociology, Syracuse U., NY, 1995, PhD in Sociology, 1998. Asst. prof. sociology Syracuse (N.Y.) U., 1998—99; asst. prof. San Jose (Calif.) State U., 1999—2004; assoc. prof. sociology George Mason U., 2004—. Faculty mentor program San Jose State U., 1999—; acad. goals com. George Mason U. Author: Prom Night: Youth, Schools and Popular Culture, 2000 (Critics' Choice award, 2002), Fast Cars, Cool Rides: The Accelerating World of Youth and their Cars, 2006; reviewer (jour.) Jour. of Gender and Society, 2002—05, Social Problems, 2002—05, Qualitative Inquiry, 2002—06. Mem. compliance com. Ams. with Disabilities Act, San Jose, Calif., 2000—04; action planning team mem. Mex. Am. Cmty. Svc., San Jose, Calif., 2000—01. Recipient Critics' Choice award, Am. Ednl. Studies Assn., 2002; grantee, San Jose State U., 1999, 2001—04;, Calif. State U. fellow,

2003, Career Devel. grantee, Jr. Faculty, 2001. Mem.: Am. Sociol. Assn. (coun. mem. children's sect. 2003—05). Democrat. Avocations: reading, gardening. Office: George Mason U Dept Sociology and Anthropology 4400 University Dr Fairfax VA 22030

BEST, JANE EVANS, retired educator, historian; b. Lancaster, Pa., Jan. 18, 1926; d. James Herbert and Florence Elizabeth (Styer) Evans; m. Albert Marlin Best, June 15, 1946; children: David Evans, Barbara Lee Ruskin, Nancy Jane Bennett, Susan Louise. BA, Hood Coll., 1946. Cert. secondary tchr., Pa. Tchr. math. Ea. Lancaster County Sch. Dist., New Holland, Pa., 1963-70, sch. bd. dir., 1979-89; contbg. editor Mennonite Family History, Elverson, Pa., 1988-97; ret. Co-author: The Groff Book, Vol. 1, 1985, Vol. 2, 1997; contbr. articles to hist. publs. Republican. Lutheran. Avocation: history. Home: 660 Willow Valley Sq # M-307 Lancaster PA 17602-4874

BEST, JUDITH A., political science professor; BA, Mich. State U., East Lansing, 1958; MA, U. Mich., Ann Arbor, 1963; PhD, Cornell U., Ithaca, NY, 1971. Rsch. assoc. Cornell U., 1971—73; asst. prof. SUNY, Cortland, 1973—75, assoc. prof., 1976—79, prof., 1980—84, disting. tchg. prof., 1984—. Presenter, spkr. in field. Author: The Case Against Direct Election of the President, A Defense of the Electoral College, 1975, The Main Stream of Western Political Thought, 1980, The Choice of the People? Debating the Electoral College, 1996; contbr. articles to profl. jours., chpts. to books; bd. editors: Presidential Studies Quar., 1984—96. Testimony on electoral coll. US Senate, Washington, 1979, 1992, US Ho. Reps., Washington, 1997. Recipient NY State Chancellors' award for Excellence in Tchg., 1977, Honor Salute for Ednl. Leadership, Am. Higher Edn. and Carnegie Found., 1986; Women's Academic and Career Choices grantee, US HEW, 1978—79. Office Phone: 607-753-4801.

BEST, KIMBERLY RENEE, psychiatrist; b. Lock Haven, Pa., June 10, 1955; d. James Edward Long and Marilyn Jane Zimmerman; m. Franklin Luther Best, May 1, 1982; children: Rebecca Suzanne, William Price. BS, Pa. State U., 1976; MD, Jefferson Med. Coll., 1978. Diplomate Am. Bd. Psychiatry and Neurology, cert. psychosomatic medicine Am. Bd. Psychiatry and Neurology, 2005. Residency training dir. in psychiatry Albert Einstein Med. Ctr., Phila., 2003—; psychoanalytic candidate Psychoanalytic Ctr. Phila., 1995—. Mem.: Pa. Psychiat. Soc. (treas. 2004—05, v.p. 2005—), Phila. Psychiat. Soc. (pres. 2000—01). Office: Albert Einstein Med Ctr 5501 Old York Rd Philadelphia PA 19141

BEST, PAMELA LAFEVER, secondary school educator; b. Arlington, Va., Feb. 19, 1952; d. Malcolm R. and Christabel P. LaFever; m. Frederick W. Best III; children: Christine, Karin. BS in Edn., Emporia State U., 1978; MBA, Rockhurst Coll., 1985; M in Ednl. Adminstrn., U. Kans., 2000, EdD in Ednl. Adminstrn., 2005. Receptionist First Va. Bank, Fairfax, 1971-72; sec. Civil Svc. Commn., Washington, 1972-73; nat. sales sec. Diddle-Glaser, Emporia, Kans., 1974-76; bus. edn. tcr. Louisburg (Kans.) H.S., 1978-99; tech. dir. Louisburg United Sch. Dist. 416, 1999—2001, dir. adminstrv. svcs., 2001—. Contbr. articles to profl. jours. Recipient 2d pl. Career Virtual Reality award Kans. City Star, 1998, 2d pl. award Kans. Ins. Edn. Found., 1998. Mem. Kans. Bus. Edn. Assn. (presenter 1991—, 1st Pl. Share-an-Idea 1995), Mountain-Plains Bus. Edn. Assn. (1st pl. Share-An-Idea award 1992). Avocations: reading, computers. Office: Louisburg USD 29020 Mission Belleview Louisburg KS 66053-6200 Office Phone: 913-837-2944. Business E-Mail: bestp@usd416.org.

BEST, SHARON LOUISE PECKHAM, retired college administrator; b. Elmira, N.Y., Aug. 4, 1940; d. Paul Arthur and Beatrice L. (Hunter) Peckham; m. Willard C. Best, Sept. 3, 1961; children: Meryl Elizabeth, Kevin Hunter. BA cum laude, William Smith Coll., 1977. Acting dir. alumnae rels. William Smith Coll., Geneva, N.Y., 1976-77; from assoc. dir. devel. to v.p. devel. Hobart & William Smith Colls., Geneva, 1977-97, v.p. devel. and gift planning, 1997—2000; ret. Cons. Nazareth Coll., Rochester, N.Y., 1985. Active Ontario County (N.Y.) rep. com., 1968-78, Geneva Hist. Soc., 1975-80; active Geneva Concerts, Inc., 1965—, bd. dir. 1974-82, pres., 1976-78; mem. planning bd. City of Geneva, 1999—; trustee Geneva Free Libr., 2002-2005, Geneva Hist. Soc., 2005-. Recipient Coun. on Advancement and Support of Edn. award capital fundraising USX Found., 1988. Mem. Coun. for Advancement and Support Edn. (bd. trustees Mid-Atlantic Dist. II 1987-89, Gold Medal-Decade Improvement in Fund Raising 1987, Circle of Excellence in Ednl. Fund Raising award 1994), Nat. Soc. Fund Raising Execs., LWV (bd. dir. 1993-97), Geneva Country Club, Phi Beta Kappa, Phi Sigma Iota. Presbyterian. Home: 859 S Main St Geneva NY 14456-3205

BEST, WANDA, career planning consultant; d. Herbert and Coretta Best; 1 child, Sharona Joy Anderson. BA in Sociology, LI U., Bklyn., 1999; M Human Svc., Lincoln U., Pa., 2006. Lic. nurse technician, Bklyn.; cert. tchr. NYC Bd. Edn. Nurse technician NY Meth. Hosp., Bklyn., 1993—2000; cons. Adolescent Career Devel. Ctr., Bronx, NY, 2000—; CEO Vocat. Career Planning, Cons., NYC, 2003—. Cons. Adolescent Career Devel. Ctr., Bronx; vocat. cons. Bronx Children's Psychiat. Ctr. Author, editor: Volunteer Training Program for At-Risk Adolescents, 2006, My Soul Awakes. Vol. Harlem C. of C., NYC, 2002—, Women in Need, NYC, 1998; mentor HS Transitions Intensive English Lang. Program, NYC; mem. Feed the Children Partnership, Oklahoma City, 2003—, Effective Tchg. Program for Exceptional Students, NYC, 2000—; outreach counselor Greater Refuge Temple Ch. of Our Lord Jesus Christ, NYC, 1995—. Named to Wall of Tolerance, Rosa Parks So. Poverty Law Ctr., Montgomery, Ala., 2004; recipient You Never Fail Until You Stop Trying award, LI U., 1997, Appreciation for Dedication and Commitment award, Adolescent Career Devel. Ctr., 2002, cert. achievement, State Senator, 4th Dist., 2006. Mem.: Nat. Alliance for Mentally Ill. Democrat. Mem. Apostolic Faith Ch. Avocations: creative writing, reading, art, travel. Home: 1875 3d Ave New York NY 10029-5407

BESTEHORN, UTE WILTRUD, retired librarian; b. Cologne, Germany, Nov. 6, 1930; arrived in U.S., 1930; d. Henry Hugo and Wiltrud Lucie (Vincentz) Bestehorn. BA, U. Cin., 1954, BEd, 1955, MEd, 1958; MS in Library Sci., Western Res. U. (now Case-Western Res. U.), 1961. Tchr. Cutter Jr. HS, Cin., 1955-57; tchr., supr. libr. Felicity (Ohio) Franklin Sr. HS, 1959-60; with libr. sci. dept. Pub. Libr. Cin. and Hamilton County, 1961-78, with libr. info. desk, 1978-91; ret., 1991. Mem. textbook selection com. Felicity-Franklin Sr. HS, 1959—60; supr. health alcove sci. dept. and ann. health lectures Cin. Pub. Libr., 1972—77. Book reviewer Libr. Jour., 1972—74, author, inventor Rainbow 40 marble game, 1971, Concominium game, 1976, patentee indexed packaging and stacking device, 1973, mobile packaging and stacking device, 1974. Mem. Clifton Town Meeting, 1988—; mem. Bookfest 90 com. Pub. Libr. Cin. and Hamilton County. Recipient cert. of Merit and Appreciation, Pub. Libr. Cin., 1986. Mem.: Greater Cin. Calligraphers Guild (reviewer New Letters pub. 1986—88), Pub. Libr. Staff Assn. (exec. bd., mem. activities com. 1965, mem. welfare com. 1966, Golden Book 25 Yr. Svc. pin 1986), Cin. Chpt. Spl. LIbrs. Assn. (archivist 1963—64, editor Queen City Gazette bull. 1964—69, archivist 1965—70), Friends of Libr., Delta Phi Alpha (nat. German hon. 1951). Republican. Mem. United Ch. Of Christ. Avocations: calligraphy, painting and sketching, writing, photography, violin. Home: 105 E 4th St Ste 300 Cincinnati OH 45202-4023

BESTON, ROSE MARIE, retired academic administrator; b. South Portland, Maine, Sept. 27, 1937; d. George Louis and Edith Mae (Archibald) Beattie; m. John Bernard Beston, Feb. 1, 1970 BA, St. Joseph's Coll., 1961; MA, Boston Coll., 1963; PhD, U. Pitts., 1967; cert. of advanced study, Harvard U., 1978. Mem. faculty St. Joseph's Coll., Maine, 1967-68, SUNY, Oneonta, 1968-69, S.E. Mo. State Coll., 1969-70, U. Queensland and Western Australian Inst. Tech., 1970-76, U. Hawaii, Manoa, 1976-77; assoc. acad. dean Worcester State Coll., Mass., 1978-80; dean for acad. affairs Castleton State Coll., Vt., 1980-84; pres. Nazareth Coll. Rochester, NY, 1984-98; ret., 1998. Former mem. Neylan Commn., Assn. Cath. Colls. and Univs., Pres. Network of Campus Compact. Contbr. articles to profl. jour. Mem. AAUW.

BETANCOURT-BRYANT, SONIA, music educator; b. Humacao, PR, Jan. 17, 1951; d. Nicasio Betancourt and Ana Gerena; m. James Bryant, Apr. 15, 2000; m. Carlos Rivera (dec. June 23, 1993); children: Danisha Rivera, Raquelisha Rivera. BA in Elem. and Music Ed., U. PR, Rio Piedras, 1972; M in Music Edn., NYU, 1975. Cert. elem. sch. tchr. Bd. Edn., PR, 1972, tchr. music Bd. Edn., PR, 1972, elem. tchr. music Dept. of Def., 1996, tchr. music mid. and high sch. Dept. of Def., 2005, humanities Dept. of Def., 2005. Elem. music tchr. Pub. Sch., Rio Piedras, PR, 1972—73, Newark, 1973—74, tchr. 2nd and 3d grades Queens, 1974—76, music tchr. Bayamon, PR, 1977—80; tchr. Spanish, English, and choir Levittown Bapt. Acad., Toa Baja, PR, 1986—92; dir. elem. music and choir Dept. of Def. - PR Dist., Ft. Buchanan Guaynabo, PR, 1992—98; dir. guitar, drama and choir Dept. of Def., PR Dist., Ft. Buchanan Guaynabo, PR, 1998—. Ch. pianist and choir dir. Christian Ch., Bayamon, 1977—. Nominee Tchr. of Yr., Dept. of Def., 2004; recipient cert. of appreciation, Dept. of the Army, 2004. Mem.: Am. Choral Dirs. Assn. (corr.), Nat. Assn. for Music Edn. (assoc.). Christian.

BETENSKY, ROSE HART, artist; b. N.Y.C., Sept. 6, 1923; d. Jacob and Clara Shainess; m. Seymour Betensky, July 11, 1943; children: Joel Benay, Richard Benay. Studied painting with Josef Presser, N.Y. Pres. N.Y. Soc. Women Artists, N.Y.C., 1970, Am. Soc. Contemporary Artists, N.Y.C., 1972—74. Exhibitions include Nat. Acad. Galleries, Royal Acad. Edinburgh, Scotland, Norfolk (Va.) Mus. Arts and Scis., Cultural Inst., Guadalajara, Mex., Palazzo Vecchio, Florence, Italy, La Napoule, France, collections, Jane Voorhees Zimmerli Art Mus. of Rutgers U. Recipient Windsor and Newton award, Grumbacher award, Bee Paper Co. award, Nat. Assn. Women Artists award, Am. Soc. Contemporary Artists awards. Mem.: Nat. Assn. Women Artists (pres. 1970—72). Home: Apt 543 100 Harbor View Dr Port Washington NY 11050

BETENSON, GAYE BRINTON, secondary school educator; b. Salt Lake City, Utah, Aug. 4, 1953; d. Brinton Phil and Helen Rae Reese Brinton; m. Donald Blaine Betenson, June 7, 1974; children: Bryan Donald, Brandon Blaine, Amber Betenson Mann, Ashley, Michelle, Michael Phil. BA in Bus. and Edn., So. Utah State Coll., 1984. Cert. tchr. Utah, 1973. Tchr. Bingham HS, South Jordan, Utah, 1973—79, Indian Hills Mid. Sch., Sandy, Utah, 1980—81; asst. coord., competency-based testing Utah State Office Edn., Salt Lake City, 1985—89, coord., competency-based testing, 1989—94; tchr. West Jordan HS, Utah, 1997—; tchr., adult HS South Pointe HS, Sandy, 2004—. Tchr. teen mother program Valley HS, Sandy, 1976—, tchr., home and hosp., 1997. Mem.: Utah Bus. Educators Assn., Utah Assn. Career and Tech. Educators. Latter-Day Saint. Avocations: sewing, quilting, embroidery. Home: 11275 Rick Cir South Jordan UT 84095-4065 Office: West Jordan HS 8136 S 2700 W West Jordan UT 84088 Office Phone: 908-256-5600. Office Fax: 801-256-5670. Personal E-mail: gayebetenson@msn.com. Business E-Mail: gaye.betenson@jordan.k12.ut.us.

BETHEA, ELIZABETH, social sciences educator, psychologist, minister; b. Hattiesburg, Miss., May 10, 1950; d. David Ball Jr. and Molly Mayo Bethea. BA, Univ. Tex., Austin; MSW, Univ. Denver, 1982; PhD, Union Inst. and Univ., Cin., 1999; ThD, Univ. Wales, Lampter, 2004—. Social worker, faculty trainer Boulder Valley Pub. Sch., 1983—94; med. social worker Adventist Health Sys., Denver, 1983—95; social work adj. faculty Univ. Denver, Denver, 1991—93; social sci. adj. faculty Front Range Cmty. Coll., Boulder, 2000—03; psychology adj. faculty Naropa U., Boulder, Colo., 2003; social work adj. faculty Colo. State Univ., Ft. Collins, Colo., 2003—04. Dir. Bether Inst. for Rsch. on the Transformation of Humanity Inc., Colo., 1994—; pyschotherapist Elizabeth Bethea, PhD, Boulder, Colo., 1983—. Author: A Critical Mass: A Primer for Personal, Social & Global Transformation, 1999; contbr. chapters to books, articles pub. to profl. jour. Chair of peace, world friendship Womens Internat. League, Boulder, Colo., 1980—85; cmty. organizer Eco Cycle, Boulder Pks. and Open Space, Doris Day Annual Leauge, Am. Humane Soc., Boulder, Colo., 1978—. Mem.: AARP, Colo. Chautquague Assn., Doris Day Animal League, Am. Humane Soc., Sierra Club. Avocations: studying Sanskirt and Hinduism, walking, spiritual ministry.

BETHEA, LOUISE HUFFMAN, allergist; b. Jackson, Miss., Mar. 27, 1947; d. Theodore G. and Frances (Allen) Huffman; m. Henry L. Bethea, Sept. 15, 1946; children: Mary, Samuel, Sarah. BS, Miss. Coll., Clinton, 1968; MD, U. Miss., 1974. Diplomate Am. Bd. Allergy and Immunology, Am. Bd. Pediatrics. Resident pediatrics U. Miss., Jackson, 1973-75; fellow allergy and immunology U. Fla., 1977-79; pvt. practice Houston, 1983—. Instr. pediatrics U. Miss., 1975-77, U. Fla., 1979-80; active staff Houston Northwest Med. Ctr., 1983—, Meml. Hermann Hosp. The Woodlands, St. Luke's Hosp. The Woodlands; cons. in field. Fellow Am. Acad. Allergy, Asthma and Immunology, Am. Coll. Allergy, Am. Acad. Pediatrics. Republican. Episcopalian. Avocations: photography, travel, arts and crafts. Home: 92 Hollymead Dr The Woodlands TX 77381-5121 Office: 17070 Red Oak Dr Ste 107 Houston TX 77090-2615 Office Phone: 281-580-6494. Business E-Mail: bethea@dbmed.net.

BETHEL, DENISE, art appraiser; MA, Courtauld Inst. Art, U. London. Dir., photography Swann Galleries, N.Y.C., 1980—90; with Sotheby's, NYC, 1990—, sr. v.p., dir., photographs. Lectr. in field. Contbr. articles to photography jours. Office: Sotheby's 1334 York Ave New York NY 10021 Office Phone: 212-894-1149. Office Fax: 212-894-1150. Business E-Mail: denise.bethel@sothebys.com.

BETHEL, JOANN D., computer programmer, analyst; b. Ardmore, Okla., Nov. 20, 1956; d. Dorvin and Marian (McKinney) B. Student, U. Okla., 1998—; AS in Computer Sci., Oklahoma City C.C., 1999, AS in Math., 1999. Computer operator Security Nat. Bank and Trust, Norman, Okla., 1978-84, programmer, 1984-87, programmer analyst, 1987-90, tech. svc. officer, 1990-95; programmer analyst C-TEQ, Oklahoma City, 1995-2000, v.p., 2000-2001; programmer InterCept, Inc., Oklahoma City, 2001—. Okla. Coun. Tchrs. of Math. scholar, 1996. Mem.: Golden Key Honor Soc., Tau Beta Pi, Phi Theta Kappa. Home: 3915 Bellwood Dr Norman OK 73072-3622 E-mail: JDBethel@ix.netcom.com.

BETHEL, MARILYN JOYCE, librarian; b. Detroit, Jan. 14, 1935; d. Thomas Agmey and Mary Helen (Lisek) Hepfner; m. Herschel Earl Bethel, June 20, 1960 (div. Mar. 1969); 1 child, Mary Joyce. BA in Edn., Fla. Atlantic U., 1974; MLS, La. State U., 1975, MEd, 1976; postgrad., Fla. Atlantic U., 1977-78. Cert. reading specialist Fla. Cons. Fla. Diagnostic and Learning Resources, Ft. Lauderdale, 1979-80; libr. Cocnut Creek (Fla.) Elem. Sch., 1980-82; cons. Fla. Coll. Bus., Pompano, 1982-84; libr. Broward County Librs., Hallandale, Fla., 1983, cataloger Ft. Lauderdale, 1983-90, br. head Deerfield, 1990-92, libr. Pompano, 1992-95, Ft. Lauderdale, 1995-2000, ret., 2000. Cons. Fla. Diagnostic and Learning Resources, 1979-80; mem. behavioral objectives writing team Broward County Spl. Edn., 1981. Advisor to periodical Biography Today, 1992—; writer newsletter Exceptional Student, 1979-80. Vol. crisis counselor Sexual Assault Treatment Ctr., Broward County, Fla., 1977-78; lectr., instr. New Covenant Ch., Pompano, 1984-87. With USAF, 1954-55. Recipient Cert. of Appreciation, Bd. County Commrs., Ft. Lauderdale, 1978. Mem. ALA (com. for cataloging for children 1989-95, liaison Freedom to Read 1979-80), Fla. Libr. Assn., Broward County Libr. Assn., Nat. Alzheimers Assn. Republican. Presbyterian. Avocations: floral arranging, snorkeling, swimming, reading. Home: 272 NE 39th Ct Deerfield Beach FL 33064-3545

BETHUNE, NIKKI, science educator; b. Billings, Mont., Mar. 1, 1968; d. Leo and Diana Wohler; m. Kevin Bethune, Sept. 4, 1966. BA in Life and Phys. Sci., Concordia U., Portland, Oreg., 1990; BS in Secondary Edn., Mont. State U., Billings, 1991; MS in Sci. Edn., Mont. State U., Bozeman, 2003. Cert. tchr. Okla., Tex., Mont. Tchr. Jersey Village H.S., Houston, 1991—92, Oak Ridge H.S., Spring, Tex., 1992—96, Sapulpa (Okla.) Jr. High, 1996—. Volleyball/soccer coach Oak Ridge H.S., Spring, 1994—96; basketball coach Sapulpa Jr. High, 1996—98, volleyball coach, 2004—; rsch. asst. Houston Advanced Rsch. Ctr., The Woodlands, Tex., 1995. Named Tchr. of Yr., Sapulpa Jr. High, 2000, Sapulpa Jr. High Student Coun., 2000. Mem.: USE, OEA, NEA, Nat. Sci. Tchrs. Assn. Avocations: bicycling, crafts, sewing. Office Phone: 918-224-6710.

BETO, DONNA L., retired elementary school educator; b. Tulsa, Okla., June 30, 1943; d. Ray William and Dorothy Estelle Legg; m. Dan Richard Beto, Aug. 16, 1969. BSc, Sam Houston State Coll., Huntsville, Tex., 1968; M in Edn., U. Conn., 1995. Cert. Gifted and Talented State of Tex., Tex. A&M U., 2003. 4th grade tchr. Long Fellow Elem., Alvin, Tex., 1968—71, Chambers Elem. Alief, Tex., 1971—79, Coll. Sta. Ind. Sch. Dist., 1979—91, gifted and talented coord., 1991—2004. Bd. sec. Tex. A&M U., 2002—. Author: (computer software) Focus on Tex., 1988. Mem. Woman's Club of Bryan, 2006—. Recipient Elem. Tchr. of Yr., Coll. Sta. Ind. Sch. Dist., 1994, Region VI of Tex., 1994, Outstanding Elem. Sci. Tchr., Tex. A&M, 1995. Mem.: Soc. Internat. for Women Educators, Tex. State Tchrs. Assn., Delta Kappa Gamma, Beta Sigma Phi (life). Luth. Avocations: travel, gardening. Home: 1316 Brook Hollow Dr Bryan TX 77802

BETTERIDGE, FRANCES CARPENTER, retired lawyer, mediator; b. Aug. 25, 1921; d. James Dunton and Emily (Atkinson) Carpenter; m. Albert Edwin Betteridge, Feb. 5, 1949 (div. 1975); children: Anne, Albert Edwin, James, Peter. AB, Mt. Holyoke Coll., 1942; JD, N.Y. Law Sch., 1978. Bar: Conn. 1979, Ariz. 1982. Tech. in charge blood banks Roosevelt Hosp. and Mountainside Hosp., N.Y.C., Montclair, NJ, 1943-49; sub. tchr. Greenwich (Conn.) HS, 1978-79; intern and asst. to labor contracts office Town of Greenwich, 1979-80; vol. referee Pima County Juvenile Ct., Tucson, 1981-85; sole practice immigration law Tucson, 1982-87; judge Pro Tempore Pima County Justice Cts., 1988-91; owner Betteridge Imports and Tours, LLC, 2004—. Commr. Juvenile Ct., Pima County Superior Ct., Tucson, 1985-87; hearing officer Small Claims Ct., Pima County Justice Cts., Tucson, 1982; mediator Family Crisis Svc., Tucson, 1982-85. vol. referee Pima County Superior Ct., 1981-85; lectr. Tucson Mus. Art, 1994—; tour leader Betteridge Imports & Tours, LLC. Pres. H.S. PTA, Greenwich, 1970, PTA Coun., 1971; mem. Greenwich Bd. Edn., 1971-76, sec. 1973-76; com. chmn. LWV Tucson, 1981, bd. dirs., 1984-85; bd. dirs., sec. Let The Sun Shine Inc., Tucson, 1981—; bd. dirs. Ariz. Sr. Acad., 2003-05; medicare vol. Pima Coun. on Aging, 2003—. Mem. ABA, Conn. Bar Assn., Ariz. Bar Assn., Pima County Bar Assn., Tucson Sr. Acad., Point o'Woods Club. Republican. Avocations: travel, folk art. Home and Office: 7659 S Vivaldi Ct Tucson AZ 85747 Personal E-mail: fmotz@aol.com.

BETTISON, CYNTHIA ANN, museum director, archaeologist; b. St. Louis, Sept. 8, 1958; d. William Leslie and Barbara Ann (Yunker) B. BA in Anthropology and Biology, Pitzer Coll., 1980; MA in Anthropology, Eastern N.Mex. U., 1983; ABD in Anthropology, U. Calif., Santa Barbara, 1986, PhD in Anthropology, 1998. Cert. profl. archaeologist Archaeol. Stds. Bd., 2004. Asst. curator dept. anthropology U. Calif., Santa Barbara, 1988-89, curator dept. anthropology, 1990-91; dir. Western N.Mex. U. Mus., Silver City, 1991—. Co-dir. Western N.Mex. U. Archaeol. Field Sch., 1992, 94, 95; lectr. Western N.Mex. U., 1992, 93, adj. asst. prof. dept. social scis., 1994—; various archaeol. positions, 1981—. Contbr. articles to profl. jours. Recipient Conservation Assessment Program grant, 1994-95, NEH, 1994; Gila Nat. Forest grantee, 1992, 94, 95, Silver City Lodgers Tax Bd. grantee, 1992, Andrew Isabell Meml. Fund grantee U. Calif., 1990, SIMSE grantee, 1994-95, 95-96. Mem. AAUW, Am. Assn. Mus., Am. Anthrop. Assn., Am. Soc. Conservation Archaeology, N.Mex. Mus. Assn. (pres. 2002-04), Soc. for Am. Archaeology, Archaeol. Soc. N.Mex., N.Mex. Archaeol. Coun. (sec. 1993-94), Coun. Mus. Anthropology (sec. 1992-94), Assn. of Coll. and Univ. Mus. and Galleries (bd. dirs. 2004—, sml. mus. adminstrn. com. bd. mem.)), Mountain Plains Mus. Assn., Univ. Women's Club, Univ. Club, Optimist Club (sec. Silver City chpt. 1992), Silver City Rotary Club (v.p. 1999-2000, pres. elect 2000-2001, pres. 2001-2002, dist. 5520 asst. gov. 2002-04), Silver City Grant County C. of C., Chpt. BR PEO, Phi Kappa Phi. Office: Western NM Univ Mus 1000 W College Ave Silver City NM 88061-4158 E-mail: bettisonc@wnmu.edu.

BETTMAN, SUZANNE, lawyer; b. June 1964; BA, Northwestern U.; JD, U. Ill. Sr. v.p., gen. counsel R.R. Donnelley & Sons Co., Chgo., 2004—. Office: RR Donnelley & Sons Co 111 S Wacker Dr Chicago IL 60606 Home: 521 W Stratford Pl Apt 2 Chicago IL 60657 Office Phone: 312-326-8000. Office Fax: 312-326-8594.

BETTRIDGE, MELINDA KAE, secondary school educator, music educator, director; d. Ed and Kae Gardner; m. Troy Bettridge, July 3, 1993; children: Carolyn, Cole. MusB in Edn., U. Nev., 1994; MS in Curriculum and Instrn., Okla. State U., 1999. Lic. tchr. music K-12 Okla., 1995. Music specialist Whitney Elem. Sch., Las Vegas, 1994—95, Bailey Elem. Sch., Owasso, Okla., 1998—2000; dir. choir Owasso (Okla.) Mid-H.S., 2000—06, Owasso (Okla.) H.S., 2006—. Chmn. music LDS Ch., Owasso, 2004—06. Named Outstanding Sr. in Music Edn., Music Dept. U. Nev., Las Vegas, 1994. Mem.: Music Educators Nat. Conf. (assoc.), Internat. Assn. Jazz Educators (assoc.), Okla. Choral Dirs. Assn. (assoc.), Am. Choral Dirs. Assn. (assoc.). Mem. Lds Ch. Avocations: music, art, travel. Office: Owasso High School 12901 E 86th St N Owasso OK 74055 Office Phone: 918-272-8082. Personal E-mail: bettridgem@owasso.k12.ok.us.

BETTS, BARBARA LANG, lawyer, real estate agent, rancher; b. Anaheim, Calif., Apr. 28, 1926; d. W. Harold and Helen (Thompson) Lang; m. Roby F. Hayes, July 22, 1948 (dec.); children: John Chauncey IV, Frederick Prescott, Roby Francis II; m. Bert A. Betts, July 11, 1962; 1 child, Bruce Harold; stepchildren: Bert Alan, Randy W., Sally Betts Joynt, Terry Betts Marsteller, Linda Betts Hansen, LeAnn Betts Wilson. BA magna cum laude, Stanford U., 1948; LLB, Balboa U., 1951. Bar: Calif. 1952, U.S. Supreme Ct. 1978. Pvt. practice, Oceanside, Calif., 1952-68, San Diego, 1960—, Sacramento, 1962—; of counsel Hayes & Assoc., 2004—. Ptnr. Roby F. Hayes & Barbara Lang Hayes, 1952-60; city atty. Carlsbad, Calif., 1959-63; v.p. Isle & Oceans Marinas, Inc., 1970-80, W.H. Lang Corp., 1964-69; sec. Internat. Prodn. Assocs., 1968—, Margaret M. McCabe, M.D., Inc., 1977-78. Co-author: (with Bert A. Betts) A Citizen Answers. Chmn. Traveler's Aid, 1952-53; pres. Oceanside-Carlsbad Jr. Chambrettes, 1955-56; vice chmn. Carlsbad Planning Commn., 1959; mem. San Diego Planning commn., 1959; v.p. Oceanside Diamond Jubilee Com., 1958; mem. steering and devel. com. Metro Air Park, 1989-2004; candidate Calif. State Legislature, 77th Dist., 1954; mem. Calif. Dem. State Ctrl. Com., 1958-66, co-chmn. 1960-62; co-chmn. 28th Congl. Dist.; alt. del. Dem. Nat. Conv., 1960; co-sponsor All Am. B-24 Liberator Collings Found. Named to Fullerton Union H.S. Wall of Fame, 1986; recipient Block S award Stanford U., Cert. Appreciation, Supreme Ct. Calif. and State Bar. Mem. ABA, AAUW (legis. com. 1958-59, local pres. 1959-60, asst. state legis. chmn. 1958-59), DAR (regent Oceanside chpt. 1960-61), DFC Soc. (assoc.), Am. Judicature Soc., Nat. Inst. Mcpl. Officers, Calif. Bar Assn., San Diego County Bar Assn., Oceanside C. of C. (sec. 1957, v.p. 1958, dir. 1953-54, 57-59), Heritage League (2d divsn. 8th Air Force), Nat. Trust for Hist. Preservation, No. San Diego County Assn. Cs. of C. (sec.-treas.), Bus. and Profl. Women's Club (so. dist. legislation chmn. 1958-59), San Diego C. of C., San Diego Hist. Soc., Fullerton Jr. Assistance League, Calif. Scholarship Fedn. (life), Loyola Guild of Jesuit H.S., Soroptimist Internat. (pres. Oceanside-Carlsbad 1958-59, sec. pub. affairs San Diego and Imperial Counties 1954, pres. pres.'s coun. San Diego and Imperial Counties, Mex. 1958-59), Barristers (Stanford, Sacramento), Disting. Flying Cross Soc. (assoc.), Stanford Mothers, Phi Beta Kappa. Home: 441 Sandburg Dr Sacramento CA 95819-2559 Office: 2508 Garfield Ave Ste E Carmichael CA 95608 Office Phone: 916-486-7575. E-mail: blbbabbetts@sbcglobal.net.

BETTS, BARBARA STOKE, artist, educator; b. Arlington, Mass., Apr. 19, 1924; d. Stuart and Barbara Lillian (Johnstone) Stoke; m. James William Betts, July 28, 1951; 1 child, Barbara Susan (dec.). BA, Mt. Holyoke Coll., 1946; MA, Columbia U., 1948. Cert. tchr. NY, Calif., Hawaii. Art tchr. Walton (N.Y.) Union Schs., 1947-48, Presidio Hill Sch., San Francisco, 1949-51; freelance artist San Francisco, 1951; art tchr. Honolulu Acad. Arts, summer

1952, 59, 63, 85, spring 61, 64; libr. aide art rm. Libr. of Hawaii, Honolulu, 1959; art tchr. Hanahauoli Sch., Honolulu, 1961-62, Hawaii State Dept. Edn., Honolulu, 1958-59, 64-84; owner Ho'olaule'a Designs, Honolulu, 1973—; art editor Scrapbook Press, 2002—, Portfolio Cons. of Hawaii, 1990—. Editor: Strategy of The Baltimore & Ohio Railroad 1930-1932; staff artist: The Arcadian newsletter, 2000—, James W. Betts & Co.; illustrator: Cathedral Cooks, 1964, In Due Season, 1986, From Nowhere To Somewhere On A Round Trip Ticket, 2003; exhibited in Hawaii Pavilion Expo '90, Osaka, Japan, State Found. Culture and Arts; exhibited ingroup shows since 1964; one-woman shows include 1991, 96, 99; represented in Arts of Paradise Gallery, Waikiki, 1990-2001, Hale Ku'ai, a Hawaiian Coop., 1998-2001, Art Exch., Hot Springs, Ark., artexchange.com, Hot Springs, Ark., 2005—, NEOCON 2006, Chgo., 2006; traveling exhbns. include Pacific Prints, 1991, Printmaking East/West, 1993-95, Hawaii/Wis. Watercolor Show, 1993-94. Mem. Hawaii Watercolor Soc. (newsletter editor 1986-90), Nat. League Am. Pen Women (art chmn. 1990-92, sec. 1992-94, 2000-02, nat. miniature art shows 1991, 92, 93, 95), Honolulu Printmakers (dir. 1986, 87), Assn. Hawaii Artists, scholarship aid programs, Mount Holyoke Coll., Mary Lyon Soc., Rutgers Univ., Col. Henry Rutgers Soc. Republican. Episcopalian. Avocations: art, travel, writing, photography. Home: 1434 Punahou St #1028 Honolulu HI 96822-4740 Office Phone: 808-955-7817. Personal E-mail: kimarail@aol.com.

BETTS, DIANNE CONNALLY, economist, educator; b. Tyler, Tex., Sept. 23, 1948; d. William Isaac and Martine (Underwood) Connally; m. Floyd Galloway Betts Jr., Feb. 14, 1973. BA in History, So. Meth. U., 1976, MA in History, 1980; MA in Econ., U. Chgo., 1986; PhD in Econ., U. Tex., 1991. Affiliated scholar Inst. for Rsch. on Women and Gender/Stanford U., 1993—; economist, tech. analyst, fin. cons. Smith Barney, Dallas, 1994—2000; economist, fin. cons. Morgan Keegan, Dallas, 2000—. Mem. women studies coun. So. Meth. U., 1993-94, Fulbright campus interviewing com. mem. 1992-93, pub. rels. and devel. liaison dept. econ., 1990-92, faculty mentor U. honors first year mentoring program, adj. asst. prof. dept. econ. and history, 1992—, vis. asst. prof. 1990-92; faculty, Oxford, summer 1991-93, adj. instr. dept. history, 1989-90, adj. instr. dept. econ., 1985-89, tchg. asst. dept. history, spring 1980; lectr. dept. polit. economy U. Tex., Dallas, summer 1988. Author: Crisis on the Rio Grande: Poverty, Unemployment, and Economic Development on the Texas-Mexico Border, 1994, Historical Perspectives on the American Economy: Selected Reading, 1995; contbr. articles to profl. jours. Rsch. Planning grant NSF, 1992; recipient Marguereta Deschner Teaching award, 1991; Humanities and Scis. Merit scholar, 1978. Mem. Am. Econ. Assn., Am. History Assn., Econ. History Assn., Cliometric Soc., Social Sci. History Assn., N.Am. Conf. on British Studies, Nat. Coun. for Rsch. on Women (affiliate), Omicron Delta Epsilon, Phi Alpha Theta. Home: 7802 Bryn Mawr Dallas TX 75225 Office: Morgan Keegan 5956 Sherry Ln # 1900 Dallas TX 75225-6531 Office Phone: 214-365-5525. E-mail: dcbetts@airmail.net.

BETTS, DOROTHY ANNE, retired elementary school educator; b. Washington, Nov. 3, 1946; d. Thomas Joseph and Elizabeth Anne (McGee) Salb; m. Jerold LeRoy Betts, July 14, 1975; 1 child, Ellen Marie. BS in Elem. Edn., U. N.Mex., 1968, MA in Edn., 1976. Cert. tchr. N.Mex. Tchr. Newman (Calif.)-Gustine Dist., 1968—69, Albuquerque Pub. Schs., 1969—79, 1980—84, 1999—2004; ret.; ednl. asst. Albuquerque Pub. Schs., 1993—99; co-owner Stork News N.Mex. Zuni Elem. Sch. coord. Pennies for Patients Leukemia and Lymphoma Soc., Albuquerque, 2001. Mem.: Delta Kappa Gamma (1st v.p. 1982—84, pres. 1984—86, 2d v.p. 2000—02). Roman Catholic. Avocations: travel, family outings, crafts. Home: PO Box 1646 Dolores CO 81323-1646

BETTS, JANET GNIADEK, lawyer; b. Chgo., Oct. 16, 1954; d. Henry M. and Betty Gniadek. BS in Dental Hygiene, Loyola U., Chgo., 1976; JD, Ill. Inst. Tech., Chgo., 1979; LLM in Taxation, Depaul U., Chgo., 1982. Bar: Ariz. 1980, U.S. Dist. Ct. Ariz. 1980, U.S. Tax Ct. Ariz. 1980, U.S. Ct. Appeals (9th cir.) Ariz. 1980. Assoc. Winston & Strawn, Phoenix, 1982-84, Streich, Lang, Weeks & Cardon, Phoenix, 1984-87; in-house counsel Brooker & Wake, Tempe, Ariz., 1987; ptnr. Gust Rosenfeld, Phoenix, 1987—99; of counsel Kutak Rock LLP, Omaha, 2000—04; mem. Jennings, Strouss & Solomon PLC, Phoenix, 2004—. Bd. dirs. Arrowhead Cmty. Bank. Past pres. ctrl div. Ariz. chpt. Am. Heart Assn., Phoenix, 1992-93, past chmn. bd. dirs. Ariz. chpt., 1994—95; bd. dirs. Ariz. Osteoporosis Coalition, Area Humane Soc., 1997-2003. Recipient Volunteer of the Year award, Amer. Heart Assn. (Ariz. affiliate), 1992-94, Fund-raising Event award, 1993-94, Devel. Chmn. award, 1992-93, Dir. Recognition award, 1991-92, Amer. Heart Assn. (Ctrl. divsn.), Polit. Excellence award, Ariz. Human Society, 2000, Mem. ABA, Ariz. Bar Assn., Maricopa County Bar Assn., Am. Heart Assn., Ariz. Humane Soc. (bd. dirs. 1997-2003). Republican. Avocations: hiking, mountain bike, golf. Office: Jennings Strouss & Salmon PLC 16427 N Scottsdale Rd #300 Scottsdale AZ 85254 Office Phone: 602-262-5927, 480-663-2162. E-mail: jbetts@jsslaw.com.

BETTS, JENNIFER LEAH, secondary school educator; b. Oneonta, N.Y., June 27, 1963; d. David Sheridan and Judith (Lewis) B.; m. Mark A. Farmer, 1998. Student, U. S.C., 1982; BA, Wells Coll., Aurora, N.Y., 1985; EdM, Harvard U., 1990. Cert. social studies tchr., N.Y. Tchr. Oneonta City Sch. Dist., 1986; tchr. history Averill Park (N.Y.) Sch. Dist., 1986-89; ednl. cons., 1990—; instr. SUNY, Oneonta, 1991; tchr. history The Galloway Sch., Atlanta, 1992-97, co-dir. The Galloway Acad., 1994-97; tchr. Atlanta Girls Sch., 2000—02; prin. lower and mid. schs. The Howard Sch., Atlanta, 2002—. Cons. Atlanta Girls' Sch., 1999-2000. Author: (activity series/curriculum) United States History Notes and Activity Series, 8 vols., 1990—. Mem. AAUW, ASCD, Am. Hist. Assn., Internat. Assn. Study of Cooperation in Edn., Soc. for History Edn. Office: The Howard Sch 1246 Ponce de Leon Ave Atlanta GA 30306 E-mail: jenniferbetts@mindspring.com.

BETTS, NICOLE LAVETTE, elementary school educator, consultant; b. Houston, Tex., Apr. 7, 1979; d. Thomas Holloway and JoAnn Kelly-James; 1 child, Nakita Morgan. BS in Criminal Justice, U. Houston, Tex., 2002; MEd, Tex. So. U., Houston, Tex., 2004. Cert. tchr. Tex. Edn. Agy., 2003. Ednl. asst. N.Q. Henderson Houston (Tex.) Ind. Sch. Dist., 1999—2002, tchr. N.Q. Henderson, 2002—, coord. after sch. program N.Q. Henderson, 2005—. Mem. tchr. adv. bd. McGovern Mus. Health and Med. Scis., Houston, 2004—05, Children's Mus., Houston, 2006—; tchr. liaison Nat. Space Found., 2006. Contbr. curriculum units. Named Tchr. of Yr., N.Q. Henderson Elem., 2006; recipient Jordan Fundamentals award, Nike and Michael Jordan, 2005; fellow, Baylor Coll. Medicine, 2004—06. Fellow: Houston (Tex.) Tchrs. Inst. (tchr. rep. 2004—, mentor 2004—); mem.: Houston Area Alliance Black Sch. Educators (named Tchr. of Yr.), Nat. Sci. Tchrs. Assn. Home: 3907 Portman Glen Houston TX 77047 Office: NQ Henderson HISD 701 Solo Houston TX 77020 Office Phone: 713-671-4195. Business E-Mail: nbetts@houstonisd.org.

BETTS, REBECCA A., lawyer; b. Memphis, Nov. 25, 1951; BA, Dickinson Coll., 1972; JD, W.Va. U., 1976. Bar: W.Va., U.S. Dist. Ct. (so. dist.) W.Va. 1976, U.S. Ct. Appeals (4th cir.) 1978, U.S. Supreme Ct. 1984. Assoc. Spilman, Thomas, Battle & Klostermeyer, Charleston, W.Va., 1976—77; asst. U.S. atty. U.S. Atty.'s Office, 1977—81, chief civil divsn., 1979—81; founding ptnr. King, Betts & Allen, Charleston, W.Va.; U.S. atty. U.S. Dist. Ct. So. Dist., W.Va., 1994—2001; ptnr. Allen Guthrie McHugh & Thomas PLLC, 2001—. Adv. com. on rules & procedures 4th Cir., 1995—2001; civil justice reform act adv. com. So. Dist. W.Va., 1991, com. for local rules and subcom. on criminal rules, 92. Mem. editl. bd.: W.Va. Law Rev. Mem.: The Legal Aid Soc. of Charleston (bd. dirs.), W.Va. State Bar (past mem. com. on legal ethics), Order of Coif. Office: Allen Guthrie McHugh & Thomas PO Box 3394 Charleston WV 25333 Office Phone: 304-345-7250. Business E-Mail: rabetts@agmtlaw.com.

BETTS, VIRGINIA TROTTER, nursing educator, researcher; b. Sevierville, Tenn., Mar. 10, 1947; d. Mell Emert and Alice (Robbins) Trotter; m. Stephen Carter Betts; children: Jennifer Susann, Jessica Alice. RN, BS in Nursing, U. Tenn.-Memphis, 1969; MS in Nursing, Vanderbilt U., 1971; JD, Nashville Sch. Law, 1978. RN; bar: Tenn. Head nurse City of Memphis Hosp., 1969-70; specialist Middle Tenn. Mental Health Inst., Nashville, 1971-72; dir. Nashville Drug Treatment Ctr., 1972-73; instr. mental health Vanderbilt U., Nashville, 1973-76, asst. prof. mental health, 1976-78, assoc. prof. mental health, 1978-91. Acad. chair behavioral scis. applied to nursing, 1981-85; quality assurance cons. Middle Tenn. Mental Health Inst., Nashville, 1976-79; exec. com. Am. Nurses Assn. Council of Specialists in Psychiat.-Mental Health Nursing, Kansas City, Mo., 1981-84. Editorial bd. Nursing Economics, 1982-84; contbr. articles to publs. Mem. Nat. Leadership Coalition on Health Reform, 1990—; bd. dirs. Womankind Health Center, Nashville, 1982-85, Nashville Opportunity House, 1983-86. Recipient Shirley Titus award for Excellence in Teaching, Vanderbilt U., 1983; named Outstanding Alumna, Coll. Nursing U. Tenn.-Memphis, 1982, Vanderbilt U., 1987; Robert Wood Johnson fellow, 1987. Mem. Am. Nurses Assn. (exec. council psychiat.-mental health nursing 1980-83, 1st v.p. 1988-92, pres. 1992—), Tenn. Nurses Assn. (pres. 1985-87), Am. Hosp. Assn. (governing council psychiat. sect. 1984—), ABA, Sigma Theta Tau. Office: Vanderbilt U Sch Nursing 503 Godchaux Hl Nashville TN 37240-0001

BETTY-SINGLETON, CHARMAINE ELIZABETH, lawyer, military officer; b. Kingston, Jamaica, Jan. 12, 1968; d. Granville Maine and Norma Elaine Betty. BA, Va. Union U., Richmond, 1989; JD, Wash. and Lee U. Sch. Law, Lexington, Va, 1992. Bar: N.J. 1993, Pa. 1992. Commissioned maj. U.S. Army, 1993; contract law atty. Office of Staff Judge Adv. West Point Mil. Acad., 1993—96; trial def. atty. Trial Def. Svcs., Würzburg, Germany, 1996—97; procurement fraud atty. USAER and 7th Army, Heidelburg, 1997—99; chief mil. justice Office of Staff Judge Adv., Ft. Gordon, Ga., 1999—2001; commd. judge advocate 513th M.I. Brigade, 2000—02; trial def. svc. Trial Def. Svc. Fort Stewart Field Office, Ga., 2002—03; chief labor and employment law 90th Regional Readiness Commd., North Little Rock, Ark., 2003—. Legal advisor Delta Sigma Theta Sorority, Inc. (Ctrl. Ark. alumnae chpt.), Little Rock, 2003. Baptist. Avocations: travel, aerobics, reading. Office: 90th Regional Readiness Commd 8000 Camp Robinson Rd North Little Rock AR 72118 Office Phone: 501-771-8962. Office Fax: 501-771-8777. E-mail: charmaine.bettysingleton@us.army.mil.

BETZ-BACON, TINA M., communications educator; b. Centerville, Ill., Mar. 28, 1966; d. Ronald John and Shirley May (Price) Betz; m. John Allen Bacon, Aug. 7, 1993. BA in Lit. and Lang., Webster U., Mo., 1991; M of Edn. and Adminstrn., S.W. Bapt. U., Mo., 2005. Tchr., speech coach Valle H.S., St. Genevieve, Mo., 1993—96; tchr. comm. arts 8th grade Farmington Mid. Sch., 1996—2000, tchr. comm. arts 9-12, 2000—. Item writer Mo. DESE-MAP, Mo., 1999, Mo., 2001, Mo., 02, test reader, scorer, Mo., 05; presenter state English conf. Write to Learn, Rsch.: A Way of Life, 2000, Color My Words: Using Color-coding to Clarify Lit., 2002. Bd. dirs. Mineral Area Coun. on Arts, Park Hills; huddle coach Fellowship of Christian Athletes, Farmington. Recipient sch. excellence grants, Mo. DESE, 1997, 1998, 1999. Mem.: NEA, Mo. Assn. Tchrs. of English. Avocations: vocal music, horseback riding. Office: Farmington H S # 1 Black Knight Dr Farmington MO 63640

BETZER, SUSAN ELIZABETH BEERS, physician, geriatrician; b. Evanston, Ill., Aug. 24, 1943; d. Thomas Moulding and Mary Ella (Waidner) Beers; m. Peter Robin Betzer, June 18, 1965; children: Sarah Elizabeth, Katherine Hannah. AB in Biol. Scis. magna cum, Mount Holyoke Coll., 1965; PhD in Oceanography, U. R.I., 1972; MD, U. Miami, 1978. Diplomate Am. Bd. Family Practice, Am. Bd. Geriat. Rsch. assoc. dept. marine sci. U. South Fla., St. Petersburg, 1973-74, rsch. scholar, scientist, 1975-76; resident in family practice Bayfront Med. Ctr., St. Petersburg, 1978-81; pvt. practice St. Petersburg, 1982—; clin. asst. prof. dept. family medicine U. South Fla., Tampa, 1982—. Cons. physician Fed. Employee Health Clinic, Honolulu, 1981-82. Contbr. articles to profl. jours. Adv. com. St. Petersburg H.S., 1996-2002; bd. dirs. Fla. Orch., Tampa, 1983-86, 88-, pres., 1985-86, mem. exec. com., 1988-, vice-chair bd. trustees 1996-2002, sec., 2002-, founder, chair audience devel. com., St. Petersburg, 1990-94; bd. dirs. Suncoast Ctr. Cmty. Mental Health, St. Petersburg, 1992-93; trustee Bayfront Health Found., 1996-2004, chmn., 2001-03; trustee Bayfront Health Svcs., 1992-96, vice-chair, 1993-96; vol. physician St. Petersburg Free Clinic, 1979-. Named Woman of Distinction, Suncoast coun. Girl Scouts U.S., 1994; recipient Golden Baton award, St. Petersburg Fla. Orch. Guild, 1994, Chmns. award, Fla. Orch., 1997, Svc. award, Pinellas County Med. Soc., 1999, Philanthropy Vol. of Yr., Tampa Bay chpt. Assn. Fundraising Profls., 2003, Humanitarian Physician of Yr., Tampa Bay Area, Fla. Med. Bus., 2004. Mem.: Fla. Acad. Family Physicians (Dr. of the Day, Fla. Legislature 1995, 1996), Am. Med. Women's Assn., Am. Acad. Family Physicians (Mead Johnson award 1980), Mount Holyoke Alumnae Assn. (alumnae honor rsch. com. 1988—91, alumnae devel. com. 1996—2003, pres. 2003—06, Alumnae medal of honor 2000), Phi Beta Kappa. Avocations: symphony, birding, cooking, reading. Home: 1830 7th St N Saint Petersburg FL 33704-3322 Office: 461 7th Ave S Saint Petersburg FL 33701-4818 Office Phone: 727-823-0402.

BEUGEN, JOAN BETH, communications executive; b. Mar. 9, 1943; d. Leslie and Janet (Glick) Caplan; m. Sheldon Howard Beugen, July 16, 1967. BS in Speech, Northwestern U., 1965. Founder, prin., pres. The Creative Establishment, Inc., Chgo., N.Y.C., San Francisco and L.A., 1969—87; founder, pres. Cresta Comm. Inc., Chgo., 1988—. Spkr. on entrepreneurship for women. Contbr. articles to profl. jours. Trustee Mt. Sinai Hosp. Med. Ctr.; del. White House Conf. on Small Bus., 1979; bd. dirs. Chgo. Network, Chgoland Enterprise Ctr., Girl Scouts Chgo. Named Entrepreneur of Yr., Women in Bus.; recipient YWCA Leadership award, 1985. Mem.: Overseas Edn. Fund Women in Bus. Com., Nat. Women's Forum, Com. of 200, Women in Film, Chgo. Film Coun., Chgo. Audio-Visual Prodrs. Assn., Midwest Soc. Profl. Cons., Chgo. Assn. Commerce and Industry, Ill. Women's Agenda, Nat. Assn. Women Bus. Owners (pres. Chgo. bhpt. 1979), Econ. Club Chgo. Office: The Cresta Group 1050 N State St Chicago IL 60610-7829

BEUTHIEN, GAYLE DAWN, special education educator, swim coach; d. Milo and Jessie Dawn Beuthien. BS, Siler Lake Coll., Wis., 1991; MS, U. Wis., Oshkosh, 2006. Cert. DVI U. Wis., Oshkosh, 1996, ednl. leadership in social justice U. Wis., Oshkosh, 2005. Spl. edn. instr., volleyball, basketball, track and swim coach Manitowoc Pub. Schs., Wis., 1991—95; spl. edn. instr., swim coach Appleton Area Sch. Dist., Wis., 1995—. Vocational specialist for sch. dist. Tech-Prep, Manitowoc, Wis., 1991—95, C. of C., Manitowoc, Wis., 1991—95. Mem.: Council for Exceptional Children. Achievements include development of apartment program to teach students with disabilites functional life skills; school-tech. work program. Avocations: water-skiing, swimming, bicycling, reading.

BEUTLER, SUZANNE A., retired secondary school educator, artist; b. Cin., Oct. 23, 1930; d. Robert and Marguerite (Pierson) Armstrong; m. Frederick J. Beutler, Jan. 5, 1969; children: Richard and Mark Ireland. BA, U. Wis., 1954; MA, U. Mich., 1966, PhD, 1974, BFA, 2000. Cert. tchr. Middle sch. tchr. Ann Arbor (Mich.) Pub. Schs. Vis. lectr. U. Mich., Ann Arbor; adj. lectr. Eastern Mich. U., Ypsilanti. Author 3 manuals with Lang. Art Projects; contbr. articles to profl. jours.; developed writing program using personal classroom experiences. Recipient Tchr. Recognition award, 1986; grantee in field. Mem. Ann Arbor Rotary Club, Phi Delta Kappa (Svc. Key award 1992). Home: 1717 Shadford Rd Ann Arbor MI 48104-4543 Office Phone: 734-663-4870. E-mail: sbeutler@umich.edu.

BEVC, CAROL-LYNN ANNE, accountant; b. Jam, N.Y., Oct. 6, 1952; d. Joseph F. and Dorothea Mae (Kirshe) Bova; m. Frank P. Bevc, May 11, 1974; children: Christine, Elizabeth. BA, U. Pitts., 1974; grad. cert. in Pub. Adminstrn., U. Ctrl. Fla., 2005. CFO Wordwise, Inc., Winter Park, Fla., 1989-2000; acct. exec. Inner/g, 2000—01. Leader Citrus coun. Girl Scouts U.S.A., 1986-96. Mem. AAUW (pres. Seminole County br. 1985-87, 95-97, bd. dirs., dir. comm. Fla. state 1998-2002), DAR (regent Sallie Harrison chpt. 2006—). Avocations: reading, writing, swimming, learning. Home: 1511 Black Bear Ct Winter Springs FL 32708-3860 Personal E-mail: clbevc@bellsouth.net.

BEVELHYMER, DARLENE PEARL, secondary school educator, lawyer; b. Napoleon, Ohio, Oct. 31, 1950; d. Herbert S. and N. Lorene (Skelton) B. BS in Edn., Ohio U., 1972, MS in Environ. Studies, 1977; JD, U. Toledo, 1987. Bar: Ohio 1987; permanent cert. comprehensive sci. tchr., Ohio. Tchr. sci. Napoleon City Schs., 1972—; pvt. practice, Bowling Green, 1987—. Mem. Napoleon Community Band, 1986—, Cantare, choral ensemble, Wauseon, Ohio, 1987-93; treas. Choral and Performing Arts Assn. N.W. Ohio, Wauseon, 1987-93; mem. Sing Out Toledo Chorus, 1996-2005. Recipient local svc. award NW Ohio Edn. Assn., 1989. Mem. NEA, Ohio Bar Assn., Ohio Edn. Assn. (legis. commn. 1991-93), Napoleon Faculty Assn. (pres., negotiator 1987-89). Democrat. Presbyterian. Avocations: choral singing, stained glass. Office: Napoleon City Schs Briarheath Dr Napoleon OH 43545 Office Phone: 419-599-1050.

BEVELS, ESTHER MARIE, medical technician, director; b. Aberdeen, Miss., June 1, 1956; d. Robert Williams and Janie Mae Brandon; children: Connelia Capote, Nyshea Simpson. Grad., Perdue U., 1992. Surgical asst. Star Inst. Tech., Stratford, NY, 2001—03; dir. sterile processing Our Lady of Lourdes Hosp., Willingboro, NJ, 1990—. Adv. bd. Harrison Career Inst., Phila., 1999—. Recipient Wall of Tolerance, So. Proverty Law Ctr., Ala., 2004. Mem.: So. Proverty Law Ctr. (leadership coun. mem. 2004), Order Eas. Star. Baptist. Avocation: reading. Office: Lourdes Med Ctr Burlington 218A Sunset Rd Willingboro NJ 08046

BEVERLEY, CORDIA LUVONNE, gastroenterologist; b. Jamaica, W.I., Oct. 19, 1950; d. Hurdley Aston and Joyce Ruby (Baker) Beverley. BA, Hunter Coll., 1971; MD, NYU, 1975. Diplomate Am. Bd. Gastroenterology, Am. Bd. Internal Medicine. Intern Columbia U., Harlem Hosp. Ctr., 1975—76, resident in medicine, 1976—78; clin. fellow divsn. gastroenterology NY Hosp./Cornell U. Med. Coll., 1979—82; asst. physician Rockefeller U. Hosp., 1978—81; pvt. practice gastroenterology, 1981—; assoc. med. staff mem. Lenox Hill Hosp., 1985—. Fellow Postdoctoral fellow, Nat. Inst. Alcohol Abuse and Alcoholism, 1980—82. Mem.: Women's Med. Assn. N.Y.C. Office: 1085 Park Ave New York NY 10128-1168 Office Phone: 212-876-1886.

BEVERLY, KELLY DEE GRAY, elementary school educator; b. Lubbock, Tex., Feb. 14, 1962; d. Burnel Laroyce and Barbara Sue (Bowman) Gray; m. Michael James Beverly, Aug. 20, 1983; children: Kurt Dennis, Kent Michael Student, South Plains Coll., Levelland, Tex., 1980—81; BEd, S.W. Tex. State U., 1984; MEd Ednl. Diagnostician, U. Tex., Tyler, 1993. Tchr. elem. Alba-Golden Ind. Sch. Dist., Tex., 1984—89, Quitman Ind. Sch. Dist., Tex., 1989—. Mem. tchr. adv. bd., grade chmn. Quitman Ind. Sch. Dist., 1990—93. Mem. Tex. Classroom Tchrs. Assn Office: Quitman Elem Sch 902 E Goode St Quitman TX 75783-1652 Office Phone: 903-763-5000. E-mail: kelbev@hotmail.com.

BEVIER, LILLIAN RIEMER, law educator; b. Washington, 1939; m. Michael BeVier; children: Nicholas, Eric, Miranda. BA, Smith Coll., Northampton, Mass., 1961; JD, Stanford U., 1965. Bar: Calif. 1966, Va. 1979. Asst. gen. sec. Stanford (Calif.) U., 1965-66, rsch. assoc., 1966-68; assoc. Spaeth, Blase, Valentine & Klein, 1968-70; now prof. law Henry L. and Grace Doherty Charitable Found. U. Va.; assoc. prof. U. Santa Clara Law Sch. Vis. scholar Nat. Constn. Ctr., Phila., 2003. Author: Campaign Finance 'Reform' Proposals: A First Amendment Analysis, 1997, Is Free TV for Federal Candidates Constitutional, 1998. Vice-chair Legal Svc. Corp, Washington, 2003—; mem. bd. Martha Jefferson Health Svc. Corp.; currently vice-chair Piedmont CASA, Va. Mem.: Local Govt. Atty.'s Assn. Va., Federalist Soc. (nat. Bd. Visitors), Order of Coif (commr.), Raven Soc. Office: U Va Sch Law Charlottesville VA 22901 Office Phone: 434-924-3132. E-mail: lrb5s@virginia.edu.

BEVIER DILL, RENE LORRAINE, secondary school educator; b. Denver, Sept. 30, 1975; d. Ray J. and Cindy K. BeVier; m. Brandon David Dill, Aug. 1, 1998; 1 child, Jackson Ray Dill. BA, U. No. Colo., Greeley, 1999. Tchg. artist TADA! (Theatre and Dance Alliance), NYC, 2000—01; dir. drama program Northglenn H.S., Colo., 2001—. Contbr. Coal Creek Comty. Theatre; choreographer, prodr. Mousique + Mosque Co. Dir.(choreographer, prodr.): The King and I, Our Town, One Acts, Kiss Me, Kate, The Mousetrap, Footloose, Rumors, Music Man, The Crucible; performer: Front Range Cmty. Theatre. Cantor, singer Nativity Our Lord Ch., Broomfield, Colo., 2006. Fellow, Globe Theatre, London. Mem.: Ednl. Theatre Assn. (life). Avocations: theater, travel, Shakespeare. Home: 11899 Quitman Street Westminster CO 80031 Office: Northglenn High School 601 W 100th Place Northglenn CO 80260 Office Phone: 720-972-4685. Home Fax: 303-466-2950; Office Fax: 720-972-4739. Personal E-mail: renebevierdill@msn.com. E-mail: rene.dill@adams12.org.

BEXTERMILLER, THERESA MARIE, architect, computer engineer; b. St. Charles, Mo., Feb. 9, 1960; d. Charles Frederick and Loretta Joan (Unterreiner) Bextermiller; m. Paul James Metzger III, Nov. 29, 2000; stepchildren: Jennifer, Michael, Stephen, Andrew. BArch, Kans. State U., 1983, MArch, 2006; MFA in Computer Graphics, Pratt Inst., 1990, degree in exptl. computer sci., engring. and interactive media, 1993, degree in digital arts, 2006. Registered arch., NY, Mo., cert. Nat. Coun. Architectural Registration Bds.; lic. real estate broker Mo. Grad. arch. Mackey/Mitchell Assocs., St. Louis, 1983-84, Fleming Corp., St. Louis, 1984-85; project arch., prototype mgr. Casco Corp., St. Louis, 1985-87; grad. arch. HBE Corp., St. Louis, 1987-88; with telecomm. Western Union, 1992-93, Lucent Techs. (formerly AT&T Network Sys.), 1993—94; contract arch. Washington Group Internat., 1994-95, Fru-Con Engring. Inc. and other firms, various locations, 1995-98; prin. TMB Architecture/Computer Graphics, 1997—, Theresa Marie Bextermiller Metzger, RA, MFA, NCARB, Broker, 2000—. Le Pique and Orne Archs.-Inc., 1998—, Hellmuth, Obata & Kassabaum, Inc., St. Louis, 1998—; planner Infante Assocs., LLC, 1999—. Substitute tchr. St. Louis Pub. Schs., 2001—02; freelance architect; cons. with 3D modeling and animation software, NY, LA, St. Louis, 1990—. Mem.: MADD, AIA, Am. Planning Assn., US Green Bldg. Coun., Couple to Couple League Internat. Roman Cath. Avocation: real estate. Home and Office: 1120 Blendon Pl Saint Louis MO 63117-1911 Office Phone: 314-645-2186. Personal E-mail: illege666@aol.com.

BEYER, BARBARA LYNN, transportation executive, consultant; b. Miami, Fla., Feb. 16, 1947; d. Morten Sternoff and Jane (Hartman) Beyer. BA, George Washington U., 1978. Supr. printing office Saudi Arabian Airlines, 1966-67; ops. coord. Modern Air Transport, Miami, 1968-70, acct. Berlin, 1970-72; rep. Johnson Internat. Airlines, Washington, 1974-75; v.p., bd. dirs. Avmark, Inc., Washington, 1975—, pres., 1989—; chmn., bd. dirs. Avmark Internat., London, 1985—; mng. dir. Avmark Asia Ltd., Singapore, 1988-89, also bd. dirs., chmn. bd. dirs. Hong Kong, 1989—; pub. Avmark Aviation Economist, London, 1986—. Mem. adv. bd. aviation bus. dept. Embry-Riddle Aero. U. Mem.: Nat. Bus. Aircraft Assn., Aviation Space Writers (internat. bd. dirs. 1986—88, award 1978), Am. C. of C., Nat. Press Club, Internat. Aviation Club, Aero Club, Fgn. Corr. Club. Avocations: reading, horseback riding, home improvement. Office: Avmark Inc 415 Church St NE Ste 203 Vienna VA 22180 Office Phone: 703-528-5610. Personal E-mail: bbeyer@avmarkinc.com.

BEYER, LA VONNE ANN, special education educator; b. Estherville, Iowa, Mar. 24, 1925; d. (George) Harold and Florence Catherine (Mulvey) Schafer; m. Gerald P. Beyer, June 7, 1943; children: Gregg Allan Beyer, Douglas Lee Beijer, Jodie Lu Beyer, Michael E. Beyer, Stefan A. Beyer. BA, Calif. State U., Northridge, 1959, MA, 1974; EdD, U. So. Calif., 1985. Cert. spl. edn. tchr., Calif. Tchr., regular and spl. edn. L.A. Unified Sch. Dist., 1959-88;

cadre mem. Beginning Tchr. Assistance Program Calif. State U., Northridge, 1992—. Faculty U. So. Calif. reading clinic, 1974-75, Valley C.C., Burbank, 1974-75, L.A. C.C. (ESL), 1976-78. Contbr. articles to profl. jours. Literacy tutor Laubach Literacy Internat. (Van Nuys, Calif. chpt.), 1967—; mem. steering com. Roosevelt Commn., 1988. Recipient Mayor's Cert. of Appreciation, L.A., 1970, Dir. of Vols. in Agencies award, Van Nuys, 1989, Community award L.A. Times, 1990. Mem. DAR, Coun. for Exceptional Children,Laubach Literacy Internat., Pi Lambda Theta (v.p., pres. 1985-91), Phi Delta Kappa. Avocations: volunteering, gourmet cooking, travel, genealogy.

BEYER, SUZANNE, advertising agency executive; b. N.Y.C. d. Harry and Jennie Hillman; m. Isadore Beyer; children: Pamela Claire, Hillary Jay. Grad., Conservatory of Mus. Art, N.Y.C., 1947; student, Nassau C. C., N.Y.C., 1963-65. Singer, tchr. piano, N.Y.C., 1947-66; asst. to v.p. media dir. Robert E. Wilson, Advt., N.Y.C., 1967-72; media planner, media buyer frank J. Corbett div. BBDO Internat., N.Y.C., 1972-77, Lavey/Wolff/Swift divsn. BBDO Advt., N.Y.C., 1977-80; sr. media planner Lavey/Wolff/Swift (divn. BBDO Advt.), N.Y.C., 1980-83, media supr., 1983-94, Lyons, Lavey, Nichel, Swift, N.Y.C., 1995-96; pharm. advt. med. media cons., 1996—. Soprano Opera Assn., Nassau, N.Y., 1976-99; soprano United Choral Soc., Woodmere, L.I., 1970-99, soprano Armand Sodero Chorale, Baldwin, Long Is., 1980-86, soprano Rockville Ctr. Choral Soc., 1986—. Mem. Pharm. Advt. Coun., L.I. Advt. Club, Healthcare Bus. Women's Assn. Home: 66 Fonda Rd Rockville Centre NY 11570-2751

BEYERLE, SUSAN D., retired elementary school educator; b. Ohio; AA, Lakeland C.C., Kirtland, Ohio, 1973; EdB, Lake Erie Coll., Painesville, Ohio, 1976; MEd, John Carroll U., Cleve., Ohio, 1983. 1-8 Elementary Ohio, 1976, K-12 LD/BD Certifiction Ohio, 1979, K-12 reading endorsement Ohio, 1985, cert. supr., adminstr. Ohio, 1998, National Board Certification Ohio, 2001. Exceptional needs specilaist Painesville City Local Schools, Painesville, Ohio, 1979—2006; ret., 2006. Recipient Human Rels. award, Holloways Commn. Award NEOEA, 1990—91. Mem.: Delta Kappa Gamma, Delta Gamma Theata (life).

BEYER-MEARS, ANNETTE, physiologist; b. Madison, Wis., May 26, 1941; d. Karl and Annette (Weiss) Beyer. BA, Vassar Coll., 1963; MS, Fairleigh Dickinson U., 1973; PhD, Coll. Medicine and Dentistry NJ, 1977. NIH fellow Cornell U. Med. Sch., 1963-65; instr. physiology Springside Sch., Phila., 1967-71; teaching asst. dept. physiology Coll. Medicine & Dentistry NJ, NJ Med. Sch., 1974-77, NIH fellow dept. ophthalmology, 1978-80; asst. prof. dept. ophthalmology U. Medicine and Dentistry NJ., NJ Med. Sch., Newark, 1979-85, asst. prof. dept. physiology, 1980-85, assoc. prof. dept. physiology, 1986—, assoc. prof. dept. ophthalmology, 1986—. Vis. assoc. prof. dept. ophthalmology and vision sci. U. Wis., Madison, 1995—; cons. Alcon Labs. Contbr. articles in field of diabetic lens and kidney therapy to profl. jours. Chmn. admissions No. NJ, Vassar Coll., 1974-79; mem. minister search com. St. Bartholomew Episcopal Ch., NJ, 1978, fund-raising chmn., 1978, 79; del. Episc. Diocesian Conv., 1977, 78; long range planning com. Christ Ch., Ridgewood, NJ, 1985-87, vestry, 1994-95. Recipient NIH Nat. Rsch. Svc. award, 1978-80, Found. CMDNJ Rsch. award, 1980; grantee Juvenile Diabetes Found., 1985-87, NIH, NEI grantee, 1980-95, Pfizer, Inc. grantee, 1985-89, 93—. Mem. Am. Physiol. Soc., NY Acad. Scis., Soc. for Neurosci., Am. Soc. Pharmacology and Exptl. Therapeutics, Assn. for Rsch. Vision & Ophthalmology, Internat. Soc. for Eye Research, AAAS, The Royal Soc. Medicine, Internat. Diabetes Found., Am. Diabetes Assn., European Assn. Study of Diabetes, Aircraft Owners and Pilots Assn., Sigma Xi. Home: 120 Ely Pl Madison WI 53726-4015

BEYMER-CHAPMAN, BRENDA MARIE, elementary school educator; b. Okmulgec, Okla., Apr. 17, 1967; d. James Walter and Barbara Jean (Cox) Beymer; m. Lance Issac Chapman, July 30, 1994; children: Ryan James Chapman, Keely Elizabeth Chapman. BS in Edn., U. Okla., Norman, 1990, JD, 1993. Bar: Okla. 1993; cert. tchr. Okla. Tchr. Carousel Corner Daycare, Norman, 1990—93; law clk. U.S. Dist. Atty.'s Office U.S. Dist. Ct. (we. dist.) Okla., Oklahoma City, 1991—93; tchr. 7-8 grades Butner Pub. Schs., Cromwell, Okla., 1993—98; tchr. 8th grade history Putnam City Schs., Oklahoma City, 1998—2004, specialist social studies curriculum, 2004—; assessor Nat. Bd. for Profl. Tchg. Stds., 2004—. Dist. 5 coord. Project Citizen Ctr. for Civic Edn., Calif., 2000—; bd. dirs. Okla. Coun. for Econ. Edn. Vol. various programs and events 1st Bapt. Ch., Norman, 1997—; mentor tchr. programs Advancing Citizenship Edn., Oklahoma City, 1995—2003. Named Tchr. of Yr., Okla. Supreme Ct., 2000, Excellent Educator, Putnam City Schs., 2001, Mid. Sch. Tchr. of Yr., Am. Lawyer's Aux., 2004; recipient Colonial Williamsburg fellowship, 1997; grantee, Putnam City Schs., 2000, 2001, 2005. Mem.: NEA, Nat. Coun. for Social Studies, Okla. Edn. Assn., Okla. Coun. for Social Studies (past pres. 2002—, Social Studies Tchr. of Yr. 2003), Okla. Bar Assn. (mem. law-related edn. com. 2000—). Democrat. Baptist. Avocations: reading, travel, history, sports, antiques. Home: 609 Branchwood Dr Norman OK 73072 Office: Putnam City Schs 540 1 NW 40th Oklahoma City OK 73122

BEYONCÉ, (BEYONCÉ GISELLE KNOWLES), singer; b. Houston, Tex., Sept. 4, 1981; d. Matthew and Tina Knowles. Mem. group Destiny's Child, Houston, 1990—. Spokesperson L'Oreal, Tommy Hilfiger for fragrance "True Star"; launched House of Dereon fashion line (with Tina Knowles), 2005. Singer: (albums) Destiny's Child, 1998, The Writing's on the Wall, 1999 (Platinum album 7 times, Grammy awards: Best R&B Song for Say My Name, 2000, Best R&B Performance By A Duo Or Group With Vocal, 2000), Survivor, 2001 (debuted at #1 Billboard Album Chart, Platinum 3 times, Grammy award: Best R&B Performance By A Duo Or Group With Vocal, 2001), 8 Days of Christmas, 2001, Destiny Fulfilled, 2004 (Am. Music Awards Favorite R&B Album, 2005), #1's, 2005, (solo albums) Dangerously in Love, 2003 (Grammy awards: Best Female R&B Vocal Performance, 2003, Best R&B Performance By A Duo Or Group With Vocals for song The Closer I Get To You, 2003, Best R&B Song for Crazy In Love, 2003, Best Contemporary R&B Album, 2003, Best Rap/Sung Collaboration for song Crazy in Love, 2003, MTV Video Music award Best Female Video for the song Naughty Girl, 2004), Live at Wembley, 2004, B'day, 2006; actor: (films) Austin Powers in Goldmember, 2002, I Know, 2003, The Fighting Temptations, 2003, The Pink Panther, 2006; composer: (films) Romeo Must Die, Charlie's Angels, Austin Powers in Goldmember, Bad Boys II, Fighting Temptations, Bridget Jones: The Edge of Reason, Soul Plane; actor: (TV Guest Appearances) Oprah Winfrey Show, 2003, 2004, The View, 2004, 20 / 20, 2004, Top of the Pops, 2004, Saturday Night Live, 2004, 106th & Park Top 10 Live, 2005. Co-recipient Best R&B Video award for Check on It, MTV Video Music Awards, 2006; named Pop Songwriter of Yr., ASCAP, 2001, Best Female R&B artist, BET awards, 2004; named one of 50 Most Influential African-Americans, Ebony Mag., 2004; recipient 4 Billboard Music awards, 2000, 2 Billboard Music awards, 2001, Am. Music award, 2000, 2 Am. Music awards, 2001, Favorite R&B Group, Am. Music Awards, 2005, MTV Music Video award, 2001, 4 World Music awards, 2001, Image award, NAACP, 2000, 2001, 2006, Sammy Davis, Jr. award, 2000, Soul Train award, 2000, World's Best-Selling Pop Group, World Music Awards, 2006, World's Best-Selling R&B Group, 2006, Best-Selling Female Group of All Time, 2006, 3 Music of Black Origin (MOBO) awards, 2006. Office: 1505 Hadley Houston TX 77002 Office Phone: 713-772-5175.*

BEZROD, NORMA R., artist; b. Phila., May 17, 1938; d. Samuel Bezrod and Bessie Roffman; m. Arthur J. Cooperman, Aug. 22, 1959 (div. Apr. 1977); 1 child, Seth Alan Cooperman; m. William D. P. Riley, July 1, 1983 (dec. Oct. 1998). BA, Queens Coll., 1960, MS, 1974; EdD, Columbia U., 1986. Lic. fine arts tchr., N.Y. Art tchr. N.Y.C. Pub. Schs., 1960-77; exec. dir. art Sr. Ctr., Human Resources Adminstrn., N.Y.C., 1977-78; instr. art edn. Queens (N.Y.) Coll., 1978-79; edn. evaluator, case mgr. N.Y.C. Bd. Edn., 1980-88. Cons. N.Y. State Coun. on the Arts, 1977-79. Author: Don't Be Afraid of the Dark, 1977, (series) Lion and Pretty Bird, 1983—85; art critic: Good Times, 1971—75; Represented in permanent collections St. John's U. Libr., Queens Coll. Mus. Teaching fellow Queens Coll., 1978-79. Home: PO Box 660125 Flushing NY 11366-0125

BHATIA, SONIA SINGH, psychologist; b. Jammu, India; m. Mohamood Bhatia, July 21, 1984; children: Sarena, Sameer. AA, Glendale Community Coll., 1980; BA, U. So. Calif., 1982; MA, U.S. Internat. U., 1984, PsyD, 1988. Designed nat. lay counselor program for Ismaili religion, 2000. Recipient Outstanding Svc. award Montgomery County Dept. Addictions, Victims and Mental Health Svcs., 1990, Vol. Svc. award Pres.'s Coun. on Svc. and Civic Participation; named Vol. of Yr. Seminole Healthy Start Coalition, 2004 Mem. Am. Assn. Marriage and Family, APA.

BHATT, MANISHA HEMENDRA, lawyer; BA in History and Spanish, Boston Coll., 1995; JD, Suffolk U. Law Sch., 1999. Intern Boston Med. Ctr.; pvt. practice civil litig.; staff atty. Family Law Unit Greater Boston Legal Services, 2001—. Office: Greater Boston Legal Services 197 Friend St Boston MA 02114 Office Phone: 617-371-1234. Office Fax: 617-371-1222.*

BHATTACHARYA, BHASWATI, preventive medicine physician; b. Calif. BA, U. Pa.; MA in pharmacology, Columbia U.; MPH in internat. health, Harvard U.; MD, Rush Med. Coll. Resident in preventive medicine Mt. Sinai Med. Ctr., NYC, with cmty. and preventive medicine dept.; pvt. practice in preventive medicine, pub. health., holistic medicine and holistic healing counseling NYC; attending physician dept. family practice and cmty. medicine Wyckoff Heights Med. Ctr., NY-Presbyn. Hosp., Bklyn., dir. rsch. dept. medicine, dir. divsn. complementary and alternative medicines; asst. prof. family practice Weill Med. Coll., Cornell U. Asian Am. health subcommittee advisor to US Senator Hillary Rodham Clinton; contbr. expert Dorland's Med. Dictionary. Founder women's health program Sakhi, NYC. Recipient Leadership award, AMA Found., 2004. Mem.: Am. Assn Physicians of Indian Origin, Am. Holistic Medicine Assn. (Nat. award 1998), S. Asian Pub. Health Assn. (bd. dir. 2004—). Office: Wyckoff Hts Med Ctr Medicine/Ob-Gyn 374 Stockholm St Brooklyn NY 11237 Office Phone: 718-907-4951. Business E-Mail: bhb9002@nyp.org.

BIALLER, NANCY, art appraiser; AB, Vassar Coll.; MA, MPhil, PhD in 16th & 17th Century Dutch Art, Yale U. With Sotheby's, London, 1976, head, Old Master Drawings NYC. Fullbright Fellow, Vienna, 1972. Office: Sotheby's 1334 York Ave New York NY 10021 Office Phone: 212-606-7230. Office Fax: 212-606-7107. Business E-Mail: nancy.bialler@sothebys.com.

BIANCHI, CARISA, advertising company executive; Formerly with Benton & Bowles, L.A., Doyle Dane Bernbach; with Chiat/Day L.A., 1989-97; mng. dir., pres., CEO TBWA/Chiat/Day, San Francisco, 1998—2002, mng. ptnr. Playa del Rey, 2002, chief strategy officer L.A., 2002—. Office: TBWA/Chiat/Day 5353 Grosvenor Blvd Los Angeles CA 90066-6319

BIANCHI, GAYLE ANN, elementary school educator; d. Victor and Vera Jean Ballerini; m. Attilin Gine Bianchi, Jan. 24, 1976; children: Christopher, Gina. AA, Ill. Valley CC, Oglesby, 1975; BE, Ill. State U., Bloomington, 1979. Tchr. art K-8th grade Holy Family, Oglesby, 1980—82; tchr. sci. 6-8th grade LaSalle Cath., Ill., 1983—87; tchr. sci. 7-8th grade Little Flower, Springfield, Ill., 1989—90; tchr. sci. 5-8th grade St. Patricks, Ottawa, Ill., 1991—2000; tchr. sci. 7-8th grade Marseilles Elem., Ill., 2000—. Named Educator of Yr., Wal-Mart, 1995. Avocations: swimming, walking, bicycling. Office: Marseilles Elem ch 201 Chicago St Marseilles IL 61341

BIANCHI, MARIA, critical care nurse, acute care nurse practitioner; b. Springfield, Mass. B of Nursing, Catherine Laboure Sch. Nursing, 1979; BSN, Fitchburg State Coll./U. Mass., Amherst, 1985. Cert. post-anesthesia care nurse; critical care clin. specialist; expert witness, Mass., Conn. Recovery as mgmt. educator; mktg. and recruitment cons.; cons. in critical care nursing; clin. faculty Am. Internat. Coll., Springfield; adminstr. dept. spl. svcs., mgr. critical care Baystate Med. Ctr., Springfield, Mass., 1980-89; recruitment adminstrn. and sr. faculty St. Francis Med. Ctr. Sch. of Nursing, Hartford, Conn., 1989-92; grad. faculty U. Mass. Med. Ctr., Worcester, 1995-97; asst. prof. Grad. Sch. U. Mass., Amherst, 1998-99; faculty U. Mass. Sch. of Nursing, Amherst, per diem nurse practitioner dept. surgery Worcester, 1995—97, 1999—; CS/NP Mass Gen. Hosp., Boston; nurse dept. emergency medicine St. Francis Hosp. and Med. Ctr., Hartford, Conn., 2006—. Pres. ProLase Medi-Spa & Clinic, Worcester and Springfield, Mass., TI Healthcare; nat. cons. critical care/post anesthesia issues; medicolegal cons.; laser med. provider; lectr. critical care and post anesthesia issues, empowerment, acute pain, holistic techniques, medicological documentation, trauma. Invited amb. del. People's for People's, Fed. Govt. Mem. AACN, Am. Soc. Post-Anesthesia Nursing (Boston chpt. editl. cons.), Soc. Critical Medicine, Mass. Gen. Hosp. Alumni Assn., Catherine Laboure Alumni Assn., Sigma Theta Tau. Achievements include research in pain, burn trauma, stress reduction, holistic methods for high risk individuals in maximum security penitentiary and critical care patients. Office: PO Box 614 Suffield CT 06078-0614 Personal E-mail: mariatih@comcast.net.

BIBAUD, RENE, artist, performer, consultant; b. Longbranch, N.J., Nov. 21, 1969; d. Richard Charles and Mildred Ellen Bibaud. Artist performer Cirque Du Soleil, Montreal, Quebec, 1996—2001; artist performer/cons. self employed, Kirkland, Wash., 2001—02. Home: 8103 39th Ave Sw Seattle WA 98136-2305 Personal E-mail: renebibaud@compuserve.com.

BIBBO, MARLUCE, physician, educator; b. Sao Paulo, Brazil, July 14, 1939; d. Domingos and Yolanda (Ranciaro) Bibbo. MD, U. Sao Paulo, 1963, ScD, 1968. Intern Hosps. das Clinicas, U. Sao Paulo, 1963, resident in morphology, 1964-66; instr. dept. morphology and ob-gyn. U. Sao Paulo, 1966-68, asst. prof., 1968-69; fellow in cytology U. Chgo., 1969-70, asst. prof. sect. cytology dept. ob-gyn., 1971-73, assoc. prof., 1973-77, assoc. prof. pathology, 1974-77, prof. ob-gyn. and pathology, 1978-92; assoc. dir. Cytology Lab., Approved Sch. Cytotech and Cytocybernetics, AMA-Am. Soc. Clin. Pathologists, 1970-91; dir. Cytology Lab., Phila., 1992—; prof. pathology and cell biology Thomas Jefferson U., Phila., 1992—, Warren R. Lane prof. pathology & cell biology, 1993—. Mem. rsch. com. Ill. divsn. Am. Cancer Soc., 1976-91. Contbr. numerous articles to profl. jours. Fellow Internat. Acad. Cytology (pres.-elect, v.p. 1987, pres. 1992, dep. editor Acta Cytologica, editor 1995), Am. Soc. Clin. Pathologists (coun. on cytopathology); mem. Am. Soc. Cytology (exec. com., pres. 1982-83), U.S. Acad. Pathology, Can. Acad. Pathology, Soc. Analytical Cytology, Coun. Cytopathology. Home: 250 S 9th St Philadelphia PA 19107-5734 Office: Cytology Lab Rm 260 Main Bldg 132 S 10th St Philadelphia PA 19107-5244 Office Phone: 215-955-6437. E-mail: bibbo@cytology-iac.org.

BIBEL, DEBRA JAN, public health scientist, editor; b. San Francisco, Apr. 6, 1945; d. Philip and Bassya (Maltzer) B. AB, U. Calif., Berkeley, 1967, PhD, 1972. Rsch. microbiologist Letterman Army Inst. Rsch., San Francisco, 1972-79; tech. writer Hoefer Sci. Inst., San Francisco, 1979; rsch. assoc. Kaiser Found. Rsch. Inst., San Francisco, 1981-83, 87-95; product mgr. Tago Inc., Burlingame, Calif., 1983-85; dir. Elie Metchnikoff Meml. Library, Oakland, Calif., 1977—2004, historian, 1986; staff rsch. assoc. dept. dermatology U. Calif., San Francisco, 1987-88, faculty rsch. assoc. dept. dermatology, 1994—99; editor AMUR Pharms., Inc., Belmont, Calif., 1997; comm. coord., exec. assoc. Alcohol Rsch. Group, Pub. Health Inst., Emeryville, Calif., 1999—. Lectr. U. Calif., Berkeley, 1975, Antioch Coll. West, San Francisco, 1975. Author: Milestones in Immunology, A Historical Exploration, 1988, Freeing the Goose in the Bottle: Discovering Zen Through Science, Understanding Science Through Zen, 1992, A Collection of Clouds. Zen Haiku and Other Poetry, 1997, Microbial Musings: A History of Microbiology, 2001; columnist Rummagings Along the Dusty Shelf, 1982-2006; contbr. articles to profl. jours. Active Ali Akbar Coll. Music, San Rafael, Calif.; instr. Berkeley Cmty. Health Project, 1971-75. Capt. U.S. Army, 1972-76. Mem. AAAS, ACLU, No. Calif. Am. Soc. Microbiology. Buddhist. Avocations: painting, photography, Asian philosophy, science history, music. Home: 230 Orange St Apt 6 Oakland CA 94610-4139 Office: Alcohol Rsch Group Pub Health Inst 6475 Christie Ave Ste 400 Emeryville CA 94608-1010 Office Phone: 510-597-3440. Business E-Mail: jbibel@arg.org.

BIBERSTINE, JOLENE BETH, medical/surgical nurse; b. Iowa City, Iowa, Feb. 17, 1967; d. Arthur Lorraine and Genevieve Rose (Ludwig) Merck; m. John Biberstine, Sept. 22, 1990; children Ashley, Sarah, Chad. BSN, Cedarville (Ohio) Coll., 1989. RN, Ind. Camp nurse, registrar East Iowa Bible Camp, Deep River, Iowa, 1989; clin. staff nurse Iowa Meth. Med. Ctr., Des Moines, 1989-90; staff nurse Adams County Meml. Hosp., Decatur, Ind., 1990; eye clinician Family Eye Clinic, Berne, Ind., 1991-93; staff nurse Swiss Village Retirement Ctr., Berne, 1994—99, program coord., 1999—2002, MDS nurse, 2002—. Children's ch. tchr., pianist, mem. music com. Evang. Mennonite Ch., Berne.

BIBLIOWICZ, JESSICA M., financial analyst; b. 1959; d. Sanford and Joan Weill; 2 children. Grad., Cornell U. Formerly with assesment mgmt. divsn. Shearson Lehman Bros.; dir. sales and mktg. Prudential Mutual Funds, 1992—94; exec. v.p., oversees mutual funds and insured investor group Smith Barney, N.Y.C., 1994—97; pres., COO John A. Levin & Co., 1997—99; pres., CEO Nat. Financial Partners, N.Y.C., 1999—. Dir. Eaton Vance Mutual Funds, Gov. Com. Scholastic Achievement, Securities Industry Assn.; mem., hedge funds adv. group, investment com. Cornell U. Gov. Boys & Girls Club of Am.; regional chair, N.E. Region. Office: NFP 787 7th Ave, 49th Fl New York NY 10019

BIBY-RUSSINA, ERIKA L., counselor; b. Springfield, Ill., Mar. 27, 1971; d. Robert Biby and N. Carolyn Wiley; m. Robert Russina; children; Gabrielle Russina, Kayla Russina. BA in Psychology, So. Ill. U., Edwardsville, 1992, MA in Clin. Psychology, 1995. Lic. profl. counselor; nat. cert. counselor. Rehab. counselor U.S. Dept. Vets. Affairs, Chgo., 1993-97; counselor Peace for Kids, St. Louis, 1997-99, Gen. Protestant Children's Home, St. Louis, 1999—2000; therapist St. Louis Effort For AIDS, 2000—05; pvt. practice, 2005—. Vol. mentor Big Bros./Big Sisters, St. Louis, 1998-2000; vol. Family Resource Ctr., St. Louis, 1993-95. Mem. ACA, APA (assoc.). Avocations: travel, hiking, camping, writing. Office: 2632 S Kingshighway St Saint Louis MO 63139 Office Phone: 314-772-0809. Business E-Mail: erika@licensedcounselor.com.

BICCUM, AMANDA, elementary school educator; b. Port Jervis, NY, Sept. 23, 1979; d. Gary and Debra Biccum. BS in Biology, SUNY, New Paltz, 2003. Cert. secondary edn. biology 7-12 NY, 2003. Seventh grade tchr. Fallsburg (N.Y.) Jr./Sr. H.S., 2003—05, eighth grade tchr., 2005—, varsity girls softball coach, 2004—06. Varsity girls soccer coach Fallsburg H.S., 2005—. Office: Fallsburg Jr/Sr High School 115 Brickman Rd Fallsburg NY 12733 Business E-Mail: abiccum@fallsburgcsd.net.

BICE, EDNA JEWEL, artist, educator; b. Bridge Port, Ala., Dec. 27, 1927; d. Edward Jack and Suzanne Reeves; m. Ronald H. Bice, June 27, 1954; children: Ronald H. Jr., Randy Reeves. Grad., Bridge Port Schs., 1945. Mothers patrol officer Charra Police Dept., Tenn., 1963—70; merchandiser Chattanooga, 1973—78; ceramics tchr. Soddy Daisy, Tenn., 1978—2004. Recipient Leadership award, Chattanooga Schs., 1965, award for commitment and svc. to elderly, City of Chattanooga, 1980. Mem.: NAACP, Nat. Hist. Soc. (life). Democrat. Presbyterian. Avocations: ceramics, arts and crafts, knitting, gardening, cross stitch. Home: 12209 Posey Hollow Rd Soddy Daisy TN 37379

BICK, JENNIE L, elementary school educator; d. Marvin J and Katherine Ruth (Croas) Austin, Margaret Austin (Stepmother); m. Jeffrey A Bick, May 13, 1983; 1 child, Jeffrey C. BS in elem. edn., Ind. U. Purdue U. Indpls., 1999—2004. Oral surgeon asst. Dr. Charles H. Redish, Indpls., 1980—86; deputation sec. Free Meth. Ch. of N.Am., Indpls., 1993—99; tchr. Indpls. Pub. Schools, 2004—. Vol. West Morris St. Free Meth. Ch., Indpls. Mem.: NSTA, Ind. State Teachers Assn. Free Methodist. Avocations: drawing, reading, travel, painting. Office Phone: 317-226-4234.

BICK, KATHERINE LIVINGSTONE, neuroscientist, educator, researcher; b. Charlottetown, Can., May 3, 1932; came to U.S., 1954; d. Spurgeon Arthur and Flora Hazel (Murray) Livingstone; m. James Harry Bick, Aug. 20, 1955 (div.); children: James A., Charles L. (dec.); m. Ernst Freese, 1986 (dec. 1990). BS with honors, Acadia U., Can., 1951, MS, 1952; PhD, Brown U., 1957; DSc (hon.), Acadia U., 1990. Rsch. pathologist UCLA Med. Sch., 1959-61; asst. prof. Calif. State U., Northridge, 1961-66; lab. instr. Georgetown U., Washington, 1970-72, asst. prof., 1972-76; dep. dir. neurol. disorder program Nat. Inst. Neurol. and Communicative Disorders and Stroke, NIH, Bethesda, Md., 1976-81, acting dep. dir., 1981-83, dep. dir., 1983-87; dep. dir. extramural rsch. Office of Dir. NIH, 1987-90; sci. liaison Centro Studio Multicentrico Internazionale Sulla Demenza, Washington, 1990-95. Cons. Nat. Rsch. Coun., Italy, 1991-97, The Charles A. Dana Found., N.Y.C., 1993-98, Edn. Commn. of the States, 1996-99. Editor: Alzheimer's Disease: Senile Dementia and Related Disorders, 1978, Neurosecretion and Brain Peptides, Implications for Brain Functions and Neurol. Disease, 1981, The Early Story of Alzheimer's Disease, 1987, Alzheimer Disease, 1994, 2d edit., 1999, Alzheimer Disease: The Changing View, 2000; contbr. articles to profl. jours. Pres. Woman's Club, McLean, Va., 1968-69; bd. dirs. Fairfax County (Va.) YWCA, 1969-70; pres. Avenel Homeowner's Assn., 1998; pres. Emerson Unitarian Ch., 1964-66; mem. Bethesda Pl. Cmty. Coun., 1992-95, pres., 1993-94; mem. Dana Alliance for Brain Initiatives, 1993—; bd. dirs. Wilmington NC Child Advocacy Commn., 1998-2002; mem. vol. guild St. John's Mus. Art, Wilmington; chair Vol. Guild Cameron Art Mus., Wilmington, 2002-03, Cameron Art Mus. Bd., 2003-06; vestry St. Andrew's on the Sound, Wilmington, 2004-06. Recipient Can. NRC award Acadia U., 1951-52, NIH Dir.'s award, 1978, Spl. Achievement award NIH, 1981, 83, Superior Svc. award USPHS, 1986, Presdl. Rank award meritorious sr. exec., 1989, Genesis award Alzheimer's Assn., 2005; Universal Match Found. fellow Brown U., 1956-57, Fed. Exec. Inst. Leadership fellow, 1980 Fellow AAAS; mem. Am. Neurol. Assn., Internat. Brain Rsch. Orgn., World Fedn. Neurology Rsch. Group on Dementias (exec. sec. Am. region 1984-86, chmn. 1986-93), Alzheimer's Disease Internat., Soc. for Neurosci. (emeritus), Acad. of Medicine Washington, Dana Alliance for Brain Initiatives.

BICKERSTAFF, MINA MARCH CLARK, retired academic administrator; b. Crowley, Tex., Sept. 27, 1936; d. Winifred Perry and Clara Mae (Jarrett) Clark; m. Billy Frank Bickerstaff, June 12, 1954 (div. 1960); children: Billy Mark, Mina Gayle Bickerstaff Basaldu. AA, Tarrant County Jr. Coll., 1982; BBA, Dallas Bapt. U., 1991. Dir. pers. svcs. Southwestern Bapt. Theol. Sem., Ft. Worth, 1976—2004; ret., 2004. Mem. Coll. and Univ. Pers. Assn., Seminary Woman's Club (past treas.), Alpha Chi. Baptist. Avocations: reading, music, genealogy. E-mail: minamb@juno.com.

BICKFORD, MARGARET WYATT, minister; b. Cleve., Nov. 3, 1936; d. Ralph Moore and Virginia Hixon Wyatt; m. William Edwin Bickford, Oct. 12, 1963; children: Virginia Musumeci, William Ralph. BA, Wellesley Coll., 1958; BArch, Boston Arch. Ctr., 1965; MDiv, Episc. Divinity Sch., 1978; DMin, Boston U. Sch. Theology, 1996. Ordained elder N.H. Conf. United Meth. Ch.; cert. grief counselor Assn. Death Edn. and Counseling. Sec. Bourne & Nichols, Archs., Boston, 1958—62, Todesco & Assocs., Boston, 1962—63, Polaroid Corp., Cambridge, Mass., 1963—64; intern Bon Secours Hosp., Methuen, Mass., 1976—77, Mass. Rehab. Hosp., Boston, 1977—78; educator Mental Health Ctr. So. N.H., 1978—81; pastor, counselor First United Meth. Ch., Methuen, Mass., 1981—89; coord. bereavement, chaplain Rockingham Hospice, Salem-Derry, NH, 1983—89; chaplain Lawrence Gen. Hosp., Mass., 1981—85; pastor Ayers Village United Meth. Ch., Haverhill, Mass., 1983—89; intern Tewksbury State Hosp., Mass., 1985—86, Elliott Hosp., Manchester, NH, 1986—87; pastoral counselor, bereavement coord. Lourdes Hospice, Paducah, Ky., 1989—93; pastor Grace United Meth. Ch.,

Canaan, Vt., 1993—98, Farnham United Meth. Ch., Pitts., NH, 1993—98, Plymouth (N.H.) United Meth. Ch., 1998—2004, Thornton (N.H.) United Meth. Ch., 1998—2004, Ashland (N.H.) United Meth. Ch., 2000—04, Milan (N.H.) Cmty. Ch., 2004—. Co-founder, pres. Rockingham Hospice, Derry, NH, 1983—89; chaplain Lawrence Gen. Hosp., NH, 1981—85, Pemi-Baker Home Health and Hospice, Plymouth, NH, 2001—, chmn. hospice com., pastoral counselor, 2001—. Author: Headwaters Harvest, 1997, Getting A Grip on Grief, 2006, United in Service, 2006. Fellow: Assn. Profl. Chaplains; mem.: Nat. Hospice and Palliative Care Orgn. Coun. Hospice Profls., Assn. Death Edn. and Counseling (grief counselor 1991—). Avocations: music, travel, history, reading. Personal E-mail: webmbkfd@emailmv.com.

BICKFORD, MELISSA A., computer scientist; b. Oakland, Calif., Oct. 22, 1964; d. Palmer Marquis and Joyce Lenore (Beeson) Oliver; m. Robert Lee Bickford, July 28, 1984 (div. July 1997). BA in Liberal Studies, Calif. State U., Hayward, 1998. CS svcs. mgr. Bay Alarm, Oakland, Calif., 1984-90, spl. project mgr. Walnut Creek, Calif., 1990-96, mgr. adanced tech., 1996-99; gen. mgr. InReach Internet, Stockton, Calif., 1999—, Cons. Integrated Telecomm Solutions, San Jose, Calif., 1999. Avocations: kayaking, camping, swimming, backpacking. Office: InReach Internet 4635 Georgetown Pl Stockton CA 95207-6203

BICKFORD, MERIS J., lawyer, bank executive; JD, Univ. Maine, 1986. Asst. v.p. Merrill Merchants Bank, Bangor, Maine; pres. MSBA, Bangor, Maine, 2005—. Mem.: Maine State Bar Found. (bd. of gov.), Maine State Bar Assn. (past dist. 5 gov., pres.-elect 2004). Office: Merrill Merchants Bank 201 Main St PO Box 925 Bangor ME 04402-0925 Business E-Mail: mbickford@merrillmerchants.com.

BICKHAM, CHARLOTTE MARIE, science educator; b. Minot, ND, Oct. 26, 1973; d. James Golden and Carmela Wallace; m. Jerry Lynn Bickham, II, Feb. 13, 1998; children: Sabrina Corrin, Jerry Lynn III. BS, Southeastern La. U., 2000. Cert. tchr. La. Tchr. Independence (La.) HS, 2000—, dept. chairperson, 2002—05. Mem.: Am. Fedn. Tchrs. (life). Baptist. Home: 50651 Abene Rd Tickfaw LA 70466 Office Phone: 985-878-9436. Personal E-mail: jbickham@bellsouth.net. Business E-Mail: charlotte.bickham@tangischools.org.

BIDDLE, FLORA MILLER, art patron, museum administrator; Granddaughter of Gertrude Vanderbilt Whitney; m. Sydney; 4 children BA, Manhattanville Coll., 1978. V.p. Whitney Mus. Am. Art, NYC, 1958—77, pres., 1978-85, chair, 1985—95, hon. trustee. Author: The Whitney Women and the Museum They Made, 1999. Mem.: NYC Art Commn. (mem. 1980—90). Home: 17 E 97th St Apt 6A New York NY 10029 Personal E-mail: florabiddle@gmail.com.

BIDDLE, JANE LAMMERT, retired English educator; b. Albany, N.Y., Oct. 10, 1926; d. Henry Christian Conrad and Elsie Annie (Arthur) Lammert; m. Thomas William Biddle, Aug. 23, 1950; 1 child, Susan Noelle. AB, U. Mich., 1947, AM, 1954. Cert. tchr. Mich., N.Y. English tchr. Haslett (Mich.) Rural Agrl. Sch., 1948-49, Slauson Jr. H.S., Ann Arbor, 1949-52, Ann Arbor H.S., 1952, John Marshall H.S., Rochester, N.Y., 1952-56, Newark Jr. H.S., 1957-61, Newark Sr. H.S., 1974-91, ret., 1991. State committeewoman N.Y. Rep. State Com., Albany, N.Y., 1976—; chmn., membership and concert com. Rochester Philharm., chmn. Wayne County Concerts, vol. coun.; pres. Newark Libr. Bd.; chmn. Wayne County Libr. Bd.; advisor Wayne County Teenage Rep., 1974—; delegate Rep. Nat. Convention, 1976; chmn. Shelter Fund Raising Wayne County Humane Soc., 1987-90; bd. dirs. Victim Resource Ctr., Newark, 1994—, Newark Wayne Cmty. Hosp., Newark, 1994—; vice chmn. Wayne County Rep. Com., 1973-76; mem. Newark Wayne Cmty. Hosp. Aux., 1999—. Named Auxilian of Yr. Newark Wayne Hosp. Aux., 1995, Citizen of the Yr. in Education Newark C. of C., 1992, George Farrell Rep. Svc. award, 1998. Avocations: interior decorating, gardening, volunteering, tutoring, working with teenagers. Home: 407 Mason St Newark NY 14513-1714

BIDWELL, KAREN RUBINO, mental health care clinician; b. Providence, Aug. 26, 1957; d. Michael Joseph and Rose Marie (Ranieri) Rubino; m. David T. Bidwell, Oct. 3, 1981; children: Kathryn Celeste, Emily Jayne. BA, Assumption Coll., 1979; cert. counselor alcohol & drug abuse, U. R.I., 1981; MS, Cen. Conn. State U., 1989. Internat. cert. alcohol and drug counselor, lic. alcohol and drug counselor. Psychol. technician Butler Hosp., Providence, 1979-81; social club dir. Genesis Ctr., Manchester, Conn., 1985-89; psychotherapist North Cen. Conn. Mental Health System, Enfield, 1989-90, Pastoral Counseling Ctr. of Manchester, Conn., 1989-94; clinician New Directions, Enfield, Conn., 1993—. Home: 31 Love Ln Manchester CT 06040-2678 Office: Inst Living 400 Washington St Hartford CT 06106

BIEBER, (ADDA) LYNN, marriage, family and child counselor; b. San Diego, Oct. 14, 1928; d. William Vere and Hazel Frances (Robinett) Nall; m. Stanley Bieber, Feb. 22, 1952; children: Danny Vere, Robinett, Davi Lynn, William (dec.). BS in Home Econs., Okla. State U., 1950; MS, Calif. State U., Hayward, 1969. Designated pupil pers. svcs.; lic. marriage, family and child counselor. Buyer Kahn's Dept. Store, Oakland, Calif., 1950-52; sch. counselor Mendenhall Jr. High Sch., Livermore, Calif., 1969-72; pvt. practice psychotherapy Livermore and Pleasanton, Calif., 1972—. Dir., founder The Alliance for Holographic Living, Pleasanton, 1991—; founder, past pres. Earth Connection, Non-Profit, Pleasanton, 1992. Founder Anthropos Counseling Ctr., Livermore, 1975, Listening Project, 1978. Recipient Recogniton of Svcs. awards Ctr. for Edn. Infant Deaf, Berkeley, 1989, Buenas Vidas Youth Svcs., Livermore, 1990. Avocations: metaphysics, reading, Scrabble. Home: 5196 Oakdale Ct Pleasanton CA 94588-3753

BIEGEL, DEBRA JEANNE, music educator; b. Billings, Mont., July 29, 1955; d. Oscar Herman and Doris Jeanne Biegel. MusB, U. Mont., 1977; M in Curriculum and Instr., Mont. State U., 1991. Music tchr. Bozeman Pub. Schools, Mont., 1980—, Ennis Pub. Schools, Mont., 1977—80. Choir dir. Hawthorne After Sch., Bozeman, Mont., 2003—; dir. piano studio Hawthorne Sch., 2000—. Recipient Mont. Tchr. of Yr., 2006, Gov. Arts award, Hawthorne Sch., 2005, Boyer Ctr. award, 2004. Mem.: Mont. Gen. Musta Tchrs. Assn., Bana Masters Assn., Music Edn. Nat. Conf., NEA. Avocations: travel, sports, movies, reading. Home: 406 Meagher Ave Bozeman MT 59718 Office: Bozeman Pub Sch 114 North Rouse Bozeman MT 59715

BIEGEL, EILEEN MAE, retired hospital executive; b. Eau Claire, Wis., Nov. 13, 1937; d. Ewald Frederic and Emma Antonia (Conrad) Weggen; m. James O. Biegel, Oct. 6, 1956; children: Jeffrey Allan, John William. Student, Dist. One Tech. Inst., 1974; corr. student, U. Wis., Madison; grad. mgmt. seminars; student, Upper Iowa U., 1984—. Cert. profl. sec. Exec. sec. to pres. Broadcaster Svcs., Inc., Eau Claire, Wis., 1969-74; exec. sec. to exec. v.p. Am. Nat. Bank, Eau Claire, 1975-77; exec. asst. to pres. Luther Hosp., Eau Claire, 1977—2000, asst. corp. sec., 1984—2000, mem. exec. staff, 1985—2000; asst. corp. sec. Luther Health Care Corp., 1984—2000; ret., 2000; sec. Dist. Atty. Offic, 2002—. Secretarial adv. council Dist. One Tech. Sch. 1975—; corp. sec. Northwest Health Ventures, 1988-92, bd. dirs. State pres. Future Homemakers Am., 1955; governance com. Wis. Hosp. Assn.; sec. bd. dirs. Chestnut Properties; sec. Christ Ch. Cathedral, Eau Claire, 2001, dist. atty., Eau Claire, 2002. Mem. Eau Claire Womens Network (founder, mem. steering com.), Profl. Secs. Internat. (chmn. goals and priorities com., pres. Eau Claire chpt. 1982-83), Wis. Hosp. Assn. (gov. com.). Home: 4707 Tower Dr Eau Claire WI 54703-8717 Personal E-mail: ebiegel23@aol.com.

BIEHL, JULIANNE, art educator; b. Pitts., Sept. 25; d. James Newton and Julia Eva (Freeauf) Addis; m. Edward Robert Biehl, June 11, 1955; children: Kathy Anne, Kimberley Anne, Kurt Edward, Karen Nancy. BS in Art Edn., Indiana U. Pa., 1952; MA in Secondary Art Edn., So. Meth. U., 1972; postgrad., U. North Tex., 1974-75. Art tchr. Titusville (Pa.) Jr. H.S., 1952-53, Langley Jr.-Sr. H.S., Pitts., 1953-55, U. Pitts. Lab. Sch., Richardson (Tex.) North Jr. H.S., 1972-78, J.J. Pearce H.S., Richardson, 1978-84, Sch. of Continuing Edn., So. Meth. U., Dallas, 1992-93, Flatbed Press, Austin, 1998—, and others. Lectr. to staff Timberlawn Psychiat. Hosp., Grand Rounds Meeting, 1989. Solo shows include So. Meth. U. Women's Ctr., 1992, U. Tex., Arlington, 1994, Flatbed Press Gallery, Austin, Tex., 1998, 20th Century Gallery, Williamsburg, Va., 1998. Estes Pk. Pub. Libr., 2006; group shows at Bradford Coll., Mass., Dartmouth St. Gallery, Albuquerque, El Dorado Gallery, Colorado Springs, Grand Prairie Visual Arts Ctr., Fine Arts Ctrn., Taos, N.Mex., Soc. Internat. Des Beaux-Arts Salon, Paris, 1993, Evelyn Siegel Gallery, Ft. Worth, 1995, Jansen-Perez Gallery, San Antonio, 1995, Salon SIBA, 1996, Westmoreland Mus. Am. Arts, Carnegie Mellon U., 2006, Regina Goucher Miller Gallery, numerous others; pvt. collections including U. Houston, N. Coast Med. Supply, Morgan Hill, Calif., Frost Bank, Ft. Worth, Tech. Studios, Dallas, and others; contbr. articles to profl. jours. Recipient Florence Art Gallery award Tex. Visual Art Assn., 1995, 2d pl. award Grand Prairie Visual Art Assn., 1990, 1st pl., 1990, Kimmel award Soc. of Watercolor Artists, Awards Fine Arts Ctr. En TAOS, 1984, 85, Nasher award Southwestern Watercolor Soc., 1991, others; Painting scholar Carnegie Tech. Mem. Dallas Womens Caucus for Art (treas. 1991, bd. dirs. 1990-92), Southwestern Watercolor Soc., Soc. of Layerists in Multi-Media, Tex. Visual Art Assn., So. Meth. U. Women's Club, So. Graphics Coun. Avocations: hiking, reading. Home: 3805 Dollar Lake Dr Estes Park CO 80517-6604

BIEHLE, KAREN JEAN, pharmacist; b. Festus, Mo., July 18, 1959; d. Warren Day and Wilma Georgenia (Hedrick) Hargus; m. Scott Joseph Biehle, Aug. 22, 1981; children: Lauren Rachel, Heather Michelle. Student of pre-pharmacy, U. Mo., Columbia, Mo., 1977-79; BS in Pharmacy, U. Mo., Kans. City, Mo., 1982. Reg. Pharmicist. Pharmacy res. U. Iowa Hosp. & Clinics, Iowa City, Iowa, 1982-83; pharmacist Jewish Hosp. of St. Louis, St. Louis, 1983-86; pharmacy mgr. Foster Infusion Care, St. Louis, 1986-88; staff pharmacist Cardinal Glennon Children's Hosp., St. Louis, 1988-90; pres. Lauren's Specialty Foods, Inc., St. Louis, 1988-89; pharmacy mgr. Curaflex Health Svcs., St. Louis, 1989-91; asst. dir. Cobb Hosp. and Med. Ctr., Austell, Ga., 1991-94; asst. dir. pharmacy Publix Supermarkets, Marietta, Ga., 1994-96; pharmacist Scottish Rite Children's Med. Ctr., Marietta, Ga., 1996—. Preceptor St. Louis Coll. Pharmacy, 1984-91, U. Ga. Sch. Pharmacy, 1992; instr. Kennesaw State U., Ga., 2005-. Recipient Roche Pharmacy Communications Award, Roche Pharmaceuticals, Kans. City, 1982, I Dare You Award, 4-H Club, Nevada, Mo., 1976. Mem. Am. Soc. Hosp. Pharmacists, Kappa Epsilon, Alpha Delta Pi (St. Louis Alumnae pres. 1989-90). Republican. Roman Catholic. Avocations: tennis, horseback riding, swimming, cooking. Home: 3200 Wicks Creek Trl Marietta GA 30062-4867 Office Phone: 404-785-2059.

BIEL, JESSICA, actress, model; b. Ely, Minn., Mar. 3, 1982; d. John and Kim Biel. Attended, Tufts U., 2000. Spokesmodel L'Oreal. Actor: (plays) Annie, Beauty and the Beast, Anything Goes, The Sound of Music; (TV series) 7th Heaven, 1996—2002; (films) Ulee's Gold, 1997, I'll Be Home for Christmas, 1998, Summer Catch, 2001, The Rules of Attraction, 2002, The Texas Chainsaw Massacre, 2003, (voice) It's a Digital World, 2004, Cellular, 2004, Blade: Trinity, 2004, Stealth, 2005, Elizabethtown, 2005, The Illusionist, 2006. Named Sexiest Woman Alive, Esquire mag., 2005. Mailing: Creative Artists Agy 9830 Wilshire Blvd Beverly Hills CA 90212-1825*

BIELKE, PATRICIA ANN, psychologist; b. Bay Shore, NY, May 11, 1949; d. Lawrence Curtis and Marcella Elizabeth (Maize) Widdoes; m. Stephen Roy Bielke, July 10, 1971; children: Eric, Christine. BA, Carleton Coll., 1971; PhD, U. Minn., 0979. Lic. psychologist, Wis.; cert. marriage and family therapist. Rsch. asst. Nat. Inst. Mental Health, Washington, 1972-74; sch. psychologist Roseville Pub. Schs., St. Paul, 1978-79; psychologist Southeastern Wis. Med. and Social Svcs., Milw., 1979-93; staff psychologist Elmbrook Meml. Hosp., 1986-2000; pvt. practice Brookfield, Wis., 1991-2000; sch. psychologist Cedarburg (Wis.) Pub. Schs., 1999—2002, New Berlin (Wis.) Pub. Schs., 2000—. Bd. dirs. LWV, Brookfield, 1984-88, Elmbrook Sch. Bd., 1989-99. Mem. Nat. Sch. Psychologist Assn., Wis. Sch. Psychol. Assn. Home: 17455 Bedford Dr Brookfield WI 53045-1301 Office: New Berlin School Dist 18695 W Cleveland Ave New Berlin WI 53146

BIELY, DEBRA MARIE, retired military officer; b. Columbus, Ohio, June 8, 1957; d. Joseph Richard and Mary Narcissus (Quin) Szulewski; m. Robert Lee Biely, July 31, 1977; children: Kevin Lee, Kelsey Lynn, Kerry Logan. BS, Ohio State U., 1979; MBA, Averett Coll., 1993. Commd. 2d lt. USMC, 1979, advanced through grades to lt. col., bn. adjutant 3d recruit tng. bn. Parris Island, S.C., 1980-82, asst. div. personnel officer 2d Marine div. Camp Lejeune, N.C., 1982-84, regimental adjutant 10th Marines, 1984-85, group adjutant 3d Force Serv SPT group Okinawa, Japan, 1986-88, squadron exec. officer hdqrs. squadron MCAS Futenma, Japan, 1988-89, div. adminstrv. officer human resources div. Washington, 1989-90, sect. mgr./adminstrv. officer requirements and programs div. HQMC, 1990-92, analyst Office Program Appraisal Sec. Navy, 1992-93; congressional fellow Office of Senator Howell Heflin, Washington, 1993-94; joint requirements oversight coun. programs/resources dept. USMC, 1994-99, ret., 1999; sr. mgr. CapGemini Ernst & Young, N.Y.C., 1999—2003; with Capgemini Govt. Solutions, N.Y.C., 2003—. Sem. XXI MIT, 1997-98. Instr. Presdl. Classroom, Washington, 1991. Mem. Women Officers Profl. Assn. (ex officio, bd. dirs.), Woodlake Country Club, Army & Navy Club (Washington). Avocation: golf. Office: Cap Gemini Govt Solutions 2250 Corporate Pk Dr Ste 410 Herndon VA 20171

BIENIAS, JULIA LOUISE, medical researcher, statistician; b. Chgo. d. Ignatius M. and Harriet L. (Huddy) B. BA in Psychology and History, Washington U., St. Louis, 1986, MA in Psychology, 1986; postgrad., U. Ill., 1986-88; ScD in Biostats., Harvard U., 1993. Rsch. asst. in gerontology and psychology Washington U., 1986; math. statistician U.S. Bur. Labor Statistics, Washington, 1987-88, U.S. Bur. Census, Washington, 1989-97; asst. prof. lectr. George Washington U., Washington, 1995-96; adj. asst. prof. U. Md., 1997; statistician Rush Coll. Medicine, Chgo., 1997—2000, asst. prof., 1997—2004, sr. statistician, 2001—, assoc. prof., 2004—. Contbr. articles to profl. jours. Mem. Spl. Svc. Area Commn., City of Chgo., 2003—; bd. dirs. Park West Condo. Assn., 1999—2005, v.p., 1999—2001, pres., 2001—05. NSF grad. fellow, 1987-92, Harvard tchg. fellow, 1992-93. Mem.: Caucus for Women in Stats. (rep.-at-large 1995—97, pres. 2005, exec. com. 2004—), Internat. Biometric Soc. (regional adv. bd. 2000—02, various coms.), Am. Statis. Assn. (various coms.), Phi Alpha Theta, Psi Chi, Pi Mu Epsilon, Phi Beta Kappa. Unitarian Universalist. Avocations: tennis, paper crafts, piano, jewelry design, interior decorating. Office: Rush Inst for Healthy Aging 1645 W Jackson Blvd Ste 675 Chicago IL 60612-3227 E-mail: jbienias@alum.wustl.edu.

BIER, KARLA, manufacturing engineer, chemical engineer, educator; d. Mary and Charles Stiefermann; m. Gregory Bier, Dec. 20, 1986; children: Kirstin, Bridget, Brandon. BS in Chem. Engring., U. Mo.- Rolla, 1988; MS in Chem. Engring., U. of Mo.- Rolla, 1994, PhD in Chem. Engring., 1998. Asst. prof. Stephens Coll., Columbia, Mo., 1999—2006; rsch. asst. U. Mo.-Rolla, 1983—89; semivolatile gc dept. chemist and mgr. Savannah Labs. and Environ. Svcs., Savannah, Ga., 1990—93; mfg. engr. 3M, Columbia, 2006—. Tchr. sci. using inquiry. Advisor Students in Free Enterprise, Columbia, 2000—04, Sigma Sigma Sigma Sorority, Columbia, 2000—06; vol. sci. workshops Stephens Natural Sci. Dept., Columbia, 2000—06; canstruction participant Ctrl. Mo. Food Bank, Columbia, 2002—06; catechist St. Thomas More Newman Ctr., Columbia, 2001—06. Mem.: Soc. Women Engrs. (pres. middle Mo. sect. 2004—06), Tau Beta Pi, Alpha Chi Sigma. Avocation: scuba diving. Office Phone: 573-886-1865.

BIERBAUM, JANITH MARIE, artist; b. Evanston, Ill., Jan. 14, 1927; d. Gerald Percy and Lillian (Sullivan) Turnbull; m. J. Armin Bierbaum, Apr. 17, 1948; children: Steve, Todd, Chad, Peter, Mark. BA, Northwestern U., 1948; student, Mpls. Art Inst., 1964; postgrad., St. Paul Art Inst., 1969-70. Rsch. asst. AMA, Chgo., 1948-49; tchr. Chgo. high schs., 1949-51; freelance artist Larkspur, Colo., 1951—. Exhibited in group shows at Foot Hills Art Ctr., 1985, 86, 87, Palmer Lake (Colo.) Art Assn., 1986-87, 88-89, Gov.'s Mansion, Bismarck, N.D., 1960; oil painting appeared in 1989 Women in Art Nat. calendar pub. by AAUW. Recipient 1st Place Purchase award, U. Minn., Mpls., 1966, Coors Classic award, Coors Beer, Golden, Colo., 1987. Mem.: Colo. Artist Assn. Republican. Avocations: cross country skiing, swimming, hiking. Home and Office: 1609 Ridgecrest Dr Loveland CO 80537-9073

BIERBAUM, ROSINA M., federal agency administrator; BS in Biology, Boston Coll., 1974, BA in English, 1974; PhD in Ecology and Evolution, SUNY, Stony Brook, 1985. Congressional fellow, 1980; sr. assoc. environ. program Office of Tech. Assessment U.S. Congress, Washington, 1991-93, sr. policy analyst Sci. Tech. Policy Office, 1993-96, asst. dir. environ. Sci. Tech. Policy Office, 1996, acting assoc. dir. Sci. Tech. Policy Office, 1996-97, apptd. assoc. dir. environ. Office Sci. Tech. Policy for the Pres., 1998—2001; dean, prof. environ. and natural resource policy and mgmt. Sch. of Natural Resources & Environment, U. Mich., 2001—. U.S. scientific expert, Permanent Ct. of Arbitration of Disputes Relating to Natural Resources and/or the Environ., in Hague, on the Bd. on Atmospheric Scis. and Climate of the Nat. Rsch. Coun. of the Nat. Academies; mem. exec. com., Inst. for Social Rsch., U. Mich.; mem. oversite com., Environ. and Energy Study Inst.; mem. design com., "The State of Nation's Ecosystems", H. John Heinz III Ctr.; lectr. in field. Mem. adv. bd. Frontiers in Ecology & the Environment, Ecological Soc. Am., mem. editl. bd. Consequences, reviewer International Panel on Climate Change; contbr. articles to profl. jours. Co-chair Def. Strategic Environ. R&D Program. Mem. Nat. Sci. & Tech. Coun. (mem. com. on environ. and natural resources), Nat. Ocean Rsch. Leadership Coun., Am. Geophysical Union (Waldo E. Smith medal, 2000), Energy Found., NAS (bd. dir. Atmospheric Chemistry and Climate); bd. dir. Fedn. Am. Scientists; fellow AAAS. Office: U Mich Sch of Natural Resources and Environment 440 Church St 2046a Dana Ann Arbor MI 48109-1041 Office Phone: 734-764-6453, 734-764-2550. Business E-Mail: rbierbau@umich.edu.

BIERDEMAN-FIKE, JANE ELIZABETH, social worker, educator; b. St. Louis, Nov. 7, 1922; d. Arthur Edward and Adele Evelyn Bierdeman; m. Don G. Fike, Aug. 5, 1978 (dec. Jan. 22, 1989). BA, Maryville Coll., St. Louis, 1944; MSW, St. Louis U., 1949; LHD (hon.), William Woods U., Fulton, Mo., 2001. LCSW Mo. Adminstrv. asst. Social Planning Coun., St. Louis, 1948—55; psychiat. social worker St. Louis State Hosp., 1955—58, supr. social work, 1958—62; dir. psychiat. social work Fulton (Mo.) State Hosp., 1962—2000. Asst. prof. social work U. Mo., Columbia, 1971—78. Mem. social work adv. bd. William Woods U., Fulton, 1989—; Elected mem. Mo. Employees Retirement Bd., Jefferson City, 1974—90; gov. appt. bd. mem. Mo. Employees Healthcare Bd., Jefferson City, 1993—2001. Named Exec. of Yr., U. Mo., 1988, Fulton State Hosp. Edn. Ctr. in her name, 2003; recipient Profl. Achievement award, Maryville Coll., 1971, Alumni Merit award, St. Louis U., 1991, Hon. Instr. Emeritus, U. Mo. Sch. Social Work, 2000. Mem.: NASW (named Pioneer 1997, Lifetime Achievement award 2004), Mo. Assn. Social Workers (pres. 1977—78). Achievements include Fulton State Hospital Education Center dedicated as the Jane Bierdeman-Fike building in 2003. Avocations: golf, painting, poetry. Home: 1318 Cedarwood Dr Fulton MO 65251-2275 Office: Fulton State Hosp 600 E Fifth St Fulton MO 65251

BIERLY, SHIRLEY ADELAIDE, communications executive; b. Waterbury, Conn., Jan. 19, 1924; d. Samuel and Frances Ada (Bogorad) Brown; m. Leroy Elwood Bierly, Jan. 19, 1946 (div. 1951); children: Lee Jr., Dennis Ray, David Lincoln. Student, Orange Coast Coll., 1963—66, L.A. City Coll., 1967—69. Mgr. Pacific Telephone, San Francisco, Calif., 1953-82; exec. dir. Sr. Power Office, San Francisco, 1982—. Cmty. activist, 1982—. Editor: Sr. Power newsletter, 1990—. Pres. Calif. Legis. Coun. for Older Am., San Francisco, 1984—, treas. Calif. Assn. of Older Am., 1984—, bd. dirs. Sr. Action Network, San Francisco, 1991—, Congress of Calif. Sr., Sacramento, 1994—; trustee Agape Found., 1994-2001; policy bd. Nat. Coun. Sr. Citizens, 1995-2001; commr. San Francisco Residential Arbitration and Stabilization Bd., 1997-2000, Calif. Commn. on Aging, 2000-03; bd. Planning for Elders in Central City, 2000-02; v.p. Yerba Buena Consortium, San Francisco, 1992—; mem. San Francisco Bd. Suprs. Pedestrian Safety Adv. Com., 2003—; exec. bd. Calif. Alliance for Ret. Ams., 2003-06, v.p., 2006—; mem. Kaiser Sr. Adv. Bd., San Francisco, 2004—; mem. adv. bd. Sr. Survival Sch., 2005—, planning com., 2004—. Mem. Am. Civil Liberties Union, Older Women's League, Gray Panthers, Alliance Ret. Ams. (charter, exec. bd., cmty. rep. 2003—). Avocations: photography, theater, reading, philately. Office: Calif Assn for Older Ams (aka Sr Power) 325 Clementina St San Francisco CA 94103-4104 Office Phone: 415-541-9629. Office Fax: 415-541-9630.

BIERMAN, AIMEE ELIZABETH, lawyer; AB, U. Mich., 1994; JD, Wayne State U., 1998. Bar: Mass. 1998, US Ct. Appeals (1st Cir.), US Dist. Ct. (Dist. Mass.). Assoc. Kirkpatrick & Lockhart, Nicholson, Graham LLP, Boston, mem. hiring com., 1999—2002. Mem.: Women's Bar Assn. Mass., Mass. Bar Assn., Boston Bar Assn., ABA, U. Mich. Alumni Assn. Office: Kirkpatrick & Lockhart Nicholson Graham LLP State Street Financial Ctr One Lincoln St Boston MA 02111-2950 Office Phone: 617-261-3166. Office Fax: 617-261-3175. E-mail: abierman@klng.com.*

BIERMAN, SANDRA, artist; b. Bklyn., N.Y., 1938; d. John Charles Riesberg and Martha Lee Blair; m. Arthur Bierman, Oct. 1, 1983; children: Cheryl, Steven, James. Represented by Contemporary S.W. Gallery, Santa Fe, 1994—, David Haslam, Boulder, Colo., 1992—, Gallery East, Loveland, Colo., 1996—, Augustine Arts, Lake Tahoe, Nev., 1997—, Bakersfield (Calif.) Mus., 2001; instr. workshop Am. Acad. Women Artists, Wickenburg, Ariz., 1997, Oil Painting with Sandra Bierman, Kauai, Hawaii, 2000. One-person shows include Contemporary S.W. Galleries, 1996, Lincoln Ctr. for the Arts, Ft. Collins, Colo., 1998, Bakersfield (Calif.) Mus. Art, 2001; group shows include C.S. Lewis Summer Inst. Show on Tour, 1994, Queens Coll. Art Gallery, Cambridge, Eng., 1994, 99th Nat. Exhbn. Nat. Arts Club, N.Y.C., 1995, 67th Grand Nat. Show, Salmagundi Club, N.Y.C., 1995, Artistes Americaines, Maison du Terroir, Genouilly, France, 1996, Colo. History Mus., 1996, Clymer Mus., Ellensburg, Wash., 1996, Desert Caballeros Mus., Wickenburg, Ariz., 1997, Colo. Gov.'s Invitational Show, Loveland (Colo.) Mus., 1997-2002, Art Expo, N.Y.C., 1998-99; works in permanent collections at City of Loveland, CSI Ltd., Cambridge, Eng., El Pomar Found., Colorado Springs, Colo., Gilford, Inc., N.Y.C., Herzog & Adams, N.Y.C., Loveland Mus., Storage Tek, Louisville, Colo., Boulder Cmty. Hosp., Colo., Telluride Gallery of Fine Art, Colo., Kaiser Permanente, Denver, Kohn Family Trust, Balt., Mfrs.-Hanover trust, N.Y.C., Mayo Women's Clinic, Scottsdale, Penrose Conf., Ctr., Colorado Springs, Philip Chamberlan Inc., Madison, Conn.; featured in Southwest Art Mag., Art Trends Mag., Mountain Living mag., Woman's Mag., Radiance mag., Sun Storm Fine Art Mag., US Art, Art World News, Art Bus. News, others. Recipient Colo. Gov.'s Purchase award, Loveland, 1988, Best of Show award Western Images, Boulder, 1993, medal of honor award Am. Artists Profl. League, N.Y.C., 1995. Mem. Am. Artists Profl. League, Bus. Coun. for the Arts N.Y.C., Nat. Mus. of Women in the Arts, Oil Painters Am., Am. Acad. Women Artists (nominating juror, exec. bd. dirs. 1997—). Office Phone: 303-447-8871. E-mail: art@sandrabierman.com.

BIERY, EVELYN HUDSON, lawyer; b. Lawton, Okla., Oct. 12, 1946; d. William Ray and Nellie Iris (Nunley) Hudson. BA in English and Latin summa cum laude, Abilene (Tex.) Christian U., 1968; JD, So. Meth. U., 1973. Bar: Tex. 1973, U.S. Dist. Ct. (we. dist.) Tex. 1975, U.S. Dist. Ct. (so. dist.) Tex. 1977, U.S. Dist. Ct. (no. dist.) Tex. 1979, U.S. Ct. Appeals (5th cir.) 1979, U.S. Ct. Appeals (11th cir.) 1981, U.S. Supreme Ct. 1981. Atty. Law Offices of Bruce Waitz, San Antonio, 1973-76; mem. LeLaurin & Adams, PC, San Antonio, 1976-81; ptnr. Fulbright & Jaworski, San Antonio, 1982—2003, head bankruptcy, reorgn. and creditors' rights sect. Houston, 1990—. Policy com. Fulbright & Jaworski, 1996-98; spkr. on creditors' rights, bankruptcy and reorganization law; lectr. Southwestern Grad. Sch. Banking, Dallas, 1980, La. State U. Sch. Banking, 1994; presiding officer, U. Tex. Sch. of Law Bankruptcy Conf., 1976, 94, State Bar Tex. Creditors' Rights Inst., 1985, 88, State Bar Tex. Advanced Bus. Bankruptcy Law Inst., 1985, State Bar Tex. Inst. on Advising Officers, Dirs. and Ptnrs. in Troubled Bus., 1987; mem. bankruptcy adv. com. 5th cir. jud. coun., 1979-80; vice-chmn. bankruptcy com. Comml. Law League Am., 1981-83; mem. exec. bd. So. Meth. U. Sch. Law, 1983-91. Editor: Texas Collections Manual, 1978, Creditor's Rights in Texas, 2d edit., 1981; author: (with others) Collier Bankruptcy Practice Guide, 1993. Del. to U.S./Republic of China joint session on trade, investment and econ. law, Beijing, 1987; designated mem. Bankruptcy Judge Merit Screening Com. State of Tex. by Tex. State Bar Pres., 1979-82; patron McNay Mus., San Antonio; rsch. ptnr. Mind Sci. Found., San Antonio; diplomat World Affairs Coun., San Antonio. Fellow: Soc. Internat. Bus. Fellows (chair bd. dirs.), San Antonio Bar Found. (life), Tex. Bar Found. (life); mem.: San Antonio Young Lawyers Assn. (pres. 1979—80, Outstanding Young Lawyer award 1979), Tex. Assn. Bank Counsel (bd. dirs. 1988—90, 2001—04), Tex. Bar Assn. (chair bankruptcy com. 1982—83, chair corp., banking and bus. law sect. 1989—90), Am. Coll. Bankruptcy Attys. (chair bd. dirs.), Zonta (Chair Z club com. 1989—90), Plaza Club San Antonio (bd. dirs. 1982—), Order of Coif. Office: Fulbright & Jaworski LLP 1301 McKinney St Ste 5100 Houston TX 77010-3031 Office Phone: 713-651-5544. Office Fax: 713-651-5246. Business E-Mail: ebiery@fulbright.com.

BIES, SUSAN SCHMIDT, bank executive; b. Buffalo, May 5, 1947; d. Louis Howard and Gladys May (Metke) Schmidt; m. John David Bies, Aug. 29, 1970; children: John Matthew, Scott Louis. BS, State U. Coll.-Buffalo, 1967; MA, Northwestern U., 1968, PhD, 1972. Banking structure economist FRS, St. Louis, 1970-72; asst. prof. econs. Wayne State U., Detroit, 1972-77; assoc. prof. Rhodes Coll., Memphis, 1977-80; tactical planning mgr. First Tenn. Nat. Corp., Memphis, 1980-81, dir. corp. devel., 1982-83, treas., 1983-84, sr. v.p., CFO, 1984-85, exec. v.p., CFO, 1985—95, exec. v.p. for risk mgmt., auditor, 1995—2001; mem. bd. govs. Fed. Res. Sys., Washington, 2001—. Mem. fin. adv. com. City of Germantown, Tenn., 1978—, also budget com.; mem. investment adv. com. Tenn. Consol. Retirement System, Nashville, 1981-86; instr. MidSouth Sch. Banking, 1985-86; mem. Com. on Corp. Reporting, Fin. Exec. Inst.; mem. Bank Adminstrn. Inst. Pres., bd. dirs. North Germantown Homewoners Assn., 1978-83; treas. Germantown Area Soccer Assn., 1985-86; treas. Fury Soccer Club, 1988—; vice chmn. task force Com. on 21st Century, Rhodes Coll., Memphis, 1986-87; mem. exec. adv. bd. Sch. Accountancy Memphis State U.; bd. dirs. Memphis Youth Initiative, 1988, Memphis Ptnrs.; mem. BAI Acctg. and Fin. Commn., 1988—, Internat. Women's Forum Fellow Ctr. for Urban Affairs, 1968-69, Fed. Res. Bank Chgo., 1970. Mem. Am. Bankers Assn. (exec. com. 1986-88), Nat. Assn. Bus. Economists, Am. Econ. Assn., End Users of Derivatives Assn., Planning Execs. Inst., Fin. Execs. Inst., (bd. dirs. Memphis chpt. 1988—), Planning Forum (Managerial Excellence award Memphis chpt. 1986), Memphis Area C. of C. (bd. dirs. 1988—, tax com. 1988—, chair 1989—), Econ. Club Memphis (bd. dirs. 1986—, vice chmn. 1987-88, chmn. 1988-89), Omicron Delta Epsilon, Lambda Alpha. Episcopalian. Avocations: gardening, golf, soccer. Office: Fed Res Sys 20th St & Constitution Ave NW Washington DC 20551

BIESEL, DIANE JANE, editor, publishing executive; b. N.Y.C., Feb. 15, 1934; d. Douglas and Runa (Patterson) Stevens; m. Donald W. de Cordova, June 24, 1956 (div. July 1971); m. David Barrie Biesel, Sept. 25, 1982. BS, Trenton State Coll., 1956; MLS, Rutgers U., 1969; MA in Edn., Seton Hall U., 1974, cert. in supervision, 1976. Tchr., libr. Arlington (Va.) Bd. Edn., 1956-58; media specialist elem. schs., librs. River Edge (N.J.) Bd. Edn., 1958-91; lectr., instr. children's lit. Alphonsus Coll., Woodcliff Lake, NJ, 1969-72; series editor Scarecrow Press, Lanham, Md., 1992—; v.p., CFO St. Johann Press, 1994—; mem. com. academically gifted River Edge Bd. Edn., 1977—83, mem. study skills com., mem. affirmative action com., 1988—90. Field svc. cons. N.J. Dept. Edn., 1969—71; cons. new books preview Baker and Taylor Co., 1972—76; adj. prof. Seton Hall U., 1978—79; mem. award com. Rutgers U. Grad. Sch. Libr. Svc., 1978—79; mem. River Dell Librs. Coop., 1988—91; cons. Pro Libra Assocs., 1992—. Editor: School Library Media Series, School Librarianship Series. Mem. Child Devel. Ctr. Bd., 1999—2005; mem. choir All Saints Ch., Bergenfield, 1971—, lay reader, 1973—, del. Diocesan Conv., 1978—, vestrywoman, 1980—83; mem. ecumenical commn. Diocese of Newark, 1992. Mem.: Divsn. Sch. Media Specialists (nat. nominating com. 1978—79, coun. 1978—79, evaluation com. 1979, steering com. 1979—80, co-chmn. liaison com. with Am. Assn. Sch. Librs. 1979—83, nat. nominating com. 1980—82, mem. awards com. 1981—89, program com. 1982—84, bd. dirs. region II 1983—84, pres. 1986, co-author: Information Power 1988, mem. task force on librs. and info. sci., White House, writing com.), River Edge Tchrs. Assn. (pres. 1964—66), Bergen County Sch. Librs. Assn. (pres. 1966—68), Ednl. Media Assn. N.J. (state chmn. recruitment 1968—69, state chmn. hospitality 1972—73, state chmn. county liaison 1973—74, co-pres. 1977—78), Bergen Button Buffs (founding grandmother 1993), N.J. Button Soc. (v.p. 1999—2002), Nat. Button Soc. Home: 315 Schraalenburgh Rd Haworth NJ 07641-1200 Office Phone: 201-387-1529. E-mail: d.biesel@att.net.

BIESINGER, MEGHAN KATHLEEN, secondary school educator; d. James and Kathleen Biesinger. BA in History and Secondary Edn. Social Studies, Pa. State U., State College, 2001. State tchg. lic. Va. Dept. Edn. Tchr. Fairfax County Pub. Schs., Alexandria, Va., 2001—05, Lorton, Va., 2005—. Jr. varsity cheerleading coach Fairfax County Pub. Schs., Lorton, 2002—. Mem.: Pa. State Alumni Assn. Roman Catholic.

BIESTEK, ELIZABETH MARY, forensic specialist; b. Chgo., Mar. 10, 1936; d. Anthony Jacob and Elizabeth Catherine Frer; m. John Paul Biestek; children: Scott Anthony, Elizabeth S. BS, Loyola U., 1965. Forensic document examiner, Arlington Heights, Ill., 1991—. Editor: (Jour.) Journal of Questioned Document Examination, 2002—. Mem.: Assn. Forensic Document Examiners, Ind. Assn. Questioned Document Examiners. Home and Office: 115 N Arlington Heights Rd Arlington Heights IL 60004 Office Phone: 847-924-3055. Business E-Mail: ebiestek@biestek.com.

BIGBEE, DARLENE MAE, retired medical/surgical nurse; b. Merna, Neb, May 12, 1939; d. Harold Franklin and Freda Mildred (Embree) Cantrell; m. Jerry W. Bigbee, Aug. 25, 1963; children: James W., Susan M. Kohlscheen, Cynthia A. Wilke, Daniel L. Diploma Nursing, St. Francis Sch. of Nursing, Grand Island, Neb, 1962; BSN, U.Nebr. Coll. Nursing, Omaha, 1986. Staff nurse, operating nurse Cmty. Hosp., Broken Bow, Nebr., 1963—71, Melham Med. Ctr., Broken Bow, 1973—79, oper. rm. supr., 1979—91, specialty clin. coord., 1991—2005, ret., 2005. Mem.: ANA, Nebr. Nursing Assn. (dist. 4 nominating com. 2004, Outstanding Achievement award 2003). Republican. United Methodist. Avocations: cooking, tropical fish, reading. Home: 736 North H St Broken Bow NE 68822

BIGBY, JUDYANN, medical educator; b. Jamaica, N.Y., 1951; children: Kenan, Naima. BA, Wellesley Coll., 1973; MD, Harvard U., 1978. Henry J. Kaiser fellow in gen. internal medicine Harvard Med. Sch. and Brigham and Women's Hosp., Boston; primary care internal medicine resident U. Wash. Affiliated Hosps., Seattle; assoc. prof. medicine Harvard Med. Sch., Boston, dir. Ctr. of Excellence in Women's Health, mem. faculty, 1983—; med. dir. Cmty. Health Programs Brigham and Women's Hosp., Boston, attending physician, 1983—. Mem. com. Assuring the Health of the Pub. in 21st Century, Inst. Medicine; mem. minority women's health panel of experts Office on Women's Health, Dept. HHS. Mem. bd. dirs. Boston Pub. Health Commn. Recipient Edna W. Smith Pioneer in Cmty. Health Care award, 2000. Office: Brigham and Womens Hosp Women Family and Cmty Programs 1620 Tremont St Boston MA 02120

BIGELOW, MARGARET ELIZABETH BARR (M.E. BARR), retired botany educator; b. Elkhorn, Man., Can., Apr. 16, 1923; d. David Hunter and Mary Irene (Parr) Barr; m. Howard Elson Bigelow, June 9, 1956 (dec.). BA with honors, U. B.C., Vancouver, Can., 1950, MA, 1952; PhD, U. Mich., 1956. Rsch. attaché U. Montreal, Que., Can., 1956-57; instr. U. Mass., Amherst, 1957-65, asst. prof., 1965-71, assoc. prof., 1971-76, prof., 1976-89, prof. emeritus, 1989—. Author: Diaporthales in N.A., 1978, Prodromus to Loculoascomycetes, 1987, Prodromus to Nonlichenized Members of Class Hymenoascomycetes, 1990; contbr. articles to profl. jours. With Can. Women's Army Corps, 1942—46. Mem. Mycol. Soc. Am. (v.p. to pres. 1980-82, editor 1975-80, Disting. Mycologist Award, 1993), Brit. Mycol. Soc., Am. Inst. Biol. Sci. (gen. chmn. ann. meeting 1986). Avocations: gardening, reading. Home and Office: 9475 Inverness Rd Sidney BC Canada V8L 5G8 Office Phone: 250-656-6732.

BIGELOW, MARTHA MITCHELL, retired historian; b. Talladega Springs, Ala., Sept. 19, 1921; children: Martha Frances, Carolyn Letitia. BA, Montevallo U., 1943; MA, U. Chgo., 1944, PhD, 1946. Assoc. prof. history Miss. Coll., Clinton, 1946-48, Memphis State U., 1948-49; Assoc. prof. history U. Miss., 1949-50; assoc. curator manuscripts Mich. Hist. Collections, U. Mich., Ann Arbor, 1954-57; prof. history Miss. Coll., 1957-71, chmn. dept. history and polit. sci., 1964-71. Dir. Bur. of History, Mich. Dept. State, 1971-90; sec. Mich. Hist. Commn., Mich. Dept. State, state historic preservation officer, 1971-90; coord. for Mich., Nat. Hist. Publs. and Recs. Commn., 1974-90. Contbr. articles to profl. publs. Fellow, Ency. Britannica, 1944—45; scholar Julius Rosenwald scholarship, 1943—44, Cleo Hearson scholarship, 1944. Mem. Am. Assn. State and Local History (v.p. 1979-80, pres. 1980-81, fellow summers 1958, 59), Orgn. Am. Historians, Nat. Assn. State Archives and Recs. Assn., So. Hist. Assn., Mich. Hist. Soc., Miss. Hist. Soc. Home: 201 Jefferson St Clinton MS 39056-4237 Office Phone: 601-924-2822. Personal E-mail: mbigelow@bellsouth.net.

BIGELOW, SHARON LEE, elementary school educator; b. Chgo., Ill., Oct. 13, 1942; d. Clarence Ellsworth and Frances Lorraine Bigelow. BA in Edn., SUNY, 1964; MA in Ednl. Psychology, N.Y.U., 1965. Tchr. Union Free Sch. Dist., Pleasantville, NY, 1966—. Art dir. Chappaqua Recreation, Chappaqua, NY, 1961—64. Named a Sharon Lee Bigelow Day, Town Bd. & Mayor, 2001. Mem.: N.Y. State Tchrs. Assn., Pleasantville Tchrs. Assn. (pres., deleg.). Avocations: reading, calligraphy, travel.

BIGELOW, VIVIAN LOU, elementary school educator, secondary school educator; b. Redding, Calif., Apr. 24, 1943; d. Lloyd Vivian and Minnie Marie Keefer; m. Robert Buckland Bigelow, Aug. 14, 1965; m. Thomas Bateman, July 24, 1992; 1 child, Christine Ann. AA, Shasta Jr. Coll., Calif., 1963; BA, Chico State U., Calif., 1966. Cert. tchr. 6-12 Calif., 1966, advanced tchg. cert. Idaho, 1972. Tchr. Fortuna Union HS, Calif., 1967—68, Parsons Jr. High, Redding, Calif., 1968—73, Lowell Scott Jr. High, Meridian, Idaho, 1973—75, Cascade HS, Idaho, 1975—77, Payette Lakes Mid. Sch., McCall, Idaho, 1977—. Developing sci. curriculum com. McCall Donnelly Sch. Dist. #421, McCall, Idaho. Avocations: hunting, hiking.

BIGGART, NICOLE WOOLSEY, dean; m. James Biggart; 1 child, Scott. BA, Simmons Coll., 1969; MA, U. Calif., Davis, 1977; PhD, U. Calif., Berkeley, 1981. Asst. prof. adminstrn. and sociology U. Calif., Davis, 1981—87, assoc. prof. mgmt. and sociology, 1987—90, prof., 1991—2002; Jerome J. and Elsie Suran chair in tech. mgmt. Grad. Sch. Mgmt., U. Calif., Davis, 2002—, dean, 2003—. Adv. bd. Sloan Found. social sci. rsch. coun. program on corp. as social instn., 1999—; mem. editl. bd. Orgn.: The Interdisciplinary Jour. of Orgn., Theory, and Soc., 1993—, Calif. Mgmt. Rev., 1993—. Co-author: (books) Governor Reagan, Governor Brown: Sociology of Executive Power, 1984, Enhancing Organizational Performance, 1997, The Changing Nature of Work, 1999; author: Charismatic Capitalism: Direct Selling Organizations in America, 1989; editor: Economic Sociology: A Reader, 2001. Mem.: Macro-Orgnl. Behavior Soc. Office: Grad Sch Mgmt Univ Calif Davis One Shields Ave Davis CA 95616-8609 Office Phone: 530-752-7366. Office Fax: 530-754-5824. Business E-Mail: nwbiggart@ucdavis.edu.

BIGGERS, CORNELIA ANDERSON, musician; b. Iowa City, Iowa, Mar. 15, 1935; d. William Arthur Anderson and Ann Maria Riddell; m. James Wesley Biggers, Jr., May 31, 1958. BA summa cum laude, U. Iowa, 1957. 3rd bassoon and contra- bassoon Tampa Philharm., Fla., 1963—68; 3rd bassoon and contra-bassoon Fla. Gulf Coast Symphony, 1968—82; 3rd bassoon and contra- bassoon Fla. Symphony, Orlando, 1967—82, The Fla. Orch., Tampa, 1982—85; prin. bassoon The Richey Cmty. Orch., Hudson, 1991—, Hernando Symphony Orch., Spring Hill, 1996—97, 2000—; 3rd bassoon and contra -bassoon Imperial Symphony Orch., Lakeland, 1998—. Substitute organist various chs.; bassoonist, mgr. Profl. Woodwind Ensembles, Clearwater; sutstitute contra-bassoon Fla. Orch., Tampa, Fla., 2005—. Author: The Contra-Bassoon: A Guide to Performance, 1977. Mem., officer Ind. Order Foresters Bounty Br., Clearwater; bldg. capt. Woodland Villas Condominium, Clearwater. Mem.: Fla. Musicians Ednl. Soc. (contra-bassoon), Internat. Double Reed Soc., Am. Fedn. Musicians (life), Mensa, Order Ea. Star, Phi Beta Kappa. Republican. Avocations: literature, Star Trek, ornithology, heckelphone.

BIGGERT, JUDITH BORG, congresswoman, lawyer; b. Chicago, Aug. 15, 1937; d. Alvin Andrew and Marjorie Virginia (Mailler) Borg; m. Rody Patterson Biggert, Sept. 21, 1963; children: Courtney Ray, Alison Mailler, Rody Patterson, Adrienne Taylor. BA, Stanford U., 1959; JD, Northwestern U., 1963. Bar: Ill. 1963. Law clk. to presiding justice US Ct. Appeals (7th cir.), Chgo., 1963-64; sole practice Hinsdale, Ill., 1964—99; mem. Ill. Gen. Assembly, 1993—98, asst. Rep. leader, 1995—98; mem. US Congress from 13th Ill. dist., 1999—, mem. fin. svcs. com., edn. and workforce com. stds. ofcl. conduct, chmn. sci. com. subcom. on energy, mem. bipartisan working group on youth violence. Mem. bd. editors Law Rev., Northwestern U. Sch. Law, 1961-63. Pres. Hinsdale Twp. HS Dist. 86 Bd. Edn., 1983-85; pres. Jr. League Chgo., 1976-78, treas., bd. mgrs., 1966—; chmn. Hinsdale Antiques Show, 1980; pres. Oak Sch. PTA, Hinsdale, 1976-78; pres.-treas. Chgo. jr. bd. Travelers Aid Soc., 1965-70; Sunday sch. tchr. Grace Episcopal Ch., Hinsdale, 1978-80, 82-85; chair, treas., 2d v.p. bd. dirs. Vis. Nurses Assn. Chgo., 1978; bd. dirs. Salt Creek Ballet, 1990-98. Recipient Servian award Jr. aux. U. Chgo. Cancer Rsch. Foun., Woman Yr. in Govt., Politics, and Civic Affairs DuPage YWCA, 1995, Hero of the Taxpayer, Am. for Tax Reform. 2000, 02, award for pub. svc., Am. Chem. Soc., 2003, Excellence in Edn., Nat. Assn. Coll. Admission Counseling, 2002, Friend of Edn., Ill. & Nat. Edn. Assn., 2002, Outstanding Leadership to Homeless and Victims of Domestic Violence, Chgo., Pub. Sch., 2002, Disting. Achiever for Protecting and Expanding Opportunities for Children and Youth Who Are Homeless, Chgo. Coalition for the Homeless, 2002, Spirit of Enterprise award US C. of C.; named one of 100 Women Making a Difference; inductee to Hinsdale Ctrl. HS Hall Fame, 1997. Mem. ABA, Ill. Bar Assn., DuPage Bar Assn., Coalition Women Legislatures. Republican. Office: US Ho Reps 1317 Longworth Ho Off Bldg Washington DC 20515-1313 also: Dist Off Ste 305 6262 S Rte 83 Willowbrook IL 60527 Office Phone: 202-225-3515.

BIGGINS, J. VERONICA, bank executive; m. Franklin Biggins; children: Dawn, Kenzie. B, Spelman Coll.; M, Ga. State U.; postgrad., U. Md. Asst. br. mgr. Citizens and So. Nat. Bank, Atlanta, affirmative action officer, compliance mgr., employee relations mgr., mgr. Atlanta personnel, exec. v.p., dir. human resources; exec. NationsBank (now Bank of Am.); asst. to Pres. The White House, Washington, dir. presdl. personnel; mng. ptnr. Heidrick& Struggles, Atlanta. Vice chair US Delegation UN's Fourth World Conf. on Women, Beijing; lectr. in field; chair Czech Slovak Am. Enterprise Fund. Bd. dirs., co-chmn. freedom fund dinner NAACP; bd. dirs. Atlanta chpt. Urban League, AirTran Airways, Avnet, NDC Health; chmn. personnel com., bd. dirs. United Way; bd. dirs., chmn. student affairs com., vice chmn. fundraising Spelman Coll.; mem. governing bd., vice chmn. Zoo Atlanta Capital Campaign; mem. exec. com. Leadership Atlanta, 1983; mem. bd. visitors Grady Hosp.; mem. bd. trustees YWCA, Exodus, Inroads Inc., Ga. Rsch. Alliance, Woodruff Arts Ctr., Down Atlanta Rotary, Internat. AIDS Fund; chmn. nominating com. NW Girl Scout Council; mem. Atlanta women's fund adv. com. Recipient Outstanding Performance award Inroads, Atlanta, 1986, Urban Bankers, 1987, trail blazer award Nat. Assn. Negro Bus. and Profl. Women's Clubs, Inc. Mem.: Internat. Bus. Fellows, Chautaugua Cir., Dogwood City Links, Am. Bankers Assn. (chmn. human resource divsn.). Episcopalian. Office: Heidrick & Struggles 303 Peachtree St NE Ste 4300 Sun Trust Plz Atlanta GA 30308

BIGGS, DIANA, elementary school educator; b. St. Louis, Mar. 3, 1946; d. David Henry and Daisy Jane Biggs. BA, Coll. William and Mary, 1968; MA, Colo. Coll., 1996. Tchr. Saunders Elem. Sch., Newport News, Va., 1968—69; campaign sec. McClure for Senate Campaign, Boise, Idaho, 1978; dist. asst. James A. McClure U.S. Senate, Boise, 1979—87; tchr. Tendoy (Idaho) Sch., 1988—89, D-11 Schs., Colo. Springs, Colo., 1990—. Mem. core team Colo. Divsn. Wildlife Tchg. Environ. Scis. Naturally tchr., Colo. Springs, 1995—; facilitator WILS Aquatic Project WILD, Colo. Springs, 2004—06. Sec. Lone Feather Inter-tribal Coun., Colo. Springs, 1990—2006; wildlife rehabilitator Colo. Divsn. Wildlife, Colo. Springs, 2004—06, transporter injured wildlife, 1995—2006; sec. Pima County Search & Rescue, Tucson, 1972—77; coaching Nat. Mid. Sch. Sci. Bowl, 2003—05; rehabilitator work Colo., 1999—; bd. dirs. Tucson Gem and Mineral Soc., 1972—77, Ariz. SPCA, Tucson, 1972—77. Fellow, Earthwatch, 2005; grantee, Colo. U., Denver, 2000; scholar, NSF, 1993—96. Mem.: Nat. Sci. Tchrs. Assn. Republican. Lutheran. Avocations: wildlife rehabilitation, nature journaling. Office: District 11 Jenkins Middle School 6410 Austin Bluffs Parkway Colorado Springs CO 80918 Office Phone: 719-328-5300. Home Fax: 719-266-5276; Office Fax: 719-266-5276. Business E-Mail: biggsd@d11.org.

BIGGS, JENNIFER M., elementary school educator; b. Peoria, Ill., Oct. 30, 1978; d. Steven R. and Marie L. Berlett; m. John R. Biggs, July 20, 2002. BS, Eureka Coll., Ill., 2000; M in Curriculum and Instrn., No. Ill. U., DeKalb, 2006. Std. tchg. cert. Ill., 2000. 6th grade tchr. Jewel Mid. Sch., North Aurora, Ill., 2000—. Advisor Leo's Club, North Aurora, 2001—03; student coun. advisor Jewel Mid. Sch., North Aurora, 2005—06. Mem.: Assn. for Curriculum and Instrn. Office: Jewel Middle School 1501 Waterford Rd North Aurora IL 60542 Office Phone: 630-801-6303. Business E-Mail: jmbiggs@sd129.org.

BIGGS, KELLY KATHLEEN, theater educator; b. National City, Calif., Sept. 3, 1969; d. Ronald Leo and Patricia Ann Buessing; m. Kevin Eugene Biggs, July 14, 1990; children: Amanda Elizabeth, Emilee Nicole, Bailee Raquel, Madison Shill, Ivory Pearl. BA in Edn., Ariz. State U., Tempe, 1992, EdM, 2001. Cert. elem. edn. Ariz. Dept. Edn., 1992, prin. Ariz. Dept. Edn., 2003. Drama tchr. Gilbert Pub. Schs., Ariz., 1994—. Student coun. advisor Gilbert Pub. Schs., 1994—. Author: (plays) Dating Predicaments, Because 'I' Said So. Named Jr. High Tchr. of Yr., Am. Legion Post 39, 2005; recipient Mid. Level Tchr. of Yr., Ctrl. Ariz. Mid. Level Assn., 1999. Mem.: Ariz. Assn. Jr. High Student Couns. (Student Coun. Advisor of Yr. 2005), Nat. Assn. Student Couns., Nat. Assn. Secondary Sch. Prins. Home: 2212 East Glencove St Mesa AZ 85213 Personal E-mail: kkbiggs@hotmail.com.

BIGGS, RUTH ANN, social studies educator; d. Richard and Helen Holleyman; m. Jason Biggs, Nov. 4, 1971; children: Talisa, Denton. BA in Edn., Northeastern State U., Tahlequah, Okla., 1995. Office worker Sears, Tulsa, Okla., 1995—99; tchr. Ctrl. Mid. Sch., Broken Arrow, Okla., 1995—2002, Centennial Mid. Sch., Broken Arrow, Okla., 2002—. Social studies dept. chair Centennial Mid. Sch., Broken Arrow, Okla., 1999—. Mem. Ch. of Christ, Broken Arrow, Okla., 1972—2006. Mem.: Nat. Honor Soc. Office: Centennial Mid Sch 225 E Omaha St Broken Arrow OK 74012 Office Phone: 918-259-4340. Business E-Mail: rbiggs@ba.k12.ok.us.

BIGHAM, MARSHA ELLIS, social studies educator, department chairman; b. Bristow, Okla., Sept. 10, 1951; d. Bill and Betty Ellis; m. Jerry Van Bigham, May 27, 1970; children: Matthew, William. BS, West Tex. A&M U., Canyon, 1980. Cert. profl. educator Tex., 1980, advanced placement instr. Advanced Placement Inst., 1995, gifted and talented instr. Tex., 1989. Social studies tchr. Canyon H.S., 1984—, chmn. social studies dept., 2001—. Pres. Canyon Pregnancy Ctr., 1998—2000. Mem.: Tex. Classroom Tchrs. Assn. Office: Canyon High School 1701 23rd St Canyon TX 79015 Office Phone: 806-677-2740.

BIGHAM, WANDA DURRETT, religious organization administrator; b. Barlow, Ky., June 19, 1935; d. Herbert Martin and Ada Florene (Baker) Durrett; m. William M. Bigham, Jr., June 7, 1958; children: William M. III, Janet Kaye, Julia Lynn. BME, Murray State U., 1956; MM, Morehead State U., 1971, MHE, 1973; EdD, U. Ky., 1978; cert., Inst. For Edn. Mgmt. -Harvard U., 1982; LittD (hon.), Loras Coll., 1989. Dir. TRIO programs Morehead (Ky.) State U., 1972-85, assoc. dean acad. affairs, dir. instructional sys., 1982-85, acting dean grad. and spl. acad. programs, 1984-85; exec. asst. to pres. Emerson Coll., Boston, 1985, v.p. for devel., 1986; pres. Marycrest Coll., Davenport, Iowa, 1986-92, Huntingdon Coll., Montgomery, Ala., 1993—2003; asst. gen. sec. for schs., colls. and univs. The United Meth. Ch., Nashville, 2003—. Bd. dirs. NAICU, 2002-03; bd. dirs., pres. Asia-Pacific Fedn. Christian Schs.; bd. dirs. Internat. Assn. Meth.-Related Schs., Colls. and Univs., Montgomery Symphony Orch., 1993-2003, Ala. Shakespeare Festival, 1996-2003, NASCUMC, 1996-2003; exec. com., pres. Univ. Senate United Meth. Ch., Ctrl. Ala. chpt. ARC, Montgomery, 1995-2003, pres, 2001-2002; mem. Leadership Ala., 1994—; co-chair Quad Cities Vision for the Future, Davenport, 1987-92. Recipient Pres.'s award Davenport C. of C., 1988, Women of Spirit and Note award Cmty. Com. of Davenport, 1991, Hope for Humanity award Jewish Fedn. of QC, Rock Island, Ill., 1993, Women's Acad. of Honor award Ala. Bus. and Profl. Women's Found., 2004; named to Alumni Hall of Fame, Morehead State U., 1988, Disting. Alumna, Murray State Coll., 1988, Woman of Distinction award Girl Scouts South Ctrl. Ala., 2001. Mem. Am. Coun. on Edn. (mem. coun. of fellows, bd. dirs. 1994-97, fellow in higher edn. adminstrn. 1983-84), Internat. Assn. Univ. Pres., Montgomery C. of C., Com. of 100, Sigma Alpha Iota (Sword of Honor 1956), Phi Kappa Phi, Kappa Delta Pi. Office: United Meth Ch Gen Bd Higher Edn and Ministry 1001 19th Ave S PO Box 340007 Nashville TN 37203-0007 Mailing: PO Box 340007 Nashville TN 37203-0007 Office Phone: 615-340-7406. Business E-Mail: wbigham@gbhem.org.

BIHARY, JOYCE, federal judge; b. Detroit, Oct. 24, 1950; BA, Wellesley Coll., 1972; JD, U. Mich., 1975. Bar: Ga. 1975. Atty. Alston, Miller & Gaines, 1975-77, Rogers & Hardin, 1977-79, ptnr., 1979-87; bankruptcy judge U.S. Dist. Ct., Atlanta, 1987—. Mem. Ga. Assn. Women Lawyers, Atlanta Bar Assn., Southeastern Bankruptcy Law Inst. (adv.); fellow Am. Coll. Bankruptcy, Lawyers Found. Ga., Ga. Consortium Personal Fin. Literacy, Coalition Debtor Edn. Office: US Bankruptcy Ct US Courthouse 75 Spring St SW Atlanta GA 30303-3309

BILANIUK, LARISSA TETIANA, neuroradiologist, educator; b. Ukraine, July 15, 1941; arrived in U.S., 1951; d. Yaroslav and Myroslava Zubal; m. Oleksa-Myron Bilaniuk, Nov. 14, 1964; children: Larissa Indira, Laada Myroslava. BA, Wayne State U., 1961, MD, 1965. Diplomate Am. Bd. Radiology, Am. Bd. Neuroradiology. Resident in radiology Hosp. of U. Pa., Phila., 1966-70; fellow Fondation Ophtalmologique, Paris, 1972; assoc. in radiology U. Pa. Sch. Medicine, Phila., 1973-74, asst. prof., 1974-79, assoc. prof., 1979-82, prof., 1982—; with Children's Hosp. of Phila., 1992—. Reviewer grants rsch. NIH, Washington, 1983—86; vis. prof. Grosshadern Clinics U. Munich, 1988; vis. prof. Inst. Med. Radiology, Kharkiv, Ukraine, 1996; lectr. in field. Co-editor: 3 radiology books; contbr. articles to profl. jours., chapters to books. Rsch. fellow, Cancer Rsch. Ctr., Heidelberg, Fed. Republic Germany, 1967—68. Fellow: Am. Coll. Radiology; mem.: Acad. Med. Sci. Ukraine (elected), Ukranian Med. Assn. N.Am., Soc. Pediatric Radiology, European Soc. Neuroradiology, Am. Soc. Neuroradiology, Radiol. Soc. N.Am., Sigma Xi. Avocations: downhill skiing, alpine hiking, glider flying, photography. Office: Childrens Hosp of Phila 324 S 34th St Philadelphia PA 19104-4345

BILDERBACK, PAMELA MARIE, elementary school educator; b. Eau Claire, Wis., Oct. 16, 1963; d. James Mathias and Barbara Jane (Geirl) Dennis; m. Steven Patrick Bilderback, June 18, 1988. BA, Coll. St. Scholastica, 1988, MA, 2004. Tchr. 4th grade Houston Ind. Sch. Dist., 1989-90, chpt. I tchr., 1990-91, tchr. 4th grade, 1992, tchr. 5th grade, 1992—, chpt. I coord., 1992—. Recipient Exceptional Edn. Tchr., Adams-Friendship Schs., 2001;

grantee Bus. and teaching grantee, 1991—92, NEA, 1997—98. Roman Catholic. Avocations: sewing, reading, camping, bicycling, gardening. Home: 1230 Port Rd Wisconsin Rapids WI 54495-9311

BILES, GLORIA C., historian, educator; d. George Graham and Lillian Oriol Crevenstene; m. Wiley Biles, June 21, 1949. BBA, U. Houston, 1947, MEd, 1957, MA, 1972; PhD, Rice U., 1979. Cert. tchr. Tex. Tchr. mid. and high sch. Houston Ind. Sch. Dist., 1957—67; lectr. U. Houston, Clear Lake, 1979—81, U. Houston, West Houston, 1979—81; adj. prof. Houston Bapt. Univ., 1984—86, asst. prof., 1986—93, assoc. prof., 1993—2002; ret., 2002. Mem. Houston Grand Opera, 1952—, Gilbert and Sullivan Soc., 1952—, Heritage Soc., 1979—, PBS, 1988—, Am. Carousel Soc., 1989—, Houston Symphony Soc., 1989—, Bush Presdl. Libr., Coll. Station, Tex., 1999—, Nat. Trust for Hist. Preservation, Mus. of Printing History, 1999—. Mem.: NEA, AAUP, Am. Hist. Assn., Phi Kappa Phi, Delta Kappa Gamma (chair coms.), Phi Alpha Theta, Phi Gamma Nu, Alpha Mu Gamma (hon.). Avocation: collecting antique carousel horses, Steuben glass and miniature animals.

BILGÉ-JOHNSON, SUMRU A., child psychiatrist; b. Ankara, Turkey, Sept. 30, 1969; arrived in U.S., 2001; d. Sait and Hulya Nezhe Bilgé; m. Charles Felzen Johnson, June 9, 2001; 1 child, Jasmin Shirin Johnson. MD, Istanbul U., Turkey, 1993; degree child and adolescent psychiatry, Istanbul Med. Sch., 1998; postgrad. in adult psychiatry, North Ohio U., Akron, 2001—. Child psychiatrist Istanbul Med. Sch., 1998—2000; pvt. practice Istanbul, 1998—2001; child psychiatrist Sisli Elfal Children's Hosp., Istanbul, Turkey, 2000—01, Project Hope (earthquake victims), Istanbul, 2000—01; resident in psychiatry NE Ohio U. Coll. Medicine, Akron, 2003—06; child psychiatry fellow Akron Children's Hosp., 2006—. Contbr. articles to profl. jour. Mem.: Istanbul Human Rights Orgn., Ohio and Am. Psychiatric Assn. Avocations: scuba diving, flute, painting, swimming, tennis. Office: Akron Children's Hosp 1 Perkins Sq Akron OH 44308

BILICH, MARION YELLIN, psychologist, writer; b. Bklyn., Feb. 14, 1949; d. Bernard Perry Yellin and Sylvia (Spector) Reveman; m. Charles Allen Bilich, Aug. 23, 1970; 1 child, Karin. BA, New Coll. of Hofstra U., 1970; MS, Columbia U., 1975; PhD, Fielding Inst., Santa Barbara, Calif., 1989. Cert. in psychology, social work. Tchr. Brookline (Mass.) Pub. Schs., 1971-72; researcher Ctr. for the Study of Anorexia and Bulimia, N.Y.C., 1984-89; psychotherapist in pvt. practice Hewlett, N.Y., 1977—. Speaker at nat. confs. Author: Weight Loss From the Inside Out: Help for the Compulsive Eater, 1983, Shared Grace: Therapists and Clergy Working Together; author articles on eating disorders and spirituality. Mem. APA. Avocations: reading, walking, learning languages.

BILLAUD, LOUISE ANN, musician, educator; b. Hamilton, Ohio, Sept. 24, 1959; d. Albert and Donna Franzmann; m. Jean-Paul Billaud; 1 child, Kéran John. MusB in Performance, U. Alaska, Anchorage, 1985; MA, Radford U., Va., 1997. Pvt. piano instr., Anchorage, 1992-95; grad. asst. Radford (Va.) U., 1995-97, instr. music, 1997—99, New River CC, Dublin, Va., 2001—. Musician (pianist): concerts and lecture-recitals, 1986—; musician: (recording) Louise Billaud, 1999, From Bartók to the Popol Vuh, 2000, Passion, 2004, (DVD) Mazeppa - An Inspirational Living Legend, 2006. Named semifinalist, Web Concert Hall Internat. Competition, 2004; recipient First prize, Internat. Bartok-Kabalevsky Piano Competition, 1987, award for Exemplary Performance, Radford U., 1997. Mem.: Music Tchrs. Nat. Assn., Phi Kappa Phi. Office: PO Box 1127 Dublin VA 24084 Office Phone: 540-674-3600 4351. Business E-Mail: nrbilll@nr.edu.

BILLAUER, BARBARA PFEFFER, lawyer, educator; b. Aug. 9, 1951; d. Harry George and Evelyn (Newman) Pfeffer. BS with honors, Cornell U., 1972; JD, Hofstra U., 1975; MA, NYU, 1982; cert. in risk scis. and pub. policy, Johns Hopkins U., 1999. Bar: N.Y. 1976, Fed. Dist. Ct. N.Y. 1977, U.S. Ct. Appeals (2d cir.) 1978, U.S. Supreme Ct. 1984. Assoc. Bower & Gardner, N.Y.C., 1974-78; sr. trial atty. Joseph W. Conklin, N.Y.C., 1978-80; assoc. dept. head Curtis, Mallet-Prevost, Colt & Mosle, N.Y.C., 1980-82; ptnr. Anderson, Russell, Kill & Olick, N.Y.C., 1982-86, Stroock & Stroock & Lavan, N.Y.C., 1986-90; ptnr., chair environ. and toxic tort practice Keck, Mahin, Cate & Koether, 1990-93; prin. Barbara P. Billauer & Assocs., Lido Beach, N.Y., 1993—. Vis. scholar Johns Hopkins U. Sch. Pub. Health, 1998-99; faculty SUNY Stony Brook Med. Sch.; adj. assoc. prof. NYU Grad. Sch., 1982-88; lectr. Rutger's U. Med. Sch.; jud. screening com. Coordinated Bar Assn., 1983-86; mem. spl panel Citywide Ct. Adminstrn. 1982-85; bd. dirs. Weizmann Inst., Am. Com. Co-author: The Lender's Guide to Environmental Law: Risk and Liability, 1993. Fellow Am. Bar Found.; mem. ABA (indoor air polution 1990-93), Met. Womens Bar Assn. (v.p. 1981-83, pres. 1983-85, chmn. bd. 1985-87), Nat. Conf. Womens Bar Assn. (bd. dirs., v.p. 1989-95), Internat. Coun. Shopping Ctrs. (environ. com.), Brit. Occupl. Hygiene Soc., Environment Toxic Torts. Home: 2867 Tilden St NW Washington DC 20008-3837 E-mail: omniscience@starpower.net.

BILLIG, ETEL JEWEL, theater director, actress; b. N.Y.C., Dec. 16, 1932; d. Anthony and Martha Rebecca (Klebansky) Papa; m. Steven S. Billig, Dec. 23, 1956 (dec. Aug. 1996); children: Curt Adam, Jonathan Roark. BS, NYU, 1953, MA, 1955; student, Herbert Berghof Studio, N.Y.C., 1955-56. Cert. elem. and high sch. tchr. Actress Washington Square Players, N.Y.C., 1950-55, Dukes Oak Theatre, Cooperstown, NY, 1955, Triple Cities Playhouse, Binghampton, NY, 1956, Candlelight Dinner Playhouse, Summit, Ill., 1970, 73, 77, 79, 90; mng. dir. Theatre 31, Park Forest, Ill., 1971-73; asst. mgr. Westroads Dinner Theatre, Omaha, 1973-76; mng. dir., actress Forum Theatre, 1973, 94; mng. dir., actress, producing dir. Ill. Theatre Ctr., Park Forest, 1976—; mng. dir., actress Goodman Theatre, Chgo., 1987, 95, Ct. Theatre, 1990, Wisdom Bridge Theatre, 1991; dir. drama Rich Ctrl. H.S., Olympia Fields, Ill., 1978-86. Del. League of Chgo. Theatres Russian Exchange to Soviet Union, 1989; actress Drury Lane, Oak Brook, Ill., 1989; mem. adj. faculty theatre program Prairie State Coll., 2004—; cons. and lectr. in field. Appeared in films including the Dollmaker, Running Scared, Straight Talk, Stolen Summer; (TV series) Hawaiian Heat, Missing Persons, Untouchables. V.p. Nat. Coun. Jewish Women, Park Forest, 1968-70; sec. Community Arts Coun., Park Forest, 1984-86; pres. Southland Regional Arts Coun., 1986-92. Recipient Risk Taking award NOW, 1982; grantee Nebr. Arts Coun., 1975, Ill. Arts Coun., 1995, 96, 2000, Athena award Matteson Area C. of C., 1997, Abby Found. award, 1997; named to Park Forest Hall of Fame, 2000. Mem. AFTRA, SAG, Actors' Equity Assn., League Chgo. Theatres, Ill. Arts Coun. Theatre Panel, Prodrs. Assn. Chgo. Area Theatre (sec. 1988-89), Bus. in the Arts Coun. of C. of C. (charter), Rotary (bd. dirs. Park Forest chpt. 1988-97, sec. 2000, hall of fame 2000). Avocations: travel, antiques. Office: Ill Theatre Ctr PO Box 397 Park Forest IL 60466-0397 Office Phone: 708-481-3510. E-mail: ilthctr@sbcglobal.net.

BILLINGS, MELANIE SPARKS, secondary school educator, department chairman; d. Ronnie and Nancy Isaacs Sparks; m. C. Darrin Billings, June 16, 1990; children: Alisha, Eli. BS in Secondary Sch. Edn., Western Carolina U., Cullowhee, NC, 1991. Cert. tchr. Class A NC. Tchr., dept. chair North Surry H.S., Mt. Airy, NC, 1991—. Clk., pianist Ladonia Bapt. Ch., Mt. Airy. Named Tchr. of Yr., North Surry H.S., 1993. Mem.: NC Sci. Tchrs. Assn., NC Assn. Educators. Office: North Surry High School 2440 West Pine St Mount Airy NC 27030 Office Phone: 336-789-5055.

BILLINGSLEY, KAREN JOYCE, music educator; b. Warwick, R.I., Aug. 24, 1962; d. Allen C. and Joyce E. Dutton; m. Lance E. Billingsley, May 20, 2006; m. George R. McKinney, July 6, 1985 (div. July 7, 2003); children: Caitlin Beth McKinney, George Andrew McKinney. MusB Edn., SUNY Potsdam, 1984; MusM Edn., SUNY Buffalo, 1989. Cert. Tchr. Music All Levels Tex., 2001, Tchr. Music K-12 N.Y., 1984. Tchr. elem. music Lyndonville Elem. Sch., NY, 1984—85; dir. orch. Grand Island Ctrl. Schools, NY, 1985—86; tchr. elem. music Oak Orchard Elem. Sch., Medina, NY, 1986—91; tchr. orch. Jessamine County Schs., Nicholasville, Ky., 1991—97; dir. orch. Hill Country Youth Orchestras, Kerrville, 1997—2001; tchr. mid. sch. band Ingram Mid. Sch., Tex., 2000—01; tchr. elem. music Nimitz Elem. Sch., Kerrville, 2001—. Dir. worship and handbells Emmanuel United Meth. Ch., Lockport, NY, 1985—91; dir. handbell choir Nicholasville United Meth. Ch., 1991—97; asst. dir. music First United Meth. Ch., Kerrville, 1998—2000; dir. choir, organist Center Point United Meth. Ch., Tex., 2000—03, First Christian Ch., Kerrville, 2003—. Chmn., scholarship com. Kerrville Performing Arts, 2004—06. Mem.: Tex. Choral Dirs. Assn., Tex. Music Educators Assn.

BILLITTERI, CARLA, literature and language professor; m. Benjamin Friedlander. Diploma (laurea, magna cum laude), U. Catania, Italy, 1989; MA, U. Buffalo, 1995, PhD, 2001. Asst. prof. U. Maine, Orono, 2002—. Office: Univ Maine 304 Neville Hall Orono ME 04469 Office Phone: 207-581-3822.

BILLNITZER, BONNIE JEANNE, nurse, gerontologist; b. Mar. 7, 1935; d. George Gottfried and Sarah Edna Elizabeth (Park) Haffelder; m. Harold R. Billnitzer, Apr. 28, 1956; children: J. Stephen, David A., John Mark, Timothy P., Michael M. BA in Psychology, U. Mich., 1977; ADN, U. Toledo, Ohio, 1989; BSN, Med. Coll. Ohio, Ohio, 1992. RN, Ohio; cert. gerontol. nurse, cert. cardiovascular nurse. Adminstrv. mgr. Med. Coll. Ohio Ambulatory Care Ctr., Toledo, 1972-79; cardiovascular nurse St. Vincent Med. Ctr., Toledo, 1988-92; case mgr. The Vis. Nurse Svc., Toledo, 1992-97; pvt. practice RN case mgr. Perrysburg, Ohio. Mem. credentialing com. for RN St. Vincent Med. Ctr., Toledo, 1991-92. Recipient Logan award for Clin. and Theoretical Excellence in Nursing, U. Toledo, 1989. Mem. AAUW, ANA, Ohio Nurses Assn., Toledo Dist. Nurses Assn. (1st v.p. 1995-96), Am. Holistic Nurses Assn., Am. Assn. Critical Care Nurses, Internat. Order St. Luke the Physician. Lutheran. Avocations: music, reading, antiques, quilting. Home: 1084 Eastbrook Dr Perrysburg OH 43551-1646

BILLONE, AMY CHRISTINE, education educator; d. Michael Charles and Christine Wahl Billone; m. Daniel Shannon Burke, June 29, 2001; 1 child, Charles Michael Burke. PhD, Princeton U., N.J., 1993—2001. Asst. prof. U. Tenn., Knoxville, 2001—. Author: (book) Little Songs: Women, Silence and the Nineteenth-Century Sonnet. Recipient Sidonie Clauss Meml. prize, Princeton U. Office: Univ Tennessee Dept English Knoxville TN 37996 Business E-Mail: abillone@utk.edu.

BILLS, JENNIFER LEAH, lawyer; b. Wichita, Kans., Feb. 10, 1969; BA, Haverford Coll., 1991; JD, Northeastern U. Sch. Law, 2001. Bar: Mass. 2002, US Ct. Appeals (1st Cir.) 2002, US Dist. Ct. (Dist. Mass.) 2002, NY 2003. Law clk. to Hon. Gene Carter US Dist. Ct. (Dist. Maine), 2001—02; atty. Law Offices of Howard Friedman PC, Boston. Mem.: Nat. Lawyers Guild, Assn. Trial Lawyers Am., Mass. Gay and Lesbian Bar Assn., Women's Bar Assn. Office: Law Offices of Howard Friedman PC 5th Floor 90 Canal St Boston MA 02114 Office Phone: 617-742-4100. Office Fax: 617-742-5858.*

BILSTAD, SANDRA A., medical/surgical nurse, home health care nurse; b. Morrisville, Vt., June 12, 1948; d. Elroy G. and Carol Carolyn (Larder) Mansfield; m. Peter R. Bilstad, Aug. 17, 1968; children: Paul, Scott, Nicole. ADN, N.D. State U., 1977. Cert. in nursing adminstrn.; cert. in healthcare quality. Insvc. edn. instr. neurol. and neurosurg. nursing St. Lukes Hosps., Fargo, N.D.; asst. mgr. neurosurgery, gynecology, urology Merit Care, Fargo, N.D., mgr. neurology/cardiology; quality mgmt. coord. Banner Health System, Fargo, clin. ops. coord. Mem. ANA, Nat. Assn. for Health Care Quality.

BIMROSE, HEIDI E., human services administrator, director; b. Schaumburg, Ill., July 27, 1967; d. Joan D. Ruppenthal. BS, No. Ill. U., Dekalb, 1989, MA, 1991. Cert. Rehab. Counselor Ill., 1999, Employee Benefit Specialist ISCEBS, 2005. Asst. dir. disability concerns Ill. State U., Normal, 1991—96; dir. disability svc. East Tenn. State U., Johnson City, 1996—2000; vocat. rehab. cons. UnumProvident, Chattanooga, 2000—02, rtw program developer, 2002—04, dir. health and productivity devel., 2004—. Vice moderator Pilgrim Congl. United Ch. of Christ, Chattanooga, 2005—06; sec. HIV Network, Johnson City, Tenn., 1998—2000. Recipient RTW Ind. Living award, UnumProvident, 2001. Mem.: IARP (corr.). Democrat. Office: UnumProvident Cos 1 Fountain Sq Chattanooga TN 37402 Office Phone: 423-294-1549. Business E-Mail: hbimrose@unumprovident.com.

BINDEMANN, LISA MARIE, mathematics educator; b. Buffalo, Mar. 29, 1978; d. Sebastian Thomas and Ella Marie Terrana; m. Scott Sebastian Bindemann, Aug. 23, 2003. MS in Edn., Buffalo State Coll., NY, 2005. Cert. pub. sch. tchr. NY, 2000. Math. tchr. Alden Ctrl. Schs., NY, 2004—. Avocation: coaching rugby. Home: 178 Waverly Ave Kenmore NY 14217 Office: Alden High School 13190 Park St Alden NY 14004 Office Phone: 716-937-9116.

BINDER, AMY FINN, public relations company executive; b. NYC, June 13, 1955; d. David and Laura (Zeisler) Finn; children: Ethan Max, Adam Finn, Rebecca Eve. BA with honors, Brown U., 1977; MBA, Columbia U. Freelance photographer, N.Y.C., 1977-78; account exec. Newton & Nicolazza, Boston, 1978-79, Agnew, Carter, McCarthy, Boston, 1979-80; dir. pub. relations City of New Rochelle, N.Y., 1980-82; dir. urban communications Ruder-Finn, N.Y.C., 1982-85, v.p., 1985-86, exec. v.p., 1986-87; pres. Ruder-Finn America, N.Y.C., 1987; CEO, exec. mng. dir. RFBinder Partners, Inc. Ruder Finn Group, 2001—. Photographer: Museum without Walls, 1975, The Spirit of Man: Sculpture of Kaare Nygaard, 1975, Knife Life and Bronzes, 1977, St. Louis: Sculpture City, 1988, The Triumph of the American Spirit: Johnstown, Pennsylvania, 1989. Mem. Internat. Ctr. of Photography (mem. pres. coun.), Pres. Assn. of Am. Mgmt. Assn. Democrat. Jewish.

BINDER, MADELINE DOTTI, retail executive; b. Chgo., Oct. 7, 1942; d. Martin and Anne (Sweet) Binder; children: Mark Nathan, Marla Susan. BEd, Nat. Coll. Edn., 1964, MS, 1972, MS in Human Svcs-Counseling, 1993. Tchr. Rochester Schs. (Minn.), 1963-64, Orange County Schs., Orlando, Fla., 1967-68; reading cons. Palatine (Ill.) Schs., 1972-73; instr. Parent Effective Tng., Wilmette, Ill., 1974-76; tchr. Effectiveness Tng., 1974-76; pres. Profls. Diversified, Wilmette, 1976-89; remedial and enrichment reading tchr. Waukegan (Ill.) Pub. Schs., 1986; pres. Lifeline, 1989-90; mgmt. cons. World Wide Diamonds Assn., Schaumburg, Ill., 1979-89; Pearl direct distbr. Amway Corp., Ada, Mich., 1976-94; exec. distbr. NU Skin, 1992; distbr. Starlight Internat., 1994—. Psychotherapist, 1993-97. Author: Organic Gardening, 1975, The Go-Getters Planner, 1986, Singles Guide to Chicagoland, 1995, Divorce: You and Your Child, 2003, Super Science Fair Projects, 2005, Children and Divorce, 2005, Toy Train Table Plans, 2005, From Bubbie's Kitchen: Jewish Recipes, 2005, Discount Movie Posters, 2006. Leader, Camp Fire Girls, Evanston, Ill., 1963, 75. Ednl. scholar Nat. Coll. Edn., 1971. Mem. Phi Delta Kappa, Alpha Delta Omega. Personal E-mail: thegoodlife@comcast.net.

BINDER, SUSAN A., chemical company executive; V.p., treas. ICC Industries, Inc., N.Y.C. Office: ICC Industries Inc 460 Park Ave New York NY 10022-1906

BINGAMAN, ANNE K., lawyer; b. Jerome, Ariz., July 3, 1943; d. William Emil and Anne Ellen (Baker) Kovacovich; m. Jeff F. Bingaman, Sept. 14, 1968; 1 child, John. BA in History, Stanford U., 1965; gen. course cert. with honors, London Sch. of Econs., England, 1964-65; LLB, Stanford U., 1968. Bar: Calif. 1969, N.Mex. 1969, Ariz. 1969, U.S. Dist. Ct. D.C. 1983. Atty. Brown & Bain, Phoenix, 1968-69, N.Mex. Bur. Revenue, Santa Fe, 1969-70, Modrall, Sperling, Roehl, Harris & Sisk, Albuquerque, 1970, N.Mex. Atty. Gen's. Office, Santa Fe, 1970-72; from asst. prof. to assoc. prof. U. N.Mex. Sch. Law, Santa Fe, 1972-76; founding ptnr. Bingaman & Davenport, Santa Fe, 1977-82; ptnr. Brown, Bain & Bingaman, Santa Fe and Washington, 1982-84, Onek, Klein & Farr, Washington, 1984-85, Powell, Goldstein, Frazer & Murphy, Washington, 1985-93; asst. atty. gen. anti-trust divsn. U.S. Dept. Justice, Washington, D.C., 1993-96; sr. v.p. LCI Internat., McLean, Va., 1997-98; CEO Valor Telecom, Irving, Tex., 1999—2002, chmn. bd., 1999—2005. Bd. dir. Lear Corp., 2004—. Contbr. articles to profl. jours. Exec. com. Stanford Law Sch. Bd. Visitors, 1978-80, 88-90; mem. for N.Mex. of 10th Cir. Jud. Nominating Panel, 1977-80. Ford Found. fellow 1975; recipient Nat. Vol. award Stanford Assocs., 1989. Fellow Am. Bar Found.; mem. ABA, N.Mex. Bar (founder, vice-chair antitrust sect. 1982-85, chair com. to rewrite comm. property & other state laws to conform to ERA), Am. Law Inst. Democrat. Episcopalian. Mailing: Lear Corp Bd Directors PO Box 5008 Southfield MI 48086

BINGHAM, JINSIE SCOTT, broadcast company executive; b. Greencastle, Ind., Dec. 28, 1935; d. Roscoe Gibson and Alpha Edith (Robinson) Scott; m. Frank William Wokoun, Jr. (dec.); children: Douglas Scott, Richard Frank; m. Richard Innes Bingham, June 24, 1964. Student, DePauw U., Greencastle, 1952-53, Northwestern U., Evanston, Ill., 1953, Coe Coll., Cedar Rapids, Iowa, 1953-54. Exec. sec. Ind. Young Dems., 1958-60; receptionist Ind. Ho. of Reps., Indpls., 1959; saleslady Avon Products, Greencastle, 1961-64; sales mgr. Sta. WJNZ (formerly WXTA), Greencastle, 1969-77, owner, pres., gen. mgr., 1977-94; owner Radio Greencastle, 1977—. Owner, pres. gen. mgr. Sta WJNZ, 1977-94; past ptnr. Sta. WVTL, Monticello, Ill., Sta. KBIB, Monette, Ark.; speaker DePauw U. Comm. Seminar, 1981-85; vis. lectr., 1986—. Co-author: Putnam County Indiana Land Patents, 2004. Com. chair Legis. Awareness Seminar, 1978—86; co-chair Greencastle Gaelic Festival, 1983—84; charter mem. Greencastle 2001, 1985—, Greencastle Civic League, 1984—, Greencastle Merchant's Assn., 1983—97, Cmty. Resources Com., 1982—87; charter mem., corp. sec. Main St. Greencastle, 1983—87, v.p., 1987—88, pres., 1989—90, chmn., 1990—91; v.p. United Way, 1996—97, bd. dirs., 1989—97, campaign chair, 1996—97, campaign advisor, 1998—99; announcer Putnam County Fair Parade, 1977—; co-chmn. centennial com. Putnam County Courthouse, 2001—05; v.p. Putnam County Mus., 2002, 2005—06, sec., 2006—, pres., 2003—04; tour guide Putnam County Conv. and Visitors Bur., 1998—; active Putnam County Coun. on Aging and Aged, 1999—; pres. Putnam County Hist. Soc., 1996—97, sec., 1998—; bd. dirs., v.p., sec., pres., hon. dir. Putnam County Found.; co-founder Greencastle H.S. Alumni Assn., 1995, founding chmn. scholarship fund, 1995—; active Govs. Commn. for a Drug Free Ind., 1991—; v.p. West Ctrl. Ind. Econ. Devel. Coun., 2003—; mem. Lilly Scholar Selection Com., 1998—; vice chmn. Putnam County Dem. Ctrl. Com., 2001—; bd. dirs. Putnam County Comprehensive Ctr., 1994—2000, Opportunity Housing, 1995—2002, Greencastle Devel. Ctr., 1988—89; charter mem., bd. dirs. Greencastle Cmty. Child Care Ctr., 1983—87; v.p. Greencastle Zoning Bd. Appeals, 1985—88, pres., 1988—; charter mem., bd. dirs. Greencastle Vol. Fire Dept., 1986. Sagamore of the Wabash, Ind. Gov. Evan Bayh, 1995; Limestone State Seal, 1996, Seal of City, Greencastle, 1996; named Hoosier Know It All Champion, Sta. WTTV, Indpls., 1998; named to Ind. Broadcasters Hall of Fame, 1999; named Outstanding Citizen Greencastle Jaycees, 1981; named one of Ind.'s Trail-Blazing Women, 2000; named to Putnam County Agr. Hall of Fame Putnam County Farm Bur., 2002; recipient Disting. Hoosier Award, conferred by Gov. Joseph Kernan, 2004 Mem. AARP (Capital City task force 2000), Nat. Soc. DAR (Centennial chmn. Washburn chpt. 2002, sec. 1994-2003, chaplain 1988-2004, chpt. regent 2003—), Broadcast Pioneers (life), Putnam County Bd. Realtors, Am. Women in Radio and TV (pres. Ind. chpt. 1979-82, Lifetime Achievement award 1996), Indpls. Network Women in Bus. (charter), Women in Comm., Inc. (bd. dirs. 1983-84, MATRIX co-chair 1984, Frances Wright award 1993), Am. Legion Aux., Nat. Assn. Broadcasters, Soc. Profl. Journalists, Ind. Broadcasters Assn. (v.p. FM 1982), Putnam County Extension Adv. Coun. (4H), Natural Resources Svc. Land Use Study Group, Greencastle Bus. and Profl. Women's Club (pres. 1975-76, 78-79, Woman of Yr. 1994), Indpls. Ad Club, Women's Press Club Ind., Indpls. Press Club, Nat. Fedn. Press Women, Ind. Dem. Editl. Assn. (sec. 1987, v.p. 1988, pres. 1990), Ind. C. of C., Greencastle C. of C. (bd. dirs. 1979-83, pres. 1982, amb. 2001—. Citizen of Yr. 1997), VFW (pres. ladies aux. 1966-68), Ind. Geneal. Soc. (bd. dirs. West Ctrl. divsn. 2005—), Packard Club Ind., Ind. Soc. Pioneers, Daus of 1812 (pres. Tippecanoe chpt. 1981, state v.p. 1982), Daus. of the Union, Internat. Order Job's Daus., Ind. DAR Chmn.'s Club (pres. 2006), Soc. Descs. of Valley Forge, Rotary (bd. dirs., pres. 1994-95, bull. editor 1995—, dist. conf. planner 1997, Paul Harris fellow 1998, del. world conf. 1998), Order Ea. Star, Women of Moose, Milestone Car Soc., Geneal. Soc. (bd. dirs., 2005-), Delta Theta Tau, Sigma Delta Chi. Mem. Christian Ch. (Disciples Of Christ). Office Phone: 765-653-3565. Business E-Mail: jinsie@ccrtc.com.

BINGHAM, JUNE, playwright; b. White Plains, N.Y., June 20, 1919; d. Max J.H. and Mabel (Limburg) Rossbach; m. Jonathan B. Bingham, Sept. 20, 1939 (dec. July 1986); children: Sherry B. Downes, Micki B. Esselstyn (dec. 1999), Timothy, Claudia B. Meyers; m. Robert B. Birge, Mar. 28, 1987; 1 stepchild, Robert R. Student, Vassar Coll., 1936-38; BA, Barnard Coll., 1940; LittD (hon.), Lehman Coll., 2002. Writer, editor U.S. Treasury, Washington, 1943-45; editorial asst. Washington Post, 1945-46; writer Tarrytown (N.Y.) Daily News, 1946. Author: Do Cows Have Neuroses?, Do Babies Have Worries?, Do Teenagers Have Wisdom?, Courage to Change: An Introduction to Life and Thought of Reinhold Niebuhr, 1961, Courage to Change: An Introduction to Life and Thought of Reinhold Niebuhr, paperback edit., 1992, U Thant: The Search for Peace, 1970, (plays) Triangles, 1986, Eleanor and Alice, 1996, You and the I.C.U., 1990; author: (with others) The Inside Story: Psychiatry and Everyday Life, 1953, The Pursuit of Health, 1985; author: (mus.) Squanto and Love, 1992, Young Roosevelts, 1993, The Other Lincoln, 1995, The Strange Case of Mary Lincoln, 2001; contbr. articles to nat. mags., newspapers and profl. jours. Bd. dirs. Riverdale Mental Health Assn., 1983-2005, Woodrow Wilson Found., Princeton, N.J., 1959-64, 83-89, Lehman Coll. Found., 1983-90, Ittleson Ctr. for Childhood Rsch., 1958-90, Franklin and Eleanor Roosevelt Inst., 1992-2002; founder T.L.C.; trained liaison comforter Vol. Program of Presbyn. Hosp., N.Y.C., mem. hosp. ethics com. Named Alumna of the Yr., Rosemary Hall, 1976. Mem. Authors Guild (nominating com. 1987-90), Dramatists Guild, PEN, Cosmopolitan Club. Democrat. Avocations: theater, movies, reading. Home: 5000 Independence Ave Bronx NY 10471-2804

BINGHAM, MARIAN, artist, printmaker; b. Oakland, Calif., July 5, 1940; d. Woodbridge and Ursula Wolcott (Griswold) Bingham; m. William Bradford Hubbell, Jr. (div. 1990); children: Drika B. Hubbell, Jonathan Bradford Hubbell; m. Kenneth George McAdams, Feb. 28, 1998. BS (magna cum laude), Conn. Coll., New London, 1991; M.Liberal Arts, Wesleyan U., Middletown, Conn., 1995. Exhibitions include Garde Arts Ctr. and Vangard Gallery, New London, Conn., 1994, Mill Gallery, 1994, Paul Mellon Arts Ctr., Wallingford, Conn., 1994, Slater Mus., Norwich, 1994, Gallery B.A.I., N.Y.C., 1995, 1997—99, Nat. Mus. Women in the Arts, Washington, 1995, New Haven Coun. Small Gallery, New Haven, Conn., 1996, Fernbank Mus. Natural History, Atlanta, 1996, New Britain Mus. Art, Conn., 1997—99, Silvermine Guild Arts Ctr., 1997—99, So Hyun Gallery, N.Y.C., 2000, 2002, Greene Art Gallery, Guilford, Conn., 1998—2001, Alexey von Schlippe Gallery of Art, Groton, Conn., 1998—2001, 2002, 2004, Conn. Graphics Art Ctr., Norwalk, 2001—06, Hotel Abbye-Ecole, Soreze, France, 2003, 4 Star Gallery, Indpls., 2004, Albany Mus. Art, Ga., 2004, Moon Gallery, Berry Coll., Mt. Berry, Ga., 2005, Bendheim Gallery, Greenwich, Conn., 2005, Opelousas (La.) Mus. Art, 2005, numerous others. Avocations: hiking, skiing, travel, poetry.

BINKOWSKI, SYLVIA JULIA, water transportation executive, consultant; b. Dearborn, Mich. d. Steve S. and Cecelia Maria (Kwiatkowski) B. BS in Psychology and Comms., Ea. Mich. U., 1978. Sr. project coord. U.S. Treas. Dept., Detroit, 1979-83; sr. legis. asst. Congressman William D. Ford, Washington, 1983-91; head purchasing Decision Support Sys., McLean, Va., 1991-93; cons. The Eagle Cos., Annandale, Va., 1993-95; data analyst Louis Berger Internat. Inc., Washington, 1995—; mgr., data analyst GWU Nat. Ports & Waterways Inst., Rosslyn, Va., 1995—. Coord. U.S. Congress/German Bundestag Staff Exch. Program, 1989; cons. STC, London, 1992-93. Fund raiser Senatorial Campaign Com., 1984—, Congl. Campaign Com., 1984—; vol. Alexandria (Va.) Jaycees, 1988. Mem. House Legis. Asst. Assn. (founder, pres. emeritus, award 1989). Roman Catholic. Avocations: photography, painting, music, writing, fund raising for charities. Office: GWU Nat Ports & Waterways Inst 1300 17th St N Ste 310 Arlington VA 22209-3801 Home: PO Box 11229 Alexandria VA 22312-0229 Fax: 703-276-7101.

BINNEY, JAN JARRELL, publishing executive, marketing professional; b. Frankfort, Ind., Aug. 16, 1941; d. Robert and Susie (Meek) Jarrell; m. Joseph M. Binney, June 23, 1962; 1 child, Robert J. BS, Purdue U., 1962; MA, Coll. N.J., 1972. Speech-lang. pathologist pub. schs., various locations, 1962-84; pvt. practice speech pathology East Brunswick, NJ, 1982-85; pres. The Speech Bin, Inc. Pub., Vero Beach, Fla., 1984—. Editor profl. publs. Deacon Presbyn. Ch., 1985-87, elder, 1987-90; bd. dirs., chpt. chmn. ARC, Indian River Country, Fla. Fellow Am. Speech, Lang. Hearing Assn. (legis. councilor 1981-89, bd. dirs. pub. info. exch. 1987-89, com. on equality 1988-90, bd. dirs. polit. action com.), N.J. Speech, Lang. Hearing Assn. (pres. 1981-82, hon. 1984), Exch. Club Indian River (sec. 1998-99, bd. dirs. 2001-2002), Exch. Club Indian River Found. (charter, sec. 2002—), Pi Beta Phi Alumnae Club (treas.). Office: The Speech Bin Inc 1965 25th Ave Vero Beach FL 32960-3000 Office Phone: 772-770-0007. Business E-Mail: jan@speechbin.com.

BINNIE, NANCY CATHERINE, retired nurse, educator; b. Sioux Falls, SD, Jan. 28, 1937; d. Edward Grant and Jessie May (Martini) Larkin; m. Charles H. Binnie. Diploma, St. Joseph's Hosp. Sch. Nursing, Phoenix, 1965; BS in Nursing, Ariz. State U., 1970, MA, 1974. Intensive care charge nurse Scottsdale (Ariz.) Meml. Hosp., 1968-70, coordinator critical care, 1970-71, John C. Lincoln Hosp., Phoenix, 1971-73; prof. nursing GateWay Community Coll., Phoenix, 1974-96; ret., 1996. Coord. part-time evening nursing programs Gateway Community Coll., 1984-97, interim dir. nursing, 1989, 91. Mem. Orgn. Advancement of Assoc. Degree Nursing, Practical and Assoc. Coun. Nursing Educators, Ariz. Coun. Nurse Educators. Avocations: gardening, golf, sewing. Personal E-mail: nancy128@wans.net.

BINNING, BETTE FINESE (MRS. GENE HEDGCOCK BINNING), athletic association official; b. Brandon, Manitoba, Canada, Sept. 20, 1927; father is an Am. citizen. d. Henry Josiah and Beatrice Victoria (Harrop) Ames; m. Gene Hedgcock Binning, May 3, 1952; children: Gene Barton, Barbara Jo, Bradford Jay. Grad., Brandon Coll., 1944; student, Brandon U., 1944—46. Exec. sec. to mgr. Gardner Denver Co., Denver, 1950—52; mem. age. group swimming com. Amateur Athletic Union U.S., 1966—68, women's swimming com., 1968—69, age group swimming objectives subcom., 1970—71, mem. age. group swimming com., 1970—72, del. Conv., 1971—77, women's swimming com., 1972—76, del. Conv., 1979—80. Okla. state chmn. age group swimming Amateur Athletic Union, 1966-68, 70-72, chmn. women's swimming com., 1968-69, 72-79, mem. Okla. exec. bd. for all amateur sports, also registration com., 1971-79; mem. U.S. Olympic com., 1972-80; nat. dir. swimming records, 1972-81; U.S. rep. to records com. Amateur Swimming Assn. Am., 1975-83, dir. records com., 1975-83; dir., sec. records com. Union Amateur de Natacion de las Americas, 1979-83; tech. ofcl. Pan Am. Games, Mex. City, 1975, San Juan, P.R., 1979; ofcl. XXI Olympiad, Montreal, PQ, Can., 1976; mem. interim organizing com. U.S. Olympic Festival, 1986; athletic adv. dir. U.S. Olympic Festival 1989, 1987-88. Team capt. YMCA fund drives, 1966-78; mem. adv. com. Internat. Gymnastics Hall of Fame, 1996-99. Mem. Kerr Mcgee Swim Club (dir. 1968-75), Quail Creek Golf and Country Club(sports dir. women's golf assn. 2003, pres. 2005), Gaillardia Country Club, Okla. City Ski Club, Vail Athletic Club Colo. Presbyterian. Home: 3101 Rolling Stone Rd Oklahoma City OK 73120-1841 also: Vail Internat 205 300 E Lionshead Cir Vail CO 81657-5204 Home Fax: 405-751-6906. E-mail: Bettebinning@yahoo.com.

BINOCHE, JULIETTE, actress; b. Paris, Mar. 9, 1964; children: Raphael, Hannah. Student, Nat. Conservatory of Drama. Appearances in films include Les Nanas, La Vie de Famille, Rouge Baiser, 1985, Rendez-Vous, 1985, Mon beau-Frère a tué ma soeur, Mauvais Sang, 1986, Un tour de Manège, The Unbearable Lightness of Being, 1988, Les amants du Pont-Neuf, 1991, Wuthering Heights, 1992, Damage, 1992, Trois Couteurs: Bleu, 1993, The Horseman on the Roof, 1995, A Couch in New York, 1995, Le Hussard Sur Le Toit, 1995, The English Patient, 1996 (Academy award, 1996), Alice et Martin, 1998, Les Enfants du Siecle, 1999, La Veuve de Saint-Pierre, 2000, Chocolat, 2000, Decalage Horaire, 2002, Country of My Skull, 2004, Cache, 2005, Bee Season, 2005, Mary, 2005. Avocation: painting.*

BINSFELD, CONNIE BERUBE, former state official; b. Munising, Mich., Apr. 18, 1924; d. Omer J. and Elsie (Constance) Berube; m. John E. Binsfeld, July 19, 1947; children: John T., Gregory, Susan, Paul, Michael. BS, Siena Heights Coll., 1945, DHL (hon.), 1977; LLD (hon.), No. Mich. U., 1998; DHL (hon.), Mich. State U., 1998, Thomas Cooley Sch. of Law, 1999; LLD (hon.), Saginaw Valley State U., 2000, Lake Superior State U., 2000; DHL (hon.), U. Notre Dame, 2000, Grand Valley State U., 2000, DHL (hon.). County commr. Leelanau County, Mich., 1970-74; mem. Mich. Ho. of Reps., 1974-82, asst. rep. leader, 1979-81; del. Nav. Conv., 1980, 88, 92; mem. Mich. Senate, 1982-90, asst. rep. leader, 1979, 81; lt. gov. State of Mich., 1990-98. Mem. adv. bd. Nat. Park Sys. Named Mich. Mother of Yr., Mich. Mothers Com., 1977; Northwestern Mich. Coll. fellow; named to Mich. Women's Hall of Fame, 1998. Mem. Nat. Coun. State Legislators, LWV, Siena Heights Coll. Alumnae Assn. Republican. Roman Catholic. E-mail: Connieltgov@mailstation.com.

BINSTOCK, SONYA (TONI) KATSH, social worker; b. Amarillo, Tex., June 26, 1930; d. Jack S. and Anna Dean Katsh; m. Robert Allen Binstock, Mar. 22, 1953 (dec.); children: Terri B. Auerbach, Jodi Lynn. BA, UCLA, 1951; MSW, U. Denver, 1979. Diplomate Am. Bd. Social Worker Examiners; LCSW. Social worker Dept. Social Svcs., LA, 1951—57; tchr. on spl. assignment integration project Denver Pub. Schs., 1974—75, social work asst., 1976—79; clin. social worker Denver and Adams County Schs., 1979—82; pvt. practice Denver, 1982—. Adv. bd. Com. Response to Abuse, Denver, 1997—2000; panelist Mayor's Commn. on Cmty. Rels., Denver, 1965—66. Contbr. articles to profl. jours. Facilitator mothers of survivors of sexual abuse Survivors United Network Hempe Found., Denver, 1992—93; pres. PTA; task force Jewish Family Svcs.; adult com. B'nai B'rith Youth. Named Vol. of Yr., Jewish Cmty. Ctr., 1983. Mem.: NASW. Avocation: exercise. Home: 160 S Glencoe Denver CO 80246

BINTLIFF, BARBARA ANN, law educator, library director; b. Houston, Jan. 14, 1953; d. Donald Richard and Frances Arlene (Appling) Hay; m. Byron A. Boville, Aug. 20, 1977 (div. 1992); children: Bradley, Bruce. BA, Cen. Wash. U., 1975; JD, U. Wash., 1978, MLL, 1979. Bar: Wash. 1979, U.S. Dist. Ct. (ea. dist.) Wash. 1980, Colo. 1983, U.S. Dist. Ct. Colo. 1983. Libr. Gaddis and Fox, Seattle, 1978-79; reference libr. U. Denver Law Sch., 1979-84; assoc. libr., sr. instr. Sch. Law U. Colo., Boulder, 1984-88, assoc. prof., libr. dir., 1989—2001, prof., 2001—, Nicholas Rosenbaum prof. law, 2002—. Legal cons. Nat. Ctr. Atmospheric Rsch., Environ. and Societal Impacts Group, Boulder, 1980; vis. prof. U. Wash., Seattle, 1996, chair U. Colo. Boulder, Faculty Assembly, 2003—. Co-author: Colorado Legal Resources: An Annotated Bibliography, 2004; editor: A Representative Sample of Tenure Documents for Law Librarians, 1988, 2nd edit., 1994, Chapter Presidents' Handbook, 1989, Representatives Handbook, 1990, Marketing Toolkit for Academic Law Libraries, 2004; assoc. editor: Legal Reference Svcs. Quarterly, Perspectives: Teaching Legal Research and Writing; contbr. articles to profl. jours. Named Disting. Alumnus, Ctrl. Wash. U., 2000; recipient Boulder Faculty Assembly Excellence Svc. award, 2001, Calhoun Svc. award, U. Colo., 2002, Frederick Charles Hicks award, Assn. of Law Librs., 2005. Mem. Am. Assn. Law Librs. (v.p./pres.-elect 2000-01, pres. 2001-02), Am. Law Inst. (elected), Colo. Bar Assn., Colo. Assn. Law Librs. (pres. 1982), Southwestern Assn. Law Librs. (pres. 1987-88, 91-92). Episcopalian. Office: U Colo Law Libr 2405 Kittredge Loop Dr Rm 190 Boulder CO 80309-0402 Business E-Mail: barbara.bintliff@colorado.edu.

BIONDI, FLORENCE, freelance/self-employed artist; b. N.Y.C., Sept. 25, 1924; d. Angelo and Frances Curreri; m. Albert Anthony Biondi, Apr. 15, 1951; children: Joseph, Albert, Thomas, Robert. Student, Bklyn. Mus. Art Sch., 1967-75, Art Student's League, New City, N.Y., 1976-79. Pen and ink illustrator Simplicity Patterns, N.Y.C., 1943-45, Reader Mail Inc., N.Y.C., 1948-86; draftsman W.L. Maxson & Co., N.Y.C., 1945-48; freelance artist, 1986—. Mem. chorus Conservatory of Music. Recipient Pen and Brush Club award, 2001. Fellow: Am. Artists Profl. League (various awards 1980—82, 1988, 2000); mem.: Catherine Lorillard Wolfe Art Club (Portrait Pastel award 1983, 1996, 2001, 2004), Pastel Soc. Am. (Kalkow award 1983, 2004), Nat. Assn. Women Artists, Audubon Artists (Gold medal 2005). Roman Catholic. Avocations: music, gardening, sewing, reading, choral music. Home: 426 Mcdonald Ave Brooklyn NY 11218-2212

BIRCH, TOBEYLYNN, librarian; BA in Psychology, U. Calif.-Santa Cruz, 1972; MA in Librarianship, U. Denver, 1976. Acquisitions asst. UCLA, 1976—79; asst. libr. Calif. Sch. Profl. Psychology, L.A., 1980—81, dir. libr., 1981; libr. Alliant Internat. U., Alhambra, Calif., 2001—04, systemwide dir. lib. svcs., 2004—. Mem. bd. dir. Statewide Calif. Elec. Libr. Consortium (SCELC), 2003—. Mem.: ALA (sec. Libr. Instrn. Roundtable 1985—86, v.p. 1987—87, pres. 1988—89), Assn. Mental Health Librs., Calif. Acad. and Rsch. Libr., Beta Phi Mu. Office: Alliant Internat U 1000 S Fremont Ave Unit 5 Alhambra CA 91803 Business E-Mail: tbirch@alliant.edu.

BIRCHARD, CATHERINE SUZANNE SIEH, artist; b. New Rochelle, NY, Jan. 20, 1964; d. Theodore and Eleanor Anne Becker Sieh; m. Richard Edward Birchard, Oct. 9, 1987; 1 child, Dylan. BA, Cornell U., Ithaca, N.Y., 1985. Painting, Munch (1938), 1997, exhibited in group shows at Westbeth Gallery, NYC, 1998, Gallery 402, 1998, Erector Sq. Gallery, New Haven, Conn., 1998, Silvermine Guild Galleries, New Canaan, Conn., 1998, The Macy Gallery, Valhalla, NY, 1999, The Art Club Gallery, NYC, 2000, NY Law Sch. Gallery, 2000, The Gallery on the Hudson, Irvington, NY, 2001, Pelham Arts Ctr. Gallery, Pelham, NY, 2002, Phoenix Gallery, NYC, 2002, The Arts Exch. Gallery, White Plains, NY, 2002—, 2003, The Macy Gallery, Valhalla, NY, 2003, Iona Coll. Arts Ctr., New Rochelle, NY, 2003. Recipient Juror's Selection Award, 1998, Cresson Pugh Award for Most Innovative, 1997; named Inaugural Westchester Biennial Artist, Castle Gallery, 1998. Mem. Mamaroneck Artists' Guild (bd. dir. 1998—, newsletter editor 1998-99, dir. programs 1998-2001, dir. publicity 2001-, membership juror 2001-), Orgn. Ind. Artists, Ctr. for Book Arts. Avocations: music, book collecting.

BIRCHER, ANDREA URSULA, psychiatric mental health clinical nurse specialist; b. Bern, Switzerland, Mar. 6, 1928; arrived in U.S., 1947; d. Franklin E. Bircher and Hedy E. Bircher-Rey. Diploma, Knapp Coll. Nursing, Santa Barbara, Calif., 1957; BS, U. Calif., San Francisco, 1961, MS, 1962; PhD, U. Calif., Berkeley, 1966. RN. Staff nurse, head nurse Cottage Hosp., Santa Barbara, 1957—58; psychiat. nurse, jr., sr. Langley-Porter Neuropsychiatric Inst., San Francisco, 1958—66; asst. prof. U. Ill. Coll. Nursing, Chgo., 1966-72; prof. U. Okla. Coll. Nursing, Oklahoma City, 1972-93, prof. emeritus, 1993—. Contbr. articles to profl. jours. Mem.: ANA, AAUP, N.Am. Nursing Diagnosis Assn., Internat. Soc. Psychiat.-Mental Health Nursing, Am. Psychotherapy Assn. (diplomate), Ventura County Writers Club, Phi Kappa Phi, Sigma Theta Tau. Republican. Avocations: indoor gardening, reading, writing. Home: 1161 Cypress Point Ln Apt 201 Ventura CA 93003-6074

BIRCHFIELD, MARTHA, librarian; b. Tallahassee, Fla., July 19, 1946; d. Merrill Charles and Bessie Christine (Dyar) Futch; m. James DeMaris Birchfield, Dec. 5, 1969. BA, Fla. State U., 1967, MA, 1969, MS, 1976. Catalog libr. Fla. State U. Law Libr., Tallahassee, 1977-78, acquisitions libr., 1978-80; libr. Coun. of State Govts., Lexington, Ky., 1980; head libr. Lexington C.C., 1980—2000, prof., 2000—. Prof. Lexington C.C. Co-chair Ky. Gov.'s Conf. on Libr. and Info. Svcs., 1991; bd. dirs. Ky. Preservation. Recipient Lexington-Fayette County Hist. Preservation award, 1994. Mem. ALA, Assn. of Coll. and Rsch. Libr. (pres. Ky. chpt. 1986-87), Southeastern Libr. Assn. (chair const. com. 1988-90), Ky. Libr. Assn. (bd. dirs. 1986-87), Phi Beta Kappa (pres. Alpha of Ky. 1991-92). Democrat. Episcopalian. Avocation: architecture. Home: 320 Linden Walk Lexington KY 40508-3020 Office: Bluegrass Cmty and Tech Coll 201 A/T Bldg Lexington KY 40506-0235 E-mail: mbirchfield@qx.net.

BIRD, CAROLINE, author; b. N.Y.C., Apr. 15, 1915; d. Hobart Stanley and Ida (Brattrud) B.; m. Edward A. Menuez, June 8, 1934 (div. Dec. 1945); 1 dau., Carol (Mrs. John Paul Barach); m. John Thomas Mahoney, Jan. 5, 1957 (dec. 1981); 1 son, John Thomas. Student, Vassar Coll., 1931-34; BA, U. Toledo, 1938; MA, U. Wis., 1939; LHD (hon.), Keene State U., 1988. Desk editor N.Y. Jour. Commerce, 1943-44; editl. rschr. Newsweek mag., N.Y.C., 1942-43, Fortune mag., N.Y.C., 1944-46; with Dudley-Anderson-Yutzy, pub. relations, N.Y.C., 1947-68; Froman Disting. prof. Russell Sage Coll., 1972-73; Mather prof. Case Western Res. U., Cleve., 1977. Author: The Invisible Scar, 1966, Born Female, 1968, rev. edit., 1970, The Crowding Syndrome, 1972, Everything a Woman Needs to Know to Get Paid What She's Worth, 1973, rev., 1982, The Case Against College, 1975, Enterprising Women, 1976, What Women Want, 1979, The Two-Paycheck Marriage, 1979, The Good Years, 1983, Second Careers, 1992, Lives of Our Own, 1995; chief writer: The Spirit of Houston, 1978; also articles in nat. mags. Mem. review bd. Dept. State, 1974. Mem. Am. Soc. Journalists and Authors, Am. Sociol. Assn. Address: The Meadows 2088 Coley Davis Rd 30 Nashville TN 37221

BIRD, MARY LYNNE MILLER, professional society administrator; b. Buffalo, Feb. 25, 1934; d. Joseph William and Mildred Dorothy (Wallette) Miller; m. Thomas Edward Bird, Aug. 23, 1958; children: Matthew David, Lisa Bronwen. AB magna cum laude, Syracuse U., 1956; postgrad., Columbia U., 1956-58. Mem. rsch. staff Ctr. for Rsch. in Personality, Harvard U., Cambridge, Mass., 1959-62, Ctr. Internat. Studies, Princeton (N.J.) U., 1962-66, Inst. Internat. Social Rsch., Princeton, 1965, Sch. Internat. Affairs, Columbia U., N.Y.C., 1966-67, Coun. Fgn. Rels., N.Y.C., 1967-69, Twentieth Century Fund, N.Y.C., 1969-72; asst. to pres. World Policy Inst., N.Y.C., 1972-74; dir. devel. Fund for Peace, N.Y.C., 1974-78; dir. fellows program Exec. Council Fgn. Diplomats, N.Y.C., 1978-79; dir. devel. Engender Health, N.Y.C., 1979—83; exec. dir. Am. Geog. Soc., N.Y.C., 1983—. Cons. Fedn. Am. Scientists, Washington, 1974-75. Trustee Bel Canto Opera Co., N.Y.C., 1975—90. Maxwell Citizenship scholar Syracuse U., 1952-56. Fellow AAAS; mem. NAS (com. on geography, liaison mem. 1984-2000), Assn. Am. Geographers, Soc. Woman Geographers, Inst. for Current World Affairs (trustee), Nat. Coun. Geog. Edn., 100-Yr. Assn. N.Y., Conf. Latin Americanist Geographers, Planning Com. for Nat. Assessment on Ednl. Progress in Geography, Nat. Music Theatre Network (bd. dirs.), St. David's Soc. (past pres.), Colonial Dames Am., Daus. of Colonial Wars, Daus. of 1812, Pilgrims of U.S., Mid-Atlantic Club N.Y.C. (bd. dirs.), Princeton Club, Welsh Women's Club NY, Am. Soc. Assn. Execs., The Bohemians, Phi Beta Kappa, Phi Kappa Phi, Eta Pi Upsilon, Phi Beta Phi. Avocations: singing, sailing. Office Phone: 212-422-5456. Business E-Mail: MLBird@amergeog.org.

BIRD, PATRICIA COLEEN, business owner; b. Wolf Point, Mont., May 10, 1953; d. Harry Sidney and Pearl Rose (Firemoon) B. AA in Fine Arts, Haskell Indian JUCO, Lawrence, Kans., 1974; student, Kans. U., 1974-78; CDC Cert., Deaconess Hosp., Glasgow, Mont., 1990. Partnership bus. owner Blue Feather Indian Store, Wolf Point, Mont., 1980—2000. Indian arts steering com. mem. Mont. Arts Coun., Helena, 1991. Exhibitions include Beauty, Honor, and Tradition: The Legacy of Plains Indian Shirts Exhibit, George Gustav Heye Ctr., N.Y., 2001. First responder ambulance Trinity Hosp., Wolf Point, 1991-92; drug and alcohol facilitator Frazer (Mont.) Sch. Dist. 2-2B, 1990-91; acting sec. Frazer Community Coun., 1991-92; N.W. accrediting assn. mem. Poplar (Mont.) Sch., 1990-91; coord. "The Longest Walk", Davis, Calif., 1978, concert dir., 1978, Outstanding Young Women of Am., Ala, 1986, 87. Named Miss Nat. Congress of Am. Indians, 1975, The Modern Ms., 1975, Miss Haskell, 1974, Oil Discovery Celebration Pres., 1974, Oil Discovery Celebration Princess, 1973, 72, 71. Achievements include design of Smithsonian Inst., Nat. Museum of the Am. Indian, ribbon shirt made in 1981 was selected to become part of the Smithsonian's permanent plains Indian shirts collection from the 19th and 20th centuries. Avocations: indian art and crafts, sewing, reading, painting, drawing.

BIRD, SHARLENE, psychologist; d. Rubin and Dina Bird. BA in Psychology & Hispanic Studies, Vassar Coll., 1979; MA in Applied Psychology, Adelphi U., 1986; MA in Human Resources Mgmt., New Sch. for Social Rsch., N.Y.C., 1987; PsyD in Clin. Psychology, Yeshiva U., 1992. Lic. psychologist, N.Y. Clin. extern St. Mary's Children and Family Svcs., Syosset, N.Y., 1980-81; behavior modifier Flower Hosp./Terence Cardinal Cooke, N.Y.C., 1981-82; clin. psychology extern Met. Ctr. for Mental Health, 1986-87; clin. psychology intern NYU Med. Ctr./Bellevue Hosp., N.Y.C., 1989-90; postdoctoral fellow in human sexuality N.Y. Hosp./Cornell Med. Ctr., 1990-92; family therapist Roberto Clemente Family Guidance Ctr., N.Y.C., 1991-93, 96-98; healthcare planning analyst Inst. for Family and Community Care, N.Y.C., 1993-96; pvt. practice N.Y.C., 1994—. Supr. NYU Med. Ctr./Bellevue Hosp., N.Y.C., 1992—; part-time clin. instr. dept. psychiatry NYU Med. Ctr., 1995—; tng. cons. Inst. for Family and Cmty. Care, N.Y.C., 1993; weekly permanent radio talk show co-host Siempre a Tu Lado, Sta. WADO 1280 AM, 1992—95. Chair bd. dirs. Mothers of Childrens with AIDS, N.Y.C., 1991-93. Mem.: APA, Assn. for Advancement of Behavior Therapy (chair pub. edn. and media dissemination com. 1996—99), Am. Group Psychotherapy Assn., Counselors and Therapists, Am. Assn. Sex Educators, Assn. Hispanic Mental Health Profls. (bd. dirs., mem.-at-large 1995—97, v.p. 1999—2001), Am. Orthopsychiat. Assn., N.Y. State Psychol. Assn., Sigma Delta Phi. Office: 112 W 56th St Rm C Ste 15 S New York NY 10019-3841

BIRD, SHELLEY, communications executive; MA in Communication Mgmt., U. South Australia. Cert. bus. communicator Internat. Assn. Bus. Communicators. With J. Walter Thompson, Toronto, Canada; mgmt. positions mktg. and comm. Asia Pacific region Motorola Electronics; with Hill and Knowlton, Hong Kong, dep. gen. mgr. Singapore office; v.p. mktg. comm. and pub. rels. Philips Consumer Comm.; chief comm. officer NCR Corp.; exec. v.p. comm. Cardinal Health. Tchr. retail mgmt. Named Corp. PR Profl. of Yr., PR News, 2004. Office: Cardinal Health 7000 Cardinal Pl Dublin OH 43017*

BIRD, SUE (SUZANNE BRIGIT BIRD), professional basketball player; b. Syosset, NY, Oct. 16, 1980; d. Herschel and Nancy Bird. Degree in comm. sci., U. Conn., 2002. Basketball player Christ the King High School, NY, U. Conn., 1998—2002; profl. basketball player Seattle Storm, WNBA, 2002—. Member USA Basketball Women's Sr. Nat. Team, 2002, 04. Named Naismith Player of Yr., 2002, AP Player of Yr., 2002, Best Female Coll. Athlete, ESPY Awards, 2002; named to Parade Mag. All-Am. first team, 1998, First Team All-WNBA, 2002, 2003, WNBA Western Conf. All-Star Team, 2002, 2003; recipient Wade Trophy, 2002, Honda Award for Women's Coll. Basketball Player of Yr., 2002. Achievements include mem.NCAA Divsn. 1 Nat. Championship Team, U. Conn., 2000, 02; mem. US Women's Basketball FIBA World Championship Gold Medal Team, 2002; Selected as the No. 1 overall pick in the 2002 WNBA Draft; mem. US Women's Basketball Team, Athens Olympics, 2004. Office: Seattle Sonics and Storm 351 Elliott Ave W Ste 500 Seattle WA 98119 Business E-Mail: StormFans@sonics-storm.com.

BIRDSALL, JEANNE, writer, photographer; married. Student, Calif. Coll. Arts & Crafts, Oakland, 1972. Photographer (permanent collections) Smithsonian Instn., Phila. Art Mus.; author: (children's books) The Penderwicks: A Summer Tale of Four Sisters, Two Rabbits, and a Very Interesting Boy, 2005 (One of Best Books of Yr., Child Mag., 2005, Nat. Book award for Young People's Lit., 2005). Mailing: care R Michelson Galleries 132 Main St Northampton MA 01060 Address: Author Mail Alfred A Knopf 1745 Broadway New York NY 10019*

BIRDSALL, LYNNE A., academic administrator; b. Canandaigua, NY, Jan. 26, 1954; d. William Cary and Geraldine Merhoff Birdsall. BA in Music/Psychology, Union Coll., 1976; MEd in Counseling, U. N.H., 2001. Med. records asst. Schenectady (N.Y.) Orthopedic Assocs., 1976-77; field rep. Child Welfare Info. Svcs., Albany, N.Y., 1977-78; asst. dir. admissions Union Coll., Schenectady, 1978-79, Rensselaer Poly. Inst., Troy, 1979-82, assoc. dir. admissions, 1982-84; account exec. Epsilon Data Mgmt., Burlington, Mass., 1984-85; asst. dir. admissions Berklee Coll. Music, Boston, 1985-87, fin. aid cons., 1988-89; asst. adminstr., editor Boston U. Sch. Law/Morin Ctr. for Banking & Fin. Law Studies, 1989-94; assoc. v.p. N.H. Tech. Inst., Concord, 1995—. Mem. ACA, Nat. Assn. Fgn. Student Advisors, N.E. Assn. for Coll. Admission Counseling, N.E. Assn. for Coll. Registrars and Admissions Officers, Pi Lambda Theta. Avocations: walking, music, reading, poetry, fine dining. Home: PO Box 1615 Concord NH 03302-1615 Office: NH Tech Inst 31 College Dr Concord NH 03301-7412 Office Phone: 603-271-7130. Business E-Mail: lbirdsall@nhctc.edu.

BIRDSALL, MELINDA R., gynecologist; d. Charles Matthew and Nancy Virginia Ropar; m. Christopher Pennock Birdsall, Sept. 19, 1987; children: Ryan, Andrew. BS, Youngstown State U.; MD, Med. U. Ohio, Toledo. Intern in gen. surgery Med. U. Ohio; resident in ob-gyn. Loyola U./St. Francis Hosp., Chgo.; physician Hale Hosp., Haverhill, Mass., Beverly Hosp., Mass., Lahey Clinic, Burlington, Mass. Asst. prof. ob-gyn. Boston U. Med. Ctr.; mem. consulting and adv. bds. contraceptive mgmt. and menopausal health. Named one of Best Drs., Boston Mag. Fellow: ACOG; mem.: AMA, Am. Assn. Gynecol. Laparoscopists, Ipswich Country Club (bd. govs., chmn.). Achievements include research in cryoblation of the uterine cavity. Avocations: golf, skiing, running. Office: Lahey Clinic Found 1 Essex Center Dr Peabody MA 01960 Office Phone: 978-538-4620. Office Fax: 978-538-4708. E-mail: melinda_r_birdsall@lahey.org.

BIRDSALL, NANCY, economist; b. Feb. 6, 1946; BA in Am. Studies, Newton Coll. of the Sacred Heart, 1967; MA in Internat. Rels., Johns Hopkins U., 1969; PhD in Econs., Yale U., 1979. Social sci. analyst Smithsonian Inst., 1972-76; economist, various policy and mgmt. positions World Bank, Washington, 1979-93; exec. v.p. Inter-Am. Devel. Bank, Washington, 1993-98; sr. assoc., dir. Econ. Reform Project Carnegie Endowment for Internat. Peace, 1998—2001; pres. Ctr. Global Devel., 2001—. Sr. adviser Rockefeller Found., 1988-89; active numerous coms. Nat. Acad. of Scis.; chair bd. dirs. Internat. Ctr. for Rsch. on Women; bd. dirs. Bd. of Population Coun., numerous others. Author numerous publs. on econ. devel. issues.

BIRDSONG, ALTA MARIE, volunteer; m. Kenneth Layne Birdsong; children: Suzanne Denise Huff, Jeffrey Layne Birdsong. BBA in Acctg. magna cum laude, U. North Tex., 1955. Cost engr. Tex. Instruments, Inc., Dallas, 1955-62; part-time acct. Atlanta, 1972—. Mem. DeKalb County Cmty. Rels. Com., 1981-93, chair, 1984-87; mem. Atlanta Regional Com. Adv. Group, 1981-88, Met. Atlanta United Way, 1985-98, resource investment vol. sch. age children; chair Sch. Age Child Care Coun., 1987-90; mem. Dekalb County Task Force on Personal Care Homes, Dekalb County Task Force on Domestic Violence; mem. steering com. for bond referendum Dekalb B. Edn.; mem. Vision 2020 Governance Stakeholders ARC, 1994-95; mem. Camp Fire Boys and Girls. Recipient John H. Collier award for Camp Fire, 1991, Luther Halsey Gulick award for Camp Fire, 1993, Frederic E. Ruccius award for Camp Fire, 1993, Mortar Bd. Alumni Achievement award, 1991, Woman of Yr. award Atlanta Alumnae Panhellenic, 1983, Women Who Have Made a Difference award DeKalb YWCA, 1985, Ember award Camp Fire, 1998, Tom Murphy State Service Good Heart Vol. award, 2002. Mem.: AAUW (rec. sec. 1982—84, mem. v.p. 1984—86, pres. elect 1986—87, divsn. pres. 1987—89, assn. nominating com. 1993—97, chair 1995—97, Atlanta chpt. pres. 2001—03, co-chair Sister-to-Sister Summit 2002, chair Woman to Woman Summit 2002, Achievement award 1999), Freedoms Found. at Valley Force (sec. 1983—85, treas. 1985—87, v.p. publicity 1988—89, v.p. 1990—91, Atlanta chpt. pres. 1991—92, ea.-so. region adv. 1994—97, treas. 1999—2000, Atlanta chpt. pres. 2000—01), Atlanta Alumnae Panhellenic (v.p. 1977—78, pres. 1978—79), Atlanta Coun. Camp Fire (region fin. officer 1989—90, v.p. 1990—92, pres. 1992—94), Delta Gamma Alumnae (treas. 1972—74, Atlanta chpt. 1st v.p. 1985—87, Oxford award 1992). Home: 5241 Manhasset Cv Atlanta GA 30338-3413

BIRDSONG, JANET LOUISE, medical/surgical nurse; b. Cushing, Okla., June 19, 1942; d. Ress Richard and Florene (Eldridge) Adams; m. Bobby Ray Birdsong, June 18, 1960; children: John Richard, David Ray. AA, Rose State Coll., 1992; BSN, U. Ctrl. Okla., 1994. Mem. U. Ctrl. Okla. Nurses Alumni Assn., Sigma Theta Tau. mem. Oklahoma Gerontological Nursing Assn. Baptist. Home: 3901 Oakbrook Del City OK 73115-3415 E-mail: jlbird1@juno.com.

BIRDWELL, SUSAN ELIZABETH SMITH, artist; b. Memphis, Jan. 27, 1948; d. Mark Black and Mildred Elizabeth (Tinsley) Smith; m. William DeWitt Whitten, Feb. 14, 1970 (dec. Dec. 1990); 1 child, Christopher Mark; m. Tony Lee Birdwell, May 17, 2003 BFA Painting, Memphis State U., 1971. Counselor Tenn. Dept. Human Svcs., Memphis, 1971—74, Nashville, 1980—81; interviewer Tenn. Dept. Employment Security, Nashville, 1981—85; portrait artist Nashville, 1980—. Works represented in pvt. collections throughout U.S.; cover designer Letters for All Seasons, 1991 Pres. Rep. Career Women, Memphis, 1976; mem. exec. com. Shelby County Rep. Com., Memphis, 1978-80, mem. steering com., 1977-80; youth counselor Belmont United Meth. Ch., Nashville, 1985— Named Miss Tennessee Young Rep., Young Reps., 1969 Mem. Hort. Soc. Davidson County, Portrait Soc. Am., Cecilia Beaux Forum, Fine Arts Blount, Townsend Bus. Assn., Alpha Phi. Avocations: fly fishing, writing, gourmet cooking, interior decorating, travel. Home: 418 Wears Valley RD Townsend TN 37882-3306 Studio: Mountainbird Studio PO Box 496 Townsend TN 37882 Office Phone: 865-448-0241. Personal E-mail: mtnbirdstudio@aol.com.

BIRDWHISTELL, JOANNE (ANNE), retired education educator, researcher; b. Evanston, Ill., Mar. 3, 1944; d. John Murdoch and Carol (Crawford) Davison; m. Ray Lee Birdwhistell, Mar. 11, 1976. Student, Columbia U., 1965; BA summa cum laude, U. Pa., 1966; MA, Stanford U., 1968, PhD, 1974. Lectr. U. Pa., Phila., 1974-75; from asst. prof. to prof. Richard Stockton Coll. NJ, Pomona, NJ, 1979—2006; profl. emeritus, 2006—. Adj. instr. Stockton Coll. N.J., Pomona, spring, 1979; article and book reviewer, 1988—; co-chair Neo-Confucian Seminar, Columbia U., 1991-93. Author: Transition to Neo-Confucianism, 1989, Li Yong (1627-1705) and Epistemological Dimensions of Confucian Philosophy; contbr. articles to profl. jours. Benjamin Franklin nat. scholar U. Pa., 1962-66; NDEA fellow Stanford U., 1966-69, Nat. Def. Fgn. Lang. fellow Columbia U., 1965, disting. faculty fellow Stockton Found., 1989, 92; valedictorian Coll. for Women, U. Pa., 1966. Mem. Am. Philos. Assn., Soc. for Comparative and Asian Philos. (bd. dirs. 1991—), Am. Hist. Assn., Assn. for Asian Studies, Soc. for the Study Chinese Religion, Am. Assn. for Chinese Studies, Phi Beta Kappa. Democrat. Avocations: wood carving, textile restoration, gardening, antiques, travel. Office: Stockton Coll of NJ Jimmie Leeds Rd Pomona NJ 08240

BIRGE, BEVERLY HARRINGTON, secondary school educator; b. St. Petersburg, Fla., Feb. 9, 1941; d. Gordon Melville and Eunice Beth Harrington; m. Gerald Kirk Birge, Feb. 23, 1962; children: Terri Lynn Mitvalsky, David Kirk. BS in Secondary Social Studies, Fla. Internat. U., Miami, 1984. Cert. peer counselor Broward C.C., Fla., 1975. Tchr. Broward Sch. Bd., Ft. Lauderdale, Fla., 1984—. S.A.D.D. sponsor Cooper City H.S., Fla., 1988—91. Develop. of 1st ethics award (an award based on character traits) The Psychology Ethics Award. Mem. DAR, St. Petersburg, Fla., 1957; contbr. The Gorilla Found., Maui, Hawaii, 1999—2006. Mem.: Kappa Delta Pi. Methodist. Avocations: family activities, teaching, research. Office: Cooper City HS 9401 Stirling Rd Cooper City FL 33328 Office Phone: 754-323-0200. Office Fax: 754-323-0330. E-mail: www.coopercityhigh.org.

BIRI, TONI ROPPOLO, elementary school educator; b. New Orleans, Sept. 21, 1957; d. Anthony Rocco and Helen Ellis (Ferguson) Roppolo; m. Gerard Michael Biri, Aug. 8, 1992; children: Michael A. Greenfield, Stephen R. Buford Jr., Kaitlyn Marie. BS, Our Lady of Holy Cross Coll., New Orleans, 1981. Cert. elem. edn. La., 1981. Tchr. 3rd grade Catherine Strehle Elem. Sch., Avondale, La., 1983—89; tchr. 6th grade Wilkerson Intermediate Sch., The Woodlands, Tex., 1989—90; tchr. 4th grade Galvez Primary Sch., Prairieville, La., 1990—. Bldg./area rep. Jefferson Fedn. Tchrs., Avondale, 1984—86; co-leader 4-H, Prairieville, La., 1995—2002. Grantee, Ascension Fund, 2000—01. Home: 40461 Myrtle St Prairieville LA 70769 Office: Galvez Primary Sch 16093 Henderson Bayou Rd Prairieville LA 70769

BIRK, PEG J., lawyer; BA, U. Houston, 1976; JD, William Mitchell Coll. Law, 1983. Bar: Minn. 1983. Sr. corp. counsel St. Paul Companies, 1990—97; city atty. St. Paul, 1997—99; gen. counsel AM. Internat. Group, Inc., 1999, Domestic Brokerage Group; sr. v.p., gen. counsel Federated Mutual Ins. Co., Owatonna, Minn., 1999—. Bd. dirs. McKnight Found., Internat. Alliance Exec. Women; U.S. delegate Asian Pacific Econ. Corp., 2002—; bd. trustees Hamline U.; dep. Minn. Bus. Partnership. Office: Federated Mutual Ins Co 121 E Park Sq Owatonna MN 55060 Office Phone: 507-455-6915. Office Fax: 507-455-5997. E-mail: pjbirk@fedins.com.

BIRK, PEGGY J., foundation administrator; BA in Philosophy, U. Houston; JD, William Mitchell Coll., St. Paul. Former asst. atty. general, Minn.; former city atty. St. Paul; former general counsel, domestic brokerage group Am. Internat. Group, Inc., NYC; sr. v.p. and general counsel Federated Insurance Co., Owatonna, 1995—2005; bd. dirs. McKnight Found., 2001—, interim pres., 2005—. Mem. Internat. Alliance of Exec. Women, 1999—2002. Trustee Hamline U.; adv. council Humphrey Inst. of Public Affairs; mem. Minn. Women's Economic Roundtable. Office: McKnight Found 710 S Second St Minneapolis MN 55401*

BIRKESTOL, ANNABELLE MOLLIE ELSIE, retired elementary school educator; b. Stanwood, Wash., May 29, 1923; d. Ole and Ingeborg Birkestol. BA in edn., Pacific Lutheran U., 1945; grad. studies U. Wash. (hon.), 1969. Elem. tchr. Woodinville Sch., Woodinville, Wash., 1945—47, Wilson Sch., Mukilteo, Wash., 1948—54, Conway Sch., Conway, Wash., 1954—76; ret., 1976. Mem. Wash. State Edn. Assn., Olympia, Wash., 1945—76, NEA, 1945—76. Mem.: Wash. State Sch. Retirees' Assn., Am. Assn. U. Women, Nat. Women's Hist. Mus., Stanwood Area Hist. Soc. (life; pres. 1978—79), Norwegian Am. Mus. Vesterheim (life), Pacific Lutheran U. Q Club, Fritjov Lodge No. 17 Sons of Norway Stanwood. Republican. Lutheran. Avocations: opera, museums, historic preservation. Home: 4515 Norman Rd Stanwood WA 98292

BIRKLE, LINDA JEAN, elementary school educator; b. Louisville, Feb. 4, 1945; d. Arthur Jacob Norgaard and June Lucille Harmer; children: William, Todd, Jason. BS in Elem. Edn., U. Wis., Madison, 1967; MEPD, U. Wis., LaCrosse; postgrad., Washburn Acad., 1995—97, postgrad., 2006. 4th and 5th grade tchr. Lapham Elem. Sch., Madison, 1967—71; tchr. pre-sch. Parkside Child Care Ctr., Kenosha, Wis., 1976—79; prin., tchr. St. Peter's Sch., Hokah, Minn., 1981—88; 5th grade tchr. St. James Sch., LaCrosse, 1988—2000, Coulee Cath. Schs./Blessed Sacrament Sch., LaCrosse, 2000—. Mem.: Nat. Cath. Edn. Assn., Eagles Club. Roman Catholic. Avocations: golf, stained glass. Home: 1311 Travis St La Crosse WI 54601

BIRMAN, RONNIE RATHKOPF, retired elementary school educator; b. NYC, Dec. 24, 1947; d. Julius and May (Levy) Rathkopf. BS in Edn., CCNY, 1969; MA in Sociology, MS in Social Rsch., CUNY, 1977, MS in Sci. Edn., 1990; cert. in adminstrn. and supervision, Bklyn. Coll., 1992; PhD in Reading, Fordham U., 2000. Cert. tchr., N.Y. Elem. sch. tchr. P.S. 316, Bklyn., 1969-84, elem. sch. sci. tchr., 1984-91; bldg. sci. mentor, 1991-92; freelance curriculum writer NYC, 1989—; staff intern, coord. tchr. workshops Impact II Grants, NYC, 1991; sci. magnet tchr. P.S. 64, NYC, 1992—93; Chpt. 1 reading tchr., 1993—94; tchr. 1st and 2d grades P.S. 19, NYC, 1995—2003; ret., 2003. Curriculum disseminator, facilitator workshops Impact II Office, Bklyn. Coll., several sch. dists. in NY, 1990—; grant writer for PIP Bklyn. Coll., 1992, adj. prof. literacy, 95; mem. Whole Lang. Inst. for Ctrl. Bd. at Dist. 8, 1992; image cons., color specialist, 2004; career/life coach, bus. coach, 2005—06; corporate trainer image and mgmt. skills, 2006; profl. makeup artist Christine Valmay, 2005. Author oral comms. curriculum "Can We Talk?"; writer for CIMS Sci. K Level Dist. 8 and Learning-Link Curiculum. Active parent workshops in communication/experimentation in sci. P.S. 316, Dist. 17, Bklyn., 1991-92. Recipient Impact II grant, 1991; grantee N.Y.C., 1992. Mem. United Fedn. Tchrs., Kappa Delta Pi. Avocations: poetry, creative writing, reading, acting, drawing. Home: 32 Gramercy Park S New York NY 10003-1707

BIRNBAUM, LINDA SHUB, retired assistant principal; b. Cleve. Heights, Ohio, Aug. 8, 1949; d. Esther and Abraham Shub; m. Neal S. Birnbaum, M.D., June 27, 1971; children: Jennifer Lynn, Lauren Beth. BS in Edn., Ohio State U., Columbus, 1971; MS in Edn., U. Pitts., 1976; MA in Edn., San Francisco State U., 1997. Cert. profl. adminstrv. Commn. Tchr. Credentialing, Calif., 2001, profl. clear single subject tchg. Commn. Tchr. Credentialing, Calif., 2001. Asst. prin. Petaluma City Sch., Calif., 1997—2006; ret., 2006. Mem., campaign kick-off maj. event women's divsn. Jewish Cmty. Fedn., San Francisco, 1977—89; mem., treas., exec. com. mem. Marin Jewish Cmty. Ctr., San Rafael, Calif., 1982—85; pres., mem. Tamalpais Union HS Dist., Larkspur, Calif., 1993—97; vol., maj. dinner co-chair Scleroderma Rsch. Found., San Francisco, 1988—2000. Tchr. Corps Internship grant, Pitts. Pub. Sch., 1974—76. Mem.: We. Assn. Coll. and Sch. (vis. team chairperson accrediting commn. 2005—06, mem. accrediting commn. 2000—06). Jewish. Avocations: dancing, travel, dance.

BIRNBAUM, LUCIA CHIAVOLA, historian, educator; b. Kansas City, Mo., Jan. 3, 1924; d. Salvatore and Kate (Cipolla) Chiavola; m. Wallace Birnbaum, Feb. 3, 1946; children: Naury, Marc, Stefan. AB, U. Calif., Berkeley, 1948, MA, 1950, PhD, 1964. Lectr. U. Calif., Berkeley, 1963-64, rsch. assoc. 1982-83, 86, 90-96; asst. prof. history San Francisco State U., 1964-69; mem. faculty Feminist Inst., Berkeley, 1981—; prof. doctoral program feminist spirituality Calif. Inst. Integral Studies, San Francisco, 1994—2000, prof., 2001—. Guest lectr. U. Sydney, Australia, 1989, U. Melbourne, Australia, 1989, U. di Padua, 1990; adj. prof. Calif. Coll. Arts and Crafts, Oakland, 1991-92. Author: La Religione e le Donne Sociulo Americane, 1981, Liberazione della Donna: Feminism in Italy, 1986 (Am. Book award 1987), 1988, Black Madonnas, Feminism, Religion and Politics in Italy, 1993, 97, 2001; Dark Mother: African Origins and Godmothers, 2001, 04, Gatherer, She is Everywhere: Anthology of Womanist/Feminist Writing in Spirituality, 2004; contbr. articles to profl. jours. Recipient Am. Book award Before Columbus Found., 1987, Anniversary award San Francisco State U., 1988, Premio Internazionale di Saggistica Salvatore Valitutti, Salerno, Italy, 1998, Enheduanna award for excellence in woman-centered lit., 2002, Founding Mother award Women's Spirituality MA and PhD programs, Calif. Inst. Integral Studies, 2003, cert. scholarly advancement 6th Ann. Cheikh Anta Diop Conf., 2004; vis. scholar Grad. Theol. Union, 1983-94, 95-96, Inst. Rsch. Women and Gender, Stanford U., 1987-94, Disting. woman scholar U. Calif., Davis, 1987; named to Internat. African Am. Multicultural Hall of Fame, 1996. Mem. ACLU, PEN Am. Ctr., Orgn. Am. Historians, Am. Italian Hist. Assn. (pres. western regional chpt. 1978-82), Nat. Women's Studies Assn., Ctr. Women and Religion Grad. Theol. Union, Women's Party for Survival. Home: 349 Gravatt Dr Berkeley CA 94705-1503 Office: Calif Inst Integral Studies 1453 Mission St San Francisco CA 94103 Office Phone: 415-575-6100 ext. 466. Business E-Mail: lbirnbaum@ciis.edu. E-mail: lucia@darkmother.net.

BIRNBAUM, S. ELIZABETH, lawyer; b. Ft. Belvoir, Va., Jan. 20, 1958; d. Myron Lionel and Emma Jane (Steiner) Birnbaum. AB, Brown U., 1979; JD, Harvard U., 1984. Bar: Colo. 1984, D.C. 1985, U.S. Dist. Ct. D.C. 1987, U.S. Ct. Appeals (D.C. cir.) 1988, U.S. Ct. Appeals (10th cir.) 1988, U.S. Ct. Appeals (4th cir.) 1990, U.S. Supreme Ct. 1990. Clk. to Justice Dubofsky Supreme Ct. Colo., Denver, 1984-85; assoc. Dickstein, Shapiro & Morin, Washington, 1985-87; counsel to water resources program Nat. Wildlife Fedn., Washington, 1987-91; counsel com. resources U.S. Ho. Reps., Washington, 1991-99; spl. asst. to solicitor U.S. Dept. of Interior, Washington, 1999-2000, assoc. solicitor for mineral resources, 2000-2001; dir. govt. affairs Am. Rivers, Washington, 2001—04, v.p. govt. affairs, 2004—, gen. counsel, 2005—. Wasserstein fellow in pub. interest law Harvard Law Sch., 2006. Editor-in-chief Harvard Environ. Law Rev., 1984. Trustee Amphibian Conservation Alliance, 1997-99; mem. Arlington Co. Environ. and Energy Conservation Commn., 2002—. Wasserstein fellow pub. interest law, Harvard Law Sch., 2006. Mem. Am. Water Resources Assn. (v.p. nat. capital sect. 1999-00), DC Bar (steering com. 1994-97, sect. environ., energy and natural resource law). Office: 1101 14th St NW Ste 1900 Washington DC 20005

BIRNBAUM, SHEILA L., lawyer, educator; b. 1940; BA, Hunter Coll., 1960, MA, 1962; LL.B., NYU Sch. Law, 1965. Bar: NY 1965. Legal asst. Superior Ct., NYC, 1965; assoc. Berman & Frost, NYC, 1965-70, ptnr., 1970-72; prof. Fordham U., NYC, 1972-78; prof. law NYU, NYC, 1978—84, assoc. dean, graduate divsn., 1982-84; ptnr. mass tort and insurance litigation Skadden, Arps, Slate, Meagher & Flom, LLP, NYC, 1984—. Chair NY State Adv. Com. on Civil Practice, 1981—86; adj. prof. law NYU Sch. Law, 1984—; mem. 2nd Cir. Com. on the Improvement of Civil Litigation, 1986—88, NY State Jud. Commn. on Minorities, 1988—91; exec. dir. Second Cir. Task Force for Racial, Ethnic and Gender Fairness, 1994—97; mem. jud. conf. adv. com. on rules and civil procedure US Supreme Ct., 1997—2004; chair, Commn. Fiduciary Appointments NY State Court System, 2000—; lectr. in field; mem. adv. com. to the Restatement of the Law of Product Liability and Complex Litigation Project. Author: (with Rheingold) Products Liability, Law, Practice Science, 1974; co-author: Practitioner's Guide to Litigating Insurance Coverage Actions; columnist NY Law Jour., Nat. Law Jour.; contbr. articles to profl. jours. First pres. and founding mem. Judges and Lawyers Breast Cancer Alert. Named one of 50 Most Powerful Women in Am. Bus., Fortune Mag., 100 Most Outstanding Members of the Legal Profession, Nat. Law Jour., 75 Most Influential Women in Bus., Crain's NY Bus.; named to, Hunter Coll. Hall of Fame; recipient John J. McCloy Meml. award, Fund for Modern Courts, 2003, Florence E. Allen award, NYU Sch. Law and NY Women's Bar Assn., Louis D. Brandeis award, Am. Jewish Congress, Law and Society award, NY Lawyers for the Public Interest, NYU Law Alumni award for Outstanding Achievement in the Legal Profession, George A. Katz Torch of Learning award, Milton S. Gould award for Outstanding Appellate Advocacy, Award for Achieving the Highest Standards of Professional Excellence, Touro Law Sch. Mem. NYC Bar Assn. (mem. exec. com. 1978—, jud. com. 1977), NY Women's Bar Assn. (pres. 1974-75), ABA (coun. of the sect. of torts and insurance practice 1982-86, spl. com. on the future of the legal profession 1996-97, House of Delegates 1997-98, chmn. product gen. liability, consumer land coms., Margaret Brent Women Lawyers of Achievement award), Am. Law Inst. (mem. coun. 1989-), Assn. of Bar of City of NY (exec. com. 1978—, 2nd century com. 1984-86, v.p. 1987), Phi Beta Kappa, Phi Alpha Theta, Alpha Chi Alpha. Office: Skadden Arps Slate Meagher & Flom LLP 4 Times Sq New York NY 10036 Office Phone: 212-735-2450. Office Fax: 917-777-2450. E-mail: sbirnbau@skadden.com.

BIRNBAUMER, DIANE MARGARET, emergency physician, educator; b. Torrance, Calif., 1958; MD, George Washington. Bd. cert. emergency medicine, bd. cert. internal medicine. Assoc. prof. clin. medicine Harbor-UCLA Med. Ctr., Torrance, Calif., assoc. residency dir. dept. emergency medicine; prof. dept. medicine UCLA Sch. Medicine. Cons. Aventis Pharmaceuticals. Assoc. editor: Jour. Watch Emergency Medicine. Fellow: Am. Coll. Emergency Physicians (award for outstanding contbn. in edn. 2003). Office: Harbor-UCLA Med Ctr Emergency Med MC 176847 Box 21 1000 W Carson Torrance CA 90509

BIRON, CHRISTINE ANNE, medical science educator, researcher; b. Woonsocket, R.I., Aug. 8, 1951; d. R. Bernard and Theresa Priscilla (Sauvageau) B. BS, U. Mass., 1973; PhD, U. N.C., 1980. Rsch. technician U. Mass., Amherst, 1973—75; grad. rschr. U. N.C., Chapel Hill, 1975—80; postdoctoral fellow Scripps Clinic and Rsch., La Jolla, Calif., 1980; fellow U. Mass. Med. Sch., Worcester, 1981—82, instr., 1983, asst. prof., 1984—87; vis. scientist Karolinska Inst., Stockholm, 1984; asst. prof. Sch. Medicine Brown U., Providence, 1988—90, assoc. prof., 1990—96, prof., 1996—, Esther Elizabeth Brintzenhoff prof., 1996—, chair Dept. Molecular Microbiology & Immunology, 1999—, dir. grad. program in pathobiology, 1995—99; sci. adv. bd. Trudeau Inst., 2004—. Mem. AIDS and related rsch. study sect. 3 NIH, 1991-93; mem. exptl. immunology study sect. NIH, 1993-97, immunology working group sci. rev.; co-organizer Keystone Symposium on Innate Immunity to Pathogens, 2005; bd. sci. counselors subcom. basic scis. Nat. Cancer Inst., 2005—. Assoc. editor: Jour. Immunology, 1990—94, 2000, bd. editors: Procs. of Soc. for Exptl. Biology and Medicine, 1993—99, sect. editor: Jour. Immunology, 1995—99; editor: Jour. Nat. Immunity, 1994—98, Jour. Leukocyte Biology, 1999—2000; mem. editl. bd.: Virology, 2001—03; contbr. articles, revs. to sci. jours.; mem. adv. bd. editors: Jour. Exptl. Medicine, 2002—, mem. editl. bd.: Immunity, 2005—. Leukemia Soc. Am. fellow, 1981, Spl. fellow, 1983, scholar, 1987; grantee NIH, 1985—; rsch. grantee MacArthur Found., 1991-96. Fellow AAAS (scholar 2002—); mem. Am. Assn. Immunologists (co-chmn. symposium 1990, 94, 95, 96, 98, 99), Am. Soc. Virology, Am. Assn. Immunology (block co-chair nat. meetings 1996-99, program com. 1998-2000), Soc. Natural Immunity (co-chair program for 2001 meeting), Sigma Xi. Office: Brown U PO Box G-B618 Providence RI 02912-0001

BIRR, CYNTHIA RUTH, special education educator; b. Elkhart, Ind., Mar. 17, 1969; d. William Robert and Jeanette Ruth Birr. BS in Elem. Edn., Manchester Coll., 1991; M in Spl. Edn., Ind. U., 1997. Substitute tchr. Concord Cmty. Sch., Elkhart, 1991—92, Goshen (Ind.) Cmty. Sch., 1991—92; daycare tchr. Kid's First, South Bend, Ind., 1993—94; spl. edn. mild disability tchr. Fairfield Cmty. Sch., Goshen, 1994—. Jr. high spl. edn. evaluator Fairfield Jr. Sr. H.S., Goshen, 2001—; bd. dirs. Fairfield jr. senoir h.s. Interdisciplinary Co-operative Edn., Goshen, 2001—. Mem. Ch. of the Bretheren, Elkhart, Ind., 1969—2005. Grantee, Fairfield Sch. Corp., 1996, 1998. Mem.: Ind. State Teachers Assn. (assoc.), NEA (assoc.). R-Consevative. Avocations: scuba diving, travel, gardening, antiques, white-water rafting. Office Phone: 574-831-2184. E-mail: cbirr@faifield.k12.in.us.

BIRREN, SUSAN J., medical educator; PhD, UCLA. Asst. prof. biology Brandeis U., Waltham, Mass. Contbr. articles to profl. jours. Mem.: Soc. for Neurosci. Achievements include research in embryonic precursor cells respond to local environmental cues during the development of the mammalian nervous system. Office: Brandeis Univ MS008 Dept Biology Neurosci PO Box 549110 Waltham MA 02454

BIRSTEIN, ANN, writer, educator; b. NYC, May 27, 1927; d. Bernard and Clara (Gordon) B.; m. Alfred Kazin, June 26, 1952 (div. 1982); 1 child, Cathrael. BA, Queens Coll., 1948. Lectr. The New Sch. Queens Coll., N.Y.C., 1953-54; writer-in-residence CCNY, 1960; lectr. The Writers Workshop, Iowa City, 1966, 72; lectr. Sch. Gen. Studies Columbia U., N.Y.C., 1985-87; dir., founder Writers on Writing Barnard Coll., N.Y.C., 1988—. Adj. prof. English Hofstra U., L.I., 1980, Barnard Coll., N.Y.C., 1981-93; film critic Vogue mag. Author: Star of Glass, 1950, The Troublemaker, 1955, The Sweet Birds of Gorham, 1966, Summer Situations, 1972, Dickie's List, 1973, American Children, 1980, The Rabbi on Forty-Seventh Street, 1982, The Last of the True Believers, 1988, What I Saw at the Fair, 2003; co-editor: The Works of Anne Frank; contbr. articles to numerous mags. Nat. Endowment of Arts grantee, 1983; Fulbright fellow, 1951-52. Mem. PEN (former mem. exec. bd., former chair admissions com.), Authors Guild (former mem. coun.), Phi Beta Kappa (hon.). Democrat. Jewish. Home: 1623 3rd Ave # 27jw New York NY 10128-3638 Personal E-mail: abirstein@aol.com.

BIRTMAN, AMY B., secondary school educator; b. Chgo., July 9, 1963; d. Seymour Jacobs and Dorri Goldgehn; m. Scott Daniel Birtman, Aug. 1, 1992; children: Joseph, Mathew, Callie. BS, U. Ill., Urbana, Ill., 1985; MS, N.E. Ill. U., Chgo., 1992; EdD, Loyola U., Chgo., 1999. Tchr. English Golf Jr. H.S., Morton Grove, Ill., 1985—88, Lake Forest (Ill.) H.S., 1988—. Office: Lake Forest High Sch 1285 N McKinley Rd Lake Forest IL 60045

BIRTWISTLE, APRIL JOY, layout artist; b. Phila., Apr. 3, 1973; d. David Norman and Mildred (Ivins) B. BS, Messiah Coll., 1995; postgrad., Villanova U. Spotter, trainer Milford Fitness Ctr., Del., 1990-91; asst. night mgr. Dairy Queen, Milford, 1988-91; customer svc. rep. JC Penney Nat. Bank, Harrington, Del., 1990-91; cashier Comp USA, Phila., 1992; teller Fidelity Fed. Savs. & Loan, Phila., 1992-94; asst. mgr. Gap, Inc., Willow Grove, Pa., 1995-98; layout artist Noble Advt., Doylestown, Pa., 1998—2004; creative planner Focus on the Family, Colo. Springs, Colo., 2004—. Publs. mgr. "The Swinging Bridge", Messiah Coll., Grantham, 1993-94, head soccer mgr., 1991-95. Vol. Mennonite Disaster Svc., Hurricane Andrew Relief, Hampstead, Fla., 1992, Girl's Club Am., Harrisburg, 1993, Spl. Olympics, Harrisburg, 1993-95, Phila. Cares, 1995. 98, Harvest Crusade, 1998; crisis counselor Choice One Pregnancy and Sexual Health Ctr.; discussion ldr. Bible Study fellowship. Mem. Am. Mktg. Assn. Avocations: reading, travel, crafts, sports. Home: 6984 Ash Creek Hts Apt 203 Colorado Springs CO 80922-2477 Office: Focus on the Family 8675 Explorer Dr Colorado Springs CO 80920

BIRTWISTLE, MONICA LYNN, secondary school educator; b. Houston, June 30, 1973; d. James Sanderson and Linda Jean Birtwistle. BA in History, U. Colo., Boulder, 1995; MEd, Houston Bapt. U., 2001. Prodn. asst. J. Walter Thompson Specialized Comm., Houston, 1997—99; tchr. Stephen F. Austin H.S., Sugar Land, TX, Tex., 2000—. World geography project facilitator Ft. Bend Ind. Sch. Dist., Sugar Land, 2002—. Fellow, Houston World Affairs Coun., 2005; grantee, Fund For Tchrs., 2005. Mem.: Tex. Coun. on Social Studies. Independent. Avocations: travel, movies, music. Office Phone: 281-634-2000. Business E-Mail: monica.birtwistle@fortbend.k12.tx.us.

BISCHEL, MARGARET DEMERITT, physician, consultant; b. Moorhead, Minn., Nov. 8, 1933; d. Connie Magnus Nystrom and Harriett Grace (Petersen) Zorner; m. Raymon DeMeritt, 1953 (div. 1958); 1 child, Gregory Raymon; m. John Bischel, 1961 (div. 1964); m. Kenneth Dean Serkes, June 7, 1974. BS, U. Oreg., Eugene, 1962; MD, U. Oreg., Portland, 1965. Diplomate Am. Bd. Internal Medicine, Nat. Bd. Med. Examiners. Resident, straight med. intern Los Angeles County/U. So. Calif. Med. Ctr., 1965-68, NIH fellow nephrology, 1968-70, asst. prof. renal medicine, 1970-74; asst. prof., instr. medicine U. So. Calif., 1968-74; instr. nephrology East L.A. City Coll., 1971-74; dir. med. edn. Luth. Gen. Hosp., Park Ridge, Ill., 1974-78, dir. nephrology sect., 1977-80, pres. med. staff, 1974-78; founding mem., med. dir., dir. med. svcs. Luth. Health Plan, Park Ridge, 1983-87; clin. assoc. prof. medicine Abraham Lincoln Sch. Medicine U. Ill., 1975-80; sr. cons. Parkside Assocs., Inc., Park Ridge, 1986-88; pvt. practice Chgo., 1974-88; physician Buenaventura Med. Clinic, Ventura, Calif., 1989-94, med. dir., 1992-94; prin. Apollo Managed Care Cons., Santa Barbara, Calif., 1988—. Trustee Luth. Health Care System, Park Ridge, 1986-90, Unified Med. Group Assn., Seal Beach, Calif., 1993-94; hon. lifetime staff mem. Luth. Gen. Hosp., Park Ridge; mem. formulary com. HealthNet, 1992-94, med. adv. com. TakeCare, 1993-94, quality assurance com. PacifiCare, 1993-94; mem. doctor's adv. network AMA, 1994-96; JCAHO advisor for behavioral health care providers. Mem. editl. adv. bd. Capitation Mgmt. Report; author 35 texts including Managing Behavioral Healthcare, 2d edit., 2006, The Credentialing and Privileges Manual, 2d edit., 2005, Medical Review Criteria Guidelines for Managed Care, 5th edit., 2006; editor: Med. Mgmt. Manual, Managed Care Bull.; contbr. chpts. to books and articles to profl. jours. Fellow: ACP (Calif. Gov.'s advisor 1993—95); mem.: Am. Coll. Physician Execs. Avocations: real estate, gardening. Office: Apollo Managed Care Cons 860 Ladera Ln Santa Barbara CA 93108-1626 Office Phone: 805-969-2606. Personal E-mail: mbischel@cox.net. Business E-Mail: mbischel@apollomanagedcare.com.

BISCHOFF, SUSAN ANN, newspaper editor; b. Indpls., July 31, 1951; d. Thomas Anthony and Betty Jean (Coons) Bischoff; m. Jim B. Barlow, June 20, 1975; 1 child, Samantha Lynn Barlow Martinez. BA, Ind. U., 1973. Rschr., reporter Congl. Quar., Washington, 1973-74; city desk reporter Houston Chronicle, 1974-75, bus. reporter, 1975-79, asst. bus. editor, 1979-84, bus. editor, 1984-86, asst. mng. editor, 1986-2000, dep. mng. editor, 2000—03, assoc. editor, 2003—. Houston corr. Kiplinger, Tex. Letter, Washington, 1980-85; juror Pulitzer Prizes in Journalism, 2004, 05. Mem. class policy Leadership Houston, 1992—94; mem. exec. com. Gulf Coast affiliate United Way, 1994—2002; pres. Friends of Houston Girl Scouts, 2002—; bd. dirs. Houston Chronicle Employees Fed. Credit Union, 1980—87, San Jacinto Coun. Girl Scouts US, 1997—2003, Child Adv., 1999—2005, US Olympic Festival VII, Houston, 1985—86, Gulf Coast Mar. of Dimes Birth Defects Found., 1989—2001, YES Coll. Prep. Sch., 1999—2002, AIDS Found., Houston, 2002—; founding bd. dir. Greater Houston Women's Found.; mem. bd. visitors Anderson Cancer Ctr. U. Tex. Named Outstanding Woman in Houston Journalism, YWCA, 1989, Fabulous Femme, Greater Houston Women's Found., 1994, Woman of Distinction, Crohn's & Colitis Found., 1996; recipient Outstanding Vol. Achievement award, Gulf Coast United Way, 1995, Outstanding Media award, Nat. Soc. Fund Raising Execs., 1997, Nat. Thanks award, San Jacinto Girl Scouts, 2001, Mayborn award, Cmty. Leadership Tex. Daily Newspaper Assn., 2001, honoree, Jewish Cmty. Ctr. of Houston Children's Scholarship Ball, 2002, Strong, Smart and Bold award, Houston Girls, Inc., 2003. Mem.: Soc. News Design (exec. com.), Am. Assn. Sunday and Feature Editors (named to Features Hall of Fame 2003), Am. Soc. Newspaper Editors (bd. dirs.). Home: 2929 Buffalo Speedway # 112 Houston TX 77098 Office: Houston Chronicle 801 Texas Ave Houston TX 77002-2996 Business E-Mail: susan.bischoff@chron.com.

BISCHOFF, THERESA ANN, not-for-profit association executive; b. Rockville Ctr., NY, Nov. 16, 1953; d. Robert and Colette (Burke) Peters. BS in Acctg. cum laude, U. Conn., 1975; MBA, NYU, 1991. Cert. CPA, 1977. Sr. dir. acctg. svcs. NYU Med. Ctr., NYC, 1984-87, v.p. fin., 1987-93, dep. provost, exec. v.p., 1993—98, pres., 1998—2003; clin. prof. health care mgmt. NYU Sch. Medicine, NYC, 1993—2003; CEO ARC in Greater NY, NYC, 2004—. Bd. dirs. Combined Coord. Coun., 1984-03, chair, 1998-02; mem. adv. com. United Hosp. Fund, 1994-03; mem. adminstrv. bd. Coun. Tchg. Hosp., 1995-03. Mem. AAMC (chair 2002-03), Greater NY Hosp. Assn. (mem. bd. dirs. 1994-03, mem. health care exec. forum 1987—, sec. 1990-92), Assn. Am. Recital Colls., Healthcare Assn. NY State (trustee 1994-02), Soc. Health Svc. Adminstrs., Mut. Am. (trustee 2001-), Dov Pharm. (trustee 2003-), U. Conn. Found. Bd. Office: ARC 520 W 49th St New York NY 10019

BISCOE, BELINDA P., academic administrator, psychologist; d. Walter Marks and Luetta Marks-Perry; children: Brandi, Ashley. BA in Sociology cum laude, Fisk U., 1971, MA in Sociology, 1973; PhD in Psychology, U. Okla., 1982. Cert. drug and alcohol dir. Okla. Drug and Alcohol Profl. Counselors Assn., prevention specialist Okla. Drug and Alcohol Profl. Counselors Assn. Evaluator, adminstr., instr. McHarry Med. Coll., Nashville, 1983—91; pres., founder Higher Horizons, Inc., Oklahoma City, 1991—; dir. Region VII Comprehensive Ctr. U. Okla., Coll. Continuing Edn., Norman, 1997—, dir. rsch. and evaluation, 2001—, asst. v.p., 2001—. Co-founder, cons. Eagle Ridge Inst., Oklahoma City, 1989; cons., trainer, rschr. U.S. Dept. Ctr. for Substance Abuse Treatment, Washington, 1996—; adj. prof. depts. advanced programs and human rels. U. Okla., 1999—; evaluation cons. Child Devel., Inc., Russellville, Ark., 1999—2001. Author/developer: psychol. assessment tool Adult Resiliency Attitudes Scale, 1994, Children's and Adolescent's Resiliency Tool, 1994; author: (tng. manual) Funding: To Be or Not To Be, 1995. Founding bd. mem. Regional Civic League, Oklahoma City, 1995—97; bd. dirs. YWCA, Oklahoma City, 1980—85. Named Woman of Yr. in Edn., Redland Chpt. of the Girl Scouts, 1992—93, Outstanding Woman of Yr., Am. Fedn. Colored Women; recipient Leadership award in edn., Women in Comm., 1995, E. Neal Stone Superior Performance award, Adminstrv. Staff Coun.-U. Okla., 2004, Making a Difference in Okla. award, Journal Record Newspaper, 2005, Continuing Edn. Profl. award, Regional U. Continuing Edn. Assn., 2006, Continuing Edn. award, Nat. U., 2006; Join Together fellow, Nat. Substance ABuse Coalition. Mem.: APA, Oklahoma County Mental Health Assn. (bd. dirs. 1984—86, 2002), U. Continuing Edn. Assn., Am. Evaluation Assn., Links (Oklahoma City chpt.). Democrat. Methodist. Avocations: hydroponic gardening, reading, crocheting, bicycling, water-skiing, snow skiing. Office: Univ Okla 555 Constitution Norman OK 73072 Office Phone: 405-325-1711. Business E-Mail: BpBiscoe@ou.edu.

BISCONTI, ANN STOUFFER, public opinion research company executive; b. Chgo., Nov. 22, 1940; d. Samuel Andrew Stouffer and Ruth Rachel McBurney; m. Raffaele Ludovico Bisconti (dec. Oct. 19, 1999); children: Alessandra Ilus Wilkes, Giulia Rachel; m. Charles William Dyke, Oct. 13, 2002. Student, Harvard U., 1958—60; BA with honors, McGill U., 1962; PhD, The Union Inst., Cin., 1978. Assoc. study dir. Nat. Commn. on Allied Health Edn., Washington, 1977—79; dir. Washington office Higher Edn. Rsch. Inst., 1979—80; ptnr. Human Resources Policy Corp., Washington, 1980; dir. Nat. Ctr. for Allied Health Leadership, Washington, 1981—83; v.p. rsch. Nuc. Energy Inst., Washington, 1983—96; pres. Bisconti Rsch., Inc., Washington, 1996—. Mem. adv. com., risk comm. program EPA, Washington, 1988; advisor tech. cooperation program in Malaysia IAEA, Vienna, 1990; mem. adv. com., risk comm. Orgn. for Econ. Cooperation and Devel., Paris, 1991. Author: College and Other Stepping Stones, 1980; co-author: Higher Education and the Disadvantaged Student, 1972, The Power of Protest, 1975, College as a Training Ground for Jobs, 1977. Pres. Congl. Award Coun., 8th Congl. Dist., Md., 1990—93; advisor long-range planning com. Town of Somerset, Chevy Chase, Md., 2002; career advisor Harvard U., Cambridge, 1996; rsch. advisor NASA Alumni League, Washington, 1998. Recipient Disting. Svc. Award, Am. Soc. Allied Health Professions (now Assn. Schs. Allied Health Profls.), 1983. Mem.: World Assn. Pub. Opinion Rsch., Am. Nuc. Soc. (bd. dirs. 1993—96, 2004—, Best Paper award 1989, Outstanding Session award 1990, 1992), Am. Assn. Pub. Opinion Rsch. Avocations: geography/travel, languages, gardening.

BISEL, MARSHA MCCUNE, elementary school educator; b. Winchester, Ind., Jan. 27, 1950; d. Floyd Elder and Vista Coral (Rust) McCune; m. Ronald G. Bisel, June 20, 1971; children: Kyle, Brooke, Kam, Robin. BS in Edn. summa cum laude, Taylor U., 1972; MA in Edn., Ball State U., Muncie, Ind., 1975. Life lic. K-8 tchr., Ind. Tchr. Ridgeville (Ind.) Elem. Sch., 1972; grade level coord. Deerfield Elem. Sch., Ridgeville. Mem. civic theatre bd. Summer Performance Co., Portland, Ind., 1997-98; bd. dirs. Habitat for Humanity, 1998; with Jay County Girls Little League, Jay County Soccer, Patriot Booster Club, Ch. choir, organist, soloist. Avocations: acting, singing. Home: 6528 S Us Highway 27 Portland IN 47371-8829

BISER, ELIZABETH GRANT, counselor, director; b. Oakland, Md., Feb. 22, 1961; d. Bowie Linn and Anne Naylor Grant. MS, Loyola Coll., Balt., 1997. Dir. residential treatment Rite Passage, Yerington, Nev., 2000—02; dir. juvenile justice Garrett Coll., McHenry, Md., 2002—. Counselor, facilitator Integrity Counseling/Mettle Workers, Oakland, Md., 1997—2000. Mem. Civic Club Oakland, Md., 1997—2006. Mem.: Md. Juvenile Justice Coalition. Office: Garrett Coll 687 Mosser Rd McHenry MD 21550 Office Phone: 301-387-3142. Office Fax: 301-387-3055. Personal E-mail: ebiser@garrettcollege.edu.

BISHOP, AMY, biology professor; b. Feb. 4, 1968; m. James Edward Anderson, Aug. 20, 1990; children: Lily Bishop Anderson, Thea Bishop Anderson, Phaedra Bishop Anderson, Seth Bishop Anderson. PhD in Genetics, Harvard U., Boston, 1993. Cardiovasc. fellow divsn. cardiovasc. rsch. Beth Israel Hosp., Boston, 1994—96; instr. dept. cancer cell biology Harvard Sch. Pub. Health, Boston, 1996—2001; instr. medicine dept. medicine Harvard Med. Sch., Boston, 2001—03; asst. prof. biology dept. biol. scis. U. Ala., Huntsville, 2003—. Cons. Cherokee Labsystems, Huntsville, 2003—; mem. Radiation Effect Team Working Group Marshall Space Flight Ctr., NASA, Huntsville, 2003—. Contbr. articles to profl. jours. Active Move On.org, Huntsville, 2005—06. Recipient Young Faculty award, U. Ala., 2003—06; Internal Rsch. and Design grantee, NASA, 2004—06, Travel fellow, Louis Stokes Alliance for Minority Participation, 2003—06. Mem.: AAAS, Internat. Soc. for Neuroscience, Soc. for Neuroscience. Achievements include discovery of phenomenon of Induced Adaptive Resistance which can be used to mitigate the effects of spinal injury, Amyotropic Lateral Sclerosis (ALS)and Multiple Sclerosis (MS); patents pending for Cell Drive-portable Incubator; Neuristor-neural electronics interface to utilize the flexibility of the neural circuit. Office: Univ Alabama Huntsville Dept Biology Wilson Hall Huntsville AL 35899 Office Phone: 1-256-824-6461. Office Fax: 1-256-824-6305. Business E-Mail: bishopa@uah.edu.

BISHOP, C. DIANE, state agency administrator, educator; b. Elmhurst, Ill., Nov. 23, 1943; d. Louis William and Constance Oleta (Mears) B. BS in Maths., U. Ariz., 1965, MS in Maths., MEd in Secondary Edn., 1972. Lic. secondary educator. Tchr. math. Tucson Unified Sch. Dist., 1966-86, mem. curriculum council, 1985-86, mem. maths. curriculum task teams, 1983-86; state supt. of pub. instrn. State of Ariz., 1987-95, gov.'s policy advisor for edn., 1995-97, dir. gov.'s office workforce devel. policy, 1996-2000; asst. dep. dir. Ariz. Dept. Commerce, 1997-2000; exec. dir. Gov.'s Strategic Partnership for Econ. Devel., 1997—2002; pres. The Vandegrift Inst., 2000—; exec. dir. Maricopa Health Found., 2002—. Mem. assoc. faculty Pima C.C., Tucson, 1974-84; adj. lectr. U. Ariz., 1983, 85; mem. math. scis. edn. bd. NRC, 1987-90, mem. new standards project governing bd., 1991; dir. adv. bd. sci. and engring. ednl. panel, NSF; mem. adv. bd. for arts edn. Nat. Endowment for Arts. Active Ariz. State Bd. Edn., 1984-95, chmn. quality edn. commn., 1986-87, chmn. tchr. crt. subcom., 1984-95, mem. outcomes based edn. adv. com., 1986-87, liaison bd. dirs. essential skills subcom., 1985-87, gifted edn. com. liaison, 1985-87; mem. Ariz. State Bd. Regents, 1987-95, com. on preparing for U. Ariz., 1983, HS task force, 1984-85, bd. dirs. Ariz. State Community Coll., 1987-95, Ariz. Joint Legis. Com. on Revenues and Expenditures, 1989, Ariz. Joint Legis. Com. on Goals for Ednl. Excellence, 1987-89, Gov.'s Task Force on Ednl. Reform, 1991, Ariz. Bd. Regents Commn. on Higher Edn., 1992; mem. governing bd. Phoenix Union HS Dist. 2005—; mem. bd. dirs. Great Heart Prep. Acad., 2005-. Woodrow Wilson fellow Princeton U., summer 1984; recipient Presdl. Award for Excellence in Teaching of Maths., 1983, Ariz. Citation of Merit, 1984, Maths. Teaching award Nat. Sci. Research Soc., 1984, Distinction in Edn. award Flinn Found., 1986; named Maths. Tchr. of Yr. Ariz. Council of Engring. and Sci. Assns., 1984, named One of Top Ten Most Influential Persons in Ariz. in Field of Tech., 1998. Mem. AAUW, NEA, Nat. Coun. Tchrs. Math., Coun. Chief State Sch. Officers, Women Execs. in State Govt. (bd. dirs. 1993), Ariz. Assn. Tchrs. Math., Women Maths. Edn., Math. Assn. Am., Ednl. Commn. of the States (steering com.), Nat. Endowment Arts (adv. bd. for arts edn.), Nat. Forum Excellence Edn., Nat. Honors Workshop, Ariz. Bioindustry Assn. (bd. dirs. 1997—, sec. 2000—), Phi Delta Kappa. Republican.

BISHOP, CAROL, oil industry executive; b. Arlington, Mass., June 5, 1956; d. Francis Joseph and Mary Ruth (Robinson) Bishop; m. Lawrence A. Balboni, May 5, 1979 (div. 1982); m. Gary L. Renick, Jan. 31, 1986 (div. 1999). Grad., Harvard U., 1991. Mgr. Larson Ins., Arlington, Mass., 1979-85, v.p., 1987-88; mgr. Merrill Lynch Realty Ins. Svcs., Boca Raton, Fla., 1985-87; pres. Essex Ins. Planners, Haverhill, Mass., 1988-98; bus. devel. strategic planner Micro Power Electronics Inc., Hillsboro, Oreg., 1998—2001, Air Brit. Petroleum, Washington, 2001—. V.p. United Internat. Ins. Agy., Inc., Braintree, Mass., 1992-94. Vol. Mus. Sci., Boston, 1988, Mus. Sci., 1988—; vol.tutor Mass. Campaign for Literacy, 1988—. Democrat. Avocations: reading, travel, equestrian events. Home: 21837 Kelsey Sq Ashburn VA 20147 Office Phone: 703-572-8419. E-mail: carol.bishop@bp.com.

BISHOP, CAROLE C., elementary school educator; b. LA, Feb. 3, 1933; d. Beverley Marshall and Marjorie (Fitch) Caister; m. David Burleson Bishop, June 16, 1956; 1 chld, Dale Brian. BS, U. So. Calif., 1955; MS, Azusa Pacific Coll., 1973. Cert. marriage and family therapist. Tchr. 3d grade Covina Unified Sch. Dist., Calif., 1955-57; tchr. 4th grade La Can. Unified Sch. Dist., La Can.-Flintridge, Calif., 1957-58, substitute tchr., 1960-66, 2000, 01, tchr. 2d and 3d grades, 1966-67, tchr. 4th grade, 1967-71, tchr. 5th and 6th grades, 1971-79, tchr. 5th grade, 1979-2000. Author: Bishop Speller, 1971. Recipient Founders Day award La Canada-Flintridge PTA, 1973, 93; honored by placement of brick at the Medal of Honor Grove, Valley Forge by Freedoms Found. Mem. Nat. Sci. Tchr. Assn., La Canada Tchr. Assn. (sec., Tchr. of Yr. 1987), Am. Assn. Marriage and Family Therapists, Am. Assn. Physics Tchr., Delta Kappa Gamma (corr. sec.). Avocations: hiking, travel, reading, cooking. Home: South Pasadena CA

BISHOP, CHRISTY B., lawyer; b. Akron, Ohio, Mar. 10, 1960; m. Dennis R. Thompson; 1 stepchild, Jeffrey Thompson. BA in Rhetoric, U. Akron, Ohio, 1985, MA in Rhetoric, 1991, JD cum laude, 2002. Journalist Village Views, Akron, 1982—85; mng. editor Great Lakes Sailor Mag., Akron, 1986—89; prof. U. Akron, 1991—94; law clk. Thompson Law Office, Akron, 1992—2002; ptnr. Thompson & Bishop, Akron, 2002—. Recipient Westlaw Excellence award, West Pub., 1998, Anderson Book award, Anderson Pub., 2001, Hon. Goldberg prize, U. Akron, 2002. Mem.: Nat. Employment Lawyers Assn. (mem. comms. com. 2003—), Ohio Employment Lawyers Assn. (mem. amicus brief com. 2002—, mem. judiciary com. 2004—, chmn. Akron chpt. 2002—). Democrat. Episc. Avocations: writing, music, boating, hiking. Office: Thompson & Bishop 2719 Manchester Rd Akron OH 44319

BISHOP, CLAIRE DEARMENT, small business owner, retired librarian; b. Youngstown, Ohio, Oct. 12, 1937; d. Eugene Howard and Ruth (Bright) DeArment; m. Carl R. Meinstereifel, 1956 (div. 1964; children: Paul, Dawn; m. Olin Jerry Dewberry, Jr., 1974 (div. 1979); m. J. Bruce Bishop, May 6, 1992 (dec. Oct. 2005). BS, Clarion State U., 1967; MLS, Ga. State U., 1977. Cert. libr. media specialist, Ga. Libr. Henry County, Stockbridge, Ga., 1967-69; head libr. Russell H.S., East Point, Ga., 1969-84; engring. libr. Rockwell Internat., Duluth, Ga., 1984-88; rep. Govt. Industry Data Exch. Program, Corona, Calif., 1984-88; libr. Raytheon Co., 1990, Missile Sys. Divsn., Bristol, Tenn., 1988-90; owner, mgr. Claire's Collectibles, rubber stamp store, St. Augustine, Fla. Author newsletter Grin and Stamp It. Sec. San Marco Avenue Mchts. Assn. Mem. St. Augustine IBM Users Group (sec.), Six-Ninety-Six Investment Club (fin. officer), Mensa. Democrat. Avocations: computers, writing, information broker. Home: 78A San Marco Ave Saint Augustine FL 32084-3258 Office Phone: 904-825-1122.

BISHOP, DELORES ANN, artist, educator; b. Balt., May 27, 1946; d. Edward James Boyle, Sr. and Norma Delores Boyle; m. John James Bishop, Jr.; children: Denise Anderson, Christine. Grad. h.s., Balt. Elite, one stroke cert. instr., cert. William Alexander instr., Jenkins, cert. instr. art. Fgn. lang. lab. asst. Baltimore County Md. Pub. Schs., Balt., 1964—71; asst. mgr. Ben Franklin Crafts, Cockeysville, Md., 1982—99; freelance decorative artist Balt., 1999—2001. Program mgr. Premises Providers, Inc (Arundel Mills Mall), Hanover, Md., 2000. Painted sculpture, The Shopper, 2000, Bushel of Crabs, 2000, Bass, 2000. Holiday vol. Cowenton Vol. Fire Dept. Sta. 200, Balt., 2000—01; Vol., asst. leader Girl Scouts Am., Balt., 1960—80. Mem.: Md. Art League, Inc., Balt. (Md.) Watercolor Soc., Decorative Painters Soc. Personal E-mail: dabishop@dabitup.com.

BISHOP, HOLLY ANN, elementary school educator; d. William Daniel and Linda Laraine Salzbrener; m. Colby Scott Bishop, May 21, 1999; children: Jillian Jo, Jespyn James Scott. BAS, Metro State Coll., Denver, 1994; EdnM, U. Phoenix, Westminster, Colo., 1996. Cert. secondary edn. Colo. Dept. Edn., 1994. Tchr. Rocky Top Mid. Sch., Thornton, Colo., 1995—. Actor: (plays) Arsenic & Old Lace, Noises Off. Independent. Office: Five Star Schs Rocky Top Mid Sch 14150 York St Thornton CO 80602 Office Phone: 720-972-2260.

BISHOP, JEANNE EMMONS, director, science educator, researcher; d. Richard Harrison and Phyllis Marie (Good) Emmons; m. Allan Roy Bishop, June 5, 1965; 1 child, Eric Paul. BS in Edn., Kent State U., Ohio, 1963; MS in Edn., U. Pitts., Pa., 1968; PhD, U. Akron, Ohio, 1981. Cert. secondary edn. Ohio. Dir. planetarium McKinley Mus., Canton, Ohio, 1963—65, Penn Hills Sch. Dist., Pitts., 1965—68; dir. planetarium, tchr. sci. Westlake Schs., Ohio, 1969—2006; ret., 2006. Guest spkr. Nat. Sci. Tchrs. Assn., Great Lakes Planetarium Assn., Internat. Planetarium Soc. Co-author: (textbook) General Science, 1982; author: numerous articles in Sci. Tchr. Planetarium, Sky & Telescope, others, 1974—. Finalist Presdl. award in Math. and Sci. Tchg., Ohio; recipient IPS Device award, Internat. Planetarium Soc., 1990, Thomas J. Brennan award for Excellence in H.S. Tchg., Astron. Soc., 1988, Galileo Svc. award, Great Lakes Planetarium Assn., 2004. Mem.: Cleve. Astron. Soc. (pres. 1992—96, sec. 1998—), Nat. Assn. Geology Tchrs., Astron. Soc. Pacific (mem. exec. bd.), Great Lakes Planetarium Assn. (pres. 1998—2000), Internat. Planetarium Soc. (exec. sec. 1975—79, pres.-elect, pres. 1982—84). Office: Westlake Schs Planetarium 24525 Hilliard Rd Westlake OH 44145

BISHOP, KATHLEEN ANN, customer service, education and communication consultant, professional speaker; b. Pueblo, Colo., Dec. 10, 1947; d. Jerome H. and I. Louise (Bird) B. AA, Brookdale Community Coll., N.J., 1971; BA in English, Stockton State Coll., 1974; MA, Century U., Calif., 1982. Accredited records technician. Supr. med. records dept. Fla. Med. Ctr., Ft. Lauderdale, 1980; med. records adminstr. Henderson Mental Health Ctr., Ft. Lauderdale, 1980-81; instr. Sheridan Vo-Tech Ctr., Hollywood, Fla., 1981-84; edn. cons. Shared Med. Systems, Hollywood, 1984-85; tng. cons. K.A. Bishop & Assocs., Fla., 1984—. Author: (personal growth and devel. workbook) Getting Out of Your Own Way: A Guide to Power and Success, 1984; co-author: (tng. manual) Learning the Ropes, 1995; contbr. articles to profl. jours.; founder World Fedn. Practical Christianity, 1998, past pres., 1998, founder Fillmore Sem., 2001, pres., 2001; Mem. Nat. Speakers Assn., Fla. Speakers Assn. (sec. 1984-85, pres. 1985-86), Am. Soc. for Tng. and Devel. Club: Toastmasters (treas. 1984-85). Avocations: reading, movies. Home and Office: 388 Piedmont I Delray Beach FL 33484

BISHOP, MILDRED ANN, literature and language educator; b. Brooksville, Fla., Sept. 14, 1947; d. Wilbur David and Mildred Hilliard Good; m. Richard Paul Bishop, Nov. 22, 1979; children: Kelly Charlotte, Mildred. B Edn., U. South Fla., Tampa, 1970. Tchr. Pasco County Sch. Bd., Land O'Lakes, Fla., 1970—. Home: 4224 Cortez Blvd Weeki Wachee FL 34607 Office: Hudson High School 14410 Cobra Way Hudson FL 34669 Personal E-mail: mannbishop@aol.com. E-mail: mbishop@pasco.k12.fl.us.

BISHOP, PAMELA JUNE, elementary school educator; d. Hubert General and Lorene Stevenson; m. Robert Rickey Bishop, Apr. 14, 1973; children: Robert Eric, Christopher William. Grad. in Early Childhood Edn., Brenau U., 1987. Cert. early childhood edn., adult edn. tchr. Ga., 1987. Early Intervention Program tchr. Murray Schs., Chatsworth, Ga., 2001—03; tchr. elem. sci. lab. Murray County Schs., Chatsworth, Ga., 2003—. Recipient Sci. Tchr. of Yr. award, North Ga. Mountains Youth Sci. Ctr., 2003-04. Office: Coker Elem Sch 1733 Leonard Bridge Rd Chatsworth GA 30070 Office Phone: 706-695-0888.

BISHOP, RUTH ANN, coloratura soprano, voice educator; b. Homewood, Ill., Feb. 21, 1942; d. George Bernard and Grace Mildred (Hoke) Riddle; m. John Allen Reinhardt, June 9, 1962 (div. 1975); children: Laura, Jonathon; m. Merrill Edward Bishop, Aug. 16, 1975; stepchildren: Mark, Lynn. BS in Music Edn., U. Ill., 1962; M of Music in Voice, Cath. U. Am., 1972; postgrad., U. Md., 1975. Music tchr. Prince Georges County (Md.) Schs., 1963-71, Yamaha Music Co., College Park, Md., 1971-73; voice tchr. Prince Georges Community Coll., Largo, Md., 1972-75, U. Md., College Park, 1975; profl. lectr. voice Chgo. Mus. Coll. Roosevelt U., 1977-82; tchr. voice McHenry County Coll., Crystal Lake, Ill., 1978-97; instr. voice Elgin (Ill.) C.C., 1981-97; pvt. voice tchr. Crystal Lake, 1975-97, Charlottesville, Va., 1997—; tchr. chorus, music and drama Burley Mid. Sch., Charlottesville, Va., 1997; asst. prof. music Piedmont Va. C.C., 1998—. Dir. music Epworth United Meth. Ch., Elgin, 1984-86, Cherub choir 1st Congl. Ch., Crystal Lake, 1986-88; mem. Camerata Singers, Lake Forest, 1988, Arts Chorale of Elgin Choral Union; performer, vocal dir. Woodstock (Ill.) Mus. Theatre Co., 1983-97; soprano soloist Internat. Band Festival, Besana Brianza, Italy, 1993; pvt. voice tchr., Charlottesville, Va., 1997—. Soprano soloist, Oratorio- The Psalms of David, 1986, opera, The Light of the Eye, 1985-86, Children's Day at the Opera, Washington, 1972, U.S. Navy Band, The White House, 1969; soloist with Crystal Lake Cmty. Choir and Band, 1987-97, 1st Congl. Ch., 1975-97, also others; performer Heritage Repertory Theatre, Charlottesville, Va., 1998, 99. Bd. dirs. Opera Soc. Charlottesville, 1998-2000. Ill. State scholar, 1959. Mem. Nat. Assn. Tchrs. Singing (rep. sec. 1984-86, bd. mem. Chgo. chpt. 1995-97), Music Tchrs. Nat. Assn., Sigma Alpha Iota, Pi Kappa Lambda, Kappa Delta. Presbyterian. Avocations: travel, camping, hiking, bicycling, wildlife. Home: 1363 Wimbledon Way Charlottesville VA 22901-0635 Personal E-mail: momrabishop@yahoo.com.

BISHOP, RUTH FRANCES, microbiologist, research scientist, educator; b. Melbourne, Victoria, Australia, May 12, 1933; d. Percival Charles William and Una Frances Armitage (Wilson) Langford; m. Geoffrey James Bishop, Dec. 8, 1956; children: Thomas Geoffrey, Anne Frances, Michael William. BSc, U. Melbourne, 1954, MSc, 1958, PhD, 1961, DSc, 1978. Rsch. fellow U. Liverpool, Eng., 1962-65, Royal Children's Hosp. Rsch. Found., Melbourne, 1968-74, CEO, 1990-91; rsch. fellow Nat. Health and Med. Rsch. Coun., Australlia, 1975-79, prin. rsch. fellow, 1980-91, sr. prin. rsch. fellow Australia, 1992-98, Murdoch Childrens Rsch. Inst., Melbourne, 1999—; profl. assoc. U. Melbourne, 1990-94, prof. Parkville, Victoria, Australia, 1995—. Dir. Australian Med. Rsch. and Devel. Co., Melbourne, 1991-92; mem. regional grants interview com. Nat. Health and Med. Rsch. Coun., Australia, 1991-98; cons. WHO, Geneva, 1983—. Editorial bd. Revs. Infectious Diseases, 1989-99; contbr. articles to profl. jours., chpts. to books. Chmn. assocs. spl. activities 8th Asian Conf. ObGyn, Melbourne, 1979-81. Decorated officer Order of Australia. Fellow Australian Soc. Microbiology; mem. Am. Soc. Microbiology, Am. Soc. Virology, Pediat. Rsch. Soc. Australia (pres. 1972), Australian Soc. Med. Rsch., Australian Soc. Infectious Diseases, Nat. Assn. Rsch. Fellows Nat. Health and Med. Rsch. Coun. (sec. 1991-93). Avocations: reading, opera, tennis, gardening. Office: Royal Childrens Hosp Flemington Rd Dept Gastroenterology Melbourne VIC 3052 Australia Business E-Mail: r.bishop@mcri.edu.au.

BISHOP, STEPHANIE ELIZABETH, theater educator; b. Petersburg, Va., July 15, 1973; d. Judy Jones Bosserman; m. Chris Lee Waugaman, Aug. 13, 2004. BA in Theatre Arts and English, Va. Tech, Blacksburg, 1995, MEd in Curriculum and Instrn., 1996; cert. in ednl. leadership, Va. Commonwealth U., Richmond, 2006. Cert. secondary tchg. Va. Dept. Edn., 1996. Theatre arts tchr., dir. Prince George H.S., Va., 1996—, fine arts dept. chairperson, 1999—, lead tchr., 2000—. Dir.: (plays) Atomic Shakespeare (Va. Theatre Assn. Champions, 2002), Riverstory (Va. H.S. League State Champions, 2004), Bionik Row (Va. H.S. League State Champions, 2006). Recipient Educator award, Milken Family Found., 2001. Mem.: Va. Milken Educator Network, Va. Theatre Assn. (assoc.). Home: 1706 Westover Ave Petersburg VA 23805 Office: Prince George High Sch 7801 Laurel Spring Rd Prince George VA 23875 Office Phone: 804-733-2720. Home Fax: 804-733-4557; Office Fax: 804-861-4530.

BISHOP, SUE MARQUIS (INA SUE MARQUIS BISHOP), retired dean; b. Charleston, W.Va., Sept. 30, 1939; d. Harold Edwin and Ina Mabel (Walkup) Marquis; m. Randal Young Bishop, Feb. 27, 1960: children: Jon Marquis, Heather Suzanne. RN, Norton Infirmary Sch. Nursing, 1960; BSN, Murray State U., 1963; MSN, Ind. U., 1967, PhD, 1983. RN, Ky., Ind., Fla., N.C. Ind. staff nurse psychiatry Norton Infirmary, Louisville, 1960-61; head nurse obstetrics, nursing supr. Murray (Ky.) Gen. Hosp., 1961-62; primary care nurse, crisis counselor infirmary Murray State U., 1962-63; staff nurse, clin. instr. Madison (Ind.) State Hosp., 1963-65; instr. through assoc. prof. Ind. U. Sch. Nursing, Indpls., 1967-89, developer child/adolescent psychiat., mental health nursing program, 1982-83, chairperson grad. dept., 1983-89; prof., asst. dean Coll. of Nursing U. South Fla., Tampa, 1989-91; dean Coll. Nursing U. N.C., Charlotte, 1992-95, dean Coll. of Nursing and Health Professions, 1995—2004, dean Coll. Health and Human Svcs., 2002—04, dean emerita, 2004—; ret., 2004. Pvt. practice marital and family therapy, 1975-89; cons. in field. Founding editor-in-chief Jour. of Child and Adolescent Psychiatric and Mental Health Nursing, 1987-91; contbr. articles to profl. jours. Bd. dirs. Carolinas blood svcs. region ARC, 1997-2002, chmn. bd. dirs., 2000—. NIMH trainee Ind. U., 1965-67, USPHS profl. nurse trainee Ind. U., 1977-78; recipient Youth Advocacy award Ind. Advs. for Child Psychiat. Nursing, 1987, Disting. Svc. award Ind. U. Sch. Nursing Alumni Assn., 1989, Nat. Youth Advocacy award Advs. for Child Psychiat. Nursing, 1990, Disting. Alumni award Ind. U. sch. Edn., 2000. Fellow Am. Acad. Nursing; mem. ANA, Psychiat. Mental Health Nursing Coun., Soc. for Edn. and Rsch. in Psychiat. Mental Health Nursing (pres. 1988-90), Am. Assn. Marital and Family Therapy, So. Nursing Rsch. Soc., So. Piedmont Alzheimer's Assn. (bd. dirs. 1999-2000), New South Hospice of Charlotte and Lincoln County (bd. dirs. 1995—2004, chair 2002-04), Sigma Theta Tau.

BISHOP, VIRGINIA WAKEMAN, retired librarian, retired humanities educator; b. Portland, Oreg., Dec. 28, 1927; d. Andrew Virgil and Letha Evangeline (Ward) Wakeman; m. Clarence Edmund Bishop, Aug. 23, 1953; children: Jean Marie Bishop Johnson, Marilyn Joyce. BA, Bapt. Missionary Tng. Sch., Chgo., 1949, Linfield Coll., 1952; MEd, Linfield Coll., McMinnville, Oreg., 1953; MA in Librarianship, U. Wash., 1968. Ch. worker U. Bapt. Ch., Seattle, 1954—56, 1959—61, tchr. parent coop presch., 1965—66; libr. N.W. Coll., Kirkland, Wash., 1968—69; undergrad. libr. U. Wash., Seattle, 1970; libr., instr. Seattle Ctrl. CC, 1970—91; co-owner small bus. Seaside, Oreg., 1972—2004. Leader Totem coun. Girl Scouts U.S., 1962-65; pres. Wedgwood Sch. PTA, Seattle, 1964-65; chair 46th Dist. Dem. Orgn., Seattle, 1972-73; precinct com. officer Dem. Party, 1968-88, 96-2000; candidate Wash. State Legislature, Seattle, 1974, 80; bd. dirs. U. Bapt. Children's Ctr., 1989-95, chair, 1990-95; vol. Ptnrs. in Pub. Edn., 1992-96. Recipient Golden Acorn award Wedgwood Elem. Sch., 1966. Mem. AAUW Seaside, LWV Seattle (2d v.p. 1994-96), U. Wash. Grad. Sch. Libr. and Info. Sci. Alumni Assn. (1st v.p. 1986-87, pres. 1987-88). Baptist. Avocations: swimming, walking, reading. Home: 3032 NE 87th St Seattle WA 98115-3529

BISHOP-GRAHAM, BARBARA, secondary school educator, journalist; b. Angwin, Calif., Apr. 22, 1941; d. Will Francis and Esther Clara (Blisséd) Bishop; children: Gregory Mark, Steven Bishop. BA in Journalism, U. Hawaii, 1975, BA in English, 1975, BA in Art History, 1975, BFA in Painting and Drawing, 1975; nat. cert. in journalism, Kans. State U., 1994; MA in Tech. Curriculum & Instrn., Calif. State U., Sacramento, 1999. Cert. tchr., Hawaii. Photography instr., art tchr. Hawaii Sch. for Girls, Honolulu, 1974-76; substitute tchr. English State Dept. Edn., Oahu, 1977-78; English and grammar instr. Hawaii Sch. for Bus., Honolulu, 1979-80; media dir., exec. asst., historian Oriental Treasures and Points West, Honolulu, 1981-82; legal asst. Goodsill, Anderson, Quinn, Honolulu, 1983-84; lang. arts and photography tchr. Lodi (Calif.) H.S., 1984-88, writing and lang. arts tchr., 1988-93, creative writing tchr., 1989-99, journalism adviser, 1993-95, lang. arts tchr., 1993—. Brit. lit. tchr., 1995—2001, tchr. rhetoric and European lit., 2001—03. Mem. curriculum coun. Lodi Unified Sch. Dist., 1989-92, 97-2000; liaison to PTSA Lodi H.S., 1991-92, mentor tchr., 1991-94; student literary mag. advisor Lodi H.S., 1989—. Sportswriter Oakland Tribune, 1957-60, Author Three Poems, 1998; contbr. articles to profl. pubis. Fundraiser chmn. Big Bros. of Am., San Francisco, 1967; media dir. Clements (Calif.) Cmty. Cares, 1985-89. Recipient Edn. Contbn. award Masons 1988-92, 20th Century Achievement award Am. Biographical Inst., 1999; grantee Nat. Endowment of Arts, rsch. Japanese Lit. 1989; social rschr. grantee Brazil, U. So. Calif. grantee, 1992; grantee S. Joaquin County Office Edn., 1996-97; champion Hawaii State barrel racing, 1980. Mem. NEA, Calif. Tchrs. Assn. (Calif. state tchrs. coun. rep. 1996-97), Lodi Edn. Assn. (conf. fund chair 1989-97). Republican. Seventh-Day Adventist. Avocations: writing, dressage riding, growing roses. Office: Lodi HS 3 S Pacific Ave Lodi CA 95242-3020

BISHOPRIC, SUSAN EHRLICH, public relations executive; b. NYC; AAS, Fashion Inst. Tech., 1965. Exec.-in-tng. Bloomingdales, Abraham & Strauss; merchandise coord. Seventeen mag.; publicity dir. Germaine Monteil Cosmetiques; account exec. Rowland Co., 1968-69, account supr., 1969-73, v.p., 1973-75, sr. v.p., creative dir., 1975-78, exec. v.p., 1979-81; pub. rels. dir. Susan Gilbert & Co., 1984-86; head pub. rels. divsn. Beber Silverstein & Ptnrs., 1986-89; founder, pres. Bishopric Agy., Coral Gables, Fla., 1989-99, NYC, 1999—. Office: The Bishopric Agy 185 E 85th St #9M New York NY 10028 E-mail: sbishopric@nyc.rr.com.

BISSELL, MINA J., lab administrator, biochemist; b. Tehran, Iran, May 14, 1940; Student, Bryn Mawr Coll., 1959-61; AB in Chemistry cum laude, Radcliff Coll., Cambridge, Mass., 1963; MA in Bacteriology and Biochemistry, Harvard U., Cambridge, Mass., 1965, PhD in Microbiology-Molecular Genetics, 1969. Milton rsch. fellow, 1969-70; Am. Cancer Soc. rsch. fellow, 1970-72; staff biochemist Lawrence Berkeley Nat. Lab. U. Calif., Berkeley, 1972-76, mem. sr. staff, 1976—, co-dir. div. biology and medicine Lab. Cell Biology, 1980—, dir. divsn., 1988-92, coord. life scis., 1989-91, assoc. lab. dir. bioscience, 1989, dir. life scis. divsn. Lawrence Berkeley Nat. Lab., 1992—, mem. faculty dept. comparative biochemistry, 1979—. Vis. prof. Kettering Inst., U. Cin. Med. Schs., 1986-88; disting. vis. scientist Queensland Inst. Med. Rsch., Brisbane, Australia, 1982; mem. coun. Gordon Rsch. Conf., 1991-94; George P. Peacock lectr. pathology U. Tex., Dallas, 1992; Dean's lectr. Mt. Sinai Med. Sch., N.Y.C., 1993; presenter numerous lectures, condr. symposia; keynote spkr. Gordon Conf. on Proteoglycans, 1994, others. Mem. editl. bd. and sect. editor In Vitro Cell and Devel. Biology Rapid Comm., 1986—; mem. editl. bd. Jour. Cellular Biochemistry, 1990-92; assoc. editor In Vitro Cellular and Devel. Biology, 1990—, Molecular and Cellular Differentiation, 1992—, Molecular Carcinogensis, 1993-97, Devel. Biology, 1993—, Cancer Rsch., 1994—, Breast Jour., 1994—; contbr. numerous articles to sci. jours. Recipient 1st Joseph Sadusk award for breast cancer rsch., 1985, Ernest Orlando Lawrence award Dept. Energy, 1996, Krakower award in Pathology, 2003, Discovery Health Channel Med. Honors, 2004; Fogarty sr. fellow NIH, Imperial Can. Rsch. Fund Labs., London, 1983-84, Guggenheim fellow, 1992-93,; honored by Susan G. Komen Breast Cancer Found. Fellow AAAS; mem. Am. Soc. for Cell Biology (mem. coun. 1989-91, Women in Cell Biology Career Recognition award 1993, pres. 1997), Internat. Soc. Differentiation (bd. dirs. 1990-96). The pioneer in postulating, and then proving that the extracellular matrix (ECM), the mass of fibrous and globular proteins that surrounds cells performs a critical role in dictating a tissue's organization and function. In 1981, Dr. Bissell formulated the concept of a "dynamic reciprocity." This communication scheme between the nucleus, the cells and their microenvironment suggests that signals are sent into the cell through ECM receptors which attach to the cell's outer skeleton and convey important information to the nucleus and the chromosomes. Office: Lawrence Berkeley Nat Lab Div Life Scis 1 Cyclotron Rd Ms 83 101 Berkeley CA 94720-8260 Business E-Mail: mjbissell@lbl.gov.*

BISSOON, CATHY, lawyer; b. NYC; married; 2 children. BA in polit. sci. summa cum laude, Alfred U., NY, 1990; JD, Harvard U., 1993; exec. leadership program, The Wharton Sch., U. Pa., 2004. Bar: Pa. 1993, US Dist. Ct. We. Dist. Pa. 1993, Supreme Ct. Pa. 1994, US Ct. Appeals 4th Cir. 1995, US Ct. Appeals 3rd Cir. 1997, US Ct. Appeals 6th Cir. 2001. Law clk. to Hon. Gary L. Lancaster US Dist. Ct. We. Dist. Pa., 1994; joined Reed Smith LLP, Pitts., 1993, ptnr., 2001—, dir. diversity, 2001—, former head employment group. Bd. mem. Girl Scouts Trillium Coun., Pitts. Zoo & PPG Aquarium. Named a Nat. Hispanic Scholar, Alfred U., Harvard U. Mem.: Pitts. Met. Area Hisp. C. of C., Hispanic Nat. Bar Assn. Office: Reed Smith LLP 435 Sixth Ave Pittsburgh PA 15219 Office Phone: 412-288-3268. Office Fax: 412-288-3063. Business E-Mail: cbissoon@reedsmith.com.

BISTRANSKY, JOYCE ELAINE, retired elementary school educator; b. Elkhart, Ind., Mar. 3, 1938; d. Albert Frederick Markas and Edith Marie (Hege) Markus; 1 child, Jennifer Lynn Bistransky-Cook. BE, Ball State Tchrs. Coll., Ind., 1956—60; MEd, Roosevelt U., Chgo., 1966—67. 2d grade tchr. Portage Twp. Sch., Ind., 1960—62; 2d & 3d grade tchr. Lake Ridge Schs., Gary, Ind., 1963—64, art tchr., 1965—2001; ret., 2001. Nat. exec. bd. mem. German-Am. Nat. Congress, 1975—; sec. Am. Fedn. Tchrs., Gary, 1974—76; vol. Portage Live Entertainment Assn., 2002—. Luth. Avocations: knitting, embroidery, sewing, painting, reading.

BITHONEY, CARMEN C. D'AMBORSIO, artistic director; b. Pelham Manor, N.Y., July 16, 1956; d. Anthony and Marian Christine D'Ambrosio; m. William G. Bithoney, Apr. 9, 1998. BA, Manhattanville Coll., 1978, MA, 1982. Exec. dir., founder First Expressions, A Nonprofit Gallery for the Arts, Inc., Boston, 1992-97; dir. Boston Film Bur. in Mayor's Office of Cultural Affairs, 1994-96; project dir. D'Ambrosio Ecclesiastical Art Studio, Onc., Mt. Kisco, N.Y., 1998—. Editor: Production Guide for Film & Video in the City of Boston, 1995. Office: DAmbrosio Ecclesiastical Art Studio Inc PO Box 656 Mount Kisco NY 10549-0656 Home: PO Box 75 Mount Kisco NY 10549-0075 E-mail: c.c.bithoney@juno.com.

BITMAN, CLARA, writer, educator; b. Montevideo, Uruguay, Sept. 29, 1935; d. David and Hela Seniak Bitman; children: Sergio Gabriel Voda, Laura Alejandra Voda. Dir. art sch. Taller Urutí, Buenos Aires, 1973—83; dir., seminars for tchrs. Inés Moreno Inst., Buenos Aires, 1980—90, Essarp Ctr., Buenos Aires, 1984—91; lectr. Bank State Coll. Edn., N.Y.C., 1994; tchr. Spanish B.B. Montessori Sch., S.I., NY, 1995—. Author: (book) El Girasol Gigante, 1998, numerous childrens books and TV programs. Vol. Ayuda Ya Inc., 1999—2003. Recipient Illustrated Poetry award, Argentinian Soc. Writers, 1980, Children's Theater Prize of Yr., Argentinian Soc. Authors, 1983. Achievements include put on stage six plays in many South Am. countries. E-mail: claser@juno.com.

BITNER, BETTY L., education educator; b. Greencastle, Pa., Feb. 7, 1945; d. Arthur Robert and Anna Elizabeth (Foreman) B. BA in Classical Langs., Thiel Coll., Greenville, Pa., 1967; MEd in Mental Retardation, Edinboro U. of Pa., 1973; EdD in Sci. Edn., U. Maine, 1983. Cert. tchr., NY, Maine, Mo. Tchr. Jamestown Pub. Schs., NY, 1967-69, 71-78, S.A.D. # 5, Rockland, Maine, 1978-81; grad. asst., instr. U. Maine, Orono, 1981-83; asst. prof. Ark. Tech. U., 1983-86; asst. prof. edn. S.W. Mo. State U., Springfield, 1986-89, assoc. prof., 1989-94, prof., 1994—2002, prof. emeritus, 2002—; prof. edn., chmn. Thiel Coll., Greenville, Pa., 2002—05; prof. edn., dir. MA in Tchg. Wilson Coll., Chambersburg, Pa., 2006—. Contbr. numerous articles to profl. jours. Founding sponsor Martin Luther King Jr. Nat. Meml. Recipient numerous grants in field. Mem. ASCD, Internat. Assn. Tech. Edn., Pa. Assn. Coll. Tchr. Educators, Nat. Assn. for Rsch. in Sci. Tchg., Nat. Audubon Soc., Nat. Sci. Tchrs. Assn. (com. on rsch. and sci. tchg. 1987-89), Southern Poverty Law Ctr., Phi Delta Kappa, Phi Kappa Phi. Avocations: the arts, hiking, reading. Office: Wilson Coll 1015 Philadelphia Ave Chambersburg PA 17201 Office Phone: 717-264-4141. Business E-Mail: bbitner@wilson.edu.

BITTEL, KIRSTIN ALICIA, science educator; d. David Hyde Dosh, Jr. and Kathryn R. Dosh; m. Clinton Neal Bittel, Mar. 15, 1972. BA in Elem. Edn. with honors, U. Ariz., Tucson, 1998; MA in Ednl. Adminstrn., Chapman U., Orange, Calif., 2001. Cert. standard elem. tchr. K-8 Ariz. Dept. Edn., 1998, bilingual endorsement Ariz., 1998. Tchr. Kellond Elem. Sch.- TUSD, Tucson, 1998—2002; sci. tchr. Mansfeld Mid. Sch., Tucson, 2002—; tech. expert U. Ariz., Tucson, 2003—. Sci. facilitator Kellond Elem. Sch.- TUSD, 1999—2002; presenter at confs. in field. Finalist Sci. Innovator of Yr., Intel, 2002; named Outstanding Arts Educator, U. Ariz., 2002; Horace Mann scholar, 2005. Mem.: AZ Sci. Tchr. Assn., AZ Earth Sci. Tchr. Assn., Nat. Sci. Tchr. Assn., Golden Key Nat. Honor Soc., Pi Lambda Theta. Office: Mansfeld Middle Sch - TUSD 1300 E 6th St Tucson AZ 85719 Office Phone: 520-225-1800. Office Fax: 520-225-1801. Business E-Mail: kirstin.bittel@tusd1.org.

BITTERMAN, MARY GAYLE FOLEY, foundation executive; b. San Jose, Calif., May 29, 1944; d. John Dennis and Zoe (Hames) Foley; m. Morton Edward Bitterman, June 26, 1967; 1 child Sarah Fleming. BA, Santa Clara U., 1966; MA, Bryn Mawr Coll., 1969, PhD, 1971. Exec. dir. Hawaii Pub. Broadcasting, Honolulu, 1974-79; dir. Voice Am., Washington, 1980-81, Dept. Commerce, Honolulu, 1981-83, E.-W. Ctr. Inst. Culture, Comm., 1984-88; cons. pvt. practice, 1989-93; pres., CEO KQED, Inc., San Francisco, 1993—2002, The James Irvine Found., 2002—03; Dtr. Osher Lifelong Learning Inst., 2003; pres. The Bernard Osher Found., 2004—. Bd. dir. Bank of Hawaii, Honolulu, Honolulu, 1984—; vice chmn. TIDE 2000, Tokyo, 1984—93; bd. dir. McKesson Corp., San Francisco, 1995—99; trustee Am.'s Pub. TV Stas., 1997—2002; bd. dir. Bernard Osher Found.; bd. dirs. Barclays Global Investors, Bay Area Econ. Forum; bd. dir. PBS, chmn.; adv. coun. mem. Stanford Inst. Econ. Policy Rsch. Prodr.: (film) China Visit, 1978; contbr. numerous articles on internat. telecomms. to various pubs. Bd. dirs. United Way, Honolulu, 1986—93; chmn. Kuakini Health System, 1991—94; trustee Santa Clara U. Recipient Candle of Understanding award Bonneville (Utah) Internat. Corp., 1985; named hon. mem. Nat. Fedn. Press Women, 1986; Doctor of Humane Letters (honoris causa), Dominican Coll. of San Rafael, 1999; Doctor of Public Svc. (honoris causa), Santa Clara U., 2003. Mem.: Pacific Forum, CSIS (bd. gov.), Commonwealth Club Calif. (bd. dir.), Nat. Acad. Pub. Admin. (fellow). Office: One Ferry Bldg Ste 255 San Francisco CA 94111 Address: 229 Kaalawai Pl Honolulu HI 96816-4435 Office Phone: 415-677-5946. Business E-Mail: mbitterman@osherfoundation.org.

BITTIKER, MARJORIE JOANNE, principal; d. James and Marjorie Swope; m. Ken D. Bittiker, June 4, 1965; children: Gayle, Brian. BS, N.W. Mo. State U., Maryville, 1963; M in Religious Edn., New Orleans Bapt. Theol. Sem., 1965. Cert. Orff music tchr.; cert. lang. and learning disabilities. Kindergarten and music tchr. St. Joseph Pub. Schs., Mo., 1965—67, music tchr., 1979—81; min. religious edn. First Bapt. Ch., Maryville, Mo., 1967—71; music tchr. East Buchanan Sch. Sys., Gower, Mo., 1975—79; spl. edn. tchr. Keene Ind. Sch. Dist., Tex., 1981—86, supr., 1986—90, prin., 1990—. Mem. Tex. Sch. Improvement Initiative, Tex. Edn. Agy., Austin, 1997—2001; mem. Effective Sch. Project, Tarleton State U., Stephenville, Tex., 1993—96. Children's Sunday sch. dir., children choir dir. Gambrell St. Bapt. Ch., Fort Worth, 1984—94; children's choir dir. Westcliff Meth. Ch., Fort Worth, 1995—2001; children's choir leader Broadway Bapt. Ch., Fort Worth, 2001—04. Named Tchr. of Yr., Keene Ind. Sch. Dist., 1986. Mem. ASCD, Assn. Tex. Profl. Educators, Tex. Elem. Prins. and Suprs. Assn. Avocations: travel, reading, choir member. Office: Keene Ind Sch Dist 401 E Fourth St Keene TX 76059-0656 Office Phone: 817-641-1482. Office Fax: 817-517-7966.

BITTINGER, CYNTHIA DOUGLAS, foundation executive; BA in Govt., Wheaton Coll., 1968; MA, Columbia U., 1970. Social studies tchr. Ridgewood (N.J.) High Sch., 1970-73; govtl. mgr. Mayor's N.Y.C. Office for Aging, 1974-76; owner, mgr. gift shop Princeton, N.J., 1978-87; exec. dir. Calvin Coolidge Meml. Found., Inc., Plymouth, Vt., 1990—. Instr. history C.C. of Vt., White River Junction, 1992—94. Commentator Vt. Pub. Radio, 2003—. Address: Calvin Coolidge Mem Found Box 97 Plymouth VT 05056

BITZER, JOAN LOUISE, psychologist; b. York, Pa., Dec. 26, 1952; d. Elwood Eugene and Betty Arlene (Smith) Fink; m. Gary N. Sipkoff, Nov. 27, 1976 (div. May 1979); m. Jeffrey T. Bitzer, May 29, 1982; children: Zachary T., Allison W. BS, York Coll. Pa., 1973; MS, Millersville State Coll., 1977. Lic. psychologist, Pa. Psychotherapist York County Mental Health Ctr., York, Pa., 1974-80; psychologist York Guidance Ctr., 1980-86; psychologist, co-owner Psychol. Assocs. Pa., P.C., York, 1986—. Cons. Children's Home of York, 1980-86, York Hosp. Nutrition and Metabolic Ctr., 1985-89, Growth, York, 1987-2002; founding bd. pres. Dream Wrights Youth and Family Theatre, 1997, bd. meme., 1997-2001. Pres. bd. dirs. Access-York Inc., 1980-87; tng. dir., vol. Contact, York, 1980—. Mem. APA, Pa. Psychol. Assn. Democrat. Avocations: restoring 1810 stone farm house, entertaining, art, creative activities. Office: Psychol Assocs PA PC 2870 Carol Rd York PA 17402-3816 Personal E-mail: joan@psychassocpa.com.

BIUNNO, THERESA, physical education educator; d. Robert Patsy and Georgiana Hope Biunno. BA, Glassboro State Coll. (now Rowan U.), NJ, 1978. Tchr. phys. edn., health Cranford Bd. Edn., NJ, 1978—. Home: 128 Westgate Dr Edison NJ 08820-1156

BIVENS, CAROLYN VESPER, former advertising executive, golf association commissioner-elect; m. Bill Bivens. Various sales and mktg. positions Xerox Corp., Dallas, Washington; with USA Today, 1982—2000, dir. nat. sales, v.p. nat. circulation sales Arlington, Va., 1985—91, sr. v.p., assoc. pub., 1991—2000; mng. dir. Western Region Initiative Media, 2000—01; pres., COO Initiative Media North Am., LA, 2001—05; commr. LPGA, Daytona Beach, Fla., 2005. Chmn. bd. govs. Children's Miracle Network; bd. dirs. Ad Coun., Nat. Steppenwolf Theatre. Named one of Most Powerful Women in TV, Electronics Media mag., 2002. Mem.: Am. Assn. Advt. Agencies (mem. Media Policy Com.), Congressional Country Club. Achievements include first female commissioner in the 55 year history of the Ladies Professional Golf Association. Avocation: golf. Office: LPGA 100 International Golf Drive Daytona Beach FL 32124-1092 Office Phone: 323-370-8000, 386-274-6200. Office Fax: 386-274-1099. E-mail: carolyn.bivens@us.initiative.com.*

BIVENS, CONSTANCE ANN, retired pre-school educator; b. Madison, Ind., June 26, 1938; d. Nelson and Virginia (Cole) B BS, George Peabody Coll. for Tchrs., now Vanderbilt U., 1960, MA, 1966; EdD, Nova Southeastern U., Ft. Lauderdale, Fla., 1982. Cert. educator. Tchr. Broward County Schs., Ft. Lauderdale, 1960—61, 1965—97, Jefferson County Schs., Louisville, 1961—62, Ft. Knox Schs., Ky., 1962—64, Madison Consol. Schs., 1964—65; ret., 1997. Chmn. K-Adult Coun., Nova Schs., Ft. Lauderdale, 1976-78; cons. 1978-80 Author: Boots, Butterflies, and Dragons, 1982, Walk to Emmaus, 1990 Mem. Women of Faith, First Christian Ch. (Disciples of Christ), Madison, 2005—, chancel choir; active Children's Cancer Caring Ctr. Inc., Broward County chpt., 1986-2004 Mem. AAUW, NEA (life), Madison Elks #524, Red Hat Soc., Hist. Madison, Inc., Jefferson County Hist. Soc., Internat. Order King's Daus. and Sons, Delta Kappa Gamma Soc. Internat. (internat. expansion com. 1986-88, chmn. internat. program of work com. 1988-90, internat. rep. World Confedn. Orgns. of Tchg. Profession 1989, chmn. S.E. regional conf. 1991, internat. nominations com. 1992-96, chmn. 1994-96, state hdqrs. adminstrv. com. 1997-2003; 1st v.p. Mu State 1993-95, Mu State pres. 1995-97, Sara Ferguson Achievement award 1990, internat. conv. credentials com. 1998), Alpha Epsilon (state rsch com. 2005—) Republican. Avocation: travel. Home: 1209 W Main St Madison IN 47250-3015

BIVENS, LYDIA RUTH, librarian; b. Victoria, Tex., May 19, 1939; d. John Wren and Nina Merle (Nolen) Higginbotham; m. Roger Wayne Bivens, Oct. 17, 1959 (div. 1970); children: Cynthia Ann, Randall Wayne. BA, Our Lady of the Lake U., San Antonio, 1966; MLS, Our Lady of the Lake U., 1974. Cert. tchr., libr., supr., Tex. Dist. libr. Georgetown (Tex.) Ind. Sch. Dist., 1966-69; libr. Harlandale Ind. Sch. Dist., San Antonio, 1970-80, Judson Ind. Sch. Dist., Converse, Tex., 1981—99; libr. coord. NE Ind. Sch. Dist., San Antonio, 1999—. Adv. bd. Adult Community Edn., Converse, 1990—; cons. Sirsi Corp., Huntsville, Ala., 1985—; mem. chpt. 75 curriculum rev. com. Tex. Edn. Agy., 1988-90. Chairperson pub. libr. bd. City of Universal, Tex., 1985-90. Mem. ALA, ASCD, Am. Bus. Women's Assn., Tex. Libr. Assn., Bexar County Libr. Assn., Tex. State Tchrs. Assn., Judson Tchrs. Assn. (pres. 1984-86), Nat. Tchrs. Assn., Tex. Assn. Sch. Libr. Adminstrs. (pres. 1993—), Tex. Assn. Librs. Tex. 100, Tex. Literacy Bd., Tex. Sch. Libr. Assn. (chair nominating com.), Delta Kappa Gamma. Avocation: painting. Home: 113 Andorra Dr Universal City TX 78148-3301 Office: 10115 Sommers San Antonio TX 78217

BIVENS, MARJORIE EARLEY, retired nursing educator; d. Robert Kelly and Edna Pearl (Jaynes) Earley; m. Arvin David Branch (div.); children: Arvin Dale Branch, Janna Arlene Branch, Rebekah Lynn Thompson; m. Gary Lee Bivens, Oct. 8, 1988. ADN, We. Piemont CC, Mortganton, NC, 1977; BSN, U. NC, Charlotte, 1984; MSN, U. NC, Greensboro, 1995. RN NC. RN Grace Hosp., Morganton, 1977—84, nursing care coord., 1984—92; RN, PRN Rutherford Hosp., 1992—95; clin. instr. Gardner Webb U., Boiling Springs, NC, 1992, mem. nursing faculty, clin. instr., 1992—95; ret., 1995. Mem., chair CFAC, Morganton, 2003—04, sec. coun., 2005—06. Republican. Baptist. Home: 1169 Burkehurst Ave Morganton NC 28655

BIXENSTINE, KIM FENTON, lawyer; b. Providence, Feb. 26, 1958; d. Barry Jay and Gail Louise (Traverse) Weinstein; m. Barton Aaron Bixenstine, June 25, 1983; children: Paul Jay, Nathan Alexis. BA, Middlebury Coll., 1979; JD, U. Chgo., 1982. Bar: Ohio 1982, U.S. Dist. Ct. (no. and so. dists.) Ohio 1983, U.S. Ct. Appeals (6th cir.) 1983. Law clk. to presiding judge U.S. Dist. Ct. (so. dist.) Ohio, Cin., 1982-83; assoc. Jones, Day, Reavis & Pogue, Cleve., 1983-90, ptnr., 1991-99; sr. counsel TRW Inc., Cleve., 1999—2001, v.p., chief litig. counsel, 2002—03; v.p., dep. gen. counsel Univ. Hosp. Health Sys., Cleve., 2003—. Sec. Planned Parenthood Greater Cleve., 1992—93, v.p., 1994—96, pres., 1996—98; chair corp. giving subcom. Cleve. Bar Found. Campaign, 2001—02; bd. dir. Planned Parenthood Greater Cleve., 1991—99; bd. dirs. Boys and Girls Club Cleve., 2001—03, chair pub. rels. com., 2002—03. Mem.: Am. Arbitration Assn. (chair comml. adv. coun. N.E. Ohio chpt. 2000—05), Cleve. Bar Assn. (commn. women in the law 1988—2001, bd. dir. 1993—96, minority outreach com. 1993—99, chair standing com. lawyer professionalism 1994—96, bd. liaison to jud. selection com. 1996, nominating com. 1997—99, chair nominating com. 1998—99, long range planning com. 2002—03, judicial selection com. 2005—), Ohio Women's Bar Assn. (chair legis. com. 1994—95, trustee 1995—97, judicial selection com. 2005—). Avocations: jogging, reading, yoga. Office: Univ Hosps Health Sys WO Walker Ctr 10524 Euclid Ave Fl 8 Cleveland OH 44106 Office Phone: 216-983-1911. Business E-Mail: kim.bixenstine@uhhospitals.org.

BIZON, EMMA DJAFAR, management consultant; b. Atlanta, July 22, 1958; d. H. and Aminah Djafar; m. Lawrence Walter Bizon, May 24, 1994; 1 child, Rimagene. BSc in City & Regional Planning cum laude, Bandung Inst. Tech., Indonesia, 1985; MBA, Harvard U., 1994. Planner, Indonesia, 1983—86; asst. dir. Investment Bd., Indonesia; team leader Amre, Inc., Livonia, Mich., 1994—97; cons. to fast food restaurants Mich., 1997—98. Avocations: sports, music, cooking, writing. Home: 10909 Melbourne Ct Allen Park MI 48101

BIZUB, JOHANNA CATHERINE, law librarian; b. Denville, NJ, Apr. 13, 1957; d. Stephen Bernard and Elizabeth Mary (Grizzle) B.; m. Scott Jeffrey Smith, 1992. BS in Criminal Justice, U. Dayton, 1979; MLS, Rutgers U., 1984. Law libr. Morris County (NJ) Law Libr., 1981-83, Clapp & Eisenberg, Newark, 1984-86; dir. libr. Sills Cummis, 1986-94; libr. dir. Montville (NJ) Twp. Pub. Libr., 1994-97; libr. dir. law dept. Prudential Ins. Co. Am., Newark, 1997—. Mem. ALA, NJ Law Librs. Assn. (treas. 1987-89, v.p./pres.-elect 1989-90, 99-2000, pres. 1990-91, 2000-01, past pres. 1991-92, 2001-02), Am. Assn. Law Librs. (pvt. law librs. SIS, vice chair 1992-93, chair 1993-94, chair awards com. 1992-93, 2005—), NJ Libr. Assn., Assoc. Libr. of Morris County (v.p. 1995, pres. 1996, treas. 1997-2001), Spl. Libr. Assn. NJ (treas. 1990-92), Am. Legion Aux. (treas. Rockden unit 175 1983-93). Democrat. Roman Catholic. Home: 11 Elm St Rockaway NJ 07866-3108 Office: Prudential Ins Co Am 22 Plz 751 Broad St Newark NJ 07102-3714 Business E-Mail: jbizub@prudential.com.

BJICK, SUZANNE CARTER, psychologist; b. New Orleans, Sept. 29, 1935; d. William Bang and Adele (Hanson) Carter; BA, Southwestern at Memphis, 1956; MA, Yale U., New Haven, Conn., 1959; PhD, Temple U., Phila., 1985; m. Ronald Lloyd Bjick, Mar. 28, 1964; children: Sarah Ellen,

Elizabeth Ann. Tchr. kindergarten Elgin (Ill) Public Schs., 1959-65; clin. intern Elgin (Ill.) State Hosp., 1958-59; tchr. elem. remedial math. Linwood (N.J.) Public. Schs., 1972-73; instr. Temple U., Phila., 1979; cons. therapist Susquehanna Assn. Family Counseling Ministry, Binghamton, N.Y., 1979-85; counselor 1st Presbyn. Ch., Endicott, N.Y., 1979—; assoc. psychologist Binghamton Psychiat. Ctr., 1985-90; pvt. practice, Choconut, Pa., 1988—; chair-elect Harper forum Binghamton U. Active Tri-Cities Opera Guild, Binghamton, Roberson Ctr. for Arts and Scis., chmn.; pres. Broome County Children and Youth Svcs. Coun., 1988-89. Mem. APA, EMDRIA, Am. Soc. for Rsch. in Child Devel., Am. Soc. for Clin. Hypnosis (cert. cons. in clin. hypnosis), Pa. Psychol. Assn., Contact Atlantic (tng. dir., exec. co-dir. 1973-76), La Leche League (founder, leader Atlantic County 1971-75). Presbyterian. Home: 35 Elmwood Dr Apalachin NY 13732-4302 Office: Box 1664 Friendsville PA 18818-9510 Office Phone: 607-625-3220.

BJÖRK, (BJÖRK GUDMUNDSDÓTTIR), singer, composer; b. Reykjavik, Iceland, Nov. 21, 1965; d. Gudmundur and Hildur; m. Thor Eldon, 1986 (div. 1988); Sindri, Isadora. Rec. artist solo album at age 11; performer with several bands; formed theatrical/rock ensemble KUKL, 1980s; rec. artist with The Sugarcubes: (albums) Life's Too Good, 1986, Here Today, Tomorrow, Next Week, 1989; solo artist: (albums) Debut, 1993, Post, 1995, Telegram, 1997, Homogenic, 1997, Selmasongs: Dancer in the Dark, 2000, Vespertine, 2001, Family Tree, 2002, Greatest Hits, 2002, Medulla, 2004; actor: (films) Juniper Tree, 1990, Dancer in the Dark, 2000 (Best Actress, Cannes Film Festival). Office: Electra Records 75 Rockefeller Plz New York NY 10019-6908

BJORKLUND, NANCY MARGARETTE WATTS, music educator; b. Maryville, Tenn., Aug. 14, 1942; d. Charles Burdett and Alma Pauline (Calhoun) Watts; m. Ralph Edward Bjorklund, June 14, 1963; children: James Andrew, Deborah Elisabeth, John Carl. AA, Manatee C.C., Bradenton, Fla., 1962; BA, MusB, Stetson U., 1964. Founder, dir. music, pianist First Bapt. Ch., Freeport, Grand Bahama Is., 1964—70; dir. Cmty. Chorus Choir, Freeport, Grand Bahama Island, 1964—70. Recipient Crystal Heart award, Girl Scouts Am., 1995. Mem.: Musical Manatee Club (treas. 2006—), Fla. State Music Tchr. Assn. (exec. bd. 1993—95, 1993—2006, pres. dist. 8 2001—06), Manatee County Music Tchr. Assn. (exec. bd. 1978—, chmn. Pianorama 1980, exec. bd. 1983—, pres. 1993—95, chmn. music spectacular 2001, 2004, 2006, pres. 2006—), Nat. Assn. Music Clubs (chmn. Fedn. Festival Manatee County 1980—), Manatee County Assn. Retarded Citizens, Fla. State Assn. Retarded Citizens. Republican. Bapt. Avocations: reading, crewel, swimming, cooking. Office: 1912 48th St W Bradenton FL 34209

BJORKLUND, VICTORIA B., lawyer; b. Glen Cove, NY, Feb. 20, 1952; BA magna cum laude & phi beta kappa, Princeton U., 1973; PhD, Yale U., 1977; JD, Columbia U., 1983. Bar: N.Y. 1984. Ptnr. Simpson, Thacher & Bartlett LLP, N.Y.C., head firm exempt orgn. group, co-chmn. pro bono com. Dir., sec., pro bono legal counsel Doctors Without Borders, 1989—2001; dir., pro bono legal counsel Robin Hood Found. Co-author: N.Y. Nonprofit Law & Practice, 1997. Recipient Commr.'s Award, Commr. IRS, 2003. Mem.: Assn. Bar City N.Y.- com. nonprofit orgn. (mem. 1991—97), ABA-sub com. international philanthropy (co-chmn.), ABA-tax sect. com. exempt orgn. (co-chmn., sub-com. private found. 1997—99, vice chmn. 1999—2001, chmn. 2001—03, co-chmn., sub-com. private found. 2003—, co-chmn., sub-com. precedential guidance 1995—97, Pro Bono Lawyer Year 2002). Office: Simpson Thacher & Bartlett LLP 425 Lexington Ave New York NY 10017-3954 Office Phone: 212-455-2875. Office Fax: 212-455-2502. Business E-Mail: vbjorklund@stblaw.com.

BJORKMAN, SYLVIA JOHNSON, psychologist; d. William A. and Alice W. Johnson; m. David R. Bjorkman, June 23, 1984; children: John, Will. MEd in Spl. Edn., UNC, 1979. Cert. sch. psychologist 1984, lic. health care provider 1993. Tchr. Mental Health Early Instrl. Program, Lumberton, NC, 1976—78; tchr., counselor Wright Sch., Durham, NC, 1979—80; tchr. Washington (N.C.) Schs., 1980—82; counselor, psychologist Pitt County Schs., Greenville, NC, 1984—86, psychologist, 1986—, specialist student svcs., 2004—; pvt. practice psychologist Ea. Carolina Behavioral and Psychiat. Specialists, Greenville, NC, 2004—. Mem. program devel. com. Pitt. County Schs., 2004—; com. safe drug free schs. Pitt County, Greenville, 2004—05; presenter in field. Mem. cmty. crisis response team Pitt County, Greenville, 1999; mem. planning com. Pitt County Vol. Summit, Greenville, 1997; mem. preschool adv. coun. East Caulino U., Greenville, 1992; mem. vestry St. Timothy's Episc. Ch., Greenville, 1994—97. Mem.: APA, N.C. Sch. Psychology Assn. Avocations: music, gardening, travel. Office: Pitt County Schools 901 Staten Rd Greenville NC 27834

BJORNCRANTZ, LESLIE BENTON, librarian; b. Jersey City, Mar. 1, 1945; d. David and Jeanne (Proctor) Benton; m. Carl Eduard Bjorncrantz, Aug. 31, 1968; 1 child, William. BA, Wellesley Coll., 1967; MLS, Columbia U., 1968. Rsch. libr. Alderman Libr. U. Va., Charlottesville, 1968-70; reference libr. Northwestern U. Libr., Evanston, Ill., 1974-78, curriculum libr., 1970—, edn. bibliographer, 1974—, psychology bibliographer, 1989—, core libr., 1989-97, mgmt. bibliographer, 1997—. Mem. libr. adv. bd. APA, 2004—. Co-editor: (book) Curriculum Material Center Collection Policy, 1984, Guide for the Development & Management of Test Collections, 1985. Bd. dir. Internat. Visitors Ctr., Chgo., 1973-76; class rep., fund raiser class of 1967, Wellesley (Mass.) Coll., 1987-92. Scholar, Wellesley Coll., 1967. Mem. ALA, APA (libr. adv. bd. 2004—), Assn. Coll. & Rsch. Librs. (sec. 1977-79, 85-87, chair curriculum materials com. 1984-85), Am. Bus. Libr. Dirs. Avocations: reading, travel, food and wine. Home: 2146 Forestview Rd Evanston IL 60201-2057 Office: Northwestern U Libr 1970 Campus Dr Evanston IL 60208-0821 Office Phone: 847-491-7602. E-mail: l-bjorncrantz@northwestern.edu.

BJORNSON, EDITH CAMERON, foundation administrator, communications consultant; b. Orlando, Fla., Sept. 12, 1937; d. Hilliard Francis and Edith Muriel (McBride) Cameron; m. Carroll N. Bjornson, Jan. 11, 1963; children: Lisa Carol, Karl Cameron (dec.). BA, U. Fla., Gainesville, 1953, MA, 1956; profl. cert., Ecole de Cuisine LaVerenne, Paris, 1983. Copywriter Sta. WGGG, Gainesville, Fla., 1953—54; exec. asst. Actors' Studio, N.Y.C., 1956—58; prodn. asst. Omnibus, N.Y.C., 1958—59; assoc. prodr. Robert Saudek Assocs., N.Y.C., 1958—60, ABC News Adlai Stevenson Reports, N.Y.C., 1960; asst. gen. mgr. Sta. WNDT-TV, N.Y.C., 1960—63; co-prodr. The Open Mind, N.Y.C., 1963—69; dir. local programming Telepromter, Inc., N.Y.C., 1979—80; corp. v.p. programming Westinghouse Broadcasting and Cable, N.Y.C., 1980—83; cons. Sta. WNYC-TV, N.Y.C., 1984—86; v.p., sr. program officer The Markle Found., N.Y.C., 1986—98. Working group Carter Commn. on Radio and TV, Atlanta, 1992—96; chmn. N.Y. New Media Assn., N.Y.C., 2002; bd. dirs. Conn. Pub. TV and Radio, 1999—, co-chair strategic planning com., 2006, bd. advisor to Culture Connect, 2003—; exec. dir. Fulfilling the Promise project on digital comm. Century Found. and Carnegie Corp., 1999—2001; sr. advisor, Morningside Ventures Columbia U., 1999—2001; project dir., website designer Fulfilling the Promise The Century Found. Carnegie Corp., 1999—2001; website editor Digital Promise Project, 2002—03; project dir., website designer The Open Mind Digital Archive Project, Columbia Tchrs. Coll., 2002—; sr. advisor Fathom.com Columbia U., 1999—2001; sr. advisor video oral history project Healthcare Chaplaincy, 2002—05; dir. oral history project The Healthcare Chaplaincy, 2003—05; prin. Recorded Oral Histories, LLC; sr. cons. Liberty Concepts LLC; cons. in field. Project advisor: (computer software) Voyager Co., 1993, SimHealth, 1994, (Internet software, multi-player online games) ReInventing America, 1995, President '96; contbr. articles to profl. jours. Vice chmn. bd. dirs. HealthCare Chaplaincy, N.Y.C., 1989-96; bd. dirs. Pro-Natura USA, N.Y.C., 1995-99; life trustee Health Care Chaplaincy, N.Y.C., 1997. Recipient Emmy award Acad. TV. Arts and Scis., 1960. Mem. Internat. Assn. Culinary Profls., Night Kitchen (computer software developers bd. dirs. 1996-98), Mortar Board, Delta Gamma. Republican. Avocation: cooking. Home: 34 E Lyon Farm Dr Greenwich CT 06831-4349 Office Phone: 212-481-3949.

BJORNSON PIERCE, SHAUNA, primary school educator; b. Dallas, Mar. 7, 1978; d. Allen Lee and Madeline Gail Bjornson; m. Jayson Pierce, Oct. 1, 2006. BS, U. North Tex., 2001. Cert. tchr. Tex. Second grade tchr. Beaver Tech. Ctr., Garland, Tex., 2001—. Tchr. liaison PTA, Garland, 2003—04; missionary worker Trinity Presbyn. Ch., Uganda, 2003, 2004. Named Tchr. of Yr., WalMart, Garland, 2003. Mem.: NSTA. Avocations: camping, scrapbooks, crafts. Home: 2121 W Campbell # 928 Garland TX 75044 Office: Beaver Elem Sch 3232 March Ln Garland TX 75042

BJORNSRUD, MARLENE, professional athletics manager; Tennis coach Grand Canyon U., Phoenix, 1979, asst. athletic dir., sr. women's adminstr.; dir. of athletics Santa Clara U.; gen. mgr. San Jose Cyber Rays Women's United Soccer Assn., San Jose, Calif. Founder Bay Area Women's Sports Initiative, San Jose, Calif., 2005—. Recipient Nat. Coach of Yr., NAIA, 1981.

BLACK, BARBARA ANN, publisher; b. Eureka, Calif., Dec. 11, 1928; d. William Marion and Letitia (Brunia) Black; m. Vinson Brown, June 18, 1950 (dec Dec. 1991); children: Tamara Pinn, Roxana Hodges, Keven Brown. BA, Western State Coll., Gunnison, Colo., 1950. Cert. tchr., Colo. Editor/proofreader Naturegraph Pubs., Los Altos, Calif., 1950-53, co-owner, mgr. San Martin, Calif., 1953-60, Healdsburg, Calif., 1960-76, owner/mgr. Happy Camp, Calif., 1976—. Author: Barns of Yesteryear, 1993; co-author: Sierra Nevada Wildlife, 1996, The Californian Wildlife Region, 1999; pub. over 100 titles on natural history and Native American subjects. Mem. Am. Booksellers Assn. Baha'i Faith. Avocations: gardening, backpacking. Home: PO Box 1045 3633 Indian Creek Rd Happy Camp CA 96039-9706 Office: Naturegraph Publishers Inc 3543 Indian Creek Rd Happy Camp CA 96039-9706 Office Phone: 800-390-5353, 530-493-5353.

BLACK, BARBARA ARONSTEIN, legal history educator; b. Bklyn., May 6, 1933; d. Robert and Minnie (Polenberg) A.; m. Charles L. Black, Jr., Apr. 11, 1954; children— Gavin B., David A., Robin E. BA, Bklyn. Coll., 1953; LLB, Columbia U., 1955; MPhil, Yale U., 1970, PhD, 1975; LLD (hon.), N.Y. Law Sch., 1986, Marymount Manhattan Coll., 1986, Vt. Law Sch., 1987, Coll. of New Rochelle, 1987, Smith Coll., 1988, Bklyn. Coll., 1988, York U., Toronto, Can., 1990, Georgetown U., 1991. Assoc. in law Columbia U. Law Sch., NYC, 1955-56; lectr. history Yale U., New Haven, 1974-76, asst. prof. history, 1976-79, assoc. prof. law, 1979-84; George Welwood Murray prof. legal history Columbia U. Law Sch., NYC, 1984—, dean faculty of law, 1986-91. Editor Columbia Law Rev., 1953-55. Active N.Y. State Ethics Commn., 1992-95. Recipient Fed. Bar Assn. prize Columbia Law Sch., 1955 Mem. Am. Soc. Legal History (pres. 1986-90), Am. Acad. Arts and Scis., Am. Philos. Soc., Mass. Hist. Soc., Supreme Ct. Hist. Soc., Selden Soc., Century Assn. Office: Columbia U Sch Law 435 W 116th St New York NY 10027-7201 Office Phone: 212-854-5735. Business E-Mail: BAB@law.columbia.edu.

BLACK, BARBARA ONDERCHEK, retired physician; b. Jamaica, N.Y., Oct. 24, 1940; d. George Stephen and Irene Elizabeth (Gaydos) Onderchek; m. Frank Snyder Black, Jr., July 12, 1969; 1 child, Frank Snyder III. BA, Trinity Coll., Washington, D.C., 1962; MD, Georgetown U., Washington, D.C., 1966. Lic. physician D.C., Md. Intern in gen. surgery Georgetown U. Hosp., Washington, 1966—67, resident in gen. surgery, 1967—68, resident in urology, 1968—71; staff urologist Group Health Assn., Washington, 1971—74; urologist Washington, 1974—92; physician Sibley Meml. Hosp., Washington, 1992—94, Mgmt. Recruiters of Washington, D.C., Silver Spring, Md., 1995—; ret. Mem.: AAUW, AMA, Am. Soc. Quality Control, Am. Coll. Physician Execs., Georgetown Clin. Soc., Sibley Med. Assn., Am. Med. Women's Assn., Med. Soc. D.C. Home: 5603 Durbin Rd Bethesda MD 20814-1013

BLACK, BEVERLY ANN MARIE LAYTON, secondary school educator, department chairman; b. Vernon, Tex., Dec. 3, 1957; d. Luther G. and Dorothy May (Koch) Layton; m. David Bryan Black, Jan. 1, 1988. BS in Secondary Math., Bus. Edn., West Tex. State U., Canyon, 1979. Cert. tchr. Tex. Math. tchr. 6-12th grades Spur Ind. Sch. Dist., Tex., 1980—81, Northside Ind. Sch. Dist., Tex., 1981—88; math. and algebra tchr. 7-8th grades Vernon Mid. Sch., Tex., 1988—99; algebra 1 and 2 tchr. Vernon HS, 1999—. Number sense coach U. Interscholastic League, Vernon, 1979—, math. coach, calculator coach, 1979—2004. Named Nobel Educator of Distinction, Nat. Soc. HS Scholars, 2004. Avocations: motorcycling, skiing. Home: 7967 Solitaire Rd Vernon TX 76384 Office: Vernon High Sch 2102 Yucca Ln Vernon TX 76384

BLACK, CAROLE, broadcast executive; b. Cin. BA in English lit., Ohio State U. With Procter & Gamble, Cin.; account supr., sr. v.p., mgmt. rep. DDB Needham, Chgo., 1983—86; v.p. worldwide mktg. home video Walt Disney Co., 1986—88, sr. v.p. mktg., TV, 1988—94; pres., gen. mgr. NBC 4, L.A., 1994—99; pres., CEO Lifetime Entertainment Svcs., 1999—2005. Named one of 100 Most Powerful Women in Entertainment, Hollywood Reporter, 2004; recipient CTAM Hall of Fame Award, 2000, Nat. Breast Cancer Coalition Leadership Award, 2000, Muse Award, NY Women in Film & Television, 2000, Impact Award, Nat. Hispanic Media Coalition, 2001, Women Who Change the World Award, NY Women in Communications, 2002, Matrix Award, 2002. Office: Lifetime Entertainment Svcs 309 W 49th St New York NY 10019-7404

BLACK, CAROLINE KAPUSTA, lawyer; b. Derby, Conn. BS, Cornell U., 1982; JD, Stetson Coll. Law, 1984. Asst. state atty. Hillsborough County State Atty.'s Office, Tampa, Fla., 1985-89; ptnr. Sessums, Mason Black & Caballero, Tampa, 1989—. Pres. Ctr. for Women, Tampa, 1995-97; chair Fla. Bar Grievance Com. 13A, Tampa, 1995. Mem. Fla. Bar (mem. exec. coun. family law sect. 1995-2002, chair 2002-03), Hillsborough County Bar Assn. (bd. dirs. family law sect. 2003—, pres.-elect 2006—). Office: Sessums Mason Black and Caballero 307 S Magnolia Ave Tampa FL 33606-2237 Office Phone: 813-251-9200.

BLACK, CATHLEEN PRUNTY, publishing executive; b. Chgo., Apr. 26, 1944; d. James Hamilton and Margaret (Harrington) Black; m. Thomas E. Harvey; children: Alison, Duffy. BA, Trinity Coll., 1966. Advt. sales rep. Holiday mag., NYC, 1966-69, Travel & Leisure mag., NYC, 1969-70, New York mag., 1970-72; advt. dir. Ms. mag., 1972-75, assoc. pub., 1975-77, New York mag., 1977-79, pub., 1979-83; pres. USA Today, 1983, pub., 1984-91; exec. v.p. mktg. Gannett Co., Inc., 1985—91, also bd. dirs.; pres., CEO Newspaper Assn. Am., Reston, Va., 1991—95; pres. Hearst Mags., NYC, 1996—. Bd. dirs. iVillage, Coca-Cola Co., 1990—91, 1993—, IBM, 1995—. Trustee U. Notre Dame. Named Pub. Exec. of Yr., Advt. Age, 2000, Corp. Pub. of Yr., Delaney Report, 2006; named one of Most Powerful Women in Am. Bus., Fortune mag., 100 Most Influential Bus. Leaders, Crain's N.Y. Bus., 2002, 100 Most Powerful Women in World, Forbes mag., 2005—06, 50 Most Powerful Women in Bus., Fortune mag., 2005, 2006; recipient Muriel Fox Award for Comm. Leadership Toward a Just Soc., NOW, 2000, Stephen P. Duggan Award, Inst. Internat. Edn., 2002, Henry Johnson Fisher award for lifetime achievements, Mag. Pub. Am., 2006. Mem.: Coun. on Fgn. Rels., Advt. Coun. (bd. mem.). Office: Hearst 250 W 55th St New York NY 10019-5201*

BLACK, CATHY TURNER, elementary school educator; d. Roscoe Johnson and Betty Shelton Turner; 1 child, Kevin Patrick. B of Music Edn., Longwood Coll., Farmville, Va., 1975. Tchr. choral music Mecklenburg County Pub. Schs., Boydton, Va., 1975—78; tchr. music, elem. edn. Bath County Pub. Schs., Warm Springs, Va., 1978—81; bank teller First Nat. Exch. Bank, Roanoke, Va., 1981—83; tchr. music Franklin County Pub. Schs., Rocky Mount, Va., 1983—. Ch. pianist Rosalind Hills Bapt. Ch., Roanoke, Va., 2002—. Mem.: Music Educators Nat. Conf. Baptist. Avocations: directing children's choir, playing piano for weddings and receptions. Office: Burnt Chimney Elem Sch 80 Burnt Chimney Rd Wirtz VA 24184 Office Phone: 540-721-2936. E-mail: katrinka521@yahoo.com.

BLACK, COBEY, journalist; b. Washington, June 15; d. Elwood Alexander and Margaret (Beall) Cobey; m. Edwin F. Black; children: Star, Christopher, Noel, Nicholas, Brian, Bruce. BA, Wellesley Coll., 1944; postgrad., U. Hawaii. Exec. sec. to Irene, designer Metro-Goldwyn-Mayer, 1944; actress Fed. Republic Germany, 1945-46; women's editor Washington Daily News, 1947-50; columnist Honolulu Star Bull., 1954-65, Honolulu Advertiser, 1969-85. Cons. HEW, Peace Corps; bd. dirs. Pacific and Asian Affairs Coun., Honolulu Com. on Fgn. Rels., Soc. Asian Art of Hawaii, Honolulu Media Coun.; pres. Black & Black, Inc. Author: Birth of A Princess, 1962, Iolani Luahine, 1986, Hawaii Scandal, 2002; travel editor Bangkok World, 1968-69; publicist CBS-TV series Hawaii Five-O, 1978. Mem. Hawaii State Commn. on Status of Women, 1978-86. Mem. Nat. Press Club, Nat. Soc. Colonial Dames, Lady of Dumbarton, Royal Bangkok Sports Club, Outrigger Canoe Club, Waialae Country Club, Garden Club of Honolulu. Democrat. Episcopalian. Office: Black & Black Inc 3081 La Pietra Cir Honolulu HI 96815-4736

BLACK, DEVERA GIGES, psychotherapist; b. Newark, Nov. 21, 1926; d. Bernard Edward and Belle (Demner) McCoy; m. Gerald Giges, July 6, 1952 (div. July 1975); children: Robert Eli, Laura Ellen; m. Stuart C. Black, Aug. 31, 1975 BA, Douglas Coll., 1948; MSW, Columbia U., 1951. LCSW, Cert. social worker N.Y.; bd. cert. diplomate social work. Med. social worker Maimonides Hosp., Bklyn., 1951—54; social work cons. Coll. Dentistry NYU, 1963—68; clin. social worker Westchester Jewish Cmty. Svcs., White Plains and Yonkers, NY, 1968—78; pvt. practice South Salem, NY, 1977—. Mem. faculty Core Energetic Inst., N.Y.C., 1981—90, Phoenica Pathwork Ctr., N.Y.C., 1982—. Nem. NASW, Soc. Clin. Social Work Psychotherapists Home and Office: 71 Twin Lakes Rd South Salem NY 10590-1012 Office Phone: 914-763-3438.

BLACK, DONNA LORD, psychologist; d. Clarence Gaither and Edith Wade Lord; m. Ronald Gregory Black, Oct. 6, 1949; children: Jason Andrew, Allison Pauline Handler. AA, San Jacinto Coll., Pasadena, Tex., 1972; BS, U. Houston Clear Lake, 1988, MA, 1992. Lic. Specialist in Sch. Psychology Tex. State Bd. Examiners of Psychologists, 1996, Psychol. Assoc. Tex. State Bd. Examiners of Psychologists, 1994, cert. instr. Nonviolent Crisis Intervention Internat. Assn. Nonviolent Crisis Intervention Cert., 2000. Caseworker, investigator Galveston County Children's Protective Svcs., Tex., 1988—90; intern Tex. Children's Hosp., Houston, 1992; lic. specialist sch. psychology Dickinson Ind. Sch. Dist., Tex., 1992—99; coord. student support svcs. Santa Fe Ind. Sch. Dist., Tex., 1999—2001; specialist sch. psychology Pasadena Ind. Sch. Dist., Tex., 2001—02; cons. Houston, 2002—04; coord. psychol. and diagnostic svcs. East Wharton County Co-Op, Tex., 2004—. Adj. faculty U. Houston Clear Lake, 2002—04. Technical assistance (sci. publ.) Demethylation in Rats Chronically Treated with Cocaine, presenter (presentation) ADHD: Taming the Beast, Prevention and Intervention: A Three-Tiered Model, Linking Assessment Data to I.E.P.s, I.E.P. Meeting Do's and Don'ts, Behavior Intervention Plans: Meeting Both the Letter and Spirit of the Law, ADHD: Do's and Don'ts for the Classroom, commentator (radio talk-show) Attack on America: A Nation Recovers, presenter (presentation) A Nation in Crisis: Helping Our Children Cope, Coping with Crisis in America: Providing a Safe and Secure Environment in the Schools, Disruptive Classroom Behavior. Vol. Wharton County Spl. Olympics; chairperson Clear Brook H.S. Project Graduation, Friendswood, Tex., 1994—95; youth coord. Cokesbury United Meth. Ch., Houston, 1991—93; chairperson Tex. Air N.G., 147th Fighter Wing Family Readiness Group, Houston, 2001—04. Named to, Nat. Dean's List, 1988—89; recipient Outstanding Coll. Students Am. award, 1989; scholar, Ch. Women United, 1986; Scholarship, Assn. Bus. and Profl. Women, Bay Area chpt., 1986, 1987. Mem.: NASP, Tex. Assn. Sch. Psychologists (newsletter editor, sec., area rep. 2000—06, Outstanding Sch. Psychologist of Yr. 2005), Tex. Coun. of Administrators of Spl. Edn. Methodist. Avocations: baseball, music, digital slideshow productions, wedding coordination. Office: Region 4 Edn Svc Ctr 7145 W Tidwell Houston TX 77092 E-mail: dblack@wharton.isd.tenet.edu.

BLACK, EILEEN MARY, retired elementary school educator; b. Bklyn., Sept. 20, 1944; d. Marvin Mize and Anne Joan (Salvia) B. Student, Grossmont Coll., El Cajon, Calif., 1964; BA, San Diego State U., 1967; postgrad., U. Calif., San Diego, Syracuse U. Cert. tchr., Calif. Tchr. La Mesa (Calif.)-Spring Valley Sch. Dist., 1967-2001, ret., 2001. NDEA grant Syracuse U., 1968. Mem.: AARP, Calif. Ret. Tchrs. Assn., Wilderness Soc., Greenpeace, San Diego Zool. Soc., Sierra Club. Roman Catholic. Avocations: reading, baseball, walking. Home: 9320 Earl St Apt 15 La Mesa CA 91942-3846 Personal E-mail: eblack44@aol.com.

BLACK, GENEVA ARLENE, social services agency administrator; b. Dazell, S.C., Apr. 30, 1932; d. Isaac and Carrie Lee (Hollimon) Sanders; children: Ronald D., Robert J., Clarissa D. Black Wells, Michael A., Steven G. Diploma Soc. Svc. Adminstrn., Temple U., 1970-73; Diploma Bus. Adminstrn., U. Detroit, 1981-82. Housing coord. Haddington Leadership Orgn., Phila., 1970-73, exec. dir., 1973; co-founder, exec. dir. Haddington Multi Svcs. for Older Adults, Inc., Phila., 1975—. Host monthly radio program Sr.'s Hour, Sta. WDAS, 1996—. Pres., block capt. 5500 Block Poplar St.; chmn. Emergency Fund Coalition; mem. human svc. com. Empowerment Zone West Phila.; 192d legis. dist. chmn. Com. on Aging, trustee, treas. inspiration choir Vine Meml. Bapt. Ch., co-chmn. ch. anniversary com., sec. Fed. Credit Union; sec. West Phila. Planning Com.; sec. bd. dirs. Spectrum Health Svcs.; bd. dirs., v.p. Housing Assn. Authority Delaware Valley; bd. dirs. Mayor's Commn. on Svcs. to Elderly, 1996—; coord. sr. programs. Recipient numerous awards, including Leon S. Rosenthal award for humanitarian and cmty. svc. West Phila. C. of C., 1983, citation for outstanding cmty. svc. Pa. Ho. of Reps., 1985, 87, 90, 95, Cmty. Svc. award Phila. chpt. Nat. Assn. Negro Bus. and Profl. Women's Club, 1989, citation for outstanding cmty. svcs. gov. State of Pa., 1990, Pa. Senate, 1990, Cmty. Svc. award Emergency Fund for Older Philadelphians, 1991, Phila. Bapt. Ch., 1993, Allan Yaffe svc. award Phila. Corp. for Aging, 1994, cert. of appreciation U. Pa., 1995; named to Afro-Am. Hall of Fame, Drexel U., 1996; named Top Ladies of Distinction, Inc. Phila. Chpt., 1998; recipient Trail Blazer award 2000 Black Women, 1998. Mem. AARP (1st sec. Overbrook chpt. 1993-96), Phila. Corp. Aging (cert. mental health, 1987).

BLACK, GINGER ELIZABETH, elementary school educator; d. Richard Temple and Mary Helen Crouch; 1 child, Caitlin Emily. BA in Edn., Lynchburg Coll., 1970; MA, U. Va., Charlottesville, 1974. Advanced profl. ednl. cert. Md. Reading specialist Montgomery County Schs., Rockville, Md., 1973—. Ednl. cons., tutor, McLean, Va., 1995—. Author: Making the Grade, 1989. Mem. Friends of the Nat. Zoo, Washington, 1993—98. Mem.: Montgomery County Edn. Assn. (Broome award for outstanding pub. 1992), Md. State Tchrs. Assn. (assoc.), Internat. Reading Assn. (assoc.), U. Va. Alumni Assn. Episcopalian. Avocations: travel, gardening, reading. Home: 7208 Evans Mill Rd Mc Lean VA 22101 Office Phone: 301-320-6555. Personal E-mail: gblack4720@aol.com.

BLACK, JULIE L., language educator; b. Woodward, Okla., Jan. 25, 1960; d. Lee W. and Julia J. Jordan; m. David Black, Aug. 4, 1982; children: Jordan, Jennifer. BS Interdisciplinary Studies, Tex. A & M, Commerce, 1993. Tchr. English Wylie H.S., Tex., 1993—. Named Tchr. of Yr., Wylie Ind. Sch. Dist., 1998.

BLACK, KATHRYN N., psychologist, educator; b. Atlantic, Iowa, Jan. 28, 1933; d. Basil John and Opal Lucille (Weaver) Norcross; children: Deirdre Rehnberg Black LeMire, Amanda Katherine Black-Pherson. BA, U. Iowa, 1954, MA, 1956, PhD, 1957. Prof. Purdue U., West Lafayette, Ind., 1965—. Mem. Phi Beta Kappa. Home: 23295 Grayshire Lane Lake Barrington IL 60010-1957

BLACK, LISA HARTMAN, actress, singer; b. Houston, June 01; m. Clint Black, Oct. 20, 1991. Grad., High Sch. Performing Arts, Houston. TV series: Tabitha, 1977-78, High Performance, 1983, Knots Landing, 1982-86, 2000

Malibu Rd., 1993; TV Movies: Murder at the World Series, 1977, Where the Ladies go, 1980, Gridlock (also released as The Great American Traffic Jam), 1980, Beverly Hills Cowgirl Blues, 1985, Roses Are for the Rich, 1987, Full Exposure: The Sex Tapes Scandal, 1989, The Operation, 1990, The Take, USA, 1990, Fire! Trapped on the 37th Floor, 1991, Not of This World, 1991, Red Wind, 1991, The Return of Elliot Ness, 1991, Without a Kiss Goodbye, 1993, Search for Grace, 1994, Someone Else's Child, 1995, Have You Seen My Son?, 1996, Out of Nowhere, 1997, Still Holding On: The Legend of Cadillac Jack, 1998; TV mini-series: Jacqueline Susann's Valley of the Dolls, 1981, Judith Krantz's Dazzle, 1995; films: Deadly Blessing, 1981, Where the Boys Are, 1984, also recorded Hold On I'm Comin', 1979, Til My Heart Stops, 1988; prodr. Have You Seen My Son?, 1996; TV guest appearances include Police Woman, 1974, Vega$, 1978, On Stage America, 1984, The Hitchhiker, 1983, Matlock, 1986.

BLACK, LISA ZAHN, elementary school educator; b. Kansas City, Mo., Oct. 1, 1958; d. F. George and Sue (Scott) Z.; children: Whitney, Rebecca. BA, Kansas City U., 1980; MS, U. Kans., 1982. Mid. sch. tchr. Kans. State Sch. for Deaf, Olathe, 1981-88, tchr., 1983-88; 4th grade tchr. Briarwood Elem. Sch., Olathe, 1988—97, Black Bob Elem. Sch., 1998—. Portfolio cons. Emporia State U., 1994—; instr. U. Kans., 1992-94; ednl. cons. Soc. Devel. Edn., 2000—. Author: Coloring Your World With Learning, 1995, The Best of Good Apple, 1995, Munchable Math, 2000, Connecting Math and Literature, 2002; contbr. articles to profl. jours. Bd. dirs. Paul Mesner Puppets, Kansas City, Mo., 1993—, com. chmn., exec. com. BOTAR, Kansas City., 1980—; chmn. Am. Royal BBQ Contest; bd. dirs. Midwest Ear Inst., Kansas City, 1988—. Recipient Presdl. award for Excellence in Tchg. Math. Office of Pres. U.S., 1994, Excellence in Tchg. Math. award Kans. Med. Soc., 1993; Christa McAuliffe fellow, 2002; named to Nat. Tchr. Hall of Fame, 2002, Mid-Am. Edn. Hall of Fame, 2003. Mem. NSTA, Nat. Supervisors of Tchrs. of Math., Nat. Coun. of Tchrs. of Math., Soc. Presdl. Awardees, Coun. Presdl. Awards for Math., Delta Kappa. Presbyterian. Avocations: bicycling, hiking, needlepoint, backpacking. Home: 5213 W 84th Ter Shawnee Mission KS 66207-1716 Office Phone: 913-780-7310. Personal E-mail: lisazblack@yahoo.com.

BLACK, MARSHA C., environmental scientist; BS in Comprehensive Sci., Converse Coll.; PhD in Ecology, U. Tenn. Acad. & postdoctoral rsch. U. Joensuu, Finland; asst. prof. zoology Okla. State U., Stillwater, Okla., 1990—94; assoc. prof. environ. health scis. Coll. Agrl. and Environ. Scis. U. Ga., Athens, Ga., 1994—. Reviewer (for several environ. toxicology pub.); mem. editl. bd.: Environ. Toxicol. Chemistry, 2000—02. Mem.: Soc. Environ. Toxicology and Chemistry (bd. dirs.). Office: Univ Ga 148 Environ Health Bldg Athens GA 30602 Business E-Mail: mblack@uga.edu.

BLACK, MARY KAY, secondary school educator; b. Winner, S.D., Jan. 10, 1960; d. Estell and Marie (Sorenson) Young; m. Fredrick Black, Aug. 10, 1979; 1 child, Heidi. AS, U. S.D., Springfield, 1981; BS in Social Sci., Dakota State Coll., Madison, S.D., 1983. Bus. and computer instr. Florence (S.D.) H.S., 1983—. Mem. S.D. Edn. Assn. (pres. 1984-86), Delta Kappa. Democrat. Lutheran. Avocations: reading, cooking, volunteer work, family. Home: PO Box 141 Florence SD 57235-0141 Office: Florence School PO Box 66 Florence SD 57235-0066

BLACK, PAGE MORTON, civic worker, vocalist, musician; b. Chgo. d. Alexander and Rose Morton; m. William Black, Mar. 27, 1962. Student, Chgo. Mus. Coll. Singer, pianist Pierre Hotel, NYC, Warwick Hotel, One Fifth Ave. Sherry Netherland Hotel; singer radio show and comml. Chock Full O'Nuts Corp.; rec. artist Atlantic Records, Den Records. Co-founder Page and William Black Post-Grad. Sch. Medicine, Mt. Sinai Med. Sch., 1965—; chmn. mem. exec. bd. Parkinsons' Disease Found., Columbia U. Med. Ctr.; mem. nat. vis. coun. Columbia U. Health Scis. Faculties; hon. chmn. Chock Full O' Nuts Corp., 1983—90; active Columbia Presbyn. Health Scis. Adv. Coun.; founding mem. ASPCA; mem. neurosci. com. Neurol. Inst. of NY at Columbia Presbyn. Med. Ctr., Columbia Presbyn. Med. Ctr. Mem. neuroscience com. Columbia Presbyn. Health Sci. Adv. Coun. Recipient Ann. award, Parkinsons' Disease Found., 1987, Police Athletic League, 1992, Manhattan Mag. award, 1992, Lifetime Achievement award, Parkinson's Disease Found., 1997, Disting. Svc. award, 2005, Humanitarian award, 2005, Dean's award for Disting. Svc., Columbia U. Coll. Physicians & Surgeons, 1998. Achievements include being honored with a laboratory and the Page & William Black Chair at Columbia U. Home: Premium Pt New Rochelle NY 10801

BLACK, REBECCA LEREE, special education educator; b. Pasadena, Calif., Sept. 15, 1954; d. James and Mary Black; m. Mario Isabella, Aug. 10, 1996. BA, San Diego State U., 1977, MA, 1987. Multiple subject tchg. credential Calif., cert. specialist credential-learning handicapped Calif., resource specialist. Substitute tchr. San Diego Unified Dist., 1978—80, Poway (Calif.) Unified Sch. Dist., 1978—79; resource specialist Coronado (Calif.) H.S., 1980—. Support provider Beginning Tchr. Support Assessment, Coronado, 2000—02; focus group leader Coronado H.S. Accreditation Com., Coronado, 2001—02. Club advisor Coronado H.S. Friday Night Live Club, Coronado, 1991—2001, Girls' Svc. Club, Coronado, 1980—83, Youth to Youth, Coronado, 1986—89. Scholar Anita Snow Meml., San Diego South County Selpa and Bonita Optimist Found., 2001. Mem.: Calif. Assn. Resource Specialists and Spl. Edn. Tchrs. Avocations: martial arts, golf, softball.

BLACK, RECCA MARCELE, elementary school educator; b. Marion, Ind., Feb. 4, 1964; d. Charles Lee and Jerry Ann Barbour. BA in Elem. Edn., Marion Coll., 1987, MEd; postgrad., Ind. Wesleyan U. Tchr. Marion (Ind.) Community Schs.; food svc. worker Marion Coll. Baldwin Food Svc.; casual clerk, cashier, sec. U.S. Post Office; audio-visual asst. VA Med. Ctr. Reporter Marion Newspaper. Contbr. numerous articles to profl. jours. Bd. dirs. YWCA. Recipient Freshman scholar, Shugar scholar. Mem.: NEA, AAUW (bd. dirs.).

BLACK, RITA DUTTON, media specialist; b. Bklyn. d. Roger and Edith Dutton; m. David M. Black, Oct. 3, 1975; 1 child, Lindsay Edith Jean. BS in History & Social Sci., Longwood Coll., 1970; M of Libr. & Info. Sci., U. S.C., 1995. Cert. tchr. SC. Bd. Edn., 1995, registered Nat. Tchg. Coun. Scotland, 1975. Tchr. Portsmouth Pub. Schools, Va., 1972—75; pub. rels. officer Crawley Borough Coun., West Sussex, England, 1978—81; dep. clk. U.S. Dist. Ct., Columbia, SC, 1982—84; tchr. Dundee Schools, Tayside, Scotland, 1975—77; info. tech. specialist Richland County Sch. Dist. One, Columbia, 1996—. Adept tchr. evaluator Richland County Sch. Dist. One, 2003—, mem. website rev. com., 2001—. Author (webmaster): (website) St. Andrews Mid. Sch. (Computer Visual Literacy Festival 1st Pl. award, 1999). Usher capt. Union United Meth. Ch., Irmo, SC, 1999—; coach SAMS Fellowship Christian Athletes, Columbia, 2002—. Wayne S. Yenawine scholar, U. S.C. Coll. of Libr. & Info. Sci. Alumni Assn., 1993. Mem.: Palmetto State Teachers Assn. (assoc.), S.C. Assn. Sch. Librarians (assoc.; regional network coord. 1998—99, mem. jr. book award com. 1997—2000), Pi Gamma Mu, Beta Phi Mu (treas. 1998—99). Conservative. Methodist. Avocations: travel, boating, reading, jazz, ballet. Office: St Andrews Mid Sch 1231 Bluefield Rd Columbia SC 29210 Business E-Mail: rblack@richlandone.org.

BLACK, RUTH IDELLA, museum curator; b. Aug. 16, 1911; BA, Hastings Coll., 1933; MA, U. Nebr., 1952. Supt. of schs. Chester (Nebr.) Pub. Schs., 1948-54; head edn. dept. Fairbury (Nebr.) Jr. Coll., 1954-70; curator Fillmore County Hist. Soc. Mus., Fairmont, Nebr., 1987—, also bd. dirs. Mem. Ret. Tchr. Assn., Nebr. State Hist. Soc., Delta Kappa Gamma Rho (chpt. pres. 1965-67, state parlimentarian 1968), Pi Gamma Mu.

BLACK, SAUNDERS PROCTOR, special education educator; b. Roanoke Rapids, N.C., July 20, 1941; d. William Hansel and Evelyn Barrett (Bridger) P. AA, Sullins Coll., 1960; BA, Sacred Heart Coll., 1975, BA, 1977; MEd, Winthrop Coll., 1985. Cert. early childhood, mental retardation and visually impaired tchr., N.C. Counselor spl. edn. Girl Scout Camp Golden Valley, Shelby, NC, 1984-89; tchr. Webb St. Sch. Gaston County Schs., Gastonia, NC, 1965-89; tchr. Fox Rd. Elem. Sch. Wake County Schs., Raleigh, NC, 1989—2000. Homebound tchr. handicapped student, Gastonia, 1988-89. Recipient Cert. of Outstanding Svc. Assn. for Retarded Citizens, Gastonia, 1982-84, Merit award Girl Scouts U.S./Boys Scouts Am., 1986; named Educator of the Yr., 1984-85, Tchr. of the Yr., Fox Road Elem. Sch., 1990-91. Mem. Assn. for Retarded Citizens, Coun. for Exceptional Children Internat., Libr. for Spl. Edn., Delta Kappa Gamma Internat., N.C. Educators Assn., Nat. Sci. Assn. Democrat. Episcopalian. Avocation: collect books and guides dealing with mentally handicapped. Home: 665 Mariposa Rd Stanley NC 28164-9655

BLACK, SHIRLEY A., healthcare educator; b. Natrona Heights, Pa., Mar. 19, 1951; d. Joseph Louis and Helen Constance Sepich; m. David Edward Black, June 24, 1978; children: Erin Marlene, Jonathan David. BS, Slippery Rock State Coll., Pa., 1973, Med, 1979. Coach. tchr. health and phys. edn. Clarion Area Sch. Dist., Pa., 1974—95; adminstrv. services mgr. Pa. Dept. Corrections, Elizabethtown, 1997—99; advisor health & phys. edn. Pa. Dept. Edn., Harrisburg, 1999—. Nat. steering com. Coun. Chief State Sch. Officers Health Edn. Assessment Project, Washington, 2003—; mem. state team Pa. Action Healthy Kids, Hershey, 2002—; dir. Govs. Inst. Health, Safety and Phys. Edn., Harrisburg, 2000—; mem. state adv. team comprehensive sch. health edn. Am. Cancer Soc., Hershey; exec. bd. Pa. State Assn. Health, Phys. Edn., Recreation and Dance, Lititz, 2000—. Organizer Clarion county autumn leaf jr. olympic program Clarion County C. of C., Pa., 1990—94. Recipient Appreciation award, Pa. State Assn. Health, Phys. Edn., Recreation and Dance, 2004. Mem.: ASCD, Assn. Advancement Health Edn., Nat. Assn. Sport and Phys. Edn., Soc. State Dirs. Health and Phys. Edn., Pa. State Assn. Health, Phys. Edn., Recreatiion and Dance, AAHPERD, Delta Psi Kappa. Achievements include development of Pennsylvania Academic Standards for Health, Safety and Physical Education. Avocations: golf, travel. Home: 1217 Chelsen Cross Mechanicsburg PA 17050 Office: Pennsylvania Department of Education 333 Market St 8th fl Harrisburg PA 17126 Office Phone: 717-772-0067. Office Fax: 717-783-3946. Personal E-mail: ssb78@comcast.net. E-mail: sblack@state.pa.us.

BLACK, SHIRLEY TEMPLE (MRS. CHARLES A. BLACK), retired ambassador, retired actress; b. Santa Monica, Calif., Apr. 23, 1928; d. George Francis and Gertrude Temple; m. John Agar, Jr., Sept. 19, 1945 (div. 1950); 1 dau., Linda Susan Falaschi; m. Charles A. Black, Dec. 16, 1950 (dec. Aug. 4, 2005); children: Charles Alden Jr., Lori Alden. Grad., Westlake Sch. Girls, 1945; D (hon.), Santa Clara Univ., Lehigh Univ. Rep. to 24th Gen. Assembly UN, N.Y.C., 1969-70; amb. to Ghana Accra, 1974-76; chief of protocol White House, Washington, 1976-77; amb. to Czechoslovakia Prague, 1989-92. Mem. U.S. Delegation on African Refugee Problems, Geneva, 1981; mem. public adv. com. UN Conf. on Law of the Sea; dep. chmn. U.S. del. UN Conf. on Human Environment, Stockholm, 1970-72; spl. asst. to chmn. Pres.'s Coun. on Environ. Quality, 1972-74; del. treaty on environment USSR-USA Joint Commn., Moscow, 1972; mem. U.S. Commn. for UNESCO, 1973; hon. U.S. Fgn. Svc. officer. Began film career at age 3 1/2; first full-length film was Stand Up and Cheer; other films included Little Miss Marker, Baby Take a Bow, Bright Eyes, Our Little Girl, The Little Colonel, Curly Top, The Littlest Rebel, Captain January, Poor Little Rich Girl, Dimples, Stowaway, Wee Willie Winkie, Heidi, Rebecca of Sunnybrook Farm, Little Miss Broadway, Just Around the Corner, The Little Princess, Susannah of the Mounties, The Blue Bird, Kathleen, Miss Annie Rooney, Since You Went Away, Kiss and Tell, 1945, That Hagen Girl, War Party, The Bachelor and the Bobby-Soxer, Honeymoon, 1947; narrator, actress: TV series Shirley Temple Storybook, NBC, 1958, Shirley Temple Show, NBC, 1960; author: Child Star: An Autobiography, 1988. Dir. Bank of Calif.; dir. Fireman's Fund Ins. Co., BANCAL Tri-State Corp., Walt Disney, Del Monte Corp.; Mem. Calif. Adv. Hosp. Council, 1969, San Francisco Health Facilities Planning Assn., 1965-69; Republican candidate for U.S. Ho. of Reps. from Calif., 1967; bd. dirs. Nat. Wildlife Fedn., Nat. Multiple Sclerosis Soc., UN Assn. U.S.A.; bd. dirs. exec. com. Internat. Fedn. Multiple Sclerosis Socs. Appointed col. on staff of Gov. Ross of Idaho, 1935; commd. col. Hawaiian N.G.; hon. col. 108th Rgt. N.G. Ill.; dame Order Knights Malta, Paris, 1968; recipient Ceres medal FAO, Rome, 1975, numerous other state decorations; Kennedy Center Honoree, 1998; recipient Chubb Fellowship Yale Univ., Screen Actors Guild Life Achievement award for career achievement and humanitarian accomplishment, 2005. Mem. World Affairs Coun. No. Calif. (dir.), Coun. Fgn. Rels., Nat. Com. for U.S./China Rels. Clubs: Commonwealth of Calif.

BLACK, SUSAN HARRELL, federal judge; b. Valdosta, Ga., Oct. 20, 1943; d. William H. and Ruth Elizabeth (Phillips) Harrell; m. Louis Eckert Black, Dec. 28, 1966. BA, Fla. State U., 1965; JD, U. Fla., 1967; LLM, U. Va., 1984. Bar: Fla. 1967. Atty. U.S. Army Corps of Engrs., Jacksonville, Fla., 1968—69; asst. state atty. Gen. Counsel's Office, Jacksonville, 1969—72; judge County Ct. of Duval County, Fla., 1973—75; judge 4th Jud. Cir. Ct. of Fla., 1975—79; judge U.S. Dist. Ct. (mid. dist.) Fla., Jacksonville, 1979—90, chief judge, 1990—92; judge U.S. Ct. Appeals (11th cir.) Fla., Jacksonville, 1992—. Faculty Fed. Jud. Ctr.; mem. U.S. Jud. Conf. Com. onInns of Ct., 1984—87; trustee Am. Inns Ct. Found., 1985—91; pres. US Dist. Judge's Assn (11th Cir.), 1987—88; mem. Jud. Improvements Com., 1987—90, Com. on Court Admin. and Case Mgmt., 1990—92, Jud. Conference Com. on Fed.-State Jurisdiction, 1998—2004. Trustee emeritus Law Sch. U. Fla.; past pres. Chester Bedell Inn of Ct. Mem.: Chester Bedell Inn of Ct. (founding mem.), Jacksonville Bar Assn., Fla. Bar Assn. Presbyterian.*

BLACK, VICTORIA LYNN, writer, artist; b. Whittier, Calif., Nov. 23, 1943; d. Raymond Witty and Dorothy Ada (Burnett) Davenport; m. Bruce Robert Black, Aug. 30, 1997; m. Richard Dee Bandlow, Sept. 16, 1961 (dec. Dec. 2, 1972); children: Lisa Lynn Bandlow Dobbins, Lincoln Dee Bandlow. Model/actress Dale Garrick Agy., Beverly Hills, Calif., 1959—78, Bronson of Calif., L.A., 1968—79; prodn. asst./casting Pub. Svc. Co., Irvine, Calif., 1979—80; theatrical agt. William Carroll Agy., Burbank, Calif., 1980—83; office mgr. Greenline, L.A., 1984—86, Napier, L.A., 1986—88, Shah Safari, L.A., 1988—93; writer, artist L.A. Author poetry, short stories, articles; artist paintings and drawings, exhibited in group shows at Verdugo Hills Art Assn., Montrose, Calif., 1999—2004, Glendale (Calif.) Coll., 1986—2002, ERA Castle, La Canada, Calif., 2004, Pasadena (Calif.) Libr., 2002, Jamboree-Art Show, Pasadena, 2003—04. Named Miss Palm Springs, 1960, Miss North Shore Beach, 1961, Miss Ma-Ha-Ya Lani, 1961, Miss Typical Teen, 1961. Mem.: Utah State Poetry Soc., W.Va. Poetry Soc., Poetry Soc. Okla., Mo. State Poetry Soc., Fla. State Poets Assn., Calif. State Poetry Soc., Ariz. State Poetry Soc., Verdugo Hills Art Assn., Alpha Gamma Sigma (life). Avocations: long walks, reading, collecting, museums and art shows. Home: PO Box 959 Sugarloaf CA 92386

BLACK, WAYNETTA GRANT, agricultural studies educator, retired counseling administrator; d. Wayman Ramsey Fagan Sr. and Vera Ella (Washington) Grant; m. Harrison Raycon Black; children: Harrison Bernarde, Christi Ranarta. BS, Tuskegee Inst., Ala., 1964; MA, U. South Ala., Mobile, 1972. Tchr., music dir. Booker T. Washington Elem. Sch., Brewton, Ala., 1964—66; tchr. Kate Shepard Elem. Sch., Mobile, Ala., 1970—72; counselor Metro Ednl. Tng., Mobile, 1972—74; counselor 9th grade S.F. Vigor HS, Prichard, Ala., 1974—80; vocational counselor Murphy HS, Mobile, 1980—99; owner Image Gallery, Mobile, 1994—2000; adminstrv. asst. Calloway-Smith Sch., Mobile, 2000; equestrian instr. Sandy Ridge Farms, Citronelle, Ala., 2000—. Owner Bak-Tari Imports, Mobile, 1972—74. Active Mobile Mus. Art., 2006, Ala. Coun. Arts, Montgomery, 2006, Keep Mobile Beautiful, Mobile, 2006. Recipient Appreciation cert., So. Poverty Law Ctr., Montgomery, 2006. Mem.: NEA (life), Ala. Edn. Assn. (life), Red Hat Soc., Kiwanis (v.p. Citronelle chpt. 2006—), Alpha Kappa Alpha (life; connection chair 2005—, Silver Star award 2006). Avocations: horseback riding, dance, antiques, reading. Home: PO Box 1197 Citronelle AL 36522

BLACKBURN, DEBBIE, elementary school educator, state representative; b. Woodward, Okla., Jan. 12, 1951; d. Norman and Laura Stevens; m. Bob L. Blackburn; 1 child, Beau. BA, Southwestern Okla. State U., 1973; postgrad studies in history, Okla. State U. Rep. Ho. Reps., State of Okla., Okla. City, 1995—. Bd. dirs. Paseo Redevelopment Corp.; chair subcom on edn, to appropriations and budget com. Okla. Ho. Reps., Okla. City, 1995—, mem. banking and fin., common edn., govt. ops., agy. oversight and adminstrv rules, human svcs. coms., 1995—. Mem. Neighborhood Alliance Okla. City. Mem.: LWV, Okla. City Leadership Alumni Assn., Okla. Acad. for State Goals, Downtown Rotary Club. Democrat. Office: 2300 N Lincoln Blvd Rm 301-A Oklahoma City OK 73105 Home and Office: 126 NW 22d St Oklahoma City OK 73103 E-mail: blackburnde@lsb.state.ok.us.

BLACKBURN, ELIZABETH HELEN, molecular biologist; b. Hobart, Australia, Nov. 26, 1948; 1 child. BSc in BioChemistry, U. Melbourne, Australia, 1970, MSc in BioChemistry, 1972; PhD in Molecular Biology, Cambridge U., Eng., 1975; post Date in Molecular and Cellular Biology, Yale U., New Haven, Conn., 1977; DSc (hon.), Yale U., 1991. Fellow in biology Yale U., New Haven, 1975-77; fellow in biochemistry U. Calif., San Francisco, 1977-78, asst. prof., dept. molecular biology Berkeley, 1978—83, prof., dept. molecular biology, 1983—86, 1986—90, chair dept. microbiology and immunology San Francisco, 1993-99, prof., depts. biochemistry and biophysics, and microbiology and immunology, 1990—. Coun. mem. President's Coun. on Bioethics, 2002—04; non-resident fellow Salk Inst.; faculty mem. Program in Biol. Sciences, U. Calif. San Francisco, Biomedical Sciences grad. PhD programs, U. Calif. San Francisco; program mem. U. Calif. San Francisco Comprehensive Cancer Ctr. Contbr. articles, scientific papers. Recipient Eli Lilly award in microbiology and immunology, 1988, le Grand Prix Charles-Leopold Mayer, 1998, Gairdner Found. award, 1998, Australia prize, 1998, Calif. Scientist of Year award, 1999, Harvey prize, 1999, AAMC Baxter award, 1999, Novartis-Drew award for Biomedical Sci., 1999, Feodor Lynen award, 2000, Am. Assn. Cancer Rsch.-G.H.A. Clowes Memorial award, 2000, Dickson prize in Medicine, 2000, Am. Cancer Soc. Medal of Honor, 2000, Am. Assn. Cancer Rsch.-Pezcoller Found. award for Cancer Rsch., 2001, Alfred P. Sloan Jr. prize, GM Cancer Rsch. Found., 2001, Ann. Bristol-Meyers Squibb award for Disting. Achievement in Cancer Rsch., 2003, Dr A.H. Heineken prize for Medicine, 2004, Benjamin Franklin medal in Life Sciences, Franklin Inst., 2005; co-recipient Albert Lasker award for Basic Med. Rsch., Lasker Found., 2006 Fellow: Am. Acad. Arts and Sciences, Royal Soc. London, AAAS; mem.: NAS (fgn. assoc. 1993, Award in Molecular Biology 1990), Genetic Soc. Am. (bd. dir. 2000—02), IOM, Am. Soc. Cell Biology (pres. 1998, Australian prize 1998, Gairdner prize 1998, Passano award 1999, Keio prize 1999, Rosensteil award 1999, E.B. Wilson medal 2001), Harvey Soc. in NY (Harvey Soc. Lectr. 1990). Office: U Calif Biochem and Biophys Box 2200 San Francisco CA 94158-2517 Business E-Mail: elizabeth.blackburn@ucsf.edu.*

BLACKBURN, JOY MARTIN, retired librarian; b. Marietta, Ohio, Oct. 28, 1925; d. Jonathan George and Helen Joy (Smith) Martin; m. Paul Edward Blackburn, Dec. 18, 1948 (dec. Dec. 1996); children: Paul Conrow, Amy Joy. BA, Ohio Wesleyan U., 1947; MA, U. Minn, 1948. Student counselor Ohio State U., Columbus, 1948—54; editor/libr. Jones & Laughlin Steel Co., Pitts., 1955—57; rsch. libr. Tech. Mktg. Assn., Concord, Mass., 1964—66; mgr. corp. libr. Washington Nat. Ins., Evanston, Ill., 1966—85; systems libr. Luth. Gen. Hosp., Park Ridge, Ill., 1986—88; info. specialist C. Berger & Co., Carol Stream, Ill., 1989—93; ret., 1993. Rschr./editor U. Pitts. Med. Sch., 1959. Author: J&L Rsch. Bull., 1955—57. Vol. Chgo. Bot. Garden Libr., Glencoe, Ill., 1997—99, U. Va. Health Sys. Mktg. and Cmty. Outreach, 2002—, U. Va. Alderman Libr., 2002—, Va. Found. Humanities, 2004—. Mem.: U. Va. Libr. Assocs. (bd. dirs. 2001—, 2004—), Cook County Hort. Soc. (hon.), Phi Beta Kappa. Avocations: history, photography, Arctic travel, art.

BLACKBURN, MARSHA, congresswoman; b. Laurel, Miss., June 6, 1952; m. Chuck Blackburn; 2 children. BS, Miss. State U., 1973. Retail mktg.; mem. Tenn. State Senate, Nashville, 1998—2002, US Congress from 7th Tenn. dist., 2003—, mem. energy and commerce com., founder Songwriters Caucus, 2003. Del. Am. Coun. Young Polit. Leaders, S.E. Asia, 1993; appointed by Gov. Don Sundquist exec. dir. Tenn. Film, Entertainment and Music Commn., 1995; chmn. Gov.'s Prayer Breakfast, 1996; bd. dirs. Benton Hall Sch., Nashville Symphony Guild, Arthritis Found., Nashville Zoo Friends; appointed Econ. Coun. on Women, 1999. Named a Small Bus. Adv., Small Bus. Survival Com., 2003; recipient Spirit of Enterprise award, US C. of C., 2004. Mem. Nat. Acad. Rec. Arts and Scis., Country Music Assn., Rotary, C. of C. Republican. Office: US Ho Reps 509 Cannon Ho Office Bldg Washington DC 20515-4305 Office Phone: 202-225-2811.*

BLACKBURN, PAMELA M., medical surgical nurse; b. Fitchburg, Mass., Sept. 12, 1948; d. Paul E. and Eugenia K. (Marsh) Gastonguay. ADN, Mt. Wachusett Community Coll., Gardner, Mass., 1975. RN, Mass., Tex. Charge nurse Leominster (Mass.) Hosp.; travel nurse Cross Country Nurses, Ga., La., Mass., Fla., Tex., Ariz.; charge nurse diabetes ctr., travel nurse Beaumont (Tex.) Med.-Surg. Hosp.; asst. dir. nursing Seymour (Mo.) Healthcare Inc.; nurse community home health Douglas County Health Dept., Ava, Mo.

BLACKBURN, PATRICIA A., elementary school educator; b. Cin., Oct. 19, 1949; d. William Earl and Ruth Mae Starks; m. Jack W. Sr. Blackburn, Aug. 26, 1967; children: Karen Biehle, Jack Jr., Philip. Degree in early elem. edn., No. Ky. U., Highland Hts., 1991, M in Elem. Edn., 1994. Sec. Dept. Solid Wastes, Cin., 1967, Retail Credit, Cin., 1968—69; mgr. Stop N Go Stores, Crescent Springs, Ky., 1970—72; tchr. Gallatin County Schs., Warsaw, Ky., 1991—2000, Grant County Schs., Crittenden, Ky., 2000—. Music minister New Bethel Bapt. Ch., 1996—. Mem.: Ky. Edn. Assn. (rep. 2005—06). Republican. Baptist. Avocations: camping, motorcycling. Home: 2492 Waller Rd Verona KY 41092

BLACKBURN, SADIE GWIN ALLEN, conservation executive; b. San Angelo, Tex., Oct. 14, 1924; d. Harvey Hicks Allen and Helen (Harris) Weaver; m. Edward Albert Blackburn Jr., Feb. 25, 1946; children: Edward III, Catherine Ledyard, Robert Allen. BA, Rice U., 1945, MA, 1975. Bookkeeper, trust dept. State Nat. Bank, Houston; tchr. elem. sch. Galveston, Tex.; mng. ptnr. Storey Creek Partnership, Houston, 1969—; dir. spl. projects San Jacinto State Park; dir. master plan State Hist. Park. Lectr. in landscape design history; spkr. in field. Co-author: Houston's Forgotten Heritage, 1822-1914, 1991; contbr. articles to gardening publs. Newsheet chmn. Jr. League, Galveston, 1950-53, art chmn., Houston Jr. League, 1957-58, chmn. garden/design com., 1991-93, mental health study com., 1959-61, 2d v.p., 1962-63, provisional chmn., 1962-63, interview chmn., 1963-64; adv. bd. Bayou Bend Gardens chmn. Mus. Fine Arts, 1973-74, Bayou Bend adv. com., 1987-89; v.p. Mental Health Assn., 1957-62, Botanic Garden Houston, 2005—; asst. treas. Child Guidance Assn., 1962-65; mem. Rice U. Hist. Commn., 1974-75; pres. River Oaks Garden Club, Houston, 1975-76; mem. adv. com. Bayou Bend Gardens, 1991—; active Buffalo Bayou Partnership, Houston Nature Conservancy, 1993, Friends of Herman Park, 1994, Meml. Park Adv., 1995, Scenic Houston Bd., 1999. Named Scenic Visionary, Scenic Houston, 2003; recipient Sweet Briar Disting. Alumna award, 1991, award, Friends of Herman Park, 2003, Stewardship Excellence award, Cultural Landscape Found., 2005, honor, San Jacinto Mus. History, 2006. Mem. Garden Club Am. (zone chmn. 1977-79, founders fund vice chmn. 1979-80, dir. 1980-82, rec. sec. 1982-84, v.p. 1984-86, archive co-chmn. 1986-87, 1st v.p. 1987-89, pres. 1989-91, Achievement medal 2002), Nat. Wildflower Rsch. Ctr. (bd. dirs.), Nat. Parks and Conservation Assn. Bd. (v.p. 1995-97, sec. 1997-99), San Jacinto Mus. History (pres. bd. 1975-77, bd. dirs.), Pi Beta Phi (Carolyn Herman Lichtenberg Crest award for disting. alumnae achievement 1998). Republican. Episcopalian. Avocations: gardening, fishing, hunting, bridge, golf. Home: 1030 Potomac Houston TX 77057-1916

BLACKBURNE-RIGSBY, ANNA, judge; b. Washington; BA in Polit. Sci., Duke U.; JD, Howard U. Sch. of Law, 1987. Assoc. atty. Hogan and Hartson, 1987—92; special counsel DC Office of Corp. Counsel, 1992—94, dep. corp.

counsel of family services div., 1994—96; hearing commsr. DC Superior Ct., 1996—2000, assoc. judge, 2000—06, DC Ct. Appeals, 2006—. Mem. judicial ed. com. DC Superior Ct.; lecturer Harvard Law Sch.; adjunct prof. U. DC David A. Clarke Sch. of Law. Recipient Women Meritorious Svc. award, Nat. Assn. of Professional Women. Mem.: Internat. Assn. of Women Judges (bd. managerial trustees), Nat. Assn. of Women Judges (v.p. dist. 4, chair nominating com.), Wash. Bar Assn. (former chair judicial council). Office: DC Ct of Appeals Moultrie Courthouse 500 Indiana Ave NW Washington DC 20001

BLACKFIELD, CECILIA MALIK, civic volunteer, educator; b. Oakland, Calif., Jan. 18, 1915; d. Benjamin Malik and Mollie Saak; m. William Blackfield, Dec. 25, 1941; children: Leland Gregory, Pamela Esther, Karen Ann. BA, U. Calif., Berkeley, 1936; MEdn., San Francisco State Tchrs. Coll., 1937. cert. elem. tchr. Calif. (lifetime). Tchr. Albany Sch. Dist., Calif., 1938-43. Rep. NEA, Alameda County, Calif., 1938-43. Pres. Calif. Tchrs. Assn., Alameda County, Calif., 1939; mem. (charter) Territorial Hosp. Aux., Kauikeolani Children's Hosp. (bd. dirs.); bd. dirs. Hastings Law Sch. Found., San Francisco, Calif., McCoy Pavilion Park, Honolulu, Hi., Daughters of the Nile, Honolulu, Temple Emmanuel; mem. Mayor's Citizen Adv. Com. for Diamond Head, Wakiki, Honolulu, Mayor's Adv. Com. for Cmty. and Urban Renewal, Beautification Com., League of Women Voters; chmn. Hawaii Cancer Fund Crusade and many more; mem. master planning com. Vision for Waikiki 2020; mem. Preservation Rev. Com. Hist. Hawaii; mem. Parks Bd., City and County of Honolulu, 2005; bd. mem. Temple Emmanuel. Named Woman of the Year for Nat. Brotherhood Week, Honolulu, 1972; recipient First Honorary Alumnus award Hastings Coll. of the Law U. of Calif., 1999. Mem. Nat. Assn. Home Builders (pres. Hawaii chpt. women's aux.), Outdoor Circle (pres.), Friends of Foster Gardens, Scenic Hawaii and Friends of Kapiolani Park (founding), Washington Palace State Capitol, Hadassah (past pres. Oakland chpt.), Women's Com. Brandeis U. (life mem.). Avocations: bridge, orchidist. Home: 901 Kealaolu Ave Honolulu HI 96816-5416

BLACKHAM, ANN ROSEMARY (MRS. J. W. BLACKHAM), realtor; b. NYC, June 16, 1927; d. Frederick Alfred and Letitia L. (Stolfe) DeCain; m. James W. Blackham Jr., Aug. 18, 1951; children: Ann C., James W. III. AB, St. Mary of the Springs Coll. (now Ohio Dominican U.), 1949; postgrad., Ohio State U., 1950. Mgr. br. store Filene & Sons, Winchester, Mass., 1950—52; broker Porter Co. Real Estate, Winchester, 1961—66; sales mgr. James T. Trefrey, Inc., Winchester, 1966—68; pres., founder Ann Blackham & Co. Inc. Realtors, Winchester, 1968—2001; v.p. Coldwell Banker, Winchester, 2001—. Bd. econ. advisors to Gov., 1969-74; participant White House Conf. on Internat. Cooperation, 1965; mem. Presdl. Task Force on Women's Rights and Responsibilities, 1969; exec. coun. Mass. Civil Def., 1965-69; chmn. Gov.'s Commn. on Status of Women, 1971-75; regional dir. Interstate Assn. Commn. on Status of Women, 1971-74; mem. Gov. Task Force on Mass. Economy, 1972; mem. Gov.'s Jud. Selection Com., 1972, Mass. Emergency Fin. Bd., 1974-75; bd. registration Real Estate Brokers and Salesman Commonwealth of Mass., 1991—, chmn. 1994—, Mass. Housing Authority, 2005—. Bd. visitors Ohio Dominican U., 1995—, nat. fund raising chair, 1998-99; corporator, trustee Charlestown Savs. Bank, 1974-84; corporator Winchester Hosp., 1983—, chair fund raising emergency room; bd. dirs. Winchester Hosp. Found., 1996—; mem. Winchester 350th Anniversary Commn.; design rev. commn. Town of Winchester, 1981-2003, Mass. Housing Authority, 2006—; bd. dirs. Phoenix Found., 1980-90, Bay State Health Care, Mass. Taxpayers Found., Speech and Hearing Found., Baystate Health Mgmt., Realty Guild Inc., v.p. 1995-96, bd. dirs. 1996-99, pres. 1997-98; regional selection panel White House Fellows, 1973-74; com. on women in svc. U.S. Dept. Def., 1977-80; 2d v.p. Doric Dames, 1971-74, founding mem., 1969; dep. chmn. Mass. Rep. State Com., 1965-66; sec. Mass. Rep. State Conv., 1970, del., 1960, 62, 64, 66, 70, 72, 74, 78, 90, 98, 2002, 06; state vice-chmn. Mass. Rep. Fin. Com., 1970; alt. del.-at-large Rep. Nat. Conv., 1968, 72, del., 1980, 84, 88, 92, 96; Rep. State Committeewoman, 1996—; pres. Mass. Fedn. Rep. Women, 1964-69; v.p. Nat. Fedn. Rep. Women, 1965-79; pres. Scholarship Found., 1976-78, Mass. Fedn. Women's Clubs; alumnae liaison The Beaumont Sch. for Girls; mem. Women for Romney, 2002; mem. Gov. Romney Inaugural Com.; mem. com. Bush Reelection, 2004; Gov.'s appointee to Housing Authority, 2006—, treas. Recipient Pub. Svc. award Commonwealth of Mass., 1978, Merit award Rep. Party, 1969, Pub. Affairs award Mass. Fedn. Women's Clubs, 1975; named Civic Leader of Yr. Mass. Broadcasters, 1962, Banker and Tradesman Leader Making a Difference, 1999; recipient Bus. Owner of Yr. award New England Women Bus. Owners, 1995, Disting. Alumnae award Ohio Dominican Coll., 1999, Disting. Service Citation Town of Winchester, 2003 Mem. Greater Boston Real Estate Bd. (hon., bd. dirs.), Eastern Middlesex Bd. Realtors (life mem. multi-million dollar club), Mass. Assn. Realtors (bd. dirs.), Nat. Assn. Realtors (women's coun.), Brokers Inst. (cert.), Coun. Realtors (cert., pres. 1983-84), Winchester C. of C. (bd. dirs.), Greater Boston C. of C., Nat. Assn. Women Bus. Owners, ENKA Soc. (treas. 2001—04), Rotary Internat., Tequesta Fla. Country Club, Capitol Hill Club, Ponte Vedra Club, Winchester Boat Club, Winchester Country Club, Wychmere Harbor Club, Womens City Club, Winton Club (sec., bd. dirs.), Hyannis Yacht Club. Office: Coldwell Banker 3 Church St Winchester MA 01890-2903 Business E-Mail: ann.blackham@nemoves.com.

BLACKMAN, DRUSILLA DENISE, dean; b. Madison, Wis., Aug. 26, 1954; d. Leonard and June (Jones) Blackman; m. Steven Baumholtz, June 28, 1987; children: Lukas Baumholtz, Adam Baumholtz. BS, Brown U., Providence; MBA, U. Pa., 1982. Dean grad. admissions and fin. aid Harvard U., Cambridge, Mass.; dean admissions and fin. aid Columbia U., N.Y.C.; dean of enrollment Culinary Inst. Am., Hyde Park, NY. Coll. cons. Vanguard Cons. Democrat. Avocations: reading, music, modern dance, cooking. Office: Culinary Inst 1946 Campus Dr Hyde Park NY 12538

BLACKMAN, GHITA WAUCHETA, natural energy consultant; b. Chgo., Feb. 19, 1932; d. William Harveston Joseph Harris and Zelda (Booth) Harris; m. David Edward Blackman, June 7, 1953 (div. Oct. 1976); children: Anasa, Anthony, Cynthia, Tracy. Student, NYU, 1949-50, U. Dayton, 1952-53. Various secretarial positions U.S. Air Force, Dayton, Ohio, Am. Humanist Assn., Yellow Springs, Ohio, 1950-64; sec. Antioch Coll., Yellow Springs, 1964-66, Fels Rsch. Inst., Yellow Springs, 1966-70; cons. direct sales Fashion Two Twenty, Dayton, 1966-72; mem. sales staff Prophet & Friends Inc., New Britain, Conn., 1972-76; customer rels. clk. Conn. Natural Gas Corp., Hartford, 1976-80, natural energy cons., 1980-98. Mem. Dayton (Ohio) Jr. Philharm. Orch., 1947-53, second violin Springfield Symphony, Ohio, 1956-64; v.p. Conn. Capitol Area chpt. Older Women's League, Hartford, 1985-87; sec. Spiritual Assembly of the Baha'is of West Hartford, Conn., 1977-78; corr. sec. Spiritual Assembly of the Baha'is of Hartford, 1982—. Independent. Mem. Baha'i Faith. Avocation: music. Personal E-mail: ghitab@juno.com. Business E-Mail: ghita@snet.net.

BLACKMAN, KENNETTE, secondary school educator; b. Alexander City, Ala., Aug. 3, 1982; d. Kenny and Cheryl Ransaw; m. Pierre Blackman, Nov. 19, 2005. BA in History, Ala. State U., Montgomery, 2004. Cert. tchr. Ala. Tchr. Loveless Academic Magnet HS, Montgomery, Ala., 2004—. Coll. ministry leader Fresh Anointing Internat. Ch., Montgomery, 2005. Leadership and Incentive scholar, Ala. State U., 2000—04. Mem.: Ala. Edn. Assn. Home: 3272 Gatsby Ln Montgomery AL 36106

BLACKMAN, LANI MODICA, copy editor; d. Salvatore Modica; m. Ronald Lewis Blackman, Sept. 17, 1969; 1 child, Lezlie Bianca Hepburn. Student, Ind. U., 1952—53; BS in Bus. Adminstrn., Bryant Coll., 1957; postgrad., SUNY, New Paltz, 1965—67; MFA in Theatre Arts, Brandeis U., 1972. Columnist Onterora Record, Woodstock, NY, 1962—64; dir. acting workshops Nashua (N.H.) and Manchester (N.H.) Inst. Arts and Scis., 1970—72; instr. acting and directing Berkshire C.C., Pittsfield, Mass., 1976—77; copy editor SUNY Press, Albany, NY, 1984—; editl. dir., copy editor, owner Renaissance Style, Ontario, NY, 1986—; editor Greenhaven Press, Mpls., 1986—87; copy editor Macmillan Pub., N.Y.C., 1988—91. Lectr. on Shakers Old Chatham (N.Y.) Mus., 1973—75; writer, editor Connections Episcopal Diocese Rochester, 1991—93; artist-in-residence Dorset (Vt.) Colony House, 2002. Author poetry, plays. Pres. Friends of the Walworth-Sealy Libr., Walworth, NY, 2005—; vestry mem. St. Luke's Episcopal, Catskill, NY, 1987, conv. del. Fairport, NY, 1989—91. Democrat. Avocations: English riding and jumping, reading, gardening. Office: Renaissance Style 641 Haley Rd Ontario NY 14519 Office Phone: 315-524-4718.

BLACKMON, BRENDA, newscaster; b. Columbus, Ga. BA in comm., Fairleigh Dickinson U., NJ, 2001. With WWOR-TV, 1990—, now co-anchor UPN 9 News Secaucus, NJ. Named Best Regularly Scheduled Newscast, AP, 1993, Best Newscast, 1998; recipient Emmy for Best Single Newscast in NY Area, Acad. TV Arts & Sci., 1995, 1997, 1998. Office: WWOR-TV/BHC Communications Inc 9 Broadcast Plz Secaucus NJ 07094-2913

BLACKMORE-HAUS, MARGARET ANN, athletic trainer, educator; b. Troy, Ohio, June 12, 1961; d. James Franklin and Doris Ann Blackmore; m. Richard Lee Haus, Dec. 23, 1989; children: Ryan Lee Haus, James Franklin Haus. BFA in Art and Health Edn., U. Cin., 1984; MA in Health and Phys. Edn., Mich. State U., Lansing, 1986. Cert. athletic trainer Nat. Athletic Tng. Assn. Asst. Athletic Trainer Wichita State U., Wichita, Kans., 1986—90; head athletic trainer and instr. health movement and leisure studies U. Cumberlands, Williamsburg, Ky., 1990—. Chair med. aspects com. Mid South Conf., 1999—2003; region XI assn. rep. Nat. Athletic Trainers Assn., 2002—; instr. std. first aid, CPR and automated external defibrillator Am. Red Cross, London, 2005—. Bookkeeper minors team Little League. Recipient 15 Yr. award, U. Cumberlands, 2005. Mem.: Coll. Univ. Athletic Trainers Soc., Nat. Strength and Conditioning Assn., Nat. Athletic Trainers Assn. Lutheran. Office: Univ Cumberlands 7790 Coll Sta Dr Williamsburg KY 40769-1388 Home: 210 S 9th St Williamsburg KY 40769

BLACKMUN, BARBARA WINSTON, art historian, educator, academic administrator; b. Merced, Calif., June 29, 1928; d. Walter Lafayette and Marian Lewelyn (Warner) Winston; m. Rupert Beall Blackmun, Apr. 16, 1951; children: Monica Blackmun Visona, William Winston, Karl Warner. BA in Fine Art, UCLA, 1949, PhD in Art History, 1984; MA in Art History, Ariz. State U., 1971. Life credentials in gen. elem. and secondary art tchg. Calif. Tchr. elem., secondary schs., Calif., 1949—64; instr. humanities Malawi Poly. Coll., Blantyre, 1965—66; lectr., chairperson arts and crafts bd. U. Malawi, Limbe, 1967—69; instr. art history San Diego Mesa Coll., 1971—76, prof. chmn. dept. art, 1976—79, 1983—85, prof. emeritus, 2000—; curator African art collection Mesa Coll., 1986—; adj. lectr. visual arts dept. U. Calif., San Diego, 1987, adj. faculty art history, 2004; adj. assoc. prof. art history dept. UCLA, 1987, vis. assoc. prof. art history, 2000. Nat. program dir. African Am. Inst., Malawi, 1968—69; mem. Nat. Craft Devel. Com., Malawi, 1968—69, Nat. Com. for Devel. O Level Syllabus in Art, Malawi, 1968—69; mem. edn. coun., contemporary arts com. San Diego Mus. Art, 1975—78, founding mem. African arts coun., 1976—, guest curator, 2003; bd. mem. San Diego Mesa Coll. Found., 1983—; curatorial cons. Chgo. Field Mus., 1990—93, Chgo. Art Inst., 1994, 2006—, Detroit Inst. Art, 2002—, Mus. fuer Voelkerkunde, Vienna, 2003—, Ethnologisches Mus. Berlin, 2003—; curator Glass Gallery exhbns. Mesa Coll., 2003—; bd. mem. African and African-Am. Studies Rsch. Program U. Calif., San Diego, 2004—. Contbr. articles, chpts. to profl. publs. Founding chmn. San Diego County Pub. Arts Adv. Coun., 1976—78. Recipient NEH Summer Rsch. Stipend, Lisbon, 1987; fellow Fulbright-Hays doctoral dissertation rsch. abroad, Benin City, Nigeria, 1981—82; grantee Calif. Cmty. Coll. Faculty rsch., Internat. Coll., Glasgow, Scotland, 1978, UCLA dept. art Dickson history of art travel, Europe, Russia, 1980; NEH fellow for coll. tchrs., 1992, Advanced Area Rsch. grantee, Social Sci. Rsch. Coun./Am. Coun. Learned Socs., 1993, Interpretive Rsch. grantee, Nat. Endowment for the Arts, 1993—99. Mem.: Arts Coun. African Studies Assn., UCLA Fowler Mus. Cultural Art, Mingei Mus. Internat. Art, San Diego Mus. Art, Archaeol. Inst. Am., African Studies Assn., Coll. Art Assn., Art Historian So. Calif., Delta Kappa Gamma (Beta Gamma chpt.). Methodist. Personal E-mail: bwblackmun@earthlink.net.

BLACKSHERE, MARGARET, labor union administrator; BS in Elem. Edn., So. Ill. Univ., Edwardsville, MS in Urban Edn. Former elem. sch. tchr., Ill.; former pres. Am. Fedn. Tchrs.; sec.-treas. Ill. AFL-CIO, 1993—2000, pres., 2000—. Del. Dem. Nat. Conv., 1980—92; mem. Dem. Nat. Com.; bd. dir. Irish Am. Labor Coalition, Unemployment Ins. Adv. Bd. Bd. dir. United Way, Ill.; Alliance for Retired Americans. Named one of 100 Most Influential Women, Crain's Chgo. Bus., 2004; named to Union Hall of Honor, Ill. Labor History Soc., 1995. Office: Ill AFL-CIO 55 W Wacker Dr Chicago IL 60601 Office Phone: 312-251-1414.

BLACKSTOCK, VIRGINIA HARRIETT, artist; b. St. Louis; d. Charles William Valentine and Ruth (Winn) Arnott; m. Ross Holcomb Blackstock, June 13, 1953; children: Susan, Kathleen, Julianne, Brian. BS, Mo. U., 1950; MA, U. Wis., 1952. Cert. tchr. Mo. Tchr. Ctrl. Mo. State U., U. of the South, Tenn., We. State Coll., Colo. Instr. watermedia painting and drawing workshops; judge, juror for art exhbns. Exhibited in 46 one person shows; group shows in Watercolor Soc. Exhbns. include Ala., Ariz., Colo., Kans., Ky., Mont., N.Mex., La., R.I., Okla., Pa., Utah, Wash., Wyo., Midwest, and San Diego Nat. Watercolor Soc., Rocky Mountain Nat. Exhbn., Nat. Watercolor Soc., Audubon Artists, Inc., N.Y., Allied Artists of Am., Adirondacks Nat., Red River Watercolor Soc., Springville Mus. of Art, C.M. Russell Mus. Auction; paintings in books include Creative Watercolor A Step-by-Step Guide, Beckwith, The Artistic Touch I and III, Unwin, Abstracts in Watercolor, Schlemm, Exploring Color (rev. edit.), Leland; commissions include cover of Ouray Summer Guide, '94, poster for the Ouray (Colo.) Chamber Music Festival (17' by 40'), cover painting, Valley Chronicle, Paonia, Colo., mural for the city of Delta, Colo.; contbr. paintings publ. to profl. jour. Quick draw artist at several fund raising auctions for non-profit orgns. Recipient Am. Artist Mag. Preserving Our Nat. Resources Contest, 1990, hon. mention Artist's Mag., won Sheep Dog Trials Poster Contest, 2006, Delta Meml. Hosp. Wine Festival Poster Contest, 2006. Mem. Colo. Watercolor Soc. (signature), N.Mex. Watercolor Soc. (signature), Pa. Watercolor Soc. (signature), Mont. Watercolor Soc. (signature), Western Colo. Watercolor Soc. (signature, exhbn. chair 1991, 92, 93, 98), La. Watercolor Soc. (signature), San Diego Watercolor Soc. (signature), Audubon Artists (signature), Kans. Watercolor Soc. (signature) Episcopalian. Avocations: skiing, biking, hiking, photography, gardening. Home: 31045 L Rd Hotchkiss CO 81419-9409 Office Phone: 970-872-4045.

BLACKSTOCK, VIRGINIA LEE LOWMAN (MRS. LEROY BLACKSTOCK), civic worker; b. Bixby, Okla., July 2, 1917; d. Joseph Arthur and Winifred (Lundy) Lowman; m. Leroy Blackstock, Dec. 29, 1939; children: Vincent Craig, Priscilla Gay Kurz, Burch Lee, Lorie Anne Mitchell; 1 child, Trena Jan. Student, Tulsa Coll. Bus., 1935-37. Legal sec. law firm, Tulsa, 1937-41. Chmn. program Internat. Students in Tulsa, 1955-65; mem. Tulsa Council Camp Fire Girls, 1963-66; mem. youth com. Tulsa Philharmonic Soc., 1969-70; now mem. women's assn.; pres. Eliot Elementary P.T.A., 1961-62, Edison High Sch. P.T.A., 1971-72; mem. Tulsa Opera Guild. Co-chmn. Democratic precinct No. 132, 1960-67. Mem. Tulsa County Bar Aux. (pres. 1954-55, sec. 1962-63, chaplain 1966-67). Clubs: Petroleum. Baptist. Home: 7213 S Atlanta St Tulsa OK 74136

BLACKSTONE, DARA, music educator, conductor; b. Conn. d. Dan and Barbara; m. Hayashi, 1995. BS, U. Conn., 1977, MusM, 1980, DPhil, 1996. Grad. asst. U. Conn., Storrs, 1978-80, 84-85; choir dir. Mansfield Bapt. Ch., Conn., 1979-87, OBesa Cantavit, 2002—. Griswold Cmty., 1997—. United Ch. Stonington, 2004—; tchr., choral dir., drama dir. Tolland HS, 1979-96; lectr., conductor U. Conn., 1985-87; cons., vocal coach, conductor pvt. practice, 1978—. Vol. instr. YMCA; bd. dirs. North Stonington Citizens Land Alliance. Mem. Am. Choral Dirs. Assn. (life), Music Edn. Nat. Conf., Internat. Fedn. Choral Musicians. Avocations: hiking, canoeing, skiing, skydiving, travel.

BLACKWELL, ANNA NELLE, medical educator, medical technician; b. Sylva, N.C., Jan. 8, 1945; d. Felix William and Nell Dodson Potts; m. Eugene Baxter Blackwell, Oct. 29, 1978; children: Denise Blackwell Nielsen, Ross Andrew Dillingham. BS in Biology, Lenoir Rhyne Coll., Hickory, N.C., 1967. Lic. med. technologist ASCP, 1970. Anatomy/physiology tchr. C.D.Owen H.S., Black Mountain, NC, 1984—; clin. chemist Mission/St. Josephs Hosp., Asheville, NC, 1988—; med. technologist Sisters of Mercy Urgent Care, Asheville, NC, 1996—2005. Prom chair person C.D.Owen H.S., Black Mountain, NC, 1984—2005. Ch. coun. St. Marks Luth. Ch., Asheville, NC, 1980—82. Mem.: NCAE, Nat. Soc. H.S. Scholars. D-Liberal. Luthern. Avocations: cooking, gardening, reading. Home: 210 Blue Ridge Rd Black Mountain NC 28711 Office: CDOwen High School 99 Lake Eden Rd Black Mountain NC 28711 Office Phone: 828-686-3852. Personal E-mail: apblackwell210@bellsouth.net. E-mail: anna.blackwell@bcsemail.org.

BLACKWELL, CARA LYNN, printing company executive; b. Waco, Tex., Nov. 17, 1964; d. Billy Hugh and Wanda Jean (Griffith) Blackwell. BSc, U. Tex., 1986; BFA, So. Meth. U., 1987; cert. in Supervisory Mgmt. Skills, McLennan C.C., 2000. Mgr. traffic Moroch & Assocs., Dallas, 1989—91; mgr. prodn. Taylor Christian, San Antonio, 1991—92; sr. mgr. prodn. Sicola Martin, Austin, Tex., 1992—2000; mgr. prodn., print buyer The Russ Reid Agy., L.A., 2001; mgr. prodn. Einson Freeman, Paramus, NJ, 2001—02, Kern Direct Mktg., L.A., 2003; mgr. material prodn. TDK Mediactive, Westlakes, Calif., 2002—03; specialist print prodn. Amgen, Inc., Thousand Oaks, Calif., 2003—04; mgr. prodn. Next Estate Comm., Monrovia, Calif., 2004. Choreographer Cheveux, Ft. Worth, Tex., 1986—90, Nat. Haircutters Am., Dallas, Tex., 1992. Vol. Blue Santa, Austin, 1978—2000, Help for Homeless, L.A., 2003, Habitat for Humanity, L.A., 2002, Walk for Life, Austin, 1994—2000. Recipient Gold award, Optima Design, 1995, 1996, Gold Addy award, Am. Advt. Fedn., 1996. Mem.: Print Prodn. Assn., Assn. Internat. Graphic Artists, Advertising Prodn. Assn. L.A., Am. Advertising Fedn. Avocations: interior decorating, jewelry making, clothing design, acting. Home: 1212 Guadalupe St # 106 Austin TX 78701-1855

BLACKWELL, DOROTHY RUTH, school system administrator; b. Culver City, Calif., Dec. 13, 1968; d. James Lee and Myra Blackwell; m. Michael Kevin Richter, Nov. 8, 1991; 1 child, David James Richter. BA, U. Mich., 1992; MA in Edn., Ea. Mich. U., 1997. Cert. tchr. Mich. Elem. tchr. Beecher Cmty. Schools, Flint, Mich.; elem. asst. prin. Carman-Ainsworth Cmty. Schools, Flint; elem. prin. Lansing (Mich.) Sch. Dist.; dir. of curriculum Waverly Cmty. Schools, Lansing, 2005—. Former bd. dirs. Girl Scouts USA, Lansing. Home: 1944 Cumberland Lansing MI 48906 Office Phone: 517-319-3028. Personal E-mail: dotblackwell@hotmail.com.

BLACKWELL, KAREN ELAINE, music educator; b. Sacramento, Apr. 25, 1954; d. Karl Lamar and Iris Elaine (McDaniel) Blackwell. BA in Music Edn., U. New Orleans, 1977, BA, 1978. Band dir. Jefferson Parish Schs., Gretna, Terrytown, Metairie, La., 1978—84, 1990—91, Higgins H.S., Marrero, La., 1984—90, Worley Mid. Sch., Westwego, La., 1991—. Honor band dir. Plaquemine Parish Schs., Belle Chasse, La., 2002, Jefferson Parish Schs., 2003; mem. New Orleans Concert Band, Jefferson Cmty. Band; sec. Summer Pops, 1978; hon. band clinician St. Charles Parish Pub. Schs., 2003. Named Worley Tchr. of Yr. Mem.: La. Band Assn., Women's Band Dirs. Nat. Assn., Nat. Band Assn., Jefferson Parish Music Educators Orgn., Dist. VI Band Dirs. Assn., La. Music Educators Assn., Music Educators Nat. Conf. Baptist. Avocations: reading, music, cross stitch, sports. Home: 472 Evergreen Dr Destrehan LA 70047

BLACKWELL, LINDA JANE, elementary school educator; b. Lawrenceburg, Ind., Mar. 28, 1938; d. Thomas Sutton and Nancy Olive Hamill; m. William J. Blackwell, Sept. 21, 1963 (dec. Aug. 1998); 1 child, William Lea. Student, Ind. U., 1956-60; BA in Anthropology, Calif. State U., 1973, MA in Anthropology, 1975. Cert. elem. tchr. Elem. sch. tchr. Park Forest (Ill.) Unified Sch. Dist., 1960-62, Torrance (Calif.) Unified Sch. Dist., 1962-64; curatorial asst., photo archivist S.W. Mus., L.A., 1975-82; elem. sch. tchr. L.A. Unified Sch. Dist., 1982—2001. Mem.: AAUW (pres. chpt. 1983—84), Phi Mu (pres. Glendale Alum chpt. 1996—2002), Delta Kappa Gamma (pres. 1998—2000). Avocation: travel. Home: 765 Prospect Dr Glendale CA 91205-3424 E-mail: merrylindakey@yahoo.com.

BLACKWELL, LOIS MOORE, fashion designer, educator, visual artist; d. Lawrence Wilbert and Ruth Jenkins Moore; m. Paul Marvin Blackwell, July 27, 1957 (dec. May 9, 1999); children: Daphne Paula, Ursula Paulette. BSc, Howard U., 1963, MSc, 1967; EdD, George Washington U., 1980. Cert. tchr. D.C. Tchr. DC Pub. Schs., Washington, 1967—74; asst. prof. Morgan State U., Balt., 1974—76, Univ. DC, Washington, 1975—77; fashion cons. Woodward & Lothrop Corp., Columbia, Md., 1978—85; cons. Westinghouse Electrical, Columbia, 1985—89; cmty. coord. Duke Ellington Sch. Arts, Washington, 1989—92; asst. prof. George Washington U., Washington, 1990—92; tchr. DC Schs., Washington, 1989—2001. Mem. English Inst. Harvard U., 1990—; mem. The Actors' Ctr., 2006—. Exhibitions include A Proud Continuum: Eight Decades of Art, Howard U., 2005; actor: HBO Cable TV series "The Wire", 2005—06; actor, actor: Twenty Questions, 2006. Recipient Merit award, All-Island Juried Art Show, 2003; fellow, Nat. Fellowships Fund, 1978. Mem.: Nat. Mus. Women in Arts. Achievements include created uniform concept designs for Oprah Winfrey's Leadership Academy for Girls, South Africa; designed sportswear for Gospel recording artist, Joii Foxx. Avocations: designing, painting, music, dramatic arts. Home Fax: 240-374-4206. Personal E-mail: lois.moore@comcast.net.

BLACKWELL-TAFFEL, CAMELLIA ANN, art educator, consultant; b. Balt., Feb. 21, 1949; BS, Morgan State U., Balt.; MFA, MEd, Md. Inst. Coll. Art, Balt.; PhD in Art Edn., U. Md. Art tchr. Balt. City Pub. Schs., 1971—76; art dir., asst. art dir. McKeldin Ctr., lectr. art dept. Morgan State U., 1971-76, art dir., asst. art dir. McKeldin Ctr. Balt., 1976-81; assoc. prof. Bowie (Md.) State Coll., 1981-83; mus. specialist Smithsonian Instn., Washington, 1984, dir. mus. publs., 1984-88; asst. prof. Howard U., Washington, 1988-89; assoc. prof. Prince George's C.C., Largo, Md., 1989-91; artist-in-residence Montpelier Cultural Arts Ctr., Laurel, Md., 1991-97; prof. U. D.C., Washington, 1991-95; exec. dir. Internat. Ctr. for Artistic Devel. Inc., 1991—; art specialist Montgomery County Pub. Schs., 1993—2004; owner art studio, gallery and gift shop Historic Savage Mill, Savage, Md., 1997—. Panelist individual artists' grants Indpls. Arts Commn., 1991; del. U.S./USSR Emerging Leaders Summit-Russia, Kazakhstan, 1990; art cons. to Cultural Ctr. of Nagyatad, Hungary, 1994, 95; owner art studio, gallery and gift shop, Historic Savage Mill, Savage, Md., 1997—. One-women shows include Blackwell Home Gallery, Balt., 1974-77, U. Ife, Ile-Ife, Nigeria, 1979, McCrillis Gardens Gallery, Bethesda, Md., 1991, Johns Hopkins Space Sci. Telescope Inst., 1992, State Fine Arts Mus. of Almaty, Kazakhstan, 1993, Howard C.C., 1996, Montpelier Cultural Art Ctr., 1996, Bowie State U., 2001; exhibited in group shows The Finnish Sch. Design, Finland, 1977, Chgo. Southside Community Art Ctr., 1991, Museu Da Gravura Cidade De Curitiba, Brazil, 1991, McCrillis Gardens Gallery, Bethesda, 1991, Katzenstein Gallery, Balt., 1991, The Print Club, Phila., 1991, James E. Lewis Mus. Art, Balt, 1992, Montpelier Cultural Arts Ctr., Morgan State U., Balt., 1992, Ctr. de Cuidad de Tres Canto, Spain, 2000, Sister City Artist Exch., Internat. Art Edn. Inst., U. Alaska, Fairbanks, 2001, Nat. Art Edn. Assn., New Orleans, 1997, San Francisco, 1988, Chgo., 1999, Washington, 2000; executed mural Howard County Rehab. Ctr., Columbia, Md., 1996. Founder, exec. dir. Internat. Ctr. Artistic Devel., Inc.; mem. cultural arts exch. France and Spain. Recipient Jurors' Choice award Md. Fedn. Art, Annapolis, 1977, NEA Grant to African Am. Mus. Assn. Conf., 1984, Merit award-design Printing Industries of Commonwealth of Va., 1985, First Pl. in Design, Printing Industries of Met. Washington, 1986, Best in Category Printing Industries of Md. Ann. Competition, 1987, Robert Rauschenberg's Learning Disabilities Workshop award, 1995, Network Jour. Mag. award, 2002, Women in Bus. award, 2002, Artist award, Prince Georges County Md. Arts Coun., 2005, Cmty. Arts award, Md. State Arts Coun. Howard County Arts Coun., 2001-04, Bus. award Network Jour. Mag., 2002, Cmty. Arts award Md. State Arts Coun., 2000-05, Individual Artist award Md. State Arts Coun., 2006; print selected to travel to the Belgium Congo Embassy, 1996; named Outstanding Advisor to Art League, Prince George's C.C., 1990; grantee to direct students to design and produce a mural for the Md. Sci. Ctr., Balt., Montgomery County Pub. Schs., 1996; Grant award for May Arts Expo Festival, Coun. Cmty. Arts, 2004, Sister City Artist Exch., Columbia, Md. and Cergy Pontrios, France, 1999. Mem. Nat. Art Edn. Assn., The Smithsonian, Md. Printmakers, So. Graphics Coun., Nat. Mus. Native Americans, Assn. Am. Museums, African Am. Museums Assn., Balt. Mus. Art, Walters Art Gallery, U. Md. Alumni Assn., Md. Inst. Coll. Art Alumni Assn., Morgan State U. Alumni Assn., Lake Clifton/Ea. High Sch. Alumni Assn. Home and Office: 6001 Jamina Downs Columbia MD 21045-3819 Studio: Hist Savage Mill 8600 Foundry St Savage MD 20763 Office Phone: 301-604-4484. E-mail: ctaffel@comcast.net.

BLACKWOOD, LOIS ANNE, elementary school educator; b. Denver, Sept. 18, 1949; d. Randolph William and Eloise Anne (Green) Burchett; m. Clark Burnett Blackwood, June 26, 1971; children: Anna Colleen, Courtney Brooke. BA, Pacific U., 1971; MA, U. Colo., 1997. Tchr. Forest Grove (Oreg.) Pub. Schs., 1971-72, Clarksville (Tenn.) Pub. Schs., 1972-73, Dept. of Defense Schs., Frankfurt, Germany, 1973-76, St. Vrain Valley Schs., Longmont, Colo., 1977—, presenter insvcs. and symposia, 1977-97, also tchr. of tchrs. Cons. Brush Pub. Schs., 1985; presenter U. No. Colo. Symposium, 1987, Greater San Diego Math. Conf., 1992-99, rural math. connections project U. Colo., 1992-94, So. sect. Calif. Coun. Math. Tchrs., 1992-98; cons. Brighton Pub. Schs., 2000-01. Recipient sustained superior svc. award U.S. Army, Frankfurt, 1975, outstanding performance award, 1976; Presdl. award for excellence in math. tchg. State of Colo., 1991, 94, Outstanding Elem. Math. Tchr. award Colo. Coun. Tchrs. Math., 1993; named Outstanding Tchr. of Yr., Longmont Area C. of C., 1992. Mem. NEA, Colo. Edn. Assn., St. Vrain Valley Tchrs. Assn., Phi Delta Kappa. Republican. Avocations: water and snow skiing, camping, tennis. Home: 1175 Winslow Cir Longmont CO 80501-5225 Office: Cen Elem Sch 1020 4th Ave Longmont CO 80501-5356 Personal E-mail: clblackwood@hotmail.com.

BLADE, MELINDA KIM, archaeologist, educator, research scientist; b. Jan. 12, 1952; d. George A. and Arline A. M. (MacLeod) Blade. BA, U. San Diego, 1974, MA in Tchg., 1975, EdD, 1986. Cert. secondary tchr. Calif., CC instr. Calif., registered profl. historian Calif. Instr. Coronado Unified Sch. Dist., Calif., 1975-76; head coach women's basketball U. San Diego, 1976-78; instr. Acad. of Our Lady of Peace, San Diego, 1976—, chmn. social studies dept., 1983—, counselor, 1984-92, co-dir. student activities, 1984-87, coord. advanced placement program, 1986-95, dir. athletics, 1990. Mem. archeol. excavation team U. San Diego, 1975—, hist. rschr., 1975—; lectr., 1981—. Contbr. hist. reports and rsch. papers to profl. jours.; editor: U. San Diego publs. Vol. Am. Diabetes Assn., San Diego, 1975—; coord. McDonald's Diabetes Bike-a-Thon, San Diego, 1977—78; bd. dirs. U. San Diego Sch. Edn. Mem.: ASCD, San Diego Hist. Soc., Register Profl. Archaeologists, Am. Hist. Assn., Medieval Assn. Pacific, Medieval Acad. Am., Assn. Scientists and Scholars, Soc. Bibl. Archeology, Calif. Coun. Social Studies, Nat. Coun. Social Studies, Internat. Shroud of Turin, Phi Delta Kappa, Phi Alpha Theta (sec.-treas. 1975—77). Office: Acad Our Lady of Peace 4860 Oregon St San Diego CA 92116-1340

BLAGDEN, SUSAN LOWNDES, retired small business owner; d. Lloyd and Marion Smith Lowndes; m. Donald Fred Blagden, Apr. 20, 1990. Student, Columbia U. Exec. sec. Living Mag., N.Y.C., 1958—60; radio announcer, newscaster Colo, Mass., Maine, Conn., 1960—71; ct. records rschr. L.C. Courthouse, Wiscasset, Maine, 1971—72; programmer Bonnar Vawter, Rockland, Maine, 1972—76; owner Data Connection, Wiscasset, 1980—91. Sec. Wiscasset Garden Club, charter mem.; moderator town meetings Town of Wiscasset, Maine, 1975—, chmn. bd. appeals, 1975—; treas. Wiscasset Pub. Libr., 1997—99, pres. bd. trustees, 1999—; bd. dirs. Lincoln County Hist. Assn., treas.; pres. Wiscasset Female Charitable Soc., treas.; charter mem. Morris Farm Trust, founding mem., treas.; sec. Merrymeeting Audubon Soc.; bd. mem. DaPonte String Quartet. Mem.: Wiscasset Yacht Club (sec.). Avocations: birding, travel, reading, music, knitting.

BLAIN, CHARLOTTE MARIE, internist, educator; b. Meadeville, Pa., July 18, 1941; d. Frank Andrew and Valerie Marie (Serafin) Blain; m. John G. Hamby, June 12, 1971 (dec. May 1976); 1 child, Charles J. Hamby. Student, Coll. of St. Francis, 1958—60, DePaul U., 1960—61; MD, U. Ill., Chgo., 1965. CLU; diplomate Am. Bd. Family Practice, Am. Bd. Internal Medicine. Intern, resident U. Ill. Hosps., 1967—70; fellow in infectious diseases U. Ill., 1968—69; pvt. practice specializing in internal medicine and family practice Elmhurst, Ill., 1969—. Instr. U. Ill. Hosp., 1969—70; asst. prof. Loyola U., 1970—71; mem. staff Elmhurst Meml. Hosp., 1970—; clin. asst. prof. Chgo. Med. Sch., 1978—95, U. Ill. Med. Sch., 1995—, Rush Med. Coll., 1997—. Contbr. articles to profl. jours., chapters to books. Bd. dirs., v.p. Elmhurst Art Mus. Fellow: ACP, Am. Acad. Family Practice; mem.: AMA, DuPage Med. Soc., Am. Profl. Practice Assn., Am. Soc. Internal Medicine, Univ. Club (Chgo.). Roman Catholic. Avocations: Hapki Do (Black Belt), Tae-Kwan-Do (Black Belt), skiing. Home: 320 Cottage Hill Ave Elmhurst IL 60126-3302 Office: 135 Cottage Hill Ave Elmhurst IL 60126-3330 Office Phone: 630-832-6633. E-mail: cblain@comcast.net, cblain@mybclinic.com.

BLAIR, BONNIE KATHLEEN, former professional speedskater, former Olympic athlete; b. Cornwall, N.Y., Mar. 18, 1964; d. Charlie and Eleanor Blair; m. David Cruikshank; 1 child, Grant B. Cruikshank Student, Mont. Tech. Univ. Mem. U.S. Olympic Team, Sarajevo, Yugoslavia, 1984; Gold medalist, 500m Speedskating, Bronze medalist 1,000m Calgary Olympic Games, 1988; Gold medalist, 500m Speedskating Albertville Olympic Games, 1992, Gold medalist, 1000m Speedskating, 1992; Gold medalist, 500m Speedskating Lillehammer Olympic Games, 1994, Gold medalist, 1000m Speedskating, 1994; pro tour speedskater, 1994-95; ret. from competitive speedskating, 1995; motivational speaker, 1995—. ABC sports commentator; motivational spkr.; founder Bonnie Blair Charitable Fund; active fundraiser Am. Brain Tumor Assn. Author: Bonnie Blair: A Winning Edge. Recipient James E. Sullivan award for Outstanding U.S. amateur athlete, 1993, Sportwoman of the Year, Sports Illustrated, 1994; named Female Athlete of Yr., AP, 1994; inducted into Nat. Speedskating Hall of Fame, Internat. Women's Sports Hall of Fame, US Olympic Hall of Fame. Achievements include 1st American woman in any sport to win gold medals in consecutive Winter Olympics; 1st American speedskater to win a gold medal in more than one Olympics. Most decorated female Olympian of all time -- five gold medals, six total. Office: Octagon Mgmt Ste 300 2 Union St Portland ME 04101

BLAIR, CYNTHIA, meteorologist, oceanographer, researcher; b. Syracuse, N.Y., Nov. 20, 1965; d. Robert Harley and Judith Anne (Scanlon) Van Ostrand; m. Charles Roy Blair, Aug. 16, 1992; 1 child, Jesse Warren. AS in Travel/Tourism Mgmt., Johnson and Wales Coll., Providence, 1985. Asst. head cashier Winn Dixie, Largo, Fla., 1987-90; joined U.S. Navy, 1990, meteorol. observer NTMOD Belle Chasse, La., 1990-94, oceanographic technician NEMOD Sigonella, Sicily, Italy, 1994-97, meteorology trainee NAVTECHTRAU Keesler AFB, Miss., 1997-98, meteorol. technician, rsch. asst. FNMOC Monterey, Calif., 1998—9. Command photographer FNMOC, USN, Monterey, 1998—; rsch. asst. Naval Rsch. Lab., Monterey, 1998—. Author poetry. Tutor, adult literacy program Monterey County Free Libr., 1998, reader, children's reading program, 1998-99. Office: Fleet Numerical Meteorology and Oceanography Ctr Stop 1 7 Grace Hopper Ave # 52 Monterey CA 93943-5598

BLAIR, KAREN ELAINE, small business owner, social psychology researcher, psychiatric consultant; b. Salem, Ohio, Mar. 11, 1948; d. Kenneth Emmanuel and Ruth Annabelle Schiller; m. Geroge LeRoy Blair, June 22, 1968 (dec. Mar. 1982); children: Princess Erin, Tiffany Alynn; m.William Larry Blaser, 1993. BS in Psychology, Calif. Luth. U., 1986, MS in Counseling Psychology, 1993. Intern, asst. in med. records Baldwin Hills Hosp., Inglewood, Calif., 1968-69; freelance fashion model LA and Ventura, Calif., 1970-72; owner Conejo Bus. Machines, The Home Office, Thousand Oaks, Calif., 1970-74, Exactel Instrument Co., Oxnard, Calif., 1975-78, Sidewinder Aircraft, Thousand Oaks, 1977—2002. Lab. asst. Neuropsychiat. Inst., UCLA, 1985—87; rsch. asst., psychiat. rehab. skills trainer and cons.; rsch. asst. UCLA-Camarillo (Calif.) State Hosp., 1989—2000; rschr. treatment of stimulant-abusing schizophrenics, 1990—91, UCLA VA, Brentwood; program dir. The Life Adjustment Team, Culver City, Calif., 1991—93; spkr. on near-death experiences, 1987—; cons. psychiat. rehab. UCLA, Brentwood, 1993—2000; pvt. cons., 1993—; guest spkr. Calif. Luth. U., Thousand Oaks, 1988—2000. Author: Tie Your Own Heartstrings, 1983. Facilitator grief edn. and grant support groups Hospice, Camarillo, 1988—90. Calif. Luth. U. scholar, 1983-86. Avocations: piano, swimming, weights, saxophone, aviation. Home: 8242 E Del Cadena Dr Scottsdale AZ 85258-2319

BLAIR, MARGARET MENDENHALL, economist, consultant, law educator; b. Bartlesville, Okla., Nov. 8, 1950; d. Harold Leroy and Mary Winifred (Simmons) Mendenhall; m. Forrest Randall Blair, May 29, 1971 (div. Sept. 1979); m. Roger Lisle Conner, June 22, 1991; 1 child, Elizabeth LeeAnn Conner. BA, U. Okla., 1973; postgrad., Harvard U., 1982-83; MA, MPhil, PhD, Yale U., 1989. Reporter Houston Chronicle, 1973-75; reporter, bur. mgr. Fairchild Publ., Houston, 1975-77; corr. Bus. Week, Houston, 1977-79, bur. chief, 1979-82; economist Fed. Res. Bank N.Y., NYC, 1985; rsch. asst. Yale U., New Haven, 1985-86, lectr., 1986-87; rsch. assoc. Brookings Instn., Washington, 1987-94, sr. fellow, 1995-99; dir. Brookings Project on Corps. and Human Capital, 1996-99; co-dir. Brookings Project on Intangible Sources of Value, 1998-2001; rsch. dir., vis. prof. Sloan-GULC project bus. inst. Georgetown U. Law Ctr, 2000—04; prof. law Vanderbilt U., Nashville, 2004—. Adj. faculty U. Md. Coll. Bus. and Mgmt., 1993—94; vis. prof. Georgetown U. Law Ctr., 1996—2004; steering com., rapporteur Woodstock Seminar Series on Bus. Ethics, Washington, 1989—90; subcoun. on capital allocation Competitiveness Policy Coun., 1993—96; rapporteur Salzburg (Austria) Seminar on Internat. Fin. Markets, 1989; steering com. time horizons project Coun. on Competitiveness, Washington, 1990; mem. Task Force on Restructuring America's Labor Market Instns., MIT/Sloan Sch. Mgmt., 1997—2001, World Econ. Forum Corp. Performance Coun., 1999—2003; non-resident sr. fellow Brookings Instn., 2000—04; bd. advisors George Washington U. Sloan Program on Bus. and Soc., 1998—2002; trustee Woodstock Theol. Ctr., 2001—04; bd. dir. Worldwide Responsible Apparel Prodn. Author: The Deal Decade Handbook, 1993, Ownership and Control: Rethinking Corporate Governance for the Twenty-first Century, 1995; co-author: Unseen Wealth: Report of the Brookings Task Force on Intangibles, 2001; editor: The Deal Decade: What Takeovers and Leveraged Buyouts Mean for Corporate Governance, 1993, Wealth Creation and Wealth Sharing: A Colloquium on Corporate Governance and Investments in Human Capital, 1996, Employees and Corporate Governance, 1999, The New Relationship Human Capital in the American Corporation, 2000; contbr. articles to profl. jours. Vol. Big Sisters Washington Met. Area, 1989-92; organizer neighborhood watch group, Washington, 1990; mem. bd. advisors Ctr. for Cmty. Interest, 1993-98; mem. bd. dir. Christ Edn. Rock Spring United Ch. Christ, 2000-03; mem. Arlington County Adv. Coun. Instrn., 1999-2003. Univ. fellow Yale U., 1983-86, Leo Model fellow Brookings Instn., 1987-88; rsch. grantee Boston U. Mfrs. Roundtable, 1990, Columbia U. Instnl. Investor Project, 1994, Alfred P. Sloan Found., 1995, 96, 98, 99. Mem.: ABA (assoc.), Am. Law Econs. Assn., Am. Econ. Assn. Avocations: ballet, religious studies, cooking. Office: Vanderbilt Univ Law Sch 131 21st St S Nashville TN 37203-1181

BLAIR, MARIE LENORE, elementary school educator; b. Maramec, Okla., Jan. 9, 1931; d. Virgil Clement and Ella Catherine (Leen) Strode; m. Freeman Joe Blair, Aug. 26, 1950; children: Elizabeth Ann Blair Crump, Roger Joe. BS, Okla. A&M Coll., 1956; MS, Okla. State U., 1961, postgrad., 1965-68. Reading specialist Pub. Schs., Stillwater, Okla., 1966-88. Past bd. dirs. Okla. Reading Coun.; active 1st Christian Ch. Mem. Internat., Okla., Cimarron (past pres.) reading assns., NEA, Okla. Edn. Assn., Stillwater Edn. Assn., Demoley Mothers Club, Rainbow Mothers Club, Lahoma Club, White Shrine Jerusalem (past worthy high priestess), Order White Shrine Jerusalem (past supreme queen's attendent), Internat. Order of Rainbow for Girls (Okla. exec. com. emeritus), Order Ea. Star (past grand Martha, past grad rep. of Nebr. in Okla., grand rep. of Manitoba in Okla.), Order of Amaranth, Kappa Kappa Iota. Democrat. Home: 51200 E 55 Rd Maramec OK 74045-6124

BLAIR, MAUDINE, psychotherapist, communications executive, management consultant; d. Eugene Goode and Della Wright Blair. MA, U. Ga., Athens, 1964; PhD, Fla. State U., Tallahassee, 1969. Diplomate Am. Psychotherapy Assn.; cert. group psychotherapist Nat. registry of Cert. Group Psychotherapists, transactional analyst, lic. psychotherapist Fla., cert. relationship specialist. Assoc. dir. of counseling and pers. svcs. Fla. State U., Tallahassee, 1964—67; dir. and founder Blair's Counseling Svc., Tallahassee, 1970—, Blair's Counseling Satellite Ctr., Tifton, Ga., 1971—92, Tenn. Comm. & Mgmt. Inst., Townsend, Tenn., 1980—89, Blair's Lodge, Townsend, Tenn., 1981—89; founder, pres. Fla. Comm. & Mgmt. Inst., Tallahassee, 1972—; co-founder, co-dir. CE Studies LLC, Tallahassee, 2005—. Co-editor: Transactional Analysis Rsch. Index vol. I, 1976, Transactional Analysis Rsch. Index vol. II, 1979; contbr. articles to profl. jours. Fellow: Am. Orthopsychiatric Assn.; mem.: APA, Fla. Assn. Marriage and Family Therapy (clin. mem.), Internat. Transactional Analysis (clin. mem.), Am. Assn. Marriage and Family Therapy (life; clin. mem.), Am. Group Psychotherapy Assn. (clin. mem.). Avocations: reading, travel, writing. Office: Blair's Counseling Svc PO Box 12697 Tallahassee FL 32317 also: CE Studies LLC PO Box 12337 Tallahassee FL 32317 Office Phone: 850-297-2190, 850-580-2600. Business E-Mail: BlairCare@att.net, CEStudies@att.net.

BLAIR, PHYLLIS E., artist; b. N.Y.C., Oct. 5, 1922; d. Franz Joseph and Marian Jane (Burke) Emmerich; m. Thomas Slingluff Blair, Sept., 17, 1946 (dec. May, 2003); children: Joan Dix, George Dike, Hadden Slingluff. Student, Skidmore Coll., 1940—42, Art Students League, 1945, Westminster Coll., 1970—72, Bennington Coll., 1989. Asst. art dept. Skidmore Coll., Saratoga Springs, NY, 1940—42; art illustrator & engring. draftsman GE, Schenectady, NY, 1942—44, Bell Labs., N.Y.C., 1944—46; tchr. elem. Clinton, Tenn., 1946—47. One-woman shows include Hoyt Inst. Fine Arts, New Castle, Pa., 1971, 93, Butler Inst. Am. Art, Youngstown, Ohio, 1982, Westminster Coll., New Wilmington, Pa., 1983, Butler Inst. Am. Art, Salem, Ohio, 1994, Cornell Mus., Delray Beach, Fla., 2004-05, Ann Norton Sculpture Gardens, West Palm Beach, Fla., 2006. Art curator Human Svcs. Ctr., New Castle, 1968-89, Jameson Health Sys., 1978-99, Jameson Care Ctr., Jameson Retirement Pl., 1978-99, Jameson Rehab Ctr., 1978-99, Almira Home, New Castle, 1990-99, Lawrence County Children and Youth Svcs., 2000, The Soup Kitchen, Boynton Beach, Fla., 2000; founding mem. Nat. Mus. of Women in the Arts, Washington, D.C. Recipient Benjamin Rush award Pa. Med. Soc., 1991. Mem. Hoyt Inst. Fine Arts (chair art com. & permanent collection 1967-99, trustee, 1967-99, Blair Sculpture Walkway named in her honor 1996), Am. Heart Assn. (Disting. Svc. award Lawrence County chpt. 1978). Avocations: golf, painting, sculpting. Home (Summer): 1611 Cold Spring Rd Williamstown MA 01267-2771

BLAIR, REBECCA SUE, English educator; b. Terre Haute, Ind., Mar. 26, 1958; d. Albert Eldon and Genevieve Virginia (Smith) B.; m. Richard Volle Van Rheeden, May 27, 1989. BA in English magna cum laud, U. Indpls., 1980; MA in Medieval Lit. with honors, U. Ill., Springfield, 1982; MA, Ind. U., 1986, PhD, 1988. Grad. asst. U. Ill., Springfield, 1980—82; dir. English language tng. Ind. U., Bloomington, 1982-83, assoc. instr., 1982-88; assoc. prof., chmn. dept. English Westminster Coll., Fulton, Mo., 1989-99, dir. writing assessment, 1989-99; assoc. prof. U. Indpls., 1999—2003, Wartburg Coll., Waverly, Iowa, 2003—, dir. inquiry studies program. Vis. prof. Webster U., St. Louis, Mo., 1988-89; writing assessment cons. Pepperdine U., Malibu, Calif., 1995, others; exec. com. of the faculty Westminster Coll.; mem. Assessment Com., College-Wide Budget Com., Profl. Stds. Com., Pers. Com., Dean's Cabinet Coun. of Chairs and Dirs., Edn. Task Force, Task Force to Reorganize the Acad. Area, Enrollment Svcs. Task Force; women's studies rep. Mid-Mo. Am. Coun. of Univs.; faculty sponsor Alpha Chi Scholastic Hon. Soc.; faculty organizer awareness of rape/domestic violence Take Back the Night Rally; presenter, spkr. in field. Author: The Other Woman: Women Authors and Cultural Stereotypes in American Literature, 1988; contbr. articles to profl. jours. Bd. dirs. Am. Cancer Soc., Callaway County, Mo., 1989-92; mem. pastor nominating com. First Presbyterian Ch., Fulton, Mo., 1990-91, elder, 1990—, session mem., elected mem., 1990-93, 97-2000, chmn. nominating com., 1993-94, chmn. music search com., 1994-95; pulpit supply Mo. Union Presbytery, 1995—, com. on ministry, 1997-2000, stated clk., 1997—; mem. Greater Mo. Focus on Leadership, 1992; vol. Habitat for Humanity, Fulton, 1993—; bd. dirs., founding mem. Coalition Against Rape and Domestic Violence, Fulton, 1995-97; bd. dirs. Friends of the Libr., Fulton, 1995-98, pres., 1997-98; sec. Fulton Art League, 1996—. Named Outstanding Faculty Mem., Westminster Coll., Fulton, 1991—92, Panhellenic Faculty Mem. of Year, Westminster Coll., 1996—97. Mem. Nat. Coun. for Rsch. on Women, Nat. Coun. Tchrs. of English, Am. Studies Assn., Midwest Modern Lang. Assn., Modern Lang. Assn., Writing Prog. Adminstrs., Coll. Composition and Comm., Fulton C. of C. (vol. 1992-96), Kiwanis (bd. dirs. 1990—, founder Circle K Club 1994, v.p. 1995-96, pres.-elect 1996-97, pres. 1997-98). Presbyterian. Avocations: gourmet cooking, reading, trains, writing. Home: 1916 Rainbow Dr Cedar Falls IA 50613 Office: Wartburg Coll 100 Wartburg Blvd Waverly IA 50677 Personal E-mail: mb326@yahoo.com. Business E-Mail: rebecca.blair@wartburg.edu.

BLAIR, ROSEMARY MILES, retired art educator, environmentalist; d. George Bernard and Kathryn Gannon Miles; m. David William Blair, Jan. 30, 1954; children: Karen, Barbara, Maria, Amanda, David Belmont, Rachel. BA, Coll. New Rochelle, 1951; MA, Columbia U. Tchrs. Coll., 1969; post grad., Princeton U., 1975. Cert. adminstrn. N.J., 1973, N.Y., 1973, art instr. K-12 N.J., N.Y., prin. NJ, 1973. Art tchr., coord. and supr. Princeton Regional Schs., NJ, 1965—96; spl. cons. tchr. preparation program Princeton U.; ret., 1996. Chair 12th dist. U.S. Congressional Art Competition. One woman and group shows, US and Can., work in corp. and pvt. collections. Founding parent, vol. Stuart County Day Sch., Princeton, 1963—; cmty. activist Princeton Cmty. Dem. Org., 1979—; lector Aquinas Found. Princeton U.; bd. trustees St. Saviour Sch., Bklyn., 1990—95; founding pres. and chmn. bd. Friends Princeton Open Space, 1979—89; mem. alumni coun. Coll. New Rochelle, NY, 1983—87; pres. Del. & Raritan Canal Coalition, 1985—; founder, trustee Del. Raritan Greenway Land Trust, Princeton, 1989—; mem. Princeton Environ. Commn., 1998—. Mem.: Montgomery Ctr. Arts, Consortium Arts Edn. (exec. dir. 1983—93), Art Educators NJ (conf. chmn. 1981, pres. 1982), Nova Scotia Nature Trust. Democrat. Avocations: painting, environment and land preservation. Home (Summer): 1371 Summerside Rd Bayfield NS Canada B0H 1A0 E-mail: rosemaryblair@cs.com.

BLAIR, RUTH REBA, retired government official; b. New Orleans, Aug. 21, 1934; d. Joseph Aloysius and Ruth (Labostrie) Porter; m. William Jennings Blair, Sept. 22, 1961 (dec.); children: Joseph Vernon, Constance Eileen. AS in Bus. Adminstrn., Loyola U., New Orleans, 1980; BA in English, U. New Orleans, 1984; masters cert. in govt. contracting, George Washington U., 1992. Cert. assoc. contracts mgr. (life); cert. mem. fed. acquisition corps. Profl. intern and various positions NASA Michoud Assembly Facility, New Orleans, 1964-84; contract specialist NASA, Marshall Space Flight Ctr, Ala., 1985-86; contracting officer USCG, New Orleans, 1986-87; contract adminstr. (supercomputers) Naval Rsch. Lab., Stennis Space Ctr., Miss., 1987-96; dir. adminstrn. Tech. Ventures, Inc., New Orleans. Author, short stories; poet, adminstr. Primary Oceanographic Prediction System quarter billion dollar contract for Navy's Large Scale Computer Supercomputer System. Recipient Special Act award Naval Rsch. Lab., 1994. Mem. ABA, AAUW, Nat. Assn. Ret. Fed. Employees (past chpt. pres.). Home: 19 Osprey Ct La Place LA 70068 E-mail: rblairtv1@aol.com.

BLAIR, SHERRY ANN, psychotherapist, educator; b. Belleville, N.J., Dec. 17, 1961; d. Edward Joseph Blair and Barbara Ann Ingham; 1 child, Michael Joseph. BA, Rutgers U., 1997; MSSW, Columbia U., 2000; postgrad., North Ctrl. U., Prescott, Ariz., 2003—. LCSW NJ. Transitional housing & fin. coord. Manavi, Inc, Union, NJ, 1998—99; social worker, psychotherapist Women's Counseling & Psychol. Svcs., Verona, NJ, 2000—01; social worker, therapist Delta T-Group, Iselin, NJ, 2000—02; psychotherapist, social worker Assocs. in Counseling, Tng. & Psychol. Svcs., Clifton, NJ, 2000—; case mgr., family violence clinician Women Rising, Inc., Jersey City, 2001; dir., adminstr. Horizon Behavioral Health Care, Prospect Park, NJ, 2001—. Corp. cons., dir. Starbound, Inc., Lanoka Harbor, NJ, 2000—; bus. cons. Synergy Life Coaching & Psychotherapy Svcs., Montclair, NJ, 2000—; adj. prof. Women's Studies Program Rutgers U., Newark, 2000—; organizer confs., workshops in field; exec. inspirational dir. Innovative Specialists Inspirational Svcs. Crisis responder-World Trade Ctr. Crisis Care Network-Delta T Group, Iselin, 2001; field organizer NASW-PACE NJ. Chpt., Hamilton, 2002. Recipient Beth Niemi award for work for women's studies, Rutgers U. Women's Studies Program, 1997; grantee Office on Women's Health, HHS, 1997. Mem.: NASW (clin. social work supr.), EMDR Inst., Internat. Critical Incident Stress Found., Am. Acad. Experts in Traumatic Stress (bd. cert. expert, diplomate), So. Poverty Law Ctr., Columbia U. Sch. Social Work Alumni Assn., Amnesty Internat., Phi Beta Kappa, Psi Chi. Office: Horizon Behavioral Health Care 316 N 6th St Prospect Park NJ 07508 Office Phone: 973-746-0333. E-mail: sherryblair@comcast.net.

BLAIR, STARLA RENEÉ, music educator; d. Stanley Vermont and Ruth U. Michael; m. Terry Lynn Blair, June 7, 1986. BS in Music Edn., SW Mo. State U., Springfield, 1979; MEd in Music, Mo. State U., Springfield, 1983. Pvt. practice, Springfield, 1979—; tchr. string class Springfield Cath. Schs., 1983—95. Dir. Suzuki violin prep. program Mo. State U., Springfield, 1990—. Violist Springfield Symphony, 1974—; state bd. dirs. Inspiration Point Fine Arts Colony, Eureka Springs, Ark., 1988—. Mem.: Suzuki Assn. Am., Nat. Fedn. Music Clubs (life; bd. dirs. 1993—, v.p. ctrl. region 1996—2000). Avocations: travel, reading. Home: 902 E Gaslight Dr Springfield MO 65810

BLAIR, SYLVIA H., aerospace engineer; BS in Physics, Lamar U., 1976. Computer resources project engr. on F-16 and F-22 fighter aircraft Ft. Worth divsn. Gen. Dynamics, 1979—89; avionics project engr. Sikorsky Aircraft Co., Stratford, Conn., 2005—. Session chmn., tutorials chmn. AIAA/IEEE Digital Avionic Systems Conf., 1983—86; conf. chmn., tech. program chmn. AIAA Aerospace Engring. Conf. and Show, L.A., 1983—85; chmn. AIAA Digital Avionic Tech. Com., 1987—89. Min. Higher Way Ministries, 1995. Recipient Navy Superior Pub. Svc. medal, U.S. Sec. of the Navy, 1988. Avocations: writing, reading, fishing, travel. Office: Sikorsky Aircraft Co 6900 Main St PO Box 9729 Stratford CT 06615-9129 E-mail: sblair@sikorsky.com.

BLAIR, TERESA TARALLO, foreign language educator; b. Lima, Peru, Feb. 23, 1951; came to U.S., 1969; d. Luis and Victoria (Cornejo) Tarallo; m. Robert E. Blair, May 11, 1976; 1 child, Byron. Student, IPCNA, Lima, 1968-69, East Stroudsburg State Coll., 1969-70; BA in English Lit. maxima cum laude, King's Coll., 1973; student, Rutger's U., 1973-74; EdM, Harvard U., 1975; postgrad., U. Valencia, Spain, 1979-80, State U. Juarez at Durango, Mex., 1981; MA in Spanish Lit., Columbia U., 1984, postgrad., 1982-86; MPhil, Columbia U., NY, 1993. Cert. tchr., Calif., Pa. Tchr. Spanish Camden (N.J.) Schs., 1973-74, Phyllips Exeter (N.H.) Acad., 1975-76, Elgin (Ill.) Acad., 1977-79, Westridge Acad., Pasadena, Calif., 1976-77; prof. Spanish Ill. Benedictine Coll., Lisle, 1987-89, Coll. Dupage, Glen Ellyn, Ill., 1989-92; instr. Spanish Columbia U., NY, 1983-86, researcher, 1992—; prof. Adlai Stevenson H.S., 1994—. Rsch. cons. CED Boston Sch., Cambridge, Mass., 1975; coord., cons. Med. Spanish Presbyn. Hosp., N.Y.C., 1983-86; cons. Diff. Pub. Co., Ill., 1987—; cons. lang. program Ill. Dept. Human Resources, Wheaton, 1988; cons., in-svc. trainer U.S. Dept. Human Resources, Wheaton, 1988; cons., cultural liaison DuPage Precision, Naperville, Ill., 1989. Mem. Internat. Com. PTA Westfield Sch., 1989-91; vol. Presdl. and Senatorial Elections, Chgo. area, 1990; advisor Latino Ethnic Awareness Coll. Dupage, 1991-92. Named scholar Inst. Internat. Edn., King's Coll., 1970-73, Harvard U., 1975-76, fellow Columbia U., 1983-86. Mem. ASCD, Am. Coun. Tchrs. Fgn. Langs. (conf. presenter Internat. Honor Soc. panel 1989), Am. Assn.

Tchrs. Spanish and Portuguese (bd. dirs. 1979—(conf. presenter 1992), Modern Lang. Assn., Ill. Coun. for Teaching of Fgn. Langs. (conf. presenter 1988, 91, workshop leader 1989), Ill. Fgn. Lang. Tchrs. Assn. (conf. presenter 1991), Alpha Delta Kappa, Alpha Mu Gamma (con. advanced Placement coll. bd. Spanish lang., 2002—; advanced placement Spanish lit. tchr. trainer leader, 2003—). Home: 1 S 235 Lloyd Ave Lombard IL 60148

BLAIR, VIRGINIA ANN, public relations executive; b. Kansas City, Mo., Dec. 20, 1925; d. Paul Lowe and Lou Etta (Cooley) Smith; m. James Leon Grant, Sept. 3, 1943 (dec. July 1944); m. Warden Tannahill Blair, Jr., Nov. 7, 1947 (dec. Apr. 2002); children: Janet, Warden Tannahill III. BS in Speech, Northwestern U., Evanston, Ill., 1948. Free-lance writer, Chgo., 1959-69; writer, editor Smith, Bucklin & Assocs., Inc., Chgo., 1969-72, account mgr., 1972-79, account supr., 1979-80, dir. pub. rels., 1980-85; pres. GB Pub. Rels., Chgo., 1985—. Judge U.S. Indsl. Film Festival, 1974, 75; instr. Writer's Workshop, Evanston, Ill., 1978; dir. Northwestern U. Libr. Coun., 1978-91, dir. alumnae bd., 1986—, John Evans Club bd., 1990-98. Author dramas (produced on CBS): Jeanne D'Arc: The Trial, 1961, Cordon of Fear, 1961, Reflection, 1961, If I Should Die, 1963; 3-act children's play: Children of Courage, 1967. Emmy nominee Nat. Acad. TV Arts and Scis., 1963; recipient Svc. award Northwestern U., 1978, Creative Excellence award U.S. Indsl. Film Festival, 1976, Gold Leaf merit cert. Family Cir. mag. and Food Coun. Am., 1977, cert. Excellence superior achievement in media rels. N.Am. Precis Syndicate, 1997, Ginny award Cremation Assn. N.Am., 2002. Mem. Pub. Rels. Soc. Am. (counselors acad.), Am. Advt. Fedn. (lt. gov. Ill. 6th dist.), Women's Advt. Club Chgo. (pres.), Publicity Club Chgo., Nat. Acad. TV Arts and Scis., John Evans Club (bd. dirs.), Woman's Club Evanston (pres.), Zeta Phi Eta (Svc. award 1978, 93), Alpha Gamma Delta, Philanthropic and Ednl. Orgn. (Ill. chpt. pres. dist. pres.). Home and Office: 2601 Central St Unit 206 Evanston IL 60201-1395

BLAIS, MADELEINE HELENA, writer; b. Holyoke, Mass., Aug. 25, 1949; d. Raymond J. and Maureen M. (Shea) B.; m. John Strong Miner Katzenbach, May 10, 1980. BA, Coll. New Rochelle, 1969; MS, Columbia U., 1970. Reporter Boston Globe, 1971-72, Trenton (N.J.) Times, 1974-76; staff writer Tropic Mag., Miami Herald, 1979-87; assoc. prof. journalism U. Mass., Amherst, 1987—. Recipient Pulitzer Prize, 1980; Nieman fellow Harvard U. Class of 1986

BLAISURE, TERRA QUINN, special education educator; b. Phillipsburg, Pa., Oct. 10, 1980; d. John Wayne and Beverly Ann Blaisure. BS, Pa. State U., 2003, MS, 2006. Special edn. tchr. Allegheny Intermediate Unit, Bethel Park, Pa., Central Dauphin Sch. Dist., Harrisburg, Pa., 2006—. Mem.: NEA, Coun. Exceptional Children, Pa. State Edn. Assn., Phi Theta Lambda. Home: 4185 Mountain View Rd Apt 106 Mechanicsburg PA 17050 Personal E-mail: terraquinn10@gmail.com.

BLAKE, CATHERINE C., judge; b. Boston, July 27, 1950; d. John Ballard and Jean Place (Adams) B. BA magna cum laude, Radcliffe Coll., 1972; JD cum laude, Harvard Law Sch., 1975. Bar: Mass. 1975, Md. Ct. Appeals 1977, U.S. Ct. Appeals (4th cir.) 1977, U.S. Dist. Ct. Md. 1977, D.C. 1979. Assoc. Palmer & Dodge, Boston, 1975-77; asst. U.S. atty. Dist. of Md., Balt., 1977-83, first asst. U.S. atty., 1983-85, 86-87, U.S. atty. (court-appointed), 1985-86; U.S. magistrate judge U.S. Dist. Ct. Md., Balt., 1987-95, U.S. dist. ct. judge, 1995—. Mem.: FBA, Fed. Judges' Assn., Nat. Assn. of Women Judges, Md. Bar Assn., Bar Assn. Baltimore City. Office: US Courthouse 101 W Lombard St Ste 7310 Baltimore MD 21201-2639

BLAKE, KIMBERLY BOSWORTH, pharmacist; b. Birmingham, Ala., Apr. 23, 1975; d. Johnny R. and Gwen Bosworth; m. Paul M. Blake, III, Aug. 2, 2003. BS, Auburn U., Ala., 1998, PharmD, 1999; MBA, W.Va. U., Morgantown, 2006. Registered pharmacist W.Va., Ala. Pharmacy practice resident Erlanger Health Care Sys., Chattanooga, 1999—2000; clin. pharmacist Carraway Meth. Med. Ctr., Birmingham, 2000—01; clin. pharmacy specialist Bapt. Montclair, Birmingham, 2001; clin. and staff pharmacist Meml. Healthcare Sys., Chattanooga, 2001—02; pharmacist, leader IV room project St. Mary's Med. Ctr., Huntington, W.Va., 2002—04; dir. pharmacy Option Care, Huntington, 2004—05, Cornerstone Hosp., Huntington, 2005—. Mem.: Cabell County Med. Soc. Alliance, Am. Soc. Health-Sys. Pharmacists, Am. Mensa, Beta Gamma Sigma, Phi Kappa Phi. Avocations: reading, hiking, playing violin. E-mail: KDBOZAU@hotmail.com.

BLAKE, LAURA, architect; b. Berkeley, Calif., Dec. 26, 1959; d. Igor Robert and Elizabeth (Denton) B. BA in Art History, Brown U., 1982; MArch, UCLA, 1985. Employee The Ratcliff Architects, Berkeley, 1986-90; architect IDG Architects, Oakland, Calif., 1990-92; assoc. ELS/Elbasani & Logan Architects, Berkeley, 1992-2000, Mark Cavagnero Assocs., San Francisco, 2000—. Organizer charity ball Spinsters San Francisco, 1988, sec., 1988-89, mem. adv. bd., 1989-92; mem. San Francisco Jr. League, 1991-2003. Recipient Alpha Rho Chi bronze medal, 1985. Mem. Soc. Calif. Pioneers. Republican. Episcopalian. Avocations: travel, photography, sport, the arts. Office: Mark Cavagnero Assocs Ste 200 1045 Sansome St San Francisco CA 94111-1315

BLAKE, LORETTA L., music educator; b. Bonham, Tex., Feb. 2, 1967; d. David F. and M. Cynthia Redding; m. Paul D. Blake, May 5, 2006; children: Hannah McGaughy, Alyssa, Audrey McGaughy, Preston, Benjamin. BS, Arlington Bapt. Coll., Tex., 1989; MA in Tchg., U. Ark., Monticello, 2003. Cert. tchr. vocal music, instrumental music, P-12, ESL P-12 Ark. Dept. Edn., 2002. Libr. asst. Arlington Bapt. Coll., 1986—88; instrumental ensemble instr. Northside Bapt. Ch., Carrollton, Tex., 1986—91; recruiter Flying Nurses, Inc., Dallas, 1989—91; pvt. voice instr. Tuscola, Tex., 1991—96; preschool tchr. Dallas Ave. Christian Acad., Mena, Ark., 2002; music tchr. K-12 Wickes Sch. Dist., Ark., 2002—06, Springfield Public Sch., Mo., 2006—. Mem.: Ark. Edn. Assn., Ark. Choral Dirs. Assn., Ark. Sch. Band and Orch. Assn. Office: Springfield Public Sch Weller Elementary 1630 Weller Ave Springfield MO 65803

BLAKE, MARGARET TATE, psychologist, educator; b. Cyril, Okla., Jan. 17, 1927; d. Joseph Clifford and Luella (Anderson) Tate; m. Duane L. Blake, Dec. 1945 (div. 1974); children: Richard Duane, Kara Barrett, Debra Dawn; m. Charles H. Jansen, Aug. 15, 1986. BS, Okla. U., 1947; MS, Iowa State U., 1963, PhD, 1966. Lic. marriage and family therapist, Colo. Asst. prof. Drake U., Des Moines, Iowa, 1964-66, Colo. State U., Ft. Collins, 1966-68; prof. psychology U. No. Colo., Greeley, 1968-89; pvt. practice Greeley, 1989—. Producer videotapes in field. Fellow Am. Assn. Marriage and Family Therapy (bd. dirs. 1989—, approved supr., pres. Colo. chpt. 1986-89); mem. Colo. Assn. Counseling and Devel. (pres. 1980-81), Rocky Mountain Coun. Family Rels. (pres. 1984-87), Am. Bd. Vocat. Experts (diplomate). Home: 1912 29th Ave Greeley CO 80634-5753

BLAKE, MIRIAM SNELL, elementary school educator, choir director, organist, pianist; b. Monterey, Ohio, May 23, 1929; d. Howard Dale and Wilma Thompson Snell; m. William Ernest Blake Jr., Dec. 18, 1949; children: Benjamin William, Michal Joan, Peter Alan. BSL, Cin. Christian U., 1953; BS, Va. Commonwealth U., Richmond, 1969; MSc in Early Childhood Edn., Va. Commonwealth U., 1976. Lic. in real estate 1985, master gardener. Dean of women Cin. Christian U., 1953—54; elem. tchr. Hanover County Schs., Mechanicsville, Va., 1961—67, Chesterfield County Schs., Richmond, 1968—88; substitute tchr. Richmond City Schs., 1988—2005. Organist, choirmaster Westside Christian Ch., 1973—97, Holly Ridge Christian Ch., Mechanicsville, 1999—2003; choirmaster, pianist Battery Park Christian Ch., Richmond, 2004—05; mem., music tchr. Shepherd's Ctr. Richmond, 2000—. Avocation: gardening. Home: 3802 Sulgrave Rd Richmond VA 23221 Personal E-mail: weblake2@verizon.net.

BLAKE, PATRICIA, writer; d. Howard W. and Lucille (Page) Blake; m. Nicolas Nabokov, 1948 (div. 1955); m. Ronnie Dugger, 1982. BA, Smith Coll., Northampton, Mass., 1946. Reporter, corr. Life Mag., N.Y.C., 1953—62; assoc. editor Time Mag., N.Y.C., 1969—87; assoc. Davis Ctr. for Russian and Eurasian Studies, Harvard U., Cambridge, Mass., 1995—. Editor: Bedbug & Selected Poetry by Vladimir Mayakovsky, 1960, Halfway to the Moon: New Writing from Russia, 1964, Antiworlds: Poetry of Andrei Voznesensky, 1967, Dissonant Voices in Soviet Literature, 1967, Writers in Russia by Max Hayward, 1980. Guggenheim Meml. fellow, 1980—81, St. Antony's Coll. fellow, Oxford U., England, 1981, Bunting Inst. fellow, Radcliffe Coll., 1998—99. Home: 115 Museum St Somerville MA 02143 Office: Davis Ctr for Russian/Eurasian Studies Harvard U 1730 Cambridge St Cambridge MA 02139

BLAKE, RENÉE, broadcast executive; b. Yonkers, NY; BA, Goddard Coll., 1973. Announcer, prodr. Sta. WCBQ-AM, Oxford, NC, 1974, Sta. WANV-AM, Waynesboro, Va., 1974; talk show host, anchor Sta. WEEZ-AM, Chester, Pa., 1974—75; reporter, anchor Sta. WWDB-FM, Phila., 1975, Sta. WMMR-FM, Phila., 1975—78; programming spl. projects Drake Chenault Enterprises, LA, 1978—79; copywriter S.M. Newmark & Assoc., LA, 1980—81; reporter, pub. affairs dir. Sta. WHLY-FM, Orlando, Fla., 1981—83; news dir. Sta. WJYO-FM, Orlando, Fla., 1983—86; program dir. Sta. WKXL-AM/FM, Concord, NH, 1986-91, Sta. KXCI-FM, Tucson, 1991—93; programmer Jerrold Comm., Concord, Tucson, 1990—94; reporter, anchor Metro Networks, Phoenix, 1995—97, news bur. chief Albuquerque, 1997—2003; owner, CEO Media IQ, Albuquerque, 1996—; continuing news dir. Sta. KUNM-FM, 2003—. Interviewer, spkr. in field. Co-editor: Westside Rapper, 1970; columnist: The Drummer, 1976-77, Steppin' Out Magazine, 1983-86; creator, prodr. Music Zone Snowbank, 1988-89 (Golden Mike Merit NH Assn. Broadcasters 1988), This Island Earth, 1990 (Best of the Best 1st Place Golden Mike NH Assn. Broadcasters 1990), NH Veterans' Memorial Wall and Scholarship Committee, 1988-90 (1st Place Golden Mike NH Assn. Broadcasters 1989), Send Our Support Day, 1990; affiliate prodr. Human Rights Now, 1989 (1st Place Golden Mike NH Assn. Broadcasters 1989); contbr. articles to profl. jours. Recipient AP First Place Newscast for Kunu, 2003, In Depth Coverage award, N.Mex. Broadcasters Assn. Div., 2004. Avocations: writing, voiceovers. Office: Media IQ 174 Calle Loma Parda NW Albuquerque NM 87120-3477 E-mail: renee_blake@yahoo.com.

BLAKELEY, LINDA, psychologist, speaker, consultant, writer; b. Bklyn., July 26, 1941; children: Stacey, Scott. BA, UCLA, 1964; MA, Calif. State U., Northridge, 1977; PhD, Calif. Grad. Inst., 1985. Founder, dir. Parents Sharing Custody, Beverly Hills, Calif., 1984—87; pvt. practice self esteem, eating disorders, leadership stress mgmt. Positive Self Images, Beverly Hills, 1984—95. Prodr., host interview/talk show. Author: ABC's of Stress Management, 1989, Do It with Love: Positive Parenting After Divorce, 1988, (audio tape) Success Strategies, 1992; one-woman show The Magic Dress, 1998. Mem. adv. bd. Nat. Coun. Alcoholism and Drug Abuse, 1991-92. Mem.: Nat. Eating Disorder Assn., Calif. Psychol. Assn. (state bd. dirs. media com. 1989—92, chair-elect media divsn.), Nat. Assn. Anorexia, Beverly Hills C. of C. (pres. women's network 1989—90, chmn. health care com. 1989). Avocation: writing. Office: 420 S Beverly Dr Ste 100 Beverly Hills CA 90212-4410 Fax: (310) 578-2434. Office Phone: 310-286-9171. E-mail: Drlindablakeley@aol.com.

BLAKEMORE, KARIN JANE, obstetrician, geneticist; b. Stockholm, Nov. 10, 1953; d. William S. and Elaine Claire (Hoover) B.; 1 child, Joseph William. BA, U. Pa., 1975; MD, Med. Coll. Toledo, 1978. Diplomate Am. Bd. Med. Genetics, Am. Bd. Ob-gyn. Resident in ob-gyn. NYU, N.Y.C., 1978-82; fellow in clin. genetics Yale U., New Haven, 1982-85; fellow in maternal-fetal medicine Washington U., St. Louis, 1985-87; asst. prof. ob-gyn. Johns Hopkins U., Balt., 1987-93, assoc. prof. ob-gyn., 1992—. Dir. Prenatal Genetics Johns Hopkins U., Balt., 1992—, dir. Maternal-Fetal Medicine, 1994—. Author chpts. to books; guest editor Obstetrics and Gynecology Clinics of N.Am., 1993. Fellow Am. Coll. Ob-gyn., Am. Coll. Med. Genetics; mem. AMA, Am. Inst. Ultrasound and Medicine, Am. Soc. Human Genetics, Internat. Soc. Ultrasound in Medicine, Soc. for Maternal-Fetal Medicine, Soc. for Gynecol. Investigation, Am. Gynecol. and Obstet. Soc. Office: Johns Hopkins Hosp Ob/Gyn Phipps 228 600 N Wolfe St Baltimore MD 21287-1228

BLAKENEY, BARBARA A., public health service officer; BS, MS, U. Mass.; diploma, Worcester City Hosp. Sch. of Nursing. Primary care nurse practitioner Amherst Med. Assoc., Amherst, Mass., Boston City Hosp., Boston; prin. pub. health nurse for homeless svcs., addiction svcs. Dept. Health and Hosp., Divsn. Pub. Health, Boston; currently dir. health svcs. for homeless Boston Pub. Health Comm.; leave of absence. Named one of 100 Most Powerful People in Healthcare, Modern Healthcare mag., 2002, 2003, 2004, 2006; recipient Pearl McIver Pub. Health Nurse award, Am. Nurses Assn., Theta Alpha chpt. Ann Kibirck Nursing Leadership award, Sigma Theta Tau. Mem.: ANA (pres. 2002—06). Office: Am Nurses Assn Ste 400 8515 Georgia Ave Silver Spring MD 20910

BLAKENEY, KAREN ELIZABETH, social service and community health program executive, consultant; b. Evanston, Ill., June 27, 1953; d. Elwood Francis and Irene Loretta (Filloon) Garlick; life ptnr. Ydalia Granado; children: Jesse Alan, Aaron Paul. Cert. in Christian edn., Angeles Bible Coll., L.A., 1972; BA in Anthropology, Calif. State U., Long Beach, 1978; MS in Counseling Psychology, Mt. St. Mary's Coll., L.A., 1992; cert. in non-profit mgmt., U. So. Calif., 1998. Commd. pastor Hosanna Ministries, 1994. Archaeologist VTM Corp., Vandenburg AFB, Calif., 1979-81; archaeologist, Arroyo Grande, Calif., 1981-82; acct. Airport Datsun/Volvo, Santa Maria, Calif., 1982-83; adminstrn. mgr. Concord Sys., Reseda, Calif., 1983-86; ins. broker Prudential Ins. Co., Torrance, Calif., 1986-87; mgr. legal compliance dept. G.J. Sullivan Cos., L.A., 1987-92; psychotherapy intern Hosanna Ministries, Santa Monica, Calif., 1990-95; children's social worker Dept. Children and Family Svcs., L.A., 1994-96; dir. social work Internat. Foster Family Agy., Carson, Calif., 1996-97; dir. youth svcs. L.A. Gay and Lesbian Ctr., Hollywood, Calif., 1997-99; dir. programs Chinatown Svc. Ctr., L.A., 1999—2002; exec. dir. Schutrum-Piteo Found., Burbank, Calif., 2002—03; CEO, pres. Blackwolf, LLC Consulting, 2001—; exec. dir. Grace Ctr., Pasadena, 2003—04, Blackwolf Gallery, 2003—; program officer First 5, L.A., 2005—. Lectr. Calif. Poly. Inst. Archaeol. Field Sch., Mission San Antonio de Padua, 1978-81; co-founder, exec. dir. Inst. for trauma Intervention, L.A., 1993-96. Author: (poetry) Sacred Journey, 1995, Ydalia's Song, 1998. Bd. dir. Art To Grow On, San Pedro, Calif., 1992-94, Desert Stream Ministries/AIDS Resource Ministry, L.A., 1985-91; mem. parent-tchr. adv. bd. Park Western Elem. Sch., San Pedro, 1993-94; dir. mem. Consortium for Homeless Youth Svcs., Hollywood, 1997-99; rep. L.A. County Svc. Planning Area Dist. 4 Coun., 1999-2002; mem. Asian-Pacific Islander police adv. com. L.A. Police Dept., 2000; mem. Nat. Network of Youth, 1997-2002; mem. Calif. Child, Youth and Family Coalition, 1998-2003; bd. dir. Coalition Against Slave Trafficking, 1999-2002, Coalition for Cmty. Health, 2001-03, Schutrum-Piteo Found., 2003-; mem. Dept. Pub. Social Svcs. long-term self sufficiency steering com. L.A. County, 2000-02. Mem. NAFE, Calif. Assn. Marriage and Family Therapists, Calif. Assn. Against Domestic Violence, Calif. Stat U.-Long Beach Anthropology Alumni Assn. (alumni bd. 1984-85). Avocations: artist, writing. Office Phone: 323-666-9566. E-mail: khlakeney90039@sbcglobal.net.

BLAKENEY, KECIA L., disability examiner; b. Balt., Jan. 21, 1964; d. Bobbie Lee and Saran (Grasty) B.; children: Michael A., Ian M., Kieren C., Myles G. BA, Sojourner-Douglas, 1986. Sr. staff tchr. Maarifa Children's Ctr., Balt.; tchrs. aide Feagin Day Care Ctr., Balt.; service rep. Social Security Adminstrn., 1989—90, claims rep., 1990—98, disability examiner, 1998—. Mem. Metro Edn. Coalition, Am. Fedn. Govt. Employees Union (steward), Nat. Assn. Disability Examiners Avocations: sewing, creating toys for children, reading, quilting, knitting.

BLAKE RAMOS, DEBRA BARBARA, writer; b. Bklyn., June 17, 1959; d. Rebecca Simmons and Jack Blake; m. Manuel Joseph Ramos, Apr. 2, 1957; children: Michael Young, Shameeka Shontele Ramos, Sarah Barbara Ramos, Abraham Joseph Ramos. Bus. degree, N.Y. Bus. Sch., 1981. Telephone technician, 1983; sec. Queensboro Correctional Facility, Queens, NY, 1984; writer, 1980—2003, 2003. Author (artist): (book) A New Birth Of Poetry (Editor's Choice award, 2001), Let Them Cry (Editor's Choice award, 2002), (CD) Serenity and Passion, 2000, Let Them Cry, 2002; songwriter Hill Top Record, 2001—03; contbr. articles to profl. jours. Mem.: Internat. Soc. Of Poets (hon. Internat. Poet of Merit award 2001).

BLAKESLEE, HELEN P., columnist; b. Coleman Falls, Va., May 14, 1919; d. Harry Lewis Peck and Mabel Starcher Northcraft; m. Theodore Edwin Blakeslee, June 3, 1945; children: Carol Carmen, Michael Edwin. BS, Ohio State U., Columbus, 1943; MA Edn., Dominican Coll. (now Dominican U.), Calif., 1966. Tchr. Mentor H.S., Ohio, 1943—45; tchr., instr. George Washington U., Washington, 1946—48; tchr. San Domenico H.S., San Anselmo, Calif., 1966—70; columnist The Gracious Grammarian Marin Ind. Jour., Novato, Calif., 1994—. Tchr. ESL Coll. Marin, Kentfield, Calif., 1972—78. Mem.: AAUW, DAR, Marin Music Chest. Republican. Methodist. Avocations: singing, reading, walking, writing poetry and prose. Home: 618 Woodbine Dr San Rafael CA 94903

BLAKESLEY, KIMBERLY KAY, art educator, consultant; b. Hampton, Iowa, Aug. 17, 1959; d. Jay Francis and Sharon Kay (Pieters) Kurth; m. Jay Kevin Hoodjer, July 22, 1977 (div. Sept. 1990); children: Joshua, Tylor, Kathryn; m. Bruce Carl Blakesley, Oct. 22, 1999. AA, Ellsworth C.C., Iowa Falls, Iowa, 1990; BA, U. No. Iowa, Cedar Falls, 1993, MA in Ednl. Leadership, 2002, postgrad. Cert. tchg. U. No. Iowa, 1997. Owner, mgr. Skay's Variety Store, Ackley, Iowa, 1983-88; mgr. Pronto Market, Ackley, 1989-90; state coord. Iowa region Nacel Cultural Exchs., St. Paul, 1994—98; art bus. instr. Waterloo, Iowa, 1998—2002; art instr., yearbook adv., coach Wapsie-Valley, Fairbanks, 2002—06; owner Revolutionary Concepts and Cons., 2006—. Artist, creator electroplated container, Container I (hon. mention 1993); exhibited in group shows at Denver Art Show (1st pl. 2002-06). Mem. NEA, ASCD, Sch. Adminstrs. Iowa, Nat. Art Educators Assn., Iowa Art Educators Assn., Phi Theta Kappa, Beta Sigma Phi. Avocations: fine arts, golf, cross country skiing. Home: 2512 Cedar Heights Dr Cedar Falls IA 50613 Office Phone: 319-939-4356. E-mail: kbangels@cfu.net.

BLAKEY, MARION CLIFTON, federal agency administrator; b. Gadsden, Ala., Mar. 26, 1948; B Internatl Studies, Mary Washington Coll., U. Va.; postgrad., Johns Hopkins U. Dir. pub. affairs NEH, 1982—84; dir. pub. affairs & spl. asst. to the sec. US Dept. Edn., Washington, 1985—87; adminstr. Nat. Hwy. Traffic Safety Adminstrn., 1992—93; prin. Blakey & Assocs., Washington, 1993—2001; chmn. Nat. Transp. Safety Bd., 2001—02; adminstr. FAA, 2002—. Office: FAA 800 Independence Ave SW Washington DC 20591-0004

BLAKNEY, JUANITA MOSLEY, psychotherapist; d. George Spellman Mosley and Clarissa Lee Whitlock; children: Denise, Donna Blakney-Williams. BS in Edn., Cheyney U., Pa., 1959; MEd, Antioch U., Yellow Springs, Ohio, 1977; EdD, Nova Southeastern U., Ft. Lauderdale, Fla., 1991. Cert. counselor Pa., lic. profl.counselor NJ. Tchr. Sch. Dist. Phila., 1959—92, Girard Coll., Phila., 1992—97; in home therapist Delaware Valley Psychol. Svcs., Moorestown, NJ, 1999—; provider Magellan Behavioral Health, 2003—. Part-time therapist CEC Counselors and Cons., Haddon Heights, NJ, 1993—96; clin. coord. Youth Advocate Programs, Camden, NJ, 2004—05; provider divsn. Youth and Family Svc., NJ, 2005—. Bd. dirs. Faces of Survivors, Arlington, Tex., Boys and Girls Club, Burlington, NJ. Recipient cert. of merit, Women in Edn., 1992. Mem.: APA, Nat. Assn. Parliamentarians, Continental Socs., Inc (Ea. regional dir. 2003—, past pres. South Jersey chpt., past v.p. South Jersey chpt., past sec. South Jersey chpt.), Order Ea. Star, Grand Chpt. (sec., PM), Alpha Kappa Alpha. Avocations: walking, dance, travel, theater, reading. Home: 322 Society Hill Cherry Hill NJ 08003 Office Phone: 609-744-2758. Business E-mail: nitablak@comcast.net.

BLALOCK, ANN BONAR, evaluation researcher; b. Parkersburg, W.Va., Apr. 16, 1928; d. Harry and Fay (Conley) Bonar; m. Hubert Blalock, Jr., 1951 (dec. 1991); children: Susan Blalock Lyon, Kathleen Blalock McCarrell, James W.; m. Gerhard E. Lenski, 1996. AB, Oberlin Coll., 1950; MA, U. N.C., 1954; MSW, U. Wash., 1978. Pvt. cons. Admiralty Inlet Consulting, Hansville, Wash. Cons. OECD, Paris, 1990, European Commn., Brussels, 1995. Author: Introduction to Social Research, 2d edit., 1982; contbg. author: Quicker, Better, Cheaper: Managing Performance in American Government, 2001; editor, reviewer: Evaluation Forum, 1986-97; editor: Evaluating Social Programs, 1990; co-editor: Methodology in Social Research, 1968; contbr. articles to profl. jours. Past pres. bd. dirs. Cmty. Mental Health Clin.; mem. Gov.'s Task Force on Accountability in Govt. Recipient Rsch. award, Partnership for Employment and Tng. Careers, 1988. Mem. NASW (past pres. Wash. state chpt.), Am. Eval. Assn. (past com. chair). Home: PO Box 409 Hansville WA 98340-0409 Personal E-mail: aglenski@earthlink.net.

BLALOCK, CARMEN, education educator; b. Birmingham, Ala., Dec. 16, 1947; d. Van Thomas Jr. and Helen Mavis (Swann) Fountain; m. Roger Blalock, Apr. 13, 1973; 1 child, Aytree. BS, MA, U. Ala., 1972, EdD, 1984. Instr. Calhoun C.C., Decatur, Ala., 1972—. Sec., treas. Bankhead Trail Riders Assn., Cullman, Ala., 1989—; pres. SHARE Club, Cullman, 1995; editor Tale of the Trail, Cullman, 1996. Avocations: horseback riding, hiking, canoeing. Home: 466 County Road 349 Logan AL 35098-1002 Office: Calhoun Cmty Coll Hwy 31 N Decatur AL 35609

BLALOCK, CAROL DOUGLASS, psychologist, educator; d. Allan Martin and Mary Louise Douglass; m. Harvey Anthony Blalock, Aug. 27, 1976; children: Jeanne, Patricia, Elizabeth. BEd, U. S.D., 1968; MEd in Edn., U. Fla., 1976, EdS in Counseling, 1976, PhD in Curriculum and Instrn., 1980; postgrad., U. Md., 1980—81. Nat. cert. sch. psychologist Fla., 1990, lic. sch. psychologist Fla., 1990. Tchr. Metcalf Elem., Gainesville, Fla., 1968, Gainesville (Fla.) H.S., 1969; coord. environ. edn. Sante Fe C.C., Gainesville, 1974—78, adj. faculty, 1974—78; grad. rsch. fellow U. Fla., rsch. assoc., 1979; chmn. sci. dept. Oak Hall Prep. Sch., Gainesville, Fla., 1981—84; guidance counselor Trenton (Fla.) HS, 1984—87; psychologist Marion County Schs., Ocala, Fla., 1987—; adj. faculty U. South Fla., Tampa, 1990. Author: (chpt.) A Futures Perspective on Instructional Design, 1980; co-author: (conf. summary) Computer Conf. on the Future, 1979, (chpt.) Learning Networks: The Next Step, 1981. Aux. officer Gainesville (Fla.) Police Dept., 1985—95; mem. Holy Faith Cath. Ch., Gainesville, Fla., 1976. Mem.: Fla. Assn. Sch. Psychologists, Nat. Assn. Sch. Psychologists, APA, Phi Delta Kappa. Republican. Roman Catholic. Avocations: travel, music, art. Office: Marion County Sch Bd Ste 5 1517 SE 30th Ave Ocala FL 34471

BLALOCK, LOUISE, librarian, public administrator; b. Neptune, N.J., Jan. 25, 1934; BS, TCNJ, 1955; MLS, SUNY, Albany, 1971; M in Pub. Adminstrn., NYU, 1987. Acting dir. Empire State Coll., NY, 1972; instr. sch. library sci. SUNY, Albany, 1973—74; coordinator children's services East Providence (R.I.) Pub. Library, 1974—77; regional coordinator Island Interrelated Library System, RI, 1977—79; dir. Barrington Pub. Library, RI, 1979—81, New Canaan (Conn.) Library, 1981—92; chief libr. Hartford (Conn.) Pub. Libr., 1994—. Chairperson State Library Standards Task Force, 1984; active Notable Books Council, 1988, Conn. Inter-Agy. Library Planning Com., 1982-86, White House Conf. Libraries and Info. Services. 1979, Recipient Outstanding Libr. award, Conn. Libr. Assn., 1999, Libr. of Yr., Libr. Jour., 2001, Nat. Award Libr. Svc., IMLS, 2002. Mem. ALA, Am. Soc. Pub. Adminstrn., Conn. Library Assn., Fairfield Adminstrs. Group (pres. 1987), New Eng. Library Assn. (exec. bd. 1975-77), R.I. Library Assn. (pres. 1979-80). Office Phone: 860-695-6280. E-mail: lblalock@hplct.org.

BLALOCK, SHERRILL, investment advisor; b. Newport News, Va., June 9, 1945; d. David Graham and Martha Lee (Bennett) B.; m. Jonathan L. Smith, Oct. 27, 1985; 1 child, Graham C.G. BA, Smith Coll., 1967. Chartered fin. analyst. Investment broker Legg Mason & Co., Washington, 1968-77,

Blyth Eastman Dillon, Washington, 1977-80; portfolio mgr., mng. dir. Mitchell Hutchins, N.Y.C., 1980-88; gen. ptnr., portfolio mgr. Weiss Peck & Greer, N.Y.C., 1988-95; gen. ptnr. Delphi Asset Mgmt., N.Y.C., 1995-98; founder, mng. mem. Chesapeake Asset Mgmt., N.Y.C., 1998—. Chair investment com., trustee Diocese of NY of Episcopal Ch., 2001—; trustee, vice chmn. bd. trustees, chair investment com. Estate and Property of Diocese Conv. of N.Y., 1996—2002; trustee Cathedral of St. John the Divine, 1998—, chair investment com., 1999—. Mem. Washington Soc. Investment Analysts, Inst. Chartered Fin. Analysts. Office: Chesapeake Asset Mgmt 1 Rockefeller Plz Rm 1210 New York NY 10020-2002 Office Phone: 212-218-4040, 212-218-4041.

BLAMER, BEVERLY A., elementary school educator; d. Gail Snell; children: Brett, Bennett, Brianna. EdB, Ill. State U., Normal, 1979; MEd, Grand Valley State Coll., Allendale, Mich., 1987. Tchg. cert. Mich. Tchr. Fremont (Mich.) Mid. Sch., 1983—. Educator assoc. Mich. Coun. Econ. Edn., 2003—; study tour to Russia Nat. Coun. Econ. Edn., 2003; study tour to Germany Goethe Inst., 2005. Leader, asst. leader Girl Scouts US, Fremont, 1999—2006; ch. youth group leader Fremont United Meth. Ch., 2004—06. Named Cool Tchr. of the Month, Sta. WGVU Pub. TV, 2003. Mem.: NEA. Methodist. Avocations: stained glass, sewing wedding gowns, travel, gardening, reading. Office: Fremont Mid Sch 500 Woodrow Fremont MI 49412 Office Phone: 231-924-8173.

BLANC, CAROL S., biology educator; d. Barbara and Carl Lundblade; m. Robert J. Blanc, Nov. 30, 1974; children: John, Kristen, Michael. BA cum laude, Whitman Coll., Walla Walla, Wash., 1974. Lic. secondary tchg. Colo., 1976, Oreg., 1996. Math/biology tchr. Northglenn Jr. H.S., Colo., 1976—78; math tchr. Pendleton Jr. H.S., Oreg., 1978—80; biology tchr. Pendleton H.S., 1995—. Pres., various other offices PEO chpt. CM, Pendleton, 1985—2006; pres. Pendleton Cultural Found., 2003—06; deacon, christian edn. bd., tchr. Presbyn. Ch., Pendleton, 2003—06; pres., various other offices PTA, Pendleton, 1985—96. Avocations: gardening, skiing, travel, tennis, golf. Home: 846 NE 3rd Pendleton OR 97801

BLANCHARD, DOROTHY HARDT, academic administrator, volunteer; b. Chgo., Apr. 12, 1930; d. Carl Frederick and Meta Jandt Hardt; m. Benjamin Seaver Blanchard, Aug. 4, 1956; children: Rebecca, Benjamin III, Lisa. BS in Edn., Concordia Tchrs. Coll., 1953; MS in Adult and Continuing Edn., Va. Tech. U., 1984. Tchr. St. Paul Luth. Sch., Patterson, NJ, 1950—51, Concordia Luth. Sch., Seattle, 1953—56; v.p., developer programs Ctr. Vol. Devel. Va. Tech. U., Blacksburg, Va., 1981—86. Adv. bd. Med. Clinic New River Valley, Christiansburg, Va., 1984—87; mem. adv. bd., trainer Ctr. Vol. Devel., Blacksburg, Va., 1981—86. Contbr. articles to profl. jours. Vol. ops. Girl Scouts U.S.A., N.Y., 1992—97; leader Genessee Valley Girl Scout Coun., Penfield, NY, 1963—71, Va. Skyline Girl Scout Coun., Roanoke, Va., 1971—75, chmn. program com., 1974—75, pres., 1975—80, past pres. adv. group, 1980—; dir. vol. programs Luther Meml. Ch., Blacksburg, Va., 1999—; founder, organizer Christ the King Luth. Ch., Nashua, NH, 1960—62; v.p., bd. dirs. Luth Campus Ministry Va. Tech. U. and Radford U., Va., 1977—80. Recipient Thanks Badge award, Va. Skyline Girl Scouts Coun., 1978, Citizen Recognition award, Rotary Internat., 1993, Cmty. Women Distinction award, 1998. Lutheran. Avocations: walking, reading, travel. Home: 301 Sutton Place Blacksburg VA 24060 Personal E-mail: dotblanchard@verizon.net.

BLANCHARD, KIMBERLY STAGGERS, lawyer, educator; b. Ann Arbor, Mich., May 17, 1954; d. Theodore R. and Bette Lee (Clark) Staggers; m. John Sears Blanchard, May 31, 1980; children: Charles Stuart, Virginia Greene. BA, Dartmouth Coll., 1976; MS, U. Wis., 1978; JD, NYU, 1981. Bar: N.Y. 1982. Assoc. Paul, Weiss, Rifkind, Wharton & Garrison, N.Y.C., 1981-83, Haythe & Curley, N.Y.C., 1983—99, ptnr., Weil, Gotshal & Manges LLP, 1999—. Pres. Pelham Pub. Libr. Mem. ABA, N.Y. State Bar Assn. (exec. com. tax sect. 1996-, 1st vice chair). Clubs: Pelham Country (Pelham Manor, N.Y.). Democrat. Avocation: golf. Office: Weil, Gothshal & Manges LLP 767 Fifth Avenue New York NY 10153

BLANCHARD, LOU, school system administrator; BS, Tex. Wesleyan, 1995; MA in Counseling, Amberton U., 1998; MEd, U. Tex., Austin, 1999. Sch. adminstr. Treetops Sch. Internat., Euless, Tex., 1988—. Office Phone: 817-283-1771. E-mail: lblanchard@esc11.net.

BLANCHARD, MARGARET MOORE, writer, educator; b. Columbus, Ga., Dec. 29, 1938; d. Robert Moore and Ann (Keller) B. BA, Incarnate Word Coll., 1960; MA, St. Louis U., 1962; PhD, Union Inst., 1990. Instr. St. Louis U., 1960-62, Grailville C.C., Cin., 1962-64, LeMoyne Coll., Syracuse, N.Y, 1964-66, U. Wis., Madison, 1967-69; asst. prof. Morgan State U., Balt., 1969-71; adminstr. Women's Growth Ctr., Balt., 1972-74; asst. prof. Towson State U., Balt., 1975-90; assoc. prof. Vt. Coll., Montpelier, 1990—; dir. The Grad. Program, Montpelier, 1995—2006; prof. The Union Inst. and Univ., 2000—. Author: Ten Irish-American Women Poets, 1987, The Rest of the Deer, 1993, From the Listening Place, 1997, (novels) Hatching, 2001, Wandering Potatoes, 2002, Who?, 2004, Queen Bea, 2005; co-author: Restoring the Orchard, 1994, Duet, 1995; author of poems; contbr. articles to profl. jours. Mem. MLA, Nat. Assn. Poetry Therapy (bd. mem.), Nat. Women's Studies Assn. (cmty. coord. 1993), Nat. Coun. Tchrs. English, Internat. Women's Writers Guild. Avocations: photography, stained glass artisan, cross country skiing. Office: The MA Program Vt Coll Montpelier VT 05602

BLANCHARD, MARY WARNER, historian, consultant; d. Raymond Chase and Twila Sigworth Warner; m. William Clifford Blanchard, Jan. 30, 1960; children: Cecily Chase, William Isaac, Clifford Wright. BA, Vassar Coll., Poughkeepsie, N.Y., 1956; MA, Rutgers U., 1989, PhD, 1994. Assoc. fellow Ctr. Hist. Analysis Rutgers U., New Brunswick, NJ, 1991—. Mem. adv. bd. Ctr. Hist. Analysis Rutgers U., 1991—; cons. in field; lectr. in field. Author: Oscar Wilde's America: Counterculture in the Gilded Age, 1998, Oscar Wilde: The Man, His Writings and His World, 2003, The Importance of Being Misunderstood: Homage to Oscar Wilde, 2003; contbr. chapters to books, articles to profl. jours. Trustee N.J. Mus. Arch., Madison, NJ, N.J. Shakespeare Festival, Madison; coord. N.J. chpt. Nat. Energy Found.; fundraiser Morristown (N.J.) Meml. Hosp.; mem. women's com. fundraiser Congressman Rodney Frelinghuysen; bd. dirs., sec. bd. trustees The Peck Sch., Morristown, NJ. Mem.: Victorian Soc. Am., Soc. Historians Gilded Age and Progressive Era, Orgn. Am. Historians, Harding Township Hist. Soc., Costume Soc. Am., Am. Hist. Assn., Am. Studies Assn. (Wise-Susman prize 1991, 1993, Annette K. Baxter grantee 1992), William Morris Soc., Edith Wharton Soc., Vassar Club, Garden Club, Colony Club. Home: 42 Glen Alpine Rd Morristown NJ 07960 Personal E-mail: mwb94@aol.com.

BLANCHARD, MARYANN N., state legislator; b. N.J., Oct. 12, 1942; d. Joseph Charles and Mary (Longo) Navatta; m. Raymond P. Blanchard, 1967; children: Mary Beth, Catherine Anne, Daniel, Frances Elizabeth. BA, St. Joseph's Coll., 1966. Mem. Rockingham County Dist. 26 N.H. Ho. of Reps., Concord, 1982-90, mem. dist. 33, 1996-2000, ranking minority mem., mem. resources, recreation and devel. com., mem. fin. com., 2000—05. Trustee Strawberry Banke, 1993-96, Portsmouth Pub. Libr., 1981-83; commr. Portsmouth Police Commn., 1991-96; mem. adv. coun. Coop-Ext., Rockingham, 1992-93; mem. Portsmouth Hosp. Guild; leader Swiftwater coun. Girl Scouts USA, 1978-82; mem. Portsmouth PTA; mem. Atlantic States Marine Fisheries Commn., 2001—. Mem. LWV (past pres., bd. dirs. 1967-71), Soc. Protection N.H. Forests, Audubon Soc., Parents Music Club. Roman Catholic. Office Phone: 603-271-2136.

BLANCHARD, PAMELA SNYDER, special education educator; b. Winston-Salem, N.C., Feb. 5, 1951; d. Roger Alexander and Marie Gobble Snyder; m. George Winborne Blanchard, July 26, 1975; children: Andrew Micah, Justin Warren, Nathan Winborne. BA in Elem. Edn., St. Andrews Presbyn. Coll., 1973; Cert. in Spl. Edn., U. Tenn., 1990; MA in Ednl. Tech. and Bible, Johnson Bible Coll., 2000. Cert. tchr. N.C., edn. and spl. edn., and Career Ladder I tchr. Tenn. Title I math. tchr. Durham (N.C.) City Schs., 1973—75; algebra tchr. Davidson County Schs., Welcome, NC, 1976; Chpt. I reading and math. tchr. Knoxville (Tenn.) City Schs., 1976—79, 1980—85; ednl. cons. Discovery Toys, Knoxville, 1989—90; spl. edn. extended resource tchr. Sevier County Schs., Sevierville, Tenn., 1990—91; spl. edn. resource specialist Knox County Schs., Strawberry Plains, Tenn., 1992—. Mem. leadership com., sch. improvement team, tech. com., webmistress Carter Elem. Sch., 1999—. Vol. counselor Sexual Assault Crisis Ctr., Knoxville, 1991—92; chairperson missions bd. Seymour (Tenn.) United Meth. Ch., 1988—90, chairperson assimilation com., 1990—92, sec. adminstrv. coun., 2000, 2001—02; missionary Charleston, SC, 2001—02, Damascus, Va., 2001—05, Zimbabwe, 2003—06, Costa Rica, 2004, Carter Elem. Sch., 2003, 2005. Recipient Tchr. Yr., 2004—05; grantee Multicultural Cooking Unit, Knoxville Jr. League, 1994, Accelerated Reader Books, East Tenn. Edn. Found., 1995. Mem.: ASCD, NEA, Internat. Reading Assn., Knox County Edn. Assn., Tenn. Edn. Assn., Children with Attention Deficit Disorder, Learning Disabilities Assn., Divsn. Learning Disabilities, Coun. for Exceptional Children, Nat. Honor Soc. Democrat. Methodist. Avocations: reading, hiking, computers, travel. Home: 705 Forest View Ct Seymour TN 37865 Office: Carter Elem Sch 9304 College Ln Strawberry Plains TN 37871

BLANCHARD, SHIRLEY LYNN, primary school educator, consultant; b. Medford, Oreg., Sept. 5, 1954; d. Richard L. Grigsby, Helen L. Grigsby; m. John T. Blanchard, Sept. 6, 1975; children: Andrew Blanchard children: Martin Blanchard, Richelle Blanchard. BA in Edn., So. Oreg. State Coll., 1975, BS, 1978; MA in Edn., So. Oreg. U., 1985. Nat. bd. cert. tchr. Nat. Bd. Profl. Tchg. Stds., 2000. Music tchr. Jackson County Sch. Dist. #6, Central Point, Oreg., 1975—81, kindergarten tchr. Eagle Point, Oreg., 1983—99; primary tchr. Jackson County Sch. Dist. #9, Eagle Point, Oreg., 1999—. Home schooling parent educator RIGGS Inst., So. Oreg., 1987—91, reading cons. for home schooling parents, 1987—91; continuing edn. presenter early childhood literacy So. Oreg. U./Medford Sch. Dist. 549C, Medford, 1995—96; site based mgmt. team chmn., mem. Glenn D. Hale Elem. Scho., Eagle Point, 1996—98; contract bargaining team mem. Eagle Point Edn. Assn., Eagle Point, 1997—98; adj. prof. edn. So. Oreg. U., 2002—. Leader Wynema Girl Scout Counsel, Medford, 1972—75; 4H leader Oreg. State Ext. Svc., Central Point, Oreg., 1997—98. Recipient Slice of Life award, Williams Bread & McKenzie Farms Bakery and KOBI-TV, 2002. Fellow: Nat. Kindergarten Alliance Network; mem.: NEA, Internat. Soc. for Tech. in Edn., Oreg. Edn. Assn., Nat. Assn. Edn. Young Children. Avocations: internet mentoring, horses, technology, writing music, birds. Home: 1939 Dry Creek Rd Eagle Point OR 97524 Office: Jackson County Sch Dist #9 PO Box 197 215 E Main Eagle Point OR 97524 Office Phone: 541-830-6121. Home Fax: (541) 826-3221; Office Fax: (541) 826-3221. Business E-Mail: blanchards@eaglepnt.k12.or.us.

BLANCHETT, CATE (CATHERINE ELISE BLANCHETT), actress; b. Melbourne, Victoria, Australia, May 14, 1969; d. Robert and June Blanchett; m. Andrew Upton, Dec. 29, 1997; children: Dashiell John, Roman Robert. Grad., Nat. Inst. Dramatic Art, Australia, 1992. Performed with Sydney Theatre Co., Belvoir St. Theatre Co. Appeared in theatre prodns. including Top Girls, Kafka Dances (Newcomer Sydney Theatre Critics Circle award 1993), Oleanna (Rosemont and Sydney Theater Critics Cir. Best Actress Award 1993), Hamlet (nominated Green Rm. award), 1995, Sweet Phoebe, The Tempest, The Seagull, The Blind Giant is Dancing, Plenty, 1999, Hedda Gabler (Prestigious Helpmann award best female actor in a play 2006), 2006; actress (films) Police Rescue, 1994, Parklands, 1996, Paradise Road, 1997, Thank God He Met Lizzie, 1997 (Australian Film Inst. award 1997, Sydney Film Critics awards best supporting actress 1997), Oscar and Lucinda (Am. Film Inst. nomination best actress 1997), 1997, Elizabeth (Golden Globe for best actress in a drama, 1999, Brit. Acad. Film and TV Arts award best actress in leading role 1999, Chgo. Film Critics Assn. award best actress 1999, London Film Critics Assn. award 1999, Toronto Fil Critics Assn. award 1999, On-line Film Critics award 1999, Variety Critics and Eng. Empire award 1999), 1998, The Talented Mr. Ripley (Brit. Acad. Film and TV Arts nomination best supporting actress 1999), 1999, An Ideal Husband, 1999, Pushing Tin 1999, The Man Who Cried (Best Supporting Actress award 2000), 2000, The Gift, 2000, Bandits (Golden Globe award nomination 2001, SAG nomination outstanding supporting actress 2001), 2001, Charlotte Gray, 2001, The Shipping News (Best Supporting Acress award 2001), 2001, Galadriel, 2001, The Lord of the Rings: The Fellowship of the Ring, 2001, Heaven, 2002, The Lord of the Rings: The Two Towers, 2002, Veronica Guerin (Golden Globe nomination best performace actress in a motion picture-drama 2003, Film Critics Assn. best actress 2003), 2003, Coffee and Cigarettes (nomination best supporting female 2005 Ind. Spirit awards), 2003, The Missing, 2003, The Lord of the Rings: The Return of the King, 2003 (SAG award outstanding performance by a cast in a motion picture 2004), The Life Aquatic with Steve Zissou, 2004, The Aviator (Acad. award best supporting acress 2004, Brit. Acad. Film and TV Assn. award 2004, SAG award 2004, Hollywood Fgn. Press Assn. nomination 2004), 2004 (Acad. Award for best actress in a supporting role, 2005, SAG award for best actress in a supporting role 2005), Little Fish, 2004, Babel, 2006, Notes on a Scandal, The Good German, 2006; (TV miniseries) Heartland, 1994, Bordertown, 1995; actor, prodr. (films) Bangers, 1999. Nominee Best Actress, SAG, Acad. Motion Picture, Arts and Scis. Office: Creative Artists Agy c/o Hylda Queally 9830 Wilshire Blvd Beverly Hills CA 90212

BLANCHETTE, BEVERLY BECKMAN, dean, theater educator; b. Pitts., Dec. 27, 1953; d. Collette Peternel Beckman; m. Edward F. Blanchette, July 12, 1975; children: Erin Michele, Megan Marie. MFA, FAU, Boca Raton, Fla., 1993. Cert. profl. Fla., 1977. Theater educator, dean AW Dreyfoos Sch. Arts, West Palm Beach, Fla. Dir.: (plays) (Ednl. Theatre Assn. Hall of Fame, 2003). Named Thespian Sponsor of the Yr., Fla. State Thespians, 2006. Mem.: Fla. Assn. for Theatre Edn. (pres. 2003—05, past pres. 2006—, Outstanding Theatre Educator 1997). Office: AW Dreyfoos School of Arts 501 S Sapodilla Ave West Palm Beach FL 33401 Office Phone: 561-802-6061. Office Fax: 561-802-6077. Business E-Mail: blanchb@palmbeach.k12.fl.us.

BLANCHFIELD, KELLY L., adult education educator; b. Ridgewood, N.J., Apr. 27, 1987; d. James Stephen and Diane Marie Blanchfield. BA, U. N.C., Wilmington, 2003. Cert. health edn. specialist Nat. Commn. Health Edn. Credentialing, 2005. Peer educator U. N.C., Wilmington, 2003; health educator Summex Corp., Indpls., 2004—. Team leader Summex Corp., Indpls., 2005—. Mem.: AAHPERD, Am. Assn. Health Edn. Democrat. Roman Catholic. Office: Summex Corp 2419 Fordham Ln Indianapolis IN 46268

BLANCO, KATHLEEN BABINEAUX, governor; b. New Iberia, La., Dec. 15, 1942; m. Raymond S. Blanco, Aug. 8, 1964; 6 children. BS in Bus. Edn., U. La.at Lafayette, 1964. Tchr. Breaux Bridge High Sch.; with La. State Legis. Dist. 45, 1984-88, mem. house edn. com., mem. house transp., hwys., and pub. works com., Pub. Svc. Commn., La., 1988-94, chair La., 1993-95; lt. gov. State of La., 1995—2003, gov., 2004—. Democrat. Catholic. Achievements include being first woman gov. of La. Office: Office of Gov PO Box 94004 Baton Rouge LA 70804-9004 Office Phone: 225-342-7015. Office Fax: 225-342-7099.*

BLANCO, LAURA, interior designer; b. Havana, Cuba, July 3, 1956; came to U.S., 1960; d. Lauro and Marina (Mardones) B.; m. Robert F. Shainheit, 1988. Studied landscape design, NY Botanical Gardens, 2000—03; studied interior design, NY Sch. Interior Design, 2002—04. Asst. box office treas., press agt. Zev Bufman Entertainment, Inc., Orlando, St. Petersburg, Fla., 1978-83; press agt. Kool Jazz Festival and Heritage Fair, Orlando, 1982; producer La. World Exposition Inc., New Orleans, 1983-84, Festival Ventures, Inc., Miami, Fla., 1985-86; producer/dir. hispanic events Festival Prodns., Inc., NYC, 1986-87; pres. Blanco Shainheit Prodns., Blanco Shainheit Music, NYC, 1988—99; ptnr. unanimo, 1992—99; pres. Laura Blanco Interiors, NYC, 2004—. Prodr. (short film) The Summer of My Dreams, 1994, La Ciudad, 1995, (feature film, award winner Havana Film Festival, 1998), Perdida, 1998. Bd. dirs. Artists Community Fed. Credit Union, 1988-90; bd. mem. Off World Theatre, 2003-05. Mem. ASCAP, Am. Latin Music Assn. Office Phone: 212-876-0053. E-mail: info@laurablanco.com.

BLAND, DEBORAH ELAINE, science educator; d. Cecil Earl Dennis and Dortha Frances Glenn Dennis; m. Benjamin Franklin Bland, Jr., July 28, 1973; children: James Eugene, Nathan Cole. BA, Adams State Coll., Alamosa, Colo., 1977, MSc, 1981. Secondary tchr. Holly Sch. Dist. Re-#, Colo., 1977—. Mem.: NEA, Nat. Sci. Tchrs. Assn. (NEWMAST award 1989), Delta Kappa Gamma (v.p. 2000—01, pres. 2001—04, membership chmn. 2004—06). Methodist. Avocation: music. Office Phone: 719-537-6512.

BLAND, DEBORAH SHAFFER, nurse; b. Tampa, Fla., Jan. 20, 1954; d. Frank Solomon and Mary Louise (Swann) Shaffer; children: Danny, Dionne. LPN, Suwanee-Hamilton Nursing Sch., Live Oak, Fla., 1984; student, St. Edwards U., 2006. LPN, Fla. Author: Skippy Goes to Ybor Square, 1998, Danny's Journey, 2004, (poetry chapbook) A Voice from Salt Springs, 2005. Chaplain Ladies Auxillary Post #10208, 2004-06, founder The Children's Book Depository, 2004; active Vet. of Fgn. Wars of U.S., Salt Springs, Fla.; mem. First Bapt. Ch., Salt Springs Christian Ch., Salt Springs; founder of A Journey in Poetry, 2003, Ocala Nat. Forest- Salt Springs newsletter, 2003, Salt Lakes Country Poets, 2004; vol. Am. Red Cross Disaster, 2003-06. Mem.: Brick City Ctr. for the Arts, Fla. State Poets Assn. Achievements include development of PAVRSTB guitar learning method, 2004. Avocations: writing, painting, photography, gardening, guitar.

BLAND, EVELINE MAE, real estate broker, musician, educator; b. Hughesville, Pa., Aug. 24, 1939; d. Burton Anthony and Mary Margaret (Mack) Morgan; m. Theodore D. Bland; 1 child, Susanna Elisabeth. BA, Mansfield U., Pa., 1961; Orff Schulwerk cert., Royal Conservatory, Toronto, Ont., Can., 1976; MBA, Century U., 1992. Tchr. Newburgh Jr. H.S., NY, 1961—62, Cedar Grove Bd. Edn., NJ, 1962—66, West Caldwell Bd. Edn., NJ, 1973—76, Covenant Christian Sch., North Plainfield, NJ, 1976—77; salesperson Janett Realtors, Verona, NJ, 1977—79; sales mgr. Degnan Boyle Realtors, Caldwell, 1979—88, Schlott Realtors, Montclair, 1988—91; realtor Coldwell Banker, Sarasota, Fla., 1992; mortgage broker Sarasota, 1992—; tchr. Faith Christian Sch., Sarasota, 1992—95, Sarasota Music Ctr., 1993—98. Prin. Camp Shawnee, Waymart, Pa., 1961-71, Melody One Music Studios Club, 1993—, Music Studio, 1995-2003; instr. Sarasota Fine Arts Acad., 1992; music arranger Mouse Mountain Toy Co., 2002-2003 Music dir. Players, Sarasota Broadway Goes to Hollywood; prof. vocal soloist, N.J., Pa. Opera, Oratorios, Broadway-type shows, 1971-91; apprentice Paper Mill Playhouse, Millburn, N.J., 1962-66, FFMC State Chmn. Composition Contest, 2006 Organist, choir dir. 1st Congl. Ch., Verona, 1978-87; organist Venice 1st Bapt. Ch., 1992-95; accompanist Sarasota Bapt. Ch., 1991; trustee Montclair Hist. Soc., 1970-87; bd. dirs. State Repertory Opera, Montclair Kiwanis, 1990-91; mem. Sarasota Opera Guild, 1992 Mem. Nat. Assn. Tchrs. Singing, Nat. Realtors Assn. (cert.), N.J. Assn. Realtors (profl. stds. and edn. coms. 1987), West Essex Bd. Realtors (v.p., sec. 1985-86, pres. 1987, career trainer 1987, Realtor of Yr. 1987), Sarasota Bd. Realtors, Fla. Assn. Realtors, Music Tchrs. Nat. Assn., Fla. State Music Tchrs. Assn. (chmn. state conf. 2000, treas. 1999), Sarasota Music Tchrs. Assn. (treas. 2002—), Christian Profl. and Bus. Women (project advisor 1992), Am. Guild Organists, West Essex C. of C., Montclair C. of C., FIABCI-USA, Gideons Aux. (various offices 1982-87), Kiwanis, Lambda Mu. Republican. Baptist. Avocations: golf, tennis, painting, reading, gardening.

BLAND, IRIS C., retired mathematics professor; d. George Dudley Clark and Mildred Callendar. BS Math., Jersey City State Coll., 1964; MA Math., U. Nebr., Lincoln, 1973; PhD Math. Edn., Walden U., Mpls., 2004. Tchr. math. Rutherford HS, NJ, 1964—66, Antilles HS, Fort Buchanan, PR, 1966—91; prof. Edison Coll., Naples, Fla., 1997—2005; ret., 2005. Pres. Dem. Women's Club Naples, 2000—02. Named Tchr. of Yr., Antilles Consol. Sch. Sys., 1977. Mem.: LWV, AAUW, Sisterhood Temple Shalom, Nat. Coun. Jewish Women. Avocations: tennis, sewing, reading. Home: 370 25th St NW Naples FL 34120

BLAND, JANEESE MYRA, editor; b. Evanston, Ill., Feb. 20, 1960; d. James Milton and Jeanette Malisa (Bryant) B. BA, U. Ark., 1980. Cert. tchr., Ark., Ill. Tutor counselor U. Ark., Pine Bluff, 1979; tchr. Pine Bluff High Sch., 1980, Chgo. Bd. Edn., 1981-84; editor, author, columnist, creator Beautiful Images Hollywood (Calif.) Gazette Newspaper, 1985—. VIP organizer People's Choice Awards, Beverly Hills, 1984—; exec. prodr. stas. Chgo. Access Corp., Century Cable Comms., L.A., BH-TV, Beverly Hills; hostess The Janeese Bland Show. Proof editor: Nursing Rsch. Jour., 1989. Polit. vol. Rep. Party, Santa Monica, 1988—; vol. organizer Windfeather, Inc., Beverly Hills, 1983—, United Negro Coll. Fund, L.A., 1984—, Sickle Cell Disease Rsch. Found., L.A., 1985—; pres., founder June Maria Bland Scholarship Found. Recipient Image award Fred Hampton Scholarship Found., 1983, Wiley W. Manuel award State Bar Calif., Cert. Merit, Bet Tzedek Legal Svcs., Ill. Cmty. Leader of the Yr. award Nat. Coun. Negro Women and Quaker Oats, 1998. Mem. SBA (pres.). Republican. Baptist. Home and office: 269 S Beverly Dr # 420 Beverly Hills CA 90212-3807 E-mail: janeesesworld@aol.com.

BLAND, PAMELA JUNE, special education educator; b. Chgo., Ill., Oct. 12, 1947; d. Arnold Richard Johnsen and June Florence Meisenhelder Johnsen; m. William Lawrence Bland, Jan. 24, 1970; children: Eric, Todd. BS, No. Ill. U., 1969; MEd, Nat. Louis U., 1996. Lead tchr. Keeler Sch. Multiply Handicapped, Aurora, Ill., 1975—78, substitute tchr., 1979—83; case mgr. Kennedy Rehab. Ctr., 1983—86; lead tchr. DeKalb County Spl. Edn. Assn., Cortland, 1986—88, Batavia Pub. Schs. Dist. 101, 1989—94, Maywood Pub. Schs. Dist. 89, Maywood, 1994—; partime faculty early childhood spl. edn. Morton C.C., Cicero, 2003—. Mem. St. Mark's Child Care Adv. Bd., Aurora, 1990—93; presenter in field. Actor: (of poems). Mem. Fox Valley Festival Chorus, Aurora, 1970—90, Naperville Chorus, 1990—; mem., Highland dancer Tunes of Glory Pipe Band, Batavia, 1980—84; high sch. youth leader St. Mark;s Luth. Ch., Aurora, 1990—98. Recipient Editors Choice award, Nat. Libr. Poetry, 1995. Mem.: ASCD, NEA, Nat. Assn. Edn. Young Children, Maywood Edn. Assn. Lutheran. Avocations: travel, camping, boating, genealogy, history. Office: Dist 89 Roosevelt Sch Maywood Pub Schs 1925 S 15th Broadview IL 60155

BLANDA-HOLTZBERG, MARIANNE LOURDES, education educator, consultant; b. Rochester, NY, Aug. 8, 1956; d. Andrew Joseph and Rosemary Reynolds Blanda; m. Richard Harry Holtzberg, Nov. 11, 1979; children: Rachael Molly Holtzberg, Vanessa Elizabeth Holtzberg, Alexandra Blanda Holtzberg. AAS, Monroe C.C., 1976; BSc in Social Sci., Nazareth Coll. Rochester, 1980; MSc in Edn., SUNY, Brockport, 1990; PhD, Union Inst. & U., Cin., 2003. Cert. Tchr. NYU, 1990, in Spl. Edn. NYU, 1992, in Sch. Adminstrn., Supervision NYU, 2002. Spl. edn. tchr. Hillside Children's Ctr., Rochester, NY, 1980—82, Rochester City Sch. Dist., 1992—2002; asst. prin. Webster Ctrl. Sch. Dist., Webster, 2002—04; adj. faculty Roberts Wesleyan Coll., Rochester, 2005—, asst. prof. spl. edn., 2006—. Ednl. cons. Holtzberg Ednl. Cons., Rochester, 2003—; lectr. in field; biennial conf. presenter Internat. Assn. Spl. Edn., 2005. Chair inclusion com. Rochester City Sch. Dist., 1994—2002. Mem.: ASCD, Coun. Exceptional Children, Learning Disabilities Assn. Am., Sch. Adminstrs. NY State. Catholic. Achievements include research in the effects of academic placements on self-esteem. Avocations: golf, tennis, photography, travel. Office: Holtzberg Ednl Cons 2586 Browncroft Blvd Rochester NY 14625 Office Phone: 585-385-8000 ext. 7292. Home Fax: 585-385-4199. Personal E-mail: mholtzberg@frontiernet.net. Business E-Mail: mholtzberg@sifc.edu. E-mail: mholtzberg4@aol.com.

BLANK, LENORE KIM, literature and language professor, consultant; b. Seoul, Republic of Korea, Apr. 17, 1930; d. Yong-Bae Kim and Dae-Ran Park; children: Kimberly, Melanie, Jonathan. BA in English Lit., Seoul Nat. U. Tchrs. Coll., 1953; MA in English Edn., N.J. State Tchrs. Coll., 1957; MA in Tchg. English to Spkrs. of other Langs., Columbia U., 1958; EdD in Curriculum and Instrn., U. San Francisco, 1981. Lifetime cert. secondary educator, std. tchg. credential State of Calif. Bd. Edn. Tchr. English Coll. H.S., 1954—55; instr. English Yun-sei U., Tong-Guk U., 1958—60; ESL tchr., resource specialist San Francisco Unified Sch. Dist., 1970—87; bilingual resource specialist U. San Francisco, 1981—98, coord. Korean lang. programs, 1995—98; ret., 1998. Korean lang. instr. U. Calif., Berkeley, 1994. Fellow, N.J. Fedn. Women, 1957—58; grantee, Nat. Fng. Lang. Ctr., Washington, 1994; scholar, Korean-Am. Found., 1955—57. Mem.: NEA, Am. Assn. Tchrs. Korean, Calif. Tchrs. Assn., Calif. Ret. Tchrs. Assn. Democrat. Achievements include development of curiculum guides for the school district as well as national academic standard tests of SAT-Korean (for students) and SSAT-Korean (for teachers). Home: 6301 Galaxy Ln Rocklin CA 95677 E-mail: lenorekblank@yahoo.com.

BLANK, MARION SUE, psychologist, educator; b. N.Y.C., Dec. 20, 1933; d. Morris David and Tillie Jean (Sherman) Hersch; m. Martin Blank, July 3, 1955; children: Donna, Jonathan, Ari. BA, CCNY, 1955, MS in Edn, 1956; PhD, Cambridge U., Eng., 1961. Asst. prof. Albert Einstein Coll. Medicine, 1965-70, assoc. prof., 1970-73; prof. dept. psychiatry Rutgers Med. Sch., Piscataway, NJ, 1973-83; mem. adj. faculty dept. psychiatry Columbia Coll. Physicians and Surgeons, N.Y.C., 1980—83; pres. Darj on Learning, Inc., 2001—; co-dir. Devel. Neuropsychiatry Program, Columbia U., N.Y.C., 2004—; dir. A Light on Literacy, 2005—. Dir. reading disabilities rsch. inst., pvt. practice, cons., 1983—; Nat. Tour lectr. Speech Pathology Assn. Australia, 1996. Author: Teaching Learning in the Preschool - A Dialogue Approach, Preschool Language Assessment Instrument, 1978, (with Rose and Berlin) The Language of Learning, 1978, Sentence Master, 1990-96, (with Berlin) A Parent's Guide to Educational Software, 1991, (with Marquis and Klimovitch) Directing School Discourse, 1994, Directing Early Discourse with Marquis and Klimovitch, 1995, The Reading Remedy, 2006. Pinsent-Darwin fellow, 1960; recipient award of commendation N.J. Speech and Hearing Assn., 1979, Spl. Edn. award Software Pubs. Am., 1990, N.J., USPHS Career Devel. award, 1965-73; named N.J. nominee Kleffner Lifetime Svc. award Am. Speech Lang. Hearing Assn., 1994, 95. Fellow APA; mem. Assn. for Children with Learning Disabilities (profl. adv. bd., instr., adv. N.J. chpt.) Home: 157 Columbus Dr Tenafly NJ 07670-1635 Office Phone: 201-567-0790. Personal E-mail: msblank@optonline.net. Business E-Mail: msb5@columbia.edu.

BLANK, REBECCA MARGARET, economist; b. Columbia, Mo., Sept. 19, 1955; d. Oscar Uel and Vernie (Backhaus) B.; m. Johannes Kuttner, 1994; 1 child, Emily. BS, U. Minn., 1976; PhD, MIT, 1983. Cons. Data Resources, Inc., Chgo., 1976-79; asst. prof. econs. Princeton U., 1983-89; assoc. prof. econs. Northwestern U., Chgo., 1989-94, prof. econs., 1994-99; sr. staff economist Coun. of Econ. Advisors, Washington, 1989-90, mem., 1998-99; dean, Henry Carter Adams prof. Gerald R. Ford Sch. Pub. Policy, U. Mich., Ann Arbor, 1999—; co-dir. Nat. Poverty Rsch. Ctr., U. Mich., 2002—. Author: It Takes A Nation: A New Agenda for Fighting Poverty, 1997, Is the Market Moral?, 2004, other books; contbr. articles to profl. jours. Vis. Professorships for Women grantee, 1988-89; Sloan Found. fellow, 1982-83; recipient Jr. Faculty Teaching award Princeton U., 1985, David Kershaw award Assn. Pub. Policy Analysis and Mgmt., 1993, Richard Lester award for best book on labor econs., 1997. Mem. Am. Acad. Arts and Scis., Nat. Bur. Econ. Rsch., Am. Econs. Assn., Assn. of Pub. Policy Analysis and Mgmt., Indsl. Rels. Rsch. Assn. United Ch. of Christ.

BLANKEN, CELESTE S., physician; b. Batesville, Ind., Oct. 4, 1961; d. Melvin C. and Alice M. (Dixon) B. BS in Engring., Wright State U., 1983; DO, Ohio U. Coll. Osteo. Medicine, 1987. Diplomate Am. Bd. Family Practice. Physician Med. Svcs. Colfax, Iowa, 1989-90, Hopeland Health Ctr., Dayton, Ohio, 1990-94, Dr. Moody & Blanken Family Practice, Dayton, Ohio, 1994-99, GMH Urgent Care, Beavercreek, Ohio, 1999—. Mem. Am. Osteo. Assn., Am. Coll. Gen. Practitioners. Avocations: tai chi, roller blading, working out, writing, embroidery.

BLANKENBURG, JULIE J., librarian; b. Madison, Wis., Dec. 22, 1956; d. Henry A. and Marjorie L. Blankenburg; m. Wayne I. Zimmerman. BA in Theatre, U. Wis., 1979, MA in LS, 1980. Asst. libr. USDA Forest Products Lab. Libr., Madison, 1988-93, libr., 1994—. Mem.: ALA, Theatre Libr. Assn., Wis. Libr. Assn., Spl. Librs. Assn. Office: USDA Forest Svc Forest Products Lab Libr One Gifford Pinchot Dr Madison WI 53726-2398 Office Phone: 608-231-9491.

BLANKENSHIP, BETSY LEE, library director; b. Marion, Ohio, Apr. 28, 1963; d. Edward Mack and Carollee Ann Flesher; m. Charles Clayton Blankenship, Sept. 21, 1985; 1 child, Wesley Lewis. AA, Ohio State U., Marion, 1983; BA in English, Ohio State U., Columbus, 1985; MLS, Kent State U., Ohio, 1997. Circulation, asst. Marion Pub. Libr., 1984—88; circulation supr., tech. svcs. OSUM/MTC Libr., 1987—98, dir. libr., 1998—. Mem. Ohio State Alumni Assn., Columbus, 1986—2006, Ohio State Alumni Assn. Marion County, 1986—2006; co-facilitator and mem. Literacy Roundtable Marion County, 2000—05; bd. mem., bd. sec., big sister Big Bros./Big Sisters of Marion County, 1986—93. Recipient Big Sister Month, Big Bros./Big Sisters Marion County, 1991, Big Sister Yr., 1993; grantee, Verizon Found., 2000, Inst. Libr. and Info. Literacy Edn., 2006. Mem.: ALA, Assn. Faculty and Profl. Women, Assn. Coll. and Rsch. Librs., Acad. Libr. Assn. Ohio (interest group chair, membership, pr/outreach coord., bd. mem. 1999—2006), Phi Delta Kappa (sec. 2000—06). Avocations: reading, walking, literacy activities. Office: Ohio State Marion/Marion Technical Coll 1469 Mt Vernon Ave Marion OH 43302 Office Phone: 740-725-6231. Office Fax: 740-725-6309. E-mail: blankenship.5@osu.edu.

BLANKENSHIP, CAROLYN ANN, elementary school educator, educator; b. Rochester, Minn., Mar. 5, 1947; d. Ervin Albert and Mayme Lexvold Glamm; children: Jena Marie, Alex Joseph. BS in Art, St.Cloud State U., Minn., 1969; BS in Elem. Edn., Winona State U., Minn., 1992. Instr. art CAL Cmty. Schs., Latimer, Iowa, 1969—75; instr. Osage (Iowa) Pub. Schs., 1975—76, Pali Preschool, Honolulu, 1976—77; sec. Willuierth & Wall Ins., Palo Alto, Calif., 1977—78; clk. new accts. Paine Webber Stock Exchange, San Jose, Calif., 1978—79; sec. rsch. Mayo Clinic, Rochester, Minn., 1979—92; instr. art Pine Island (Minn.) Pub. Schs., 1992—. Mem.: Nat. Art Educators Assn., Pine Island (Minn.) Edn. Assn. (sec. 2004—), Pine Island (Minn.) Area People for Arts. Avocations: painting, hiking, antiques, reading. Office: Pine Island Pub Schs 223 1st Ave SE Pine Island MN 55963

BLANKENSHIP, COLLEEN MARIE-KRICK, secondary school educator, writer; b. Myrtle Beach, S.C., Feb. 19, 1962; d. Roger Lenwood and Barbara Holbrook Krick; children: Allen Reeves, Emily Catherine, Rebecca Lynne. BA, Berry Coll., Mt. Berry, Ga., 1984; MEd, U. Ga., Athens, 1997. Tchr. Shiloh H.S., Gwinnett County Schs., Snellville, Ga., 1988—2000, Brookwood H.S., Gwinnett County Schs., Snellville, 2000—. Writer Prentice Hall, Boston, 2005—; curriculum writer Ga. Online Sch., Atlanta, 2005—. Chmn. election campaign Com. to Elect Phyllis Miller to State Legislature, Snellvillle, 2004; chmn. election com. Campaign to Elect Warren Auld to State Legislature, Snellville, 2005. Nominee Disney Hand Tchr., Disney Co., 2006; named Tchr. of Yr., Shiloh H.S., 2000, Gwinnett County Law Tchr. of Yr., Gwinnett Bar Assn., 2000. Office: Brookwood High School 1255 Dogwood Rd Snellville GA 30078 Office Phone: 770-972-7642.

BLANKENSHIP, CYNTHIA L., bank executive; Pres., COO Bank of the West, Irving, Tex. Mem.: Independent Bankers Assn. of Tex. Office: Bank of the West 2111 W Airport Freeway Irving TX 75062

BLANKENSHIP, LINDA LOU, education educator; b. Grundy, Va., June 11, 1951; d. Theodore Roosevelt and Delphia Jewell Thompson; m. Millard Eugene Blankenship, Feb. 12, 1983 (dec. 2004); 1 child, Jessica Lynn Moore. AS, Southeast Va. Cmty. Coll., 1970; BSc, East Tenn. State U., 1973, M in edn., 1982. Tchr. D.A. Justus Elem. Sch., Hurley, Va., 1973—82, Hurley Elem. Mid. Sch., 1982—2005; part time faculty Southwest Va. Cmty. Coll., 1982. Recipient Commissioned a Ky. Col., Gov. Paul E. Patton, 1999. Mem.: Nat. Edn. Assn., Buchanan Edn. Assn. (sec., treas. 1976—77). Avocations: theater, travel, art, music. Home: Rte 1 Box 350 Grundy VA 24614 Office: Hurley Elem Sch P O Box 111 Hurley VA 24620 Personal E-mail: jakes1@naxs.net.

BLANTON, BELIA, secondary school educator; b. San Jose Ranch, Tex., May 4, 1943; m. Horace Lee Blanton; children: Carlos Kevin, Celina Kay, Lucas Scott. PhD, Tex. A&I, Kingsville, 1982. HS English tchr. Freer Ind. Sch. Dist., Tex., 1964—. Adj. instr. Coastal Bend Coll., Beeville, Tex. Recipient Adv. award, Tex. Future Tchrs. Am., 1998, 2005. Mem.: Tex. State Tchrs. Assn. (assoc.; local sch. dist. pres.). Home: PO Box 878 Freer TX 78357 Office Phone: 361-394-7046. Business E-Mail: bblanton@freerisd.esc2.net.

BLANTON, ELIZABETH ANNE, secondary school educator; b. Saint Louis, Nov. 30, 1975; d. Christopher Michael and Pamela Greer Blanton. BA, Washington U., 1997; MS, St. Louis U., 2001, Miss. State U., 2006. Educator Villa Duchesne/Oak Hill Sch., St. Louis, 1998—. Home: 128 Hollywood Ln Saint Louis MO 63122 Office: Villa Duchesne/Oak Hill Sch 801 South Spoede Rd Saint Louis MO 63131 Office Phone: 314-810-3412. Personal E-mail: blantonea@aol.com. Business E-Mail: eblanton@vdoh.org.

BLANTON, FAYE WESTER, legislative official; b. Tallahassee, Nov. 9, 1946; m. Edwin F. "Ed" Blanton; children: Wade, Doug, Laurel McDaniel. Staff asst. govtl. efficiency com. Fla. Senate, Tallahassee, asst. to dir. mgmt. staff, asst. sec., sec., 1996—. Advisor, counselor Girls State, Boys State, YMCA Youth Legislature, Silver-Haired Legislature; pres. PTO Leon County Sch. Dist., mem. adv. bd. Mem. Am. Soc. Legis. Clks. and Secs. (exec. com., past assoc. v.p., mem. exec. and nominating com.; chair, vice-chair, mem. various coms.) Baptist. Avocations: gardening, walking, reading. Home: 610 Summerbrooke Dr Tallahassee FL 32312 Office: Fla Senate 404 S Monroe St Tallahassee FL 32399-1100 Fax: 850-487-5174. E-mail: blanton.faye@flsenate.gov.

BLANTON, PATRICIA LOUISE, periodontal surgeon; b. Clarksville, Tex., July 9, 1941; d. Ben E. and Mildred L. (Russell) B. MS, Baylor U., 1964, PhD, 1967, DDS, 1974, cert., 1975. Diplomate Am. Bd. Oral Medicine. Tchg. asst. Baylor Coll. of Dentistry, Dallas, 1963-67, asst. prof., 1967-70, spl. instr., 1970-73, assoc. prof., 1974-76; resident periodontics VA Hosp., Dallas, 1975; prof. Baylor Coll. of Dentistry, Dallas, 1976-85, Baylor U. Grad. Sch., Dallas, 1976—; prof., chmn. Baylor Coll. of Dentistry, Dallas, 1983-85, prof. emeritus, 1994—, disting. alumni, 2005. Cons. VA Hosp., Dallas, 1979-82; adj. prof. Baylor Coll. of Dentistry, Dallas, 1985—; cons. Commn. on Dental Accreditation and Coun. of Dental Edn., 1981—; v.p. State Anatomical Bd., Tex., 1983-85; mem. ADA-AADS Liaison Com., 1983—; chmn. Nat. Insts. Health, Oral Biology and Medicine Study Sect. II, 1985-86. Author: Periodontics for the G.P., 1977, Current Therapy in Dentistry, 1980, An Atlas of the Human Skull, 1980 (1st place honors 1981). Invited participant Am. Coun. on Edn., Austin, 1984; mem. liaison com. Dallas County Dental Soc.-Am. Cancer Soc., Dallas, 1976-78; bd. dirs. Dallas Dental Health Programs, 1992-93, S.W. Med. Found., 1992-93; bd. devel. Hardin-Simmons U., 1995—. Named one of Outstanding Young Women in Am., 1976; named Disting. Alumna, Baylor Coll. Dentistry, 2005. Fellow Am. Coll. Dentists (pres. Tex. sect. 2003-04, regent), Internat. Coll. Dentists; mem. ADA (alt. del., pres. 2002-2003), Tex. Dental Assn. (bd. dirs. 1995-97, v.p., pres.-elect 2003, pres. 2003—), Am. Assn. Anatomists, Am. Acad. Periodontology, Am. Acad. Oral Medicine, Am. Acad. Osseointegration, Tex. Soc. Periodontists (pres. 1998-99), S.W. Soc. Periodontology (pres. 1999-00), Dallas County Dental Soc. (pres. 1992-93), Xi Psi Phi, Omicron Kappa Upsilon (pres. 1992-93). Avocations: reading, travel. Office: 4514 Cole Ave Ste 902 Dallas TX 75205-4172 E-mail: pblanton@email.net.

BLANTON, VALLYE J., elementary school educator; b. Valdosta, Ga., Sept. 4, 1953; d. Louie Sloan and Tomie Jean (Roberts) B. BS in edn., U. Ga., 1975; MEd, Valdosta State Coll., 1977, cert., 1977-79. Tchr. Lowndes County Sch. System, Valdosta, Ga., 1975-89; assessment specialist Coastal Plains Regional Assessment Ctr., Valdosta, Ga., 1989-90; tchr. Lowndes County Sch. System, Lake Park, Ga., 1990—. Bd. dirs. Ga. Partnership for Excellence in Edn., Atlanta, 1994—; tchr. adv. com. Southeastern Regional Vision for Edn., Greensboro, N.C., 1994—; editorial bd. Tchr. Learning Resource Ctr., Dayton, Ohio, 1994—; scholarship selection com. U.S. Space & Rocket Ctr., Huntsville, Ala., 1994—. Bd. dirs. Valdosta Jr. Svc. League, 1985—, Valdosta State U. Alumni Bd., 1993—, U. Ga. Booster Club, 1982—. Named Ga. Tchr. of Yr. Ga. Dept. Edn., 1994; recipient Milken Nat. Educator award Milken Family Found., 1994. Mem. Ga Assn. Educators (profl. devel. chmn. 1975-94), Profl. Assn. Ga. Educators, Ga. Coun. Tchrs. Math., Nat. State Tchrs. of Yr. Orgn., Kappa Delta Pi, Phi Delta Kappa. Baptist. Avocations: reading, walking, volunteer work. Home: 2832 Fawnwood Cir Valdosta GA 31602-4105 Office: Lake Park Elementary School 604 W Marion Ave Lake Park GA 31636-5068

BLASCHKE, ROSE ANN, elementary school educator; d. Joseph and Jennie Castellani; children: Mark D., Jennifer L. Macias. BA, U. No. Colo., Greeley, 1965; MA, U. Colo., Denver, 1992. Tchr. Denver Pub. Schs., 1966—72; pre-sch. tchr. Jefferson County Schs., Golden, Colo., 1979—82, tchr., 1982—. Mem.: NEA, Am. Guild English Handbell Ringers (C.H.I.M.E. chmn. 2004—06), Jefferson County Edn. Assn., Colo. Edn. Assn., Music Educators Nat. Conf., Delta Omicron (life; treas. 1998—2006, Zeta Zeta chpt.). Office: Stevens Elementary School 4001 Reed St Wheat Ridge CO 80033 Office Phone: 303-982-2198.

BLASE, NANCY GROSS, librarian; b. New Rochelle, NY; d. Albert Philip and Elsie Wise (May) Gross; m. Barrie Wayne Blase, June 19, 1966 (div.); m. Charles M. Goldstein, July 25, 1999; 1 child, Eric Wayne. BA in Biology, Marietta (Ohio) Coll., 1964; MLS, U. Ill., 1965. Info. scientist brain info. svc. Biomed. Libr., UCLA, 1965-66; libr. Health Sci. Libr., U. Wash., Seattle, 1966-68, Medlars search analyst, 1970-72, coord. Medline, 1972-79, head Natural Scis. Libr., 1979—. Mem. libr. adv. com. Elizabeth C. Miller Libr., Ctr. for Urban Horticulture, Seattle, 1986-90. Contbr. articles to profl. jours. Mem. Bet Chaverim, Seattle, pres., 1998—2000. NSF fellow interdept. tng. program for sci. info. specialists U. Ill., 1964-65. Mem.: Internat. Tng. in Comm. (pres. Pacific N.W. region 1994—95), Am. Soc. Info. Sci. (pres. personal computer spl. interest group 1993—94, chair constn. and bylaws com. 1994—97, chair med. informatics spl. interest group 1998—99, rsch. grantee Pacific N.W. chpt. 1984—85), Phi Beta Kappa (pres. U. Wash. chpt. 1993—97, pres. Puget Sound Assn. 2001—03, mem. com. on chpts. 2002—). Avocations: walking, reading. Home: 10751 Durland Ave NE Seattle WA 98125-6945 Office: U Wash Natural Scis Libr Box 352900 Seattle WA 98195-2900 Personal E-mail: nancy@blases.org. Business E-Mail: nblase@u.washington.edu.

BLASING, MUTLU KONUK, English language educator; b. Istanbul, Turkey, June 27, 1944; arrived in U.S., 1963; d. Mustafa Celal Konuk and Muzeyyen (Uzun) Dursunoglu; m. Randolph Charles Blasing, Aug. 21, 1965; 1 child, John Konuk. Student, Carleton Coll., 1963-65; BA, Coll. William and Mary, 1969; PhD, Brown U., 1974. Lectr. English U. Mass., Mass., 1974-76; asst. prof. Pomona Coll., Claremont, Calif., 1977-79, Brown U., 1979-83, assoc. prof., 1983-88, prof., 1988—. Dir. Copper Beech Press, Providence. Author: The Art of Life, 1977, American Poetry: The Rhetoric of Its Forms, 1987, Politics and Form in Postmodern Poetry, 1995; translator: Human Landscapes (N. Hikmet), 1982, Epic of Sheik Bedreddin (N. Hikmet), 1975, Things I Didn't Know I Loved, (N. Hikmet), 1975, Rubaiyat (N.Hikmet), 1985, Selected Poetry (N. Hikmet), 1986, Poems of Nazim Hikmet, 1994, Human Landscapes from my Country (N. Hikmet), 2002, Poems of Nazim Hikmet, 2002. Fellow, U. Mass., 1974—76. Office: Brown U English Dept PO Box 1852 Providence RI 02912-1852 Office Phone: 401-863-3744. Business E-Mail: mutlu_blasing@brown.edu.

BLASINGAME, JANET LYNN, primary school educator; b. Dallas, July 28, 1961; d. Melvin and Carolyn Rethmeier; m. Jerry Michael Blasingame, June 12, 1982; children: Jay, Jeffery, Jarrett. BS, Tex. Tech. U., 1983. Tchr. 1st grade Wright Elem. Sch., Perryton, Tex., 1984—2003, tchr. 2d grade, 2003—05. Mem. fellowship, edn. and youth coms. 1st Christian Ch. Mem.: Delta Kappa Gamma. Republican. Avocations: baking, walking. Home: 12500 FM3045 Perryton TX 79070 Office: James L Wright Elem Sch PO Box 1048 Perryton TX 79070-1048 E-mail: jblasingame@perrytonisd.com.

BLASKO, BARBARA ANN, secondary school educator; b. Pitts., Nov. 17, 1957; d. Roy Edward and Shirley Marie Newbould; m. Robert Stephen Blasko, Jr., Aug. 4, 1990. BS in Secondary Edn. Biology, Calif. U., Pa., 1979, BS in Earth Sci., 1985, EdM in Guidance Counseling, 1995. 8th grade sci. tchr. Bethel Park Schs., Pitts., 1979—80; HS tchr. Bentworth Schs., Bentleyville, Pa., 1980—. Jr. class sponsor, advisor Bentworth Sch. Dist., Bentleyville, Pa., 1982—, advisor, sponsor student coun., 1985—89, counselor student assistance team, 1993—, co-dir. HS musicals, 2002—. Worthy advisor, grand officer Order of Rainbow, Pitts., 1970—88, grand officer; coord. blood drive ARC, Mon Valley, Pa., 1982—94; coord., vol. Am. Cancer Soc., Washington County, Pa., 1984—; treas. Sunday sch., mem. adult choir Concord Presbyn. Ch., 1977—79; deacon First Presbyn. Ch., California, 1988—, moderator, 1992—95. Recipient Grand Cross award for svc., Internat. Order of Rainbow, 1974—77, Second Pl. Donors award, ARC, 1985—93; grantee, Sci. in Medieval Times Consortium, 1997—99. Mem.: Bentworth Edn. Assn. (treas., rep.), Pa. State Tchrs. Assn., Nat. Tchrs. Assn., Friends Nat. Park, Nat. Air Disaster Support League (life), Order of Eastern Star, Alpha Xi Delta (pres., treas. 1976—79). Avocations: walking, forensics, swimming, crafts, singing. Home: 1961 Rostraver Rd Belle Vernon PA 15012 Office: Bentworth Sch Dist 75 Bearcat Dr Bentleyville PA 15314 Business E-Mail: bblasko@bentworth.k12.pa.us.

BLASSBERG, FRANCI J., lawyer; b. Sept. 28, 1953; m. Joseph Rice III, 1991. BA, Cornell U., 1975, JD magna cum laude, 1977. Bar: NY 1978. Ptnr., co-head Private Equity Group, mem. Mgmt. Com. Debevoise & Plimpton LLP, NYC. Editor-in-chief Debevoise & Plimpton Private Equity Report; co-editor: The Debevoise & Plimpton European Private Equity Handbook, 2004. Bd. trustees Cornell U., NY City Ballet, New Sch. U. Named a Dealmaker of the Yr., Am. Lawyer mag., 2006. Mem.: NY County Lawyers Assn., Assn. Bar of City of NY (mem., com. on corp. law 1985—89). Office: Debevoise & Plimpton LLP 919 Third Ave New York NY 10022 Office Phone: 212-909-6531. Business E-Mail: fjblassberg@debevoise.com.

BLATT, MELANIE JUDITH, small business owner; b. Phila., Sept. 29, 1946; d. Jack and Rose (Ginsburg) Weinberger; children: Marnie, Keath, Lindsay. BA, Antioch U., 1980; MA, U. Phoenix, 1989. Sales rep. Sharp Products, Tempe, Ariz., 1982—92, Hobart Corp., Tempe, 1984—92; pres. Merit Enterprises, Fountain Hills, Ariz., 1992—; dir. bus. devel. Leggett & Platt, Inc. Bd. dirs. Bucks County Jewish Family Service, Bucks City, 1982. Mem. Retail Grocers Assn. Ariz., U. Phoenix Alumni Network (bd. dirs.). Avocations: dance, children's rights. Home: 15807 N Eagle Nest Dr Fountain Hills AZ 85268-1437 Office: 16605 E Palisades Blvd Ste 124 Fountain Hills AZ 85268-3716

BLATTNER, FLORENCE ANNE, retired music educator; b. Rockford, Ill., Nov. 27, 1935; d. Keith F. and Grace L. (Turney) Perkins; m. Lewis Olof Blattner, Mar. 28, 1959; children: Gloria Grace Blattner Mundt, Gayle Mary Blattner Ludwig. BA, Carroll Coll., Waukesha, Wis., 1958; studied piano with Vladimir Levitski, 1984—95; studied piano with Weekly and Arganbright, U. Wis. LaCrosse, 1995, U. Ind., 1997, studied piano with Weekly and Arganbright, 1998; studied piano with Joanne Tierney, 1995—2002. Elem. and jr. high sch. libr. Racine (Wis.) Pub. Schs., 1958—60, elem. substitute tchr., 1961—62, elem. and jr. high tchr., 1962; pvt. practice piano instr. Indpls., 1970—78; data processor OMS Internat., Greenwood, Ind., 1978; pvt. practice piano and theory instr. Des Moines, 1980—83; piano and theory instr. Prelude Piano Studio, Apple Valley, Minn., 1983—2003; ret., 2003. Duettist concerts duet lit., Racine, Wis., 1996, 1999, Apple Valley, Minn., 1996, 1998—2002, White Bear Lake, Minn., 1996, Dodge City, Kans., 2001, Bloomington, Minn., 1996—97, 2001, Godfrey, Ill., 1998, 2000, Alton, Ill., 1998, 2000, solo perfomer, Hot Springs Village, Ark., 2003, 2004; musician (pianist): Village String Ensemble, 2005, 2006. Ch. pianist, accompanist, 1970—; vol. Rep. Party-Minn., Apple Valley, 1992, 94, 96, 98. Mem. Music Tchrs. Nat. Assn., Minn. Music Tchrs. (assoc. cert., state ensemble festival chair 1994-97, cert. com. 1997-2001), South Suburban Music Tchrs. Assn. (1st v.p. 1995-97, pres. 1998-2000, newsletter editor 1995-2001, yearbook editor 2001-2002), Nat. Guild Piano Tchrs., Am. Fedn. Music Clubs. Avocations: canoeing, hiking, piano performance, quilting, knitting. E-mail: flblattner@usfamily.net.

BLATTNER, MEERA MCCUAIG, computer scientist, educator; b. Chgo., Aug. 14, 1930; d. William D. McCuaig and Nina (Spertus) Klevs; m. Minao Kamegai, June 22, 1985; children: Douglas, Robert, William. BA, U. Chgo., 1952; MS, U. So. Calif., 1966; PhD, UCLA, 1973. Rsch. fellow in computer sci. Harvard U., 1973-74; asst. prof. Rice U., 1974-80; assoc. prof. applied sci. U. Calif.-Davis, Livermore, 1980-91, prof. applied sci., 1991-99, prof. emeritus, 2000—; pres. Color Wheel Creations, Las Vegas, Nev., 2001—, Digital Touch Media, LLC, Las Vegas, 2004. Adj. prof. U. Tex., Houston, 1977—99; vis. prof. U. Paris, 1980; program dir. theoretical computer sci. NSF, Washington, 1979—80. Co-editor: (with R. Dannenberg) Multimedia Interface Design, 1992; contbr. articles to profl. jours. NSF grantee, 1977-81, 93-99. Mem. Assn. Computing Machinery, Computer Soc. of IEEE. Office: 8516 Glenmore Dr Las Vegas NV 89134 Business E-Mail: meera.blattner@cvi.net.

BLATZ, KATHLEEN ANNE, former state supreme court justice; BA summa cum laude, U. Notre Dame, 1976; MSW, U. Minn., 1978, JD cum laude, 1984; LHD (hon.), Hamline U., 1999. Psychiat. social worker, 1979—81; mem. Minn. Ho. of Reps., St. Paul, 1979—93, chmn. crime and family law, fin. instns. and ins. coms., 1985—86; judge Dist. Ct., Henne Pin County, 1993—96; justice Minn. Supreme Ct., 1996—98, chief justice, 1998—. Asst. minority leader Minn. House of Reps., 1987—90, 1993; dir. employee assistance prog. Fairview Community Hospital, 1979—81; assoc. atty. Popham, Haik, Schnobrich & Kaufman, 1984—88; asst. county atty. Hennepin County Attorney's Office, 1992—93; mem. Health and Human Services Com., Rules and Legislative Administration Com., Judiciary, Gen. Legislation Veterans Affairs and Elections Com., Taxes Com.; chair Nat. Ctr. for State Cts. Rsch. Advisory Council; mem. Conference of Chief Justices; bd. dirs. Riversource Funds, 2006—. Trustee Fairview Southdale Hospital; former mem. Children's Defense Fund Advisory Council, Governor's Task Force on Fetal Alcohol Syndrome; former vice-chair Minn. Supreme Ct. Foster Care and Permanency Task Force; former bd. mem. Big Brothers Big Sisters of Greater Minneapolis. Recipient Women in State Govt. "A Minn. Treasure" award, 27th Annual Women & Bus. Conference Career Achiev. award, 1999, Minn. Women Lawyers Myra Bradwell award, 2002, Minn. Council of Child Caring Agencies Disting. Service award, 2004. Mem.: Minn. State Bar Assn.*

BLATZ, LIDIA, music educator, elementary school educator; d. Fidias Jaffet and Georgina Echevarria; m. Richard Harris Blatz, Oct. 28, 1976. BA, Temple U., Phila., 2000. Music dir. Zion Luth. Ch. and Sch., Deerfield Beach, Fla., 2000—05; band dir. Zion Luth. Sch., Deerfield Beach, 2000—02, musical theatre tchr., 2001—05, gen. music tchr., 2004—. Profl. soloist, Deerfield Beach, 2000—06; profl. chorister Accapella Singers, Coral Springs, Fla., 2006—; ind. accompanist, Pompano Beach, Fla., 2006. Office Phone: 954-421-3146 234.

BLATZ, LINDA JEANNE, sales manager; d. William Edmund and Jeanne Grace (Hyman) B. BS, U. Md., 1972. Mgr. sales Milliken & Co., N.Y.C., 1972-81; retail market mgr. Greenwood Mills Mktg. Co., N.Y.C., 1981-89; dist. mgr. Steelcase Inc., N.Y.C., 1989-94, tng. cons., 1994-95, tng. mgr.,

1995-2000, tng. dir., 2000—03, sales tng. cons., 2003; regional sales mgr. Nat. Bus. Furniture, N.Y.C., 2003—. Contbr. articles to profl. jours. Mem. N.Y.C. Ballet Guild; corr. sec., v.p., pres. PEO; mem. jr. com. N.Y.C. Ballet; v.p. membership, bd. mgrs. exec. com. N.Y. Jr. League (Outstanding Vol. award 1991-92); nominating dir. Assn. Jr. Leagues Internat., 1997, centennial adv. bd., 1999—. Recipient Outstanding Vol. of the Yr. award N.Y. Jr. League, 1992. Mem.: ASTD, AAUW, Am. Woman's Econ. Devel. Corp., N.Y. Women's Agenda, U. Md. Alumni Assn., Nat. Arts Club, Women's City Club N.Y., East River Rowing Club, Alpha Gamma Delta. Congregationalist. Avocations: ballet, aerobic dancing, swimming, reading. Personal E-mail: ljbeje@aol.com.

BLAU, FRANCINE DEE, economics professor; b. NYC, Aug. 29, 1946; d. Harold Raymond and Sylvia (Goldberg) B.; m. Richard Weisskoff, Aug. 1969 (div. 1972); m. Lawrence Max Kahn, Jan. 1, 1979; children: Daniel Blau Kahn, Lisa Blau Kahn. BS, Cornell U., 1966; AM, Harvard U., 1969, PhD, 1975. Vis. lectr. Yale U., New Haven, 1971; instr. econs. Trinity Coll., Hartford, Conn., 1971-74; research assoc. Ctr. for Human Resource Research, Ohio State U., Columbus, 1974-75; asst. prof. econs. and labor and indsl. relations U. Ill., Urbana, 1975-78, assoc. prof., 1978-83, prof., 1983-94; Frances Perkins prof. indsl. and labor rels. Cornell U., 1994—. Cons. law firms, 1979, 81-83, EEOC, 1981-85, U.S. Commn. on Civil Rights, 1976, 20th Century Fund Task Force on Working Women, 1970-71; mem. Nat. Acad. Scis. Panel on Technology and Women's Employment, 1984-86; mem. Nat. Acad. Scis. Panel on Pay Equity Rsch., 1985-89; rsch. assoc. Nat. Bur. Econ. Rsch., Cambridge, Mass., 1988—; vis. scholar Russell Sage Found., 1999-2000. Author: Equal Pay in the Office, 1977, (with Marianne Ferber) The Economics of Women, Men and Work, 1986, 2d edit., 1992, (with Marianne Ferber and Anne Winkler) The Economics of Women, Men and Work, 3rd edit., 1998; editor Jour. Labor Econs., 1992-95; assoc. editor Jour. Econ. Perspectives, 1994—; mem. editorial bd. Social Sci. Quar., 1978-94, Signs: Jour. Women in Culture and Soc., 1979—, Women and Work, 1984—, Indsl. Rels., 1989-97; bd. editors Am. Econ. Rev., 1998-2002; editor (with Ronald Ehrenberg) Gender and Family Issues in the Workplace, 1997; contbr. articles to profl. jours. Recipient Burligton Northern faculty achievement award, 1993; Harvard U. fellow, 1966-68; U.S. Dept. Labor grantee, 1977-80. Mem. Am. Econ. Assn. (v.p. 1993), Indsl. Rels. Rsch. Assn. (exec. bd. 1987-89, pres. 1997), Midwest Econ. Assn. (v.p. 1983-84, pres. 1991-92, exec. com. 1990-93), Population Assn. Am. Office: Cornell U 265 Ives Hall Ithaca NY 14853-3901

BLAU, HELEN MARGARET, pharmacology educator; b. London, May 8, 1948; (parents Am. citizens); d. George E. and Gertrude Blau; m. David Spiegel, July 25, 1976; children: Daniel Spiegel, Julia Spiegel. BA in Biology, U. York (Eng.), 1969; MA in Biology, Harvard U., 1970, PhD in Biology, 1975; Doctorate (hon.), U. Nijmegen, Netherlands, 2003. Predoctoral fellow dept. biology Harvard U., Cambridge, Mass., 1969-75; postdoctoral fellow div. med. genetics, dept. biochemistry and biophysics U. Calif., San Francisco, 1975-78; asst. prof. dept. pharmacology Stanford (Calif.) U., 1978-86, assoc. prof. dept. pharmacology, 1986-91, prof. dept. molecular pharmacology, 1991—99, prof. dept. microbiology and immunology, 2002—, chair dept. molecular pharmacology, 1997—2001, dir. gene therapy tech., 1997—, Donald E. and Delia B. Baxter prof., 1999—, dir. Baxter Lab. in Genetic Pharmacology, 2002—. Rolf-Sammet-Fonds vis. prof., U. Frankfurt, 2003; plenary talk on stem cells, Academic des Sci. della France at Pontifical Acad., the Vatican, Modern Biotech. Symposium, 2003; co-chmn. various profl. meetings; spkr. in field. Mem. editorial bd. 14 jours. including Jour. Cell Biology, Somatic Cell Molecular Genetics and Exptl. Cell Rsch., Molecular and Cellular Biology, Genes to Cells, Molecular Therapy; contbr. articles to profl. jours. Mem. ad hoc molecular cytology study sect. NIH, 1987-88; mem. five-yr. planning com genetics and teratology br. NICHHD/NIH, 1989. Recipient Rsch. Career Devel. award NIH, 1984-89, SmithKline & Beecham award, 1989-91, Women in Cell Biology Career Recognition award, 1992, Excellence in Sci. award FASEB, 1999, McKnight Endowment Fund for Neurosci. award, 2001; Mellon Found. faculty fellow, 1979-80, William H. Hume faculty scholar, 1981-84; grantee NIH, NSF, Ellison Med. Found., Muscular Dystrophy Assn., March of Dimes, 1978—; Yvette Mayent-Rothschild fellow for vis. profs. Inst. Curie, Paris, 1995. Fellow AAAS, Havard Overseers; mem. NAS (del. to China 1991), Internat. Soc. Differentiation (pres. 2002-04), Am. Soc. for Cell Biology (nominating com. 1985-86, program com. 1990), Soc. for Devel. Biology (pres. 1994-95), Inst. Medicine Nat. Acad. Scis., Am. Soc. Gene Therapy (bd. dirs. 1999-2002). Avocations: skiing, swimming, hiking, music, theater. Office: Stanford U Sch Medicine 269 Campus Dr CCSR 4215 Stanford CA 94305-5175 Fax: (650) 736-0080. E-mail: hblau@stanford.edu.

BLAUHORN, CATHY A., music educator; b. Yankton, S.D., July 3, 1977; d. Stanley A. and Violet W. Pinkelman; m. Brian L. Blauhorn, Dec. 15, 2001; children: Faith, Blaze. AA in Music, Northeast C.C., Norfolk, Nebr., 1998; BS in Music Edn., Wayne State Coll., Nebr., 2000. Tchr. music Fullerton Pub. Sch., Nebr., 2001—. Dir. jazz band, Fullerton, 2001—; jr. class sponsor, 2005—. Choir dir., organist/pianist St. Peter's Cath. Ch., Fullerton, 2001—. Mem.: Music Educators Nat. Conf., Nebr. Edn. Assn., Fullerton Edn. Assn. Roman Catholic. Avocations: exercise, sewing, crafts, gardening, music. Home: 861 T Rd Archer NE 68816 Office: Fullerton Pub Sch 606 4th St Fullerton NE 68638 Business E-Mail: cblauhorn@esu7.org.

BLAUVELT, BARBARA LOUISE, nutritionist; d. Starr Chester and Dorothy (Schofield) Blauvelt. PhD, U. Mass., 1969. Nutrition program supr. divsn. pub. health nutrition Va. Dept. Health, Roanoke, 1970-95. Pvt. cons., 2002—. Co-author: Kitchen Memories, 1998.

BLAXALL, MARTHA OSSOFF, economist; b. Haverhill, Mass., Feb. 2, 1942; d. Michael M. and Eve Joan (Kladky) Ossoff; m. John Blaxall, May 15, 1970 (div. 1989); children: Jenifer, Johanna. BA, Wellesley Coll., 1963; PhD, Tufts U., 1971. Economist Abt Assocs. Inc., Cambridge, Mass., 1965-68; budget examiner Office Mgmt. and Budget, 1969-72; sr. profl. assoc. Inst. Medicine NAS, 1972-76; dir. rsch. Health Health Care Fin. Adminstrn., U.S. HHS, 1976-79; dir. Office Utilization and Devel., Nat. Marine Fisheries Svc., Dept. Commerce, 1979-82; assoc. prof. dept. cmty. and family medicine Georgeteown U. Med. Sch., 1982; pres. BBH Corp., 1982-87; prin. Chase, Brown & Blaxall, Inc., 1983-87; v.p. ICF Inc., Washington, 1987-89; economist Hill and Knowlton Econs. Group, Washington, 1990-91; dir. agribus. trade and investment group Devel. Alternatives Inc., Bethesda, Md., 1991-93, dir. mktg. devel. group, 1993-95, v.p., 1995—2001; dir. Ctrl. Asia and Caucasus Project Yale U. Ctr. Study Globalization, 2001—02; vis. scholar Nitze Sch. for Adv. Internat. Studies John Hopkins U., 2002—03; strategic devel. officer econs. studies Brookings Inst., 2004—. Treas. Fedn. Orgns. Profl. Women, 1974—76, 1983—84, exec. coun., 1982. Co-editor: Women in the Workplace: The Implications of Occupational Segregation, 1976. Trustee Sheridan Sch., Washington, 1978—86, Coun. for Excellence in Govt., 1991—; mem. Inst. Women's Policy Studies, 1993—2002, chair, 1998—2002; mem. Woolly Mammoth Theatre Co., 1997—2005, vice chair, 1999—2005; active Leadershp Forum Internat., 2002—06; bd. dirs. Washington-Moscow Exch., 1990—93, Children's Health and Environ. Ctr. NDEA fellow, 1964—65. Mem.: Md. Fedn. Art (treas. 2005—, bd. dirs. 2006—), Nat. Economists Club (v.p. 1990—91), Am. Econ. Assn. Home: 3960 Birdsville Rd Davidsonville MD 21035 Office Phone: 202-797-6306. E-mail: mblaxall@brookings.edu.

BLAYDES, SOPHIA BOYATZIES, English language educator; b. Rochester, N.Y., Oct. 16, 1933; d. James George and Helene (Bougdanos) Boyatzies; m. David Fairchild Blaydes, June 4, 1961; children: Stephanie Anne, Jeffrey Glenn. BA, U. Rochester, 1955; MA, Ind. U., 1958, PhD, 1962. Teaching asst. English Ind. U., 1955-62; instr. to asst. prof. Am. Thought and Lang. dept. Mich. State U., 1962-65; instr. to prof. English W.Va. U., Morgantown, 1966-99, chair faculty senate, 1990-91, coord. program for sr. and retired faculty, 1994—; pres. Carolinas Symposium for British Studies, 1990-91. Co-dir. Lit. Discussion Group for Sr. Citizens, 1978—; mem. faculty Elderhostel, 1985, 87, 88, 90, 94; mem. ctrl. exec. com. Folger Inst., 1992-99; chair faculty senate, bd. advisors W.Va. U., 1990-91, rep. to adv. coun. to bd. trustees, 1993-99; state del. to the 1995 White House Conf. on Aging; bd. trustees Univ. Sys., 1998-99, Women in Sci. and Health, Robert C. Byrd Health Scis. Ctr., 2004-. Author: Christopher Smart as a Poet of His Time: A Re-Appraisal, 1966, (with others) Sir William Davenant, 1981, Sir William Davenant: An Annotated Bibliography, 1986; editor: (with others) Selected Papers from the W.Va. Shakespeare and Renaissance Association, 1976, The Literary Discussion Group, 1982, 85; contbr. chpts. to books, articles to profl. jours., encys., dictionaries, bibliographies. Mem. cen. exec. com. Folger Inst., 1992-99. Recipient Disting. Manuscript award Mich. State U., 1965, Gerontology Ctr. award, 1983; named Disting. West Virginian, W.Va. Gov., 1995; grantee W.Va. Found., 1973, W.Va. Humanities, 1980; W.Va. U. Senate rsch. grantee, 1984, 89; Folger fellow, 1981, Folger grantee, 1988, 91; recipient Sigma Tau Delta Outstanding Tchg. award, 1996. Mem. Am. Soc. 18th Century Studies, MLA, W.Va. Assn. Coll. English Tchrs. (pres. 1977), Shakespeare and Renaissance Soc. W.Va. (chmn. 1978, 84), Carolinas Symposium on Brit. Studies (chair program 1989, pres. 1990, conf. chair 1993), Women in Sci. and Health (WISH), W. Va. U. Health Scis. Ctr. Home: 652 Bellaire Dr Morgantown WV 26505-2421 Office: W Va U PO Box 6296 Morgantown WV 26506-6296

BLAZ, DEBORAH, secondary school educator, writer; b. St. Charles, Ill., Apr. 27, 1951; d. Walter Emmett and Lois Mary Best; m. Michael Blaz, Aug. 4, 1976; children: Nathaniel, Suzanne. BA, Ill. State, 1973; MA, U. Ky., Lexington, 1974. Cert. tchr. Ind., 1977. Tchr. Fremont HS, Ind., 1978—88; tchr., chmn. dept. Angola HS, Ind., 1989—. Presenter, spkr. in field. Author (translator): Foreign Language Teacher's Guide to Active Learning, 1998; author: A Collection of Performance Assessments and Rubrics: Foreign Languages, 2000, Bringing the Foreign Language Teaching Standards to Life, 2002, Foreign Language Teachers Guide to Differentiated Instruction, 2006. Recipient Excellence in Edn. award, Project E, 2000, Hon. mention, All Am. Tchr. Team, USA Today. Mem.: Ind. Assn. Tchrs. French (list mgr. 2006, French Tchr. of Yr. 1987). Avocations: handicrafts, gardening. Office: Angola HS 350 S John McBride Ave Angola IN 46703 Office Phone: 260-665-2234.

BLAZAK, PAIGE GAYLE, psychotherapist, school counselor; b. Rochester, N.Y., Feb. 16, 1947; d. Morry and Diane (Jacobs) Storm; m. Robert S. Blazak, Apr. 22, 1967; children: Robin, Eric. BSW, Keuka Coll., Keuka Park, N.Y., 1978; MS, SUNY, Brockport, 1988. Cert. sch. counselor; nat. cert. mental health counselor; credentialed substance abuse counselor, hypnotist. Realtor Sail Realty, Canandaigua, N.Y., 1975-89; weight counselor Nutri-Systems, Rochester, N.Y., 1986-87; dir. Cultured Concepts, Canandaigua, 1982-90; chem. dependency counselor Park Ridge Chem. Dependency, Canadaigua, 1987-89; sch. counselor Geneva (N.Y.) Middle Sch., 1989—2002; psychotherapist in pvt. practice Canandaigua Lake, NY, 1989—. Cons. Cultural Concepts, Canandaigua, 1982-90; dir. Geneva Middle Sch. Theater Group, 1989-2002; part-time therapist Clifton Springs Hosp., 2003— Coord. Am. Cancer Soc., 1975. Breakfast Club grantee geneva Sch. Dist., 1990-91, GMS Theatre Group grantee, 1990—; Creative Works grantee Canandaigua Nat. Bank, 1985. Mem. Am. Assn. Counseling and Devel., N.Y. State Assn. Counseling & Devel., N.Y. State Tchrs. Assn. Avocations: sailing, skiing, tennis, white-water rafting, golf. Home: 4963 Walnut Cove Dr Canandaigua NY 14424-4203 Office: 23 Sly St Canandaigua NY 14424

BLAZEJ, PENNY ANNETTE, clinical social worker, writer, artist; b. San Francisco, Sept. 2, 1954; d. Edmond Hugo and Betty Rae (Marvin-Mallory) Realini; m. Roger Noel Bybee, May 28, 1978 (div. June 1983); m. Anthony John Blazej, Oct. 12, 1985; 1 child, Kathryn Anne (dec. Feb. 1989). BS in Biol. Sci., U. Calif., Davis, 1976; MSSW, MPH in Mgmt. and Policy, Columbia U., 1996. Cert. clin. social worker, N.Y., Conn., Calif.; LCSW Am. Bd. Examiners; bd. cert. diplomat. Chemist Seroyal Brands, Concord, Calif., 1976-78; chemist, salesperson, mgmt. specialist Varian Assocs., Concord, Calif., 1978-80; dr. Smith Kline Beckman, Berkeley, Calif., 1980-82; mgmt. cons. IBM, 1982-92; bereavement counselor Hospice Care, Inc., Stamford, Conn., 1999—99; clin. social worker Cancer Care, Inc., 1993-95, Four Winds Hosp., Katonah, N.Y., 1995-96, Family and Children's Agy., Norwalk, Conn., 1997—99; sch. social worker Westchester Jewish Cmty. Svcs., White Plains, N.Y., 1996-97; med. social worker Hospice Care, Inc., Stamford, Conn., 1997-99; pvt. practice Valley Center, Calif., 2003—. Vol. Hospice, 1989—; founder, CEO, North County Psychotherapy Referral Svc., 2005. Contbr. articles to profl. jours. Vol. Hospice Care, Inc., Stamford, 1989-92, Cancer Care, Inc., Norwalk, 1994-95; vol., CCT tchr. St. John's Ch., Darien, Conn., 1992-93, program dir. for Reach Out, 1989-92; vol., bereavement counselor St. Alouisa Ch., New Canaan, Conn., 1989-91; mem. pred. coun. on Cancer, 2000. Recipient 1st prize photog., Silvermine Gallery Show, 1999. Mem. NASW (v.p. referral svc. 2004-05), Exec. Nat. Pub. Health Orgn., Nat. Hospice Orgn., Nat. Orgn. Aging., Families of Spinal Muscular Atrophy (vol. 1989—), Calif. Clin. Social Workers Assn. Roman Catholic. Avocations: painting, writing, cooking, gardening, photography. Office Phone: 760-685-3403. Personal E-mail: pblazej@vcweb.org.

BLAZEJOWSKI, CAROL A., professional sports team executive, retired professional basketball player; b. Elizabeth, NJ, Sept. 29, 1956; Grad., Montclair State Coll., 1978. Player Montclair State U., 1974—78, Allentown Crestettes, Pa., 1978—80, NJ Gems, 1980-81; dir. licensing NBA, 1990—95, dir. women's basketball programs, 1995—96; dir. basketball devel. WNBA, 1996—97; promotional rep. Adidas; v.p., gen. mgr. NY Liberty WNBA, 1997—2000, sr. v.p., gen. mgr., 2000—. Named Kodak All-Am., Montclair State Coll., 1976—78, Converse Women's Player Yr., 1977, Women's Basketball Player Yr., 1978; named to Naismith Basketball Hall Fame, 1994, NJ Sports Hall Fame, 1995; recipient Wade Trophy, 1978. Achievements include All-Am. selection, 1976, 77, 78; single season and career women's basketball scoring records, 1976; mem. World Univ. Gold Medal team, Mexico City, 1979; Pan Am. Silver medal team, 1979; leading scorer Women's Basketball League, 1980-81. Office: New York Liberty 2 Penn Plz New York NY 10121-0101 also: c/o Basketball Hall of Fame PO Box 179 Springfield MA 01101-0179

BLAZEK-WHITE, DORIS, lawyer; b. Easton, Md., Nov. 17, 1943; d. George W. and Nola M. (Buterbaugh) Defibaugh; m. Thacher W. White; children: Christine T., Judson M. BA, Goucher Coll., 1965; JD, Georgetown U., 1968. Bar: DC 1969, VI 1969, Md. 1978, registered: US Ct. Appeals (3rd cir.) 1969, US Ct. Appeals (DC cir.) 1971. Gen. practice with Judge Warren H. Young, St. Croix, VI, 1968-70; assoc. Covington & Burling, Washington, 1970-76, ptnr., 1976—, chmn. Estates & Trust Practice Group. Mem.: ABA (tax sect.), DC Superior Ct. (adv. com., probate and fiduciary rules), Washington DC Estate Planning Coun., Am. Coll. Trust & Estate Counsel. Office: Covington & Burling 1201 Pennsylvania Ave NW Washington DC 20004 Office Phone: 202-662-5490. Office Fax: 202-778-5490. Business E-Mail: dblazek-white@cov.com.

BLAZINA, JANICE FAY, pathologist; d. Joseph and Cordelia Evelyn B. BS, Youngstown State U., 1975; MD, Ohio State U., 1978. Diplomate Am. Bd. Pathology. Resident in anat. and clin. pathology U. Ala. Med. Ctr., Birmingham, 1978-82; assoc. pathologist various hosps., Bryan, Tex., 1982-83, High Plains Bapt. Hosp., Amarillo, Tex., 1983-84; fellow in blood banking Baylor U. Med. Ctr., Dallas, 1984-85; asst. prof. dept. pathology Ohio State U., Columbus, 1985-93, asst. prof. Sch. Allied Med. Professions, 1987-93. Asst. dir. transfusion svc. Ohio State U. Hosp., 1985-89, assoc. dir., 1989-90, dir., 1990-93, med. dir. histocompatibility, paternity, apheresis and phlebotomy svcs., 1987-93, divsn. med. tech., 1987-93; asst. med. dir. Carter Blood Ctr., Ft. Worth, 1993-95, med. dir., 1995-96. Contbr. articles to profl. publs. Bremer Found. grantee, 1987. Mem. AMA, Am. Soc. Apheresis, Am. Soc. Histocompatibility and Immunogenetics, Am. Assn. Blood Banks (insp. 1987—), Ohio Assn. Blood Banks (trustee 1990-93, sec. 1992-93), Assn. Women Sci. Cen. Ohio (v.p. 1989-90, pres. 1990-91), Nat. Alliance Mentally Ill Tarrant County (sec. 2003). Mem. Church of Christ. Avocation: gardening. Personal E-mail: bbpathd1@yahoo.com.

BLEAM, LAURA JANE, pediatrics nurse, educator; b. New Britain, Pa., Mar. 27, 1940; d. Andrew Y. Jr. and Edna (Tagert) Michie; m. Brian L. Bleam, Apr. 8, 1978 (dec. Oct. 1996); 1 child, Jennifer Lynn. BSN, Alderson-Broaddus Coll., Philippi, W.Va., 1963; MA, Villanova (Pa.) U., 1971, postgrad., 1991; MSN, Gwynedd-Mercy Coll., Gwynedd Valley, Pa., 1985. RN, W.Va., N.J., Pa.; cert. pediatrics nurse, elem. counselor, Pa. Instr. Grand View Hosp. Sch. Nursing, Sellersville, Pa., 1963-67; instr. nursing Gwynedd-Mercy Coll., 1967-69; assoc. prof. pediat. nursing Montgomery County C.C., Blue Bell, Pa., 1972—2004, prof. emeritus, 2003—. Contbr. articles to newspapers. Admission counselor Pa. Masonic Villages; bd. deacons New Britain Bapt. Ch., 1992—, vice chmn., 1993—95, chmn., 1995—96, chmn. 250th anniversary, 1997—2004, ch. clk., 2000—05; past bd. dirs. Bucks County Am. Lung Assn. Mem. DAR, Nat. League for Nursing, Pa. League for Nursing, Alderson-Broaddus Nursing Alumni Assn. (life), Gwynned-Mercy Coll. Nursing Honor Soc. Sigma Theta Tau, Order of Eastern Star (bd. dirs. 1987-93, chmn. 1991-93, Doylestown chpt. Worthy Matron). Personal E-mail: janie1376@verizon.net.

BLEAM, NANCY KAY, physical education educator; b. Adrian, Mich., May 17, 1957; d. Donald Fay and Evelyn Ruth Bleam. BA in Elem. Edn., Adrian Coll., Mich., 1980; MEd in Athletic Adminstrn., Austin Peay State U., Clarksville, Tenn., 1984. Cert. athletic trainer Nat. Athletic Trainer's Assn., 1987. Tchr., athletic trainer Unified Sch. Dist. 495., Larned, Kans., 1980—81; rehab. aide Herrick Meml. Hosp., Tecumseh, Mich., 1982—83; tchr., athletic trainer Greenville (Mich.) Pub. Schs., 1985—90; athletic trainer, instr. Culver-Stockton Coll., Canton, Mo., 1990—94; athletic trainer Hannibal (Mo.) Regional Hosp., 1994—96; athletic trainer, instr. Keene (N.H.) State Coll., 1996—. Avocations: travel, photography, reading. Home: 20 Gates Road 15 Marlborough NH 03455 Office: Keene State College 229 Main Street Keene NH 03435 Office Phone: 603-358-2825. Personal E-mail: nbleam@hotmail.com. Business E-Mail: nbleam@keene.edu.

BLEDEL, ALEXIS (KIMBERLY ALEXIS BLEDEL), actress; b. Houston, Sept. 16, 1981; d. Martin and Nanette Bledel. Attended, Page Parkes Ctr. of Modeling and Acting; studied Film, NYU Tisch Sch., NYC, 1999—2000. Actor: (TV series) Gilmore Girls, 2000—; (films) Rushmore, 1998, Tuck Everlasting, 2002, DysEnchanted, 2004, Bride & Prejudice, 2004, The Orphan King, 2005, Sin City, 2005, The Sisterhood of the Traveling Pants, 2005; guest appearances The Late Late Show with Craig Kilborn, 2003, Late Show with David Letterman, 2005, The View, 2005. Named one of 25 Hottest Stars under 25, Teen People mag., 2002; recipient Family Friendly Forum Award, best actress in a drama, 2002. First language Spanish. Office: 17 Little West 12th St #333 New York NY 10014-1311

BLEDSOE, ADALENE HAY, family counselor, retired elementary school educator; b. Jeff, Ala., Feb. 14, 1929; d. Thompson Rucker and Adalene Rhyne Kelly; m. John Carroll Hay Jr. (dec.); children: John Carroll Hay III, Susan Hay Woodroof, David Kelly Hay; m. Theodore Thomas Bledsoe, June 24, 2000. AA, Stephens Coll., Columbia, Mo., 1948; BS in Edn., U. Ala., Tuscaloosa, 1950; MS in Counseling Psychology, Ala. A&M, Huntsville, 1974. Elem. tchr. Crestline Elem. Sch., Birmingham, Ala., 1950—53, Fifth Ave. Elem. Sch., Huntsville, 1953—55, Lake Forest Day Sch., Ill., 1955—56; family counselor Episcopal Ch. of the Nativity, Huntsville, 1976—2001. Pres. Mental Health Assn., Huntsville, 1972—73; mem. adv. bd. Huntsville Madison County Mental Health Ctr., 1974; chmn. fundraising campaign Sapp Shelter for Homeless Women and Children, Huntsville, 1999—2002; tutor Adult Learning Ctr., Huntsville, 2005—06; bd. dirs. Downtown Rescue Mission, Huntsville, 1996—2006. Mem.: Jr. League, Huntsville Garden Club (pres. 1991). Democrat. Episcopalian. Avocations: church activities, travel, golf, reading. Home: 1006 Carmelian St SE Huntsville AL 35897

BLEDSOE, CYNTHIA WYRICK, sales executive, consultant; b. Greensboro, N.C., Oct. 12, 1961; d. Bobby Joe and Norma Jean Wyrick; m. Martin Lewis Bledsoe, Mar. 10, 1950. Student, U. N.C., Greensboro, 1982—83; AA in Paralegal Studies, Guildford Tech. C.C., Jamestown, N.C., 1987; trainer cert., Tchg. Skills Inst., 1981. Dir. sch.-cmty. rels. Asheboro (N.C.) City Schs., 1987—88; v.p. Vinson-Starr Advt., Greensboro, 1988—90; area exec. dir. Am. Heart Assn., Greensboro, 1990—97; paralegal office adminstr. Richard Shope Atty. at Law, Greensboro, 1997—98; dir. market devel. Douron, Inc., Balt., 1998—2003; v.p. sales Project Masters Inc., Balt., 2003—05; exec. dir. Greater Towson Com. Inc., Md., 2005—; vol. chair, comm. Tomorrow's Towson Inc., 2006—. Pres. Ireland House Preservation, Greensboro; chair ambs. C. of C., Greensboro, 1990. Named Heart Assn. of Yr., Am. Heart Assn., 1991. Mem.: Thoroughbred Owners and Breeders Assn., Project Mgmt. Inst. Avocations: thoroughbred racing, architectural history, furniture design, writing. Office Phone: 410-825-2549.

BLEI, LAURIE N., counseling administrator; b. Evergreen Park, Ill., Nov. 11, 1956; d. John Earl and Carol Virginia Nolan; m. Jeffrey Elmer Blei, July 7, 1984; children: David, Jennifer. BS in Spl. Edn., Ill. State U., Normal, 1978; MS in Counselor Edn., No. Ill. U., DeKalb, 1988. Cert. guidance counselor, spl. edn. tchr. Ill. Spl. edn. tchr. Argo H.S., Summit, Ill., 1979—80, Downers Grove South H.S., Ill., 1980—88, guidance counselor, 1995—, guidance counselor/career cons., 2005—. Co-author: Developmental Guidance Curriculum Focus, 1998—. Mem. LWV. Mem.: Ill. Assn. of Coll. Admissions Counselors, Ill. Counseling Assn. Avocations: travel, reading, gardening, hiking. Office: Downers Grove South High School 1436 Norfolk Downers Grove IL 60516

BLEIER, CAROL STEIN, writer, researcher; b. N.Y., Jan. 31, 1942; d. Shelley and Ruth (Brown) Stein; m. Michael Bleier, Oct. 9, 1966; children: Thomas, Lisa, Mark. BA in English Lit., Syracuse U., 1963; MLS, U. Pitts, 1986. Pub. info. specialist IRS, Washington, 1964-68; columnist Springfield (Va.) Ind., 1977-78; mktg. cons. Greater Pitts. Mus. Coun., 1986-88; pub. rels. dir. Greater Pitts. Literacy Coun., 1988-89; writer, 1985—. Author: (corp. history books) To Good Health and Life: L'Chaim A History of Montefiore Hospital of Pittsburgh, 1898-1990, 1997, Tradition in Transition: A History of the School of Information Sciences, 2001; co-author: (corp. history book) The Ketchum Spirit: A History of Ketchum Communications Inc., 1992; contbg. author: Encyclopedia of Library History, 1994, (history book) A Century of Heroes, 2004; contbr. articles to periodicals. Mem. ALA, Beta Phi Mu. Democrat. Jewish. Avocations: reading, travel. Home: 214 Lynn Haven Dr Pittsburgh PA 15228-1821

BLEKE, DIANE K., music educator, director; b. Springfield, Mo., Jan. 10, 1951; d. Karl William Engeking and Mary Ida Cotler; m. Earl Howard Bieke, Mar. 20, 1982; children: Christine, John, Angela; 1 child, Tanya. MusB, S.W. Mo. State U., 1972; MusM, U. Austin, 1979; degree in Organ, Concordia U., 1995. Pvt. music tchr., Oconomowoc, Wis., 1965—90; social worker Dept. Human Resources, Austin, Tex., 1975—83; dir. choir H.S. St. Paul's Evang. Luth. Ch., Austin, 1982—90; min. music Hope Luth. Ch., Milw., 1990—91; tchr. music Lake Bluff and Atwater Elem. Schs., 1990—91; dir. music St. Paul's Evang. Luth. Ch., Oconomowoc, 1990—. Dir. children's choir King of Kings United Meth. Ch., Sprinfield, Mo., 1970—72; dir. choir Crest View United Meth. Ch., Austin, 1975—82; coach, accompanist U. Tex., Austin, 1972—73; dir. choir, accompanist Austin (Tex.) Children's Choir Concordia Coll., 1987—90. Mem.: Choral Dirs. Assn., Nat. Assn. Tchrs. Singing, Oconomowoc Music Club. Luth. Avocations: harp, guitar, drums, gardening. Home: W358 N5971 Misty Ct Oconomowoc WI 53066-2436 Office: St Pauls Church and School 210 E Pleasant Oconomowoc WI 53066-3050 Office Phone: 262-567-5001 x242. Business E-Mail: ebleke@wi.rr.com.

BLENDELL, ELIZABETH A., lawyer; BA, Mt. Holyoke Coll., 1972; JD, Boston Coll., 1980. Bar: Calif. 1980. With Latham & Watkins, L.A., 1980—, ptnr., 1988—. Mem. faculty Practising Law Inst., 1990—. Mem.: ABA, Calif. Bar Assn. Office: Latham and Watkins LLC 633 W Fifth St Ste 4000 Los Angeles CA 90071

BLESCH, K(ATHY) SUZANN, small business owner; b. Evansville, Ind., Dec. 14, 1951; d. Robert Lee McBride and E. Jean (Oliver) Schumacher; m. Larry J. Blesch, Aug. 17, 1974; children: Nicholas R., Spencer A., Clayton W. Grad. Grad. Realtors Inst., Ind. U., 1979; cert. residential specialist, Nat. Assn. Realtors, 1980. Waitress, hostess Skyway & Pete's, Evansville, Ind., 1971-73; operator, asst. mgr. Stecklers T.A.S., Evansville, 1969-71; salesperson, broker Midwest Realty, Evansville, 1973-78; broker, owner Blesch Realty, Evansville, 1978-80; broker, salesperson Brand Realty, Evansville, 1980-83; owner, operator Nick Nackery Pl., Evansville, 1985—. Bd. dirs. Hope of Evansville, 1976-79. Mem. Nat. Costumers Assn., Am. Taekwondo Assn. (1st degree black belt). Avocation: reading. Home and Office: 201 E Virginia St Evansville IN 47711-5529 Office Phone: 812-423-6425.

BLESS, MARTHA M., secondary school educator, department chairman; b. Framingham, Mass., Mar. 10, 1963; d. Paul John and Marguerite Ann Mailhot; m. Thomas Laurence Grosmann (div.); children: Sarah Ashley Grossman, Alexander Nicholas Grossman; m. William Joseph Bless, Sept. 4, 1999. AS, Teikyo Post U., 1998, BA, 1999; MS, So. Conn. State U., 2001, postgrad., 2005. English tchr. Regional Sch. Dist., Woodbury, Conn., 2001—, chmn. English dept., 2004—. Coord. Trick or Treat for Charity event, 2003—05. Recipient award, Women in Bus. Assn., Waterbury, Conn., 1999. Mem.: ASCD, Nat. Coun. Tchrs. English, Alpha Chi. Avocations: singing, running, bicycling, reading. Office: Nonnewaug HS 5 Minortown Rd Woodbury CT 06798

BLESSING, CAROLE ANNE, human resources manager; b. Phila., Nov. 27, 1945; d. Walter Francis and Margaret Jane (Hindman) Thompson; m. William Blessing, May 26, 1991. BA, Temple U., Phila., 1978; MA Univ. Pa., 1986. Cert. occupational health and safety, Temple U., Villanova U. Asst. safety supr. Phila. Coke Co. Inc., Phila., 1969-71, safety supr., 1971-73, dir. personnel and safety, 1973-78; div. mgr. safety and security Kelsey Hayes Co., Phila., 1978-86, mgr. human resource, Heintz Corp., 1986-91; mgr. human resources Jefferson Smurfit Corp. Phila., 1991-2000, regional human resources, 2000-; exec. v.p., dir. Powell Envirn., Inc., 1988-93; pres., chmn. Data Research, Inc., Phila., 1983-91; dir. Affiliated Med., Phila., 1983-90; lectr. Drexel U., 1983-84; cons in field Contbr. articles to profl. jours. Chmn. first aid and safety programs ARC, Phila., 1974-76. Recipient safety achievement awards Phila. Safety Council. Mem. AAUW, NAFE, Am. Soc. Safety Engrs. (treas. Phila. chpt. 1978-79, 80), Nat. Safety Mgmt. Soc., Soc. for Human Resource Mgmt., Am. Mgmt. Assn. Republican. Home: 1602 Northview Blvd Plymouth Meeting PA 19462-2651

BLESSING, MAXINE LINDSEY, secondary school educator; b. Skirum, Ala., Mar. 27, 1920; d. John Amos and Lizzy Maude (Croft) Lindsey; m. Alvin Reed Blessing, June 24, 1939; 1 child, Deanna Dawn Blessing Gilbert. BS in Secondary English Edn., Jacksonville (Ala.) U., 1956; postgrad., Auburn U., 1974-75. Tchr. DeKalb County (Ala.) Schs., 1943-97; ret., 1997. Beta Club sponsor Crossville (Ala.) H.S., 1960—, drama dir. jr. and sr. plays, 1960—, interim counselor. Sunday sch. tchr., pianist, organist Skirum Bapt. Ch., Crossville. Mem. AAUW, NEA, Nat. Coun. Tchrs. English, Ala. Coun. Tchrs. English, Ala. Edn. Assn., DeKalb County Edn. Assn. (mem. English textbook com. 1988-89), Ea. Star (worthy matron 1944-45), Skirum Cmty. Club (various coms.). Democrat. Baptist. Avocations: music, church and community activities, bridge, reading, attending plays. Home: 2314 County Road 46 Dawson AL 35963-3400 Office: Crossville HS PO Box 38 Crossville AL 35962-0038

BLESSING-MOORE, JOANN CATHERINE, allergist, pulmonologist; b. Tacoma, Sept. 21, 1946; d. Harold R. and Mildred (Benson) Blessing; m. Robert Chester Moore; 1 child, Ahna. BA in Chemistry, Syracuse U., 1968; MD, SUNY, Syracuse, 1972. Diplomate Am. Bd. Pediatrics, Am. Bd. Allergy Immunology, Am. Bd. Pediatric Pulmonology. Pediatric intern, then resident Stanford U. Sch. Medicine, Palo Alto, Calif., 1972-75, allergy pulmonology fellow, 1975-77; co-dir. pediatric allergy pulmonology dept. Stanford U. Children's Hosp., Palo Alto, Calif., 1977-84; clin. asst. prof. dept. Allergy Immunology Respiratory Disease (AIR) Stanford U. Sch. Medicine, Palo Alto, Calif., 1977-84, co-dir. pediatric pulmonology lab., 1977-84; clin. asst. prof. dept. immunology Stanford U. Hosp., 1984—; allergist Palo Alto Med. Clinic, 1984-90; pvt. practice allergy immunology-pediatric-pulmonary Palo Alto, San Mateo, Calif., 1990—. Dir. ednl. program for children with asthma Camp Wheeze, Palo Alto, 1975-90; cons. FDA, Allergy Pulmonary Adv. Bd., 1992-97; cons. in field. Author handbooks, camp program manuals; co-editor jour. supplements; mem. edit. bd. Allergy jours.; contbr. articles to sci. pubs. Fellow Am. Acad. Allery, Asthma, Immunology (various offices 1980—, joint task force parameters of care asthma and allergy 1989—, Outstanding fellow 1998, Women in Allergy award 2000), Am. Coll. Chest Physicians (com. mem. 1980—), Am. Coll. Asthma, Allergy and Immunology (mem. regent com. 1995-98); mem. Am. Thoracic Soc., Am. Lung Assn., No. Calif. Allergy Found. (bd. dirs., pres.), Peninsula Women's Assn., Santa Clara and San Mateo County Med. Soc. (bd. dirs. 1999-2004), Chi Omega. Republican. Presbyterian. Avocations: music, sailing, skiing, horseback riding, scuba diving. Office: 780 Welch Rd Ste 204 Palo Alto CA 94304-1518 also: Stanford Univ Hosp Dept Immunology Palo Alto CA 94304 Office Phone: 650-688-8480. Personal E-mail: j_blessingmoore@hotmail.com.

BLETHEN, SANDRA LEE, pediatric endocrinologist; b. San Mateo, Calif., May 16, 1942; d. Howard Albion and Laura Katherine (Wolf) B.; m. Fred I. Chasalow, Nov. 26, 1966. BS in Biochemistry, U. Chgo., 1961; PhD in Biochemistry, U. Calif., Berkeley, 1965; MD, Yeshiva U., 1975. Diplomate Am. Bd. Pediat. Fellow biochemistry Brandeis U., Waltham, Mass., 1965-68; instr. biochemistry U. Calif., San Diego, 1968-69; asst. prof. San Francisco State U., 1969-71; resident in pediat. Columbia Presbyn. Med. Ctr., N.Y.C., 1975-77; fellow pediatric endocrinology U. N.C., Chapel Hill, 1977-79; asst. prof. pediatrics Washington U., St. Louis, 1979-84; assoc. prof. pediat. SUNY, Stony Brook, 1985-96; assoc. attending pediatrician L.I. Jewish Med. Ctr., New Hyde Park, NY, 1984-90; attending pediatrician Univ. Hosp., Stony Brook, 1991-96; cons. Genentech, Inc., South San Francisco, Calif., 1985-96, sr. endocrinologist, 1996—99, assoc. dir. product experience, 1997-2000, sr. clin. scientist, 1999—2002; v.p. med. affairs metabolic endocrinology Serono, Inc., Rockland, Md., 2002—. Cons. Diagnostic Systems Labs., Webster, Tex., 1989-96. Mem. editl. bd. Steroids, 1990—, Jour. of Endocrinology and Metabolism, 1995-98; contbr. more than 90 articles to profl. jours. Predoctoral fellow NSF, 1961-63, Postdoctoral fellow USPHS, 1965-67. Mem. Am. Pediatric Soc. (program com. 1994), Endocrine Soc., Lawson Wilkens Pediatric Endocrine Soc. (membership chair 1994-95), Soc. for Pediatric Rsch., Phi Beta Kappa, Alpha Omega Alpha. Avocation: sailing. Office: Serono Inc 1 Tech Pl Rockland MA 02370 Office Phone: 781-681-2433. Personal E-mail: sandra.blethen@serono.com.

BLETHYN, BRENDA ANNE, actress; b. Ramsgate, Kent, England, Feb. 20, 1946; m. Alan James Blethyn (div.). LittD (hon.), Kent U., 1999. Actress Royal Nat. Theater, U.K., 1975-89. Appeared in films, including The Witches, 1990, A River Runs Through It, 1992, Secrets & Lies (Best Actress award Cannes Film Festival, 1996, Golden Globe award, Acad. award nominee, Best Actress winner Brit. Acad. award), Music From Another Room, 1998, In the Winter Dark, 1998, Girls Night, 1998, Little Voice (Acad. award nominee), 1998, Saving Grace, 2000, Yellow Bird, 2001, Daddy and Them, 2001, Sonny, 2002, (voice) The Wild Thornberrys Movie, 2002, Plots with a View, 2002, The Sleeping Dictionary, 2003, Blizzard, 2003, Beyond the Sea, 2004, A Way of Life, 2004, On a Clear Day, 2005, (voice) Pooh's Heffalump Movie, 2005, Pride and Prejudice, 2005; television includes Outside Edge (Best Comedy Actress award British Comedy Awards, 1994), Grown-Ups, 1980, King Lear, 1982, Death of an Expert Witness, 1983, Chance in a Million, 1984, The Labours of Erica, 1989-90, The Buddha of Suburbia, 1993, Outside Edge, 1994-96, The Bullion Boys, 1993, RKO 281, 1999, Between the Sheets, 2003, Belonging, 2004; Broadway shows include Absent Friends (Outstanding New Talent award Theater World Awards, 1991).*

BLEVINS, ELAINA GWEN, music educator, director; d. Calvin Ray and Irma Nell (Burkhalter) Blevins. MS in Edn., Nat. U., L.A., 1998. Cert. tchr. Fla. Dept. Edn., 1987, Calif. Dept. Edn., 2002, lic. Nev. Dept. Edn., 2006. Dir. bands Bassett H.S., La Puente, Calif., 1996—98, Rosamond H.S., Calif., 1998—. Dir. bands Forest H.S., Ocala, Fla., 1987—91; dir. of bands Flemming Jr. High and Lincoln H.S., L.A., 1991—92; dir. bands Burbank H.S., Calif., 1992—94; music tchr./music mgmt. tchr. David Starr Jordan H.S., Long Beach, Calif., 1994—96. Bd. mem. Royal Family Kids Camp, Lancaster, Calif., 2005—06. R-Consevative. Christian. Avocations: studying the lives and performing styles of successful musicians and the correlation between the two, history. Home Fax: 702-361-8105.

BLEY, CARLA BORG, composer; b. Oakland, Calif., May 11, 1938; d. Emil Carl and Arlene (Anderson) Borg; m. Paul Bley, Jan. 27, 1959 (div. Sept. 1967); m. Michael Mantler, Sept. 29, 1967 (div. 1992); 1 dau., Karen. Student public schs., Oakland. Mem. adv. bd. Jazz Composers Orch. Assn. Freelance jazz composer, 1956—, pianist, Jazz Composers Orch., N.Y.C., 1964—, European concert tours, Jazz Realities, 1965-66; founder, WATT, 1973—, toured Europe with Jack Bruce Band, 1975; leader, Carla Bley Band, touring, U.S. and Europe, 1977—; composed, recorded: A Genuine Tong Funeral, 1967, (with Charlie Haden) Liberation Music Orch., 1969; opera Escalator Over the Hill, 1970-71 (Oscar du Disque de Jazz 1973), Tropic Appetites, 1973; composed: chamber orch. 3/4, 1974-75; film score Mortelle Randonnèe, 1983; recorded: Dinner Music, 1976, The Carla Bley Band: European Tour, 1977, Musique Macanique, 1979, (with Nick Mason) Fictitious Sports, 1980, Social Studies, 1980, Carla Bley Live!, 1981, Heavy Heart, 1984, I Hate to Sing, 1985, Night Glo, 1985, Sexted, 1987, Duets, 1988, Fleur Carnivor, 1989, The Very Big Carla Bley Band, 1991, Go Together, 1993, Big Band Theory, 1993, Songs with Legs, 1995, Goes to Church, 1996, Fancy Chamber Music, 1998, Are We There Yet?, 1999, 4x4, 2000, Looking for America, 2003, The Lost Chords, 2004. Named winner internat. jazz critics poll Down Beat mag., 1966, 71, 72, 78, 79, 80, 83, 84; Best Composer of Yr., Down Beat Readers' Poll, 1984, composer/arranger of yr., 1985-92; Guggenheim fellow, 1972; Cultural Coun. Found. grantee, 1971, 79; Nat. Endowment for the Arts grantee, 1973, Oscar du Disque de Jazz (for Escalator Over the Hill) 1973; named Best in Field Jazz Times critics poll, 1990, Best Arranger, Downbeat Critics Poll, 1993, 94, Best Arranger, Downbeat Readers' Poll, 1994; recipient Prix Jazz Moderne from Academie du Jazz for The very Big Carla Bley Band album, 1992. Office: Watt Works PO Box 67 Willow NY 12495-0067 E-mail: watt@ulster.net.

BLIGE, MARY JANE, recording artist; b. Yonkers, NY, Jan. 11, 1971; d. Cora Blige; m. Kendu Isaacs, Dec. 7, 2003; 3 stepchildren. Singer: (albums) What's the 411?, 1992, (NY Music award for Best R&B Album, 1993), My Life, 1994 (Billboard Music award for R&B Album of Yr., 1995), Mary Jane, 1995, Share My World, 1997 (Am. Music award for Favorite R&B Album, 1998, Soul Train Lady of Soul award for R&B Soul Album of Yr., 1998), Mary, 1999 (Soul Train Music award for Best R&B Album & Lady of Soul award for Album of Yr., 2000), The Tour, 1999, No More Drama, 2001, Dance For Me, 2002, Love & Life, 2003, The Breakthrough, 2005 (songs) I'll Do For You, 1991, Real Love, 1991 (Soul Train Music award for Best Female Single, 1993), I'll Be There for You/You're All I Need (with Method Man), 1995 (Grammy award for Best Rap Duo Performance, 1996, named one of 100 Greatest Videos Ever Made, MTV, 1999), Not Gon' Cry, 1996, No More Drama, 2001 (Best R&B Video, MTV Video Music awards, 2002), He Think I Don't Know, 2001 (Grammy award for Best Female R&B Vocal Performance, 2003), Whenever I Say Your Name (with Sting), 2003 (Grammy award for Best Pop Collaboration With Vocals 2004), Be Without You, 2005 (BET Video of Yr. award, 2006); actress: (films) Angel, 2001, Prison Song, 2001. Recipient Soul Train Music award for Best New Artist 1993, Best Debut R&B Artist & Rising Star award, NY Music Awards, 1993, Source award for R&B Artist of Yr., 1994, 1995, Heroes award, RIAA, 1999, Patrick Lippert award, Rock the Vote, 2001, Best Female R&B award, Black Entertainment TV (BET), 2001, 2006, Favorite R&B Female Artist, Am. Music Awards, 2003, Legend award, Vibe mag., 2005.*

BLINN, JOHNA See DORSEY, HELEN DANNER

BLISS, MELISSA MOORE, chemistry educator; b. West Columbia, SC, Apr. 9, 1976; d. Henry C. and Harriet M. Moore; m. Patrick F. Bliss, Dec. 1, 2001; 1 child, Jordan Lane Elizabeth. BS in Chemistry, St. Andrews Pres. Coll., Laurinburg, NC, 1998. Resident asst. St. Andrews Pres. Coll., 1997—98; tchg. substitute Charlotte Mecklenburg Schs., NC, 1999; chemistry tchr. Independence HS, Charlotte, NC, 1999—. Recipient Thomas R. Blackburn award, St. Andrews Pres. Coll., 1998. Mem.: Classroom Tchrs. Assn. (assoc.). Office: Independence HS 1967 Patriot Dr Charlotte NC 28227 Office Phone: 980-343-6900. Office Fax: 980-343-6907.

BLISSITT, PATRICIA ANN, medical/surgical nurse; b. Knoxville, Tenn., Sept. 23, 1953; d. Dewitt Talmadge and Imogene (Bailey) Blissitt. BSN with high honors, U. Tenn., 1976, MSN, 1985; PhD in Nursing, U. Wash., 2002; postgrad., U. Pa., 2003—05. RN, cert. case mgmt., trauma nurse course, ACLS. Staff nurse neurosci. unit City of Memphis Hosp., 1976-78, head nurse neurosci. unit, 1978-79; physician's asst. Dr. John D. Wilson, Columbus, Miss., 1979-81; staff nurse med.-surg.-trauma ICU U. Tenn. Meml. Hosp., Knoxville, 1982-83; staff nurse neurosci. ICU Bapt. Meml. Hosp., Memphis, 1985-86, clin. nurse specialist neurosci., 1986-94, trauma coord., 1991-93, neuro case mgr., 1993-94; staff nurse neurosurg. ICU Harborview Med. Ctr., Seattle, 1994—2000, 2001—02; NIH postdoctoral fellow neuro critical care U. Pa., Phila., 2003—05; neurotrauma staff nurse surg. ICU Hosp. U. Pa., 2003—05; staff nurse neurosci. ICU Duke U. Med. Ctr., Durham, NC, 2005—. Nurse cons. neurosci. VA Hosp., Memphis, 1986; mem. adv. com. Tenn. Bd. Nursing Practice; mem. test devel. com. Am. Bd. Neurosci. Nursing, 1996—2001, trustee, 2000—03, treas., 2002—03, chair test devel. com., 2003—06; lectr. in field. Author: AACN Advanced Critical Care, 2006; author: (with others) Critical Care Nursing in Clinics in North America, 1990, 2006, Guidelines for Critical Care Nursing, Care Management, 2001; mem. editl. bd. Focus on Critical Care, 1990—92, abstractor Nursing SCAN in Critical Care, 1995—99; author, reviewer, editor with others: Core Curriculum for Neuroscience Nursing, 4th edit., 2004; contbr. chapters to books, articles to profl. jours. Mem. rev. com. Neurosci. Nursing Found./AANN Scholarship com., 2001. Grantee, NIH/NINR/U. Wash., 1999—2002; scholar, Wash. State Nurses Found., 1998, Am. Assn. Neurosci. Nurses, 1999, AANN Scholar Com., 2001. Mem.: ANA (mem. coun. med.-surg. nurses), AACN (life; pres.-elect Greater Memphis area chpt. 1989—90, CCRN corp. exam. devel. com. 1989—92, pres. 1990—91, editl. cons. bd. 1990—92, past pres., chair nat. critical care awareness week 1990—93, chpt. cons. Region II 1991—93, NTI spkr. 1992—93, chpt. of yr. com. chair 1992—94, chair-elect Puget Sound chpt. program 1995—96, chair program com. 1996—97, editor elect newsletter Puget Sound chpt. 1997—98, program com. 1997—2003, newsletter editor Puget Sound chpt. 1998—99, pres.-elect 1999—2001, pres. 2002—03, edn. com. Southea. Pa. chpt. 2003—05, publs. chair, newsletter editor 2003—05, AACN Procedure Manual for Critical Care, 5th edit. 2005, contbr. articles to jour., cert., cert. med.-surg. clin. nurse specialist), Soc. of Critical Care Medicine, Neurocritical Care Soc. (charter), Tenn. Nursing Congress (pres. 1990—94), Western Inst. Nursing, Tenn. Nurses Assn. (com. practice 1992—93), NC Nurses Assn., Am. Assn. Spinal Cord Injury Nurses, Am. Assn. Neurosci. Nurses (pres. local chpt. 1989—90, program/seminar chair local chpt., mid-south chpt. 1990—93, chair nat. resource devel. com. 1992—94, pres. Memphis chpt. 1995—98, editor newsletter 1998—2000, chair role delineation study task force 2000—01, editor newsletter 2001—02, chair test devel. com. 2003—, mem., edn. coord. Triangle Chpt. 2005—, pres.-elect Triangle chpt., edn. chair 2005—, chmn. resource devel. com., nurse practice com., contg. edn./ann. sci. program com., cert.), Am. Assn. Neurol. Surgeons (assoc.), Sigma Theta Tau. Methodist. Avocation: music. Home: 2616 Erwin Rd Apt 1536 Durham NC 27705-3880 Business E-Mail: bliss007@mc.duke.edu, pbliss@u.washington.edu.

BLISSITTE, KAREN DAWN, elementary school educator; b. Rantoul, Ill., Mar. 2, 1966; d. Jackie Eugene and Alice Ruth Mann; m. Tommy Alan Blissitte, June 6, 1987; children: Alicyn Grace, Alexandria Rose. A Music, Weatherford Jr. Coll., 1987; MusB, Tarleton State U., 1995. Cert. tchr. Accompanist Mineral Wells Ind. Sch. Dist., Tex., 1987—99, substitute tchr., 1987—94; music tchr. Palo Pinto, 1996—. Musician First Bapt. Ch., Mineral Wells, 1988—, childrens choral dir., coord., 1997—, mem. orch., choir, handbells. Mem.: Tex.Music Educators Assn. Baptist. Avocations: puzzles, reading, antiques, crafts. Home: 1306 SE 22d St Mineral Wells TX 76067 Office: Palo Pinto Ind Sch Dist PO BOX 280 Palo Pinto TX 76484 E-mail: kblissitte@escll.net.

BLIZARD, MARJORIE CLAIRE, small business owner; b. Mineola, N.Y., Mar. 10, 1950; d. Robert Brooks and Jane Lucille (Berggren) Blizard; m. John Sturgis Ayer, Dec. 13, 1975 (div. 1998), Robert Elliot Davidson, Aug. 7, 2005; children: Amelia Grace, Michael Daniel. BA, U. Colo., 1971. With Am. Thread, Willimantic, Conn., 1972-73; lab technician Rogers (Conn.) Corp., 1973-76; lab mgr. Kali Inc., Lebanon, Conn., 1977-82; owner Blizard Profl. Cleaning, Franklin, Conn., 1983—96; asst. dir. Entrepreneurial Ctr., 1994—97; owner, prin. cons. MCB Assoc., 1996—; gen. mgr. Hillyer Realty, 2003—05; bus. mgr. Distributed Digital Signage, 2006—. Bd. dirs. Kali Inc., corp. sec., 1980—. Mem. Ea. Conn. C. of C. (bd. dirs. 1989-95, chmn. bus. edn. coun. 1989-95), Norwich Redevelopment Agy. Mem. Baha'i. Office Phone: 860-892-1231. Business E-Mail: blizard@mcbassociates.com.

BLIZNAKOV, MILKA TCHERNEVA, architect, educator; b. Varna, Bulgaria, Sept. 20, 1927; came to U.S., 1961, naturalized, 1966; d. Ivan Dimitrov and Maria Kesarova (Khorozova) Tchernev; m. Emile G. Bliznakov, Oct. 23, 1954 (div. Apr., 1974). Architect-engr. diploma, State Tech. U., Sofia, 1951; PhD, Engring.-Structural Inst., Sofia, 1959; PhD in Architecture, Columbia U., 1971. Sr. researcher Ministry Heavy Industry, Sofia, 1950-53; pvt. practice architecture Sofia, 1954-59; assoc. architect Noel Combrisson, Paris, 1959-61; designer Perkins & Will Partnership, White Plains, NY, 1963-67; project architect Lathrop Douglass, N.Y.C., 1967-71; assoc. prof. architecture and planning Sch. Architecture, U. Tex., Austin, 1972-74; prof. Coll. Architecture, Va. Poly. Inst. and State U., Blacksburg, 1974-98, prof. emerita, 1998—; prin. Blacksburg, 1975—. Bd. dirs. founder Internat. Archives Women in Architecture, Va. Poly. Inst. and State U., The Parthena award, 1994. Prin. works include Speedwell Ave. Urban Renewal, Morristown, N.J., 1967—69, Wilmington (Del.) Urban Renewal, 1968—70, Springfield (Ill.) Ctrl. Area Devel., 1969—71, Arlington County (Va.) Redevel., 1975—77; author (with others): Utopia e Modernitá, 1989, Reshaping Russian Archtecture, 1990, Russian Housing in the Modern Age, 1993, Nietzsche and Soviet Culture, 1994, New Perspectives on Russian and Soviet Artistic Culture, 1994, The Eastern Dada Orbit: Russia, Georgia, Ukraine, Central Europe, 1996, Signs of Times, Culture and the Emblems of Apocalypse, 1998, Women Architects in Eastern Europe: The Contributions of the Bulgarians, 1997, International Archive of Women in Architecture, 1997; author: (with others) 5th edit., 2003; author: (with others) Encyclopedia of Eastern Europe, 2000, Centropa, 2001; author: (with others) 2d edit., 2003; author: (with others) Women Architects in Japan, 2002, Housing in Russia: 20th Century, 2002; author: (with others) Encyclopedia of Twentieth Century Architecture, 2003. William Kinne scholar, 1970, vis. scholar Inst. Advanced Russian Studies, The Wilson Ctr. of Smithsonian Instn., 1988; NEA grantee, 1973-74, Am. Beautiful Found. grantee, 1973, Internat. Rsch. and Exch. Bd. grantee, 1984, 93; Fulbright Hays rsch. fellow, 1983-84, 91; recipient Parthena award, 1994. Mem. Internat. Archive Women in Architecture (founder, chair bd. dirs.), Am. Assn. Tchrs. Slavic and East European Langs., Soc. Archtl. Historians, Nat. Trust Hist. Preservation, Am. Assn. Advancement of Slavic Studies, Assn. Collegiate Schs. of Planning, Inst. Modern Russian Culture (chairperson architecture, co-founder, dir.), Bulgarian Studies Assn., Assn. Collegiate Schs. of Architecture. Home: 2813 Tall Oaks Dr Blacksburg VA 24060-8109 Office: Va Poly Inst and State U Coll Architecture Blacksburg VA 24061 Business E-Mail: mbliznak@vt.edu.

BLOCH, JULIA CHANG, educational association administrator; b. Mar. 2, 1942; came to U.S., 1951, naturalized, 1962; d. Fu-yun and Eva (Yeh) Chang; m. Stuart Marshall Bloch, Dec. 21, 1968. BA, U. Calif., Berkley, 1964; MA, Harvard U., 1967, postgrad. in Mgmt., 1987; DHL (hon.), Northeastern U., Boston, 1986. Vol. Peace Corps, Sabah, Malaysia, 1964-66; tng. officer East Asia and Pacific region, Washington, 1967-68, evaluation officer, 1968-70; mem. minority staff U.S. Senate Select Com. on Nutrition and Human Needs, Washington, 1971-76, chief minority counsel, 1976-77; dep. dir. Office of African Affairs U.S. Internat. Comm. Agy., Washington, 1977-80; fellow Inst. Politics Harvard U., Cambridge, Mass., 1980; asst. adminstr. Bur. for Food For Peace and Voluntary Assistance AID, Washington, 1981-87; asst. administr. Bur. for Asia and Near East, 1987-88; assoc. U.S.-Japan Rels. Program, Ctr. for Internat. Affairs Harvard U., Cambridge, Mass., 1988-89; amb. Kingdom of Nepal, 1989-93; group exec., v.p. Bank Am., San Francisco, 1993-96; pres. The U.S.-Japan Found., 1996-98; dir. Am. West Airlines, 1994-98, Penn Mut. Life Ins., 1997; prof. Am. studies Beida U., Beijing, 1998; amb. in residence U. Md., 2000—; pres. US-China Edn. Trust, Washington, 2004—. Trustee Eisenhower Exch. Fellowship, 1995-97, Nat. Com. U.S. China Rels., 1998—; U.S. Senate rep. World Conf. on Internat. Women's Yr., Mex., 1975; advisor U.S. Del. to Food and Agr. orgn. Conf., Rome, 1975; rep. Am. Coun. Young Polit. Leaders, Peoples Republic China, 1977; charter mem. Sr. Exec. Svc., 1979; head U.S. del. Biennial Session World Food Programme, Rome, 1981-86, Devel. Assistance Com. Meeting on Non-Govtl. Orgns., Paris, 1985, Intergovtl. Group on Indonesia, The Hague, Netherlands, 1987, World Bank Consultative Group Meeting, Paris, 1987, mem. exec. women in govt., 1988-93, mem. coun. fgn. rels., 1991—; vis. prof. internat. rels. Peking U., 1998—; Starr sr. fellow U.S. China Rels. Fudan U., Shanghai, adj. prof. Author: A U.S.-Japan Aid Alliance, 1991; co-author: Chinese Home Cooking, 1986. Exec. bd. mem. Internat. Ctr. for Rsch. on Women, 1974-81; mem. adv. bd. Women's Campaign Fund, 1976-78; mem. nat. adv. coun. Experiment in Internat. Living, 1981-83; mem. U.S. Nat. Com. for Pacific Econ. Cooperation, 1984—, Nat. Presdl. Debate Forum, 1987-92; bd. trustees Atlantic counsel, 2004-; mem. presdl. adv. couns. Peace Corps, 1988-89; mem. com. to visit art mus. Harvard U., 1989; founder Women Fgn. Policy Group; mem. Am. Refugee Com. Bd., 1993; mem. Am. Himalayna Found. Bd., 1994; commr. Asian Art Mus., San Francisco, 1994; trustee, bus. leadership cir., 1994—; bd. trustees Coun. Am. Ambs., 2003-; chmn. bd. dirs. F.Y. Chang Found. Hon Fulbright fellow, 1996, Woodrow Wilson fellow, 2000-; recipient Hubert Humphrey award for internat. svc., 1979, Humanitarian Svc. award AID, 1987, Leader for Peace award Peace Corps, 1987, Asian Am. Leadership award, 1989, Brotherhood/Sisterhood award NCCJ, 1996; named Outstanding Woman of Color, Nat. Inst. for Women of Color, 1982, Woman of Distinction, Nat. Conf. for Coll. Women Student Leaders and Women of Achievement, 1987, Disting. Pub. Svc. award Nat. Assn. Profl. Asian Pacific Am. Women, 1989; Ford Found. Study fellow for internat. devel. Harvard U., 1966, Paul Harris award Rotary, 1992, Award of Honor Narcotic Enforcement Assn., 1992. Fellow Nat. Acad. Pub. Adminstrn.; mem. Orgn. Chinese Am. Women (founder, chair 1977—, bd. dirs., Woman of Yr. 1987), Asia Soc. (pres. coun. 1989, trustee, 1994), Am. Studies Ctr. (vice-chair), Prytannean Honor Soc., Coun. Fgn. Rels., Mortar Bd., Cosmos Club. Republican. Avocations: ceramics, gourmet cooking, collecting art. Office Phone: 202-884-8533. E-mail: jcbloch@aol.com.

BLOCH, SUSAN LOW, law educator; b. NYC; d. Ernest and Ruth Low; m. Richard I. Bloch; children: Rebecca, Michael. BA in Math., Smith Coll., 1966; MA in Math., U. Mich., MA in Computer Sci., PhC, 1972, JD, 1975. Bar: D.C. 1975. Law clk. to chief judge U.S. Ct. Appeals, Washington, 1975-76; law clk. to assoc. justice Marshall U.S. Supreme Ct., Washington, 1976-77; assoc. Wilmer, Cutler & Pickering, Washington, 1978-82; prof. Georgetown U. Law Ctr., Washington, 1983—. Legal analyst for impeachment procs. CBS, 1998; impeachment expert U.S. Ho. of Reps. Jud. Com., 1998. Author: Supreme Court Politics: The Institution and Its Procedures, 1994; contbr. Constl. Commentary, Duke Law Jour., Mich. Law Rev., Am. U. Law Rev., Wis. Law Rev., Law and Contemporary Problems, Georgetown Law Rev., St. Louis U. Law Jour., ABA Jour., Supreme Ct. Preview, Voice of

Am., Supreme Ct. Hist. Soc. Yearbook, 1987, Supreme Ct. Hist. Soc. Yearbook, 1992, Oxford Companion to the Supreme Ct. of the United States, 1992, Biology, Culture and Law, 1993. Active Common Cause, Women's Legal Def. Fund. Recipient Smith Coll. medal, 2005. Mem. ABA, Am. Bar Found., Am. Law Inst., D.C. Bar (Bicentennial of Constn., mem. ethics com., jud. evaluation com.), D.C. Cir. Judicial Conf. (prog. chair 1993, 96), U. Mich. Com. Visitors, 1982—, Inst. Pub. Representation (bd. dirs.), Order of Coif, Phi Beta Kappa, Sigma Xi. Home: 4335 Cathedral Ave NW Washington DC 20016-3560 Office: Georgetown U Law Ctr 600 New Jersey Ave NW Washington DC 20001-2075 Office Phone: 202-662-9063. Business E-Mail: bloch@law.georgetown.edu.

BLOCHOWIAK, MARY ANN, retired cultural organization administrator; b. Shawnee, Okla., Dec. 18, 1943; d. Casimir Joseph Blochowiak, Mary Roberta Blochowiak. BA in History, U. Ctrl. Okla., 1979, MA in History, 1984. RN. Staff nurse Mercy and Deaconess Hosps., Oklahoma City, 1964—90; asst. editor Okla. Hist. Soc., Oklahoma City, 1988—89, asoc. editor, 1990—99, pub. divsn. dir., 1993—2005, editor The Chronicles of Oklahoma, 2000—05, ret., 2005. Book awards judge Okla. Ctr. for the Book, Oklahoma City, 1998—. Contbr. articles to profl. jours. Mem.: Okla. Mus. Assn., Okla. Assn. Profl. Historians, Western History Assn. Avocations: history, reading, needlecrafts. Office Phone: 405-522-5243. Office Fax: 405-/521-2492. Business E-Mail: mablochowiak@ok-history.mus.ok.us.

BLOCK, AMANDA ROTH, artist; b. Louisville, Feb. 20, 1912; d. Albert Solomon and Helen (Bernheim) Roth; m. Gordon J. Wolfe, June 16, 1931 (div. 1947); 1 child, Joseph G. Wolf; m. Maurice Block, Jr., July 15, 1949. Student, Smith Coll., 1930-31, U. Cin., 1933, Art Acad. Cin., 1933-40; BFA, Ind. U.-Purdue U., Indpls., 1960. Instr. Herron Sch. Art, Ind. U. Purdue U., Indpls., 1969-73; instr. lithography Indpls. Art Ctr., 1974. Adv. bd. Indpls. Art League Found., 1979-81. One-woman shows, 1444 Gallery, Indpls., 1962, Sheldon Swope Art Gallery, Terre Haute, Ind., 1963, 73, Park Avenue Gallery, Indpls., 1964, Harriet Crane Gallery, Cin., 1965, Talbot Gallery, Indpls., 1967, Merida Gallery, Louisville, 1967, Herron Mus. Art, Indpls., 1969, Editions Ltd. Gallery, Indpls., 1972, 79, Franklin (Ind.) Coll., 1973, Tucson Mus. Sch., 1977, Indpls. Art League, 1992; two-woman shows, Jason Gallery, N.Y.C., 1964, Orange County Coll., Middletown, N.Y., 1964, Washington Gallery, Frankfort, Ind., 1975, Edits. Ltd. Gallery, Indpls., 1983; exhibited in group shows, Chgo. Art Inst., 1941, Butler Inst. Am. Art, Youngstown, Ohio, Burr Gallery, N.Y.C., Hanover Coll., Wabash, Ind., De Pauw U., Soc. Am. Graphic Artists AAA Gallery, Purdue U., Istan Gallery, Tokyo, Phila. Print Club, Pa. Acad. Fine Arts, 1969, Imprint Gallery, San Francisco, 1972, Van Straaten Gallery, Chgo., 1973, McNay Inst., San Antonio, 1972, Pratt Graphics, N.Y.C., 1976, Ind. State Mus., 1976, Indpls. Mus. Art, 1977, Tucson Mus. Art, 1978, internat. traveling exhbn., Soc. Am. Graphic Artists, 1974-75, traveling exhbn., 1977, 78; represented in permanent collections, Continental Ill. Bank, Chgo., De Pauw U., Ind. State Coll., Terre Haute, Ind., Med. Soc., Indpls., Sheldon Swope Art Gallery, Stevens Coll., Boston Public Library, USIA, Lafayette (Ind.) Art Center, Lippman Assos., architects, Indpls., J.B. Speed Mus., Louisville, IBM Bldg., Indpls., Phila Mus. Art, Bklyn. Mus., Cin. Art Mus., N.Y. Public Library, Columbua U. Gallery, N.Y.C., Biodynamics Inc., Indpls., Fidelity Bank, Carmel, Ind., Tuscon Mus. Art, Indpsl. Mus. Art, Indianapolis Art Ctr. Retrospective Print and Drawing Exhib., 1992. Recipient award Ben and Beatrice Goldstein Found., N.Y.C., 1971. Mem. Soc. Am. Graphic Artists. Jewish. E-mail: minblock@cs.com.

BLOCK, ESTELL LENORA, educational consultant; b. Schenectady, NY, Dec. 21, 1938; d. Jack Kaufman and Zelda Schwartz-Kaufman; m. Frederic Block, Dec. 18, 1960; children: Neil, Nancy Block Bannister. BS, SUNY, Albany, 1960; MA in Counseling, C. W. Post Coll., Brookville, NY, 1969. Cert. tchr. NY, counselor NY. Tchr. Union Free Sch. Dist. #6, Port Jefferson, NY, 1969—73, counselor, 1973—78, guidance dept. head, 1978—95; cons., co-founder Coll. Dirs., Port Jefferson, 1995—. Spkr., participant Round Table SUNY, Stony Brook. Adv. bd. Planned Parenthood, Smithtown, NY, 1996—2004; mem. Port Jefferson Arts Coun., 1990—; creater scholarship program Port Jefferson; committee person Brookhaven Dems., East Setauket, NY, 1997—, fundraiser, 2000—. Named Humanitarian of the Yr., Hope House Ministries, 1995; named to Wall of Fame, Port Jefferson HS, 2005. Mem.: Suffolk County Guidance Assn., Round Table, Port Jefferson Ret. Tchrs. Assn. (pres. 1996—2002), Hadassah. Jewish. Avocations: hiking, aerobics, opera, theater, reading. Home: 15 Stern Dr Port Jefferson NY 11777

BLOCK, FRANCESCA LIA, writer; b. Hollywood, Calif., Dec. 3, 1962; d. Irving Alexander and Gilda Rona (Klein) B.; m. Chris Schuette; children: Jasmine Angelina Schuette, Samuel Alexander Schuette. BA in English Lit., U. Calif., Berkeley, 1986. Author: Weetzie Bat, 1989 (ALA Best Book award, 1989), Witch Baby, 1991 (Sch. Libr. Jour. Best Book award), Cherokee Bat and the Goat Guys, 1992 (ALA Best Book award, N.Y. Times Book Rev. Notable Book), Ecstasia, 1993, Missing Angel Juan, 1993 (ALA Best Book award, 1993), Primavera, 1994, The Hanged Man, 1994, Baby Be Bop, 1995 (Pub.'s Weekly Best Book award, 1995, ALA Best Book award, 1995), Girl Goddess # 9, 1996, Dangerous Angels, 1998 (L.A. Times Rev. Best Seller), I Was a Teenage Fairy, 1998; author: (with Hillary Carlip) Zine Scene, 1998, Violet and Claire, 1999 (L.A. Times Rev. Best Seller), The Rose and the Beast, 2000 (L.A. Times Rev. Best Seller, Pub.'s Weekly Best Book award, 2000), Nymph, 2000, Echo, 2002; author: Guarding the Moon, 2003 (L.A. Times Rev. Best Seller, 2003), Wasteland, 2003, Goat Girls, 2004, Beautiful Boys, 2004;: Necklace of Kisses, 2005, Psyche in a Dress, 2006; author: (with Carmen Staton) Ruby, 2006; author: various translations into French, Italian, German, Japanese, Czech, Danish, Finnish and Norwegian. Recipient Margaret A. Edwards Lifetime Achievement award, ALA, 2005. Mem. Phi Beta Kappa. Democrat. Jewish. Office: c/o Lydia Wills Paradigm Agy New York NY 10019-5206

BLOCK, HOLLY, museum director; Programs coord. Washington Project for the Arts (WPA); curator The Brox Mus., Bronx, NY, 1985—88; exec. dir. Art in General, NYC, 1988—2006, The Bronx Mus., 2006—. Co-commr. Cairo Biennial U.S. Dept. of State, 2003; advisor Nat. Assn. of Aritsts Orgns.; bd. dirs. ArtTable; co-studio theme chair Coll. Art Assn. Nat. Conf., NYC, 1997; mem. steering com. NYC Arts Coalition. Author: Art Cuba: The New Generation, 2001. Office: The Bronx Mus of the Arts 1040 Grand Concourse at 165th St Bronx NY 10456-3999*

BLOCK, LANISE, secondary school educator; d. Ron Belvin and Gwen Onumah-Onikoro; m. Carlos Block, Feb. 3, 1969. MEd, U. St.Thomas, St. Paul, 1999. Cert. learning tech. U. of St. Thomas, 2004. Social studies tchr. North H.S., Mpls., 1996—2002, Interdistrict Downtown Sch., Mpls., 2002—. Choir dir. Gospel Temple Ch. of God in Christ, St. Paul. Office Phone: 612-752-7116.

BLOCK, MARIAN S., lawyer; b. Dayton, OH, 1953; BA, Kenyon Coll., 1975; M in History, Brown U., 1976; JD, U. Va., 1981. Bar: Ga. 1981. Assoc. Arnold & Porter, Washington, Reed, Smith, Shaw & McClay (now Reed Smith); v.p., assoc. gen. counsel Lockheed Martin Corp., Bethesda, Md. Mem.: Washington Met. Area Corp. Counsel Assn. (pres. 2005—, former program chair, pres.-elect). Office: Lockheed Martin Corp 6801 Rockledge Dr Bethesda MD 20817-1877 Office Phone: 301-897-6704. Office Fax: 301-897-6704. E-mail: marian.block@lmco.com.

BLODGETT, ELSIE GRACE, small business owner, property manager; b. Eldorodo Springs, Mo., Aug. 2, 1921; d. Charles Ishmal and Naoma Florence (Worthington) Robison; m. Charles Davis Blodgett, Nov. 8, 1940; children: Carolyn Doyel, Charleen Bier, Lyndon, Daryl(dec.). Student, Warrensburg State Tchrs. Coll., Mo., 1939—40; BA, Fresno State Coll., Calif., 1953. Tchr. schs., Mo., 1940—42, Calif., 1947—72; owner, mgr. rental units, 1965—; exec. dir. San Joaquin County Rental Property Assn., Stockton, Calif., 1970—81; prin. Delta Rental Property Owners and Assoc., 1981—82; propr. Crystal Springs Health World, Inc., Stockton, 1980—86. Active PTA, Girl Scouts U.S., Boy Scouts Am., Vols. in Police Svc., 1993—2004; capt. Delaware Alpine Neighborhood Watch, 1994—2003; past bd. dirs. Stockton Better Bus. Bur.; bd. dirs. Stockton Goodwill Industries, 1994—2003. Named (with husband) Mr. and Mrs. Apt. Owner of San Joaquin County, 1977. Mem.: Nat. Apt. Assn. (state treas. women's divsn. 1977—79), Calif. Ret. Tchrs. Assn., Mil. Wives, DAV Aux., Stockton Zonta Lodge. Republican. Methodist. Home: 4350 St Andrews Dr Stockton CA 95219 Office Phone: 209-954-1638.

BLODGETT, HARRIET, retired language educator; b. N.Y.C., Sept. 4, 1932; d. Morris and Fannie (Cohen) Horowitz; m. William Edward Blodgett, Sept. 4, 1955; 1 child, Bruce. BA, Queens Coll., 1954; MA, U. Chgo., 1956; PhD, U. Calif., Davis, 1968. Lectr. in English and comparative lit. U. Calif., Davis, 1973-85, 86-87, lectr. in English Irvine, 1985-86; lectr. in English, humanities and women's studies Calif. State U., Sacramento, 1982-87; lectr. Calif. State U. Stanislaus, Turlock, 1989-92, asst. prof., then assoc. prof., 1992-98, prof., 1998—2005, prof. emerita, 2005. Lectr. Stanford U., U. Calif. Santa Cruz, 1988; vis. scholar Inst. for Rsch. on Women and Gender, Stanford U., 1983, affil., 1984-92. Author: Patterns of Reality: Elizabeth Bowen's Novels, 1975, Centuries of Female Days: Englishwomen's Private Diaries, 1988; editor, compiler Capacious Hold-All: An Anthology, 1991; essayist, article writer, contbr. South-Atlantic Quar., Critique, N.Y. Times Book Rev., Internat. Fiction Rev., 19th-Century Prose, James Joyce Quar., others. Mem. Phi Beta Kappa, Phi Kappa Phi. Avocations: painting, gardening, reading. Home: 781 Mulberry Ln Davis CA 95616-3430

BLOM, NICOLE JAN, magazine advertising executive; b. Seattle, Oct. 3, 1958; d. Daniel Charles and Ellen Lavon (Stewart) Blom. Attended, Am. Conservatory Theatre, 1978; BA in Theatre, U. Wash., 1981. Profl. dancer, actress, Seattle, 1976—80; assoc. dir. devel. pub. rels. officer The Bush Sch., Seattle, 1981—83; acctg. rep., advt. dir. Pacific Northwest mag., Seattle, 1983—86; assoc. advt. mgr. Esquire mag., N.Y.C., 1986—88, mgr. eastern advt., 1988—90, U.S. advtg. dir., 1990—. Fund raising co-chmn. Bob Ellis for Wash. State Legis., 1982. Mem.: Advt. Women of N.Y., U. Wash. Alumni Assn., Jr. League of N.Y., Women's Univ. Club, Gamma Phi Beta Alumni Assn. Avocations: sailing, reading, travel, skiing.

BLOMQUIST, MARYLANE NEUBAUER, secondary school educator; d. John Jacob Neubauer and Betty Magdalena Bladel Neubauer; m. Clark D. Blomquist, Dec. 30, 1972; children: Laurel, Holly, Jacob, Justin, Kate. BA, Clarke Coll., 1972; MS, Marquette U., 1990, Cardinal Stritch U., 2000. Tchr. math. Aldrin Jr. High Sch., Barstow, Ill., 1972—73; tchr. grades 6-8 math Mother of Perpetual Help Sch., Milw., 1986—88; dir. theater Dominican High Sch., 1988—90; tchr. grades 9-12 math. St. Joan Antida High Sch., 1990—99; tchr. grades 10-12 math. Kewaskum High Sch., 2001—. Adj. faculty math. Mt. Mary Coll., Milw., 1999—2001. Mem. adv. bd. Kids Korps, Inc., Milw., 1994—. Recipient Bank One award, Milw., 1995; fellow, Herb Kohl Found., 1996; grantee, Milw. Found., 1988. Mem.: ASCD, Wis. Math. Coun., Nat. Coun. Tchrs. Math. Avocations: reading, crocheting, needlecrafts, tap dance. Office: Kewaskum High Sch 1510 Bilgo Ln Kewaskum WI 53040

BLONDER, BARBARA IRENE, biologist; b. Framingham, Mass., Mar. 24, 1961; d. Fred Daniel and Margery Sharon B.; m. David Arthur Haynes, May 9, 1993. BA in Zoology, U. N.H., 1981; MS in Marine Biology, Fla. Tech., 1985. Marine sci. tchr., divemaster Internat. Field Studies, Andros, Bahamas, 1982-83; biologist Bionetics Corp., Kennedy Space Ctr., Fla., 1985-86; fishery biologist Nat. Marine Fisheries Svc., Panama City, Fla., 1986; biol. sci. II Fla. Dept. Natural Scis., Marathon, Fla., 1986-89, environ. specialist II Apopka, Fla., 1989-91; land steward The Nature Conservancy, Kill Devil Hills, NC, 1991—99; biologist, steward NC Nat. Estuarine Rsch. Reserve, 1999—2001; biologist The Nature Conservancy, Fla., 2001—03; asst. prof., coord. natural scis. Flagler Coll., St. Augustine, 2003—. Vol. firefighter Town of Kill Devil Hills, N.C., 1991-93. Avocations: windsurfing, bicycling, travel. Office: The Nature Conservancy 701 W Ocean Acres Dr Kill Devil Hills NC 27948-8848

BLONDIN-ANDREW, ETHEL D., Canadian government official; b. Tulita, N.W.T., Can., Mar. 25, 1951; d. Cecilia Modeste, adopted d. Joseph and Marie Therese Blondin; children: Troy Zanl, Tanya, Timothy Townsend. BEd, U. Alta., 1974, LLD, 2001. Tchr. Tuktoyaktuk, Ft. Franklin, Ft. Providence, 1974-81; tchr. lang. spl. dept. edn. Yellowknife, 1981-84, asst. dep. min., culture & comm., 1986—88; tchr. U. Calgary & Arctic Coll., 1983; mgr., then acting dir. Pub. Svc. Commn., Canada, 1984-86; sec. state tng. and youth Can., 1993-97, sec. state children and youth, 1997—. Mem. bd. dirs. Arctic Inst. N.Am., Nat. Steering Ctr., Aboriginal Lang. Policy Dvel.; chair Indigenous Lang. Devel. Rev. Ctr. Recipient Culture and Heritage Preservation award MLA, 1987, Hilroy Scholar award R.C. Hill Char. Found., 1982. Liberal. Roman Catholic. Office: Ste # 102 51 02-50 Ave Yellowknife NT Canada X1A 3S8 also: House of Commons Ottawa ON K1A 0A6 Canada

BLOODWORTH, GLADYS LEON, elementary school educator; b. Natchitoches, La., July 9, 1946; d. Rudolph and Mary (LeRoy) Leon; m. John Edward Bloodworth, Aug. 14, 1971; children: John, Jeremy. BA, Southern U., Baton Rouge, 1968; MA, Calif. State U., Dominguez Hills, 1989. Nat. bd. cert. tchr. mid. childhood generalist NBCT/MC, 2001. Lang. arts tchr. grades 6-10 Natchitoches Parish Schs.; categorical program adviser LA Unified Schs., mentor tchr., 1999—, coord. gifted coord., 1988. Named Outstanding Math Tchr., 1987-88. Mem. NEA, United Tchrs. LA, Calif. Tchrs. Assn., Women in Ednl. Leadership, Kappa Kappa Iota. Methodist.

BLOODWORTH, VELDA JEAN, librarian, educator; b. Campobello, SC, June 28, 1929; d. Lloyd Ernest and Nora Frances (McNeal) Burke; m. Clifford Burton Bloodworth, Aug. 14, 1949; children: Jill Henderson, Jackie Herschberger. BA, So. Coll., Collegedale, Tenn., 1967; MS, Fla. State U., 1968; MAT, Rollins Coll., 1979. Libr. Forest Lake Acad., Apopka, Fla., 1968-74, Rollins Coll., Winter Park, Fla., 1974—99, assoc. prof. emerita; ret., 1999. Cons. libr. Forest Lake Acad., Apopka, 1987-88. Editor, curator: (catalog for art mus. exhibit) Jessie B. Rittenhouse Poetry Collection, 1984. Mem. Beta Phi Mu. Home: 3162 Holliday Ave Apopka FL 32703-6634 Office: Rollins Coll Olin Libr 1000 Holt Ave Winter Park FL 32789-4499 E-mail: jbloodworth@rollins.edu.

BLOOM, CLAIRE, actress; b. London, Feb. 15, 1931; d. Edward Max and Elizabeth (Grew) B.; m. Rod Steiger, Sept. 19, 1959 (div. Jan. 1969); 1 child, Anna Justine; m. Philip Roth, Apr. 29, 1990 (div. Mar. 1995). Student, Badminton Sch., Bristol, Eng., Fern Hill Manor, New Milton, Eng., Guildhall Sch. Music and Drama, London. Disting. vis. prof. Hunter Coll., N.Y.C., 1989-90. Appeared as Ophelia, Stratford-Upon-Avon, 1948; plays include Ring Around the Moon, London, 1949-51, Romeo and Juliet, also as Juliet in Old Vic tour of U.S., Six Lessons in Six Weeks, 2006; film roles in Limelight, Richard III, 1956, Alexander the Great, 1956, The Brothers Karamazov, 1958, Look Back in Anger, 1958, The Brothers Grimm, 1962, The Chapman Report, 1962, The Haunting, 1963, 80,000 Suspects, 1963, Alta Infidelita, 1963, Il Maestro di Vigeevano, 1963, The Outrage, 1964, The Spy Who Came in from the Cold, 1965, The Illustrated Man, 1969, Three into Two Won't Go, 1969, A Severed Head, 1971, A Doll's House, 1973, Islands in the Stream, 1976, Clash of the Titans, 1981, Always, 1984, Sammy and Rosie, 1987, Crimes and Misdemeanors, 1989, Daylight, 1995, The Book Eve, 2002, Imagining Argentina, 2002, Daniel and the Superdogs, 2003; Broadway prodns. include Rashomon, 1959; other theatre appearances include Duel of Angels, London, 1958, Altona, Royal Court Theatre, London, 1960, Ivanov, London, 1964, A Doll's House, Hedda Gabler, 1971, Vivat! Vivat Regina!, 1972; N.Y. appearance The Innocents, 1976; London appearances A Doll's House, 1973, A Streetcar Named Desire, 1974, Rosmersholm, 1977, The Cherry Orchard, 1981, These are Women, 1982-83, When We Dead Awaken, 1990, Daughters, Wives and Mothers, 1991, Silenced Voices, 1992, Women in Love, 1993, The Cherry Orchard, 1994, Long Days Journey into Night, 1996, Electra, 1998, Conversations After a Burial, 2000, A Little Night Music, 2001, A Little Night Music NYCO, 2003, Whistling Psyche, 2004, Six Dance Lessons in Six Weeks, 2006-; many roles Brit. and U.S. TV including In Praise of Love, 1975, A Legacy, 1975, Henry VIII, 1979, Hamlet, 1979, The Ghost Writer, 1983, Cymbeline, 1983, King John, 1983, Brideshead Revisited, 1981, Shadowlands, 1984, Time and the Conways, 1985, miniseries Queenie, 1987, Anastasia, 1987, Shadow in the Sun, 1988, The Camomile Lawn, 1991, The Mirror Crack'd, 1992, Remember, 1993, Village Affairs, 1994, Family Money, 1996, When the Dead Man Heard, 1997, The Lady in Question, 1999, Law and Order, 2003, Ten Commandments, 2005, Trial and Retribution, 2005, Miss Marple, 2005, Doc Martin, 2005, Lady Chatterley, 2006; author: Limelight and After, 1982, Leaving A Doll's House, 1996. Recipient Evening Standard award, London, 1974, Brit. Film and TV award, London, 1984; nominee Tony award, 1998, 99, Ibsen award, Oslo, 2006. Office: Marion Rosenberg Agy 1345 N Hayworth Ave Ste 104 Los Angeles CA 90046 Home: 14 Rosaville Rd London SW6 7BL England

BLOOM, JANE MAGINNIS, emergency physician; b. Ithaca, NY, June 22, 1924; d. Ernest Victor and Miriam Rebecca (Mansfield) M.; m. William Lee Bloom, Mar. 31, 1944; children: David Lee, Jan Christopher, Carolyn Wells, Eric Paul, Joseph William, Robert Carl, Mary Catherine, Thomas Mark, Patrick Martin (dec.), Arthur Emerson. BS, U. Mich., 1968, MD, 1974. Diplomate Am. Bd. Internal Medicine. Rotating intern Wayne County Gen. Hosp., Eloise, Mich., 1974-75; resident in internal medicine St. Mary's Hosp., Rochester, NY, 1975-77; emergency physician Emergency Physicians Med. Group, Ann Arbor, 1986—2003. Fellow: Am. Coll. Emergency Physicians (life); mem.: AMA, Mich. State Med. Soc., Am. Coll. Physicians, Am. Med. Womens Assn., Am. Assn. Women Emergency Physicians, Washtenaw County Med. Soc. Avocations: bird watching, planting trees, classical music, walking. Home and Office: 537 Elm St Ann Arbor MI 48104-2515 Office Phone: 734-761-2435. Personal E-mail: jbmdfacep@aol.com.

BLOOM, KATHRYN RUTH, public relations executive; d. Morris and Frances Sondra (Siegel) B. BA, Douglass Coll.; MA, U. Toronto, Can. Dir. spl. projects United Jewish Appeal, NYC, 1973-78; mgr. pub. affairs Bristol-Myers-Squibb Co., NYC, 1978-86; mgr. pub. rels. pharm. and nutritional Bristol-Myers Squibb Co., 1986-90, dir. pharm. and rsch. comms., 1990-91; dir. comms. Biogen Idec, Inc., 1992—2001, sr. dir. pub. affairs Cambridge, Mass., 2001—05; dir. Biogen Idec Found., 2005—. Bd. overseers Beth Israel Deaconess Med. Ctr., 2000—, Hebrew Coll., 2004—. Mem.: Am. Technion Soc. (v.p. NE regional bd. dirs. 2004—), The Boston Club, Phi Beta Kappa. Office: Biogen Idec 14 Cambridge Ctr Cambridge MA 02142-1481

BLOOM, LISA READ, lawyer; b. Phila., Sept. 20, 1961; d. Peyton Huddleston Bray and Gloria Allred; children: Sarah Wong Bloom, Samuel Bloom Wong. BA, UCLA, 1983; JD, Yale U., 1986. Bar: N.Y., 1987, Calif., 1992; U.S. Dist. Ct. (so. and ea. dists.) N.Y., 1987, U.S. Dist. Ct. (cen. dist.) Calif. 1992. Assoc. Meister, Leventhal & Slade, N.Y.C., 1986-87, Robinson, Silverman, Pearce, Aronsohn & Berman, N.Y.C., 1987-91, Allred, Maroko & Goldberg, L.A., 1992—2001; co-host Closing Arguments Court TV, 2001—03, co-anchor Trial Heat, 2003—. Spkr. in field. Numerous TV and radio appearances. Recipient Cert. of Merit, Courage to Tell Found., Calif., 1993. Office: Court TV Network LLC 600 Third Ave New York NY 10016

BLOOM-FESHBACH, SALLY, psychologist, educator; b. Balt., Feb. 11, 1953; d. Jordan and Carol (Wallerstein) Bloom; m. Jonathan Feshbach, Aug. 29, 1976 (dec. June 1999); children: Alison, Kimberly; m. Donald Evans, July 2002. AB, Brown U., 1975; MS, Yale U., 1977, MPhil, 1979, PhD, 1980. Lic. clin. psychologist, Washington. Staff psychologist Am. U. Ctr. for Psychol. and Learning Svcs., Washington, 1980-84, dir. postgrad. tng., 1982-84; pvt. practice psychotherapy, Washington, 1982—; rsch. cons. com. on child devel. NAS-NRC, Washington, 1980-83. Assoc. clin. prof. dept. psychiatry and behavioral sci. George Washington U., Washington, 1985—; mem. faculty Inst. for Contemporary Psychotherapy and Psychoanalysis, 1996—, Washington Sch. Psychiatry, 2001—; cons. in field. Co-editor: Psychology of Separation and Loss, 1987; contbr. articles to profl. jours., chpts. to books. Fellow Yale U., 1975-77, NIMH, 1977-80; travel grantee NATO, APA, 1981, 82, rsch. grantee Sigma Xi, 1978. Mem. APA (bd. dirs. sect. on women and psychoanalysis), Brown U. Club, Yale U. Club, Phi Beta Kappa, Sigma Xi. Home: 2919 Garfield St NW Washington DC 20008-3504 Office: 1301 20th St NW Ste 608 Washington DC 20036-6016 Office Phone: 202-293-1036. E-mail: salbf@aol.com.

BLOOMFIELD, CLARA DERBER, oncologist, educator, medical institute administrator; b. Flushing, L.I., N.Y., May 15, 1942; d. Milton and Zelda (Trenner) Derber; m. Victor A. Bloomfield, June 11, 1962 (div. 1983); m. Albert de la Chapelle, Jan. 1, 1984. Student, U. Wis., 1959-62; BA, San Diego State U., 1963; MD, U. Chgo., 1968. Diplomate Am. Bd. Internal Medicine, Nat. Bd. Med. Examiners. Intern in medicine U. Chgo. Hosps. and Clinics, 1968-69, resident internal medicine, 1969-70, U. Minn., Mpls., 1970-71, med. oncology fellow, 1971-73, chief resident in medicine, Jan.-June, 1972, instr., 1972-73, asst. prof. medicine, 1973-76, assoc. prof., 1976-80, prof. medicine div. oncology, 1980-89, dir. fellowship program med. concology, 1987—89, mem. univ. senate, 1986-89, mem. all univ. Commn. on Women, 1988-89; prof. medicine, chief div. oncology SUNY, Buffalo, 1989—97; head dept. medicine Roswell Pk. Cancer Inst., Buffalo, 1989—97; William G. Pace III prof. cancer research Ohio State U. Coll. Med. & Pub. Health, 1997—, dir., div. hematology & oncology, dept. Internal Medicine, 1997—. Mem. Kettering selection com. GM Cancer Rsch. Found., 1986-87; cons. Office Tech. Assessment, U.S. Congress, 1988; participant, chair various coms. Internat. Human Gene Mapping Workshops, Helsinki, Finland, 1985, France, 1987, Internat. Workshops Chromosomes in Leukemia, Lund, Sweden, 1980, Chgo., 1982, Tokyo, 1984, London, 1987, Buffalo, 1991; mem. nat. and sci. adv. bds. NIH, 1977—, mem. bd. sci. counselors divsn. cancer treatment, 1991—, organizer Internat. Hodgkins Disease Symposium, 1981; bd. dirs. cancer and leukemia group B, 1982—, mem. other coms., 1973— sponsored clin. trial groups, Nat. Cancer Inst., cons. S.W. oncology group; mem. nat. and sci. adv. bd. Don and Sybil Harrington Cancer Ctr., Amarillo, Tex., 1979—, Med. Coll. Pa., 1988—; bd. trustees Berlex Oncology Found., 1992—; vis. prof. dept. medicine W.Va. U., 1973, U. Ariz., Tucson, 1979, U. Fla., Gainesville, 1979, Emory U., Atlanta, 1980, U. Chgo., 1982, George Washington U., Washington, 1982, U. Tex., San Antonio, 1982, Brown U., Providence, 1982, Mayo Clinic, Rochester, Minn., 1982, U. Zurich, Switzerland, 1983, U. P.R., 1984, U. Witwatersand, S. Africa, 1984, Nihon U., Tokyo, 1984, Leukemia Soc. Mass., 1991; frequent invited speaker, guest lectr. symposia, workshops, continuing edn. courses, seminars, med. congresses, univs. in U.S., Europe, S. Am., Scandinavia, Eng., Japan, Republic of South Africa, New Zealand. Author: (with others) Recent Advances in Bone Marrow Transplantation, Vol. VII, 1983, New Prespectives in Human Lymphoma, 1984, Neoplastic Diseases of the Blood, 1985, Current Therapy in Hematology/Oncology 1984-85, 1985, Medical Genetics: Past, Present, Future, 1985, Directions in Oncology, Vol. 1, 1985, Medical Oncology, Basic Principles and Clinical Management of Cancer, 1985, Tumor Aneuploidy, 1985, Malignant Lymphomas and Hodgkins Disease: Experimental and Therapeutic Advances, 1985, Current Therapy in Internal Medicine, 1987, Genetic Maps, Vol. 4, 1987; contbr. over 250 articles, abstracts to profl. jours.; editor ann. Adult Leukemia series in Cancer Treatment and Rsch., 1979-85; cons. editor Leukemia and Lymphoma Yearbook of Cancer, 1980—; assoc. editor Cancer Rsch., 1981-88, editor, 91, Leukemia Rsch., 1984-87, Leukemia, 1987-89; mem. editorial bd. Jour. Clin. Oncology, 1983-88, Cancer Genetics and Cytogenetics, 1983-87, Directions in Oncology, 1984-86, Cancer Rsch. Bull., 1984-85, Med. and Pediatric Oncology, 1987—, Blood, 1988—, Annals of Medicine, 1989—, Seminars in Oncology, 1989—; editorial bd. Am. Jour. Hematology, 1985, assoc. editor, 1988—; reviewer 23 med. jours. Recipient Nat. Bd. award Med. Coll. Pa., 1981, Past State Pres.' Bus. and Profl. Women award U. Tex. System Cancer Ctr., M.D. Anderson Hosp. and Tumor Clinic, Houston, 1987, Joseph H. Burchenal Clinical Rsch. award, Am. Assn. Cancer Rsch., 2004; prin. or co-prin. investigator 8 grants, NIH, 1975—, also ACS, 1980-84, Minn. State Spl. Coleman Leukemia Rsch. Fund, 1981-89, Coleman Leukemia Rsch. Fund Endowment, 1981—, Baltzar W.A. von Platen Found., 1984-85, Genentech/Hoffman -LaRoche, 1988—. Mem. ACP, AAAS, Am. Assn. Cancer Rsch., Am. Soc. Hematology, Am. Soc. Clin. Oncology (bd. dirs. 1991—), Am. Fedn. Clin. Rsch., Cen. Soc. Clin. Rsch., N.Y. Acad. Scis., Inst. Medicine, Internat. Assn. Comparative Rsch.

Leukemia and Related Diseases, Med. Soc. Finland (external mem.), Phi Beta Kappa, Alpha Omega Alpha, Sigma Delta Epsilon. Office: Comprehensive Cancer Ctr 320 W 10th Ave Columbus OH 43210

BLOOMFIELD, SARA J., museum director; BA in English Lit., Northwestern Univ.; MA in Education. V.p. Cleveland Financial Group; dep. dir. for ops. U.S. Holocaust Meml. Coun., Washington, 1986—88, exec. dir., 1988—94; assoc. dir. for mus. programs U.S. Holocaust Memorial Museum, Washington, 1994—98, acting dir., 1998—99, dir., 1999—. Established the first Learning Disability Program for the Shaker Heights City School System. Recipient of the Young Leadership award from the American Jewish Com., 1986, Jan Karski award from the Anti-Defamation League, Washington Chap. Bd. mem, Women's Political Caucus, the Cleveland City Club and the American Jewish Com. Office: US Holocaust Meml Mus 100 Raoul Wallenberg Pl SW Washington DC 20024-2126

BLOOMFIELD, SUSANNE GEORGE, language educator, writer; b. Minden, Nebr., Mar. 6, 1947; d. Thomas Carter and Imogene P. Flack; m. Terry Bloomfield, Dec. 29, 1999; children: Tamara Wagman, Chad Lindau. BA cum laude, U. Nebr., Kearney, 1968, MA in Edn., 1979; PhD in English, U. Nebr., Lincoln, 1988. Tchr. English, French Axtell Pub. Sch., Nebr., 1968—73; tchr. English U. Nebr., Kearney, 1979—87, prof. English, 1988—. Author: The Adventures of the Woman Homesteader: The Life and Letters of Elinore Pruitt Stewart, 1992, Kate M. Cleary: A Literary Biography with Selected Works, 1997 (Susan Koppelman award, 1998), (monograph) Absolutely No Manners: On Having the Audacity to Write Biography, 2003; co-editor: The Platte River: An Atlas of the Big Bend Region, 1993, A Prairie Mosiac: An Atlas of Central Nebraska's Land, 2000, A Presidential Visit, 2002; co-author: From the Beginning: A Century of Excellence at the University of Nebraska at Kearney, 2005; editor: Wellsprings: Poems by Six Nebraska Poets, 1995, Impertinences: Selected Editorials of Elia W. Peattie, A Journalist in the Gilded Age, 2005. Recipient Mari Sandoz award, Nebr. Libr. Assn., 1998, Holdt Disting. Faculty award, U. Nebr. Kearney, 2002, Martin Disting. Professorship, 2005—. Fellow: Ctr. for Great Plains Studies (mem. governing bd.); mem.: Willa Cothen Pioneer Meml. and Ednl. Found. (mem. governing bd.), We. Lit. Assn. (pres. 1996). Avocations: horseback riding, camping. Office: Univ Nebr 109D Thomas Hall Kearney NE

BLOOMGARDEN, KARENNE JO, elementary school educator, small business owner; b. N.Y.C., July 5, 1951; d. Kermit and Carol (Lane) B. BS, Bradley U., 1973; M Secondary Edn., Mercy Coll., 2000. Health and phys. edn. tchr. N.J. Bd. Edn., Plainfield, 1973-76, phys. edn. tchr. Orange, 1976-79; camp dir. Orange YWCA, 1977-85; health and phys. edn. tchr. Newark Bd. Edn., 1980-83; exec. dir. Am. Camping Assn., N.Y.C., 1984-87; tchr., trainer N.Y.C. Bd. Edn., 1988-90, adaptive phys. edn. tchr., 1990—; pres. KB Camp Svc., Inc., 1985—. Camp dir. Balt. Cancer Soc., 1977-85, 86-91; dir. The Summer Camp, N.Y.C., 1985-92; stds. accreditation vis. Am. Camping Assn., N.Y.C., 1980—; spokesperson Children and Adults with Attention Deficit Disorder, N.Y.C., 1993—; pres. KB Camp Svc., Inc., 1985—. Contbr. articles to mags. Vol. Starlight Found., N.Y.C., 1989—, Ronald McDonald House, N.Y.C., 1990-92, Coalition for the Homeless, N.Y.C., 1990—, Yorkville Pantry Shelter, N.Y.C., 1993—, Kwazulu Natal-Mduku Cmty., South Africa, 2000—; founder Girl Club of Am., Peoria, Ill., 1973. Named Tchr. of Yr., P.U.S.H., N.J., 1975; featured in Time Mag., 1986, N.Y. Times,1994, LA Times, 2001. Mem. Am. Camping Assn. (cert. camp dir.). Home and Office: 351 E 84th St New York NY 10028-4423 Office Phone: 212-772-6633. Personal E-mail: kbcamp@rcn.com.

BLOOMGARDEN, KATHY FINN, public relations executive; b. NYC, June 9, 1949; d. David and Laura (Zeisler) Finn; m. Zachary Bloomgarden; children: Rachel, Keith, Matthew. BA, Brown U., 1970; MA, PhD, Columbia U.; cert., East Asian Inst. Pres. Rsch. & Forecasts, N.Y.C.; pres., dir. Ruder-Finn, Inc., N.Y.C., 1988—98, pres., 1998—, co-CEO, 2001—. Mem. comm. com. Brown U. Mem. comms. com. Brown U., Providence. Recipient PR Industry's All-Star award. Mem.: Women's Forum, Fgn. Policy Assn., Coun. Fgn. Rels., Am. Mgmt. Assn. (bd. dirs.), Pub. Rels. Soc. Am. Jewish. Office: Ruder Finn 301 E 57th St New York NY 10022-2900

BLOS, JOAN W., writer, critic, educator; b. NYC, Dec. 9, 1928; m. Peter Blos, Jr., 1953; 2 children, 1 deceased. BA, Vassar Coll., 1950; MA, CCNY, 1956; DHL (hon.), Bank St. Coll. Edn., 2001. Asso. publs. div., mem. tchr. edn. faculty Bank St. Coll. Edn., N.Y.C., 1958-70; lectr. Sch. Edn., U. Mich., Ann Arbor, 1972-80; U.S. editor Children's Literature in Education, 1976-81. Author: "It's Spring!" She Said, 1968, (with Betty Miles) Just Think!, 1971, A Gathering of Days: A New England Girl's Journal, 1830-32, 1979 (Newbery medal ALA, Am. Book award 1980, Best Book of Yr., Sch. Libr. Jour.), Martin's Hats, 1984, Brothers of the Heart: A Story of the Old Northwest, 1837-38, 1985, Old Henry, 1987 (Honor book Boston Globe Horn Book award 1991), Lottie's Circus, 1989, The Grandpa Days, 1989, One Very Best Valentine's Day, 1990, The Heroine of the Titanic (Juvenile Fiction award 1991, For Exch. in Lit. Arts 1992), 1991, A Seed, A Flower, A Minute, An Hour, 1992, Brooklyn Doesn't Rhyme, 1994, The Days Before Now, 1994, Hungry Little Boy, 1995, Hello, Shoes (Best Book award Bank St. Coll. Edn. 1999). Office Phone: 212-473-5400.

BLOSE, RUTH ELAYNE, language educator; b. Waynesburg, Pa., July 9, 1952; d. John William and Julia Helen Yesenosky; m. Phillip Richard Blose, Aug. 11, 1973; children: Scott Todd, Phillip Alan, Amanda Lee. BS Edn., Indiana U. Pa., 1974. Cert. Spanish, French tchr. Pa., tchr. Gifted Carlow Coll. Tchr. Avella Sch. Dist., Pa., 1974—. Sponsor Nat. Honor Soc. Avella H.S., 1974—, sponsor sr. class, 1990—, coord. Gifted and Talented, 1977—. Named to Whos Who Am. H.S. Tchrs. Office: Avella Area High Sch 1000 Avella Rd Avella PA 15312

BLOSKY, ELIZABETH ANNE, science educator; d. George Franklin and Eileen Ann Fausnaught; m. Bernard Joseph Blosky, July 26, 2003. Degree in secondary edn. biology, U. Scranton, Pa., 2002. Cert. PDE Level I tchg. Derry Township Sch. Dist. Tchr. biology Derry Township Sch. Dist., Hershey, Pa., 2002—. Co-advisor Key Club, Hershey, 2004—; team mem. Student Assistance Team, Hershey, 2005—. Mem.: Kiwanis. Republican. Catholic. Avocations: exercise, reading. Office: Derry Township Sch Dist PO Box 898 Homestead Rd Hershey PA 17033 Business E-Mail: eblosky@hershey.k12.pa.us.

BLOSSER, PAMELA ELIZABETH, metaphysics educator, counselor, minister; b. Norman, Okla., Dec. 12, 1946; d. William Bernard and Emma Elizabeth (Ambrister) Carpenter; m. William Richard Stewart, June 10, 1969 (div. Apr. 1979); m. Paul Gerald Blosser Jr., Sept. 24, 1994 (div. Apr. 2006). BA, Tex. Christian U., 1969; DDiv, Interfaith Ch. Metaphysics, Windyville, Mo., 1992; DMetaphysics, Sch. Metaphysics, Windyville, 1994; degree with honors, Maria Montessori Tng. Divsn., London, 1977. Ordained to ministry Interfaith Ch. of Metaphysics, 1992; cert. in counseling. Dir. metaphysics ctrs. Sch. Metaphysics, various locations, 1979-89; directress Golden Moments Montessori, Columbia, Mo., 1987-89; instr. metaphysics Sch. Metaphysics, various locations, 1977-89, readings coord. Windyville, 1989—98, dir. printing, 1989—, instr. metaphysics, 1991—; min. of music Interfaith Ch. Metaphysics, Windyville, 1990-96, min., 1995—; area dir. Sch. Metaphysics, North Area, 2004—. Dir. Camp Niangua for Young People, Sch. Metaphysics, Windyville, 1995-2004; ordination bd. Interfaith Ch. of Metaphysics, 1993—; bd. govs. Sch. Metaphysics, 1997—, pres., 2002—06. Author: Power of Structure, 1988, Total Recall, 1993, Motivation: From Existence to Fulfillment, 1997, The 7 Steps to Deepen Meditation, 2001, Essay in Interpreting Dreams for Self-Discovery, 2001; contbr. articles to profl. jours. Mem. Dallas County Homemakers (sec.-treas. 1995-96, sec. 2000-01, pres. 2001-03), Homemaker Club Windyville (v.p. 1995, 98, pres. 1996, 99-2001, sec. 2002). Independent. Avocations: reading, playing celtic harp. Home and Office: Sch of Metaphysics 163 Moon Valley Rd Windyville MO 65783-9703

BLOSSOM, BEVERLY, choreographer, educator; b. Chgo., Aug. 28, 1926; d. Theodore and Florence (Pfeiffer) Schmidt; m. Roberts Blossom, 1966 (div.); 1 child, Michael. BA, Roosevelt U., 1950; MA, Sarah Lawrence, 1953. Dancer Alwin Nikolais Co., N.Y.C., 1952-62; instr. Adelphi U., L.I., NY, 1964-66; prof. dance dept. U. Ill., Urbana, 1967-90. Choreographer Festival Theatre, Krannert Ctr., Urbana, Radio Show, 1985, Quick-Step, 1985, Heartbeat, 1985, Interlude from Veranda, 1985; choreographer: Rehearsal for a Class Act, 1983, You Are Still With Me, Fred, 1983, Dad's Ties, 1983, Ordinary Heartbreak, 1984, Egg, 1984, Weatherwatch, 1986, Potpourri, 1986, Eye of the Beholder, 1986, Russian Tea Room, 1986, Entitled, 1987, Grass Widow, 1987, Inch, 1987, Castles in Spain, 1988, Swansong, 1989,.Exit, 1990, The Cloak, 1990, Onward, 1991, Shards, 1993, Dead Monkey, 1996, Cynicism, 1996, Cello Lessons, 2003, The Incomplete Lament of an Old Dancer, 2005, others. Choreography grantee Nat. Endowment for the Arts, 1986-90, 92-95, Ill. Arts Coun. Choreography grantee, 1980-82; recipient Bessie award, 1993. Mem.: Am. Guild of Musical Artists (cert.), Screen Actors Guild (cert.), Union of Profl. Employees (cert.). Office Phone: 312-347-0981. E-mail: bblossom@jps.net.

BLOUNT, JACKIE MARIE, educator; b. Tullahoma, Tenn., Dec. 19, 1959; d. Edward Buck and Gwendolyn Maude (Merritt) B. B.Music Edn., U. N.C., 1983, MAT in Physics Tchg., 1989, PhD in Social Found. of Edn., 1993. Cert. tchr. music, physics, N.C. Tchr. physics Lexington (N.C.) H.S., 1985-90; asst. prof. Iowa State U., Ames, 1993-98, assoc. prof., 1998—2004, assoc. dean, 2000—03, 2006—, prof., 2004—. Author: Destined to Rule the Schools, 1998, Fit To Teach, 2005; contbr. articles to profl. jours. Woodrow Wilson Found. Spencer Dissertation fellow, 1992-93, Dean Smith Scholarship Found. scholar, 1991-92, John Motley Morehead Found. scholar, 1978-82; recipient Thomas Urban Rsch. award F.I.N.E. Found., 1997, Iowa State U. award, 1998, Critics' Choice award, 1998, 2005; inducted into Iowa Acad. Edn., 2004. Mem. Am. Ednl. Rsch. Assn., History of Edn. Soc. Democrat. Office: Iowa State U Coll Human Sci E262 Lagomarcino Hall Ames IA 50011-0001 Business E-Mail: jblount@iastate.edu.

BLOUNT, YOLANDA DENISE, social services administrator, psychologist; m. Osborn Blount, Oct. 21, 1989; 1 child, Osborn LaVonte. BA, Columbia Coll., Mo., 1996; MA Clin. Psychology, Ctr. Humanistics Studies, Detroit. Lic. psychologist Mich. Therapist N.W. Behavioral Health Svcs., Jacksonville, Fla., 1998—99, Child Guidance Ctr., Jacksonville, 1999, Renaissance Behavioral Health Sys., Jacksonville, 2000; social svc. specialist Cmty. Hospice N.E. Fla., Jacksonville, 2001—; psychol. specialist Fla. State Prison, Raiford, 2002—03. Psychologist Disaster Med. Assistance Team, Jacksonville, 2004—. With USNR. Decorated various mil. awards. Office: Comty Hospice NE Fla 4266 Senbeam Rd Jacksonville FL 32257

BLOWE, ARNETHIA, religious studies educator; b. Sussex County, Va., Aug. 4, 1924; d. Reverend Willie Green and Mary Lue Blowe. BS, Va. State Coll., Ettrick, 1947. Asst. dir. Christian edn. Am. Bapt. Conv. USA, 1962; cert. home econs. tchr. Va. State Dept. of Edn., 1947, tchr. K-8 N.J. Dept. of Edn., 1962, Storyteller Maplewood Adult Sch., 1991. Storyteller N.J. Storyteller's Guild, Montclair, NJ, 1990—, Nat. Black Storytellers Assn., Baltimore, Md., 1992—. Elem. tchr. Newark Pub. Sch. Sys., 1968—91. Performer: (storytelling) Black History Presentations (Black History Cert. of Appreciation, Elizabeth Urban League, 2002). Pres. Congress of Christian Edn. New Hope Missionary Bapt. Assn. Inc, Newark, 2000—. Recipient Cert. of Appreciation, Middlesex Ctrl. Bapt. Assn. N.J., 1993, award, Nat. Coun. Negro Women, 2003. Mem.: NAACP (life; exec. bd. mem. 1998—2002). Home: 930 Flora St Elizabeth NJ 07201

BLOXSON, PHYLLIS JANE, art educator; b. Hampton, Va., Dec. 7, 1961; d. John Richard Sr. Bloxson and Barbara Ellen Shepherd/ Bloxson; 1 adopted child, Jacob Earl. BS in Art, Writing, Christian Edn., Bryan Coll., 1985; MEd, Nova Southeastern U., 2006. Cert. Art K-12 Tenn. Kindergarten tchr. Calvary Bapt. Sch., Graysville, Tenn., 1986—88; nursing asst. Graysville Nursing Home, Tenn., 1986, Spring City Healthcare, 1988—89, Mid-SouthHome Health, 1990—95, Scotia Village, Laurinburg, NC, 1995—96, Continued Care, 1996—97, Home Health East Tenn., 1997—99, nursing asst. spl. needs children Chattanooga, 1994—99; art tchr. Rhea County Bd. Ed, Dayton, Tenn., 1999—. Art tchr., developer Home Schoolers, Dayton, 1987—96. Illustrator The Best of Character, Best of Character Two, researcher Character Counts, Character Gems. Pub. rels. com. First Bapt. Ch., Dayton, 2003—05. Named Tchr. of Yr., Walmart, 2005. Mem.: NEA, Dayton Art League (v.p. 2003—04). Republican. Southern Baptist. Avocations: fishing, singing, photography, painting, drawing. Home: 812 Blythe Ferry Rd Dayton TN 37321

BLUE, CATHERINE ANNE, lawyer; b. Boston, Feb. 17, 1957; d. James Daniel and Angela Devina (Savini) Mahoney; m. Donald Sherwood Blue, 1980 (dec. 2001); children: Mairead Catherine, Edward Pierce. BA, Stonehill Coll., 1977; JD, Coll. William and Mary, 1980. Bar: Pa. 1980, N.Y. 1999, Mass. 2000, DC 2006. Atty. Aluminum Co. Am., Pitts., 1980-83, Pa. Dept. Revenue, Harrisburg, 1983-85, State Workmen's Ins. Fund, Pitts., 1985-87, Met. Pitts. Pub. Broadcasting (now QED Comm. Inc.), 1987-91, gen. counsel, 1991-95; regional gen. counsel ctrl. region AT&T Wireless Svcs., Paramus, NJ, 1995-97, dir. N.E. region, 1997-98, chief counsel land use, 1998-2000, v.p. land and comml. trans., 2000—05; chief counsel land use Cingular Wireless, Paramus, 2004—05; sr. counsel Holland & Knight, Washington, 2005—06; ptnr. Donohue & Blue, Alexandria, Va., 2006—. Mem. Pa. Bar Assn., Mass. Bar Assn. Democrat. Home: 1200 1st St Apt 1123 Alexandria VA 22314 Office: 801 N Fairfax St Ste 209 Alexandria VA 22314 Office Phone: 703-549-5382. Business E-Mail: catherine.blue@donohueblue.com.

BLUE, LISA A., lawyer, psychologist; b. Atlanta, Oct. 12, 1952; m. Fred Baron. BS Ed., Univ. Ga., 1973; Ed. S., Univ. Va., 1974, M. Ed., 1976; PhD counseling & psychology, No. Tex. State Univ., 1978; JD, So. Tex. Coll. Law, 1980. Bar: Tex. 1981, US Dist. Ct. (no., we. dist. Tex.), US Supreme Ct.; lic. psychologist Tex., 1978, cert. Am. Bd. Forensic Psychology, Am. Bd. Profl. Psychology. Asst. dist. atty., Dallas, 1981—85; atty. Baron & Budd PC, Dallas, 1985—; counseling & forensic psychologist private practice. Contbr. articles to profl. jours. Named one of Top 50 Women Litigators in U.S., Nat. Law Jour., 2002, Top 100 Lawyers in Tex., Top 100 Lawyers in Dallas, Top 50 Women Lawyers, Law & Politics Media, Dallas Best Lawyers, D Mag., 2001—05. Mem.: Am. Bd. Trial Advocates (past pres. Tex. chpt., Dallas chpt., Trial Lawyer of the Year, Tex. chpt. 1999), ABA (mem. judiciary task force), Assn. Trial Lawyers Am., Trial Lawyers for Public Justice (bd. dir.), Tex. Bar Found., Tex. Trial Lawyers Assn. (mem. exec. com., head amicus com.), Dallas Bar Assn. (bd. dir., chmn. CLE com.), Dallas Bar Found., Dallas Trial Lawyers Assn., Am. Thoracic Assn., Tex. Psychol. Assn., Dallas Psychol. Assn., Am. Psychol. Assn., Am. Assn. Sex Educators. Office: Baron & Budd Ste 1100 3102 Oak Lawn Ave Dallas TX 75219 Office Phone: 214-521-3605. Office Fax: 214-520-1181. Business E-Mail: lblue@baronbudd.com.

BLUE, ROSE, writer, educator; b. N.Y.C., 1931; d. Irving and Frieda (Rosenberg) Bluestone. BA, Bklyn. Coll., 1953; postgrad., Bank St. Coll. Edn., 1967. Tchr. N.Y.C. Pub. Schs., 1967—. Writing cons. Bklyn. Coll. Sch. Edn., 1981-83. Author: A Quiet Place, 1969, Black, Black Beautiful Black, 1969, How Many Blocks Is The World, 1970, Bed-Stuy Beat, 1970, I Am Here (Yo Estoy Aqui), 1971, A Month of Sundays, 1972, Grandma Didn't Wave Back, 1972 (teleplay 1983), Nikki 108, 1973, We are Chicano, 1973, The Preacher's Kid, 1975, Seven Years from Home, 1976, The Yo Yo Kid, 1976, The Thirteenth Year, 1977, Cold Rain on the Water, 1979, My Mother The Witch, 1981 (teleplay 1984), Everybody's Evy, 1985, Heart to Heart, 1986, Goodbye Forever Tree, 1987, The Secret Papers of Camp Get Around, 1988, Barbara Bush First Lady, 1990, Colin Powell Straight to the Top, 1991, Barbara Jordan-Politician, 1992, defending Our Country, 1993, Working Together Against Hate Groups, 1993, People of Peace, 1994, The White House Kids, 1995, whoopi Goldberg Entertainer, 1995, Bring Me A Memory, 1996, Good Yontif, 1997, Who's That In the White House?, 1998, Staying Out of Trouble in a Troubled Family, 1998, Madeline Albright U.S. Secretary of State, 1999, You're the Boss: Positive Attitude and Work Ethic, 1999, Who Lived In The House Divided, 2000, Chris Rock, 2001, Benjamin Banneker--Mathematician and Stargazer, 2001, Monica Seles, 2002; lyricist: Drama of Love, 1964, Let's Face It, 1961, Give Me a Break, 1962, My Heartstrings Keep Me Tied To You, 1963, Homecoming Party, 1966; contbg. editor: Tchr. mag., Day Care mag. Mem. PEN, Authors Guild Am., Authors League Am., Mensa, Profl. Womens Caucus, Broadcast Music, Inc.

BLUEMER, BEVAN, acrobatics company executive; b. 1970; married. Owner, ind. cons. Arbonne Internat.; owner, dir. Ariz. Acrobatics. Prog. facilitator GEARUP, Amphitheater High Sch.; dir. campus campaign, The Vagina Monologues. Mem. Beowolf Alley Theatre. Named one of 40 Under 40, Tucson Bus. Edge, 2006. Office: The Honors College Slonaker House 1027 E 2nd St Tucson AZ 85721*

BLUESTEIN, EVE, plastic surgeon; d. June Buchalter and Richard Bruce Cohen; m. Philip Mark Bluestein, Jan. 11, 1998; children: Solomon, Isaac. MD, U. Cin., Ohio, 1994—2000. Cert. Maxillofacial Surgeon Am. Bd. Oral & Maxillofacial Surgery, 2002. Maxillofacial surgeon Bluestein Surg. Arts, P.C., Louisville, Colo., 2001—. Clin. asst. prof. U. Colo. Health Scis. Ctr., Denver, 2001—; pres. Boulder County Med. Soc., 2005—; scope of practice subcom. Colo. Med. Soc., Denver, 2004—, grievance rev. com., 2004—, front range president's coun.; biomedical ethics com. Boulder Cmty. Hosp., 2000—05; president-elect Boulder County Med. Soc., Boulder, Colo., 2004—05; lectr. in field. Mem. C. of C., Louisville, Colo., 2004—06; sponsor North Boulder Little League, 2005. Fellow: Am. Dental Soc. Anesthesiology, Am. Acad. Cosmetic Surgery (mem. Webster Soc. 2005—, Excellence in Cosmetic Surgery Edn. award 2006). Avocations: tennis, running, skiing, bicycling. Office: Bluestein Surgical Arts PC 864 W South Boulder Rd Ste 100 Louisville CO 80027 Office Phone: 303-938-1161.

BLUESTEIN, VENUS WELLER, retired psychologist, educator; b. Milw., July 16, 1933; d. Richard T. and Hazel (Beard) Weller; m. Marvin Bluestein, Mar. 7, 1954. BS, U. Cin., 1956, MEd, 1959, EdD, 1966. Diplomate Am. Bd. Profl. Psychology. Psychologist-in-tng. Longview State Hosp., Cin., 1956-58; sch. psychologist Cin. Pub. Schs., 1958-65; asst. prof. psychology U. Cin., 1965-70, assoc. prof., 1970-79, prof., 1979-93, prof. emerita, 1993—, dir. sch. psychology program, 1965-70, co-dir. sch. psychology program, 1970-75, dir. undergrad. studies, 1976-91, dir. undergrad. advising, 1991-93. Cons. child psychologist. Sec., U.S. exec. com. rsch. Children's Internat. Summer Villages, 1964—68; chmn. Ohio Interuniv. Coun. Sch. Psychology, 1967. Editor Ohio Psychologist, 1961-68, co-editor, 1972-79; contbr. articles to profl. publs. Vol. Hamilton County Parks, 1982—, vol. naturalist, 1995—; vol. educator Cin. Zoo, 1982— Recipient George B. Barbour award, 1985, 20 Yrs. of Svc. award Cin. Zoo, 2002, Hamilton County Parks Dist., 2002. Mem. AAUP, APA, Nat. Assn. School Psychologists, Ohio Psychol. Assn. (citation 1972, Disting. Svc. award 1968), Southwestern Ohio Sch. Psychol. Assn., Cin. Psychol. Assn. (sec. 1961-62), Sch. Psychologists Ohio, Forum for Death Edn. and Counseling, Kappa Delta Pi, Sigma Delta Pi, Psi Chi (award for outstanding mentor 1985, award for outstanding contbns. to undergrad. psychology students 1994). Avocations: horseback riding, photography. Office: U Cin Dept Psychology Ml 376 Cincinnati OH 45221-0001

BLUESTONE, ELLEN HOPE, literature, writing, and women's studies professor, writer; b. Miami, Fla, Oct. 8, 1950; d. Alexander Herbert and Shirley Anne (Kalin) Bluestone; m. Christopher Albert Wilmot (div.); children: Jessica Dawn Wilmot, Richard Alexander Wilmot, Andrew S. H. Wilmot. BA in Art History, Wellesley Coll., Mass., 1971; MA in English, Villanova U., Pa., 1986; grad. Philosophy and Appreciation of Art, The Barnes Found., Merion, Pa.; doctoral cand. in English, Rutgers U., New Brunswick, N.J. Instr. English Harcum Coll., Bryn Mawr, Pa., 1981—82, União Cultural Brasil- U.S., Sao Paulo, Brazil, 1982—84, Harcum Coll., Bryn Mawr, Pa., 1984—86; tchg. asst. and English instr. Rutgers U., New Brunswick, NJ, 1987—92, Douglas Coll., 1991; instr. English West Chester U., Pa., 1997—99, Pa. State U., Media, 1999—2001, West Chester U., 2000—02, 2003—05, Immaculata U., 2003—04, Widener U., 2004—05; instr. English and women's studies Pa. State U., Media, 2004—06; instr. bus. writing Strayer U., 2006—. Conf. organizer Edn. in New Communities, Washington, 1972; corp. English instr. Banco Crefisul, Sao Paulo, Brazil, 1982—84; dir. Main Line Arts Ctr., 1986; instr. tech. writing Rohm and Haas, Ft. Washington, Pa., 1999; instr. writing Am. Inst. Chartered Property Casualty Underwriters, Malvern, Pa., 2000; tchr. art history Acad. Learning in Retirement Widener U., Exton, Pa., 2004—05; tech. writer InGrid, Inc., 2006; fellow Pa. Writing and Lit. Project, 2005, Nat. Writing Project, 2005; freelance writer, 1975—; resume cons., Gladwyne, Pa., 1979—81. Juried Art Exhibition, Delaware County C.C., 2000. Jr. Great Books tchr. The Gladwyne Sch., Pa., 1983, 1987; inner city vol. Phila., 1996. Named Outstanding Faculty Mem., Interfraternity and Panhellenic Council, West Chester U., 2005; recipient Margaret Esmonde award, Grad. Sch. Arts and Scis. Villanova U., 1986. Mem.: Sisters in Crime (Del. Valley chpt.). Avocations: painting, writing, gardening, swimming, pets. Home: A 508 750 Old Lancaster Rd Berwyn PA 19312 Office Phone: 484-913-1490.

BLUH, BONNIE, scriptwriter, actress, novelist, playwright; b. NYC, Mar. 29; d. Morris and Mary (Steinberg) Bluh; children: Craig, Kenn, Brian. Cons. Lincoln Repertory Theater, N.Y.C., 1962; dir. improvisational theater East Brunswick (N.J.) Jr. H.S., 1965; creative drama tchr., Phila., 1968-71; Emmy judge, 1989—; mentor Young Writers Inst., West Hartford, Conn., 1995—; lectr. in field. Author: Woman to Woman, 1974, Banana, 1976, The Old Speak Out, 1979, The Eleanor Roosevelt Girls, 1979, (plays) N, My Name is Nicki, 1962, Light a Candle for Charlie, 1964, Lifetime Policy, 1975, The Day God Died, 1992; co-editor: Broadway's Fabulous Fifties, 2002; actor: Many Wonder, 1989, Jesus Christ is Alive, 1990, One Woman Show, 1991, and assorted TV roles. Recipient Best Actor award, Festival Short Films, N.Y., 1990. Mem. AFTRA, Authors Guild, New Dramatists (alumna exec. com.), Dramatists Guild. Jewish. Home: 55 Bethune St New York NY 10014-2010 Personal E-mail: bbluh@aol.com.

BLUHM, BARBARA JEAN, communications agency executive; b. Chgo., Mar. 5, 1925; d. Maurice L. and Clara (Miller) B. Student Coll. William and Mary, 1943-45; BS, U. Wis., 1947. Exec. tng. program Carson Pirie Scott & Co., Chgo., 1947-52; home economist Lever Bros. Co., Chgo., 1952-57; field rep. The Merchandising Group, Chgo., 1957-62, v.p. N.Y.C., 1962-82, pres., 1982-87, chmn., 1987-90. Publicity chmn. James Lenox House Assn., N.Y.C., 1980—90; vol. Venice Little Theatre; active Coll. Club of Venice, Venice Art Ctr., Venice Symphony, Friends of the Venice Libr. Mem. Venice Yacht Club, Venice Area Hist. Soc. Republican. Presbyterian. Home: 1470 Colony Pl Venice FL 34292-1550 Personal E-mail: bbluhm@iopener.net.

BLUITT, KAREN, information technology executive; b. NYC, Oct. 25, 1957; d. James Bertrand and Beatrice (Kaufman) B.; m. Kenneth Mark Curry, Nov. 24, 1979 (div. Dec. 1991). BS, Fordham U., 1979; MBA, Calif. State Poly. U., 1982; postgrad., George Mason U., 1994-98; PhD, Kennedy Western U., 2000. Software engr. Hughes Aircraft Co., Fullerton, Calif., 1979-81; microprocessor engr. Beckman Instruments Co., Fullerton, 1981-82, Singer Co., Glendale, Calif., 1982-83; sr. software engr. Sanders Assoc., Nashua, NH, 1983-85; software project mgr. GTE Corp., Billerica, Mass., 1985-86; sr. software engr. Wang Labs., Lowell, Mass., 1986-87; project task leader Vanguard Rsch., Lexington, Mass., 1987-88; program mgr. Applied Rsch. & Engring., Bedford, Mass., 1989-91, Sparta, McLean, Va., 1992-93; prin. software engr. Sci. Applications Internat., Arlington, Va., 1993-94; tech. mgr. CACI, Arlington, 1994, Booz-Allen & Hamilton, Vienna, Va., 1995, MRJ Tech. Solutions, Inc., Fairfax, Va., 1996-97, Softek Systems, Inc., Fairfax, 1998—2001; pres. QSCI, Ashburn, Va., 2001—. 1st lt. U.S. Army, 1979-88. Scholar Gov. N.Y. Scholarship Com., 1975-79, Beta Gamma Sigma, 1978—. Mem. IEEE, AAUW, Am. Women in Sci., Am. Brokers Network, Assn. Computing Machinery, Soc. Women Engrs., Wash. Soc. of Engrs. Office Phone: 703-328-9661. Personal E-mail: karens-mail2007@yahoo.com.

BLUM, BARBARA DAVIS, investor; b. Hutchinson, Kans. d. Roy C. and Jo (McKinnon) Davis; children: Devin, Hunter, Ragan, Davis. BA, Fla. State U., 1960, MSW, 1961. Founder, ptnr. Mid-Suffolk Ctr. for Psychotherapy, Hauppage, L.I., NY, 1965-67; v.p. Restaurant Assocs. Ga., Inc., Atlanta, 1967-75; dep. adminstr. U.S. EPA, Washington, 1977-81; mem. Pres.'s Interagy. Coordinating Coun.; chair, pres., CEO Abigail Adams Nat. Bancorp and Adams Nat. Bank, Washington, 1983-98; CEO BDB Investment Partnership, 1998—; chair MainSt. Bank, 2003—. Chair U.S./Japan Environ. Agreement, 1977—81; head 1st U.S. Environ. Del. to China, 1978; chmn. Environ. Policy Inst., 1981—84; sr. advisor UN Environ. Program, 1981—84; pres. UN Univ. Peace, 1986—89; chair emeritus Ctr. for Policy Alternatives; trustee Fed. City Coun., 1988—99; nat. adv. bd. U.S. SBA, 1993—2001; chmn. D.C. Econ. Devel. Fin. Corp., 1986—2002. Del. UN Mid Decade Conf. on Women, 1980; Presdl. appointee trustee and treas. Inst. Am. Indian Art, 1992—; founder, chmn. Leadership Washington, 1989—; trustee, treas. Southeastern U.; trustee, chmn. investment com. DC Retirement Bd.; bd. chmn. Main St. Bank; dep. dir. Carter-Mondale U.S. Presdl. campaign, 1976; dir. Carter-Mondale Transition Team, Washington, 1976—77; panelist Clinton-Gore Econ. Conf., Little Rock and Atlanta; bd. dirs., chmn. performance com. Kaiser Found. Health Plan Mid Atlantic, 1989—2004; bd. dirs., chair compensation com. Kaiser Found. Health Plan, Inc., 2001—05; bd. dirs., chair exec. com. Kaiser Found. Hosp., 2002—04; bd. dirs., treas. Stimpson Ctr., 2002—. Decorated comdr.'s cross Order of Merit W. Ger.; recipient Disting. Svc. award Federally Employed Women, Spl. Conservation award Nat. Wildlife Fedn., Orgn. of Yr. award Ga. Wildlife Fedn., 1974, Disting. Svc. award Americans for Indian Opportunity; named Bus. Woman of Yr. Nat. Assn. Bus. Women, Leukemia Soc., Assn. Women Contractors, Vol. of Yr., Leadership Grerden, Washington, 2006. Mem. Washington Women's Forum, Internat. Women's Forum, Cosmos Club. Democrat. Personal E-mail: bdavisblum@verizon.net.

BLUM, BETTY ANN, footwear company executive; Student, Vanderbilt U. Various positions Zayre Dept. Store, Framingham, Mass., 1970-75; divsn. pres. Mootsie Tootsies, pres. Jones N.Y., exec. v.p. Maxwell Shoe Co., Hyde Park, Mass., 1976-88, exec. v.p., 1988—. Mem. bd. women's study group Brandeis U., 1998. Trustee Dana Farber Cancer Inst., 1998; dir. 210 Internat. Found., 1991.

BLUM, DIANE S., human services manager; Bachelor's Degree, U. Rochester; Master's Degree, SUNY, Buffalo. Social work supr. Meml. Sloan-Kettering Cancer Ctr. and the Dana Farber Cancer Inst.; joined Cancer Care, Inc., N.Y.C., 1984, dir. social svc., exec. dir. Co-founder Nat. Breast Cancer Awareness Month; bd. mem. The Cure for Lymphoma Found.; com. mem. Cancer Info. Svc., Nat. Cancer Inst., Am. Assn. Ret. Persons, Rose Kushner Award, United Way N.Y., ECOG, Intercultural Cancer Coun., United Hosp. Fund; fellow Brookdale Ctr. on the Aging, Hunter Coll., CUNY; lectr. in field. Contbr. articles to profl. jours. Recipient Lifetime Achievement award, Nat. Breast Cancer Awareness Month Bd. Sponsors, Spl. Recognition award, Nat. Coalition for Cancer Survivorship, award, Republic Bank Breast Cancer Rsch. Found. Mem.: NASW, Nat. Alliance Breast Cancer Orgns. (co-founder), Am. Soc. Clin. Oncology (sr. editor OnLine, com. mem.), Assn. Oncology Social Workers (com. mem.). Office: Cancer Care Inc 275 7th Ave Fl 22 New York NY 10001

BLUM, EVA TANSKY, lawyer; b. Pitts., July 29, 1949; d. Harry and Jeanette N. Tansky; 1 child. BA, U. Pitts., 1970, JD, 1973. Bar: Pa. 1973. Atty. U.S. Dept. Commerce, Washington, 1973-76, U.S. Air, Washington, 1976-77; sr. v.p., dir. cmty. devel. PNC Fin. Group, Pitts., 1990—, chair PNC Found., 2002—, dir. PNC Grow Up Great, 2003—. Mem. com. Pitts. Health and Welfare Planning Assn., 1985-89; bd. dirs. Family Health Coun., Pitts., 1987-94, Forbes Health Found., 1992-96, WQED, Pitts., 1994—, U. Pitts. Alumni Assn., 1992-98, 2000—, The Ellis Sch., 1996-2002; bd. dirs., sec. ARC Western Pa. chpt. 1992-94; trustee Am. Jewish Com., Pitts., 1977—. Mem. ABA, Pa. Bar Assn., Allegheny County Bar Assn. Office: PNC Fin Svcs Group One PNC Plaza 249 5th Ave Pittsburgh PA 15222-2709 Office Phone: 412-762-2748. Business E-Mail: eva.blum@pnc.com.

BLUM, JOAN KURLEY, not-for-profit fundraiser, marketing executive, consultant; b. Palm Beach, Fla., July 27, 1926; d. Nenad Daniel and Eva (Milos) Kurley; m. Robert C. Blum, Apr. 15, 1967 (dec. Apr. 2001); children: Christopher Alexander, Martha Jane, Louisa Joan. BA, U. Wash., 1948. Cert. fund raising exec. U.S. dir. Inst. Mediterranean Studies, Berkeley, Calif., 1962-65; devel. officer U. Calif., Berkeley, 1965-67; pres. Blum Assocs., Fund-Raising Cons., San Anselmo, Calif., 1967-92; ptnr. Philmark Australia, 1980—2001; pres. The Blums of San Francisco, 1992-2001, ret., 2001. Mem. faculty U. Calif. Extension, Inst. Fund Raising, S.W. Inst. Fund-Raising U. Tex., U. San Francisco, U.K. Vol. Movement Group, London, Australasian Inst. Fund Raising. Contbr. numerous articles to profl. jours. Mem. Marin County Civil Grand Jury, 2004—05. Recipient Golden Addy award Am. Advt. Fedn., Silver Mailbox award Direct Mail Mktg. Assn., Best Ann. Giving Time-Life award, others; decorated commdr. Sovereign Order St. Stanislas. Mem. Nat. Soc. Fund-Raising Execs. (dir.), Nat. Assn. of Hosp. Devel., Women Emerging, Rotary, Fund Raising Inst. (Australia), Tahoe Yacht Club. Office: 202 Evergreen Dr Kentfield CA 94904-2708 Business E-Mail: sugarblum@aol.com.

BLUM, LENORE, mathematician, computer scientist, educator; m. Manuel Blum; 1 child, Avrim. PhD, MIT, 1968; LLD Mills Coll. (hon.), 1999. Postdoctoral fellow, lectr. U. Calif., Berkeley, 1968—73; faculty mem. Mills Coll., 1974—99; prof. computer sci. Carnegie Mellon U., Pitts., 1999—. Vis. prof. math. and computer sci. City U. Hong Kong, 1996—98; vis. prof. CUNY, 1985—86; vis. scientist TJ Watson Rsch. Ctr. IBM, 1987; spkr. in field. Author (with F. Cucker, M. Shub, S. Smale): Complexity and Real Computation, 1997; contbr. articles to profl. jours. Recipient Career Advancement award, NSF, 1983. Mem.: AAAS (chair math. sect. 1998—99), Am. Math. Soc. (pres., coun. 1990—92), Math/Sci. Network, Assn. for Women in Math. (pres. 1975—78), Math. Scis. Rsch. Inst. (co-dir. 1975—81), Internat. Computer Sci. Inst. Office: Dept Computer Sci Wean 4105 Carnegie Mellon Univ Pittsburgh PA 15213-3891

BLUM, LISA CARRIE, social worker, researcher; b. N.Y., Nov. 11, 1961; BA magna cum laude, Douglass Coll., 1983; MSW, Rutgers U., 1985, PhD, 1996. LCSW Bd. of Social Work Examiners, N.J., 1994. Clin. program coord. Women Aware, Inc. Abused Women's Svcs., New Brunswick, NJ, 1986—94; planning rsch. cons. Atlanta (Ga.) Jewish Fedn., 1994—98; grants evaluator Friedman Supporting Found., Atlanta, 1996—98; coord. outpatient geriatric svcs. Jewish Family and Vocat. Svc., Edison, NJ, 2000—03; trainer Women Aware, Inc. Abused Women's Svcs, 2001—; sr. program coord. Highland Park Sr./Youth Ctr., NJ, 2004—. Adj. faculty Sch. Social Work Rutgers U., New Brunswick, 1985—91; cons. in field. Adv. bd. Project SPAN, Edison, 1989—; commr. Middlesex County Commn. on Missing and Exploited Children, New Brunswick, 1990—92; mem. Middlesex County Child/Adult Protection Coalition, New Brunswick, 1986—94. Grantee, Fahs-Beck Found., 1992; scholar, Rutgers U., 1986—89. Mem.: NASW, N.J. Coalition Battered Women, Nat. Coun. Family Rels., Phi Beta Kappa. Achievements include development of National Model for Domestic Violence Response Teams now mandated under New Jersey Law. Office: Highland Park Sr Youth Ctr 220 S Sixth Ave Highland Park NJ 08904

BLUM, TERRY C., dean; b. Bklyn., Dec. 25, 1953; m. Paul M. Roman; children: Lue, Faith Elisabeth. BA in sociology with honors, Bklyn. Coll., 1976; MA, Columbia U., 1978, MPhil, 1980, PhD, 1982. Asst. prof. orgnl. behavior and human resource mgmt. Ga. Inst. Tech. Coll. Mgmt., 1986—88, assoc. prof., 1988—92, prof., 1992—, dir. Ctr. Entrepreneurship and New Venture Devel., 1996—2000, Tedd Munchak chairholder in entrepreneurship, 1996—, dean, 1999—. Mem. Prevention and Epidemiology Initial Review Group Nat. Inst. Alcohol Abuse and Alcoholism, 1988—92; mem. cmty. prevention and control study section NIH, 1997—2000. Grantee, Nat. Inst. Alcohol Abuse and Alcoholism, 1982, 1983, 1987, 1988, Nat. Inst. Drug Abuse, 1991, 1999, NIH, 1993, 1994, Coleman Found., 1999; special opportunities grant, Whitaker Found., 1998. Office: Ga Inst Tech Coll Mgmt 800 W Peachtree St NW Atlanta GA 30332-0520 Office Phone: 404-894-4924. Office Fax: 404-894-6030. Business E-Mail: terry.blum@mgt.gatech.edu.

BLUMBERG, ADELE ROSENBERG, volunteer; b. Harrisburg, Pa., Jan. 19, 1916; d. Robert and Mary (Katzman) Rosenberg; m. Leonard Blumberg, June 16, 1940; children: Joyce Kozloff, Bruce, Allen. AB, Dickinson Coll., Carlisle, Pa., 1937; grad. cum laude, Froelich Sch. Music, Harrisburg, 1932. Tchr. piano, various cities, 1933-47; with Pa. Dept. Pub. Assistance, Harrisburg, 1937—40; assoc. pubr. Somerset Star, Somerville, NJ, 1951-55; sec. Raritan Valley Pub. Co., Manville, NJ, 1951—55. Pres. Somerville Coun., 1954—55, Rolling Hill Girl Scouts U.S., 1966—72, Bridgewater Raritan High Sch. PTO; pres., sec., bd. dirs. Bridgewater (N.J.) Local Assistance Bd., 1957—94; bd. dirs. Somerset County Jewish Family Svc., 1980—89, Inst. Arts and Humanities Edn., NJ, 1983—94, People Care Ctr., Finderne, NJ, 1985—91, Arts Found. N.J., New Brunswick, 1986—93, George St. Playhouse, 1997—2000, Bridgewater Com. Creative Arts, 1995—, Brook Art Ctr., 2001—, Somerset County Cmty. Concerts, Opera Theater N.J., Jewish Home for Aged, Somerset County, 1995—99; chmn. Printmakers Coun. N.J., 1975—79; past bd. dirs. Manville Red Cross, Somerset County Homemakers Svc., Somerset County Vis. Nurses, Bound Brook AAUW; pres. Somerset chpt. Hadassah, 1950—52, Jewish Fedn. Somerset County, 1974—76; past bd. dirs. Temple Shalom. Named Adele Blumberg Day in her honor, Mayor of Bridgewater, 1983, hon. alumna, Dickinson Law Sch., 1998; recipient Hannah G. Solomon award, Nat. Coun. Jewish Women, 1969, Israel Freedom award, 1976, Cmty. Patriot, Bridgewater Edn. Assn., 1976, Tercentenary award, Bd. Freeholders and Cultural and Heritage Commn. Somerset County, 1988, Good Scout award, Boy Scouts Am., 1993, award, Leonard and Adele Blumberg Edn. Found. Bridgewater-Raritan, 1995, Citizen of the Yr. award, Somerset C. of C., 1998, Hon. award, Dickinson Law Sch., 1998. Mem.: AAUW, Zonta (v.p. 1970—71). Democrat. Jewish. Avocations: music, piano, needlecrafts, travel, photography. Address: 1820 Woodland Ter Bound Brook NJ 08805-1449

BLUMBERG, BARBARA SALMANSON (MRS. ARNOLD G. BLUMBERG), retired state housing official, housing consultant; b. Bklyn., Oct. 2, 1927; d. Sam and Mollie (Greenberg) Salmanson; m. Arnold G. Blumberg, June 19, 1949 (dec. June 1989); children: Florence Ellen Schwartz, Martin Jay, Emily Anne. BA, De Pauw U., 1948; postgrad., New Sch. for Social Rsch., N.Y.C. Mem. pub. rels. dept. Nate Fein & Co., N.Y.C., 1948-51; freelance pub. rels. cons., 1960—; councilwoman North Hempstead, N.Y., 1975-82; adviser to energy com. N.Y. State Assembly, N.Y.C., 1982-84; dir. spl. needs housing Divsn. Housing and Cmty. Renewal, State of N.Y., 1984-89, ret., 1989. Mem. bd. visitors Pilgrim State Hosp. Pres. UN Assn. Great Neck, N.Y., 1967-69, chmn. China Study Workshop, 1966-67; pres. Shalom chpt. Hadassah, 1955-57; exec. v.p. Lakeville PTA, Great Neck, 1963-65, Great Neck South Jr. H.S., 1965-66; co-chair UNICEF, Great Neck, 1968-70, spkrs. bur., 1971—; v.p. Herricks Cmty. Life Ctr., 1976-77, B'nai B'rith, Lake Success, N.Y.; coord. 6th Congl. Dist., N.Y. McGovern for Pres.; bd. dirs. New Dem. Coalition Nassau, Am. Jewish Congress, Day Care Coun. Nassau County, Citizens Sch. Com., Great Neck; active Reform Dem. Assn. Great Neck; platform com. Nassau Dem. Com.; del. Dem. Nat. Conv., 1992; adv. com. to spkr. N.Y. State Assembly; resource coun., housing devel. com. Cmty. Advocates; chair North Hempstead Housing Authority; trustee L.I. Power Authority, 1994-96. Recipient award Anti-Defamation League, New Hyde Park, N.Y., 1975, Alumni award DePauw U., 1977, Hadassah New Life award, 1980, Women's Pole of Honor, North Hempstead, 1994. Mem. North Shore Archeol. Assn. (chmn. study group), Women in Comm., Internat. Platform Assn., L.I. Womens Network (co-convenor), Interfaith Nutrition Network (v.p.), Cmty. Advocates (bd. dirs.), Mental Health Assn. Nassau County (bd. dirs.), North Shore NAACP, N.Y. Alumni Club DePauw U. (trustee), Alpha Lambda Delta.

BLUMBERG, BETTY LOU, education educator; b. New Haven, July 20, 1936; d. Adolph and Sylvia (Levine) Perlroth; m. Joseph Richard Blumberg, Dec. 20, 1956; children: Nancy Mae, Debra Lee. BA, Vassar Coll., Poughkeepsie, N.Y., 1957; MS, So. Conn. State Coll., New Haven, 1967; CAS, Wesleyan U., Middletown, Conn., 1981, M in Humanities, 1995. Tchr. English Hillhouse H.S., New Haven, 1957-59; lectr. English Albertus Magnus Coll., New Haven, 1965-71; tchr. English Hamden Hall County Day Sch., Hamden, Conn., 1971—2001, dept. chair English, coord. 7-12, 1982—92, chmn., 1985; adj. prof. English Quinnipac U., 2001—. Tchr. docent com. Yale U., Brit. Art Mus., 1992—; student tchr. supr. Albertus Magnus/Hamden Hall, Yale U., 1973, 86; book reviewer Hadassah, Tower One, B'nai Jacob Synagogue, Hamden Libr., Branford Libr., Temple Emanuel. Bd. dirs. Tower One, Tower East, New Haven, 1986; mem. bd. edn. B'nai Jacob Synagogue, 1990-91; lead tchr. New Haven Holocaust Tchr. Group. Shakespeare Studies fellow Yale U., summer 1958; recipient citation Women in Leadership, YWCA, 1991, Disting. Tchr. commendation Hamden Hall, 1983. Mem. New Haven Vassar Club (bd. dirs., alumni rep. to coun. 1986—), Cum Laude Soc. Hamden Hall (sec. 1986—2001). Democrat. Jewish. Avocations: reading, art, tennis. Office: Quinnipiac Univ Adjunct Office Hamden CT 06517 Business E-Mail: bettylou.blumberg@quinnipiac.edu.

BLUMBERG, GRACE GANZ, lawyer, educator; b. NYC, Feb. 16, 1940; d. Samuel and Beatrice (Finkelstein) Ganz; m. Donald R. Blumberg, Sept. 9, 1959; 1 child, Rachel. BA cum laude, U. Colo., 1960; JD summa cum laude, SUNY, 1971; LLM, Harvard U., 1974. Bar: N.Y. 1971, Calif. 1989. Confidential law clk. Appellate Divsn., Supreme Ct., 4th Dept., Rochester, NY, 1971-72; tchg. fellow Harvard Law Sch., Cambridge, Mass., 1972-74; prof. law SUNY, Buffalo, 1974-81, UCLA, 1981—. Reporter Am. Law Inst., Prins. of the Law of Family Dissolution, 2002. Author: Community Property in California, 1987, Community Property in California, rev. edit., 1999, 2003, Blumberg's California Family Code Annotated; contbr. articles to profl. jours. Office: UCLA Sch Law Box 951476 Los Angeles CA 90095-1476

BLUMBERG, SHERRY HELENE, Jewish education educator; b. Mar. 7, 1947; BA in Drama Edn., U. Ariz., 1969; MA in Librarianship, San Jose State U., 1973; MA in Jewish Edn., Hebrew Union Coll., L.A., 1976, PhD in Jewish Edn., 1991. Cert. Reform Jewish educator. Sr. reference specialist Stanford (Calif.) U. Libr., 1969-73; dir. edn. B'nai Israel, Sacramento, 1976-79, Temple Israel, Long Beach, Calif., 1979-85; assoc. prof. Jewish edn. Hebrew Union Coll.-Jewish Inst. Religion, N.Y.C., 1985-99; vis. assoc. prof. Jewish edn. Gratz Coll., York, Pa., 1999; dir. edn. Congregation Shalom, Milw., 1999—2004, Congregation Am Echod, Lindenhurst, Ill., 2004—; adj. prof. St. Francis Sem., Milw., 2002—, lectr., 2002—; adj. prof. U. Wis., Milw., 2004—. Participant 1st internat. sem. on interreligious dialogue, Beijing, 1998. Author: God: The Eternal Challenge, 1980, A Teacher's Guide To Rooftop Secrets and Other Stories of Anti-semitism, 1987; co-author: Death, Burial and Mourning in the Jewish Tradition, 1978, Divorce in the Jewish Tradition, 1979, Teaching About God and Spirituality: A Resource for Jewish Settings, 2002. Mem. exec. bd. Coalition for Jewish Learning, Milw., 2001—; mem. editl. and adv. bd. for women's Torah commentary project Women of Reform Judaism. Mem. Internat. Seminar on Religious Edn. and Values, Assn. Profs. and Rschrs. in Religious Edn. (mem. nat. bd. 1993-96), Religious Edn. Assn. (exec. bd. 1991-2000, acting pres. 1995-96, pres. 1999-2000), Union Am. Hebrew Congregations (exec. bd. com. Jewish edn. 1997-2000), ASCD, Nat. Assn. Temple Educators, Coalition on Advancement Jewish Edn. (v.p. ednl. resources 2004—). Office: Congregation Am Echod 2945 Falling Water Blvd Lindenhurst IL 60046 Office Phone: 847-265-1818. E-mail: blumberg@teacher.com, education@amechod.org.

BLUME, GINGER ELAINE, psychologist; b. Lock Haven, Pa., Apr. 8, 1948; d. Martin Luther and Virginia Ruth (Rudy) B. BA, U. Fla., Gainesville, 1970, MA, 1975, PhD, 1979. Predoctoral intern in psychology VA Hosp., West Haven, Conn., 1976-77; postdoctoral intern in psychology Elmcrest Psychiat. Inst., Portland, Conn., 1977-78; pvt. practice clin. psychology Dr. Ginger E. Blume and Assocs., Middletown, Conn., 1978—. Assoc. Harrison Assocs., Inc., Cons., Berkeley, Calif.; co-owner, program dir. PMT Assocs. Inc.; co-owner/trainer TeamMasters; mem. affiliated faculty New Eng. Type Inst.; mem. adj. psychology faculty Middlesex C.C., Antioch Grad. Sch., Keene, N.H.; bd. dirs. Gilead House, halfway facility, SAFE, sexual assault clinic, Family Resource Ctr.; developer Doc-U-Chart; cons. in field. Host daily AM radio talk show, 1996-2000; monthly columnist on psychology Middletown Press, 1996—; co-author 3 workbooks on managing violence. Recipient President's award, CPA, 2003, 1st 2d, and 3d prize adults, Patton Writing Contest, 2002, 2003, 2004, 2005. Fellow APA (bus. of practice network, rep. for state of Conn. 1997-2003), mem. ASTD, Conn. Psychol. Assn. (chmn. mktg., Disting. Contbn. in Media award 1996), Orthopsychiatry Assn., Internat. Imagery Assn., AAUW (chmn. edn. found. program), Soroptimists, Exch. Club, Phi Kappa Phi, Kappa Delta. Achievements include being world's youngest twin engine female pilot at age 17. Home: 77 Oak Ridge Dr Haddam CT 06438-1053 Office: 300 Plz Middlesex 2d Fl Middletown CT 06457-5153 Office Phone: 860-346-6020 x1. E-mail: gblumeasso@aol.com.

BLUME, JUDY, author; b. Elizabeth, N.J., Feb. 12, 1938; d. Rudolph and Esther (Rosenfeld) Sussman; m. John M. Blume, Aug. 15, 1959 (div. Jan. 1975); children: Randy Lee, Lawrence Andrew; m. George Cooper, June 6, 1987; 1 stepchild, Amanda. BA in Edn., NYU, 1960; LHD (hon.), Kean Coll., 1987, Endicott Coll., 1995. Author: (fiction) including The One in the Middle is the Green Kangaroo, 1969, Iggie's House, 1970, Are You There God? It's Me, Margaret (selected as outstanding children's book 1970), Freckle Juice, 1971, Then Again, Maybe I Won't, 1971, It's Not the End of the World, 1972, Tales of a 4th Grade Nothing, 1972, Otherwise Known as Sheila the Great, 1972, Deenie, 1973, Blubber, 1974, Forever, 1975, Starring Sally J. Freedman as Herself, 1977, Superfudge, 1980, Tiger Eyes, 1981, The Pain and the Great One, 1984, Just As Long As We're Together, 1987, Fudge-A-Mania, 1990, Here's to You, Rachel Robinson, 1993, Double Fudge, 2002 others; (adult novels) Wifey, 1977, Smart Women, 1984, Summer Sisters, 1998; (other writings) Letters to Judy: What Kids Wish They Could Tell You, 1986; exec. producer (25 min. film) Otherwise Known As Sheila The Great, Barr Films, 1988. Founder, trustee The Kids Fund, 1981. Recipient Carl Sandburg Freedom to Read award Chgo. Pub. Libr., 1984, The Civil Liberties award ACLU, 1986, John Rock award Ctr. for Population Options, 1986, Margaret A. Edwards for lifetime achievement ALA, 1996, medal for disting. contbn. to Am. letters, Nat. Book Found., 2004; numerous Children's Choice award, U.S.A., Europe, Australia. Mem. Authors Guild (bd. dirs.), Nat. Coalition Against Censorship (adv. bd.), Soc. Children's Book Writers (bd. dirs.). Jewish. Office: c/o William Morris Agy 1325 Ave of Ams New York NY 10019

BLUME, WENDY M., dean; d. Solomon and Shirley Malkoff; m. Charles Barnett Blume, May 19, 1974; children: Jonathan, Jeffrey, Seth. BSc, Case Western Res., 1973; MSc, Thomas Jefferson U., 1977; EdD, Temple U., 1994. Program dir. Manor Jr. Coll., Jenkintown, Pa., 1986—87; faculty C.C. Phila., 1987—2000, dept. chair, 1991—98, acting dean, 1998—2000; dean, math, sci. health careers Camden C.C., Blackwood, NJ, 2000—. Bd. govs. health acad. Phila. Sch. Dist., 1998—2000; bd. mem. Nat. Network NN2, 2003—04; participant Nat. Inst. Leadership Devel. Author: (textbook) The Phlebotomy Text, 2001; peer reviewer: Jour. Allied Health, 2003—04, co-author articles in field. Office: Camden County Coll Box 200 Coll Dr Blackwood NJ 08012

BLUMENFELD, ANITA, community relations consultant; b. London; came to U.S. d. Samuel and Eva (Lehrman) Leigh; m. George Blumenfeld; children: Michael Russell, Vincent Joseph. Student, City of London Coll. Adminstrv. asst. Jewish Nat. Fund & Mogen David Adom (Israeli Red Cross), London, 1951-55; field cons. AMIT Women, L.A., 1978-81; pub. rels. rep. Mercury Savs. & Loan, Long Beach, Calif., 1981-84; cmty. rels. dir. Ams. AMIT Women for Torah & Israel, L.A., 1986-90. Editor, collator: British Evacuees during World War II, 1977-79; compiler: Social Action Conference Reports, 1977, 79, 85. Social action chmn. Temple Menorah, 1970-79; co-pres. Vols. for Israel, 1988-89; del. to Soviet Union, Refusniks, 1990—; active various other civic orgns. Recipient Humanitarian award, Temple Menorah, L.A., 1994. Mem. Amnesty Internat., Ams. for Safe Israel, Hadassah. Jewish. Avocations: reading, travel, interpretive dance. Home: 2743 W 233rd St Torrance CA 90505-3111

BLUMENFELD, JOAN, architect; m. Bob Krone; 2 children. BA in Philos. Psychology, U. Chgo.; MArch, Harvard U. Prin. Swanke, Hayden, Connell Archs., N.Y., 1999—. Active N.Y. New Visions; bus. bd. dirs. Pro Mujer. Mem.: AIA (com. planning and urban design), IFMA, Soc. Am. Registered Archs., Comml. Real Estate Women. Office: SHCA 295 Lafayette St New York NY 10012

BLUMENTHAL, KAREN, newspaper executive; Bus. editor Dallas Morning News, 1992-94; dep. bur. chief Dallas bur. The Wall St. Jour., 1994-96, bur. chief Dallas bur., 1996—2004; sr. editor WSJ Reports, 2004—. Author: Six Days in October: The Stock Market Crash of 1929, 2002, Let Me Play, 2005. Office: The Wall St Jour 1201 Elm St Ste 5050 Dallas TX 75270-2141

BLUMENTHAL, RONNIE, lawyer; b. Passaic, N.J., Nov. 27, 1944; d. Paul and Marga (Stern) B. BA, George Washington U., 1966, JD, 1969. Bar: D.C. 1969. Gen. atty. EEOC, Washington, 1969-71, spl. asst. to commr., acting chmn., 1971-78, sr. atty., 1978-82, dir. spl. svcs. staff, 1982-85, dir. compliance programs, 1985-91, acting dir. Office of Communications-Legis. Affairs, 1991-92; spl. asst. U.S. atty. Dept. Justice, Washington, 1992, dir. Office Fed. Ops., 1992-99, mediator, 1999—. Legis. fellow U.S. Senate, 1982; chmn. Performance Review Bd., Exec. Resources Bd; lectr., cons. in field. Mem. ABA, D.C. Bar Assn., Fed. Bar Assn., Exec. Women in Govt., Womens Bar Assn., Soc. Profls. in Dispute Resolution. Home: 853 Vanderbilt Beach Rd # 327 Naples FL 34108-8746 Office Phone: 202-297-1191. Personal E-mail: ronnieblum@aol.com.

BLUMENTHAL, SUSAN JANE, psychiatrist, educator; m. Edward John Markey. BA, Reed Coll., Portland, Oreg., 1971; MD, U. Tenn., 1976; MPA, Harvard U., Cambridge, Mass., 1982; PhD (hon.), Trinity Coll., Washington, 1996, Ben Gurion U., Israel, 2005, Pine Manor Coll., Chestnut Hill, Mass. Diplomate Am. Bd. Psychiatry and Neurology. Intern. Stanford U. Sch. Medicine, 1976-77, residency and fellowship, 1977-80; fellow NIMH, 1980-81, assoc. dir. Psychiatry Tng. Rev., head suicide rsch. unit and coord. of project depression, 1982-85, chief behavioral medicine program, 1985-93, chief behavioral and basic prevention rsch. br., 1991-93; clin. asst. prof. Tufts Med. Ctr., 1981-82; clin. asst. prof. psychiatry George Washington Sch. Medicine, 1982-86; clin. assoc. prof. psychiatry Georgetown Sch. Medicine, 1986-91, clin. prof. psychiatry Washington, 1991—; first dep. asst. sec. women's health HHS, Washington, 1993—97, asst. surgeon gen., 1996—2005, sr. med. and e-health advisor, 2002—05, sr. sci. advisor, 2002—05, sr. global health advisor, 2003—05, sr. advisor for health and medicine Ctr. for the Study of the Presidency, 2006—; clin. prof. psychiatry Tufts Sch. Medicine, 1995—; assoc. v.p. for health affairs George Washington U. Med. Ctr., 1998; pres. Global Health Inst. LLC, Washington, 2006—; sr. advisor for sci., health and medicine Ctr. Study of the Presidency, 2006—. Vis. prof. ob-gyn. George Washington U. Med. Ctr., 1998-99; disting. vis. prof. women's studies Brandeis U., 1999—; vis. prof. Stanford U., 2004-; hon. prof. Ben Gurion U. Sch. Medicine, 2004-, med. dir. discovery/AFI global health series, 2006—; chair NIH Coord. Com. on Health and Behavior, 1991-94; co-chair NIH Reunion Task Force, 1992-94; chair Fed. Coord. Com. Breast Cancer, fed. coord. com. women's health and the environ., co-chair nat. breast cancer action plan; coord. Com. Women's Health Issues and Domestic Violence, 1994-98; mem. Pres.'s Interagy. Coun. on Women; sr. advisor pub. health White House Coun. on Youth Violence, 2000-02, sr. advisor on pub. health and sci. to the sec., USDA, 2000-02; vis. fellow Harvard U. Sch. Govt., 2004-05; pres. Global Health Inst., LLC 2006-; vis. prof. Mayo Clinic, 2005. Editor: Suicide Over the Life Cycle, 1989, Premenstrual Syndrome, 1985; mem. editl. bds.: Jour. Women's Health, Depression, health columnist: Elle Mag., Ladies Home Jour., U.S. News and World Report; med. dir.: Discovery/AFI global health film series; chief med. advisor: PBS Health Initiative; contbr. articles to sci. jours. Mem. Nat.

Commn. on Sleep Disorders Rsch., workgroup on mental health Pres. Task Force on Health Care Reform; U.S. rep. global commn. on Women's Health WHO; trustee Meridian Internat. Ctr., 2005—, Save the Children, Acad. Achievement, Hadassah HMO. Capt. USPHS, 1992-94, rear adm., 1994—. Recipient Outstanding Svc. medal, 1989, Commendation medal, 1990, Meritorious Svc. medal, USPHS, 1992, Sec.'s Honor award for Domestic Violence, 1996, Asst. Sec. for Health's award for Breast Cancer, 1996, Am. Med. Writers award, 1996, Gretchen Poston award, The Nat. Race for the Cure, 1996, Founder's award, 1996, Pub. Svc. award, Nat. Alliance for the Mentally Ill, 1996, Surgeon Gen.'s Exemplary Svc. medal, 1997, Gracie award, Assn. Women Radio and TV Profls., 1997, Inspiration Leader award, Pa. Diabetes Assn., 1997, Spl. Assignment Svc. medal, 1998, 2002, Women of Distinction award, Nat. Assn. Women in Higher Edn., 1998, Woman of Valor award, United Jewish Fedn., 1999, Mosaic award, Komen Found., 2000, Founder's award, 2000, Feminist First award for Health, Feminist Majority, 2000, Congl. award, 2001, Congl. citation, 2002, Achievement medal, 2002, Women's Ctr. Leadership award, 2003, Leadership award, Save the Children, 2004, Nat. Breast Cancer Awareness Pub. Svcs. Leadership award, 2004, Disting. Svc. award, Spirit of Life Found., 2004, Presdl. Sacher Medallion, Brandeis U., 2005, Disting. Svc. medal, USPHS, 2006; fellow, Harvard U. Sch. Govt., 2004. Mem. AMA, Am. Psychiat. Assn. (cons. Joint Coun. on Pub. Affairs, Francis Braceland award for pub. svc. 1998), Am. Coll. Psychiatrists, Am. Med. Women's Assn. (past chair com. on publicity and pub. rels., Pres.'s citation, 1996), Congl. Club, Nat. Assn. Bus. and Profl. Women (Magnificent Seven award 1996), Internat. Club, Internat. Women's Forum, Am. Suicide Found. (past bd. dirs. Washington divsn., pres.), Starlight Found. (past chmn. sci. adv. bd.). Office: Global Health Inst PO Box 6298 Washington DC 20015 Office Phone: 240-432-0281.

BLUMSTEIN, RENEÉ J., educational research and evaluation consultant; b. Bklyn., Apr. 1, 1957; d. Robert and Rosalie (Burak) B.; m. Vic DiVenere, May 12, 1996; children: Robert Victor DiVenere, Joseph Dante DiVenere. BA, Queens Coll., N.Y., 1978; MA, Columbia U., 1980, MEd, 1982, MPhil, 1984, PhD, 1986. Rsch. psychologist CCNY, 1980-85; rsch. cons. AT&T, N.Y.C., 1986; rsch. analyst Citibank, N.Y.C., 1986-87, ednl. rsch. cons., 1987—, rsch. and statis. cons. L.I.; adj. prof. rsch. methods CUNY, 1990—99. Scholar Columbia U., 1981. Mem. APA, AAUW, Nat. Assn. Women Bus. Owners, Am. Edn. Rsch. Assn. Avocations: travel, biking, swimming. Home and Office: 14 Ingold Dr Dix Hills NY 11746-7804 Office Phone: 631-427-1661. E-mail: rjb@researchforeducation.com.

BLUNT, JOYCE OMEGA, special education educator; d. Herbert and Rosemary Blunt. BA, So. U. New Orleans, 1978; MA, Xavier U., 1982; postgrad., Southeastern U., 1986. Chair, black history, grade, student coun. advisor Harahan, La., 1998—2004; mem. spl. edn. adv. coun. Jefferson Parish, Harvey, 1995—; tchr. Granville T. Woods Elem. Sch., Kenner, La. Parent tchr. rep. Harahan, 1998—2003, dollars for scholars, 1998—2004. Named Outstanding Young Educator, Metairie Jaycees, 1994, Walmart Tchr. Yr., 2002, Reading Tchr. Yr., La. Reading Coun., Jefferson, 2002. Mem.: Nat. Assn. Univ. Women (edn. chair), Jefferson Fed. Tchrs. Union (mem.-at-large 1986—). Baptist. Avocations: travel, shopping. Home: 7924 Macon St Metairie LA 70003

BLUNT, KATHRYN LONDON, writer, scriptwriter; b. Aug. 31, 1934; Student, Midwestern U., Tex. Author: The Universe Would Have No Reason to Exist Without Man to Comprehend It, 1993, Gossemer's Wings, 1993, A Lamp Needs Not Another Lamp for Its Illumination, 1993, Born of an Angel's Seed_natured in the Womb of Time, 1993, Wings Within, 1994, Remnants For Your Pleasure-Soaring Above the Heights of Life, 1994, Cogito-Ergo-Sun, 1995, Last Tasty Morsels to be Savored as Your Palate Will Allow, 1995, (with John Edward Blunt) Anteres, 1999-01, (with John Edward Blunt) Mutation's of Evolutions's, 2002: author: (screenplays) The Eighth Day, 1999, The Golden Luster, 1999, Vigil of Venus, 1999, Mountains of the Moon, 1999, Visa Tergo, 2001, The Fairy Stone, 2001, The Last Manuscript, 2003, Studio Secretary, 2004, Under Four Flags, 2005, The Fifth World, 2005, New Age, 2005, Exordian, 2006. Mem. Nat. Resources Def. Coun., World Wildlife Fund, Nature Conservancy, Guissepe Armani Sculptors, Ocean Conservancy, Nat. Trust Hist. Preservation, Hollywood Arts Coun., Smithsonian Inst., Nat. Trust Hist. Preservation, U.S. Sailing Club.

BLUNTZER, CHISPA HERNÁNDEZ, artist, educator; b. Caracas, Venezuela, Mar. 31, 1932; came to the U.S., 1948; d. Jose Benigno and Anita (Espinal) Hernández; m. Robert Dougherty Bluntzer, Aug. 23, 1952; children: Mary Ellen, Christopher, Dianna. AAS in Interior Design, Nat. Art Sch., 1952; BFA in Painting with highest honors, Tex. A&M U., 1991; postgrad., NYU, 1995. Watercolor instr. Art Ctr. Corpus Christi, 1989, Victoria (Tex.) Art Assn., 1991,. Smith Art Workshops, Caracas, 1993, Ateliers san Frontiers, Les Cerqueux s/Passavant, France, 1998; gallery lectr. Art Mus. South Tex., Corpus Christi, 1991; instr. children's summer art program Creative Art Ctr., Corpus Christi, 1992; adj. prof. art Tex. A&M U., Corpus Christi, 1992, 95; trustee Art Mus. South Tex., Corpus Christi, 1986—. One-woman shows Corpus Christi Mus., 1981, Josek's of Tex., Corpus Christi, 1981, Bay Front Plaza Arts and Sci. Ctr., Corpus Christi, 1985, Thomason Gallery, Ft. Worth, 1985, Corpus Christi Pub. Libr., 1987, Corpus Christi State U., 1991, Art Ctr. Corpus Christi, 1993, Kucera Gallery, 2004; group exhbns. include Bonner/White Gallery, Corpus Christi, 1983, Tiburon Gallery, Austin, 1986, Zanesville (Ohio) Art Ctr., 1987, Western Colo. Ctr. for the Arts, Grand Junction, 1988, S.W. Craft Ctr., San Antonio, 1988, Art Mus. South Tex., Corpus Christi, 1992, 98, U. Tex. Health Sci. Ctr., San Antonio, 1992, Weil Gallery Tex. A&M U., Corpus Christi, 1995, Art Ctr. Corpus Christi, 1995, 97, 2003-04 (award 2004), Transco Towers Galleries, Houston, 1995, Multicultural Ctr., Corpus Christi, 1996-98, Art Mus. South Tex., Corpus Christi, 1997, 99, Rockport (Tex.) Art Ctr., 1998-99, Tex. Inst. for the Arts, Corpus Christi, 1998, Wilhelmi/Holland Gallery, Corpus Christi, 1998, Cain Meml. Gallery Del Mar Coll., Corpus Christi, 1999, 2003, Victoria Regional Mus., 2004, others; represented in permanent collections Art Mus. South Tex., Corpus Christi Mus. Sci. and History, Commerce Bank, Corpus Christi Bank & Trust, Corpus Christi Cathedral, Nations Bank, Corpus Christi, Saumur Oil, Corpus Christi, Porter Oil, Corpus Christi, Landmark Condominiums, Corpus Christi. Pres. PTA S. Cyril and Methodius Sch., Corpus Christi, 1962-63; leader Girl Scouts Am., Corpus Christi, 1969-70. Mem. Nat. Watercolor Soc., Watercolor Soc. South Tex. (pres. 1978-79), Soc. Layerists in Multi Media, Western Fedn. Watercolor Socs. Roman Catholic. Avocations: gardening, reading, travel, writing. Home: 230 Circle Dr Corpus Christi TX 78411-1233

BLUTH, B. J. (ELIZABETH JEAN CATHERINE BLUTH), sociologist, aerospace technologist; b. Phila., Dec. 5, 1934; d. Robert Thomas and Catherine Cecelia (Boxman) Gowland; m. Thomas Del Bluth, Aug. 20, 1960 (dec. Aug. 6, 1980); children: Robert Thomas, Richard Del. BA in Sociology (Washington semster fellow), Bucknell U., 1953; MA, Fordham U., 1960; PhD, UCLA, 1970. Teaching fellow in methods of social research Fordham U., 1957-58; reading instr. St. Margaret's High Sch., Tappahannock, Va., 1958-59; instr. history, civics and English, Rosary High Sch., San Diego, 1959-60; successively instr., asst. prof. sociology Immaculate Heart Coll., Los Angeles, 1960-65; prof. sociology Calif. State U., Northridge, 1965-87; grantee NASA Ames Research Ctr., Moffett Field, Calif., 1982-83; grantee space sta. program NASA, Washington, 1983-87, aerospace technologist system engring. div. space sta. program office Reston, Va., 1987-90, spl. asst. to dep. program dir. space sta. freedom program and ops., 1990-94, spl. tech. asst. to dir. edn. divsn., mgr. edn. evaluation Washington, 1994—2006, program mgr. on-line edn. evaluation program, 1994—2006. Cons. Immaculate Heart Cmty., L.A., 1967-69; engring. rsch. NASA Space Sta. design Boeing Aerospace Co., 1982-83; mem. Presdl. Citizens Adv. com. on Space, Coun. Nat. Space Policy, Nat. Tech. Com. on Soc. and Tech., UN team on relevance of space activities to econ. and social devel.; professor emeritus Calif. State U., 1987—; computational scis. and informatics inst. dir.'s search com. George Mason U., 1992-93. Editor: (with others) Search for Identity Reader, vol. I and II, 1973, (with S.R. McNeal) Update on Space, vol. I, 1961, Parson's General Theory of Action, 1982, Space Station Habitability Report, 1983, Soviet Space Station Analog, 1983, Space Station Human Productivity Study NASA, 1986, Russian Mir Space Station Analog, 1993, Marching with Sharpe, 2001; contbr. articles to profl. jours. Recipient Alpha Omega faculty awards, 1966, 1974. Fellow Am. Astronautical Soc.; mem. AIAA (chpt. award for outstanding program 1980), Am. Sociol. Assn., L5 Soc., Brit. Interplanetary Soc., Inst. Social Sci. Study of Space (acad. adv. bd.), Space Studies Inst., Internat. Acad. Astronautics (com. on space econs. and benefits), Phi Beta Kappa. Republican. E-mail: bjb@patriot.net.

BLY-MONNEN, APRIL M., quality assurance professional; b. Akron, Ohio, Apr. 15, 1949; d. Chester Thomas Monnen and Rita M. Cassinelli; m. Charles A. Bly. BS in Edn., Miami U., 1970; PhD in Instrnl. Tech., U. Va., 1983. Cert. ISO internal quality auditor. Sr. instrnl. designer Applied Sci. Assocs., Butler, Pa., 1986-92; tech. info. mgr., quality assurance mgr. INOVA Corp., Charlottesville, Va., 1995—2005. Mem. ASTD, Am. Soc. for Quality (chmn. sect. 1108 Blue Ridge 2002-04, treas. 2005—), Acad. Am. Poets, N.Y. Acad. Sci. Avocations: handcrafts, amateur botany. Home: 777-D Mountainwood Rd Charlottesville VA 22903 Office: Sperry Marine 1070 Seminole Tr Charlottesville VA 22901

BLYSTONE, DEBRA A., social studies educator; b. Indiana, Pa., May 29, 1953; d. Donald E. and Jane L. (Prescott) Blystone. BS in Edn. (hon.), Youngstown State U., Ohio, 1975, MS in Edn., 1979. Cert. Tchr. Grades 1-8 Ohio Dept. Edn., 1975. Tchr. grades 2d, 4th, 6th and 8th Austintown Local Schs., Ohio, 1976—96, 7th grade social studies tchr., 1996—. Lead mentor tchr. Austintown Local Schs., Ohio, 2000—, lead social studies tchr., 2002—; sec. Austintown Edn. Assn., Ohio. Mem.: NEA, Ohio Edn. Assn. (assoc.). Office Phone: 330-797-3923.

BLYTH, ANN MARIE, retired secondary school educator; b. Sharon, Pa., June 18, 1949; d. Chester Stanley and Mary Clara (Romian) Kacerski; m. Lynn Allan Blyth, June 26, 1976 (dec. June 1983); 1 stepchild, Breton Alan Blyth; 1 child, Amanda Lynn. BS in Edn., Kent State U., Ohio, 1971; postgrad., Loyola U., New Orleans, 1973-74; MS in Teaching, John Carroll U., University Heights, Ohio, 1978. Cert. comprehensive sci., maths. and physics tchr., Ohio. Jr. high math. tchr. New Philadelphia Bd. of Edn., Ohio, 1971-72; high sch. sci. and math. tchr. Hubbard Exempted Village Bd. of Edn., Ohio, 1972-76, Painesville City Local Bd. Edn., Ohio, 1976—2006; head dept. sci. Harvey H.S., 2001—06; ret., 2006. Instr. math. Morton Salt, Painesville, 1979-80; part-time faculty Lake Erie Coll., 1992. Mem. Adv. Bd. Western Res. br. Am. Lung Assn. of Ohio, Painesville, 1986-89, sec, 1988-89, Northeastern br., Youngstown, Ohio, 1989-99; judge state level Nat. Pre-teen and Pre-Teen Petite Pageants, 1990. Martha Holden Jennings Found. scholar, 1984-85; named Tchr. of the Yr., Harvey High Sch. Key Club, 1981-82. Mem. NEA, Ohio Edn. Assn., Northeastern Ohio Edn. Assn., Painesville City Tchrs. Assn., Am. Assn. Physics Tchrs. (Ohio sect.), Nat. Sci. Tchrs. Assn., Sci. Edn. Coun. Ohio, Cleve. Regional Coun. of Sci. Tchrs. Democrat. Episcopalian. Avocations: travel, gourmet cooking, baking, gardening, music. Home: 7243 Scottsdale Cir Mentor OH 44060-6408

BLYTH, MYRNA GREENSTEIN, publishing executive; b. NYC, Mar. 22, 1939; d. Benjamin and Betty (Austin) Greenstein; m. Jeffrey Blyth, Nov. 25, 1962; children: Jonathan, Graham. BA, Bennington Coll., Vt., 1960. Sr. editor Datebook mag., N.Y.C., 1960-62, Ingenue mag., N.Y.C., 1963-68; book editor Family Health mag., 1968-71; book and fiction editor, then assoc. editor Family Circle mag., N.Y.C., 1972-78, exec. editor, 1978-81; editor-in-chief Ladies' Home Jour., 1981—2002, pub. dir., sr. v.p., 1987—2002, former editor-in-chief, pub. dir.; editor-in-chief, pub. dir. More Mag., 1998—2002, v.p., editl. dir., 2002—03; with new product devel. Meredith Corp., 2002—03; freelance writer. Chmn. Pres.' commn. White House Fellows, 2002—; mem. adv. com. for ORIWH, NIH. Author: Cousin Suzanne, 1975, For Better and For Worse, 1978, Spin Sisters, 2004; columnist: Nat. Rev. Online, NY Sun; contbr. articles to New Yorker mag., New York mag., Redbook mag., Cosmopolitan mag., Readers Digest. Del. White House Conf. on Aging; mem. nat. adv. bd. Susan G. Komen Breast Cancer Found.; mem. adv. com. ORWH at NIH; mem. Pres.' Commn. on White House Fellows, chmn. Recipient Headliner award Women in Comms., Inc., 1992, Human Rels. award, Am. Jewish Com.'s Pub. Divsn., 1992, Henry Johnson Fisher award, 1999. Mem.: Women's Forum, Women's Media Group, N.Y. Women in Comm., Inc. (past pres., Amb. of Excellence, Matrix award 1988), Am. Soc. Mag. Editors, Overseas Press Club (bd. govs.), Authors League. Personal E-mail: myrnablyth@aol.com.

BLYTHE, MARY SUSAN, retired elementary school educator; b. Berkley, Calif., Dec. 15, 1945; d. Roy William and Mary Josephine (Burks) Corriston; (div. 1973); m. Holly John Blythe, Mar. 24, 1984. Assoc., Kansas City Community Coll., 1965; BSE, Emporia State U., Kans., 1968; M., Emporia State U., 1975. Cert. elem. tchr., Kans. Tchr. Kansas City Pub. Schs., 1968-74, elem. sci. coord., 1974—2001, sch. improvement facilitator, 2002—03, coach math. instrn., 2003—05, ret., 2005. Instr. Avila Coll., Kansas City, Mo., 1986—; faciliator State Kans. Sci. Outcome Writing Team, 1992-93, state sci. stds. writer, 1996; devel. sci. materials ctr. Kansas City (Kans.) Public Schs. 1991-92; Kans. state sci. assessment writer, 2000; adj. prof. Park U., Emoria State U. Co-writer and editor elem. sci. curriculum guide. Mem. Kansas City Zoo Docent Orgn., 1984-1993. Recipient Environ. award MACD, 1977, Allis-Chalmers Environ. Conservation award NACD, 1978, Disting. Svc. award Sci. Pioneers Orgn., 1990, Outstanding Sci. Educator award-Adminstr. Adv. Sci. Health Assn. Reaching Excellence, 1991; grantee State of Kans., 1991. edn. program enhancement, 1991-92. Mem. Nat. Sci. Tchrs. Assn. (conv. mgr. nat., regional 1990, 93), Kansas Assn. Tchrs. Sci. (bd. dirs. 1976-78), Kansas City Jaycees (v.p. 1981, Outstanding Dir. 1980), Friends of Zoo, Delta Kappa Gama. Democrat. Mem. Cmty. Christ Ch. Avocations: fossil collecting, camping, shopping. Office: John F Kennedy Elem 2600 North 72nd Kansas City KS 66109

BLYWISE, BARBARA, mental health services professional; b. Cleve., Nov. 17, 1947; d. Robert Taussig Blywise and Ruth Eleanor Schimberg; m. Richard Erwin Porter (div.); 1 child, Michael Blywise Porter. BA, U. Wash., Bothell, 1996; MA, Seattle U., Wash., 2000. Lic. mental health counselor Wash. Mgr. Martin of London, LA, 1974—81; office mgr. Kings Cabinet, LA, 1981—83; adminstrv. asst. Bear Stearns, LA, 1983—88, Shearson Lehman, Seattle, 1989—90; adminstrv. asst., human resources Oppenheimer Co., Seattle, 1990—93; adminstrv. asst. Merrill Lynch, Bellevue, Wash., 1993—96; clinician III Federal Way Youth and Family, Wash., 1999—2004; pvt. practice, 2004—. Mem.: Am. Mental Health Counselor Assn., Am. Psychol. Assn. Democrat. Jewish. Avocation: jewelry making. Home: 31849 48th Cir SW Federal Way WA 98023 Office: Agy Ctr 402 S 333d St Ste 129 Federal Way WA 98003 Office Phone: 253-929-1529. Office Fax: 253-874-4382. Business E-Mail: b.blywise@comcast.net.

BOAC, THELMA BLANTUCAS, principal; b. Bohol, Philippines, Feb. 13, 1950; d. Diego Campos and Crispina Blantucas de Vera; m. Danilo Sales Boac, July 7, 1973; children: Roland Culajara, Maria Rosalie Culajara. BA, San Francisco State U., 1972; MA in Edn., San Jose State U., 2001. Professional Clear Adminstrv. Credential Calif., 2002. Resource specialist Independence H.S., San Jose, Calif., 1981—90, h.s. villa prin., 2001—05; prin. Silver Creek H.S., San Jose, Calif., 2005—. Edn. cons. Northside Cmty. Ctr., San Jose, 1999—. Bd. mem. Benevolent Assn. Eastside Employees, San Jose, 2005, Human Develop. Internat., 2005. Recipient Dr. Martin Luther King, Jr. Good Neighbor award, Martin Luther King Assn. of Santa Clara County, 2005. Mem.: Nat. Assn. of Secondary Sch. Prins. (assoc. Dr. Jose Rizal Heroes Award 2001). Roman Catholic. Avocations: playing the piano, singing, dancing, travel, kickboxing. Home: 839 Clearview Dr San Jose CA 95133 Office: Silver Creek High Sch 3434 Silver Creek Rd San Jose CA 95121 Office Phone: 408-347-5811. Home Fax: 408-937-0358. Personal E-mail: dboac@comcast.net. Business E-Mail: boact@esuhsd.org.

BOADLE-BIBER, MARGARET CLARE, physiologist, educator; b. Melbourne, Australia, Jan. 18, 1943; arrived in U.S., 1967; d. Campbell Dean and Constance Ellen (Browne) Boadle; m. Thomas Ulrich Leonard Biber, Oct. 8, 1969; 1 child, Eric Gustav Nicholas Biber. BS, U. Coll. London, 1964; DPhil, Oxford (Eng.) U., 1967. Rsch. assoc. pharm. dept. Yale U. Sch. Medicine, New Haven, 1968-69, instr. pharm. dept., 1969-71, asst. prof. pharm. dept., 1971-75; assoc. prof. physiology dept. Va. Commonwealth U., Richmond, 1975-87, prof., 1987—, interim chair, 1991-93, chair, 1993—. Contbr. articles to profl. jours. Mem.: Soc. Neuroscience, Am. Soc. Pharm. and Exptl. Therapeutics, Am. Soc. Neurochemistry. Office: Va Commonwealth U 1101 E Marshall St Richmond VA 23298-0551 Office Phone: 804-828-9756. Business E-Mail: mbiber@vcu.edu.

BOAL, MARCIA ANNE RILEY, clinical social worker; b. Carthage, Mo., Sept. 29, 1944; d. William Joseph and Thelma P. (Simpson) Riley; m. David W. Boal, Aug. 12, 1967; children: Adam J. W., Aaron D. Boal. BA, U. Kans., 1966, MSW, 1981. Lic. clin. social worker. Child therapist Gillis Home for Children, Kansas City, Mo., 1981; social worker Leavenworth (Kans.) County Spl. Edn. Cooperative, 1981-84; sch. social worker, dir. health and social svcs. Kans. State Sch. for the Blind, Kansas City, Kans., 1984—2004. Pvt. practice individual and family counseling and workshops, 1981—; field instr. Sch. of Social Welfare Kans. U., 1986—. Author: Surviving Kids, 1983, Teaching Social Skills to Blind and Visually Impaired Children, 1987, Kansas Sate School for the Blind Social Skills Curriculum, 2002. Nat. networking chmn. Jr. League Kansas City, 1977—81; bd. dirs. Wyandotte House Inc., 1973—81, Kans. Action for Children, Topeka, 1981, Gov.'s Commn. on Parent Edn., Topeka, 1984—. Named Kans. Sch. Social Worker of Yr., 1989. Mem. Council Exceptional Children, Nat. Assn. Social Workers, Kans. Assn. Sch. Social Workers, Am. Orthopsychiat. Assn., Kans. Conf. Social Welfare, R.P. Found., Internat. Critical Incident Stress Found., Phi Kappa Phi. Home: Lake Of The Forest Bonner Springs KS 66012 Office: 10601 Kaw Dr Ste B Edwardsville KS 66111 Office Phone: 913-441-3030. Personal E-mail: mboal@marciaboal.com.

BOALER, JO, education educator; BSc in Psychology, U. Liverpool, Eng., 1985; MA in Math. Edn., London U., 1991, PhD in Math. Edn., 1996. Tchr. secondary sch. math., Camden, London, 1986—89; dep. dir. math. assessment project King's Coll., London U., 1989—93, lectr., rschr. on math. edn., 1993—98; assoc. prof. Stanford (Calif.) U., 2000—. Mem. Math. Edn. Study Panel; bd. dirs. Gender and Edn. jour. Mem.: Internat. Orgn. for Women in Math. Edn. Office: Stanford U Sch Edn 485 Lasuen Mall Stanford CA 94305-3096

BOARDMAN, EUNICE, retired music educator; b. Cordova, Ill., Jan. 27, 1926; d. George Hollister and Anna Bryson (Feaster) Boardman. B. Mus. Edn., Cornell Coll., 1947; M. Mus. Edn., Columbia U., 1951; Ed.D., U. Ill., 1963; DFA (hon.), Cornell Coll., 1995. Tchr. music pub. schs., Iowa, 1947-55; prof. music edn. Wichita State U., Kans., 1955-72; vis. prof. mus. edn. Normal State U., Ill., 1972-74, Roosevelt U., Chgo., 1974-75; prof. mus. edn. U. Wis., Madison, 1975-89, dir. Sch. Music, 1980-89; prof. music, dir. grad. program in music edn. U. Ill., Urbana, 1989-98; ret. Author: Musical Growth in Elementary School, 1963, 6th rev. edit., 1996, Exploring Music, 1966, 3d rev. edit., 1975, The Music Book, 1980, 2d rev. edit., 1984, Holt Music, 1987; editor: Dimensions of Musical Thinking, 1989, Dimensions of Musical Thinking: A Different Kind of Music, 2002, Up the Mississippi: A Journey of the Blues, 2002. Named to MENC Hall of Fame, 2004. Mem. Soc. Music Tchr. Edn. (chmn. 1984-86), Music Educators Nat. Conf. Avocations: reading, antiques.

BOARDMAN, MAUREEN BELL, community health nurse, educator; b. Hartford, Conn., June 11, 1966; d. Jack Russell and Mary Elizabeth (Brumm) Bell; m. Byron Earl Boardman, June 4, 1988; children: Meghan Elizabeth, Cameron Phillip. BSN, U. Maine, Orono, 1988; MSN, U. Tenn., 1991. RN, Tenn.; ACLS; cert. family nurse practitioner. Charge nurse med.- surg. divsn. Scott County Hosp., Oneida, Tenn., 1988-89, employee health nurse, 1989-92; nurse team leader Oneida Home Health, 1989, Quality Home Health, Oneida, 1989-90; FNP Straightfork Family Care Clinic, Pioneer, Tenn., 1992-96, Huntsville (Tenn.) Family Care Clinic, 1996-98, Oak Grove Primary Care Clin., 1998-2001, Cmty. Health Ctr., Hanover, NH, 2001—04, Bradford Health Svcs., 2004—. Mem. child abuse rev. team Dept. Human Svcs., Huntsville, Tenn., 1993-2001; adj. prof. Coll. Nursing U. Tenn., 1997-2001; instr. cmty. and family medicine Dartmouth Med. Sch., 2001—. Med. advisor, liaison Scott County (Tenn.) Sch. Systems Sci. Fair Com., 1992-2001; bd. dirs., editor newsletter Appalachian Arts Coun., Oneida, 1993-2001, v.p., 1996-98, del., 1997; com. on health policy TNA, 1998-2000. Mem. Sigma Theta Tau (sec. Gamma Chi chpt. 1996-2000). Roman Catholic. Avocations: reading, biking, swimming, dance. Home: PO Box 958 Bradford VT 05033 Office: Bradford Health Svcs 437 S Main St Bradford VT 05033 also: Bradford Health Svcs 437 S Main ST Bradford VT 05033 Office Phone: 802-222-9317. Personal E-mail: maureen.b.boardman@hitchcock.org. Business E-Mail: maureen.b.boardman@dartmouth.edu.

BOAST, MOLLY SHRYER, lawyer; b. Cin., Apr. 10, 1948; d. Davis Maxwell Shryer and Mary Stratton (Bowlby) Baird; m. Thomas Hansen Boast, Sept. 4, 1971; 1 child, Emma Alice. BA with gen. honors, Coll. William & Mary, 1970; MS in Journalism, Columbia U., 1971, JD, 1979. Bar: N.Y. 1980, U.S. Dist. Ct. (so. dist.) N.Y., U.S. Dist. Ct. (ea. dist.) N.Y., U.S. Ct. Appeals (1st cir.), U.S. Ct. Appeals (2d cir.), U.S. Ct. Appeals (3d cir.), U.S. Supreme Ct. Teaching asst. Columbia U. Grad. Sch. Journalism, NYC, 1971-72; writer, pub. rels. George Jr. Republic, Dryden, NY, 1973-76; assoc. Le Boeuf, Lamb, Leiby & MacRae, NYC, 1979-87, ptnr., mem. exec. com., chmn. litigation dept., 1988; sr. dep. dir. and dir. Bur. of Competition, FTC, 1999—2001; ptnr., mem. litig. dept. Debevoise & Plimpton LLP, NYC, 2001—. Sec., bd. dirs. N.Y. Lawyers for the Pub. Interest, N.Y.C., 1989-99; bd. dirs. Vols. Legal Svc., Inc., N.Y.C. Named Harlan Fiske Stone scholar Columbia U. Sch. Law, N.Y.C., 1979; recipient Jane Marks Murphy prize Columbia U. Sch. Law, N.Y.C., 1979. Mem. ABA (chair ins. industry com. antitrust sect. 1992-95, coun. 1995-98, editl. vice-chmn. Antitrust Law Jour. 1990-92), Fed. Bar Coun. (chair com. on second cir. cts. 1990-93, v.p. 1991-94, trustee 1995-99), City Bar Assn. (chair fed. ctr. com. 2004—), Mortar Bd. Avocations: bicycling, swimming, gardening, reading, music. Office: Debevoise & Plimpton LLP 919 Third Ave New York NY 10022 Office Phone: 212-909-1069. Fax: 212-909-6836. E-mail: msboast@debevoise.com.

BOATWRIGHT, CHARLOTTE JEANNE, marketing professional, public relations executive; b. Chattanooga, Dec. 12, 1937; d. Clifton Jerry and Veltina Novella (Braden) Blevins; m. Robert W. Boatwright; children: Lynn Kay, Janis Ann, Karen Jean, Mary Ruth, Melody Susan, April Celeste. Diploma, Erlanger Sch. Nursing, Chattanooga, 1963; BS, U. Tenn., Chattanooga, 1976, MEd, 1981; student in Ministry, U. South, Sewanee, Tenn., 1984; PhD, Columbia Pacific U., San Rafael, Calif., 1987. Diplomate Nat. Assn. Forensic Counselors, Nat. Bd. Addiction Examiners; cert. domestic violence counselor Nat. Assn. Forensic Counselors; mediator Mediation Assn., Tenn. Supreme Ct., 1999. Surgeon's asst. William Robert Fowler, M.D., Chattanooga, 1963—64; instr. med.-surg. nursing Baroness Erlanger Hosp. Sch. Nursing, Chattanooga, 1964—67, instr. fundamentals nursing, 1971—74, chmn. dept. mental health-psychiat. nursing, 1977—81; staff nurse Meml. Hosp., Chattanooga, 1967—68, supr. nursing, 1968—70; dir. inservice edn. Hutcheson Med. Ctr., Ft. Oglethorpe, Ga., 1970—71; youth work cons. Sewanee Dist. Episcopal Chs., Chattanooga, 1975—76; dir. spl. projects N. Park Hosp., Chattanooga, 1984—87, dir. mktg. and pub. rels., 1987—. Pres. CBB Comm.; freelance writer; expert witness in field. Mem. editl. bd.: Rsch. Mag. Founder, pres. Domestic Violence Coalition Greater Chattanooga, 1994; bd. dirs. Family Violence Shelter Com., Sexual Abuse Resource Ctr., Child Abuse Prevention Coun.; mem. Cmty. Ptnrs. Neighborhood Change-Crime and Neighborhood Safety; crisis intervention homes prevention com. Partnership Families, Children and Adults, residential adv. com.; mem. fair housing roundtable Chattanooga; mem. endeavors re-entry roundtable Chatanooga; mem. coalition eliminate homelessness Faith Cmty. Svc. Network, Chatanooga; founding mem. Family Justice Alliance of Chattanooga, 2004; mem. dept. youth work Episcopal Diocese Tenn., 1975—77, mem. violence in soc. resource team, pres. diaconate formation com., 2002, mem. crisis response team; bd. dirs. Partnership Families, Children and Adults, Opportunity Home, Chattanooga; mem. oversight bd. Hamilton County Domestic Violence Task Force; bd. dirs. Crisis/Homelessness Prevention Svcs., Partnership Families, Children and Adults; vice chmn. Brynewood Park Cmty. Assn., 1985, 1986; coord. Chattanooga (Tenn.) Family Justice Alliance, 2004. Recipient Liberty Bell award, Chattanooga Bar Assn., 1997, Advocacy for Children award, S.E. Tenn. Coun. Children and Youth, 2000. Mem.: Nat. Assn. Forensic Counselors, Chattanooga C. of C., Chattanooga Press Assn., Tenn. Soc. Hosp. Mktg. and Pub. Rels., Tenn. Hosp. Assn., Am. Coll. Healthcare Execs. (nominee), U. Tenn. Alumnae Assn. Republican. Avocations: music, reading, gardening, travel. Personal E-mail: cbb1955@yahoo.com.

BOAZ, BETHANY L., secondary school educator; b. Springfield, Mo., Jan. 11, 1979; d. Clinton Roy and Judy Conrad; m. Keith Boaz. BS in English Edn., S.W. Mo. State U., Springfield, Mo., 2002. Cert. tchr. 5-12 English edn. Mo., 2002. Tchr. comm. arts H.S. Marionville (Mo.) Pub. Schs., 2002—. Mem.: Mo. State Tchrs. Assn. Office: Marionville Public Schools College & O'Dell Marionville MO 65705 Office Phone: 417-258-2521.

BOBAY, JENNIFER ANN, elementary school educator; b. Chgo., Apr. 21, 1973; d. Dennis Leo and Sandra Eileen Koziol; m. Patrick Joseph Bobay, June 30, 2001. BS in Edn., Ind. U., Bloomington, 1995; postgrad., Northeastern U., Chgo., 2003—. Tchr. 7th & 8th grade Diocese Ft. Wayne/South Bend, Ind., 1995—97; tchr. mid. sch. Diocese Chgo., 1997—98; cons., trainer Success for All Found., Balt., 1998—99; tchr. mid. sch. Chgo. Pub. Schs., 1999—2005, Glenview Dist. #34, 2005—. Local sch. coun. rep. Chgo. Pub. Schs., 2000—03; coord. sci. fair Cath. Schs., Ft. Wayne, 1995—2003, Chgo. Pub. Schs., 1995—2003; with Gear Up Inner City Mentoring Program, 2002—05. Co-planner golf outing Am. Cancer Soc., South Bend, Ind., 2004; vol. Am. Brain Tumor Assn., Des Plaines, Ill., 2004. Mem.: NEA, Nat. Sci. Tchrs. Assn. Democrat. Roman Catholic. Avocations: reading, walking, yoga, interior decorating. Office: Glenview Dist #34 2500 Chestnut Ave Glenview IL 60025 E-mail: pbobay@sbcglobal.net.

BOBB, CAROLYN RUTH, science writer; b. Flint, Mich., Jan. 9, 1955; d. Clarence Edward Bobb and Martha Elizabeth Maxwell; m. David A. Bazzett, June 25, 1977 (div. Feb. 1980); m. Theodore D. Spear. BS, Mich. State U., 1979; postgrad., U. Mich., Flint. Lab. med. technician Furda Biochem. Biopsy, Lansing, Mich., 1979; lab. technician Mich. Dept. Agr., East Lansing, 1979-81; forensic scientist Mich. State Police, East Lansing, 1981-89; writer Flint, 1991—. Forensic cons., Lansing, 1988-89. Mem. NAFE. Avocation: piano. Home: 939 Major St Flint MI 48507-2564

BOBB, MARIE L., mathematics educator; d. William and Antionette Maddison; children: Andrew Willian Tynon, Justin Cory Tynon. Associates, SUNY, Morrisville, 1988; BS, SUNY, Potsdam, 1990; MA, SUNY, Brockport, 1994. Permanent tchr. certification NY, 1995. Secondary math. tchr. Webster (NY) Thomas H.S., 1994—, dept. leader math., 2001. Cons. NY State Dept. Edn., Albany, 2006—, McDougal Littel, Evanston, Ill., 2006. Sec. Webster Athletic Assn., 2002—05. Mem.: ASCD (assoc.). Office: Webster Thomas High School 800 Five Mile Line Rd Webster NY 14580 Office Phone: 585-670-8000. Business E-Mail: marie_bobb@websterschools.org.

BOBEK, NICOLE, professional figure skater; b. Chgo., Aug. 23, 1977; Competitive history includes: mem. of 1st place team Hershey's Kisses Challenge, 1997, placed 13th in World Championships, 1997, 3rd in Nat. Sr., 1997, 2nd (team) U.S. Postal Svc. Challenge, 1996, 3rd (team) Hershey's Kisses Challenge, 1996, 10th place Centennial on Ice, 1996, 1st place Starlight Challenge, 1995, 3rd in World Championships, 1995, 1st in Nat. Sr., 1995, 2d place, World Pro Championship, 2000, 3d place, Canadian Open, 2001, numerous others. Champions on Ice Tour, 2000-. Avocations: dance, drawing, poetry, modeling, designing clothes. Office: USFSA 20 1st St Colorado Springs CO 80906-3624

BOBER, JOANNE L., lawyer; b. NYC, Dec. 14, 1952; BA, Wash. U., 1974; JD, Georgetown U., 1980. Bar: Tex. 1980. Assoc. Moore & Peterson, 1980—82, Jones, Day, Reavis & Pogue, NYC, 1983—88, ptnr., 1989—96; sr. v.p., gen. counsel, sec. Gen. Signal Corp., Stamford, Conn., 1997—99; sr. v.p., gen. coun. Chubb Corp., Warren, NJ, 1999—2005; sr. v.p., gen. counsel, sec. J.C. Penney Corp. Inc., Plano, Tex., 2005—. Mem.: ABA, Tex. Bar Assn., Phi Beta Kappa. Office: JC Penney Corp Inc 6501 Legacy Dr Plano TX 75024

BOBERG, DOROTHY KURTH, author; b. Lincoln, Nebr., Mar. 17, 1930; d. Herman R. and Regina E. Kurth; m. John Elliott Boberg, Sept. 17, 1951; 1 child, Mark. BA, U. Nebr., 1951; postgrad., Calif. State U., Northridge, 1959-62, U. So. Calif., 1981. Libr. Nebr. Legis. Coun., Lincoln, 1952; child welfare worker L.A. County, 1953-57, 67-68; rsch. assoc. Nuclear Facilities/Radiation Monitoring in Calif. Another Mother for Peace, Beverly Hills, Calif., 1975; exec. v.p. So. Calif. divsn. UN Assn., L.A., 1977-78. Author: Evolution and Reason Beyond Darwin, 1993; editor Nebraska Blue Book. Resolutions chair L.A. County Dem. Cen. Com.; chair UN Internat. Solar Exhibition, L.A., 1978, Mayor's Lifeline Com., Earthquake Prediction Task Force; pres. Northridge Civic Assn., 1971-73; founding bd. mem. Northridge East Neighborhood Coun., 2004; bd. dirs. Alliance for Democracy, 2004-05. Recipient Achievement award Nebr. Sec. State, 1993, Admiral, Nebr. Navy/Gov. State Nebr., 1993. Mem. AAAS, Soc. Study Evolution, AAUW (pres. San Fernando Valley Br. 1966-67), Phi Beta Kappa, Psi Chi, Alpha Kappa Delta. Home: 10912 Nestle Ave Northridge CA 91326-2849

BOBERG, LARON CAPBARAT, importer, retailer; b. San Rafael, Calif., May 2, 1947; d. Joseph Lauren and Anna Marion (Schlosser) Capbarat; m. Robert Arthur Boberg, Oct. 2, 1976; 1 child, Lauren Lynn. Student, No. Ariz. U., 1965-68, U. Hawaii, 1972, Hong Kong U., 1984. Realtor Frank Howard Adams Co., Novato, Calif., 1972-75; property mgr. R&B Devel. Co., Los Angeles, 1975-76; realtor Willoughby & Assocs., Portland, Oreg., 1980-82; owner Far East Shoppers, Hong Kong, 1983-85, Oriental Merc. Co., Raleigh, N.C., 1985—. Residential real estate broker Coldwell Banker; pres. NC Equity, 1990. Facilities chmn. N.C. Women's Resource Ctr., Raleigh, 1988; active in Women's Forum N.C., 1988. Named to Pres. Cir., Coldwell Banker. Mem. Triangle Chpt. N.C. World Trade Assn., N.C. Nat. Assn. Women Bus. Owners (pres. 1987-88). Avocation: travel. E-mail: roni@roniboberg.com.

BOBINO, RITA FLORENCIA, psychologist; b. San Francisco, June 18, 1934; d. Arthur Mortimer and Urania Theodorcia Cummings; m. Felix Joseph Bobino (dec.); children: Sharelle Hagg, Michael J, Mauricio J, Malaika J. AA, Laney Coll., 1973; BS in Sociology, Coll. of the Holy Names, 1975; MS, Calif. State U., Hayward, 1977; PhD, Wright Inst., 1985. Cert. Marriage Therapist State of Calif., 1980. Mental health therapist Berkeley Mental Health, Berkely, Calif., 1977—80; dir. alternative prog Cities in Schools Fremont H.S., Oakland, Calif., 1980—81, counselor, 1981—83; on-call sexual assault therapist Highland Hosp., Oakland, 1980—90; counselor Oakland Tech. H.S., 1983—87; prin. Far West H.S., Elmhurst Mid., Oakland, 1987—99; psychotherapist pvt. practice, Oakland, 1980—; prof. Calif. State U., Hayward, 1999—. Admin. asst. Oakland Poverty Program, 1960—71; dir., WIC program Children's Hosp., Oakland, 1973—76; co-founder and dir. Black Women and Men United, 1978—85, Relationship Strategists, 1979—88; juvenile diversion program Juvenile Hall, San Leandro, 1983—85; cons. Black Family Inst., Oakland, 2004—05, Dept. Defense Soldier and Family Life, MHN, Germany, 2005. Recipient Pi Gamma Mu. Soc. Sci. Honor award, Holy Names Coll., 1975, Charlene V. Carodine Unique Profl. Achievment award, Alpha Kappa Alpha, 63d Far Western Regional Conf., 1992. Democrat. Christian. Avocations: walking, yoga, reading, travel, writing. Home: 3833 Elston Ave Oakland CA 94602 Office: P O Box 27545 Oakland CA 94602 Office Phone: 510-569-3267.

BOBKA, MARLENE S., publishing executive; d. Rudolph J. and Marilyn E. Bobka; life ptnr. Glen H. Klag. BS in Biology, U. Albany, 1979, MLS, 1980. V.p. FOI Svcs., Gaithersburg, Md., 1985—. Rsch. grantee, AAAS, 1979. Mem.: Spl. Librs. Assn. (com. mem. 1980—2004). Office: FOI Svcs Inc 704 Quince Orchard #275 Gaithersburg MD 20878 Office Phone: 301-975-9400.

BOBNAK, MARSHA CORE, music educator; b. Martins Ferry, Ohio, Jan. 22, 1959; d. Marshall Barton and Gwendolyn I. (Reynard) Core; m. George Stephen Bobnak. BA in Music Edn. summa cum laude, Bethany (W.Va.) Coll., 1981; MusM in Choral Conducting, Westminster Choir Coll., Princeton, N.J., 1992. Cert. music educator, Pa. Tchr. gen. music, chorus Drexel Hill (Pa.) Middle Sch., 1983-88; choral dir. Haverford H.S., Havertown, Pa., 1987—; tchr. music Lynnewood Elem. Sch., Havertown, Pa., 1988—. Profl. flutist Tre Voci-Chamber Trio, Ardmore, Pa., 1986—; curriculum writer Haverford Music Dept., Havertown, 1988—; profl. soprano opera chorus Festival Dei Due Mondi, Charleston, S.C., 1992—; sponsor Tri-M Music Soc., Havertown, 1994—. Author: (directory) District 12 Music Tchrs., 1995. Mem. Am. Choral Dirs. Assn., Am. Guild of Organists, Pa. Music Edn. Assn., Iota Kappa Alpha Music Honor Soc., Lambda Epsilon Kappa Acad. Frat. Avocations: history, medieval history, acapella vocal music. Office: Haverford H S 200 Mill Rd Havertown PA 19083-3718

BOBO, GENELLE TANT (NELL BOBO), retired office administrator; b. Paulding County, Ga., Oct. 31, 1927; d. Richard Adolph and Mary Etta (Prance) Tant; m. William Ralph Bobo, May 1, 1948; children: William Richard, Thomas David (dec.). Student, Berry Coll., Mt. Berry, Ga., 1945—47. Exec. sec. Macon (Ga.) Kraft Co., 1951-54; med. sec. Drs. Loveman & Fleigleman, Louisville, 1954-55; tchr. Fulton County Schs., Palmetto, Ga., 1960-68; exec. sec. Rayloc, Atlanta, 1968-70; adminstrv. coord. U. Ga., Athens, 1970-77; assoc. to dir. Mission Svc. Corps, Home Mission Bd. So. Bapt. Conv., Atlanta, 1977-94; ret., 1994. Rschr., writer Sta. 11-TV, Atlanta, 1989. Author: Driven by a Dream, 1992. Philanthropy chmn. Exec. Women, Inc., Atlanta, 1968-69; mem. adv. coun. Baylor U., Waco, Tex., 1993-99; missionary, nat. sr. adult cons. N.Am. Mission Bd., 1994—. Mem. NAFE. Baptist. Avocations: public speaking, teaching, music, sewing, reading. Home: 87 Vickers Rd Fairburn GA 30213-1139 Office Phone: 770-969-8566.

BOBRUFF, CAROLE MARKS, radio producer, radio personality; b. N.Y.C., Nov. 11, 1935; d. Morris Frank and Harriet (Lehman) Marks; m. Jerome Bobruff, June 20, 1954 (div. 1986). Student, Quinnipac Coll., 1954-55, U. N.C., 1955-56; AS, U. New Haven, 1981; BS in Human Services, N.H. Coll., 1982. Founder, dir. Tyndall Air Force Daycare Ctr., Panama City, Fla., 1957-60; med. asst. Digestive Disease Assocs., New London, Conn., 1974-82; program coord. Pre-Trial Release Program, Norwich, New London, Conn., 1982-84; case mgr., counselor residential criminal justice program Cochegan House, Montville, Conn., 1984-85; exec. dir. Ret. Sr. Vol. Program So. New London County, 1984-91; producer, host nat. radio program A Touch of Grey, Groton, Conn., 1990-97; prodr., host Senior Focus Talk Am. Radio Network, Groton, Conn., 1997—; CEO Focus Commn. Treas. Dir. Vols. in Agys., New London, 1986—, Conn. RSVP Dirs., 1987; bd. dirs. Cochegan House, Widowed Persons Service, Waterford, Conn. Editor: Senior Citizens Guide to Discounts and Services, 1988; editor, author: RSVP Newsletter, 1984—; columnist: The Day, 1987. Pres. women's aux. New London County Med. Assn., 1986-87; bd. dirs. League Women Voters, New London, HOSPICE, New London, Am. Cancer Soc. New London County. Recipient Proclamation Community award Town of Waterford, 1989, Community Service award The Connection, Inc., 1987. Mem. Women's Network New London County, Children and Family Services, Pub. Relations Network, Nat. Assn. Female Execs., Brandeis U. Jewish. Home: 3 Pondside Ct Mystic CT 06355-3124 Fax: 860-572-8239. E-mail: carole@atouchofgrey.com.

BOBZIEN, CATHERINE HARDY, mathematics educator; b. Providence, Apr. 4, 1947; d. Francis Wilfred and Frances Baker Hardy; m. David Paul Bobzien, Sept. 6, 1969; children: David Paul Bobzien (Jr.), Brendan Francis. BA in Math., Newton Coll. of the Sacred Heart, Newton, Mass., 1968; MA in Math., U. of Va., Charlottesville, 1971. Cert. secondary tchr. Va., 1984. Adj. prof. No. Va. C.C., Sterling, Va., 1975—; math tchr. Herndon H.S., Va., 1984—. Ap calculus reader Coll. Bd., Ft. Collins, Colo., 2000—. Tchr. sponsor Team 116, HHS FIRST Robotics Team, Herndon, 1999—2006, Varsity Math Team and Math Honor Soc., Herndon. Mem.: Va. Math. Assn. of Two Yr. Colls., No. Va. Coun. of Tchrs. Math., Va. Coun. of Tchrs. Math., Nat. Coun. of Tchrs. Math. (assoc.), Kappa Gamma Pi. Roman Catholic. Home: 2022 Durand Dr Reston VA 20191 Office: Herndon High School 700 Bennett St Herndon VA 20170 Office Phone: 703-810-2200. Personal E-mail: catherine.bobzien@fcps.edu.

BOCCARDO-DUBEY, GENNY MERCEDES, art dealer; b. Miami, Fla., Sept. 29, 1970; d. Humberto Jose Boccardo and Maria Josefina Bertrán; m. Frank Dubey, Mar. 10, 1998; 1 child, Thomas. BA in Internat. Rels., U. San Francisco, 1991, MBA in Internat. Bus., 1996. Acct. mgr. Consolidated Bank, Caracas, Venezuela, 1991—93; pub. rels. mgr. Laguna Art Mus., Laguna Beach, Calif., 1996—98; sales mgr. St. Gobain, Paris, 1999—2002; gallery dir. La Cachette Gallery, Chagrin Falls, Ohio, 2004—. Mktg. assoc., web maintenance Valley Art Ctr., Chagrin Falls, 2004—. Editor (editor-in-chief): USF Bus. Jour. Mem.: Internat. Women's Group Cleve., French-Am. C. of C. Avocations: ceramics, writing, watercolors, scuba diving. Home: 87 May Ct Chagrin Falls OH 44022 Office: La Cachette Gallery 20 Ea Orange St Chagrin Falls OH 44022

BOCCIA/STACY, JUDY ELAINE, home health agency executive, consultant; b. San Diego, Aug. 29, 1955; d. Robert Garrett and Jerry Athalee (Carruth) Stacy; 1 child, Jennifer Lynn. BSN, Calif. State U., San Diego, 1978. RN, Calif.; lic. pub. health nurse, Calif. Staff nurse Univ. Hosp., U. Calif., San Diego, 1978-80, 81-82, Moffitt Hosp., San Francisco, 1980—81, Humana Hosp., Huntington Beach, Calif., 1982—84; intravenous and hospice vis. nurse Town & Country Nursing, Garden Grove, Calif., 1984—85; vis. nurse Vis. Nurse Assn., Orange, Calif., 1985—86; v.p. Doctors and Nurse Med. Mgmt., Newport Beach, Calif., 1986—89; dir. nursing HMSS, So. Calif., 1989—90; pres. Premier Care, Irvine, 1990—91, Homelife Nursing & Staffbuilders, Lake Forest, Calif., 1991—96. Cons., Calif., 1987—1996; pres., adminstr. Homelife Nursing-Staff Builders, O.C., 1991-97; AIDS educator; presenter in field; guest radio spkr. Parish nurse. Mem. Oncology Nursing Soc., Intravenous Nurse Soc., Calif. Nurses Assn. Avocations: singing, gardening. Home and Office: 22712 Wood Lake Ln Lake Forest CA 92630 Office Phone: 949-697-6296.

BOCHERT, LINDA H., lawyer; b. East Orange, N.J., May 13, 1949; BA, U. Wis., 1971, MS, 1973, JD, 1974. Bar: Wis. 1974. Dir. environ. protection unit Wis. Atty. Gen. Office, 1978-80; exec. asst. to the secy. Wis. Dept. Natural Resources, 1980-91; ptnr. Michael, Best & Friedrich, Madison, Wis., 1991—. Mem. ABA, Wis. State Bar Assn. Office: Michael Best & Friedrich PO Box 1806 Firstar Plaza 1 S Pinckney St Madison WI 53701-1806 Office Phone: 608-283-2271. Business E-Mail: lhbochert@michaelbest.com.

BOCK, CAROLYN A., writer, consultant, small business owner; b. Jan. 25, 1942; d. Wilfred Ignatius and Marcella Mary (Birkemeier) Gerschutz; m. Donald Charles Bock, Sept. 7, 1974 (dec. Nov. 1997); 1 child, Jonathon Edward. Student, Notre Dame Coll., 1960—62, John Carroll U., 1962—66. With sales and purchasing depts. Schaffer Diversified Corp. and other cos., Cleve., 1962-74; owner Dynamic Living Assocs., 1986—. Author: Authors, Artists and Auras, 1988, Gerschutz Family History, 1989. Co-founder, trustee Cmty. Action Team, Westlake, Ohio, 1980—85; co-founder Westlake Arts Coun., 1983—84, pres., 1984—85, Westlake PTA Coun., 1980—82; active Boy Scouts Am., Clague Playhouse, Westlake Hist. Soc., 1985—98; chmn. Morning Sem., Rocky River, Ohio, 1981—85. Named hon. life mem., Ohio PTA, 1982; recipient Outstanding Svc. award, Boy Scouts Am., 1980. Mem.: Soc. Profl. Journalists, Word Works, Westfield Ctr. Hist. Soc. Unitarian-Universalist. Avocations: travel, reading, history, gardening. Home: 9183 S Leroy Rd Westfield Center OH 44251 also: PO Box 240 Lodi OH 44254-0240

BOCK, JANINE SCHMELZER, music educator; b. Nelsonville, Ohio, June 14, 1963; d. Maurice David Schmelzer and Jeanne Marie Flemming; m. James David Bock, Sept. 6, 1953; children: Christopher David McCabe, LeeAnn Marie McCabe. MusB in Edn., Ohio State U., 1985, MA, 2004. Cert. tchg. Ohio, 1985. Band dir. Franklin Local Sch. Dist., Duncan Falls, Ohio; dir. of bands Licking Valley Local Sch., Newark, Ohio, 1991—2001, music tchr., 2001—. Guest condr., clinician Zanesville Meml. Concert Band, Zanesville, Ohio, 2001—; tuba soloist Women in Music, Columbus, Ohio; tuba player, guest conductor Muskingum Valley Winds, 2004—; area clinician, guest condr. wind bands. Musician tuba performance, (concerto soloist) Tubby in Tubby the Tuba, Wind Band Music, 2005. Sec. Zanesville Meml. Concert Band, Ohio, 1996—2003; pres. St. Benedict Cath. Sch. Home & Sch. Assn., Cambridge, Ohio, 2002—04; mem. Rep. Club of Guernsey County, Cambridge, Ohio, 1997—. Mem.: Music Educators Nat. Conf., Licking Valley Edn. Assn., Ohio Music Edn. Assn., Ohio State U. Marching Band TBDBITL Alumni Club. R-Conservative. Roman Cath. Achievements include i dotter-first female to dot the i in the Script Ohio Marching manuever in a single script in front of a home football crowd while a member of The Ohio State Univ Marching Band, Fall 1984. Avocations: travel, sewing, sports. Personal E-mail: jbock@muskingum.edu.

BOCKENKAMP, KAREN ANN, bank administrator; b. St. Louis, Dec. 19, 1960; d. Joseph John and Constance M. (Bernabe) Clifford; divorced; children: Megan Elizabeth Clifford, Mallory Anne Clifford; m. William L. Bockenkamp, Nov. 8, 1996. BA in Polit. Sci., St. Louis U., 1983; MA in Legal Studies, Webster U., 1996, MBA, 1996; cert. in paralegal studies, Meramec C.C., St. Louis, 1984; cert. in bus. leadership, St. Louis U., 1997. Legal asst. Husch, Eppenberger, St. Louis, 1986-88, Nat. Bus. Owners, St. Louis, 1988-92, Deutsche Fin. Svcs., St. Louis, 1995-96; contract adminstr. Spectrum Healthcare Svcs., St. Louis, 1997, Nations Bank, 1997—. Mem., vol. St. Louis Zoo Friends, 1990—; mem. St. Louis Art Mus., 1994—, St. Louis Sci. Ctr., 1994—, YWCA of Met. St. Louis, 1994—, St. Louis Ambs., 1992—, St. Louis Women's Polit. Caucus, 1997—; mem., leader Girl Scouts USA, St. Louis, 1989—. Mem. AAUW (chmn. St. Louis chpt. 1997—), Bar Assn. St. Louis, Ga. Assn. Legal Assts. (cert.). Democrat. Roman Catholic. Avocation: volunteering. Office: NationsBank NA 910 N 11th St Saint Louis MO 63101-2914

BOCKHORST, BARBARA ALICE, retired secondary school educator; b. St. Louis, Feb. 2, 1939; d. Harold Calvert and Lillian Amelia (Smith) Cox; m. William Dreon Bockhorst (div.); children: William Dreon Jr., Walter Richard. BEd, U. Mo., 1961; MEd, Washington U., 1972. Tchr. sci., phys. edn. RIII Sch. Dist., Troy, Mo., 1961—64; tchr. Ft. Zumwalt Sch. Dist., O'Falllon, Mo., 1965—2006; ret., 2006. Coach track and field Ft. Zumwalt Sch. Dist., 1983—95. Rosalia Tilles Non-Sectarian Fund scholar, Mo. U., 1957—61. Mem.: Lions, Mensa. Independent. Avocations: reading, embroidery, paper cutting.

BOCOBO-BALUNSAT, DALISAY, librarian, journalist; b. Metro Manila, Philippines, Jan. 22, 1926; d. Jorge Bocobo; m. Anthony Anton Balunsat. PhB, U. Philippines, 1950. Faculty mem. Adamson U., Manila, 1950—53; corr., columnist Philippine-Am. press, 1953—; ref. libr. San Francisco Pub. Libr., 1958—84. Founder, dir. Philippine-Am. Cultural Celebration, San Francisco, 1973—. Named Outstanding Filipino-Am. of No. Calif. award in field of culture and art, 1984, Outstanding Filipino-Am. Journalist award, 1986, June 8, 1991 Dalisay Bocobo-Balunsat Day, San Francisco Mayor Art Agnos, 1991, Top Fgn. Contbr., Philippines Free Press; named to KGO-TV's Salute to Prominent Asian-Pacific-Am. San Francisco Bay Area list, 2002; recipient Recognition award, Philippine-Am. Press and Media, 1973—2005, Calif. State Senators George Moscone and Milton Marks, 1975, Calif. State Assembly, 2005, Honor award, Mayor and Bd. Suprs. San Francisco and Calif. Legislatures, 1973—2005, Salutes to Asian-Am. award, 2002, Outstanding Achievement award, 2004—05, Cert. of Appreciation, Philippine Consulate-Gen., 1975, Asian-Am. Role Model award, US Navy Filipino Employees, 1975, US Bicentennial award, Filipino Arts Fiesta, 1976, Outstanding Pub. Svc. award, Mayor Dianne Feinstein of San Francisco, 1984, Fiesta Islands Recognition award, Philippine Tourism, 1989, Commendation award, San Francisco Pub. Libr. Commn. and City Librarian, 1998, Bd. Supr. City and County of San Francisco, 2006, Outstanding Cmty. Svc. award, San Francisco Bd. of Supr. and Legis., 2004, Hon. cert., City and County of San Francisco, 2004, Commendation cert., Mayor and City Coun. Daly City, Calif., 2004—05, Literary and Cmty. Svc. Calatagan award, Philippine-Am. Writers and Artists, 2004—05, Commendation award, Calif. Governor Jerry Brown, Woman Warrior award, Pacific Asian Am. Women, Outstanding Sch. Vol. award, San Francisco Pub. Sch. Mem.: ALA (Dana Nat. Libr. award 1975), Phillipine-Am. Press Corr., Filipino Artists, Writers, and Performers (founder 1973—, dir. 1973—, various Recognition awards 1973—2005). Avocations: travel, writing, reading, movies. Office: Filipino Artists Writers and Performers 1437 19th Ave San Francisco CA 94122

BODA, VERONICA CONSTANCE, lawyer; b. Phila., Oct. 8, 1952; d. Louis Paul and Helen Anna (Zwigaitis) B. AB, Wilson Coll., 1974; JD, Vt. Law Sch., 1978; LLM in Taxation, Villanova U., 1989. Bar: Pa. 1978, U.S. Dist. Ct. (ea. dist.) Pa. 1982, U.S. Tax Ct. 1984. Staff atty. Cape-Atlantic Legal Services, Atlantic City, 1978-79; sole practice Phila., 1980—95; tchr. Am. Inst. for Paralegal Studies, Phila., 1982-86; instr. bus. adminstrn. program Pa. State U., Media, Pa., 1987-88; ins. agt. Prudential Ins. Co., Wayne, Pa., 1985-86; investment and tax adv. V C Boda & Co., 1986—. Planned giving cons. Wilson Coll., Chambersburg, Pa., 1985—91. Author: (with others) Newberg on Class Actions, 1985; editor Women Lawyers Jour., 1993-97; contbr. articles to profl. jours. Bd. dirs. Emergency Aid of Pa. Found., 1994-96; bd. dirs. Colonial Phila. Hist. Soc., 1983, pres., 1984-89. Mem. Nat. Assn. Women Lawyers (treas., pres.), Phila. Bar Assn. (chair com. real estate sect. 1984-86). Democrat. Avocations: tennis, gardening, chess, photography, art. Office Phone: 609-839-7244.

BODDEN, LISA, theater educator; d. Chuck and Kathy Cook; m. Charlie Bodden, June 14, 2003. BS in Theatre Edn., No. Ariz. U., Flagstaff, 1999; MA in Theatre Edn., U. Ariz., Tucson, 2006. Theatre tchr. and dir. St. Gregory Sch., Tucson, 2000—; drama instr. Live Theatre Workshop, Tucson, 2001—. Tchr. grades 3 and 4 Palo Christi Elem. Sch., Kingman, Ariz., 2000; theatre camp dir. Tucson Parks and Recreation, 2006—. Actor: Sweet Charity, (play) Much Ado About Nothing, Dial M For Murder, The Mousetrap, Crimes of the Heart, As You Like It, The Perfect Party, Ah, Wilderness!, All My Sons, Antigone. Scholar Mary L. Ashton, U. Ariz., 2003—04. Mem.: Ariz. Theater Alliance, Ariz. Alliance for Arts Edn., Arts and Learning Spl. Interest Group, SW Theatre Assn., Theatre Comm. Group, Inc. Office Phone: 520-327-6395.

BODEN, KATHERINE L., utilities executive; Grad., Poly. U., 1990; MBA, Hofstra U., 1998. Intern Consol. Edison Co. N.Y. Inc., N.Y.C., 1990, dept. mgr. Manhattan Electric Control Ctr., 2001—03, chief engr. distbn., 2003—. Named to, Crain's N.Y. Bus. "40 under 40", 2004. Office: Consol Edison Co NY Inc 4 Irving Pl New York NY 10003

BODENHAUSEN, JUDITH ANNE, school system administrator; Phd with honors, U. Calif., Berkeley, 1993. Head math. dept. Berkeley (Calif.) HS, 2001—. Mem.: Nat. Bd. Profl. Tchg. Standards. Office: Berkeley HS Math Dept 2223 Martin Luther King Jr Way Berkeley CA 94704

BODENHEIMER, SALLY NELSON, reading educator, retired; b. Bedford, Ind., Aug. 31, 1939; d. Paul Edwin Sr. and Sarah Kathryn (Scott) Nelson; m. Robert Edward Bodenheimer, June 24, 1961; children: Robert Edward, Marc Alan, Bryan Lee. BS, U. Tenn., Knoxville, 1961, postgrad., Northwestern U., Carson Newman Coll., Johnson Bible Coll. Cert. tchr. K-3, 1-9, K-12, music. Interni Crow Island Elem., Winnetka, Ill., 1961-62; tchr. 1st grade Wilmot

Elem Sch., Deerfield, Ill., 1962-63, Vestal Elem. Sch., Knoxville, 1981-82; 7th grade math. tchr. Knox County Schs., Doyle Middle Sch., Knoxville, 1982-83; kindergarten tchr. Mt. Olive Sch., Knoxville, 1983-93, chpt. I lang, reading, reading recovery tchr., 1993—95, tchr. kindergarten, 1995—2001. Recipient Knoxville Arts Coun. Art in Edn. award, Golden Apple award Knoxville News Sentinel, Outstanding Environ. Edn. award. 21st Century Classroom. Mem. NEA, ASCD, Tenn. Edn. Assn., Knox County Edn. Assn., Smoky Mountain Reading Assn., Internat. Reading Assn., Nat. Coun. Tchrs. Math., Smoky Mountain Math. Educators Assn., Nat. Sci. Tchrs. Assn., Music Educators Nat. Conf., East Tenn. Foxfire Tchrs. Network (steering com.), Greater Knoxville C. of C. (Leadership Edn., Best Tchr. award 1989, 1996), Delta Kappa Gamma, Pi Lambda Theta, Sigma Alpha Iota. Home: 3335 Tipton Station Rd Knoxville TN 37920-9565

BODENSTEINER, KARIN JOHANNA, biology professor, researcher; d. Joseph Adams Bodensteiner and Emily Beth Homstad; m. Mark Jaden Emerson, Aug. 11, 1995; children: Anna Faye Emerson, Sophie Elizabeth Emerson. BA in Biology and Psychology magna cum laude, Luther Coll., Decorah, Iowa, 1991; MS in Endocrinology, U. Wis., Madison, 1995; PhD in Reproductive Physiology, Colo. State U., Ft. Collins, 1999. Postdoctoral rschr. Colo. State U., Ft. Collins, 1999—2000; asst. prof. St. Lawrence U., Canton, 2000—05, assoc. prof., 2005—. Com. mem. St. Lawrence U., Canton, 2000—, trained adv. women, 2002—, safe zone ally, 2003—; presenter in field. Contbr. articles to profl. jours. Recipient NIH Nat. Rsch. Svc. award, Colo. State U., 1999, William B. Bradbury, Jr. Faculty award, St. Lawrence U., 2003; PEO scholar, 1997—98. Mem.: Soc. Study Reproduction (mem. edn. com. 2001—04), Beta Beta Beta, Psi Chi, Phi Beta Kappa. Avocations: bicycling, gardening, furniture restoration, running, swimming. Office: Saint Lawrence U 23 Romoda Dr Canton NY 13617 Office Phone: 315-229-5137.

BODENSTEINER, LISA M., utilities executive, lawyer; BS Bus. Adminstrn. & Acctg., U. Nev., 1985; JD, Santa Clara U., 1989. Assoc. Thelen, Reid & Priest, 1994—96; assoc. counsel Calpine Corp., 1996—99, v.p., gen. counsel, 1999—2001, sr. v.p., gen. counsel, 2001—02, asst. sec., exec. v.p., gen. counsel, 2002—. Office: Calpine 50 W San Fernando St 5th Fl San Jose CA 95113

BODI, SONIA ELLEN, library director, educator; b. Chgo., June 24, 1940; d. Franz Frithiof and Elsa (Noren) Bergquist; m. Peter Phillip Bodi, July 30, 1966; 1 child, Eric Christopher; stepchildren: Glenn Peter, John Jeffrey. Student, U. Edinburgh, Scotland, 1960-61; BA, Augustana Coll., Rock Island, Ill., 1962; MA Libr. Sci., Dominican U., River Forest, Ill., 1977; MA, Northwestern U., Evanston, Ill., 1986. Tchr. English and history Gemini Jr. H.S., Niles, Ill., 1962-64, Nagoya (Japan) Internat. Sch., 1964-65; tchr. English, Old Orchard Jr. H.S., Skokie, Ill., 1965-67; reference libr. Wilmette (Ill.) Pub. Libr., 1977-79, Kendall Coll., Evanston, Ill., 1979-81; head reference and instructional libr. North Park U., Chgo., 1981—, asst. prof. bibliography, 1985-87, assoc. prof., 1988-92, prof., 1992—2005; prof. emeritus, 2005—; chmn. divsn. humanities North Park U., Chgo., 1988-99, interim libr. dir., 1996-98, libr. dir., 1998—2005; instr. Dominican U. Grad. Sch. Libr. and Info. Sci., River Forest, Ill., 2004—. Contbr. articles to profl. jours. Pres. PTA, Lincolnwood, Ill., 1977—79; active Bd. Edn., Lincolnwood, 1980—91, sec., 1981—84, pres., 1984—87, LIBRAS, 2001—02; chair Ill. Coop. Collection Mgmt. Program, 2002—03; elder First Presbyn. Ch. of Evanston, 1989—, Stephen ministry leader, 1992—98; bd. dirs. Chgo. Libr. Sys., 1999—2004, Ill. Libr. Computer Sys. Orgn., 2003—05. Mem. Ill. Libr. Assn., ALA, Am. Assn. Coll. and Rsch. Librs., Beta Phi Mu. Democrat. Avocations: reading, bicycling, opera, knitting, piano. Home: 6710 N Trumbull Ave Lincolnwood IL 60712-3740 Office: Dominican U 7900 Divsn River Forest IL 60305 Business E-Mail: sbodi@northpark.edu.

BODIE, PHYLLIS JEAN, art educator, watercolorist; b. Beatrice, Nebr., Apr. 11, 1950; d. Donald Charles and Harriet M. (Wilms) Cacek; divorced; children: Brook C., Aaron B., Paige M. BS cum laude, Peru State U., Nebr., 1971. Tchr. Antilles Consol. Schs., P.R., 1972-73, Fajardo (P.R.) Acad., 1973-74; prof. artist Miami, Fla., 1971—; tchr. Tropical Christian Sch., Miami, 1988—; owner art gallery Coconut Grove, Fla., 1995-96. Exhibited work in shows in Miami and Miami Beach. Recipient Outstanding Educator's award Kappa Delta Pi, 1969, awards for watercolors Old Island Days, Fla., 1993, 97. Mem. One Ear Soc., Nat. Mus. Women in the Arts. Christian.

BODILY, KIM GAYLEN, secondary school educator; d. Gaylen L. and Marie Bodily. BS in Recreation, Kinesiology/Phys. Edn., Calif. State U., Hayward, 1974; M. in Phys. Edn., Idaho State U., 1976, BA in Sociology, 1987. Instr./coach Valparaiso (Ind.) U., 1977-79; supr. Lamb-Weston, American Falls, Idaho, 1980-89; tchr./coach Sch. Dist. #25, Pocatello, 1990—. Named to Athletic Hall of Fam, Calif. State U.-Hayward, 1994. Mem. AAHPERD (life). Office: Franklin Jr High Sch 2271 E Terry St Pocatello ID 83201-2704

BODIN, KATE, dean; BFA, Boston U.; MEd in Creative Arts and Learning, Endicott Coll. Dean of faculty Montserrat Coll. Art, Beverly, Mass., 1992; acad. dean Oreg. Coll. Art and Craft, Portland, Oreg., 2005—. Office: Oreg Coll Art and Craft 8245 SW Barnes Rd Portland OR 97225 Office Phone: 502-397-5544 x 125. E-mail: kbodin@ocac.edu.

BODINE, SUSAN P., federal agency administrator; AB, Princeton U., 1983; JD, U. Penn., 1988. Atty. Covington & Burling, Washington, 1988—95; counsel Subcommittee on Water Resources & the Environment, Com. on Transportation & Infrastructure, US Ho. Reps., Washington, 1995—2002, staff dir., sr. counsel, 2002—05; asst. admin. for solid waste & emergency response EPA, Washington, 2005—. Office: EPA Rm 3146 1200 Pennsylvania Ave NW Washington DC 20460 Office Phone: 202-566-0200. Office Fax: 202-566-0207.*

BODINI, DANIELE DAMASO, real estate company executive; b. Erba, Italy, Dec. 20, 1945; arrived in U.S., 1971; d. Franco and Cesarea (Martano) Bodini; m. Toni Allen Kramer, June 9, 1979. MArch, U. Rome, 1970, M Engring., 1968; MBA, Columbia U., 1972. Lic. arch., engr., Italy; real estate broker NY. Asst. prof. Sch. Engring. U. Rome, 1968—70; trainee Blyth, Eastman Dillon, N.Y.C., 1973, v.p. realty, 1975—78; U.S.A. mgr. SGI, N.Y.C., 1974; exec. v.p., prin. Am. Continental Properties Inc., N.Y.C., 1978—80, pres., 1981—. Lt. Italian Air Force, 1969—70. Mem.: Racquet and Tennis Club. Home: 800 5th Ave New York NY 10021-7216 Office: Am Continental Properties Inc 400 Park Ave 7th Fl New York NY 10022

BODKIN, RUBY PATE, real estate broker, educator; b. Frostproof, Fla., Mar. 11, 1926; d. James Henry and Lucy Beatrice (Latham) P.; m. Lawrence Edward Bodkin Sr., Jan. 15, 1949; children: Karen Bodkin Snead, Cinda, Lawrence Jr. BA, Fla. State U., 1948; MA, U. Fla., 1972. Lic. real estate broker Fla. Banker Barnett Bank, Avon Park, Fla., 1943-44, Lewis State Bank, Tallahassee, 1944-49; ins. underwriter Hunt Ins. Agy., Tallahassee, 1949-51; tchr. Duval County Sch. Bd., Jacksonville, Fla., 1952-77; pvt. practice realty Jacksonville, 1976—; tchr. Nassau County Sch. Bd., Jacksonville, 1978-83; sec., treas., v.p. Bodkin Corp., R&D/Inventions, Jacksonville, 1983—. Author: 100 Teacher Chosen Recipes, 1976, Bodkin Bridge Course for Beginners, 1996, (autobiography) Grandma Bodkin, 2000, Essay on Death, 2003; author numerous poems. Mem. Jacksonville Symphony Guild, 1985—, Southside Bapt. Ch. Recipient 25 Yr. Svc. award Duval County Sch. Bd., 1976, Tchr. of Yr. award Bryceville Sch., 1981, 30 Yr. Svc. award State of Fla. Dept. Edn. Mem. Am. Contract Bridge League, Nat. Realtors Assn., Southside Jr. Woman's Club, Garden Club Sweetbriar (bd. dirs.), Oak St. Woman's Club Jacksonville (fin. dir. 1991-92, 3rd v.p. social dir. WCOJ, 1992-99), UDC (Martha Reid chpt. #19), Fla. Edn. Assn. (pers. problems com. 1958), Duval County Classrooms Tchrs. (v.p. membership 1957), Woman's Club Jacksonville Bridge Group, Fla. Ret. Tchrs. Assn., Fla. Realtors Assn., N.E. Fla. Realtors Assn., Jacksonville Geneal. Soc. (practicing genealogist, family historian 1986—), Friday Musicale of Jacksonville, San Jose Golf Country Club, Jacksonville Sch. Bridge. Baptist. Avocations: reading, writing, genealogy, photography, club bridge. Home: 1149 Molokai Rd Jacksonville FL 32216-3273 Office: Bodkin Jewelers & Appraisers PO Box 16482 Jacksonville FL 32245-6482 Personal E-mail: larubodkin@aol.com.

BODNAR-BALAHUTRAK, LYDIA, artist, educator; b. Cleve., May 6, 1951; d. Wolodymyr and Luba M. (Hurko) Bodnar; m. Michael B. Balahutrak, Jan. 8, 1977. BS, Kent State U., 1973; postgrad., Corcoran Sch. Art, Washington, 1976-77; MFA, George Washington U., 1977. Art specialist Parma (Ohio) City Pub. Schs., 1973-75; instr. San Jacinto Coll., Houston, 1977-79; art exhbns. coord. U. Houston, Clear Lake, Tex., 1981-82, lectr., 1979-82, 86-87, 92-94. Vis. guest lectr. U. Pitts., 1983; guest artist/lectr. La. State U., 1989; guest lectr. Stephen F. Austin State U., Nacogdoches, Tex., 1991; guest lectr./artist residency Lviv State Inst. Fine and Applied Arts, Ukraine, 1991, 2d Internat. Painters' Symposium, Ukraine, 1993. One-woman shows include U. Houston at Clear Lake, 1985, Graham Gallery, Houston, 1988, Galveston (Tex.) Arts Ctr., 1993, Dallas Visual Arts Ctr., 1995, The Nave Mus. of Art, Victoria, Tex., 1995; exhibited in group shows at Bowling Green State U., 1995, Edith Baker Gallery, Dallas, 1991, 92, 93, Sherry French Gallery, N.Y.C., 1990, numerous others; represented in numerous pub. and pvt. collections; featured in newspapers and profl. publs. Grantee Scurlock Found., 1979, Harris and Eliza Kempner Fund, 1979, La Napoule (France) Art Found., 1985, La. State U. Guest Artist Series, 1989, Internat. Rsch. and Exchs. Bd., 1991; recipient Purchase award George Washington U., Washington, 1976, 1st Place award Nat. Small Painting and Drawing Competition, N.Y.C., 1983, Purchase award Hoyt Inst. Fine Arts, Pa., 1984, NEA Artist Hon. award Art League Houston, 1985, Creative Artist Program award Cultural Arts Coun. Houston, 1993.

BODWELL, LORI, lawyer; b. Oct. 1966; AB, Bowdoin Coll., 1988; JD, Boston Coll., 1991. Bar: Alaska 1992, Maine 1993, Mass. 1992, Dist. of Alaska (US Dist. Ct.) 1994, 9th Air 1995. Mem.: Tananeu Valley Bar Assoc., Nat. Assoc. of Criminal Def. Lawyers, Alaska Bar Assn. (pres. 2002—03). Address: 712 8th Ave Fairbanks AK 99701

BOECKMAN, PATRICIA ELLEN, writer, educator; b. Chgo., June 23; d. Levi and Juanita Kennelly; m. Charles Boeckman; 1 child, Sharla. BA, North Tex. State U., 1962; MA, Tex. A&I U., 1972. Cert. tchr., Tex. Tchr. pvt. and pub. schs., Corpus Christi, Tex., 1962-72; instr. Tex. A&I U., Kingsville, 1970-72, Del Mar Coll., Corpus Christi, 1986-93; writer, novelist Corpus Christi, 1972—; tchr. Spanish St. James Episcopal Sch., 1992-97. Spkr. various regional and nat. writers' confs., 1979-86; tchr. Richard Milburn Acad., 1999—. Author: Captive Heart, 1980, The Beachcomber, 1980, Louisiana Lady, 1981, Angry Lover, 1981, Love's Treacherous Journey, 1981, Spotlight to Fame, 1982, Daring Encounter, 1982, Mermaid's Touch, 1982, Forbidden Affair, 1983, Time for Us, 1984, On Stage, 1985, Someday My Love, 1988, Bitter Victory, 1982, Tender Deception, 1982, Enchanted Surrender, 1983, Thunder at Dawn, 1983, Storm Over the Everglades, 1984, Nashville Blues, The Movie, Odds Against Tomorrow, 1985, Dateline: Washington, 1985, Summer's Storm, 1986, Danger in His Arms, 1987, Please Let Me In, 1981, With the Dawn, 1984; newspaper columnist, 1990—; bass player, 1970—. Newsletter pub. St. James Episcopal Sch., Corpus Christi, 1992-93. Mem. Romance Writers Am., Tex. Press Women, Nat. Fedn. Press Women, Am. Christian Fiction Writers. Avocations: public speaking, music, drawing, travel, gardening.

BOEHMER, ANN, mathematics professor; d. Donald and Nancee McCarthy; 1 child, Max. BA in Math., U. Mo., St. Louis, 1997, MA in Math., 2000. Asst. prof. East Ctrl. Coll., Union, Mo., 2000—. Faculty assn. v.p. East Ctrl. Coll., Union, 2006—, faculty devel. co-chair, 2005—06. Mem.: Am. Math. Assn. Two Yr. Colls., Nat. Assn. Devel. Edn. Office: East Central College 1964 Prairie Dell Rd Union MO 63084 Office Phone: 636-583-5193. Business E-Mail: boehmera@eastcentral.edu.

BOEHMER, RAQUEL DAVENPORT, newsletter editor; b. Bklyn., Feb. 24, 1938; d. John Joralemon Davenport and Fanny (Barberis) Allison; m. Peter Joseph Boehmer; children: Kristian Ludwig, Louisa Boehmer Wickard, Timothy Joralemon. BA, Wells Coll., 1959. Radio producer Maine Pub. Broadcasting Network, Bangor, 1977—; developer, editor consumer newsletter Seafood Soundings, Monhegan, Maine, 1986-92; columnist, editor newsletter New Monhegan Press, Monhegan, Maine, 1989-96, chief editor, 1995—. Speaker Seafare, L.A., 1986; keynote speaker Beyond Wells Day, Wells Coll., Aurora, N.Y., 1988; founder, pres. bd. dirs. Monhegan Artists' Residency Corp., 1995-2003. Writer, prodr. (radio commentary) Whole Foods for All People, 1977-91; prodr., host (TV cooking program) Different Kettle of Fish, 1984; prodr./host TV cooking program Great Tastes of Maine, Maine Pub. TV, 1996; author: A Foraging Vacation, 1982, Raquel's Maine Guide to New England Seafoods, 1988, Raquel's Maine Guide to Northeast Winter Vegetables, 1993. Writer legislation, Maine legis., 1985, 87, 91; treas. Monhegan Plantation, 1970-72, chair bicentennial com., 1976; chair Monhegan Sch. Bd., 1973-74; co-chair Monhegan Solid Waste Com., 1988-98; commr. Maine State Liquor and Lottery Commn., 1996—; mem. edn. task force Nat. Alcohol Beverage Control Assn., 1998—. Recipient Pub. Svc. award Maine Nutrition Coun., 1987, Alumnae award Wells Coll., 1992, Ptnrs. in Prevention award, 2005; named Gt. New Eng. Cook, Yankee mag., 1986. Mem. Women's Fisheries Network (bd. dirs. N.E. chpt. 1992-94, sec. to nat. bd. dirs. 1994-97, v.p. 1997-98, pres. nat. bd. dirs. 1998-2000), Colonial Dames Am., Women's Strike for Peace. Avocation: long distance walking. Home: 4 Madokawando Rd Falmouth ME 04105-1632 E-mail: raquel@monhegan.com.

BOEHNE, PATRICIA JEANNE, foreign languages educator, department chairman; b. Paris, Feb. 4, 1940; (parents Am. citizens); d. Jean Atlee and Mary Anna (McFarland) Graffis; m. Edward George Boehne, Jan. 24, 1960; children: Lisa Elena, Edward Mark (dec.). BA, Ind. U., 1961, MA, 1962, PhD, 1969. Cert. tchr. Spanish and French. Tchg. asst. Ind. U., Bloomington, 1961-62, 65-66; tchr. Spanish Martinsville (Ind.) H.S., 1962-63; instr. French and Spanish Bradley U., Peoria, Ill., 1963-65; asst. prof. Spanish Franklin and Marshall Coll., Lancaster, Pa., 1968-70; assoc. prof. French, Spanish and Russian Ea. Univ., St. Davids, Pa., 1970-78, prof. romance langs., 1978—2000, chairperson romance langs., 1975—, prof. emeritus, 2000—. Humanist evaluator for pub. com. Humanities in Pa., 1978—; chairperson orgnl. mgmt. Ea. Univ., 1988—, chairperson faculty devel, 1989—, chairperson various coms.; chairperson conf. Les Pays Africains Francophones, 1988, strategic planning chairperson on global awareness, 1988, mem. strategic planning acad. com., 1988-89, mem. task force to internat. acad. program. Author: Dream and Fantasy in 14th and 15th Century Catalan Prose, 1975, An Introduction to Catalan Literature, 1977, J.V. Foix, 1980, The Renaissance Catalan Novel, 1989; contbr. articles to profl. jours. Bd. dirs. Basic Needs Internat., 1987—, Jenkins Arboretum, Devon, Pa., 2002—. Episcopal Cmty. Svcs., 2002—; former mem. vestry, alt. deanery del., lic. lay leader, chalice bearer, other positions Ch. of the Good Samaritan, Paoli, Pa., to 1992; Washington Meml. Chapel, Valley Forge, Pa., bd.Washington Meml. Heritage; lic. layreader chalist Carillon Restoration Com. Washington Meml. Chapel, Valley Forge, Pa., lay eucharistic minister, pastoral chaplin; chairperson Hispanic ministry com., mem.fin. and property com., Diocese of Pa., 1978-81, 88-89; Dem. committeeperson Easttown Twp. Pa. 7th precinct, 1974-80; Dem. candidate for twp. supr., 1975, 77; chairperson Easttown Dem. Com., 1975-79; del. candidate Birch Bayh-Dem. Nat. Conv., 1979. Recipient NDEA Title IV and VI fellowships, 1963, 65-68; Mellon fellowship Vatican Microfilm Libr., 1982, Am. Philos. Soc. fellowship, 1982, NEH grant, 1983, Del. Valley Faculty Exchange fellowship U. Pa., 1984, Lindback award for oustanding teaching, 1988. Mem. MLA (mem. exec. com. Catalan-Provencal discussion group 1977-80, 90-92), Am. Assn. Tchrs. of Spanish and Portuguese, World Affairs Coun. Greater Valley Forge (bd. dirs. 1990—, pres. 1991-92, v.p. 1992-93), N.Am. Catalan Soc. (bd. dirs. 1978-85, sec. 1982—, v.p. 1990-93, pres. 1993-95), Jenkins Arborturm, Ea. Univ. Friends of Libr. (bd.), Phi Sigma Iota (chpt. founder, Iota Pi advisor), Sigma Delta Pi, Kappa Delta Pi., Chi Omega. Democrat. Episcopal. Avocations: gardening, tennis, writing. Office: Ea Univ 1300 Eagle Rd Saint Davids PA 19087-3619 Personal E-mail: phoehne@msn.com.

BOEHS, SARAH TEACHWORH, lawyer; b. Southfield, Mich., 1977; AB with honors, Davidson Coll., 1998; JD, U. Conn., 2001. Bar: Mass. 2002. Law clk. Jackson, O'Keefe & Phelan, Travelers Bond; summer intern Hon. Dominic J. Squatrito US Dist. Ct. (Dist. Conn.). Mem.: Women's Bar Assn., Mass. Bar Assn. Office: Nixon Peabody LLP 100 Summer St Boston MA 02110 Office Phone: 617-345-6035. Office Fax: 866-947-1938. E-mail: sboehs@nixonpeabody.com.*

BOEKHOUDT-CANNON, GLORIA LYDIA, finance educator; b. Portsmouth, Va., Jan. 18, 1939; d. William and Clara (Virgil) Boekhoudt; m. George Edward Cannon, Dec. 27, 1959. AB in Sociology/Psychology, Calif. State U., San Diego, 1977; MA in Spl. Edn./Learning Disabilities, Calif. State U., Sacramento, 1981; EdD in Orgn. and Leadership of Higher Edn. and Curriculum and Instrn., U. San Francisco, 1989. Instr. bus. edn. Midway Adult Sch. extension San Diego City Coll., San Diego, 1974-78, San Diego City Coll., 1974-78; prof. bus. edn. Sacramento City Coll., 1979—2003; ret., 2003. Author: Fundamentals of Business English, 1986. Mem. Women in Community Colls., Phi Delta Kappa. Democrat. Jewish. Avocations: golf, needlepoint. Office: Sacramento City Coll Dept Bus 3835 Freeport Blvd Sacramento CA 95822-1318

BOEPPLE, BETTIE ANN, elementary school educator; d. Frank J. and Bessie M. Juranek; m. Thomas M. Boepple, Jr., Aug. 25, 1979; children: Stephanie Suzanne, Matthew Judson. BA summa cum laude in Interdisciplinary Studies, U. Houston, Tex., 1999. Cert. tchr. elem. edn. State Bd. Educator Certification, Tex., 1999, tchr. elem. math. State Bd. Educator Certification, Tex., 1999. Corp. sec., office mgr. Bep's Auto Supply & Svc., Inc., Ganado, Tex., 1981—94; clk. ins., front desk, ins. Ronnie L. Andress, D.D.S., Freeport, Tex., 1995—99; tchr. title one math. Walt Disney Elem. Sch. Alvin Ind. Sch. Dist., Tex., 1999—2000; tchr. Madge Griffith Elem. Sch. Brazosport Ind. Sch. Dist., Clute, Tex., 2000—01; tchr. Lamar Jr. H.S. Lamar Ctrl. Ind. Sch. Dist., Rosenberg, Tex., 2001—, chmn. Dept. Math. Lamar Jr. H.S., 2001—.

BOER, LINDA KAREN, medical/surgical nurse; b. Lynwood, Calif., Sept. 12, 1952; d. Tom and Aldora (Eichert) Ponder; m. Richard Boer, Sept. 19, 1970; children: Andrea, Sonja, Jennifer, Linda Rae. LVN with honors, Chaffey Coll., 1983, AS, 1985; ASN, U. State N.Y., 1987; BS in Health Sci., Chapman U., 1999. RN, Calif.; cert. adv. med./surg. care nurse. Nurse med./surg. unit Kaiser Perm Hosp., Fontana, Calif., nurse urgent care/emergency rm. addition medicine dept. Mem. United Nursing Assn. Calif.

BOERSMA, P. DEE, marine biologist, educator; b. Mt. Pleasant, Mich., Nov. 1, 1946; d. Henry W. and Vivian (Anspach) B. BS, Ctrl. Mich. U., 1969; PhD, Ohio State U., 1974; DSc (hon.), Ctrl. Mich. U., 2003. From asst. prof. to prof. Inst. Environ. Studies U. Wash., Seattle, 1974—88, prof. zoology, 1988—, assoc. dir., 1987—93, acting dir., 1990—91, adj. prof. women's studies, 1993—2003, prof. biology, womens studies, 2003—, Wadsworth endowed chair in conservation sci., 2006—, acting chair biology, 2005—; mem. sci. adv. com. for outer continental shelf Environ. Studies Program, Dept. Interior, 1980—83; prin. investigator Magellanic Penguin Project Wildlife Cons. Soc., 1982—. Evans vis. fellow U. Otago, New Zealand, 1995, Pew fellow in marine conservation, 1997-2000; naturalist Lindblad Expdns., 2001-04. Assoc. editor Ecological Applications, 1998-2001; exec. editor Conservation in Practice, 2000—; contbr. articles to profl. jours. Mem. adv. U.S. del. to UN Status Women Commn., N.Y.C., 1973, UN World Status Women Commn., N.Y.C., 1973, UN World Population Conf., Romania, 1974; mem. Gov. Lowry's Task Force on Wildlife, 1993; sci. adv. EcoBios, 1985-95; bd. dirs. Zero Population Growth, 1975-82, Washington Nature Conservancy, 1995-98; adv. bd. Walt Disney World Animal Kingdom, 1993—, Island press, 1999—, Compass, 2000-04; bd. dirs. Peregine Fund, Bullitt Found., 1996-00, Islandwood, 2000-04; mem. scholar diplomatic program Dept. State, 1977. Recipient Outstanding Alumni award Ctrl. Mich. U., 1978, Matrix award Women in Comm., 1983; named to Kellogg Nat. Leadership Program, 1982-85; recipient Top 100 Outsiders of Yr. award Outside Mag., 1987, Outstanding Centennial Alumni award Ctrl. Mich. U., 1993; sci. fellow The Wildlife Conservation Soc., 1982—, Aldo Leopold Leadership fellow, 2000-01. Fellow AAAS, Am Ornithol. Union (regional rep. Pacific seabird group 1981-85); mem. AAAS, Ecol. Soc. Am., Wilson Ornithol. Soc., Cooper Ornithol. Soc., Soc. Am. Naturalists, Soc. Conservation Biology (bd. govs. 1991-94, pres-elect 1995-97, pres. 1997-99, Disting. Svc. award 2006), Ecol. Soc. Am. (mem.-at-large 2003-06), Internat. Union Biol. Scis., Gopher Brokers Club (pres. Seattle chpt. 1982-83). Office: U Wash Dept Biology PO Box 351800 Seattle WA 98195-1800 Business E-Mail: boersma@u.washington.edu.

BOERSTE, DOROTHY, psychotherapist; b. East Islip, N.Y., Mar. 1, 1955; d. Albert James and Vita Boerste; m. Jeffrey Meeker, June 4, 1988 (div. Dec. 1995); 1 child, Molly Maxx BA, Rutgers U., 1989; MA, Pepperdine U., 1993. Cert. marriage and family therapist. Freelance writer, Geneva, 1976—85; case worker Child Welfare Adminstrn., N.Y.C., 1990—92; pvt. practice psychotherapist San Francisco, 1995—. Resource cons. Norma Morris Ctr. for Healing from Child Abuse, San Francisco, 1995—, bd. dirs., 1999-2001 Clin. dir. S.A.G.E. Project, 2003— Democrat. Office: 1537 Franklin St Ste 307 San Francisco CA 94109-4581 Office Phone: 415-674-8744. E-mail: Boerste123@jps.net.

BOESE, MICHELLE LYNNE, accountant, consultant; b. Lafayette, Ind., July 19, 1955; d. Robert (Fritz) Lawrence Lowery and Dorothy Jean (Lowery) Toops; m. Stephen Craig Boese, Dec. 26, 1977. Diploma, Ind. Bus. Coll., Ind., 1974; AA in Acctg., Cypress Coll., Calif., 1992; BS in Acctg., Colo. Tech. Coll, 2006. Exec. sec. Sargent Industries, El Segundo, Calif., 1976—79; salesperson Dietzgen Corp., Cerrtios, Calif., 1979—81; sr. acct. Olympic Graphics, Irvine, Calif., 1981—83, Tech. Duplicator Svc., Santa Ana, Calif., 1983—85; contr. Huntington Beach Bus. Svc., Huntington Beach, Calif., 1985—95; owner Boese Consulting, Anaheim, Calif., 1985—2001, Puzzleme Records, Huntington Beach, 1995—97; sr. acct. M.E. Howell & Assocs., Evergreen, Colo., 1997—2002; owner MSB & Assocs., Conifer, Colo., 2001—. Rural carrier US Postal Svc., Conifer, 2002—. Contr. Rancho Westwood Village Homeowners Assn., Anaheim, 1992—96; adminstr. Elizabeth Bowen Childrens Home, Evergreen, 2002. Mem.: Assn. For Ind. Music (AFIM) (assoc.), Ind. State Jr. Bowlers Assn. (assoc.; sec. 1974—75), Wash DC Mus. of Women in Art (assoc.), Nat. Scholars Honor Soc. Achievements include 1996-Letter of Acknowledgement on exemplary service and dedication in my work on Agent Orange Class Assistance Program (National Project for Vietnam Vets and families). Avocations: bicycling, dirt biking, canoeing. Home: PO Box 858 Conifer CO 80433 Office: MSB & Assocs P O Box 838 Conifer CO 80433 Office Phone: 303-916-0085. Home Fax: 303-816-5595. Personal E-mail: mboese1@msn.com.

BOESING, MARTHA, theater artist; b. Providence, Jan. 24, 1936; d. Harold Bancroft Gross and Mary Elizabeth Jones; life ptnr. Sandy Boucher; m. Paul Dennis Boesing (div.); children: Curtis Pierce, Rachel, Jennifer. BA, Conn. Coll. for Women, 1957; MA, U. Wis., 1958. Founder, artistic dir. Mpls. At the Foot of the Mountain, 1974—84. Author produced over 40 plays throughout the country and Europe. Leadership team, pres. bd. dirs. Buddhist Peace Fellowship, Berkeley, 2002—04; active Faithful Fools St. Ministry, San Francisco. Home: 3912 Forest Hill Ave Oakland CA 94602 Office Phone: 510-530-6188.

BOESKY, LISA, child/adolescent psychologist, writer, speaker, consultant; d. Doris and Howard Boesky. BA magna cum laude with distinction, U. Calif., Santa Barbara, CA, 1988; MA, Wayne State U., Mich., 1991, PhD,

1995. Lic. clin. psychologist Wash. Psychol. intern Western State Hosp., Seattle, 1994—95; post-doctoral fellow King County Juvenile Detention, 1995—96; clin. prof. U. Wash., 1996—2000; pvt. practice San Diego, 1997—. Cons., spkr. in field. Author: Juvenile Offenders With Mental Health Disorders: Who Are They and What Do We Do With Them?; contbr. chapters to books. Bd. dirs. Compeer San Diego, 2003—. Mem.: APA, San Diego Psychol. Assn., Calif. Psychol. Assn. Avocations: travel, music. Office: 4019 Goldfinch St #205 San Diego CA 92103 Office Phone: 619-993-2570. Business E-Mail: drlisab@drlisab.com.

BOESL, BETH MARIE, music educator; b. Langdon, ND, Aug. 23, 1974; d. Floyd Richard and Deanne Catherine Boesl. BS Elem. Edn. and Music, U. N.D., Grand Forks, 1998; MS Edn., U. N.D., 2004. Cert. tchr. N.D., Minn. Tchr. 1st grade Rossman Elem. Sch., Detroit Lakes, Minn., 1998—99; tchr. music and reading Schroeder Mid. Sch., Grand Forks, 1999—. Instr. pvt. piano lessons, Grand Forks, 1996—; accompanist Schroeder Mid. Sch., Grand Forks, 1999—, Holy Family Ch., Grand Forks, 2002—. Coord. Schroeder Mid. Sch. United Way, Grand Forks, 2002—. Named to Who's Who Among Am. Tchrs., 2006; recipient Sword of Honor, Sigma Alpha Iota, Chpt. and Province Leadership award, Coll. Honor award. Avocations: reading, crafts. Office: Schroeder Mid Sch 800 32d Ave S Grand Forks ND 58201

BOESZ, CHRISTINE C., science foundation administrator; b. Bridgeton, N.J., May 26, 1944; d. Stanley Marion and Cecilia Marie (Cantillon) Clark; m. Daniel Lester Boesz, June 26, 1965. AB, Douglass Coll., New Brunswick, N.J., 1966; MS, Rutgers U., 1967; DPH, U. Mich., 1997. Asst. prof. Math. Valdosta (Ga.) State Coll., 1967-69; statistical analyst Alamo Area Coun. Govts., San Antonio, 1969-71, Bexar County Med. Found., San Antonio, 1971-74, exec. dir., 1974-78; dep. dir. compliance office HMO U.S. Govt., Rockville, Md., 1978-86; sr. program and policy analyst Prepaid Health Care Health Care Financing Adminstrn., Washington, 1986-87, dir. compliance divsn. Prepaid Health Care, 1987-92, dir. ops. Office of Managed Care, 1992-95; v.p. govt. programs NYLCare Health Plans, N.Y.C., 1995—98; insp. gen. Nat. Sci. Found., 2000—; head regulatory accountability Aetna US Healthcare (AUSHC), 1998—99. Faculty preceptor George Washington U., 1995. Contrb. chpts. to books, articles to profl. jours. Pres. Scientists Cliffs Assn., Pt. Republic, Md., 1985-86. Recipient Pew Meml. Trust fellowship U. Mich., 1990-92. Mem. AAUW, APHA, Am. Statis. Assn., Nat. Assn. Managed Care Regulators (pres. 1985-86, sec. 1981-84, Lifetime Achievement award 1994), Zonta. Avocations: reading, travel. Office: Nat Sci Found 4201 Wilson Blvd Arlington VA 22230

BOETTGER, NANCY J., state legislator; b. Chgo., May 1, 1943; m. H. David Boettger; 4 children. BS, Iowa State U., 1965; BA, Buena Vista Coll., 1982. Owner farm, 1965—; spl. edn. tchr., 1965-66; tchr. jr. H.S., 1982-86; dir. edn. Myrtue Meml. Hosp., 1986-99; mem. Iowa Senate from 41st dist. (now 29th dist.), 1994—2004, asst. majority leader, 1996—2004. Mem. Midwest Legis. Coun., 1996-2000. Mem. First Bapt. Ch., People Who Care; former bd. dirs. Harlan Cmty. Libr.; former mem. dean's adv. bd. Iowa State U. Ext. Mem. PEO, Am. Legis. Exchange Coun., Midwest Coun. State Govts. (chair health and human svcs. 1997-99), Coun. State Govts. (mem. drug task force 1998), Iowa Coun. Internat. Understanding Bd., Shelby County Found. for Edn. (former exec. dir.), Farm Bur., Pork Prodrs. Republican. Home: 926 Ironwood Rd Harlan IA 51537-5308 Office: State Capitol Dist 41 3 9th And Grand Des Moines IA 50319-0001 E-mail: nancy_boettger@legis.state.ia.us.

BOETTICHER, HELENE, retired lawyer; b. Syracuse, N.Y., Mar. 26, 1920; d. Ford and Emily (Bennett) Zogg; m. William Donald Boetticher, Oct. 18, 1958 (dec. July 1990); children: John, Amy, Sally. BA, U. Wis., 1941, LLB, 1943. Bar: Wis., Ill. Atty. NLRB, Chgo., 1951—57, OSHA Rev., Washington, 1972—73, Dept. Labor, 1973—95, counsel for litigation, 1978—95; ret. Contbr. articles to profl. jours. Democrat. Episcopalian. Avocation: travel. Home: 15204 Carrolton Rd Rockville MD 20853 Office Phone: 301-929-1297. Personal E-mail: hzb3099@att.net.

BOFFA, LISA SAUNDERS See BAUGH, LISA

BOGACZ, DOLORES ROSALIE MARIE, retired elementary school educator, paralegal; b. Chgo., Ill., Nov. 26, 1938; d. Joseph C. and Rose Therese Bogacz. BA, Dominican U., River Forest, Ill., 1966; MS Edn., No. Ill. U., De Kalb, 1978; student, DePaul U., 1956—59; postgrad. studies, Gov's State U., Univ. Park, Ill., 1995, Carthage Coll., Kenosha, Wis., 2005. Cert. paralegal. Tchr. Ill. Pub. Schs., 1966—81; editor Riverside Press, Chgo., 1981; dean, asst. prin. Ill. Pub. Schs., 1982—84; prin. Ill. & Wis. Pub. Schs., Cath. Schs., Chgo. and Joliet, Ill., 1984—2004; paralegal Kenosha, Wis., 2005; ret. Author (editor) Curriculum Guide. Grantee Reading First grant, U.S. Govt., 2002. Mem.: Phi Delta Kappa. Roman Catholic. E-mail: drbogacz@wi.net.

BOGAN, ELIZABETH CHAPIN, economist, educator; b. Morristown, N.J., Aug. 22, 1944; d. Daryl Muscott and Tirzah (Walker) Chapin; m. Thomas Rockwood Bogan, June 5, 1965; children: Nathaniel Rockwood, Andrew Allerton. AB, Wellesley Coll., 1966; MA, U. N.H., 1967; PhD, Columbia U., 1971. Mem. faculty Fairleigh Dickinson U., Madison, NJ, 1971-92, prof. econs., 1982-92, chmn. merit scholarship com., 1981-82; reviewer univ. press Farleigh Dickinson U., Madison, NJ; mem. faculty Princeton (N.J.) U., sr. lectr. in econs., 1992—. Vis. prof. Princeton U., 1991. Author articles and macroecons. text Recipient Outstanding Tchr. award Fairleigh Dickinson U., 1979, 86, 87, Richard Quandt award for tchg. econs. Princeton U., 1997, 2005; NSF fellow, Pres'. fellow, Earhart fellow Columbia U., 1968-71. Mem. AAUP, Am. Econ. Assn., Ea. Econ. Assn., Atlantic Econ. Soc. Clubs: Wellesley, Beacon Hill. Congregationalist. Home: 41 Windermere Ter Short Hills NJ 07078-2254 Office: Princeton U 109 Fisher Hall Princeton NJ 08544

BOGAN, MARY ELLEN, draftsman, educator; b. Crowley, La., July 22, 1951; d. Lynn F. Lyons and Betty L. Chauvin; m. John C. Bogan, Sept. 13, 1975; children: John L., Charles N. M, U. Phoenix, 2006. Draftsman, Houston, 1995—2006; prof. drafting San Jacinto Coll. North, Houston, 2000—. Chair dept. San Jacinto Coll. North, Houston, 2001—. Mem.: Am. Soc. Engring. Educators (assoc.). R-Consevative. Episcopal. Home: 203 Wickhamford Way Houston TX 77015 Office: San Jacinto College North 5800 Uvalde Rd Houston TX 77049 E-mail: mary.bogan@sjcd.edu.

BOGAN, MARY FLAIR, stockbroker; b. Providence, July 9, 1948; d. Ralph A.L. and Mary (Dyer) B. BA, Vassar Coll., 1969. Actress Trinity Sq. Repertory Co., R.I., Gretna Playhouse, Pa., Skylight Comic Opera, Milw., Cin. Playhouse, Playmakers' Repertory, N.C.; mem. nat. co. No Sex, Please, We're Brit.; also TV comms., 1970-77; acct. exec. E.F. Hutton & Co., Inc., Providence, 1977-86; act. v.p. Paine Webber, 1986-97; v.p. investments Prudential Securities, Providence, 1997—2003, Wachovia Securities, 2003—; econ. reporter Sta. WPRI-TV, 1982-85, Sta. WJAR-TV, 1987—. Recipient Century Club award, 1980, 81, 82, 83, 85, Blue Chip Sales award, 1983, 85, Pacesetter Sales award, 1986-90; named Woman of Yr. Profl. Bus. and Rep. Women's Assn. Mem. Univ. Club, Brown Faculty. Home: 18 Cooke St Providence RI 02906-2023 Office: Wachovia Securities 900 Fleet Ctr 50 Kennedy Plz Providence RI 02903-2393

BOGARD, CAROLE CHRISTINE, soprano; b. Cin. d. Harold and Helen Christina (Whittlesey) Geistweit; m. Charles Paine Fisher, Dec. 30, 1966; children: Christine, Pamela. Student, San Francisco State U. Debuts include: Despina in Cosi fan Tutte (Mozart), San Francisco, 1965, Poppea in Coronation of Poppea (Monteverdi), Netherlands Opera, 1971; other appearances include, Boston Opera, N.E.T., orchs. Boston, Madrid, Minn., Phila., Pitts., San Francisco, summer festivals, Mostly Mozart, N.Y., Tanglewood, Carmel, Aston Magna, Gt. Barrington, Mass., appeared in concerts throughout Europe and with Smithsonian Chamber Players, 1976-; recorded numerous albums including 1st rec. of songs of John Duke for his 80th birthday, 1979, recital of Groupe des Six; premiered songs of Dominic Argento in, Holland, 1978, songs of Richard Cumming (in collaboration with Donald Gramm); regular participant rec. and scholarly projects, Smithsonian Instn.; judge regional auditions, Boston; tchr., with emphasis on technique as taught in last Century; recs. have been re-issued on CDs during the 1990s including Baroque Cantatas and Arias, Mozart C minor Mass, Mozart Coronation Mass., 2 CD collection American Songs, 2000; female lead 3 CD Handel opera Tamerlano, 2002. Mem. Sigma Alpha Iota Home: 161 Belknap Rd Framingham MA 01701-3886

BOGARD, EILEEN JUDITH, investor, retired small business owner, retired education administrator; b. Chgo., Sept. 18, 1945; d. John Joseph and Helen Agatha (Hoy) Kennedy; m. Robert L. Bogard Jr., Aug. 20, 2003; 1 child, Diana Marie Parks. BA, Northea. Ill. U., 1966, MA, 1976, postgrad., 1980-81, Nat. Coll. Edn., 1981, 83, No. Ill. U., 1987—. Tchr. Canty Elem. Sch., Chgo., 1967-76, St. Raymond's Sch., Mt. Prospect, Ill., 1976-78; pvt. practice diagnosis, remediation learning disabilities; cons. spl. edn. Des Plaines, Ill., 1976-78; prin. Angel Town Pvt. Sch., Des Plaines, 1978-79; tutoring, coop. work tng. coord. Nipper Sch., Des Plaines, 1979-86; tchr. acad. resources Oak Terr. Sch., Highwood, Ill., 1986-87; vocat. coord. North and West regions Sch. Assn. Spl. Edn. Du Page County, Roselle, Ill., 1987-89; prin. Sch. Assns. Spl. Edn./Du Page N. Alternative Sch., 1989-91, Aura Extended Day Sch., 1990-91; asst. prin. Stratford Jr. H.S., Bloomingdale, Ill., 1991-94, Foley Intermediate Sch., Foley, Ala., 1999-2001. Founder, pres. Handy Ma'ams, Inc., Allegan, Mich., 1994-99, Heartfelt Creations, S augatuck and Allegan, Mich., 1996; tchr. parent-edn. classes; cons. in field to pvt. schs., various groups and agys. Past chmn. Smiles Campaign; past mem. Glen Lakes Beautification Com. 1999-2002; mem. St. Matthew's Ch. Parish Events Com., 2006, Episcopal Ch. Women, 2005-06, Chapel Hill Homeowners's Assn., 2005-06; chairperson Relay for Life 2005-06. Mem.: TRADE Industries (parent group), Assn. U.S. Army, Hunstville Botanical Gardens, Newcomers Club Greater Huntsville (decoration Com. 2006, asst 3rd v.p.). Home and Office: 214 Avian Ln Madison AL 35758 Office Phone: 256-325-2040. Business E-Mail: leeny@knology.net.

BOGARD, MARGARET JOAN, nurse; b. New Castle, Pa., Apr. 5, 1933; d. Frank James and Anna Dorothy (Gonda) Smilek; m. John H. Bogard, Sept. 4, 1954; children: Cheryl Ann, Brian, Kenneth. RN, Providence Hosp., Beaver Falls, Pa., 1954. Med.-surg. nurse Providence Hosp., 1954-56, delivery rm. nurse, 1956-57; RN in home care, 1967-85; nurse continued edn. Harmerville (Pa.) Rehab., 1985, rehab. nurse, asst. phys. therapist to home care patients, 1986-94; office coord. in home care Med. Ctr., Beaver, Pa., 1994—2000, INCARE Home Health Agy., North Myrtle Beach, SC, 2000—.

BOGAS, KATHLEEN LAURA L., lawyer; b. Detroit, Mar. 4, 1951; d. Edward Joseph and Eleanor Laura (Hughes) B.; m. Frank Kavanaugh Rhodes III, Jan. 2, 1982; children: Katherine Bogas, Frank Kavanaugh IV. AB U. Detroit, 1972, JD 1975. Bar: Mich. 1975. Assoc. law firm Sachs, Nunn, Kates, Kadushin, O'Hare, Helveston & Waldman, P.C. (now Sachs, Waldman), Detroit, 1975-80, ptnr., 1981-2001, mng. dir., 1993, now ptnr. Eisenberg & Bogas PC. Mng. editor Jour. Urban Law, 1974-75. Mem. ATLA, Mich. Trial Lawyers Assn. (exec. bd. 1981—, chmn. jud. qualifications com. 1981—, chmn. ct. rules com. 1983-84, treas. 1993-94, sec. 1994-95, v.p. 1995, pres.-elect 1996-97, pres. 1997-98), Am., State Bar of Mich. (jud. qualifications com. 1983-89, 2003—, negligence coun., 1984-93, chair 1992-93, advanced tech. task force 1987-93), Women Lawyers of Mich. (labor and employment coun. 2002—), Detroit Bar Assn., Oakland County Bar Assn., Mich. Civil Rights Commn. (hearing referee 1983—), Am. Arbitration Assn., U. Detroit Sch. of Law Alumni Assn. (bd. dirs. 1986-92), Met. Trial Lawyers Assn. (bd. dirs. 1987-91), Nat. Employment Lawyers Assn. (co-chair trial practice com. 1994, exec. bd., 1999-, v.p. 2004-05, 1st v.p. 2005-2006), Women's Econ. Club of Detroit. Democrat. Office: Eisenberg & Bogas Ste 145 33 Bloomfield Hills Pkwy Bloomfield Hills MI 48304 Office Phone: 248-258-6080. Office Fax: 248-285-9212. Business E-Mail: klb@ebpclaw.com.

BOGDAN, CAROLYN LOUETTA, financial specialist, retired small business owner; b. Wilkes-Barre, Pa., Apr. 15, 1941; d. Walter Cecil and Ethna Louetta (Kendig) Carpenter; m. James Thomas Bogdan, May 5, 1961; 1 child, Thomas James. Head bookkeeper Forty Ft. (Pa.) State Bank, 1959-63, U.S. Nat. Bank, Long Beach, Calif., 1963-65; office mgr. United Parts Exch., Long Beach, 1976-81; contract adminstr. Johnson Controls, Inc., Rancho Dominguez, Calif., 1981-88, credit coord., 1989-98; co-owner, acct. Bogdan Elec. R & D, Lakewood, Calif., 1981—98; ret., 1998. Mem. Radio Amateur Civil Emergency Svc., L.A. County Sheriff Dept., 1974—, records keeper, 1988—93, radio comm. officer, 1994—2002. Mem. Tournament of Roses Radio Amateurs (pin chmn. 1975-2005), Calif. State Sheriffs Assn. (assoc.), Calif. State Office Emergency Svcs. Republican. Avocations: crocheting, gardening, electronics, amateur radio. Home: 3713 Capetown St Lakewood CA 90712-1437

BOGDANOWICZ, LORETTA MAE, artist, educator; b. West Palm Beach, Fla., Aug. 11, 1940; d. James Paul and Bessie Margaret (Smith) Cone; m. Lawrence Robert Bogdanowicz, July 18, 1959; children: Laura June Ford, Michael David, Denise Ann Pharris. AA, Ocean County Coll., Toms River, N.J., 1982; BFA, U. Ariz., 1996. Cert. art tchr., Ariz. Art instr. Ariz. Theatre Co., Tucson, 1997-98, Catalina Foothills Cmty. Sch., Tucson, 1997-98, Tucson Mus. Art Edn., 1997—2004; incorporator Floorcloths and More, Inc., 2001; art instr. Pima CC, Tucson, 2002—. Exhibited in solo and group shows. Vis. artist Devon Gables Health Care Ctr., Tucson, 1997-2001; instr. neighborhood classes; artist in residence Acacia Elem. Sch., Vail. Recipient Liquitex Paint Exch. award, 1996. Mem.: Tucson/Pima Arts Coun., Tucson Mus. Art, Phi Kappa Phi. Avocations: hiking, photography, gardening, reading, travel.

BOGEN, NANCY, writer, English educator; b. Bklyn., Apr. 24, 1932; d. George Meyer and Rose (Zwaifler) Warshaw; m. Hyman Bogen, May 1965 (div. 1969); m. Arnold Greissle-Schönberg, Jan. 13, 1989. BA, NYU, 1952; MA in English Lit., Columbia U., N.Y.C., 1962, PhD in English Lit., 1968. Asst. prof. English Richmond Coll., CUNY, S.I., N.Y., 1967-76; prof. English Coll. of S.I., 1976—. Artistic dir. The Lark Ascending, N.Y.C., 1997. Author: A Critical Edition of William Blake's book of Thel, 1971; (novels) Klytaimnestra Who Stayed at Home, 1980, Bobe Mayse, A Tale of Washington Square, 1993, Bagatelle.Guinevere, 1995; (play) Coeur de Lion, Mon Coeur, 2000, Twelve-Tone Blues, 2005, Lost Morning Eyes, 2005; (textbook) How to Write Poetry, 1990, 3d edit., 1998. Fellow Va. Ctr. Creative Arts, 1987; grantee Poets and Writers, 1995—. Mem. PEN, Dramatists Guild Am. Home: 31 Jane St Apt 17B New York NY 10014-1982 Office Phone: 212-741-2417. Personal E-mail: nancyrbogen@cs.com.

BOGER, CHERYL LYNN, academic administrator, education educator; b. Columbia, Ky., Aug. 8, 1962; d. Dale Mann and Betty Lou Riggs; m. Mike Boger, July 3, 2004; children: Wes Whitehead, Kelly Whitehead. Assoc. Early Childhood Edn., Lindsey Wilson Coll., 2000, B Human Svcs., 2002, M Mental Health Counseling, 2004. Tchr. KCEOC Head Start, Manchester, Ky., 1987—96, Lake Cumberland Head Start, Russell Springs, Ky., 1997—2002; coord., advisor, instr. Lindsey Wilson Coll., Columbia, Ky., 2002—. Bd. dirs., treas. Lake Cumberland Children Advocacy Ctr., Jamestown, Ky.; presenter in field. Named Tchr. Who Made a Difference, U. Ky. Coll. Edn., 2006. Mem.: ACA, Ky. Mental Health Counseling Assn., Ky. Counseling Assn. Avocations: gardening, remodeling, reading. Office: Lindsey Wilson Coll 210 Lindsey Wilson St Columbia KY 42728

BOGER, GAIL GREEN PARSONS, educator; b. Worthington, Ind., June 8, 1914; d. Byron Tennison and Bula (Taylor) Green; m. Alva B. Parsons, June 8, 1935; children: Donald Alva, Robert Bradley, Gail Marie Parsons Michel, Helen Jean Parsons Czuba; m. Clarence O. Boger, Aug. 10, 1974; stepchildren: Donald Boger, Maxine Rideout, Sandra Plummer. BS, Ind. U., 1950, MS, 1959; postgrad., U. Internat., Santandar, Spain, 1968; PhD, U. Utah, 1969. Instr. Fresno (Calif.) State Jr. Coll., 1948-54; asst. prof. Purdue U. Extension, Michigan City, Ind., 1955-58; tchr. Jr.-Sr. High Sch., Michigan City, 1954-59; instr. Ind. U., Bloomington, 1959-64; prof. dept. edn. and Sch. Engring. Ohio No. U., Ada, from 1964, now prof. emeritus. Adj. instr. world geography Defiance Coll., Ohio, earth sci. Blufton Coll., Ohio; chmn. internat. research com. Children's Internat. Summer Villages, Inc., 1980-85, chmn. nat. research com., trustee, hon. life mem. 1988; researcher comparative ednl. systems in Cairo, Teheran, Iran, Iceland, Can., 1974. Author lab. manuals on physical, human geography and engring. geology; cons. Internat. Rsch. and Devel. Jour.; contbr. articles to profl. jours. Dupont fellow, 1957; NSF fellow, 1961, 63; NSF-AEC fellow, 1960 Mem. Am. Assn. for Supervision and Curriculum Devel., Am. Assn. Coll. Tchrs. of Edn., AAUP, Nat. Assn. Edn. of Gifted (dir., past v.p.), Nat. Assn. Creative Children and Adults (nat. trustee), Ohio Assn. Gifted Children, NEA, Ohio Edn. Assn., N.W. Ohio Edn. Assn., Ohio Acad. Sci., Gifted Children's Study Club, Kappa Delta Pi, Kappa Sigma Pi, Kappa Phi Clubs: Federated Women's. Democrat. Episcopalian. Office: Ohio No U 315 Dukes Ada OH 45810

BOGER, GAIL LORRAINE ZIVNA, reading specialist; b. Portland, Oreg., Sept. 15, 1946; d. Stephen Edward and Harriet Lucille (Laws) Zivna; m. Dan Calvin Boger, June 23, 1973; children: Gretchen, Gregory. BS in Edn., Oreg. State U., Corvallis, 1968; MA in Edn., Stanford U., Calif., 1973; MA in Reading, U. LaVerne, 1982. Cert. reading and lang. arts specialist, Calif. Elem. tchr. Monterey (Calif.) Peninsula Unified Sch. Dist., 1968-72, 73-75, lang. arts tchr., 1979-81; elem. tchr. San Ramon (Calif.) Unified Sch. Dist., 1976-79; Miller-Unruh reading specialist Monterey (Calif.) Peninsula Unified Sch. Dist., 1983—, reading specialist Title 1, lit. coach, 2004—, literacy coach, reading specialist, 2005—. Mem.: Reading is Fundamental Program, Monterey County Reading Assn., Calif. Reading Assn., Internat. Reading Assn., Delta Kappa Gamma (rec. sec. 1992—94, 2002—04). Avocations: music, piano, reading, golf. Home: 27 Cramden Dr Monterey CA 93940-4145 Personal E-mail: dngboger@sbcglobal.net.

BOGGAN, AMY L., secondary school educator, education educator; b. Meridian, Miss., Oct. 21, 1973; d. Robert E. and Voncile A. Boggan. BA, U. So. Miss., Hattiesburg, 1996; MA, U. Md., College Park, 2000. Secondary composite social studies cert. Tex. Tchr., PACE/humanities and pre-AP/IB geography Clark HS, Plano, Tex., 2000—; assoc. prof. Collin County C.C., Plano, 2003—. Mem. site-based improvement com. Clark HS, 2004—; mem. social studies curriculum devel. com. Plano Ind. Sch. Dist. Dep. voter registrar Collin County Elections Dept., McKinney, Tex., 2004; mem. Plano Civic Chorus. Islamic Cultural Studies scholar, U. Tex., Austin. Mem.: Tex. Assn. Gifted and Talented, Nat. Coun. Social Studies. Avocations: music, games. Office: Clark HS 523 W Spring Creek Pky Plano TX 75023 Office Phone: 469-752-7200.

BOGGESS, CAROL BROWNSCOMBE, language educator, writer; d. Clement Dale and Evelyn McIver Brownscombe; m. Samuel Forest Boggess, Aug. 24, 1977; children: Laura McIver, William Cowan. MA in TESL, U. Ill., Urbana, 1977; MA in English, Syracuse U., NY, 1972; PhD in English, U. Ky., Lexington, 1995. Tchg. lic. secondary English NC. English tutor U. Adelaide, South Australia, Australia, 1972—73; asst. dir. girls' English program King Faisal U., Dammam, Saudi Arabia, 1977—83; English instr. Mayland CC, Spruce Pine, NC, 1984—87; prof., chair divsn. humanities Mars Hill (NC) Coll., 1987—, Jefferson Pilot prof., 1999. Bd. dirs. Together We Read, NC, 2005—06, NC Humanities Coun., 2002—. Recipient Gibbs Outstanding Tchr. award, Mars Hill Coll., 2001; grantee, NEH, 2001; John Stephenson fellow, Appalachian Coll. Assn., 2002—03. Mem.: NC Humanities Coun., Appalachian Studies Assn., Nat. Coun. Tchrs. English, Sigma Tau Delta, Phi Kappa Phi, Phi Beta Kappa. Avocations: travel, gardening, hiking.

BOGGS, BETH CLEMENS, lawyer; b. Dubuque, Iowa, July 28, 1967; d. Theodore Alan and Mary Ann (Fleckenstein) Clemens; m. T. Darin Boggs, Mar. 9, 1991. BA, Govs. State U., 1987; JD, So. Ill. U., 1991. Bar: Ill. 1991, Mo. 1992, U.S. Dist. Ct. (so. dist.) Ill. 1991, U.S. Dist. Ct. (ea. dist.) Mo. 1992, U.S. Dist. Ct. (we. dist.) Mo. 2002, U.S. Dist. Ct. (cen. dist.) Ill. 1997. Clk. R. Courtney Hughes & Assocs., Carbondale, Ill., 1990-91; lawyer Sandberg Phoenix & von Gontard, St. Louis, 1991-93; assoc. LaTourette, Schlueter & Byrne, St. Louis, 1993-95; mng. ptnr. Landau, Omahana & Kopka, P.C., St. Louis, 1995-99; mng. and founding ptnr. Boggs, Backer & Bates, LLC, St. Louis, 1999—2002, Boggs, Boggs & Bates, LLC, St. Louis, 2002—. Adj. prof. Webster U., 1995-; former vice-chair A.B.A. Law and Medicine Sect. and Corp. Counsel Com. Editor student articles So. Ill. U. Law Jour., 1991; contbr. articles to profl. jours; speaker and author: insurance and legal/medical topics; published articles in the S.I.U. Law Journal, the Illinois Bar Jour., The Jour. Mo. Bar and the ABA Mag., Contbr. Rights & Remedies and Litig. Settlements. Named one of Lawyers of the Year, Mo. Lawyers Weekly, 2005. Mem. Young Lawyers divsn. of ABA (vice chair corp. counsel com. 1991-92, editor Corp. Counsel Newsletter 1991-92), Bus. Women St. Louis, Women Lawyers Assn., Def. Rsch. Inst., Mo. Orgn. Def. Lawyers; Am. Bar Assn., Tort & Ins. Sect. and Health Care Law Sect., Mo. Bar, Ill. State Bar Assn., Bar Assn. of Metropolitan St. Louis, Lawyers Assn. of St. Louis, St. Clair County Bar Assn., Nat. Assn. Ins. Women, Transp. Lawyers Assn. Avocations: tennis, softball, golf. Office: BBB 7912 Bonhomme Ave Ste 400 Saint Louis MO 63105-3512 Office Phone: 314-726-2310. Office Fax: 314-726-2360. Personal E-mail: bbblawyers@aol.com. Business E-Mail: bboggs@bbblawyers.com.

BOGGS, CATHERINE J., lawyer; b. Denver, 1954; BA, U. Denver, 1976; MS, Mich. State U., 1977; JD, U. Denver, 1981. Bar: Colo. 1982, Oreg. 1991, Calif. 1993. Atty. Sherman & Howard, 1982—90, Stoel Rives, 1991—93, Baker & McKenzie, Chgo., 1993—. Trustee Rocky Mountain Mineral Law Found., 2001—. Mem.: ABA, Soc. Mining, Metallurgy and Exploration, Soc. Mining, Oreg. State Bar Assn., Colo. Bar Assn., Calif. State Bar Assn. Office: Baker & McKenzie One Prudential Plz 130 East Randolph Dr Chicago IL 60601 Office Phone: 312-861-8000.

BOGGS, PAULA ELAINE, lawyer; b. Washington, May 2, 1959; d. Nathaniel Boggs Jr. and Janice C. (Anderson) Barber. BA, Johns Hopkins U., 1981; JD, U. Calif., Berkeley, 1984. Bar: Pa. 1986, D.C. 1988, Wash. 1992, U.S. Dist. Ct. (we. dist.) Wash. 1988, U.S. Ct. Appeals (9th cir.) 1990, U.S. Ct. Appeals (D.C. and fed. cirs.) 1995. Sr. law clk. Office of Army Gen. Counsel, Arlington, Va., 1984-85; spl. asst. Office of Dep. Under Sec. of the Army, Arlington, 1985-86; staff atty. White House Iran-Contra legal task force, Washington, 1987-88; asst. U.S. atty. we. dist. U.S. Atty.'s Office, Seattle, 1988-93; staff dir. adv. bd. investigative capability dept. def. Dept. Def., Arlington, 1994; ptnr. Preston Gates & Ellis, Seattle, 1995—97; v.p. legal Dell Computer Corp., 1997—2002; exec. v.p., gen. counsel, sec. Starbucks, Seattle, 2002—. Mem. faculty Nat. Inst. for Trial Advocacy, 1995; adj. prof. law U. Wash., Seattle, 1993. Vol. instr. presdl. classroom for young Ams., Washington, 1991; bd. dirs. ctrl. dist. YMCA, Seattle, 1991-93, Greater Seattle YMCA, 1995—; nat. chair Johns Hopkins U. Second Decade Soc., Balt., 1995-96. With U.S. Army, 1981-88. Recipient Sec. Def. award for Excellence William J. Perry, 1994; Presdl. svc. badge Pres. Ronald Reagan, 1988; Def. Meritorious Svc. award, 1987, Spl. Achievement award Dept. Justice, 1990, 91. Mem. ABA (ho. of dels., litigation sect. co-chair bus. torts com., bus. crimes com., criminal justice sect. white collar crimes com., standing com. on constn. and bylaws), Nat. Bar Assn., Wash. State Bar Assn. (corrections com.), King County Bar Assn., Fed. Bar Assn., Wash. Women Lawyers (bd. dirs. 1991-93), Loren Miller Bar Assn. Avocations: running, bicycling, reading. Office: Starbucks 2401 Utah Ave S PO Box 34067 Seattle WA 98134

BOGGUS, TAMARA, elementary school educator; d. Sarah M. Grantham; m. Jon C. Boggus, Oct. 22, 1983; children: Cullen, Marshall, Livesay. BS in Geology, Millsaps Coll., Jackson, Miss., 1982; MA in Tchg. and Learning, Nova Southeastern U., Ft. Lauderdale, Fla., 2002. Tchr. secondary sci. Suwannee H.S., Live Oak, Fla., 1983—. Coord. sci. fair Suwannee County

Sch. Bd., Live Oak, Fla., 2003—; presenter in field. Mem. St. Lukes Episcopal Ch., Live Oak, Fla. Recipient Tchr. Yr., Suwannee H.S., 2002. Mem.: Alpha Delta Kappa (treas. 1996—2006). Office Phone: 386-364-2639.

BOGHOSSIAN, JOAN THOMPSON, artist; b. Newport, R.I., Mar. 6, 1932; d. Joseph and Hope (Bliss) Thompson; m. Paul O. Boghossian Jr., 1952 (dec. July 1995); children: Carol Boghossian Spencer, Paul O. III, David M., Nancy Boghossian Staples. BS, U. R.I., 1953. One person shows at Attleboro Mus., Newton Libr. Gallery, Charlestown Gallery; two-person shows at Providence Art Club (J. Banigan Sullivan prize 1984, David Aldrica award 2005), Dodge House Gallery; group exhbn. at RI Watercolor Soc. (1st in watercolor 1988, 91, Block Artists Merchandise award 1989, Grumbacher Gold Medallion 1990, 93, 94, Dr. Edwin Dunlop award 1997), Mystic Art Assn. (1st in watercolor 1990, 92, 93, 95, Mystic Manor spl. award for aquatint 1992), Wickford Art Assn. (1st in watercolor 1986, 1st in all-media 1993, 2d in oil 1995), South County Art Assn. (award 1987, Florence B. Kane award 1989, Herbert Richard Cross award 1992, C. Gordon Harris award 1993, 1st prize award 1997), Peel Gallery-Danby, Vt., New Eng. South Shore Artists (Best in Show 1986), Cape Cod Art Assn. (1st in watercolor 1987, 90, 1st in graphics 1987, 2d in watercolor 1988, 92, Juror's award of merit 1994), Warwick Arts Found. (1st in watercolor 1985); RI Watercolor Soc. David Marsland Meml. Award, Providence Art Club, Wm. S. Brigham Award and Juror's Choice Award, Warwick Mus.Open, Am. Frame Award, 2002; others. Recipient Hon. mention award, Newport Art Mus., 2006. Mem.: others, New Eng. Watercolor Soc. (James W. Duffy award 1998), South County Art Assn. (1st prize Open Annual South County award 1997, Kinney award Best Floral Painting 1996, C. Gordon Harris award 1993, Herbert Richard Cross award 1992, Best Marine Painting Loring award 1990, Florence B. Kane award 1989, Art Assn. award 1987), Wickford Art Assn. (1st pl. in show 1996, 2nd pl. in oil 1994, 1st pl. all-medal 1993), Mystic Art Assn. (1st pl. watercolor Annual Regional Exhbn. 1990, 1992, 1993, 1995, Mystic Manor Spl. award for Aquatint 1992), R.I. Watercolor Soc. (Dr. Edwin Dunlop Meml. award 1997, Grumbacher gold medallion 1990, 1993, 1994, 1st pl. Watercolor Soc. Open 1987, 1988, 1991), Providence Art Club (Frederick Sisson award 1988), Copley Soc. Boston, Catherine Lorillard Wolfe Art Club (Anna Hyatt Huntington medal 1996, Mary Hill Meml. award 1998). Home: 640 East Ave Pawtucket RI 02860-6158 Studio: 7 Thomas St Providence RI 02903-1314

BOGLE, KIMBERLY LAYNG, physical education educator; d. Warren Fredrick and Susan Layng Bogle. BS in Bus. and Exercise Sci., Skidmore Coll., Saratoga Springs, NY, 1996; MS in Movement Sci., Fla. State U., Tallahassee, 1998, PhD in Sport Mgmt., 2002. Asst. prof. sport mgmt. Daniel Webster Coll., 2004—05; asst. prof. So. NH U., Mancester, 2005—. Office Phone: 603-668-2211.

BOGLE, MELISSA ANNE, dermatologist, educator; d. John and Helen Bogle. BS, Stanford U., Calif., 1995; MD, U. Tex., Houston, 1999. Resident in dermatology U. Tex. Health Sci. Ctr. Houston, 2004; post-residency fellow lasers and cosmetic surgery SkinCare Physicians (Boston, MA), Boston, 2005; dir. Laser and Cosmetic Surgery Ctr. Houston; clin. asst. prof. U. Tex. MD Anderson Cancer Ctr., Houston. Cons. laser, cosmetic surgery and gen. dermatology; lectr. in field. Contbr. over 10 book chpts., over 31 articles to profl. jours.; chair (texas dermatological society) Commitee on Mentoring and Leadership, member (american society of dermatologic surgery) Resident Education Work Group, (women's dermatologic society), award recipient (research) Humanities and Technology in Health Care Scholar. Fellow: Am. Soc. Dermatologic Surgery, Am. Soc. Laser Medicine and Surgery, Am. Acad. Dermatology (Young Leaders in Dermatology award 2006). Achievements include development of new techniques for radiofrequency skin tightening; research in glass laser for inflammatory facial acne; effect of thermage treatment over dermal fillers, plasma skin rejuvination; effect of volume on the diffusion and efficacy of botulinum toxin type A in the treatment of lateral orbital rhytids; pulsed dye laser versus KTP laser for reduction of facial telangiectasias. Avocations: travel, art, books, history. Office: Laser and Cosmetic Surgery Ctr Houston 3700 Buffalo Speedway Ste 700 Houston TX 77098 Office Phone: 713-622-1720.

BOGSTAHL, DEBORAH MARCELLE, market research consultant; b. Irvington, NJ, June 5, 1950; d. Marcel and Helena Christina (de Jaroszynsky) Bogstahl; children: Alexandra Boman, Michelle Boman. BA in English Edn., The Coll. of NJ, 1972. Cert. tchr., NJ Project dir. US Testing Co., Hoboken, NJ, 1973-75; project dir. J. Walter Thompson Co., NYC., 1975-77; rsch. account exec. Dancer Fitzgerald Sample, NYC, 1977-80; group rsch. mgr. Bristol-Myers Co., NYC, 1980-87; dir. rsch. Med. Econs. Co., Inc., Oradell, NJ, 1987-90; mktg. rsch. mgr. The Mennen Co., 1991-92, Reckitt & Colman, Inc., Wayne, NJ, 1992-2000, Kraft Foods, 2000—. Contbr. poetry to anthology. Mem. Am. Mktg. Assn., Product Devel. and Mgmt. Assn. Democrat. Roman Catholic. Avocations: sailing, reading, writing, music. Home: 45 Lapis Cir West Orange NJ 07052

BOHAN, GLORIA, travel company executive; BA, Marymount Manhattan Coll., LLD with hon., 2003. With Forbes Mag.; pres. Omega World Travel, Fairfax, Va., 1972—. Bd. dirs. Am. Bus. Conf., Greater Washington Bd. Trade. With Race for the Cure, Suited for Change, Leukemia Lymphoma Soc., Salvation Army; bd. mem. Fairfax County Edn. Found, Enterprising Women Mag, C. of C., Va. Found. Independent Coll. Recipient Woman Yr., Network Entrepreneurial Women, 1990, Entrepreneurial Visionary award, 2003; named Businesswoman of Yr., Office Depot, 2004; named to Enterprising Women Hall of Fame, 2005. Mem. Nat. Assn. Women Bus. Owners, Am. Soc. Travel Agts. (Travel Agt. of Yr. award 2004), Soc. Govt. Travel Profls. (pres. 1986-87). Office: Omega World Travel Inc 3102 Omega Office Park Fairfax VA 22031-2400 Fax: 703-350-8880. Office Phone: 703-359-0200. E-mail: gbohan@owt.net.

BOHAN, RUTH LOUISE, art educator; b. Galesburg, Ill., Dec. 27, 1946; d. John Lynch and Ethel Margaret (Gillmor) B. BA, U. Ill., 1969; MA, U. Md., 1972, PhD, 1980. Rsch. assoc. Yale U. Art Gallery, New Haven, 1979-80; Mellon fellow Washington U., St. Louis, 1980-81; asst. prof. art history U. Mo., St. Louis, 1981-87, assoc. prof., 1987—2006, prof., 2006—. Chairperson U. Mo., St. Louis, 1995-1998, 1999-2003. Author: The Société Anonyme's Brooklyn Exhibition: Katherine Dreier and Modernism in America, 1982; contbg. editor: The Société Anonyme Collection and The Dreier Bequest at Yale University: A Catalogue Raisonné, 1984, Looking Into Walt Whitman, 1850-1920, 2006; also articles. Grantee Smithsonian Instn., 1975-76, 87, NEH, 1984, J. Paul Getty Trust, 1985-86. Mem. MLA, Am. Studies Assn., Coll. Art Assn., Mid-Am. Am. Studies Assn. Office: Univ Mo Dept Art and Art History One University Blvd Saint Louis MO 63121-4499

BOHANNON, SARAH VIRGINIA, personnel professional; b. Roanoke, Va., Mar. 1, 1947; AA in Bus. Adminstrn. Mgmt., Nat. Bus. Coll., 1983. Pers. appointment clk. IRS, Richmond, Va., 1983—84; pers. technician Commonwealth of Va., Richmond, Va., 1985—97, pers. asst., 1997—98, pers. technician, 1999—2000, pers. adminstrv. specialist dept. human resource mgmt., 2001—02; human resources rep. City of Richmond, 2004. Mem. Am. Biog. Inst. (life, dep. gov. 1991, mem. women's inner circle of achievement 1991). Home: 8006 Anoka Rd Richmond VA 23229-3308

BOHANON, KATHLEEN SUE, neonatologist; b. Mpls., 1951; BA summa cum laude, U. Minn., 1973, MD, 1977. Diplomate Am. Bd. Pediat., Am. Bd. Neonatal-Perinatal Medicine. Commd. 2d lt. USAF, 1973, advanced through grades to col., 1995; resident in pediats. Case Western Res. U., Cleve., 1977-80; gen. pediatrician USAF, 1980-85; fellow in neonatology Wilford Hall Med. Ctr., San Antonio, 1985-87; neonatologist, dir. neonatal ICU USAF Med. Ctr., Wright-Patterson AFB, Ohio, 1987-95, chmn. dept. pediat., 1995-98, chief med. staff, 1998-2000; ret., 2000; locum tenens neonatologist, 2001—03; staff neonatologist St. Mary's Hosp. and Med. Ctr., Grand Junction, Colo., 2004—06; ret., 2006. Asst. clin. prof. pediat. U. N.D. Sch. Medicine, Grand Forks, 1981-82; assoc. Wright State U. Sch. Medicine, Dayton, Ohio, 1987-2000, Uniformed Svc. U. Health Scis., Washington, 1988-2000; mem. com. Infant Bio-Ethics Com., Dayton, 1990-2000. Fellow Am. Acad. Pediat.

BOHEN, BARBARA ELIZABETH, archaeologist, retired museum director; b. Bradford-on-Avon, Eng., Apr. 24, 1941; arrived in US, 1960; d. Charles Henry and Rhoda Victoria (Chenery) Jones; m. Robert D. Bohen (div.); 1 child, Leonora La Peter. Cert., Mus. Mgmt. Inst., 1982; BA in Classics, CUNY, 1969; MA in Fine Arts, NYU, 1973, PhD in Classical Art and Archaeology, 1979. Lectr. archaeology NYU, NYC, 1972—73; lectr. art history Queens Coll. CUNY, NYC, 1973; lectr. archaeology Am. Cmty Schs., Athens, Greece, 1975; from asst. to dir. to rsch. assoc. Kerameikos Mus., Athens, 1977—81; mus. dir. World Heritage Mus., Champaign, Ill., 1981—97; rsch. archaeologist German Archaeol. Inst., Athens, 2004—. Adj. prof. classics U. Ill., Champaign, 1992—98. Business E-Mail: bohen@uiuc.edu.

BOHI, LYNN, state legislator; b. Cleve., Feb. 20, 1947; m. Charles W. Bohi. BA, Olivet Coll., 1970; postgrad., Plymouth State U. State rep. Vt. Ho. of Reps., 1989—90, 1993—98, 2001—; chair local govt. com., 1997—98; vice chair local govt. com., 2003—04; vice chair govt. ops. com., 2005. Active Conn. River Joint Commn. Upper Valley River Subcom., Human Svcs. Coun., 1987-89, United Way Upper Valley, 1981-88, Hartford Recycles, Workforce Investment Bd., Adult Edn. Coun., 1997-2003, Cmty. Partnership of Orange and Windsor Counties; trustee EarthRight, 1991-94. Mem. No. Light Quilting Guild, Hartford Garden Friends. Address: 156 Manning Dr White River Junction VT 05001-8075 Office Phone: 802-828-2228. E-mail: lbohi@leg.state.vt.us.

BOHLE, SUE, public relations executive; b. Austin, Minn., June 23, 1943; d. Harold Raymond and Mary Theresa (Swanson) Hastings; m. John Bernard Bohle, June 22, 1974; children: Jason John, Christine K. BS in Journalism, Northwestern U., 1965, MS in Journalism, 1969. Tchr. pub. high schs, Englewood, Colo., 1965-68; account exec. Burson-Marsteller Pub. Relations, Los Angeles, 1969-73; v.p., mgr. pub. relations J. Walter Thompson Co., Los Angeles, 1973-79; founder, pres. The Bohle Company, L.A., 1979—; pres., CEO The Bohle Co., L.A.; former exec. v.p. Ketchum Pub. Rels., L.A. Free-lance writer, instr. communications Calif. State U. at Fullerton, 1972-73; instr. writing Los Angeles City Coll., 1975-76; lectr. U. So. Calif., 1979—. Contbr. articles to profl. jours. Dir. pub. rels. L.A. Jr. Ballet, 1971-72; pres. Panhellenic Advisers Coun., UCLA, 1972-73; mem. adv. bd. L.A. Valley Coll., 1974-75, Coll. Communications Pepperdine U., 1981-85, Sch. Journalism U. So. Calif., 1987-95, Calif. State U., Long Beach, 1988-93; bd. visitors Medill Sch. Journalism Northwestern U., 1984—. Recipient Alumni Svc. award Northwestern U., 1995; Univ. scholar, 1961-64, Panhellenic scholar, 1964-65; named to Hall of Achievement, Medill Sch. Journalism, 1997, charter mem. Hall of Fame; named to 50 Top Women in PR, PR Week, mag., 2001. Fellow Pub. Rels. Soc. Am. (bd. dirs. L.A. chpt. 1981-90, v.p. 1983, pres. 1989, del. nat. assembly 1980, 94, 95, 96, co-chmn. long-range strategic com. 1990, pres.'s adv. coun. 1991, exec. com. Counselors Acad. 1984-86, sec.-treas. 1990, chmn. 1992, sec. Coll. Fellows 1993, vice chair 1994, chmn. 1995, Silver Anvil award 1994); mem. Worldcom PR Network (bd. dirs. 2002—), World Com., Women in Comm., Shi-ai, Delta Zeta (editor The Lamp 1966-68, Woman of Yr. award 1993), Kappa Alpha Tau. Office: 1900 Avenue of the Stars # 200 Los Angeles CA 90067-4301 Office Phone: 310-785-0515 ext. 223. E-mail: sue@bohle.com.

BOHMAN, CAROL ELIZABETH, secondary educator; b. Erie, Pa., Oct. 9, 1962; d. Frederick Elmer and Sally Ann (Lindy) Buck; m. Mark Allen Bohman, Aug. 11, 1990; 1 child, Alex Andrea, Brian Allen. BA, Edinboro (Pa.) U., 1985, MEd, 1991. Cert. tchr. II, Pa. Secondary tchr. social studies Smethport (Pa.) Area Sch. Dist., 1986-87, Millcreek Twp. Sch. Dist., Erie, 1987—. Avocations: reading, tennis, crafts, cooking, music. Office: Millcreek Twp Sch Dist 901 W 54th St Erie PA 16509-2505

BOHRER, JANE ROTHROCK, controller; b. Teaneck, NJ, Sept. 4, 1957; d. Charles Edward and Rose Marie Rothrock; m. James Michael Bohrer; children: Jessica, Matthew. Bacholor of Science, Virginia Tech, Blacksburg, Virginia, 1975—79; MS, Fairfield (Conn.) U., 1990. Cert. mgmt. acct., 1987. Mgr. Arthur Andersen, LLP, N.Y.C., 1996—97; corp. controller RBC Am., Inc., Fairfield, Conn., 1997—. Treas. Va. Tech. SGA, Blacksburg, 1978—79; adj. prof. U. Conn., Stamford, 1985—87; v.p. RBC Fgn. Sales Corp, Bridgetown, Barbados, 1997—. Mem.: NAFE, Inst. Mgmt. Accts. Roman Catholic. Avocations: reading, sports, travel. Office: RBC of America Inc 60 Round Hill Road Fairfield CT 06430 Home: 3508 Cedar Grove Cir Virginia Beach VA 23452-6030 Office Fax: 203-256-0775. Personal E-mail: bohrerbc@aol.com. Business E-Mail: jbohrer@rbcbearings.com.

BOHRER, TEREZIE S., human service consultant; b. Mar. 28, 1939; d. Carl Straka and Viola Straka-Valone; m. Norman K. Bohrer, June 14, 1959; children: Jan. Sheri, Thia, Shelli. Diploma, Mt. Sinai Hosp. Sch. Nursing, N.Y.C., 1959; BS Sociology/Social Work magna cum laude, Bowie (Md.) State Coll., 1976; MSW, U. Md., Balt., 1978. RN, N.Y.; cert. legal nurse cons., Vicki Millazo Inst. 2005. Head nurse, instr. Mt. Sinai Hosp., 1960-62; staff nurse Bowie Internal Medicine Assocs., 1964-70; staff nurse, supr. Prince George's Hosp. and Med. Ctr., 1970-76; exec. dir. Prince George's County Office Coord. Svcs. to Handicapped, 1978-85; facility rights advisor and supr. Dept. Health and Mental Hygiene, State of Md., 1986-92; human svcs. pvt. cons. and trainer, 1989—; dir. Prince George's County Dept. Family Svcs., 1992-99; propr. Terezie S. Bohrer & Assocs., Human Svcs. Cons., Bowie, Md., 1999—. Contbr. articles to profl. jours. Disaster mental health coord., ARC, 2006-; served on numerous task forces. Mem. ACLU, Am. Heart Assn., LWV, Nat. Jewish Dem. Coun., Mental Health Assn. Prince George's County, Mental Health Assn. Md. (pres.), Alpha Delta Mu, Phi Kappa Phi, Alpha Chi, Alpha Kappa Delta. Address: 16304 Bawtry Ct Bowie MD 20715-4367 Office Phone: 301-262-2772. E-mail: tshohrer@yahoo.com.

BOHRMAN, CATHERINE LEUCHS, sculptor; d. Frederick L. Leuchs and G. Marie Bidwell; m. David E. Bohrman, June 9, 1976; children: Amber Bohrman Warrington, Harrison Zerr. Bachelors in Edn., Stanford U. Sculpture, Dawn Series, Dubai, United Arab Emirates, Legacy, Constitution Hall, Washington, Joan Scarangelo Found. award. Mem.: DAR, Wash. Sculptors Group, Conn. Women Artists, Nat. Sculpture Soc. (colleague 1996), Greenwich Art Soc. (life; v.p. publicity 1985—2000), Nat. League Am. Pen Women (life; local and nat. bds. 1994). Personal E-mail: catherine@bohrman.com.

BOICE, MARTHA HIBBERT, writer, publishing executive; b. Toledo, Oct. 1, 1931; d. George Wilfrid and Gladys (Harbage) Hibbert; m. William V. Boice, Nov. 26, 1955; children: Ruth Celeste Boice Oake, Thomas Wilson, Judith Lynette. BA, Ohio Wesleyan U., 1953; MSW, U. Mich., 1955. Caseworker Travelers Aid, Toledo, 1955-57; pub. Knot Garden Press, Dayton, Ohio, 1986—. Author, compiler: Shaker Herbal Fare, 1985, The Wreath Maker, 1987, The Herbal Rosa, 1990, Maps of the Shaker West, 1997 (award of excellence Ohio Assn. Hist. Societies and Museums 1998); organizer, compiler: A Sense of Place, 1977. Pres. Nat. Assn. Monnett Clubs Ohio Wesleyan U., Delaware, Ohio, 1971-72; chmn. Washington Twp. Zoning Appeals Bd., 1980; trustee Ohio Preservation Alliance, Columbus, 1988-94; chair lit. com. Celebrate Dayton '96, 1995-96. Recipient Disting. Svc. award Nat. Assn. Ohio Wesleyan Monnett Clubs, Delaware, 1974, Centerville Mayor's award for cmty. svcs., 1988; named Vol. of the Yr., Dayton-Montgomery County Park Dist., 1985. Mem.: Herb Soc. Am. (libr. chmn. 1988—90, curator rosemary collection 1997—), Western Shaker Study Group (program chair 1988—91, 1999—2000, sec. 2001—02, program chair 2003—04, chair 2005—), Nat. Trust for Hist. Preservation, Friends of White Water Shaker Village, Inc. (trustee 2002—, sec. 2003—04), Centerville-Washington Twp. Hist. Soc. (landmark chair 1974—78, 1980—94, 1997—99), Landmarks Found. (trustee 1995—, chair 1997—2001), Flower and Herb Exch., Cox Arboretum and Gardens (vol.), Phi Beta Kappa. Avocations: gardening, slide lectures on gardens and historic preservation topics. Home: 7712 Eagle Creek Dr Dayton OH 45459-3414 E-mail: marthaboice@aol.com.

BOIMAN, DONNA RAE, artist, art academy executive; b. Columbus, Ohio, Jan. 13, 1946; d. George Brandle and Donna Rae (Rockwell) Hall; m. David Charles Boiman, Dec. 8, 1973 (div. Aug. 1990). BS in Pharmacy, Ohio State U., 1969; student, Columbus Coll. Art & Design, 1979-83. Registered pharmacist, Ohio. Pharmacist, mgr. various retail stores, Cleve., 1970-73, Columbus, 1973-77; owner L'Artiste, Reynoldsburg, Ohio, 1977-81; pres. Cen. Ohio Art Acad., Reynoldsburg, 1981—2002, Art Acad. Ctrl. Ohio, Reynoldsburg, 1990—; owner Big Red Designs, Reynoldsburg, 1989—; pub. rels. mgr. Freedom Farm Equestrian Ctr., Pataskala, Ohio, 1991—; design dir., v.p. Sterling Automotive Mgmt., Inc. Cons. to Mayor City of Reynoldsburg, 1986-87, webmaster, 1999—; owner Ctrl. Ohio Art Graphics/Design/Website Design; jewelry designer Zarah Co. Calif., 2001. Represented in permanent collections including Collector's Gallery Columbus Mus. Art, Gallery 200, Columbus Art Exch., The Huntington Collection, Dean Witter Reynolds Collection, Zanesville Art Ctr., Mt. Carmel East Hosp., Columbus, Corp. 2005, Radisson Hotels, Mich. and Ohio, Fifth 3d Bank, Bexley, Ohio, On Line Computer Libr., Dublin, Ohio, Columbus Torah Acad.; author: Anatomy Made Easy: Draw, Color and Learn, Anatomy and Structure: A Guide for Young Artists, 1988, Shadow of the Queen; creator Warriors line of cat jewelry and Shadow of the Queen children's book series. Mem. Columbus Better Bus. Bur.; founder Forest Warrior Project, 2002. Recipient John Lennon Meml. Award for the Arts, Internat. Art Challenge com., 1987. Mem. Pa. Soc. Watercolorists, Nat. Soc. Layerists in Multimedia, Allied Artists of Am. (assoc.), Nat. Wildlife Fedn., Ohio State U. Alumni Assn., Ohio State U. Pharmacy Alumni Assn. (charter), U.S. Dressage Fedn., Internat. Arabian Horse Assn., Soc. Concerned Scientists. Avocations: showing horses, skiing, white water river running, ice skating. Office: Cen Ohio Art & Graphics PO Box 209 7347 E Main St Reynoldsburg OH 43068-2105 Office Phone: 614-864-5973. E-mail: ohioart@infinet.com.

BOIS, DEBORAH LYNN, special education educator; d. Douglas Lawrence and Barbara Lois Bois; m. James Richard Bonner, Dec. 5, 1998 (div.); 1 child, Finnegan James Bonner. BA, U. NH, 2004, M Elem. Edn., 2005. Cert. elem. tchr., learning disabilities tchr., spl. edn. tchr. NH. Tchr. Kingston (NH) Children's Ctr., 2001—02; tchg. asst. U. NH, Durham, 2002; spl. edn. intern McDonough Elem. Sch., Manchester, NH, 2004, elem. edn. intern, 2004, learning disabilities specialist, 2004—. Presenter in field. Vol. Newmarket (NH) Elem. Sch., 2002—03. Mem.: NEA, Coun. for Exceptional Children. Avocations: snowboarding, gardening, home improvement, painting. Office: McDonough Elem Sch 550 Lowell St Manchester NH 03101 Home: 37 Alice Dr Unit 68 Concord NH 03303 Personal E-mail: dbois@verizon.net.

BOISE, AUDREY LORRAINE, retired special education educator; b. Hackensack, NJ, Feb. 12, 1933; d. Paul George and Lillian Rose (Goedecker) B. BA, Wellesley (Mass.) Coll., 1955; MA, Fairleigh Dickinson U., 1977. Cert. tchr. K-8, learning disabilities, supervision. Tchr. Township of Berkeley Heights, N.J., 1958-67; learning cons. Borough of New Providence, N.J., 1978-82, 86-00, ret., 2000; learning cons. Scotch Plains/Fanwood, N.J., 1984-86; instr. Fairleigh Dickinson U., Madison, N.J., 1975-78. Several other short-term tchg. positions; supr. student tchrs., 1968, 1975-78, 2000-02; lectr. on fgn. countries and areas of U.S.; part-time travel agt. Life mem. Rep. Nat. Com. (Pres. Club 2003-06); mem. Nat. Rep. Senatorial Com., Washington, Rep. Presdl. Task Force, Washington, Rep. Congl. com., Washington, N.J. State Rep. Com., Trenton, Nat. Fedn. Rep. Women, Washington; attended presdl. inauguration, 2005 Recipient Rep. of Yr. Gold medal, Nat. Rep. Com., 2002, 2003, 2006. Mem. NEA, AAUW, N.J. Assn. Learning Cons., Assn. for Children with Learning Disabilities, N.J. Edn. Assn., Internat. Platform Assn., Fortnightly Club, Hist. Soc. Summit, Canoe Brook Country Club Methodist. Avocations: travel, photography.

BOISITS, REGINA MARIE, elementary school educator; b. Jersey City, June 18, 1945; d. Cisberto Ricciardelli and Domenica Castellano; m. Christian J. Boisits, June 17, 1967; children: Sherri Lynn, Christian Jr., Lisa Marie. BS, Fairleigh Dickinson U., Rutherford, NJ, 1967; MEd, William Paterson U., NJ, 1993. Elem. tchr. Washington Sch., Lodi, NJ, 1967—72, Meml. Sch., Paramus, NJ, 1988—, tchr.-in-charge, 1991—. US rep. US Edn. Program, Japan, 2004. Recipient Family Sci. Instr. award, Rutgers U., Gov.'s Tchr. Recognition award, State of NJ, 1994; Dream grantee, Paramus Bd. Edn., 2001. Mem.: Edn. Assn. Paramus (mem. exec. bd. 2000—), Paramus Garden Club (master gardener 2000—). Roman Catholic. Avocations: tutoring, bicycling, gardening, travel. Home: 188 Morningside Rd Paramus NJ 07652

BOISSEAU, JANE, lawyer; BA, U. New Orleans, 1967; MA, U. Calif. Berkeley, 1968, Columbia U. Teachers Coll., 1978; JD, NYU, 1985. Bar: NY 1986. Ptnr., chmn. life ins./healthcare dept. LeBoeuf, Lamb, Greene & MacRae LLP, NYC. Contbr. articles to profl. jour. Office: LeBoeuf Lamb Greene & MacRae LLP 125 West 55th St New York NY 10019-5715 Office Phone: 212-424-8644. Office Fax: 212-424-8500. Business E-Mail: jane.boisseau@llgm.com.

BOISVERT-BUSCHBAUM, M. NOELLA, music educator; d. Alcide A. and Regina M. (Champigny) Boisvert; m. Charles J. Buschbaum; children: Susan Buschbaum Romano, Jon Charles. BS in Music Edn. summa cum laude, Western Conn. State U., 1972, MS in Music Edn., 1976; Profl. Diploma in Adminstrn., So. Conn. State U., 1981; PhD in Music, U. Conn., 1990. Cert. tchr., music tchr., adminstr. Tchr. music Redding (Conn.) Sch., 1972—; ednl. cons. Prof. Devel., 2000—. Assessor Conn. State Dept. Edn.-Beginning Educator Support and Tng. Program, 1989—, trainer of mentor and cooperating tchrs., 1993—, cooperating tchr., 1988—, mentor, 1988—; mem. Conn. Educator Talent Pool, 1988—; seminar lectr. Music Portfolio Scorer, adjudicator, Nat. Piano Playing Auditions Recipient fellowship and grant U. Conn., 1988, 89, Oustanding Music Student award Western Conn. State U., 1972, Tchr. Recognition award Union Carbide, 1987. Mem. NEA, ASCD, Nat. Guild of Piano Tchrs., Adminstrn. and Supervision Assn. So. Conn., Conn. Edn. Assn., Conn. Music Educators Assn., Redding Edn. Assn. (award 1987), Music Educators Nat. Conf., Kappa Delta Pi, Phi Delta Kappa, Pi Kappa Lambda. Home: 868 Alstread Ctr Rd Alstead NH 03602

BOIVIN, CAROL JANE, retired secondary school educator; b. Pittsfield, Mass., Oct. 10, 1945; d. Alice Louise and Lawrence Albert Boivin. BA in Biology and Secondary Edn., Coll. St. Rose, Albany, NY, 1967, MS in Edn., 1986, MA in Biology, 1972. Sci. and math. tchr. Babylon Jr./Sr. HS, NY, 1967—69; biology and chemistry tchr. Pittsfield Pub. Schs.-Taconic HS, Mass., 1969—87; mid-sch. sci. tchr. Annunciation Sch., Albuquerque, 1987—90; sci. tchr. Albuquerque Pub. Schs.-Harrison Middle Sch., 1991—93; biology and chemistry tchr. Albuquerque Pub. Schs.-La Cueva HS, 1993—2006; ret. Continuing edn. faculty Berkshire CC, Pittsfield, 1979—80, adj. faculty, 1985; sci. dept. chairperson Pittsfield Pub. Schs.-Taconic HS, 1982—87; developmental studies tchr. Albuquerque Tech.-Vocat. Inst., 1988—91. Lector Ch. of the Risen Savior, Albuquerque, 1990—, Eucharistic min., 1990—. Named Outstanding Educator in Math. and Sci., Hughes Aircraft Corp., 1990; recipient Disting. Svc. award, Thomas Edison Found., 1971; grantee, NSF, 1972, 1985—86. Home: 7112-217 Pan American Frwy NE Albuquerque NM 87109

BOJSZA, JOAN E., elementary school educator; b. Orange, N.J., Jan. 3, 1949; d. Stephen William and Josephine Rosemary (Sulpy) Horkay; m. Walter Joseph Bojsza, June 20, 1970; children: Elizabeth Joy, Katherine Anne. BS in Early Childhood Edn., U. Md., 1971. Cert. elem. edn. and nursery tchr. N.J. Preschool tchr. Woodyard Rd. Ctr., Clinton, Md., 1971—72, YWCA-Ridgeview Ctr., West Orange, NJ, 1982—91; 2d grade tchr. St. Bernard Sch., Riverdale, Md., 1972—73; title I tchr. Rockaway (N.J.) Twp. Schs., 1973—74, 4th grade tchr., 1974—75; 1st grade tchr. St. Thomas More Sch.,

Fairfield, NJ, 1975—77; kindergarten tchr. Newton St. Sch., Newark, 1991—99, Quitman St. Sch., Newark, 1999—2002, pre-kindergarten tchr., 2002—03, kindergarten tchr., 2003—. Project, new beginnings tchr. Summer Inst., Newark, 1998; presenter in field. Contbr. chpt. to book. Mem. coun., PTA officer, pres. various, West Orange, 1986—99; PTA officer pres. West Orange HS, 1995—98; active leadership assocs. Montclair State U., 2005—; comitteewoman West Orange Dems., 1991—96; mem. Democratic County Com. Recipient Outstanding Leaders award, Girl Scouts U.S., 1990, Best Practices award, SLT I - Teamwork Colloquim, 2005. Mem.: Nat. Assn. Edn. Young Children, Comer Whole Sch. Reform Model (chairperson mem. parent/staff com. 2000—01), Newark Early Childhood Educators Assn. (v.p. 1993—2001, sec., newsletter editor), Essex Hudson Assn. Edn. Young Children (corr. sec. 2001—, v.p. programs 2004—), Kappa Delta Pi. Avocations: gardening, singing, crafts. Home: 25 Harvard Ter West Orange NJ 07052

BOK, JOAN TOLAND, utilities executive; b. Grand Rapids, Mich., Dec. 31, 1929; d. Don Prentiss Weaver and Mary Emily Toland; m. John Fairfield Bok, July 15, 1955; children: Alexander Toland, Geoffrey Robbins. AB, Radcliffe Coll., 1951; JD, Harvard U., 1955. Bar: Mass. 1955. Assoc. Ropes & Gray, Boston, 1955-61; pvt. practice Boston, 1961-68; atty. New England Electric Sys., Westborough, Mass., 1968-73, asst. to pres., 1973-77, v.p., sec., 1977-79, vice-chair, 1979-84, pres., CEO, 1988-89, chair, 1984-98, chair emeritus, 1998—. Past pres. bd. overseers Harvard U.; bd. dirs. Boston Adult Literacy Fund, Vt. Hist. Soc., Woods Hole Oceanog. Inst., Mass., The Bold Initiative. Fellow Am. Bar Found.; mem. Boston Bar Assn., Am. Acad. Arts and Scis., Phi Beta Kappa. Unitarian Universalist. Home: 53 Pinckney St Boston MA 02114-4801 Office: 25 Research Dr Westborough MA 01582-0001

BOK, SISSELA, philosopher, writer; b. Stockholm, Dec. 2, 1934; d. Gunnar and Alva (Reimer) Myrdal; m. Derek Bok, May 7, 1955; children— Hilary, Victoria, Tomas BA, George Washington U., 1957, MA, 1958, LHD (hon.), 1986; PhD, Harvard U., 1970; LLD (hon.), Mt. Holyoke Coll., 1985; LHD (hon.), Clark U., 1988, U. Mass., 1991, Georgetown U., 1992. Lectr. Simmons Coll., Boston, 1971-72; lectr. Harvard-MIT Div. Health Scis. and Tech., Cambridge, 1975-82, Harvard U., Cambridge, 1982-84; assoc. prof. philosophy Brandeis U., Waltham, Mass., 1985-89, prof. philosophy, 1989-92; fellow Ctr. for Advanced Study, Stanford, Calif., 1991-92; Disting. fellow Harvard Ctr. Population and Devel. Studies, Cambridge, Mass., 1993—. Mem. ethics adv. bd. HEW, 1977-80; bd. dirs. Population Coun., 1971-77; mem. Pulitzer Prize Bd., 1988-97, chmn., 1996-97. Author: Lying: Moral Choice in Public and Private Life, 1978 (Melcher award, George Orwell award), Secrets: On the Ethics of Concealment and Revelation, 1982, Alva: Ett kvinnoliv, 1987, A Strategy for Peace, 1989, Alva Myrdal: A Daughter's Memoir, 1991 (Melcher award), Common Values, 1996, Mayhem: Violence as Public Entertainment, 1998; mem. editl. bd. Ethics, 1980-85, Criminal Justice Ethics, 1980—, Contention, 1990-96, Common Knowledge, 1991—, (with others) Euthanasia and Physician-Assisted Suicide, 1998. Bd. dirs. Inst. for Philosophy and Religion, Boston U.; mem. Pulitzer Prize Bd., 1989-97. Recipient Abram L. Sachar Silver medallion Brandeis U., 1985, Radcliffe Coll. Grad. Soc. medal, 1993, Barnard Coll. medal of distinction, 1995, centennial medal Harvard Grad. Sch. Arts & Scis., 1998. Fellow Hastings Ctr. (dir. 1976-84, 94-97); mem. Am. Philos. Assn.

BOKHARI, ROBINA MAQBOOL, physician; b. Lahore, Punjab, Pakistan, Feb. 1, 1963; Came to U.S., 1991; d. Syed and Khadija Maqbool; m. Syed Asif Umar, Feb. 16, 1989; children: Syed Zeesham Asif, Sehr Asif, Syed Alina. MBBS, King Edward Med. Coll., 1987; cert. Ednl. Commn. for Fgn. Med. Grads., U. Punjab; MD, 1994. Intern Lady wallington Hosp., Lahore, Pakistan, 1988-89; resident U. South Dakota, Sioux Falls, 1999—. Author: Post Partum Psychosis, 1998. Mem. Pakistan Human Rights Soc., 1978. Mem. Am. Psych. Assn., AMA.

BOLAND, DEBORAH CATHERINE, music educator; b. Columbia, S.C., Feb. 7, 1954; d. Andrew Stephen and Mary Catherine Boland. MusB in Edn., U. Ga., Athens, 1976. Music specialist Fulton County Schs., Atlanta, 1976—. Tchr. ctr. asst. Fulton County Schs., 1982—84. Musician: Atlanta Symphony Orch. Chorus (recipient several Grammy awards). Choral dir./mem. various ch. choirs, Atlanta, 1970—. Recipient Tchr. of Yr., various Fulton County schs. Business E-Mail: boland@fulton.k12.ga.usa.

BOLAND, WINNIFRED JOAN, retired librarian; b. Watrous, Sask., Can., Sept. 5, 1931; arrived in U.S., 1961; d. Charles Frederick Fisher and Mary Jane Little; m. William Guy Boland, Feb. 16, 1968; children: Thomas Richard, James Patrick. BA, U. Sask., 1952; BLS, McGill U., 1955; MLS, U. Wash., 1965. Reference libr. Provincial Libr., Regina, Canada, 1955—57, U. Sask., Canada, 1957—61, Seattle (Wash.) Pub. Libr., 1962—65; reference libr. Undergraduate Libr. U. Wash., Seattle, 1966—68, head reference libr. Undergraduate Libr., 1968—70, instr. Libr. Sch., 1969—70; vol. reference libr. Wash. State Libr., Olympia, Wash., 1990—2000. Mem. citizen's adv. com. Wash. State Libr., Olympia, 2002—. Precinct com. officer Thurston County Dems., Olympia, 1998—2002; lobbyist Washington Coalition Against Censorship, 1984—. Recipient John L. McKinnon trophy, Sask. Tech. Collegiate, 1949;, Sask. Govt. scholar, 1954. Mem.: ACLU (contact person Thurston County 1995—2002), Friends of Clinton Presdl. Found., Wash. Libr. Assn. (lobbyist 1984—), Friends of Wash. State Libr., So. Poverty Law Ctr., People for Am. Way, Nat. Coalition Against Censorship, Beta Phi Mu. Democrat. Protestant. Avocations: reading, public speaking. Home: 5035 Donnelly Drive SE Olympia WA 98501-5009

BOLANDRINA, GRETHEL RAMOS, nurse; b. Reina Mercedes, Isabela, Philippines, Dec. 11, 1966; arrived in U.S., 1989; d. Teodolo Collantes and Estrella Luyun Ramos; m. Joseph Maximino Bolandrina, Jan. 11, 1991; children: Jessica Dawn, Gino Ray, Lilly Amber, Max Joseph. BSN, U. Santo Tomas, Manila, Philippines, 1987; BS in Creative Journalism, Harvard U., 2001. RN; CRRN; lic. notary pub., Mass. Charge nurse Philippine Gen. Hosp., Manila, 1988-89, St. John of God Hosp., Brookline, Mass., 1989-91, nursing supr., 1991-94, Milford Meadows, Milford, Mass., 1994-95; dir. quality imp. SunRise for Milford, 1995-99, charge nurse, 1999-2000; nurse mgr. SunBridge for Milford, 2002—; asst. mgr. Motyka Art & Frame Gallery Inc., Central Falls, RI, 2000—02. Mem. QA/QI Network Group, Newton, Mass., 1995-99. Contbr. numerous articles to profl. jours. Active parent Iskwelahang Pilipino, Boston, 1997-99; press rels. Philippine Cmty. N.E. Area, 1997, Mrs. Philippine Centennial, Found., R.I., 1998, Nat. Fedn. Filipo Am. Assns., 1998; leader, asst. troop 290 Brownies, 1997-99. Recipient Excellence award 10 yrs Girl Scouts USA, Milford, 1997. Mem. Philippine Nurses Assn. New Eng. (editor newsletter 1997, rec. sec. 1994-96, corr. sec. 1996-98, v.p. 1998-2000, Mem. of Yr. 2001). Avocations: painting, gardening, writing, arts and crafts, embroidery. Home: 14 Smith Hill Way Douglas MA 01516 Office: 79 Chestnut St Central Falls RI 02863-2005

BOLDEN, KRISTIN ELIZABETH, secondary school educator; b. Marietta, Ohio, May 17, 1939; d. Howard Alfred Spindler and Thelma Kathryn (Totman) Williamson; m. Norman William Holt II, June 2, 1959 (div. Feb. 1966); m. James William Bolden, Oct. 8, 1966; children: James William, Bruce Douglas, Cynthia Sue. BS in Edn., Ohio No. U., 1961. Cert. elem. and secondary tchr. Ohio. Tchr., Spanish Ohio No. U., Ada, 1961; tchr. Ada Elem. Sch., Ohio, 1961—62; tchr., Spanish and English Warren H.S., Vincent, Ohio, 1962—99. Mem. Southeastern Ohio Fgn. Lang. Alliance, 1983—99. Pianist Royal Highlands Chorus and Kitchen Band. Jennings Scholar, 1973—74. Mem.: Delta Kappa Gamma. Republican. Presbyterian. Avocations: swimming, singing, piano, reading, bridge. Home: 4524 Glen Coe St Leesburg FL 34748-7583

BOLDING, KANDY DENESE MYNEAR, special education educator; b. Pampa, Tex., Oct. 31, 1960; d. Carl Andrew and Eva Nell Mynear; m. Timothy Stewart Bolding, June 14, 1980; 1 child, Brandon Traye. A in Edn., Western Tex. Coll., 2000; BA in Humanities, U. Tex., Odessa, 2000, Tchg. Cert., 2002. Youth dir. Southside Bapt. Ch., Perryton, Tex., 1989—91; tchg. asst. Perryton H.S., 1991—94, Snyder (Tex.) Jr. H.S., 1994—98, James Brooks Mid. Sch., Midland, Tex., 1998—2000; spl. edn. tchr. Greenwood H.S., Midland, Tex., 2000—. Mem. campus ednl. improvement com. James Brooks Mid. Sch., 1999—2000; mem. dist. ednl. improvement com. Greenwood H.S., 2000—. Mem.: Assn. Tex. Profl. Educators, Coun. for Exceptional Children. Republican. Baptist.

BOLDOVITCH, GERRI, art educator; d. Joseph and Esther Boldovitch. AA, Miami Dade C.C., 1971; BA, Fla. Atlantic U., 1971—73; MS, St. Thomas U., 1980. Cert. profl. educator in art edn. K-12, prof. educator in specific learning disabilities K-12, profl. educator in varying exceptional edn. K-12, endorsement ESOL, educator English to spkrs. of other langs. Art instr. grades 10-12 Miami Norland Sr. H.S., Dade County Pub. Schs., Miami, 1973—74; art instr. K-6 Oak Grove Elem., Miami, 1974—78, Bay Harbor Elem., 1977—84; art instr. K-5 Greynolds Park Elem., Miami, 1984—87, Ojus Elem., Miami, 1987—89, North Beach Elem., Miami, 1989—91, Highland Oaks Elem., North Miami, 1991—94, Madie Ives Elem., Miami, 1994—2000, Hibiscus Elem., Miami, 1977—; art instr. k-5 Hubert O. Sibley Elem., Miami, Fla., 2003—. Mem. PTA, Dade County Pub. Schs., Miami, 1977—2000; participant South Fla. State Cmty. Safe Sch. Summit, Ft. Lauderdale, Fla., 1998. Etchings exhibited in London, sculpture exhibited in Mexico City, crafts exhibited in Can. Founding mem. Nat. Campaign for Tolerance; mem. Friends of the Everglades, Miami, 2003; contbr. United Way, Miami, 1973—2002. Named to Wall of Tolerance, Civil Rights Meml. Ctr., Montgomery, 2005. Mem.: PTA, NEA, Nat. Art Edn. Assn., United Tchrs. of Dade County, SierraClub. Avocations: theater, music, reading, art-related activities.

BOLDT, PATRICIA C., social worker; b. Jersey City, July 16, 1955; d. Edward J. and Agnes Brajczewski; m. Harry Boldt, Nov. 5, 1978. MSW, NYU, 1982. Lic. clin. social worker, social worker, N.J., N.Y.; cert. supr. in edn. Social worker Div. Youth and Family, Jersey City, 1983-86; sch. social worker Montville (N.J.) Bd. Edn., 1986-87, Barnegat Bd. of Edn., 1987—. Mem. Acad. Cert. Social Workers. Avocations: boating, stained glass. Office Phone: 609-698-5880 4040.

BOLDUC, DIANE EILEEN MARY BUCHHOLZ, psychotherapist; b. Elizabeth, N.J., May 1, 1953; d. Howard Robert and Barbara Ann (Bowen) Buchholz; m. David Vianney Buchholz Bolduc, May 21, 1977; children: Elizabeth, Katharine. BA cum laude in Psychology, U. N.H., 1975, MEd Counseling, 1976. Lic. clin. mental health counselor. Counselor, asst. supr., social worker III Divsn. Children & Youth Svcs., Manchester/Salem, NH, 1978—88; supr. Child Health Svcs., Manchester, NH, 1987—88; program coord. N.H. Task Force on Child Abuse & Neglect, Concord, 1988—91; dir. youth & family svcs. Luth. Social Svcs. New England, Concord, NH, 1992—94; home/sch. coord. Raymond Schs., NH, 1994—96; counselor Pelham H.S., NH, 1996—. Mem.: ACA, Am. Mental Health Counselors Assn., N.H. Sch. Counselors Assn., N.H. Mental Health Counselors Assn. (treas. 2001—), Women*Spirit*Song. Home: 189 Ray St Manchester NH 03104

BOLEN, BETTYE SUE, academic administrator; b. Princeton, W.Va., Aug. 31, 1945; d. James Willard Conner and Trixie Gladys (Hill); m. Daniel Wayne Farley, Aug. 21, 1966 (div. 1983); children: Kathy Jo Quesenberry, Julia Anne Noland; m. Larry E. Bolen, Sr., Nov. 21, 1984. B in bus. edn., Concord Coll., 1966; M in counseling, guidance, W.Va. U., 1971; ednl. specialist degree, W.Va. Grad. Coll., 1996, M in adminstrn., 1996. Exec. sec. Kersey Mfg. Co.-Figie, Internat., Bluefield, Va., 1971-73, W.Va. Conf. United Meth. Ch., Princeton, 1973-78; couns. spl. edn. Mercer County Schs., Princeton, 1981—; coord., cons. Concord Coll., Athens, W.Va., 1994—. Adj. faculty Bluefield State Coll., 1983-91; bd. dirs. Appalachian OH-9, Inc.; co-coord. Mercer County Crisis Intervention Team; mem. prevention, edn. com. Mercer County Child Abuse; mem. Mercer County Sch. Health Coun., Mercer County Adolescent Health Task Force, Mercer County Spl. Edn. Adv. com.; coord. Mercer County Link, W.Va. Statewide Transition Sys. Change Project. Presenter in field. Bd. dirs. Civitan Internat., 1990-92, pres.-elect, 1997-98, pres., 1998—; mem. Internat. Grants and Scholarship Com., 1994-97, chair, 1995-96; mem. admin. bd. First United Meth. Ch. Recipient Internat. Honor Key Civitan Internat., 1994, Disting. Lt. Gov. award W.Va. Dist. 1982-83, Honor Key, Princeton Civitan Club 1982-83, Honor Key, W.Va. Dist. 1983-84, Gov.'s Honor Key, W.Va. Dist. 1987, Superior Recruitment award Civitan Internat. 1991; named Civitan-of-Yr., W.Va. Dist., 1982-83; inductee Jr. Civitan Internat. Hall of Fame, 1993. Mem. Assn. for Supervision and Curriculum Devel., Nat. Vocational Assn., W.Va. Vocational Assn., Delta Kappa Gamma Internat. Edn. Soc. (exec. com. mem., 2nd v.p. 1996-98, chairperson, scholar. com. 1994-96). Methodist. Avocation: travel. Home: 304 Cardinal Ave Princeton WV 24740-4212 Office: Mercer County Schs 1403 Honaker Ave Princeton WV 24740-3065 Personal E-mail: civitan@charter.net.

BOLEN, JANE M., music teacher, organist, choir director; b. Montgomery, Punjab, India, Mar. 17, 1928; d. Ralph Erskine and Ida (Saville) Moore; children: Nan Ellis, Dwane E. AB, Erskine Coll., Due West, S.C., 1948; MMus in Piano Theory/Composition, Converse Coll., Spartanburg, S.C., 1970; PhD in Musicology, Fla. State U., 1974; cert. arts mgmt., Harvard U. Tchr. gen. sci. and physics Pub. Schs., Abbeville, S.C., 1948-49; pvt. piano tchr. Abbeville, 1949-73, Greenwood Jr. Conservatory, 1974—; choir dir. Greenwood AR Presbyn. Ch., 1990—. Exec. dir. Greenwood Coun. Arts, 1977-79; part-time tchr. dept. music Lander U., Greenwood, 1974, 96. Mem. Greenwood Music Tchrs. Assn. (pres. 1998—), Greenwood Organists Guild, Am. Guild Organists (Greenwood dean 1990-92), Delta Kappa Gamma, Phi Kappa Lambda, Delta Omicron. Avocations: genealogical research, gourmet cooking, french hand sewing, houseplants. Address: 210 W Cambridge Ave Greenwood SC 29646-2236

BOLES, LENORE UTAL, nurse psychotherapist, educator; b. N.Y.C., July 3, 1929; d. Joseph Leo and Dorothy (Grosby) Utal; m. Morton Schloss, Dec. 17, 1955 (div. May 1961); 1 child, Howard Alan Schloss; m. Sam Boles, May 24, 1962; children: Anne Leslie, Laurence Utal; stepchildren: Harlan Arnold, Robert Gerald. Diploma in nursing, Beth Israel Hosp. Sch. Nursing, 1951; BSN, Columbia U., 1964; MSN, U. Conn., 1977. Bd. cert. clin. specialist in adult psychiatry/ mental health nursing, advanced practice registered nurse. Staff nurse Beth Israel Hosp., N.Y.C., 1951, Kingsbridge VA Hosp., Bronx, N.Y., 1951-55; night supr. Gracie Square Hosp., N.Y.C., 1959-60; head nurse Elmhurst City Hosp., Queens, N.Y., 1960-62; nursing instr. Norwalk (Conn.) Hosp., 1966-74; asst. prof. U. Bridgeport, Conn., 1976-78; nurse psychotherapist Nurse Counseling Group, Ltd., Norwalk, 1979—2003, Changing Perspectives, LLP, Westport, 2003; nursing faculty Western Conn. State U., Danbury, 1978-80. Adj. asst. prof. Sacred Heart U., Bridgeport, Conn., 1983-89; adj. faculty Western Conn. State U., Danbury, 1994, 96-2000; lectr. Yale U. Sch. Nursing, 2000-02; nurse cons. Bradley Meml. Hosp., Southington, Conn., 1982, Lea Manor Nursing Home, Norwalk, 1982, St. Vincent's Hosp., Bridgeport, 1982-92; staff devel. nurse Silver Hill Hosp., New Canaan, Conn., 1980-86, 94; cons. in field, 1980—. Author: (book chpt.) Nursing Diagnoses for Psychiatric Nursing Practice, 1994. V.p. Sisterhood Beth El, Norwalk, 1969-71; bd. dirs. religious sch. Congregation Beth El, Norwalk, 1971-75, 79-80, rec. sec. bd. trustees, 1975-77, v.p. congregation, 1977-80, bd. trustees, 1980-83. Named Speaker of Yr., So. Fairfield County chpt. Am. Cancer Soc., 1976. Mem. ANA, Northeastern Nursing Diagnosis Assn. (chair N.E. region conf. 1985, chair planning com. 1984-85, chair nominating com. 1989-91), N.Am. Nursing Diagnosis Assn., Coun. Psychiat./Mental Health Clin. Specialists, Conn. Nurses Assn. (Del. to convs. 1975-2000, legis. com. dist. 3 1984-86, nominating com. 1988-90, Florence Wald award 1984, Conn. Nursing Diagnosis Conf. Group 1980-87), Conn. Soc. Nurse Psychotherapists (founding mem.). Democrat. Jewish. Avocations: travel, reading, gardening, spending time with grandchildren. Home: 173 E Rocks Rd Norwalk CT 06851-1715 Office: Changing Perspectives LLP 468 Post Rd E Ste A Westport CT 06880

BOLES, SHARON ISABELLE O'SHIELDS, mathematics educator; d. Richard L. and Shirley Isabelle O'Shields; children: Amy Rose BolesWagner, Anne Patience Marshall. BS Elem. Edn., Kans. State U., Manhattan, 1981; MS Edn., Newman U., Wichita, 2005. Cert. Educator K-9 and ESL K-12 Kans. State Dept. Edn., 2005. Tchr. sixth grade MacArthur Elem. Sch., Liberal, Kans., 1981—89; tchr. sci. West Mid. Sch., Liberal, 1989—2001; tchr. math., sci. Cottonwood Intermediate Sch., Liberal, 2001—04; tchr. algebra 1 Liberal H.S., 2004—. Coach math. team Unified Sch. Dist. 480, Liberal, 1983—89; chmn. sci. fair MacArthur Elem., Liberal, 1983—89, West Mid. Sch., Liberal, 1992—94, mem. drug/alcohol prevention team, 1991—93, sponsor student coun., 1992—94, sponsor sci. club, 1993—2001, mem. qpa stakeholders com., 1999—2001; chmn. problemsolving com. Cottonwood Intermediate Sch., Liberal, 2002—04, mentor tchr., 2002—03; mem. problemsolving tag team Liberal H.S., 2004—; tchr. math, tutor LATER at Liberal H.S., 2005—; v.p. profl. devel. coun. Unified Sch. Dist. 480, Liberal, 1999—2001, chmn. Friends Edn. Com., 1993—94, mem. mid. sch. strategic planning com., 1987—91. Mem., chaplain, sec. IB Chpt. PEO, Liberal, 1975—2006; leader Girl Scouts U.S.A., Liberal, 1977—80; mem. Friends of Baker Arts; mem., v.p. Beta Sigma Phi, Liberal, 1970—78; mem., chmn. Vacation Bible Sch., sponsor Meth. Youth Fellowship, tchr. Sun. Sch., chmn. Cir. First United Meth. Ch., Liberal, 1970—2006. Named Girl of Yr., Beta Sigma Phi, 1978; recipient Outstanding Young Women Am., Outstanding Young Women Am., 1974, Who's Who Among Am. Tchrs., Who's Who Among Am. Tchrs., 1994, Life Membership award, Liberal PTA, 1987, Outstanding Project Leader award, Seward County 4-H Coun., 1985, Conservation Edn. Svc. award, Seward County Conservation/Ext. Office, 1984, Super Tchr. award, Mac Arthur Elem. Sch., 1982. Mem.: NEA, Liberal Edn. Assn. (sec. 1986—87), Kans. Assn. Math., Delta Kappa Gamma. Avocations: interior decorating, landscape design, exercise, travel, music. Office: Math Dept Liberal High School Liberal KS 67901

BOLEY, ANDREA GAIL, secondary school educator; b. Lewistown, Pa., July 27, 1956; d. Robert Banks and Marjorie Katheryn (Shearer) Henry; m. Richard C. Shiley, m. May 13, 1978 (dec. June 1996); 1 child, Evan Andrew; m. Daniel M. Boley, Feb. 6, 1999. BS in Music Edn., Indiana U. of Pa., 1978; Jr. High Sci. Cert., Brevard Community Coll., Melbourne, Fla. Choral dir./tchr. S.W. Jr. High Sch., Brevard County Sch. Dist., Palm Bay, Fla., 1988—. Contbr. articles to profl. jours. Named Stone Middle Sch. tchr. of the Yr., 1984-85. Mem. ASCD, AAUW, Music Educators Nat. Conf., Fla. Music Educators Assn. (bd. dirs.), Fla. Vocal Assn., Brevard Fedn. Tchrs., Am. Fedn. Tchrs., Tri-M (Fla. chmn.), Nat. Tri-M Adv. Com. Home: 241 Devlin Ct Se Palm Bay FL 32909-2322 E-mail: aboley@cfi.rr.com.

BOLEY, ANNA MARIE, literature and language educator; b. Hannibal, Mo., July 25, 1953; d. James Thomas and Marie Marie Griffith; m. Clayton Edward Boley, June 4, 1977; children: James David, Jessica Diane. BSE, N.E. Mo. State U., Truman, 1971—75, MA, 1981. English tchr., 7-8 & 11th grades Wellsville-Middletown R-1, Wellsville, Mo., 1975—77; English tchr., 7-12 grades Gethsemance Christian Sch., Louisville, Ky., 1977—78; tchr., English/Ky. history & geography 9th & O Christian Sch., Louisville, 1978—79; English, speech/drama tchr. Lincoln County R-II HS, Elsberry, Mo., 1979—. Office: Lincoln County R-II HS 138 Tomahawk Dr Elsberry MO 63343

BOLGER, DOREEN, museum director; BA, Bucknell U., 1971; MA, U. Del., 1973; PhD, CUNY, 1983. Mem. curatorial staff Am. Wing Met. Mus. Art, N.Y.C., 1976—88, curator Am. painting and sculpture, 1989; curator painting and sculpture Amon Ctr. Mus., Ft. Worth, 1989-94; dir. RISD Mus., Providence, 1994-98, Balt. Mus. Art, 1998—. Panelist NEA, NEH; field reviewer Inst. for Mus. and Libr. Svcs.; curator women artists exhbn. for Govt. House, Annapolis, Md.; Ailsa Mellon Bruce vis. sr. fellow Ctr. for Advanced Study in the Visual Arts Nat. Gallery of Art; lectr. in field. Bd. dirs. several orgns. Chester Dale fellow Met. Mus. Art; grantee NEH, Met. Mus. Art Office: Balt Mus Art 10 Art Museum Dr Baltimore MD 21218-3898 Office Phone: 410-396-6460. E-mail: dbolger@arthma.org.

BOLGER, DORITA YVONNE FERGUSON, librarian; b. Sharon, Pa., Apr. 18, 1951; d. Harold Edward Ferguson and Pauline May McQueen Ferguson; m. Terrence James Bolger, Sept. 24, 1977; children: Sarah Catherine Pauline, Matthew Terrence. BA, Pa. State U., 1973; MLS, Clarion U., 1978. English tchr. Greenville Area Schs., Pa., 1974—75; libr. asst. Pa. State U., Sharon, 1975—81; prof. and ref. interlibrary loan and info. literacy libr. Westminster Coll., New Wilmington, Pa., 1981—. Mem. industry review bd. Sage Pubs., Inc., Thousand Oaks, Calif., 2001—; book rev. editor, contbr. Jour. Interlibr. Loan, Document Delivery & Electronic Access Haworth Press, Binghampton, NY, 1999—. Co-author: (novels) Church and Social Action, 1990; contbr. chapters to books. Founding mem., chair Mercer County (Pa.) Commn. for Women, 1989—93. Mem.: ALA. Office: Westminster Coll McGill Libr 319 S Market St New Wilmington PA 16172 Office Phone: 724-946-7330. Business E-Mail: dbolger@westminster.edu.

BOLHUIS, DOREEN, recreational facility executive, physical education educator; d. Victor Ray and Elizabeth Claire Corpron; m. Mark Henry Bolhuis, June 17, 1972; children: Blythe, Paige. BS in Edn., Ctrl. Mich. U., Mt. Pleasant, Mich., 1973. Tchr. East Grand Rapids (Mich.) H.S., 1973—77; dir. Oak Gymnastics, Zeeland, Mich., 1977—80; prin., owner Gymco Sports, Grand Rapids, 1980—. Prof. Aquinas Coll., Grand Rapids, 2003—; regional dir. USA Gymnastics, Indpls., 1980—89; chmn. Bus. Alliance for Families, Grand Rapids, 2004—06; expert in field; spkr. in field. Author: (films) Gymtime, 2006. Named Top Women Owned Bus., Grand Rapids (Mich.) Bus. Jour., 2005; named one of 101 Best and Brightest Businesses, Mich. Bus. Assn., 2005. Mem.: Am. Assn. Health, Phys. Edn. and Recreation, Alliance Women Entrepreneurs (spkr.), Grand Rapids (Mich.) C. of C. (bd. dirs. 2004—06, named Small Bus. of Yr. 2004, nominee Athena award 2005), Grand River Investors (pres. 2005—06), Univ. Club, Inforum Women's Econ. Club. Avocations: running, bicycling, water-skiing, skiing, cello. Office: Gymco Sports 2306 Camelot Ridge Ct Grand Rapids MI 49546

BOLIN, JULIE PAUL, secondary school educator; b. Alexandria, La., Oct. 16, 1973; d. Elaine Hutson and Hershal L. Paul; m. Brett William Bolin, Nov. 18, 1995; children: Cade William, Emma Corrin. BA in History, La. Coll., Pineville, 1997. Cert. secondary edn., history tchr. La., 2002, libr. media Specialist La., 2006. Coord. presch. outreach program Rapides Parish Libr., Alexandria, La., 1998—99; tchr. Pineville Jr. HS, La., 1999—. Leadership team for So. Assn. of Colls. and Schs., Pineville Jr. H.S., La., 2001—02; cons. La. Social Studies INTECH Pilot, Baton Rouge, 2002—02; leadership team Pineville Jr. H.S., La., 2005—. Free Methodist. Home: 263 Q Stockman Rd Deville LA 71328 Office: Pineville Jr HS 501 Edgewood Dr Pineville LA 71360 Office Phone: 318-640-0512. Personal E-mail: bolinj@rapides.k12.la.us.

BOLINGER, KAY LYNN, literature and language educator; d. Arthur Arnold and Norma Rennels; m. Michael Dale Bolinger, Apr. 30, 1975; 1 child, Ashley Lynne. BA, Ind. State U., 1972. Cert. French and English tchr. Quality control analyst Columbia House, Terre Haute, 1972—85; English tchr. Marshall (Ill.) Cmty. Unit Sch., 1991—. Vol. Cmty. Theatre, Terre Haute, 2004—; sec. bd. dirs. First Preferred Health Care. Recipient Tchr. of Yr., Walmart, Marshall, 2002. Mem.: NEA, Marshall Edn. Assn., Ill. Edn. Assn. (Personal and Profl. Devel. award 1998). Democrat. Avocations: reading, fishing, travel. Home: 8349 E Milner Ave Terre Haute IN 47803 Office: Marshall High Sch 806 N 6th St Marshall IL 62441 Office Phone: 217-826-2395. Business E-Mail: kbolinger@marshall.k12.il.us.

BOLLA, KAREN IRENE, neuropsychologist, educator; b. Bainbridge, Md., Mar. 26, 1955; d. Frank V. and Irene (Galletta) B. BA, U. Vt., 1977; MA, SUNY, Stony Brook, 1979, PhD, 1983. Lic. psychologist, Md. Postdoctoral fellow Johns Hopkins U., Balt., 1984-85, instr., 1985-87, assoc. prof. neurology, 1988—. Reviewer Jour. Nervous and Mental Disease, Jour.

Occupational Medicine, Neuropsychology. Contbr. abstracts to sci. jours. Grantee NIH, others. Mem. Internat. Neuropsychol. Soc., Am. Psychol. Assn., Am. Acad. Neurology. Avocations: dance, skiing, golf.

BOLLEN, SHARON KESTERSON, artist, educator; b. Cin., Apr. 27, 1946; d. Marc J. and Regina (Mills) Kesterson; m. Jerry H. Bollen, June 22, 1968; children: Heather, Christopher. BA in Art, Coll. of Mt. St. Joseph, Cin., 1968; MA in Art Edn., U. Cin., 1970, EdD in Art Edn., 1980. Tchr. art Marian H.S., Cin., 1968-77; prof. art Coll. of Mount St. Joseph, Cin., 1977—. Fabric surface design art works in juried and invitational regional and nat. exhbns.; book reviewer Nat. Art Edn. Assn. Women's Caucus newsletter, 1985—. Recipient Alumni Appreciation award Coll. of Mount St. Joseph, 1993, Disting. Teaching award, 1981. Mem. Nat. Art Edn. Assn. (Student Chpt. Sponsor award 1994, Outstanding Ohio Art Educator of Yr. 1990, Western Region Higher Edn. Art Educator of Yr. 2001), Ohio Art Edn. Assn. (Outstanding Art Educator 1988, Higher Edn. Art Educator of Yr. 2000), Nat. Surface Design Assn., Am. Crafts Coun., Nat. Mus. for Women in the Arts (charter), Georgia O'Keeffe Mus. Roman Catholic. Home: 1138 Cryer Ave Cincinnati OH 45208-2803 Office: Coll of Mount St Joseph Art Dept 5701 Delhi Rd Cincinnati OH 45233-1670

BOLLES, SUSAN, production designer; b. Boston, May 25, 1960; d. Peter Piper and Jacqueline Maoria (Gilmore) B. BA in Theater, U. Mass., 1982; MFA, NYU, 1985; cert., L'Univ. Cath. L'ouest, Angiers, France, 1980. Vis. lectr. Tisch Sch. of Arts NYU, 1997. Prodn. designer (feature films) The Suburbans, Myth of Fingerprints, His & Hers, Illtown, Denise Calls Up, Me & the Mob, Wide Sargasso Sea (AD), (TV) The Kids' Choise Awards, House of Buggin', ESPN's 2 Minute Drill, The MTV Beach House, The Rolonda Show, Inside the Comedy Mind, Night After Night, Turn It Up!, The Ben Stiller Show, Remote Control, also numerous Tn spls. and pilots. Recipient Broadcast Designers' award, 1989, 90. Mem. United Scenic Artists local 829 (exam judge 1986—, exam. com. 1991—), Art Dirs. Guild (local 876, nominated for excellence in prodn. design). Democrat. Unitarian Universalist. Fax: 213- 629-4692.

BOLLEY, ANDREA, artist; d. Hildo and Laura Bolley. BFA, U. Windsor, 1975. Tchr. Activity Ctr. Art Gallery Ont., 1979, 80, Arts Sake, Toronto, 1982. One-woman shows include IDA Gallery York U., 1976, Art Gallery Brant, 1977, Pollock Gallery, Toronto, 1977-78, 80, Agnes Etherington Art Ctr., Kingston, 1981, Gallery One, Toronto, 1984-86, Klonaridis Gallery, Toronto, 1989-91, Upper Can. Brewing Co., 1993, Studio Show, 1994-2006, 02, Masterworks Found., Bermuda, 2004, Thames Art Gallery, Ont., 2004; group exhbns. include Grapestake Gallery, San Francisco, 1980, Alta. Coll. Art, Calgary, 1980, Art Gallery Ont., 1981, Art Gallery Hamilton, 1981, Gallery One, 1984-86, Triangle N.Y., 1985, 91, Klonaridis Gallery, 1988, John Schweitzer Gallery, Montreal, 1989, Mississauga Civic Ctr. Art Gallery, 1990, Magnum Books, Ottawa, 1991, Bennington Coll., Vt., 1991, Upper Can. Brewing Co., 1992, Robert Kidd Gallery, Birmingham, Mich., 1999, Group of Ten Corkin-Shopland, Toronto, Can., 2003, McGill U., Montreal, 2003, Guild Hall, London, 2004, Masterworks, Bermuda, 2004, Ocad, Toronoto, 2005, Gibbs Mus., Charleston, James Bard Gallery, Nfld., RW Norton Gallery Gallery, LA, others; represented in permanent collections Can. Coun. Art Bank, Art Gallery Windsor, Labatt's Can. Ltd., Citicorp Ltd., Can., Can. Imperial Bank Commerce, Max Factor Ltd., Chatelaine Mag., J.E. Seagram Ltd., McGill Club, Imperial Oil, Citibank Can., Toronto-Dominion Bank, Casey House, Am. Express, Guaranty Trust, Abitibi Paper, Triangle, Toronto Sund, Arthur Gelgoot and Assoc., Premiere Mag., Bells & Whistles, Masterworks Found., Bermuda, and various pvt. collections. Grantee Ont. Arts Coun., 1975, 76, 78, 79, 84, 85, Can. Coun., 1976, 80; recipient Ont. Soc. Artists Purchase award J.E. Seagram and Son Ltd., 1980. Office: 132 Jarvis St Toronto ON Canada M5B 2B5 Office Phone: 416-955-0660. E-mail: andrea@andreabolley.com.

BOLLHEIMER, (CECILIA) DENISE, marketing professional, finance company executive; b. Memphis, Sept. 8, 1950; d. Parker Cecil Jr. and Kathleen Alice (Reinhart) Henderson; m. Philip Anthony Bollheimer Jr., June 10, 1972. Student, Rhodes Coll., 1968-69; BBA in Mktg., Memphis State U., 1972, MBA in Fin., 1979; cert. in Banking, Rutgers U., 1983; cert. in Trust Ops., So. Trust Sch., 1984. Research analyst, mgr. Union Planters Corp., Memphis, 1973-75, asst. to mktg. dir., 1975-76, asst. v.p., 1976-77, v.p. mktg. div., 1977-83; sr. v.p. trust group Union Planters Nat. Bank, Memphis, 1983-84; sr. v.p. fin. mgmt. group Union Planters Corp. (now Regions Bank/Morgan Kegan), Memphis, 1984-86; dir. advt., promotions, mktg. communications Meth. Health Systems, Memphis, 1986-87, dir. mktg., 1987-88; v.p. mktg. and planning UT Med. Group, Inc., Memphis, 1988-96; dir. mktg. U. Tenn. Med. Ctr., 1989—; v.p. mktg. and managed care UT Med. Group, Inc., 1996—. Instr. health care fin. Memphis State U., 1988-90. Mem. planned giving com. Rhodes Coll., Memphis, 1985-86, alumni fund-raising com. 1987; mem. Leadership Memphis, 1985—, class rep., 1985-93, 99-2004; chmn. world championship barbecue cooking contest Memphis in May Internat. Festival, 1986-88, mktg. steering com., 1990, speakers bur., 1991-93; chmn. advt. com. entertainment com. Am. Heart Assn., Memphis, 1986, 87, advt. and communications com., Memphis, 1990—; bd. dirs. Commitment Memphis, 1984-87, pres., 1987; bd. dirs. Memphis Lit. Coun., 1986-90, chmn. bd., 1989-90, Lupus Found. Am., Memphis, 1987-88; mem. fin. com., bd. dirs. Memphis/Shelby County chpt. ARC, 1990-96; group leader YWCA Capital Campaign, Memphis, 1990; trustee Hemophilia Found., Memphis, 1990-95; bd. dirs. U. Memphis Soc., Inc., 1995-98; chmn. bd. Mid-South region ARC, 1996-99, bd. dirs., 1996—, mem. fin. com., 1998—; bd. dirs. Womens Leadership Coun., U. Memphis, 1996-2001; Mobilizing Memphis Shelby County Regional Health Coun., 2003-05; chair Healthy Memphis Common Table, 2006—. Recipient Isis award, Memphis Bus. Women, 2001, 50 Women Who Make a Difference award, City of Memphis Women Mag., ARC Vol. Yr. award for Excellence in Mgmt. and Governance, 2000. Mem. Am. Inst. Banking (Banker of Yr. Memphis region 1981-2002), Kiwanis (sec. bd. dirs. Kiwanis Charities 1988-90, 92-04, membership com. 1990-98, program com. 1993-98, bd. dirs. 1994-2004), Beta Gamma Sigma, Alpha Omicron Pi. Avocations: skiing, jogging, reading. Home: 1542 Harbert Ave Memphis TN 38104-4903 Office: UT Med Group Inc 66 N Pauline St Memphis TN 38105-5122 Business E-Mail: denise.bollheimer@utmg.org.

BOLLHOFER-WHITE, JOANNE, pharmacist; b. Jamaica, NY, Nov. 10, 1962; d. William Harry and Joan Anne Bollhofer; m. Douglas William White, July 20, 2002. BS in Pharmacy, St John's U., 1985, MS, 1989; MBA, U. West Fla., 1999. Registered pharmacist N.Y., 1985, N.J., 1993, Md., 2005. Commd. USAF, 1991, chief pharmacy svcs. 305th Med. Group McGuire AFB, NJ, 1991—95, chief pharmacy svcs. 64th Med. Group Reese AFB, Tex., 1996—97, chief inpatient pharmacy element 96th Med. Group Eglin AFB, Fla., 1997—2000, pharmacy flight comdr. 377th Med. Group Kirtland AFB, N.Mex., 2000—04, diagnostics and therapeutics flight comdr. 11th Med. Group Bolling AFB, DC, 2004—. Question writer, editor Pharmacy Technician Cert. Bd., 2005—, mem. std. setting bd., 2006—. Maj. Air Force, 1999. Decorated Achievement medal with one oak leaf cluster USAF, Commendation medal, Meritorious Svc. medal with one oak leaf cluster. Mem.: Soc. Air Force Pharmacy, Am. Pharmacists Assn. Avocations: reading, travel, cross stitch. Personal E-mail: joannerph@comcast.net.

BOLLINGER, SHARON MOORE, psychotherapist; b. Cape Girardeau, Mo., May 27, 1949; d. Raymond V. and Lucille (Broshuis) Moore; m. Skip Bollinger, Aug. 30, 1968; children: Kristell, Amber. AA, St. Louis C.C., 1988; BA in Psychology, Lindenwood Coll., St. Charles, Mo., 1990, MA in Profl. Counseling, 1992; postgrad., St. Louis U., 1996—2001; PhD in Counseling Psychology, EarthNet Inst., 2004. Lic. profl. counselor; nat. cert. counselor. Computer operator Clothworld/Brown Group, St. Louis, 1986-88; grad. asst. Lindenwood Coll., St. Charles, 1990-92, St. Louis. U., 1999—2000; dir. social svcs. Wentzville (Mo.) Park Care Ctr., 1993-98; pvt. practice psychotherapy St. Peters, Mo., 1998—; clin. therapist Provident Counseling, 2000—02; outpatient clinician Crider Ctr. for Mental Health, 2002—. Presenter in field. Newsletter editor Long Term Care Social Svcs. Mo., Social Svcs. Assn. Mo. Vol. counselor St. Joseph's Health Ctr.-Hospice, St. Charles, 1991, All Saints Ch., St. Peters, Mo., 1992. Mem.: ACA, Mo. Counseling Assn., Alpha Sigma Tau, Phi Theta Kappa. Avocations: languages, reading, crafts, dance, scuba diving.

BOLLS, IMOGENE LAMB, English language educator, poet; b. Manhattan, Kans., Sept. 25, 1938; d. Don Q. and Helen Letson (Keithley) Lamb; m. Nathan J. Bolls, Jr., Nov. 24, 1962; 1 child, Laurel Helen. BA, Kans. State U., 1960; MA, U. Utah, 1962. Instr. French Kans. State U., Manhattan, 1959-60; instr. English U. Utah, Salt Lake City, 1960-62; instr. to prof. Wittenberg U., Springfield, Ohio, 1963—. Poet-in-residence, dir. journalism program Wittenberg U.; tchg. poet Antioch Writers' Workshop Antioch Coll., summers, 1992—93; intensive seminar poet Antioch Writers' Workshop Antioch Coll., summer, 1994; poetry tchr. Ohio Poet-in-the-Schs. program, 1972—82; poetry instr. acad. camp; state and nat. poetry judge. Author: (poetry) Glass Walker, 1983, Earthbound, 1989, Advice for the Climb, 1999, works represented in anthologies; contbr. more than 600 poems to mags. Recipient Individual Artist award Ohio Arts Coun., 1982, 90, Poetry prize S.D. Rev., 1983, Poetry award Kans. Quarterly, 1985, Ohioana Poetry award Ohioana Libr. Assn., 1995; finalist Vassar Miller Prize in Poetry, 1994; grantee Ireland, 1986, France, 1990, Am. Southwest. Mem. Acad. Am. Poets (assoc.), Poetry Soc. Am., Women in Comm. Avocations: Native American cultures, hiking, photography, music, travel. Address: PO Box 2917 Taos NM 87571

BOLM, DEBORAH DELL, elementary school educator, consultant; b. Austin, Tex., Nov. 19, 1951; d. Herbert Straube and Ruby Dell (Lewis) B. BS in Elem. Edn., S.W. Tex. State U., 1974; MEd, U. Tex., 1987. Cert. elem. tchr., ESL tchr. Tchr. Jarrell (Tex.) Ind. Sch. Dist., 1974-77, Del Valle (Tex.) Ind. Sch. Dist., 1977—. Workshop presenter, cons. Edn. Svc. Ctr. Region XV, San Angelo, Tex., 1990, Edn. Svc. Ctr. Region XIV, Abilene, Tex., 1991. Mem. Assn. Tex. Profl. Educators. Avocations: music, movies, travel. Home: Apt 306 4201 Monterey Oaks Blvd Austin TX 78749-1025 Office: Hillcrest Elem Sch 6910 E William Cannon Dr Austin TX 78744-8312

BOLOGNIA, JEAN LYNN, academic dermatologist; b. Hammond, Ind., July 1, 1954; d. John Paul and Jo Ann (Dill) B.; m. Dennis Lawrence Cooper, Aug. 25, 1985. BA summa cum laude, Rutgers U., 1976; MD cum laude, Yale U., 1980. Diplomate Nat. Bd. Med. Examiners. Intern, resident in internal medicine Yale-New Haven Hosp., 1980-82, resident in dermatology, 1982-85; rsch. fellow dermatology Yale U. Sch. Medicine, New Haven, 1985-87, asst. prof. dermatology, 1987-93, assoc. prof. dermatology, 1993-97, prof. dermatology, 1997—, dir. residency tng. program, 1994-2000. Lectr. at over 100 univs. and internat. meetings; bd. dirs. Am. Bd. Dermatology. Author: Harrison's Principles of Internal Medicine, 1991, 5th edit., 2004, Textbook of Medicine, 2004. Mem.: Med. Dermatology Soc. (pres. 2000), Pan Am. Soc. for Pigment Cell Rsch. (coun. 1998—2000), Dermatology Found. (med. and sci. com. 1997—2000, bd. trustees 2003—), Soc. for Investigative Dermatology (v.p. 2003—04, bd. dirs. 2004—), Women's Dermatol. Soc. (newsletter editor 1999—2001, bd. dirs. 1999—2003, v.p. 2004—05, pres. 2005—), Am. Dermatol. Assn. (membership com. 2000—06, bd. dirs. 2003—), Am. Acad. Dermatology (environment coun. 1997—2001, bd. dirs. Sulzberger Inst. 1998—2003, nominating com. 2000—02, chair, audit com. 2003—, bd. dirs. 2004—06). Achievements include patent for enhancing depigmentation therapy; research in depigmentation therapy, characteristics of nevi and melanoma, disorders of pigmentation.

BOLOMEY, ROSE L., secondary school educator; b. Longview, Tex., May 13, 1950; d. Jessebee H. McIlveene and Stella M. Rogers McIlveene; m. Stephen L. Bolomey, May 27, 2000; m. Rudolph E. Maldonado, Mar. 20, 1976 (dec. Nov. 3, 1983); children: Rudolph E. Maldonado, II, Jamie C. Maldonado, Adam G. Maldonado. BA, U. Tex., Tyler, 1990—96. Cert. Tchr. Tex. Dept. Edn., 1996. Tchr. Pine Tree HS, Longview, 1997—. Office: Pine Tree HS PO Box 5878 Longview TX 75608 Office Phone: 903-295-5031. Business E-Mail: rbolomey@ptisd.org.

BOLSTER, JACQUELINE NEBEN (MRS. JOHN A. BOLSTER), communications consultant; b. Woodhaven, N.Y. d. Ernest William Benedict and Emily Claire (Guck) Neben; m. John A. Bolster, May 8, 1954. Studied, Pratt Inst., Columbia U. Promotion mgr. Photoplay mag., 1949—53; merchandising mgr. McCall's, N.Y.C., 1953—64; dir. promotion and merchandising Harper's Bazaar, 1964—71; dir. advt. and promotion Elizabeth Arden Salons, 1971—76; dir. creative svcs. Elizabeth Arden, Inc., 1976—78; dir. comm. Elizabeth Arden Salons, 1978—87; comm. cons., 1987—. Recipient Art Dir.'s award, 1961, 1966. Mem.: Fashion Execs. Roundtable, Fashion Group, Advt. Women N.Y. (life), Women's Nat. Rep. Club (life). Episcopalian. Home and Office: 8531 88th St Woodhaven NY 11421-1308 also: Halsey Neck Ln Southampton NY 11968 Office Phone: 718-849-0975.

BOLSTERLI, MARGARET JONES, English professor, farmer; b. Watson, Ark., May 10, 1931; d. Grover Clevel and Zena (Cason) Jones; m. Mark Bolsterli, Dec. 30, 1953 (div. Dec. 1964); children: Eric, David. BA with honors, U. Ark., 1952; MA, Washington U., St. Louis, 1953; PhD, U. Minn., 1967. Asst. prof. Augsburg Coll., Mpls., 1967-68; prof. English, U. Ark., Fayetteville, 1968-93, prof. emeritus, 1993—, dir. Ctr. for Ark. and Regional Studies, 1984-87. Fulbright lectr., Portugal, 1986; vis. rsch. fellow Yale U., 1997-98; bd. dirs. Ark. Humanities Coun., 1992-94. Author: The Early Community at Bedford Park, 1977, Vinegar Pie and Chicken Bread, 1982, Born in the Delta, 1991, A Remembrance of Eden, 1993; contbr. articles and stories to Jour. Modern Lit., So. Quar., others. NEH Younger Humanist grantee, 1970-71; Ark. Endowment for Humanities grantee, 1980, 81 Mem. MLA (pres. women's caucus), South Cen. MLA. Democrat. E-mail: mbolster@alltel.net.

BOLT, DAWN MARIA, financial planner; b. Bklyn., June 12, 1949; d. Gulick Arthur B. and Georgette Helen (Werner) Bolt-Wiggs; widowed; children: Robert B. Williams, Wesley A. Williams. BA, Bklyn. Coll., 1971. Cert. fin. planner; chartered fin. analyst. Fin. analyst Blyth Eastman Dillon, N.Y.C., 1971—77; rating agy. analyst Fitch Investors Svc., N.Y.C., 1977—78; bank analyst Merrill Lynch, N.Y.C., 1978—80; fin. analyst Moodys Investors Svc., N.Y.C., 1980—86; real estate sales agt. J.R. Silvers Realty, N.Y.C., 1987—95, Coldwell Banker Hunt Kennedy, N.Y.C., 1995—98; pvt. practice fin. planning and coaching, 1998—. Avocations: bowling, tennis, skiing, reading, coaching. E-mail: jodiedawn49@hotmail.com.

BOLT, EUNICE MILDRED DEVRIES, artist; b. Clifton, N.J., Oct. 31, 1926; d. Lambert H. and Cora DeVries; m. Maurice L. Bolt (dec. Nov. 1989); children: Macyn Bolt, Tamsen Bolt, Valerie Bolt Wegner. Grad., Pratt Inst. Art & Design, Bklyn., 1949; BA, Calvin Coll., 1952; MA, Western Mich. U., 1973. Book illustrator Fideler Pubs., Grand Rapids, Mich., 1952-53, Zondervan Pub. Co., Grand Rapids, Mich., 1953-56; prof. Calvin Coll., Grand Rapids, Mich., 1962-67, Grand Rapids C.C., 1968-91. Internat. art study tours coord. and guide, 1978-2005; fine art exhbn. juror, 1987—; lectr. art history, 1991—, presenter watercolor workshops, 1991—; artist-in-residence, 1995—. Exhibited in group shows at Grand Rapids Art Mus., Kalamazoo Inst. Art, U. Mich. Schlusser Gallery, Pitts. Ctr. for the Arts, Westmoreland Mus. Art, Detroit Inst. Art. Home and Studio: 2481 Autumn Ash Dr Grand Rapids MI 49512

BOLT, LYNDA ELAINE, alcohol/drug abuse services professional; b. Beverly, Mass., Feb. 5, 1941; d. Emil Henry and Gladys Evelyn (Crane) Forss; m. William Coventry Henderson II, Jan. 12, 1980 (div. Aug. 1989); m. Chris Bolt, Feb. 14, 1992. BSc in Mgmt. Studies, U. Md.; MSc in Counseling & Human Devel., Troy State U. Lic. mental health counselor Fla., cert. addiction profl. Fla., cognitive-behavioral therapist Nat. Assn. Cognitive Behavioral Therapy, registered addiction specialist Fla., cert. alcohol drug counselor Internat. Cert. & Reciprocity Consortium. Social svc. asst. USN, Naples, Fla., Italy, 1987—88, facilitator, 1988—89; from addiction counselor to program dir. Twelve Oaks, Navarre, 1989—94, program dir., 1994—95; outpatient program dir. APOGEE, Ft. Walton Beach, 1995—97; substance abuse coord. ALTACARE, 1998—99; pvt. practice Destin Counseling, 1997—2002, Elen P. Gajo M.D. & Assoc., Ft. Walton Beach, 1999—; outpatient program mgr. N.W. Fla. Counsel Alcohol and Drug Dependencies, 2000—02; dir. Lifestyle Solutions and Counseling Ctr., Navarre, 2002—03. Facilitator Intervention Project for Nurses, 1993—; presenter in field. Mem.: Nat. Assn. Cognitive Behavioral Therapy, Fla. Counseling Assn., Fla. Mental Health Counselors Assn., Fla. Alcohol and Drug Abuse Assn., Gulf Coast Mental Health Counselors Assn., Am. Counseling Assn., Am. Mental Health Counselors Assn. Avocations: tennis, swimming. Office: 68 Beal Pwy SW Fort Walton Beach FL 32548 Office Phone: 850-243-7035.

BOLTJES, CONNIE CLOY, music educator; b. Cozad, Nebr., May 30, 1951; d. Junior Edson Van Cleave and Evelyn Mae Barnes, Rose Van Cleave (Stepmother) and Earl Barnes (Stepfather); m. Marion Larkin Rossitter, June 29, 2002; children: Melody Marie Schreiner, Tyler Dana Schreiner, Amber Ann Schreiner, Amy Lynn. MA in Edn., No. Ariz. U., Flagstaff, 1998. Cert. tchr. Ariz., 1991. Elem. tchr. Bayard Elem. Sch., Nebr., 1974—78; music tchr. Melbeta Sch., Nebr., 1983—85; grades K-12 music tchr. Minatare Sch., Nebr., 1985—90; elem. music tchr. Nogales Unified Sch. Dist., Ariz., 1991—. Organist, ch. musician, pianist, choir dir. Missionary work, musician United Ch. of Christ, Nogales, 1991—2006. Mem.: NEA (assoc.), Music Educators Nat. Conf. Democrat-Npl. United Church Of Christ. Avocation: singing and playing instruments. Home: 403 Poston St Rio Rico AZ 85648 Office: Robert Bracker Elem Sch Plum St Nogales AZ 85621 Personal E-mail: cloybaby@hotmail.com.

BOLTON, ANN P., music educator; b. Cleve., Sept. 5, 1962; d. Thomas Edward and Jane Snyder Peeling; m. Calvin Alonzo Bolton, July 7, 1984; children: Daniel, David. BA in Music Edn., Ohio State U., Columbus, 1984; MusM, U. NC, Greensboro, 1991. Music tchr. Rutherford County Schs., Rutherfordton, NC, 1984—88, Mebane Elem. Sch., NC, 1988—89, Spartanburg Christian Acad., SC, 1999—; choral dir. Ea. Almance HS, Mebane, 1990—91; band dir. Guilford Coll., Greensboro, NC, 1990—91. Panelist edn. symposia U. NC, Greensboro, 1991. Mem.: Music Educators Nat. Conf. (judge 2005). Baptist.

BOLTON, BETTY J., medical/surgical nurse, poet; b. Lusedale, Miss., Sept. 2, 1952; d. Saul Jones and Mary Hurley Fairley; m. Joe N. Bolton, July 28, 1968; children: Terry, Benilda, Timiki; 1 child, Joe Jones. AAS, Miss. Gulf Coast Jr. Coll., 1986; postgrad., Coastal Tng., Pascagoula, Miss., 1989. Libr. ref. aide Pascagoula Libr., Miss., 1986—89; program specialist I Salvation Army Domestic Violence Women, Pascagoula, Miss., 1986—90; owner B&J Vending, Moss Point, Miss., 1990—92; home health nurse Profl. Home Health, Biloxi, Miss., 1992—97; supr. South Miss. Regional Ctr., Long Beach, Miss., 1997—99; pvt. duty nurse Jackson County and South Miss., 2000—03. Author (poetry): Best Poems of 2002, 2002 (Editors Choice award, 2002), Across the Abyss, 2002 (Editors Choice award, 2002), Best Poems of 2003, 2003 (Editors Choice award, 2003). Recipient Pres. award, Iliad Press, 2003. Mem.: Ri Rsch., Acad. Am. Poets, Internat. Soc. Poets. Ch. Of Christ. Avocations: arts and crafts, sewing, walking, creative cooking, poetry. Home: 3809 Jeffery Dr Moss Point MS 39562 E-mail: joebet51@bellsouth.net.

BOLTON, DEBORAH A., ambassador; b. Phila. BA, St. Joseph's U., 1974; diploma in Security Studies, USAF Coll., Maxwell Air Force Base, 1992—93. Joined Fgn. Svc., US Dept. State, 1974, assigned to Am. Embassy Hungary, Ecuador, Argentina, Spain, country officer for Uruguay and Paraguay, 1986, European affairs officer Office of Amb.-at-Large for Counterterrorism, chief consular sect., US Interests Section Havana, Cuba, 1990, dep. dir. internat. security and peacemaking ops. Bur. of Political-Military Affairs, 1993, dep. chief of mission, charge d'affairs Valetta, Malta, acting and dep. prin. officer Consulate Gen. Ho Chi Minh City, Vietnam, chief of mission, consul gen. to Netherlands Antilles and Aruba, 2001—. Office: US Consulate Gen 3160 Curacao Pl Washington DC 20521-3160

BOLTON, MARTHA O., writer; b. Searcy, Ark., Sept. 1, 1951; d. Lonnie Leon and Eunice Dolores Ferren; m. Russell Norman Bolton, Apr. 17, 1970; children: Russell Norman II, Matthew David, Anthony Shane. Freelance writer for various comedians, 1975-86; newspaper columnist Simi Valley Enterprise, Simi, Calif., 1979-87; staff writer Bob Hope, 1986—, The Mark and Kathy Show, 1995-96. Author: A Funny Thing Happened to Me on My Way Through the Bible, 1985, A View from the Pew, 1986, What's Growing Under Your Bed?, 1986, Tangled in the Tinsel, 1987, So. How'd I Get To Be in Charge of the Program?, 1988, Humorous Monologues, 1989, Let My People Laugh, 1989, If Mr. Clean Calls Tell Him I'm Not In, 1989, Journey to the Center of the Stage, 1990, If You Can't Stand the Smoke, Get Out of My Kitchen, 1990, Home, Home on the Stage, 1991, TV Jokes and Riddles, 1991, These Truths Were Made for Walking, 1991, When the Meatloaf Explodes It's Done, 1993, Childhood Is a Stage, 1993, Honey, It's Time To Weed the Carpets Again, 1994, Walk A Mile in His Truths, 1994, The Cafeteria Lady on the Loose, 1994, On the Loose, 1994, If the Pasta Wiggles, Don't Eat It, 1995, Bethlehem's Big Night, 1995, Club Family, 1995, When the Going Gets Tough, The Tough Start Laughing, 1995, Who Put The Pizza in the VCR?, 1996, And Now a World from Our Maker, 1997, A Lamb's Tale, 1998, (lyrics) Mouth in Motion, Sermon on the Stage, 1998, Never Ask Delilah For A Trim, 1998, (with Mark Lowry) Piper's Night Before Christmas, (with Gene Perret) Talk About Hope, The Twelve Plays of Christmas, 1999, Don't Jump to Conclusions Without a Bungee Cord, 1999, I Love You.Still, 2000, Didn't My Skin Used to Fit, 2000, Piper Steals the Show, 2000, The "Official" Book series, 2002—, I Think Therefore I Have a Headache, 2003, Cooking with Hot Flashes, 2004, Growing My Own Turtleneck, 2005, My Life As A Bystander (co-written with Jeff Allen), 2005. Pres. Vista Elem. Sch. PTA, Simi, 1980-81. Recipient Emmy nomination for outstanding achievement in music and lyrics, 1988, Internat. Angel award, 1990, 91, 2001, 02, Amb. award Media Fellowship Internat., 1995. Mem. ASCAP, NATAS, Nat. League Am. Pen Women (pres. Simi Valley br. 1984-86, 96-98, Woman of Achievement award 1984, Pen Woman of Yr. award 1995, pres. 1996-98), Writers Guild Am. West. Avocation: travel. Office: PO Box 3046 Brentwood TN 37024 E-mail: marthabolton@marthabolton.com, boltonha@aol.com.

BOLTUCK, MARY A., retired psychologist, educator; b. Yellow Springs, Ohio, Nov. 2, 1924; d. Clyde Stewart and Sarah (Walker) Adams; m. Charles J. Boltuck, July 16, 1950; children: Richard Dale, Jane Ellen. BA, Miami U., Oxford, Ohio, 1946; MA, State U. Iowa, 1948. Clin. psychologist Wichita Guidance Ctr., 1948-50; psychologist/probation Monroe County, Bloomington, Ill., 1950-53; clin. psychologist Galesburg (Ill.) State Residential Hosp., 1953-55, Kent (Ohio) State U., 1957-64; from asst. prof. to assoc. prof. psychology St. Cloud (Minn.) State U., 1964-90. Tchr., workshop facilitator, spkr., 1990—. Mem.: APA, AAUW (life), Assn. Prevention Elder Abuse, Assn. Prevention of Child Abuse, Minn. Women Psychologists, Minn. Psycol. Assn., Midwest Psychol. Assn., Nat. Coun. on Aging, Ctrl. Minn. Psychol. Assn., Psi Chi (life; psychol. hon. advisor 1978—90). Avocations: travel, reading, knitting, walking, conservation.

BOLTZ, MARY ANN, aerospace materials company executive, travel company executive; b. Far Rockaway, NY, Jan. 12, 1923; d. Thomas and Theresa (Domanico) Caparelli; m. William Emmett Boltz; children: Valerie Ann Boltz Austin, Beverly Theresa, Cynthia Marie Boltz O'Rourke. Publicist CBS, N.Y.C., 1943-48; mgr. Coast-Line Internat. Distbrs. Ltd., Lindenhurst, N.Y., 1961-80, v.p., 1980-86, pres., 1987-90, CEO, 1990—; chief exec. officer Air Ship 'N Shore Travel, Woodmere, N.Y. and Marco Island, Fla., 1978—. Pres. Bangor Realty, 1975. Formerly radio and TV editor local publs., writer Gotham Guide mag. Sec. Inwood Civic & Businessmen's Assn., 1952-64, pres., 1964-66, chmn. bd., 1967-68; pres. Lawrence Pub. Schs. System PTA, 1956-58; pres., life mem. Cen. Coun. PTA, 1958-60; founder Inwood Civic Scholarship Fund, 1964; v.p. Econ. Opportunity Coun., Inwood; fundraising bd. yearly ball St. Joachim Ch., Cedarhurst, NY; gift chmn. L.I. Bd. Boys Town of Italy; bd. dirs. Marco Island Cancer Fund Dr.; dir., promoter Marco Island Philharmonic Symphony; dir. polit. campaign William Sieffert, Oceanside, N.Y.; chmn. 30 yr. reunion Class of 41, 1971, 50 yr. reunion, 1991, 55th yr. Lawrence H.S. reunion Class of 1938-42; asst. chmn. 50 yr. reunion Class of 42, 1991, Lawrence H.S. 55th Reunion Class of 1941, 1996; fundraiser Stecker and Horowitz Sch. Music Dinner Com., 1978, Am. Bus. Women's Assn., Long Island charter chptr., Rockville Centre, N.Y., 1990-92, United Fund, Red Feather Ball, 1992 Recipient award Nassau Herald Newspaper, Cedarhurst, Inwood Civic Assn., PTA Life Membership award, 25 Yr. Silver Medallion Boys Town of Italy, gold medal, 1995, Citizen of Yr. Bronze Plaque award Inwood Civic Assn., 1996; named Woman of the Year Boys Town of Italy, 1997. Mem. Am. Bus. Women's Assn. (L.I. charter chpt.), Nissoquogue Golf Club, Sun 'N Surf Beach Club, Island Country Club (Marco Island, Fla.), Desert Mountain Country Club. Republican. Roman Catholic. Home: 149 Hempstead Ave Rockville Centre NY 11570-2904 Office: Coast-Line Internat Distbrs 274 Bangor St Lindenhurst NY 11757-3633 Office Phone: 631-226-0500.

BOMAL, CHERYL ANN, secondary school educator; d. Richard and Mary Bomal. BA in History, U. Lowell, Mass., 1989; MEd in Curriculum, U. Mass., Lowell, 1991. Personnel coord. Hannaford, Dracut, Mass., 1986—97; tchr. history Greater Lowell Tech. H.S., Tyngsboro, Mass., 1988—. Named Local Hero, Lowell Sun, 2005. Office: Greater Lowell Tech HS 250 Pawtucket Blvd Tyngsboro MA 01879

BOMAR, GAIL MARIE, language educator; d. Gerald Eugene and LaVetta Helen Janicek; m. Melvin Leroy Bomar, July 22, 1978; children: Scott, Michael, Justin, Lukas. BA in Edn., U. Nebr., Lincoln, 1973, MEd, 1997. Tchr. Spanish Holdrege City Schs., Nebr., 1973—75; tchr. Spanish/English So. Pub. Schs., Wymore, Nebr., 1975—78; tchr. English Humphrey Pub. Schs., Nebr., 1978—83, Scotus Ctrl. Cath., Columbus, Nebr., 1983—84; tchr. Spanish Schuyler Ctrl. H.S., Nebr., 1985—. Student coun. advisor Schuyler Ctrl. H.S., 1988—. Pres., treas. St. Peter's PCCW, Bellwood, Nebr., 1988—89, 2004—; mem. bd. Aquinas Alumni Bd., David City, Nebr. Named Tchr. of Yr., Humphrey Pub. Schs., 1979, Schuyler Ctrl. H.S., 1987, Nebr. Assn. Student Coun., 1999. Business E-Mail: gbomar@esu7.org.

BOMAR, LAURA BETH, music educator; b. Atlanta, Ga., Feb. 24, 1965; d. Alvie Troy and Mary Elizabeth Elliott; m. Robert Linton Bomar, June 27, 1987; 1 child, Sarah Beth. AA, Brewton-Parker Coll., 1985; BA, Tift Coll., 1987; MusM, Ga. State U., 1993. Music tchr. Butts County Schools, Jackson, Ga., 1987—. Team leader North Mulberry Elem. Sch., Jackson, Ga., 1999—, sch. coun. mem., 2003—. Mem.: Music Educators Nat. Conf., PA of Ga. Educators (bldg. rep. 2001—). Protestant. Avocations: hiking, camping, biking, reading. Office: North Mulberry Elem Sch 820 N Mulberry St Jackson GA 30233

BOMBARDIERI, MERLE ANN, psychotherapist; b. Atlanta, Mar. 16, 1949; d. Sol and Sadie (Drucker) Malkoff; m. Rocco Anthony Bombardieri, Jr., Aug. 22, 1971; children: Marcella, Vanessa. B.A. in Psychology, Mich. State U., 1971; M.S.W., San Diego State U., 1976. Cert. clin. social workers, Mass., clin. hypnosis Am. Soc. Clin. Hypnosis; Diplomate Nat. Assn. Social Workers, Am. Bd. Examiners in Clin. Social Work. Crisis intervention worker and trainer Listening Ear, East Lansing, Mich., 1969-71; tchr. English as 2d lang. Instituto Brasil Estados Unidos, Rio de Janeiro, 1971-73; supr. infant unit Married Student Day Care Ctr., Mich. State U., East Lansing, 1973-74; psychotherapist/family life educator Family Svc. Assocs., San Diego, 1975-77; psychotherapist Dade Wallace Mental Health Ctr., Nashville, 1977-78; psychotherpist/workshop leader Met. Beaverbrook Mental Health Ctr., Waltham, Mass., 1980-81; pvt. practice psychotherapy, Acton-Belmont, Mass., 1982—; clin. dir. Resolve, Inc., infertility orgn., Belmont, 1982-84; clin. cons., 1984—; cons. HealthData Internat., Westport, Conn., 1983—, Open Door Soc., Newton, Mass., 1983—, First Day Film Corp., 1985—, Mass. Dept. Social Svcs., 1987; sec. Boston Fertility Soc., 1995, others; psychology seminar leader; radio and TV appearances. Author: The Baby Decision, 1981, (cassettes) Your Mind's Own Medicine, 1998; founder, editor, pub. Wellspring newsletter; contbr. articles to profl. and med. jours. N.Y. State Regents scholar, 1967; NIMH trainee, 1970. Mem. Acad. Cert. Social Workers, Phi Beta Kappa, Phi Kappa Phi. Home: 4 Broadview Rd Acton MA 01720-4202 Office: 33 Bedford St Lexington MA 02420-4319

BOMBOY, JENNIFER MARIE, social studies educator, coach; b. Allentown, Pa., Oct. 22, 1976; d. James and Carol Snyder; m. Eric William Bomboy, Jan. 20, 1973. MEd, East Stroudsburg U., Pa., 2004. Cert. tchr. grades 8-12 Pa., 1998. Tchr. Stroudsburg H.S., Pa., 1999—, coach varsity softball, 2005—06. Coach varsity field hockey Stroudsburg H.S., 1999—. Named Hockey Coach of Yr., Stroudsburg H.S., 2003. Mem.: Stroudsburg Area Edn. Assn. (corr.; coun. rep. 2005—06). Office Phone: 570-421-1991.

BOMCHILL, FERN CHERYL, lawyer; b. Chgo., Feb. 25, 1948; BA, U. Mich., 1969; JD, U. Chgo., 1972. Bar: Ill. 1972, U.S. Dist. Ct. (no. dist.) Ill. 1972, U.S. Ct. Appeals (7th cir.) 1986, U.S. Dist. Ct. (ea. dist.) Mich. 1999. Ptnr. Mayer, Brown & Platt, Chgo. Mem. ABA, Fed. Bar Assn. (bd. dirs. Chgo. chpt.), Chgo. Coun. Lawyers, Law Club Chgo., Legal Club Chgo., The Menomonee Club for Boys and Girls (bd. dirs., pres. 1993-94). Office: Mayer Brown & Platt 190 S La Salle St Ste 3100 Chicago IL 60603-3441 Office Phone: 312-701-7331. Office Fax: 312-706-8608. Business E-Mail: fbomchill@mayerbrown.com.

BOMHAN, RUTH WALKER, social studies educator; b. Wilmington, N.C, Dec. 17, 1955; d. Robert Henry and Edna (Barritt) Walker; m. Kenneth Earl Bomhan (div.); 1 child, Kenneth Earl Jr. BA, U. N.C., Wilmington, 1984. Cert. tchr. social studies. Tchr. New Hanover H.S., Wilmington, 1984-85, Hoggard Night Sch., Wilmington, 1985-88, Lakeside H.S., Wilmington, 1988-2000, Roland-Grise Mid. Sch., Wilmington, 2000—. Mem. Smithsonian Instn., Civil War Trust, Nat. Geog. Soc., Mus. of Confederacy, World War II Meml., N.C. Coun. Social Studies, Libr. Congress, Nat. Trust Historic Preservation, Friends of Nat. Park Gettysburg, N.C. Assn. Educators, Nat. Honor soc. Polit. Sci., Colonial Williamsburg Found. Avocations: bowling, lapidary, reading, travel, martial arts. Office: Roland-Grise Mid Sch 4412 Lake Ave Wilmington NC 28403

BOMHOF, ROBYN, artist, educator; b. Chgo., June 19, 1952; d. Emmett Earl and Ruth Carolyn Miller; m. James Alan Bomhof, Dec. 27, 1974; children: Russell, Allyson, Jessica. BFA with honors, Kendall Coll. Art and Design, Grand Rapids, Mich., 1997; MFA, Western Mich. U., Kalamazoo, 2001; Academia De Belle Arte de Pietro Vanucci, Perugia, Italy, 1999. Youth program dir. West YMCA, Grand Rapids, 1968-72; program dir. Vic Tanny, Inc., Detroit, 1974-76; creative dir., artist Genesis Advt., Grand Rapids, 1977-79; artist self employed, Grand Rapids, 1970—; tchr. Western Mich. U., Kalamazoo, 1998—2001, asst. dir. exhbns., 1999—2001. Mem. exec. bd. Westside Christian Sch., Grand Rapids, 1988-91; charter mem. Rivertown Artists Guild, Grand Rapids, 1990—; dir. word fellowship Sunshine Ministries, Grand Rapids, 1988-89. One-woman shows include Kendall Coll. Art and Design, 1997, Riley Galleries/Rapture, 1999, Western Mich. U., 2000, Newago Coun. for Arts 2002, exhibited in group shows at Fine Arts Gallery, 1998, Great Lakes Regional Competition, 1997, 1998, 1999, 2000, Lowell Coun. for the Arts Regional Show, 1997, Ferris State U., 1996, Muskegon Mus. Art, 1998 (Curator's award), Festival Regional, Grand Rapids, 1999, ARC Gallery, Chgo., 1999, Battle Creek Ctr. for the Arts, 1999, Carnegie Ctr. for Arts, 1999 (Best of Show), Kalamazoo Inst. of Art, 2000, works in various pub. and pvt. collections. Vol. disaster relief Am. Red Cross. Recipient awards for art and design; Vt. Studio Ctr. grantee, 1999; Western Mich. U. grantee, 1999; travel grantee Dietre Heineke. Mem. AAUW, Coll. Art Assn., Grand Rapids Kennel Club (bd. dirs. 1976-85), Friesian Horse Assn. N.Am., Am. Driving Soc., Carriage Assn. N.Am., Mich. Horse Drawn Vehicle Assn., Metamora Carriage and Driving Assn. Avocations: reading, dogs, cats, Friesian horses, driving. Office: Black Oak Farm 14 Mile Rd NE Sparta MI 49345-1701

BONACORSI, ELLEN E., lawyer; BA, Stanford U., 1976; JD, Harvard U., 1979. Bar: Mo 1979, Ill 1981. Ptnr. Bryan Cave LLP, St. Louis. Mem.: Phi Beta Kappa. Office: Bryan Cave LLP One Metropolitan Square 211 N Broadway, Ste 3600 Saint Louis MO 63102 Office Phone: 314-259-2804. E-mail: eebonacorsi@bryancave.com.

BONACORSI, MARY CATHERINE, lawyer; b. Henderson, Ky., Apr. 24, 1949; d. Harry E. and Johanna M. (Kelly) Mack; m. Louis F. Bonacorsi, Apr. 23, 1971; children: Anna, Kathryn, Louis. BA in Math., Washington U., St. Louis, 1971; JD, Washington U., 1977. Bar: Mo. 1977, Ill. 1981, U.S. Dist. Ct. (ea. dist.) Mo., U.S. Dist. Ct. (so. dist.) Ill., U.S. Ct. Appeals (8th cir.), U.S. Supreme Ct. 1995. Ptnr. Thompson Coburn, St. Louis, 1977—. Chairperson fed. practice com. eastern dist., St. Louis, 1987—, eight cir. jud. conf. com., St. Louis, 1987—. Fellow Am. Bar Found.; mem. ABA, ATLA, Mo. Bar Assn., Met. St. Louis Bar Assn., Am. Bd. Trial Advocates (assoc.), Order of Coif. Office: Thompson Coburn LLP One US Bank Plz Saint Louis MO 63101 Office Phone: 314-552-6014. E-mail: mbonacorsi@thompsoncoburn.com.

BONANNI, VICTORIA, writer; b. Jersey City, N.J., Dec. 13, 1952; d. Joseph Salvatore and Dolores DiMaria (Aidala) B. BA in English/Secondary Edn., SUNY, Stony Brook, 1974. Cert. ESL tutor, electronics technician. Sec., retail newsletter editor Zayre, Inc., Framingham, Mass., 1974; temporary sec., adminstrv. asst. Manpower, Inc., Salem, Mass., 1975; reporter/photographer The Beverly (Mass.) Times, 1976; mktg. comm. coord. United Shoe Machinery Corp., Middleton, Mass., 1977-79; adminstrv. writer HBH Co., Rosslyn, Va., 1979-80; technical writer Teradyne, Inc., Boston, 1981-89; sr. technical writer Panametrics, Inc., Waltham, Mass., 1989, EMC Corp., Hopkinton, Mass., 1991; owner, prin. writer VB Documentation Enterprises, Natick, Mass., 1991—. Author, editor: A Blue Perfume, 1993; editor: Dolorata: Looking To The Future (Dolores Fiore), 1995, Burning Heads (Lawrence Carradini), 1996, A Bowl of Cherries: Just Spit The Pits (Mark Willman), 1996, I Wish That My Room Had a Floor Living With An Emotional Disorder (Rafael Woolf), 1996, A Pen Is Like A Piece (Gary Hicks), 1997, Hot Moon Night (Ann Murphy Fletcher), 1998, Of Rare Design (William J. Barnum), 1999; author: Ad Vivum, 2001. Direct mail fund raiser-coord. Kennedy Sr. Ctr., Natick, 1997. Recipient honorable mention "Writer's Digest", Cin., 1993, 2001, 80 Hrs. Cmty. Svc. award Natick Vis. Nurse Assn., 1996; recipient Cambridge Poetry Award, 2nd prise, Mass., 2001. Mem. NAFE, Soc. Am. Poets, Natick Ctr. Assocs. Roman Catholic. Avocations: original greeting cards, miniatures, historical perspectives, theology, songwriting. E-mail: vnatick@aol.com.

BONASSI, JODI, artist, marketing professional, consultant; b. LA, Aug. 22, 1953; d. Julian and Sara (DeNorber) Feldman; m. Raymond Gene Bonassi, June 7, 1986; 1 child, Spencer. Student, Otis Art Inst., L.A., 1972, Calif. State U., 1983-85, Calif. State U., Northridge, 1985-86. Participating artist Concern Found. and World Cup Soccer Gala Event for Cancer Rsch., Beverly Hills, Calif., 1994; lectr., guest spkr. L.A. Pub. Libr., Canoga Park, 1999, Pierce Coll., 2003; mem. adv. bd. Park LaBrea Art Coun.; guest spkr. Pierce Coll., 2003; art tchr. Learning Tree, Chatsworth, Calif., 2004. Artist, Creative With Words Publs., 1987, greeting cards, 1994—; one-woman shows include Pt. Adesa Gallery, Rancho Mirage, Calif., 1996, Orlando Gallery, 1999, Performing Arts Gallery, Calif. State U., Northridge, 2002; exhibited in group shows at Bowles-Sorokko Gallery, Beverly Hills, 1994, ChaChaCha, Encino, Calif., 1994—, Lyn/Bassett Gallery, L.A., 1994, Topanga (Calif.) Canyon Gallery, 1994, Hartog Fine Art Gallery, L.A., 1995, Charles Hecht Gallery, Tarzana, Calif., 1995, New Canyon Gallery, Topanga, 1995, Made With Kare, West Hills, Calif., 1995, Gail Michael Collection, Northridge, 1995, Mythos Gallery, Burbank, 1995-96, Nicole Brown Simpson Found., 1996, Orlando Gallery, Sherman Oaks, Calif., 1998, West Gallery, U. Calif., Fullerton, 1998, The Century Gallery at Mission Coll., 1998, Orlando Gallery, 1998-99, Christie's Beverly Hills Silent Auction, 1999, Palos Verdes Art Ctr. Gallery, 1999, White Meadows Gallery, 2000, St. Louis Artist Guild Gallery, 2000, Bank of Am., Laguna Beach, 2000, Almost Paradise Gallery, Laguna Beach, 2d City Gallery, Long Beach, 2002-03, Cambridge Nat. Prize Show, 2002-03, Beckstrand Gallery, Palos Verdes, 2003, Pierce Art Gallery, Woodland Hills, Calif., 2003, Lankershim Art Gallery, North Hollywood, Calif., 2003-04, Finegood Art Gallery, West Hills, Calif., 2004, Pelican Arts Gallery, 2004, Long Beach Art Gallery, 2005, Upstream People Gallery, 2005, Grey McGear Modern, Inc. Gallery, Santa Monica, 2005-06, Satellite Gallery, Long Beach, 2005, CRA Gallery, North Hollywood, 2005, LAWA Exhibit, Tom Bradley Terminal, LAX, 2005, Grey McGear Modern Inc. Gallery, Santa Monica, 2005-06, Warner Ctr. Marriott, Woodland Hills, 2006, Beckstrand Gallery, Palos Verdes, Calif., 2006, Creative Arts Workshop, 2006, Korean Cultural Ctr., 2006, others; on-line exhbn. Upstream Peoples gallery; represented in pvt. collections; commd. works include Von's Corp., Alhambra Bus. Assn., North Hollywood Revitalization Program, MTA of N. Hollywood Fence Panel Project, 2003; illustrator All About Us, 1996; featured in books including Living Artists, 13th edit., 2003, New Art Internat., 4th edit., 2003, Community of Angels Book, 2001; featured in articles and art revs. including Pasadena Star News and Pasadena Weekly, The Chronicle Rev., LA Daily News, Harpers Mag., Boston Globe, 2003, also Showtime Cable-TV Film: Trust Me, 1997, Chandler Outdoor Gallery Documentary, 2002, others; featured artist in Living Artist, 2003; cover art for Art Calendar Mag., 2005, Daily News, 2006. Art tchr. K-12 West Valley Christian Ch. Schs., 1997—2001, Woodcrest Elem. Sch., 2004-06. Recipient Best Banner 2d prize LA County Mus. Art, Park LaBrea Arts Couns. for PLB/LACMA Family Art Fund, 1997, World Peace Tour, 1997, Spl. Judges Art award Park LaBrea Art Coun., 1998, nat. prize Cambridge Art Assn., 2002, Outstanding Painting award Nat. Portrait Gallery, Washington, 2003, Smithsonian Nat. Portrait Gallery. Mem. Calif. Women Bus. Owners, L.A. Mcpl. Art Gallery Registry, So. Calif. Women's Caucus for Art, Soc. Children's Bookwriters and Illustrators. Avocations: hiking, reading, swimming. Office Phone: 818-274-7393. Personal E-mail: jbonassi@aol.com.

BONATTI, CHRISTINE ANNE, elementary school educator; b. New Haven, July 24, 1978; d. Joseph Edward and Sandra Jane Bonatti. BA, Mass. Coll. Liberal Arts, North Adams, 2000; MEd, Boston Coll., Chestnut Hill, Mass., 2006. Lic. educator State of Conn., State of Mass. Tchr. grade 6 Beaver Country Day Sch., Chestnut Hill, Mass., 2001—04; tchr. grades 7 and 8 Cmty. Day Charter Pub. Sch., Lawrence, 2004—05, tchr. grade 4, 2005—06. Asst. basketball coach U. Mass., Boston, 2001—04; girls soccer and lacrosse coach Beaver Country Day Sch., Chestnut Hill, 2001—04; varsity basketball coach Cmty. Day Charter Sch., Lawrence, 2004—06. Home: 11 Skylark Dr Northford CT 06472

BONAUTO, MARY, lawyer; b. 1961; BA, Hamilton Coll.; JD, Northeastern U. Civil rights project dir. Gay and Lesbian Advocates & Defenders (GLAD), 1990—. Mem. Mass. Atty. Gen. Working Group on Racial Profiling. Mem.: ABA (sub.-com. sexual orientation & gender identity, vice-chair), Boston Bar Assn. (mem. family law steering com.). Office: Gay and Lesbian Advocates & Defenders Ste 800 30 Winter St Boston MA 02108

BONAZINGA, MARIE THERESE, manufacturing executive; b. Bklyn., May 10, 1948; d. Bartholomew and Ann Bonazinga. AA, Gloria K. Bus. Sch., 1967. Adminstrv. asst. Gallard-Schlesinger Chem. Mfg. Corp., Carle Place, N.Y., 1967-75; v.p. Accurate Chem. & Sci. Corp., Westbury, NY, 1975—; pres. Accurate Surg. & Sci. Instruments Corp., Westbury, 1979—, Leeches USA Ltd., Westbury, 1986—. Recipient Boli award, L.I. Advt. Club, 1981. Mem.: Nat. Assn. Women Bus. Owners (award L.I. chpt. com. 100 1996), Roslyn Heights Civic Assn. Avocations: gardening, reading, antiques. Office: Accurate Surg & Sci Instruments 300 Shames Dr Westbury NY 11590-1736

BONAZZI, ELAINE CLAIRE, mezzo soprano; b. Endicott, NY; d. John Dante and Zina (Rossi) Bonazzi; m. Jerome Ashe Carrington, Sept. 21, 1963; 1 child, Christopher Carrington. BM (George Eastman scholar), Eastman Sch. Music. Currently artist-in-residence SUNY, Stonybrook; pvt. voice studio N.Y.C. Past faculty Peabody Conservatory; vis. prof. Eastman Sch. Music, Rochester, NY, 1979; judge nat. and internat. competitions. Singer: Santa Fe Opera, 1958, Opera Soc. Washington, 1960, NYC Opera, 1965, Opera Internacional, 1966, Met. Opera at Forum, 1973, Europe, West Berlin Festival opera, 1961, Spoleto Festival, 1974, Castel Franco Festival Venetian Music, 1975, Berlin Bach Festival, 1976, Pks. Radio TV Difusion, 1980—, Netherlands Opera, 1978, Minn. Opera, 1985, Artpark Festival, 1987, Opera Theater St. Louis, 1988, New Orleans Opera, 1988, 1990, Spoleto-Charleston Festival, 1981, Edmonton Opera, 1990, 1992, Winnipeg Opera, 1993, Libr. Congress concerts, (Operas) Pique Dame, 1989, Vanessa, 1988, Carlson's Midnight Angel, 1993, Glimmergalss Opera La Calisto, 1995, NYC Opera, NY Philharm., Phila. Orch., Boston Symphony, Cleve. Orch., Can. Broadcasting Corp., PBS NET Opera Theatre, NBC, ABC, CBS TV networks, (albums) Candide, Vanguard, Folkways, Grenadilla, The Art of Elaine Bonazzi, 2005, over 40 world permier of major works by leading composers with maj. orchs. and opera cos. Named Bonazzi scholar fund in her honor, SUNY Stony Brook, 2005; named one of 6 honored alumni 50th Anniversary Yr., Eastman Sch. Music, 1971; recipient Concert Artists Guild award, 1960; William Matheus Sullivan grantee. Mem.: Mu Phi Epsilon.

BOND, CHRISTINA M., judge; b. Washington, Dec. 9, 1967; d. Eugene M. and Ann Marie (Berik) Bond. BA, Youngstown State U., 1989; JD, U. Akron, Ohio, 1989-92. Cert. to serve as co-counsel on death penalty cases. Clk. CIA, Langley, Va., 1990-91; rsch. asst. U. Akron, 1991-92; paralegal instr. Bus Sch., Ravenna, Ohio, 1993-95; hearing officer, trial and appellate Child Support Enforcement, Youngstown, Ohio, 1995-97; magistrate Mahoning County Ct. of Common Pleas, Youngstown, 1997—. Named to Outstanding Young Women of Am., 1997. Mem. ABA, Ohio Bar Assn. (bd. govs. Women in the Profession and Young Lawyers), Mahoning County Bar Assn. (newsletter editor 1995—), Ohio Assn. Magistrates, Youngstown Panhellenic Assn., Youngstown Women's Polit. Caucus, Cleve. Mus. Art, Butler Mus. Art, Friends of Nat. Zoo, Delta Zeta (newsletter editor). Office: Ste 200 1040 S Commons Pl Youngstown OH 44514-1959 Home: 4610 E Cerro De Aguila Tucson AZ 85718-6931

BOND, ENRIQUETA CARTER, science administrator; b. Buenos Aires, May 22, 1939; d. James Prescott and Harriette Mortley (Bovard) Carter; m. Langhorne Bond, Aug. 26, 1962; children: Langhorne Carter, Prescott McCook. BA in Zoology and Physiology, Wellesley Coll., 1961; MA in Biology and Genetics, U. Va., 1963; PhD in Molecular Biology and Biochem. Genetics, Georgetown U., 1969. Asst. prof., acting chmn. biology Chatham Coll., Pitts., 1970-73; asst. prof., dept. exec. dept. med. scis. So. Ill. U., Springfield, 1974-78; staff officer Nat. Acad. Scis., Inst. of Medicine, Washington, 1979-80, divsn. dir., 1981-88, exec. officer, 1989-94; pres. Burroughs Wellcome Fund, Durham, NC, 1994—. Bd. regents Nat. Libr. Medicine, Bethesda, Md., 1996—; bd. sci. counselors Nat. Ctr. Infectious Disease Control and Prevention, Atlanta, 1997—; bd. mem. health sci. policy Inst. Medicine, Washington, 1994-97, Nat. Academies' Com. on Sci., Engrng., and Pub. Policy Contbr. articles to profl. jours. Bd. dirs. NC Biotech Ctr., Research Triangle Park, NC, 1995—, pres., 1998; bd. dirs. Rsch. Triangle Found., 1996—; mem. leadership coun. Rsch. America!, Alexandria, Va., 1996—. Recipient Profl. Staff award Nat. Acad. Sci., 1985. Mem. AAAS, APHA, Inst. Medicine (mem. coun. 1999—), Am. Soc. Microbiology, Soc. for Advancement of Women's Health Rsch. (sec. bd. dirs. 1995—), Sigma Xi. Episcopalian. Avocations: needlepoint, reading. Office: Burroughs Wellcome Fund PO Box 13901 Research Triangle Park NC 27709-3901

BOND, KARLA JO, elementary school educator; b. Abilene, Tex., Oct. 11, 1951; d. David Lipscomb and Elizabeth Rosalie (Henthorn) Kennamer; m. Dennis Earl Bond, July 28, 1979; children: Ryan Jeffrey, Blake Justin. BS in Edn., Abilene Christian U., 1972; MA, Maryville U., 1994. Tchr. Abilene (Tex.) Christian Campus Sch., 1972-73, LaMarque (Tex.) Pub. Schs., 1973-78, Kansas City (Kans.) Unified Sch. Dist. 500, 1979-90, Ft. Zumwalt Pub. Schs., O'Fallon, Mo., 1990—, coord. elem. sch. math., 1993—. Instr. math. Math. Learning Ctr., Portland, 1990-92; leader math. insvc. Ft. Zumwalt Pub. Schs., 1990-94. Mem. NEA, Nat. Coun. Tchrs. Math., Mo. Coun. Tchrs. Math., Math. Educators Greater St. Louis. Republican. Mem. Ch. of Christ. Avocations: water-skiing, reading, piano, sports. Office: Mid Rivers Elem 7479 Mexico Rd Saint Peters MO 63376

BOND, KRISTA SUZETTE, secondary school educator; b. LaJara, Colo., July 26, 1979; d. Steven Kay and Denise Miller; m. Bart Bond, May 25, 2000; 1 child, Texa Chalee. Degree in Secondary English Edn., Adams State Coll., Alamusa, Colo., 2001. Sec. Adams State Coll.; tchr. English Del Norte Schs., Colo., Sanford Schs., Colo. Sponsor Nat. Honor Soc., drama club Sanford Schs., 2005—. Mem.: Sanford Tchr. Orgn. Home: 1686 State Hwy 15 S Monte Vista CO 81144 Office: Sanford Sch PO Box 39 Sanford CO 81151

BOND, MARY LLEWELLYN, movement education educator; b. LA, June 8, 1942; d. Arthur Llewellyn and Zoe Thompson Bond; m. Renardo John Barden (div.); children: Rohana Barden, Michael Barden. BA, Smith Coll., Northampton, Mass., 1964; MA, UCLA, 1968. Cert. structural integration practitioner Rolf Inst., Boulder, Colo., 1986. Pvt. practice structural integration therapist, LA, 1969—; instr. Immaculate Heart Coll., Los Angeles, Calif., 1969—71, Touch Therapy Inst., Encino, Calif., 1993—, Rolf Inst., 1998—. Author: Balancing Your Body, The New Rules of Posture. Mem.: Rolf Inst., Nat. Certification Bd. Therapeutic Massage and Bodywork, Internat. Assn. Structural Integrators. Avocations: travel, yoga, dance. Office: Touch Therapy Inst 15720 Ventura Blvd Encino CA 90041 Office Phone: 818-788-0824. E-mail: touch@touchtherapyinstitute.com.

BOND, VICTORIA ELLEN, conductor, composer; b. LA, May 6, 1945; d. Philip and Jane (Courtl) B.; m. Stephan Peskin, Jan. 27, 1974. B Mus. Arts, U. So. Calif., LA, 1968; M Mus. Arts, Juilliard Sch. Music, 1975, D Mus. Arts, 1977; DFA (hon.), Washington and Lee U., 1992, Hollins Coll., 1995, Roanoke Coll., 1995. Condr., composer. Mem. NY State Coun. Arts Music Panel, 1987-90; bd. dirs. NY Women Composers; pres., artistic dir. Welltone New Music, Inc., 2004. Guest condr. numerous orgns. including most recently Warsaw Symphony, Poland, York Symphony, Pa., Music from Penn's Woods, Pa., 1999-00, NYC Opera Showcasing Am. Composers, 2001, Norwalk Symphony, 2002, Da Corneto Opera Co., 2003, Dallas Symphony Ray Charles Concert, 2003, Central Opera, Beijing, 2004, Ctr. for Contemporary Opera, 2004, 06, Music Festival of the Hamptons, 2004, Chamber Opera, Chgo., 2005, 06; music dir. New Amsterdam Symphony Orch., NYC, 1978-80, Pitts. Youth Symphony Orch., 1978-80, Empire State Youth Orch., 1982-86, Southeastern Music Ctr., 1983-84, Bel Canto Opera, 1983-86, Roanoke Symphony Orch., Va., 1986-95; artistic dir. Bel Canto Opera Co., 1986-88, Harrisburg Opera, 1998-03, Cutting Edge Concerts, NYC, 1999-; artistic adv., Wuhan Symphony, China, 1997-2000; artistic dir. Opera Roanoke, 1989-95; Exxon/Arts Endowment condr., Pitts. Symphony, 1978-80, recs. include Twentieth Century Cello, Two American Contemporaries, The Frog Prince, An American Collage, Live from Shanghai, Victoria Bond: Compositions, The American Piano Concerto, Yes, 2003; commd. by Pa. Ballet, 1978, Jacob's Pillow Dance Festival, 1979, Am. Ballet Theater, 1981, Empire State Inst. Performing Arts, 1983-84, Stage One, Louisville, 1986, Ga. State U., 1986, L'Ensemble, 1990, Renaissance City Winds, 1990, Audubon String Quartet, 1990, Women's Philharm., San Francisco, 1993, Va. Explore Park and The Shanghai Symphony, 1994, D Day Found., 1994, Linda Plaut, 1994, Pianofest, 2005, Duo Gelland, 2005, Ethel, 2005, Am. Piano Concertos, Albany, 2006, Billings Symphony, Mont., Elgin Symphony, Ill., Elements String Quartet, Indpls. Chamber Orch., Composers' Conf., Jade String Trio, others; commns. include Gettysburg Chamber Orch., 2006, Fontana Chamber Arts, 2006. Bd. dirs. Am. Music Ctr. Recipient Victor Herbert award 1977, Perry F. Kendig award, 1988, ASCAP Composition award 1973—; Nat. Inst. for Music Theater grantee in opera conducting NYC Opera, 1985, Martha Baird Rockefeller grantee, 1978-79, Meet-The-Composer grantee in Composition, 1973—; Juilliard scholar, 1972-77; Juilliard fellow, 1975-77, Aspen Music Festival fellow, 1973-76; named Exxon/Arts Endowment Conductor, 1978-80, Woman of Yr. in Va., 1990, 91; featured on NBC Today show, 1990, profiled in C.S. Monitor, 1987, Wall Street Jour., 1987, others. Mem. ASCAP (awards 1975—), Am. Symphony

Orch. League, Am. Fedn. Musicians, Condrs. Guild (bd. dirs. 1994—98), Internat. Alliance Women in Music, NY Women Composers, Mu Phi Epsilon. Avocations: horseback riding, sailing, hiking. Business E-Mail: victoria@victoriabond.com.

BONDAREFF, JOAN M., lawyer, retired government agency administrator; b. Utica, N.Y., Jan. 7, 1944; 1 child. Student, Cornell U., 1961-64; BA in Polit. Sci. cum laude, George Washington U., 1965; JD magna cum laude, Am. U., 1975. Bar: Md. 1975, D.C. 1978, U.S. Supreme Ct. 1979. Clk. Md. Ct. Spl. Appeals, 1975; atty. advisor for legis. and regulation Office Gen. Counsel, Dept. Commerce, Washington, 1975-76, atty. on detail to Dept. Justice, 1976-77; staff atty. NOAA, Washington, 1977-80, sr. counsel to nat. earth satellite svc., 1980-82, asst. gen. counsel for adminstrn., 1981-82, asst. gen. counsel for ocean svcs., 1982-87; sr. counsel Coast Guard and Mcht. Marine group U.S. Ho. of Reps. Mcht. Marine and Fisheries Com., Washington, 1987-94; chief counsel and acting dep. maritime adminstr. Maritime Adminstn., Dept. Transp., Washington, 1994—99; counsel maritime/marine dept. Dyer Ellis & Joseph, Washington, 2001—02; counsel maritime/marine transp. group Blame Rome LLP, Washington, 2003—. Legal counsel Nat. Safe Boating Coun. Contbr. articles to law jours., including Territorial Sea Jour., Coastal Mgmt. Jour., Internat. Ship Registry Rev. Former chmn. Women's Aquatic Network. Mem.: Bar Assn. DC, Md. State Bar Assn., Women's Bar Assn. DC, ABA (marines resouces com. 1989—, vice chair marine resouces com. nat. resources enivronmental law sect. 1994—98). Avocations: hiking, running, music, travel. Office: Blank Rome LLP The Watergate Bldg 600 New Hampshire Ave NW Washington DC 20037*

BONDI, KATHLEEN, social worker; b. Hammond, Ind., Sept. 7, 1952; d. Del and Anna (Uher) Bondi. BA, Purdue U., 1974; MSW, Ind. U., Indpls., 1987. Caseworker Youth Svc. Bur., Kokomo, Ind.; hotline dir. Voluntary Action Ctr., South Bend, Ind.; social worker No. Ind. State Devel. Ctr., South Bend; therapist Madison Ctr., South Bend. Mem. Alpha Delta Mu. Office: Madison Ctr 801 E Washington St South Bend IN 46617 Office Phone: 574-283-0581.

BONDINELL, STEPHANIE, counselor, academic administrator; b. Passaic, N.J., Nov. 22, 1948; d. Peter Jr. and Gloria Lucille (Burden) Honcharuk; m. Paul Swanstrom Bondinell, July 31, 1971; 1 child, Paul Emil. BA, William Paterson U., 1970; MEd, Stetson U., 1983. Cert. elem. educator Fla., guidance counselor grades K-12 Fla. Tchr. Bloomingdale (N.J.) Bd. Edn., 1971-80; edn. dir. Fla. United Meth. Children's Home, Enterprise, 1982-89; guidance counselor Volusia County Sch. Bd., Deltona, Fla., 1988—. Coord. sch. improvement svcs., Deltona Lakes, 1996—98, Deltona Lakes, 2002—05. Sec. adv. com. Deltona Jr. HS, 1996—98, sec. PTA, 1982; vice-chmn. adv. com. Deltona Mid. Sch., 1988, chmn., 1991—92, 1991—92; mem. adv. com. Deltona HS, 1995—96; secondary sch. task force Volusia County Sch. Bd., 1986—; team leader Volusia County Sch. Accreditation Quality Assurance Team, 2003—06; mem. exec. com. Volusia County Reps.; mem. Rep. Presdl. Task Force; mem. state adv. bd. Fla. Future Educators Am., 1990—92, 2003—06. Named Deltona Lakes Tchr. of Yr., Volusia County Sch., 1991, 1996, Volusia County Sch. Dist. Accreditation Steering Com. Team Leaders, 2003—06, Volusia County Guidance Counselor of Yr., 2006; recipient Outstanding Ednl. Partnership award, S.W. Volusia C. of C., 1998, Sunshine State Medallion award, Fla. Pub. Rels. Assn., 1998, award, Volusia/Flagler Alcohol and Drug Abuse Prevention Coun., 1998—2006, Fla. Lottery Creative Tchg. award, 2002; Acad. scholar, Becton, Dickinson & Co., 1966, N.J. State scholar, 1966—70. Mem.: AAUW, ASCD, Fla. Edn. Assn., Internat. Platform Assn., Volusia Tchrs. Orgn., N.J. Edn. Assn., Fla. Assn. Counseling and Devel., Disvn. Learning Disabilities, Coun. Exceptional Children, Stetson U. Alumni Assn., Deltona Civic Assn., 4 Townes Federated Rep. Women's Club (sec., v.p.), Deltona Rep. Club (v.p. 1991—93). Avocations: painting, creative writing, dance. Home: 1810 W Cooper Dr Deltona FL 32725-3623 Office: Volusia County Sch Bd 2022 Adelia Blvd Deltona FL 32725-3976 E-mail: sbondine@mail.volusia.k12.fl.us.

BONDS, GEORGIA ANNA, writer, educator; b. N.Y.C., Dec. 30, 1917; d. Alex Matthews and Mattie Ethel (Stephens) Arnett; m. Alfred Bryan Bonds Jr., Feb. 23, 1939; children: Anna Belle, Alfred Bryan III, Alexandra Burke, Stephen Arnett. BA, U. N.C., Greensboro, 1938; MA, La. State U., 1940; postgrad., U. N.C., 1940—42, Baldwin-Wallace Coll., 1960. Editl. asst. The So. Rev., Baton Rouge, 1938-39; editor Abstracts of Theses La. State U., Baton Rouge, 1940; editl. asst. pub. sch. curricula State of La., 1941; freelance writer, lectr., 1943—; editor dist. newspaper United Meth. Ch., Cleve., 1979-91. Lectr. on Egyptian days and ways, 1956-70, internat. concerns, 1970-85, Cherokee Indian heritage, 1985—. Editor: (English transl.) Wheat Growing in Egypt, 1954; author: The Lake Erie Girl Scout Council, the First Seventy-Five Years, 1987, Who Killed Bob Lawson?, 2003; contbr. articles to popular mags. Active Girl Scouts USA, 1928—, leader, organizer troop 1, Cairo, 1953-55, mem. Lake Erie coun., Cleve., 1956—, leader, organizer Mounted troop, 1957-80, coun. bd. dirs., 1966-70, 79-87, coun. pres., 1979-84, mem. nat. coun., 1966-72, 78-83, troop leader internat. encampment, 1968, condr. world tour nat. and internat. ctrs., 1972, world conf. asst., 1984, organizer troops, Volgograd, Russia, 1991—; mem. Dist. United Meth. Women, Cleve., 1956—, bd. dirs., 1965-78, pres., 1974-78, com. on dist. superintendency, 1977-81, chair, 1978-81, mem. World Meth. coun., London, 1966; mem. Ch. Women United in Ohio, 1960—, state bd. dirs., 1966-72; active YWCA, Little Rock, 1950—, bd. dirs., 1950-53, bd. dirs. Cleve. chpt., 1977-79; active Philanthropic Ednl. Orgn., 1950—, bd. dirs. Ohio state chpt., 1965-71, pres., 1971. Recipient Outstanding and Dedicated Svc. award Girl Scouts of Lake Erie Coun., 1979, Thanks Badge, 1971, Thanks Badge II, 1997, World Friendship and Understanding Through Girl Scouting award Girl Scouts of Lake Erie Coun., 1984, award of honor for fund raising S.W. Gen. Hosp. Found., 1996, Outstanding Intellectual of the 20th Century Internat. Biographical Ctr., Cambridge, England. Mem. AAUW (bd. dirs. 1984-89), Baldwin-Wallace Coll. Women's Club (hon. life mem.), Order of Ea. Star, Delta Zeta, Kappa Phi, Phi Beta Kappa (Cleve. assn. bd. dirs. 1964-69, pres. 1968). Avocations: swimming, travel. Home: PO Box 768 Berea OH 44017-0768

BONDURANT, AMY LAURA, investment company executive; b. Union City, Tenn., Apr. 20, 1951; m. David E. Dunn III; 1 child. BA, U. Ky., Lexington, 1978; JD, Am. U. Bar: D.C. 1978, Ky. 1978. Legis. aide Office of Senator Wendell Ford, Washington, 1975—78; sr. counsel Senate Com. on Commerce, Sci. and Transp., Washington, 1978—88; sr. shareholder Verner, Liipfert, Bernhard, McPherson & Hand, Washington, 1987—97; amb. Orgn. for Econ. Cooperation and Devel., Paris, 1997—2001; mng. dir. Bozman Ptnrs., Paris and Washington, 2001—. Chmn., mem. comml. space transp. adv. com. Dept. Transp. Contbr. articles to profl. jours. Mem. adv. bd. Forum 21 Conf. on Transatlantic Dialogue, Washington and Paris, 2001; mem. vestry Am. Cathedral of Paris, 2002; bd. govs. Am. Hosp. of Paris, 2001—02. Mem.: Coun. Am. Ambs., Coun. on Fgn. Rels., Cosmos Club. Episcopalian. Office: Bozman Ptnrs 1340 31st St NW Washington DC 20037 Home Fax: 01 45 00 19 56. Personal E-mail: albond@attglobal.net.

BONDY, ALISON A., music educator; d. Alson Landon and Gloria Ehrlichmann Bondy. BS in Music Edn., U. Minn., Mpls., 1986; M Human Devel., U. St. Mary's, Mpls., 1996. Lic. tchr. Iowa. Music tchr. Mpls. Pub. Schs., Mpls., 1986—2001, Sioux City Cmty. Schs., Iowa, 2001—. Min. music Immanuel Luth. Ch., Sioux City, 2003—; organist, worship leader, choir dir. Bethlehem Luth. Ch., Zion Luth. Ch., St. Mark's Luth. Ch., Oakland Ave. United Meth. Ch., Luth. Campus Ministries, Ctrl. Luth. Ch.; presenter in field. Registrar Reforming Ch., Mpls., 1994—94. Mem.: Am. Orff-Schulwerk Assn. (life; v.p. local chpt. 2005—06), Iowa State Educator's Assn. (life), So. Poverty Law Ctr. (life), Alpha Delta Kappa (life). Office Phone: 712-279-6811.

BONEAU, JANNE MARIE, music educator; d. Richard Alan Boneau and Bernice Droege Boneau. BA in Music, U. Ark., Fayetteville, 1976; MusM, U. So. Miss., Hattiesburg, 1978; BS in Info. Sys., Maryville U., St. Louis, 1984. Cert. tchr. Mo., 2004. Accompanist Marquette H.S., St. Louis, 1998—2002; tchr. asst. spl. edn. Spl. Sch. Dist., St. Louis, 2002—03; music tchr. Archdiocese of St. Louis, 2003—04, St. Clair Sch. Dist., Mo., 2006—; vocal music tchr. Washington Sch. Dist., Mo., 2004—06. Music theater instr. Ctr. Contemporary Arts, St. Louis, 2000—; grad. asst. U. So. Miss., 1976—78. Recipient Musician Musician's award, U. So. Miss., 1978, Honorarium, Interlochen Arts Acad., 1980. Mem.: Music Educator's Nat. Conf. (assoc.).

BONEBRAKE, TARA JANE, elementary school educator; b. St. Louis, Aug. 26, 1977; d. Albert James and Stevia Bonebrake. BA, Drury U., Springfield, Mo., 2000; MA in Tchg., Wash. U. St. Louis, Mo., 2005. Cert. tchr. Mo., 2004. Tchr. 8th grade sci. Jennings Sch. Dist., Mo., 2004—. Instr. deckhand Catalina Island Marine Inst., Long Beach, Calif., 2003—03. Vol. Acad. Prep Ctr. Edn., St. Petersburg, Fla., 2001—04. Fellow, Notre Dame Americorps, St. Petersburg, 2001—04; scholar, Wash. U. Sch. Arts and Scis., 2004—05. Mem.: Nat. Sci. Tchrs. Assn. Personal E-mail: h2obug2677@hotmail.com.

BONEMERY, ANNE M., language educator; b. Springfield, Mass., Nov. 1, 1950; d. Alley and Radie Bonemery. BA, Am. Internat. Coll., 1972, MAT, 1974; AS, Springfield Tech. C.C., 1993. Cert. tchr. in English and Bilingual English Mass., tchr. French and Bilingual French Mass., tchr. Spanish and Bilingual Spanish Mass. Tchr. Northampton Pub. Schs., Mass., 1972—85; prof. Springfield Tech. C.C., 1985—; acct., office mgr. Emery Devel., Ltd., Mass., 1985—. English lang. cons. Springfield Instn. Savings (now First Mass. Bank), 1996—97; treas. Emery Devel., Ltd., 1985—, bd. dirs. Vol. U.S. citizenship studies and English lang. studies Springfield Literacy Network, 1987—; bd. dirs. Am. Internat. Coll. Alumni Bd., Mass., 1997—2000, bd. dirs. Springfield chpt., 2000—. Recipient Nat. Inst. Staff and Orgnl. Devel. Excellence award, U. Tex. Austin, 1997, 2000, Ptnr. in Philanthropy award, We. Mass. chpt. Assn. Fundraising Profls., 2001. Mem.: TESOL, MLA, NEA, Springfield Tech. C.C. Profl. Assn. (bldg. rep.), We. Mass. Fgn. Lang. Assn., Mass. Fgn. Lang. Assn., Mass. Assn. TESOL, Mass. Tchrs. Assn., Am. Coun. Tchg. Fgn. Langs., Am. Assn. Tchrs. French, Springfield Libr. and Mus. Assn., Sigma Lambda Kappa (sec. 1985—2000). Avocations: travel, reading, photography, hiking. Office: Springfield Tech CC One Armory Sq Springfield MA 01105

BONET, LISA (LILAKOI MOON, LISA MICHELLE BONEY), actress; b. San Francisco, Nov. 16, 1967; d. Allen and Arlene Boney; m. Lenny Kravitz, Nov. 19, 1987 (div. Apr. 1993); 1 child, Zoe. Studied acting, Celluloid Actor's Studio, North Hollywood, Calif. Actress TV series The Cosby Show, 1984-87, A Different World, 1987-88, also appearances in The Cosby Show, 1987-91, Tales From the Darkside, St. Elsewhere, NBC-TV, The Two of Us (recurring role), New Eden, 1994; films include Angel Heart, 1987, Tales From the Darkside 2, 1991 Bank Robber, 1993, Dead Connection, 1994, Serpent's Lair, 1995, Enemy of The State, 1998, High Fidelity, 2000, Lathe of Heaven, 2002, Biker Boyz, 2003, Whitepaddy, 2006; dir. music videos Let Love Rule, 1988, The Gentleman Who Fell, 1993, Revelation Sunshine, 1999. Recipient Youth in Film award.*

BONETTI, SUSANNA, administrative director; b. Alfonsine, Italy; d. Enzo Bonetti and Hedda Melandri; m. Rico Peter Solinas, Dec. 17, 1998; 1 child, Nina Solinas. Lit. Major, U. Bologna, 1983; Libr. Tech., City Coll. of San Francisco, 1990. Libr. tech. San Francisco Psychoanalytic Inst. and Soc., 1990—94, sr. libr. asst., 1994—98, adminstrv. dir., 2000—. Home: 2730 23rd St San Francisco CA 94110 Office: San Francisco Psychoanalytic Inst and Soc 2420 Sutter St San Francisco CA 94115 Office Phone: 415-563-4477. Business E-Mail: library@sfpis.org.

BONFANTE, LARISSA, classics educator; b. Naples, Italy; arrived in U.S., 1939, naturalized, 1951; d. Giuliano and Vittoria (Dompé) B.; m. Peter B. Warren, Sept. 1950 (div. 1962); children: Sebastian Raditsa, Alexandra Benfante-Warren; m. Leo Ferrero Raditsa, May 2, 1973 (dec. 2001). Student, Radcliffe Coll., 1950, U. Rome, 1951; BA, Barnard Coll., N.Y.C., 1954; MA, U. Cin., 1957; PhD, Columbia U., N.Y.C., 1966. Mem. faculty NYU, 1963—, prof., 1978—, chmn. dept. classics, 1978—84, 1987—90. Cons. in field; vis. mem. Inst. for Advanced Study, 1980. Author: Etruscan Dress, 1975, paperback, 2003, Out of Etruria, 1981, Reading the Past, Etruscan, 1990; author: (with Giuliano Bonfante) The Etruscan Language (transl. into Italian 1985, into Romanian 1996), 1983, 2d edit., 2002; author: Etruscan Life and Afterlife, 1986, translated to Romanian, 1996, Corpus Speculorum Etruscorum, N.Y. The Metropolitan Museum of Art, 1997; author: (with Judith Swaddling) Etruscan Myth, 2006; editor (with Francesco Roncalli): Antichità dall'Umbria a New York, 1991; editor: (with Judith Sebesta) The World of Roman Dress, 1994; editor: (with Vassos Karageorghis) Italy and Cyprus in Antiquity: 1500-450 BC, 2000; editor: (with Blair Fowlkes) Classical Antiquities at New York U., 2006; translator: Chronology of the Ancient World (E.J. Bickerman), 1967; translator: (with Alexandra Bonfante Warren) The Plays of Hrotswitha of Gandersheim, 1979; contbr. articles to profl. jours. Mem. Archaeol. Inst. Am. (gov. bd. 1982-88), Inst. di Studi Etruschi (fgn., pres. US sect.), German Archaeol. Inst. (corr. mem.). Home: 50 Morningside Dr New York NY 10025-1739 Office: NYU Classics Dept 25 Waverly Pl New York NY 10003-6701 Office Phone: 212-998-8594. Business E-Mail: lb11@nyu.edu.

BONFIELD, BARBARA GOLDSTEIN, non-profit organization administrator; b. Lincoln, Ala., Jan. 12, 1937; d. Samuel Jacob and Margaret (Embry) Goldstein; m. Robert Lawrence Bonfield, Feb. 26, 1959; children: Barney, Susan. BA, Ala. Coll., 1958; MSW, U. Ala., 1976. Lic. cert. social worker, Ala. Social worker Jefferson County Dept. Pub. Welfare, Birmingham, Ala., 1958-59; child welfare worker Children's Aid Soc., Birmingham, 1960-71; human resources officer Jefferson County Commn., Birmingham, 1976-77, dir. area agy. on aging, 1977-96; founder, dir. Human and Natural Resources, Inc., Birmingham, 1996—. Editor Care Notes, 2005—; freelance writer Builder/Architect Mag., 2000-04, Med. Profl. Mag., 2004. Dir. Ms. Sr. Am. Ala., Inc., 1995-99; bd. dirs. Jewish Family Svcs. Birmingham, 1996-2005, chmn. sr. svcs. com. 1999, 2000, mem. exec. bd., 1999-2005, v.p., 1999-2005; bd. dirs. Am. Classics, Inc., 1997-98, Birmingham Jewish Found., 2003—, advisor Assistance League of Birmingham, 1996-2005; mem. Birmingham Holocaust Edn. Com., 2003—; bd. dirs. Temple Beth-El, 2004—, chmn. cemetery com.; mem. alumni bd. U. Montevallo. Recipient Cmty. Svc. award B'nai B'rith Women, Birmingham, 1983, Social Worker of Yr. award Ala. Conf. Social Work, 1993, CARTS Transp. award; named to State of Ala. Sr. Citizen Hall of Fame 1993, Ala. Social Work Hall of Fame, 2002. Mem. NASW (chair PACE com. 1997-2004, Social Worker of Yr. Birmingham chpt. 1978, 99, Lifetime Achievement in Social Work Ala. chpt. 1999), Ala. Gerontol. Soc. (Profl. of Yr. 1986), Nat. Assn. Area Agys. on Aging, Southeastern Assn. Area Agys. on Aging (sec., bd. dirs. 1981), Acad. Cert. Social Workers, Hadassah (nominating com. 2002, fundraising com. 2002—, exec. bd. asst. treas. 2003). Democrat. Jewish. Avocations: reading, gardening, interior decorating, photography, volunteer work. Home and Office: 233 Beech Cir Birmingham AL 35213-2021 E-mail: BBonfield@bellsouth.net.

BONHAM-CARTER, HELENA, actress; b. Golders Green, London, Eng., May 26, 1966; 1 child. Student, Westminster. TV appearances include A Pattern of Roses, Miami Vice, A Hazard of Hearts, The Vision, Arms and the Man, Beatrix Potter, Dancing Queen, Fatal Deception, A Dark Adapted Eye; films include Lady Jane, A Room with a View, Maurice, Francesco, The Mask, Getting It Right, Hamlet, Where Angels Fear to Tread, Howard's End, Mary Shelley's Frankenstein, A Little Loving, Mighty Aphrodite, Margaret's Museum, 1994, Portraits Chinois, 1995, Twelfth Night, 1995, Wings of a Dove, 1996, Revengers Comedies, 1996, Keep the Aspidistra Flying, 1997, The Theory of Flight, 1997, Fight Club, 1998, Women Talking Dirty, 1999, Novacaine, 2000, Til Human Voices Wake Us, Planet of the Apes, 2001, Heart of Me, 2001, Live from Baghdad, 2002, Big Fish, 2003, Henry VIII, 2003, (voice) Corpse Bride, 2004, (voice) Wallace & Gromit, 2004, Conversations with Other Women, 2004, Charlie and the Chocolate Factory, 2004. Office: Adam Isaccs United Talent 9560 Wilshire Blvd Beverly Hills CA 90212-2427 also: Conway Van Gelder 18-21 Jermyn St London SW1Y 6HP England

BONIFACHO, BRATSA, artist; b. Belgrade, Yugoslavia, 1937; arrived in Can., 1973, naturalized, 1976. Student Sumatovachka Sch. Art, Belgrade, 1957-59; BArch, MFA, U. Belgrade, 1965; postgrad., Acad. di Belle Arti, Italy, 1966-68, Atelier Kruger, West Germany, 1966-68. Tchr. painting and drawing Sch. Fine Arts, Belgrade, 1967-68; pvt. tutor, 1979-87. One-person shows Gallery Scollard, Toronto, 1978, Contemporary Art Gallery, Vancouver, 1979, Richmond Art Gallery, B.C., 1982, 93, 97, Heffel Gallery Ltd., Vancouver, 1988, 90, 91, Quan-Schieder Gallery, Toronto, 1989, 90, Fran Willis Art Gallery, Victoria, B.C., Can., 1992, 93, 94, 95, 2000, Patrick Doheny Fine Art Gallery, Vancouver, 1992, 93, 94, Artropolis, 1993, Seattle Art Fair, 1993, Threshold Gallery, Vancouver, 1993, Bau-Xi Art Gallery, Vancouver and Toronto, 1995, 96, 99, 2001, 02, 03, 04, Kimzey Miller Gallery, Seattle, 1996, Mus. History and Art, Anchorage, 1997, Gallerijk Progres, Belgrade, 2000, Contemporary Art Gallery, Zrenjanin, Yugoslavia, 2001, Gallery of the Matica Srpsick, Novi Sad, Yugoslavia, 2002, Foster/White Gallery, Seattle, 2004, 05, Art Fair, Toronto, 2004, Cologne Art Fair, Germany, 2005, Bau Xi Gallery, Vancouver, B.C., 2006, Art Fair, Toronto, 2006; exhbn. Richmond Art Gallery, B.C., Bali-Xi Gallery, Vancouver, 2006, Foster/White Gallery, Seattle,2006; juried group exhbns. in B.C., 1974-93; represented in numerous pub. and pvt. collections. Grantee, B.C. Arts Coun., 1996, 1998, 2000, Can. Coun., 1996, 1998, 1999; travel grantee, 2000, 2001, 2002, B.C. travel grantee, 1999. Office: PO Box 549 Sta A Vancouver BC Canada V6C 2N3 Office Phone: 604-254-1405. Business E-Mail: bonifacho@telus.net.

BONIFAS, JANE MARIE, psychologist; b. Ottoville, Ohio, Jan. 18, 1935; d. George P. and Lucinda (Miller) Hilvers; m. Richard J. Bonifas, Nov. 28, 1953; children: James, Debra, Daniel, Linda, Carl, Darlene. BA with high honors, Lourdes Coll., Sylvania, Ohio, 1989; MEd, U. Toledo, 1990; PhD in Clin. Psychology, Union Inst., 1994. Bookkeeper Ottoville Bank, 1953-55; seamstress Landeck, Ohio, 1960-76; dir. religious edn. St. John Ch., Landeck, 1976-85, Lima, Ohio, 1985-87; coord. religion programs Cath. Lay Ministry, Toledo, 1988-90; psychol. asst. Comprehensive Psychol. Svc. Inc., Lima, 1990-97; clin. psychologist Comprehensive Psych. Svc. Inc. and Nursing Homes, Lima, 1997—2000, Alternative Behavioral Svc. Ltd., 2000—. Advisor 4-H, Landeck, 1964-78; den mother Cub Scouts, Boy Scouts Am., Landeck, 1964-78; organizer cmty. parade, Landeck, 1973; mem. AIDS Task Force, Lima, 1990-93. Mem. OPA, APA, Kappa Gamma Pi. Home: 13731 Converse Roselm Rd Venedocia OH 45894-9532 Office: Alternative Behavior Svc Ltd 2050 N Eastown Rd Lima OH 45807

BONIN, SUZANNE JEAN, artist; b. Oakland, Calif., Nov. 12, 1955; d. Charles Freeman and Dorice Ruth (Brown) B.; m. John Aime Mearle, Mar. 1976 (div. 1980); m. Donald George Winchester, May 16, 1986 (div. Nov. 1990); m. Joseph Bogusis, Nov. 2, 1996. Owner, mgr. Bonin Gallery, Wolfeboro, NH, 1983-94, Bonin Studio, Wolfeboro, NH, 1994—. Spl. needs art instr. Kingswood Regional Sch. System, Wolfeboro, 1982. Designer logo Audubon Soc. of NH, 1982; exhbn. The Art Place, Wolfeboro; illustrator: The Best Plants for New Hampshire Gardens and Landscapes, 2003; artist, collections at Nat. Mus. Women in Arts, Corcoran Gallery of Art, DC.; illustrator for Nov./Dec. issue ACCENT Home & Garden mag., 2005 Charter mem. Gov. Wentworth Arts Coun., Wolfeboro, 1980, vol., 1980—; donor NH Public TV, Durham; silent auction donor, Am. Lung Assn. NH, Bedford, 2004, 05, Great Waters Music Festival, Wolfeboro, 2005; initiator of art collection for silent auction Hospice, Wolfeboro, 1982—; donor Lakes Region Humane Soc., 1999—; mem. Cmty. Ch. of Alton, 1962—. Mem. League of NH Craftsmen, Washington Area Printmakers, No. NH Arts Alliance. Avocations: gardening, fishing, swimming, cross country skiing, kayaking. Studio: Bonin Studio PO Box 801 Wolfeboro NH 03894-0801 Office Phone: 603-569-5397. Business E-Mail: boninstudio@msn.com.

BONINA, SALLY ANNE, principal; b. Stamford, Conn., Jan. 30, 1951; d. Salvatore Edward and Mary Dolores (Giancola) Bonina; children: Vincent Salvatore, Michael Christopher. BA in Spanish with honors, Coll. New Rochelle, 1972; MS in Reading Cons., Bridgeport U., 1975; 6th yr. degree adminstrn., So. Conn. State U., 1994. Spanish tchr. Westhill H.S., Stamford, 1973-78; pvt. tutor John Jay Middle and High Schs., Katonah, N.Y., 1978-89; substitute tchr. Katonah (N.Y.)/Lewisboro Schs., 1990-91; Spanish tchr. Cloonan Middle Sch., Stamford, 1991-2001, Shelton (Conn.) H.S., 2001—06; prin. Derby Mid. Sch., Conn., 2006—. Scheduling com. mem. Cloonan Sch., Stamford, 1992-95, student-of-the-month com., 1993-94, character counts com., 1998—; active middle sch. confs., Champion Internat., Stamford, 1991-94; mem. fgn. lang. curriculum writing team Stamford Pub. Schs., 1997-99, character counts com., 1998-2001, prof. devel. com., 1999-2001; mem. world lang. curriculum team Shelton Pub. Schs., 2004-05; ednl. adv. Nat. Young Leaders Conf., Washington, D.C. Religious edn. tchr. St. Aloysius Ch., New Canaan, Conn., 1984-91; lector St. Margaret Mary Parish, 2003—; pub. ctr. coord. Meadow Pond Sch., Katonah, 1988-90, book fair co-chairperson, 1989-90; schedule co-coord. Westchester (N.Y.) Putnam Baseball Assn., 1992-94; mem. Cloonan Site Based Com., 1997-98; mentor Connecticut BEST program, 2000—; mem. exec. bd. Rivendall Condo Assn., 2004—. Mem.: ASCD, Stamford Edn. Assn. (negotiations team 1999—2000), Shelton Edn. Assn. (negotiations team 2002), Am. Coun. Tchg. Fgn. Langs., N.E. League Mid. Schs., Adminstrn. and Supervision Assn. So. Conn. State U. Roman Catholic. Avocations: swimming, reading, walking, cooking, theater. Office: Derby Mid Sch 8 Nutmeg Ave Derby CT 06418 E-mail: sbonina@derbyps.org.

BONINO, FERNANDA, art dealer; b. Torino, Italy, Jan. 5, 1927; arrived in U.S., 1963; d. Francesco Pogliani and Marina Collino; m. Alfredo Bonino, July 29, 1925 (dec. Jan. 1981). M in Art, U. Italy, Torino, 1942. Dir. Galeria Bonino Ltd., N.Y.C., 1963-90, dir., pres., 1981—. Mem. Art Dealers Assn. Am. Office: Galeria Bonino Ltd 48 Great Jones St New York NY 10012-1133 Office Phone: 212-598-4262.

BONN, ETHEL MAY, psychiatrist, educator; b. Cin., Oct. 14, 1925; d. Stanley Ervin and Ethel May (Cliffe) B. BA, U. Cin., 1947; MD, U. Chgo., 1951. Asst. chief, then chief women's neuro-psychiat. services VA Hosp., Topeka, 1956-61, chief north service, 1961-62; assoc. dir. for clin. services Ft. Logan Mental Health Ctr., Denver, 1962-67, dir., 1967-76; clin. instr. psychiatry U. Colo. Sch. Medicine, 1963-76; field rep. Joint Commn. on Accreditation of Hosps., 1976-78; assoc. clin. prof. psychiatry UCLA Sch. Medicine, 1978-81; chief of quality assurance VA Med. Ctr.-Brentwood, L.A., 1978-81; chief psychiatry service VA Med. Ctr., Albuquerque, 1981-89; assoc. prof. psychiatry U. N.Mex. Sch. Medicine, 1981-89; prof. emeritus psychiatry sch. medicine U. N.Mex., 1989—. Cons. Fitzsimons Army Hosp., Denver, 1963-67, U. Calif. Dept Biobehavioral Scis., Los Angeles, 1978-81, VA Hosps., Ft. Lyon, Colo., Sheridan, Wyo., Tuscaloosa, Ala., 1963-67. Contbr. chpts. to books, articles to profl. jours. Recipient Dirs. commendation, VA, 1962, 81, 89, Psychiat. Adminstrs. award Am. Assn. Psychiat. Adminstrs., 1976. Fellow Am. Coll. Psychiatrists (emeritus), Am. Psychiat. Assn. (life; program com. insts. for hosp. and cmty. psychiatry 1977-81), Am. Coll. Mental Health Adminstrn. (founding), Am. Coll. Utilization Rev. Physicians; mem. AMA, Am. Hosp. Assn. (chmn. psychiat. sect. 1972-74). Avocations: travel, gardening, oil and watercolor painting, collecting rocks and minerals, photography.

BONNEAU, WENDY SUE, special education educator; b. Blue Island, Ill., Oct. 24, 1969; d. Michael Robert and Mary Catherine Bonneau. BS in Edn., No. Ill. U., DeKalb, 1995; MS in Edn., No. Ill. U., 2001. Spl. educator Indian Prairie Sch. Dist. 204, Naperville, Ill., 1995—2001, DeKalb Sch. Dist. 428, 2001—. Instr. No. Ill. U., DeKalb, 2002—; coach Spl. Olympics Indian Prairie Sch. Dist. 204, Naperville, 1996—2001, Open Door Rehab. Ctr., Sandwich, Ill., 1992—93.

BONNELL, VICTORIA EILEEN, sociologist, educator; b. NYC, June 15, 1942; d. Samuel S. and Frances (Nassau) B.; m. Gregory Freidin, May 4, 1971. BA, Brandeis U., 1964; MA, Harvard U., 1966, PhD, 1975. Lectr. politics U. Calif., Santa Cruz, 1972—73, 1974—76, asst. prof. sociology Berkeley, 1976—82, assoc. prof., 1982—91, prof., 1991—. Chair Berkeley

Ctr. for Slavic and East European Studies, U. Calif.-Berkeley, 1994-2000, dir. Inst. Slavic, East European, and Eurasian Studies, 2002-04. Author: Roots of Rebellion: Workers' Politics and Organizations in St. Petersburg and Moscow, 1900-1914, 1983; editor: The Russian Worker: Life and Labor Under the Tsarist Regime, 1983, (with Ann Cooper and Gregory Freidin) Russia at the Barricades: Eyewitness Accounts of the August 1991 Coup, 1994, Iconography of Power: Soviet Political Posters Under Lenin and Stalin, 1997, Identities in Transition: Eastern Europe and Russia After the Collapse of Communism, 1996, Beyond the Cultural Turn: New Directions in the Study of Society and Culture, 1999, (with George Breslauer) Russia in the New Century: Stability or Disorder, 2004, (with Thomas Gold) New Entrepreneurs of Europe and Asia: Russia, Eastern Europe and China, 2004; contbr. articles to profl. jours. Recipient Heldt prize in Slavic women's studies, 1991; AAUW fellow, 1979; Regents Faculty fellow, 1978, Fulbright Hays Faculty fellow, 1977, Internat. Rsch. and Exch. Bd. fellow, 1977, 88, Stanford U. Hoover Instn. nat. fellow, 1973-74, Guggenheim fellow, 1985, fellow Ctr. Advanced Study in Behavioral Scis., 1986-87, Pres.' Rsch. fellow in Humanities, 1991-92; grantee Am. Philos. Soc., 1979, Am. Coun. Learned Socs., 1976, 90-91. Mem.: Am. Assn. Advancement Slavic Studies, Am. Sociol. Assn. Business E-Mail: vbonnell@berkeley.edu.

BONNELL-MIHALIS, PAMELA GAY SCOGGINS, library director; b. Monterey, Calif., Feb. 2, 1948; d. Dewey L. and Marlyce I. (Hansen) Scoggins; m. Verneil S. Henerson, June 18, 1966 (div. 1971); 1 child, V. Samuel Henerson III; m. Chrisman E Bonnell, Mar. 2, 1974 (div. 1983); m. Hugh R. McElroy, Nov. 10, 1990 (div. 1996); m. Stephan S. Mihalis, Oct. 5, 2002. BA, Cameron U., Lawton, Okla., 1972; MLS, U. Okla., 1972—73; CPM, S.W. Tex. State U., 1998. Libr. Met. Libr. Sys., Oklahoma City, 1974—75, Office of City Mgr., Dallas, 1977—80; dir. audience devel. Dallas Symphony Orch., 1980—81; libr. Dallas Morning News, 1981—83; libr. mgr. Plano (Tex.) Pub. Libr. Sys., 1983—91; dir. libr. svcs. Waco-McLennan County Libr. System, Waco, Tex., 1992—2001; exec. dir. Elyria (Ohio) Pub. Libr., 2002—05; realtor Scoggins Realty, Lawton, Okla., 2006—. Bd. trustees Lawton Pub. Libr., 2006—. Author: Fund Raising for Small Libraries, 1983; contbr. chapters to books, articles to profl. jours. Gala chair Easter Seal Soc., Dallas, 1988; bd. dirs. Women's Shelter, Plano, 1991; exec. bd. Am. Heart Assn., 1997—99; chmn. Lorain County Librs. Coun., 2003—04; trustee Freedom to Read Found., 1999—, liaison, 2004—; chmn.Oboler award com. Intellectual Freedom Round Table, 2004—; mem. program com. Fund, 2004—; mem. ops. com. Main St. Elyria, 2004—05; trustee Dallas Symphony Orch., 1981; bd. dirs. Salvation Army, 2003—; pres. Townbluff Homeowners Assn., Plano, 1984—90, Hippodrome Theatre Guild, 1996; treas. YWCA, 1995—96. Recipient Telecom. Excellence award, Ctrl. Tex. Edn., 1997. Mem.: ALA (councilor-at-large 1990—99, pres. Intellectual Freedom Round Table 1993—94, constn. and bylaws chair 1994—97, Shirley Olofson Meml. award 1974, cert. of Spl. Thanks 1986, John Phillip Immroth award 1990), Ctrl. Tex. Women's Alliance (bd. dirs. 1992—96), Tex. Libr. Assn. (chmn. Adminstrs. Roundtable 1994—95, trustee Leroy C. Merritt Trust Fund 1997—2000, chair intellectual freedom com. 2000—02, SIRS Intellectual Freedom award 1990), Tex. Mcpl. Librs. Dirs. (pres. 1994—95), Jr. League, Leadership Waco Alumni Assn., Rotary. Avocations: reading, travel. Office: Scoggins Realty Co 1401 W Gore Blvd Lawton OK 73501 Home: 825 NW 44th St Lawton OK 73505 Office Phone: 580-357-5700, 580-583-8046. Personal E-mail: pbonnell39@hotmail.com.

BONNER, BESTER DAVIS, school system administrator; b. Mobile, Ala., June 9, 1938; d. Samuel Matthew and Alma (Davis) Davis; m. Wardell Bonner, Nov. 28, 1964; children: Shawn Patrick, Matthew Wardell. BS, Ala. State Coll., 1959; MS in Library Sci., Syracuse U., 1966; PhD, U. Ala., 1982. Cert. tchr. Librarian Westside High Sch., Talladega, Ala., 1959-64; librarian, tchr. lit. Lane Elem. Sch., Birmingham, Ala., 1964-65; head librarian Jacksonville (Ala.) Elem. Lab. Sch., 1965-70; asst. prof. library media Ala. A&M U., Huntsville, 1970-74; adminstv. asst. to pres. Miles Coll., Birmingham, 1974-78, chmn. div. edn., 1978-85; specialist media Montgomery County Pub. Schs., Md., 1987-88; dir. libr. and media svcs. div. curriculum and ednl. tech. Dist. of Columbia Pub. Schs., 1988—. Forum leader Nat. Issues Forum, Domestic Policy Assn. U. Ala., Birmingham, 1983-84; mem. Libr. Svcs. Construction Act Adv. Com.; head judge spelling bee D.C., 2003, 04; adv. bd. sch. libr. media U. Md., 2004. Contbr. writer The Developing Black Family, 1975. Chmn. ethics comm. St. Ala., Montgomery 1977-81; radiothorn site coordinator United Negro Coll. Fund, Birmingham 1981. Mem. ALA, Ala. Instructional Media Assn. (pres. dist. II 1971-72), Assn. Women Deans and Adminstrs., Com. 100, D.C. Assn. Sch. Librs., D.C. Libr. Com., Am. Assn. Sch. Librs., Nat. Assn. State Ednl. Profls. Democrat. Methodist. Avocations: writing, speaking, consulting, piano. Home: 9601 Burgess Ln Silver Spring MD 20901-4701 Office Phone: 202-576-6317. Business E-Mail: bester.bonner@k12.de.us.

BONNER, JUDY L., academic administrator; BS, MS, U. Ala.; PhD, Ohio State U. Faculty mem. U. Ala., Tuscaloosa, 1981—, asst. acad. v.p., 1985—90, dean Coll. Human Environ. Scis., 1990—2003, provost, v.p., 2003—. Office: Univ Ala Office of Provost and Vp Tuscaloosa AL 35487 Office Phone: 205-348-4892. Business E-Mail: judy.bonner@ua.edu.

BONNER, MICHELLE, music educator; m. Jerome Bonner. MusB, Ariz. State U., Tempe, 1995. Cert. tchr. Ariz., 1995. Music tchr. Santa Fe Elem., Peoria, Ariz., 1996—. Office: Santa Fe Elem 9880 N 77th Ave Peoria AZ 85345 Office Phone: 623-486-6475. E-mail: mbonner@peoriau.k12.az.us.

BONNER, PATRICIA JANE, retired physical education and special education educator; b. Painesville, Ohio, Apr. 8, 1935; d. Charles Leonard and Marie Estelle (Burridge) B. BA, Milligan Coll., 1957; MEd, U. Ariz., 1963; MRE, Emmanuel Sch. Religion, Johnson City, 1970; EdS, G. Peabody Coll., Nashville, 1975; EdD, Highland U., 1978. Cert. tchr., Tenn. Asst. instr. Happy Valley Elem. Sch., Elizabethton, Tenn., 1956-57; tchr. Riverside (Ohio) High Sch., 1957-62; grad. asst. U. Ariz., Tucson, 1962-63; tchr. Thomas Jefferson High Sch., Calif., 1963-64; instr. Fullerton Jr. Coll., Calif., 1964-65; chair, dept. human performance and exercise sci. Milligan Coll., Tenn., prof. spl. edn. and phys. edn., dir. testing and career ctr. Tenn., 1966—98; ret. Contbr. articles to Christian mags. Mem. choir, tchr., chairperson missions com. 1st Christian Ch., Johnson City; chairperson Family Ministries Com., Task Force on Missions of Christian Chs.; missionary Mex. Philippines, Austria. Mem. AAHPERD (life, exec. sec., state rep., coord. state reps. Nat. Intramural Sprots Coun.), S. Dist. AAHPERD, Tenn AAHPERD (honor award 1978), Nat. Assn. Phys. Edn. for Higher Edn., Soc. Assn. Phys. Edn. for Coll. Women, Coun. for Exceptional Children, Pi Lambda Theta, Delta Kappa Gamma (charter, pres. 1988-90, Xi state rec. sec. 1991-93, treas. 1993—). Republican. Avocations: cross-stitch, tennis, swimming, writing. Home: 180 Bentley Parc Johnson City TN 37615-4916

BONNETT, LOU ANN HUMPHREY, education educator; b. Pitts., July 31, 1959; d. Milo and Josephine Humphrey; m. Tim Bonnett, June 26, 2004; children: Lindsay, Cody. BS, Slippery Rock State Coll., Pa., 1981; MEd, Slippery Rock U., Pa., 1986; PhD, U. Denver, Colo., 2001. Cert. elem. and spl. edn. tchr. Pa., 1981, early childhood edn. Pa., 1986. Mem. staff residential program Assn. Retarded Citizens, Butler, Pa., 1981—86; tchr., dir. United Cerebral Palsy, Butler, Pa., 1986—96; instr. U. Colo., Denver, 1997—2001; asst. prof. Clarion U., Pa., 2001—06, assoc. prof., 2006—. Home: 20639 Route 68 Clarion PA 16214 Office Phone: 814-393-2591. Business E-Mail: lhumphrey@clarion.edu.

BONNEY, JO, theater director; b. Sydney, Australia; arrived in US, 1979; m. Eric Bogosian; 2 children. Grad. Fine Arts, Sydney Coll. Arts. Dir. (plays) Funhouse, 1983, Sex, Drugs, Rock & Roll, 1990, Pounding Nails in the Floor with My Forehead, 1994, Some People, 1994, At Midnight and Morning Rain, 1995, Stray Cats, 1997, The Flatted Fifth, 1997, The Fastest Clock in the Universe, 1998, Stop Kiss, 1998, Jails, Hospitals & Hip-Hop, 1998, Look Back in Anger, 1999, Wake Up & Smell the Coffee, 2000, References to Salvador Dali Make Me Hot, 2001, Slanguage, 2001, Good Thing, 2001, Humpty Dumpty, 2002, Fat Pig, 2004, Fifth of July (Lortel award), A Soldier's Play, 2005, The Seven, 2006; directorial cons. (play) House Arrest, 2000; editor: Extreme Exposure: An Anthology of Solo Performance Texts From the 20th Century, 1999. Recipient Obie award, sustained excellence of direction, 1998; grantee Jerome Found., 1980. Mem.: Soc. Stage Dirs. and Choreographers.*

BONO, MARY WHITAKER, congresswoman; b. Cleve., Oct. 24, 1961; d. Clay and Karen Whitaker; m. Sonny Bono, Feb. 1986 (dec.); children: Chesare Elan, Chianna Maria. BFA in Art History, U. So. Calif., 1984. Cert. personal fitness instr. Mem. U.S. Congress from 45th (formerly 44th) Calif. dist., 1998—; mem. energy and commerce com. Bd. dirs. Palm Springs Internat. Film Festival. Active D.A.R.E. Program, Olive Crest Home Abused Children, Tiempos de Los Ninos. Named Woman of the Yr., San Gorgonio (Calif.) chpt. Girl Scouts U.S., 1993. Republican. Avocations: outdoor activities, computer technology. Office: US House of Reps 405 Cannon Ho Office Bldg Washington DC 20515-0545

BONOSARO, CAROL ALESSANDRA, professional society administrator, retired federal agency administrator; b. New Brunswick, N.J., Feb. 16, 1940; d. Rudolph William and Elizabeth Ann (Betsko) B.; m. Donald D. Kummerfeld, Sept. 8, 1962 (div. Jan. 1970); m. Athanasios Chalkiopoulos, Nov. 21, 1976 (div. Dec. 1991); 1 child, Melissa. BA, Cornell U., 1961; postgrad., George Washington U., 1961-62. Analytical statistician Office Mgmt. and Budget, Exec. Office of Pres., Washington, 1961-66; asst. dir. fed. programs div. U.S. Commn. on Civil Rights, Washington, 1966-68, dir. Office Fed. Programs, 1968-69, dir. tech. assistance div., 1969-71, spl. asst. to staff dir., 1972, dir. women's rights program, 1972-79, asst. staff dir. for program planning and evaluation, 1979-80, asst. staff dir. congressional and public affairs, 1980-86; pres. Sr. Execs. Assn., Washington, 1986—. Mem. adv. com. Asian Am. Govt. Execs. Network, 1996—; mem. Nat. Partnership Coun., 1997-2001. Vice chmn. Nat. Com. on Asian Wives of U.S. Servicemen, 1975-85; pres. Catholics for a Free Choice, 1980-83; chmn. bd. dirs. William Jump Found., 2003—. Mem. Exec. Women in Govt., Sr. Exec. Assn. (dir. 1981-86, chmn. bd. dirs. 1983-86) Democrat. Home: 5504 Jordan Rd Bethesda MD 20816-1366 Office: Sr Execs Assn PO Box 44808 Washington DC 20026-4808 E-mail: SEAPresident@seniorexecs.org.

BONSACK, ROSE MARY HATEM, state legislator, physician; b. Havre de Grace, Md., Oct. 24, 1933; d. Joseph Thomas and Nasma (Joseph) Hatem; m. James P. Bonsack, Aug. 24, 1957; children: Jeanette, Karen, Thomas, David, James J. BS in Chemistry cum laude, Washington Coll., 1955; MD, Med. Coll. Pa., 1960. Intern Easton (Pa.) Hosp., 1961; physician outpatient clinic Kirk Army Hosp., Aberdeen Proving Ground, Md., 1962-74, chief outpatient clinic, 1968-72, chief dept. hosp. clinics, 1972-74; contract physician Harford County Dept. Health, Md., 1975-78; utilization rev. officer Harford Meml. Hosp., Havre de Grace, 1981-82; pvt. practice Aberdeen, Md., 1981—; mem. Md. Gen. Assembly, 1991-99, chmn. house rules and exec. nominations com., 1991-94, mem. house ways and means com., 1995-99. Coord. clinics Hypertensive Coun. Md., 1977-81; reviewer quality assurance for nursing homes in Harford County, Md. Licensing Div., 1977-81; utilization rev. officer Harford Meml. Hosp., Havre de Grace, 1981-82; med. dir. Ashley Alcoholic Rehab., Havre de Grace, 1983-84; mem. Bd. Med. Examiners Md.; mem., exec. sec. Commn. on Med. Discipline, 1985-88. V.p. St. Joan of Arc Home-Sch. Assn., 1968, pres., 1969, mem., 1968-85; v.p. No. Md. Heart Assn., 1969, pres., 1970, bd. dirs., 1973; bd. dirs. Mann House, Bel Air, Md., 1973-82, Harford County Cancer Soc., 1973-86; mem. John Carroll Home-Sch. Assn., 1974—, 1st v.p., 1975, pres., 1975; bd. dirs. John Carroll H.S., 1975—, pres. bd. dirs., 1979-85; mem. Harford County Dem. Cen. Com., 1987-90; mem. chief exec.'s coun. Harford C.C., 1990; trustee Washington Coll., 1992-99, Harford C.C., 1999—. Recipient Outstanding Contbn. to Md. Traffic Safety citation State of Md., 1969, Cert. of Merit for svc. Md. Cancer Soc., 1977, Women Helping Women award Soroptomists Harford and Cecil Counties, 1983-84, V. McCrory award for significant contbn. to enhancement of eye care in Md., Md. Optometric Assn., 1995, Alumni Citation for outstanding achievement and svc. in field of pub. svc. Washington Coll., 2000; named one of Top 100 Women in Md., Daily Record, 1996; named Harford County Living Treasure, 2004. Mem. Am. Acad. Family Physicians (bd. dirs. 1997-99, alt. del. 1990-94, del. from Md. 1994-96, chmn. chpt. affairs com. 1992—, commn. on regulations 1993-96, found. bd. dirs. 1999—), Med. Chirurgical Fac. Md., Hartford County Med. Soc. (sec. 1967, pres. 1968, v.p. 1978, Outstand Cmny. Svc. citation 1979), Md. Acad. Family Physicians (v.p. 1987, pres. 1988, Lifetime Achievement award 2003).

BONTEMPO, ELAINE, language educator; b. Lima, Peru, May 19, 1946; came to U.S., 1948; d. H. Ellis and Esther Plyler; m. Blaine Bontempo, Jun. 15, 1968; children: Brian, Kari. BA, Baldwin-Wallace Coll., 1968; MS in Edn., N. Ill. U., 1994. Coord. Spanish-English lang. prog. Metropolitan Life Ins. Co., N.Y.C., 1968-71; ESL tchr. Project Lift, Dallas, 1978-80, Literacy Vols. of Am., Norwalk, CT, 1984-86, Ctrl. Piedmont C.C., Charlotte, NC, 1989-90; non-native literacy tchr., workforce ESL tchr. William Rainey Harper Coll., Palatine, IL, 1991—. Presenter IL/TESOL Conv., Chgo, 1999, Adult Learning Resource Ctr./Adult Edn. Conf., Rosemont, Ill., 1999; missionary Vols. in Mission, various locations in S. Am., 1999. Mem. Hunter's Ridge Homeowners Assn., Ill., (treas. 1991-93, social chair 1997-99). Mem. New Oratorio Singers (bookkeeper 1990—), Elgin Choral Union, Four Seasons Garden Club (membership chair 1990—), Ill. TESOL. Christian. Office: William Rainey Harper Coll Workforce ESL 1200 W Algonquin Rd Palatine IL 60067-7373

BONZO, DEBORAH L., dietician, educator; d. James D. Miller and Nancy L. Barone; m. Michael L. Bonzo, Aug. 13, 1986; children: Stephan, Leah. BS, Purdue U., West Lafayette, Ind., 1984; MS, Kent State U., Ohio, 1991. Nutritionist Jordon Health Ctr., Rochester, NY, 1992, Monroe County Health Dept., Rochester, 1992—; prin., owner Premier Cheer, Inc., Rochester, 2002—. Adj. prof. Monroe C.C., Rochester, 1993—. Mem.: Genesee Valley Dietetic Assn. (pres. 1998—99, mem. cmty. rels. com. 1995—96), N.Y. State Dietetic Assn., Am. Dietetic Assn.

BOOHER, ALICE ANN, lawyer; b. Indpls., Oct. 6, 1941; d. Norman Rogers and Olga (Bonke) B. BA in Polit. Sci., Butler U., Indpls., 1963; LLB, Ind. U., Bloomington, 1966, JD, 1967. Bar: Ind. 1966, U.S. Dist. Ct. (so. dist.) Ind. 1966, U.S. Tax Ct. 1970, U.S. Ct. Customs and Patent Appeals 1969, U.S. Ct. Mil. Appeals 1969, U.S. Ct. Appeals (D.C. cir.) 1969, U.S. Supreme Ct. 1969; cert. tchr., Ind. Rsch. asst., law clk. Supreme and Appellate Cts. Ind., Indpls., 1966; legal intern, atty., staff legal advisor Dept. State, Washington, 1966-69; staff legal adviser Bd. Vets. Appeals, Washington, 1969-78, sr. atty., 1978—, counsel, 1991—. Former counselor D.C. Penal Facilities and Shelters. Author: The Nuclear Test Ban Treaty and the Third Party Non-Nuclear States, also children's books; contbr. articles to various publs., chpts. to Whiteman Digest of International Law; exhibited crafts, needlepoint in juried artisan fairs; originator U.S. postage stamps Women in Mil. Svc., 1980-97, POWs/MIAs, 1986-96. Pres., legal advisor VA Employees Assn.; mem. sec.'s mus. task force Dept. Va; founding sponsor Nat. Mus. of US Army; patron Vietnam Vets. Art Mus.; bd. dirs. cmty. groups including DC Women's Commn. for Crime Prevention, 1980—81, Friends of Nat. Vets. Mus. Named Ky. Col., 1988; recipient various awards, Diisting. Svc. award, Contrbn. of Merit awards. Mem. DAV (life), VFW Aux. (life), D.C. Sexual Assault Coalition (chmn. legal com.), Life Mem. Judge Advocates Assn., U.S. Supreme Ct. Hist. Soc., U.S. Naval Inst., Nat. Mus. Women in Arts, Kennedy Ctr. Stars, Sackler/Freer Galleries (patron), Women in Mil. Svcs. to Am. Found., Bus. and Profl. Women (pres. D.C. 1980-81, nat. UN fellow 1974, nat. bd. dirs. 1980-82, 87-94, Woman of Yr. award D.C. 1975, Marguerite Rawalt award D.C. 1986), USO (DVA sec), Navy League U.S.A. (life), Am. Legion Aux. (life), Women Officers Profl. Assns., Nat. Vets. Mus. Task Force, Nat. Task Force on Women of the Mil. and Women Mil. POWS (chair Esther Peterson Tribute 1995, panel, paper moderator conf. 1997, book reviewer, contbr. to Stars & Stripes, Ex POWs Bull., others), Assn. Former Intelligence Officers (assoc.), Am. News Womens Club, Cons., Saigon Tourist, Inc., Alliance Nat. Def. (editor Advocate), OSS Soc. (assoc.), Nat. Mus. US Army (founding sponsor), Nat. Vietnam Vets. Art Mus., Winterthur.

BOOKER, DELOIS FONDON, art educator; b. Parkin, Ark., Jan. 21, 1964; d. Fred Frank and Mary Lee Fondon; m. Roy A. Booker, July 1, 1989; children: Edgar, Royden, Caleb. BS, S.E. Mo. U., 1987; M in Curriculum and Instrn., Willian Woods U., Fulton, Mo., 2002. Tchr. Portageville (Mo.) Sch. Dist. Youth pastor Victory Unity Refuge Ch., Portageville, Mo., 2000—; spkr. women's ministry various chs. and confs., 2005—. Named Educator of Yr., Milkin Family Found., 2002, Portageville Sch. Dept., 2002. Mem.: Portageville Dist. Tchrs. Assn., Student Assist Team (recorder 2004—). Avocations: reading, singing. Office: Portageville Sch Dist 904 King Ave Portageville MO 63873 Office Phone: 573-379-5706. Business E-Mail: dbooker@portageville.k12.mo.us.

BOOKER, NANA LAUREL, art gallery owner, honorary consul; b. Waco, Tex., Aug. 5, 1946; d. Karl and Helen Dorothy (Keene) B. BA, Baylor U., 1968; MA, U. Fla., 1970; MBA, Pepperdine U., 1980. Asst. prof. comm. U. New Orleans, 1970-74, 1977-78; pub. rels. cons. New Orleans, 1974-78; dir. pub. rels. Touro Infirmary, New Orleans, 1976-78; dir. comm. Lifemark Corp., Houston, 1978-81; pres. Comm. Alliance, Houston, 1981-82; dir. internat. rels., comm. Mayor's Office, City of Houston, 1982-84; pres. Nana Booker & Assocs. (now Booker/Hancock & Assocs.), Houston, 1984—2004; owner Booker-Lowe Gallery of Australian Aboriginal Art, 2002—. Hon. consul of Australia, State Tex., 1999—. Co-author: Introduction to Theatrical Arts, 1972. Mem. South Tex. Dist. Export Coun., Houston, 1988-92; press aide campaign K. Whitmire for Mayor, Houston, 1982; mem. exec. adv. bd. coll. bus. adminstrn. U. Houston, 1990-95; bd. dirs. Escape Ctr., 1990-93, YWCA, Houston, 1991-92, Greater Houston Partnership, 2003—, Asia Soc. Tex., 1999--. Recipient Internat. Assn. Bus. Communicators awards, Women in Comms. awards, Crystal award Am. Mktg. Assn., Outstanding Pub. Rels. Practitioner award Tex. Pub. Rels. Assn., 1996, Vol. of the Yr. award Houston Area Women's Ctr., 1998, Order of Australia, 2005. Mem. Pub. Rels. Soc. Am. (accredited, chairperson internat. sect. 1993-95, Excalibur award 1988, Cert. of Appreciation 1993, 94, 95; mem. U.S. coun. 1994-96), Internat. Pub. Rels. Assn., Houston World Trade Assn. (bd. dirs. 1986—), Houston-Shenzhen Sister City Assn. (bd. dirs. 1987-94), Swiss-Am. C. of C. (bd. dirs. 1987-90), River Oaks Breakfast Club (bd. dirs. 1997), The Asia Soc. of Tex. (bd. dirs. 1995—). Avocations: hot air ballooning, photography, design, collecting art. Business E-Mail: bookerlowegallery@houston.rr.com.

BOOKMAN, ANN EDITH, director; b. N.Y.C., Apr. 28, 1948; d. John Jacob and Ruth Louise (Lowe) B.; m. Eric P. Buehrens, July 5, 1981; children: Nicholas, Emily. BA with honors, Barnard U., 1970; MA, Harvard U., 1973, PhD, 1977. Asst. dir. The Bunting Inst./Radcliffe Coll., Cambridge, Mass., 1983-89; rsch. assoc. in child and family policy Lesley Coll., Cambridge, 1990-92; dir. Ctr. for Interdisciplinary and Spl. Studies Coll. of the Holy Cross, Worcester, Mass., 1992—93; policy and rsch. dir. U.S. Dept. Labor-Women's Bur., Washington, 1993-96; exec. dir. Commn. on Family and Med. Leave, Washington, 1995-96; dir. Ctr. for Interdisciplinary and Spl. Studies Coll. of the Holy Cross, 1996—2000; vis. scholar MIT Sloan Sch. Mgmt., 2000—01; exec. dir. MIT Workplace Ctr. Sloan Sch. Mgmt., 2001—. Editor: Women and the Politics of Empowerment, 1988; author Starting In Our Own Backyards: How Working Familites Can Build Cmty and Survive the New Economy, 2004. Gubernatorial appointee Commn. on TDI and Ins., Boston, 1988-89, Gov.'s Day Care Partnership Task Force, Boston, 1991-92; presdl. appointee U.S. Dept. Labor, Washington, 1993-96. Fellow Am. Anthropol. Assn. Democrat. Jewish. Avocation: gardening.

BOONE, DEBORAH ANN (DEBBY BOONE), singer; b. Hackensack, NJ, Sept. 22, 1956; d. Charles (Pat) Eugene and Shirley (Foley) Boone; m. Gabriel Ferrer, Sept. 1, 1979; children: Gabriella, Dustin Boone, Tessa Rose, Jordan. Student Calif. schs. Singer: with father, Pat Boone, and family group, 1970—, (albums) You Light Up My Life, 1977, Midstream, 1978, Debby Boone, 1979, Love Has No Reason, 1980, With My Song, 1980, Savin' It Up, 1981, Surrender, 1983 (Dove award, 1983), Choose Life, 1985, Friends For Life, 1987, Be Thou My Vision, 1989, Home For Christmas, 1989, (soundtrack) Reflections of Rosemary, 2005; numerous appearances (TV series) TV talk and variety programs, appeared (ABC-TV Movie of the Week TV films) Sins of the Past, 1984, star children's video Hug Along Songs; author: Debby Boone--So Far, 1988, (children's book) Bedtime Hugs for Little Ones, 1988; co-author: Tomorrow is a Brand New Day, 1989; starred in nat. tour (Broadway plays) Seven Brides for Seven Brothers, 1981—82, nat. tour Sound of Music, 1987—88, The King and I, actress (plays) Camelot, 2005, tribute show Reflections of Rosemary, 2005. Named Singing Star of Yr., Am. Guild Variety Artists, 1978, Working Mother of Yr., 1982; recipient Am. Music award, song of yr., 1977, Grammy award, best new artist, 1977, Grammy award, best inspirational performance, 1980, Grammy award, best Gospel performance for Keep the Flame Burning, 1984, Nat. Assn. Theatre Owners award, best new personality, 1980, Dove award, 1980, Country Music award, best new country artist, 1977. Mem.: Ch. on the Way. Address: 4334 Kester Ave Van Nuys CA 91403-4135

BOONE, DONNA CLAUSEN, physical therapist, statistician, researcher; b. Nebraska City, Nebr., Dec. 12, 1932; d. Otto Ralph and Hallie Rae Clausen; m. Robert William Boone, Apr. 3, 1965. BA in Zoology, U. Wyo., 1954; MS in Phys. Therapy, U. So. Calif., 1980, MS in Biometry, 1983. Lic. phys. therapist, Calif. Phys. therapist Ill. Hosp. Sch., Chgo., 1955—59, Calif. Hosp., L.A., 1959—63; hemophilia specialist in phys. therapy Orthop. Hosp., L.A., 1963—78, rschr., project dir. Hemophilia Ctr., 1967—78; instr. rsch. methods U. So. Calif., L.A., 1982—83, Calif. State U., Long Beach, 1982—83; biostatistician immunulogy U. So. Calif., L.A., 0983—1987, coord., statistician Nat. Clin. Trial, Silicone Study, 1987—93; phys. therapist Huntington Meml. Hosp., Pasadena, Calif., 1993—98; cons. Hemophilia Continuous Quality Improvement, Lompoc, Calif., 1998—. Internat. lectr., cons. World Fedn. Hemophilia, Montreal, Can., 1970-78; cons. biostatis. dentistry and pharmacology U. So. Calif., L.A., 1982-83, cons. orthop., U. Buffalo, 1982-83; continuous quality improvement coach Doheny Eye Inst., L.A., 1990-92, Huntington Meml. Hosp., Pasadena, Calif., 1993-97; cons. phys. therapy working group Nat. Hemophilia Found., 2000—. Editor: Comprehensive Management of Hemophilia, 1976, (internat. newsletter) World Hemophilia AIDS Ctr., 1984-93; contbr. articles to profl. jours. Co-chair United Way Campaign Orthopaedic Hosp., L.A., chair, 1975—75; mem. Lompoc Rep. Women, 1998—, legis. chair, 2000—; vol. Rep. Campaign for Ho. of Reps., Glendale, Calif., 1996; recording sec. Santa Barbara County Rep. Women, 2000—01; lay leader St. Mary's Episcopal Ch., 1998—; bd. dirs. World Hemophilia Alliance, sec., 1996—; mem. alumni com. U. Wyo., 1999—; mem. med. adv. bd. Hemophilia Found. So. Calif., L.A., 1974—78. Grantee Fed. Govt. Agys., 1967, 73; recipient Dr. Murray Thelin award Nat. Hemophilia Found., 1976, Disting. Alumna award U. Wyo., 1979, Achievement award Alpha Chi Omega, 1980, Spl. Achievement award for treatment advances 50th Anniversary of Nat. Hemophilia Found., 1998, Donna Clausen Boone ann. award Nat. Hemophilia Found. to Phys. Therapist, 1999—. Mem. Antique Automobile Club. Republican. Episcopalian. Avocations: gardening, antique autos, travel, reading, jazz music clubs.

BOONSHAFT, HOPE JUDITH, public relations executive; b. Phila., May 3, 1949; d. Barry and Lorelei Gail (R ienzi) B. BA, Pa. State U., 1972; postgrad. Del. Law Sch, Kellogg Inst. Mgmt. Tng. Program writer Youth Edn., N.Y.C., 1972; legal aide to judge Phila., 1975; dir. spl. projects Guiffre Med. Ctr., Phila., 1975; senatorial campaign fin. dir. Arlen Specter, Phila., 1975; presdl. campaign fin. dir. Jimmy Carter, Atlanta, 1976; fin. dir. Dem. Nat. Com., 1977—79; dir. devel. World Jewish Congress, N.Y.C., 1978, Yeshiva U., L.A., 1979; dir. comm. Nat. Easter Seal Soc., Chgo., 1979-83; CEO Boonshaft-Lewis & Savitch Pub. Rels and Govt. Affairs, L.A., 1983-93; sr. v.p. Edelman Worldwide, 1993-95; exec. v.p. external affairs Sony Pictures Entertainement, L.A., 1995—. Spl. adv. cmty. rels. The White House, 1977-80; guest lectr. U. Ill., 1982, May Co.'s Calif. Women in Bus. Bd. dirs. L.A. Arts Coun., Los Angeles County Citizens for Economy and Efficiency in Govt. Commn., Calif. Film Commn., Spkrs. Commn. Calif. Initiative. Home: 1967 Mandeville Canyon Rd Los Angeles CA 90049-2235 Office: Sony Pictures Entertainment 10202 Washington Blvd Culver City CA 90232-3119

BOOTH, ADA SOKAL, retired education educator; b. Lvov, Poland, Apr. 1, 1921; arrived in US, 1924; d. Henry B. and Ethel Torten Sokal; m. Robert Edward Booth, 1995; children: Barbara, Elaine, Thomas, James. Student, Barnard Coll., NY, 1936—37; AB, Bklyn. Coll., NYC, 1940; postgrad., Columbia U., 1943, MIT, 1944, Harvard U., 1944; MA, Stanford U., Palo Alto, Calif., 1946; postgrad., San Jose State U., 1952. Commd. ensign USN, 1944, advanced through grades to lt., 1958; hs tchr. San Jose, Calif., 1959—66; adj. prof. Santa Clara U., 1966—90; ret., 1990. Contbr. articles to profl. jours. Democrat. Avocations: gardening, reading.

BOOTH, ANNA BELLE, accountant; b. Homesville, Ohio, Jan. 15, 1912; d. John Wilson and M. Pearl (Toomey) B.; m. Guy DiAmbrosio, Apr. 29, 1930; 1 child, Guy Booth. BA, Taylor Coll., 1930. Office mgr. in charge of mfg. Jacobs Tailored Clothes, Inc., Phila., 1931-41; acct., corp. cashier Lehigh Coal and Navigation Co., Phila., 1941-55; acct. Bishop & Hedberg, Phila., 1955-57; acct., office mgr. The Camax Co., Phila., 1957-60; office mgr., cashier New Eng. Mutual Life Ins. Co., Phila., 1960-67; acct. Wall & Ochs, Inc., Phila., 1967-71; comptr. Bisler Packaging Div./Pet, Inc., Phila., 1971-82; ret. Mem. Am. Soc. Women Accts. (Phila. pres. 1956-58, dir. 1952-54, 62-64, 73-75), LWV (Phila.). Home: 135 S 20th St Apt 1002 Philadelphia PA 19103

BOOTH, BARBARA RIBMAN, civic worker; b. N.Y.C., May 2, 1928; d. Benjamin C. and Ceclia (Lowe) Ribman; m. Mitchell B. Booth, July 13, 1952; 1 child, Brian S. AA, Centenary Jr. Coll., Hackettstown, N.Y., 1948; BA, Barnard Coll., 1950. Pres. women's alliance, chmn., Christmas fair 1st Congl. Ch. of City of N.Y., 1959-63; mem. vol. com. Sheltering Arms Children's Svc., N.Y.C.; vol., coord. high sch. visits, pres. aux. N.Y. Hosp., 1989-91, co-chmn., 1995—; trustee Florence K. Griswold Meml. Fund. Com., All Souls Unitarian Ch., N.Y.C., United Hosp. Funds Auxiliary for N.Y. Hosp., 1996; bd. dir. women's div. Jefferson Dem. Club. N.Y.C.; committee-woman N.Y. County Dem. Com.; bd. govs., v.p. N.Y. Fruit and Flower Mission, Inc.; del. city conv., chmn. East Manhattan br. LWV. Recipient Auxilian of N.Y. Hosp. award, 1996. Mem. City Gardens Club N.Y.C. (mem. grants com.). Home: 75 E End Ave New York NY 10028-7909

BOOTH, BETTY JEAN, retired daycare administrator, poet; b. St. Louis County, Mo., Dec. 27, 1944; d. Richard Augustus and Leoma Thelma (Atchison) Woods; m. Alfred Lee Pope Jr., Aug. 20, 1962 (div. Apr. 14, 1975); children: Wayman Maurice Woods, Aundrea Denise Walker, Juanita Rosetta Pope-Miller, Victoria Lynn Pope, Daniel Jerome Pope, Alfred Lee III Pope; m. Robert Lee Booth, Mar. 3, 1984; 1 stepchild, David Lee Griffin. Cert., United Bus. Coll., North St. Louis, Mo., 1987. Baby nurse, Ladue, Mo., 1984—89; home care worker and provider Clayton, Mo., 1989; adminstrv. asst. Grateful Home Homeless Shelter, Detroit, 1992; day care asst. Time for Happy Land Care, Detroit, 1999—. Author: Traveling on the Wing's of Life's Inner Circle, 2005; contbr. poetry to lit. publs. Recipient numerous awards for poetry. Mem.: Internat. Soc. Poets and POetry. Avocations: writing, gardening, taping, reading, creating. Home: 14503 Hazelridge St Detroit MI 48205-3619

BOOTH, CATHERINE KEENER, music educator, director; b. Cin., Feb. 28, 1975; d. David Lee and Karen Kiser Keener; m. David Martin Booth, June 26, 1999. MusB in Music Edn., Wright State U., Fairborn, Ohio, 2001. Cert. tchr. music State of Ohio. Pvt. tchr. music, 1992—; band and choir dir. Ridgeville Christian Schs., Springboro, Ohio, 2001—04; dir. bands Valley View Local Schs., 2005—. Mem.: Ohio Music Educators Assn.. Avocations: boating, water-skiing. Home: 1012 Foxshire Pl Centerville OH 45458

BOOTH, JANE SCHUELE, real estate company officer, real estate broker; b. Cleve. d. Norman Andrew and Frances Ruth (Hankey) Schuele; m. George Warren Booth, Dec. 6, 1968. AA, Stephens Coll., 1946; student, U. Mo., 1946—47. Lic. real estate broker, Fla. Assoc. J.M. Mathes Inc., N.Y.C., 1947-48; dept. supr. Lord and Taylor, Scarsdale, N.Y., 1948-50; art coord. J. Walter Thompson, Inc., N.Y.C., 1953-58; art buyer SSC&B Inc. Advt., N.Y.C., 1959-80; pres. Jane Schuele Booth Realty, Ocala, Fla., 1982—. Mem. Fla. Thoroughbred Fillies, Ocala, 1980—; charter mem., trustee Royal Dames for Cancer Rsch., Inc., Ocala, 1986—; treas. Ladies Aux. Fla. H.C.H. Inc., Ocala, 1986-90; bd. visitors Fla. Horsemen's Children's Home, Inc., 1983-90. Mem. Ocala/Marion County Assn. Realtors, Ocala/Marion County C. of C. (agribus./equine com.), Nat. Assn. Realtors, Fla. Assn. Realtors. Home: 1771 SW 55th Street Rd Ocala FL 34474-5933 Office: PO Box 5538 Ocala FL 34478-5538 Personal E-mail: janeschuelebooth@aol.com.

BOOTH, KAREN LEE, elementary school educator; b. Refrom, Ala., Mar. 28, 1970; d. Percy Hobson and Nancy Thaxton Lee; m. Steven McCoy Booth, Mar. 26, 1994; children: John David, James Michael. BS, Miss. U. for Women, Columbus, 1991; EdM, U. West Ala., Livingston, 1994. Classroom tchr. Gordo Elem. Sch., Ala., 1992—. Active First United Meth. Ch., Carrollton, Ala., 1976—2006. Partners in Edn. grantee, Ala. Power Co., 1997. Home: PO Box 97 Coker AL 35452 Office: Gordo Elementary School 535 4th Street NW Gordo AL 35466 Office Phone: 205-364-8480.

BOOTH, KORTNEY DIANA, music educator; b. Salt Lake City, Sept. 18, 1976; d. Rick A. Booth and Penny Lee Jones. MusB, Utah State U., Logan, 2001; MA in Music Edn., U. Wyo., Laramie, 2006. Tchr. music Uinta County Sch. Dist. #1, Evanston, Wyo., 2001—. Coach color guard Evanston H.S. Band, Wyo., 2004—06. Office Phone: 307-789-3106. E-mail: kbooth@uinta1.k12.wy.us.

BOOTH, RACHEL ZONELLE, nursing educator; b. Seneca, S.C., Feb. 10, 1936; m. Richard B. Booth, Feb. 13, 1957; 1 child, Kevin M. Student, Furman U., 1953-54; diploma in nursing, Greenville Gen. Hosp., SC, 1956; student, U. Alaska, 1964-66; BS in Nursing, U. Md., Balt., 1968; MS in Nursing, U. Md., 1970, PhD in Adminstrn. Higher Edn., 1978; D of Nursing Sci. (hon.), Chiang Mai U., Thailand, 1999. RN. Staff nurse VA Hosp., Murfreesboro, Tenn., 1956-57, U. Colo. Med. Ctr., Denver, 1957-58; nurse psychiatry dept. Patton State Hosp., Calif., 1958-59; staff nurse USAF Dispensary, Iraklion, Greece, 1959-60; charge nurse psychiatry Santa Rose Med. Ctr., San Antonio, 1961; staff nurse Shannon S.W. Tex. Meml. Hosp., San Angelo, 1962; supervisory clin. nurse, head nurse U.S. Dept. Health, Edn., and Welfare/USPHS/Indian Health Service, Anchorage, 1962-66; staff nurse U.S. Dept. Health, Edn., and Welfare/USPHS, Balt., 1966, 68; assoc. dir. dept. nursing U. Md. Hosp., 1970-76, dir. primary care nursing svc., 1976-81; asst. prof. Sch. Nursing U. Md., 1972-76, asst. prof. Sch. Pharmacy, 1972-80, acting assoc. dean Sch. Nursing, 1979-81, assoc. prof. Sch. Nursing, 1979, assoc. prof. clin. pharmacy, 1980-83, assoc. dean for undergrad. studies Sch. Nursing, 1981-83, co-dir. nurse practitioner program Sch. Nursing, 1972-76, chairperson grad. program dept. primary care, 1974-79; dean, Sch. of Nursing and asst. v.p. for health affairs Duke U., Durham, N.C., 1984-87; dean Sch. Nursing U. Ala. at Birmingham, University Station, 1987—. Instr. Sch. Medicine U. Md., 1972-83, program dir. primary care nurse practitioner program continuing edn., 1976-82, project dir. Robert Wood Johnson Nurse Faculty Fellowship program, 1977-82; mem. joint practice com. Med. and Surg. Faculty Md., 1974-77, mem. tech. adv. com. for physician's assts. Bd. Med. Examiners Md., 1975-80; mem. adv. com. nursing program Community Coll. Balt., 1976-79; mem. Joint Commn. on Accreditation of Hosps., pres. Md. Council Dirs. of Assoc. Degree, Diploma, and Baccalaureate Programs, 1982-83; mem. adv. bd. nursing Essex Community Coll., 1983; mem. peer rev. panel advanced nurse edn. nursing div. U.S. Dept. Health and Human Services, 1987—. Editor (with others) Hospital Pharmacy, 1971-72; asst. editor Jour. Profl. Nursing, 1984-87; contbr. articles on nursing to profl. jours. Bd. dirs. Health and Welfare Coun. Ctrl. Md., Inc., 1974-78, v.p., 1975-78; mem. health adv. com. to Pres. of Pakistan, 1981—. Recipient numerous grants for nursing adminstrn., 1972—. Mem. ANA (mem. nat. rev. com. 1975-78, v.p. 1977, chair 1978), Internat. Coun. Nurses (observer conf. 1981), Nat. Acad. Practice for Nursing (vice chairperson 1984-89), Nat. Orgn. for Nurse Execs., Nat. League for Nursing, Coun. Nat. Acad. Practice, Am. Assn. Colls. in Nursing (dean's summer seminar com. 1984-85, edn. and credentialing com. 1985-86, nominating com. 1986-87, bd. dirs. 1989-96, pres.-elect 1992-94, pres. 1994-96), N.C. Orgn. Nurse Execs. (bd. dirs. 1986-87), So. Coun. Collegiate Edn. for Nursing (exec. com. 1986-91, v.p., bd. dirs. 1991-94, pres. 1997-99), Sigma Theta Tau (chairperson nominating com. 1974, mem. 1975, rec. sec. 1980-83). Avocations: genealogy, travel, swimming. Office: U Ala at Birmingham 1530 3rd Ave S Birmingham AL 35294-0002

BOOTH, SUSAN, educational association administrator, product designer, marketing professional, researcher; d. Kyung Hi Yang and John Kent Booth; m. Martin Johnson, Jan. 4, 2002; 1 child, Makani Booth Johnson. BS, Lewis and Clark Coll., Portland, Oreg., 1984; MEd, Lesley Coll., Cambridge, Mass., 1988. Cert. elem. edn. Mass., 1988. Edn. and tech. devel. specialist Coun. for Advancement and Support of Edn., Washington, 1993—98; mgr., edn. tech. programs Nat. Sch. Bds. Assn., Alexandria, Va., 1998—2000; dir. of products and svcs. devel. Nat. Assn. of Ind. Schs., Washington, 2000—. Mem.: Am. Mktg. Assn., Greater Wash. Soc. of Assn. Exec., Am. Soc. of Assn. Exec.

BOOTH CORWIN, TAMI, publishing executive; Editor health and medicine category Little Brown, 1994—97; exec. editor health and lifestyle books IDG Books, NYC and Chgo., 1997—2000; dir. new title devel. Rodale, Inc., NYC, 2000, exec. editor Women's Health Books, 2000—01, editor-in-chief Women's Health Books NYC, 2001—, pres., books divsn., 2005—. Named one of 50 Women to Watch, Wall Street Journal, 2005. Office: Rodale Inc 733 3rd Ave 15th Fl New York NY 10017-3204 also: Rodale Inc 33 E Minor St Emmaus PA 18098-0099*

BOOZ, GRETCHEN ARLENE, marketing executive; b. Boone, Iowa, Nov. 24, 1933; d. David Gerald and Katherine Bevridge (Hardie) Berg; m. Donald Rollett Booz, Sept. 3, 1960; children: Kendra Sue (dec.), Joseph David, Katherine Sue. AA, Graceland Coll., 1955. Med. asst. Robert A. Hayne M.D., Des Moines, 1955-61; mktg. dir. Herald Pub. House, Independence, Mo., 1975—. Author: (book) Kendra, 1979. Mem. Citizens Adv. Bd., Blue Springs, Mo., 1979-91, Independence Mayor's Christmas Concert Com., 1987-91; bd. dirs. Comprehensive Mental Health, 1981-83, Child Placement Svcs., Independence, 1987-94, Hope House, Inc., Independence, 1987-91, Ctr. for Profl. Devel. and Life-long Learning, Inc., 1995-96; trustee Graceland U., Lamoni, Iowa, 1984-96. Mem. Leadership Edn. Action Devel. (L.E.A.D.), Independence C. of C. (diplomat, Outstanding Mem. award 1981), Rotary. Republican. Mem. Community of Christ Ch. Avocation: writing and presenting monologues of women in history. Home: 1000 NW Cedar Ln Grain Valley MO 64029 Office: Herald Pub House 1001 W Walnut PO Box 390 Independence MO 64051-0390 Office Phone: 816-521-3015 1481. E-mail: gbooz@heraldhouse.org, gbooz3@comcast.net.

BOOZER-BLASCO, CLAUDIA RUTH, family and consumer resources educator; b. St. Louis, Sept. 16, 1950; d. Howard Rae and Frances Kintner Boozer; m. George Blasco Jr., July 30, 1994 (dec. Nov. 15, 2005); stepchildren: Michelle Blasco Smith, Paul Blasco. BS in Home Econs. Edn., U. RI, Kingston, 1972; MEd in Counseling, U. NH, Durham, 1988. Health edn. tchr. St. Joseph's Indian Sch., Chamberlain, SD, 1972—73; home econs. tchr. Guilford Mid.-High Sch., NH, 1974—77; cmty. health educator Manchester Area Family Planning, NH, 1977—83; ext. educator family and consumer resources U. NH Coop. Ext., Brentwood, 1983—. Com. mem. Inst. for Health and Recovery, Cambridge, Mass., 2004—05. Founding mem. Fetal Alcohol Spectrum Disorder Adoptive Parents Support Group, Manchester, 2000—. Recipient Outstanding Family and Consumer Scis. Specialist award, NH Assn. Family and Consumer Scis., 1999. Mem.: Nat. Coun. Family Rels., Am. Assn. Family and Consumer Scis. (cert.), Nat. Ext. Assn. Family and Consumer Scis. (Nat. Comm. award for TV feature 1995, Continued Excellence award 1996, Disting. Svc. award 1995). Unitarian Universalist. Avocations: travel, hiking, miniature dollhouses. Office: U NH Coop Ext 113 North Rd Brentwood NH 03833 Office Phone: 603-679-5616.

BOPP, ANNETTE LEE, mathematics educator; b. WheatRidge, Colo., May 19, 1965; d. Gary Lynn and Jackie Lee Gray; m. Robert Daniel Bopp, June 24, 1989; children: Craig Daniel, Jarrett Lee. BS in Math., Colo. State U., Ft. Collins, 1987. Cert. tchr. State of Tex., 2001, State of Calif., 1998, State of Pa., 1989, State of Colo., 1987. Math. tchr. Westlake Jr. High, Northglenn, Colo., 1988—89, Broughal Mid. Sch., Bethlehem, Pa., 1989—91, East Hills Mid. Sch., Bethlehem, 1991—98, Ruth Musser Mid. Sch., Rancho Cucamonga, Calif., 1998—2000, Conroe H.S., Tex., 2001—02, Magnolia H.S., Tex., 2002—. Ofcl., starter and clk. of course Rivershire Rattlesnakes Swim Team, Conroe, Tex., 2002—06. Mem.: Nat. Coun. Tchrs. Math. (assoc.), Kappa Mu Epsilon. R-Conservative. Methodist. Avocations: sewing, water skiing, swimming. Office: Magnolia High School PO Box 428 Magnolia TX 77353 Office Fax: 281-252-2092. E-mail: abopp@magnoliaisd.org.

BOQUIST, DIANA D., mayor, real estate agent; b. Columbus, Ohio, Mar. 26, 1940; d. Cleo Lewis and Elizabeth Katherine (Fry) Dumaree; m. Edwin Russell Boquist, June 9, 1961; children: Kimberly, Kelly, Kerry. BSc in Edn., Ohio State U., 1961. 4th grade tchr. Long Beach (Calif.) Unified Sch. Dist., 1961-63; real estate sales staff Schlott & Coldwell Banker Realtors, Bernardsville, N.J., 1983-95; mgr. real estate office Coldwell Banker, Basking Ridge, N.J., 1995-98; asst. mgr. Weichert Realtors, Bernardsville, N.J., 1998—. Pres. Boeing Wives Club, Cape Canaveral, Fla., 1967, PTA, Greensburg, Pa., 1973, Welcome Wagon, Somerset Hills, 1978, Sch. Bd., Bernards Twp., 1986, 87; coun. mem. Town Coun., Bernards Twp., 1992—, mayor, 1995, 99; elder Basking Ridge Presbyn. Ch., 1999—. Named Woman of Yr., Bus. and Profl. Women, Bernardsville, 1995, Basking Ridge, 1995. Mem. N.J. Assn. Realtors (Disting. Realtor award 1993). Republican. Avocations: bridge, travel, golf. Office: Weichert Realtors 62 Morristown Rd Bernardsville NJ 07924-2305 also: Collyer Ln Basking Ridge NJ 07920

BORAS, KIM, lawyer; BA, Rollins Coll., 1986; JD, Harvard U., 1989. Bar: Calif. 1989, Fla. 1990, N.Y. 2001. Jud. clk. to Hon. Peter T. Fay, Judge, U.S. Ct. Appeals (11th cir.), 1989—90; with Latham & Watkins, L.A., 1990—, ptnr., 2001—. Office: Latham and Watkins LLC 633 W Fifth St Ste 4000 Los Angeles CA 90071

BORCHARDT, BETSY OLK, artist; b. Clintonville, Wis., June 5, 1953; d. James Howard and Bernice Durben (Olk); m. Andrew Peter Borchardt, Dec. 27, 1980. Student, Lawrence U., Appleton, Wis., 1971; BA Sociology, St. Norbert Coll., De Pere, Wis., 1980; postgrad., U. Tenn., Nashville, 1981. Home health aide Upjohn, Oshkosh, Wis., 1989, Oshkosh, 90; pvt. practice, Omro, 1990—93; program aide United Cerebral Palsy, Oshkosh, 1996—97; artist, participant electronic transmission art Ariz. State U. project shown at UN 4th World Conf. on Women, Beijing, 1995; recruiting asst. U.S. Census Bur., Stevens Point, Wis., 2000; line therapist Autism and Behavioral Cons., Fond du Lac, Wis., 2002—03. Author: (poetry) A Personal Struggle, 1987; one-woman shows include U. Wis. Ctr., Marinette, 2003, exhibited in group shows at Kansas City S/B Civic Ctr., Kans., Pub. Libr., The Country Club Plz., Kansas City, Mo., 1987—88, Neville Pub. Mus., Green Bay, Wis., 1990, The Art Barn Gallery, Green Lake, Wis., 1995, Wis. Ctr., Madison, 1996, Our Savior Luth. Ch., Oshkosh, Wis., 1998, Art for All, Menominee, Wis., 2002, Howard Young Med. Ctr., Woodruff, Wis., 2004. Vol. Franklin Ctr. Coffee Shop, Kansas City, 1984; activity aide Omro Care Ctr., 1988—89; visual arts leader Winnebago County 4-H, Omro, 1991, 1992; vol. tutor Redgranite Elem. Sch., 1995—2000; vol. reader, leader art activities Redgranite Libr., 2005—; mem. chorus, drama cast, handbell choir Maestro Prodns., Inc., Oshkosh, 1991—2000; scientist pen-pal Sci. By Mail Mus. Sci., Boston, 1996—2000; founding mem. Wildlife Land Trust Human Soc. U.S., Wildlife Guardian for Defenders of Wildlife, 1999—; mem. and legis. activist The Wilderness Soc. Mem. Wis. Regional Artists Assn. (Kenneth and Marie Kuemmerlein award 1992, Obermiller Edn. award, 1996), Wilson Ctr. Assocs., Nat. Arbor Day Found., Lions (sec. 2001—) Avocations: reading, camping, fishing, bird watching. Home: 231 Wood St Redgranite WI 54970-9342 Office Phone: 920-290-2595. Personal E-mail: betsyborchardt@hotmail.com.

BORCHERS, JANET MARISE, elementary school educator, counselor; b. Miami, Fla., July 1, 1955; d. James Hilliard and Janet Marise Cole; m. Kenneth Fred Borchers, May 8, 1976; 1 child, Russell James. AA, Edison C.C., Ft. Myers, Fla., 1989; BA, U. South Fla., Ft. Myers, 1992; MA, Fla. Gulf Coast U., Estero, 2001. Cert. tchr. ESOL Fla., tchr. English 5-9 Fla., primary edn. K-3 Fla., elem. edn. 1-6 Fla., guidance and counseling PK-12 Fla. Tchr. Sch. Dist. of Lee County, Ft. Myers, 1992—2001, sch. counselor, 2001—. Mem. Island Coast FEA Coun., Ft. Myers, 2006—. Named Elem. Sch. Counselor of Yr., Lee County, 2006. Mem.: Fla. Edn. Assn., Fla. Gulf Coast Nat. Writing Project (fellow 2001—, grantee 2006), Tchrs. Assn. Lee County (assoc.; sch. rep. 1992—, Area VII coord. 2002—), Lee County Counselors Assn. (assoc.), Am. Sch. Counselor Assn. (assoc.). Avocation: meditation. Home: 12550 Tower Rd Bonita Springs FL 34135 Office: Spring Creek Elem 25571 Elementary Way Bonita Springs FL 34135 Office Phone: 239-947-0001. Office Fax: 239-947-4690. Personal E-mail: jtortures2@aol.com. E-mail: janetmb@leeschools.net.

BORCHERS, MARY AMELIA, middle school educator; b. Miles City, Mont., July 6, 1935; d. Earl Gordon and Lulu Irene (Ankerman) Forgaard; m. Justus Charles Borchers, Nov. 25, 1960; 1 child, James Gordon. AA, Lassen Jr. Coll., 1955; BA, Chico State Coll., 1960. Cert. tchr., Calif. Tchr. Loyalton (Calif.) High Sch., 1957-60, Point Arena (Calif.) High Sch., 1960-64, Nelson Ave Sch., Oroville, Calif., 1965-81; math. tchr. Weaver Elem. Sch., Merced, Calif., 1986—. Mem. math. educators del. People to People, Russia and Estonia; AIMS trainer Fresno (Calif.) Pacific Coll., 1988-90. Mem. Calif. Tchrs.' Assn., Weaver Tchrs.' Assn., Phi Delta Kappa. Personal E-mail: maryb190@aol.com.

BORCHERT, CATHERINE GLENNAN, minister; b. L.A., Dec. 6, 1936; d. Thomas Keith and Ruth Haslup Adams Glennan; m. Frank R. Borchert Jr., Sept. 12, 1959 (dec. Sept. 1997); children: Frank R. III, Anne Matthews, Thomas Adams. BS, Swarthmore Coll., 1958; MSLS, Western Res. U., 1959; MDiv, McCormick Theol. Sem., 1991; postgrad., Case Western Res. U. Ordained to ministry, Presbyn. Ch., 1991. Serial records libr. U. Chgo. Libr., 1959-61; ref. libr., head outreach Cleveland Heights (Ohio) Pub. Libr., 1979-86; stated clk. Presbytery of Western Res. U., Cleve., 1984-94; interim pastor Lyndhurst (Ohio) Cmty. Presbyn. Ch., 1993-94; coord. adv. com. social witness policy Gen. Assembly of Presbyn. Ch., Louisville, 1994-97; adj. faculty McCormick Theol. Sem., Chgo., 1987—, interim dean doctoral programs and continuing edn., 2000-01. Mem. exec. com. Permanent Judicial Commn. Contbr. articles to profl. jours. Bd. dirs. United Protestant Campus Min., Cleve., 1999—2002, History Assocs., Cleve., 1999—; mem. steering com. Woman 2000 Case Western Res. U., 1998—2000; alumni interviewer Swarthmore (Pa.) Coll., 1965—; mem. exec. com. Chs.' Ctr. for Theology and Pub. Policy, Washington. Mem.: Mortar Bd., Phi Alpha Theta, Beta Phi Mu. Democrat. Avocations: reading, birdwatching, choir, bike riding. Home: 13415 Shaker Blvd #9C2 Cleveland OH 44120

BORDALLO, MADELEINE MARY (MRS. RICARDO JEROME BORDALLO), congresswoman; b. Graceville, Minn., May 31, 1933; d. Christian Peter and Mary Evelyn (Roth) Zeien; m. Ricardo Jerome Bordallo, June 20, 1953; 1 daughter, Deborah Josephine. Student, St Mary's Coll., South Bend, Ind., 1952; AA, St. Katherines Coll., St. Paul, 1953; AA hon. degree for community service, U. Guam, 1968. Presented in voice recital Guam Acad. Music, Agana., 1951, 62; mem. Civic Opera Co., St. Paul, 1952-53; mem. staff KUAM Radio-TV sta., Agana, 1954-63; freelance writer local newspaper, fashion show commentator, coordinator, civic leader, 1963; nat. Dem. committeewoman for Guam, 1964—2004; 1st lady of Guam, 1974-78, 81-85; senator 16th Guam Legislature, 1981-82, 19th Guam Legislature, 1987-88, 20th Guam Legislature, 1989-90, 21st Guam Legislature, 1991-92, 22nd Guam Legislature, 1993-94; Dem. Party candidate for Gov. of Guam, 1990; lt. gov. of Guam, 1994—2002; del. US Congress from Guam, 2002—03, 2004—; mem. armed svcs., resources and small bus. coms. Del. Nat. Dem. Conv., 1964, 68, 72, 76, 80, 84, 88-92, 96, 2000-04, pres. Women's Dem. Party Guam, 1967-69; rep. Presdl. Inauguration, Washington, 1965, 77, 85, 2005; del. Dem. Western States Conf., Reno, 1965, L.A., 1967, Phoenix, 1968, conf. sec., 1967-69; del. Dem. Women's Campaign Conf., Wash., 1965, Dem. Inauguration, 1992. Pres. Guam Women's Club, 1958-59; del Gen. Fedn. Women's Clubs Convs., Miami Beach, Fla., 1961, New Orleans, 1965, Boston, 1968; v.p. Fedn. Asian Women's Assn., 1964-67, pres., 1967-69, pres. 1996-98; pres. Guam Symphony Soc., 1967-73, del. convs., Manila, Philippines, 1959, Taipei, Formosa, 1960, Hong Kong, 1963, Guam, 1964, Japan, 1968, Taipei, 1973; chmn. Guam Christmas Seal Drive, 1961; bd. dirs. Guam chpt. ARC, 1963, sec., 1963-67, fund dr. chmn., 2000; pres. Marianas Assn. For Retarded Children, 1968-69, 73-74, 84—; bd. dirs. Guam Theatre Guild, Am. Cancer Soc.; mem. Guam Meml. Hosp. Vols. Assn., 1966—, v.p., 1966-67, pres., 1970-71; chmn. Hosp. Charity Ball, 1966; pres. Women for Service, 1974—, Beauty World Guam Ltd., 1981—, First Lady's Beautification Task Force of Guam, 1983-86; pres. Palace Restoration Assn., 1983—; nominee Dem. party for Gov. of Guam, 1990. Mem. Internat. Platform Assn., Guam Rehab. Assn. (assoc.), Guam Lytico and Bodig Assn. (pres. 1983-98), Spanish Club of Guam, Inetnon Famalaoan Club (pres. 1983-86), Guam Coun. of Women's Club (pres. 1993-95), Nat. Conf. Lt. Govs. (exec. com. 1998—). Democrat. Home: Watergate E 305 N 2510 Virginia Ave NW Washington DC 20037 Office Phone: 202-225-1188. Business E-Mail: madeleine.bordallo@mail.house.gov, roseanne.meno@mail.house.gov.

BORDELON, CAROLYN THEW, elementary school educator; b. Shelby, Ohio, Dec. 28, 1942; d. Burton Carl and Opal Mae (Harris) VanAsdale; m. Clifford Charles Spohn, Aug. 28, 1965 (div. Feb. 1982); m. Al Ramon Bordelon, Oct. 26, 1985. BA in History and Polit. Sci., Otterbein Coll., 1966; MA in Edn., Bowling Green State U., 1972; postgrad., Ohio State U., 1986—. Cert. tchr. grades 1-8, Ohio. Elem. tchr. Allen East Schs., Harrod, Ohio, 1966—68, Marion (Ohio) City Schs., 1968—78, chpt. I reading tchr., 1978—86, reading recovery tchr., 1986—88, Dublin (Ohio) City Schs., 1988—. Adj. instr. reading dept. grad. studies Ashland (Ohio) U., 1996. Author: The Parent Workshop, 1992, Octopus Goes to School, 1995. Vol. Am. Heart Assn., Worthington, Ohio, 1991; mem. Rep. Nat. Com., Washington, 1994-95; mem. Royal Scots Highlanders, Mansfield, Ohio, 1976—; deacon Covenant Presbyn. Ch., Upper Arlington, Ohio, 2006—. Recipient Excellence in Edn. award Dublin City C. of C., 1991-93, 96, 97; Dublin City Schs./Ohio Dept. Edn. Tchr. Award grantee, 1993; Martha Holden Jennings Found. scholar, 1978. Mem. Archaeol. Inst. Am., Ohio Edn. Assn., Reading Recovery Coun. N.Am., Columbus Opera Assn., Columbus Mus. Art, Phi Delta Kappa, Phi Alpha Theta. Avocations: bagpiping and scottish activities, archaeology, interior design, harpsichord. Home: 3958 Fairlington Dr Columbus OH 43220-4531 Office: Griffith Thomas Elem Sch 4671 Tuttle Crossing Blvd Dublin OH 43017-3575 Personal E-mail: c.bordelonread@aol.com.

BORDELON, DENA COX YARBROUGH, retired special education educator, director; b. Gorman, Tex., June 20, 1933; d. William Thomas and Imogene (Dunlap) Cox; m. James Edgar Yarbrough, June 20, 1950 (dec.); m. Cecil J. Bordelon, Sept. 24, 1999. BA, Nicholls State U., 1964, MEd, 1971, postgrad., 1978. Supr. profl. pers., prin. schs., elem. tchr. Terrebonne Parish Sch. Bd., Houma, La., 1964-79, dir. spl. edn. svcs., 1980-91; ret., 1991. Mem.: La. Ret. Tchrs. Assn. Democrat. Methodist. Avocations: reading, theater. Home: 202 White St Houma LA 70364-2934 E-mail: cbordelon@sw.rr.com.

BORDELON, SUZANNE MACKIE, writing and rhetoric educator; b. Brampton, Can., Mar. 12, 1962; d. Ian and Eileen Patience (Weaver) Mackie; m. Robert Michael Bordelon, July 16, 1989; 1 child, Nicholas Ian. BA in Journalism and History, U. Wash., 1984; MA in Lit. and Lang., Calif. State U., Chico, 1992; PhD in Rhetoric and Composition, U. Oreg., 1998. Reporter Skagit Valley Herald, Mt. Vernon, Wash., 1986—87, Record Searchlight, Redding, 1987—92; asst. prof. English U. Alaska, Fairbanks, 1998—2002; coord. upper divsn. writing San Diego State U., 2002—. Recipient Outstanding Faculty and Staff award, San Diego State U., 2004, Demmert Appreciation and Recognition award, U. Alaska, 2002. Mem.: Modern Lang. Assn., Nat. Women's Studies Assn., Writing Program Adminstrn., Rhetoric Soc. of Am., Nat. Coun. of Teachers of English. Personal E-mail: sbordelon2@cox.net.

BORDERS, SARAH ROBINSON, lawyer; b. Ariz. JD, U. Va., Charlottesville, 1988. Bar: Ga. 1989. Assoc. King & Spalding, Atlanta, 1989—95; ptnr. King & Spalding LLP, Atlanta, 1996—. Active Alliance Theatre, Atlanta. Office: King & Spalding LLP 1180 Peachtree St Atlanta GA 30309

BORDNER, PATRICIA ANNE, insurance agent, writer; b. Red Wing, Minn., Mar. 29, 1946; d. Harold Arthur and Cecilia Helen Rodman; m. Thomas Ottis Bordner, May 18, 1981. AA, U. Minn., 1966. Cert. commercial rater U.S. Fidelity and Guaranty Co. Tchr. St. Albert the Great Elem. Sch., Mpls., 1967—68; tchr. Epiphany Edn. Ctr., Coon Rapids, Minn., 1968—70; comml. rater and acctg. clk. U. S. Fidelity and Guaranty Co., Mpls., 1971—85; ind. comml. ins. rater Coon Rapids, 1985—. Author: (poems) Hands of Time, 2000; contbr. poems to poetry contests and mags. Named Internat. Profl. of Yr., Internat. Biographical Ctr., England, 2005; named to Internat. Poetry Hall of Fame, 1996; recipient Golden Poet award, 1990, 1991, 1992, Editor's Choice award, 1993—98, 21st Century award for achiev., Internat. Biographical Ctr., England. Roman Catholic. Home: 1010 94th Ave NW Coon Rapids MN 55433-5501

BORDOFF, SHERRI BETH, social worker; b. N.Y.C., Sept. 5, 1955; d. Abraham and Lillian Dobroff; m. Nils Bordoff, Aug. 18, 1985; children: Justin Keith, Samantha Joy. BA, Queens Coll., 1976; MSW, NYU, 1978. Cert. social worker. Group work supr. Samuel Field YM-YWHA, Little Neck, NY, 1978-82; asst. clin. dir. Summit Sch., Flushing, NY, 1982—. Mem. NASW, Coun. for Exceptional Children, Phi Beta Kappa, Kappa Delta Pi. Office: 183-02 Union Tpk Flushing NY 11366

BORELL, MARY PUTNAM, language educator, playwright; d. Max Clyde and Elizabeth Maynard Putnam; m. Melvin George Borell, Sept. 9, 1979; m. Ronald Reiner Wempen (div.); children: Rex Reiner, Eric Putnam. BA in English, Wellesley Coll., Mass., 1961; MA in Am. studies, U. So. Calif., LA, 1968, MA in profl. writing, 2004; PhD in ednl. adminstrn., Northwestern U., Ill., 1974. Cert. tchr., adminstr. Instr. English San Antonio USD, San Antonio, 1968—69, Barat Coll., Lake Forest, Ill., 1970—73; asst. prof. English Calif. State U., Carson, 1975—78; assoc. prof. English LA Southwest Coll., 1979—81, dean of instrn., 1981—92; dir. econ. devel. LA CC, 1992—98; prof. English LA Harbor Coll., Wilmington, Calif., 1998—. Edn. bd. mem. Pvt. Industry Council, LA, 1992—98, Rebuild LA, 1993—95. Author: (plays) In the Nude, 2002, Murder Ahoy, 2004, Gerald, 2006. Pres. Palos Verdes Women's Club, Calif.; v.p. Nat. Women's Polit. Caucus, South Bay, Calif. Recipient Chancellor's award, LA CC Dist., 1994, Mayor of LA award, City of LA, 1996, 1998. Mem.: Rotary (past pres.), Calif. CC Adminstrs., AAUW. Office: LA Harbor Coll 1111 Figueroa Pl Wilmington CA 90744 Personal E-mail: mary_borell@yahoo.com.

BORELLI, MYRIAM, social worker, educator; b. Buenos Aires, Apr. 5, 1937; arrived in U.S., 1960; d. Francisco Rosnati and Angela Martin; children: Maggie Cummings, Ricardo, Virginia Sampson, Carla McCall. BS, Licee No 3, Buenos Aires, 1954; M in History, Instituto Nat. Profesoreton, Buenos Aires, 1960; MSW, Loyola U., Chgo., 1978; PhD in Edn., Ill. State U., Normal, 1996. Socialworker CPS in Region Spl. Edn. and Gifted Programs, Chgo., 1978—. Founder Hispanic Profls. Orgn., Chgo., 1980; co-founder Minority Admision, Loyola U., Chgo., 1980—2005. Mem. Hispanic Gifted Programs, Chgo. Pub. Schs.; docent Hy, Archeology, Egyptology Field Mus., Chgo., 1999—2006. Recipient 20 Yr. Svc. award, Sch. Soc. Workers, 2001. Mem.: Field Mus. Avocation: archaeology. Home: 1450 Brickell Bay Dr 1109 Miami FL 33131

BOREN, LYNDA SUE, gifted education educator; b. Leesville, La., Apr. 1, 1941; d. Leonard and Doris (Ford) Schoenberger; m. James Lewis Boren, Sept. 1, 1961; 1 child, Lynda Carolyn. BA, U. New Orleans, 1971, MA, 1973; PhD, Tulane U., 1979. Prof. Northwestern State U., Natchitoches, La., 1987-89; propr. Colony Country House, New Llano, La., 1992-94; tchr. of gifted Leesville (La.) H.S., 1992—. Vis. prof. Newcomb Coll., Tulane U., New Orleans, 1979-83, U. Erlangen-Nuremburg, Germany, 1981-82, Middlebury (Vt.) Coll., 1983-84, Ga. Inst. Tech., Atlanta, 1985-87, Srinakharinwirot U., Bangkok, 1989-90; mem. planning com. 1st Kate Chopin Internat. Conf., Natchitoches, La., 1987-89; Fulbright lectr. USIA and Bd. Fgn. Scholars, 1981-82, 89-90. Author: Eurydice Reclaimed: Language, Gender and Voice in Henry James, 1989; co-editor, author: Kate Chopin Reconsidered, 1992; contbg. author: Encyclopedia of American Poetry, 1998; contbr. numerous articles to profl. jours. Founding mem. John F. Kennedy libr. Recipient awards for watercolors; Mellon fellow Tulane U., 1977-78; NEH seminar fellow Princeton U., 1986. Mem. MLA, AAUW, DAR, AFT, Fulbright Alumni Assn. Avocations: painting, video film documentaries, photography. Home: 1492 Fords Dairy Rd Newllano LA 71461-4530 Office Phone: 337-239-3464. Personal E-mail: alborn@peoplepc.com, schoenberger@bellsouth.net. Business E-Mail: lboren@vpsb.k12.la.us.

BORETZ, NAOMI MESSINGER, artist, educator; b. Bklyn. BA, Bklyn. Coll.; MA in Fine Arts, CUNY; MA in Art History, Rutgers U.; postgrad., Art Students League N.Y. Exhibitions include Westminster Arts Coun. Arts Ctr., London, 1971, Hudson River Mus., N.Y., 1975, Katonah Gallery, 1976, Condeso-Lawler Gallery, N.Y.C., 1987, Carnegie-Mellon Art Gallery, Pitts., 1989, The Nelson Atkins Mus. of Art, St. Louis, 1994, Westbeth Gallery, N.Y., 1996, Mishkin Gallery, Baruch Coll., 1997, Rutgers (N.J.) U. Art Gallery, 1998, Hillwood Art Mus., N.Y., 2000, Muhlenburg Coll. Art Gallery, 2002, others, Represented in permanent collections Met. Mus. Art, NYC, Solomon R. Guggenheim Mus., Whitney Mus. Am. Art, Mus. Modern Art, DeLand Art Mus., Fla., Brit. Mus., London, Nat. Mus. Am. Art, Washington, Yale U. Art Gallery, Joslyn Art Mus., Omaha, Walker Art Ctr., Mpls., Miami U. Art Mus., Oxford, Ohio, Fogg Art Mus. Harvard U., Cambridge, Mass., Glasgow (Scotland) Mus., San Jose (Calif.) Art Mus., Asheville (N.C.) Art Mus., Princeton U. Graphic Arts Collection, N.J., Mus. S.W., Midland, Tex., Swope Art Mus., Terre Haute, Ind., others; contbr. to arts publs. Artist-fellow Va. Ctr. Creative Arts, 1973, 86, Ossabaw Found., 1975, Tyrone Guthrie Arts Ctr., Ireland, 1987, Writers-Artists Guild Can., 1988; grantee N.J. State Coun. on Arts, 1985-86. Studio: Princeton NJ

BORG, RUTH I., home nursing care provider; d. Axel Gunner and Charlotte (Benston) B. Diploma, West Suburban Sch. Nursing, 1956; tchr.'s degree, Chgo. Conservatory, 1958; BSN, Alverno Coll., 1981. Staff nurse Boath Meml. Hosp., Chgo.; head nurse psychiatry, head nurse long-term medicine VA North Chgo. Med. Ctr.; staff nurse, night supr. intermediate care VA Clement Zabiocki Med. Ctr., Milw.; pool nurse, in-home nursing care provider Milw. County Mental Health Complex; home nurse care provider Dr. Ghonsham Sooknandan, Kenosha, Wis., 1994—99. In-home nursing care provider. Contbr. articles to profl. jours. Recipient Mary D. Bradford Disting. Alumni award, 1998. Mem.: Wis. Nurses Assn. (nominations com.). Avocation: teaching and performing music.

BORGEN, IRMA R., music educator; b. McPherson, Kans., Jan. 15, 1911; d. Nels J.W. Nelson and Ida Elizabeth Shallene; m. Clifford E. Borgen, July 6, 1942 (dec. Oct. 1967); children: David John, Elizabeth Marie. BA, Gustavus Adolphus Coll., St. Peter, Minn., 1932; postgrad., U. Colo., 1964—65. Tchr. Am. Sch. for Dependents, Essen, Germany, 1950—51; pvt. music tchr. Colorado Springs, Colo., 1969—. Mem.: Mil. Widows, Fountain Valley Sr. Orgn. Democrat. Lutheran. Avocations: music, fitness classes. Home: 114 Harvard St Colorado Springs CO 80911

BORGER, ANN WORK, communications professional, webmaster; b. Elkhart, Ind., Dec. 26, 1941; d. James Anderson III and Marie Ethlyn (Church) Work; m. Erik William Pottala, Mar. 1965 (div. Apr. 1975); 1 child, James Viktor; m. Barrie Lee Borger, Feb. 14, 1982. BA in Psychology, Ind. U., 1963; MS in Computer Sci., U. Md., 1971. Programmer Nat. Security Agy., Ft. Meade, Md., 1963-65; analyst Control Data Corp., Washington, 1966-68; rsch. assoc. U. Md., College Park, 1969-73; mgr. software devel. Simcon Inc., Washington, 1974-75; cons. Deltak, Inc., Washington, 1976-80; cons., analyst Air Products and Chems., Allentown, Pa., 1981-88; pres. Ann Borger Comm., Allentown, 1989—. Adj. prof. Muhlenberg Coll., 1985—86, DeSales U., 1996. Bd. dirs. Allentown YWCA, 1992-94; chair comm. com. Coalition for a Smoke-Free Valley, Allentown, 1994-99; loaned exec. United Way of the Greater Lehigh Valley, 1996. Named winner GLVWG Flash Contest, Pa. Poetry Soc. Mem.: Greater Lehigh Valley Writer's Group. Presbyterian. Avocations: choral music, bridge, travel. Home and Office: 3131 Hillcrest Ave Allentown PA 18103-6909 E-mail: awborger@yahoo.com.

BORGFORD, NORMA JEANNE, minister; b. Seattle, July 16, 1933; d. Ulvar George and Olga Helene (Olsen) B. BSN, Pacific Luth. Coll., Tacoma, Wash., 1956; MDiv, Luther N.W. Sem., St. Paul, 1986. Ordained to ministry Luth. Ch., 1986. Commd. 2d lt. USAF, 1957, advanced through grades to maj., 1972, ret., 1979; pastor Trinity Luth. Ch., Wibaux, Mont., 1986-90; interim pastor Valier Luth. Ch., Mont., 1990—91, Raymond, South Bend, Wash., 1990—91, Stevenson, Wash., 1990—91, Chinook, Wash., 1990—91, Tukwilla, Wash., 1990—91, Tacoma, 1990—91, Aberdeen, Wash., 1990—91, Wilbur, Wash., 1990—91. Home: 8613 Zircon Dr SW Apt G4 Lakewood WA 98498-4007

BORHI, CAROL, data processing executive, finance company executive; b. N.Y.C., Oct. 23, 1949; d. Carl and Elsie Elizabeth (Varady) Chaky; m. Nicholas Anthony Borhi, Sept. 23, 1972; children: Christy Nicole, Nicholas James. Assoc. in Applied Sci., Manhattan Community Coll., 1970; student, Hunter Coll., 1967-68, 70-71. Programmer asst. N.Y. Telephone, N.Y.C., 1970-73, programmer, 1974-76, programmer analyst, 1976-83; staff analyst Nynex Svc. Co., N.Y.C., 1984-87; systems analyst Nynex Corp., N.Y.C., 1987, assoc. dir., 1987-90, staff dir., 1991—97, Bell Atlantic, 1997—2000; sr. staff cons. Verizon, 2000—. Pres. Personal Touch Computing, N.Y.C., 1981-86. Mem. Telephone Pioneers Am. (charter), Creative Investors Am. Clubs: Sacred Heart. Republican. Roman Catholic. Avocations: real estate investing, coin collecting/numismatics, dance, guitar, piano. Office: Verizon Comms 1095 Ave of the Americas New York NY 10036

BORIS, RUTHANNA, dancer, educator, choreographer, dance therapist; b. Bklyn., Mar. 17, 1918; d. Joseph Jay and Frances (Weiss) B.; m. Frank W. Hobi (dec.) Student, Profl. Children's Sch., N.Y.C. Dir. Boris-Hobi Concert Co., 1955—57. Prin. dancer Am. Ballet, N.Y.C., 1934, Ballet Caravan, N.Y.C., 1936; prima ballerina Met. Opera Co., N.Y.C., 1939-41, Ballet Russe de Monte Carlo, N.Y.C., 1942-49; prima ballerina, choreographer-in-residence Royal Winnipeg Ballet of Can., 1957-59, dir. 1957-58; choreographer Ballet Russe de Monte Carlo, 1947, N.Y.C. Ballet, 1951; prof. dance U. Wash., Seattle, 1965-83, prof. emeritus, 1983—; adj. prof. psychiatry U. Wash., 1982; pres. exec. dir. Ctr. for Dance Devel. & Research, Albany, Calif., 1986—; choreographer: Cirque de Deux, 1947, Quelques Fleurs, 1948, Cakewalk, 1951, Kaleidoscope, 1951, Will O' The Wisp, 1951, Pasticcio, 1955, Wanderling, 1957, Ragtime, 1975, Tape Suite, 1976, Four All, 1980. Mem. adv. bd. Seattle Psychoanalytic Inst., 1975-82. Mem. Am. Guild Mus. Artists (award 1964, gov. 1942-64), Am. Dance Therapy Assn. (pres. Calif. chpt. 1986-88, mem. dance therapy credentials com. 1990-92). Office: Ctr Dance Devel & Rsch Apt 1334 555 Pierce St Albany CA 94706-1009 Office Phone: 510-528-2188.

BORKO, HILDA, education educator; BA in Psychology, UCLA, 1971, MA in Philosophy of Edn., 1973, PhD in Ednl. Psychology, 1978. Elem. tchg. credential Calif., specialization in mental retardation U. So. Calif. Asst. and assoc. prof. Coll. Edn., Va. Poly. Inst. and State U., 1980—85; assoc. prof. Coll. Edn., U. Md., College Park, 1985—91, Sch. Edn., U. Colo., Boulder, 1991—94; prof. Sch. Edn. U. Colo., Boulder, 1994—. Co-author (with M. Eisenhart): (book) Designing Classroom Research: Themes, Issues, and Struggles, 1993 (Outstanding article award, 1992); contbr. articles to profl. jours. and chpts. to books. Recipient grants in field. Mem.: APA, Nat. Acad. Edn., Nat. Coun. for Tchrs. of Math., Invisible Coll. for Rsch. on Tchg., Am. Assn. Colls. of Tchr. Edn., Am. Ednl. Rsch. Assn. (pres. 2003—04), Pi Gamma Mu, Phi Beta Kappa, Phi Delta Kappa. Office: U Colo Sch Edn CB249 Boulder CO 80309 Office Phone: 303-492-8399.

BORKOVEC, VERA Z., literature and language professor; b. Brno, Czechoslovakia, Aug. 13, 1926; came to U.S., 1952; d. Josef Zanda and Jarmila (Tuscher) Martinasek; m. Alexej B. Borkovec, Aug. 29, 1951. BA, Charles U., 1949; MA, Hollins Coll., 1961, The Am. U., 1966; PhD, Georgetown U., 1973. Secondary sch. tchr. English, French Montgomery County Pub. Schs., Md., 1961-64; from asst. prof. to assoc. prof. Russian studies The Am. Univ., Washington, 1966-91, prof. emerita. Recipient Artis Bohemiae Amicis medal, Czech Ministry of Culture, 2003. Mem. Czechoslovak Soc. of Arts and Scis. (v.p. 1994—). Avocations: theater, music, poetry. Home: 12013 Kemp Mill Rd Silver Spring MD 20902-1515

BORKOW, MARY P., small business owner, consultant; d. Theodore James Pappas and Assunta Caputo; m. Joel E. Borkow; children: David T., Jason E., Michelle M., K. Andrew, Philip S. Diploma in liberal arts, Sacramento State U., 1973, U. Pitts., 1993. Wth circulation dept. Johnstown Tribune Democrat, Pa., 1962—63; exec. sec. WJAC-TV, Johnstown, 1963—65, Shell Oil Co., Sacramento, 1971—72; adminstr. asst. C. of C., Johnstown, 1983—90; bus. owner Martins Fashions and Footwear, Johnstown, 1990—98; bus. advisor Plastic Surg. Assocs., Johnstown, 1999—. Pres., bd. dirs. YWCA, Johnstown, 1983—89; pres. com. C. of C. Bus. Alliance, Johnstown, 1988—96; pres. bd. dirs. Johnstown Symphony Orch., 1992—2002, pres., 1994—96, aux. mem.; pres. bd. dirs. Main Street Mgr. Program, 1996—98; bd. dirs. Johnstown Area Heritage Assn.; bd. trustees So. Alleghenies Mus. Art; co-founder Tribute to Women Award for YWCA; mem. McCort Sch. Bd., 1988—98; trustee YWCA; pres. Johnstown Symphony Aux.; founder Johnstown Cultural Trust; bd. dirs. Lee Initiatives. Recipient Tribute to Women award, YWCA, 1992, Hall of Fame award, Johnstown C. of C., 2002, Vol. in Arts award, 2005, Dominion People's Vita award, WQED Radio, 2006. Mem.: Meml. Hosp. Aux., Jaha Guild, Roxbury Bandshell Preservation Alliance (pres. 2006), Lee Hosp. Aux., Cultural Affair Com C. of C. (chair 1998—), Pres. Johnstown Investment Club, Johnstown Investment Club (pres. 2005—). Roman Catholic. Achievements include overseeing the building of Johnstown Gazebo in Central Park; responsible for the re-development of the Kernville Revitalization project. Avocations: travel, yoga, golf. Home: 1618 Sunshine Ave Johnstown PA 15905 Office: Plastic Surg Assocs of Johnstown 415 Napoleon Pl Johnstown PA 15901

BORLAND, KATHRYN KILBY, writer; b. Pullman, Mich., Aug. 14, 1916; d. Paul Melbourne and Vinnie (Bensinger) Kilby; m. James Barton Borland, May 16, 1942; children— James Barton, Susan Lee. BS in Journalism, Butler U., 1937. Editor North Side Topics, Indpls., 1938-42. Author: (all with Helen Ross Speicher) Southern Yankees, 1960, Allan Pinkerton, 1962, Miles and the Big Black Hat, 1963, Everybody Laughed, 1964, Eugene Field, 1964, Phillis Wheatley, 1968, Harry Houdini, 1969, Clocks from Shadow to Atom, 1969, Good-Bye to Stony Crick, 1975, The Third Tower, 1974, Stranger in the Mirror, 1974, Good-bye, Julie Scott, 1975, To Walk the Night, 1976, These Tigers' Hearts, 1978, Irena, 1979, Pseudonyms: Alice Abbott, Jane Land. Co-recipient award for most distinguished children's book pub. by Ind. author Ind. U., 1969 Mem.: P.E.O., Theta Sigma Phi, Kappa Alpha Theta. Home: 1050 S Maish Rd Frankfort IN 46041-3213

BORN, BROOKSLEY ELIZABETH, retired lawyer; b. San Francisco, Aug. 27, 1940; d. Ronald Henry and Mary Ellen (Bortner) Born; m. Alexander Elliot Bennett, Oct. 9, 1982; children: Nicholas Jacob Landau, Ariel Elizabeth Landau, Andrew E. Bennett, Laura F. Bennett, Peter J. Bennett. AB, Stanford U., 1961, JD, 1964. Bar: DC 1966. Law clk. U.S. Ct. Appeals, Washington, 1964—65; legal rschr. Harvard Law Sch., 1967—68; assoc. Arnold and Porter, Washington, 1965—67, 1968—73, ptnr., 1974—96, 1999—2002; chair U.S. Commodity Futures Trading Commn., Washington, 1996—99. Lectr. law Columbus Sch. Law, Cath. U. Am., 1972—74; adj. prof. Georgetown U. Law Ctr., Washington, 1972—73; mem. D.C. Jud. Nominating Commn., 2005—. Pres.: Stanford Law Rev., 1963—64. Chair bd. visitors Stanford Law Sch., 1987; trustee Ctr. Law and Social Policy, Washington, 1977—96; bd. dirs. Nat. Legal Aid and Defenders Assn., 1972—79, Washington Legal Clinic for Homeless, 1993—96, Lawyers Com. for Civil Rights Under Law, 1993—96, Am. Bar Found., 1989—99, Washington Lawyers Com. for Civil Rights and Urban Affairs, 1992—96, ALI-ABA, 2005—; chmn. bd. dirs. Nat. Women's Law Ctr., 1981—96, 2003—. Recipient Lifetime Achievement award, Am. Lawyer mag., 2005. Mem.: ABA (chair sect. ind. rights and responsibilities 1977—78, chair fed. judiciary com. 1980—83, chair consortium on legal svcs. and the pub. 1987—90, bd. govs. 1990—93, chair resource devel. coun. 1993—95, state del. from DC 1994—2005, chair coun. Fund for Justice and Edn. 1995—96), Southwestern Legal Found. (trustee 1993—96), Am. Law Inst., DC Bar (sec. 1975—76, mem. bd. govs. 1976—79), Order of Coif. Office: Arnold & Porter 555 12th St NW Washington DC 20004-1206 Office Phone: 202-942-5832. Business E-Mail: brooksley_born@aporter.com.

BORN, DANA H., dean, career military officer; BS, USAF Acad., 1983; MS, Trinity Univ., 1985; MA, Univ. Melbourne, Australia, 1991; PhD in indsl. & org. psychol., Pa. State Univ., 1994. Commd. 2d lt. USAF, advanced through grades to brig. gen., 2004; job analyst, exec. officer Occupational Measurement Ctr., Randolph AFB, Tex., 1983—86; personnel measurement psychol. USAF Exch. & Liaison office, Australian Royal Air Force, Melbourne, Australia, 1986—89; asst. prof., dept. behavioral sci. USAF Acad., Colo., 1989—91; liaison officer Pa. State Univ., 1991—94; asst. dir., recruiting rsch. & analysis Office of Asst. Sec. of Def. for Force Mgmt. Policy, Washington, 1994—97; policy analyst, aide to Sec. Office of Sec. of the Air Force, Washington, 1997—98; dep. chief, personnel issues team Office of Dep. Chief of Staff for Personnel, Washington, 1998—2000; comdr. 11th Mission Support Squadron, Bolling AFB, DC, 2000—02; prof., head Dept. Behavioral Sci. & Leadership USAF Acad., Colo., 2002—04, dean of the faculty Colo., 2004—. Decorated Def. Meritorious Svc. Medal, Meritorious Svc. Medal with 3 oak leaf clusters, Air Force Commendation medal with oak leaf cluster, Air Force Org. Excellence award, Nat. Def. Svc. medal with bronze star. Office: Dean of the Faculty U S A F Academy CO 80840

BORN, ETHEL WOLFE, religious writer; b. Kasson, W.Va., Jan. 6, 1924; d. Otto Guy and Nancy Grace (Nestor) Wolfe; m. Harry Edward Born, Apr. 4, 1944 (dec. Aug. 1992); children: Rosemary Ellen (dec.), Barbara Anne Born Craig. Student, Ecumenical Inst., Geneva, 1983; BA, Mary Baldwin Coll., 1991. Author: A Tangled Web--A Search for Answers to the Question of Palestine, 1989, By My Spirit, Methodist Protestant Women in Mission, 1879-1939, 1990, From Memory to Hope, A Narrative History of the Areas of the World Federation of Methodist Women, 2000, Candlesticks, Methodist Women Putting Faith to Work in Virginia; contbr. articles to religious publs. Va. pres. United Meth. Women, 1972-76; bd. dirs. United Meth. Gen. Bd. Global Ministries, N.Y.C., 1976-84, v.p. women's divsn., 1980-84, v.p. com. on relief, 1980-84, Mid. East cons. women's divsn., 1984-88; chmn. N.Am. Coordinating Com. for Non-govtl. Orgns. UN Symposium, N.Y.C., 1986, 87; pres. N.Am. area, asst. world treas. World Fedn. Meth. Women, 1986-91, archivist, 1992-2001; mem. United Meth. Gen. Comm. Christian Unity and Inter-Religious Concerns, N.Y.C., 1988-96; mem. interfaith commn. Nat. Coun. Chs. of Christ, 1996-2000; mem. Pan-Meth. Commn. on Cooperation, 1996-2000. Recipient Stanley S. Kresge award, 1995, John Wesley Disting. Edn. award, 2004. Mem. AAUW (Pioneer Women Breaking Barrier Achieving Positive Change award 2005), Nat. League Am. Pen Women, Nat. Assn. Parliamentarians. Avocation: crafts.

BORN, FRANCES EMMARY HOLLICK, middle school art educator; b. The Philippines, Philippine, July 24, 1948; d. Francis Haas and Wanda Mae (Kirch) Hollick; m. Philip L. Born, Dec. 22, 1973; 1 child, Frank Edward. BS in Edn., No. State Coll., 1970; MEd, U. Tex., El Paso, 1982. Cert. art and lang. arts edn., curriculum and instruction. Art and lang. arts tchr. Grand Junction (Colo.) H.S., 1970-82, East Middle Sch., Grand Junction, 1982—2004; ret., 2004. Judge Asst. Art Exhibits, Grand Junction, 1970-82; art curriculum com. Sch. Dist. #51, Grand Junction, 1988-93. Choir First United Meth. Ch., 1973—. Recipient Colo. Art Edn. Mid. Sch. Tchr. of the Yr., 2004. Mem. NEA, Mesa Valley Edn. Assn. (bldg. rep. 1974-92, area dir. 1991, 92, 94, 95), Colo. Edn. Assn. (del. assembly 1991, 92, 95), Nat. Art Edn. Assn., Colo. Art Edn. Assn., Parent Tchr. Student Assn. (sec. 1994, 95), Delta Kappa Gamma (1st v.p., 2d v.p., pres., scholarship 1982, 83). Democrat. Methodist. Avocations: art, music, writing, reading. Home: 2215 N 13th St Grand Junction CO 81501-4204 Office: East Middle Sch 830 Gunnison Ave Grand Junction CO 81501-3295 Personal E-mail: art2teach2@aol.com.

BORNHOLDT, LAURA ANNA, academic administrator; b. Peoria, Ill., Feb. 11, 1919; d. John and Barbara (Kohl) B. AB, Smith Coll., 1940, MA, 1942; PhD, Yale U., 1945. Asst. prof. history Smith Coll., Northampton, Mass., 1945-52; internat. relations asso. AAUW, Washington, 1952-57; dean Sarah Lawrence Coll., Bronxville, NY, 1957-59; dean women, adj. prof. history U. Pa., Phila., 1959-61; dean coll., prof. history Wellesley (Mass.) Coll., 1961-64; v.p. Danforth Found., St. Louis, 1964-73; sr. program officer Lilly Endowment Inc., Indpls., 1973-76, v.p. for edn., 1976-84; dir. office univ.-sch. rels. U. Chgo., 1984-94. Nat. adv. com. on black higher edn. and black colls. and univs. Dept. Edn., 1977-82; mem. Yale U. Council, 1977-82; emerita life trustee Coll. of Wooster, Ohio, 1967-77; trustee St. Louis U., 1971-75. Recipient Yale U. Wilbur Cross medal, 1976, Smith Coll. Alumnae medal, 1987. Mem.: Phi Beta Kappa. Home: 925 Juniper Pl Bloomington IN 47408-1285

BORNSTEIN, BARBARA MARKEY, psychologist; m. Ronald Bornstein. BS in Comm. Arts, U. Wis., 1974, PhD in Urban Edn., 1986; MA in Ednl. Psychology, Calif. State U., 1978. Nat. cert. sch. psychologist, cert. pub. instrn. Wis. Ad-hoc instr. U. Wis., Milw., 1982—83; psychometrist Milw. Pub. Schs., 1983—85; sch. psychologist Waukesha Sch. Dist., Wis., 1985—88, Nicolet HS, Glendale, Wis., 1991—; psychologist Stress Mgmt. & Mental Healt Clinics, Glendale, 1988—92. Adv. com. Wis. Dept. Pub. Instrn., Wis., 2004—. Exec. bd. mem. Nicolet Chpt. North Shore United Educators, Glendale, 2004—. Mem.: APA, Nat. Assn. Sch. Psychologists, Suburban Sch. Psychologists Assn. (pres. 1995—96), Wis. Sch. Psychologists Assn. (mem. Profl. Practices Com. 1993—96), Phi Delta Kappa. Office Phone: 414-351-7564.

BORNSTEIN, MIMI, writer, social scientist; b. N.Y.C., Sept. 15, 1945; d. Irving and Zelda Zinman Bornstein. BA, CCNY, 1966; MLS, San Jose State U., 1973. Caseworker N.Y.C. Dept. Social Svcs., 1967-71; social scientist Am. Insts. for Rsch., Palo Alto, Calif., 1974—94; cons., ind. scholar, 1974—; poet and playwright, 1976—; freelance writer N.Y.C., 1976-88; founder Renaissance II, N.Y.C., 1991—. Mem.: Acad. Am. Poets, NY Acad. Scis., Mensa. Avocation: cooking. Office Phone: 212-706-9702.

BORNSTEIN, RITA, academic administrator; b. NYC, Jan. 2, 1936; d. Carl and Florence (Gates) Kropf; m. Harland G. Bloland; children from previous marriage: Rachel, Mark, Per. BA in English, Fla. Atlantic U., 1970, MA in English, 1971; PhD in Ednl. Leadership and Instrn., U. Miami, 1975. Tchr., adminstr. Dade County Pub. Schs., Fla., 1971-75; adminstr. dept. edn. U. Miami, Coral Gables, Fla., 1975-81, adminstr. divsn. devel., 1981-85, v.p., 1985-90; pres. Rollins Coll., Winter Park, Fla., 1990—2004, pres. emerita, 2004—. Bd. dirs. tupperware Corp.; cons. in field. Author: (book) Freedom or Order: Must We Choose?, 1976, Title IX Compliance and Sex Equity: Definitions, Distinctions, Costs and Benefits, 1981; contbr. articles to profl. jours., to numerous profl. jours. Recipient George D. and Harriet W. Cornell Chair of Distinguished Presidential Leadership, 2001. Mem.: So. Univ. Conf. (exec. com. 1998—2003, pres. 2001—02), So. Assn. Colls. and Schs. (commn. colls. 1998—2000, exec. coun. 1999—2000, appeals com. 2002—), Ind. Colls. and Univs. of Fla. (coun. pres. 1990—, chair 1997—98), Fla. Coun. of 100, Assoc. Colls. of the South (bd. dirs. 1992—2001, treas.

1993—95, sec. 1995—97, vice chair 1997—99, chair 1999—2001), Nat. Assn. Ind. Colls. and Univs. (bd. dirs. 1992—95, chair govt. rels. com. 1994—95), Am. Coun. on Edn. (com. leadership devel. 1991—93, bd. dirs. 1995—98), Annapolis Group (exec. com. 1999—2001). Office: Rollins Coll Office of Pres 1000 Holt Ave # 2711 Winter Park FL 32789-4499

BOROS, DEBORAH THERESA, elementary school educator; b. Little Falls, Minn., Mar. 26, 1955; d. John Joseph and Elaine Theresa Gau Boros. BS, St. Cloud State U., 1977; MA magna cum laude, St. Mary's U., 1995. Tchr. Pasco County Sch. Bd., Dade City, Fla., 1981—87, Anoka-Hennepin, Coon Rapids, Minn., 1988—. Creator kindergarten sci. curriculum Anoka-Hennepin Dist.; mem. expert panel NSF, 1999—2003; mem. nat. adv. bd. Macmillan/McGraw Hill, 2004—. Parish coun. St. Stephen's Cath. Ch., Anoka; pres. Women of St. Stephen's, Anoka. Named San Antonio Tchr. of Yr., Pasco County Sch. Bd., 1982; recipient Outstanding Contbn. award, Pasco County Libr. Assn., 1985, Presdl. award for excellence in math. and sci. tchg., White Ho., 1998, Exemplary Elem. Sci. Tchr. award, Coun. Elem. Sci. Internat./Ciba Specialty Chem., 2005, Outstanding Educator award, Ctr. for Acad. Excellence WEM, 2005, Assoc. Master Tchr., Fla., 1985, 1986. Mem.: NSTA (assoc.; awards and recognition com. 2004—), ASCD (assoc.), Nat. Coun. of Tchrs. of Math. (assoc.), Minn. Coun. of Tchrs. of Math. (assoc.), Minn. Sci. Tchrs. Assn. (assoc.; elem. metro rep. 1999—2005, Elem. Sci. Tchr. Yr. 1997), Minn. Acad. of Sci. (assoc.), Nat. Sci. Edn. Leadership Assn. (assoc.), Coun. Elem. Sci. Internat. (assoc. Exemplary Elem. Sci. Tchg. 2005), Edn. Minn. (assoc.), Assn. for Childhood Edn. Internat. (assoc.), Minn. Kindergarten Assn. (assoc.), Soc. of Elem. Presdl. Awardees (life; pres. 2004—). Office: Mississippi Elem 10620 Direct River Dr NW Coon Rapids MN 55433 Office Phone: 763-506-3535. Office Fax: 763-506-3503. E-mail: deb.boros@anoka.k12.mn.us.

BOROVICKA, MARSHA LORRAINE, music educator; b. Las Vegas, Nev., July 21, 1951; d. Arlo Fielding and Carrie Graff Beatty; m. Robert L. Borovicka. BA, U. Nev., 1973, MEd, 1979. Music tchr. CCSD/Jo Mackey Elem. Sch., La Vegas, Nev., 1973—75; dir. choral activities CCSD/Basic H.S., Henderson, Nev., 1975—82, CCSD/Cannon Mid. Sch., Las Vegas, Nev., 1983—85, Clark County Sch. Dist./Chaparral H.S., Las Vegas, Nev., 1985—. Choral dir. LDS Ch., Las Vegas, Nev., 1971. Musician (conductor) various choral groups. Named Tchr. of the Yr., Clark County Sch. Dist./Southland Corp., 1991. Mem. Lds Ch. Avocation: golf. Office: Chaparral HS 3850 Annie Oakley Dr Las Vegas NV 89121 Office Phone: 702-799-7580 ext. 4050. Personal E-mail: mlh554@interact.ccsd.net.

BOROWSKI, JENNIFER LUCILE, corporate administrator; b. Jersey City, Oct. 23, 1934; d. Peter Anthony and Ludwika (Zapolska) B. BS, St. Peter's Coll., 1968; postgrad., Pace Coll., 1976-77. Mgr. benefits Amerada Petroleum Corp., N.Y.C., 1951-66, Mt. Sinai Hosp., N.Y.C., 1966-67; mgr. payroll and payroll taxes Haskins & Sells, N.Y.C., 1967—73, Cushman & Wakefield, Inc., N.Y.C., 1973—89. Mem. Am. Payroll Assn. (bd. dirs. 1979-81, cert.), Am. Mgmt. Assn., Am. Soc. Payroll Mgrs., Internat. Platform Assn. (hon.), Am. Soc. Profl. Exec. Women, NAFE. Avocations: golf, opera, boating. Home: 36 Front St North Arlington NJ 07031-5822

BORRA, SUSAN T., dietician, medical association administrator; Grad., U. Md. Dir. health profl. svcs. Dairy Coun. of the Upper Chesapeake Bay, Towson, Md., 1976—83; dir. consumer affairs Food Mktg. Inst., Washington, 1983—93; sr. v.p., dir. nutrition Internat. Food Info. Coun., Washington, 1993—. Lectr. in field; instr. nutrition Anne Arundel C.C., Arnold, Md., 1978—80; mem. subcom. on interpretation and uses of dietary ref. intakes NAS Inst. Medicine. Contbr. articles to profl. jours. Mem. industry nutrition adv. com. Am. Heart Assn., mem. health edn. com. Recipient Pres.'s Cir. for Nutrition Edn. award, Am. Dietetic Assn. and Found., 1985, 1995, honor, Susan T. Borra Nutrition Comms. Fellowship, IFIC Found., 1999. Mem.: Soc. Nutrition Edn. (former chmn. corp. relations com.), Dietitians in Bus. and Comms. and Nutrition Edn. for the Pub., Food and Culinary Profls., D.C. Met. Dietetic Assn. (former recording sec.), Md. Dietetic Assn. (pres., rep. to ADA ho. of dels.), Am. Dietetic Assn. (bd. dirs. 1991—, pres. 2001—02, past chair legis. and pub. policy com.). Office: Internat Food Information Coun 1100 Connecticut Ave NW Ste 430 Washington DC 20036

BORROFF, MARIE, English language educator; b. N.Y.C., Sept. 10, 1923; d. Albert Ramon and Marie (Bergersen) B. Ph.B., U. Chgo., 1943, MA, 1946; PhD, Yale U., 1956. Teaching asst. U. Chgo., 1946-47; instr. dept. English Smith Coll., 1948-51, asst. prof., 1956-59, asso. prof., 1959; vis. asst. prof. English Yale U., 1957-58, vis. asso. prof., 1959-60, asso. prof. English, 1960-65, prof., 1965-71, William Lampson prof., 1971-92, Sterling prof. English, 1992-94; Sterling prof. English emeritus, 1994—; Phi Beta Kappa vis. scholar, 1973-74. Fellow Ezra Stiles Coll., Yale. Author: Sir Gawain and the Green Knight: A Stylistic and Metrical Study, 1962, (with J. B. Bessinger, Jr.); recorded dialogues read in Middle English, 1965, Sir Gawain and the Green Knight: A New Verse Translation, 1967, Pearl: A New Verse Translation, 1977, Language and the Poet: Verbal Artistry in Frost, Stevens, and Moore, 1979, Sir Gawain and the Green Knight, Patience and Pearl: Verse Translations, 2000, Stars and Other Signs: Poems, 2002; essay collection: Traditions and Rewewals Chaucer, the Gawain-Poet, and Beyond, 2003; editor: Wallace Stevens, A Collection of Critical Essays, 1963; videotaped lectures: To Hear Their Voices, Chaucer, Shakespeare and Frost, Assn. of Yale Alumni Great Tchrs. Series, Chapter Headings: Remarks Made at the Annual Initiation Ceremonies of Phi Beta Kappa, Alpha Chapter of Connecticut, 1989-1994, 1996. Bd. Govs. Yale U. Press, 1988-98. Recipient James Billings Fiske poetry prize U. Chgo., 1943; Eunice Tietjens Meml. prize Poetry mag., 1945; Margaret Lee Wiley fellow AAUW, 1955-56; Guggenheim fellow, 1969-70 Fellow Am. Acad. Arts and Scis.; mem. MLA, Acad. Am. Poets, Medieval Acad. Am., Phi Beta Kappa. Home: 311 St Ronan St New Haven CT 06511-2328 Office Phone: 203-432-2233. Business E-Mail: marie.borroff@yale.edu.

BORSCHEL, VALERIE LYNN, medical/surgical nurse; b. Kenmore, N.Y., Sept. 16, 1956; d. Richard N. and Patricia A. (Gowland) Graser; children: Scott Keven, Eric Dennis. BSN, D'Youville Coll., 1977. Staff nurse Roswell Park Meml. Hosp., Buffalo, 1977-84, St. Elizabeth's Hosp., Utica, N.Y., 1984-87; head nurse St. Luke's Meml. Hosp., Utica, 1987-89; staff nurse St. Francis Hosp., Poughkeepsie, NY, 1989—2001; cuurent staff Candler Hosp., Savannah, Ga., 2001—. Project mgr. Nat. Surg. Breast and Bowel Project, 1992-94. Bd. dirs. Am. Cancer Soc., 1993-99. Mem. Oncolog. Nurses Assn. (past pres., treas. Mohawk Valley chpt.). Home: 8903 Ferguson Ave Savannah GA 31406-6364

BORTELL, LINDA LEE, clinical psychologist; b. Harrisburg, Pa., Jan. 25, 1963; d. Joseph Thomas and Ruth Janet (Mengel) B. BA, Ind. U. Pa., 1985; MA, Fairleigh Dickinson U., Morristown, N.J., 1987; PsyD in Psychology, Calif. Sch. Profl. Psychology, 1993. Charge person, psychiat. emergency team Kimball Med. Ctr., Lakewood, N.J., 1988-89; counselor Chabad Rehab., Culver City, Calif., 1989-92; hotline counselor Open Quest Inst., Pasadena, Calif., 1990-91; intern The Switzer Ctr., Torrance, Calif., 1991-92, The Wright Inst., L.A., 1992-93; hotline counselor Child Help USA, Hollywood, Calif., 1991-96; postdoctoral assoc. The Wright Inst., L.A., 1993-94; psychologist Santa Anita Family Svc., Monrovia, Calif., 1993—2003; pvt. practice, 1994—; assoc. prof. Calif. State U., 1996—. Mem. adj. faculty Calif. Sch. Profl. Psychology, Alhambra, 1994-2002; cons. "The Leeza Show", 1996—, Children's Inst. Internat., 1995—; faculty Wright Inst., L.A., 2001—, Healing Hearts Counseling Ctr., 2001-03; bd. dirs. Wright Inst., Rose City Counseling Ctr. Mem. mental health team. ARC, 1996—. Mem. APA, Calif. State Psychol. Assn., Pasadena Area Psychol. Assn., Div. 39 Psychoanalysis, LA County Psychological Assn. (pres. 2004-05, bd. dirs. 2001—). Office: 625 Fair Oaks Ave Ste 270 South Pasadena CA 91030-5801 Office Phone: 626-799-7941. E-mail: lborkilpsyd@sbcglobal.net.

BORYSEWICZ, MARY LOUISE, editor; b. Chgo. d. Thomas J. and Mabel E. (Zeien) O'Farrell m. Daniel S. Borysewicz, June 11, 1955 (dec. 2005); children: Mary Adele, Stephen Francis (dec. 1997), Paul Barnabas. BA, Mundelein Coll., 1970; postgrad. in English lit., U. Ill, 1970—71; grad. exec. program, U. Chgo., 1982. Editor sci. publs. AMA, Chgo., 1971—73; exec. mng. editor Am. Jour. Ophthalmology, Chgo., 1973—95; media cons. Fox-Wahls Design, Chgo., 1999—2004; editl. svc. cons. A.T. Kearney, Chgo., 2004. Asst. sec., treas. Ophthalmic Pub. Co., 1985—95; guest lectr. U. Chgo. Med. Sch., 1979, Harvard U. Med. Sch., 1978, Northwestern U. Med. Sch., 1979, Am. Acad. Ophthalmology, 1976, 81, Northwestern U. Joseph Medill Sch. Journalism, 2002. Editor: Ophthalmology Principles and Concepts, 7th edit., 1992, 8th edit., 1996, Documenta Ophthalmologica History Issue, 1997, 98; contbg. writer Chicago Shops, 2002, 03, 06; contbr. articles to sci. publs. Mem. Coun. Biol. Editors (bd. dirs. 1988-91, fin. com. 1985-88, teller com. 1992-95). Personal E-mail: mbory@aol.com.

BORZIO, STEPHANIE JEAN, secondary school educator; b. Middletown, NY, June 3, 1978; d. Lori Jean and Lawrence Ronald Marshall; m. Matthew Daniel Borzio, Sept. 22, 2001; 1 child, Zachary Matthew. BS in Biology, Bucknell U., Lewisburg, Pa., 2000; M in Edn., Wilkes U., Wilkes-Barre, Pa, 2004. Sci. tchr. Valley Ctrl. HS, Montgomery, NY, 2000—01, Ctrl. Bucks Sch. Dist., Doylestown, Pa., 2001—. Office: Tohickon Mid Sch 5051 Old Easton Rd Doylestown PA 18901

BOSCH, MICHELE C., lawyer; b. Washington, Apr. 29, 1968; BA, U. Va., 1990; JD, Coll. William & Mary, 1993. Bar: Va. 1993, DC 1997, US Patent & Trademark Office. Ptnr. Finnegan, Henderson, Farabow, Garrett & Dunner LLP, Washington, mem. mgmt. com. Mem.: Am. Chem. Soc., Fed. Cir. Bar Assn., DC Bar Assn., Va. Bar Assn., Am. Intellectual Property Assn., ABA. Fluent in French. Office: Finnegan Henderson Farabow Garrett & Dunner LLP 901 New York Ave NW Washington DC 20001-3315 Office Phone: 202-408-4000. Office Fax: 202-408-4400. Business E-Mail: michele.bosch@finnegan.com.

BOSCHOK, JACKIE, labor union administrator; b. Kansas City, Mo., Apr. 24, 1952; d. John and Margaret Robey; m. Alex Boschok, July 30, 1983. Student, Culver Stockton Coll., 1970—71; BS, U. Mo., 1977. Materials facilitator Boeing Comml. Airplane Group, Seattle, 1980—2001; bus. rep. Aerospace Machinists Dist. 751, Seattle, 2001—. Chair labor and trades campaign cabinet Snohomish County United Way, Everett, Wash., 1994—97; mem. Snohomish County chpt. ARC, Everett, 2000—01. Recipient Spirit of Labor award, Snohomish County United Way, 1998; fellow, U. Mo. Columbia Sch. Agr., 1977. Mem.: Snohomish County Labor Coun. (exec. bd. 2000, v.p. 2005), Wash. State Labor Coun. (women's com. 1994—2005), Coalition Labor Union Women (nat. exec. bd. 1991—2005, rec. sec. Puget Sound chpt. 1993—2005). Office: Aerospace Machinists Dist 751 8729 Airport Rd Everett WA 98204 Personal E-mail: jackieboschok@hotmail.com.

BOSCO, MARY BETH, lawyer; b. Jersey City, Feb. 23, 1956; BA cum laude, Yale Univ., 1978; JD with honors, George Washington Univ., 1983. Bar: DC 1983, US Dist. Ct. (ea. Ark., so. Tex., Wyo. dist.), US Ct. Appeals (8th, 10th & Fed. cir.), US Supreme Ct. Ptnr., head Govt. Contracts & Fed. Marketing practices, mem. mgmt. com. Patton Boggs LLP, Washington. Contbr. articles to profl. jours.; author (contributing): Environ. Law Handbook, 1994. Mem.: ABA. Office: Patton Boggs LLP 2550 M St NW Washington DC 20037-1350 Office Phone: 202-457-6420. Office Fax: 202-457-6315. Business E-Mail: mbbosco@pattonboggs.com.

BOSDELL, MELONY, special education educator; b. Prosperity, S.C., Apr. 22, 1958; d. Jacob Frank and Janie Blondell Bickley; m. Francis Alvin Bosdell Jr., Oct. 17, 1981; children: Francis Alvin III, Martina Lee, Melony Danielle. BA in Edn. cum laude, Clemson U., 1979, M in Reading, 1981. Tchr. educable mentally retarded Palmetto Mid. Sch., Williamston, S.C., 1981-82; tchr. trainable mentally retarded, 5th grade Lexington (S.C.) Intermediate Sch., 1982-86; tchr. educable mentally retarded Johnsonville (S.C.) Elem. Sch., 1986; tchr. trainable mentally retarded Pee Dee Regional Ctr., Florence, S.C., 1987, New Kent (Va.) Primary Sch., 1989-92; tchr. elem. emotionally disturbed Va. Randolph Spl. Edn. Ctr., Glen Allen, Va., 1998—. Lutheran. Home: 9133 Epps Rd Mechanicsville VA 23111-6018 Office: Va Randolph Spl Edn Ctr 2206 Mountain Rd Glen Allen VA 23060-2232 E-mail: bosdell@juno.com.

BOSE, MEENA, political science professor; b. Pitts., June 30, 1970; d. Nirmal Kumar and Chandra Bose; m. Colin Churchill Barr, Aug. 7, 1994. BA, Pa. State U., 1990; MA, Princeton U., 1992, PhD in Politics, 1996. Asst. prof. polit. sci. Hofstra U., Hempstead, NY, 1996—2000, acting dir. Honors Program, 1999—2000, Peter S. Kalikow Chair for Presdl. Studies, 2006—; asst. prof. polit. sci. US Mil. Acad., West Point, NY, 2000—01, assoc. prof., 2001—06, dir. Am. Politics Program. Commentator The NewsHour with Jim Lehrer, Rep. Nat. Convention, NYC, 2004. Author: Shaping and Signaling Presidential Policy: The National Security Decision Making of Eisenhower and Kennedy, 1998; co-editor: From Cold War to New World Order: The Foreign Policy of George H.W. Bush, 2002, Making the Grade: Uses and Abuses of Presidential Ratings, 2003. Non-resident fellow, Centre for Pub. Mgmt., Brookings Inst., 1996—97. Mem.: Am. Polit. Sci. Assn. Office: Hofstra U Peter S Kalikow Ctr for Study of Am Pres Hempstead NY 11549-1000*

BOSE, MICHELLE DENISE, secondary school educator; b. Conroe, Tex., Mar. 10, 1982; d. Stephen Craig and Melissa Gale Byrd; m. Jason Robinson Bose, Jan. 15, 2002; children: Madison Michelle, McKenzie Carter. BS in Math., U. Tex. Permian Basin, Odessa, 2003. Cert. tchr. Tex., 2003. Algebra 1 tchr. Midland (Tex.) Freshman H.S., 2004—. Bldg. coord. Stonegate Fellowship, Midland, 2003—06. Republican. Baptist. Office Phone: 432-689-1200.

BOSHIER, MAUREEN LOUISE, health facilities administrator; b. Elizabeth, N.J., Oct. 1, 1946; d. John Henry and Mary Hanora (McGarry) B.; m. Robert Hall Rea, May 23, 1987. BSN, Coll. Misericordia, Dallas, Pa., 1968; MS in Psychiat. Nursing, U. Colo., 1973; MBA, U. Phoenix, 1987. Cert. healthcare exec. Clin. specialist psychiat. nursing Denver Gen. Hosp., 1973-74; dir. rehab. svcs. N.Mex. Cancer Control, Albuquerque, 1976-80; exec. dir. N.Mex. State Bd. Nursing, Albuquerque, 1980-84; exec. v.p. N.Mex. Hosp. Assn., Albuquerque, 1984-88; adminstr. surg. svcs., sr. nursing adminstr. U. N.Mex. Hosp., Albuquerque, 1988-94; CEO, pres. N.Mex. Hosps. and Health Sys. Assn., Albuquerque, 1994—2004; v.p. op. E. Va. Med. Sch., 2006—. Dir. Profl. Seminar Cons., Inc., Albuquerque, 1982—; v.p. exec. bd. N.Mex. Health Resources, Albuquerque, 1981—, pres., 1989; vice chmn., bd. dirs. Hosp. Home Health Care, Albuquerque, 1978—; dir. Acad. Seminars, Inc., 1982—; mem. governing coun. for small and rural hosps. Am. Hosp. Assn., 1996—, women's dir. devel. program Kellogg Sch. Mgmt. Ctr. for Exec. Devel., 2003. Mem. adv. bd. N.Mex. Bus. Jour., 1995—; contbr. articles to profl. jours. Sec. N.Mex. Ballet Co., Albuquerque, 1982-87; vice chmn. Gov.'s Task Force on Nursing Issues, Albuquerque, 1982-88; adv. bd. Sub-area Coun. Health Sys., Albuquerque, 1980-84; mem. Leadership N.Mex. Class of 2000, alumni com. 2001—. Capt. U.S. Army, 1967-71. Recipient Woman on the Move award YWCA, 1992, Wharton Sch. of Bus. fellowship for health care execs., 1993, Gov.'s award for Outstanding N.Mex. Woman, 1997, Frank Gabriel award for outstanding achievement N.Mex. Hosps. and Health Sys., 2004; named Nurse of Yr., March of Dimes, 2002; fellow Johnson & Johnson, 1993 Mem. Am. Orgn. Nurse Execs. (vice chmn. legis. advocacy com. 1992-94, chmn. 1993-94), Am. Coll. Healthcare Execs. (diplomate, Regent's award 2000), N.Mex. Orgn. Nurse Execs. (treas. 1988-89, pres. 1990), N.Mex. League for Nursing, N.Mex. Nurses Assn. (Nurse Adminstr. award 1984), The N.Mex. Hosps. and Health Systems Assn. (Frank Gabriel award 2004), Rotary (Albuquerque bd. dirs. 2001—), Albuquerque C. of C. (mem. quality of life com. 1994—), Sigma Theta Tau (pres.-elect 1994, pres. 1995—, Mentor award Gamma Sigma chpt. 1994). Democrat. Avocations: music, dance, travel. Home: 375 Middle St Portsmouth VA 23704

BOSKIN, CLAIRE, psychotherapist, educator; b. Bklyn., Apr. 25, 1933; d. Benjamin and Frieda (Brofman) G.; m. Joseph Boskin, Aug. 5, 1955 (div. Feb. 1982); children: Julie Lise, Lori Kem, Deborah Jo. BA, Bklyn. Coll., 1956; MSW, U. Minn., 1959. Tchr. Ctr. for Tng. U. So. Calif., L.A., 1965—69; program developer, trainer Dept. Urban Affairs UCLA, 1962—65; pvt. practice spiritually oriented tchg. and counseling Chestnut Hill, Mass., 1973—. Ptnr. Stan 2 Selib, 1992. Avocations: choral singing, photography, gardening. Office: 18 Quincy Rd Chestnut Hill MA 02467-3935 E-mail: clairebenf@aol.com.

BOSLEY, KAREN LEE, language educator, communications educator; b. Beech Grove, Ind., Sept. 23, 1942; d. Lowell Holmes and Kathryn Gertrude (Drake) Foley; m. Norman Keith Bosley, Dec. 21, 1964; children: Mark Harold, Rachael Kathryn, Keith Lowell, Sidney Clark. AB in Lang. Arts summa cum laude, U. Indpls., 1965; MA in English, Northwestern U., 1967; MA in Journalism, Ball State U., 1984; postgrad. (Newspaper Fund fellow), U. Mo., 1973; postgrad., Ohio U., 1977. Copy editor, reporter Indpls. News, 1963-65; English tchr., yearbook adviser Beech Grove (Ind.) Jr. H.S., 1965-66; English tchr. So. Regional H.S., Manahawkin, N.J., 1967-68; prof. humanities, journalism, and English Ocean County Coll., Toms River, N.J., 1971—, student newspaper adviser, 1971—, yearbook adviser, 1999—. Part-time reporter Daily Times-Observer, Toms River, 1972—77, part-time copy editor, 1993. Contbr. articles to publs. in field. Trustee Long Beach Island Hist. Assn., Friends of Island Libr., 1975-79; pres. Long Beach I PTA; chmn. Long Beach Twp. Dem. Mcpl. Com., 1971-78; Dem. committeeman Long Beach Twp. Dist. 2, 1971-78, 85—; mem. Long Beach Twp. Recreation Commn., 1972-75; bd. dirs. Ocean County Red Cross, 1972-78, Ocean County Family Planning, Inc., 1972-78, bd. dirs. Student Press Law Ctr., 1987-2002, sec., 1998-2000, mem. adv. coun., 2002—; chmn. Cub Scout pack 32, Ocean County Coun. Boy Scouts Am.; founder, bd. dirs. Long Beach I Hist. Assn., Island Dems., Inc.; mem. adminstrv. bd. First United Meth. Ch. Beach Haven Terrace (N.J.); So. Regional H.S. Band Parent Orgn., 1995-96, pres., 1996-97, corr. sec; So. Regional Jazz Band Parents Assn., charter mem., 2001—. Mem. AAUW (pres., dir. Barnegat Light Area br.), NEA, N.J. Edn. Assn., Ocean County Edn. Assn., Faculty Assn. Ocean County Coll. (v.p. 1984-85), Coll. Media Advisers, Inc. (disting. newspaper adviser for U.S. 2-yr. colls. 1978, dir., sec.), Assn. Edn. in Journalism and Mass Comms., C.C. Journalism Assn. (dir., v.p.), Soc. Profl. Journalists, Internat. Platform Assn., Sigma Delta Chi. Home: 9 E Old Whaling Ln Long Beach Township NJ 08008-2930 Office: Ocean CC PO Box 2001 College Dr Toms River NJ 08754-2001 Office Phone: 732-255-0400 ext 2237. E-mail: kbosley@mac.com.

BOSLEY, VALERIE LYNNE, elementary school educator; b. Clarksville, Tenn., Nov. 6, 1967; d. William and Georgia Bosley. BS in Edn., Austin Peay State U., Clarksville, Tenn., 1990. Cert. tchr. Tenn., 2004. Ins. clk. Nebben Chiropractic Ctr., Clarksville, Tenn., 2002—04; tchr. CMCSS, Clarksville, Tenn., 2004—. Mem.: Tenn. Edn. Assn. Office Phone: 931-648-5620. Personal E-mail: vbosley@hotmail.com.

BOSNIAK, KANTA, artist; b. Phila., June 22, 1950; d. Richard Dengler and Dorothy Geraldine Stine; m. Murray Eli Bosniak; 1 child, Joshua Joseph. Student, U. Pa.; DD, Omega U., 2003, PhD in hypnotherapy, 2004. Ordained to ministry Sanctuary of the Beloved, 1990; cert. clinical hypnotherapist N.Eng. Inst. Hypnotherapy, 2002, hypnosis trainer Nat. Assn. Transpersonal Hypnotherapists, 2005, impaired childbirth Holistic Healing Ctr., Chestnut Ridge, N.Y., 2005, hypnosis trainer Nat. Assn. Transgressional Hypnosis, 2005. Artist-in-residence Omega Inst. for Holistic Studies, Rhinebeck, NY, 1999, 2000. Founder, dir. Alpha Learning Inst., Floyd, Va., 2003. Contbg. artist Beautiful Necessity: The Art and Meaning of Women's Altars, 1999; exhibited in solo shows at Urban Artware, Winston-Salem, Omega Inst., Heritage Ctr., Virginia Beach, Assn. for Rsch. and Enlightenment, U. N.C., Wilmington, Blue Ridge Pub. TV, Wilmington, NC, NC Public Radio, others; contbr. articles to Magical Blend Mag., Studies in Edn., Point of Light and Sagewoman Mag.; slide show Blue Ridge Pub. TV, 2005-presenter workshops in churches, healing ctrs., alternative ednl. instns., pub. and pvt. ednl. schs. Recipient Walter E. Brackelmann's award for Extraordinary Dedication, Assn. of Advanced Ethical Hypnosis, 2005. Avocations: film studies, screenwriting mystery and suspense books. Office: Alpha Learning Inst PO Box 777 Floyd VA 24091-0777 Office Phone: 540-745-3335. Personal E-mail: info@alphalearninginstitute.com.

BOSQUEZ, JOY DENISE, elementary school educator; b. New Braunfels, Tex., May 20, 1972; d. Harold William and Kathleen Marie Buck; m. Frank Bosquez, July 31, 1999; children: Seth, Simon. BS in Interdisciplinary Studies, SW Tex. State U., San Marcos, 1995. Tchr. music Carrillo Elem., San Antonio, 1995—97, tchr. 1st grad, 1997—99, tchr. 2d grade, 1999—2001, tchr. 1st grade, 2001—02, tchr. kindergarten, 2002—03, tchr. 1st grade, 2003—04; tchr. music Kindred Elem., San Antonio, 2004—. Workshop South San Antonio Ind. Sch. Dist., 2003. Dir.: (ballet with 150 K-5th grade students) The Nutcracker. Mem.: Am. Orff-Schulwerk Assoc. Avocation: cake decorating. Office: Kindred Elem 7811 Kindred Rd San Antonio TX 78224 Office Phone: 210-977-7575. E-mail: jbosquez@southsanisd.net.

BOSS, AMELIA HELEN, lawyer, educator; b. Balt., Apr. 3, 1949; d. Myron Theodore and Loretta (Oakjones) B.; m. Roger S. Clark, Mar. 3, 1979; children: Melissa, Seymour, Edward, Ashley. Student, Oxford (Eng.) U., 1968; BA in Sociology, Bryn Mawr, 1970; JD, Rutgers U., 1975. Bar: N.J, Pa., U.S. Dist. Ct. (ea. dist.) N.J., U.S. Dist. Ct. (ea. dist.) Pa., U.S. Supreme Ct., U.S. Ct. Appeals (3d cir.). Law clk. Hon. Milton B. Cranford N.J. Supreme Ct., 1975-76; assoc. Pepper, Hamilton & Scheetz, Phila., 1976-78; assoc. prof. law Rutgers U. Sch. Law, Camden, NJ, 1983-87, Temple U., Phila., 1989-91; prof. law Temple U. Sch. Law, Phila., 1991—, Charles Klein prof. law, 1999—. Vis. prof. law U. Miami Sch. Law, Coral Gables, Fla., 1985—86; Leo Goodwin disting. vis. prof. law Nova U., Sch. Law, 1998; mem. coms. Nat. Conf. Commrs. on Uniform State Laws; U.S. rep. to UN Commn. on Internat. Trade Law; dir. Inst. for Internat. Law and Pub. Policy, 2001—. Author: (books) Electronic Data Interchange Agreements: A Guide and Sourcebook, 1993, ABCs of the UCC: Article 2A, ABCs of the UCC: Article 5; editor-in-chief The Data Law Report, 1993-97, The Business Lawyer, 1998-99, ABCs of the UCC; mem. permanent editl. bd. Uniform Comml. Code; contbr. articles to profl. jours. Named among top 50 women lawyers in U.S. Nat. Law Jour., 1998. Fellow Am. Bar Found.; mem. ABA (chmn. bus. law sect. 2000-01, chmn. sect. officers conf. 2001—), Internat. Bar Assn., Am. Law Inst. (coun. 2000—), Am. Bankruptcy Inst., Am. Coll. Comml. Fin. Lawyers, Nat. Assn. Women Lawyers. Home: 309 Westmont Ave Haddonfield NJ 08033-1714 Office: Temple U Sch Law 1719 N Broad St Philadelphia PA 19122-6002 Office Phone: 215-204-8947.

BOSS, MARYLIN JEANETTE, elementary school educator; b. Gooding, Idaho, Nov. 11, 1949; d. Don Raymond and Mary Lillian Bauscher; m. Charles Edward Boss, Mar. 22, 1987; 1 child, Jason Job. BA in Elem. Edn., Albertsons Coll. Idaho, Caldwell, 1972. Cert. elem. tchr. Idaho. Tchr. 2d grade Elem. Pub. Sch., Gooding, 1972—76, tchr. phys. edn. Fulton, 1978, tchr. kindergarten, 1979, 1979—80; tchr. combined first and second grade Cath. Sch., Trinidad, Colo., 1984—85; tchr. fifth grade Elem. Pub. Sch., Hollister, Idaho, 1985—86, tchr. second grade Filer, Idaho, 1986—87, tchr. third grade Hollister, Idaho, 1987—89; tchr. kindergarten Agape Christian Sch., Twin Falls, 1995—96, tchr. 2d grade, 1996—97; tchr. kindergarten-8th grade Three Creek Sch., Rogerson, Idaho, 2003—. Governess Pvt. Family, Mt. Caroll, Ill., 1980—82; substitute tchr. in Wash., Ill. and Iowa Kindergarten-Twelfth Grades in various Pub. Schools, 1976—79, substitue tchr., Colo., 1983—84; substitute tchr. Kindergarten-Sixth Grades in various Pub. Schools, Idaho, 1993—95; tutor Labor Camp, Marsing, Idaho, 1968—72. Supporter and vol. helper DAV, 1995—2006. Named Super Servant of yr., Cornorstone Bapt.

Ch., 1994. Mem.: Idaho Farm Bur. (assoc.), NRA (assoc.), Twin Falls Bridge Club (life). Republican. Baptist. Avocations: bridge, visiting and helping the elderly, travel, collecting readings. Home: 2341 US Highway 93 Twin Falls ID 83301 Office: Three Creek School 49909 Three Creek Road Rogerson ID 83302

BOSSE, MARGARET FISHER ISHLER, education educator; b. Bellefonte, Pa., Oct. 19, 1934; d. Fred Raymond Fisher and Margaret (Hoffmeister) Fisher Hess; m. Richard Eves Ishler, Dec. 27, 1956 (div. June 1978); children: Frederick, Theodore; m. Richard C. Bosse, June 26, 1999. BA in English Edn., Pa. State U., 1956, MA in English, 1960; EdD, U. Toledo, 1972. English tchr. Bald Eagle (Pa.) H.S., 1956-57, Marion (N.Y.) Ctrl. Sch., 1957-59, York (Pa.) Suburban H.S., 1959-60; adj. instr. English Pa. State U., York, 1962-64; instr. York Coll., 1964-65; adj. inst. English U. Toledo, 1966-68, grad. asst., 1968-71; from asst. prof. to prof. Bowling Green (Ohio) State U., 1972-90, dir. field experiences and stds. compliance, 1985-90; head dept. curriculum and instrn., prof. U. No. Iowa, Cedar Falls, 1990-96, prof. curriculum and devel., 1997-2000, acting dir, teacher edn., 1998-99, prof. emeritus, 2000—. Mem. Nat. Coun. for Accreditation of Tchr. Edn. Bd. Examiners, 1998—. Co-author: Creating the Open Classroom, 1974, Teaching in a Competency-Based Program, 1977, Dynamics of Effective Teaching, 5th edit., 2003; contbr. articles to profl. jours. Bd. dirs. Wittenberg (Ohio) U., 1984-86, Luth. Student Chapel, Bowling Green, 1988-91, Ohio Luth. Campus Ministry, Columbus, 1986-87, Christian Cmty. Devel. Bd., Waterloo, Iowa, 1992-96. Recipient Christa McAuliff Showcase for Excellence award, 1990. Mem.: Iowa Assn. Tchr. Educators (pres. 1992—94), Ohio Assn. Tchr. Educators (exec. sec. 1980—87, pres. 1982, Disting. Educator 1982), Am. Assn. Colls. Tchr. Edn. (rep. 1985—, cons. 2000—), Assn. Tchr. Educators (nat. pres. 1996—97, named One of 70 Top Tchr. Educators 1990), Mortar Board, Phi Gamma Mu, Pi Lambda Theta, Phi Kappa Phi. Avocations: travel, golf, poetry. E-mail: mishlerbosse@msn.com.

BOSSERT, JILL AUDREY, author; b. NYC, Aug. 10, 1949; d. William Thomas and Audrey Anthony (Blum) B. AA, Am. U., Paris, 1971; BA magna cum laude, NYU, 1994; MFA, Columbia U., 1997. Assoc. pub. Madison Sq. Press, N.Y.C., 1985-92; editor Rotovision, Switzerland, 1991—97. Cons. Schutz & Co. Fine Art, N.Y.C. and Greenwich, Conn., 1992-2005, Winter Antiques Show, 2003— Author: Pro-Illustration Series vol. 1, 1997, vol. 2, 1998, John LaGatta, An Artist's Life, 2000, Mark English, 2003, Fred Otnes Collage Paintings, 2003, Malcom Liepke, 2005, short stories. Vol. Mark Green for Mayor, N.Y.C., 1994. Philip Guston fellow Columbia U., 1996; named Herbert C. Jaffa Alumni, NYU, 1994. Mem. AAUW, Soc. Illustrators (citations of merit 1992-2005, Dean Cornwell award 2006), Alpha Sigma Lambda Home: 52 Garden Pl Brooklyn NY 11201

BOSSUAT, JUDY WEIGERT, music educator; d. Edward Raymond and Edith Mabel Weigert; m. Christophe Raphael Louis Bossuat, Nov. 13, 1978 (div. June 27, 1994); 1 child, Joshua Edward Joseph. MusB magna cum laude, SUNY, Potsdam, 1975; M in Suzuki Method Pedagogy, Talent Edn. Inst., Matsumoto, Japan, 1978, postgrad., 1982. Eminence tchr. credential Calif. Suzuki violin tchr. Potsdam Suzuki Talent Edn., 1973—77; dir., tchr., condr., tchr. trainer Ecole de Musique Suzuki de Lyon, Lyon, France, 1978—94; lectr. music edn. U. of the Pacific, Stockton, Calif., 1994—2005; dir., tchr. Bossuat Music Sch., Stockton, 1994—2005; string tchr. Pacific Sch., Lincoln Unified Sch. Dist., Stockton, 1995—2000; lectr. music edn. master tchr. String Project Calif. State U., Sacramento, 2002—05; instr. string pedagogy, dir. Cmty. Music Inst. U. Oreg., Eugene, 2005—. Founding mem., bd. dirs. European Suzuki Assn., 1979—94, Fedn. Musical Suzuki de France, 1980—94; v.p. Assn. Ecoles Musique Rhone, Lyon, 1984—90; European violin-viola rep. Internat. Suzuki Assn., Dallas, 1992—93; condr. Ctrl. Valley Youth Symphony Jr. Strings, 2004—05; presenter in field. Author: Learning to Read Music for the Violin, 1991, Exercises for Left Hand Devel., 2000, 2d edit., 2003, composer; contbr. articles to profl. jours. Recipient medal of honor for exceptional contbn. to edn., Nat. Assembly France, 1983, medals of the city, Marseille, France, 1983, Lyon, France, 1986, Duluth, Minn., 1993, 1st prize, Regional Youth Orch. Competition, France, 1993, 2d prize, 1994. Mem.: Music Educators Nat. Conf. (Calif. Bay sect. orch. rep. 2001—02), Oreg. Music Educators Assn., European Suzuki Assn. (hon. life), Fedn. Musical Suzuki de France (hon. life), Suzuki Assn. Ams. (Suzuki method tchr. trainer), Am. String Tchrs. Assn. (Calif. state pres. 2003—05, nat. bd. 2006—). Office: U Oreg Cmty Music Inst 1225 University of Oregon Eugene OR 97403-5693 Office Phone: 541-346-5694. Business E-Mail: jbossuat@uoregon.edu.

BOST, JANE MORGAN, psychologist; b. Corpus Christi, Aug. 20, 1953; d. Clayton Aquilla and Eleanor (Hoving) M.; m. David Edward Bost, June 16, 1984; children: Christopher David, Morgan Jane. BS, Okla. State U., 1976, MS, 1980, PhD, 1984. English tchr. Perry High Sch., Okla., 1976-78; acad. advisor Okla. State U., Stillwater, 1980-82, staff therapist, 1982-83; counseling psychology intern Tex. A&M U., College Station, 1983-84; dir. counseling svcs. Southwestern U., Georgetown, Tex., 1984-92; asst. dir. counseling and mental health ctr. U Tex., Austin, 1992-98, assoc. dir. counseling and mental health ctr., 1998—. Contbr. articles to profl. jours. Mem. collegue status faculty Creative Problem Solving Inst., Buffalo, 1985-86, 88, 91, 92, 93, 94. Named Outstanding Young Women of Am., 1988, 91 Merit award for Outstanding Staff, U. Tex. Parents Assn., 2003-04; grantee Combat Violence against Woman on Campus, U.S. Dept. Justice, 2000, 02, 05. Mem. APA, Am. Coll. Pers. Assn., Tex. Psychol. Assn., Nat. Register Health Service Providers in Psychology. Methodist. Avocations: hiking, photograph, reading, artwork, gardening. Office: U Tex Counseling & Mental Health Ctr Austin TX 78712

BOSTON, BETTY LEE, investment company executive, financial consultant, financial planner; b. Agana, Guam, Dec. 21, 1935; d. Homer Laurence and Bessie Margarete (Leech) Litzenberg; m. Filibert Roth Boston, Aug. 12, 1956; children: William Litzenberg, Beth Boston Tedesco, Brent Litzenberg. BA, U. Mich., Ann Arbor, 1958. CFP®. Stockbroker I.M. Simon & Co., Murray, Ky., 1976—78, 1st of Mich. Corp., Murray, Ky., 1978—86; fin. cons. J.J.B. Hilliard, W.L. Lyons, Inc., Murray, Ky., 1986—; v.p. Hilliard Lyons Inc., Murray, Ky., 1998—. Instr. adult edn. investment classes Murray State U., 1977—2000; investment commentaror Sta. WKMS, Murray, 1987—2006. Author: (fin. columnist) Murray Ledger and Times, 2000—06. Chmn. Inter-Faith Coalition Congregations, Ann Arbor, 1971-73; pres. Need Line Ch. and Cmty. Ministry, Murray, 1981-83; mem. Murray regional bd. Ky. Coun. on Econ. Edn., 1987—. Recipient Woman of Yr. award, Murray Bus. and Profl. Women, 1988. Mem. AAUW (treas. Murray br. 1982-87, pres. 1991-97), Rotary (sec. Murray club 1990-95, pres. 1998-99, Paul Harris fellow). United Methodist. Home: 917 N 16th St Murray KY 42071-1523 Office: JJB Hilliard WL Lyons Inc 414 Main St Murray KY 42071-2059

BOSTON, BILLIE, costume designer, costume history educator; b. Oklahoma City, Sept. 22, 1939; d. William Barrett and Margaret Emeline (Townsend) Long; m. William Clayton Boston, Jr., Jan. 20, 1962; children: Kathryn Gray, William Clayton III. BFA, U. Okla., 1961, MFA, 1962. Asst. to designer Karinski of N.Y., N.Y.C., 1966-67; prof. costume history Oklahoma City U., 1987—. Rep. Arts Coun., Oklahoma City, 1987-90, Arts Festival, Oklahoma City, 1972-80; dir. ETC Theater, Oklahoma City SW Coll., 1979-83; actress Lyric Theatre, Oklahoma City, 1979-81; designer Casa Mahara Theatre, Ft. Worth, 1998. Exhibited in group shows at Taos, N.Mex., Santa Fe; represented in permanent collections in Dallas, Taos, Santa Fe, Tulsa, N.Y.C., La Jolla; costume designer Ballet Okla., Oklahoma City, 1979-84, Agnes DeMillie's Rodeo Ballet Okla., 1982, Royal Ballet Flanders, 1983, Pitts. Ballet, 1983, BBC's Childrens Prodn., 1984, 86, Lyric Theatre, Oklahoma City, 1987-95, Red Oak Music Theatre, Lakewood, N.J., 1988, Winter Olympics, 1988, Miss Am. Pageant, 1988, for JoAnne Worley in Hello Dolly, San Francisco Opera Circus, 1991, Jupiter (Fla.) Theatre, 1991-92, Mobile (Ala.) Light Opera, 1992, The Boy Friend, Temple U., Japan, 1995, The Sound of Music, Lyric Stage, Dallas, 1995, Annie Get Your Gun, Guys and Dolls with Vic Damone, 1995, Westbury Flash Valley Forge Music Fair, Oklahoma and Sound of Music, Casa Manana, Theatre, Ft. Worth, 1997, Singing in the Rain, Lone Star Theatre, Galveston, Tex., 1997, Most Happy Fellow, Lyric Stage Dallas, 1997, To Gillian on her 37th Birthday, Watertower Theatre, Dallas, 1998, Carousel, Annie Get Your Gun, Cinderella, Casa Manana, 1998; designer Titanic, Irving, Tex., 2003, Specture Bridegroom, Irving, 2003, Opal, Lyric Stage, Irving, 2003; designer (play) Finian's Rainbow, Lyric Stage, Dallas, Tex., 2004, Ragtime, Lyric Stage, 2004 (Leon Rabin award costume design, 2005). Rep. Speakers Bur. Oklahoma City for Ballet, 1979-85; judge State Hist. Speech Tournament, Oklahoma City, 1985-87; chmn. State of Okla. Conf. on Tchr./Student Relationships, Oklahoma City, 1981. Recipient Gov.'s Achievement award, 1988, Lady in the News award, 1987; Excellence in Costume Design award Kennedy Ctr. Am. Coll. Theatre Festival XXXIV, 2001, Leon Rubin Costume Design award Dallas Theatre League, 2005. Mem. Alpha Chi Omega (house corp. bd. 1986-90). Methodist. Avocation: watercolorist. Home: 1701 Camden Way Oklahoma City OK 73116-5121 Office Phone: 405-521-5050. E-mail: bboston@okcu.edu.

BOSTON, LORRAINE, bank executive; Joined Kennebunk Savings Bank, Maine, 1992, exec. v.p. Comml. Svcs. Maine, 2002—. Mem. So. Maine Econ. Devel. Dist.'s Revolving Loan Com. Bd. dirs. York Hosp.; mem. York County CC Found. Bd. Named Fin. Svcs. Champion of Yr., US Small Bus. Assn., 2005. Office: Kennebunk Savings Bank 104 Main St PO Box 28 Kennebunk ME 04043-0028 Office Phone: 207-985-4903. E-mail: Lorraine.Boston@kennebunksavings.com.

BOSTON, PENELOPE J., science educator, researcher; BS, MS, PhD, U. Colo. Rsch. assoc. prof., cave and karst sci. N. Mex Tech., Socorro, N.Mex.; dir., cave and karst studies program N.Mex. Inst. Mining and Technology, Socorro, N.Mex. Contbr. articles to profl. jours. Explored the Lechuguilla cave in New Mexico at 1,567 feet down the deepest limestone cave in the US; lived for two weeks with five other chambernauts in a self-contained 24 foot capsule in the Utah desert to simulate working conditions on Mars. Office: Dept Earth & Environ Sci MSEC 346 New Mexico Tech 801 Leroy Place Socorro NM 87801 Office Fax: 505-835-5657. Business E-Mail: pboston@nmt.edu.

BOSTROM, SUSAN L., marketing executive; b. 1960; 3 children. BS, U. Ill.; MBA, Stanford U. Acct. exec. AT&T Corp., 1982; with McKinsey & Co., Nat. Semiconductor; sr. v.p. global mktg. and strategic planning FTP Software; with Cisco Systems, Inc., San Jose, Calif., 1997—, v.p. Internet bus. solutions, 1998—2000, sr. v.p., 2000—06, sr. v.p., chief mktg. officer worldwide govt. affairs, 2006—. Exec. sponsor women's initiative Cisco Systems, Inc., 2001—04. Bd. dirs. Varian Med. Systems, 2004—, Stanford Hospitals and Clinics; mem. adv. bd. Stanford Inst. Econ. Policy Rsch. Office: Cisco Systems Inc 170 W Tasman Dr San Jose CA 95134*

BOSWELL, MARTHA LEE, elementary school educator; b. Lynchburg, Va., Dec. 30, 1945; d. Robert Terrell and Annette Foote (Judd) Lee; m. John Smith Boswell Jr., Aug. 14, 1965; children: Anna-Carter, Amanda-Lee, J. Smith III. BA in Botany, U. So. Fla., 1967; MS in Microbiology, Clemson U., 1971. Cert. secondary sci. tchr., S.C. Tchr. various middle schs., S.C., 1967-74; instr. N.W. Miss. Jr. Coll., Senatobia, 1981-82, U. S.C.-Salkehatchie, Allendale, 1982-83; tchr. Clarendon Dist. Two, Manning, S.C., 1984—. Recipient Presdl. award for excellence in sci. tchg. Nat. Sci. Tchrs. Assn. and NSF, Washington, 1994-95. Methodist. Avocations: environmental education, travel, canoeing. Office: Manning Mid Sch Hwy 261 W Manning SC 29102

BOSWELL, VIVIAN NICHOLSON, protective services official; b. Brewton, Ala., Mar. 27, 1950; d. Nathaniel Irving Nicholson, Ethel Mae Nicholson; m. Leonard Boswell, Jan. 30, 1981. BA in Sociology, Stillman Coll., 1972. Correctional officer D.C. Dept. Corrections, Washington, 1973—2000. Recipient award of excellence, 9-5 Working Women's Assn., 1997, Lifetime Achievement award, 9 to 5 Working Women, 2002. Mem.: Mothers Against Drunk Driving, AARP, NAACP, Women's World Peace Family, Working Women's Assn., Am. Assn. Retired Persons, Harriet Tubman Assn., Diabetic Assn. Democrat. Baptist. Avocations: singing, art, mentoring, cooking, philantropic activities.

BOSWORTH, KATE, actress; b. L.A., Jan. 2, 1983; Actor: (films) The Horse Whisperer, 1998, Remember the Titans, 2000, The Newcomers, 2000, Blue Crush, 2002, The Rules of Attraction, 2002, Wonderland, 2003, Advantage Hart, 2003, Win a Date with Tad Hamilton, 2004, Beyond the Sea, 2004, Bee Season, 2005, Superman Returns, 2006; (TV series) Young Americans, 2000. Mem.: Nat. Honor Soc. Office: United Talent Agy 5th Fl 9560 Wilshire Blvd Beverly Hills CA 90212*

BOSWORTH, MARY JANE, retired music educator; d. Millard William and Dorothy Kimball Bosworth. BS in Edn., Castleton State Coll., Vt., 1966; Diploma, Kodaly Mus. Tng. Inst., Wellesley, Mass., 1975. Cert. tchr. Mass., Vt., N.Y. Elem. music tchr. Addison-Rutland Dist., Fair Haven, Vt., 1966—67, Green St. Sch., Cazenovia, NY, 1967—72, Sherborn Sch., Mass., 1975—76, Town of Rockingham, Bellows Falls, Vt., 1977—2003. Elem. choral dir. Madison County Music Assn., Madison, NY, 1969; handbell dir. Saxtons River Ringers, Vt., 1990—. Treas. Kodaly in Keene, NH, 1985—2006; sec.-treas. Saxtons River Hist. Soc., 1997—. Mem.: Orgn. of Am. Kodaly Educators (treas. 1985—2006), Am. Guild English Handbell Ringers (treas. 2001—). Home: PO Box 265 18 Clark Ct Ext Saxtons River VT 05154

BOTKA, BETSY JEAN, industrial arts and career awareness instructor; b. Freeport, NY, Nov. 25, 1956; d. Herman and Ruth Bender Rubenstein; m. Brian Joseph Botka, Aug. 19, 1999. BA, Trenton State Coll., Ewing Twp., NJ, 1979. Cert. Tchr. Idsl. Arts NJ, Elem. Sch. Tchr. NJ. Woodshop instr. Pemperton Twp. HS, Pemberton, NJ, 1979—82; indsl. arts/ career awareness instr. Somerdale Pk. Sch., Somerdale, NJ, 1982—. After sch. sports dir. Somerdale Pk. Sch., Somerdale, NJ, 1995—2005. Mem.: NEA, Somerdale Edn. Assn., Camden County Edn. Assn., NJ Edn. Assn. Avocations: antiques, travel, gardening, interior decorating. Office: Somerdale Pk Sch 301 Grace St Somerdale NJ 08083

BOTSFORD, MARY HENRICH, retired ophthalmologist; b. Buffalo, Aug. 22, 1915; d. John William and Margarethe Ingeborg (Kähler) Henrich; m. Daniel Ray Botsford, Feb. 11, 1943 (dec. Dec. 1970); children: Daniel Jr., Janet B. Thrush, William H., Thomas H. BA, Mount Holyoke Coll., 1937; MD, U. Buffalo, 1941. Diplomate Am. Bd. Ophthalmology. Assoc. Ivan J. Koenig M.D., Buffalo, 1943-46, 56-60; pvt. practice Buffalo, 1960-84; retired, 1984. Staff St. Francis Hosp., Buffalo, 1962-72, Vets. Hosp., Buffalo, 1962-72, Gowanda State Hosp., Helmuth, N.Y., 1962-80, Buffalo Children's Hosp., 1943-96, Buffalo Gen. Hosp., 1943-96. Founding bd. dirs., vol. Habitat for Humanity, Buffalo, 1985-2005; vol. Meals on Wheels, Buffalo, 1985-96, Am. Cancer Soc., Buffalo, 1985-96. Recipient Outstanding Achievement in Medicine citation, SUNY, Buffalo, 1984. Mem. Am. Acad. Ophthalmology, Buffalo Ophthal. Club, N.Y. State Ophthal. Soc., Common Cause. Democrat. Lutheran. Avocations: bridge, classical music, travel, theater, reading.

BOTT, PATRICIA ANN, medical/surgical nurse; b. Washington, Jan. 24, 1946; d. Vincent F. and Jessie (Prince) Lopresti; m. Frederick W. Bott, Jan. 7, 1973; children: Jennifer Moller, Rebecca Moller, Michael. Diploma, All Souls Hosp. Sch. Nursing, 1967; student, Cochise Coll., 1979-80. Staff and charge nurse Monmouth Med. Ctr., Long Branch, N.J., 1972, Galion (Ohio) Community Hosp., 1974-76, Sierra Vista (Ariz.) Community Hosp., 1979-81, St. Mary's Hosp., Tucson, 1982—.

BOTTARI, MARIANNA TERESA, public relations executive; b. Phila., Nov. 17, 1941; d. Guido Albert and Malvina Rose (Seccia) Bottari. Attended, U. Pa., 1962—64, Charles Morris Price Sch. Journalism and Advt., 1964—66. News rels. asst. Smith Kline & French Labs., Phila., 1962—64; pub. rels. asst. St. Luke's and Children's Med. Ctr., Phila., 1964—66, Thomas Jefferson U. Hosp., Phila., 1969—71; pub. rels. dir. Albert Einstein Med. Ctr., Phila., 1971—74, John Muir Meml. Hosp., Walnut Creek, Calif., 1974—77, Peralta Hosp., Oakland, Calif., 1977—80; cmty. rels. and devel. dir. Sequoia Hosp., Redwood City, Calif., 1980—82; cmty. rels. and mktg. dir. Valley Meml. Hosp., Livermore, Calif., 1982—84. Owner PR Woman & Co. Bd. dirs. Coop. Ctr. Coun., 1976—77; v.p. Sun Country Homeowners Assn., 1977—79; bd. dirs. Yqnacio Terr. Homeowners Assn., 1986—. With USNR, 1979—81. Recipient MacEachern Nat. citation, 1973, MacEachern cert. of merit, 1976. Mem.: Nat. Assn. Female Execs., Nat. Assn. Hosp. Devel., Internat. Assn. Bus. Communicators, Hosp. Pub. Rels. Assn. No. Calif., Acad. Hosp. Pub. Rels.

BOTTENBERG, JOYCE HARVEY, writer, social services administrator; b. Melrose, Mass., June 29, 1945; d. Robert Willis and Amy Sheppard (Wood) Harvey; 1 child, Joanne Harvey; m. Norman G. Bottenberg, 1985. BA, U. Mass., 1967, diploma grad. journalism program, 1969; diploma, Simmons Coll. Grad. Sch. Mgmt., 1984. Lic., cert. social worker, Mass. Sr. tech. writer Itek Corp., Lexington, Mass., 1967-70; dir. pub. info. Walla Walla (Wash.) C.C., 1970; profl. interviewer McGraw Hill Rsch., N.Y.C., 1971-73; coord. pub. rels. James B. Rendle Assocs., Malden, Mass., 1973-76; exec. dir. ARC, Melrose, Mass., 1976-80, regional mgr., 1980-84, Lynn, Mass., 1984-85; tech. writer Municipality of Met. Seattle, 1985-86; exec. dir. Epilepsy Assn. Western Wash., Seattle, 1986-87; dir. devel. ARC, Seattle, 1988-97, mgr. svc. ctr., 1994—96; exec. dir. Medic One Found., Seattle, 1997-2000; devel. dir. Success Mktg. Inc., Seattle, 2000—03; dir. devel. Starlight Starbright Children's Found., Redmond, 2004—. Chief devel. officer Child Care Resources, Seattle, 2001-03; v.p. resource devel. Boys and Girls Clubs of King County, 2003-04. Instr. 1st aid, CPR, ARC Recipient Cert. of merit ARC, 1981; named Profl. Fund Raiser of Yr., ARC, 1994; New Eng. Newspaper fellow, 1969. Mem. AAUW, DAR, NAFE, Soc. Mayflower Descs., Nat. Ski Patrol System, N.W. Devel. Officers Assn., Wash. Planned Giving Coun., Puget Sound Grantwriters Assn. Episcopalian. Avocation: amateur radio. Office: 4536 150th Ave NE Redmond WA 98052 Home: 3020 Issaquah Pine Lake Rd SE # 500 Sammamish WA 98075-7253 Office Phone: 425-861-7827. Personal E-mail: bberg@oz.net. Business E-Mail: joyce@starlight-washington.org.

BOTTOLFSON, WAHNITA JOAN, parochial school educator; b. Sharon, Pa., Aug. 23, 1952; d. Jerald Russel and Verlene Estelle Barr; m. Larry Alan Bottolfson, Aug. 30, 2003; children: Corine Hannah Knutson, Christina Joan Cope, James Ryan Cope. BS, Ohio State U., Columbus, 1974. Cert. early and mid. childhood edn. tchr. Ariz., 2001. Tchr. Grace Cmty. Christian Sch., Tempe, Ariz., 1988—. R-Liberal. Christian. Avocations: reading, travel. Office Phone: 480-966-5022.

BOTTOMS, REBECCA LYNN, literature and language educator; b. Grand Haven, Mich., July 30, 1958; d. William Vance and Sally Ane Strebig; m. Randall Grayson Bottoms, July 6, 1985; children: Jonathan Edwards, Robert E. Lee. BA in Speech, Bob Jones U., Greenville, S.C., 1980, MA in Comms., 1982. Tchr. speech Bob Jones U., Greenville, SC, 1980—82; tchr. English Woodland Christian Sch., Winston-Salem, NC, 1982—. Speech chmn. elem. divsn. NCCSA, NC, 1998—2006; sponsor Nat. Honor Soc., Winston-Salem, NC, 2000—06. Host Summer Tours Abroad EF Tours, 1985—2005. Mem.: DAR (regent 1996—2000), Children of the Am. Revolution (state chmn. 2004—06). Republican. Baptist. Avocations: travel, reading, cooking. Office: Woodland Christian Sch 3665 N Patterson Ave Winston Salem NC 27105

BOTTONE, JOANN, health services executive; b. Bklyn., June 20, 1943; d. Anthony and Claire (Bisesti) B.; m. William Recevuto, Feb. 12, 1989; children: Matthew, Sandra. RN, Kings County Hosp. Ctr., Bklyn., 1963; BS, St. Francis Coll., Bklyn., 1980; MPA, Russell Sage Coll., Albany, N.Y., 1986; PhD in Pub. Adminstrn. magna cum laude, Kensington U., 1995. Bd. cert. Health Care Mgmt. Am. Coll. Health Care Execs., 1997. From staff nurse, head nurse, quality assurance coord. Victory Meml. Hosp., Bklyn., 1961-81; instr. infection control Community Hosp. Bklyn., 1981-82; dir. quality assurance Profl. Stds. Rev. Orgn., Bklyn., 1982-85; devel. and coord. HIV post-test counseling program Greater N.Y. Blood Ctr., N.Y.C., 1985-88; dir. HIV/AIDS programs Health Sci. Ctr. SUNY, Bklyn., 1988—2000. Tchr. SUNY Coll. Health Related Professions; mem. working group to develop statewide policies and procedures for health care workers involved in potential HIV exposures N.Y. State Health Commr., 1990; mem. tech. adv. group to develop guidelines for OSHA's bloodborne pathogen standard Greater N.Y. Hosp. Assn., 1992, N.Y.C. Mayor's HIV and Human Svcs. planning coun., 1999; lectr. in field. Contbr. articles to profl. jours. Mem. Am. Coll. Health Care Execs (diplomate), Greater N.Y. Hosp. Assn. (tech. adv. group). E-mail: dr.jbr@msn.com.

BOTTS, LILLIAN SULLIVAN, elementary school educator; b. Smithville, Miss., Sept. 14, 1945; d. Tremon and Elvie Weaver Sullivan; m. Billy Wayne Botts, July 6, 1963; children: Sandra Botts Owen, Steve. AA, Itawamba Jr. Coll., Fulton, Miss., 1965; BA, U. Miss., 1967, MEd, 1978. Intermediate spl. edn. tchr. Lee County Schs., Belden, Miss., 1975—76, elem. tchr. Shannon, Miss., 1981—2004, primary tchr., 2004—. Named Tchr. of the Yr., Shannon Primary, 2005—06. Mem.: Miss. Assn. Profl. Educators, Internat. Reading Assn., Nat. Sci. Tchrs. Assn. Baptist. Avocations: reading, gardening, travel. Home: 785 Palmetto Rd Tupelo MS 38801

BOTWAY, JACLYN COOPER, antiques dealer, consultant; b. St. Louis, Sept. 14, 1935; d. Sterling Ellis and Thelma Adeline (Kinder) Cooper; m. Clifford Alan Botway, July 29, 1950; children: Cooper Alan, Jill Robyn-Sterling. BA, MA, U. Ga., 1947; MSW, N.Y. Sch. Social Work, 1950. Med. social worker Met. Hosp., N.Y.C., 1950-55; owner, mgr. Jaclyn J. Inc. (doing bus. as Rainbarrel), Salt Point, N.Y., 1980—. Pres., dir. Hist. Hudson Valley Antiquity, Clinton Corners, N.Y., 1980—; dir. Dutchess County Hist. Roads, Poughkeepsie, N.Y., 1985—. Author: Finding Art Treasures at Home, 1979, Auctions Mania, 1980, Money in the Attic, 1985, The Ancients Collectively, 1986. Mem. Clinton Hist. Road Commn.; founder Clinton Hist. Soc., 1989; v.p. New Rochelle (N.Y.) League for Svc., 1955-81; vol. Internat. Garden Club, Pelham, N.Y., 1955—; sec. Women's Manor Club, Pelham, 1955-57; v.p. Little Guild of St. Francis for Animals, Key West, Fla., 1982—; founder Art and Hist. Soc., Key West, 1982, Martello Mus., Key West, 1982, Tennessee Williams Arts Ctr. and Theatre, Key West, 1982—. Named Rep. Woman of Dutchess County, Nat. Rep. Com., 1963. Mem. Oldest House Mus., Mus. Modern Art, Mus. Natural History, Clinton Hist. Soc., Phi Beta Kappa. Avocations: pilot, gardening, skiing, fox hunting, scuba diving, sea mobile racing. Home: 460 Beechmont Dr New Rochelle NY 10804-4613 Office: Rainbarrel No 2 Salt Pt Tpke Salt Point NY 12514

BOUCHARD, LYNNE KATHERINE, music educator; b. L.A., June 24, 1955; d. Thomas Joseph and Anne Katherine (Gurmatakis) Bouchard; m. Daniel Ernest Winans, Apr. 6, 1985 (div.); children: Collette Jeanine Winans Engle, Ashley Anne Winans; m. Timothy Ervin Junette, May 2, 1997 (div.). Lic. practical nurse, Ariz. We. Coll., 1981. LPN; lic. instr. Kindermusik Internat. LPN Dr. David Buster, Yuma, Ariz., Dr. Abraham Injean, Yuma, Yuma County Health Dept.; pvt. piano instr. Yuma, 1987—99; tchr. music Grace Brethren Christian Sch., Waldorf, Md., 1999—2001, tchr. drama, 2000—03. Pvt. piano instr. Ivory Moon Piano Studio LLC, Waldorf, 1999—. Mem.: Md. State Music Tchrs. Assn., Port Tobacco Players, Nat. Guild Piano Tchrs. Avocations: acting, interior decorating, gardening, antiques. Home: 4575 Grouse Pl Waldorf MD 20603

BOUCHARD, WENDY ANN BORSTEL, language educator; m. Douglas K. Bouchard, Aug. 6, 1983. BA, SUNY, Geneseo, 1978; MA, Hofstra U., Hempstead, N.Y., 1982. Cert. secondary English tchr. N.Y. English tchr. Oneida (N.Y.) Sr. H.S., 1978—80, Mineola Jr. H.S., 1980—81, Thompson Jr. H.S., Syosset, NY, 1981—83, Roslyn (N.Y.) Jr. H.S., 1983—84, Garden City (N.Y.) Mid. Sch., 1984—2000, Garden City (N.Y.) Sr. H.S., 2000—. Life mem. Girls Scouts Am. Mem.: N.Y. State English Coun., L.I. Lang. Arts

Coun., N.Y. State United Tchrs., Nat. Coun. Tchrs. English. Avocations: travel, reading, swimming. Office: Garden City Sr High Sch 170 Rockaway Ave Garden City NY 11530 Office Phone: 516-478-2000. Business E-Mail: bouchardw@gcufsd.net.

BOUCHONVILLE, SUSAN JOANNE, public health service officer, medical technician; b. Albuquerque, N.Mex., Feb. 28, 1975; d. Kenneth Lehman and Linda Yoder; m. Matthew Frederick Bouchonville, July 22, 1976. BA in Biology, Ea. Mennonite U., Harrisonburg, Va., 1997; MPH, Ea. Va. Med. Sch., Norfolk, 2005. Cert. med. technologist Am. Soc. Clin. Pathologists, 2000. Med. technologist Rockingham Meml. Hosp., Harrisonburg, Va., 2000—02, Bon Secours Hampton Roads, Norfolk, Va., 2002—; rsch. assoc. Ea. Va. Med. Sch., Norfolk, 2005—. Mem.: Delta Omega. Avocation: environmental conservation.

BOUDREAU, LYNDA L., state agency administrator; m. Jim Boudreau. Rep. Minn. Ho. of Reps., 1994—2004, speaker pro tempore. Chair, health and human svc. policy com. Office: 559 State Office Bldg 100 Rev Martin Luther Ling Jr Blvd Saint Paul MN 55155 Office Phone: 651-201-5807. E-mail: lynda.boudreau@state.mn.us.

BOUDREAU, SHARON KAY, special education educator; b. Norfolk, Va., Oct. 26, 1956; d. Henry Crawford and Ida Ruth (Fantone) Roberson; m. James Anthony Boudreau, Aug. 2, 1980; children: Allison Leigh, Ethan Gray. BS in Edn., Old Dominion U., 1978, MS in Edn., 1985. Cert. tchr., Va. Elem. tchr. Norfolk City Schs., 1978-83, spl. edn. tchr., 1983-90, Va. Beach City Schs., 1990—, Kings Grant Elem. Sch., Va.; tchr., curriculum devel. specialist Chance program Old Dominion U., Norfolk, 1983-86. Mem. Va. Reading Coun., Delta Kappa Gamma (Beta chpt.). Roman Catholic. Avocations: gardening, needlecrafts, weights and working out, beach. Home: 533 Ingram Rd Virginia Beach VA 23452-7142 Business E-Mail: sharon.boudreau@vbschools.com.

BOUFFORD, JO IVEY, health administrator, educator; b. Durham, NC, July 2, 1945; BA in Psychology magna cum laude, U. Mich., 1967, MD with distinction, 1971; DSc (hon.), SUNY, Bklyn., 1992. Diplomate Nat. Bd. Med. Examiners, Am. Bd. Pediats. Resident in social pediats. medicine Montefiore Hosp. and Med. Ctr., Bronx, N.Y., 1971-74, asst. attending physician, 1975-97, co-dir. Inst. for Health Team Devel., 1975-82, dir. residency program in social medicine, 1975-82; adminstrv. dir. Valentine Lane Family Practice, Yonkers, N.Y., 1975-82; v.p. med. ops. N.Y.C. Health and Hosps. Corp., 1982-83, v.p. med. and profl. affairs, 1983-85, exec. v.p., 1985, acting pres., 1985, pres., 1985-89; internat. fellow in comparative health sys. mgmt. King's Fund Coll., London, 1989-91, dir., 1991-93; prin. dep. asst. sec. for health Dept. Health and Human Svcs., Washington, 1993-97, acting asst. sec., 1997; dean Robert F. Wagner Grad. Sch. of Pub. Svc., New York Univ., 1997—2002; clin. prof. peds. NYU, 1997—, prof. pub. svc. health policy and mgmt., 2003—. Adj. prof. Lehman Coll. Nursing, Bronx, 1974-80; mem. Nat. Adv. Coun. for Health Professions Edn. US-DHHS, 1976-80; mem. tech. panel on the ednl. environ. Grad. Med. Edn. Nat. Adv. Coun., 1979-80; cons. on manpower programs divsn. medicine bur. Health Professions Edn. HRSA-DHHS, 1980-88; mem. N.Y. State Coun. on Grad. med. Edn., 1987-89, N.Y. State Commn. on Grad. Med. Edn., 1985-86; rep. of U.S. on exec. bd. WHO, 1994-97; U.S. staff dir. Gore-Chernomyrdin Commn. Health Com., 1994-97; various consulting positions. Mem. editl. bd. Jour. Med. Edn., 1980-86; mem. editl. adv. bd. The New Physician, 1979-89; contbr. articles to profl. jours.; presenter in field. Mem. Nat. Adv. Coun. of Agy. for Healthcare Quality and Rsch., 2000—04; bd. dirs. United Hosp. Fund, 1999—; chair sub-bd. on pub. health, Open Soc. Inst., 1998-2004; mem. N.Y. State Coun. on Grad. Med. Edn., 1987-89. Fellow Am. Acad. Pediats.; mem. APHA, NAS Inst. Medicine Coun. (Robert Wood Johnson health policy fellow 1979-80), Soc. Med. Adminstrs., Med. Adminstrs. Conf. Office: NYU Robert F Wagner Grad Sch Pub Svc 295 Lafayette St 3rd Fl New York NY 10012 Office Phone: 212-998-7410. E-mail: jo.boufford@nyu.edu.

BOUGHAN, ZANETTA LOUISE, music educator; b. Grantham, Eng., Mar. 22, 1959; arrived in U.S., 1964; d. Peter Leonard and Alyda Venita Maria (Bellord) Snowden; m. Robert William Boughan, Nov. 3, 1995. AAS, Cochise Coll., 2003—; BS with honors, Wayland Bapt. U., 2005. Pvt. piano and violin instr., Sierra Vista, Ariz., 1988—. Concertmaster Cochise Coll. Orch., Sierra Vista, 1999—2001, Pima Coll. Orch., Tucson, 2001—02; first violinist Sierra Vista Sym. Orch., 2001—02. Vol. Sierra Vista Police Dept., 2002—06; ct. apptd. spl. adv. vol. State Ariz., 2002—; vol. in Police Svc., 2002—06; mem. Citizens Police Acad. Assocs., 2003—; vol. Cochise County Juvenile Ct., 2003—, Vol. Interfaith Caregiver Program, 2005—. With USN, 1979—84. Mem.: Ariz. Music Tchrs. Assn., Nat. Music Tchrs. Assn., Cochise Music Tchrs. Assn. (chmn. fundraising com. 1997—, sec. 1998—2000, treas. 2001—03, pres. 2003—05, Profl. Develop. grant 2001), Phi Theta Kappa. Avocations: photography, travel, music, swimming, tennis, walking, reading. Home: 4924 Marconi Dr Sierra Vista AZ 85635 Personal E-mail: zboughan@earthlink.net.

BOUGHNER, MARTHA REED, music educator; b. New Brunswick, N.J., Aug. 8, 1949; d. James George and Patricia Elizabeth Boughner. BA in music performance, Douglass Coll., N.J., 1971; MusM in clarinet, Syracuse U., N.Y., 1973; MEd in supervision and adminstrn., Rutgers U., N.J., 1986; M in Theological studies, Drew U., N.J., 1997. Cert. tchr. N.J., N.Y., Pa., Del., prin. N.J. Music sales JW Pepper & Sons, Inc., Valley Forge, Pa., 1973—76; band tchr., supr. Music for Am., Elkhart, Ind., 1977—79, Future Musicians, Inc., Cranford, NJ, 1979—85, 1987—; co-op edn., career counselor Jersey City State Coll., 1985—86; orchestra/theory tchr. Roxbury HS, NJ, 1986—87. Musician Suburban Symphony, Cranford, NJ, 1980, New Brunswick Chamber Orch., NJ, 1976—90, Silver Starlite Orch., Caldwell, NJ, 1986—. Composer: (concert band music) March to the Future, 1988. Alumnae bd.mem. Douglas Coll., New Brunswick, NJ, v.p. alumnae program; verger St. James Episcopal Ch., Upper Montclair, NJ, 1988—, vestry mem., 1993—96, 2002—. Recipient Margaret T. Corwin award, 2005. Mem.: Rutgers Univ. Alumni, Music Educators Nat. Conf. Episcopal. Avocations: golf, reading, music. Home: 1 Laurel Pl West Caldwell NJ 07006 Office: Future Musicians Inc PO Box 882 Cranford NJ 07016

BOUGHTER, BARBARA B., mathematics educator; b. Sellersville, Pa., June 16, 1947; d. Luther Thomas and Adele Sterner Barndt; m. Charles Robert Moyer, 1971 (div. 1976); m. Frederick Wayne Boughter (dec. 1994); children: Jonathan Brian, Jeffrey Ryan. BSc, Kutztown State U., Pa., 1969; EdM, Kutztown State U., 1978. Math tchr. Indian Valley Jr. H.S., Harleysville, Pa., 1969—71, Mary Potter Mid. Sch., Oxford, NC, 1971—73, Pennridge H.S., Perkasie, Pa., 1973—98; substitute tchr. Ctrl. Middle Sch., 1998—2005; ret., 2005. Cheerleading adv. Indian Valley Jr. H.S., 1969—71; adv. Pennridge H.S. Class of 1976, 1973—76; mentor student tchrs. Pennridge H.S., 1978—87. Deacon on consistory St. Stephen's United Ch. of Christ, 2006—, treas., 2006—; mem. bd. dirs. Harleysville Soccer Assn., 1986—88; officer, coord. Souderton H.S. Soccer Parents Assn., 1994—98. Named to Wall of Tolerance, Southern Poverty Law Ctr., 2005. Mem.: NEA, Pa. Assn. of Sch. Retirees, Southern Poverty Law Ctr., Nat. Coun. of Teachers of Math. Home: 990 Long Mill Rd Telford PA 18969

BOUGHTON, LILIAN ELIZABETH, secondary education educator, retired; b. Cumberland, Md., May 15, 1913; d. Orble Brooks and Christine (McAlpine) B. Student, Potomac State Coll., 1930-32; BA, Western Md. Coll., 1934; MA, Columbia U., 1938. Tchr. English Pennsylvania Ave. Jr. High Sch., Cumberland, Md., 1934-36, Ft. Hill High Sch., Cumberland, 1936-73. Sch. evaluation team mem. Md. State Sch. System for N.E. Evaluation Team, Baltimore City, 1940s; chairperson bylaws com. Md. State Tchrs. Assn., Balt., 1950s; conv. com. mem. Md. Retired Tchrs. Assn. Conv., Ocean City, 1983. Elder, circle leader Presbyn. Ch. Recipient cert. March of Dimes, 1983, plaque, 1984, Presbyn. Women's Hon. Life Membership award, 1996. Mem. AAUW (pres. 1975-77, 83-86, activities chair 1985—, publicity com., name honored 1983-84, 2 plaques Cumberland br. 1993), Allegany County Ret. Tchrs. Assn. (pres. 1982-83, newsletter editor 1983-94, publicity com.), Hist. Soc. (life, curator 1980, vol. 1985—), Women's Civic Club (edn. chair 1992—). Avocations: meals-on-wheels, gardening, travel, church choir member.

BOUKNIGHT, FRAN SHOOLBRED, science educator; d. Richard Fowler and Mary Britton Shoolbred; m. Ricky W. Bouknight, June 15, 1985; children: Richard W., Beth. BS in Secondary Sci. Tchg., Clemson U., SC, 1982; EdM in Secondary Edn., U. SC, Columbia, 1987, EdM in Secondary Adminstrn., 2002. Sci. tchr., dept. chmn. Columbia H.S., 1982—2000; adminstrv. asst. Brookland-Cayce H.S., SC, 2000—03, sci. tchr., 2003—. Ch. coun. mem., coun. sec. Mt. Hermon Luth. Ch., West Columbia, SC, 2002—05. Named Tchr. of Yr., Columbia H.S., 1987, Outstanding Biology Tchr. of Yr., SC Biology Tchrs. Assn., 1994—95. Mem.: SC Sci. Coun., Palmetto State Tchrs. Assn. (STAR Tchr. of Yr. 1993), Phi Delta Kappa (hon.; historian 2001—03). Office: Brookland-Cayce High School 1300 State St Cayce SC 29033 Office Phone: 803-791-5000.

BOULANGER, CAROL SEABROOK, lawyer; b. NYC, Sept. 14, 1942; d. John M. and Anne (Schlaudecker) Seabrook; m. Jacques P. Boulanger, June 1, 1974; children: Rodolphe, Adriana. BA, Swarthmore Coll., 1964; LLB, U. Pa., 1969. Bar: N.Y. 1970, U.S. Tax Ct. 1970. Assoc. Baker & McKenzie, N.Y.C., 1969-71, Wender, Murase & White, N.Y.C., 1971-75, ptnr., 1975-82, Boulanger, Finley & Hicks, N.Y.C., 1982-84, Drinker, Biddle & Reath, N.Y.C., 1984-89, Boulanger, Finley & Hicks, P.C., N.Y.C., 1989—96, Winthrop Stimson Putnam & Roberts, N.Y.C., 1996—2000, Pillsbury Winthrop, LLP, N.Y.C., 2001—05, Pillsbury Winthrop Shaw Pittman LLP, NYC, 2005—. Founding mem. ARCS Found. Inc., N.Y.C., sec. 1973-75, v.p. 1975-80; bd. dirs. Swarthmore Coll., 1977-81; trustee, treas. Am. Friends of the Victoria and Albert Mus., Inc., 1999—. Mem. ABA (tax sect., real property, probate and trust sect.), Assn. Bar City of N.Y. (internat. law com. 1980-84, fgn. and comparative law com., 1984-85, chmn. 1985-88).

BOULDING, ELISE MARIE, sociologist, educator; b. Oslo, July 6, 1920; came to U.S., 1923, naturalized, 1929; d. Joseph and Birgit (Johnsen) Biorn-Hansen; m. Kenneth Boulding; Aug. 31, 1941; children: John Russell, Mark David, Christine Ann, Philip Daniel, William Frederic. BA, Douglass Coll., 1940; MS, Iowa State Coll., 1949; PhD, U. Mich., 1969. Rsch. assoc. Survey Rsch. Inst., U. Mich., 1957-58, Mental Health Rsch. Inst., 1959-60; rsch. devel. sec. Ctr for Rsch. on Conflict Resolution, 1960-63; prof. sociology, project dir. Inst. Behavioral Sci., U. Colo., Boulder, 1967-78; Montgomery vis. prof. Dartmouth Coll., 1978-79, chmn. dept. sociology, 1979-85; prof. emerita, 1985; sec. gen. Internat. Peace Rsch. Assoc., 1989-91; pres. IPRA Found., 1992-96. Mem. program adv. council Human and Social Devel. Program, UN Univ., 1977-80; mem. governing council, 1980-86. Author: (with others) Handbook of International Data on Women, 1976, Bibliography on World Conflict and Peace, 1979, Social System of Planet Earth, 1980, Women and the Social Costs of Economic Development, 1981; author: The Underside of History: A View of Women Through Time, 1975, rev. edit., 1992, Women in Twentieth Century World, 1977, Children's Rights and the Wheel of Life, 1979, Building a Global Civic Culture: Education for an Interdependent World, 1988, 90, One Small Plot of Heaven, 1990, Cultures of Peace: The Hidden Side of History, 2000; (with Kenneth Boulding) The Future: Images and Processes, 1994; editor: Peace Culture and Society: Transnational Research and Dialogue with Clovis Brigagao and Kevin Clements (eds.), 1990; New Agendas for Peace Research: Conflict and Security Reexamined (ed.), 1992; Building Peace in the Middle East: Challenges for States and Civil Society, (ed.), 1993. Internat. chair Women's Internat. League for Peace and Freedom, 1967-70; mem. Exploratory Project on Conditions for Peace, 1984-90; mem. U.S. Commn. for UNESCO, 1978-84; mem. UNESCO Peace Prize jury, 1980-87; chair bd. Boulder Cmty. Parenting Ctr., 1988-92; bd. dirs. Am. Friends Svc. Com., 1990-94, Wayland MA Coun. on Aging, 1988-2000; councillor Interfaith Peace Coun., 1995—. Recipient Disting. Achievement award Douglass Coll., 1973, Ted. Lentz Peace award, 1976, Athena award, 1983, Nat. Women's Forum award, 1985, Inst. of Def., Disarmament, Peace and Democracy award, 1990, Jack Gore Meml. Peace award Denver Am. Friends Svc. Com., 1992, Global Citizen award Boston Rsch. Ctr., 1995, Peacemaker of Yr. award Rocky Mountain Peace and Justice Ctr., 1996, World Futures Studies Fedn. award, 1997, Jane Addams Peace Activist award Women's Internat. League for Peace and Freedom, 2000; named to Rutgers Hall of Disting. Alumni, 1994; Danforth fellow, 1965-67; named Peacemaker Elder, Nat. Conf. on Peacemaking and Conflict Resolution, 1999; chosen as one of 1000 Women for the Nobel Peace Prize, 2005. Mem. Am. Sociol. Assn. (Jessie Bernard award 1982, Peace and War sect. award 1994), Internat. Peace Rsch. Assn. (newsletter editor 1983-87), World Future Studies Fedn., Colo. Women's Forum. Mem. Soc. Of Friends. Home: N Hill 865 Central Ave Apt I 301 Needham MA 02492-1361

BOULIANE, MARY STEPHANIE, elementary school educator; d. Johnny E. and Judy E. Procell; m. Matthew H. Bouliane, Jan. 15, 2000; 1 child, Annemarie Elise. BS in Zoology, Tex. A&M U., College Station, 2000. Cert. tchr. Tex. Mgr. Loupot's Bookstore, College Station, 1999—2002; sci. tchr. Truman Mid. Sch., Grand Prairie, Tex., 2002—. Curriculum writer Lucent Technologies/NASA, Houston, 2003—04; sea camp counselor Tex. A&M, Galveston, 2004; vertical alignment team Grand Prairie Ind. Sch. Dist., Grand Prairie, 2004—; camp counselor math and computer engring. U. Tex., Arlington, 2006—. Teach for Tex. grant, Tex. Bd. Higher Edn., 2004. Mem.: Nat. Sci. Tchr. Assn. (assoc.), Tex. Classroom Tchrs. Assn. (assoc.; campus rep. 2005—06). Office: Truman Mid Sch 1501 Coffeyville Tr Grand Prairie TX 75052 Office Phone: 972-641-7676. Business E-Mail: stephanie.bouliane@gpisd.org.

BOULLY, LAJUAN BONNIE, minister, religious studies educator; b. Sanford, Fla., Oct. 11, 1930; d. Ira and Charity Pearl (Ellis) Brewer; children: James Robert, Leroy, Olan W., Mildred. Degree, Polk Cmty. Coll. Cert. day care. Sec. tng. dept. Publix Supermarket, Lakeland, Fla.; pastor, tchr. Faith Harbor Ch., Lakeland, Fla.; evangelist Taiwan, 1978, various locations, 2002—. Author: Miracles of Faith Harbor, 2006. Mem.: Morris Cerullo World Evangelism. Home: 4516 Redwood St Winter Haven FL 33880-1633 Office Phone: 863-294-6158. Personal E-mail: lajuanboully@aol.com. E-mail: ljboully@cs.com.

BOULOS, NADIA EBID, medical/surgical nurse; b. Sanhag, Egypt, Feb. 15, 1938; came to U.S., 1967; d. Eberd Hanna and Lisa (Saleh) Assad; m. Romshdy Sahfik Boulos, Jan. 31, 1965; children: Nader Romshdy, Mona Mary. BSN, U. Alexandria, Cairo, Egypt, 1960; MSN, Wayne State U., Detroit, 1966; PhD, U. Mich., 1974. Staff nurse ICU U. Alexandria, 1960-62, supr. Med. Ctr., 1962-64; instr. Alexandria Coll. Nursing, 1966-68; rsch. asst. Wayne State U., 1968-69; asst. prof. Oakland U., Rochester, Mich., 1979-82, assoc. prof. tenured, 1982-86; dir. dept. nursing Oakland C.C., Union Lake, Mich., 1986—. Author abstracts. Chair Arab Mgmt. in Am., Detroit, 1986—, Youth Group Alternative, 1988—. Mem. ANA, Mich. Nurses Assn., Mich. League Nurses, Nat. League Nurses, Oakland Dist. Nurses assn. (by lawc com. 1984-86), Coun. Nurse Rschrs. Orthodox. Home: 730 Westview Rd Bloomfield Hills MI 48304-2474

BOULTON, BONNIE SMITH, assistant principal, special education educator; b. Galliano, La., June 27, 1960; d. Kenneth Joseph and Geraldine Ledet Smith; m. Ross E. Boulton, May 11, 2001. BA, Nicholls State U., 1982, EdM, 1985; PhD, La. State U., 2003. Spl. edn. tchr. Lafourche Parish Schs., Thibodaux, La., 1982—87, Jefferson Parish Pub. Schs., Metairie, La., 1987—90, St. Charles Parish Schs., Destrehan, La., 1990—99; grad. asst. La. State U., Baton Rouge, 1999—2000; edn. program coord. La. Dept. Edn., Baton Rouge, 2000—01; asst. prin., spl. edn. campus supr. Eanes Ind. Sch. Dist., Austin, Tex., 2002—. Bd. dirs. La. Dyslexia Assn., 1994—98. Named to, Outstanding Young Women Am., 1985. Mem.: ASCD, Coun. for Exceptional Children. Avocations: reading, travel, gardening, cooking. Home: 11007 Major Oaks Dr Baton Rouge LA 70815-5449

BOULWARE, CAROL CARTER, retired music educator; d. Hoke Smith and Mary Griffin Carter; m. Robert MacDowell Boulware Jr., Dec. 27, 1960; children: Rob, Michelle Holseth. B Music Edn., Fla. State U., Tallahassee, 1961. Cert. Orff Level 1, Kodaly Level 1. Music tchr. Taylor County Sch. Dist., Perry, Fla., 1961—62, Polk County Sch. Dist., Lakeland, Fla., 1973—2004; ret., 2004. Children's choir dir. 1st Presbyn. Ch., Lakeland, 1971—2003. Mem. Lakeland Choral Soc.; driver Am. Cancer Soc. Named Tchr. of Yr., Polk County Sch. Bd., 1998. Mem.: FEMFA, PEA, Fla. Music Educators Assn., Music Educators Nat. Conf., Delta Kappa Gamma (pres. Delta Beta chpt.). Avocations: reading, knitting, sewing, piano. Home: 1752 Clarendon Ave Lakeland FL 33803

BOUMA, LYN ANN NICHOLS, music educator; b. Lincoln, Nebr., Jan. 5, 1963; d. Raymond Joseph and Margaret Ann (Gewacke) Nichols; m. Stephen George Bouma, Jan. 25, 1964; 1 child, Claire. BMus, Nebr. Wesleyan U., Lincoln, 1985; MMus, U. Nebr., Lincoln, 1991. Choral dir. West Point (Nebr.) Pub. Schs., 1985—93, Omaha Ctrl. HS, 1993—. Mem. music ad hoc com. Nebr. Dept. Edn., Lincoln, 2000. Mem. Omaha Chamber Singers. Recipient Outstanding Tchr. award, Alice Buffett Found., 1999, Outstanding Music Alumni award, Nebr. Wesleyan U., 2002. Mem.: NEA, Music Educators Nat. Conf., Am. Choral Dirs. Assn. (life; Nebr. sec. 1992—94, chair Nebr. women's chorus 2000—04, conducted featured choirs at convs., Outstanding Young Choral Dir. 1989). Democrat. Congregationalist. Avocations: exercise, contract bridge. Home: 5123 Decatur Omaha NE 68104 Office: Omaha Ctrl HS 124 N 20th St Omaha NE 68102 Office Phone: 402-557-3361. Business E-Mail: lyn.bouma@ops.org.

BOUMENOT, STACY LEAH, school psychologist; b. Leominster, Mass., Sept. 22, 1978; m. Christopher Boumenot; 1 child, Colin. BA cum laude, Assumption Coll., 1996—2000; MA, U. of Hartford, 2000—02. Lic. School Psychologist Mass. Dept. of Edn., 2004. Residential counselor Cmty. Health Link, Youth Opportunities Upheld, Henry Lee Willis, Worcester, Grafton, Hudson, Mass., 1997—2001; intern/clinician Johnson Meml. Hosp., Stafford Springs, Conn., 2001—02; clinician Northeastern Family Inst., Westboro, Mass., 2002—03; sch. psychologist Lunenburg Pub. Schools, Mass., 2003—. Mem. Greater Enfield Youth Suicide Prevention Group, Enfield, Conn., 2002. Presdl. scholar, Assumption Coll., 1996—2000. Mem.: NASP, APA (assoc.), Psi Chi (life). Achievements include first psychology graduate intern to cofacilitate a hospital-wide seminar at Johnson Memorial Hospital. Avocations: kickboxing, skiing, dance, Karate, scrapbooks.

BOUNDS, RENEE P., secondary school educator; b. Gulfport, Miss., Apr. 3, 1958; m. Mitchell Bounds, Dec. 17, 1977; 1 child, Olivia. BS in Social Studies, Miss. Coll., Clinton, 1980, EdM, 1984. Nat. bd. cert. tchr. Nat. Bd. for Profl. Tchg. Stds., 2005, advanced placement cert. U.S. govt. and politics Coll. Bd. AP, 2003, advanced placement cert. econs. Coll. Bd. AP, 1995. Secondary tchr. Tri County Acad., Flora, Miss., 1981—84, Jackson Pub. Schs. Provine H.S., Miss., 1984—92, Jackson Pub. Schs. Forest Hill H.S., 1992—. Active First Bapt. Ch., Clinton. Republican. Baptist. Avocations: travel, reading. Home: 112 Countrywood Circle Clinton MS 39056 Office: Forest Hill High School 2607 Raymond Rd Jackson MS 39212 Office Phone: 601-371-4313. Personal E-mail: rbounds@yahoo.com. Business E-Mail: rbounds@jackson.k12.ms.us.

BOUNDS, SARAH ETHELINE, historian; b. Nov. 5, 1942; d. Leo Deltis and Alice Etheline (Boone) Bounds. AB, Birmingham-So. Coll., 1963; MA, U. Ala., 1965, EdS in History, 1971, PhD, 1977. Tchr. social studies Huntsville City Sch., 1963, 65-66, 1971-74; residence hall adv., dir. univ. housing U. Ala., Tuscaloosa, 1963-65, 68-71; instr. history N.E. State Jr. Coll., Rainsville, Ala., 1966-68, U. Ala., Huntsville, 1975, 78-80,85—. Dir. Weeden House Mus., 1981-83, com. mem., 1981-2000; asst. prof. edn., supr. student tchr. U. North Ala., Florence, 1978. Mem.: AAUW, NEA, Assn. Tchr. Educators, Huntsville Music Study Club, Historic Huntsville Found., Huntsville Hist. Soc., Twickenham Study Club, Huntsville Pilot Club (pres. 1990—91, club builder 1991—93, Ala. dist. lt. gov. 1995—96, Ala. dist gov. elect 1996—97, Ala. dist gov. 1997—98), Aladdin Club (pres. 2004—05), Phi Alpha Theta, Kappa Delta Pi, Alpha Delta Kappa (state pres. Ala. 1990—92, regional sec. 1991—93, mem. internat. com. 1993—97, chmn. internat. com. 1995—97). Methodist. Home: 1100 Bob Wallace Ave SE Huntsville AL 35801-2807

BOUNDS-SEEMANS, PAMELLA J., artist; b. Milton, Del., Nov. 5, 1948; d. James Wilson Bounds and Marguerite Edna (Rickards) Bounds Carey; m. Jeffrey Wayne Seemans, Mar. 20, 1984; children: Misty Autumn, Sterling Hunter, Jordan Windsor. BA, N.Mex. Highlands U., 1971, MA, 1972. Tchr. elem. art Indian River Sch. Dist., Frankford, Del., 1973-79. Lectr. U. Md., 1981, U. Del., 1986, Del. Tech. and C.C., 1988, 75th Del. Women's Day Conf. at U. Del., U. Del. Coll. Arts and Mineralogy, 1999. Exhibited in group shows including Rehoboth (Del.) Art League, 1980, 89, 90, 92, 93, Tideline Gallery, Rehoboth Beach, Del., 1980—, Greenville, Del., 1993, Wicomico Art League, 1980, Del. Tech. and C.C., Georgetown, 1981, U. Md., 1981, Bluestreak Gallery, Wilmington, Del., 1989—, Blue Streak Art Gallery, Wilmington, 1993, Jamison Gallery, Santa Fe, 1993—, Del. Art Mus., 1996, Biennal 96 and 98 Del. Art Mus., U. Del., 1999, Am. Mus. Visionary Arts, Balt., 2000, numerous others; represented in permanent collections including Wilmington (Del.) Trust Co., Del. Nat. Bank, Sussex County Courthouse, Del. Parks and Recreation Bldg., Del. State Folklore Collection, also numerous pvt. collections; poster for mayor's office Clifford Brown Jazz Festival, Wilmington, 1998; mem. cmty. adv. editl. bd. News Jour., Gannett Papers, Wilmington, 1997-98; artist Dino Doys Rennaissance Corp. Donated art work to oncology ctr. Beebe Hosp. Found., 1995, Multiple Sclerosis Found. Del., Ronald McDonald House Del.; mem. cmty. adv. bd. News Jour. editl. Staff, 1997—; mem. parental adv. bd. U. Del., 2005. Recipient award for outstanding body of work Torpedo Factory, Alexandria, Va., 1982; fellow State of Del. Divsn. of the Arts, 1995. Mem. Nat. Mus. of Women in the Arts, Del. Art Mus., Tunnel 2d place award for most outstanding work in exhibit 1990, Popular Vote award 1980, 93, 94, 95, 96, 1st place award 1993, hon.), Del. Ctr. for Contemporary Arts, Del. Ctr. for Creative Arts, Newark Arts Alliance, Del. Nature Soc., Mothers Multiple Births (v.p. 1987), Wicomo Art League (hon. mention 1981), Univ. and Whist Club (Wilmington). Avocations: criminology, fashion, psychology, gourmet cooking. Home: 1203 Greenbank Rd Wilmington DE 19808-5842

BOURDON, CATHLEEN JANE, professional society administrator; b. Sparta, Wis., July 13, 1948; d. Cletus John and Josephine Marie (Bourdon) Scheurich; children: Jill Krzyminski, Jeff Krzyminski. BA in Polit. Sci., U. Wis., 1973, MLS, 1974. Tchr. Peace Corps, Arba Minch, Ethiopia, 1969-72; asst. prof., dir. Alverno Coll. Libr., Milw., 1974-83; dep. exec. dir. Assn. Coll. and Rsch. Librs., Chgo., 1983-93; exec. dir. Ref. and User Svcs. Assn. divsn. ALA Assn. Specialized and Coop. Libr. Agys., Chgo., 1993—. Mem. ALA (pres. Staff Assn. 1987-88). Avocations: movies, reading. Office: Assn Specialized & Coop Libr Agys 50 E Huron St Chicago IL 60611-5295 Office Phone: 312-280-4395. E-mail: cbourdon@ala.org.

BOURGEOIS, KIMBERLY BETH, mathematics educator; b. Albany, N.Y., Aug. 12, 1973; d. Richard and Barbara Jerard; m. Gary Paul Bourgeois, Nov. 27, 1965; children: Renee Nicole, Kristina Lynn. BS, SUNY, Oneonta, 1995; MS, SUNY, Albany, 2005. Cert. tchr. math. 7-12 NY State Dept. of Edn., 1996. Math tchr. Schalmont H.S., Rotterdam, NY, 1996—98, Bishop Maginn H.S., Albany, NY, 1998—99, Stillwater H.S., NY, 1999—. Class advisor 2006 and 2003 Stillwater H.S., 2000—, yearbook advisor, 2001—. Named Tchr. of the Yr., Stillwater H.S., 2004—05. Home: 18 Fieldstone Dr Clifton Park NY 12065 Office: Stillwater High School 334 North Hudson Ave Stillwater NY 12170 Office Phone: 518-373-6100. E-mail: kbourgeois@scsd.org.

BOURGEOIS, LOUISE, sculptor; b. Paris, 1911; arrived in US, 1938, naturalized, 1953; m. Robert Goldwater, 1938 (dec. 1973); 3 children. Student, Sorbonne U., 1932-35; baccalaureate, Ecole des Beaux Arts, 1936-38; postgrad., Ecole du Louvre, 1936-37, Acad. Grande Chaumiere;

D.F.A. (hon.), Yale U., 1977, Calif. Coll. Arts and Crafts, 1988, Moore Coll. Art, Mass. Coll. Art, 1983, Md. Art Inst., 1984, The New Sch., 1987. Instr. Md. Art Inst., Balt., 1984, New Sch. Social Rsch., N.Y.C., 1987. One-woman shows include Norlyst Gallery, 1947, Peridot Gallery, 1949, 50, 53, Allan Frumkin Gallery, Chgo., 1953, White Art Mus., Cornell U., Ithaca, N.Y., 1959, Stable Gallery, 1964, Rose Fried Gallery, 1963, 112 Greene St., N.Y.C., 1974, Xavier Fourcade Gallery, N.Y.C., 1978-80, Max Hutchinson Gallery, N.Y.C., 1980, Renaissance Soc., 1981, Mus. Modern Art, N.Y.C., 1982, retrospective Contemporary Art Mus., Houston, 1983, Daniel Weinberg Gallery, L.A., 1984, Robert Miller Gallery, 1982, 84, 87-89, 91, Serpentine Gallery, London, 1985, Maeght-Lelong, Zurich, 1985, Paris, 1985, Taft Mus., Cin., 1987-89 (travelled to The Art Mus. at Fla. Internat. U., Miami, Fla., Laguna Gloria Art Mus., Austin, Tex., Gallery of Art, Washington U., St. Louis, Henry Art Gallery, Seattle, Everson Mus. Art, Syracuse, N.Y.), Mus. Overholland, Amsterdam, The Netherlands, 1988, Dia Art Found., Bridgehampton, N.Y., retrospective Frankfurter Kunstverein, Frankfurt, Fed. Republic Germany, 1989 (travelled to Städtische Galerie im Lenbachhaus, Munich, 1990, Riverside Studios, London, 1990, Musée d'Art Contemporain, Lyon, 1990, Fondacion Tapies, Barcelona, Spain, Kunstmuseum, Berne, Switzerland, Kröller-Müller Mus., Otterlo, The Netherlands), Linda Cathcart Gallery, Santa Monica, Calif., 1990, Barbara Gross Gallerie, Munich, 1990, Karsten Schubert, London, 1990, Galerie Krinzinger, Vienna, 1990, Karsten Greve Gallery, Cologne, 1990, Ginny Williams Gallery, 1990, Monika Sprüthe Gallerie, Cologne, 1990, Robert Miller Gallery 1986, 1987, 1988, 1989, 1991, Galerie Lelong, Zurich, 1991; solo exhbns. include Parrish Art Mus., Southampton, N.Y., Ydessa Hendeles Found., Toronto, 1991, 92, Milwaukee Art Mus., 1992, The Fabric Workshop, Phila., Galerie Karsten Greve, Paris, Linda Cathcart Gallery, Santa Monica, Calif., Second Floor, Reykjavik, Iceland; exhibited in numerous group shows, U.S., Europe including Sculpture Ctr., 1997, Jim Kempner Fine Art, 1997, Steinbaum Krauss Gallery, 1998, Mary Boone Gallery, 1998, Am. Craft Mus., 1998; represented in permanent collections Mus. Modern Art, N.Y.C., Whitney Mus., Met. Mus. Art, Hirshorn Mus., Musée Nat. D'Art Moderne, Paris, R.I. Sch. Design, NYU, Albright-KnAustralian Nat. Gallery, Canberra, Musée d'Art Moderne, Paris, Mus. Fine Arts, Houston, Guggenheim Mus., N.Y.C., Kunstmus. Bern, stmus. Lucerne, Albertina, Vienna, Mus. Modern Art, Vienna, Walker Art Ctr., Mpls., Storm King Art Ctr., Mountainville, N.Y., New Mus. Contemporary Art, N.Y.C., DC Moore Gallery, N.Y.C., Cheim & Read Gallery, N.Y.C., Denver Art Mus., Colo.; appeared in Limited Edition Artists Books 1990—. Recipient Outstanding Achievement award Women's Caucus, 1980, Pres.'s Fellow award R.I. Sch. Design, 1984, Skowhegan medal sculpture Skowhegan (Maine) Sch. Painting, and Sculpture, Gold medal of honor Nat. Arts Club, 1987, Creative Arts Medal award Brandeis U., 1989, Grand Prix Nat. de Sculpture French Ministry of Culture, 1991, Nat. medal arts, 1999, Wolf prize in arts Wolf Found., Israel, 2003; recipient Lifetime Achievement award Coll. Art Assn., 1989, Internat. Sculpture Ctr., 1991; named Officer of Arts and Letters French Ministry of Culture, 1984. Fellow Am. Acad. Arts and Scis.; mem. Am. Acad. and Inst. Arts and Letters, Sculptors Guild, Am. Abstract Artists, Coll. Art Assn. (Disting. Artist award for lifetime achievement 1989). Office: Robert Miller Gallery 524 W 26th St Ground Fl New York NY 10001-5541*

BOURGEOIS, PATRICIA ANN, middle school educator; b. N.Y.C., Aug. 25, 1952; d. John Patrick and Ellen Patricia (Park) Roche; m. Bruce David Bourgeois, Aug. 26, 1972; children: Larisa, Sean, Nicole. BS, Fairleigh Dickinson U., 1974; M., U. Houston, 1990. Cert. spl. edn. tchr., Tex. Life skills tchr. Humble (Tex.) Ind. Sch. Dist., 1989-92; tchr. students with autism Aldine (Tex.) Ind. Sch. Dist., 1992—. Mem. Tex. Assn. for Persons with Severe Handicaps (bd. dirs. 1991-94), Assn. for Persons with Severe Handicaps, Coun. for Exceptional Children. Roman Catholic. Avocation: research. Home: 8706 Donys Dr Houston TX 77040-1547

BOURGEOIS, PATRICIA MCLIN, academic administrator, women's health and pediatrics nurse, educator; b. Hammond, La., Mar. 12, 1941; d. Lannie McLin and Mary (Lossett) Nicolay; m. Charles Bourgeois, June 10, 1962; children: Deborah, Cynthia, Terry Kay, Lori, Betsy. BSN, McNeese State U., 1962; MSN, Northwestern State U., Natchitoches, La., 1980. Cert. clin. nurse specialist, nursing child assessment, La. Office nurse pediatrics Green Clinic, Ruston, La., 1962-63; staff nurse ob-gyn. Lincoln Gen. Hosp., Ruston, 1963-64; staff nurse nursery St. Francis Cabrini Hosp., Alexandria, La., 1966-67; prof. maternal/child nursing La. Tech. U., Ruston, 1975—, faculty senate v.p., 2005—, faculty senate pres., 2006. Part-time office nurse Green Clinic, 1975-93; part-time resident nurse Methodist Children's Home, Ruston, 1990-97. Vice chairperson La. Coalition for Maternal/Infant Health, Baton Rouge, 1989-91; pres. Ruston Civic Guild, 1990. Recipient Inst. Regulatory Excellence fellow, Nat. Coun. State Bd. Mem. ANA (del. 1991-93), La. State Nurses Assn. (sec. 1991-93, pres. 1994-95), La. State Bd. of Nursing (apptd. mem., v.p. 2004, pres. 2005). Democrat. Roman Catholic. Office: La Tech Univ PO Box B 152 Ruston LA 71272-3178

BOURGEOIS, SHARON E., mechanical engineer; b. Beverly, Mass., June 11, 1955; d. Perry Bradford and Claire Arnold; m. Edwin H. Griffen, Apr. 12, 1977 (div.)l children: David, Michelle. BSME, U. New Orleans, 1981. Assoc. engr. La. Power & Light, New Orleans, 1982-84, engr., 1985-88, maintenance engr., 1988-90, Va. Power, Mineral, 1990-92, staff engr., 1992—. Served with U.S. Army, 1976-79. Mem. ASME (assoc.). Avocations: painting, home renovation, skiing. Home: 6909 W 34th St Little Rock AR 72204-4724

BOURGOIN, MARY BETH NIVISON, social studies educator; b. Waterville, Maine, Oct. 10, 1968; d. Jack A. and JoAnn W. Nivison; m. Jim Bourgoin, June 27, 1992; children: Conner J., JoAnn K. BS, U. Maine, Orono, 1991. Tchr. lang. arts grade 7 Winslow Jr. H.S., Maine, 1991—96, tchr. social studies grade 8, 1996—. Coach field hockey Winslow Jr. H.S., 1991—94, 2005—, student coun. advisor, 1999—2002. Dir./coach field hockey Town of Winslow Parks & Recreation, 2002—, basketball coach, 2005—; softball coach Winslow Little League, Winslow, 2004—; sch. bd. chairperson/mem. St. John Regional Cath. Sch., Winslow, 2002—. Mem.: Winslow Edn. Assn. (assoc.; v.p. 2000—06). Catholic. Avocations: travel, walking, golf. Office: Winslow Jr HS 6 Danielson St Winslow ME 04901 Office Phone: 207-872-1973.

BOURGUIGNON, ERIKA EICHHORN, anthropologist, educator; b. Vienna, Feb. 18, 1924; d. Leopold H. and Charlotte (Rosenbaum) Eichhorn; m. Paul H. Bourguignon, Sept. 29, 1950. BA, Queens Coll., 1945; grad. study, U. Conn., 1945; PhD, Northwestern U., 1951; DHL, CUNY, 2000. Field work Chippewa Indians, Wis., summer 1946; field work Haiti; anthropologist Northwestern U., 1947-48; instr. Ohio State U., 1949-56, asst. prof., 1956-60, assoc. prof., 1960-66, prof., 1966-90, acting chmn. dept. anthropology, 1971-72, chmn. dept., 1972-76, prof. emeritus, 1990—; dir. Cross-Cultural Study of Dissociational States, 1963-68. Bd. dirs. Human Relations Area Files, Inc., 1976-79 Author: Possession, 1976, rev. edit., 1991, Psychological Anthropology, 1979, Italian transl., 1983; editor, co-author: Religion, Altered States of Consciousness and Social Change, 1973, A World of Women, 1980; co-author: Diversity and Homogeneity in World Societies, 1973; adv. editor: Behavior Sci. Rsch., 1976-79; assoc. editor Jour. Psychoanalytic Anthropology, 1977-87; mem. editl. bd. Ethos, 1979-89, 97—2005, 2005—, Jour. Haitian Studies, 2000—, Anthropology of Consciousness, 2002—; editor: Margaret Mead: The Anthropologist in America—, Occasional Papers in Anthropology, No. 2, Ohio State U. Dept. Anthropology, 1986; (with Barbara Rigney) Exile: A Memoir of 1939 by Bronka Schneider, 1998; contbr. articles to profl. jours. Fellow Am. Anthrop. Assn.; mem. Ctrl. State Anthrop. Soc. (treas. 1953-56, exec. com. 1995-98), Ohio Acad Sci., World Psychiat. Assn. (transcultural psychiatry sect.), Am. Ethnol. Soc., Current Anthropology (assoc.), Soc. for Psychol. Anthropology (nominations com. 1981-82, bd. dirs. 1991-93, lifetime achievement award 1999), Soc. for the Anthropology of Religion, Phi Beta Kappa, Sigma Xi. E-mail: bourguignon.1@osu.edu.

BOURKE-FAUSTINA, MARLENE FRANCES, music educator; b. Honolulu, Mar. 10, 1944; d. Francis Patrick and Violet Kahale Bourke; m. Manuel Edward Faustina, Jan. 3, 1990; children: Aaron Faustina, Christian Faustina, Shane Faustina. B.Mus.Edn., Walla Walla Coll., College Place, Wash., 1970; Profl. Diploma in Music Edn., U. Hawaii, Honolulu, 1973. Music tchr. Umatilla County #31/K-8, Milton-Freewater, Oreg., 1970—72; chorus/band/vocal coach Hawaiian Mission Acad., Honolulu, 1974—76; chorus, music tchr. Hawaiian Mission Elem. Acad. K-12, Honolulu, 1974—76, Waianae Intermediate Sch., Waianae, 1977—84, Highlands Intermediate Sch., Pearl City, Hawaii, 1984—88, Wahiawa Intermediate Sch., 1988—92, Waianae Intermediate Sch., 1992—. Vocalist Royal Hawaiian Band, Honolulu, 1972—77, Ctrl. Union Ch., Honolulu, 1977—84, Kawaihao Ch., Honolulu, 2005—06. Dir., coord. Roses Waianae Charity WIS Campaign for Homeless. Named Outstanding Secondary Educators of Am. award, 1978, Hawaii Leeward State Tchr. of the Yr., 1985, 2003; recipient Outstanding Alumni award, Kamehameha Schs., 1970. Mem.: Am. Choral Dirs. Assn., Music Educators Nat. Conf. Democrat. Seventh-Day Adventist. Avocations: designing Hawaiian floral arrangements, gardening, arranging music. Home: 85-223 C Ala Akau St Waianae HI 96792 Office: Waianae Intermediate Sch 85-626 Farrington Hwy Waianae HI 96792 Business E-Mail: marlene-bourke-faustina@notes.k12.hi.us.

BOURNE, JOANN M., bank executive; Mgr. Comml. Deposit Svcs. Div. Union Bank of Calif., LA, 1997—2002, exec. v.p., 2000—, head Comml. Banking Group, 2002—03, group head Comml. Deposits and Treasury Mgmt. Group, 2003—. Bd. mem. LA County Econ. Develop. Corp. Office: Union Bank of Calif 400 California St San Francisco CA 94104-1302

BOURNE, KATHERINE DAY, journalist, educator; b. Lynn, Mass., Sept. 11, 1938; d. Schuyler Vandervort and Elsie Marie (Mayo) Day; m. William Nettleton Bourne; children: William Alexander, Katherine Loring. BS in Edn., Keene Tchrs. Coll., 1960; MEd, Harvard U., 1984. Tchr. Wachusett Regional High Sch., Holden, Mass., 1960-61; arts editor Bay State Banner, Boston, 1966—2006; dir. edn. Suffolk County House of Correction, Boston, 1979-84; edn. coord. Dept. Transitional Asst., Mass., 1984—2002, ret., 2002—; lead critic Kay Bourne Arts Report, 2006—. Adj. scholar Northeastern U., 2006—. Contbr. music revs. to Christian Sci. Monitor. Dir. rels. Crime-out, Boston, 1983; mem. Gov.'s Commn. on Status of Women, 1970-74; co-founder, dir. Harvard-Radcliffe Forum Theatre, Cambridge, 1964-68; bd. dirs., mem. ARC Greater Boston, 1987-95, NAACP Boston, 1978-81. NEH journalism fellow, 1978; recipient Melnea A. Cass award Greater Boston YMCA, 1984. Mem. NAACP (life). Avocations: collecting african-american literature, aerobics, photography, stamps, art relating to black history and life. Home: 52 High St Brookline MA 02445-7707

BOURNE-BUSBY, ELISE BERNADETTE, principal; b. Port-of-Spain, Trinidad and Toabgo, May 30, 1942; arrived in U.S., 1963; d. Reginald Adalbert and Ivy Muriel Bourne; m. Winston Allen Thomas (div.); children: Nakeisha Hills, Trinay Thomas, Charisse Torres; m. Kenneth Talbot Busby, July 3, 1997. AA, Mt. Aloysius Jr. Coll., Cresson, Pa., 1965; EdB, Coll. Misericordia, 1967; EdM, Howard U., 1973; EdD, Nova South Ea. U., 1997. Cert. tchr. N.Y., N.J., adminstrn./supervision N.Y., N.J. Metrication specialist Trinidad and Tobago Metrication Bd., 1977—82; elem. sch. tchr. St. Anthony of Padua Cath. Sch., Passaic, NJ, 1982—84, N.Y.C. Bd. Edn., Bronx, 1984—86; elem. sch. prin. St. Anthony of Padua Sch., Passaic, 1986—92; elem. sch. tchr. Hawthorne Sch.-Teaneck (N.J.) Pub. Schs., 1992—94; elem. sch. prin. Longfellow Sch.-Teaneck Pub. Schs., 1994—97, Whittier Sch.-Teaneck Pub. Schs., 1997—. Chairperson Communities-In-Schs., Passaic, 1990—, More Than Friends, Passaic, 1995—; Cancer Survivor Reach to Recovery vol. Am. Cancer Soc. Recipient Woman of Achievement award, Congressman Bill Pascrell, 2004, Cmty. Svc. award, Phi Delta Kappa, 2005; Dodge Project grant, N.J. Network for Edn. Renewal, Montclair State U., 2005. Mem.: N.J. Prins. and Suprs. Assn., N.J. Assn. for Supervision and Curriculum Devel. Roman Catholic. Avocations: travel, reading, designing educational tools. Home: 350 Sherman St Passaic NJ 07055 Office: Whittier Elem Sch 491 W Englewood Ave Teaneck NJ 07666

BOURQUE, LOUISE, film director, film instructor; BA in Comm., Univ. de Moncton, 1986; BFA in Film Prodn., Concordia Univ., 1990; MFA in Filmmaking, Sch. Art Inst. Chgo., 1992. Film instr. Sch. Mus. Fine Arts, Boston. Dir.: (films) The People in the House, 1994, Going Back Home, 2000, Self Portrait Post Mortem, 2002, The Bleeding Heart of it, 2005. Achievements include appearing in Whitney Biennial, Whitney Mus. Art, NYC, 2006. Office: SMFA Boston 230 The Fenway Boston MA 02115*

BOURQUE, PEGGY SUE, emergency nurse practitioner; b. Pt. Arthur, Tex., Apr. 9, 1958; d. Carl Raymond Fischer and Jewel Lavern Nolan; m. Dwayne David Bourque, June 30, 1978. BSN, Tex. Woman's U., 1984; MSN, U. Tex., Houston, 1996. RN, Tex.; acute care nurse practitioner. Emergency nurse practitioner Emcare@Meml. Hosp.-S.E., Houston, 1997, Bapt. Hosp., Orange, Tex., 1997-98, Meml. Hermann N.W. Hosp. Emergency Physicians, LLP, Houston, 1998—. Mem. adv. com. for emergency/ambulatory nurse practitioner program U. Tex., Houston, 1996—. Mem. Am. Acad. Nurse Practitioners, Emergency Nurses Assn., Sigma Theta Tau. Avocations: reading, dance. Office: Meml Hermann NW Hosp Emergency Physicians LLP 1635 North Loop W Houston TX 77008-1532 E-mail: peggysb@juno.com.

BOUSKA LEE, CARLA ANN, nursing and health care educator; b. Ellsworth, Kans., Nov. 26, 1943; d. Frank J. and Christine Rose (Vopat) Bouska; m. Gordon Larry Lee, July 8, 1967. RN, Marymount Coll., Salina, Kans., 1964; BSN, U. Kans., 1967; MA, Wichita State U., 1972, EdS, 1975, M in Nursing, 1984; PhD, Kans. State U., 1988. RN, cert. family and adult nurse practitioner, health edn. specialist, advanced nurse adminstr. Staff, charge nurse Ellsworth (Kans.) County Vet. Meml. Hosp., 1964—65; critical, coronary, and surg. nurse Med. Ctr. U. Kans., Kansas City, 1966—67, Watkins Meml. Hosp. and Student Health Ctr., 1965—66; asst. dir., chief instr. Wesley Sch. Nursing, Wichita, Kans., 1967—74; asst prof., chair nurse clinician/practitioner dept. Wichita State U., 1974—84, asst. prof. grad. health adminstrn. program, 1984—92; assoc. prof., dir. nurse practitioner program Ft. Hays State U., Hays, Kans., 1992—95; assoc. prof., coord. postgrad. nursing studies Clark Coll., Omaha, 1995—, nursing health svcs. mgmt. and allied health, 1994—; cons., v.p. devel. GRCIs Industries, Inc., 1994—; coord. nurses continuing edn. Providers - Kans. Mo. Nurses Assn. EMT, physician asst. HCA; lectr. Wichita State U., 1972—74, mem. grad. faculty, 1993—95; cons. Hays Med. Ctr.-Family Healthcare Ctr., 1993—96, Baker U., Northeastern U., Boston; mem. adv. coun. Kans. Newman Coll.; mem. adv. bd. Kans. Originals, Kans. Dept. Econ. Devel. Project, Wilson; mem. grad. faculty U. Kans., 1993—95; rschr. in field; bd. advisors Who's Who in Am. Nursing; bd. rsch. advisors Internat. Biog. Ctr., Cambridge, England. Author (with Ig & Barrett): Fluids and Electrolytes: A Basic Approach, 1996; author: Delman's Fundamental and Advanced Nursing Skills, 2000, (poetry) Seasons: Marks of Life, 1991 (Golden Poet award, 1991); actor: (poetry) Winter Tree, 1995 (Internat. Poet of Merit award, 1995); author: (booklet) Czechoslovakian History, 1988 (honor room Czech Mus. and Opera House, Wilson); author: (and editor) History of Kansas Nursing, 1987; contbr. articles to profl. jours. Co-founder Kans. Nurses Found., pres., trustee, 1978—93; vol. ARC, 1967—92, bd. dirs., 1977—90; mem., rschr. Gov.'s Commn. Health Care, Topeka, 1990; vol., lectr. Am. Heart Assn., 1967—, Am. Cancer Soc., 1967—; chair Nat. Task Force on Core Competence of Nurse Practitioners, 1994—95; mem. State of Kans. health care agenda Kans. Pub. Health Assn., 1995; city coord. campaign Sec. State, 1986; election judge Sedgwick County, Kans., 1989—94. Named Outstanding Cmty. Leader, Jaycees, Alumnus of Yr., Kans. U., 1979, Marymount Coll., 1987, Poet of the Yr., 1995; recipient Tchr. award, Mortar Bd.; grantee Nurse Practitioner Tng. grantee, U.S. Health and Human Svcs., 1966—67. Fellow: Am. Acad. Nursing, Am. Acad. Nursing; mem.: Internat. Soc. Poets (disting.), Gt. Plains Nurse Practitioners Soc. (founder, pres. 1993—), Kans. Nurse Found. (pres., dir., dist. alt. rep. 1978), Kans. Alliance Advanced Nurse Practitioners (founder, pres. 1986—, pres., dir., dist. alt. rep. 1992), Kans. Nurses Assn. (bd. dirs., treas.), Nat. Commn. on Credentialing of Health Edn. Specialists, Am. Bus. and Profl. Women's Assn. (Hall of Fame 1999), Am. Acad. Nurse Practitioners, Nat. League Nursing, ANA (nat. and site visitor ANCC), Sigma Theta Tau (Internat. Woman of the Yr. 1998), Alpha Eta (pres. chpt.). Republican. Roman Catholic. Avocations: poetry, music, gardening, writing, sewing. Home: 1367 N Westlink Ave Wichita KS 67212-4238 Office: Holy Names College Dept Nursing 3500 Mountain Blvd Oakland CA 94619-1699 Fax: 510-436-1376. E-mail: lee@hnc.edu.

BOUSLOG, ROBBIN RAYE, performing arts educator, art educator; b. Fullerton, Calif., July 17, 1952; d. Roger Leslie and Wanda Lee (Culpepper) Acton; m. Richard Bouslog, Mar. 28, 1998; 1 stepchild, Summer Nicole; m. Allan Lee Morrow, June 26, 1971 (div. Dec. 17, 1997); children: Samuel Eli Morrow, Israel Allan Morrow. AA, San Jacinto CC, Calif., 1985; BA in Liberal Studies, Calif. State U., San Bernardino, 1987; MA in Edn., Claremont Grad. Sch., Calif., 1989. Cert. Collaborative Design Inst., 2003, Collaborative Design Inst. Leadership, 2006. Musician and choir dir. Canyon Lake (Calif.) Cmty. Ch., 1982—87; worship leader and musician Elsinore Valley Friends Ch., Lake Elsinore, Calif., 1987—97; elem. tchr. Lake Elsinore Unified Sch. Dist., 1987—96; adj. prof. Edn. dept. Hope Internat. U., Fullerton, 2001; mid. sch. tchr. Lake Elsinore Unified Sch. Dist., 1996—. Presenter visual and performing arts Lake Elsinore Unified Sch. Dist., 1987—; presenter Calif. League of Mid. Schs., San Francisco, 1996—, San Diego, 1996—. Author: (projects) Weaving in the Arts, 2000, LEUSD Visual and Performing Arts Stds., 2001. Com. mem. Tuscany Hills Homeowners Assn., Lake Elsinore, 2001; dir. Canyon Lake Choraleers, Canyon Lake, 1992. Nominee Bravo award, L.A. Music Ctr. Edn., 1994, 2002; scholar Tchrs. Honor Soc., San Jacinto C.C., 1985; Apple grant, Claremont Grad. Sch., 1987. Mem.: Calif. Music Edn. Assn., Calif. Tchrs. Assn., Calif. Art Project. Republican. Achievements include direction of nationally recognized mid. sch. choirs. Avocations: acting, music, hiking, travel, reading. Office: Lake Elsinore Unified Sch Dist 545 Chaney St Lake Elsinore CA 92530 Home: 30431 Harbor Cir Canyon Lake CA 92587-7718 E-mail: rickandrobbin@msn.com.

BOUSQUET-MONK, NANCY KATHRYN, elementary school educator; b. Knoxville, Iowa, Feb. 15, 1945; d. Joseph Pierre Bousquet and Frances Marie Hansen; m. Charles Cowley Monk, Apr. 1, 1994; m. Joel Bernard Swetish (div.); children: Joel Frederick, Laurel Jane. BS, Ctrl. Coll., 1967; M in Edn., Nat. Louis U., 1987. Elem. sch. tchr. Gower Sch., Hinsdale, Ill., 1967—69, Oak Creek Franklin Sch., 1969—2001. Avocations: genealogy, reading. Home: 5751 Finch Lane Greendale WI 53129

BOUSTEAD, DIANE DOLORES, secondary school educator, chemistry educator; d. Donald Robert and Martha Dolores Behnke; m. Charles Oren Boustead, June 18, 1976; children: Jared Nathan, Lynn Collins Amanda, Kristen Rene. BS in Chemistry, Westminster U., 1976. Cert. tchr. Pa., 1987. Chemist, indsl. hygenist Mobay (Now Bayer), Pitts., 1976—79; ind. cons. in field Pitts., 1979—84; industial hygenist NUS Corp., Pitts., 1984—89; tchr. chemistry West Allegheny H.S., Imperial, Pa., 1989—. Coach, event supr. Sci. Olympiad, New Wilmington, Pa., 1990—; coach Hometown Hi Q, Pitts., 1999—. Active Clinton (Pa.) Buckle Up Baby, 1981—98; planner agrl. fair Findlay Twp. Fair Bd., Clinton, 1985—2005. Named All Star Educator, U. Pitts. Sch. Edn., 1998; recipient Governor's Hwy. Safety award, State of Pa., 1984. Mem.: West Allegheny Edn. Assn., Key Club (faculty advisor 2001—). Republican. Presbyn. Avocations: travel, needlecrafts, gardening. Home: 257 Main Street Imperial PA 15126 Office: West Allegheny High School 205 West Allegheny Road Imperial PA 15126 Business E-Mail: dboustead@westallegheny.k12.pa.us.

BOUTIETTE, VICKIE LYNN, elementary school educator, reading specialist; b. Valley City, N.D., Mar. 13, 1950; BS in Elem. Edn., Valley City State U., 1972; MS in Reading, Moorhead State U., 1997; postgrad., U. S.D., 1998—. 4th-5th grade tchr. Pillsbury Pub. Sch., 1973-74; 3rd grade tchr. West Fargo Pub. Schs., 1984-90, remedial reading tchr., elem. tchr., 1993-98, Reading Recovery tchr. leader, 1998—. Sunday sch. tchr., 1975—, ch. newsletter editor, 1993—; vol. U. Minn. Hosps. and Clinics, 1991-93. Recipient Nat. Educator Award Milken Family Found., 1998, Courage award N.D. Edn. Assn., 1994, Disting. Alumni award Minn. State U. Moorhead, 2002, Alumni Merit award Valley City State U., 2000; Christa McAuliffe fellowship, 2000; named N.D. Tchr. of Yr., 1998, West Fargo Tchr. of Yr. 1997-98. Mem. NEA, West Fargo Edn. Assn. (exec. bd. 1989-90, elem. chairperson 1988-89, pub. rels. chairperson 1988-90), N.D. Edn. Assn., Valley Reading Assn. (rec. sec. 1997—), N.D. Reading Assn., Phi Delta Kappa, Alpha Mu Gamma (pres. 1972). Home: 7103 64th Ave S Fargo ND 58104-5715 Office: Westside Elem Sch 945 7th Ave W West Fargo ND 58078-1429 Fax: 701-356-2119.

BOUTROS, LINDA NELENE WILEY, medical/surgical nurse; b. New Orleans, Aug. 31, 1951; d. Robert Vernon and Marye Dell (Adcock) Wiley; m. Eddy Boutros, Dec. 23, 1972; children: Scott, Mark, Natalie. BS in Nursing, U. S.W. La., 1973. Cert. health care risk mgr. RN, relief charge, charge nurse, med./surgical flr. Bap. Hosp., Beaumont, Tex., 1973—76; RN, coord./supr. of nursing Kelsey Seybold Clinic, Missouri City, Tex., 1982-86; RN, head nurse S.W. Pediatric Ctr., Sugarland, Tex., 1986-87; RN, nursing supr. Westshore Hosp., Tampa, Fla., 1988-89; med.-surg. nurse Centurion Hosp., Carrollwood and Tampa, 1989-90, asst. head nurse med., 1990-91, relief supr., 1991, dir. surg. nursing svcs., 1992-93; nurse mgr. surg. floor, relief house supr. Univ. Cmty. Hosp. Carrollwood, Tampa, Fla., 1993-99, RN adminstrv. supr., 1999—2005, relief supr., 2005—. Adj. faculty U. So. Fla. Coll. Nursing; clin. instr. for RN nursing students U. Cmty. Hosp. Carrollwood. Mem. ANA, Fla. Nurses Assn. Office: Univ Cmty Hosp Carrollwood 7171 N Dale Mabry Hwy Tampa FL 33614-2670 Personal E-mail: lwboutros@hotmail.com.

BOUTWELL, ANNE DIELSCHNEIDER, artist, painter; b. Portland, Oreg., Mar. 12, 1932; d. William Norwood and Edra Anne Dielschneider; m. Burr North Boutwell, Sr., Aug. 22, 1955 (dec. Jan. 20, 1977); children: Burr North Boutwell, Jr., Meade Norwood, Noell Seufert. BFA in Portraiture, Pacific NW Coll. Art, PNCA, 1980; BS in Drawing and Painting, U. Oreg., Sch. Architecture and Allied Arts, 1954. Artist Anne Boutwell Studios, Portland, 1981—86; mktg. support Print Right (now Lazerquick), Willsonville, Oreg., 1986—87; assoc. dir. Argus Fine Arts Corp., Portland, 1987—88. Program editor, various coms., chmn. of Oreg. hist. soc. vol. progam Portland Jr. League, Portland, 1961—72; pres. Womens League, 1972—75; arts and cultural standing com., arts and humanities, land use and zoning, land use study standing committees City Club, 1977—88; visual arts chmn., spl. events com. Art Quake Bd. of Dis., 1982—85; pres. Portland Beautification Assn., 1986—88; regent Mutlnomah Chpt., DAR, 1998—2000; organizing sec. for state of oreg. Oreg. State Soc. DAR, Oreg., 2002—04. Wall mural, Vista St. Claire, 2 wall murals, LazerQuick Corp. Exec. Hdqrs., Willsonville, Represented in permanent collections Oreg. Hist. Soc., Portland, Dr. Francis J. Newton. Collection, Portland Art Mus., Rental Sales. Mem. Rep. Party. Recipient 50 Yr. Pin, Kappa Kappa Gamma, 1951-2001, Order of the Emerald Soc. 50 Yr. Pin, U. Oreg., 2004. Mem.: DAR, Portland Art Mus., Contemporary Art Coun., Jr. League Garden Club, Women's Archtl. League, Trinity Catherdral Iconography Inst. (icon painter 2004—05), Arnold Bennett Hall Soc. Episcopalian. Home: 2309 SW 1st Ave #441 Portland OR 97201-5039 Personal E-mail: anneboutwell@aol.com.

BOUTWELL, SHARON MARIE, school system administrator, educator; 2 children. BS in Secondary Edn., U. Tex., 1973; MEd in Curriculum and Instrn., U. Houston, 1981, EdD in Adminstrn. and Supervision, 1995. Cert. English, history, gifted and talented tchr., mid-mgmt., supt. Tex. Tchr. Spring Branch Ind. Sch. Dist., Houston, 1974—92, 1993—95, dir. tech., 1992—93, grad. sch. facilitator, rsch. and evaluation staff appraisal, staff devel., 1995—96, facilitator, staff and orgnl. devel., 1996—99, lead area instrnl. specialist Stratford Learning Cmty., 1999—2002, adminstr. strategic planning and profl. devel., 2002—05; adminstrn. spl. projects, 2005—. Cons. Ministry of Edn., Singapore, 1998; adj. prof. Houston Bapt. U., U. St. Thomas, Tex. A&M U.; pres. Region IV Tex. Coun. Women Sch. Execs., 2003—04; presenter in field; mem. Nat. Staff Devel. Coun. Graduate Acad. VIII, 1999—; mem. alumni bd. U. Houston, Coll. Edn., 2002—; regional rep. State Level Tex. Coun. Women's Sch. Execs., 2004—. Author, co-dir. (video) Learning Organization Initiative, 1996 (Matrix award, 1996). Chair h.s. drill team events, Houston, 2000—04; PTA treas., 2005—; mem. ch. leadership Meml. Drive United Meth., Houston, 1997—2001. Mem.: Tex. Staff Devel. Coun., Assn. Supervision, Curriculum and Instrn., Tex. Assn. Gifted and Talented, Tex. Assn. Sch. Adminstrs., Nat. Staff Devel. Coun., Phi Delta Kappa. Methodist. Avocations: gardening, interior decorating, antiques, reading. Office: 955 Campbell Rd Houston TX 77024 Office Phone: 713-464-1511.

BOUVÊ, JANET SAAR, secondary school educator; b. Iowa City, Iowa, Jan. 6, 1947; d. Jesse Lee Saar and Gertrude Conrad; m. David Clement Bouvé, July 27, 1974; children: Kristen Saar Bouvé, Andrew David Bouvé. BA, Am. U., Washington, DC, 1968; MAT, U. Iowa, Iowa City, 1971. Publs. ofcl. World Bank, Washington, 1968—69; h.s. tchr. Montgomery County, Md., 1969—70, 1981—, Fairfax County, Va., 1971—81. Mem. selection com. chpt. NHS Col. Zadok Magruder H.S., 2000—, sponsor Juan Rulfo chpt. Sociedad Hispanica, 2006—; trustee Oakdale Emory United Meth. Ch., Olney, Md., 1993—99. Mem.: NEA, Montgomery Ednl. Assn., Phi Kappa Phi. Republican. Office: Col Zadok Magruder HS 5939 Muncaster Mill Rd Derwood MD 20855

BOUVIER, LINDA FRITTS, publishing executive; b. Dover, N.J., Nov. 8, 1946; d. Fletcher Loomis and Dorothy Evelyn (Lukens) Fritts; m. Alan Moylan, May 30, 1971 (div.); m. John Emerson Ross, Dec. 28, 1985 (div.); m. Claude Edward Bouvier, Nov. 12, 1994 (div.); m. Alan Jay Dressler, Oct. 11, 2005. BFA in Advt. Design, Visual Comm., Pratt Inst., Bklyn., 1968. Designer MD Med. News Mag., N.Y.C., 1968-71; art dir. Miami (Fla.) Mag., 1973-74; ind. cons. Linda Moylan Design, Miami, 1974-84; prodn. mgr. U. Miami, 1984-85; product devel., sales The Mazer Corp., Dayton, Ohio, 1986-89; sales mgr. TSI Graphics, Cranford, N.J., 1989-92; product mgr., electronic svcs. RR Donnelley and Sons, N.Y.C., Waltham, Mass., 1992-94; v.p. emerging pub. technologies Simon & Schuster, N.Y.C., 1994-95; v.p. prodn., mfg., inventory sch. divsn. Houghton Mifflin Co., Boston, 1995-97; sr. acct. exec. Ames On-Demand, Woburn, Mass., 1998-99; v.p. content devel. and pub. rels. RoweCom, Inc., Cambridge, Mass., 1999-2000; cons. Boston, 2000—. Adv. bd. The Heller Report: Internet Strategies for Education Markets, 1995—. Co-chair N.Y. Book Show, 1989. Enabling technologies com. Am. Assn. Publ., 1995. Recipient award Soc. Pub. Designers, 1970-82. Mem. Bookbuilders of Boston. Avocations: photography, gourmet cooking, art, horticulture. Personal E-mail: lbouvier@aol.com.

BOVEROUX, LORIE ANN HANSEN, secondary school educator, graphics designer; b. Mt. Vernon, N.Y., Dec. 10, 1966; d. Thede Martin Hansen and Margaret Gertrude Neave Hansen; m. Benjamin Apthorp Gould Boveroux, Apr. 20, 1996; 1 child, Elisabeth Ashleigh. BArch, Cornell U., 1988; MS in City and Regional Planning, Pratt Inst., 2001. Lic. graphic arts tchr. N.Y. Layout artist Hagedorn Coram, New Rochelle, NY, 1982—86; prodn. coord. Lillian Vernon, Mt. Vernon, 1986—88; office asst. supt. Spencer Press of Maine, N.Y.C., 1988—90; sr. prodn. mgr. Harrison Svcs., N.Y.C., 1990—92; lead tchr. graphics Mt. Vernon H.S., 1992—98, Saunders Trades and Tech. H.S., Yonkers, NY, 1998—. Occupl. ednl. adv. coun. Mt. Vernon City Schs., 1992—98; designer St. Paul's Epistle St. Pauls Episcopal Ch., Fairfield, Conn., 1999—. Sponsor NAACP, Mt. Vernon, 1998. Named Outstanding Student, Am. Planning Assn., 2000. Mem.: Vocat. Indsl. Clubs Am. (state and regional chairperson adv. design 1992—98, advisor 1998—). Avocations: historic preservation, community development, urban planning. Home: 670 Reid St Fairfield CT 06430-3467 Office: Saunders Trades and Tech HS 183 Palmer Rd Yonkers NY 10701

BOWARD, DIANA LARSON, medical/surgical nurse; b. Savannah, Ga., June 22, 1949; m. Robert E. Boward, July 10, 1971; children: Rebecca, Katherine. BSN, U. Iowa, 1971. Cert. nutritional support nurse, Oncology Nurse., Cancer Care Coord. Clin. instr. Sauk Valley Coll., Dixon, Ill.; staff RN, ICU KSB Hosp., Dixon, RN, nutritional support nurse. Mem.: Mem. Oncology Nursing Soc.

BOWDEN, LAURA ANN, retired secondary school educator, retired counselor; b. Superior, Wis., Apr. 22, 1915; d. Herbert Lincoln Beglinger and Dea Anne Biglow; m. Clayton George Bowden, June 30, 1937 (dec.); children: Dea JuVette, Clayton George Bowden, Jr.(dec.), Beth Good, John. BEd in Social Scis., English & German, Superior Tchrs. Coll., 1935; MEd in Counseling, U. Wis., 1966. Tchr. Hawkins Sch. Dist., Wis., 1935—37; psycho-therapist Treatment Ctr. Seriously Disturbed Children, Superior, 1966—68; tchr., counselor Superior Sr. HS, 1968—76; ret., 1976. Founder Tchr.-Mom Program Superior Sch. Dist., 1965—77, chair, 1976—80; presenter workshops in field. Ch. youth counselor, vol. Divsn. Corrections, 1952—61; adv. com. Superior Vocations Ctr., 1979—85; mem. Youth Task Force, Superior, 1993; advocate vol. Boys & Girls Club, Superior, 1995—; cert. lay spkr. Faith U. Meth. Ch., Superior, 1990—; bd. dirs. Douglas County Human Resource Ctr., 1979—84. Recipient Woman of Yr., Wis. Mental Health Assn., 1964, Citizen of Yr., Douglas County Commn., 1979, Presdl. Citation award, Pres. Reagan, DC, 1985, award, Superior Area Ret. Educators Assn. Mem.: Mental Health Assn. (charter pres. 1963, inst. chair 1977), Wis. Retired Educators Assn., Phi Delta Kappa (edn. chair 1966—68). Achievements include founding The Health Care Clinic in Superior, a reproductive health program for youth and young adults in 1979; pioneering a teen-suicide prevention program in Douglas County, Wisconsin in 1985, where legislation mandated prevention information within the schools. Avocations: gardening, canoeing, swimming, baking. Home: 1013 N 19th St Superior WI 54880 Office: Health Care Clinic 2231 Catlin Ave Superior WI 54880

BOWDEN, LINDA, diversified financial services company executive; b. New Jersey; BA in Edu., Rowan U.; MA in Institutional Counseling, William Paterson U.; MBA, Fairleigh Dickinson U.; grad., Nat. Trust Sch., Northwestern U. Cert. Trust Fin. Advisor. Former teacher, Wyckoff, NJ; various positions including NW sales mgr., private banking group Citibank, 1983—91; various positions including portfolio mgr., trust and investment officer, and private banking officer Wachovia, NYC, 1991—2000; dir. wealth mgmt. for NY, NJ and Conn. Wachovia Wealth Mgmt., NYC, 2000—04, wealth mgmt. exec., 2004—. Named one of 25 Women to Watch, US Banker mag., 2005. Office: Wachovia Wealth Mgmt 12 E 49th St New York NY 10017*

BOWDEN, SALLY ANN, choreographer, educator, dancer; b. Dallas, Feb. 27, 1943; d. Cloyd MacAnally and Sally Estelle. Student, Boston U., 1960-62. Mem. Paul Sanasardo Dance Co., N.Y.C., 1963-67; pvt. tchr., choreographer N.Y.C., 1968-70; faculty Merce Cunningham Dance Studio, N.Y.C., 1971-76; faculty, co-dir. Constrn. Co. Dance Studio, N.Y.C., 1972-77; choreographer Constrn. Co. Theater/Dance Assocs., N.Y.C., 1972—. Artist-in-residence U. Wis., Madison, fall, 1975, N.C. Sch. of Arts, winter, 1978, U. Minn., Duluth, 1979, 1981-82, Kenyon (Ohio) Coll., fall 1980 Choreographer: Three Dances, 1969, Sally Bowden Dances and Talks at the New School, 1972, The Ice Palace, 1973, White River Junction, 1975, The Wonderful World of Modern Dance or The Amazing Story of the Plie, (1976) Wheat, 1976-77, Kite, 1978, Voyages, 1978, Morningdance, 1979, Crescent, 1980, Diverted Suite, 1983, Baby Dance, 1984. Recipient Creative Artists Public Service award for choreography, 1976-77; Nat. Endowment for the Arts Choreography fellow, 1975 Office: Theater/Dance Assocs 41 E 1st St New York NY 10003-9307

BOWDEN, VIRGINIA MASSEY, librarian; b. Houston, Tex., July 22, 1939; d. Calvin Scott and Juanita Barlow Massey; m. Charles Lee Bowden, July 2, 1960; children: Sharon Scott Bowden Davis, Ellen Maureen Bowden McIntyre. BA, U. Tex., 1960, PhD, 1994; MSLS, U. Ky., 1970. Programmer Texaco Inc., Houston, 1960-64; sr. programmer AMA, Chgo., 1964-65, C.E.I.R. Inc., N.Y.C., 1965-66, Bambergers, Newark, 1967-68; systems analyst, asst. to dir. U. Tex. Health Sci. Ctr., San Antonio, 1970-78, assoc. libr. dir., 1978-85, libr. dir., 1985—2003, libr. dir. emeritus, 2004—. Author: (with others) Handbook of Medical Library Practice, 1983; contbr. articles to profl. jours. Prse. Friends Pub. Libr., San Antonio, 1989-90. Recipient numerous grants Nat. Libr. Medicine, 1982-2003, Julia Grothaus award Bexar Libr. Assn., 1983; fellow Coun. Libr. Resources, 1978-79. Fellow Med. Libr. Assn. (Louise Darling medal 1990); mem. ALA, LWV (bd. dirs. 1983-85, 2004-2005), Acad. Health Info. Profls, Assn. Acad. Health Sci. Libr. Dirs. (bd. dirs. 1995-98), Nat. Network Librs. Medicine (bd. dirs. South Ctrl. region 1995-97), Amigos Bibliographic Coun. (trustee 1986-89), Nat. Libr. Medicine (cons. 1983-88), Tex. Libr. Assn., Coun. Rsch. and Acad. Librs. (pres. 1986-87), Tex. Coun. State Univ. Librs. (pres. 1996-98), Daus. Rep. Tex., Phi Beta Kappa (pres. San Antonio Assn. 1979). Unitarian Universalist. Home: PO Box 2968 Canyon Lake TX 78133-0016

BOWDISH, COLETTE ELIZABETH, secondary school educator; b. Denver, Dec. 31, 1949; d. William Bickett and Marguerite Katherine (Tank) Bastien; m. David Spencer Bowdish, Feb. 20, 1971; 1 child, Lara Elise. BA in Psychology, U. Colo., Boulder, 1970; BA in Biology with distinction, U. Colo., Denver, 1986, MA in Biology with distinction, 1988. Cert. tchr., Colo. Mgr., v.p. Bastien's Restaurant, Inc., Denver, 1971—; tchg. asst. U. Colo., Denver, 1986-88; tchr. Denver Pub. Sch., 1984-89; rating bd. specialist VA, Denver, 1989—. Troop leader Girl Scouts Am., Denver, 1986—. Recipient Regent's scholarship, U. Colo., 1967, Colo. Scholars' scholarship, 1985-87. Republican. Roman Catholic. Avocations: training horses, collecting and pressing flowers, camping, travel. Home: 15720 E Mercer Pl Aurora CO 80013-2540 also: 144 Van Gordon St Denver CO 80225-1808

BOWDITCH, RACHEL EMILY, theater educator; b. Rome; arrived in U.S., 1994; d. James and Christine Bowditch; m. John Tzelepis. BA, Skidmore Coll., Saratoga Springs, N.Y., 1998; MA, post grad., N. Y.U., N.Y.C., 2003—. Edn. assoc. PERFORMA, N.Y.C., 2003—06; adj. prof. N.Y. U., 2003—06; asst. prof. Ariz. State U., Tempe, 2006—. Artistic dir. and performer Vessel, N.Y.C., NY, 1998—2006. Dir.: (plays) City of Bells, 2000, Majtaba, 2003, Arcana, 2006. Recipient Margaret Clifford Eller Meml. prize, Skidmore Coll., 1998, Paulette Goddard pre-doctoral grant, N.Y.U., 2006; grantee, 2005, Humanities Coun., 2006. Mem.: Off Off Broadway Cmty. Dish, Actor's Equity. Democrat. Avocations: yoga, painting, mask making, travel. Office: Ariz State Univ 300 E Univ Dr Tempe AZ 85287

BOWDLER, JANE MAXON, mathematics educator; d. Homer Andrew and Eleanor Maxon; m. Thomas Edward Bowdler, Aug. 8, 1970; children: Jeffrey Thomas, Gregory Andrew. BS, Heidelberg Coll., Tiffin, Ohio, 1968; MA, Montclair State Coll., Upper Montclair, N.J., 1970. Cert. tchr. math. 7-12 N.Y. State Edn. Dept., 1971. Math. tchr. West Can. Valley H.S., Newport, NY, 1969, Wayne Valley H.S., Wayne, NJ, 1970—72, Albion H.S., NY, 1973—80, Brockport H.S., 1996—. Tech. for All Students instr. Tex. Instruments, 2004—. Mem.: Assn. Math Tchrs. N.Y. State, Nat. Coun. Tchrs. Math. Office: Brockport HS 40 Allen St Brockport NY 14420 Office Phone: 585-637-1870. E-mail: jbowdler@bcs1.org.

BOWE, MARY ANN, small business owner, art educator; b. Fond du Lac, Wis., Mar. 13, 1955; d. Leo Clement and Carol May Brown; m. Michael Alvin Bowe, June 12, 1976; children: Bill, Angela, Brian, Andy. BA in Art Edn., U. Wis.-Oshkosh, 1977. Owner Bowe's Pit Stop, Mt. Calvary, Wis., 1980—, B & B Express, Malone, Wis., 1995—, B & B on 4th, Fond du Lac, 2005—. Tchr. art Shepherd of the Hills Sch., Eden, Wis., 2002—. Vol. various ch. activities. Avocations: gardening, golf, reading.

BOWEN, ALICE FRANCES, retired school system administrator; b. Worcester, Mass., Apr. 14, 1948; d. Vincent Francis and Alice Frances (Gray) B. BS in Edn., Worcester State Coll., 1971, MS in Math. Edn., 1973, MS in Computer Sci. Edn., 1985. Cert. prin., math. and social studies tchr., Mass. Tchr. math. Worcester Pub. Schs., 1971-83, tchr. computer sci., 1983-92, asst. prin., 1992—2006; ret., 2006. Instr. SAT prep. Ctrl. New Eng. Coll., Worcester, 1980-85; mem. Greater Worcester Urban Math. Collaborative Alliance for Edn., 1992-95. Leader Montachusetts coun. Girl Scouts U.S.A., 1968-85. Recipient St. Anne award Montachusetts coun. Girl Scouts U.S.A., 1978. Mem. ASCD, AAUW (bd. dirs. Worcester br. 1972-75, 90-96, Eleanor Roosevelt tchr. fellow 1991, Turtle award Worcester br.), Alliance for Edn., Delta Kappa Gamma, Phi Delta Kappa (Adminstr. of Yr. 2002). Democrat. Roman Catholic. Avocations: travel, crafts, reading. Home: 30 Lower Brook Rd South Yarmouth MA 02664 E-mail: afbowen2@hotmail.com.

BOWEN, BARBARA CHERRY, French and comparative literature educator; b. Newcastle-upon-Tyne, Eng., May 4, 1937; came to U.S., 1962; d. Harold E. and Hilda Edith (Meech) Cannings; m. Vincent E. Bowen, Jan. 12, 1963; children: Sarah, Tessa. MA, Oxford U., Eng., 1962; D in French Lit., U. Paris, 1962. Instr. French U. Ill., Urbana, 1962-63, asst. prof., 1963-66, assoc. prof., 1966-73, prof., 1973-87; prof. French and comparative lit. Vanderbilt U., Nashville, 1987—2002. Author: Les Caractéristiques Essentielles de la Farce Française, 1964, The Age of Bluff, 1972, Words and the Man in French Renaissance Literature, 1983, One Hundred Renaissance Jokes, 1988, Rabelais in Context, 1994, Enter Rebelais Laughing, 1998, Humour and Humanism in the Renaissance, 2004. Guggenheim fellow France, 1974-75; NEH summer seminar, 1980, 91; NEH fellow Italy, 1981-82; Villa I Tatti fellow Florence, Italy, 1981-82; NEH fellow France, 1988-89. Mem. MLA (mem. exec. coun. 1978-81), Ctrl. Renaissance Conf. (mem. orgn. com.), Medieval Assn. Midwest (mem. exec. coun.), Renaissance Soc. Am. (pres. 1996—98). Episcopalian.

BOWEN, CLOTILDE MARION DENT, retired military officer, psychiatrist; b. Chgo., Mar. 20, 1923; d. William Marion Dent and Clotilde (Tynes) D.; m. William N. Bowen, Dec. 29, 1945 (dec.). BA, Ohio State U., 1943, MD, 1947. Intern Harlem Hosp., N.Y.C., 1947-48; resident and fellow in pulmonary diseases Triboro Hosp., Jamaica, L.I., 1948-50; resident in psychiatry VA Hosp., Albany N.Y., 1959-62; asst. resident in psychiatry Albany Med. Ctr. Hosp., 1961-62; pvt. practice N.Y.C., 1950-55; chief pulmonary disease clinic N.Y.C., 1950-55; asst. chief pulmonary disease svc. Valley Forge Army Hosp., Pa., 1955—59; chief psychiatry VA Hosp., Roseburg, Oreg., 1962-66, acting chief of staff, 1964-66; asst. chief neurology and psychiatry Tripler Gen. Hosp., Hawaii, 1966-68; psychiatr. lcons. and dir. Rev. Br. Office Civil Health and Med. Program Uniform Svcs., 1968-70; commd. capt. U.S. Army, 1955, advanced through ranks to col., 1968, neuropsychiat. cons. USA Vietnam Medcom Vietnam, 1970—71, chief dept. psychiatry Fitzsimons Army Med. Ctr., 1971-74, chief dept. psychiatry Tripler Army Med. Ctr., 1974-75; assoc. clin. prof. psychiatry U. Hawaii, 1974-75; comdr. Hawley Army Clin., post surgeon U.S. Army, Ft. Benjamin, Harrison, Ind., 1977-78, chief dept. primary care and cmty. medicine, 1978-83, chief psychiat. consultation svc. Fitzsimons Army Med. Ctr., 1983-85; chief psychiatry svc. med./regional office ctr. VA, Cheyenne, Wyo., 1987-90; staff psychiatrist Denver VA Satellite Clin., Colorado Springs, Colo., 1990-96; ret., 1996. Locum Tenens practice psychiatry, 1996—; surveyor Joint Commn. on Accreditation Healthcare Orgns., 1985-92; assoc. clin. prof. psychiatary U. Colo. Med. Ctr., Denver, 1971-2006; spkr. Vietnam Vets. Meml. Wall, 2001. Decorated Legion of Merit, Bronze Star, Vietnam, others; recipient Colo. Disabled Am. Vets. award, 1994-95, Pres.'s 300 Commencement award Ohio State U., 1987, Profl. Achievement award Ohio State U. Alumni Assn., 1998, Cert. of Appreciation, VFW, 2000, Am. Assn. Emergency Psychiat. award, 2001. Fellow Am. Psychiat. Assn. (disting. life), Acad. Psychosomatic Med.; mem. AMA, Nat. Med. Assn., Menninger Found (charter), Ctrl. Neuropsychiat. Assn. (Peter Bassoe fellow), S.W. Assn. of Buffalo Soldiers, Inc. Home: 1020 Tari Dr Colorado Springs CO 80921-2257

BOWEN, FERN CHAMBERS, artist, educator; b. Orange Cove, Calif., May 3, 1917; d. Robert Malcolm Chambers and Mary Ether Montgomery; m. Howard Clee Willcox, Dec. 24, 1935 (div.); m. Walter Johnson Bowen, Feb. 19, 1946 (dec. Mar. 29, 1985); 1 child, Stephen Llane. Student, Soldini Sch. Art, Long Beach, Calif., 1957—67, Laguna Beach Sch. Art, Calif., 1968—80, Calif. State U., Chico, 1967—76, Calif. State U., San Diego, 1977, Inst. San Miguel de Allende, Mex., 1981; studied with Arnold Schiffrin, Italy, 1970—71. Artist, Bellflower, Calif., 1960—83; artist, lectr. for internat. travel L.A. County Mus. Art, 1972—81; dir. arts and crafts Cunard Princess Lines, NJ, 1984—85; art history lectr. local svc. clubs L.A., 1975—85. With prodn. illustration/engring. dept. U.S. Mil., Long Beach, Calif., 1942—43. One-woman shows include Long Beach Comty. Playhouse Gallery, 1968, San Diego State U. Exhbn., Malcolm Love Libr., 1970, exhibitions include Pacific Asia Mus., 1974, Long Beach Mus., 1976, Downey Mus. Art, 1977—78 (1st Pl. award, 1977), Palm Springs Desert Mus. Art, 1984—85, Represented in permanent collections Long Beach Mus. Art. Mem. Civic Art Assn. Palm Springs Desert Mus., Nat. Trust for Hist. Preservation. Named Esteemed Artist, Westminster (Eng.) Gallery award, 2001; recipient Award of Excellence, Cerritos Coll., 1970, 1972, Best of Show award, Arteasel.com., Inc., 2001, 1st Pl. award, Nat. Acrylic Painters' Assn., 1998. Mem.: Nat. Mus. Women in Arts, L.A. Art Assn., Women Painters West. Home: Unit 109 1750 E Ocean Blvd Long Beach CA 90802

BOWEN, GINGER ANN, artist; b. Amarillo, Tex., Feb. 16, 1953; d. Emmitt Lewis and Rose Hales; m. James A. Bowen; 1 child, Christian. Grad. h.s., Amarillo. Dir. adminstrns. Warner Bros. Records, Nashville, 1980—84. Exhibited in group shows at Ctrl. South Art Exhibit, 1994 (Chromatic Photo-imaging Svc. award), Catherine Lorillard Wolfe Art Club, 1995, Am. Artist Profl. League, 1995 (award, 1995), 2000—01 (Honorable Mention, 1999, Frank C. Wright Meml. award, 2001), Art Maui, 1997—98 (Purchase Pledge award, 1997), San Bernadino County Mus., 1999 (Honorable Mention, 2001), exhibitions include Calif. Art Club, 2004. Recipient First Pl. Profl., Scottsdale Artist Sch Best and Brightest Competition, 2003. Mem.: Nat. Mus. Women in Arts, Am. Artist Profl. League, Oil Painters Am. (assoc.), Calif. Art Club, Catherine Lorillard Wolfe Art Club. Avocations: travel, music. E-mail: gbowen7@cox.net.

BOWEN, JEAN, retired librarian, consultant; b. Albany, NY, Mar. 23, 1927; d. John W. and Grace Lester (Quier) B.; m. Henry F. Bloch, June 26, 1962; 1 child, Pamela A. Bloch. AB, Smith Coll., Northampton, Mass., 1948, AM, 1956; MS, Columbia U., N.Y.C., 1957. Curator Rodgers & Hammerstein Archives of Recorded Sound, N.Y.C., 1962-67; asst. chief music divsn. N.Y. Pub. Libr., N.Y.C., 1967-85, chief music divsn., 1986-96, dir. Humanities and Social Scis. Libr., 1996-2000. Cons. Rockefeller Bros. Found., N.Y.C., 1963, N.Y.C., 67, N.Y. Philharm., N.Y.C., 1984, Schubert Archives, N.Y.C., 1982; mem. faculty Rare Book Sch. Columbia U., N.Y.C., 1984, N.Y.C., 87, N.Y.C., 91; bd. dirs. Amphion Found., N.Y.C.; mem. bd. New World Records, N.Y.C. Contbr. articles to High Fidelity, Opera News, Am. Record Guide, Saturday Rev., MLA Notes, New Grove Dictionary of Am. Music. Mem.: Rare Book Sch. (mem. faculty, Columbia U., NYC 1984, 1987, 1991).

BOWEN, LINNELL R., director; b. Orlando, Fla., June 16, 1940; m. Paul Ivan, Jr. Bowen; children: Julia Anne, Paul Ivan III. Student, U. Md., 1962; fundraising and devel. mgmt. program, Goucher Coll., 1990; leadership tng. course, Nat. Trust for Hist. Preserve, 1991. Tchr. U.S. history Annapolis H.S., 1962—65; dir. devel./pub. rels., dir. edn., ednl. cons. Hist. Annapolis Found., 1976—94; adj. tchr. Colonial Md. Experience Anne Arundel C.C., 1989—91; adj. tchr. fundraising for hist. preservation Goucher Coll. Ctr. for Continuing Studies, 1993—95; exec. dir. Annapolis 300, A Capital Celebration, 1994—95, Md. Hall for Creative Arts, 1996—. Bd. pres. Cultural Arts Found. Anne Arundel County, 1995—96, Jr. League Annapolis Adv. Bd., 1995—96; County exec. appt. Scenic and Hist. Rds. Commn., 1986—96; pres. Scholarship for Scholars Inc., 1991—93; steering com. Millennium Legacy Trail Art Competition, City of Annapolis Whitbread Race; active Cultural Heritage Alliance Com.; founder, dir. Annapolis Arts Alliance, 2004—05; bd. dirs. Scholarship for Scholars Inc., 1991—93, Annapolis and Anne Arundel County Conf. and Visitors Bur.; adv. com. Mitchell Gallery at St. John's Coll., 1995—2005. Named one of Md.'s Top 100 Women, 1998, 2001; recipient City of Annapolis award of commendation, Annapolis 300 Celebration, 1995, Cmty. award for Annapolis 300 Celebration, Hist. Annapolis Found., 1996, Leadership Anne Arundel Cmty. Trustee award, 1996, Lifetime Achievement award, Pub. Rels. Soc. Annapolis and Anne Arundel County, 1999; fellow Paul Harris fellow, Rotary Found., 1997. Mem.: Annapolis/Anne Arundel County (chpt. trustee), Pub. Rels. Soc. Am., Annapolis and Anne Arundel County C. of C., Anne Arundel Trade Coun. Office: 801 Chase St Annapolis MD 21401 Office Phone: 410-263-5544. Personal E-mail: anna300@aol.com. Business E-Mail: lbowen@mdhallarts.org.

BOWEN, PATRICIA LEDERER, dental educator; b. Evanston, Ill., July 5, 1943; d. John Arthur and Edna Virginia Lederer; m. Clarence Henry Metzner, Jr., June 1, 1963 (div. Feb. 1972); children: Donald Frederick Metzner, John Henry Metzner; m. Steven Casto Bowen, Mar. 31, 1973. Dental Hygienist, U. Louisville, Ky., 1972; B in Health Edn., U. Ky., Ft. Knox, 1982; MPA, We. Ky. U., Bowling Green, 1985. Pvt. practice dental hygienist, various locations, 1972-75; pub. health dental hygienist U.S. Army, Berlin, 1975-78; cmty. health dental hygienist U.S. Army Dental Activity, Ft. Knox, Ky., 1978-95, U.S. Army Health Svcs. Command, Ft. Knox, Ky., 1981-95; pub. health dental hygienist Meade County (Ky.) Sch. Sys., 1995-96, LaRue County (Ky.) Sch. Sys., 1995-96; instr. pub. dental health Elizabethtown (Ky.) C.C., 1996-97; asst. dir. Meade County Tourism, 1996-97, dir., 1997—2004. Reporter Meade County Messenger, 1998, news editor, 1999—2003; lectr. in field. Contbr. articles to profl. jours. Pub. health dental hygienist Lebanon Sch. Sys., Ohio, 1974—75; pub. health dental program presenter Grand Junction, Colo., 1973—74; CPR instr./instr.-trainer Am. Heart Assn., Ft. Knox, 1985—98, ARC, Ft. Knox, 1978—87; vol. libr. and literacy West Point Ind. Sch., 2004—; PR/Edn. chmn. Pets In Need Soc., bd. dirs., 2005—, Decorated Order of Mil. Med. Merit U.S. Health Svcs. Command; recipient Patriotic Civilian Svc. award, Dept. of Army, 1986, award for Excellence, Delta Dental Ins. Co., 1991, 1994. Mem.: Ky. Oral health Consortium (exec. sec.-treas. 1991—96, chair 1995—96), Ky. Dental Hygiene Assn. (chair pub. health dental hygiene 1980—84), Louisville Dental Hygiene Assn. (chair legislation 1982), Am. Assn. Pub. Health Dentistry, Am. Dental Hygiene Assn. (pub. health cons. Ky. 1979—80), Meade County C. of C. (dir. 1998, Vol. of the Yr. 1998), Assn. U.S. Army (v.p. publicity 1994—2004). Avocations: photography, travel, snorkeling, hiking, reading. Home: 67 Greenbriar Ct Brandenburg KY 40108-9153 E-mail: pbowen@bbtel.com.

BOWEN, RHYS See QUIN-HARKIN, JANET

BOWEN, SHARON Y., lawyer; BA, U. Va., 1978; MBA, JD, Northwestern U., 1982. Bar: NY 1984. Ptnr., corp. dept. Latham & Watkins LLP, NYC. Mem. adv. counsel NY Women's Bar Assn. Found., Northwestern U. Law Bd. Mng. editor Northwestern Jour. Internat. Law and Bus. Bd. dirs. NY Lawyers Pub. Interest, Inc., Harlem Sch. Arts, NYC Econ. Devel. Corp., Urban-America, Inc. Named one of Am. Top Black Attys., Black Enterprise, 2003. Mem.: ABA (mem. ho. del.), NY State Bar Assn., Bar Assn. City of NY (mem. com. corp. law). Office: Latham & Watkins LLP 885 Third Ave Ste 1000 New York NY 10022-4802 Office Phone: 212-906-1332. Office Fax: 212-751-4864. Business E-Mail: sharon.bowen@lw.com.

BOWENS, GLORIA FURR, educational administrator; b. Detroit, Apr. 15, 1927; d. Leon Lewis and Iva Rose (Talbot) Furr; B.S., Tufts Coll., 1947; Ed.M., State Coll. Boston, 1968; Ed.D., Harvard U., 1975; 1 dau., Stephanie T. Sci. tchr. Boston Pub. Schs., 1961-71, asst. to the dir. orientation for integration, 1971-73, acting dir. personnel mgmt., 1981-82, instr. med. tech., 1982—; asst. supt. schs. Roosevelt (L.I., N.Y.) Sch. Dist., 1974-77; asst. dir. urban schs. collaborative Northeastern U., Boston, 1977-79, dist. IX coordinator curriculum and competency resources, 1979-81; ptnr. antique shop, Pickering Wharf, Salem, Mass., 1982—; pres. Horizons Extended Ednl. Consulting, 1992-98. Mem. Nat. Council Adminstrv. Women Edn. (exec. bd. 1970-73), Am. Assn. Sch. Adminstrs., North Shore Antiques Assn. (treas.), Phi Delta Kappa, Alpha Kappa Alpha.

BOWER, BARBARA JEAN, nurse, consultant; b. Akron, Ohio, Aug. 25, 1942; d. William Howard and Maxine (Goodykoontz) Sturm; m. Howard Bower, Aug. 25, 1961 (dec. 1989); children: Nancy, Janet. BA, Elmhurst Coll., 1974, postgrad., 1987; diploma, Evang. Sch. Nursing, 1970; PhD, U. Chgo., 1993. Bd. cert. legal RN cons. Critical care nurse, supr. nursing Loyola U. Med. Ctr.; critical care nurse Med. Staffing Svcs., Oak Park, Ill., 1978—84;

pres. Heart Care Unltd., Oak Brook, Ill., 1982—. Creator ednl. programs for cardiac patients, families and staff, 1971—. Stephen min. Christ Ch. of Oak Brook, Ill.; Republican election judge, DuPage County. Mem. AAUW, ANA, Am. Assn. Critical Care Nurses, Am. Heart Assn., Elmhurst Coll. Alumni Assn., U. Chgo. Alumni Assn., Oak Brook Exec. Breakfast Club. Avocations: rose gardening, cooking, candymaking. Office: Heart Care Unlted PO Box 3275 Oak Brook IL 60522-3275 Office Phone: 630-920-1122.

BOWER, CATHERINE DOWNES, management consultant; b. Balt., Dec. 29, 1947; m. Réjean Pierre Proulx, Apr. 28, 1990. BA, Kent State U., 1969. Editor East Ohio Gas Co., Cleve., 1971-74, Personnel Administrator mag., Berea, Ohio, 1974-79, dir. communications, 1979-84; v.p. communications, pub. Am. Soc. Pers. Adminstrn. (name Soc. Human Resource Mgmt.), Alexandria, 1984-86, v.p. communications and pub. relations, 1986-91; sr. ptnr. Tecker Cons., Trenton, N.J., 1991-96, prin. ptnr., 1996—; pres. Cate Bower Communications, Alexandria and West River, Md., 1991—. Project dir. Work in the 21st Century, 1984. Editor: Work Life Visions, 1987. Pres. Oak Cluster Community Council, Alexandria, 1985-89. Recipient Monument award Great Washington Soc. Assn. Execs., 1996. Fellow Am. Soc. Assn. Execs. (cert.; vice chmn. comms. sect. coun. 1986-87, chmn. 1987-88, planning com. 1989-91, bd. dirs. Found. 1989-93, chair rsch. com. 1995-96, chmn. strategic leadership forum 2003, Best Pub. Rels. Program award 1984); mem. Greater Washington Soc. Assn. Execs. (chmn. visibility task force 1994-95, Monument award 1996), West River Sailing Club. Avocations: sailing, gardening. Office: Cate Bower Comms 5109 Holly Dr West River MD 20778-9744 Personal E-mail: catecomm@aol.com. Business E-Mail: cbower@tecker.com.

BOWER, FAY LOUISE, academic administrator, nursing educator; b. San Francisco, Sept. 10, 1929; d. James Joseph and Emily Clare (Andrews) Saitta; children: R. David, Carol Bower Tomei, Dennis James, Thomas John. BS with honors, San Jose State Coll., 1965; MSN, U. Calif., 1966, DNSc, 1978. Cert. pub. health nurse, sch. nurse, Calif. Office nurse Dr. William Grannis, Palo Alto, Calif., 1950-55; staff nurse Stanford Hosp., 1964-72; asst. prof. San Jose (Calif.) State U., 1966-70, assoc. prof., 1970-74, prof., 1974-82, coord. grad. program in nursing, 1977-78, chairperson dept. nursing, 1978-82; dean U. San Francisco, 1982-89, v.p. acad. affairs, 1988-89, dir. univ. planning and instl. rsch., 1989-91; pres. Clarkson Coll., 1991-97; cons. in field, 1997—; chair dept. nursing Holy Names U., 2000—. Vis. prof. Harding Coll., 1977, U. Miss., 1976; lectr. U. Calif., San Francisco, 1975; nat. exec. adv. bd. Nurse Week, 1999—; spkr., cons. in field. Author: Approaches to Teaching Primary Care, 1981, The Newman Systems Model: Application to Nursing Education and Practice, 1982, Managing a Nursing Shortage: A Guide to Recruitment and Retention, 1989, Cracking the Wall: Women in Higher Education Administration, 1993, Nurses Taking the Lead., 2000, Care and Management of Alzheimers, vols. 1-5, 2002, Developing and Managing a Career in Nursing, 2003; (with Em O. Bevis) Fundamentals of Nursing Practice: Concepts, Roles and Functions, 1978, (with Margaret Jacobson) Community Health Nursing, 1978, The Process of Planning Nursing Care, 3d edit., 1982, (with Mae Timmons) Medical Surgical Nursing, 1995, (with others) Concepts & Issues in Nursing, 3d edit., 1996, Creating Nursings' Futures: Issues, Opportunities & Challenges, 1999; contbr. articles to profl. jours. Fellow Am. Acad. Nursing; mem.APHA (Calif. chpt.), Nurses Assn., Western Gerontol. Assn., Jesuit Deans in Nursing (chair 1982-85), Rotary (Omaha), Sigma Theta Tau (internat.pres., 1993-95, magnet appraiser 2006—). Democrat. Roman Catholic. Home: 1457 Indianhead Cir Clayton CA 94517-1239 Office Phone: 510-436-1024. Personal E-mail: fbower1@sbcglobal.net. Business E-Mail: bower@hnu.edu.

BOWER, JANET ESTHER, writer, educator; b. National City, Calif., Apr. 14, 1943; d. Murvel and Esther Eva (Clark) Newlan; m. Robert S. Bower Jr., Nov. 23, 1968; children: Llance Clark, Esther Elizabeth. BA in History and Psychology, Calif. We. U., San Diego, 1965; MA in History, UCLA, 1966; MA in Edn., U.S. Internat. U., 1970. Std. jr. coll. credential, elem. credential, Calif. Instr., mem. adj. faculty San Diego C.C. Dist., 1969—, Grossmont/Cuyamaca Coll. Dist., El Cajon, Calif., 1973, 1997—, Palomar Coll. Dist., San Marcos, Calif., 1993, Palomar Coll. dist., San Marcos, 1997—, Midlands Tech. Coll., Columbia, SC, 1995—96, Mira Costa Coll., 2001—. Adj. faculty mem. Nat. U., 1999—, Union Inst., 2000—; hist. cons. pub. Contbg. author: Women in the Biological Sciences, 1997; contbr. articles to periodicals; pub. editor Friends of the Internat. Ctr. Newsletter, U. Calif., San Diego, 1984-85. Bd. dirs. Women of St. Paul's Episcopal Ch., San Diego, 1983-86, Oceanids, U. Calif., San Diego, 1980-85. Grantee U.S. Dept. Edn., 1968-69. Mem. Am. Hist. Assn., Calif. Hist. Soc., Project Wildlife (hon. life mem.), Soroptomists Club, Internat. Club LaMesa. Republican. Avocations: cooking, travel. Business E-Mail: jbower@palomar.edu.

BOWER, JEAN RAMSAY, lawyer, writer; b. NYC, Nov. 25, 1935; d. Claude Barnett and Myrtle Marie (Scott) Ramsay; m. Ward Swift Just, Jan. 31, 1957 (div. 1966); children: Jennifer Ramsay, Julia Barnett; m. Robert Turrell Bower, June 12, 1971 (dec. June 1990). AB, Vassar Coll., 1957; JD, Georgetown U., 1970. Bar: D.C. 1970. Exec. dir. D.C. Dem. Ctrl. Com., Washington, 1969-71; pvt. practice Washington, 1971-78, 94—; dir. Counsel of Child Abuse and Neglect Office D.C. Superior Ct., 1978-94. Mem. Mayor's Com. on Child Abuse and Neglect, 1973-94, vice chmn., 1975-79; mem. Family Div. Rules Adv. Com., 1977-94; pres., bd. dirs. C.B. Ramsay Found., 1984—; cons. child welfare issues, writer. Contbr. poetry to In a Certain Place. Mem. D.C. Child Fatality Rev. Com., 1992-; bd. dirs. Friends D.C. Superior Ct., 1994—, pres. bd. dirs., 2002-05; bd. dirs. Family and Child Svcs., Washington, 1995-2003, bd. dirs., 2004-; chair Folger Poetry Bd., 2002-06, Folger Shakespeare Libr., 1998-. Named Washingtonian of the Yr. Washington Mag., 1978. Mem. Women's Bar Assn. (bd. dirs. 1993-96, found. 1986-91, Woman Lawyer of Yr. 1986), D.C. Bar Assn. (election bd. 1994-96, Beatrice Rosenberg award sect. com. 1994—), Women's Bar Assn. Found. (bd. dirs. 1986-91). E-mail: JBower3714@aol.com.

BOWER, LAUREL LEE, education educator, researcher; b. San Antonio, Tex., Jan. 8, 1951; d. James Hamilton and Carol Doris Hunt; m. Stephen Paul Bower, Apr. 2, 1970; children: Shawn Matthew, Angela Rose Watts. AA, Great Falls C.C., 1972; BA, Boise State Univ., Idaho, 1996, MA, 1998; PhD, Univ. Nev., Reno, Nev., 2003. Office mgr. House of Flowers, Boise, Idaho, 1974—76; bus. owner Riding Instr., Boise, Idaho, 1985—88, Words Unlimited, Boise, Idaho, 1987—90; acctg. supr. Warm Springs Ctr., Boise, Idaho, 1990—93; acad. adv. Coll. of Bus. Boise State Univ., Boise, Idaho, 1993—96; tchg. asst. Boise State Univ., Boise, Idaho, 1996—98, Univ. Nev., Reno, 1998—2002. Basic writing coord. Univ. Nev., 2000—01, corewriting com., 2000—01, editl. bd., 2000—01. Contbr. articles to numerous profl. jour., to numerous profl. conf. Mem.: Modern Language Assn., Nat. Coun. of Tchrs. of English, Sigma Tau Delta, Phi Kappa Phi. Republican.

BOWERMAN, ANN LOUISE, writer, secondary school educator, genealogist; b. Branch County, Mich., June 4, 1933; d. George Allen and Mary (Thomas) Hubbard; m. Virgil Lee Bowerman, June 4, 1954 (div. 1977); children: William Lee, Sally Ann; m. Virgil Wayne Dunkel, Jr., May 23, 1987 (div. Dec. 1996). BA, We. Mich. U., 1966, MSLS, 1971, MA, 1976. Cert. tchr. K-8 Mich., libr. sci. Tchr. Bethel #6 Sch. Dist., Coldwater, Mich., 1953—55; tchr. kindergarten Union City Schs., Mich., 1963—64; children's libr. Sturgis Pub. Libr., Mich., 1971—72; libr./media specialist Coldwater H.S., 1972—91; field rep. U.S. Census Bur., 2000—02, 2003—; media specialist libr. Union City Schs., 2002—03; ret., 1991. Mem. programming com., mem. ann. scholarships telethon com., camera staff, video editor Calbe TV Channel 31, Coldwater, 1983—90. Author: The Bater Book, 1987, A Bowerman Family History, 1998, Historic Howe, Indiana Walking Tour, 1998, The William Bowerman Family of Conneaut Township, 1998; co-author: Recommendations for High School Media Centers in Michigan, 1980; contbr. articles to profl. jours. Leader All Around 4-H Club, Union City, 1954—74; mem. Sullivan Lady's Aid Soc., Union City, 1955—74, Coldwater Hist. Preservation Assn., 1978—86, Twin Lakes Cmty. Assn., 1997—, Mich. Assn. Computer Users in Learning, 1975—91; mem. adv. coun. Calhoun and Branch Counties Regional Ednl. Media Ctr., Marshall, Mich., 1972—91; mem., chair governing bd. Woodlands Libr. Coop., Albion, Mich., 1973—74, 1983—86; chair winter program com. Tibbits Arts Found., Coldwater, 1980—90; com. mem. So. Mich. Region Coop., Albion, 1989—91; mem. cultural arts com., mem. walking tour com. Howe (Ind.) Cmty. Assn., 1996—2005, pres., 2003—05; del. Mich. Rep. State Conv., Detroit, 1986; candidate Branch County Commr., Coldwater, 1988. Recipient cert. of Appreciation, Mich. Assn. Media Edn., 1980, 1991, Golden Apple Retirement award, Coldwater HS, 1991. Mem.: DAR (mem. good citizen selection com., treas. Coldwater br. 1997—2002, registrar 2003—04, regent 2003—05), Howe Philmath Soc., Coldwater Edn. Assn. (sec. 1980—90), Crawford County Geneal. Soc., Union City Geneal. Soc., Ctrl. N.Y. Geneal. Soc., New Eng. Hist. Geneal. Soc., Soc. Genealogists (London), St. Joseph County Hist. Soc. (advisor to Land Office Mus. com. 1997—), Old Brutus Hist. Soc., Schenectady County Hist. Soc., Mich. Assn. Ret. Sch. Pers., Descs. Founders of Ancient Windsor, Beta Phi Mu. Avocations: travel, coin collecting/numismatics, tennis. Home: 1820 W 600 N Howe IN 46746-9406

BOWERS, ANDREA, artist; b. Wilmington, Ohio, 1965; BFA, Bowling Green State U., 1987; MFA, Calif. Inst. Arts, 1992. One-woman shows include Damaged Goods, Bliss, Pasadena, Calif., 1994, Spanish Box, Santa Monica, Calif., 1996, Spectacular Appearances, Santa Monica Mus. Art, Calif., 1998, Moving Equilibrium, Sara Meltzer Gallery, NY, 1999, Intimate Strangers, 2000, Box with Dance of Its Own Making, Chouakri Brahms, Berlin, 2002, From Mouth to Ear, Goldman Tevis, LA, 2002, Virtual Arena, Sara Meltzer Gallery, NY, 2002, Magical Politics, Chouakri Brahms, Berlin, 2003, Nonviolent Civil Disobedience Training, Sara Meltzer Gallery, NY, 2004, Magazin 4 Voralberger Kunstverein, Austria, 2004, Mary Goldman Gallery, LA, 2004, exhibited in group shows at Whitney Biennial Am. Art, Whitney Mus. Am. Art, 2004, 100 Artist See God, Laguna Art Mus., San Francisco, 2003—04, Rendered, Sara Meltzer Gallery, NY, 2003, C.O.L.A. 2003, Municipal Art Gallery, Barnsdale Art PK., LA, 2003, Time-Share, Sara Meltzer Gallery, NY, 2002, Everybody Now, Bertha & Karl Leubsdorf Gallery, NY, 2001, Subject Plural, Contemporary Arts Mus., Houston, 2001, Moving Pictures, Galerie Tommy Lund, Copenhagen, Denmark, 2000, Me Mine, Luckman Fine Arts Gallery, Calif., 1999, Unfinished History, Walker Art Ctr., Mpls., 1998—99, Dave's Not Here, Three Day Weekend, LA, 1994. Regional Fellowship Visual Arts Sculpture, Western States Arts Fedn./Nat. Endowment Arts, 1995—96, Fellowship Visual Arts, City LA, 2003.

BOWERS, BEGE KAYE, literature educator, communications educator, academic administrator; b. Nashville, Aug. 19, 1949; d. John and Yvonne Bowers. BA in English cum laude, Vanderbilt U., 1971; student, U. Mich., 1985; MACT, U. Tenn., 1973, PhD, 1984. Asst. loan officer Ctr. for Fin. Aid and Placement, Baylor U., Waco, Tex., 1975-76; editorial asst. Wassily Leontief, NYU, N.Y.C., 1976-78; instr. bus. English Florence-Darlington Tech. Coll., Florence, SC, 1979-80; tchr. English and French St. John's High Sch., Darlington, SC, 1980-82; teaching asst. dept English U. Tenn., Knoxville, 1982-84; from asst. prof. English to prof. Youngstown (Ohio) State U., 1984—92, prof., 1992—, asst. to dean Coll. Arts and Scis., 1992-93, dir. profl. writing and editing, 1996-2000, assoc. to the dean Coll. Arts and Scis., 2001—02, asst. provost acad. programs and planning, 2002—05, interim provost, 2005, v.p. acad. affairs, 2005, assoc. provost acad. programs and planning, 2005—. Part-time freelance editor MLA, N.Y.C., 1978-80; cons. Project Arete, Youngstown and Mahoning County Pub. Schs., 1984-87, Youngstown Pub. Schs., 1986, 87-88, 90-91, Macmillan Pub. Co., 1986, Trumbull (Ohio) County Schs., 1988, Akron Beacon Jour., 1994-95, Ohio Dept. Edn., 1998-2001, Ohio Bd. Regents, 2002—; chair Mahoning Area Consortium Tech. Prep. Governing Bd., 2002—. Co-editor: CEA Critic, 1998—2002, CEA Forum, 1988—2004; co-editor: (with Barbara Brothers) Reading and Writing Women's Lives: A Study of the Novel of Manners, 1991; co-editor: (with Chuck Nelson) Internships in Technical Communication, 1991; co-editor: (with Mark Allen) Annotated Chaucer Bibliography, 1986—96, 2002 (MLA award for disting. bibliography, 2004); mem. editl. bd. South Atlantic Rev., 1987—89; editor: more than 40 pamphlets, 7 children's books, and 1 videoscript. Alumni Found. Rsch. fellow U. Tenn., 1978, dissertation fellow U. Tenn., 1983, Davis editl. fellow U. Tenn., 1984; Grad. Rsch. Coun. grantee Youngstown State U. Mem.: MLA, Gould Soc. (pres. faculty com. 1991—93), No. Ohio Soc. for Tech. Comm., Soc. for Tech. Comm. (Jay R. Gould award for excellence in tchg. tech. comm. 1999, Disting. Chpt. Svc. award 2001, Assoc. fellow award 2002), Assn. Tchrs. Tech. Writing, New Chaucer Soc. (asst. bibliographer 1986—), Coll. English Assn. Ohio, Coll. English Assn. (exec. bd., Disting. Svc. award 1996, Lifetime Achievement award 2005), Phi Beta Kappa, Phi Kappa Phi (web mgr. 2005—, pres. 1991—92, sec. 1994—98, exec. bd. 1998—). Office: Youngstown State U Office of the Provost Youngstown OH 44555-0001 Office Phone: 330-941-1560. E-mail: bkbowers@ysu.edu.

BOWERS, CHRISTI C., mediator, lawyer, educator, writer, poet; b. Hagerstown, Md., Nov. 4, 1970; BA in Psychology, BS in Bus., Shepherd Coll., 1993; JD, MS, U. Balt., 1998, MBA, 2000. Bar: Md. 2000, cert.: Md. Inst. Continuing Profl. Edn. Lawyers (mediator), Md. Inst. Continuing Profl. Edn. Lawyers (domestic, custody and visitation mediator), Md. Inst. Continuing Profl. Edn. Lawyers (domestic property, fin. issues mediator) 2000, Md. Inst. Continuing Profl. Edn. Lawyers (advanced transformative mediator) 2002, Md. Inst. Continuing Profl. Edn. Lawyers (worker's compensation mediator) 2002, Dist. Ct. of Md. (advanced mediator) 2002. Freelance mediator - custody/visitation, civil disputes, landlord/tenant/neighbors, marriage/relationships, tng. programs for businesses, Hagerstown, 2000—; tchr.,presenter co-parenting workshop for adults and children Children of Separation and Divorce (now Nat. Family Resiliency Program), Balt., 2000—; case mgr., staff mediator family divsn. Cir. Ct. for Prince George's County, Upper Marlboro, Md., 2003—. Vol. mediator civil large and small claims cases Dist. Ct. Md., Annapolis, 2000—; vol. faculty critiquer Md. Inst. Continuing Profl. Edn. Lawyers Mediation Tng., Balt., 2001—; substitute tchr. Bd. Edn. Washington County, Hagerstown, 1999—. Author: Mediation In Maryland; editor: Resolving Issues newsletter. Exec. bd.- mem. at large Md. Coun. Dispute Resolution, Balt., 2002; bd. dirs., sec. Washington County Cmty. Mediation Ctr., Hagerstown, 2002—03. Recipient cert. appreciation for vol. mediation, Dist. Ct. of Md., 2002. Mem.: ABA, Assn. Conflict Resolution, Washington County Bar Assn., Md. State Bar Assn., Sigma Iota Epsilon (hon.). Avocations: writing, singing, travel, writing- poems, songs, guidebooks, fiction, creating things. Office Phone: 301-730-6244. Personal E-mail: christicbo@aol.com. Business E-Mail: ccbowers@co.pg.md.us.

BOWERS, JANE MEREDITH, retired music educator; b. Mpls., Sept. 17, 1936; B in Music, Wellesley Coll., 1958; MA in Music History, U. Calif., Berkeley, 1962, PhD in Music History, 1971. Instr. U. N.C., Chapel Hill, 1968-72; asst. prof. dept. music history and musicology Eastman Sch. Music, Rochester, N.Y., 1972-73, 74-75; lectr., instr. women's studies, music and continuing edn. Portland (Oreg.) State U., 1977—81; instr. flute Reed Coll., Portland, 1979-81; from asst. prof. dept. music to prof. U. Wis., Milw., 1981—2001, prof., 1993—2001, chmn. music history and lit. area, 1997—2001, mem. faculty senate, 1997—2000, ret., 2000. Lectr. women's studies program Cornell U., Ithaca, N.Y., spring 1979; vis. asst. prof. dept. music Oreg. State U., 1980-81; lectr. in field, 1969—; flutist Am. Wind Symphony, summer 1958, Cabrillo Music Festival, 1963-64; asst. prin. flutist Oakland Symphony Orch., 1962-65; free-lance Baroque flutist, N.Y.C., 1975-77; numerous recitals and chamber music concerts on modern and Baroque flute, 1964-85. Editor: Michel de La Barre: Pieces pour la Flute Traversiere, 1978, Joseph Boden de Boismortier: Petites Sonates pour 2 Flutes Traversieres, 1993, (with Judith Tick) Women Making Music: The Western Art Tradition, 1150-1950, 1986, paperback edit., 1987 (Deems Taylor award ASCAP 1987, Pauline Alderman prize 1987), François Devianne's Nouvelle Méthode Théorique et Pratique pour la Flute, 1999; contbr. articles and revs. to profl. jours. and anthologies. Bd. dirs. Early Music Guild Oreg., 1981, Early Music Now, Milw., 1989-92. Alfred Hertz meml. travel scholar, 1965-66; postdoctoral fellow AAUW, 1973-74, 78-79, fellow Ctr. for 20th Century Studies, U. Wis.- Milw., 1982-83, Humanities Inst., U. Wis.-Madison, 1988-89; grantee NEH, summers 1980, 84. Mem. Am. Mus. Instrument Soc. (rev. editor Jour. 1976-81, bd. govs. 1988-91), Am. Musicological Soc. (coun. 1982-84, chmn. performance com., 1998-2000, mem., chmn. Noah Greenberg award com. 1987-89), Coll. Music Soc. (sec. com. on status of women 1972-74, mem. com. 1992-96, tchr. Summer Inst. 1993), Soc. for Ethnomusicology (coun. 1995-98, chmn. constn. revision com. 1996-2000), Am. Women Composers (editl. bd. 1992-94), Internat. Assn. Women in Music (editl. bd. 1995-2002), Assn. Women in Edn. (vice chmn., chmn. U. Wis.- Milw. 1985-87). Home: 2516 E Stratford Ct Shorewood WI 53211-2634

BOWERS, KIM, lawyer, energy executive; b. Ohio; BA, Miami U., Ohio; MA, Baylor U., Waco, Tex.; JD, U. Tex. Sch. Law, Austin. With Kelly, Hart & Hallman, Ft. Worth; corp. counsel to sr. comml. counsel Valero Energy Corp., San Antonio, 1997—2002, mng. counsel, 2002—03, v.p. legal svcs., 2003, sr. v.p., gen. counsel, 2006—. Office: Valero Energy Corpn One Valero Way San Antonio TX 78249

BOWERS, LINDA, educational association administrator; b. Lancaster, S.C., Aug. 11, 1950; d. Vernon Ray and Betty Elliott Bowers. BA in Elem. Edn., U. S.C., 1972, MA in Instnl. Design/Media, 1987. Cert. elem. tchr., S.C. Tchr. Orangeburg Sch. Dist., Springfield, S.C., 1972-73, Richland Sch. Dist., Columbia, S.C., 1973-86, elem. curriculum cons., 1986-97, dir. Richland Clicks!, 1998—. Adj. prof. U. Charleson, 1993, 94; cert. trainer Covey/Franklin; accelerated schs. project coach Stanford (Calif.) U., 1994; presenter in field. Author video script: Effective Teacher/Effective Teaching, 1996. Mem. Forest Hills Assn., 1987—; mem. testbook selection com. S.C. State Dept. Edn., Columbia, 1991; mem. violence prevention com. Columbia C. of C., 1989; mem. sch. improvement coun. A.C. Flora H.S., Columbia, 1994-96. Mem. S.C. ASCD, S.C. Coun. Tchrs. Math., S.C. Suprs. Math. (bd. dirs. 1994), Columbia Area Reading Coun. (bd. dirs. 1995-97), Delta Kappa Gamma, Phi Delta Kappa. Avocations: boating, photography, cooking, reading. Home: 225 Lake Vista Dr Chapin SC 29036-8471

BOWERS, MADELINE KATHERINE JENTE, elementary school educator; b. St. Louis, June 30, 1959; d. Richard Charles and Madeline Mary (Haertter) Jente. BA in Edn., Maryville Coll., 1981; MA, Webster U., 1982; cert., Washington U., St. Louis, 1981. Cert. elem. edn., reading, testing. Tchr. Rohan Woods Sch., St. Louis. Mem. Pi Lambda Theta. Office Phone: 314-821-6270. E-mail: Mbowers@rohanwoods.org.

BOWERS, PATRICIA ELEANOR FRITZ, economist; b. NYC, Mar. 21, 1928; d. Eduard and Eleanor (Ring) Fritz. Student scholar, Goucher Coll., 1946-48; BA, Cornell U., 1950; MA, NYU, 1953, PhD, 1965. Statis. asst. Fed. Res. Bank NY, NYC, 1950-53; lectr. Upsala Coll., East Orange, NJ, 1953-59; researcher Fortune mag., NYC, 1959-60; teaching fellow NYU, NYC, 1960-62, instr., 1962-64; mem. faculty Bklyn. Coll., CUNY, 1964-00, prof. econs., 1974-2000, chair dept. econs., 1996-99, prof. emerita, 2000—. Author: Private Choice and Public Welfare, 1974. Sec. Friends of the Johnson Mus., Cornell U., 1989-91; Cornell Fund rep. Class of 1950, Cornell U., 2004—. Mem. Am. Econ. Assn., Econometric Soc., Met. Econ. Assn. (sec. 1963-68, pres. 1974-75), Am. Statis. Assn. (univs. chmn. ann. forecasting confs. 1970-71, 71-72), Cornell Club NY, Kappa Alpha Theta. Home: 145 E 16th St Apt 11-L New York NY 10003-3405

BOWERS, SUSAN BAILEY, secondary school educator; b. Clarksville, Tenn., Aug. 14, 1952; d. Wylie F. Bailey and Opal Ralls-Bailey; m. James Michael Bowers, Dec. 16, 1982; 1 child, Kate Suzanne. BS, Austin Peay State U., Clarksville, Tenn., 1974; MA, Murray State U., Ky., 1980. Cert. tchr. Tenn. Tchr. sci. dept. Stewart County Bd. Edn., Dover, Tenn., 1974—80; water chemist Tenn. Valley Authority, Cumberland City, 1980—84; tchr. sci. dept. Hawkins County Bd. Edn., Church Hill, Tenn., 1984—. Tchr. sci. dept. Vol. H.S., Church Hill, 1984—. Master gardener U. Tenn. Ext. Svc., Church Hill, Tenn., 2004; active Houskins County Dem. Women. Democrat. Methodist. Avocations: gardening, hiking, bicycling, woodworking, cooking. Office: Volunteer HS PO Box 247 Church Hill TN 37642

BOWERS, ZELLA ZANE, real estate broker; b. May 24, 1929; Real estate broker Haley Realty Inc, Colorado Springs. Home: 128 W Rockrimmon Blvd Apt 104 Colorado Springs CO 80919-1876 Office: Haley Realty Inc 109 E Fontanero St Colorado Springs CO 80907-7494 Office Phone: 719-535-9325. Personal E-mail: 221889@yahoo.com.

BOWES, BETTY MILLER, painter, art consultant; b. Phila, July 30, 1911; d. George Washington and Elizabeth (Dawson) Miller; m. Thomas David Dowes, June 22, 1946 (div. 1981). ED., Moore Coll. Art., Phila., 1932. One-man shows, Phila. Art Alliance, 1954, 60, 65, Woodmere Gallery, 1958-64, group shows; art cons., Sun Oil Co., Radnor, Pa., 1975—, mem. exhbn. com, Woodmere Gallery, Designer tapestry, (paintings reproduced in art books). George W. Elkins European fellow, 1932; Dolphon fellow; recipient numerous awards Mem. Am. Watercolor Soc., Phila. Art Alliance, Phila. Watercolor Soc. Republican. Roman Catholic. Home: 301 Mcclenaghan Mill Rd Wynnewood PA 19096-1012

BOWES, ROSEMARY TOFALO, psychologist, consultant; b. Boston, Nov. 14, 1948; d. Francis and Margaret (Kaim) Tofalo; m. David Bigelow Bowes, Oct. 29, 1988. BA, U. Md., 1970; MS, Howard U., 1972, PhD, 1975. Lic. psychologist, D.C., Md. Tng. fellow NIMH, Rockville, Md., 1971; pvt. practice Stress Mgmt. Focus, Washington, 1990—; clin. faculty family practice program Georgetown Med. Sch., Washington, 1990—; asst. clin. prof. George Wash. U., 2004—. Mem. med. staff Columbia Hosp. for Women, Washington, 1990-2000; bd. mem. Nat. Women's Health Resource Ctr., Washington, 1990-2000. Mem. APA, Md. Psychol. Assn., N.Am. Menopause Soc., Women of Washington, Psi Chi. Home: The Oaks Box 180 Keedysville MD 21756-0180 Office: 2300 M St NW Washington DC 20037-1434

BOWICK, SUSAN D., retired computer company executive; Bus. analyst Hewlett-Packard Co., Loveland, Colo., 1972-85, pers. mgr. Lake Stevens instrument divsn. Everett, Wash., 1985-89, group pers. mgr. computer sys. orgn., 1989-93, pers. mgr. San Diego, 1993-95, pers. mgr. computer orgn., 1995-98, exec. v.p. human resources Palo Alto, Calif., 1998—2003. Fax: 650-813-3003.

BOWKER, EILEEN GUNSON, athletic trainer, educator; d. Frank Brooke and Kathleen Miriam Gunson; m. Brian John Bowker, Dec. 12, 1989; children: Kayle, Emily, Brian, Sean. BS, Castleton State Coll., Vt., 1984; MA, Western Mich. U., Kalamazoo, 1985; grad. in Ednl. Adminstrn., Rutgers U., New Brunswick, NJ., 2006. Realtor State of N.J., tchr. health, phys. edn., 1984. Athletic trainer USA Wrestling, Colorado Springs, 1996—2006. Author: Eat, Wrestle and Win, 1998. Coach Burlington County Recreational Softball, NJ, 1995—2004; pres. Burlington County Athletic Assn., NJ, 2001—03. Named to Hall of Fame, NJSIAA, 1993. Mem.: Athletic Tng. Soc. N.J. (sec. 1993—95), Nat. Athletic Trainer Assn. (continuing edn. com. 2003—, cert. trainer). Roman Catholic. Avocations: kayaking, climbing, running, quilting. Office: PTHS 148 Arneys Mount Rd Pemberton NJ 08068 Office Phone: 609-893-8141 ext, 2063. E-mail: ebowker@pemb.org.

BOWKER, MARGARET SHEARD, artist; b. Dordrecht, South Africa, Oct. 31, 1938; BA, Tchr.'s U., Grahamstown, S. Africa, 1960. Tchr. Cape Edn. Dept., E. London, 1961—64, Natal Edn. Dept., Durban, 1965—97. Achievements include specialization in painting of women from the 1920-30 and unique portraits by commission. Office: Margie Bowker Art 429 Monterey Rd Santa Maria CA 93055 Office Phone: 805-937-0665.

BOWLER, MARIANNE BIANCA, federal judge; b. Boston, Feb. 15, 1947; d. Richard A. and Ann C. (Daly) B. BA, Regis Coll., 1967; JD cum laude, Suffolk U., 1976, LLD (hon.), 1994; LD (hon.), Regis Coll., 2003. Bar: Mass. 1978. Rsch. asst. Harvard Med. Sch., Boston, 1967-69; med. editor Mass. Dept. of Pub. Health, Boston, 1969-76; law clk. Mass. Superior Ct., Boston, 1976-77, dep. chief law clk., 1977-78; asst. dist. atty. Middlesex Dist. Atty.'s Office, Cambridge, Mass., 1978; asst. U.S. atty. U.S. Dept. of Justice, Boston,

1978-90, exec. asst. U.S. atty., 1988-89, sr. litigation counsel, 1989-90; magistrate judge U.S. Dist. Ct. Mass., Boston, 1990—2002, chief U.S. magistrate judge, 2002—. Chmn. bd. trustees New England Bapt. Hosp., Boston, 1990-95. Trustee Suffolk U., Boston, 1994—, Discovering Justice, 2003—; bd. dirs. The Boston Found., 1995—; dir. South Cove Nursing Facilities Found., Inc., 1995—; co-pres. Boston Coll. Inn of Ct., 1998—2002; bd. dirs. Discovering Justice, 2003-; overseer U.S.S. Constn. Mus., 2005-. Mem. Jr. League Boston, Suffolk Law Sch. Alumni Assn. (pres. 1979-80), Vincent Club, Isabel O'Neil Found., Save Venice. Democrat. Roman Catholic. Avocations: faux finishing, trompe l'oeil painting. Office: 1 Courthouse Way Ste 8420 Boston MA 02210-3010 Office Phone: 617-748-9219. Business E-Mail: honorable_marianne_bowler@mad.uscourts.gov.

BOWLES, BARBARA LANDERS, investment company executive; b. Nashville, Sept. 17, 1947; d. Corris Raemone Landers and Rebecca (Bonham) Jennings; m. Earl Stanley Bowles, Nov. 27, 1971; 1 son, Terrence Earl. BA, Fisk U., 1968; MBA, U. Chgo., 1971. Chartered fin. analyst. From bank official to v.p. First Nat. Bank of Chgo., 1968-81; asst. v.p. Beatrice Cos., Chgo., 1981-84; v.p. investor rels. Kraft Inc., Chgo., 1984—89; pres., founder The Kenwood Group Inc., Chgo., 1989—2005; vice chair The Project Investment Group, 2006—. Bd. dirs. Black & Decker Corp., Hyde Pk. Bank. Bd. dirs. Children's Meml. Hosp., Wis. Energy, and Dollar Gen. Corp. The Chgo. Urban League; mem. Grad. Sch. Bus. U. Chgo. Scholar United Negro College Fund, 1989. Mem. NAACP (life), Assn. Investment Mgmt. and Rsch., Chgo. Fisk trustee (1998-). Mem. United Ch. of Christ. Avocations: tennis, bridge. Office Phone: 312-368-1666. E-mail: kenwoodg@aol.com.

BOWLES, CRANDALL CLOSE, textiles executive; m. Erskine Bowles. B in Econ., Wellesley Coll.; MBA, Columbia U. Fin. analyst Springs Industries, Inc., 1973—78, exec. v.p. growth and devel., 1992, exec. v.p. textile prodn., 1993, pres. bath fashions group, 1995, pres., COO, 1997—98, CEO, chmn., 1998—; exec. v.p. Springs Co., 1978—82, pres., 1982; also bd. dirs. Bd. dirs. Deere & Co. Bd. trustees African Wildlife Found.; bd. dirs. Juvenile Diabetes Rsch. Found., Charlotte Inst. for Tech. Innovation. Mem.: Palmetto Bus. Forum, Bus. Roundtable, Bus. Coun., Am. Textile Mfrs. Inst., Excellence in Edn. Coun. Office: Springs Global PO Box 70 205 N White St Fort Mill SC 29715-1654

BOWLES, LIZA K., construction executive; BA in Polit. Sci., Mary Washington Coll.; M in Urban Affairs, Va. Tech. Pres. NAHB Rsch. Ctr., Upper Marlboro, Md., 1991—2002; gen. mgr. Newport Ptnrs., Davidsonville, Md., 2002—. Office: Newport Ptnrs LLC 3760 Tanglewood Lane Davidsonville MD 21035 Office Phone: 301-889-0017. Business E-Mail: lizabowles@newportpartnersllc.com.

BOWLES, VICKY LYNN HILL, elementary school educator; b. Russellville, Ark., Oct. 6, 1953; d. Charles LaVan and Jimmie Sue (Goates) Hill; children: James Robert, Jennifer Rae. BS in Music Edn., Ark. Tech. U., Russellville, 1975; MS in Edn., Ark. State U., Russellville. Tchr. Desha Drew Sch. Dist., Tillar, Ark., 1976—85, South Conway County Sch. Dist., Morrilton, Ark., 1985—. Ednl. cons. Compton, Inc., Morrilton. Treas. City of Tillar, 1977—85; mem. bd., treas., coach Morrilton Youth Assn., 1995—2003. Avocations: sports, music, reading.

BOWLIN, STEPHANIE D., university dean; b. Union Town, Ala., Dec. 8, 1959; d. Bertha Oliver; m. Ronnie Arnez Bowlin, June 20, 1981; children: Sheri Diana, Ronnie Arnez II. Physician Asst., Charles Drew U., 1983; MS in Health and Profl. Edn., Western U. of Health Sci., Pomona, Calif., 1992; EdD, U. Laverne, Calif., 1998. Cert. physician asst., Calif. Physician asst. in pediats. Commerce Med. Group, L.A., 1983-84; family practice physician asst. Cmty. Health Found., L.A., 1984-85; urgent care physician asst. Kaiser Permanent, Bellflower/Anaheim, Calif., 1988-92; physician asst. pediats. Friendly Hills Med. Group, 1992-94, Tower Med. Group, Riverside, 1988—, Kaiser Permanent, Riverside, 1996—; chair physician asst. edn. dept. Western U. Health Sci., Pomona, dean Coll. Allied Health Professions. Chair Accreditation rev. Com. on Physician Assts., 1998—. Editor CLER, 1999, Perspective Physician Asst. Edn., 1998—; mem. editl. bd. Perspective on Physician Asst. Edn., 1997—. Bd. dirs. ARC, Claremont, Calif., 1998—. Recipient Excellence in Tchg. award Sch. Allied Health Professions, Pomona, 1995, Don and Jean Oriva Meml. award Western U., 1992, Honor award Charles R. Drew Postgrad. Med. Sch., 1983. Mem. Am. Acad. Physician Assts., African Heritage Caucus, Soc. for Physician Assts. in Pediats. (physician asst./nurse practitioner subcom. 1995—), Am. Assn. Physician Assts., Calif. Acad. Physician Assts. Avocation: aerobics. Office: Western Univ Health Sci 309 E 2nd St Pomona CA 91766-1854 Home: 7871 Mission Grove Pkwy S Apt 84 Riverside CA 92508-5032 E-mail: sbowlin@westernu.edu.

BOWLING, RITA JOAN, medical/surgical nurse; b. Martins Ferry, Ohio, Feb. 20, 1949; d. Edgar Lee and Pauline Winifred (Bernard) Wilson; m. Chester John Bowling, Jr., Dec. 23, 1978 (div.); 1 child, Melissa Ann. BSN, Wayne State U., 1972, MSN, 1978; MBA, Baldwin-Wallace Coll., 1989. Med. surg. clin. nurse specialist, ANA, cert. profl. healthcare quality. Staff nurse Grace Hosp., NW, Detroit, 1972-73, Providence Hosp., Southfield, Mich., 1973-76; staffing supr. Health Care I, Inc., Southfield, 1976-78; cardiac clin. nurse specialist St. Joseph Mercy Hosp., Pontiac, Mich., 1978-81, Aultman Hosp., Canton, Ohio, 1982-88, hosp., nursing home and physician rels. coord., 1988—98; project mgr. Peer Rev. Sys., Westerville, Ohio, 1998—99, Ohio KePRO, Seven Hills, 1999—, dir. acute care svcs., 2002—. Mem. rev. bd.: Clin. Nurse Specialist Jour., 1986—91. Mem.: Ohio Assn. Healthcare Quality, Medina County Nurses Assn. (pres. 1983—86), Ohio Soc. Physician Svcs. (founder, dist. coord. 1994—98), Delta Zeta, Sigma Theta Tau. Episcopalian. Avocations: sailing, skiing, reading, hand crafts, martial arts. Home: 400 Abbyshire Rd Akron OH 44319-3806 Office: Ohio KePRO Rock Run Ctr Ste 100 5700 Lombardo Center Dr Seven Hills OH 44131 Office Phone: 216-447-9604. E-mail: rjb136@aol.com.

BOWMAN, BARBARA TAYLOR, early childhood educator; b. Chgo., Oct. 30, 1928; d. Robert Rochon and Dorothy Vaugn (Jennings) Taylor; m. James E. Bowman, June 17, 1950, 1 child, Valerie Bowman Jarrett. BA, Sarah Lawrence Coll., 1950; MA, U. Chgo., 1952; DHL (hon.), Bankstreet Coll., 1988, Roosevelt U., 1998, Dominican U., 2002, Gov.'s State U., 2002, Wheelock Coll., 2005. Tchr. U. Chgo. Nursery Sch., 1950—52, Colo. Women's Coll. Nursery Sch., Denver, 1953—55; mem. sci. faculty Shiraz U. Nemazee Sch. Nursing, Shiraz, Iran, 1955—61; tchr. spl. edn. Chgo. Child Care Soc., 1965—67; mem. faculty Erikson Inst., Chgo., 1967—, dir. grad. studies, 1978—94, pres., 1994—2002, prof. early edn., 2002—; chief officer early childhood edn. Chgo. Pub. Schs., 2004—. Mem. early childhood com. Nat. Bd. Profl. Tchg. Stds., 1998-2002; cons. early childhood edn., parent edn.; chair com. on early childhood pedagogy NRC, 1998-99. Contbr. articles to profl. jours. Bd. dirs. Ill. Health Edn. Com., 1969—71, Inst. Psychoanalysis, 1970—73, Ill. Adv. Coun. Dept. Children and Family Svcs., 1974—79, Child Devel. Assoc. Consortium, 1979—81, Chgo. Bd. Edn. Desegregation Commn., 1981—84, Bus. People in Pub. Inst., 1980—, High Scope Ednl. Rsch. Found., 1986—93, Gt. Books Found., 1988—, Cmty.-Corp. Sch., 1988—90; mem. Family Resource Coalition, 1992—96, mem. nat. bd. profl. tchr. stds., 1996—2002. Mem. Ill. Assn. Edn. Young Children, Nat. Assn. Edn. Young Children (pres. 1980-82), Chgo. Assns. Edn. Young Children (pres. 1973-77), Black Child Devel. Assn., Am. Ednl. Rsch. Assn. Achievements include research in early education teaching and school improvement. Office: Erikson Inst 420 N Wabash Ave Chicago IL 60611-3568 E-mail: bbowman@erikson.edu.

BOWMAN, CHRISTINE DIANE, middle school educator; b. San Francisco, Jan. 1, 1953; d. Earl M. and Patricia A. Homan; m. Kenneth Michael Bowman, June 7, 1975; children: Jeffrey Michael, Scott M.E. BA, San Francisco State U., Calif., 1975. Tchr., coach Jefferson UHSD, Daly City, Calif., 1976, Campbell UHSD, San Jose, Calif., 1976—81; tchr. San Bruno Pk. Sch. Dist., Calif., 1981—95, athletic dir., 1995—, dept. chairperson, 1995—. Gymnastics coach Jefferson, Campbell, DC, San Jose, Calif., 1971—81, Sequoia YMCA Club, Redwood City, Calif., 1976—81. Recipient Outstanding Phys. Edn. Tchr. award, Calif. State Senate, 1991. Mem.: NEA, Calif. Tchrs. Assn., SBEA, CAHPER. Avocations: water sports (skiing, swimming), gymnastics, gardening. Home: 2740 Carmel Dr San Bruno CA 94066

BOWMAN, CYNTHIA GRANT, law educator; BA with honors, Swarthmore Coll., 1966; PhD in Polit. Sci., Columbia U., 1972; JD cum laude, Northwestern U., 1982. Law clk. to Hon. Richard D. Cudahy US Ct. Appeals (7th cir.), 1982—83; assoc. Jenner & Block, Chgo., 1983—88; vis. asst. prof. Northwestern U. Sch. Law, Chgo., 1988—89, asst. prof. law, 1989—92, assoc. prof., 1992—95, prof. law, 1995—, prof. gender studies, 2000—. Co-author: Cases and Materials on Feminist Jurisprudence: Taking Women Seriously, 2001, Women and Law in Sub-saharan Africa, 2003; contbr. articles to profl. jours. Mem.: ABA, Soc. Am. Law Tchrs., Law and Society Assn. Office: Northwestern U Sch Law 357 E Chicago Ave Chicago IL 60611 Office Phone: 312-503-6607. Office Fax: 312-503-2035. E-mail: cgbowman@law.northwestern.edu.

BOWMAN, DELORES, medical cost management administrator; b. Irmo, S.C., Aug. 7, 1948; d. Willie Bowman and Geneva Bowman-Nelson. AS, Allegheny C.C., 1970; BSN, NYU, 1975. RN; cert. risk mgr. Dir. HRA Medicaid/EPSDT Program/Medicaid HMO, 1978-80; project mgr., dir. Bradford Nat. Corp. McAuto Sys. Group, 1980-83; v.p. med. svcs. and programs NYLCARE Health Plan, 1983-98; cons. pres. Bowman Mgmt., 1998-99; v.p. PSI Medica, Elm Wood Park, N.J., 1999—. Home: 21-07 Greenwood Dr Fair Lawn NJ 07410-4537

BOWMAN, DOROTHY LOUISE, artist; b. Hollywood, Calif., Jan. 20, 1927; d. Bruce L. and Dorothy L. (Kalkman) B; m. Howard Hugh Bradford, Dec. 30, 1949 (div. 1965); children: Brock, Cyndra, Tal Scott, Heather, Delia, Callia. Student, Chouinard Art Inst., Calif., 1945-48, Jepson Art Inst., L.A., 1948-49; BA, Webster U., 1979. One-woman show Ventana Gallery, Big Sur, 1998; serigrapher, printmaker, painter: represented in permanent collections: Immaculate Heart Coll., L.A. County Mus., Bklyn. Mus., Long Beach Mus., Crocker Art Gallery, Mus. Modern Art, Phila., Mus. Fine Arts, San Jose State Coll., De Cordova and Danna Mus., Boston Pub. Libr., Boston Mus. Fine Arts, N.Y. Pub. Libr., Rochester Meml. Gallery, U. Wis., U. Hawaii, U. Ill., U. Kans., Santa Barbara Mus., Achenbach Found. Legion of Honor, Mus. Modern Art, Monterey, Calif., Libr. Congress, Calif. State Libr. Archives, Arquivos Historicos De Arte Contemporanea Museu De Arte Moderna, San Paulo, Brazil, Ch. of Latter Day Saints History Mus., Salt Lake City, 1987, Nat. Mus. of Women in the Arts, Washington, 2000—; twice juried internat. show 27 countries, 1987; creator animation films The Mobius World, 2000, Really O'Reiley, 2002, Never Seen Fox, 2003, Cry Baby Lion!; Traveling show Smithsonian Inst., Nat. Collection of Fine Arts, 1952; movie prodr. hist. film, Big Sur, 2002. Address: Nat Mus of Women in the Arts Archives 1250 New York Ave NW Washington DC 20005-3970 Office Phone: 831-375-5170. E-mail: dorothybowman@redshift.com.

BOWMAN, ESTHER RUTH-KAZIAN, music educator; b. West Covina, Calif., Aug. 30, 1972; d. John Mark and Mary Ellen Kazian; m. David Arthur Bowman, Feb. 14, 2004; children: Benjamin David, Rosalie Susan Carol. Student, Excelsior U. Family assistance ctr. coord. Maine Army N.G., Augusta, Maine, 2003—; music educator SAD #48, Newport, Maine, 2005—. Freelance music educator, Plymouth, Maine, 1996—. Staff sgt. Army Nat. Guard, 2003—06, Augusta, Maine. Mem.: Mensa (corr.). Republican. Avocations: music, crafts, running, exercise. Home: 656 Clark Rd Plymouth ME 04969 Office: Maine Army National Guard 33 State House Station Augusta ME 04333 Office Phone: 207-650-8601. Business E-Mail: esther.bowman@us.army.mil.

BOWMAN, HAZEL LOIS, retired English language educator; b. Plant City, Fla., Feb. 18, 1917; d. Joseph Monroe and Annie (Thoman) B. AB, Fla. State Coll. for Women, 1937; MA, U. Fla., 1948; postgrad., U. Md., 1961-65. Tchr. Lakeview HS, Winter Garden, Fla., 1939-40, Eagle Lake Sch., Fla., 1940-41; welfare visitor Fla. Welfare Bd., 1941-42; specialist U.S. Army Signal Corps, Arlington Hall, Va., 1942-43; recreation work, asst. procurement officer ARC, CBI Theater, 1943-46; lab. technician Am. Cyanamid Corp., Brewster, Fla., 1946-47; instr., asst. prof. gen. extension divsn. U. Fla., Fla. State U., 1948-51; freelance writer, editor, indexer NY, 1951-55, Fla., 1951—55; staff writer Tampa Morning Tribune, Fla., 1956; staff writer, telegraph editor Winter Haven News-Chief, Fla., 1956-57; registrar, admissions officer U. Tampa, 1957-59; coll. counselor Atlantic States, 1959-60; registrar, freshman advisor Towson State Tchrs. Coll., Balt., 1960-62; dir. student pers., guidance, admissions Harford Jr. Coll., Bel Air, Md., 1962-64; instr., asst. prof. English, journalism York Coll., Pa., 1965-69; tchr. S.W. Jr. HS, Lakeland, Fla., 1969-70; tchr. learning disabled Vanguard Sch., Lake Wales, Fla., 1970-82; libr. asst. Polk County Hist. and Geneal. Libr., Bartow, Fla., 1986-91. Editor Fla. Flambeau, 1936-37, Tampa Altrusan, 1958-60, Polk County Hist. Calendar, 1986-90. Mem. Polk County Hist. Commn., 1992-99. Recipient Mayhall Music medal, 1933, Excellence in Cmty. Svc. award Nat. Soc. DAR, 1994, Outstanding Achievement award Fla. State Geneal. Soc., 2002. Mem.: AAUW (hon. 50 yr. life), Polk County Hist. Assn., Imperial Polk Geneal. Soc., Nat. Geneal. Soc., Mortar Board, Chi Delta Phi, Alpha Chi Alpha. Home: 1001 Fifth St NE Mulberry FL 33860-2608

BOWMAN, KARMIEN C., art educator, artist, sculptor, ceramist; d. Charles Brown and Ethel Rowena Carsey; m. Alton Joseph Bowman III, July 22, 1984; children: Ada, Alton Joseph IV, Ariel. BFA, U. Tex., 1969; MA in Ceramics, Art Metals, Sculpture, Tex. Women's U., 1975. Cert. all-level tchr. Tex., 1980. Tchg. asst. ceramics Tex. Women's U., Denton, 1974—75; artist in schs. Tex. Commn. Arts, City of Tyler, 1976, artist in residence City of Dallas, 1978; project dir. Cmty. Edn. Tng. Adminstrn. City Arts: Prodn. Ceramics & Youth, 1979; art faculty Lewisville Ind. Sch. Dist. Millican Mid. Sch., 1979—82; dir. Yarmouth Gallery, 1970—83; assoc. prof. art Tarrant C.C., Hurst, Tex., 1990—. Adj. instr. ceramics and jewelry Brookhaven Coll. Dallas County C.C. Dist., 1979—89; guest artist technician Joe Schaefer Art Bronze Foundry, Ft. Worth, 2000; vis. artist Flower Mound HS, 2000, Lamar Jr. HS, Flower Mound, 2002; guest artist and presenter Greater Denton Arts Coun., 2003, Visual Art Soc. Tex., Denton, Tex., 2003; guest artist lectr. Paris Jr. Coll., 2003; guest artist scout coord. Trinity Ceramic Supply inc., 2004. Exhibitions include Okla. Eight State Show, 1972 (Painting award), Voertman Show, 1974 (Best of Show in Painting award), Grad. Exhbn., Tex. Woman's U., 1975, Women in Action Tour Sculpture, Tex., 1976, Tex. Fine Arts Assn. Sculpture, 1976 (Best in Show), New City Hall Dallas, 1978, Tex. Assn. Schs. Art One Sq. Foot Confs., 1991—2005, Tex. Assn. Schs. Art One Sq. Foot, McAllen, Tex., 2001, Ft. Worth, 2002, San Antonio, 2003, Dallas, 2005, State Fair, Tex. Sculpture Assn., 1993, 1995—97, Jesuit Scholarship Exhibit, 1994, Osteo. Medicine Ctr., 2000, Bank One, Ft. Worth, 1997, Form Function Boogiewoogie Blues Permian Basin Nat. Invitational, Odessa, Tex., 2002, Cowgirl Hall of Fame Inaugural Exhibit, 2002, Old Modern Retrospective duo exhibit, 2003, FireHouse Gallery, Ft. Worth, 2004, CrossTimbers Cultural Arts, ArtHouse Open Studio Tour, Denton County, Tex., 2004—, Phillip Combs Design, 2004, Tex. Clay Festival, Rimas Rippoff, Gruene, Tex., 2004, one-woman shows include North Lake Coll., 1980, Farmers' and Merchants' Gallery, 1981, Ctr. Art Gallery, 1990, NE Tex. A&M, Mt. Pleasant, 2006, Paris Gallery on the Square, Paris, Tex., 2006, exhibited in group shows at Fortieth Hour Invitational Group Show, Ft. Worth Cmty. Arts Ctr., 2003, Represented in permanent collections U. Tex., Austin, Ceramics, Southland Corp., pvt. collections to numerous individuals; contbr. articles to jours., books and mags. in field. Mem. Nat. Cowgirl Mus. Hall of Fame, Nat. Mus. Women Art, Nat. Geog., Dallas Mus. Art, Meadows Mus., Kimbell Art Mus., Modern Art Mus., Fort Worth, Tex. Smithsonian; vol. benefit artist to numerous orgns.; vol Grapevine Hist. Ctr. Foundry, 2005; art bible sch. tchr. Argyle Meth. Ch., 1993, 1998. Nominee Thatcher-Hoffman Smith award, 2002; recipient Faculty Devel. Leave award, Tarrant C.C., 2006. Mem.: Am. Ceramic Edn. Rsch. Soc. (founders potters coun.), Am. Crafts Coun., Am. Ceramic Soc. Cross Timbers Cultural Arts Assn. (founding chair 1984—2005), Potters Coun., Nat. Conf. Edn. in Ceramics Arts Assn., Dallas Ctr. Contemporary Art (Critics choice exhibit 2003), Internat. Sculpture Assn., Dallas Area Clay Artists Assn. (fundraising com. 2003), Tex. Clay Art Assn., Tex. CC Tchrs. Assn. (art section chair 1994—), Tex. Assn. Schs. Art (bd. mem. 1999—), Tex. State Tchrs. Assn., Tex. Fine Arts Assn. (collectors cir. 2003). Avocations: horseback riding, sculpting. Office: Tarrant County Coll Northeast Campus 828 Harwood Hurst TX 76054 Office Phone: 817-430-3032. Business E-Mail: karmien.bowman@tccd.edu.

BOWMAN, KATHLEEN GILL, academic administrator; BS English & Spanish, U. of Minn., 1964, MA English Edn., 1967, PhD English Edn., 1977. Rsch. assoc. Legis. Adv. Coun. on the Econ. Status of Women, St. Paul, 1976-77; asst. dir. of grad. studies, asst prof. of edn. Reed Coll., Portland, OR, 1977-79, exec. asst. to the pres., dir. of spl. programs, 1979-82; assoc. dir., program officer Fred Meyer Charitable Trust, Portland, OR, 1982-84; assoc. v.p. for rsch. U. of Oreg., Eugene, OR, 1985-89, vice-provost for internat. affairs, 1989-94; pres. Randolph-Macon Woman's Coll., Lynchburg, VA, 1994—. Fullbright Sr. Scholar award, Japan & Korea, 1993. Office: Randolph-Macon Womans Coll Office of the Pres 2500 Rivermont Ave Lynchburg VA 24503-1555

BOWMAN, LEAH, fashion designer, consultant, photographer, educator; b. Chgo., Apr. 21, 1935; d. John George and Alexandra (Colovos) Murges; m. Veron George Broe, Aug. 31, 1954; 1 child, Michelle; m. John Ronald Bowman, Feb. 28, 1959 Diploma, Sch. of Art Inst., Chgo., 1962. Designer Korach Bros. Inc., Chgo., 1962-65; costume designer Hull House South Theatre, Chgo., 1966-67, Wellington Theatre, Chgo., 1966-67; from instr. to prof. emeritus Sch. of Art Inst., Chgo., 1967—2001, prof. emeritus, 2001—. Prodr. fashion performances and style exhbns.; vis. prof., cons. SNDT Women's U., Bombay, 1980, 85, 92, Ctrl. Acad. Arts and Design, Beijing, People's Republic of China, 1987; faculty sabbatical exhbn. Sch. of Art Inst., 1986, 93. Recipient Fulbright award, Coun. for Internat. Exchange for Scholars, India, 1980, Pres. award, Art Inst. Chgo., 1991, Honoror's award, Sch. of Art Inst., Chgo., 1998, Disting. Faculty award, Sch. Art Inst. Chgo., 2005. Office: Sch of Art Inst Chgo 37 S Wabash Ave Chicago IL 60603-3002

BOWMAN, LYNNE BARNETT, medical librarian; b. Shelbyville, Ky., Apr. 12, 1954; d. James Robert and Alice Louise (Harrison) Barnett; m. Howard Wayne Bowman, Mar. 5, 1987. AB, U. Louisville, 1976; MSLS, U. Ky., Lexington, 1978. Med. libr. U. Ky., Lexington, 1978—. Mem. Health Scis. OCLC Users Group (recording sec. 1991-92, 97-98), Med. Libr. Assn., Ky. Libr. Assn. Spl. Librs. Sect. (sec. 1981-82, 90-91, treas. 1985-86), Midwest Chpt. Med. Libr. Assn., Beta Phi Mu, Phi Kappa Phi. Avocations: cross stitch, needlepoint, gardening.

BOWMAN, MARJORIE ANN, physician, educator; b. Grove City, Pa., Aug. 18, 1953; d. Ross David and Freda Louise (Smith) Williamson; m. Robert Choplin; children: Bridget Williamson Foley, Skyler Weston Williamson Choplin. BS, Pa. State U., 1974; MD, Jefferson Med. Coll., 1976; MPA, U. So. Calif., L.A., 1983. Intern, then resident in family practice Duke U., Durham, NC, 1976-79; med. officer USPHS, Hyattsville, Md., 1979-82; clin. instr. uniformed svcs. U. Health Scis., Bethesda, Md., 1980-83; dir. family practice residency, prof. Georgetown U. Sch. Medicine, Washington, 1983-86; chmn. dept. family practice, prof. Wake Forest U., Winston-Salem, NC, 1986—96; prof., chmn. dept. family medicine & cmty. health U. Pa., Phila, 1996—. Author: (Book) Stress and Women Physicians, 1985, 1990, Women in Medicine: Life and Career, 2002; editor: Archives Family Medicine, 1992—2000, Jour. Women's Health, 2001—05, Jour. Am. Bd. Family Medicine, 2003—; contbr. articles to profl. jours. Fellow Am. Acad. Family Physicians; mem. AMA, Soc. Tchrs. Family Medicine (bd. dirs. 1984-88, bd. dirs. Found. 1984-99, v.p. 1988-91, pres. 1991-92), Am. Pub. Health Assn. Republican. Unitarian Universalist. Office: Univ Pa 2 Gates 3400 Spruce St Philadelphia PA 19104-4283 Business E-Mail: bowmanm@uphs.upenn.edu.

BOWMAN, PATRICIA LYNN, lawyer; b. Mpls., July 5, 1956; d. Robert Lee and Delores Helen (Roberts) B. BA in History with distinction, Stanford U., 1978; JD cum laude, Harvard U., 1981; MA, Grad. Theol. Union, 1999. Assoc. Perkins Coie, Seattle, 1981-84, Foster, Pepper & Shefelman, Seattle, 1984-89; v.p., assoc. counsel Washington Mut. Bank, Seattle, 1989-97. Pastoral asst. for social outreach, St. James Cathedral, Seattle, 2000—. Bd. dirs., vice chair Common Ground, Seattle, 1987-93; bd. dirs. Elderhealth Northwest, Seattle, 1994-97. Mem. ABA, Wash. State Bar Assn., Seattle-King County Bar Assn., Seattle Mortgage Bankers Assn. (mem. legal com.), Phi Beta Kappa.

BOWMAN, SARAH, librarian; b. Ferriday, La., June 4, 1948; d. Willie Bowman and Clara Bowman Woodruff; 1 child, Marcus E. Kennedy. BS, Grambling State U., La., 1970; MS, U. So. Miss., 1976; postgrad., Auburn U., Ala., 1978. Cert. in-tech coord. La. Libr. Rosston (Ark.) Sch. Dist., 1970—71, Natchez Jr. Coll., Natchez, Miss., 1974—75; bus. tchr. Concordia Parish Sch., Ferriday, La., 1972—74, libr. Vidalia, La., 1976—88, Ferriday, 1988—. Sec.-treas. St. Paul Bapt. Ch., Ferriday, 1992—. Mem.: Am. Fedn. Tchrs. (membership chmn. 1999—2005), N.E. La. Libr. Network (sec.-treas. 1989—91), Phi Delta Kappa. Democrat. Baptist. Avocations: reading, cooking, entering sweepstakes. Home: 802 10th St Ferriday LA 71334 Office: Ferriday Upper Elem School PO Box 524 Ferriday LA 71334

BOWNE, MARTHA HOKE, editor, consultant; b. Greeley, Colo., June 9, 1931; d. George Edwin and Krin (English) Hoke; children: Gretchen, William, Kay, Judith. BA, U. Mich., 1952; postgrad., Syracuse U., 1965. Tchr. Wayne (Mich.) Pub. Schs., 1953-54, East Syracuse and Minoa Cen. Schs., Minoa, NY, 1965-68; store mgr. Fabric Barn, Fayetteville, NY, 1969-77; store owner Fabric Fair, Oneida, NY, 1978-80; prodr., owner Quilting by the Sound, Port Townsend, Wash., 1987—2000, Quilting by the Lake, Cazenovia, NY, 1981—. Organizer symposium Am. Quilters Soc.; founder, pres. Quilter's Quest confs., 1994—. Mem., pres. Minoa Library, 1960-75; mem. Onondaga County Library, Syracuse, 1968-71. Mem.: Am. Quilters Soc. (editor Am. Quilter mag. 1985—95). Avocations: reading, hiking, travel, bridge, Scrabble. Home: 478 Oden Bay Dr Sandpoint ID 83864-6499 E-mail: martyidaho@sandpoint.net.

BOWNE, SHIRLEE PEARSON, credit manager; b. High Shoals Twp., NC, Mar. 11, 1936; d. Lloyd E. Pearson and Parnell (James) Garland; divorced; 1 child, Gregory Charles. Grad. h.s., Gaffney, S.C. Various secretarial positions, 1955-64; sales repr., pres. Real Estate Marketers, Inc., Tallahassee, 1964-80; chief exec. officer Shirlee Bowne Mktg. & Devel. Inc., Tallahassee, 1980-91; vice chmn. Nat. Credit Union Adminstrn., Washington, 1991-97. Cons. in field. Treas. Rep. Party Fla., 1988-91. Episcopalian. Avocation: bridge. Personal E-mail: shirleebrowne@earthlink.net.

BOWSER, SHIRLEY, volunteer; b. Williamsport, Ohio; BA in Ed., Ohio State U. Mem. Nat. Agricultural Rsch., Extension, Ed., and Economics Adv. Bd., 2000—. Mem. of food and soc. com. Nat. Assn. of Land-Grant Coll. and U.; bd. treasurer Pickaway County Community Found.; trustee W.K. Kellogg Found., 1982—, chair, 1990—91, 2000—01; mem. W.K. Kellogg Trust, 2002. Office: WK Kellogg Found One Michigan Ave E Battle Creek MI 49017-4012

BOXER, BARBARA, senator; b. Bklyn., Nov. 11, 1940; d. Ira and Sophie (Silvershein) Levy; m. Stewart Boxer, 1962; children: Doug, Nicole. BA in Economics, Bklyn. Coll., 1962. Aide to Congressman John L. Burton, 1974—76; stockbroker, econ. rschr. N.Y. Securities Firm, N.Y.C., 1962-65; journalist, assoc. editor Pacific Sun, 1972-74; congl. aide to rep. 5th Congl. Dist. San Francisco, 1974-76; mem. 98th-102d Congresses from 6th Calif. dist., mem. armed services com., select com. children, youth and families; majority whip at large; co-chair Mil. Reform Caucus; chair subcom. on govt. activities and transp. of house govt. ops. com., 1990-93; US Senator from Calif. US Senate, 1993—. Mem. Presdl. Advisory Commn. on Holocaust Assets in the US; mem. com. commerce, sci. and transp. US Senate, com. environment and public works, com. fgn. relations. Author (with Nicole

Boxer): Strangers in the Senate: Politics and the New Revolution of Women in America, 1993; (with Catherine Whitney) Nine and Counting: The Women of the Senate, 2000, (with Mary-Rose Hayes) (novels) A Time to Run, 2005. Mem. Marin County Bd. Suprs., 1976-82, pres. 1980-81; mem. Bay Area Air Quality Mgmt. Bd., San Francisco, 1977-82, pres., 1979-81; bd. dirs. Golden Gate Bridge Hwy. and Transport Dist., San Francisco, 1978-82; pres. Dem. New Mems. Caucus, 1983. Recipient Open Govt. award Common Cause, 1980, Rep. of Yr. award Nat. Multiple Sclerosis Soc., 1990, Margaret Sanger award Planned Parenthood, 1990, Women of Achievement award Anti-Defamation League, 1990, Star Legis. award LA Women's Legis. Coalition, 1991, Elected Official of the Year Stonewall Democratic Club, 1997, Edgar Wayburn award Sierra Club, 1997, Demetris Bouhoutsos award Hellenic-Am. Coun. So. Calif., 1998, Pres. award for the Advancement of Women Nat. Assn. Women Lawyers, 1998, Alumnae of the Year, Bklyn. Coll., 1999, Reg. Elected Official of the Year Sacramento Area Coun. Governments., 1999, Vision award Highwood Online Girlsite, 1999, Pub. Servant award Nat. Orgn. on Fetal Alcohol Syndrome, 1999, Every Action Counts Congl. award Hadassah, 1999, Spirit of Achievement Albert Einstein Coll. Med., 2000, Paul E. Tsongas award Lymphoma Rsch. Found. Am., 2000, Peter H. Behr award Friends of the River, 2000, Environmental Leadership award Calif. League of Conservation Voters, 2003. Mem.: Marin Community Video, Marin Nat. Women's Polit. Caucus, Marin Edn. Corps. Democrat. Jewish. Office: US Senate 112 Hart Senate Office Bldg Washington DC 20510-0001 also: District Office Ste 2240 600 B St San Diego CA 92101-4508 Office Phone: 202-224-3553, 619-239-3884. Office Fax: 619-239-5719.*

BOXX, RITA MCCORD, retired banker; b. Greenwood, S.C., Aug. 10, 1930; d. John Thomas Logan and Dempsie (Dixon) McCord; m. John Douglas Boxx, Apr. 17, 1949; children: John Stephen, Eric Wesley, Merry Christine. Student, pub. schs. Asst. mgr. Greenwood Ins. Agy., 1961-65, mgr., 1967-80; with Bankers Trust S.C., Greenwood, 1981—2006; asst. v.p. charge ins. dept. NCNB (formerly Bankers Trust S.C.), 1980—2006; ret., 2006. Tchr. ins. seminars. Mem. Nat. Assn. Ins. Women, Ind. Ins. Agts. Am., Greenwood Assn. Ins. Women, Greenwood C. of C. (dir. 1974-76, chmn. environ., energy and conservation com. 1974), chmn. edn. com. 1977), Greenwood Country Club. Baptist. Home: 434 Dogwood Dr Greenwood SC 29646-9210

BOYCE, CORRIE MOSBY, music educator; b. Columbia, S.C., Apr. 7, 1953; d. Rufus Levi and Emma Jo Mosby; m. W. Ray Boyce, June 21, 1975; 1 child, Ray D'Mitry. BA, Columbia Coll., 1974; MEd, Cambridge Coll., 1995. Tchr. Richland Sch. Dist. 1, Columbia, 1974—; instr. Middle Sch. Sci. Enrichment Program, Benedict Coll., Columbia, 1996—. Cluster leader Keenan Cluster Sch.'s Music Program, Columbia, 1989—90; choral music curriculum com. Richland Sch. Dist. 1, Columbia, 1998; Curriculum Leadership in the Arts participant S.C. State Dept. Edn., Columbia, 2003. Rhomania co-chairperson Beta Epsilon Sigma chpt. Sigma Gamma Rho, 1991—2002. Named Outstanding Club Woman of Yr., S.C. Fedn. of Women and Youth Clubs, Inc., 1990, United Meth. Woman of Yr., I. DeQuincey Newman United Meth. Women, 1995, Living the Legacy honoree, Nat. Coun. Negro Women, Inc., 1998. Mem.: Music Educators Nat. Conf. and affiliates, NEA and affiliates (mem. S.C. del. assembly 1993—98). United Methodist. Home: 204 Torwood Dr Columbia SC 29203 Office: Richland County Sch Dist 1 1616 Richland St Columbia SC 29201 E-mail: corrie0407@aol.com.

BOYCE, DOREEN ELIZABETH, foundation administrator, educator; b. Antofagasta, Chile, Apr. 20, 1934; d. George Edgar and Elsie Winifred Vaughan; m. Alfred Warne Boyce, Aug. 11, 1956; children: Caroline Elizabeth, John Trevor Warne. BA with hons., Oxford (Eng.) U., 1956, MA with hons., 1960; PhD, U. Pitts., 1983; DHL (hon.), Westminister Coll., 1986, Washington and Jefferson Coll., 1993, Franklin and Marshall Coll., 2005. Lectr. and tutor in econs. U. Witwatersrand, South Africa, 1960-62; provost and dean of faculty, Mary Helen Marks prof. econs. Chatham Coll., Pitts., 1963-79; prof. econs., chmn. dept. econs. and mgmt. Hood Coll., Frederick, Md., 1979-82; pres. Buhl Found., Pitts., 1982—. Dir. and vice chair DQE Duquesne Light Co., Dollar Bank, FSB, Coun. Ind. Colls., Carnegie Mus.; co-founder, dir. Microbac Labs., Inc.; Pa. Gov.'s Sports and Exposition Facilities Task Force, 1995; del. White House Conf. on Small Bus., 1980; mem. Gov.'s Conf. Small Bus., 1979-82; mem. devel. com. Somerville Coll., 2005— Chmn. bd. dirs., emerita trustee Franklin and Marshall Coll., 1982-04, Frick Edn. Commn., 1980-94, Carnegie Sci. Ctr., 1982—, Carnegie Inst., 2005-; mem. Fed.Jud. Nominating Commn., 1977-79, Pa. Gov.'s Commn. on Financing of Higher Edn., 1983-85; bd. dirs. World Affairs Coun., 1984-96; mem. appeal com. Somerville Coll., Oxford, Eng., devel. com., 2005-. Recipient Medallion of Distinction, U. Pitts., 1987, Univ. Laureate, U. Pitts., 2004; named Disting. Dau. Pa., 1996, Hon. Fellow Somerville Coll., U. Oxford, Women Who Make A Difference award, Internat. Women's Forum, 1998. Mem. Am. Econs. Assn., Am. Assn. Higher Edn., Grantmakers of Western Pa. (pres. 1984), Internat. Women's Forum, Assn. Governing Bds. Univ. and Coll. (coun. bd. chairs 2002—), Duquesne Club (bd. dirs. 2000-03, chmn. found. 2005-). Office: Centre City Tower 650 Smithfield St Ste 2300 Pittsburgh PA 15222-3912

BOYCE, EMILY STEWART, retired library and information science educator, retired library and information scientist; b. Raleigh, N.C., Aug. 18, 1933; d. Harry and May (Fallon) B. BS, East Carolina U., 1955, MA, 1961; MS in Libr. Sci., U. N.C., 1968; postgrad., Cath. U. Am., 1977. Libr. Tileston Jr. H.S., Wilmington, NC, 1955-57; children's libr. Wilmington Pub. Libr., 1957-58; asst. libr. Joyner Libr. East Carolina U., Greenville, NC, 1959-61, libr. III, 1962-63; ednl. supr. II ednl. media divsn. N.C. State Dept. Pub. Instrn., Raleigh, 1961-62; assoc. prof. dept. libr. and info. scis. East Carolina U., 1964-76, prof., 1976-92, chmn. dept., 1982-89; retired, 1992. Cons. So. Assn. Colls. and Schs., Raleigh, 1975-92. Active Asheville YWCA, Mediation Ctr., Botanical Gardens, Literacy Coun. Buncombe County. Mem. ALA, AAUW, N.C. Libr. Assn., Assn. Libr. and Info. Sci. Educators, Spl. Librs. Assn. Democrat. Home: 3000 Galloway Ridge C107 Pittsboro NC 27312 Personal E-mail: esboyce30@charter.net.

BOYCE, MARIA WYCKOFF, lawyer; b. Houston, Tex., Aug. 30, 1963; BA cum laude, Conn. Coll., 1985; JD, Northwestern Univ., 1988. Bar: Tex. 1988, US Dist. Ct. (so., ea., no., we. dist. Tex., Colo.), US Ct. Appeals 5th cir., US Supreme Ct. Ptnr. litigation dept. & mem. exec. com. Baker Botts LLP, Houston. Editor (in chief): Jour. Criminal Law & Criminology. Mem. adv. bd. Girls Inc. of Greater Houston; bd. dir., Houston chpt. Tex. Gen. Counsel Forum. Mem.: Am. Intellectual Property Law Assn., Houston Bar Assn., Fed. Bar Assn. (pres.elect). Office: Baker Botts LLP One Shell Plz 910 Louisiana St Houston TX 77002-4995 Office Phone: 713-229-1922. Office Fax: 713-229-2722. Business E-Mail: maria.boyce@bakerbotts.com.

BOYCE, MARTHA JO, artist, educator; b. Hartingen, Tex., Mar. 16, 1953; d. Larry Burton and Trellis Lorraine (Trotter) Ledbetter; m. Richard Jude Boyce, Aug. 10, 2001; children: Christopher Broadway, Samuel Broadway, Sarah Broadway Greenville. BS in Edn., U. Tex., Tyler, 1985; BS in Art Edn., U. Tex., 1985. Art instr. Sabine Ind. Sch. Dist., Gladewater, Tex.; 4th grade tchr. Overton Ind. Sch. Dist., Overton, Tex.; art instr., pre-K tchr. Holy Trinity Sch., Jefferson, Tex. Mem.: Tex. Art Edn. Assn. Avocations: painting, photography, travel, hunting, fishing.

BOYCE, MARY C., mechanical engineer, educator; BS, Va. Polytechnic Inst., 1981; MS, MIT, 1983, PhD, 1987. Asst. prof. mechanical engring. MIT, 1987—92, assoc. prof. mechanical engring., 1992—99, prof. mechanical engring., 1999—2000, disting. alumnae prof. mechanical engring., 2000—. Named MacVicar Faculty fellow, 2000—10; recipient ALCOA Found. award, 1988, 1991, Presidential Young Investigators award, NSF, 1991—96, DuPont Faculty award, 1992—95, GenCorp Signature U. award, 1998, Keenan Innovation in Teaching award, 1998. Fellow: Am. Acad. Arts & Scis.; mem.: Materials Rsch. Soc., Am. Physics Soc., Am. Acad. of Mechanics, Am. Soc. of Mechanical Engineers (Special Achievement award 1998). Office: MIT 1-304 Mechanical Engring 77 Mass Ave Cambridge MA 02139

BOYCE, TIFFANY MARIE, literature and language educator; b. Mount Pleasant, Pa., Aug. 12, 1981; d. Barry Lee and Cynthia Ann Huffine; m. Jason Ryan Boyce, June 21, 2003; 1 child, Logan Rylee. BA in English, Seton Hill U., Greensburg, Pa., 2004. Cert. secondary English tchr. Pa., 2004. Tchr. English, dir. of edn. Agape Day Treatment, Monessen, Pa., 2004—05; tchr. English, Charleroi Area H.S., Pa., 2005—. Yearbook co-sponser Charleroi H.S., Monessen, Pa., 2005—; student forum co-sponser Charleroi Area H.S., Pa., 2005—. Recipient John L. Weiss Award for Cmty. Leadership, Seton Hill U., 1999-2000. Mem.: NEA. Democrat. Roman Catholic. Avocations: traveling, outdoor activities, creative writing, swimming. Office Phone: 724-483-3573. Personal E-mail: tiffanyboyce22@yahoo.com. E-mail: tboyce@charleroisd.org.

BOYD, AMANDA D., elementary school educator; b. Washington, Dec. 18, 1979; d. Diane Ruth and John Michael Boyd. AA, Prince George's CC, Md., 2000; BS cum laude, Towson U., Md., 2001—03; postgrad. (hon.), Loyola U., 2003—. Std. Profl. 1 Md. State Dept. Edn., 2003, Cert. of Achievement in Life Sci. CC of Balt. County and Balt. County Pub. Sch., 2004, Cert. Completion of NASA Program Md. State Tchrs. Assn., 2003, Profl. Devel-.Cert. Tchg. Sci. Balt. County Pub. Sch., 2003. Fourth and fifth grade tchr. Charlesmont Elem., Balt., 2003—04, fourth grade tchr., 2004—. Sci. liason Charlesmont Elem., Balt., 2003—. Recipient Outstanding Tchr. award, Fourth Grade Parents, 2003-2004. Mem.: Tchrs. Assn. Balt. County. Office: Charlesmont Elem 5463 Princess Dr Baltimore MD 21237 Home: 5463 Princess Dr Rosedale MD 21237-4020 Office Phone: 410-887-7004. Personal E-mail: aboyd@bcps.org.

BOYD, ANN FISHER, office administrator; b. Corpus Christi, Oct. 2, 1933; d. King and Jewel (Tanner) Fisher; m. Waymon Lewis Boyd, July 8, 1956; children: Wayne Allen, Randy Lynn. Student, Durham Bus. coll., 1956. Operator Gen. Telephone Co., Port Lavaca, Tex., 1954-56; bookkeeper Champ Traylor Meml. Hosp., Port Lavaca, 1955-56; sec., payrol clk. King Fisher Marine Svc., Port Lavaca, 1956-58; sec., asst. sec., treas. King Fisher Marine Svc., Inc., Port Lavaca, 1961-64, asst. sec., treas., 1964—2001; ret. 2002. Home: PO Box 27 134 Harbor Dr W Port Lavaca TX 77979

BOYD, BE (BELINDA) CAROLYN, theater educator; m. John Wayne Shafer. BS in Comm. and Theater, Austin Peay State U., 1982; MFA in Acting, U. Louisville, 1986. Voice/ acting instr. U. of Louisville, 1986—89; asst. prof. of theater U. of Vt., Burlington, Vt., 1989—91; assoc. prof. if theater U. N.C., Greensboro, 1991—98; assoc. prof. of theater Tex. Christian U., Ft. Worth, 1998—2002, U. of Ctrl. Fla., Orlando, 2002—. Dir., dir.: La Lorona; actor: (actor in fires in the mirror) Fires in the Mirror (Best Actress, 2000); author: (play) Dream Keeper, Mother Of Civil Rights, In Focus: A Recollection of Black Thought. Mem.: Ctrl. Fla. Performing Arts Alliance, Assn. for Theatre in Higher Edn., Voice and Speech Trainers Assn., Am. Coll. Theatre Festival, Actor's Equity Assn., Southeastern Theatre Conf. (culteral diversity com. 1998—2000), Dramatist's Guild (assoc.). Office: U Ctrl Fla PO Box 162372 Orlando FL 32816-2372

BOYD, CAROLYN PATRICIA, history professor; b. San Diego, June 1, 1944; d. Peter James and Patricia Mae (de Soucy) B.; m. Frank Dawson Bean, Jan. 4, 1975; children: Peter Justin Bean, Michael Franklin Bean. AB with great distinction and with honors in History, Stanford U., 1966; MA, U. Wash., 1969, PhD, 1974. Tchg. asst. dept. history U. Wash., 1970-71; from instr. to prof. dept. history U. Tex., Austin, 1973-95, prof. history, 1995-99, assoc. dean Grad. Studies, 1986-88, 90-92, chair history dept., 1994-99; dir. univ. honors program, assoc. prof. history U. Md., College Park, 1989-90; prof. history U. Calif., Irvine, 1999—, chair history dept., 2004—06, dean Grad. Studies, 2006—. Lectr. in field. Author: Praetorian Politics in Liberal Spain, 1979, La política pretoriana en el reinado de Alfonso XIII, 1990, Historia Patria: Politics, History and National Identity in Spain, 1875-1975, 1997, Spanish edit., 2000; mem. editl. bd. Essays, 1992-95, Ayer, 2005-; author chpts. to books; contbr. articles to profl. jours. Recipient Summer award U. Tex. Rsch. Inst., 1997; Woodrow Wilson hon. fellow, 1966, Fulbright-Hays fellow, 1966-67, NDEA Title IV fellow, 1968-72, AAUW fellow, 1972-73, ACLS fellow, 1985; ACLS Grant-in-Aid, 1977, Am. Philos. Soc. grant, 1978, URI Rsch. grant, 1985, New Del Amo Program grant, 2000-02; fellow Woodrow Wilson Internat. Ctr. for Scholars, 2002-03. Mem. Am. Hist. Assn. (James Harvey Robinson prize com. 1992-94, John Fagg prize com. 2001-03), Soc. Spanish and Portugese Hist. Studies (gen. sec. 2000-04, mem. exec. com. 1978-80, 83-85, 96-98, chair local arrangements, program chmn. conf. 1987), Coun. European Studies, Internat. Inst. in Spain, Assn. Contemporary History. Office: U Calif Irvine Dept History Irvine CA 92697-0001 Business E-Mail: cpboyd@uci.edu.

BOYD, DEBORAH ANN, pediatrician; b. Urbana, Ohio, Jan. 30, 1955; d. John A. Sr. and Juanita Jean (Routt) B. BA cum laude, Wittenberg U., 1977; MD, U. Cin., 1982. Diplomate Am. Bd. Pediatrics, Nat. Bd. Med. Examiners. Intern Children's Hosp. Med. Ctr., Cin., 1982—83, pediat. resident, 1982—85; pediatrician Nat. Health Svc. Corps, Springfield, Ohio, 1985—89; former pediatrician Cmty. Hosp. Health Care Ctr., Springfield, 1989—97; staff pediat. primary care ctr., clin. faculty Children's Hosp. Med. Ctr., Cin., 1998—. Mem. Continuing med. edn. com. Mercy Med. Ctr., Springfield, 1989—, infection control com., 1987—. Adv. com. Miami Valley Child Devl. Ctr., Springfield, 1985—, New Parents as Tchrs., 1986—. Mem. Assn. of Clinicians for the Underserved, Am. Acad. Pediats., Ambulatory Pediat. Assn. Democratic. Avocations: bicycling, photography, basketball, music, church activities. Home: 12132 S Pine Dr Apt 240 Cincinnati OH 45241-1743 Office: Dept Gen Com Pediatrics Children's Hosp Med Ctr 3333 Burnet Ave Fl 4 Cincinnati OH 45229-3026 Office Phone: 513-636-7594.

BOYD, HAZEL, minister; b. Huntingdon, Tenn., Sept. 09; d. Marion Homer Barnett and Lennie Victolia Hawkins; married; 6 children. Student in real estate, Columbus State Coll., Ohio. Ordained clergy Anderson Ind. Ch. of God, Ohio; cert. health aide Columbus State Coll., profl. activity dir. Cosmetologist, Columbus, Ohio; area commr. Columbus City Coun.; prison minister Columbus. Pres. PTA, 1960; judge Bd. Election; Sunday Sch. tchr., Bible tchr. Recipient various awards and citations, various orgns., including NAACP. Mem.: Greater SLAC, 50 Plus Club, Linden Kiwanis. Home: 1264 E 16th Ave Columbus OH 43211

BOYD, HELEN M. (S. HELEN R. BOYD), education educator; b. N.Y.C., Oct. 7, 1938; d. Robert Joseph Boyd and Helen Ann Jockell. BS in Edn., St. Thomas Aquinas, Sparkill, N.Y., 1961; MA in European History, St. John's U., Jamaica, N.Y., 1971, DA in Modern World History (hon.), 1999. Cert. tchg. and adminstrn. N.Y. Elem. tchr. Archdiocese of N.Y., 1958—69; prin. St. Catherine of Siena, Binghamton, NY, 1969—70, St. Augustine's, New City, NY, 1971—79, St. Thomas Canterbury, Cornwall, NY, 1979—89, Alperns Melanus, Bardonia, NY, 1989—96; prof. Iona Coll., New Rochelle, NY, 1999—. Trustee, mem. edn. com., nominations com. St. Thomas Aquinas Coll., 1990—2002. Author: (book) The Future of Tibet, 2004. Recipient Blue Ribbon award for Excellence in Edn., U.S. Dept. Edn., 1989. Mem.: Assn. Curriculum Devel. Democrat. Roman Catholic. Avocations: travel, painting, swimming. Home: 175 Rt 340 Sparkill NY 10976 Personal E-mail: profboyd@msn.com.

BOYD, JULIANNE MAMANA, theater director, educator; b. Easton, Pa., Dec. 22, 1944; d. Joseph and Julia (Cericola) Mamana; m. Norman Wingate Boyd Jr., July 9, 1966; children: Sarah, Norman III, Emily. BA, Beaver Coll., 1966; MA, Adelphi U., 1968; PhD, CUNY, 1986. Lectr. NYU, 1987-91; artistic dir. Berkshire Theatre Festival, Stockbridge, Mass., 1992-94; artistic dir., founder Barrington Stage Co., Great Barrington, Mass., 1995—. Conceiver and dir. Broadway musical Eubie, 1978 (Audelco award Outstanding Dir 1978), off-Broadway play A.My Name is Alice, 1984 (Outer Critics award), A.My Name is Still Alice, 1992; dir. Onward Victoria, 1980, Ring Around the Moon, 2006; worked extensively in NY and regional theatres including Old Globe, LaJolla Playhouse, McCarter Theatre, and Coconut Grove Playhouse. Mem. adv. bd. Women's Project, Inc., NY, 1988-92. Recipient Golden Disc award Beaver Coll., 1981, Outstanding Young Entrepreneur award Citicorp, N.Y., 1980, Outstanding Alumni award CUNY, 1995. Mem. Soc. Stage Dirs. and Choreographers (pres. 1992-98). Office: Barromgtpm Stage Co 30 Union St Pittsfield MA 01201 E-mail: jboyd@barringtonstageco.org.*

BOYD, MARY FRANCES, retired school nurse, pastor; b. Stockton, Md., Feb. 18, 1944; d. Alonzo Willard and Polly Frances Wilson; m. Eddie Boyd, July 29, 1972; children: Nathanael Ivan, Stephen Eddie. RN Salisbury U., 1965. Staff nurse Peninsula Gen. Hosp., Salisbury, Md., 1965—67; sch. nurse Wicomico City Bd. Edn., Salisbury, 1967—68, 1975—82, Worcester County Bd. Edn., Newark, Md., 1985—2006; indsl. nurse Buddy Bay Processing Plant, Snow Hill, Md., 1968—74, Worcester County Penal Sys., Snow Hill, 1982—85. Pastor First Corinthians Holiness Ch. Inc., 1979—; overseer Glorious Mt. Sinai Holy Ch., 2005—. Mem.: NAACP. Avocations: cooking, sewing, quilting, reading, singing.

BOYD, MARY H. (MARY H. MERRILL), social services administrator; b. Winnetka, Ill., Sept. 11, 1929; d. Harold Gatton and Martha Emily (Lawson) Heberling; children: Constance Anne Boyd Mazares, Richard Parker Jr. At, Long Beach City Coll., 1956, UCLA, 1973; cert. in Human Svcs., U. Calif., Riverside, 1974; BS with honors, LaVerne U., 1982. Exec. sec. Ontario-Pomona Assn. Retarded Citizens, Montclair, Calif., 1962—65, exec. dir., 1965—93, CEO, 1993—94; ret., 1994. Founder Mental Retardation Svc. Coun. of San Gabriel Valley, 1965; trainer Kellogg Found., OPARC Aux. Found., 1969; mem. Area 12 Calif. Developmental Disabilities Area planning bd., 1970—76, chmn. profl. adv. counsel, 1977—80; mem. steering com. for development regional ctrs. Inland Counties, 1969—70; mem. steering com. for development of regional ctrs. San Gabriel Valley; instr. Chaffey Coll., Alta Loma, Calif., 1972—76, coord. classes for disabled, 1972—76; instr. weekend series LaVerne U., 1974, vis. lectr., 1969—74, U. Calif. at Riverside, 1972, Mt. San Antonio Coll., 1976, UCLA, 1981—82; lectr. in field. Author (with J. Cook, J. Travers): Parents as Natural Helpers to Physicians at Time of Diagnosis of Developmental Disability, 1979. Active Girl Scouts U.S.A., 1960—68; leader and advisor Tri-Hi-Y, 1968—71; chmn. Mt. Baldy United Way Conf. Execs, 1983, 1986—87; pastoral care City of Hope; counselor, elder ministry, facilitator discovery classes Crystal Cathedral; trustee Inland Counties Regional Ctr.; bd. dir. PTA, 1958—62; mem. adv. bd. L.A. United Way, 1966—85, Chaffey Coll., 1972—78, Mt. San Antonio Coll. Allied Health, 1975—80, Calif. Inst. for Men, 1968—72, San Bernardino County Child Health and Disability Prevention, 1975—78, chmn., 1977—78. Recipient award of Merit, San Bernardino County Coun. of Cmty. Svcs., 1966, Hon. Svc. award, Ontario Montclair Sch. Dist., 1971, Humanitarian award, Humanitarian award, 1976, Chaffey Cmty. Rep. Women Federated Recognition award, 1977, Cmty. Svc. award Lioness award, 1977, 1984, Cmty. Svc. award, U. LaVerne, 1982, Svc. award, ARC, 1983, 1985, Calif. CCE Leadership award, 1983, 1985, Outstanding Leadership award, United Way, 1987—88; grantee, HEW, 1968, 1969, 1970, 1972, 1973, 1974, 1975, 1976, 1979, Calif. Cmty. Found., 1968, Price Found., 1969, 1972, Calif. Dept. Rehab., 1972, 1973, 1974, 1975, 1979, 1981, Calif. Dept. Health, 1976, 1977. Mem.: Coun. Agy. Execs., Conf. Execs.-Calif. (chmn. 1982—83), Conf. Execs. of Assns. for Retarded U.S. (charter 1965), Assn. for Retarded-Calif. (v.p. 1979—81, pres. 1981—82), Assn. for Retarded-U.S. (chmn. 1976—77, pres. S.W. chpt. 1987). Republican. Home: 940 W 5th St Ontario CA 91762-1534 Office: Ste H 8939 Vernon Ave Montclair CA 91763-1612

BOYD, VELENA, retired community health nurse, consultant; b. Lebanon, Ind., Nov. 11, 1911; d. Floyd Frank and Lula Mae (Gates) B. Diploma, Ind. U. Sch. Nursing, 1941; PHN, U. Calif., 1949; MPH, U. Calif. Sch. Pub. Health, 1956; postgrad. in sociology, U. Calif., Berkeley, 1962-63. Cert. braillest Libr. of Congress. Community health nurse Contra Costa County (Calif.) Health Dept., 1949-59; asst. prof. community health nursing U. Calif., 1959-65; cons. community health nursing and nursing adminstrn. WHO, South America, 1965-67; asst. prof. community health nursing U. Md. Sch. Nursing, 1967-77, ret., 1977. Vol. cons., prof. community health nursing U. P.R., Mayaguez, 1977-78, Shavaji U.-Miraj Med. Ctr., India, 1979-80; vol. cons. preventive care Sch. Nursing and Med. Ctr., Lahore, Pakistan, 1972; cons. to nursing program WHO Counterpart, Porto Alegre, Brazil, 1973; vol. cons. community health nursing, Istanbul, Miraj, Taipei, 1975; former cons. to Sixth Army Surgen Gen. Co-author: Nursing Examination Review Book, 2d edit., 1974; contbr. articles to profl. publs. Vol. reader, transcriber, book taper Balt. Reading Svc., 1981—; active Life Support Program, City of Balt., Levindale Geriatric Ctr., 1982—, tchr. English to Russian patients and residents. Col. Nurse Corps, U.S. Army, 1941-46, full col. USAR, 1946-71, ret., 1971. USPHS grantee U. Md., 1967-72; named to Md. Sr. Citizen's Hall of Fame, 1992; recipient Salute to Excellence award, Gov. State of Md., 1994, Disting. Alumna award Ind. U. Sch. of Nursing Alumni Assn., 1997. Mem. ANA (Md. Constituency), Nat. League Nursing, APHA, Sigma Theta Tau. Avocations: braille, studying spanish.

BOYDSTON, RESA ODETTE, mental health services professional; d. C. Daniel and Dorothy Jean Boydston; 1 child, Sylvia R. Degree in sociology, Washburn U., Topeka, Kans., 1999. Cert. CNA/CMA/DTSI Kans. CNA/CMA/MHDD-tech. Kans. Neurol. Inst., Topeka, 1980—. Home: PO Box 1111 Topeka KS 66601 Office: State of Kan-Kans Neurol Inst 3107 SW 21st Topeka KS 66603 Office Phone: 785-296-5631. Personal E-mail: rothelion@excite.com.

BOYEA, RUTHE W., retired education educator; b. Waltham, Mass., Sept. 22, 1918; d. George Walter and Ethel Maude Wright; m. Douglas Paul Boyea, 1944; children: Ruthe Priscilla Boyea-Boiczyk, Douglas Paul. B Social Sci., Boston U., 1940; MEd, Ctrl. Conn. State U., 1960; cert. in polit. sci., Trinity Coll., 1970. Cert. elem. tchr., Conn. Dir. religious edn., Springfield, Mass., 1945; tchr. New Britain, Conn., 1945-51; prof. edn. Ctrl. Conn. State U., New Britain, 1951-65, dir., founder Women's Ctr. (now Ruthe Boyea Women's Ctr.), 1965-85, prof. emeritus, 1985, lectr. on women's issues; ret. Adj. prof. Tunxis C.C., Mattatuck C.C., 1960-70. Commr. Human Rights and Opportunity, City of New Britain; vol., chair bd. dirs. ARC, New Britain; elected mem. Vets. Commn., City of New Britain, 1999. Lt. (j.g.) USN, 1942-45. Named Women's Educator of Yr., YWCA, 1975, Vol. of Yr. United Way, 1999; recipient Women Helping Women award Soroptimist Internat., 1982, Disting. Alumni award Boston U. Sch. Theology, 2002, Cmty. Svc. award, NAACP. Mem. AAUW (officer), LWV (bd. dirs.), Nat. Women's Mil. Meml. (founder), Nat. Women's Art Mus., Nat. Women's Hall of Fame. Mem. United Ch. of Christ. Office: Ctrl Conn State U Stanley St New Britain CT 06053 also: 126 New Britain Ave Apt Z2 Plainville CT 06062-2047

BOYER, AURELIA G., information technology executive; M in Nursing, MBA. RN. Project mgr. clinical info. sys. NY Hosp., 1993—96; cons. PriceWaterhouse; dir. NY Hosp., 1996—98, v.p., 1998; sr. v.p. NY Presbyterian Hosp. (formerly NY Hosp.), chief info. officer. Office: NY Presbyterian Hospital 525 East 68th St New York NY 10021 Office Phone: 212-585-6427.*

BOYER, CAROL A., elementary school educator; b. Port Angeles, Wash., May 11, 1954; d. Frank Gilbert and Ruth Beverly (Hay) Peterson; m. Terry Boyer, Nov. 12, 1977; children: Karen, David, Felicia, Sally. BA in Edn. magna cum laude, Pacific Luth. U., Tacoma, Wash., 1975, BA in Spanish magna cum laude, 1977, MA in Reading Edn. magna cum laude, 1980. Cert. tchr. K-12, K-12 spl. edn. Wash. Elem. migrant tchr. Pasco (Wash.) Sch. Dist., 1976; K-adult migrant tchr. Wash. State Dept. Migrant Edn., Sunnyside, 1976—78; K-12 music tchr. Mary M. Knight Sch. Dist., Matlock, Wash., 1978—79; Indian edn. and music tchr. Hood Canal Sch. Dist., Union, Wash., 1979—80; edn. supr. Migrant Mini-Corps, Tacoma, 1980—82, Grays Harbor Head Start, Aberdeen, Wash., 1984; elem. migrant tchr. Prosser (Wash.) Sch. Dist., 1986—87; spl. edn. tchr. Hoquiam (Wash.) Sch. Dist., 1987—93; spl. edn. and 5th grade tchr. Elma (Wash.) Sch. Dist., 1993—. Choir dir. Montesano (Wash.) Meth. Ch., 1978—; youth leader for team bldg. 3 hos. for impoverished families Meth. Ch. and Amor Ministries, Tijuana, Mexico, 1999, 2001, 2004; bd. dirs. Chehalis Basin Edn. Consortium, Olympia, Wash., 1999—; Spanish interpreter various law enforcement agys., Grays

Harbor, Wash., 1982—. Recipient Teach to the Future award, Intel Corp., Seattle, 2001, Disney Am. Tchr. award, 2004; Tchr. Leadership grantee, Bill and Melinda Gates Found., Seattle, 2000, Tapestry grantee, Toyota Corp./Nat. Sch. Tchrs. Assn., 2003. Mem.: Wash. Sci. Tchrs. Assn., Nat. Sci. Tchrs. Assn. Avocations: piano, cello, quilting, birdwatching, reading. Home: 208 Monte-Brady Rd Montesano WA 98563 Office Phone: 360-482-2632 ext 494. Office Fax: 360-482-4565. E-mail: cboyer1@eagles.edu.

BOYER, CAROLYN MERWIN, school psychologist; b. New Haven, Conn., Oct. 4, 1936; d. Richard Treat Merwin and Elsie Mae (Donaldson) Schuyler; m. Kenneth Sutton Boyer, Aug. 19, 1961; 1 child, Kenneth Merwin. BA in Spanish, Bucknell U., 1958; MS, So. Conn. State U., 1991. Nat. cert. sch. psychologist Milford Bd. Edn. Claims approver Equitable Life Assurance, NYC, 1961—63; libr. asst. Milford Pub. Libr., Conn., 1973—74; archtl. reporter Dodge/McGraw Hill, 1974—84; sec. Milford Bd. Edn., 1984—92, sch. psychologist, 1992—2003; ret. Reporter neighborhood news Milford Citizen, 1973—76. Exhibitions include oil paintings Firehouse Art Gallery, Milford, 2004—05. Mem. diaconate bd. 1st Ch. Christ, 1980—83, 1999—2002; bd. dirs. Miles Merwin Assn., Milford, 1974—75; bd. dirs., membership chair Nat. Assn. Women Constrn., 1975—78. Mem.: Nat. Assn. Sch. Psychologists, Conn. Assn. Sch. Psychologists. Republican. Avocations: gourmet cooking, tennis, reading, birdwatching, art. Home: 11 Anderson Ave Milford CT 06460

BOYER, CHERYL, finance company executive; b. Bklyn., 1966; BS Hotel Mgmt., Cornell Univ. With InterContinental Hotels, Laventhal & Horwath; v.p. Landauer Assoc.; pres., sales mktg. Hotel Ptnrs.; mng. dir. capital markets group Insignia Hotels; with PricewaterhouseCoopers, NYC, 1999—, dir. hospitality and leisure industry, 2004—. Office: PricewaterhouseCoopers 300 Madison Ave 26th Fl New York NY 10017 Office Phone: 646-471-5706. Fax: 646-471-8869.

BOYER, JOAN SUE, liberal arts educator, social sciences educator; b. Winamac, Ind., Mar. 10, 1940; d. Fred M. and Eldonna P. Graffis; m. R. David Boyer, June 3, 1962; children: Katherine, R. David II, S. Elizabeth, S. Thomas. BA, Taylor U., 1961; MEd, Ind. U., 1969. Cert. secondary tchr. language arts and social scis. Jr. HS tchr. Pulaski County Schs., Ind., 1961—62, Cherry Hill Schs., NJ, 1962—64; tchr. 5th grade Hamilton County Schs., Fishers, Ind., 1964—65; tchr. 8th and 9th grade English E. Allen County Schs., New Haven, Ind., 1965—71; tchr. 8th-12th grade English and Social Scis. Ft. Wayne Christian, Ind., 1981—2002, counselor, 1981—2002. Tchr., mentor Brookside Ch. Leadership Council, Fort Wayne, 1994—. Docent Lincoln Mus., Fort Wayne, 2004—05; mentor Brookside Ch., Fort Wayne, 2004—05, good sense counselor, 2005. Mem.: Brookside Women's Group (pres. ladies' soc. 1971—72), Cedar Creek Women's Club (sec. 1979). Republican. Protestant. Avocations: travel, reading, camping.

BOYER, KAYE KITTLE, association management executive; b. Peoria, Ill., July 5, 1942; d. Keith Howard and Evelyn Pearl (Benson) Kittle; m. Jon Frederick Boyer, Mar. 20, 1965; children: Tristan Boyer Binns, Kristine Monique Hitchens. Student, Merrill Palmer Inst., Detroit, 1964; BS in Home Econs., Pa. State U., University Park, 1964; MA in Sociology, Rutgers State U., New Brunswick, 1967. Cert. assn. exec.; cert. in family and consumer scis. Creative rschr. Nat. Inst. Drycleaning, Silver Spring, Md., 1963; extension home economist Md. Coop. Extension Svc., Westminster, 1964-65; coord. human resources N.J. Coop. Extension Svc., New Brunswick, 1966-67; instr. Douglass Coll., Rutgers U., New Brunswick, 1967-70; coord., instr. pilot project Urban Coalition of Met. Wilmington (Del.) Inc., 1972; asst. to chmn. 4-H Youth Devel. Dept., Cook Coll., 1973-74; feasibility study dir. Ocean County Coll., Toms River, N.J., 1975; exec. dir. N.J. Home Economics Assn., Manalapan, 1975-86; pres. Boyer Mgmt. Svcs., Manalapan, N.J., Earleville, Md., 1984—, Palm Coast, Fla., 1984—. Mgr. Costume Soc. Am., Palm Coast, Fla., 1984-2006, exec. dir., 2006-; cons. Plumpton Pk. Zool. Gardens Rising Sun, 1988-89, bd. dirs., 1990-92; cons. N.J. White House Conf., Trenton, 1980, Baltimore County Med. Assn., 1995-96, Md. Acad. Family Physicians, 1994, 97, Textile Soc. Am., 1998—; adv. com. Dept. Cmty. Edn. Rutgers U., 1979-84 Editor Exchs. Newsletter; resource dir., N.J. Programs and Svcs. Related to Adolescent Pregnancy. Vol. Soroptimist Internat. of Elkton, Md., 1987-94; bd. dir. Cmty. Libr. Cecilton, 1986-92; player US Pub. Links Amateur, 1986; trustee Cecil County Bd. Libr., 1998-2002. Couples Champion Grand Haven Golf Club, 2005, Sr. Women's Club Champion, 2005. Mem. AAUW (v.p. program devel. NJ divsn. 1984-86), Am. Assn. Family and Consumer Scis. (cert., Ruth O'Brien project grantee), Am. Soc. Assn. Execs. (cert.), Fla. Soc. Assn. Execs. (edn. com, 2006-), Profl. Conv. Mgmt. Assn. (edn. and profl. devel. com. 1996-2001, edn. and profl. devel. working com., 2002), Internat. Assn. of Facilitators, Fla. Assn. Family and Consumer Scis., Profl. Conv. Mgmt. Assn. Edn. Found. (transition team product/svc., 2001, design task force 2000, learning ctr. task force 2000-2001, trustee 2000-2003), Penn State Alumni Assn.(chmn. strategic planning Daytona-Palm Coast chpt. 2003—), Kappa Omicron Nu (v.p. fin. 1992-93, chair constn. and bylaws com. 1994-97). Democrat. Avocation: golf. Home and Office: 107 Front St Palm Coast FL 32137

BOYER, LISA, basketball coach; Degree, Ithaca Coll., 1979. Asst. coach Davidson Coll., 1980-82, East Carolina, 1983-84, Miami of Ohio, 1984-95, Va. Tech., 1985-86; coach Bradley Univ., 1986-96, Phila. Rage. Named Gateway Conf. Coach of Yr., 1990.

BOYER, M. CHRISTINE, architecture educator; BA, Goucher Coll.; MS in Computer and Info. Sci., U. Pa.; M in City Planning, MIT, PhD. William R. Kenan Jr. prof. arch. and urbanism Princeton (N.J.) U. Sch. Arch. Lectr. in field. Author: Draming the Rational City: The Myth of City Planning 1890-1945, 1983, Manhattan Manners: Architecture and Style 1850-1890, 1985, The City of Collective Memory: Its Historical Imagery and Architectural Entertainments, 1994, CyberCities: Visual Perception in the Age of Electronic Communication, 1996; contbr. articles to profl. jours. Office: Sch Arch Princeton Univ Princeton NJ 08544-5264

BOYER, PATRICIA W., publishing executive, editor; b. Weaverville, N.C., Oct. 12, 1925; d. William Malcolm and Katherine Lotspeich Waters; m. Clyde M. Boyer, June 28, 1946 (dec. Aug. 10, 1997); children: John Gregory, Abigail, Judd Meredith, Clyde Merrill. Co-owner Boyer Ranch, Calif., 1963—97; CEO Got Solar, Inc., Oreg., 2001—; CFO H2Nation Pub. Inc., Brookings, Oreg., 2003—, Nev., 2003—; editor H2Nation Mag., Nev., 2003—. Bd. dirs. H2Nation Pub. Inc., Sparks, Nev., 2003—, Got Solar, Inc., Oreg., 2000—. Author: The Last Free Chief of the Modoc Nation: An Allegory, 2001. Mem.: Women Writing the West, Nat. Mus. of the Am. Indian at the Smithsonian, Toastmasters Internat. Avocations: music, poetry, gardening, writing, history. Office: H2Nation Publishing Inc PO Box 52080 Sparks NV 89435 Office Phone: 775-356-8411. Business E-Mail: pat@h2nation.com.

BOYER, SUSAN ELAINE, psychotherapist, consultant, speaker; b. Detroit Lakes, Minn., Aug. 1, 1948; d. Chauncey Alcott and Lucille Mildred (Aull) B.; 1 child, Belden George Sadler BA, U. Minn., 1972, postgrad., 1986—87; MS Counseling Psychology, Chaminade U. Honolulu, 1990; postgrad. Marriage and Family Therapy, Adler Grad. Sch., 2000—02. Lic. profl. counselor, Colo., 1993, Minn., 2004, lic. assoc. Marriage and Family Therapist, 2003; cert. employee assistance profl., 2003; lic. marriage family therapist, 2006. Case aide Ottertail County Welfare, Fergus Falls, Minn., 1973—74; social worker/sr. social worker Hennepin County, Mpls., 1974—85; pvt. practice counselor Mpls., 1986—87; psychiat. social worker State of Hawaii, Honolulu, 1988, substitute tchr. Oahu, 1989—90; clin. social worker/cmty. liaison Salvation Army, Honolulu, 1990—91; clin. social worker Teen Intervention Program, Honolulu, 1991—92; counselor, cons. AT&T-NSD, Denver, 1992—96; group facilitator Adoptees in Search, Denver, 1993—98. Spkr. in field of adoptive triad, search, and reunion, adult children of alcoholics, reparenting inner child, co-dependency, 1986—; house dir. Sigma Delta Tau, Mpls., 1978-79, Delta Gamma, Boulder, Colo., 1998-99, Pi Beta Phi, Mpls., 1999-2000, Kappa Kappa Gamma, Mpls., 2000-01; specialist home studies Contract-Cath. Svcs., Honolulu, 1989; group facilitator Parents United, Honolulu, 1990-92 Frear and Leemosynary scholar Chaminade U. Honolulu, 1988, C.T.C. Ching Meml. scholar, 1989, Janice Wishart scholarship, 2001 Mem. Employee Assistance Program Assn., Colo. Mental Health Counselors Assn., Concerned United Birth Parents, Adoptees in Search-Facilitator-Support Group (bd. dirs.), Minn. Assn. Marriage and Family Therapists, Minn. Counseling Assn., Am. Adoption Congress, Minn. Employee Assistance Program Adminstrs. and Counselors Avocations: swimming, movies, music, reading, theater. Home: 4301 Park Glen Rd #103 Saint Louis Park MN 55416 Office: PO Box 62342 Minneapolis MN 55426 Office Phone: 952-945-9179.

BOYES, MELANIE JOAN, secondary school educator; b. Williston, N.D., Dec. 18, 1964; d. Kenneth Wayne and Ida Marie (Schaan) Kirchmeier; m. Mark Ian Boyes, June 18, 1988; children: Malorie, Acacia, Laykin. BS in English, Minot State U., N.D., 1987; MA in Tchg., Grand Canyon U., Phoenix, 2001. English tchr. Grenora H.S., ND, 1987—89; journalist, reporter Williston Dialy Herald, ND, 1989—90; English/journalism tchr. Williston H.S., 1990—91; English/lang. arts educator Cy Jr. H.S., Casper, Wyo., 1991—. Facilitator/trainer for differentiated instrn. Natrona County Sch. Dist., Casper, 2001—, dist. mentor for new faculty, 2002—, portfolio assessor, 2005—. Vol., supr. Relay for Life, Casper, 2002—; vol. March of Dimes, Casper, 2004—. Recipient Significant Educator award, Natrona County Sch. Dist., 1998—2006, Medallion of Excellence, 2002, Golden Apple award, Arch Coal, 2002—03. Mem.: Nat. Coun. for Tchrs. English. Roman Catholic. Avocations: writing, reading, softball, jewelry making, story telling. Office: Cy Jr HS 2211 Essex Ave Casper WY 82604

BOYETT, JOAN REYNOLDS, performing company executive; b. L.A., May 2, 1936; d. Clifton Faris Reynolds and Jean Margaret (Howard) Hauck; m. Harry William Boyett, Oct. 5, 1956; children: Keven William, Suzanne Marie Boyett. Student, Occidental Coll., 1954-55, Pasadena Playhouse, 1955-57. Mgr. youth activities LA Philharm. Orch., 1970-79; dir., founder edn. divsn. The Music Ctr. LA County, 1979-2001, v.p. edn., 1988-2001. Mem. supt.'s task force on arts edn. Calif. State Dept. Edn., 1997; cons. NEA, Washington; chmn. arts edn. task force Calif. Arts Coun., Sacramento, 1993-95; arts edn. mem. Nat. Working Group, Washington, 1992-95; mem. U.S. Sec. of Edns. Com. on Am. Goes Back to Sch. Active various cms. and task forces, L.A., Sacramento. Named Woman of Yr. L.A. Times, 1976; recipient Labor's award of honor County Fedn. Labor, L.A., 1984, Susan B. Anthony award Bus. and Profl. Women, 1986, Gov.'s award Calif. Arts Coun., 1989, R.O.S.E. Outstanding Svc. to Edn. award, U. So. Calif., 1999, Outstanding Arts Educator award Calif. Arts Coun., 2001, Music Ctr. Club 100 Spl. Tribute award, 2001, Women in Ednl. Leadership award, 2002, Ovation award for cmty. svc. Theatre League Alliance, 2002. Mem. Calif. Art Edn. Assn. (Behind the Scenes award 1985), Calif. Dance Educators Assn. (Svc. award 1985), Calif. Ednl. Theatre Assn. (Outstanding Contbn. award 1990, nominated for Nat. Medal Arts 1996, 97). Republican. Presbyterian. Avocations: reading, attending arts events, gardening, swimming. Home: PO Box 1805 Studio City CA 91614-0805 Personal E-mail: jarboyett@sbcglobal.net.

BOYETT, LINDA MARIE, music educator; d. Avent and Lanier Gross; children: Amy Marie, Kelly Anne. BS in Music Edn., Ga. So. U., Statesboro, Ga., 1973; BS in Early Childhood, Valdosta State U., Ga., 1980; MAT in Music, Jacksonville U., Fla., 1992; EdD in Curriculum and Instrn., Argosy U., Sarasota, Fla., 2004. Music tchr. Ware County H.S., Waycross, Ga., 1972—78; reading tchr. title I Hoboken Elem. Sch., Ga., 1978—79; music tchr. Brantley County Schs., Hoboken and Nahunta, Ga., 1978—89, Matilda Harris Elem. Sch., Kingsland, Ga., 1989—; adj. prof. Ga Mil., Kings Bay Naval Base, 1993—2000, Valdosta State U., Kings Bay Naval Base, 1993—2000, Armstrong Coll., Savannah, Ga., 1993—2000. Treas. Kingsland Cmty. Betterment Program. Recipient Tchr. of Yr., Camden Co./Matilda Harris Elem. Sch., 1993. Mem.: Profl. Assn. Ga Educators, North Fla. Orff Chpt. (pres. 2005—), Ga. Music Educators Assn. Home: 475 Lanier Ave Kingsland GA 31548 Office Phone: 912-729-2940. Business E-Mail: mboyett@camden.k12.ga.us.

BOYKIN, ANNE JANE, dean; BSN, Alverno Coll., 1966; MSN, Emory U., 1972; PhD, Vanderbilt U., 1981. Asst. prof. Marquette U., Milw., 1973-74; assoc. prof., asst. dir. Valdosta (Ga.) State Coll., 1975-80; in-svc. educator Holy Cross Hosp., Ft. Lauderdale, Fla., 1980-81; assoc. prof. Fla. Atlantic U., Boca Raton, 1984—, dean Coll. Nursing, prof., 1996—. Dir. Christine E. Lynn Ctr. for Caring. Co-author: Nursing as Caring: a Model for Transforming Practice, 1993, 2d edit., 2001; editor: Living a Caring-Based Program, 1993, Power, Politics and Public Policy: A Matter of Caring, 1995; co-editor: Caring as Healing; Renewal through Hope, 1994; contbr. chpts. to books, articles to profl. jours. Mem. Internat. Assn. for Human Caring, Fla. Nurses Assn. (Nursing Educator award 1991), Sigma Theta Tau, Phi Kappa Phi. Office: Fla Atlantic U Christine E Lynn Coll Nursing 777 Glades Rd PO Box 3091 Boca Raton FL 33431-0991 Office Phone: 561-297-3206. Business E-Mail: boykina@fau.edu.

BOYKIN, GLADYS, retired religious organization administrator; b. N.Y.C., Dec. 10, 1929; d. Jacob Allen and Annie Mae (Alston) McClendon; m. Eugene S. Callender (div. 1963); 1 child, Renee Denise; m. John R. Strachan (dec. 1982); m. Elton Boykin, 1996. Student, NYU, 1947-49. Dep. asst. Presbyn. Ch. of East Africa, Nairobi, Kenya, 1964-67; assoc. for women's program Presbyn. Ch. of U.S., N.Y.C., 1970-83; exec. dir. United Presbyn. Women, N.Y.C., 1983-97; ret., 1997. Cons. Peace Corps, Nairobi, 1964-67, Operation Crossroads Africa, Nairobi, 1964-67, Afro-Am. Ednl. Inst., Teaneck, N.J., 1977-79, various women's orgns. in Asia, Australia, Europe, Africa. V.p. Addicts Rehab. Ctr. Bd., N.Y.C., 1957—; mem. N.Y. Coalition of 100 Black Women, N.Y.C., 1972—; v.p., bd. dirs. La. Internat. Cultural Ctr.; bd. dirs. aging resource ctr. Sister Cities of Louisville. Recipient Cert. of citation borough pres. N.Y.C., 1977, Harlem Peacemaking award Harlem Peacemaking Com., 1983, Vol. award Louisville Internat. Culture Ctr., 1996. Mem. La. C. of C., River City Assn. Bus. and Profl. Women, Downtown Resident Assn. (pres.), Jefferson Club (bd. govs.). Avocations: music, reading, travel, needlepoint, theater. Home: 800 S 4th St Apt 2202 Louisville KY 40203-2132

BOYKIW, NORMA SEVERNE, retired nutritionist, educator; b. Coalmont, Ind., Feb. 3, 1918; d. Charles Edward Goble and Ressa Naomi Johnson; m. Russel Yaroslav Alexis Boykiw, 1948 (dec. Sept. 4, 1992); children: Russel Alexis II, Mark Emerson. BS, Ind. State U., 1941. Registered Mem. Asst. 1950. Dietitian asst. Ind. State U., Terre Haute, Ind., 1939—40; tchr. home econ. Wawaka Sch. Sys., Wawaka, Ind., 1941—42; nutrition tchr. Crown Point Sch., Crown Point, Ind., 1942—43; mem. staff patient diabetic diets Wesley Meml. Hosp., Chgo.; writer of diet manuals Pa., 1945—48; office mgr. Russel Boykiw, MD, Clearfield, 1948—92, ret., 1992. Ombudsman Area Agy. on Aging, Clearfield, Pa., 1999—2002. Compilation author Genealogy for the Goble Family, 1976;, author diet manuals Hosps. Active cmty. devel. Pa. State U., Clearfield, Pa., 1959, 1966; den mother Presbyn. Ch., Clearfield, 1967; bd. dirs. Shaw Pub. Libr. Named Woman of the Yr., Bus. and Profl. Women, 1974, Outstanding Citizen of the Yr., Clearfield Rotary Club, 1987; grantee, Ctrl. Pa. Dist. Libr. Bd., 1968—79. Mem.: AAUW (life; founder, Outstanding Woman award 1983), Nat. Soc. Daus. of Founders and Patriots of Am., Nat. Soc. DAR, Clearfield County Hist. Soc. (grant), Heritage Found. (founder), Hobby Garden Club. Democrat. Avocation: yoga. Home: 364 Bailey Settlement Hwy Clearfield PA 16830-3505

BOYLAN, ELIZABETH SHIPPEE, academic administrator, biologist, educator; b. Shanghai, Nov. 29, 1946; d. Nathan M. and Elizabeth (Little) Shippee; m. Robert J. Boylan, Oct. 2, 1971; children: Elizabeth B., Emily A. AB, Wellesley Coll., 1968; PhD, Cornell U., 1972. Postdoctoral fellow U. Rochester (N.Y.) Sch. Medicine, 1972-73; asst. prof. Queens Coll. CUNY, Flushing, 1973-78, assoc. prof., 1978-82, prof. biology, 1983-95, acting asst. provost, 1988-89, asst. provost, 1989-90, assoc. provost, 1990-92; acting provost Queens Coll. CUNY, Flushing, 1992-93; assoc. provost acad. programs and planning Queens Coll., Flushing, 1994-95; provost and dean of faculty Barnard Coll., N.Y.C., 1995—, prof. biology, 1995—. Chmn. Queens Coll. Acad. Senate, 1985-88; mem. grad. faculty Grad. Ctr. CUNY, N.Y.C., 1977-95; vis. investigator Sloan-Kettering Inst. Cancer Rsch., N.Y.C., 1979-80; trustee N.Y. Met. Ref. and Rsch. Libr. Agy., Manhattan, 1989-97, chmn. fin. com. 1991-97; co-chmn. bd. trustees study com. on secondary edn. CUNY, 1987-88, co-chair vice chancellor's task force on sci., engring., tech. and math., 1988-89; panelist NSF grad. fellowship program, 1992-93; cons. to Nat. Cancer Inst., N.J. Commn. on Cancer Rsch., Endocrine Soc.; mem. breast cancer task force NCI, 1980-84; mem. adv. com. Am. Cancer Soc., 1981-85; Am. Coun. Edn. fellow Pace U., 1993-94; commr. Commn. on Higher Edn., Mid. States Assn. Colls. and Schs., 1999-2004. Contbr. and reviewer articles to profl. publs.; patentee in field. Grantee Nat. Cancer Inst., 1975-83, Am. Inst. Cancer Rsch., 1987-90, Am. Fedn. Aging Rsch., 1988-89. Mem. AAAS, Soc. Devel. Biology, Am. Assn. Cancer Rsch., N.Y. Acad. Scis., Sigma Xi. Office: Barnard Coll Office of Provost 3009 Broadway New York NY 10027-6501 Office Phone: 212-854-2708. Business E-Mail: eboylan@barnard.edu.

BOYLAN, TONYA R., banker, consultant; b. LaGrange, Ga., Apr. 29, 1957; d. Joel Hudson and Shirley Wright Bowen; m. Philip R. Boylan, Dec. 17, 1977; children: Philip Adam, Thomas Joel. BEd in Home Econs., Longwood Coll., Farmville, Va., 1983; student in Art Edn., Berry Coll., Mt. Berry, Ga., 1975—77; degree in Mortgage Loans, Capstone Inst. Mortgage Fin., Marietta, Ga., 2005. Instr. art Berry Coll., Mt. Berry, Ga., 1975—77; instr. home econs. Longwood Coll., Farmville, Va., 1983; specialist mortgage loans Capstone Inst. Mortgage Fin., Marietta, Ga., 2005—; dir. mus. ho. Ga. Trust Hist. Preservation, Monroe, Ga., 1995—96; mortgage cons. Home Tech Mortgage, Alpharetta, Ga., 2005—. Comdr. squadron Civil Air Patrol, Rome, Ga., 2003—04, pub. affairs officer Ga., 2004—05, inspector gen., 2005—06, group comdr., 2006—. Mem.: DAR, Lavendar Mt. Quilt Guild. Home: 3974 Old Rockmart Rd PO Box 109 Silver Creek GA 30173

BOYLE, ANN M., dean, dental educator; BA, Case Western Reserve U., 1971; DMD, Fairleigh Dickinson U., 1975, MA in Ednl. Psychology, 1984. Cert. gen. practice Hackensack Hosp., 1976; managament cert. Harvard U., 1999. Mem. faculty Coll. Dental Med. Fairleigh Dickinson U., 1976—90, chair restorative dept., 1988—90; chair restorative dept. to assoc. dean acad. affairs Sch. Dentistry Case Western Reserve U., Cleveland, 1991—94; assoc. dean Sch. Dental Med. So. Ill. U., 1995—2002, acting dean, 2002—03, dean, prof. restorative dentistry, 2003—. Extramural pvt. practice. Fellow: Pierre Fauchard Acad., Am. Coll. Dentists; mem.: ADA (mem. commn. on Dental Accreditation), Internat. Assn. Dental Rsch., Am. Assn. Dental Rsch., Am. Dental Edn. Assn., Acad. Operative Dentistry. Office: So Ill U Sch Dental Med 2800 College Ave Bldg 273/2300 Alton IL 62002*

BOYLE, ANNE C., state commissioner; b. Omaha, Dec. 22, 1942; m. Mike Boyle; children: Maureen, Michael, James, Patrick, Margaret. Chmn., co-chmn. various polit. campaigns, Omaha, 1974-78; office coord. for U.S. Senator James Exon., 1979-81; corp. and polit. fundraiser, 1983-85, 88; campaign mgr. pub. rels. firm, Omaha, 1990-91; pres. Universal Rev. Svcs., Omaha, 1992—; mem. Nebr. Pub. Svc. Commn., Lincoln, 1996—. Active Clinton for Pres. Campaign, organizer fund raisers, host open house, Omaha, 1992; cons., lobbyist, 1994-95. Former nat. committeewoman Nebr. Young Dems.; chmn. Douglas County Dem. Ctrl. Com.; mem. jud. nominating com. for Douglas County Juvenile Ct.; chmn. inaugural ball invitation com. for gov. of Nebr., 1982; co-chmn. Midwestern Govs. Conf., 1984, Jefferson-Jackson Day Dinner, 1976, 82; del. Dem. Nat. Conv., 1988, 92, 96; mem. Nebr. Rev. com. for Fed. Appts. to U.S. Atty., U.S. Marshall and 8th Dist. Ct. Appeals Fed. Judgeship, 1993-95; mem. Nebr. Dem. Ctrl. Com.; mem. Fin. Com. to Reelect Gov. Ben Nelson; mem. Nebr. Interagy. Coun. on Homeless, President's Adv. Com. on Arts, 1995; Nebr. authorized rep. '96 Clinton-Gore Campaign; Bd. dirs. Bemis Ctr. for Contemporary Arts, Omaha; chmn. Nebr. Dem. Party, 1999-2001. Mem. Nat. Assn. Regulatory Utility Commrs. and Mid-Am. Regulatory Commrs. Democrat. Office: PO Box 94927 Lincoln NE 68509-4927

BOYLE, ANTONIA BARNES, writer, editor; b. Detroit, May 21, 1939; d. James Merriam and Florence (Maiullo) B.; 1 child, Caitlin Merriam. BS in Speech, Northwestern U., Evanston, Ill., 1962. Staff announcer WEFM-FM, Chgo., 1975-78; pres. Boyle Communications, Chgo., 1978-85; exec. producer Nightingale-Conant Corp., Chgo., 1985-90, Cassette Prodns. Unltd., Irwindale, Calif., 1990-92; pres. Antonia Boyle & Co., 1992—; v.p. content acquisition Youachieve.com, Inc., 1997—. Author: The Optimal You, 1990, Taping Yourself Seriously, 1991; co-author (with Jay Gordon): Good Food Today, Great Kids Tomorrow, 1994; co-author: (with Scott McKain) Just Say Yes, 1994; co-author: (with William McCurry) Guerrilla Managing for the Imaging Industry, 1997; co-author: (with William McCurry and Harold Lloyd) It's Your People.Really!, 2005; co-author: (with K.D. Sullivan) The Gremlins of Grammar, 2005. Chmn., bd. dirs. Horizons for the Blind, Chgo., 1984; bd. dirs. WNUR FM Alumni, Northwestern U., Evanston, 2002-03. Mem. AFTRA, NU Club (Chgo.). Home: 3119A Lake Ave Wilmette IL 60091-1157 Personal E-mail: aboyleco@earthlink.net.

BOYLE, BARBARA DORMAN, film company executive; b. NYC, Aug. 11, 1935; d. William and Edith (Kleiman) Dorman; m. Kevin Boyle, Nov. 26, 1960; children: David Eric, Paul Coleman. BA in English with honors, U. Calif., Berkeley, 1957; JD, UCLA, 1960. Bar: Calif. 1961, N.Y. 1964, U.S. Supreme Ct. 1964. Atty. bus. affairs dept, corp. asst. sec. Am. Internat. Pictures, L.A., 1960-65; ptnr. Cohen & Boyle, L.A., 1967-74; exec. v.p., gen. counsel, chief op. officer New World Pictures, L.A., 1974-82; sr. v.p. prodn. Orion Pictures Corp., L.A., 1982-85; exec. v.p. prodn. RKO Pictures, L.A., 1986-87; pres. Sovereign Pictures, Inc., L.A., 1988-92, Boyle and Taylor Prodns., 1993-99, Valhalla Motion Pictures, L.A., 2000—03; chair film, TV and digital media dept. UCLA, 2003—. Lectr. in field. Exec. prodr. (film) Eight Men Out, 1987, Bottle Rocket, 1995, Campus Man; prodr. (films) Mrs. Munck, 1995, Phenomenon, 1996, Instinct, 1999; exec. prodr. The Hi Line, 1998; co-prodr. Phenomenon II, 2002; contbr. chpts. to books. Bd. dirs. UCLA Law Fund Com., L.A. Women's Campaign Fund; pres. Ind. Feature Project/West; founding mem. entertainment adv. coun. sch. law UCLA, co-chmn. 1979-80, co-chair, 2002-03. Named UCLA Law Sch. Alumni of Yr, 1999, Women in Film Crystal award, 2000. Mem. Acad. Motion Picture Arts and Scis. (exec. com.), Acad. TV Arts and Scis. (exec. com.), Women in Film (pres. 1977-78), Hollywood Women's Polit. Com., Calif. Bar Assn., N.Y. State Bar Assn. Office: UCLA Sch of Theater Film & TV 203 E Melnitz Box 951622 Los Angeles CA 90095-1622 Office Phone: 310-825-7741. Business E-Mail: boyle@tft.ucla.edu.

BOYLE, GERTRUDE, sportswear company executive; b. Augsberg, Germany, 1924; came to U.S., 1938; d. Paul and Marie Lanfrom; m. Neil Boyle, 1948; children: Tim, Kathy, Sally. BA in Sociology, Univ. Ariz., 1947. Pres., CEO Columbia Sportswear Co., Portland, Oreg., 1970-88, CEO, 1988-94, chmn. bd., 1994—. Named one of Best Mgrs. Bus. Week Mag., 1994, Am.'s Top 50 Women Bus. Owners Working Woman mag., Woman of Yr. Oreg. chpt. Women's Forum, 1987. Office: Columbia Sportswear Co 14375 NW Science Park Dr Portland OR 97229-5418

BOYLE, JANE J., federal judge, lawyer; b. Sharon, Pa., Dec. 15, 1954; BS, U. of Tex., Austin, 1977; JD, So Meth. U., Dallas, 1981. Asst. dist. atty. Dist. Atty.'s Office, 1981-87; asst. U.S. atty. U.S. Dist. Ct. (no. dist.) Tex., 1987-90, magistrate judge U.S. Dallas, 1990—2002, U.S. atty., 2002—04; judge US Dist. Ct. (no. dist) Tex., 2004—. Office: US Courthouse 1100 Commerce St Rm 1452 Dallas TX 75242

BOYLE, KAMMER, financial planner, investment advisor, research analyst, options trader; b. New Orleans, June 17, 1946; d. Benjamin Franklin and Ethel Clair (Kammer) B.; m. Edward Turner Barfield, July 23, 1966 (div. 1975); children: Darren Barfield, Meloe Barfield. BS in Mgmt. magna cum laude, U. West Fla., 1976; PhD in Indsl./Organizational Psychology, U. Tenn., 1982. Lic. psychologist, Ohio, Tenn.; reg. securities rep. InterSecurities, Inc., Nat Assn. Securities Dealers. Pvt. practice mgmt. psychology, Knoxville, 1978-81; tchg. and rsch. asst. U. Tenn., Knoxville, 1977-81; mgmt. trainer U.S. State Dept., Washington, 1978; cons. PRADCO, Cleve., 1982-83; pres., cons. Mgmt. and Assessment Svcs., Inc., Cleve., 1983-90; pres. Kammer Investment Co., Cleve., 1989-96; fin. asst. advisor O'Donnell Securities Corp., Cleve., 1997-98; registered securities prin., investment advisor rep. and retirement specialist Wealth Charter Group of InterSecurities, Inc., 1998—2004, asset mgr., options trader, rsch. analyst, 2005—. Mem. editl. rev. bd. Jour. of Managerial Issues, 1987; author and presenter ann. Conf. APA, 1980, Southeastern Psychol. Conf., 1979, ann. Conf. Soc. Indsl./Orgnl. Psychologists, 1987, ann. conf. Am. Soc. Tng. and Devel., 1988. Mem. Jr. League Am., Pensacola, Fla., 1970-75; treas. Bar Aux., Pensacola, 1971. Recipient Capital Gifts Stipend U. Tenn., 1976-80; Walter Bonham fellow, 1980-81. Mem. APA, Cleve. Psychol. Assn., Orgn. Devel. Inst., Acad. of Mgmt., Soc. Advancement Mgmt. (pres. 1974-75), Am. Soc. Tng. and Devel. (chpt. rep. career devel. 1984-86), Cleve. Psychol. Assn. (bd. dirs. 1987-88), Real Estate Investor's Assn. (Cleve., trustee/sec. 1992-94), Mensa. Office: Wealth Charter Group 1154 Castleton Rd Cleveland OH 44121

BOYLE, LARA FLYNN, actress; b. Davenport, IA, Mar. 24, 1970; Actress: appeared in films made for TV and for movie house distbn.: Amerika, 1987, Poltergeist III, 1988, Terror on Highway 91, 1989, How I Got into College, 1989, The Preppie Murder, 1989, The Rookie, 1990, Mobsters, 1991, Wayne's World, 1992, Where the Day Takes You, 1992, The Temp., 1993, Three of Hearts, 1993, Red Rock West, 1993, Threesome, 1994, Baby's Day Out, 1994, The Road to Wellville, 1994, Three IFS and a Maybe, 1996, Dogwater, 1997, Twin Peaks, 1989, Dead Poets Society, 1989, Men in Black II, 2002; TV appearances include The Practice, 1997-2003, Las Vegas, 2005-; host Saturday Night Live, 2001.

BOYLE, MARCIA, medical association administrator; BA, Skidmore Coll.; MS, Columbia Univ. Co-founder Immune Deficiency Found., 1980, CEO, pres., 1980—95, chair, 1980—2001, CEO, chair, 2005—; dir. devel., Neurology and Brain Sci. Johns Hopkins Medicine; dir., dept. programs, capital projects, dir. prin. gifts Fund for Johns Hopkins Medicine; dir. devel. Wilmer Eye Inst. Office: Immune Deficiency Found Ste 308 40 W Chesapeake Ave Towson MD 21204 Office Phone: 410-321-6647.

BOYLE, OLABISI ARIYO, manufacturing engineer; m. John Boyle; 1 child, Robert John. BS, Fordham U., Columbia U. Sch. Engring., 1988, MS, 1991. Various engring. position Ford Motor Co., Wayne, Mich., 1995—98, supr. vehicle ops. quality, 1998—2001, mgr. mfg. strategy & bus. planning, 2001—04; sr. mgr. product strategy DaimlerChrysler Corp., Auburn Hills, Mich., 2004—. Recipient Most Promising Engr., Women of Color Tech. Awards, 2005. Office: DaimlerChrysler Corp 1000 Chrysler Dr Auburn Hills MI 48326-2766*

BOYLES, NORMA JEAN, elementary school educator; b. Wilkensburg, Pa., Mar. 22, 1951; d. Matthew and Emily Zatko; m. Ronald Gene Boyles, July 11, 1987; 1 child, Bradley Gene. BS in Edn., Calif. U. Pa., 1973. Tchr. remedial reading Gilmer County Pub. Schs., Glenville, W.Va., 1973—80; tchr. mid. sch. Upshur County Pub. Schs., Buckhannon, 1980—86; tchr. 6th grade Prince William County Pub. Schs., Manassas, Va., 1986—. Recipient Governor's Sch. Disting. Tchr., Lynchburg U., Va., 2004. Mem.: Nat. Tchrs. Assn., Va. Edn. Assn. Methodist. Home: 12163 Loft Court Bristow VA 20136 Office: Prince William County Public Schools 8602 Mathis Avenue Manassas VA 20110 Office Phone: 703-361-3106. Office Fax: 703-361-8993. Personal E-mail: greatbear12@aol.com. E-mail: boylesnj@pwcs.edu.

BOYNTON, LEIGH ANNE, secondary school educator; b. Warren, Mich., Apr. 15, 1970; d. Ted and Joyce Gillam; 1 child, Kennedy Lee. BS in Secondary Edn., Stephen F. Austin State U., Nacogdoches, Tex., 1992. Tchr. Lewisville Ind. Sch. Dist., Carrollton, Tex., 1992—. Office: Lewisville Ind Sch Dist 2109 Arbor Creek Carrollton TX 75010 Office Phone: 972-350-2526. E-mail: boyntonl@lisd.net.

BOYNTON, SANDRA KEITH, illustrator, cartoonist, stationery products executive; b. Orange, NJ, Apr. 3, 1953; d. Robert Whitney and Jeanne Carolyn (Ragsdale) B.; m. James Patrick McEwan, Oct. 28, 1978; 1 dau., Caitlin Boynton McEwan. BA in English, Yale U., 1974, postgrad. Sch. Drama, 1976-77; postgrad., U. Calif.-Berkeley Drama Grad. Sch., 1974-75. Designer Recycled Paper Products, Inc., Chgo., 1974—, v.p., 1980—; illustrator greeting cards, 1975—. Illustrator/author: Hippos Go Berserk, 1977, If At First, 1979, Gopher Baroque, 1979, The Compleat Turkey, 1980, Chocolate: The Consuming Passion, 1982, Moo, Baa, La La La, 1982, The Going to Bed Book, 1982, But Not the Hippopotamus, 1982, Opposites, 1982, A is for Angry, 1983, Blue Hat, Green Hat, 1984, Doggies, 1984, Chloë and Maude, 1985, Christmastime, 1987, Oh My, Oh, My, Oh Dinosaurs, 1993, One, Two Three, 1993, Barnyard Dance, 1993, Birthday Monsters, 1993, Pajama Time, 2000, Yay, You!: Moving Out, Moving Up, Moving On, 2001 (Publishers Weekly picture book bestseller, 2005), Philadelphia Chickens, 2002, Snuggle Puppy, 2003, Fuzzy, Fuzzy, Fuzzy!, 2003, Belly Button Book, 2005, (with Jamie MacEwan) Story of Grump and Pout, 1983, The Heart of Cool, 2001; Albums: Grunt: Pigorian Chant, 1999 (Amazon.com bestseller), (with Michael Ford): Rhinoceros Tap, 1996, Philadelphia Chickens, 2002. Mem. Soc. Of Friends. Known for creating famed birthday card greeting "Hippo Birdies Two Ewes.".

BOYSEN, JONEA GENE, marketing executive, copywriter; d. Robert Dee and Linda Susan Boysen. BS in Mktg., Mgmt. and Psychology, Calif. Luth. U., 2004, MBA in Mktg. and Fin., 2005; grad. Global Bus. Program in Internat. Mgmt., FH-Joanneum, Graz, Austria, 2003. Profl. cert. marketer Am. Mktg. Assn., 2005, cert. bus. communicator Bus. Mktg. Assn., 2005. Mktg. comm. specialist and copywriter UBS Fin. Svcs. Inc., Ventura, Calif., 2003—04; pub. rels. copywriter NBC, Universal and Calif. Luth. U., Burbank, Calif., 2004—04; mgmt. cons., copywriter Jonea Gene Copywriting & Consulting, Myrtle Beach, SC, 1999—; mng. editor The Breeze, Myrtle Beach, 2006—; writer Coastal Bus. Life, 2006—. Author (copywriter): (mktg. plan) DECA Learn & Earn Project (11th Pl. in Nation, 2000). Mem.: Am. Advt. Fedn., Am. Mktg. Assn., Myrtle Beach C. of C. (amb.), Conway Area C. of C. (amb. chair, bd. dirs.), Sigma Beta Delta, Psi Chi. Achievements include Youngest MBA Grad. at Calif. Luth. U. to date. Avocations: feng shui, time with family, fiance and friends, exercise. Office Phone: 843-267-9977. Personal E-mail: joneagene@hotmail.com.

BOYSEN, MELICENT PEARL, finance company executive; b. Houston, Dec. 1, 1943; d. William Thomas and Mildred Pearl (Walker) Richardson; m. Stephen M. Boysen, Sept. 10, 1961 (dec. 1973); children: Marshella, Stephanie, Stephen. Student, Cen. Mo. State, 1973-75. Owner, pres. Boysen Enterprises, Kansas City, Mo., 1973-93; fin. cons., underwriter New Eng. Life Ins. Co., Kansas City, 1978-81; owner, pres. Boysen Agri-Svcs., Kansas City, 1984-94; pres. Boysen & Assocs., Inc., Kansas City, 1987—; stockholder, pres. Am. Crumb Rubber, Inc., Kansas City, 1996—; prin. Initiatives Worldwide, Inc., Kansas City, 2002—. Cons. San Luis Rey (Calif.) Tribal Water Authority, Wind River (Wyo.) Reservation, Cheyenne River (S.D.) Sioux, Iroquois Nations (N.Y.), 1983—; founding bd. dirs., pres. Am. Indian Youth Orgn., Visible Horizons, 1987—. Founding bd. dirs. Rose Brooks Ctr. Battered Women, Kansas City, 1979-87, treas., 1979-81; exec. dir. The Flame Spirit Run, 1992; citationist, 1993; mem. Pres.'s Vol. Action Awards Program; mem. Pres.'s Bus. Adv. Coun., 2001. Recipient Women of Conscience award Panel Am. Women of Greater Kansas City. Mem. DAR, Kans. C. of C. and Industry, Kansas City C. of C. Methodist. Avocations: stamp collecting/philately, sports cars. Office: Boysen & Assocs 4112 Pennsylvania Ave Ste 202 Kansas City MO 64111-3057 Office Phone: 816-960-1900. E-mail: mboysen@boysencompanies.com.

BOYTER, JUDY B, music educator; b. Tulsa, Okla., Nov. 24, 1948; d. M. H. and Boots Butler Benson; m. Dennis G. Boyter, June 6, 1998; children: Weston R. Hurt, Kristy L. Hurt. MusB, Tex. Tech U., 1971. Secondary Music Education Tex., 1971. Pvt. voice and piano instr. Pvt. Studio, Spring, Tex., 1971—; choir dir., tchr. Hildebrandt Intermediate Sch., Spring, Tex., 1982—84, Strack Intermediate Sch., Spring, Tex., 1984—90, Klein Oak H.S., Spring, Tex., 1990—98, Conroe H.S., Tex., 1998—99, Cy-Fair H.S., Cypress, Tex., 1999—2005. Choir dir. State St. Christian Ch., Valdosta, Ga., 1971—72, Cypress Creek Christian Ch., Spring, Tex., 1979—85, Christ Ch. United Meth. Ch., The Woodlands, Tex., 1991—97; asst. music dir. St. John Luth. Ch., Cypress, Tex., 1997—2002. Sr. Music scholarship, Tex. Tech U. Music Dept., 1970—71. Mem.: Tex. Music Educators Assn., Am. Choral Directors Assn., Tex. Choral Directors Assn., Tex. Music Adjudicators Assn., Nat. Assn. of Teachers of Singing, Cypress Creek Music Teacher's Assn., Music Teachers Nat. Assn. Avocations: travel, reading, pets. Office Phone: 281-655-0914. Personal E-mail: jboyter@sbcglobal.net.

BOYUM (BALL), JENNIFER MARIE, music educator; b. Orange, Calif., Jan. 31, 1975; d. Gary A. and Linda L Boyum; m. Andrew James Ball, Jan. 18, 2003. MB, U. Ariz., 1997; MusM, Northwestern U., Evanston, Ill., 2003. Dir. choral activities WD Johnson Jr. High, Las Vegas, 1997—99, Rolling Meadows HS, Ill., 1999—2002, La Jolla Country Day Sch., Calif., 2002—. Alto sect. leader St. James by the Sea Epsicopal Ch., La Jolla, Calif., 2002—. Dir.(music dir.): (theater) A Wake for Chorus and Soloists (San Diego Union Tribune Top Ten Performances of 2005, 2005). Mem.: So. Calif. Vocal Tchrs. Assn., Am. Choral Dirs. Assn., Music Educators Nat. Conf. Achievements include Oustanding Choral Dir., World of Music Festivals, 1998; nominee for Most Outstanding First Year Teacher, Clark County Schools, 1998; nominee for Disney's Outstanding Teachers Award, 1999. Office Phone: 858-453-3440. Personal E-mail: jboyum@ljcds.org.

BOZA, CLARA BRIZEIDA, marketing executive; b. Havana, Cuba, Apr. 18, 1952; came to U.S., 1957; d. Eduardo Otmaro and Hubedia Marta (Garcia) B. BA in English summa cum laude, Barry Coll., 1973, MS in Comm. Media, 1988. Program adminstr. Dade County Coun. Arts and Scis., Miami, Fla., 1980-82; dir. program devel. Nat. Found. for Advancement in Arts, Miami, 1982-85; exec. dir. Bus. Vols. for Arts/Miami, 1985-86; dir. mktg. Steel Hector & Davis, Miami, 1986-96; dir. practice devel. Arnold & Porter, Washington, 1996-98; chief mktg. officer Kirkpatrick Lockhart Nicholson Graham LLP, Washington, 1998—2006; mktg. and mgmt. cons., 2006—. S.E. regional cons. Arts and Bus. Coun., N.Y.C., 1986-88; panelist and spkr. various local, state and nat. orgns. and assns. Recipient ednl. scholarship Barry Coll., Miami, 1969-73, Fla. Bd. Regents, 1969-73. Mem. ABA (mem. commn. on advt. 1994-97), Legal Mktg. Assn. (bd. dirs. and officer 1993, 94, 96, bd. dirs. Mid-Atlantic chpt. 1997-99), Am. Mktg. Assn. (bd. dirs. Miami chpt. 1992-96), Fla. Bar (standing com. on advt. 1993-96). Office: 1601 K St NW Washington DC 20006 E-mail: cboza@vna1.com.

BOZARTH, STEPHANIE BELLE MAYS, social worker; b. San Antonio, Sept. 25, 1971; d. Howard Wright and Lula Belle (Maddox) Mays. B Social Work, U. Miss., 1994; MSW, Our Lady of the Lake U., San Antonio, 1999. LCSW Washington, lic. master social worker Tex. Rep. customer svc. Dun & Bradstreet, Austin, Tex., 1995—97; counselor crisis response team San Antonio Police Dept., 1997—98; intern social work pediat. intensive care Tex. Children's Hosp., Houston, 1999; counselor, social worker U. Tex. MD Anderson Cancer Ctr., Houston, 1999—2000; clin. social worker Children's Nat. Med. Ctr., Washington, 2000—. Bereavement program developer Children's Nat. Med. Ctr., Washington, 2000—. Advocate Stand for Children, Washington, 2000—02, Young Profls. for Children, Houston, 1999—2000; bd. dirs. Assn. for Death Edn. and Counseling, Houston, 1999—2000, Tex. Alliance for End of Life Care, Houston, 1999—2000. Mem.: NASW, Phi Alpha. Office: Children's Nat Med Ctr 111 Michigan Ave NW Washington DC 20010 Personal E-mail: stephmays@yahoo.com. Business E-Mail: smays@cnmc.org.

BOZO, MOLLY CATHERINE, elementary school educator; b. Spokane, Wash., May 17, 1954; d. Michael and Margarite O'Brien; m. Joseph L. Bozo, Mar. 17, 1973; children: Anne Marie, Joseph M., Nicholas C., Samantha A., Christopher M. BE, EWU, Cheney, Wash., 1973; MA, EWU, 1991. K-4 thcr. Spokane Schs., 1990—98, tchr. coach, 1998—2006, reading recovery tchr., 1998—2005, reading recovery tchr. leader, 2005—, dist. coach, 2005—. Recipient Dist. Disting. Tchr., Spokane Schs., 2006. Office: Spokane Schs N 200 Bernard Spokane WA 99207

BOZOYAN, SYLVIA, elementary school educator; b. Aleppo, Syria, Feb. 18, 1953; arrived in U.S., 1953; d. Edward Yervant and Takouhi (Knnablian) B. BA, St. Peter's Coll., 1975; MEd, William Paterson Coll., 1978. Cert. elem. tchr. NJ, nursery sch. tchr. NJ. 1st grade tchr. Thomas A. Edison Sch., Union City, NJ, 1975—. Armenian sch. tchr. Holy Cross Armenian Ch., Union City, 1972—80, Sunday sch. tchr., 1969—. Named Outstanding Tchr. Govs. Tchr. Recognition Program, N.J., 1987-88, Outstanding Young Woman of Am., Ala., 1982, 87. Mem. Armenian Gen. Benevolent Union of Am. (sec. N.Y./N.J. Met. chpt. 1985-1995, sec., dancer ANTRANIG Dance Ensemble/exec. com. 1979—), N.J. Edn. Assn., Hudson County Edn. Assn., Union City Edn. Assn., Kappa Delta Pi, Pi Lambda Theta. Home: 1812 West St Union City NJ 07087-3311

BRAASCH, BARBARA LYNN, banker, consultant; b. Santa Monica, Calif., Apr. 14, 1958; d. C. Duane and René Barbara (Siegel) B. Student, Golden Gate U., 1989-91. Cert. Compensation Professional, 1999. Ops. officer Bank of Am., Fresno, Calif., 1976-87; v.p., mgr. Wells Fargo Bank, San Fransisco, 1987-96; v.p., mgr. fin. MIS Bank of Am., San Fransisco, 1996-2000, catalyst bus. cons., owner, 2000—; mgr. investment sys.; mgr. devel. Wells Fargo Bank, 2000—. Mentor Jr. Achievement, L.A., 1980-83. 1st class scout Girl Scouts Am., 1976, leader, asst. leader, 1976-79, 84-87; vol. Open Hand, San Francisco, 1991-92, San Francisco AIDS Found., various women's groups, 1989—. Mem. Am. Compensation Assn., Bay Area Compensation Assn., Fin. Tech. Forum. Democrat. Jewish. Avocations: music, movies, theater. Office: Wells Capital Mgmt 525 Market St 10 B Fl San Francisco CA 94105 Home: 77 Dow Pl Apt 904 San Francisco CA 94107-4186 E-mail: braascba@wellscap.com.

BRABEC, ROSEMARY JEAN, retail executive; b. St. Paul, Apr. 5, 1951; d. Peter Michael and Mary Jane (Nigro) Jacovitch; m. Loren W. Brabec, Sept. 16, 1972; children: Brenda Marie, Daniel Joseph. BS in Elem. Edn., St. Cloud State U., 1973. Tchr. Ind. Sch. Dist. 314, Braham, Minn., 1975-78; owner, mgr. Rosemary's Quilts and Baskets, Braham, 1988-97. Dir. Community Edn. Adv. Coun., Braham, 1978-95, chmn., 1992-95. Designer quilt block representing Minn. div. AAUW for display at Internat. Fedn. Univ. Women conv., Calif. Chmn. P.I.C.K. Immunization Clinic, Braham, 1978—85; vol. driver coord. Home Delivered Meals, Braham, 1984—; vol. coord. Com. to Build Robert Leathers Playground, Braham, 1985; mem. Braham Pie Day Com., 1990—, chmn., 2005—; mem. Braham City Pk. Bd., 2001—, chmn., 2002—. Mem. AAUW (sec.Cambridge Area Branch, 1985-87, 98-99, v.p. 1987-88, historian 1997-98, pres. 1999-2002), Minn. Quilters.

BRABECK, MARY MARGARET, dean, psychology professor; BA, U. Minn., 1967, PhD, 1980; MS, St. Cloud U., 1970. Tchr. Bryant Jr. H.S., 1968—71; instr. U. Minn., 1971—75; instr. psychology Salve Regina Coll., Newport, RI, 1976—80; asst. prof., coord. The Human Devel. Program Boston Coll., Chestnut Hill, 1980—86, assoc. prof., 1986—92; assoc. prof., divsn. dir. Lynch Sch. Edn., Boston Coll., 1988—90, prof., chair dept. counseling, devel. psychology and rsch. methods, 1990—92, assoc. dean, 1992—95, dean, 1996—2003, prof., 1996—2003; dean The Steinhardt Sch. Edn., NYU, 2003—, prof. psychology, 2003—. Vis. prof. Brown U. Ctr. Human Devel., 1995—96; chmn. bd. Am. Assn. Colls. Tchr. Edn. Recipient Kuhmerker award, Assn. Moral Edn., 1996, Boston Higher Edn. Partnership Svc. award, 2002, Alumni Achievement award, U. Minn., 2006. Fellow: APA (bd. ednl. affairs 2004—06, com. on women leadership award 2006, Presdl. citation 2006, Presdl. award 2005). Office: Steinhardt Sch Edn Joseph & Violet Pless Hall NYU 82 Washington Sq E New York NY 10003 Office Phone: 212-998-5003. Business E-Mail: mary.brabeck@nyu.edu, mmb7@nyu.edu.

BRACCO, LORRAINE, actress; b. Bklyn., Oct. 2, 1954; m. Daniel Guerard, 1979 (div. 1982); 1 child, Margaux; m. Harvey Keitel, 1982 (div. 1993); 1 child, Stella; m. Edward James Olmos, Jan. 28, 1994 (dec. Mar. 1, 2002). Studied, Actors Studio; studied with Stella Adler, Ernie Martin, John Strasberg. Actor (films) Duos sur canape, 1979, What Did I Ever Do to the Good Lord to Deserve a Wife Who Dinks in Cafes with Men?, 1980, Commissaire Moulin, 1980, Fais gaffe a la gaffe, 1981, A Complex Plot About Women, Alleys and Crimes, 1986, The Pick-Up Artist, 1987, Someone to Watch Over Me, 1987, Sing, 1989, The Dream Team, 1989, As Long as It's Love, 1989, Sea of Love, 1989, Goodfellas, 1990 (Acad. award nominee for best supporting actress 1990, LA Film Critics Assoc. award for best sup. actress, 1990), Talent for the Game, 1991, Switch, 1991, Medicine Man, 1992, Radio Flyer, 1992, Traces of Red, 1992, Being Human, 1994, Even Cowgirls Get the Blues, 1994, The Basketball Diaries, 1995, Hackers, 1995, Les Menteurs, 1996, Silent Cradle, 1997, Ladies Room, 1999, Tangled, 2000, Your Aura is Throbbing, 2000, Riding in Cars With Boys, 2001, Tangled, 2001, Death of a Dynasty, 2003, Max and Grace, 2004, My Suicidal Sweetheart, 2005; (TV movies) Scam, 1993, Getting Gotti, 1996, Lifeline, 1996, The Taking of Pelham One Two Three, 1998, Custody of the Heart, 2000, Sex in our Century, 2001, Dinner with the FoodFellas, 2006; (TV series) The Sopranos, 1999-,(SAG award for Outstanding Performance by an Ensemble in a Drama Series, 2000); (TV appearances) Crime Story, 1986, Law & Order: Trial By Jury, 2005; (off-Broadway plays) Goose and Tom-Tom; (Broadway plays) The Graduate, 2002; (dir. films) AutoMotives, 2000; Author: On the Couch, 2006 Mem.: bd. of dir. Riverkeeper, NY Council for the Humanities. Office: First Artists Assoc 12 W 57th St #PH New York NY 10019-3900*

BRACKBILL, NANCY LAFFERTY, retired elementary school educator; b. Lancaster, Pa., Sept. 7, 1938; d. Jacob Martin and Erma Irene Lafferty; m. Albert Landis Brackbill Jr., Aug. 6, 1960; children: Lynn Elizabeth, Lisa Ann. BS in Elem. Edn., Millersville U., 1960, cert. reading specialist, 1981. Tchr. kindergarten Hempfield Sch. Dist., Landisville, Pa., 1960-63; tchr. nursery sch. Zion U.C.C. Nursery Sch., Millersville, Pa., 1971-72; tchr. elem., reading Annville (Pa.)-Cleona Sch. Dist., 1978-79; tchr. reading Palmyra (Pa.) H.S., 1980-81; elem. tchr., reading specialist East Stroudsburg (Pa.) Area Sch. Dist., 1981—2002, chmn. elem. reading, 1991—2002; ret., 2002. Mem. Nazareth Area Cmty. Chorus, St. John's Evang. Luth. Ch. Mem.: NEA (ret. life mem.), KeyStone State Reading Assn., Pa. Edn. Assn. (ret.), Colonial Area Reading Educators (legis. chair 1992—), Internat. Reading Assn. Avocations: reading, music, yoga/Pilates, bicycling. Home: 188 Brookside Ln Nazareth PA 18064-9109

BRACKEN, LINDA DARLENE, medical/surgical nurse; b. Muncie, Ind., May 7, 1948; d. Russell Lloyd and Ina Fern (Blaich) Enyeart; m. Norman Harold Bracken, Apr. 15, 1972; children: Aaron Lee, Dana Lynn. ADN, Ind. U., 1968. RN, Ind. Staff nurse, night charge Meth. Hosp., Indpls., 1968-69; office nurse ob/gyn Muncie Clinic, 1969-70; asst. supr. OR Marion (Ind.) Gen. Hosp., 1970-72; staff nurse OR and float Anderson (Ind.) Community Hosp., 1972-83, staff nurse, OR, cardiac cath. lab., 1987-88; office nurse, surgeon Robert McCurdy, Anderson, 1983-84; staff nurse, crit. care McPherson Hosp., Howell, Mich., 1984-87; staff nurse Favorite Nurse, Indpls., 1988-90; staff nurse OR St. John's Health Systems, Anderson, 1992—. Pres.: Talking Tours, 1990—. Republican. Avocations: reading, music. Home: 2016 N 900 W Anderson IN 46011-9121

BRACKEN, LYNDA, physical education educator; AS, Orange County CC, N.Y., 1975; BS, East Stroudsburg U., N.Y., 1980, M in Edn., D in Edn., Columbia U., N.Y., 2003. Asst. rsch. dir. Crystal Run Village, Middletown, NY, 1981—83; health rschr, dean of students Jeff-Youngsville Ctrl. Sch., Jefferson, NY, 1983—86; physical edn. tchr. Sullivan West Ctrl. Sch., Jefferson, NY, 1986—. Recipient Tchr. Recognition award, Jeff-Youngsville Nat. Honor Soc., 1995. Mem.: NYSHPERD, AAHPERD. Home: PO Box 415 Youngsville NY 12791

BRACKEN, MARY PARKER, biologist, educator; b. Columbia, Mo., Nov. 11, 1950; d. Robert Parker Hulett and Sarah Louise Bird. AA, Stephens Coll., Columbia, Mo., 1970; BS, U. Mo., Columbia, Mo., 1972; MS in Edn., U. N. Tex., Denton, 1979; MS in Biology, U. Tex., Arlington, 1990. Tchr. Park Hill Sch. Dist., Kansas City, Mo., 1972—76, Plano Ind. Sch. Dist., Tex., 1976—86; instr. Richland Coll., Dallas, 1986—91; prof. dept. biology Trinity Valley C.C., Terrell, Tex., 1987—. Named Tchr. of the Yr., Plano Sch. Dist., 1981—82, Phi Theta Kappa, 2003. Mem.: Human Anatomy and Physiology Soc. (bd. dirs. 1989—), Nat. Assn. Biology Tchrs. (sec.), Tex. Assn. Biology Tchrs. Avocations: scuba diving, hiking, gardening, bicycling. Office: Trinity Valley Community College PO Box 668 Terrell TX 75160

BRACKEN, PEG, writer; b. Filer, Idaho, Feb. 25, 1918; d. John Lewis and Ruth (McQuesten) B.; m. John Hamilton Ohman, June 15, 1991; 1 child from previous marriage, Johanna Bracken. AB, Antioch Coll., 1940. Author: The I Hate to Cook Book, 1960, The I Hate to Housekeep Book, 1962, I Try to Behave Myself, 1963, Peg Bracken's Appendix to The I Hate to Cook Book, 1966, I Didn't Come Here to Argue, 1969, But I Wouldn't Have Missed It for the World, 1973, The I Hate to Cook Almanack - A Book of Days, 1976, A Window Over the Sink, 1981, The Compleat I Hate to Cookbook, 1986, On Getting Old for the First Time, 1996. Office Phone: 503-294-0443. Personal E-mail: akafeller@aol.com.

BRACKENRIDGE, N. LYNN, not-for-profit developer; b. Youngstown, Ohio, Sept. 9, 1957; d. John Bruce and Mary Ann (Rossi) Brackenridge; m. Harry Lee Carrico, July 1, 1994. BA, Lawrence U., 1978; MS, Georgetown U., 1980. Tchg. asst. Georgetown U., Washington, 1979-81, admissions officer, 1984-85, editor, writer devel., 1985-87, asst. dir. devel., 1987-89; dir. devel. Cath. Charities U.S.A., Washington, 1989-91, Johns Hopkins U. Bologna (Italy) Ctr., 1991-92; dir. devel. and pub. rels. Nat. Ctr. for State Cts., Williamsburg, Va., 1993-97; v.p. for devel. Gateway Homes Greater Richmond (Va.), Inc., 1998-99, pres., 1999—2004; exec. dir. John Marshall Found., 2004—. Vol. Richmond Ballet, 1993-95, Leukemia Soc. Am., Hampton, Va., 1996—; bd. dirs. Ctrl. Va. chpt. Alliance for Mentally Ill, 2005. Georgetown U. fellow, 1979-81; recipient diplome d'etudes Inst. d'Etudes Francaises de Touraine, 1976. Mem.: Nat. Soc. Fund Raising Execs. (cert. fund raising exec., chair program com., pres. 1997). Democrat. Avocations: flying small aircraft, running, reading, films, languages. Home: 9303 Cragmont Dr Richmond VA 23229-7610 Office: John Marshall Found 209 W Franklin St Richmond VA 23220 Office Phone: 804-775-0861. Business E-Mail: lynnb@johnmarshallfoundation.org.

BRACKETT, PRILLA SMITH, artist, educator; b. New Orleans, Nov. 8, 1942; d. Wilson Fitch and Hannah Balch (Coffin) Smith; m. George Conrad Brackett, Sept. 28, 1968; children: Ethan Samuel, Matthew Aaron. BA in Psychology and Sociology, Sarah Lawrence Coll., 1964; MA in Sociology, U. Calif., Berkeley, 1967; MFA in Painting and Drawing, U. Nebr., 1981. Grad. tchg. asst. U. Nebr., Lincoln, 1979-81; adj. prof. Simmons Coll., Boston, 1989; instr. DeCordova Mus. Sch., Lincoln, 1992-93; adj. prof. U. Mass. Harbor Campus, Boston, 1993, Salem (Mass.) State Coll., 1993; instr. landscape workshops Arts Pro Tem, Hancock, N.H., 1993-95, 97, West Yellowstone, Mont., 1993-95. Panel coord., moderator Nat. Women's Caucus for Art, San Francisco, 1989, 95, Boston, 1996; panelist Coll. Art Assn. Nat. Conf., Chgo., 1992; guest lectr. and spkr. in field. One-woman shows include Winfisky Gallery, Salem (Mass.) State Coll., 1989, Gallery 57, Cambridge, 1989, The Bunting Inst., Radcliffe Rsch. and Study Ctr., Cambridge, 1990, Soho 20 Invitational Space, N.Y.C., 1990, Wessell Libr., Tufts U., Medford, Mass., 1990, DeCordova Mus. and Sculpture Park, Lincoln, Mass., 1993, Gallery 57, Cambridge, Mass., 1994, UMF Gallery, Farmington, Maine,

1999, duPont Gallery, Washington and Lee U., Lexington, Va., 1999, Soc. for the Protection of N.H. Forests, Concord, 2000, Berman Mus. Art, Ursinus Coll., Collegeville, Pa., 2000, Watson Gallery, Wheaton Coll., Norton, Mass., 2000, Housatonic Mus. Art, Bridgeport, Conn., 2000, Cress Gallery, U. Tenn., Chattanooga, 2001, Inst. Ecosys. Studies, Millbrook, N.Y., 2001, others; two-person exhbn. Mark Gallery, Cambridge, Mass., 2003, 04, Art Complex Mus., Duxbury, Mass., 2005; group exhbns. include Portland (Maine) Mus. Art, 1998, Creiger-Dane Gallery, Boston, 1998, Fitchburg (Mass.) Art Mus., 1998, St. Lawrence U., Canton, N.Y., 1998, U. Oreg., Eugene, 1998, Virginia Lynch Gallery, Tivarton, R.I., 2000, Berkshire Art Mus., Pittsfield, Mass., 2001, Elliot Smith Contemporary Art, St. Louis, 2002, Sonia Zaks Gallery, Chgo., 2003, Arnot Art Mus., Elmira, N.Y., Boston Printmakers Exch. Portfolio, 2005, China Art Acad., Hangzhou, 2005, Danforth Mus. Art, Framingham, Mass., 2006, A.I.R. Gallery, NYC, 2006, others. Co-pres. Boston chpt. Amigos de las Americas, Boston, 1993-95. Recipient fellowship in painting Bunting Inst., Radcliffe Rsch. and Study Ctr., Cambridge, 1989-90, The Francine Frank fellow residency Millay Colony of the Arts, Austerlitz, N.Y., 1994, residency at Ragdale Found., Lake Forest, Ill., 1997, 98, 2nd place cash award Lancaster Mus., 1997, Lois Neelie Gill award and residency Ucross Found., Clearmont, Wyo., 1998, residency Va. Ctr. for Creative Arts, Sweet Briar, Va., 2001, 03; Vision Fund grantee, Boston Found., 1998. Mem. Coll. Art Assn., Women's Caucus for Art (coord. for exhbns. nat. conf. 1986, co-chair Boston chpt. 1987-88). Avocations: gardening, hiking, opera, theater, dance and chamber music concerts. Home: 171 Lake View Ave Cambridge MA 02138-2131 Office: 75 Richdale Ave Ste 11 Cambridge MA 02140-2608 Business E-Mail: psb@luceatlux.com.

BRACY, CECELIA WIGGINS, primary school educator; b. Ahoskie, N.C., Dec. 9, 1958; d. Cecil Dewey Wiggins, Jr. and Doris Deane Taylor Wiggins; m. Anthony (Tony) Roger Bracy, July 11, 1982; children: Adam Ryan, Amber Dawn. BS, East Carolina U., Greenville, N.C., 1980. Cert. tchr. N.C. Dept. Pub. Instrn., 1981. Tchr. Hertford County Pub. Schs., Winton, NC, 1998—. Steering com. family chairperson Spl. Olympics Hertford County, Ahoskie, 2001—06. Cub scout den leader Boy Scouts Am.-East Carolina Coun., Ahoskie, 2000—04; troop leader Girl Scouts Am.-Hertford County Svc. Unit, Ahoskie, 2001—06; bowling coach Spl. Olympics Hertford County, Ahoskie, 2003—06. Named Family of Yr., Spl. Olympics-N.C.-Hist. Albemarle Area, 2004. Mem.: Profl. Educators N.C. Baptist. Avocations: reading, singing, word puzzles, bowling, crafts. Home: 236 Hollowell Rd Aulander NC 27805 Office: Hertford County Public Schools Bearfield Primary Sch 145 Hertford County High Rd Ahoskie NC 27910 Office Phone: 252-209-6140. Business E-Mail: bracyc@hertford.k12.nc.us.

BRADARIC, SUZANNE JOY, music educator, theater director; b. Burbank, Calif., Nov. 15, 1979; d. Michael A. and Diane Marie Bradaric. BA in Theater, Anderson U., Ind., 2001; postgrad., Calif. State U., Long Beach, 2004—. Asst. children's dir., youth counselor Magnolia Bapt. Ch., Anaheim, Calif., 1997—2001; pvt. voice tchr. Cypress, Calif., 1999—; 7th-11th grade English tchr., long-term substitute Anaheim Discovery Christian Sch., Anaheim, 2002—03; substitute tchr., tchrs. aide Anaheim Discovery Christian Sch. and Brethren Chritstian HS, Anaheim and Huntington Beach, Calif., 2002—03; producing artistic dir. Pacific Art Theatre and Abstract Productions, Inc., Cypress, 2002—; adj. faculty voice tchr. Sch. Music Calif. Bapt. U., Riverside, 2003—04; tchr. Sylvan Learning Ctr., Huntington Beach and Downey, Calif., 2004—05; instr., grad. asst. dept. theater arts Calif. State U., Long Beach, 2004—. Acting apprentice Barn Theatre, Augusta, Mich., 2000. Dir.: (play) The Vagina Monologues; actor: The Diary of Anne Frank, (opera) The Magic Flute, (musical) Godspell, (play) As You Like It, (operetta) The Gondoliers (Voices of Angels award, 2002); asst. dir. (play) Medea (Polly Warfield award for Best Season, LA Drama Critics Cir., 2006); composer (and music director): (music for play) Cloud Nine; dir.: (play) Much Ado About Nothing; actor: (world premiere musical) Fool of Hearts; dramaturg (world premiere play) (M)asking Questions: The Life Stages of Humanitas Persona; singer: (concept recording) Old Timer-The Musical; prodr.: (children's theatre programs) Pacific Art Theatre's Theatre Camp; actor, dir., singer: (fundraising event/showcase performance) Till There Was You; author: (dramatic reading) Daily Bread, (one-act play) Balance; singer: (worship band) Elements band; author: (short plays and sketches) Various works; actor: (plays and musicals) Various productions; author: (poems, songs, stories, scripts, essays) Various works; actor(amanda wingvalley): (play) For Whom the Southern Belle Tolls; dir.(producer): The Star-Spangled Girl, (choreographer) (muscial) Scrooge's Christmas, (producer) (one-act play-west coast premiere) Benny and Cameron, (play) Sister Mary Ignatius Explains It All For You; actor: (musical) Evita; singer (actor): (caberet) Various shows at Barn Theatre; composer: (string quartet) Variations on Finlandia; actor(city her): (musical) Gifts of the Magi, Antony and Cleopatra; actor, actor: A Midsummer Night's Dream; actor, asst. dir.: Hamlet; actor: (musical) Into the Woods; dir., actor: muscial Songs for a New World; actor(widow douglas): (musical) Big River, (play) The Crucible, In Love With Shakespeare, (musical) Ragtime, Nine; dir., prodr., sound designer: play Peter Pan. Worship dir. mem. leadership/planning team Open Door, Anderson, Ind., 1998—2000; spl. forces/creative team mem., theater dir. God's Ho., Huntington Beach, Calif., 2001—04; pres. Pacific Art Theatre/Abstract Productions, Inc., Cypress, 2003—06. Grantee, Geisbauer Found. and So. Calif. Ctr. Nonprofit Mgmt., 2005. Mem.: Theatre Comm. Group (hon.), Phi Lambda Sigma, Alpha Psi Omega (v.p. Lambda Theta cast 2000—01). Independent. Avocations: theater, opera, music, literature, photography. Office: Pacific Art Theatre P O Box 488 Cypress CA 90630 Office Phone: 714-536-6322. Business E-Mail: info@pacificarttheatre.com.

BRADBURY, BETTY MARIE, history and music educator; b. Madison, Ind., Mar. 5, 1933; d. Lawrence Allen and Elsie Margret (Spivey) Bladen; m. Robert Lesley Bradbury, Aug. 23, 1952; children: Robert A., Jonathan R., Randall E., Daryl R., Robert II. Diploma, Sherwood Music Sch., 1966; Assoc. in Gen. Studies, Ind. U., Kokomo, 1989, B Gen. Studies with distinction, 1990, MS in Edn., 1995. Cert. tchr., adminstr. Tchr. Malta (Ohio) Christian Sch., 1971-73, Beaver Valley Wesleyan, Vanport, Pa., 1973-77; pvt. piano tchr. Madison, Ind., 1977-80; tchr. Bible Wesleyan Acad., Crab Orchard, W.Va., 1980-82, Beckley (W.Va.) Pentecostal Acad., 1983-84; tchr., prin. Bible Wesleyan Acad., Crab Orchard, 1984-87; tchr. Union Bible Acad., Westfield, Ind., 1989-90, prin., 1990-92; prof. Union Bible Coll., Westfield, 1992—. Seminar leader-tchr. Evang. Bible Mission, Haiti, 1993, 95, 98, 2000; mem. exec. com. Union Bible Coll., Westfield, 1990-92; chmn. Union Bible Coll. edn. dept., 2000-04 Author: The Walls Talk, 1993. Jr. ch. leader Pilgrim Holiness Ch., Indpls., 1993-94; sec.-treas. Pilgrim Holiness Ch., Muncie, Ind., 1969-71; den mother Cub Scouts, Middletown, Ind., 1966-69; missionary pres. Bible Wesleyan Ch., Crab Orchard, 1984-86. Mem. Alpha Chi. Republican. Avocations: reading, music, puzzles. Home: 507 S Walnut St Westfield IN 46074-8956

BRADDOCK, NONNIE CLARKE, religious organization administrator; b. Rye, N.Y. d. Peter Benedict and Nora Bridget (Devins) Clarke; m. Eugene Stephen Braddock, Sept. 7, 1962; children: Stephen E., Brian B., Glenn C. Adminstr. Beaver Farm Retreat and Conf. Ctr., Yorktown Heights, N.Y.; deputy city clk. City of Rye, N.Y. Founder, pres. Celebrations; dir. Security Enforcement Bur.; part-time therapist; with Marriage Encounter movement, co-founder, chmn. bd., team leader No. Westchester-Putnam (N.Y.) Interfaith Marriage Encounter, 1981-87. Vol. Boy Scouts Am., numerous polit. orgns. and cmty. groups, 1970—; chair Warmth for Christmas clothing drive, N.Y.C. shelters; facilitator mil. family support group; organizer food collections for needy, Heart to Heart, coord. Angel Fund; organizer, sponsor Weekly Cable TV program featuring peace, 1991; bd. dirs. Homeless Shelter; adv. com. Comty. Mem. Interfaith Clergy Coun., Rite Christian Initiation for Adults, Right to Life, North Am. Retreat Dirs. Assn., Pax Christi Metro, Westchester Assn. Vol. Adminstrs., Feminists for Life, Fedn. Christian Ministries, Internat. Platform Assn. Avocations: music, travel, reading. Office: Beaver Farm Retreat Ctr Underhill Ave Yorktown Heights NY 10598

BRADDY, CAROLYN MORTON, pastor; b. Biloxi, Miss., Mar. 31, 1936; d. James Harvey and Ione Seymour Morton; children: Sharon Salsberry, Jay, Ann Chambers. BS in Natural Scis., Lee U., Cleveland, Tenn., 1975; postgrad., Emory U., Atlanta, 1989. Tchr. sci. and math. Cleveland Mid. Sch., 1979—98; pastor United Meth. Chs., Meigs and Bradley Counties, 1983—. Tchr. remedial math., 1981. Spiritual dir. Cleveland Emmaus Comty.; counselor New Hope Pregnancy Care Ctr., Cleveland, 2001—; telephone counselor CONTACT Telephone Crisis, Cleveland, 1973—95; facilitator jail ministry Promised Land Found., Cleveland, 2005—; judge sci. fair projects Cleveland Mid. Sch., 1999—2005. Recipient Mustard Seed award for outstanding small ch., Holston Conf., 2002. Republican. United Methodist. Avocations: travel, bridge, reading, walking.

BRADEN, BETTY JANE, legal association administrator; b. Sheboygan, Wis., Feb. 5, 1943; d. Otto Frank and Betty Donna (Beers) Huettner; children: Jennifer Tindall, Rebecca Leigh; m. Berwyn Bartow Braden, Nov. 5, 1983. BS, U. Wis., 1965. Cert. elem. tchr., Wis. Tchr. Madison (Wis.) Met. Sch. Dist., 1965-70, 71-72, sub. tchr., 1972-75; adminstrv. asst. ATS-CLE State Bar Wis., Madison, 1978, adminstrv. asst. Advanced Tng. Seminars-Continuing Legal Edn., 1979, coordinator, 1980, adminstr. coordinator, 1980-84, adminstrv. dir., 1984-87, dir. adminstrn., bar svcs., membership, 1987—; mem. rels. and pub. svcs. dir. Legal Edn., 1992—. Speaker Bar Leadership Inst. of ABA. Mem.: LWV, Nat. Assn. Bar Execs. (program chair 1995—96, sec. 1996—98, v.p. 1998—99, pres. elect 1999—2000, pres. 2000—01), Wis. Soc. of Assn. Execs., Am. Soc. of Assn. Execs., Am. Soc. for Personnel Adminstrn., Am. Mgmt. Assn., Adminstrv. Mgmt. Soc., Meeting Planners Internat. (sec. Wis. chpt. 1981—82, pres. 1982—83). Avocations: tennis, scuba diving, reading, skiing. Home: 41 Golf Pkwy Madison WI 53704-7003 Office: State Bar of Wis 5302 Eastpark Blvd Madison WI 53718-2101 Office Phone: 608-250-6104. Business E-Mail: bbraden@wisbar.org.

BRADEN, JOAN KAY, mental health counselor; b. Easton, Pa., Apr. 14, 1934; d. W.F. and J.H. (Snover) Ebner. AA, George Washington U., 1973, BA in Gen. Studies, 1976; MA, Hood Coll., Frederick, Md., 1979. Cert. nat. clin. mental health counselor; cert. profl. counselor, Md. Staff psychologist Gt. Oaks Ctr. Md. Dept. Health and Mental Hygiene, Silver Spring, 1980-86; instr. Cath. Univ. Am., 1981-82; behavioral cons. U. Md. Hosp., Balt., 1986-87; therapist Montgomery County Abused Persons Program, Bethesda, Md., 1987-94; pvt. practice mental health counseling Kensington, Md., 1979—2005; ret. Cons., group leader Am. Lung Assn., Rockville, Md., 1983-85, Lupus Found., Alexandria, Va., 1984-87. Author: The Family Providing Training in Violence: A Counseling Challenge, 1992; editor: Help for Families of Chronic Lung Disease, 1985. Mem. Md. Assn. Counseling and Devel., Md. Mental Health Counseling Assn. (pres. 1988-89), Am. Mental Health Counselors Assn. (profl. recognition award 1989), Psi Chi, Alpha Sigma Lambda. Avocations: boating, painting.

BRADEN, KATIE ELIZABETH, elementary school educator; b. Wichita, Kans., Nov. 13, 1978; d. Jack W. and Mary A. Wilder; m. John Eric Braden, May 8, 2004. BS, U. North Tex., 2000; MS, Tex. A&M U., Commerce, 2004. Cert. tchr. Tex. Fifth grade tchr. Mesquite (Tex.) Ind. Sch. Dist., 2000—05; sixth grade sci. tchr. Rockwall (Tex.) Ind. Sch. Dist., 2005—. Roman Catholic. Avocations: volleyball, reading, hiking, walking. Home: 2109 Cedar Park Dr Forney TX 75126

BRADFORD, BARBARA REED, retired lawyer; b. Cleve., June 13, 1948; d. William Cochran and Martha Lucille (Horn) Bradford; m. Warren Neil Davis, Oct. 9, 1976 (div. 1989); m. S. Jack Odell, Dec. 12, 1991. BA, Pitzer Coll., 1970; JD, Georgetown U., 1975, MBA, 1985. Bar: N.Y. 1976, DC 1976. Staff asst. Sen. Edward M. Kennedy, Washington, 1970-71; assoc. Breed, Abbott & Morgan, N.Y.C., 1975-76, Verner, Liipfert Law Firm, Washington, 1976-78; atty. AID, Washington, 1978-83; pres. Georgetown Export Trading, Inc., Washington, 1984-86; regional dir. U.S. Trade and Devel. Agy., Washington, 1986-2000, agy. dep. dir., 2000—05; ret., 2005. Bd. dirs. Jr. League, Washington, 1977—78. Democrat. Avocations: art, golf, reading.

BRADFORD, BARBARA TAYLOR, writer, journalist; b. Leeds, Eng. arrived in U.S., 1964; d. Winston and Freda (Walker) Taylor; m. Robert Bradford, Dec. 24, 1963. Student pvt. schs., Eng.; LittD (hon.), Leeds U., Eng., 1990, U. Bradford, West Yorkshire, Eng., 1995; LHD (hon.), Teikyo Post U., Waterbury, Conn., 1996. Women's editor Yorkshire (Eng.) Evening Post, 1951-53, reporter, 1949-51; editor Woman's Own, 1953-54; columnist London Evening News, 1955-57; exec. editor London Am., 1959-62; editor Nat. Design Center Mag., 1965-69; syndicated columnist Newsday Spls., L.I., 1968-70; nat. syndicated columnist Chgo. Tribune-N.Y. (News Syndicate), N.Y.C., 1970-75, LA Times Syndicate, 1975-81. Author: Complete Encyclopedia of Homemaking Ideas, 1968, A Garland of Children's Verse, 1968, How to Be the Perfect Wife, 1969, Easy Steps to Successful Decorating, 1971, Decorating Ideas for Casual Living, 1977, How to Solve Your Decorating Problems, 1976, Making Space Grow, 1979, Luxury Designs for Apartment Living, 1981, (novels) A Woman of Substance, 1979, Voice of the Heart, 1983, Hold the Dream, 1985, screen adaptation, 1986, Act of Will, 1986, To Be the Best, 1988, The Women in His Life, 1990, Remember, 1991, Angel, 1993, Everything to Gain, 1994, Dangerous to Know, 1995, Love in Another Town, 1995, Her Own Rules, 1996, A Secret Affair, 1996, Power of a Woman, 1997, A Sudden Change of Heart, 1999, Where You Belong, 2000, The Triumph of Katie Byrne, 2001, Three Weeks in Paris, 2001, Emma's Secret, 2003, Unexpected Blessings, 2004, Just Rewards, 2005. Recipient Dorothy Dawe award, Am. Furniture Mart, 1970, 1971, Matrix award, N.Y. Women in Comm., 1985, Spl. Jury prize for body of lit., Deauville Festival Am. Film, 1994, Just award. Mem.: Am. Soc. Interior Designers, Authors Guild Am. (mem. coun. 1989—), Nat. Soc. Interior Designers (Disting. Editl. award 1969, Nat. Press award 1971), Coun. Authors Guild. Office: Bradford Enterprises 450 Park Ave New York NY 10022-2605 Personal E-mail: bradford.ent@att.net.

BRADFORD, DOLLI MARIA, music educator; b. Durham, NC, May 25, 1976; d. Harold R.T. and Inell Lyons Bradford; 1 child, Marcus Alexander Craig-Bradford. BA, St. Augustine's Coll., Raleigh, NC, 2001. Cert. music edn. K-12 NC. Sales assoc. Hecht's (May Co.), Durham, 1996—; sales assoc., reciever Staples Office Supply, Durham, 1998; music tchr. Butner Stem Elem. Granville County Schs., NC, 2001—03; music instr. Walltowns Children's Theatre, Durham, 2004—05; music tchr. J.W. Neal Mid. Sch. Durham Pub. Schs., 2003—. Mem. music adv. bd. Macmillan-MacGraw Hill, NC; fine arts dept chair J.W. Neal Mid. Sch. V.p. young adult choir 1st Calvary Bapt. Ch., Durham, 2005. Mem.: Music Educators Nat. Conf., NC Assn. Educators, Nat. Educators Assn. Democrat. Baptist. Avocations: personal shopping, reading, travel. Home: 526 Cotton St Creedmoor NC 27522 Office: JW Neal Mid Sch 201 Baptist Rd Durham NC 27701 Office Phone: 919-560-3955. Office Fax: 919-560-3451. Personal E-mail: alexmcb@msn.com. E-mail: dolli.bradford@dpsnc.net.

BRADFORD, JOANNE K., computer software company executive; Mgmt. tng. RH Macy, 1986; dist. sales mgr. Engrng. News Record; acct. mgr. Bus. Week Mag., 1989, tech. mktg. mgr., v.p. sales Western region, 1997, v.p. sales N. Am. Mktg.; v.p., chief media revenue officer MSN, Redmond, Wash., 2001—06; corp. v.p. global sales & trade mktg Microsoft Corp., Redmond, Wash., 2006—. Office: Microsoft Corp 1 Microsoft Way Redmond WA 98052-6399 Office Phone: 425-882-8080. Office Fax: 425-936-7329.

BRADFORD, JUDITH LYNNELL, journalist, artist; b. Denver, Jan. 27, 1946; d. Robert Benjamin and Frances Mildred (Wolfe) B.; m. Gary Paul Zimmerman, Jul. 5, 1985; 1 child, Katherine. BA, East Carolina Univ., 1972. Columnist Keynoter, Fla., 1996—; freelance, 1988—; editor Fgn. Broadcast Info. Svc., 1994-95; weekly arts columnist Solares Hill Newspaper, Key West, 1988—96. Ptnr., sec. Guild Hall Gallery, 1987-98; adminstrv. asst., vol. coord. Durham Arts Coun., 1975-76; ind. tchr. painting at Images Art Camp, East Martello Mus., Key West, 1996-97; taught painting and drawing classes, 1991—; tchr. painting Audubon Ho. & Gardens Mus., Key West, 2000—. Author: Lizard Licks: A Comic History of Key West, 2003; invented Lizard Licks, 1979, founder Key West Plein Air Painters, 2002. Coord. Fantasy Fest Parade, 1995—, Chicken Fest Key West Parade, 2004, 05; founded Pathfinders Bicycle Advocacy Group, 1992, Key West, coord. Street Arts Fair, Hemingway Days St Fair, 1994; bd. dirs. Waterfront Playhouse, Last Stand Environ. Group, Montessori Children's Sch., 1991-96. Named Mem. of Yr., Last Stand Environ. Group Key West Cultural Preservation Soc., 1995, Artist of Yr., 1985; recipient Non-Fiction award Am. PEN Women, 2002. Mem. Am. Mensa. Home and Office: PO Box 1844 Key West FL 33041-1844

BRADFORD, LOUISE MATHILDE, social work administrator; b. Alexandria, La., Aug. 3, 1925; d. Henry Aaron and Ruby (Pearson) B. BS, La. Poly. Inst., 1945; cert. in social work, La. State U., 1949; MS, Columbia U., 1953; postgrad., Tulane U., 1962, 64, La. State U., 1967; cert., U. Pa., 1966. Diplomate NASW, Am. Bd. Clin. Social Work; cert. social worker Acad. Cert. Social Workers; La. Bd. Approved Clin. Suprs. With La. Dept. Pub. Welfare, Alexandria, 1945-78, welfare caseworker, 1950-53, children's case supr., 1957-59, child welfare cons., 1959-73, social svcs. cons., 1973-78, state cons. day care, 1963-66; dir. social svcs. St. Mary's Tng. Sch., Alexandria, 1978-2000; adoption splst. Vols. of Am., 2000—. Del. Nat. Day Care Conf., Washington, 1964; mem. early childhood edn. com. So. States Work Conf., Daytona Beach, Fla., 1968; mem. La. adv. com. 1970 White House Conf. on Children, also del.; mem. So. region planning com. Child Welfare League Am., 1970-73; mem. profl. adv. com. Cenla chpt. Parents Without Partners, 1970-95; adj. asst. prof. sociology La. Coll. Pineville, 1969-85; lectr. Kindergarten Workshop, 1970-72; mem. La. 4-C Steering Com.; social svcs. cons. La. Spl. Edn. Ctr., Alexandria, 1980-86; del. Internat. Conf. on Social Welfare, Nairobi, 1974, Jerusalem, 1978, Hong Kong, 1980, Brighton, 1982, Montreal, 1984; del. White House Conf. on Children. Bd. dirs. Cenla Cmty. Action Com., Alexandria, 1966-68; mem. kindergarten bd. Meth. Ch., 1967-87, ofcl. bd., 1974-75, 77-81, 83-85, 96-98, 2000-03. Recipient Social Worker of Yr. award, Alexandria br. NASW La. Conf. Social Welfare, 1974, Lifetime Achievement award, La. Chpt. Nat. Assn. of Social Workers, 2003. Mem.: DAR, NASW (Lifetime Achievement award, La. chpt. 2003), Ctrl. La. Pre-Sch. Assn. (dir. 1967—70), Am. Assn. on Mental Retardation (La. social work chair 1989—94, Meritorious Contbn. award 1999, La. chpt. Svc. award 2001, Region V Svc. award 2001), Internat. Coun. on Social Welfare, La. Conf. Social Welfare (George Freeman award 1987, Hilda C. Simon award 1987), So. La. Assn. Children Under Six, Acad. Cert. Social Workers, Alexandria Golf and Country Club, Lions.

BRADFORD, MARIAH, elementary school educator, consultant; b. Bay Springs, Miss., Sept. 23, 1929; d. Glasco Hunter Bender and Georgianna Holloway; m. Demond Bradford, Sr., Apr. 15, 1960 (div. Sept. 1984); children: Anita, Demond Jr., Kelvin. BS in Home Econs., Jackson Coll., 1953; MS in Edn., Ind. U., 1973; LHD (hon.), Martin U., 1994. Cert. tchr. Miss., 1953, Ind., 1962, Ariz., 1997. Tchr. Scott County Pub. Schs., Forest, Miss., 1953—57, Meridian (Miss.) Mcpl. Separate Schs., 1957, 1959—61; county ext. agent Coop. Ext. Dept., Kosciusko, Miss., 1958—59; tchr. Ind. Pub. Schs., Indpls., 1963—92; sub. tchr. Peoria and Dysart Unified Schs., Peoria, El Mirage, Ariz., 1997—. Sec., bd. dirs. Martin U., Indpls., 1989—94; mem. bd. dirs. Indpls. Edn. Assn., 1970—78; mem. desegregation task force Ind. State Tchrs. Assn., Indpls., 1975—80. Contbr. poems to literary pubs. and jours. (Editors' Choice award, 1996). Commr. Planning and Zoning, Surprise, Ariz., 1997—99; big sister Big Brothers/Big Sister, Indpls. and Phoenix, 1987—; supt. Sunday sch. Gideon Missionary Bapt. Ch. Recipient Sagamore of the Wabash, State of Ind., Gov. Evan Bayh, 1994, Golden Apple award, Indpls. Power and Light Co. and Cmty. Leaders Allied for Superior Schs., 1992, Special Human Rights award, Indpls. Edn. Assn. Human Rights Com., 1993, Human Rights award, Indpls. Edn. Assn., 1983; grantee, Indpls. Pub. Schs. Found., 1986, DePauw U. and Dept. of Health Edn. and Welfare, 1977. Mem.: NAACP (life), Assn. Negro Bus. and Profl. Women's Clubs (founder, pres. Madame Walker chpt. 1979—89, Sojourner Truth award 1982), Ch. Nurses Auxiliary (first v.p., nat. missionary Bapt. Conv. Am., Svc. award 1998), Zion Rest Dist. Ch. Nurses Auxiliary (cons.), Household of Ruth (#6851, Grand United Order of Oddfellows). Democrat. Baptist. Avocations: writing, reading, travel, volunteering, sewing. Home: 18019 N 145th Dr Surprise AZ 85374-4222 Personal E-mail: bradfordsurp@aol.com.

BRADFORD, MARY ROSEN, lawyer; b. Chgo. d. Ralph John and Joan (McMahon) Rosen; m. William H. Bradford; children: Jennifer, Lillian. BA, U. Md.; MS in Mgmt., Stanford U., 1980; JD, Georgetown U., 1982. Bar: D.C. Pk. ranger Nat. Pk. Svc., Md., Calif., Washington, atty.; spl. asst. Dept. Interior, Washington; dep. regional dir. Nat. Pk. Svc., Santa Fe, assoc. dir., CFO Washington; prin. Cardinal Strategies, Washington. Adv. bd. Stanford U., Stanford, Calif.; dir. Ea. Nat., Pa., Global Govt. Strategies, Washington. Co-founder Hands Across the Pks., Md.; co-chair Long Br. Revitalization Task Force, Silver Spring, Md.; dir. parks Montgomery County, Nat. Capital Park and Planning Commn., Md.

BRADFORD, SUSAN ANNE, management consultant, writer; b. Pasadena, Calif., Dec. 2, 1969; d. Wesley Gene and Nancy Cornelia (Dixon) B. Student, Coll. Cevenol, 1985, St. Andrews U., 1989—90; BA in English, U. Calif., Irvine, 1992; MA in Internat. Rels., Essex U., 1996, postgrad. Editor-in-chief Gandalf's Gazette, Irvine, 1987—88; news editor New Univ., Irvine, 1987—88; intern Sta. CBS-TV News, L.A., 1989; host, exec. prodr. Witness the News TV show, Irvine, 1990—92; prodn. asst. PBS Red Car Film Project, L.A., 1982—83; intern in news writing Sta. KNX News, L.A., 1993; reporter City News Svc., L.A., 1994—95; founder/editor European Rev., 1995—98; coord. VA media outreach Kerry-Edwards Presdl. Campaign, 2004; prin., owner Bradford Consulting, 2005—. Sr. rsch. fellow, polit. cons., councillor Atlantic Coun. U.K., 1996—2002; speechwriter U.K. Shadow Fgn. Sec. Michael Howard, 1998; prodr. Fox News Channel, 2000; speechwriter Korean Amb. Sung Chul Yang, 2002—03; Va. pub. rels. dir. Clark presdl. campaign, 2003—04; cons., 2005; pres., CEO Bradford Con., 2005—; columnist Palos Verdes Peninsula News. Author poems; contbr. articles to profl. jours. Mem., spkr., media liaison UN Assn., 2000—; mem. adv. com. NATO U., 1996—99. Recipient Writing awards Palos Verdes Nat. Bank, 1987, AFL-CIO, 1987, 3d Pl. award Nat. Fedn. Press Women, 1992. Mem. Calif. Press Women (pub. rels. chair 1991-92), Hollywood Women's Press Club (bd. dirs. 1989-94, bd. dirs. Scholarship Found., 1992-93), European Movement (com., London strategy group media coord. 1995-98), Irvine Women's Crew (founder, pres.), English Speaking Union, Federalist Soc. (internat. law com.), UN Assn. (media cons., spkr., writer), Creative Coalition, Federalist Soc. Mem. United Ch. Of Christ. Office Phone: 705-536-1413. Personal E-mail: susanbradford7@aol.com. Business E-Mail: susan@susanbradford.info.

BRADLEY, ANN WALSH, state supreme court justice; b. Richland Center, Wis. married; 4 children. BA, Webster Coll., 1972; JD, U. Wis., 1976. Former high school tchr.; atty. priv. practice, 1976—85; judge Marathon County Circuit Ct., Wausau, Wis., 1985—95; justice Wis. Supreme Ct., Madison, Wis., 1995—. Former assoc. dean and faculty mem. Wis. Judicial Coll.; former chair Wis. Jud. Conference; lecturer ABA Asia Law Initiative; commr. Nat. Conference on Uniform Laws. Bd. of visitors U. Wis. Law Sch. Fellow: Am. Bar Found.; mem.: ABA, State Bar of Wis. (Bench Bar Com.), Am. Law Inst., Am. Judicature Soc. (Harley award 2004). Office: Wis Supreme Ct PO Box 1688 Madison WI 53701-1688*

BRADLEY, BARBRA BAILEY, musician, educator, accompanist; b. Windsor, Ont., Can., Dec. 27, 1944; d. Charles David Bailey and Mary Alice Calow; m. Joseph Patrick Bradley, Sept. 19, 1981. BA in Honours Music Edn., U. Western Ont., London, Can., 1967; A of Music in Piano, West. Ont. Conservatory Music, London, 1967; MM in Piano, Ind. U., 1969. Freelance performer, adjudicator, 1974-81; tchr. piano, performer Brigham Young U., Provo, Utah, 1973-74; accompanist concert tour Mu Phi Epsilon Found., various cities, 1974-76; tchr. piano, performer St. Clair divsn. Royal Hamilton Coll. Music, Windsor, Ont., 1975-79; tchr. piano, performer music dept. St. Clair Coll., Windsor, 1979-81; freelance performer piano and harp Washington, 1981—; tchr. piano, performer Leidzen Sch. Music, Fairfax, Va., 1987-88, Nat. Cathedral Sch., Washington, 1988—. Composer (music for children's theater): Cricket on the Hearth, 1989, Goldilocks and the Christmas Bears, 1991. Doctoral fellowship for grad. study Ind. U., Can. Coun., 1970. Mem.: Am. Fedn. Musicians, Internat. Soc. of Folk Harpers and Craftsmen, Am. Harp Soc., Fri. Morning Music Club (chamber music performer 1986—), Mu Phi Epsilon (pres. Washington alumni chpt. 1990—94, dist. dir. Atlantic-2 dist. 1994—96, internat. officer, alumni advisor 1996—2003, Sterling Staff Internat. Competition winner 1974). Mem. Lds Ch. Avocations: ballet, photography, walking, genealogy. Office: Nat Cathedral Sch Mount St Albans Washington DC 20016 E-mail: barbra_bradley@cathedral.org.

BRADLEY, BECKY SUE, music educator; d. Francis and Joyce Jamison; m. Jon Bradley, June 10, 1978; children: Christine Eckhardt, Thomas, Nathan. B of Music Edn. K-12 and Elem. Edn., U. of Denver, 1978; M in Creative Arts, Lesley U., Cambridge, Mass., 2004. Tchr. Colo. Dept. of Edn. Music tchr. Jefferson County Pub. Schs., Lakewood, Colo., 1979—. Pvt. voice tchr., Lakewood, 1978—; chorister Opera Colo., Denver, 1982—. Named Opera Colo. Educator of the Yr., Opera Colo., 2002; recipient Cen. City Opera Educator award, Cen. City Opera, 2002, My Tchr., My Hero award, Jefferson Found., 2006. Mem.: Music Educators Nat. Conf. (assoc.). Office Phone: 303-982-8324.

BRADLEY, BETSY, museum director; BA, Millsaps Coll.; MA in English, Vanderbilt U. Dep. dir. and cmty. arts dir. Miss. Arts Commn., exec. dir., 1995—2001, Miss. Mus. Art, Jackson, 2001—. Bd. mem. Nat. Assembly of State Arts Agencies; panelist Nat. Endowment for Arts; adv. panel mem. Miss. Sch. Arts. Pres. Miss. Ctr. for Nonprofits. Named one of Top 50 Bus. Women, Miss. Bus. Jour. Office: Miss Mus Art 201 E Pascagoula St Jackson MS 39201 E-mail: mmart@netdoor.com.

BRADLEY, BETTY HUNT, psychologist, consultant; b. Oelwein, Iowa, Dec. 17, 1932; d. Hollis Nelson and Mildred (Wilkins) Hunt; m. Ray P. Bradley, Apr. 21, 1962 (dec. May 1995); 1 child, Teresa Bradley Taylor. BA, Coe Coll., 1954; MA, Ohio State U., 1955. Licensed psychologist, Ohio. Psychologist Columbus (Ohio) Devel. Ctr., 1954-94, Overbrook Clinic, Columbus, 1994—. Co-author Teaching Moderately and Severely Retarded Children, 1971; contbr. articles to profl. jours. Mem. Cat Welfare Soc., Columbus, Columbus Zoo. Mem. Phi Kappa Phi, Phi Beta Kappa. Methodist. Avocation: collecting postcards. Home: 90 E Henderson Rd Columbus OH 43214-2742 Office: Overbrook Clinic 4100 N High St Columbus OH 43214-3252 Office Phone: 614-263-2113. Personal E-mail: bbetty857@aol.com.

BRADLEY, BONITA MAE, psychotherapist; b. Chgo., Oct. 20, 1949; d. Joseph Eric and Janell (Wimer) Barfuss; B.A. with high honors, U. Mich., 1971, MA in COunseling Psychology Framing State Coll.; Ed.M. in Counselor Edn., Lesley Coll., 1977; m. James W. Bradley, Jan. 12, 1974; 1 dau., Aurea Mae. Adminstr., Boston VA Hosp., 1971; clin. research technician Children's Hosp. Med. Center, Boston, 1972-76; counselor Lesley Schs. for Children, Cambridge, Mass., 1976-77; guidance counselor Douglas Sch., Acton, Mass., 1976-77; group and individual psychotherapist Charles River Hosp., Wellesley, Mass., 1977-80; pvt. practice group and individual psychotherapy, West Newton and Marlboro, Mass., 1980—; cons. juvenile diversion program Norfolk County Dist. Atty.'s Office. Lic. cert. social worker; Contbr. article in field to sci. publ. Home and Office: 363 Millham St Marlborough MA 01752-1028

BRADLEY, CAROL ANN, nursing consultant, editor; b. Genoa, Nebr., July 7, 1953; d. John Martin and Marguerite (Leonard) Brower; m. Jonathan R. Bradley, Nov. 30, 1985; children: Amanda, Emma. Assoc. Nursing, U. Nebr., Omaha, 1974, BSN, 1977; MSN, U. Ariz., 1978. Staff charge nurse U. Nebr., Omaha, 1974—77; mem. faculty, staff nurse U. Ariz., Tucson, 1977—78; clin. nurse specialist VA, San Diego, 1978—80; dir. nursing med. Good Samaritan Med. Ctr., Phoenix, 1980—85; v.p. patient care United Western Med. Ctr., Santa Ana, Calif., 1986—87; chief nursing officer Rancho Los Amigos Med. Ctr., Downey, Calif., 1987—92; v.p. patient care svcs. Huntington Meml. Hosp., Pasadena, Calif., 1992—99; regional v.p./editor Nurseweek Pub. Co., Sunnyvale, Calif., 2000—03; prin., owner Careforce Consulting Group, S. Pasadena, Calif., 1999—; faculty The Governance Inst., LaJolla, Calif.; regional CNO Tenet Healthcare, Inc., 2003—. Contbr. articles to profl. jours. Wharton/J & J fellow, 1991. Mem. Am. Orgn. Nurse Execs. (bd. dirs. 1994-97, chmn. edn. comm., pres. elect 1998, pres. 1999), Assn. Calif. Nurse Leaders (bd. dirs. 1988-90, sec. 1990-92, pres. 1992). Democrat. E-mail: cabradley7753@msn.com.

BRADLEY, CHRISTINE OWEN, secondary school educator; b. Indpls., Oct. 29, 1957; d. Donald McPhail and Rillah Jean Owen; m. Glenn Harvey Bradley, June 26, 1982; children: Colin James, Owen Patrick. BA, U. Va., Charlottesville, 1980; MA in Humanities, Pa. State U., Harrisburg, 1992. Tchr. English Elizabethtown Area HS, Pa., 1986—. Violinist Hershey Symphony Orch., Pa., 1986—2006. Mem.: Nat. Coun. Tchrs. English. Office: Elizabethtown Area HS 600 E High St Elizabethtown PA 17022 Personal E-mail: chris_bradley@etown.k12.pa.us.

BRADLEY, DEBORAH J., music educator; b. Frankfurt, Germany, Nov. 28, 1953; d. Chelse A. and Rose M. Bradley. B in Music Edn., Troy (Ala.) State U., 1975, MS in Edn., 1977, specialist degree in edn., 1999. Band dir. Clarke County H.S., Grove Hill, Ala., 1975—76; music sales rep. Art's Music Shop, Inc., Dothan, Ala., 1976—77; band dir. Calhoun County H.S., Edison, Ga., 1977—78, Valdosta (Ga.) Jr. H.S., 1978—88; asst. dir. Valdosta H.S. band, 1978—88; band dir., music dir. Patrick Henry State Jr. Coll., Monroeville, Ala., 1988—90; band dir. Clarke Ctrl. H.S., Athens, Ga., 1990—91, Max Bruner Jr. Mid. Sch., Ft. Walton Beach, Fla., 1991—92, Cook H.S., Adel, Ga., 1992—2004, Lowndes Mid. Sch., 2004—; asst. dir. Ga. Bridgemen Lowndes H.S., Valdosta, Ga. Honor band chmn. Sousa Found., 2003. Alumni pres. Sound of the South Alumni Band. Named Tchr. of Yr., Cook H.S. and Cook County, 2000; named to Sudler Order of Merit, John Philip Sousa Found., 1984. Mem.: Ga. Music Educators Assn. (dist. 8), Women Band Dirs. Internat. (indsl. chmn. 1975—2001, pres. elect 2004, pres. 2005, Silver Baton award 2003), Alumni Assn. South Ga. Troy State U. (pres. 1986—2001), Tau Beta Sigma (charter pres. Tau Beta Sigma chpt., regional dir. John Philip Sousa Jr. Hons. Band, Outstanding Svc. to Music award 2000). Avocations: travel, volleyball, tennis, bowling, golf. Personal E-mail: booradlee@ureach.com.

BRADLEY, DEIDRA D., elementary school educator; d. Willene A. Denis and Lester John Denis Sr.; m. Felton Thomas Bradley Jr.; children: Jyron Howard Gautreaux, Tahj Julien, Shelby Olivia. BA in Elem. Edn., So. U. New Orleans, 1995. Tchr. New Orleans Pub. Schs., New Orleans, 1996—2003, St. Tammany Pub. Schs., Slidell, 2003—05. Tchr. Dekalb County Schs., Decatur, Ga., 2005.

BRADLEY, DONDEENA G., consumer products company executive; b. Dec. 28, 1964; m. Allen Bradley; children: Madison, Keaton. Prin. Health Bus. Partners Consulting; founder Conceptual Ventures; dir., applied innovation and strategy McNeil Nutritional, LLC, a Johnson & Johnson Co., New Brunswick, NJ. Mem. editl. bd. Nutraceuticals World. Named one of 25 Masters of Innovation, BusinessWeek. Office: McNeil Nutriotionals LLC 501 George St New Brunswick NJ 08903 Business E-Mail: dbradley1@mcnus.jnj.com.*

BRADLEY, JANICE JEANENNE, retired medical technician; b. Decatur, Ill., June 17, 1938; d. George Alfred and Hazel Bernice (Nie Toll) Smith; m. Robert Ellison Bradley, Dec. 26, 1964; children: Shayne Guylaine, Craig Andre, Blayne Pierre. BS, Fresno State Coll., Calif., 1960, postgrad., 1963; diploma in edn. for ministry, U. of the South, Tenn., 1994. Lic. med. technologist Calif. Med. technologist Fresno VA Hosp., Calif., 1960—63; radioisotope technologist San Francisco Gen. Hosp., 1963; med. technologist Project Hope Ship, Guyaquil, Ecuador, 1963—64, Pvt. Lab., San Luis Crispo, Calif., 1964—65, Anglican Ch. of Can., Kangra, India, 1965—67; cmty. activist, vol. Dadgriga, Belize, 1977—. Rsch. technologist Fresno VA Hosp., Calif., 1962—63. Author: (syllabus) Radioisotope Laboratory Syllabus, 1962. Sec. Battle Ground Soccer Club, Wash., 1979; den mother, advisor Cub and Boy Scouts, Wash., 1980—90; pres., treas. Parent Tchr. Student Assn., Wash., 1982; treas. Clark County Med. Alliance, Vancouver, Wash., 1982; meet offcl. Jr. Olympics and Hershy Track, Oreg., 1983—90; treas. Clark County Young Audiences, Vancouver, Wash., 1983; vol. Friends In Svc. to Humanity, Vancouver, Wash., 1996—; bible study leader Ch. of Holy Spirit, 2005—, lic. eucharistic minister, 1989—. Mem.: Christian Prison Ministry, Christian Ministry. Episcopal. Avocations: genealogy, bridge, travel, running, weightlifting. Personal E-mail: janbrad44@aol.com.

BRADLEY, JEAN IRENE, elementary school educator; d. Lawrence Carl and Mildred Eleanora Stuehringer; m. Danforth Tremain Bradley, Dec. 31, 1977. BS Edn., Cleve. State U., 1966, MS Edn., 1970; post grad., U. Pitts., 1970—72. Tchr. math Bonita Mid. Sch., Bonita Springs, Fla., 1989—96, Gulf Mid. Sch., Cape Coral, Fla., 1983—89, 1996—. Mem. budget com. Gulf Mid. Sch., Cape Coral, 1996—, mem. sch. leadership com., 1996—, facilitator focus group, 2005—, leader 7th grade team, 2005—, coach math team, 1988—89; mem. sch. steering com. Bonita Mid. Sch., Bonita Springs, 1989—96, mem. budget & curriculum committees, 1989—96. Migrant tutor Lee County Schs., Ft. Myers, Fla., 1990—93, mentor drop out prevention program, 1997—2000. Nominee Golden Apple Tchr. Recognition award, Student Nominations, 1995—2006; named Mid. Sch. Math. Tchr. of Yr., Lee County Math. Coun., 1999. Mem.: Tchrs. Assn. Lee County (sch. rep. 1983—2006), Lee Sci. Edn. Assn., Fla. Coun. Tchrs. Math., Lee County Math Coun. Avocations: sudoku, crossword puzzles. Home: 1446 Medoc Lane Fort Myers FL 33919 Office: Gulf Middle Sch 1809 SW 36th Ter Cape Coral FL 33914 Personal E-mail: dtbdl@earthlink.net.

BRADLEY, JENNETTE B., state official, former lieutenant governor; b. Oct. 2, 1952; m. Michael C. Taylor. BA in Psychology, Wittenberg U. Lic. registered rep. Nat. Assn. Securitites Dealers. Exec. dir. Columbus Met. Housing Authority; sr. v.p. pub. fin. banker Kemper Securities; sr. v.p., pub. funds mgr. Huntington Nat. Bank; councilwoman Columbus (Ohio) City Coun., 1991—2002, chair parks and recreation com., chair utilities and energy generation coms., chair safety com., mem. safety and judiciary com., mem. adminstrn. com., mem. recreation and parks com., mem. health, housing and human svcs. com., mem. zoning com.; lt. gov. State of OH, 2003—05, treas., 2005—; dir. OH Dept. Commerce, 2003—05. Mem. fin., adminstrn. and intergovernmental rels. steering and policy coms. Nat. League Cities. Grad. Leadership Columbus; trustee Wittenberg U.; bd. mem., former chair Joint Columbus and Franklin County Housing Adv. Bd. Recipient Woman of Achievement award, YWCA. Republican. Office: OH Dept Treasury 30 E Broad St 9th Fl Columbus OH 43215*

BRADLEY, MARILYNNE GAIL, advertising executive, educator; b. Rockford, Ill., Apr. 12, 1938; d. Sherwin S. and Lillian (Leopold) Gersten; m. Charles S. Bradley, 1959 (div. Feb., 1994); children: Suzanne, Scott. BFA, Washington U., 1960; MAT, Webster U., St. Louis, 1975; MFA, Syracuse U., 1981; postgrad., St. Louis Tchrs. Acad., 1990. With Essayons Studio, St. Louis, 1968-69; tchr. Webster Groves (Mo.) H.S., 1970-98; instr. Webster Univ., Webster Groves, 1973-82, 97—, supr., 2002—; instr. U. Mo., 1980—, St. Louis U., 1978-99, Washington U., St. Louis, 1984-87. Sec. Mo. Art Edn., State of Mo., 1986-87; mem. Tchrs. Acad. 1990-92. Author, illustrator: Arpens and Acres, 1976, Packets on Parade, 1980, illustrator: St. Louis Silhouettes, 1977; editor: (videos) 12 Water Color Lessons, 1987, Techniques of American Watercolor, 1990, The Santa Fe Trail Series, 1993, Over Gauguin's Shoulder, 1994, Aboriginal Art Techniques, 1994, City of Century Homes, 1995, Australian Dreamings, 1996, Aboriginal Art - Past, Present and Future, 1996, Drawing and Painting Techniques, 1997, Line, Shape, Value, 1998, Molas, Snip and Sew: The Kuna Indians, Molas: Panamanian Traditions, 1999, The Katy Trail Series, 2000, Art Along the Katy Trail, 2000, Apre's Paris, 2001, Lewis and Clark Trail, 2001, It's Somewhere in St. Louis, 2002, St. Louis World's Fair, 2004, The Mathematics of Moorish Mosaics, 2004, Sidewalks of St. Louis, 2005. Bd. govs. Webster Groves Hist. Soc., 1965-72, 94—; mem. St. Louis Philharm. Soc., 1956-72; commr. City of Webster Groves, 1995—; co-chair Hist. Preservation Com., 2002, v.p., 2002—; active Arts Commn., 2005—. Named Tchr. of Yr., 1987, Best of Show, Mo. Watercolor Soc., 2000, Educator of Yr. award, 2006. Mem.: Mo. Watercolor Soc. (bd. mem. 2001—), St. Louis Artist Guild (sec. 1985—86, pres. 1989—92, v.p. pres.'s coun. 1995—, treas. 2004, Disting. Woman 1987), St. Louis Woman Artists, So. Watercolor Soc. (life; sec. 1978—80, v.p. 2002—04, pres. 2004—, chair 26th ann. exhibit, chair 28th ann. exhibit, Silver Brush award, Exceptional Salute to the Masters award), Monday Club (chmn. 1979—83). Avocations: music, art, travel. Home and Office: Bradley & Assocs 817 S Gore Ave Saint Louis MO 63119-4023 Office Phone: 314-968-1439. Personal E-mail: mgbrad@aol.com.

BRADLEY, MARY RENEE, research analyst; b. Charleston, S.C., Mar. 11, 1964; d. William Philip and Mary Dalby (Hair) B. BA, Coll. of Charleston, 1986, M in Edn., 1990; PhD, U. S.C., 1999. Spl. edn. tchr. Charleston (S.C.) County Schs., 1986-94; rsch. asst. U. S.C. Policy Ctr., Columbia, 1994-95; clin. instr. U S.C., Columbia, 1995-97; rsch. analyst Dept. of Spl. Edn., Washington, 1997—99; spl. asst. dir. rsch. to practice U.S. Office of Spl. Edn. Programs, Washington, 1999—. Cons. Ednl. Cons. Tng., Columbia, 1988-97, Coun. for Children with Behavior Disorders S.E. Coord., 1994-97. Contbr. articles to profl. jours. Mem.: ASCD, Coun. for Children with Behavior Disorders (divsn. learning disabilities, divsn. of rsch.), Coun. for Exceptional Children, Phi Delta Kappa. Episcopalian. Avocations: equestrian sports, jack russell terriers, gardening. Home: 8310 Geller Cir Manassas VA 20112-3163 Office: U S Office Of Spl Edn 400 Maryland Ave SW Washington DC 20202-0001 Office Phone: 202-245-7277. Business E-Mail: renee.bradley@ed.gov.

BRADLEY, NANCY ELIZABETH, elementary school educator; b. Madrid, Jan. 13, 1961; d. Wayne Wendell and Marian Elizabeth Cox; m. Dewayne Lyle Bradley, June 5, 1981; children: Scott Dewayne, Stephanie Elizabeth. BA in History/Edn., U. Ctrl. Okla., Edmond, 1983. Cert. elem. tchr. Okla., 1983. Tchr. grade 3 Mid-Del Pub. Schs., Midwest City, Okla., 1996—98; tchr. grade 5 Holly Creek Schs., Broken Bow, Okla., 1998—2000, Broken Bow Pub. Schs., 2000—02; tchr. grade 7 Chickasha Pub. Schs., Okla., 2002—06; tchr. grades 6, 7, and 8 Calumet Pub. Schs., Okla., 2006—. Asst. softball coach Chickasha Pub. Schs., 2002—06, asst. girls basketball coach, 2004—05. Grantee, Chickasha Pub. Schs. Found., 2002—04. Mem.: NEA (assoc.), Okla. Ednl. Assn. (assoc.; rep. 2001—02). Liberal. Avocations: travel, sports. Home: PO Box 261 Calumet OK 73014 Office: Calumet Public Schools 110 N Freehome Calumet OK 73014 Office Phone: 405-893-2222. Office Fax: 405-893-8019.

BRADLEY, NANCY LOVETT, retired medical and surgical nurse, administrator; b. Woonsocket, R.I., Jan. 30, 1937; d. Harold D. Sr. and Rena M. (Daigle) Gould; m. Joseph F. Bradley, Feb. 4, 1961; children: Joseph F., Naomiruth, Joellen, Johnna, Nobilee, Nannette, Nadine. Diploma, David Hale Fanning Sch., Worcester, Mass., 1978; ADN, Community Coll. R.I., Lincoln, 1983; BSN, Framingham State Coll., 1992. Cert. med.-surg. nurse, CPR instr., gerontol. nurse, diabetic instr. LPN, primary staff nurse Milford (Mass.)-Whitinsville Regional Hosp., 1978-83, RN, 1983-89; asst. nurse mgr. Landmark Med. Ctr., Woonsocket, 1989—. Chmn. profl. edn. Am. Cancer Soc; mem. bd. Aging Public Safety Bldg. Comm., Mass., bd. educators Tri Valley Inc. Mem. Nat. Gerontol. Nursing Assn., R.I. Coun. Nurse Mgrs. Home: 28 Maple St Mendon MA 01756-1247

BRADLEY, PATRICIA ELLEN, professional golfer; b. Arlington, Mass., Mar. 24, 1951; d. Richard Joseph and Kathleen Maureen (O'Brien) B. Assoc. in Phys. Edn, Miami-Dade North Jr. Coll., 1971; BS, Fla. Internat. U., 1974. Mem. Sun-Star Japan-U.S. Team Matches, 1975-76, All-Am. Collegiate Team, 1971, U.S.A. Com., 1974, 76, Golf Mag.'s All Am. Team, 1976, 77-78, 79-81; qualified for Colgate Triple Crown Tournament, 1975, 76, 77, 78. Staff mem. Dunlop Golf Co.; under contract with Nabisco. Winner N.H. Womens Amateur Championship, 1967, 69, Fla. Collegiate Championship, 1970, Mass. Womens Amateur Championship, 1972, New Eng. Amateur Championship, 1972, 73, Colgate Far East Tournament, 1975, Girl Talk Classic Tournament, 1976, Bankers Trust Classic Tournament, 1977, Lady Keystone Open, Hoosier Classic, Rail Charity Classic, 1978, 91, J.C. Penny Classic, 1978, 89, Balt. Classic, Peter Jackson Classic, 1980, U.S. Womens Open, 1981, Du Maurier Classic, 1985, LPGA Pro-Am, 1985, Rochester Invitational, 1985, Turquoise Classic, 1990, Centel Classic, 1991, Safeco Classic, 1991, MBS Classic, 1991, HEALTHSOUTH Inaugural, 1995; recipient Most Improved Player award Golf Digest, 1976; named Player of Yr., 1986, Mazda Series, 1986, Vare Trophy, 1986; named to Ladies Profl. Golf Hall of Fame, 1991; mem. U.S. Solheim Cup Team, 1990, 92, 96, named capt., 2000; named on of the LPGA's top 50 players all-time, 2000. Mem. Ladies Profl. Golf Assn. Roman Catholic. Achievements include playing exhbn. golf match with Pres. Ford, Vail, Colo., 1976; first woman golfer to win all four USGA Womens Open, LPGA Championship, Du Maurier Classic and Nabisco/Dinah Shore Tournaments; leading money winner PGA, 1986, 91.

BRADLEY, PAULA E., former state legislator; b. New Haven, Oct. 11, 1924; d. Richard Travis and Harriett (Bogenhagen) Elliott; m. William L. Bradley, 1947; children: James R. Choukas-Bradley, Dwight C., Paul W. BA, Hiram Coll., 1945; postgrad., Middlebury Coll., 1946, Hartford Seminary, 1963-64. Ret. rsch. assoc. univ. devel. Yale U.; mem. N.H. Ho. of Reps., 1992—98, 2000—02. Treas. Coos County Dem. Com., 1992—, Randolph Dem. Party, 1992—2004; chair bd. adjustment Town of Randolph, 2000—01, mem. planning bd., 2003—06; mem. Gorham (N.H.) Congregational Ch.; bd. dirs. Coos County Family Health Svcs., Berlin, NH, 1993—2001, 2004—06, Weeks Meml. Hosp., Lancaster, NH, 1993—95, No. Forest Heritage Park, Berlin, NH, 2001—, No. Country Coun., 2003—06. Mem.: Randolph Mountain Club (bd. dirs. 1986—91, treas. 1989—91, bd. dirs. 1992—97, pres. 1995—96). Democrat. Avocations: walking, gardening, choral singing. Office: # 324 149 East Side Dr Concord NH 03301

BRADLEY, VANESSA LYNN, management consultant; b. Saginaw, Mich., Apr. 8, 1967; BS in Indsl. Engring., Northwestern U., 1989; MBA, U Pa., 1993. Project engr. Gen. Motors Corp., 1989—91; project cons. Ctr. for Applied Rsch., 1992—93; v.p. Bradley Automotive Group, Ann Arbor, Mich., 1996—98; prin. A.T. Kearney, Inc., Chgo., 1993—96, 1998—. Bd. trustees Sherwood Conservatory of Music, Chgo., Providence St. Mel Coll. Prep. Sch., Chgo. Mem.: NAFE, Northwestern Alumni Club of Chgo. Office: AT Kearney Inc 222 W Adams St Chicago IL 60606 Office Phone: 312-961-1219. E-mail: vanbrad67@aol.com.

BRADLEY, WANDA LOUISE, librarian; b. Havre de Grace, Md., June 6, 1953; d. William Smith and Josephine Viola (Miller) B. BA, U. Md., 1975; MSLS, Atlanta U., 1976; postgrad., Cath. U.; MPA (scholar), U. Balt., 1986. Libr. Harford County Pub. Libr., Bel Air, Md., 1976, Harford County Bd. Edn., Bel Air, Md., 1977-81, Nat. Grad. U., Arlington, Va., 1982, Md. State Dept. Edn., Balt., 1982-83, U.S. Dept. Labor, Washington, 1984, Balt. Gas and Electric Co., 1984-85, Morgan State U., Balt., 1985, Coppin State Coll., Balt., 1985-86, Montgomery County Pub. Sch. System, Rockville, Md., 1985-86, Community Coll., Balt., 1987-88; grant adminstr. Howard County Pub. Libr., 1988; libr., media specialist Balt. City Pub. Sch. System, 1992—. Acad. advisor George Mason U., Fairfax, Va., 1981-82. Dept. Edn. fellow, 1983-84; U. Balt. Merit scholar, 1984, Atlanta U. scholar, 1976, U. Md. scholar, 1971; Howard County Pub. Libr. grantee, 1988. Mem. ALA, ASIS, Md. Libr. Assn., Spl. Librs. Assn., Med. Libr. Assn. Methodist. Office: Diggs Johnson Mid Sch 1300 Herkimer St Baltimore MD 21217 Office Phone: 410-396-8700.

BRADLEY GARDNER, JANICE, federal agency administrator; BA, Wake Forest U.; MA, American U. Econ. officer U.S. Embassy to Japan, 1990—92; br. chief Persian Gulf Office Leadership Analysis, 1993—95; dir. ctrl. intelligence rep. to nat. sec. coun. Exec. Office of Pres., 1995—96; spl. advisor internat. affairs Office of V.P., 1996; chief East Asia group Fgn. Broadcast Info. Svc., dep. dir.; sr. intelligence liaison US Dept. Treasury, dep. asst. sec. intelligence and analysis, asst. sec. intelligence and analysis, 2005—. Office: Dept of Treasury 1500 Pennsylvania Ave NW Washington DC 20220 Office Phone: 202-622-1841. Office Fax: 202-622-1829.

BRADSHAW, DOVE, artist; b. NYC, Sept. 24, 1949; d. David Nelson and Jean Kathryn (Cormack) B. BFA, Boston Mus. Sch. Fine Arts, 1973. Co-artistic advisor The Merce Cunningham Dance Co., N.Y.C., 1984—. Artist in residence Pier Ctr., Orkney, Scotland, Sirius Art Ctr., Cork, Ireland, Niels Borch Jensen, Copenhagen, 1999, 2005, Statens Vaerksteder for Kunst, Copenhagen, 2000 One-man shows include Alan Stone Gallery, N.Y.C., 1979, Graham Gallery, NY, 1979, Ericson Gallery, 1982, NY Wave Hill, NY, 1983, Sandra Gering Gallery, N.Y., 1988, 89, 91, 93, 95, 98, PSI Mus., NYC, 1991, Mattress Factory Mus., Pitts., 1990, 99, Pier Ctr., Orkney, Scotland, 1995, Stalke Gallery, Copenhagen, 1995, 96, 98, 99, 2001, 03, 04, Barbara Krakow Gallery, 1997, Mus. Contemporary Art, LA, 1998, Larry Becker Contemporary Art, Phila. 2000, 05, Stark Gallery, NY, 2001, Baruch Coll., CUNY, 2003, Diferenca Gallery, Lisbon, 2003, Volume Gallery, NY, 2004, SolwayJones, L.A., 2005, Spirit of Discovery, Trancoso, Portugal, 2006, Radio Rocka, Bolognano, Italy, 2006, Gallery 360, Tokyo, 2006, Murato Factory Mus., Kochi, Japan, 2006, 6th Gwangju Biennale, Republic of Korea, 2006, Senzatitolo, Rome, 2006, others; group shows include Am. Ctr., Paris, Science Mus., Tokyo, 1982, Mus. Modern Art, NYC, 1989, Carnegie Internat., Pitts., 1991, Met. Mus. NY, 1992, Art Inst. Chgo., 1992, 96, Aldrich Mus., Ridgefield, Conn., 1993, 2004, Phila. Mus., 1993, 98, 2000, Swiss Inst., NYC, 1995, Baumgartner Gallery, Washington, 1998, Carnegie Mus. Art, 1997, Whitney Mus. Am. Art, NY, 1997, Millennium Film Theatre, 1998, Mus. Contemporary Art, LA, 1998, U. Calif., San Diego, Radio Rocks, 1999, U. Mass. Amherst, 1999, UBU Gallery, NYU, Univ. Art Mus., U. Va., Charlottsville, 2000, 05, Anastasi Bradshaw Cage Mus. Contemporary Art, Roskilde, Denmark, 2001, 04, Rooseum Contemporary Art Ctr., Malmo, Sweden, Nikolaj Contemporary Art Ctr. Copenhagen, 2002, Baruch Coll., NY, Volckers and Freunde Gallery, Berlin, Tanya Bonakdar, NY, 2003, Stalke Gallery, Copenhagen, 2004, Anastasi Bradshaw Cage Cunningham, Shering Fine Art, Berlin, 2005, Salt Mountain, 2006, Marine Maritime Mus., Staten Island, NY, others; represented in permanent collection at Met. Mus. Art, NYC, Mus. Modern Art, NYC, Bklyn. Mus. Art, Whitney Mus. Am. Art, Art Inst. Chgo., Phila. Mus. Art, Ark. Art Ctr., Little Rock, Fogg Art Mus., Cambridge, Mass., Harvard U., Getty Ctr., LA, Mus. Contemporary Art, LA, Nat. Gallery, Washington, Carnegie Mus Art, Pitts., Mattress Factory Mus., Pitts., Internat. Le Pompidou Ctr., Paris, Pier Ctr. Orkney, Scotland, Mus. Art, Bilboa, Spain, Kunst Mus., Dusseldorf, Germany, Modern Mus., Stockholm, Russian State Mus., St. Petersburg, Self Interest, 1999, Six Continents, 2003, Angles 12 Rotatiions, 2003, One of the Boys, 2004, And So And All, 2004, They were and Went, 2004, (outdoor sculpture) Material/Immaterial, 2005, (photography) One of the Boys, And So And All, Angles 12 Rotations, 2003, Radio Rocks, Bolognano, Italy, 2006; prodr., dir., artist: (film) Indeterminacy, 1995; prodr. Met. Mus. postcard, 1976, 92, Met. Mus. guerilla postcard, 1978, (outdoor sculpture) Indeterminancy, 1993, Passion, 1993, (paintings) Boundary, Full, 1991, Contingency, 1984-, others; artist, prodr. handmade books, including Plain Air (installation with live birds 1969, 88, 91, documentation 1991), 1969-91 Recipient Pollock-Krasner award, 1985; grantee Nat. Endowment Arts, 1975. Mem.: Larry Becker Contemporary Art, Phila., Ressle Fine Art, NY, Stalke Gallery, Copenhagen, Solway Jones Gallery, LA. Avocations: meditation, yoga, running, reading, gardening, landscape gardening. Home and Studio: 924 W End Ave New York NY 10025-3534 Personal E-mail: dbradshaw1@nyc.rr.com.

BRADSHAW, PHYLLIS BOWMAN, historian, historic site staff member; b. Cumberland, Ky., June 19, 1929; d. Lawrence David and Ann Rees Bowman; m. Glenn Lewis Bradshaw, June 30, 1949 (dec. Feb. 2000)); children: Charles Lewis, David Bowman. Student, Ctr. Coll., Danville, Ky., 1947-50, N.Y Sch. Speed Writing, 1967. Sec. to dir. and asst. dir. Shakertown, Pleasant Hill, Ky., 1967-68, asst. food dir., 1968-70, mus. dir. dept. interpretation, 1970-72; mus. hist. interpreter Old Fort Harrod State Pk., Harrodsburg,

Ky., 1993-98. Rschr.: book Beyond Shenandoah, 2001. Mem. Harrodsburg Hist. Soc., Ky. Hist. Soc., Girl Scouts Am., Nat. Trust, Libr. Congress, Washington; tchr. Sunday sch. Harrodsburg Presbyn. Ch.; life mem. Women's Soc., Burgin Meth. Ch., bd. dirs., tchr./leader H.S. group; pres., sec. Burgin PTA; den mother cub scouts Boy Scouts Am.; life mem. Ky. PTA, Shakertown at Pleasant Hill; founding mem. Harlan (Ky.) Musettes; active Mercer County Blood Bank; assisted in creation of The Ky. Classic Sauces-Bluegrass Trade Assn. Mem. DAR (Jane McAfee chpt.), Lewis and Clark Assn., N.W. Territory Assn., Hite Family Assn., Ky. History Tchrs. Assn., Colonial Dames Ct. of Honor (Ky. chpt.), Ctr. Coll. Alumni Assn., Lions Club. mem. Va. Hist. Soc., 2002. Home: 876 Beaumont Ave Harrodsburg KY 40330

BRADY, ADELAIDE BURKS, public relations agency executive, giftware catalog executive; b. N.Y.C., June 27, 1926; d. Earl Victor and Audrey (Calvert) Burks; m. James Francis Brady, Jr., June 22, 1946 (div. 1953); 1 child, James Francis. BS, Boston U., 194. Exec. v.p. Media Enterprises, 1952—55; dir. group rels. Save the Children Fedn., N.Y.C., 1955-59; dir. pub. affairs divsn. Girl Scouts U.S.A., N.Y.C., 1959-69; pres. Comm. Internat., Inc., Washington, 1969-73, Burks Brady Comm., Washington, 1972—, Adelaide's Angel Shopper Catalog Inc., Wilton, Conn., 1976—. Exec. v.p. Arts in Parks Inc., Washington, 1971—. Past bd. dirs. Lenox Hill Hosp., N.Y.C., Achievement Rewards for Coll. Scientists Found.; pres. Animal Lovers Inc. Decorated comdr. Order of St. John of Jerusalem (Eng.); recipient Silver Reel award for film The Children of Now, Save the Children Fedn. Mem. NAFE, NEA, AAUW, Nat. Assn. Women Bus. Owners, Pub. Rels. Soc. Am., Am. Women in Radio and TV, Nat. Ednl. Broadcasters Assn., Am. Soc. Profl. and Exec. Women, Women Execs. in Pub. Rels., N.Y. Press Women, Nat. Fedn. Press Women (state pres.),Women's Econ. Roundtable, DAR, Capitol Hill Club (Washington), Yacht and Country Club (Fla.), MDW Officers Club (Washington). Republican. Episcopalian. also: Yacht Country Club 3664 SE Fairway E Stuart FL 34997-6116 Office: 785 Park Ave New York NY 10021-3552

BRADY, CAROLE ANN, physical education teacher; b. Aransas Pass, Tex., Aug. 1, 1950; d. James Ray and Jacklyn Marie Broussard; children: Lance, Kimberly Brady Termain. BS in Edn., U. Ariz., 1972. Phys. edn. tchr. Safford (Ariz.) Unified Sch. Dist., 1990—92, 1993—97, cooperating tchr., 1995—, 4th grade tchr., 1997—99. Mem.: AAHPERD, Ariz. Profl. Educators, Ariz. Assn. Health, Phys. Edn., Recreation and Dance (pres., CEO 2005—, governing bd. 1994—97, 2000—, Elem. Phys. Edn. Tchr. of Yr. 2005). Office: Lafe Nelson Sch 734 11th St Safford AZ 85546 Office Phone: 928-348-7020. E-mail: cbrady@saffordusd.k12.az.us.

BRADY, DARLENE ANN, artist, designer; b. Ft. Hood, Tex., Aug. 4, 1951; d. Egbert Leo, Jr. and Eleanor Rose Marie (Wollenhaupt) B.; m. Mark M. English, 1984. BFA summa cum laude, Ohio U., 1976; MLS summa cum laude, U. Pitts, 1978, MA summa cum laude, 1980; MS in Architecture summa cum laude, U. Cin., 1986; MArch summa cum laude, Carnegie-Mellon U., 1990. Registered arch. Ohio, 2000. Ptnr. Archi-Textures, Cin., 1984—. Painter, stained glass artist, 1976-; tchg. asst. arch. studies Inst. Continuing Edn. Ohio U. West, 1976, U. Pitts., 1978-79; guest curator Stained Glass from Mellon Collection, U. Pitts., 1979; curatorial asst. Three Essays in Exhibition, U. Pitts., 1980; fine arts bibliograher Tulane U., 1981-83; grad. and teaching asst. U. Pitts., 1977-80; asst. curator fine arts slide library, 1973-77; curator BFA grad. Exhibit, Ohio U., 1976; asst. prof. architecture Ball State U., 1993—; vis. adj. 1991; fine arts bibliographer Tulane U., 1981-83; vist. asst. prof. Sch. Arch. & Interior Design U. Cin., 1990-91; adj. prof. arch. Chgo. Sch. Arch. U. Ill., 1991; asst. prof. arch. Ball State U., 1993-95; vist. asst. prof. arch. U. Ill. Urbana-Campaign, 1996-98; adj. prof. Art Acad. Cin., 2003-04; academic com. mem. Ind. MA Program, Antioch U., 2004. Group exhbns. include Fest for All '81, Broussard Galleries, Baton Rouge, 1981, Assocs. Exhibit, Stained Glass Assn. Am., 1980-84, Glass on Holiday, Gazebo Gallery, Gatlinburg, Tenn., 1981, Ark.-La.-Tex. Glass Invitational, La. Tech. U. Art Gallery, 1981, Nat. Exhbn., Royal Ont. Mus., Toronto (best use of antique glass award), 1985, "Vitraux des U.S.A," Micheline Loire Gallery, Chartres, France, 1985, Corning Mus. of Glass, 1987, U. Edinburgh, 1997, Off-The-Avenue Gallery, Cin., 1998, Internat. Festival for Arch. in Video of Florence, Italy, 1999, Cath. U. Wash., 2000, Chidlaw Gallery, Art Acad. Cin., 2003, Carnegie Mellon U., 2006; commns. include stained glass panel Athens Humane Soc., 1976, Athens Landscape painting for McDonald's Restaurant, 1976, Transitions stained glass windows Tompson residence, Athens, 1977. La. Cypress stained glass panels entrance door Hainesworth residence, Ruston, La., 1979, stained glass triptych Marybell Holstead residence, Ruston, 1981, solar room with 7 stained glass panels wollenhaupt residence, Lima, Ohio, 1984, skylight Union Bank, Columbus, Ind., 1985, others. Author: Stained Glass Index, 1906-77, 1979; Stained Glass: A Guide to Information Sources, 1980; Le Corbusier: An Annotated Bibliography, 1985; contbg. editor Architecture Week, 2000-02. Contbr. articles to profl. jours. Grantee Graham Found., Ball State U.; recipient hon. mention Stairway to Heaven Graphisoft Internat. Design Competition, 1998; finalist Place of Contemplation, ACSA/AM Wood Coun. Nat. Competition, 1990; Scholastic award of Excellence AIA, 1990. Scholar Phi Kappa Phi, 1977, J.W. Morgan, 1977, Deans fall 1978, Provost, 1978. Mem. Boyer Guild of Women in Architecture, eCAADe, ACADIA, Glass Arts Soc., Stained Glass Assn. Am. (assoc., rep. 1980-81), Beta Phi Mu, Phi Kappa Phi. Home: 1665 Pullan Ave Cincinnati OH 45223-2049

BRADY, DONNA ELIZABETH, sales executive, marketing executive, performing company executive; b. Rockville Centre, NJ, Nov. 17, 1955; d. Frank A. and Dorothy Eleanor (Munden) B. BA, Knox Coll., 1976. Stage mgr., lighting designer Dance Edn. Svcs., Inc., Northport, NY, 1973—86; coord. Am. Dance Festival Tech. Assistance Project, NYC, 1981—85; exec. dir. Performing Arts Resources, Inc., NYC, 1986—, also pres., bd. dirs.; fiscal/mktg. specialist Monterey Bay Aviation, 2002—05, dir. sales and mktg., 2005—. Project staff Tech. Assistance Group/TAG Found., Ltd., N.Y.C., 1980-81; treas. N.Y. Tech. Assistance Providers Network, 1995, 96, co-chair 1997; lighting designer, stage mgr. Solomons Co. Dance, 1978-81; asst. stage mgr. Pilobolus, 1978. Bd. dir. Artists Cmty. Fed. Credit Union, 1992-2001, sec., 1993-2000; bd. dir., treas. Acanthus Dance, 1997—. Mem. Am. Dance Guild (bd. dirs. 1980-87, treas. 1983-87). Office Phone: 831-883-8994. E-mail: dbradypar@aol.com.

BRADY, JEAN STEIN, retired librarian; b. Concord, Mass., Nov. 4, 1930; d. Walfred and Mary Selina (Jussila) Stein; m. Maurice Goodrich Klein, Feb. 22, 1957 (div. 1982); 1 child, Audrey Elaine; m. Lawrence Kevin Brady, Oct. 15, 1988. BS, Simmons Coll., 1952; cert. d'Etudes, U. Grenoble, France, 1954; MA, Northwestern U., 1957. Cert. pub. libr., N.Y. Sr. libr. N.Y. Pub. Libr., 1952-53, 57-60; cataloger Columbia U., N.Y.C., 1954-55; reference asst. Northwestern U., Evanston, Ill., 1955-57; cataloger U. W.Va., Morgantown, 1960-61; book reviewer ALA, Chgo., 1961-63; sr. cataloger Cleve. Pub. Libr., 1964-70; sr. catalog libr. Yale U. Libr., New Haven, Conn., 1970-92; cataloger Columbia U., N.Y.C., 1993-95; ret., 1995. Revision asst. Bibliographical Guide to Romance Langs. and Lits., 1956-57; reviewer: Booklist and Subscription Books Bulletin, 1961-63. Mem.: Simmons Coll. Club Cape Cod. Democrat. Episcopalian. Avocations: reading, travel, walking, swimming.

BRADY, JEAN VICK, education educator; b. Rocky Mount, N.C., Mar. 4, 1937; d. Ernest Telfair and Carrie Elizabeth (Baker) Vick; m. William Thomas Brady, Apr. 2, 1939; children: Arlan Thomas, William Tyler. AB in Eng. & Elem. Edn., Atlantic Christian Coll., Wilson, N.C., 1961; MA in Edn., East Carolina U., Greenville, 1963. Cert. Tchr., N.C. Tchr. Fayetteville (N.C.) City Schs., 1960-61, Rocky Mount City Schs., 1961-64, Raleigh (N.C) City Schs., 1964-66, Campbell County Schs., Brookneal, Va., 1966-68; dir. Homeplace Inc., Laurinburg, N.C., 1972-74; tchr. Scotland (N.C.) County Schs., 1981-82, Nash County (N.C.) Schs., 1981-82, Round Rock (Tex.) Schs., 1982-84; instr. Coll. Lake County, Grayslake, Ill., 1986-92. Author, Editor: Directory, Adult Edn. Classes in Lake County 1988. Elected mem. bd. edn. Libertyvill (Ill.) High Sch., 1989-95. Recipient Scotland County Mental Health Assn. award, Laurinburg, N.C., 1974. Republican. Baptist. Home: PO Box 1466 Carthage NC 28327-1466

BRADY, LAUREN JEAN, corporate communications specialist; b. Youngstown, Ohio, Oct. 12, 1951; d. Charles Henry and Maryon Ellen (Johnson) Joachim; m. Paul Matthew Brady, June 21, 1975. BA with hons., Calif. Poly. State U., 1973. Pub. affairs asst. Standard Oil Co., Calif., 1973—77, audio visual prodns. asst. Calif., 1977—79; pub. affairs asst., staff writer Chevron Chem. Co., San Francisco, 1979—80; editor The Catalyst, San Francisco, 1980—84; comms. specialist Standard Oil Co. Calif., San Francisco, 1984—. Recipient Merit award, Pub. Rels. Soc. Am., 1983. Mem.: Internat. Assn. Bs. Communicators (Internat. Gold Quill award merit 1982, Silver Six award 0821, Gold Qull commendation 1983, Gold Quill award merit 1984). Home: 1454 45th Ave San Francisco CA 94122-2935 Office: 225 Bush St Ste 1127 San Francisco CA 94104-4207

BRADY, M. JANE (MURIEL JANE BRADY), judge, former state attorney general; b. Wilmington, Del., Jan. 11, 1951; d. William Henry Brady Jr. and Edith Brady; m. Michael E. Neal, 1989. BA, U. Del., 1973; JD, Villanova U., 1976. Dep. atty. gen. State of Del., 1977—90; chief prosecutor Sussex County, 1987—90; solo law practice, 1990—94; atty. gen. State of Del., Wilmington, 1994—2005; judge Del. Superior Ct., Wilmington, 2005—. Bd. dirs. Nat. Dist. Attys. Assn., Kent/Sussex Industries. Past chair Rep Attys. Gen. Assn.; bd. dirs. Nat. Org. Victim Assistance; founder KINfolk; bd. dirs. Del. Children's Trust Fund; advisory bd. Big Bros./Big Sisters Sussex County. Named Delaware's Top Fraud Fighter, AARP Del., 1998; recipient Del. Humane Assn. award, Kent County SPCA's Animal Kindness award, Woman of the Yr. award, Del. Federation of Bus. and Professional Women, Leadership and Excellence award, Coordinating Council Against Sexual Assault in Del. Mem.: Nat. Assn. Attys. Gen. (exec. com.). Republican.*

BRADY, MARSHA MCCANDLESS, secondary school educator; b. Connellsville, Pa., Nov. 2, 1963; d. William Randall and Geraldine Robbins McCandless; m. David Leonard Brady, Jr., Feb. 4, 1989 (div. Apr. 1996); 1 child, Grant David. BS Music Edn., Ind. U. Pa., 1987. Cert. tchg. cert. 1998, choral music experience cert. 1998. Accompanist Pitts. Boys/Girls Choir, 1988—91, choral dir. tng. choir, 1990—91; choral dir. all star chorus Connellsville (Pa.) Schs., 1991—, choral tchr., 1993—; childrens choir dir. Asbury U.M. Ch., Uniontown, Pa., 1999—, Greater Uniontown Chorale, Uniontown, Pa., 1999—. Substitute tchr. Connellsville Schs., Pa., 1988—93; pvt. piano and voice lessons, Connellsville, Pa., 1993—2001; accompanist, organist for weddings, Connellsville, 1982—; accompanist for local theater, choirs, and soloists, Connellsville, 1982—. Recipient Treble Choir Judge's Choice award, Heritage Music Festivals, Williamsburg, Va., 1995, Music in the Parks, Sandusky, Ohio, 1997, Heritage Music Festivals, Jackson, N.J., 1996, Heritage Music Festivals, Hershey, Pa., 1994. Mem.: Connellsville Area Educators Assn., Pa. Music Educators Assn., Choristers Guild, Am. Choral Dirs. Assn., Music Educators Nat. Conf. Avocations: dancing instructor, music technology instructor, choral touring, accompanying, travel. Office: Connellsville HS 201 Falcon Dr Connellsville PA 15425 Home: 317 S 9th St Connellsville PA 15425-2911 Personal E-mail: marsharb@helicon.net.

BRADY, MARY ROLFES, music educator; b. St. Louis, Nov. 26, 1933; d. William Henry and Helen Dorothy (Slavick) Rolfes; m. Donald Sheridan Brady, Aug. 29, 1953; children: Joseph William, Mark David, Douglas Sheridan, John Rolfes, Todd Christopher. Student, Stanford U., 1951—54, UCLA, 1967, U. So. Calif., 1972—73; pvt. studies with, Roxanna Byers, Dorothy Desmond, and Rudolph Ganz. Pvt. piano tchr., L.A., 1955—; TV and radio performer. Pres. Jr. Philharm. Com. L.A., 1975-76; legis. coord., bd. dirs. Philharm. Affiliates, L.A., 1978-80. Life mem. Good Samaritan Hosp., St. Vincent Med. Ctr., L.A.; trustee St. Francis Med. Ctr., 1984-88; bd. dirs. Hollygrove-L.A. Orphans Home, Inc. Mem. Am. Coll. Musicians Club, Stanford Women's Club (past bd. dirs., pres. L.A. chpt. 1977—), The Muses, Springs Country Club.

BRADY, SHELAGH ANN, elementary school educator; b. Lowell, Mass., Aug. 4, 1943; d. Frank William and Margaret (Foye) B. BA in Tchr. Edn. and Social Studies, Emmanuel Coll., Boston, 1966; MEd, Fitchburg State Coll., 1983. Cert. tchr. elem. edn. Commonwealth of Mass. Dept. Edn. Tchr. grade 3 St. Joseph Elem. Sch., Somerville, 1965-69, tchr. grade 6, 1969-70; tchr. grade 5 St. Bridget Elem. Sch., Maynard, Mass., 1970-73, Norman E. Day Sch., Westford, Mass., 1973-76, lang. arts tchr. grade 6, 1976-90, Abbott Middle Sch., Westford, 1990-92, Blanchard Middle Sch., Westford, 1992—2000, Norman R. Day Sch., 2000—01; ret., 2001. Mem. NEA, Westford Edn. Assn. Democrat. Roman Catholic. Avocations: genealogical research, reading, gardening, birding, hiking. Home: PO Box 1201 Westford MA 01886-0901

BRADY, TERRIE, political organization executive; Student, Polit. Leadership Tng. Sch., Washington, 1979, 85. Tchr., Jacksonville, Fla.; chair Fla. State Dem. Party, 1993—98; pres. Duval Teachers United. Mem. Fla. State Dem. Platform Com., 1978, 80, 82, 89, 92; del. Nat. Dem. Conv., 1980, 84, 88, 92; mem. Dem. Nat. Com., 1989—; polit. dir., legis. liaison Duval Tchrs. United. Recipient Hubert H. Humphrey award for Fla.'s outstanding Dem., 1987, Golden Gavel award, 1989, 91, Frontier award Fla. Dem. Party, 1992, Mary Nolan award NOW, Jacksonville, 1996. Mem. Spina Bifida Assn., March of Dimes. Office: DTU 1601 Atlantic Blvd Jacksonville FL 32207

BRADY-BORLAND, KAREN, retired reporter, columnist; b. Buffalo, Mar. 13, 1940; d. Charles A. and Mary Eileen (Larson) B.; m. Gregg Robinson Borland, Sept. 6, 1969 (div. July 1985); children: Caitlin Luise, Kristin Robinson, Leila Nell. BA in English, Daemen Coll., 1961; MS in Journalism, Columbia U., 1962. Summer reporter Buffalo News, 1961, reporter, 1965-68, columnist, 1968-81; editor Prentice-Hall, Inc., Englewood, NJ, 1962-65; press officer for Rep. Max McCarthy U.S. Ho. Reps., Washington, 1967; gen. assignment & features reporter Buffalo News, 1981—91, higher education reporter, 1991—2002; ret., 2002. Book reviewer Buffalo News, 2006—. Recipient numerous awards Buffalo Newspaper Guild, 1969-79, N.Y. State award for Major Dailies Mag. Writing AP, 1982, numerous community awards, Hilbert Coll. medal, 2002.

BRAGG, CHERYL, museum director; d. Dewey and Bonnie Huddleston; m. Coy Bragg; 2 children. BA, Jacksonville State U. Bus. mgr. Anniston (Ala.) Mus. Natural History, 1985—90, asst. dir., 1990—98, dir., 1998—. Office: PO Box 1587 Anniston AL 36202

BRAGG, LYNN MUNROE, trade association administrator, former federal commissioner; b. Ft. Leonard Wood, Mo., June 15, 1954; d. Irving William and Elaine Frances (Heath) Munroe; m. Raymond Frank Bragg, Jr., Aug. 12, 1989; children: Hudson, Rachael, Braxton. BA in English, Mary Washington Coll., 1976; MS in Pub. Rels., Boston U., 1978. Speech and fin. writer Potomac Electric Power Co., Washington, 1978-80; legis. dir., legis. asst. Office of U.S. Senator Malcolm Wallop, Washington, 1981-91; dir. govtl. affairs Edison Electric Inst., Washington, 1991-94; commr. U.S. Internat. Trade Commn., Washington, 1994—2002, vice chmn., 1996-98, chmn., 1998-2000; pres. Chocolate Mfrs. Assn., McLean, Va., 2003—. Republican. Episcopalian. Avocation: golf.

BRAGGIO, SHERRYLL ANN MORRIS, retired elementary school educator, volunteer; b. Biloxi, Miss., Feb. 28, 1944; d. James Carlton and Mary Julia Morris; m. John Thomas Braggio, Mar. 15, 1973; 1 child, G. Edward Robertson. ARRT, Piedmont Hosp. Sch. Radiologic Tech., Atlanta, 1963; BA, U. N.C., Asheville, 1979; EdM, U. Ctrl. Okla., Edmond, 1985. Cert. radiologic technologist Am. Radiologic Tech. Assn. Ga., 1963; mid. sch. educator N.C., 1979, sch. counselor U. Ctrl. Okla., 1982. Tchr. Okla. City Pub. Schs., 1982—94; sch. counselor Classen Sch. Advanced Studies, 1994—2004; ret., 2004. Vol. docent Walters Art Mus., Balt., 2005—. Achievements include research in learning and teaching styles. Avocations: golf, walking, travel, museums. Home: Apt A 640 N Calvert St Baltimore MD 21202 Personal E-mail: sherryllb@hotmail.com.

BRAGGS, PATRICIA, account manager; Assoc., Computer Learning Ctr., 1983; B in Orgnl. Adminstrn., Ctrl. Mich. U., 2003. Cert. account devel. strategies SBC and AT&T, 2002, security products and svcs. SBC and AT&T, 2003, PremierServe total IP solutions SBC and AT&T, 2004, negotiating to win SBC and AT&T, 2002. Spl. events coord. office philanthropy Henry Ford Health Sys., Detroit, 1994—96; med. mgmt. assoc. Health Alliance Plan, Detroit, 1997—98, mktg. specialist Southfield, Mich., 1998—2000; field svc. mgr. AT&T, Southfield, 2000—02; account mgr. II SBC, Southfield, 2002—. Mem. Southwestern Bell Co. Cmty. Network Profls., Southfield, Mich., 2002—; pioneer Southwestern Bell Co., Southfield, 2002—. TV prodn. vol. Greater Grace TV Prodn. Ministry, Detroit, 2002—05. Mem.: Women Tech. Internat. (assoc.). Democrat-Npl. Avocations: travel, tennis.

BRAHAM, DELPHINE DORIS, accountant, government official; b. L'Anse, Mich., Mar. 16, 1946; d. Richard Andrew and Viola Mary Aho; m. John Emerson Braham, Sept. 23, 1967 (div. Aug. 1988); children: Tammy, Debra, John Jr. BS summa cum laude, Drury Coll., 1983; M in Mgmt., Webster U., 1986. Bookkeeper Cmty. Mental Health Ctr., Marquette, Mich., 1966—68; acctg. technician St. Joseph Hosp., Parkersburg, W.Va., 1972—74; mgr. material U.S. Army, Ft. Leonard Wood, Mo., 1982—86; acct., 1986—92; supervisory acct. Dept. Def., Indpls., 1992—. Instr., adj. faculty Columbia Coll., 1987-92, Park Coll., 1988-92. Leader Girl Scouts U.S., Williamstown, W.Va., 1972-74, Hanau, Germany, 1977-79. Mem. AAUW (treas. Waynesville br. 1986-90), Am. Soc. Mil. Comptrs., NAFE, Assn. Govt. Accts., Waynesville Bus. and Profl. Women's Orgn. Home: 2752 Pawnee Dr Indianapolis IN 46229-1418

BRAIGHTMEYER, JANET HUBER, elementary school educator, music educator; d. David Swisher and Charlotte Shoemaker Huber; m. Brian Lee Braightmeyer, June 14, 1984; children: Eric Wesley, Kelli Renee, Kyle Ryan. BS in Music Edn., Lebanon Valley Coll., Annville, Pa., 1982. Tchr. elem. music Solanco Sch. Dist., Quarryville, Pa., 1982—. Ch. organist Chestnut Level Presbyn. Ch., Quarryville, Pa. Mem.: Music Educators Nat. Conf. (corr.). Office: 211 S Hess Street Quarryville PA 17566 Office Phone: 717-786-2546.

BRAILEY, AMY LYNORA, secondary school educator, language educator; b. Xenia, Ohio, June 3, 1973; d. William Eben and Mary Rosalind Brailey. BS in Edn., Taylor U., Upland, Ind., 1995. Tchr. 7-12 grade English, history The King's Acad., Marion, Ind., 1995—2002; tchr. 8th grade English Thomas Edison Jr./Sr. High Sch., Lake Station, 2002—. Actor: (civil war reenactment). Team leader Fuel Internat., Crown Point, Ind., 1997—2005. Recipient Youth Leader Yr., Living Stones Fellowship, 2003—04. Mem.: Alpha Psi Omega (life), Kappa Delta Phi (life; mem.). Conservative. Home: 25 Meadow Lane Merrillville IN 46410 Personal E-mail: abrailey@hotmail.com.

BRAILOW, NORMA LIPTON, artist; b. N.Y., Apr. 30, 1916; d. Leon Israel Lipton and Estelle (Laiken) Rich; m. Alexander A. Brailow, Apr. 26, 1941; children: Anthony George, David Gregory. BA, Keuka Coll., 1963; MA, State U., 1970. Lic. tchr. Fashion artist Berger's Dept. Store, Buffalo, 1941-44; tchr. II, Penn Yan Acad., 1967-69; sculptor, Keuka Park, N.Y., 1970—. One woman shows include Lightner Gallery, Keuka Coll., N.Y., 1978, 82, Arnot Art Mus., Elmira, N.Y., 1979, Yates County Arts Coun., Penn Yan, N.Y., 1988; exhibited in numerous group shows Keuka Coll., Penn Yan County, Geneva, N.Y. Bd. dirs. Yates County Arts Coun., Yates Performing Arts. Mem. AAUW (bd. dirs. Yates County) Home and Office: 1714 Decourcy Ln Franklin IN 46131-7237

BRAINARD, BARBARA, artist; b. Boston, Mar. 21, 1952; d. Snelling Robinson Brainard and Tatiana (Holmsen) Rhinelander; children: Alexandra, Berry. BFA, Newcom Coll., 1985; MFA, Tulane U., 1988; BA, U. Coll., 1991. Instr. Tulane U., New Orleans, 1986-89; asst. prof. Loyola U., New Orleans, 1989—. Solo shows include: Still-Zingel Gallery, New Orleans, 1996, 98, Art Who, Ocean Springs, Miss., 1997, Sulaune Zinsel Gallery, New Orleans, 2000, Gautier, Miss., 2002, Cole Pratt Gallery, New Orleans, 2002, 03, 05, Delgado Gallery, 2004. Mem. Newport Hist. Soc., Arts Coun. New Orleans, L.A. Printmaking Soc. Avocations: swimming, cats. Mailing: 4728 Perrier St New Orleans LA 70115

BRAINARD, MELISSA, accountant; b. Buffalo, Jan. 11, 1969; d. Peter Anthony and Mary Agnes (Lazarus) Arena; m. Kevin Joseph Brainard, Sept. 25, 1993; children: Jacob Leon, Zachary Martin. BS, SUNY, Buffalo, 1991. CPA, N.Y., 1993. From staff mem. to mgr. KPMG, Buffalo, 1991-97; CFO Goodwill Industries Western N.Y., 1997-98; mgr. Deloitte & Touche, Buffalo, 1999—2002; contr. Albright-Knox Art Gallery, Buffalo, 2002—. Avocation: running marathons. Personal E-mail: mab1696@cs.com. Business E-Mail: mbrainard@albrightknox.org.

BRAINERD, MARY, small business owner; b. Denver, Apr. 25, 1963; d. John and Jane B. B in Music, U. Colo., 1985, M in Music, 1988, MBA, 1988. Freelance musician, Denver, 1975—; rsch. assoc. CSM, Golden, Colo., 1988-95; ind. prospect rschr. Colo. Pub. Radio, Children's Hosp., Mile High United Way, Denver, 1995-98; owner Golden Music Ctr., 1996—. Bd. dirs. Jefferson Symphony Orch., Golden, 1997-98. Office: Golden Music Ctr 2430 East St Golden CO 80401-2418 E-mail: goldenmusiccenter@home.com.

BRAININ, STACY L., lawyer; b. Houston, Jan. 3, 1959; BA with high honors, U. Tex., 1981, JD with high honors, 1984. Bar: Tex. 1984, admitted to practice: US Dist. Ct. (No. Dist.) Tex. 1986, US Ct. Appeals (5th Cir.) 1986, US Dist. Ct. (Ea. Dist.) Tex. 1987, US Supreme Ct. 1991. Ptnr., antitrust & white collar criminal defense Haynes and Boone LLP, Dallas. Assoc. editor Tex. Law Rev., 1983—84. Mem.: Dallas Bar Assn. (Antitrust & Trade Regulation Sect.), ABA (Litig. Sect., Criminal Justice Sect. white collar crime com. healthcare fraud subcom), Phi Beta Kappa, Order of Coif. Office: Haynes and Boone LLP 901 Main St Ste 3100 Dallas TX 75202-3789 Office Phone: 214-651-5584. Office Fax: 214-200-0373. Business E-Mail: stacy.brainin@haynesboone.com.

BRAISTED, MADELINE CHARLOTTE, artist, retired financial planner, military officer; b. Jamaica, N.Y., Nov. 23, 1936; d. Melvin Vincent and Charlotte Marie (Klos) B. AAS, Nassau C.C., 1968; BA, Hofstra U., 1973, MA, 1975; grad., U.S. Command and Gen. Staff Coll., 1985. Cert. fin. planner, 1991. Reservations agt. Airline Industry, N.Y.C., 1957-64; reservations contr. Auto Lease Industry, N.Y.C., 1964-66; nuclear medicine technician Queens Gen. Hosp., Jamaica, N.Y., 1969-70; lab. mgr. CUNY, 1970-80; owner Energy Etcetera, Flushing, N.Y., 1979-85; active duty with U.S. Army Health Profl. Support Agy., Office of Surgeon Gen., Washington, 1980-92. Author, pub. Energy Etcetera catalog, 1981-85; artist On Shore painting (honorable mention 1974). Merit badge counselor Boy Scouts Am., Queens County, N.Y., 1980-83; active PTA, Jamaica, 1980-84. Served with USMC, 1954-57, from sgt. to maj. USAR, 1975-96. Decorated Legion of Merit, Army Commendation medal with one oak leaf, Army Achievement medal with one oak leaf cluster, expert field med. badge. Mem. NAFE, APHA, Am Acad. Med. Adminstrs., Fin. Planners Assn., Am. Assn. Individual Investors, Assn. Mil. Surgeons U.S., Res. Officers Assn., Ret. Officers Assn., Nat. Art League, Rockaway Artists Alliance, Queens Coun. Arts. Roman Catholic. Avocations: painting, sculpting. E-mail: westeggstudios@msn.com.

BRAISTED, MARY JO, elementary school educator; b. Rochester, Minn., July 28, 1937; d. George Richard and Maxine Helen Hays; 1 child from previous marriage, Jennifer. BBA, Fla. Atlantic U., Boca Raton, 1981, BA in Elem. Edn., 2001, postgrad., 2006—. Mgr. mktg. adminstrn. IBM Corp., Boca Raton, 1982—84, mgr. product scheduling, 1985—88; vol. St. Joan of Arc, Boca Raton, 1989—96; tchr. Boca Raton Elem. Sch., 2001—. Sch. adv. com. chair, mem. profl. devel. com., PTA/faculty liaison Boca Raton Elem. Sch.,

2003—06; instr. Sci. IDEAS, Boca Raton, 2005. Mem. Rep. Women's Club, 2003—06. Named Tchr. of the Yr., Rotary, 2006. Mem.: Nat. Sci. Tchrs. Assn. (presenter 2005). Roman Catholic. Avocations: travel, reading, walking. Home: 1100 Pepperidge Ter Boca Raton FL 33486 Office: Boca RatonElem Sch 103 SW 1st Ave Boca Raton FL 33432

BRAITERMAN, THEA GILDA, economics professor, state legislator; b. Balt., Sept. 11, 1927; d. Isaac E. and Clara (Fink) Bloom; m. Marvin Braiterman, Mar. 21, 1948; children: Kenneth, Marta, David. BS, Johns Hopkins U., 1949; MA, U. Md., 1966; PhD, Union Inst., 1977. Assoc. prof. econs. Balt. Coll. of Commerce, 1966-73; prof. econs. New England Coll., Henniker, NH, 1973—; mem. N.H. Ho. of Reps., 1988-94. Cons. on retirement, 1988—; selectman Town of Henniker, 1997-2005. Author: Workbook on Economic Theory, 1966; contbr. articles to profl. jours. Sec., bd. govs. United Way of Merrimack County, Concord, N.H., 1984-90; v.p., bd. govs. Cmty. Svcs. Coun., Concord, 1980-84. Jane Addams Peace Assn. grantee, 1976-77; Gilmore grantee New Eng. Coll., 1988-90. Mem. Am. Econ. Assn., Ea. Econ. Assn. Home: PO Box 686 Henniker NH 03242-0686 Office: New England Coll Henniker NH 03242 E-mail: theabrait@conknet.com.

BRAITHWAITE, BARBARA JO, retired secondary school educator; BA, Ctrl. Mich. U., 1959; MA, U. Mich., 1960. Geography tchr. Pocono Mountain Sch. Dist., Swiftwater, Pa., 1980—2001; ret., 2001. Recipient 1st Place award Am. Express geography competition for tchrs., 1990, Outstanding Secondary Level Tchr. of the Year award Pa. Coun. Social Studies, 1992, Innovative Tchg. award State Farm Ins. Co., 1995, US, Russia, Ukraine Tchr. Excellence award Am. Couns. for Internat. Edn., US State Dept., 1997, Pa. Tchr. of Yr. award Dept. Edn., 1999. Mem. Pa. Geog. Alliance (steering com., tchr. cons.), Pocono Regional Geog. Alliance (co-founder, chair), Nat. Coun. Geog. Edn., Pa. Geog. Soc. (Tchr. Recognition award 1993). Home: 65 Stones Throw East Stroudsburg PA 18301-9694 also: Pocono Mountain Sch Dist Swiftwater PA 18370-0200 Personal E-mail: bjb65@aol.com.

BRAITHWAITE, MARILYN JEAN, realtor; b. Winchester, Va., Jan. 24, 1948; d. Charles Wilson and Bette (Dickson) B. AS in English, Ferrum Coll., 1969; cert. in real estate, Merrill Lynch Inst., 1987; cert., Real Estate Sch. W.Va., 1992; grad. Realtor Inst., W.Va. U., 1995. Cert. residential specialist; accredited buyer rep. Acctg. officer Nat. Pub. Affairs Ctr. for TV, Washington, 1972-76; office mgr. Nat. Consumers Union, Washington, 1976-78; pers. dir. Urban Environment Conf., Washington, 1978-84; dir. of adminstrn. Human Rights Campaign Fund, Washington, 1984-87; realtor Barbara Held/City Sites, Washington, 1987-92, Long & Foster Real Estate, Martinsburg, W.Va., 1992-2000; with RE/MAX Enterprises, Hedgesville, W.Va., 2000—. Instr. real estate principles and law Shepherd Coll., Shepherdstown, W.Va., 1993-98; field trainer Long & Foster Real Estate, Martinsburg, W.Va., 1996-2000; chair Ea. Panhandle Bd. Profl. Standards Com., Martinsburg, 1999. Contbg. author: Patterns: An Anthology of Modern Poetry, 1970. Donation solicitor Shenandoah Women's Shelter, 1994—. Mem. Profl. Bus. Women's Assn. (founder), Ea. Panhandle Bd. of Realtors (pres. 2000), Nat. Assn. Realtors, W.Va. Assn. Realtors, Nat. Trust for Hist. Preservation. Democrat. Methodist. Avocations: reading, cooking, attending auctions, bird watching. Home: 1004 Candi Ct Martinsburg WV 25401-2407

BRAKAS, NORA JACHYM, education educator; b. Schenectady, N.Y., Aug. 9, 1952; d. Thaddeus Michael and Theresa Mary (Patnode) J.; m. Jurgis Brakas, June 15, 1996. BS in Elem. Edn., Plattsburg State U. Coll., 1974; MS in Reading, SUNY, Albany, 1977, Cert. Advanced Study in Reading, 1986, PhD in Reading, 1990. Cert. elem. sch. tchr., reading tchr. Elem. sch. and reading tchr. Lee (Mass.) Ctrl. Sch., 1976-82; reading specialist Guilderland (N.Y.) Sch. Dist., 1988-89; rsch. asst., tchg. asst. SUNY, Albany, 1985-88, instr. reading dept., 1989-90; asst. prof. tchr. edn., reading specialist Southeastern La. U., Hammond, 1990-91, Marist Coll., Poughkeepsie, NY, 1991—. Presenter, spkr. in field. Contbr. articles to profl. jours. Student Literacy Corp. grantee U.S. Dept. Edn., 1991, IBM/Marist Joint Study Project grantee, 1992. Mem. Internat. Reading Assn., Soc. Children's Book Writers and Illustrators. Avocations: drawing, writing children's books, collecting antique children's books. Home: PO Box 176 Rhinecliff NY 12574-0176 Office: Marist Coll 388 F Dyson Poughkeepsie NY 12601 E-mail: Nora.Brakas@Marist.edu.

BRAKEBILL, JEAN NEWTON, military officer, nurse, educator; b. Mobile, Ala., Sept. 4, 1953; d. James Harold and Eleanor (Mrotek) Newton; m. James Arden Brakebill, Dec. 15, 1985; 1 child, Justin James. BSN, West Tex. State U., 1975; MS, Corpus Christi U., 1982; MBA in Health Adminstrn., Nat. U., 1987. RN, Tex. Staff nurse Southwestern Gen. Hosp., El Paso, Tex., 1975—76; commd. ensign U.S. Navy, 1976, advanced through grades to capt., 1998, staff nurse Naval Hosp., Charleston, SC, 1976, staff nurse Okinawa, Japan, 1978, head nurse ICU Corpus Christi, Tex., 1980-83, head nurse, clin. cons., ednl. program adminstr. Naval Hosp. San Diego, 1983-89; divsn. head med. surg. ward Naval Hosp., Long Beach, Calif., 1989-90, clin. nurse specialist inpatient nursing, 1990-91, head dept. inpatient nursing, 1991-92, head dept. command edn. and tng., 1992-93; command edn. and tng. program adminstr. Naval Med. Ctr., Portsmouth, Va., 1993-95; head dept. command staff edn. and tng. Twenty-Nine Palms Naval Hosp., Marine Corps Air Ground Ctr., Calif., 1995-98; dir. nursing svcs. Twenty-Nine Palms Naval Hosp., Calif., 1998-2001; instr. first aid, CPR ARC, 1998—. Instr. trainer BLS Am. Heart Assn., various locations, 1985—2003; advanced trauma life support educator, San Diego, 1987—91; nurse ARC, 1980—, mem. bd. execs. Morongo Basin chpt., 2001—05, chair health and safety com., 2002—05. V.p. Blessed Sacrament Elem. Sch. Bd., 2001—02, pres., 2000—02, cathecist, 2003—. Mem.: Kappa Delta. Roman Catholic. Avocations: guitar, needlecrafts, reading, swimming, art. Personal E-mail: brakebill002@earthlink.net.

BRALEY, OLETA PEARL, community health nurse, writer; b. Rochester, NY, July 19, 1944; d. Horace Everet and Ruby Doris Sullivan; m. Edward Walter Plow, June 24, 1967 (dv. Jan. 10, 1990); children: James Edward Plow, John Patrick Plow; m. Franklin John Braley, Mar. 17, 1990 (dec. 1992). Lic. in cosmetology, Continental Sch. Beauty, 1966; student, Sch. Visual Arts, N.Y.C., 1963. Prodn. Kodak Park, Rochester, 1964—66; hairdresser local salons Rochester, 1966—80; money room oper. AMSA, Rochester, 1986—90; home health aide Tender Loving Care, Rochester, 1990—97; home health caretaker Via Health II, Rochester, 1992—2004, Home Care Plus, 2004—. Author: (poetry book) Best of the 90's, 1996, Best Poetry and Poets, 2002; composer: (songs) Remember, 1997, Wondering, 1997, Here to Stay, A Country Letter; featured (on-air interview) with Brian Jobel, N.Y.C., 1999, author various poems in field; lyricist: Our American Vet, 2005, staff writer: Countrywine Pub., 2005—. Recipient Editor's Choice award, Internat. Soc. Poetry, 1995—98, 2002. Avocations: music, art, writing, playing piano and cello. Home: 91 B Green Leaf Meadows Rochester NY 14612-4347

BRALY, ANGELA F., lawyer, insurance company executive; b. 1961; BBA, Tex. Tech. U.; JD, So. Meth. U. Bar: Mo. 1985. Ptnr. Lewis Rice & Fingersh LC, St. Louis; gen. counsel RightCHOICE Managed Care Inc., St. Louis, 1999—2003; pres., CEO Blue Cross Blue Shield of Mo., St. Louis, 2003—05; exec. v.p., gen. counsel, chief pub. affairs officer WellPoint, Inc., Indpls., 2005—. Named one of 25 Most Influential Women in Bus., St. Louis Bus. Jour., 2000. Mem.: ABA, Am. Health Lawyers Assn., State Bar Mo., Bar Assn. Met. St. Louis, St. Louis Health Lawyers Network. Office: WellPoint Inc 120 Monument Cir Indianapolis IN 46204 Office Phone: 317-532-6000.

BRAMBLE, PAMELA CHACE LEUBA, artist, educator; b. Ft. Meade, Md., Nov. 29, 1955; d. Edward Russell and Millicent (Chace) Leuba; m. Francis Laurence John Bramble, June 27, 1981. BFA, U. Conn., 1979; MFA, Columbia U., 1986. Dir. Carlson Gallery U. Bridgeport, Conn., 1981-84; adj. faculty Sacred Heart U., Fairfield, Conn., 1987-89; assoc. prof. art U. Conn., Torrington, 1989—. Juror various art orgns., 1990—. Exhibited at New Britain Mus. of Art Am., Conn., 1992, Paesaggio Gallery, Canton, Conn., 1993, Bowery Gallery, N.Y.C., 1993, Artspace, New Haven, 1993, 95, John Slade Ely House, New Haven, 1994, Slater Meml. Mus., Norwich, Conn., 1994, 100 Pearl Gallery, Hartford, 1995. Recipient Emerging Artist/Pres.'s Gold Medallion award Grumbacher Co., 1986, Honorable Mention award New Britain (Conn.) Mus. Am. Art, 1993; U. Conn. Rsch. Found. grantee, 1990. Avocations: bicycling and bike touring, travel, gardening. Office: U Conn 855 University Dr Torrington CT 06790-2635

BRAMHALL, DEBRA A., information technology manager, consultant; d. Ronald C. Bramhall, Sr.; 1 child, Benjamin R. Solo. Assoc. Degree, Westmoreland County C.C., Youngwood, Pa.; Bachelor Degree, U. Phoenix, San Jose, Calif.; Masters Degree, Columbus U. Info. tech. sys. adminstr., contr. Syntrax, Provo, Utah, 1989—90; sys. mgr. Novell, San Jose, Calif., 1990—96; LAN mgr. Kaiser Permanent, Stockton, Calif., 1996—98; NSD mgr. Am. Century, Mountain View, Calif., 1998—2000; dir. Cyber Ctr. Qwest, Columbus, Ohio, 2000—02; ind. sr. cons., sr. IT advisor Columbus, 2002—04; v.p., program mgr. JP Morgan/Bank One, Columbus, 2004—. Mem.: NAFE, PTA. Avocations: volunteering, playing tenor saxophone.

BRAMLETT, SHIRLEY MARIE WILHELM, interior designer, artist; b. Scottsboro, Ala., June 14, 1945; d. Robert David and Alta (Reeves) Wilhelm; m. Paul Kent Bramlett, June 5, 1966; children: Paul Kent II (dec.), Robert Preston. BS, David Lipscomb U., 1966; postgrad., U. Miss., 1966-68; pvt. study art, 1976—. Decorator The Anchorage House, Oxford, Miss., 1966-67, Interiors by Shirley, Tupelo, Miss., 1971-80; tchr. Oxford City Schs., 1967-69; decorator, buyer Donald Furniture, Tupelo, 1969-71; owner, importer Bramblewood Interiors & Antiques, Belden, Miss., 1976-80; owner, decorator, artist The Cottage on Caldwell, Inc., Nashville, 1980—. Sec.-treas. Kent Bramlett Found., Inc., 1992—. Represented in art galleries Hundred Oaks Castle, Winchester, Tenn., Lyzon Gallery, Nashville; introduced and presented painting House of Parliament, Luxembourg; commd. for watercolor print fortnightly Musicale of Miss., 1991-92; European representation by Internet Internat. Bd. dirs. Found. for Christian Edn., 1988—, Ea. European Missions, Vienna, Austria, 1986— (commd. for watercolor print used in internat. fundraising); del. Miss. Dem. caucus, 1970; fundraiser Agape Artist, 1991; sec., treas., bd. dirs. Kent Bramlett Found., Inc.; curator Hundred Oaks Castle, Winchester, Tenn. Named Woman of Decade, David Lipscomb Coll., 1986, one of Outstanding Young Women of Am., 1979; selected Centennial Artist, David Lipscomb U., Nashville, 1991, one of ten Master Tenn. Artists, Lyzon Gallery, Nashville, 1991. Mem. Nat. Mus. Women in Arts, Tenn. Watercolor Soc., Nat. Soc. Tole and Decorative Painters, Green Hills Garden Club (cover artist for nat. conv. garden clubs 1985), Assoc. Ladies Lipscomb (bd. dirs. 1991-92). Mem. Ch. of Christ. Avocation: restoring historic castle. Home: 930 Caldwell Ln Nashville TN 37204-4016

BRAMSON, PHYLLIS HALPERIN, artist, educator; b. Madison, Wis., Feb. 20, 1941; d. Herman and Ester (Goldberg) Halperin. BFA with high honors, U. Ill., 1963; MA in Painting, U. Wis., 1964; MFA, Sch. of Art Inst. Chgo., 1974. Prof. studio arts U. Ill., Chgo. One-woman shows include Gallerie Farideh Cadot, Paris, 1980, Marilyn Butler Gallery, Scottsdale, Ariz., 1983, Hewlett Gallery Carnegie-Mellon U., Pitts., 1985, The Renaissance Soc., Chgo., 1986, Monique Knowlton Gallery, N.Y.C., 1986, Brody's Gallery, Washington, 1987, Victorian Coll. Arts, Melbourne, Australia, 1988, G.W. Einstein Gallery, N.Y.C., 1991, Dart Gallery, Chgo., 1992, Brody's Gallery, Washington, 1993, Phyllis Kind Gallery, Chgo., 1994, Printworks Gallery, Chgo., 1997, Chgo. Cultural Ctr., 1998, Ft. Wayne Mus, Ind., 2001, Ind. U., Bloomington, 2002, Carl Hammer Gallery, Chgo., 2004, Printworks, Chgo., 2004, Littlejohn Contemporary, NY, 2004, Boulder Art Mus, Bolder, Colo., 2004, Gallery of Art U. No. Iowa, 2004, Claire Oliver Fine Arts NY, 2005, others; group shows include The Renwick Gallery, Washington, 1976, The New Mus., N.Y.C., 1979, 96, Musee De Toulon (France), 1983, Seattle Art Mus., 1985, Walter Bischoff Galeries, Stutgardt, Germany, 1990, Smart Mus., Chgo., 1991, Andrew Zarre Gallery, N.Y.C., 1992, Corcoran Mus. Art, Washington, 1993, U. Art Gallery, Vermillion, S.D., 1994, P.P.O.W. Art Gallery, N.Y.C., 1995; group exhbns. include Gallery A, Chgo., 1995, David Bietzel Gallery, N.Y.C., 1995, Associated Am. Artists, N.Y.C., 1996, Mus. Contemporary Art, Chgo., 1996, Southeastern Ctr. for Contemporary Painting, 1996, Carl Hammer Gallery, Chgo., 1999, 03, Brenda Taylor Gallery, N.Y.C., 1999, The New Mus. Contemporary Art, N.Y., N.Y., 2000, Block Mus. Northwestern Ill. U., Evanston, Ill., 2000, Exit Art, N.Y.C., N.Y., 2002, Emily Davis Gallery, Myers Sch. Art U. Akron, Ohio, 2002, Zolla Lieberman Gallery, Chgo., Ill., 2002, Palm Springs (Calif.) Mus., 2002, Sheppard Gallery, U. Nev., Reno, Nev., 2002, Frist Ctr. Visual Arts, Nashville, Tenn., 2003, Nat. Acad. Mus., N.Y., N.Y., 2004 Louis Comfort Tiffany grantee, 1980, Ill. Arts Coun. grantee, 1981, 88, NEA grantee, 1976, 83, 93, Johns Simon Guggenheim grantee, 1993; Sr. Fulbright scholar, Australia, 1988; recipient Rockefeller Found. grant/residency, 1997, Artadia: The Fund Art and Dialog Jury award, 2004.

BRAMWELL, MARVEL LYNNETTE, nursing administrator, social worker; b. Durango, Colo., Aug. 13, 1947; d. Floyd Lewis and Virginia Jenny (Amyx) Bramwell. LPN, Durango Sch. Practical Nursing, 1968; ADN, Mt. Hood CC, 1972; BSN, BS in Gen. Studies cum laude, So. Oreg. State Coll., 1980; cert. in edn. grad. sch. social work, U. Utah, 1987, cert. in counselor alcohol, drug abuse, 1988, MSW, 1992. RN Utah, Oreg., Ind.; LCSW Utah, Ind., Nev. Staff nurse Monument Valley (Utah) Seventh Day Adventist Mission Hosp., 1973-74, La Plata Cmty. Hosp., 1974-75; health coord. Tri County Head Start Program, 1974-75; nurse therapist, team leader Portland Adventist Med. Ctr., 1975-78; staff nurse Indian Health Svc. Hosp., 1980-81; coord. village health svcs. North Slope Borough Health and Social Svc. Agy., Barrow, Alaska, 1981-83; nurse, supr. aides Bonneville Health Care Agy., 1984-85; staff nurse LDS Adolescent Psychiat. Unit, 1985-86; coord. adolescent nursing CPC Olympus View Hosp., 1986-87, 91; charge and staff nurse adult psychiatry U. Utah, 1987-88; nurse MSW Cmty. Nursing Svc., Salt Lake City, 1989-90, Willow Springs Ctr., Reno, 1996—2002; resident scvs. coord., dir. nursing Arden Cts., Reno, 1998-99—; med. social worker Meth. Home Health, Indpls., 1994-96; psychiat. nurse Willow Springs Ctr., 1996—2002; DON, resident svc. coord. Arden Cts., Reno, 1998-99; per diem nurse N. Nev. Med. Ctr., 2000—01; discharge planner Carson-Tahoe Hosp., 2003; bed control coord. Washoe Med. Ctr., Reno, 2004—. Cons. design and constrn. 6 high tech. health clinics Alaska Arctic, 1982—83; per diem nurse Reno VA Med. Ctr., N. Nev. Med. Ctr., 1998—99; psychiat. nurse specialist Cmty. Nursing Svc.; vol. cons. Grief Solace Tree, 2006—. Contbr. articles to profl. jours. Recipient cert. appreciation, U.S. Census Bur., Colo., 1970, Barrow Lion's Club, 1983, others. Mem.: NASW, NOW, Assn. Women Sci. Achievements include designed software for TRAC- treatment and reporting abacus for case management. Avocations: watercolor painting, photography, hiking, horseback riding. Home: Apt 349 6200 Meadowood Mall Circle Reno NV 89502-6621 Personal E-mail: anp3943@aol.com. Business E-Mail: marvel@bhr.reno.nv.us.

BRANCH, FELECIA ANN-SELDON, elementary school educator; d. Willie George and Doris Juanita Seldon; 1 child, Justin Michael Alexander. BA in Liberal Arts, U. Detroit, 1991. Cert. provisional tchg. U. Detroit, 1995, profl. tchg. 7-12 in speech & English U. Detroit, 2001. Lang. arts tchr. Hutchins Mid. Sch., Detroit, 1991—. Debate coach Detroit Pub. Schs., 1992—2001; narrative contest judge Area D, 1997; tchr. liason Mid-East/West Fest, 1997—2001, mem. planning com., 1997—2001; tchr. participant Inside Out, 1997—; leader Reading for Real Tchr., 1999—2000, Jr. Great Books, 2000—02, Soar to Success, 2001; accelerated reader tchr. leader Renaissance Reading, 2005. Mem. planning com. Mid East/West Fest, 1997—2001; participant W.K. Kellogg Found. Youth Initiative, 1998—99; mem. Site-based Mgmt. Com. Hutchins Mid. Sch., 1999—; vol. donor Great Book Leader for Reading Detroit Pub. Libr., 2000—02; asst. girl scout troop leader Girl Scouts Am., 1997—; leader Jr. Great Books Detroit Pub. Libr., 2000—02; tchr. Wednesday Night Children's Bible Study, 2004—. Recipient Cert. Recognition, Detroit Middle Schs. Debate League, 1992—2001. Avocations: reading, writing, poetry, skating, weightlifting. Office Phone: 313-873-2787.

BRANCH, LAURA MICHELLE, science educator; b. National City, Calif., Sept. 9, 1971; d. James Howard and Diane Marie Bradbury; m. Brian Kiest Branch, June 22, 1996; 1 child, Oscar James. AA in Geol. Scis., Santa Barbara City Coll., Calif., 1994; BS in Geol. Scis., San Diego State U., 1996; MEd in Edn., U. Calif., Santa Barbara, 1999. Sci. educator Ernest Righetti H.S., Santa Maria, Calif., 1999—. Named Coast Geol. Soc. Tchr. of Yr., 2003; recipient Tech-2-Go grant, Santa Barbara County Edn. Office, 2002; grantee, PTSA, 2003. Mem.: Women Educators of Sci. and Tech., Calif. Sci. Tchr. Assn., Nat. Sci. Tchr. Assn. Avocations: camping, hiking, cooking, jazz dancing.

BRANCH, MARY FLETCHER COX, secondary school educator; b. Jackson, Tenn., May 20, 1938; d. John Fletcher and Helen Wood (Henderson) Cox; m. William Terrell Branch, 1964; 1 child, Ashley Tucker. Office: Holy Trinity Luth Sch 3712 W El Prado Blvd Tampa FL 33629-8700

BRANCH, MICHELLE, musician; b. Flagstaff, Ariz., July 2, 1983; d. David and Peggy Branch; m. Teddy Landau, May 23, 2004; 1 child, Owen Isabelle. With Maverick Records, Beverly Hills, Calif., 2001—. Musician: (CD) Broken Bracelet, 2000, The Spirit Room, 2001, Breathe - The Remixes, 2002, Hotel Paper, 2003, (single) Everywhere, 2001, All You Wanted, 2001, Goodbye to You, 2003, Are You Happy Now, 2003, Breathe, 2003, (with Santana) The Game of Love, 2002 (Grammy award for Best Pop Collaboration with Vocals, 03). Recipient Grammy award for Best New Artist, 2003. Office: Maverick Recording Co 3300 Warner Blvd Burbank CA 91505-4632

BRANCIFORT, JANET MARIE, hospital administrator, respiratory therapist; b. New Britain, Conn., Dec. 3, 1956; d. Thomas Joseph and Ann Marie (Montanile) Thibodeau; 1 child, Jessica Marie Brancifort. AS in Respiratory Care, Manchester (Conn.) C.C., 1977; BS in Respiratory Care, Quinnipiac Coll., 1987; postgrad. in MPH program, U. Conn., 1991—. Cert. Nat. Bd. Respiratory Care, 1980, registerd, 1981, lic. respiratory care practitioner, Conn., 1995. Staff therapist New Britain Meml. Hosp., 1977-84, per diem respiratory therapist, 1981-84, asst. chief respiratory care, 1984-88; respiratory clin. specialist Hosp. for Spl. Care (formerly New Britain Meml. Hosp.), 1988-94, clin. outcomes mgr., 1994—. Chair-elect Conn. Pulmonary Care Respiratory Com., 1992, chair, 1993; presenter in field. Contbr. papers to profl. conf. procs. Asst. scout leader Conn. Yankee Girl Scouts Am., Berlin, 1992—. Recipient Conn. Yankee Girls Scout Leader award, 1993. Mem. Am. Assn. Respiratory Care (mem. ad hoc com. for pulmonary rehab. reimbursement, Dallas, 1993-94, mem. long term mech. ventilation task force 1993-95, clin. practice guidelines reviewer 1990-96), Nat. Bd. Respiratory Care, Conn. Thoracic Soc. (program com. 1994-95), Conn. Soc. Respiratory Care (legis. com. 1994-95), Conn. Pub. Health Assn., Alpha Sigma Lambda. Democrat. Roman Catholic. Avocations: reading, exercise, theater, basketball. Office: Hosp for Spl Care 2150 Corbin Ave New Britain CT 06053-2298

BRAND, DONNA J., career consultant, mental health counselor; b. St. Louis; d. Richard Matthew and Esther (Shipley) Tully; m. Tom Krebs; children: Michelle, Todd, Kevin, Brian; m. Herb Brand, May 14, 1983. BA in Psychology, SUNY, Albany, 1987; MA in Counseling and Psychology Svcs., Marymount U., 1989. Cert. career counselor Nat. Bd. Cert. Counselors. Counselor Fairfax (Va.) County Pub. Schs., 1987-90, George Mason U., Fairfax, Va., 1990; career counselor Montgomery County Commn. for Women, Rockville, Md., 1990-95; owner consulting firm, career coach McLean, Va., 1995—. Cons., facilitator Women's Ctr. No. Va., Vienna, 1995—; guest commentator on career issues radio stas. WGAY-FM, WGTS-FM, WBIG-FM, Washington and met. area, 1990—. Bd. dirs. Pinecrest Cmty. Assn., Alexandria, Va., 1995—, Woodburn Mental Health Ctr., Fairfax, 1996, Vol. Emergency Families for Children, Fairfax, 1990-93. Recipient Women Making a Difference award Sta. WCOA-TV and Nat. Mus. Women in the Arts, 1995. Mem. Am. Counseling Assn. (cert.), Nat. Career Devel. Assn, Va. Counseling Assn., Psi Chi.

BRAND, RACHEL L., federal agency administrator, lawyer; BA, U. Minn., 1995; JD, Harvard U., 1998. Law clk. to Justice Charles Fried Mass. Supreme Judicial Ct., 1998—99; law clk. to Justice Anthony Kennedy U.S. Supreme Ct.; assoc. Cooper, Carvin & Rosenthal; assoc. counsel to Pres. The White House, Washington; prin. dep. asst. atty gen. Office of Legal Policy, U.S. Dept. Justice, Washington, 2003—05, acting asst. atty. gen., 2005, asst. atty. gen., 2005—. Editor-in-chief Harvard Jour. Law and Pub. Policy. Office: Office Legal Policy Rm 4234 Main Justice Bldg 950 Pennsylvania Ave NW Washington DC 20530-0001 Office Phone: 202-514-4601.

BRAND, VICKI L., elementary school educator; d. Jacob Charles and Freda Marie Brand; children: Amilee Marie Kramer, David Jung Mark Kramer. BA, Ctrl. Coll., Pella, Iowa, 1972. Cert. tchr. Iowa Bd. Ednl. Examiners, 1972. Tchr. phys. edn. Grinnel-Newburg Ctrl. Sch. Dist., Iowa, 1972—. Coach Grinnell-Newburg Ctrl. Sch. Dist., 1974—. City clk. Oakland Acres, Iowa, 1989—91, mem. city coun., 1992—99. Mem.: NEA, Iowa State Edn. Assn., Grinnell Newburg Edn. Assn. Avocations: gardening, yardwork, reading, fitness, golf. Office: Grinnell Newburg CSD 132 East St S Grinnell IA 50112

BRAND-BUCHANAN, MICHELLE CATHY, elementary school educator; d. John and Linda Brand; m. Justin B uchanan, Dec. 16, 2000. BS, U. North Tex., Denton, 1998. Cert. tchr. La. Sci. tchr. DeSoto East Jr. H.S., DeSoto, Tex., 1999—2000; gifted tchr. Pineville Jr. H.S., La., 2001, Alexandria Mid. Magnet Sch., Alexandria, La., 2001—01, sci. tchr., 2002—. Master tchr. ARMADA Project, Narraganset, RI, 2005—. Named Tchr. of the Yr., Sam's Club, 2004—05, Alexandria Mid. Magnet Sch., 2004—05. Mem.: La. Sci. Tchrs. Assn. (region VI rep. 2001—). Office: Alexandria Middle Magnet 122 Maryland Ave Alexandria LA 71301

BRANDENBURG, ANNABEL JUNE, retired small business owner; b. Beaver Dam, Wis., June 6, 1936; d. Charles George and Sylvia Agnes (Woolery) Marthaler; m. Orville F. Brandenburg (dec. July 1986); children: Cindy, Russel, Krystal, Charles, Sujen. Owner, truck driver Brandenburg Trucking, Beaver Dam, 1964-89; owner Sew & So Shop, 1990—2004, Annabel's Bridals, 1991—2004, Annabel's Inches Away, 1994—2005; ret., 2005. Lutheran. Avocations: sewing, crocheting, handy crafts. Home: N8034 State Road 33 Beaver Dam WI 53916-9769

BRANDES, JO ANNE, lawyer; BA, U. Wis., Eau Claire; JD, Willamette U. Assoc. Herz, Levin, Teper, Chernof & Sumner, SC, 1978—81; exec. v.p., CAO, gen. counsel Johnson Diversey, Inc., Sturtevant, Wis. Dir. Johnson Family Funds, Andersen Corp. Inc. Regent emeritus U. Wis., Wis., 1996—; past mem. Gov.'s Commn. on Glass Ceiling; chmn. Wis. Child Care Coun.; past president Racine (Wis.) Area United Found.; dir. Bright Horizons Family Solutions, Johnson Family Funds. Named Working Mother of Yr., Working Mother mag., 1994. Office: Johnson Diversey Inc 8310 16th St PO Box 902 Sturtevant WI 53177-0902

BRANDI, KRISTINA, professional tennis player; b. San Juan, P.R., Mar. 29, 1977; d. Joe and Jane Brandi. Grad., Bradenton Acad., 1995. Winner Futures, Indpls., 1994, Heinetzen Trophy, The Netherlands, 1999; ranked 44 in 1999. Avocations: biking, jet-skiing, reading, modern dance, going to plays and musicals. Office: US Tennis Assn 70 W Red Oak Ln White Plains NY 10604-3602

BRANDIS, BERNARDINE, lawyer; b. San Francisco; d. Sidney Norman and Sheva Diane (Braunstein) B.; m. Jeffrey Peter Alperin, Mar. 27, 1982; 1 child, Shaun Lee Alperin. BA, UCLA, 1975, JD, 1978. Bar: Calif. 1978. Counsel 20th Century Fox, L.A., 1981-83; dir. bus. affairs Universal Pictures, Universal City, Calif., 1983-85; v.p. bus. affairs Walt Disney Pictures and TV, Burbank, Calif., 1985-88; sr. v.p. bus./legal affairs Hollywood Pictures Co., Burbank, 1988; exec. v.p. bus. and legal affairs Walt Disney Studios. Mem. Phi Beta Kappa. Office: Walt Disney Studio TD202F 500 S Buena Vista St Burbank CA 91521-0006*

BRANDLER, MARCIELLE Y., poet, educator; b. Riverside, Calif., June 27, 1950; d. Cecil U. and Luverne M. (Lieb) Parks. M of Profl. Writing, U. So. Calif. LA, 1994; BA, U. Utah, 1981. Cert. lectr. LA CC, 1988. Vis. poet Calif. Poets in Schs., LA, 1988—2000; educator various colls., LA, 1988—; dir. poetry workshop, mentor Performing Tree, LA, 2002—. Condr. seminars in publishing, tchg., poetry and grammar; spkr. in field; guest poet. Singer, composer, producer (CD) The Breathing House, pub. (book of poems), 2006;, author poems published internationally; featured singer/poet/emcee (various benefit performances), entertainment writer Sierra Madre Vista & Creative Line Magazine, writer Religion & Ethics Digest, 1997; prodr.: (pub. access TV program with Adelphia TV,) Marcielle Presents!. Vol. Unitarian Universalist Ch., Pasadena, Calif., 1999—2003; mem. Foothill Enrichment Ctr., Sci. of Mind. Recipient First Pl. for poem, Eden, Mt. San Antonio Coll., 1997. Mem.: Am. Fedn. Tchrs. (assoc.), Alameda Writers Group (assoc.; former bd. mem.), Ams. United Separation Ch. and State (former bd. mem.), Pasadena Opera Guild (assoc.; mem.). Achievements include producing a film for American Film Institute; producing a variety show for LA Coalition to End Hunger; producing a benefit performance for the Literacy Campaign; producing an event to celebrate banned books. Avocation: poetry. Office Phone: 626-791-5867. E-mail: marcielle@dslextreme.com.

BRANDON, KATHLEEN ALMA, director; b. Cincinnati, Ohio, July 11, 1946; d. Arthur Hubert Brandon and Alma Martha Vorwerck; m. James Lee Frost, Apr. 15, 1987 (dec. June 13, 2000). BS, Ohio State U., 1969; MA, Calif. State U., Northridge, 1983, Calif. State U., L.A., 1997. Tchr., spl. edn. Franklin County Program for the Mentally Retarded, Columbus, Ohio, 1969—76, Atwater Ave. Sch., L.A., Calif., 1979—95, categorical program advisor, 1996—98; asst. prin. Los Angeles Unified Sch. Dist., L.A., Calif., 1998—99; coord. spl. edn., orthop. impaired L.A. Unified Sch. Dist., 1999—. Mem.: Computer Using Educators, Assn. Supervision and Curriculum Design, Coun. for Exceptional Children, Calif. Speech Lang. Hearing Assn., Am. Speech Lang. Hearing Assn. Avocations: reading, travel, decorating. Office: Los Angeles Unified Sch Dist 333 S Beaudry 17th Fl Los Angeles CA 90017 Personal E-mail: kate.brandon@lausd.net.

BRANDON, KATHLEEN VIRGINIA, social studies educator; b. La Jolla, Calif., July 2, 1945; d. Kathryn Elizabeth and William Brandon; m. Daniel Warren McEnulty, Oct. 17, 1970 (div.); 1 child, Megan Kathryn McEnulty. BA Polit. Sci., U. Utah, Salt Lake City, 1968; Secondary Social Studies Certification, Westminster Coll., Salt Lake City, 1994, MEd, 2003. Cert. Tchr. Secondary Social Studies Utah State Bd. Edn., 1995. Advisor student activities Colo. State U., Ft. Collins, Colo., 1968—69; dir. student activities and campus ctr. Holy Cross Coll., Worcester, Mass., 1969—72; counselor and mgr. ctr. Nutri Sys., Salt Lake City, 1988—91; tchr. social studies Park City Sch. Dist., Utah, 1995—. Leader ninth grade team Treasure Mountain Internat. Sch., Park City, Utah, 2005—; mem. curriculum devel. com. Project Archaeology, Bozeman, 2002—; lead tchr. Cmty. of Caring, Park City, 1997—2000; rep. Park City Edn. Assn., 1998—2000; advisor student coun. Ecker Hill Mid. Sch., Park City, 1997—99; facilitator Project Archaeology, Bozeman, Mont., 1995—. Chmn., regional dir. Collegiate Coun. UN, Salt Lake City, 1963—68; mem.youth adv. coun. Park City Govt., 1996—2000; advisor Builders/Key Club, Park City, Utah, 2005—06; leader Girl Scouts U.S.A., Mukilteo, Wash., 1978—81; mem. Nature Conservancy, Salt Lake City, 2004—06; mem., organizer Utah Population Coalition, Salt Lake City, 2003—06; v.p. Young Dem., Salt Lake City, 1966—67; elected student govt. rep. Westminster Coll., Salt Lake City, 1993—94; leader Boy Scouts Am., Salt Lake City, 1984—86. Named Tchr. of Excellence, Park City Edn. Found., 2003; named to Dean's List, Westminster Coll., 1992—94; recipient, U. Utah, 1991—92, Spur Scholastic and Svc. Hon., 1964—65, Cwean Scholastic and Svc. Hon., 1965—66; scholar, Gilder Lehrman Inst., 2005, U. Utah, 1963—67. Mem.: ASCD, Geography Alliance, Utah Edn. Assn. (rep.), Planned Parenthood Utah (coord. edn. 2003—04), Nat. Assn. for Mentally Ill, Phi Mu (life; pres. of chpt., Scholarship Honor Pledge 1963-1964). Avocations: travel, archaeology, swimming, hiking, bicycling. Home: PO Box 680173 Park City UT 84068 Office: Treasure Mountain International School 2530 Kearns Blvd Park City UT 86060 Office Fax: 435-645-5649. Personal E-mail: kvb0702@msn.com. E-mail: kbrandon@pcschools.us.

BRANDON, KATHRYN ELIZABETH BECK, pediatrician; b. Sept. 10, 1916; d. Clarence M. and Hazel A. (Cutler) Beck; children: John William, Kathleen Brandon McEnulty, Karen (dec.). MD, U. Chgo., 1941; BA, U. Utah, 1937; MPH, U. Calif., Berkeley, 1957. Diplomate Am. Bd. Pediats. Intern Grace Hosp., Detroit, 1941-42; resident Children's Hosp. Med. Ctr. No. Calif., Oakland, 1953-55, Children's Hosp., L.A., 1951-53; pvt. practice La Crescentia, Calif., 1946-51, Salt Lake City, 1960-65, 86—. Med. dir. Salt Lake City public schs., 1957-60; dir. Ogden City-Weber County (Utah) Health Dept., 1965-67; pediatrician Fitzsimmons Army Hosp., 1967-68; coll. health physician U. Colo., Boulder, 1968-71; student health physician U. Utah, Salt Lake City, 1971-81; occupational health physician Hill AFB, Utah, 1981-85; child health physician Salt Lake City-County Health Dept., 1971-82; cons. in field; clin. asst. U. Utah Coll. Medicine, Salt Lake City, 1958-64; clin. asst. pediatrics U. Colo. Coll. Medicine, Denver, 1958-72; active staff emeritus Primary Children's Hosp., LDS Hosp., and Cottonwood Hosp., 1960-67. Fellow APHA, Am. Pediat. Acad., Am. Sch. Health Assn.; mem. AMA, Utah Coll. Health Assn. (pres. 1978-80), Pacific Coast Coll. Health Assn., Utah Med. Assn., Salt Lake County Med. Soc., Utah Pub. Health Assn. (sec.-treas. 1960-66), Intermountain Pediat. Soc.

BRANDON, LIANE, filmmaker, educator; Student, St. Lawrence U., U. Edinburgh, Scotland; exchange student, U. Moscow; AB, MEd, Boston U. Ski instr., Mt. Tremblant, Que., Canada; actress Children's Theatre, Cambridge, Mass.; film project dir. English dept. Quincy pub. schs., Mass.; prof. film-TV prodn. and media studies Sch. Edn. U. Mass., Amherst, 1973—; co-founder, mem. New Day Films, 1971—, Filmwomen of Boston, 1974—; co-dir. UMass Ednl. TV, U. Mass., Amherst, 1994—2004; dir. Sch. Edn. Ednl. Tech. Program, U. Mass., 1998—. Film cons. Mass. Gov.'s Commn. on Status of Women, 1974; cons. Mass. Artists Found., 1975, 82, WGBH-TV, 1992-97; judge Regional Student Acad. Awards, 1991, New Eng. Regional Emmy Awards,1992; trustee Theaterworks, 1981-83; bd. dirs. Boston Film-Video Found., 1983-87, ACLU of Mass., 1988-97; mem. adv. bd. Children's Media Found. Boston, 1993-97; guest lectr. various confs. on edn. and film to colls. and art schs. in US. Exhibited film, Mus. Modern Art, Whitney Mus. Am. Art, Chgo. Art Inst., Nat. Film Theatre, London, Internat. Womens Film Festival, Paris, Mus. Fine Arts, Boston, Libr. Congress, Washington, John F. Kennedy Ctr. Performing Arts, Washington; dir., prodr. (film) Anything You Want to Be, 1971 (Blue Ribbon Am. Film Festival award), Betty Tells Her Story, 1972, Once Upon a Choice, 1980 (Silver medal Houston Internat. Film Festival), How to Prevent a Nuclear War, 1987 (Blue Ribbon award Am. Film Festival 1988); prodr. (video) Goodnight Amherst, 1995, Fine Print, 1995, Try This At Home, 1998 (Judge's Choice award Hometown Video Festival 1999), Fresh Ink, 1998, Try This At Home: Nature Series, 2000 (award of Distinction, Communicator award); still photographer: Murder at Harvard, 2002, Act Your Age, 2002, (PBS) The Most Dangerous Woman in America, 2005. Recipient Creative Artist award AAUW, 1975, Disting. Alumni award Boston U., 1985; Careth Found. grantee, 1988, Funding Exchange grantee, 1989, Mass. Found. for Humanities and Pub. Policy grantee, 1975, Film Fund grantee, 1985. Try this at Home: Nature Series (Award of Distinction, Communicator Awards), 2000 Mem. New Eng. Screen Edn. Assn. (v.p. 1972-83), Assn. Ind. Video and Filmmakers, Women in Film and Video New Eng. (founding mem. 1981-). E-mail: brandon@educ.umass.edu.

BRANDON, MICHELLE MARIE, marketing executive; b. Tallmadge, Ohio, Nov. 8, 1976; d. Timothy Roy Brandon and Judy Ann Ripple. BS, Cornell U., Ithaca, N.Y., 1999. Mktg. asst. Hanger Thacker, Ithaca, 1995—99; promotions asst. N.Y.C. Opera, 1999—2000; dir. mktg. Pearl Theatre Co., N.Y.C., 2000—03, Signature Theatre Co., N.Y.C., 2003—05; mktg. cons. N.Y.C., 2005—.

BRANDT, ASTRID, elementary school educator; b. Buenos Aires, Mar. 31, 1947; d. Clemens Antonius Hendrious and Johanna Wilhelmina Wever Brandt; m. Rodolfo Augusto Lértora, Oct. 1, 1972; 1 child, Astrid L. Novak. Student, Harris County CC, Houston, 1988—89; BS in Math., Sam Houston State U., Huntsville, Tex., 1990—91, MA in Math., 1998—2000. Cert. Secondary Tchr., Math., Bilingual, ESL Tex. Dept. Edn., 1991. Math. tchr., lead tchr. Burbank Mid. Sch., Houston Ind. Sch. Dist., 1993—97; prof., devel. math. Sam Houston State U., 1998—2000, liaison math. dept., bilingual edn., 1999—2002. Prof., devel. math. Prison Sys., Ferguson Unit, Huntsville, 1998; algebra I trainer for new tchrs. Houston Ind. Sch. Dist., 2002—. Sec. Pi Mu Epsilon, Huntsville, 1999—2000. Recipient Tchr. of Yr., Burbank Mid. Sch., 1997. Mem.: Am. Math. Soc., Math. Assn. Am., Nat. Coun. Tchrs. Math. Avocations: drawing, motorcycling. Office: Houston Ind Sch Dist 310 Perry Rd Houston TX 77020

BRANDT, CAROLE, theater educator, department chairman; b. Lincoln, Ill., Oct. 22, 1937; d. Clifton Perry and Mary Helen (Mitchell). BS in Speech Edn., U. Ill., 1959, MA in Theatre Art, 1962; postgrad., U. Iowa, 1968-69; PhD in Directing and Dramatic Lit., So. Ill. U., 1976. Tchr. speech and drama, play dir. pub. schs., Oak Lawn, Joliet, Maywood, Ill., 1959-65, 66-68; teaching asst. in speech U. Ill., Urbana, 1961-62; teaching asst. in rhetoric, then instr. edn. play prodn. U. Iowa, Iowa City, 1968-69; asst. prof. theatre Ill. State U., Normal, 1969-74; assoc. prof. drama Ill. Wesleyan U., Bloomington, 1975-82, dir. Sch. Drama, 1977-82; artistic dir. Cen. Sta. Dinnner, Bloomington, 1982-83, Co. ONSTAGE, Bloomington, 1983-84; prof., chmn. dept. theatre U. Fla., Gainesville, 1984-88; prof., head dept. theatre arts, exec. producer, artistic dir. Pa. State U. and Pa. Centre Stage, University Park, 1988-94; dean Meadows Sch. of the Arts, So. Meth. U., Dallas, 1994—, prof. Vis. artist, prof. Idaho State U., Pocatello, 1984; critic Am. Coll. Theater Regional and State Festivals; guest critic numerous univs. and theatres; mem. Pa. Adv. Coun. for Arts in Edn., 1990-92; exec. producer, bd. dirs. Pa. Centre Stage, 1988-92; mem. nat. com. Am. Coll. Theatre Festival, Kennedy Ctr. for Performing Arts, Washington, 1978-89, 91-93, mem. nat. exec. com., 1982-89, 91-93, nat. chmn., 1985-87. Co-author: (video tape) Adjudication 1987; dir. Nat. Evening of Scenes, Kennedy Ctr. for Performing Arts, 1986, A Chorus Line, Hippodrome State Theatre, 1987. Convener Nat. Think Tank for Change, Washington, 1990; trustee Twin Cities Ballet, Bloomington, 1982; panel mem. Ill. Arts Coun., Chgo., 1978-81; mem. reading panel Nat. Endowment for Arts, 1991-92. Recipient Theatre Educator of Yr. award Fla. Assn. for Theatre Edn., 1988; AMOCO medal of excellence Am. Coll. Theatre Festival, 1981, Kennedy Ctr. medal, 1989, 91, 93, Disting. Alumni awrd Dept. Theatre/So. Ill. U., 1996, Coll. Arts and Scis./So. Ill. U., 1997, Encomienda de la Orden de Isabel La Catolica, King Juan Carlos, 2001, Creative Arts award for excellence Dallas Hist. Soc., 2002. Fellow Coll. Fellows Am. Theatre (former dean); mem. Assn. for Theatre in Higher Edn. (founding, bd. govs. 1991—, pres. 1993-95), Nat. Assn. Schs. Theatre (panelist, evaluator 1987, 89-92, bd. dirs. 1991—, treas., v.p., pres.), Soc. for Stage Dirs. & Choreographers, Nat. Theatre Conf. (life, v.p., pres.), Fla. Theatre Conf. (pres.), Ill. Theatre Assn. (pres.). Avocations: reading, listening to music, cultural events. Office: Meadows Sch Arts/So Meth U Offfice of the Dean PO Box 750356 Dallas TX 75275-0001 Office Phone: 214-768-2880. Business E-Mail: cbrandt@mail.smu.edu.

BRANDT, ELSA LUND ERICKSON, music educator; b. Bklyn., Oct. 3, 1932; d. Ernst Ansgar Erickson and Astrid Osestad; m. Carl David Brandt, Apr. 25, 1964; children: Karen, Erik. BMus, Manhattan Sch. Music, N.Y., 1953; MMus, Manhattan Sch. Music, 1963; BMusE, Hartt Coll. Music, Hartford, Conn., 1957. Violinist Hartford Symphony Orch., 1954—57; instrumental instr. pub. schs., New Rochelle, NY, 1958—60; violinist New Orleans Symphony Orch., 1960—61; violin tchr., prep. dept. Manhattan Sch. Music, N.Y.C., 1961—63; freelance musician Washington, 1967—89; asst. prof. music Howard U., Washington, 1968—90; pvt. studio Silver Spring, Md., 1985—. Founder Maggini String Quartet, Silver Spring; past adjudicator string festivals Md. State Tchrs. Assn.; tape audition com. Johansen Internat. String Competition, 1997, 2000, 03. Performer: (violin solo recital) Carnegie Recital Hall, 1966. Mem.: Am. String Tchrs. Assn. (curriculum com. Am. String Tchrs. Assn. Md.-DC chpt., pres. Md. DC chpt., Outstanding Tchr. of Yr. Am. String Tchrs. Assn. Md.-DC chpt. 2000), Coll. Music Soc. (life), Photographic Soc. Am., Friday Morning Music Club (soloist, violin and viola 1967—). Home and Studio: 819 E Franklin Ave Silver Spring MD 20901-4709 Personal E-mail: ElsaBrandt@aol.com.

BRANDT, JENNIFER ANNE, lawyer; b. Perth Amboy, N.J., July 26, 1969; d. Sanford D. and Joan M. (Klein) B. BA highest honors, Rutgers U., 1991; JD, U. Pa., 1994. Bar: Pa. 1994, N.J. 1994, D.C. 1996. Assoc. Dilworth, Pakson, Kalish & Kauffman, LLP, Phila., 1994—98; mem. Cozen O'Connor, Phila., 1998—. Editor (sr.): Jour. Internat. Bus. Law, 1994. Named one of Lawyers on the Fast Track, Am. Lawyer Media, 2004; Arthur Littleton Fellowship, U. Pa. Mem.: ABA, N.J. Bar Assn., Pa. Bar Assn., Phila. Bar Assn. (co-chair, mem. comm.). Office: Cozen O'Connor 1900 Market St Philadelphia PA 19103

BRANDT, KATHLEEN **See WEIL-GARRIS BRANDT, KATHLEEN**

BRANDT, LEOTA FAY, medical/surgical nurse; b. Hamburg, Iowa, June 22, 1940; d. Ralph Lester and Dorothy O. (Folkes) Melton; m. J. Merril Brandt, July 26, 1960; children: Forrest, Clifford, Merrilee, Stephen. ADN, Iowa Western Community Coll., 1985; student, Bethany Nazarene Coll., 1959, 86. RN, Iowa. Staff nurse Grape Community Hosp., Hamburg, Iowa, 1986-90, Glenwood (Iowa) State Hosp., 1987—.

BRANDT, PAMELA ANN, art educator, special education educator; b. Manitowoc, Wis., Sept. 13, 1962; d. Jerome Nicholas and Patricia Ann Gresenz; m. Robert Martin Brandt, June 18, 1988; children: Adam Jerome, Eric Robert, Elise Patricia. BA, Alverno Coll., 1984. Cert. art & spl. edn. tchr. Dept. Pub. Instrn., Wis., 1984. Art, art spl. edn. tchr. Hartford Joint No. 1 Sch. Dist., Wis., 1984—. Art dept. curriculum chairperson Hartford Joint 1 Sch. Dist., 1994—. Leader Girl Scouts Am., Slinger, Wis., 2002—; troop com. mem. Boy Scouts Am., Slinger, 1999—. Recipient Scouter's Tng. award, Boy Scouts Am., 2002, Scouter's Key, 2002, Arrowhead Honor award, 2002. Mem.: NEA, Wis. Edn. Assn., Cedar Lake United Educators, Hartford Elem. Edn. Assn., Wis. Assn. Mid- Level Educators, Am. Art Therapy Assn., Wis. Art Therapy Assn., Nat. Art Edn. Assn., Wis. Art Edn. Assn., Delta Kappa Gamma. Avocations: crafts, camping, hiking, swimming, fishing. Home: 603 Highview Dr Slinger WI 53086 Office: Central Mid Sch 1100 Cedar St Hartford WI 53027 Office Phone: 262-673-8040. Office Fax: 262-673-7596. Business E-Mail: brandt@hartfordjt1.k12.wi.us.

BRANDT, SARA JANE, elementary school educator; b. Hutchinson, Kans., Mar. 14, 1964; d. Rollin and JoNel (Diggs) Lohmeyer; m. Larry J. Brandt, June 29, 1985 BS summa cum laude, Ft. Hays State U., 1986. Cert. in early childhood edn., English as 2d lang., Calif. Tchr. kindergarten Green Acres Sch., Dumas, Tex., Hillcrest Sch., Dumas. Mem. Assn. Tex. Profl. Educators., Phi Kappa Phi (named Moore County Tchr. Yr. 2005) Personal E-mail: lbrandt03@valornet.com.

BRANDT, TRACI LYNN KELLER, music educator, musician; d. John Allen and Linda Mae Keller; m. Eric George Brandt, Oct. 20, 2001; children: Jared Parker, Emma Nicole. MusB in Edn., The Ohio State U., Columbus, Ohio, 1993, MA in Music Edn., 2001. Lic. profl. tchr. Ohio, 2004. Asst. dir. band Lakewood Local Sch., Hebron, Ohio, 1993—2000; tchr. mid. sch. instrumental music Reynoldsburg City Schs., Ohio, 2000—01; dir. bands Heath City Schs., Ohio, 2001—. Musician: Brass Band Columbus, 2000—. Mem. com. Hosanna Luth. Ch., Pataskala, Ohio, 2005—06. Mem.: N.Am. Bras Band Assn., Ohio Music Edn. Assn., Heath Edn. Assn. Luth. Home: 101 Purple Finch Loop Pataskala OH 43062 Office: Heath City Schools 300 Licking View Dr Heath OH 43056 Office Phone: 740-788-3300. Personal E-mail: tbrandt70@gmail.com. Business E-Mail: tbrandt@laca.org.

BRANDT-SHAPIRO, IRENE HILDEGARD, retired secondary school educator; b. Meriden, Conn., June 6, 1942; d. Walter M. and Hildegard E. Brandt; married Robert Shapiro, Aug. 20,2005. BS, Ctrl. Conn. State U., New Britian, 1964, MS, 1969, cert. 6th yr. degree, 1989, postgrad., 1989. Cert. 7-12 math. tchr., K-12 adminstrn. and supervision, intermediate supervision, Conn. Tchr. math. Jefferson Jr. H.S., Meriden, 1964-67, Platt H.S., Meriden, 1967-99; ret., 1999. Substitute tchr. Platt H.S. Active Summit Club, Meriden, 1972-99. Yearbook dedicated to her Platt H.S., 1971, named Oustanding Tchr. by SRS., 1990, 91, 92, 96, 98, 99, 2000, 05, 06. Mem. ASCD, Nat. Coun. Tchrs. Math., New Eng. Math. Tchrs. Assn., Assn. Tchrs. Math. in Conn. (conv. presider 1990-98), Am. Fedn. Tchrs., Conn. Fedn. Tchrs., Meriden Fedn. Tchrs. (sec. 1982-90). Avocations: travel, reading, crossword puzzles, gardening.

BRANDVOLD, AURORA PAULINE, nursing researcher; b. Wadena, Sask., Can., Aug. 15, 1941; d. Skulmindar Einar and Aurora Beatrice Thorsteinson; m. Duane George Brandvold; children: James, Donnelle (dec.), Joseph, Johnathan, Jason. BSN, Seattle Pacific U., 1985; MSN, Seattle U., 1996. Cert. oncology nurse. Staff nurse Foam Lake (Sask.) Union Hosp., 1962—63; office nurse, internist Clinic, Everett, Wash., 1962—65; staff nurse Everett Gen. Hosp., 1965—68; staff nurse, inservice dir. Long Term Care Facilities, Snohomish, Wash., 1972—76; gen. duty nurse physician's office, Everett, 1976—81; staff nurse (including ICU) Bone Marrow Transplant Unit Swedish Hosp. Med. Ctr., Seattle, 1981—96; clin. rsch. nurse Fred Hutchinson Cancer Rsch. Ctr., Seattle, 1996—. Mem. steering com. Coord. Clin. Trials, U. Wash. and Fred Hutchinson Cancer Rsch. Ctr., 2000; mem. ethics com. Fred Hutchinson Cancer Rsch. Ctr., 1996—2003; chairperson Clin. Trials Coordinating Group, 1998—2000; mem. reunion 2000 com. Fred Hutchinson Cancer Rsch. Ctr., 1998—2000; mem. stem cell spl. interest group Oncology Nursing Soc.; mem. ethics com. Swedish Hosp. Med. Ctr., 1985—96; mem. reunion 2005 com. Fred Hutchinson Cancer Rsch. Ctr. Mem.: Assn. Clin. Rsch. Profls., Puget Sound Oncology Nurses Assn. (mem. organizing com. ann. symposium 1994—95, rsch. com. 2003—), Oncology Nurses Soc., Snohomish County Nurses Assn., Wash. State Nurses Assn. (PAC bd. trustees), ANA. Republican. Roman Catholic. Avocation: family. Home: 5307 139th Ave S E Snohomish WA 98290 Office: Fred Hutchinson Cancer Rsch Ctr LF-240 PO Box 19024 1100 Fairview Ave N Seattle WA 98109-1024 Personal E-mail: res04j9c@gte.net.

BRANHAM, JENNIE JONES, artist; d. Charles Alfonzo and Louise Kilgo Jones; m. Mack Carison Branham, Dec. 17, 1953; children: Kenneth Gary, Charles Michael, Keith Robert, Laurie Lynn. BA in Art and Art Mgmt., Columbia Coll., 1986. Art gallery dir. Columbia Coll., Columbia, 1986—90; supt. of fine arts S.C. State Fair, Columbia, 1997—2000. Exhibitions include, Crooked Creek Art League, Trenholm Artists Guild, Hilton Head Art League, SC State Fair, Sumter Gallery Art, Carolina Gallery, McKissick Mus, Gallery at Nonnah's, Anastasio's Pawleys Island, represented in corporate and private collections. Com. mem. Endorsing Com. for Luth. Chaplains of, Washington, 1975—81; mem. Religion & Art, Salisbury, NC, 1983—89; pres. Officers Wives Assn., Air University (Maxwell AFB), Ala., 1971—72. Mem.: Crooked Creek Art League (founding pres. 1995, Mem. of the Yr. 1995). Republican. Lutheran. Avocations: travel, reading, aerobics. Home: 109 Laurent Way Irmo SC 29063 Office: Circa Art 109 Laurent Way Irmo SC 29063 Personal E-mail: jennie2839@hotmail.com.

BRANHAM, REGINA JEANETTE, elementary school educator; b. Chattanooga, Mar. 28, 1975; d. Bernard Lee and Jimmie Louise Branham. BS, Lee U., Cleveland, Tenn., 1998. Sch. tchr. Lake Forest Middle Sch., Cleveland, 1998—.

BRANICK, TERRY LYNN, secondary school educator; b. Wakenney, Kans., Oct. 19, 1959; d. Richard Lee Stewart and Vera Frances Karst; m. Frederick Walter Azeltine, Jan. 6, 1979 (div. Aug. 1982); children: Misty Dawn, Dustin Lee; m. Joseph Dennis Branick, Nov. 29, 1986; children: Joseph Clay, Westin Stewart, Desiree Danae. A in Gen. Studies, Barton County C.C., 1990; BA in Art, Ft. Hays State U., 1997. Cert. K-12 art 2002, 7-12 psychology 2004. Substitute tchr. various schs., Kans., 1990—. Deines Cultural Ctr., Russell, Kans., 2004; set designer: play, summer play, 2004. Mem. Bickerdyke Elem. Site Coun., Russell, Kans., 2000—; leader Girl Scouts Am., 2000—03, mem. transp. com., 2000—, Boys Scouts Am., 1995; block chairperson Am. Heart Assn., 2001; play park com. Russell, 2002—03; vol. Russell Dream Theatre, 2002—; Sunday sch. tchr., 1997—98; edn. com. Trinity United Meth. Ch., 2002—; Sunday sch. tchr., 2003—04. Mem.: Venture Club (leader 2001—03). Methodist. Avocations: poetry, photography, bicycling, art, hiking. Home: 513 S Kansas St Russell KS 67665

BRANIGAN, HELEN MARIE, educational consultant, administrator; b. Albany, NY, Sept. 24, 1944; d. James J. and Helen (Weaver) B. BS in Bus. Edn., Coll. St. Rose, Albany, 1967, MA in English, 1972; postgrad., SUNY, Albany, 1973—81. Tchr., chair dept. bus. edn. S. Colonie Sch. Dist., Albany, 1968-81; assoc. Bur. Bus. Edn. NY State Edn. Dept., Albany, 1981-87; assoc. Bur. Occupl. Edn. Program Devel., Albany, 1987-91, Bur. Occupl. Edn. Innovation and Quality, Albany, 1991-93, Ctrl./So. Regional Field Svcs., Albany, 1993-95, North Country/Regional Field Svcs., 1995-98, Regional Sch. Improvement Team, 1998—2003. Bd. trustees St. Catherine's Found., 1993-97; sr. cons. Internat. Ctr. for Leadership in Edn., Schenectady, NY, 1991—; facilitator Champlain Valley Ednl. Ctr., Plattsburgh, NY, 2004-; cons. Inst. Learning Centered Edn., Potsdam, NY, 2004-; ednl. cons. Students First, Albany, 2004—; bd. dirs. Adirondack Curriculum Project, 2003—. Editor: Glencoe Pub., 1986—; contbr. articles to profl. jours. Lay vol. Archdiocese of Anchorage, 1967-68; mem. NY State Staff Devel. Coun. Mem.: ASCD, Delta Pi Epsilon. Roman Catholic. Avocations: skiing, mountain climbing, golf, reading. Home: 540 New Scotland Ave Albany NY 12208-2318 Office Phone: 518-482-3189. E-mail: hbranigan@aol.com.

BRANN, EVA TONI HELENE, philosophy educator; b. Berlin, Jan. 21, 1929; came to U.S., 1941; d. Edgar and Paula (Sklarz) B. BA, Bklyn. Coll., 1950; MA, Yale U., 1951, PhD, 1956; HHD (hon.), Whitman Coll., 1995, Middlebury Coll., 1999. Instr. archaeology Stanford (Calif.) U., 1956-57; tutor St. John's Coll., Annapolis, Md., 1957—, dean, 1990-97; mem. Inst. for Advanced Study, 1958. Mem. U.S Adv. Commn. for Internat. Edn., 1975-77; vis. prof. Whitman Coll., Walla Walla, Wash., 1978-79; honors prof. U. Del., Newark, 1984-86. Author: Protoattic Pottery from the Athenian Agora, 1962, Paradoxes of Education in a Republic, 1979, The World of the Imagination, 1991, The Past Present, 1997, What, Then, Is Time, 1999, The Ways of Naysaying, 2001, Homeric Moments, 2002, The Music of the Republic, 2004, Open Secrets, 2004; translator: Greek Mathematics and the Origin of Algebra, 1968; co-translator: Plato's Sophist, 1996, Plato's Phaedo, 1998. Mem. state adv. com. U.S. Commn. on Civil Rights, Md., 1988-96. Recipient Pres. Nat. Humanities medal, 2005; grantee, NEH, 1987; Woodrow Wilson Ctr. fellow, 1976. Mem. Phi Beta Kappa. Democrat. Jewish. Office: St John's Coll 60 College Ave Annapolis MD 21404-2800 Office Phone: 410-263-2371.

BRANNAN, PATRICIA A., lawyer; b. Milw., Nov. 1953; BA summa cum laude, Marquette U., 1975; JD cum laude, Harvard U., 1979. Bar: D.C. 1980, MD 1996, U.S. Ct. Appeals D.C., eleventh cir., seventh cir., U.S. Supreme Ct. Law clk. to Hon. John M. Ferren, D.C. Ct. Apeals, 1979—80; assoc. Hogan & Hartson LLP, Washington, 1980, ptnr.-in-charge, Pro Bono Program, cmty. svc. practice group dir. Author: Implications Mo. vs. Jenkins Mcpl. & Sch. Dist. Fin., 1991, Critical Details: Amending U.S. Constitution, 1979; co-author: Adverse Impact Ednl. Opportunity Cases Challenging State Sch. Financing Schemes, 1991. Fellow: Am. Bar Found.; mem.: MD State Bar Assn., D.C. Bar (Disciplinary System Study Com.). Office: Hogan & Hartson LLP Columbia Sq 555 Thirteenth St NW Washington DC 20004-1109 Office Phone: 202-637-8686. Office Fax: 202-637-5910. Business E-Mail: pabrannan@hhlaw.com.

BRANNICK, ELLEN MARIE, retired management consultant; b. Rochester, Minn., Aug. 10, 1934; d. Daniel Ryther and Grace Ellen (Mills) Markham; m. Thomas L. Brannick. BS in Health, Phys. Edn., MacMurray Coll., 1956, MS, 1959. Elem. phys. edn. Ritenour Consol. Sch. Dist., Overland, Mo., 1958-61; head tchr., summer dir. Civic League Day Nursery, Rochester, 1961-64; recreation therapist Rochester State Hosp., 1964-68; rehab. dir. Rochester State Hosp., 1968-70; rehab. therapist Napa State Hosp., Calif., 1971, indsl. therapy con. Calif., 1971-73, community liaison rep. Calif., 1973—2000; ret., 2001. Mem. Friends Napa County Libr., 1977. Mem.: Rogue Valley Geneal. Soc., Napa County Hist. Soc. Democrat. Avocations: antique post cards, genealogy, military history, travel. Personal E-mail: ebrannick@medford.net.

BRANNON-PEPPAS, LISA, chemical engineer, researcher; b. Houston, Sept. 19, 1962; d. James Graham and Patricia Ann (Hightower) Brannon; m. Nicholas A. Peppas, Aug. 10, 1988. BS, Rice U., 1984; MS, Purdue U., 1986, PhD, 1988. Sr. formulations chemist Eli Lilly & Co., Indpls., 1988-91; pres., founder Biogel Tech., Indpls., 1991—2002; rsch. prof. dept. biomed. engring. U. Tex., Austin, 2002—, dir. Ctr. of Biol. and Med. Engring., 2003—. Author, editor: Absorbent Polymer Technology, 1990, mem. editl. bd.: Jour. Applied Polymer Sci., 1995—2001, Jour. Controlled Release, 1997—2001, Jour. Nanoparticle Rsch., 1998—, Biomaterials, 1999—2003, Drug Development and Industrial Pharmacy, 2003—. Vol. Indpls. Mus. Art, 1990—98, Humane Soc. Indpls., 1990—98, Indpls. Zoo, 1994—2000; trustee Chem. Engring. Found., 1999—2000. Recipient Harold B. Lamport award Biomed. Engring. Soc., 1989; named Outstanding Young Alumna, Kinkaid Sch., 1998. Fellow Am. Inst. of Med. and Biol. Engring.; mem. AIChE (dir. 1998-2000, exec. bd. programming coun., dir. materials divsn., chmn. subcom. biomaterials divsn. 1990-93, dir.-at-large food, pharm. and bioengring. divsn. 1992-94, 2d vice chair materials divsn. 1994-95, 1st vice chmn. materials divsn. 1995-96, chmn. 1996-97, bd. dirs. 1998-2000), Am. Chem. Soc. (membership com. 1990—), Controlled Release Soc. (treas. 1995-98, internat. planning com. 1991, bd. govs. 1992-95), Jr. League Indpls. (bd. dirs. 1992-94). Avocations: fine art, dance, travel. Office: U Tex Austin CPE 3-168a Austin TX 78712 E-mail: peppas@mail.utexas.edu.

BRANSFORD-YOUNG, ANGHARAD ANN, counselor, educator; d. Byron Everett and Frankie C. Bransford; children: Alison Koi Howard, Stephanie Ann Parker. BA, N. Tex. U., Denton, 1965; MA, Northeastern State U., Tahlequah, Okla., 1968; EdD, U. Tulsa, Okla., 1982. Sr. Diplomate Am. Bd. Disability Analysts, lic. Profl. Counselor Okla. Dept. Health, Family Therapist Okla. Dept. Health. Counselor Oral Robert U. Counseling, Tulsa, 1981—84, asst. dir., 1984—86; counselor Tulsa CC, 1986—87; counselor, dir. Counseling Care Assn., 1987—90; dir. Oral Roberts U. Counseling, 1990—98; counselor/cons., pvt. practice Tulsa, 1996—; assoc. prof. Oral Roberts U., 1998—. Address: PO Box 52492 Tulsa OK 74152

BRANSTETTER, ANN DYCHE, psychology professor; b. Springfield, Mo., Sept. 2, 1971; d. William Calvin and paulene May Dyche; 1 child, Margaret May. BS magna cum laude in Psychology, Southwest Mo. State U., Springfield, 1993; MS in Clin. Psychology, ND State U., Fargo, 1995; PhD in Clin. Psychology, U. Kans., Lawrence, 2001. Tchg. asst. Dept. Psychology U. Kans., 1996—97, instr. Dept. Psychology, 1998; resident psychology U. Ill. Med. Ctr., Chgo., 1999—2000; clin. health psychology intern U. Ill., 2000—01; instr. in medicine Wash. U. Sch. Medicine, St. Louis, 2000—03; prin. investigator ACS, 2001—03; asst. prof. Mo. State U., Springfield, 2003—. Guest reviewer Jour. Abnormal Psychology, 2001; editl. bd. mem. Online Behavior Analyst, 2005—06; guest lectr. various sch., 1999—2005. Recipient Excellence in Psychology award, Southwest Mo. State U., 1991, Winner Rsch. Competition, Mo. Psychological Assn., 1993, Grad. Study Rsch. Enhancement award, ND State U., 1995, Presidential award, Assn. for Advancement Behavior Therapy, 2000, Citation award, Soc. Behavioral Medicine, 2004. Mem.: ACS (chair 2005—, ambassador 2006), Am. Psychological Assn., Am. Pain Soc., Assn. Behavioral and Cognitive Therapies, Assn. Behavior Analysis, Clin. Behavior Analysis Spl. Interest Group (pres. 2003—06), Golden Key, Phi Kappa Phi, Psi Chi. Office: Mo State U Dept Psychology 901 S Nat Ave Springfield MO 65897-0001 Office Phone: 417-836-5406. Business E-Mail: annbranstetter@missouristate.edu.

BRANT, DORRIS ELLEN STAPLETON, bacteriologist, music educator; b. Southard, Mo., Jan. 21, 1933; d. John Ross Stapleton and Sylvia Cleo Boren; m. James Chesney Brant, Sept. 1, 1953; children: Solveig, Sonja Brant Betzen. BA, U. of Wichita, Wichita, KS, 1954, MS, 1956. Cert. tchr. Okla., 1966. Tchg. fellow Wichita U., Wichita, Kans., 1954—55; bacteriologist Hyde Pk. (Borden) Dairy, Wichita, Kans., 1955—56; asst. bacteriologist Wichita / Sedgwick Co. Dept. of Pub. Health, Wichita, Kans., 1956—59; educator Unified Sch. Dist. 382, Pratt, Kans., 1966—96; adj. prof. music St. Mary of Plains Coll., Dodge City, Kans., 1987—89. State bd. Kans. ORFF Assn., Kans., 1995—2000; exec. bd. Delta Kappa Gamma Soc. Internat., Kans., 1980—. Internat. chmn. of travel study com. Delta Kappa Gamma Soc., Kans., 1998—2000; nominating com. Delta Kappa Gamma Soc., Kans., 2002—; pres. Delta Kappa Gamma Soc., Kans., 1991—93; cmty. / foods leader Kans. Farm Bur. Youth Seminar, Manhattan, Kans., 1966—81; sr. counselor Pratt County 4-H Club, Pratt, Kans., 1960—90; pres. Pratt Regional Med. Ctr. Aux., Pratt, Kans., 2000—01; ctrl. com. mem. Rep. Party, Pratt, Kans., 1960—90, 1998—2002. Recipient Delta Epsilon (Hon. Sci.), Ft. Hays U., 1955, Phi State Achievement Award, Delta Kappa Gamma Soc. Internat., 2000, Golden Gift Leadership / Mgmt., Delta Kappa Gamma Soc. Internat., 1985. Mem.: Nat. Assn. of Parliamentarians, Pratt Music Club (pres. 1960—2002), AAUW (vice-president 1990—2002), AAUW (vice-president 1960—80), Phi Delta Kappa. R-Consevative. Methodist. Avocations: music, reading, geneology, ice skating (figure), cooking. Home: 70215 SE 100th Avenue Isabel KS 67065 Personal E-mail: jdbrant@havilandtelco.com.

BRANT, JACQUELYN LOIS, secondary school educator, history educator, department chairman; b. Holdenville, Okla., Sept. 24, 1946; d. Orrin Leonard Swinbart and Doris Medill Tynan; children: Stephanie Gore, Randall Gore, Cynde Gore Larkins. BA, U. N.C., 1979, MA in Tchg. History, 1992. Tchr., dept. chmn., coach East Columbus H.S., Lake Waccamaw, NC, 1980—96; tchr., coach Cmty. Mid. Sch., Nevada, Tex., 1996—97, LBJ H.S., Johnson City, Tex., 1997—99; tchr., dept. chmn. Mabank (Tex.) H.S., 1999—2005; tchr. Burke (Va.) ALC, 2005—, chmn. Dept. History, 2005—. Supt. adv. coun. Fairfax County Pub. Schs. Chmn., organizer Vets. Meml. Garden, Mabank, 2003—05. With USN, 1964—66. Named Tchr. of Yr., VFW, 2004, Citizen of Yr., DAR, 2004; recipient Citizenship Bronze medal, Sons Am. Revolution, 2004. Mem.: NHE, NCSS. Home: 10206 Colston Ct 304 Burke VA 22015 Office: Burke ALC 9645 Burke Lake Rd Burke VA 22015

BRANT, RENEE S. TANKENOFF, psychiatrist; b. St. Paul, Minn., Oct. 23, 1946; d. Oliver H. and Mollie F. (Tishler) Tankenoff; m. Jonathan Brant, July 11, 1970; children: Simone, Justin. BA, Brandeis U., Waltham, Mass., 1958; MD, Harvard U., Cambridge, 1972. Diplomate Child and Adolescent Psychiatry Am. Bd. Psychiatry, 1974, Gen. Psychiatry Am. Bd. Psychiatry, 1979. Intern pediatrics Mass. Gen. Hosp., Boston, 1971—73; resident child psychiatry Childrens Hosp., Boston, 1973—75; resident adult psychiatry Beth Israel Hosp., Boston, 1975—77; clin. instr. Harvard Med. Sch., Boston, 1977—90, asst. clin. prof., 1990—. Founder Sexual Abuse Team Childrens Hosp., Boston, 1978—87. Pres. Boston chpt. Am. Profl. Soc. on the Abuse of Cbildren, 1992—94. Recipient Women Who Dared award, Boston Jewish Women's Archive, 2001. Mem.: Am. Acad. Child and Adolescent Psychiatry, Mass. Psychiatric Soc. Office: 30 Lincoln St Newton Highlands MA 02461 Office Phone: 617-964-6982. Office Fax: 617-969-7803. Personal E-mail: rjbrant@comcast.net.

BRANTINGHAM, ANDRYA J., special education educator; b. Libertyville, Ill., May 27, 1965; d. John David and Betsy Ann Luther; m. Eric Lawrence Brantingham, May 24, 1997; children: Kade Pierre, JD Luke. BS, Fla. State U., 1987; MA, U. No. Colo., 1994; PhD in Curriculum Instrn., U. Wyo., 2001. Tchr. Littleton Pub. Schs., Colo., 1989—94; tchr. spl. edn. North Park Schs., Walden, Colo., 1994—96; tchr. Ouray R-1, Ridgway, Colo., 2001—03; staff devel. contractor pvt. practice, Norwood, 2004—. Bd. dirs. Wright's Mesa Ctr., Norwood; mem. exec. bd. Voyager Youth Program, Ridgway, 2003—04. Coach Spl. Olympics, Ft. Collins, Colo., 1985—87. Mem.: ASCD, Colo. Assn. Sch. Bds. Avocations: horseback riding, skiing. Home: PO Box 451 Norwood CO 81423

BRANTLEY, WILLA JOHN, educational association administrator; b. Carthage, Miss., Aug. 24, 1956; d. Rena John; m. Harlon Dwight Bell, May 15, 1974 (div. 1979); children: Chassidy Georgina, Gerrard Dwight; m. Nicky Paul Brantley, Jan. 5, 1985 (div. 1991). Student, East Cen. Jr. Coll., 1975, Wood Jr. Coll., 1975-76; BEd magna cum laude, Jackson State U., 1979; postgrad., Miss. State U., 1979-81, 83—. Cert. elem. tchr., Miss. Counselor Miss. Band Choctaw Indian, Philadelphia, Miss., 1979; elem. tchr. Standing Pine Sch., Walnut Grove, Miss., 1979-81, prin. Philadelphia, 1983-87; ednl. specialist Chocotaw Agy., Phila., 1981-83, 87—, acting agy. supr. for edn. Philadelphia, 1981-88, agt. supt. for edn. Phila., 1990—; tchr. evaluator Pa. Dept. Edn., Philadelphia, 1990—; dir. Choctaw Dept. Edn., Philadelphia, 1990—96; substitute tchr. Oxford Elem. Sch., Batesville Job Corp., Attalla County Sch. Dist., 1996—98; legis. analysis and rsch. asst. Office of Tribal Coun., 1998—2003, exec. adminstr., 2003—. Trainers of tng. Nat. Indian Sch. Bd., Philadelphia, 1987—; curriculum specialist Bur. Indian Affairs-Choctow, Philadelphia, 1987—, staff devel. coord., 1986—; chmn. bd. ESEA, 1991; bd. dirs. Southeastern Region Visions for Edn. Vol. program implementation Save the Children Fedn., Cherokee, N.C., 1981—; planning participant nat. issues forum Kettering Found., Dayton, Ohio, 1987; mem. task force com. Office of Indian Edn. Program, Washington, 1985. Recipient cert. of recognition Save the Children Fedn., 1986. Fellow Internat. Reading Assn., Miss. Staff Devel. Coun.; mem. ASCD, Minn. Edn. Computer Consortium, Choctaw Dept. Educators (bd. dirs.), Red Water Basketball Club, Red Water Community Devel. Club, Phi Theta Kappa. Democrat. Methodist.

BRANTON, SUSAN CAMILLE, education educator, department chairman; d. Don Otho and Sara (Sally) Lee (Gosopasture) Baker; m. Harry W. Branton, Jr. (div.); children: Sarah Katherine Keith, Susan Irene Hall. BS in Edn., Miss. State U., Starkville, 1972; MEd, Delta State U., Cleve., Miss., 1987; PhD, Miss. State U., Starkville, 1989. Lic. profl. counselor Miss. Bd. Examiners for Lic. Profl. Counselors, tchr. Miss. Prof. Delta State U., 1989—2005; prof./chair Miss. Valley State U., Itta Bena, 2005—. Pvt. counselor, Cleve. and Indianola, Miss. Author: (articles) Delta Edn. Jour., 2003. Vol. Breast Cancer Soc., Indianola, 1990—2003; counselor pro bono for underpriveleged children Sun Flower Co., Bolivia. Recipient Outstanding Student Rsch., CEC, 1989—90. Mem.: MSERA, ACEI, Phi Delta Kappa. Avocations: reading, sewing. Home: 305 E Gresham St Indianola MS 38751 Office: Miss Valley State Univ 14000 Hwy 82 W Box 7243 Itta Bena MS 38941 Personal E-mail: camille.branton@gmail.com.

BRANYAN, CHERYL MUNYER, museum administrator; b. Vincennes, Ind., Apr. 27, 1970; d. Edward A. and Janet E. Munyer. BA, Ea. Ill. U., 1992, MA, 1995. Asst. curator Coles County Hist. Soc., Charleston, Ill., 1994-95, Manship Ho. Mus., Jackson, Miss., 1995-96, The Hermitage, Nashville, 1996-97; mus. adminstr. Rosalie Miss. State Soc. DAR, Natchez, 1999—2003; v.p Miss. Museums Assn., 2001—02, pres., 2002—04; dir. Hist. Jefferson Coll., Washington, Mo., 2003—. Newsletter editor Historic House Museums Affinity Group, 2000-05; bd. dirs. Natchez Hist. Soc., 2000-04. Editor SERA News, 1998-2002; co-founder, contbr. jour. Historia, 1992 Mem. Nat. Assn. Jr. Aux. (Natchez chpt. pres. 2005), Phi Alpha Theta, Sigma Tau Delta Democrat. Episcopalian. Avocation: visiting museums. Office: Hist Jefferson Coll PO Box 700 Washington MS 39190 E-mail: cbranyan@mdah.state.ms.us.

BRASEL, JO ANNE, pediatrician, educator; b. Salem, Ill., Feb. 15, 1934; d. Gerald Nolan and Ruby Rachel (Rich) B. BA, U. Colo., 1956, MD, 1959. Diplomate in pediatrics and pediatric endocrinology Am. Bd. Pediatrics. Pediatric intern, resident Cornell U. Med. Coll.-N.Y. Hosp., N.Y.C., 1959-62; fellow in pediatric endocrine Johns Hopkins U. Sch. Medicine, Balt., 1962-65, asst. prof. pediats., 1965-68; asst. prof., then assoc. prof. pediatrics Cornell U. Med. Coll., N.Y.C., 1969-72; assoc. prof., then prof. pediats. Columbia U. Phys. and Surg., N.Y.C., 1972-79; prof. pediats. Harbor-UCLA Med. Ctr./UCLA Sch. Medicine, 1979—, program dir. Gen. Clin. Rsch. Ctr., 1979-93, prof. medicine, 1980—2005; Joseph W. St. Geme, Jr. prof. pediats. UCLA Sch. Medicine, 1999—2005, prof. emeritus pediatrics, 2005—. Mem. adv. com. FDA, Rockville, Md., 1971-75; mem. nutrition study sect. NIH, Bethesda, Md., 1974-78; mem. select panel for promotion of child health HEW, Washington, 1979-80; mem. life scis. adv. screening com. Fulbright-Hays program, Washington, 1981-84; mem. digestive disease and nutrition grant rev. group NIADDK, 1985-89; mem. U.S. Govt. Task Force on Women, Minorities and the Handicapped in Sci. and Tech., 1987-89. Recipient Rsch. Career Devel. award NIH, 1973-77, Irma T. Hirschl Trust Career Sci. award, 1974-79, Sr. Fulbright Sabbatical Rsch. award, 1980. Mem. Soc. Pediatric Rsch. (sec.-treas. 1973-77, v.p. 1977-78, pres. 1978-79), Am. Fedn. Clin. Rsch., Endocrine Soc., Am. Soc. Clin. Nutrition, Am. Inst. Nutrition, Western Assn. Physicians, Lawson Wilkins Pediatric Endocrine Soc. (bd. dirs. 1972-74, v.p. 1991-92, pres. 1992-93), Western Soc. Pediatric Rsch., Phi Beta Kappa, Alpha Omega Alpha. Office: Harbor-UCLA Med Ctr Box 446 1000 W Carson St Torrance CA 90509-2910 Office Phone: 310-222-1971. Business E-Mail: brasel@labiomed.org.

BRASHARES, ANN, writer; b. Chevy Chase, Md. m. Jacob Collins; children: Sam, Nathaniel, Susannah. B in philosophy, Barnard Coll. With Daniel Weiss Associates, NYC, editor-in-chief; co-pres., editor-in-chief 17th St. Productions, NYC. Author: Steve Jobs: Thinks Different, 2001, Linus Torvalds: Software Rebel, 2001, The Sisterhood of the Travelling Pants, 2001, The Second Summer of the Sisterhood, 2003, Girls in Pants: The Third Summer of the Sisterhood, 2005 (Quills award for young adult/teen book, 2005). Office: c/o Random House Inc 1745 Broadway New York NY 10019

BRASHER, TERRIE WALKER, secondary school educator; b. Leeds, Ala., June 20, 1960; d. Ernest Hershel and Ellen Imojean Walker; m. Donald Ray Brasher, July 19, 1986; children: Trey Donald, Cody Ray. MA in Edn., U. Ala., Birmingham, 1998; MS in Biology, Samford U., Birmingham, 1982. Lab technician Samford U., Birmingham, 1980—82, U. Ala., Birmingham, 1982—83; lab instr. Samford U., Birmingham, 1983—91; sci. tchr. Moody (Ala.) H.S., 1997—. Grantee, St. Clair County Ednl. Assn., 2005, St. Clair Ednl. Assn., 2006. Home: 2738 Sunrise Dr Moody AL 35004 Office: Moody High Sch 714 High School Dr Moody AL 35004 Office Phone: 205-640-5127.

BRASHER, TREASURE ANN KEES, physics professor; b. Maypearl, Tex., May 12, 1938; d. Leslie and Ora Odell (Segars) K.; m. Charles Albert Brasher, Sept. 5, 1959; 1 child, Cynthia Lynn Brasher Baker. BS, West Tex. State Coll., Canyon, 1960; MS, West Tex. State U., Canyon, 1967; postgrad., No. Ariz. U., Flagstaff, 1970, U. Houston, 1979, Tex. Tech. U., Lubbock, 1983. Cert. tchr. Tex. Instr. math. West Tex. State Coll., Canyon, 1961-62, tchg. asst. math., 1963-65, instr. physics, 1980—; physics/phys. sci. tchr. Canyon Ind. Sch. Dist., 1962-63, earth/life sci. tchr., 1965-66, physics/chemistry tchr., 1966-80. Dir. West Tex. A&M U. Regional Jets Contest, Canyon, 1983-99, dir. U. Interscholastic Sci. Contest Canyon, 1990—, coord. Pantex Dept. Energy, Canyon Sci. Bd., 1994—, dir. traveling chemistry show, Canyon, 1997-2000; dir. Panhandle JASON Project, 1998—; mem. Acad. Educator Devel. Tex. A&M U. Sys., 2000—. Author: Elementary Physics With Activities, 1995, Elementary Chemistry With Activities, 1995; contbg. editor: (with Gerald Skoog) Activities for Middle School Teachers, 1996. Sunday sch. tchr. First Bapt. Ch., Canyon, 1980—, mem. sanctuary choir, 1956—; mem. Panhandle chpt. Singing Women of Tex., 1992—. Named Eisenhower Tchr. Enhancement grantee, West Tex. State U., 1990—94, Eisenhower grantee, Tex. Edn. Agy., 1994—99, Sid Richardson Tchg. fellow, Tex. A&M U.Sys. and Tex. Edn. Agy., 1998—2000; recipient Outstanding Prof. award, Scribes/Mortar Bd., 1991—92, Outstanding Univ. Faculty award, Regl. Alliance Sci. Engring. Math., 2002; grantee, NSF, 1991—93, Amarillo Nat. Resource Ctr., 1996—98, ANRC, 1998—2000, New Century Energies, 2000—01, Xcel Energy Co., 2002—, W. Mem. NEA, Am. Assn. Physics Tchrs., Nat. Sci. Tchrs. Assn., Tex. State Tchrs. Assn. (regional pres. 1978-80, state bd. dirs. 1983-87), Tex. Assn. Coll. Tchrs. (pres. 1986-88), Acad. for Educator Devel. Avocations: reading, needlecrafts, travel. Home: 83 Country Club Dr Canyon TX 79015-1821 Office: West Tex A&M U Dept Math Phys Scis & Engrin Canyon TX 79016-0001 E-mail: tbrasher@mail.wtamu.edu.

BRASOVEANU TARPY, ALEXANDRA, mathematics professor; b. Bucharest, Romania, May 16, 1958; arrived in US, 1992; d. Alexandru and Felicia Sandulescu; m. Cliff Tarpy, June 15, 2002. MA in math., U. Bucharest, Romania, 1981; MA in applied math., U. Md., 1998. Cert. math. grades 7-12 Md., 1999. Math tchr. Pub. Sch., Bucharest, Romania, 1981—92, Odenton Christian Sch., Odenton, Md., 1993—99, Thomas S. Wootion HS MCPS, Rockville, Md., 1999—. Coach math team Thomas S. Wooton HS, Rockville, Md., 1999—, City Sch., Bucharest, Romania, 1984—92. Contbr. articles various profl. jours. Mem.: NEA, Md. Coun. of Tchrs. of Math., Nat. Coun. of Tchrs. of Math. Avocations: reading, travel, tennis, hiking, swimming. Personal E-mail: a_brasoveanu@hotmail.com.

BRASSARD, JANICE ALINE, retired secondary school educator; b. Harlingen, Tex., Oct. 7, 1949; d. Gaston Paul Jr. and Jewel Aline (Davis) Jennett; m. Raymond Maurice Brassard, June 3, 1972; children: Brenden Eugene, Bryan Edward, Britten Elliott BS Secondary Edn., U. Tex., 1971; MEd Supervision, Lamar U., 1975. Cert. tchr., Tex. Tchr. English and lang. arts Silsbee Ind. Sch. Dist., Tex., 1971—72; tchr. 8th grade Our Mother of Mercy Cath. Sch., Houston, 1972—73; tchr. h.s. English South Park/Beaumont Ind. Sch. Dist., Tex., 1973—2005; ret., 2005; owner, instr. Miz B's Tutorials, Beaumont, 2005—. Mem. Tex. state sch. improvement initiative Tex. Edn. Agy., Austin, 1996-97; in-svc. trainer Beaumont Ind. Sch. Dist., 1980, 94, 96 Author: High School Basic Curriculum, 1975; co-author 10th grade gifted and talented curriculum, 1997 Bd. trustees Beaumont Ind. Sch. Dist.; troop leader Girl Scouts U.S.A., Beaumont, 1979-95; del. Dem. State Conv., Beaumont, 1976, 82, 92 Named Outstanding Tchr. of Yr., South Park Ind. Sch. Dist., 1980, Beaumont Ind. Sch. Dist., 1993; named one of 10 outstanding tchrs. Quality Edn. Beaumont, 1986 Mem. NEA, AAUW, Tex. State Tchrs. Assn., Beaumont Classrm. Tchrs. Assn., Tex. Humanities Alliance, Nat. Coun. Tchrs. English, Tex. Coun. Tchrs. English Lutheran. Avocations: reading, cooking, swimming. Home: 820 Chatwood Dr Beaumont TX 77706-5404 Office: Miz B's Tutorials 1450Wellington Cir Ste 102 Beaumont TX 77706

BRASSEUR, IRMA FAYE, special education educator; b. Flint, Mich., Apr. 18, 1961; d. Ermen Massie and Gearldine Herbst; m. Curtis James Brasseur (div. Jan. 25, 1996); 1 child, Cali Jean. BS in Spl. Edn., Ctrl. Mich. U., Mt. Pleasant, 1984; MA in Spl. Edn., Eastern Mich. U., Ypsilanti, 1990; postgrad., U. Kans., 1998—. Cert. tchr. Mich. Tchr. Area Edn. Agy. #7, Waterloo, Iowa, 1984—86, Davison (Mich.) Cmty. Schs., 1986—98; project coord. U. Kans., Lawrence, 2000—. Student rep. Divsn. Learning Disabilities, 1999—2002, v.p., 2001—03, pres., 2003—04. Student Initiated grantee, Office Spl. Edn. Programs, 2001. Avocations: reading, bicycling, aerobics. Office: U Kans Ctr Rsch Learning 1122 W Campus Rd Lawrence KS 66045 Business E-Mail: ibrasser@ku.edu.

BRASSIL, JEAN ELLA, psychologist; b. New Haven, Conn., June 4, 1933; d. Joseph Eugene and Ella Eve (Lindhardt) B. BS, So. Conn. State U., 1955; MA, Columbia U., 1957; PhD, Adelphi U., 1971. Cert. tchr., Conn., N.Y. Tchr. pub. schs., North Haven, Conn., 1955-58, 60-62, Casper, Wyo., 1958-59, Montebello, Calif., 1959-60; psychol. examiner Meriden (Conn.) Pub. Schs., 1962-63; instr. Adelphi U., Garden City, N.Y., 1964-67; asst. prof. So. Conn. State U., New Haven, 1967-68; psychologist Child Guidance Clin. Greater Bridgeport (Conn.), 1968-73; psychologist, counselor Fairfield (Conn.) Pub. Schs., 1973-94; pvt. practice psychology Derby, Conn., 1972—. Bd. govs. Inst. Learning in Retirement Albertus Magnus Coll., 1998—, sec. Inst. Learning in Retirement, 2002—. Mem. Am. Psychol. Assn., Conn. Psychol. Assn. (bd. dirs. 1971-81, sec. 1981-82, pres. 1983), Jane Austin Soc. N.Am. (regional coord. Conn. chpt. 2003—). Home and Office: 7 Orangewood W Derby CT 06418-2614

BRASWELL, JACKIE BOYD, state agency administrator; b. Leon County, Fla., Feb. 15, 1938; d. Chalmer Parks and Kathryn Iris (Johnson) Boyd; m. Fletcher Braswell, Nov. 28, 1957; children: Flecia Lori, Carmen Ethelee. BS, Fla. State U., 1964; M in Ednl. Adminstrn., 1976. Cert. educator Valdosta State Coll., 1968, lic. real estate sales assoc. Fla., 2005, cert. Rayner Real Estate, Tallahassee, Fla. Lic. tchr., adminstr. Fla. single mgr., ammunition, base clothing fund, security clearance USAF, Moody AFB, 1958-61; tchr. bus. edn. Berrien H.S., Nashville, Ga., 1966-69, Rickards H.S., Tallahassee, 1970-75; bus.-vocat. tchr., chmn. dept. career edn. Lincoln H.S., 1975—99; dir. ednl. affairs and policy Fla. Lottery, 1999—2005; real estate assoc. Rayner Real Estate, 2005—. Co-owner, fin. mgr. Rundown Farms, Tallahassee, 1969—; pres. Eight Out Investment Group, 1993-2003; mem. Gov.'s Mentoring Initiative Lottery Mentoring Program, 1999-2005. Editor: In Touch, 1979-80; contbr. articles to profl. jours. Apptd. to Fla. State Bd. Pub. Schs., Gov. Fla., 1987-90, vice chmn., 1990-91; chmn.; apptd. mem. by Spkr. of Ho. of Reps. to Fla. Commn. Edn. Reform and Accountability, Spkr. Fla. Ho. Reps., 1991-93; invited del. Citizens Amb. Program People Internat., Beijing, Hangzhou, Shanghai, China, 1995; fundraising chmn. Dist. Sch. Supts. Campaign, 1996; sponsorship chair Capital Cultural Ctr., Chukker Challenge, 1997-98; mem. fundraising com. ann. dinner Boys and Girls Club Big Bend, 2005-06; mem. ann. fundraiser com. Pace Ctr. for Girls, 2005, 06. Recipient Merit award Future Farmers Am., 1974; selectee Harvard Inst., 1991. Mem. Nat. Mus. Women in the Arts (charter), Nat. Bus. Edn. Assn., Fla. Vocat. Assn., Fla. Bus. Edn. Addn., Leon Vocat. Assn. (pres. elect 1987-88, pres. 1988-89), Leon Classroom Tchrs. Assn. (sec.-treas. 1987-88, chair pub. rels., parliamentarian 1988-89, govtl. rels. 1991), Dance Arts Guild, Leon County Farm Bur., Capital Gains Club (treas., 2000), Quill and Scroll, Phi Kappa Phi. Republican. Home and Office: 7006 N Meridian Rd Tallahassee FL 32312-8017

BRASWELL, JODY LYNN, gifted and talented educator; b. Cin., Aug. 30, 1955; d. Edward George and Willadene B. Kraemer; m. Jimmy Billings Braswell, Dec. 22, 1974; children: Cynthia, Gina. BS in Edn., West Tex. State U., 1985; MA in Edn., Sul Ross State U., 2000. Cert. elem. edn. grades 1-8, generic spl. edn. all levels, gifted/talented endorsement, reading specialist, master reading tchr. Tchr. spl. edn. Amarillo Ind. Sch. Dist., Tex., 1985—86; elem. tchr. Ector County Ind. Sch. Dist., Odessa, 1989—91, St. John's Episcopal Sch., 1991—95; tchr. spl. edn. Ector County Ind. Sch. Dist., 1995—2000, curriculum specialist, 2000—01, gifted/talented program tchr., 2001—06, tchr. 3d grade, 2006—. Lead mentor Ector County Ind. Sch. Dist., Odessa, 1998—2003, trainer, facilitator, 2000—. Vol. Home Hospice, Odessa, 1995—; pres. Permian Basin Reading Coun., Odessa, 2000—03; bd. mem. Read Odessa, 2003—05. Recipient Lifetime Achievement award, PTA, Odessa, 2000. Mem.: Tex. Classroom Tchrs., Tex. Reading Assn., Internat. Reading Assn., Delta Kappa Gamma Iota (pres. 2004—06). Presbyterian. Avocations: reading, music, needlecrafts, gardening. Home: 1514 E 10th Odessa TX 79761 E-mail: jjcgbraz@cableone.net.

BRASWELL, LAURA DAY, periodontist; b. Bowling Green, Ky., July 22, 1958; d. Lawson Moyers and Bettye (Wall) Braswell; children: DeFord Lawson Smith, Ashley Smith, Alison Smith, Jeanette Smith. DDS, U. N.C., 1982; cert. periodontology, Emory U., 1988. Diplomate Am. Acad. Periodontology. Staff dentist Sam Rudd DDS, Raleigh, N.C., 1982-83; mem. faculty Emory U., Atlanta, 1983-93; assoc. scientist Yerkes Regional Primate Ctr., Atlanta, 1984-98; zoo dentist Zoo Atlanta, 1986—; pvt. practice Atlanta, 1988—. Vol. Healing for the Poor, Kingston, Jamaica, 1986, Ctrl. Presbyn. Health Ctr., Atlanta, 1986-91, Grant Park Family Health Ctr., 1989-93, dentist Ga. Part for Caring; 1st vice chmn. Arthritis Found., Ga., 1997; dental coord. Face-to-Face. Master Acad. Laser Dentistry (charter); fellow Internat. Coll. Dentistry, Am. Soc. Vet. Dentistry (hon.), Pierre Fouchard Acad.; mem. ADA, Internat. Assn. Dental Rsch., Am. Assn. Dental Rsch., Ga. Dental Assn., No.

Dist. Dental Soc. (pres. Buckhead br. 2000), Psi Omega. Methodist. Avocations: skeet shooting, hiking, fishing, kayaking, camping. Office: Ste 622 2970 Peachtree Rd Atlanta GA 30305 Office Phone: 404-261-9593. E-mail: ldb3312@mindpspring.com.

BRASWELL, MARY PAUL GIBSON, elementary school educator; b. Rule, Tex., Dec. 18, 1933; d. Derwood Reginald and Loudell (Bell) Gibson; m. Roy French Braswell, May 29, 1955 (div. June 1989); children: Roy Bennett II, Paul Bradford, Donald Hodges Bowman, Neal Blake BA, U. North Tex., Denton, 1957; MPA, West Tex. State U., Canyon, 1983. Cert. tchr., Tex. Tchr. St. Mark's Sch. Tex., Dallas, 1957—62; part-time tchr. Wayland Bapt. U., Pampa, Tex., 1985—86, 1988, Clarendon Coll., Pampa, 1983—85, 1988; tchr. appraiser Scholastic Analysis Corp., Lubbock, Tex., 1987—89; tchr. Alice Ind. Sch. Dist., Tex., 1989—90; tchr. 4th grade Mineral Wells Ind. Sch. Dist., Tex., 1990—93, tchr. 5th grade math. and sci., 1993—2000; ret., 2000. Trustee Pampa Ind. Sch. Dist., 1982-85, pres. sch. bd., 1984-85; bd. dirs., treas. Pampa Cmty. Concert Assn., 1985-88; bd. dirs., sec. Pampa Area Found. for Outdoor Art, 1986-88; mem. Jr. Svc. League Pampa, 1973-83, pres., 1979-80; lic. lay reader St. Matthews Episcopal Ch., Pampa, 1984-89; pres. Women of St. Matthews Episcopal Ch., 1976-78; trustee St. Matthews Episcopal Day Sch., 1973-78; mem. vestry St. Luke's Episcopal Ch., Mineral Wells, 1993-96, Eucharist lay min., 1994-2000; pres. Women of St. Luke's, 1994-96 Named Sr. Clubwoman of Yr., Key Dist.-Tex. Federated Women's Clubs, 1970-71, Sr. Mother of Yr., 1972-73; grantee Eisenhower math. and sci. found. U. North Tex., 1992 Mem. NSTA, Tex. Classroom Tchrs. Assn., Tex. Sci. Tchrs. Assn., Nat. Soc. DAR (Ralph Ripley chpt.), Sigma Tau Delta, Alpha Delta Kappa (Delta Tau chpt. treas. 1994-96, pres. elect 1996-98, pres. 1998-2000) Avocations: travel, reading, walking. Home: 13695 Goldmark Dr Apt 2314 Dallas TX 75240-4213

BRASWELL, PAULA ANN, artist; b. Decatur, Ala., May 6, 1955; d. Andrew Leon and Dorothy Faye (Fretwell) B.; m. Roger Armand Robichaud, June 22, 1990. BA, Jacksonville State U., 1978; postgrad., New Orleans Acad. Fine Arts, 1987, U. New Orleans, 1987-88; MFA, Fla. State U., 1990. Instr. art Butler Sch., Marrero, La., 1984, Fla. Keys Coll., Tavernier, 1985; grad. instr. Fla. State U., Tallahassee, 1989-90; adj. prof. Calhoun Coll., Decatur, Ala., 1990, Chattanooga State Coll., 1991, Cleveland (Tenn.) State Coll., 1991; studio artist Knoxville, Tenn., 1991-96, Toronto, Ont., Can., 1996—. One-woman shows include Contemporary Arts Ctr., New Orleans, 1992, ARC Gallery, 1997, Propeller Gallery, 2000—01, WARC Gallery, Toronto, 2003—04, Melt Loop Gallery, 2004, Kabat/Wrobel Gallery, 2004, Hysteria Festival of Women, 2004, Luz Gallerie, 2005, Loop Gallery, Toronto, Can., 2006, exhibited in group shows at Knoxville (Tenn.) Mus. Art, 1994—95, Combined Talents Fla. Nat., 1995, Transforming Tradition, 1996, New American Talent, 1996, Fla. State U., Mus. of the Ams., Washington, 1997, Mus. of Fine Arts, 1998, FSU Mus., 1998, Propeller Gallery, Toronto, 2000—02, WARC Gallery, 2000, 2003, Sculpture Soc. Can., 2000—01, Gallery 121, Toronto, 2000, Soul Ecology Exhibit, 2000, Propeller Ctr. for the Visual Arts, 2000—02, Sculpture Soc. Gallery, 2001, 2004, John B. Aird Gallery, 2001, 2003, Windsor (Ont.) Gallery Art, 2002, Ontario Arts Coun., 2004 (Exhbn. Assn. grant, 2004), Maison de la culture, Cote-des-Neiges, 2005—, 5th Anniversary Loop Gallery, Toronto, 2005. Grantee, Nat. Endowment Arts, 1991, Ont. Arts Coun., 1997, 2000, 2001—02, 2003, 2004, 2006, Can. Coun., 2002. Mem. AAUW, NOW, Women's Caucus for Arts (exhibitor), Knoxville Mus. Art (exhibitor), Knoxville Arts Coun. (exhibitor), Coll. Art Assn., Contemporary Arts Ctr. (exhibitor), People for Protection of Animals, Humane Soc. U.S., Mercier Union Art Ctr., Propeller Arts Ctr., Loop Gallery, Red HEad Gallery. Democrat. Mem. Ch. of Christ. Avocations: gardening, environmental concerns, animal care, skiing, camping. Address: 221 Winona Dr Toronto ON Canada M6C 3S4 Office Phone: 416-654-0051. Personal E-mail: paulabrasw@aol.com.

BRATNELY, MARCIA J., music educator; b. Greenville, SC, Oct. 3, 1950; d. Edith H. Jones; m. Ronald Edward Brantley, July 14, 1950; children: Edward Wellington Brantley, James Matthew Brantley. MusB, Furman U., Greenville, SC, 1972. Cert. tchr. State SC Bd. Edn., 1996. Choral music tchr. Oconee County Sch. Dist., Seneca, SC, 1973—75; elem. music tchr. Charleston County Schs., SC, 1976—78; ch. pianist/handbell coord. Summerville Bapt. Ch., SC, 1986—, interim music min., 2006—; handbell tchr. Dorchester Dist. Two Schs., Summerville, 1996—. Founder, dir. Palmetto Bronze, Summerville, 2003—. Author: (tchg. materials) Made for Praise Vol. 3; musician (artistic/lighting/music exec. prodr.): (musical presentation) The Low Country Singing Christmas Tree. Mem.: Am. Guild English Handbell Ringers (bd. mem. area IV 2006—, SC chair area IV 2006—). Baptist. Avocation: handbells. Home: 202 Caveson Dr Summerville SC 29483 Office Phone: 843-873-3610. Personal E-mail: bellwoman@yahoo.com.

BRATT, PEGGY L., personal trainer; b. Indpls., Nov. 20, 1967; d. Carolyn Sue Soules and adopted d. Joe Black. BA, Maryville Coll., Tenn., 1991. Cert. Atc Nat. Athletic Trainer's Assn., Tenn., 2000, EMT Nat. Registry of Emergency Med. Technicians, Tenn., 2002, Emt-Iv Tenn., 2004. Phys. therapy technician Appalachian Therapy Ctr., Maryville, Tenn., 1987—99; psychol. asst. Peninsula Village, Louisville, Tenn., 1991—95; program dir., case mgr. Cornerstone of Recovery Monitoring Ctr., Knoxville, 1995—96; program coord. Cornerstone of Recovery Behavioral Ctr., Knoxville, 1996—97; utilization rev., counselor Child and Family Svcs., Lakeway Acad., Maryville, Tenn., 1997—99; dir. outreach svcs., head athletic trainer Alcoa HS, Appalachian Therapy Ctr., Maryville, Tenn., 1999—. Secondary schs. com. Tenn. Athletic Trainer's Soc., 2004—06, chair pub. rels. com., 2006—, women in athletic tng. com., 2006—; adv. bd. Lincoln Meml. U., Athletic Tng., Harrogate, Tenn., 2005—06. Youth basketball coach Maryville/Alcoa/Blount County Parks and Recreation, Tenn., 1992—93. Mem.: Tenn. Athletic Trainer's Soc., SE Athletic Trainer's Assn., Nat. Athletic Trainer's Assn. Avocations: reading, motorcycling, athletic activities. Office: Appalachian Therapy Ctr 829 E Lamar Alexander Pkwy PO Box Maryville TN 37804 Office Phone: 865-977-8282. Home Fax: 865-982-0143; Office Fax: 865-982-0143. Business E-Mail: peggybratt@appalachiantherapy.com.

BRATTEN, MILLIE MARTINI, editor-in-chief; m. John Bratten. With merchandising dept. Mademoiselle mag., 1975; assoc. editor Bride's mag. Conde Nast Pubs., NYC, fashion coord. menswear Bride's mag., editor accessories, fashion and beauty assoc. Bride's mag., exec. editor Bride's mag., 1991—94, editor-in-chief Bride's mag., 1994—; editl. dir. Conde Nast Bridal Group, 2002—. TV appearances in Weekend Today, Good Morning Am., Good Day N.Y., Network News, Family Values, Weddings of a Lifetime; host Romance Classics A Day of Diana; interviewed in USA Today, N.Y. Times, Washington Post, Wall Street Journal, Boston Globe, Forbes, ABC Radio Network. Mem. Am. Soc. Mag. Editors (bd. dir.), Fashion Group Internat., NY Women in Comms., Inc. (program coun. NY, past bd. dirs., v.p. membership). Office: Conde Nast Pubs 4 Times Sq 6th Fl New York NY 10036 Business E-Mail: editorinchief@bridesmag.com.*

BRATZLER, MARY KATHRYN, web services manager; b. Albuquerque, Sept. 16, 1960; d. William James and Nancy Jane (Hobbs) Colby; m. Zim Emig, May 30, 1987 (div. Nov. 1990); 1 child, Aeriel Kaylee Emig; m. Steven James Bratzler, Mar. 16, 1996, 1 child, Cody Benjamin. B of Univ. Studies, U. N.Mex., 1995. Comml. artist Modern Press, Albuquerque, 1978—80; asst. composition supr. Graphic Arts Pub., Albuquerque, 1980—84, composition supr., 1984—85, asst. plant mgr., 1985—86; typesetter Universal Printing and Graphics, Albuquerque, 1986—87, Bus. Graphics, Albuquerque, 1988—90; office asst. UNM Gen. Honors, Albuquerque, 1992—93; desktop pub., 1990—; computer specialist NEDA Bus. Cons., Inc., 1996—98; electronic prepress Acad. Printers, Albuquerque, 2002—03; publs. and web svcs. mgr. Albuquerque Acad., 2003—. Cons. Mary Kay Cosmetics, 1991—96. Participant N.Mex. Pub. Utilities Commn., Santa Fe, 1993; coord. clothing bank PTA Zia Elem. Sch., 1995—96; parent rep. Unified Student Centered Classroom, 1996—98; gen. bd. mem. Albuquerque Acad. Parent Assn., 2000—05. Mem. Golden Key, Phi Beta Kappa. Avocations: piano playing, bicycling, hiking, camping.

BRAUDY, SUSAN ORR, writer; b. Phila. d. Bernard and Blanche (Malin) Orr. BA cum laude, Bryn Mawr Coll.; postgrad., U. Pa., Yale U. Editor, writer The New Jour. Yale U., New Haven; assoc. editor Newsweek Mag., N.Y.C.; editor, writer Ms. Mag., N.Y.C.; freelance writer N.Y. Times, Vanity Fair Mag., N.Y.C.; v.p. Warner Bros., N.Y.C., L.A., Michael Douglas Prodns., N.Y.C., L.A. Author: (memoir) Between Marriage and Divorce, 1975, (novels) Who Killed Sal Mineo, 1984, What the Movies Made Me Do, 1984, (nonfiction) This Crazy Thing Called Love, 1991, Family Circle: The Boudins and the Aristocracy of the Left, 2003; screenwriter: (films) Scorsese Co.; Am. Zeotrope; Ixtlan; Disney; contbr. articles to mags. Mem.: NOW, Authors' Guild, Writers Guild of Am., PEN Club Internat., Vet. Feminists Am. Home: 240 Central Park S Apt 16B New York NY 10019-1413

BRAUER, CAMILLA THOMPSON (KIMMY THOMPSON BRAUER), civic leader; b. St. Louis, Apr. 8, 1946; m. Stephen F. Brauer; children: Blackford, Rebecca, Stephen Jr. Grad., Mary Inst., Bennett Coll., Millbrook, N.Y., 1966. Dir. St. Louis Arts & Edn. Coun., 1988-2001; dir., exec. com. Opera Theater of St. Louis, 1986—; dir. exec. com. Sheldon Arts Found., 1991—; trustee St. Louis Art Mus., 1989-94, chmn. bd. trustees, 1991-94, commr., 1996-2002; trustee Webster U., 1994—; exec. com., 1995-2002; chair Alexis de Tocqueville Soc., 1995, 96, 2001, 05; v.p. exec. com. United Way of St. Louis, 1996—; bd. trustees St. Louis Symphony, 1994-2001, exec. com., 1995-2001. Recipient Internat. Barker award Variety Club, 2000; named St. Louis Post Dispatch Woman of Achievement, 1996. Mem. Naat. Soc. Fund Raising Execs. (Vol. of Yr. St. Louis 1994, Vol. of Yr. U.S. 1996), Variety Club (exec. bd. dirs. 1992—, Woman of Yr. 1992, Mo. Hist. Soc. (dir. 1991—, exec. com. 1991—). Home: 9630 Ladue Rd Saint Louis MO 63124-1311 Fax: (314) 994-1441. E-mail: camillabrauer@aol.com.

BRAUER, RHONDA LYN, publishing executive, lawyer; b. Gary, Ind., Nov. 23, 1959; d. Hugh Donald and Charlotte Gloria (Danzig) B.; m. Gregory John Holch, Sept. 7, 1989; children: Jillian Brauer Holch, Justin Brauer Holch. BA magna cum laude, Cornell U., 1981; JD magna cum laude, Ind. U., 1984. Bar: N.Y. 1985, U.S. Dist. Ct. (so. and ea. dist.) N.Y. 1991, U.S. Supreme Ct. 1992. Assoc. Cleary, Gottlieb, Steen & Hamilton, N.Y.C., 1984-86, 89-92, Brussels, 1986-88; counsel The N.Y. Times Co., N.Y.C., 1992—94, sr. counsel, 1994—2006, asst. sec., 1996—2002, corp. sec., 2002—, corp. governance officer, 2006—. Contbr. articles to profl. jours. Pro bono work Lawyers Com. for Human Rights, NYC, 1984-86, ACLU, 1989-90, Vol. Lawyers for the Arts, NYC, 1989-92, NY Lawyers for the Pub. Interest, 1992-95. Recipient Anne MacIntyre Litchfield prize of history Cornell U. Coll. Arts and Scis., 1981; Salzburg (Austria) Seminar fellow, 1988. Mem. Assn. Bar City N.Y., N.Y. Women's Bar Assn., Soc. Corp. Secs. and Governance Profls. Avocations: swimming, hiking, films, jogging, sculling.

BRAULT, G. LORAIN, health facility administrator; b. Chgo., Jan. 3, 1944; d. Theodore Frank and Victoria Jean (Pribyl) Hahn; m. Donald R. Brault, Apr. 29, 1971; 1 child, Kevin David. AA, Long Beach City Coll., 1963; BS, Calif. State U.-Long Beach, 1973, MS, 1977. RN, Calif; cert. nurse practitioner. Dir. nursing Canyon Gen. Hosp., Anaheim, Calif., 1973-76; dir. faculty critical care masters degree program Calif. State U., Long Beach, 1976-79; regional dir. nursing and support svcs. Western region Am. Med. Internat., Anaheim, Calif., 1979-83; v.p. Hosp. Home Care Corp. Am., Santa Ana, Calif., 1983-85; pres. Hosp. Home Health Care Agy. Calif., Torrance, 1986-92; v.p. Healthcare Assn. So. Calif., L.A., 1993—98; dir. student health svc. Fullerton Coll., 1999—. Invited lectr. China Nurses Assn., 1983; cons. AMI, Inc., Saudi Arabia, 1983; guest lectr. dept. pub. health UCLA, 1986—87; assoc. clin. prof. U. So. Calif., 1988—93; chair editl. adv. com. RN Times, Nurseweek, 1988—2000; advisor Nursing Inst., 1990—91; lectr. Calif. State U., L.A., 1996—99, Fullerton, Calif., 1999—2003; bd. dirs. Health and Human Svcs., Long Beach, Calif., 1997—, chmn., 2002—03; writer, dir. grants, State & Local. Contbr. articles to profl. jours., chpts. to books. Commr. HHS, Washington, 1988. Grantee Health and Human Svcs. Advanced Nurse Tng., pub., county, pvt. and state, 1998—. Mem. Women in Health Adminstrn. (sec. 1989, v.p. 1990), Nat. Assn. Home Care, Am. Orgn. Nursing Execs., Calif. Assn. Health Svcs. at Home (task force chmn. 1988, bd. dirs. 1988-93, chmn. bd. dirs. 1990-93), Calif. League Nursing (bd. sec. 1983, program chmn. 1981-82), Am. Coll. Health Care Execs., Am. Orgn. Nurse Execs., Healthcare Svc. Adminstrn. Calif. Cmty. Colls. (sect. pres. 2003-2004, state pres. 2004-05), Phi Kappa Phi, Sigma Theta Tau, Soroptomist Internat. Republican. Methodist. Personal E-mail: ldbrault@earthlink.net. Business E-Mail: lbrault@fullcoll.edu.

BRAUN, LILIAN JACKSON, writer; Author: The Cat Who Could Read Backwards, 1966, The Cat Who Ate Danish Modern, 1968, The Cat Who Turned On And Off, 1968, The Cat Who Saw Red, 1986, The Cat Who Played Brahms, 1987, The Cat Who Played Post Office, 1987, The Cat Who Knew Shakespeare, 1988, The Cat Who Sniffed Glue, 1988, The Cat Who Had Fourteen Tales, 1988, The Cat Who Went Underground, 1989, The Cat Who Talked to Ghosts, 1990, The Cat Who Lived High, 1990, The Cat Who Knew A Cardinal, 1991, The Cat Who Wasn't There, 1992, The Cat Who Moved A Mountain, 1992, The Cat Who Went Into The Closet, 1993, The Cat Who Came to Breakfast, 1994, The Cat Who Blew the Whistle, 1995, The Cat Who Smelled a Rat, 2001, The Cat Who Went Up the Creek, 2002, The Cat Who Talked Turkey, 2004, The Cat Who Went Bananas, 2005.

BRAUN, MARY E., elementary school educator; d. John F. and Genevieve H. Vogel; m. Edward D. Braun, June 24, 1967; children: Michael E., Jennifer K. Canfield, Melissa A. Rubinich. BS in Elem. Edn., Kutztown U., 1966. Fourth grade tchr. Reading Sch. Dist., Pa., 1966—67; second grade tchr. Middletown Sch. Dist., 1967—69; pre-sch. tchr. Half Day Play Nursery Sch., Harrisburg, Pa., 1974—83; second and third grade tchr. Holy Name of Jesus, Harrisburg, 1984—89; first grade tchr. North Side Elem. Sch. Ctrl. Dayton Sch. Dist., Harrisburg, 1989—. Mem. CD Dist. Math. Com., 1998—; chairperson North Side Social Com., 1992—2004. Pres. Civic Club Suburban Harrisburg, 1985; sch. coord. Daffodils Days Am. Cancer Soc., Harrisburg, 1985—; vol. Hershey Children's Garden and Butterfly House, 2006. Mem.: North Side Scholarship Com., Pa. State Edn. Assn. Avocation: reading to children. Office: Central Dauphin Sch Dist 4520 Devonshire Rd Harrisburg PA 17109

BRAUN, SUSAN J., foundation administrator; married; 1 child, Alex. BA in English and Sociology, George Mason U.; MA in Health Scis., U. Md.; postgrad. in Internat. Mktg., U. Muenster, Germany. Exec. Pracon Inc. and Ctr. Econ. Studies in Medicine; various positions, Oncology/Immunology Divsn. Bristol-Myers Squibb, Princeton, NJ; pres., CEO Susan G. Komen Breast Cancer Found., 1996—. Bd. mem., staff liaison Intercultural Cancer Coun. Mem. editl. bd.: Breast Jour., C.U.R.E. Mag. Active Americorps NCCC. Recipient Frances Williams Preston award for breast cancer awareness, Vanderbilt-Ingram Cancer Ctr., 2001. Mem.: Am. Soc. Clin. Oncology, World Soc. Breast Health, Am. Soc. for Breast Disease (chair pub. policy com.). Office: Susan G Komen Breast Cancer Found 5005 LBJ Freeway Ste 250 Dallas TX 75244

BRAUNSTEIN, TERRY MALIKIN, artist; b. Washington, Sept. 18, 1942; d. Hiram and Dorothy (Malakoff) Malikin; m. David R. Braunstein, Jan. 17, 1965; children: Samantha, Matthew. BFA, U. Mich., 1964; MFA, Md. Inst. Art, 1968. Vis. prof. Calif. State U., Long Beach, 1989; asst. prof. Corcoran Sch. Art, 1978-86; lectr. in field. One-woman shows include Franklin Furnace, N.Y.C., 1977-79, Fendrick Gallery, Washington, 1980, Washington Project for Arts, 1976-82, Marcuse Pfeifer, N.Y.C., 1987, Tartt Gallery, Washington, 1986, 88, U. Mich., Ann Arbor, 1990, Hampshire Coll., Amherst, Mass., 1990, Hampshire Coll., Amherst, Mass., 1990, Almediterranea '92, Almeria, Spain, 1990, Long Beach (Calif.) Mus. of Art, 1991, Krull Gallery, L.A., 1992, 94, 95, 97, Troyer Fiktzpatrick, Lassman Gallery, Washington, 1995, U. Salamanca (Spain), 1996, Centro Exposicione Rodalquilar, Spain, 1998, Centro Andaluz De La Fotografia, America, Spain, 2002, Piazza del Erbe, Montecassiano, Italy, 2005—, Museo Civico, Villa Colloredo Mels di Recanati, Italy, 2005-06; exhibited in group shows at Bronx Mus., 1976, Corcoran Gallery of Art, 1973, 85, Gallery Miyzazki, Osaka, Japan, 1983, Bertha Urdang Gallery, N.Y.C., 1985, Calif. State U., Long Beach, Calif., 1987, Ctr. Georges Pompidou, Paris, 1985, Calif. Mus. Photography, Riverside, 1990, Long Beach Mus. Art., 1992, Sala Arcs Gallery, Barcelona, Spain, 1990, Salas de Arenal and traveling exhibition, Seville, Madrid, Spain and Marseille, France, 1992—, Centro Esposito della Rocca Paotina, Italy, 1994, L.A. County Mus. Art, 1995, Armand Hammer Mus., 1996, Salas De Arenal, Seville, Spain, 1997, Palazzo Del Consoli, Gubbio, Italy, 1998, Long Beach Mus. of Art, Calif., 2001, Nat. Mus. Woman in the Arts, 2003; commd. pub. art works include Dirty Windows, Berlin, Germany, 1996, L.A. County Met. Transp. Authority MetroRail, 1992, L.A. County Mus. Art, 1997, 1st St. Facade, Long Beach, Calif., 1999, Bluff Erosion & Enhancement project, Long Beach, 2000—, City Hall, Long Beach, 2003, Navy Meml., 2004, 50th Ann. Sculpture, Cerritos, Calif; represented in permanent collections at Mus. Modern Art, N.Y.C., Corcoran Gallery of Art, Washington, Long Beach Mus. Art, Mus. Contemporary Art, Chgo., Bibliotheque Nationale, Paris, Libr. of Congress, Washington, Bruce Peel Spl. Collections Libr., U. Alberta, Can., Nat. Mus. Am. Art, Washington, Mills Coll. Spl. Collections Libr., Oakland, Calif., U. Art Mus., Calif. State U., Long Beach, Getty Ctr. for Arts & Humanities, Victoria and Albert Mus., others. Recipient Visual Artists fellowship Nat. Endowment for Arts, 1985, Disting. Artist award City of Long Beach, 1992, video grant Long Beach Mus. Art, 1992, Nat. Artist's Book award Nat. Mus. Women in Arts, 1994; named disting. Vis. Prof., Calif. State U., 1989; Yaddo Artists resident, 1997, 99, 03, 05. Home: 262 Belmont Ave Long Beach CA 90803-1522 Personal E-mail: terrybraun@hotmail.com.

BRAUTIGAM, DEBORAH ANNE, political science professor; b. Madison, Wis., Nov. 28, 1954; d. Richard Kensing and Anne Hall Brautigam; life ptnr. David Hirschmann. BA, Ohio Wesleyan U., 1972—76; MA in Law and Diplomacy, Tufts U., Medford, Mass., 1980—83, PhD, 1983—87. Asst. prof. Columbia U., NYC, 1987—92, assoc. prof., 1992—94, Am. U., 1994—. Mem. bellagio com. Rockefeller Found., NYC, 1999—2004; cons. World Bank, 1987, Nigeria, 91, Lesotho, 91, 96, UN, Cambodia, 1993, NY, 2003, US AID, The Gambia, 1983, Sri Lanka, 86, The Gambia, 89, Egypt, 2000. Author: (books) Chinese Aid and African Development, 1998, Aid Dependence and Governance, 2000; contbr. articles to profl. jours. Internat. Affairs Fellowship award, Coun. Fgn. Rels., 1990—91, Fulbright Regional Rsch. award, Dept. of State, 1999, Resident Fellowship award, Woodrow Wilson Internat. Ctr. Scholars, 2001—02, Fulbright-Hays Fellowship award, Dept. Edn., 2004—05. Mem.: Phi Beta Kappa. Office: Am Univ Sch Internatl Svc 4400 Mass Ave NW Washington DC 20016

BRAUTIGAN, JUNE MARIE, artist, poet; b. Syracuse, N.Y., Apr. 2, 1952; d. Ward Ernest Shaut and Frances Mary Craig; m. Thomas Francis Brautigan, Nov. 24, 1995; children: Timothy, Chad, Nathan, Crystal. Assoc. Degree, Corning C.C., Corning, N.Y., 1994. Author: (poetry) Goldenrod, 1993 (Winner in SCOP jour., 1993), Hometown, 1995, Perpetuate, 1997, Seacast, 1997, Purgation, 1998, Reign, 1999, the coming of Age, 2000, Unify, 2001, I Can See Things I Cannot See, 2002, Weathering The Layoff, 2002, The Same Sameness, 2002, (short stories) A Room I Remember, 1992 (First place in Scop jour., 1992), Judgments, 2002, Red Light, Yellow Light, Green Light, 2003, As If In A Dream.I Sleep Awake, 2006. Mem.: Internat. Poet Soc. Avocations: interior decorating, gardening. Home: 3 Warden St Bath NY 14810-1227 Personal E-mail: jmbrautigan@yahoo.com.

BRAVERMAN, CAROLE GAE, literature and language educator; b. N.Y.C. d. Harry and Edith Braverman; 1 child, Daniel Feng. BA, Bklyn. Coll., 1964; MA, Purdue U., West Lafayette, Ind., 1966. Instr. English Phillips Acad., Andover, Mass., 1979—. Playwright in residence Berkeley (Calif.) Repertory Theater, 1983—85. Author: (play) The Yiddish Trojan Women (Plays on Stage award London Weekend TV, 1993), The Margaret Ghost (Prodn. award Berkeley Repertory Theater, 1984), The Girl With a Sense of Fair Play (Prodn. award Am. Repertory Theater, 1976), (short story) Originat Tenant (Pubn.award Jewish Quar., London), (play) In Tiber Melting (Prodn. award, N.Y.C., 1982). Achievements include Production of plays in New York, London, Los Angeles, San Francisco, Boston. Home: 3 Stonehedge Rd Andover MA 01810 Office: Phillips Acad 180 Main St Andover MA 01810 Office Phone: 978-749-4000. Personal E-mail: cbraverman@andover.edu.

BRAVO, ROSE MARIE, apparel executive; b. NYC, Jan. 13, 1951; d. Biagio and Anna (Bazzano) LaPila; m. William Selkirk Jackey, Oct. 9, 1983. BA in English, Fordham U., 1971. Exec. trainee, dept. mgr. A&S, Bklyn, 1971—74; assoc. buyer Macy's, N.Y.C., 1974—75, buyer, 1975—79, councilor, 1979—80, adminstr., 1980—84, group v.p., 1984—85, sr. v.p., 1985—88; chmn., CEO I. Magnin, San Francisco, 1988—92; pres. Saks Fifth Ave., Inc., N.Y.C., 1992—97; CEO Burberry Group plc, London, 1997—2006, vice chmn., 2006—. Bd. dirs. Tiffany & Co., Burberry Group plc. Named one of the Most Powerful Women in Bus., Forbes mag., 2005, 50 Most Powerful Women in Global Bus., Fortune mag., 2005. Office: Burberry Group plc 18-22 Haymarket London SW1 4DQ England*

BRAWNER, CYNTHIA D., elementary school educator; b. Chgo., Oct. 30, 1962; d. Lloyd and Berdena Brawner. BA, Columbia Coll., 1986; MA Early Childhood Edn., Nat.-Louis U., 2000; MA Sch. Adminstrn., Concordia U., 2000. Ordained min. Pentecostal Assemblies of World, 2000; cert. tchr. early childhood edn. Ill., gen. adminstr. Ill., nat. bd. cert. tchr. EC/GEN. Proofreader Visual Tech. Inc., Chgo., 1987—89; ednl. instr. Chgo. Pub. Schs., 1989—. Cons. in field. Editor: (newsletter) The Call; author: (short stories) Invitations. Study group team Chgo. Found.; study group coach Chgo. Found. Edn. Tchrs. Network Leadership Inst., 2002—04; 2d v.p. Internat. Single People's Alliance of PAW, Inc., 2005—; ordained min. Pentecostal Assemblies of World, Indpls., 2000—05. Recipient Emerging Leader award, ASCD, 2005; fellow Action Rsch., Chgo. Found. Edn. Tchrs. Network Leadership Inst., 2003, 2004; mentor, 2001, 2002, 2003. Mem.: Nat. Coun. Tchrs. English, Nat. Assn. Edn. of Young Children, Internat. Reading Assn., Phi Lambda Theta. Avocation: writing. Office: Brawnerview PO Box 805122 Chicago IL 60680 Office Phone: 773-805-0434. Office Fax: 773-288-8595. Business E-Mail: brawnerview@sbcglobal.net.

BRAXTON, TONI, popular musician; b. Severn, Md., Oct. 7, 1967; m. Keri Lewis; children: Denim Cole Braxton Lewis, Diezel Ky Braxton Lewis. Albums Toni Braxton, 1993, Heat, 2000, Snow Flakes, 2001, More Than a Woman, 2002, Platinum & Gold Collection, 2004, Please, 2005, Libra, 2005, appeared in (films) Kingdom Come, 2000, contbr. Boomerang soundtrack, 1992, Secrets, 1997; actor: (Broadway musical) Aida, 2003. Recipient Grammy award Best Female R&B Vocal, 1994, 1995, 2001, Aretha Franklin Soul Train award, 2000, BET Black Oscar, 2000, 3 time Amer. Music award.

BRAY, CAROLYN SCOTT, education educator; b. May 19, 1938; d. Alonzo Lee and Frankie Lucile (Wood) Scott; m. John Graham Bray Jr., Aug. 24, 1957 (div. May 1980); children: Caron Lynn, Kimberly Anne, David William. BS, Baylor U., 1960; MEd, Hardin-Simmons U., 1981; PhD, U. North Tex., 1985. Registered med. technologist. Dir. career placement Hardin-Simmons U., 1979-82, adj. prof. bus. comm., 1981-84, assoc. dean students, 1982-85; assoc. dir. career planning and placement U. North Tex., Denton, 1985-95, adj. prof. higher edn. adminstrn., mem. Mentor program; dir. Career Ctr., U. Tex. at Dallas, Richardson, 1995-2000, prof. edn., 2000—, tchr. devel. ctr. assessment officer, 2000—. Mem. Consortium State Orgn. Tex. Tchr. Edn., 1999—; mem. adv. bd. TxBESS, 2000—; adv. com. Accountability Sys. for Edn. Performance, 2003—, Tex. Edn. Assn., 2006—. Adult Bible study tchr., mem. personnel com., coord. new mem. com., 1st Bapt. Ch., Richardson, Tex., 2000—. Mem.: North Ctrl. Tex. Assn. Sch. Pers. Adminstrs. and Univ. Placement Pers. (pres. 1987—88, sec. 1988—95), Nat. Assn. Colls. and Employers (co-chair nat. conf. planning com. 1996—98), Tex. Assn. for Employer Edn. and Staffing (v.p. 1986—87, pres. 1987—88), Am. Assn. for Employment in Edn. (bd. dirs. 1989—94, treas. 1994—95, nat. conf. com. 1999, conf. com. local arrangements 1999, Priscilla A. Scotlan award for disting. svc. 1999), S.W. Assn. Colls. and Employers (life; chair ann. conf. registration 1991—92, vice chair ops. 1992—93, 4-yr. coll. dir. 1998—99, pres.-elect 1999—2000, co-chmn. tech. com.), Leadership Denton (co-dir. curriculum 1988—89, chair membership selection com., steering com. 1990, 1993—94), Denton C. of C. (pub. rels. com. 1988—95), Kappa Kappa Gamma (chpt. advisor, chair adv. bd. Zeta Sigma chpt. 1987—93). Republican. Avocations: skiing, tennis, golf, reading. Office: U Tex at Dallas PO Box 830688 GR22 Richardson TX 75083-0688 Business E-Mail: csbray@utdallas.edu.

BRAY, PATRICIA SHANNON, music educator, musician, small business owner; b. Elkton, Md., Sept. 4, 1953; d. Francis William Shannon and Mary Elizabeth Gardner; m. William Joseph Bray Jr., July 31, 1976; children: Mark William, Eric Joseph. BMEd magna cum laude, East Carolina U., 1975; MS summa cum laude, Med. Coll. Va., Va. Commonwealth U., 1995. Lic. tchr. Va. Tchr., dir. orch. Chesterfield County Pub. Schs., Chesterfield, Va., 1975—. Cellist Richmond Philharm. Orch., Va., 1975—82, Petersburg Symphony, Va., 1987—94, Lynchburg Symphony, Va., 1998—; chair dept. music Salem Ch. Mid. Sch., Richmond, 1998—; owner Talent Edn. Chesterfield, 2000—; adjucator Richard Bland Lions Club, Music Scholarship Competition, Chester, Va., 2000; adjucator Jr. Festival Va. Fedn. of Music Clubs, 2003; presenter in field, 00; co-presenter Suzuki Assn. of the Ams. Conf., 2002; presenter Chesterfield County Pub. Schs. Leadership Conf., 2002; cons. Suzuki violin edn.-autism rsch. project Pa. State U., 2004. Faculty sponsor Salem Music Boosters, Richmond, 1998—; sch. crisis team Chesterfield County Pub. Schs., 1995—2004, sch. improvement planning com., 2002—04. Scholarship, Theodore Presser Publ. Co. Scholarship, 1973. Mem.: Va. Mid. Sch. Assn. (conf. presenter 2003—04), NEA, Am. String Tchrs. Assn., Music Educators Nat. Conf., Suzuki Assn. Americas, Sigma Alpha Iota, Kappa Delta Pi, Phi Kappa Phi. Avocations: hiking, reading, gardening. Home: 3318 Brewton Way Midlothian VA 23113-3793 Office: Salem Ch Mid Sch 9700 Salem Church Rd Richmond VA 23237 Personal E-mail: intuitpsb@aol.com. Business E-Mail: patricia_bray@ccpsnet.net.

BRAYER, EDITH MARIE, marriage and family therapist, consultant; d. Edgar A. Silies and Marie Lucille Caumont; m. Roger Charles Brayer, Dec. 27, 1947 (dec.); children: Michael, Mark, Patrick, Anne-Marie. B in Liberal Studies, St. Louis U., 1981, MA, 1984, PhD, 1991. Rsch. asst. Wash. U., St. Louis, 1981—82; tchg. asst. Spl. Sch. Dist., St. Louis County, 1981—85; marriage and family therapist St. Elizabeth Med. Ctr., Granit City, Ill., 1987—2001; bereavement group facilitator Hospice Madison County, Ill., 1989—2001; cons. St. Louis, 2001—. Named First Lady of Day, Sta. WRCH, Hartford, Conn., 1966. Mem.: Am. Assn. Marriage and Family Therapy, Am. Counseling Assn. Roman Catholic. Avocations: hiking, tennis, genealogy, painting.

BRAYMEN-LAWYER, REBECCA KAY, psychologist; b. Lincoln, Nebr., Aug. 21, 1956; d. Dale Eugene and Margaret (Hunt) Fahrnbruch; m. William Joe Braymen, Mar. 8, 1975 (div. 1983); children: Charles Byron, Christina Danielle; m. Mark D. Kipper, Apr. 7, 1990 (div. 1991); 1 child, Cassandra Danielle; m. William Lawyer, Sept. 3, 2005. BS, Nebr. Wesleyan U., 1977; MS, U. Nebr., 1979, PhD, 1988. Lic. psychologist, Nebr., nationally cert. sch. psychologist, Lancaster County, Pa. Adj. instr. psychology Bellevue Coll., Omaha, 1979-82; instr. U. Nebr., Omaha, 1980-82, teaching asst. Lincoln, 1986; psychology intern Nebr. Consortium for Profl. Psychology, Lincoln, 1987-88; sch. psychologist Nebr. Ctr. for Children and Youth, Lincoln, 1988; postdoctoral fellow in clin. psychology Charlton Assocs., P.C., Lincoln, 1988-90; pvt. practice Child & Family Svcs., Lincoln, 1990—. Alt. mem. Lancaster County Mental Health Bd. Contbr. articles to profl. jours. Willard scholar Nebr. Wesleyan U., 1973-74; achievement scholar Nebr. Wesleyan U., 1973-77. Mem. APA, Nebr. Sch. Psychologists Assn., Assn. Nat. Cert. Sch. Psychologists, Phi Gamma Mu. Republican. Mem. Covenant Ch. Office: 4706 S 48th St Lincoln NE 68516-1276 Office Phone: 402-432-6810.

BRAZEAL, AURELIA ERSKINE, former ambassador; b. Chgo., Nov. 24, 1943; BS, Spelman Coll., 1965; M of Internat. Affairs, Columbia U., 1967; postgrad., Harvard U., 1972. With Foreign Svc., 1968; consular and econ. officer U.S. Embassy, Buenos Aires, 1969-71; econ. reports officer Econ. Bureau U.S. State Dept., 1971-72, watch and line officer Office of Secretariat, 1973-74, desk officer Uraguay, Paraguay, 1974-77; review officer Office of Secretariat U.S. Dept. Treasury, 1977-79; econ. officer Tokyo, 1979-82; officer ECON Bur. U.S. Dept. State, 1982-84; dep. dir. Econ. Office Japan, 1984-86; mem. sr. seminar, 1986-87; min. counselor econ. affairs U.S. Embassy, Tokyo, 1987-90; U.S amb. to Micronesia, 1990-93; U.S. amb. to Kenya, 1993-96; deputy asst. sec. East Asian & Pacific Affairs, 1996-98; dean sr. seminar Fgn. Svc. Inst., Arlington, Va., 1998-99, dean leadership and mgmt. sch. and sr. seminar, 1999—2002; U.S. amb. to Ethiopia, 2002—05; diplomat-in-residence Howard U., Washington, 2005—. Office: Howard Univ 2218 6th St NW Washington DC 20059

BRAZEAL, DONNA SMITH, psychologist; b. Greenville, SC, Feb. 10, 1947; d. G.W. Hovey and Ollie Occena (Crane) Smith; m. Charles Lee Brazeal, June 27, 1970 (div. May 1980). BA, Clemson U., 1971, MEd, 1975; postgrad., Western Carolina U., 1974, Furman U., Greenville, 1977; PhD, Columbia Pacific U., 1994. Lic. sch. psychologist, SC, NC. Instr., head med. record dept. Greenville Tech. Coll., 1971-73; N.E. area chief psychologist Greenville County Schs., 1975-80; coord. psychol. svcs. Union County Schs., Monroe, NC, 1980-97; ret., 1997; pvt. practice psychology Monroe and Charlotte, NC, 1986—. Mem. learning disabilities com. Greenville County Schs., 1978-79; co-founder, bd. dirs. Ctr. for Spiritual Awareness of NC, Monroe, 1982—. Co-author, co-editor: School Psychologist, 1980. Child find program coord. Union County, 1980-85; mem. various coms. Assn. for Retarded Citizens, Monroe; mem. Union County Assn. for Retarded Citizens; mem. interagy. coun. Piedmont Mental Health, Monroe, 1983-97; mem. adult edn. com. River Hills Cmty. Ch., 1985-86. Catawba Bus. Women scholar, 1965; NC Dept. Pub. Instrn. Pre-Sch. Incentive grantee, 1984. Mem. Nat. Assn. Sch. Psychologists, NC Assn. Sch. Psychologist (mem. pub. rels. com. 1984-85), Greenpeace, Humane Soc. U.S., Am. Mensa, Delta. Democrat. Interdenominational Christian. Home: PO Box 240173 Charlotte NC 28224-0173 Personal E-mail: donny210@aol.com.

BRAZELL, GLORIA RUTH, art educator, elementary school educator; d. Wilson L. and Gloria Katharine Weyand; children: Charles Scott, Robert Thomas. BS in Art Edn., N.E. Mo. State U., Kirksville, 1969; MA in Tchg., Lindenwood U., St. Charles, Mo., 2002; MEd in Diverse Learners, Fontbonne U., St. Louis, 2006. Tchr. art Pattonville Sch. Dist., St. Louis, 1969—77, St. Louis Archdiocese, 1985—97, St. Louis Pub. Schs., 1997—99, Mehlville Sch. Dist., St. Louis, 1999—. Mem. safe schs. adv. com. Mehlville Pub. Schs., 1992—; presenter in field. Contbr. articles to websites and mags. Del. Dem. Nat. Conv., L.A., 2000; pres. bd. edn. Mehlville, 1997. Recipient Disting. Svc. award, Mehlville Sch. Dist., 2000; grantee, Mehlville Sch. Dist. Found., 2001—02, Internat. Edn. Consortium, 2003—04, Cooperating Sch. Dists., 2003. Mem.: Mo. State Tchrs. Assn. Avocations: travel, reading. Office: Margaret Buerkle Mid Sch 623 Buckley Rd Saint Louis MO 63125

BRAZELL, KAREN WOODARD, literature educator; b. Buffalo, Apr. 25, 1938; d. Charles Cary and Josephine Mary (Bordonaro) Woodard; m. James Reid Brazell, Aug. 27, 1961 (div. 1978); children: Katherine Ann Brazell Rivera, Stephen Reid. Student, Coll. Wooster, 1956—58, Internat. Christian U., Tokyo, 1958—60; BA, U. Mich., 1961, MA, 1962; PhD, Columbia U., 1969; D Lit (hon.), U. Puget Sound, 1993. Asst. prof. Japanese lit. Princeton U., 1969—74; assoc. prof. Cornell U., Ithaca, NY, 1974—79, prof., 1979—2000, Goldwin-Smith prof. Japanese lit. and theatre, 2000—, chmn. dept. Asian studies, 1977—82, dir. East Asia program, 1987—91, dir. Global Performing Arts Consortium, 2000—. Vis. prof. U. Calif., Berkeley, 1984, Nat. Inst. Japanese Lit., Tokyo, 1988-89, Kyoto Ctr. Japanese Studies, 2001-02; vis. Shinchôsha prof. Japanese Lit., Columbia U., 1996; disting. vis. prof., Nat. U. Singapore, 2000; dir. Global Performing Arts Consortium, 2000-. Author: Confessions of Lady Nijo, 1973 (Nat. Book award 1974), Noh as Performance, 1977, Dance in the Noh Theater, 1981; editor: Twelve Plays of the Noh and Kyôgen Theaters, 1988, re-printed edit., 1997, Traditional Japanese Theater: An Anthology of Plays, 1998; assoc. editor: Jour. Japanese Studies, 1978—; contbr. articles and book revs. to profl. jours. Trustee Cornell U., 1979-83; bd. dirs. U.S.-Japan Soc. Ithaca, N.Y., Japan Soc. N.Y.C. Performing Arts Adv. Com., 1993-2005, Japan-U.S. Partnership for Performing Arts Inc., N.Y.C., 1994-98 Fulbright-Hayes fellow, 1972-73, NEH fellow, summer 1974, Cornell U. Soc. Humanities fellow, 1976-77, Japan Found. fellow, 1978, 85, Nat. Inst. Japanese Lit. rsch. fellow, Tokyo, 1988-89. Mem. Assn. Asian Studies, Assn. Tchrs. of Japanese (exec. com. 1981-83, bd. dirs. 1989-92), Phi Beta Kappa (senator at large 1976-82, trustee found. 1977-82). Office: Cornell U Dept Asian Studies Ithaca NY 14853 Business E-Mail: kwb3@cornell.edu.

BRAZELL, TINA ARNING, actress, executive recruiter; b. Winfield, Ill., Oct. 27, 1968; d. Holger Kristian and Maria Kallimopoulou Arning; m. Jason Aaron Brazell, Nov. 21, 2004; children: Bowdoin Harold, Barrett Yannis. BS, Boston U., 1990. Actress various starring and support roles, film and TV, L.A., 1994—2000; actress off-Broadway and Broadway Ghosts of 1492, N.Y.C., 1991—93, Dreamtime, N.Y.C., 1991—93; actress, guest star TV Frasier, Newsradio, Ned and Stacy, others, L.A., 1995—99; actress leading role TV Young and Restless, L.A., 1995—97; actress recurring role TV Everybody Loves Raymond, L.A., 1996—99; rsch. assoc. Morgan Samuels Co., Beverly Hills, Calif., 2000—04; exec. recruiter DHR Internat., L.A., 2004—. Author: Dating 101 - For Women, 2002. Child sponsor Worldvision Internat., 2004—; donor makeachildsmile.org, 2002—; big sister Big Bro./Big Sisters, L.A., 1998—. Mem.: Mensa, AFTRA, Screen Actors Guild. Democrat. Avocations: reading, ballet, theater, skiing, children's charities. Office: DHR International 2029 Century Park E #1010 Century City CA 90067

BRAZIL, AINE M., engineering company executive; Student, Univ. Coll., Galway, Ireland; BS in Engring., U. Coll. Galway, Ireland, 1977; MS in Engring., Imperial Coll. Sci. and Tech., London, 1980. Structural engr. Thornton-Tomasetti Engrs., N.Y.C., 1982, sr. assoc., 1992—97, prin., 1997—. Adj. prof. dept. civil engring. and engring. materials Columbia U. Named one of Women of Achievement, Profl. Women in Constrn., 2001.

BRAZILE, DONNA, advocate; b. New Orleans; B, La. State U. Regional dir. Hands Across Am., 1985; nat. coord. housing Housing Now, 1989; founder, exec. dir. Nat. Polit. Congress Black Women; chief staff to Eleanor Holmes Norton, DC del. to US House Reps.; former host, prodr. A View From the Hill, Radio One News; campaign mgr. for Al Gore presdl. campaign, 2000; founder, mng. dir. Brazile and Assocs., LLC. Adj. prof. Georgetown U.; sr. fellow James MacGregor Burns Acad. Leadership, U. Md.; at-large mem. Dem. Nat. Com.; polit. commentator CNN; columnist Roll Call Newspaper; contbg. writer Ms. mag. Nat. student coord. Martin Luther King, Jr. Holiday Com., 1981; nat. mobilization dir. 20th Anniversary Commemoration 1963 March on Wash., 1983; nat. chair Voting Rights Inst., 2003. Named one of Outstanding Young Achievers, Ebony mag., 100+ Most Influential Black Americans, 2006, 100 Most Powerful Women in Wash., Washingtonian mag., 2001; recipient Congl. Black Caucus Youth award, Nat. Women's Student Leadership award. Office: Acad Leadership Univ Md College Park MD 20742-7715 Office Phone: 301-405-6100. Office Fax: 301-405-6402. Business E-Mail: dbrazile@academy.umd.edu.*

BRAZILE, ORELLA RAMSEY, library director; b. Leesville, La., May 28, 1945; d. Dave Ramsey and Lue Bertha Harris; m. Rodgers Henry Brazile, June 4, 1966. BS, Grambling State U., 1967; M in Libr. Sci., U. North Tex., 1973; MEd, So. U., La., 1976; MS, U. North Tex., 1982, PhD, 1991. Libr. Caddo Parish Sch. Bd., Shreveport, La., 1968—68; circulation libr. So. U. at Shreveport, La., 1968—78, interim vice chancellor, 1993—94, libr. dir., 1978—. Bd. of trustees Shreve Meml. Libr., Shreveport, 1985—2004; bd. mem. YMCA, 1986—88; site evaluator So. Assn. Colls., Atlanta, 1987—2003. Mem. NAACP, 1985—2005, Am. Legion Women Aux., Shreveport, 1975—2005, YWCA, 1980—2005. Fellow, Nat. Assn. of U. Women, 1988; grantee, La. Edn. Quality Support Fund, 1992, 1995. Mem.: Nat. Assn. of U. Women (life; sponsor 1990—2005), Delta Sigma Theta Sorority (life; journalist 1985—86). Baptist. Avocations: bowling, walking, aerobics. Home: 4396 Worth Cir Shreveport LA 71109 Office: So Univ at Shreveport 3050 Martin Luther King Jr Drive Shreveport LA 71107 Office Phone: 318-674-3401. Office Fax: 318-674-3403. E-mail: 318 674-3403.

BRAZZEL, REGINA GAYLE, secondary school educator; b. Houston, Aug. 28, 1976; d. Gary and Jenny Bowman; m. Lee Alexander Brazzel, Apr. 8, 1995; children: Aaron Connor, Lucas Dillard, Samuel Lee. MS, Stephen F. Austin, Nacogdoches, Tex., 2006, BS (hon.) cum laude, 2001. Cert. math. 8-12 Tex., early childhood Tex. Spl. ed tchr. Wells (Tex.) Ind. Sch. Dist., Wells, Tex., 2000—01; spl. ed tchr. 6-8 Garrison (Tex.) Ind. Sch. Dist., 2001—03; third grade tchr. Nacogdoches Ind. Sch. Dist., Nacogdoches, Tex., 2003—04; math tchr. Ctr. HS, Center, Tex., 2004—. Algebra curriculum writer Ctr. HS, Center, Tex., 2005—. Home: 170 Shady Acres Dr Nacogdoches TX 75965 Office: Center HS 658 Roughrider Dr Center TX 75935 Office Phone: 936-598-6173. Personal E-mail: brazzelr@yahoo.com. Business E-Mail: rbrazzel@centerisd.org.

BRAZZLE, SARA, publishing executive; b. St. Louis, May 1, 1964; d. William James and Carol Gaddis, Donna Gaddis (Stepmother); m. Robert Brazzle, Oct. 28, 2000; children: Ethan William, Ryan Edward. EdM, Webster U., St. Louis. Cert. tchr. Mo. Tchr. Univ. Sch. Dist., St. Louis, 1989—2000; mgr, custom assessment Riverside Pub. Co., Chgo., 2000—. Mem. day care bd. First United Meth. Ch., DeKalb, Ill., 2005—06. Mem.: Nat. Sci. Tchrs. Assn. Methodist. Home: 1105 Highpointe Dr Dekalb IL 60115 Office: Riverside Pub Co 425 Spring Lake Dr Itasca IL 60143-2079 Office Phone: 630-467-6052. E-mail: sara_gaddis-brazzle@hmco.com.

BRDLIK, CAROLA EMILIE, retired accountant; b. Wuerzburg, Germany, Mar. 11, 1930; came to U.S., 1952; d. Ludwig Leonard and Hildegard Maria (Leipold) Baumeister; m. Joseph A. Brdlik; children: Margaret Louise, Charles Joseph. BA, Oberrealschule Bamberg, Fed. Republic Germany, 1948; MA, Bavarian Interpreter Coll., Fed. Republic Germany, 1949; Cert., Internat. Accts. Soc., Chgo., 1955. Interpreter, exec. sec. NCWC Amberg, Schweinfurt, Ludwigsburg and Munich, Fed. Republic Germany, 1949-52; exec. sec. Red Ball Van Lines, Jamaica, N.Y., 1952; interpreter Griffin Rutgers Inc., N.Y.C., 1952-53; office mgr., exec. sec. Rehab. Ctr. Summit Co., Inc., Akron, 1953-56; pvt. practice acctg. Cuyahoga Falls, Ohio, 1956-61, Uniontown, Ohio, 1961-81; sec., treas. Omaca, Inc., Uniontown and Deerfield Beach (Fla.), 1981-86, pres. Uniontown and Jupiter, 1986-2000, ret., 2000. Sec.-treas. Shipe Landscaping, Inc., Greensburg, Ohio, 1968-92, Sattler Machine Products, Copley, Ohio, 1981-88; asst. treas. Mar-Lynn Lake Park, Inc., Streetsboro, Ohio, 1969-97. Bd. dirs., trustee Czechoslovak Refugees, Cleve. and Cin., 1968. Mem.: Nat. Assn. Tax Profls., Nat. Soc. Accts. Roman Catholic. Avocations: sewing, swimming, travel. E-mail: ceb0311@bellsouth.net, brdlikj@bellsouth.net.

BREARLEY, CANDICE, fashion designer; b. Trenton, N.J., Jan. 2, 1944; d. Joseph William and Lillian (Mieler) Szalay; m. Purvis Brearley, Sept. 2, 1965. BFA, Mus. Sch., Phila., 1965, MFA, 1968; BFA, Parsons Sch. Design, 1975, New Sch. Social Rsch., 1975. Freelance portrait artist, Trenton, 1965-72; asst. designer Malcolm Starr, N.Y.C., 1974-75; designer Originala, N.Y.C., 1975-77, Vignette, N.Y.C., 1977-78; pres., designer Candice Brearley, Inc., Trenton, 1978—; pres. Wickford Corp. of N.J., Trenton, 1986—. Bd. dirs. Beta Con Corp., Lawrenceville, N.J. One-woman shows Nat. State Bank, N.J., 1971, R.F. Gallery, Trenton N.J., 2004; exhibited in group show at N.J. State Mus., Trenton, 1970. Mem. devel. com. Restoration of "The Brearley House," Lawrenceville, N.J. Recipient award Lane Bryant Design Competition, 1974. Fellow Phila. Mus. Art, Met. Mus. Art, Princeton U. Mus., N.J. State Mus.; mem. Lawrence Hist. Soc. Roman Catholic. Avocations: collecting art, vintage cars, antique refinishing, opera, cooking. Office: Candice Brearley Inc 128 Buckingham Ave Trenton NJ 08618-3314 Office Phone: 609-393-8724.

BREATHITT, LINDA K., energy advisor, former federal energy commissioner; b. Hopkinsville, Ky. BA in Edn., U. Ky., 1975; cert. state-local govt. exec. mgmt. pro., Harvard U. Exec. dir. Washington Office, Commonwealth of Ky., 1980-92; commr. Ky. Pub. Svc. Commn., 1993-95, chmn., 1996-97; commr. FERC, 1997—2002; sr. energy advisor Thelen Reid & Priest LLP, Washington, 2002—. Bd. dirs. Martin Sch. Pub. Policy, U. Ky., Tata Energy Rsch. Inst. Regulatory Studies and Governance, New Delhi. Mem.: U. Ky. Alumni Assn. Methodist. Avocations: photography, scuba diving, gardening. Office: Thelen Reid & Priest LLP 701 8th St NW Washington DC 20001

BREAUX, CHERYL, counselor; b. New Orleans, Oct. 6, 1945; d. Wilson John and Velma (Rodriguez) B.; children: Michael Jr., Nicole. BA, Nicholls State U., 1966, MEd, 1979, MA, 1981. Cert. classroom tchr.; cert. sch. psychologist; lic. profl. counselor. Tchr. East Baton Rouge Sch. Bd., 1966-67, Orleans Parish Sch. Bd., New Orleans, 1967-68, Jefferson Parish Sch. Bd., Marrero, La., 1968-73; sch. psychologist Terrebonne Parish Sch. Bd., Houma, La., 1981-85, Lafourche Parish Sch. Bd., Thibodaux, La., 1985-90; profl. counselor Jo Ellen Smith Psychiat. Hosp., Raceland, La., 1988—; at risk program mgr. La. Dept. Edn., Thibodaux, 1990—. Conf. presenter La. Dept. Edn., Baton Rouge, 1990—91; adminstr. Lafourche Parish Drug Treatment Court, 2000—04; counselor Terrebonne Parish Sch. Bd., 2005—06. Bd. dirs. Bayou Coun. for Alcoholism and Substance Abuse. Mem. Nat. Assn. Sch. Psychologists, La. Assn. Lic. Counselors. Republican. Roman Catholic. Avocations: painting, needlecrafts, horseback riding.

BREAUX, MONICA LEBLANC, elementary school educator; b. Houma, La., May 4, 1968; d. Hubert Charles and Lynette Dupre LeBlanc; m. Ted Michael Breaux, Nov. 29, 1986; children: Derek Michael, Tyler James. BA in Elem. Edn., Nicholls State U., Thibodaux, La., 1999, MEd in Curriculum and Instrn., 2004. Nat. bd. cert. tchr. La., cert. reading specialist La., tchr. La. 1st grade tchr. Southdown Elem. Sch., Houma, La., 1999—2006, k-3 reading and math content leader, master tchr., 2006—. Named Tchr. of the Yr., Southdown Sch., 2003. Mem.: NEA (assoc.), Nat. Conf. Tchrs. English (assoc.), Ind. Reading Assn. (assoc.). Republican. Roman Catholic. Office: Southdown Elem Sch 1124 Saint Charles St Houma LA 70360 Office Phone: 985-872-9429.

BRECHT, SALLY ANN, quality assurance executive; b. Trenton, N.J., Aug. 5, 1951; d. Charles L. and Helen (Orfeo) B. BBA, Coll. William and Mary, 1973; MBA, Rider Coll., 1981. Cert. quality engr., software quality engr.; quality auditor, quality mgr., project mgr. Project Mgmt. Inst. Electronic data processing auditor McGraw Hill, Inc., Hightstown, N.J., 1976-79, State of N.J., Mercerville, 1979-80, NL Industries, Hightstown, 1980-84; systems tech. planning specialist Ednl. Testing Svc., Princeton, N.J., 1984-85, acting div. dir. application devel., 1985-87, mgr. computer standards and security, 1987-88, asst. dir. office corp. quality assurance, 1988-98; dir. software quality assurance Y2K Renovation, 1998—; portfolio project mgr. IT Project Mgmt. Office, 2000—02; project mgr. CMM Metrics Implementation, 2002—03. Contbr. articles to popular publs. Mem. Am. Soc. for Quality Control (cert. quality engr., mgr., auditor and software quality engr.); pmi cert. project mgmt. profl. Avocation: dressage. E-mail: sbrecht@ets.org.

BRECKEL, ALVINA HEFELI, librarian; b. Chgo., Dec. 6, 1948; d. William Christ and Liselotte (Herrmann) Hefeli; m. Theodore A. Breckel, Feb. 10, 1973. BFA cum laude, Bradley U., Peoria, Ill., 1970; MALS, Rosary Coll. (now Dominican U.), River Forest, Ill., 1973. Cert. art tchr., media libr., Ill. Tchr. art Chgo. Pub. Schs., 1971—84; libr. Oakton C.C., Des Plaines, Ill., 1988—. Co-chmn. Winnetka Antiques Show, 1999, chmn., 2000, dealer chmn., 2000—; mem. North Shore Bd. Gads Hill Ctr., corr. sec., 2000—04, pres., 2004—06; mem. Com. Gallery 37 in Schs., 2001—06; mem. visual arts com. Chgo. Cmty. Trust Gallery Northwestern U. Settlement Assn., 2001—05. Author: Looking for Glass on the Internet, 1996; editor News & Notes, 1988-89. Rep. election judge New Trier Twp., Ill., 1988; com. mem. Villagers for a Safe Winnetka, 1989; mem. women's bd. Howard Area Cmty. Ctr., 1990-95; chmn. Fuller Lane Cir., Winnetka, 1991-92, 94-95; mem. Midwestern Antiques Club, 1993—; mem. women's bd. Winnetka Cmty. House, 1995—03, historian, 1997—2003, mem. steering com., 1999—; dealer chmn. Winnetka Antiques Show, 2001-. Mem. AAUW (bd. dirs. New Trier chpt. 1989-90), Sandwich (Mass.) Hist. Soc., Winnetka Hist. Soc., Art Inst. Chgo. (life), Nat. Greentown Glass Assn., Nat. Am. Glass Club (life, founding mem. James H. Rose chpt., chpt. sec. 1992-97), Greater Chgo. Glass Collectors Club (v.p. 1995-97, pres. 1998-2000, chmn. bylaws com. 2001, chmn. nominating com. 2002), Early Am. Pattern Glass Soc. (nominating com. 1998, nat. seminar spr., 1999, spkr. Mid-States conf. 2001), Chgo. Area Shaker Interest Group, Pi Lambda Theta (life, art editor chpt. Notes 1977-84), Delta Zeta (v.p. Chgo. North Shore chpt. 1987-90), Phi Delta Kappa. Avocation: collecting and researching early American decorative arts, especially glass. Home: 185 Fuller Ln Winnetka IL 60093-4212 Office: Oakton CC 7701 Lincoln Ave Skokie IL 60077-2800

BRECKENRIDGE, BETTY GAYLE, management development consultant; b. Austin, Tex., Dec. 8, 1945; BA, Baylor U., 1966; MA, So. Meth. U, 1984. Cons. Devel. Dimensions Internat., Pitts., 1984—. Office: 3447 N Druid Hills Rd Ste P Decatur GA 30033-3765 Office Phone: 404-321-1071. Personal E-mail: bg.breckenridge@comcast.net.

BRECKENRIDGE, JUDITH WATTS, writer, educator; b. Knoxville, Tenn., Jan. 30, 1948; d. William Robert and Mary Kathryn (Ault) Watts; m. Rufus Gentry Breckenridge, June 26, 1977; children: Kathryn Suzanne, Mary Audra, Caroline Irene, Judith Gentry. BA in English, Carson-Newman Coll., 1970; MA in English, West Ga. Coll., 1972. Instr. Augusta (Ga.) Coll., Walter State C.C., Morristown, Tenn., 2002—; columnist Greeneville (Tenn.) Sun, 1993—; freelance writer. Author: Simple Physics Using Everyday Materials, 1993; author, creator (radio spots) Momtrax Minutes, 1999; author: (song) LA Cop: Cop of Lower Alabama, 1991. Mem.: First Families Tenn., Greeneville Arts Coun., Tuesday Morning Book Club. Baptist. Achievements include copyright Grammar Sticks; copyright Momtrax. Avocations: hiking, photography. Home: 506 Whisperwood Dr Greeneville TN 37743 Personal E-mail: jbreckenridge@xtn.net.

BREDEHOFT, ELAINE CHARLSON, lawyer; b. Fergus Falls, Minn., Nov. 22, 1958; d. Curtis Lyle and Marilyn Anne (Nesbitt) Charlson; m. Keenan P. Frank; children: Alexandra Charlson, Michelle Charlson. BA, U. Ariz., 1981; JD, Cath. U. Am., 1984. Bar: Va. 1984, DC 1994, admitted to practice: US Ct. Appeals (4th Cir.) 1984, US Bankruptcy Ct. (Ea. Dist.) Va. 1987, US Ct. Appeals (DC Cir.) 1994. Assoc. Walton and Adams, McLean, Va., 1984-88, ptnr., 1988-91, Charlson Bredehoft, PC (now Charlson Bredehoft & Cohen PC), Reston, Va., 1991—. Spkr. Fairfax Bar Assn. CLE, 1992—, spkr. VB Assn., 1993—; spkr. Labor and Employment Law Update, 1993—, Va. Women's Trial Lawyers Assn. Ann. Conf., 1998, Va. Bar Assn. Labor and Employment Conf., 1994—97, 1999—, Va. Trial Lawyers Assn., 1995, 97, Va. Law Found., 1995—, 1995—, Va. Assn. Def. Attys., 1996, 2001; mem. faculty Va. State Bar Law Student Professionalism Com.2, 2001—; invitee 4th Cir. Jud. Conf., 1997—99, permanent mem., 1999—; invitee Boyd Graves Conf., 1999—; substitute judge 19th Jud. Dist., 1998—. Bd. dir. Va. Commn. on Women and Minorities in the Legal Sys., 1987—90, sec., 1988—90. Named an 12 top Employment Lawyers in the Washington Met. Area, Legal Times, 2004; named one of The Best Lawyers in America, 1997, 50 Best Lawyers in Washington, Washingtonian mag., 1997, 40 Top Lawyers Under 40, 1998, 75 Best Lawyers in Washington, 2002, top employment lawyers, 2004; recipient The Best Lawyers in America, 1998, 1999, 2000, 2001, 2002, 2003, 2004. Fellow: Internat. Acad. Trial Lawyers, Am. Coll. Trial Lawyers; mem.: Fairfax Bar Assn. (chair diversity taskforce 1998—99, co-chair subcom. on minorities, Pres.'s Vol. award 1998, 1999), Minn. State Soc., Va. Trial Lawyers Assn. (mem. com. on long-range planning 1996—97, vice chmn. ann. conv. 1996—98), Va. Bar Assn. (spkr. 1995, 1997, mem. exec. com. young lawyers sect., mem. litig. com., mem. nominating com., chmn. model jud. com.), George Mason Inns of Ct. (master 1996—). Office: Charlson Bredehoft & Cohen PC 11260 Roger Bacon Dr Ste 201 Reston VA 20190-5252 Office Phone: 703-318-6800. E-mail: ebredehoft@charlsonbredehoft.com.

BREDEMEIER, MARY ELIZABETH, counselor, educator; b. Eden, N.C., Sept. 4, 1924; d. William Thomas and Cora May (Lewis) Robertson; m. Harry C. Bredemeier, Nov. 16, 1953; 1 child, Suzanne Leaphart. BS, James Madison U., 1944; MA, Columbia U., 1946; EdD, Rutgers U., 1972. Instr. Finch Coll., N.Y.C., 1945-46; tchr. Ben Franklin Jr. H.S., Yonkers, N.Y., 1949-53; instr. Douglass Coll., New Brunswick, N.J., 1953-54; tchr., counselor Middlesex County Vocat. and Tech. H.S., Woodbridge, N.J., 1955-67; prof. edn. Montclair State Coll., Upper Montclair, N.J., 1967-88, prof. emeritus, 1988—. Cons. Miami (Fla.)-Dade Pub. Schs., 1989—. Author: Labor Problems in America, 1970, Social Forces in Education, 1980, Urban Classroom Portraits, 1988; contbr. numerous articles to profl. jours. Democrat. Avocations: tennis, swimming, reading, jewelry-making. Home: 7441 Wayne Ave Apt 15C Miami Beach FL 33141-2566

BREDESON, BRENDA PENNISTON, secondary school educator; b. Monroe, Wis., Dec. 12, 1960; d. Charles Ardell and Teresa Flannery Penniston; m. Ronald Dean Bredeson, Sept. 5, 1981; children: Charles, Russell, Andrea. Bachelor's, U. Wis., Platteville, 1993; Master's, U. Wis., LaCrosse, 2004. Elem. libr. Etiwanda Sch. Dist., Fortana, Calif., 1994—96; tchr. English Stockton Mid. Sch., Ill., 1997—98, Juda HS, Wis., 1998—. Mem. liturgy com. St. Victor's Cath. Ch., Monroe, Wis., 1996—. Home: 304 N State St Argyle WI 53504 Office: Juda HS N2385 Spring St Juda WI 53550 Business E-Mail: bb@juda.k12.wi.us.

BREDESON, CHERYL, elementary school educator; b. Albuquerque, N.Mex., Aug. 18, 1945; d. Herbert Paul Fritze and Valiera Juanita Heim; m. Jon G. Bredeson, Aug. 5, 1987; m. Gerald Dan Lawson (div.); children: Jonathan Matthew Lawson, Julie Leann Lawson. BS in Edn., U. Ctrl. Okla., 1967; MS in Edn., U. Okla., 1972. MCSE. Tchr. Putnam City Schs., Oklahoma City, 1967—74; counselor Noble Pub. Schs., Okla., 1977—79, tchr., 1985—88; tchr. elem. sch. Tuscaloosa County Schs., Ala., 1988—99, Lubbock Ind. Sch. Dist., Tex., 1998—; reading first coach Stewart Elem. Sch., 2005—. Pres. campus planning and orgn. com. Lubbock (Tex.) Ind. Sch. Dist., 2003—04; sect. leader Lubbock (Tex.) Chorale; campus rep. East Lubbock Task Force. Contbr. MENC mag. Helpline vol., Norman, Okla., 1980; caseworker Ct. Appointed Spl. Advocate, Lubbock, 1998—99; fundraiser, chairperson Adopt an Eagle, Lubbock, 2003; organizer for relief drive Tsunami Relief, Lubbock, 2005; Ruby Payne trainer The Framework in Poverty; leader Lubbock Chorale Soc., 2000—05; mem. East Lubbock Task Force, 2000—05; Reading First coach Lubbock Ind. Sch. Dist., 2005; trainer Voyager Universal Literacy, 2006. Finalist Elem. Tex. Tchr. of Yr. award, 2004; nominee Disney Tchr. of Yr., 2005; recipient Jacksonville Hall of Fame, 1974, Oustanding Tchr. in Am., 1991. Mem.: Music Educators Nat. Conf., Nat. Arts in Edn., Tex. Music in Edn. Assn., Tex. Arts in Edn. Assn., Tex. Classroom Tchrs. Assn. Home: 9802 Uxbridge Ave Lubbock TX 79424 Office: Stewart Elementary 4815 46th St Lubbock TX 79414 Business E-Mail: cbredeson@juno.com, cbredeson@lubbockisd.org.

BREDHOFF, STACEY ANNE, curator; b. N.Y.C., Mar. 24, 1955; d. Saul J. and Florence Meadow Bredhoff. BA, Trinity Coll., Hartford, Conn., 1976; MAT, George Washington U., Washington, 1983. Bilingual clk. UN, N.Y.C., 1976—79; curatorial asst. Corcoran Gallery Art, Washington, 1983—85; curator Nat. Archives, Washington, 1986—. Author: American Originals, 2001, A New World is at Hand, 2004, Eyewitness, 2006. Avocations: piano, swimming, yoga. Office: National Archives 700 Pennsylvania Ave NW Washington DC 20408 Office Phone: 202-357-5484. Business E-Mail: stacey.bredhoff@nara.gov.

BREEDEN, CAROLYN SULLIVAN, dean, educator, interior designer, consultant; b. Great Bend, Kans., Apr. 6, 1943; d. T. R. and Lillian Oleta (Weaver) Sullivan; m. Ronald Gene Breeden, Dec. 23, 1961; children: Ronald Gene, Jon Charles. BA in Home Econ., Kans. State U., 1966; MA in Textile Sci. and Design, Calif. State U., Long Beach, 1976; EdD, U. So. Calif., 1985. Instr. and dept. chmn. Anaheim Union High Sch. Dist., Calif., 1966—73; instr. pub. rels. Southwestern Bell Telephone, Hays, Kans., 1965—66; instr. and dept. chmn. family and consumer studies Santa Ana C.C., Calif., 1974—82, curriculum coord. and instr., 1982—85, coord. media svcs. and curriculum devel., 1985—87, coord. instructional resources, 1987—88, dean learning resources, 1988—. Adj. prof. Calif. State U., Long Beach, 1989—92; v.p. exec. bd. Intelecom, Calif., 1989; v.p. publ. Nat. Coun. Staff Profl. and Organizational Devel., 1993. Author: Designing Home Interiors: A Study Guide of Telecourses, 1979, A Matter of Taste, 1980, Light Cuisine, 1981. V.p. exec. bd. Orange County High Sch. Arts Found., 1990—. Recipient Outstanding Designer award, Calif. State U.-Long Beach, 1976, Outstanding Citizen award, Rotary Club, 1965, Leaders of 80s award, Women in C.C. Adminstrn., 1981, Merit award, Nat. Coun. Staff Profl. and Organizational Devel., 1987, Adminstrv. Excellence award, So. Calif. Telecom Consortium, 1991. Mem.: Am. Assn. C.C., Interior Design Edn. Coun., Assn. Coll. Profs. Textiles and Clothing, Calif. Home Econ. Assn., Am. Home Econ. Assn., Am. Assn. Rsch. Postsecondary Edn., Am. Assn. Women in Cmty. and Jr. Colls., Kappa Omnicron Phi. Home: 6909 E Sycamore Glen Dr Orange CA 92869-1016 Office: Rancho Santiago College Santa Ana Campus 1530 W 17th St Santa Ana CA 92706-3398

BREEN, KATHERINE ANNE, speech and language pathologist; b. Chgo., Oct. 31, 1948; d. Robert Stephen and Gertrude Catherine (Bader) Breen. BS, Northwstern U., 1970; MA, U. Mo., Columbia, 1971. Cert. speech pathologist. Speech/lang. pathologist Fulton (Mo.) Pub. Schs., 1971-73; co-dir. Easter Seal Speech Clinic, Jefferson City, Mo., summer 1972, 73; speech/lang. pathologist Shawnee Mission (Kans.) Pub. Schs., 1973-96; staff St. Joseph's Hosp., Kansas City, Mo., 1978-81, Midwest Rehab. Ctr., Kansas City, 1985; pvt. practice speech therapy Deborah A. King & Assocs., 2003—. Cons. East Ctrl. Mo. Mental Health Center; guest lectr. Fontbonne Coll., St. Louis. Vol., Mid Am. Rehab. Hosp. Mem. NEA, Am. Speech and Hearing Assn., Kans. Speech and Hearing Assn., Mo. State Tchrs. Assn., Kansas City Alumni Assn. of Northwestern U. (dir. alumni admissions coun., Outstanding Leadership award 1981, Svc. award 1991), Friends of Art Nelson/Atkins Art Gallery and Mus. (vol.), Nat. Trust Historic Preservation, Kansas City Hist. Found., Zeta Phi Eta. Methodist. Home: 8318 Mackey St Shawnee Mission KS 66212-2728

BREGA, KERRY ELIZABETH, physician, researcher; b. Denver, Sept. 8, 1961; d. Charles Franklin and Betty Jean Brega. BA, U. Colo., 1983, MD, 1989. Diplomate Am. Bd. Spine Surgery, Am. Bd. Neurol. Surgery. Resident in neurosurgery U. Colo., Denver, 1990-95, asst. prof. neurosurgery, 1995—; dir. neurosurgery Littleton Adventist Hosp., Denver, 1998—; asst. prof. neurosurgery U. Colo., Denver, 1995—2005, assoc. prof. neurosurgery, med. dir. Stroke Ctr., 2006—, assoc. dir. neurosurg. residency tng. program, 2006—. Bd. dirs. Donor Alliance, Denver, 1994—. Mem. Am. Coll. Spine Surgery, Am. Assn. Neurol. Surgeons, Congress Neurol. Surgeons, Colo. Neurol. Soc., Alpha Omega Alpha. Office: 4200 @ 9th Ave Denver CO 80262 Office Phone: 303-315-1429.

BREGOLI-RUSSO, MAUDA RITA, language educator; b. Iesi-Ancona, Italy; came to U.S., 1965; d. Antonio Bregoli and Libe Maria Scipioni; m. Franco Gino Russo, June 27, 1964; 1 child, Antonella. Laurea, Bologna (Italy) U., 1963; PhD in Romance Langs., U. Chgo., 1978. Vis. asst. prof. Northwestern U., Chgo., 1981-83; asst. prof. U. Ill., Chgo., 1984-90, assoc. prof., 1990—. Author: Boiardo Lirico, 1979, Renaissance Italian Plays, 1984, Impresa Come Ritratto, 1990, Teatro D'Isabella D'Este, 1997. NEH grantee, 1981. Mem. MLA, Renaissance Soc. Am., Associazione Italiana per Gli Studi Di Lingua E Letteratura Italiana. Home: 100 E Walton St Apt 19de Chicago IL 60611-1448 Office: U Ill Chgo 601 S Morgan St Chicago IL 60607-7100 E-mail: mabrer@uic.edu.

BREHM, LORETTA PERSOHN, retired art educator, librarian, consultant; b. New Orleans, Jan. 31, 1954; d. Edwin Joseph and Loretta (Persohn) B. BA, Nicholls State U., Thibodaux, La., 1975, MEd, 1979, postgrad., 1980. Cert. tchr., La. Substitute tchr. Jefferson Parish Sch. Bd., Gretna, La., 1971-74; tchr. art John Ehret Sch., John Ehret High Sch., Marrero, La., 1974-95; art tchr., libr. Westbank Cathedral Acad., 1995-98; cons. Ventures Edn. Sys., 1998—; pub. rels. rep. Jefferson West Higher Edn. Ctr., 1999—. Trustee, chmn. bd. emeritus Jefferson Parish Coun. on Aging; assessor La. State Dept. Edn., 1997—. Ladies Aux. Westwego Vol. Fire Co.; historian Westwego Bicentennial; vol. Westwego Com. on Aging, Gumbo Festival, Bridge City, La., ARC, Operation Mainstream, others; founding mem. Jefferson Parish Cmty. Arts Commn.; alumni pres., former sch. advisor Jefferson Parish 4-H Clubs; art dir. Knights of King Arthur Mardi Gras Orgn.; libr. asst. Westbank Cathedral Acad.; choir, set designer Holy Guardian Angels Ch.; trustee Jefferson Parish Coun. on Aging, 1993—; bd. dirs. Westwego Hist. Soc., Jefferson Parish Hist. Soc.; commnr. Westwego Law Enforcement Commn., Westwego Zoning Commn., treas. Westwego Tourist Commn.; vice-chmn. Bridge City Cmty. Com. on Aging. Recipient awards from Jefferson Parish Sch. Bd., 1978, Westwego Vol. Fire Co., 1982, 4-H Club, 1983, Am. Automobile Assn. Nat. Sch. Traffic Safety Program, 1987-92, others. Mem. Nat. Art Edn. Assn., La. Art Edn. Assn., Internat. Reading Assn. (chmn. Jefferson Parish coun.), Jefferson Parish Hist. Soc. (charter), New Orleans Mus. Art, La. Children's Mus., Nicholls State U. Alumni Assn., Delta Kappa Gamma (pres. Epsilon State), Kappa Kappa Iota, Phi Delta Kappa. Democrat. Avocations: travel, gardening, social work, freelance art work. Home: 250 Louisiana St Westwego LA 70094-4114

BREHM, PATRICIA CHRISTMAN, principal; b. Richmond Hill, N.Y., Mar. 4, 1943; d. Franklin Peter and Veronica Leonard Christman; m. John Louis Brehm, May 10, 1969. BA, Coll. of Mt. St. Vincent, Riverdale, N.Y., 1964; MS, Hofstra U., 1967. Ednl. leadership Nova U. Tchr. East Lake Elem. Sch. Massapequa (N.Y.) Pub. Schs., 1964—82; tchr. Highland Elem Sch. Palm Beach County Schs., Lake Worth, Fla., 1982—85; tchr. Coral Sunset Elem., Boca Raton, Fla., 1985—94; asst. prin. Berkshire Elem., West Palm Beach, Fla., 1994—2000; prin. Waters Edge Elem. Sch., Boca Raton, 2000—. Participant Rep. Edn. Adv. Coun., Pompano Beach, Fla., 1988—89, Edn. Partnership of Palm Beach County - Leadership Forum, West Palm Beach, Fla., 1994—96, Cmty. Found. of Palm Beach and Martin County, West Palm Beach, 1995; facilitator Palm Beach County Instrnl. Forum, West Palm Beach, 1992—93; judge ednl. grants Citibank, West Palm Beach, 1994—98; mem. screening com. Palm Beach County Tchrs.' Guild, West Palm Beach, 1995—97; participant S.E. Fla. Vision 2025, Fort Lauderdale, 1995—95. Mem., treas., v.p., pres. Soroptimist Internat., Pompano Beach, Fla., 1988—94. Named Outstanding Tchr., Rotary Club Boca Raton, 1993; recipient Excellence in Edn. award, Palm Beach County Dwyer, 1993, Fla. Master Tchr. award, 1986. Mem.: Fla. Assn. Sch. Adminstrs., Nat. Assn. Elem. Sch. Prins., Palm Beach County Prin.s' Assn. Roman Catholic. Avocations: travel, sailing, tennis, reading. Home: 21824 Mountain Sugar Ln Boca Raton FL 33433 Office: Waters Edge Elem Sch 21601 Shorewind Dr Boca Raton FL 33428 Office Fax: 561-883-8068. Business E-Mail: brehmp@palmbeach.k12.fl.us.

BREHM, SHARON STEPHENS, psychology professor, former academic administrator; b. Roanoke, Va., Apr. 18, 1945; d. John Wallis and Jane Chappel (Phenix) Stephens; m. Jack W. Brehm, Oct. 25, 1968 (div. Dec. 1979) BA, Duke U., 1967, PhD, 1973; MA, Harvard U., 1968. Clin. psychology intern U. Wash. Med. Ctr., Seattle, 1973-74; asst. prof. Va. Poly. Inst. and State U., Blacksburg, 1974-75, U. Kans., Lawrence, 1975-78, assoc. prof., 1978-83, prof. psychology, 1983-90, assoc. dean Coll. Liberal Arts and Scis., 1987-90; prof. psychology, dean Harpur Coll. of Arts and Scis. SUNY, Binghamton, 1990-96; prof. psychology and interpersonal comm., provost Ohio U., Athens, 1996—2001; v.p. acad. affairs Ind. U., 2001—03, sr. advisor to pres., 2004—05; chancellor Ind. U. Bloomington, 2001—03, prof. dept. psychology, 2001—. Vis. prof. U. Mannheim, 1978, Istituto di Psicologia, Rome, 1989; Fulbright sr. rsch. scholar Ecole des Hautes Etudes en Sciences Sociales, Paris, 1981-82; Soc. for Personality and Social Psychology rep. APA's Coun. of Reps., 1995-2000; chair governing bd. Ohio Learning Network, 1998-99 Author: The Application of Social Psychology to Clinical Practice, 1976, (with others) Psychological Reactance: A Theory of Freedom and Control, 1981, Intimate Relationships, 1985, 2d edit., 1992, (with others) Social Psychology, 1990, 4th edit., 1999, also numerous articles, and chpts. Mem. APA (fin. com. 1999-2001, 2002-04, pres. elect, 2005-). Office: Ind U 1101 E 10th St Bloomington IN 47405-7000 Personal E-mail: sbrehm@indiana.edu.*

BREHM-GRUBER, THERESE FRANCES, minister, consulting psychologist; b. Milw., July 6, 1932; d. Stanley Leo and Frances Hedwig (Kulasiewicz) Maternowski; m. James Monroe Brehm, Aug. 17, 1968 (dec. Feb. 1983); children: Frank X. Brehm, Gretchen Brehm Duran, Eric Brehm; m. Harold John Gruber, July 2, 1994. BS, Marquette U., 1961, MEd, 1963; D of Ministry, Grad. Theol. Found., 1993. Cert. state sch. psychologist, Wis.; ministerial cert. Fedn. Christian Mins. Counselor, sch. psychologist Germantown (Wis.) St. Sch. Dist., 1963-68; sch. psychologist Neenah (Wis.) St. Sch. Dist., 1968-91; lay min. Green Bay Diocese/Parish, Neenah, 1973—. Cons., Wis., 1990-94. Co-author: (with Irene Dill) The Sharing of Power in the Catholic Church, 1993. Vol. follow-up worker Best Friends, Neenah and Menasha, 1994-2000; dir. mem. bd. dir s. Big Bros./Big Sisters, screeners of vols., 1970-80. Named Dutch Uncle, Big Bros./Big Sisters, 1972, Vol. of Yr., 1975. Mem. Bd. Total Cath. Educators of Green Bay Diocese (bd. dirs., nominating com. 1993-99), Altrusa Club Neenah Menasha (pres. 1990-92). Democrat. Roman Catholic. Avocations: swimming, exercise programs, gardening, reading mystery books. Home: 711 Congress St Neenah WI 54956-3419

BREIDENBACH, TONYA D., educator; b. Tiffin, Ohio, July 20, 1977; d. Thomas W. and Denice M. Daniel; m. Eric S. Breidenbach, Nov. 3, 1971; children: Macy G., Jada L. M in Indsl. Tech., Bowling Green State U., Ohio, 2003. Engr. Tiffin (Ohio) Metal Products, 1998—99; assoc. prof. Terra C.C., Fremont, Ohio. Higher edn. chairperson Ohio Fedn. Tchrs., Columbus, 2004—06. Mem.: Soc. Mfg. Engrs. Republican. Office: Terra Community College 2830 Napoleon Rd Fremont OH 43420 Office Phone: 419-559-2450.

BREITBART, BARBARA RENEE, psychologist, administrator, writer; b. N.Y.C. d. Bernard John and Sally Etta (Horwitz) Garson; m. Sheldon Lewis Breitbart; children: Stacey Jana, Kevin Harrison. AB, Syracuse U., 1973; MA, Adelphi U., 1975, PhD, 1978. Lic. psychologist, N.Y. Pvt. practice, Great Neck, N.Y., 1979-89; pres. Rsch. Inst. Psychophysiology, Sedona, Ariz., 1980—; editor-in-chief Who's Who in Biobehaviorial Scis., 1983—. Cons. on wellness; columnist, lectr. on behavioral medicine and psychophysiology, 1978—; guest on radio talk shows; lectr. life, exec. coach: emotional intelligence, stress mgmt. and life transitions mediation, 2005—. Mem. Am. Psychol. Assn. Avocations: chess, classical music, tennis.

BREITENBACH, DEBORAH JONES, language educator; d. Tracey K. and Martha Jones; m. John C. Breitenbach, Jr., Aug. 27, 1977; children: Katherine, John. BS in Secondary Edn., Bucknell U., Lewisburg, Pa., 1972—76; MS in Lit., Coll. St. Rose, Albany, NY, 1980—83. Cert. tchr. NY, 1983. Creative writing tchr. Ticonderoga Ctrl. Schs., NY, 1979—. Recipient Sr. Project Program of Excellence award, NY Tchrs. English, Tchr. of Excellence award; grantee Arthur Vining Davis fellow, Found. Excellent Schs., 2000—04. Office: Ticonderoga Ctrl Schs Calkins Pl Ticonderoga NY 12883 Office Phone: 518-585-6661. E-mail: dbreit@ticonderogak12.org.

BREKKE, KATHRINE LYDIA, music educator; d. Henry Peter Johnson and Delores Ann Hilde Johnson; m. Shawn Brekke, June 19, 1993; 1 child, Daniel. Student, U. Oreg., 1988—89; BSc, Minn. State U., 1991, MSc in Music Edn., 1993. Tchr. music Moorhead (Minn.) Schs., 1995—98, Detroit Lakes (Mich.) Schs., 1998—99; bandleader, singer Ramada Plaza Stes., Fargo, ND, 1999—. Instr. piano Minn. State U., Moorhead, 2001—; dir. vocal jazz ensemble Concordia Coll., Moorhead, 2002—. Composer, musician: (albums) Snow, 1999, Apostles Blues Band, 2000, Song of Praise, 2003. Avocations: bicycling, skiing, walking. Office: Music Dept Minn State Univ 1104 7th Ave S Moorhead MN 56563

BRELAND, ELAINE, webmaster, retired education specialist, special education educator, webmaster; b. Orangeburg, S.C., June 29, 1948; d. Jacob Murray Jr. and Annie Laurie (Rogers) B. BS, Charleston So. Bapt. Coll., 1980. Cert. tchr. Va. Tchr. mid. sch. Berkeley County Schs., Moncks Corner, S.C., 1979-85; tchr. maths. Charleston (S.C.) County Schs., 1985-86, Norfolk (Va.) Pub. Schs., 1988-90; edn. specialist Tidewater Psychiat. Inst., Virginia Beach, Va., 1990-91; edn. therapist Norfolk (Va.) Psychiat. Ctr., 1991-92; ednl. therapist The Pines, Portsmouth, Va., 1992—96, First Corrects Corp., Wilmington, Del., 1996—97; ret., 1997; webmaster designonline.com, Inc., 1999—. Mem. NAFE, Coun. for Exceptional Children, Coun. for Children with Behavioral Disorders, Nat. Coun. Tchrs. Math. Avocations: music, writing, drawing, water sports. Home: 100 Fallon Ave Wilmington DE 19804-1917

BRELSFORD, MARY J., music educator; b. Osage, Iowa, Aug. 2, 1948; d. Robert Duane Mark and Marjorie June Saline; children: Jason E., Nathan E. MusB, Simpson Coll., 1970; MEd, Winona State U., Minn., 1998. Music tchr. Harmony (Minn.) Pub. Schs., 1975—76, Wabasha (Minn.)-Kellogg Pub. Schs., 1979—. Pvt. piano and voice tchr., 1966—; tchr. theatre and music (summers) Am. Sch., Leysin, Switzerland, 1980—84; music adjudicator Minn. State H.S. League, 1985—; music arranger, 1966—. Charter mem. River Junctions Arts Coun., Wabasha, 1980—; ch. organist St. Agnes Cath. Ch., Kellogg, Minn., 1st Bapt. Ch., Osage, Iowa, 1962—2000, United Meth. Ch., Kellogg, Minn., 1962—2000. Home: PO Box 103 Kellogg MN 55945 Office: Wabasha-Kellogg Pub Schs 2113 Hiawatha Dr E Wabasha MN 55981

BREMER, CELESTE F., judge; b. San Francisco, 1953; BA, St. Ambrose Coll., 1974; JD, Univ. of Iowa Coll. of Law, 1977; EdD, Drake U., 2002. Asst. county atty. Scott County, 1977-79; asst. atty. gen. Area Prosecutors Div., Iowa, 1979; with Carlin, Liebbe, Pitton & Bremer, 1979-81, Rabin, Liebbe, Shinkle & Bremer, 1981-82; with legal dept. Deere and Co., 1982-84; corp. counsel Economy Forms Corp., 1985-89; magistrate judge U.S. Dist. Ct. (Iowa so. dist.), 8th cir., Des Moines, 1984—; ed. D. Drake U. Sch. of Edn., 2002. Instr. Drake Univ. Coll. of Law, 1985—88, 2005—06. Mem. ABA, Fed. Magistrate Judge Assn., Nat. Assn. Women Judges, Am. Judicature Soc., Iowa State Bar Assn. (bd. govs., 1987-90), Iowa Judges Assn., Iowa Supreme Ct. Coun. on Jud. Selection (chmn. 1986-90), Iowa Orgn Women Attys., Polk County Bar Assn., Polk County Women Attys. Office: US Courthouse Ste 435 123 E Walnut St Des Moines IA 50309-2036 Office Phone: 515-284-6200.

BREN, KARA L., chemistry professor; b. Minn. BA, Carleton Coll., Northfield, Minn., 1991; PhD, Calif. Inst. Tech., Pasadena, 1995. Assoc. prof. chemistry U. Rochester, NY, 2003—. Named Paul Saltman Meml. Lectr., Paul Saltman Meml. Fund, 2004; Alfred P. Sloan Rsch. fellow, Alfred P. Sloan Found., 2003—05. Office: Dept Chemistry University of Rochester Rochester NY 14627-0216 Office Phone: 585-275-4335.

BRENCHLEY, JEAN ELNORA, microbiologist, researcher, science administrator; b. Towanda, Pa., Mar. 6, 1944; d. John Edward and Elizabeth (Jefferson) B.; m. Bernard Asbell, July 21, 1990 (dec. Feb. 2001). BS, Mansfield U., 1965; MS, U. Calif., San Diego, 1967; PhD, U. Calif., Davis, 1970; degree (hon.), Lycoming Coll., 1992. Rsch. assoc. biology dept. MIT, Cambridge, 1970-71; from asst. prof. to assoc. prof. microbiology Pa. State U., Univ. Pk., 1971-77, head. dept. molecular and cell biology, dir. Biotech. Inst. University Park, 1984-87, prof. microbiology, dir. Biotech. Inst., 1984-90, prof. microbiology and biotech., 1990—; assoc. prof., then prof. biology Purdue U., West Lafayette, Ind., 1977-81; research dir. Genex Corp., Gaithersburg, Md., 1981-84. Mem. Nat. Biotech. Policy Bd., 1990-93; trustee Biosis, 1983-88; vis. scholar NIH, 1991. Editor Applied and Environ. Microbiology, 1981-85; mem. editorial bd. Jour. Bacteriology, 1974-84, Butterworth Biotech. Series, 1988-92; editor Microbiol. Revs., 1992-97. Recipient Outstanding Alumni award Manfield U., 1983; Waksman award Theobald Smith Soc., 1985; named to Pa. Hall of Fame, 1988. Fellow AAAS (nominating com. 1990-92), Am. Acad. Microbiology; mem. NAS (bioprocess com.), Am. Soc. Microbiology (pres. 1986-87, ASM Found. lectr. 1975, Alice Evans award 1996), Assn. Women in Sci., Am. Soc. Biol. Chemists, Am. Chem. Soc., Found. for Microbiology (trustee 1988-95), Sigma Delta Epsilon (hon.). Office: Pa State Univ Frear Lab University Park PA 16802

BRENDAHL, MARCIA, artist, illustrator; b. Battle Creek, Mich., Mar. 2, 1953; d. Ray LaVerne and Iris Donna (Hawkins-Eckhart) Leonard; m. Mark Eric Brendahl, Mar. 7, 1985; children: Mallorae E., Maureen E. AD in Liberal Arts, Lansing (Mich.) C.C., 1985. Ceramic tchr. Leonard's Ceramics, Lansing, 1972-83; fine artist Lansing, 1983—; art designer Lansing Sch. Dist./Kendon Elem. Sch., 1999—. Children's art tchr. Lansing Art Gallery, 1998-99, Lansing Parks and Recreation, 1999. Designer murals for stage performances, 1997—; fine art portraits of children and authors, 1989—. Vol. worker, artist Mich. Rep. Party, Lansing, 1999. Mem. Nat. Women of the Arts, Lansing Art Guild. Avocations: painting, writing short stories, photography. Home: 6888 Londal Cir Lansing MI 48911-7044

BRENKEN, HANNE MARIE, artist; b. Duisburg, Germany, July 6, 1923; arrived in U.S., 1977; d. Hermann and Luise (Werth) Tigler; m. Hans Brenken, Mar. 28, 1942 (div. 1985); children: Karin Brenken Schneider-Henn, Berndt; m. Ricardo Wiesenberg, May 20, 1986. Grad., Landschulheim, Holzminden, Germany, 1941; studied in pvt. art schs., Munich and Bonn, Germany. One-person shows include Contra Kreis Gallery, Bonn, Germany, 1958, Galerie Junge Kunst, Fulda, Germany, 1959, Universa-Galerie, Nurenberg, Germany, 1960, Galleria Monte Napoleone, Milan, 1961, Galerie Niedlich, Stuttgart, Germany, 1961, 63, Galerie am Jakobsbrunnen, Stuttgard, 1964, 67, Kunst und Kunstverein Mus. Pforzheim, Germany, 1969, Kunstverein Mus., Munich, 1972, Galerie Dorothea Leonhart, Munich, 1974, I.C.L. Gallery, East Hampton, N.Y., 1980, Anne Reid Gallery, Princeton, N.J., 1981, Adagio Gallery, Bridgehampton, N.Y., 1982, 84, Queens Mus., N.Y., 1983, Ericson Gallery, N.Y.C., 1984, 85, Benton Gallery, Southampton, N.Y., 1986, Vered Gallery, East Hampton, N.Y., 1988, Gallery Rodeo, Lake Arrowhead, Calif., Taos, N.Mex., Beverly Hills, Calif., 1990, Brian Logan Art Space, Washington, 1991, The Gallery, Leesburg, Va., 1992, Amerika Haus, Frankfurt, Germany, 1993, Ganser Haus Gallery, Wasserburg, Germany, 1993, Ann Norton Sculpture Gardens, West Palm Beach, Fla., 1994, Jean Chisholm Gallery, West Palm Beach, 1994, Okuda Internat. Gallery, Washington, 1995, Misia Broadhead Studio/Gallery, Middleburg, Va., 1996, Millennium Gallery, East Hampton, N.Y., 1997, Reynolds Gallery Westmont Coll., Santa Barbara, Calif., 1998, Svitozor Fine Arts, Santa Barbara, Calif., 2000, L.A. Artcore, Los Angeles, 2001; group shows include Duisburg (Germany) Mus., 1959, Baden-Baden Mus., Germany, 1961, 62, Haus der Kunst, Munich, 1963, 64, 69, 70, 71, 72, 73, Kunstgebäude, Stuttgart, 1963, 71, Acad. Fine Arts, Berlin, 1964, 73, Forum Stadtpark, Graz, Austria, 1965, Folkwang Mus., Essen, Germany, 1965, Munich City Mus., 1967, Karlsruhe (Germany) Kunstverein, 1967; permanent collections include Solomon R. Guggenheim Mus., New York, Queens Mus., Phoenix Art Mus., Guild Hall Mus, several mus. in Europe. Avocations: travel, visiting galleries and musuems, reading.

BRENNAN, CARRIE, principal; b. 1967; BA, Darthmouth Coll., Hanover, NH; MA, U. Ariz. Founding faculty mem. Catalina Foothills High Sch.; prin. City High Sch., Tucson. Co-dir. Southern Ariz. Writing Project's Tchr. Inst.; workshop instructor curriculum design and collaborative profl. devel.; chair Symposium on Sch. Improvement. Involved with Tucson Small Sch. Project. Named one of 40 Under 40, Tucson Bus. Edge, 2006. Office: City High School PO Box 2608 Tucson AZ 85702 Office Phone: 520-623-7223. Office Fax: 520-547-0680. Business E-Mail: carrie@cityhighschool.org.*

BRENNAN, DEBORAH ANN, artist; b. Dumas, Tex., Dec. 26, 1954; d. Ralph Elden and Mary Dell (Burros) Turner; 1 child, Shay Weston Turner. BS Interior Design, S.W. Mo. State U., 1977. Cert. draftsman Am. Design

Drafting Assn., 1998. Adelstein dome, Addison Jewelry Store, 1981, beveled glass, St. George & the Dragon, Van Buren, Mo., stained and lead glass windows, Breathe of the Spirit, Holy Trinity I & II, Father, Son & Holy Spirit, Piedmont, Mo., Mary & Child, Springfield, Grapes & Wheat, Mountain View, Mo., Yellow Ribbon window, Branson, Mo., Springfield-Cape Girardeau Diocese, and others. Office: 1020 E Edgewood Springfield MO 65807 Office Phone: 417-886-2997. Personal E-mail: debbiebrennan@sbcglobal.net.

BRENNAN, DEBORAH DIKEMAN, assistant principal; b. Buffalo, Feb. 3, 1948; d. Wilfred Clark and June Mary Dikeman; m. Jeffrey Hastings Brennan, Dec. 16, 1967; children: Michelle Elizabeth, Jennifer Elaine. BS, U. Cen. Okla., Edmund, 1997; MA in Spl. Edn. and Ednl. Leadership, U. No. Colo., Greeley, 2004. Lic. adminstr. Colo., lifetime tchg. cert. Tex. Tchr. San Marcos (Tex.) Consol. Ind. Sch. Dist., 1991—97, coord. gifted and talented, 1994—99; constrn. coord. GDA Real Estate, Greenwood Valley, Colo., 2000—01; tchr. Douglas County Sch. Dist., Highland Ranch, Colo., 2001—05, asst. prin., 2005—. Co-author: (white papers) Stemming the Tide: A Coorado Response to the Crisis in Science, Technology, Technology, Engineering and Math Education. Named San Marcos Tchr. of Yr., San Marcos CISD, 1989. Mem.: Colo. Assn. for Gifted and Talented (pres. 2006). Office: Thunder Ridge H S 1991 Wildcat Pkwy Highlands Ranch CO 80129 E-mail: deborah_brennan@yahoo.com.

BRENNAN, DONNA LESLEY, public relations company executive; b. Washington, Mar. 13, 1945; d. Don Arthur and Louise (Tucker) B.; m. James L Bergey, Mar. 6, 1999. BA, Denison U., 1967. Tchr. Souderton Area H.S., Pa., 1967—69; mgr. media rels. Ins. Co. N.Am., Phila., 1969—72; dir. press rels. Colonial Penn Group, Phila., 1972—75, 1975—81, dir. comm., 1981—83; v.p. corp. comm. Norstar Bancorp, Albany, NY, 1983—85; v.p. comm. Meritor Fin. Group, Phila., 1986—87; prin. Donna Brennan Assocs., 1988—. Bd. dirs. A Chance to Heal. Bd. dirs. A Chance to Heal, 2005—, French & Pickering Creeks Conservation Trust, 2006—. Mem. Pub. Rels. Soc. Am. (pres. Phila. chpt. 1988), Phila. Women's Network (founder, bd. dirs.), Pathways Pa. (vice-chmn. 1995—, bd. dirs.), Forum of Exec. Women (pres. 1992-93, bd. dirs. 1989-97). Office Phone: 610-469-8765. E-mail: db@brennanpr.com.

BRENNAN, JANICE M., medical/surgical nurse, nursing educator; b. Balt., Dec. 5, 1956; MS, U. Md., Balt. Cert. med./surg. nurse, ANCC, 2006. Nursing instr. Johnston Sch. Practical Nursing, Balt., 1993—96; assoc. prof. nursing C.C. of Balt. County, Balt., 1998—. Presenter in field. Recipient Nat. Nurse Traineeship award, U. Md., 1993. Mem.: Sigma Theta Tau (Cmty. Leader award 1999), Phi Kappa Phi. Office: CC Balt County 800 S Rolling Rd Baltimore MD 21228 Business E-Mail: jbrennan@ccbcmd.edu.

BRENNAN, MAUREEN, lawyer; b. Morristown, N.J., Aug. 7, 1949; BA magna cum laude, Bryn Mawr Coll., 1971; JD cum laude, Boston Coll., 1977. Bar: Pa. 1977, U.S. Dist. Ct. (ea. dist.) Pa. 1978, Ohio 1989. Atty. U.S. EPA, Washington, 1977-80; asst. dist. atty. Phila. Trial and Appellate Divs., 1980-84; in-house environ. counsel TRW Inc., 1985-87; assoc. Baker & Hostetler LLP, Cleve., 1987-91, ptnr., 1991—. Adj. prof. Case Western Res. U., Cleve., 1990-92, 00-06. Active Cleve. Tree Commn., 1991-96, co-chair, 1993-95; trustee Clean-Land Ohio, 1990-2000; rep. Canal Heritage Corridor Com., 2000—; mem. Cuyahoga County Greenspace Working Group, 1999-2002; bd. dirs. Crown Point Ecology Ctr., 2001--. Recipient Bronze Medal for Achievement, U.S. EPA, 1980. Mem. ABA (natural resources and environ. sect., standing com. environ law 1996-98), Pa. Bar Assn. (environ. law com.), Ohio State Bar Assn. (environ. law com.), Cleve. Bar Assn. (environ. law sect., chair wetlands com. 1991-92, sect. chair 1996-97, mem. steering com. adv. OEPA on Brownfield regulations 1995-97). Office: Baker & Hostetler LLP 3200 Nat City Ctr 1900 E 9th St Ste 3200 Cleveland OH 44114-3475 Office Phone: 216-861-7957. Business E-Mail: mbrennan@bakerlaw.com.

BRENNAN, NOELLE C., lawyer; JD, DePaul U., 1995. Assoc. Katten Muchin & Zavis; trial atty., supervisory atty. Equal Employment Opportunity Commn.; ptnr. Brennan & Monte Ltd. Adj. prof. employment discrimination. Named one of 40 Under 40, Crain's Chgo. Bus., 2005. Office: Brennan & Monte Ltd Ste 1530 20 South Clark St Chicago IL 60603 Office Phone: 312-422-0001. Office Fax: 312-422-0008. E-mail: nbrennan@brennan-monte.com.*

BRENNAN, NORMA JEAN, professional society administrator, director; b. Helena, Mont., Apr. 16, 1939; d. Harland Sanford Herrin and Elizabeth (Wardlaw) Brumfield; m. Anthony E. Brennan, Dec. 4, 1964 (div. Mar. 1986); children: Christopher E., Kimberly A. BA, U. Pacific, 1960. Editl. asst. Am. Rocket Soc., N.Y.C., 1961-62, asst. mng. editor, 1962-65; mng. editor AIAA, N.Y.C., 1978-80, publs. divsn. dir. N.Y.C., Washington, Reston, Va., 1980—. Mem. Young Republicans, Stockton, Calif., 1958-60; vol. Mt. Sinai Hosp., N.Y.C., 1962-64. Fellow: AIAA (Space Shuttle Flag award); mem.: Washington Women's Info. Network, N.Am. Serials Interest Group, Coun. Engring. and Sci. Soc. Execs., Assn. Am. Pubs., Coun. Sci. Editors, Soc. for Scholarly Pub. (bd. dirs.). Avocations: reading, travel, gardening. Home: 11551 Links Dr Reston VA 20190-4820 Office: AIAA 1801 Alexander Bell Dr Reston VA 20191-4344 E-mail: normab@aiaa.org.

BRENNAN, SUSAN MALLICK, utilities executive; BS, U.S. Air Force Acad., 1981; MBA, Nat. U., 1989. Fin. analyst and investor rels. analyst Nev. Power Co., Las Vegas, 1992—93, mgr. reogrn. project, 1993—94, mgr. performance mgmt. and analysis, 1993—95, dir. human resources, 1995—97, dir. industry restructuring and strategic planning, 1997—99; exec. dir. customer svc. and industry restructuring Sierra Pacific Resources, 1999—2001; v.p., chief info. officer Sierra Pacific Power and Nev. Power, 2001—. Active Leadership Las Vegas, 1998, Workforce 2010 Task Force; regional pres. Am. Diabetes Assn.; bd. mem. United Blood Svcs., Found. Bd. Opportunity Village. With USAF, 1981—88. Mem.: Las Vegas C. of C. Office: Sierra Pacific/Nev Power PO Box 10100 6100 Neil Rd Reno NV 89520

BRENNAN-BERGMANN, BRIDGET CATHERINE, special education educator; b. San Antonio, June 10, 1955; d. Eugene Anthony and Evelyn Joyce Brennan; m. Ernest Bergmann, Jr., Dec. 29, 1997. BS, Stephen F. Austin State, Nacogdoches, Tex., 1978; MEd, North Tex. State U., Denton, 1981. Cert. tchr. for life in areas ednl. diagnostican, physically handicapped, elem. and psychology tchr. Tchr. Stoneleigh Day Sch., Denton, 1978, Hartford County, Md., 1987—90; tchr., diagnostician Lewisville I.S.D., Tex., 1978—84, diagnostician, 1985—87; tchr., counselor Am. Sch., Guadalajara, Mexico, 1984—85; tchr., spl. edn. dept. chair Randolph Field Elem. Sch., Randolph AFB, 1990—. Vol. Therapeutic Horseback Riding, San Antonio, 2003—05; leader support group Alzheimer's Assn., Schertz, Tex., 2004—. Named Tchr. of Game, San Antonio Spurs/Rampage, 2003; recipient Carol Gray award tchr. outstanding students, Future Horizons, Arlington, Tex., 2004. Mem.: Assn. Tex. Profl. Educators, Phi Delta Kappa, Alphi Chi. Avocations: doll collecting, antiques, gardening. Office: Randolph Field Elem Sch Bldg 146 Randolph Afb TX 78148 Office Fax: 210-357-2346.

BRENNEMAN, AMY, actress; b. New London, Conn., June 22, 1964; m. Brad Silberling, Sept. 30, 1995; children: Charlotte Tucker, Bodhi Russell. BA in Comparative Religion, Harvard U., 1987. Mem. Cornerstone Theater Co. Actress (films) Bye, Bye Love, 1995, Heat, 1995, Casper, 1995, Fear, 1996, (TV series) Middle Ages, 1992, NYPD Blue, 1993—94, actress and co-creator Judging Amy, 1999—2005, (TV films) Mary Cassatt: An American Impressionist, 1999, Things You Can Tell Just By Looking at Her, 2000, Off the Map, 2003, Nine Lives, 2005, actress (plays) Saint Joan of the Stockyards, 1992, (off Broadway) The Learned Ladies, God's Heart, 1997, (plays) A Nervous Smile, 2006. Founder Cornerstone Theater Co., Conn. Office: Creative Artists Agy 9830 Wilshire Blvd Beverly Hills CA 90212-1825 Address: Travel Entertainment 9171 Wilshire Blvd Ste 700 Beverly Hills CA 90211 also: PMK/HBH Pub Rels 8500 Wilshire Blvd Ste 700 Beverly Hills CA 90211*

BRENNEN, ANNA B., theater producer, director, playwright, actor; d. Chester Alyn and Helen (Boice) Brennen; 1 child, Lisa Deal. BA, U. Calif., 1964; postgrad., Hunter Coll., NYU. Founder, producing dir. Stageworks, Tampa, Fla., 1983—. Fellowship panel Fla. State Theatre; cons. in field. Author: (plays) Sleepless Dancer, 1980, Echo Nevada, 1987. Named Best Dir., Weekly Planet and Tampa Tribune, 1992—2004. Mem.: Dramatists Guild, Actors Equity Assn., Theatre Comms. Group. Avocations: movies, cooking, reading.

BRENNER, BETH FUCHS, publishing executive; Grad., U. Vt., 1980. Sales promotion coordinator Chanel, Inc., 1980-83; promotion mgr. M mag., 1983-86; adv. sales rep. New York mag., 1986-91, adv. dir., 1991-93, SELF mag., 1993-94, pub., 1994-2001, v.p., pub., 2001—04; v.p., pub. domino mag., 2004—. Office: Domino Mag 4 Times Sq New York NY 10036-6562 E-mail: Beth_Brenner@condenast.com.

BRENNER, BETTY ESTHER BILGRAY, social worker; b. Providence, Feb. 13, 1943; d. Albert Theodore and Clara (Simon) Bilgray; m. Douglas Brenner, Sept. 1, 1968; children: Steven, Michael, Deborah. BA, U. Mich., 1965, MSW, 1967. Lic. clin. social worker, N.J. Social worker Peter Bent Brigham Hosp., Boston, 1967-69, Union County Psychiat. Clinic, Summit, N.J., 1969-71, Mental Health Resource Ctr., Montclair, N.J., 1977-83, Jewish Family Svc. N. Jersey, Wayne, N.J., 1983-91; pvt. practice N. Haledon and Livingston, N.J., 1991—. Home: 61 E Sherbrooke Pkwy Livingston NJ 07039-3133 Office: 546 High Mountain Rd North Haledon NJ 07508-2606

BRENNER, BONNIE SUE, singer, artist, educator; b. Chgo., Dec. 8, 1954; d. Richard S. and Iris Brenner; m. Jeffrey M. Thompson, Aug. 4, 1984 (div. Jan. 1995). MS, U. Ill., Champaign-Urbana, 1987—87. Cert. tchr. Ill., 2004. Electron microscopist VA Med. Ctr., Loma Linda, Calif., 1987—92; rsch. asst. VA Lakeside, Chgo., 1993—94; instr. Wilbur Wright Jr. Coll., Chgo., 1994—97; sci. tchr. Niles West H.S., Skokie, Ill., 2000—. Summer rsch. technician Northwestern U., Evanston, Ill., 2001. Sponsor Niles West S.A.V.E. Club, Skokie, 2002. Mem.: Soc. for Neurosci., Microscopy Soc. of Am., Nat. Sci. Tchrs. Assn., Nat. Assn. of Biology Tchrs. Office: Niles West High School 5701 W Oakton St Skokie IL 60077 Office Phone: 847-626-2780. E-mail: bonbre@niles-hs.k12.il.us.

BRENNER, ELIZABETH (BETSY BRENNER), publishing executive; b. Bellevue, Wash. m. Steven Ostrofsky. BJ, MBA, Northwestern U. City news reporter The Chgo. (Ill.) Tribune, 1977, bus. news reporter, columnist, 1978; with mktg. dept. The New York Times; with retail advt. and circulation posts Miami Herald, Rocky Mountain News, Denver, sr. v.p. sales and mktg., 1994—96; pub. Bremerton Sun, 1996—98, The News Tribune, Tacoma, 1998—. Bd. dirs. Econ. Devel. Bd, Tacoma, Mus. Glass, Greater Tacoma Cmty. Found., exec. coun.; mem. Tacoma adv. coun. U. Wash.; co-chmn. campaign Olympic Coll. Libr. Kitsap County. Office: The News Tribune 1950 S State St Tacoma WA 98405-2817 Mailing: PO Box 11000 Tacoma WA 98411 E-mail: betsy.brenner@mail.tribnet.com.

BRENT, HELEN TERESSA, school nurse; b. Grand Rapids, Mich., Oct. 4, 1946; d. William Henry and Anita Broyles Burress; m. Robert Lee Brent, June 10, 1967. AS, Grand Rapids C.C., 1966; diploma, Butterworth Hosp. Sch. Nursing, 1968; BSN summa cum laude, U. Mich., 1981; MPA, Western Mich. U., 1992. RN, Mich. Staff nurse Butterworth Hosp., Grand Rapids, Mich., 1968-69, head nurse psychiat. unit, 1969-72; DON Forest View Psychiat. Hosp., Grand Rapids, Mich., 1972-75; asst. DON, staff devel. coord. Kent Oaks Psychiat. Unit Kent Community Hosp., Grand Rapids, Mich., 1975-80; DON Kent Community Hosp. Complex, Grand Rapids, Mich., 1980-94; psychiat. nurse Pine Rest Christian Mental Health Svcs., Grand Rapids, 1994—; health planner Kent County Pub. Health Dept., Grand Rapids, 1996-97; sch. nurse Grand Rapids Pub. Schs., 1997—. Adj. faculty nursing divsn. Grand Rapids C.C., 1999—. Mem. adv. coun. Mich. Family Planning Mich. Dept. Cmty. Health, 1991-99, Family Outreach Ctr., Grand Rapids, 1980-95; mem. hospice care study panel United Way Kent County, 1984; vol. nursing health svcs. Kent County chpt. ARC, Grand Rapids, 1974—; vol. mediator West Mich. Dispute Resolution Ctr., 1995—. Recipient Outstanding Svc. award Family Outreach Ctr. Kent County Comty. Mental Health, 1988, Helen Barnes award for outstanding vol. contbns. in nursing svcs. Kent County chpt. ARC, 1994, Eugene Browning Med. Svc. award Giants Orgn., Grand Rapids C.C., 1995. Mem. Vis. Nurses Assn. West Mich.(bd. dirs. 1991-2000), Nat. Black Nurses Assn. (local chpt. 1999—), Harambe Black Nurses Assn. Grand Rapids. Democrat. Avocations: travel, reading. Home: 3834 Old Elm Dr SE Kentwood MI 49512-9523 Office: Grand Rapids Pub Schs KEC Mayfield 225 Mayfield Ave NE Grand Rapids MI 49503-3768 E-mail: hbrent5558@webtv.net, BrentH@grps.k12.mi.us.

BRENT, PATRICIA LEE, health facility administrator, writer; d. Charles Robert and Marion Helen Brent; m. George Dewey Sorenson, Mar. 12, 1988. BS, Vt. Coll., 1968; MPH, Emory U., 1981; JD, Vt. Law Sch., 1997. Cert. med. technologist Am. Soc. Clin. Pathology, 1968. Dir. profl. svcs. Alice Peck Day Meml. Hosp., Lebanon, NH, 1981—87, v.p., strategic planning, 1987—94; pres. Morgan Hill Assocs., Meriden, NH, 1998—; rsch. asst. Dartmouth Med. Sch., Hanover, NH, 1968—70, rsch. assoc., 1972—79, Stanford U. Sch. Medicine, Palo Alto, Calif., 1970—72. Mem. editl. adv. bd. compliance CCH, Inc., Chgo., 2003—. Author: (book-medicare hosp. financing policy) Inside Medicare Outliers: Keys to Policy, Payment and Compliance, (book-medicare reimbursement policy) Understanding Reimbursement for Investigational Drugs and Devices, (web-based book) Critical Access Hospitals: The Application Process, 2005; content editor, cons. (web-based ednl. product) Medicare and Medicaid Now; contbr. articles to profl. jours. and newsletters. Mem. med. ethics com. Alice Peck Day Meml. Hosp., Lebanon, 1996—; chair rev. and allocations com. United Way Upper Valley, Lebanon, 1992—94, bd. mem., 1992—95, Am. Lung Assn., Manchester, 1984—92; pres. Human Svc. Coun. Upper Valley, 1988—92. Mem.: Healthcare Fin. Mgmt. Assn., Healthcare Compliance Assn. (region 1 planning com. 2000—05), Am. Health Lawyers' Assn. Episcopalian. Avocations: downhill skiing, birdwatching, hiking, antiques. Office: Morgan Hill Assos PO Box 176 Meriden NH 03770 Office Phone: 603-469-3536.

BREON, NANCY G., music educator; b. Midland, Tex., Feb. 19, 1962; d. Charles W. and Rogene Miller; m. John A. Breon, June 22, 1985; children: Rachel, Eric, Eli. MusB, U. Ctrl. Okla., Edmond, 1984. Tchr. music Choctaw Pub. Schs., Okla., 1984—85; pvt. piano instr., 1988—2003; tchr. music Timberlake Pub. Schs., Helena, Okla., 1997—98; asst. tchr. music Beaver Pub. Schs., Okla., 1999—2000; tchr. music Forgan Pub. Schs., Okla., 2001—03, Eufaula Pub. Schs., Okla., 2003—. Mem.: Okla. Choral Dirs. Assn., Okla. Music Educators Assn. Meth. Home: 110 North L Eufaula OK 74432

BRESCHI, KAREN LEE, artist, image consultant, educator; b. Oakland, Calif., Oct. 29, 1941; d. Leo John and Delores F. (Swenson) B. BFA with distinction, Calif. Coll. Arts and Crafts, 1963; MA, San Francisco State U., 1965; postgrad., San Fancisco Art Inst., 1966-69; PhD, Calif. Inst. Intergral Studies, 1988. Mem. faculty San Francisco Art Inst., 1970-75, 85, San Francisco State U., 1974-81; prin. Karen Breschi-Image Cons., San Francisco, 1981-83; vis. artist Banff Ctr. Sch. Fine Art, Alta., Can., 1984, San Francisco Acad. Art, 1985; mem. faculty St. Mary's Coll., Moraga, Calif., 1985—. Vis. artist U. Mont., Missoula, 1979, Calif. Coll. Arts and Crafts, Oakland, 1980, U. Calif., Davis, 1981-82. Exhibited group shows, U. Calgary, 1973, Whitney Mus., N.Y.C., 1974, Everson Mus., Syracuse, N.Y., 1979, Smithsonian Inst., Washington, 1980. Mem. Am. Fedn. Tchrs., Am. Soc. Tng. and Devel., Am. Psychol. Assn., Assn. for Humanistic Psychology Democrat. Unitarian Universalist. Office: care Braustein Gallery 254 Sutter St San Francisco CA 94108-4403

BRESCIA, ALICIA, science educator, vice principal; b. Reading, Pa., Jan. 19, 1947; d. Joseph John and Alice B. Heine; m. Frank J. Brescia, June 29, 1985. BA in Elem. Edn. and Biology, Coll. of St. Elizabeth, Convent Sta., NJ, 1969; MA in Sci. Edn., Columbia U., NYC, 1976. Profl. Diploma in Secondary Edn. Adminstrn. Fordham U., NYC, 1994. Tchr. Assumption Sch., Morristown, NJ, 1968—72, St. Teresa Sch., Summit, NJ, 1972—77; prin. St. Vincent Martyr Sch., Madison, NJ, 1977—81; tchr. biology and sci. Gov. Livingston HS, Berkeley Heights, NJ, 1982—85; faculty sci. in elem. edn. Coll. of St. Elizabeth, 1983—85; tchr. sci. and biology Somers (NY) HS, 1986—93; spl. GE tchr. program Ossining (NY) HS, 1993—94; vice prin. Port Chester (NY) HS, 1994—96, chair sci. dept., 1994—98; tchr. biology The Living Environment Marine Sci. and Paleontology, 1994—. Prin. summer sch. Port Chester HS, 1996—99, mem. scholarship com., 1994—, mem. sch. improvement com., 1999—, small learning cmtys. com., 2002—, mem. faculty senate, 2005—; bereavement and grief related issues Calvary Hosp., Bronx, NY, 2002; freshman acad. team Edn. Alliance and Brown Univ., 2004—. Mem. vis. com. Mid. States Assn. Colls. and Schs., 1999; bd. dirs. Heritage Hills Condo 7, Somers, 1996—2002, pres. bd., 1991, sect. leaders chair, 1996—2002. Named Outstanding Elem. Tchr. of Am., Outstanding Elem. Tchrs. Am., 1974; grantee, NSF, 1971. Fellow: Assn. Supervision and Curriculum Devel., Sci. Tchrs. of N.Y. State; mem.: N.J. Sci. Tchrs. Assn., Hastings Inst. of Ethics, United Fedn. Tchrs. Roman Catholic. Avocations: gardening, travel, cooking. Office: Port Chester High School 1 Tamarack Rd Port Chester NY 10573 Office Phone: 914-934-7952. Personal E-mail: abres@portchesterschools.org.

BRESLIN, WYNN BOIN, artist; b. Hackensack, NJ, Nov. 6, 1932; d. Clinton Edward and Elsie (Dubelbeiss) Boin; m. William Walsh Breslin, June 25, 1953; 1 child, William Walsh IV. BFA, Ohio Wesleyan U., 1954; MEd, U. Del., 1961. Cert. tchr. Ohio, Del., NJ. Instr. art Georgetown (Del.) Sch. Dist., 1954-56, Newark Sch. Dist., 1956-60; supr. art Alexis I. duPont Dist., Wilmington, Del., 1960-63; instr. art Tatnall Sch., Wilmington, 1964, Del. Art Mus., Wilmington, 1956-76; visual artist residency program Del. State Arts Coun., Divsn. Arts, Wilmington, 1980—. Art cons. Gore Assocs., Inc., Elkton, Md., 1981—; condr. painting workshops Del. Ctr. Contemporary Art, Wilmington, 1982-93; judge art exhbns., Del., Md., 1971-81. Mem. edn. com. Del. Art Mus., 1966-71; mem. Del. Ctr. Contemporary Art, 1980-93. Scholar Haystack Sch. Art, Maine, 1960, Benedictine Art award Nat. Arts Club, N.Y.C., 1967, Frist Prize Oil and Best-in-Show NOW, Wilmington, Del., 1972, First Prize Acrylic Painting U. Del., 1988, Permanent Collection award Del. Divsn. Librs., 1981, 83, Acad. of Italy award with gold medal, 1989. Mem. Nat. League Am. Pen Women (treas. 1971-73), Del. Assn. Art Edn. (pres. 1960-62). Avocations: European travel, painting. Home and Office: Wynn Breslin Studio Gallery 470 Terrapin Ln Newark DE 19711-2118 Studio: 470 Terrapin Ln Newark DE 19711-2118 E-mail: wynnbreslin@wynnbreslin.com.

BRESLOW, ESTHER MAY GREENBERG, biochemistry professor, researcher; b. NYC, Dec. 23, 1931; d. Harry Daniel and Lillian (Solomon) Greenberg; m. Ronald Charles David Breslow, Sept. 4, 1955; children: Stephanie Ruth, Karen Ann. BS with distinction, Cornell U., 1953; MS in Biochemistry, NYU, 1955, PhD in Biochemistry, 1959; postgrad., Radcliffe Coll., 1954-55. Postdoctoral fellow Cornell U. Med. Coll., N.Y.C., 1959-61, rsch. assoc., 1961-64, asst. prof., 1964-72, assoc. prof., 1972-78, prof. biochemistry, 1978—, acting chmn. dept. biochemistry, 1992-95. Mem. rev. panels NIH, Bethesda, Md., 1973—77, Bethesda, 1994—97, NSF, Bethesda, 1981—84. Mem. editorial bd. Jour. Biol. Chemistry, 1982-87, Internat. Jour. Peptide and Protein Rsch., 1981—87; contbr. articles to profl. jours. Mem. Englewood (N.J.) Bd. Health, 1986-94; mem. Dem. Mcpl. Com., Englewood, 1985-91. Fellow, Eli Lilly, 1954—55, USPHS, 1959—61; grantee, NIH, 1961—. Fellow AAAS; mem. Am. Soc. for Biochemistry and Molecular Biology, Am. Chem. Soc. (sec. div. biol. chemistry 1972-76), Harvey Soc., Sigma Xi. Home: 44 W 77th St New York NY 10024 Office: Joan and Sanford I Weill Med Coll Cornell U 1300 York Ave New York NY 10021-4805 Office Phone: 212-746-6428. Business E-Mail: ebreslow@med.cornell.edu.

BRESLOW, STEPHANIE R., lawyer; b. NYC, June 20, 1960; d. Ronald and Esther Breslow. BA cum laude, Harvard U., 1981; JD, Columbia U., 1984. Bar: Ohio 1984, NY 1986. Assoc. Cleary Gottlieb Steen & Hamilton, NYC, 1985-93; ptnr., corp. dept. Schulte Roth & Zabel LLP, NYC, 1993—, hiring ptnr., recruiting com. Spkr. in field; co-author: New York Limited Liability Companies and Partnerships, NY & Del. Business Entities: Choice Formation Operation Financing and Acquisitions. Bd. trustees The Joyce Theater, NY. Harlan Fiske Stone Scholar, 1982—84. Mem.: Pvt. Investment Fund Forum (founding mem.), Wall St. Hedge Fund Forum (steering com.), Assn. Bar City NY. Office: Schulte Roth & Zabel LLP 919 Third Ave New York NY 10022-4774 Office Phone: 212-756-2542. Office Fax: 212-593-5955. Business E-Mail: stephanie.breslow@srz.com.

BRESLOW, TINA, public relations executive; b. Phila., Feb. 18, 1946; d. Harry and Doris (Stein) Horowitz; m. Alan Breslow, Aug. 28, 1965 (div. 1970); children: Peter, Jennifer, Brett. Office mgr. Temple U. Ctr. City, Phila., 1976-79; publicist Temple U. Theater, Phila., 1979-81; mgr. pub. rels. Hershey Phila. Hotel, 1981-83; dir. pub. rels. Franklin Plaza Hotel, Phila., 1983-84; account mgr. Sommers Rosen, Inc., Phila., 1984-85; prin. Breslow Partners, Phila., 1985—. Pub. rels. cons. Dock St. Beer, Phila., 1986-87, Sheraton Soc. Hill Hotel, Phila., 1985-86. Chmn. pub. rels. com. Phila. Convention and Vis. Bur., 1985; pub. rels. cons. Phila. City Planning Commn., 1988, Phila. Commn. on AIDS, 1988. Recipient Super Communicator award Women in Communication, 1984, Best New Bus. Intro. award Phila. Better Bus. Bur., 1986, Community Svs. award Hotel Sales and Mktg. Assoc. Internat., 1988, Golden Bell award, 1988, Breakfast for Champions and Olymic Fundraiser The Alexander Hotels, 1988, Woman of Distinction award, 2002; named to Wall of Fame. N.E. H.S., 2002. Mem. Phila. Pub. Rels. Assn., Pub. Rels. Soc. Am. Jewish. Office: Tina Breslow Pub Rels 2042 Rittenhouse Sq Philadelphia PA 19103-5621*

BRESNAHAN, PAMELA ANNE, lawyer, mediator, arbitrator; b. Washington, Ohio, Nov. 21, 1954; d. Richard and Margaret (McBride) Bresnahan; m. Theda Sersen, Sept. 6, 1941. Student, Wayne State U., 1946—47; LLB, Detroit Coll. Law, 1950; BA magna cum laude, U. Md., 1976; post grad, 1976—77, JD (hon.), 1980. Bar: Md. 1980, US Dist. Ct./Md 1980, DC 1982, US Supreme Ct. 1984, NY 1988. Atty. Dearborn Twp., Mich., 1956—62; corp. counsel Town Dearborn Heights, Mich., 1962—63; mcpl. judge, 1963—69; judge 20th Dist. Ct. Mich., Dearborn Heights, 1969—75, 3d Jud. Cir. Mich., Wayne County, 1975; chief judge, 1977—87; exec. chief judge Wayne Cir. Ct., 1981—87; prin. Seidenman & Bresnahan, PA, Balt., 1980—82; assoc. Finley, Kumble et al, Washington; ptnr. Laxalt, Washington, Perito and Dubuc, Semmes, Bowen & Semmes, Washington, 1991—95, Vorys, Sater, Seymour and Pease, Washington, 1995—; mediator/arbitrator DC and Md. ct. and pvt. arbitrations. Recipient Gov. and Mayor Citations for Pub., Svc., 1988; fellow Am. Bar Found., Md. Bar Found. Mem.: Anne Arundel County Bar Assn., Md. State Bar Assn. (exec. com., bd. gov. 1986—87, chair jud. appointments 1991—92), Women's Bar Assn. Md. (pres. 1987—88), Young Lawyers Md. State Bar Assn. (chmn. 1986—87), Young Lawyers Exec. Coun. (Dist. 7 rep. 1987—88), ABA (chair tellers com. 1994—96, chair 1995—97, chair house com. on membership 1996—97, select com. of The House 1996—97, lawyers responsibility for client protection com.), Am. Judicature Soc., Mich. Judges Assn., Conf. Met. Ct., Detroit Assn. Def. Counsel, Mich. Assn. Trial Lawyers, Mediation Tribunal Assn., Detroit Coll. Law, Jud. Dispute Resolutions, Inc., Sponsor US Naval Acad. Plebe Sponsor Program, United Fund, Eastport Yacht Club, Elks, Washtenaw Country Club, Alpha Omicron Pi, Phi Beta Kappa. Roman Catholic. Office: Vorys Sater Seymour and Pease LLP 1828 L St NW Ste 1111 Washington DC 20036-5109

BRESNAN, JOAN W., literature and language professor; life ptnr. Marianne Brem. Sadie Dernham Patek Prof. in Humanities Stanford U., 2000—; Erskine Fellow U. Canterbury, Christchurch, 2005. Fellow: Am. Acad. Arts & Sci., 2004; mem.: Linguistic Soc. Am. (pres. 1999). Avocations: bicycling, photography. Office: Stanford University Builing 420 Room 22 Stanford CA 94305-2150 Office Phone: 650-723-0144. Office Fax: 650-723-5666. Business E-Mail: bresnan@stanford.edu.

BRESSMAN, SUSAN BERLINER, health facility administrator; b. Bronx, N.Y., Jan. 29, 1951; d. Joseph and Dorothy Berliner. BA, Barnard Coll., 1973; MD, Columbia U., 1977. Cert. Am. Bd. Psychiatry and Neurology. Resident Columbia Presbyn. Med. Ctr., N.Y.C., 1978-81; prof. neurology Albert Einstein Coll. Medicine, N.Y.C.; chair Mirken dept. neurology Beth Israel Med. Ctr., N.Y.C. Movement Disorders fellow Neurol. Inst., Columbia Presbyn. Med. Ctr., 1981-83. Office: Beth Israel Med Ctr Phillips Ambulatory Care 10 Union Sq E Ste 2Q New York NY 10003

BRESTEL, MARY BETH, librarian; b. Cin., Feb. 5, 1952; d. John Wesley and Laura Alice (Knoop) Seay; m. Michael Charles Brestel, Aug. 3, 1974; 1 child, Rebecca Michelle. BS, U. Cin., 1974; MLS, U. Ky., 1984. Libr. asst. history and lit. dept. Pub. Libr. Cin. and Hamilton County, 1974-78, children's asst. Pleasant Ridge br., 1978-81, children's asst. Westwood br., 1981-84, reference libr. sci. and tech. dept., 1984-90, 1st asst. sci. and tech. dept., 1990-92, mgr. dept., 1992—. Mem. Ohio Libr. Coun., Columbus, 2001—. Mem. United Methodist Ch. Office: Pub Libr Cin and Hamilton County Sci and Tech Dept 800 Vine St Cincinnati OH 45202-2071 Office Phone: 513-369-6938. Business E-Mail: marybeth.brestel@cincinnatilibrary.org.

BRETON, TRACY ANN, journalist; b. N.Y.C., July 16, 1951; BA in Journalism, Polit. Sci., Syracuse U., 1973. Reporter Danbury (Conn.) News-Times, summer 1972; reporter in legal affairs Providence Jour.-Bull., 1973-99, investigative reporter, 1999—. Vis. prof. dept. English and pub. policy Brown U., 1997—. Contbr. articles to N.Y. Times, New Woman mag., other profl. and popular publs. Mem. R.I. Supreme Ct. Com. on Cameras in Courtroom, Providence. Recipient Best Feature Story for large met. newspaper award UPI, 1976, Service to Women in R.I. award Gov.'s Permanent Adv. Commn. on Women, 1977, Pulitzer Prize for investigative reporting, 1994, Master Reporter award New Eng. Soc. Newspaper Editors, 1995; Rosalynn Carter Mental Health Journalism fellow, 2006. Mem. U.S. Tennis Assn. (R.I. bd. dirs.), Phi Kappa Phi. Avocations: tennis, gourmet cooking, theater, travel. Home: 174 Columbia Ave Cranston RI 02905-3800 Office: Providence Jour 75 Fountain St Providence RI 02902-0050 Office Phone: 401-277-7362. E-mail: tbreton@projo.com.

BRETT, JAN CHURCHILL, illustrator, author; b. Hingham, Mass., Dec. 1, 1949; d. George and Jean (Baxter) Brett; m. Daniel Bowler, Feb. 27, 1970 (div. Jan. 1979); 1 child, Lia Bowler; m. Joseph Hearne, Aug. 18, 1980. Student, Colby Jr. Coll., 1968-69, Boston Mus. Fine Arts Sch., 1970; DHL (hon.), Fitchburg State Coll., 1996. Author, illustrator Fritz and the Beautiful Horses, 1981 (Parent's Choice award, 1981), Good Luck Sneakers, 1981, Annie and the Wild Animals, 1985, The First Dog, 1988, Beauty and the Beast, 1989, The Wild Christmas Reindeer, 1990, The Twelve Days of Christmas, 1990, The Mitten, 1990, Goldilocks and the Three Bears, 1990, The Owl and the Pussycat, 1991, Berlioz the Bear, 1991, The Trouble With Trolls, 1992, Christmas Trolls, 1993, Town Mouse, Country Mouse, 1994, Armadillo Rodeo, 1995, Comet's Nine Lives, 1996, The Hat, 1997 (Am. Booksellers Abby award, 1998), The Night Before Christmas, 1998, The Gingerbread Baby, 1999, Hedgie's Surprise, 2000, illustrator Woodland Crossings, 1978, Inside a Sand Castle and Other Secrets, 1979, The Secret Clocks Time Senses of Living Things, 1979, St. Patrick's Day in the Morning, 1980 (Parent's Choice award, 1981), Young Melvin and Bulger, 1981, In the Castle of the Cats, 1981, Some Birds Have Funny Names, 1981 (Amb. Honor award English Speaking Union U.S., 1983), I Can Fly, 1981, Prayer, 1983, The Valentine Bears, 1983, Some Plants Have Funny Names, 1983, Where Are All the Kittens, 1984, Old Devil is Waiting, 1985, The Mother's Day Mice, 1985, Scary, Scary Halloween, 1986, Noelle of the Nutcracker, 1986, The Enchanted Book, 1987, Happy Birthday, Dear Duck, 1988, Hedgre's Surprise, 2000, Daisy Comes Home, 2002. Mem. bd. overseers Boston Symphony Orch., 1991—99, trustee, 1999—, Thayer Acad., Braintree, Mass. Mem.: Nat. Soc. Colonial Dames Am., Chilton Club. Office: 132 Pleasant St Norwell MA 02061-2523 E-mail: janbrett@janbrett.com.

BRETT, NANCY HELÉNE, artist; BFA, Wayne State U., 1969; MFA, Cranbrook Acad. of Art, 1972. One-woman shows include Gallery Seven, Detroit, 1976, Ericson Gallery, N.Y.C., 1980, Harm Bouckaert Gallery, N.Y.C., 1982, Hillwood Art Mus., C.W.Post, Long Island U., N.Y., 1987, L'Ecole Gallery, N.Y.C., Victoria Munroe Gallery, N.Y.C., 1989, 91, 93, Victoria Munroe Fine Art, N.Y.C, 1993, Lake George Arts Project, N.Y., 1996, The Painting Ctr., N.Y.C., 1997, Cranbrook Art Mus., 1998, Hyde Collection Art Mus., Glen Falls, N.Y., 1999; group shows include Mich. Focus, Detroit Inst. of Art and Grand Rapids Mus. of Art (Catalog), 1974, Mus. of Modern Art, Touchstone Gallery, N.Y.C., 1979, Susan Caldwell, N.Y.C., 1979, Landscape Anthology, Grace Borgenicht Gallery, N.Y.C., 1988, Lines of Vision: Drawings by Contemporary Women, Blum Helman Warehouse and Hillwood Art Mus., Long Island U. Catalog, N.Y., 1989, Notions of Place: Paintings and Drawings, Victoria Munroe Gallery, N.Y.C., 1990, The Painters, 1991, Summer Salon, 1992, Celebrating Nature, Champion Internat. Corp. Collection Exhibit., Stamford, Conn., 1991, Landscape Not Landscape, Gallery Camino Real, Boca Raton, Fla. Catalog, 1994, Bklyn. Mus. Art, Gasworks Gallery, London, Cornerstone Gallery, Manchester, U., Gallery Camino Real, Boca Raton, Fla., 1994, U. Art Mus., 1994, Gallery at Hastings-on-Hudson, Mcpl. Bldg., N.Y., 1995, West Eng., Bristol, 1996, Parsons Gallery, 1996, Bklyn. Mus. Art, 1997, Hyde Collection Art Mus., Glens Falls, N.Y., 1998, Exit Art/The first World, N.Y., 1999, Wendy Cooper Gallery, Madison, Wis., 2000, Williamsburg Art and Hist. Ctr., Bklyn., 2000, Akus Gallery, Ea. Conn. State U., Willimantic, Conn., 2000, Exit Art/The First World, N.Y.C., 2002, Sperone Westwater Gallery, N.Y.C., 2002, Courthouse Gallery, Lake George, N.Y., 2002, A.I.R., N.Y.C., 2002, numerous others; represented in pub. collections: J.P. Morgan, Morgan Guaranty Trust Co., N.Y., Champion Internat., Stamford, Conn., Amerada Hess Corp., GE, Manhattan Savings Bank, Milbank, Tweed, Hadley and McCloy, N.Y.C., Herbert F. Johnson Mus. of Art, Cornell U., Prudential Ins., Best Products, IBM, Morgan Stanley, N.Y.C., Cranbrook Acad of Art Mus., Kidder Peabody, Inc., Hosp. Corp. Am., Power Inst. of Fine Arts, Sydney, Australia, IBM, GE, Princess Cruise Lines, Marsh and McClennan Cos. Inc., Libr. of Congress, Washington. Studio: 457 Broome St New York NY 10013-2681

BRETTSCHNEIDER, CATHIE I., editor; b. Balt., Nov. 29, 1947; d. William Henry and Mary Irene (Kyle) B. BA in Religion and Philosophy, Catawba Coll., 1969; MA in Religion and Culture, Syracuse U., 1970, MPhil. in Religion and Culture, 1975. Promotion copywriter Princeton U. Press, N.J., 1977-80, manuscript editor N.J., 1983-91, religion acquisitions editor N.J., 1987-91; prodn. editor APA, Arlington, Va., 1981-83; humanities acquisitions editor Univ. Va. Press, Charlottesville, 1991—. Consulting editor (mag. book rev.) Belles Lettres, Gaithersburg, Md., 1985-95. Bd. dirs. Ctr. for Faith and the Arts, Salisbury, N.C., 1997-2002. Mem. MLA, Am. Acad. Religion. Office: Univ of Virginia Press PO Box 400318 Charlottesville VA 22904-4318

BRETZ, KELLY JEAN RYDEL, actuary, consultant; b. Wadena, Minn., Oct. 30, 1962; d. Edmund Leroy and Glenyce Clara (Andrie) B.; m. Daniel Mark Bretz Rydel; children: Michael Charles Bretz Rydel, Alexa James Bretz Rydel. BA in Math., Moorhead State U., 1984. Chartered fin. analyst. Asst. actuary Northwestern Nat. Life Ins. Co. (now ING Reliastar), Mpls., 1984-92; assoc. actuary TMG Life Ins. Co. (Clarica part of Sun Life), Fargo, ND, 1993-94, MSI Life Ins. Co., Arden Hills, Minn., 1994, MidAm. Mut. Life Ins. Co., Roseville, Minn., 1994-95; actuarial officer Fortis Fin. Group, Woodbury, Minn., 1996—2001; v.p. and sr. portfolio mgr. US Bank, Mpls., 2001—02; ind. cons. Minn., 2002—03; dir. pricing and fin. evaluation Thrivent Fin. for Lutherans, Mpls., 2003—. Grader Soc. Actuaries' Exam 220, 1992, 93. Contbr. articles to co. jours. Organizer blood drive Mpls. Blood Bank, 1992; meal deliverer Meals on Wheels, Fargo, 1993; meal server Sharing and Caring Hands, Mpls., 1992. Fellow Soc. Actuaries (mem. fin. and investment mgmt. practice edn. com. 1995-96); mem. Am. Acad. Actuaries, Twin Cities Actuarial Club, Life Ins. Mktg. and Rsch. Assn. (fin. mktg. and svcs. com. 1993). Avocations: scuba diving, outdoor and indoor physical activies, reading. Office: 625 Fourth Ave S Minneapolis MN 55415-1665 Office Phone: 612-340-7193. E-mail: kellybretz@aol.com.

BRETZFELDER, DEBORAH MAY, retired museum staff member; b. Hazelton, Pa., Sept. 21, 1932; d. Joseph and Rose (Smulyan) Hirsh; m. Robert Bretzfelder, Dec. 24, 1955; children: Karl, Marc. Student, Syracuse U., 1950-53. Textile colorist, designer Cohn-Hall-Marx, N.Y.C., 1954-55; fashion coordinator Hecht's Dept. Store, Washington, 1956; freelance artist Washington, 1956-58; exhibits technician Smithsonian Instn., Washington, 1958-59, supr. exhibits prodn., 1959-63, exhibits specialist Nat. Mus. Am. History, 1963-75, visual info. specialist, project mgmt. officer, 1975-83, acting chief design, 1983, chief design, 1983-87, assoc. asst. dir. exhibits and pub. spaces, 1987-88; ret., 1988. Cons. various firms., orgns., mus. personnel; instr. mus. programs; freelance photographer and exhibit designer; project dir. Contbr. works to various publs.; musician: violin sect. Capital Symphony Orch. (formerly George Washington U. Orch.), 1965—2003, violin sect. Georgetown Symphony Orch., 2003—, violin sect. Capital Symphony Orch., 2005—. Mem.: Am. Craft Coun., Fiber Arts Study Group, Nat. Mus. Women in Arts, Nat. Soc. Hist. Preservation, Am. Assn. Mus., Tau Sigma Delta. Jewish. Home: 2748 Woodley Pl NW Washington DC 20008-1517 Office Phone: 202-232-7665. Personal E-mail: drbretzfelder@hotmail.com.

BREUER, JOANN GREEN, theater director; d. Louis A. and Mathilde Soloff; m. Miklos M. Breuer; children: Shoshanna, Jonas. BA, Wellesley Coll., 1959; MA in Tchg., Harvard U., 1960. Artistic dir. Cambridge (Mass.) Ensemble, 1970—79; instr. Harvard U., Cambridge, 1979—84; play dir. Am. Repertory Theatre, Cambridge, 1981—84; artistic assoc. Boston Shakespeare, Boston, 1985—86, Am. Nat. Theater, Washington, 1986—87, Vineyard Playhouse, Tisbury, Mass., 2000—. Play dir., adaptor short stories numerous cos., including Theatre of the Deaf, 1970—. Author: The Small Theatre Handbook, 1970 (Best Play awards). Recipient award, Boston Critics' Cir., 1970—80, Continued Excellence in Directing award, 1999. Mem.: Soc. Stage Dirs. and Choreographers. Jewish. Avocation: social service. Home: 1501 Beacon St # 804 Brookline MA 02446 Office: Vineyard Playhouse 24 Church St Vineyard Haven MA 02568 Office Phone: 508-693-6450. Personal E-mail: jgbreuer@comcast.net.

BREUNING, PAMELA, music educator; b. Joliet, Ill., Apr. 13, 1952; d. David Raymond Burd and Roberta Mae Hann-Burd; m. Scott E. Breuning, July 12, 1975; children: Jeffrey S., Elizabeth A. Breuning-Ruttencutter. B in Music Edn., Ill. State U., Normal, 1974. Orch. dir. Joliet G.S. Dist. #86, 1993—2000, Joliet Twp. H.S. #204, 2000—. Pres., performer Joliet Cmty. Orch., 2005—. Named Outstanding Tchr. of Yr., 1995, Outstanding Chicagoland Music Educator of Yr., 2003. Mem.: Ill. Fedn. Tchrs., Nat. Music Educators Assn., Am. String Tchr. Assn. (Outstanding Tchr. award 2005). Avocations: reading, travel, golf.

BREVOORT, DEBORAH B., librettist; b. Columbus, Ohio; d. Gordon and Virginia Brevoort; life ptnr. Chuck Cooper. BA in English, Kent State U., Ohio, 1976; MA in Polit. Sci., Kent State U., 1977; MFA in Playwriting, Brown U., Providence, 1993; MFA in Mus. Theatre Writing, NYU, N.Y.C., 1995. Adj. prof. Eugene Lang Coll./New Sch. U., N.Y.C., NY, 1998—; faculty Goddard Coll., Plainfield, Vt., 2004—; adj. prof. Columbia U., N.Y.C., 2004—; tchg. guest artist NYU, N.Y.C., 1997—. Playwright (stage play) The Women of Lockerbie (Kennedy Ctr. Fund for New Am. Plays award, 2001), (Silver medal, Onassis Internat. Playwriting Competition, 2001), librettist (musical) King Island Christmas (Frederick Loewe Award in Musical Theatre, 1998), Coyote Goes Salmon Fishing (Frederick Loewe Award in Musical Theatre, 2001), playwright (stage play) Signs of LIfe (Jane Chambers Playwriting Award, 2002), The Poetry of Pizza (Ruby Lloyd Aspey Playwriting award, 2005), The Blue Sky Boys (Ensemble Studio Theatre/Alfred P. Sloan Found. Sci. & Tech. project commn., Galileo prize, 2004), (noh drama about elvis presley) Blue Moon Over Memphis (Lee Korf Playwriting prize, 1994), (stage play) Into the Fire (L. Arnold Weissberger award, 1999). Co-founder and core mem. Theatre Without Borders, N.Y.C., NY, 2004—06. Recipient Legacy award, Rites & Reason Theatre, 1993, Gold Medalist, Pinter Rev. prize for Drama, 2004, Joe Calloway award, New Dramatists, 2001, L. Arnold Weissberger award, Weissberger Found., 1999, Paul Green award, Nat. Theatre Conf., 1999; fellow Paulette Goddard fellow, NYU, 1993, Individual Artist fellow, N.Y. Found. on the Arts, 2001, Alaska State Coun. on the Arts, 1991, Yip Harbug fellow, NYU, 1993, Playwriting fellow, Brown U., 1991, Danish Am. Nationals Cultural Exch. fellow, Danish Am. Soc. & New Dramatists, 1998, Sumner Locke Elliott Australian Exch. fellow, New Dramatists, 1997, McDowell fellow, McDowell Colony, 1994; grantee, Ludwig Vogelstein Found., 2004, Residency in Mex., Nat. Endowment for the Arts, 1994, Playwriting grantee, Rockefeller Found., 1989, CEC Artslink, 2004. Mem.: ASCAP, New Dramatists, Dramatist Guild.

BREWER, AIDA M., treasurer; BS in bus., LeMoyne Coll., Syracuse. With Key Bank, 1976—83; investment officer, asst. investment officer Treasury Divsn., NY, 1983—2000; dep. treas. NY, 2000—; dep. commr. NY, 2002—. Recipient First Woman Treas., N.Y., 2000. Mem.: Nat. Assn. State Treas., Assn. for Fin. Profls. Office: NY State Dept of Taxation and Fin Divsn Treasury PO Box 22119 Albany NY 12201-2119 E-mail: aida-brewer@tax.state.ny.us.

BREWER, ANGELA SUE, middle school educator; b. Knoxville, Tenn., Nov. 13, 1962; d. Fred David and Constance Sue Wyrick; m. Mark Alan Brewer, July 27, 1985; children: Ashley Michelle, Destiny Cheyenne. BS, U. Tenn., Knoxville, 1985, MS, 1988. Tchr., dept. head Knox County Schs., Knoxville, 1985—88, Cobb County Schs., Marietta, Ga., 1988—91; tech. writer, trainer Roane State Coll., Oak Ridge, Tenn., 1992—93; tech trainer sampling and environ. group Sci. and Tech. Inc., 1993—94; tchr. Cobb County Schs., 1994—96, Paulding County Schs., Dallas, 1996—98, tchr., dept. head, 1998—. Recipient Tchr. Yr., Paulding County Schs., 2003. Avocations: travel, reading, photography, cooking. Office Phone: 770-443-7028.

BREWER, CHERYL ANN, obstetrics and gynecology educator; b. New Rochelle, NY, Oct. 31, 1959; d. John Paul and Marie Elizabeth (Royance) B. BS, Miss. U. for Women, 1981; MD, Ind. U., Indpls., 1985. Resident in ob-gyn. SUNY Health Scis. Ctr., Syracuse, 1985-89, asst. prof. ob-gyn., 1989-91; asst. prof. dept. ob-gyn. Ind. U., Indpls., 1991-92; fellow in gynecologic oncology U. Calif., Irvine, 1992-96; asst. prof. ob-gyn., dir. gynecologic oncology Sch. Med. So. Ill. U., 1996-98; asst. prof. U. Ill., Peora, 1998—2004; assoc. prof. ob-gyn. U. Miss. Med. Ctr., Jackson, 2005—. Dir. divsn. gyn. oncology U. Ill., Peoria, 2000—04. Fellow Am. Coll. Ob-Gyn. Office: Univ Miss Med Ctr Jackson MS Home: 508 Beacon Cove Brandon MS Office: 2500 N State St Jackson MS 39216 Office Phone: 601-984-5321. Business E-Mail: bactd@uic.edu, cabrewer3@ob-gyn.umsmed.edu.

BREWER, JANICE KAY, state official; b. Hollywood, Calif., Sept. 26, 1944; d. Perry Wilford and Edna Clarice (Bakken) Drinkwine; m. John Leon Brewer, Jan. 1, 1963; children: Ronald Richard, John Samuel, Michael Wilford. HHD (hon.), LA Chiropractic Coll., 1970. Cert med. asst. Valley Coll., Burbank, Calif., 1963, practical radiol. techician cert. Valley Coll., Burbank, Calif., 1963. Pres. Brewer Property & Investments, Glendale, Ariz., 1970—; mem. Ariz. Ho. of Reps., Phoenix, 1983—86, Ariz. State Senate, Phoenix, 1987—96, majority whip, 1993—96; mem. Maricopa County Bd. Supr., 1997—2002; sec. of state State of Ariz., Phoenix, 2003—. State committee woman Rep. Party, Phoenix, 1970, Phoenix, 83; legis. liaison Arrowhead Republic Women; treas. Nat. Assn. Lt. Gov., 2004; bd. dir. Motion Picture & TV Commn. Named Woman of Yr., Chiropractic Assn. Ariz., 1983, Legislator of Yr., Behaviour Health Assn. Ariz., 1991, NRA, 1992; recipient Freedom award, Veterans of Ariz., 1994. Mem.: Am. Legis. Exch. Coun., Nat. Fedn. Rep. Women, NOW. Republican. Lutheran. Office: Office of Sec of State 7th Fl State Capitol 1700 W Washington Phoenix AZ 85007-2808 Office Phone: 602-542-3012. Office Fax: 602-542-1575.*

BREWER, JUSTINE ADRIANNE, zoological park administrator; b. Woonsocket, RI, Mar. 24, 1936; d. Justin Adrian and Clarice Daniels Southwick; m. Robert Galliford Brewer, June 25, 1955 (dec.); children: David, Peter, Betsey, Robert Scott, Cindy Clarice. AS, Becker Coll., 1955. Sec. Southwick Wild Animal Farm, Inc., Mendon, Mass., 1965—70, pres., treas., 1995—; treas. Santa's Land Inc., Putney, Vt., 1970—98, pres., 1995—98. Pres. Daniels Farmstead Found., Blackstone, Mass., 2004—; corporator UniBank, Whitinsville, Mass., 2003. Vol. Make A Wish Found., Boston, 2005; mem. Chestnut St. Meeting House, Millville, Mass., 1981; bd. dirs. Ctrl. Mass. Convention and Visitors Bur., Worcester, 2003—. Recipient Women of Distinction award, Girl Scouts Mass., Worcester, 2005. Mem.: New Eng. Assn. Amusement Parks and Attractions, Zool. Assn. Am., Mendon Hist. Soc., Nat. Trust for Hist. Preservation, Millville Women's Club. Congregationalist. Avocations: genealogy, gardening. Office: Southwick's Zoo 2 Southwick St Mendon MA 01756

BREWER, KAREN, librarian; b. Janesville, Wis., Apr. 29, 1943; d. Gordon A. and Charlotte (Warren) Schultz; m. Eugene N. Brewer, June 22, 1963. BA, U. Wis., 1965, MA, 1966; PhD, Case Western Res. U., 1983. Libr. Middleton Med. Libr. U. Wis., Madison, 1966-67; libr. Med. Libr. U. Tenn., Memphis, 1968-69; libr. Cleve. Health Sci. Libr. Case Western Res. U., Cleve., 1970-76; dir. libr. Coll. Medicine Northeastern Ohio U., Rootstown, 1976-88; dir. libr. Med. Ctr. NYU, 1988—. Mem. editl. bd. Ann. Stats. Acad. Health Sci. Libr., 1986—91. Fellow N.Y. Acad. Medicine; mem. Assn. Acad. Health Sci. Librs. (sec.-treas. 1986-89, pres. 1995), Med. Libr. Assn. (bd. dirs. 1991-94), Acad. Health Info. Profls. (disting. mem.), Am. Med. Informatics Assn. Office: NYU Med Ctr Libr 550 1st Ave New York NY 10016-6402

BREWER, KAREN ELAINE LAUTERBACH, secondary school educator; b. Peoria, Ill., Feb. 12, 1950; d. Gordon Lee and Elaine Marie (Mularoni) Holliday; m. Robert Lee Lauterbach, July 18, 1970 (div.); children: Scott Robert, Andrea Renea; m. Ronald E. Brewer, July 11, 1993. BE, Ill. State U., 1972, MEd, 1990. Tchr. Elmwood HS, Ill., 1972-74, Gardner So. Wilmington HS, Ill., 1981-91, Minooka HS, Ill., 1992-94, Joliet HS, Ill., 1994—2003, Branson HS, Mo., 2004—. Math. cons., calculator trainer Ednl. Svc. Ctr. 10, Channahon, Ill., 1990-99; question evaluator Nat. Assessment Evaluation Project, 1991; participant NSF/Nat. Coun. Tchrs. of Math. Geometry Seminar, 1991; sci. literacy coord. Tri-County Ednl. Svc. Ctr., 1991; adj. instr. math. Joliet Jr. Coll., 1992-2001; Mo. assessment evaluator, MAP, 2006. Recipient Disting. Tchr. award Western Ill. U., 1987; grantee Ill. Math and Sci. Acad., 1990, Impact II award, 1990. Mem. Nat. Coun. Tchrs. of Math., Ill. Coun. Tchrs. of Math., Delta Kappa Gamma. Presbyterian. Avocations: swimming, sewing, water-skiing, reading, crocheting. Home: 102 Cabana Ct Reeds Spring MO 65737-8919 Office Phone: 417-334-6511. Personal E-mail: kbrewer50@hotmail.com.

BREWER, LESLIE KAY, elementary school educator; b. Ft. Worth, Tex., Aug. 1, 1963; d. Ronald Perry and Karon Lee Coffey; m. Les G. Brewer, Aug. 17, 1984; children: Andrew, Mark, Mitchell, Macy. BS in Edn., Lubbock Christian U., Tex., 1985. Cert. elem. edn. K-8 Tex. Tchr. Frenship Ind. Sch. Dist., Lubbock, 1991—. Mem.: Assn. Tex. Profl. Educators. Church Of Christ. Avocations: reading, writing, travel, painting.

BREWER, LYNN, energy executive; d. Alan E. and Judith E. Morris; m. Douglas Richard Brewer, Nov. 9, 2000. Cert. Bus. Ethics Colo. State U., 2003. Corp. devel. exec. Ralston Purina, St. Louis, 1993—96; cons. Peterson Consulting LLC, Houston, 1996—98; exec. Enron Corp., Houston, 1998—2001; pub. spkr., author Seattle, 2002; founding chmn. Integrity Inst., Inc., Portland, 2004—. Leadership coun. Open Compliance and Ethics Group (OCEG), Phoenix. Author: (book) Confessions of an Enron Executive: A Whistleblower's Story, House of Cards: Confessions of an Enron Executive, SportsVision: Athletic Excellence through Visualization. Endowment fund-raising chairperson Lakewood Skating Found., Tacoma, 2004; bd. mem. Columbia Tower Club, Seattle, 2005. Paul Harris fellow, Rotary Found. of Rotary Internat., 2004. Mem.: Columbia Tower Club (assoc.; bd. mem. 2005). Achievements include first to Standardized Model for Measuring Structural Integrity of Organizations. Avocations: equestrian, trap shooting, snowmobiling, skiing, bicycling. Office Phone: 253-843-0202. Personal E-mail: lynn@theintegrityinstitute.org.

BREWER, LYNNE ORAHOOD, elementary school educator; b. Havre, Mont., Nov. 12, 1960; d. Wesley Jackson and Marlyn Orahood; m. Don Earl Brewer, Sept. 6, 1980; children: Drew Jasper, Casey Earl. BS in Elem. Edn., MSU-N, 1982; MA in Edn., Lesley U., Boston, MA, 2000. Instr. grades k-8 Tie Creek, Ekalaka, Mont., 1982—85; instr. grade k Dodson Pub. Sch., Mont., 1986—87, instr. grades 5-6, 1987—90; instr. grade 5 Malta Pub. Sch., Mont., 1990—95, instr. grade 6, 1995—. Lead integration specialist North East Tech. Edn. Consortium, Malta, 2003—. Mem.: MEA/MFT, Delta Kappa Gamma (Alpha Zeta Chpt.) (corr. sec. 1998—2000). Avocations: technology, photography, reading, outdoor activities. Office: Malta Pub Schs 7th St Malta MT 59538 Office Phone: 406-654-2320.

BREWER, MARILYNN B., psychology professor; PhD social psychology, Northwestern U., 1968. Dir. Inst. Social Sci. Research, UCLA; prof. psychology UCLA, Ohio State U., 1993. Editor Personality & Social Psychology Rev. Jour. Recipient Kurt Lewin Award, SPSSI, 1995, Donald T. Campbell Award for Distinguished Research Social Psychology, 1992. Fellow: Am. Acad. Arts & Sci.; mem.: Soc. Psychol. Study Social Issues (pres. 1984—85), Soc. Personality & Social Psychology (pres. 1990—91), Am. Psychol. Soc. (pres. 1993—95). Office: Dept Psychology Ohio State U 1885 Neil Ave Columbus OH 43210-1222 Office Phone: 614-292-9640. E-mail: Brewer.64@osu.edu.

BREWER, MARTHA JOHNSTON, gynecologist, educator; d. Norman Craig and Martha Manly Brewer. BA, Sweet Briar Coll., Va., 1969; MD, U. Miss., Jackson, 1977. Diplomate Am. Bd. of Obstetrics and Gynecology, 1985. Pvt. practice ob/gyn, New Orleans/Metairie, 1984—2005; assoc. prof. Univ. of Ark. for Med. Sci., Little Rock, 2006—. Recipient Robert S. Caldwell award, Miss. State Med. Soc./Med. Assurance Co of Miss., 1984. Fellow: ACOG (licentiate); mem.: Winifred L. Wiser Soc. (pres. 1988—90). Office: UAMS-Dept Ob/Gyn 4315 W Markham St #518 Little Rock AR 72205-7199 Office Phone: 501-526-6834.

BREWER, NEVADA NANCY, elementary school educator; b. Balt., Jan. 21, 1949; d. Leo and Rebecca (Johnson) Brewer. BS, Coppin State Coll., 1973, MEd, 1974, MEd, 1981; postgrad., C.C. Balt., 1985. Cert. elem. tchr., spl. edn. tchr. Tchr. Balt. County Adult Edn., Towson, Md., 1973-88; coord. Just Say No to Drugs program Balt. City Sch. Sys., tchr., 2000—01, mgr. summer sch., 2000—02, acad. coach math. and sci., 2002—03, coord. math. elem. lab., 2003—04; tchr. supr. Pratt Sch.- Dept. Juvenile Svcs., 2004—. Coord. Heads Up Program, 1980, math-a-thon program St. Jude Rsch. Ctr., 1993—, 24 Challenge Math. Tournament, 1996—, elem. math. lab., 2003—; supr. tchr. for student tchrs. Towson State U., Coll. Notre Dame, Coppin State Coll., 1989—; leadership tchr. STARS sci. program, 1995; participant in Project Future Search Phone-a-Thon to recruit minority students U. Md., College Park., Write to Learn Program, Balt. City Sch. Sys., 1990-91; acad. coach math and sci. grades Pre-K-5, 2002—; coord. Echo Hill Outdoor Sch., 1998-2003. Coord. Echo Hill Outdoor Sch., 1988—, mem. adv. bd., 2003—. Recipient Freedom Found. award, 1974. Home: 1616 Wentworth Ave Baltimore MD 21234-6125 E-mail: nbrewe@verizon.net.

BREWER, ROGENNA WYNNE, writer; b. Fon du Lac, Wis., Apr. 12, 1961; d. Roger Wayne Bean and Gloria Ann (Amend) Madien; m. Jeffrey Reagan Brewer, Jan. 22, 1986; children: Todd Eugene, Tyler Wayne, Troy Roger. Interior design diploma, Southern Coll., Orlando, Fla., 1984. Bookseller, reviewer, Colo., 1990—98; writer Colo., 1998—. Author: (book) Midway Between You and Me, 2002, Sign, Seal, Deliver, 2001 (Romantic Times Top Pick, 2001), Seal It with a Kiss, 1999 (Romantic Times Top Pick, 1999, Romantic Times Reviewers Choice nominee, 2000, Booksellers Best nominee, 2000, 3d pl. Blue Boa, 2000), Aspen Gold, 2000 (1st pl. Long Contemporary, 2000), Heart of the Rockies (working title: Puss in Boots),

1997 (1st pl. Long Contemporary, 1997). With USN, 1980—85. Mem.: Colo. Romance Writers (pres. 1997), Heart of Denver Romance Writers (founding pres. 1998), Romance Writers of Am. Avocations: reading, gardening.

BREWER, TRACI LYNN, secondary school educator; b. Cleve., Dec. 11, 1975; m. Chris Brewer, Aug. 2, 2003. BEd, U. Dayton, Ohio, 1998, MTech, 2005. Tchr. Bethel H.S., Tipp City, Ohio, 1998—2001, 2004—, Fairborn H.S., Ohio, 2001—03. Drama advisor, newspaper advisor Bethel H.S., 2004—, yearbook advisor, 2005—. Office: Bethel HS 7490 State Rte 201 Tipp City OH 45371 Personal E-mail: tracimed@yahoo.com.

BREWER, VALERIE D., science educator, secondary school educator; d. Michael and Carolyn Brown; m. Charles D. Brewer, Dec. 27, 1986; children: Connor, Ethan. BSChemE, U. Ark., Fayetteville, 1989. Type 09 cert. Rockford Coll., Ill., 2004. Engr. Dixie Cups and Plates, Fort Smith, 1990—92; traveling sci. educator High Touch High Tech., Coral Springs, Fla., 2000—02; sci. tchr. South Beloit HS, Ill., 2004—06, Harlem HS, Ill., 2006—. Grantee, Ecolab, 2005. Mem.: NSTA (assoc.). Office: Harlem HS 1 Husky Cir Machesney Park IL 61103 Business E-Mail: vbrewer@harlemlzz.org.

BREWSTER, ELIZABETH WINIFRED, literature educator, poet, writer; b. Chipman, N.B., Can., Aug. 26, 1922; d. Frederick John and Ethel May (Day) Brewster BA, U. N.B., 1946, DLitt, 1982; MA, Radcliffe U., 1947; BLS, U. Toronto, 1953; PhD, Ind. U., 1962. Cataloger Carleton U., Ottawa, Ont., 1953—57, Ind. U. Libr., Bloomington, 1957—58, N.B. Legis. Libr., 1965—68, U. Alta. Libr., Edmonton, Canada, 1968—70; mem. English dept. Victoria U., B.C., 1960—61; reference libr. Mt. Allison U. Libr., Sackville, N.B., 1961—65; vis. asst. prof. English U. Alta., 1970—71; mem. faculty U. Sask., Saskatoon, Canada, 1972—, asst. prof. English, 1972—75, assoc. prof., 1975—80, prof., 1980—90, prof. emeritus, 1990—. Author: East Coast, 1951, Lillooet, 1954, Roads, 1957, Passage of Summer, 1969, Sunrise North, 1972, In Search of Eros, 1974, Sometimes I Think of Moving, 1977, The Way Home, 1982, The Sisters, 1974, It's Easy to Fall on the Ice, 1977, Digging In, 1982, Junction, 1982, A House Full of Women, 1983, Selected Poems 1944-84, 2 vols., 1985, Visitations, 1987, Entertaining Angels, 1988, Spring Again, 1990, The Invention of Truth, 1991, Wheel of Change, 1993, Away from Home, 1995, Footnotes to the Book of Job, 1995, Garden of Sculpture, 1998, Burning Bush, 2000, Jacob's Dream, 2002, Collected Poems, Vol. 1, 2003, Vol. 2, 2004, Bright Centr, 2005. Recipient E.J. Pratt award for poetry, U. Toronto, 1953, Pres. medal for poetry, U. We. Ont., 1980, Lit. award, Can. Broadcasting Corp., 1991, Lifetime award excellence in arts, Sask. Arts Bd., 1995, Short List award, Gov. Gen., 1996, Sask. Book award for poetry, 2003, Sask. Centennial medal, 2005. Mem. League Can. Poets (life), Writers' Union Can., Assn. Can. Univ. Tchrs. English, Order of Can.

BREWSTER, JAMIE SUSAN, theater educator; b. Appleton, Wis., Mar. 6, 1961; d. James H. and Peggy A. Brewster; m. James Trya, Oct. 1, 1959. BA in Oral Comm. Edn., U. Ctrl. Okla., Edmond, 1982, BA in English, 1983; M in Gifted Edn., Okla. City U., 1994. Cert. Tchr. Okla. Dept. Edn., 1982. Tchr. Capitol Hill HS, Oklahoma City, 1987—92; drama tchr. Summit Mid. Sch., Edmond, 1993—. Dir. Korean Student Exch. Program, Edmond, 2000—03. Actor: (cmty. theatre) Lost in Yonkers (Best Actress, 1998); founding mem. (profl. theatre) CityRep Theatre Co. Recipient Educator of Yr., Teen Ink Mag., 2001—02, Tchr. of Yr., Capitol Hill HS, 1992, Summit Mid. Sch., 2004, Dr. Pepper Educator of Yr., 1992; scholar, Quartz Mountain Arts Program, 1992. Mem.: OEA. Democrat. Avocations: reading, crafts, writing, theater. Personal E-mail: jamesnjamie6@aol.com.

BREWSTER, LOUISE BOONE, artist, educator; b. Comanche County, Okla., July 5, 1925; d. Raymond Jennings and Annie Faye (Brazil) Wimple; m. Robert Lee Boone, July 8, 1969 (dec. Jan. 1982); m. Curtis Evan Brewster, July 19, 1992; children: James Dale Hall Jr., Margaret Elaine Heimlich, Lynda Louise Carnes. Student, Acad. Fine Arts, Vienna, 1982. Sales agt. Fidelity Life Ins., Irving, Tex., 1954-60; advt. mgr. Radio Sta. KVWC, Vernon, Tex., 1961-63; v.p. La Velle Labs., Oklahoma City, 1963-67; regional sales rep. Mr. Fine - Dallas, Sweet Adeline - Chgo., Midwest, 1967-70; art tchr. Rolla (Mo.) Sheltered Workshop, 1973-76; dir. Hobbit Hill Studio, Rolla, Mo., 1974—; actor Regional Opera Co., Newburg, Mo., 1989-92. Spkr. Rep. Women, Rolla, 1972-82. Mem. Philanthropic Ednl. Orgn., Order of Ea. Star (worthy matron 1973—). Baptist. Avocations: gardening, horsemanship. Home: HC 33 Box 101 Rolla MO 65401-9808

BREWSTER, MARGARET EMELIA, artist; b. Kaukauna, Wis., July 18, 1932; d. Eathen Edward and Emelia Josepha (Jennick) B. Attended, U. Wis., Fox Valley, 1951-53. Photographer, graphic artist Appleton Papers, Inc., Combined Locks, Wis., 1954-90. Exhbns. include Appleton Gallery Arts, 1965-94, Bank of Kaukauna, 1974-2003, Frances Hardy Gallery, Ephraim, Wis., 1984, 86, 93, 95, Neville Pub. Mus. Brown County, Green Bay, 1986-87, 90, 92-95, Minn. State Capital, St. Paul, 1987, Brown County Libr., Green Bay, 1988, Ctr. Visual Arts, Wausau, Wis., 1991, Milw. Art Mus., 1991-92, Outagamie County Hist. Mus., 1991-95, Bank One Lobby Gallery, Neenah, Wis., 1993-94, 96, Wis. Arts Bd. Gallery, 1994, U. Wis., Platteville, 1996, William F. Boniface Arts Ctr., Escanaba, Mich., 1996, Anderson Art Ctr., Kenosha, Wis., 1997, Atrium Gallery, Indpls., 1997, Mason St. Gallery, Green Bay, Wis., 1997-98, Colorado Springs Art Ctr., 1998, U. Wis., Marinette, 2000, Chgo. Windy City Artists, 2000, U. Wis., Oshkosh, 2001, White Bear Art Ctr., Minn., 2002, Portalwisconsin.org, 2002, Lambeau Field Atrium, 2004 Bd. dirs. Friends of the 1000 Islands Environ. Ctr., Kaukauna, 1986—, chair art fair, 1986-2005, sec., 1988-93. Mem. Kaukauna Creative Artists Group (sec. 1991-2003, chair exhibit and publicity 1991—), Nat. Mus. Women in Arts, Bay Area Watercolor Guild. Avocations: photographer, needle arts, gardening, walking, nordic skiing. Studio: 400 W Division St Kaukauna WI 54130-1120

BREWSTER, MARY MOORHEAD, retired educational association administrator; b. Fitzgerald, Ga., May 11, 1924; d. Henry Augustus and Grace Haynes Moorhead; m. Joseph Screver Brewster, June 28, 1947 (dec.); children: Linda Brewster Ayers, Joseph S. Jr., John G. II. BS in Edn., West Ga. Coll., Carrollton, 1962; M in Adminstrn., West Ga. U., 1990; M in Bus. Edn., Ga. State U., Atlanta, 1970. Semi profl. War Dept., South Eastern States, 1943—45; exec. sec. Polk County Tuberculosis Assn., Cedartown, Ga., 1952—55; tchr. Polk County Bd. Edn., 1962—78, asst. supt., 1978—89. Mem. State Textbook Com., 1970—75. Pres. Polk Ret. Educators, Cedartown, Ga., 1991—92, Polk Hist. Soc., Cedartown, 1989—90; mem. sec. Jury Selection Comm., Cedartown, 1985—90; tchr. First Bapt. Ch. Sun. Sch., Cedartown, 1980—. Recipient Outstanding Educator, Ga. Vocat. Assn., 1975—76. Mem.: Resaissance Honors Program. Avocations: travel, gardening, reading.

BREYER, PAMELA PETERSON, writer; b. L.A., June 28, 1941; d. Loyl Leonard and Dorothy Helen Peterson. BA in Journalism, U.Calif., Berkeley, 1963; MA, Columbia U., N.Y.C., 1970. Cert. tchr. basic edn. Calif., 1987. ESL tchr. Centro Colombo Americano, Bogota, Colombia, 1964—65, Japanese Tchrs. Program, NYC, 1968—69, Columbia U., NYC, 1969—70; tchr. tng. instr. Coun. on Internat. Ednl. Exch., UN, 1970, 1974; esol tchr. Centro Norteamericano, Seville, Spain, 1970—71; asst. prof. Pace U., NYC, 1973—77; editor Regents Pub. Co., 1977—80; editl. dir. Grolier Video Project, Drew/Fairchild Inc., NYC, 1989—91; ESL tchr. Braille Inst. Am., L.A., 1995—2002. Cons. CUNY Children's TV Workshop, 1976. Author: Grammar Work, 1981; co-author: Write by Yourself, 1976, Milk and Honey Teachers Manuals, 1985. Mem., 2d v.p. Welcome Wagon of North Orange, 2005. Recipient Pres.'s award for innovation in improving ESL techniques, Braille Inst., 1996, award, Pearson Longman, 2005. Mem.: Tchg. English to Speakers of Other Languages, Inc. (publs.com. 1989—91, chair 1987—88). Avocations: reading, bridge, tennis. Home: 2158 Flame Flower Lane Fullerton CA 92833

BREYNE, MICHELE K, mathematics educator; d. Sandra K. and Lawrence M. Linden. A, Waubonsee CC, Ill., 1997—99; B, Ill. State U., 1999—2001; M, Walden U., Minn., 2003—05. Tchr. St. Anne Cmty. HS Dist. #302, Ill., 2001—02; HS math tchr. Yorkville Cmty. Unit Sch. Dist. #115, Yorkville, 2002—. Grantee Gen. Assembly scholarship, Patricia Reid Lindner, 1999—2000, Steven J Rauschenberger, 2000—01; Lucille Gustafson Scholar, Waubonsee CC, 1997—99.

BRHEL, KAREN MOLLITOR, elementary school educator, music educator; AA, Elgin C.C., Ill., 1975; MusB, No. Ill. U., DeKalb, Ill., 1978; MEd on Music, VanderCook Coll. Music, Chgo., 2000. Specialist elem. music Sch. Dist. U-46, Elgin, Ill., 1990—; dir. choral South Elgin H.S., Ill., 2005—. Tchr. sunday sch. Holy Trinity Luth. Ch., Elgin, 1989; dir. music and theatre Bartlett Pk. Dist., Ill., 2000—06; dir. music Children's Theatre of Elgin, Elgin, Ill., 1988—2002. Mem.: NEA, Am. Fedn. Musicians, Ill. Edn. Assn., Music Educators Nat. Conf., Boys Scouts Am. (mem adult com. Carol Stream chpt. 2003—06). Avocations: musical theatre, bicycling, hiking, gardening, baseball. Office: South Elgin High School 760 E Main Street South Elgin IL 60177 Office Phone: 847-289-3760. Business E-Mail: karenbrhel@u-46.org.

BRIA, JANICE, secondary school educator, sports official; b. Reno, Nev., Aug. 27, 1954; d. Beverly and Rudy Bria. BA, U. Ariz., Tucson, 1976. Tchr. Sparks H.S., Nev., 1990—. Game ofcl. Washoe County Sch. Dist., Reno, 1990—; mgr. tour World Sport Internat. Sports Tour, L.A., 1999—. Mem. City of Reno Bicycle Coun., 1993—95. Named Who's Who Am. Tchrs., 1998, 2000, 2003, 2005, 2004; recipient Best of Edn. Cert. of Merit, Reno Gazette-Journal, 2000. Avocations: bicycling, hiking, travel, gardening. Office: Sparks High School 820 15th Street Sparks NV 89431 Personal E-mail: jbria@softcom.net.

BRIAN, MARY H., librarian; b. Breckenridge, Tex., Dec. 17, 1929; d. Thomas Henry and M. Loyce Davis Hailey; m. Jack Brian, Dec. 26, 1953 (dec. Sept. 1983); children: Crystal Lee, Rosemary Hope, Tommy Wilson. BA, North Tex. State U., 1949; grad. in Libr. Sci., U. Tex., 1953. Tchr., libr. Dumas Jr. HS, Tex., 1949-94. Fin. chair Moore County Libr. Bd., Dumas, 1959-60, chair, 1960-62. Named among outstanding leaders in elem. & secondary edn., 1976; Defender of the constitution award. Mem. Tex. Ret. Tchr. Assn. (20th Century tchr. award 1997), Tex. Farm Bur.; Rep. Nat. Com., Eisenhower Commission, 2002, Nat. Rifle Assn., 2003. Republican. Baptist. Avocations: travel, opera, gardening, history. Home: 5278 Fm 722 Channing TX 79018-3312

BRIAND-RYAN, DONNA MARIE, artistic designer; b. Inglewood, Calif, Aug. 16, 1957; d. Roland Joseph and Mary Ann (Plunkett) Levesque; m. Kenneth Leo Briand Sr., Mar. 3, 1975 (div. Feb. 1982), children: Kenneth Leo Briand Jr., Keith Allen Briand; m. Gordon Clinton Ryan, Sept. 9, 1999; 1 stepchild, Shawn Marie Ryan. A in Engring. and Fine Arts, Bristol Community Coll., Fall River, Mass., 1986; student in fashion design, Newbury Coll., 1987. Cert. artistic designer. Theatre designer Bristol Cmty. Coll. Repertory Theatre, Fall River, Mass., 1983-87; graphic freelancer Bristol Cmty. Coll. Art Ctr., Fall River, Mass., 1983-88; stage designer Bristol Cmty. Coll. Theater, Fall River, Mass., 1985—88; designer, illustrator Design-A-Line, Swansea, Mass., 1988; freelance artist Inglis, Fla., 1988—; fashion designer pvt. practice, Inglis, Fla., 1991—; printing tchr. Zula's Pl., Yankeetown, Fla., 1990—. Mem. art student adv. com. Bristol C.C. Art Ctr., Fall River, 1984-86; art tchr. Salvation Army, Fall River, 1984, Sheriff Youth Camp, Levy County, Fla., 1989. Author numerous poems. Art tchr. Salvation Army, Fall River, 1984, Sheriff's Youth Camp, Levy County, Fla., 1990. Recipient awards for individual paintings. Avocation: creations.

BRIANS, MICHELLE SUZANNE, music educator, musician; b. Longview, Tex., July 19, 1979; d. Robin Hood and Suzanne Brians. MusB in Gen. Instrumental Music, U. North Tex., 2003. Cert. tchr. music all levels Tex., 2003. Assoc. dir. orchs. Denton (Tex.) H.S., 2003—05; dir. orchs John Guyer H.S., Denton, 2005—. Advisor Tri-M Music Honor Soc., Denton, 2004—05; adjudicator Denton Ind. Sch. Dist.; performer Baroque violin Dallas Bach Soc. Musician: Henry Mancini Inst., LA, CA, (master class performer/concurrent event) Boston Early Music Festival, (co-concertmaster, soloist) UNT Music in the Mountains, Crested Butte, CO, (convention performer- jazz violin) First Jazz String Caucus at IAJE in NYC, NY, (performer- baroque violin) Longy International Baroque Inst., Oberlin Baroque Performance Inst., (vocals, rock/country/jazz fiddle) Country/Rock Band, (founding mem, performer) U. of North Texas Jazz Strings, (section violin) East Texas Symphony Orch. Recipient Nat. Performance scholar Alt., Early Music Am., 2001; Adkins String scholar, U. of North Tex., Charn Uswachoke Music scholar. Mem.: Tex. Music Educators Assn. (region 2 orch. divsn. chair 2006—), Nat. Assn. for Music Edn., Pi Kappa Lambda Music Honor Frat., Phi Kappa Phi Nat. Honor Soc. Episcopalian. Avocations: painting, swimming, songwriting.

BRICARD, YOLANDA BORRAS, music educator, music program administrator; b. Santo Domingo, Dominican Republic, Apr. 6, 1959; d. Alvaro Borrás and Ileana Viñas de Borrás; m. Philippe F. Bricard, Jan. 18, 1985; children: François, Henri. B in Music, Piano performance, Peabody Conservatory Johns Hopkins U., Balt., 1985; MA in Ednl. Aminstrn., Columbia U., 1998. Elem. music tchr. Atlanta Internat. Sch., 1985—87, St. Ignatius Loyola, NY, 1988—89, Hong Kong Internat. Sch., 1992—93; vol. music tchr. Lycee Français Hong Kong, 1990—91; music tchr. Diller-Quaile Sch. Music, N.Y.C., 1997—99; program founder, adminstr. Mus. Kids Internat., N.Y.C., 1999—. Mem.: Music Educators Nat. Conf., Orgn. Am. Kodaly Educators, Kappa Delta Pi. Roman Catholic. Avocation: reading. Home: 200 E 66th St Apt C1203 New York NY 10021-9186 Office Phone: 212-996-5898. Business E-Mail: yolanda@musicalkids.net.

BRICE, JACQUELINE (JACKIE BRICE), landscape artist; b. Miami, July 11, 1935; d. Alvin Fletcher and Limmie Claudie Holliday; m. Herman Wood Brice, Feb. 27, 1954; children: Debra Lynn Corry, Herman Jr.(dec.). Exhibitions include The Mus. Sci., Miami, A.E. Bean Backus Gallery & Mus, Ft. Pierce, Fla., The Riviera Country Club, Coral Gables, Fla., Rod & Reel Club, Hibiscus Island, Miami Beach, Fla., Govs. Club, West Palm Beach, Fla., Governmental Ctr., West Palm Beach, Northwood U., Loxahatchee Hist. Mus., Jupiter, Fla., State Capitol Bldg., Tallahassee, Richard B. Russell Senate Bldg., Washington, Ann Norton Sculpture Gardens, West Palm Beach, Ct. Ho. Cultural Ctr. Galleries, Stuart, Fla., Govs. Office, State Capitol Bldg., Tallahassee, Hart Senate Bldg., Washington, Jupiter Town Hall Gallery, Lighthouse Ctr. Arts, Tequesta, Fla., Represented in permanent collections Palm Beach County, Mcpl. Juno Beach, Fla., Town of Jupiter, Barry U., Miami, Bascom-Palmer Eye Inst., Palm Beach, Jupiter Med. Ctr., Allen Morris Corp., Hill-York Corp., Hav-A-Tampa/Phillies Corp., Barnett Banks, Cmty. Savs., Coconut Grove Bank, Comerica, Burt Reynolds, Greg Norman, U.S. Senator and Mrs. Bob Graham, U.S. Congressman and Mrs. E. Clay Shaw, The White House; contbr. to covers of mags. Mem. Palm Beach Cultural Coun., Fla. History Ctr. and Mus., Norton Mus. Art. Mem.: Nat. Mus. Women in Arts, Nat. Assn. Women Artists. Office Phone: 561-575-2499. E-mail: jhbric@msn.com.

BRICEÑO, CANDACE MICHELE, artist; b. Austin, Tex. MFA, Sch. of Art Inst. of Chgo., Ill., 2002. Cert. K-12 art tchr. Tex. Art instr. Austin Ind. Sch. Dist., Tex., 2003—. Numerous exhbns. Named one of 22 to Watch, Austin Mus.

BRICE-O'HARA, SALLY, career military officer; b. Annapolis, Md. m. Bob Brice-O'Hara; 2 children. BA in Sociology, Goucher Coll., 1974; grad., Officer Candidate Sch., 1975; MA in Public Admin., Harvard U.; MS in Nat. Security Strategy, Nat. War Coll.; LittD (hon.), Goucher Coll., 2002. Former asst. dir. of admissions Coast Guard Academy. Former dir. personnel mgmt., fifth coast guard dist. US Coast Guard, former commanding officer of training ctr. in Cape May, former comdr. Station Cape May & Group Baltimore, former dep. comdr. of activities at Baltimore, comdr. fifth coast guard dist., 2003—05, dir., reserve and training, 2005—, mem., reserve forces policy bd., 2005—. Decorated Legions of Merit, Meritorious Service Medal, Coast Guard Commendation Medals, Coast Guard Achievement Medal. Office: US Coast Guard 2100 2nd St SW Washington DC 20593

BRICE ROSS, CARLA YVETTE, school counselor; d. Rutherford Jack Brice and Barbara Eloise Gohanna Brice; children: Rashida Lawanna Ross Andrews, Kaymi Yvette Ross. BA, Clark Coll., 1969—71; Med, Ga. State U., 1972—74, Med, 1983—85, Edn. Specialist, 1991—95; postgrad., Ga. Southern U. Professional Counselor Composite Bd. Profl. Counselors Marriage and Family Therapists, 2004, Georgia Educator Certificate/Teacher Support Specialist Ga. Profl. Standards Commn., 2002, Mediator Justice Ctr. of Atlanta, 1998, Licensed Professional Counselor Ga. Composite Bd. of Profl. Counselors, 1997, National Counselor Certification Nat. Bd. for Cert. Counselors, 1997, National Certified School Counselor Nat. Bd. for Cert. Counselors, 2002, Georgia Educator Certificate/Data Collection Ga. Profl. Standards Commn., 2002, Georgia Educator Certificate/Eary Childhood Education (P-5) Ga. Profl. Standards Commn., 2002, Georgia Educator Certificate/Educational Leadership (P-12) Ga. Profl. Standards Commn., 2002, Georgia Educator Certificate/Middle Grades (4-8) English Language Arts Ga. Profl. Standards Commn., 2002, Georgia Educator Certificate/Middle Grades (4-8) Social Science Ga. Profl. Standards Commn., 2002, Georgia Educator Certificate/School Counseling (P-12) Ga. Profl. Standards Commn., 2002. Social sci./reading tchr. St. Anthony Cath. Sch., Atlanta, 1971—72; tchr. Walton County Schs., Loganville, Ga., 1973—74; tchr., team supr. Turner Mid. Sch., Lithia Springs, Ga., 1979—85; asst. prin., tchr. Marion Smith Elem. Sch., East Point, Ga., 1985—89; guidance counselor Atlanta Pub. Schs., 1989—; grief counselor Carl M. Williams Funeral Directors, Atlanta, 1996—; trainer, cons. Clark Atlanta U./Allied Health Services Dept., 1985—; officer of the ct. Fulton County Juvenile Ct., Atlanta, 2000—. Social sci. curriculum writer Douglas County Schools, Douglasville, Ga., 1975—77, master tchr. for support and assessment, 1979—89, student tchr. supr., 1975—79; tchr. and counselor mentor Atlanta Pub. Schools, 1990—; master tchr. for assessment and support Fulton County Schools, East Point, Ga., 1986—89; counselor internship and practicum supr. Atlanta Pub. Schools, 1997—, workshop presenter, 1990—. Citizens rev. panel mem. Fulton County Juvenile Ct., Atlanta, Ga., 2000—05. Recipient Elem. Sch. Counselor of the Yr., Atlanta Sch. Counselor Assn., 2002, Atlanta Pub. Schools Counselor of the Yr., Am. Fedn. of Teachers, 2002. Mem.: Ga. Sch. Counselor Assn. (region 3 chair 2002—03, co-chair mentoring com. 2003—05), Am. Sch. Counselor Assn. (profl. devel. chair 2003—05), Pi Lambda Theta, Delta Sigma Theta (life; chair phys. and mental health com. 2000—05). Roman Catholic. Avocation: writing. Home: 181 Saddleview Trail Riverdale GA 30274-4090 Office: Atlanta Public Schools 211 Memorial Dr Atlanta GA 30312 Office Phone: 404-330-4672.

BRICKER, CAROL JEAN, biology educator; d. Louis Allen and Phyllis Ruth Cowan; m. Bret Norman Bricker, July 11, 1987; children: Erik Taylor, Sean Nicholas. BS, U. Ark., Fayetteville, 1984, MS, 1990. Biology tchr. Southside HS, Ft. Smith, Ark., 1984—, sci. dept. chmn., pathwise mentor. Women's ministry com. Heritage United Meth. Ch., Van Buren, Ark., 2006. Office: Southside High Sch 4100 Gary St Fort Smith AR Office Phone: 479-646-7371.

BRICKER, RUTH, national foundation administrator, real estate developer; b. Oak Park, Ill., Mar. 23, 1930; m. Neal S. Bricker; children: Daniel Baker, Cary, Dusty, Suzanne. Student, UCLA, 1945; postgrad. in Art, U. So. Calif.; BA in Urban Planning, Antioch U., MA in Urban Planning, 1978. Cert. mediator. Staff Artforum Mag., L.A., 1966—69; we. dir. Experiments in Art and Tech., L.A., 1969—75; owner Empire Real Estate and Devel., L.A., 1975—76; mng. gen. prtnr. Orchard Pk. Devel., Loma Linda, Calif., 1988—; prodr., "Headline", "The Doc. are in" Inland Empire, Cable Sys., Calif., 2000—. Designer Trade-Off; developed programs in art and tech. for Calif. State Coll.-Long Beach, U. So. Calif., UCLA; designer laser light wall Calif. Inst. Tech.; lectr. and cons. in field. Author: Getting Rich in Real Estate Partnerships, 1983; editor, contbg. author: Experiments in Art and Technology/L.A. Jour., 1974-79; prodr. (monthly TV program) Headline; publr. Warner Books. Mem. Mayor's Housing Task Force, L.A.; Internat. Inst. Kidney Diseases; founding mem. exec. com. Sav. and Preserving Archtl. and Cultural Environment; bd. mem. Am. Found. for Pompidou Mus., Paris, Getty Mus., Archival Sec. Achievements include development of art and technology programs for the first moon landing in 1969. E-mail: ruthbricker@comcast.net.

BRICKER, VICTORIA REIFLER, anthropologist, educator; b. Hong Kong, June 15, 1940; arrived in US, 1947, naturalized, 1953; d. Erwin and Henrietta (Brown) Reifler; m. Harvey Miller Bricker, Dec. 27, 1964. AB, Stanford U., 1962; A.M., Harvard U., 1963, PhD, 1968. Vis. lectr. anthropology Tulane U., 1969-70, asst. prof., 1970-73, assoc. prof., 1973-78, prof., 1978—2005, chmn. dept. anthropology, 1988—91, 2003—05. Author: Ritual Humor in Highland Chiapas, 1973, The Indian Christ, The Indian King: The Historical Substrate of Maya Myth and Ritual, 1981 (Howard Francis Cline meml. prize Conf. Latin Am. History), A Grammar of Mayan Hieroglyphs, 1986, (with Gabrielle Vail) Papers on the Madrid Codex, 1997, (with Eleuterio Po'ot Yah and Ofelia Dzul de Po'ot) A Dictionary of the Maya Language as Spoken in Hocaba, Yucatan, 1998, (with Helga-Maria Miram) An Encounter of Two Worlds: The Book of Chilam Balam of Kaua, 2002; book rev. editor: Am. Anthropologist, 1971-73; editor: Am. Ethnologist, 1973-76; gen. editor: Supplement to Handbook of Middle American Indians, 1977—. Guggenheim fellow, 1982; Wenner-Gren Found. Anthropol. Rsch. grantee, 1971; Social Sci. Rsch. Coun. grantee, 1972; NEH grantee, 1990. Fellow Am. Anthrop. Assn. (exec. bd. 1980-83); mem. NAS, Am. Philos. Soc., Am. Soc. Ethnohistory (exec. bd. 1977-79), Linguistic Soc. Am.

BRICKER-BONE, JENNIFER K., athletic trainer; b. Anderson, Ind., July 17, 1972; d. Stephen Paul and Betty Jean Bricker; m. Kyle Matthew Bone, Sept. 4, 2004. BA, Anderson U., Ind., 1997; MS, U. Memphis, 2005. Cert. atheltic trainer Tenn. Bd. Med. Examiners. Staff athletic trainer St. Johns Hosp., Anderson, 1997—98, Campbell Civic Orthop., Memphis, 1998—2000; grad. asst. U. Memphis, 2000—02, asst. athletic trainer men's basketball, 2002—. Recipient Melvin Humphries award, U. Memphis, 2005. Mem.: Nat. Athletic Trainers Assn. (cert.). Baptist. Avocations: quilting, sewing, scrapbooks. Home: 6566 Sungate Cir Bartlett TN 38135 Office: U Memphis 109 Athletic Business Office Memphis TN 38152

BRICKEY, SUZANNE M., editor; b. Grand Rapids, Mich., Apr. 4, 1951; d. Robert Michael and Elizabeth (Rogers) Stankey; m. Homer Brickey, Jr. BA, Ohio U., Athens, 1973; B.J., U. Mo., Columbia, 1977. Editor Living Today, The Blade, Toledo, 1980-82, Toledo Mag., The Blade, 1982-92; asst. editor Features, Toledo, 1992—. Mem. Toledo Press Club, Toledo Rowing Club. Home: 2510 Kenwood Blvd Toledo OH 43606-3601 Office: The Blade 541 N Superior St Toledo OH 43660-0001 E-mail: suebrickey@theblade.com.

BRIDE, NANCY J., lawyer; b. Oct. 7, 1970; BA, Bowdoin Coll., 1992; JD, Notre Dame Law Sch., 1997. Bar: Ohio, US Dist. Ct. Southern Dist. Ohio, US Ct. of Appeals, Sixth Cir. Team in tng. mentor Leukemia & Lymphoma Soc.; vol. The Point, Wills for Heroes Prog.; mentor Cin. Youth Collaborative; orgnaizer Am. Breast Cancer Soc.; hostess Bacchanalian Soc. Wine Tasting Fundraiser. Named one of Ohio's Rising Stars, Super Lawyers, 2006. Mem.: Cin. Bar Assn. (Ct. Common Pleas Com.), Ohio State Bar Assn., ABA, Notre Dame Club of Cin. Office: Greenebaum Doll & McDonald PLLC 2800 Chemed Ctr 255 E 5th St Cincinnati OH 45202-4728 Office Phone: 513-455-7600. Office Fax: 513-455-8500.*

BRIDGE, BOBBE JEAN, state supreme court justice; b. 1944; m. Jonathan J. Bridge; children: Rebecca, Don. BA magna cum laude, U. Wash; MA, U. Mich., PhD in Polit. Sci.; JD, U. Wash., 1976. Superior Ct. judge King County, Wash., 1990-1999; chief judge King County Juvenile Ct., Wash., 1994-97, asst. presiding judge Wash., 1997-98, presiding judge Wash.,

1998-99; justice Wash. State Supreme Ct., 1999—. Chmn. Judicial Info. Sys. Comm, Legislative Comm.; co-chmn. Unified Family Ct. Bench-Bar Task Force. Bd. dirs. YWCA, Becca Task Force, State Commr. on Children in Foster Care, Seattle Children's Home, Catalyst for Kids Youth Care, Tech. Adv. Com. Female Juvenile Offenders, Adv. Com. Adolescent Life Skills Program, Street Youth Law Program, Northwest Mediation Svc., Woodland Pk. Zoological Soc., Wash. Coun. Crime and Delinquency, Women's Funding Alliance, Alki Found., Privacy Fund, Seattle Arts Commn., U. Wash. Arts and Sci. Devel., Greater Seattle C. of C., Metrocenter YMCA, Juvenile Ct. Conf. Com.; mem. King County Task Force on Children and Families, Wash. State's Dept. Social and Health Svcs. Children., Youth, Family Svcs. Adv. Com., Child Protection Roundtable, Govs. Juvenile Justice Adv. Com.; chmn. State Task Force on Juvenile Issues, Coun. Youth Crisis Work Group, Families-at-Risk sub-com., Bd. Dirs. Ctr. Career Alternatives, Candidate Evaluation Com. Seattle-King Mcpl. League, Law and justice Com. League Women Voters; co-chmn. Govs. Coun. on Families, Youth, and Justice; pres. Seattle Women's Commn., Seattle Chpt. Am. Jewish Com.,bd. dirs., asst. sec.-treas. Jewish Fedn. Greater Seattle, chmn., vice chmn. Cmty. Rels. Coun. Named Judge of Yr. Wash. Women Lawyers, 1996; recipient Hannah G. Solomon award Nat. Coun. Jewish Women, 1996, Cmty. Catalyst award Mother's Against Violence in Am., 1997, Women Making a Difference award Youthcare, 1998, Annual Family Advocate award, 2002; honored "woman helping women" Soroptimist Internat. of Kent, 1999. Mem. Nat. Kidney Found., Ctr. Women and Democracy, Phi Beta Kappa. Office: Wash Supreme Ct PO Box 40929 Olympia WA 98504-0929*

BRIDGE, KAREN SUE, microbiologist, laboratory administrator; b. Wayne, Nebr., Jan. 3, 1944; d. Dale Victor Anderson and Alice Lorraine Johnson; m. Michael Franklin Johnson, Apr. 20, 1969 (div. Dec. 5, 1986); 1 child, Brett D. Johnson; m. David Lance Bridge, Sept. 8, 1990; children: Traci, Shawn. BS, Bethany Coll., 1966; Med. Technology, Trinity Luth. Hosp., 1967; MS, Wichita State U., 1976. Sec. Bethany Coll., Lindsborg, Kans., 1963-65; asst. supr. Trinity Luth. Hosp., Kansas City, Mo., 1966-71; supr. Women's Clinic Lab, Wichita, Kans., 1971-72; technologist R&D lab St. Francis Regional Med. Ctr., Wichita, 1976-94; tech. dir. Ctr. Infectious Diseases, Wichita, 1994—. Cons. Infectious Disease Cons., Wichita, 1986-94; presenter in field. Contbr. articles to profl. jours., chpt. to book. Scorekeeper Littel League Baseball, Wichita, 1977-84; treas. Christ Ch. Luth. Ch., Wichita, 1980-84. Study grantee Pfizer Corp., 1998-99, Bristol-Myers Squibb, 1999—. Mem. Am. Soc. Clin. Pathologists (cert. med. technologist), Am. Soc. Microbiology, Southwestern Assn. Clin Microbiologists (area dir. 1998—, editor newsletter 1997—), Wichita State Alumni Assn., Literacy Soc. (tutor 1991-93). Republican. Lutheran. Avocations: collecting antiques, water-skiing, cooking, baking, gardening. Office: Ctr Infectious Diseases 1100 N Saint Francis St Ste 120 Wichita KS 67214-2865

BRIDGEFORTH, CHRYSTL L., former labor union administrator; Former exec. dir. Coalition Labor Union Women, Washington. Office: Coalition Labor Union Women 1925 K St NW Ste 402 Washington DC 20006

BRIDGES, CHRISTINE E., elementary school educator; b. Springfield, Mass., Nov. 4, 1954; d. Claude Thomas and Rita Christina (Banim) Myers; m. Garry C. Bridges, Sept. 25, 1976; 1 child, Kevin Michael BS Edn., Westfield State U., 1986. Cert. early childhood edn., kindergarten to 3d. Tchr. DeBerry Elem. Sch., Springfield, Homer St. Elem., Springfield, Milton Bradley Elem. Sch., Springfield. Sec. decision-making team; faculty liaison and student coun. coord. PTO; cert. megaskills leader Home and Sch. Inst Mem. Mass. Tchrs. Assn., Springfield Edn. Assn. (union rep.), Springfield Tchrs. Club (early childhood curriculum com.), Kappa Delta Pi Office Phone: 413-787-7475. Personal E-mail: chris650@comcast.net.

BRIDGES, CYNTHIA ELAINE, music educator; b. Chgo., Dec. 25, 1960; d. Horace Alcus and Hettie Malone Bridges; 1 child, Orlando Pierre McLin. B in Music Edn., Roosevelt U., Chgo., 1985; M in Musical Arts, Northwestern U., Evanston, Ill., 2002. Cert. music tchr. Ill. Tchr. Kinder Kare Preschool, 1985—86; music tchr. Unity Cath. HS, Chgo., 1986—88, St. Martin de Porres HS, Chgo., 1988—91, Kipling Elem. Sch., Chgo., 1991—. Dir., chaplain Doris Ward Workshop Chorale, Chgo., 1985—2001; asst. condr. All City Elem. Youth Chorus, Chgo., 1997—99, Chgo., 2003—05; vocal coach ch. singers Vocal Boot Camp, Chgo., 2004—. Asst. pastor 1st Pentecostal Cmty. Ch., Calumet, Ill., 1984—. Named Outstanding Music/Drama Tchr., Beulah A. G. Smith Found., 1997; fellow, Northwestern U., 1999. Mem.: Music Educator Nat. Conf. Avocations: movies, spa. Home: 1016 W 108th St Chicago IL 60643 Office: Kipling Sch 9351 S Lowe Ave Chicago IL 60620

BRIDGES, LISA JANE, psychology educator; b. San Pedro, Calif., May 18, 1958; d. Earl LeRoy and Lois Orvilla (Bolton) B. BA, Pitzer Coll., Claremont, Calif., 1980; MA, U. Rochester, 1985, PhD, 1988. Asst. prof. devel. psychology U. Calif., Riverside, 1988—. Contbr. articles to profl. jours. Recipient outstanding dissertation award div. 7 APA, 1990. Mem. Soc. for Rsch. in Child Devel., Internat. Soc. for Infant Studies, Am. Psychol. Soc. Democrat. Office: U Calif Dept Psychology Riverside CA 92521-0001

BRIDGES, MARGARET ELIZABETH, physician; b. Brevard, N.C., Jan. 26, 1947; d. James Oliver B. and Mary Elizabeth Allison. BS, Coll. Charleston, 1969; MD, U. S.C., 1973. Intern Med. U. S.C., 1973-74, resident, 1974-76, fellow gastroenterology, 1977-79; physician Diagnostic Clin. Houston, 1979—; asst. clin. prof. Baylor Coll. Medicine, Houston, 1984—. Bd. trustees Diagnostic Hosp., Houston, 1994-97; vol. faculty Ben Taub Gen. Hosp., Houston, 1981—. Contbr. articles to profl. jours. Founder, advisor Lucky Livers Support Group, Houston, 1989—; bd. trustees Coll. Charleston (S.C.) Coll. Found., 1978-79. Fellow Am. Coll. Physicians; mem. Am. Assn. Study Liver Disease, Am. Coll. Gastroenterology, Am. Gastroen. Assn., Am. Soc. Gastroen. Endoscopy, Alpha Omega Alpha. Episcopalian. Avocations: scuba diving, bird watching, skiing. Home: 13114 Hermitage Ln Houston TX 77079-7201

BRIDGES, MARY JO, music educator; b. Russellville, Ark., Apr. 16, 1946; d. Ernest Christopher Graves and Mary Glynn Overbey-Graves; m. David Merrill Bridges, Dec. 22, 1967; children: David Christopher, Jolyn. BA in Music Edn., Northeastern State Coll., Tahlequah, Okla., 1968. Tchr. music and drama Andrew Jackson Elem. Sch., Tulsa, Okla., 1968—71; tchr. music, choir accompanist Tulsa Jr. Coll., Okla., 1980—83; tchr. music, drama, Spanish, Robert E. Peary Elem. Sch., Tulsa, Okla., 1990—. Ch. choir accompanist Ch. of the Shepherd United Meth.Ch., Tulsa, Okla., 1977—. Recipient Tulsa Tchr. award, Tulsa Pub. Schs., 2006. Avocations: camping, playing the piano, crossword puzzles. Home: 1016 E 18th St Tulsa OK 74128-6310 Office: Robert E Peary Elem Sch 10818 E 17th St Tulsa OK 74128 E-mail: 2mjtoday@cox.net.

BRIDGES, SHIRLEY WALTON, air transportation executive; BA in math., Clark Atlanta U.; M in project mgmt., George Washington U. Positions with Bridgehaus Inc., Norfolk So. R.R.; sr. project mgr. Delta Air Lines, Inc., 1990; v.p. airline ops. systems Delta Tech., Inc., sr. v.p. ops., now COO; acting chief info. officer Delta Air Lines, Inc. Named one of the Premier 100 IT Leaders, Computerworld, 2005. Office: Delta Tech Inc 1001 Internat Blvd Atlanta GA 30354-1801

BRIDGEWATER, DEE DEE, jazz singer, diplomat; b. Memphis, May 1927; Lead vocalist Thad Jones and Mel Lewis Orch., 1971-75; appeared in theatrical prodns. The Wiz (Tony award), Sophisticated Ladies, Lady Day (L. Oliver nomination), Carmen Jazz, others; albums include Afro Blue, 1974, Dee Dee Bridgewater, 1976, 1980, Just Family, 1977, Bad for Me, 1979, Live in Paris, 1986, In Montreux, 1990, Keeping Tradition, 1992, Love and Peace: A Tribute to Horace Silver, 1995 (Grammy award), Dear Ella, 1997 (Grammy awards), Victim of Love, 1998, Live at Yoshi's, 2000 (Grammy nomination), This is New, 2002. Amb. U.N. Food and Agr. Orgn., 2002—.

BRIDGEWATER, PAMELA E., ambassador, former federal agency administrator; b. Fredericksburg, Va., Apr. 1947; BA in Polit. Sci., Va. State U., 1968, LLD (hon.), 1997; MA in Polit. Sci., U. Cin., 1970; postgrad., Am. U., 1976. Tchr. Voorhees Coll., Denmark, SC, Bowie (Md.) State U., Morgan State U., Balt.; vice-consul US Dept. State, Brussels, labor attache/polit. officer Kingston, Jamaica, polit. officer Pretoria, South Africa, 1990—93, consul gen. Durban, South Africa, 1993—96, dep. chief of mission Nassau, Bahamas, 1996—99, mem., pres. 42nd Sr. Seminar, 1999—2000, US amb. to Benin, 2000—03, dep. asst. sec. for African affairs Washington, 2003—05, US amb. to Ghana, 2005—. Office: DOS Amb 2020 Accra Pl Washington DC 20521

BRIEN, LOIS ANN, psychologist, educator; b. Cleve., Sept. 24, 1928; d. Alexander and Anne Lois (Katz) B.; m. Melvin Lintz, June 1961 (div. June 1964). BFA, Ohio U., 1950; MA, U. Ala., 1953; PhD, U. Iowa, 1959. Instr. Auburn (Ala.) U., 1953-55; clin. instr. Baylor Coll. Medicine, Houston, 1959-64; diagnostician Houston Speech and Hearing Ctr., 1959-64; faculty, speech com. Case Western Reserve U., Cleve., 1965-69; faculty, psychology San Francisco State U., 1970-72; pvt. practice San Francisco, 1969-79; faculty Calif. Sch. Profl. Psychology, Berkeley, 1971-79; pvt. practice Palm Springs, 1981-82; faculty, women's studies San Diego State U., 1983-86; pvt. practice Encinitas, Calif., 1982—; prof. psychology Nat. U., San Diego, 1984-87, dean Sch. Psychology, 1987-91, dean emeritus, assoc. faculty, 1991—. Contbr. articles to profl. jours. and textbooks. Commr. Marin County Commn. on the Status of Women, 1974-77. U.S. Office Edn. grantee, 1970-71. Mem. NOW, Am. Psychol. Assn., Calif. Assn. Marriage, Family Therapy, Am. Assn. Marriage, Family Therapy, Am. Acad. Psychotherapists. Democrat. Jewish. Avocations: tennis, gardening, hiking, bicycling, skiing. also: Nat U Dept Psychology University Park San Diego CA 92108

BRIENZA, PAULA KENAH, retired chemist; b. Montclair, N.J., May 24, 1931; d. Joseph Albert Kenah and Agnes Fabian Tighe; m. Walter Brienza (div.). BA in Chemistry, Caldwell Coll., NJ, 1952. Chemist, mgr. Engelhard Corp., Newark, 1952—86; quality assurance mgr. Engelhard, Seneca, SC, 1986—90; ret. Pres. East Orange Jr. Womans Club, NJ, 1966—67, 1967—68; Eucharistic min. St. Catharines/St. Margarets Ch., Spring Lake, 1990—, mem. adults edn. group, 1990—. Mem.: Garden Club Spring Lake. Democrat. Roman Catholic. Achievements include patents for coated film of catalytically active oxide on a refractory support; patents in field. Avocation: gardening.

BRIER, BONNIE SUSAN, lawyer; b. Oct. 19, 1950; d. Jerome W. and Barbara (Srenco) B.; m. Bruce A. Rosenfield, Aug. 15, 1976; children: Rebecca, Elizabeth, Benjamin. AB in Econs. magna cum laude, Cornell U., 1972; JD, Stanford U., 1976. Bar: Pa. 1976, U.S. Dist. Ct. (ea. dist.) Pa., U.S. Tax Ct., U.S. Ct. Appeals (3d cir.), U.S. Supreme Ct. Law clk. to chief judge U.S. Dist. Ct. Pa. (ea. dist.), Phila., 1976-77, asst. U.S. atty. criminal prosecutor, 1977-79; from assoc. to ptnr. Ballard, Spahr, Andrews & Ingersoll, Phila., 1979-90; gen. counsel Children's Hosp. of Phila., Phila., 1990—. Legal counsel Womens Way, 1979—1999; lectr. U. Pa. Law Sch., 1988-95; lectr., speaker various orgns. and seminars. Editor Stanford Law Rev., 1974-76; contbr. articles to profl. jours. Bd. dirs. U.S. Com. for UNICEF, 1994—2000, vice chmn., 1998-2000. Recipient Woman of Achievement award, March of Dimes, 2003, Leadership award, Women's Way, 2004. Fellow Am. Coll. Tax Counsel, Am. Law Inst., Am. Health Lawyers Assn. (bd. dirs. 1991-96); mem. ABA (exempt orgn. com. on tax sect., chair 1991-93, mem. health law sect., bd. dirs. 1998-, chair 2003-), Pa. Bar Assn. (tax sect., health law sect., mem. com. charitable orgn., children's rights), Phila. Bar Assn. (tax sect., health law com.). Home: 132 Fairview Rd Narberth PA 19072-1331 Office: Children's Hosp of Pa 34th St and Civic Ctr Blvd Philadelphia PA 19104

BRIERLEY, CORALE L., geological and biomining engineer; b. Mont. m. Jim Brierley. Student, Mont. State U.; BS in Biology, N.Mex. Inst. Mining & Tech., MS in Chemistry; PhD in Environ. Scis., U. Tex., Dallas, 1981. With N.Mex. Bur. Mines; founder Advanced Mineral Techs., 1983-87; chief environ. process devel. Newmont Mining Co., 1989-91; founder, prin. Brierley Cons. LLC, Highlands Ranch, Colo., 1991—. Office: Brierley Consultancy LLC PO Box 260012 Highlands Ranch CO 80163-0012 E-mail: clbrierley@msn.com.

BRIERRE, MICHELINE, artist; b. Jeremie, Haiti; d. Luc Brierre and Simone Lataillaide; m. Charles Lopez (div.); children: Liza Berntein, Charles Lopez; m. Barry Kaplan. Studied with, Mr. Ramponeau, Haiti, 1951-53; student, Academie Nehemie Jean, Haiti, 1958-60, Miraflores Art Ctr., Peru. Author: I am Eve, 1980, Spanish translation, 1980; solo show Commonwheel, Manitou Springs, Colo., 1995; exhibited in group shows at Galerie Hotel Rancho, Haiti, 1961, Galerie Brochette, Haiti, 1962, Onze Femmes peintres, Haiti, 1963, Gallerie Brochette, Haiti, 1964, Brierre/Castera, Haiti, 1965, Musee d'Art, Haiti, 1980, Galeria 70, Bogota, Colombia, S. Am., 1980, Galeria San Diego, Colombia, 1980, Woman's Way, Miami, Fla., 1982, Un Regard Soleil, Port-au-Prince, Haiti, 1983, Reflection On The Past, Aureus, Miami, 1983, Un Mundo Para Compartir, Lima, Peru, 1983, Festival Arts Gallery, Port-au-Prince, 1984, An Evening With The Artists, Naples, Fla., 1986, 87, Art in Jewelry, Island House, Bayside, Fla., 1987, Mixed Media Studio Show, Miami, 1989, 91, Collective Show, Commonwheel, Manitou Spings, Colo., 1994, Douglas County Art Ctr., Roby Mills Gallery and Bus. of Art Ctr., 1995. Mem. Fine Arts Ctr. Colo. Springs, Bus. of Art Ctr., Commonwheel Co-op. Home: All Things Beautiful 8050 Woody Creek Dr Colorado Springs CO 80911-8332 Personal E-mail: mbrierre@michelinebrierre.com.

BRIERTON, CHERYL LYNN, lawyer; b. Hartford, Conn., Nov. 11, 1947; d. Charles Greenwood and Elizabeth (Grechko) Wootton; m. David Martin Black, Oct. 12, 1968 (div. 1978); m. John Thomas Brierton, Sept. 6, 1982 (div. 1988); 1 child, John Greenwood. BA, Wellesley Coll., 1969; JD, U. San Diego, 1982. Bar: Calif. 1983. Tchr., libr. Anglican High Sch., Grenada, West Indies, 1972-74; dep. dir. Transalpino Student Travel, Paris, 1975-76; asst. dir. adminstn. Project OZ, YMCA, San Diego, 1976-78; asst. coord. policy and advocacy Community Congress San Diego, 1978-81; field dir. Calif. Child, Youth and Family Coalition, San Diego, 1981-83; asst. exec. dir. Community Congress San Diego, 1984-85; exec. dir. Calif. Child, Youth and Family Coalition, Sacramento, 1985-86; gen. atty. Def. Logistics Agy., Def. Depot Tracy, Calif., 1986-88; atty.-advisor Dept. of the Navy, Mare Island Naval Shipyard, Vallejo, 1988-89; staff atty. San Diego Superior Ct., 1989—. Mem. faculty Nat. Juvenile Judges Conf. Dispositional Alternatives Serious Offenders, 1982, 6th and 7th Nat. Confs. Juvenile Justice, 1979-80; cons. San Diego Youth Involvement Project, 1983-84, San Diego Youth and Community Svcs., 1983-84, South Bay Community Svcs., Chula Vista, 1983. Mem. Juvenile Justice Commn., Golden Hill Neighborhood Justice Cen. Planning Bd.; mem. com. jud. process Regional Criminal Justice Planning Bd. Scholar U. San Diego 1979. Mem. MENSA. Avocations: yachting, travel. Home: 1329 Bancroft St San Diego CA 92102-2429

BRIGDEN, ANN SCHWARTZ, mediator, educator; b. East Aurora, N.Y., Oct. 15, 1932; d. John G. and Mildred (Glaser) Schwartz; m. John Kraig Brigden, June 17, 1953 (div. Nov. 1974); children: Nancy Brigden, Barbara Brigden Victor; m. Steve Nemeth, Dec. 31, 1983 (div. Nov. 1996); children: Kyra Nemeth Akins, Abel Nemeth. BS in Human Ecology, Cornell U., 1954; MA in Behavioral Scis., Calif. State U., Dominguez Hills, 1977, grad. cert. in negotiation/conflict res., 1991, MS in Marriage and Family Counseling, 1993. Cert. mediator, L.A. County. Dist. dir. Girl Scouts of Erie County, Buffalo, 1954-55; recreation leader City of Phila., 1955-56; field dir. Angeles Girl Scout Coun., L.A., 1956-58, 69-79; dir. vols. Children's Home Soc. Calif., L.A., 1979-84, dir. Human Maturity Program, 1984-90; counselor-intern Dolores St. Sch., Carson, Calif., 1990-95; developer and dir. Conflict Resolution Programs Dolores and Catskill Schs., Carson, Calif., 1994—. Adv. bd. L.A. Unified Sch. Dist. Health Edn., 1985-87; chair Maternal, Child & Adolescent Health Coun. L.A. County West, L.A., 1988-93. Author (textbooks): Maturing as Humanly as Possible, 1986, Becoming a Teenager, 1988; co-author (jr. h.s. curriculum) Curriculum in Human Maturity, 1980, revised 1986, 94. Aux. mem. Children's Hosp. San Diego, 1962-68; Girl Scout leader, bd. mem. Girl Scout Coun. San Diego, 1964-68; com. chair Peninsula Action for Youth, Palos Verdes, Calif., 1971-76; vol. mediator L.A. County, 1992—; bd. dirs. Dispute Resolution Ctr. Calif. State U. Dominguez Hills/L.A. County, 1987—. Grantee Soc. Psychol. Study of Social Issues, 1994-96, L.A. County Dept. Edn., 1996—. Mem. So. Calif,. Mediation Assn., Calif. State U. Dominguez Hills Marriage, Family and Child Counseling Alumni Assn. Avocations: volunteering, piano, friends. Home: 3162 Crownview Dr Palos Verdes Estates CA 90275-6414

BRIGGS, BONNIE SUE, school librarian, minister; d. Charles and Joyce Baldwin; m. Ronald Briggs, Jan. 26, 1986; children: Dawn Elaine Kauffman, Kristy Lynn Heath, Joy Ellen Hilderbrand, Mistie Sue Stephenson. AA, Liberty Bible Coll., 1989. Cert. gen. bible Liberty Bible Coll., 1989. Libr. Ohio Valley Local Schs., West Union, Ohio, 1994—; min. Refuge Ministries, West Union, 1995—. Missionary Internat. Focus Ministries, Columbus, Ohio, 2004—. Author (poet): (anthology) Best 200 Poets of 2003. Ch. liason Christian Coalition Am., DC, 2004—. Mem.: Refuge Ministerial Fellowship (licentiate). R-Consevative. Protestant. Avocations: travel, writing, gardening.

BRIGGS, CAROLE A., elementary school educator; b. Dec. 28, 1936; BS in Elem. Edn., Clarion U., 1972; MEd, Ind. U. of P., 1976; Sixth Yr. Cert., U. Conn., 1988. Bilingual tchr. Pars Internat. Sch., Abadan, Iran, 1967-71; tchr. DuBois Area Sch. Dist., Reynoldsville, Pa., 1972-75; elem., gifted support tchr. Brookville Area Sch. Dist., Pa., 1975—2001; Exec. Dir/Curator Jefferson County Hist. Ctr., Pa., 1989—. Author: The Presbyterian Church of Brookville, 1999, An Old-Fashioned Feller: Charles Albert Bowdish, 2003; co-author: Creamed Onions for Supper, 2001, Jefferson County, Pennsylvania: An Illustrated History, 2004. Recipient Outstanding Cmty. Social Equity award, Clarion U. of Pa., 1998, Robert Lee Stowe award, 2000, Walter Dick award, Brookville C. of C., 2002. Mem. AAUW (local pres., state bd. 1980-86), Nat. Assn. Gifted Children, Pa. State Edn. Assn. (mem. state com. 1996-97), Brookville Area Edn. Assn. (pres. 1988-90). Home: 45 Richards St Brookville PA 15825-1633

BRIGGS, CYNTHIA ANNE, educational administrator, clinical psychologist; b. Berea, Ohio, Nov. 9, 1950; d. William Benajah and Lorraine (Hood) B.; m. Thomas Joseph O'Brien, Nov. 28, 1986; children: Julia Maureen, William Thomas. B Music Edn., U. Kans., 1973; MusM, U. Miami, 1976; D. Psychology, Hahnemann U., 1988. Lic. psychology, Mo.; bd. cert. music therapist. Music therapist Parsons (Kans.) State Hosp., 1973-74; grad. asst. U. Miami, Coral Gables, Fla., 1974-76; asst. prof., dir. Hahnemann U., Phila., 1976-85, asst. prof., 1985-91; psychology resident Assocs. in Psychol. and Human Resources, Phila., 1988-91; clin. dir. Child Ctr. of Our Lady, St. Louis, 1991—2004; adj. faculty Lindenwood U., 2000—04; dir. music therapy Maryville Univ., 2004—. Mem. editl. bd. Jour. Music Therapy, 1997—2001; contbr. articles to profl. jours., chapters to books. Mem. Am. Assn. Music Therapy (pres. 1987-89), Nat. Coalition Arts Therapies Assns. (chair 1991-93). Democrat. Avocations: cooking, piano, music, theater. Office: Maryville Univ Sch Health Professions 13550 Conway Rd Saint Louis MO 63141 Office Phone: 314-529-9441. Business E-Mail: cbriggs@maryville.edu.

BRIGGS, ETHEL DELORIA, federal agency administrator; BA, N.C. Ctrl. U., 1971; M in Counseling, U. N.C., 1972. Dir. adult svcs. Nat. Coun. Disability, Washington, 1985—, dep. dir., acting exec. dir., exec. dir. Named one of Top 100 African Am. Bus. and Profl. Women, Dollars and Sense Mag., 1989. Office: Nat Coun Disability 1331 F St NW Ste 850 Washington DC 20004-1138 Business E-Mail: ebriggs@ncd.gov.

BRIGGS, GERALDINE HACKWORTH, reading specialist eduator; b. Lake City, Tenn., Apr. 12, 1936; d. Clarence Everett and Flora Edith (Law) Hackworth; children: Denise Briggs Chaney, Elizabeth Briggs Mudge. BS, Western Ky. State Coll., 1965; MEd, U. Md., 1976. Cert. advanced profl. Md. State Dept. Edn. Tchr. Head Start Hamilton County Pub. Sch., Chattanooga, 1965—66, tchr. home econs., sci., English, 1966—74; reading specialist Prince George Pub. Schs., Upper Marlboro, Md., 1976—98; ret., 1998. Mem. coord. com. specific lang./reading Prince George Schs., 1978—82, liaison multicultural affairs, 1993—98, coord. Md. state testing com., 1994—98. Vol. Dem. Party, Blount County, Tenn., 2004, Shannondale Health Ctr., Maryville, Tenn., 2004; vol. hospice Bloung Meml. Hosp., 2004—; vol., reading tutor Blount County Sch. Sys., 2004—. Mem.: Sam Houston Hist. Sch. House Guild. Democrat. Theist. Avocations: metaphysical pursuits, gardening, storytelling, creative writing. Home: 951 Shannondale Way Maryville TN 37803

BRIGGS, LAURA, education educator; AB in Women's Studies, Mt. Holyoke Coll., South Hadley, Mass.; MTS in Theology and Secondary Edn., Harvard Div. Sch.; PhD in Am. Civilization, Brown U., Providence, RI. Assoc. prof. U. Ariz., Tucson, 2003—. Acting head dept. women's studies U. Ariz., 2006—. Author: (book) Reproducing Empire: Race, Sex, Science and U.S. Imperialism in Puerto Rico. Jr. warden Grace St. Paul's Episcopal Ch., Tucson; mem. com. on the status of women in the hist. profession Orgn. Am. Historians, 2001—04; mem. com. Rourke prize Am. Studies Assn., 2004; dir. faculty mentoring youth program Ariz. Humanities Coun. Project, 2002—03. Recipient Constance A. Rourke prize, Am. Studies Assn., 2001; fellow, Harvard U. Warren Ctr., 1999, Mexico-North Transnationalism, 2005. Business E-Mail: lbriggs@email.arizona.edu.

BRIGHAM, NICOLETTE BAINBRIDGE, educational consultant; b. St. Albans, Eng., Sept. 29, 1965; d. Roland Everard Bainbridge, Kathleen Treacy Bainbridge; m. Michael J. Brigham, Sept. 24, 2005. BA in Psychology, Wichita State U., 1989; MS in Edn., U. Kans., 1999. Early childhood spl. edn. tchr. Rainbows United, Wichita, Kans., 1994—96; infant-toddler program dir. Spl. Svcs. Coop., Wamego, Kans., 1996—2000; rsch. asst. Vanderbilt U., Nashville, 2000—04; edn. cons. Vanderbilt Children's Hosp., 2004—05; coord. outreach program Kennedy Treatment Rsch. Inst. Autism Spectrum Disorders, 2005—. Chair Interagency Coordinating Coun., Wamego, 1996—2000; mem. Parents as Teachers Adv. Bd., Wamego, 1996—2000; autism cons. Spl. Svc. Coop., Wamego, 1998—2000; adj. instr. Highland C.C., Wamego, 2000. Contbr. articles to profl. jours. Chair Interagency Coord. Coun., Wamego, Kans., 1996—2000; mem. United Way Pottawatomie and Wabaunsee Counties, Wamego, 1998—2000, Parent as Tchrs. Adv. Bd., Wamego, 1996—2000; Member Graduate Student Council of Vanderbilt University, Nashville, 2000—00. Recipient Grad. Rsch. assistantship, Vanderbilt U., 2000, 2001, 2002, 2003. Mem.: Autism Soc. Am. Independent. Roman Catholic. Avocations: travel, literature. Office: Vanderbilt Kennedy TRIAD 1207 18th Ave S Nashville TN 37212 Office Phone: 618-936-2163. Business E-Mail: nicolette.l.bainbridge@vanderbilt.edu.

BRIGHT, MARGARET, sociologist; b. Bentonville, Ark., Nov. 19, 1918; d. William Ray and Edna May (Woolwine) B.; m. Herman Binder, 1983. AB, U. Calif., Berkeley, 1941; MA, U. Mo., 1944; PhD, U. Wis., 1950. Lectr. rural sociology U. Mo., 1944-47; asst. project dir. U. P.R., 1950-51; acting assoc. prof. Cornell U., 1951-52; social affairs officer population br. UN, N.Y.C., 1952-54; research assoc. Bur. Applied Social Research Columbia U., N.Y.C., 1954-57; sociologist-demographer UN Tech. Assistance, Bombay, India, 1957-59; asst. prof. chronic diseases Johns Hopkins U., Balt., 1959-63, assoc. prof., 1963-68; dir. research Center for Urban Affairs, 1968-72, assoc. prof. behavioral scis., 1968-70, prof., 1970-83, prof. emerita, 1983—. Mem. U.S. Mission Coop. Health and Sanitation to, Brazil, 1960. Author: Cooperativas de Consumo de Puerto Rico: Análisis Socio-Económicó, 1957; co-author: Graduates of American Schools of Public Health, 1976; contbr. articles to profl. jours. Mem. Balt. Mayor's Task Force on Polit. Redistricting, 1971; mem. Rockefeller Commn. on Population and the Am. Future, 1970-72. Mem. Am. Pub. Health Assn. Democrat. Office: 624 N Broadway Baltimore MD 21205-1900 Home: 105 W 39th St Apt P-1 Baltimore MD 21210

BRIGHT, SHERYL ANN, special education educator; b. Hot Springs, Ark., Jan. 1, 1949; d. Alfred A. and Opal Owens; m. Darrell Lindrell Bright, Apr. 20, 1973; children: Victoria Ann, Elizabeth Angeline. BS in Phys. Edn., Henderson State Coll., 1969; MS in Spl. Edn., U. Ark., 1983. Cert. spl. edn. tchr., Ark., Ala. Placement specialists Dept. of Rehab., Industry and Bus., Little Rock, 1988-89; educator spl. edn. grades 1-5 Benton (Ark.) Pub. Sch. Sys., 1989-90; counselor, adminstr. North Little Rock Alternative Sch., 1990-91; owner Bright Balloons and Baskets, North Little Rock, 1992-96; educator spl. edn. grades 10-12 Baldwin County Pub. Sch. Sys., Bay Minette, Ala., 1996—97; educator spl. edn. grades 10-12 mildly handicapped Mobile (Ala.) Pub. Sch. Sys., 1997—2003; educator elem. edn. grades 5-8 Atlantic Undersea Testing and Evaluation Ctr., Andros, Bahamas, 1998-99; educator spl. edn. grades 7-8 Fairfax Co. Pub. Schs., Alexandria, Va., 2003—. Spl. edn. cons. Millcreek of Ark., Fordyce, 1988-89; chmn. unit family support group USAR, 1988-92; cons. to mgmt. team for choices program Southwestern Bell Telephone Co., Little Rock, 1988-89. Methodist. Avocations: skiing, scuba diving, decorating, designing, music. E-mail: sherylbright@hotmail.com.

BRIGHT, TRINA LYNN, secondary school educator; d. Al and Donna McCorkle; children: Brianna Belote, Bethany Belote. MS in Edn., U. Ctrl. Ark., Conway, 2001. Nat. bd. cert. tchr. Tchr. Conway Sch. Dist., 2002—03; literacy coach Little Rock Sch. Dist., 2003—. Tchr. Mt. Vernon-Enola Sch. Dist., Ark., 1997—2001. Author: (memoir) Marathon Memories, (non-fiction) A Mother's Legacy. State bd. dirs. Ark. Coun. Tchrs. English Lang. Arts, Little Rock, 2002. Fellow: Nat. Writer's Project of Ctrl. Ark. (corr.); mem.: Ark. Reading Assn. (assoc.; local pres. 2002—03, state chmn. studies and rsch. 2004, Diamond award 2003—04, Jo Flanigan award 2006), Internat. Reading Assn. (assoc.), Phi Lambda Theta, Delta Kappa Gamma (2d v.p. 2006). Roman Catholic. Avocations: running, travel, reading, weightlifting. Office: Hall HS 6700 H St Little Rock AR 72205 Office Phone: 501-447-2047.

BRIGHTBILL, JANET M., music educator; b. Lebanon, Pa., Jan. 8, 1954; d. Gurney I. and Harriet E. Eisenhauer; m. Gary G. Brightbill, Sept. 2, 1972; children: Jeremy J., Jessica M. Brightbill-VonCrist, Jamie L. BA in Music Edn., U. of Charleston, W.Va., 1986. Cert. Profl. Tchr. W.Va. Dept. of Edn., 2002. Piano tchr. Grace Christian Sch., Myerstown, Pa., 1977—81, Bible Ctr. Christian Sch., Charleston, W.Va., 1983—86; music tchr., k-12 Cross Lanes Christian Sch., W.Va., 1986—97; piano instr. U. of Charleston, W.Va., 1998—. Accompanist Charleston Civic Chorus, W.Va., 1992—2002; pianist Bible Ctr. Ch., Charleston, W.Va., 1995—; accompanist U. of Charleston Concert Choir/U. Singers, W.Va., 1999—, W.Va. Symphony Chorus, Charleston, 2000—. Home: 5122 Lone Pine Ln Cross Lanes WV 25313 Office: U of Charleston 2300 MacCorkle Ave SE Charleston WV 25304 Office Phone: 304-357-4905.

BRIGHTMAN, CAROL, writer; Author: (with Larry Rivers) Larry River's Drawings and Digressions, 1988, Writing Dangerously: Mary McCarthy and Her World, 1992 (Nat. Book Critics Circle award for biography 1993).

BRIGHTMAN, SARAH, singer, actress; b. Berkhampstead, England, Aug. 14, 1960; d. Grenville and Paula (Hall) Brightman; m. Andrew Lloyd Webber (div. 1990). Student, Elmhurst Ballet Sch., Arts Edn. Sch., London. Stage appearances include (musicals) I and Albert, 1973, Cats (original cast), 1981, Nightingale, 1982, Song and Dance, 1984, Phantom of the Opera, 1986 (Drama Desk award), Aspects of Love, 1990, (requiem) Andrew Lloyd Webber's Requiem, 1985 (Grammy nomination), (operettas) Pirates of Penzance, 1983, Merry Widow, 1985; dancer, singer (dance group) Hot Gossip, 1978 (#1 record 1978); albums include: Dive, 1993, Timeless, 1997, Time To Say Goodbye, 1997, As I Came of Age, 1998, Fly, 1998, Surrender, 1998, Sings the Music of Andrew Lloyd Webber, 1998, Trees They Grow So High, 1998, Eden, 1998, La Luna, 2000, Harem, 2003. Avocations: singing, driving, swimming, writing.

BRIGHTWELL, WENDY SUE, biology educator; b. Mt. Arlington, N.J., Jan. 24, 1955; d. Marvin Perry and Ethel Belle Forsythe; m. Eric Dean Brightwell, Feb. 18, 1995; children: Justin Ouray Nez, Shane Perry Nez. BS, Athens State Coll., Ala., 1978. Cert. tchr. Ala. Dept. Edn., 1979. Tchr. Ctrl. Consol. Schs., Shiprock, N.Mex., 1981—88; tchr. biology Huntsville (Ala.) City Schs., 1988—. Bd. dirs. Huntsville (Ala.) Crimestoppers, 1992—2000, Huntsville (Ala.) Area Safe Kids, 1989—2000. Mem.: NEA (assoc.; chmn. membership 1982—88). Independent. Meth. Avocations: gardening, swimming. Office: Grissom High School 7901 Bailey Cove Road Huntsville AL 35802 Office Phone: 256-428-8000. Business E-Mail: wbrightwell@hsv.k12.al.us.

BRILES, JUDITH, writer, consultant; b. Pasadena, Calif., Feb. 20, 1946; d. James and Mary Tuthill; children: Shelley, Sheryl, Frank (dec.), William (dec.). MBA, Pepperdine U., 1980; PhD, Nova U., 1990. Brokers asst. Bateman, Eichler, Hill, Richards, Torrance, Calif., 1969-72; account exec. E. F. Hutton, Palo Alto, Calif., 1972-78; pres. Judith Briles & Co., Palo Alto, 1978-85, Briles & Assocs., Palo Alto, 1980-86; ptnr. The Briles Group, Inc., 1987—. Instr. Menlo Coll., 1986-87, Skyline Coll., 1981-86, U. Calif.-Berkeley Sch. Continuing Edn., U. Calif.-Santa Cruz Sch. Continuing Edn., U. Hawaii; mem. adv. coun. Miss Am. Pageant, 1989-95, No-nonsense Panty Hose, 1989-92, Colo. Women's News, 1993-97; founder Colo. Authors Hall of Fame, 2005-. Author: The Woman's Guide to Financial Savvy, 1981, Money Phases, 1984, Woman to Woman: From Sabotage to Support, 1987, Dollars and Sense of Divorce, 1988, Faith and Savvy Too!, 1988, When God Says No, 1990, The Confidence Factor, 1990 (Bus. Book of Yr, 2003), Money Guide, 1991, The Workplace Factor, 1990, Money Guide, 1991, The Workplace: Questions Women Ask, 1992, Financial Savvy for Women, 1992, The Briles Report on Women in Healthcare, 1994, Money Sense, 1995, Gender Traps, 1996, Raising Money Wise Kids, 1996, When God Says No, 1997, The Dollars and Sense of Divorce, 1998, Woman to Woman 2000, 1999 (chgo. Tribune Bus. Book of Yr.), 10 Smart Money Moves for Women, 1999(Book of Yr., 2002), Smart Money Moves for Kids, 2000 (Best How to Parenting, 2001), The Confidence Factor—Cosmic Goose Lay Golden Eggs, 2001, Stop Stabbing Yourself in the Back, 2001, Zapping Conflict in the Healthcare Workplace, 2003, Money Smarts, 2005; columnist Colo. Woman News, Denver Bus. Jour., MsMoney.com, Men in Nursing. Pres., v.p., sec., bd. dirs. foothill-DeAnza Coll. Found., Los Altos Hills, Calif., 1979-90; bd. dirs. Col. Nurses Task Force, Col. League Nursing, 1994-95; mem. adv. bd. Flint Ctr., Cupertino, Calif. Mem. NAFE (adv. bd. bus. woman's mag. 1981-86), Peninsula Profl. Women's Network, Nat. Speaker's Assn. (bd. dirs.), WISH List (bd. dirs. 1998-2002), Colo. Ind. Pubs. Assn. (bd. dirs. 2000-, pres. 2002-05), Gilda's Club (Denver bd. dirs. 2001-04, pres., v.p.). Independent. Office Phone: 303-627-9179. Personal E-mail: DrJBriles@aol.com. Business E-Mail: judith@briles.com.

BRILL, MARILYN, community-based collaboration consultant; b. Inglewood, Calif., July 11, 1947; d. Glenn Edwin and Dorothea Maxine (Burling) Facka; m. David R. Brill, June 17, 1972. BA, Austin Coll., Sherman, Tex., 1969; MAT, Duke U., 1970; MA, Bloomsburg (Pa.) U., 1982. Pres. LWV of Pa., Harrisburg, 1987-91; bd. dirs. LWV of U.S., Washington, 1992-96, 1st v.p., 1996-98; ptnr., internat. observer 1996 Bosnia election Groupworks Cons., Lewisburg, Pa., 1998—. Sec., bd. dirs. Pa. Women's Campaign Fund, Harrisburg, 1991—. Deacon, Grove Presbyn. Ch., Danville, Pa., 1984—. Recipient Outstanding Woman award Columbia/Montour Counties Women's Conf., 1984. Mem. LWV of Danville Area (Anna E. Strawbridge honor 1991). Democrat. Avocations: running, tennis, swimming, biking. Office: 202 S 3rd St Lewisburg PA 17837-1912 Home: 119 S 3rd St Lewisburg PA 17837-1909 E-mail: MFBrillgroupworks@worldnet.att.net.

BRILL, YVONNE CLAEYS, engineer, consultant; b. St. Norbert, Manitoba, Can., Dec. 30, 1924; d. August and Julienne (Carette) Claeys; m. William Franklin Brill, Dec. 15, 1951; children: Naomi, Matthew, Joseph. BS, U. Manitoba, Canada, 1945; MS, U. So. Calif., 1951. Mathematician Douglas Aircraft, Santa Monica, Calif., 1945-46; research analyst Rand Corp., Santa Monica, 1946-49; group leader Marquardt Corp., Van Nuys, Calif., 1949-52; staff engr. UTC Research, East Hartford, Conn., 1952-55; project engr. Wright Aeronautical, Wood Ridge, NJ, 1955-58; mgr. propulsion systems RCA AstroElectronics, Princeton, NJ, 1966-81, staff engr., 1983-86; mgr. solid rocket motor NASA Hdqrs., Washington, 1981-83; with space engring segment Internat. Maritime Satellite Orgn., London, 1986-91; cons. Brill Assocs., Skillman, NJ, 1991—. Mem. USAF Sci. Adv. Bd., Washington, 1982-83, Nat. Acad. Engring.; Com. on Internat. Orgns. and Programs, 1992-96; apptd. mem. aerospace safety adv. panel NASA, 1994-2001. Contbr. articles to sci. jours.; patentee in field. Recipient Engr. of Yr. award, Ctrl. Jersy Engring. Couns., 1979, Diamond Superwoman award, Harpers Bazaar/DeBeers Corp., 1980, Disting. Pub. Svc. medal, NASA, 2001, Judith A. Resnik award, IEEE, 2002. Fellow AIAA (Marvin C. Demlar award 1983, WYLD award in rocket propulsion 2002), Soc. Women Engrs. (dir. student affairs 1979-80, 83-84, treas. 1980-81, Engring. Achievement award 1986, Resnik Challenger medal 1993); mem. Nat. Acad. Engring., Internat. Astronautical Acad. (academician, edn. com. 1983-85), Sigma Xi, Tau Beta Pi. Home and Office: 914 Route 518 Skillman NJ 08558-2616

BRILMAYER, R. LEA, lawyer, educator; b. 1950; BA, U. Calif.-Berkeley, 1970, JD, 1976; LLM, Columbia U., 1978. Bar: Tex. 1978. Assoc. in law Columbia U, 1976—78; asst. prof. law U. Tex., 1978—79, U. Chgo., Chgo., 1979—81, prof., 1991; vis. prof. Yale U., New Haven, 1981—82, Nathan Baker prof., 1986—91, Howard M. Holtzmann prof. Internat. Law, 1998—; Benjamin F. Butler prof. NYU, NYC, 1991—97. Author: Justifying International Acts, 1989, American Hegemony: Political Morality in a One Superpower World, 1994, Conflict of Laws: Foundation and Future Directions, 1995. Office: Yale U Dept Law PO Box 208215 New Haven CT 06520 E-mail: lea.brilmayer@yale.edu.

BRINDEL, JILL RACHUY, cellist; b. Chgo., Jan. 17, 1950; d. Bernard A. and June (Rachuy) B.; m. William Louis Klingelhoffer, July 30, 1972; children: Sarah Brindel Klingelhoffer, Louis Brindel Klingelhoffer. Student, Ind. U., 1968-70; B.M. (Tanglewood scholar), Roosevelt U., 1974. Asst. prin. cellist Chgo. Lyric Opera, 1974-76; mem. Chgo. Grant Park Orch., 1974-78; prin. cellist Chgo. Contemporary Chamber Players, 1974-77, Chgo. performances Joffrey Ballet, Am. Ballet Theater, N.Y.C. Ballet and Internat. Ballet Festival, 1975-79; mem. Houston Symphony, 1979-80; prin. cellist Joffrey Ballet, San Francisco, 1981; cellist San Francisco Symphony, 1981—; appeared on 5 nationally broadcast chamber concerts Chamber Music Sundaes, 1982; recitalist Chgo. Musical Coll., ann. 1972-75, 78, North Shore Music Ctr., 1971, Houston, 1978, 79, Old First Series, San Francisco, 1982, 83; prin. cellist Mendocino Music Festival, 1987—94; mem. Navarro Trio in residence Sonoma State U., 1990—. Recipient prizes Union Civic League, 1978; recipient prizes William C. Byrd competition, 1976, prizes Chgo. Musical Coll. Concerto competition, 1972, 73, prizes Dumas String award, 1972, prizes Evansville competition, 1972, prizes Crescendo Music Club, 1972, Farwell award, 1972 Mem. Am. Fedn. Musicians Office: care San Francisco Symphony Van Ness And Hayes St San Francisco CA 94102

BRINDEL, JUNE RACHUY, writer; b. Little Rock, Iowa, June 5, 1919; d. Otto L. and Etta Mina (Balster) Rachuy; m. Bernard Brindel, Aug. 26, 1939; children: Sylvia Mina, Paul, Jill. BA, U. Chgo., 1945, MA, 1958. Prof. English Wright Coll., Chgo., 1958-81. Tchr. drama Nat. Music Camp, Interlochen, Mich., 1957—67. Author: Luap, 1971, Ariadne, 1980 (nominee Pultizer prize), Phaedra, 1985, Nobody is Ever Missing, 1984; editor: Bernard Brindel, Who Wore at His Heart the Fire's Center, 1999; contbr. short stories and poems to jours. Recipient C. S. Lewis prize, Ind. U., 1973, Lit. award, Ill. Arts Coun., Chgo., 1985; fellow, 1984, 1985. Mem.: The Writers, Soc. Midland Authors, Phi Beta Kappa. Home: 2740 Lincoln Ln Wilmette IL 60091-2234

BRINGMAN, DEBRA ANN, music educator; b. Fostoria, Ohio, Jan. 13, 1959; d. Donald Henry and Doris Maxine Bringman. BA in Music Edn., Bowling Green State U., Ohio, 1981; MEd in Leadership, Wright State U., Dayton, Ohio, 1996. Vocal music tchr. Tipp City Schs., Ohio, 1981—; asst. dir., sect. leader Gear City Sweet Adelines, Dayton, Ohio, 1985—; music leadership team Sweet Adelines Region 4, Ohio, Ind., Ky. Mem.: Am. Choral Dirs. Assn., Ohio Choral Dirs. Assn., Music Edn. Nat. Conf., Ohio Music Edn. Assn. (vocal/choral adjudicator 1996—, pres. dist. XI, chair Choral 2007 Conf., mem. choral selection com.). Avocations: travel, barbershop quartets, reading.

BRINK, EMILY RUTH, music educator; b. Grand Rapids, Mich., Oct. 21, 1940; d. Ralph Jacob and Minnie Brink. BA, Calvin Coll., Grand Rapids, Mich., 1962; MusM, U. Mich., Ann Arbor, 1964; PhD, Northwestern U., Evanston, Ill., 1980. Tchr. Manhattan Christian Sch., Mich., 1964—66; asst. prof. music SUNY, New Paltz, 1966—67, Trinity Christian Coll., Palos Heights, Ill., 1967—74; asst. prof. music theory U. Ill., Champaign-Urbana, 1974—83; editor CRC Pubs., Grand Rapids, 1983—2004; sr. rsch. fellow Calvin Inst. Christian Worship, 2002—. Dean Am. Guild Organists, Grand Rapids, 2005—06. Editor: Psalter Humnal, 1987, Sing! Anew Creation, 2001. Fellow: Hymn Soc. U.S. and Can. (pres, 1990—92). Office: Calvin Inst Christian Worship 1855 Knollcrest Cir Grand Rapids MI 49546-4402

BRINK, MARION ALICE, retired human resources specialist; b. Boston, Feb. 15, 1928; d. Martin Bernhard and Astrid Marie (Bjaastad) Windedal; m. A. Rudie Shobaken, Feb. 5, 1947 (div. 1963); children: Richard Michael Shobaken, Ron Eric Shobaken; m. James A. Brink, Jan. 29, 1977. Student, Cambridge Jr. Coll., 1945—47, Framingham State Coll., 1967, Boston U., 1967—69; BA, U. N.H., 1983, MLS, 2001; M in Theol. Studies, Harvard U., Cambaridge, Mass., 1987. From lab tech. to chemist Liberty Mut. Rsch., Hopkinton, Mass., 1963-77; asst. to mgr. Rec. Sec. Office Harvard U., 1977-79; sec. Sloan Sch. MIT, 1980-82; owner tech. typing svc. New Castle, NH, 1982-84; counseling intern Green Pastures Counseling Ctr., Dover, NH, 1984-85; alcohol educator Freedom From Chem. Dependency Found., Inc., Needham, Mass., 1985-87, dir. devel., editor News Bulletin, 1987-88; ptnr. Palmerbrink, Charlestown, Mass., 1989-90; founder MB Assocs., Charlestown, 1991-96; ret., 1996. Mem. Harvard Inst. Learning in Ret., U. N.H. Marine Docent Program. Bd. dirs. Friends Metro Boston, Inc.; counselor Women's Resource Ctr., Portsmouth, 1980. Democrat. Unitarian Universalist. Avocations: sailing, women's studies, reading, spiritual development. Home: 579 Sagamore Ave Unit 15 Portsmouth NH 03801-5567

BRINKER, NANCY GOODMAN, social services administrator, former ambassador; b. Peoria, Ill., 1946; m. Norman Brinker; 1 child, Eric. B in Sociology, U. Ill., 1968; PhD (hon.), Southern Meth. U. Founder Susan G. Komen Breast Cancer Found., 1982—, Race for the Cure fitness/walk fundraising event, 1983—; founder, chair, CEO In Your Corner, Inc., 1994—98; US amb. to Hungary US Dept. State, Budapest, 2001—03. Spkr. in field; advocate for women's health issues in Congress; collaborating ptnr., Nat. Dialogue on Cancer; bd. dirs. LHC Group, Inc., 2006- Author: The Race is Run One Step at a Time, 1995; co-author: 1000 Questions About Women's Health; articles published in nat. and internat. media. Bd. dirs. Physicians Reliance Network, Harvard Sch. Pub. Health, NYU Med. Sch. Found., Nat. Surg. Adjuvant Breast Project, Susan Komen Breast Cancer Found., Palm Beach Fellowship of Christians and Jews, Manpower, Inc., 2004-, US Oncology, Inc., Netmarket, Inc., Meditrust Corp.; mem. Nat. Cancer Adv. Bd.; bd. govs. Nat. Jewish Coalition.; mem. adv. bd. Harvard Ctr. for Cancer Prevention, Women's Health Initiative, Nat. Coalition of Cancer Suvivorship, Nat. Cancer Inst. Recipient Jefferson award for Hero award Coping Mag., 1996, Pub. Svc. award Oncology Nursing Soc., 1996, Greatest Pub. Svc. by a Pvt. Citizen, Am. Inst. Pub. Svc., 1997, Lifetime Achievement award Nat. Breast Cancer Awareness Month, 1997, Albert Einstein's Sarnoff Vol. award, Humanitarian of Yr. award Mt. Sinai, James Ewing Layman's award, Soc. Surg. Oncology, Humanitarian of Yr. award Rep. Women's Leadership Forum, Healthcare Humanitarian award, Global Conf. Inst., Tex. Gov. award, outstanding nat. svc., the first Salomon Smith Barney Extraordingary Achievement award, Champion of Prevention award, Nat. Found. for Ctrs. for Disease Control, internat. achievements in support of breast cancer rsch., Sword of Ignatius Loyola award, St. Louis Univ., Spl. Recognition award, Am. Soc. Clin. Oncology, Caring award, 1999, Cino del Duca award, 2000, Toastmasters Internat. Top Five Speakers award, 2001, Lifetime Achievement award, Sisters Network, 2001, Mary Woodward Lasker Pub. Svc. award in Support of Med. Rsch. & the Health Sciences, Lasker Found., 2005, Global Pathfinder award, Am. Soc. Breast Disease, 2006; named EVIE Profl. of the Yr., Profl. & Bus. Forum, 2005; named one of 100 Most Important Women of 20th Century, Ladies Home Jour., 25 Most Powerful Women in Am., Biography Mag., Top 10 Champions of Women's Health, Ladies Home Jour.; named to Cancer Rsch. and Treatment Fund, Inc. Cancer Survivors Hall of Fame. Mailing: Susan G Komen Breast Cancer Foundation PO Box 650309 Dallas TX 75265-0309*

BRINKLEY, AMY WOODS, bank executive; b. Franklin, Va., Jan. 19, 1956; d. Samuel Baker and Iris (Lankford) Woods; m. Robert Gentry Brinkley, Jan. 2, 1988; 2 children. BA, U. NC, Chapel Hill, 1978. Credit analyst NCNB, Charlotte, NC, 1978-79, internat. banking officer, 1979-80, comml. banking officer Greensboro, NC, 1981-84, credit policy officer, 1985-87; sr. consumer credit policy exec. NationsBank (formerly NCNB), Greensboro, 1988—93; exec. v.p., sr. consumer credit policy exec. NationsBank, 1990—99, mktg. grp. exec., 1993—99; pres. consumer products. Bank Am. (formerly NationsBank), 1999—2001; chmn. risk policy Bank Am., 2001—02, dep. head risk mgmt., 2001—02, global risk exec., 2002—. Bd. dirs. Carolinas HealthCare Sys., Pvt. Export Funding Co.; bd. trustees Princeton Theol. Sem. Bd. trustees Princeton Theol. Seminary; bd. advisors Partners in Out-of-Sch. Time, NC Dance Theatre, former chmn., bd. trustees; mem. U. NC bd. visitors. Named one of The 25 Most Powerful Women in Banking, US Banker mag., 2004, 2005, Most Powerful Women in Bus., Fortune mag., 2005, 50 Most Powerful Women in Bus., 2006. Mem. Women's Profl. Forum, Risk Mgmt. Roundtable, RMA Consumer Credit Execs., Phi Beta Kappa. Office: Bank Am 100 N Tryon St 18th Fl Charlotte NC 28255*

BRINKLEY, CHRISTIE, model, spokesperson, designer; b. LA, Feb. 2, 1954; d. Don and Marge B.; m. Jean François Allaux, 1974 (div. 1981); m. Billy Joel, 1985 (div. 1994); 1 child, Alexa Ray; m. Ricky Taubman, 1995 (div. 1995) 1 child Jack Paris; m. Peter Cook, 1996 (separated 2006); 1 child Sailor Lee. Attended, U. Calif., Northridge, La Grande Chaumiere. Model Elite Model Mgmt., Ford Models Inc., 1982—; co-owner Christie Brand Cosmetics, 1995—. Spokeswoman Nuskin Internat. Modeled for over 500 mag. covers incl. Sports Illustrated's annual swimsuit issue, 1979, 80, 81; product promotions incl. longest cosmetic contract with Cover Girl, Prell, Chanel No. 19 perfume; pub. Christie Brinkley's Outdoor Beauty and Fitness Book, 1983; appearance (film) National Lampoon's Vacation, 1983, Vegas Vacation, 1997, (video) Billy Joel's "Uptown Girl", River of Dreams, Keepin the Faith, Matter of Trust, (TV) Mad About You, 1994; designed album cover Billy Joel's "River of Dreams"; active infomercials Total Gym; past host Living in the 90's with Christie Brinkley CNN, others. Office: Ford Models Inc 142 Green St New York NY 10012 also: William Morris Agy 1325 Avenue Of The Americas New York NY 10019-6026*

BRINKLEY, EDNA, psychologist, consultant; b. Warthen, Ga., Sept. 4, 1959; d. Hugh Matthew and Lillie Mae (Reese) Brinkley; m. Katherine Michelle Davis, Dec. 18, 2003. AAS, North Harris C.C., Houston, 1980; BA Psychology cum laude, U. Tex., 1994, PhD Counseling Psychology magna cum laude, 2001. Lic. psychologist Tex., cert. trainer for anti-discrimination response tng. U. B.C., Vancouver, 2005. Field svc. technician Panafax Corp., Houston and Los Alamitos, Calif., 1980—83; tchr. EFL Tokyo Ctr. For Lang. and Culture, Kawai Juku, 1984—88; intern Temple, Tex., 2000—01; resident psychology Southwestern U./Fed. Correctional Inst.-Bastrop, Georgetown and Bastrop, Tex., 2001—03; lectr. Tex. State U., San Marcos, 2004; pvt. practice Austin, 2004—; founder, owner Cultural Solutions, 2005—. Presenter in field. Author: Managing Stress in Interpersonal Relationships for Female Students, 2000. Fellow, U. Tex., Austin, 1995—98. Mem.: ACA, APA (named Minority Undergraduate Student of Excellence 1994), Nat. Inst. Multicultural Competence, Diversity Inst., Tex. Psychol. Assn. Avocations: travel, hiking, languages, genealogy, gardening. Office: Cultural Solutions PO Box 204404 Austin TX 78720-4404 Office Phone: 512-680-2874. Personal E-mail: drbrinkley@austin.rr.com.

BRINKLEY, GLENDA WILLIS, medical, surgical, and women's health nurse; b. Gore Springs, Miss., Dec. 23, 1961; d. Stark Willis and Loree Conley; m. Timothy L. Brinkley, Sept. 15, 1984; children: Victoria Celeste, Tia Danielle. BSN, Miss. U. for Women, 1987; BS in Biology, Miss. Valley U., 1984. RN Miss. Nurse mgr. Clay County Med. Ctr. Named to Outstanding Young Women of Am., 1987. Mem. Miss. Nurses Assn., Assn. Women's Health, Obstetrics, and Neonatal Nursing.

BRINSON, MONICA EVETTE, mental health specialist, pharmaceutical sales representative; b. Hackensack, NJ, Feb. 19, 1971; d. Attichous and Gladys Brinson. BA, Rowan U., 1994. Lic. health and life ins. Acct. exec. Total Media, Hackensack, NJ, 1994—98; ins. sales rep. Aetna U.S. Health Care, Fairfield, NJ, 1998—99; profl. sales rep. Solvay Pharms., mental health specialist. Mem.: Women in Careers, Delta Zeta. Avocations: travel, golf, running. Office: Sanofi-Synthelabo Pharms 90 Park Ave New York NY 10016 Home: Unit 1H 3050 Edwin Ave Fort Lee NJ 07024

BRINSON, VIDA L., counselor; b. Valparaiso, Fla., Feb. 26, 1950; d. Rosier Eugene and Mary Belle Cuchens; m. Aaron D. Brinson, Oct. 20, 1972; children: Adam D., Amy L. Rasz. BA, U. West Fla., 1972, MEd, 1986, MA in Psychology, 2002. Lic. mental health counselor Fla., cert. tchr. Fla. Tchr. Freeport (Fla.) H.S., 1981—88; mathmetician Eglin AFB, Fla., 1988—99; mental health counselor Chautauqua Offices Psychotherapy and Evaluation, Inc., DeFuniak Springs, Fla., 2001—. Mem. adv. bd. Bd. Edn., Freeport, 1985—88. Named Outstanding Tech. Civilian of Yr., 1st Space Wing, U.S. Space Commd., 1990. Mem.: Am. Assn. Christian Counselors, Am. Counseling Assn., Gamma Beta Phi. Methodist. Office: Chautauqua Offices Psychotherapy and Evaluation 3686 Hwy 331 South Defuniak Springs FL 32435

BRINTNALL, CHARLENE MAY, special education educator; b. Alva, Okla., Feb. 21, 1938; d. Charles W. and May E. (Walker) Cunningham; m. Dean W. Brintnall, May 14, 1960; children: Ray, Sheila. BS in Edn., N.W. Okla. State U., 1960; MS in Spl. Edn., Wichita State U., 1974. Tchr. Kiowa (Kans.) Elem. Sch., 1960-63; tchr. spl. edn. South Ctrl. Kans. Spl. Edn. Coop., Iuka, Kans., 1971—. Home: 809 S 5th St Kiowa KS 67070-9100

BRINTON, LOUISE A., cancer epidemiologist; MPH in Epidemiology, U. NC, Chapel Hill; PhD in Epidemiology, Johns Hopkins Sch. Hygiene and Pub. Health, 1979. Staff fellow Nat. Cancer Inst., 1976, acting chief environ. studies sect., 1984, chief environ. epidemiology br., 1996, sr. investigator, chief hormonal and reproductive epidemiology br.; postdoctoral rschr. U. Oxford. Contbr. articles to profl. jours. Recipient Spl. Recognition award, Pub. Health Svc., Director's award, NIH. Mem.: Soc. Epidemiologic Rsch. (pres. 1990). Office: Nat Cancer Inst Divsn Cancer Epidemiology and Genetics 6120 Exec Blvd MSC 7242 Exec Plz S Rm 7068 Bethesda MD 20892-7335 E-mail: brintonl@mail.nih.gov.*

BRIODY, LYNN, municipal official; b. Bklyn., Sept. 30, 1941; d. Arthur and Marie (Fitzgerald) Skur; m. James Francis Briody, May 28, 1966; children: Jennifer, Kevin. BS, Fordham U., 1966; MA, NYU, 1969; postgrad., Harvard U., 1983. Adminstrv. asst. NYU, N.Y.C., 1967—69; budget coord. U. So. Calif., LA, 1969—70; rsch. analyst U. Santa Clara, Calif., 1970—72; coun. mem. City Coun., Sunnyvale, Calif., 1979—81, vice mayor, 1981—83, mayor, 1983—84; vice chmn. cmty., housing and econ. devel. com. League Calif. Cities, Sacramento, 1980—. Vice chmn., mem. cmty. and econ. devel. steering com. Nat. League Cities, Washington, 1983—. Chmn., mem. Local Agy. Formation Commn. Santa Clara County, Calif., 1980—82; planning commn. City of Sunnyvale Calif., 1977—79; bd. dirs. LWV, Cupertino-Sunnyvale, Calif., 1973—75. Mem.: Calif. Elected Women in Edn. and Rsch. Democrat. Roman Cath. Office: City of Sunnyvale City Of Sunnyvale 456 Sunnyvale CA 94086

BRION, NORMA M., real estate broker; arrived in U.S., 1967; d. Jose Mendoza and Consolacion Pesongco Mendoza; m. Benny Brion (div.); 1 child, Werner. BS in Pharmacy, U. Santo Tomas, Philippines, 1960; cert., Elyria Meml. Hosp., Ohio, 1962; lic. in real estate, Am. Real Estate Acad., 1980, lic. in broker, 1980. Lab. supr. St. Anne's Hosp., Fall River, Mass., 1984—86; broker Pacheco Real Estate, Fall River. Mem.: Nat. Assn. Realtors, Mass. Assn. Realtors, Greater Fall River Bd. Realtors. Avocations: gardening, aerobics, swimming, photography. Home: 3200 County St 328B Somerset MA 02726 Office: Pacheco Real Estate 411 Columbia St Fall River MA 02721

BRIOSO-MESA, MAUREEN DIANE, mental health services professional; b. Queens, N.Y., Aug. 24, 1975; d. Esther Estela and Hugo Alberto Brioso. MSc with distinction, Carlos Albizu U., Miami, 2002. Lic. mental health counselor, cert. nat. counselor. Outpatient counselor Children's Psychiat. Ctr., Miami, 2001—02; counselor Family Resource Ctr., Miami, 2002—03; child therapist The Village, Miami, 2003—04; behavioral health therapist Family Counseling Svcs., Miami, 2004, clin. supr., 2005—06; care mgr. Magellan Behavioral Health Svcs., Doral, Fla., 2006—. Mem.: Nat. Bd. Cert. Counselors, Fla. Assn. Play Therapy (corr.; Miami-Dade chpt. chair profl. devel. 2006), Assn. Play Therapy (corr.), Fla. Mental Health Counselor Assn. (corr.), Am. Mental Health Counseling Assn. (corr.). Office: Magellan Behavioral Health Svcs Doral FL Office Phone: 800-424-1693.

BRISBON, ADA VANESSA, assistant principal; d. John Bernard and Ada Lovinia Holliday; children: Juanita Nicole, Sierra Bernadette Scott. BS, Coppin State Coll., Balt., Md., 1982; MS, Cavelier Coll., Towson, Md., 1983. Tchr. spl. edn. Balt. City Pub. Schs., 1983—2003, asst. prin., 2003—. Office: Woodlawn Mid Sch 3033 St Lukes Ln Baltimore MD 21207-4498

BRISCAR-MARTEL, NANCY MARIE, agent, musician, educator; b. Cleve., Nov. 4, 1966; d. Richard Vincent and Rosanna Marie Briscar; m. Robert Michael Martel, Nov. 26, 1994. MusB, Baldwin Wallace Coll. Conservatory Music, 1990. Agt., mgr. Apollo String Quartet, Cleve., 1985—; pvt. instr. violin, viola and voice Cleve., 1986—; dir. Great No. Mall Christmas Choir, N. Olmsted, Ohio, 1988—91; pres., co-owner Tritone Prodns. Inc., Cleve., 1990—95; dir. music Rockport United Meth. Ch., Rocky River, Ohio, 1995—; adjudicator Omea Solo and Ensemble Competitions, Ohio, 1997—. Vocal soloist St. John's Cathedral, Cleve., 1987—89, Swing Time Big Band, Cleve., 1989—90; vocalist Cleve. Chamber Singers, 1996—97; violist in concert with Roberta Flack, Peabo Bryson, Jeffrey Osborne and Patty Austin, Cleve., 1992, in concert with Rosemary Clooney and Debby Boone, Erie, Pa., 1996, Apollo String Quartet, Cleve., 1985—2001, in concert with Roy Clark, Mansfield, Ohio, 1996, in concert with Yes, Richfield, 2001, in concert with Irish Tenors, Cleve., 2001; mem. symphony, Mansfield, Ohio, 1990—96, Wheeling, W.Va., 1990—96; violist in concert with Tony Bennett, 2002. Dir.: (theatrical production) Red, Hot and Cole, 1996, Anything Goes, 1997; author: numerous poems. Recipient Editor's Choice award, Nat. Libr. Poetry, 1999. Mem.: Nat. Assn. Music Educators, Ohio Music Educators Assn., Am. Fedn. Musicians, Nat. Assn. Women's Bus. Owners, Omicron Delta Kappa. Roman Catholic. Avocations: scrapbooks, rubber stamping, reading. Office: 3301 Wooster Rd Rocky River OH 44116-4181 Personal E-mail: nancy@apollostrings.com. Business E-Mail: RUMC44116@aol.com.

BRISCOE, ANNE M., retired science educator; b. N.Y.C., Dec. 1, 1918; m. William A. Briscoe, Aug. 20, 1955 (dec. Dec. 1985); m. Theodore H. Heinly Sr., Jan. 21, 1989 (dec. Dec. 2002). MA, Vassar Coll., 1945; PhD, Yale U., 1949. From rsch. assoc. to asst. prof. Cornell U. Med. Coll., N.Y.C., 1950-56; faculty Columbia U. Coll. Physicians and Surgeons, N.Y.C., 1956—, prof. emeritus, 1987. Spl. lectr., 1987-89; lectr. Harlem Hosp. Center Sch. Nursing, 1968-77; adj. asst. prof. Hunter Coll., 1951-64, 73-75; mem. N.Y.C. Commn. on Status of Women, 1979-93, vice chair, 1982-93; non-govtl. orgn. del. to UN; adv. coun. Inst. Nuc. Power Ops., 1979-84. Contbr. articles to profl. jours. Sterling Jr. fellow, USPHS fellow, Yale U., 1949; recipient Yale medal, 1986, Susan B. Anthony award, 1989, Wilbur Cross medal Yale Grad. Sch. Sesquicentennial Convocation, 1997, Yale Fund Chmns. award, 2000. Fellow: AAAS (mem. coun. 1982—85, chmn.'s award Yale Alumni Fund 2001), Assn. Women in Sci. (editor newsletter 1971—74, nat. pres. 1974—76), N.Y. Acad. Sci. (chair women in sci. com. 1978—92, bd. govs. 1981), Am. Inst. Chemists (sec. N.Y. chpt. 1981—83); mem.: ACS, Assn. Women in Sci. Ednl. Found. (pres. 1978—82), Fedn. Orgns. for Profl. Women (treas. 1978—80), Harvey Soc., Am. Fedn. Clin. Rsch., Am. Soc. Clin. Nutrition, Yale Grad. Sch. Alumni Assn. (pres. 1981—86), Assn. Yale Alumni (assembly rep. 1978—, bd. govs. 1982—85). Home: 2116 Sea Cres Ruskin FL 33570-6128 E-mail: drannieb@aol.com.

BRISCOE, MARY BECK, federal judge; b. Council Grove, Kans., Apr. 4, 1947; m. Charles Arthur Briscoe. BA, U. Kans., 1969, JD, 1973; LLM, U. Va., 1990. Rsch. asst. Harold L. Haun, Esq., 1973; atty.-examiner fin. divsn. ICC, 1973—74; asst. U.S. atty. for Wichita and Topeka, Kans. Dept. Justice, 1974—84; judge Kans. Ct. Appeals, 1984—95, chief judge, 1990—95; judge U.S. Ct. Appeals (10th cir.), Topeka, 1995—. Named to Women's Hall of Fame, Univ. Kans., 2001; recipient Univ. Kans. Law Soc. Disting. Alumnus award, 2000. Fellow: Kans. Bar Found., Am. Bar Found.; mem.: ABA, Women Attys. Assn. Topeka, Kans. Bar Assn. (Outstanding Svc. award 1992), Topeka Bar Assn., Nat. Assn. Women Judges, Am. Judicature Soc., U. Kans. Law Soc., Kans. Hist. Soc., Washburn Law Sch. Assn. (hon.). Office: US Ct Appeals 10th Cir 645 Massachusetts Ste 400 Lawrence KS 66044-2235 also: US Ct Appeals 10th Cir Byron White US Courthouse 1823 Stout St Denver CO 80257*

BRISKIN, JACQUELINE ELIZABETH, author; b. London; came to U.S., 1938, naturalized, 1944; d. Spencer and Marjorie Orgell; m. Bert Briskin, May 9, 1948; children— Ralph, Elizabeth, Richard. Author: (novels) California Generation, 1970; Afterlove, 1974; Rich Friends, 1976; Paloverde, 1978; The Onyx, 1982; Everything and More, 1983; Too Much Too Soon, 1985, Dreams Are Not Enough, 1987, The Naked Heart, The Other Side of Love, 1991, The Crimson Palace, 1995. Recipient LMV Peer award, 1985. Mem. Authors Guild, PEN.

BRISKIN, MADELEINE, oceanographer, paleontologist; b. Paris, Sept. 4, 1932; came to U.S., 1951, naturalized, 1956; d. Michel and Mina B. BS, CCNY, 1965; MS, U. Conn., 1967; PhD, Brown U., 1973. Prof. geology Geology-Physics Bldg., U. Cin., 1980—. Recipient award Rsch. Support, 1971-72, Support award NSF, 1978. Mem. AAAS, Am. Geophys. Union, Am. Quaternary Assn., Climap, Cin. Engrs. and Scientists Soc., Planetary Soc., Soc. Sci. Exploration, Woods Hole Oceanographic Instn., Lamont-Doherty Geol. Obs., N.Y. Acad. Scis., Sigma Xi. Achievements include discovery of 430,000 plus years astronomical cycle in deep-sea sediments; development of pulsating earth model. Office: U Cin Dept Geology Cincinnati OH 45221-0001

BRISMAN, JENNIFER, event planning executive; BA in Exercise & Sport Sci., George Wash. U. Event planner GANZI Prodns., Prodn. Group Internat., NYC; sr. conf. prodr. Internat. Comm. Mgmt., summit dir. fin., banking & ins. divsn.; founder, pres. jennifer brisman weddings newyork inc., NYC. Mem.: NY Women in Comm. Office: Jennifer Brisman Weddings NY Inc 128 E 62d St No 1 New York NY 10021 Office Phone: 212-588-0007. E-mail: info@theweddingplanner.com.

BRISSETTE, MARTHA BLEVINS, lawyer; b. Salisbury, Md., Apr. 30, 1959; d. Reuben Wesley and Miriam Rebecca (Walters) Blevins; m. Henry Joseph Brissette III, May 24, 1980; children: Madeline Rose, William Roy. BA, U. Richmond, 1981, JD, 1983. Bar: Va. 1983, U.S. Supreme Ct. 1987. Law clk. Supreme Ct. Va., Richmond, 1983-84; atty. Dept. Justice, Washington, 1984-88; staff atty. Office of the Exec. Sec., Supreme Ct. Va., Richmond, Va., 1988; asst. atty. gen. Office of the Atty. Gen. of Va., Richmond, 1989-92; atty., v.p. counsel Lawyers Title Ins. Corp., Richmond, 1992-97; asst. counsel State Farm Ins. Cos., 1997-99; asst. atty. gen. Office of Atty. Gen. of Va., Richmond, 1999—2001; pvt. practice Richmond, 2002—05; assoc. Ukrops Supermarkets, Inc., 2004—05; atty. Va. Divsn. Legis. Svcs., Richmond, 2005—. Mem.: Richmond Bar Assn. Roman Catholic. Avocation: cake decorating. Home: 8307 Forge Rd Richmond VA 23228-3127 Office Phone: 804-786-3591. Business E-Mail: marthabbrissette@justice.com, mbrissette@leg.state.va.us.

BRISTAH, PAMELA JEAN, librarian; b. Highland Park, Mich., May 13, 1956; d. James Werner and Emily Ann (Josif) B.; m. David Dukehart Wright, July 20, 1984. MusB, Westminster Choir Coll., 1978; MLS, Columbia U., 1985. Cataloger Manhattan Sch. Music, N.Y.C., 1985-88, head libr., 1988—. Author: A Basic Music Library, 3d edit., 1997. Mem. Music Libr. Assn. Avocation: photography. Office: Manhattan Sch Music 120 Claremont Ave New York NY 10027-4698

BRISTER, GLORIA NUGENT, small business owner, elementary school educator; b. Dry Prong, La., Apr. 10, 1926; d. Floyd P. and Vergie W. Nugent; m. C. W. Brister, Jr., Mar. 28, 1946; 1 child, Mark Allen. BS, La. Coll., Pineville, 1947; postgrad., Columbia U., NYC, 1962; MEd, Tex. Christian U., Ft. Worth, 1973; postgrad., U. London, 1974. Tchr. home econs. La Fargue HS, Effie, La., 1947—49, Rosemont Mid. Sch., Ft. Worth, 1958—62; tchr. DeZavala Elem. Sch., Ft. Worth, 1964—68, J.T. Stevens Elem. Sch., Ft. Worth, 1968—71; math. clinician, resource tchr. Ft. Worth Ind. Sch. Dist., 1971—81; founder, CEO Patterns for Living, Ft. Worth, 1980—. Lectr., presenter in field, 1980—. Home: 7905 Vista Ridge Dr N Fort Worth TX 76132-4528

BRISTO, MARCA, human services administrator; b. Albany, N.Y., June 23, 1953; d. Earl C. and Dorothy (Moore) B.; m. J. Robert Kettlewell, Oct. 15, 1988; children: Samuel Clayton Kettlewell, Madeline Elizabeth Kettlewell. BA in Sociology, Beloit Coll., 1974; BSN, Rush Coll. Nursing, Chgo., 1976. Cert. nursing. RN Rush Presbyn. St. Luke's Med. Ctr., Chgo., 1976-77, Northwestern Meml. Hosp., Chgo., 1977, family planning nurse specialist, 1978-79; exec. dir., co-founder Access Living Met. Chgo., 1979-84, pres., CEO, 1984—. Chair Nat. Coun. Disability, Washington, 1994-2002, Ill. Pub. Action Coun., 1989-94, U.S. delegate U.N. world summit on urban living and shelter, 1996, bd. dirs. Disability Funders Network, 2002-. Mem. Pres.'s Com. on Employment of People with Disabilities; mem. Pres.'s Task Force on Employment of Adults with Disabilities; bd. dirs. Rehab. Inst. Chgo.; mem. Leadership Greater Chgo.; mem. The Chgo. Network. Avocations: cooking, travel. Office: Access Living of Metropolitan Chicago 614 W Roosevelt Rd Chicago IL 61614

BRISTOR, KATHERINE M., lawyer; b. Hampton, Va., 1953; BA magna cum laude, Carleton Coll., 1975; JD, Columbia U., 1980. Bar: N.Y. 1981. Ptnr. Skadden, Arps, Slate, Meagher & Flom, N.Y.C. Harlan Fiske Stone scholar. Office: Skadden Arps Slate Meagher & Flom 4 Times Sq Fl 24 New York NY 10036-6595

BRITT, DEBRA L., medical/surgical nurse; b. Corpus Christi, Tex., Mar. 7, 1954; d. Floyd Morris and Thurena B. (Holley) McNutt; children: Jamie Lealan, Nancy Elizabeth; m. Jack Britt, June 18, 2000 (div. Mar. 2005). Diploma, St. John's Sch. Nursing, Springfield, Mo., 1984; student, S.W. Mo. State U., 1982-83. RN, Mo.; cert. med.-surg. nurse, ACLS. Staff nurse Venice (Fla.) Hosp.; staff/charge nurse Tuomey Regional Med. Ctr., Sumter, S.C.; staff nurse S.W. Fla. Regional Med. Ctr., Ft. Myers, St. John's Regional Ctr., Joplin, Mo.; staff/charge nurse Springfield (Mo.) Gen. Hosp., med./surg. nurse; staff/charge nurse Cox Med. Ctr. North, Springfield; nurse Mid South Comprehensive Home Care, Memphis; clin. supr. First Am. Home Care, Arcadia, Fla.; charge nurse Bates Med. Ctr., Bentonville, Ark.; med.-surg. and stepdown supr. Northwest Health Sys.-Benton County, 2003—; staff/charge nurse NW Med. Ctr., Benton City, 2004—05. Recipient Outstanding Ednl. Devel. award, 1984, dist. 9 nominee for Edn. Nurse of the Yr., 1999.

BRITT, DONNA MARIE, school nurse; b. Phila., Oct. 27, 1950; d. Joseph D. and Margaret M. (Cullen) Finn; children: Colleen Marie, Patricia Ann, Joseph James. BA in Biology, Holy Family Coll., 1972, BSN, 1974. Cert. sch. nurse, N.J. Staff nurse Jeannes Hosp., Phila., 1975; tchr. Archdiocese of Phila., 1985-91; sch. nurse Camden City Bd. Edn., NJ, 1991-93; sch. nurse, health tchr. Riverside (N.J.) Bd. edn., 1994-95; sch. nurse City of Burlington, NJ, 1995—. Co-chairperson mid. states com. Camden City Sch., 1991—93. Cons. (book) Tough Love for Teachers, 1989. Merit badge counselor Boy Scouts Am. Frontier Dist., Phila., 1990—; chairperson mid. states com. Our Lady Help Christians, Phila., 1988—91. Named Sch. Nurse of Yr., Burlington County, 2001. Mem.: NEA, Burlington County Edn. Assn., N.J. Edn. Assn., N.J. State Sch. Nurses Assn., Nat. Sch. Nurses Assn., Burlington County Sch. Nurses Assn. Roman Catholic. Avocations: needlecrafts, gardening, art. Home: 9 Primrose Pl Delran NJ 08075-2817 Office: Capt James Lawrence Sch 315 Barclay St Burlington NJ 08016-1737 Office Phone: 609-387-5861.

BRITT, JULIA MOODY, secondary school educator; d. Charles Truman Moody and Lily Hazel (Calloway) Moody Cabe; m. William M. Britt, June 28, 1958; children: Bronwyn Elizabeth Britt Springer, William James, Jeffrey Morris. BS in English/Journalism with high hons., We. Carolina U., 1957; MEd in Guidance/English, U.N.C., 1959; postgrad., U. Tenn., Queens Coll., 1972—. Cert. tchr., N.C. Tchr. high sch. English and journalism East Mecklenburg High Sch., Charlotte, N.C., 1957-58, South Mecklenburg High Sch., Charlotte, 1959-60; kindergarten tchr. U.S. Army DEG Schs., Toul, France, 1960-61; tchr. English, guidance counselor Augsburg Jr. High, Germany, 1961—62; kindergarten tchr. Munich Elem. Sch., Germany, 1962-63; chmn. English dept. Carmel Acad., Charlotte, N.C., 1977-80, Charlotte Country Day Sch., 1980—2002; ret., 2002. Dir. pubs., archivist Ind. Sch., NAIS, 1980-02. Author/editor parent and alumni pubs. for Charlotte Country Day Sch. 1982-88; contbg. author: Rich and Enriching: A Manual for AP English, 1985, USIA Project: American Portfolio, 1988, N.C. State Univ./Russian workshop text, 1990; author: Charlotte Country Day School: The First 50 Years, 1991. Reader AP English exams, Ednl. Testing Svc., Princeton, N.J., 1988-94. J.R. Williams Summer Travel fellow, Trinity Coll., Dublin, 1999. Fellow Cum Laude Soc. (sec. 1992-2002); mem. N.C. English Tchrs. Assn. (ind. sch. rep., bd. dirs. 1990, program chmn./presenter state conf. 1994, pres. 1997-98), Nat. Coun. Tchrs. English (coord. achievement awards in writing 1992-96), Delta Kappa Gamma (mem. world fellowship profl. affairs 1983, pres. 1988-90). Presbyterian. Avocations: reading, writing, travel.

BRITTAIN, NANCY HAMMOND, accountant; b. Athens, Pa., Oct. 29, 1954; d. Charles Avery Hammond and Leona May (Rolls) Mc Creary; m. Edward M. Brittain, Sept. 6, 1975. AS in Bus., Elmira Coll., 1989, BS in Acctg. summa cum laude, 1994. Legal sec. Friedlander, Friedlander, Reizes, Joch & Littman, P.C., Waverly, N.Y., 1973-84; bus. mgr., bd. dirs., pres. Foundry divsn. Ajax X-Ray, Inc., Sayre, Pa., 1984—; pres., bd. dirs. Ajax Leasing Corp. Mem. Athens Borough Zoning Bd., 1991-97. Mem. Inst. Mgmt. Accts., Rotary Internat., Alpha Sigma Lambda (mem. exec. com. Beta Tau chpt., various offices 1988-95). Republican. Methodist. Avocations: gardening, skiing. Home: PO Box 948 132 Vista Dr Sayre PA 18840-1107 Office: Ajax X-Ray Inc Foundry Divsn PO Box 98 Sayre PA 18840-0098

BRITTIN, MARIE E., retired communications, psychology, speech-language and hearing science educator; b. Wichita, Kans. d. F. E. and A. M. Brittin. BS, Northwestern U., 1941; MA, U. Iowa, 1942; PhD, Northwestern U., 1949. Lic. speech pathologist Ohio, Wash. Instr. U. Wis., Madison, 1950—53; coord. comm. disorders Tacoma Pub. Schs., 1956—64; dir. speech-lang. and hearing Coll. Edn. Ohio State U., Columbus, 1964—73, assoc. prof. speech-lang. and hearing sci., 1973—89; ret., 1989. Cons. Kent (Wash.) Pub. Schs., 1991; chair Chauncey D. Leake award for excellence in pharmacology, 1978-90; elected mem. compensation and benefits com. Ohio State U., 1985-89; adj. faculty comm. U. Wash., 1994—; adj. prof. U. Puget Sound, U. Wash., Tacoma; cons., spkr., presenter in field Editor: Ohio Jour. Speech and Hearing, 1984-85; author Family Medicine Management, 2005; contbr. articles to profl. jours. Pres., com. chair Zonta Internat., Tacoma, Columbus. Fellow Am. Speech-Lang.-Hearing Assn. (legis. coun. 1989, 90, 91, site visitor 1982-84, Ace award 1986); mem. APA, Internat. Assn. Logopedics and Phoniatrics, AAAS, Nat. Aphasia Assn., PEO, Christian Med. and Dental Assn., Ohio State U. Faculty Women's Club (pres. 1966-67), Pi Lambda Theta (pub. adv. bd. 1983-85), Delta Kappa Gamma (pres. Alpha Tau chpt. 1964, 2002-04), P.E.O. (chaplain 2002-03). Avocations: gardening, photography, reading. Home: PO Box 1201 Puyallup WA 98371 Office Phone: 253-845-0088.

BRITTON, EMILY MADDOX, sales executive; b. Harris County, Ga., June 21, 1915; d. Charles Baker Maddox and Sara Brown Hudson; m. Joe Britton, June 25, 1935; children: Charles Wayne, Joe Maddox. Diploma, La Grange Bus. Coll., La Grange, Ga. Retail salesperson J.C. Penney, La Grange, Ga., Ala. Vol. with numerous church missions with United meth. Ch. Mem.: Paint Pushers Art Group, DAR, Anchorage Womans Club. Avocation: homemaker, family activities. Home: 1003 D St Anchorage AK 99501

BRITTON, KIM BARNETT, medical/surgical nurse; b. Lubbock, Tex., July 5, 1957; d. Dennison Jones and Carmaleta (Campbell) Barnett; m. Patrick Carl Britton, May 19, 1979; children: Brian Alan, Julie Denise. BSN, West Tex. State U., 1979; MSN, Tex. Tech. U., 2006. RN, Tex. Staff nurse oper. rm. Good Shepherd Med. Ctr., Longview, Tex., 1979-84, staff devel. nurse, coord. health sch., 1984-87, med.-surg. staff nurse, 1989—. Mem.: Am. Nurse Practitioners, Jr. League Longview (pres. 1999—), Sigma Theta Tau. Republican. Baptist. Avocations: reading, walking, volunteering. Personal E-mail: kbbritton@sbcglobal.net.

BRITTON, RUTH ANN WRIGHT, elementary school educator; b. Ft. Smith, Ark., Apr. 4, 1943; d. Ralph M. and Margaret E. (Reising) Wright; m. Joseph D. Britton, Sept. 25, 1965; children: Beth, Meg, Jo. BA in Elem. Edn., Concordia Tchrs. Coll., River Forest, Ill., 1965; MS, Kans. State U., 1978. Cert. in reading K-12, elem. 1-6, developmental reading K-12, developmental edn. Tchr. 5th grade Pickens (S.C.) Sch. Dist., 1966-68; Tchr. grades 5 and 2 Manhattan (Kans.) City Schs., 1969, 77-78; Chpt. I reading tchr. Montgomery County Schs., Christianburg, Va., 1982-86; Dir. Jr. HS reading lab. Hillsborough County Schs., Tampa, Fla., 1986-92; Instr., dept. head Cochise Coll., Douglas, Ariz., 1993—. Co-author: Reading Handbook for Parents, Making Connections, a sociology and reading handbook. Recipient Helping Hands award for vol. svc. U.S. Army 7th Corps in Germany, 1980, Excellence in Edn. by Nat. Inst. for Staff and Organizational Development, 1997-98; named Outstanding Instr. Cochise Coll., 1999-2000, Tchr. of Yr. TCJS, 1989-90. Mem. Internat. Reading Assn., Literacy Vols., Coll. Reading and Learning Assn., Governor's Commn. for Svc. Learning and Volunteerism, 2002-. Office: Cochise Coll 4190 West Highway 80 Douglas AZ 85607

BRITTON, SANDRA LOUCILLE MARY, artist, gallery owner; b. Morelia, Michoachan, Mexico, Apr. 22, 1948; d. Jose Trinidad Absalon Martinez y Ramirez and Rikki Marie Elizabeth (Anderson) Britton. BA, San Diego State U., 1983. came to U.S., 1948. Karate instr. Karate-Do Centre, Del Mar, Calif., 1986-93; graphic artist, project mgr. Ecol. Rsch. Assoc., Del Mar, Calif., 1988-88; artist, gallery owner Sandra Britton Studio/Gallery, Del Mar, Calif., 1988-93; owner Sandra Britton Studio, Pagosa Springs, Colo., 1993—. Judge Carlsbad (Calif.) Art League, 1991; artist, illustrator Jundokan Internat., Spokane, 1987—; instr. Karate Southwest Martial Arts, Pagosa Springs, 1993—; co-owner Western Bio Cons. Represented in five galleries throughout Southwest and Japan; prin. works include ltd. edition print Intergalactic Passage, 1991, An Ancient Point of View, 1994. Mem.: U.S. Karate Assn. Internat. Independent. Avocations: painting, martial arts, hiking, gourmet vegetarian cooking, organic gardening. Home and Studio: 613 Woodgreen Way Nipomo CA 93444 Office Phone: 805-234-3381. Personal E-mail: sandrabritton@verizon.net.

BRITZ LOTTI, DIANE EDWARD, investment company executive; b. York, Pa. June 15, 1952; d. Everett Frank and Billie Jacqueline (Sherrill) Britz; m. Marcello Lotti, Sept. 9, 1978 (dec. Apr. 1990); children: Ariane Elizabeth Lotti, Samantha Alexis Lotti. BA, Duke U., 1974; MBA, Columbia U., 1982. Asst. mgr. Columbia Artists, N.Y.C., 1974-76; gen. mgr. Ea. Music Festival, Greensboro, NC, 1977-78; v.p. Britz Cobin, N.Y.C., 1979-82; pres. Pan Oceanic Mgmt., Inc., 1983-90, Pan Oceanic Advisors, Ltd., 1988-94; chair Pan Oceanic Mgmt. Ltd., 1994-2001; mng. dir. Am. Capital Ptnr., Ltd., 1996—, Erafo Ltd., 2000—; chmn. Trinity Investors Fund Inc.; founding ptnr. Circle Fin. Group LLC, 2003—, vice chmn., 2003—. Bd dirs Trinity Investors Fund Inc, Cir. Fin. LLC. Bd. advisors Turtle Bay Music Sch.; pres. Marcello Lotti Found.; bd. dirs. exec. com. Am. Acad. in Rome; chair Trinity bd. visitors Duke U. Mem.: Explorers Club, Columbia Bus Sch Club NY. Mem. Soc. Of Friends. Office: Circle Financial 17th Fl 650 Madison Ave New York NY 10022

BRIZIUS, JANICE JANE, producer, owner; b. Bainbridge, Ohio, Mar. 21, 1935; d. Robert John and Cora Adina (Head) Judkins; m. David Boone Brizius, July 24, 1954; children: David A., Carol Sue, Barbara Ann, Rebecca Lyn. Student, Ohio U., 1953-54. Part owner The 7 Caves, Bainbridge, Ohio, 1950-80; ptnr. Magi-Promotions, Gahanna, Ohio, 1970—, Magic Motivations, Gahanna, Ohio, 1980—; promoter The Haunted Hills, Bainbridge, 1988—; dir. C.A.M.P., Gahanna, 1956—; promoter, owner Christmas at the Cabin, Bainbridge, 1983—; producer, owner Magic Waters Theatre, Bainbridge, 1985—. Author History of the 7 Caves: composer 40 theme songs for C.A.M.P.; author (musical) Make Her a Star, Broadway on Cave Holler; playwright Head in' West: The Story of Daniel Boone, Mystery of the Apple Orchard: The Story of Johnny Appleseed, It Happened in Greenfield; publisher Happenings in the Hills, 1992- (commendation from Pres. George Bush, Svc. to Youth award 1990). Pres. Chapelfield Elem. PTA, Gahanna, 1968-69; leader Girl Scouts, Gahanna, 1965-66; youth sponsor Gahanna Community Ch., 1956-79, bd. dirs. Recipient Gov.'s award 1973, Svc. to Youth Commendation, 1974, 80, 90, Humanitarian award Successful Meetings Mag., 1993. Mem. South Ohio Tourism Assn. (mktg. dir. 1988-90, v.p. 1990-91). Avocation: music. Home: 7757 Cave Rd Bainbridge OH 45612-9501 Office: Magic Waters Theatre 7757 Cave Rd Bainbridge OH 45612-9501 Office Phone: 513-365-1388. Personal E-mail: dbbjjb@bright.net.

BRO, RUTH HILL, lawyer; b. Brookings, S.D., July 9, 1962; BA, Northwestern U., 1984; JD, U. Chgo., 1994. Atty. McBride Baker & Coles (now Holland & Knight), 1994—99, Baker & McKenzie LLP, Chgo., 1999—2001, ptnr., 2001—. Editor: The E-Bus. Legal Arsenal: Practitioner Agreements and Checklists, 2004; co-author: Online Law, 1996, 6th edit., 2000; mem. editl. bd.: The SciTech Lawyer, ABA, 2004—, Internet Law & Strategy, Am. Lawyer Media, 2005—, exec. editor, chair bd. dir.: The Privacy & Data Protection Legal Reporter, Am. Lawyer Media, 2005—; contbr. articles to profl. jours. Mem.: ABA (founder e-privacy law com., vice chair sci. and tech. law sect., mem. info. security com.), Ill. Bar Assn., Chgo. Bar Assn. (computer law com.). Office: Baker & McKenzie LLP One Prudential Plz 130 East Randolph Dr Chicago IL 60601 Office Phone: 312-861-7985. Business E-Mail: bro@bakernet.com.

BROAD, MARGARET CORBETT (MOLLY BROAD), academic administrator; b. Wilkes-Barre, Pa., Feb. 22, 1941; d. Stanley A. and Margaret (Kelly) Corbett; m. Robert William Broad, Aug. 25, 1962; children: Robert W. Jr., Matthew David. BA in Econs., Syracuse U., 1962, postgrad., 1971; MA in Econs., Ohio State U., 1965. Rsch. assoc. to comptr., v.p. finance Ohio State U., Columbus, 1963—65; budget and planning officer Syracuse U., NY, 1971—76; dep. dir. State Commn. Future of Postsecondary Edn. in N.Y., Albany, 1976—77; v.p. govt. and corp. rels. Syracuse U., 1977—85; exec.

dir., chief exec. officer Ariz. Bd. Regents, Phoenix, 1985—92; sr. vice chancellor adminstrn. and fin. Calif. State U., 1992—93, exec. vice chancellor, COO, 1993—97; chair bd., CEO Calif. State U. Inst., 1994—97; pres. U. N.C., Chapel Hill, 1997—. Mem. bd. trustees Nat. Humanities Ctr., Research Triangle Park; hon. mem. Chapel Hill Preservation Soc., 1997; mem. bd. advisors NC Blumenthal Performing Arts Ctr.; 2000 campaign chairperson Rsch. Triangle United Way, Morrisville, NC. Named Disting. Alumna, Syracuse U.; recipient Woman of Achievement award, Syracuse, 1979, 1990 Leadership Am. award, Leadership Am., 1990, Ann. award, Leadership Calif., 1996, Arents award, Syracuse U., 1999, Tar Heel of Yr. award, U. (Chapel Hill) NC, 2001, Woman of Achievement award, Gen. Fedn. Women's Clubs (Raleigh) NC, Inc., 2003, Alexander Meiklejohn award, AAUP, 2003; fellow, Ohio State U., Syracuse U.; GM scholar. Mem.: Beta Gamma Sigma (coun. pres.), Phi Beta Kappa. Roman Catholic. Avocations: tennis, bicycling, gardening. Home: 400 E Franklin St Chapel Hill NC 27514-3707 Office: U NC Gen Adminstrn Bldg 910 Raleigh Rd Chapel Hill NC 27514-3916 Business E-Mail: mbroad@northcarolina.edu.

BROADBENT, AMALIA SAYO CASTILLO, graphic arts designer; b. Manila, May 28, 1956; came to U.S., 1980, naturalized, 1985; d. Conrado Camilo and Eugenia de Guzman (Sayo) Castillo; m. Barrie Noel Broadbent, Mar. 14, 1981 (div. Apr. 1999); children: Charles Noel Castillo, Chandra Noel Castillo. BFA, U. Santo Tomas, 1978; postgrad., Acad. Art Coll., San Francisco, Alliance Francaise, Manila, Karilagan Finishing Sch., Manila Computer Ctr.; BA, Maryknoll Coll., 1972. Designer market rsch. Unicorp Export Inc., Makati, Manila, 1975-77; asst. advt. mgr. Dale Trading Corp., Makati, 1977-78; artist, designer, pub. rels. Resort Hotels Corp., Makati, 1978-81; prodn. artist CYB/Young & Rubicam, San Francisco, 1981-82; freelance art dir Ogilvy & Mather Direct, San Francisco, 1986; artist, designer, owner A.C. Broadbent Graphics, San Francisco, 1982—. Faculty graphic design and advt. depts. Acad. Art U., San Francisco. Works include: Daing na Isda, 1975, (Christmas coloring) Pepsi-Cola, 1964 (Distinctive Merit cert.), (children's books) UNESCO, 1973 (cert.). Pres. Pax Romana, Coll. of Architecture and Fine Arts, U. Santo Tomas, 1976-78, chmn. cultural sect., 1975; v.p. Atelier Cultural Soc., U. Santo Tomas, 1975-76; mem. Makati Dance Troupe, 1973-74; vol. spl. events San Francisco Mus. of Modern Art. Recipient Merit cert. Inst. Religion, 1977. Mem. Alliance Francaise de San Francisco. Roman Catholic. Office: 4380A Eagle Peak Rd Concord CA 94521-3427 E-mail: amybroadbent@comcast.net.

BROADDUS, ANDREA LYNN, environmental services administrator; b. Washington, D.C., Dec. 27, 1971; d. Ashton Gustave and Carolyn Edith (nee Viens) Broaddus. BS in Geology and Geophysics, U. N.C., 1996; postgrad., Harvard U., 2004—06. Organizer trainee Green Corps, Madison, Wis., 1996—97; campaign coord. Wisconsin's Environ. Decade, Madison, 1997—98; state coord. New Transp. Alliance, Madison, 1997—99; Milw. mgr. Bicycle Fedn. Wis., Milw., 1999—2001; cons., Grassroots organizer Citizens for a better Environment, Milw., 1999—2000; self employed Environ. Law and Policy Ctr. of the Midwest, Chgo., 1999—2000. Bd. dirs. Am. Walks, Portland, Oreg., 2003—, Walk D.C., 2003—04. Author: (report) Troubled Waters, 1997, The State of the Nation's Rail, 2004. Mem. Adv. Neighborhood Commn., 2002—04; mem. steering com. Program Dane, Madison, 1996—97; bd. dirs. Pro-Rail, Madison, 1999—2000; pres. bd. dirs. Madison Hostel, 1999—2001. Fellow, U. N.C., 1995—96; grantee, Am. Pub. Power Assn., Washington, 1995—96; scholar, Alexander von Humboldt Found., 2006—. Avocations: bicycling, running, swimming, yoga, chess. Business E-Mail: andrea_broaddus@ksg06.harvard.edu.

BROADDUS, KRISTIE JONES, elementary school educator; b. Lexington, Ky., June 4, 1975; d. Cron Jones and Sharlene Broaddus. BA, Western Ky. U., 1997; M in Art Edn., U. Louisville, 2002. Cert. K-5 tchr. Ky., nat. profl. tchrs. cert. New asst. WLKY, Louisville, 1997; reporter WKAG, Hopkinsville, Ky., 1997—98; tv prodr. Fox 41, Louisville, 1998—2001; tchr. New Haven (Ky.) Sch., 2003—04, Goshen Elem., Prospect, Ky., 2004—. Facilitator Population Connection, Washington, 2003—; mem. Student Support Com., Goshen, Prospect, 2004—. Youth leader Bloomfield Bapt. Ch., Ky., 2004. Mem.: Nat. Coun. Soc. Studies, Ky. Sci. Tchrs. Assn. Avocations: yoga, reading, scrapbooks. Office: Goshen Elem 12518 Ridgemoor Dr Prospect KY 40059 Office Phone: 502-228-0101. Business E-Mail: kristie.broaddus@oldham.kyschools.us.

BROADWAY, NANCY RUTH, landscape company executive, consultant, model, actress; b. Memphis, Dec. 20, 1946; d. Charlie Sidney and Patsy Ruth (Meadows) Adkins. BS in Biology and Sociology cum laude, Memphis State U., 1969; postgrad., Tulane U., 1969—70; MS in Horticulture, U. Calif.-Davis, 1976. Lic. landscape contractor, Calif. Claims adjuster Mass. Mut. Ins., San Francisco, 1972—73; coord. cmty. garden City of Davis, Calif., 1976; supr. seed propagation Bordier's Wholesale Nursery, Santa Ana, Calif., 1976—78; owner, founder Calif. Landscape Co., 1978—88, Design & Mgmt. Cons., 1988—; pres. N.R. Broadway, Inc., 1998—; founder, operating mgr. Property Devel. LLC, 2006—. Actress: Visions of Murder, 1993, Eyes of Terror, 1994. NDEA fellow Tulane U., 1969-70. Fellow Am. Hort. Soc.; mem. Nat. Assn. Gen. Contractors, Calif. Native Plant Soc., Stockton C. of C. Democrat. Home and Office: 2801 Jackson St #301 San Francisco CA 94115-2156 Personal E-mail: nrbway@aol.com.

BROBECK, SUSAN WILLIAMS, private school educator; b. N.Y.C., Sept. 9, 1943; d. Hermann Warner Williams and Alice Barrett Farley; m. Stephen James Brobeck, May 7, 1971. BA, Skidmore Coll., 1965; MA, Care Western Res. U., 1971. Art tchr. Troy Pub. Schools, Troy, NJ, 1965—66; registrar, curator of edn. Allentown Art Mus., Allentown, Pa., 1966—67; art tchr., apprentice Potomac Sch., McLean, Va., 1967—69, tchr., 1969—70; head tchr. Ind. Sch. in East Cleve., Ohio, 1971—77; third grade tchr. Hathaway Brown Sch., Shaker Heights, 1977—80, Beauvoir Sch., Wash., 1980—. Chair, sci. curriculum com. Beauvoir Sch., Wash., 2001—. Chair edn. com., bd. dir. Bright Beginnings. Inc., Wash. Democrat. Avocations: tennis, golf, yoga. Home: 4700 Conn Ave NW #501 Washington DC 20008 Office: Beauvoir Sch 3500 Woodley Rd NW Washington DC 20016 Office Phone: 202-537-5230.

BROCK, CAROLYN PRATT, chemist, educator; b. Chgo., July 25, 1946; d. Charles Stebbings and Grace (Goodman) Pratt; m. Louis Milton Brock, July 22, 1972. BA, Wellesley (Mass.) Coll., 1968; PhD, Northwestern U., 1972. Asst. prof. chemistry U. Ky., Lexington, 1972-78, assoc. prof. chemistry, 1978-87, prof., 1987—. Vis. scientist organic chemistry lab. Swiss Fed. Inst. Tech., Zurich, 1980—81, Zurich, 1988—89; bd. govs. Cambridge Crystallographic Data Centre, 2001—, vice chmn., 2003—05, chmn., 2005—. Co-editor: Acta Crystallographica, 1993; editor: Sect. B of Acta Crystallographica, 2002—; contbr. articles to profl. jours. Mem. Am. Chem. Soc., Am. Crystallographic Assn., U.S. Nat. Com. for Crystallography (sec.-treas. 1989-91), Phi Beta Kappa, Sigma Xi. Home: 133 Sycamore Rd Lexington KY 40502-1841 Office: U Ky Dept Chemistry Lexington KY 40506-0055 Office Phone: 859-257-1959. Business E-Mail: cpbrock@uky.edu.

BROCK, DEE SALA, television executive, educator, writer, consultant; b. Covington, Okla., June 7, 1930; d. Lester Edward and Vera Mae (Bowers) Sala; m. Robert Wesley Brock, June 8, 1952 (div. 1979); children: Baron Sala, Bishop Chapman, Bevin Bowers. BA, U. North Tex., 1950, MA, 1956, PhD, 1985. Tchr. high sch. Dallas Ind. Sch. Dist., 1952-66; dir. Dallas Cowboy Cheerleaders, 1960-75; mem. faculty, adminstr. Dallas County Community Coll. Dist., 1966-74, telecourse writer, producer, adminstr., 1974-75, dir. mktg. info., 1975-80; dir., v.p. PBS, Washington, 1980-89, sr. v.p. edn. Alexandria, Va., 1989-90; pres. Dee Brock & Assocs., Plano, Tex., 1991-98; pub. FAQs Press, 1999—. Bd. dirs. Pub. Svc. Satellite Consortium, U.S. Basics; adv. bd. Learning Link, 1987-90, Telcon Industry, 1990-91; chair exec. coun. U. of the World, 1989-91; adv. coun. Triangle Coalition, 1989-91; spkr. in field. Author: Writing for a Reason: Study Guide, 1974; author: (with Jeriel Howard) Writing for a Reason, 1978; author: (with Laura Derr) The World of F. Scott Fitzgerald, 1980; author: (with Deborah Burkett and Carole Wilson) Troup Goes to War: World War II, A Collection of Memories, 1999; author: (with Linda Resnik) Food FAQs: Substitutions, Yields & Equivalents, 2000; author: (with JoAnna Lewis) 100 Great Fundraising Ideas Celebrating 100 Years of Texas Library, 2002; mem. editl. bd.: Am. Jour. Distance Edn., 1987—90; prodr.: (internat. teleconf.) Out of the Red, 1991; prodr., writer: TV series and workbook Communicating in English in the Healthcare Workplace, 1994; contbr. articles to profl. jours. Trustee Coun. for Adult and Experiential Learning, 1989—99; chair spl. task force Mcpl. Libr. Friends of Libr., 1996, pres., 1997—; lay rep. N.E. Tex. Libr. Sys., 1996—, chair planning to plan com., 1997—98, adv. coun., 1998—, vice chair, 1998—2000, chair, 2000—04; chmn. Strategic Planning Com., 1999; fund-raising co-chair Komen Tyler Race for the Cure, 1999; active PTA, Dallas; pres. Littera, 2002—04, Friends of the Troup Libr., 1998—; chair Libr. Friends, Trustees and Advs., 2001—03; bd. dirs. Tyler Civic Theatre Ctr., Coalition for the Advancement of Citizenship, 1988—90. Reynolds Econ. fellow U. N.C., 1966; Literacy award N. Tex. Reading Coun., 1980, Nat. Person of Yr. award Nat. Coun. on Community and Continuing Edn., 1985, Award for Excellence in TV Programming NEA, 1986; recipient Outstanding Career Achievement award ITC Am. Assn. Community and Jr. Colls., 1990. Mem. NEH (nat. bd. cons. 1980-85), LWV (bd. dirs., v.p. cmty. rels. Tyler chpt. 2002-03, pres. 2003—), U.S. Distance Learning Assn. (bd. dirs. 1989-91, adv. bd. 1989), So. Assn. Colls. and Schs. (project 1990 task force 1984-86), Nat. Assn. Ednl. Broadcasters (steering com. 1979-81), Assn. Ednl. Comms. Tech., Nat. Coun. Tchrs. English (pres. S.W. regional coun. 1972-74), Tex. Libr. Assn. (legis. com. 1999—, chair roundtable 2001-2003, chair pub. rels. com. 2005—). Methodist. Achievements include being co-patentee video indexing system; design of and management of PBS Adult Learning Service and PBS Adult Learning Satellite Service. Home and Office: 3529 Woods Blvd Tyler TX 75707

BROCK, DOROTHY DIXON, psychologist, psychology professor; b. St. Louis, Nov. 16, 1954; d. Arthur Roy and Dorothy Arnett Dixon. BS, Oral Roberts U., 1978; MEd, Ga. State U., 1980, PhD, 1991. Lic. psychologist Ga.; cert. tchr. Okla. Doctoral intern Altanta Network for Individual and Family Therapy, Dunwoody, Ga., 1989—91; tchr. Clinton Jr. HS, Tulsa, Okla., 1978—79; co-founder Landmark Counseling Ctr., Norcross, Ga., 1981—83; contract therapist Rapha, Dunwoody, Ga., 1994—96; pvt. practice psychologist Norcross, Ga., 1995—97, 2001—04, 2005—; adj. instr. Toccoa Falls (Ga.) Coll., 1995—96, instr., 2001—02, asst. prof., 2002—, coll. counselor, 2003—04; clin. coord. New Life Clinics, Smyrna, Ga., 1997—2000. Mem.: APA, Am. Assn. Christian Counselors. Office: Toccoa Falls Coll Toccoa Falls GA 30598 Office Phone: 770-843-9077.

BROCK, HELEN RACHEL MCCOY, retired mental health and community health nurse; b. Cromwell, Okla., Dec. 10, 1924; d. Samuel Robert Lee and Ire Etta (Pounds) McCoy; m. Clois Lee Brock, Sept. 29, 1963; children: Dwayne, Joyce, Peggy, Ricki, Stacey. AS, Southwestern Union Coll., Keene, Tex., 1968; BS in Nursing, Union Coll., Lincoln, Nebr., 1970; postgrad., Vernon Regional Jr. Coll., Tex., 1972—76; MPH, Loma Linda U., Calif., 1983. Cert. ARC nurse. Dir. nursing Chillicothe (Tex.) Clinic-Hosp., 1970-77, Pike County Hosp., Waverly, Ohio, 1977-79, Marion County Hosp., Jefferson, Tex., 1979-81; nurse III, nursing unit supr, patient health educator Vernon State Hosp., Maximum Security for Criminally Insane, 1981-96; retired, 1996; nurse, admissions and assessments Texhoma Community Health Svcs., 1987-94. Mem.: ANA, Tex. Nurses Assn. Home: PO Box 238 Chillicothe TX 79225-0238

BROCK, HOLLY MELINDA, marketing professional; b. Terceria, Azores, Portugal, Aug. 28, 1973; d. Edwin L. Cox Jr. and Mary Elizabeth Cox; 1 child, Taylor Robert. Degree in Human Svc. Mgmt. (hon.), U. Phoenix, 2003. Cert. alcohol and drug counseling State of Nev., 2003, HIPAA regulations State of Nev., 2004, HIV/AIDS educator ARC, 2000. Recreation and activity leader Clark County Pk. and Recreation, Las Vegas, 1993—96; activity asst. Desert Ln. Care Ctr., Las Vegas, 1996; domestic violence, children's adv. SAFEHouse, Henderson, Nev., 1996—98; case mgr. Lighthouse Compassionate Care, Las Vegas, 1999—2000; housing coord. Caminar, Inc., Las Vegas, 2000—03; counselor Ctr. Behavioral Health, Las Vegas, 2003; case mgmt. supr. State of Nev. Bur. Cmty. Health, Las Vegas, 2003—04; mktg. dir. The Plz. at Sun Mountain, Las Vegas, 2004—. Mem. So. Poverty Law Ctr., Montgomery, Ala., 2003—04; bd. mem. City of Henderson, Cmty. Devel. Bldg. Grant Adv. Bd., 2003—05; mem. MADD, Las Vegas, 2003—05; edn. chair Susan G. Komen Breast Cancer Found., Las Vegas, 2003—05. Achievements include Name added to the Wall of Tolerance at the Civil Rights Memorial Center in Montgomery, Alabama. Office: The Plaza at Sun Mountain 6031 W Charleston Las Vegas NV 89108 Office Phone: 702-658-5882. Office Fax: 702-658-5842.

BROCK, KARENA DIANE, dancer, educator; b. L.A., Sept. 21, 1942; d. Orville DeLoss and Sallie Alice (Anderson) B.; m. Ted Kivitt, Apr. 16, 1965 (div. 1978); m. John Robert Carlyle, June 28, 1985; 1 child, Timothy John. Grad. H.S., Kansas City, Mo. Tchr. master classes Radford (Va.) Coll., U. Louisville, U. Tampa; staff tchr. Bklyn. Coll.; mem. faculty SUNY-Purchase; artistic dir., choreographer, tchr. and founder Hilton Head Dance Theater and Sch., Hilton Head Island, SC, 1985—. Guest tchr. S.C. Dance Inst., Columbia, 1993-94, Walnut Hill Sch., Boston, Savannah Ballet, Cleve. Ballet; tchr. master classes Florence, S.C., Columbia; guest choreographer Towson (Md.) U., 2000, 05, Carolina Ballet Theatre, Greeville, S.C., 1998, Island Dance Theatre Ga., 2005, Ron Jones Dance, Ga., 2004. Dancer, David Lichine Concert Group, L.A., 1960-61, Netherlands Nat. Ballet Co., Amsterdam, 1961-62, mem. corps, Am. Ballet Theatre, N.Y.C., 1963-68, soloist, 1968-73, prin. ballerina, 1973-79, artistic dir., prima ballerina, choreographer, Savannah (Ga.) Ballet Co., 1979-85; co-artistic dir. and choreographer Ballet South, Savannah, 1992-96; guest artist, Miami (Fla.) Civic Ballet, Macon (Ga.) Civic Ballet, Tampa (Fla.) Civic Ballet, U. Ill. Ballet Co., Champaign, San Jose (Calif.) Civic Ballet, Ballet de San Juan, P.R., Gala Ballet, Amarillo (Tex.) Civic Ballet, Maywood Ballet Co., Phila., U. Wis., Milw. Civic Ballet, Stars of Am. Ballet, various TV shows, White House, 1966, 69. Mem. adv. bd. S.C. Arts Commn., Columbia, 1988—; hon. mem. bd. dirs. Columbia City Ballet. Mem.: AFTRA, AGVA, Am. Guild Mus. Artists. Office: Hilton Head Dance Theater and Sch 24 Palmetto Business Park Rd Hilton Head Island SC 29928-3234 Office Phone: 843-785-5477. Personal E-mail: balletkbc@yahoo.com.

BROCK, KATRINA RAE, music educator; b. Montgomery, Ala., Aug. 18, 1977; d. Kathreen Louis and Ray Von Straughn; m. Joey Thomas Brock. BA in elem. edn., Huntingdon Coll., 2001, BA in early childhood edn., vocal choral performance, 2001. Cert. elem. tchr. Ala., 2001, cert. vocal, choral, music tchr. grades K-8 2005. Sales assoc. Big B/ Revco / CVS, Montgomery, Ala., 1995—98; work study Huntingdon Coll. Performing Arts Dept., Montgomery, Ala., 1995—98, Huntingdon Coll. Libr., Montgomery, Ala., 1997—98; camp counselor Strinfellows Camp - Huntingdon Coll. and Montgomery Symphony Orch., Montgomery, Ala., 1999—2000; choir singer St. John's Episcopal Ch., Montgomery, Ala., 1995—2001; libr. page Montgomery City/ County Libr., 1998—2000, libr. asst., 2001; music specialist at Brewbaker Primary Montgomery County Pub. Schs., Montgomery, Ala., 2001—. Tutoring Montgomery City County Pub. Libr., Montgomery, Ala., 2000—02; childrens pastor's wife Bethel Assembly of God, 2002—, choir and praise team mem., 2001, puppet team co-dir., 2002; camp counselor Assembly of God Camp, Springville, Ala., 2003, 2004, 2005; truth in action drama team Bethel Assembly of God, 2005—. Mem.: NEA, Montgomery County Edn. Assn., Ala. Edcation Assn., Music Educators Nat. Conf., Student Ala. Educators Assn., Collegate Music Educators Nat. Conf. (treas. 1997—2000), Cir. K. Pentacostal. Avocations: singing, acting, puppetry, travel, teaching and tutoring. Home: 231 Landmark Dr Montgomery AL 36117 Office: Brewbaker Primary 4445 Brewbaker Dr Montgomery AL 36116 Personal E-mail: kat4cows@hotmail.com.

BROCK, ROSLYN MCCALLISTER, association executive; BS magna cum laude, Va. Union U., 1987; M in Health Svcs. Adminstrn., George Washington U., 1989; MBA, Northwestern U., 1999. Dir. sys. fund devel. Sisters of Bon Secours Health Sys. Inc.; vice chair nat. bd. dirs. NAACP, Balt., 2001—. Vol. elem. sch. instr. Jr. Achievement; host local cable access program Cmty. Voices. Named a Future Leader, Ebony mag., 1989; named Outstanding Alumna, Va. Union U., hon. chairperson, Nat. Black Family Summit, Young Leaders fellow, Nat. Com. on U.S.-China Rels., 2003; named one of 100 Young Women of Promise, Good Housekeeping, 1987; recipient Martin Luther King, jr. medal for human rights, George Washington U. Mem.: APHA, Nat. Assn. Health Svc. Execs., The Links, Inc., Nat. Black MBA Assn., Alpha Kappa Alpha Sorority, INc. Office: NAACP 4805 Mt Hope Dr Baltimore MD 21215

BROCKETT, FRANCESCA L., retail executive; BA, Harvard U., 1982; MBA, Stanford U., Calif., 1986. Cons. Booz-Allen and Hamilton, Atlanta, 1982—85, McKinsey and Co., Houston, 1986—92; with PepsiCo, New Eng., 1994—95, Irvine, Calif., 1995—97, Tricon Global Restaurants, Louisville, 1997—98; from sr. v.p. strategic planning and bus. devel. to exec. v.p. Toys "R" Us, Inc., Wayne, NJ, 1998—2000, exec. v.p. strategic planning and bus. devel., 2000—. Office: Toys R Us Inc 1 Geoffrey Way Wayne NJ 07470-2030 Business E-Mail: brocketf@toysrus.com.

BROCKETT, RAMONA, criminologist, educator; b. Bklyn., Sept. 25, 1962; d. William Edwin and Virginia Mae Brockett. BA, Coll. St. Elizabeth, Convent Station, NJ, 1985; JD, Boston Coll., Newton Centre, Mass., 1989; PhD, Rutgers U., Newark, 1998. Lectr. justice studies Kent State U., Ohio, 1997—98, asst. prof. justice studies, 1998—2000; asst. prof. criminal justice No. Ky. U., Highland Heights, 2001—04, U. Md. Ea. Shore, Princess Anne, 2004—06, assoc. prof. criminal justice, 2006—, chair dept. criminal justice, 2006—. Talk show host (Legal Talk with Dr. Ramona Brockett) Nat. Pub. Radio, WEMS, 2006—; contbr. chapters to books, articles to profl. jours. Broadcast cons. Nat. Pub. Radio/ WHYY, Phila., 1995—96; contbr. Black Issues in Higher Edn., Washington, 2002—05; cons., presenter African Criminology Conf. Columbia U., Manhattan, NY, 2003; contbr., broadcast cons., commentator CBS, NewsMakers, Cin., 2003; inspirational/motivational spkr. Ea. Correctional Facility, Princess Anne, 2004—06; trustee bd. mem., exec. bd. mem. Media Bridges, Cin., 2001—04, exec. bd. mem., 2001—04. Named Woman of Yr., Black Cultural League, Rowan U., 1996, Alpha Rho Chpt., Zeta Phi Beta, No. Ky. U., 2004; recipient Outstanding Contbns. in the Field of Drug Law Enforcement award, Drug Enforcement Adminstrn., 1993, 1994, 1995; grantee Law Forum for Pre Law Students, Law Svcs. Admission Coun., 2005. Mem.: Phi Alpha Delta (assoc.; pre law advisor U. Md. Ea. Shore 2004—, Advisor award U. Md. Ea. Shore chpt. 2005, 2006, mini-grant 2005), Acad. Criminal Justice Scientists (assoc.; nat. exec. counselor 2004—, Evelyn Gilbert Unsung Hero award 2006), Am. Soc. Criminology (assoc.; vice chair 2000—02, nat. exec. counselor 2003—05, Outstanding Svc. award 2004, Outstanding Contbns. in Field of Drug Law Enforcement, Divsn. People of Color on Crime 2003), Am. Soc. Criminologists (assoc.; chair membership divsn. people of color on crime 2004—). Conservative. Avocations: bicycling, beaches, travel, music, theater. Office: Univ Maryland Eastern Shore 1 Backbone Rd Princess Anne MD 21853 Office Phone: 410-651-8914. Office Fax: 410-651-8098. Business E-Mail: rbrockett@umes.edu.

BROCKINGTON, CAROLYN, neurologist; MD, Albany Med. Coll., NY, 1994. Resident, neurology Mount Sinai Med. Ctr., NY, 1999—2000; fellow, acute intervention U. Calif., San Diego, 1998—99; fellow, stroke prevention therapies Beth Israel Med. Ctr., NY, 1999—2000, attending physician, dept. neurology NY; dir. Yarmon Stroke Center, Hyman-Newman Inst. for Neurology and Neurosurgery (INN), Beth Israel Med. Ctr. Achievements include cerebrovascular disease (stroke, TIA, stenosis, aneursym, and ateriovenous malformations).

BROCKMEYER, KRISTIE LEE, secondary school educator; b. Mason City, Iowa, May 27, 1949; d. Edward Lee and Betty Grace Elizabeth Theesfeld; m. Paul Brockmeyer, Apr. 1, 1972; children: Amber Kristine, Eric Paul. BS, Minn. State U., 1970. Cert. tchr. chemistry, physics, math. Iowa, 1982. Tchr. chemistry, physics, electronics Sheffield - Chapin (Iowa) Consol. Sch. Sys., 1986—2001; tchr. chemistry, physics Nora Springs - Rock Falls (Iowa) Consol. Sch. Sys., 2001—. Sec. Sheffield (Iowa) Pub. Libr., 1985—89. Mem.: NEA (life), Lake Area Quilt Guild (pres. 2005—06). Democrat. Luth. Avocations: quilting, golf, travel, knitting. Office: Nora Springs Rock Falls Schools 501 Iowa Street Nora Springs IA Office Phone: 641-749-5301.

BROCKOVICH-ELLIS, ERIN, legal researcher; b. Lawrence, Kans., June 1960; m. Eric Ellis, 1999; 3 children. MA (hon.), Jones Internat. U.; LLD (hon.), Lewis A. Clark Law Sch., 2005. Management trainee K-Mart, Calif.; electrical engineer trainee Fluor Engineers and Constructors; sec. E.F. Hutton, Reno; former file clerk Masry & Vititoe, Westlake Village, Calif., dir. rsch.; pres. Brockovich Rsch. and Cons., 2006—. Lectr. in field. Author: Take It From Me, Life's a Struggle, But You Can Win; actor: (films) Erin Brockovich, 2000, (TV series) Challenge America, 2001, Final Justice, 2003. Named Ms. Pacific Coast, 1981; recipient Scales of Justice award, Ct. TV, Spl. Citizen award, The Children's Health Environmental Coalition, Mothers & Shakers award, Redbook mag., Lifesaver award, Lymphoma Rsch. Found. Am., World Social Nominations award, 2004, 2005, Julius B. Richmond award, Harvard Sch. Pub. Health, 2005, Profiles in Courage award, Santa Clara Trial Lawyers Assn. Achievements include spearheaded largest toxic tort injury settlement in U.S. history, 1996; subject of hit movie "Erin Brockovich", 2000. Office: c/o William Morris Agy 151 El Camino Dr Beverly Hills CA 90212

BROCK-SERVAIS, RHONDA LEE, literature and language professor; b. Kenosha, Wis., June 30, 1967; d. James Eugene Brock and Bernice Julia Nelson; m. Antone Michael Servais, Oct. 9, 1995. PhD, U. SC, Columbia, 1999. Assoc. prof. dept. English, Longwood U., Farmville, Va., 2001—; vis. assoc. prof. Hollins U., Roanoke, Va., 2005. Grad. coord. English, Longwood U., Farmville, Va., 2005—. Recipient Jr. Faculty Achievement award, Longwood U., 2005. Avocations: women's issues, reading. Office: Longwood Univ 201 High St Farmville VA 23909 Office Phone: 434-395-2695. Office Fax: 434-395-2145. E-mail: brockservaisrl@longwood.edu.

BROCKWAY, LAURIE SUE, editor-in-chief, journalist, writer, minister; b. N.Y.C., Dec. 18, 1956; d. Lee L. and Shirley Ruth Brockway; 1 child, Alexander Kent Garrett; m. Vic Fohrman, Jan. 18, 2005. AA, Laguardia C.C., 1978; student in Arts, Hunter Coll. CUNY, 1978-81; MSC, The New Seminary, 1999. Features editor, crime reporter The Bklyn. Paper, 1978-81; editor-in-chief The Iniator, N.Y.C., 1982-83; pub., editor The Transformer, N.Y.C., 1983-84; co-prodr., writer The Brockway Good News Report, N.Y.C., 1984-85; N.Y. bur. chief Women's News, N.Y.C., 1983-85, Manhattan corr., 1985—2000, mng. editor, 1990; account supr. Brockway Assocs., Inc., N.Y.C., 1985-88. Tchr. women's sexuality, spirituality, 1990—; mem. faculty The Seminar Ctr., 1998—2003; mgr. Bridal Survival Club, 2004-05. Author: Network Your Way to Endless Romance, 1998, How to Seduce a Man and Keep Him Seduced, 1999, A Goddess Is a Girl's Best Friend, 2002, Wedding Goddess, 2005; editor: Playgirl, 1994—97; editor: (editor in chief) Single Living, 1997; spirituality editor Hitchny.com, 2005—; editor (and guide): Wedding Goddess Wisdom, —. Recipient LaGuardia Meml. award, 1978, LaGuardia Student Coun. scholar, 1978, Expository Writing award, LaGuardia English Dept., 1978, Woman of Achievement award Women's News, 1997. Home and Office: 83-27 159th St Jamaica NY 11432 Office Phone: 212-631-3520. E-mail: revlauriesue@aol.com.

BROCKWAY-HENSON, AMIE, producing artistic director; b. Warren, Ohio, Oct. 13, 1938; d. Raymond Horatio and Amabelle Virginia (Willard) Woodworth; m. Ronald F. Brockway, June 3, 1956 (div. 1980); children: Adrienne J., Ginny A.; m. Richard G. Henson, June 30, 1984. BFA, SUNY, Purchase, 1975; MFA, Rutgers U., 1978. Adminstrv. asst. Ashtabula (Ohio) Arts Ctr., 1967-69; exec. asst. McCarter Theatre, Princeton, N.J., 1969-72; artistic dir. St. Theatre, Princeton, 1970-72, Creative Theatre Unlimited, Princeton, 1975-78; dir. audience devel., resident dir. The Open Eye: New Stagings, N.Y.C., 1980-82, assoc. artistic dir., 1982-84, artistic dir., 1984-94, producing artistic dir., 1994—. Editor TYA Today, 1991-94; author: stage adaptation of The Odyssey by Homer; co-author stage adaptation The Nightingale (Hans Christian Anderson), 1999. Trustee U.S. chpt. Internat. Assn. Theatres for Children and Young People (ASSITEJ/USA), 1991-94, U.S. rep. 22nd Danish Children's Theatre Festival, Denmark, 1992. Recipient Paul Green Found. award, 1991, Performers at Work Artistic Visionary award, 1994, Internat. Travel Incentive award Internat. Assn. Theatres for Children and Young People, 1999, Berrilla Kerr award New Am. Plays, 1999, 2000, 01. Mem. League Profl. Theatre Women (co-pres. 1992-94), Soc. Stage Dirs. and Choreographers, Dramatists Guild. Home and Office: The Open Eye Theater PO Box 959 Margaretville NY 12455-0959 E-mail: openeye@catskills.net.

BRODA-HYDORN, SUSAN, entomologist; b. Newton, N.J., Sept. 2, 1947; d. William E. and Margaret G. Hydorn. BS in Entomology with honors, U. Mass., 1969; MS in Entomology with honors, U. Fla., 1971; PhD in Entomology, U. Calif., 1977. Tchg. asst. dept. entomology U. Calif., 1973, rsch. asst. biol. control, 1974—76; rsch. assoc. dept. entomology U. Maine, 1977—79; adj. prof. dept. entomology U. Fla., 1979; instr. entomology, preventive medicine divsn. U.S. Army Acad. Health Sci., San Antonio, 1979—82; nematologist, quarantine officer, plant protection and quarantine Animal Plant Health Inspection Svc., USDA, West Hampton Beach, NY, 1984—87, identifier, entomology, 1987—95, nat. thysanoptera specialist, 1995—. Mem.: Am. Arachnological Soc., Md. Entomol. Soc., Entomol. Soc. D.C., Fla. Entomol. Soc. (hist. com. 1993—95), Entomology Soc. Am. (student awards com. 1993—96, internat. affairs com. 1997—2000). Avocations: music, organ. Home: 8319 Snowden Oaks Pl Laurel MD 20708 Office: USDA APHIS PPQ 2200 Broening Hwy Ste 140 Baltimore MD 21224 Office Phone: 410-631-0073. Office Fax: 240-568-0433. Business E-Mail: susan.broda@aphis.usda.gov.

BRODBECK, MARY LOU, artist, furniture designer; b. Hastings, Mich., Nov. 25, 1958; d. Willard Nathan and Margaret Grace (Balduf) Brodbeck; m. John Joseph Schmitt, May 20, 1995; 1 stepchild, Jack Schmitt. BFA, Mich. State U., 1982; MFA, Western Mich. U., 1999. Assoc. indsl. designer Haworth, Holland, Mich., 1985-90; freelance designer, woodblock printmaker Kalamazoo, 1990—. Cons. indsl. designer Steelcase, Inc., Grand Rapids, Mich., 1993—94. One-woman shows include UpJohn Corp., Kalamazoo, 1992, Kingscott Gallery, 1998, Carnegie Ctr. for Arts, Three Rivers, Mich., 1998, Cmty. Arts Ctr., Hancock, Mich., 1999, New Moon Gallery, Benton Harbor, Mich., 2000, Oasis Gallery, Marquette, Mich., 2002, Lansing Art Gallery, 2003, Southwestern Mich. Coll., Dowagiac, 2003, Studio 23, Bay City, Mich., 2004, Pine Tree Gallery, Ironwood, Mich., 2005, Forest Hills Fine Art Ctr., Grand Rapids, Mich., 2006. Vol. leader Campfire Girls, Douglas, Mich., 1988—89; mem. Douglas Planning Commn., 1995—98. Recipient Purchase award, Holland Arts Coun., 1990, Krasl Art Ctr., St. Joseph, Mich., 1991, Hunterdon Mus. Art, NJ, 2004, Cash award, Artlink, Ft. Wayne, Ind., 2002, 3d pl., Internat. Print Competition, Hollywood, Fla., 2002, Best Series award, Peninsula Art Sch., Fish Creek, Wis., 2002, Juror's Choice award, Md. Fedn. Art, 2004, 1st prize, Am. Color Print Soc., 2005; Bunka-Cho fellow, Japanese Govt., 1998. Achievements include patents for for furniture designs. Avocation: swimming. Home: 471 W South St Apt 503 Kalamazoo MI 49007-4677 Office Phone: 269-344-6654. Personal E-mail: mary@marybrodbeck.com.

BRODERICK, JO STEWART, academic administrator; b. Northampton, Mass., Aug. 28, 1955; d. Richard Henry and Patricia Ann (Maynard) S.; children: Adelyn, Page; m. Philip M. Broderick, Oct. 8, 2005. BA, U. Mass., 1978. Gen. assignment reporter Salem Evening News, Mass., 1978—88; dir. pub. rels. Montserat Coll., Beverly, Mass., 1989-96; dir. coll. rels. Montserat Coll. Art, Beverly, 1996-2000, dir. coll. advancement, 2001—02, dir. coll. rels. and external affairs, 2002—, assoc. v.p. cmty. rels., 2003—. Co-founder, past pres. North Shore Press Club, Salem, Mass., 1979-81. Bd. dirs. North Shore Coun. for Children, Danvers, Mass., 1987-90; co-leader Girl Scouts U.S., Middleton, Mass., 1991-94; chmn. Trinity Episcopal Ch. Parish Life Commn., 1994-99; mem. membership com. Beverly C. of C., 1996-97, bd. dirs., 2000—, v.p. 2003—, pres., 2004—; pres. Beverly Main Streets (co-pres., 2005); mem. Beverly Arts Festival com., 2002—. Mem.: Coun. for Advancement and Support Edn., Beverly Rotary (bd. dirs. 2005). Office: 23 Essex St Beverly MA 01915-4508 Office Phone: 978-921-4242 1113. Business E-Mail: jbroderick@montserrat.edu.

BRODERICK, LAURA ANNE, federal official; b. Phoenix, Feb. 25, 1953; d. George Donald and Barbara Ann (Huls) Broderick. BA, Ohio Wesleyan U., 1975. Comms. dir. to Congressman Dick Schulze U.S. Ho. of Reps., Washington, 1976—78, press sec. to Congressman Phil Crane, 1978—81; dir. multimedia outreach dept., editor Source Rep. Nat. Com., Washington, 1981—82; dir. pub. affairs mgmt. Office Mgmt. and Budget, Exec. Office of Pres., The White House, Washington, 1982—84; drp. dir. Pres.'s Commn. on White House Fellowships, Washington, 1984—. Mem. Task Froce on Corp. Volunteerism, Jr. League, Washington, 1984. Republican. Roman Catholic. Office: 712 Jackson Pl NW Washington DC 20006-4901

BRODERSON, THELMA SYLVIA, retired marketing professional; b. St. Louis, Feb. 6, 1932; d. Harry and Lillian (Fishman) B. BA, U. Denver, 1953; postgrad., Washington U., St. Louis, 2001—. Marketer Marsh & McLennan, Inc., St. Louis, 1966—85; account exec. Daniel & Henry Co., St. Louis, 1985—87; marketer G. Steven DeMaster, Inc. at Crane Agy., St. Louis, 1987—99; ret., 1999. Prodr. Harry Fender Program Sta. KMOX-CBS, St. Louis, 1968-74; columnist The Oil Can, 1972-75. Tchr. religious sch. United Hebrew Temple, St. Louis, 1956—63. Donor Harry Fender Memorabilia to St. Louis Pub. Libr. Media Archives and Rare Books Collection, 1997. Mem.: Phi Beta Kappa. Avocations: theater, arts.

BRODEUR, CATHERINE RECKART, artist; b. L.A., May 6, 1927; d. John Charles Reckart and Catherine Hyland Burns; m. Raymond Roy Brodeur, Apr. 17, 1948; children: George, Anne, Arthur, Martha, Frances Student, Art Student's League, N.Y.C., 1975; studied with, Daniel Greene, N.Y.C., John Howard Sanden, Jack Callahan, John Phelps, Rockport and Springfield, Mass. Art instr. Holyoke (Mass.) Home Info. Ctr., 1979, 80, 81, Wistariahurst Mus., Holyoke, 1988, 89, 90; lectr. W. Springfield C. of C., 1981, Holyoke Hosp., 1993; ofcl. artist USCG, 1981-91 Exhibited in group shows at Nat. Arts Club, N.Y.C., Federal Hall, N.Y.C., World's Fair, New Orleans, City Hall, Boston, New Eng. Air Mus., Windsor Locks, Conn., Berkshire Mus., Pittsfield, Mass., Governor's Island, N.Y., The Prestige Gallery, Toronto, Can., 1992, Wistariahurst Mus., Holyoke, 1992, Mus. Fine Arts, Springfield; ann. exhibits Vt. Inst. Natural Sci., Woodstock, Nature Ctr., Westport, Conn.; represented in numerous pub. and pvt. collections including Permanent Naval Art Collection, Washington, First Nat. Bank, Boston, Dominican Monastery, West Springfield; contbr. popular mags Recipient Merit award Springfield (Mass.) Art League Nat., 1986 Mem. Pastel Soc. Am., Copley Soc. Boston, Acad. Artist's Assn. (v.p., Wilkins award 1990), Hudson Valley Arts Assn. (Margaret Fernald Dole award 1982), North Shore Art Assn Roman Catholic. Avocation: antiques.

BRODEUR, ESTHER CORINNE, educator; d. Anthony Eugene and Josephine Carmela Campo; m. Michael Robert Brodeur, July 21, 1979; children: Melissa Marie, Kristin Nicole. BS, U. NH, Durham, 1978, MEd, 1980. Tchr. City of Nashua, NH, 1979—. Leader Nashua Girl Scouts, NH, 1994—2000; tchr. Immaculate Conception, 1990—2001. Mem.: Nashua Tchrs. Union. Roman Catholic. Avocations: scrapbooks, reading, travel. Office: City of Nashua Nashua High North 10 Chuck Druding Drive Nashua NH 03063 Office Phone: 603-589-8229. Personal E-mail: brodeure@nashua.edu.

BRODIE, ANGELA M., biomedical researcher, educator; b. Manchester, Lancashire, Eng., Sept. 28, 1934; d. Herbert Kent and Ann (Hargreaves) Hartley; m. Harry Joseph Brodie, Apr. 25, 1928; children: Mark, John. BS in Biochemistry with honors, Sheffield (Eng.) U., 1956, MS in Biochemistry, 1958; PhD in Chem. Pathology, Manchester (Eng.) U., 1961. Jr. scientific officer Nat. Blood Transfusion Svc., Manchester, 1956-57; rsch. asst. dept. hormone rsch. Christie Hosp. and Holt Radium Inst., Manchester, 1957-59; predoct. fellow Med. Rsch. Coun., Eng., 1959-61; steroid tng. program NIH, 1961-62; postdoct. tng. program in steroid biochemistry Clark U./Worcester Found. Exptl. Biology, Shrewsbury, Mass., 1962; staff scientist Worcester Found. for Exptl. Biology, Shrewsbury, 1962-68, 70-78, sr. scientist, 1978-79; res. assoc. prof. dept. pharmacology and exptl. therapeutics U. Md. Sch. Medicine, Balt., 1979-83, assoc. prof. dept. pharmacology and exptl. therapeutics, 1983-86, prof., 1986—; prof. divsn. reproductive endocrinology dept. physiology U. Md., 1985—. Invited presenter Am. Assn. Cancer Rsch., 1987; program leader prostate cancer divsn. oncology dept. medicine The Marlene and Steart Greenebaum Cancer Ctr. U. Md., 1988—; mem. ad-hoc biochem. endorcrinology study sect. NIH, 1982, 83, 85, spl. cons. social scis. and population dynamics, 1982, 84-88, 91, reproductive endocrinology, 1998—; mem. selection com. Roussel Prize, 1985-92; mem. nominating com. Women in Endocrinology, 1991-94, 97-99; chmn. liaison com. Am. Soc. Andropology, 1988-91; site visitor Cancer Rsch. Campaign Program Projects, Eng., 1993, 94, 95; reviewer Nat. Action Plan on Breast Cancer, 1995; mem. integration panel breast cancer program U.S. Army, 1998; chmn. numerous symposia; cons. in field. Editor, contbr. Jour. Enzyme Inhibition, 1990, proceedings 3rd Internat. Aromatase Conf., 1992, Breast Cancer Rsch. and Treatment, 1994; co-editor: Clin. and Biol. Rsch., 1986; rev. Endocrinology, Sci. Steroids, Biology of Reproduction, Cancer Rsch., Jour. Clin. Endocrinology and Metabolism, numerous others; mem. editl. bd. Steroids, 1964-66, 95—, Jour. Steroid Biochemistry, 1985—, Jour. Enzyme Inhibition, 1992—; abstractor Biol. Abstracts, 1968-70. Recipient Pharmacia Upjohn Internat. award for excellence in clin. rsch., 1998, Brinker Internat. award for breast cancer rsch. The Susan Co. Komen Breast Cancer Found., 2000, Kettering prize Gen. Motors, 2005. Mem. AAAS, Am. Assn. Cancer Rsch. (mem. program com. 1988-89, membership com. 1997—), Internat. Soc. Comparative Oncology, Soc. Study Reproduction (mem. pubs. com. 1985, membership com. 1987, nominations com. 1990, awards com. 1995—), Endocrine Soc., Soc. Andrology. Achievements include 4 patents; research, development of formestane aromatase inhibitors, first selective aromatase and first specifically designed for treatment of breast cancer; research in new treatments for prostate cancer, steroid biochemistry, endocrinology of breast and prostate cancer and other estrogen mediated diseases, reproductive endocrinology. Office: U Md Sch Medicine 655 W Baltimore St Baltimore MD 21201 Address: PO Box 263 Fulton MD 20759

BRODIE, SUSAN GERRISH, special education educator; d. George Bachelder and Jean Sutherland Gerrish; m. Robert W. Brodie, Nov. 30, 1985; children: Jonathan B., Jeffrey M. MS in Communicative Disorders, John's Hopkins U., Balt., 1985. Tchr. spl. edn. Montgomery County Schs., Rockville, Md., 1978—85, Groton Pub. Schs., Conn., 1987—, head tchr., 2005—. Making stds. work trainer Ctr. Performance Assessment, Denver, 2003—. Mentor, facilitator Westerly Innovations Network, RI, 2002—06. Recipient Earth Day award, State of RI, 2005; grantee, RI Found., 2005. Mem.: Coun. Exceptional Children, Womens Investment Network (pres. 2002—05), Westerly Coll. Club.

BRODIE-BALDWIN, HELEN SYLVIA, retired college and human services administrator; d. Adolphus T. and Myrtilla Brodie; m. Wilmer Baldwin, Sept. 6, 1966; 1 child, Trevor Adolphus Avery Baldwin. BA, Hunter Coll., 1956; MA, Columbia U., 1963. Asst. prof. Queensborough C.C., Bayside, NY, 1965—82, dir. counseling-student pers.; asst. prof. CUNY, 1965—82; exec. dir. Minisink Town Ho. and Camp, N.Y.C., 1979—91; asst. to the pres. York Coll. CUNY, Jamaica, NY, 1993—94; exec. dir. The Harlem Cmty. Inc., N.Y.C., 1995—97; pres., ceo Catalyst Consulting Group Internat., N.Y.C., 1999—. Cons. Nat. Conf. of Black Mayors, Atlanta, 2001—; bd. dirs. Louis Aug. Jonas Found., Rhinebeck, NY; cons. Murphy Fine Arts Ctr. Morgan State U., Balt., 2002—; adv. coun. N.Y. Women's Found., N.Y.C., 1988—94. Prodr.: (films) Lucky Devil, 2002; editor (founder): UPTOWN: The Voice of Ctrl. Harlem, 1979—84; prodr.: (plays) Show of Shows. Bd. dirs. Cmty. Bd. 10, N.Y.C., 1989—97; chmn. NYCMS Cadet Corps, Bronx, NY, 1970—79; com. chmn. N.Y.C. Mission Soc., The Cathedral Sch. of St. John the Divine, N.Y.C., YWCA-West Side, N.Y.C., 1970—74; nat. v.p. Am. Camping Assoc., 1988—90, 1992—94. Grantee, Hart Found., 1970, Am. Forum For African Studies, 1970; scholar, NYC Mission Soc., 1952—56. Mem.: NAFE, Nat. Assn. Fgn. Student Advisors (com. chmn. 1970—77), Internat. Women's Club, Delta Sigma Theta (life; v.p.rho chpt. 1954—56). Democrat. Avocations: writing, travel. Home and Office: Catalyst Consulting Group International POBox 250786 Columbia Univ Station New York NY 10025-1509 E-mail: hsbbest@msn.com.

BRODKIN, ADELE RUTH MEYER, psychologist; b. NYC, July 8, 1934; d. Abraham J. and Helen (Honig) Meyer; m. Roger Harrison Brodkin, Jan. 26, 1957; children: Elizabeth Anne Brodkin Brauer, Edward Stuart. BA, Sarah Lawrence Coll., 1956; MA, Columbia U., 1959; PhD, Rutgers U., 1977. Lic. psychologist N.J. Sch. psychologist pub. schs., 1961—73; assoc. dir. Infant Child Devel. Ctr. St. Barnabas Med. Ctr., Livingston, NJ, 1977-79; clin. asst. prof. dept. psychiatry U. Medicine and Dentistry N.J., Newark, 1979-90, clin. assoc. prof., 1990-2001. Vis. scholar Hasting Ctr. for Life Scis., NY, 1979; sr. child devel. cons.; cons. Scholastic, Inc., 1988—. Author: Between Teacher and Parent, Supporting Young Children As They Grow, 1994, The Lonely Only Dog, 1998, Fresh Approaches to Working with Problematic Behavior, 2001, Raising Happy and Successful Kids, 2006; co-author (with A.T. Jersild and E.A. Lazar): The Meaning of Psychotherapy in the Teacher's Life and Work, 1962; author, prodr.: (documentaries) Competing Commitments, 1984 (Best Ednl. Videotape award N.J. Cable); co-author, prodr.: (ednl. videos) Passage to Physicianhood, 1985; The Insidious Epidemic, 1986; columnist Between Tchr. and Parent, Pre-K Today mag., 1988—93, Early Childhood Today, 1993—, Scholastic Parent and Child mag., 1988—, child devel. columnist, 1991—92, columnist You and Today's Child, Instr. mag., 1992—93, Kids in Crisis, 1993—96, Ask Dr. Brodkin, Scholastic.com, 1997—, Scholastic Network, 1995—, Instr. mag., 1990—; contbr. articles to profl. jours. Fellow, NIMH, 1962; Adelaide M. Ayer fellow, Columbia U., 1962—63, Louis Bevier fellow, Rutgers U., 1976—77. Mem.: APA, Am. Sociol. Assn., N.J. Psychol. Assn. Home and Office: 2 Trevino Ct Florham Park NJ 07932-2724

BRODOWSKI, DEBRA LEE, consumer sciences educator; b. Steubenville, Ohio, Sept. 1, 1954; d. William E. Cozart and Shirley O'Leary; m. Daniel Lee Brodowski, Dec. 17, 1977; children: Richard, Michael. BS in Home Econs. Edn., Ohio State U., Columbus, 1976; MEd in Family and Consumer Scis. Edn., Berry Coll., Rome, Ga., 1994. Tchr. family and consumer scis. Paulding County H.S., Dallas, Ga., 1994—2002; early childhood edn. instr. West Ctrl. Tech. Coll., Carrollton, Ga., 2005—. Dist. rep. Ga. Assn. Young Children, Atlanta, 2003—06. Recipient Family and Consumer Sciences Tchr. of Yr., Ga. Assn. Family and Consumer Scis., 2000, Nat. Top Ten Tchr. of Yr. award, Am. Assn. Family and Consumer Scis., 2000. Mem.: Nat. Assn. for Edn. of Young Children, Am. Assn. Family and Consumer Scis. (v.p. membership 2003—04), Phi Upsilon Omicron, Phi Delta Kappa. Avocation: genealogy. Office Phone: 770-836-4702.

BRODRICK, SHERI MARY-ANN, secondary school educator; b. Toledo, Mar. 15, 1943; m. Malcolm Brodrick, June 11, 1966; children: C.J., Brooks. BS, Northwestern U., 1965; MA, Adelphi U., 1971. Tchr. drama and English Seaside (Calif.) HS, Hollister, Calif., 1988-92, San Benito HS, Hollister, Calif., 1992—98, Mohave HS, Bullhead, Calif. Tchr. English and drama Mohave CC, Lake Havasu, Ariz., speech and debate Saratoga HS, Calif., 1998-2004; bd. mem. framework com. Lake Havasu Sch.; past bd. dirs., Libr. Bd. Mellon fellow, 1993. Mem. AAUW, Calif. Tchrs. Assn., Ednl. Theatre Assn., Nat. Forensic League (Diamond coach). Democrat. Roman Catholic. Avocation: community theater. Home: 525 Valley Rd Charlottesville VA 22903

BRODSKY, BEVERLY, artist; b. Bklyn., Aug. 16, 1941; Student, The Bklyn. Mus., 1954; BA in Art, Bklyn. Coll., 1965, postgrad., 1966, Sch. Visual Arts, N.Y., 1969-70, The New Sch., 1969-70. Tchr. Parsons Sch. Design, 1979—, Adelphi U., 1980-85, Vt. Grad. Sch., Vt. Coll., others; lectr. in field. Author, illustrator: The Crystal Apple, A Russian Folktale, 1974, Sedna, An Eskimo Myth, 1975, The Golem, A Jewish Legend, 1976 (Caldecott honor medal 1977, Notable Book award 1977), Jonah, 1977, Secret Places, 1979, The Story of Job, 1986; illustrator: Forest of the Night, 1975), Gooseberries to Oranges, 1982 (Notable Book award 1983), The Purim Players, 1984, Buffalo, 2003 (Henry Bergh Honor Book award, ASPCA; Best Children's Book of the Yr., Bank St. Coll.; Notable Book award, Teacher's Nat. Coun. for Social Studies, Social Studies Trade Book Assn.); one woman shows include B.E.L. Gallery, Westport, Conn., 1979, Washington (Conn.) Art Assn., 1979, SUNY, Plattsburgh, 1980, Wilson Arts Ctr., Rochester, N.Y., 1982, Open Gallery Parsons Sch. Design, N.Y.C., 1986, Kimberly Gallery, N.Y.C., 1990, Elizabeth Stone Gallery, Birmingham, Mich., 1991, Westbeth Gallery, N.Y.C., 1998, Heller Archives Gallery, Hebrew Union Coll., N.Y.C., 1996, Telcom, N.Y.C., 2001, Studio 18 Gallery, N.Y.C., 2005, Etra Fine Arts, Miami, 2005; group shows include 92nd St. YMCA, N.Y.C., 1982, N.Y. Pub. Libr., N.Y.C., 1982, Ruth S. Harley U. Ctr. Gallery Adelphi U., 1983, Yeshiva U. Mus., N.Y.C., 1983, City Gallery, N.Y.C., 1984, Houghton Gallery Cooper Union, N.Y.C., 1985, Internat. Gallery, San Diego, 1987, Triangle Artists' Workshop, Pine Plains, N.Y., 1988, Jewish Mus., N.Y.C., 1988, Parsons Sch. Design, N.Y.C., 1989, LÖrhl Gallery, MÖnchengladbach, Germany, 1990, M-13 Gallery, N.Y.C., 1992, Galerie Berhard Steinmetz, Bonn, Germany, 1992-93, Blondies' Contemporary Art, High, N.Y.C., 1992, Janice Scharry Epstein Mus., West Bloomfield, Mich., 1992, Art Ctr. Battle Creek, Mich., 1992, Painting Ctr., Soho, N.Y.C., 1994, 96, ALJIRA Found., Newark, 1994, Elsa Mott Ives Gallery, N.Y.C., 1994, Abney Gallery Internat., Soho, N.Y.C., 1997, Broome Street Gallery, Soho, N.Y.C., 1997-98, Westbeth Gallery, 1997-98, Whitney Mus., 2000, Whitney Mus. Westbeth Gallery, 2001, Studio 18 Gallery, 2001, Guild Hall, East Hampton, 2001, Sotheby's Exhbn., N.Y., 2001, Tribeca Rooftop, 2002, Studio 18 Gallery, 2002-03, Etra Fine Art, Miami, Fla., 2005, Flinn Gallery, Conn., 2005, Art Basel, Miami, 2005, Barbara Paci Gallery, Pietrasanta, Italy, 2005, Art Fair Verona (with Barbara Paci Gallery), Italy, 2005. Conn. Commn. on the Arts fellow, N.Y. Found. Arts fellow, 2000; Triangle Artists Workshop resident, 1988, Nat. Endowment for the Arts cmmn., 1988. Office: Etra Fine Art 50 NE 40th St Miami FL 33137 Personal E-mail: bbrodynyc@aol.com.

BRODY, CAROL Z., artist, educator; b. Bklyn., July 5, 1941; d. Morris and Augusta Zimmerman; m. Elliott Brody, June 30, 1962; children: Evan, Susan, David. BA cum laude, Bklyn. Coll., 1962; postgrad., Parsons Sch. Design, 1982-86. Lic. tchr., N.Y. Tchr. Bd. Edn., N.Y.C., 1963-65, art tchr., 1991-96; instr. watercolor Armory Art Ctr., West Palm Beach, Fla., 1997-98. Instr. watercolor Art Lab. at Snug Harbor, N.Y.C., 1987-96; instr. art edn. Coll. S.I., N.Y.C., 1991-96. Exhibitions include Nat. Watercolor Soc., Calif., 2001, NAD, N.Y.C., 1994, Nat. Arts Club, 1987—2002, Salmagundi Club, 1987—2002, Pen and Brush Club, 1988—99, Met. Mus. Art, Lever house, Fed. Ct. House, Borough Hall, S.I., St. Johns U., Wagner Coll., Newhouse Gallery, Soc. for the Four Arts, Fla., 1997, Coral Springs City Ctr., 1997—2005, Cornell Mus., 1977—79, Ann Norton Sculpture Garden, 1999, Watercolor Mag., 1990, 2004, Vutler Inst., Ohio, 2001, Best of Acrylic Painting, 1996; (works appeared in) CBS-TV Ctrl. Park West, 1996; author: The Art of Layering: Making Connections. Mem. Nat. Watercolor Soc., Nat. Collage Soc., Allied Artists Am., Soc. Layerists in Multi-Media, Catharine Lorillard Wolfe Art Club (v.p., bd. dirs. 1995-96), Salmagundi Club (jury awards 1990-91, admissions com. 1991-94), Audubon Artists, Nat. Assn. Women Artists. Avocations: gardening, swimming. Home: 801 Caraway Ct West Palm Beach FL 33414-8211

BRODY, JACQUELINE, editor; b. Utica, N.Y., Jan. 23, 1932; d. Jack and Mary (Childress) Galloway; m. Eugene D. Brody, Apr. 5, 1959; children: Jessica, Leslie. AB, Vassar Coll., 1953; postgrad., London Sch. Econs., 1953-56. Assoc. editor Crowell Collier Macmillan, N.Y.C., 1963-67; writer Coun. Fgn. Rels., N.Y.C., 1968-69; mng. editor Print Collector's Newsletter, N.Y.C., 1971-72, editor, 1972-96, art writer, 1996—; dir., v.p. Picanet, Inc., N.Y.C., 1996—. Office: 2765 Deerfield Rd Sag Harbor NY 11963

BRODY, JANE ELLEN, journalist, researcher; b. Bklyn., May 19, 1941; d. Sidney and Lillian (Kellner) B.; m. Richard Engquist, Oct. 2, 1966; children: Lee Erik and Lorin Michael Engquist (twins). BS, N.Y. State Coll. Agr., Cornell U., 1962; MS in Journalism, U. Wis., 1963; HHD (hon.), Princeton U., 1987; LHD (hon.), Hamline U., 1993, SUNY Hlth. Sci. Ctr., 1999; LHD U. Minn. (hon.), 2000. Reporter Mpls. Tribune, 1963-65; sci. writer, personal health columnist N.Y. Times, N.Y.C., 1965—; mem. adv. council N.Y. State Coll. Agr., Cornell U., 1971-77. Author: (with Richard Engquist) Secrets of Good Health, 1970; (with Arthur Holleb) You Can Fight Cancer and Win, 1977, Jane Brody's Nutrition Book, 1981, Jane Brody's The New York Times Guide to Personal Health, 1982, Jane Brody's Good Food Book, 1985, Jane Brody's Good Food Gourmet, 1990; (with Richard Flaste) Jane Brody's Good Seafood Book, 1994, Jane Brody's Cold and Flu Fighter, 1995, Jane Brody's Allergy Fighter, 1997, The New York Times Book of Health, 1997, The New York Times Book of Women's Health, 2000, The New York Times Guide to Alternative Health, 2001. Recipient numerous writing awards including Howard Blakeslee award Am. Heart Assn., 1971, Sci. Writers' award ADA, 1978, J.C. Penney-U. Mo. Journalism award, 1978, Lifeline award Am. Health Found., 1978 Jewish. Office: NY Times 229 W 43d St New York NY 10036-3913

BRODY-LEDERMAN, STEPHANIE, artist; b. NYC; d. Maxwell and Ann Brody. BS in Design, Finch Coll., 1961; MA in Painting, LI U., 1975. One-person exhbns. include James Yu Gallery, 1976, Nassau County Mus. Fine Arts, Roslyn, NY, 1978, Harriman Coll., 1979, Franklin Furnace, NYC, 1979, 55 Mercer Gallery, NYC, 1979, Kathryn Markel Fine Arts, NYC, 1979, 81, 83, Anderson Gallery, Va. Commonwealth U., 1980, Bengt Torvall, Stockholm, 1982, Katzen/Brown Gallery, NYC, 1988, 89, Real Art Ways, Hartford, Conn., 1984, San Francisco Internat. Airport, 1986, Rastovski Gallery, NYC, 1987, Hal Katzen Gallery, NYC, 1988-89, 1991, Alfred U., 1990, Queensboro CC, NY, 1990, Hillwood Art Mus., LI U., Brookville, NY, 1992, Casements Mus., Ormond Beach, Fla., 1994, Broward CC, Ft. Lauderdale, Fla., 1994, Renee Fotouhi Gallery, East Hampton, NY, 1994, Hebrew Home for the Aged, Riverdale, NY, 1994, Galerie Caroline Corre, Paris, 1995, La. State U., Shreveport, 1995, Marc Miller Gallery, East Hampton, NY, 1996, Pierogi 2000, Bklyn., 1996, Arlene Bujese Gallery, East Hampton, NY, 1997, 2001-03, 123 Watts Gallery, NYC, 1998, Edison CC, Fort Myers, Fla., 2001, Hudson Opera House, NY, 2001, Cleary, Gottlieb, Steen & Hamilton Artists Program, NYC, 2003, OK Harris Fine Art, NYC, 2004, Guild Hall Mus., East Hampton, NY, 2004; exhibited in numerous group shows including Cont Art Mus., 1976, Mus. Modern Art, NYC, 1976, 78, 80, 86, Cooper Hewett Mus., NYC, 1978, Susan Caldwell Gallery, NYC, 1978, Phila. Coll. Art, 1979, Alex Rosenberg Gallery, NYC, 1980, U. Colo., 1981, Freedman Gallery, Albright Coll., Reading, Pa., 1981, Franklin Furnace, NYC, 1981, Galerie Bar de l'aventure, Paris, 1982, Newark Mus., 1983, U. Gallery, U. Mass., 1984, Holly Solomon Gallery, NYC, 1984, OH State U., 1986, The Clocktower, NYC, 1986, Henry Street Settlement, NYC, 1987, 2000, Blum Helman Gallery, NYC, 1989, Queens Mus., 1989, Basel Art Fair, 1989, Ctr. Cultural de boulogne-Billancourt, France, 1989, Pub. Sch. 1 Mus., Queens, NY, 1989, So. Alleghenies Mus. Art, Loretto, Pa., 1990, RI Sch. Design-Mus. Art, Providence, 1990, Libr., Mus. Modern Art, NYC, 1990, Midtown Payson Gallery, NYC, 1990, Hillwood Art Mus., Brookville, NY, 1991, 2001, Sculpture Ctr., NYC, 1992, Heckscher Mus., Huntington Mus., 1992, Am. Acad. Arts and Letters, NYC, 1992, Guild Hall Mus., East Hampton, NY, 1993, 2004, Ind. U., Terre Haute, 1993, Jewish Mus., NYC, 1994, Nat. Mus. Women in Arts, Washington, 1994, 2003, Ronald Feldman Gallery, NYC, 1995, Alt. Mus., NYC, 1995, 1997, Eugenia Cucalon Gallery, NYC, 1995, Rotunda Gallery, Bklyn., 1995, Redfern Gallery, London, 1995, Espace Eiffel-Branly, Paris, 1996, Fotouhi Cramer Gallery, NYC, 1996, 123 Watts Gallery, NYC, 1996, Mediateque, Les Mureaux, France, 1996, San Francisco State U., 1997, Bklyn. Mus., 1997, Weatherspoon Gallery, U. NC, 1997, Gasworks Gallery, London, 1997, HarperCollins Exhbn. Space, NYC, 1997, Parrish Art Mus., Southampton, NY, 1998, Neuburger Mus., Purchase, NY, 1998, Librairie Nicaise, Paris, 1998, Conn. Coll., 1998, Arlene Bujese

Gallery, East Hampton, 1998, 2000, 05, Generous Miracles Gallery, NYC, 1999, Montclair Art Mus., NJ, 1999, Minn. Ctr. BA, 1999, Mpls. Coll. Art, 1999, Musee Bourdelle, Paris, 1999—, U. of the Arts, Phila., 1999, Limn Gallery, San Francisco, 1999, Bklyn. Mus., NYC, 2000, Nassau CC, Garden City, NY, 2000, Ctr. Artistique, Verderonne, France, 2000, 02, U. Bridgeport, 2000, Hungarian Consulate, NYC, 2001, Coll. Art and Design, Bristol, Eng., 2001, Ctr. Book Arts, NYC, 2001, 04, 06, Sevran Svc. Culturel, France, 2001, Woodstock Guild, NY, 2002, Metaphor Contemporary Art, Bklyn., 2002, Meridian Inernat. Ctr., Washington, 2002, Topkapi Mus, Istanbul, 2002, Gracie Mansion Gallery Chelsea, NYC, 2002, Robert Wilson-Byrd Hoffman Waterill Ctr., Bridgehampton, NY, 2002, Rotunda Gallery, Bklyn., 2002, Ind. State U., 2002, Bradley U., Ill., 2002, Brussels Art Fair, 2002, Snug Harbor, Staten Island, NY, 2002, Kentler Internat. Drawing Space, Bklyn., 2002, 06, 450 Art Gallery, NYC, 2002, Gracie Mansion Booth, Javits Galleria, NYC, 2003, Chelsea Art Mus., NY, 2003,Berliner Kunstproject, Berlin, 2003, OK Harris Gallery, NYC, 2003, Bklyn. Pub. Libr., Kentler Internat. Drawing Space, NYC, 2003, Mus. Biblioteque Forney, Paris, 2004, Mediateque F. Mitterand, Argentan, France, 2005, OK Harris Booth, Chelsea Piers, NY, 2005, Pratt Inst., Skylight Gallery, Bklyn., 2005, Gilbert Pavilion, HHR, Riverdale, NY, 2006, Ctr. Artistique de Verderonne, Manoir du Boulanc, France, 2006, Bklyn. Arts Coun., 2006; represented in permanent collections including Newark Mus., Mus. Modern Art, Prudential Ins., Bertelsmann Music Group, Guild Hall Mus., East Hampton, LI, Cooper Hewitt Mus., NYC, Grafikhuset Futura, Stockholm, Sweden, Atlanta Coll. Art, Art Gallery of Peale, Brampton, Ont., Yale U. Libr. Art and Arch., New Haven, Conn., The Jewish Mus., NYC, Carnegie Mellon Libr., Pitts., Archive Concrete & Visual Poetry, Miami Bech., Chase Manhattan Bank, NY Health and Hosp. Corp., Newark Mus., NJ, Victoria & Albert Mus., London, Doubleday Books, Saks 5th Ave. Corp., Vero Beach Ctr. for the Arts, Fla., Bklyn. Mus., Montclair Art Mus., NJ, Librairie Arcade, Osaka, Japan, ArmsteaCentre Du Livre D'Artiste, Verderonne, France, Hancock Info. Group, Orlando, Fla., 2002, others; represented in public collections including the Edward Albee Found., Montauk, NY, Am. Womans Econ. Devel. Corp., NYC, Amherst Coll, Mass., Archive Concrete & Visual Poetry, Miami Beach, Fla., Art Gallery Peale, Brampton, Ontario, Can., ASCAP, NYC, Atlanta Coll. Art., Barnes Hosp., St. Louis, Bass Mus. Art Mus. Shop, Miami Beach, Bertelsmann Music Group, NYC, Bklyn. Mus. Art, Bklyn. Union Gas, Carnegie Mellon Lib., Pitts., Ctr. for Arts, Vera Beach, Fla., Ctr. du Livre d'Artiste, Verderonne, France, Chase Manhattan Bank, NYC, Cooper Hewitt Mus., NYC, Cumberland Health Facility, Bklyn., Doubleday Books, Garden City, NY, Erasmus Haus, Basel, Switzerland, Harvard Bus. Sch., Boston, Grafikhuset Futura, Stockholm, Sweden, Guild Hall Mus., East Hampton, NY, Hebrew Home for Aged, Riverdale, NY, Ins. N.Am., NYC, Libraire Arcade, Osaka, Japan, The Jewish Mus., NYC, Med. Coll. Va., Richmond, Montclair Art Mus., NJ, Mus. Fine Art, RI Sch. Design, Providence, Mus. Contemporary Art, LA, Mus. Modern Art, NYC, Nat. Mus. Women in Arts, DC, Nelson-Atkins Mus., Kansas City, Mo., Newark Mus., Print Divsn., NY Pub. Lib., NY Health & Hosps. Corp., Prudential Ins. Co., Newark, Saks 5th Ave. Corp. Collection, Troy, Mich., SUNY-Cortland, Sydney U., Australia, Tate Mus., London, Tesseract Early Sci. Instruments, NY, Paris, Victoria & Albert Mus., London, Wadsworth Athenium Lib., Hartford, Conn., WPA Bookstore, DC, Yale U. Lib. Arts & Architecture, New Haven, Conn.; contbg. artist: Postcards, Series II, JM Kaplan Fund and Pub. Art Fund, 1978, Paris Rev., 1979, ArtistMultiplesProject, 1980, WhiteWalls Mag., 1983, L'Oreil Mag., 1983, Huess House Project, Lower Manhattan Cultural Coun., 1992, Arts in the Hosps., MCV Program, Richmond, 1994, Neuberger Mus., Purchase, NY, 1998, Pub. Art, Cowparade NY, 2000, Project Purgatory Pie Press, NYC, 2001, UNFRAMED Artists Respond to Aids, powerHouse Books, NY, 2002, NUTUREart Multiple Project, 2002, Cover for Paris Rev. 2002, Gastronomica, Jour. Food and Culture, 2003; (paintings for TV) (film) The Heidi Chronicles, 1995, The Apprentice, 2004. Recipient Hassam and Speicher Purchase award Am. Acad. and Inst. Arts and Letters, 1988, Purchase award Arts in Hosps., Richmond, Va., 1994, Ann. award Guild Hall Mus., 1997, Exhbn. award, 2003; grantee Creative Artists Pub. Svc. NYS Coun. Arts, 1979, Ariana Found. for Arts, 1983, LINE grant NYS Coun. Arts, NEA, 1984, Poster Commn. NEA InterArts Program and Alt. Mus., NYC, 1984, Artists grant Artists Space, 1987, Project grant E.D. Found., 1991, USA Commn. award Lancaster Group, 1991, Spl. Opportunity stipend NY Found. Arts and East End Arts Coun., 1992, Drawing Commn., CRIA, 1999. Studio: 822 Madison Ave Fl 4 New York NY 10021 Office Phone: 718-938-1185. Personal E-mail: sbrodyl@aol.com.

BROE, CAROLYN WATERS, conductor, music educator, violist; b. Santa Monica, Calif., July 6, 1957; d. Warren Palmer and Lois Virginia Waters; m. Steve Broe, Apr. 26, 1980; children: JeanRené Waters Broe, Jasmine Elizabeth. MusB, Chapman Coll., 1979; MFA, Calif. State U., 1984; DMA, Ariz. State U., 2001. Co-prin. violist Mozart Camerata, Irvine, Calif., 1980-85; prin. violist Capistrano (Calif.) Valley Symphony, 1986-90; artistic dir. Capistrano Valley Chamber Players, Newport Beach, Calif., 1986-90; founder Orange County Four Seasons Orch., Newport Beach, 1990-93; condr., faculty violin Glendale (Ariz.) C.C., 1993—95; condr. Paradise Valley C.C., Phoenix, 1993—2003; condr., artistic dir. Four Seasons Orch., Scottsdale, Ariz., 1991—. Assoc. condr. master class Tanglewood (Mass.) Music Inst., 1995. Author: J.S. Bach's Treatment of the Viola, 1984; composer (chamber music score): Rebirth of the Goddess, 1992; prodr.(Four Seasons String Quartet): Wedding Album; dir., violist:; author: The String Compositions of Louise Lincoln Kerr: Analysis and Edition of Five Solo Viola pieces; dir.: (Four Seasons Orch.), 2000; composer: (album) Just Wishing On The Moon, 2000 (nominated Grammy award in 2 categories, 2000). Bd. dirs. Chapman Music Assn., Orange, Calif., 1985-86, Fiske Instrument Mus., Claremont, Calif., 1986-87, Capistrano Valley Symphony, 1987-88, Four Seasons Orch., Scottsdale, 1991—. Named Dream Catcher 1995, Indian Women in Progress, Phoenix, 1995; Cultural Arts grantee Scottsdale Cultural Arts Coun., 1995, 96, 2003, Artist award Phoenix Office of Cultural Arts, 2005. Mem. Am. String Tchr. Assn. Republican. Unitarian Universalist. Avocations: photography, roses, ancient history. Home and Office: Four Seasons Orch 4972 E Paradise Ln Scottsdale AZ 85254-9623 Office Phone: 602-923-0300.

BROER, EILEEN DENNERY, management consultant; b. Phila., Sept. 7, 1946; d. Vincent Paul and Jane Dorothy (Knight) Dennery; m. Paul Alan Broer, Nov. 26, 1970 (div. 1976); m. Charles Kenneth ReCorr, Sept. 10, 1981 (div. 1991); 1 child, Matthew Vincent ReCorr; m. John W. Lipe, Dec. 2, 2000. BA, Coll. Mt. St. Vincent, 1969; degree in orgn. and sys. devel., Gestalt Inst. Cleve., 1989. Dir. media, mgr. control Merrill Anderson Co., N.Y.C., 1970—72; exec. asst. fin. McCall Pattern Co., N.Y.C., 1972—74, pers. specialist, 1974—77, mgr. employee rels., 1978; dir. pers. Notions Mktg. Inc., N.Y.C., 1978—79; 2d v.p. pers. Manhattan Life Ins. Co., N.Y.C., 1979, v.p. human resources, 1980—82; corp. v.p. human resources McM Corp., Raleigh, NC, 1982—85; pres. Human Dimension, Castle Rock, Colo., 1985—. Adj. faculty bus. writing NYU, N.Y.C., 1975—78; sr. cons. PDS, Inc., Clearwater, Fla., 1990—98; cons. orgn. devel., supr. exec. coaching Lore Internat. Inst., 2001—; bd. dirs. Ctr. Health Edn. Inc. Recipient Best Application Psychol. Type award, Jour. Psychol. Type, 1999. Mem.: ASTD, Assn. Psychol. Type (chair 1992—, pres. N.C. chpt. 1995—96, pres. Rocky Mt. chpt. 2005—06), Gestalt Inst. Cleve., Nat. Assn. Women Bus. Owners (pres. N.C. chpt. 1988—89), Orgn. Devel. Network. Mailing: 2275 Sandhurst Dr Castle Rock CO 80104-2397 Office Phone: 303-660-4598. Business E-Mail: ebroer@humandimension.org.

BROERING, NAOMI CORDERO, librarian; b. N.Y.C., Nov. 24, 1939; d. Julius and Emily (Perez) Cordero; B.A., Calif. State U., 1961, M.A. in history, 1963; postgrad. UCLA, 1964, M.L.S. in Library Sci., 1966, postgrad. (NIH fellow), 1967; postgrad. Sch. of Law, U. West Los Angeles, 1970; m. Arthur J. Broering, 1971 (dec. 1992). Acquisitions and reference librarian U. So. Calif., 1967-68; chief librarian Children's Hosp., Los Angeles, 1968-71; asst. librarian Walter Reed Gen. Hosp., Washington, 1972; chief reader services, grant officer VA, Washington, 1972-75; assoc. libr. Med. Ctr., Georgetown U., Washington, 1975-78, libr., 1978—; Med. Ctr. libr. Dahlgren Meml. Library, dir. Biomed. Info. Resources Ctr., 1983—, P.I. Georgetown, Integrated Acad. Info. Mgmt. System, 1986—; mem. adj. faculty Cath. U. Editor: Bull. Med. Libr. Assn. Fellow Am. Coll. Med. Informatics, Med. Libr. Assn. (dir. 1979-82); mem. ALA, Am. Med. Informatics Assn., Am. Soc. Info. Sci., AAAS, Assn. Acad. Health Sci. Library Dirs., Spl. Library Assn., Acad. Health Info. Profls. (disting. mem.). Author, editor: High Performance Medical Libraries, 1993; contbr. articles to profl. jours. Office: Georgetown U Med Ctr Libr 3900 Reservoir Rd NW Washington DC 20007-2188

BROERS, BRENDA ANN, chemistry professor; 1 child, Maddy. MS in Chemistry, Ctrl. Wash. U., Ellensburg, 2002. Chemsitry prof. Wenatchee Valley Coll., Wash., 1999—; chemistry prof. Clark Coll., Vancouver, Wash., 2005—. Office Phone: 360-992-2981.

BROGAN, LISA S., lawyer; b. Chgo., Apr. 23, 1963; BA, Northwestern U., 1984, JD, 1987. Bar: Ill. 1987, U.S. Dist. Ct. (no. dist.) Ill. 1988, U.S. Ct. Appeals (fed. cir.) 1989, U.S. Ct. Appeals (7th cir.) 1994. Atty. Baker & McKenzie, Chgo., 1987—. Mem.: ABA, Ill. State Bar Assn., Chgo. (Ill.) Bar Assn. Office: Baker & McKenzie One Prudential Plz 130 East Randolph Dr Chicago IL 60601

BROGDEN-STIRBL, SHONA MARIE, writer, researcher; b. Tuscaloosa, Ala., Sept. 3, 1948; d. Edward Henry Jr. and Esther Ruth (Coleman) Brogden; m. Robert Clark Stirbl, Mar. 30, 1990. BA, U. South Ala., Mobile, 1972; MA in English (Poetics), NYU, 1982, postgrad. Adult protective social worker Mobile County Dept. Pensions and Security, 1972-74; child protection social worker Cumberland County Child Protective Svcs., Fayetteville, NC, 1975-76; cmty. placement specialist S.I. Devel. Ctr., 1976-78, Manhattan Borough Devel. Svc., NYC, 1978-80; adminstr. Coun. on Internat. Ednl. Exch., NYC, 1981, Office of Univ. Devel., Advt. and Pub. Affairs, NYU, NYC, 1982-85; dir. advt. Office of Advt. and Pub. Affairs, NYU, NYC, 1986; cons. Meml. Sloan-Kettering, NDRI, NYU, NYC, 1986-97. Voice recorder Book on Tape, Jewish Braille Inst., NYC, 1996; adminstrv. support Gay Men's Health Crisis, NYC, 1986; vol. Serendipity Sch. for Emotionally Disturbed Children, Sacramento, 1975; Strasberg Theatre Inst., 1977-78; founding mem. Tell It Like It Was, 1999, Ft. Bragg Semi-Reperatory Theatre Co., 1975-76, Dixie Darlings, 1966-67. Scholar NYU, 1978-82, U. So. Miss., 1966-68. Mem.: Caltech Women's Club. Christian. Achievements include patent photographic films with multiple ASA and associated camera. Avocations: poetry, art, acting, baroque violin, options trading. Home and Office: 465 S Madison #109 Pasadena CA 91101 E-mail: s.brogden.1@alumni.nyu.edu.

BROGLIATTI, BARBARA SPENCER, retired television and motion picture executive; b. LA, Jan. 8, 1946; d. Robert and Lottie Spencer; m. Raymond Haley Brogliatti, Sept. 19, 1970. BA in Social Scis. and English, UCLA, 1968. Asst. press. info. dept. CBS TV, L.A., 1968-69, sr. publicist, 1969-74; dir. publicity Tandem Prodns. and T.A.T. Comm. (Embassy Comm.), L.A., 1974-77, corp. v.p., 1977-82; sr. v.p. worldwide publicity, promotion and advt. Embassy Comm., L.A., 1982-85; sr. v.p. worldwide corp. comm. Lorimar Telepictures Corp., Culver City, Calif., 1985-89; pres., chmn. Brogliatti Co., Burbank, Calif., 1989-90; sr. v.p. worldwide TV publicity, promotion and advt. Lorimar TV, 1991-92; sr. v.p. worldwide TV publicity, promotion and pub. rels. Warner Bros., Burbank, 1992-97; sr. v.p. corp. comm. Warner Bros., Inc., 1997-2000; sr. v.p., chief corp. comm. officer Warner Bros. Entertainment Inc., 2000—04; exec. v.p., chief corp. comm. officer Warner Bros., 2004—05. Adv. com. acad. advancement program UCLA; bd. govs. UCLA Found., 2003—; adj. prof. comm. Bradley U., Peoria, Ill., 2006—. Mem. bd. govs. TV Acad., L.A., 1984-86, UCLA Found., 2003—; bd. dir. Nat. Acad. Cable Programming, 1992-94; mem. Hollywood Women's Polit. Com., 1992-93; mem. steering com. L.A. Free Clinic, 1997-98. Recipient Gold medal Broadcast Promotion and Mktg. Execs., 1984. Mem. Am. Diabetes Assn. (bd. dir. L.A. chpt. 1992-93), Am. Cinema Found. (bd. dir. 1994-98), Dir. Guild Am., Publicists Guild, Acad. TV Arts and Scis. (vice chmn. awards com.); adv. com. UCLA Acad. Advancement Prog.

BROHAWN, VIRGINIA BRIDGEMAN, retired music educator; b. Lockport, NY, Feb. 8, 1943; d. Ross George Bridgeman and Helene Elizabeth Mac Donald; m. Philip Brohawn, Jr., June 13, 1964; children: Jennifer, Bridget. B in music edn., West Va. Wesleyan Coll., 1964. Cert. APC tchr. Md. Music tchr. Cambridge (Md.) HS, 1964—67; choir dir. St. Paul's United Meth., Cambridge, 1968—81; music specialist St. Claire Elem., Cambridge, 1970—72; music tchr. S. S. Peter and Paul Cath., Easton, Md., 1977—81; pvt. tchr. French horn Cambridge, 1980—87; dir. choral music Cambridge-South Dorchester HS, Cambridge, 1983—2005; ret., 2005. Found., dir. Chorus of Dorchester, Cambridge, 1975—; adj. Md. All State MMEA, 1983—2005; music adv. coun. Chesapeake Coll., Wye Mills, Md., 1986—91. Recipient Md. State Eastern Region Choral award, Md. Music Educators Assn., 1997. Mem.: NEA, Md. State Tchrs. Assn., Ea. Shore Choral Dirs. Assn., Dorchester Educators, Dorchester Arts Ctr., Dorchester Garden Club, Cambridge Yacht Club, Alpha Xi Delta. Republican. Episcopal. Achievements include Govs. Salute To Excellence for the Md. You Are Beautiful Chorus Dir. 8 citations 1993-2001. Avocations: gardening, reading, cooking, genealogy. Home: 207 Oak St Cambridge MD 21613 Personal E-mail: cookiebrohawn@comcast.net.

BROMANTE, CHRISTINA GARCIA, mathematics educator; d. Victor and Ella Garcia; m. Scott Anthony Bromante, Feb. 28, 1961; children: Stephanie Christina, Christopher Scott. BBA, Fla. Atlantic U., Boca Raton, 1985. Cert. tchr. Fla., 2005. Gt. exploration in math. tchr. Sch. Bd. of Broward County, Ft. Lauderdale, Fla., 1993—. Office: Indian Ridge Mid Sch 1355 South Nob Hill Rd Davie FL 33324 Office Phone: 754-323-3300.

BROMSTAD, ANGELA, broadcast executive; married; 2 children. B, U. So. Calif. Asst. Telepictures Productions; dir. creative affairs Freyda Rothstein Productions, 1988—91, v.p. creative affairs, 1991—94; dir. miniseries & motion pictures for television NBC Entertainment, 1994—96, v.p. miniseries & television, 1996; v.p. miniseries & motion pictures for television NBC Studios, 1997—99, v.p. primetime series, 1999—2000, v.p. drama devel., 2000, sr. v.p. drama devel., 2000—03, exec. v.p., 2003—04; co-pres. NBC Universal Television Studio, 2004—05, pres., 2005—. Office: NBC Univeral Studios 100 Universal City Plz Universal City CA 91608 Office Phone: 818-777-1000.*

BROMUND, ALICE A., retired elementary school educator; b. Mar. 24, 1943; d. Frank and Louise Vobora; m. Henry A. Cannon, Feb. 14, 1969 (div. July 1979); 1 child, Tracy Ann Young. BA in Humanities, Biola U., 1966. Primary grades tchr., Allendale, 1967—68; tchr. grades 1-2 San Ysidro Sch. Dist., Calif., 1968—70; tchr. sch. dist. grades 1-8 Gorman, Calif., 1970—76; tchr. grade 2 Alpharetta, Ga., 1976—77; kindergarten tchr. Menifee Sch. Dist., Sun City, Calif., 1980—96, 1997—2001; kindergarten tchr., bilingual resource tchr. North Sacramento Sch. Dist.; kindergarten tchr. San Bernardino (Calif.) Unified Sch. Dist., 2001—03; pre-sch. tchr. North Sacramento Sch. Dist., 2005—. Nominee Walt Disney Tchr. Am., 1999. Mem.: NEA, Calif. Ret. Tchrs. Assn. Personal E-mail: grammaalice@sbcglobal.net.

BROMWELL, LINDA ANNE, librarian, writer; m. William A Winter, Feb. 14, 1981. BA in Recreation Adminstrn., Calif. State U., 1974; BA in Education, Western Wash. U., 1977; MA in Nonprofit Mgmt., Regis U., 2003. Cert. tchr. Wash., 1977. Tchr. Archdiocese Seattle, Mount Vernon, Wash., 1977—81; academic instr. Cascades Job Corps Ctr., Sedro-Woolley, Wash., 1988—91; adminstr. Skagit Valley Regional Ministry, Mount Vernon, Wash., 1994—98; coord. tng. ChildCare Resource & Referral, Everett, Wash., 1999—2001; libr. JD Ross Libr., Rockport, Wash., 2002—05; ind. writer Soap Lake, Wash., 2005—. Author: English Grammar Basics, 2005. Chmn. Girl Scouts - Totem Coun., Mt. Vernon, W.Va., 1988—94; liturgy chair Immaculate Heart of Mary Ch., Sedro-Woolley, Wash., 1990—96. Mem.: Alpha Sigma Nu. Independent. Roman Catholic. Avocations: reading, outdoors, travel, theater.

BRONAUGH, DEANNE RAE, home health care administrator, consultant; b. Cameron, Mo., Feb. 3, 1952; d. Myron McMillin and Kathryn Marie (Ogden) Bell; m. Richard N. Bronaugh, July 18, 1987; 1 child, Elisabeth Catherine. BSN magna cum laude, Avila Coll., 1974; MBA, U. Mo., Kansas City, 2006. Cert. nursing adminstr., ANA. Staff nurse Bapt. Meml. Hosp., Kansas City, Mo., 1974-77; nurse clinician North Kansas City (Mo.) Meml. Hosp., 1977-78; asst. dir. Bethany Med. Ctr., Kansas City, 1978-79, spl. projects dir., 1979-80, dir. critical care, 1980-81; DON Lee's Summit (Mo.) Community Hosp., 1981-84; asst. adminstr. Muskogee (Okla.) Regional Med. Ctr., 1984-86; cons. Creative Nursing Mgmt., Mpls., 1986-87; pres. Liberty Cons., Muskogee, 1992-93; state liaison for accreditation affairs ABC Home Health, 1993-94; regional adminstr. 1st Am. Home Care (formerly ABC Home Health), 1994-96; regional dir. clin. svcs. Integrated Health Svcs., Overland Park, Kans., 1996-97; assoc. Corridor Group, Inc., Overland Park, Kans., 1997; sr. assoc. Curran Care, North Riverside, Ill., 1997-98; gen. mgr. VNA Plus, Lenexa, Kans., 1998-99; design cons. Norwalk Furniture, Lenexa, Kans., 1999—; clin. outcomes specialist St. Luke's South Hosp., Overland Park, Kans., 2001—03; nursing adminstrv. coord. U. Kans., 2002—. Health care cons., 2000—; mem. adv. bd. Am. Heart Assn., Kansas City, Kans., 1979-81; clin. outcomes specialist St. Lukes South Hosp., Overland Park, Kans., 2001—. Mem. Rep. Women's Club, Muskogee, 1988, P.E.O., Muskogee, 1992. Mem. Sigma Theta Tau. Home: 11502 W 127th Ter Overland Park KS 66213-3534

BRONKAR, EUNICE DUNALEE, artist, educator; b. New Lebanon, Ohio, Aug. 8, 1934; d. William Dunham and Helen Kate (Hypes) Connor; m. Charles William Bronkar, Jan. 26, 1957; 1 child, Ramona. BFA, Wright State U., 1971, M in Art Edn., 1983, postgrad. art studies, 1989, Dayton Art Inst., 1972. Cert. art tchr., Ohio. Part time tchr. Springfield Mus. Art, Ohio, 1967—77; adj. instr. Clark State C.C., Springfield, 1974—84, lead tchr., 1984—94, adj. asst. prof., 1998—2000, asst. prof., 1989—94; ret., 1994; artist Urbana, Ohio, 1995—. Edn. chmn. Springfield Mus. Art, 1973-74; image banks participant, Ohio Arts Coun., Columbus, Visual Arts Network, Dayton, Ohio, 1994—; affiliated with The Art Ctr. of St. Augustine, Fla. Art Scene, Little Gallery, Springfield, Ohio, The Frame Haven Gallery and Frame Craft Gallery, Springfield, Ohio. One-woman shows include, Springfield, Ohio, Polo Club, Upper Valley Mall Cinema, Security Nat. Bank, Mr. C's Beauty Salon, Lakewood Beach (1st drawing, 2006), Springfield Mus. Art, Clark State C.C., Dayton, Ohio, Miami Valley Hosp., High St. Gallery, Stoeffer's Restaurant, Wegerzyn Garden Ctr., Meml. Hall, Wright State Univ., Urbana, Ohio, Champaign County Arts Coun., Urbana Cinema, South Charleston, Ohio, Cmty. Park Dedication, Phillip Caldwell spl. guest spkr., exhibited in group shows at Springfield Mus. Art, 1999 (1st drawing, 2005), Zanesville Ohio Art Ctr., 2000, accepted in over 100 area, state, regional, and nat. juried exhbns. including Wilson Gallery, Sidney Ohio and Ohio Water Color Soc. Ann. Travelling shows, 1983—84, 1986—87, We. Ohio Watercolor Soc. (Hon. Mention, 1983, 2001, Chase Patterson award, 1985, Spl. Merit award, 1990, 1st, 1995, 3d Pl., 2005, 1st, 2000, Merit award, 1997, 1998), Dayton Soc. Painters and Sculptors (Best of Show, 1974, 2000, 1st painting, 2nd painting, 3rd drawing, 1978, Hon. Mention, 1979, 3rd graphic, 1980, Best of Show drawing, 1981, 1st pastel, 1981, 1st drawing, 1991, 3rd painting, 1993, 2nd drawing, 1993, Spl. Merit award for balance, 2001, Merit award, 2001, 2003), Champaign County Fair (Best of Show drawing, 1968, 1st pastel, 1968), 1st Painting, Miamisburg, Ohio, 2003 (1st Oil, 2003, Best of Show Drawing, 2003), Represented in permanent collections, drawings and paintings in Am. Artist Renown, 1981, Shades of Gray, 1983, 1984, 1986, 1987, 1990, 1991, 1993, 1994, 1997, Miamisburg (Ohio) Gallery. Cleaned and restored art collections at Springfield Pub. Schs., Hist. Soc. in Springfield, Logan County Hist. Soc., Champaign County Hist. Soc., Warder Pub. Libr., Foos Manor Bed & Breakfast, Masonic Temple, Penn House, Mus. Art in Springfield, 1970-2006, and Calumet Antiques, Yellow Springs, Ohio, other groups and numerous pvt. collections, 1970—; mem. adv. com. comml. art, Clark County JVS Sch., Springfield, 1991-2003; judge more than 10 pub. h.s. art shows, 1970s-90s; judge Logan County (Ohio) Fair Fine Art Show profl. and amateur, 1998, Champaign County Fair Art Show, 2001. Recipient medal Bicentennial Com. of Clarke County and 4H Found. of Ohio, Springfield, 1976, Outstanding Tchr. award Clark State C.C., 1992, commd. to paint 2 past pres. Generals of the Natl. Soc. Daughters of the Amer. Revolution, which hangs in Continental Hall, Washington. Mem. Western Ohio Water Color Soc, Springfield (Ohio) Mus. of Art, Dayton Soc. Painters and Sculptors, Cin. Art Club, Ohio Water Color Soc., Nat. Mus. Women in Arts, Ohio Plein Air Painters, Audubon Artists Soc., Pastel Soc., St. Augustine (Fla.) Art Assn., Portrait Soc. Ames, others. Avocations: swimming, walking, sewing, flower arranging, travel.

BRONKESH, ANNETTE CYLIA, public relations executive; b. Vineland, N.J., Dec. 18, 1956; d. Manasha and Miriam (Kutlan) B.; m. Steven Silver Schwartz, Aug. 18, 1985; children: Sarah, Emily, Julie. BA, NYU, 1979. Sr. editor Instnl. Investor, N.Y.C., 1979; chief editor McGraw-Hill, N.Y.C., 1980-85; dir. Am. Stock Exchange, N.Y.C., 1985-87; v.p. pub. rels. Nikko Securities, N.Y.C., 1987-90; pres. Bronkesh Assocs., Clifton, NJ, 1990—. Mem. 100 Women in Hedge Funds. Mem. Securities Industry Assn. (pub. rels. roundtable), Fin. Women's Assn. N.Y., Phi Beta Kappa. Avocation: piano. Office: Bronkesh Assocs 23 Virginia Ave Clifton NJ 07012-1222

BRONSON, CAROL E., health facility administrator; b. St. Louis, Sept. 11, 1944; d. Whitfield R. and Ruby E. (Graham) B.; m. Andre Pierre Duplessis, Sr. Nov. 16, 1980; children: Carl, Carol Lynne, Sterling, Andre, Jr., William, Andra, K'rin. BBA, Nat. U., San Diego, 1978; MA, U.S. Internat. U., San Diego, 1993; MA in Culture and Human Behavior, Calif. Sch. Profl. Psychology, San Diego, 2000; student, The Fielding Inst., Atlanta. Adminstrv. coord. Calif. Sch. Profl. Psychology, San Diego, 1989—2001; mgr., owner Any Necessary Typing Svc., San Diego, 1988-93; tchr. in bus. Calif. Cmty. Colls.; tchr. San Diego City Schs., 2001. Instr. San Diego C.C., 1997, instr. 1979-2000; spkr. Cath. Diocese of San Diego, 1995, San Diego Black Nurses Assn., 1994. Author: (book) A History of Christ: The King Catholic Church 1932-95, 1996. Co-dir. nat. conf. comty. and justice, 1998-2001; probation asst. San Diego Dept. of Probation, 1994-95, tutor, 1987; children's advocate Voices for Children, San Diego, 1992-93; vol. coord. United Negro Coll. Fund, San Diego, 1985-95. Recipient 1st place runner-up award Writers Guild, San Diego, 1992. Mem. Nat. Assn. Multicultural Educators. Democrat. Roman Catholic. Avocations: reading, writing short stories. Home: 4400 Spur Look Xing Douglasville GA 30135-8656

BRONSON, MERIDITH J., lawyer; b. N.Y.C., Dec. 4, 1958; d. Ira D. and Carolyn Bronson; children: Logan Alexa, Jordan Alanna. BA, Drew U., 1980; JD, Seton Hall U., 1984. Cert. matrimonial law atty., Supreme Ct. N.J. Jud. law clk., Newark, N.J., 1984-85; ptnr. Stern Steiger Croland, Paramus, 1985-95, Shapiro & Croland, Hackensack, N.J., 1995—. Master Family Law Inns of Ct., N.J., 1996-2004. Mem. ABA, ATLA, N.J. Bar Assn., Phi Beta Kappa. Office: Shapiro & Croland 411 Hackensack Ave Fl 6 Hackensack NJ 07601-6365 Office Phone: 201-488-3900.

BRONSTEIN, LOIS HELENE, marketing professional; b. Bklyn., Sept. 2, 1950; d. Bertram Lester and Elaine (Hoch) B.; m. Howard David Glicksman, Mar. 26, 1988. BS in Math., Pa. State U., 1972; MS in Info. Sci., Drexel U., 1973; MBA, Widener U., 1982. From mem. staff to mktg. rsch. cons. DuPont, Wilmington, Del., 1973—2000; mktg. rsch. cons. DuPont Electronic Techs., Rsch. Triangle Pk., NC, 2000—. H.W. Wilson Found. fellow, Drexel U., 1972. Mem.: Am. Mktg. Assn. Avocation: painting. Office: DuPont Electronic Technologies 14 TW Alexander Dr Research Triangle Park NC 27709 Office Phone: 919-248-5080. Business E-Mail: lois.h.bronstein@usa.dupont.com.

BRONSTER, MARGERY S., retired state attorney general, lawyer; b. NY, Dec. 12, 1957; married; 1 child. BA in Chinese Lang., Lit. and History, Brown U., 1979; JD, Columbia U., 1982. Bar: N.Y. 1983, Hawaii 1988, U.S. Dist Ct. (So. & Ea. N.Y. & Hawaii dist.), U.S. Tax Ct., U.S. Ct. Appeals (Ninth & Eleventh cir.). Assoc. Sherman & Sterling, NY, 1982—87; ptnr. Carlsmith, Ball, Wichman, Murray, Case & Ichiki, Honolulu, 1988—94; atty. gen. State of Hawaii, 1994—99; ptnr. Bronster Crabtree & Hoshibata, Honolulu,

1999—. Co-chair planning com. Citizens Conf. Jud. Selection, 1993; chair State of Hawaii Tobacco Prevention & Control Adv. Bd. Author: Litigating a Class Action Suit in Hawaii, 2001. Mem. Violence Against Women's Act; mem. nat. gov. bd. Common Cause. Recipient Fellow of the Pacific award, Hawaii Pacific Univ., 2000, Profiles in Courage award, SW Bell Conf. We. Atty. Gen., 2000, Advocate of the Year, Hawaii Cancer Soc., 1999, Kelley-Wyman Atty. Gen. of Yr. award, Nat. Assn. Atty. Gen., 1999, Top Cop award, State of Hawaii Law Enforcement Coalition, 1999, Hawaii Woman Lawyer of the Year, Hawaii Women Lawyers, 1998, Tommy Holmes award, Sex Abuse Treatment Ctr., 1998; scholar Harlan Fisk Stone. Office: Bronster Crabtree Hoshibata Suite 2300 Pauahi Tower 1001 Bishop St Honolulu HI 96813 Office Phone: 808-524-5644. Business E-Mail: mbronster@bchlaw.net.

BRONWELL, NANCY BROOKER, writer; b. Columbia, SC, Oct. 11, 1921; d. Norton Wardlaw and Lucile Duty (Michaux) Brooker; m. Alvin Wayne Bronwell, June 21, 1943 (div. Mar. 1975); children: Betsy Randolph Bronwell Jones, Cynthia Alison (dec.). BS, Mary Washington Coll., 1942; postgrad., U. Ky., Lexington, 1942-43, Tex. Tech. U., 1965, 87. Tchr. English, phys. edn. Louisville Pub. Schs., 1943-46; sec. edn. dept. Jos. S. Seagram & Sons Inc., Louisville, 1945-46; sec. to sales mgr. Marshall Field Corp., Chgo., 1946; sec. to dir. purchases Jos. E. Seagram & Sons., Inc., 1946-48; freelance writer Lubbock, Tex., 1978—. Author: Lubbock: A Pictorial History, 1980; contbr. articles to mags. Co-founder, bd. dirs. Young Women's Christian Assn., Lubbock, 1953; vol. Lubbock Jr. League, Lubbock Symphony Orch., Palsy Ctr., ARC, Tech. Mus., St. Paul's Ch. Mem. South Plains Writers Guild, Lubbock Heritage Assn. (Excellence award 1981), DAR, Huguenot Soc., Friends of Libr. (life). Republican. Episcopalian. Avocations: reading, word games. Home and Office: 4108A 18th St Lubbock TX 79416-6009 Office Phone: 806-795-5731.

BRONZAFT, ARLINE L., psychology consultant; b. N.Y.C., Mar. 26, 1936; d. Morris and Ida Cohen; m. Bertram Bronzaft, Oct. 7, 1956; children: Robin, Susan. BA, Hunter Coll., 1956; MA, Columbia U., 1958, PhD, 1966. Lectr. Hunter Coll., N.Y.C., 1958-65; instr. Finch Coll., N.Y.C., 1965-67; prof. psychology Lehman Coll., N.Y.C., 1967-92, prof. emerita, 1992—. Cons. N.Y. Transit Authority, N.Y.C., 1977-85. Author: Top of the Class; contbr. chpts. to books, articles to profl. jours. and popular mags. Bd. dirs. N.Y. C. Coun. on the Environment, 1985—; bd. dirs. Hunter Coll. scholarship and welfare com. Recipient Cert. of Appreciation, U.S. EPA Region 2, 1976, Outstanding Woman of Bklyn. Cert. from Bklyn. NOW, 1974, Service to Bronx Cert., Bronx NOW, 1988. Mem. APA, Phi Beta Kappa (senator, 2000-).

BROOKE, AVERY ROGERS, publisher, writer; b. Providence, May 28, 1923; d. Morgan Witter and Lucy Avery (Benjamin) Rogers; m. Joel Ijams Brooke, Sept. 14, 1946; children— Witter, Lucy, Sarah. B.F.A., R.I. Sch. Design, 1945, Union Theol. Sem., 1970. Founder Vineyard Books, Inc., Noroton, Conn., 1971-88; pub., v.p. Seabury Press, N.Y.C., 1980-83. Mentor Annand Program in Spiritual Growth, Yale/Berkeley Div. Sch., 1991—96. Author: Youth Talks with God, 1959, Doorway to Meditation, 1973, How To Meditate without Leaving the World, 1975, Plain Prayers for a Complicated World, 1975, 93, Roots of Spring, 1975, As Never Before, 1976, Hidden in Plain Sight, 1978, Cooking with Conscience (under pseudonym Alice Benjamin), 1975, The Vineyard Bible, 1980, Celtic Prayers, 1981, Trailing Clouds of Glory, 1985, Finding God in the World, 1989, 2d edit., 1994, Plain Prayers in a Complicated World, 1993, Healing in the Landscape of Prayer, 1996, 2d edit., 2004; contbr. articles to religious jours. Mem. The Author's Guild, Oblate Order of the Holy Cross, Spiritual Dirs. Internat. Democrat. Episcopalian. Home: 27 Pasture Ln Darien CT 06820-5618 Office Phone: 203-655-6102. Personal E-mail: AveryRBR@aol.com.

BROOKE, LINDA HUNDLEY, human resources specialist; b. Chattanooga, Aug. 9, 1943; d. Howard Derwent and Leola Ruth (Taylor) Hundley; m. James Edmondson Brooke, Feb. 21, 1970. BS, U. Tenn., 1965. Buyer trainee Foley's, Houston, 1965—66; adminstrv. asst. Cameron Iron Works, Houston, 1966—67; placement dir. M. David Lowe, Houston, 1968—69; employment cons. Met. Life Ins. Co., NYC, 1969—73; EEO cons., 1973—78; v.p., dir. affirmative action Chem. Bank, NYC, 1978—87, v.p. human resources subs. liaison, 1987—89; v.p. human resources Creditanstalt, NYC, 1989—94, Sunkyong Am., NYC, 1995—98, Nat. Audubon Soc., NYC, 1999—. Home: 44 Gramercy Park N # 14D New York NY 10010-6310 Office Phone: 212-979-3010.

BROOKE, MELODY, counselor, marriage and family therapist; b. Oklahoma City, Sept. 7, 1955; d. Jerry Lee Gill and Mary Lynn Million Crowe, Laird Willis Crowe (Stepfather); m. Michael Roy Henricks, June 19, 1999; children: Athena Brooke Walker, Hayley Michelle Hahn, Heather Marie Hahn, Jennifer Michelle Henricks, Wayne Michael Henricks. Studied acting and directing, U. Okla., Norman, 1973—76; BA in Theatre, U. Tex. at Dallas, Plano, 1979; MA in Counseling and Guidance, Tex. Womans U., Denton, 1989. Lic. profl. counselor Tex. State Bd. Examiners, 1991, marriage and family therapist Tex. State Bd. Examiners, 1991, cert. adj. tchr. Radix Inst., 1999, tchr. InterPlay, 2006, faciliator Right Use of Power, 2006. Therapist The Beacon Ctr., Sherman, Tex., 1989—90, Arbor Creek Hosp., Sherman, 1990—92, The Country Pl. Adolescent Treatment Ctr., Wylie, Tex., 1992—95, John Jacobs, PhD, Plano, 1998—2001; pvt. practice Richardson, Tex., 2001—; care mgr. Charter Hosp. Dallas, Plano, 1996—97; co-dir. Timberlawn Dissociative and Traumatic Stress Unit, Dallas, 1997—98. Presenter in field. Author: (book) Cycles of the Heart: A Way Out of the Egocentrism of Daily Life, 2006. Mem.: ACA, Am. Soc. Clin. Hypnotists, Right Use of Power Tchrs. Guild, InterPlay Leaders Cir., Radix Inst., Internat. Soc. Study Dissociation. Avocations: singing, skiing, reading, travel. Office: 1221 Campbell Rd Ste 271 Richardson TX 75080 Business E-Mail: melody@melodybrooke.com.

BROOKE, SANDRA LEE, painter; b. Bremerton, Wash., Oct. 9, 1947; d. Milton John and Alberta Marguerite Griffith; m. James William Brooke; 1 child, Christen Michelle Brooke Gladu; m. Henry Marshall Sayre, Nov. 3, 1990; stepchildren: Robert F. Sayre, John P. Sayre. BFA, U. Oreg., 1972, MFA, 1993. Art instr. Ctrl. Oreg. CC, Bend, 1987—89, Oreg. State U., Corvallis, 1990—2000; asst. prof. Oreg. State U.-Cascade, 2001—. Author: Drawing as Expression, 2003, Techniques and Concepts, 2003, Hooked on Drawing, 2003, Hooked on Painting, 2003; exhibitions include Portland Art Mus., Gango, Portland, Maveety Gallery, Gleneden Beach, Oreg. Bd. dirs. High Desert Jour., Bend, 2005, Arts Ctrl., Bend, 2001—05. Mem.: Nat. Mus. for Women in the Arts (charter), Coll. Art Assn. Democrat. Buddhist. Avocations: skiing, bicycling, golf. Office: Oreg State Univ Cascade Hall 2600 NW College Way Bend OR 97702 Business E-Mail: sandy.brooke@osucascades.edu.

BROOKER, FERN G., healthcare educator; b. Chgo., July 7, 1948; m. Michael Brooker; 1 child, Erin; 1 child from previous marriage, Phil. BA, Northeastern Ill. U., Chgo., 1969. Tchr. Sawgrass Springs Mid. Sch., Coral Springs, Fla., Silver Lakes Mid. Sch., North Lauderdale, Fla. CPR, 1st aid instr. Am. Heart Assn., Ft. Lauderdale; mem. health curriculum evaluation team Fla. Dept. Edn. Ptnr. Children's Diagnostic and Treatment Ctr., Fla. Named Mid. Sch. Health Educator of Yr., Broward County, 2006. Mem.: AAHPERD, Broward County Assn. Health, Phys. Edn., Recreation and Dance, Fla. Assn. Health, Phys. Edn., Recreation and Dance. Avocations: exercise, reading, baking. Office: SSMS 12500 W Sample Rd Pompano Beach FL 33065

BROOKER, LENA EPPS, human services administrator, consultant; b. Lumberton, NC, Oct. 13, 1941; d. Frank Howard and Grace Evelyn (Smith) Epps; m. James Dennis Brooker, July 30, 1966; children: Lora, Lindsey. AB, Meredith Coll., Raleigh, N.C., 1962. Cert. elem. sch. tchr., N.C. Elem. sch. tchr., Charlotte, Robeson County, N.C., Winchester, Va., Chevy Chase, Md., Raleigh, 1962-75; coord. human svcs. program N.C. Commn. Indian Affairs, Raleigh, 1975-78; planner, adminstr. human svcs. program N.C. Dept. Natural Resources and Community Devel., Raleigh, 1978-86; dir. diversity mgmt. The Women's Ctr., Raleigh, 1990-96; mgr. Diversity prog. First Citizens Bank, Raleigh, 1996-97; human rels. and diversity mgmt. cons., 1998-99. Developer model program U.S. Dept. Labor, Raleigh, 1976; presenter Pres.'s Commn. on Status of Women, Raleigh, 1979; facilitator Internat. Yr. of Woman, Winston-Salem, N.C., 1977; speaker in field. Contbg. writer The Carolina Call, The Carolinian. Chaplain, entertainment chmn. Dem. Women Wake County, Raleigh, 1989-91; mem. Task Force on Native Am. Ministry NC Conf. United Meth. Ch., chmn. ethnic minority local ch. concerns com., 1988-91, bd. evangelism, 1986-91, audit com. coun. fin. and adminstrn., 1990-91, coun. ministries, 1992-94, mem. bishops task force on staff and structure, 1993-95, cert. lay spkr., 2006; mem. Wake County Mammography Task Force, 1990-93; cultural diversity com. Wake County Arts Coun., 1990; bd. dirs. Internat. Festival Raleigh, 1990-91, Triangle OIC, 1991-93, N.C. Civil Liberties Union, 1992-94, United Arts Coun. Wake County, 1996-97, sec. 1996; mem. steering com. for Yr. of native Am., NC Mus. Natural History, 1986; mem. city of Raleigh Human Resources and Human Rels. Commn., 1990-93; pres. bd. dirs. Women's Fund of NC, 1993-97; bd. advisors Heritage Arts Found., 1993, N.Am. Health Edn. Fund, 1994-98, Women's Leadership Inst., Bennett Coll., 1995-96; active NC Coun. on Women, 1999-2002; bd. dirs. Carteret County Domestic Violence Program, 1999; adminstrv. bd. Weaverville United Meth. Ch., 2003. Recipient Personal Advocacy for Women in N.C. Carpathian award N.C. Equity, 1993, Martin Luther King Jr. Light of Hope award Wake County Pub. Schs., 1998, N.C. Woman of Achievement Award N.C. Gen. Fedn. Women's Clubs, 2004; grantee N.C. Arts Coun., Duke-Seminars Fine Arts Found., 1986. Mem. N.C. Natural Scis. Soc. (bd. dirs. 1987-90), Triangle Native Am. Soc. (past coord. spl. projects), Meredith Coll. Alumne Assn. (bd. dirs. 1994-95),The Women's Forum of N.C. Avocations: tennis, reading, writing, collecting american indian art and objects, gardening. Address: 120 Leisure Mountain Rd Asheville NC 28804-1117 E-mail: lbrooker00@cs.com.

BROOKER, NANCY, literature and language educator; b. Hinsdale, Ill., Sept. 23, 1950; d. Raynold Mathson and Winifred Kowalski; m. Richard Brooker, Jan. 3, 1970; children: Craig, Michelle. B in English, Ind. U., Bloomington, M in Edn. Tchr. English Hebron H.S., Ind., 1980—. Home: 639 N County Line Rd Hobart IN 46342 Office: Hebron HS 509 S Main St Hebron IN 46341 Office Phone: 219-996-4771.

BROOKER, SUSAN GAY, employment consulting firm executive; b. Washington, Sept. 4, 1949; d. Robert Morris and Mildred Ruby (Parler) B. BA, St. Mary's Coll., St. Mary's City, Md., 1971. News editor WPGC Radio, Lanham, Md., 1971; mgr. trainee Household Fin. Corp., Silver Spring, Md., 1972; career counselor Place-All, Bethesda, Md., 1972-73; exec. v.p. New Places, Inc./ Get-A-Job, Washington, 1973-89; employment cons., owner, pres. SGB Consultants, Reston, Va., 1989—. Mem. Emploibank, Washington, 1978-79; guest condr. LGCW 15th Aniv. Concert, 1999. Conservation chairperson Silver Spring Woman's Club, 1993—94; watch capt. Sawyer's Neighborhood, 1997—2001; crisis crew mem. Avon Breast Cancer, 2000; outreach vestry chair Grace Episcopal Ch., 1992—94. Recipient Cert. Appreciation U.S. Fish and Wildlife Assn., 1985, Cert. of Recognition Chaplaincy Assocs., Howard Gen. Hosp, Letter of Appreciation Pres. Bill Clinton, 1996; 2d Pl. Jim McDonnell 1-mile Lake Swim, Reston, Va., 2004. Mem. Pell-Capital Pers. Svc. Asssn. (cert.), St. Mary's Coll. (Md.) Alumni Assn. (bd. dirs. 1987-91). Democrat. Avocations: swimming, travel, kayaking, strength training. Home and Office: 2209 Coppersmith Sq Reston VA 20191-2305 Office Phone: 703-758-7111. Personal E-mail: suebrooker@aol.com.

BROOKS, A. TAEKO, historian; d. Mitsuo and Haruko Oshiro; m. E. Bruce Brooks, July 23, 1964; 1 child, E. Clement. BA, U. Hawaii, 1958, MA, 1961. Rsch. assoc. Warring States Project/U. Mass., Amherst, Mass., 1993—. Co-author: The Original Analects, 1998; contbr. chapters to books, articles to profl. jours. Mem.: Soc. for the Study of Early China, Assn. for Asian Studies, Am. Hist. Assn. Office: Warring States Project/U Mass 201C Goodell Amherst MA 01003 Business E-Mail: atbrooks@research.umass.edu.

BROOKS, ANDRÉE AELION, journalist, educator, writer; b. London, Feb. 2, 1937; d. Leon Luis and Lillian (Abrahamson) Aelion; m. Ronald J. Brooks, Aug. 16, 1959 (div. Aug. 1986); children: Allyson, James. Journalism cert., N.W. London Poly., 1958. Reporter Hampstead News, London, 1954—58; story editor Photoplay mag., N.Y.C., 1958—60; N.Y. corr. Australian Broadcasting Co., N.Y.C., 1961—68; elected rep. Elstree, England, 1973—74; contbr. columnist N.Y. Times, N.Y.C., 1978—95; freelance journalist, 1978—. Adj. prof. journalism Fairfield U., Conn., 1983—87; assoc. fellow Yale U., 1989—, founder, pres. Women's Campaign Sch., 1993—96; v.p. Minuteman Media, 1995—96; coord., dir. Out Spain hist. curriculum, 2000. Author: Children of Fast Track Parents, 1989 (Best Non-Fiction Book award, 1990), The Women Who Defied Kings: The Life and Times of Dona Gracia Nasi, 2002 (Mark Twain award, 2003, finalist Nat. Jewish Book awards, 2003), Russian Dance, 2004 (1st pl. Nat. Fedn. Press Women, 2005), Spanish lang. edit., 2006. Exec. bd. Am. Jewish Com., 1987—91; trustee Temple Israel, Westport, Conn., 1991—97. Named one of Am. Women Achievement, Am. Jewish Com., 1989; recipient 1st pl. news writing, Conn. Press Women, 1980, 1983, 1985—86, 1987, 1994, Outstanding Achievement award, Nat. Fedn. Press Women, 1981, 1st pl. award mag. writing, 1983, 1st pl. award, Fairfield County chpt. Women Comm., 1982—83, 1986—87, 1992, 1993, 1997, 2d pl. award in mag. writing, Nat. Assn. Home Builders, 1983, Spl. Svc. award, Conn. chpt. Am. Planning Assn., 1983, Mark Twain award, Conn. Press Club, 2003, Pioneer award, Gomez House Found., 2003, honor, Am. Sephardi Fedn., 2001. Mem.: Conn. Press Women (chmn. nominating com. 1983—86), Women Comm. (contest co-chmn. 1983—84). Personal E-mail: andreebrooks@hotmail.com.

BROOKS, ANITA HELEN, public relations executive; b. NYC; d. Arthur and Bertha (Stewart) Sayle; m. Arnold Brooks, July 1, 1954 (div.). BA, Hunter Coll., 1950; MA, Columbia U., 1952, MLS, 1954. Tchr. Latin Hunter Coll. H.S., N.Y.C., 1955; publicity rep. WOR Radio, N.Y.C., 1955; writer King Features Syndicate, N.Y.C., 1955-59; pub. rels. exec. NBC-TV, N.Y.C., 1956; dir. pub. rels. N.Y. State Mental Health Fund Campaign, 1956, WMCA Radio, N.Y.C., 1957; account exec. various pub. rels. agys., N.Y.C., 1957-65; pres. Anita Helen Brooks Assocs., Pub. Rels., N.Y.C., 1965—. Lit. agt. Anita Brooks Lit. Agt., N.Y.C., 1956—. Writer radio-TV shows. Vice chmn. Sinatra for Meml. Sloan-Kettering Cancdr Hosp. Benefit; mem. patroness com. Harkness Ballet Found.; mem. benefit com. Mannes Coll. Music, N.Y.C.; mem. legis. adv. com. of Senator Roy M. Goodman, N.Y. State Senate. Decorated dame comdr. Knights of Malta; named hon. citizen Venezuela. Mem. Am. Women in Radio and TV, Pub. Rels. Soc. Am., Internat. Radio and TV Soc., Publs. Publicity Assn., Assn. Motion Picture Advertisers, Mystery Writers Am., Columbia U. Alumni Assn., Sisters in Crime Soc., Smithsonian Assocs., N.Y. Press Club, Eta Sigma Phi, Latin/Greek Honor Soc. Home and Office: 155 E 55th St New York NY 10022-4038 Office Phone: 212-755-4498.

BROOKS, SISTER ANNE, osteopath; b. Washington; BA cum laude, Barry U., 1970; DO, Mich. State U., 1982. Tchr., Fla.; founder Tutwiler Clinic, Tutwiler, Miss., 1983, physician, exec. dir.; physician Clarksdale Hosp.; chief of staff Northwest Miss. Regional Med. Ctr., 2000—02. Entered Sisters of the Holy Names of Jesus & Mary, 1955. Tutor Clearwater Free Clinic, Fla. Recipient Martin Luther King Jr. award, Internat. Fellowship of Reconciliation, Outstanding Commitment and Devotion to Serving Humanity award, Tallahatchie Devel. League, Pride in the Profession award, Miss. State Ho. of Reps, 2005; Nat. Health Svc. Corps Scholar, 1978. Catholic. Office: Tutwiler Clinic 205 Alma St Tutwiler MS 38963*

BROOKS, BARBARA CARRK, registered nurse, administrator; b. Albany, N.Y., Mar. 23, 1948; d. Frank C. and Nancy C. Carrk; m. Charles W. Brooks, Sept. 30, 1966; children: M. Tammy, M. Tracey, M. Tricia. AAS, Hudson Valley Cmty. Coll., 1978; BSN, Russell Sage Coll., 1991, MSc, 1993. Cert. prof. healthcare quality nurse. Staff ICU nurse Albany (N.Y.) Med. Ctr. Hosp., 1979-89; discharge planner Saint Mary's Hosp., Troy, N.Y., 1989-93; clin. quality assurance coord. Ellis Hosp., Schenectady, N.Y., 1991-94; dir. quality resource mgmt. Lanier Park Regional Hosp., Gainesville, Ga., 1994-95; dir. Cmty. Gen. Hosp. Sullivan County, Harris, N.Y., 1995-96; quality nurse specialist Eddy Visiting Nurse Assn., Troy, N.Y., 1996-98, Vis. Nurse Assn., Troy, N.Y., 1998—; mgr. Healthcare Assn. N.Y. State, Albany. Spkr. in field. Trustee St. Patrick's Ch. Mem. Northeast N.Y. Healthcare Quality (pres.). Roman Cath.

BROOKS, BETTY ANN, retired obstetrician, retired gynecologist; b. May 22, 1921; d. Frederick Param and Sarah Wallace. BA, Agnes Scott Coll., Decatur, Ga.; MD, Med. Coll. Ga., Augusta. Pvt. practice, Decatur, 1952—85; physician Ryan White Clinic, Brunswick, Ga., 1991—2000, Coastal Gen. Health Dept., Brunswick, Ga., 1986—2000; ret., 2000. Bible moderator St. Simons Parish. Fellow: Am. Coll. Ob-gyn. (life); mem.: Coastal Ga. Hist. Soc. Home: 117 Tolomato Trce Saint Simons Island GA 31522

BROOKS, DEBORAH JUNE, art educator; b. Brighton, Colo., Jan. 29, 1966; d. Ivan Lloyd and Sheryl June Brooks. BFA, Met. State Coll., Denver, 1991; MA in Edn., U. Colo., 1996. Lic. tchr. Colo. Elem. art tchr. Adams 12 Five Star Schs., Thornton, Colo., 1992—. Contract artist, instr. Butterfly Pavilion, Westminster, Colo., 2002—. Designer, painter (tidepool mural) Butterfly Pavilion, 2001; illustrator: (children's book) Tarantula Tracks: Rosie's Wild Adventure, 2004; solo exhbn., Better Framer Gallery, Lakewood, Colo., 2000, exhibited in group shows at Fairplay (Colo.) Art Festival, 1996, Adams County Fair, 1996, 1998, All About Art Festival, 2004, 2005, Friends and Family of the Butterfly Pavilion, 2006. Vol., contbr. Butterfly Pavilion, Westminster, 2000—; edn. dir. Yellow Ribbon Suicide Prevention Program, Westminster, Colo., 2003—. Named Colo. Elem. Art Tchr. of Yr., 2005; recipient Hon. Mention award, Kennedy Ctr. Schs. Excellence in Arts, 2005; grantee, Colo. Sch. to Career Partnership, 2001. Mem.: Artsource Colo., Colo. Art Edn. Assn. (nominee art tchr. of yr. 2001, 2002, 2005), Nat. Art Edn. Assn. Avocations: art, travel, teaching, learning.

BROOKS, DEBRA L., healthcare executive, neuromuscular therapist; b. Cedar Rapids, Iowa, Dec. 10, 1950; children: Brei, Benjamin, Bryan. BA, Coe Coll., 1973; MS, Clayton Coll., 1999, PhD, 2000. Cert. neuromuscular therapy Fla., natural therapeutics specialist N.Mex. Tchr. Cedar Rapids Cmty. Sch. Dist., Iowa, 1973—92; COO NeuroMuscular Therapy Ctr., Walford, Iowa, 1994—. Educator Helping Hands Seminars, Cedar Rapids, 1992—2000, Debra Brooks' Seminars, Walford, 1993—; bus. and edni. cons. Brooks Consults, Cedar Rapids, 1990—; mem Iowa Bd. Examiners, 2001—03; chair adv. bd. ABLE, 2001—02; mem., chair Nat. Alliance State Bds., 2001—02; editl. bd. Momentum Media. Contbr. articles to profl jours and newsletters. Fundraiser, performer in musicals St Luke's Hosp, Cedar Rapids, 1978—91; fundraiser, performer in Follies Cedar Rapids Symphony, 1981—99; fundraiser, performer in telethons Variety Clubs Am, Cedar Rapids, 1989—91; mem Walford Cmty. Devel., 1994—98; editl. bd. Tng. and Conditioning Mag.; bd. dirs. Cedar Rapids Concert Chorale, 2005—, chmn. fundraising, 2005—. Named Outstanding Mentor of Yr., YWCA, 2001; recipient First in Nation Edn. Award, State of Iowa, 1991, Tribute Women of Achievement award, YWCA, 2001. Mem.: Am. Coll. Healthcare Execs., Am. Massage Therapy Assn. (state v.p., edn. dir. 1992—94, nat. trustee Found. 1994—98, nat. bd. dirs. 1994—2002), Profl. Women's Network (chmn. 2002—03). Avocations: singing, painting, pianist, power walking, philosophy. Office: NeuroMuscular Therapy Ctr PO Box 277 Walford IA 52351-0277 Personal E-mail: montanadebrabrooks@yahoo.com.

BROOKS, DIANA B., former auction house executive; b. 1950; m. Michael C. Brooks; 2 children. Grad., Miss Porter's Sch., Farmington, Conn., 1968, Yale U., 1973. Lending officer Nat. Banking Group, Citibank, N.Y.C., 1973—79; sr. v.p. to pres., CEO Sotheby's North Am., 1979—80; pres., CEO Sotheby's North and South Am., 1990—2000, Sotheby's Holdings, Inc., N.Y.C., 1994—2000. Trustee Yale U., Deerfield Acad., The Allen-Stevensen Sch.; pres. coun. assocs. Frick Art Ref. Libr.; adv. bd. dirs. Old Westbury Gardens; bd. dirs. N.Y.C. Partnership. Office: Sotheby's 1334 York Ave New York NY 10021-4806

BROOKS, DONNA JEAN, counselor, educator; b. San Francisco, Apr. 26, 1935; d. Carter Oswell and Doris Elizabeth (Birt) Garver; children: Deborah Gay Marston, Nancy Jean Littlewood, Paula Sue Giles, Jerry Wayne Brooks, Barry Glenn Brooks. BA in Bus. and Psychology, Webster U., MA in Counseling; postgrad. women's studies, Ariz. State U. Career counselor Maricopa County Health Dept., 1977—97. Instr. Williams AFB Coll. Author: Celebrate Your Choices, Poetry Anthology, 1986. Pres. Chandler Unified Sch. Dist. Governing Bd., Ariz., 1988—, pres., 1991-92, clk., 1990-91; chmn. bd. Chandler United Way, Mesa C.C. Lifelong Learning, Chandler Hist. Soc., East Valley Charity Ball; adv. bd. ARC, YMCA; past v.p. and bd. dirs. Human Action for Chandler and Celebration of Women; vol. Desert Caballeros Mus., Wickenburg, Ark. Recipient Chandler Chamber Club award for contbns. to community, 1989; named Woman of the Yr. City of Chandler Celebration, 1989. Mem.: Elks, Soroptimists (pres. 1986), Wickenburg (Ariz.) Lions. Home: PO Box 21036 Wickenburg AZ 85358-6036

BROOKS, ELLYN HERSH, retired special education educator; b. Bklyn., Mar. 25, 1943; d. Leonard and Midge Roth Hersh; m. John William Brooks, Aug. 14, 1999; children: Ross Benjamin Hochen, Allison Dawn Israel. BA, U. Fla., 1964; MEd., Trinity Coll., 1975. Cert. advanced spl. edn. tchr. Md. Spl. edn. tchr. Montgomery County Pub. Schs., Rockville, Md., 1975—2005; ret., 2005. Mem.: Montgomery County Ret. Tchrs. Home: 30 Mountain Willow Ln Murphy NC 28906

BROOKS, GAIL DENISE, school system administrator, consultant; b. Camden, N.J., Oct. 24, 1951; d. Russel John and Marie Alverta (Jenkins) Brooks; 1 child, Adrienne. BA, Hofstra U., 1973; MEd, U. Pa., 1983, EdD, 1997. Tchr. Camden Bd. Edn., 1973—87, asst. prin., 1987—93, dir. curriculum & assessment, 1993—98; asst. supt. Monroe (N.J.) Twp. Bd. Edn., 1998—2004; supt. Pleasantville (N.J.) Bd. Edn., 2004—. Adj. prof. Rowan U., Glassboro, NJ, 1987—93, Rutgers U., Camden, 2004—. Mem.: Pi Lambda Theta, Phi Delta Kappa. Methodist. Home: 1596 Ormond Ave Camden NJ 08103-2941

BROOKS, GERALDINE, writer, reporter, news correspondent; b. Sydney, Australia, Sept. 14, 1955; arrived in Eng., 1989; d. Lawrie and Gloria (Van Boss) B.; m. Anthony Lander Horwitz, Dec. 15, 1984. BA with honors, U. Sydney, 1979; MS in Journalism, Columbia U., 1983. Reporter Sydney Morning Herald, 1979-82, The Nat. Times, NSW, Australia, 1985-86; Australasian corr. Asian Wall Street Jour., NSW, 1986-87; reporter Wall Street Jour., Cleve., 1983-84, Mid. East corr. Cairo and London, 1987—. Author: Nine Parts of Desire, Foreign Correspondence Year of Wonders, 2001, March, 2005 (Pulitzer Prize for fiction, 2006); contbr. articles to mags. Recipient Montague Grover award Australian Journalists Assn., 1979; Hal Boyle award for print reporting Overseas Press Club, N.Y.C., 1990, citation, 1991; Greg Shackleton scholar Australian Fgn. Corrs. Award Com., 1982.*

BROOKS, GLADYS SINCLAIR, retired public affairs consultant; b. Mpls., June 8, 1914; d. John Franklin and Gladys (Phillips) Sinclair; m. Wright W. Brooks, Apr. 17, 1941; children: Diane Brooks Montgomery, John, Pamela (Mrs. Jean Marc Perraud). Student, U. Geneva, Switzerland, 1935; BA, U. Minn., 1936; LLD, Hamline U., 1966. Dir. Farmer's and Mechanics Bank, 1973-82; pres. Brooks/Ridder & Assocs., 1983-94; ret. Lectr. world affairs, 1939—, lectr. on world tour as Am. specialist U.S. Dept., State, 1959-60; instr. continuing edn. for women U. Minn.; del. Rep. Nat. Conv., 1952; state chmn. Citizens for Eisenhower, 1956; founder, pres. Rep. Workshop. Mem. YWCA (pres. 1953-57, 62-65, mem. nat. bd., 1959-71, del. world mtg., Denmark), Mpls. Charter Commn., 1948-51, Mpls. City Coun., 1967-73, Coun. Ch. Women (pres. 1946-48), Nat. Coun. of Chs. (mem. gen. bd., v.p. 1961-69), Minn. Coun. of Chs. (1st woman pres. 1961-64, Christian service award 1967), Mpls. Coun. of Chs. (v.p. 1946-48), United Ch. Women (bd. mgrs.), Minn. UN Assn. (dir.), Nat. League Cities (human resources steering com. 1972-73, coun. fgn. rels.), U.S. Com. for UNICEF, 1959-68, Gov.'s Adv.

Com. Children and Youth, 1953-58, Minn. Adv. Com. Employment and Security, 1948-50, Midwest adv. com. Inst. Internat. Edn., nat. com. White House Conf. Children and Youth, 1960, Midwest Selection Panel, White House Fellows, 1981; trustee United Theol. Sem., YWCA, Met. State U., Hamline U. Met. State U.; mem. pres.'s adv. coun. St. Catherine's Coll.; bd. dirs. Hamline U. Midwest China Ctr., Walker Health Services; chmn. Gov.'s Human Rights Commn., 1961-65, Minn. Women's Com. for Civil Rights, 1961-64, Mpls. Adv. Com. on Tourism, 1976-82, Ctr. Women in Govt., 1987-92, adv. com. Office World Trade, 1988-92; vice chmn. Nat. Community Partnerships Seminars, 1977-82; co-chmn. Mpls. Bicentennial Commn., 1974-76; dir. Citizens Com. Delinquency and Crime, 1969-93, Minn. Alumni Assn.; pres. Internat. Ctr. for Fgn. Students. Recipient Centennial Women of Minn. award Hamline U., 1954, Woman of Distinction award AAUW, Mpls., 1956, Outstanding Achievement award U. Minn., 1962, Woman of Yr. award YWCA, 1973, Brotherhood award NCCJ, 1975, State Bar award for community leadership, 1976, Service to Freedom award Minn. State Bar Assn., 1976, Community Leadership award YWCA, 1981, Svc. Beyond Self award Rotary, 1990. Mem. AAUW, World Affairs Coun. (pres. 1942-44), Minn. LWV (dir. 1940-45), Am. Acad. Polit. Sci., Minn. Women's Polit. Caucus, Minn. Women's Econ. Roundtable, Horizon 100, Women's Club, Delta Kappa Gamma (hon.). Home: 1023 Mount Curve Ave Minneapolis MN 55403-1126

BROOKS, HELEN BOUSKY, literature and language professor, performing arts educator; d. Richard Isadore and Mary Presley Bousky; m. William Richard Brooks, Sept. 6, 1952; children: James Richard, Andrew Thomas, Steven William. BA in English, San Francisco State U., Calif., 1968, MA in English, 1971; PhD in English and Humanities, Stanford U., Calif., 1980. Sr. lectr. English Stanford U., Calif., 1994—2002, assoc. dir. Interdisciplinary Studies in Humanities, 2000—, prof. (acting) English, 2002—. Guest lectr. English dept. U. St. Louis, Madrid, 2005; del. Oxford Round Table, 2004, 05; invited spkr. and presenter in field. Co-contributing editor: The Variorum Edition of the Poetry of John Donne: The Holy Sonnets, vol. 7, 2005; mem. editl. adv. bd. Forum on Pub. Policy Jour.; contbr. to books and essays. Del. Citizens' Diplomacy Tours, 1989; lector St. Mark's Episcopal Ch., Palo Alto, Calif., 1980—. Recipient Dinkelspiel award, Stanford U., 1994. Mem.: MLA, No. Calif. Renaissance Soc., John Donne Soc. (sec.-treas., mem. exec. bd. 2005—06). Office: Stanford U Interdisciplinary Studies in Humanities Bldg 250 Rm 251-F Stanford CA 94305-2020 Office Phone: 650-723-0813.

BROOKS, HELENE MARGARET, editorial consultant; b. Jersey City, Apr. 1, 1942; d. Sinclair Duncan and Helen Margaret (McDermott) B.; m. Joseph F. Olivieri, Dec. 10, 1987 (dec. July 1991). BA, C.W. Post Coll., 1977; MBA, Dowling Coll., 1992; grad. cert. paralegal studies, Hofstra U., 1998. Asst. editor McCall's mag., N.Y.C., 1969-72, assoc. editor, 1972-75, editor features and travel, 1975-83; managing editor 50 Plus mag. Whitney Commn., N.Y.C., 1983; exec. editor 50 Plus mag. Whitney Comm., N.Y.C., 1983-87; editor in chief/mktg. mgr. Internat. Air Transport Assn., N.Y.C., 1987—2000; dir. pub. affairs and prof. Vaughn Coll., LaGuardia Airport, Flushing, NY, 2000—. Editorial cons. Am. Hairdressing Industry, N.Y.C. 1983. Mem. Am. Soc. Mag. Editors, Delta Mu Delta, Phi Eta. Republican. Avocations: cooking, reading, piano, floral design. Home: 16 Vermont St Long Beach NY 11561-1410 Office: Vaughn College LaGuardia Airport 86-01 23d Ave Flushing NY 11369 Business E-Mail: helene.brooks@vaughn.edu.

BROOKS, HILLARY AFTON, social worker; b. Radford, Va., June 10, 1947; d. Ray C. and C. Louise (Altic) Absher. BS, Madison Coll., 1970; MSW, Va. Commonwealth U., 1974. Lic. clin. social worker. Clin. social worker Cen. State Hosp., Petersburg, Va., 1970-76, So. Va. Mental Health Inst., Danville, 1976-77; social worker VA Med. Ctr., Salem, Va., 1977-80, Richmond, Va., 1980-86, Martinsburg, W.Va., 1988-98, ret., 1998; coord. outpatient clinic St. John's Hosp., Richmond, 1987-88; case mgr. AIDS Network Martinsburg (W.Va.) Social Svcs., 2006—. Cons. Alcohol Safety Action Program, Richmond, 1981-82, appointed information security ofcr. for Martinsburg UAMC. Formed and organized Women's Spirituality Grp., 1992, initiated as priestess of Avalon of the Chalice Well in Glasdonbury, Eng., 1998. Avocations: music, reading, cross-stitch.

BROOKS, JACKIE DANIEL, social studies educator; b. Raleigh, N.C., Sept. 27, 1948; d. Joan Richardson and Jack Harman Daniel; m. James Anderson Brooks, Jr., May 23, 1986; children: Beryl Kelsi Young, Emily Blake Little. BA History, East Carolina U., Greenville, N.C., 1970; MEd History, East Carolina U., 1982. Cert. tchr. level G N.C., 2005. Tchr. mid. sch. social studies St. Peters Sch., Greenville, 1974—80; tchr. 8th grade social studies Ligon Mid. Sch., Raleigh, NC, 1982—. Author: (Libr. of Congress Am. memories) Was the New Deal North Carolina's Reconstruction?. Contbr. Nat. Assessment Governing Bd., 1994—94; mentor Wake County Schools, Raleigh, 1985—2006. Recipient Nat. Honor Recognition, Save Our History; grantee Save Our History, History Channel, 2006. Fellow: Nat. Bd. Tchg. Stds. (lic. Nat. Bd. Tchg. Fellows 1999). Independent. Anglican. Avocations: travel, reading, coaching novice teachers. Office: Ligon GT Magnet Mid Sch 706 E Lenoir Street Raleigh NC 27601 Office Fax: 919-856-3745. E-mail: jbrooks@wcpss.net.

BROOKS, JANE K., real estate agent, educator; b. NYC, Feb. 5, 1921; d. Louis B. Kochmann and Nesta Bell Weicker; m. Samuel Hutchison Beer, June 3, 1989; children: Alison Spence, Roger Angus, Camilla Jane; m. Robert Angus Brooks, 1943 (dec.). BA, Smith Coll., Mass., 1942, MA, 1943. Cert. tchr. Mass., 1950, lic. real estate DC, Md., 1979. Rsch. asst. Dept. English Edn., GS English, Harvard U., Cambridge, 1958—61; coll. tchr. Dept. English., Pine MAN Coll., Wellesley, Mass., 1962—65; lectr. Dept. Literature, Am. U., Washington, 1967—69, 1979—88; sales agt. real estate HA Gill, Washington, 1979—2004; ret., 2004. Exec. interviewer Lewis Harris Poll, N.Y.C., 1976—78; editor, publicity dir. Textile Mus., Washington, 1978—79. Editor: Smith College Handbook, 1941—42, Audience Mag., 1959—62, Guide to Part-time Study and Employment in Washington, 1967. Mem.: Literary Soc. of Wash. (corr. sec.), Smithsonian Women's Com. (steering com. 1973—). Avocations: reading, singing, writing, poetry, theater. Home: 2912 - 32 St NW Washington DC 20008

BROOKS, JANET PFOHL, social studies educator, department chairman; b. Oswego, NY, Aug. 20, 1948; d. Bernard Edward and Edith Rapp Pfohl; m. Charles P. Brooks, Jr., Dec. 28, 1974; children: Charles P. III, Elaine Barbara, Stephen Andrew. BA in History, Agnes Scott Coll., Decatur, Ga., 1970; MS in Secondary Social Studies and Edn., SUNY, Oswego, 1977. Cert. tchr. NY. Math tchr. Ft. Caroline Jr. HS, Jacksonville, Fla., 1970—71; social studies tchr., student activities coord. Sandalwood Jr./Sr. HS, Jacksonville, 1971—74; social studies tchr., dept. chair Liverpool HS, NY, 1975—. Curriculum writer Colonial Williamsburg Found., Va., 1995—; AP US history reader, table leader Ednl. Testing Svc., 2001—. Christian edn. coord. Baldwinsville 1st United Meth. Ch., NY, 2004—. Avocations: tennis, camping. Office: Liverpool HS 4338 Wetzel Rd Liverpool NY 13090

BROOKS, JOAE GRAHAM, psychiatrist; b. Boston, June 14, 1926; d. Collins and Hannah Slade (Benton) Graham; m. Bernard Charles Brooks, Jan. 11, 1976; children by previous marriage: Anne Benton Millman, Jane Graham Selzer. Nursing degree, Mass. Gen. Hosp. Sch. Nursing, 1947; AB with distinction, U. Rochester, 1950, MD, 1954. Diplomate Am. Bd. Psychiatry and Neurology. Intern in medicine Duke Hosp., Durham, N.C., 1954-55; resident in psychiatry Mass. Mental Health Ctr., Boston, 1955-57; resident in child psychiatry Beth Israel Hosp., Boston, 1957-59, mem. staff, 1959-97; pvt. practice Brookline, Mass., 1959-97. Cons. New Eng. Home for Little Wanderers, Boston, 1959-75, Kimberly Clark Corp., 1983-97; asst. clin. prof. psychiatry Harvard U. Med. Sch., Boston, 1978-97; vol. psychiatrist Sr. Friendship Ctr. Health Clinic, Naples, Fla., 1998—; mem. Bd. Registration in Medicine of Mass., 1991-95. Author: No More Diapers! A Guide to Toilet Training, 1971, 2d edit., 1991, When Children Ask About Sex-A Guide for Parents, 1975, I'm A Big Kid Now! A Guide to Toilet Training for Children and Parents, 1989. Distinguished fellow APA (life), Acad. Child and Adolescent Psychiatry (life); mem. Mass. Psychiat. Soc., New Eng. Coun. Child Psychiatry (bd. dirs. 1979-82, pres. 1987-89). Home: 5950 Almaden Dr Naples FL 34119-4627 Office Phone: 239-263-7425.

BROOKS, JUANITA ROSE, lawyer; b. Merced, Calif., May 9, 1954; BA, San Diego State U., 1974; JD, Yale U., 1977. Bar: Calif. 1977, Supreme Ct. Calif., U.S. Supreme Ct., U.S. Ct. Appeals (9th cir.). Atty. Fed. Defenders San Diego, Inc., San Diego, 1977-80; pvt. practice, 1980-93; ptnr. McKenna & Cuneo, L.L.P., San Diego, 1993-2000; prin. Fish & Richardson, P.C., San Diego, 2000—. Adj. prof. Calif. Western Sch. Law, 1984-86, Nat. Criminal Defense Col. 1979—, Nat. Inst. Trial Advocacy, 1982—. Contbr. articles to profl. jours. Appeared numerous television programs including Good Morning Am., Today, CBS Morning News. Recipient Silver Tongue award, San Diego, 1999; Named One of the Best Lawyers in Am., San Diego Mag, 2001, 2005, One of the Top Women Litigators in Calif., San Francisco Daily Journ. & LA Daily Journ., 2002-05, One of Calif. Top 25 IP Lawyers, San Francisco Daily Journ., 2003, 2005. Mem. ABA, Calif. Bar Assn., Nat. Assn. Criminal Defense Lawyers (bd. dirs. 1993—), Am. Trial Lawyers Assn., Am. Acad. Healthcare Attys. Office: Fish & Richardson PC 12390 El Camino Real San Diego CA 92130-2081 Office Phone: 858-678-4377. Business E-Mail: brooks@fr.com.

BROOKS, LILLIAN DRILLING ASHTON (LILLIAN HAZEL CHURCH), adult education educator; b. Grand Rapids, Mich., May 27, 1921; d. Walter Brian and Lillian Church; m. Frederick Morris Drilling, 1942 (div. Apr. 1972); children: Frederick Walter, Stephen Charles, Lawrence Alan, Lynn Anne; m. Richard Moreton Ashton, Aug. 25, 1973 (dec. 1990); m. Ralph J. Brooks, May 21, 1994. Student, Grand Rapids Jr. Coll., 1939-41, Wayne State U., 1941-42, Grand Rapids Art Inst., 1945-49, UCLA, 1964-69, Loyola Marymount Coll., Westchester, Calif., 1970-73; life tchg. credential, U. So. Calif., Long Beach, 1973. Life teaching credential, Calif. Decorator John Widdicomb Furniture Co., 1945-49; tchr. art Inglewood Sch. Dist., Calif., 1965-73; tchr. adult edn. art Downey Unified Sch. Dist., 1973-95; tchr. art Assn. Retarded Citizens and Mentally Disadvantaged Students Downey Cmty. Health Ctr., 2003—04. Art tchr. institutionalized adults ages 18 to 60, 2000-2004; lectr. Downey Art League, 1990-92, Whittier (Calif.) Art Assn., 1991, h.s. and mid. sch. lectr., 1994-95; judge Children's Art Exhibit, Downey, 1992; participant Getty Found., San Francisco, 1993, Getty Found., Cranbrook, 1994, Getty Conf. on Aesthetics, 1995, Cin. U., 1992, El Segundo, 1994; mem. state accreditation com. Inglewood and Downey United Sch. Dists., 1966-70, 75-80, 85—; owner A & B Furniture Svc. Ctr., 1995—. One-woman shows include El Segundo Mcpl. Libr., 1965, Pico Rivera Art Gallery, 1978, Downey Art Mus., 1999; exhibited in group shows at Fairlane Show, Dearborn, Mich., 1959, Jane Lessing Art Gallery, 1966, Westchester Mcpl. Libr., 1971, Inglewood City Hall, 1973, Aegina Sch., Greece, 1973, Downey Mus. Art, 1992, 99-2000; represented in permanent collection U. Mich., Calif. Senate Bldg. Pres. bd. dirs. Downey Art Mus., 1996-2002, dir. Mus., 1998, vol. dir., 1999, bd. dirs. 1998-2000; art commr. City of Dearborn, Mich., 1954-59; former pres. Dearborn Art Inst., Pacific Art Guild; pres. Downey Art League, 1991-94, v.p., 1999-2000; pres. Exhbn. Ch., 1995, v.p. 1996-98; vol. dir. Art Mus., 1998-99; lectr. on art as a career local Downey high and mid. schs.; juried children's art shows; vol. tchr. basic art; judge art shows. Recipient Certs. of Appreciation for contbn. of leadership Coord. Coun. Downey, Downey Governing Bd., Downey Bd. Edn., 1997, 2002, Cmty. Svc. award for Outstanding Svc. Downey Rotary, 1994, Cert. of Recognition Calif. State Assembly, 1999, Downey Coord. Coun., 1998-99, award 2002; named Tchr. of Yr., Masons, Downey, 1986; painting chosen to represent dist. in state capital, 1999-2001. Mem. Calif. Coun. on Art Edn. (parliamentarian Downey 1990-92, Calco Excellence in Tchg. award 1991, various certs.). Avocations: reading, hiking, international travel, photography, painting. Home: 9318 Fostoria St Downey CA 90241-4020

BROOKS, LORRAINE ELIZABETH, retired music educator; b. Port Chester, NY, Mar. 10, 1936; d. William Henry Brooks and Marion Elizabeth Brooks. BS in Music Edn., SUNY, Potsdam, 1958; M of Performance, Manhattan Sch. Music, 1970; cert. in Religion EPS, Trinity Coll., 2001. Dir. Camp Spruce-Mountain Lakes, North Salem, N.Y., 1964-73; youth adviser St. Peter's Episcopal Ch., Port Chester, N.Y., 1964-65, St. Andrew's-St. Peter's Ch., Yonkers, N.Y., 1970-73; v.p. South Yonkers Youth Council, 1970-76; assoc. Sisters Charity of N.Y., Scarsdale, 1978—; eucharistic min., lector Our Lady of Victory Ch., Mt. Vernon, NY, 1981-93, 1981—93; asst. chaplain White Plains Hosp. Ctr., NY, 1981—2000. Cons. Quincy Tenants Assn., Mt. Vernon, 1986—; Cath. spiritual dir., 1986—; workshop presenter in kidney hemodialysis transplant; choral dir. Elem. Middle Sch.; cons. in field. Soloist Greenhaven Correctional Facility retreat, N.Y., 1994; recital St. Mary's Ch. Outreach Program, 1994. Vestrywoman St. Andrew's Episc. Ch., Yonkers, 1971-75; contralto soloist St. Peter's Episc. Ch., Port Chester, 1959-69, Cape Cod Roman Cath. Charismatic Conf., 1993; mem. Collegiate Chorale, NYC, 1958-68; svc. team mem. Charismatic Cmty., Scarsdale, 1975-91; v.p. Willwood Tenant Assn., Mt. Vernon, 1981-82, pres., 1982-84; vol. speaker NY Regional Transplant Program, 1992—; active Montefiore Med. Ctr. TRIO, 1991—, presenter kidney transplant program, 1995; active Teen/Twenty Encounter Christ, 1995-97; soloist concert Holy Spirit Episcopal Ch., Orleans, Mass.; facilitator Our Lady of the Cape, Brewster, Mass.; inspirational spkr. St. Joan of Arc, Orleans, Mass., 2002; lector, eucharistic min., workshop presenter, leader of prayer group, cons. St. Mary's Roman Cath. Ch., 1993—, facilitator RENEW program, 1994—, CORE team mem., 1996, coord. prayer group Day of Reflection, elected leader prayer group, 1998—, adviser young adults ministry, 1998-2002; asst. coord. RENEW, St. Mary's Ch., Mt. Vernon, NY, leader Charismatic Prayer Group, 1998-2000, cons. to Charismatic group, 2000—; coord. Life in the Spirit Program, 1997; trustee Edn. Parish Svc. Program, Trinity Coll., 2000; vol. chaplain for renal patients St. Joseph's M.C., Yonkers, NY, 2001—; team mem. Women's Cursillo-English, NY Archdiocese; active Christopher Leadership course Gabriel Richard Inst., NY, 2000; dir. EPS Local Task Force, 2003-; mem. Assn. Christian Therapist, McLean, Va., 2003—. Mem. Westchester County Sch. Music Assn. (exec. bd.), Scarsdale Tchrs. Assn. (exec. bd.), Music Educators Nat. Conf., West Cmty. Sch. Music Assn (exec. bd. 1967-70). Democrat. Roman Catholic. Avocations: swimming, reading, walking, organic cooking, concerts. Personal E-mail: brookhem@aol.com.

BROOKS, LYNDA BARBARA, psychologist; b. Seattle, May 4, 1953; d. James Spiro and Anna Lois David; m. Steven Lawrence Brooks, Aug. 25, 1974; children: Joseph Steven, Bryan James. BA cum laude, San Diego State U., 1994, MA in Devel. Psychology, 1996; MA in Clin. Psychology, Calif. Sch. Profl. Psychology, 1998, PhD, 2001; cert., Nat. U., San Diego, 2003. Diplomate Am. Bd. Psychology. Intern Bayview Hosp., Chula Vista, Calif., 2000—01; counselor, therapist Bio-Psyco-Social Rehab., Vista, Calif., 2001—02, The EYE, San Marcos, Calif., 2001—02; counselor Cmty. Rsch. Found., Oceanside, Calif., 2002—04; intern Oceanside Unified Sch. Dist., 2002—03; counselor crisis, referrals United Health Group, San Diego, 2004—05; psychologist Psychiatric Ctrs. at San Diego, Escondido, Calif., 2005—. Tchg. asst. intelligence testing Calif. Sch. Profl. Psychology, 1997—98; presenter in field. Editor: Calif. Sch. Profl. Psyh-newspaper, 1997—98; mem. editl. bd.:, 1996—97; contbr. chapters to books. Vol. Trauma Intervention Program, Fallbrook, 2003—05; vol., counseling ministry St. Peter's Cath. Ch., Fallbrook, Calif., 1999—2003. Recipient Poster Presentation award, Psi Chi, 1995, Nat. Honor Soc. in Psychology, 1995; scholar, Phi Theta Kappa, 1991. Mem.: APA, San Diego Psychol. Assn. Democrat. Roman Catholic. Avocations: art, theater.

BROOKS, MARSINAH L., performing arts educator; d. Brooks and Roy. BA in Dance, U. Md., College Park, 2002. Cert. tchr. Prince George's County, 2005. Dance dir. Colours performing arts group, Adelphi, Md., 2002—; tchr. dance Andrew Jackson Mid. Sch., Forestville, Md. Named Outstanding Dance Dir., Colours. Office: Andrew Jackson Middle School 3500 Regency Pkwy Forestville MD 20747 Office Phone: 301-817-0310.

BROOKS, PATRICIA SCOTT, principal; b. St. Louis, July 19, 1949; d. John Edward and Doris Louise (Webb) Scott; m. John Robert Brooks, May 22, 1986; 1 child, Ollie. BS, W.Va. State Coll., 1971; MA, Marshall U., 1974; cert. in adminstrn., Ind. U., 1990. Cert. tchr., Ind. Tchr. spl. edn. Huntington (W.Va.) State Hosp., 1971; tchr. elem. edn. Kanawha County Sch., Charleston, W.Va., 1971-78, Washington Twp., Indpls., 1979-82, tchr. mid. sch., 1982-90, adminstrv. intern, 1989-90, asst. coord., 1990, 92, asst. prin., 1990-93; prin. Pike Twp., Indpls., 1993-2000, New Pike Twp. Sch.-Snacks Crossing Elem., 2001. Participant Ind. U. Tchr. as a Decision Maker Program, Bloomington, 1989; mem. Human Rels. Com., Indpls., 1996; presenter U.S. Dept. Edn. Panelist State PTA Conv. Recipient Tchr. Spotlight award Topics Newspaper, 1983; named one of 100 Outstanding Black Women in State of Ind., Nat. Coun. Negro Women, 1990, Ctr. for Leadership Devel. award, 2002; Danforth fellow Ind. U., 1989. Mem. Ind. Assn. for Elem. and Mid. Sch. Prins., Phi Delta Kappa, Delta Sigma Theta. Methodist. Avocations: tennis, cooking, reading, dance. Home: 2432 Laurel Lake Blvd Carmel IN 46032-8902 Office Phone: 317-295-7206.

BROOKS, RENANA ESTHER, clinical psychologist, consultant, researcher; b. Bethesda, Md., July 18, 1956; d. David Abraham and Harriet (Kahn) B.; m. Robert Benjamin Rovinsky, Jan. 1, 1989. Student, Princeton U., 1978; BA, Barnard Coll., 1980; PhD, George Washington U., 1989. Clin. fellow Harvard Med. Sch., Cambridge, Mass., 1985-88; dir. psychol. svcs. Skyline Psychiat. Assocs./Commonwealth Mental Health Assocs., Va., 1989-91; founder, dir. Sommet Inst. for the Study of Power 8 Persussion, Va., 1990—. Author: Breaking the Cycle of Intergenerational Rage, Blame and Shame, 1996, A Nation of Victims, 2003, Character Myth, 2003; contbr. articles to profl. jours. Diplomate, Fellow Am. Bd. Med. Psychotherapy (also div. of cons. psychologists, clin. psychologists); mem. Am. Assn. Marriage and Family Therapy (clin.). Home: 3547 Brandywine St NW Washington DC 20008-2912 Office Phone: 202-783-0775. Personal E-mail: renanabrooks@starpower.net.

BROOKS, SHARON DIANE, lawyer; d. Bernard Edward and Alice Lillian Brooks. BA, U. Ill., 1984; MPH, Yale U., 1986; JD, Georgetown U., 2000. Bar: (Washington, D.C.) 2001, (Md.) 2000. Data base mgr./analyst Cardiac Arrhythmia Ctr., Wash. Hosp. Ctr., Washington, 1986—88; epidemiologist CSR, Inc., Washington, 1988—92; sr. data analyst U. Rsch. Corp., Bethesda, Md., 1992—94; policy analyst Project HOPE, Ctr. for Health Affairs, Bethesda, Md.; law clk. Am. Cancer Soc., Washington, 2000; atty. Olsson, Frank and Weeda, Washington, 2000—04, Alston & Bird LLP, Washington, 2004—. Contbr. reports to pub. health publs. Mem., instl. rev. bd. Project Hope, Ctr. for Health Affairs, Bethesda, Md., 1996—2003. Office: Alston & Bird LLP The Atlantic Bldg 950 F St NW Washington DC 20004 Personal E-mail: sdbrooks1@verizon.net.

BROOKS, SHERRY MOORE, medical/surgical nurse; b. Hillsville, Va., Sept. 8, 1954; d. Sylvon Ervin and Donna Lou (Jennings) Moore; divorced; children: Melissa Dawn, Connie Renae. LPN, Twin County Sch. Prac. Nursing, Hillsville, 1990. Staff nurse Twin County Regional Hosp., Galax, Va., 1992—. Avocations: cooking, country/gospel music, dance. Home: 120 Hanes Rd Lot 60 Galax VA 24333-2528 Office: Twin County Regional Hosp 200 Hospital Dr Galax VA 24333-2227

BROOKS, SUSAN W., prosecutor; Grad., Miami U.; JD, Ind. U., 1985. Ptnr. McClure, McClure & Kammen, 1985—97; dep. mayor City of Indpls., 1998—99; of counsel Ice Miller Law Firm, Indpls., 2000—01; US atty. (so. dist.) Ind. US Dept. Justice, 2001—. Chair United Way's Violence and Safety Impact Coun.; protocol chair World Police & Fire Games, Indpls., 2001; nominating com. Hoosier Capitol Girl Scouts Coun.; adv. bd. Marion County Commn. on Youth; mem. Ind. Fed. Cmty. Defender Bd.; bd. mem. Jr. League of Indpls., Little Red Door Cancer Agy., Marion County Commn. on Youth, Network of Women in Bus., Greater Indpls. Progress Com. Named Influential Woman of Indpls, Indpls. Bus. Jour., 1999, Who's Who in Law, 2002; named to 40 under 40 list. Office: US Attys Office 10 W Market St Ste 2100 Indianapolis IN 46204 Office Phone: 317-226-6333.

BROOKS, VELMA, entrepreneur, small business owner; Grad., Madam C.J. Walker Beauty Coll., Dallas, 1968; student, Bethune Cookeman Coll., Daytona Beach, Fla., Prairie View A&M U., Tex.; AA, El Centro C.C., Dallas, 1970; student, Internat. Aviation Travel Acad., Arlington, Tex., Loreal Sch. of Color, Paris, 1976. Cosmetology instr., ednl. dir. Madam C.J. Walker Beauty Coll., Dallas, 1974; salon owner, mgr. Velma B's Coiffures, Dallas; operator Neighborhood Beauty Salon, Dallas; tchr., technician Mme C.J. Walker Products Mfg. Co., Chgo.; artistic ednl. dir. Simpson's Labs., Houston; mktg. and sales dir. Diamite Direct Sales Corp., Santa Barbara, Calif.; outside sales rep. Mayo Travel Svcs., Dallas, Oak Cliff Travel Agy., Dallas. Named Legends in Bus., Ban of Am., 1997, Bus. Woman Against the Odds, Smithsonian Inst., Bus. Woman of the Yr., Theta Nu Sigma; recipient 1st place Rose D'or Championship, The Golden Rose Paris Festival, Vienna, Austria, 1974, Bus. Woman of the Yr., South Dallas Bus. and Profl. Women's Club, Pylon nat. Businessman's League, Psi Lambda, Trail Blazer award, Venture Advisors, Inc./Tex. State Assn. Beauty Culturist League, Outstanding Ednl. Contbn. award, Internat. Beauty Show Group/Advanstar Prodns., award for dedicated mentor and svc., Dallas Ind. Sch. Dist., 25 Yrs. Svc. in Indsl. Career Tech., Tex. Cosmetology Assn./Nat. Cosmetology Assn., Legacy award, Urban League Greater Dallas, 2004.

BROOKS-KORN, LYNNE VIVIAN, artist; b. Detroit, July 6, 1951; d. Loren Edward and Edith Zona (Gaub) Brooks; m. Howard Allen Korn, Apr. 17, 1977. BFA magna cum laude, U. Mich., 1973, MFA, 1976. Teaching fellow U. Mich. Sch. Art, Ann Arbor, 1976. Vis. lectr. various history of art depts.; over 280 solo and group shows since 1992. Numerous one-woman shows, including Grants Pass (Oreg.) Mus. Art, 1993, Red River Valley Mus., Vernon, Tex., 1993, Coll. Ea. Utah, 1994, Carlsbad (N.Mex.) Mus., 1994, Aberdeen (Scotland) Arts Ctr., 1995, Napa County Librs., 1996, MacLaurin Art Gallery, Ayr, Great Britain, 1996, Calif. State U., Chico, 1997, S.D. State U., 1998, Coll. Ea. Utah, 1999, Columbus Cultural Arts Ctr., 2000; group shows include Foster City (Calif.) Mus. Gallery, 1993, San Bernadino County Mus., Redlands, Calif., 1993, Ohio State U., 1994, Bryn Mawr (Pa.) Coll., 1995, Haggin Mus., Stockton, Calif., 1996, Smithsonian Instn., 1997, San Jose (Calif.) Inst. Contemporary Art, 1998, Lake Forest (Ill.) Coll., 1999, U. Bridgeport, Conn., 2000; represented in permanent collections San Bernadino County Mus., Longwell Mus., Downey Mus. Art, Red River Valley Mus., Yosemite Mus., Brit. Mus., Bryn Mawr Coll., others; work reviewed in numerous publs.; various commns. Recipient numerous awards for art, including Internat. Art Competition, 1987, 88, 89, Nepenthe Munki Soc., Wichita, Kans., 1989, Haggin Mus., Stockton, Calif., 1990, Menlo Park Civic Ctr., 1991, San Bernardino County Mus., 1992, Sweetwater County Art Guild, 1993, East Tex. State U., 1993, Breckenridge Fine Arts Ctr., 1993, Lake Worth Art League, Inc., 1993, 94, Amador County Arts Coun., 1993, Coastal Ctr. for Arts, St. Simons Island, Ga., 1993, Soc. We. Artists Signature Mem., 1994, Ea. Washington WC Soc., 1994, San Jacinto Coll., Pasadena, Tex., 1995, Peninsula Art Assn., Burlingame, Calif., 1996, San Jose Inst. Contemporary Art, 1998; Rackham grantee U. Mich., 1975. Mem. Coll. Art Assn., Soc. Western Artists (signature). Democrat. Avocations: classical choral singing, Karate. Studio: 700 Loma Vista Ter Pacifica CA 94044-2425 Office Phone: 650-355-2081, 650-355-0284. Personal E-mail: lynneart@aol.com.

BROOKS SHOEMAKER, VIRGINIA LEE, librarian; b. Oklahoma City, Sept. 16, 1944; d. Leo B. and Eloise Gilreath; m. Phil Ashley Brooks, Aug. 10, 1972 (dec. Oct. 1982); 1 child, Philip Brooks; m. Gene Darrel Shoemaker, Feb. 16, 1986; children: Rob Shoemaker, Julie Shoemaker, Donna Shoemaker, Gary Shoemaker. Student, Oklahoma City C.C., 1980; BS, U. Ctrl. Okla., 1988, M in Sch. Media, 1991, postgrad., 2000—; attended, Okla. State U. With Dept. Human Svcs., Oklahoma City, 1970-75, State Dept. Librs., Oklahoma City, 1980-87; substitute tchr. Oklahoma City Schs., 1989-91, 1995; vol. libr. Children's Libr., Children's Hosp., Oklahoma City, 1992—; libr. vol. Corpus Christi Sch. Libr., 1998—; vol. children's sect. First Bapt.

Libr.; vol. Libr. for Blind. Sponsor World Vision, Seattle, 1994—; active cub scouts Boy Scouts Am.; vol. Habitat for Humanity, Vista Care Hospice; dir. project transformation summer reading program First Bapt. Good Shepherd Children's Dental Clinic; vol. Vista Care Hospice, 2002—; project transformation reading program Wesley Meth.; reading sch. libr. tutor First Bapt. Good Shepherd Children's Dental Clinic; active, life mem. Meth. Ch. of the Servant; women mission groups Wesley Meth., First Bapt. Ch.; vol. children's sect. First Bapt. Libr. Recipient Adopt-a-Park award, 1985, 1986, 1987, Oklahoma City Beautiful award, 1985—88, Omniplex Sci. Mus., Oklahoma City, 1986—89. Mem.: Omniplex Sci. Mus. (Adpot-a-Park award 1986—89), Internat. Reading Assn. (reading tutor city schs.), Coun. Exceptional Children, Zool. Soc., Classen Alumni Assn., U. Ctrl. Okla. Alumni Assn. Baptist. Avocations: piano, reading, creative writing, making greeting cards. Office Phone: 405-171-4947. Personal E-mail: doggytown14@webtv.net.

BROOKS-TURNER, MYRA, music educator; b. Knoxville, Tenn., Jan. 13, 1933; d. Paul David and Lilli Ray Brooks; m. Ronald J. Turner, June 11, 1960; children: Stacy Turner Steele, Cheryl Turner Walker, Teresa Turner Basler. Student of piano, voice and composition, Juilliard Sch. Music, 1945—51; BMus in Piano, So. Meth. U., 1955, MusM in Theory and Composition, 1956, postgrad. in Piano, 1957—58. Educator Dallas Indep. Schs., Tex., 1956—60; choral music specialist Knoxville City Schs., Tenn., 1960—65; composer-in-residence Birmingham Children's Theatre, Ala., 1965—68; music instr. Mercer U. Music Prep. Sch., Atlanta, 1975—77; instr. composition Maryville Coll. Prep. Sch. of the Arts, Tenn., 1978—80; music instr. U. Tenn., Knoxville, 1990—92; owner Myra Brooks Turner Studio of Music, Knoxville, Tenn., 1992—. Freelance writer, pub. MBT Prodns., Knoxville, 1993—; French instr. Ossoli Cir., 2004—; composer Schaun Pub., Inc., 2000—. FJH Music Co. Inc., 2000—. Composer, prodr.: (musicals) Make Way for Love, 1955; Uh-Uh, 1956; Javaho Junction, 1958; composer, dir. The Green Dragon, 1965—68 (Seattle Nat. Playwriting First Place award); 450 music pieces, 1993—2006; contbr. columns to mags., articles to profl. jours. Music worship leader Epis. Ch. of Ascension, Knoxville, Tenn., 1992—93. Recipient Cultural Arts award, Tenn. Arts Commn., 1982. Mem.: Chopin Soc. (dir. 1993—), Beethoven Soc. (dir. 1993—), Tenn. Fedn. Music Clubs (officer, state bd. 1978—89, Ea. Tenn. divsn. jr. counselor 2002—05, Ea. Tenn. divisional v.p. 2002—, officer, state bd. 2002—, editor State Piano Competition Book 2003, 2004—06, state jr. counselor 2005—, 2005—), Nat. Fedn. Music Clubs (jr. festivals bulletin advisor 1982—90), Knoxville Music Tchrs. Assn. (sec., bd. dirs 2000—01, Composer of Yr. 1978, 2001), Tenn. Music Tchrs. Assn., Nat. Music Tchrs. Assn., Ossoli Circle (bd. dirs. 2005—, lang. dept. chmn. 2005—), Knoxville Writers Group (exec. bd., sec. 2005—), Camelot Fine Arts Club, Camelot Fine Arts Club (pres. 2005—,), U. Tenn. Faculty Women's Club, Tuesday Morning Musical Club (pres. 1990—91), Pi Kappa Lambda, Mu Phi Epsilon (pres. 1973—74, pres. Atlanta Alumnae, Music Therapy award 1974), Alpha Delta Pi. Republican. Episcopalian. Avocations: study of French, study of Italian, photography, interior decorating. Business E-Mail: MyraBrooksTurner@aol.com.

BROOTEN, DOROTHY, retired dean, nursing educator; b. Hazleton, Pa. married; two children. BSN, U. Pa., 1966, MSN, 1970, PhD in Ednl. Adminstrn., 1980. Assoc. prof. nursing Thomas Jefferson U., 1972-77; from asst. to assoc. prof. nursing U. Pa., 1977-88, prof. nursing, chair Health Care of Women & Childbearing, 1980-93, dir. Ctr. for Low Birthweight, Sch. Nursing, 1990-96, Overseers prof. perinatal nursing, 1990-96; dean, prof. Frances Payne Bolton Sch. Nursing Case Western Res. U., Cleve., 1998—2000; prof. Florida International Univ., 2001—, assoc. dir. graduate program, School of Nursing, 2003—. Cons. Sch. Medicine, U. Utrecht, The Netherlands, 1989, Ministry of Health, Malawi, Africa, 1991. Recipient Contbrn. to Nursing Sci. award ANA, 1988. Mem. Inst. Medicine-NAS, Am. Acad. Nursing (mem. gov. coun. 1988-91). Achievements include research on low birthweight prevention, postdischarge care of low birthweight infants, health care delivery. Office: Fl Internat U Rm ACII230 11200 SW 8th St Miami FL 33199

BROPHY, DEBORAH SUSAN, secondary school educator; b. Washington, Nov. 3, 1967; d. Rene J. and Anita B. Barretto (Stepmother); m. Stephen J. Brophy, Apr. 3, 2004; 1 child, Hannah Jane. MA, The George Wash. U., 2002. Tchr. Falls Ch. (Va.) H.S., 2002—, West Potomac H.S., Alexandria, Va., 2002—, sch. counselor, 2002—. Nominee Agnes Myer Tchr. of Yr., The Wash. Post, 1993. Roman Catholic. Home: 484 W Taylor Run Parkway Alexandria VA 22314 Office: Fairfax County Public Schools 6500 Quander Rd Alexandria VA 22307 Office Phone: 703-718-2500. Personal E-mail: dsbrophy@hotmail.com. Business E-Mail: deborah.brophy@fcps.edu.

BROPHY-ANTONEZ, DEBORAH SUE, special education educator; b. Bennington, Vt., Mar. 30, 1960; d. Harvey V. and Dorothy M. (Thompson) Brophy; m. John Peter Antonez, Apr. 16, 1988; children: Christopher Brophy Antonez, Jessica Lauren Antonez. BSE, Coll. St. Joseph the Provider, Rutland, Vt., 1982, MA in Spl. Edn., 1985. Spl. edn. tchr., head tchr. B.O.C.E.S., Hudson Falls, N.Y., 1982-87; learning specialist Bennington Rutland Supervisory Union, Manchester Center, Vt., 1987-94, Dorset Sch., Vt., 1994—, Dir. of spl. edn./learning specialist. Mem. Delta Kappa Gamma. Avocations: reading, sports, horseback riding, crafts. Home: 1474 Vt Rt 7A Manchester Center VT 05255-9606 Office: Dorset Elem Sch Morse Hill Rd Dorset VT 05251

BROSIUS, KAREN, museum director; Attended, Butler U., Ecoles d'arts Americaines, Juilliard Sch. Music; MA summa cum laude, Hunter Coll., CUNY. Rschr. Rsch. Found. of City of NY; pub. affairs officer Pierpont Morgan Libr.; sr. philanthropic, arts, and comm. exec. Altria Group, Inc, NYC, dir. corp. affairs, dir. corp. contbns. and pub. affairs, dir. media rels.; dir. Columbia Mus. Art, SC, 2004—. Bd. dirs. Arts & Bus. Coun., ArtTable. Bd. mem. Funders Concerned About AIDS, Nat. AIDS Fund, City Harvest. Mem.: Am. Assn. Mus., Nat. Endowment Arts. Office: Columbia Mus Art PO Box 2068 Columbia SC 29202 E-mail: Kbrosius@columbiamuseum.org.

BROSNAN, CAROL RAPHAEL SARAH, retired art association administrator; b. Paterson, NJ, July 19, 1931; d. Basil Roger and Mary Ellen Carroll (McDonald) B. Piano student of, Iris Brussels, 1940—53; student, George Washington U., Washington, 1956—61, U. Va., 1975, U. Oxford, Eng., 1975; BA in History, George Washington U., 1981, MA in History, 1987. Adminstrv. clk. Dept. Army, Def., Pentagon, Office asst. chief staff intelligence, Washington, 1955-58; clk. fgn. sci. info. program NSF, Washington, 1958-60, adminstrv. clk., 1960-65, adminstrv. fellowship clk. grad. fellowship program, 1965-72; staff asst. to Jane Alexander, chmn. Nat. Endowment Arts, Washington, 1972-94; ret., 1994. Music tchr. (piano), Paterson, 1945—53; pianist at recitals U.S., Heidelberg, Germany. With WAC U.S. Army, 1953—55. Recipient Young People's Concerts award, 1945. Hon. fellow Harry S. Truman Libr. Inst. Nat. Internat. Affairs, 1975. Mem. Am. Legion, Am. Hist. Assn., Nat. Assn. Uniformed Svcs., Acad. Polit. Sci. (contbg. 1978-81), Am. Classical League, Friends Bodleian Libr. (Oxford U.), Luther Rice Soc. George Washington U. (life), Heritage Soc. (life), Phi Alpha Theta. Home: 6030 Sunset Ridge Ct Centreville VA 20121-3051 Office: Nat Endowment for Arts 1100 Pennsylvania Ave NW Washington DC 20004-2501

BROSNICK, LISA A., science educator; b. Buffalo, June 2, 1971; d. Bernard J. and Elizabeth L. Radomski; m. Randy B. Brosnick, July 12, 1997; children: Zachary Alan, Noah Ryan. BA in Biology, SUNY, Buffalo, 1993, MS in Edn., 1997. Cert. sci. tchr. N.Y., 1993. Sci. tchr. Mt. Mercy Acad., Buffalo, 1993—95, North Collins Ctrl. Schs., NY, 1995—. Biology mentor N.Y. State Biology-Chemistry Profl. Devel. Network, 2004—. Confirmation coord. Immaculate Conception Parish, Eden, NY, 2004—06. Mem.: North Collins Tchr.'s Assn. (sec. 2004—06, Leadership award 2005), Sci. Tchr.'s Assn. of N.Y. State. Roman Catholic. Avocation: travel. Office: North Collins Ctrl Schs 2045 School St North Collins NY 14111

BROSS, KATHLEEN, elementary school educator; d. Edward Andrew and Eleanor Grace Zagata; m. Albert Louis Bross III, Sept. 12, 1987; children: Clifford Bryan, Albert IV Louis, Tempe Ann, Peter Michael. BS in Edn. and Sociology, Caldwell Coll., N.J., 2005. Cert. tchr. N.J., 2006. Student coun. advisor Lebanon Borough Sch., Lebanon, NJ, 1999—, music tchr., 2003—05, art tchr., 2004—05. Rebel 2 advisor Lebanon Borough Sch., 2000—. Life mem. N.J. Ladies Aux., Hamilton, NJ, 1987—2006; vol. Habitat for Humanity, Raritan, NJ, 2005—06, Am. Heart Assn., NJ, 1999—2006; relay for life coord. Am. Cancer Soc., Flemington, NJ, 1999—2006; vol. Am. Heart Assn., New Brunswick, NJ, 1999—2006, Mar. of Dimes, New Brunswick, 2000—06; vol. - pop top coord. Ronald McDonald Ho., Long Branch, NJ, 1999—2006; July 4th king and queen chairperson Lebanon 4th of July Celebration Com., 1987—2000; vol. Big Bros./Big Sisters of Hunterdon and Somerset County, Annandale, NJ, 1999—2006; bicycle safety coord. Lebanon Borough Sch., 1999—2006; bd. of health chairperson Borough of Lebanon, 1999—2006; vol. United Way of Hunterdon County, Lebanon, 1999—2006, NORWESCAP Food Bank, Phillipsburg, NJ, 1999—2006; ladies aux. life mem. Lebanon Borough Vol. Fire Co., 1987—2006; rep. chairperson Hunterdon County Reps., Lebanon, 2000—06. Grantee Bicycle Safety grantee, Hunterdon County Area Rural Transit, 2005—06, Pedometer grantee, Hunterdon Area Rural Transit, 2005—06, Walking Sch. Bus grantee, 2005—06, Tel. Book Recycling, R. H. Donnelly, 2006. Mem.: Kappa Delta Gamma. Avocation: photography. Office Phone: 908-236-2448. Personal E-mail: kbross@ctsd.k12.nj.us.

BROTHERS, JOYCE DIANE, television personality, psychologist; b. NYC; d. Morris K. and Estelle (Rapoport) Bauer; m. Milton Brothers, July 4, 1949; 1 child, Lisa Robin. BS, Cornell U., 1947; MA, Columbia U., 1950, PhD, 1953; LHD (hon.), Franklin Pierce Coll., Gettysburg Coll., Lehigh U., 1994, Mt. St. Mary Coll., 1998. Asst. in psychology Columbia U., N.Y.C., 1948-52; instr. psychology Hunter Coll., N.Y.C., 1948-52; ind. psychologist, writer, 1952—. Co-host: TV program Sports Showcase, 1956; appearances: TV program Dr. Joyce Brothers, 1958-63, Consult Dr. Brothers, 1960-66, Ask Dr. Brothers, 1965-75; hostess (TV syndication) Living Easy with Dr. Joyce Brothers, 1972-75; columnist TV syndication, N.Am. Newspaper Alliance, 1961-71, Bell-McClure Syndicate, 1963-71, King Features Syndicate, 1972—, Good Housekeeping mag., 1962—; appearances Sta. WNBC, 1966-70; radio program Emphasis, 1966-75, Monitor, 1967-75, Sta. WMCA, 1970-73, ABC Reports, 1966-67, NBC Radio Network Newsline, 1975—; news analyst radio program, Metro Media-TV, 1975-76, news corr., TVN, Inc., 1975-76, Sta. KABC-TV, 1977-82, Sta. WABC-TV, 1980-82,, 86-88, Sta. WLS-TV, 1980-82, NIWS Syndicated News Service, 1982-84, The Dr. Joyce Brothers Program, The Disney Channel, 1985, Sta. KCBS-TV News, 1987—; contbr. CBS News, 2003—, MSNBC, 2003—; spl. feature writer Hearst papers, UPI; current affairs spl. corr. Fox TV Syndication, 1990-97; featured on A&E's Biography, 1999; author: Ten Days to a Successful Memory, 1959, Woman, 1961, The Brothers System for Liberated Love and Marriage, 1975, How to Get Whatever You Want Out of Life, 1978, What Every Woman Should Know About Men, 1982, What Every Woman Ought to Know About Love and Marriage, 1988, The Successful Woman, 1989, Widowed, 1990, Positive Plus: The Practical Plan to Liking Yourself Better, 1994. Co-chmn. sports com. Lighthouse for Blind; door-to-door chmn. Fedn. Jewish Philanthropies, N.Y.C.; mem. fund raising com. Olympic Fund; mem. People-to-People Program. Winner $64,000 Question TV Program, 1956, $64,000 Challenge, 1957; recipient Mennen Baby Found. award, 1959, Newhouse Newspaper award, 1959, Am. Acad. Achievement award, Am. Parkinson Disease Assn. award, 1971, Deadline award Sigma Delta Chi, 1971, Pres.'s Cabinet award U. Detroit, 1975, Woman of Achievement award Women's City Club Cleve., 1981, award Calif. Home Econs. Assn., 1981, award Distrubutive Edn. Clubs Am., 1981, Golden Gavel Excellence in Comm. award Toastmasters, 1982, Pub. Svc. award Ridgewood Women's Club, 1987, Women Who Make a Difference award Sen. Bill Bradley, 1990, Gt. Am. award Bards of Bohemia, 1993, Diamond award, 1994, George M. and Mary Jane Leader Healthcare Achievement award, 1995, Nat. Cmty. Svc. award McQuade Children Svcs., 1998, Presdl. citation Am. Psychol. Assn., 2002. Mem. Sigma Xi. Office: NBC Westwood One Radio Network 1700 Broadway New York NY 10019-5905

BROTHERS, LYNDA LEE, lawyer; b. Palo Alto, Calif., Nov. 21, 1945; BS in genetics, U. Calif., Berkeley, 1968; MS in biochemical genetics, U. Va., 1971; JD, Golden Gate U., 1976. Bar: Calif. 1976, Wash. 1986. Counsel com. sci. and tech. subcom. environment and atmosphere US Ho. of Reps., Washington, 1977-79; dep. asst. sec. for environment US Dept. Energy, Washington, 1979-81; asst. dir. solid, hazardous and radioactive waste and air pollution Wash. Dept. Ecology, Olympia, 1984-86; with Heller, Ehrman, White & McAuliffe, Seattle, 1986-90; ptnr. Davis, Wright & Tremaine, Seattle, 1990—2000, Sonnenschein Nath & Rosenthal LLP, San Francisco, 2000—. Mem. bd. on Radioactive Waste Mgmt. NRC, 1989—96. Mem. editorial bd. Golden Gate U. Law Rev., 1976; contbr. articles to sci. and legal jours. Mem. N.W. Citizens' Forum on High Level Nuclear Waste at Hanford, 1986-88; pres. Washington Environ. Found., 1983-90. Office: Sonnenschein Nath & Rosenthal LLP 685 Market St, 6th Fl San Francisco CA 94105 Office Phone: 415-882-0344. Office Fax: 415-543-5472. Business E-Mail: lbrothers@sonnenschein.com.

BROTMAN, BARBARA LOUISE, journalist, writer; b. N.Y.C., Feb. 23, 1956; d. Oscar J. and Ruth (Branchor) Brotman; m. Chuck Berman, Aug. 28, 1983; children: Robin, Nina. BA, Queens Coll., 1978. Writer, columnist Chgo. Tribune, 1978—. Recipient Ill. Newspapers Column Writing award, UPI, 1984, Peter Lisagor award, Sigma Delta Chi, 1984; John S. Knight fellow for profl. journalism, 2004. Avocation: broomball. Office: Chgo Tribune Co 435 N Michigan Ave Chicago IL 60611-4066

BROTMAN, PHYLLIS BLOCK, advertising executive, public relations executive; b. Balt., Mar. 23, 1934; d. Sol. George and Delma (Herman) Block; m. Don N. Brotman, Aug. 16, 1953; children: Solomon G., Barbara Brotman Kaylor. Student, Balt. Jr. Coll., U. Va., Mary Washington Coll. Assoc. Channel 13 TV, 1953-55; free-lance pub. rels., 1960-66; coord. pub. rels. Md. Coun. Edn. TV, 1965-66; pres., CEO Image Dynamics, Inc., Balt., 1966—. Lectr., cons. Md. Gen. Assembly Legis. Info. Program, 1968-70; panelist TV and radio; bd. dirs., trustee Notre Dame Coll., Md.; bd. visitors Elon Coll., N.C.; vice chair bd. visitors Towson U., Md. Columnist Balt. Bus. Jour., 1965. State chair U.S. Olympics Com. Mid-Atlantic Region, 1989-92; chair, com. mem. Greater Balt. Com., 1985-87, econ. devel. coun., 1990-91; adv. bd. Nat. Aquarium Balt., 1988—; bd. dirs. Nat. Adv. Rev. Bd., 1988-89, Balt. Symphony Orch., 1989-2001, mktg. com. 75th ann. season, 1991; active Balt. Pub. Rels. Coun.; chair adv. bd. Children and Youth Trust Fund, 1989—; bd. dirs. Internat. Visitors Ctr., co-chair mktg. com., 1990—; founding mem. Chamber Symphony San Francisco, 1984, bd. dirs., 1984-91; pub. rels. com., pres. adv. coun. U. Md. Sys., 1988—; 20th ann. conf. com. Internat. Urban Fellows Program Johns Hopkins Inst. Policy Studies, 1989-90; cmty. resources bd. Jr. League Balt., 1982-87; bd. dirs. New Directions for Women, 1979, 87-90, Stella Maris Hospice Oper. Corp., 1985-87, Jewish Family and Childrens Soc., 1980-83, Nat. Coun. Jewish Women; mem. comm. United Way Ctrl. Md., 1981-83; mktg. and pub. rels. com. Balt. Mus. Art, 1982-84, hon. com. Joshua Johnson Coun. and Endowment Fund, 1988; active U. Md. Endowments Com., 1978-79; nat. commr. B'nai B'rith Youth Commn.; bd. electors Balt. Hebrew Congregation, pres. parents assn., religious sch. com., bd. congregation; past bd. dirs. Assoc. Placement and Guidance Bur., Levindale Home and Infirmary Ladies Aux., Sinai Hosp. Aux., Nat. Jewish Welfare Fund; chair Balt. County Econ. Devel. Commn., 1987-91; appointed commn., 1980; appointed Mayors Commn. Telecomm., 1987-90; appointed State of Md. Legis. Compensation Commn., 1979—, Mayor Balt. Bus. Delegation for Balt. Conv. Ctr., 1979; bd. trustees Loyola Coll. Balt., 1986-93, treas., 1981, 82-83; bd. adv. Towson State U., 1989-, bd. vice-chair, 2004-, bd. vis., mem. adv. coun. Sch. Bus. & Econs., 1983-85; Found. bd. dirs. Mary Washington Coll., 1985-87, 88-92, speaker jr. class ring ceremony, 1981; mem. exec. com. Inst. Politics and Govt. Coll. Continuing Edn. U. So. Calif.; commencement speaker U. Ky. Coll. Dentistry, 1982; chmn. panel State Dept. Edu., 2001-2002; mem. Bd. Edn. Visionary Panel, 2001—, chmn. support task force; bd. visitors Towson U.; chmn. Sch. Comms. Recipient Cert. Achievement, Young Womens Leadership Coun., Cert. Appreciation for svc. to Md. Gen. Assembly by Md. Senate, Cert. Achievement in profession Md. Ho. Dels., Legis. Info. Program Pub. Rels. Soc. Am. Md. Chpt., Cert. Appreciation pub. svc. Md. Area Residences Youth, Pub. Rels. award Great Chesapeake Balloon Race Pub. Rels. Soc. Am., Md. Chpt., Leadership award nat. svc. to profession Internat. Orgn. Women Execs., 1980, Dedicated Svc. award Jewish Family and Children, 1983, Pres. Citation pvt. sector initiatives, 1985, Guardian of Menorah Internat. award B'nai B'rith, 1986; named one of Balt. Most Powerful Women, Balt. Mag., Balt. Outstanding Women Mgts. WMAR-TV, U. Balt., 1983, Woman of Yr., Arlene Rosenbloom Wyman Guild-U. Md. Cancer Ctr., 1984, B'nai B'rith Internat., 1985, 94, Avon Products, Inc., 1990, Media Advocate of Yr. for Md. U.S. Small Bus. Adminstrn., 1985, Most Admired company Balt. Mag., 1987-89, Entrepreneur of Yr. Balt. County Econ. Devel., 1990, Save-A-Heart Humanitarian of Yr., 1991, Balt. County Woman of Yr., 2004. Mem. Am. Assn. Adv. Agencies (chair mid-Atlantic region 1981-82, gov. eastern region 1982-84, chair 1986-87, bd. dirs., gov. rels. com. 1982-87), Am. Assn. Polit. Cons. (pres. 1976-80, bd. dirs. 1974-76, 80—), Nat. Coun. Jewish Women (life, bd. dirs.), Pub. Rels. Soc. Am. (Md. chpt nat. chair rountable 1987-88, co-chair nat. conf. 1980, v.p. 1968, Silver Anvil award 1988, Lifetime Achievement award 1993), Am. Adv. Fedn. (co-chair pub. rels. com. 1986-88, nat. govt. rels. coun. 1982—, chair legis. com. 1981), Meeting Planners Internat. (co-chair pub. rels. 1978-80, task force election by-laws 1979), Adv. Assn. Balt. (bd. dirs. 1974-76), Md.-DC-Del. Press Assn. (co-chair assocs. sect. 1982-83), Am. Trauma Soc. (nat. bd. dirs. 1981-87, Md. bd. dirs. 1982-89), Balt. County C. of C. (co-chmn. pub. rels. 2003—, mem. legis. com., 2002—), Beta Gamma Sigma, Alpha Sigma Nu, Balt. Md. C. of C. (v.p. membership 1991—, v.p. leadership Md. bd. govs. 1992-93, v.p. ctrl. dist. 1985-91, legis. conf. chair 1990, exec. com. 1986—, bd. dirs. 1984—), Balt. County C. of C. (bd. dirs. 2004-, Woman of Yr. 2004), Ctr. Club Balt. (bd. dirs., comm. chair 1983—, pres. 2003—). Avocations: tennis, flying, wine tasting. Home: 8105 Mcdonogh Rd Baltimore MD 21208-1005 Office: Image Dynamics Inc 8105 Mcdonogh Rd Baltimore MD 21208-1005 Office Phone: 410-363-1565. Personal E-mail: pbbrotman@comcast.net.

BROUGHTON, HAZEL CALLEN, rehabilitation counselor, consultant; b. Avant, Okla., Feb. 13, 1920; d. Melvin Harvey and Dorothy Lee (Avant) C.; m. Seldon Broughton, Jan. 15, 1944 (div. Oct. 1978); children: Nancy, Richard, Carol. AA, Del Mar Coll., Corpus Christi, Tex., 1975; BA magna cum laude in Comm.-Sociology, Tex. A&I State U., 1976, MA in Comm., 1976. Cert. rehab. counselor, vocat. expert, Tex. Ind. field interviewer, Corpus Christi, 1965-70; owner, mgr. Broughton Market Rsch. Field Svc., Corpus Christi, 1970-79; pers. cons. Barron Pers., Houston, 1980-83; mgr. Heakin Market Rsch., Houston, 1983-84; job readiness trainer and counselor Tex. Rehab. Commn., Houston, 1984—, impartial hearings officer, 1994—; rehab. med. & vocat. case mgr. Resource Opportunities, 1995—. Tex. del. Nat. Rehab. Govtl. Affairs Seminar, Washington, 1990—91; network vocat. rehab. counselor Union Pacific Railroad, 2003—. Mem. Women's Polit. Caucus, Corpus Christi, 1973-78; pres. Women's Equity Action League, Corpus Christi, 1976. Mem. Tex. Rehab. Assn. (pres. job placement div. 1988-89, bd. dirs. 1990-92, Bottom Line award 1989), Teal Run Investment Club (founder, pres. 1994—), Phi Theta Kappa. Avocations: creative writing, travel, photography, reading.

BROUGHTON, MARGARET MARTHA, mental health nurse; b. London, Ky., Feb. 1, 1926; d. Edward Broughton and Stella Alice Johnson; m. Louis Kurt Henkel, May 17, 1947 (div. Nov. 1957); children: Gretchen Maria Henkel Clark, Suzanne Henkel Guthrie, Elizabeth Henkel Stark, David Lawrence Henkel, John Arthur Henkel. RN, Christ Hosp. Sch. Nursing, Cin., 1947; BA in Religious Studies, U. Calif., Santa Barbara, 2003. Staff nurse, psychiatric nurse to asst. supt. psychiatric nurse and instr. Camarillo (Calif.) State Hosp., 1958—70; mental health nurse I and II, insvc. instr. Ventura County Mental Health, Calif., 1973—88; part-time spiritual group facilitator Hillmont Psychiatric Ctr., Ventura, Calif., 1995—. Democrat. Universalist Unitarian. Avocations: singing, reading, walking. Home: 980 Terracina Dr Santa Paula CA 93060 Personal E-mail: phoenixrise3@verizon.net.

BROUN, ELIZABETH, art historian, curator; b. Kansas City, Mo., Dec. 15, 1946; d. Augustine Hughes and Roberta Catherine (Hayden) Gibson. BA, U. Kans., 1968, PhD, 1976; cert. advanced study, U. Bordeaux, France, 1967. Curator prints and drawings Spencer Mus. Art, Lawrence, Kans., 1976-83; asst. prof. U. Kans., Lawrence, 1978-83; asst. dir. chief curator Nat. Mus. Am. Art, Washington, 1983-88, acting dir., 1988-89; dir. Smithsonian Am. Art Mus. (formerly Nat. Mus. Am. Art), Washington, 1989—. Author: exhbn. catalogues Prints of Zorn, 1979, Prints and Drawings of Pat Steir, 1983, Patrick Ireland; Drawings 1965-85, 1986, Albert Pinkham Ryder, 1989; co-author: Benton's Bentons, 1980, Engravings of Marcantonio Raimondi, 1981. Woodrow Wilson fellow, 1968-69; Ford. Found. fellow, 1970-72 Mem. Phi Beta Kappa Office: MRC 970 PO Box 37012 Washington DC 20013-7012 Office Phone: 202-275-1515.

BROUSSARD, CAROL MADELINE, writer, consultant, photographer; b. Calif. children: Valerie Madeline, Sean Hunter Rutledge. Student, West Hill Coll., Coalinga, Calif., Coll. Sequoias, Visalia, Calif., Inst. Metaphysics, La Brea, Calif., Fresno City Coll., Calif., 1995-97. Cert. human svcs. Former pub. and investigative journalist; pub. TV Watch, Tyler, Tex., 1969-74; resource sec. John C. Fremont Sch., Corcoran, Calif., 1974-77; editor Coalinga (Calif.) Record, 1978-81; pub., prodn. mgr. Kern Valley Chronicle, Lake Isabella, Calif., 1981-84; freelance writer, 1990—. Featured TV show Writing Procedures, 1992; instr. home pub. Calif. State U. Adult Edn., Fresno, 1992, 95; instr. photography Clovis (Calif.) Adult Edn., 1993—, instr. ethnic watercolors, 1993-94, instr. investigative photo-journalism. 1994, instr. freelance photo-journalism, 1995; tchr. photog. lab. Clovis Teen Summer Sch., 1992. Author poetry; composer lyrics for Cajun Hoedown Man Century T.V., summer 1990, theme song Karma for Cinnimin Skin, Lance Mungia film, 1994. Vol., Literacy Program for WIN/WIN, Fresno Unified Sch. Dist., 1992, Trained Domestic Violence Response Team, Marjoree Mason Ctr., 1996-2003; staff: crisis intervention specialist II Shelter for Abused Women and Children; crisis hotline counselor, adv., 2001-03 Recipient Photo-Journalist award Calif. Newspaper Assn., 1983, Best Feature Photo award Calif. Justice System, 1984, World of Child Photo award Fresno City and County Offices, 1980, Poetic Achievement award Amherst Soc., 1990, award of merit World of Poetry, 1990, Golden Poet award, 1990, 91, Iliad Literary award, 1990, Poetry Editor's Choice award, 1992-93; spotlight TV interview Writers' Journal, 1992 Mem. Writers Internat. Network (speaker 1991, 92, coord. Vols. Conf. awards 1991). Avocation: writing.

BROWAR, LISA MURIEL, librarian; b. NYC, Jan. 22, 1951; d. Elliott Andrew and Shirley (Kahn) Browar. B in English Lit., Ind. U., 1973, MLS, 1977; M in English Lit., U. Kans., 1976; Exec. MA in Philanthropic Studies, Ind. U.-Purdue. U., Indpls., 2005—. Cert. in fund raising mgmt. 2001. Asst. curator Beinecke Libr. Yale U., New Haven, 1979-81, archivist Sterling Meml. Libr., 1981-82; curator spl. collections Vassar Coll. Libr., Poughkeepsie, NY, 1982-87; asst. dir. rare books and manuscripts N.Y. Pub. Libr., N.Y.C., 1987-96; dir. The Lilly Libr., Ind. U., Bloomington, 1996-2001; libr. for English and Am. lit., philosophy and film studies Main Libr., Ind. U., Bloomington, 2001—02; univ. libr. New Sch. U., N.Y.C., 2002—. Editor RBM: A Jour. of Rare Books, Manuscripts, and Cultural Heritage, 1999-2003. Mem. ALA, Assn. Coll. and Rsch. Librs. (sec. rare books and manuscripts sect. 1987-89, chair, 1994-95, editor 1999—), Soc. Am. Archivists, Bibliog. Soc. Am., Grolier Club. Democrat. Avocations: opera, theater, photography. Office: Fogelman Libr 65 Fifth Ave New York NY 10011 Office Phone: 212-229-5598 ext. 3149. Business E-Mail: browarl@newschool.edu.

BROWER, ANNE CLAYTON, radiologist; b. Plainfield, NJ, July 5, 1938; d. Charles Hendrickson and Elizabeth Nelson Brower; m. Glenn Allen Scott, Sept. 29, 2001; m. James Edward Culver (div.); children: Catherine Leigh, James Linwood. BA, Smith Coll., Northampton, Mass., 1960; MD, Coll. of Physicans and Surgeons, NYC, 1964. Ordained Episcopal priest 2001.

Radiology instr. U. Va. Hosp., 1973—74, asst. prof. radiology, 1974—76, U. Kans., 1976—77; assoc. prof., dept. radiology and nuc. medicine Va. Commonwealth U., 1977—79, Uniformed Svcs. of the Health Sci., 1979—81, prof., dept. radiology and nuc. medicine Bethesda, 1981—82; prof., dept. radiology George Wash. U., 1982—83; prof., dept.radiology Georgetown U. Hosp., Wash., DC, 1984—87; prof. radiology and orthop. surgery Duke U. Med. Ctr., 1987; prof., dept. radiology and nuc. medicine Uniformed Svcs. U. of the Health Sci., Bethesda, Md., 1988—93; prof., chair and program dir. Eastern Va. Med. Sch., Norfolk, 1993—97. Program dir. residency tng. Med. Coll. of Va., Richmond, George Wash. U. Med. Sch., Georgetown Med. Sch., Wilmington, NC. Author: (book) Arthritis in Black & White, 1981—, I'm Not Ready to Die Just Yet, 2005; mem. editl. bd. Jour. of Arthritis and Rheumatism, 1981—, Radiology, 1983—, Am. Jour. of Roentgenology, 1983—, Radiograhics, 1984—, rev. Jour. of Rheumatology, 1990—. Mem.: AMA, Am. Assn. for Women Radiologists, Am. Coll. Rheumatology, Med. Soc. Va., Am. Soc. Emergency Radiology, Eastern Radiological Soc., Am. Rheumatism Assn., Southeastern Soc. of Skeletal Radiology, Internat. Skeletal Soc., Assn. of U. Radiologists, Am. Roentgen Ray Soc., Radiological Soc. N. Am., Am. Coll. Radiology. Republican. Episc. Avocations: music, theater, writing. Home: 1016 Baldwin Ave Norfolk VA 23507

BROWER, JANICE KATHLEEN, library and information scientist; b. Chgo., July 29, 1952; d. Gerald B. (dec. Dec. 2000) and Emily (Kavicky) B. AA, Lincoln Coll., 1973; BS, Ill. State U., 1975; postgrad., U. Okla., 1984-86. Libr. assoc. Chgo. Pub. Libr., 1975-80, 81-83; libr. technician U. Okla. Biol. Sta., Norman, 1987; libr. technician III Jim E. Hamilton Correctional Ctr. Okla. Dept. of Corrections, Hodgen, 1987—. Lutheran. Avocations: reading, walking, visiting historical sites and museums, architecture. Office: Jim E Hamilton Correctional Ctr 53468 Mineral Springs Rd Hodgen OK 74939-3064 Office Phone: 918-653-7831 372. Business E-Mail: janice.brower@doc.state.ok.us. E-mail: jkbrower@alltel.net.

BROWN, ADRIANE M., aerospace transportation executive; b. Richmond, Va; BS in Environ. Health, Old Dominion Univ.; MBA, M.I.T. With Corning Inc., 1980—99, v.p., gen. mgr. environ. products divsn., 1994—99; v.p., gen. mgr. Aircraft Landing Systems Honeywell, Inc., South Bend, Ind., 1999—2001, v.p., gen. mgr. Honeywell Engine Systems & Accessories Tempe, Ariz., 2001—05, pres., CEO, Honeywell Transp. Systems Torrance, Calif., 2005—. Ariz. Gov. Coun. Innovation & Tech.; adv. coun. grad studies rsch. Univ. Notre Dame; bd. dir. Jobs for Am. Grads. Mem.: Ariz. Women's Forum. Office: HoneywellTransp Systems 2525 W 190th St Torrance CA 90504*

BROWN, ALICE ELSTE, artist; b. Balt., Nov. 5, 1922; d. Albert John and Anna Emily (Rosenbauer) Elste; m. Charles Hammond Brown, Nov. 30, 1946 (dec. Sept. 1994); children: Charles Hammond Jr., Barbara Brown Lander, Laurie Ellen. RN, U. Md., 1944; BS in Nursing Edn., Johns Hopkins U., 1949; BA in Art, Coll. Notre Dame, Balt., 1978; MA in Painting and Art Edn., Towson U., 1984. RN Md. Nurse, head nurse U.S. Army Nurse Corps, U.S., Europe, 1944-46; pub. health nurse Balt. Health Dept., 1950-52; artist Balt., 1960—; artist-in-residence Pyramid-Atlantic Studios, Balt., 1987-92. Adj. instr. drawing and design Coll. Notre Dame, 1980. One-woman shows include Roland Park Libr., 1965, Greater Balt. Med. Ctr., 1964, exhibited in group shows at Md. Fedn. Art, 1970—79, Jewish Cmty. Ctr., 1970, Towson YMCA, 1960, Easton (Md.) Acad. Arts, 1977, Coll. of Notre Dame, 1980, Western Md. Coll., Westminster, 1990, Pyramid Atlantic, Washington, 1990, Rehoboth (Del.)Art League, 1996—. Home nursing tchr. ARC, Balt., 1950s; asst. leader, leader Girl Scouts Am., Balt., 1960s; vol. docent Balt. Mus. Art, 1970s. 1st lt., U.S. Army Nurse Corps, 1944-46. Recipient Pi Lambda Theta award, Johns Hopkins U., 1949, Steinbugler award in art, Coll. Notre Dame, 1978. Mem. Nat. Mus. Women in the Arts (charter mem.), Md. Art Place, Rehoboth Art League (Thomas McFarland Skelly Meml. award 1998, Best in Show 2003), Johns Hopkins U. Alumni Club. Democrat. Avocations: walking, reading, archaeology, environmental concerns.

BROWN, ALVENICE HORTENSE BRYAN, educator; b. Portsmouth, Va., Apr. 17, 1931; d. James and Bessie Olga (Smith) Bryan; m. William Hiliary Brown, Sr., Aug. 16, 1958 (div. Jan. 1991); children: William Henry Jr., LaEunice Olga. BS, Hampton U.; MA in Speech, U. Mich.; EdD, NYU. Cert. tchr. Fla., Va., N.Y. Tchr./chairperson English Blanche Ely and I.C. Norcom, Pompano, Fla., Portsmouth, Va.; English tchr. N.Y.C. Pub. Schs., Jamaica, NY; prof. speech/composition Norfolk (Va.) State U., 1969—85; lectr. composition U. Mich., Ann Arbor, Tidewater C.C., Portsmouth, Va.; substitute tchr. Portsmouth Pub. Schs.; writer Inst. for Children's Writing, West Redding, Conn. Chair/cons. Portsmouth Pub. Schs. Editor (critic): (anthology) Dreams and Memories. Active Delacardos, Portsmouth. Mem.: Alpha Kappa Alpha Sorority Inc. (epistoleus). Republican. Baptist. Avocations: quilting, reading, singing. Mailing: 5800 Bernhowe Manor Suffolk VA 23435-0593

BROWN, AMIRA KHALILA, neuropsychologist, researcher; d. Leonard Mason Brown and Aisha M. Robinson-Cobbs; 1 child, Turhan Taliaferro. BA in Psychology, U. D.C., 1998; MS in Neuropsychology, Howard U., 2000; PhD in Exptl. Neuropsychology, 2003. Behavior modification specialist St. Elizabeth's Hosp., Washington, 1997; clin. neuropsychology intern Ctr. for Mental Health, Washington, 1999—2000; neuropsychology intern Mt. Wash. Pediat. Hosp., Balt., 2001—02; rschr. Molecular Imaging Br. NIMH/NIH, Bethesda, Md., 2004—. Adj. prof. Howard U., Washington, 2001—02, Trinity U., Washington, 2003—04, Prince Georges C.C., Largo, Md., 2003—. Rape crisis hotline and companion counselor D.C. Rape Crisis Ctr., Washington, 1994—98. Recipient Ruth L. Kirschstein Nat. Rsch. Svc. award, Vanderbilt U. Neurosci. Dept. Sch. of Medicine, Nat. Intramural Rsch. Tng. award, NIMH/NIH. Fellow: Acad. Molecular Imaging (corr.); mem.: APA (assoc.), Women in Neurosci., Inc. (corr.), Internat. Neuropsychol. Soc. (assoc.), Beta Kappa Chi (life), Psi Chi (life), Alpha Kappa Alpha (life). Avocations: travel, reading. Office Phone: 301-435-1695.

BROWN, AMY CHRISTINE, art educator; d. Donald Brown and Lillian Vorbeck, Lowell Vorbeck (Stepfather). BA, Madonna U., 2001; MA (hon.), Nova Southeastern U., 2003. Cert. elem. tchr. Mich. Art educator Airport Cmty. Schs., Newport, Mich., 2001—. Exhibitions include sr. art exhibit, Madonna U., 1999, pvt. collection, plaster sculpture, 2000, Lucille Dedene. Mem.: PTO (sch. rep. 2001—05). Office Phone: 734-586-2676. Home Fax: 734-242-3416. Personal E-mail: amybrown@wwnet.net.

BROWN, ANGELA MCHANEY, editor; b. Fresno, Calif., July 28, 1973; d. Leon Tony McHaney and Marilyn Nall. BA in English, Calif. State U., Fresno, 1996; MA in Lit., DePaul U., Chgo., 2001. Bookstore mgr. Crown Books, Chgo., 1996—98; assoc. editor InContext, Evanston, Ill., 1998—2000; editor Heinemann Libr., Chgo., 2000—02, McDougal Littell, Evanston, 2004—; supervising editor Heinemann-Raintree, Chgo., 2002—04. Author: (children's book) Carpenter, 2000, Produce Manager, 2000, Months of the Year, 2005. Avocations: reading, travel, photography, movies, poetry. Office Phone: 847-424-3302.

BROWN, ANGELIA, poet; b. Barnesville, Ga., Jan. 5, 1968; d. Charlie Fred and Elizabeth Brown; children: Demarius, Marcus, Jalessa Freeman, David Freeman. Poet: Nature, 1992, In Memory of Those We Love and Cherish, 1993, Love That Is Meant to Be, 1994, Love, 1997, Our Love, 1997, A Friendship, 1998 (Accomplishment of Merit award, 1998), Life, 1998 (Editors Choice award, 1998), All About Angelia and the Lord, 1998, Watch Them Dogs, 2003 (Editors Choice award, 2003). Mem.: Internat. Soc. Poets, Assn. Black Women Entrepreneurs Inc. Methodist. Avocations: gardening, art, baking, bookmaking. Home: 128 Roger Brown Dr Barnesville GA 30204 Personal E-mail: browna2365@aol.com.

BROWN, ANN W., not-for-profit developer; m. Donald Brown, 1959; 2 children Student, Smith Coll., 1955-58; BA, George Washington U., 1959; LLD (hon.), Smith Coll., 2000. Past v.p. Consumer Fedn. Am.; chmn. bd. Pub. Voice, 1983-94; chmn. U.S. Consumer Product Safety Commn., 1994—2001, Safer Am. for Everyone, Palm Beach Gardens, Fla., 2001—. Nat. and local chmn. consumer affairs com. Ams. for Dem. Action; past chmn. adv. bd. Washington Consumer Protection Office. Named Washingtonian of Yr., Washingtonian Mag., 1989, Govt. Communicator of Yr., Nat. Assn. Govt. Communicators, 1995, Outstanding Alumna, George Washington U., 1996; recipient Champion of Safe Kids award, Nat. Safe Kids Campaign, 1994, Philip Hart Pub. Svc. award, Consumer Fedn. Am., 1999, Excellence in Pub. Svc. award, Am. Acad. Pediat., 2000, Nat. Working Parent award, Lokoff Found., 2000, Crystal Slipper award, 2002. Avocations: tennis, movies. Home and Office: SAFE Safer Am for Everyone 2734 Rhome Dr Palm Beach Gardens FL 33410 Office: SAFE Safer Am for Everyone 1776 I Street NW Ste 900 Washington DC 20006

BROWN, ANNE SHERWIN, speech pathologist, educator; b. Denver, Oct. 15, 1952; d. John Frederick and Barbara Toft Sherwin; m. Max Dennis Brown, June 15, 1985; children: Jack Steven, Michael Patrick. BA, Adams State Coll., 1974, MA, 1975. Tchr. Aurora (Colo.) Pub. Schs., 1978—. Author: Adopt-A-Cop, 1994. Bd. mgrs. YMCA, Aurora, 1996-98. Pub. Svc. Co. grantee, Denver, 1996-97, 98-99; Excel Energy Found. grantee, 2002-03. Mem. ASCD, Aurora Edn. Assn., Internat. Reading Assn. Avocations: reading, dance, sewing, guitar, motorcycles. Home: 416 S Victor Way Aurora CO 80012-2447 Office: Aurora Pub Schs 395 S Troy St Aurora CO 80012-2472

BROWN, ARLENE PATRICIA THERESA See BROWN, RENI

BROWN, BARBARA ANN, county extension agent; b. Jefferson City, Mo., May 15, 1949; d. Barbara Eloise and Raymond George Frank Hirschvogel; m. Robert David Brown, Sept. 30, 1967; children: Charles, Christopher. M in Internat. Rels., U. So. Calif., London, 1984. Youth program§ports dir. USAF, RAF Mildenhall, Eng., 1981-82, media specialist, 1983-84; pubs. rels./rsch. dir. H&S Wholesalers, Sumter, S.C., 1985-88; mgmt. analyst USAF, Shaw AFB, Sumter, 1989-90; county ext. agt. Clemson U. Coop. Ext. Svc., 1990—. Mem. editl. bd. CYFERNet, U.S. Facilitator Nat. Issues Forum, S.C., 1988—; del. People to People, China, 1988, 94; coord. Cmty. Youth Devel. Join Hands Day, 2000 (award 2000, 01). Drug Supply/Demand Reduction grantee Shaw AFB, 1995-96, Networks in Communities grantee S.C. United Way and S.C. Dept. Edn., 1997-99, Strenghtening Families grantee Sumter United Way, 1999, Children, Youth, Families at Risk grantee USDA, 1999-2004, Drug-Free Cmty., 2002—, Svc. Learning, Dept. Edn., 2002-2005, New Communities, USDA, 2005—, Operation Mil. Kids, USDA, 2004—; recipient Excellence in Teamwork award Nat. Assn. Ext. 4-H Agts., 2002. Mem.: LWV, Nat. Assn. Cmty. Econ. Devel. Profl., 4-H Assn., Epsilon Sigma Phi. Methodist. Avocations: travel, reading. Home: 20 Naomi Ct Sumter SC 29154 Office Phone: 803-773-5561. Office Fax: 803-773-0070. Business E-Mail: babrwn@clemson.edu.

BROWN, BARBARA BERISH, lawyer; b. Washington, June 26, 1946; d. Alfred Edward and Sylvia (Kaufman) B.; m. Robert F. Berish, Mar. 26, 1988; 1 child, Jared. BA, Radcliffe-Harvard, 1968; JD, Yale U., 1971. Law clk. to Hon. J. Joseph Smith US Ct. Appeals (2d cir.), 1971—72; ptnr. Paul Hastings Janofsky & Walker, LLP, Washington, 1984—, chair, 2000—. Co-author: Legal Guide to Human Resources, 1984, supplement, 2005. Fellow Coll. Labor and Employment Lawyers; mem. ABA (vice chair labor and employment law sect.). Office: Paul Hastings Janofsky & Walker 875 15th St NW Washington DC 20005 Office Phone: 202-551-1717. Office Fax: 202-551-0117. Business E-Mail: barbarabrown@paulhastings.com.

BROWN, BARBARA JUNE, hospital and nursing administrator; b. Milw., Aug. 17, 1933; d. Carl W. and Nora Anne (Damrow) Rydberg; children: Deborah, Robert, Andrea, Michael, Steven, Jeffrey. BSN, Marquette U., Milw., 1955, MSN, 1960, EdD, 1970. RN, Wis.; cert. nurse adminstr. advanced. Adminstr. patient care Family Hosp., Milw., 1973-78; assoc. clin. prof. U. Wash., Seattle, 1980-87; assoc. adminstr. nursing Virginia Mason Hosp., Seattle, 1980-87; assoc. exec. dir. King Faisal Specialist Hosp., Riyadh, Saudi Arabia, 1987-91; adj. prof. Univ. Ariz., 2001—. Project dir. NIH, Sexual Assault Treatment Ctr., Milw., 1975-78; lectr., cons., 1974—. Founder, editor-in-chief: Nursing Adminstrn. Quar., 1976—; editor-in-chief, regional v.p. Nurse Week, Mountain West, 2000—04; editor-in-chief: Modern Nurse, 2005—06. Vol. ski instr. for disabled, Winter Park, Colo. Fellow: Nat. Acad. Practice, Am. Acad. Nursing (governing coun.); mem.: ANA, Grand County Pub. Health and Emergency Svcs. (chmn. health adv. com. 1994—96), Nat. League Nursing (bd. govs. 2002—05, bd. dirs.), Am. Orgn. Nurse Execs., Sigma Theta Tau. Office Phone: 520-825-5629. Personal E-mail: naqbb@aol.com.

BROWN, BARBARA SPROUL, retired librarian, consultant, writer; b. Salem, Jan. 12, 1934; d. Robert Hugh Sproul and Bernadette Elizabeth Marsolais; m. Bernard Peter Friesecke, Feb. 18, 1955 (div. Nov. 1975); children: Richardine, Rachel, Julie; m. Wallace Robert Brown, Jan. 16, 1988. AB magna cum laude, Boston U., 1967; MLS, Simmons Coll., 1971; cert. advanced grad. studies, Northeastern U., 1978. Cert. sch. libr. media specialist, instrnl. tech. specialist, Mass. Libr. Watertown (Mass.) Sch. Dept., 1969-97, profl. developer for faculty, 1990-96; instr. Watertown Adult Edn., 1983-87. Intern, cons. women's alcohol program CASPAR, Inc., Cambridge, Mass., 1977-79; cons. on database devel. Mindware Inc., Natick, Mass., 1982-83, Coleco Industries, Natick, 1983-84. Essay columnist Watertown Sun, 1990-02; author adult computer courses, 1983-96; contbr. short stories to lit. periodicals. Mem. Lexington (Mass.) Civil Rights Orgn., 1963-68; campaign worker Boston Dem. Com., 1985-93; bd. dirs. Coronado Unitarian Ch., 1999—. Mem. ACLU, Phi Beta Kappa, Beta Phi Mu. Democrat. Avocations: weight training, camping, motorcycling, competitive rifle shooting. Home: 1636 Donax Ave San Diego CA 92154-1003

BROWN, BERNICE LEONA BAYNES, foundation administrator, secondary school educator, consultant; b. Pitts., June 19, 1935; d. Howard Leon and Henrietta Lydia (Hodges) Baynes; m. James Brown, May 4, 1964; 1 child, Kiyeseni Anu. BFA, Carnegie Mellon U., 1957; MEd, U. Pitts., 1966. Tchr. Pitts. Pub. Schs., 1957-65; lectr. Carlow Coll., Pitts., 1964-67; edn. specialist Bay Area Urban League, San Francisco, 1967-68; asst. prof. San Francisco Coll. for Women, 1968-72; dean students Lone Mountain Coll., San Francisco, 1972-76; dir. San Francisco Pub. Schs. Commn., 1976; program exec. San Francisco Found., 1977-86; ednl. cons. San Francisco, 1987—; found. adminstr. Clorox Co. Found., 1989-91; dean of faculty and staff devel. City Coll. of San Francisco, 1991-98; dean Workforce Edn./Calworks Edn. and Tng., 1998—2002. Vis. scholar Stanford (Calif.) U., 1987-88. Mem. bd. govs. Calif. Cmty. Colls., 1975-81, Calif. Post Secondary Edn. Commn., Sacramento, 1978-80, State Supt's Adv. Com. on Black Am. Affairs, Calif., 1985—; chair Found. Cmty. Svc. Cable T.V., San Francisco, 1982-84; trustee Schs. of Sacred Heart, San Francisco, 1982-87; bd. dirs. Urban Econ. Devel. Corp., 1988-2000, High/Scope Ednl. Rsch. Found., 1990-98, Network for Elders, 1997—, Cmty. Bds., Inc., 2000—, Presidio World Coll., 2000—; trustee Howard Thurman Ednl. Trust, 1989-94, Uprising Cmty. Credit Union, San Francisco, 2001—. Recipient Milestone award Citizen's Scholarship Found. Am., 1995, Profl. Woman of Yr. award San Francisco Bus. and Profl. Women, Inc., History Makers award, 2002, Image award in Edn. Delta Sigma Theta, Inc., 2003. Mem. San Francisco LWV (bd. dirs. 2000-02), Women and Founds. Corp. Philanthropy (bd. dirs. 1985-87), Assn. Black Found. Execs. (bd. dirs. 1978-82), Commonwealth Club of Calif. (bd. govs. 1988-91). Home: 886 Junipero Serra Blvd San Francisco CA 94127-2850 E-mail: bbrown@ccsf.edu.

BROWN, BETTY J., retired elementary school educator; b. Red Bluff, Calif., Apr. 19, 1934; d. Hugh Jerry and Lena Belle (Dobkins) Moran; m. Richard Owen Brown, Nov. 26, 1958; children: Karen, Gretchen, Heidi. BA in Edn., Calif. State U., Chico, 1956. Cert. tchr., Calif. Tchr. Gridley Elem. Dist., Calif., 1956-61; reading tchr. Richfield Elem. Dist., Corning, 1968, tchr., 1970—2003. Bd. dirs. Sch. Site Coun., Corning, 1990-2000; mem. County Lang. Arts Com., Red Bluff, 1987-99; mem., sec. Learning Coun., Red Bluff, 1995-99. Mem. Home Town Christmas, Corning, 1996-2000; vol. Shrine Hosp., Sacramento, 1998-2000; mem. adv. bd., mother adv. dep. Rainbow Girls, Corning, 1975-87; writing contest coord. Tehama County, 1992— Recipient Nat. Educator award Milken Family Found., 1994, Literacy award Tehama County Reading Coun., 1995, 2001. Mem. AAUW, Tehama County Reading Coun. (pres. 1991-93), Corning C. of C., Order Eastern Star, Tehama County Shrine Club Wives (pres. 1990, 96, 2001-02, treas. 1989—), Delta Kappa Gamma (pres. 2004-06, legis. chair 2003—). Avocations: reading, biking, skiing, travel. Home: 1406 Butte St Corning CA 96021-2408

BROWN, BETTYE, librarian, educator; b. Ft. Valley, Ga., Mar. 14, 1945; d. Tom and Lucinda (Holt) B. BS in Secondary Edn., Ft. Valley State Coll., 1967; MSLS, Atlanta U., 1975. Cert. secondary tchr., Ga. Tchr. Pearl Stephens HS, Warner Robins, Ga., 1967-69, Perry (Ga.) HS, 1969-70; libr. Vienna (Ga.) Elem. Sch., 1971-72; libr. tech. asst. Ill. State CC, East St. Louis, Ill., 1972-75, ref. libr., 1975—96, prof., 1983—; ref. libr. Southwestern Bell Libr. and Tech. Ctr. Harris-Stowe State U., St. Louis, 1997—. Historian, mem. pub. rels. com. Nat. Coun. Negro Women, East St. Louis, 1985, corr. sec., 1990—, newsletter editor, 1990—. Mem. AAUP (sec. 1983-85, v.p. 1988—), AAUW (fin. sec. 1987-90, sec. 1990—), NOW, Am. Fedn. Tchrs. (sec. 1980-82), Nat. Assn. U. Women, Ill. Libr. Assn., Bus. and Profl. Women East St. Louis (chmn. libr. com. 1987—), Women of Essence (treas. 1985-89), Women Organized for Community Survival (v.p. 1988—), Alpha Kappa Alpha. Democrat. Pentecostal. Avocations: reading, sewing, travel, aerobics, drama. Office: Harris-Stowe State U Southwestern Bell Libr and Tech Ctr 3026 Laclede Ave Saint Louis MO 63103 Office Phone: 314-340-3506. Business E-Mail: brownb@hssu.edu.

BROWN, BEULAH LOUISE, retired elementary school educator; b. Warren County, Ohio, Feb. 21, 1917; d. Fred Austin and Roba E. (Doughman) Birmingham; m. William Dale Brown, Aug. 14, 1942 (dec. Apr. 1984). Student, Ohio U., 1937-39, BS in Edn. cum laude, 1957. Cert. tchr., Ohio. Tchr. 2d grade Bainbridge (Ohio) Village Sch., 1939-43; rsch. lab. asst. Mead Paper Corp., Chillicothe, Ohio, 1944-45; tchr. 2d grade Chillicothe City Schs., 1945-46, Marysville (Ohio) Schs., 1946-49; tchr. 1st grade Riley Twp. Sandusky County Schs., Fremont, Ohio, 1951-52; tchr. 2d grade Fremont City Schs., 1952-59, Lancaster (Ohio) City Schs., 1959-64, tchr. 1st grade, 1966-75; tchr. 2d grade Ashland (Ohio) City Schs., 1964-66. Supervising tchr. Bowling Green (Ohio) State U., 1955-59, Ohio U., Athens, 1960-64, 66-75, Ashland Coll., 1964-66. Mem. AAUW, Farifield County Ret. Tchrs., Ohio Ret. Tchrs., Clionian Literary Club, Kappa Delta Pi, Delta Kappa Gamma. Republican. Methodist. Avocations: reading, travel.

BROWN, BEVERLY JEAN, retired elementary school educator; b. Pensacola, Fla., Jan. 24, 1943; d. Elisha and Melanie Alfreda (Creal) Jones; m. Ozie Marion Portis, May 1, 1963 (div. Apr. 1976); 1 child, Diedra LaShalle; m. Ernest Arnell Brown, Oct. 13, 1979. BS, Fla. A&M U., 1966; M of Edn., U. North Fla., 1986. Cert. in adminstrn. and supervision. Tchr. Meriwether County Sch. Dist., Greenville, Ga., 1966-67, Hamilton County Sch. Dist., Jasper, Fla., 1968-69, Duval County Sch. Dist., Jacksonville, Fla., 1969-82, primary resource tchr., 1982-87; adminstrv. intern Duval County Sch. Bd., 1987-88, tchr. instructional support, 1988-90, vice prin., 1990—95, prin., 1995—2000; re., 2000. Mem. Retired Duval Adminstrs., Fla. Ret. Educators, Duval Ret. Educators. Democrat. Home: 11133 Aristides Way Jacksonville FL 32218-6217

BROWN, BEVERLY MICHELLE, music educator; b. Tupelo, Miss., Sept. 27, 1966; life ptnr. Tina Y Brown, Sept. 1, 1995. MusB, U. Miss., Oxford, 1988; MusM, Youngstown State U., Ohio, 1991. Cert. tchr. music K-12 Ohio, Calif., Miss. Tchr. Brentwood Union Sch. Dist., Calif., 1997—2004, Knightsen Elem., Calif., 2005—. Mem.: Calif. Tchrs. Assn. Office Phone: 925-625-0073. E-mail: mbrown@knightsen.k12.ca.us.

BROWN, BILLYE JEAN, retired nursing educator; b. Damascus, Ark., Oct. 29, 1925; d. William A. and Dora (Megee) B. BSNEd, U. Tex. Med. Br., Galveston, 1953; MSNEd, St. Louis U., 1958; EdD, Baylor U., 1975. Asst. prof. U. Tex. Med. Br. Sch. Nursing, 1958-60; assoc. prof. U. Tex. Nursing Sch., Austin, 1960-67, assoc. dean, prof., 1968-72, dean, prof., 1972-89; prof. emeritus Sch. Nursing U. Tex., 1989—; mem. Nat. Adv. Council Nurse Tng., 1982-87. Nat. League for Nursing fellow, 1957-58; recipient Alumni Merit award St. Louis U., 1981; Am. Acad. Nursing fellow, 1984. Mem. ANA, Am. Assn. Colls. Nursing (pres. 1982-84, Sister Bernadette Armiger award 1990), Tex. League Nursing, Tex. Nurses Assn. (Nurse of Yr. 1980), Sigma Theta Tau (pres. 1989-91, Internat. Mary T. Wright Founders award 1999), Phi Kappa Phi (life).

BROWN, BLANCHE Y., secondary school educator, genealogist, researcher; b. Saint Mary's, W.Va., Feb. 2, 1918; d. Lewis Frederick and Edna Clara (Walker) Yost; m. Vincent Robert Brown, June 1, 1946; children: Susan Elizabeth, Roberta Ann Brown Pugh. BA, Marietta Coll., 1939; postgrad., Columbia U., 1946, 47. Cert. secondary tchr. in sci. and English. Pers. supr. Packard Electric divsn. Gen. Motors Corp., Warren, Ohio, 1940-44; tchr. bus. edn. New Matamoras (Ohio) H.S., 1945-49; fin. sec. St. Paul's United Meth. Ch., Houston, 1949-50; pers. dept. Olin Chem. Corp., Pasadena, Tex., 1951-53; tchr. biology Pasadena H.S., 1958-78. Co-editor: Grandview Township's First Trustees Journal--1803-1843, 1991; editor Matamoras Area Hist. Soc. Newsletter, 1987-99. Recipient First Families of Ohio award Ohio Geneal. Soc., 1989, Award of Achievement Ohio Hist. Soc. for Matamoras Area Hist. Soc. Newsletter, 1992. Mem. Tex. Ret. Tchrs. Assn. (life), Nat. Soc. DAR (Marietta, Ohio chpt. schs. chmn. 1988-94, corr. sec. 1995-99, nat. Photography award 1989), Matamoras Area Hist. Soc. (genealogy and local history coord. for Sesquicentennial Celebration 1846-1996, Bicentennial Celebration 1797-1997), VFW Aux. (life), AAUW. Republican. Methodist. Avocations: photography, artwork with shells, writing. Home: 733 Main St New Matamoras OH 45767-6013

BROWN, BRENDA BERNADINE, education educator; b. N.Y.C., Feb. 21, 1939; d. Stephen Anderson and Audrey Juanita (Cheatham) Bell; m. Harold Brown, Feb. 10, 1962; children: Gordon Avery, Bruce Anderson. BA, CCNY, 1961; MA, Atlanta U., 1976; postgrad. Columbia U., 1962, CUNY, 1962-68, U. Bridgeport (Conn.), 1974; Ed.D, Harvard U., 1988. Pub. sch. tchr., Bronx, N.Y., 1961-65, 73-74; English tchr. Salem (Mass.) State Coll., 1971-72; reading tchr./coordinator Capitol View Elem. Sch., Atlanta, 1976-77; tchr. secondary social studies Shenendehowa High Sch., Clifton Park, N.Y., 1978-79; staff/curriculum developer Cambridge (Mass.) Public Schs., 1980-87; tenured assoc. prof. edn. emerita, Merrimack Coll., North Andover, Mass., 1987-2002, chairperson dept. edn., 1994-2001, ret. 2002; mentor to sch. adminstrn. Sarasota Sch. Dept., Fla., 2004—; Mem. Assn. for Study of African-Am. Life and History, Harvard Club of Sarasota, Howard Club of Southwest Fla., Delta Sigma Theta. Episcopalian. E-mail: hbrown20@tampabay.rr.com.

BROWN, C. ALISON, counselor; d. William Thomas Wynn Jr. and Rose E. Wynn; m. Jim D. Brown, Nov. 22, 1986; children: Steven Brett Wallis, Aaron Thomas. BA in Psychology, U. Mo., St. Louis, 1992, MEd in Counseling, 1995. Lic. profl. counselor Mo., nat. cert. counselor. Domestic violence counselor Bridgeway Women's Ctr., St. Charles, Mo., 1995—2000; dir. Bridgeway Alternatives to Violence and Abuse Program, St. Charles, Mo., 2000—. Co-chairperson St. Charles County Family Violence Coun., 2001—; Mo. state bd. rep. Mo. Coalition Against Domestic Violence, St. Louis, 2003—. Mem.: Assn. for Batterer Intervention Providers (pres. 2002—04). Office: Bridgeway Alternatives to Violence/Abuse 1570 South Main St Saint Charles MO 63303 E-mail: avaprogram@sbcglobal.net.

BROWN, CAMPBELL, commentator; m. Dan Senor, Apr. 2, 2006. BA in Polit. Sci., Regis Coll. Polit. reporter KSNT-TV, Topeka, WWBT-TV, Richmond, Va., WBAL-TV, Balt., WRC-TV, Wash.; corr. NBC News, 1996—98, White Ho. corr., 1998—; co-anchor NBC Weekend Today, 2003—. Office: Weekend Today NBC News 30 Rockefeller Plz New York NY 10112*

BROWN, CAROL, make-up artist; b. Stockholm, Nov. 26, 1949; d. Julius C. and Violet (Moten) B. Student, Mt. St. Mary's Coll., 1968-72, European Exch. Program, 1972-74, L.A. Valley Coll., 1974-76. Cert. make-up artistry tchr., Calif. Makeup-artist Spelling Entertainment, Paramount, Disney, NBC, others, L.A., 1977—; CEO Natural to Knockout.com., L.A., 1996—; founder, CEO Carol Brown Natural Empowerment Found., L.A., 2000—. Aesthetic cons. C.B. Enterprises, 1990—; instr. Fred Segal Beauty, 1990—; spkr. in field; mem. adv. bd. Denise Roberts Found.; mem. speakerservices.com. Author: Natural to Knockout Makeup Application Beauty Guide, 2001. Vol. L.A. Mission, 1989—, Jenesee Ctr., L.a., 1996—, Sickle Cell Disease Assn. Am., L.A., 1996—. Recipient Outstanding Tech. Achievement award L.A. Black Media Coalition, 1989. Mem.: NATAS (mem. Emmy awards com. 1985—90, mem. show com. 1985—90, mem. exec. peer group com. 1985—93, 3 Emmy awards, 7 Emmy award nominations), NAACP, Assn. Image Cons. Internat., Colour Soc. Australia, Internat. Alliance Stage and Theatrical Emmployees, Aesthetics Internat. Assn. Office: Carol Brown Natural Empowerment Found PO Box 79083 Los Angeles CA 90079

BROWN, CAROL ANN, librarian, director; b. Denver, Mar. 7, 1948; d. Truman Veach and Mary Margaret Yowell; m. Robert Ray Brown, Sept. 15, 1974; 1 child, Nancy Ann. AA, Western Wyo. Coll., Rock Springs, 1969; BA, Western State Coll., Gunnison, Colo., 1971; MLS, Emporia State U., Kans., 1998. From libr. technician to assoc. libr. Western Wyo. Coll., 1972—2005, assoc. libr., interim libr. dir. Hay Libr., 2005—, libr. dir. Hay Libr., 2006—. Pres. Western Wyo. Coll. Para-Profl. Assn., 2003—04. Pres. Bus. and Profl. Women, Rock Springs, 2001—03. Recipient Performance Incentive award, Western Wyo. Coll., 2004—05; grantee, Wyo. State Libr., Cheyenne, 2003, 2005. Mem.: ALA, Wyo. Libr. Assn. (section chair 2003—04, exec. coun. 2003—04), Mountain Plains Libr. Assn. Avocations: reading, ATV riding, horseback riding, snow mobiling. Office Phone: 307-382-1702. Business E-Mail: cabrown@wwcc.wy.edu.

BROWN, CAROL ROSE, artist; BFA, Cornell U. Solo shows include The Witkin Gallery, N.Y.C., Charles Lucien Gallery, N.Y.C., Rettig Y Martinez, Santa Fe, Korn Gallery, Drew U., Madison, N.J.; exhibited in group shows at Missoula (Mont.) Mus. Fine Arts, Parrish Mus., Southampton, N.Y., Provincetown (Mass.) Art Assn. and Mus., Whitney Mus. at Stamford (Conn.), The Torrey (Utah) Gallery; represented in collections U.S. Embassy, Athens, Greece, Rabat, Morrocco, Ashgabat, Turkmenistan. Individual fellow Nat. Endowment for the Arts, 1994. Personal E-mail: carolrosebrown@mac.com.

BROWN, CAROL SUE, minister; b. Pitts., May 20, 1950; d. George William and Carolyn Mae (McClelland) B. BA, Slippery Rock U., 1972; MDiv, Pitts. Theol. Sem., 1975; D Min, San Francisco Theol. Sem., 2002. Ordained to ministry Presbyn. Ch., 1975. Pastor Garrard and Manchester (Ky.) Presbyn. Chs., 1975-83; assoc. pastor First Presbyn. Ch., Stroudsburg, Pa., 1983—. Del. Gen. Assembly, 1982; accredited visitor World Coun. Chs., Canberra, Australia, 1991. Cons. Girl Scouts U.S., Stroudsburg, 1989—; commr. gen. assembly Presbyn. Ch. U.S.A., 2004. Mem. Internat. Assn. Women Mins. (treas. 1979—). Office: First Presbyn Ch 579 Main St Stroudsburg PA 18360-2003

BROWN, CAROLYN P., retired librarian; b. Newton, Miss., Jan. 24, 1923; d. Roscoe C. and Eva Alice (Alexander) Pugh; m. Thomas Kite Brown III, Oct. 15, 1949; 1 child, Susanna Shelby BA, U. Miss., 1942, MA, 1945; MLS, U. Md., 1968. Libr. div. computer rsch. NIH, Bethesda, Md., 1968-72; libr. Naval Med. Rsch. Inst., Bethesda, 1972-75; chief info. svcs. Nat. Bur. Standards, Gaithersburg, Md., 1975-77; chief user svcs. NOAA, Rockville, Md., 1977-80; dir. info. mgmt. and svcs. Exec. Office of Pres., Washington, 1980-82; chief libr. NIH Libr., Bethesda, 1982-92. Mem. exec. adv. coun. Fed. Libr. and Info. Network, 1981-84. Mem. Md. Gov.'s Conf. on Libraries and Info. Sci., 1979, 90. Coun. on Libr. Resources fellow, 1977. Mem. AAAS, ALA (bd. dirs. Fed. Librs. Roundtable 1985-88), Spl. Librs. Assn. (chmn. documentation div. 1979-80), Med. Libr. Assn.

BROWN, CATHERINE ALLETTO, elementary school educator; b. Chgo., Apr. 30, 1964; d. William Charles and Frances (Brown) Alletto; m. James Ronald Brown, April 24, 1993; 1 child, Emily Lauren. BA in edn., U. Ill., Chgo., 1987, MEd, 1990. Tchr. Archdiocese of Chgo. Bridgeport Cath. Acad., Chgo., 1987-91, Chgo. Bd. Edn.-Carson Sch., Chgo., 1991-95, Chgo. Bd. Edn.-Everett Sch., Chgo., 1995—2001, McClellan Sch., 2001—. Cheerleading coach Carson Sch., 1991-95, Everett Sch., 1995-1996. Choir dir. Bridgeport Cath. Acad., 2002—. Nominated for Thanks to tchr. award, WBBM-TV, 1995; named Internat. Woman of Yr. in Edn., 1997. Mem. AAUW, Internat. Reading Assn., Ill. Coun. for Affective Reading Edn. Roman Catholic. Avocations: reading, singing, aerobics. Office: Chgo Bd of Edn Everett Sch 3419 S Bell Ave Chicago IL 60608-6010

BROWN, CECILY, artist; b. London, 1970; Attended, NY Studio Sch., 1992; BA in Fine Arts, First Class Honors, Slade Sch. Art, London, 1993; B-TEC Diploma in Art & Design, Epsom Sch. Art, Surrey, England, 1987; attended Drawing & Printmaking classes, Morley Coll., London, 1987—89. Exhibitions include Fete Worse Than Death, Laurent Delaye, London, 1994, Eagle Gallery, London, 1995, Taking Stock, NY, 1996, Deitch Projects, NY, 1997, Janice Guy Gallery, NY, 1997, Vertical Painting, P.S. 1 Contemporary Art Ctr., NY, 1999, Pleasure Dome, Jessica Fredericks Gallery, NY, 1999, Facts & Fictions, Galleria in Arco Turin, Italy, 1999, At Century's End: John P. Morrissey Collection 90's Art, Mus. Contemporary Art, Fla., 1999, Deitch Projects, NY, 2000, The Skin Game, Gagosian Gallery, Beverly Hills, Calif., 2000, Serenade, Victoria Miro Gallery, London, 2000, Gagosian Gallery, NY, 2000, Emotional Rescue: Contemporary Art Project Collection, Ctr. Contemporary Art, Seattle, 2000, Days of Heaven, Contemporary Fine Arts, Berlin, 2001, Directions, Hirshhorn Mus. & Sculpture Garden, Washington, DC, 2002, Off, Murray Guy, NY, 2003, Whitney Biennial Am. Art, Whitney Mus. Am. Art, 2004. Mailing: c/o Gagosian Gallery 555 West 24th St New York NY 10011

BROWN, CINDY LYNN, family practice nurse practitioner, critical care nurse; b. Washington, July 11, 1956; d. Harry Carl and Betty (Gable) Sampson; m. Wayne Brown, 1998; children: Justin, Jesse. BSN, George Mason U., 1991; MSN, Marymount U., 1995. RN, Va.; CCRN; cert. family nurse practitioner; cert. clin. nurse specialist in critical care; cert. prescriptive authority; cert. ACLS, CPR instr./trainer, EMT; cert. chemotherapy adminstr. Coord. ARC, Honesdale, Pa., 1985-88; instr. CPR Fair Oaks Hosp., Fairfax, Va., 1988-97, extern critical care, 1990-91, trainer CPR instrn., 1991—; nurse critical care Washington Hosp. Ctr., 1991-94; flight nurse World Access Inc., 1993-94; emergency dept. nurse Mt. Vernon Hosp., Alexandria, Va., 1994-96; emergency nurse practitioner Potomac Hosp., Woodbridge, Va., 1996-97; family practice nurse practitioner Advanced Med. Ctr., Naples, Fla., 1997—. Lectr. in field; instr. sign lang. Fairfax County Schs., 1989-90; tissue and organ donation educator Nat. Student Nurses Assn., George Mason U., 1990-91, pres., 1990-91; 1st aid corps mem. ARC, Fairfax, 1988—92; mem. Nurse Practitioner Coun. Collier County, 1998—. Active nat. disaster relief health svc. team for Hurricane Andrew, ARC, Homestead, Fla., 1992, Miss. River Flood, 1993, Hurricane Marilyn, St. Thomas, V.I., 1995, Tropical Storm Jerry, Bonita Springs, Fla., 1995, Hurricane Fran, N.C., 1996, Hurricane George, Naples, Fla., 1998, Hurricane Charley, Naples, Fla., 2004. Named Nursing Student of Yr. Nursing Student Assn. Va., 1991, Student Leader of Yr. George Mason U., 1991. Mem. AACN (Essay award 1991), Am. Acad. Nurse Practitioners, Golden Key Honor Soc., Sigma Theta Tau (Leadership award Epsilon Zeta chpt. 1991), Alpha Chi, Delta Epsilon Sigma. Avocations: country western dancing, water sports. Home: 3231 60th St SW Naples FL 34116

BROWN, CORRINE, congresswoman; b. Jacksonville, Fla., Nov. 11, 1946; 1 child, Shantrel. BS, Fla. A&M U., 1969, MS, 1971; EdS, U. Fla., 1974. Prof. Fla. Community Coll., 1977—82, guidance counselor, 1982—92; mem. Fla. Ho. of Reps, 1982—92; del. Nat. Dem. Conv., 1988; mem. U.S. Congress from 3rd Fla. dist., 1993—, mem. transp. and infrastructure com., vet. affairs com. Named one of Most Influential Black Americans, Ebony mag., 2006. Mem. Sigma Gamma Rho. Democrat. Baptist. Home: 314 Palmetto St Jacksonville FL 32202-2619 Office: US Ho of Reps 2444 Rayburn Ho Office Bldg Washington DC 20515-0903 also: Dist Office Ste 202 101 E Union St Jacksonville FL 32202*

BROWN, CRYSTAL JEANINE, writer; b. Bay Minette, Ala., Sept. 26, 1978; d. John M. Bolding and Kathy Lou Abbott; children: Megan Elizabeth, Ashland Victoria Bryan, Cassandra Jeanine Bryan. A in Social Sci., Faulkner State C.C., Bay Minette, 2000; B in Social Sci., Wash. State U., 2001. Children's pastor Salvation Army, Saraland, Ala., 2002—. Author: Embedded Dreams, 1997, A Prism of Thoughts; contbr. poetry to anthology. Vol. Deep South Coun. Girls Scouts of Am., Ala., 2001—02; fundraising coord., sec. women's home league Salvation Army, Ala. Recipient Editors Choice award, Nat. Libr. Poetry, 1997. Avocations: poetry, genealogy, crafts, photography, sports.

BROWN, DALE PATRICK, retired advertising executive; b. Richmond, Va., Aug. 11, 1947; d. Thomas Windom and Helen (Curtis) Patrick. BA in Journalism, U. Richmond, 1968, MA in English, 1978. Reporter city news sect. Richmond Times-Dispatch, 1968-71; free-lance writer, 1971-73; v.p., supr. pub. rels. account The Martin Agy., Richmond, 1973-77, account supr. advt., v.p., 1977-79, v.p., supr. advt. account, then group v.p. and sr. v.p., 1983-89; mgr. communications svcs. Mobil Chem. Co., Richmond, 1979-81; mgr. communications Whittaker Gen. Med., Richmond, 1981-83; exec. v.p. The Stenrich Group, Richmond, 1989-90; pres., chief exec. officer Sive/Young & Rubicam, Cin., 1990-98. Trustee U. Richmond, 1992-2004, hon. trustee, 2004—, mem. exec. com., 1999-2001, vice chair acad. program com., 2002-04; mem. devel. bd. Good Samaritan Hosp., 1992-95, Leadership Cin.; bd. dirs. Met. Growth Alliance, 1997-99, Downtown Cin. Inc., 1995-98, Midwest Strategic Trust, 1993-97, Ohio Nat. Life Ins. (exec. com.), bd. dirs. Frisch's Inc., 1998—, Mercantile Libr., 2000—, Cin. C. of C., 1995-98; chair Acad. Career Women of Achievement, 1996-2001; bd. govs. Cin. chpt. Am. Assn. Advt. Agys., 1990-98. Recipient 2 AAF Silver medals, 1988, 96, Richmond Advt. Person of Yr. award Advt. Club Richmond, 1988, Woman of Achievement award Cin. YWCA, 1993, Human Rels. award Am. Jewish Com., Cin. chpt., 1996, various others including Addy, Effie, Clio awards N.Y. Art Dirs. Club. Mem. Pub. Rels. Soc. Am., Advt. Club Cin., Queen City Club (bd. dirs.), Comml. Club of Cin. Avocations: reading, travel, arts. Home: 1231 Martin Dr Cincinnati OH 45202-1737

BROWN, DALE SUSAN, retired federal agency administrator, academic administrator, consultant, writer; b. NYC, May 27, 1954; d. Bertram S. and Beatrice Joy (Gilman) Brown. BA, Antioch Coll., 1976. Rsch. asst. Am. Occupl. Therapy Assn., Rockville, Md., 1978—79; writer Pres.' Com. on Employment of People with Disabilities, Washington, 1979—82, program mgr. handicapped concerns com., 1982—85, program mgr. labor com., 1985, Washington, 1996—98, program mgr. work environment and tech. com., 1988—94, program mgr. com. on libr. and info. svcs., 1984—86, youth devel com., 1986—88, mem. team new products devel., 1987—90, agy. rep., 1991—93, with interagy. tech. assistance coordinating team, 1992—94; program mgr. Job Accomodation Network, 1997—99; mgr. Nat. Conf. of Youth with Disabilities, 2000; policy advisor Office Disability Employment Policy Dept. Labor, 2001—05, mem. youth team, 2002—05, ret., 2005. Cons. in field, gen. assembly spkr. nat. conv. Gen. Fedn. Women's Clubs, 1981, mem. Rehab Svcs. Adminstrn. Task Force on Learning Disabilities, 1981-83. Author: Pathways to Employment for People with Learning Disabilities, 1991, Working Effectively with People Who Have Learning Disabilities and Attention Deficit Hyperactivity Disorder, 1995, I Know I Can Climb the Mountain, 1995, Learning Disabilities and Employment, 1997, Learning A Living Guide to Planning Your Career and Finding A Job for People with Learning Disabilities, Attention Deficit Disorder and Dyslexia, 2000, Job-Hunting Tips for the So-Called Handicapped, 2001, Steps to Independence for People with Learning Disabilities, 2005, (films) They Could Have Saved Their Homes, 1982; dir.: (videotape) Part of the Team People with Disabilities in the Workforce, 1990; co-editor: Learning Disabilities Quar. Americans with Disabilities Act and Learning Disabilities, 1992; mem. editl. bd. Perceptions, 1981—83, Learning Disabilities Focus, 1988—90, In the Mainstream, 1994—98; guest editor: Learning Disabilities Rsch. and Practice, 1990—96; guest editor Learning Disability and Career Development, 2002; guest editor: Career Planning and Adult Devel. Jour., 2002. Rep. interagy. com. Handicapped Employees, 1998—99; adv. com. Learning Disability Online web site, 2005—; bd. dirs. Closer Look Nat. Info. Ctr., Washington, 1980—83, Am. Coalition for Citizens with Disabilities, 1985—86; mem. Congl. Task Force Rights and Empowerment of Ams. with Disabilities, 1988—90; profl. adv. bd. Nat. Attention Deficit Disorder Assn., 1996—99; bd. dirs. Coun. on Quality and Leadership, 2001—05; adv. bd. Internat. Ctr. for Disability Resources on the Internet, 2003—; chair Conf. on Info. Tech. for User With Disabilities, 1989; spl. asst. for people with disabilities Federally Employed Women, 1991—92; mem. blue ribbon panel Nat. Telecomm. Access for People with Disabilities, 1989—94; pres. Assn. Learning Disabled Adults, Washington, 1979—80; del. Nat. Writer's Union, 1999; rep. com. on fed. govt. as model employer, com. on youth with disabilities Presdl. Task Force on Employment of Adults with Disabilities, 1999—2002; judge, Ten Outstanding Young Ams. U.S. Jr. C. of C. Jaycees, 2003. Named one of Ten Outstanding Young Ams., U.S. Jr. C. of C. Jaycees, 1994; recipient, Margaret Byrd Rawson award, 1989, Personal Achievement award Women's Program USDOL, 1989, Individual Achievement award, Nat. Coun. on Comm. Disorders, 1991, Spl. Achievement award, Pres.'s Com. on Employment of People with Disabilities, 1991, Gold Screen award, Nat. Assn. Gov. Communicators, 1991, Arthur S. Fleming award, 1992, Voices Campaign award, 2004, Honor award, Dept. Labor, 2004; grantee, Found. for Children with Learning Disabilities, 1982. Mem.: ALA, Inter Agency. Com. on Handicapped Employees (rep. 1989—91), Learning Disabilities Assn. Am. (bd. dirs. 1986—91), Nat. Assn. Govt. Communicators (Blue Pencil award 1986), Nat. Network of Learning Disabled Adults (founder, pres. 1980—81). Democrat.

BROWN, DEBORAH ELEANOR, priest; b. Carmel, Calif., Jan. 20, 1940; d. Charles Edward and Lois Eleanor French; m. Ronald Earl Brown; children: Cynthia Leigh Brown Cockrill, Gregory Scott. BA, Occidental Coll., 1961; MDiv, Episc. Theol. Sem. Southwest, 1989. Ordained priest Episc. Ch., 1990. Tchr. primary elem. Long Beach Unified Sch. Dist., Calif., 1961—62; tchr. Pueblo Unified Sch. Dist., Colo., 1965—66, New Ulm Sch. Dist., Minn., 1970—77; assoc. rector St. Christopher's Episcopal Ch., Roseville, Minn., 1992—96, interim rector, 1996—98; asst. interim rector St. John the Evangelist Episcopal Ch., Mpls., 1998—99; interim rector St. Luke's Episcopal Ch., Mpls., 2000—01; pre-interim rector St. Clement's Episcopal Ch., St. Paul, 2005—, co-interim rector, 2005—. Supply priest Episcopal Diocese of Minn., Mpls., 1992—; chaplain Eagan Police Dept., Minn., 1995—, coord. chaplain program, 1999—; co-coord. vol. Gen. Coun. of Episc. Ch., Mpls., 2003; co-coord. deacon/laity Episcopal Diocese of Minn., Mpls., 2002—. Rep. Eagan Police Dept. Eagan Health Cmty. Init., 2001—03, Eagan Park and Recreation Master Plan, 2005; mem. Metro Critical Incident Stress Mgmt. Team, 2001—. Recipient Award of Merit, Eagan Police Dept., 2000. Democrat. Episcopalian. Avocations: reading, knitting, art.

BROWN, DEBORAH ELLEN, gifted and talented educator, writer; d. Murphy and Mary Brown. BA, Calif. State U., Northridge, Calif., 1977; cert. in Multiple Subject Credentials, U. Calif., Riverside, Calif., 1978. Tchr. Fairfield Sch., Van Nuys, Calif., 1978—83, 1991—95, L.A. (Calif.) Unified Sch. Dist., 1988—90, Countryside Prep. Sch., Northridge, 1990—91, Mirman Sch. for Gifted, L.A., 1995—. Lectr. in field. Editor: MERIDIAN, 1995—; contbr. articles to profl. jours. and mags. Nominee Tchr. award, Disneyland. Mem.: Nat. Tchrs. Math., Calif. Assn. for Gifted. Democrat. Office: Mirman School for Gifted 16180 Mulholland Dr Los Angeles CA 90049

BROWN, DEBRA, elementary school educator; b. Sacramento, May 4, 1952; d. Robert Gates and Ramona Irene (Evans) B.; m. Steve Quayle Cannon, Nov. 3, 1978; children: Emily Fay Cannon-Brown, Bonnie Quayle Cannon-Brown. BA, U. Calif., Berkeley, 1974. Cert. tchr., Calif. 1st grade tchr. Am. Sch., Tegucigalpa, Honduras, 1975-78; 1st and 2d grade tchr. Bahi Sch., Siguatepeque, Honduras, 1978-79; 4th grade and kindergarten tchr. Amador County Unified Schs., Pine Grove, Calif., 1981-88; kindergarten, 1st, 2d, 3d, 5th and 6th grade tchr. Lodi Unified Sch. Dist., Victor, Calif., 1991—. Sec. Dem. Women. Amador County, 1982; mem., vol. Operation Care Crisis Line, treas., 1981-82, phone vol., 1980-88, 93-96. Mem. AAUW, NOW, Calif. Tchrs.' Assn., Amnesty Internat. Avocations: reading, gardening, travel.

BROWN, DELLA HEWETT, elementary school educator; b. Chickasha, Okla., Nov. 6, 1954; d. Hugh Andrew and Alma Jane Hewett; m. William Charles Brown, Jan. 20; children: Andrew Charles, Eric Cuchulain. MusB in Edn., West Tex. State (A&M) U., Canyon, Tex., 1977; MA in Guidance and Counseling, Ball State U., Athens, Greece, 1981. Registered Music Therapist NAMT, 1978, National Board Certified Teacher Nat. Bd. for Profl. Tchg. Standards, 2005. Admin. asst. to embassy/peace corp. med. unit, Mbabane, Swaziland, 1993—96; tchr. elem. strings Fairfax County Pub. Schools, Reston, Va., 1996—. Vol. embassy chorus dir. US Embassy, Tel Aviv. Music dir., Asuncion, Athens, Tel Aviv, Paraguay. Mem.: Am. String Teachers Assn. (licentiate). Home: 302 Missouri Ave Herndon VA 20170 Office: Forest Edge Elem Sch 1501 Becontree Lane Reston VA 20190 Office Phone: 703-925-8000. Personal E-mail: della.brown@fcps.edu.

BROWN, DELORES RUSSELL, health management company official; b. Phila., Sept. 20, 1947; d. William and Jean (Nichols) Russell; children: Brendell F., William A. Jr. Student, Temple U., 1969-71; BA, Antioch U., Phila., 1988; MSW, U. Pa., 1991. Lic. real estate salesperson, Pa.; cert. residential appraiser, Pa. Real estate cons. Ball Real Estate, Inc., Phila., 1976-86; publ. word processor Magnavox (GAC), Wymoor, Pa., 1982-83; real estate closing clk. Merrill Lynch Relocation, Bala Cynwyd, Pa., 1983-84; med. and tech. sec. U. Pa., Phila., 1984-86, adminstrv. asst., 1986-89; social worker for aged Episcopal Community Svcs., Phila., 1989-90, dir. social svc., 1991-92; sr. svc. coord., rsch. interviewer Phila. Health Mgmt. Corp., 1992—, facilitator, 1992. Mem. Phila. Mayor's Adv. Bd. on Aging, 1987; tutor Phila. Mayor's Literacy Program, 1988; asst. dir. social svcs. Zion Cares Ministry, Phila., 1991—; mem. Zion Bapt. Outreach Ministry, 1985—; mem. family planning bd. Temple U., 1970-76. Recipient svc. award Temple U., 1988, Rosa Wessell Outstanding MSW award, U. Pa., 1991. Mem. Nat. Assn. Real Estate Brokers (2d v.p. women's coun. Washington 1991-92, Disting. Local Chpt. Presdl. award 1993), Phila. Women's Coun. of Assn. Real Estate Brokers (pres. 1991-93, Outstanding Presdl. award 1993), Alliance of Black Social Workers, Women of Color Coalition. Avocation: bowling. Home: 8101 Fayette St Philadelphia PA 19150-1214

BROWN, DENISE, poet; b. Chgo., Oct. 7, 1963; d. Earl L. and Dorothy Grier; married; 3 children. Author: (poetry) A Treasury of Great Poems, 1998, poems. Recipient Editor's Choice award, 1999, Cert. of Recognition, 2001, The Diamond Homer award, 1998.

BROWN, DENISE SCOTT, architect, urban planner; b. Nkana, Zambia, Oct. 3, 1931; arrived in U.S., 1958, naturalized, 1971; d. Simon and Phyllis (Hepker) Lakofski; m. Robert Scott Brown, July 21, 1955 (dec. 1959); m. Robert Charles Venturi, July 23, 1967; 1 child, James C. Student, U. Witwatersrand, South Africa, 1948—51; diploma, Archtl. Assn., London, 1955; M of City Planning, U. Pa., 1960, MArch, 1965; DFA (hon.), Oberlin Coll., 1977, Phila. Coll. Art, 1985, Parsons Sch. Design, 1985; LHD (hon.), N.J. Inst. Tech., 1984, Phila. Coll. Textiles and Sci., 1992; DEng (hon.), Tech. U. N.S., 1991; HHD (hon.), Pratt Inst., 1992; DFA (hon.), U. Pa., 1994; LittD (hon.), U. Nev., 1998; D. Arch. (hon.), U. Miami, 1997; DFA (hon.), Lehigh U., 2002. Registered architect, U.K. Asst. prof. U. Pa., Phila., 1960—65; assoc. prof., head urban design program UCLA, 1965—68; with Venturi, Rauch and Scott Brown, Phila., 1967—, ptnr., 1969—89; prin. Venturi, Scott Brown and Assocs. Inc., Phila., 1989—. Asst. prof. U. Pa., 1960—65, vis. prof. Sch. Fine Arts, 1982, 83, mem. bd. overseers U. Librs., 1995—2004; vis. prof. arch. U. Calif., Berkeley, 1965, Yale U., 1967—70; mem. visitors com. MIT, 1973—83; mem. adv. com. dept. arch. Temple U., 1980—2001; Eliot Noyes design critic in arch. Harvard U., Cambridge, Mass., 1989—90, mem. jury Prince of Wales Prize in Urban Design, Grad. Sch. Design, 1993, mem. com. to rev. policies and practices Grad. Sch. Design, 2006, William E. Massey Sr. lectr history Am. civilization, 03; cons. to dean search com. Sch. Arch. Washington U., St. Louis, 1992; mem. adv. bd. dept. arch. Carnegie Mellon U., 1992—; master builder lectr. Carpenters' Co., 2005; Kassler lectr., Whitney J. Oats fellow in Humanities Coun. and Sch. Arch. Princeton U., NJ, 2006. Author: Urban Concepts, 1990; co-author: Learning from Las Vegas, 1972, (rev. edit.), 1977, A View from the Campidoglio: Selected Essays, 1953-84, 1985, Architecture as Signs and Systems for a Mannerist Time, 2004; contbr. numerous articles to profl. jours.; prin. works include campus plans U. Mich., Dartmouth Coll., Tsinghua U., Beijing, prin. works include city plans Miami Beach, Memphis, prin. works include plans U. Pa. Perelman Quadrangle, U. Mich., Palmer Dr. Sci. Complex, Life Scis. Inst., Parking Garage, Brown U., Baker/Berry Libr. & Carson Hall, Dartmouth Coll. (Phase 1), Baker/Berry Libr. & Carson Hall, Dartmouth Coll. (Phase 2), Nat. Gallery, London, Hotel du Dept. de la Haute Garonne, Toulouse, France, prin. works include many others. Policy panelist design arts program NEA, 1981—83; mem. bd. adv. Architects, Designers and Planners for Social Responsibility, 1982—; mem. capitol preservation com. Commonwealth of Pa., Harrisburg, 1983—87; trustee Chestnut Hill Acad., Phila., 1985—89; hon. vice patron The Royal Soc. for the Encouragement of Arts, Manufacture and Commerce in the U.S., 2004; active Civil Alliance Planning and Design Workshop for Lower Manhattan, 2002, Penn's Landing Pub. Forums, 2003; US patron The Friends of Benjamin Franklin House, London, 1996—; mem. curriculum com. Phila. Jewish Children's Folkshul, 1980—86; bd. dirs. Ctrl. Phila. Devel. Corp., 1985—, Urban Affairs Partnership, Phila., 1987—91. Decorated commendatore Order of Merit Italy, chevalier de l'Ordre des Arts et des Lettres France; co-recipient The Phila. award, 1993, Luminary award, 2005, The Founder's award, Hist. Soc. Pa., 2006; named to Germantown Hall of Fame, Germantown Hist. Soc., Pa., 2002; recipient Chgo. Architecture award, 1987, U.S. Presdl. award, Nat. Medal of Arts, 1992, Hall of Fame award, Interior Design mag., 1992, The Benjamin Franklin medal, Royal Soc. for Encouragement of Arts., Mfg. and Commerce, 1993, Topaz medal, Am. Coll. Schs. of Architecture/AIA, 1996, Giants of Design award, House Beautiful Mag., 2000, Joseph Pennell medal, Phila. Sketch Club, 2000, Vincent J. Scully Prize, Nat. Bldg. Mus., 2002, Edith Wharton Women of Achievement award for Urban Planning, 2002, Soc. for Environ. Graphic Design Fellow award, 2003, Visionary Woman award, Moore Coll. Art and Design, 2003, The Franklin Founder Bowl, The Franklin Celebration, 2005, Harvard Radcliffe Inst. medal, 2005, Carpenters Co. Master Builder award, 2005. Mem.: Germantown Historical Soc. of Phila., Germantown Jewish Centre (Germantown Hall of Fame 2002, Soc. for Environ. Graphic Design Fellow award 2003), Royal Soc. Encouragement of Arts, Mfg. and Commerce (hon. vice patron 2004), Soc. Archtl. Historians (bd. dirs. 1981—84), Soc. Coll. and Univ. Planning, Archtl. Assn. London, Am. Planning Assn., Archs. Designers and Planners for Social Responsibility, Am. Acad. Arts and Scis., Royal Inst. Brit. Archs., Athenaeum of Phila., Carpenters Co. of City and County of Phila., Internat. Women's Forum. Democrat. Jewish. Office: Venturi Scott Brown & Assocs Inc 4236 Main St Philadelphia PA 19127-1696

BROWN, DIANA L., elementary school educator; b. Bklyn., Oct. 9, 1946; d. Elva Jane Brown. AAS, N.Y.C. Community Coll., Bklyn.; BS, CCNY, 1980; postgrad., Nova U., Ft. Lauderdale, Fla. Cert. educator, Fla.; class cert.

behavior analysis. Asst. dir. Toddlers Country Club, Orlando, Fla.; tchr. Friends Sem., N.Y.C.; supr. outpatient clinics N.Y. Health and Hosps. Corp.; tchr. grade 3 Dover Shores Elem. Sch./Orange County Sch. Bd., Orlando, Fla.; 3d grade tchr. Shingle Creek Elem. Sch., 1993, 5th grade tchr., 1993—95, curriculum resource tchr., dean, 1995—97; alternative edn. tchr. for at-risk students grades 4-5 Dover Shores Elem. Sch., 1997; 5th grade tchr. Tangelo Park Elem., 1997—2002; behavior specialist resource tchr. Rock Lake Elem. Sch., 2002—, dean, 2002—. Sch.-based care team at-risk students Orange County Schs., Orlando, Fla., mem. state sci. textbook adoption com., 1994—95, mem. county sci. curriculum writing team, 1994—95; trainer new tchrs. Great Beginnings Program, 2001—; dean sch.-wide discipline Rock Lake Elem. Sch., 2001—, SAFE coord., 2001—. Co-author: Afro-American Artists: A Bio-Bibliographical Directory, 1973. Named Tchr. of Yr. Dover Shores, 1990-91; Coun. of Black Faculty and Staff scholar. Mem.: NEA, Nat. Sci. Tchrs. Assn. Office: Rock Lake Elem School 408 N Tampa Ave Orlando FL 32839 Office Phone: 407-245-1880 2264. E-mail: brownd@ocps.net.

BROWN, DOROTHY M., academic administrator; Prof. history Georgetown U., Washington, 1966—98, interim provost, 1998—99, provost, 1999—. Former chair history dept. Georgetown U. Office: Georgetown U Office of the Provost Box 571014/ ICC 650 Washington DC 20057-1014

BROWN, ELIZABETH, health science association administrator, educator; d. Earlene Ruth and adopted d. Eunice Syretha Brown. AA in Gen. Edn., Roane State C.C., Harriman, Tenn., 1988; BS in Health Care Adminstrn. and Planning, Tenn. State U., Nashville, 1991; MS in Pub. Health, Meharry Med. Coll., Nashville, 1994. Cert. health edn. specialist Nat. Commn. for Health Edn. Credentialing, Inc., nursing home adminstr. Tenn. Asst. dir. occupl. and preventive medicine dept. Meharry Med. Coll., Nashville, 1996—2001; adj. instr. Tenn. State U., Nashville, 1998—2001; grad. tchg. assoc. U. Tenn., Knoxville, 2001—; safety intern Dept. Instrnl. Tech., Health and Cultural Studies, Lenoir City, Tenn., 2006—. Mem. Gov.'s Task Force for Environ. Justice, Nashville, 1998—99; mem. quality of life subcom. Rockwood (Tenn.) Indsl. Bd., 2006—. Named to Chancellor's List, Ednl. Comm., Inc., 2004—05; recipient Profl. Promise award, Chancellor, 2004; June Gorski scholar, June Gorski and Coll. of Edn., Health and Human Scis., 2005. Mem.: AAHPERD, APHA, Soc. Pub. Health Edn. Avocations: reading, travel. Home: PO Box 535 Rockwood TN 37854 Office: U Tenn 1914 Andy Holt Ste 390 Knoxville TN 37996

BROWN, ELIZABETH ANN, foreign service officer; b. Portland, Oreg., Aug. 15, 1918; d. Edwin Keith and Grace Viola (Foss) B. AB, Reed Coll., 1940; postgrad. (teaching fellow), Wash. State Coll., 1940-41; A.M., Columbia, 1943. Exec. asst. to chmn. 12th region WLB, Seattle, 1943-45; internat. affairs officer Dept. State, 1946-56; joined U.S. Fgn. Service, 1956; assigned Office UN Polit. Affairs, Dept. State, 1956-60; 1st sec. Am. embassy, Bonn, Germany, 1960-63; dep. dir. Office UN Polit. Affairs, 1963-65, dir., 1965-69; mem. State Dept. Sr. Seminar in Fgn. Policy, 1969-70; counselor for polit. affairs Am. embassy, Athens, Greece, 1970-75, dep. chief mission The Hague, Netherlands, 1975-78; sr. insp. Dept. State, 1978-79, cons., 1980—; ret., 1979. Adviser U.S. del. UN Gen. Assembly, 1946-50, 53, 55, 57-59, 64-65 Recipient 7th ann. Fed. Woman's award, 1967 Mem. Am. Fgn. Service Assn., Phi Beta Kappa. Home: 4848 Reservoir Rd NW Washington DC 20007-1561 Office: Dept State Washington DC 20007

BROWN, ELIZABETH MCCARTHY, social services administrator; b. Omaha, Oct. 3, 1941; d. James John and Mary Theresa McCarthy; m. V.K. Brown, Aug. 3, 1974; children: V.K. III, Steven. BA, Ohio State U., 1963; MASW, U. Chgo., 1968. Cert. social worker Acad. Cert. Social Workers; lic. clin. social worker, Ill. Acting intake supr. Franklin County Welfare Dept., Columbus, Ohio; social worker Hull House Assn., Chgo.; unit dir. homebound programs Abraham Lincoln Centre, Chgo., dir. social work svc. dept.; exec. dir. coun. of internat. programs Loyola Univ. Chgo., 2004—05, pres. coun. internat. programs, 1989—91, 2005—06. Dir. program ops. Little Bros.-Friends of the Elderly; dir. social work svcs. Abraham Lincoln Ctr., 2001, cons. Recipient Svc. award Chgo. Osteo. Hosp. Pediatric and Adolescent Comprehensive Care and Prevention Program, Svc. award Coun. Internat. Programs, Loyola U., Chgo., 1987; named for Outstanding Field Work Supr., Valparaiso U., 1975-76. Fellow Am. Orthopsychiat. Assn.; mem. NASW. Home: Apt 2516N 4800 S Chicago Beach Dr Chicago IL 60615-2170 Office Phone: 773-415-2888. Business E-Mail: ag9803@ameritech.net.

BROWN, ELIZABETH SCHMECK, fashion historian; b. Ancon, Panama, Sept. 7, 1918; d. Henry Penuel and Pansy Blossom (Logan) Schmeck; m. Walter Daniel Brown, July 29, 1944; children: David Henry, Walter Daniel Jr., Edward Logan, Kenneth Maclin. Student, U. Tex., 1935—37; BS, Cornell U., 1940, MS, 1945; student, Art Students League N.Y. Cert. family and consumer scis. AAFCS. Instr. textiles and clothing, curator costume collection Coll. Home Econs. Cornell U., Ithaca, NY, 1941—45; assoc. home economist McCall Pattern Co., N.Y.C., 1963—65; assoc. Uno Pattern Co., N.J. and Pa., 1972—74; lectr. on hist. dress, 1972—; appraiser of hist. dress, 1978—. Contbr. articles to profl. publs.; curated exhbns., NJ Divsn. on Women, Trenton, Kemmerer Mus., Bethelehem, Pa., Antiques at the Armory, Phila., Rutgers Inst. for Rsch. on Women, New Brunswick, N.J., N.J. Hist. Commn. Mem. Montgomery Twp. Bd. Edn., Skillman, NJ, 1969—81, various offices, including pres., 1975—77; legis. chmn., pres. Somerset County Sch. Bds. Assn., Somerville, NJ, 1977—80; testified to State Legis. and Bd. Edn. for mandate of Family Life Edn.; active N.J. Network Family Life, 1983—2002; mem. adv. coun. Family, Career, and Cmty. Leadership Am., 2001—; bd. dirs. Costume and Textile Group N.J., 2001—; bd. dir. (former treas.) Wesley Found., 1984—, Princeton U.; mem. PTA, Pitts.; pres. Whittier Sch., Park Ridge, Ill.; founding com. River-Ridge Council, Broomall, Pa. Fellow: Costume Soc. Am. (treas. 1980—86, bd. dirs. several terms 1982—, Bd. of Dir., several terms 1982—2004, corr. sec. 1986—92, pres. region II 1993—97, v.p. internal rels. 1998—2003, parliamentarian, bd. dirs.); mem.: AAUW (pres. Princeton br. 1973—75), N.J. Assn. Family and Consumer Scis. (state pres.'s unit nom. com., divsn. chair, apparel and textiles, archives and history), Am. Assn. Family and Consumer Scis. (nat. leader 1992), Van Harlingen Hist. Soc. (former trustee), Hist. Soc. Princeton (collections com.), Internat. Textile and Apparel Assn., N.J. Assn. Mus., PTA Pitts. (various offices), Internat. Sewing Machine Collectors Soc., Am. Assn. State and Local History, Cornell Alumni Assn., Princeton YWCA (vol. Friday Club 1968—2000), Y Canoe Club, Cornell Woman's Club (Pitts.) (pres., chair sec. sch. com.), Friday (com. mem. 2000—), Cornell Woman's Club (Chgo.), Cornell Woman's Club (Phila.), Phi Kappa Phi, Kappa Omicron Nu, Alpha Lambda Delta. Avocations: costume collection of over 2000 items, collecting antique paper patters, collecting antique sewing machines and other sewing items. Home and Office: 45 Whippoorwill Way Belle Mead NJ 08502 E-mail: ebrown@nerc.com.

BROWN, ELLYN L., lawyer, consultant; b. Detroit, Mar. 20, 1950; AB with honors, Vasser Coll., 1972; MS, John Hopkins U., 1975; JD, U. Md., 1980. Securities commr. State of Md., 1987—92; atty. in residence U. Md. Sch. Law, 1993—95; pres. Brown & Assocs., Balt., 1995—; visiting prof. Villanova U. Sch. Law, 2003—05. Dir., officer N. Am. Securities Administrators Assn., 1988—92; bd. mem. Nat. Assn. Securities Dealers Regulation, Inc., 1995—98; mem. Editorial Bd. Villanova Jour. Law and Investment Mgmt., 1998—; mem. CFP Bd. Standards, 2000—04; bd. dirs. NY Stock Exch., NYC, 2005—06, NYSE Group, Inc., 2006—. Mem. Balt. Symphony Orch., Planned Parenthood Md., U. Md. Law Sch. Alumni Assn. Mem.: ABA, Md. State Bar Assn. Office: Brown and Assocs 11055 Greenspring Ave Annex A Lutherville Timonium MD 21093 also: NYSE Group Inc c/o Corp Sec 11 Wall St New York NY 10005*

BROWN, ELMIRA NEWSOM, retired elementary school educator; b. Proctor-Crittenden, Ark., May 31, 1907; d. Emanuel Newsom and Tennessee Johnson; m. James Jefferson Brown, Nov. 19, 1942. BS, U. Ark., Pine Bluff, 1950; MS, U. Ark., Fayetteville, 1954. Tchr. Wynoka (Ark.) Elem. Sch., 1930-34, Mildred Jackson Elem. Sch., Hughes, Ark., 1934-42; prin. McCrory (Ark.) Elem. Sch. (now Elmira N. Brown H.S.), 1943-50; tchr. Scipio A. Jones H.S., North Little Rock, Ark., 1950-53, Howard Elem. Sch., Ft. Smith, Ark., 1954-60, Goldstein Elem. Sch., Hot Springs, Ark., 1960-67, Langston H.S., Hot Springs, 1967-68; ret., 1968. Interim exec. dir. Coun. Econ. Opportunity, Hot Springs, 1968—. V.p. Woodland Shores Cmty. Action, Royal, Ark., 1983-92; mem. Dem. Nat. Com., Washington, 1992-97; chairperson task force Dem. Congl. Campaign Com., Royal, 1992-96; mem. women's missionary soc. African Meth. Episcopal Ch., dir. connectional skill shops WMS, 1980. Mem. AAUW, LWV, Ch. Women United, U. Ark. Alumni Assn., Zeta Phi Beta. Mem. African Meth. Episcopalian Ch. Avocations: softball, basketball, fishing, boating, gardening.

BROWN, EVA EVERLEAN, business executive; d. Robert Lee Creacy and Alzora Lee Bass; m. Royal Guy Brown, Apr. 14, 1963 (dec.); 1 child, Royal Guy Jr. BS, SUNY, Albany, 1979. Adminstrn. mgmt. IBM Corp., Albany, 1968—87; founder, pres. Get Smart, Inc., Sanford, NC, 1991—98, founder, COO, 1998—. Pres. NAACP, Sanford, 1989—93. Recipient IBM Master's award, IBM Corp., 1986, Vol. award, N.C. Govs. Office, 1991, Outstanding Citizen's award, Sanford Area C. of C., 1994, Razor Walker award, U. N.C., Wilmington, 1997, Image award, Lee County Chpt. NAACP, 1999, Sanford Rotary 4-Way Test award, Sanford Rotary Club, 1999, Lifetime Achievement award, The Sanford Herald, 2005. Mem.: Delta Kappa Gamma Theta (hon.; Delta Rho chpt.), Delta Sigma Theta. Democrat. Methodist. Avocations: writing, cooking, collecting cookbooks. Home: 2207 Spring Ln Sanford NC 27330 Office: Get Smart Inc 1309 Washington Ave Sanford NC 27330 Office Phone: 919-776-6119. Office Fax: 919-776-7905. Personal E-mail: eebrow@earthlink.net. Business E-Mail: getsmart@wave-net.net.

BROWN, FAY, editor, writer; b. Patterson, La., Aug. 5, 1925; d. Alvan Paul Gautreau and Mari2 Stella Seghers; m. Hilton J. Brown, Aug. 12, 1950 (dec.); children: Patrick Ronald, Robert Allan(dec.). BA with highest distinction, U. Southwestern La., 1945. Editor weekly newspaper Franklin (La.) Banner Tribune, 1945-50; editor diocesan newsletter for older adults Diocese of La., Franklin, 1991—. Author: Franklin through the Years, 1972, St. Mary's Episcopal Church-Yesterday and Today. Past sec. St. Mary Landmarks; past chmn. St. Mary Coun. on Aging, Franklin, 1999-2001; mem. bd. St. Mary Literacy Coun., 1999—; mem. St. Mary Civil War Commn., 1999—. Recipient civic award Franklin Bus. and Profl. Women's Club, 1950. Independent. Episcopalian. Avocations: reading, music.

BROWN, FLORENCE S., librarian, administrator; b. Phila., Feb. 11, 1937; d. Andrew Wilson and Inez Ellegood (Sutton) Simkins; m. James Albert Brown, Jr., Jan. 1, 1963 (div. Feb. 1982); 1 child, Catherine Inez. Student, Bennett Coll., Greensboro, N.C., 1954-56; BA, Benedict Coll., Columbia, S.C., 1958; MSL.S., Syracuse U., 1959. Asst. reference librarian Morgan State U., Balt., 1959-64; head librarian Md. State Dept. of Health, Balt., 1965-73; librarian R.F. Kennedy Elem. Sch., Providence, 1973-75; head librarian Concord Pike Public Library, Wilmington, Del., 1975-82; dir. New Castle County Dept. of Libraries, Wilmington, Del., 1982-87; chief extension div. Enoch Pratt Free Library, Balt., 1987—. Mem. White House Conf. on Libraries and Info. Services Task Force, 1980—; adv. com. Read Aloud Del.; chmn. pub. relations com. Del. Coalition for Literacy. Bd. dirs. Police Athletic League of Del., Wilmington, 1984-87; county chmn. United Negro College Fund, New Castle County, Del., 1985-86. Mem. Del. Library Assn. (Disting. Pub. Librarian award 1982, chmn. legis. com. 1986-87), ALA (chpt. relations com. 1983—, LAMA (pub. relation services to libraries com. 1984—), Black Caucus of ALA (mem. exec. bd. 1980-82, co-chmn. membership com. 1980-84) Democrat. Episcopalian. Avocations: gardening, reading. Home: 2301 S Ocean Dr Apt 707 Hollywood FL 33019-2622 Office: Enoch Pratt Free Library 400 Cathedral St Baltimore MD 21201-4401

BROWN, FRANCES LOUISE (GRANDMA FRAN), artist, art gallery director; b. Indpls., Oct. 19, 1925; d. Harley and Lenore (Spencer) Netherland; m. C.G. Clarkson, July 24, 1943 (div. Aug. 1967); children: James E. Clarkson, John B. Clarkson, Deborah L. Cromis. Thomas L. Currey, June 9, 1972 (dec. May 1978); m. George L. Brown, Jr., Mar. 3, 1982; 1 stepchild, Nancy Snow. BS in Edn., Miami U., 1968; MA in Edn., Ball State U., 1970. Tchr. elem. sch. Liberty Elem. Sch., Ind., 1968—71; tchr. Ball State U., Muncie, Ind., 1971—72; instr. Colby C.C., Kans., 1972—75; gallery owner, primitive artist Grandma Fran Art Gallery (formerly Currey Studio Gallery), Berryville, Ark., 1975—. Author: Now Hear This, 1974; works exhibited at Nat. Mus. Am. Art, Washington, Wichita (Kans.) Art Assn. Gallery, Ark. Coll., Batesville, South Ark. Art Ctr., El Dorado, Harding Coll., Searcy, Ark., U. Ark., Fayetteville, Eureka Springs (Ark.) Hist. Mus., Western State Coll. Colo., Gunnison, MacMurray Coll., Jacksonville, Ill., Colby (Kans.) Coll., Claremore (Okla.) Coll., Warren Hall Coutts, III, Meml. Art Gallery, Inc., El Dorado, Kans., Masur Mus. Art, Monroe, La., Nebr. State Hist. Soc. Mus., Lincoln, Ind. State Mus., Indpls., Ozark Folk Ctr., Mountain View, Ark., Ft. Smith (Ark.) Art Ctr., Ctr. for So. Folklore, Memphis, Rogers (Ark.) Hist. Mus., Albrecht Art Mus., St. Joseph, Mo., Shiloh Mus., Springdale, Ark., Intenrat. Ctr. Contemporary Art, Paris, John Judkyn Meml. Mus., Eng., Mykonos (Greece) Folklore Mus., Musees Royaux des Beaux-Arts de Belgique, Brussels, Setagaya Art Mus., Tokyo, Fukuoka (Japan) Art Mus.; represented in permanent collections Smithsonian Instn., Washington, Mus. Am. Folk Art, N.Y.C., Nebr. State Hist. Soc. Mus., Lincoln, Ind. State Mus., Indpls., Ozark Mountain Folk Ctr., Mountain View, Ctr. for So. Folklore, Memphis, Setagaya Art Mus., others; paintings recognized in various books, newspapers and articles. Avocations: pilot, sewing, reading, fishing, cooking. Home and Office: Grandma Fran Art Gallery 3331 Highway 62 W Berryville AR 72616-8948 Office Phone: 870-423-2073. Business E-Mail: grandmafran@hbeark.com.

BROWN, GAIL, secondary school educator; b. Columbia, Tenn., Dec. 17, 1949; d. William Mayfield and Sarah Evelyn (Blackburn) Chunn; m. Thomas H. Brown, Apr. 16, 1971 (div. Mar. 1999); 1 child, Micah. MEd, Mid. Tenn. State U., Murfeesboro, 1974, postgrad., 1997. Profl. lic. and career ladder I. Tchr. Franklin (Tenn.) H.S., 1971-72; tchr., coach Northside Jr. High, Brentwood, 1972-77, Warren Ctrl. High, Bowling Green, Ky., 1979-82, Lakeview-Ft. Oglethorpe (Ga.) High, 1982-83; math. dept. chair Ooltewah (Tenn.) H.S., 1983-88, Franklin H.S., 1988—. Adv. bd. mem., treas. Tenn. Assn. Student Coun., Nashville, 1988-91; presenter in field. Mem. DAR, Nat. Coun. Tchrs. Math., Tenn. Edn. Assn., Mensa, Delta Kappa Gamma. Republican. Mem. Ch. of Christ. Avocations: reading, cross stitch. Home: 656 Watson Branch Dr Franklin TN 37064-5130

BROWN, GERALDINE REED, lawyer, management consultant; b. LA, Feb. 18, 1947; d. William Penn and Alberta Vernice (Coleman) Reed; m. Ronald Wellington Brown, Aug. 20, 1972; children: Kimberly Diana, Michael David. BA summa cum laude, Fisk U., 1968; JD, Harvard U., 1971, MBA, 1973. Bar: N.Y. 1974, U.S. Dist. Ct. (so. and ea. dists.) N.Y. 1974, U.S. Ct. Appeals (2d cir.) 1974, U.S. Supreme Ct. 1977, N.J. 1992, U.S. Dist. Ct. N.J. 1992, Pa. 1993. Assoc. White & Case, N.Y.C., 1973-78; atty. J.C. Penney Co., Inc., N.Y.C., 1978-88; pres. The Reed-Brown Cons. Group., Montclair, NJ, 1989—; counsel Spooner & Burnett, N.Y.C., 1993-98. Asst. prof. bus. law Montclair State Coll., 1990-92; adj. prof. bus. law Kean Coll. NJ, 1989-94; adj. prof. Law Sch. Seton Hall, 1995; dir., sec., gen. counsel Renaissance Jr. Golf, Inc., Newark; instr. Hudson County C.C., Bergen C.C., Entrepreneurial Tng. Inst.; mem. com. on women and the cts. NJ Supreme Ct., com. on fee arbitration. Bd. dirs. Coun. Concerned Black Execs., N.Y.C., 1977-88, Studio Mus. in Harlem, N.Y.C., 1980-81; mem. Montclair (N.J.) Devel. Bd., 1985-88, ad hoc com. on Montclair Econ. Devel. Corp., 1985-88; sec., bd. trustee Montclair YWCA, 1989-97, United Hosps. Med. Ctr., vice chmn., 1991-93, trustee, 1989-97, exec. com., chair bylaws com., chair strategic planning com., pers. com.; former sec. bd. trustees, chair human resources com. Ramapo Coll., 1993-04, trustee, 1993-04; chair bylaws com., N.J. United Minority Bus. Brain Trust; trustee Essex County Ct. Apptd. Spl. Advocates, 1989-93, Jr. League of Montclair, Newark Mental Health Resources Ctr., Montclair, N.J., 1991-96; trustee, sec. Montclair Early Childhood Corp., 1997-98; trustee, sec. St. Marks United Meth. Ch., Pineridge Corp., United Meth. Homes; mem. bd. dirs. Equal Opportunity Fund NJ Commn. Higher Edn. Fellow NY State Bar Found.; mem. ABA (several coms. sect. corp., banking and bus. law, sect. internat. law and practice), NJ Bar Assn. (mem. bus. orgns. com.), Essex County Bar Assn., NY State Bar Assn. (mem. Ho. of Dels. 2005-, exec. com. CLE, legis. liason 1981-90, vice chmn. 1988-90, exec. com. of corp. counsel sect., chmn. com. on SEC, fin. corp. law and governance, chair com. atty. professionalism 1994-97, mem. task force on profession, com. rev. of cts. and professions), Assn. of Bar of City of NY (corp. law com. 1978-81), NY County Lawyers Assn. (corp. law com.), Exec. Women of NJ, Harvard Bus. Sch. Club, Harvard Law Sch. Assn. (trustee, v.p. NJ chpt.), Coalition 100 Black Women, Harvard Bus. Sch. Black Alumni Assn., Harvard Law Sch. Black Alumni Assn., Phi Beta Kappa, Delta Sigma Theta (past chair social action com. Montclair alumnae chpt., past chair rules com., parlimentarian)

BROWN, GLENDA ANN WALTERS, ballet director; b. Buna, Tex., July 22, 1937; d. Jesse Olaf and Kathryn Jeanette (Rogers) Walters; m. David Dann Brown, Dec. 13, 1958 (div. 1995); children: Kathryn, Jean, Vanessa Lea. Grad. h.s., Beaumont, Tex. Mem. Melody Maids, Beaumont, 1950-60; asst. tchr. Widman Sch., Beaumont, 1952-55; owner, tchr. Walters Sch. of Dance, Jasper, Tex., 1955-59; assoc. tchr. Emmamae Horn Sch., 1964-81, artistic dir., 1981—; assoc. dir. Allegro Ballet Houston, 1974-81, artistic dir., 1981—; owner, dir. Allegro Acad. Dance, Houston, 1981—. Dir. Regional Dance Am., Nat. Craft Choreography Conf., 1987—2001; mem. adv. bd. Dance Tchr. Mag., 1998—2003; founder, dir. Glenda Brown Choreography Project, 2002—. Dance panel Cultural Arts Coun., Houston, 1979, Tex. Commn. on the Arts, 1988-90; sec. Riedel Estates Civic Club, Houston, 1975-78; Rep. poll worker, Houston, 1970-81; bd. dirs. Austrian Alps Performing Arts Festival, 1996-98; coord. First Nat. Regional Dance Am. Festival, 1997, bd. dirs. Tanzsommer/Austria, 1998—; dir. Young Tanzsommer, 2006-. Mem. Dance Masters Am. (exam. chair chpt. 3 1980-86), Regional Dance Am. S.W. (exec. v.p. 1981-2001), Dance Am., Nat. Assn. Regional Ballet (bd. dirs. 1985-88), Regional Dance Am. (nat. bd. dirs., v.p. 1988-95, pres. 1995-2001, dir. emeritus 2002—). Methodist. Avocations: camping, singing, golf, travel. Office: Allegro Ballet and Dance Acad 1570 S Dairy Ashford St Ste 200 Houston TX 77077-3870 Office Phone: 281-496-4670. Personal E-mail: glendabrown@ev1.net.

BROWN, GLORIA DIANE, elementary school educator; d. Earl and Joyce Taylor; m. Bobby Lee Brown, June 29, 1977 (dec. May 15, 2005); children: Danielle Marie Patterson, Bobby Lee Brown, II, Bradford Leverette. BA, Grambling State U., 1970; MA, Wayne State U., 1975, Edn. Specialist, 1997. Cert. Continuing Tchr. Wayne State. Remedial reading and reading lab Detroit (Mich.) Pub. Schs., 1972—73, tchr. social studies, 1973—74, tchr. homeroom, 1975—88, kindergarten and reading lab, 1988—89, tchr., 1989—94, tchr. sci., 1994—2000; tchr. in charge Vernor Elem. Sch., 2004—; tchr. grade 1 Detroit (Mich.) Pub. Schs., 2005—. Tutor; cons. Title I workshops. Mem. sci. edn. delegation to Russia People to People Ambassador Program, 2006; treas. St. Michael Ch., Detroit, 1977—2005, sec. Finalist Tchr. of Yr., State Mich. Dept. Edn., 1993-1994; named, Detroit Pub. Schs., 1993-1994; recipient Innovative Tchr. of Yr., Phi Delta Kappa Internat., 1988, Golden Apple Tchr. award, Wayne Intermediate Sch. Dist., 1994, Booker T. Wash. Bus. award, Booker T. Wash. Bus. Group, 1998, Air Force award, Selfridge AFB, 1998-1999; grantee Mich. Dept. Edn., State Mich., 1989-1990, Dwight D. Eisenhower Grant award, Detroit Pub. Schs., 1993; Title One Mini grant, 1991-1992. Mem.: Mich. Reading Assn., Nat. Sci. Tchr. Assn., Phi Delta Kappa Internat., Alpha Kappa Alpha Sorority (del. Boulefor Alpha Kappa 2006). Achievements include Master Tchr. for the Detroit Public Schs; Mich. Educator Exchange Opportunity Abroad Program. Avocations: reading, line dancing, travel, writing. Home: 20549 Bentler Ct Detroit MI 48219-1268 Office: Vernor Elem Sch 13726 Pembroke Detroit MI 48235 Office Phone: 313-494-7342. Personal E-mail: broglori@comcast.net.

BROWN, GRETA KAY, psychologist; b. Dothan, Ala., Nov. 16, 1970; d. Donald Rayo and Nina Loretta Brown. EdS in Sch. Psychology, Fla. State U., Tallahassee, 1998, MS in Counseling, 1998. Sch. psychologist Bay Sch. Dist., Panama City, Fla., 1998—. Baptist. Avocations: reading, piano. Office: Bay Sch Dist 1311 Balboa Ave Panama City FL 32401

BROWN, GWENDOLYN WILLIAMS, music educator; b. Danville, Ky., Aug. 3, 1945; d. Edward Pendleton Williams, Sr. and Mattie (Pride) Williams; m. Albert Sylvester Brown, Jr., Feb. 14, 1976; 1 child, Lydia Ruth; m. John Davidson Reynolds, Aug. 4, 1964 (div. Aug. 1, 1968). BA, CSULA, Los Angeles, Calif., 1964—67, tchg. credential, 1994. Banker Wells Fargo Bank, Pasadena, Calif., 1968—75, Oakland, Calif., 1968—75, Berkeley, Calif., 1968—75; sales clk., music dept. Marshall Fields, Skokie, Ill., 1976—78; clerical substitute Arcadia Unified Sch. Dist., Arcadia, Calif., 1987—89; bible class, tchr. First A.M.E. Ch., Pasadena, Calif., 1989—92; substitute tchr. Pasadena Unified, Pasadena, Calif., 1989—93, Arcadia Unified, Arcadia, Calif., 1989—93; children's choir dir. First A.M.E. Ch., Pasadena, Calif., 1990—94; choral music tchr. Monrovia Unified Sch. Dist., Calif., 1993—. Soloist, opera workshop Merritt Coll., Oakland, Calif., 1971—75; Western Opera Co. chorus San Francisco Opera, San Francisco, 1981; Phil Reeder Oakland Choraleers Oakland Choraleers, Oakland, Calif., 1986. Mem. First A.M.E. Ch., Pasadena, Calif., 1984—, First A.M.E. Heritage Com., Pasadena, Calif., 2000—. Recipient Outstanding Student Tchr., Calif. State Univ./Los Angeles, Calif., 1993—94, African Am. Artist award, First A.M.E. Ch., Pasadena Youth Usher Bd./ Calif., 2000. Mem.: Am. Choral Dir. Assn. (mem. 1994—), Music Educators Nat. Conf. (mem. 1994—), Kappa Delta Pi (mem. 1995—, v.p. 1996—98). Democrat. African Methodist Episcopalian. Avocations: reading, photography, sewing, knitting, crocheting. Home: 44 W La Sierra Drive Arcadia CA 91007-4019 Office: 325 E Huntington Drive Monrovia CA 91016

BROWN, HELEN GURLEY, editor-in-chief; b. Green Forest, Ark., Feb. 18, 1922; d. Ira M. and Cleo (Sisco) Gurley; m. David Brown, Sept. 25, 1959. Student, Tex. State Coll. for Women, 1940—41, Woodbury Coll., 1942; LLD, Woodbury U., 1987; DLitt, L.I. U., 1993. Exec. sec. Music Corp. Am., 1942—45; exec. sec. William Morris Agy., 1945—47; copywriter Foote, Cone & Belding (advt. agy.), Los Angeles, 1948—58; advt. writer, account exec. Kenyon & Eckhardt (advt. agy.), Hollywood, Calif., 1958—96; editor-in-chief Cosmopolitan mag., 1996—, Cosmopolitan Internat. Edits, 1997—. Author 8 books. Named 1 of 25 most influential women in U.S., World Almanac, 1976—81; recipient Francis Holmes Achievement award for outstanding work in advt., 1956—59, Disting. Achievement award, U. So. Calif. Sch. Journalism, 1971, Spl. award for editl. leadership Am. Newspaper, Woman's Club, Washington, 1972, Disting. Achievement award in journalism, Stanford U., 1977, Matrix award in mag. category, N.Y. Women in Comm., 1985, Henry Johnson Fisher award, Mag. Pubs. of Am., 1995, Helen Gurley Brown Rshc. Professorship established name, Northwestern U. Medill Sch. Journalism, 1986, inducted into Pubs.' Hall of Fame, 1988. Mem.: AFTRA, Am. Soc. Mag. Editors (Hall of Fame award 1996), Authors League Am., Eta Upsilon Gamma. Office: Cosmopolitan The Hearst Corp 300 W 57th St New York NY 10019 Office Phone: 212-649-3555.

BROWN, HILARY SUSANNE, music educator, photographer; b. Charleroi, Pa., Aug. 19, 1974; d. John Howard and Cheryl Bakori Holmes; m. Jeffery Wayne Brown, June 20, 1998; 1 child, Sydney Allison. BS in Music Edn., Clarion U., Pa., 1996. Cert. instrnl. level II tchg. Pa., 2004. Music tchr. and band dir. Albany County Sch. Dist. #1, Laramie, Wyo., 1997—2000, Charleroi Area Sch. Dist., Pa., 2000—02, Ringgold Sch. Dist., Monongahela, 2002—. Developer H.S. jazz ensemble curriculum Charleroi Sch. Dist.; developer H.S. guitar class curriculum Ringgold Sch. Dist., Pa. Sphere (First pl., 2006). Recipient Outstanding Tchr. of Week, Laramie Area Cmty., 1999. Mem.: Pa. State Educators Assn., Ringgold Educators Assn., Pa. Music Educators Assn., Music Educators Nat. Conf. Achievements include first woman High School band director in Wyoming, 1997; played on semi-pro women's football team, Pittsburgh Passion, 2004. Avocations: photography, sports, music, walking. Home: 214 Diane Dr Monongahela PA 15063 Office: Ringgold Sch Dist 1 Ram Dr Monongahela PA 15063 Office Phone: 724-258-2200. E-mail: hbrown@ringgold.org.

BROWN, HOLLACE ANN HOLLY, advertising executive; b. NYC, June 1, 1946; d. Sidney H. and Muriel (Smukler) Brown; m. Lewis M. Wallensky, June 26, 1982. BS, Boston U., 1968; student, Hunter Coll., 1970—72. Publicity asst. Vidal Sassoon Co., NYC, 1970—71; sec., statis. rschr. Roth, Gerard and Co., NYC, 1971—73; publicity asst. MGM Records, Hollywood, Calif., 1974—75, publicity dir., 1975; mgr. sales comms. Max Factor and Co., Hollywood, 1975—80; v.p. advt. and sales promotion Paramount Home Video, Hollywood, 1980—88, sr. v.p., 1988—96. Bd. dirs. John Wayne Cancer Inst. Aux. E-mail: wallenskyfamily@yahoo.com.

BROWN, IFIGENIA THEODORE, lawyer; b. Syracuse, N.Y., Mar. 14, 1930; d. Gus and Christine Theodore; m. Paul Frederick Brown, Sept. 16, 1956; 1 child, Paul Darrow. BA, Syracuse U., 1951, LLB, JD, 1954. Bar: N.Y. 1956. Acting police justice Village of Ballston Spa, NY, 1960—62; sr. ptnr. Brown & Brown, Ballston Spa, 1958—95; ptnr. Brown Brown & Peterson Esqs, Ballston Spa, 1995—2000; of counsel Brown, Peterson, Craig and Thomas, Ballston Spa, 2000—. Chmn. N.Y. State Bd. Real Property Svcs., Albany, 1996—. Mem. Charlton Sch. Bd., 1989-93, Ballston Spa Libr. Bd., 1991-94; founder, pres. Saratoga County Women's Rep. Club; vice-chmn. Saratoga County Rep. Com., 1958-72. Mem. N.Y. State Bar Assn., Saratoga County Bar Assn. (treas. 1983-84, pres. 1984-85), Zonta (pres. Saratoga County 1962, 90), Order Ea. Star. Republican. Greek Orthodox. Avocations: church choir, piano. Home: 42 Hyde Blvd Ballston Spa NY 12020-1608 Office: Brown Peterson Craig and Thomas One E High St Ballston Spa NY 12020 Office Phone: 518-885-9292, 518-885-7496.

BROWN, ILENE DE LOIS, special education educator; b. Wichita, Kans., Aug. 17, 1947; d. Homer DeWitt and Estella Lenora (Cleland) Rusco; m. Gale Robert Aaroe, Nov. 23, 1967 (div. July 1983); 1 child, Candice Yvonne. BEd in Elem. Edn., Washburn U., Topeka, 1969; MS, Nazareth Coll. Rochester, 1979. Cert. tchr. Idaho. Emotionally disturbed trainer Rochester Mental Health Ctr., Greece, N.Y., 1970-71, West Ridge, Greece, 1971-72; tutor kindergarten through grades 6 Craig Hill, Greece, 1978-79; resource rm. tchr. math. English Village, Greece, 1979-80; resource rm. tchr. grades 4-6 Lakeshore, Greece, 1980; tutor, translator Guadalajara, Mex., 1980-82; tchr. grade 1 English John F. Kennedy Sch., Guadalajara, 1982-83; tchr. various grades Greenleaf (Idaho) Friends Acad., 1983-89; resource tchr., high sch. spl. edn. community work coord. Middleton (Idaho) Primary Sch., 1989-91, tchr., 1991—, tchr. 2d grade, 1990—. Sunday sch. tchr. Mem. Coun. for Exceptional Children, Coun. for Children with Behavior Disorders and Learning Disabilities (officer, sec. state chpt. 1991-92), Middleton Profl. Devel. Com. (chairperson profl. devel. com. 1992-95—), Idaho Edn. Assn., Middleton Edn. Assn., Phi Delta Kappa. Avocations: bicycling, travel, reading, birdwatching. Office: Mill Creek Elem Sch 500 N Middleton Rd Middleton ID 83644-5499 E-mail: ibrown@msd134.org.

BROWN, JACLYN, elementary school educator; d. Joan Brown. BS, U. Findlay, Ohio, 1999—2003. Mid. sch. tchr. math & sci. Toledo Accelerated Acad., 2003—05; sci. tchr. Lee Mid. Sch., Fort Myers, Fla., 2005—. Supr. Sylvania Conservation Corps, Ohio, 2001—04. Office: Lee Mid Sch Fort Myers FL

BROWN, JACQUELINE ELAINE, obstetrician, gynecologist; b. Houston, Sept. 20, 1948; d. Issac Cleve Brown and Hazel Eva (Mullen) Hill; m. Felton Watkins, Dec. 31, 1971 (div. Jan. 1974); 1 child, Alan Christopher Watkins; m. Ronald Hayes, Nov. 9, 1985. BA, North Tex. State U., 1970; postgrad., Tex. So. U., 1971-72; MD, U. Tex., Dallas, 1980; MPH, Johns Hopkins U., 1985. Intern in ob-gyn Pa. Hosp., Phila., 1980-84, resident in ob-gyn, 1980-84; ob-gyn physician Johns Hopkins Health Plan, Balt., 1984-85, Kaiser Permanente Health Plan, Washington, 1985-87; former asst. med. dir. ob-gyn Johns Hopkins Health Plan, Balt.; founder Total Women Health Care Ctr., 1991—. Advisor Black Women's Health Project, Phila., 1983-84; former cons. Women's Resource and Devel. Ctr., Balt., former Teen Parenting Prevention Program, Balt., Straight Talk, Washington, 1987. Mem. bd. trustees Bethel African Meth. Episcopal Ch., Balt., 1985. Southwestern Found. scholar, Dallas, 1976. Fellow Am. Coll. Ob-Gyn (jr.); mem. Am. Med. Women's Assn., Alpha Kappa Alpha. Avocations: bicycling, walking. Office: Total Woman Health Care Ctr 11821 East Freeway Ste 300 Houston TX 77029 Office Phone: 713-453-6773. E-mail: totalwomanhealth@yahoo.com.

BROWN, JANICE ROGERS, federal judge, former state supreme court justice; b. Greenville, Ala., May 11, 1949; m. Allan Brown (dec.); 1 child, Nathan; m. Dewey Parker. BA, Calif. St. U., Sacramento, 1974; JD, UCLA, 1977; LLM, U. Va., 2004. Bar: Calif. 1977. Dep. legis. counsel Calif. Legis. Counsel Bur., 1977—79; dep. atty. gen. Calif. Dept. Justice, 1979—87; deputy sec., gen. counsel Calif. Business, Transportation & Housing Agy., 1987—90; sr. assoc. Nielsen, Merksamer, Parrinello, Mueller & Naylor, Sacramento, 1990—91; legal affairs sec. to Gov. Pete Wilson State of Calif., Sacramento, 1991—94; assoc. justice Calif. Ct. Appeals (3rd dist.), Sacramento, 1994—96, Calif. Supreme Ct., San Francisco, 1996—2005; judge US Ct. Appeals (DC cir.), 2005—. Adj. prof. law U. Pacific, 1998—99. Achievements include being the first African-American woman to serve on the Calif. Supreme Court. Office: US Ct Appeals 333 Constitution Ave NW Washington DC 20001*

BROWN, JANINE, lawyer; b. Wheeling, W.Va., Oct. 5, 1961; BA with distinction, Univ. Mich., 1982; JD high honors, Duke Univ., 1986. Bar: Ga. 1986. Ptnr., chair, tech. group Alston & Bird LLP, Atlanta. Named a Ga. Super Lawyer, 2004; named one of the Top 50 Female Super Lawyers., 2004. Office: Alston & Bird LLP One Atlantic Ctr 1201 W Peachtree St NW Atlanta GA 30309-3424 Office Phone: 404-881-7834. Office Fax: 404-881-7777. Business E-Mail: jbrown@alston.com.

BROWN, JEAN WILLIAMS, former state supreme court justice; b. Birmingham, Ala. m. E. Terry Brown; 2 children. Grad. with honors, Samford U., 1974; JD, U. Ala., 1977. Bar: Ala. 1977, U.S. Ct. Appeals (11th cir.), U.S. Supreme Ct. Law clerk Tucker, Gray & Thigpen; asst. atty. gen. criminal appeals divsn., chief extradition officer Ala. Atty. Gen.'s Office; judge Ala. Ct. Criminal Appeals, 1997-99; justice Supreme Ct. Ala., 1999—2005. Mem.: Bench and Bar Legal Honor Soc. Office: Ala Supreme Ct 300 Dexter Ave Montgomery AL 36104-3741 Office Phone: 334-221-6488.

BROWN, JEANETTE GRASSELLI, retired director; b. Cleve., Aug. 4, 1928; d. Nicholas W. and Veronica Gecsy; m. Glenn R. Brown, Aug. 1, 1987. BS summa cum laude, Ohio U., 1950, DSc (hon.), 1978; MS, Western Res. U., 1958, DSc (hon.), 1995, Clarkson U., 1986; D Engring. (hon.), Mich. Tech. U., 1989; DSc (hon.), Wilson Coll., 1994, Notre Dame Coll., 1995, Kenyon Coll., 1995, Mt. Union Coll., 1996, Cleveland State U., 2000, Kent State U., 2000, Ursuline Coll., 2001; DSc, Youngstown State U., 2003; DSc (hon.), U. Pecs, Hungary, 2002. Project leader, assoc. Infrared Spectroscopist, Cleve., 1950-78; mgr. analytical sci. lab. Standard Oil (name changed to BP Am., Inc. 1985), Cleve., 1978-83, dir. technol. support dept., 1983-85, dir. corp. rsch. and analytical scis., 1985-88; disting. vis. prof., dir. rsch. enhancement Ohio U., Athens, 1989-95; ret., 1995. Bd. dirs. AGA Gas, Inc., USX Corp., McDonald Investments, BDM Internat., BF Goodrich Co., Nicolet Instrument Corp.; mem. bd. on chem. sci. and tech. NRC, 1986-91; chmn. U.S. Nat. Com. to Internat. Union of Pure and Applied Chemistry, 1992-94; mem. joint high level adv. panel U.S.-Japan Sci. and Tech., 1994-2001, Ohio Bd. Regents, 1995—, chmn., 2000-2002; vis. com. Nat. Inst. Stds. and Tech., 1988-91. Author, editor 8 books; editor: Vibrational Spectroscopy; contbr. numerous articles on molecular spectroscopy to profl. jours.; patentee naphthalene extraction process. Bd. dirs. N.E. Ohio Sci. and Engring. Fair, Cleve., Martha Holden Jennings Found., Cleve. Clinic Found., Sci. Svc. Inc.; chair bd. dirs. Cleve. Scholarship Programs, Inc., 1994-2000; trustee Holden Arboretum, Cleve., 1988—, Edison Biotech Ctr., Cleve., 1988-95, Cleve. Playhouse, 1990-96, Garden Ctr. Greater Cleve., 1990-93, Mus. Arts Assn., 1991—, Gt. Lakes Sci. Ctr., 1991—, Rainbow Babies and Children's Hosp., 1992-95, Nat. Inventors' Hall of Fame, 1993—, Ohio U., 1985-94, chmn. 1991-92; chair steering com. Mellen Ctr. Cleve. Clinic, 1996—, Cleve. Orchestra, 2000-; chair bd. dirs. ideastream, PBS, NPR, Ideastream Pub. Radio, 2003-; vice chair Great Lakes Sci. Ctr., 2004-. Recipient Disting. Svc. award Cleve. Tech. Soc. Coun., 1985; named Woman of Yr. YWCA, 1980; named to Ohio Women's Hall of Fame State of Ohio, 1989, Ohio Sci. & Tech. Hall of Fame, 1991, Humanitarian award Nat. Conf. Cmty. Justice, 2000, Medal of Honor, Ellis Island, 2002. Mem. Am. Chem. Soc. (chair analytical divsn. 1990-91, Garvan medal 1986, Analytical Chem. award 1993, Encouraging Women into Careers in Sci. award 1999), Soc. for Applied Spectroscopy (pres. 1970, Disting. Svc. award 1983), Coblentz Soc. (bd. govs. 1968-71, William Wright award 1980), Royal Soc. Chemistry (Theophilus Redwood lectr. 1994), Phi Beta Kappa, Iota Sigma Pi (pres. fluorine chpt. 1957-60, nat. hon. mem. 1987). Republican. Roman Catholic. Avocations: swimming, dance, music. Home: 150 Greentree Rd Chagrin Falls OH 44022-2424

BROWN, JENNIFER KAY, lawyer; b. 1956; BA, Antioch Coll.; JD, Yale U., 1993. Bar: 1995. Pres., exec. dir. NOW; law clk. U.S. Ct. Appeals (2d cir.); asst. U.S. atty. So. dist NY; dir. reproductive rights unit Office NY State Atty. Gen., N.Y.C., 1999—; v.p., legal dir. legal def. and edn. fund. NOW, 2004—. Recipient Nova award, Planned Parenthood, 2002.

BROWN, JENNIFER LEIGH, music educator, musician; b. Sioux Falls, S.D., Sept. 11, 1976; d. Joel Richard and Nancy Rae Brown. BMus, U. Nebr., Lincoln, 1995—2000. Band dir. Hamburg Pub. Schs., Iowa, 2000—02, Huron Pub. Schs., SD, 2002—06, Omaha South Pub. HS, 2006—. Musician Huron Symphony Orch., 2002—05, Huron Mcpl. Band, 2003—06; musician vocal dept. Omaha Pub. Schs., 2006—. Recipient The Sudler Trophy, John Philip Sousa Found., 1996. Mem.: Kappa Kappa Psi (pres. 1999—2000). Republican. Baptist. Avocations: reading, writing, drawing, music, sports. Office: Omaha S Pub HS Vocal Dept 4519 S 24th St Omaha NE 68107 Office Phone: 402-557-3648. Personal E-mail: quietwolf1@hotmail.com.

BROWN, JERRI L., performing arts educator, choreographer; d. John J. and Jean K. Oleniacz; m. Jarod P. Brown. BFA in Dance magna cum laude, Marymount Manhattan Coll., NYC, 1996. Cert. fitness instr. Dance instr., ballet mistress Star Maker Sch. Performing Arts, Flemington, 1996—, studio mgr., 1998—. Dance instr. Roger Atkinson Ballet Ctr., Frenchtown, NJ, 1997—2001; aerobics instr. Health Fitness Corp., Branchburg, NJ, 2002—, Powerhouse Gym, Bridgewater, NJ, 2005—, Health and Wellness Ctr., Whitehouse, NJ, 2006—; adjudicator, choreographer Ticket to Broadway, Pittstown, NJ, 2003—; model A Wish Come True, Bristol, Pa., 2005—. Choreographer, dir. (ballets) A Business Man's Daydream, 2002, Journey of a Gift, 2004, Common Variables, 2006. Recipient Top Tchr. award, Star Sys. Dance Corp., Lawrenceville, NJ, 2001, 2005, Choreography award, Nat. Dance Showcase Dance Competition, 2006, Star Quest Dance Competition, 2006, Odyssey award, 2006. Avocations: crafts, baking, scrapbooks, crocheting. Home: 434 Liberty Blvd Phillipsburg NJ 08865

BROWN, JERRI LYNNE, history educator; d. Thomas and Bobbie Brown. BA, U. of the South, Sewanee, Tenn., 1979. Cert. tchr. Fla. Tchr. Dvual County Sch. Bd., Jacksonville, Fla., 1992—; dept. chair Duval County Sch. Bd., Jacksonville, 2003—. Mem. Fla. Social Studies Coun., 2000—06. Independent. Episcopalian. Avocations: reading, cooking, travel, power walking, Bunko. Home: 6239 Pottsburg Plantation Blvd Jacksonville FL 32216 Office: Duval County Schs Twin Lakes Acad 8050 Point Meadows Dr Jacksonville FL 32256 Office Phone: 904-538-0825. Business E-Mail: brownj@educationcentral.org.

BROWN, JESSI EDEN, mental health services professional; b. Port Jefferson, NY, Dec. 5, 1973; d. Martin Barry Katz and Vivian Ione Brown. Assoc. Gen. Studies in Outdoor Recreation Leadership, Colo. Mountain Coll., 1998; BS in Psychology cum laude, Colo. State U., 1996; MS in Counseling Psychology, Ctrl. Washinton U., 2001. Lic. profl. counselor Colo., mental health counselor Wash. Wilderness therapist Obsidian Trails Outdoor Sch., Bend, Oreg., 2002, SageWalk, Wilderness Sch., Redmond, Oreg., 2002—03; clin. dir. program co-dir. Penrith Farms Young Adult Program, Newport, Wash., 2003—05; at-risk program coord., counselor Lake County Sch. Dist., Leadville, Colo., 2005—. At-Risk Student Svcs. grantee, Colo. Dept. Edn., 2005—. Mem.: ACA, Assn. Experiential Edn., Phi Beta Kappa, Phi Chi. Green Party. Avocations: adventure therapy, animal training, parenting skills instruction, camping, backpacking, skiing. Office: Lake County Sch Dist 1000 W 6th St Leadville CO 80461 Office Phone: 719-486-6913. Office Fax: 719-486-6880. Personal E-mail: aussierastus@hotmail.com. Business E-Mail: jbrown@lakecountyschools.net.

BROWN, JOAN TERESA, writer, retired language educator; d. George James and Theresa McAndrews; m. Donald Douglas Brown, Aug. 7, 1954; children: Cathy, Jim, Nancy. BA magna cum laude, Coll. New Rochelle, N.Y., 1953. English tchr. Schuylerville HS, Schuylerville, NY, 1953—54; tchr. Ursuline Acad., New Rochelle, NY, 1954—55. ESL tchr., advisor, Tacoma, 1977—79, Belleville, Ill., 1979—80; spkr. women's orgns. nationwide, 2002—. Author: Colors of France: A Painting Pilgrimage, 2002, editor women's magazines; contbr. articles to publs. Advisor, vol. Am. Red Cross, Tacoma, 1976—79, Family Svcs., Tacoma, 1976—79, women's orgns., Vacaville, Calif., 1984—87; bd. mem. Connexion, Tacoma, 1988—90. Mem.: Pacific NW Writer's Assn. (seminar leader 2003—).

BROWN, JOBETH GOODE, food products executive, lawyer; b. Oakdale, La., Sept. 15, 1950; d. Samuel C. Goode and Elizabeth E. (Twiner) Baker; m. H. William Brown, Aug. 4, 1973; 1 child, Kevin William. BA, Newcomb Coll. Tulane U., 1972; JD, Wash. U., 1979. Assoc. Coburn, Croft & Putzell, St. Louis, 1979-80; staff atty. Anheuser-Busch Cos. Inc., St. Louis, 1980-81, exec. asst. to v.p. sec., 1982-83, asst. sec., 1983-89, sec., v.p., 1989—. Trustee Anheuser-Busch Found., St. Louis, 1989—, Girls, Inc., St. Louis; bd. dirs. Jr. Achievement Miss Valley, Inc., Met. Assn. Philanthropy. Mem.: ABA, Am. Soc. Corp. Secs. (pres. 1992), Bar Assn. Met. St. Louis, Mo. Bar Assn., Mo. Women's Forum, Algonquin Golf Club, Order of Coif. Republican. Office: Anheuser-Busch Cos Inc One Busch Pl 202-6 Saint Louis MO 63118-1852

BROWN, JOY ALICE, social services administrator; b. Redmesa, Colo., Mar. 19, 1917; d. Ezra E. and Alice M. (Pinkerton) Walker; m. Clayton Henry Brown, Apr. 9, 1941; children: Kimleigh Clayton, Loraleigh Joy. BA, Highlands U., 1958; MA, U. No. Colo., 1967, EdD, 1970. Tchr. La Plata County, Colo., 1936-41; prin. Bayfield (Colo.) pub. schs., 1942-46; tchr. Aztec (N.Mex.) pub. schs., 1946-63; spl. edn. coordinator primary schs. Palmer, Alaska, 1963-67; lab. sch. supr. U. No. Colo., 1967-70; assoc. prof. edn. N.Mex. State U., 1970-75; dir. Open Door Center, Las Cruces, N.Mex., 1975—. Cons. Tex. Edn. Service Center, Roswell (N.Mex.) schs.; sec. Dona Ana Human Services Consortium, 1977. Contbr. articles on edn. to profl. jours. Recipient Community Service award Las Cruces Eastside Center, 1972; Outstanding Contribution award N.Mex. Council of Exceptional Children, 1977. Mem. NEA, Council for Exceptional Children, Nat. Assn. Retarded Citizens, Phi Delta Kappa. Home: 34081 Country Rd M Mancos CO 81328

BROWN, JOY WITHERS, music educator; b. Louisville, Ky., Jan. 29, 1955; d. Harold B. and Sarah B. Withers; m. Robert O. Brown Jr., Mar. 20, 1982; 1 child, Sarah Teresa. BA in Music & Christianity, Mercer U., 1976; M in Ch. Music, So. Bapt. Theol. Sem., 1980; postgrad., U. Louisville, 1981, Ga. State U., 1993; cert. in music, State U. W. Ga., 2000. Youth dir. YMCA, Waycross, Ga., 1976—77; music intern 2d Presbyn. Ch., Louisville, 1978—79; music therapist Children's Treatment Svcs., Louisville, 1979—81; program dir. YWCA Greater Atlanta, Riverdale, Ga., 1982—83; sr. caseworker Clayton County Dept. Family & Children's Svcs., Jonesboro, Ga., 1983—87; retirement counselor Tchrs. Retirement Sys. Ga., Atlanta, 1987—97; music tchr. Hickory Flat Elem. Sch., MCDonough, Ga., 1997—. Mem.: Ga. Music Educators Assn., Music Educators Nat. Conf. Baptist. Home: 107 Windsong Dr Stockbridge GA 30281-6423 Office: Hickory Flat Elem Sch 841 Brannan Rd Mcdonough GA 30253 Office Phone: 770-898-0107.

BROWN, JOYCE F., academic administrator; b. N.Y.C., July 7, 1946; d. Robert E. and Joyce Cappie Brown; m. H. Carl McCall, Aug. 13, 1983. BA, Marymount Coll., 1968; MA, NYU, 1971, PhD, 1980. From vice chancellor to prof. emeritus CUNY, 1983—98, prof. emeritus, 1998—. Dep. mayor pub. and cmty. affairs, N.Y.C., 1990; pres. Fashion Inst. Tech. SUNY, 1998—; bd. dirs. Polo Ralph Lauren. Dir. N.Y.C. Outward Bound Ctrl. Pk. Conservancy, women's com., Paxar Corp.; trustee Marymount Coll.; dir. Boys Harbor Inc., 1987—. Office: Fashion Inst Tech Seventh Ave at 27th St New York NY 10001-5992

BROWN, JUDITH, academic administrator; BA, U. Calif., Berkeley, 1968, MA, 1971; PhD in History, Johns Hopkins U., 1977. Asst. prof. history U. Md., Balt. County, 1977—82, Stanford U., Palo Alto, Calif., 1982—92, prof., 1991—95; Allyn and Gladys Cline prof. history, dean Sch. Humanities Rice U., Houston, 1995—2001; v.p. acad. affairs, provost Wesleyan U., Middletown, Conn., 2001—. Author: In the Shadow of Florence: Provincial Society in Renaissance Pescia, 1982, Immodest Acts: The Life of a Lesbian Nun in Renaissance Italy, 1986. Office: Wesleyan U 3d Fl North Coll 237 High St Middletown CT 06459

BROWN, JUDITH OLANS, retired lawyer, educator; b. Boston, May 29, 1941; d. Sidney and Evelyn R. (Lefkowitz) Olans; m. James K. Brown, Oct. 5, 1969. AB magna cum laude with distinction, Mt. Holyoke Coll., 1962; LL.B. cum laude, Boston Coll., 1965. Bar: Mass. 1965. Law clk. Supreme Jud. Ct., 1965-66; assoc. Foley, Hoag and Eliot, Boston, 1966-69; chief counsel Mass. Dept. Cmty. Affairs, Boston, 1969-70; atty. adv. Office Regional Counsel, HUD, Boston, 1970, asst. regional counsel, 1971, assoc. regional counsel, 1971-72; instr. Boston U. Law Sch., 1971, Northeastern U. Sch. Law, Boston, 1972, assoc. prof., 1972-75, prof., 1975-98; prof. emeritus Faculty Inst. Lifelong Edn. Dartmouth, 1998—. Vis. prof. Law Sch., Boston Coll., 1992. Contbr. articles to legal jours.; article and book rev. editor: Boston Coll. Indsl. and Comml. Law Rev., 1964-65. Mem. steering com. Lawyers Com. for Civil Rights under Law (emeritus); trustee Kimball Union Acad.1993-2003. Loeb fellow, 1972—73. Mem.: Order of Coif, Phi Beta Kappa. Home: PO Box 82 Plainfield NH 03781-0082 Personal E-mail: jkbjob@verizon.net.

BROWN, JULIA, museum director; b. Washington, Mar. 9, 1951; d. Winthrop Gilman and Peggy (Bell) Brown; m. James Archie Turrell; children: Sophia, Arlan. BA, Sarah Lawrence Coll., 1972. Docent Nat. Gallery Art, Washington, 1973-74; art historian GSA, Washington, 1974-75, project mgr., 1975-80; curator Hudson River Mus., Yonkers, N.Y., 1980-81, Mus. Contemporary Art, L.A., 1981-83, sr. curator, 1983-86; dir. Des Moines Art Ctr., 1986-91, Am. Federation Arts, 2000—. Mem. Assn. Art Mus. Dirs. Democrat. Mem. Soc. Of Friends.

BROWN, JUNE DYSON, retired elementary school educator, principal; b. Petersburg, Va., July 28, 1949; d. James Elmer Sr. and Clara (Foster) Dyson; m. Robert Wendell Brown, Apr. 10, 1971; children: Jason, Joshua, James-Robert. BA in English, Emory & Henry Coll., 1971; MEd in Early Childhood Edn., U. Ga., 1993; EdS, U. Ga, 1998. Cert. elem. tchr., Ga. Tchr. DeKalb County Schs., Decatur, Ga., 1971-72, 76-78, Newton County Schs., Covington, Ga., 1972-74, 80-84, 85-88, Henry County Schs., McDonough, Ga., 1984-85; tchr., grade mgr. Gwinnett County Schs., Berkeley Lake, Ga., 1988-90; tchr., learner support strategist Cobb County Schs., Marietta, Ga., 1990-96, asst. adminstr., 1996—2000; Prin. Lamar County Elem. Sch., 2000—; prof. Piedmont Coll., 2000—. Active North Ga. Conf. Min.'s Wives, Atlanta, 1990-93; pres. Atlanta/Marietta Min.'s Wives, 1991-93 Mem. ASCD, DAR (John Houston chpt.), Internat. Reading Assn., Profl. Assn. Ga. Educators, Kappa Delta Pi, Phi Kappa Phi. Methodist. Avocations: sewing, reading, beachcombing. Home: 385 Whitney Ln Mcdonough GA 30253-7767

BROWN, JUNE GIBBS, retired government official; b. Cleve., Oct. 5, 1933; d. Thomas D. and Lorna M. Gibbs; children: Ellen Rosenthal, Linda Windsor, Victor Janezic, Carol Janezic. BBA summa cum laude, Cleve. State U., 1971, MBA, 1972; postgrad., Cleve. Marshall Law Sch., 1973-74; JD, U. Denver, 1978; postgrad. Advanced Mgmt. Program, Harvard U., 1983. Cert. govt. fin. mgr., 1995; CPA, Ohio. Real estate broker, officer mgr. N.E. Realty, Cleve., 1963-68; staff acct. Frank T. Cicirelli, C.P.A., Cleve., 1970-71; asst. to comptr. S.M. Hexter Co., Cleve., 1971; grad. tchg. fellow Cleve. State U., 1971-72; dir. internal audit Navy Fin. Ctr., Cleve., 1972-75; dir. fin. sys. design Bur. of Land Mgmt., Denver, 1975-76; project mgr. Bur. of Reclamation, 1976-79; insp. gen. Dept. Interior, Washington, 1979-81, NASA, Washington, 1981-85; v.p. fin. and adminstrn. Sys. Devel. Corp., a Burroughs Co., 1985-86; assoc. adminstr. for mgmt. NASA, 1986-87; insp. gen. U.S. Dept. Def., Arlington, Va., 1987-90; dep. insp. gen. USN-CINCPACFLT, 1990; insp. gen. USN Pacific Fleet, Pearl Harbor, Hawaii, 1991-93, HHS, Washington, 1993-2001; inspector gen. HHS, SSA, Washington, 1995-96; ret., 2001. Bd. dirs. Fed. Law Enforcement Tng. Ctr., 1984-85, Interagy. Auditor Tng. program Dept. Agr. Grad. Sch., 1983-85; chmn. interagy. com. on Info. Resource Mgmt., 1984-85; mem. bd. advisors Nat. Contract Mgmt. Assn., 1987-89, NSF, 2002-05; mem. Pres.'s Coun. on Integrity and Efficiency, 1993-2001, vice chair, 1994-97, 1998-2001, rep. Nat. Intergovtl. Audit Forum, 1994-98; bd. dirs. Insps. Gen. Auditor Tng. Inst. Mem. bd. advisors Howard U. Sch. Bus., 1987-89. Recipient award Am. Soc. Women Accts., 1969, 70, 71, Raulston award Cleve. State U., 1971, Pres.'s award Cleve. State U., 1971, Outstanding Achievement award U.S. Navy, 1973, Career Svc. award Chgo. region Fed. Exec. Bd., 1974, Outstanding Contbn. to Fin. Mgmt. award Denver region Fed. Exec. Bd., 1977, Donald L. Scantlebury award Joint Fin. Mgmt. Improvement Program, 1980, Outstanding Svc. award Nat. Assn. Minority CPA Firms, 1980, NASA Exceptional Svc. medal, 1985, Outstanding Achievement in Aerospace award, 1987, Woman of Yr. award, YWCA 1988, Bur. Land Mgmt., Dept. Interior, 1975, Disting. Pub. Svc. award Dept. Def., 1989, Meritorious Civilian Svc. award U.S. Navy, 1993, Nat. Capital Area chpt./Govt. Exec. Mag. award for leadership, 1994, George Washington U. Pi Alpha Alpha Pub. Svc. award, 1996; named Disting. Alumni Cleve. State U., 1990, named Outstanding Fellow of Coun. for Ethical Org. for Creating the Standards for Healthcare Compliance, 2001 Fellow Nat. Acad. Pub. Adminstrn. (standing panel exec. orgn. and mgmt., pub. svc. panel); mem. AICPA (mem. govt. auditing stds. 1996-99), Assn. Govt. Accts. (nat. pres. 1985-86, nat. exec. com. 1977-87, vice chmn. nat. ethics com. 1978-80, 90, chmn. fin. mgmt. standards bd. 1981-82, service award 1973, 76, 93, outstanding achievement award 1979, Robert W. King Meml. award 1988, dir. Hawaii chpt. 1991-93, Nat. Pres.'s award 1999, Disting. Fed. Leadership award 1998), Hawaii Soc. CPAs (bd. dirs. 1991-93), Am. Accts. Assn., Nat. Contract Mgmt. Assn. (bd. advisors 1988-90), NASA Alumni Assn., Women in Aerospace, ASPA (at-large mem. nat. coun. 1994-98, Profl. Responsibility Exemplary Practice award 1990, pres.-nat. capital area chpt. 1989), Exec. Women in Govt., Nat. Sci. Found. (adv. panel 2003-05), Beta Alpha Psi. Personal E-mail: igjgb@yahoo.com.

BROWN, JUNE IRIS, retired librarian, artist; d. Carl M. and June (Whiting) Slaughter; m. Jim E. Brown, July 16, 1961; 1 child, Julian L. BFA, U. Ala., 1964; MS in Art Edn., U. Tenn., 1977, MLS, 1983. Tchr. art Mobile (Ala.) County Schs., 1964—65; tchr. elem. sch. Jackson County Schs., Scottsboro, Ala., 1967—81; tchr. art RoaneState Coll., Harriman, Tenn., 1977—82; libr. Harriman (Tenn.) H.S., 1985—86, Tulane U., New Orleans, 1983—84, State Libr. Ala., Montgomery, Ala., 1989—2002, ret., 2002. Organizer art shows, 2000—01. One-woman shows include L.B. Wallace Coll., 1996, Auburn at Montgomery (Ala.) Technacenter, 1997, Ala. Pub. Libr. Svc., 2001, exhibited in group shows at Ala. Landscapes, 1998—99, 33d So. Artist Show, 1999—2000, Biennials Montgomery (Ala.) Mus. Art, 1997—2005, Nightingale Biennial, 1998—2006, Ala. Artists Show, Rosa Parks Libr., 2005, honorarium, Montgomery (Ala.) Mus. Fine Arts, 2003. Mem.: Ala. Watercolor Soc., Montgomery (Ala.) Art Guild, Capri Cmty. Film Soc., Montgomery (Ala.) Mus. Fine Arts. Avocations: reading, travel, birdwatching, gardening, swimming. Home: 955 Autumn Ridge Rd Montgomery AL 36117 Personal E-mail: juneiris@charter.net.

BROWN, KAORI AKAMINE, principal; b. Suzuka City, Japan, Apr. 27, 1967; d. Yasuhiko and Keiko Akamine; m. Douglas Everett Brown, Dec. 23, 1993; 1 child, Jae-Sun Chan-Young. BA in Elem. Edn., Fla. State U., Tallahassee, 1989. Elem. grade tchr. W.T. Moore Elem., Tallahassee, 1990—2000; tchr., prin. Seagull Elem., Kapolei, Hawaii, 2000—02; lower sch. prin. Le Jardin Acad., Kailua, Hawaii, 2002—. Author: (humor) Bad Dogs: True Tails of Trouble Only a Best Friend Can Get Away With, 2000. Office: Le Jardin Academy 917 Kalanianaole Hwy Kailua HI 96734 Office Phone: 808-261-0707. Office Fax: 808-262-9339. Business E-Mail: kbrown@lejardinacademy.com.

BROWN, KAREN KENNEDY, judge; b. Houston, May 23, 1947; BA, U. Pa., 1970; JD, U. Houston, 1973. Bar: Tex. 1973, U.S. Ct. Appeals (5th cir.) 1974, U.S. Dist. Ct. (so. dist.) Tex. 1975, U.S. Supreme Ct. 1980, U.S. Ct. Appeals (11th cir.) 1981. Law clk. to Hon. John Brown, Houston, 1973-75; law clk. to Hon. Woodrow Seals, 1975-76; asst. fed. pub. defender So. Dist. Tex., Houston, 1976—82; pvt. practice Houston, 1982—83; magistrate judge U.S. Dist. Ct. (so. dist.) Tex., 1984-90, bankruptcy judge Houston, 1990—. Episcopalian. Office: US District Court PO Box 61252 Rm 4202 515 Rusk Ave Houston TX 77208

BROWN, KATHLEEN, diversified financial services company executive; b. 1946; d. Edmund G. and Bernice Brown; m. George Rice (div. 1979); children: Hilary, Alexandra, Zebediah; m. Van Gordon Sauter, 1980; 2 stepsons. BA in History, Stanford U., 1969; JD, Fordham U., 1985. Mem. L.A. Bd. Edn., 1975-80; atty. O'Melveny & Myers, N.Y.C., LA; commr. L.A. Bd. Pub. Works, 1987-89; treas. State of Calif., 1990-94; exec. v.p. Bank of Am., L.A., 1994-99, pres. Pvt. Bank for Investment Mgmt. Group, 1999—2001; sr. pvt. wealth adv. investment mgmt. divsn. Goldman, Sachs & Co., L.A., 2001—03, sr. adv., head of pub. fin. We. region, 2003—. Co-chmn. Capital Budget Commn., Washington, 1997—. Mem. Pacific Coun. on Internat. Policy, Stanford Inst. for Internat. Studies; dir. Children's Hosp. L.A., San Francisco Ballet, Calif. Endowment, LA C. of C. Democrat. Office: Goldman Sachs & Co Fox Plz Ste 2600 2121 Ave Stars Los Angeles CA 90067*

BROWN, KATIE, columnist; b. Petosky, MI, 1963; m. William Corbin, Nov. 25, 2003; 1 child. BA art history, Cornell U. Propr. GOAT antique stores, LA, Mackinac Island, Mich. Host (TV series) Next Door with Katie Brown, Lifetime, 1998, All Yr. Round with Katie Brown, A&E, 2003, Simple Solutions with Katie Brown, PBS, 2006, frequent contbr. Oprah!, Good Morning America, Live with Regis & Kelly; author: Katie Brown Entertains, 2000, Katie Brown Decorates, 2002, Katie Brown's Weekends, 2005, (syndicated column) Domestic Dilemmas, 2005—. Office: NY Times Syndication Sales Corp 14th Fl 122 E 42nd St New York NY 10168 Office Phone: 212-499-3411. Office Fax: 212-499-3382.*

BROWN, KAY (MARY KATHRYN BROWN), retired state official, consultant, political organization worker; b. Ft. Worth, Dec. 19, 1950; d. H. C., Jr. and Dorothy Ruth (Ware) Brown; m. William P. Dougherty, Dec. 15, 1978 (div. 1984); m. Mark A. Foster, Aug. 24, 1991; 1 adopted child, Kathryn Yucui. BA, Baylor U., 1973. Reporter UPI, Atlanta, 1973-76; reporter, feature writer Anchorage Daily Times, 1976-77; reporter, co-owner Alaska Adv., Anchorage, 1977; aide, rschr. Alaska State Legislature, Juneau, 1979-80; dep. dir. divsn. of oil and gas (formerly divsn. minerals and energy mgmt.) Alaska Dept. Natural Resources, Anchorage, 1980-82, dir., 1982-86; elected Alaska Ho. of Reps., 1986-96; exec. dir. Alaska Conservation Alliance and Voters, 1997-2000; prin., owner Kay Brown Comms., 2000—05; Alaska comms. dir. Dem. Nat. Com., 2005—. Del. White Ho. Conf. Libr. and Info. Svcs., 1991. Co-author: (book) Geographic Information Systems: A Guide to the Technology, 1991; talk radio host, 1996—2000. E-mail: kaybrown@alaska.net.

BROWN, L. ELIZABETH, judge; b. Ft. Smith, Ark., Aug. 4, 1969; d. Theresa D. Comer; m. Craig L. Brown; 1 child, Seth. AA, Carl Albert State Coll., Poteau, Okla., 1988; BS, Northeastern State U., Tahlequah, Okla., 1991; JD, Okla. City U., 1997. Bar: U.S. Supreme Ct. 2001. Assoc. Andrews Davis, Okla. City, 1998—2002; assoc. dist. judge State of Okla., Stilwell, 2002—. Bd. dirs. Kiwanis, C. of C. Mem.: Okla. Indian Bar Assn., Okla. Bar Assn., ABA.

BROWN, LAIMA ADOMAITIS, art therapist, artist, writer; b. Balt., June 6, 1960; d. Vytautas Albin and Ona Miliauskas Adomaitis; m. Thomas William Brown, Aug. 3, 1985. BA in Journalism magna cum laude, U. ND, 1982; MA in Art Therapy, George Washington U., 1995. Graphic artist The Viguerie Co., Falls Church, Va., 1983—85; art dir. Absolutely Art, Inc., Herndon, Va., 1986—90; clin. art therapist Graydon Manor, Psychiat. Residential Treatment Ctr., Leesburg, Va., 1994—96, supr. expressive therapy program, 1996—99; supr. clin. program, clin. art therapist Safe Haven Youth Shelter, Pensacola, Fla., 2000—02; dir. therapeutic activity, clin. art therapist BayPointe Hosp./Mobile Mental Health Ctr., Ala., 2003—. Participant Nat. Hon. Student Exchange Humboldt State U., Arcata, Calif., 1981; field supr. MA art therapy interns George Washington U., 1996—98; art therapy cons., Orange Beach, Ala., 2000—03; presenter in field. Exhibitions include Art with a Southern Drawl, Mobile, 2001, 621 Gallery, Tallahassee, 2000; artist, writer: essay and acrylic painting H20 Project (included in juried collection promoting clean water and conservation, U.S. tour), contbg. writer, poet, art therpist: Word Pictures: The Poetry and Art of Art Therapists; author: Essay: Creativity is Supernatural. Mem. Nat. Coun. of Cath. Woman, Arlington, Va., 2003, Nat. Mus. of Women in Arts, Washington, 1996; supporter Lithuanian Heritage, Lemont, Ill., Parabola Soc., N.Y.C., 1996. Mem.: Assn. Humanistic Psychology, Am. Art Therapy Assn. (registered art therapist). Roman Catholic. Avocations: painting, folkcrafts, creative writing. Personal E-mail: laimabrown@hotmail.com.

BROWN, LILLIE HARRISON, music educator; b. Cin., July 7, 1937; d. James Albert and Lucille Elizabeth Harrison; m. Frederick Brown, Apr. 12, 1958 (dec. June 1996); children: Kevin Frederick(dec.), Gyll Renee Simpson, Carla Y. BS in Music Edn., U. Cin. Coll. Conservatory of Music, 1961. Music specialist Cin. Pub. Schs., 1961—91, 1999—2002; minister of music, ch. musician Bethel Bapt. Ch., Cin., 1956—. Nominating com. chmn. Coll. Conservatory Alumnae Bd., Cin., 1995—2001; music com. chmn. Hamilton County Ret. Tchrs., Cin., 1992—; mem. NAACP, 1994—. Mem.: Alpha Kappa Alpha (regional music chmn., dir., pres. 1972—76). Home: PO Box 12735 Cincinnati OH 45212-0735

BROWN, LINDA CURRENE, small business executive; b. Clovis, N.Mex., Oct. 28, 1942; d. Currie Oscar and Minnie Irene (Rodgers) Bell; m. Harvey Robert Brown, June 11, 1961; 1 child, Christopher Robert. Student, Ea. N.Mex. U., 1960-63. Youth dir. Sandia Bapt. Ch., Clovis, 1969-76; pres. Linda's Orna-Metal, Clovis, 1974—; portrait cons. Triangle Home Ctr., Clovis, 1977-81, dept. supr., 1979-81, customer rels. rep., 1981-82, advt. dir., 1982-83; merchandising mktg. dir., advt. dir., customer relations rep. Hollands Office Equipment, Clovis, 1983-85; office mgr. Poka Lambro Telecommunications, Clovis, 1985. Patentee in field. Active life mem. Clovis High Plains Hosp. Aux., 1983, pres. Home Owner's Assn., Clovis, 1999-2002, exec. officer, 2003. Democrat. Baptist. Avocations: bowling, fishing, designing, gardening. Home and Office: 225 Sandzen Dr Clovis NM 88101-2320 Office Phone: 505-762-1367.

BROWN, LINDA HARPER, bookkeeping company executive; b. Dallas, Mar. 20, 1948; d. Harold Eugene and Opal Lee Gooch; m. Charles Michael Harper (div.); children: Timothy Drake Harper, Terry Christopher Harper; m. William E. Brown III; 1 child, William Craig. Cyma cert. computer cons. Acct. W.E. Brown III CPA, Duncanville, Tex., Brown & Hildebrand CPA, DeSoto, Tex.; comptr. Prism Graphics, Inc., Dallas; pres. H & H Bookkeeping, Inc., Irving, Tex., 1990—. Trustee Duncanville Sch. Bd., 1985-91, v.p., 1989-90; mem. Irving City Coun., 1997-2002, mayor pro tem, 1998-99; treas., bd. dirs. Dallas Regional Mobility Coalition, 1997—; bd. dirs. North Ctrl. Tex. Coun. of Govts., 1998—, Irving Heritage Soc.; founding mem. Irving Lyric Stage, treas., 1995-95; bd. dirs. Irving Schs. Found., pres., 1997-98; mem. steering com. Nat. League of Cities Crime Prevention and Pub. Safety, 1998-2002; mem. Tex. Ho. of Reps., 2002, 2004, vice chair select com. on state healthcare expenditures, 2004, mem. transp. com. and elections com., interim com. for child welfare and adoption, 2005, vice chmn. land and resource mgmt. com.; mem. Tex. Higher Edn. Coordinating Bd., 2006Y—; mem. Tex. Legis. Coun., 2006. Named Entrepreneur of Yr., Las Colinas Bus. and Profl. Women, 1993, Irving Women of the Yr., Irving Cancer Soc., 1995, Outstanding Woman in Govt., YWCA, 1998, Nat. Rep. Freshman Legislator, Nat. Rep. Legislators Assn., 2003; recipient Irving High Spirited Citizen award, 1994, Leader of Excellence award Rep. Caucus, 2003, Fighter of Free Enterprise award Tex. Assn. Bus., 2003, 06. Avocations: reading, research, travel, hunting, walking. Office: H & H Bookkeeping Inc Ste 250 125 E John Carpenter Fwy Irving TX 75062

BROWN, LINDA SUE, elementary school educator; b. Hillsboro, Ill., Nov. 6, 1962; d. James and Dorothy Funk; m. Paul M. Brown, Aug. 17, 1985; children: Kayla Elizabeth, Claire Aldene. BS in Edn., Ill. State U., Normal, 1984; MA in Tchr. Leadership, U. Ill., Springfield, 2005. Math tchr. Sparta Sch. Dist., Ill., 1984—85; jr. high math tchr. Virginia Cmty. Unit Sch. Dist., Ill., 1985—. Cross country coach Porta Jr. H.S., Petersburg, Ill., 2002—. Mem.: Va. Edn. Assn. (treas. 2005—06), Nat. Coun. Tchrs. of Math. Office Phone: 217-452-3387.

BROWN, LISA M., academic administrator; d. Robert and June Galloway; children: Mitch R., Morgan M. M in Ednl. Adminstrn., Western Ill. U., Macomb, 2000. Dir. campus activities Scott C.C., Bettendorf, Iowa, 1990—2000, dean of students, 2000—. Alderman at large Bettendorf City Coun., 2000—. Home: 5331 Taylor Ave Bettendorf IA 52722 Office: Scott Community Coll 500 Belmont Rd Bettendorf IA 52722 Office Phone: 5634414016.

BROWN, LOIS HEFFINGTON, retired health facility administrator; b. Little Rock, Mar. 28, 1940; d. Carl Otis and Opal (Shock) Heffington; M. Ivy Roy Brown, June 21, 1984; children: Carletta Jo Rice, Roby Lynn Rice, Pherby Allison Graham, Phelan Missy Graham. Student, Guilford Tech. Community Coll., Jamestown, N.C., 1974-75, 77, 80. Cert. hearing aid specialist. Sec. Berger Enterprises, West Memphis, Ark., 1962-65; office mgr. Beltone Hearing Aid Ctr., Greensboro, N.C., 1975-81; owner Hearing Care Ctr., Cullman, Ala., 1982-85, Miracle-Ear Ctr., Cullman, Decatur, Fultondale, Jasper and Birmingham, Ala., 1985-87; pres. L&I Corp., Cullman, Decatur, Fultondale, Jasper and Birmingham, 1987-90, L & I Corp. Miracle Ear Ctr., Cullman, Decatur, Jasper, Ala., 1991-93; owner Conway (Ark.) Hearing Aid Ctr., 1994—2006, Beltone Hearing Aid Ctr., Conway, 1995-96; ret., 2006. Distbr. Showcase Distbg. Co., Conway, North Little Rock. Gov.-appointed Ala. Bd. Hearing, 1989-91. Mem. Nat. Hearing Aid Soc., Ark. Hearing Soc. (sec. 1996—), Ala. Hearing Aid Dealers Assn. (sec. 1984-86, 96-2002, v.p. 1986-88, bd. dirs. 1988-91), Ark. Hearing Aid Dealers Assn. (appt. by gov. to Ark. hearing aid bd. 2002—). Republican. Baptist. Avocations: music, swimming, gardening, tennis, golf. Home: 6 Ryans Way CV Greenbrier AR 72058-9358 Office Phone: 501-329-7979.

BROWN, LORA ALICE, entertainment company executive, educator; b. Nashville, Oct. 23, 1975; d. Barry Lee and Susan James Brown. BA in Music cum laude, U. Tenn., 1997; MusM, Belmont U., 2003. Dir. string methods and music edn. The Renaissance Ctr., Dickson, Tenn., 2000—03; pres., founder Amadeus Entertainment, Inc., Dickson, Tenn., 2003—. Musical dir. Amadeus Cmty. Orch., Dickson, 2004—. Prodr.: (annual musical benefit) A Home Town Christmas. Tchr. Poplar Grove Ch. of Christ, McEwen, Tenn., 1998—. Mem.: Suzuki Assn. Am., Music Educators Nat. Conf., Conductor's Guild, Am. String Tchrs. Assn., Dickson Area Women in Bus. (founding 50 mem.), Phi Kappa Lamda, Golden Key Honor Soc., Sigma Alpha Iota (life; pres. 1994—95). Office Phone: 615-446-4340. E-mail: amadeusentertainment@yahoo.com.

BROWN, LORENE B(YRON), retired library educator; b. Plant City, Fla., Nov. 9, 1933; d. Benjamin and Sallie (Barton) Byron; m. Paul L. Brown, Aug. 1, 1974. BS, Fort Valley State Coll., 1955; MSL.S., Atlanta U., 1956; PhD, U. Wis., 1974. Cataloguer N.C. Central U., Durham, 1956-58, Gibbs Jr. Coll., St. Petersburg, Fla., 1958-60, Fort Valley State Coll., Ga., 1960-65, Norfolk State U., Va., 1965-70; assoc. prof., dean Atlanta U., 1970-89, prof., 1989—2003; dir. Info. Retrieval Workshops, Atlanta, 1976-78; evaluator Coop. Coll. Library Ctr., Atlanta, 1979-82; cons. United Bd. Coll. Devel., Atlanta, 1976-79. Mem. southeastern/Atlantic regional adv. coun. Nat. Network Librs. Medicine, 2001—03. Author: Subject Access for African American Material, 1995. Mem. Friends of Library, Atlanta, 1982. Recipient Rachel Schenk award Library Sch. U. Wis., Madison, 1971; So. Fellowship Found. fellow Atlanta, 1972-74 Mem. ALA, Am. Soc. for Info. Sci., Assn. Library and Info. Sci. Edn., Ga. Library Assn., Met Atlanta Library Assn., Beta Phi Mu. Democrat. Baptist. Home: 855 Flamingo Dr SW Atlanta GA 30311-2402

BROWN, LORRAINE A., literature educator; b. Grand Rapids, Mich., Apr. 3, 1929; d. Benjamin Franklin Dundas and Eva Elizabeth Campbell; m. William Liller; 1 child, Tamara Kay Liller. BA in English and Edn., U. Mich., 1952, MA, 1962; PhD, U. Md., 1968. From asst. prof. to prof. English George Mason U., 1980—. Home: 11322 Westbrook Mill Ln Apt 103 Fairfax VA 22030 E-mail: lbrown@aol.com.

BROWN, LUCY L., neurology and neuroscience professor, researcher; BA in Psychology, NYU, 1968, PhD in Psysiological Psychology, 1973. Post-doctoral position, neurology dept. Albert Einstein Coll. Medicine, Yeshiva U., 1973—76, instructor, dept. neurology, 1976—79, asst. prof., dept. neurology, with joint appt., dept. neuroscience, 1979—85, assoc. prof., neurology and neuroscience, 1985—95, prof., dept. neurology and neuroscience, 1995—, principal investigator, functional neuroanatomy and basal ganglia rsch. lab. Co-dir., Interdepartmental Inst. for Tng. in Rsch. in the Behavioral and Neurological Sciences Albert Einstein Coll. Medicine, Yeshiva U., 1980. Office: Albert Einstein Coll Medicine 1300 Morris Park Ave K810 Bronx NY 10461 Office Phone: 718-430-3728, 718-430-3632 (lab). Office Fax: 718-430-8821. Business E-Mail: brown@accom.yu.edu.*

BROWN, LYNETTE RALYA, journalist, publicist; b. Beloit, Wis., Dec. 15, 1926; d. Lynn Louis and Ethel Clara (Meeker) Ralya; m. Donald Adair Brown, Jr., Dec. 20, 1947; children: Donald Adair III, Alison Laura, Julia Carol. BA in Journalism, Mich. State U., 1948, MA in Journalism, 1985; MA in Mass Comm., Wayne State U., 1983. Actress, publicist Grand Traverse Playhouse, Traverse City, Mich., 1946 (summer), N.Y. Summer Playhouse, Mackinac Island, Mich., 1947 (summer); writer WILS Radio, Lansing, Mich., 1947-48; writer, performer WJBK Radio, TV, Detroit, 1948-49; editor Denby Ctr. News, Detroit, 1949-51; freelance writer Oakland County, Mich., 1952-78; editor Henry Ford Mus., Dearborn, Mich., 1979-81; writer, reporter Legal Advertiser Newspaper, Detroit, 1983-85; publicist Bloomfield (Mich.) and Birmingham (Mich.) Pub. Librs., 1986-89; freelance writer, publicist Lynette Brown Comm., Birmingham, Mich., 1989—. Columnist: (newspaper) At the Libraries, 1986-89; solo performer Elizabeth Cady Stanton, 1995—. Probation sponsor Dist. Ct. Mich., 1960-70; publicist Oakland County Vol. Bur., 1979-82; leader sr. high/jr. high youth group Drayton Ave. Presbyn. Ch., Oakland County, 1952-54, 62-66, Pine Hill Congl. Ch., Oakland County, 1968-71, Northbrook Presbyn. Ch., Oakland County, 1976-77; polit. campaign worker Rep. candidates and non-partisan jud. candidates, 1952—; Cub Scout leader Royal Oak Emerson Sch., Oakland County, 1961-64; Girl Scout troop leader Bloomfield Twp. Meadow Lake Sch., Oakland County, 1966-71; dir. Martha Griffiths Project, 1989-. Grantee N.Y. State's Thanks Be To Grandmother Winifred Found., 1996, Elizabeth Kummer Award AAUW Mich., 2002. Mem. AAUW (chair women's issues, pub. info. dir. 1995-2000, state projects dir. 2000—), Oakland County C. of C. (Athena award 1995), Mich. Women's Studies Assn. (bd. dirs. 1999—). Home and Office: 6120 Westmoor Rd Bloomfield Township MI 48301 Office Phone: 248-626-5414.

BROWN, MABEL WELTON, lawyer; b. Geneseo, Ill., Dec. 7, 1916; d. Harry E. and Mabel (Welton) B. BA, Oberlin Coll., 1938; JD, U. Chgo., 1941. Bar: Ill. Ptnr. Brown and Brown, Geneseo, 1941-44; sole owner Brown & Brown, Geneseo, 1944-81; sr. ptnr. Brown and Ray, Geneseo, 1981—. Atty. Green River Spl. Drainage Dist., Henry and Bureau Counties, Ill.; chmn. Geneseo Planning Commn., 1961-68, bd. dirs. Geneseo Hist. Assn., 1987—. Mem. ABA, Ill. Bar Assn., Henry County Bar Assn. (pres. 1973-76). Republican. Methodist. Office: Brown and Ray 115 N State St Geneseo IL 61254-1345 Office Phone: 309-944-5115.

BROWN, MADELINE MORGAN, internist; b. Marlton, N.J., Dec. 4, 1976; d. Wallace Francis and Dianne Edythe Brown; m. Donald John Bitto, Jr., Oct. 10, 2004. BA in Molecular Biology, Rosemont Coll., 1998; MD, MCP Hahnemann (Drexel) Med., Phila., 2002. Internal med. internship Med. U. S.C., Charleston, 2002—03, internal medicine resident, 2003—04, Temple U. Hosp., Phila., 2004—05; gen. internist/physician Fountainville Med. Specialists, Doylestown, Pa., 2005—. Resident rep., infection ctrl. com. Med. U. S.C., 2003—04. Author: (invention) Patient Data Cards, 2002, (book) The Intern Survival Guide, 2003. Trainer for standardized patients Nat. Bd. Med. Examiners, Phila., 2005. Mem.: ACP, AMA. Democrat. Avocations: piano, drums, ice skating, reading, bicycling. Office: Fountainville Med Specialists 1456 Ferry Rd Ste 600 Fountainville PA 18923 Office Phone: 215-230-8390.

BROWN, MARCIA JOAN, author, artist, photographer; b. Rochester, NY, July 13, 1918; d. Clarence Edward and Adelaide Elizabeth (Zimber) B. Student, Woodstock Sch. Painting, summers 1938, 39; student painting, New Sch. Social Research, Art Students League; BA, N.Y. State Coll. Tchrs., 1940; student Chinese calligraphy, painting, Zhejiang Acad. Fine Arts, Hangzhou, Peoples Republic China, 1985, 87; studied painting with Judson Smith, Stuart Davis, Yasuo Kuniyoshi, Julian Levi; LHD (hon.), SUNY, Albany, 1996. Tchr. English, dramatics Cornwall (N.Y.) High Sch., 1940-43; library asst. N.Y. Pub. Library, 1943-49; tchr. puppetry extra-mural dept. U. Coll. West Indies, Jamaica, B.W.I., 1953. Tchr. workshop on picture book U. Minn.-Split Rock Arts Program, Duluth, 1986, workshop on Chinese brush painting Oriental Brush Artists Guild, 1988; sponsor Chinese landscape painting workshops with Zhuo HeJun, 1988-89; sponsored workshops Chinese caligraphy with A. Wang Dong Ling, 1989-90, 92; invited speaker exhbn. illustrations, Japan, 1990, 94. Illustrator: The Trail of Courage (Virginia Watson), 1948, The Steadfast Tin Soldier (Hans Christian Andersen), 1953 (Caldecott Honor Book award), Anansi (Philip Sherlock), 1954, The Three Billy Goats Gruff (Asbjornsen and Moe), 1957, Peter Piper's Alphabet, 1959, The Wild Swans (Hans Christian Andersen), 1963, Giselle (Théophile Gautier), 1970, The Snow Queen (Hans Christian Andersen), 1972, Shadow (Blaise Cendrars), 1982 (Caldecott award 1983), How the Ostrich Got His Long Neck (Aardema, Mainichi Japan Picture Book award 1997, Translation Winner' prize Mainichi Newspapers and Sch. Libr. Assn. 1997), 1995, (with others) Sing a Song of Popcorn, 1988, Of Swans, Sugar Plums and Satin Slippers (Violette Verdy); author, illustrator: The Little Carousel, 1946, Stone Soup, 1947 (Caldecott Honor Book award), Henry Fisherman, 1949 (Caldecott Honor Book award), Dick Whittington and His Cat (retold), 1950 (Caldecott Honor Book award), Skipper John's Cook, 1951 (Caldecott Honor Book award), The Flying Carpet (retold), 1956, Felice, 1958, Tamarindo, 1960, Once a Mouse (retold), 1961 (Caldecott award), Backbone of the King, 1966, The Neighbors, 1967, The Bun (retold), 1972, All Butterflies, 1974 (Boston Globe Honor Book, Horn Book), The Blue Jackal (retold), 1977, Walk Through Your Eyes, 1979, (with photographs) Touch Will Tell, 1979; (with photographs) Listen to a Shape, 1979, Lotus Seeds; Children, Pictures and Books, 1985; (with others) From Sea to Shining Sea, 1993; translator, illustrator: Puss in Boots, 1952 (Caldecott Honor Book award), Cinderella (Charles Perrault), 1954 (Caldecott award 1955), How, Hippo!, 1969 (honor book Book World Spring Book Festival); author, photographer: film strip The Crystal Cavern, 1974; exhibited at Bklyn. Mus., Peridot Gallery, Hacker Gallery, Library Congress, Carnegie Inst., Phila. Print Club, Hammond Mus., North Salem, NY, 1988; one-woman show include: U. Albany, SUNY, 1997; represented in permanent collections Library of Congress, NY Pub. Library, Mazza Gallery Findlay (Ohio) Coll.; pvt. collections. Recipient Disting. Svc. to Children's Lit. award, U. So. Miss., 1972, Regina medal Cath. Libr. Assn., 1977, Disting. Alumnus medal SUNY, 1969, Laura Ingalls Wilder award, 1992; U.S. nominee Internat. Hans Andersen award illustration, 1966, 76; career rsch. material in spl. libr. collection, SUNY, Albany, de Grummond Collection, U. So. Miss., Hattiesburg, Kerlan Collection, U. Minn.; named Marcia Brown Rsch. Rm. in her honor SUNY, Albany, 2001. Fellow Internat. Inst. Arts and Letters (life); mem. Author's Guild, Print Coun. Am., Art Students League, Oriental Brush Artists Guild, Sumi-e Soc. Am, Am. Artists of Chinese Brush Painting. E-mail: lotusseed2@aol.com.

BROWN, MARGARET ANN, lawyer; b. Mobile, Ala., 1952; BA, Univ. Va., 1974, JD, 1977. Bar: La. 1977, Va. 1986. Ptnr., practice group leader, real estate fin. Troutman Sanders LLP, McLean, Va. Mem.: ABA, Fairfax Bar Assn., La. State Bar Assn. Office: Troutman Sanders LLP Ste 500 1660 Industrial Dr Mc Lean VA 22102 Office Phone: 703-734-4336. Office Fax: 703-448-6506. Business E-Mail: ann.brown@troutmansanders.com.

BROWN, MARGARET CATHERINE, artist; b. Washington, Oct. 16, 1939; d. Joseph Brown Pearson and Helen Minnie Dusenberry; m. Tyler T. Brown (div.). BS, W. Va. U., 1961. Tchr. Fairfax Pub. Schs., Va., 1961—65; program analyst Fed. Govt./Dept. Navy/NOAA, Washington, 1974—99. One-woman shows include Richard Byrd Libr., Rachael M. Schlesinger Concert Hall and Arts Ctr., 2003, Greater Atlanta Bank, exhibited in group shows at Nat. Exhbn. River Rd., Baton Rouge, 2003—04, Nat. Exhbn. NC, Southport, 2003, Nat. Exhbn. Barnsite Gallery, Kewannee, Wis., 2003, Internat. Exhbn. Fine Art Miniatures, Bethesda, Md., 2003—05, Nat. Exhbn. Calif. Watercolor Assn., 2006, Art League of Alexandria, Springfield Art Guild, Art at the Mill, Millwood, Va., Four Seasons of Oatlands, Reston Art League, Gallery 222, Leesburg, many others, Fairfax County Govt. Ctr., Fairfax City Hall and Cobblestone Gallery, numerous pvt. collections. Recipient Equal award, Art League of Alexandria, Famous Artisans of the 21st Century Show, Peoples Choice award, Old Town Hall Gallery, numerous 2d place awards various art shows, Grand Prize award, Art Supply Warehouse Catalog Contest, 2003—04. Mem.: Miniature Painters Soc. (juried instr. 2006), Prince William Art Soc., Vienna Art Soc., No. Va. Watercolor Group, Potomac Valley Watercolorists, Art League of Alexandria, Nat. League of Am. Pen Women, Washington Watercolor Assn. (bd. dirs.), Springfield Art Guild (v.p.), Fairfax Art League (v.p.), Va. Watercolor Soc. (assoc.), So. Watercolor Soc. (assoc.), Nat. Watercolor Soc. (assoc.), Am. Watercolor Soc. (assoc.). Avocations: piano, reading, aerobics, travel. Home and Office: 7765 Shooting Star Dr Springfield VA 22152-3105 Personal E-mail: peggy-brown@msn.com.

BROWN, MARGARET DEBEERS, lawyer; b. Washington, Sept. 24, 1943; d. John Sterling and Marianna Hurd (Hill) deBeers; m. Timothy Nils, Aug. 28, 1965; children: Emeline Susan, Eric Franklin. BA magna cum laude, Radcliffe Coll., 1965; postgrad., Harvard U., 1965-67; JD, U. Calif., Berkeley, 1968. Bar: Calif. 1969, U.S. Ct. Appeals (9th cir.) 1971, U.S. Ct. Appeals (D.C. cir.) 1986, U.S. Ct. Appeals (2d cir.) 1987, U.S. Supreme Ct. 1972. Assoc. White, Hamilton, Wyche, Shell & Pollard, Petersburg, Va., 1968-70, Heller, Ehrman, White & McAuliffe, San Francisco, 1970-73; sole practice San Francisco, 1973-77, 98—; atty. Pacific Telephone (name changed to Pacific Bell), San Francisco, 1977-83, sr. atty., 1983-85; sr. counsel Pacific Telesis Group, 1985-98, ret. 1998. Elder, deacon, sec.-treas. of deacons Calvary Presbyn. Ch., San Francisco; bd. dirs. No. Calif. Presbyn. Homes and Svcs chmn. 2003-. Mem. Calif. State Bar (mem. com. bar examiners 1994-98, chair subcom. on petitions and litigation 1996-98), San Francisco Bar Assn. (chmn. corp. law dept. sect. 1993, judiciary com. 1993-96, nominating com. 1993), Harvard Club of San Francisco (v.p. schs. 1998—2003, bd. dirs.), Radcliffe Club of San Francisco (bd. dirs.), Phi Beta Kappa. E-mail: mdbk@pge.com.

BROWN, MARGUERITE JOHNSON, music educator; b. El Paso, Tex., Mar. 31, 1940; d. Don Lee and Eloise (Watson) Johnson; m. R. Don Lumley, Dec. 1961 (div. July 1982); children: Jessica Lumley Rodela, Jeffrey Tate Lumley; m. Gilbert Bivins Brown, Oct. 27, 1989; 1 stepchild, Erich Michael. MusB in Piano Pedagogy with honors, U. Tex., 1962; M in Liberal Arts with honors, So. Meth. U., 1974. Tchr., group piano Dallas Ind. Sch. Dist., 1965-72; tchr. music theory Canal Zone Coll., Panama Canal Zone, 1977-79, musical theater accompanist, 1975-79; tchr. class piano Del Mar Coll., Corpus Christi, Tex., 1980-82; tchr., edn. dir. piano & keyboard Coast Music Co., Corpus Christi, Tex., 1982-87; tchr. class piano, theory Del Mar Coll., Corpus Christi, Tex., 1987-90, performance accompanist, 1993-94; owner, piano tchr. pvt. Studio 88, Corpus Christi, Tex., 1994—2001; resident music dir. Monastery St. Clare, Brenham, Tex., 2001—. Mem.: Nat. Guild Piano Tchrs. (adjudicator), Nat. Guild Piano Tchrs., Dallas Music Edn. Assn. (pres. piano divsn. 1969—71), Music Tchrs. Nat. Assn., Corpus Christi Music Tchrs. Assn. (pres. 1995—97), Nat. Fedn. Music Clubs. Office: Monastery Saint Clare 9288 Hwy 105 Brenham TX 77833-7269 Home: 9280 Highway 105 Brenham TX 77833-7269 E-mail: margueritejohn@cs.com.

BROWN, MARILYN BRANCH, retired educational administrator; b. Richmond, Va., Apr. 11, 1944; d. Elbert LeRoy and Edna Harriett (Eley) Branch; m. Winfred Wayland Brown, Jr., June 19, 1982; 1 dau., Lesli Antoinette; 1 dau. by previous marriage, Kara Rachelle Lancaster-Gay. B.S., Va. State U., 1966; M.S., U. Nebr., 1968; postgrad. U. Ala., Va. Commonwealth U. Nat. Tchr. Corps intern U. Nebr. at Omaha and Omaha Pub. Schs., 1966-68; tchr. McKlenburg County Pub. Schs., Boydton, Va., 1968-71; community organizer model cities health planning Capital Area Comprehensive Health Planning Coun., Richmond, Va., 1971-72; asst. dir. com. mental health mental retardation svcs. bd. Va. Dept. Mental Health and Mental Retardation, Richmond, 1972-75, spl. edn. dir., 1975-76; civil rights coord. Va. Dept. Social Svcs., Richmond, 1976-88, chmn. EEO adv. com., 1984-88; supr. spl edn. compliance Va. Dept. Edn., 1988-92; chmn. adv. com. on Black adoption Va. Dept. Social Svcs. Program coord. Swansboro Bapt. Ch., Richmond, 1979—; mem. Swansboro Mass Choir, 2002—. Swansboro Mass Choir, 2002—; coord. One Ch. One Child; pres. Swansboro Deaconess Ministry, 2004—. Recipient Youth Motivation Commendation, Nat. Alliance of Bus., 1983. Fellow Am. Orthopsychiat. Assn.; mem. Am. Assn. Affirmative Action (fed. program grant reviewer 1994-2002), Black Adminstrs. in Child Welfare, Alliance for Black Social Welfare, Regional Youth Coord. National Tots & Teens, Inc., Ea. Star (Elizabeth Harris chpt.), Alpha Kappa Alpha, Psi Chi. Home: 5500 Larrymore Rd Richmond VA 23225-6020

BROWN, MARTA MACÍAS, legislative staff member, executive assistant; b. San Bernardino, Calif., Nov. 29, 1944; m. George E. Brown Jr., Mar. 27, 1989. BA, Calif. State U., San Bernardino, 1970; postgrad., U. Calif., Riverside, 1971. Publ., editor El Chicano Cmty. Newspaper, San Bernardino, 1968-75; cmty. edn. specialist human resources agy. County of San Bernardino, 1972-73, dir. of info. and referral svcs., 1973-75; student affirmative action officer U. Calif., Riverside, 1975-80; exec. asst., dist. press sec. to Congressman George Brown, Calif., 1980-99; field rep. Senator Barbara Boxer, 1999—. Bd. dirs. Casa Ramona Inc., San Bernardino, Ramona Sr. Complex, San Bernardino; pres. George and Marta Brown Found. Mem. Senator Barbara Boxer's judicial appts. com., 1992-94; adv. bd., sponsor, Peacebuilders, 1994—; mem. Calif. Dem. Party Ctrl. Com., 1994-99, family preservation planning com. County of San Bernardino, 1995-99; adv. bd. Children's Spine Found. U. Calif. grad. fellow, 1970. Mem. LWV, Democratic Spouses, Kiwanis (bd. dirs. greater San Bernardino chpt. 1990—). Roman Catholic. Avocation: water gardens. Home: 873 Bernard Way San Bernardino CA 92404-2413 Office: Senator Barbara Boxer 201 N E St Ste 10 San Bernardino CA 92401-1517

BROWN, MARY, nursing educator; b. Hastings, Nebr., Dec. 7, 1945; d. Edsel Waldo Glass and Dorothy Eloise McPherson; m. James Cleo Brown, Apr. 17, 1970; children: Michael, Stephanie, Carrie. BSN, Ariz. State U., 1968; cert. travel agt., Arapahoe C.C., Littleton, Colo., 1989; MSN, U. No. Colo., 1996; MEd in counseling, U. Phoenix. Head nurse, staff nurse Good Samaritan Hosp., Phoenix, 1968-70; pvt. care nurse St. Francis Hosp., Grand Island, Nebr., 1969-70; ICU nurse Sun Towers Hosp., El Paso, Tex., 1970-72; insvc. edn. and staff nurse, IV nurse Swedish Med. Ctr. Health One, Englewood, Colo., 1972-98; nurse instr. Arapahoe-Douglas Area Career and Tech. Sch./Arapahoe C.C., Littleton, 1980—; prof. Arapahoe C.C. Mem. ACC Nurse Aide Adv. Bd., Littleton, 1999—; chmn. Med. Prep. Adv. Bd., Littleton, 1980—; mem. Colo. Med. Prep. Adv. Bd., Denver, 1996—. Author curriculum materials in field; contbr. articles to profl. publs. Chmn. Santa shop ARC, Englewood, Colo., 1986; mem. Colo. Reps., Littleton. Mem. Assn. for Career and Tech. Edn., Colo. CPR Assn., ARC Educators, Colo. Nurses Assn., Health Occupation Students Am. (hon., mem. state adv. bd. 1990—, chmn. competitive events 1979-95, Outstanding Svc. award 1991, 2004, Outstanding State Advisor award 1982, 96), Clin. Nurse Specialist, Lions Club (v.p., emergency response instr.). Republican. Methodist. Avocations: fishing, boating, reading, travel, camping. Office: Arapahoe-Douglas Area Career and Tech Sch 3784 S Logan Lowell Annex Englewood CO 80110 Personal E-mail: mbrown7266@msn.com.

BROWN, MARY ANNE, childcare advocate; Exec. dir. Hephzibah Children's Assn., Chgo., 1976—. Mem. Cook County Public Guardian Com., 1997—. Named one of Chicago's 100 Most Influential Women, Crain's Chicago Business mag., 2004; recipient Excellence in Cmty. Leadership award, Concordia Univ., 2003. Office: Hephzibah Children's Assn 946 N Blvd Oak Park IL 60301

BROWN, MARY ELLEN, former state legislator, accountant; b. Hartland, Maine, July 26, 1952; d. Justin O. and Ernestine (Garnett) Humphrey; m. Gary R. Brown, June 6, 1971; children: John A., Jessica I. AA, Franklin Pierce C.C., Concord, N.H., 1978. Pvt. practice Automated Bookkeeping Svcs., Pittsfield, NH, 1976—; realtor historic properties and distinctive homes Pembroke. Author: Out of Season, 1997, Messages From Mothers to Daughters, 2001, The Impeachment Trial of the New Hampshire Surpreme Court Justuce, 2002, Promoting Your Book in New Hampshire, 2004, others; contbr. articles to newspapers, mags. State legislator, N.H., 1995-96; pres. Chichester (N.H.) PTO, 1979, Tax Payers Assn., 1996. Mem. Internat. Women's Writers Guild, Nat. Soc. Pub. Accts., N.H. Wildlife Fedn., Go N.H. (polit. group), N.H. Writers Project. Avocations: writing, fishing, gardening.

BROWN, MARY ELLEN, retired humanities educator; b. Vicksburg, Miss., Jan. 6, 1939; d. Samuel Evans and Janie Stevens Brown; children: Perrin Wardlaw Rubin, Torrence Evans Lewis. BA, Mary Baldwin Coll., 1960; MA, U. Pa., 1963, PhD, 1968. Tchg. fellow in English U. Pa., 1962—63; asst. prof. English Ind. State U., 1970—72; vis. asst. prof. Ind. U., Bloomington, 1972—73, asst. prof. folklore, 1974—79, assoc. prof., 1979—85, prof., 1985—2003, dir. women's studies, 1985—91, prof. women's studies, 1988, adj. prof. English, 1989, dir. Inst. Advanced Study, 1998—2003, prof. emerita, 2003—. Vis. tutor Sch. Scottish Studies, Edinburgh U., Scotland, 1973—74. Author: Burns and Tradition, 1984, Encyclopedia of Folklore and Literature, 1998, The Bedesman and the Hodbearer: The Epistolary Friendship of James Child and William Walker, 2001, William Motherwell's Cultural Politics 1797-1835, 2001; editor: Jour. Folklore Rsch., 1992—2004; contbr. articles, revs. to profl. jours., chpts. to books. Fellow, John Simon Guggenheim Found., 2004—05; grantee, Am. Coun. Learned Socs., 1979, Ind. U. Coll. Arts and Scis., 1980—82; rsch. fellow, Inst. Advanced Studies in Humanities, Edinburgh U., 1978, 1979, travel grantee, Ind. U., 1979, 1984, 1989, 1996, 1998, 2001, summer faculty fellow, Ind. U., Rsch. and Grad. Devel., 1975, 1976, 1982, 1984, travel grantee, Am. Coun. Learned Socs., 1984, Title VI summer lang. fellow, 1991, 1993, Mid-Career/Sr. Faculty fellow, 1991—92, Fulbright rsch. fellow, 1998, Joan Nordell fellow, Houghton Libr., Harvard U., 2002—03, traveling fellow, Ind. U. Coll. Arts and Humanities Inst., 2003, emeritus fellow, Andrew W. Mellon Found., 2005. Fellow: Am. Folklore Soc. (exec. bd. 1979—82, chmn. nominating com. 1976—77); mem.: Internat. Folk Narrative Soc., Assn. Scottish Literary Study. Episcopalian. Office: Ind U Dept Folklore and Ethnomusicology 504 N Fess Bloomington IN 47401 Home: 818 S Stull Ave Bloomington IN 47401

BROWN, MARY JANE, history educator; b. Columbus, Ohio, Mar. 25, 1939; d. Oreste and Clara (D'Andrea) Ricci; m. Michael W. Fallon, Aug. 5, 1961 (dec. Sept. 1971); children: Paul Matthew, Quinn Patrick, Kathleen Erin, Erin Suzanne; m. Donald L. Brown, Oct. 21, 1972; 1 child, Megan Elizabeth. BA summa cum laude, Otterbein Coll., Westerville, Ohio, 1987; MS, Ohio State U., 1989, PhD, 1998. Adj. faculty Otterbein Coll., 1992-96, Columbus State U., 1992—. Author: (book) Eradicating This Evil: Women in the American Anti-Lynching Movement, 1892-1940, 2000; contbg. author Peace and Change, vol. 28, no. 3, 2003. Mem. adv. bd. United Healthcare, Columbus, 1993—. Mem. AAUW, Orgn. Am. Historians, Sybilla Soc. Avocations: gardening, water sports, skiing, reading, cooking. E-mail: mjb@columbus.rr.com.

BROWN, MARY LOUVINIA, literature and language professor, lawyer; d. Herbert and Chairety Elizabeth Brown; 1 child, Charity Marie. BA, Lincoln U., Oxford, Pa., 1971; MAT, U. Pitts., 1972; JD, Columbus Sch. Law, Washington, 1981. Bar: Pa. 1984. Prof. English Prince George's C.C., Largo, Md., 1972—; assoc. prof. U. D.C., Washington, 1982—86; equal employment specialist U.S. Dept. Agr., Washington, 1988—89; dir., founder The Book Bridge Project, Largo, 1996—. Project coord. Coll. Success Program, Upper Marlboro, Md., 1986—87; diversity cons. NIH, Bethesda, Md., 1998—99. Pres., bd. dirs. Literacy Coun. Prince George's County, Hyattsville, Md., 2003—05; bd. dirs., pub. rels. Prince George Hosp. Guild, Bladensburg, Md., 1992—; pres. PTA, nat. PTA bd. Pullen K-8, Landover, Md., 1991—93; mem. Com. of 100 Prince George County Pub. Schs., Upper Marlboro, 1995—97; mem. Police Chief Adv. Com., Landover, 2004—05; apptd. by gov. Md. Commn. on African Am. History and Culture; v.p. Unity Ch., Washington, 1999—2002. Recipient Pres.'s award, NAACP, Cmty. Svc. award, Prince George Human Rels. Commn., Largo, Md., 1997, Palette & Pen award, Delta Sigma Theta, 2000, Hesburgh cert. of excellence, TIAA/CREF, N.Y.C., 2002. Mem.: J. Franklyn Bourne Bar Assn. (youth chair 1982—83), Nat. Trust for Historic Preservation, Senegalese Friendship Com. (life; edn. chair 1992—94), Nat. Coun. Negro Women (life). Achievements include being first woman and community college professor to head the National Congress of Black Faculty. Avocations: reading, research, tennis, public speaking, writing. Home: 15615 Everglade Ln # 304 Bowie MD 20716 Office: Prince George's CC 301 Largo Rd Upper Marlboro MD 20772 Office Phone: 301-322-0575. E-mail: brownml@pgcc.edu.

BROWN, MARY ROSE, energy executive; B in Comm., S.W. Tex. State U. V.p. pub. rels. Atkins Agy., 1983—97, Valero Corp., San Antonio, 1997, sr. v.p. corp. comm., 1997—. Trustee Our Lady of The Lake U. Recipient Women's Leadership award, San Antonio Bus. Jour., Silver Anvil award, Pub. Rels. Soc. Am. Mem.: Pub. Rels. Soc. Am., Tex. Pub. Rels. Assn. (nearly 20 Silver Spur and Best of Texas awards). Office: Valero PO Box 696000 San Antonio TX 78269-6000

BROWN, MARY WILKES, secondary school educator; d. Jackson Wilkes Jr. and Thelma McDonald Wilkes; m. James H. Brown Jr., Oct. 12, 1974; children: Raena Antoinette, James Henry III, Ryan Jackson. BA in Spanish, Norfolk State U., Va., 1974, endorsement in adminstrn. and supervision, 2005; MA in Edn., Old Dominion U., Norfolk, 1998. Endorsement in English. Spanish tchr. Smithfield HS, Va., 1974—80, Lake Taylor HS, Norfolk, 1980—87, 1996—, Chesterfield Heights Elem. Sch., Norfolk, 1987—96. Named Tchr. of Yr., Lake Taylor HS, 1984, Chesterfield Heights Elem. Sch., 1990; scholar, Valencia, Spain, 1989. Mem.: NEA (assoc.), Fgn. Lang. Assn. Va., Edn. Assn. Norfolk (assoc.), Am. Assn. Tchrs. of Spanish and Portuguese (assoc.). Avocation: exercise. Home: 4782 Christopher Arch Virginia Beach VA 23464 Office: Lake Taylor HS 1384 Kempsville Rd Norfolk VA 23502 Office Phone: 757-892-3200. Office Fax: 757-892-3210. Business E-Mail: mwbrown@nps.k12.va.us.

BROWN, MAUREEN JILL, elementary school educator; d. Maureen Jill Jordan; m. Brian Keith Brown, Dec. 26, 1997. BA, Calif. State U., Fullerton, 1996; MS, Nat. U., 2001. Cert. ednl. specialist Calif. Resource specialist tchr. Rowland Unified Sch. Dist., Rowland Heights, Calif., 1996—98, Capistrano Unified Sch. Dist., San Juan Capistrano, Calif., 1998—. Cert. key trainer cons. Project GLAD, Costa Mesa, Calif., 2002—06. Office Phone: 949-234-5966.

BROWN, MEHRI I., psychiatrist, educator; b. Rome, June 2, 1969; d. Benjamin and Khorshid Ostowari Brown; m. Jolyon Miller, Oct. 15, 2005. BA, Brown U., 1992, MD, 1996. Diplomate Am. Bd. Psychiatry & Neurology. Resident Northwestern Meml. Hosp., Chgo., 1998—2002; asst. clin. prof. U. Calif., San Francisco, 2002—. Mem.: Am. Psychiat. Assn., Am. Med. Student Assn. (assoc.; officer task force on disabilities 1994—96). Avocations: travel, hiking. Office: 388 Market St Ste 1010 San Francisco CA 94111 Office Phone: 415-981-8085. Personal E-mail: mehri_brown@yahoo.com. E-mail: mehri.bown@ucsf.edu.

BROWN, MELISSA, secondary school educator; d. Richard E. and Lynne E. Brown. M, U. Utah, Salt Lake City, 2001. Tchr. Riverton H.S., Riverton, Utah, 2001—. Mem.: Jordan Edn. Assn. (assn. rep. 2005—06). Office Phone: 801-256-5800.

BROWN, MICHELLE ALISE, elementary school educator; b. Bronx, N.Y., June 17, 1966; d. Albert Charles Jr. and Sherry Ann (Arrington) B. BS, Cornell U., Ithaca, N.Y., 1988; MA, Columbia U., N.Y.C., 1991, EdM, 1993. Elem. tchr. N.Y.C. Bd. Edn., 1988-91; tchr. Teaneck Pub. Schs., NJ, 1991—99; adminstr. Englewood Bd. Edn., 1999—2002; dir. Syney J. Walker Meml. Learning Ctr., 2003; facilitator, coord. New Tchrs' Acad. Tchrs. Coll. Columbia U., N.Y.C., 2003—04; dir. instrn. Harlem Childrens' Zone Promise Acad., 2004—; prin. Harlem Childrens' Zone Promise Acad. II, 2005—. Researcher in field. Mem. ASCD, Nat. Coun. Negro Women, Nat. Staff Devel. Coun., Nat. Alliance Black Sch. Educators, Nat. Assn. Elem. Prins., Delta Sigma Theta. Personal E-mail: shellbrown@aol.com.

BROWN, MYRA SUZANNE, school librarian; b. Gainesville, Fla., Jan. 6, 1949; d. Samuel Jackson and Myra Frances (Whiddon) B.; m. Roman Jonas Yoder, Jan. 5, 1973 (dec.); m. Jeremy Gallaudet Hole, May 3, 1986. Student European divsn., U. Md., West Berlin, 1967-69; BA, U. South Fla., 1971; MSLS, Fla. State U., 1972; postgrad., U. Cin., 1974. Libr. asst. Strozier Libr., Fla. State U., Tallahassee, 1973, libr. serials dept., 1973; libr. sci. and tech. dept. Pub. Libr. of Cin. and Hamilton County, 1973-74; libr. assoc. II Coll. Design, Architecture and Art Libr. U. Cin., 1975-77; assoc. univ. libr. State U. Sys. of Fla. Extension Libr., St. Petersburg, Fla., 1979-81, Edn. Libr. U. Fla. Librs., Gainesville, 1982-84, head and edn. bibliographer, 1984-90; asst. dept. chair humanities and social scis. svcs. dept. Smathers Librs. U. Fla., Gainesville, 1990—92, head and edn bibliographer Edn. Libr., 1992—2002, asst. edn. libr., 2002—, univ. libr., 2002—. Mem. reference liaisons discussion group Rsch. Librs. Group, Inc., 1990-92; reviewer Gale Rsch. Co., Inc., 1988—Ednl. Librs., 1995—; participant rsch. panel Univ. Microfilms Internat., 1992; mem. nat. user group Libr. of Congress Cataloging Distbn. Svc., 1992-96; cons. Mus. Fine Arts Libr., St. Petersburg, Fla., 1981-82, Design, Architecture and Art Libr., U. Cin., 1975-77; participant focus group ISI, 1998, 99; participant rsch. panel Libr. Supplies, 1999; cons. New Bus. Devel. Edn. titles Gale Rsch., 1998, 99. Mem. editl. bd. Edn. Librs., 1999—; contbr. World Architecture Index: A Guide to Illustrations, 1991; contbr. chpts. to books, articles to profl. jours. Aux. mem., vol. Shands Hops. of U. Fla., Gainesville, 1993-96, nominating com., 1995-96, sustaining mem., 1997—; advocate for homeless; mem. outreach com., evangelism com., implementation team VIA media program Holy Trinity Episcopal Ch.; advocate for animal rights; vol. Interfaith Hospitality Network, 2003—; co-chair Holiday Bazaar-Jewelry Room, 2004—; mem. exec. bd. Cedar Creek Homeowners Assn., 2004—, v.p., 2004-2005. Mem. ALA (chmn., planner, moderator preconf. and conf. program, mem. divsns. 2000—, reference svcs. in medium-sized rsch. librs. discussion group 1992—2001, presenter), ALA/Assn. Coll. and Rsch. Librs. (edn., behavioral and social scis. sect., mem. ERIC users discussion group 2005—), Spl. Librs. Assn. (info. tech. divsn., 1979-93, edn. divsn. Fla. chpt. 1979—, discussion list mgr., developer 1994-2000, chair nominations com., 2004, editl. referee Edn. Librs. 2004—), presenter at ann. confs.), Am. Ednl. Rsch. Assn., Fla. Ednl. Rsch. Assn., U. Fla. Librs. Assn. (v.p. 1983-84), U. Faculty Fla. (U. Fla. chpt. sec. 2004-05, v.p. 2005—), Phi Delta Kappa (historian 1993-94). Democrat. Episcopalian. Avocation: art. Office: Smathers Librs of U Fla Edn Libr 1500 Norman Hall PO Box 117016 Gainesville FL 32611-7016 Office Phone: 352-392-0759. Business E-Mail: msbrown@ufl.edu.

BROWN, NAN MARIE, retired minister; b. Winton, NC, Jan. 2, 1931; d. Richard and Aberdeen Elizebeth (Clanton) Watford; m. Joseph Linwood Blunt, June 9, 1947 (dec. Sept. 1970); children: Linette, Joseph Linwood Jr., Alvin; m. Frank Coolige Brown, Oct. 2, 1972; stepchildren: Ameedah Ali, Sami Nuridden. BS, D.C. Tchrs. Coll., 1972; MDiv magna cum laude, Va. Union U., 1982, D Ministry in Ch. Adminstrn., 1993; PhD in Pastoral Leadership (hon.), Va. U., 2003. Ordained to ministry Bapt. Ch., 1980. Clk., sec., adminstr. Dept. Commerce and AEC, Suitland, Germantown, Md., 1960-65; program analyst Job Corps, U.S. Office Econs., Washington, 1965-67; licensing asst. U.S. Nuclear Regulatory Commn., Bethesda, Md., 1967-72, pers. mgmt. analyst, 1972-74; mgr. nat. fed. women's program U.S. Dept. Energy, Germantown, 1974-76; nat. dir. fed. women's program U.S. Dept. Interior, Washington, 1979; asst. pastor Pleasant Grove Bapt. Ch., Columbia, Va., 1975-83; pastor Mt. Level Bapt. Ch., Dinwiddie, Va., 1983-87, New Hope Bapt Ch., Esmont, Va., 1987-89; founder, pastor The Way of Cross Bapt. Ch., Palmyra, Va., 1989—2003; vice moderator, moderator Albemarle Bapt. Assn., 1996-98; moderator Slate River Bapt. Assn., 1997-99; ret., 2003. Bd. dir. AIDS Svcs. Group, 1989-99, Women's Health, Va.; cons. Nan M. Brown Assocs., bus. cons.; vol. cons., reviewer AIDS proposals for funding Va. Health Dept., Richmond, 1979-89; founder, dir. Children's Saturday Enrichment Program, Palmyra, 1990—; gen. bd. Bapt. Gen. Conv. Va., social concerns com., 1990; vice moderator Slate River Bapt. Assn., 1995—; cert. AIDS trainer; adj. professor, Va. Union U., Samuel Dewitt Sch. Theology, Evans-Smith Leadership Inst. 1982—; founder, CEO The Way of the Cross Comm. Devel. Corp., Inc., 1998—; com. mem. Va. State Health Dept., 1995-97. Author: (devotionals) The Word in Season, 1986, The Patience To Wait, Vol. I, 1988, Vol. II, 1992; contbg. author: Wise Women Bearing Gifts, 1988, Those Preachin' Women, 1988, Sister to Sister, 1995, My Soul Explodes, 2005. Founder, pres. Black Women in Sisterhood for Action, Washington, 1979-82; vol. chaplain Martha Jefferson Hosp., Charlottesville, Va., 1993—; bd. dirs. AIDS Support Group, Charlottesville, 1990; active Fluvanna County Minority Health Coalition, 1993—, Fluvanna County Commn. on Youth, 1999—; U.S. del. to Internat. Women's Yr. Conf. on Women, Mexico City, 1975; participant First All-Africa Theol. Conf./Bapt. World Alliance, Zimbabwe; selected by Women's Internat. Dem. Fedn. to represent U.S. as del. to World Congress on Women, Moscow, 1987, others. Named Disting. Black Woman, Black Women in Sisterhood for Action, 1982; recipient recognition for cmty. svc. Interfrat. Coun., Charlottesville, 1993, award for excellence Sister Care Internat., 1995, spl. achievement and cmty. svc. award Charlottesville Tribune, 1996, Disting. Svc. award for pastoral leadership and care U. Va. Health Scis. Ctr., 2003. Mem. NAACP (pres. Fluvanna County chpt. 1979-81, cert. of appreciation 1994), Va. Women in Ministry (founder, pres. 1983-88, chaplain, Founder's award 1986, 90, 95). Avocations: reading, listening to music, sewing, travel, playing piano. Home: PO Box 39 18 Tabscott Rd Kents Store VA 23084 Office Phone: 424-589-3641.

BROWN, NANCY CHILDS, marriage and family therapist; b. Butler, Ga., Feb. 17, 1938; d. Preston Bussey and Essie Lou (Jones) Childs; m. Luther Edward Brown (dec. Oct. 6, 1988); children: Melanie B. Ketchum, Catherine B. Tucker, Anthony E. Brown. BA in English with honors, Mercer U., 1960, MS, 1998. Lic. assoc. marraige and family therapist. Stockbroker/sales asst. Evans & Co./Robinson-Humphrey Co., Augusta, Ga., 1961-64; real estate owner/mgr. Macon, Ga., 1975-98; exec. dir. Macon Arts Alliance, 1985-92; assoc. marriage and family therapist in pvt. practice, 1998—. Bd. leaders Atlanta Internat. Mus. Art and Design, 1994—; bd. dirs. Ga. Coun. for the Arts (gov. appointee), 1994-97. Treas. Hay House, 1995-96, adv. bd., 1996—; pres. Macon Heritage Found., 1979-80; mem. founding bd. City Club of Macon, 1989-91; v.p. legislation Assocs. to Ga., Soc. Ophthalmology, 1985; chmn. City of Macon Cmty. Devel. Inner City Adv. Com., 1979-82; bd. dirs. tourism devel. com. Macon Conv. and Visitors Bur., 1990-97; mem. MAPS (City of Macon) Policy Com. (mayoral appointee ward 3), 1994-99; former pres. Bibb County Med. Soc. Alliance; choir of Vineville United Meth. Ch., 1988—; bd. dirs. Macon Symphony Orch., 1998—. Recipient Macon Cultural award Macon Arts Alliance and City of Macon, 1992; named Woman of Achievement Career Women's Network, Macon, 1990; winner Algernon Sydney Sullivan award, 1960, Alumni Meritorious Svc. award Mercer U., 1977. Mem. Career Women's Network, City Club of Macon, Ga. Trust for Hist. Preservation, Am. Assn. for Marriage and Family Therapy, Phi Kappa Phi. Avocations: choral singing, golf, culinary arts, piano playing, travel. Home: 937 Walnut St Macon GA 31201-1918

BROWN, NANCY FIELD, editor; b. Troy, N.Y., Feb. 20, 1951; d. Robert Grant and Barbara Katherine (Field) B. BS in Journalism, Mich. State U., East Lansing, 1974. Asst. editor Mich. Am. Legion, Lansing, 1974-76, State Bar of Mich., Lansing, 1976-78, editor, 1976—, sr. dir. pubs., 1995-98, asst. exec. dir. publs., 1998—. Mem. Nat. Assn. Bar Execs. (cons. pubs. com. Chgo. chpt. 1989—), Mich. State U. Alumni Assn., Nat. Assn. Desktop Pubs., Am. Soc. Assn. Execs. Presbyterian. Avocations: reading, writing, photography, travel. Office: State Bar of Mich 306 Townsend St Lansing MI 48933-2012

BROWN, NORA M., elementary school educator; Tchr. Dr. James H. Naylor Sch., Hartford, Conn., 1973—; area coord., sec., third v.p. Hartford Fedn. Tchrs., 1994—2000; serves on Nat. Bd. Profl. Tchg. Stds. Office: Dr James H Naylor Sch 639 Franklin Ave Hartford CT 06114-3089 Office Phone: 860-695-4620. E-mail: norabrown1@aol.com.

BROWN, ORAL LEE, real estate company executive, entrepreneur; b. Batesville, Miss. 3 children. BS, Univ. San Francisco. Lic. Realtor Calif., Real Estate Broker Calif. Mgr. Blue Cross Ins. Co.; now owner Nationwide Realty/TPI Corp., Oakland; and owner/chef Cobbler's Restaurant. Co-author (with Caille Millner): The Promise: How One Woman Made Good on Her Extraordinary Pact to Send a Classroom of First Graders to College, 2005. Bd. dir. Oakland Cmty. Housing Resource Bd.; past commr. Alameda County Assessment Appeal Bd.; mem. Harmony Missionary Baptist Ch. Named an honoree at Black History Month awards, Union Bank of Calif. and KQED; named one of Glamour Magazine's Women of the Yr., 2002, 10 Most Influential People, San Francisco Mayor Willie Brown; recipient Hero In Education award, Calif. State Lottery, Madame C.J. Walker award. Mem.: Assoc. Real Property Brokers, Oakland Bd. Realtors, Cal-Pak Assn. Achievements include promising a college education to first graders at Brookfield Elementary Sch. in 1987-of 23 students, 19 graduated and enrolled in college. In 2001 she made the promise to 60 more students. Office: Oral Lee Brown Found Nationwide Realty 9901 MacArthur Blvd Oakland CA 94605

BROWN, PAMELA S., former attorney general; BA in Cultural Anthropology, U. Wash., 1982, JD with honors, 1988. Tech. dir, news dir., news ed. KOMO TV, ABC, Seattle, 1981—85; Rule 9 atty., King County prosecutors and Wash. State, atty. gen., consumer protection div., 1986—87; criminial def. atty. Seattle, 1987—89; criminal prosecutor, off. of atty. gen. No. Mariana Islands, 1989—90, chief sen. legal counsel, 1990—94; ptnr. Long & Brown, attys. at law, 1994—98; pvt. practice, 1998—99; fed. ombudsman, off. of ombudsman, off. of insular affairs US Dept. of Interior, Saipan, 1999—2001; of counsel Teker Civille Torres and Tang attys. at law and MP mng. atty. for

Saipan Off., Labor, Immigration and Civil Litig., Saipan, 2001—02; legal counsel to gov. No. Mariana Islands, Saipan, 2002—03, atty. gen., 2003—06. Mem. Am. Bar Assn., Commonwealth Bar Assn.

BROWN, PAMELA WEDD, artist; b. Cauderan, Gironde, France, Nov. 21, 1928; came to U.S., 1953; d. William Basil and Nora Marsh (van Nostrand) Wedd; m. Charles Freeman Brown, Nov. 29, 1952; children: Penelope Susan, Nicholas Wedd. Student, Ecole des Beaux Arts, Paris, 1947-48, Academie Julian, 1946-51. Free lance fashion illustrator, Paris, 1947-48; dir. arts and crafts YWCA, Toronto, Ont., Canada, 1951; dir. Washington Womens Arts Ctr., 1987-88; dir., pres., founding mem. Washington Printmakers Gallery, 1990-91; co-pres. Studio Gallery, 1992-94; founding mem. Wash. Printmakers Gallery. Artist in residence The Art Barn, Washington, 1986. Designer book plate Nat. Mus. Women in Arts Libr., 1985; represented in permanent collections Libr. of Congress, NIH, Nat. Mus. Am. History, Nat. Mus. Women in Arts. Precinct capt. Bd. of Elections and Ethics, Washington, 1970-80. Recipient First prize drawing, Academie Julian, Paris, 1947, Purchase award, Jr. League, Newport News, Va., 1971. Mem. Studio Gallery D.C. (assoc.), Art League (Equal award 1980, 82, 85, 88, 2000, 02), Woman's Nat. Dem. Club. Avocations: music, tennis, sailing, dance. Home: 3050 Military Rd NW # 636 Washington DC 20015 E-mail: cfbrown@his.com.

BROWN, PATRICIA A., customer service representative; b. Lynchburg, Va., Jan. 23, 1952; d. William Andrew Jr. and Josephine Jackson Paige; m. Arthur Landrum III, May 1, 1970 (div. Apr. 1977); 1 child, Michelle Evonne; m. Bobby G. Brown, Jr., Jan. 6, 1989; 1 child, Bobby Gordon III. A in Bus., Ctrl. Va. C.C., Lynchburg, 1979; cert. microcomputer applications, John Tyler C.C., Richmond, Va., 1994; B in Bus., Averette Coll., 1998. Operator AT&T, Richmond, 1976—. Job stewart Comm. Workers Am., Richmond, 1985—, social com. co-chair, 1995—; co-chair alliance AT&T, Richmond, 1986-97, chair Christmas children wish list, 1993. Active Chesterfield (Va.) Voters League, 1994; vol. Providence Elem., Richmond, 1995. Mem. Women With Vision (pres. 1997—). Democrat. Baptist. Avocations: travel, reading, volunteer work with children. Home: 1703 Winters Hill Cir Richmond VA 23236-2378

BROWN, PATRICIA MARY CLARE, health facility administrator; b. N.Y.C., Jan. 30, 1960; m. Joseph Paul Gill; stepchildren: Mallory R. Gill, Natalie R. Gill. BA, U. Richmond, 1982; JD, U. Balt., 1986. Asst. atty. gen. Office Atty. Gen., Dept. Health and Mental Hygiene, 1984—94; sr. counsel Johns Hopkins Health Sys., 1994—; acting pres. Johns Hopkins Health Care LLC, 2000, pres., 2000—, also bd. dirs. Sr. dir. managed care Johns Hopkins Medicine, 1997—2000; v.p. managed care Johns Hopkins Health Care LLC, 1997—2000; bd. dirs. Priority Ptnrs., Inc. Trustee Maryvale Prep. Sch., 1992—2000; bd. dirs. Glenwood Life Ctr., Inc., 1997—2000. Mem.: Am. Heart Assn. Md. Coun. (pub. policy and advocacy com. 1997—98), Md. State Bar Assn. (sec./treas. health care law sect. coun. 1993—94, vice chairperson health care law sect. coun. 1994—95, chairperson health care law sect. coun. 1995—96).

BROWN, PEARLIE MURRAY, school librarian; b. Kings Mountain, NC, Mar. 24, 1940; d. Sloan George and Mary Lee Murray; m. Marvin Brown, June 27, 1964; children: Vincent Allen, Adrienne Brown Lee. BS, N.C. Ctrl. U., 1961, MLS, 1971; EdD, Nova Southeastern U., 1982; post grad., U N.C.-Charlotte, 1975. Libr. Carver HS, Spindale, NC, 1961—64; tchr. Pleasant Ridge Elem., Gastonia, 1964—65; libr. Gaston Coll., Dallas, NC, 1966—. Mem. Gaston Coll. Assn. Educators, 1970—, Gaston Coll. Personal Assn., 1985—; bd. mem. Gaston County's Children Coun., 1990—91. Trustee bd. Vestibule AME Zion Ch., young adult ministries; mem. United Arts Coun., Gastonia, 1998—. Mem.: NEA, Black Caucus of Am. Libr. Assn., NCCC Learning Resources Assn., Zeta Phi Beta Sorority. Methodist. Avocations: reading, bowling. Office: Gaston Coll Morris Libr 201 Hwy 321 S Dallas NC 28034

BROWN, PEGGY ANN, language educator, writer; d. Clyde and Nadine Chittenden; m. James Troy Brown, Oct. 29, 1960; children: Lori Steiger, Camille Maren, Matthew, Mandi Loggains. AA, Richland Coll., 1978; BA in English, U. Tex., 1980, MA, 1985, PhD, 1990. Prof. English & humanities Collin Coll., Plano, Tex., 1987—. Author: (novel) Strangler Figs, 2005, (instr. manual) Humanities Through the Arts, 2004. Office: Collin Coll 2800 East Spring Creek Plano TX 75074

BROWN, PEGGY LEE, academic administrator, consultant, singer; b. Trenton, N.J. d. Fitzhugh and Mary Susan Brown. BS cum laude, The Coll. N.J., 1987. Pres. PLB Tng. Consultants, Trenton, 1991—2002; asst. dir. ednl. talent search Mercer County CC, Trenton, 2003—. Singer: (recital) Carnegie Hall, Hotel Fiuggi Terme, Italy, N.J. State Mus., (concert) Trenton War Meml., Opera Internat.-Princeton U., Teatro Della Fonti, Italy, (opera performance) Rider U., Fine Arts Series throughout N.J. and Pa., (CD) Simply Peggy, Good News. Mem. Mercer County Youth Svcs. Commn., Trenton, 1994—96; mem. bd. Trenton YWCA Bd., 1986. Recipient alt. semi-finalist, Queens Opera Ninth Ann. Vocal Competition, 1994, semi-finalist, N.Y. Vocal Artists Competition, 1997. Mem.: ASTD. Christian-Church Of Christ. Avocation: travel. Office: Mercer County Community Coll North Broad & Academy Sts Trenton NJ 08608 Office Phone: 609-586-4800 6677. Personal E-mail: plbrown@surfree.com. E-mail: brownpl@mccc.edu.

BROWN, REBECCA, writer, educator; b. San Diego, Mar. 27, 1956; d. Vergil Neal Brown Jr. and Barbara Ann (Wildman) Brown; life ptnr. Christine Galloway. BA, George Washington U., 1978; MFA, U. Va., 1981. Tchr. Pacific Luth. U., Tacoma, 1997—98; writer-in-residence Hugo House, Seattle, 1997—99; tchr. MFA program Goddard Coll., Plainfield, Vt., 1999—. Creative dir. lit. Centrum. Author: (short stories) Annie Oakley's Girl, 1992, What Keeps Me Here, 1996, (fiction) The Dogs: A Modern Bestiary, 1998, (novels) The Gifts of the Body, 1994, The End of Youth, 2003, Excerpts From a Family Medical Dictionary, 2003, The Last Time I Saw You, 2006. Recipient award, Boston Book Review, 1994, Pacific N.W. Booksellers, 1994, Wash. State Gov.'s Arts, 1995, Lambda Lit., 1995. Mem.: PEN West, Phi Beta Kappa. Democrat.

BROWN, REBECCA SUE, director; d. Hewell Fred and Shirley Mae Brown; m. Steve Arnold. AS in Animal Sci., Imperial Valley Coll., 1978; BA in Internat. Agr. Devel., U. Calif., Davis, Calif., 1982, MEd, 1987; PhD in Agr. Edn., Iowa State U., 1991. Faculty, coord. Earth U., Costa Rica, 1992—95; dir. internat. and intercultural edn. Maricope C.C., Tempe, Ariz., 1995—2001; dir. Internat. Studies Office U. Va., Charlottesville, Va., 2001—. Adv. nat. security edn. program, Washington, 2002—04. Mem.: Assn. Internat. Educators. Office: Univ Va Internat Studies Office PO Box 400165 Charlottesville VA 22904 Office Fax: 434-982-3011. Business E-Mail: rebeccabrown@virginia.edu.

BROWN, RENEE, sports association executive; b. Henderson, Nev. Grad., U. Nev., Las Vegas. Asst. coach women's basketball U. Kans., Stanford U., Calif., San Jose State U., Calif.; asst. coach USA Basketball Women's Nat. Team, Colorado Springs, Colo., 1995—96; dir. player pers. Women's Nat. Basketball Assn., N.Y.C., 1996—99, sr. dir. player pers., 1999—2000, v.p. player pers., 2000—. Office: Women's Nat Basketball Assn Olympic Tower 645 Fifth Ave New York NY 10022

BROWN, RENI (ARLENE PATRICIA THERESA BROWN), artist; b. Jan. 3, 1953; d. William J. and Adelaide Elizabeth Brown. Student, Union Coll., 1971; BA Visual Comm., BA Occupl. Therapy, Kean Coll., 1980; student, Union Coll., $D71. Cert. personal trainer, health fitness instr. Am. Coll. Sports Medicine, water safety instr., ARC, swim instr., ARC, lifeguard, ARC, CPR, ARC, first aid, ARC, workplace safety instr., ARC, yoga instr., ARC, yoga synthesis instr., ARC, U.S.A. water safety ski coord., ARC, regis. yoga instr., Yoga Alliance. Owner, pres. Reni Co., Roselle Park, N.J., 1979—; profl. faux surface finishes artist residential and comml. Pvt. tchr. art, Glass and Mirror Abrasive Etching, comml. carved glass designs and creation, air brush artist designer, pinstripper metal and wood, crystal engraving and carving, Roselle Park, 1979—; owner Twinks Trademark and Associated Characters; performance nutrition specialist Internat. Sports Sci. Assn. Exhibited in The Children's Mus., Ind.; patentee in field. Recipient 3d Pl. award Custom Car and Van Show, Meadowlands, N.J., 1981, 2d Pl. award Custom Car and Van Show, Asbury Park, N.J., 1982. Mem. Artists' Equity Assn., Summit Art Assn., Princeton Art Assn., Am. Women's Econ. Devel. Assn., Found. Christian Living, Positive Thinkers Club, N.J. Art Dirs. Club, Morris County C. of C., N.J. Jewelers Assn., Internat. Jet Sports Boating Assn. (standup womans' ski pts. champion 1996), Assn. Jensen Owners, Westfield Art Assn., Alumni Assn. Kean Coll. Office Phone: 908-451-1195. Personal E-mail: R777eni@aol.com.

BROWN, RHONDA JEAN, special education educator; b. Montgomery, Ala., May 25, 1947; d. R.C. and Essie Belcher Brown. AB magna cum laude, Benedict Coll., 1969; MEd, Ga. State U., 1977, EdS, 2001. Cert. tchr. English Ga. Dept. Edn., 1969, tchr. learning disabilities Ga., 1983, tchr. interrelated spl. edn. Ga., 1984, data collection Ga., 1989, behavior disorders Ga., 1990, dir. spl. edn. Ga., 1992. Tchr. H.S. English Atlanta Pub. Sch. Sys., 1970—77; tchr. learning disabled Dekalb County Sch. Sys., Decatur, Ga., 1978—82, tchr. interrelated spl. edn., 1986—89, lead tchr. spl. edn. and ednl. diagnostician, 1990—, exceptional edn. instructional specialist; tchr. interrelated spl. edn. Fulton County Sch. Sys., Coll. Park, Ga., 1983—85. Specialist spl. edn. support and diagnostics Dekalb County Sch. Sys., 1990—, instr. staff devel. courses, 1999—, collector behavior analysis data, 2001—. Named Woman of Yr., Am. Bus. Women's Assn. Northlake chpt., 1982; named to Civil Rights Meml. Wall of Tolerance, Montgomery, Ala., 2005. Mem.: Coun. Exceptional Children, Pi Lambda Theta, Alpha Kappa Mu, Zeta Phi Beta. Democrat. Baptist. Home: 3447 Cobbs Ferry Dr Decatur GA 30032 Office: Dekalb County School Dept Exceptional Edn 5839 Memorial Dr Stone Mountain GA 30083 Office Phone: 678-676-2041. Personal E-mail: rjbrown5@bellsouth.net.

BROWN, RHONDA ROCHELLE, chemist, health facility administrator, lawyer; b. Shelbyville, Ky., July 13, 1956; d. Clifton Theophilus and Fannie Mae (Lawson) B. BA in Chemistry, U. Md., 1978; MA, Ctrl. Mich. U., 1983; JD, No. Va. Law Sch., 1992. Bar: D.C. 1998, Md. 2004, U.S. Dist. Ct. D.C., U.S. Dist. Ct. Md., Ind. 2004. Analytical chemist Dept. Health and Mental Hygiene, Annapolis, Md., 1978-83, epidemiologist Balt., 1983-88; patent examiner U.S. Patent and Trademark Office, Xtal City, Va., 1989-90; freelance rschr. New Carrollton, Md., 1990—; lawyer, pvt. practice Washington, 1998—. Mem. Am. Chem. Soc., Washington, 1978-82; mem., exec. bd. Nat. Lawyers Guild, Washington, 1987—; pres. Voucher Express, 1993—; mediator Superior Ct., Washington, 1993—; legal advt. mgr. Sentinel Newspaper. Subcom. chmn. Anne Arundel County Task Force for Drug and Alcohol Abuse, 1979-80; pres., bd. mem. Md. Ornithol. Soc., 1979-82; mem., exec. bd. Md. Condominium and Homeowners Assn., Rockville, Md., 1988-91. Named Outstanding Young Women of Am., 1983. Mem. ABA, ATLA (family divsn. 1999—), Nat. Assn. Criminal Def. Lawyers, Superior Ct. Trial Lawyers Assn. (criminal and family divsn.), Nat. Intellectual Property Law Assn., Anne Arundel County Tennis Assn., Sigma Iota Epsilon. Office Phone: 202-220-3111.

BROWN, RITA MAE, writer; b. Hanover, Pa., Nov. 28, 1944; d. Ralph and Julia Ellen B. AA, Broward Jr. Coll., 1965; BA, NYU, 1968; cinematography degree, Sch. Visual Arts, NYC, 1968; PhD, Inst. Policy Studies, 1976; DLitt, Wilson Coll., 1992; LLD (hon.), William Woods U., Fulton, Mo., 2000; LLD (hon.), York Coll., Pa., 2003; LHD (hon.), Franklin Pierce Coll., 2002. Photo editor Sterling Pub., N.Y.C., 1969-70; lectr. Fed. City Coll., Washington, 1970-71; rsch. fellow Inst. Policy Studies, Washington, 1971-73; pres. Am. Artists Inc., Charlottesville, Va., 1980—. Vis. mem. faculty in feminist studies Goddard Coll., Plainfield, Vt., 1973—; mem. lit. panel NEA, 1978-81; Hemingway judge for 1st fiction PEN Internat., 1983; blue ribbon panelist Prime Time Emmy Awards, 1984, 86; tchr. Nebr. Summer Writers Conf., U. Nebr., Lincoln, 2003, 04. Author: (translator) Hrotsvitra: Six Medieval Plays, 1971, (novels) The Plain Brown Rapper, 1972, The Hand That Cradles the Rock, 1971, Songs to a Handsome Woman, 1973, Rubyfruit Jungle, 1974, In Her Day, 1976, Six of One, 1977, Southern Discomfort, 1982, Sudden Death, 1983, High Hearts, 1986, Starting from Scratch, 1987, Bingo, 1988, Wish You Were Here, 1989, Rest in Pieces, 1991, Murder at Monticello, 1993, Venus Envy, 1993, Dolley, 1994, Paydirt, 1995, Riding Shotgun, 1996, Murder, She Meowed, 1996, Loose Lips, 1998, Outfoxed, 2000, Mrs. Murphy Mysteries, 2001, Outfoxed, 2000, Alma Mater, 2001, Hotspur, 2002, Full Cry, 2003, Whisker of Evil, 2004, Cat's Eyewitness, 2005, The Hunt Ball, 2005; (poetry) The Poems of Rita Mae Brown, 1987; TV series include I Love Liberty, 1982, Long Hot Summer, 1985, My Two Loves, 1986, The Alice Marble Story, 1986, Southern Exposure, 1990, Cat on the Scent, 1999, Loose Lips, 1999, Outfoxed, 2000, Pawing Through The Past, 2000; TV films include The Girls of Summer, 1989, Selma, Lord, Selma, 1989, Passing Through, 1993, A Family Again, 1994, others; (cable TV) The Mists of Avalon, 1986, The Nat Turner Story-African American Anthology, 1993, The Wall, K-9, 1993; (films) Slumber Party Massacre, 1982, Sweet Surrender, 20th Century Fox, 1986, Table Dancing, 1987, Mary Pickford, 1998. Former exec. officer NOW; bd. dirs. Human Rights Campaign Fund, N.Y.C., 1986; co-founder Radical Lesbians; founder Redstockings Radical Feminist Group, Nat. Gay Task Force, Nat. Women's Polit. Caucus. Recipient Award for Best Variety Show on TV Writers Guild Am., 1982, Outstanding Alumni, Am. Assn. Cmty. Colls., 1999, Outstanding Alumna, Broward Cmty. Coll., 1999, Literary Lion award N.Y. Pub. Library, 1986, Emmy award nomination for The Long Hot Summer, ABC mini-series, 1985; Emmy nomination for best variety show I Love Liberty, 1982; named Charlottesville favorite author The Observer, 1990, Athlete of the Week, The Observer, 1990. Mem. PEN Internat., Oak Ridge Foxhunt Club (Master of Foxhounds). Office: care of The Wendy Weil Agy 232 Madison Ave Ste 1300 New York NY 10016-2901 E-mail: waywardwomen@aol.com.

BROWN, ROSELLEN, writer; b. 1939; BA, Barnard Coll., 1960; MA, Brandeis U., 1962. MS prof. in am. and English lit. Tougaloo Coll., 1965—67; prof. creative writing Goddard Coll., Plainfield, Vt., 1976; vis. prof. creative writing Boston U., 1977—78; prof. creative writing U. Houston, 1982—85, 1989—96; prof. Grad. Creative Writing Program Sch. Art Inst. Chgo., 1997—. Author: The Autobiography of My Mother, 1976, Tender Mercies, 1978, Before And After, 1992, Civil Wars, 1994 (Janet Heidinger Kafka award for best novel), Half a Heart, 2000, short stories, poetry. Recipient award in Lit., Am. Acad. Arts and Letters; fellow, Radcliffe Inst., MacDowell Colony, Guggenheim Found., Ingram Merrill Found., Bunting Inst., Howard Found. Office: Sch Art Inst Chgo 4th Fl 37 S Wabash Chicago IL 60603-3103

BROWN, RUTH PAYNE, retired elementary school educator, retired principal; b. Cannelton, W.Va., Jan. 1, 1933; d. Andrew and Nancy Payne; m. Harts Morrison Brown (div.); children: Nancy V., Ellyne. BS, Bluefield State Coll., W.Va., 1955; MEd, The Johns Hopkins U., Balt., 1958; PhD in Edn., U. Md., College Park, 2005; cert. of advanced study, Johns Hopkins U., Balt., 1978. Elem. sch. tchr. All Sts. Parish Sch., Virgin Islands, 1955—57, Balt. City Pub. Schs., 1957—59, demonstration tchr., 1959—72, staff devel. assoc., 1972—74, ednl. specialist, 1974—76, asst. principal, 1976—78, principal, 1978—92, ctrl. office adminstr., 1992—98. Home: 3701 Bowers Ave Baltimore MD 21207-7004

BROWN, SALLY DAY, minister, literature and language educator, preschool educator; b. Boston, Mar. 14, 1943; d. Charles Hoben and Helen Dearing Day; m. Roger Davis Brown, Aug. 17, 1968; children: Jonathan Charles, Jeffrey Roger. BA with highest distinction, U. Main, 1965; MA in Edn., St. Joseph Coll., Conn., 1989; MDiv., Yale U., 2000. Ordination tchg. cert. Mass., Conn., Maine, 2003. Pre-sch. tchr. Sci. Mus. of Conn., West Hartford, Conn., 1987—91; parish adminstr. St. James Episc. Ch., West Hartford, 1991—94; lay pastor All Saints Episc. Ch., Ivoryton, Conn., 1994—98; student pastoral intern St. Mark's Episc. Chr., New Britain, Conn., 1998—2000, lay patoral assoc., 2000—01; parish vis. Asylum Hill Congo Christ Ch., Hartford, 2002; assoc. pastor 1st Congl. United Ch. Christ, Ocala, Fla., 2003—. Tutor English and secondary sch. West Hartford Pub. Schs., 1980—87; tutor SAT and coll. bds., 1975—90. Author of poems. Mem.: LWV, Fla. Conf. United Ch. Christ, Jr. League of Greater Hartford, Phi Kappa Phi, Phi Beta Kappa. Democrat. United Church Of Christ. Avocations: reading, walking, movies. Home: 539 North Cherry Pop Dr Inverness FL 34453 Office: First Congl United Ch Christ 7171 SW SR 200 Ocala FL 34476

BROWN, SANDRA, writer; b. Waco, Tex., Mar. 12, 1948; m. Michael Brown; children: Ryan, Rachel. Mgr. Merle Norman Cosmetics Studios, Tyler, Tex., 1971-73; weather reporter KLTV-TV, Tyler, 1972-75, WFAA-TV, Dallas, 1976-79; model Dallas Apparel Mart, 1976-87. Author: (romance novels) Breakfast in Bead, 1983, Heaven's Price, 1983, Relentless Desire, 1983, Tempest in Eden, 1983, Temptation's Kiss, 1983, Tomorrow's Promise, 1983, In a Class by Itself, 1984, Send No Flowers, 1984, Bittersweet Rain, 1984, Sunset Embrace, 1984, Words of Silk, 1984, Riley in the Morning, 1985, Thursday's Child, 1985, Another Dawn, 1985, 22 Indigo Place, 1986, The Rana Look, 1986, Demon Rumm, 1987, Fanta C, 1987, Sunny Chandler's Return, 1987, Adam's Fall, 1988, Hawk's O'Toole's Hostage, 1988, Slow Heat in Heaven, 1988, Tidings of Great Joy, 1988, Long Time Coming, 1989, Temperatures Rising, 1989, Best Kept Secrets, 1989, A Whole New Light, 1989, Another Dawn, 1991, Breath of Scandal, 1991, Mirror Image, 1991, French Silk, 1992, The Silken Web, 1992, Honor Bound, 1992, A Secret Splendor, 1992, Shadows of Yesterday (also published as Relentless Desire), 1992, Three Complete Novels, 1992, Charade, 1994, The Witness, 1995, "TEXAS!" series: Texas! Lucky, 1990, Texas! Sage, 1991, Texas! Chase, 1991, Texas! Trilogy, 1992, (as Laura Jordan) Hidden Fires, 1982, The Silken Web, 1982, (as Rachel Ryan) Love Beyond Reason, 1981, Love's Encore, 1981, Eloquent Silence, 1982, A Treasure Worth Seeking, 1982, Prime Time, 1983, (as Erin St. Claire) Not Even for Love, 1982, A Kiss Remembered, 1983, A Secret Splendor, 1983, Seduction By Design, 1983, Led Astray, 1985, A Sweet Anger, 1985, Tiger Prince, 1985, Above and Beyond, 1986, Honor Bound, 1986, The Devil's Own, 1987, Two Alone, 1987, Thrill of Victory, 1989, Exclusive, 1996, Fat Tuesday, 1997, Unspeakable, 1998, The Alibi, 1999, Stand Off, 2000, The Switch, 2000, The Crush, 2002 (NY Times Bestseller), Hello Darkness, 2003, White Hot, 2004 (Publishers Weekly Bestseller, 2005), Chill Factor, 2005, Ricochet, 2005. Recipient Am. Bus. Women's Assn's Disting. Circle of Success award, B'nai B'rith's Disting. Literary Achievement award, A. C. Greene award, Romance Writers Am. Lifetime Achievement award. Mem.: Literacy Partners, Novelists, Inc, Internat. Assn. Crime Writers, Mystery Writers Am., Author's Guild.

BROWN, SANDRA ANN, psychology educator; b. Grayling, Mich., Feb. 21, 1953; d. Albert Kingsley and Catherine (Fiel) B.; m. Martin Alan Magy, Feb. 18, 1984; children: Daniel Magy, Kathleen Magy. BA in Math., Psychology, Hope Coll., 1975; MA in Clin. Psychology, Wayne State U., 1978, PhD in Clin. Psychology, 1981. Intern Vets. Affairs Med. Ctr., San Diego, 1979-80; staff psychologist Del Mar Psychiat. Ctr., Calif., 1981-82; asst. prof. grad. faculty No. Ill. U., DeKalb, 1982-84; assoc. chief psychology Vets. Affairs Med. Ctr., San Diego, 1987-88; asst. prof. U. Calif., San Diego, 1984-90, assoc. prof. dept. psychiatry, 1990-93, prof. dept. psychiatry, 1996—; dir. psychol. svcs. for alcohol and drug treatment program VA Med. Ctr., San Diego, 1984-93, chief, 1993—2000. Chair Nat. Inst. on Alcohol Abuse and Alcoholism Instl. Rev. Group, Washington, 1991-93; chair R&D VA Med. Ctr. Grantee Nat. Inst. on Alcohol Abuse and Alcoholism, U. Calif., San Diego, 1986—, VA Merit grantee, 1984—, Nat. Inst. Drug Abuse, 2000—; New Investigator Rsch. award Nat. Inst. on Alcohol Abuse and Alcoholism, U. Calif., San Diego, 1983-86. Mem.: APA (pres. divsn. 50 1998—99). Roman Catholic. Avocations: jogging, swimming, skiing, gardening. Office: VA Med Ctr Psychology Svc 3350 La Jolla Village Dr # 116B San Diego CA 92161-0002

BROWN, SANDRA LEE, art association administrator, consultant, artist; b. Chgo., July 9, 1943; d. Arthur Willard and Erma Emily (Lange) Boettcher; m. Ronald Gregory Brown, June 21, 1983; 1 child, Jon Michael. BA in Art and Edn., N.E. Ill. U., 1966; postgrad., No. Ill. U. Cert. K-9 tchr., Ill. Travel agt. Weiss Travel Bur., Chgo., 1959-66; tchr. Chgo. Sch. Sys., 1966-68, Schaumburg (Ill.) Sch. Dist. 54, 1968-94, creator coord. peer mentoring program for 1st-yr. tchrs., 1992-96; cons. Yardstick Ednl. Svcs., Monroe, Wis., 1994—2003; exec. dir. Monroe Arts Ctr., 1996—2001, Monroe Area Coun. for the Arts, Madisonville, Tenn., 2002—03; arts mgmt. cons. Helping Hands, Non-Profit Consulting, Knoxville, Tenn., 2003—, Tenn. Arts Commn. Arts cons.; mem. adv. bd. Peer Coaching and Mentoring Network, Chgo. suburban region, 1992-94; peer cons. Schaumburg Sch. Dist. 54, 1988-94. Exhibited in solo and group exhibitions, Court House Gallery, Woodstock, Ill., Millburn (Ill.) Gallery, Gallerie Stefanie, Chgo., Monroe Arts Ctr., Athens Art Ctr., Athens, Tenn., Chumley/Orr Gallery, Cleve., Tenn. Campaign chmn. for mayoral candidate, Grayslake, Ill., 1989; campaign chmn. for trustee Citizens for Responsible Govt., Grayslake, 1991. Mem. Lakes Region Watercolor Guild, Delta Kappa Gamma (chmn. women in arts Gamma chpt. Ill. 1992-94, Alpha Mu chpt. 1995-97), Cmty. Arts League (Athens, Tenn.). Avocations: gardening, musician for barn dances, pre-war Appalachian, blues and cajun music, research collecting 78 rpm records. Home and Office: Helping Hands Non-Profit Consulting PO Box 1456 Athens TN 37371

BROWN, SHANNON ELIZABETH, mathematics educator; b. Greenwich, Conn., July 4, 1982; d. Robert and Mary Louise Brown. BS in Math. cum laude, Fairfield U., Conn., 2004. 7th grade math. tchr. Saxe Mid. Sch., New Canaan, Conn., 2004—. Mem.: Omnicron Delta Epsilon. Home: 42 Richland Rd Greenwich CT 06830 Office Phone: 203-594-4500.

BROWN, SHARI K., special education educator; b. Detroit Lakes, Minn., Nov. 5, 1973; d. Kermit and Marie Schultz; m. Christopher A. Brown, June 20, 1998. BA, Concordia Coll., 1996; postgrad., Moorhead State U., 1997. Lic. specific learning disabilities. Tchr. specific learning disabilities Moose Lake (Minn.) Cmty. Schs., 1997—98, Sebeka (Minn.) Pub. Schs., 1999—. Mem.: Edn. Minn.-Sebeka. Office Phone: 218-837-5101.

BROWN, SHARON WEBB, art educator; b. Whitesburg, Ky., Nov. 20, 1942; d. Chester and Doris Adams Webb; m. Bob Brown, May 19, 1973; children: Alyn, Ashley Susan. BA, Georgetown Coll., Ky., 1964. Art tchr. Jefferson County Schs., Louisville, 1964—72; art coord. Louisville City Schs., Louisville, 1972—73; tchr. fine arts, dept. chair Marshall County Schs., Benton, Ky., 1975—. Editor: Hallowed Hollows, 2001, Women in God's Word, 2001, God's Specialty, 2002; actor: (plays) Harvey, 2001, 2002, Do Not Go Gentle, 2002. Elder Presbyn. Ch., Calvert City, Ky. Mem.: Women in the Arts, Speed Mus. (bd. dirs. 1972—73), Commonwealth Yacht Club (rec. sec. 1993—2004). Republican. Avocations: travel, literature, painting. Home: POBox 641 Calvert City KY 42029 Office: Marshall County Schools 416 High School Road Benton KY 42025 Personal E-mail: sbrown@marshall.k12.ky.us.

BROWN, SHEBA ANN, elementary school educator; b. Miss., 1951; married; 1 child, Joshua. BS in Elem. Edn., U. So. Miss., 1973. Tchr. 4th grade Biloxi (Miss.) Pub. Schs., 1973-74; tchr. 3d grade Ferncrest Acad., New Orleans, 1974-75, Cifton Ganus Pvt. Sch., New Orleans, 1975-78; tchr. 4th grade Putnam County Schs., Palatka, Fla., 1986-87; tchr. multi-age primary class Biloxi Pub. Schs., 1987—. Condr. workshops; presenter in field. Recipient Beverly Briscoe award Biloxi Schs., 1990, Enhancement award City of Biloxi, 1995, Leo Seal Tchr. Recognition award, 1999; named Miss. Tchr. of Yr., 1995, Women at the Top Coast Mag., 1996. Mem. Internat. Reading Assn., Nat. Coun. Tchrs. English, Jeff Davis PTA (treas.), Delta Kappa Gamma. Home: 135 Travia Ave Biloxi MS 39531-5328

BROWN, SHERI LYNN, artist, poet, educator; b. Bluefield, W.Va., Nov. 22, 1968; d. James H. and Rosa B. Wilkes; m. Gene A. Wyatt Jr. BA in Comml. Art and Advt., Concord Coll., 1992. Writer Hill Top Records, Hollywood, Calif., 2001; owner T.J. Cool Advt., 1992—. Model Magic Mart Stores,

2005—. Author: numerous poems. Mem. I Am His choir Scott St. Bapt. Ch., 1983—87. Mem.: Internat. Soc. Poets. Avocations: art, writing, trumpet, french horn, mellophone. Home and Office: 120 Russell Terr Bluefield WV 24701-2932

BROWN, SHIRLEY ANN, speech-language pathologist; b. Bklyn., Oct. 9, 1935; d. Hyman and Lillian (Fuhrer) Rubak; m. Ronald Wallace Brown, Sept. 29, 1956; children: Abbie Howard, Daniel Mark. BA, Bklyn. Coll., 1956, MA, 1961. Lic. speech/lang. pathologist, N.Y., N.J. Speech pathologist Richmond County CP Treatment Ctr., S.I., N.Y., 1956-59, Coney Island Hosp., Bklyn., 1959-61, Mendham Boro Schs. and Chatham Twp. Schs., 1962-67; pvt. practice home care speech pathologist various hosps. and med. facilities, 1967-79; dir. speech pathology dept. Englewood (N.J.) Hosp., 1974-92; speech pathologist Holy Name Hosp., Teaneck, N.J., 1992-96, chief speech-lang. pathology dept., 1996-2000; speech pathologist Home Health Care Agys., Bergen County, 1992—. Clin. supr. comm. disorders grad. program Kean Coll., NJ, 1993—2000, Montclair State U., 1996—2000; project leader speech-lang. pathology Multiple Sclerosis Consortium website editl. bd., 1999—2001; website project dir. Consortium of Multiple Sclerosis Ctrs., 2001—. Editl. bd. Internat. Jour. Multiple Sclerosis Care, 1999—. Chair svc. and rehab. Am. Cancer Soc., Hackensack, N.J. Recipient Nat. Honor citation for Profl. Edn., Am. Cancer Soc., 1985, Crimson Sword award Am. Cancer Soc., 1989. Mem.: Nat. Multiple Sclerosis Soc. (Greater North Jersey chpt., clin. chpt. programs, adv. com. 1998—), N.J. Speech, Lang., Hearing Assn. (Disting. Svc. award), Am. Speech., Lang. Hearing Assn. (cert., congl. action com., state chair career info., Continuing Edn. award 1983—, Outstanding Clin. Achievement award 1985). Avocation: cooking. Home and Office: 200 Winston Dr Cliffside Park NJ 07010

BROWN, SHIRLEY MARGARET KERN (PEGGY BROWN), interior designer; b. Ellensburg, Wash., Mar. 30, 1948; d. Philip Brooke and Shirley (Dickson) Kern; m. Ellery Kliess Brown, Jr., Aug. 7, 1970; children: Heather Nicole Coco, Rebecca Cherise, Andrea Shirley Serene, Ellery Philip. BA in Interior Design, Wash. State U., 1973. Apprentice then interior designer L.S. Higgins & Assocs., Bellevue, Wash., 1969-72; interior designer ColorsPlus Interiors, Inc., Bellevue, Wash., 1972, Strawns Office Furniture & Interiors, Inc., Boise, 1973-75, Empire Furniture, Inc., Tulsa; owner Inside-Out Design Co., Ltd., Boise, 1973-82; interior designer Architekton, Inc., Tulsa, 1984-86, Johnson Brand Design Group, Inc., 1986-87, Ellery Brown & Assocs. Arch., 1987—, Seattle Design Ctr.-Visions & Studio Programs, Scottsdale, Ariz., 1998—, Mehagian's Fine Furniture, Scottsdale, Am. Soc. Interior Designers Showhouse, 2000, Ladlows Fine Furniture, 2003—05; with Dept. Design Robb & Stucky Interiors, Scottsdale, 2006—. Lectr. in field. Featured designer Ariz. Lifestyle mag., 2002, 06; contbr. articles to profl. jours. Pres. PTA, co-chair capital bond prin. sel. com., enrollment rev. com., 1989-95; bd. dirs. Paradise Valley Young Life; designer West Valley Child Crises Ctr., Inc.; contributing designer West Valley Child Crisis Ctr. Recipient Seattle Design Ctr. Marjorie Siegel award, 1997, Phoenix Home and Garden Mag. ASID Showhouse, 2000. Mem.: AAUW, Nat. Soc. Interior Designers, Am. Soc. Interior Designers (dir. chpt. 1976—77, presdl. citation Oreg. chpt. 1977, chmn. Boise subchpt. 1977—79, sec. 1980—81, chmn. Wash. chpt. step workshop chmn. 1993—97, NCIDQ chmn. 1993—97, Wash. state presdl. citation 1995, presdl. citation Oreg. chpt. 1995—96, Wash. state presdl. citation 1996, 1997, bd. dirs. North Ariz. chpt. 2003—, pres.-elect 2006—, chmn. awards banquet 2006, Showhouse Mehagian's Designer award Phoenix Home and Garden Mag. 2000, bd. dirs. Ariz. chpt. 2003—), Jr. League Phoenix, Wash. State U. Alumni Assn., Idaho Hist. Co., Jr. League Seattle, Zonta, Alpha Gamma Delta. Republican. Presbyterian. Office: Robb & Stucky Interiors 15440 N Scottsdale Rd Scottsdale AZ 85254 Office Phone: 480-321-8108. Personal E-mail: az_browns@hotmail.com, ekbrownjr@cox.net. Business E-Mail: shirley.kernbrown@robbstucky.net.

BROWN, SHONA, information technology executive; BS in computer systems engring., Carleton U.; MA in econ. and philosophy, Oxford U.; Phd in indsl. engring. and engring. mgmt., post-doctorate in indsl. engring. and engring. mgmt., Stanford U. Prof. dept. indsl. engring. and grad. sch. bus. Stanford U.; former ptnr. Global Strategy Practice McKinsey and Co.; sr. v.p. bus. ops. Google Inc., 2003—. Author: Competing on the Edge: Strategy as Structured Chaos. Office: Google Inc 1600 Amphitheatre Pky Mountain View CA 94043 Office Phone: 650-623-4000. Office Fax: 650-618-1499.*

BROWN, TINA, journalist, television personality; b. Maidenhead, Eng., Nov. 21, 1953; d. George Hambley and Bettina Iris May (Kohr) Brown; m. Harold Evans, Aug. 20, 1981; children: George Frederick, Isabel Harriet. MA, Oxford U.; D (hon.), The London Inst., 2001. Columnist Punch Mag., London, 1978; editor in chief Tatler Mag., London, 1979—83, Vanity Fair Mag., N.Y.C., 1984—92; editor New Yorker mag., N.Y.C., 1992—98; chmn., editor-in-chief Talk Media, 1998—2002; weekly columnist The Wash. Post, 2003—, Salon.com, 2003—; host, Topic A with Tina Brown CNBC, 2003—. Author: (plays) Under the Bamboo Tree, 1973 (Sunday Times Drama award), Happy Yellow, 1977, (book) Loose Talk, 1979, Life As A Party, 1983. Named Most Promising Female Journalist, Young Journalist of Yr., 1978, Comdr. Brit. Empire, Her Royal Highness Queen Elizabeth, 2000; recipient Kathrine Pakenham prize, Sunday London Times, 1973, Mag. Editor of the Yr., Age Mag., 1988, USC Disting. Achievement in Journalism award, USC Journalism Alumni Assoc., 1994. Office: Attn Betty Greif 447 E 57th St New York NY 10022

BROWN, TOMMIE FLORENCE, social work educator; b. Rome, Ga., June 25, 1934; d. Phillip and Mary Louise (Murden) B. BA, Dillard U., 1957; MSW, Washington U., St. Louis, 1964; DSW, Columbia U., 1984. Social svc. supr. Tenn. Dept. Pub. Welfare, Chattanooga, 1964-67, dir. tng., 1967-71; asst. prof. sociology U. Tenn., Chattanooga, 1971-73, head social work dept., 1973-82, UC Found. assoc. prof. social work, 1982—; mem. Tenn. Ho. of Reps., Nashville, 1992—, mem. commerce, conservation and environ. coms., 1992-94, mem. edn. com., 1995—, sec. fin. ways and means com., 1995—. Named Nat. Social Worker of Yr., NASW, 1971. Democrat. Baptist. Home: PO Box 3258 Chattanooga TN 37404-0258 Office: Tenn Gen Assembly Legislative Plz Ste 36 Nashville TN 37243-0128

BROWN, TONI, health and physical educator; BS, Gardner-Webb U., 1993; MEd, George Mason U., 2005—. Health and phys. educator J.L. Simpson Mid. Sch., Leesburg, Va., 1996—. Scholar Tchr. Endorsement Scholarship, Loudoun Edn. Found., 2006. Mem.: Va. AAHPERD, NEA, Am. AAHPERD. Office: JL Simpson Mid Sch 490 Evergreen Mill Rd Leesburg VA 20175 Office Phone: 703-771-6640. Business E-Mail: tbrown@loudoun.k12.va.us.

BROWN, TRISH EILEEN See VERNAZZA, TRISH

BROWN, TRISHA, dancer; b. Aberdeen, Wash., Nov. 25, 1936; BA in Dance, Mills Coll., Calif.; D (hon.), Mills Coll., 1997; PhD in Fine Arts (hon.), Oberlin Coll. Founder, artistic dir. Trisha Brown Dance Co., N.Y.C., 1970—; founding mem. Judson Dance Theater; choreographer Grand Union Improvisation Group, 1970-76. Lectr. Mills Coll., Calif., Reed Coll., Oreg., NYU, N.Y.C., Goucher Coll., Md., Carnegie Mellon U., Pa.; condr. workshops and seminars throughout world. Choreographer Untitled, 1961, Trillium, 1961, Lightfall, 1963, Untitled Duet, 1963, Part of a Tango, 1963, Target, 1964, Rulegame Five, 1964, Motor, 1965, Homemade, 1965, Inside, 1966, Skunk Cabbage, 1967, Saltgrass and Waders, 1967, Medicine Dance, 1967, Snapshots, 1968, Ballet, 1968, Falling Duet, 1968, Sky Map, 1969, Dance with Duck's Head, 1968, Yellow Belly, 1969, Leaning Duets, 1970, The Stream, 1970, Man Walking Down the Side of a Building, 1970, Accumulation 4 1/2, 1971, Walking on the Wall, 1971, Leaning Duets II, 1971, Falling Duet II, 1971, Rummage Sale and the Floor of the Forest, 1971, Planes, 1968, Roof Piece, 1971, Primary Accumulation, 1972, Accumulating Pieces, 1973, Group Accumulation, 1973, Roof and Fire Piece, 1973, Spanish Dance, 1973, Structured Pieces, 1973, Figure 8, 1974, Drift, 1974, Spiral, 1974, Pamplona Stones, 1974, Locus, 1975, Line Up, 1976, Water Motor and Splang, 1978, Glacial Decoy, 1979, Opal Loop, 1980, Son of Gone Fishin', 1981, Set and Reset, 1983 (N.Y. Dance and Performance award, 1984), Lateral Pass, 1985 (N.Y. Dance and Performance award, 1986), Carmen, 1986, Newark, 1987, Astral Convertible, 1989, For M.G.: The Movie, 1991, Astral Converted, 1991, Another Story as in Falling, 1993, If you couldn't see me, 1994, Foray Forêt, 1990, You Can See Us, 1995, M.O., 1995, Twelve Ton Rose, 1996; featured (TV series) M.O., Sta. WNET-TV, N.Y.C., Dance in America, Sta. WGBH-TV, Boston, Dancing on the Edge, Making Dances; exhibitions include Venice Biennale, Toulon Mus., exhibited in group shows at Musée de Marseille, Numerals: Math. Concepts in Contemporary Art, The Pluralist Decade, New Notes for New Dance, Art and Dance: Images From the Modern Dialogue. Mem. Nat. Coun. on Arts, 1994. Decorated chevalier Ordre des Arts et des Lettres; recipient Creative Arts award, Brandeis U., 1982, Dance Mag. award, 1987, Samuel H. Scripps Am. Dance Festival award, 1994, Prix de la Danse la Société des Auteurs et Compositeurs Dramatiques award, 1996, Nat. medal of Art, 2003; fellow, Guggenheim Found., 1975, 1984, NEA Creative Artists Svc. Program, 1977, 1981—84; grantee, NEA, N.Y. State Coun. on Arts; MacArthur fellow, 1991. Mem.: Am. Acad. Arts and Letters (Nat. medal of Art 2003). Office: Trisha Brown Co care Rebecca Davis 625 W 55th St New York NY 10019-3560

BROWN, TYESE ANDREA, music educator; d. Andrew Percy and Elois Smith Brown. B of Music Edn., Howard U., 1993; MA, NYU, 1999. Cert. tchr. music K-12. Telemarketer Americana Portraits, West Orange, NJ, 1992; substitute tchr. Orange Bd. Edn., Orange, NJ, 1994—95, South Orange and Maplewood (N.J.) Bd. Edn., 1994—95; music dir. Jersey Explorer Mus., East Orange, 1997—99; music tchr. K-4 Jersey City (N.J.) Bd. Edn., 1999—2000; music tchr. grades 3-5 Montclair (N.J.) Bd. Edn., 2000—02; music tchr. grades 7-8 North Plainfield (N.J.) Bd. Edn., 2002—03; music tchr. grades K-7 Roselle (NJ) Bd. Edn., 2003—. Music competition judge NAACP ACT-SO Competitions, Charlotte, N.C. and Atlanta, Ga., 1996—98; soprano vocal judge Ctrl. Jersey Music Educators Assn. Jr. Competitions, 2002, NJ Music Educators Assn., 2002; music dir. Hillside's Traveling Troupe, Montclair, 2000—02. Composer: (songs) The Winds of Yesterday, 1984 (Instrns. Experience Exposures award, 1984), The Ancient Springs, 1985. Music dir. AmeriCorps, Jersey City, 1997—99. Named Gifted Musician of Essex County, Instrns. Experience Exposure, 1984; recipient Gifted Student scholarship, Geraldine R. Dodge Found., 1984, Musician of Yr. award, Newark Comty. Sch. Arts, 1982—88. Mem.: ASCAP (songwriter/pub. mem.), Music Educators Nat. Conf., NYU Alumni Assn., Howard U. Alumni Assn., Kappa Delta Pi, Pi Lambda Theta. Avocations: drawing, reading, composing music, swimming, bowling. Office: ASCAP 1 Penn Plz New York NY 10019 also: Roselle Bd Edn 710 Locust St Roselle NJ 07203 E-mail: tyenote@aol.com.

BROWN, VALERIE ANNE, psychotherapist, social worker, educator; b. Elizabeth, N.J., Feb. 28, 1951; d. William John and Adelaide Elizabeth (Krasa) B. BA summa cum laude (fellow), C.W. Post Coll., 1972; MSW (Silberman scholar), Hunter Coll., 1975; PhD, Am. Internat. U., 1996. Diplomate Am. Bd. Examiners, Am. Bd. Clin. Social Work, Nat. Assn. Social Work; cert. addictions specialist; cert. master hypnotherapist; cert. psychophilogic integration therapist. Social work intern Greenwich House Counseling Ctr., N.Y.C., 1973-74, Metro Cons. Ctr., N.Y.C., 1974-75; sr. psychiat. social worker, co-adminstr. Essex County Guidance Ctr., East Orange, NJ, 1975-80; pvt. practice psychiat. social work, psychotherapy, 1979—. Sr. psychiat. social worker John E. Runnells Hosp., Berkeley Heights, N.J., 1980-86; dir. social work Northfield Manor, West Orange, N.J., 1987; clin. coord. Project Portals East Orange Gen. Hosp., 1987-88; asst. dir. ARS/Century House Riverview Med. Ctr., Red Bank, N.J., 1988-93; sr. clin. case mgmt. specialist Prudential Ins. Co., Woodbridge, N.J., 1993; clin. dir. Greenhouse-KMC, Lakewood, N.J., 1994-2000, Shoreline-KBH, Toms River, N.J., 1996-2000; tech. advisor Nat. Comm. Network, 1988—; mental health clinician III UMDNJ-UBHC, Edison, N.J., 2000—; instr. Brookdale Coll., 1991—; co-founder Women's Growth Ctr., Cedar Grove, N.J., 1979; counselor Passaic Drug Clinic, 1978-80; field instr. Fairleigh Dickinson U., Madison, N.J., 1981-86, Brookdale Coll., 1989-92; field supr. Union Coll., Cranford, N.J., 1986; instr. Sch. Social Work, NYU, N.Y.C., 1980-83, asst. prof., 1983-85; evaluator Intoxicated Driver Resource Ctr., Essex County, N.J., 1987-88. Alt. Monmouth County profl. adv. bd.; founding mem. Nat. Campaign Tolerance of So. Poverty Law Project, 2004. Recipient Congl. Order of Merit, Nat. Rep. Congl. Com., 2005; named Dist. Alumnae Mother Seton Regional H.S., Clark, N.J., 1997. Mem. NASW (Whittman Lifetime Achievement nominee 1997-98), Psi Chi, Pi Gamma Mu, Sigma Tau Delta. Avocations: reading, swimming, travel. Office: 20 Ellsworth Ct Red Bank NJ 07701-5403

BROWN, VIVIAN ANDERSON, retired government agency administrator; b. Manor, Tex., Aug. 27, 1920; d. Carl Robert Anderson and Edna Belle Elizabeth Johnson Anderson; m. Karl Patrick Brown, Aug. 29, 1970 (dec. July 1976); stepchildren: Patrick Thomas, Peggy Ann, David Brian. Student, U. Tex., 1938—39, Mayfair Taylor Secretarial Sch., 1940—42. Purchasing clk. USAF, Bergstrom AFB, Tex., 4357, contracting officer, 1957—73; ret., 1973. Contbr. articles to profl. publs. (Outstanding award). Pres. women's orgn. Prince of Peace Luth. Ch., Austin, Tex. Recipient Vivian A. Brown Spl. Day honor, Mayor of Marshall, Tex., 1990, Gov. of Tex., 1990. Mem.: DAVA (state comdr. 1980—89), Nat. Assn. Ret. Fed. Employees (pres. 1979—81), Swedish Orgn. Carl-Widen Lodge (sec. 1998—2000). Democrat. Lutheran. Avocations: public speaking, reading, writing. Home: 11406 Rustic Rock Dr Austin TX 78750-3505

BROWN, WENDY WEINSTOCK, nephrologist, educator; b. NYC, Dec. 9, 1944; d. Irving and Pearl (Levack) Weinstock; m. Barry David Brown, May 2, 1971 (div. Sept. 1995); children: Jennifer Faye, Joshua Reuben, Julie Aviva, Rachel Ann. BA, U. Mass., 1966; MD, Med. Coll. of Pa., 1970; MPH, St. Louis U., 1999. Diplomate Am. Bd. Internal Medicine. Intern U. Ill. Affiliated Hosps., Chgo., 1970-71; resident in internal medicine The Med. Coll. Wis. Affiliated Hosps., Milw., 1971-74; gen. practitioner Vogelweh (W. Germany) Health Clinics, 1975-76; fellow in nephrology Med. Coll. of Wis. Milw. County Med. Complex, Milw., 1976-78; staff physician St. Louis VA Med Ctr., 1978—2003, acting chief, hemodialysis sect., 1983-85, chief dialysis/renal sect., 1985-90, dir. clin. nephrology, 1990—2003; staff physician St. Louis U. Hosps., 1978—2003, St. Louis City Hosp., 1982-85, St Mary's Health Ctr., St. Louis, 1994—2003; chief of staff VA Tenn. Valley Healthcare Sys., Nashville, 2003—06, Jesse Brown VA Med. Ctr., 2006—. Assoc. prof. internal medicine St. Louis U. Health Sci. Ctr., 1985—98, prof. internal medicine, 1998—2003; prof. medicine Meharry Med. Coll. Vanderbilt Univ., 2003—. Reviewer Clin. Nephrology, Nephrology, Dialysis and Transplantation, Am. Jour. Nephrology, Am. Jour. Kidney Disease, Jour Am. Geriatric Soc., Jour. Am. Soc. Nephrology, Geriatric Nephrology and Urology, Kidney Internat.; med. editor NKF Family Focus; mem. editl. bd. Clin. Nephrology, Geriatric Nephrology, Internat. Urology and Nephrology, Advances in Renal Replacement Therapy; editor-in-chief: Advances in Chronic Kidney Disease, 2004-; contbr. articles to profl. jours. Mem. adv. coun. Mo. Kidney Program, 1985-91, chmn., 1988-89; numerous positions Nat. Kidney Found., 1984—, nat. chmn., 1995-97; bd. dirs. United Way, St. Louis, 1994-2003, Nat. Kidney Found. Ea. Mo. and Metro East, Inc., 1980-94; bd. dirs. Combined Health Appeal Greater St. Louis, Inc., 1988, pres., 1989-92; bd. dirs. Combined Health Appeal Am., 1991-98, sec., 1992-96, vice chmn., 1996-98. Named Casual Corner Career Woman of Yr., 1986, Combine Health Appeal of Am. Vol. of Yr., 1991, Olympic Torch Bearer, 1996, St. Louis Health Profl. of Yr., 1997; recipient Upjohn Achievement award, Med. Coll. Wis. Affiliated Hosps., 1972, Cert. of Leadership, St. Louis YWCA, 1989, Chmn.'s award, Nat. Kidney Found. of Ea. Mo. and Metro East, 1990, award of excellence, 2002, Chmn.'s award, Nat. Kidney Found., Washington, 1990, Martin Wagner award, Nat. Kidney Found., 1999, award of excellence, Nat. Kidney Found. Ea. Mo. and Metro East, 2002. Fellow ACP, AHA; mem. Am. Soc. Nephrology, Internat. Soc. Nephrology, Coun. on Kidney in Cardiovascular Disease, Am. Heart Assn., St. Louis Soc. Am. Med. Women's Assn., St. Louis Internists (v.p. 1983-84, pres. 1984-85), Women in Nephrology (pres. 2000-02), Internat. Soc. for Peritoneal Dialysis, Am. Geriatrics Soc., Soc. for Exec. Leadership in Acad. Medicine (bd. dirs., program chair 1999—), Alpha Omega Alpha. Jewish. Home: 1728 Glen Echo Rd Nashville TN 37215-2910 Office: VA Tenn Valley Healthcare Sys 1310 24th Ave S Nashville TN 37212-2637 Office Phone: 615-327-5330. Business E-Mail: wendy.brown@va.gov.

BROWN, WILMA ELAINE, elementary school educator, artist; d. Elizabeth Hayes and Ernest Wayne Brown. BS, Winthrop U., Rock Hill, S.C., 1965—68; Cert. in Art, Furman U., Greenville, S.C., 1989—92. Cert. Techr. S.C. Dept. Edn., 1992, Nat. Cert. in Art Nat. Bd. Profl. Tchg. Stds., 2005. Dietitian Greenville Hosp. Sys., SC, 1970—72; tchr. Anderson Sch. Dist. #1, Williamston, SC, 1992—. Pres. Sunset Farms, Inc., Easley, SC, 1985—91. Exhibitions include pvt. The People's Market, 1974, oil, pastels, watercolors. Sunday sch. tchr. Leawood Bapt. Ch., Greenville, 1980—83. Mem.: Foothills Reading Coun. (assoc.). Office Phone: 864-269-4571.

BROWN, YVONNE THERESA, retired writer; b. LA, Oct. 29, 1935; m. Donald A. Brown, Jan. 5, 1957; children: Jeffrey Allen, Cynthia Kay, Debra Joy, Douglas Gerard, Todd Patrick. BS in Written Comms., Ea. Mich. U., 1986, MA in Written Comms., 1996. Tech. writer Enrico Fermi Power Plant, Monroe, Mich., 1986—89, Madison, Madison Inc., Detroit, 1989—93, Horiba Instruments, Inc., Ann Arbor, Mich., 1997—2001, ret., 2001. Contbr. articles to jours. and mags. Mem. St. Irene Cath. Ch., Dundee, Mich., 1953—89, soloist, 1953—89; chmn. St. Anthony Cath. Ch., Belleville, Mich., 1989—, cantor, 1989—. Home: 45515 Harmony Lane Belleville MI 48111 Personal E-mail: donbon55@provide.net.

BROWNA, JO MCINTYRE, nurse; d. Cornelius Daniel McIntyre and Josephine Rafferty McIntyre; children: Marc L., Patrick J. Diploma in Nursing, Albert Einstein Med. Ctr., Phila., 1972. Cert. oper. rm. nurse, Assn. of Oper. Rm. Nurses, 1992, RN 1st asst., Assn. of Oper. Rm. Nurses, 1998. Mgr., staff Virtua Health Sys., Voorhees, NJ, 1993—2003; tech. support rep. Medtronic Neurol., Phila., 2000—03. Nurse 1st asst. various hosp. affiliations, NJ, 2001—. Recipient Excellence Leadership award, Dale Carnegie, 1997. Mem.: Assn. of Oper. Rm. Nurses, Am. Assn. of Neurol. Surgeons (assoc.). Achievements include working with other RNFAs to change N.J. laws prohibiting RNFAs to work in N.J; having N.J. ins. cos. value our roles and have mandatory reimbursement from all ins. cos; support of legislature to vote for Medicare reimbursement. Home and Office: Jo Browna PC 13 Dori Court Erial NJ 08081

BROWNBACK, LINDA MASON, health company executive; b. Columbus, Ohio, Mar. 31, 1947; d. Lloyd Walter and Ann Elizabeth (Seely) Mason; m. Clifford A. Bridges, Sept. 14, 1968 (div. Dec. 1982); 1 child, David Lloyd Bridges; m. Thomas S. Brownback, Oct. 28, 2001. BA summa cum laude, Ohio U., 1969; MA, Kutztown (Pa.) U., 1985. Diplomate Am. Psychotherapy Assn., Peak Performance-Neurotherapy Bd., cert. EEG biofeedback Biofeedback Cert. Inst. Am. Ptnr. Brownback, Masons & Assocs., Allentown, Pa., 1982—. Co-author: (novels) Neurotherapy in Dissociative Disorders, Introduction to Quantitative EEG and Neurofeedback, 1999. Bd. dirs. Lehigh Valley Nursing Mothers, 1993—98, Allentown Rescue Mission, 1996—99. Recipient Outstanding Alumni award, Kutztown U., 1995. Mem.: Assn. Applied Psychophysiology and Biofeedback (presenter 1992, 1998, 2000, 2001), Am. Bd. Forensic Examiners, Acad. Cert. Neurotherapists, Internat. Soc. for Study of Dissociation (co-presenter 1985, 1986, 1989), Mortar Bd., Phi Beta Kappa. Home: 1702 W Walnut St Allentown PA 18104-6741 Office: Brownback Mason & Assocs 1702 W Walnut St Allentown PA 18104-6741 E-mail: brownbackmason@enter.net.

BROWN-BARTON, GRACE OLIVE, music educator; b. Kingston, Jamaica, Apr. 15, 1942; arrived in U.S., 1968; d. Wilfred Owen and Lucille May Brown; children: Babafemi Barton, Nayo Barton. BS, NYU, 1979, MA, 1980. Music coord. Jamaica Cult. Devel. Corp., Kingston, 1983—85; tchr. Bd. Edn., N.Y.C., 1985—87; music tchr. Yonkers Bd. Edn., NY, 1987—. Founder, dir. The Bronx Chorale, NY. Recipient Spl. Mother Award, UN, 2004. Baptist. Avocations: stamp collecting/philately, coin collecting/numismatics. Personal E-mail: grabro@msn.com.

BROWN-BLACK, LILLIAN (RUSTY BROWN-BLACK), volunteer; b. Ft. Leavenworth, Kans., Oct. 10, 1920; d. Charles Robert and Lillie (Irvin) Brown; m. Robert Russell Black, Mar. 25, 1991. Club-recreation worker ARC, Philippines-Japan, 1945-47, Germany, 1947-48, Japan-Korea, 1950-52; sec.-civilian U.S. Army, Washington, 1952-53; sec. The White House, Washington, 1953-61; personal-pvt. sec. Pres. Dwight D. and Mamie Eisenhower, Gettysburg, Pa., 1961-68; claims authorizer Social Security, Kansas City, Mo., 1968-73; caretaker The Brown Family, Kansas City, Kans., 1973-91. Spkr. Eisenhower Years/Life on an Old Indian Fort/Philately, 1990—. Bd. mem. Eisenhower Soc., Gettysburg, 1991—; state contact Kans. ARC Overseas Assn., 1992—. Mem. Nat. Mus. Women in Arts. Republican. Baptist. Avocations: genealogy, golf, travel, stamp collecting/philately. Home: 8541 Muirfield Cir Hollins VA 24019 E-mail: lhrbb@cox.net.

BROWN-DANIELS, PATRICIA, budget analyst, wedding planner; b. Washington, June 25, 1953; d. Jesse and Katherine Austin; m. Joseph Lee Daniels, Aug. 25, 1990; children: Dionnah, James, Freddie. Assoc. in Bus. Adminstrn., Washington Saturday Coll., 1999; B in Ministry, Faith Christian U., Washington, 2002. Clk. typist IRS, Washington, 1972—75; procurement clk. U.S. GPO, Washington, 1975—78; acctg. technician Dept. of Navy - NSS, Washington, 1978—83, Dept. of Navy - BUMED, Washington, 1983—88; budget analyst Dept. of Navy - NNMC, Bethesda, Md., 1988—. Profl. wedding cons. Assn. Bridal Consultants, Stamford, Conn., 1999—; trustee, chair budget com. Mt. Rona Bapt. Ch., Washington, 1997—; mem., min. Thank God for Jesus Ministries, 2005—; Mary Kay cons., 2004—. Organizer Langdon / Woodridge Outreach Ministries, Washington, 2000—; founder A Tribute to 'Black' Male Choir, Washington, 2005; organizer Red Hat Diva Angels, 2005—, Women in the Bible, Washington, 2005—; debutante com. Shiloh Bapt. Ch., Washington, 1999—. Recipient Mary M. Bethune recognition Award, Nat. Coun. Negro Women, 1999-2001. Mem.: NAACP (life; sec. 1999—), LJM Toastmasters Club (sec. 1997—, ATM-B 2000), Nat. Coun. Negro Women (life; membership chair 1999—). Baptist. Home: 2429 Hamlin Street NE Washington DC 20018 Office Phone: 301-319-4523. Personal E-mail: pbdaniels0@aol.com.

BROWN-DUGGAN, GLORIA LORENE, health facility administrator; b. Alpine, Utah, July 22, 1927; d. George Alfred and Alice Cleora (Adams) Brown; m. George F. Duggan, Jr., Aug. 25, 1972; 1 child, Gregory P. Maynard. BS with honors, San Diego State U., 1957, postgrad., 1964—74. Sch. nurse, tchr. Sweetwater Union H.S., National City, Calif., 1966—68; resident head nurse Mary C. Wheeler Sch., Providence, 1968—70; subregional trainer Calif. State Drug program, Calif. Dept. Edn., 1970—71; hearing conservation program San Francisco Schs., San Francisco Dept. Pub. Health, Maternal and Child Welfare, 1974; clin. lab. instr. cmty. health R.I. Coll., Providence, 1975—76; exec dir. Pawtucket (R.I.) Neighborhood Health Ctrs., Inc., 1976—90; regional rep. Nat. Assn. Cmty. Health Ctrs., Inc., 1985—90. Lectr. in field; publicity dir. LaJolla aux. San Diego Symphony Orch., 1966—68, chmn. summer music festivals, 1967—. Past chmn. health adv. com. Dept. Human Svcs., State of R.I.; assoc. R.I. Health Ctr. Mem.: APHA, AAUW (publicity dir. 1966), New Eng. Pub. Health Assn., New Eng. Cmty. Health Ctr. Assn., R.I. Health Ctr. Assn. (exec. com., publicity dir. 1978, bd. dirs., legis. com., data evaluation com., sec. 1989—), Nat. Assn. Cmty. Health Ctrs., Inc. (past treas. region 1, program planning com. 1978—88), Phi Kappa Phi. Ch. Jesus Christ Of Latter-Day Saints. Home: 7 Gilbert St Warwick RI 02886-4403

BROWNE, A. PAULINE, accountant, writer; b. Topeka, June 26, 1918; d. James Paul and Alice Bertha (Crabb) Sweeney; m. Raymond Smetzer, Jan. 4, 1948 (div. Jan. 1957); children: Jerry, Raymond, Jonathan, Patricia. BBA, U. Miami, 1975; JD, Atlanta Law Sch., 1980. Owner Smetzer Airport, Castalia, Ohio, 1948-58, Greenwood Inn, Castalia, Ohio, 1956-57; freelance legal sec., 1958-89. Owner Sweeney's Tax Svc., 1948—, Photographs By Pauline; legal word processor Steel Hector Davis, West Palm Beach, Fla., 1989-2003; spkr. in field. Artist (shows) Coral Gables, Fla., 1970, West Palm Beach, 1985, Valencia Gardens, Coral Gables, Fla., Methodist Ch., West Palm Beach, Fla., Orchid Show, Miami, Fla., 1995; exhibits include: Arts and Crafts Show, West Palm Beach; contbr. articles to profl. jours. Activist Fighting for Our Rights Under the Constitution, Alcoholics Anonymous. Mem. Women in Arts, U. Miami Alumni Assn. Avocations: golf, travel, whitewater rafting, hiking, scuba diving, yoga. Home: 1124 Lauren Ln Apt 1114 Tarpon Springs FL 34689 Office Phone: 727-934-0688. Personal E-mail: apauline@verizon.net.

BROWNE, AUTUMN LEE, theater educator, actress, theater director; b. North Hollywood, Calif., Sept. 21, 1957; d. Harry Browne and Gloria Maxwell; m. Michael C. Buss, July 22, 1999; m. Barry Fasman; m. William Wilson. BA in Comms., Calif. State U., Fullerton, 1978; tchg. credential, Chapman U., Orange, Calif., 1995; MA in Theater Prodn., Ctrl. Wash. U., Ellensburg, 2005. Drama tchr. Brookhurst Jr. HS, Anaheim, Calif., 1996—; actress TV commls., theatrical prodns. Bd. dirs. New Voices Playwrights Theatre. Dir.: (plays) Pure as the Driven Show, 1998, Brighton Beach Memoirs, 1999, Toyer, 2004, Social Security, 2006, numerous others. Mem. edn. com. South Coast Repertory Theatre, 2003—; Libertarian Party candidate Calif. State Assembly, 1998, 2000. Recipient Theatre Educator of Yr. award, 2001. Mem.: Toastmasters Internat. (area gov. 1994—96). Address: 601 N Brookhurst St Anaheim CA 92801-3832

BROWNE, BONNIE ESTHER, minister; d. Howard Edward Browne and Mabel Leezer; 1 child, Deborah Dudley Zumberge. BS in nursing, U. of Cin., 1941—46; M in pub. adminstrn. health svcs., U. of Ariz., 1968—74. Registered Nurse, Ariz. and Ohio; Minister Living Bible Ctr., 1986, Interfaith Minister Emerson Theol. Inst., 2003. Counselor, children's clinic Arthritis Found., Tucson, 1973—74; hosp. co-founder and adminstr. Americare Hosp., Tucson, 1975; practitioner Religious Sci., Tucson, 1978—2003; ceo Sewage Treatment Rsch. & Devel., Tucson, 1979—81; facilitator/counselor Bonnie Browne Seminars, Tucson, 1983—2003; min. Celebration of Life Ctr., Tucson, 1988—2001; staff min. Cmty. Ch. of Positive Living, Tucson, 2001—; faculty, dir., founder Emerson Theol. Inst., Satellite Campus, Tucson, 2005. Cons. - pain mgmt. U. Med. Ctr., Tucson, 1979—80; bd. mem. Governor's Adv. Bd. of So. Ariz. Mental Health Ctr., 1973—75; mem. of adv. com. to dir. Coll. of Nursing, U. of Ariz., 1967—68; chmn. Cmty. Coun. Health and Hosp. Planning Com., Tucson, 1961; fin. com. mem. Barry Goldwater Campaign, Tucson, 1964; vol. Am. Cancer Soc., Ariz. Heart Assn., Tucson Festival Soc., Women's Symphony Assn., Combined Hosp. Fund Dr., Kiwanis Women's Organizations, Asthmatic Found., Adv. Com. polit. candidates, Tucson, 1955—75; bd. mem. Ariz. Sch. of Acupuncture and Oriental Medicine, 2003—; sales dir. Mary Kay Cosmetics, Tucson, 1981—86. Del./officer LWV, Tucson, 1958—65; fundraising and candidates' vol. Rep. Party, Tucson, 1960—65. Recipient Outstanding Leadership award, Dale Carnegie, 1979. R-Liberal. Religious Science. Avocations: travel, reading, teaching, research.

BROWNE, JOY, psychologist, radio personality; b. New Orleans, Oct. 24, 1950; d. Nelson and Ruth (Strauss) B.; Carter Thweatt, June 9, 1966 (div. 1979); 1 child, Patience. BA, Rice U.; PhD, Northeastern U.; postgrad., Tufts U. Registered psychologist, Mass. With rsch./optics dept. Sperry Rand, Boston, 1966-68; engr. space program Itek, Boston, 1968-70; head social svcs. dept. Boston Redevel. Authority, 1970-71; staff psychologist South Shore Counselling Assocs., Boston, 1971-82; on-the-air psychologist Sta. WITS, Boston, 1978-82, Sta. KGO, San Francisco, 1982-84; host, news Sta. KCBS, San Francisco, 1984-85; on-air psychologist Sta. WABC, N.Y.C., 1985-87, ABC Talkradio, N.Y.C., 1987-92, WOR Radio Network, N.Y.C., 1992—, Sta. WABC-TV, 1995-97, Dr. Joy Browne Show, Syndicated Eyemark Entertainment, 1999—. On-air psychologist WCBS-TV Five O'Clock News, 1999; dir. Town of Hull Adolescent Outreach Program; cons. human sexuality PBS, 1994—. Author: The Used Car Game, 1971, The Research Experience, 1976, Nobody's Perfect, 1988, Why They Don't Call When They Say They Will and Other Mixed Signals, 1989, Dating for Dummies, 1998, 2d edit., 2006, 9 Fantasies That Will Ruin Your Life, 1998, It's a Jungle out There Jane! Understanding the Male Animal, 1999, Getting Unstuck: 8 Simple Steps To Solving Any Problem, 2002, Dating Disasters and How to Avoid Them, 2005, The Dr. Joy Browne Show Live on Discovery Health Network, 2006. Named One of 25 Outstanding Broadcasters USA Today, 1995-96, 100 Most Influential Talkers, Legend La., 1996, Best Female Talk Show Host, Nartash, 1996, 97, Female Talk Show Host of Yr., Vanity Fair Hall of Fame, 1996. Mem. APA (bd. dirs. 1994-97), Phi Kappa Phi (Communicator of Yr. award 1992). Office: care WOR Radio 111 Broadway 3d Fl New York NY 10006 E-mail: drjoybrowne@compuserve.net.

BROWNE, MARIJANE LEILA BENNER, lawyer; BA summa cum laude, Bowdoin Coll., 1983; JD magna cum laude, Harvard U., 1987. Bar: Mass. 1987, D.C. 1989. Nat. hiring ptnr. Bingham McCutchen LLP, Boston, chairperson Boston hiring com., co-chairperson com. assoc., dep. chairperson pro bono com. Mem.: Boston Adv. Bd. Posse Found., Bowdoin Coll. (trustee), Boston Lawyers Group (vice chairperson, chairperson, hiring & edn. com.). Office: Bingham McCutchen LLP 150 Federal St Boston MA 02110-1726 Office Phone: 617-951-8228. Office Fax: 617-951-8736. Business E-Mail: mb.browne@bingham.com.

BROWNELL, BLANCHE P., retired secondary school educator; b. Waterbury, Conn., Oct. 27, 1934; d. Gustavo Mario and Philomena Marie (Santoro) Parisi; m. Edwin Rowland Brownell; children: Elizabeth R., Elaine B. Dorrans, Evelyn B. Mika. BBA, U. Miami, Coral Gables, 1956. Cert. tchr. U. Miami, 1962. Sec. Radio and Electronic Equipment Co., Miami, Fla., 1952; classified, display ad rep. Miami Herald Pub. Co., 1953—56, 1962; sec. advt. dept. Burdines Dept. Store, Miami, 1961; tchr. bus. edn. Miami Jackson Sr. HS, 1962—68; corp. sec. E.R. Brownell & Assoc. Inc., Miami, 1968—92; ret., 1992. Founder ladies aux. Fla. Soc. Surveying and Mapping, Tallahassee, 1973, Dade County Soc. Surveying and Mapping, Tallahassee, 1973. Named Sponsor of Yr., Future Bus. Leaders Am., Tallahassee, 1965—66; recipient Outstanding Svcs. award, Am. Congress Surveying and Mapping, Washington, 1973. Mem.: U. Miami Woman's Gulid, Garden Club Coral Gables (corr. sec. 2005—), Woman's Club City of Coral Gables, Elkettes. Roman Catholic. Avocations: crafts, ballroom dancing, gardening, travel, computers.

BROWNELL, NORA MEAD, former commissioner; b. Erie, Pa., May 18, 1947; d. George J. and Mary E. (Burke) Mead; m. Frederic M. Brownell, Sept. 9, 1972 (div.); children: Samantha, Peter, Alexa. Student, Manhattanville Coll., 1965-66, U. Syracuse, N.Y., 1966-69. Auction dir. channel 12 Stas. WHYY, Phila., 1980-81; inaugural dir., campaign cons. Re-election Campaign for Gov. Thornburgh, Harrisburg, 1981-82; dep. exec. asst. Gov. Richard Thornburgh, Harrisburg, Pa., 1982-87; v.p. corp. community rels. Meridian Bancorp, Inc., Phila., 1987-92; sr. v.p. corp. affairs Meridian Bancorp, Inc., Corestates Bancorp., 1992-96; acting exec. dir. Regional Performing Arts Ctr. Inc., 1997; commr. Pa. Pub. Utility Commission, 1997—2001, Fed Energy Regulatory Comm., US Dept. Energy, Washington, 2001—06. Bd. dirs. NARUC, Times Pub. Co., Pa. Free Libr., Need Indeed, Please Touch Mus., Pa. Humanities Council, Susquehanna Art Mus., NRRI, Millennium Bank. Mem. Greater Phila. Cultural Alliance, Harmony House, Bus. Vols. for the Arts.*

BROWNELL, PATRICIA JANE, social worker, educator; b. Platteville, Wis., July 14, 1943; d. Richard and Thelma (Rowe) B.; m. James Gale Collins, Mar. 5, 1996. BA, U. Wis., 1967; MSW, Fordham U., 1978, PhD, 1994. Cert. social worker, N.Y. Caseworker dept. social svcs. Human Resources Adminstrn., N.Y.C., 1967-73, project coord. office spl. housing svcs., 1973-77, project mgr. office adminstrv. svcs., 1977-78, grants mgr., rsch. asst., sr. planner policy/program devel., 1978-83, exec. asst. to exec. dep. and dep. commr. home care svcs., 1983-90, dir. spl. projects office exec. dep. commr. family support, 1990-94, dep. dir. non-residential svcs. domestic violence program, 1994, adv. to exec. dep. commr. family support adminstrn., 1995—; from instr. to adj. prof. Fordham U. Grad. Sch. Social Svc., N.Y.C., 1990-94, asst. prof., 1995—. Vis. prof. behavioral sci. dept. Police Acad./N.Y.C. Police Dept., 2001—; adv. bd. Mary's House, 2000—; sec. DW Fin. Mgmt. Agy., 1995-97; cons. N.Y.C. Dept. for the Aging, 1998—; rsch. assoc. Ctr. for Hispanic Mental Health Rsch., 2000—; ad hoc coord. Fordham-St. James Field Placement and Cmty. Practice Project, 2000—; steering com. Interdisciplinary Ctr. for Family and Child Advocacy, 1997—; dir. profl. devel. Interdisciplinary Tng. for Pub. Child Welfare Workers and Supr. to Improve Child Welfare Svcs., 1997-2000; liaison Influencing State Policy, 1997— Co-author: Work with Older People: Challenges and Opportunities, 1994, Helping Battered Women: New Perspectives and Remedies, 1996, Social Work in Juvenile and Criminal Justice Settings, 2d edit., 1997, Multicultural Perspectives in Working with Families, 1997; (with E.P. Congress and I. Abelman) Battered Women and their Families: Intervention and Treatment Strategies, 1998; (with J. Berman) To Grandmother's House We Go and Stay: Perspectives on Custodial Grandparents, 2000; (with M. Moch) Social Work in the Era of Devolution: Toward a Just Practice, 2001; mem. editl. bd. (newsletter) Victimization of the Elderly and Disabled: Preventing Abuse, Mistreatment and Neglect, 1997—; contbr. articles to profl. jours. Bd. dirs. Fund for the Advancement Social Svcs., 1998—; steering com. N.Y.C. Elder Abuse Coalition, 1995—. Faculty Rsch. grantee Fordham U., 1996-97, 99—, N.Y.C. Dept. for the Aging grant, 1999—; Ravazzin scholar Ravazzin Ctr. for Social Work Rsch. in Aging, 1998—; Rational Emotive Inst. fellow, 1995; recipient Linda Mills Meml. award N.Y. State Divsn. Parole, 1993, Faculty Merit award, 1996-2000. Mem. NASW (welfare reform task force N.Y. chpt. 1994—, nominating com., del. assembly 2000—), State Soc. on Aging N.Y. (nominating com. 1999—, exec. com., co-chair social policy com. 2001—) Avocations: reading, yoga, drawing. Office: Fordham U Grad Sch Social Svc 113 W 60th St New York NY 10023 E-mail: brownell@fordham.edu.

BROWNELL, VICKIE MARIE, elementary school educator; b. Las Vegas, July 28, 1959; d. G.L. Cowan and Linda Brownell. BS in Edn., Mo. Western U., Saint Joseph, Mo., 1982; MA. in Edn., East Carolina U., Greenville, N.C., 1983. Lic. tchr. phys. edn. and health Mo., 1982. Instr. elem. phys. edn. St. Joseph (Mo.) Sch. Dist., 1986—. Co-coord. site Project Fit Am., Saint Joseph, Mo., 1997—; footwear assoc. Dicks Sporting Goods, Kans. City, Mo., 2005—. Named Nat. All Star Tchr., Project Fit, 2000; recipient award, Gov.'s Coun. Health Leadership, Jefferson City, Mo., 2001; grantee, Project Fit Am., 1997, Mo. Dept. Elem. and Secondary Edn., 1999, WalMart, 2005. Mem.: NEA (assoc.), Tchrs. Credit Union (assoc.), Mo. Assn. Health, Phys. Edn. Recreation and Dance (assoc. named Mo. State Phys. Edn. Tchr. of Yr. 2004), Humane Soc. Office: Pershing Elementary School 2610 Blackwell Rd Saint Joseph MO 64505 Office Phone: 816-671-4320. Office Fax: 816-671-4457. Personal E-mail: vbrownell@kc.rr.com. Business E-Mail: vickie.brownell@sjsd.k12.mo.us.

BROWNER, CAROL M., management consultant, former federal agency administrator; b. Fla., Dec. 16, 1955; d. Michael Browner and Isabella Harty Hugues; m. Michael Podhorzer; 1 child, Zachary. Grad., U. Fla., 1977, JD, 1979. Gen. counsel govt. ops. com. Fla. Ho. of Reps., 1980; with Citizen Action, Washington; chief legis. aide environ. issues to Sen. Lawton Chiles US Senate, 1986—88, legis. dir. to Sen. Al Gore, Jr., 1988-91; sec.Dept. Environ. Regulation State of Fla., 1991-93; administr. EPA, Washington, 1993—2000; prin. The Albright Group L.L.C., Washington, 2001—. Mem. adv. coun. Harvard Med. Sch., Ctr. for Health and the Global Environment. Recipient Mother of the Yr. award, Nat. Mother's Day Com., 1997, Lifetime Achievement award, NY State Bar Assn., Woman of the Yr. award, Glamour mag., Guy M. Bradley Lifetime Achievement award, Audobon Soc. (S. Fla. chapter). Democrat. Office: The Albright Group 901 15th St NW Ste 1000 Washington DC 20005*

BROWN-HRUSKA, SHARON, federal agency administrator; m. Donald Hruska; 1 child, Jacob. PhD in Econ., Va. Tech., 1994. Asst. prof. fin. AB Freeman Sch. Business, Tulane Univ., 1995—98, George Mason Univ., 1998—2002; commr. CFTC, 2002—, acting chmn., 2004—05. Contbr. articles to numerous profl. jours. Recipient Key Women in Energy's Global Leadership award, 2004. Office: CFTC Three Lafayette Ctr 1155 21st St NW Washington DC 20581 Office Phone: 202-418-5000. Office Fax: 202-418-5514.*

BROWNING, BECKY BECK, elementary school educator; b. Lufkin, Tex., July 3, 1944; d. H.V. and Jo Marie (Nerren) Beck; m. Grayson Douglas Browning, July 15, 1972. BS, U. Tex., 1971, MEd, 1976. Cert. in spl. edn. (visually impaired and emotional disturbance), Tex. Spl. edn. tchr. Ortega Elem. Sch., Austin, Tex., 1971-85; tchr. 5th grade, Philosphy for Children program facilitator Lee Elem. Sch., Austin, 1985-98; ret., 1999. Vis. scholar Tex. Wesleyan U., Ft. Worth, summer 1993, Creative and Critical Tchg. Ctr., Ft. Worth, summer 1994. Contbr. chpt. to book, articles to profl. jours.

BROWNING, CANDACE, corporate financial executive; B in Hist., Brandeis U., 1977; MBA in Mktg., Columbia U., 1979. Analyst airline industry; rsch. analyst Merrill Lynch and Co., NYC, 1990, dir. equity rsch. for Ams. region, 2001—03, sr. v.p., head global securities rsch. and econs. group, 2003—; dep. dir. global rsch. product Pan-Europe MLEMEA Rsch. Mgmt., London, 2000—01. Mem.: Soc. Airline Analysts, Wings Club (bd. dirs.). Office: Merrill Lynch & Co Inc 4 World Fin Ctr 250 Vesey St New York NY 10080

BROWNING, CHARLOTTE ELISABETH, social studies educator; d. Carol Redfield Vizzini and Edward Tracy Browning. Student, Dalhousie U., Halifax, Nova Scotia, 1990—92; BA (hon.), Conn. Coll., New London, 1994; MA, Coll. N.J., Ewing, 1997. Lic. secondary edn. N.J., 1997. Houseparent, non-resident Am. Boychoir Sch., Princeton, NJ, libr., 1994—2003, tour tutor, 2000—, asst. english tchr., resource tchr., 2000—03, acad. advisor, 2000—, social studies tchr. grades 6-8, 2003—. Avocations: canoeing, crafts, gardening. Office: American Boychoir Sch 19 Lambert Dr Princeton NJ 08540 Office Phone: 609-924-5858.

BROWNING, EMILY ROSE, science educator; b. Hialeah, Fla., Mar. 21, 1977; d. Timothy James and Rose Marie Browning. BS in Biology, W.Va. U. Tech., Montgomery, 1999; MA in Biol. Sci., Marshall U., Huntington, W.Va., 2001. Internship coord. career ctr. Marshall U., Huntington, 2000; adj. biology instr. U. Charleston, W.Va., 2001; adj. anatomy and physiology instr. W.Va. U. Tech., Montomery, 2001—02; vis. instr. biology Glenville (W.Va.) State Coll., 2002—03, vis. instr. environ. sci., 2003—06. Mem. adv. bd. Gilmer Watershed Coalition, Glenville, 2003—06; advisor GSC Environ. Orgn., Glenville, 2005—06. Recipient Renaissance of Shared Values Fairness award, Glenville State Coll., 2003. Mem.: Nat. Assn. Biology Tchrs., Nat. Sci. Tchrs. Assn., Chi Beta Phi (sec. alpha iota chpt. 2005—06). Business E-Mail: emilybrowning2002@yahoo.com.

BROWNING, JANE LOUISE, social services administrator; b. Omaha, Dec. 7, 1947; d. Dale Paul and Esther Lucille (Quick) Schmidt; m. John William Browning III, July 29, 1978; children: John William IV, Paul Cornelius. Student, Northwestern U., 1966-68; BA in English Lit. cum laude, U. Tex., Dallas, 1978. Citizen advocacy coord. The Arc of Denver, 1972-74; pub. info. specialist The Arc of the U.S., Arlington, Tex., 1974-78; asst. dir. Ark. Endowment for Humanities, Little Rock, 1979-82, exec. dir., 1982-89; pres., CEO Word Work, Little Rock, 1989-90; dir. devel. The Arc of Md., Annapolis, 1991-95; exec. dir. Md. Coalition for Inclusive Edn., Balt., 1995-96; dir. divsn. membership & publs. NASW, Washington, 1997-98; exec. dir President's com. on mental retardation, Washington, 1999—2000; dep. dir. Nat. Assn. Women Judges, 2001; exec. dir. Learning Disabilities Assn., 2001—05, Internat. Cmty. Corrections Assn., 2005—. Exec. com. Ark. Developmental Disabilities Coun., Little Rock, 1982-87; appointee, mem. Pres.'s Com. on Mental Retardation, Washington, 1994-2000; mem. nominating com. The Arc-U.S., The Arc-U.S. Congress States, 1997-99; treas. Arc-Anne Arundel County, 2004—. Co-author: (textbook) An Arkansas History for Young People, 1991, 3d edit., 2002. Mem. PEO, Am. Soc. Assn. Execs. Democrat. Episcopalian. Business E-Mail: jbrowning@iccaweb.org.

BROWNING, SARA LOUISE, science educator; b. Aurora, Ill., Sept. 2, 1973; d. Robert Edward and Nancy Catherine Jung; m. Fred Joseph Browning, June 18, 1994; children: Alice Catherine, Jill Olivia. AS, Waubonsee C.C., Sugar Grove, Ill., 1993; BS in Liberal Arts magna cum laude, U. Ill., Champaign/Urbana, 1995; MS, No. Ill. U., DeKalb, 1997. Biology instr. Judson Coll., Elgin, 1998, Elgin C.C., Ill., 1998—99; sci. instr. Westminster Christian H.S., Elgin, 1998—2001; biology instr. Palm Beach Atlantic U., West Palm Beach, Fla., 2004—. Sponsor World Vision, 1993—; group leader La Leche League Internat., West Palm Beach, 2004—; conf. spkr. La Leche League, West Palm Beach; master gardener U. Fla. Master Gardener Ext., West Palm Beach, 2004—; conf. spkr. La Leche League Internat., Orlando, 2005, pub. spkr. Palm Beach Gardens, Fla., 2005. Christian. Avocation: gardening. Office: Palm Beach Atlantic Univ 901 S Flagler West Palm Beach FL 33401 Office Phone: 561-803-2285. Business E-Mail: sara_browning@pba.edu.

BROWNING, SINCLAIR, writer; b. Long Beach, Calif., Nov. 17, 1946; d. George William Sinclair, Rowena Mae Morse; m. William Docker Browning, Dec. 17, 1974; 1 child, Benjamin Sinclair stepchildren: Christopher, Logan, Courtenay; m. Allyn D. Bates, Sept. 2, 1966 (div. Aug. 1974). BA in Lit. and Creative Writing, U. Ariz., Tuscon, 1970. Judge Shamus Awards Pvt. Eye Writers, 2001; judge Edgar Awards Mystery Writers of Am., N.Y.C., 2002; judge best 1st novel St. Martin's Press, 2000; judge best novel Edgar, 2002, Shamus, 2005. Author: Enju, 1983, America's Best, 1995, The Last Song Dogs, 1999, The Sporting Club, 2000, Rode Hard, Put Away Dead, 2001, Crack Shot, 2002, Tragady Ann, 2003; co-author: Lyons on Horses, 1991; editor: Feathers Brush My Heart, 2002; contbr. various anthologies. Nominee Ariz. Arts award, 2000, Shamus award for best paperback novel, 1999, 2000, Barry award for best paperback novel, 1999, 2001. Mem.: Internat. Thriller Writers, Private Eye Writers of Am., Internat. Assn. of Crime Writers, Sisters in Crime, Mystery Writers of Am., Authors Guild. Avocations: horseback riding, reading. Mailing: PO Box 1007 Sonoita AZ 85637

BROWNLEE, DELPHINE, actress, musician; b. Paris, July 19, 1930; d. John Donald and Carla (Oddone) B.; m. Dan Oluf Eriksen, Apr. 24,1954 (div. June 1958); 1 child, Lynn Michele; m. Theodore Robert Bashkow, Sept. 12, 1960. Grad., Neighborhood Playhouse, N.Y., 1949. Tchr. pvt. studio, 1977—; adj. prof. Montclair State U., 1981-84; faculty Conservatory Hackley Sch., 1985-90, Mt. Kisco Sch. Music. Several voice overs for TV and radio commercials, recitals at Carnegie Recital Hall, opera performances with Singers Theatre; original cast of Man of La Mancha, Fade-Out, Fade-In, Here's Love, Carnival, others. Mem. N.Y. Singing Tchrs. Assn., N.Y. State Music Tchrs. Assn., Nat. Coun. Jewish Women (past pres. No. Westchester sect. 1971-73), Actor's Equity Assn., Screen Actors Guild, Am. Federations TV and Radio Artists. Avocations: gardening, reading, birdwatching. Home: 92 Jay St Katonah NY 10536-3729 Personal E-mail: delkatonah@verizon.net.

BROWNLEE, PAULA PIMLOTT, higher education consultant; b. London, June 23, 1934; came to US, 1959; d. John Richard and Alice A. (Ajamian) Pimlott; m. Thomas H. Brownlee, Feb. 10, 1961; children: Kenneth Gainsford, Elizabeth Ann, Clare Louise. BA with honors, Somerville Coll., Oxford U., Eng., 1957, PhD in Organic Chemistry, 1959. Postdoctoral fellow U. Rochester, NY, 1959-61; rsch. chemist Am. Cyanamid Co., Stamford, Conn., 1961-62; lectr. U. Bridgeport, Conn., 1968-70; asst. prof., then assoc. prof. Rutgers U., NJ, 1970-76, assoc. dean, then acting dean Douglass Coll. NJ, 1972-76; dean faculty, prof. chemistry Union Coll., Schenectady, NY, 1976-81; pres., prof. chemistry Hollins U., Va., 1981-90; pres. Assn. Am. Colls. and Univs., Washington, 1990-98; prin. Pres.' Group, LLC, 1997—2003; founding prin. Nat. Acad. for Acad. Leadership. Bd. dirs. Acad. Search Consultation Svc. Contbr. articles to profl. jours., chapters to books. Sr. trustee U. Rochester; trustee Wilson Coll., Pa. Hon. fellow Somerville Coll., Oxford, Eng., 1996—. Mem. Am. Chem. Soc., Sigma Xi. Episcopalian. Office Phone: 540-869-7066. E-mail: pbrownlee@hughes.net.

BROWN-OLMSTEAD, AMANDA, public relations executive; b. Oct. 7, 1943; Founder ABOA (formerly a divsn. Shandwick PLC), 1972; pres., CEO A Brown Olmstead Assocs., Atlanta. Mem. Atlanta Pub. Rels. Seminar Group. Bd. dirs. Ctrl. Atlanta Progress, Councilors for The Carter Ctr., Atlanta Bot. Garden; mem. adv. bd. Sheperd Spinal Ctr., U. Miss. Bus. Sch.; mem. adv. guild Clark U.; pres. Ga. chpt. Internat. Women's Forum; mem. exec. com. Regional Bus. Coalition, bd. dirs., Atlanta Regional Health Forum; mem. exec. com. Robinson Coll. Bus., chair Hall of Fame program. Named a Recognized Woman of Achievement, Internat. Women's Forum; named one of The Ten Outstanding Atlantans; named to Georgia Pub. Rels. Hall of Fame; recipient Gold medal, N.Y. Film and TV Festival; YWCA honoree, Salute to Women of Achievement. Fellow: Pub. Rels. Soc. Am. (mem. Counselors Acad., mem. eligibility bd., Silver Anvil award); mem.: Order of the Phoenix, Leadership Atlanta. Achievements include being featured in Mademoiselle magazine, Business Week, Savvy, Atlanta Weekly, Atlanta magazine, and Movers and Shakers in Georgia. Office: A Brown Olmstead Assocs 274 W Paces Ferry Rd NW Atlanta GA 30305-1167

BROWNSON, MARY LOUISE, counselor, educator, artist; b. Detroit, Dec. 8, 1927; d. Max Curt Poppe and Hilda Caroline Larson; m. Elwyn James Brownson, Dec. 30, 1950 (div. Sept. 1979); children: Elwyn James, Richard, Matthew, Mary. B of Design, U. Mich., Ann Arbor, 1950; MS, No. Mont. Coll., Havre, 1976. Cert. secondary sch. tchr. Mont., 1972. Instr. Wittenburg U., Springfield, Ohio, 1950—53, No. Mont. Coll., Havre, 1963—71; drug and alcohol counselor Alcohol Svcs. Ctr., Boise, Idaho, 1979—80; migrant career placement counselor Boise State U., Idaho, 1981—85; mgr. Ctr. Use, Boise Sr. Ctr., Idaho, 1985—88; employment counselor Fed. Cmty. Treatment Ctr., Boise, Idaho, 1988—90; mgr. activities Hillcrest Retirement Ctr., Boise, Idaho, 1990—94. Represented in permanent collections, Kent State U. Collection. Pres. PTA, Havre, Mont.; Dem. candidate for state legislature Havre, Mont. Mem.: AAUW (pres.), LWV (pres. 1999—2003). Democrat. Unitarian-Universalist. Avocations: gourmet cooking, swimming, reading, painting. Home: 3820 Sheringham Dr Boise ID 83704 Personal E-mail: mlbrownson@hotmail.com.

BROWNSTEIN, BARBARA LAVIN, geneticist, educator, director; b. Phila., Sept. 8, 1931; d. Edward A. and Rose (Silverstein) Lavin; m. Melvin Brownstein, June 1949 (div. 1955); children: Judith Brownstein Kaufmann, Dena. Asst. editor Biol. Abstracts, Phila., 1957-58; research fellow dept. microbial genetics Karolinska Inst., Stockholm, 1962-64; assoc. Wistar Inst., Phila., 1964-68; assoc. prof. molecular biology, dept. biology Temple U., Phila., 1968-74, prof., 1974-96, prof. emeritus, 1996—, chmn. dept., 1978-81, provost, 1983-90; sr. assoc. Ctr. Ednl. Rsch. U. Wash., Seattle, 1994—. Vis. scientist dept. tumor cell biology Imperial Cancer Rsch. Fund Labs., London, 1973-74; bd. dirs. Univ. City Sci. Ctr., Greater Phila. Econ. Devel. Coun., Forum Exec. Women; program officer NSF, 1992-93; sr. assoc. Inst. Ednl. Inquiry, Seattle, 1994—. Bd. dirs. Lopez Island Sch., 2001—. Recipient Liberal Arts Alumni award for excellence in teaching Temple U., 1980; recipient Outstanding Faculty Woman award Temple U., 1980 Fellow AAAS; mem. Am. Soc. Cell Biology, N.Y. Acad. Sci., Assn. Women in Sci., NSF (program officer 1992-93). Home: PO Box 835 Lopez Island WA 98261 Personal E-mail: bbrownst@msn.com.

BROWNSTEIN, ELIZABETH SMITH, writer; d. Frank Edward and Grace Hanrahan Smith; m. Arnold Wallace Brownstein, Oct. 12, 1967 (div. 1973). BA in Polit. sci., Wellesley Coll., 1952; MSc in Internat. Rels., London Sch. Econs. and Polit. Sci., 1967. Chief TV rschr. CBS, 1952—56, chief TV rschr. Meet the Press, 1958—60; dir. The Experiment in Internat. Living, N.Y.C., 1960—66; assoc. prodr., writer Evening Edit. with Martin Agronsky, 1971—76; exec. prodr., program devel. mgr., asst. program mgr. WETA-TV, Washington, 1976—82. Author: If This House Could Talk, 1999, Lincoln's Other White House, 2005; dir. rsch.: (TV series) Smithsonian World, 1982—87; coord. prodr.: Smithsonian Video Collection, 1989—92. Mem.: Soc. Woman Geographers (sec. nat. exec. coun. 1990—96, Washington Group rep. 1996—2002, 2004—05, v.p. 2005—), Alumni and Friends of

London Sch. Econs. (exec. v.p. 1977—80, bd. dirs. 1977—, pres. 1980—82), Washington Press Club (bd. govs. 1979—83), Nat. Press Club. Democrat. Unitarian. Avocations: walking holidays, swimming, reading, films.

BROWN THOMAS, RYNN, elementary school educator; b. Fort Lauderdale, Fla., Aug. 1927; d. Shelia Green and Joseph Brown; m. Thomas, Nov. 20, 2005; children: Olivia R. Thomas, Ashleigh A. Thomas. MBA, AIU, Plantaion, Fla., 2003. Cert. tchr. Fla., 2004. Tchr. Broward County Sch. Bd./ Millenium Mid., Tamarac, Fla., 2004—. Mem. Abyssinian Bapt. Ch., Pompano Beach, Fla., 1995. Home: 471 Banks Rd Margate FL 33063 Office: Millennium Mid Sch Tamarac FL

BROWN-WAITE, VIRGINIA (GINNY BROWN-WAITE), congresswoman; b. Albany, NY, Oct. 5, 1943; m. Harvey Waite; children: Jeannine Bradford, Danene Mitchell, Lorie Sue Busiere. BS, SUNY, 1976; MS, Russell Sage Coll., 1984. Legis. dir. NY State Senate, 1970—87; commr. Hernando County Bd. of Commr., 1991—93; mem. Fla. State Senate, 1992—2002, US Congress from 5th Fla. dist., 2003—; mem. fin. svcs. com., govt. reform com., vet. affairs com. Adj. prof. Springfield Coll.; owner Mr. Donut franchise. Active W Hernando GOP, United Way; bd. dirs. Hernando County Spouse Abuse Ctr. Mem. Bus. and Profl. Women's Club, Suncoast MG Club. Republican. Roman Catholic. Office: Dist Office 38008 Meridian Ave Dade City FL 33526 Office Phone: 202-225-1000.

BROWN WEISS, EDITH, law educator; b. Salem, Oreg., Feb. 19, 1942; d. Leon M. and Edith E. Brown; m. Charles Weiss, Jr., July 24, 1969; children: Jed, Tamara. AB, Stanford U., 1963; JD, Harvard U., 1966; PhD, U. Calif., Berkeley, 1973; DDL (hon.), Chgo.-Kent Coll. Law, 1993. Bar: DC 1967, US Ct. Claims 1967. Atty. advisor ACDA, Washington, 1966-68; rsch. assoc. Columbia U., NYC, 1970-72, Brookings Instn., Washington, 1972-74; asst. prof. civil engring. and politics Princeton U., 1974-78; prof. law Georgetown U., Washington, 1978—, Francis Cabell Brown prof. internat. law, 1996—. Cons. UN Environ. Program, 1974—78, 1994—97, 2000—01, UNU, 1983—98; assoc. gen. counsel internat. law EPA, 1990—92; chmn. com. on rsch. on global environ. change Social Sci. Rsch. Coun., 1989—94; spl. legal advisor, N.Am. Commn. Environ. Coop., 1995—2002; bd. trustees Ctr. Internat. Environ. Law, 2001—02; mem. inspection panel World Bank, 2002—07, chmn. inspection panel, 2003—. Author: (with Jacobson) Engaging Countries: Strengthening Compliance with International Environment Accords, 1998, (with Jackson) Reconciling Environment and Trade, 2001, In Fairness to Future Generations: International Law, Common Patrimony and Intergenerational Equity, 1989, Environmental Change and International Law, 1992, (with Boisson de Cazournes and Bernasconi-Osterwalder) Fresh Water and International Economic Law, 2005; mem. bd. editors Am. Jour. Internat. Law, Jour. Internat. Econ. Law, Environment, Transnat. Press, Global Environ. Politics, Internat. Environ. Agreements, Politics, Law and Econs., Berkeley Jour. Internat. Law; contbr. articles to profl. jours. Recipient Dinkelspiel award Stanford U., 1963, Leland T. Chapin award, 1962, Mellinkoff award, 1963; Harold and Margaret Sprout award, 1979, Elizabeth Haub prize, 1994, Prominent Woman in Internat. Law award Am. Soc. Internat. Law, 1996; Woodrow Wilson fellow, 1968. Mem. ABA (vice chmn. internat. environ. law com., Individual award for disting. achievement environ. law and policy, 2003), Am. Soc. Internat. Law (chmn. ann meeting 1979, exec. coun. 1981-85, v.p. 1983-85, pres. 1994-96, Cert. Merit 1990), NAS (environ. studies bd. 1981-84, vice chair US nat. com. for SCOPE 1984-85, water sci. and tech. bd. 1985-88, commn. on geoscis., environment and resources 1992-95), Internat. Inst. Applied Sys. Analysis (vice chair US nat. com. 1993-98), Coun. Fgn. Rels., Am. Law Inst., Internat. Coun. Environ. Law, Cousteau Soc. (coun. advs. 1992-2002), Japanese Inst. Global Environ Strategies (bd. dirs. 1996-2003), Nat. Ctr. for Atmospheric Rsch. (adv. coun. 2001-04), Phi Beta Kappa, Sigma Xi. Office: Georgetown Univ Law Ctr 600 New Jersey Ave NW Washington DC 20001 Office Phone: 202-662-9000.

BROWN-ZEKERI, LOLITA MOLANDA, elementary school educator; b. Stephens County, Mar. 15, 1963; d. James and Doris (Phillips) Brown; m. Austin Zekeri, Nov. 21, 1998; 1 child, Annabelle Lola. BS with honors, North Ga. Coll., 1985, MEd, 1989, EdS, 1994. Cert. tchr. Tchr., 2nd grade Jackson County Bd. Edn., Nicholson, Ga., 1985-87, chpt. 1 tchr., 1987—98, third grade tchr., 1998—. Chmn. grade level Jackson County Bd. Edn., 2002—03. Author: Exploring Blue Highways, 1995; co-author: Making Learning Funner, So People Want To Learn, A Longitudinal Study of Students' Perceptions About Schooling. Active Paradise AME Ch. trustee 1986-99, asst. Sun. Sch. sec. 1986-99, Sun. Sch. sec., 1999—, young adult choir mem. 1987-2001, Christian Edn. Youth Dept. 2d v.p. 1988—, Vacation Bible Sch. art coord. and tchr. 1986—. Mem. Ga. Edn. Assn., Assn. Childhood Educators Internat., North Ga. Coll. Union Bd. (chmn. decorations/hospitality com. 1983-84, sec. 1984-85), Benton Parent/Tchr. Orgn.

BROXTERMAN, LISA, secondary school educator; d. Eddie and Shirley Spangler; m. Terry Broxterman, Aug. 7, 1982; children: David, Jordan, Caleb, Jacob, Mariah. EdB, Kans. State U., Manhattan, 1991, M in Secondary Edn., 2001. Cert. tchr. Kans., 1992. English tchr. Frankfort H.S., Kans., 1992—95, Axtell H.S., Kans., 1995—. Office: Axtell High School 504 Pine Axtell KS 66403 Office Phone: 785-736-2237.

BROYLES, BONITA EILEEN, nursing educator; b. Ross County, Ohio, Sept. 29, 1948; d. Arthur Runnels and Mary Elizabeth (Page) Brookie; m. Roger F. Broyles, Dec. 29, 1984; children: Michael Richard Brown, Jeffrey Allen Brown. BSN, Ohio State U., 1970; MA with honors, N.C. Cen. U., Durham, 1988; EdD summa cum laude, LaSalle U., 1996; PhD, St. Regis U., 2004. ADN instr., CPR instr. Piedmont C.C., Roxboro, N.C.; instr. nursing Watts Sch. Nursing, Durham; res. float staff nurse Durham County Gen. Hosp., Durham; dir. practical nursing edn., instr. Piedmont C.C., Roxboro, N.C.; maternity patient tchr. Mt. Carmel Med. Ctr., Columbus, Ohio. Second-level coord. assoc. degree nursing faculty Piedmont Community Coll., 1990—. Co-author: Test Manual for Bowden, Dickey, Greenberg Children and Their Families: The Continuum of Care, 1998; author: Clinical Companion for Ashwill and Droske Nursing of Children: Principles and Practice, 1997; author: (with Reiss and Evans) Pharmacological Aspects of Nursing Care, revised 6th edit., 2002; author: Dosage Calculation Practice for Nurses, 2003, Medical-Surgical Nursing Clinical Companion, 2005, Clinical Decision Making: Case Studies in Pediatrics, 2005, Thomson Delmar Learning's Case Studies Series: Pediatrics, 2005. Named ADN Educator of Yr. N.C. Assoc. Degree Nursing Coun., 1993; recipient nat. tchg. excellence award Nat. Inst. Staff Orgnl. Devel., U. Tex., Austin, 1998, Faculty Excellence award Piedmont C.C., 2001, 04. Office: Piedmont CC Sch Nursing College St Roxboro NC 27573 Office Phone: 336-599-1181. Business E-Mail: broyleb@piedmontcc.edu.

BROYLES, CHRISTINE ANNE, art educator; d. H.C. and Dorothy E. Lippstreuer; m. Robert E. Broyles, Dec. 30, 1989. BFA, B in Art Edn., U. South Fla., 1981. Cert. tchr. Fla., Nat. Assn. Underwater Instrs. Intern Charlotte County Pub. Schs., Port Charlotte, Fla., 1981, sci. tchr. Lemon Bay H.S., 1981—83, art instr. grades 6-8 L. A. Ainger Mid. Sch. Rotonda West, Fla., 1984—; adult edn. tchr. (arts and GED) Charlotte County Adult and Cmty. Edn., Englewood, Fla., 1982—85; adult edn. tchr. (arts) Sarasota (Fla.) Vocat. and Tech. Sch., 1982—85, Venice (Fla.) Area Art League, 1982—86; freelancer, guest writer Suncoast Media Group, Venice, 1982—. Layout editor Charlotte County Lit. and Fine Arts Mag., Port Charlotte, 1999—2001; mem. supt.'s roundtable forum Charlotte County Pub. Schs., Port Charlotte, 1999—2001, secondary fine arts liason, 1998—, dept. head (elective subjects) L. A. Ainger Mid. Sch., Rotonda West, 2000—, EXCEL mentor tchr., Port Charlotte, 1999—, mem. code of student conduct com., 1999, mem. pupil progression plan com., 99, mem. student assistance team, 2000; trainer Beacon Learning Ctr., Panama City, Fla., 2001—; webmaster, co-creator, editor The Art Web; dir. instrnl. pers. Charlotte County Classified and Tchrs. Assn., Punta Gorda, 1995—96, v.p., 1996—98; mem. specification and validation com. Fla. Tchr. Certification Exam, 1984, 2004, tech. and lit. coun., 1999—; facilitator Profl. Learning Cmty., 2004—; presenter in field. Author: (teacher resource book) Art Across the Curriculum. Named Educator of Yr., Sunshine Rotary of Englewood, 1998, Tchr. of Yr. (local), Wal-Mart, 1998, Sam's Club, 1998; recipient Best of Show award, Arts and Humanities Coun. Port Charlotte, 1999; grantee, Fla. Arts and Humanities Coun., 1996—98, Fla. Arts and Humanities Coun., 2002—04; scholar, Am. Legion Aux., 1975—80; arts program scholar, Fla. Ctr. for Tchrs., 2000. Mem.: Fla. Art Edn. Assn., Fla. League Tchrs. (mem. league bd. 1999—, 2004—), Nat. Art Edn. Assn. Avocations: scuba diving, travel, arts, antiquing. Office: L A Ainger Mid Sch 245 Cougar Way Rotonda West FL 33947 Office Phone: 941-697-5800. Business E-Mail: christine_broyles@ccps.k12.fl.us.

BROYLES, DEBORAH J., lawyer; b. Worcester, Mass., July 8, 1963; BA, Mt. Holyoke Coll., 1985; JD, Harvard U., 1993. Bar: Calif. 1993, US Ct. Appeals (9th Cir.), US Dist. Ct. (No. Dist.) Calif., US Dist. Ct. (Ea. Dist.) Calif., US Dist. (Ctrl. Dist.) Calif., US Dist. Ct. (So. Dist.) Calif. Ptnr., Diversity Com. Thelen Reid & Priest LLP, San Francisco. Mem.: Charles Houston Bar Assn., Nat. Bar Assn., Nat. Employment Law Coun., Calif. Minority Counsel Program (steering com. 2004—05), Calif. Assn. of Black Lawyers (ann. convention co-chmn. 1996, v.p.-north 1998—99, jud. appointments com. 1999—2002), Bar Assn. San Francisco, ABA. Office: Thelen Reid & Priest LLP 101 Second St Ste 1800 San Francisco CA 94105-3601 Office Phone: 415-369-7203. Office Fax: 415-371-1211. Business E-Mail: djbroyles@thelenreid.com.

BROYLES, JENNIFER KAYE, elementary school educator; b. Naples, Fla., Feb. 12, 1978; d. James B. and Marilyn L. Broyles. BA, Clemson U., S.C., 2000. 3d grade tchr. Whitehall Elem. Sch., Anderson, SC, 2001—. Sec. Electric City Playhouse, Anderson, SC, 2006; local exec. dir. Miss Anderson County Pageant, 2005. Avocations: community theater, singing. Home: 116 Reed Pl Anderson SC 29621 Office: Whitehall Elementary School 702 Whitehall Rd Anderson SC 29625

BROZMAN, TINA L., federal judge; b. 1952; BA, NYU, 1973; JD, Fordham U., 1976. Ptnr. Anderson Russell Kill & Olick, 1976—85; judge U.S. Bankruptcy Ct. So. Dist. N.Y., N.Y.C., 1985—96, chief judge, 1996—2000; ptnr. Bingham McCutchen LLP, N.Y.C., 2000—, chairperson fin. restructuring practice group. Lectr. Practicing Law Inst., 1987. Fellow: Am. Coll. Bankruptcy (second cir. nominating com.); mem.: Bankruptcy Appellate Panel U.S. Ct. Appeals, second cir., Assn. Bar City N.Y. (bankruptcy & corp. reorganization com.), Am. Bankruptcy Inst., Nat. Conf. Bankruptcy Judges (former second cir. governor), Internat. Insolvency Inst. (elected), Am. Law Inst. (elected), UN Commn. Internat. Trade Law, INSOL Internat. (founder & former chairperson Judge's divsn.). Office: Bingham McCutchen LLP 399 Park Avenue New York NY 10022-4689 Office Phone: 212-705-7756. Business E-Mail: tina.brozman@bingham.com.

BRUBACH, HOLLY BETH, writer; b. Pitts., Dec. 7, 1953; d. David J. and Dorothy Elizabeth (DeRusha) B. BA in English and History, Duke U., 1975. Freelance writer, 1975-78; staff writer Vogue mag., N.Y.C., 1978-82, contbg. editor, 1983-87; staff writer The Atlantic, Boston, 1982-87; fashion editor The New Yorker, N.Y.C., 1988—94, The New York Times Mag., N.Y.C., 1994—98; dir. home design Prada, N.Y.C., 1998—2001. Author: (with others) Choura: The Memoirs of Alexandra Danilova, 1986 (De La Torre Bueno award), Girlfriend: Men, Women and Drag, 1999, A Dedicated Follower of Fashion, 1999; scriptwriter Dance in America, 1980. Recipient Nat. Mag. award Am. Soc. Mag. Editors, 1982. Mem. Dance Critics Assn., Writers Guild Am. Presbyterian.

BRUBAKER, KAREN SUE, small business owner; b. Ashland, Ohio, Feb. 5, 1953; d. Robert Eugene and Dora Louise (Camp) Brubaker; m. Philip J. Potter, Oct. 10, 2003. BSBA, Ashland U., 1975; MBA, Bowling Green State U., 1976. Supr. tire ctr. ops. B.F. Goodrich Co., Akron, Ohio, 1976-77, supr. tire ctr. acctg., 1977-79, asst. product mgr. radial passenger tires, 1979-80, product mgr. broadline passenger tires, 1980-81, group product mgr. broadline passenger and light truck tires, 1981-83, mktg. mgr. T/A high tech radials, 1983-86; product mktg. mgr. B.F. Goodrich T/A radials The Uniroyal Goodrich Tire Co., Akron, Ohio, 1986-91; product mktg. mgr. Michelin performance tires Michelin Americas Small Tires, Akron, Ohio, 1991-95; ind. EcoQuest Internat. distbr. DBA Indoor Air Repair & Water, Fairlawn, Ohio, 1996—. Sect. chmn. indsl. divsn. United Way, Akron, 1983-86; mem. adv. coun. to trustees Coll. Bus. and Econs, Ashland U., 1990-92; vol. Hospice Vis. Nurses Svcs., 1995--; fund raiser Nat. Heart Assist and Transplant Fund/Judi Reali Transplant Fund, 1996. Recipient Alumni Disting. Service award Ashland Coll., 1986; Alpha Phi Clara Bradley Burdette scholar, 1975. Mem. Am. Mktg. Assn. (pres. Akron/Canton chpt. 1982-83, Highest Honors award 1983, nat. bd. dirs., v.p. bus. mktg. 1984-86, v.p. profl. chpts. 1987-89), Sales and Mktg. Execs. (v.p. membership, 1998-99), Akron Women's Network, Zonta Internat. (membership dir. 1987-94, 96—), Beta Gamma Sigma, Omicron Delta Epsilon. Home: 822 Village Pkwy Fairlawn OH 44333-3297 Office Phone: 330-666-9330. Personal E-mail: airwaves@bigplanet.com.

BRUBECK, MARCIA ELLEN, psychotherapist; b. Balt., Mar. 1, 1948; d. William Hurst and Margaret Bramwell Brubeck. Attended, Swarthmore Coll., Pa., 1965—69; BA, George Washington U., Wash., DC, 1970; JD, U. Conn., Hartford, 1992; MSW, U. Conn., West Hartford, 1995. Bar: Conn.; diplomate clin. forensic counseling Am. Coll. Certified Forensic Counselors; cert. sch. social worker Conn., lic. clin. social worker Conn., cert. social work field instr. U. Conn., parent assistor Learning Disabilities Assn. Promotion mgr. Temple U. Press, Phila., 1971—74; promotion assoc. Princeton U. Press, NJ, 1974—77; manuscript editor Yale U. Press, New Haven, 1979—81; primary therapist Elmcrest Psychiat. Inst., Portland, Conn., 1995—96, Children's Ctr., Hamden, Conn., 1996—98, Village for Families and Children, Hartford, Conn., 1998—2000; pvt. practice Hartford, 2000—. Contbr. articles various profl. jours.; prodr.: Great Kids, Great Families. Starr fellowship, U. Conn. Sch. Law, 1990. Mem.: Learning Disabilities Assn., Conn. Soc. Clin. Social Work, Nat. Assn. Forensic Counselors, Am. Group Psychotherapy Assn., Nat. Assn. Social Workers. Avocations: antiques, gardening, writing, strategy games, nature. Office: 674 Prospect Ave 3RR Hartford CT 06105 Office Phone: 860-231-1997. Office Fax: 860-231-1960.

BRUCE, BRENDA, pianist; b. Nov. 26, 1942; d. Leo Allen and Dorotha Mae (Russell) Bruce; m. Emmett W. Windham, Feb. 21, 1976 (div. Aug. 1988); m. Alvin Mark Fountain II, June, 2003. BMusic Edn., Ctrl. Meth. Coll., Fayette, Mo., 1964; MMus, New Eng. Conservatory, Boston, 1966; student piano master class, Claude Debussy Conservatory, St. Malo, France, 2000-01. Mem. faculty Dana Sch. Music, Wellesley, Mass., 1965-76, Campbell U., Buies Creek, N.C., 1977-79, Meredith Coll., Raleigh, N.C., 1979-90; pianist SAS Inst., Cary, NC, 1989—2001. Mem. adv. bd. Capitol Area Cmty. Chorus, Raleigh, 1999—; participant Master Class Pro Musica, St. Malo, France, 2000, 01, Sopron, Hungary, 2004; bd. dirs. Raleigh Chamber Music Guild. Performer, recitalist, 1964—, montage and piano, flute duo, 1992. Emerging Artists grantee City of Raleigh, 1992, Emerging Artists grantee United Arts, 1995, State Arts Coun. grantee, 1995—, regional artists grantee, 1999-2001, NCMTA grantee. Mem. Nat. Music Tchrs. Assn., Nat. Guild of Piano, Raleigh Piano Tchrs. Assn., Cary-Apex Piano Tchrs. Assn.; Pi Kappa Lampda. Mem. Christian Ch. Avocations: bicycling, travel, Polish dancing. Home: 103 Birkhaven Dr Cary NC 27511 Office Phone: 919-233-5200. E-mail: brendabruce@mindspring.com.

BRUCE, CAROL ELDER, lawyer; b. East Orange, NJ, June 7, 1949; BA, George Washington U., 1971, JD, 1974. Bar: DC 1975. Law clk. to Hon. Harold H. Greene, Chief Judge DC Superior Ct.; asst. atty. U.S. Dist. Atty. Office, Washington, 1975—85; ptnr. comml. litig. and white collar criminal def. Venable LLP, Washington; dep. ind. counsel in field. Mem., Lawyer Counseling Panel US Dist. Ct. (Dist. DC); faculty Georgetown U., Washington. Bd. adv. George Washington U. Law Ctr., Washington. Named a Top Washington Lawyer, criminal def., Washingtonian Mag., 2004, Leading Lawyer, litig., Legal Times, 2003. Master: Edward Bennett Williams Am. Inn of Ct. (charter mem.); fellow: Am. Coll. Trial Lawyers (internat. affairs com.); mem.: DC Bar Assn. (bd. gov.). Office: Venable LLP 575 7th St NW Washington DC 20004 Office Phone: 202-344-4717. Office Fax: 202-344-8300. Business E-Mail: cebruce@venable.com.

BRUCE, CHRYSTAL DAWN, chemistry professor; b. Hazard, Ky., Oct. 22, 1975; d. Phyllis Ann Ludtke; m. Robert Todd Bruce; 1 child, Rohan Sofia. BS, U. Tenn., Chattanooga, 1997; PhD, U. N.C., Chapel Hill, 2003. Rsch. lab. mgr. Microbial Insights Inc., 1997—98; rsch. asst. U. N.C., Chapel Hill, 1999—2003; asst. prof. Erskine Coll., Due West, SC, 2003—. Presenter in field. Contbr. articles to profl. jours. Recipient William E. Brock scholarship, U. Tenn., 1993; Grad. fellowship, NSF, 1999. Mem.: Am. Chem. Soc., Omicron Delta Kappa. Avocations: reading, gardening. Home: 4 Lindsay Ln Due West SC 29639 Office: Erskine Coll PO Box 338 Due West SC 29639 Office Phone: 864-379-6573. Business E-Mail: cbruce@erskine.edu.

BRUCE, JUDITH ESTHER, retired music educator, elementary school educator; b. St. Louis, Oct. 16, 1945; d. Charles Edward and Helen Ruth (Yost) Poleos; m. Roy N. Bruce; children: Rory, Robert, Joshua. BS in Edn., Southeast Mo. State U., 1967; MA in Theatre, Lindenwood U., 1992, MFA in Theatre, 1994. Tchr. vocal music Springdale Elem. Sch., Mo., 1967—77, DeSmet Elem. Sch., Florissant, Mo., 1977—85; tchr. vocal and MIE Yamaha Walnut Grove Elem. Sch., Ferguson, Mo., 1985—2002. Talent chmn., benefit charity shows, Christian Hosp. Aux., St. Louis, 1977-2000 Recipient Hall of Fame award, St. Louis Suburban Music Educators Assn., 2002—03. Mem.: St. Louis Suburban Music Educators Assn., Music Educators Nat. Conf., St. Louis Suburban Music Edc. Assn. (Hall of Fame award 2002—03, 2002—03), Ferguson-Florissant Cmty. Tchrs. Assn., Mo. State Tchrs. Assn. (treas. Ferguson-Florissant dist. chpt. 1985—2002), Raintree Arts Coun. of Lincoln and Pike Counties, White Shrine. Home: 17534 Highway NN Bowling Green MO 63334 E-mail: bruce45@earthlink.net.

BRUCE, MARY HANFORD, academic administrator, educator, writer; d. Francis Hamilton Baldy and Frances Lawson Waterfield; m. Guy Steven Bruce, Mar. 23, 1991; m. David Allan Terry, Oct. 6, 1962 (div. Jan. 8, 1980); children: David Hamilton Terry, John Hanford Terry. PhD, Ariz. State U., Tempe, 1986. Cert. tchr. Ariz., Tenn., Tex. Lectr. Memphis State U., 1968—69, Ariz. State U., Tempe, 1982—85; sr., Fulbright scholar Ecole Normale Superieure, Yaomde, Cameroon, 1988—90; dir. internat. children's reading, writing and tchg. program Monmouth Coll., Reading, England, 2001—04. Dir. Associated Programs of Midwest Program, Harare, Zimbabwe, 1995; writer-in-residence U. Dar es Salaam, Tanzania, 2004; tchr. Am. Cultural Studies Ctr. Moscow State U., 2006. Author: Holding to the Light, 1992, Dr. Sally's Voodoo Man, 2003, (short stories) Twin Bead, Echoes, Voodoo Faust, Swaying, C'est Le Parfum, They Only Laughed Later, numerous poems, articles. Recipient Fulbright scholarship, Russian State U. for Humanities, 2006; grantee, Mellon Found. Global Ptnrs., Kenya, 2000, 2002, Mellon Found. Global Ptnrs., Tanzania, 2004—. Mem.: AAUP, Associated Writing Programs. Home: 511 E Boston Monmouth IL 61462 Office: Monmouth Coll 700 E Broadway Monmouth IL 61462 Office Phone: 309-457-2183. Business E-Mail: mary@monm.edu.

BRUCE, MARYANN, bank executive; Grad., Duke Univ. Sr. v.p. OppenheimerFunds, 1985—97; sales exec. Allstate Ins. Co., 1998—99; pres., retail, high net worth sales, mktg. First Union Evergreen Investment Svcs. (now Wachovia), Boston, 1999—. Named one of Most Powerful Women in Banking, USBanker Mag., 2005. Office: Evergreen Investment Svcs 17th fl 200 Berkeley St PO Box 2121 Boston MA 02106 also: Evergreen Investment Svcs 401 S Tryon St Charlotte NC 28288

BRUCE, MELODY ANN, obstetrician-gynecologist; b. New Orleans, Apr. 26, 1953; d. John Markey and Irma Drusilla (Weisdorffer) B.; m. David Allan Ray, July 18, 1982; children: Isaac Michael Ray, Margaret Rose Ray, Arielle Elizabeth Ray. B.S., La. State U., Baton Rouge, 1975; M.D., La. State U.-New Orleans, 1978. Diplomate Am. Bd. Obstetrics and Gynecology. Intern, Albany (N.Y.) Med. Ctr., 1978-79, resident, 1979-81, chief resident, 1981-82; teaching cons. Kasturba Med. Coll., Manipal, Karnataka, India, 1982; practice medicine specializing in ob-gyn, Troy, N.Y., 1983-84; mem. med. adv. bd. Planned Parenthood, Upper Hudson Valley, N.Y. State, 1994—; chief dept. ob/gyn Samaritan Hosp., 1996-2005, pres. med. staff, 1997; med. dir. women health svcs., N.E. Health, 1997; chmn. adult edn. B'nai Sholom Synagogue, Albany, 1984-85; bd. dirs. Albany Symphony Orch., 1995—. Named Outstanding Young Woman of Am., Albany, 1980; named Outstanding Woman Resident Am. Med. Women's Assn., Albany Med. Ctr., 1981; recipient Physician of Yr. award N.E. Health Found., 2004. Fellow Am. Coll. Obstetricians/Gynecologists; mem. AMA, N.Y. State Med. Soc., Rensselaer County Med. Soc. Democrat. Home: 4 S Lyons Ave Menands NY 12204 Office: 2001 5th Ave Troy NY 12180-3340 Office Phone: 518-274-0476. Personal E-mail: mbruce@obgynhca.com.

BRUCE, NADINE CECILE, internist, educator; b. Oak Park, Ill., Apr. 6, 1942; d. Roy Alford and Henrietta Hedwige (Denk) B. BS in Chemistry, Coll. St. Francis, 1964; MD, U. Ill., 1970. Diplomate Nat. Bd. Internal Medicine, Nat. Bd. Med. Examiners. Resident in internal medicine St. Francis Integrated Med. Program, Honolulu, 1970-74; pvt. practice Honolulu, 1974-77; assoc. program dir. med. residency program U. Hawaii, Honolulu, 1974-87, dep. program dir., 1987-90, program dir., 1990-91; cons. internist Rehab. Hosp. of the Pacific, 1992—94. Mem. ACGME Internal Medicine Residency Rev. Com., 1994-2001, ACGME Transitional Rev. Com., 2001-, chmn., 2002-2004; asst. prof. U. Hawaii John A. Burns Sch. Medicine, 1974-89, assoc. prof., 1989-94; assoc. prof. medicine Case Western Reserve Sch. Medicine, 1995-2000, Northeastern Ohio Univs. Coll. Medicine, 2000-; program dir. internal medicine residency program Mt. Sinai Med. Ctr., Cleve., 1994-2000, St. Elizabeth Health Ctr., 2000-. V.p. bd. trustees Hawaii Bound Sch., 1977-80; bd. govs. Hawaii Med. Libr., 1980-85, Hawaii Blood Bank, 1983; mem. drug product selection bd. State of Hawaii, 1984-92, chmn., 1987-89. Fellow ACP (master; bd. govs. 1989-93); mem. N.Y. Acad. Scis., Soc. Gen. Internal Medicine, Am. Geriatrics Soc., Assn. Program Dirs. in Internal Medicine (councilor 2002-05), Am. Med. Dirs. Assn. Republican. Roman Catholic.

BRUCE, RAE MARIE, retired language educator; b. Waitsfield, Vt., Apr. 6, 1937; d. Kenneth Wilton and Esther Montgomery (Young) Cota; m. Rev. W. Ralph Bruce, July 7, 1979; children from previous marriage: Kenneth J. Stewart, Heather Stewart. BA in English Edn., U. N.H., Durham, 1959; MA, Rivier Coll., Nashua, N.H., 1988; MFA, Vt. Coll., 2004. Tchr. English Winthrop Sr. H.S., Mass., 1959—64, Rundlett Jr. H.S., Concord, NH, 1978—83, 1983—89, Merrimack H.S., NH, 1983—99. Tchr. rsch. and writing Rivier Coll., 1988, tchr. lit. to adolescents, 89; poetry chair New Eng. Assn. Tchrs. of English, 1998—2004; conf. co-chair N.H. Assn. Tchrs. of English, 1999—2002; mem. bd. N.H. Poetry Soc. Author: (poetry) various jours. including Jour. So. N.H. Coll., Poetry Rev., Spoon River, others; co-author: (book chpt.) Writing to Learn Sciences: Programs and Practices Writing Across the Curriculum, 1994; contbr. poetry to lit. publs. Leader poetry discussion Merrimack Pub. Libr., 2002—05; faciliator group devotional meditations writers Main St. United Meth. Ch., Nashua, 2003—. Finalist Tchr. of Yr., N.H., award for Excellence in Edn.; recipient Poet of Yr., New Eng. Assn. Tchrs. of English, 1996. Mem.: N.H. Pastel Soc., N.H. Poetry Soc., AWP. Avocation: painting. Home: 8 Burberry Ct Merrimack NH 03054 Personal E-mail: rae-marie.bruce@verizon.net.

BRUCE, VERNA LEE SMITH HICKEY, media specialist, librarian; b. Corbin, Ky., Feb. 16, 1935; d. William Abaslom and Ruthie Marie (McKeehan) Smith; m. Ralph Milton Hickey, June 2, 1956 (dec. Sept. 1981); m. Edward Bruce, June 22, 1991; stepchildren: Judy, Gary, Alisa. BA in Bus., Cumberland Coll., 1955, BS in Edn., 1968; MA in Libr. Sci., Union Coll., 1970; cert. in supervision, Ea. Ky. U., 1977. Cert. media specialist, libr., tchr., Ky. Typist Whitley County Court Clerk Office, Williamsburg, Ky., 1955-62; head bookkeeper Harlan (Ky.) Daily Enterprise, 1963-65; elem. tchr. Harlan County Bd. Edn., 1966-70; reading tchr. Boone County Bd. Edn., Florence,

Ky., 1970, media specialist, libr., 1970-95. Coach girls basketball, Burlington (Ky.) Elem. Sch., 1974-79, coord. girls basketball, 1979-94. Active Florence Bapt. Ch., 1970-95, mem. single adult ministry, 1970-90, choir mem., 1970-91; active Corinth Bapt. Ch., 1935-62, Calvery Bapt. Ch., Loyall, Ky., 1963-68, Chevelot Bapt. Ch., 1968-70; pres. PTA, Loyall, 1967-69, active other chpts.; mem. salary/contract com. Boone County Edn. Assn., 1990-94, mem., clerk, choir mem., Corinth (Ky.) Missionary Baptist. Recipient Lifetime Membership award PTA, 1994, No. Ky. Sch. Libr./Media Specialist award, 1995. Mem. NEA, Ky. Edn. Assn., No. Ky. Libr. Assn., Ky. Libr. Assn., Ky. Sch. Media Assn., Boone County Libr. Assn. (sec. 1980-91), Boone County Homemakers. Republican. Avocations: sports, crafts, travel, reading, entertaining. Home: 100 Birch Rd Corbin KY 40701-7956 Office Phone: 606-528-2581. E-mail: bruvl@juno.com.

BRUCH, CAROL SOPHIE, law educator; b. Rockford, Ill., June 11, 1941; d. Ernest and Margarete (Willstätter) B.; m. Jack E. Myers, 1960 (div. 1973); children: Margarete Louise Myers Feinstein, Kurt Randall Myers. AB, Shimer Coll., 1960; JD, U. Calif.-Berkeley, 1972; Dr. honoris causa, U. Basel, 2000. Bar: Calif. 1973, U.S. Supreme Ct. 1980. Law clk. to Justice William O. Douglas U.S. Supreme Ct., 1972-73; acting prof. law U. Calif., Davis, 1973—78, prof., 1978—2001, rsch. prof., prof. emeritus, 2001—05, chair doctoral program in human devel., 1996—2001, disting. rsch. prof., disting. prof. emeritus, 2005—. Acad. vis. law dept. U. Munich, 1978-79, 92, U. Cologne, 1990, U. Cambridge, 1990, London Sch. Econs. and Polit. Sci., 1991, Kings Coll., London, 1991; vis. prof. U. Calif., Berkeley, 1983, Columbia U., 1986, U. Basel, 1994, vis. Fulbright prof. Hebrew U., Jerusalem, 1996-97; vis. fellow Fitzwilliam Coll., Cambridge, Eng., 1990, U. Calif. Humanities Rsch. Inst., Irvine, 1999, vis. scholar Inst. for Advanced Legal Studies (Univ. London), 1991, UCLA Ctr. Study of Women, 2004-05; cons. to Ctr. for Family in Transition, 1981, Calif. Law Revision Commn., 1979-82, NOW Legal Def. and Edn. Fund, 1980-81; lectr., legis. drafting and testimony, 1976—; mem. U.S. del. 4th Inter-Am. Specialized Conf. on Pvt. Internat. Law, OAS, 1989. Contbr. articles to legal jours. Editor Calif. Law Rev., 1971; editorial Bd. Family Law Quar., 1980-87; Representing Children, 1995—, Am. Jour. of Comparative Law, 2001—; lectr. in field. Mem. adv. com. child support and child custody Calif. Commn. on Status of Women, 1981-83, child support adv. com. Calif. Jud. Coun., 1991-94, adv. com. on private internat. law U.S. Dept. State, 1989—, internat. child abduction steering com. Internat. Ctr. for Missing and Exploited Children (London), 1999-2001; host parent Am. Field Service, Davis, 1977-78. Max Rheinstein sr. rsch. fellow Alexander von Humboldt Found., Fed. Republic Germany, 1978-79, 92, Fulbright fellow, Western Europe, 1990, Fulbright Sr. Scholar, Israel, 1997, Disting. Pub. Svc. award U. Calif. Davis Acad. Senate, 1990. Mem. ABA, Calif. State Bar Assn., Am. Law Inst., Internat. Soc. Family Law (exec. coun. 1994-2000, 2002—), Internat. Acad. Comparative Law, Order of Coif. Democrat. Jewish. Office: U Calif Sch Law 400 Mrak Hall Dr Davis CA 95616-5201

BRUCH, DEBRA LYNN, theater educator; b. Olds, Alberta, Canada, June 21, 1951; d. John King Galloway and Elsa Jean (Reid) Ambrose, adopted d. Robert Page Bruch. BS, NW Mo. State U., Maryville, 1974; MA, U. Mo., Kansas City, 1977; PhD, U. Mo., Columbia, 1987. Asst. prof. theatre Mich. Tech. U., Houghton, 1987—94, assoc. prof. theatre, 1994—. Adjudicator Kennedy Ctr./Am. Coll. Theatre Festival, Mich., 1991—93. Author: (book) Creating Theatre for Worship, (playscripts) In: Scenes for Drama Ministry; editor: Jour. Religion and Theatre, 2003—; contbr. articles to profl. jours.; dir.: (performance) The Mousetrap, The Dividing Line, The Odd Couple, Taming of the Shrew, Death of a Salesman, A Moon for the Misbegotten, Deathtrap, Macbeth, Dial M for Murder, A Midsummer Night's Dream, Arsenic and Old Lace, Steel Magnolias; actor: Sancho in Man of La Mancha, Bertha in Pippin, Lotte in Lettice and Lovage. Leader various workshops Calumet Players, Mich., 1994—2005; profl. theatre advisor Cmty. Christ, Independence, 1976, pastor, elder Houghton, 1993. Mem.: Assn. Theatre Higher Edn. (chair nat. playwriting competition 1996—2000, chair, focus rep, religion and theatre focus group 2002—04, conf. planner religion and theatre focus group 2002—04, chair info. bank subcom. 2005—). Community Of Christ. Avocations: making computer games, painting, carpentry, travel. Office: Michigan Technological University 1400 Townsend Dr Houghton MI 49931

BRUCH, RUTH E., information technology executive; BA in fin., U. Iowa. Contr. Davenport Bank and Trust Co., Iowa; with ctr. bus. innovation Ernst & Young; v.p. and dir. IT planning First Bank Sys. (now US Bank), St. Paul; v.p. and mng. dir. info. sys. Continental Bank (now Bank Am.), Chgo.; prin. JGA Consulting, Barrington, Ill., 1991—93; from dir. info. tech. strategic planning to v.p. and CIO Union Carbide Corp., Danbury, Conn., 1993—99; pres. and COO Zonetrader.com, Chgo., 1999—2000; v.p. and CIO Visteon Corp., Dearborn, Mich., 2000—02; sr. v.p. and CIO Lucent Tech., Murray Hill, NJ, 2002—. Bd. dir. Mellon Fin. Corp., 2003—; tech. adv. bd. Blue Star Solutions. Office: Lucent Tech Inc 600 Mountain Ave Murray Hill NJ 07974

BRUCK, ARLENE FORTE, secondary school educator; b. Kingston, N.Y., June 26, 1945; d. Machileo and Lillian (Turco) Forte; m. Laurence J. Bruck; children: Jennifer Lynn, Jason Scott. BA in Latin, Coll. Mt. St. Vincent, Riverdale, N.Y., 1967; MS in Psychology, SUNY, New Paltz, 1971. Cert. in social studies, Latin, elem. edn. Tchr. 2d grade Kingston Schs. Consol., 1967-74, tchr. Latin, psychology and sociology, 1984—. Mem. Mid-Hudson Social Studies Coun., 1992—. Placement chair Jr. League, Kingston, 1982-84; vol. Girl Scouts, Tillson, N.Y., 1981-86, Athletes Against Drugs, Kingston, 1984-87. NEH fellow, 1992; recipient Gender Equity fellowship, Mary Dodge McCarthy award for gen. excellence, 1967, Mid-Hudson Social Studies Coun. Excellence in Tchg. award, 1994, Nat. Honor Soc. Tchr. Recognition award, Wall of Tolerance honoree, Southern Poverty Law Ctr.; named Outstanding Young Woman, 1974, Internat. Biog. Ctr. Woman Yr., 1996-97; N.Y. State Regents scholar, 1963-67, AAUW scholar, 1963-67. Mem. APA, AAUW (v.p. 1970-74, sec. 1975-77, pres. program 1994, pres. 1995-96), N.Y. State Assn. Fgn. Lang. Tchrs. Roman Catholic. Avocations: reading, gourmet cooking, travel. Home: 39 Beth Dr Kingston NY 12401-6148 Office: Kingston High Sch 403 Broadway Kingston NY 12401-4617

BRUCK, CONNIE JANE, reporter; b. Newark, May 22, 1946; d. Carl and Edith Mora (Bornstein) B.; m. Ben Schlossberg, Dec. 8, 1970 (div. 1978); 1 child, Ari. Student, Wellesley Coll., 1964-66; BA, Barnard Coll., 1968; MS, Columbia U. Sch. Journalism, 1969. Reporter Am. Lawyer Mag., NYC, 1979-89; staff writer New Yorker mag., 1989—. Author: The Predators' Ball, 1988, Master of the Game, 1994. Recipient Gerald Loeb award for excellence in bus. reporting, 1991, Nat. Mag. award for reporting, 1991, 1996, Front Page award Newswomen's Club NY, 1990, 1997.*

BRUCKERHOFF, THERESA, business owner, educational researcher; b. Manchester, Vt., Apr. 9, 1961; d. Daniel Xavier Sr. and Alice Winifred Stannard; m. Charles E. Bruckerhoff, Dec. 21, 1986; children: Matthew Charles, Michael Charles. BS in Elem. Edn., Coll. St. Joseph, Rutland, Vt., 1983; MA in Curriculum and Instrn., Cleve. State U., 1991. Day care provider Sugar Maple Day Care, Rutland, 1979-83; classrm. tchr. Rutland Pub. Schs., 1983-85, Shaker Heights (Ohio) Pub. Schs., 1985-91; ops. mgr., asst. rschr. Curriculum Rsch. and Evaluation, Chaplin, Conn., 1995—. Pres. Storrs (Conn.) Cmty. Nursery Sch., 1994-95; treas. Beaver Pond Child Devel. Ctr., Chaplin, 1993-94; chair SMSJ Sch. Family Assn., Willimantic, Conn., 1998-2005. Office: Curriculum Rsch and Evaluation 237 Singleton Rd Chaplin CT 06235-2223 E-mail: theresa@creus.com.

BRUCK LIEB PORT, LILLY, retired advocate, columnist, commentator; b. Vienna, May 13, 1918; came to U.S., 1941, naturalized, 1944; d. Max and Sophie M. Hahn; m. Sandor Bruck, Mar. 7, 1943; 1 child, Sandra Lee (Mrs. John David Evans III); m. David L. Lieb, Dec. 7, 1985; m. Charles S. Port, Nov. 22, 1998. PhD in Econs., U. Vienna; postgrad., Sorbonne, Paris, Sch. of Econs., London, Sch. of Bus., Columbia U., 1941-42, Sch. of Social Work, NYU, 1964-66. Dir. consumer edn. Dept. Consumer Affairs, City of N.Y., 1969-78; project dir. Am. Coalition of Citizens with Disabilities, 1977-78; consumer advisor, broadcaster In Touch Networks, N.Y.C., 1978-90; consumer affairs commentator Nat. Pub. Radio, 1980-82; ret. Author: Access, The Guide to a Better Life for Disabled Americans, 1978; contbr. articles to disability and rehab. to books, ency. and mag. Presid. Scarsdale Hadassah, 1960-68. Chmn. Westchester county, Bonds for Israel, 1960-68; trustee Kol AMI-JCC, White Plains, N.Y.; assoc. Jewish Mus.; sponsor Lilly Bruck Lieb Creative Writing Program, Purchase Coll., SUNY; mem. pres.'s coun. White Plains (N.Y.) Hosp. Recipient Woman of Yr. award Anti Defamation League, 1972. Democrat. Home: 25 Murray Hill Rd Scarsdale NY 10583-2829 E-mail: lblone@aol.com.

BRUCKNER, MARTHA, academic administrator; B, M, U. Nebr., Omaha; Doctorate, U. Nebr., Lincoln. Assoc. supt. for ednl. svcs. Millard (Nebr.) Pub. Schs.; tchr. h.s,. asst. prin., prin. pub. schs.; assoc. prof., chairperson ednl. adminstrn. U. Nebr., Omaha. Contbr. articles to profl. jours. Recipient award, Nebr. Coun. Sch. Adminstrs., Nebr. Schoolmasters Orgn. Mem.: ASCD (pres. 2005—06, bd. dirs., budget liaison, organizer student chpt. U. Nebr., Omaha). Office: Don Stroh Adminstrn Ctr 5606 S 147th St Omaha NE 68137 Office Phone: 402-895-8301. E-mail: mmbruckner@mpsomaha.org.

BRUCKNER, MATILDA TOMARYN, romance language and literature educator; b. Abington, Pa., Nov. 9, 1946; d. Michael Paul and Mary Gwendolyn (Stoutenburgh) Tomaryn; m. Edward Bruckner, Aug. 24, 1969; children: Raphael, Daniel. Student, L'Academie, Paris, 1966-67; AB magna cum laude, Bryn Mawr Coll., 1968; postgrad., Ctr. de Estudios Hispánicos, Madrid, 1968; PhD, Yale U., 1974, MPhil, 1971. Teaching asst. French Yale Coll., 1971-72; adj. asst. prof. French and Spanish Medgar Evers Coll.-CUNY, 1974-75; lectr., asst. prof. Romance langs. and lits. Princeton U., 1975-83; asst. prof. Boston Coll., Chestnut Hill, Mass., 1983-85, assoc. prof., 1985-94, prof., dir. grad. studies, Romance langs. and lits., 1987-90, chmn., 1991—95, coord. intermediate French, 1983-84, coord. medieval forum, 1991—; acting assoc. dean Grad Sch. of A&S, 1999—2000. Vis. lectr. U. Mich., 1979; vis. assoc. prof. Boston U., 1986; lectr. in field Western Mich. U., Medieval Club N.Y., U. Toronto, also others. Author: Narrative Invention in Twelfth-Century French Romance: The Convention of Hospitality (1160-1200), 1980, Shaping Romance: Interpretation, Truth and Closure in 12th Century French Fictions, 1993, Songs of the Women Troubladours, 1995; mem. editorial bd. Speculum, 1987-91, book editor, 1991—; contbr. chpts. to collective vols., articles to profl. jours. Procter and Gamble scholar Bryn Mawr Coll., 1964-68, Elizabeth S. Shippen scholar in langs., 1968; Woodrow Wilson fellow, 1968, Yale U. fellow, 1968-72, Princeton U. rsch. fellow, 1982, Am. Coun. Learned Socs. fellow, 1985-86, NEH fellowship, 2006, Boston Faculty fellowship, 2006; travel grantee Am. Coun. Learned Socs., 1985, rsch. grantee Boston Coll., 1987, 89, 91, 93, 94. Mem. MLA (speaker confs., exec. com. Arthurian lit. discussion group 1987-91, medieval French lang. and lit. divsn. 1992—), Internat. Courtly Lit. Soc., Internat. Arthurian Lit. Soc., Am. Assn. Tchrs. of French, Medieval Acad. Am., New Eng. Medieval Conf. (steering com. 1988-92).

BRUDER, JUDITH, writer; b. Bklyn., Nov. 6, 1934; d. Harry and Libby Mandell; m. Franklin Bruder, Feb. 28, 1960; children: Jane Kennedy, John Bruder. BA with honors, Wellesley Coll., 1956; MA, L.I. U., 1973. Assoc. editor Merrill Lynch, N.Y.C., 1956-62; campus min. Fordham at Lincoln Ctr., N.Y.C., 1989-97. Adj. instr. SUNY, Stony Brook, 1975-79. Author: Going to Jerusalem, 1979, Convergence, 1993; contbr. articles to profl. publs. Creative fellow AAUW, 1979. Mem. Jane Austen Soc. (life), Friends of Uther Pendragon (co-founder). Avocations: reading, travel. Home: PO Box 1954 Lenox MA 01240-4954 E-mail: tsarinajb@hotmail.com.

BRUDNER, HELEN GROSS, social sciences educator; b. NYC; d. Nathan and Mae (Grichtman) Gross; children: Mae Ann, Terry Joseph, Jay Scott. BS, NYU, 1959, MA, 1960, PhD, 1973. Tchr. NYC Bd. Edn., 1959-60; instr. Pratt Inst., Bklyn., 1959-61; asst. prof. history NY Inst. Tech., NYC, 1961-63, dir. guidance, 1962-63; assoc. prof. Fairleigh Dickinson U., Rutherford, NJ, 1963-73, prof. history, polit. sci. Teaneck, NJ, 1974—, dir. Honors Coll. Rutherford, NJ, 1972-84, chmn. dept. social sci., 1980-88, pres. univ. senate, 1975-78, asst. provost, 1983—, dean, 1984, dir. grad. programs, assoc. dir. Sch. History, Polit., Internat. Studies, 1995—, dir. lang. grad. studies, pres. acad. senate, 1996—; v.p. HJB Enterprises, Highland Park, NJ, 1970—. Vice-chmn. bd. dirs. WLC Inc., Highland Park, 1990-, Casitas De Monte Corp., Calif., treas., 2005; vice-chmn. Casitas De Monte Assoc., Palm Springs, Calif., 2000-04, treas., 2005; cons. auto ednl. systems, 1971-; participant bd. trustees F.D.U.; spkr. NJ Com. Humanities. Contbr. articles to profl. jours. constl. law, transfer tech., futurism. Active women politics project NSF, 1981; active consortium project women Am. history NEH Woodrow Wilson Found., 1980, Consortium Global Interdependence, Princeton, 1984; bd. dirs. Options Spkrs. Bur., NJ Credit Union League, NJ Credit Union Shared Network, WLC Inc.; mem. Mcpl. Alliance Highland Park, Hist. Preservation Commn., Highland Park; chmn. bd. dirs. Fairleigh Dickinson U. Fed. Credit Union, 1987—; vice chmn. NJ Adv. Com. on Women Vets., 1993-; design selection com. NJ Korean Vets. Meml.; mem. N.J. VA Women's Health Com., 2005—. Recipient Woman Yr. award Am. Businesswomen's Assn., 1980, Meritorious Svc. award NJ Credit Union League, 1997, Cert. Spl. Congrl. Recognition, 2000, NJ Divsn. Mil. and Vet. Affairs award, 2004 Mem. Am. Judicature Soc., Am. Hist. Soc., Acad. Polit. Sci., Phi Alpha Theta, Phi Sigma Alpha. Office: Fairleigh Dickinson U Sch History, Polit Internat Studies Teaneck NJ 07666 Address: PO Box 1407 Highland Park NJ 08904

BRUECKNER, LESLIE A., lawyer; b. 1961; AB, U. Calif.; JD magna cum laude, Harvard U. Assoc. Berle, Kass & Case; staff atty. Pub. Citizen's Lit. Group, 1991—93, Trial Lawyers Pub. Justice, Wash., DC, 1993—. Guest prof. appellate advocacy Wash. Coll. Law, Am. U., Georgetown Law Ctr. Office: Trial Lawyers Pub Justice PC 1717 Massachusetts Ave NW Washington DC 20036

BRUEL, IRIS BARBARA, psychologist; b. N.Y.C., June 10, 1933; d. Herman and Anna (Cohen) Goldstein; m. Robert Bruel, Apr. 1953 (div. 1957); adopted children: Michael Abraham, Russell Emanuel. BA in Psychology, CCNY, 1956, MS in Sch. Psychology, 1961; PhD in Clin. Psychology, U. Miami, Fla., 1972. Cert. profl. psychologist, Fla. Child supr. Linden Hill Sch., Hawthorne, N.Y., 1957-59; tchr., therapist The League Sch. for Severely Disturbed Children, Bklyn., 1959-61, Assn. for Mentally Ill Children, Yonkers, N.Y., 1961-63; assoc. psychology rsch. U. Miami, Coral Gables, Fla., 1964-67; trainee VA Hosp., Miami, 1967-68; intern diagnostic testing and psychotherapy Henderson Clinic, Ft. Lauderdale, Fla., 1968-69; intern child psychol. svcs. San Fernando Valley Child Guidance Clinic, Van Nuys, Calif., 1970-71; cons. Sorensen Group, N.Y.C., 1972; clin. psychologist Dade County Dept. Youth and Family Devel., Miami, 1972-77; co-dir. Ctr. for the Whole Family, Inc., Coral Gables, 1976-79; pvt. practice clin. psychology, South Miami, Fla., 1979—; clin. psychologist Juvenile Ct. Assessment Ctr., Miami, 1989—2004. Cons. Jewish Vocat. Svc., 1980-85; mem. affiliate staff Grant Ctr. Hosp., 1977—; med. staff Charter Hosp., 1991—; allied health staff Highland Park Hosp., 1988—; adj. prof. Nova U., Ft. Lauderdale, 1977; field supr. practicum students So. Fla. Sch. Profl. Psychology, Miami, 1978-80; cons. Guardian Ad Litem program, 1988—. Sec. Reform Dem. Club, N.Y.C., 1962-63. Mem. APA, Am. Soc. Clin. Hypnosis, Nat. Acad. Neuropsychology, Fla. Soc. Clin. Hypnosis (sec. editor newsletter), Dade County Mental Health Assn., Cousteau Soc., N.Y. Acad. Scis., Assn. for Play Therapy, Am. Bd. Profl. Disability Cons. (diplomate), Seaton Found., Amnesty Internat., Am. Bd. Assessment Psychology, Am. Coll. Forensic Examiners, Am. Acad. Experts in Traumatic Stress, EMDR Internat. Assn. Jewish. Home: 2869 Shipping Ave Miami FL 33133-8602 Office: 7800 S Red Rd Ste 310ph Miami FL 33143-5528 Office Phone: 305-444-6005. E-mail: dririsbruel@bellsouth.net.

BRUENE, BARBARA JANE, artist, educator; b. Waterloo, Iowa, June 22, 1936; d. Hazen M. and Mary Lisle Fallgatter; m. Roger Julius Bruene, June 10, 1956; children: Jim, Bruce. BA, U. No. Iowa, Cedar Falls, 1958; MA, Iowa State U., Ames, 1978; MFA, Drake U., Des Moines, Iowa, 1986. Gallery dir. Coll. of Design Gallery, Iowa State U., Ames, 1988—98; faculty Dept. Art and Design, Iowa State U., Ames, 1975—98, assoc. prof. emeritus, 1998—. One-woman shows include Calligraphic Paintings and Artist's Books, Ball State U., Muncie, Ind., 2000, exhibitions include Alpha Mark traveling exhbn., 1999—2001, Artist's Books, Corcoran Gallery of Art, Washington, 1999, numerous other group and solo exhbns. Avocations: reading, travel. Home: 2122 Greeley St Ames IA 50014

BRUESEWITZ-LOPINTO, GAIL C., marketing professional; b. N.Y.C., May 17, 1956; d. Arthur George and Blanche Juliana (Dobos) Bruesewitz; m. Joseph LoPinto, Sept. 1990; children: Frank Joseph LoPinto, Joseph Arthur LoPinto. BA in Eng. Lit., SUNY, Binghamton, 1978. Mem. promotion and artist devel. staff Columbia Records/CBS Records, Inc., N.Y.C., 1979-82, dir. nat. dance music mktg., 1982-89; nat. dir. Ear Candy Records, 1990-91; prodn. coord. AIG Risk Mgmt., Inc. divsn. Am. Internat. Group, Inc., N.Y.C., 1991-96, Swiss Reins. Am. Alternative Risk Transfer Div., N.Y.C., 1996-98; meeting and event specialist corp. comm. Swiss Re New Markets, N.Y.C., 1999-2000; mktg. coord. Am. Home Assurance Co. AIG, 2004—. Rep. record divsn.Women's Orgn. coun. CBS, Inc., N.Y.C., 1980—82; mem. adv. bd. dance/music New Music Seminar, N.Y.C., 1989—; auction benefit co-chair First Presbyterian Ch., Sag Harbor, NY, 2002; mem. adv. bd. dance/music LoPinto Prodns., N.Y.C., 2000—04; meeting and event planning cons., 2000—04; co-chair catalog com. Grace Ch. Sch Scholarship Benefit Auction, 2002. Editor: (newsletter) Brueser's Boogie Backpage, 1983—90. Active Big Sisters, Binghamton (N.Y.) Social Svcs. Dept., 1975—78; bd. dirs. Camp Wilbur Herrlich, Pawling, NY, 1990, Mt. Tremper (N.Y.) Luth. Camp and Retreat Ctr., 1976—78; asst. Sunday sch. tchr. 1st Presbyn. Ch., Sag Harbor, 2000—. Named N.Y. rep., Mademoiselle mag., 1975. Democrat. Avocations: sailing, ballet, jazz. Office: Am Home Assurance Co 20th Fl 175 Water St New York NY 10038 Office Phone: 212-458-5815. Office Fax: 212-458-1300. Business E-Mail: gail.lopinto@aig.com.

BRUGGE, JOAN S., medical educator; BA in Biology, Northwestern U.; PhD in Virology, Baylor U. Postdoctoral rschr. U. Colo. Med. Ctr.; mem. faculty SUNY, Stony Brook, 1979—88; prof. microbiology Sch. Medicine U. Pa., 1989—92; investigator Howard Hughes Med. Inst., 1989—92; sci. dir. ARIAD Pharm., Inc., Cambridge, Mass.; prof. dept. cell biology Med. Sch. Harvard U., Boston, 1997—. Mem.: NAS (mem. Inst. Medicine). Office: Dept Cell Biology Harvard Med Sch 240 Longwood Ave Boston MA 02115

BRUHN, JOANN MARIE, radiologic technologist, writer, speaker; b. Perham, Minn., Oct. 3, 1952; d. Raymond Ellsworth and Donna Jeanne (Peterson) Bruhn; children: Mark Schermerhorn, Justin, Craig Schermerhorn-(dec.). Student, Bernice Robe Studio, Detroit Lake, Minn., 1981; cert., Meritcare Sch. Radiologic Tech., Fargo, N.D., 1987. Registered technologist Am. Registry Radiologic Technologists. Piano tchr., Vergas and Moorhead, Minn., 1978—86; music coord. Moorhead Healthcare Ctr., Moorhead, 1985—86; registered radiologic technologist Healtheast/St. John's Hosp., St. Paul, 1987—. Presenter original music. Author: Sundance, The Story of Craig, 2002; composer: piano compositions, 1986—. Vol. pianist Leukemia and Lymphoma Soc., Wayzata, Minn., 2003; vol. spkr. Am. Cancer Soc., Minn., 2004; vol. pianist, spkr. White Bear Lake (Minn.) United Meth., 1987—; vol. pianist, organist Vergas United Meth. Ch., 1968—81. Mem.: Am. Registry Radiol. Technologists, Am. Soc. Radiologic Technologists. Avocations: songwriting, piano and vocal performance, kayaking, swimming, bicycling. Home and Office: Sundance Project 4372 Greenhaven Dr Saint Paul MN 55127 Personal E-mail: joannbruhn@hotmail.com.

BRUMBAUGH, MELISSA BETH, elementary school educator; b. Dayton, Ohio, Jan. 15, 1956; d. Eugene Paul Brumbaugh and Suzanne Kessler Limehouse. BS, Berry Coll., 1978; MS in Edn., Walden U., 2003. Cert. tchr. Ga. Tchr. Ballground (Ga.) Sch., 1978—79, Cass Mid. Sch., Cartersville, Ga., 1979—82, Hayesville (NC) H.S., 1986—88, Towns Co. Mid. Sch., Hiawassee, Ga., 1996—; personal asst. to chmn. bd. dirs. Interstate North Bank, Houston, 1982—86; admissions advisor Young Harris (Ga.) Coll., 1988—96. Bd. dirs. Towns Co. C. of C., Hiawassee, Ga., 1990—94. Mem.: Ga. Sci. Tchrs. Assn., Profl. Assn. Ga. Educators. Home: 770 Amethyst Ln Hiawassee GA 30546-2400 Office: Towns Co Mid Sch 1400 US Hwy 76 Hiawassee GA 30546 Office Phone: 706-896-4131 1116. Business E-Mail: melissab@towns.k12.ga.us.

BRUMIT, JO ANN, sheet metal manufacturing executive; 4 children. With KARLEE, 1982—, CEO & chmn. Garland, Tex. Recipient Entrepreneur of Yr. for Mfg. by INC. Mag., Ernst & Young, 1991, Amb. of Yr. Award, Hogan Ctr. for Performance Excellence, 1994, 1999, Dir. of Yr., Garland Chamber of Commerce, 1997, Athena Award, 2000, Malcolm Baldridge Nat. Quality Award, 2000. Mem.: Hogan Quality Roundtable, Garland Ind. Sch. Dist. (bus. sch. ptnr.), Richland Cmty. Coll. Middle Mgmt. Prog. (adv. bd. mem.), Baylor Healthcare System Found. (bd. dirs.), Sch. to Career Bd., Tex. Work (source bd. mem.), Tex. Quality Found. (adv. bd., Tex. Quality award 1999). Office: Karlee PO Box 461207 Garland TX 75046-1207 E-mail: jabrumit@karlee.com.

BRUMMETT, SHIRLEY ANN, art educator; b. Oklahoma City, Okla., Mar. 29, 1948; d. Roy Bennie and Marguerite Ann Dickerson; m. Verne Edwin Brummett, Dec. 16, 1977; 1 child, Brandon. Bachelor's degree, Oklahoma City U., 1971. Art tchr. Putnam City Cen. Jr. H.S., Oklahoma City, 1973—81, Hilldale Elem., Oklahoma City, 1985—89, Windsor Hills Elem., Oklahoma City, 1989—. Sponsor honors art club Windsor Hills Elem., Oklahoma City, 1989—. Named Tchr. of Yr., Hilldale Elem., 1989, Windsor Hills Elem., 1997. Mem.: NEA, Okla. Edn. Assn. Democrat. Methodist. Avocations: pen and ink drawings, reading, gardening, calligraphy. Home: 4965 NW 30 Pl Oklahoma City OK 73122 Office: Windsor Hills Elem 2909 N Ann Arbor Oklahoma City OK 73127 E-mail: ladybugart@aol.com.

BRUNDAGE, GERTRUDE BARNES, pediatrician; b. Neptune, N.J., May 13, 1941; d. John Holt and Mary Downey (Chatham) B. BS in Chemistry, Marietta Coll., 1964; MD, Jefferson Med. Coll., 1971. Diplomate Am. Bd. Pediatrics. Chemist Lederle Labs., Pearl River, NY, 1964-67; intern pediatrics Harrisburg (Pa.) Polyclinic Hosp., 1971-72; resident pediatrics Wilmington (Del.) Med. Ctr., 1972-74; pediatrician St. Barnabas Med. Ctr., Livingston, NJ, 1974—. Chief dept. pediat. Hosp. Ctr. At Orange, 1990—98. Moderator Presbytery of Newark, 1996; active 1st Presbyn. Ch., elder, trustee, 1982—87, 1989—92, 2004—. Mem. AMA, N.J. Med. Women's Assn., Am. Med. Women's Assn., Essex County Med. Soc., Med. Soc. N.J., Alpha Gamma Delta. Republican. Presbyterian. Avocations: choral singing, needlecrafts, gardening. Home: 18 Farrington St West Caldwell NJ 07006-7716 Office: Gertrude B Brundage MD 572 Park Ave East Orange NJ 07017-1904 Office Phone: 973-678-1214. E-mail: trudyb18@comcast.net.

BRUNDAGE, MARJORIE UNDERWOOD, academic administrator; b. Bellefontaine, Ohio, Feb. 5, 1940; d. James Madison and Mary Louise (Mustaine) Underwood; m. Richard Keith Brundage, Dec. 20, 1967; children: Jennie Lee, Judith Lynn. BS, Bowling Green State U., 1962. Systems trainee IBM, Toledo, 1962-63; systems analyst Kaiser Jeep Corp., Toledo, 1963-64, Lazarus Dept. Store, Columbus, Ohio, 1964-66; rsch. assoc. Ohio State U., Columbus, 1966-67, supr. computer dept., 1967-79, dir. computer dept., 1979—99; ret. Cons. U.S. Post Office, Columbus, 1972, labor reseach service, Columbus, 1971-79, local bank, Columbus, 1978-79; owner, Brundage Cottage Rental. Author (with others) Accounting Review, 1969; contbr. articles to profl. jours. Trustee and violinist Met. Chamber Orch., Columbus, 1979—; elder and tchr. Cen. Presbyn. Ch., Columbus, 1966—; com. mem. Scioto Valley Presbytery, Columbus, 1985—; mem. Columbus Landmarks Nat. Trust, 1980—. Mem. Logan County Hist. Soc., Indian Lake Area Hist. Soc. (charter mem., trustee, treas), Logan County Landmarks Preservation Assn. (charter mem., founder, trustee), Athenian Club, Indian Lake C. of C. Republican. Avocations: sewing, music, swimming, reading.

BRUNDAGE, MAUREEN, lawyer; b. 1957; m. Terence Brundage; children: Katie, Brian. BA, Fordham U., 1978; JD, NYU, 1981. Assoc. White & Case LLP, ptnr., 1988—2006, co-head worldwide securities practice group, chief corp. securities practice; exec. v.p., gen. counsel The Chubb Corp., 2006—. Office: The Chubb Corp 15 Mountain Valley Rd Warren NJ 07059 Office Phone: 908-903-2000. Office Fax: 908-903-2027.*

BRUNE, CATHERINE S., insurance company executive; BS, Univ. SC, 1974. Mgmt. positions through v.p. tech. shared services Allstate Ins. Co., Northbrook, Ill., 1976—2002, sr. v.p., chief info. officer, 2002—. Bd. mem. Chgo. & worldwide Junior Achievement. Named one of Premier 100 IT Leaders, Computerworld mag.; named to Academy of Women Achievers, YWCA; recipient Excellence in Corp. IT Leadership award, Women in Tech. Internat. Office: Allstate Ins Co 2775 Sanders Rd Northbrook IL 60062*

BRUNE, MICHELLE L., literature and language educator; b. Ft. Riley, Kans., July 20, 1971; d. Fredrick Henry Brune and Donna Louise Blodgett. BS in Phys. Edn., U. LaVerne, Calif., 1993, tchg. credential, 1994. Swim coach Bonita Unified Sch. Dist., San Dimis, Calif., 1997—99, tchr., 1998—99, Roaring Fark Sch. Dist., Glenwood, Colo., 2001—, swim coach, 2005—. Mem.: Nat. Coun. Tchrs. of English, Sierra Club. Avocations: white-water rafting, skiing, backpacking. Office: Basalt High Sch 600 Southside Dr Basalt CO 81621 Office Phone: 970-384-5936. Business E-Mail: mbrune@rfsd.k12.co.us.

BRUNELL, KATERI TABLER, performance excellence executive, consultant; b. Hamilton, Ohio, Oct. 1, 1959; d. William John and Marian Winkeljohann Tabler; m. David Joseph Brunell, Feb. 20, 1982. AA, Manatee C.C., Bradenton, Fla., 1980; BA in Mass Comm., U. South Fla., Tampa, 1981; MBA, Fla. Atlantic U., Boca Raton, 1990. Cert. quality engr., Am. Soc. for Quality, Wis., 2000; quality mgr. Am. Soc. for Quality, Wis., 1997, Myers-Briggs Type Indicator profl. Ctr. for Application of Psychol. Type, Fla., 2003, Six Sigma Black Belt Am. Soc. for Quality/Wis., 2003, Six Sigma Master Black Belt Tyco Internat., N.J., 2004. Dir. Qualtec Quality Svcs., Inc. (FPL Group Co.), North Palm Beach, Fla., 1993—96; v.p./ptnr. Six Sigma-Qualtec, Inc., Tempe, Ariz., 1996—99; mng. dir./owner Conceptual Dynamics, Inc., West Palm Beach, Fla., 1999—2004; mgr., continuous improvement Sensormatic Electronics, Inc., Boca Raton, Fla., 2001—02; performance excellence cons. II, Nat. Coun. on Compensation Ins., Inc., Boca Raton, Fla., 2002—04; dir. of operational excellence ADT Security Svcs., Inc., Boca Raton, Fla., 2004—. V.p., mem. com. Am. Mktg. Assn., Ft. Lauderdale, Fla., 1983—85; bd. of examiners Fla. Sterling award for performance excellence Fla. Sterling Coun., Tallahassee, 1997—2000; bd. of examiners Malcolm Baldrige Nat. Quality award U.S. Dept. of Commerce/Nat. Inst. of Stds. and Tech., Gaithersburg, Md., 2000—02; presenter in field. Co-author: (book chpt.) Service Quality Handbook; co-author and lead rschr.: Designing Services for Customer Satisfaction. Mem. Prospect Pk. Hist. Neighborhood Assn., West Palm Beach, Fla., 1998—2006, Rep. Party, West Palm Beach, Fla., 1982—2006; v.p. Palm Beach Noon Toastmasters, West Palm Beach, Fla., 1983—85, pres., 1985—86. Mem.: Am. Soc. for Quality (vice-chairman (svc. quality divsn.) 1991—95, bd. dirs. internat. edn. and tng. devel. 2000—02, Outstanding Svc. award 1992), Assn. for Psychol. Type. Achievements include Created first Service Design methodology using Quality Function Deployment in the United States. Avocations: reading, poetry/short story writing, jewelry making. Home: 200 Avila Rd West Palm Beach FL 33405 Office: ADT Security Svcs Inc 1 Town Center Rd Boca Raton FL 33486 Office Phone: 561-981-4367. Personal E-mail: ktbrunell@cdinc.com. E-mail: kbrunell@adt.com.

BRUNELLO-MCCAY, ROSANNE, sales executive; b. Cleve., Aug. 26, 1960; d. Carl Carmello and Vivan Lucille (Caranna) B.; m. Walter B. McCay, Feb. 26, 1994; children: Angela Breanna, Mikala Bell. Student, U. Cin., 1978—81, Cleve. State U., 1981—82. Indsl. sales engr. Alta Machine Tool, Denver, 1982; mem. sales./purchases Ford Tool & Machine, Denver, 1982-84; sales/ptnr. Mountain Rep. Enterprises, Denver, 1984-86; pres., owner Mountain Rep. Ariz., Phoenix, 1986—; pres. Mountain Rep. Oreg., Portland, 1990—, Mountain Rep. Wash., 1991—, Mountain Rep. Calif., Sunnyvale, 1997—, San Clemente, 1998—, Port Clinton, Ohio, 1999—; we. regional sales mgr. Offshore Internat., Inc., Tucson, 2002—. Sec. Computer & Automated Systems Assoc., 1987, vice chmn., 88, chmn., 89. Active mem. Rep. Party, 1985—; mem. Phoenix Art Mus., Grand Canyon Minority Coun., 1994; vol. fundraiser Make-A-Wish Found., 1995—, Leukemia Soc., 2006; founder Ariz. Sonora Corridor Network. Named Mrs. Chandler Internat., Mrs. Ariz. Internat. Orgn., 1996, Mrs. East Valley U.S., 1997; finalist Mrs. Ariz. Internat., 1996, Ms. Ariz. 2000, Ms. U.S. Continental Pageant; nominated The 19th Ann. Athena award Greater Phoenix C. of C., 2006. Mem. NAFE, Soc. Mfg. Engrs. (pres. award 1988), Computer Automated Assn. (sec. 1987, vice chmn. 1988 chmn. 1989), Manufacturers and Agents Nat. Assn. (chair-elect 2002), Nat. Hist. Soc., Italian Cultural Soc., Tempe C. of C., Vocat. Edn. Club Am. (mem. exec. bd., pres. 1987—). Roman Catholic. Avocations: sports, aerobics, dance, skiing, golf, tennis. Office: Mountain Rep 254 S Lakeview Blvd Chandler AZ 85225-5792 Office Phone: 480-899-1900. Business E-Mail: rosanne@mtnrep.com.

BRUNETT, MIRANDA JO, systems administrator; b. Johnstown, Pa., Dec. 17, 1975; d. Bruce Mark and Barbara Jean Brunett. BS, Pa. State U., Univ. Pk., 1999. GIS tech. Adams County Govt., Gettysburg, Pa., 1999—2001; GIS analyst Carroll County Govt., Westminster, Md., 2001—04; GIS project mgr. homeland security Ctr. Geographic Info. Sys. Towson U., Towson, 2004—05; GIS coord. Md. Emergency Mgmt. Agy., Reisterstown, 2004—05; GIS analyst City of Balt., 2005; GIS specialist Keystone Internat. and Dept. Energy, Germantown, Md., 2006—. Mem. Maritime Security Task Force, Balt., 2005; chair Megin Outreach, Towson, 2005; mem. MSGIC Exec. Com., Md., 2005. Vol. Carroll Hospice Care, Westminster, Md., 2003. Mem.: Pa. State Alumni Assn., Am. Mensa. Republican. Roman Catholic. Avocations: knitting, reading, hiking, camping. Office: Dept Energy 19901 Germantown Rd Germantown MD 20874

BRUNING, NANCY PAULINE, writer; b. N.Y.C., Nov. 7, 1948; d. Nicholas Cornelius Bruning and Anne Marie (Liebenberg) Jacelon. BA, Pratt Inst., 1969. Author: Breast Implants, 1995, Coping With Chemotherapy, 1995, Healing Homeopathic Remedies, 1996, Ayurveda: The A-Z Guide to Healing Techniques from Ancient India, 1997, The Real Vitamin & Mineral Book, 1997, The Mend Clinic Guide to Natural Medicines for Menopause and Beyond, 1997, Natural Medicines for Colds and Flu, 1998, Natural Relief for Your Child's Asthma, 1999, Methylation Miracle, 1999, Effortless Beauty, 1999, Dare to Lose, 2002, The Way of the Belly, 2006. Bd. dirs. Breast Cancer Action, 1990-91, Urban Ecology, Oakland, 1992-97; pres. Friends of Fort Tryon Park, 2002-06. Office: 250 Cabrini Blvd Apt 9G New York NY 10033-1163 Business E-Mail: nbruning@aol.com.

BRUNKE, DAWN BAUMANN, writer, editor; b. Madison, Wis., Nov. 6, 1959; d. Richard Joseph and Carol Edler Baumann; m. Bob Brunke, May 25, 1991; 1 child, Alyeska Isabela. BA, Lawrence U., 1977—81. Massage Therapist AMTA, Wash. D.C., 1985. Instr. Potomac Inst. of Myotherapy, Washington, 1986—88; massage therapist Gaithersburg, Md., 1986—88; editor Alaska Wellness Mag., Anchorage, 1995—; massage therapist Alaska Club, Wasilla, 2001—06. Author: In God's Garden (Grand Prize; Anchorage Daily News/ U. of Alaska Creative Writing Contest, 1997), Before She Was the Queen of Syrup (Editors Choice, Anchorage Daily News/ U. of Alaska Creative Writing Contest, 1998), Animal Voices: Telepathic Communication in the Web of Life, 2002, Awakening to Animal Voices: A Teen Guide to Telepathic Communication with All Life, 2004. Home: P O Box 877229 Wasilla AK 99687 Personal E-mail: akdawn@mtaonline.net.

BRUNKE, KATHLEEN ELIZABETH, adult education educator; m. Bruce Anderson, June 0, 1979. PhD, Mont. State U., Bozeman, Mont., 1982. Assoc. prof. Christopher Newport U., Newport News, Va., 1993—. Office: Christopher Newport U 1 University Pl Newport News VA 23606 Personal E-mail: kbrunke@cnu.edu.

BRUNNER, LILLIAN SHOLTIS, nurse, writer; b. Freeland, Pa. d. Andrew J. and Anna (Tomasko) Sholtis; m. Mathias J. Brunner, Sept. 8, 1951; children: Janet Brunner Cramer, Carol Ann Brunner Burns, Douglas Mathias. RN, diploma, U. Pa., 1940, BS, 1945, LittD (hon.), 1985; MS in Nursing, Case-Western Res. U., 1947; ScD (hon.), Cedar Crest Coll., 1978. RN, Pa. Head nurse U. Pa. Hosp., Phila., 1940-42, operating room supr., 1942-44, head, fundamentals of nursing dept., 1944-46; asst. prof. surgical nursing Yale U. Sch. Nursing, New Haven, Conn., 1947-51; surgical supr. Yale-New Haven Hosp., 1947-51; Lillian Sholtis Brunner chair med.-surg. nursing U. Pa., 2001. Rsch. project dir. Sch. Nursing Bryn Mawr (Pa.) Hosp., 1973-77; co-founder History of Nursing Mus., Pa. Hosp., Phila., 1974; mem. bd. overseers Sch. Nursing U. Pa., 1982-88; bd. overseers emeritus, 1988—; chmn. nursing adv. Presbyn.-U. Pa. Med. Ctr., Phila., 1970-88, 90-93, trustee, 1976-88, 90-95, vice chmn. bd. trustees, 1985-88; mem. com. profl. advisory Vis. Nurse Assn., Lancaster, Pa., 1996-99; sec. Glen Coun., Willow Valley Manor North, 1997-2000. Author: Manual of Operating Room Technology, 1966, (with others) Lippincott Manual of Nursing Practice, 1974, 4th edit., 1986, Textbook of Medical and Surgical Nursing, 1964, 6th edit., 1988; mem. editl. bd. Jour. Nursing and Health Care, Nursing 1978-1999, Nursing Photobook Series, 1978-90. Bd. dirs. Presbyn. Found. for Phila., 1995-99. Recipient Disting. Alumnus award Frances Payne Bolton Sch. Nursing, Case Western Res. U., 1980, Alumni award for merit Soc. Alumni Assns., U. Pa., and Am. Dream Achievement award Class of '45, U. Pa., 1995, Mentor award, Millersville U. Sch. Nursing, 2004. Fellow: Am. Acad. Nursing (Living Legend award 2002); mem.: Nurses Alumni Assn. U. Pa. Hosp., Philanthropic Ednl. Orgn., Nat. League for Nursing (judge nat. writing contest 1982—84, Disting. Svc. award 1979), ANA, Acad. U. Pa., Ben Franklin Soc., Internat. Old Lacers Soc., Nat. League Am. Pen Women (sec. Phila. chpt. 1972—76, nat. sec. 1984—88), Pi Lambda Theta, Pi Gamma Mu, Sigma Theta Tau. Home and Office: Apt J-411 645 Willow Valley Sq Lancaster PA 17602-4871 Office Phone: 717-464-6247.

BRUNNER-MARTINEZ, KIRSTIN ELLEN, pediatrician, psychiatrist; b. Allentown, Pa., July 26, 1959; d. John Wilson and Ulla Brita (Arvide) Brunner; m. Fred F. Martinez. BS, Muhlenberg Coll., Allentown, Pa., 1981; DO, Phila. Coll. Osteo. Medicine, 1986. Diplomate Am. Bd. Pediatrics, Am. Bd. Psychiatry and Neurology in child and adolescent psychiatry and adult psychiatry. Resident U. Ky., 1992; dept. dir. Integra Health Family Devel. Ctr., Cedar Rapids, Iowa, 1993-98; with Hamot Inst. for Behavioral Health, Erie, Pa., 1998-2001; med. dir. Hamot Child and Adolescent Psychiat. Unit, Erie, 1999-2001, Sarah Reed Children's Ctr., Erie, 2001—. Fellow Am. Acad. Pediatrics; mem. AMA, Am. Acad. Child and Adolescent Psychiatry, Am. Psychiat. Assn. Avocations: cross country skiing, soccer (outdoor and indoor). Office: Sarah Reed Children's Ctr 1020 E 10th St Erie PA 16503 Business E-Mail: kbrunner@sarahreed.org.

BRUNO, ANTOINETTE, food service executive; married; 2 children. MBA, Harvard Bus. Sch.; post-grad. degree, London Sch. Econ. Founder, mgr. retail store chain; securities negotiator Salomon Brothers; CEO, editor-in-chief StarChefs, 1999—. Organizer, moderator, celebrity chef panels Wine & Cuisine Soc. Harvard Bus. Sch. Featured in Bus. Week, Venture Wire, Nation's Restaurant News. Office: StarChefs 9 East 19th St Fl 9 New York NY 10003 Office Phone: 212-966-3775. Office Fax: 212-477-6644.*

BRUNO, CAROL JEANETTE, library media specialist, gifted and talented education educator, innkeeper; b. Phila., Dec. 21, 1949; d. Everette Noble and Gertrude Mae (Weaver) Cliff; m. C. Gus Bruno, Aug. 28, 1971; children: Peter Everette, Jason Eugene. AA, Wesley Coll., 1969; BA, Davis & Elkins Coll., 1971; postgrad., St. Joseph's U., 1994—, Rowan U., 1997—. Elem. tchr. Ocean City (N.J.) Primary Schs., 1971-72; instr. Atlantic C.C., Mays Landing, 1979-80; reading tchr. Egg Harbor Twp. (N.J.) Schs., 1980-82; coord. gifted edn. Sea Isle City (N.J.) Pub. Schs., 1982—, adviser student yearbook, Nat. Jr. Honor Soc. Local pres., county pres., mem. state bd. dirs. N.J. PTA, Trenton, 1978-90; founder After-Sch. Care Program, Ocean City, 1984, Ocean City Safe Homes Project, 1984; den mother Boy Scouts Am., Ocean City, 1980-82; mem. Mayor's Task Force on Drug and Alcohol Abuse, Ocean City; pres., bd. dirs. Cape Ednl. Fund, Cape May County, N.J., 1980—. Named Role Model, Sun Newspaper, 1988, Cape May County Tchr. of Yr., 1993. Mem. ASCD, Sea Isle City Edn. Assn. (sec.). Avocations: reading, travel, decorating bed and breakfast, cooking. Office: Sea Isle City Pub Sch 4501 Park Rd Sea Isle City NJ 08243-1896 Home: 500 Bay Ave Apt 401S Ocean City NJ 08226-3965

BRUNO, CATHY EILEEN, management consultant, former state official, social sciences educator; b. Binghamton, N.Y. d. Martin Frank and Beverly Carolyn (Hamlin) Piza; m. Frank L. Delaney (div.); m. Paul R. Bruno, May 5, 1990. BA, SUNY, Binghamton; MSW, Syracuse U. Psychiat. social worker Broome Devel. Ctr., Binghamton, 1973-74, 76, congl. legis. aide, 1975; asst. dir. Bur. Program and Fiscal audits N.Y. State Office Mental Retardation and Devel. Disabilities, Albany, 1976-80; statewide coord. Intermediate Care Facilities for Developmentally Disabled, 1980; cert. coord. Western County Svc. Group, 1980-83, Upstate unit dir. Bur. Cert. Control, 1983-85; dir. ICF/DD Survey and Rev., 1985-89; area dir. Bur. Program Cert., 1989-95; dir. Bur. Transitional Svcs., 1995-97, mgmt. cons., 1997—. Adj. instr. SUNY Sch. Social Welfare, Albany, 1982-83; adj. faculty C.C. of Southern Nev., Las Vegas, 1998. Vol. U. Nev. Coop. Ext. Master Gardener program, 1997—; bd. dirs. Worldwide AIDS Movement, 2000—01. Mem. Am. Mgmt. Assn. Home and Office: 293 Canyon Spirit Dr Henderson NV 89012-3472

BRUNO, MARIA FRANCES, writing and cultural educator; b. Highland Park, Mich., Aug. 14, 1948; d. Philip Paul and Mary Bruno; m. Ronald Lee Holley, June 14, 1969 (div. Dec. 1987); children: Emily Beth, Rebeccah Lynn; m. George Robert Cook, Apr. 29, 1999. BA, Mich. State U., 1970, M, 1982, PhD, 1986. Assoc. prof. Mich. State U., East Lansing, 1986—. Contbr. chapters to books Charlotte Perkins Gilman: The Woman and Her Work, 1989, The Gulf War: A Broader Perspective, 1992, Doing Feminism: Teaching and Research in the Academy, 1997, Spectacle: Women on Popular Culture, 1997, articles to profl. jours.; author short stories, screenplays. Fellow, Mich. State U., 1985. Office: Mich State U 235 Bessey Hall East Lansing MI 48824

BRUNO, PHYLLIS, school system administrator; b. Middletown, NY, Aug. 5, 1954; d. Herbert I. and Lillian Grodin; m. Robert E. Bruno, July 7, 1975; children: Jessica Bruno-Raiz, Heather. BA in Am. Studies, Ramapo Coll. of NJ, 1976; M Ednl. Leadership Fairleigh-Dickinson U., 04. Social studies tchr. Franklin Twp. Bd. Edn., Somerset, NJ, 1986—2005, dir. social studies and work readiness, 2005—. Cons. on internet safety, 2005—. Scholar for holocaust studies, Seton Hall U. Judeo-Christian Studies Inst. Mem.: ASCD, NJ Social Studies Supr., Nast. Coun. Social Studies Tchrs. Avocations: walking, reading, bicycling. Home: 644 Viscaya Ct Somerset NJ 08873

BRUNO, SHERRIE L., science educator; b. Pitts., Sept. 30, 1959; d. Charles R. and Shirley J. Mansfield; m. Pierre W. Bruno, Aug. 4, 2001. BS, Ashland Coll., Ohio, 1982; MS, Akron U., Ohio, 1988. Geologist, prodn. analyst F.P.I. Antrino Ore, Lansing, Mich., 1988—90; asst. geologist Patrick Petroleum, Jackson, NY, 1990—93; adj. sci. instr. Hesser Coll., Manchester, NH, 1993—2000, N.H. Coll., Manchester, 1995—2000, Coll. for Life Long Learning, Manchester, 1998—2000, Notre Dame Coll., Manchester, 1999—2000; sci. tchr. Manchester Ctrl. H.S., 1999—. Advisor S.E.A. (Students for Environ. Action), Manchester, 2000—; mem. ctrl. pride post-card com. Ctrl. H.S., Manchester, 2005—. Mem.: Nat. Sci. Tchrs. Assn. Home: 63 Lyndeboro Rd New Boston NH 03070 Office: Central High School 207 Lowell St Manchester NH 03040

BRUNS, CHRISTINE, music educator; b. NY; m. Robert Bruns. MusB, Ithaca (NY) Coll., 1997, MusM, 2002. Cert. permanent tchr. music K-12 NY, clear renewable tchr. music PreK-12 Ga., clear renewable tchr. mid. level reading Ga. Music tchr. Groton Ctrl. Schs., NY, 1997—2005, Rockdale County Schs., Conyers, Ga., 2005—. Dir. Intergenerational Cmty. Choir, Groton, 2002—04. Fundraising chair Ithaca Concert Band, 2003—05; 1st v.p. programs Ithaca Music Club, 2003—05. Mem.: Am. Choral Dirs. Assn., Music Educators Nat. Conf., Phi Kappa Phi (life), Sigma Alpha Iota (life; Tau A province officer 2005—06). Office Phone: 770-483-3371. Business E-Mail: cbruns@rockdale.k12.ga.us.

BRUNSWICK, ANN FINKENBERG, social psychologist, health researcher; b. N.Y.C., July 1, 1926; d. Leo and Erna (Eiseman) Finkenberg; m. J. Peter Brunswick, Sept. 14, 1950 (div. June 1976); children: Debra, Naomi. AB, Hunter Coll., 1946; MA, Clark U., 1947; PhD, Columbia U., 1976. Asst. dir. study NORC U. Chgo., 1951—60, dir. study, 1960—65; sr. rsch. assoc. CUNY, 1966; rsch. assoc., co-dir. adolescent health project Columbia U., 1966—71, prin. investigator, dir., 1972—73, sr. rsch. assoc., sociomed. area Ctr. Cmty. Health Sys., 1973—74, sr. rsch. scientist, prin. investigator, dir. longitudinal Harlem health study, 1974—. Author book chpts. in field; contbr. numerous articles to profl. jours. Fellow APA, Am. Psychol. Soc.; mem. AAAS, APHA, Soc. Psychologists in Substance Abuse, Am. Assn. Pub. Opinion Rsch., Soc. Psychol. Study of Social Issues, Am. Sociol. Assn., Soc. Study of Social Problems, Assn. Social Scis. in Health Office: Columbia U Sch Pub Health 722 W 168th St New York NY 10032-3722

BRUSCO, TERESA EILEEN, special education educator; b. Springfield, Vt., Apr. 23, 1950; d. Mark John and Carlie May Sullivan; m. Raymond Brusco, Mar. 9, 1974; 1 child, Nicole Balkind. BS in Edn., So. Conn. State Coll., New Haven, 1972; MS in Edn., Coll. St. Rose, Albany N.Y., 1977. Cert. exceptional needs specialist/early childhood through young adulthood Nat. Bd. for Profl. Tchg. Stds., 2005. Spl. educator Wappingers Ctrl. Sch. Dist., Wappingers Falls, NY, 1972—. Advisor landscaping and nature dept. Oak Grove Elem. Sch., Poughkeepsie, NY, 1998—2006; level 1 cert. Wilson Reading Sys., Oxford, Mass., 2005—06. Vol. COVERTS Program N.Y. State Master Forest Owners, Poughkeepsie, 1998—2006. Recipient Edn. award, Nat. Arbor Day Found., 2003, Best of Hudson Valley Environ. Edn. award, 2004. Mem.: ASCD. Avocations: stained glass, travel, sewing, gardening, hiking. Office: Myers Corners Elem Sch Myers Corners Rd Wappingers Falls NY 12590 Office Phone: 845-298-5260 ext. 118. Personal E-mail: the3bees2002@hotmail.com. Business E-Mail: teresa.brusco@wappingersschools.org.

BRUSH, FLORENCE CLAPHAM, kinesiologist, exercise physiologist, physical education educator; b. Little Rock, May 16, 1928; d. Thomas Wilson and Clara Sumpter Clapham; children: Robert Charles, Elizabeth Wrenne. BS, BA, Tex. Women's U., 1950, MA, 1951; PhD, U. Md., 1966. Instr. U. Ark., Fayetteville, 1950—53; assoc. prof., aquatics dr. Northwestern State Coll., Natchitoches, La., 1953—54; asst. prof. U. Md., 1954—59, Temple U., 1963—64; rsch. assoc. divsn. rsch. Lankenau Hosp., Phila., 1962, 1963; assoc. prof. Direct Execise Physiology Lab. Portland State U., Oreg., 1965—69; assoc. prof. SUNY Coll. Cortland, 1971—92, assoc. prof. emeritus. Vis. scholar dept. growth and devel. Inst. Child Health U. London, 1970—71; vis. scholar Emory U., 1976; tutor math. Editor: Jour. Phys. Edn., Oreg. Assn. Health Phys. Edn. Recreation, 1969—70; contbr. articles to profl. jours. Tchr. swimming YWCA. Recipient several grants. Mem.: ACLU, Nat. Strength and Conditioning Assn. Am. Assn. Health Phys. Edn. Recreation and Dance, Internat. Soc. Electrophysiological Kinesiology, United U. Professions, Environ. Orgn., Am. Coll. Sports Medicine. Democrat. Presbyterian. Achievements include research in anthropometric, physiological, neurological and electromyographic correlates of motor performance. Avocations: piano, kayaking, birdwatching. Home: 773 Blue Creek Rd Cortland NY 13045 Personal E-mail: brushf@cortland.edu.

BRUSH, JULIANNA R., marine biologist; married. MS in Marine Sci. for Coral Pathology, U. SC, 2003. West Nile virus technician; marine mammal and sea turtle stranding coord. Md. Dept. Natural Resources; fellow Office Protected Resources Nat. Marine Fisheries Svc.; with Nat. Ocean Svc. NOAA. Contbr. articles to profl. jours. Recipient W.P. Carey Field Rsch. award, Wings WorldQuest Women of Discovery Awards, 2006; grantee Sea Grant fellowship. Office: NOAA Nat Ocean Svc SSMC Bldg 4 1305 East-West Hwy Silver Spring MD 20910 E-mail: julianna.brush@noaa.gov.*

BRUTON, REBECCA ANN, mayor, commissioner; b. Arkansas City, Kans., Dec. 12, 1949; d. Robert Thomas and Gloria JoAnn (Jackson) Bush; m. Ronald Dean Bruton, Sept. 23, 1973. BS, Southwestern Coll., Winfield, Kans., 1975; grad. Inst. Mcpl. Leadership, Wichita State U., 2001. Elem. tchr. USD #471, Dexter, Kans., 1977—88; owner, sec. Bruton's Towing and Salvage, Arkansas City, 1988—; mayor, city commr. City of Arkansas City, 1999—2003; founder A Piece of the Garden Ministries, 1989—. Bd. trustees S. Ctrl. Kans. Regional Med. Ctr., Arkansas City, 2000—03; bd. dirs. Strother Field Commn., Arkansas City, 2000—03. Preacher Medicalodge East, Arkansas City, 1992—2001. Named Vol. of Yr., Medicalodge East, 1999—2000. Mem.: Kans. Sunshine Coalition Open Govt. (charter mem.), Kans. Taxpayers Assn. Avocations: Bible study, reading. Office: Bruton's Towing and Salvage 1800 South Fourth Arkansas City KS 67005 E-mail: actycomm@ArkCity.org.

BRUTTOMESSO, KATHLEEN ANN, dean, nursing educator, researcher; b. Torrington, Conn., Apr. 28, 1935; d. Thomas F. and Margaret (Gleeson) McMahon; div.; children: Raymond I. Jr., Cheryl A., Robert I., Charles A., Douglas A. BS, St. Joseph Coll., West Hartford, Conn., 1956; MS, Boston Coll., 1959; DNSc, Boston U., 1987. RN, Conn., Mass., Ill., N.J. Staff nurse, head nurse, supr. Mass. Gen. Hosp., Boston, 1956-59; supr. Charlotte Hungerford Hosp., Torrington, 1963-64; instr. Seton Hall U., South Orange, N.J., 1975-77; assoc. prof. U. Conn., Storrs, 1977—, interim dean. Researcher in field. Contbr. articles to profl. jours. Boston U. scholar, 1980-81. Mem. ANA, Conn. Nurses Assn., Conn. Nurses Found. (charter mem.), Ea. Nursing Rsch. Soc., Sigma Theta Tau (Mu chpt. Gamma Nu chpt., charter mem.).

BRUVOLD, KATHLEEN PARKER, retired lawyer; BS in Math., U. Denver, 1965; MS in Math., Purdue U., 1967; JD, U. Cin., 1978. Bar: Ohio 1978, U.S. Dist. Ct. (so. dist.) Ohio 1978, U.S. Dist. Ct. (ea. dist.) Ky. 1979. Mathematician bur. rsch. and engring. U.S. Post Office, 1967; instr. math. Purdue U., West Lafayette, Ind., 1967-68, asst. to dir., tng. coord., programmer Administrv. Data Processing Ctr., 1968-71; instr. math. Ind. U., Kokomo, 1969-70; pvt. practice Cin., 1978-80; asst. dir. Legal Adv. Svcs. U. Cin., 1980-89, assoc. gen. counsel, 1989—2002; asst. atty. gen. State of Ohio, 1983—2002; ret., 2002. Chair Ohio pub. records com. Inter-univ. Coun. Legal Advisors, 1980-84; presenter various confs. and symposiums. Active com. group svcs. allocation United Way and Community Chest; v.p. Clifton Recreation Ctr. Adv. Coun., 1983-84; vice chair Cin. Bilingual Acad. PTA, 1989-90. U. Denver scholar, Jewel Tea Co. scholar; Nat. Merit finalist. Mem. ABA, Nat. Assn. Coll. and Univ. Attys. (bd. dirs., co-chair taxation sect., com. ann. meeting arrangements, program com., publs. com., bd. ops. com., JCUL editl. bd. nominations com., honors and award com., intellectual property sect., com. continuing legal edn. 1992-2002), Ohio Bar Assn., Cin. Bar Assn. (com. taxation, program chmn. 1985-86, sec. 1986-87, com. computer law). Home: 536 Evanswood Pl Cincinnati OH 45220-1527

BRUZEK, PATRICIA ANN, elementary school educator; b. La Grange, Ill., Feb. 12, 1956; BS in Elem. Edn., U. Ill., Champaign, Ill., 1978. Cert. tchr. Ill., 1978. Primary edn. tchr. trainer U.S. Peace Corps, Baimma, Sierra Leone, 1978—80; tchr. math. Field Mid. Sch., Northbrook, Ill., 1981—84; tchr. math. mid. sch. Am. Sch. Japan, Tokyo, 1984—87; tchr. math. Lombard (Ill.) Jr. H.S., 1988—90, Glenn Westlake Mid. Sch., Lombard, 1993—. Treas. Lombard (Ill.) Newcomer's and Neighbors, 1992—94. Mem.: Friends Sierra Leone (fundraiser 2005—06), Nat. Assn. Peace Corps (assoc.), Chgo. (Ill.) Area Peace Corps Vols. (assoc.; coord. global edn. returned vols. 1988—93,

Global Educator of Yr. award 1992), U. Ill. Alumni Assn. (life). Roman Cath. Avocation: swimming. Home: 354 Cimarron Road Lombard IL 60148-1480 Office: Glenn Westlake Middle School 1514 S Main Street Lombard IL 60148 Office Phone: 630-827-4500. Home Fax: 630-620-3791; Office Fax: 630-620-3791. Business E-Mail: pbruzek@sd44.org.

BRYAN, BARBARA DAY, retired librarian; b. Livermore Falls, Maine, May 20, 1927; d. Lorey Clifford and Olga Elvira (Bergquist) Day; m. Robert S. Bryan, June 24, 1950. BA in Psychology, U. Maine, 1948; MS in Library Sci., So. Conn. State U., 1964. Catalog dept. asst. Yale U. Library, New Haven, 1948-49; departmental library cataloger Harvard U., Cambridge, Mass., 1949-51; descriptive cataloger Yale U. Library, New Haven, 1951-52; cataloger Fairfield (Conn.) Pub. Library, 1952-54, reference librarian, 1954-57, asst. librarian, order librarian, 1957-65; asst. dir. libraries Fairfield U., 1965-74, university librarian, 1974-96, u. librn. emerita, 1996—. Mem. Conn. State Libr. Bd., Hartford, 1978—92, chair, 1987—92; bd. dirs. Bibliomation, Inc., Stratford, Conn., 1987—91. Pres. Friends Nyselius Libr., Fairfield U., 1998-2000, mem. exec. bd., 2001—; commr. Fairfield Hist. Dist. Commn., 2003—. Named Conn. Libr. Assn. Libr. of Yr., 1988; recipient Disting. Alumnus award, So. Conn. State U. Sch. of Libr. Sci., 1979. Mem. ALA (life, Conn. chpt. councilor 1977-80), Assn. Coll. and Rsch. Librs. (constn. and by-laws com. 1986-90, mem. coll. libr. sect. stds. com. 1991-95), New Eng. Libr. Assn. (mem. com. 1981-85, coun. mem. 1975-77), Conn. Libr Assn. (legis. com. 1996—), Fairfield Hist. Soc. (libr. vol.), Conn. Audubon Soc., Oak Lawn Cemetery Assn. (bd. dirs. 1994—), Assn. Conn. Libr. Bds. (bd. dirs., chair legis. com. 1996—), Inst. Ret. Profl. (adv. bd. 1998-2001, 05-), Fairfield U. Retirees Assn. (pres. 2003-04), Phi Beta Kappa, Phi Kappa Phi. Democrat. Avocations: reading, walking. Home: 999 Merwins Ln Fairfield CT 06824-1919

BRYAN, BETH ANN, educational association administrator; BA in Elementary Edn. & English, Houston Baptist U., 1969; MA in Edn. Guidance & Counseling, U. Houston. Psychological assoc. pvt. practice; program dir. Laura Bush's Family Literacy Initiative, Tex.; adv. Tex. Gov.'s Bus. Coun.; edn. policy dir. Gov. George W. Bush, Tex., 1985; sr. adv. to edn. sec. US Dept. Edn., Washington, 2001—03; exec. dir. Laura Bush Found. for Am.'s Libraries, 2003—. Mem., mayor pro tem City of West University Place City Coun., 1985—89; regional coord. Houston area Tex. Bus. & Edn. Coalition. Office: Laura Bush Found for Am Libraries c/o Cmty Found Nat Capital Region 1201 15th St NW Ste 420 Washington DC 20005 Office Phone: 202-955-5890.

BRYAN, BILLIE MARIE (MRS. JAMES A. MACKEY), retired biologist; b. Norfolk, Va., Dec. 30, 1932; d. William B. and Marie (Fortescue) Bryan; m. James A. Mackey. BA in Biology, U. Richmond, 1954; MEd, Am. U., 1966. Bacteriologist Arlington County Health Dept., Arlington, Va., 1954-58; med. bacteriologist Walter Reed Army Inst. Rsch. Walter Reed Army Med. Ctr., Washington, 1959-62; tchr. Fairfax (Va.) H.S., 1962-66; biologist NIH, Washington, 1966—2004; ret. Contbr. articles to profl. jours. Mem. AAAS, DAR, Internat. Soc. for Polit. Psychology. Home: 6025 Arlington Blvd Falls Church VA 22044

BRYAN, CAROLYN J., music educator, saxophonist; b. Dubois, Pa., Dec. 7, 1963; d. Frank H. and Elizabeth J. (Moyer) Bryan. BME, Baldwin-Wallace Coll., Berea, Ohio, 1985; MMusic, Ind. U., 1987, DMus, 1997. Cert. K-12 music tchr., Ohio, Minn. Band dir., area coord. Musicl Youth, Inc., Cleve., 1987-92; lectr. music theory and edn. Baldwin-Wallace Coll., 1990-92; dir. bands Dakota Meadows Middle Sch./ISD 77, Mankato, Minn., 1995-97; assoc. prof. music Ga. So. U., Statesboro, 1997—. Performing artist Yamaha Corp., 1997—; vis. prof. saxophone Youngstown (Ohio) State U., 1991; vis. instr. music Gustavus Adolphus Coll., St. Peter, Minn., 1993-94; presenter in field. Author lit. and rec. revs.; performer audio rec. Winds of Ind., 1995. Fellow 11th Ann. Summer Inst. Holocaust and Jewish Civilization. Spl. Initiatives grantee Coll. Liberal Arts and Social Scis., Ga. So. U., 1999, 2001, Faculty Rsch. grantee Ga. So. U., 1999. Fellow 11th Inst. on Holocuaust and Hewish Civilization; mem. Music Educators Nat. Conf., N.Am. Saxophone Alliance, Pi Kappa Lambda, Mu Phi Epsilon, Phi Kappa Phi. Avocations: reading, music, travel. Office: Ga So U PO Box 8052 Statesboro GA 30460-8052 Office Phone: 912-681-5669. Business E-Mail: cbryan@georgiasouthern.edu.

BRYAN, KAREN SMITH, lawyer; BA in Psychology, Bryn Mawr Coll., 1972; MA, UCLA, 1973; JD, U. So. Calif., 1979. Bar: Calif. 1979. With Latham & Watkins LLP, L.A., 1979—, ptnr., 1987—. Mem. planning com. U. So. Calif. Tax Inst. Named So. Calif. Super Lawyer, 2003—06; named one of Am.'s Leading Bus. Lawyers, Chambers & Ptnrs., 2003—06. Mem.: ABA (corp. tax com. and ind. income tax com.). Office: Latham & Watkins LLP 633 W Fifth St Ste 4000 Los Angeles CA 90071 Office Phone: 213-485-1234. Business E-Mail: karen.bryan@lw.com.

BRYAN, KAY MARIE, retired minister; b. Independence, Mo., Oct. 16, 1936; d. Joseph Price and Naoma Muriel (Upham) Price Scott; m. William Burgess (div. Nov. 1976); children: Deborah Tinker, William Burgess, Phillip Burgess; m. Travis Johnson; 1 child, Steve Johnson; m. Marlan William Bryan, July 28, 1984. BA in Health Care Mgmt., Park U., 1978. Accredited records technician; cert. profl. healthcare quality. Records technician St. Luke's Hosp., Kansas City, Mo., 1973-76; asst. dir. med. records U. Health Sci., Kansas City, Mo., 1976-78; dir. med. records Toledo (Ohio) Hosp., 1978-84; dir. med. records and quality assurance Gateway Rehab. Ctr., Aliquippa, Pa., 1985-97, ret., 1997; min. Cmty. of Christ, 1999—2006, ret., 2006. Officiating coord. Aaronic Mins., Aaronic priesthood; field instr. U. Pitts., 1985-97, Allegheny C.C., Pitts., 1994-97; cons. Pa. Health Info. Mgmt., 1987-97; mem. curriculum coun. Ind. Dist. Sci. Coun., 2002. Mem. Am. Assn. Healthcare Quality, Western Pa. Assn. Healthcare Quality, Am. Health Info. Mgmt. Assn., Western Pa. Health Info. Mgmt. Assn., Beaver Valley Piecemakers, Ohio Assn. Health. Avocations: piano, quilting, doll making, crocheting. Home: 17800 Bolger Rd Apt 408B Independence MO 64055-6775

BRYAN, MARY JO W., realtor, artist, art educator; b. Dumas, Tex., Apr. 12, 1944; d. Edwin Franklin and Martha Lou (Workman) Williams; m. Gary W. Bryan, June 4, 1966; children: Mark William, Stacy Lynn. BS in Edn., Tex. Tech U., 1966; MEd in Guidance and Counseling, North Tex. U., 1969; MA in Art, West Tex. A&M U., 1994. Cert. tchr., all-level counselor, Tex. Tchr. Lubbock (Tex.) Ind. Sch. Dist., 1966, Irving (Tex.) Ind. Sch. Dist., 1966-68, Dallas Ind. Sch. Dist., 1968-69, counselor, 1969-71; bus. mgr. Gary W. Bryan, M.D., P.A., Amarillo, Tex., 1977—2002; artist Amarillo, 1994—; mgr. Prudential Ada Realtors, 2003—. Organizer Healthtreat, Med. Alliance, 1988; speakers chmn. Med. Alliance AIDS Program, 1992-96; mem. Leadership Amarillo, C. of C., 1989-90; Mem. Polk Street United Meth. Ch., class program com., 1988, 90, 93, 95, 96, chair Role and Status of Women feminist theology, 1995-2001; bd. friends Amarillo (Tex.) Pub. Libr., 1997-2003, v.p., 2001-02; bd. dir. Panhandle Art Ctr., 2003. Mem.: Amarillo Watercolor Assn. (pres. 2002—04), Lone Star Pastel Soc., Amarillo Fine Arts (chair Fall Art Show 2002), Potter-Randall County Med. Alliance (pres. 1988—89, sec.-treas. healthreat, Svc. award 1989), Tex. Med. Alliance (chair AIDS and sexually transmitted disease 1995—99), Am. Med. Alliance, Med. Mgrs. (v.p. 1989—90, Svc. award 1989).

BRYAN, PEGGY, mathematics educator; b. Latrobe, Pa., June 9, 1961; children: Matthew Borza, Justin Borza, James Borza. BA, Seton Hill U., Greensburg, Pa., 1983; MBA, East Carolina U., 1987. Cert. in math. Pa. Math tchr. Greater Latrobe (Pa.) Sch. Dist., 1994—96, Norwin Sch. Dist., North Huntingdon, Pa., 1996—. Jr. class sponsor Norwin Sch. Dist., North Huntingdon, 2000—05. Mem.: Assn. Supervision and Curriculum Devel. Home: 2940 Seminary Dr Greensburg PA 15601 Office: Norwin HS 251 McMahon Dr North Huntingdon PA 15642 Office Phone: 724-861-3005. Personal E-mail: pbryan@norwinsd.org.

BRYAN, SHARON E., literature and language educator; b. Portland, Oreg., Oct. 14, 1956; d. William Milton Bryan and Beverly Jean Alvord; m. Patrick Alan Scott, Aug. 16, 1980; 1 child, Anthony. BA in English, U. Oreg., Eugene, 1978, M of Curriculum and Instrn., 1985. Cert. K-12 continuing edn. Wash. Tchr. English La Ctr. HS, 1979—. Chairperson English dept. La Center H.S., 1983—. Author: (book) La Center High School: Its History and Its Graduates, 2001. Named Most Influential Tchr., Clark Coll., 1986; recipient Tchr. Leadership Project grant, Microsoft Inc., 2000, Secondary Award of Excellence, Whitman Coll., 2001. Mem.: La Center Edn. Assn. (pres. 1979—), Am. Film Inst., Wash. Edn. Assn. Avocations: films, literature. Office: La Center H S 725 Highland Rd La Center WA 98629 E-mail: shbryan@adelphia.net.

BRYANT, ANNE LINCOLN, educational association executive; b. Jamaica Plain, Mass., Nov. 26, 1949; d. John Winslow and Anne (Phillips) B.; m. Peter Harned Ross, June 15, 1986; stepchildren: Charlotte Ross, George Ross. BA in English, Secondary Edn., Simmons Coll., 1971; EdD in Higher Edn., U. Mass., 1978. Intern U. Mass., Amherst, 1972; asst. to dean Springfield Tech. C.C., 1972-74; dir. Nat. Assn. Bank Women Ednl. Found., Chgo., 1974-86; v.p. P.M. Haeger, Chgo., 1978-86; exec. dir. AAUW, Washington, 1986-96, also exec. dir. Ednl. Found., Legal Advocacy Fund; exec. dir. Nat. Sch. Bds. Assn., Washington, 1996—. Contbr. articles to profl. jours. Mem. exec. com. Simmons Coll., Boston, 1971—; adv. commr. Edn. Commn. States, 1986—; mem. bd. govs. UNA of U.S.A., 1991—97, Ind. Sector, 1988-94, Hosp. Corp. Am., 1993-94. Recipient William H. Cosby Jr. award U. Mass., 1983; named Woman of Yr. for Edn., YWCA, 1976. Fellow Am. Soc. Assn. Execs. (bd. dirs. 1985-88, Key award 1992); mem. Am. Assn. for Higher Edn. (bd. dirs. 1980-87). Episcopalian. Avocations: tennis, skiing, reading, walking. Office: NSBA 1680 Duke St Alexandria VA 22314 E-mail: alb3@nsba.org.

BRYANT, BARBARA EVERITT, academic administrator, researcher, retired marketing professional, retired federal agency administrator; b. Ann Arbor, Mich., Apr. 5, 1926; d. William Littell and Dorothy (Wallace) Everitt; m. John H. Bryant, Aug. 14, 1948; children: Linda Bryant Valentine, Randal E., Lois. AB, Cornell U., 1947; MA, Mich. State U., 1967, PhD, 1970; HonD, U. Ill., 1993. Editor art Chem. Engring. mag. McGraw-Hill Pub. Co., N.Y.C., 1947-48; editl. rsch. asst. U. Ill., Urbana, 1948-49, free-lance editor, writer, 1950-61; with continuing edn. adminstrn. dept. Oakland Univ., Rochester, Mich., 1961-66; grad. rsch. asst. Mich. State U., East Lansing, 1966-70; sr. analyst to v.p. Market Opinion Rsch., Detroit, 1970-77, sr. v.p., 1977-89; dir. Bur. of the Census, U.S. Dept. Commerce, 1989-93; rsch. scientist Ross Sch Bus., U. Mich., 1993—. Author: High School Students Look at Their World, 1970, American Women Today & Tomorrow, 1977, Moving Power and Money: The Politics of Census Taking, 1995; contbr. articles to profl. jours. Mem. U.S. Census Adv. Com., Washington, 1980—86, Mich. Job Devel. Authority, Lansing, 1980—85; state editor LWV of Mich., 1959—61; bd. dirs. Roper Ctr. for Pub. Opinion Rsch., 1993—2004; mem. nat. adv. com. Inst. for Social Rsch., U. Mich., 1993—. Fellow: Am. Statis. Assn.; mem.: Am. Assn. Pub. Opinion Rsch., Am. Mktg. Assn. (pres. Detroit 1976—77, midwestern v.p. 1978—80, v.p. mktg. rsch. 1982—84, found. trustee 1993—2001), Rotary, Cosmos Club. Republican. Presbyterian. Avocation: swimming. Home: 1505 Sheridan Dr Ann Arbor MI 48104-4051 Office: Ross Sch of Business U Mich Ann Arbor MI 48109-1234 Office Phone: 734-763-9062. Business E-Mail: bryantb@umich.edu.

BRYANT, BERTHA ESTELLE, retired medical/surgical nurse; b. Va., Jan. 11, 1927; d. E.F. and Julia B. Diploma, Sibley Meml. Hosp., Washington, 1947; BS, Am. U., 1948; MA, Tchrs. Coll., Columbia U., 1962. Staff nurse, head nurse NIH, Bethesda, Md., 1954-59; asst. dir. nursing USPHS Alaska Native Hosp., Mt. Edgecumbe, 1959-61; instr. Sch. Nursing, U. Mich., 1962-64; chief div. clin. nursing Bur. Nursing, D.C. Dept. Public Health, Washington, 1964-65; commd. Nurse Corps, USPHS, 1965, nurse dir., capt., 1974—. Nurse cons., hosp. facilities services br., div. hosps. and med. facilities Bur. Health Services, HEW, Silver Spring; nurse cons., social analysis br., div. health services research and analysis Nat. Center Health Services Research, Health Resources Adminstrn., HEW, Rockville, Md.; nurse cons. div. extramural research Nat. Center Health Services Research, Office Asst. Sec. Health, HHS, Hyattsville, Md., 1977-81 Contbr. articles to profl. jours. Mem. AAUW, Assn. Mil. Surgeons U.S., Commd. Officers Assn. USPHS

BRYANT, BETTY JEAN, bank executive; b. Mountain Grove, Mo., Oct. 9, 1940; d. James A. and Joyce D. (Cramer) Bryant; m. Fernando Guzman, Apr. 1, 1981. JD, Whittier Coll., 1968. Bar: Calif., U.S. Dist. Ct. (ctrl. dist.) Calif. 1969. Clk. LA County Clk.'s Office, 1963—69; assoc. trust counsel Security Pacific Nat. Bank, LA, 1969—73; assoc. counsel Union Bank, LA, 1973—77; asst. sec. gen. counsel Calif. Bus. and Transp. Agy., Sacramento, 1977—78; dir. Calif. Dept. Econ. and Bus. Devel., Sacramento, 1978—80; sr. v.p., dir. Am. City Bank, LA, 1980—83; dir. govt. and pub. affairs LA (Calif.) County Transp. Commn., 1983—85; mgr. pub. affairs E. Bay Mcpl. Utility Dist., Oakland, Calif., 1985—. Mem. adv. com. on revenue Mayor of LA, 1975; mem. task force on women's rights Calif. Atty. Gen., 1974, 75; dir., officer job creation bd. LA (Calif.) County Econ. Devel. Coun.; mem. adv. coun. LA County Dist. Atty.; pres. Ctrl. Adv. Coun. LA City Sch. Dist. for Girl's Week. Recipient Outstanding Career Woman award, 1973, Outstanding Vol. Svc. to Cmty. award, 1976, Ernestine Stahlhut award, 1978, Alumnus of Yr. award, Whittier Coll., 1978. Mem.: ABA, Nat. Assn. Women Lawyers (regional dir. S. Pacific), Calif. Banker's Assn., Am. Inst. Banking, Women Lawyer's Assn. LA (past pres.), Calif. Women Lawyers, Nat. Bus. and Profl. Women Lawyers (past pres., named woman of achievement 1978), Calif. State Bar (joint com. on structures of judiciary), LA (Calif.) County Bar Assn. (trustee 1975—77), Women's Assn., Calif. C.of C.

BRYANT, CARMEN JULIA, missionary, educator; b. Redding, Calif., Apr. 25, 1943; d. Ray Kenneth Michaels and Nettie Pearl Bradley; m. Donald Roy Bryant, June 1, 1963; children: Julia Lynn Webster, Brenda Sue Dodd, James Robert. BA in Spanish, Pacific U., Forest Grove, Oreg., 1964; MA in Exegetical Theology, Western Sem., Portland, 1992, ThM, 2000. Lic. Oreg., 2000. Tchr. Forest Grove (Oreg.) Pub. Sch., 1964—65; missionary, Bible translator CB Internat., Borneo, Indonesia, 1969—92, missionary educator Isabela, Philippines, 1992—97; missionary Mission to the Ams., Portland, 1997—; adj. prof. theol. writing Western Sem., Portland, 1998—2000; adj. prof. writing and Spanish Multnomah Bible Coll., Portland, 1999—. Mem.: Evang. Theol. Soc. Conservative. Baptist. Achievements include first to reduce two Dayak tribal languages to writing and developed dictionaries for the languages (Borneo). Avocation: piano. Home: 1285 SE Maple St Hillsboro OR 97123 Office: Multnomah Bible Coll 8435 NE Glisan St Portland OR 97220 Personal E-mail: carmenhills@comcast.net. E-mail: cjbryant@multnomah.edu.

BRYANT, COLLEEN CANNINGTON, history educator; b. Alexandria, Va., Aug. 9, 1956; d. Curtis Frederick and Doris Jean Cannington; m. William Gary Bryant, Oct. 28, 1978; children: Craig William, Jacqueline Brooke Tuck. BA, North Ga. Coll., Dahlonega, 1978; MA in Edn., Western Carolina U., Cullowhee, NC, 1986; postgrad., Coll. William and Mary, 2006—. Tchr. Dept. Def. Dependent Schs., Heidelberg, Germany, 1987—89, Chesterfield County Pub. Schs., Va., 1990—2001; instrnl. specialist history Va. Dept. Edn., Richmond, 2001—04; instrnl. specialist history and social sci. Chesterfield County Pub. Schs., 2004—. Nursery worker, substitute Sunday sch. tchr. Ironbridge Bapt. Ch., Chesterfield. Maj. U.S. Army, 1978—98. Decorated Army Commendation medal U.S. Army. Mem.: Va. Consortium Social Studies Specialists and Coll. Educators (treas. 2005—06). Office: Chesterfield County Public Schools 2318 McRae Rd Richmond VA 23235 Office Phone: 804-560-2759. Office Fax: 804-560-9182. E-mail: colleen_bryant@ccpsnet.net.

BRYANT, DEANNE, music educator; b. Grand Rapids, Mich., Mar. 30, 1943; d. Harold Frederick and Lillie Edna Hauser; m. Gerald I Bryant, June 29, 1968; stepchildren: Gerald Michael, Gary Alan, Linda Renee Smith. MusB, Ill. State U., 1965, MusM, 1970. Music tchr. Carbondale Pub. Sch., 1965—66; orch. instr. Elmhurst Elem. Dist., 1967—68; dir. orch. program Unit #5 Sch., Normal, Ill., 1968—93; condr. and mgr. Bloomington Normal Youth Symphony, 1994—; adj. music faculty Ill. Wesleyan U., 1994—. Orch. mentor Music Educators Nat. Conf., 2003, 05. Vol. BroMenn Health Care Cr., 1993—. Mem.: Ill. Music Educators Assn., Music Educators Nat. Conf., Am. String Tchrs. Assn. (Disting. Svc. award 2006). Avocations: travel, needlecrafts, walking. Office: Ill Wesleyan U Music Dept Bloomington IL 61702 Business E-Mail: dbryant@iwu.edu.

BRYANT, IRENE MELBA, retired elementary school educator, artist; d. Leon Lawrence and Dorothea Irene Spottswood; m. S.L. Bryant (div.). BFA, U. Cin., 1973, MFA, 1975, MA, 1993; MEd, Xavier U., 1992. Permanent tchg. cert. Ohio. Classroom art specialist Cin. Pub. Schs., 1984—91, 1992—2005; Montessori art specialist Lackland Elem. Sch., Ohio, 1992—93; ret., 2005. Represented in permanent collections U. Cin., numerous pvt. collections. Mem. adv. coun. Pub. Rels. Commn., Cin., 1980—88; trustee Comm. of the Arts, Cin., 1997—98; vol. Cin. Art Mus., 1994—; bd. dirs. Crayons to Computers, Cin., 1997—99. Fellow U. Cin., 1983; scholar, 1973, 1977. Avocations: painting, swimming. Home: 17 Merzen Ct Cincinnati OH 45217-2002

BRYANT, JONANNA ROCHELLE, registered nurse; b. Cinn., Nov. 12, 1969; d. Jonathan and Martha (Anderson) R. BSN, Coll. New Rochelle, 1991; MSB, Phila. Biblical U., 2005. RN. RN pvt. duty HSSI, Phila., 1991-92; RN homecare MCW Healthcare Providers, Phila., 1993, Hahnemann Univ. Hosp., Phila., 1994-98, RN staff nurse, 1991-99; case mgr. Intracorp., 1999—2003, Cheltenbaun Nursing and Rehab. Ctr., 2003—04; unit mgr. Gen. Healthcare Resources, 2003—; staff nurse Albert Einstein Med. Ctr. Willowiest Divsn., 2005—06, Centennial Village Nursing and Rehab., 2006—. Mentor Hahnemann Univ. Hosp., 1994, youth supervisor, Jones Meml. Baptist Ch. Democrat. Baptist. Home: 6529 N 20th St Philadelphia PA 19138 Personal E-mail: mrsjobryant@aol.com.

BRYANT, JOSEPHINE HARRIET, library executive; b. Oshawa, Ont., Can., Dec. 3, 1947; d. Donald Joseph and Margaret Mary (Quilty) B.; children: David Joseph, Michael Andrew. BA, U. Toronto, Ont., 1969, BLS, 1970, MLS, 1974; diploma in Pub. Adminstrn., U. Western Ont., London, 1988. Libr. Ont. Hydro, Toronto, 1970-74; libr. supr. Brampton Pub. Libr. and Art Gallery, Ont., 1974-77, br. head Ont., 1977-79; regional dir. Fairview North York Pub. Libr., Ont., 1983-85, mgr. century libr. Ont., 1986, dep. dir. Ont., 1986-88, CEO Ont., 1988-98; city libr. Toronto Pub. Libr., Ont., 1998—. Co-chair faculty info. sci. fundraising com., dean's adv. com. U. Toronto. Mem. ALA, Can. Libr. Assn., Ont. Libr. Assn., Inst. Pub. Adminstrn., Urban Libr. Coun., Public Libraries Internat. Network. Avocation: golf. Office: Toronto Pub Libr 789 Yonge St Toronto ON Canada M4W 2G8 Office Phone: 416-393-7032. Business E-Mail: jbryant@torontopubliclibrary.ca.

BRYANT, LA KESHA JOY, physical education educator; b. Pa., June 27, 1980; d. Percy J. Bryant III and Darlene Smith Bryant. BA, Rowan U., Glassboro, N.J., 2004. EMT Nat. Registry of EMTs; std. cert. tchr. of health and phys. edn. State Bd. of Edn., basic mil. tng. course USAF. Cashier Dollar Store, Washington, NJ, 1996—98; dispatcher C.O.P.S. Monitoring, Williamstown, NJ, 1998—2005; asst. sec. Inst. of Bus. Mgmt., Rowan U., Glassboro, 1998—2000; mem. phys. and recreation asst. staff EOF/MAP Pre-Coll. Inst., Rowan U., Glassboro, 2001, 177th Figther Wing, Air N.G., Egg Harbor Township, NJ, 2002—; substitute tchr. Wash. Twp. Bd. of Edn., NJ, 2004—05; tchr. of health and phys. edn. Gloucester County Inst. of Tech., Sewell, NJ, 2005—. Coach jr. varsity cheerleading Gloucester County Inst. of Tech., Sewell, NJ, 2005—; adviser Christian Fellowship of Athletes, Gloucester County Inst. of Tech., Sewell, 2005—; mem. Airmen's Coun., Egg Habor Township, NJ, 2002—. Mem., treas. NAACP, Glassboro, 1999—2004; mem., corr. sec., parliamentarian Black Cultural League, Rowan U., Glassboro, 1999—2002; vol. coach Glassboro Midget Football / Cheerleading Assn., 2002—03; mem., historian, treas. Nat. Panhellenic Coun., Rowan U., Glassboro, 2000—04; mem., historian 3-D Dance (Dangerously Diverse Dancers), Rowan U., Glassboro, 1998—2004; mem., sr. yr. capt. Clayton H.S. Field Hockey, 1994—98; mgr. Clayton H.S. Girls Basketball, 1995—96; v.p., mem. Students United for Racial Equality Club, Clayton, 1993—98. Named Student of the Month, Clayton Pub. Sch., 1994—96, Airman of the Quar., 177th Fighter Wing Air N.G., 2005; recipient Honors Acad. awards, Clayton Pub. Schs., 1994—97, Student Excellent awards, 1994—97, USAF Cert. of Appreciation Sheppard AFB Chapel Squadron Program, Sheppard AFB Chapel Rope Program Dir., 2004. Mem.: AAHPERD (assoc.), Alpha Kappa Alpha (assoc.). Office Phone: 856-468-1446.

BRYANT, LAURA MILITZER, artist; b. Detroit, Mar. 3, 1955; d. Paul Herman and Kanella (George) Militzer; m. Matthew T. Bryant, May 25, 1980. BFA summa cum laude, U. Mich., 1978. Pres., owner, founder Prism, Buffalo, 1983-92, pres., owner St. Petersburg, Fla., 1992—. Active Emily's List, 1990—, Mus. Fine Arts, St. Petersburg, 1992—. Fla. Gulf Coast Art Ctr., 1994—. Individual artist grantee State of Fla., 1994; individual artist fellow Nat. Endowment for Arts, 1992; recipient Best of Show award Hilton Head Art League, 1995, award of excellence Craft Art, 1997. Mem. Am. Craft Coun., Knitting Guild Am. (tchr. 1995-96), Nat. Needlework Assn., Fla. Craftsmen (mem. various coms. 1993—). Office: Prism Arts 3140 39th Ave N Saint Petersburg FL 33714-4530

BRYANT, MARIAN ALANNA, electric company consultant; b. Riverside, Calif., Apr. 5, 1955; d. Alan L. Bryant and Dorothea Sara Marie Ellington; children: Collin, Erin. BSBA, U. Ariz., 1983; MBA, U. Phoenix, 1990. Mgr. acctg. DM Fed. Credit Union, Tucson, Ariz., 1983-85; fin. analyst Carondelet Health Care, Tucson, 1985-93; fin. mgr. U. Med. Ctr., Tucson, 1993-97; internal bus. cons. Tucson Electric Power Co., 1997—. Bd. dirs. Tucson Urban League, 1997-99, Frontier Little League, Tucson, 1998-99; vol. mayoral campaign Bruce Wheeler, Tucson, 1995. Mem. Assn. of Internal Mgmt. Cons., Internal Mgmt. Accts. Avocations: hiking in mountains, weightlifting, racquetball, biking, swimming. Home: 6461 W Box Canyon Dr Tucson AZ 85745-9460 Office: Tucson Electric Power PO Box 711 Tucson AZ 85702-0711

BRYANT, MOLLIE ANNETTE, counselor; b. Columbus, Ga., Apr. 5, 1949; d. Nathan and Lula Pearl Bryant; children: Reginald Dennard Bush, Erica Denise Bush. MEd, Ga. State U., 1978. Lic. counselor, mental health profl., substance abuse profl. Ga. Rehab. counselor Ga. Divsn. Rehab. Svcs., Decatur, 1980—95; dir. Comprehensive Vocat. Svcs., Atlanta, 1994—95; counselor New Horizons Cmty. Svc. Bd., Columbus, Ga., 2000—02; clin. dir. Ga. Therapy Assoc., Columbus, 2002—. Social resources cons. L.I.F.E., Inc., Stone Mountain, Ga., 1992—2006. Sponsoring founder Martin Luther King, Jr. Nat. Meml., Washington, 2006; mem. So. Poverty Law Ctr., Montgomery, Ala., 2005; sponsoring founder Civil Rights / Wall of Tolerance, Montgomery, 2005. Mem.: ASPCA, Nat. Assn. Negro Bus. and Profl. Women's Club, Inc., Humane Soc., Alpha Kappa Alpha. Home: 5280 Kingsberry St Columbus GA 31907-4233 Office: Georgia Therapy Assoc 1301 Wynnton Ct Columbus GA 31906 Office Phone: 706-576-4033. Home Fax: 706-576-4230. Office Fax: 706-576-4230. Personal E-mail: bryantmollie@bellsouth.net. Business E-Mail: mbryantgtacol@bellsouth.net.

BRYANT, MYNORA JOYCE, not-for-profit fundraiser; EdD, U. Md. Coord. counseling svcs. and student activities No. Va. CC; internat. grand basileus Sigma Gamma Rho. Named one of 100 Most Influential Black Americans, Ebony mag., 2006. Office: Ste 200 1000 Southhill Dr Cary NC 27513 Office Phone: 919-678-9721. E-mail: Mbryant@nvcc.edu.*

BRYANT, PAULA JEAN, music educator; b. Cleve., June 6, 1947; d. Fred and Jean Kuta; m. Barry W. Bryant, Aug. 20, 1971; children: Jason Allen, Jeremy Michael, Christy Lynn, Melissa Jean. BS in Music Edn., Kent State U., Ohio, 1971; postgrad., Shenandoah U., Winchester, Va., 2000—02. Pvt. violin, viola, guitar tchr., 1970—; music tchr. Sterling Park Mid. Sch., Sterling, Va., 1971—72; music and dance instr. Shenandoah Coll., 1984—86;

K-8 music tchr. Powhatan Sch., Boyce, Va., 1986—. Violinist Manila Symphony, 1968—70, Philippine Nat. Philharmonic, 1968—70; dancer Harariya Dance Co., Philippines, 1969—70. Office: Powhatan Sch 49 Powhatan Ln Boyce VA 22620-2207

BRYANT, PEGGY JEAN, editor, journalist; b. Amarillo, Tex., Apr. 24, 1931; d. Harry R. and Gertrude J. (Culwell) Williams; m. Ira Ludwig Bryant, May 1953; children: Tim, Holly. Student, Mary Hardin-Baylor Coll., 1948—49; BA in Journalism, Ariz. State U., 1952. Editor woman's page Mesa (Ariz.) Daily Tribune, 1952—53; editor Chandler Arizonian, 1953—54, eloy Enterprise, Ariz., 1955—58; reporter, news editor, mng. editor Tempe (Ariz.) Daily News, 1959—79, editor, 1980—. Bd. dirs. Tempe (Ariz.) United Way, Tempe (Ariz.) St. Lukes Hosp., Tempe (Ariz.) Cmty. Coun. Mem.: Tempe (Ariz.) Bus. and Profl. Women (past pres.), Zonta Club. Office: Tempe Daily News-Tribune 120 W 1st Ave Mesa AZ 85210-1312

BRYANT, RUTH ALYNE, banker; b. Memphis, Jan. 12, 1924; d. James Walter and Leola (Edgar) B. Student, Rhodes Coll. (formerly Southwestern Coll.), Memphis, 1941-43; LHD (hon.), U. Mo., St. Louis, 1990. Clk. Fed. Res. Bank of St. Louis (Memphis Br.), 1943-47, exec. sec., 1947-68, asst. cashier, 1968-69, asst. v.p., 1969-73, v.p., 1973-90. Trustee chancellor's coun. U. Mo., St. Louis, 1979—, chmn., 1985-88; pres. Premiere Performances, 1990-96, vice chmn., 1996-98, bd. dirs., 1998; mem. adv. bd. Salvation Army, St. Louis, 1983-91, DePaul Health Ctr., St. Louis, 1984-87; adv. coun. Hope Ctr., St. Louis, 1987, chmn., 1990-91; chmn. adv. coun. Riverway Sch., 1989-95; bd. dirs. Assocs. of St. Louis U. Librs., 1977—, pres., 1983-85; bd. dirs. The Vanderschmidt's Sch., 1980-86, Internat. Edn. Consortium, 1988-92; bd. dirs. St. Louis Merc. Libr., 1989—, sec., 1990-92, v.p., 1992-94, pres., 1994-2000; trustee Mo. Coun. on Econ. Edn., 1989-93; bd. dirs. Dance St. Louis, 1992—2003, v.p., 1993-94, English Lang. Sch., 1993-97; mem. devel. bd. U. Mo. Press, 2002—; bd. dirs. Ctr. French Colonial Studies, 1994-, pres. 2003-. Fellow: Winston Churchill Meml.; mem.: Bank Mktg. Assn. (dir. Mo.-Ill. chpt. 1976—79), English Speaking Union (bd. dirs. 1989—, 1989—, v.p. 1992—96, nat. bd. dirs. 1995—96, pres. 1997—, nat. bd. dirs. 1998—2004), Nat. Assn. Bank Women (editor Woman Banker 1959—62, v.p. so. region 1967—68, pres. 1970—71, trustee ednl. found. 1974—75), Mo. Bankers Assn. (mktg. and pub. rels. com. 1974—76), Am. Inst. Banking (nat. women's com. 1962—63, pres. Memphis chpt. 1968—69), Alliance Francaise of St. Louis (exec. v.p. 2001—03, pres. 2003—), Nat. Soc. Arts and Letters, Rhodes Coll. Internat. Alumni Assn. (exec. bd. 1999—2000), Univ. Club (St. Louis), The Venerable Order of St. John in Jerusalem (comdr.). Home: 625 S Skinker Blvd Apt 202 Saint Louis MO 63105-2301

BRYANT, SUSAN V., academic administrator; m. David Gardiner. BSc, King's Coll. London U., 1964; PhD in Developmental Biology, St. Mary's Hosp. Med. Sch. U. London, 1967. Postdoctoral fellow Case Western Reserve U., Cleve.; with U. Calif. Irvine, 1969—, asst. vice chancellor for plans and programs, 1973—75, acting dean, sch. biol. sciences, 1979—80, chair, developmental & cell biology, 1995—97, prof., developmental & cell biology, sch. biol. sciences, dean, sch. biol. sciences, 2000—06, vice chancellor for rsch., 2006—. Mem. Calif. Independent Citizen's Oversight Com., Calif. Regenerative Medicine; mem. adv. bd. VA office Regeneration Programs; program dir., developmental biology program NSF, 1981—82; spkr. in field. Contbr. scientific papers; mem. editl. bd. Developmental Biology, Regenerative Medicine, Journal Experimental Zoology. Mem. Ind. U. Axolotl Colony. Fellow: Assn. Women in Sci.; mem.: Am. Soc. for Cell Biology, Soc. for Developmental Biology, AAAS. Office: U Calif Sch Biol Sciences 100 BSA Mail Code 1450 Irvine CA 92697 Office Phone: 949-824-5316. Office Fax: 949-824-3035. Business E-Mail: svbryant@uci.edu.*

BRYCHTOVA, JAROSLAVA, sculptor; b. Semily, Czechoslovakia, 1924; m. Stanislav Libensky (dec. Feb. 2002). Student, Acad. Applied Arts, Prague, Czechoslovakia, 1945—51, Acad. Fine Arts, Prague, 1947—50. Designer Zeleznobrodské sklo, Zelezny Brod, Czech Republic, 1950—84. Guest lectr. Pilchuck Summer Sch., Stanwood, Wash., Ctr. Creative Studies, Detroit, others; presenter in field. also: Heller Gallery 420 W 14th St New York NY 10014-1064 Office Phone: 212-414-4014.

BRYJAK, JACQUELINE MAE, elementary school educator; b. Chgo., July 21, 1937; d. Emil Carl and Lucille Rose (Tanke) George; m. Richard Joseph Bryjak, Aug. 21, 1965. BS in Edn., No. Ill. U., 1959; MA in Edn., Governors State U., University Park, Ill., 1988. Cert. reading specialist, elem. tchr. Tchr. Sch. Dist. 108, Highland Park, Ill., 1959-60, Sch. Dist. 124, Evergreen Park, Ill., 1960-96; ret. Mem. Internat. Reading Assn., Ill. Reading Assn., South Suburban Reading Assn., Am. Fedn. Tchrs., Ill. Fedn. Tchrs. (Local 943 coun. past recording sec., 1st and 2d v.p., pres.), Ill. PTA (life, Disting. Svc. award 1984, Tchr. of Yr. 1989-90). Avocations: travel, hiking, gardening, reading, singing in church choir.

BRYNIE, FAITH HICKMAN, writer, educator; b. Bluefield, W.Va., July 7, 1946; d. Cleland Henry and Helen Freda (Belcher) Mace; m. Lloyd Earl Brynie, July 28, 1989. BA, W.Va. U., 1967; MA, U. Colo., 1981, PhD, 1983. Project dir. biol. scis. curriculum study, Boulder, Colo., 1969-82; asst. prof. U. Colo. Sch. Edn., 1982-86; tchr. Dept. Def. Dependents Schs., Eng., 1986-91; freelance writer, 1991—. Author: Genetics and Human Health: A Journey Within, 1995, Six-Minute Science Experiments, 1996, AIDS: Facts, Issues, Choices, 1997, Six-Minute Nature Experiments, 1998, Painless Science Projects, 1998, 101 Questions Your Brain Has Asked About Itself but Couldn't Answer.Until Now, 1998, 101 Questions About Skin that got Under Your Skin.Until Now, 1999, 101 Questions About Your Immune System, 2000 (Best of Yr. award), 101 Questions about Blood and Circulaiton, 2001 (Editor's Choice award), 101 Questions about Food and Digestion, 2002 (Best of Yr. award), 101 Questions about Sex and Sexuality, 2003 (Outstanding Sci. Trade Book, 2004), 101 Questions about Human Reproduction, 2005, Parents' Crash Course in Science Projects, 2005, 101 Questions about Sleep and Dreams, 2006; editor: Odyssey (tchrs. guide), 1997—; contbr. articles to profl. jours. Recipient Presl. Scholar award, Washington, 1964. Mem. NSTA, Nat. Assn. Biology Tchrs. (past v.p., treas.), Colo. Biology Tchrs. Assn. (life). Home: 556 W Village Dr Bigfork MT 59911-6151 E-mail: fbrynie@centurytel.net.

BRYN-JULSON, PHYLLIS, soprano, music educator; m. Donald S. Sutherland. BMus, Syracuse U., 1967, MMus in Voice, 1969; PhD (hon.), Concordia Coll., Moorhead, Minn., 1995. Solo debut Lulu Suite, Boston Symphony Orch., 1966; opera debut Montezuma, 1976. Mem. faculty Kirkland-Hamilton Coll., Clinton, NY, 1969—70, Am. U., Washington, 1971, U. Md., College Park, 1971—84; mem. faculty, chair dept. Voice Peabody Conservatory, Johns Hopkins U., Balt., 1984—; tchr., summer programs at Yale, Cin., Aix-en Provence in France, the Royaumont Sch. in Paris, and Tanglewood. Singer: more than 100 recordings and CDs. Nominee Grammy award for performance in Dallapicolla's opera Il Prigioniero, Grammy for Best Vocalist in the classical music category, 1998; recipient Disting. Alumni award, Syracuse U., Paul Hume award, 1995, Amphion award, 1995, Catherine Filene Shouse award, 1995, Performance of Erwartung by Arnold Schoenberg, best opera Gramaphone award, 1995, Prix du Monde for performance in Dallapicolla's opera Il Prigioniero, Arts award, Dickinson Coll., 1997. Mem.: Minn. Composers Forum (mem. adv. panel for composers commissioning program 1981), Am. Classical Music Hall of Fame (mem., nat. artistic directorate), Am. Women Composers, Inc., Nat. Assn. Tchrs. of Singing, Southwest Chamber Orch., NEA Composer/Librettist Panel, The Theater Chamber Players of Kennedy Ctr., Pro Musicis Found., Mu Phi Epsilon (artist chmn., internat. competition 1992—). Achievements include first to give a master class at the Moscow Conservatory in 1988; first musician to receive the U.S.-U.K. Bicentennial Exch. Arts Fellowship; inducted into the Scandinavian-American Hall of Fame in 2000. Office: The Peabody Inst of the Johns Hopkins Univ One E Mount Vernon Pl Baltimore MD 21202

BRYSON, LOUISE HENRY, broadcast executive; m. John E. Bryson; 4 children. BA, Univ. Wash.; MAT, MBA, Stanford Univ. V.p. Nat. Broadcasting Co.; sr. v.p. FX Networks; exec. v.p., distbn. & bus. devel. Lifetime Television, 1999—2005; exec. v.p. gen. mgr. Lifetime Movie Network, 2005—; pres. distbn. & bus. develop. Lifetime Television, 2005—. Past dir. & chmn. KCET TV, LA; past dir. So. Calif. Public Radio; dir. Investment Co. of Am.; past. mem. PBS Nat. Bd. Mem. bd. councilors Annenberg Sch. for Comm., Univ. So. Calif.; trustee J. Paul Getty Trust, 1998—, chmn., 2006—. Recipient Excellence in Public TV Leadership award, 1998. Office: Lifetime Television 309 W 49th St New York NY 10019*

BRZEZINSKI, MIKA, TV news anchor; b. N.Y.C., May 2, 1967; m. Jim Hoffer; 2 children. B of English, Williams Coll., 1989. Desk asst. World News This Morning ABC-News, 1990; assignment editor, futures editor Sta. WTIC-TV, Hartford, 1990-91, gen. assignment reporter, 1991-92; New Haven bur. chief, substitute anchor WFSB-TV, Hartford, 1993-95, anchor Eyewitness News This Morning, At Noon, At Six, 1995-97; co-anchor Up To The Minute CBS-TV News, NYC, 1997—2000; anchor, reporter, co-anchor host Home Page MSNBC; correspondent CBS-TV News, NYC, 2001—. Recipient Excellence in Journalism award Soc. Profl. Journalists, 1996. Office: 524 W 57th St New York NY 10019-2902*

BRZOZOWY, KANDY DORIS, behavioral health writer; b. Torrington, Conn., May 7, 1962; d. Doris Marie Daigle-Menti; m. Barry Frank Brzozowy; children: Jessica, Nicole, Katherine. Various pharmacy positions throughout N.W. corner, Torrington, Conn., 1979—82; front sec. Harbour Med. Sterilization Facility, Sanford, Fla., 1985—86; front staff sec.-organizer, coord. Petrovits, Barron, Co. CPA, Torrington, 1986—88; team leader Seitz Corp., Torrington, 1990—92; radiation tech. aide, radiation oncology dept. Charlotte Hungerford Hosp., Torrington, Conn., 1992—95, constant observer, 1999—2002, psychiat. asst., adult psychiat. tech. adolescent extended day program, 2003—; office coord. Spa at Litchfield Hills, Conn., 1995—98; with guest rels. Wisdom House Retreat and Conf. Ctr., Litchfield, 1998—99. Contbr. poems. to profl. jour. Office Phone: 860-485-0542. Personal E-mail: kandyd@email.com.

BUALAT, MARIA G., computer engineer; Computer engr. NASA Ames Rsch. Ctr. Avocations: ceramics, painting, needlepoint, bicycling, hiking. Office: NASA Ames Rsch Ctr Bldg 269 Rm 122 Moffett Field CA 94035

BUBECK, MARGARET ANN, mathematics educator; b. Mt. Clemens, Mich., Dec. 9, 1965; d. Edward Thomas and Reva Elizabeth Bubeck. BA in Math Edn., U. Detroit, 1990; MA in Ednl. Leadership, Saginaw Valley State U., Mich., 1995. Tchr. mid. sch. math. St. Peter Cath. Sch., Harper Woods, Mich., 1990—93, Detroit Pub. Schs., 1993—94, East Detroit Pub. Schs., Eastpointe, 1994—99, Grosse Pointe Pub. Schs., 1999—. Personal E-mail: margaret.bubeck@gpschools.org.

BUBLITZ, DEBORAH KEIRSTEAD, pediatrician; b. Boston, Feb. 28, 1933; d. George and Dorothy (Kingsbury) Keirstead; m. Clark Bublitz, June 1, 1958; children: Nancy B. Dyer, Susan B. Schooleman, Philip K. Bublitz, Caroline D. Bublitz, Elizabeth E. Bublitz. BS, Bates Coll., 1955; MD, Johns Hopkins U., 1959. Resident St. Louis Children's Hosp., 1959-60, U. Colo. Health Sci. Ctr. and Dept. Health and Hosps., Denver, 1968-74; pvt. practice Littleton, Colo., 1974—; asst. clin. prof. pediatrics U. Colo. Health Sci. Ctr. and Children's Hosp., 1975-87, assoc. clin. prof. pediatrics, 1987—. Credentials com. Swedish/Porter Hosp., Englewood, Colo., 1985-87, chief dept. pediatrics, 1985-87; med. assoc., advisor LaLeche League, 1975—. Author: (with others) Clinical Pediatric Otolaryngology, 1986. Fellow Am. Acad. Pediatrics; mem. AMA, Colo. Med. Soc. (women's governing coun. 1990-96, asst. chair women's governing coun. 1993-94, chair, 1994-95), Arapahoe Med. Soc., Am. Women's Med. Assn. Episcopalian. Avocations: painting, gardening, bird watching. Home: 5621 Blue Sage Dr Littleton CO 80123-2713 Office: Littleton Pediatric Med Ctr 206 W County Line Rd Ste 110 Highlands Ranch CO 80129-2319 E-mail: littletonpeds@uswest.net.

BUC, NANCY LILLIAN, lawyer; b. Orange, NJ, July 27, 1944; d. George L. and Ethel Buc. AB, Brown U., 1965, LLD (hon.), 1994; LLB, U. Va., 1969. Bar: Va. 1969, N.Y. 1977, D.C. 1978. Atty. Fed. Trade Commn., Washington, 1969-72; assoc. Weil, Gotshal & Manges, N.Y., 1972-77, ptnr., 1977-78, Washington, 1978-80, 81-94, Buc & Beardsley, Washington, 1994—; chief counsel FDA, Rockville, Md., 1980-81. Mem. recombinant DNA adv. com. NIH, 1990-94, reduced risk tobacco products core com. Life Scis. Rsch. Office, 2005-; consensus panelist NIH Consensus Devel. Conf. on Effective Med. Treatment of Heroin Addiction, 1997; adj. prof. law Georgetown U. Law Ctr., 2000-02; bd. dirs. Dynavax Techs. Corp., Food and Drug Law Inst. Mem. editl. bd. Food Drug and Cosmetic Law Jour., 1981-87, 94-97, Jour. of Products Liability, 1981-92, Health Span: The Jour. of Health, Bus. & Law, 1984-95. Mem. adv. com. on new devels. in biotech. 1986-89, mem. adv. com. on govt. policies and pharm. R & D, 1989-93, Office of Tech. Assessment, Washington, mem. com. to study drug abuse medications devel. and rsch., 1993-95; mem. com. on contraceptive R&D, Inst. Medicine, Washington, 1994-96; trustee Brown U., 1973-78, 1998-2004, fellow, 1980-92. Recipient Disting. Svc. award Fed. Trade Commn., Washington, 1972, Award of Merit FDA, Rockville, 1981, Sec.'s Spl. citation HHS, Washington, 1981, Ind. award Associated. Alumni of Brown U., 1991. Mem. ABA (mem. spl. com. to study FTC 1988-89), Nat. Partnership for Women and Families (bd. dirs.). Office: Buc & Beardsley 919 18th St NW Ste 600 Washington DC 20006-5507 Office Phone: 202-736-3610. Business E-Mail: nlb@bucbeardsley.com.

BUCCI, MARY D., lawyer; BA summa cum laude, Trinity Coll., 1996; JD, Northeastern U., 1999. Bar: Mass., US Dist. Ct. (Dist. Mass.), US Ct. Appeals (1st Cir.). Mem. Turnaround Mgmt. Assn., Internat. Women's Insolvency & Restructuring Confederation. Mem.: Women's Bar Assn., Boston Bar Assn. (mem. pro bono com., Bankruptcy Sect.), Mass. Bar Assn., ABA. Office: Brown Rudnick One Financial Ctr Boston MA 02111 Office Phone: 617-856-8134. Office Fax: 617-289-0478. E-mail: mbucci@brownrudnick.com.*

BUCEY, CONSTANCE VIRGINIA RUSSELL, retired elementary school educator, education educator; b. Miami, Aug. 22, 1936; d. Mose and Lillian (Jones) Russell; m. Henry Lee Bucey. BS Virginia State Coll., 1959, postgrad. U. Miami, 1961—63; postgrad. Fla. A&M U., Tallahassee, 1962—63; postgrad. UCLA, 1970; MA and Reading Specialist Credential, Pepperdine U., 1976. Tchr. J.R.E. Lee Elem. Sch., South Miami, Fla., 1959—67, Margaret Duff Elem. Sch., Rosemead, Calif., 1974—82, Hillcrest Elem. Sch., Monterey Park, Calif., 1982—95; ret., 1995; part-time prof. Calif. State U. Charter Sch. Edn., L.A., 1998—, univ. supr. in divsn. curriculum and instrn., 1998—. Bd. pres., v.p., dir. First Fin. Fed. Credit Union, 1973—82, dir., 1985—. Los Angeles Ct. juror docent. Recipient Vol. Achievement Filene award, 1997, awards for oil paintings, various exhbns. Mem.: AAUW, NEA, Nat. Assn. Credit Union Presidents, Ret. Tchrs. Calif., Garvery Sch. Tchrs., Calif. Tchrs. Assn., Reading Specialists of Calif., Southland Art Assn., Bus. and Profl. Womens Club, Am. Legion Aux., Alpha Kappa Alpha. Home: 871 Ashiya Rd Montebello CA 90640

BUCHANAN, ALICE MOORE, education educator; PhD, Tex. A&M U., College Station, 1996. Assoc. prof. Auburn U., Ala., 1997—. Contbr. articles to profl. jours. Mem.: AAHPERD, Assn. Tchr. Educators. Office: Auburn Univ 2050 Memorial Coliseum Auburn University AL 36849 Office Phone: 334-332-0540.

BUCHANAN, CAROLEE HORSTMAN, special education educator, consultant; b. Sheridan, Wyo., Oct. 16, 1944; d. Carl Edgar and Marjorie Rowell Horstman; divorced; children: Carl Jeffries, P. Kent Jeffries, Jennie L. Anderson. BE, Black Hills State Univ., Spearfish, S.D., 1983; cert. in resource specialist, U. Calif., 1994. Cert. Special Edn. Black Hills State Univ., 1988, tchg. endorsement Wyo., 2001. Special edn. profl. Spearfish S.D. Pub. Sch., 1986—88; special edn. tchr. Albuquerque Pub. Sch., Albuquerque, 1988—90, Alvord Pub. Sch., Riverside, Calif., 1990—94, Bedford Pub. Sch., Mass., 1994—95, Turqoise Trail Charter Sch., Santa Fe, 1995—96, Ayer Pub. Sch., Mass., 1996—98; special edn. cons. Wyo. Dept. of Edn., Cheyenne, Riverton, Wyo., 1998—. State coord. McKinney Veto Homeless Edn., Wyo., 2000—. Mem.: P.E.O. Ednl. Orgn. Meth.

BUCHANAN, EDNA, writer, retired journalist; b. Paterson, NJ; Journalist Miami Beach (Fla.) Daily Sun, 1965-70; became journalist The Miami (Fla.) Herald, 1970. Author: Carr: Five Years of Rape and Murder, 1979, The Corpse Had a Familiar Face: Covering America's Hottest Beat, 1987, Nobody Lives Forever, 1990, Never Let Them See You Cry: More From Miami, America's Hottest Beat, 1992, Contents Under Pressure, 1992, Miami, It's Murder, 1994, Suitable for Framing, 1995, Act of Betrayal, 1996, Margin of Error, 1997, Pulse, 1998, Garden of Evil, 1999, You Only Die Twice, 2001, Cold Case Squad, 2004, Shadows, 2005; contbr. articles to popular mags. Recipient Green Eye Shade award Soc. Profl. Journalists, 1982, Pulitzer prize for gen. reporting, 1986, George Polk Career award, 2001. Mem. United Ch. of Christ. Office: care Don Congdon Assocs 156 5th Ave Ste 625 New York NY 10010-7002

BUCHANAN, ELIZABETH SPOON, assistant principal, language educator; b. Ashboro, N.C., June 7, 1942; d. Ernest Clyde and Ada Roanna Spoon; 1 child from previous marriage, Amy Louise Buchanan-Feinberg. BA in History, Winthrop U., Rock Hill, S.C., 1962; MA in French, U. S.C., Columbia, 1973; PhD in Applied Linguistics, Georgetown U., Washington; EdM in Adminstrn. and Supervision, George Mason U., Fairfax, Va., 1990. Tchr. Charleston County Schs., SC, 1962—68, Wake County Schs., Raleigh, 1968—72, Fairfax County Schs., Reston, Va., 1978—98; asst. prin. and tchr. ESL Tabernacle Elem. Sch., 1998—; instr. Randolph Cmty. Coll., Asheboro, NC, 1999—. Bilingual interpreter Randolph Hosp., Asheboro, NC, 1999—. Author poetry, (plays) Death of an American Dream, 1996. Sec.-treas. Randolph Hist. Soc., Asheboro, NC, 1998—; treas. Gamecock Alumni Club of Triad, High Point, 2000—; com. mem. Undergrad. Admissions Bd., Asheboro, 1999—. Recipient Golden Eagle award, Fairfax County Schs., 1996, Disting. Educator award, Randolph County Schs., 2001, 2002; Fulbright scholar Argentina, U.S. Govt., 1986, Fulbright scholar Mexico, 1992, Fulbright scholar Scotland, 2003. Mem.: ASCD, N.C. Assn. Prin. and Asst. Prin. Baptist. Avocations: pottery, quilting, travel, theater. Office: Tabernacle Elem Sch 4901 Tabernacle Sch Rd Asheboro NC 27205-2859 Office Phone: 336-629-3633.

BUCHANAN, LOUISE, political organization worker, consultant; d. James Ellis and May (Hall) Buchanan. BA, Blue Mountain Coll., 1958; MA, Carver Sch. Missions and Social Work, 1960. Exec. dir. Bapt. Good Will Ctr., Charleston, SC, 1960—65; comty. organizer Inner City Meth. Coun., Louisville, 1965—66; neighborhood coord. Comty. Action Commn., Louisville, 1966—71; supr. comty. resources Ky. Dept. Child Welfare, Louisville and Frankfort, Ky., 1971—74; exec. asst. to Rep. Jack Kemp U.S. Ho. Reps., Washington, 1974—76, exec. asst. to Rep. Joe Early, 1976—93; cons. child advocacy Washington, 1993—; mem. adv. bd. Efforts from Ex-Convicts, Washington, 1978—96; exec. bd. pres. Life Pieces to Masterpieces, Washington, 1997—; mem. adv. bd. Congl. Chorus, Washington, 1989—. Organizer Capitol Hill Staffers for Hungry and Homeless, Washington, 1976—93; trainer benefit walks For Love of Children, Washington, 1988; active Arlingtonians for Better County, 1997; mem. Common Cause, 1989—; coord. Capitol Hill Women's Polit. Caucus, Washington, 1976—83; mem., v.p. Park Spring Bd. Park Spring Condo Assn., 1999—. Recipient Keys to City of Worcester, Mass., Worcester City Coun., 1986, 1988, outstanding Svc. award, Efforts from Ex-Convicts, 1992, Leadership award, Life Pieces to Masterpieces, 2002. Democrat. Presbyterian. Avocations: music, writing, travel, tennis, being a loyal friend. Home: # 201 5075 7th Rd S Arlington VA 22204 Office: Consulting for Creative Change # 201 5075 7th Rd S Arlington VA 22204 Office Phone: 703-820-7293. Personal E-mail: lbuch44@msn.com.

BUCHANAN, MARY BETH, prosecutor; BA, Calif. U. Pa., 1984; JD, U. Pittsburgh Sch. Law, 1987. Assoc. Strassburger, McKenne, Gutnick and Potter, Pittsburgh, 1987—88; asst. US atty. civil divsn. (we. dist.) Pa. US Dept. Justice, 1988—92, asst. US atty. criminal divsn. (we. dist.) Pa., 1992—2001, US atty. (we. dist) Pa., 2001—, dir. exec. office US Attorneys Washington, 2004. Mem. adv. com. U.S. Sentencing Commn., 2002—03; chair adv. com. U.S. Attys., 2003—04. Pres. bd. dir. Am. Heart Assn.; chairperson Crimes Against Children Task Force; v.p. Parental Stress Ctr.; sec. Found. Calif. U. of Pa. Recipient Susan B. Anthony award, Women's Bar Assn., 2002, Vectors Pitts. Person of Yr. award, law and govt., 2003, Athena award, Pitts. C. of C., 2004. Mem.: Internat. Women's Forum, Pa. Commn. on Women in the Profession, Women's Bar Assn. of Western Pa. (pres.), Am. Inns of Court (pres., U. Pitts. Chapt.), Allegheny County Bar Assn. (chair, judiciary com., chair, criminal practice com., Fed. Ct. Sect.). Office: US Attys Office 633 US Post Office & Courthouse Pittsburgh PA 15219*

BUCHANAN, PATRICIA O'NEILL, retired social worker; b. Sacramento, Sept. 25, 1928; d. Leland Francis O'Neill and Clare Gertrude Rooney; m. Duncan F. Buchanan, May 16, 1953; children: Mary Clare, Maureen(dec.), Paul, Kate, Margaret. BA, U. Calif., Berkeley, 1951. Ins. agt. Liberty Mut., San Francisco, 1951—53; social worker Alameda County Social Svcs., Oakland and Hayward, Calif., 1952—54, 1966—89; substitute tchr. Union City Unified Sch. Dist., Calif., 1963—66; ret., 1989. Mem. Social Svcs. Com., Oakland, 1991—93. Mem. Hayward Environ. Quality Commn., 1980—87; leader Girl Scouts USA, Knights Landing, Calif., 1940—50, Hayward, 1957—60; mem. Hayward Citizens Adv. Coun., 1987—90; leader Secular Franciscans, San Leandro, Calif., 2003—; mem. Pax Christi, Fremont, Calif., 1996—. Mem.: AAUW (mem. nominating com. 2006—). Democrat. Avocations: travel, gardening, writing, hiking, bicycling. Home: 30847 Prestwick Ave Hayward CA 94544-7505

BUCHANAN, THERESA CARROLL, judge; b. Alexandria, Va., Aug. 27, 1957; BS, U. Va., 1979; JD, Coll. of William and Mary, 1982. Pvt. practice law, 1983-91; asst. U.S. atty. U.S. Dist. Ct. (ea. dist.) Va., Alexandria, 1991-96, magistrate judge, 1996—. Mem. Fed. Bar Assn., Va. State Bar Assn., Alexandria Bar Assn.

BUCHANAN, VALERIE RUSSO, nursing administrator, critical care nurse, entrepreneur, consultant; b. New Haven, Feb. 23, 1949; d. Alfred D. and Sherry (Florio) Russo; m. George F. Buchanan, 1966; children: George F. III, Gregory. AA, Middle Tenn. State U., 1980; BS, Ea. Ill. U., 1990; MPA, Albany State Coll., 1993. RN, Ill., Tenn., Ga.; cert. CCRN, nursing adminstr. Staff nurse U. Miss. Med. Ctr., Jackson, Rutherford Hosp., Murfreesboro, Tenn., S.E. Lackey Meml. Hosp., Forest, Miss.; staff nurse, asst. mgr., nurse mgr. Carle Found. Hosp., Urbana, Ill.; nurse mgr. surg. ICU, progressive care unit Phoebe Putney Meml. Hosp., Albany, Ga., 1990-92; dir. critical care nursing So. Ga. Med. Ctr., Valdosta, Ga., 1992-93; pres. The Buchanan Cos. Inc., Albany, Ga., 1994—. Affiliate faculty Albany State Coll. Contbr. articles to profl. jours. Mem. AACN, Am. Heart Assn. (cardiopulmonary and critical care nursing couns.), Am. Trauma Soc., Am. Orgn. Nurses Execs., Am. Coll. Healthcare Execs., Soc. of Critical Care Medicine, Am. Soc. Pub. Adminstrs., Ga. Hosp. Assn., Ga. Orgn. Nurse Execs., Alpha Sigma Lambda, Sigma Theta Tau. Home: 1201 N Davis St Albany GA 31701-1843 Office: The Buchanan Cos Inc PO Box 491 Albany GA 31702-0491

BUCHANOWSKI, TERESA LORRAINE, retired elementary school educator; b. Ithaca, NY, Aug. 1, 1939; d. Carl Potter and Julia Bridget Lyman; m. Robert Wiertel Buchanowski; children: Robert S., Patrick J., Teresa S., Christoper C., Gregory W., Michelle A. BS in Edn., Buffalo State U., 1973; MS in Edn., SUNY, 1978. Ins. co. receptionist, Buffalo, 1957—59; elem. tchr. West Seneca Cntrl. Sch. Sys., NY, 1973—2002; ret., 2002. Union rep. West Seneca Tchr. Assn., 1987—92, 1996—2001; coord. Gabriel Project, Sarasota, Fla., 2005—06; coord. Respect for Life ministry St. Michael the Archangel

Parish, Sarasota, 2003—06, legis. chmn. Coun. Cath. Women. Mem.: NY State Ret. Tchrs. Roman Catholic. Avocations: reading, volunteer work, travel, golf. Home: 5792 Ferrara Dr Sarasota FL 34238

BUCHAR, KAREN, mathematics educator; b. Paterson, NJ, Dec. 19, 1964; adopted d. Joseph and Terry Buhler; m. Rodney Buchar, Sept. 24, 1989; 1 child, Ariana. BA, Montclair State U., NJ, 1987. Asst. mgr. br. United Jersey Bank, NJ, 1990—94; tchr. math. Pascack Valley H.S., Hillsdale, 1996—97, Glen Rock H.S., 1997—. Mem.: Nat. Coun. Tchrs. Math. Office: Glen Rock High School 400 Hamilton Ave Glen Rock NJ 07452 Office Phone: 201-445-7700.

BUCHBINDER, ELLEN MAUD, allergist; b. N.Y.C., 1950; MD, Tulane U., 1978. Diplomate Am. Bd. Allergy and Immunology. Intern New England Deaconess Hosp., Boston, 1978-79, resident Bsoton, 1979-81; with Mt. Sinai Hosp., N.Y.C. Asst. clin. prof. Mt. Sinai Sch. Medicine. Allergy & Immunology fellow Mass. Gen. Hosp., Boston, 1981-83. Fellow ACP, Am. Acad. Allergy and Immunology, Am. Coll. Allergy and Immunology; mem. AMA. Office: 111 E 88th St Ph B New York NY 10128-1173

BUCHEISTER, PATRICIA LOUISE (PATT PARRISH), writer, artist; b. Waterloo, Iowa, Mar. 27, 1942; d. David Melvin and Elaine Rebecca Fluharty; m. Raymond Cecil Bucheister, Jan. 14, 1961; children: Scott Raymond, Todd David. Author: Make the Angel Weep, 1979, Summer of Silence, 1980, Feather in the Wind, 1981, The Sheltered Haven, 1981, The Amberley Affair, 1983, Lifetime Affair, 1985, The Dragon Slayer, 1986, Night and Day, 1986, Two Roads, 1987, The Luck of the Irish, 1988, Flynn's Fate, 1988, Touch the Stars, 1988, Time Out, 1988, Fire and Ice, 1989, Near the Edge, 1989, Elusive Gypsy, 1989, Once Burned, Twice as Hot, 1990, Relentless, 1990, The Rogue, 1990, Tropical Heat, 1990, Tropical Storm, 1991, Hot Pursuit, 1991, Island Lover, 1992, Mischief and Magic, 1992, Struck By Lightning, 1992, Tilt at Windmills, 1992, Island Lover, 1992, Stroke by Stroke, 1992, Tame a Wildcat, 1993, Unpredictable, 1995, Strange Bedfellows, 1994, Instant Family, 1995, Hot Southern Nights, 1995, Instant Family, 1995, Wild in the Night, 1994, Gypsy Dance, 1997, Below the Salt, 1999, others. Recipient Silver Palette award, 1986. Mem. Romance Writers Am., Published Authors Network, Nat. Soc. of Tole and Decorative Painters.

BUCHENHORNER, MARIANNE, psychotherapist, psychoanalyst; b. Budapest, Hungary, Sept. 15; d. Tibor and Agnes Aczel (Marks) de Nagy; m. Walter Buchenhorner, Aug. 16, 1965 (div.); m. Thomas Jacobs, Oct. 19, 1990 (dec. Dec. 1997). B.A., Vassar Coll.; M.S.W., Columbia U., 1966; D in Psychology, Internat. U., 1983; cert. in psychotherapy and psychoanalysis Postgrad. Center for Mental Health, 1975, cert. mental health cons., 1976, cert. in supervision, 1977. Rsch. asst., librarian Psychoanalytic Inst., Columbia U., N.Y.C., 1960-61; asst. to dir. of social sci. and humanities textbooks McGraw Hill Co., N.Y.C., 1961-63; case aide Youth House, N.Y.C., 1963-64; social worker Community Svc. Soc. N.Y.C., 1966-69; supr. State U. Hosp., Bklyn., 1969-71; dir. Multiple Svc. Ctr., Big Bros. Inc., N.Y.C., 1971-72; dir. counseling svcs. Postgrad. Center for Mental Health, N.Y.C., 1976-81, tchr., 1974—, supr., pvt. practice psychotherapy, N.Y.C.; supr. Inst. Contemporary Psychotherapy, N.Y.C., Ctr. Study of Anorexia and Bulimia, N.Y.C. Mem. Nat. Assn. Social Workers, Soc. Clin. Social Work Psychotherapists, Postgrad. Psychoanalytic Soc. Office: 196 E 75th St Apt 2B New York NY 10021-3256 Office Phone: 212-737-7606.

BUCHERT, STEPHANIE NICOLE, music educator; b. Seaford, Del., Sept. 2, 1976; d. John George; m. Todd Michael Buchert; children: Colby Skyler, Alyse Olivia. Student, West Chester U., 1998, BS in Music Edn., 1998. Cert. music tchr. Choir dir., asst. band dir. Cape Henlopen HS, Lewes, Del., 1998—2002; choir dir., music tchr. Lewes Mid. Sch., 1998—2001, 2002—03, Beacon Mid. Sch., 2003—. Mem.: Del. Jr. All State Choirs Com., Del. State Educators Assn., Del. Music Educators Assn. Avocations: singing, reading, drawing. Office: Beacon Mid Sch 19483 John J Williams Hwy Lewes DE 19958 Home: 31 Clover Dr Georgetown DE 19947 Office Phone: 302-645-6288 ext. 6020. Business E-Mail: sbuchert@cape.k12.de.us.

BUCHIN, JACQUELINE CHASE, psychologist; b. Providence, Nov. 27, 1935; d. Leslie Thurber and Mary Hillyer (Lyon) Chase; m. Stanley Ira Buchin, Sept. 14, 1957; children: Linda Chase Sullivan, David Lyon, Gordon Tomlinson. BA, Wellesley Coll., 1957; MEd in Counseling Psychology, Antioch U., 1979; PsyD, Mass. Sch. Profl. Psychology, Boston, 1990. Lic. clin. psychologist Mass. Dir., coord. emergency housing program Multi-Svc. Ctr., Newton, Mass., 1978-81; family therapy intern Newtom Guidance Clinic, 1981-82, Framingham (Mass.) Youth Guidance, 1982-84; psychology intern The Arbour Hosp., Boston, 1984-85, Solomon Carter Fuller Hosp., Boston, 1985-86, Behavior Assocs., Boston, 1986-90; staff psychologist Biobehavioral Treatment Ctr., Brookline, Mass., 1990—; fellow in clin. cognitive therapy program Mass. Gen. Hosp., Boston, 1993-95, clin. assoc., 1995—, rsch. clinician, 1995—; clin. assoc. dept. psychology Ctr. for Anxiety and Related Disorders, Boston U., 2005—. Clin. instr. Psychology Dept. Harvard Med. Sch., Boston, 1995—; faculty mem. Inst. Cognitive Therapy Mass. Gen. Hosp., Boston, 1996—99; founding mem. Acad. Cognitive Therapy, 2000. Pres. Wellesley Jr. Svc. League, 1972—73; mem., bd. dirs. Jr. League of Boston, 1975—77; bd. dirs. Wellesley Cmty. Chest and Coun., 1972—73, Wellesley Friendly Assoc., 1972—73, Family Counseling Region W, 1969; bd. dirs. Wellesley chpt. ARC; bd. dirs. Wellesley Cmty. Child Care, 1976, Human Rels. Svc.; trustee Mass. Sch. Profl. Psychology, 1991—. Mem.: Assn. Advancement Cognitive Behavior Therapy. Episcopalian. Home: Union Wharf Boston MA 02109-1206 Office: Biobehavioral Treatment Ctr 1051 Beacon St Brookline MA 02446-3282 Office Phone: 617-738-4814. Personal E-mail: jbuchin@att.net.

BUCHMANN, MOLLY O'BANION, choreographer, educator; b. Baton Rouge, Nov. 22, 1949; d. James Dennis and Annie Laurie (Joffrion) O'Banion; m. Fred J. Buchmann, Aug. 23, 1969; children: F. Jason (dec.), Dennis Andrew. BS in Secondary Edn., La. State U., 1971, MS in Dance, 1973. Artistic dir. Baton Rouge Ballet Theatre, 1976—; choreographer Baton Rouge Little Theatre, 1983—; tchr. dance Baton Rouge Magnet H.S., 1979-85; owner, mgr. The Dancers' Workshop, Baton Rouge, 1973—; dir. dance Scotlandville Magnet H.S., 1986-98; dance dir., profl.-in-residence dept. theatre La. State U., Baton Rouge, 1999—. Vis. artist Arts and Humanities Council of Greater Baton Rouge, 1976; choreographer Aubin Lane Dinner Theatre, Baton Rouge, 1980-82; mem. cultural caucus steering com. La. State Div. of Arts, cons., 1986. Editor La. Dance News, 1976-77. Choreographer numerous ballets. State of La. Div. Arts Choreographic grantee, 1982; Baton Rouge Alumni Fedn. scholar, 1967; recipient Mayor-Pres.'s award for excellence in the arts. Mem. Southwest Regional Ballet Assn. (bd. dirs., sec. 1984-88, parliamentarian 1993). Democrat. Roman Catholic. Office: Baton Rouge Ballet Theatre PO Box 82288 Baton Rouge LA 70884-2288 Business E-Mail: mbuchml@lsu.edu.

BUCHNER, AMANDA ELIZABETH, secondary school educator, coach, athletic trainer; b. Evanston, Ill., Oct. 26, 1975; d. Moira Kelleher; m. Marc Stephen Buchner, June 11, 2004; 1 child, Ryann Elizabeth. BA in Psychology & Fine Arts, St. Michael's Coll., Colchester, Vt., 1994—98; MEd in Athletic Tng., Plymouth State U., NH, 2001—03. Cert. athletic trainer Bd. Cert. Nebr., 2003. Cmty. life tchr., tennis coach Peddie Sch., Hightstown, NJ, 2004—. Cert. athletic trainer Ind. Contractor, NJ, 2005—. Mem.: Nat. Athletic Trainer's Assn. Avocations: knitting, beading, reading, snowboarding, tennis.

BUCHSBAUM, BETTY CYNTHIA, clinical psychologist; b. N.Y.C., May 27, 1927; d. Joseph and Kate (Havel) B.; m. William Weinstein; 1 child, Daniel James. BA, Cornell U., 1948; MA, U. Pa., 1950; PhD, Yeshiva U., 1965. Sch. psychologist N.Y.C. Bur. Child Guidance, 1954-57; staff psychologist Kings County Hosp., Bklyn., 1957-58; from instr. to asst. clin. prof. Jacobi Hosp.-Albert Einstein Coll. Medicine, Bronx, N.Y., 1958-67; chief psychology Ctr. for Preventive Psychiatry, White Plains, N.Y., 1967-68; asst. prof. Bellevue Hosp-N.Y. Med. Coll., N.Y.C., 1968-69; pvt. practice clin psychology Rye, N.Y., 1969—. Clin. asst. prof. N.Y. Hosp.-Cornell Med. Ctr., Westchester Div., White Plains, 1976-82, adj. clin. asst. prof., 1982-98; asst. clin. prof. Albert Einstein Coll. Medicine, 1981-86; dir. psychology tng. program Ctr. for Preventive Psychiatry, 1986-97, co-dir., 1997-99, cons., supr., tchr., 1999—. Contbr. chpts. to books and articles to jours.; researcher in parent loss in childhood. Mem. Am. Psychol. Assn., Westchester County Psychol. Assn., Phi Beta Kappa, Psi Chi, Phi Kappa Phi. Democrat. Avocations: classical music, reading, travel, theater, art. Address: 515 Greenhaven Rd Rye NY 10580-1016

BUCHWALD, EMILIE DAISY, publisher, editor; b. Vienna, Sept. 6, 1935; came to U.S., 1938; d. Norbert N. and Maryla (Knebel) Bix; m. Henry Buchwald, June 6, 1954; children: Jane Nicole, Amy Elizabeth, Claire Gretchen, Dana Alexandra. BA, Barnard Coll., 1957; MA, Columbia U., 1961; PhD, U. Minn., 1971. Editor Sloane Jour. Obstetrics, NYC, 1957-58; freelance editor NYC, 1958-60; instr. English U. Minn., Mpls., 1960-69; instr. Continuing Edn. for Women, Mpls., 1969-71, The Loft, Mpls., 1978-80; publisher, editor Milkweed Editions, Mpls., 1980—2003, Gryphon Press children's books, Mpls., 2006—. Author: Gildaen, 1973 (Best Book of Yr. 8-12-yr.-olds 1973), Floramel and Esteban, 1982 (Notable Book); editor: The Poet Dreaming in the Artist's House, 1984, This Sporting Life, 1988, Mixed Voices, 1991, Transforming a Rape Culture, 1993; co-editor: The Most Wonderful Books, 1997. Bd. dirs., chmn. The Loft, Mpls., 1979-84; bd. dirs. Hennepin County Libr. Found., Mpls., 1991-96, Minn. Ctr. for the Book, 1996—. Recipient The Lyric Meml. award The Lyric, 1976, W.A. White award finalist Children's Book Coun., 1984; named Marvelous Minn. Woman, Gov.'s award, 1991; finalist LMP Trade Book Editor of Yr., 1993. Mem. Minn. Wome's Econ. Round Table.*

BUCHWALD, NAOMI REICE, federal judge; b. Kingston, NY, Feb. 14, 1944; BA cum laude, Brandeis U., 1965; LLB cum laude, Columbia U., 1968. Bar: N.Y. 1968, U.S. Ct. Appeals (2d cir.) 1969, U.S. Dist. Ct. (so. and ea. dists.) N.Y. 1970, U.S. Supreme Ct. 1978. Litigation assoc. Marshall, Bratter, Greene, Allison & Tucker, N.Y.C., 1968-73; asst. U.S. atty. So. Dist. N.Y., N.Y.C., 1973-80, dep. chief civil divsn., 1976-79, chief civil divsn., 1979-80; U.S. magistrate judge U.S. Dist. Ct. (so. dist.) N.Y., N.Y.C., 1980-99, chief magistrate judge, 1994-96, U.S. dist. judge, 1999—. Editor Columbia Jour. Law and Social Problems, 1967-68. Recipient spl. citation FDA Commrs., 1978, Robert B. Fiske Jr. Assn. William B. Tendy award, Outstanding Pub. Svc. award Seymour Assn., Columbia Law Sch. Class of 1968 Excellence in Pub. Svc. award, 1998. Mem. Fed. Bar Coun. (trustee 1976-82, 97-00, v.p. 1982-84), Assn. of the Bar of the City of NY (trademarks and unfair competition com. 1988-89, mem. long range planning com. 1993-95, litig. com. 1994-96, ad hoc com. on jud. conduct 1996-99, prof., jud. ethics com. 2002-04), Phi Beta Kappa, Omicron Delta Epsilon.

BUCICCHIA, CAROLANNE STEPHANIE, elementary school educator; b. Rockville Centre, NY, Dec. 25, 1982; d. Vincent James and Carol Bucicchia Jr. BS in Music Edn., Hartwick Coll., Oneonta, NY, 2004; postgrad., Five Towns Coll., Dix Hills, NY, 2005—. Cert. music tchr. NY. Music educator Hampton Bays (NY) Union Free Sch. Dist., 2004—. Fellow: Hampton Music Educators Assn.; mem.: NY State United Tchrs., Music Educators Nat. Conf., NY State Sch. Music Assn., Suffolk County Music Educators, Hampton Bay Tchrs. Assn. Office: Hampton Bays Elem Sch 72 Ponquogue Ave Hampton Bays NY 11946

BUCK, BERNESTINE BRADFORD, retired school counselor; b. Altheimer, Ark., July 25, 1924; d. Henry Walker and Dora Lois Bradford; BA, Stowe Tchrs. Coll., 1950; MEd, U. Mo., 1973; m. Joseph Wellington Buck, Oct. 1, 1950; children: Stanley W., Linda Carol, Debra Lois. Tchr. pub. schs., St. Louis, 1950-73, sch. counselor, 1973-87. Committeewoman, St. Louis 20th Ward, 1988-89; mem. U. Mo. scholarship com., 1974-84, Antioch Bapt. Ch. scholarship com., 1980-86, Coro Reinvest Program, 1988. Mem. Am., Mo. personnel and guidance assns., St. Louis Guidance Assn. (pres. 1979-80), Mo. Guidance Assn. (exec. council 1980-81, v.p. elem. sect.), Alpha Kappa Alpha. Baptist.

BUCK, D. RUTH, legal research and writing educator; b. 1952; BA, U. Va., 1974; MEd, U Va., 1976; JD, U. Va., 1985. Bar: Ga. 1986, Va. 1986. Assoc. Neely & Player, Atlanta, 1985—86; asst. dir. com. continuing legal edn. Va. Law Found., 1986—88; instr. legal writing U. Va. Sch. Law, 1988—90, asst. prof., 1990—94, assoc. prof., 1994—2000, prof., 2000—, co-dir. legal rsch. & writing program, 1988—. Office: U Va Sch Law 580 Massie Rd Charlottesville VA 22903-1789 Office Phone: 434-924-1042. E-mail: drb7c@virginia.edu.

BUCK, DOROTHY CECELIA, psychotherapist, writer; b. St. Louis, June 2, 1940; d. Martin and Cecelia (Bishop) B.; m. Achille Snyder, Mar. 10, 1967 (div. 1979, dec. 1993); children: Raoul David, Ariane Marie. MA, Emmanuel Coll., 1987; PhD, Boston U., 1990. Ballet performer, tchr. internat. ballet cos., 1958-71; dir. Classical Ballet Acad., New Haven, 1971-85; pvt. practice psychotherapy, pastoral counseling Boston, 1990—. Bd. dirs. L'Associations Dos Amis de Louis Mossignon, Paris. Author: The Dance of Life, 1987, Dialogues with Saints and Mystics: In The Spirit of Louis Massignon, 2002; contbr. articles to profl. jours. Mem. Am. Mental Health Assn., Mass. Mental Health Counseling Assn., New Eng. Soc. Group Psychotherapy. Roman Catholic. Avocations: french language translation, church activities, travel, inter-religious prayer and reconciliation.

BUCK, JANE LOUISE, retired psychology professor; d. C. Robert and Viola Louise (Berger) B.; m. Leo Laskaris, Oct. 7, 1954 (div. Aug. 1978); 1 child, Julie. BA, U. Del., 1953, MA, 1959, MEd, 1966, PhD, 1971. Instr. U. Del., Newark, 1964-66; rsch. assoc. Rsch. for Better Schs., Phila., 1967-68; asst. prof. Del. State U., Dover, 1969-73, assoc. prof., 1973-77, prof. psychology, 1977-98; ret., 1998; pvt. cons. Cons. in stats. E.I. duPont de Nemours, Wilmington, Del., 1983-93; vis. prof. Ctr. for Sci. and Culture, U. Del., 1986; bd. dirs. The Blvd. and Beyond, Wilmington. Author: Specifying the Risk, 1985; contbr. articles to profl. jours. Speaker, evaluator Del. Humanities Forum, 1980-88; pres. Del. Gerontol. Soc., Newark, 1987-88; mem. town coun. Chesapeake City, Md., 1998-2000; commr. parks and recreation, Chesapeake City, Md., 1998-99; bd. dirs. Friends of Cecil County Libr., 2000. Mem. AAAS (mem. sr. scientists and engrs.), AAUP (nat. coun. 1987-90, 93-99, pres. Del. State U. chpt. 1976-80, 95-98, chief negotiator 1982-98, mem. nat. com. on historically Black instns. and scholars of color 1988-91, 98-2000, interim sec. Del. Conf 1991-92, pres. Del. conf. 1993-2000, mem. nat. com. govt. rels. 1994-97, Sternberg award for collective bargaining 1994, nat. pres. 2000-2006, mem. exec. com. nat. coun. 2006—), Am. Psychol. Soc., Coun. Tchrs. Undergrad. Psychology, Humanities and Tech. Assn., Am. Statis. Assn. (v.p. Del. chpt. 1999-2000), Danforth Assocs., Kappa Delta Pi, Psi Chi. Avocations: reading, gardening, sewing, computer graphics. Personal E-mail: buck@count.com.

BUCK, LINDA DEE, executive recruiting company executive; b. San Francisco, Nov. 8, 1946; d. Sol and Shirley D. (Setterberg) Press. Student, Coll. of San Mateo, Calif., 1969—70. Head hearing and appeals br. Dept. Navy Employee Rels. Svc., The Philippines, 1974-75; dir. human resources Homestead Savs. & Loan Assn., Burlingame, Calif., 1976-77; mgr. VIP Agy., Inc., Palo Alto, Calif., 1977-78; exec. v.p., dir. Sequent Pers. Svcs., Inc., Mountain View, Calif., 1978-83; founder, pres. Buck & Co., San Mateo, 1983-91. Publicity mgr. for No. Calif., Osteogenesis Imperfecta Found. Inc., 1970-72; cons. Am. Brittle Bone Soc., 1979-88; mem. Florence (Oreg.) Area Humane Soc., 1994—, Friends of Libr., Florence, 1994—; bd. dirs. Florence Festival Arts, 1995; bd. dirs., dir. women Rhododendron Scholarship Program, Florence, 1995. Jewish.

BUCK, LOUISE ZIERDT, psychologist; b. Edgewood, Pa., Nov. 21, 1919; d. Conrad Henry and Nancy Leora (Harshberger) Zierdt; div. 1954; children: David Randall, Susan Buck Sutton. BS, Pa. State U., 1940; MEd, U. Pitts., 1954; EdD, Columbia U., 1978; advanced cert., Bklyn. Coll., 1984. Lic. sch. psychologist, clin. psychologist, N.Y. Tchr., dir. Chatham Village Nursery Sch., Pitts., 1953-55, Yellow Springs (Ohio) Community Nursery Sch., 1955-58; tchr. Oak Lane Country Day Sch., Phila., 1958-59, Walden Sch., N.Y.C., 1959-60, Bank St. Sch. for Children, N.Y.C., 1960-61; early childhood tchr., coord. sch. psychology Bd. Edn., City of N.Y., 1961-87; asst. prof. Bklyn. Coll., 1978-80; rsch. fellow Albert Einstein Coll. Medicine, Bronx, N.Y., 1988-89; psychotherapist Fifth Ave Ctr. for Psychotherapy, N.Y.C., 1989, Met. Ctr. for Mental Health, N.Y.C., 1990—2006. Psychologist cons. Bd. Edn. City of N.Y., 1987-88; pvt. practice, N.Y.C. Contbr. articles to profl. jours. Mem. APA, N.Y. State Psychol. Assn., Soc. for Psychoanalytic Psychotherapy. Democrat. Avocations: travel, swimming, the arts. Home: 444 E 86th St Apt 34C New York NY 10028-6459 Office: 27 W 96th St Ste 1A New York NY 10025-6515 Office Phone: 212-749-3867. Personal E-mail: louisebuck@rcn.com.

BUCK-BACON, LOUISE JOHN, education educator; b. Norwich, Conn., June 14, 1955; d. John Kirkham and Sophie D. Buck; m. Donald F. Bacon, Oct. 21, 1978; children: Amanda Bacon, Cheyanne Bacon-Thompson. AS in Cytotechnology, Quinnipiac U., Hamdon, Conn., 1976; BA in Psychology, U. NH, Durham, 1992, MEd, 1994. Pvt. practice, Newfields, NH, 1996—. Adj. prof. NH Cmty. Tech. Coll., Stratham, 2003—. Author: How to Love Someone to Death, 2006. Vol. Seacoast Hospice, Exeter, NH, 1994—; active ARC, NH, 2003—, bd. dirs. NH, 2003—, Am. Soc. Tng. Devel., NH, 2000—03. Avocation: Karate. Home: PO Box 313 Newfields NH 03856

BUCKBEE, MALINA, music educator; d. James and Carolyn Buckbee. MusB in Music Edn., Eastman Sch. Music, Rochester, NY, 2006, postgrad., 2006—. Cert. tchr. NY, 2004. Tchr. Greece Ctrl. Sch. Dist., Rochester, 2004—. Mem.: Mu Phi Epsilon. Office: Greece Central School District 750 Maiden Ln Rochester NY 14615 Office Phone: 585-966-8612.

BUCKINGHAM, BARBARA RAE, social studies educator; b. Union City, Ind., Jan. 27, 1932; d. Ray E. and Edith A. (Wagner) B. BA cum laude, Hanover Coll., 1954; MA, Ind. Univ., 1956. Tchr. City Sch. Dist., Marion, Ohio, 1956-64, social studies educator Rochester, NY, 1966—. Editor: Revonah, 1954; art work Aldelphean, 1959. Vol. Peace Corps, Ethiopia, 1964-66, Mary Cariola Children's Ctr., Christian Heritage Homes, Hope Hall, Congresswomen Louise Slaughter Campaign, 1996-97, 96-98; mem. governing bd. Rochester Returned Peace Corps Vols., 1968-76; com. mem. Councilwoman Letvin, Gates, N.Y., 1980; steering com. Pub. Affairs Forum, Hanover, 1952, DAR. Mem. AAUW (pres. 1958-59), DAR, Rochester Tchrs. Assn., Nat. Peace Corps Assn., Friends of Ethiopia, Rochester Tchr. Assn. (election com.), Pi Gamma Mu (Outstanding Grad. award 1954), Gamma Sigma Pi, Alpha Phi Gamma. Democrat. Presbyterian. Avocations: travel, art work. Home: 64 Lyellwood Pkwy Rochester NY 14606-4532

BUCKINGHAM, DEIDRE LYN, writer, musician; b. Endicott, N.Y., Apr. 18, 1973; d. Richard Paul and Doris May (Mlynar) Moore; m. Jeff K. Buckingham, June 9, 1995. AA in Office Tech., Cedarville (Ohio) Coll., 1993, BA in Profl. Writing, 1995. Tech. writer Ont. Sys. Corp., Muncie, Ind., 1995-97. Author: Snapdragon's Dance, 2004. Caption editor Deaf Video Comm. Am., Lisle, Ill., 1997-99. Recipient Pres.'s award for lit. excellence Iliad Press, 1997, Editor's Choice award Internat. Libr. Poetry, 2003; Mari Heyduck scholar Women in Comm., 1994. Avocations: writing poetry and essays, recording original music.

BUCKINGHAM, ELIZABETH C., lawyer; b. 1964; AB magna cum laude, Smith Coll., 1985; JD, Harvard Univ., 1988. Bar: DC 1988, Minn. 1994. Ptnr., co-head, trademark and litig. group Dorsey & Whitney LLP, Mpls. Articles editor Harvard Jour. on Legis., 1987—88, lectr., writer in field. Mem.: Minn. Intellectual Property Lawyers Assn., Internat. Trademark Assn., Midwest Intellectual Property Inst., WomenVenture (bd. dir. 2000—), Phi Beta Kappa. Office: Dorsey & Whitney LLP Ste 1500 50 S Sixth St Minneapolis MN 55402-1498 Office Phone: 612-343-2178. Office Fax: 612-340-8856. Business E-Mail: buckingham.elizabeth@dorsey.com.

BUCKINGHAM, LORIE, automotive executive; BA in Math. and Chemistry, SUNY, Potsdam. Dir. enterprise IT solutions Union Carbide Corp., Danbury, Conn., 1993—99; former chief info. officer Zonetrader.com, Chgo.; dir. global software solutions Visteon Corp., Dearborn, Mich., 2000—02, v.p., chief info. officer, 2002—. Office: Visteon Corp 1700 Rotunda Dr Dearborn MI 48120

BUCKLEY, ELEANOR JANE, retired elementary school educator; b. Pitts., Pa., Jan. 23, 1936; d. Jesse Anderson and Virginia (Gillespie) Hiller; m. Richard Dale Buckley, June 19, 1965 (dec.). BSc, Ind. State Tchrs. Coll., Ind., Pa., 1958; MEd, U. Pitts., Pitts., Pa., 1960. Cert. Elem. Edn. K-8. 1st elem. tchr. Dept. Instruction Evaluation Team, Wis., 1972—77; ret. Blood drive coord. Am. Red Cross, 2000—06; citizens adv. ARC, 2000—06; pres. Delta Kappa Gamma hon. Educators Assn., 1974—75, Oshkash Educators Assn., 1984—85; bd. Oshkosh Symphony, Oshkosh, 2001—03; pres. Oshkosh Symphony League, 2002—03. Recipient Expectional Vol. Svc., Am. Red Cross, 2002, Outstanding Vol., United Meth. Women, 2002. Mem.: Oshkosh Educators Assn., Nat. Edn. Assn., Wis. Edn. Assn. Avocations: travel, painting, reading.

BUCKLEY, JOAN N., retired literature and language professor; b. Mpls., Jan. 27; d. Carl J. and Helene (Groth) Naglestad; m. Wendell D. Buckley, June 7, 1957; children: David, Julie. BA, St. Olaf Coll., Northfield, Minn., 1952; MA, U. Chgo., 1956; PhD, U. Iowa, 1976. Instr. English Concordia Coll., Moorhead, Minn., 1956-63, asst. prof., 1963-69, assoc. prof., 1969-76, prof. English, 1976—2005, ret., 2005. Named Flaat Disting. Prof., Concordia Coll., Glydenvand Prof.; NEH grantee 1977, 1980, 1983. Mem.: Norwegian-Am. Hist. Assn. (bd. dirs.), Delta Kappa Gamma (Tau State 1st v.p., U.S. forum chair, Woman of Achievement 2001). Home: 2317 Rivershore Dr Moorhead MN 56560 Office: Concordia College Dept English Moorhead MN 56562 E-mail: buckley@cord.edu.

BUCKLEY, NANCY MARGARET, retired research scientist; b. Phila., Pa., Dec. 2, 1924; d. Thomas and Margaret Craig Buckely; m. John H.E. Fried, May 22, 1984; 1 child, Jacqueline Fried Thomann. BA, U. Pa., 1948; MD, U. Pa., 1950. Cert. Medical License Pa., NY, NJ. Asst. prof. physiology Ohio State U., Columbus, 1952—56; assoc. prof. physiology and biophysics Albert Einstein Coll. of Medicine, NY, 1958—74, prof. physiology and biophysics, 1974—89; ret. Prin. investigator Nat. Inst. Health, 1958—88. Contbr. articles to profl. jours. Mem.: Physicians for Social Responsibility, NY Acad. of Sci., Women's City Club of NY. Avocations: music, travel, literature. Home: 372 Ctrl Pk W New York NY 10025

BUCKLEY, PRISCILLA LANGFORD, magazine editor; b. NYC, Oct. 17, 1921; d. William Frank and Aloise (Steiner) B. BA, Smith Coll., 1943. Copy girl, sports writer UP, N.Y.C., 1944; radio rewrite staff mem. U.P., 1944-47, Paris corr., 1953—56; news editor Sta. WACA, Camden, S.C., 1947-48; reports officer CIA, Washington, 1951-53; with Nat. Rev. Mag., N.Y.C., 1956—, mng. editor, 1959-86, sr. editor, 1986-99. Mem. U.S. Adv. Commn. Pub. Diplomacy, 1984-91. Editor: The Joys of National Review, 1995; columnist One Woman's Voice Syndicate, 1976-80; author: String of Pearls, On the Newsbeat in New York and Paris, 2001. Mem. Sharon Country Club (Conn., sec. 1973-77, pres. 1978-80, 94-95). Office: Nat Review 215 Lexington Ave New York NY 10016-6023 E-mail: pbuckley@mohawk.net.

BUCKLEY, REBECCA HATCHER, allergist, immunologist, pediatrician, educator; b. Hamlet, NC, Apr. 1, 1933; d. Martin Armstead and Nora (Langston) Hatcher; m. Charles Edward Buckley, III, July 9, 1955; children: Charles Edward IV, Elizabeth Ann, Rebecca Kathryn, Sarah Margaret. BA, Duke U., 1954; MD, U. NC, 1958. Intern Duke U. Med. Ctr., Durham, NC, 1958-59, resident, 1959-61, pediat. allergist and immunologist, 1961—. Dir., chair exam. com. Am. Bd. Allergy and Immunology, Phila., 1971—73, co-chair bd. dirs., 1982—84; chair Diagnostic Lab. Immunology, 1984—88;

mem. staff Duke U. Med. Ctr., asst. prof. pediat. and immunology, 1968—72, assoc. prof. pediat., 1972—79, prof. pediat., 1976—79, prof. immunology, J. Buren Sidbury prof. pediat., 1979—. Contbr. articles to profl. jours. Fellow: AAAS (chair med. scis. sect. 2001—03); mem.: NAS, Inst. Medicine of NAS, Am. Pediat. Soc. (coun. mem. 1991—, pres. 1999—2000, chmn. immune deficiency found. med. adv. com. 2003—), Southeastern Allergy Assn. (pres. 1978—79), Am. Acad. Pediat. (Bret Ratner award 1992), Soc. Pediat. Rsch., Am. Assn. Immunologists, Am. Acad. Allergy and Immunology (exec. com. 1975—82, pres. 1979—80, hon. fellow award 1999). Republican. Episcopalian. Home: 3621 Westover Rd Durham NC 27707-5032 Office: Duke U Med Ctr PO Box 2898 Durham NC 27710 Office Phone: 919-684-2922. Business E-Mail: buckL003@mc.duke.edu.

BUCKLEY, SUSAN, lawyer; b. Rockville Center, N.Y., Dec. 24, 1951; BA, Mt. Holyoke Coll., 1973; JD, Fordham U., 1977. Bar: N.Y. 1978, D.C. 1980. Ptnr. Cahill Gordon & Reindel LLP, N.Y.C., 1985—. Mem. ABA, N.Y. State Bar Assn. (com. on media law 1992-95), Bar Assn. N.Y.C. (com. comm. law 1986-89). Office: Cahill Gordon & Reindel LLP 80 Pine St Fl 17 New York NY 10005-1790 Office Phone: 212-701-3000.

BUCKLEY, VIRGINIA LAURA, editor; b. NYC, May 11, 1929; d. Alfred and Josephine Marie (Manetti) Iacuzzi; m. David Patrick Buckley, July 30, 1960; children: Laura Joyce, Brian Thomas. BA, Wellesley Coll., 1950; MA, Columbia U., 1952. Tchr. English Bennett Coll., Millbrook, NY, 1954-56, Berkeley Inst., Bklyn., 1956-58; copy editor World Pub. Co., N.Y.C., 1959-69; children's book editor Thomas Y. Crowell, N.Y.C., 1971-80; editl. dir. Lodestar Books, N.Y.C., 1980-97; contbg. editor Clarion Books, N.Y.C., 1997—. Author: State Birds, 1986; contbr. articles to profl. jours. Mem. ALA Home: 33 Brook Ter Leonia NJ 07605-1504 Office: Clarion Books 215 Park Ave S New York NY 10003-1603 E-mail: vlbuckley@verizon.net.

BUCKLO, ELAINE EDWARDS, United States district court judge; b. Boston, Oct. 1, 1944; married. AB, St. Louis U., 1966; JD, Northwestern U., 1972. Bar: Calif. 1973, U.S. Dist. Ct. (no. dist.) Calif. 1973, Ill. 1974, U.S. Dist. ct. (no. dist.) Ill. 1974, U.S. Ct. Appeals (7th cir.) 1983. Law clk. U.S. Ct. Appeals (7th cir.), Chgo.; pvt. practice, 1973-85; U.S. magistrate judge U.S. Dist. Ct. (no. dist.) Ill., Chgo., 1985-94, judge, 1994—. Spkr. in field. Contbr. articles to profl. jours. Mem. jud. conf. com. on adminstrn. Magistrate Judge Sys., 1998-2004; mem. vis. com. No. Ill. U. Sch. Law, 1994—; mem. Northwestern U. Law Bd., 1996-99. Mem. ABA (standing com. law and literacy 1995-98, assoc. editor Litigation), FBA (v.p. 1990-92, pres. Chgo. chpt. 1992-93), Women's Bar Assn. Ill. (bd. dirs. 1994-96), Chgo. Coun. Lawyers (pres. 1977-78). Office: US Dist Ct No Dist Everett McKinley Dirksen Bldg 219 S Dearborn St Ste 1446 Chicago IL 60604-1794

BUCKMAN, DEBRA ANN, science educator; b. Williamsport, Pa., Sept. 9, 1950; d. Dorsey Eugene and MaryJane Ringler; m. James Watson Buckman; children: Nicholas, Sean. BA, Mansfield U., Pa., 1972; M in Edn., Arcadia U., Glenside, Pa., 1977. Hazardous Waste Operator Pa. Coll. of Tech., 2005, cert. tchr. Pa. Tchr. physics and biol. scis. Sch. Dist. Phila., 1974—79; chemist Avco Lycoming, Williamsport, Pa., 1979—83; sr. chemist Litton Electron Devices, Williamsport, 1984—91; environ. engr. Textron Lycoming, 1991—95; asst. prof. environ. tech. Pa. Coll. of Tech., Williamsport, 1995—; tchr. of phys. and biol. sciences Sch. Dist. of Phila. Mem. Lycoming County Local Emergency Planning Com., Williamsport, Pa., 1985—; regional dir. Pa. Assn. of Environ. Educators. Pres. local chpt. NGA, Inc., Warminster, Pa., 1991—2006; pres., treas. Williamsport Civic Chorus, 1975—2006; author emergency response plan Litton. Environ. Edn. grant, Pa. Dept. of Environ. Protection, 2002. Mem.: Water Environment Fedn. Achievements include development of curriculum for the environmental technology program at Pennsylvania College of Technology. Avocations: music, theater. Office: Pa Coll of Tech One College Ave Williamsport PA 17701 Office Phone: 570-320-2400 ext. 3526. Business E-Mail: dbuckman@pct.edu.

BUCKMAN, LISA PAULINE, psychotherapist; b. Newburgh, NY, Aug. 26, 1963; d. William Harry and Irene Evelyn Buckman; m. Timothy Joseph Smith (div.); children: Thomas Jason Smith, Gregory Edward Smith. BA, U. Mass., 1996; MEd, Springfield Coll., 1998. Clinician Lake Grove Sch., Wendell, Mass., 1998—2001; therapist Gandara Mental Health Agy., Springfield, Mass., 2001—04; pvt. practice psychotherapy Amherst and West Springfield, Mass., 2004—. With U.S. Army, 1981—83. Mem.: Am. Mental Health Counselor Assn. (licentiate). Avocations: meditation, reading, walking, bicycling. Home: 1040 N Pleasant St Apt 12 Amherst MA 01002-1327 Office: 10 Central St Ste 30 West Springfield MA 01089 also: 664A Main St Amherst MA 01002 Personal E-mail: buckman44@hotmail.com.

BUCKMAN, TRACEY ANN, political finance director; b. Berkeley, Calif., May 25, 1964; d. Charles Albert and Tracey (Tighe) B. BA, Vanderbilt U., 1986; student, Am. U., 1988. Adminstrv. asst. Majority Whip, U.S. Senate, Washington, 1987-89; cons. The Com. for a Dem. Consensus, Washington, 1989-90; fundraising asst. Cranston for Senate, Washington, 1989-90; fundraising cons. Women's Legal Def. Fund., Washington, 1990; dep. nat. fin. dir. Senator Daniel Akaka Campaign, Washington, 1990-91; dir. membership programs Dem. Senatorial Campaign Com., Washington, 1991-93; nat. fin. dir. Senator Richard Bryan Campaign, Washington, 1993-94; nat. dir. fin. Senator Max Baucus Campaign, Washington, 1994-97; nat. fin. dir. Dem. Senatorial Campaign Com., Washington, 1997-99, Senator Joseph Lieberman campaign, Washington, 1999—. Spl. events vol. D.C. Spl. Olympics, Washington, 1988-91; vol. park guide Smithsonian Nat. Zool. Park, Washington, 1987-89; vol. Washington Humane Soc., 1995-98. Mem. NAFE, Nat. Dem. Club, Friends of the Nat. Zoo, Vanderbilt U. Washington Alumni (bd. dirs. 1991-92). Avocations: tennis, skiing, bicycling, photography, softball, scuba diving.

BUCKNAM, MARY OLIVIA CASWELL, artist, educator; b. Modesto, Calif., Feb. 6, 1914; d. Charles Henry and Helen Anne (Cross) Caswell; m. William Nelson Bucknam, June 22, 1946 (dec. 1966); children: William Nelson Jr., Charles Henry. BA, Calif. State U., San Jose, 1936; postgrad., U. Calif., Berkeley, 1938, Calif. State U., Stanislaus, 1968-75, U. San Francisco, 1968-75. Tchr. Stanislaus County (Calif.), 1936-38, Modesto (Calif.) Schs., 1938-43, San Bernardino (Calif.) City, 1943-46; art tchr. Klamath Union Schs., Klamath River, Calif., 1960-61; co-owner Bigfoot Ranch and Resort, Klamath River, 1960-66; art tchr., tchr. Riverbank (Calif.) City Schs., 1966-79; art cons. Riverbank Elem., 1986; gallery artist Cen. Calif. Art League, Modesto, 1986—. One-person show C.C.A. Ctr., 1998; exhibited in group shows at Siskiyow Artists Assn., 1961-66 (Best of show, First award, others), Stanislaus County Shows, 1975-90 (Best of show, First award, others), Caswell Park Remembered, 2000, Great Valley Mus., Modesto, 2002; Three Sisters Show Gallery, 1991-93, Travels with my Paintbrush, 1991-2003; retrospective show Ctrl. Calif. Art Ctr., Mistlin Gallery, 2004; represented in permenant collections. Donor with Caswell family of land for Caswell State Park, San Joaquin County, Calif., 1995; pres. Caswell Sch. PTA, Ceres, Calif., 1956-57, Ceres Study Club, 1952-53; v.p. Siskiyou Artists Assn., Yreka, Calif., 1963-65; pres. Modesto Tchrs. Assn., 1940-41; vol. tchr. adult watercolor classes; active Trinity Singers Choirm 1990—. Named Woman of Distinction Soroptimist Internat., Ceres, Calif., 1992, Outstanding Woman of Stanislaus County Stanislaus County Commn. for Women, 1994; recipient Outstanding Achievement in Visual Arts, Stanislaus Arts Coun., 2000. Mem. AAUW (Modesto br., fellowships chair 1959-60, historian 1956), Ctrl. Calif. Art League (chmn. bank shows Modesto 1988-94, co-chair young artists show Modesto 1986, 88, 89, 90, head art gallery docent 1994-99), Calif. Ret. Tchrs. Assn., Stanislaus County Hist. Soc., Sierra Club, Tuolumne River Lodge, Delta Kappa Gamma (hist.-photography 1985-94, v.p. chpt. 1969-71), Kappa Delta Pi. Republican. Presbyterian. Avocations: painting, world travel, art gallery docent, church service. Home: 2704 La Palma Dr Modesto CA 95354-3229

BUCKNER, JOYCE, psychologist, educator; b. Benton, Ark., Sept. 25, 1937; d. Waymond Floyd Pannell and Willie Evelyn (Wright) Whitley; m. John W. Buckner, Aug. 29, 1958 (div. 1970); children: Cheryl, John, Chris. BA, Ouachita Bapt. Coll., 1959; MS in Edn., Henderson State U., 1964; PhD, North Tex. State U., 1970. Lic. psychologist, Tex., marriage and family therapist; cert. Nat. Registry Health Svc. Providers in Psychology; master trainer in imago relationship therapy. Assoc. prof. U. Tex., Arlington, 1970-80, chmn. dept. edn., 1976-78; pvt. practice Arlington, 1974—. Dir., chief profl. officer Southwest Inst. Relationship Devel.; appeard on tv shows including Oprah; spkr. in field. Author: Making Real Love Happen: The New Era of Intimacy. Mem. APA, Nat. Assn. for Imago Relationship Therapy (pres.), Nat. Speakers Assn., Am. Assn. Marital and Family Therapy. Avocations: dance, travel, art. Home: 4118 Bishop Creek Court Arlington TX 76016 Office Phone: 817-478-5257. Personal E-mail: joybuckner@aol.com.

BUCKNER-BROWN, JOYCE, allied health instructor; b. Greenwood, Miss. BS, Tougaloo Coll., 1977; M in Health Sci., Miss. Coll., 1991; PhD, Miss. State U., 1995. Registered respiratory therapist. Asst. prof. U. So. Miss., Hattiesburg, 1995-97; interim chair Jackson (Miss.) State U., 1997-98, asst. prof., 1998—2003, assoc. prof., 2003—. Cons. Joyce Buckner-Brown & Assocs., Ridgeland, Miss., 1999—. Seminar leader on health and wellness comm. chs., 1998-99. Grantee Ctrs. Disease Control, 1998, Miss. Tobacco Pilot Program, 1998-2000. Mem. APHA, ASPA, Nat. Assn. African Am. Studies (bd. dirs. 1997, leadership award 1999, 2000), Miss. Soc. Respiratory Care, Nat. Rural Health Assn., Nat. Minority Health Assn. Avocations: reading, travel. Office: Jackson State U Sch Allied Health Scis 350 W Woodrow Wilson Ave Jackson MS 39213-7681 E-mail: joyce.buckner-brown@jsums.edu.

BUCKSBAUM, MELVA, foundation administrator; m. Martin Bucksbaum (dec.); 1 child, Mary; m. Raymond J. Learsy. Mgr. Martin Bucksbaum Family Found., 1995—; dir. Robert I. Goldman Found., 1996—; bd. mem. Am. Friends of Israel Mus., NY, The Jewish Mus., NY, Hirshhorn Mus. & Sculpture Garden, Washington, Save Venice, New York & Venice; visiting com. Grad. Sch. Design, Harvard U. Named one of top 200 collectors (with Raymond Learsy), ARTnews Mag., 2004; recipient Gertrude Vanderbilt Whitney Award for outstanding arts patronage & philanthropy, 2004. Mem.: Whitney Mus. Am. Art (trustee 1996—, vice chmn. 2004—), Tate Gallery (Internat. Com.). Avocation: collector of contemporary art. Mailing: 646 Willoughby Way Aspen CO 81611 also: c/o Whitney Mus Am Art 945 Madison Ave New York NY 10021

BUCKSTEIN, CARYL SUE, writer; b. Denver, Aug. 10, 1954; d. Henry Martin and Hedvig (Neulander) B. BS in Journalism, U. Colo., 1976. Editor Rifle (Colo.) Telegram, 1976; corr. So. Colo. Pueblo (Colo.) Star-Jour. and Chieftain, 1977-84; corr. The Denver Post, 1985; staff editor Nat. Over-the-Counter Stock Jour., Denver, 1985-89; writer Rocky Mountain News, Denver, 1990-92; editor Urban Spectrum, Denver, 1993; contbg. writer Boulder (Colo.) County Bus. Report, 1992—. Bd. mem. Holiday Project, Denver, 1996; mem. exec. bd. Denver Newspaper Guild, 1998. Recipient 1st Place Gen. Assignment Bus. Articles, Colo. Press Women, Denver, 1985, 90, 91. Mem. Colo. Soc. Profl. Journalists (sec.-treas. 1988), Denver Newspaper Guild (bd. dirs. 1998). Avocations: inventing, writing. Home: 9995 E Harvard Ave Apt 0215 Denver CO 80231-3906 Personal E-mail: doewrite1701@comcast.net.

BUCOLO, GAIL ANN, biotechnologist; b. Port Chester, N.Y., July 27, 1954; d. Joseph Anthony and Jennie (Tomassetti) Bucolo. BS in French, Oneonta State Coll., 1976; MA in French, Middlebury Coll., 1977; postgrad., Columbia U., 1981—82; MS in Biotech., Manhattan Coll., 1995. Technician N.Y. Hosp., N.Y.C., 1983-86; rsch. technician NYU Hosp., N.Y.C., 1986; sr. rsch. technician Meml. Sloan Kettering, N.Y.C., 1986-88, Columbia U., N.Y.C., 1988-2001; tchr. Cathedral HS, N.Y.C., 2001—04; rsch. tech. N.Y. Meth. Hosp., Bklyn., 2004—. Corr. Scienceport, Rye, NY, 1994—96; adj. prof. Mercy Coll., Dobbs Ferry, NY, 1996—2004; summer rsch. intern Rockefeller U., 2003. Mem.: AAAS, Am. Chem. Soc., N.Y. Acad. Scis., Sigma Xi. Roman Catholic. Achievements include research in factor VIII inhibitor and discovery that it inhibited reverse transciptase of HIV; spinal cord injury and neuronal regeneration which was implemented at the Miami Project in Florida. Home: 1025 Louise Ave Basement Apt Mamaroneck NY 10543 Office: NY Methodist Hosp Brooklyn NY Personal E-mail: gailbucolo@aol.com.

BUDD, BERNADETTE SMITH, lawyer, newspaper executive, public relations consultant; b. N.Y.C., Feb. 23, 1948; d. Stanley Allen and Toby (Percak) Smith; m. Thomas Witbeck Budd, July 4, 1988; children: Amanda Rose Kronin Gregurich, Karen Wendy Kronia Campisi, Paige Elizabeth Glickman, Kelly Lynn Budd Tinsley. BA in History and English, Bucknell U., 1964; MA in Liberal Studies, SUNY, Stony Brook, 1971; EdM, Columbia U., 1982; JD, Jacob D. Fuchsberg Law Ctr., 1998. Tchr. history N.Y., 1964-69; innovator pre-sch. programs Shoreham, N.Y., 1975-79; editor, pub. Cmty. Jour., Wading River, N.Y., 1978—, advt. mgr., 1978—; editor Shoreham-Wading River Newsletter, 1978-88; editor-in-chief Restatement Touro Law Ctr., 1997-98. Profl. breeder, shower A.K.C. golden retriever dogs; cons., workshop leader, 1979—; exec. dir. Suffolk County chpt. NYCLU, 1998-2000. Editor: C. of C. Directory, Shoreham, 1983, 84; contbr. articles N.Y. Times, Reader's Digest, Psychology Today Mag.om., 1979-82. Advisor Teen Recreation Adv. Com., Shoreham-Wading River, 1979-82; mem. Nuclear Emergency Evacuation Com., 1979-82; pres. PTA, Wading River, 1980-83; v.p. Spl. Edn. PTA, Wading River, 1979-80, Am. Civil Liberties Union Student Chpt. Touro Law Ctr.; active Com. Gifted and Talented Children, Wading River, 1979-80, Occupational Edn. Commn., 1979-80; mem. Suffolk County Human Rights Commn. Recipient Disting. Service award Am. Cancer Soc., 1982-83; award of merit N.Y. State Pub. Relations Assn., 1982-83; award of honor Nat. Sch. Pub. Relations Assn., 1981. Mem. Wading River C. of C. (bd. dirs. 1979-80), Suffolk County Bus. and Profl. Women's Assn., Women's Equal Rights Congress, East End Women's Network, N.Y.C. Press Assn., Rocky Point C. of C. (bd. dirs.), Soc. Profl. Journalists, L.I. Press Club, Sigma Delta Chi, Kappa Kappa Gamma. Roman Catholic. Home and Office: Cmty Jour PO Box 619 Wading River NY 11792-0619 E-mail: bernadettesbudd@aol.com.

BUDDE, MITZI MARIE JARRETT, librarian; b. Salisbury, N.C., Aug. 7, 1961; d. James Curtis and Donna Lee (Kluttz) J.; m. John August Budde, Apr. 23, 1994. BA, Lenoir-Rhyne Coll., 1982; MA, Luth. Theol. Sem., 1984; M in Librarianship, U. S.C., 1985. Asst. libr. Luth. Theol. So. Sem., Columbia, S.C., 1985-87, libr. dir., 1987-91; libr. Va. Theol. Sem., Alexandria, 1991—. Sec. Luth./Meth. Campus Ministry, U. S.C., Columbia, 1988-91. Mem. ALA, Am. Theol. Libr. Assn. (bd. dirs. 1992-95), Beta Phi Mu (Beta Omega chpt. pres. 1989-90). Office: Va Theol Sem Bishop Payne Libr 3737 Seminary Rd Alexandria VA 22304-5202

BUDDINGTON, OLIVE JOYCE, shop owner, retired education educator; b. Norwich, Conn., June 11, 1925; d. William and Viola Jane (Turnbull) B. BS, Ea. Conn. State U., 1947; MA, Columbia U., 1951. Cert. tchr. nursery-6th grade, Conn. Tchr. Bd. Edn., Greenwich, Conn., 1947-49, 51-84; tchr. Agnes Russell Ctr. Tchr.'s Coll. Columbia U., N.Y.C., 1949-51; owner, mgr. 1840 House-Antiques, Norwich, Conn., 1965—. Bd. dirs. TVCCA (pres.), Rose City Land Trust, Woman's City Club, Hist. Norwichtown Day, United Cmty. and Family Svcs., Inc.; bd. corporators Norwich Free Acad.; cons. in early childhood edn.; pres. Thames River Family Program, Martin House Corp.; chmn. UCF Mktg. and Devel. Com., Tourism Com.; trustee Slater Mus. Photographer tourism and promotion, 1994. Chair Parking Commn. City Coun., Norwich, Conn., 1989-91, Tourism Commn., 1990—; chmn. environ. com., Norwich, 1989-91; vol. United Way, Am. Red Cross, Leukemia Soc., Am. Heart Assn., Am. Cancer Soc.; mem. Norwich Downtown Renewal Com., Norwich Slum and Blight Com., Norwich City Hall Renovations Com., UCF Health Svcs. Com., Rose Sr. Ctr. Bldg. Com. (chmn.), Dem. Town Com., Dept. Children and Families Regional Adv. Coun. Positive Youth Devel. Com., Sch. Breakfast Com., Sch. Readiness Com., Children's First Initiative, Norwich tourism Task Force; host (cable program) RSVP Why Not Read??; bd. dirs. Greeneville Neighborhood Resource Ctr., 2002—. Named Vol. of Yr., Citizen of Yr. Ea. Conn. C. of C., 1997; recipient Caroline Bidwell Award, Greenwich (Conn.) Assn. Pub. Schs., 1984, Svc. Above Help Norwich Rotary Club, 1995, Woman of Achievement award, Woman's Internat. Fed., 1997, Sam Walton Leadership award, 1998, Cmty. Svc. award, DAR, 1998, Successful Aging award, Conn. Cmty. Care, Inc., 2000, Pub. Svc. award, Conn. Sec. of State, 2002. Mem. Nat. Edn. Assn., Conn. Edn. Assn., Norwich Hist. Soc. (life, ednl. dir., bd. dirs. 2001-05). Democrat. Avocations: reading, travel, knitting, photography, arts and crafts. Home and Office: 47 8th St Norwich CT 06360-3834 Office Phone: 860-887-2808.

BUDHISETIAWAN, BARBARA CRAWFORD, music educator; d. William and Rebecca Crawford; m. Aaron O.L. Budhisetiawan; 1 child, Aaron. BA in Music Edn., Carson Newman Coll., Jefferson City, Tenn., 1997. Music tchr. East Albemarle Elem. Sch., Albemarle, NC, 1997—2002; faculty Stanly C.C., 1998—2002; music tchr. North Windy Ridge Sch., Weaverville, 2002—. Dir. childrens choir First Presbyn. Ch., Albemarle, NC, 1998—2002. Recipient Tchr. of Yr., North Windy Ridge Sch., 2007. Mem.: Music Educators Nat. Conf. Avocations: scuba diving, swimming, travel. Office: North Windy Ridge Sch 20 Doan Rd Weaverville NC 28787 Office Phone: 828-658-1892.

BUDIG, JEANETTE, special education educator; b. Hays, Kans., Apr. 18, 1947; d. Ignatius F. Gross and Lydia B. Mermis; m. Arthur E. Budig, Aug. 13, 1981 (dec.); children: Mary M. Lewis, Melissa A. O'Reagan, Rodney A. BS in Elem. Edn., Ft. Hays State U., 1972, MS in Spl. Edn., 1985, cert. in elem. sch. counseling, 1989. 2d grade tchr. Stockton (Kans.) Elem. Sch., 1972—74; 6th grade tchr. Sts. Peter and Paul Elem. Sch., Tucson, 1974—75; spl. edn. tchr. Hays (Kans.) Unified Sch. Dist., 1975—79, traveling tchr. emotionally disturbed classes K-5, 1979—80; tchr. K-5 self-contained classroom, emotionally disturbed students Jefferson Elem. Sch., Hays, 1980—82; tchr. K-5 grade self-contained classroom, emotionally disturbed students Lincoln Elem. Sch., Hays, 1982—89, interrelated resource rm. tchr. grades K-5, 1989—97, interrelated resource rm. tchr. grades K-3, 1997—2001, interrelated resource rm. tchr. grades K-2, 2001—. Home: PO Box 13 Hays KS 67601 Office Phone: 785-623-2500.

BUDIN, WENDY C., nursing educator, researcher; m. Arnold I. Budin, June 13, 1973; children: Barri, Sarah, Jill. BSN, Adelphi U., Garden City, NY, 1973; MSN, Seton Hall U., South Orange, NJ, 1986; PhD, NYU, N.Y.C., 1996. Cert. perinatal nurse, ANCC, 2002; Lamaze childbirth educator Lamaze Internat., 1998. Assoc. prof. nursing Seton Hall U. Coll. Nursing, South Orange, NJ, 1986—2002, program dir.-Lamaze childbirth educator program, 1994—, assoc. dean grad. nursing programs and rsch., 2002—; acad. dir. online MSN program SetonWorldWide-Seton Hall U., South Orange, NJ, 2001—. Co-chair nursing/ psychosocial adv. group N.J. State Commn. on Cancer Rsch., Trenton, 1994—; cons. rsch. in nursing Excelsior Coll., Albany, NY, 1996—; med. adv. bd. North Jersey Affiliate of Susan G. Komen Breast Cancer Found., Summit, NJ, 1999—; collateral reviewer Sigma Theta Tau Internat., Indpls., 2001—. Author (co-author with j. hott): (book) Notter's Essentials of Nursing Research (Brandon/Hill Selected List of Nursing Books for Rsch., 2000); author: (co-author with c. hoskins and j. haber) Breast Cancer: Journey to Recovery; editor (contributing editor): Journal of Perinatal Education; contbr. articles to profl. jours. Recipient Rudin Family award doctoral student achievement, NYU, 1994, Arch award, NYU Sch. Edn., 1996, Sigma Theta Tau Internat. Regional Rsch. Dissertation Award, Sigma Theta Tau Internat., 1997, NJ Gov.'s Nursing Merit award nurse rschr., NJ Dept. of Health and Sr. Svcs., 1999, N.J. Nurse of Yr. award, AWHONN, 2004, CARE award for nursing rsch., NJ State Nurses Assn., 2004, Disting. Alumnae award, NYU divsn. nursing, 2004; grantee Co-Investigator & Project Dir. Stress and Coping in Caregivers of AIDS Children, NIH - NINR, 1991, Am. Nurses Found., 1994, Co-Investigator and Nurse Interventionist for Breast Cancer: Edn., Counseling and Adjustment, AREA Grant - NINR, 1998, Fed. Nurse Traineeship, Divsn. of Nursing -Dept. of Health and Human Svcs., 2002-03; Doctoral scholarship, Sigma Theta Tau Internat., 1992, Erline P. McGriff Doctoral scholarship, NYU - Divsn. of Nursing, 1995, N.J. Breast Cancer Rsch. Vis. Scholar fellowship, N.J. Commn. on Cancer Rsch., 1996. Mem.: Oncology Nursing Soc., Assn. for Woman's Health, Obstet. & Neonatal Nursing-AWHONN, Ea. Nursing Rsch. Soc., Lamaze Internat. (certification coun.), Sigma Theta Tau (past president-gamma nu chpt.). Achievements include research in breast cancer. Office: Seton Hall Univ College of Nursing South Orange NJ 07079 Business E-Mail: budinwen@shu.edu.

BUDNIAKIEWICZ, THERESE, writer; b. Mons, Belgium, Sept. 28, 1948; came to U.S., 1961; naturalized, 1967; d. Tadeusz Eugeniusz and Janina Antonina (Więckowska) B.; m. Bart S. Ng, July 6, 1972. BA in Math., U. Chgo., 1971; MA in Comparative Lit., U. Mich., 1972, PhD in Comparative Lit., 1986. Lectr. English, Ind. U.-Purdue U., Indpls., 1987-92. Author: Fundamentals of Story Logic, 1992; contbr. Ency. of Semiotics, 1998. Mem. MLA, Semiotic Soc. Am., Can. Semiotic Assn., Internat. Assn. for Semiotics of Law, Internat. Assn. for Semiotic Studies. Avocation: publishing technologies. Home and Office: 5823 Dapple Trace Indianapolis IN 46228-1698 E-mail: tbudniakiewicz@math.iupui.edu.

BUDNY, LORRAINE, newspaper reporter, freelance writer; b. Chicopee, Mass., July 18, 1917; d. Marcel Girouard and Cecile Babineau; m. J. Travers Ward, Dec. 31, 1941 (div. June 1946); m. Bernard S. Budny, Aug. 15, 1947 (dec. Aug. 1981). Student, N.Y. Theater Sch. Dramatic Art, Traphagen Sch. Fashion Design, N.Y.C. Asst. designer to Bonnie Cashin Adler & Adler, N.Y.C.; publicist Claire McCardell, N.Y.C.; dir. fashion promotion Lord & Taylor, N.Y.C., 1945-47; fashion editor Harper's Bazaar, N.Y.C., 1947-48; fashion designer Lorraine Budny Inc., N.Y.C., 1948-55; publisher, editor, writer South Kent, Conn., 1987-97; columnist, freelance writer Housatonic Publs., New Milford, Conn., 1997—. Mem. adv. com. New Milford Bank and Trust. Roman Catholic. Avocations: art museums and galleries, reading, travel, travel writing, double crostic puzzles. Office Phone: 860-567-6619 ext. 219.

BUDOFF, PENNY WISE, retired physician, author, researcher; b. Albany, N.Y., July 7, 1939; d. Louis and Goldene Wise. BA, Syracuse U., 1959; MD, SUNY-Upstate Med. Sch., 1963. Intern St. Luke's Meml. Hosp., Utica, N.Y., 1963-64; practice medicine specializing in family practice, women's health, Woodbury, N.Y., 1964-85; clin. assoc. prof. family medicine SUNY, Stony Brook, 1980—97. Founder, dir. emeritus North Shore U. Hosp. Women's Healthcare (formerly Penny Wise Budoff, MD Women's Health Svcs.), 1985-97, Bethpage, N.Y., 1985, ground-breaking women's health care facility; attending dept. ob/gyn. North Shore U. Hosp., 1992-97; asst. prof. ob/gyn. Cornell U. Med. Coll., 1993-96, pres. Bonne Forme Vitamins and Skin Care, divsn. Vitamins for Women, Farmingdale, N.Y., 1983—; TV guest on women's medicine and health issues; mem. spl. menopause NIH, 1993; clin. rsch. on menstrual pain, premenstrual syndrome, menopause, breast cancer and osteoporosis. Author: No More Menstrual Cramps and Other Good News, 1980, No More Hot Flashes and Other Good News, 1983, No More Hot Flashes and Even More Good News, 1998, World Book Health and Medical Annual, 1994; med. reviewer Jour. JAMA; contbr. articles to profl. jours. Bd. dirs. Coalition Against Domestic Violence. Named Woman of Yr. C.W. Post Coll., 1981; recipient Nat. Consumers League award, 1983, Max Cheplove award Erie chpt. N.Y. State Acad. Family Physicians, 1983, Women of Distinction award Soroptimist Internat. of Nassau County, L.I., 1990, award for promoting better understanding of menopause N.Am. Menopause Soc., 1999; honoree Nassau County Coalition Against Domestic Violence, 1992. Fellow Nassau County Med. Soc., Am. Acad. Family Physicians (chmn. com. on pub. rels.); mem. NOW (Equality award in Health 1988, Unsung Heroine award), Am. Med. Women's Assn. (co-chmn. nat. women's health com., liaison), Nassau Acad. Family Physicians (past pres.).

BUECHLING, LINDA, language educator; m. Steve Buechling. BA in History/Fine Arts, Coll. of William and Mary, Williamsburg, Va., 1980; MA in Linguistics, George Mason U., Fairfax, Va., 1990. Cert. ESL George Mason U., 1990. Instr. ESL No. Va. CC, Annandale, 1990—92; instr. English Darton Coll., Albany, Ga., 2001—. Personal E-mail: gapoo@bellsouth.net.

BUEHLER, SALLY SALMEN, clinical social worker; b. Newton, Mass., July 31, 1938; d. Stanley and Margaret (Green) Salmen; m. John A. Buehler, Aug. 24, 1971; 1 child, Daniel. AB, U. N.H., 1960; MSW, U. Calif., 1963. Lic. clin. social worker, Calif. Social worker psychiat. Child Guidance Clinic Children Hosp., San Francisco, 1965-69, supt. social worker psychiat., 1968-69; social worker psychiat. Family Service Agy., Pittsfield, Mass., 1970-71; social worker clin. Kentfield, Calif., 1971—. Cons. Pacific Recovery Ctr., Larkspur, Calif., 1983—. Fellow Soc. Clin. Social Work (bd. cert. diplomate in Clin. Social Work). Home: 18 Turnagain Rd Kentfield CA 94904-2717 Office Phone: 415-461-5277. E-mail: saljac@msn.com.

BUEHNER, ANDREA RUTH, small business owner; b. Cleve., Feb. 29, 1948; d. Andrew Steve and Ruth (Gamary) H.; m. Larry John Buehner, May 12, 1988. Student, Dyke Coll., Cleve., 1971-72, Cuyahoga Community Coll., Parma, Ohio, 1984-88. Acct. C.E. Basic, Inc., Cleve., 1973—83; office mgr., acct. Bassichus Co., Cleve., 1983—85; office mgr. Ross Equipment, Cleve., 1985—89, contr., 1988—90; sec.-treas. Associated Equipment Corp., Cleve., 1985—90; owner, sec.-treas. G.A.L. Family Corp., 1988—97; owner, operator Bean's Pl., Cleve., 1998—2002; compliance adminstr., traveling retail auditor Wireless Phone divsn. GTE, Cleve., 1997—2002; pres., chief fund raiser Cottonwood Civic Ctr. Renovation com. Cottonwood Civic Ctr., Ariz., 2002—04. Treas. Cottonwood Ranch Club Assn. Del Webb Cottonwood Ranch, 2002-03; mem audit and budget coms. St. Patrick's Ch., 2004—; mem. St. Patrick's Ch. Audit and Budget Com., 2004—. Mem. Profl. Women's Assn., Cleve. Women Working (past v.p.). Democrat. Catholic. Avocations: reading, swimming, travel. Home: 5002 Sand Ripples Ln Colorado Springs CO 80922

BUELL, EVANGELINE CANONIZADO, advocate; b. San Pedro, Calif., Aug. 28, 1932; d. Estanislao (C.) and Felicia (Stokes) Canonizado; m. Ralph D. Vilas, 1952 (dec.); m. Robert Alexander Elkins, July 1, 1961 (dec.); children: Nikki Vilas, Stacey Vilas, Danni Vilas Plump; m. William David Buell, Feb. 21, 1987. Student, San Jose State Coll., 1952—53; grad., U. San Francisco, 1978. With Consumers Coop. of Berkeley (Calif.) Inc., 1958—, edn. asst. for cmty. rels., 1964—73, supr. edn. dept., 1973—76, asst. to edn. dir., 1976—78, program coord. edn. dept, 1980—81, pers. tng. coord., 1981—92; ret. Events coord. Internat. House, U. Calif., Berkeley, 1984; also guitar tchr. Columnist Coop. News, 1964—; contbr. articles to profl. jours. and mags.; author, co-editor (anthology) Seven Card Stud with Seven Manangs Wild. Pres. Berkeley Cmty. Chorus and Orch.; co-chair Berkeley Art Commn., 1992—94; dir. various activities YMCA, YWCA, Oakland City Recreation Dept., Oakland, 1959—73; bd. dirs. Philippine Ethnic Arts and Cultural Exch.; mem. cmty. adv. com. Bonita House, Berkeley, 1974; mem. steering com. for cultural and ethnic affairs Guild of Oakland Mus., 1973—74; bd. dirs., v.p. Berkeley Art Ctr., pres., 1998. Recipient Honor award, U. Calif. Student Coop., 1965, Outstanding Staff award, U. Calif. Berkeley Chancellor, 1992, Nat. Philanthropy Disting. Vol. award, 1993, Outstanding Instrn. Program Support award, Cole Sch. Visual & Performing Arts, Outstanding Berkeley Woman award, Berkeley Commn. on the Status of Women, 1996, others. Mem.: Coop. Educators Network Calif., Filipino Am. Nat. Hist. Soc. (pres. East Bay chpt. 1996, Silver Arts & Music award 1994). Democrat. Unitarian Universalist. Home: 516 Santa Barbara Rd Berkeley CA 94707-1746 E-mail: vangiec@uclink.berkeley.edu.

BUES, SUSAN DENISE WILDERMUTH, academic administrator; b. Hudson, N.Y., Oct. 3, 1950; d. Frank Edward Wildermuth and Ruth Erhlen (Corson) Demler. BS, SUNY, New Paltz, 1973; MBA, Bernard Baruch Coll., 1987. Tchr. Brevard County Sch. Dist., Cocoa Beach, Fla., 1973-76; asst. adminstr. St. Luke's/Roosevelt Hosp., New York, 1978-82; asst. to v.p. Ptnrs. in Care, Inc., N.Y.C., 1983-85; dir. adminstrv. svcs. Polytechnic Univ., Bklyn., 1986-93; bus. adminstr. Adams-Cheshire Regional Sch. Dist., Adams, Mass., Chatham (N.Y.) Ctrl. Sch., 1993-96; chief fin. officer, treas. N.Y. province Sisters of the Holy Names of Jesus and Mary, Albany, 1997—. Mem. Commn. Stewardship & Mission Interpretation, United Ch. of Christ; treas. Canaan Congregational Ch.; bd. dirs. N.Y. Interfaith Power and Light, 2004—, Karuna Tendai Dharma Ctr.; advisor Bklyn. Econ. Devel. Corp.; mem. investment com. Interfaith Ctr. for Corp. Responsibility, 2006—. Mem. Nat. Assn. Coll. and Univ. Bus. Officers, NACAS, CUPA, IPMA, NAPM, Sierra Club, Berkshire Bot. Garden. Democrat. Congregationalist. Avocations: painting, drawing, photography, gardening. Home: 599 County Route 34 East Chatham NY 12060-2408 E-mail: susanwbues@yahoo.com.

BUESING, LESLIE MARIE, theater educator, director; b. Austin, Dec. 4, 1970; d. Mary Frances and Theodore Frederick Burger; m. Brian James Buesing, May 27, 2001; children: Adrian Frederick, Krystalynn Marie. BA in Theatre, St. Edward's U., Austin, 1994. Cert. Secondary Theatre Arts in Edn. Tex. Edn. Agy., 1997. Videographer Beautiful Moments Video Prodns., Gonzales, Tex., 2004—. Actor: (supporting character) The Whole Wide World. Scholar Theatre, East Tex. State U., 1989—92. Avocation: Tae Kwon Do. Office: Gonzales HS and Jr High PO Box M Gonzales TX 78629 Office Phone: 830-672-8641. Business E-Mail: leslie.buesing@gonzales.txed.net.

BUFFLER, PATRICIA ANN, epidemiologist, educator, dean; b. Doylestown, Pa., Aug. 1, 1938; d. Edward M. and Evelyn G. (Axenroth) Happ; m. Richard T. Buffler, Jan. 20, 1962; children: Martyn R., Monique L. BSN, Cath. U. Am., 1960; MPH, U. Calif., Berkeley, 1965, PhD in Epidemiology, 1973. Prof. epidemiology sch. pub. health U. Tex. Health Sci. Ctr., Houston, 1979—91; prof. U. Calif., Berkeley, 1991—, dean sch. pub. health, 1991—98, dean emerita, 1998—. Mem. expert adv. panel on occupl. health WHO, 1985—2002; mem. environment, safety and health adv. com. U.S. DOE, 1992—95; mem. bd. on water sci. and tech. NRC, 1992—94; chair, bd. dirs. Mickey Leland Nat. Urban Air Toxics Rsch. Ctr., 1994—97, Societal Inst. of Math. Scis.; mem. Nat. Commn. on Superfund, Keystone Ctr., 1992—94; mem. adv. panel on mng. nuc. materials from warheads U.S. Congress Office Tech. Assessment, 1992—93; bd. sci. counselors Nat. Inst. for Occupl. Safety and Health, 1991—93; mem. sci. adv. bd. radiation adv. com. subcom. on cancer risks associated with electric and magnetic fields U.S. EPA, 1990—93, mem. sci. adv. bd., 1996—98; mem. Nat. Adv. Coun. on Environ. Health Scis., 1995—98, NAS, Nat. Coun. Radiation Protection. Contbr. articles to profl. jours. Fellow: AAAS, Inst. Medicine of NAS, Am. Coll. Epidemiology (pres.-elect 1990—91, pres. 1991—92); mem.: APHA (epidemiology sect. 1964—), Internat. Soc. for Environ. Epidemiology (pres.-elect 1989—91, pres. 1992—94), Soc. of Toxicology, Internat. Commn. on Occupl. Health, Internat. Soc. for Exposure Assessment (charter, bd. internat. councillors 1993—98), Internat. Epidemiol. Assn., Soc. for Occupl. and Environ. Health, Am. Epidemiol. Soc., Soc. for Epidemiol. Rsch. (pres.-elect, pres., past pres. 1984—88), Collegium Ramazzini. Office: U Calif Sch Pub Health 714-F Univ Hall 140 Earl Warren Hl Berkeley CA 94720-0001

BUFFUM, KATHLEEN D., artist; b. Abington, Pa., Dec. 5, 1925; d. Leroy Adolph Frederick and Julia Elizabeth (Suwall) Droescher; m. John McEntee Bowman Jr., Dec. 17, 1961 (dec. Dec. 1970); 1 child, Alexandra Kip Bowman; m. George Allen Buffum, Oct. 2, 1972 (dec. Oct. 2002); stepchildren: George Allen, Price. Grad., Harcum Coll., Bryn Mawr, Pa., 1944; student, Pa. Acad. Fine Arts, Phila., 1957-59, Barnes Found. Pvt. Mus. Sch., Merion, Pa., 1971-72. Solo shows include Phila. C.C., 1998, Beaumont Gallery, Bryn Mowr, Pa., 2004; exhibited in juried shows at Pa. Acad. Fine Arts, The Art Alliance, Smithsonian Inst., The Sketch Club, Woodmere Mus., Am. Coll., Bryn Mawr, Art Studnets League, Rehoboth Beach, Del., Villanova (Pa.) U., others; more than 160 paintings in pvt. collections. Mem. maternity com. Thomas Jefferson U. Hosp. Womans Bd.; active Phila. Antiques Show Com. U. Pa. Hosp. Recipient Violet Oakely prize, 1972. Mem. Wayne Art Ctr., Pa. Acad. Fine Arts (womans bd.), Phila. Acad. Fine Arts, Woodmere Mus. Republican. Episcopalian. Address: 200 N Wynnewood Ave Wynnewood PA 19096-1433

BUFORD, EVELYN CLAUDENE SHILLING, retired consumer products company executive; b. Ft. Worth, Sept. 21, 1940; d. Claude and Winnie Evelyn (Mote) Hodges; m. William J. Buford, Mar. 1982; children by previous marriage: Vincent Shilling, Kathryn Lynn Shilling. Student, Hill Jr. Coll., 1975-76, Tarrant County Jr. Coll, Tex., 1992-93. With Imperial Printing Co., Inc., Ft. Worth, 1964-70, corp. sec., 1977-79, gen. sales mgr. coml. divsn., 1982—89; with Tarrant County Hosp. Dist., Ft. Worth, 1973—76, asst. to asst. adminstr., 1975—76; merch. asst. J.C. Penney Co., Hurst, Tex., 1989—96; ret., 1996. Mem. Exec. Women Internat. (life, dir., publs. chair, v.p. 1984, pres. 1985, chair adv. com. 1986-87, scholarship dir. 1988-93, corp. publ. com. 1988-89, dir. South ctrl. region 1993-94). Republican. Methodist. Home: 1025 Kenneth Ln Burleson TX 76028-2246 E-mail: claudenebuford@yahoo.com.

BUGBEE, JOAN BARTHELME, retired corporate communications executive; b. Galveston, Tex., Dec. 31, 1932; d. Donald and Helen (Bechtold) Barthelme; m. George A. Bugbee, Apr. 2, 1966; children: Richard, John. BA in Journalism, U. Colo., 1955. Pub. rels. rep. Philco Corp., Phila., 1957-60; account exec. Jacobs Keeper Newell Assoc., Houston, 1960-63; pub. rels. rep. Tex. Ea. Corp., Houston, 1963-66; assoc. editor Oil and Gas Digest Mag., Houston, 1978-79; mgr. corp. comms. Pennzoil Co., Houston, 1980-87, dir. corp. comms., 1987-90, v.p. corp. comm., 1990-96; ret., 1996; pub. rels. cons. Bd. dir., mem. bd. exec. com. Blue Ridge Pub. TV.; book reviewer for The Roanoke Times. Mem. Radio Reading Svc., Sta. WVTF; publicity chmn. Roanoke chpt. Brady/Million Mom Mar.; publicity chmn., hosp. vol. St. Elias Ch. Recipient Outstanding Presentation award, Phila. chpt. Pub. Rels. Soc. Am., 1959. Mem.: Red Hat Soc., Roanoke Times Book Club, Phi Beta Kappa. Maronite Catholic.

BUGBEE-JACKSON, JOAN, sculptor, educator; b. Oakland, Calif., Dec. 17, 1941; d. Henry Greenwood and Jeanie Lawler (Abbot) B.; m. John Michael Jackson, June 21, 1973; 1 child, Brook Bond. BA in Art, U. Calif., San Jose, 1964, MA in Art and Ceramics, 1966; student, Nat. Acad. Sch. Fine Arts, N.Y.C., 1968-72. Instr. pottery Greenwich House Pottery, NYC, 1969-71, Craft Inst. Am., NYC, 1970-72, Cordova Ext. Ctr., U. AK, 1972-79, Prince William Sound Cmty. Coll., 1979—. One-woman exhbn. in Maine, NYC, Alaska, Calif.; group exhbns. include Allied Artists Am., 1970-72, Nat. Acad. Design, 1971, 74, Nat. Sculpture Soc. Ann., 1971, 72, 73, Alaska Woman Art Show, 1987, 88, Cordova Visual Artists, 1991-96, Alaska Artists Guild Show, 1994, Am. Medallic Sculpture Nat. Travelling Exhbn., 1994-95, pres. Cordova Arts and Pageants Ltd., 1975-76; commns. include Merle K. Smith Commemorative plaque, 1973, Eyak Native Monument, 1978, Anchorage Pioneer's Home Ceramic Mural, 1979, Alaska Wildlife Series Bronze Medal, 1980, Armin F. Koernig Hatchery Plaque, 1985, Cordova Fishermen's Meml. Sculpture, 1985, Alaska's Five Gov., bronze relief, Anchorage, 1986, Reluctant Fishermen's Mermaid, bronze, 1987, Charles E. Bunnell, bronze portrait statue, Fairbanks, 1988, Alexander Baranof Monument, Sitka, Alaska, 1989, Wally Noerenberg Hatchery Plaque, Prince William Sound, Alaska, 1989, Russian-Alaskan Friendship Plaque (edit. of 4), Kayak Island, Cordova, Alaska and Vladivostok & Petropavlovsk-Kamchatskiy, Russia, 1991, Sophie-Last Among Eyak Native People, 1992, Alaska Airlines Medal Commn., 1993, Hosp. Aux. plaque, 1995, La Cirena, Mex., 1998, Alaska Vets. Monument lifesize bronze, Anchorage, 2001, Alaska R.R.: Sheffield Plaque, 2002, Joe Redington Sr., Father of the Iditarod, statue, Wasilla, Alaska, 2003, Pioneer Aviator Monument, Anchorage, 2005; also other portraits. Bd. dir. Alaska State Coun. Arts, 1991-95. Scholar, Nat. Acad. Sch. Fine Arts, 1969-72; recipient J.A. Suydam Bronze medal, 1969, Dr. Ralph Weiler prize, 1971, Helen Foster Barnet award, 1971, Daniel Chester French award, 1972, Frishmuth award, 1971, Allied Artists Am. award, 1972, C. Percival Dietsch prize, 1973, citation Alaska Legis., 1981, 82; named Alaskan Artist of Yr., 1991; Alaska Gov. Award, 2002. Fellow Nat. Sculpture Soc. Address: PO Box 374 Cordova AK 99574-0374 E-mail: artworks@ctcak.net.

BUGG, CAROL DONAYRE, interior designer; b. N.Y.C., June 8, 1937; d. Carlos G. and Frances M. (Burkhart) Donayre; m. James S. Bugg, Dec. 24, 1968; step-children: Karen, Ken, Darlene, Jim, Whitney. AA, Georgetown Visitation Coll., Washington D.C., 1957; student in Spanish, Georgetown U., Washington D.C., 1960; student interior design, Internat. Inst. of Interior Design, Washington, 1967; interior decorator, Parsons Sch. Design, Paris, 1984. Design asst. W&J Sloane, Washington D.C., 1967-68, The H. Chambers Co., Washington D.C., 1968-69; dir. design Internat. Cosmetic Co., Washington D.C., 1970-72; interior decorator Stix, Baer & Fuller, St. Louis, 1972-73, Burklew Design Assocs., Md., 1973-76; pres. Carol Donayre Bugg & Assocs., 1976-85; v.p., dir. design Decorating Den Systems, Inc., Bethesda, Md., 1984—. Author: (book) Dream Rooms For Real People, 1990, Divine Design, 1994, Smart & Simple Decorating, 1999, Creating Great Guest Rooms, 2005; lectr. in field. Mem. decorating com. Congl. Women's Club, Washington D.C.; sponsor Leader Dogs For the Blind, Rochester, Mich.; active gourmet gala March of Dimes, Washington D.C. Mem. Am. Soc. Interior Design (Washington D.C. chpt. chmn. ways and means com. 1979), Color Mktg. Group. Home: 8659 Commerce St Easton MD 21601 Office: Decorating Den Systems Inc 8659 Commerce St Easton MD 21601 Office Phone: 410-822-9001.

BUGGLIN, CAROL STEPHANIE, clinical psychologist, psychotherapist; b. Rockville Ctr., N.Y., Dec. 20, 1958; d. George Raymond and Helen Ann B.; m. Mark Steven Borer, Aug. 1, 1987; children: Eric Daniel Bugglin-Borer, Brett Joseph Bugglin-Borer, Leana Marie Bugglin-Borer, Gwendolyn Alayne Bugglin-Borer. BA, SUNY, Binghamton, 1981; MA, U. Conn., 1986, PhD, 1987. Lic. psychologist, Del. Child psychologist Upper Shore Mental Health Ctr., Chestertown, Md., 1987-89; child and family psychologist Tressler Ctrs. Del., Dover, 1987-90, Psychiat. Assess for Cen. Del., Dover, 1990—. Coord. Profls. Educating for and Advocating for Children, Dover, 1989—; radio talk show guest. Contbr. articles to profl. jours. Mem. APA, Del. Psychol. Assn., Phi Beta Kappa. Roman Catholic. Avocations: travel, swimming, dance, reading, prayer. Office: Psychiat Access Ctrl Del 846 Walker Rd Ste 32-2 Dover DE 19904-2756

BUGGS, ELAINE S., financial analyst; b. Trenton, N.J., Aug. 18, 1954; d. Moses and Hattie (Mitchell) S.; m. Richmond Akumiah, Dec. 1982 (div. Aug. 27, 1987); m. James A. Buggs, Sr., Oct. 2, 1996; 1 child, James A., Jr. BS, Rochester Inst. Technol., 1976; MBA, Atlanta U., 1985. Mktg. rep. Mobil Oil Corp., 1976-77; mfg. analyst Reader's Digest, Pleasantville, N.Y., 1977-80; mgr. fin. instns. Am. Express, N.Y.C., 1980-83; sr. market analyst Ryder Systems Inc., Miami, 1985-86; dir. recruiting Atlanta U., 1986; cons. Consultants & Assocs., Washington, 1987-89; mgr. fin. analysis Blue Cross Blue Shield of Va., Roanoke, 1989-90; dir. group fin. reporting & analysis Blue Cross Blue Shield of Md., Owings Mills, 1990-93; sr. med. group analyst mid-Atlantic states region Kaiser Permanent, Rockville, Md., 1993-95; asst. mgr. Johns Hopkins U., Balt., 1995-98; mgr. bus. ops. Dingman Ctr. for Entrepreneurship, U. Md., College Park, 1998-2000; dir. fin. and adminstrn. Arts and Humanities Coll., U. Md., College Park, 2000—. Named IBM scholar, 1983. Mem. NAFE, Md. New Directions (bd. dirs. 1994-96), Internat. Soc. Strategic Planners, Nat. Assn. MBA Execs., Nat. Assn. of Black MBAs. Democrat. Methodist. Avocations: tennis, aerobics, antique hunting. Office: Univ Md College Park Arts and Humanities Coll 1211B Art/Sociology Bldg College Park MD 20742 Home: 13702 Colgate Way Apt 1043 Silver Spring MD 20904-4850 E-mail: eb148@wmail.umd.edu.

BUHAGIAR, MARION, editor, writer; b. N.Y.C., Oct. 27, 1932; d. George and Mae (Pietrzak) B.; 1 child, Alexa Ragozin. BA cum laude, Hunter Coll., 1953; postgrad., Mt. Holyoke Coll., 1954. Economist U.S. Dept. Commerce, 1954-57; bus. reporter Time mag., 1957-59; assoc. editor Fortune mag., 1960-73, story devel. editor, 1970-73; text editor Time-Life Books, N.Y.C., 1973-76; v.p. Boardroom Inc., 1977-84; editor Boardroom Reports, 1977-84; exec. editor Bottom Line/Personal, 1980-84; pres. Expert Connections, N.Y.C., 1994—2002; editor Street Smart Investing, 1987-89; ret., 2003. Author: How to Build a College Fund for Your Child, 1989, Battle Plan for American Business, 1992, I-Power, 1992; editor: The Book of Secrets, 1989. Adv. bd. Scientists Inst. for Pub. Info., N.Y.C. E-mail: buhmarion@yahoo.com.

BUHL, CYNTHIA MAUREEN, advocate, educator; b. L.A., Apr. 14, 1952; d. Albert Buhl and Dorothy Jane (Loth) Henry. BA, Lewis & Clark Coll., 1974. Dir. Resource and Counseling Ctr., Portland Youth Advs., Oreg., 1971-72; resource coordinator S.E. Youth Service Ctr., Portland Action Coms. Together, 1975-77; sec., asst. Human Rights Office Nat. Council Chs. Christ, N.Y.C., 1977-78; human rights coordinator Coalition for a New Fgn. and Mil. Policy, Washington, 1978-85; cons. Fgn. Policy Edn. Fund, Washington, 1986; nat. adv. bd. Caribbean Basin Info. Project, 1983-85; bd. dirs., legis. dir. Pax Am.'s/Priorities-PAC, 1986-90; legis. dir. Ctrl. Am. Working Group, 1990-93; dir. Indigenous Peoples Program, Bank Info. Ctr., 1994-96; legis. dir. U.S. Rep. James A. McGovern, 1997—. Author: Citizen's Guide to the Multilateral Development Banks and Indigenous Peoples: The World Bank, 1994, Spanish transl., 1995, Bahasa transl., 1996, Russian transl., 1996; co-editor: Central America 1985: Basic Information and Legislative History on U.S.-Central American Relations, 1985. Contbr. articles to various jours., mags. Co-chmn. Human Rights Working Group, Washington, 1978-81, chmn., 1982-85; chmn. Central Am. Lobby Group, 1983-85. Office Phone: 202-225-6101.

BUHLER, JILL LORIE, editor, writer; b. Seattle, Dec. 7, 1945; d. Oscar John and Marcella Jane (Hearing) Younce; 1 child, Lori Jill Moody; m. John Buhler, 1990; stepchildren: Christie Reynolds, Cathie Zatarian, Mike. AA in Gen. Edn., Am. River Coll., Sacramento, 1969; BA in Journalism with honors, Sacramento State U., Calif., 1973. Reporter Carmichael (Calif.) Courier, 1968-70; mng. editor Quarter Horse of the Pacific Coast, Sacramento, 1970-75, editor, 1975-84, Golden State Program Jour., 1978, Nat. Reined Cow Horse Assn. News, Sacramento, 1983-88, Pacific Coast Jour., Sacramento, 1984-88, Nat. Snaffle Bit Assn. News, Sacramento, 1988; pres., CEO Comm. Plus, Port Townsend, Wash., 1988—; bd. sec. N.W. Maritime Ctr., 2001—; editor-in-chief Peninsula Lifestyle mag., 2006—. Mag. cons., 1975—. Interviewer Pres. Ronald Regan, Washington, 1983; mng. editor Wash. Thoroughbred, 1989-90; editor-in-chief Peninsula Lifestyle Mag., 2005-. Mem. 1st profl. communicators mission to USSR, 1988; bd. dirs. Carmichael Winding Way, Pasadena Homeowners Assn., 1985-87; mem. scholarship com. Thoroughbred Horse Racing's United Scholarship Trust; mem. governing bd. Wash. State Hosp. Assn., 1996-2000, mem. legis. policy com., 1999—, hosp. commr. Jefferson Healthcare, 1995—, chair bd. dirs. 1997-2000, 2006-, sec., 2004; mem. Jefferson County Bd. Health, 1997—, vice chmn., 1998, chmn. 2001; mem. Wash. State Health Care Leadership Com., 2003-. Recipient 1st pl. feature award, 1970, 1st pl. editl. award Jour. Assn. Jr. Colls., 1971, 1st pl. design award WCHB Yuba-Sutter Counties, Marysville, Calif., 1985, Photography awards, 1994, 95, 96. Mem. Am. River Jaycees (Speaking award 1982), Am. Horse Publs. (1st Pl. Editl. award 1983, 86), Port Townsend C. of C. (trustee, v.p. 1993, pres. 1994, officer 1996, 97, 98), Mensa (bd. dirs., asst. local sec., activities dir. 1987-88, membership chair 1988-90), Kiwanis Internat. (chair maj. emphasis program com., treas. 1992—), 5th Wheel Touring Soc. (v.p. 1970). Republican. Roman Catholic. Avocations: sailing, photography. Home: 440 Adelma Beach Rd Port Townsend WA 98368-9280 Office Phone: 360-379-1385. Personal E-mail: jillb@olypen.com.

BUHLER, LESLIE LYNN, museum director; BA in History and Art History with honors, Syracuse U., 1969; postgrad., New Sch. for Social Rsch., 1971, Am. U., 1980. Asst. for cmty. programs Met. Mus. Art, N.Y.C., 1970-72; resident assoc. program Smithsonian Instn., Washington, 1972-75; instl. devel. officer Nat. Archives and Records Svc., Washington, 1975-78; cons. Alban Inst., Inc., Bethesda, Md., 1978—95; exec. dir. Tudor Place Hist. House and Garden, Washington, 2000—. Grant reviewer Office of Mus. Programs, NEH, Washington, 1973-74. Bd. dirs. Mus. of City of Washington, 1980-84; vol. advisor Nat. Mus. for Bldg. Arts, Washington, 1977-79. Recipient cert. of appreciation Am. Revolution Bicentennial Adminstrn., 1976. Office: Tudor Place Found 1644 31st St NW Washington DC 20007

BUHRO, NATALIE JO, mathematics educator; d. Noel L. and Ilene M. Whitis; m. Dennis W Buhro, Aug. 18, 1973; children: Bradley R., Joshua A. BA, Olivet Nazarene U., Kankakee, Ill., 1964—68; MEd, Ind. U. Lic. Math. Tchr. Ind. Dept. Edn., 1983. Math. tchr. East Noble Sch. Corp., Kendallville, 1983—, DeKalb Ea. Schs., Butler, Ind. Dir., instr. Kendallville Pk. Dept. Nursery Sch.; math. tchr. Stanley-Boyd Jr. High & HS, Stanley, Wis., Scotch Plains-Fanwood Jr. High, Scotch Plains, NJ, Jerstad-Agerholm Jr. HS, Racine, Wis. Tchr., dir. of jr. ch., bd. mem., dir. of mission edn., dir. of teen bible quizzing, etc. First Ch. of the Nazarene, Kendallville, Ind. Fellow, NSF, 1971—72. Mem. Christian Ch. Avocations: travel, antiques. Office Phone: (260) 347-0100.

BUINGER, MARY KAY, history professor; d. Glenn and Vivian Mapes; m. Gene Buinger, Jan. 25, 1969; children: Ann, Douglas. BA in History, Ft. Hays State U., Hays. Kans., 1969; MA in History, U. Mo., Kans. City, Mo., 1971. Assoc. prof. history Odessa Coll., Tex., 1993—96; instr. history Tarrant County Coll., Ft. Worth, 2002—. Named Outstanding Faculty Mem. Cmty. Svc., Odessa Coll. Faculty Senate, 1995, Outstanding Divsn. Faculty Mem., Tarrant County Coll. Divsn. Bus. & Social Sci., 2006. Mem.: Tex. C.C. Tchr.'s Assn., Orgn. Am. Historians. Presbyn. Avocations: reading, travel, museums, gardening. Office: Tarrant County College 828 Harwood Hurst TX 76054 Office Phone: 817-515-6537.

BUISHAS, KRISTIN MAUREEN, elementary school educator; b. Harvey, Ill., Jan. 1, 1980; d. John Martin and Mary Louise Buishas. BA, Ea. Ill. U., 2002. Cert. elem. educator Ill., 2003. Tchr. St. Kieran, Chicago Heights, Ill., 2003—. Recipient Spl. Edn. Achievement award, Ea. Ill. U., 1999. Mem.: ASCD (assoc.). Office: St Kieran School 700 W 195th St Chicago Heights IL 60411 Office Phone: 708-754-8999. Personal E-mail: kbuishas@hotmail.com.

BUISSONNIÈRE, MARINE, international organization administrator; physician; Korea rep. Doctors Without Borders/Médecins Sans Frontières, now sec. gen. Office: Doctors Without Borders 2nd Floor 333 7th Ave New York NY 10001-5004

BUJOLD, LOIS MCMASTER, writer; b. Columbus, Ohio, Nov. 2, 1949; d. Robert Charles and Laura Elizabeth (Gerould) McMaster; m. John Fredric Bujold, Oct. 9, 1971 (div. Dec. 1992); children: Anne Elizabeth, Paul Andre. Author: (novels) Shards of Honor, 1986, The Warrior's Apprentice, 1986, Ethan of Athos, 1986, Falling Free, 1988 (Nebula award, 1989), Brothers in Arms, 1989, Borders of Infinity, 1989, The Vor Game, 1990 (Hugo award, 1991), Barrayar, 1991 (Hugo award, 1992, 1st place Locus poll, 1992), Mirror Dance, 1994 (Hugo & Locus awards, 1995), Cetaganda, 1996, Memory, 1996, Komarr, 1998 (Minn. book award, 1999), A Civil Campaign, 1999, The Curse of Chalion, 2001 (Mythopoeic award, 2002), Diplomatic Immunity, 2002, Paladin of Souls, 2003 (Hugo award, 2004, Locus award, 2004, Nebula award, 2005), The Hallowed Hunt, 2005, The Sharing Knife, 2006, (novellas) The Borders of Infinity, 1987, The Mountains of Mourning, 1989 (Nebula and Hugo awards, 1990), Labyrinth, 1989 (Best Novella/Novelette Analytical Lab., 1990), Weatherman, 1990 (Best Novella Analytical Lab., 1991), Winterfair Gifts, 2004; contbr. short stories to sci. fiction mags., articles to profl. jours. Mem.: Sci. Fiction and Fantasy Writers Am. Office: Spectrum Literary Agency 320 Central Park W Ste 1D New York NY 10025-7659 Personal E-mail: lois@dendarii.com.

BUKER, ELOISE ANN, political science educator; b. Jan. 3, 1941; d. Thomas R. and Eloise L.; m. Robert Cahill. BA in English, Capital U., 1963; MA in Polit. Sci., U. Hawaii, 1978, PhD in Polit. Sci., 1981. Dir. internat. studies Gonzaga U., Spokane, Wash., 1985-88, co-dir. women's studies,

1988-91, asst. prof. polit. sci., 1981-88, assoc. prof. polit. sci., 1988-91; dir. women's studies program U. Utah, Salt Lake City, 1991-93, assoc. prof. polit. sci., 1991-93; dir. women's studies Denison U., Granville, Ohio, 1993-95, prof. polit. sci. & women's studies, 1993—, assoc. prof. women's studies, 1993—. Author: Politics Through A Looking Glass: Understanding Political Cultures Through a Strucutralist Interpretation of Narratives, 1987 (Jesuit Nat. Book award 1987), Taking Parts: Ingredients for Leadership, Participation and Empowerment, 1994. Mem. various tasks forces; active cmty. orgns. for women's edn. Mem. Am. Polit. Scis. Assn. (awar 1989), Western Polit. Sci. Assn., Nat. Women's Studies Assn., N.W. Women's Studies Assn., Midwestern Polit. Sci. Assn., Alpha Sigma Nu. Office: Denison U 106 Fellows Hall Granville OH 43023

BUKER, VIRGINIA FRANCES, elementary school educator; b. Miami, Fla., June 9, 1951; d. Archibald Elmore and Anna Frances Buker; children: Regina Danielle Cassara, Nicholas Andrew Cassara. Assocs. Degree, Miami-Dade Jr. Coll., Fla., 1971; EdB, Fla. Atlantic U., Boca Raton, 1973. Cert. elem. edn., middle sch. sci. Fla., Nat. Bd. for Profl. Tchg. Stds. Sci. tchr. Gifford Middle Sch., Vero Beach, Fla., 1973—79; 5th grade tchr. Osceola Elem. Sch., Vero Beach, 1979—82; 6th-8th grade sci. tchr. Cartersville Middle Sch., Ga., 1982—86; 3rd-5th grade tchr. Citrus Elem. Sch., Vero Beach, 1986—97; sci. tchr. Oslo Middle Sch., Vero Beach, 1997—, sci. dept. head, 1999—. Mem. edn. bd. Edn. Found., Vero Beach, 1998—; dir. sci. fair Indian River Co., Vero Beach; ednl. cons., workshop presenter Sci. Kit and Boreal Labs., 2002—03. Author: Projects, 1997; co-author: Raintree Illustrated Science Encyclopedia, 1998, 1999. Recipient award of excellence, Edn. Found., 1998. Mem.: NEA, Indian River County Tchrs. Union, Fla. Assn. Sci. Tchrs. (Elem. Sci. Tchr. of Yr. 1992). Avocations: power walking, gardening. Home: 2801 8th St Vero Beach FL Office: Oslo Middle Sch 480 20th Ave SW Vero Beach FL 32962

BUKOWSKI, ELAINE LOUISE, physical therapist, educator; b. Phila., Feb. 18, 1949; d. Edward Eugene and Melanja Josephine (Przyborowski) B. BS in Phys. Therapy, St. Louis U., 1972; MS, U. Nebr., 1977; D in Phys. Therapy, Drexel U., 2006. Lic. phys. therapist, NJ; diplomate Am. Bd. Disabilities Analysts (sr. analyst, profl. adv. coun. 1995—). Clk. City of Phila., 1967; staff phys. therapist St. Louis Chronic Hosp., 1973, Cardinal Ritter Inst., St. Louis, 1973-74; dir. campus ministry musicals Creighton U., Omaha, 1974-75; tchg. asst. U. Nebr. Med. Ctr., Omaha, 1975-76; lectr. in anatomy U. Sci. and Tech., Kumasi, Ghana, 1977-78; chief phys. therapist Holy Family Hosp., Berekum, Ghana, 1978-79; coord. info. & guidance The Am. Cancer Soc., Phila., 1979-81; staff phys. therapist Holy Redeemer Vis. Nurse Assn., Phila., 1981-83, rehab. supr. Swainton, NJ, 1983-87; asst. prof. phys. therapy Richard Stockton Coll. NJ, Pomona, 1987-96, assoc. prof., 1996—2002, prof., 2003—, assoc. dir. post-profl. D of Phys. Therapy program, 2006—. Bd. dirs. The Bridge, Phila., 1979-80; vacation relief phys. therapist, NJ, summer 1988—; mem. profl. adv. coun. Holy Redeemer VNA, Swainton, 1982-93, chmn., 1985-91, mem. pers. com., cons. hospice program, 1985-87, rehab. cons., 1987-88; legis. adv. coun. subcom. on edn. and health care Cape May & Cumberland Counties, 1988-90; utilization rev. cons. rehab. svcs., 1990; mem. fitness screening team NJ State Legislature, 1990; mem. geriatric rehab. del. Citizen Amb. Program, China, 1992; mid. states accreditation team evaluator, 1997-98. Co-author slide study program, (video) Going My Way? The Low Back Syndrome, 1976; author: Muscular Analysis of Everyday Activities, 2000; contbr. chpts. to book. Vol. Am. Cancer Soc., Phila., 1979-82, Walk-a-Day-in-My Shoes prog. Girl Scouts Am., Cape May County, NJ, 1983-86; task force phys. therapy program Stockton State Coll., Pomona, 1985-88. Recipient Vol. Achievement award, Am. Cancer Soc., 1981; U.S. Govt. trainee, 1971, 1972, Physical Therapy Fund grantee, 1975—76. Mem. Am. Phys. Therapy Assn. (edn. sect., orthop. sect., vice chmn. so. dist. 1993-96, 99-2001, chmn. 1996-98, bd. dirs., ho. of dels. 1994-97, key contact voting dist. 2, mem. NJ legis. network 1989-96, 1999-2002, mem. mentoring program 1998—, chair nominating com. 2002-04), Phys. Therapy Club (sec. 1971-72), NJ Phys. Therapy Assn. (rsch. com. 1995-97, Outstanding Svc. award, 2004). Avocations: gardening, music, reading, poetry. Office: Richard Stockton Coll NJ Phys Therapy Program Jim Leeds Rd Pomona NJ 08240 Office Phone: 609-652-4416. Business E-Mail: elaine.bukowski@stockton.edu.

BUKTA, POLLY, state representative; b. Greenville, Pa., Apr. 3, 1937; m. Michael Bukta. BS, Mercyhurst Coll., 1962; postgrad., U. No. Iowa, 1967. Elem. tchr., Clinton, Iowa, 1967—2000; ret., 2000—; mem. Iowa Ho. Reps., DesMoines, 1997—, mem. various comms. adminstrn. and rules, edn. and transp., asst. minority leader, 2001—02, 2003—04, 2005—. Mem.: NEA, NACCP, AAUW, Clinton Area C. of C., Clinton Edn. Assn., Iowa State Tchrs. Assn., Clinton Womens Club, Delta Kappa Gamma. Democrat. Office: State Capitol East 12th and Grand Des Moines IA 50319 also: 604 S 32nd St Clinton IA 52732 Office Phone: 515-281-7331. Personal E-mail: pollyb03@msn.com.

BULBA-CARVUTTO, SUSAN DIETZ, rabbi; b. Newton, Mass., Oct. 7, 1946; d. Ernest Frederick and Jean (Pinanski) Dietz; m. Daniel Bulba (dec.); 1 child, Eli Bulba; m. James Robert Carvutto, July 16, 1988. BA, Radcliffe Coll., Cambridge, Mass., 1968; MAT, Harvard Sch. Edn., Cambridge, Mass., 1970. Rabbi Hebrew Union Coll., Cin., 1997. Rabbi Temple Bethel, Augusta, Maine, 1997—. Pres. Augusta Clergy Assn. Office: Temple Bethel Woodlawn St Augusta ME 04330 E-mail: rabbisue@gw.net.

BULGER, RAYMONDE ALBERTINE, French language educator; b. Lyon, France, July 13, 1921; came to U.S., 1946; d. Francis Alexandre and Alice Jeanne (Bianchi) Saliou; m. Wallace F. Bulger, Sept. 15, 1945 (div. 1977); children: Patrick, Thomas, Michelle, John, Jeffrey. BS, Ecole Tech. Lyonnaise, France, 1941, U. N.D., 1963; MA, Ecole Francaise, Middlebury, Vt., 1970; D Modern Lang., Ecole Francaise, 1976. Tchr. Grand Forks (N.D.) Pub. Schs., 1963-69; asst. prof. N.D. State U., Fargo, 1976-77, U. Minne., Mpls., 1977-78; asst. prof. French and Spanish S.D. State U., Brookings, 1978-79; vis. prof. U. Nebr., Omaha, 1979-80; from asst. prof. to prof. French Graceland Coll., Lamoni, Iowa, 1980-88, emerita prof., 1992—. Author: Letters to Julie Victoire Daubié, 1992; contbr. articles to profl. jours. Mem. Modern Lang. Assn. Am., Assn. Tchrs. French, Romanian Studies Assn. Am. (treas. 1982-92), Am. Romanian Acad. Arts and Scis., Soc. Profs. French, Women in French, Friends of George Sand, XVII th Century French Studies, Blaise Cendrars Internat. Soc., Internat. Coun. Francophone Studies. Democrat. Roman Catholic. Avocations: swimming, skating, walking, scuba diving, theater. Home: 1381 Berry Ridge Rd Apt 603 Eagan MN 55123-1488

BULKELEY, CHRISTY CLAIRE, foundation administrator; b. Galesburg, Ill., Feb. 10, 1942; d. Geraldand Clough and Patricia Ann (Pettingell) Bulkeley; m. Perry David Finks, Sept. 6, 1975. BJ, U. Mo., 1964. Reporter The Times-Union, Rochester, NY, 1964—72, editl. page editor, 1973—74; pres., pub., editor Saratogian, Saratoga Springs, NY, 1974—76, 1984, Comml. News, Danville, Ill., 1976—84; v.p. cen. region newspaper div. Gannett Co. Inc., 1981—84, v.p. spl. corp. projects, 1984; v.p. Gannett Found., 1985; dir. WRI Inc., Albany and N.Y.C. Contbr. New Guardians of the Press, 1983. Bd. dirs. Danville Area Econ. Devel. Corp., Cmty. Coll. Found., Danville, Vermilion County OIC, Danville, Travers Com., Saratoga, NY; leadership giving capt., nominating com Greater Rochester United Way, 1986—89; adv. bd. U. Mo. Sch. Journalism, 1986; v.p. Rochester Grantmakers Forum, 1986—88; mem. steering com. Rochester Womens Fund, 1986—88. Recipient awards Gannett Co. Inc., 1984, Outstanding Contbns. Ill., Mcpl. Human Rels. Assn., 1981, Young Achiever Nat. Coun. Women, 1976. Mem.: Danville Area C. of C. (bd. dirs. 1980—84), Soc. Profl. Journalists, Inland Daily Press Assn. (bd. dirs. 1983—84), Am. Soc. Newspaper Editors (bd. dirs. 1983—84), Women in Comm. Inc. (pres. 1975—76, headliner 1978), Women and Found/Corp. Philanthropy (program com. 1988—89), AP (nominating com. 1979—84), Carolina Trace Club. Home: 1717 Margarita Ln Sanford NC 27332-8301 Office: The Freedom Forum 1101 Wilson Blvd Ste 2300 Arlington VA 22209-2265

BULL, INEZ STEWART, retired music educator, curator, director, singer, writer, musician; b. Newark, Apr. 13, 1920; d. Johan Randulf and Aurora (Stewart) B. Artist diploma in piano, Juilliard Sch., N.Y.C., 1946; cert., Chautauqua Inst. Sch. Music, 1940-46; diploma, U. Oslo Grad. Sch., Norway, 1955; MusB, N.Y. Coll. Music, 1965; MA, NYU, 1972, EdD, 1979. Piano tchr. Juilliard Inst. Musical Art, NY, NY, 1942-43; chmn. music dept. Casement's Coll., Ormond Beach, Fla., 1949-50; dir. music Essex County Girls Vocat. & Tech. HS, Newark, 1953-57; dir. music, organist State of N.J. Institution for Retarded Girls North Jersey Tng. Sch., Totowa, NJ, 1953-68; spl. edn. gifted coord. Jefferson Magnet Sch. Pub. Sch. Sys., Union City, NJ, 1956-95; dir. Upper Montclair Music Sch., Montclair, NJ, 1945—, Ole Bull Music Sch., Potter County, Pa., 1952-68. Pres. N.J. Music Educators Assn. Aux. 1935-48; adjudicator Lycoming Coll., Williamsport, Pa., 1948—; conductor Whippany Symphony Orch., 1951-52; curator, builder Ole Bull Mus., Galeton, Pa., 1968—; dir. youth chorus Jefferson Sch., Union City, N.J., 1956-95; dir. Hudson County Elem. Choral Festival, 1971—; artist-in-residence, Union City; guest lectr. Columbia U., NYC, Yale U. Grad. Sch. Music, Hartford, Conn., NYU, Lycoming Coll., Williamsport, Pa., Mansfield U., Pa., Princeton U., NJ, U. Scranton, Pa., Jersey City State Coll. Author: 32 books; editor: various newsletters and mag.; author: (song) Evening Prayer, 1934, I Will Bow and Be Humble, 1954, Voice of Am., 1952; recording artist Educo Records, soloist WFMB radio sta., Daytona Beach, Fla., 1949—50, NBC, Hartford, Conn., WNJR, Union, N.J., 1952—68, WNBT-ABC, Wellsboro, Pa., 1997—2006, Norsk Rikskringkasting, Oslo, Radio and TV Francaise, Paris, recitals, France, Norway, Eng., Switzerland, S. Am., US. Choir dir. First Congl. Ch., 1940-43, Holy Trinity Luth. Ch., Nutley Luth. Ch., 1953-55; organist, choir dir. North Jersey Tng. Sch. Chapel, 1952-68; founder, dir. Ole Bull Music Festival, Galeton, Pa, 1952—; dep. gov. and mem. rsch. bd. advisors Am. Biog. Inst., Raleigh; US State Dept amb. of goodwill to Norway by order of Pres. Dwight D. Eisenhower, 1953, Norwegian Goodwill amb. to US by order of King Haakon VII, 1953. Recipient Freedom medal-Eisenhower medal, 1953, Sterling Silver plaque King Olav V of Norway, 1966, NJEA award, 1970, Performing Arts Prestige award in Edn., 1976, Olympic Gold medal Norwegian Govt., 1992, Silver medal of Honor, 1991, Gold medal of Honor, 1992, Pa. Senate Legis. citation, 1992, Outstanding Tchr. of the Handicapped in the U.S. Nat. Rsch. Coun., 1970, Woman of Distinction honorable mention award Girl Scout Coun. of Greater Essex County, 1996, Artisan award Oakeside Bloomfield Cultural Ctr., 1996, 50 Women You Should Know award Internat. YWCA, 1996, St. Olav medal King Harald V (Norway), 1999, Outstanding Woman in Arts award World History Project/Twp. of Montclair, 2000, Key to City of Renovo award, Pa., 2000, 2002, Am. Medal of Honor award Pres. of U.S., 2001, Nobel Peace prize, 2002, Congl. Medal of Merit, 2003, Congl. Medal of Excellence, 2003, Amb. of Grand Eminence, 2004, Legion of Honor medal United Cultural Conv., 2005, Spl. Alumni Svc. award NYU, 2005; Fulbright scholar U. Oslo (Norway) Grad. Sch., 1955; film made in her honor A Child is Waiting, 1963. Mem. Ole Bull Hist. Soc. (pres. 1972—), Phi Delta Kappa (pres. 1984-86, newsletter editor 1984-92), Kappa Delta Pi (pres. 1984—, newsletter editor 1984—, counselor NYU Beta Pi chpt. 1996), Pen & Brush Club, Internat. Percy Grainger Soc. (v.p.), NYU Alumnae Club Inc. (bd. dirs., rec. sec., newsletter editor, 1979—), Swedish Cultural Soc. (hon.), Sons of Norway (hon.), Edvard Grieg Soc. (hon.), Alliance Francaise de Montclair, Victorian Soc., Montclair Women's Club, Montclair Cosmopolitan Club. Republican. Avocations: piano, singing, writing. Home (Summer): 79 S Cherry Springs Rd Galeton PA 16922

BULL, MARTHA, artist, educator; d. Charles and Phyllis Smead; m. James Bull, July 28, 1973; 1 child, Caitlin. EdB in Art Edn., No. Ill. U., Dekalb, 1975, MA in Studio Art Drawing, 1986, MFA in Studio Art Drawing, 1990. Exhibitions include Harper Coll. (Hon. Mention, 1987), Elgin CC (2nd Pl., 1988), Norris Cultural Vicinity, Elgin Bubotto Salon, 1990—95, Norris Art Shows, one-woman shows include McHenry County Coll., Campbell House Art Gallery, Parlor Art Gallery St. Charles Congregational Ch. Grantee, Greater St. Charles Edn. Found., 2000, 2001, 2004—05. Mem.: St. Charles Edn. Assn. (assoc.), Ill. Art Edn. Assn. (assoc.), Nat. Art Edn. Assn. (assoc.). Office: Haines Mid Sch 305 S 9th St Saint Charles IL 60174

BULL, VIVIAN ANN, retired academic administrator, educator; b. Ironwood, Mich., Dec. 11, 1934; d. Edwin Russell and Lydia (West) Johnson; m. Robert J. Bull, Jan. 31, 1959; children: R. Camper, W. Carlson. BA, Albion (Mich.) Coll., 1956, DEcons (hon.), 1999; postgrad., London Sch. Econs., 1957; PhD, NYU, 1974; DHL (hon.), Drew U., 2003, Alhion Coll., U. Portland. Economist Nat. Bank Detroit, 1955-59; with Bell Telephone Labs., Murray Hill, NJ, 1960-62; dept. econs. Drew U., Madison, NJ, 1960-92, assoc. dean, 1978-86; pres. Linfield Coll., McMinnville, Oreg., 1992—2005, ret., 2005, emeritus. Bd. dirs. Chem. Bank N.J., Morristown; trustee Africa U., Zimbabwe; treas. Joint Expedition to Caesareu Maritima Archaeology, 1971—. Author: Economic Study The West Bank: Is It Viable?, 1975. Trustee, assoc. Am. Schs. Oriental Rsch., 1982-90; trustee Colonial Symphony Soc., 1984-92, The Albright Inst. of Archaeol. Record; commr. Downtown Devel. Commn., Madison, 1986-92; mem. Univ. Sen. United Meth. Ch., 1989-96, 2000-, gen. bd. higher edn., 1988-92; mem. planning bd. Coll. Bus. Adminstrn., Africa U., Zimbabwe, 1990-91; exec. com. Nat. Assn. Commns. on Salaries, United Meth. Ch., 1986-92. Fulbright scholar, 1956, Paul Harris fellow Rotary Internat., 1988; named Disting. Alumna Albion Coll., 1979; recipient Salute to Policy Makers award Exec. Women in N.J., 1986, John Woolman Peacemaking award George Fox Coll., 1994, Equal Opportunity award Urban League of Portland, 1995. Mem. Nat. Assn. Bank Women, N.W. Assn. Colls. and Univs. (exec. com. 2000—), Phi Beta Kappa. Avocations: archaeology, travel, music. Home: 54 Prospect St Madison NJ 07940 Personal E-mail: vbull@armigerint.com.

BULLARD, BETTIE CATHERINE POSEY, adult education educator; b. Brookhaven, Miss., May 27, 1938; d. Charlie Lee and Hattie Woolley Posey; children: Sherri Slusher, Charla, Shanna Boyer, Shawn. BA, Miss. Coll., 1959; MA, U. So. Miss., 1977, PhD, 1998. Cert. Gifted Edn. Miss., 1978. Tchr. Jackson County Schs., Biloxi, Miss., 1970—98; asst. prof. U. South Ala., Mobile, Ala., 1999—. Cons. gifted music various orgn., Biloxi, 1998—2001; pvt. music tchr., 1970—; founder Epsilon Sigma Delta, 2003. Mem. First Bapt. Ch., Gulfport, 1994—. Named a Notable Americans, 1976—77; named one of Outstanding Leaders in Elem. and Secondary Edn., 1976; recipient Parents Appreciation award, St. Martin Parents for Gifted Edn., 1988; grantee Arts Workshop grant, Miss. Arts Commn., Artists in the Schools grant, Odyssey of the Mind grant, Miss. Power Found., The Sun-Herald. Mem.: Nat. Assn. Gifted and Talented, World Coun. Gifted and Talented, Miss. Inst. Arts and Letters, Ala. Assn. Gifted and Talented, Coun. Exceptional Children, Crescendo Club, Sigma Tau Delta, Kappa Delta Pi, Phi Kappa Phi. Office: Univ South Ala Ucom 3810 Mobile AL 36688 Home: 5906 Reams Dr South Mobile AL 36608 also: 3684 Lakeland Ln Apt C1 Jackson MS 39216-4711 Office Phone: 251-380-2766. Office Fax: 251-380-2724. Personal E-mail: bettiecb@excite.com. Business E-Mail: bbullard@usouthal.edu.

BULLARD, CHRISTINE ADELE DOUTT, retired physical education educator; d. Charles Raymond and Margaret Elizabeth Doutt, Nellie Delores Doutt (Stepmother); m. Gerald Dean Bullard, Nov. 24, 1978 (dec. Nov. 12, 2003); children: Jeri Lu Allsup, Dene Anne Rizley, Starley Gaye Moore. BS, M Tchg., U. Tulsa, 1974; cert. adminstr., Colo. State U., Fort Collins, 1996. Cert. adminstr. Colo., 1997. Curriculum coord. phys. edn. Holland Hall Sch., Tulsa, 1971—75; girls athletics dir., asst. dir. admissions Kent Denver Sch., Englewood, Colo., 1975—90; coord. athletics Jefferson County Pub. Schs., Golden, Colo., 1990—92, dir. athletics and activities, 1993—2006. Sec./treas. SW Prep. Conf., Tulsa, Okla., 1973—75; exec. com. Colo. chpt. Nat. Football Found. and Coll. Hall of Fame, Denver, 1990—94; bd. dirs. Colo. chpt. Nat. Girls and Women in Sports Day, Denver, 1990—98. Dir.: (conference) Jeffco Women In Sports Conference. Bd. dirs. YMCA, Wheat Ridge, Colo., 1994—97. Named Athletic Dir. of Yr., Nat. HS Athletic Coaches Assn., 2004; recipient Outstanding Achievement in Field Hockey, Sportswomen of Colo., 1990, Coach of the Yr., Basketball, Met. League, 1982, Hall of Fame, 1986, Nat. Fedn. of H.S. Assn. Citation Award, Nat. Fedn. of H.S. Associations, 2006, Nat. H.S. Athletic Coaches Assn., Athletics Dir. of the Yr., Nat. H.S. Athletic Coaches Assn., 2004, Outstanding Female Athletic award renamed Christine D. Bullard award, Kent Denver Sch., 1990, Gerald D. Bullard and Christine D. Bullard Gymnasium named in her honor, 1996, Coaches award, 1986, Sportswomen of Colo. Leadership award, Jeffco Women in Sports Conf., 2000, citation award, Nat. HS Athletic Coaches Assn., 2006. Mem.: Nat. Interscholastic Athletic Adminstrs. Assn. (Hall of Fame com. 2004—07, State award of Merit 1991), Nat. Fedn. HS Assns. (mem. field hockey com. 2004—06), Colo. HS Activities Assn. (mem. soccer com. 1982—88, budget com. 1983—96, tournament playoff and fin. com. 1989—92, bd. control 1994—97, exec. com. 1997—2001, chmn. field hockey com. 1999—2004, Athletics Dir. of Yr. 2004), Colo. Athleltics Directors Assn. (bd. dirs. 1982—2006, sec. 1987—88, pres. 1989—90, mem. field hockey com. 1997—2004, pres. 2004—05, Svc. Award 1995-96 and 1999-2000). Office: Jefferson County Public Schs 1829 Denver West Drive Building 27 Golden CO 80401 Office Phone: 303-982-6634. Personal E-mail: gerbullard@msn.com. Business E-Mail: cbullard@jeffco.k12.co.us.

BULLARD, CYNTHIA L., elementary school educator; m. Timothy Bullard. BS in Math., Truman State U., Kirksville, Mo., 1993—97; MA in Edn., Truman State U., Kirksville, 1997—98. Math. tchr. Nev. R-5, Mo., 1998—2006. Recipient Tchr. of Yr., Nev. R-5, 2004.

BULLARD, JUDITH EVE, psychologist, systems engineer; b. Oneonta, N.Y., Oct. 5, 1945; d. Kurt and Herta (Deutsch) Leeds; divorced; children: Nicholas A., Elizabeth A. BA in Polit. Sci., Spanish U., Oreg., 1966, MA in Psychology, 1973; MBA, George Washington U., 1994. Cert. Project Mgr. 1993, lic. realtor N.J. Supr. residential program Skipworth Juvenile Home, Eugene, Oreg., 1966-68; research asst. Oreg. Research Inst., Eugene, 1968-69, 83-85; supr. residential program Ky. Correctional Facility, Lexington, 1969-70; research asst. U. Oreg., Eugene, 1970-73; asst. dir. Regional Mental Health Clinic, Frankfort, Ind., 1974-76; dir. mental health Lane County Mental Health, Eugene, 1977-80; cons. Managerial Communications, Eugene, 1980-83; sys. engr. AT&T Bell Labs., Holmdel, N.J., 1985-91, mgr. strategic/tech. planning, 1992-95, mgr. reliability, customer satisfaction, process engring., 1996—; dir Lucent/Bus. Comm. Sys., 1998—2000; tech. mgr. Sys. Test Quality Configuration Processes, Alameda, Calif., 1999—2001; ret., 2001; art tchr. St. Agnes Cath. Sch., 2002—03; cons., 2002—05; nat. svcs. mgr. Avaya, Inc., 2005—. Mem. strategic bus. planning task force Globa Bus. Comm. Sys., chairperson customer focus groups-new products edn. forum, 1991-95, mgr. forward looking work/tech. coord. tech. bus.-customer partnership program, 1994—, chairperson 2-day software symposium, tech. chmn. strategy conf., 1995, chmn. Breakthru Tech. project, 1996, software design project, 1999-2000, coord. planned and executed Rsch. Tech. Exch. Symposium, mem. leadership team Cultural Change project; exec. prodr. 13TV Broadcast Solutions, 1996. Prodr. (video) The World is Our Work Place, 1991. Bd. dir. Asbury Park 10K, Jersey Shore 1/2 Marathon, 1985—, Women's Resource and Survival Ctr., Keyport, N.J., 1986—; chairperson Area Affirmative Action Com., 1990—; pres. Affirmative Action Diversity Coun.; active Alliance Neighbors 9/11 Support Group, 2002—. Mem. Women's Profl. Network (trustee Holmdel br. 1987—), N.J. Bd. Realtors, Nat. Bd. Realtors, Nat. Art Collectors Assn., Partnership in Edn. & Bus., Corrections in Mental Health, Human Factors Soc. Avocations: running, biking, swimming, tennis, cooking. Office Phone: 408-456-5178. Business E-Mail: jbullard@avaya.com.

BULLARD, MARCIA, publishing executive; b. Springfield, Ill., Aug. 28, 1952; d. Clark Wesley and Eileen (Kloppenburg) B. AA, Springfield (Ill.) Coll., 1972; BS, So. Ill. U., 1974; MBA, George Washington U. Reporter Democrat and Chronicle newspaper, Rochester, N.Y., 1974-79, mag. editor, 1979-82; dep. mng. editor Life sect. USA Today, Washington, 1982-85; mng. editor USA WEEKEND mag., Washington, 1985-89, editor, 1989—, pres., CEO, 1996. Tutor 2 schs. D.C., 1984-89, Literacy Vols., Washington, 1987. Mem. AP Mng. Editors, Newspaper Assn. Am., Am. Soc. Newspaper Editors. Office: USA WEEKEND 7950 Jones Branch Dr Mc Lean VA 22107

BULLARD, MARY ELLEN, retired religious organization administrator; b. Elkin, N.C., Jan. 12, 1926; d. Roy Brannoch and Mattie Reid (Doughton) H.; m. John Carson Bullard Sr., Apr. 27, 1957; children: John Carson Jr., Roy Harrell. BS, U. N.C., Greensboro, 1947; postgrad., Union Theol. Sem., N.Y.C., 1956; MA, Troy State U., Montgomery, Ala., 1979. Dir. women's and girls' work Gilvin Roth YMCA, Elkin, 1947-49; dir. Christian edn. 1st United Meth. Ch., Salisbury, N.C., 1949-51, Charlotte, N.C., 1951-55; dir. youth ministry United Meth. Ch., Western N.C. Conf., 1956-57; dir. ednl. ministries, div. continuing edn. Huntingdon Coll., 1979-88; dir. U.S. office Bibl. Resources Study Ctr., Inc., Jerusalem, 1988-92. Bd. dirs. Ch. Women United Ala., 1970-71; del. World Meth. Coun., 13th World Meth. Conf., Dublin, 1976; mem. 15th World Meth. Conf., Nairobi, Kenya, 1986, 16th World Meth. Conf., Singapore, 1991, exec. com., 1991—, 17th World Meth. Conf., Rio de Janeiro, World Evangelism Inst., 1991—; del. Gen. Conf. United Meth. Ch., St. Louis, 1988, Louisville, 1992; del. Southeastern Jurisdictional Conf., United Meth. Ch., Lake Junaluska, N.C., 1988, 92, 96; mem. gen. coun. fin. and adminstrn. United Meth. Ch., 1992-2000. Bd. dirs. LWV, Montgomery, 1966-70, Am. Cancer Soc., Montgomery, 1975-81, Ala. Dept. Youth Svcs., Mt. Meigs Campus Chapel, 1984-86; mem. Montgomery Symphony League, 1984—; mem. adv. bd. Resurrection Cath. Mission, 1993—; mem. Nat. Vision 2000 Long-Range Dream Team, United Meth. Ch., 1995; del. Southeastern Jurisdictional Conf., The United Meth. Ch., 1988, 92, 96; bd. trustees Ala. West Fla. Con. The United Meth. Ch., 1995-96. Recipient award of recognition Bd. Edn. We. N.C. Conf. The United Methodist Ch., 1956, Christian Higher Edn., Ala.-West Fla. Conf. United Meth. Ch., 1975, Conf. Coun. on Ministries, Ala. West Fla. Conf., 1987, Candler Sch. of Theology, Emory U., 1990, Alice Lee award Ala. West Fla. Conf. United Meth. Ch., 1994. Mem. Christian Educators Fellowship, Kappa Delta Pi. Home: 3359 Warrenton Rd Montgomery AL 36111-1736

BULLARO, GRACE RUSSO, literature, film and foreign language educator, critic; b. Salerno, Italy, July 11, 1949; arrived in U.S., 1958; d. Salvatore and Carmela (Paciello) Russo; m. Frank John Bullaro, Sept. 19, 1971; children: Christian, Adrian Alexander. BA magna cum laude, CCNY, 1971; MA, SUNY, Stony Brook, 1989, PhD in Comparative Lit., 1993. Grad. tchg. asst. SUNY, Stony Brook, 1988-92; adj. asst. prof. SUNY-Nassau C.C., Garden City, 1990—, CUNY-Lehman Coll., Bronx, 1991-2000, adj. assoc. prof., 2000—02, asst. prof., 2002—06, assoc. prof., 2006—. Mem. acad. senate CUNY, 1997—, mem. libr. com., 1998, mem. exec. com. of the faculty, acad. senate, 1998—, liaison English Dept. Libr. Acquisitions, 2000—, sec. Faculty Exec. Com., 2004—, chair English dept. honors com., 2004—06, faculty advisor English honors program, 2004—06; with Lincoln Ctr., N.Y.C., NY, 1998; mem. Exec. Com. Faculty Lehman Coll., Bronx, NY, 1999—; English dept. libr. acquisitions liaison Lehman Coll., 2000—, mem. tchr. of yr. selection com.; acad. senate Lehman Coll. CUNY, 1997—99, 2001—; mem. Exec. Com. Faculty CUNY, 1999—, elected sec., 2004—; cons. Pub. Libr. Fgn. Lang. Acquisitions, Syosset, NY, 2002—; mem. profl. adv. bd. Am. Biog. Inst., 2002—; book reviewer in field. Author: Beyond Life is Beautiful: Comedy and Tragedy in the Cinema of Roberto Benigni, 2005, Man in Disorder: The Cinema of Lina Wertmiller in the 1970's, 2006; contbr. chapters to books, articles to profl. jours. Recipient Excellence in Tchg. award, Excellence in Tchg. Selection Com., SUNY, Stony Brook, 1992, Adj. Tchr. Yr. award, conferred by Tchr. Yr. Selection Com., CUNY, Lehman Coll., 2001. Mem. MLA, Popular Culture Assn./Am. Culture Assn., N.E. Modern Lang. Assn., Nat. Coun. Tchrs. English, Assn. Italian-Am. Educators, Inst. Français, Soc. Profs. Français, Phi Beta Kappa (elected sec. 2004—). Avocations: fitness trainer, tennis, travel, swimming, horseback riding. Office: CUNY Lehman Coll English Dept Bedford Park Blvd W Bronx NY 10468 Office Phone: 718-960-8362. E-mail: grace.bullaro@lehman.cuny.edu.

BULLER, CAROL H., secondary school educator; b. Pontiac, Mich., Nov. 17, 1948; d. Basil Clarence and Ida Mae H.; m. Michael J. Buller, Apr. 24, 1970; children: Jeremy J., Annamarie H. BA, Oakland U., 1970; MA, Ctrl. Mich. U., 1974. Tchr. English and German Saginaw (Mich.) Twp. Cmty.

Schs., 1971-86; tchr. German Midland (Mich.) Pub. Schs., 1986—2001. Adj. prof. Saginaw Valley State U., 2002—03, Delta Coll., 2003. Mem. Swan Valley Bd. Edn., Saginaw, 1975-77. Named Tchr. of Yr., Saginaw Valley League, 1994; recipient Gerstacker award for tchg. excellence, 2000. Mem. Am. Assn. Tchrs. German, Mich. Fgn. Lang. Assn. Avocations: travel, reading, music, theater.

BULLERDICK, KIM H., lawyer, petroleum executive; b. Richmond, Ind., 1953; BA, Wittenberg U., 1975; JD, U. Va., 1978. Legal dept. dir. Giant Industries, Inc., Scottsdale, Ariz., 1998—2000, v.p., corp. sec., subs. officer, 1998—, gen. coun., 2000—. Office: Giant Industries Inc 23733 N Scottsdale Rd Scottsdale AZ 85255-3466

BULLETT, VICKY, former professional basketball player; b. Oct. 4, 1967; Grad., U. Md., 1989. Forward-center, Italy, 1990—93, Cesna, 1993—97, WNBA - Charlotte (N.C.) Sting, 1997—99, Washington Mystics, 1999—. Named to, Italian League All-Star Teams, 1992, 1995, 1996, 1997, Goodwill Games Team, 1989, World Championship Qualifying Team & USA Select Team, 1986, All-ACC Tournament Team, 1989, Kodak All-Am. Team, 1989; recipient U.S. Olympic gold medal, 1988, Bronze medal, 1992. Avocations: softball, tennis, tap dancing, keyboards, reading. Office: Washington Mystics MCI Ctr 601 F St NW Washington DC 20004-1605

BULLIN, CHRISTINE NEVA, art association administrator; b. New Plymouth, New Zealand, Apr. 13, 1948; d. Kenneth and Hazel Iris Bullin. BA, Wellesley Coll., 1969; MLA, Simmons Coll., 1973. Dir. Opera New England, Boston, 1974—78; with San Francisco (Calif.) Opera, 1978—81; mgr. San Francisco (Calif.) Opera Ctr., 1981—94.

BULLINGTON, GAYLE ROGERS, writer, researcher; b. Watsonville, Calif., May 17, 1923; d. Manley Duane and Gladyce Thelma (Horton) Rogers; m. Keith Charles Brown, Nov. 26, 1944 (div. Feb.4, 1963); children: Kendall Keith, Kevin Doran; m. Jack William Bullington, Dec. 23, 1978. BA, UCLA, 1949; postgrad., Northridge U., 1962; MA, Calif. Luth. U., 1974. Cert. tchr., secondary tchr. Calif. Tchr. Southgate (Calif.) Jr. H.S., 1947-48, Virgil Jr. H.S., L.A., 1948-50, North Hollywood (Calif.) H.S., 1950-52, Van Nuys (Calif.) H.S., 1953-54, Thousand Oaks (Calif.) H.S., 1963-79. Author: The Second Kiss, 1972, NAKOA's Woman, 1975—81, Gladyce With a C, 2000, Dark Corners, 2002, My Name Was Mary, 2003, Mary's Little Lamb, 2004, For Love's Sake Only, 2005. Mem. ACLU, Pub. Citizen, Common Cause, Nation Assocs. Home: 23119 19th Ave NE Arlington WA 98223-7631 Office Phone: 360-435-4622. Personal E-mail: gayle.rogers@verizon.net.

BULLIS, JO LOUISE, social services administrator, educator; d. Robert E. Bullis and Mary M. Bullis Hoyt. BS in Phys. Therapy, U. N.D., 1976, JD, 1983. Bar: N.D. 1983, Mich. 1989. Program dir. Women's Resource Ctr., Traverse City, Mich., 1992—. Adj. instr. Northwestern Mich. Coll., Traverse City, 1995—; mem. Governor's Domestic Violence Law Implementation Task Force, Lansing, Mich., 1995—96, Best Practices for Law Enforcement Tng. - Violence Against Women Tng. Inst., Lansing, 1998—99, Mich. State Planning Body - Civil Legal Services for the Poor, Lansing, 2001—, Domestic Violence Trial Manual Com. - Pros. Attorney's Assn. of Mich., Lansing, 2002—03; mem. instrs. com. Mich. Law Enforcement Acad., Lansing, 1999—; peer reviewer Mich. Domestic Violence Prevention & Treatment Bd., Lansing, Mich., 2001—; mem. adv. group Safe Haven Supervised Visitation and Safe Exch. Nat. Demonstration Project, Traverse City, 2003—. V.p., chair fin. com. Addiction Treatment Services, Inc., Traverse City, 1998—. Named Woman of the Yr., Traverse City Zonta Club, 1997, Sarah Hardy Humanitarian of the Yr., Traverse City Human Rights Commn., 2000; recipient Domestic Violence Summit III Govs. award, Mich. Domestic Violence Prevention & Treatment Bd., 1997. Mem.: Women Lawyers Assn., Antrim-Grand Traverse-Leelanau Bar Assn., Order of the Coif, Phi Delta Phi (life Internat. Grad. of the Yr. 1983). Avocations: gardening, reading, travel, music. Office: Women's Resource Ctr Ste 2 720 S Elmwood Traverse City MI 49684 Office Phone: 231-941-1210. Business E-Mail: jbullis@wrcgt.com.

BULLOCK, ANNA MAE See TURNER, TINA

BULLOCK, MARY BROWN, former academic administrator; m. George Bullock; children: Ashley, Graham. BA, Agnes Scott Coll., Atlanta, 1966; MA in Chinese history, Stanford U., 1968, PhD in Chinese history, 1973. Profl. assoc. Com. on Scholarly Comm. with People's Republic of China, 1973—77, dir., 1977—88; dir. Asia program Woodrow Wilson Internat. Ctr. Scholars, Washington, 1988—95; pres. Agnes Scott Coll., Decatur, Ga., 1995—2006. Trustee China Med. Bd. of N.Y.; dir. Nat. Com. on U.S.-China Rels., Am. Coun. Edn.; mem. adv. coun. on U.S.-China cooperation in sci., policy, rsch. and edn. NSF; chair Nat. Assn. Ind. Colls. and Univs., 2002—04, Women's Coll. Coalition; bd. dirs. Am. Coun. on Edn., Sun Trust Bank, Atlanta, Genuine Parts Co.; treas. Atlanta Regional Consortium Higher Edn. Recipient Elizabeth Luce Moore Visionary Leadership award, Dist. Svc. award, NAS; fellow, Woodrow Wilson Internat. Ctr. Scholars, Rockefeller Conf. Ctr., Bellagio, Italy; grantee, Ford Found., Henry Luce Found., Rockefeller Found., NSF. Mem.: Coun. on Fgn. Rels., Carter Ctr. Bd. of Councilors. Business E-Mail: mbb@agnesscott.edu.

BULLOCK, MOLLY, retired elementary school educator; d. Wiley and Annie M. Jordan; m. George Bullock; children: Myra A. Bauman, Dawn M. BS in Edn., No. Ariz. U., 1955, postgrad., 1958, LaVerne U., 1962, Claremont Grad. Sch., 1963, Calif. State U. L.A., 1966. Tchr. Bur. Indian Affairs, Kaibeto, Ariz., 1955-56, Crystal, N.Mex., 1956-59, Covina (Calif.) Valley Unified Sch. Dist., 1961-95, supervising master tchr. trainees LaVerne U. and Calif. State U. - L.A., 1961-71, mem. curriculum devel. adv. bd., 1977-79; ret., 1995. Cons. Bauman Curry Co., PR; mem. voting com. Excellence in Edn. awards Lawry's Foods; attendee reading conf. Claremont (Calif.) Grad. Sch. Author: (poems) A Tree (Golden Poet, 1991), What is Love (Golden medal of honor), The Change of Seasons (Dimond Homer trophy, 1999, Poet of the Yr. medallion). Vol. visitor area convalescent hosps.; mentor to former students. Mini grantee, Hughes/Rotary Club/Foothill Ind. Bank, 1986—90. Mem.: NAFE, Covina Unified Edn. Assn., Internat. Platform Assn., Internat. Soc. Poets (hon.). Avocations: poetry, collecting jewelry, dolls, paintings.

BULLOCK, SANDRA (SANDRA ANNETTE BULLOCK), actress; b. Arlington, Va., July 26, 1964; d. John and Helga Bullock; m. Jesse James, July 16, 2005; stepchildren: Chandler, Jesse Jr., Sunny. Attended, East Carolina U. Actor (films) Hangmen, 1987, Fire on the Amazon, 1991, Religion Inc., 1989, Love Potion #9, 1992, When the Party's Over, 1992, Who Do I Gotta Kill, 1992, The Vanishing, 1993, Demolition Man, 1993, The Thing Called Love, 1993 (also composer for Song Heaven Knocking On My Door), Wrestling Ernest Hemingway, 1993, Speed, 1994 (Best Female Performance, Most Desirable Female MTV Movie awards), While You Were Sleeping, 1995 (Favorite Actress in a Motion Picture award People Choice Awards 1996), The Net, 1995, Two if by Sea, 1996, A Time to Kill, 1996, In Love and War, 1996, Speed 2: Cruise Control, 1997, Practical Magic, 1998, Forces of Nature, 1999, Exactly 3:30, 1999, 28 Days, 2000, Divine Secrets of the Ya-Ya Sisterhood, 2002, Crash, 2004, Loverboy, 2005, Infamous (Hollywood award for Best Supporting Actress Hollywood awards, 2006) 2006; actor, dir., writer Making Sandwiches, 1998; actor, prodr. Gun Shy, 1999, Miss Congeniality, 2000, Two Weeks Notice, 2002, Miss Congeniality 2: Armed and Fabulous, 2005, The Lake House, 2006 (with Keanu Reeves Movie-Choice Liplock, Teen Choice Awards, 2006); actor, exec. prodr. Hope Floats, 1998, Murder By Numbers, 2002; actor (TV movies) Bionic Showdown: The Six-Million Dollar Man and the Bionic Woman, 1989, Who Shot Patakango, 1989, The Preppie Murder, 1989; (TV series) Working Girl, 1990; (TV mini-series) Lucky/Chances, 1990; prodr. (films) Our Father, 1996, Trespasses, 1999; exec. prodr. (TV series) George Lopez, 2002- Recipient Best Actress MTV's Big Picture, 1994 and 1995, Best Actress US Mag., 1995, Favorite Actress in a Comedy/Drama Theatrical and Favorite Actress-Comedy Video awards BlockBuster Entertainment Awards, 1996, Favorite Actress People's Choice award, 1997, 1999, ShoWest Female Star of the Year, 2001, Am. Comedy Award for Funniest Female Performer in a Motion Picture, 2001, Favorite Female Movie Star, People's Choice Award, 2006, Outstanding Performance by a Cast in a Motion Picture, SAG awards, 2006; named Woman of the Yr. Glamour mag, 2006; named one of 50 Most Beautiful People, People Mag., 1996, 1999.*

BULLY-CUMMINGS, ELLA M., police chief; b. Japan; d. Daniel Lee Bully; m. William Cummings. BA with hons. in Pub. Adminstrn., Madonna State U., 1993; JD cum laude, Mich. State U., 1998. Bar: Mich. 1998. From police officer to chief police Detroit (Mich.) Police Dept., 1977—2003, chief police, 2003—; assoc. Miller, Canfield, Paddockand Stone, PLC, 1999—2000, Foley & Lardner, 2000—02. Mem.: Mich. Assn. Chiefs Police, Nat. Orgn. Black Law Enforcement Execs., Internat. Assn. Chiefs Police, Wolverine Bar Assn., Nat. Bar Assn. Office: Detroit Police Dept 1300 Beaubien Detroit MI 48226

BULMER, CONNIE J., film librarian; b. Seattle, Jan. 22, 1931; d. George Arthur and Helen Harriet (Braman) Bulmer. Librarian Republic Studios, Studio City, Calif., 1950-54; head librarian Revue Prodns.-Universal Studios, Studio City, 1954-61, Twentieth Century Fox, Beverly Hills, Calif., 1961-62, Selmur Prodns., Culver City, Calif., 1963-68, Hope Enterprises, Burbank, Calif., 1968-71, Paramount Studios, Hollywood, 1972—. Mem. Acad. TV Arts and Scis., Motion Picture-Videotape Editors, Am. Film Inst.

BULTROWICZ, TARA LYNN, school psychologist; b. Mayfield, Ohio, Sept. 21, 1974; d. Gerald Paul and Mary Catherine Kohanski; m. Mark Bultrowicz, Apr. 9, 2005. BA, Hiram Coll., 1996; MEd, Kent State U., 1998, EdS, 2000. Cert. Nat. Sch. Psychologist NASP, 2001, Sch. Psychologist OH Dept. Edn., 2000. Sch. psychology intern Mayfield City Schs., Ohio, 1999—2000; sch. psychologist Canton City Schs., 2000—01, Cuyahoga Falls City Schs., 2001—. Practicum sch. psychology supr. Cuyahoga Falls City Schs., Kent State U., 2002—, intern sch. psychology supr., 2003—; presenter in field. Mem.: Kent Akron Assn. Sch. Psychologists, OH Sch. Psychol. Assn., NASP. Roman Catholic. Avocations: travel, swimming, reading. Home: 877 Heath Ln Streetsboro OH 44241 Office: Cuyahoga Falls City Schs 2222 Issaquah Cuyahoga Falls OH 44221

BUMBLIS, KRISTIN N., music educator; b. Rochester, Pa., Oct. 16, 1977; d. Harry B. and Joyce I. Fry; m. Jason Bumblis, Aug. 2, 2002; 1 child, Domenic B. BA in Music Edn., Indiana U. Pa., 2000. Cert. music edn. grades K-12 Pa., 2000. Elem. music Salem City Schs., Ohio, 2001—02, Hampton Twp. Sch. Dist., Allison Park, Pa., 2002—. Baptist. Avocations: reading, walking. Office: Hampton Township School District 4100 Middle Rd Allison Park PA 15101 Office Phone: 412-486-6000.

BUMBRY, GRACE, soprano; b. St. Louis, Jan. 4, 1937; d. Benjamin and Melzia (Walker) B. Student, Boston U., 1954-55, Northwestern U., 1955-56, also fgn. countries, Music Acad. West, 1956-59; studied with Lotte Lehmann, 1956-59; HHD (hon.), St. Louis U.; HD (hon.), Rust Coll., Holly Spring, Miss., U. St. Louis, U. Mo.; MusD (hon.), Rockhurst Coll. Operatic debut, Paris Opera, 1960; debut Basel Opera, 1960, Bayreuth Festival, 1961, Vienna State Opera, 1963, Royal Opera House, Covent Garden, 1963, Salzburg Festival, 1964, Met. Opera, 1965, La Scala, 1964, Les Troyens, Paris, 1990, Turandot, Wembley Arena, 1991; has appeared all major opera houses worldwide, S.Am., Japan, U.S.; command performances The White House; recs. for Deutsche Grammophon, Angel, London and RCA. Recipient John Hay Whitney award, Richard Wagner medal, 1963, Grammy award, 1979, Royal Opera House medal, 1988, Puccini award, 1990, Commandeur de l'Ordre des Arts et Lettres, France, 1996, Music Acad. West Distinguished Alumna, 2004. Mem. Zeta Phi Beta, Sigma Alpha Iota.

BUMBRY-BRONSON, VENETTA, music educator; b. Washington, July 12, 1957; d. Lillian Holmes Myrick and Ventura Bumbry; m. Kevinll Willard Bronson, Feb. 3, 1990; children: Venetta Lucille Bronson, Katrina Jean Bronson. MusB Edn., U. D.C., 1982; MS, McDaniel Coll., Westminister, Md., 2004. Cert. Adminstr. McDaniel Coll., 2005, Advance Profl. Prince George's County Pub. Schs., 2005. Tchr. gen. music D.C. Pub. Schs., 1983—95, Prince George's County Pub. Schs., Suitland, Md., 1996—. Instr. piano Charles Houston Magnet Sch., Washington, 1988—95. Mem.: Music Educators Nat. Conf. Personal E-mail: vbumbry@msn.com.

BUMGARDNER, JULIE, music educator; b. Vallejo, Calif., Nov. 28, 1976; d. Michael and Geneen Cummings; m. William Bumgardner, July 1, 2000; 1 child, Morgan. MusB in Music Edn., U. Nev., Reno, 2000. Cert. tchr. Nev., 2000. Music tchr. Dayton (Nev.) H.S., 2000—. Pres. Sigma Alpha Iota, Reno, 2002—04. Named Employee of Yr., Dayton H.S., 2004. Mem.: Music Educator's Nat. Conf. (life). Republican. Office: Dayton High School 335 Old Dayton Valley Rd Dayton NV 89403 Office Phone: 775-246-6240.

BUMP, ELIZABETH BERTHA, music educator; d. Earl Harald and Lillian May Bump. BA in Music, Rivier Coll., Nashua, NH, 1978. Recorder ensemble dir.; cantor trainer; band dir., choir dir. Ascension Sch., Melbourne, Fla., 2002—. Dir. bell choir Ascension Sch.; advisor Tri-M Nat. Music Hon. Soc., Nat. Band Acad. Nominee Disney Tchr. of Yr., 2004; named Tchr. of Yr., Wal-Mart, 2006. Mem.: Fla. Band Masters Assn., Nat. Assn. Women in Music, Schawn Keyboard Soc., Nat. Fedn. Music Clubs, Music Educators Nat. Conf., Nat. Cath. Edn. Assn. (Orlando diocesan religion com., music curricilum com.). Business E-Mail: ebump@ascensioncatholicsch.org.

BUMPUS, JEANNE, lawyer; JD, Univ. Calif., Berkeley, 1993. Legislative counsel U.S. Senator Slade Gorton, 1995—2000; counsel Comm. Subcommittee, U.S. Senate; staff dir. & gen. counsel Com. Commerce, Sci. & Tech., U.S. Senate. Office: Committee on Commerce Science and Transportation Room 254 Senate Russell Office Building Washington DC 20510-6125

BUNCH, CHARLOTTE, advocate; b. Ashe County, N.C., Oct. 13, 1944; d. Pardue and Marjorie Bunch. BA in History magna cum laude, Duke U., 1966; postgrad., Inst. Policy Studies, Washington, 1967-68. Founder Ctr. Women's Global Leadership Rutgers U., New Brunswick, NJ, 1989—, dir., disting. prof. women's and gender studies. Spkr. in field. Creator, editor: Quest: A Feminist Quar., 1974, 1980. Office: Ctr Womens Global Leadership Douglass Coll Rutgers U 160 Ryders Ln New Brunswick NJ 08901-8555 Office Phone: 732-932-8782. Business E-Mail: cwgl@igc.org.

BUNCH, KATHY LYNN, secondary school educator; b. Louisville, June 29, 1956; d. Herbert H. and Jean (Harper) B. BS, Western Ky. U., Bowling Green, 1978, MA, 1981, postgrad., 1984, 86. Cert. Home Econs., edn. adminstrn. level I, 2000, level II, 2002. Nutritionist So. Ky. Headstart, Bowling Green, 1978-79; home econs. tchr. Metcalfe County High Sch., Edmonton, Ky., 1979—; teen parent coord. Metcalfe County Bd. Edn., Edmonton, 1985—; dir., owner Kid's World Day Care, Glasgow, Ky., 1990—2001; asst. prin. McCean County Mid. Sch., Calhoun, Ky., 2001—02; prin. Hardinsburg Elem. Sch., Ky., 2002—04, Tompkinsville Elem. Sch., Ky., 2004—. Asst. prin. McLean County Mid. Sch., Calhoun, Ky., 2001-02; prin. Hardinsburg Elem. Sch., Ky., 2002-04, Tompkinsville Elem. Sch., Ky., 2004-. Mem. Nat. Assn. for Edn. Young Children, Ky. Assn. for Early Childhood Edn., Child Care Coun., Nat. Certification Day Care Ctrs. (treas. Region IV), Am. Home Econs. Assn., Am. Vocat. Assn., Ky. Vocat. Assn., Ky. Assn. Vocat. Home Econs. Tchrs., Am. Spl. Vocat. Edn. Assn., Ky. Spl. Vocat. Assn., Metcalfe County Edn. Assn. (bldg. rep. 1980-81, 85-86, chmn. evaluation com. 1989-90), Ky. Home Econs. Tchrs. Assn., Phi Eta Sigma, Phi Upsilon Omicron. Democrat. Methodist. Avocations: cooking, sewing, bicycling, skating, dance. Home: 24 Love Knob Rd Glasgow KY 42141-9521 Office: Metcalfe County Bd Edn Edmonton KY 42129

BUNDCHEN, GISELLE, model; b. Horizontina, Rio Grande do Sul, Brazil, July 20, 1980; d. Valdir and Vania Bundchen. Model appearing on covers of various magazines including Vogue USA, Vogue Italia GQ, Harper's Bazaar, W, Rolling Stone, marie claire, ELLE, i-D, Allure, Big, Arena, The Face; model Christian Dior, Missoni, Ralph Lauren, Celine, Victoria's Secret, ZARA, Dolce & Gabbana, Strenesse, Versace, Valentino, Gianfranco Ferre, Chloe, Forum, Alphorria, Daslu, Hering, Lycra, Cori; featured in Pirelli Calendar, 1997. Actor: (films) Taxi, 2004. Achievements include highest paid model in the world. Office: IMG Models Penthouse North 12th Fl 304 Park Ave South New York NY 10010

BUNDY, ANNALEE MARSHALL, library director; b. Chgo., Feb. 11, 1938; d. Warren Elmer and Marie Thresa (Madden) Marshall; m. John Willard Bundy, Mar. 11, 1961. BA, U. N.H., 1960; MLS, Simmons Coll., 1961. Assoc. head libr. Coll. Guam Libr., Agana, 1961-62, head libr., 1962-63; tech. libr. E.I. duPont de Nemours & Co., Maydown Works, Londonderry, No. Ireland, 1963-65; head libr. children's rm. Schenectady County (N.Y.) Libr., 1965-66; documents and periodicals libr. Grad. Sch. Pub. Affairs, SUNY, Albany, 1966-67; asst. dir. Medford (Mass.) Pub. Libr., 1967-73; dir. librs. Somerville (Mass.) Pub. Libr., 1973-78; dir. Providence Pub. Libr., 1978-88; program dir. EPA Librs. and Records Ctrs., 1990-91; exec. dir. Ames Free Libr., Easton, Mass., 1992—. Adj. faculty U. R.I. Grad. Libr. Sch.; cons. libr. bldgs., automation, govt. rels.; mem. adv. com. R.I. Sch. Design; mem. accreditation vis. team New Eng. Bd. Higher Edn.; challenge grant panelist NEH. Compiler: Alternatives in Print, II, 1972; mem. editl. bd. The Bottom Line: A Fin. Mag. for Librs.; contbr. articles to profl. jours. Mem. Mass. Cable TV Commn., 1975-79; bd. corporators Butler Hosp., 1983-2004; bd. dirs. Leadership R.I., 1984-88, R.I. Film and Video Competition. Recipient David E. Sweet award Leadership R.I., 1987, Disting. Leadership Alumni award Nat. Assn. Cmty. Leadership Orgns., 1987; Brown Humanities Inst. fellow, 1985-87. Mem. ALA (PLA/MLS sect. pres. 1981-82, chmn. Allie Beth Martin award com. 1986), Agawam Hunt Club, Providence Art Club, Am. Libr. Assn., Pub. Libr. Assn. Office: 53 Main St North Easton MA 02356-1496

BUNDY, BARBARA KORPAN, former college president; b. Chgo., May 13, 1943; husband dec.; 1 child. B.A., U. Ill., 1964; Ph.D. in Comparative Lit., Ind. U., 1970. Asst. prof. Slavic and comparative lit., U. Calif., Berkeley, 1966-69; lectr. Russian and German, U. Calif., Santa Cruz, 1969-71; with Dominican Coll. of San Rafael, Calif., 1971-87, prof., pres., 1980-87. Contbr. articles to profl. jours.

BUNDY, JANE BOWDEN, artist, educator; b. Jersey City, N.J., Mar. 14, 1922; d. John Stanley and Caroline (White) Bowden; m. Wendell Stimpson Brown Jr., June 20, 1942 (dec. Aug. 1992); children: Wendell S. Brown, Caroline E. Calbos, Barbara J. Valentine, Jeffrey L. Brown, Cynthia J. Brown; m. Donald Lawson Bundy, Oct. 15, 1999 (dec. Sept. 2000). BS in Phys. Edn., Douglass Coll., 1942; studies with Betty Abel, Little Silver, N.J., 1962; studies with John Terelak, Marblehead, Mass., 1968-70; studies with Amelia James, Atlanta, 1975-82, studies with Ouida Canaday, 1982-94, studies with Joseph Perrin, 1994. Cert. tchr. phys. edn. and sci. K-12. Substitute tchr. Elem. Sch., Little Silver, N.J., 1965-68, Title I tchr., 1967-68; substitute tchr. Marblehead and Lynn, Mass., 1968-70, DeKalb County, Decatur, Ga., 1970—2002. Publicity chmn., sec., v.p. DeKalb County Art Ctr., Atlanta, 1976—; sec., v.p. Artists Atelier of Atlanta, 1993—. Exhibitions include Artists Atelier, 1999, 2000, 2002, 2003, 2004, A.R.T. Station, Atlanta Artists Ctr., Callanwolde Art Ctr., 2002—03; contbr. articles to profl. jours. V.p., sec., bd. dirs. PTA, Little Silver, 1958-70; bd. dirs. AAUW, Little Silver, 1960-70. Mem. Callanwolde Guild (bd. dirs. 1976—), Atlanta Artists Club (Merit award 1995). Republican. Presbyterian. Avocations: tennis, bridge, reading, gardening, bowling. Home: 2110 Gunstock Dr Stone Mountain GA 30087-1621 Studio: Artists Atelier Atlanta 800 Miami Cir NE Ste 200 Atlanta GA 30324-3048 Office Phone: 404-231-5999. E-mail: janebundy@peoplepc.com.

BUNDY, SUZANNE, human services administrator; b. Arlington Heights, Ill., Feb. 24, 1977; d. William Patrick Bundy and Laura Suzanne Schmahl. Dep. canvass dir. Am. Coming Together, Lauderhill, Fla., 2004; adj. sociology instr. Keiser Coll., Ft. Lauderdale, Fla., 2005; sr. grants rsch. specialist Broward County Human Svcs., Ft. Lauderdale, 2005—. Vol. ARC, Fla., Head Start, Deerfield Beach, Fla.; team leader Making Strides Against Breast Cancer, Boca Raton, Fla. Grantee Grad. Rsch. fellowship, Loyola U. Chgo., 2002—03, Grad. Tchg. assistantship, Fla. Atlantic U., 2003—04. Mem.: Am. Sociol. Assn., Am. Assn. Grant Profls. Avocations: photography, dance aerobics, rollerblading, kayaking, travel.

BUNDY-DESOTO, TERESA MARI, language educator, vocalist; d. Jose Jesus Avila-Carrillo and Maria del Pilar Lozano Avila; m. Glendon B. Bundy, Oct. 15, 1972 (div. May 20, 1987); children: Pete Hernandez Bundy, Angelita Dianne Bundy, Crystal Lorraine Bundy-Schwabenland, Ivan Glen Bundy; m. John B. Soto, Mar. 31, 1996. AA magna cum laude, Fresno City Coll., 1976; BA summa cum laude, Calif. State U., Fresno, 1978; Spanish and bilingual tchg. credential, Calif. State U. Fresno, 1979. Master tchr., trainer Proteus Adult Edn., Visalia, Calif., 1967—73; tchr. trainer Fresno City-County Manpower Commn., Calif., 1973—76; tchr. Spanish, mentor tchr. Ctrl. Unified Sch. Dist., Fresno, 1979—86; dept. chairperson Madera Unified Sch. Dist., Calif., 1986—89; tchr. Spanish, English Hoover H.S./Fresno Unified Sch. Dist., 1989—. Rschr., trainer Office of Edn., Washington, 1968—74; adult edn. tchr. Chavez Adult Edn. Ctr.; alt. chief examiner ofcl. GED testing ctr. Gen. Ednl. Devel. Testing Svc., 1999—; spkr. in field. Singer: recorded 2 CDs and mus. videos under stage name Luz De Luna. Profl. radio announcer Spanish Radio Stas., Fresno, 1978—96; TV model Spanish TV Univision, Fresno, 1980; judge Miss Laverkin, Utah, 1982. Recipient Miss El Futuro C.U., 1967, 1972. Mem.: Am. Coun. on Edn., Calif. Tchr. Assn. Democrat. Mem. Lds Ch. Home: 1149 E San Bruno Ave Fresno CA 93710 Office Phone: 559-225-4880. Business E-Mail: tadesot@fresno.k12.ca.us.

BUNDY FARAH, SANTHA RARNA RAU, science educator; b. Phila., Pa., Mar. 11, 1946; d. Frank Harold and Elayne Mayo Bundy; children: Bruce Perry, Faool Jama Farah, Haweya Katarina Farah. BA, William Penn. Coll., 1968; MA, St. John's Coll., 1993. Ednl. asst. Wash. DC Pub. Sch., 1970—85, sci. tchr., 1985—90, Sidwell Friends, Wash., 1990—2004, Briggs Chaney, Montgomery City, Md., 2004—06. Bd. dirs. alumni St. John's Coll., Annapolis, Md., 1994—2000; cons. Nat. Geographic Soc., Wash., 1995—2000; adv. Mini Med. Sch. Math and Sci. Tech. Acad., Wash., 1998. Co-pres. Urban Nation Hip Hop Choir, 2002—. Mem.: Biotechnology Edn. Tchr. Assn., Nat. Sci. Tchr. Assn. (mid level com. 2000—03). Avocations: coin collecting/numismatics, camping, Scrabble. Home: 1131 Univ Blvd W #1202 Silver Spring MD 20902 Office: Briggs Chaney Mid Sch 1901 Rainbow Dr Silver Spring MD 20905

BUNE, KAREN LOUISE, state agency administrator; b. Washington, Mar. 6, 1954; d. Harry and Eleanor Mary (White) B. BA in Am. Studies cum laude, Am. U., Washington, DC, 1976, MS in Adminstrn. of Justice with distinction, 1978. Diplomate in traumatic stress, bd. cert. in domestic violence. Case mgr. Arlington (Va.) Alcohol Safety Action Program, 1979-94; victim specialist Office of Commonwealth's Atty., Arlington, 1994—2004; cons. victim issues Dept. Justice, Office for Victims, 2001—; victim specialist, legal asst. States Attys. Office for Prince George's County, Md., 2004—. Case mgr. regional rep. of case mgmt. com. of Dirs. Assn. Commn. on Va. Alcohol Safety Action Program, Richmond, 1980-81, 84-85, 88-89, mem. subcom. studying treatment issues, 1988-94; chair career guidance subcom. alumni adv. com. Sch. Pub. Affairs Am. U., Washington, 1991-94; participant IACP Summit on Victims of Crime, 1999, nat. forum on terrorism, NCJA, 2002; adj. prof. George Mason U., Fairfax, Va., Marymount U., Arlington. Author: nycop.com Online Mag. Bd. vis. Marymount U. Named Woman of Yr., Am. Biog. Inst., 1990; named to Outstanding Achievement in Case Mgmt. Hall of Fame; recipient Spl. Achievement award, Dept. Navy, 1973, Merit award, Arlington County, 1986, 1997, cert. Recognition Svc. to Crime Victims, 3d Ann. Neighborhood Day, 1999, cert. Appreciation, US Dept. Justice, 2000, 2004, Carl T. Earles Meml. Cmty. Svc. award, No. Va. Crime Prevention Assn., 1999, 2001, cert. Appreciation, Peddlers for Peace, 2004, Stacie award for dedicated svc. to homicide victims, 2006. Fellow: Am. Acad. Experts in Traumatic Stress (cert. in domestic violence); mem.: AAUW (nat. and Arlington, Va. chpt.), APHA, NAFE, Am. Soc. Pub. Adminstrn. (pres. No. Va.

chpt. 2003—04, Kathy Hensley Disting. Svc. award No. Va. chpt. 2005, exec. coun. bd. mem. 2005—), D.C. Sociol. Soc., Am. Soc. Victimology, Va. Network for Victims and Witnesses of Crime, Md. Coalition Against Sexual Assault, Justice Studies Assn., Am. Criminal Justice Assn., Nat. Dist. Atty.'s Assn., Internat. Assn. Forensic Mental Health Svcs., Am. Acad. Experts in Traumatic Stress, Am. Sociol. Assn., Am. Pub. Human Svcs. Assn., Am. Profl. Soc. on Abuse of Children, Nat. Ctr. Women in Policing, Am. Probation and Parole Assn., Soc. for Study of Social Problems, Va. Assn. Female Execs., No. Va. Fraternal Order Police, No. Va. Crime Prevention Assn., Soc. Profl. Journalists, Va. Crime Prevention Assn., Internat. Narcotic Enforcement Officers Assn., Va. Sheriffs Inst., Am. Soc. Criminology, So. Criminal Justice Assn., Acad. Criminal Justice Scis., Am. Police Hall of Fame (cert. of appreciation 1985), Nat. Assn. Women Law Enforcement Execs., Nat. Ctr. Victims of Crime, Nat. Orgn. Victim Assistance, Nat. Criminal Justice Assn., Nat. Assn. Chiefs Police (award of merit 1986), Internat. Assn. Chiefs of Police (nat. adv. bd. on police-based victim response 2000—), MD Network Against Domestic Violence, Washington Ind. Writers, Am. U. Alumni Assn. (immediate past pres. sch. pub. affairs chpt. 1994—96), World Affairs Coun., Nat. Air Disaster Alliance Found., Lambda Alpha Epsilon, Phi Delta Gamma (1st v.p. 1981—82), Phi Alpha Alpha, Phi Kappa Phi. Avocations: concerts, dance, travel, theater, writing. Home: 926 16th St S Arlington VA 22202-2606 Office Phone: 703-472-5811. Business E-Mail: kbune@gmu.edu.

BUNGE, MARY BARTLETT, medical educator; PhD, U. Wis., 1960. Postdoctoral fellow in neurobiology Columbia Coll. Physicians and Surgeons, N.Y.C., 1960—62; rsch. assoc. neurobiology Harvard U., Cambridge, Mass., 1968—69; rsch. assoc. anatomy Columbia U., N.Y.C., 1963—70; prof. anatomy/neurobiology Washington U., St. Louis, 1970—89; vis. rschr. MRC Cell Biophysics Unit, King's Coll., London, 1984; prof. cell biology/anatomy/neurol. surgery U. Miami, 1989—. Contbr. articles to profl. jours. Mem.: Soc. for Neurosci. Achievements include research in neural tissue, particularly the cell-cell and cell-extracellular matrix interactions that occur during peripheral nerve development; Schwann cell ensheathment and myelination and during axonal growth and regrowth. Office: Univ Miami Sch Medicine Dept Cell Biology/Anatomy 1600 NW 10th Ave Miami FL 33136

BUNGUM, CHERYL NANCY, music educator, director; b. Providence, May 9, 1963; d. Richard Leonard and Jean Wentworth Bratt; m. Brett Charles Bungum, Aug. 16, 1986; children: Samuel, Joshua. BA, Gustavus Adolphus Coll., St. Peter, Minn., 1981—85; EdM, St. Mary's U., Winona, Minn., 2000—02. Cert. tchg. K-12 Minn., 1985. Vocal music tchr. grades 5-12 Paynesville Area Schools, Paynesville, Minn., 1986—. Ch. choir dir. Paynesville Luth. Ch., Paynesville, Minn., 1994—; sect. leader Minn. All State Women's Choir, St. Peter, Minn., 2001. Author: (co-project planner for M) Fostering and Improving School Harmony, 2001—02. Planning com. mem. for new auditorium, Paynesville, Minn., 2000—01; dir. cmty. musical for Foodshelf, Paynesville, Minn., 1990—91; bd. mem. Minn. Music Educator's Assn., 2006—. Recipient Tchr. of the Yr., Minn. Edn. Paynesville Area, 1996, Tchr. of Excellence, Minn. Edn., 1996. Mem.: Am. Choral Director's Assn., Music Educators Nat. Conf., Minn. Music Educators Assn. Lutheran. Achievements include 7th and 8th grade performing at Minn. Music Educators Assn. State Convention 1991. High sch. choir performing at Minn. Am. Choral Directors Assoc. State Convention 1991 and MMEA 1994. Avocations: singing, golf, reading, scrapbooks, camping. Home: 418 W Mill St Paynesville MN 56362 Office: Paynesville Area High Sch 795 Hwy 23 W Paynesville MN 56362 Business E-Mail: cbungum@paynesville.k12.mn.us.

BUNKER, BERYL H., retired insurance company executive, volunteer; b. Chelsea, Mass., Aug. 18, 1919; d. Albert Crocker and Eva Agnes Hardacker; m. John Wadsworth Bunker, Oct. 31, 1942. Student, Simmons Coll., 1936—38, Boston Coll. Law, 1948—49; grad., Bentley Sch. Acctg., 1958; BBA with highest honors, Northeastern U., 1962, MBA, 1967; D of Humane Svc. (hon.), Simmons Coll., 2001. CFA, CFA Inst. Legal rsch. clk. Frank Shepard Co., NYC, 1938—43; cost acct. Johns Manville Corp., Pittsburg, Calif., 1943—46; studio mgr. Wheelan Studios, Boston, 1946; clerical supr. Columbian Purchasing Group, Boston, 1946—48; office mgr. Wellesley Coll., Mass., 1948—51; statistician Eastman Kodak Co., Rochester, NY, 1951—53; investment officer John Hancock Mut. Life, Boston, 1953—74; sr. v.p. John Hancock Advisers, Boston, 1974—84; ret., 1984. Mem. Ct. Women in Politics and Public Policy, Assocs. of the Boston Pub. Libr. Bd., Coll. Club Boston, 1998—, Cambridge YWCA, Neighborhood Assn. of the Back Bay; mem. world svc. coun. YWCA USA, 1992—, nat. bd. dir., 1988—94, hon. bd. dir., 1998—; pres. bd. dir. YWCA, Boston, 1985—87, active, 1977—96; bd. dir. Old South Meeting House Mus., 1989—92; mem. women's coun. Pine St. Inn, 1992—; trustee Simmons Coll., 1994—2000, chair centennial com., 1999—2000, corporator, 2000—05, hon. trustee, 2005—; chair bd. Vis. Nurses Assn. Cape Cod Found., South Dennis, 1995; mem. adv. com. On the Rise, 1997—, Boston Women's Fund, 2001—; mem. adv. com; Inst. Leadership & Change Simmons Coll., 2004—. Recipient Philanthropy award Women in Devel., 1990, Disting. Alumni award Bentley Coll., 1994; named Woman of Achievement, Cambridge YWCA, 1991, Lifetime Service to Women award, On The Rise, 1998, Lifetime Achievement award, College Club of Boston, 1998, Outstanding Alumna Northeastern U., 2000, Cmty. Cornerstone award, Woman in Devel., 2005; honoree Pine St. Inn Women's Coun., 2000. Mem. AARP, LWV, NOW, AAUW, CFA Inst., Mass. Action for Women, Mass. Women Polit. Caucus, Boston Security Analysts Soc. (treas. 1973-76), Simmons Coll. Alumnae Assn. (pres. 1989-91, Alumnae Svc. award 1984, Planned Giving award 1993), Older Women's League, Harwich Hist. Soc., Project Vote Smart, Crittenton Women's Union, Friday Forum, Eire Soc., Wellesley Ctrs. for Women. Avocations: fundraising, theater, reading. Home: 790 Boylston St Apt 22F Boston MA 02199-7921 Personal E-mail: beryllb@mailstation.com.

BUNNELL, LINDA HUNT, academic administrator; d. Byron and Bobbye Bunnell. BA in English and Comm., Baylor U., 1964; MA in English Lang. and Lit., U. Colo., 1967, PhD in English Lit., 1970. Asst. prof. English U. Calif., Riverside, 1970-77, asst. dean coll. humanities, 1972—77; from asst. dean to dean academics Calif. State U. Sys., 1977-87; vice chancellor acad. affairs Minn. State U. Sys., St. Paul, 1987-93; chancellor U. Colo., Colorado Springs, 1993—2001; sr. v.p. higher edn. Coll. Bd., 2001—02; CEO Bunnell Assocs., Colo. Springs, Colo., 2002—04; chancellor U. Wis., Stevens Point, 2004—. Active Minn. Women's Econ. Round Table, 1989-93; mem. exec. com. Nat. Coun. for Accreditation Tchr. Edn., 1996-99; bd. dirs. Aspirus Health Care, 2005-. Mem. St. Paul chpt. ARC; mem. cmty. bd. Norwest Bank, Colorado Springs, 1997—, mem. El Pomar awards for Excellence com., 1997—; mem. leadership commn. Am. Coun. Edn., 1997-2000; mem. subcom. ROTC; mem. edn. com. U.S. Army, 1998-2001. Recipient Disting. Alumni award Baylor U., 1995; named leader of yr., Colo. Springs Econ. Devel. Coun., 2001; Woodrow Wilson dissertation fellow, Univ. Colo. Avocations: gardening, baseball, cooking, sable burmese cats. Office: U Wis Stevens Point 2100 Main St Stevens Point WI 54481-3897 Office Phone: 715-346-2123. Business E-Mail: lbunnell@uwsp.edu.

BUNTE, MANDY KAY, principal, education educator; b. Chicago Heights, Ill., Feb. 6, 1975; d. Dennis Clarence and Kay Lynn (Wehling) Bunte. BA in English lit., Northwestern U., Evanston, Ill., 1997; MA in Reading, Lang. and Specialized Instrn., DePaul U., Chgo., 2001. Type 9 cert. Ill. State Bd. Edn., type 10 cert. Ill. State Bd. Edn., type 75 cert. DePaul U., 2006. Tchr. Bloom H.S., Chicago Heights, Ill., 1997—99; grad. asst. DePaul U., Chgo., 1999—2001, learning specialist, 2000—01; tchr. Bella Vista Sch., Maracaibo, Venezuela, 2001—03, Hyde Park Day Sch., Chgo., 2003—04, prin., 2004—; adj. faculty instr. DePaul U., 2006—. Pvt. practice learning specialist and tutor, Chgo., 2003—. Participant AIDS Marathon, Chgo., 2005; organizer meml. fund. Mem.: Coun. Exceptional Children, Phi Delta Kappa, Alpha Chi Omega. Democrat. Lutheran. Avocations: reading, jogging, tennis, travel, scuba diving. Office Phone: 773-834-5082.

BUNTING, CAROLYN ANNE, writer; b. Waltham, Mass., Sept. 17, 1949; d. Lawrence Earl and Josephine Ann (MacPherson) Rogers; m. Richard Dennis Bunting, Sept. 27, 1975; children: Dennis Richard, Christine Marie. Author: (anthology books) Poem, 1986, 89, 90, 92, Poetic Song, 1989. Roman Catholic. Avocation: poetry. Home: 49 Nelson St # 3 Quincy MA 02169-4806

BUNYAN, ELLEN LACKEY SPOTZ, retired chemist; b. Clark Mills, Pa., Aug. 14, 1921; d. Scott Richard and Mary Ellen (Beal) Lackey; m. Robert J. Spotz, 1944 (div. 1976); m. Arthur H. Bunyan, 1978 (dec. 1996); children: Mark Stephen Spotz, Leslie Claire Spotz, Elizabeth Grace O'Rourke Xavier. BS, U. Pitts., 1942; PhD, U. Wis., 1950. Sr. technologist Eastman Kodak Co., Kingsport, Tenn., 1942-44; instr. chemistry U. Wis., Milw., 1946-47, rsch. assoc. dept. chemistry Madison, 1950-52; instr. physics St. Agnes Acad., Houston, 1965; Welch fellow chemistry Rice U., Houston, 1968-69; lectr. Montgomery Coll., Rockville, Md., 1970-72; asst. prof. chem. tech. Univ. D.C., Washington, 1972-78, assoc. prof., 1978-91; ret., 1991. Guest worker Nat. Bur. Stds., 1976; adj. prof. continuing edn. Walter Reed Army Med. Ctr. U. D.C., Washington, 1991—94, adj. prof., 1995—2000, mem. adv. coun. mortuary sci. program, 2002; curriculum developer Allied Health Chemistry. Contbr. articles to profl. jours. Bd. dirs. Takoma Pk. Symphony, 1988—2001; mem. adv. bd. Cambodian Children's Assn., Inc., 1991—2000. Fellow, Nat. Urban League Eastman Kodak Co., 1976. Mem.: Am. Chem. Soc., Sigma Delta Epsilon, Sigma Xi. Methodist.

BUNZA, LINDA HATHAWAY, editor, writer, composer, director; b. Hartford, Conn., Feb. 23, 1946; m. Geoffrey J. Bunza; children: Stephen, Matthew. BA, Bates Coll., 1968; MA, The Hartford Sem. Found., 1971; PhD, Syracuse U., 1974. Editl. asst. The Harvard Ednl. Rev., Cambridge, Mass., 1974—76; mng. editor The Andover Rev., Andover, Mass., 1976—79; dir. Columbia Rsch. Inst. Arts and Humanities, Portland, Oreg., 1998—2002. Editor Renaissance Mag., Hartford, 1963—64; editl. asst. Symposium Mag., Syracuse, NY, 1973—74; editor Soc. Arts, Religion, and Contemporary Culture, N.Y., NY, 1974—78; lectr. in field. Composer: (Classical Music Composition) There is Something Still Floating, 1999, Report From A Spiral, 1998, Snow Mountain, 2000, RiverMusic, 1995, Mythology of Clouds, 1993, Sphere, 1992, Cascadia, 1989, Widmanstatten Lines, 1987, View from a Mobius Strip, 1986, Sounds from the Olympic Peninsula, 1998, Electric Night, 1984, Odalisque, 1982, Awakening Night, 1981; editor: (Book) Adventures and Misadventures of Dr. Sonjee by Dr. Prasanna Pati, Snehalata Press, 2001, (Novel) Against Parched Winds by Kanta Luthra, (Book) Art of Literary Criticism, 2000; author: Theories of Modern Art-I, 1972, Theories of Modern Art-II, 1973, Theories of Modern Art-III, 1973; author: (catalog) Blue Note: The Art of Bruce Warner, 2000, Air, 2001, Where Art Reveals Itself in Symbols, Words are Hard to Find, 2001; mem. editl. bd. Anima Mag., 1973—95. Bd. dirs. Fear No Music 20th Century Ensemble, 2000—02, Third Angle New Music Ensemble, Portland, 2000—04, Contemporary Art Coun., Portland Art Mus., 2001—04, Portland Baroque Orch., 2000—04; arts and culture com. City Club of Portland, 2000—04, arch. com., 1999—2002. Recipient Pres.'s award, Beaverton Arts Commn., 2000. Mem.: Portland Inst. Contemporary Art, European and Am. Art Coun., Portland Art Mus., Northwest Bookfest (program com.), Ancient Egypt Studies Assn., The Coll. Music Soc., Soc. Composers Internat., Friends William Stafford Assn. (life). Office: Columbia Rsch Inst Arts and Humanities PO Box 25316 Portland OR 97298 Personal E-mail: bunza@teleport.com. Business E-Mail: columbiaarts@aol.com.

BUONAMICI, APRIL GRAHAM, elementary school educator, music educator; b. Maumee, Ohio, Apr. 16, 1950; d. John and Claudine Graham; m. James Buonamici, May 31, 1975; children: Domenick, Brett, Byron. MusB, Bowling Green State U., Ohio, 1972, MEd, 1973. Cert. music and elem. tchr. Ohio. Tchr. Toledo City Schs., 1972—73, Euclid City Schs., Ohio, 1973—74, Lyndhurst City Schs., Ohio, 1974—76, Colegio Internacional, Caracas, Venezuela, 1976—78, Solon City Schs., Ohio, 1978—2005. Composer: (percussion ensemble) Boredom, 1969. Pres. 1st Ch. of Christ, Scientist, Painesville, Ohio, 1983, 1986, bd. dirs. Chagrin Falls, Ohio, 2003—05. Mem.: Solon Edn. Assn. (pres., v.p., grievance chmn., trustee 1979—2005). Christian Scientist. Avocations: skiing, piano. Home: 110 Bennett Dr Bozeman MT 59715 Personal E-mail: abuonamici@aol.com.

BURAU, JENNETTE ANNE, music educator; d. Robert Allen Eckert and Kathleen Mary Behrens; m. Daniel Allen Burau, Oct. 15, 2005. MusB in edn. (cum laude), Ill. U., Normal, 2004. Strings tchr. Scottsdale Unified Sch. Dist., Ariz., 2004—. Coord. Festival and Honors Orch., Scottsdale, Ariz., 2005—06. Recipient Dean's List, Ill. State U., 2003—04. Mem.: Music Educator Nat. Assn., Am. String Tchrs. Assn. Avocation: scrapbooks.

BURBANK, JANE RICHARDSON, historian, educator; b. Hartford, Conn., June 11, 1946; d. John and Helen Lee (West) B.; m. Frederick Cooper, Sept. 3, 1985. BA, Reed Coll., 1967; MLS, Simmons Coll., 1969; MA, Harvard U., 1971, PhD, 1981. Asst. prof. Harvard U., Cambridge, Mass., 1981-85, U. Calif., Santa Barbara, 1985-86, assoc. prof., 1986-87, U. Mich., Ann Arbor, 1987-95, prof., 1995—2002, NYU, 2002—. Reviewer Kritika, 1983, Russian Rev., 1984, 98, Am. Hist. Rev., 1988, 91, 96, Jour. Modern History, 1989, 92, 94, Slavic Rev., 1990, Harvard Ukrainian Studies, 1991; presenter in field; dir. ctr. Russian E. European studies U. Mich., 1992-95, 98. Author: Intelligentsia and Revolution: Russian Views of Bolshevism, 1917-1922, 1986, Russian Peasants Go To Court: Legal Culture in the Countryside, 2004; editor: Perestroika and Soviet Culture, 1989, Imperial Russia, New Histories for the Empire, 1998; editor Kritika, 1978-80; mem. editl. bd. Ind.-Mich. Series in Russian and East European Studies, Kritika, 1999-2001; contbr. articles to profl. jours. Fulbright-Hayes Rsch. award, 1991, Krupp Found. fellow, Ctr. for European Studies, Harvard U., 1977-78, Whiting fellow, 1980-81, Am. Coun. Learned Socs. fellow, 1983-84, Hoover Inst. Postdoctoral fellow, 1990-91; grantee NEH, 1984, 97, Harvard U., 1982-84, Internat. Rsch. and Exchs. Bd., Acad. Exch. with the USSR, 1987-88, 91, U. Mich., 1990, 91, 93, 94, 97; fellow Ctr. for Advanced Study in the Behavioral Scis., 2002-03. Mem. Am. Hist. Assn., Am. Assn. for the Advancement of Slavic Studies, Social Sci. Rsch. Coun. (joint com. on Soviet studies 1988-93), Nat. Coun. for Eurasia and East European Rsch., Phi Beta Kappa. Office: NYU 53 Washington Sq South New York NY 10012 Office Phone: 212-998-8628. Business E-Mail: jane.burbank@nyu.edu.

BURBANK, LYNDA A., painter; b. Burbank, Calif., Apr. 18, 1943; d. Norman Alfred and Glendora McComb Mactaggart. BA in Psychology, U. So. Calif. Prodn.designer (films) Born In East L.A., Quiet Cool, Sid And Nancy, The Wrestling Movie, Repo Man, The Slayer, Happy Birthday, Roadside Prophets, Highway To Hell, Body Rock, The Lady In Red, The Hitcher, Flicks, Losin' It, Walker, (TV Cable) True Tales, Love Kills, My Life As A Man, The Weathergirls, set decorator (TV series) Less Than Perfect, According to Jim, Geena Davis Show, Shasta Mcnasty, Mad About You, Ellen, John Ridley Pilot, Less Than Perfect Pilot, Bette Midler Pilot, Wish You Were Here Pilot, Over The Top Pilot, (TV films) The Taxman, Ride The Wind, When Love Kills, A Murderous Affair: The Carolyn Warmus Story, Running Mates, Alison Gertz Story, Keep The Change, Keeper Of The City, Call Me Anna (The Patty Duke Story), Rainbow Drive, Billy Crystal's Midnight Train To Moscow, A Summer To Remember, Doing time: Women In Prison. Home: 3205 Weldon Ave Los Angeles CA 90065

BURBIDGE, E. MARGARET, astronomer, educator; b. Davenport, Eng. d. Stanley John and Marjorie (Stott) Peachey; m. Geoffrey Burbidge, Apr. 2, 1948; 1 child, Sarah. BS, PhD, U. London; Sc.D. hon., Smith Coll., 1963, U. Sussex, 1970, U. Bristol, 1972, U. Leicester, 1972, City U., 1973, U. Mich., 1978, U. Mass., 1978, Williams Coll., 1979, SUNY, Stony Brook, 1985, Rensselaer Poly. Inst., 1986, U. Notre Dame, 1986, U. Chgo., 1991. Mem. staff U. London Obs., 1948-51; rsch. fellow Yerkes Obs. U. Chgo., 1951-53, Shirley Farr fellow Yerkes obs., 1957-59, assoc. prof. Yerkes Obs., 1959-62; rsch. fellow Calif. Inst. Tech., Pasadena, 1955-57; mem. Enrico Fermi Inst. for Nuclear Studies, 1957-62; prof. astronomy dept. physics U. Calif. San Diego, 1964—89; dir. Royal Greenwich Obs. (Herstmonceux Castle), Hailsham, Eng., 1971-73; univ. prof. U. Calif., San Diego, 1984-91, prof. emeritus, 1991—, rsch. prof. dept. physics, 1990—. Lindsay Meml. lectr. Goddard Space Flight Ctr., NASA; Abby Rockefeller Mauze prof. MIT, 1968; David Elder lectr. U. Strathclyde, 1972; V. Gildersleeve lectr. Barnard Coll., 1974; Jansky lectr. Nat. Radio Astronomy Observatory, 1977; Brode lectr. Whitman Coll., 1986; Hitchcock lectr. U. Calif., Berkeley, 2001. Author (with G. Burbidge): Quasi-Stellar Objects, 1967; editor: Observatory mag., 1948—51; mem. editl. bd.: Astronomy and Astrophysics, 1969—85. Co-recipient Warner prize in Astronomy, 1959; recipient Bruce Gold medal, Astronomy Soc. Pacific, 1982, U.S. Nat. medal of Sci., 1984, Sesquicentennial medal, Mt. Holyoke Coll., 1987, Einstein medal, World Cultural Coun., 1988; fellow hon. fellow, Univ. Coll., London, Girton Coll., Lucy Cavendish Coll., Cambridge. Fellow: Royal Astron. Soc. (Gold medal 2005), Am. Acad. Arts and Scis., Nat. Acad. Scis. (chmn. sect.12 astronomy 1986), Royal Soc.; mem.: Internat. Astron. Union (pres. commn. 28 1970—73), Am. Astron. Soc. (v.p. 1972—74, pres. 1976—78, Henry Norris Russell lectr. 1984), Grad. Women Sci. (hon.). Office: U Calif-San Diego Ctr Astrophysics Space Scis Mail Code # 0424 La Jolla CA 92093 Office Phone: 858-534-4477. Business E-Mail: mburbidge@ucsd.edu.*

BURCH, BARBARA G., academic administrator; BA in English, Western Ky. U.; MA in Edn., PhD in Edn., U. Ind. Dir. curriculum devel. and rsch. Shelby County Schs., Memphis; asst. v.p. U. Memphis, acad. affairs, interim dean, assoc. dean, dir. grad. studies; dean Sch. Edn. and Human Svcs. Calif. State U., Fresno; v.p. for acad. affairs Western Ky. U., Bowling Green, 1996—, provost, 1998—. Mem.: Am. Assn. for Colls. Tchr. Edn. (pres.). Office: Provost & VP for Acad Affairs Western Ky Univ 1 Big Red Way Bowling Green KY 42101-3576

BURCH, CLAIRE RITA, writer; b. NYC, Feb. 19, 1925; d. Albert I. and Dorothy (Denhoff) Cohen; m. Bradley A. Burch, Apr. 24, 1944 (dec. 1967); children: Laurie (dec.), Thomas (dec.), Emily, Elizabeth. BA, Washington Square Coll., N.Y.C., 1947. Editor, writer, N.Y.C., 1947-50; freelance writer, 1950-68; adj. prof. Union of Experimenting Colls., Antioch, N.Y., 1970-73; editor, freelance writer various nat. mags., N.Y.C., 1974-78; contbg. editor No. Calif. Psychiat. Network News, Berkeley, 1978-83; artistic dir. Art and Edn. Media Inc., Berkeley, Calif.; distbr. Regent Press, Oakland, Calif. Distbr. Facets Multimedia, Chgo., Tapeworm, Calif., Solid Entertainment, San Francisco; conducted numerous workshops in field. Author: Stranger in the Family, 1972, Shredded Millions, 1980, Homeless in the Eighties, 1988, Goodbye My Coney Island Baby, 1989, Solid Gold Illusion, 1991, Homeless in the Nineties, 1994, You Be the Mother Follies, 1994, Stranger on the Planet: Charles Darwin in Cyberspace, 1996; filmmaker (documentaries) James Baldwin: Entering Oakland (People's Choice award), Alfonia (People's Choice award), Thumbed a Ride to Heaven, Baby Don't Cry, Oracle Rising, People's Park Then and Now, Street Survivors, The Telegraph Ave., Street Calendar Live, Remembering the Summer of Love, Oracle Rising, Ghost of the S.F. Oracle Meets Tim Leary, How Timothy Leary Changed My Life; author (folk opera) It's a Blues to Be Called Crazy When Crazy's All There Is; assoc. prodr. (film) Tim Leary's Dead, 1997. Grantee City of Berkeley, 1989-2005, Calif. Arts Coun., 1991-94, Seva Found., 1996, San Francisco Found., 1999, Alameda Arts Coun., 1997, Puffin Found., 1999, Winfred Found.; recipient Carnegie award, 1978-79, Lifetime award Bay Area Film Festival, 2003 Office: Art and Edn Media Inc 2747 Regent St Berkeley CA 94705-1212 Address: c/o Regent Press 60208 Adeline St Ste A Oakland CA 94608-1446 Office Phone: 510-547-7602. Personal E-mail: claire_burch@yahoo.com. Business E-Mail: info@claireburch.com.

BURCH, JULIE S., science educator; b. Indpls., June 28, 1965; d. James Albert and Belva Joan Burch. B in Chemistry Edn., Purdue U., West Lafayette, Ind., 1987; M in Environ. Studies, So. Ill. U., Edwardsville, 1996. Chemist Shell Oil Co., Wood River, Ill., 1988—92; instr. The Magic Ho.: St. Louis Children's Mus., 1992—93; sci. tchr. Belleville West H.S., Ill., 1993—. Seasonal instr. St. Louis Zoo, 1989—. Home: 212 S 74th St Belleville IL 62223 Office: Belleville West High School 4063 Frank Scott Parkway West Belleville IL 62223 Office Phone: 618-222-7610. Personal E-mail: julburch@stclair.k12.il.us.

BURCH, LORI ANN, obstetrics nurse; b. Charleston, Ill., Jan. 27, 1967; d. Lawrence Lee and Leslie Ann (Biddle) Pedigo; m. Steven Wayne Burch, Oct. 16, 1987 (div. June 1992); 1 child, Colby Steven. Diploma, Bapt. Sch. Nursing, Springdale, Ark., 1992. RN, Ark., Mo. Staff nurse Sprindale Meml. Hosp., 1992-94; agy. RN Healthstaf, Inc., Branson, Mo., 1994-98; sch. nurse Kirbyville (Mo.) Sch. Dist., 1998—. Educator, spkr. in field. Avocations: swimming, running, travel, golf.

BURCH, PAULA USERY, special education educator; b. Greenfield, Tenn., Dec. 26, 1955; d. Leonard Lee and Patricia Ann (Huffstetler) Usery; m. Thomas Burch, Sept. 30, 1979; children: Michael, Jennifer. BS, U. Tenn., Martin, 1977, MS. Cert. tchr., Mo. Tchr. Caruthersville (Mo.) Sch. Dist., 1977-82, Pemiscot County Spl. Sch. Dist., Hayti, Mo., 1984—. Avocations: reading, camping. Home: 208 E 6th St Caruthersville MO 63830-1608

BURCHENAL, JOAN RILEY, science educator; b. NYC, Dec. 11, 1925; d. Wells Littlefield and Bertha Barclay (Fahys) Riley; m. Joseph Holland Burchenal, Mar. 20, 1948; children: Elizabeth Payne Burchenal Paul (dec.), Joan Littlefield Burchenal Nycum, Barbara Fahys Burchenal Landers, Caleb Wells, David Holland, Joseph Emory Barclay; 1 stepchild, Mary Holland Burchenal Nottebohm. BA, Vassar Coll., Poughkeepsie, N.Y., 1946; MAT, Yale U., New Haven, Conn., 1971; MA, Fairfield U., Conn., 1981. Sci. tchr. New Canaan (Conn.) Country Sch., 1968-69, Low Heywood Sch., Stamford, Conn., 1968-69, The Thomas Sch., Rowayton, Conn., 1972-73, Darien Bd. Edn., Conn., 1973-91, ret. Conn. Mem. panel on grants for tchrs. enhancement program NSF, 1987, 92; K-12 sci. curriculum com., 1994-2000. Hon. chmn. Darien Sci. Fair, 1986; mem. steering com. Holly Pond Saltmarsh Conservation Com., 1968—71; mem. acad. courses com. Darien Cmty. Assn., 1964—71, chmn., 1971; trustee Garrison Forest Sch., 1959—62; rep. Town Meeting Darien, 1993—2003, mem. edn. com., 1993—2003, chair edn. com., 1995—97, rules com., 2000—03; cmty. rep. K-12 Sci. Curriculum Com., 1994—2000; bd. dirs. Darien LWV, 1951—62; elder First Presbyn. Ch. of New Canaan, 1994—97, Stephen min., 1994—; bd. dir., chmn. standards com. A Better Chance, Darien, Conn., 1985—99; bd. dir. Darien Nature Ctr., 1975—91, Darien Audubon Soc., 1978—86; mem. Darien LWV, 1951—2004; bd. dir. Alumnae and Alumni Vassar Coll. Recipient Presdl. award for excellence in sci. teaching, Nat. Sci. Tchrs. Assn., NSF, Washington, 1985. Mem. AAAS, N.Y. Acad. Sci., Assn. Presdl. Awardees in Sci. Teaching (nominating com. 1987-90), Cosmopolitan Club, Ausable Club, Phi Beta Kappa. Democrat. Presbyterian. Avocations: reading, travel, trekking, birding. Home: Kendal at Hanover #432 80 Lyme Rd Hanover NH 03755 Personal E-mail: jhbjrb@valley.net.

BURCHFIELD, ELLA LOGGINS, science educator; d. Sylvester and Para Lee Loggins; children from previous marriage: MaSonya Janika, Aisha Jamila. Post grad., Ctrl. Mich. U., Mt. Pleasant, MI, 2006—. Cert. T-5 in sci. edn. grades 7-12 GA Performance Stds., 1976. Tchr. Clayton County Pub. Schs., Jonesboro, Ga., 1982—. Leader Girl Scouts USA, Atlanta, 1982—89; mem. Crusade fellowship United Meth. Ch., 1974—75. Mem.: Ga. Sci. Tchr. assn. (assoc.). Democrat. Avocations: travel, reading, music. Office: Clayton County Pub Schs 1597 McDonough Rd Lovejoy GA 30250 Office Phone: 770-473-2920. Office Fax: 770-473-2920. E-mail: eburchfiel@clayton.k12.ga.us.

BURCHFIELD, SUSAN, psychologist; b. Columbus, Ohio, Nov. 16, 1951; d. James Ralph and Dorothy Burchfield; m. William Chapman Holliday, May 31, 1980; children: William Burchfield, Jessica Renée. BSN, Ohio State U., 1974; PhD in Psychology, U. Wash., 1978. Lic. psychologist, Wash.; RN, Wash. Nurse U. Wash. Hosps., Seattle, 1974-78; asst. prof. U. Ky., Lexington, 1979-81; pvt. practice Seattle, 1984—. Editor: Stress: Psychological and

Physiological Interactions, 1984. Mem. Wash. State Psychol. Assn. (chpt. pres. 1989-91), Am. Psychol. Assn., Am. Psychosomatic Soc., Sigma Theta Tau. Office: 4026 NE 55th St Ste B Seattle WA 98105-2254

BURCH-MARTINEZ, BERKELEY ALISON, primary school educator; b. Santa Monica, Calif., Nov. 20, 1967; d. Robert Dale and Joann Hansen B.; m. Gilbert Jesse Martinez, June 24, 1998; children, Sterling Alexander, Carsen Aren. BA, U. Calif., Irvine, 1992; MA, Pepperdine U., 1993. Tchr. spl. edn. King City (Calif.) Union Sch. Dist., 1997-98; tchr. kindergarten, 1st grade Ocean View Sch. Dist., Oxnard, Calif., 1998—. Mem. NEA, Calif. Tchrs. Assn., Internat. Reading Assn., Calif. Kindergarten Assn., So. Calif. Kindergarten Assn Avocations: writing, education.

BURD, BARBARA R., mathematics educator; d. Richard G. and Ruth F. King; m. James J. Burd, June 3, 1972; children: James J., Jason M., Alicia D. BA, Rowan U., Glassboro, N.J., 1972, MA, 1990. Cert. tchr. math. N.J., 1972. Adj. faculty/tutor coord. Rowan U., 1977—90; tchr. math. Pitman H.S., NJ, 1984—. Dept. chair Pitman H.S., 2000—. Grantee, PEA, 2002. Mem.: Computer Sci. Tchr. Assn. (assoc.), Nat. Coun. Tchrs. of Math. (assoc.). Avocations: tennis, kayaking, hiking, bicycling, travel. Office Phone: 856-589-2121.

BURD, JOYCE ANN, librarian; d. James Edgar and Azile Danehower Odom; m. Robert Banks Burd, Mar. 29, 1983 (dec. Nov. 15, 2001); 1 child, Sarah Azile Fratta. MLS, U. Tenn., 1976. Elem. and secondary edn. Va., 1981. Tech. services mgr. Suffolk Pub. Libr., Va., 2002—, cataloger, 2000—02; media specialist/resource tchr. Houston Ind. Sch. Dist., 1982—87; audio visual cataloger Norfolk Pub. Schools, Va., 1978—81; cataloger York Pub. Libr., Va.; original materials/govt. docs. cataloger Chesapeake Pub. Libr., Va., 1988—2000; tech. svcs. mgr./network adminstr. Suffolk Pub. Libr., Va., 2000—. Libr. rep. Suffolk Civil War Days, Va., 2004—05; girl scout liason/com. mem. Chesapeake Civil War Days, 1994—2000; coord. Native Am. Gathering / Chesapeake Pub. Libr., 1996—98. Mem.: Va. Libr. Assn. (assoc.), ALA (assoc.), NAFE (assoc.). Independent. Church Of Christ. Avocations: travel, computers, knitting. Office: Suffolk Public Library 443 W Washington St Suffolk VA 23434 Business E-Mail: jburd@city.suffolk.va.us.

BURDEN, SHERRI LYNN ERICKSON, secondary school educator; m. Robert John Burden, May 30, 1980; children: Erica Lynn, John Edward. Bachelor's, U. Okla., Norman, 1979. Cert. tchr. Okla. Classroom English tchr. McAlester Pub. Schs., Okla., 1979—. Docent Italian Festival, McAlester, 1985—90; ch. deacon First Presbyn. Ch., McAlester, 1990—2006. Mem.: NEA, McAlester Edn. Assn., Okla. Edn. Assn. Republican. Presbyterian. Office: McAlester HS 1 Buffalo Dr Mcalester OK 74501 Office Phone: 918-423-4771.

BURDETT, BARBRA ELAINE, biology professor; b. Lincoln, Ill., Mar. 18, 1947; d. Robert Marlin and Klaaska Johanna Baker; m. Gary Albert Burdett, Sept. 27, 1968; children: Bryan Robert, Heather Lea, Amanda Rose. AA, Lincoln Coll., 1981; postgrad., Ill. State U. Edn. Core, 1982-83; BS, Millikin U., 1985; postgrad., Western U., 1994-95, U. Ill., Springfield, 1997, Quincy (Ill.) U., 1998. Cert. tchr., Ill. Tchr. advanced placement biology, botany and human physiology Brown County H.S., Mt. Sterling, Ill., 1985-95; tchr. zoology, botany, environmental sci. Pleasant Plains (Ill.) H.S., 1995-97; tchr. biology Quincy (Ill.) H.S., 1997-98; owner Wild Winds Pub. Co., 1999—. Dir. Drama Club, Brown County H.S., 1988-90, dir. sci. fairs; edn. advisor Nat. Young Leaders Conf. Author: Misty White, 1991, Possums Sing, 1994; co-author: The Last Button on Gabe's Coat, 1999, Derthro—Meet Mrs. Claus, 1999. Sponsor Children, Inc., Richmond, Va., 1985—, Internat. Wildlife Coalition, North Falmouth, Mass., 1991—; commdr. club, silver leader., 1988—. Mem. ASCD, Nat. Assn. Biology Tchrs. (Biology Tchr. of Yr. in Ill. 1994), Ill. Sci. Tchrs. Assn., Phi Delta Kappa (newsletter editor 1990), Phi Theta Kappa. Episcopalian. Avocation: classical guitar.

BURDETTE, JANE ELIZABETH, former nonprofit association executive, consultant; b. Huntington, W.Va., Aug. 17, 1955; d. C. Richard and Jewel Kathryn (Wagner) B. AAS, Parkersburg CC, W.Va., 1976; BA, Glenville State Coll., 1978; MA, W.Va. U., 1984; DD (hon.), U. Life Monastery, 2000. Fund raiser, recruiter Muscular Dystrophy Assn., Charleston, W.Va., 1973, 74, 75; sec., bookkeeper Nationwide Ins. Co., Parkersburg, 1975; v.p. Burdette Funeral Home, Parkersburg, 1976-85; intake and referral specialist Wood County Sheltered Workshop, Parkersburg, 1985-91; cons. in field, 1991—. Bd. dirs. Sheltered Workshop, Parkersburg, 1982-86; past pres. Western Dist. Guidance Ctr., Parkersburg, 1984-94; vol. St. Joseph's Hosp., 1991-96; mem. W.Va. Coun. Ind. Living, 1992-94; mem. W.Va. Muscular Dystrophy Assn. task force on disability issues, 1992—; bd. advisors, vice chmn. Parkersburg C.C., 1980-89, Domestic Violence Interdisciplinary Adv. Com., 1987, Just Say No, 1987-91; mem. Wood County Commn. on Crime, Delinquency and Corrections, Parkersburg, 1985—, chmn., 1995-99; chmn. Mid Ohio Valley United Fund Agy., 1986 Heads; v.p. Jr. League of Parkersburg, 1989—; mem. Sanctuary Soc., 1991—, All Saints Guild, 1991-95, St. Margaret Mary Parish Coun., 1992-97; bd. dirs. Cmty. Svc. Coun., 1985—; v.p. Parkersburg Transit Authority, 1994-98; past chmn. W.Va. Statewide Rehab. Adv. Cou., 1998—, pres., 2000; liaison Gov. Commn. on Disabled Persons, Charleston, W.Va., 1981-85; mem. Career Adv. Network, 1987-91; treas. W.Va. Women's Conf., 1987, Children's Discovery Ctr. Mus., 1998-01; exec. com. W.Va. chpt. Muscular Dystrophy Assn., 1987—, past pres.; mem. We've Been There Parent Support Group, 1987-90; v.p. A Spl. Wish Found., 1988-98; mem. Parkersburg Consumer Adv. Group; mem. founding com. Banquet of Wealth, 1988-91; bd. dirs. Horizon's Ind. Living Ctr., 1990—, past pres.; past transition plan team leader Wood County Bd. Edn.; past liason Internat. Yr. Disabled Persons; past treas., program chmn. Gov.'s Conf.; former pres. Y Teen Club, YWCA; former adv. com. Mountwood Pk. White Oak Village, Organ Donor Com., 1989, and others; mayoral candidate City of Parkersburg, 1997; mem. Girls Night Out, Nebr., 2004-; sec. Parkersburg Mcpl. Dem. Com., 2004-; v.p. Dem. exec. com. Wood County, 2002-. Named Miss Wheelchair W.Va., 1981, Outstanding Young Woman of Yr. for W.Va., 1981, Outstanding Young Woman of the Yr., 1986; recipient Kenneth Hieges award Muscular Dystrophy Assn., 1982, Outstanding Citizen award Frat. Order of Police, 1984, Cmty. Svc. award Moose Lodge, 1995, Cert. Appreciation, State W.Va., Gov. Jay Rockefeller, Cert. Appreciation, Am. Legion Aux., Trail of New Beginning award Banquet of Wealth Trail Blazer award YWCA/Altrusa, 1989, Personal Achievement award for W.Va., MDA, 1993, 94, 97, Mary Harriman Cmty. Leadership award Jr. League Internat., 1994, Jennings Randolph award W.Va. Rehab. Assn., 1996, Good Neighbor award Supermarket Comm./Big Bear, 1997, Jefferson award Sta. WCHS-TV, 1998; named W.Va.'s Disabled Profl. Woman of Yr. Pilot Internats., 1989, Hometown Hero Sta. WSAZ-TV, 1993, One Who Makes a Difference, Sta. WTAP, 1994, Profl. and Bus. Woman's Internat. Hall of Fame, 1995, Nat. Hall of Fame for Persons with Disabilities, 1998, W.Va. Women Hall of Fame, 1999, Cover Girl Women At their Best award, 1999, Dem. of Yr. award Wood County, 2001. Mem. NAFE, Toastmasters (Comm. and Leadership award 1989). Democrat. Roman Catholic. Avocation: designing. Home: 2500 Brooklyn Dr Parkersburg WV 26101-2913 Personal E-mail: jane13@charter.net.

BURDICK, GINNY MARIE, state senator; b. Portland, Oreg., Dec. 3, 1947; BA, U. Puget Sound, 1969; M in Journalism, Oreg. U., 1973. Reporter, editor Port Angeles (Wash.) Daily News, Eugene (Oreg.) Register-Guard, AP, Bur. Nat. Affairs, Legal Times of Washington, 1969—79; environ. issues mgr. Atlantic Richfield Co., 1981—84; self-employed crisis mgmt. specialist, 1989—2004; v.p., sr. counsel Gard & Gerber Advt. and Pub. Rels., 2004—; mem., chair, senate judiciary comm. Oreg. Senate, Salem, 1996—. Democrat. Home: 4641 SW Dosch Rd Portland OR 97239-1244 Office: S 317 State Capitol Salem OR 97301 E-mail: sen.ginnyburdick@state.or.us.

BURDICK, MARGARET SEALE (MARGE BURDICK), interior designer; b. Ft. Worth, Tex., July 24, 1919; d. Walter Braton and Ivy (McCleskey) Seale; m. Donald K. Bennett (dec. May 1943); 1 child, Donald Jr.; m. William J. Walsh, Dec. 1, 1945 (div. June 1959); children: Susan S. Lynch, William J. Jr., Margaret J. Tannery; m. Lorence Connable Burdick, Oct. 21, 1961 (div. Aug. 1979); children: Michael, John, Timothy (dec.). Student, So. Meth. U., 1937-38. Interior redesigner Kalamazoo (Mich.) Country Club, 1948; interior desiger Child Guidance Ctr. Jr. League (formerly Service Club), Kalamazoo, 1956, designer nearly new shop, 1955; co-owner, interior designer Red Lion Inn, Vail, Colo., 1962-80; owner MSB Designs, 1980-2001; interior designer Outstanding Homes in Vail, 1981-99. Co-organizer 1st Sch. Bd. Vail, 1963; charter bd. dirs. Vail Inst Performing Arts, 1973-84; pres. Vail Inst., 1979-84, also hon. bd. dirs. 1984-87; mem. Art Selection Com. Vail, 1981-84; bd. dirs. Gerald R. Ford Commemorative Com., Vail, 1980-85; charter mem. bd. dirs. Bravo! Colo. Music Festival, Vail and Beaver Creek, 1987-95, adv. bd., 1995-2005; bd. dirs. Betty Ford Alpine Carden Found., 1986-97, nat. adv. bd., 1997-2001; bd. dirs. Vail Religious Found. Endowment Com., 1995-2004, Bravo! Music Festival Endowment Com., 1991-98, Ctr. for the Arts Com. (now Vilar Ctr.), Beaver Creek, Vail Valley Arts Coun., 1991—, pres., 1993-97. Honoree Bravo! Colo. Music Festival, 1997. Mem.: Racquet Club (charter), Homestead Ct. Club, Vail Athletic Club (charter). Republican. Episcopalian. Home and Office: 2833 Newport Cir Grand Junction CO 81503 E-mail: msb@vail.net.

BURDINE, LINDA SHARON, secondary school educator, writer; b. Milw., July 23, 1950; d. Carl and Ruby (Dirk) Wiedmann; m. Stephen Michael Burdine, May 16, 1975; children: Scott, Kristine. BS, Ball State U., 1973; MS, Ind. U., Bloomington, 1979. Cert. secondary tchr. St. Bd. Examiners Ind., career and tech. info. Nat. Bd. Profl. Tchg. Stds., 2003, tchr. Nat. Bd. Profl. Tchg. Stds. Tchr. bus. edn. Washington H.S., Indpls., 1974—76, Perry Meridian H.S., 1976—. Chairperson textbook adoption State of Ind., 1976; state tchr. mentor; grad. Tchr. Leadership Acad. Author: Typing Bulletin Board Projects, 1985, Awards, Rewards Coupons, 1985, Learning General Business, 1985, Learning Shorthand Learning Typing, 1985, Creations, Inc., A Typewritng Simulation, 1986. Recipient Grand prize, Nat. Amateur Advt. Contest, 1990, 1st pl. display, Ind. Bus. Ednl. Assn., 1990, 1991, 1992, 1st pl. newsletter, 1992, 1st pl., Sta. WZPL Kelloggs City Wide Radio Contest, 1993, Golden Apple award, Indpls. Power & Light, 1996, Creativity award, Nat. "Got Milk" Dairy Assn., 1999, Tchr. Excellence award, Project e., 2001. Mem.: Perry Edn. Assn. (mem. negotiation team 1977, bldg. rep. 1985—), Indpls. Bus. Edn. Assn., Ind. State Tchrs. Assn., Pi Beta Lambda, Phi Delta Kappa, Kappa Delta Pi. Avocations: reading, writing, swimming. Office: Perry Meridian High Sch 401 W Meridian School Rd Indianapolis IN 46217-4215 Office Phone: 317-789-4454. Personal E-mail: smile1000@aol.com.

BURDMAN, JACQUELINE BERMEL, retired special education educator; b. Buffalo, Apr. 8, 1943; d. Milton Paul and Dorothy Helen Bermel; m. Phillip Allan Burdman, June 17, 1973; children: Laurie, Rachelle. BS in Edn., SUNY, Buffalo, 1965, MS in Edn., 1969, EdD, 1978. Cert. tchr., supr., adminstr. NY. Tchr. spl. edn. Clarence Ctrl. Sch., NY, 1965—70, Amherst Cen. Schs., NY, 1970—2004; ret., 2004. Tchr. Buffalo State Hosp., 1966, 77; instr. SUNY, Buffalo, 1978—79; diagnostic evaluator Childrens Psychiatric Ctr., West Seneca, NY, 1980. Mem.: Amherst Ret. Tchrs. Assn., NY State Ret. Tchrs. Assn., Mensa. Avocations: reading, gardening, swimming.

BURESH, LAURA LYNN, literature educator; b. Cedar Rapids, Iowa, Oct. 1, 1980; d. David James and Donna Kay Buresh. BA in Edn., U. No. Iowa, 2003. English tchr. Oskaloosa (Iowa) Sr. HS, 2004—. Storybook players sponsor Oskaloosa Sr. HS, 2005—. Stage manager Angels in America Part 1 (Kennedy Ctr. Am. Coll. Theatre Festival Meritorious Achieve. award, 2003). Mem.: Profl. Educators Iowa. Office: Oskaloosa HS 1816 N 3rd St Oskaloosa IA 52577 Office Phone: 641-673-3407. Office Fax: 641-672-2440. Business E-Mail: bureshl@oskaloosa.k12.ia.us.

BURFEIND, BETTY RUTH, science educator; b. Chgo., Feb. 10, 1947; d. William Frederick Burfeind and Ruth Pauline Amanda Batzer; m. Joseph Andres Ibanez, June 8, 1992. BS in Phys. Edn., Ea. Ill. U., 1969, MS in Phys. Edn., 1977; paralegal cert., Roosevelt U., 1982; type 75 adminstrv. cert., Govs. State U., 1994. Tchr. health and phys. edn. James Hart Jr. H.S., Homewood, Ill., 1969—80; tchr. sci. and phys. edn. Carl Sandburg H.S., Orland Park, Ill., 1980—83, Victor J. Andrew H.S., Tinley Park, Ill., 1983—2004; ret. Coach swimming Victor J. Andrew H.S., Tinley Park, 1983—, coach water polo, 1998—; mem. governing bd., Dist. 230 NEA, Orland Park, 1980—. Instr. ARC, Chgo., 1969—. Mem.: Nat. Sr. Games Assn., U.S. Water Polo Assn., Am. Swim Coaches Assn., Nat. Intercollegiate Swimming Coaches Assn. Lutheran. Avocations: softball, golf, bicycling, travel, writing. Home: 10601 Brookridge Dr Frankfort IL 60423 Office: Consol Sch Dist 230 15100 W 94th Ave Orland Park IL 60462 Office Phone: 708-342-5800.

BURGE, CONSTANCE M., television producer; d. Phil. MFA in Playwriting, UCLA. Cons. prodr.: (TV series) Ally McBeal, 1997—2002; Ed, 2000—04; prodr.: Savannah, 1996—97, Charmed, 1998—2000, Boston Public, 2003; author: The Power of Three: A Novelization, 1999, The Crimson Spell, 2000, Haunted By Desire, 2000, Kiss of Darkness: An Original Novel, 2000, Voodoo Moon, 2000, Whispers from the Past, 2000, Beware What You Wish, 2001, The Gypsy Enchantment, 2001, The Legacy of Merlin, 2001, Soul of the Bride, 2001, Charmed Again, 2002, Spirit of the Wolf, 2002.*

BURGER, ANNA, labor union administrator; b. Phila. m. Earl F. Gohl; 1 child. Grad., Penn. State U. Former union activist & caseworker Service Employees Internat. Union- Local 668, Pa., former pres. Pa., dir., field ops. Pa., 1988—90; nat. dir., field programs and ops. Service Employees Internat. Union, 1990—95, former dir. of Ea. ops, 1995—2001, sec.-treas., 2001—. Head Change to Win coalition. Office: Service Employees Internat Union 1313 L St NW Washington DC 20005

BURGER, MARY LOUISE, psychologist, educator; b. Chgo., Nov. 03; d. Robert Stanley and Margaret Agnes (Brennan) Hirsh; m. William Bronson Burger, Mar. 16, 1968. BA, Mundelein Coll., 1954; MEd, Loyola U., Chgo., 1957; EdD, No. Ill. U., 1973. Tchr. Chgo. Bd. Edn., 1954-68; mem. faculty DePaul U., 1960-61, Roosevelt U., 1967-70; cons. psychologist Worthington-Hurst & Assos., Headstart Program, Chgo., 1972-74; asst. prof. early childhood edn. Northeastern Ill. U., Chgo., 1968-71, assoc. prof., 1972-79, prof., 1979-85, chmn. dept. early childhood, 1970-80, coord. early childhood programs, 1985—2000, prof. curriculum and instrn., 1985-95, prof. divsn. tchr. edn., 1995—, prof. internat./intercultural dept., 1990—, chmn. faculty assembly Coll. Edn., 1980; chmn. subcom. Chgo. region White House Conf. on Children, 1979-81; ednl. dir., owner Childhood Edn. Nursery and Day Care Center, Evanston, Ill., 1974-86. Cons. Chgo Mayor's Office Child Care Svcs., 1970-82; ednl. psychologist, cons. Burger Cons., Ltd., 1983—. Editor: bull. and pamphlets Assn. Childhood Edn. Internat, 1975-77. Bd. dirs. Univ. Cmty. Care Ctr., 1975-80, chmn. bd. dirs.; aux. bd. v.p. N.W. Cmty. Hosp., 1999-2004; mem. Loyola U. Woman's Bd., 1999-2000. Mem. Assn. Childhood Edn. Internat. (pres. Ill. br. 1978-80, pres. Chgo. br. 1976-78, chmn. internat. nominating com. 1980, internat. tchr. edn. com. 1981, v.p. internat. exec. bd. 1983-86, v.p. rep. infancy, 1983-86, mem. exec. bd. 1988-92, internat. pres.-elect 1988-89, internat. pres. 1989-91, past pres. 1991-92), Nat. Coun. Accreditation Tchr. Edn. (unit accreditation bd. 1988-92, exec. bd. 1992-95), Nat. Assn. Edn. Young Children, Assn. Higher Edn., N.W. Assn. Nursery Schs., AAUP, Zonta Internat. (pres. Chgo. Loop 1986-88, 92-93, 95—), Phi Delta Kappa, Delta Kappa Gamma (pres. Gamma Alpha chpt. 1974-76, pres. Cook County corrdinating coun. 1991-93, chair 1994-96, chair nominations Chgo. loop 1986-91, 92-94, 95—). Home: Fairfax Village 1 Kittery On Auburn St Rolling Meadows IL 60008-2317 also: Burger Cons Ltd 1701 E Woodfield Rd Schaumburg IL 60173-5905

BURGESON, JOYCE ANN, travel company executive; b. Jamestown, N.Y., Sept. 10, 1936; d. Walter Edward and Marion (Cree) Van Horn; m. David G. Burgeson, Sept. 10, 1955; children: Kathalene, Donna, Jeffrey, Karen, Christine. AS, Empire State Coll., SUNY, Saratoga Springs, 1990. Bookkeeper Burgeson Wholesale, Jamestown, 1962—88; realtor assoc. Kote Realty, Jamestown, 1982—89; travel saleswoman, tour escort Cert. Travel Tours, Jamestown, 1983—90; real estate appraiser Goldome Bank, Jamestown, 1986—89; mgr. payroll Resource Ctr., Jamestown, 1988—95; travel saleswoman, tour escort Travelhost of Jamestown, 1990—95, Cert. Travel Tours, Jamestown, 1996—98; tour dir. Globus/Cosness, Littleton, Colo., 1999—2000. Prin. Burgeson Bus. Seminars, Jamestown, N.Y., 1990—; bd. dirs. Monet Acres Assn., 1999-2003. Vol. Alamanda Elem. Sch.; mem. adminstrv. bd. 1st United Meth. Ch., Jamestown, NY, 1985—95; cert. lay spkr. United Meth. Ch., 1987—97; mem. bd. Maple Grove HS, Bemus Point, NY, 1979—82. Mem. Toastmasters, Order of Vikings. Avocations: travel, lay speaking, camping. Home and Office: 622 Monet Acres Palm Beach Gardens FL 33410 Office Phone: 561-307-6680. E-mail: dgb622@yahoo.com.

BURGESS, ANN WOLBERT, nursing educator; Van Ameringen prof. nursing U. Pa., Phila.; prof. of psychiat. and mental health nursing Boston Coll. Author: Advanced Practice Psychiatric Nursing, 1998, Psychiatric Nursing: Promoting Mental Health, 1997, Child Trauma I: Issues & Research, 1992, Community Mental Health: Target Populations, 1976, Rape: Victims of Crisis, 1974; co-editor: (with Robert K. Kessler and John E. Douglas) Sexual Homicide: Patterns and Movies, 1988, Rape and Sexual Assault II, 1985; co-author: (with Robert R. Hazelwood) Practical Aspects of Rape Investigation: A Multidisciplinary Approach, 3d edit., 1993, (with Robert Ann Prentsky) Forensic Management of Sexual Offenders, 2000, (with Robert R. Hazelwood and Park Elliott Dietz) Autoerotic Fatalities, 1983, (with Bruce A. Baldwin) Crisis Intervention Theory and Practice: A Clinical Handbook, 1981, (with Nicholas Groth and Suzanne M. Sgroi) Sexual Assault of Children and Adolescents, 1978. Mem.: Inst. Medicine, NAS. Office: Boston Coll Sch Nursing Cushing Hall 414 140 Commonwealth Ave Chestnut Hill MA 02467

BURGESS, CLARA SKIPWITH, retired principal; b. Newburgh, N.Y., Nov. 3, 1930; d. Luther Kerman and Clara Bell (Pickens) Skipwith; m. Joseph Edward Burgess, May 14, 1966 (dec. Sept. 1968). BA, Hunter Coll., 1953, MA, 1954; Profl. Diploma Adminstrv. Supervision, Fordham U., 1970, PhD, 1975. Early childhood instr. N.Y. Inst. Blind, Bronx, 1953—54; tchr. kindergarten, early childhood tchr. trainer, exceptional edn. Pub. Sch. 43, Bronx, 1954—69; supr. Headstart Dist. 7, Bronx, 1970; evaluator Headstart and Pre-Kindergarten Funding, 1970—71; dir. Morrisania Early Childhood Learning Ctr. 3 Dist. 9, Bronx, 1971—72; prin. Cmty. Elem. Sch. 236, Dist. 9, Bronx, 1972—91, ret., 1991. Recreational counselor Pub. Sch. 43, Bronx, 1955—61; tchr. piano Pub. Sch. 18, Bronx, 1960—61, dir. ctr., 1961, tchr. dance, 1961—63; adj. instr. early childhood curriculum devel. CCNY, 1972—; rep. Non-Govtl. Orgn. at UN, 1980—; presenter in field. Women's editor Cmty. Jour. of Air, Radio Sta. WLIB, 1964—69. N.Atlantic rep. Ednl. Advancement Found.; workshop presenter Women's Conf., Nairobi, Kenya, 1985, Beijing Plus Ten, UN, 2005; bd. dirs. Wiltwyck Sch. Boys, 1967—. Named Tchr. of Yr., Bronx Boro Pres.; grantee, Ford Found., 1970. Mem.: Fordham Assn. Sch. Suprs. and Adminstrs., Coalition Assns. Black and Puerto Rican Educators and Suprs., Urban Educators Comparative Studies (founder), Bronx Reading Coun., N.Y. Assn. Black Educators, Nat. Soc. Edn. Young Children, Nat. Soc. Study Edn., Alpha Kappa Alpha. Home: 609 W 147th St New York NY 10031

BURGESS, LYNNE A, lawyer; BA, William Smith Coll.; JD, Fordham U. Asst. gen. counsel Am. Nat. Can Co.; of counsel Colier, Shannon, Rill & Scott, Washington, 1992—94; sr. v.p., gen. counsel Entex Info. Services, 1994—2000; gen. counsel, sec. Oliver, Wyman & Co. LLC, 2001—02; v.p., gen. counsel Asbury Automotive Group, 2002—. Office: Asbury Automotive Group 622 Third Ave 37th Fl New York NY 10017

BURGESS, MARJORIE LAURA, retired protective services official; b. Whitakers, N.C., Nov. 24, 1928; d. Benjamin and Laura Lenora (Ford) Harrison; m. Bonus David Dixon, July 24, 1948 (div. Apr. 1970); children: David Kingsley (dec.), Terence David, Michael Jerome; m. William A. Burgess, June 6, 1970 (div. July 1976). AS in Correction Adminstrn., John Jay Coll. Criminal, Justice, N.Y.C., 1971; BA in Social Scis., John Jay Coll Criminal Justice, N.Y.C., 1972, postgrad., 1973-75. Correction officer N.Y. State Dept. Correction, Bedford Hills, NY, 1959-67, correction sgt., 1967-73, correction lt., 1973-82, 86-90, capt., 1982-86; ret., 1990. Adv. coun. divsn. sr. svcs. Bergen County, 1997. Author: (poetry) Walking on the Road of Life, 1997, Life! It's More Than A Notion, libr. of congress Watermark press, 2000. Vol. intergenerational program Martin Luther King Srs. Ctr. Mem. AAUW, Am. Correctional Assn., Alumni Assn. John Jay Coll., The Smithsonian Assocs., Retired Pub. Employees Assn., AARP. Democrat. Baptist. Avocations: writing, singing, playing scrabble, reading.

BURGHARDT, LINDA FEUERBERG, writer; b. Nov. 11, 1946; BA, CUNY, 1968, MA, 1998. Writer, editor N.Y. Daily News, N.Y.C., 1972-78; editor JCPenney Co., N.Y.C., 1975—78, Burghardt Zomm, Great Neck, N.Y., 1981—; reporter N.Y. Times, N.Y.C., 1989—; publs. mgr. St. Regis Paper Co. Office: 300 Northern Blvd Great Neck NY 11021-4810 E-mail: burgcomm@aol.com.

BURGHART, LYNDA R., chemistry educator; d. James Philip and Velma Mae (Tasset) Liebl; m. Timothy James Burghart, Jan. 7, 1978; children: Maggie, Jacob, Ben. BS in Behavioral Sci. Edn., Bethany Coll., Lindsborg, Kans., 1982; BSc in Biology, St. Mary of the Plains, Dodge City Kans. Tchr. Kinsley (Kans) HS, 1993—. Mem.: Nat. Coun. Tchrs. of Math., Kans. Assn. Tchrs. of Sci. Office: Kinsley-Offerle Jr and Sr HS 716 Colony Ave Kinsley KS 67547-1155

BURGHER, PAULINE MENEFEE, retired marriage and family therapist; b. Houston, July 25, 1930; d. Henry Kirkpatrick and Pauline Menefee Arnold; m. Ballard Macdougal Burgher II (div. July 2981); children: Mary Steward, Ballard III, Martha Burgher Plunkett; m. Henry Irving Schweppe Jr., Jan. 6, 1998; stepchildren: Katharine Randall Schweppe(dec.), Jane Schweppe Scott. BA, Smith Coll., Northampton, Mass., 1952; M, U. Houston, 1987. Lic. profl. counselor 1989, marriage and family therapist 1989. Therapist Houston Child Guidance Clinic, 1975—88; marriage and family therapist pvt. practice, 1989—99. Ruling elder Presbyn. Ch., Houston, 1979—81; mem. vestry Christ Ch. Cathedral, 1991—93. Democrat. Episcopalian. Avocations: music, travel, ballet.

BURGIO, JANE L., pathologist, writer; d. John and Doris Lee Belton; m. Joseph Joseph Burgio, Oct. 9, 1999; children: Victoria Anne, Alexandria Lee. BS, Oral Roberts U., Tulsa, Okla., 1984; MS Edn., State U. Coll., Buffalo, N.Y., 1989. Cert. Clin. Competence in Speech Lang. Pathology Am. Speech & Hearing Assn., 1990, lic. Speech Lang. Pathology N.Y. State Edn. Dept., 1990. Speech lang. pathologist Buffalo Hearing and Speech Ctr., Buffalo, 1989—91, Erie County Early Intervention, Buffalo, 1990—93; speech lang. pathology clinic supr. State U. Coll. at Buffalo, Buffalo, 1998—2000; tchr. of the speech and hearing handicapped Buffalo Pub. Sch., Buffalo, 1991—. Adv. bd. mem. Speech Lang. Clinic at State U. Coll. at Buffalo, Buffalo, 2001—04. Author: (book, edn. program) Strategies for Learning in the Classroom for Kids (SLICK); editor: (book) Resource for the School Based Speech Language Pathologist, (edn. program) Say and Sign Language Program. Dir. handwritten bible project Pure For God Ministries, Inc., Getzville, NY, 2004—05; coord. Good Deed Bible Club, Buffalo, 1999—2000; group leader on internat. missions trips Repossession Co., Inc., Getzville, NY, 1999—2001. Recipient An Apple for the Tchr., Iota Phi Lambda Sorority, Inc., Beta Phi Chpt., 1999. Mem.: Am. Speech-Language Hearing Assn. Achievements include development of participated in devel. of video. Avocations: travel, flute, painting, reading, write children's stories. Office Phone: 716-816-3240.

BURGMAN, DIERDRE ANN, lawyer; b. Logansport, Ind., Mar. 25, 1948; d. Ferdinand William Jr. and Doreen Walsh Burgman. BA, Valparaiso U., 1970, JD, 1979; LLM, Yale U., 1985. Bar: Ind. 1979, U.S. Dist. Ct. (so. dist.)

Ind. 1979, N.Y. 1982, U.S. Dist. Ct. (so. dist.) N.Y. 1982, U.S. Ct. Appeals (7th cir.) 1982, U.S. Ct. Appeals (D.C. and 2d cirs.) 1984, U.S. Supreme Ct. 1985, D.C. 1988, U.S. Dist. Ct. (ea. dist.) N.Y. 1992. Law clk. to chief judge Ind. Ct. Appeals, Indpls., 1979-80; prof. law Valparaiso U., Ind., 1980-81; assoc. Dewey, Ballantine, Bushby, Palmer & Wood, NYC, 1981-84, Cahill Gordon & Reindel, 1985-92; sr. v.p., gen. counsel NY State Urban Devel. Corp., 1992-95; dep. insp. gen. State NY, 1992-95; of counsel Vandenberg & Felieu, NYC, 1995-99; cons. Salans, 1999—2000, counsel, 2000—04, Sullivan & Worcester, 2004—06. Note editor Valparaiso U. law rev., 1978-79; contbr. articles to law jours. Mem. bd. visitors Valparaiso U. Sch. Law, 1986—95, chmn., 1989—92, mem. nat. coun., 2001—. Ind. Bar Found. scholar, 1978. Mem. ABA (trial evidence com. 1983-86, profl. liability com. 1986-89, ins. coverage litigation com. 1990-92), Assn. Bar City N.Y. (com. profl. responsibility 1988-91, com. profl. and jud. ethics 1991-95, mem. coun. jud. adminstrn. 1997-99), New York County Lawyers Assn. (com. Supreme Ct. 1987-94, chmn. 1990-93, bd. dirs. 1991-97, 2002-03, exec. com. bd. dirs. 1992-95, fin. and pers. com. 2003, mem. found., 2003-), N.Y. State Bar Assn. (mem. Ho. Dels. 1994-98, mem. com. on profl. stds. of atty. conduct 2002-). Home: 345 E 56th St Apt 5C New York NY 10022-3744

BURGOS-SASSCER, RUTH, chancellor emeritus; b. N.Y.C., Sept. 5, 1931; m. Donald Sasscer, June 14, 1958; children: Timothy, James, Julie, David. BA, Maryville (Tenn.) Coll., 1953; MA, Columbia U., 1956; PhD, Fla. State U., 1987. Mem. faculty Inter-Am. U., P.R., 1968-71; dept. chair U. P.R., Aguadilla, 1972-76, dir. non-traditional programs Cen. Adminstrn. Regional Coll., 1976-81, dir., dean, chief exec. officer Aguadilla, 1981-85; v.p. faculty and instrn. Harry S. Truman Coll., Chgo., 1988-93; pres. San Antonio Coll., 1993-96; chancellor Houston C.C. Sys., 1996-2000; sr. fellow U. Houston Law Ctr. Inst. of Higher Edn Law and Goverance, 2001—03. Bd. dirs. Nat. Postsecondary Edn. Coop., Maryville Coll. Nat. Adv. Coun., Montgomery County Coalition for Adult Literacy and ESOL. Mem. Am. Assn. C.C. Presbyterian. Home: 15115 Interlachen Dr Apt 403 Silver Spring MD 20908 Office Phone: 301-598-2288. E-mail: ruthburgossas@hotmail.com.

BURGOYNE, MOJIE ADLER, clinical social worker; b. Abilene, Tex., Apr. 26, 1942; d. Leonard A. and Mojie W. (Jennings) Adler; m. Wallace Carr Burgoyne, June 27, 1964 (div. Dec. 1974); children: Kristina, Pamela, Carr. BA, Tex. Woman's U., 1964; MSW, U. Houston, 1979. Lic. master social worker-advanced clin. practitioner, Tex.; diplomae Am. Bd. Cert. Managed Care Providers, Am. Bd. Examiners. in Clin. Social Work. Clin. social worker Post Oak Psychiatry & Assocs., Tomball, Tex., 1986-90, Raul R Gomez & Assocs., Tomball, 1990-91; owner, clin. social worker Affiliated Mental Health Svcs., Tomball, 1991—. Pres. Home Health Adv. Bd., Tomball, 1979-84. Contbg. author: Social Work Treatment with Abused and Neglected Children, 1985. Polit. activist Child Welfare Bd., Montgomery County, Tex., 1974-77. Named Woman of Yr., Montgomery County (Tex.) YWCA, 1981. Mem. NASW (diplomate in clin. social work). Avocations: reading, restoring an antique barn in farm country of south central texas. Office: Affiliated Mental Health Svcs Ste 2 701 W Main Tomball TX 77375-4451

BURGOYNE, NOEL JAEGER, retired secondary school educator; b. Erie, Pa., Jan. 2, 1935; d. Harry Max and Carolyn Blakely Jaeger; m. Charles Joseph Burgoyne, July 2, 1966. BA, Merryhurst Coll., 1957; MA, Case We. Res. U., 1962. Cert. tchr. Pa., 1957. Tchr. Millcreek Sch. Dist., Erie, Pa., 1957—60; tchg. fellow Case We. Res. U., Cleve., 1960—62; instr. Mercyhurst Coll., Erie, 1962—64; tchr. Erie (Pa.) Sch. Dist., 1964—93, lead tchr., 1986—93, chair Acad. H.S. English Dept.; ret., 1993. Instr. Villa Maria Coll., Erie, 1975—77; sec. Northwest Pa. Lead Tchr. Consortium, Erie, 1990—93. Mem. editl. bd.: Pa. Lead Tchr. Mag., 1991—95. Vol., coord. Erie (Pa.) Philharmonic, 1994—2002; vol. Flagship Niagara League/Mus., Erie (Pa.) Pub. Libr., United Way Allocation Panel; v.p. Erie Dwellings and Advocacy for Women in Need, 2006—; bd. dirs. Friends of Philharmonic, Erie, 1996—2001, Erie Philharm., 2000—, bd. govs., 2000—, chmn. bd. govs., 2004—; chmn. steering com. Erie Jr. Philharm., 2001—; bd. dirs. Erie Dwellings and Advocacy for Women in Need, 2004—, v.p., 2004—; sec. adv. bd. Gannondale for Girls, Erie, 2004—. Named Tchr. of Yr., Acad. H.S., 1989, Star Tchr., GE Found., 1990, Vol. of Yr., Flagship Niagara League, 1995, Erie Philharm., 1997; recipient, 2006, Scholarship Devel. award, Villa Maria Ctr., 2000. Mem.: Cleve. Mus. Art, Jazzerie, Erie Art Mus., Erie Hist. Soc., Friends of Libr., Erie Club, Delta Kappa Gamma. Avocations: travel, reading, concerts, plays, pets. Home: 4020 Trask Ave Erie PA 16508 Personal E-mail: ncburg35@aol.com.

BURGOYNE, SUZANNE, theater educator, writer; b. St. Joseph, Mich., Oct. 25, 1946; d. Leon Edward and Betty Louise Burgoyne. Cert., Belgian Nat. Theatre Inst. (L'INSAS), Brussels, 1969; BA, Mich. State U., 1968; MA, Ohio State U., 1970; PhD, U. Mich., 1975. Vis. asst. prof. theatre N.E. Mo. State U., Kirksville, 1973—74; head dept. dramatic art So. Sem. Jr. Coll., Buena Vista, Va., 1975—77; from asst. to assoc. prof. fine and performing arts Creighton U., Omaha, 1977—89; vis. prof. directing and dramaturgy L'INSAS, Brussels, 1986—87; assoc. prof. theatre U. Mo., Columbia, 1989—97, prof. theatre, 1997—, Catherine Paine Middlebush chair fine and performing arts, 2005—. Dir.: (student-authored play) Survival Dance (show selected for performance at regional Kennedy Ctr. Am. Coll. Theatre Festival (KCACTF), 2003), (play) Oleanna (show selected for regional KCACTF-meritorious achievement award for directing (regional); Hon. Mention Award for Directing (Nat.), 1999), (and translator) La Vita Breve (by Paul Willems) (show selected for performance at regional KCACTF; Meritorious Achievement Award for Directing (regional), 1996), The Fool's Journey, 2005 (Meritorious Achievement award for directing KCACTF, 2005); co-author: Teaching and Performing: Ideas for Energizing Your Classes, revised edit.; translator: (play) Paul Willems' The Drowned Land and La Vita Breve.; translator: (of 2 of 4 plays, vol. editor) Four Plays of Paul Willems: Dreams and Reflections; contbr. articles to profl. jours., chapters to books. Recipient Author of the Month awrd, Highlights for Children Mag., 1986; Kellogg Nat. fellow, W.K. Kellogg Found., 1981—84, Summer Rsch. fellow, U. Mo. Rsch. Coun., 1992, Summer salary and travel grantee, 1994, Carnegie scholar, Carnegie Acad. for the Scholarship of Tchg. and Learning, 2000—01, NEH Summer Seminar fellow, 1979, 1985, U. Mo. Kemper fellow, 2004. Mem.: Pedagogy and Theatre of the Oppressed, Kennedy Ctr. Am. Coll. Theatre Festival (regional playwriting awards chair 1978—80), Mid-America Theatre Conf. (v.p., pres. 1991—95), Assn. for Theatre in Higher Edn. (editor, theatre topics 1993—95, v.p. for profl. devel. 1999—2003, pres. elect 2005, award as editor of Theatre Topics 1995, Outstanding Tchr. award 2003). Avocations: water aerobics, reading, gardening, swimming. Home: 103 Tracy Dr Columbia MO 65203 Office: Dept Theatre U Missouri 129 Fine Arts Columbia MO 65211 Office Phone: 573-882-0528. Personal E-mail: burgoynes@missouri.edu.

BURINGRUD, LISA MARIE, music educator; b. Brawley, Calif., Jan. 16, 1961; d. Joseph Paul McKim and Mary Legakes-McKim; m. Joel Dean Buringrud, Nov. 30, 1991; children: Rebecca Danae, Deanna Marie. BA in Music with cert. in music therapy, Calif. State U., Long Beach, 1987; MusM in Instrumental Conducting, Calif. State U., Sacramento, 2001. Cert. profl. clear single No. subject Calif., bd. cert. music therapy Calif. Bd. Music Therapy, tchg. credential in music Calif. Music therapist, band dir. L.A. GOAL, Santa Monica, Calif., 1986—90; music therapist Fairview Developmental Ctr., Costa Mesa, Calif., 1987—90, Stockton (Calif.) Developmental Ctr., 1990; music dir. Vanden H.S., Fairfield, Calif., 1993—99; band dir. Armijo H.S., Fairfield, 1999—2000; assoc. condr. wind studies dept. Calif. State U., Sacramento, 2000—01; instrumental music dir. Mendocino (Calif.) Unified Sch. Dist., 2001—03; band dir. Calaveras H.S., San Andreas, Calif., 2003—. Prin. flutist Solano Winds, Fairfield, 1995—2001; condr., artistic dir. North Coast Wind Symphony, Mendocino, 2002—03; assoc. condr. Opera Fresca, Mendocino, 2001—03; condr. children's concert series Symphony of the Redwoods, Mendocino, 2002—. Author: (book) American Women Composers of Band Music: A Biographical Dictionary and Catalogue of Works: An Addendum and Update, 2001. Music min. St. Marks Luth. Ch., Fairfield, 2000—01; bd. dirs. St. Marks Pre-Sch., Fairfield, 1999—2001. Recipient Cert. of Appreciation for Performance, Travis AFB, 1997. Mem.: Nat. Band Dirs. Assn., Calif. Music Educators Assn. (Hon. Recognition Band Concert/Clinic Pres. 2002), Calif. Band Dirs. Assn. (Hon. Recognition Band Concert/Clinic Pres. 1999, 2003), Women Band Dirs. Internat., Am. Sch. Band Dirs. Assn., Phi Kappa Lambda. Avocations: bicycling, jogging, reading, flute performance. Office: Calaveras H S PO Box 607 San Andreas CA 95249 Office Phone: 209-754-1811. Business E-Mail: lburingrud@calaveras.k12.ca.us.

BURINI, SONIA MONTES DE OCA, apparel manufacturing executive, public relations executive; b. Havana, Cuba, Apr. 28, 1935; d. Francisco and Nilda (Diaz) Montes de Oca; m. Franco Burini, Apr. 5, 1959. Student, U. Havana, 1954-57, Georgetown U., 1958; BA in History cum laude, U. Miami, Coral Gables, Fla., 1971. Adminstr. Roma Fashions, Inc. D/B/A Franco B., Coral Gables, 1976-95; entrepreneur, pub. rels. exec., 1995—; dir. promotions and special events Social Mag., 2004—. Founder Nat. Parkinson Found., 1986—; v.p. Vizcayans Fund Raising Orgn., 1990—, chmn. fine arts events, 1993-95; co-chmn. 1st annual fund raising event Am. Cancer Soc. Winn-Dixie Hope Lodge Ctr.; mem. women with heart group Heart Assn. Greater Miami, Fla., 1981—; founder, bd. dirs. Cancer Link program U. Miami Comprehensive Cancer Ctr., 1987; chmn. spring fantasy luncheon Am. Cancer Soc., 1988; founding chmn. Rose Group, Am. Lung Assn., chmn. Rose Ball, 1989; amb. Mercy Hosp. Found., 1987-95; bd. dirs. Newborn program U. Miami, 1978, bd. dirs., 1982-87, amb. category years; vol. guide Viscaya Mus., Dade County, Fla., 1972-79, chmn. various coms., 1979—, found. bd. dirs., steering com., mem. com. of 100; bd. dir., Young Patrons of the Opera, 1979-87; grand patron Greater Miami Opera, 1986-95, bd. dirs., 1978—, chmn. opera gala, 1987, mem. opera guild, 1988; founding bd. mem. Ears Dears U. Miami, 1986—, chmn. 1990 gala; mem. Dade County Performing Art Ctr. Trust, 1993—; spl. chmn. fine arts events Vizcayans, 1993—; mem. sister cities com. Cities of Miami, Fla. and Nice, France, 1994—, Nat. Trust Hist. Preservation, 1997—. Named Oustanding Woman of Yr. Mayor of Dade County, 1986, Woman of Yr. Heart Assn. Greater Miami, 1986, named to Miss Charity Biscayne Bay Marriott Hotel and Marina, 1987, One of the Leading Ladies for the March of Dimes, 1998. Mem. Nat. Trust Historic Preservation, Ballet Soc. Miami (bd. dirs. 1979-80, named one of Miami's Oustanding Women 1986), Confrerie de la Chaine des Rotisseurs, NAFE, Am. Children's Orch. for Peace (bd. adv. 2001—), Opera Guild Fla. Grand Opera (bd. dirs. 2003—). Home: 5401 Collins Ave Apt 1016 Miami Beach FL 33140 Office: Roma Fashions Inc 3311 Ponce De Leon Blvd Coral Gables FL 33134-7210 Address: 4730 SW 67th Ave Miami FL 33155 Fax: 305-864-2047. Office Phone: 305-663-0473. Office Fax: 305-663-4644. E-mail: strokespokes@aol.com.

BURK, MARTHA GERTRUDE, political psychologist; b. Tyler, Tex., Oct. 18, 1941; d. Ivan Lee Burk and Dorothy May (White) Dean; m. Eddie C. Talley, Sept. 2, 1960 (div. Sept. 1985); children: Edward, Mark; m. Ralph Estes, July 3, 1986. BS, U. Houston, 1962; MS, U. Tex., Arlington, 1968, PhD, 1974. Lic. psychologist, Tex. Asst. prof. mgmt. U. Tex., Arlington, 1976-79, rsch. dir. Grad. Sch. Social Work, 1974-76, ptnr. Sch. Psychology Cons., 1979-80; pres. A.U. Software, Inc., Wichita, Kans., 1981-90, Ctr. for Advancement of Pub. Policy, Washington, 1990—; now chair Nat. Coun. of Women's Organizations, Washington. Syndicated columnist. Author (software) Talley Spl. Edn. Mgmt. System, 1984, Testlab 2000, 1988, (books) Cult of Power: Sex Discrimination in Corporate America and What Can Be Done About It, 2005. Mem. Commn. Responsive Democracy, Washington, 1990, Nat. Task Force on Pay Equity, 1993—. Rsch. grantee U.S. Dept. Edn., 1989-94, named Woman of Yr., Ms Mag., 2003. Mem. NOW (nat. bd. dirs. 1988-90). Democrat. Office: Nat Coun Women's Orgns Ste 250 1050 17th St NW Washington DC 20036 Office Phone: 202-293-4505.

BURKARD, PATRICIA, writer; b. Saginaw, Mich., Sept. 28, 1942; d. Edward John Burkard and Catherine Hard; m. Gordon Larsen, May 1, 1965 (div. June 1974); children: Leif Edward Larsen, Eric Armand Larsen, Bridgit Larsen. BA in Math., U. Mich., 1963, MA in Math., 1966. Computer programmer Uniroyal Tire, Detroit, 1963—65, Bendix Aerospace, Ann Arbor, Mich., 1967, U. Mich., Ann Arbor, 1968—70, 1973—75; artist Saginaw and London, 1977—97; freelance writer Saginaw, 1981—. Author (under pseudonym Kate Jackson): Matriarchy Strikes, 1991, Dark Side of the Sun, 1992, Running Bear, 1998. Del. conv. Dem. Party, Mich., 1970, del. conf. Mich., 1974; state treas. Shirley Chisholm campaign, Mich., 1972; nat. del. New Dem. Coalition, Chgo. Named to nat. cross country team, AAU; recipient Helen Newberry scholarship, Regents Alumnae Scholarship. Achievements include patents for scientific subroutine package. Avocations: astronomy, knitting, painting, math tables.

BURKE, ANNE M., state supreme court justice; b. Chgo., Feb. 3, 1944; m. Edward M. Burke; children: Jennifer, Edward, Emmett, Sarah; 1 foster child. BA in Edn., DePaul U., 1976; JD, IIT/Chgo.-Kent Coll. Law, 1983. Bar: Fed. Ct. No. Dist. Ill. 1983, U.S. Ct. Appeals (7th cir.) 1985, cert.: Trial Bar Fed. Dist. Ct. 1987. Phys. edn. tchr. Chgo. Park Dist.; pvt. practice, 1983—94; judge Ill. Ct. Claims, 1987—94; spl. counsel to Gov. Child Welfare Services State of Ill., 1994—95; judge Ill. Appellate Ct. (1st dist.), Chgo., 1995—96, 1996—2006; justice Ill. Supreme Ct., Chgo., 2006—. Founder of the first Special Olympics. Grantee, Kennedy Found. Avocations: dance, antiques. Office: Ill Supreme Ct 160 N LaSalle St Chicago IL 60601*

BURKE, BETTY JANE, retired real estate manager; b. Houston, Dec. 30, 1918; d. Loren Joseph and Bess Eva (Bontz) Patton; m. Thomas Francis Vickers, Aug. 11, 1942 (dec. Aug. 1944); 1 child, Thomas Francis III; m. Elmo James Burke Jr., Oct. 7, 1955 (dec.); 1 child, Elmo James III. BS, U. Houston, 1940; MSW, Tulane U., 1953. Juvenile probation worker Harris County Probation, Houston, 1940-42; case worker Depelchin Faith Home, Houston, 1945-56; v.p. Burke Homes, San Antonio, 1966-83; pres. Burke Devel., San Antonio, 1983-92, ret., 2004. Mem. airport adv. com. City of San Antonio, 1970-72; mem. planning commn. City of San Antonio, 1986-89. Mem. NASW, AAUW (pres.). Democrat. Episcopalian. Avocations: gardening, camping, travel. Office: PO Box 23247 San Antonio TX 78223-0247

BURKE, BEVERLY J., lawyer, utilities executive; m. Gregory Saunders. BA, Brown U.; JD, George Washington U. Law clerk to Judge Norma Holloway Johnson U.S. Dist. Ct.; atty. civil litigation & appellate advocacy D.C. Govt., 1982—92; with Office Gen. Counsel Washington Gas & Light Co., 1992-96, dept. head, 1996-98, v.p., asst. gen. counsel, 1998—2001, v.p., gen. counsel, 2001—. Mediator U.S. Dist. Ct., D.C. Mem. D.C. Courts Gender Bias Task Force; bd. mem. Wash. Performing Arts Soc.; second v.p. Lafayette Elementary Home & School Assn. Mem.: ABA, D.C. Bar Assn. (Children's Initiative Com., Legal Ethics Com., Nominations Com., Screening Com.). Office: Washington Gas and Light Co 1100 H St NW Washington DC 20080-0002

BURKE, BROOKE, actress, model; b. Hartford, Conn., Sept. 8, 1971; d. George and Donna; m. Garth Fisher, 2001 (div. 2005); children: Neriah Fisher, Sierra Sky Fisher. Studied bus. advertising and broadcast journalism, Santa Monica Coll. and UCLA. Has calendar and swin-wear line. Host Wild On, 1999—2002, co-host (infomercial) Peterson's Core Secrets workouts, 2005, 2006, Rock Star: INXS, 2005, Rock Star: Supernova, 2006—, guest appearances That's Life, 2002, Rock Me Baby, 2003, Monk, 2004, Less Than Perfect, 2004, The Hazing, 2004, It's All Relative, 2004, Knuckle Sandwich, 2004, Eve, 2005, Las Vegas, 2006, The Bernie Mac Show, (off-broadway) Pieces, (video game) Need For Speed: Underground 2 (Spike TV Video Game award, Best Performance by a Human-Female), (commercials) Burger King, voice-celebrity host, People and Places category (video game) Trivial Pursuit Unhinged (Atari), judge Pet Star, 2005. Photographed for charity book project, PRECIOUS Starlight Children's Found. Avocations: yoga, pilates, walking, cooking, watching movies and plays.*

BURKE, CARLA MICHELLE, lawyer; b. Slaton, Tex., Aug. 17, 1969; BA, So. Meth. U., 1991, MA, 1994, JD, 1999. Bar: Tex. 1999, US Ct. Appeals (5th cir.) 2000, NY. Atty. water contamination litig. sect. Baron & Budd, P.C., Dallas, 2000—. Adj. clin. instr. law So. Meth. U. Legal Clinic, 2001. Contbr. articles to profl. publs. Recipient Rising Star, Tex. Super Lawyers mag., 2006. Fellow: Dallas Bar Found.; mem.: Dallas Bar Assn., Dallas Trial Lawyers Assn., Tex. Trial Lawyers Assn., Bar Assn. of 5th Fed. Ct., Trial Lawyers for Pub. Justice, Assn. Trial Lawyers of Am. Office: Baron & Budd PC 3102 Oak Lawn Ave Ste 1100 Dallas TX 75219 Office Phone: 214-521-3605.*

BURKE, CAROL A., lawyer; b. 1951; children: Stephen, Louisa. BA, Smith Coll., 1973; JD, George Wash. U., 1976. Bar: DC 1976, Okla. 1977, Calif. 1977, Ill. 1983. Atty. Baker & McKenzie, Rome, Econ. Crime Project, Chgo.; spl. counsel, assoc. gen. counsel legal dept. Chgo. Bd. of Trade, sr. v.p., gen. counsel, 1994—95, exec. v.p., chief of staff, gen. counsel, 1995—. Mem.: ABA (former co-chmn. contracts markets subcom.). Office: Chgo Bd of Trade 141 W Jackson Blvd Ste 600 Chicago IL 60604 Office Phone: 312-435-3500. Office Fax: 312-435-3623.

BURKE, DELTA, actress; b. Orlando, Fla., July 30, 1956; m. Gerald McRaney, May 28, 1989. Educated, London Acad. Music & Dramatic Arts. Clothing designer & mgr. Delta Burke Design, NYC. Appeared in TV movies Charleston, A Last Cry for Help, Mickey Spillane's Mike Hammer: Murder Me, Murder You, A Bunny's Tale, Where the Hell's That Gold?!!?, A Promise to Carolyn, 1996, Melanie Darrow, 1997, What Women Want, 2000; appeared in TV mini-series The Seekers, 1979; appeared in TV series The Chisholms, 1980, Filthy Rich, 1982, First and Ten, 1984; guest appearance on series Simon & Simon; regular role on series Designing Women, 1986-91; star own series Delta, 1992-93, The Women of the House, 1995; (film) Maternal Instincts, 1996; appeared on broadway Thoroughly Modern Millie, 2003, Steel Magnolias, 2005. Named Miss Fla., 1974, later competed in Miss Am. Pageant. Mailing: c/o Lyceum Theatre 247 West 44th St New York NY 10036

BURKE, JAN HELENE, writer; b. Houston, Aug. 1, 1953; d. John Francis and Velda Marie Fischer; m. Timothy Edward Burke, May 28, 1988. BA, Calif. State U., Long Beach, 1978. Author: (novels) Goodnight, Irene, 1993, Hocus, 1997, Harm, 1999, Bloodlines: An Irene Kelly Novel, 2005. Recipient readers award and Macavity award for short story Ellery Queen Mystery Mag., 1994, Ellery Queen Mystery Mag. award, Agatha award. Mem. Mystery Writers Am., Am. Crime Writers League, Internat. Crime Writers Assn., Sisters in Crime. Fax: 562-429-1811. E-mail: jan@janburke.com.

BURKE, KAREN A., medical/surgical nurse; b. Ariz., Jan. 23, 1945; d. Halder John and Virgie Lee (Harris) Rex; children from previous marriage: Virgie Ann, Lori Jan. AS, Cen. Ariz. Coll., 1974. RN, Ariz.,, CPR; ACLS; cert. crisis intervention and trauma nurse, Ariz. Charge nurse med. surg., emergency rm., ob. Miami Inspiration Hosp., Ariz., 1974-84; med./surg. nurse Gila Gen. Hosp., Globe, Ariz., 1980-81; relief charge nurse ob. Yavapai Regional Med. Ctr., Prescott, Ariz., 1984—2006, interim unit dir., 1988-89, charge nurse, emergency rm., med./surg., others, 1990—, clin. nurse I, 2004—. Med. mission, Papalote, Mexico, 1993; mem. Med. Res. Corps. Homeland Security Yavapai County, 2004—.

BURKE, KATHLEEN B., lawyer; b. Bklyn., Sept. 2, 1948; BA, St. John's U., 1969, JD, 1973. Bar: Ohio 1973. Ptnr. Jones Day, Cleve. Chair Notre Dame Coll. of Ohio, 2002-06. Pres. Cleve. Skating Club, 2000-02. Named a Woman of Achievement, Cleve. YWCA, 2004; recipient Ohio Bar medal, 2002. Fellow Ohio State Bar Found. (pres. 2000); mem. Ohio State Bar Assn. (pres. 1993-94). Office: Jones Day North Point 901 Lakeside Ave E Cleveland OH 44114-1190 Office Phone: 216-586-3939. Business E-Mail: kbburke@jonesday.com.

BURKE, KATHLEEN J., music director, writer; b. Detroit, Mich. d. Arthur Reginald and Lois Genevieve Brooks; married, Apr. 17, 1982; children: Sean Patrick, Conor Timothy. A in History, Butte Jr. Coll., Calif., 1975; BS in History, Calif. State U., Fullerton, 1977. Pub. rels. sports Burke Sports Mktg., Eugene, Oreg., 1977—79, Burke Comms., Irvine, Calif., 1983—90, pub. rels. gen. Mission Viejo, Calif., 1991—98, pub. rels. music, 1999—2002, Parodudes Inc., Pitts., 1999—2002, mgr. booking, 2001—02. Author, editor: PSA for Project Independence, 1988 (2d pl., Calif. Press Women, 1988). Vol. Rep. Party, Calif., 1991—92; vol. meals ministry S.V.C.C., Calif., 1991—2002, vol. christian missions Calif., 2000—. Mem.: Recording Acad., Women in Comms., Nat. Mus. of Women in Arts, Nat. Assn. Rock Radio, Gospel Music Assn. Avocations: distance running, biking, hiking, triathlons. Office: Burke Comms 24161 Saiero Ln Mission Viejo CA 92691-4131 E-mail: music4filmbiz@cox.net.

BURKE, LAURA ANNE, elementary school educator; b. Mt. Cisco, N.Y., Oct. 7, 1962; d. James William and Dierdre Lena Thomson; m. Edward Boruam Burke, Jr., July 20, 1985; children: Helen, Richard, Mary. BA, Kean Coll., 1984; MAT, Marygrove Coll., 1999. Cert. tchr. of handicapped. Tchr. Damon House H.S., New Brunswick, NJ, 1984—85; tchr. resource ctr. Cranbury (N.J.) Elem. Sch., 1985—. Creator before-sch. homework program The Learning Club (T.L.C.), 2005. Named Gov.'s Tchr. of Yr. for Cranbury Sch., 2004; scholar, Alpha Delta Pi, 1984. Mem.: Cranbury Edn. Assn. Presbyterian. Avocations: reading, skiing, photography. Home: PO Box 487 Tennent NJ 07763 Office: Cranbury Elem Sch 23 N Main St Cranbury NJ 08512

BURKE, LILLIAN WALKER, retired judge; b. Thomaston, Ga., Aug. 2, 1917; d. George P. and Ozella (Daviston) Walker; m. Ralph Livingston Burke, July 8, 1948 (dec.); 1 son, R. Bruce. BS, Ohio State U., 1947; LLB, Cleve. State U., 1951, postgrad., 1963-64; grad., Nat. Coll. State Judiciary, U. Nev., 1974. Bar: Ohio 1951. Gen. practice law, Cleve., 1952-62; asst. atty. gen. Ohio, 1962-66; mem., vice chmn. Ohio Indsl. Commn., 1966-69; judge Cleve. Mcpl. Ct., 1969-87, chief judge, 1981, 85, vis. judge, 1988-97; ret., 1997. Guest lectr. Heidelburg Coll., Tiffin, Ohio, 1971; cons. Bur. Higher Edn., HEW, 1972. Pres. Cleve. chpt. Nat. Coun. Negro Women, 1955-57; sec. East dist. Family Service Assn., 1959-60; mem. coun. human rels. Cleve. Citizens League, 1959-79; mem. Gov.'s Com. on Status of Women, 1966-67; pres. Cleve. chpt. Jack and Jill of Am., Inc., 1960-61; v.p.-at-large Greater Cleve. Safety Coun., 1969-79; mem. Cleve. Landmarks Commn., 1990-97; woman ward leader 24th Ward Republican Club, 1957-67; mem. Cuyahoga County Ctrl. Com., 1958-68; sec. Cuyahoga County Exec. Com., 1962-63; alt. del. Rep. Nat. Conv., Chgo., 1960; bd. dirs., chmn. minority div. Nat. Fedn. Rep. Women, 1966-68; life mem., past bd. dirs. Cleve. chpt. NAACP; bd. dirs. Greater Cleve. Neighborhood Ctrs. Assn., Cath. Youth Counselling Svcs.; trustee Ohio Commn. on Status of Women, 1966-70, Consumers League Ohio, 1969-75, Cleve. Music Sch. Settlement; bd. mgmt. Glenville YWCA, 1960-70; mem. project com. Cleve. Orch.; apptd. mem. City Planning Comm. Cleve., 1997-2002. Recipient achievement award Parkwood Christian Meth. Episcopal Ch., 1968, Martin Luther King Citizen's award, 1969, outstanding achievement award Ta-Wa-Si Scholarship Club, 1969, Outstanding Svc. award Morning Star Grand chpt., Cleve., 1970, award of honor Cleve. Bus. League, 1970, svc. award St. Paul AME Ch., Lima, Ohio, 1972, Woman of Achievement award Inner Club Coun., Cleve., 1973, cert. of award Nat. Coun. Negro Women, 1969, Cleve. Found. Golf Philanthropic Leadership award, 1997; named Career Woman of Yr., Cleve. Women's Career Clubs, 1969, Jewel of Yr., Women's City Club, 2002, award for hist. preservation So. African Hist. Soc., 2002, Woman of Achievement award YWCA, 2003. Mem. ABA, Nat. Assn. Investment Clubs (pres. Dynasty Investors Club 1992-96, bd. dirs. N.E. Ohio Coun. 1993-2003), Nat. Bar Assn., Ohio Bar Assn., Cuyahoga County Bar Assn., Cleve. Bar Assn., Am. Judicature Soc., Am. Judges Assn. (bd. govs. 1982-86, chmn. conv. agenda com. 1981-83), Phillis Wheatley Assn., Women Lawyers Assn. (hon. adviser), Ohio State U. Alumni Assn. (life), Cleve. Marshall Law Sch. (life), Am. Bridge Assn. (life), Women's City Club of Cleve. (life), Altrusa, Alpha Kappa Alpha. Anglican. Home: 1357 East Blvd Cleveland OH 44106-4018

BURKE, LINDA BEERBOWER, lawyer, mining executive, metal products executive; b. Huntington, W.Va., June 19, 1948; d. William Bert and Betty Jane (Weddle) Beerbower; m. Timothy F. Burke, Jr., Aug. 26, 1972; children:

Ryan Timothy, Hannah Elizabeth. BA in Govt., Coll. of William and Mary, 1970; JD, U. Pitts., 1973. Bar: Pa. 1973. Tax atty. legal dept. Aluminum Co. Am., Pitts., 1973-77, gen. tax atty. tax dept., 1977-80, mgr. legal and planning taxes, 1980-86, tax counsel, 1987-2000, asst. officer, 1992-2000, dir. taxes, 1993-2000; now v.p. Suriname Aluminum Co., Pitts., Alcoa Minerals of Jamaica, Inc., Pitts., Alcoa Steamship Co., Inc., Pitts.; with Alcoa Svc. Corp., Pitts., to 2000; v.p. Northwest Alloys, Inc., Pitts.; oper. divsn. counsel large and mid-size bus. IRS, Washington, 2000—. V.p. various Alcoa subs.; presenter on fields internat. and employee benefits taxation, IRS audit procedures, atty.-client privilege. Note editor U. Pitts. Law Rev., 1972-73. Bd. dirs. YWCA Greater Pitts., 1987-95, 97-2000, v.p., 1989-92, pres., 1993-94; Alcoa co-chmn. Taylor Allderdice-Alcoa Partnership in Edn., 1982-84, chmn., 1985-88; mem. law fellows com. U. Pitts. Law Sch., 1988—, chmn. class ann. giving fund for law sch. class, 1982-94, chmn. law fellows, 1998—; bd. dirs. Soc. Alumni Coll. William & Mary, 2000—; mem. rev. com. United Way, 1987-94; bd. dirs. Vol. Action Ctr., 1982-85; mem. pers. com. Woman's Ctr. and Shelter Greater Pitts., 1986-94; trustee St. Edmund's Acad., 1986-94, sec., 1989-90, treas., 1990-92, mem. fin. com., 1986-93, chmn. enrollment com., 1988-90, co-chmn. ann. giving, 1986-87; mem. Leadership Pitts., 1990-91, bd. dirs., 1997-2000, sec., 1999-2000; bd. trustees Am. Tax Policy Inst., 1996-2000; mem. program com. Tax Found., 1996-2000; mem. adv. group to commr. Internal Revenue, 1996-98. Recipient tribute in corp. tax Triangle Corner, 1982, Asst. Commr.'s award IRS, 1992 Mem. ABA, Allegheny County Bar Assn., Am. Corp. Counsel Assn., Pitts. Internat. Tax Soc. (program com. 1988-94), Tax Execs. Inst. (bd. dirs. Pitts. chpt. 1981-86, pres. 1985-86, nat. bd. dirs., nat. exec. com. 1988-89, 90-91, 92-95, nat. chmn. IRS adminstrv. affairs com. 1989-90, 91-92, nat. sec. 1992-93, nat. sr. v.p. 1993-94, v.p. region VI 1990-91, internat. pres. 1994-95), Pitts. Tax Club (bd. dirs. 1989-95, pres. 1993-94), Duquesne Club. Democrat. Avocations: skiing, bridge, cooking, golf.

BURKE, MARGARET ANN, computer company executive, communications executive; b. N.Y.C., Feb. 25, 1961; d. David Joseph and Eileen Theresa (Falvey) B. BS in Computer Sci., St. John's U., Jamaica, N.Y., 1982; MBA, U. Md., 1994. Cert. data processor. Software specialist Bell Atlantic Corp., Washington, 1983—. Active Friends of Hillwood Mus., Washington. Mem. NAFE, Alliance Francaise, Nat. Fedn. Rep. Women, Am. Film Inst. Roman Catholic. Home: 6652 Hillandale Rd Unit A Bethesda MD 20815-6406 Office: Bell Atlantic 13100 Columbia Pike Silver Spring MD 20904-5296

BURKE, MARIANNE KING, state agency administrator, finance company executive, consultant; b. Douglasville, Ga., May 30, 1938; d. William Horace and Evora (Morris) King; divorced; 1 child, Kelly Page. Student, Ga. Inst. Tech., 1956-59, Anchorage C.C., 1964-66, Portland State U., 1968-69; BBA, U. Alaska, 1976. CPA, Alaska. Sr. audit mgr. Price Waterhouse, 1982-90; v.p. fin., asst. sec. NANA Regional Corp., Inc., Anchorage, 1990-95; v.p. fin. NANA Devel. Corp., Inc., Anchorage, 1990-95; sec.-treas. Vanguard Industries, J.V., Anchorage, 1990-95, Alaska United Drilling, Inc., Anchorage, 1990-95; treas. NANA/Marriott Joint Venture, Anchorage, 1990-95; v.p. fin. Arctic Utilities, Inc., Anchorage, 1990-95, Tour Arctic, Inc., Anchorage, 1990-95, Purcell Svcs., Ltd., Anchorage, 1990-95, Arctic Caribou Inn, Anchorage, 1990-95, NANA Oilfield Svcs., Inc., Anchorage, 1990-95, NANA Corp. Svcs., Inc., Anchorage, 1992-95; dir. divsn. ins. State of Alaska, 1995-99; pres. Marianne K. Burke Cons., 1999—. Cons. Ins. Regulatory and Devel. Authority of India, 2002—, Superintendencia de Banca y Seguros de Peru, 2004, Ins. Supervisory Commn. Republic of Albania, 2004; cons. Bosnia and Herzegovina ins. sector Fin. Svcs. Vol. Corps, 2003, cons. assessment mission in Kosovo, 05, cons. assessment of ins. cos. supervision, Croatia, 05; mem. State of Alaska Medicaid Rate Commn., 1985—88, State of Alaska Bd. Accountancy, 1984—87; bd. dirs. Nat. Assn. Ins. Commrs. Edn. and Rsch. Found.; chair Bd. Equalization Municipality of Anchorage, 2004—; instr. IAIS Core Ins. Principles, Croatia, 2006. Bd. dirs. Alaska Treatment Ctr., Anchorage, 1978, Alaska Hwy. Cruises; treas. Alaska Feminist Credit Union, Anchorage, 1979-80; mem. fund raising com. Anchorage Symphony, 1981. Mem. AICPA, Internat. Assn. Ins. Suprs. (funded mem.), Alaska Soc. CPAs, Govtl. Fin. Officers U.S. and Can., Fin. Execs. Inst. (bd. dirs.), Nat. Assn. Ins. Commrs. (bd. dirs.). Avocations: travel, reading. Home: 3818 Helvetia Dr Anchorage AK 99508-5016 Office Phone: 907-563-9790. Personal E-mail: mkburke@gci.net.

BURKE, MARJORIE TISDALE, retired special education educator; b. Chase City, Va., May 27, 1926; d. Henry and Sallie Keene; m. Willie Tisdale, 1948; children: Michael S., Carita F., Lydia R.; m. William C. Vaughn, 1966 (div. 1976); m. Faxie Burke, May 22, 1993. BS, Va. State Coll., 1956. Tchr. elem. edn. Newark (N.J.) Bd. Edn., 1951-53, tchr. spl. edn., 1954-64, Elizabeth (N.J.) Bd. Edn., 1964—92, Fauquier Bd. Edn., Warrenton, Va., 1992—; tutor, subs. tchr. Va.; ret., 1992. Cmty. parent advocate in spl. edn.; Mary Kay beauty cons., 1973—. Mem. Mt. Pleasant Bapt. Ch., Gainesville, Va., also choir mem., usher, sec., v.p. women's aux., pres. scholarship fund, asst. supt. Sunday sch., chairperson of greeters. Mem. AAUW, AARP, NAACP (chmn. edn. com. Prince William County 1994—), Nat. Coun. Negro Women (sr. caretaker), Garden Club Va., Nat. Congress Black Women, Inc. (Prince William chpt.), Housekeepers Club of Aldie (v.p.). Avocations: yoga, poetry, singing, volunteer work at hospital and church. Home: PO Box 3 Gainesville VA 20156-0003

BURKE, MARY GRIGGS (MRS. JACKSON BURKE), art collector; b. St. Paul; m. Jackson Burke (dec.). BA, Sarah Lawrence Coll.; MA in Clin. Psychology, Columbia U.; postgrad., New Sch. for Social Rsch. Pvt. collector Japanese art, St. Paul, 1966—; founder The Mary & Jackson Burke Found., N.Y.C., 1972—. Mem. vis. com. Freer Gallery Art, Smithsonian Instn.; mem. Met. Mus. Art; pres. The Mary and Jackson Burke Found. Mem. nominating com., mem. membership com., mem. exec. com., mem. activities com. The Japan Soc., 1959-77, chmn. student and visitors com., 1957-63, chmn. art gallery adv. com., 1970-73, bd. dirs., 1968-77, also hon. life trustee; chmn. friend mem. Japan House Gallery, 1969-75, 87—; bd. dirs. The Cable (Wis.) Natural History Mus., 1968-92, also hon. life trustee, Sarah Lawrence Coll., Bronxville, N.Y., 1968-78, also hon. life trustee, The Internat. Crane Found., Baraboo, Wis., 1978-90, The Hobe Sound (Fla.) Nature Ctr., 1987—; mem. adv. coun. dept. art history and archeology Columbia U., N.Y.C., 1970—; mem. internat. coun. Mus. Modern Art, N.Y.C., 1970—; mem. vis. com. Freer Gallery of Art, Smithsonian Instn., Washington, 1971—, vice chmn., 1989-92; mem. vis. com. dept. Asiatic art Mus. Fine Arts, Boston, 1972-90, also friend, 1972-90; mem. vis. com. dept. Islamic art, mem. vis. com. dept. Asian art, mem. edn. com., mem. acquisitions com., bd. dirs. Met. Mus. Art, N.Y.C., 1976—, also friend Far Ea. dept., 1984—; mem. Smithsonian Assocs. nat. bd. Smithsonian Instn., Washington, 1977-83; mem. art gallery adv. com., mem. exec. com., mem. devel. com., bd. dirs. The Asia Soc., 1978-88, also hon. life trustee; friend Bklyn. Mus. Art, 1982—, Friends of Asian Art, Freer and Sackler Galleries, 1991—; William Beene fellows N.Y. Zool. Soc., 1986—. Decorated Order of The Sacred Treasure (Japan), Second Leve Gold and Silver Star (Japan), named one of top 200 collectors, ARTnews Mag., 2004. Achievements include The Mary Griggs Burke Collection of Japanese Art at Met. Mus. of Art in NY is the largest ptv. collection of Japanese art outside Japan. Avocation: collector of Japanese art. Mailing: Mary Livingston Griggs & Mary Griggs Burke Foundation 1400 Fifth Street Ctr Saint Paul MN 55101

BURKE, MICHELLE C., lawyer; b. Cleve., Oct. 2, 1952; d. Andrew L. and Catherine L. (Sedlak) Matlak; m. Michael E. Burke, Dec. 29, 1971. BA with honors, Lake Forest Coll., 1980; JD cum laude, Harvard, 1983. Bar: Ill., 1983; U.S. Dist. Ct. (no. dist.) Ill., 1984; U.S. Ct. Appeals (3rd. cir.), 1994. Assoc. Sidley & Austin, Chgo., 1983-86, McDermott, Will & Emery, Chgo., 1986-88, ptnr., 1989—. Mem. Phi Beta Kappa. Office: McDermott Will & Emery 227 W Monroe St Ste 3100 Chicago IL 60606-5096

BURKE, RACHAEL J., art educator; b. Pottstown, Pa., Sept. 27, 1954; d. Vincent Robert and Lillian Mabel Jacobs. BFA in Painting, Western Ky. U., 1977; MFA in Painting, Miami U., Oxford, Ohio, 1983. Instr. Arts Consortium, Cin., 1986; adj. instr. Art Acad. of Cin., 1984—90, Miami U., Oxford, 1990; asst. prof. art Edinboro U., Pa., 1990—97, assoc. prof., 1997—. Exhibitions include New American Painting, vol. 15 and 27, 1998, 2000, exhibited in group shows at Butler Inst. of Am. Art, Youngstown, Ohio, 1998, 2000, one-woman shows include Lowe Gallery, Atlanta, 1995, 1996, Cummings Gallery, Mercy Hurst Coll., 1999, Erie Art Mus., 2004. Named Featured Artist of the Yr., Multiple Sclerosis Soc., Erie, Pa., 2000; recipient Purchase award, Carnegie Mus. Art, Pitts., 2000, Jurors award, Erie Art Mus., 2000, Chautauqua Inst. award, Art Inst. Chautauqua, 1991. Office: Edinboro Univ of Pa Dept Art Edinboro PA 16444 Studio: 629 Parade St Erie PA 16503

BURKE, RACHEL E., lawyer; b. Newcastle Upon Tyne, Eng., Aug. 31, 1971; BS, Miami U., 1993; JD, Coll. of William & Mary, 1996. Bar: Ohio 1996, US Dist. Ct. Southern Dist. Ohio 1997, US Dist. Ct. Northern Dist. Ohio 2006. Of counsel Porter Wright Morris & Arthur LLP, Cin. Trustee Cin. Fire Mus. Named one of Ohio's Rising Stars, Super Lawyers, 2006. Mem.: Order of Coif, ABA, Ohio State Bar Assn., Cin. Bar Assn. Office: Porter Wright Morris & Arthur LLP 250 E Fifth St Ste 2200 Cincinnati OH 45202-5118 Office Phone: 513-369-4236. Office Fax: 513-421-0991.*

BURKE, RHONDA WILLIAMS, counselor; d. Charles O. and Rebekah Sue Williams; m. William H. Burke, Apr. 21, 1984; children: Ashley Elizabeth, Courtney Celeste. BS in Edn. cum laude with hons., Winthrop Coll., 1984; MEd, The Citadel, 1989. Lic. profl. counselor, nat. cert. counselor. Tchr. Berkeley County Schs., SC, 1984—87, Dorchester County Schs., 1987—90; counseling assoc. Summerville, 1989—, Charter Hosp., Charleston, 1994—95, Summerville Behavioral Health, 1999—. Troop leader Summerville Girl Scouts, 1991, 1996; bd. mem. Robert Ivey Young Profls., Summerville, 2003—04; state dir. for SC/NC Am.'s Nat. Teenager Scholarship Orgn.; Sunday sch. leader Bethany Meth. Ch., Summerville, 1995—2001; mem. bd. YMCA, 1996; bd. dirs. Create-a-Smile-Team Program, 2004—. Named Tchr. of Yr, Berkeley Country Schs., 1988. Mem.: Phi Kappa Phi. Methodist. Avocations: reading, scuba diving, photography, travel. Office: Summerville Behavioral Health 709 Trolley Rd Summerville SC 29485 Office Phone: 843-821-2480. Personal E-mail: id28532673@aol.com.

BURKE, SANDRA E., information technology executive; b. Libertyville; AB, Boston U.; M in Physiology, Fairleigh Dickinson U.; PhD in Physiology, Thomas Jefferson U. Postdoctoral rschr. Robert Woods Johnson Cardiovascular Rsch. Inst., NJ; dir. cardiovascular systems rsch. Abbot Laboratories, Volwiler assoc. rsch. fellow. Founding mem. Black Bus. Network, exec. coun. mem. Named a Woman of Achievement, YWCA of Lake County, 2004; named to Hall of Fame, Women in Tech. Internat., 2005. Mem.: Volwiler Soc. Office: Abbott Laboratories 100 Abbott Park Rd Abbott Park IL 60064-6400*

BURKE, SHEILA P., federal agency administrator; b. San Francisco, Jan. 10, 1951; d. George Abbott and Mary Joan (Winfield) B.; m. David Chew, Jan. 1983; children: Daniel, Kathleen, Sarah. BSN, U. San Francisco, 1973; MA in Pub. Adminstrn., Harvard U., 1982. Staff nurse Alta Bates Hosp., Berkeley, Calif., 1973-74; dir. student affairs Nat. Student Nurses Assn., NY, 1974-75, dir. program and field svcs., 1975-77; legis. asst. Senator Bob Dole, 1977-78; profl. staff mem. Senate Com. Fin., U.S. Senate, 1979-82, dep. staff dir., 1982-85; dep. chief of staff Senate Majority Leader Bob Dole, U.S. Senate, 1985-86; chief of staff Senator Bob Dole, 1986-96; sec. U.S. Senate, Washington, 1995; undersec. Am. Mus. and nat. programs Smithsonian Instn., Washington, 2000—03, dep. sec., COO, 2004—. Adj. nursing faculty Georgetown U.; rsch. asst. J.F. Kennedy Sch. Govt., Harvard U., 1980-81, advisor to dean, 1996, exec. dean, lectr. pub. policy, 1996-2000, adj. lectr., 2000—. Mem.: Inst. Medicine. Republican. Address: 1323 Merrie Ridge Rd Mc Lean VA 22101-1826

BURKE, TARA LEANN, music educator; b. Newberg, Oreg., Mar. 15, 1968; d. Hardie Richard Rollins and Lorna Lee Gosson; m. David George Burke, May 14, 1993; children: Kendall, Heidi, Kaela, Hannah, Kara. AA, Ricks Coll., 1988; BA, George Fox Coll., 1994. Foreign church rep. Ch. Jesus Christ or Latter Day Saints, Duesseldorf, Germany, 1989—91; human resources adminstr. Evergreen Internat. Aviation, McMinnville, Oreg., 1991—92, sr. human resources adminstr., 1992—93, EEO, anti-drug program coord., 1993—94; property mgr. Westridge Construction, Newberg, 1994—97; pvt. violin tchr. Hillsboro, Oreg., 1997—. 1st violinist Oreg. Pro Arte Chamber Orch. Cmty. svc. coord. Ch. of Jesus Christ of Latter-Day Saints, Hillsboro, Oreg., 2005. Named Oreg. Young Mother of Yr., 2005; recipient AMI Nat. Violin Contest, 2006. Mem.: Violin/Piano Unlimited (violinist), Eastwood Elem. PTA (treas.), Classic String Quartet (1st violinist). Republican. Avocation: basketball. Home: 491 NE 17th Ave Hillsboro OR 97124 Personal E-mail: woodenquartet@juno.com.

BURKE, YVONNE WATSON BRATHWAITE (MRS. WILLIAM A. BURKE), lawyer; b. LA, Oct. 5, 1932; d. James A. and Lola (Moore) Watson; m. William A. Burke, June 14, 1972; 1 child, Autumn Roxanne; 1 stepchild, Christine. AA, U. Calif., 1951; BA, UCLA, 1953; JD, U. So. Calif., 1956; Doctorate (hon.), Pepperdine U. Bar: Calif. 1956. Mem. Calif. Assembly, 1966-72, chmn. urban devel. and housing com., 1971, 72; mem. 93d-95th Congresses, 1973—79, House Appropriations Com.; chmn. Congl. Black Caucus, 1976; Los Angeles county supervisor 4th dist., 1979—80; ptnr. Jones, Dan, Reagis & Pogue, 1987—92. Dep. corp. commr., hearing officer Police Commn., 1964-66; atty., staff McCone Commn. (investigation Watts riot), 1965; past chmn. L.A. Fed. Res. Bank; U.S. adv. bd. Nestle. Vice chmn. 1984 U.S. Olympics Organizing Com.; bd. dirs. or bd. advisers numerous orgns.; former regent U. Calif., Bd. Ednl. Testing Svc.; Amateur Athletic Found.; former bd. dirs. Ford Found., Brookings Inst.; mem. bd. supr's. 2d Dist., L.A. County Bd. of Supr's., 1992—, chair, 1993-94, 97-98, 2002-03; bd. govs. L.A. Met. Transp. Authority; pres. So. Calif. Assn. Govts., 2006, LA Coliseum Commn., 2006. Recipient Profl. Achievement award UCLA, 1974, 84; named one of 200 Future Leaders Time mag., 1974, Alumni of Yr., UCLA, 1996; recipient Achievement awards C.M.E. Chs.; numerous other awards, citations.; fellow Inst. Politics John F. Kennedy Sch. Govt. Harvard, 1971-72; Chubb fellow Yale, 1972 Office: 500 W Temple St Rm 866 Los Angeles CA 90012 Office Phone: 213-974-2222. Business E-Mail: yburke@bos.co.la.ca.us.

BURKE-FANNING, MADELEINE, artist; b. New Orleans, Feb. 12, 1941; d. Henry Raymond Burke Sr. and Ella Mae Falgout-Burke; children: Denise Angele Duizend-Hargis, Michele Renee Duizend-Meyer, Jeanne Monet Duizend-Fillman; m. Joel Cornell Fanning, Mar. 28, 1981. Student, Pensacola (Fla.) Jr. Coll., 1988-96. Coord. New Orleans World Trade Ctr., Pensacola Cultural Ctr.; adj. prof. advanced watercolor Pensacola Jr. Coll.; tchr. nat. and internat. workshops; instr. advanced watercolor City of Pensacola, Vickrey Ctr., Fla. One-woman shows include Michele Dion Gallery, 1994, Soho Gallery, 1994, Wise Choice Gallery, 1996, The Wright Place, 1997, Awakenings, Gulf Breeze, Fla., 1997—98, The Shoppe Gallery, 1998, Pensacola Mus. Art, 1998—2003, Adams Street Gallery, 1998, Ducks Unltd., Pensacola, 1998, Right Angles Gallery, 1999, Kate Holmes-Branton Gallery, 1999—2002, The Art Market, Gulf Breeze, Fla., 2000, Art and Design Soc., Ft. Walton Beach, Fla., 2000, White Cloud Gallery and Gifts, Pensacola, 2000, Sam Houston Racetrack, Houston, 2001, Corner Copia, Orange Beach, Ala., 2000—03, N.W. Fla. Laser and Skincare Inst., Laurie Grizzard Gallery, 2001—, The MANE Event Expressions Gallery, Pensacola, 2001—, Kotlarz Gallery, 2002—, Stockamp Gallery, 2002—05, Woodcock Interiors and Gallery, Pensacola, 2003—04, Roger Scott Tennis Ctr., 2003—06, Michelle Ray Gallery, 2004, Sanger Theatre, 2004—06, Moza Tile, Pensacola, Fla., 2005, Michelle Ray, 2005—06, exhibited in group shows at Pensacola Jr. Coll., 1988—96, 2003, Gnu Zoo, 1995—96, Eastern Shore Mus. Art, Fairhope, Ala., 1994—96, Pensacola Regional Airport, 1996, World Trade Ctr., 1996, Schmidt's Gallery, 1996, Pensacola Cultural Ctr., 1997, Adams Street Gallery, 1998, Artel Gallery, 1999—2005, Vickney Ctr., 1999—, Visual Art Ctr. of N.W. Fla., Panama City, 2001, The Avenue, St. Paul's Roman Cath. Ch., Pensacola, Fla., 2001—03, Woodcock Interior and Gallery, 2004—05, Escambia County Equestrian Ctr., Pensacola, 2003—04, Sacred Heart Found., Miracle Camp, 2005—06; host (TV show) Art and Healing, 1997, (TV feature) Inside Scope, New Orleans, 1993, (TV show) Art Vision, 1994, Culture Center BLAB TV, 1996; host: (TV show) Everything Old is New Again, Pensacola Heritage Assn., 2002; TV appearance N.W. Fla. Arts Coun. Art Auction, Sanger Theatre, Pensacola, 2001; exhibitions include Sanger Theatre, 2003, Five Flags Stallion Assn. Horse Show, Pensacola, 2003—05, exhibited in group shows at Woodcock Gallery, 2003—05, Am. Heart Assn. Ala. Art for Heart, 2005—06, Sacred Heart Hosp., 2005, Miracle Camp, 2005, Moza Tile; contbr. articles and art in Pensacola Opera League Publication; Banquet at the Opera, 2003. Art judge Just Say No Program, 1996—97, PTA Reflective Program, 1997—98; art chair Pensacola chpt. Ducks Unltd., 1998—2004; instr. Ctr. Ind. Living, Pensacola, 1998—2000, Vickery Ctr., Pensacola, 2000—06, Pensacola Jr. Coll., 2000—05. Recipient Rockport Pubs. award of distinction for inclusion in Best of Watercolor: Painting Texture, 1997, Collected Best of Watercolor, 2002. Mem.: Artel.Art with an Edge, Bay Cliff Watercolor Soc. (founder), Woodbine Figure Painters, Pensacola Mus. Art, N.W. Fla. Arts Coun., Tallahassee Watercolor Soc., La. Watercolor Soc., Fla. Watercolor Soc., Nat. Mus. Women in Arts, Am. Soc. Portrait Artists. Avocations: gardening, horseback riding, travel, sailing, photography. Home and Office: Palm Cottage Studio 4160 Rommitch Ln Pensacola FL 32504-4490 Office Phone: 850-434-3598.

BURKEMPER, JENNIFER A., secondary school educator; b. Elmhurst, Ill., June 28, 1978; d. Joseph and Diana Tompa; m. Andrew Burkemper, June 3, 2006. B in Music Edn., Ind. U., Bloomington, 2001; M in Choral Conducting, Mich. State U., East Lansing, 2006. Choir dir. Glenbard North H.S., Carol Stream, Ill., 2001—04, Glenbard West H.S., Glen Ellyn, Ill., 2004—05. Mem.: Ill. Music Educators Assn., Am. Choral Dirs. Assn. Office: Glenbard West HS 670 Crescent Blvd Glen Ellyn IL 60137

BURKEN, RUTH MARIE, utilities executive; b. Kenosha, Wis., Sept. 25, 1956; d. Richard Stanley and Anne Theresa (Steplyk) Wojtak; m. James H. Burken, Oct. 15, 1988. AAS, Gateway Tech. Inst., 1976; BA, U. Wis., Parkside, 1980; AAS, Coll. of DuPage, 1995. Transp. aide Kenosha Achievement Ctr., 1977; libr. clk. U. Wis.-Parkside, Kenosha, 1978-80, lifeguard, 1980; asst. mgr. K Mart Corp., Troy, Mich., 1980-88, regional office supr., 1988, internal auditor, 1989-92, sr. field auditor, 1992-98; gen. auditor Nicor Gas, Naperville, Ill., 1998-2000, billing splist., 2000—. Mem. Defenders of Wildlife, World Wildlife Fund. Mem.: NAFE, VFW, Am. Gas Assn., U. Wis.-Parkside Alumni Assn., Distributive Edn. Clubs Am. (parliamentarian 1976). Roman Catholic. Office: Nicor Gas 1844 W Ferry Rd Naperville IL 60563-9600 Office Phone: 630-388-2412. Business E-Mail: rburken@nicor.com.

BURKETT, JANICE MAYO, science educator; d. Robert and Catherine Mayo; children: Ryan, Sean. BS, Pace U., White Plains, 1977; MS, Manhattanville Coll., Purchase, N.Y., 1985. Sci. tchr. Good Counsel Acad. H.S., White Plains, NY, 1977—79, Maria Regina H.S., Hartsdale, NY, 1979—81, Westlake Mid. Sch., Thornwood, NY, 1981—83, Lawrence Mid. Sch., Cedarhurst, NY, 1983—93, Lawrence H.S., Cedarhurst, 1993—99, Garden City (N.Y.) H.S., 1999—. New tchr. mentor, 2005—06. Recipient Richard Gazzda Tchr. fellowship, NY State PTA; fellow, Am. Meteorol. Soc., 2006. Home: 98 Cherry Valley Ave Garden City NY 11530

BURKETT, JULIE ANN, science educator; b. DuBois, Pa., July 12, 1973; d. George R. and Roberta J. Bedell; m. Brian Keith Burkett, Nov. 6, 1999; 1 child, Olivia Madison. Degree in biology, Pa. State U., Erie, 1995; degree in edn., Clarion U. Pa., 1999. Tchr. 7th grade sci. DuBois Area Mid. Sch., Pa., 2001—. Home: 216 Pennsylvania Ave Big Run PA 15715 Office: DuBois Area Sch Dist 400 Liberty Blvd Du Bois PA 15801 Office Phone: 814-375-8770.

BURKHALTER, MYRA SHERAM, retired marketing professional; b. Ringgold, Ga., Feb. 3, 1945; d. Benjamin Porter and Imogene (Bandy) Sheram; m. Alva Prentice Burkhalter, Dec. 19, 1965. BS, U. Ga., 1966; MEd, Auburn U., 1968; EdD, Fla. State U., 1981. Tchr. Barrow County Sch. Bd., Winder, Ga., 1965-66, Lee County Sch. Bd., Opelika, Ala., 1966-67, vocat. home econs. tchr., 1968-69; teaching asst. Auburn (Ala.) U., 1967-68; prof. interior design Ga. So. U., Statesboro, Ga., 1969-70; ednl. supr. State Fla. Dept. Edn., Tallahassee, 1971-77, chief cons. tchr. cert., 1977-81; adminstr. B.H. Margolis & Co., Houston, 1981-82; mktg. adminstr. petrolite Corp., St. Louis, 1984-89; adminstrv. mgr. Lifescapes, Inc., Atlanta, 1990-92; retired. Active Humane Soc., 1984—. Mem. U. Ga. Alumni Soc., Auburn U. Alumni Assn., Fla. State U. Alumni Soc., Phi Delta Kappa. Avocations: travel, crafts, gardening. Home: 1300 Ten Mile Still Rd Bainbridge GA 39817

BURKHARDT, JOANNA MARIE, librarian; b. Worcester, Mass., July 16, 1954; d. Edgar Severns and Roberta Margaret Burkhardt; m. F. Michael Wakefield, Oct. 3, 1992; 1 child, Katherine Taft Burkhardt. BA, U. Wis., 1975, MA, 1981; M.Libr.Info.Svcs., U. R.I., 1986. Libr. asst. U. Conn. Law Sch. Libr., Hartford, 1981-82; asst. libr. U. Conn.-Avery Point, Groton, 1982-87; head libr. U. Conn., Torrington, 1987-92, U. RI, Providence, 1992—. Libr. cons. Watch Hill Improvement Soc., 1981—. Author: Teaching Information Literacy, 2003, Creating a Comprehensive Plan for Information Literacy, 2005; contbr. articles to profl. jours. Champlin grantee, 1994, Found. grantee URI, 1996, Rsch. Office grantee, 2005, Student Assessment Office grantee, 2006. Mem. ALA (pres. 1993-94), New Mems. Round Table (pres. 1993-94). Avocation: lighthouses.

BURKHARDT, MARY SUE D., secondary school educator; b. Frankfort, IN, Aug. 19, 1948; d. Marshall Clifton and Opal Marie Davis; m. Ronald John Burkhardt, June 13, 1970; children: John Thomas, Kristine Marie. BS, Purdue U., 1971, MS, 1974. Cert. Cert. family and consumer scis. Educator Twin Lakes H.S., Monticello, Ind., 1972—. Adj. faculty Ivy Tech State Coll., Lafayette and Logansport, Ind.; lectr. Purdue U., West Lafayette, Ind. Author: Developing Career and Living Skills, 2005. Mem.: numerous profl. assns. Home: 1510 E 500 N West Lafayette IN 47906 Office: Twin Lakes High Sch 300 S Third St Monticello IN 47960 Office Phone: 574-583-7108. Business E-Mail: mburkhar@twinlakes.k12.in.us.

BURKHART, CATHERINE RAY, secondary school educator; b. Tucson, Mar. 2, 1939; m. Bruce Burkhart; children: Lee, Katy, Dottie. BA, U. Ariz., Tucson, 1961, MEd, 1966. Tchr. Tucson Sch. Dist., 1961—66, Whittier (Calif.) HS Dist., 1966—98. Mentor tchr.; cons. ETS, instr., Rio Hondo Coll., 1974-04, Nogales HS, Rowland, 2003-05; guest spkr. at various confs. Editor Southland Coun. Tchrs. English newsletter. Home: 2530 Cardillo Ave Hacienda Heights CA 91745-4441 Personal E-mail: bwburkhart@aol.com.

BURKHART, KATHERINE WEST, music educator, adult education educator; b. Roanoke, Va., Feb. 12, 1944; d. James Lemuel Wills and Kate Bradley West; m. Harold Eugene Burkhart, June 12, 1971; 1 child, Anna Katherine. BA in Music, Mary Baldwin Coll., 1966; MA in Humanities-Liberal Studies, Hollins U., 1976. Cert. basic literacy tchr. Literacy Vols. Am., ESL tchr. Literacy Vols. Am., collegiate tchr. Va. Freelance organist Va. Tech. Meml. Chapel, Blacksburg, 1964—2000, St. Luke's Anglican Ch., Rotorua, New Zealand, 1976—77; elem. sch. music tchr. Montgomery County Schs., Va., 1967—68, Va., 1970—73; elem. music tchr. Virginia Beach (Va.) City Schs., 1968—69; ch. organist Blacksburg Presbyn. Ch., 1973—79, 1984—2000; pvt. piano tchr. Christiansburg/Blacksburg, 1973—84, 1990—; ESL program mgr. Literacy Vols. Am., Christiansburg, 1999—2000; ESL lead tchr. Rowe Furniture Co./Literacy Vols. Am., Elliston, Va., 2002—04. Tutor, cons. Literacy Vols. Am., Christiansburg, 1999—. ESL cons., com. chair Task Force on Refugee Resettlement, Blacksburg, 1999. Mem.: Va. Music Tchrs. Assn. (Highlands chpt., pres. 1993—95), Nat. Guild Piano Tchrs., Am. Guild Organists (Highlands chpt., newsletter editor 1984—86, sub-dean 1992—93, Newsletter grant 1984). Presbyterian. Avocations: reading, foreign language films, travel, tutoring. Office: Literacy Vols Am New River Valley 195 W Main St Christiansburg VA 24073

BURKHART, SANDRA MARIE, art dealer; b. Cleve., Dec. 29, 1942; d. John Joseph Norris and Audrey Eleanor Kegg McGuire Marshall; m. Thomas Henry Burkhart, Oct. 29, 1960 (div. Sept. 26, 1979); children: Bryan, Brad, Lisa, Michelle. Student, Evergreen Valley Coll., San Jose, 1978-80, San Jose City Coll., 1978-80, West Valley Coll., Saratoga, Calif., 1978-79. Med. technician Eye Med. Clinic, San Jose, 1980-83; ind. corp. art salesperson San Jose, 1983-92; corp. sales dir. Phoenix Gallery, San Jose, 1986-88; v.p. mktg. Whittlers Mother, San Francisco, 1989-90; dir. Martin Lawrence Galleries, Santa Clara, Calif., 1990-97. Avocations: watercolors, crafts, tennis, skiing, horses. Home and Office: 115 Cheltenham Way San Jose CA 95139 Office Phone: 408-972-1060. Personal E-mail: sb_art_consulting@yahoo.com.

BURKHEAD, CYNTHIA ANNE, literature and language professor; b. San Antonio, Tex., Dec. 14, 1957; d. A.W. and Helen Ruth Paris; m. John S. Burkhead. BA, Fontbonne U.; MA, So. Ill. U., 1997. Instr. U. North Ala., Florence, Ala., 2000—. Author: (book) Student Companion to John Steinbeck, 2002. Bd. mem. Shoals Habitat for Humanity, 2004—06. Mem.: Popular Culture Assn. Home: 1104 E Pryor St Athens AL 35611 Office: U North Ala UNA Box 5050 Florence AL 35632

BURKHOLDER, KELLY LEANN, elementary school educator; d. Wayne and JoAnne Mucke; m. Kent Allen Burkholder, June 7, 1986; children: Jacob Allen, Allison Paige. BS in Edn., SW Mo. State U., Springfield, 1983; MS in Edn. (hon.), Ctrl. Mo. State U., Warrensburg, 1990. Cert. elem. tchr. grades 1-6, spl. edn. K-8. Tchr. 5th grade Heber Hunt Elem. Sch., Sedalia, Mo., 1990—95; spl. edn. tchr. Sedalia Mid. Sch., Mo., 1985—90, tchr. math., 1995—. Mem. various commns. Sacred Heart Cath. Ch., Sedalia. Mem.: Mo. State Tchrs. Assn. Office Phone: 660-829-6549.

BURKLOW, KATHLEEN ANN, psychologist; b. Evansville, Ind., Oct. 23, 1964; d. Donald Ray and Kyung Ai Burklow; m. John Michael Berlier, May 1999; children: Grace Berlier, Claire Berlier. BA, Vanderbilt U., 1987; MA, U. Cin., 1990, PhD, 1994. Lic. psychologist Ohio, 1997. Intern Children's Hosp., Columbus, 1993—94; postdoctoral fellow Cin. Children's Hosp. Med. Ctr., 1994—97, asst. prof. psychology, 1997—, assoc. prof. psychology, 2004—. Contbr. articles to profl. jours. Recipient K23 Career Devel. award, NIH/Nat. Ctr. for Rsch. Resources, 2000. Mem.: APA. Office: Cincinnati Children's Hosp Med Ctr Divsn of Psychology ML3015 3333 Burnet Ave Cincinnati OH 45229-3026 Business E-Mail: kathleen.burklow@cchmc.org.

BURKO, DIANE, artist, educator; b. N.Y.C., Sept. 24, 1948; d. David and Doris Burko; m. Edwin B. Goldberg, Sept. 4, 1966 (div. Sept. 1993); 1 child, Jessica Burko; m. Richard Ryan, May 6, 1999. BS in Painting, Skidmore Coll., 1966; MFA, U. Pa., 1969. Prof. C.C. Phila., 1969—. Vis. prof. Princeton U., NJ, 1985; vis. instr. Anderson Ranch Arts Ctr Snowmass Coll., 1996; mem. Phila. Art Commn., 1992—96. Represented in permanent collections Art Inst. Chgo., DeCordova Mus., Pa. Acad. Fine Arts, Phila. Mus. Art, Reading Pub. Mus., Locks Gallery, Phila., Frederick R. Weisman Art Mus., U. Minn., Mpls. Mem. Mayor's Cultural Adv. Coun., Phila., 1987—91; bd. dirs. Phila. Vol. Lawyers for the Arts, 1985—89, Nat. Women's Caucus for Art, 1984—87, Coll. Art Assn., 1994—98. Recipient Bessie Berman award, Leeway Found., 2000; fellow Rockefeller Found. residency fellow, Bellagio, Italy, 1993, Visual Arts fellow, Nat. Endowment for Arts, 1985—86, 1991—92, Readers Digest Found. residency fellow, Giverny, France, 1989; grantee Pa. Coun. on the Arts individual grantee, 1981, 1995. Home: 275 S 19th St Philadelphia PA 19103-5769 Office Phone: 215-334-9969. E-mail: burko@bellatlantic.net.

BURKS, BRENDA ROUNSAVILLE, retired music educator, council member; b. Summerville, Ga., Nov. 7, 1944; d. Clifford and Louise McCutchins Rounsaville. BA in Music Edn., Spelman Coll., 1966; M in Music Edn., Ga. State U., 1974; postgrad., Fisk U., 1975, Emory U., 1976. Lifetime cert. music tchr. K-12. Choir dir. ladies singing ensemble W. 5th St. Ch. of Christ, Summerville, Ga., 1960-81; pvt. music tchr. Atlanta, 1966-84; music tchr. adult night sch., 1966-84; city coun. mem. City of Summerville, 1997—. Mentor Summerville Mentoring Com., 1997—. Mem. Adminstrv. Headstart Bd., Summerville, 1995—99, Literacy Bd. of Chattanooga County, Summerville, 1995—97; career advisor Consol. Base Pers. Office, Dobbins AFB, Marietta, 1983—84; sec. Martin Luther King Jr. Commn., Summerville, 1998—99; mem. City Coun., 2005—, Leadership Inst. Mcpl. Elected Ofls., 2005; sec. Ladies Bible Study; bd. dirs. Downtown Devel. Authority, Summerville, 1999—; trustee Chattooge County Libr. Bd., 2002—06. Recipient Tng. award, U. Ga. and Ga. Mcpl. Assn., 2003, Jefferson-Jackson Pres. award, 2003, cert. Appreciation award, Ga. Mcpl. Assn., 2003, cert. recognition award, 2003, Excellence award, 2006, award, Leadership Inst. Mcpl. Elected Ofcls., 2005. Mem.: Small Bus. Retail Assn. Democrat. Mem. Ch. of Christ. Avocations: bicycling, gardening, sewing, baking, movies.

BURKS, REBECCA ANN, music educator; b. Little Rock, July 29, 1963; d. James W. and Betty Ann Lyons; m. Andrew Alan Burks, Dec. 23, 1984; children: Elizabeth Ann, William Andrew. B in Music Edn., Ouachita Bapt. U., Arkadelphia, Ark., 1985; MS in Edn., Henderson State U., Arkadelphia, Ark., 1995. Cert. K-12 music, K-6 counseling Ark., 2006. Music tchr. grades K-12 Carthage Pub. Schs., Ark., 1985—87; music tchr. grades K-5 Glen Rose Elem., Malvern, Ark., 1999—. Assoc. music dir. First Bapt. Ch., Malvern. Baptist. Home: 2139 Taylor Malvern AR 72104 Office: Glen Rose Public Schools 14334 Hwy 67 Malvern AR 72104 Office Phone: 501-332-3694. Personal E-mail: praisemusic2@lycos.com. Business E-Mail: bburks@gr1.dsc.k12.ar.us.

BURKS, ROBIN J., psychologist; b. Tiffin, Ohio, July 13, 1960; d. Dave and Rose Burks; m. Frederick Carl Ames, Sept. 7, 1991; children: Travis Carl, Jessie Joy. BA, Bowling Green State U., 1982, MA, PhD, Bowling Green State U., 1987. Dir. of psychology svc. Bowling Green State U., Ohio, 1985—86; psychology intern Baylor Coll. Medicine, Houston, 1986—87; psychotherapist Rosewood Med. Ctr., Houston, 1987—88; clin. coord. Ctr. for Stress Mgmt., Houston, 1987—92; clin. psychologist pvt. practice, Houston, 1988—. Parent edn. co-chmn. Annuciation Orthodox Sch., Houston, 2001—, ann. fund class co-chair., 2004—05, gala underwriting co-chmn., 2002—03. Disaster mental health svc. com. mem. Am. Red Cross, Greater Houston Area, 2002—; asst. baseball coach United Christian Athletic League, 2004—05, asst. soccer coach Houston, 2003. Recipient Houston Group Psychotherapy Soc. scholarship, Baylor Coll. Medicine, 1987, Psychologist of the Yr., Houston Psychol. Assoc., 2002, Outstanding Visionary, 2002; U. Nonservice Fellowship award, Bowling Green State U., 1985. Avocations: running, writing, reading. Office: 9525 Katy Freeway #210 Houston TX 77024

BURLAGE, DOROTHY DAWSON, clinical psychologist; b. San Antonio, Sept. 13, 1937; d. Joseph M. and Virginia (Hendrix) Dawson. BA, U. Tex., 1959; EdM, Harvard U., 1972, PhD, 1978. Lic. psychologist, Mass. Horace Lentz lectr. Harvard Coll., 1972-73; rsch. assoc. in psychiatry Harvard Med. Sch., Cambridge, Mass., 1976-78; rsch. assoc. Children's Hosp. Med. Ctr., Boston, 1978-79; clin. fellow psychology Harvard Med. Sch., 1978-80; staff psychologist Eliot Community Mental Health Ctr., Concord, Mass., 1980-85; instr. dept. psychiatry Harvard Med. Sch., 1984-88; mem. staff dept. psychiatry Newton Wellesley Hosp., 1986-92; now with Harvard U. Health Svcs.; pvt. practice clin. psychologist Cambridge; clin. supr. Children's Hosp., Boston, 1994-96. Co-author: Deep in Our Hearts, 2000; contbr. articles to profl. jours. Bd. dirs. Children's Mus., Boston, 1988-94, Profls. for Parents and Families, 1994; mem. scientist adv. bd. Mind Sci. Found., 1994. Grantee HEW, Bus. and Profl. Women's Found., 1976; fellow NIMH, 1972-73, 73-74, Zeta Tau Alpha, 1972-73; Woodrow Wilson fellow in Women's Studies, 1976-77. Mem. Am. Psychol. Assn., Mass. Psychol. Assn., AOA. Home: 166 Oakleigh Rd Newton MA 02458-2224 Office Phone: 617-969-2442. Personal E-mail: burlaged@aol.com.

BURLEND, VIRGINIA ANN, elementary school educator; d. Nellie Pearl Williams; m. Melvin Vincent Burlend, Dec. 21, 1969; children: Traci Deanne Seal, Matthew David, Tricia Renee Johnson. BS, Olivet Nazarene U., Kankakee, Ill., 1970. Cert. tchr. elem. edn. Ill., 1970. Operator in home day care, Bourbonnais, Ill., 1981—89; tchr. elem. sch. math. and social studies Manteno (Ill.) Mid. Sch., 1990—. Supr., tchr. nursery First Ch. Nazarene, Kankakee, Ill., 1986—2006. Scholar, U. Ill., 1996. Nazarene. Office: Manteno Middle School 250 N Poplar Street Manteno IL 60950

BURLESON, EMILY JANE, nursing educator; b. Fayette, Ala., June 12, 1968; d. Paul Wilburn and Dianne Woods; children: Ashley, Alisyn. ADN, SUNY, 1995; BS in Mgmt. Human Resources, Faulkner U., 1999; M in Nursing, U. Phoenix, 2005. RN Ala., 1995. Clin. coord. and staff devel. coord. Fayette Med. Ctr. Home Care, 1994—2000; LPN scrub nurse Fayette (Ala.) Med. Ctr., 1993; nursing adminstr. Lamar Healthcare Svcs. Inc., Sulligent, Ala., 2000—. Mem.: ANA, Ala. Nurses Assn., Assn. Operating Room Nurses. Avocations: gardening, swimming, walking, water-skiing. Office: Beveill State CC 2631Temple Ave N Fayette AL 35555 Office Phone: 205-932-3221 x 5618. Business E-Mail: eburleson@bscc.edu.

BURMAN, DIANE BERGER, career management and organization development consultant; b. Pitts., Dec. 7, 1936; d. Morris Milton and Dorothy June (Barkin) Berger; m. Sheldon Oscar Burman, Dec. 15, 1926; children: Allison Beth, Jocelyn Holly, Harrison Emory Guy. BA, Vassar Coll., 1958; MA, Middlebury Coll., 1961. Tchr. French Allderdice H.S., Pitts., 1960-61, Mamaroneck (NY) H.S., 1961-64; pers. specialist G.D. Searle & Co., Skokie, Ill., 1972-77, orgn. devel. tng. cons., 1977-78; personnel and orgn. devel. cons. Abbott Labs., North Chgo., 1978-82; orgn. devel. cons., v.p., mgr. career devel. Harris Bank, Chgo., 1982-97; ind. mgmt. cons. in orgn. devel., career devel., 1997—; pres. Dee Burman & Assoc., Highland Park, Ill., 1997—; pres., co-founder RetireRight Ctr., 2004—. Mem. editl. bd. Orgn. Devel. Jour., 1987. Bd. advisors Grad. Sch. Bus. No. Ill. U. Mem. ASTD (bd. dirs. Chgo. career devel. profl. practice area 1987—), Internat. Quality Leadership Inst. (sec., bd. dirs. 2000), Orgn. Devel. Network (founder, exec. dir. Chgo. chpt. 1986-89), Assn. Psychol. Type-Nat. Conf., Orgn. Devel. Inst. (adv. bd. 1987-91, chmn. nat. conf. 1990), Nat. Assn. Bank Women, Assn. Career Profls. Internat. (bd. dirs. Chgo. chpt. 1999-2001, co-chair pub. com. 1999), Am. Counseling Assn., Vassar Club (bd. dirs. 1975-80, 95—, chair career assistance com. 1997—, co-sec. 2000-2001, co-chmn. ann. scholarship benefit 2002, v.p. Class of 1958 Vassar Coll., co-chair class reunion 2005). Jewish. Avocations: biking, playing flute, travel. Home and Office: 247 Prospect Ave Highland Park IL 60035-3357 Office Phone: 312-673-3842. E-mail: deeburman@aol.com.

BURMASTER, ELIZABETH, school system administrator; b. Balt., July 26, 1954; m. John Burmaster; 3 children. B in Music Edn., U. Wis., 1976, M in Edn. Adminstrn., 1984. Vocal music and creative dramatics dir. Longfellow Elem. and Sennett Middle Sch., Madison, Wis., 1976—78; choral and drama dir. East H.S., Madison, 1978—85; asst. prin. Marquette Middle Sch., Madison, 1985—88; fine arts coord. Madison Sch. Dist., 1988—90; prin. Hawthorne Elem., Madison, 1990—92, Madison West H.S., 1992—2001; state supt. pub. instrn. State of Wis., Madison, 2001—. Mem. Govs. Econ. Growth Coun., Coun. Chief State Sch. Officers, chair task force on early childhood learning, bd. dirs.; chair-elect Nat. Ctr. for Learning and Citizenship. Mem. bd. regents U. Wis.; mem. Edn. Commn. of the States, Wis. Tech. Coll. Sys. Bd., Ednl. Comms. Bd., Very Spl. Arts Wis., Gov.'s Work-Based Learning Bd.; bd. dirs. TEACH Wis. Mem.: Coun. of Chief State Sch. Officers, SAI-Music Assn., Tempo Internat., Assn. Wis. Sch. Adminstrs. Mailing: Wis Dept Pub Instrn PO Box 7841 Madison WI 53707-7841

BURMEISTER, VIRGINIA ELIZABETH, retired secondary educator; b. Danville, Ill., Oct. 27, 1926; d. Carl J. and Ruby M. (Ludwig) B. BSEd, Eastern Ill. U., 1949; MA, U. Colo., 1960. Tchr. sci. Cumberland Unit Dist., Toledo, Ill., 1949—54, Bellwood Sch. Dist., 1954—59, Ladue Sch. Dist., St. Louis, 1959-89; ret., 1989. Mem. PEO, Mo. State Tchrs. Assn. (past pres.), Delta Kappa Gamma, Kappa Kappa Iota. Home: 1610 Redbird Cv Saint Louis MO 63144-1122

BURN, BARBARA LOUISE, literature and language educator; d. Edgar George Nuss and Jeanette Pauline Nuss Mennenga; m. Doyle Dohn Burn, June 4, 1965; children: Twila, John, David. BA, Wartburg Coll., Iowa, 1965; MA, Viterbo U., Wis., 2002. Girls' phys. edn. educator Saydel HS, Des Moines, 1965—66; phys. edn., English educator Des Moines Christian Sch., 1967—68, 1971—73, phys. edn. and English educator, girls' dean, girls' basketball coach, yearbook adviser, 1980—97; phys. edn. educator Des Moines Pub. Schs., 1974—77; English educator, yearbook Nat. Honor Soc., Grandview Park Bapt. Sch., Des Moines, 1997—. Profl. educators DEI, 1970; adv. bd. Des Moines Pub. Schs., 1975—77; adj. grammar instr. AIB Coll. Bus., Des Moines, 2000—03. Libr. bd. mem. City Libr., Carlisle, Iowa, 1980—82; bd. mem. Alpha Women's Ctr., Des Moines, 1992—93; vol. Rep. Party, Iowa, 2004; mem. Grandview Park Bapt. Ch., 1996—; mem. adv. panel, Christian edn. dept. FBBC, Ankeny, Iowa. Mem.: ACSI (conv. workshop facilitator 1985—95), Kappa Delta Pi. Republican. Baptist. Avocations: sports, dramas, concerts. Office: Grandview Park Bapt Sch 1701 E 33d Des Moines IA 50317

BURNER, CLARA MILLER, librarian; b. Gettysburg, Pa., May 27, 1943; d. Herbert and Ruth (Myers) Miller; m. Emory C. Bogle, March 21, 1970 (div. March 1991); 1 child, Andrew Miller Ibrahim Bogle; m. Robert Henry Burner, Aug. 20, 1995 (dec.). BA in Spanish, Pa. State U., 1965; MLS, Pratt Inst., 1968. Reference libr. Richmond (Va.) Pub. Libr., 1970-76, branch libr., 1977-85, deputy city libr., 1985—, acting city libr., 1996-97. Mem. Am. Libr. Assn. (Va. chapt.). Methodist. Office: Richmond Public Library 101 E Franklin St Richmond VA 23219-2107

BURNETT, AMY LOUISE, artist, art gallery owner; b. Bremerton, Wash., Nov. 3, 1944; d. George Allen and Violet (Morris) Bjorgen; m. Lee Arthur Burnett, Sept. 25, 1971 (div. 1981); m. Earl O. Sande, Mar. 26, 1989. AA, Olympic Coll., 1965; BBA, Cen. U., 1967, BA in Edn., MA, 1969. Cert. tchr., Wa. Plumber B.H. Allen Plumbing, Bremerton, Wash., 1975-78; plumber, mech. inspector Kitsap County, Wash., 1978-90; owner Amy Burnett Gallery, Bremerton, 1991—. Instr. Olympic Coll., Bremerton, 1977-90; lectr. in field. Author: Something About Art, 1977, Nordbee The Norsthing; co-author (pub.): Life Threads Northwest, 1988, Amy's Bremerton Window, 2005; contbr. columns in newspapers. Named Woman of the Yr. YWCA, 1989; recipient Bus. Achievement award Main St. USA, 1992. Mem. Young Womans Christian Assn., Bremerton C. of C., Hood Canal Salmon Enhancement Group. Avocations: bridge, interior design, cooking, art museums, drawing. Office: Amy Burnett Gallery 408 Pacific Ave Bremerton WA 98337-1915

BURNETT, BARBARA DIANE, retired social worker; b. Charleston, W.Va., Aug. 20, 1928; d. LeRoy Sparks and Hallie Catherine (Walker) Montague; m. Clyde Ray Burnett, Sept. 20, 1947 (div. Nov. 1972); children: Beverly O'Reilly, Pamela Hurd, Marcia Montague(dec.), Janet Summers, Craig. BS, U. Wis., 1949; MS, Pa. State U., 1963; MSW, Va. Commonwealth U., 1977. LCSW Fla. Spl. edn. tchr. Palm Beach County Sch. Bd., various locations, 1964-75; social worker Project Peace Elizabeth Falk Found., Boca Raton, Fla., 1977-78; social worker Cmty. Home Health, Boynton Beach, Fla., 1978-90, Hospice Care Broward Inc., Ft. Lauderdale, Fla., 1986-91; pvt. practice supr. MSW profls. Broward County, Fla., 1991—; with Fresenius Med. Care, Ft Lauderdale, Fla., 1997—2005; ret., 2005. Field instr. sch. social work Barry U., 1986—91, Fla. Internat. U., 1986—91, Fla. Atlantic U., 1986—91, Nova U., 1986—91. Crucible jr. hon. U. Wis., 1948, mortar bd. sr. hon., 1949; active Dem. Party, Broward County, 1977—. Named Fla. Renal Social Worker of the Yr., Nat. Kidney Found., Tampa, 1998. Mem.: LWV, Common Cause, Nat. Kidney Found. (coun. nephrology social workers), Am. Assn. Kidney Patients (bd. mem.), Omicron Nu, Phi Lambda Theta. Democrat. Episcopalian. Avocations: reading, walking, swimming, attending grandchildrens special events, travel.

BURNETT, CAROL, actress, comedienne, singer; b. San Antonio, Apr. 26, 1933; d. Jody and Louise (Creighton) B.; m. Joseph Hamilton, 1963 (div.); children: Carrie Louise, Jody Ann, Erin Kate; m. Brian Miller, 2001. Student, UCLA, 1952-54. Introduced comedy song I Made a Fool of Myself Over John Foster Dulles, 1957; Broadway debut in Once Upon a Mattress, 1959; regular performer in Garry Moore TV show, 1959-62; appeared several CBS-TV spls., 1962-63; star Carol Burnett Show, CBS-TV, 1966-77, Carol & Co., 1990-91; appeared on Broadway, Once Upon a Mattress, 1960, Plaza Suite, 1970, I Do, I Do, (musical) 1973, Same Time Next Year, 1977, Moon Over Buffalo, 1995 (Tony nomination), co-wrote play (with Carrie Hamilton), Hollywood Arms, 2001; films include Who's Been Sleeping in My Bed, 1963, Pete 'n' Tillie, 1972, Front Page, 1974, A Wedding, 1977, Health, 1979, Four Seasons, 1981, Chu Chu and the Philly Flash, 1981, Annie, 1982, Noises Off, 1992, Moon Over Broadway, 1997, Get Bruce, 1999, The Trumpet of the Swan (voice), 2001; TV movies Friendly Fire, 1978, The Grass is Always Greener Over the Septic Tank, 1979, The Tenth Month, 1979, Life of the Party, 1982, Between Friends, 1983, Hostage, 1988, Men, Movies, and Carol, 1994, Seasons of the Heart, 1994, The Marriage Fool, 1998 (American Comedy award, 1998), Grace, 1998, Once Upon a Mattress, 2005; club engagements, Harrah's Club, The Sands, Caesar's Palace, MGM Grand; TV specials Julie and Carol: Together Again, 1989, Happy Birthday Elizabeth: A Celebration of Life, 1997, Putting it Together, 2000, Carol Burnett: Show Stoppers, 2001; TV series Mad About You, 1996-1998; TV miniseries Fresno, 1986, A Century of Women, 1994; dir., writer The Universal Story, 1995, also prodr. Southern Star: Portrait of Atlanta, 1996; prodr. Fred Astaire: Puttin' On His Top Hat, 1980, Fred Astaire: Change Partners and Dance, 1980, Bacall on Bogart, 1988, Fred Astaire Songbook, 1991, Southern Star: A Portrait of Atlanta, 1996, others. Recipient outstanding comedienne award Am. Guild Variety Artists, 5 times, Emmy award for outstanding variety performance Acad. TV Arts and Scis., 5 times, Emmy award for best supporting actress in a comedy series for Mad About You, 1997, TV Guide award for outstanding female performer, 1961, 62, 63, Peabody award, 1963, Golden Globe award for outstanding comedienne of year Fgn. Press Assn., 8 times, 12 People's Choice awards, 1st ann. Nat. TV Critics Circle award for outstanding performance, 1977, San Sebastian Film Festival award for best actress for A Wedding, 1978, 1st Ace award Best Actress Between Friends, 1983, Horatio Alger award Horatio Alger Assn. Disting. Ams., 1988, Presdl. Medal of Freedom, The White House, 2005, Career Achievement award, TV Critics Assn., 2006; named One of 20 Most Admired Women Gallup Poll, 1977; named Woman of Year award Acad. TV Arts and Scis. Address: ICM 8942 Wilshire Blvd Fl 2 Beverly Hills CA 90211-1934*

BURNETT, ELIZABETH B., lawyer; b. 1955; married; 2 children. BA, Brown U., 1976; JD cum laude, U. Mich., 1979. Bar: Mass. 1979, US Dist. Ct. (Dist. Mass.), US Ct. Appeals (1st Cir.). Ptnr., chair, Litig. Sect. Mintz Levin Cohn Ferris Glovsky & Popeo PC, Boston. Founding bd. mem. Jane Doe Safety Fund.; bd. dir. NewFund, Greater Boston YMCA; active Brown U. Sports Found. Named a Super Lawyer, Boston Mag. Office: Mintz Levin Cohn Ferris Glovsky & Popeo PC One Financial Ctr Boston MA 02111 Office Phone: 617-348-1613. Office Fax: 617-542-2241. Business E-Mail: eburnett@mintz.com.

BURNETT, IRIS JACOBSON, corporate communications specialist; b. Bklyn., Nov. 14, 1946; d. Milton and Rose (Dubroff) Groman; m. Allan Jacobson; 1 child, Seth Jacobson; m. David Burnett, Jan. 29, 1984; 1 child, Jordan Burnett. BS, Emerson Coll., 1968, MS in Commn. Theory, 1971. Instr. Boston U., 1971-73; dir. press and pub. rels. Dept. Parks and Recreation, Boston, 1975-77; dir. internat. visitors U.S. Dept. State, Washington, 1977-80; dir. security Dem. Nat. Conv., N.Y.C., 1980; sr. v.p. Arrive Unltd., Washington, 1980-84; pres. In Advance, Arlington, 1984-87; asst. prof. Am. U., Washington, 1987-90; pres. Sound Remarks, Arlington, 1990-92; exec. dir. Debates '92, Washington, 1992; chief staff USIA, Washington, 1993-96; sr. v.p for corp. comm. USA Network, N.Y.C., 1997-99; prof. Am. U. Sch. Comm., 1999—. Co-founder, co-chair, pres. Count Mein for Women's Econ. Ind., 2002; pres. Kai Prodns. Author: Hart for Pres., 1984, Nat. Surrogate Schedule, 1984, Inauguration, Transition: Clinton Gore Campaign, 1992, (novels) Schlepper! A Mostly True Tale of Presidential Politics, 2004; prodr.: (documentary) The Gefilte Fish Chronicles. Active McGovern presdl. campaign, Boston, 1972; mem. nat. staff Udall for Pres., Washington, 1974-76, Carter-Mondale '76, 1976-77; bd. dirs. Tap Am. Project, 1994—; official del. 4th World Conf. on Women; bd. gov.'s USO.; founder Broad Confidence in Chair Women; bd. dirs. Erase the Hate Found.; mem. Bretton Woods Com. Named Presdl. appt. to Bd. Govs. USO. Mem. Women's Fgn. Policy Group, Emily's List, Nat. Jewish Dem. Coalition.

BURNETT, JEAN B. (MRS. JAMES R. BURNETT), biochemist; b. Flint, Mich., Feb. 19, 1924; d. Chester M. and Katheryn (Krasser) Bullard; B.S., Mich. State U., 1944, M.S., 1945, Ph.D. (Council fellow), 1952; m. James R. Burnett, June 8, 1947. Research assoc. dept. zoology Mich. State U., East Lansing, 1954-59, dept. biochemistry, 1959-61, acting dir. research biochem. genetics, dept. biochemistry, 1961-62, assoc. prof., asst. chmn. dept. biomechanics, 1973-82, prof. dept. anatomy, 1982-84, prof. dept. zoology, Coll. Natural Sci. and Coll. Osteo. Medicine, 1984—; assoc. biochemist Mass. Gen. Hosp., Boston, 1964-73; prin. research assoc. dermatology Harvard, 1962-73, faculty medicine, 1964-73, also spl. lectr., cons., tutor Med. Sch.; vis. prof. dept. biology U. Ariz., 1979-80. USPHS, NIH grantee, 1965-68; Gen. Research Support grantee Mass. Gen. Hosp., 1968-72; Ford Found. travel grantee, 1973; Am. Cancer Soc. grantee, 1971-73; Internat. Pigment Cell Conf. travel grantee, 1980; recipient Med. Found. award, 1970. Mem. AAAS, Am. Chem. Soc., Am. Inst. Biol. Sci., Genetics Soc. Am., Soc. Investigative Dermatology, N.Y. Acad. Scis., Sigma Xi (Research award 1971), Pi Kappa Delta, Kappa Delta Pi, Pi Mu Epsilon, Sigma Delta Epsilon. Home: PO Box 805 Okemos MI 48805-0805

BURNETT, SUSAN W., academic administrator; d. Vernon I. and Gladys Segal Wides; life ptnr. Jim C. Frishe; m. Donald C. Burnett, Jan. 30, 1971 (dec. May 20, 1991); children: Alison Burnett Nichols, Jennifer Nicole. AA, St. Petersburg Jr. Coll., 1966; BA, U. South Fla., Tampa, 1969, MEd, 1980. HS tchr. Pinellas County Schs., St. Petersburg, 1969—74, 1984—96; tech prep coord. St. Petersburg Coll., St. Petersburg, Fla., 1996—. Sec. bd. trustees Temple Beth-El, St. Petersburg, 1975—80. Mem.: Fla. Assn. Career and Tech. Edn., Assn. Career and Tech. Edn. (awards chmn. 2004—05), Fla. Tech Prep Network (pres. 2000—01), Fla. Assn. Cmty. Colls. Avocations: reading, exercise. Office Phone: 727-3411-3392.

BURNETT, SUSAN WALK, personnel service company owner; b. Galveston, Tex., Aug. 21, 1946; d. Joe Decker and Ruth Corinne (Lowe) Walk; m. Rusty Burnett, Dec. 27, 1973; stepchildren: Barbara, Sara. BA in Journalism, U. Ark., Fayetteville, 1968. Asst. pub. rels. mgr. Sta. KATV, Little Rock, 1968-69; speech writer Assoc. Milk Producers, Inc., Little Rock, 1969-70; mgr. Allied Personnel, Houston, 1970-74; owner, pres. Burnett Pers. Svcs., Houston, 1974—. Exec. bd. dirs. Arthritis Found.; bd. dirs. Goodwill, Better Bus. Bur. Recipient Appreciation awards Lyndon Johnson Space Ctr., NASA, 1983, State of Tex., 1984, Top Houston Woman Bus. Owner award Nat. Assn. Women Bus. Owners, 1996, Blue Chip award U.S. C. of C., Philanthrophy award Houston Bus. Jour., Better Bus. Bur. Pinnacle award, 2006; named one of 10 Women on the Move in Houston, Houston Chronicle, 1996, Most Outstanding Woman in Bus. YWCA, 1997, Entrepreneur of Yr., Ernst & Young, 1998; named 2001 Woman Bus. Entrepreneur, Women's Bus. Enterprise Alliance; named to 2000 Women of Excellence, Women's Enterprise. Mem.: Am. Staffing Assn. (bd. dirs.), Houston Assn. Pers. Cons. (v.p. 1985, pres. 1986, Outstanding Contbn. to Placement Industry and Cmty. award 1995), Tex. Assn. Pers. Cons. (v.p. 1985), Nat. Assn. Pers. Cons., Chi Omega Alumnae. Avocations: reading, golf, travel. Office: Burnett Staffing Specialists Inc 9800 Richmond Ave Ste 800 Houston TX 77042-4548

BURNETTE, ADA M. PURYEAR, program coordinator; b. Darlington, SC; d. Theodore and Floia (King) Peoples; m. Paul Lionel Puryear, March 27, 1954 (div. 1975); children: Paul Lionel, Jr., Paula Lynn. BA in Math., Talladega Coll., 1953; postgrad., Chgo. State U., 1954-56; MA in Reading, U. Chgo., 1958; PhD, Fla. State U., 1986; postgrad., Fla. A&M U., 1994, Oxford U., 2005. High sch. math tchr., Winston-Salem, NC, 1953-54; elem. tchr. Chgo. Pub. Schs., 1954-58; reading clinician U. Chgo., 1958; dir. reading clinic, asst. prof. Norfolk State U., 1958-61, Tuskegee Inst., 1961-66; coord. freshman math., asst. prof. math. Fisk U., 1966-70; adminstr. early childhood basic skills and elem. edn. State of Fla. Dept. Edn., Tallahassee, 1973-88; assoc. prof., program dir., grad. studies dir. Bethune-Cookman Coll., Daytona Beach, Fla., 1988-90; dir., supt. Fla. A&M U. Devel. Rsch. Pub. Sch. Dist., Tallahassee, 1990-93; coord., prof., dept. chmn., dir. PhD program devel. Fla. A&M U., 1993-98, coord., prof., 1998—2003, prof., dir. Robert H. Anderson Ednl. Leadership Libr., 1998—2003, prof. emerita, 2003—; assoc. prof., coord. off campus programs Valdosta State U., 2005—. Hostess radio talk show, 1977—79; sec.-treas. Afro-Am. Rsch. Assocs., 1968—74; tutor, diagnostician, lectr., cons., planner, 1958—; cons. Job Corps, N.C. Advancement Sch., pub. co.; lectr. univ. classes; trustee Fla. A&M U., 2003, pres. faculty senate, 1999—2003, adj. prof., 2003—05. Regular columnist profl. jours., 1974—; writer grants proposals; weekly columnist Capital Outlook, 1991-97; contbr. articles to profl. publs. Pres. PTA, 1975—76, v.p., 1983—84; edn. commentator Sta. WFSU, 1993—94; mem. United Fund com., Leon County 4C Bd.; pres. Norfolk Women's Interracial Coun., 1960; mem. Dem. Exec. Com. Leon County, 1981—88, 1991—93; deacon Presbyn. Ch., 1981—2004, AME ch. grief chmn., 2004—; bd. dirs. Tallahassee Coalition for the Homeless, 2002—, sec., 2004—. Mem.: AAUW (regional dir. 2003—, pres. Tallahassee chpt. 2005—, dir. Fla. 2005—), Am. Acad. Cert. Pub. Mgmt., Fla. Assn. Cert. Pub. Mng. NF (bd. dirs. 2004—), Nat. Assn. African Am. Studies (coord. 1999—), Fla. Soc. Cert. Pub. Mgrs. (newsletter bd., pres. North Fla. chpt. 2004, pres. North Fla. chpt. 2004—, state bd. 2004—), Am. Assn. Sch. Adminstrs., Socs. Docta Inc. (co-founder, sec. 1987—93), So. Assn. Colls. and Schs. (elem. and mid. sch. commn.), Assn. Childhood Edn. Internat., Leon Assn. Children Under Six (pres. 1977), So. Assn. Children Under Six, Fla. Assn. Children Under Six, Nat. Assn. Edn. Young Children, Nat. Assn. Elem. Sch. Prins., Internat. Reading Assn. (pres. Concerned Educators Black Students 1983—86, nat. early childhood com., nat. textbook com., libr./media com., nat. med. com., nat. awards com., nat. media com.), Fla. ASCD (regional dir. policy rev. jour. editl. bd. 1995—), Alliance of Black Sch. Educators, Assn. State Cons. on Early Childhood Edn., Fla. State Reading Assn., Fla. Coun. Elem. Edn., Fla. Assn. Suprs. and Adminstrs., The Holidays (nat. sec. fin. 1993—97, nat. v.p. 1997—2001, nat. pres. 2001—, chpt. pres.), Drifters (nat. membership chmn. 1977—79, Nat. Now Black Woman 1984, historian, reporter 1992—94, pres. 1994—99, cluster coord. 2000—), FAMU Ladies Art and Social Club (pres.), Alpha Kappa Alpha (treas., summer sch. dir., undergrad. adv., parliamentarian, sec.), Pi Lambda Theta, Phi Kappa Phi (pres. 1985—86, v.p. pub. rels. chair), Phi Delta Kappa (advisor 2004—). Home: PO Box 1513 Valdosta GA 31603 Office: Valdosta State U 1800 N Patterson St Valdosta GA 31698 Office Phone: 229-333-5622. Personal E-mail: draburnette@wmconnect.com. Business E-Mail: amburnette@valdosta.edu.

BURNHAM, SHANNON L., elementary school educator; b. Warner Robins, Ga., Jan. 14, 1980; d. Randall H. and Dialphia T. Lanier; m. Benjamin Joshua Burnham, June 29, 2002. BS in Mid. Grades Edn., Ga. So. U., Statesboro, 2002. Tchr. Bonaire Mid. Sch., Ga., 2002—. Mem., youth councilor, adminstrv. bd. Eastman First United Meth. Ch., 2002—06; mem. Ga. So. Wesley Found., Statesboro, 2006. Mem.: Ga. Coun. Tchrs. Math.

BURNLEY, JUNE WILLIAMS, secondary school educator; b. St. Augustine, Fla., Mar. 13, 1936; d. Marcellus Henry Gilford and Ella (Broadus) Williams. BS, N.C. Agrl. and Tech. State U., 1958; MA, Villanova U., 1975, St. John's Coll., Annapolis, Md., 1993; student, Oxford U., London, 1995. Cert. English tchr., counseling psychologist. Grade sch. tchr., 1958-59; lang. arts supr. Wharton Ctr., Phila., 1967-68; English/French lang. tchr. Hatch. Jr. H.S., Camden, NJ, 1962-68; English tchr. George Washington H.S., Phila., 1968-93, secondary counseling intern, 1975. Mem. Pa. State Coun. English Tchrs., 1968-93, Educators to Africa, Phila., 1993-97; tutor Temple-New Career Ladders, 1975-76. Mem. Germantown Civic League, Phila., 1993, West Mt. Airy Neighbors, Phila., 1968—, Social Action Com., Phila., 1993-95, Germantown Hist. Soc., Unitarian Soc. Germantown; vol. guide in tng. Phila. Mus. Art, 1996—. Pa. State Bd. Edn. fellow, 1985, Arco & Exxon fellow, 1991, St. John's Coll. fellow, 1992-93. Fellow Commonwealth Partnership; mem. Nat. Coun. English Tchrs. (Svc. award 1972), Eleanor Trailor Readers (co-founder), Literary Group (founder), Literati (founder), Amnesty Internat., Phi Delta Kappa, Delta Sigma Theta. Avocations: reading, knitting, sewing, word games, travel. Home: 700 Elkins Ave Apt E3 Elkins Park PA 19027-2315 Personal E-mail: alithaevol@aol.com.

BURNS, AMY MARGARET, music educator; d. Robert W. and Ruth H. Willis; m. Christopher R. Burns, June 26, 1999. B in Music Edn./Performance, Ithaca Coll., Ithaca, N.Y., 1995; MS in Music Edn., Ctrl. Conn. State U., New Britain, Conn., 2006. Technology Institute for Music Educators (TI:ME) Level 1 Tech. Inst. for Music Educators (TI:ME), 2001, Technology Institute for Music Educators (TI:ME) Level 2 Tech. Inst. for Music Educators (TI:ME), 2004, Orff-Schulwerk Level 1 Am. Orff-Schulwerk Assn. (AOSA), 2001. Music educator Musically Yours, Millburn, NJ, 1996—97; pvt. flute and clarinet instr. Mendham, NJ, 1996—; music educator for grades prekindergarten through three Far Hills Country Day Sch., Far Hills, NJ, 1997—, founder, dir. philharm., 1998—2006, founder, dir. conservatory, 2002—04. Com. mem. NJ. Assn. Ind. Schs., Edison, NJ, 2002—04; presenter in field. Author: (lesson plans) Nine Lesson Plans that Integrate Technology into the Music Classroom; contbr. articles pub. tro profl. jour. Recipient Tchr. of the Yr., Tech. Inst. for Music Educators (TI:ME), 2005. Mem.: NJ. Music Educators Assn., Music Educators Nat. Coun., Tech. Inst. Music Educators. Home: PO Box 612 Far Hills NJ 07931 Office: Far Hills Country Day Sch Rt 202/ Box 8 Far Hills NJ 07931 Office Phone: 908-766-0622 484. Personal E-mail: awillis2@aol.com.

BURNS, ANGELA KAYE, secondary school educator; d. Thomas George and Grace Burns. B, Sam Houston State U., Huntsville, Tex., 2001. Cert. tchr. State of Tex., 2002. Tchr. h.s. Humble Ind. Sch. Dist., Tex., 2001—. Grantee, Humble Edn. Found., 2005. Mem.: Tex. Coun. Social Studies, Assn. Tex. Profl. Educators. Liberal-Conservative. Avocation: travel. Office: Humble ISD 1301 Wilson Road Humble TX 77388 Office Phone: 281-641-6078. E-mail: angela.burns@humble.k12.tx.us.

BURNS, BARBARA BELTON, investment company executive; b. Fredericktown, Mo., Dec. 10, 1944; d. Clyde Monroe and Mary Celestial (Anderson) Belton; m. Larry J. Bohannon; Mar. 27, 1963 (div.); 1 child, Timothy Joseph; m. Donald Edward Burns, Nov. 1, 1980; stepchildren: Brian Edward, David Keone (dec.). Student, Ohio State U., 1970-75. Dir. nat. sales Am. Way, Chgo., 1976-77; recruiter Bell & Howell Schs., Columbus, Ohio, 1978-80; pres., founder Bardon Investment Corp., Naples, Fla., 1980-90; founder Cambridge Mgmt. Co., Columbus, 1983-86; pres., CEO Charter's Total Wardrobe Care, Columbus, 1984-89; founder, exec. Phoenix Bus. Group, Inc., 1990—; founder, pres. Celestial Group Inc., Las Vegas, 1999—; pres., Bondtech Direct Nutraceuticals, 2002—. Treas. Vicace-Columbus Symphony, 1981—82; fundraiser Grant Hosp., Columbus, 1986; chmn. Impresarios/Opera Columbus, 1986—87; founding mem. Columbus Women's Bd., 1986—87; mem. devel. com. Babe Zaharias/Am. Cancer Soc.; auction chmn. Opera Ball-Opera/Columbus, 1989; tennis tournament chmn. NABOR Scholarship Fund, 1990—91; mem. Philharm. Chorale, Naples, Fla., 1992, First Presbyn. of Las Vegas Chancel Choir, 1998—; spokesman Diabetes Found. Collier County, Fla., 1992—, pres. Fla., 1994, Diabetes Found., 1994—; pres. CEO Bond Direct NutraCeuticals; elder Vanderbilt Presbyn. Ch., 1994; mem. Jubilee Gospel Singers, 2005—. Named Entrepreneur of Yr. Arthur Young/Venture mag., 1988, Outstanding Vol. Opera Columbus, 1986, Vol. of Yr. Diabetes Found., 1994; recipient Design award Reynoldsburg C. of C., 1988. Mem. Naples C. of C. (new bus. com. 1990—), Las Vegas C. of C. Republican. Avocations: tennis, boating, travel, music. Office Phone: 702-281-0780. Business E-Mail: info@bondtechdirect.net.

BURNS, B(ILLYE) JANE, museum director; b. Yeager, Okla., Nov. 1, 1940; d. William O. and Berniece (Floyd) French; m. Richard D. Burns, June 12, 1960 (div. 1990); children: Jennifer, Richard, Timothy, Daniel. AS, Okla. State U., 1960; BA in Bus., Goshen Coll., 1988. Treas. Woodlawn Nature Coun., Inc., Elkhart, Ind., 1975-82; cons. Am. art Midwest Mus. Am. Art, Elkhart, 1978-81, founding trustee, 1978—, dir., 1980—2003. Cons. Heritage Fine Arts, Elkhart; bd. dirs. Key Bank. Mem. Woodlaw Nature Coun., Inc., Elkhart, 4-Arts Club, Elkhart, Ind. Advs. for Art, Elkhart County Symphony; bd. dirs. No. Ind. Partnership Arts, 1997—, Elkhart Ctr., 1997—, Ind. U. Arts Found.; mem. Hoosier Millennium Com., 1999—. Mem. LWV (bd. dirs. 1985-2003, v.p. 1990-2003), Michiana Arts and Scis. Coun., Concert Club. Democrat. Methodist. Avocations: collecting art, antiques, skiing, curling, travel. Home: 300 E Stratford Pl Elkhart IN 46516 Office: MW Mus Am Art 429 S Main St Elkhart IN 46516-3210 Office Phone: 574-293-6660. E-mail: bjbfrench@aol.com.

BURNS, CASSANDRA STROUD, prosecutor; b. Lynchburg, Va., May 22, 1960; d. James Wesley and Jeanette Lou (Garner) Stroud; m. Stephen Burns; children: Leila Jeanette, India Veronica. BA, U. Va., 1982; JD, N.C. Cen. U., 1985; MBA candidate, Regis U., 2005. Bar: Va. 1986, N.J. 1986, U.S. Dist. Ct. (ea. dist.) Va. 1987, U.S. Ct. Appeals (4th cir.) 1987, U.S. Bankruptcy Ct. (ea. dist.) Va. 1987; cert. in criminal law. Law clk. Office Atty. Gen. State of Va., Richmond, summer 1984; law intern Office Dist. Atty. State of N.C., Durham, 1985; staff atty. Tidewater Legal Aid Soc., Chesapeake, Va., 1987-89; asst. atty. Commonwealth of Va., Petersburg, 1989-90; assoc. atty. Bland and Stroud, Petersburg, 1990; asst. pub. defender City of Petersburg, 1990-91, Commonwealth's atty. Va., 1991—; adj. prof. Va. Commonwealth U., 2003, Va. State U., 2004—. Founder BED Task Force on Babies Exposed to Drugs, 1991, Buddies of Petersburg Program, 1997—. Sec. Chesapeake Task Force Coun. on Youth Svcs., 1987-89; ch. directress and organist; mem. NAACP; chair Petersburg-Dinwiddie Cmty. Criminal Justice Bd.; bd. dirs. Mary Carter Beacon House, 2004—; mem. leadership coun. United Way, 2004—. Mem. Va. Bar Assn. (mem. coun. 1993-99), Old Dominion Bar Assn., Va. Assn. Commonwealth Attys. (bd. dirs., mem. coun. 1993-2000), Legal Svcs. Corp. Va. (bd. dirs.), Nat. Bd. Trial Advocacy (cert.), Nat. Dist. Attys. Assn., Southside Va. Legal Aid Soc. (bd. dirs.), Petersburg Bar Assn., Nat. Black Prosecutors Assn. (regional dir.), Petersburg Jaycees, Order Eastern Star, Peterburg C. of C., Kiwanis, Internat., Buddies Club, Phi Alpha Delta, Alpha Kappa Alpha. Democrat. Baptist. Avocations: piano, organ, volleyball, needlework, pets. Home: 326 N Park Dr Petersburg VA 23805-2442 Office: Commonwealth's Atty 150 N Sycamore St Petersburg VA 23803 Office Phone: 804-861-8899. E-mail: bossyda@aol.com.

BURNS, CATHERINE L., lawyer; b. 1970; BS cum laude, Boston U., 1994; JD cum laude, Suffolk U., 1997. Bar: Mass. 1998. Sr. assoc. Seyfarth Shaw LLP, Boston. Mem.: New England Women in Real Estate, Women's Bar Assn., ABA, Mass. Bar Assn., Boston Bar Assn. Office: Seyfarth Shaw LLP World Trade Center East Two Seaport Lane Ste 300 Boston MA 02210-2028 Office Phone: 617-946-4972. Office Fax: 617-946-4801. E-mail: cburns@seyfarth.com.*

BURNS, CLARE MARIE, retired elementary school educator; b. Providence, Aug. 31, 1953; d. Eugene Joseph and Virginia Louise Trainor; m. Thomas Joseph Burns, Apr. 26, 1980. AA, C.C. R.I., Warwick, 1974; BA, R.I. Coll., Providence, 1976, M, 1999. Cert. reading specialist - cons. RI, 1999. First grade tchr. St. James Sch., West Warwick, RI, 1982—90, Blessed Sacrament Sch., Providence, 1990—99; reading specialist Globe Pk. Elem. Sch., Woonsocket, 1999—2002; first grade tchr. Woonsocket Sch. Dept., 2002—04; ret., 2004. Vol. Dysart Unified Sch. Dist., Surprise, Ariz., 2006—. Named Wal-Mart Tchr. of Yr., 1999. Home: 17109 W Ironwood St Surprise AZ 85388-1246

BURNS, DORIS ELEANOR, retired elementary school educator; b. Phila., Pa., June 7, 1934; d. Alfred Carmen and Eleanor Mi Bilotta; m. Raymond C. Baileau (div.); children: JeanAnne, Philip, Debbie, Patti. BS, U. Pa. 4th grade tchr. Cheltenham Twp., Pa., 1955—59; 2d grade tchr. Interboro Twp., Prospect Pk., Pa., 1959—60; tchr. Phila. Sch. Dist., 1975—88. Chmn. study group L.W.V., Carlsbad, Calif., 2005—06. Avocations: travel, reading, cooking, movies, baseball. Home: 1937 Dove Lane #203 Carlsbad CA 92009

BURNS, DRUSILLA LORENE, microbiologist; b. Manhattan, Kans., Feb. 14, 1953; BS in Chemistry, Tulane U., 1975; PhD, U. Calif., Berkeley, 1980. Fellow lab cellular metabolism NIH, 1980-84; from sr. fellow to rsch. chemist FDA Ctr. for Biologics Evaluation and Rsch., Bethesda, 1984-94, chief lab. pertussis, 1994-99, chief lab. respiratory and spl. pathogens, 1999—. Ad hoc reviewer in field. Mem. editl. bd. Infection and Immunity, 1989-98, Jour. Biol. Chemistry, 1995-2000; editor Infection and Immunity, 1998—; contbr. articles to profl. jours. Recipient Am. Inst. Chemists award, 1975, FDA Commrs. Spl. Citation, 1989. Mem. AAAS, Am. Acad. Microbiology, Am. Soc. Microbiology (internat. activities com., pub. and sci. affairs bd. 1989-92, councilor divsn. B 1999), Phi Beta Kappa. Achievements include patents for process for isolation of the B oligomer of pertussis toxin; process for the purification of a 69,000 da outer membrane protein of Bordetella pertussis. Office: Ctr for Biologics Eval 8800 Rockville Pike Bldg 29 Bethesda MD 20892-0001 Business E-Mail: drusilla.burns@fda.hhs.gov.

BURNS, SISTER ELIZABETH MARY, retired hospital administrator; b. Estherville, Iowa, Mar. 3, 1927; d. Bernard Aloysius and Viola Caroline (Brennan) B. Diploma in Nursing, St. Joseph Mercy Sch. Nursing, Sioux City, Iowa, 1952; BS in Nursing Edn, Mercy Coll., Detroit, 1957; M.Sc. in Nursing, Wayne State U., 1958; Ed.D., Columbia U., 1969. Joined Sisters of Mercy, Roman Cath. Ch., 1946; nursing supr. Mercy Med. Ctr., Dubuque, Iowa, 1952-55; supr. orthopedics and urology St. Joseph Mercy Hosp., Sioux City, 1955-56; dir. Sch. Nursing, 1958-63; chmn. dept. nursing Mercy Coll. of Detroit, 1963-73; dir. health svcs. Sisters of Mercy, 1973-77; pres., CEO Marian Health Ctr., Sioux City, 1977-87; sabbatical leave, 1988; ret., 2006. Coord. life planning Sisters of Mercy, 1989-90, mem. province adminstrv. team, 1990-98; cons. Trinity Health, 2001—. Bd. dirs. Mercy Sch. Nursing of Detroit, 1968-77, Mercy H.S., Farmington Hills, Mich., 2000-05; mem. exec. com. Greater Detroit Area Hosp. Coun., 1973-77; trustee St. Mary Coll., Omaha, 1981-82, Briar Cliff Coll., Sioux City, 1981-87, Battle Creek Health Sys., 1998-2000, 02-04, Mercy Med. Ctr., Sioux City, Iowa, 2001-05; chmn. Mercy Health Adv. Coun., 1978-80. Mem. Western Iowa League for Nursing (pres. 1960-62), Nat. League for Nursing, Sisters of Mercy Shared Svcs. Coordinating Com., Cath. Hosp. Assn. (trustee 1977-80), Sisters of Mercy Health Corp. (trustee 1988-90, governance coord. 1998-2001), Mercy Health Svcs. (chair bd. 1990-95, membership bd. 1995-98, historian 1998-2004). Address: 28554 Eleven Mile Farmington MI 48336-1507 Business E-Mail: eburns@mercydetroit.org.

BURNS, ELIZABETH MCMAHON, dairy scientist, psychologist; b. Chattanooga, Tenn., Nov. 9, 1953; d. Everett Keith McMahon and Martha L. Grahm. BA, U. Ga., 1975; MA, U. Colo., 1992; PhD, U. Nebr., 2002. Asst. program dir. Valley Hope Assn., Parker, Colo., 2000—02, program dir. Bronville, Mo., 2002—. Contbr. articles to profl. jours. Mem.: APA. Avocations: dog training, travel, photography. Office: Valley Hope Assn 1415 Ashley Rd Boonville MO 65233

BURNS, ELIZABETH MURPHY, media executive; b. Superior, Wis., Dec. 4, 1945; d. Morgan and Elizabeth (Beck) Murphy; m. Richard Ramsey Burns, June 24, 1984. Student, U. Ariz., 1963-67. Promotion and programming sec. Sta. KGUN-TV, Tucson, 1967-68; programming and traffic sec. Sta. KFMB-TV, San Diego, 1968-69; owner, operator Sta. KKAR, Pomona, Calif., 1970-73; co-owner, pres. Evening Telegram Co. (parent co. Murphy Stas.); pres. Morgan Murphy Stas., Madison, Wis., 1976—. Bd. dirs. Nat. Guardian Life Ins. Co., Republic Bank, Nat. Assn. Broadcasters, various media stas. and corps. Mem. Wis. Broadcasters Assn., Madison Club, Northland Country Club (Duluth), Boulders Country Club (Carefree, Ariz.), Bishop's Bay Country Club, Silverleaf Golf Club (Scottsdale, Ariz.). Roman Catholic. Avocations: golf, travel. Home: 180 Paine Farm Rd Duluth MN 55804-2609 Office: Sta WISC-TV 7025 Raymond Rd Madison WI 53719-5053 Personal E-mail: emb@embtv.com.

BURNS, ELLEN BREE, federal judge; b. New Haven, Conn., Dec. 13, 1923; d. Vincent Thomas and Mildred Bridget (Bannon) Bree; m. Joseph Patrick Burns, Oct. 8, 1955 (dec.); children: Mary Ellen, Joseph Bree, Kevin James. BA, Albertus Magnus Coll., 1944, LLD (hon.), 1974; LLB, Yale U., 1947; LLD (hon.), U. New Haven, 1981, Sacred Heart U., 1986, Fairfield U., 1991. Bar: Conn. 1947. Dir. legis. legal svcs. State of Conn., 1949-73; judge Conn. Cir. Ct., 1973-74, Conn. Ct. of Common Pleas, 1974-76, Conn. Superior Ct., 1976-78, U.S. Dist. Ct. Conn., New Haven, 1978—, chief judge, 1988-92, sr. judge, 1992—. Trustee Fairfield U., 1978-85, Albertus Magnus Coll., 1985—. Recipient John Carroll of Carrollton award John Barry Council K.C., 1973, Judiciary award Conn. Trial Lawyers Assn., 1978, Cross Pro Ecclesia et Pontifice, 1981, Law Rev. award U. Conn. Law Rev., 1987, Judiciary award Conn. Bar Assn., 1987, Raymond E. Baldwin Pub. Svc. award Bridgeport Law Sch., 1992. Mem.: ABA, Conn. Bar Found., Conn. Bar Assn., New Haven County Bar Assn., Am. Bar Found. Roman Catholic. Office: US Dist Ct 141 Church St New Haven CT 06510-2030

BURNS, ELLEN JEAN, distance education administrator; b. Memphis, Sept. 1, 1953; d. Eugene Harold and Elizabeth Josephine Burns; m. Daniel Bruce Eisenberg, July 25, 1986. BM, BME, U. Memphis, 1976; MSLS, U. Tenn., 1977; MM, Fla. State U., 1982, PhD, 1994. Asst. prof. Ala. State U., Montgomery, 1991-92; instr. Fla. State U., London, 1994, asst. prof. Tallahassee, Fla., 1994-95; instr., asst. prof. Northern Ariz. U., Flagstaff, 1996-98; dir. DistanceLearn Regents Coll., Albany, 1999—. Editor: Texts on Texts and Textuality, 1999; editor H-Net, 1993—; clarinet soloist Germantown Symphony Orch., 1979; clarinet recitalist Ballet South, 1981, La Camara transatlantica, 1995. Recipient Young Artist award Beethoven Club, 1980. Mem. Am. Musicol. Soc., Am. Soc. of Aesthetics, Lyrica Soc. for Word-Music Rels. (v.p. 1996-98, pres. 1998-2000, assoc. editor 1984-94), Phi Eta Sigma (hon.), Pi Kappa Lambda. Avocation: taoist tai chi.

BURNS, ERICA MARIE, orthopedist, surgeon; b. Enterprise, Ala., Sept. 23, 1976; d. John Fredrick and Sandra Ann Timm; m. Chad Christopher Burns, July 7, 2000. BA, Ctrl. Wash. U., Ellensburg, 1999; MD, Creighton U., Omaha, 2004. Resident U. Nebr., Omaha, 2004—. Mem.: Ruth Jackson Orthopaedic Soc., Alpha Omega Alpha. Roman Catholic. Avocations: volleyball, travel, piano, baking. Home: 3309 S 44th St Omaha NE 68105

BURNS, ERIN CATHLEEN, lawyer; b. Lancaster, Pa., Aug. 10, 1977; d. Francis Patrick Burns, Jr. and Sara Louise Burns. BA, U. of Del., Newark, 1999; JD, Villanova U., Villanova, Pa., 2002. Bar: Pa. 2002, U.S. Dist. Ct. (ea. dist.) Pa. 2003, U.S. Ct. Appeals (D.C. cir.) 2005. Law clk. to the hon. Louis J. Farina Lancaster County Ct. of Common Pleas, Lancaster, Pa., 2002—04; assoc. RodaNast, P.C., Lancaster, 2004—. Leader Law Explorers Post Learning for Life, Lancaster, 2004—06. Mem.: ATLA, ABA, Lancaster Bar Assn. (chair Young Lawyers sect. 2005, bd. dir. 2005, pres., Pres.'s award 2005), Pa. Bar Assn. Office: RodaNast PC 801 Estelle Dr Lancaster PA 17603 Office Phone: 717-892-3000. Office Fax: 717-892-1200. E-mail: eburns@rodanast.com.

BURNS, JUDITH O'DELL, library assistant, educator; b. Lenoir, NC, May 28, 1941; d. James Horace and Mary Douglas O'Dell; m. David Capps Creech, Apr. 2, 1989 (div.); children: Laurel Anne, Mary Carolynn. MusB, Greensboro Coll., 1963; certificate in Edn., Sacred Heart Coll., 1976; student, Appalachian State U., 1988—94. Cert. Educator K-6 NC, 1976. Tchr. Gaston County Schs., Gastonia, NC, 1976—87; presch. coord. Watauga County Schs., 1990—94; tchr. Gaston County Schs., 1994—2000; libr. asst. Gaston County Pub. Libr., 2001—. Piano & voice instr., Gastonia, 1964—; parent counselor, Gastonia, 1994—; cons. Watauga County Children's Coun., 1990—, pres., Boone, NC, 1988—94; mem. Watauga County Interagy. Bd., Boone, 1990—94. Singer; author: various parent handbooks, 1990—94, poetry and short stories. Sec. Gastonia Dist. United Meth. Women, 2002—06; nat. del. Pioneer Girl Scout Coun., Gastonia, 2002; pres. Nat. Assn. Edn. of Young Children, Boone, 1990—91, Christ Ch. United Meth. Women, Gastonia, 2001—02; choir dir. various chs., Gastonia, 1965—82; founder, dir. Christ United Meth. Ch. After Sch. Care, Gastonia, 2000. Mem.: AAUW, Gaston County Friends of Libr. (v.p. 2000—01, com. chmn. 2000—01), Sharps & Flats Music Club (former pres., com. chmn.). Methodist. Avocations: writing, reading, needlecrafts, music, walking. Home: 855 Nottingham Dr #65 Gastonia NC 28054

BURNS, KARA ALLYN, education educator; b. Birmingham, Ala., Mar. 15, 1980; d. Robert Starr and Gloria Langford Allyn; m. Micheal Woodrow Burns. BEd, U. Missouri, Columbia, 2002. Cert. tchr. Mo., 2002. Instr. St. Louis CC, 2004—, ednl. asst., 2004—. Youth group adult vol. Meml. Presbyn. Ch., St. Louis, 2003—06. R-Consevative. Presbyterian. Home: 2745 Old Hanley Rd Saint Louis MO 63114 Office: St Louis CC 5600 Oakland Ave Saint Louis MO 63110 Office Phone: 314-644-9915. Personal E-mail: knmb323@hotmail.com. Business E-Mail: kaburns@stlcc.edu.

BURNS, KATHLEEN ADLEY, educational consultant; b. Boston, Mass., Apr. 17, 1947; d. Edward Myles and Marguerite Frances (Garten) Adley; m. Thomas Michael Burns, June 30, 1973; 1 child, Bridget Michaela. BEd, Framingham State Coll., 1970; MEd, Univ. Mass., Boston, Mass., 1975; MEd summa cum laude, Salem State Coll., Salem, Mass., 1999. Cert. tchr., guidance counselor, guidance dir., prin. Tchr. Burlington Pub. sch., Burlington, Mass., 1970—85, guidance counselor, 1985—90, asst. prin., 1993—2002, prin., 2002—. Exec. bd. mem. Burlington Educators Assn., Burlington, Mass., 1975—82; sec. Burlington Sch. Adminstrn. Assn., Burlington, Mass., 1995—2000. Recipient Svc. award. Democrat. Roman Cath. Avocations: golf, photography, travel, sports, theater. Business E-Mail: burns@burlington.mec.edu.

BURNS, KATHLEEN DEMEO, art and photography educator; d. Louis Michael DeMeo and Joan Irene Sichler; m. Robert Lewis Burns, 1985; children: Mary-Kate, Noelle. BFA, U. Bridgeport, Conn., 1977; MA, C.W. Post U., N.Y., 1985. Art/photo instr. St. John the Baptist D.H.S., West Islip, NY, 1979—. Asst. leader Girl Scouts, 2002—. Mem.: Nat. Art Edn. Assn., Nat. Art Honor Soc. (moderator 1995—). Avocations: bicycling, photography. Office: St John the Baptist DHS 1170 Montauk Hwy West Islip NY 11795 Office Phone: 631-587-8000 ext. 201.

BURNS, KITTY, playwright; b. Chgo., Feb. 1, 1951; d. Joseph Lewis and Evelyn Marian (Smith) B. Creator Vampire Trous, LLC. Author: (plays) Terminal Terror, 1991 (Silver award San Mateo Playwriting Contest 1991), Psycho Night at the Paradise Lounge, 1994, If God Wanted Us to Fly He Would Have Given Us Wings!, 1996; pub. Samuel French, Inc.; creator, performer The Vampire Tour of San Francisco. Mem.: Dramatists Guild. Avocations: writing children's books, poetry, short stories, acting, horseback riding. Office Phone: 650-279-1840. E-mail: sfvamptour@yahoo.com.

BURNS, LINDA D., elementary school educator; b. Sapulpa, Okla., Oct. 1, 1948; d. Leonard Leo and Frances Jordan Dyer; m. John Thomas Burns; 1 child, Malinda. BA, McNeese State U., 1972, M, 1974, postgrad., 1976. Bd. dirs. Sch. Employees of Allen Parish Credit Union, 1988—94. Relay for Life chair Am. Cancer Soc., Oakdale, La., 2005; mem. Friends of Glenmora Libr., 2004—. Recipient Award of Merit for Regional Publs., Antique Automobile Club Am., 2002, 2003, 2004, 2005, Nike award, L.A. Bus. Profl. Women Club, 2005. Mem.: ASCD, La. Fedn. Bus. and Profl. Women (exec. bd. mem.

2000—, pres. 2003—04), Oakdale Bus. Profl. Women Club (Woman of Yr. award 1985), Cenla Old Car Club, Bus. Profl. Women Club USA (bd. dirs. 2003—04). Home: 1424 Evangeline Rd Glenmora LA 71433

BURNS, M. MICHELE, human resources company executive; b. Rincon, Ga. B in bus. adminstrn. summa cum laude, U. Ga., M. Accountancy. Mgmt. Arthur Anderson, 1981-84, mgr., 1984-91, ptnr., 1991-99; v.p. corp. taxes, treas. Delta Airlines, 1999, sr. v.p. fin., treas., 2000, exec. v.p., CFO, 2000—04; exec. v.p., CFO, chief restructuring officer Mirant Corp., Atlanta, 2004—06; exec. v.p., CFO Marsh & McLennan Companies, Inc., NYC, 2006, chmn., Mercer Human Resource Consulting, 2006—. Bd. dirs. Wal-Mart Stores Inc., 2003—, Cisco Systems, Inc., Ivan Allen Co., Atlanta Symphony Orch. Recipient Distinguished Alumna award, U. of Ga. Terry Coll. of Bus., 1993. Office: Marsh & McLennan Companies Inc 1166 Avenue of the Americas New York NY 10036-2774*

BURNS, MARCELLINE, retired psychologist, researcher; BA in Psychology, San Diego State U., 1955; MA, Calif. State U., L.A., 1969; PhD, U. Calif., Irvine, 1972. Co-founder So. Calif. Rsch. Inst., LA, 1973—2003, ret., 2003. Cons., expert witness alcohol and drug effects on performance, FSTs, HGN, and drug recognition; lectr. in field. Contbr. articles to profl. jours. Recipient Public Svc. award U.S. Dept. Trans., 1993. Achievements include research on alcohol and drug effects, field sobriety tests and drug recognition. Office Phone: 805-382-4696. Business E-Mail: mburns4430@adelphia.net.

BURNS, MARIAN LAW, human resources specialist, legal association administrator; b. Pa., Jan. 10, 1954; d. Vincent Charles and Agatha M. Law; m. Lawrence Joseph Burns, Sept. 29, 1979; children: Peter Andrew, Rita Marie. Paralegal, legal sec. Tuso & Gruccio, Vineland, NJ, 1972—74; legal sec. Swartz, Campbell & Detweiler, Phila., 1974—80; adminstrv. mgr. Drinker Biddle & Reath (formerly Smith, Lambert, Hicks & Beidler, P.C.), Princeton, NJ, 1980—88; legal adminstr. Sherr, Joffe & Zuckerman, P.C., West Conshohocken, Pa., 1988—90, Groen, Laveson, Goldberg & Rubenstone, Bensalem, Pa., 1990—99; v.p. adminstrn. Brintnall & Nicolini, Inc., Phila., 1999—. Adj. prof. paralegal program Bucks County Cmty. Coll. Newtown, Pa. 1998—99, mem. paralegal studies adv. com., 1996-99. Mem.: Independence Chpt. Assn. Legal Adminstr. (sec. 1991—93, pres.-elect 1993—95, pres. 1995—96, founding mem.), Soc. Human Resources Mgmt., Train Ladies Investment Club (pres. 2006—), WWF Investment Club (pres. 2004—05). Office: Brintnall & Nicolini Inc 1880 JFK Blvd 16th Fl Philadelphia PA 19103 Business E-Mail: marian.burns@brintnall.com.

BURNS, MARY, performing arts educator; BA in arts/dance, Barnard College; MA in dance education, Columbia U. V.p. fin. Am. Dance Guild, N.Y.C.; dir dance prog and Acad of Dance Tyler Jr Coll, Tyler, Tex., 2003—. Mem.: Natl Dance Ed Org bd dir. Office: Tyler Jr Coll Academy of Dance PO 9020 Tyler TX 75711-9020

BURNS, MARYANN MARGARET, retired elementary school educator; b. Portland, Maine, Mar. 4, 1944; d. William and Emma (Greco) B. Finishing sch. grad., Chandler Sch. for Women, Boston, 1963; BS in Edn. and English summa cum laude, U. Maine, 1974. Cert. elem. tchr., Maine. Pvt. sec. IBM, L.A., 1968-70; learning lab. tchr. Sch. Adminstrv. Dist. # 6, Bar Mills, Maine, 1974—2001, Frank Jewett Sch., West Buxton, Maine. Mem. NEA, Maine Tchrs. Assn., U. Maine Alumni Assn., Polit. Action Com. Democrat. Roman Catholic. Home: 17 Wild Rose Ave South Portland ME 04106-6619 Office: Sch Adminstrv Dist 6 PO Box 38 Bar Mills ME 04004-0038 Office Phone: 207-929-3836. Personal E-mail: maryann.burns22@verizon.net.

BURNS, MELINDA, journalist; BA in English, Harvard U.; MS in Education, U. Southern Calif. Reporter L.A. Times, 1984—85; with Santa Barbara News Press, 1985—, sr. writer, regional affaris, housing, transportation, Latino issues. Recipient Science Journalism award, AAAS, 2004. Achievements include several awards for reporting on farm-workers and the environment. Office: Santa Barbara News Press 715 Anacapa St Santa Barbara CA 93101 Address: Santa Barbara News Press PO Box 1359 Santa Barbara CA 93102 Office Phone: 805-564-5262. Office Fax: 805-966-6258. Business E-Mail: mburns@newspress.com.

BURNS, NOËLLE ANN, art educator; b. Elkhorn, Wis., Dec. 26, 1955; d. Robert F. and Christiane T. Marszalek; m. Edward William Burns, June 2, 1979; children: Amanda Louise, Cassandra Anne. BS, Carroll Coll., 1978; MS in Edn., U. Wis., Whitewater, 1993. Cert. art tchr. K-12 Wis. Child care counselor II Wis. Sch. Deaf, Delavan, 1978—85, tchr. asst., 1985—90; tchr. Watertown (Wis.) Unified Sch. Dist., 1990—. Asst. troop leader Girls Scouts U.S., Lake Hills, Wis., 1989—2006; bd. dirs., CPA Jefferson Performing Arts Ctr., 2001—04; tchr. St. Francis Xavier Ch., Lake Hills, 2000—05. Recipient W. T. Graham award, W. T. Graham/Youth Art Month, 1997, 2003, 2005. Mem.: Watertown Arts Coun., Wis. Art Edn. Assn., Nat. Art Edn. Assn., Phi Kappa Phi. Republican. Roman Catholic. Avocations: travel, art, gardening, reading. Home: 219 Woodland Ct Lake Mills WI 53551 Office: Watertown Unified Sch Dist 111 Dodge St Watertown WI 53094 Office Phone: 920-262-1480 2303.

BURNS, REBECCA ANN, elementary school educator, librarian; b. Waynesboro, Pa., Dec. 28, 1946; d. John Albert and Betty Jane (Mason) Castelluccio; m. Terry Lee Burns, 1966; children: Todd Darin, Derick Jason. BS, Shippensburg U., 1968, postgrad., 1969, 70, 75, Pa. State U., 1973-74, 87, 89, U. Wyo., 1989. Cert. elem. tchr., libr. sci. tchr. Pa. Migrant educator Waynesboro (Pa.) Sch. Dist., 1971-72, elem. tchr., 1968-71, 74-79, Mifflin County Sch. Dist., Lewistown, Pa., 1972-74; test examiner Office Personnel Mgmt. U.S. Govt., State College, Pa., 1982-83; instr. Adult Basic Edn.- Gen. Edn. Devel. and Career Tng. Mifflin County Job Tng. Partnership Act, Lewistown, 1985-86; libr. State Correctional Inst.-Rockview, Bellefonte, Pa., 1983-85, Midd-West Sch. Dist., Middleburg, Pa., 1986-89; edn. adminstrn. assoc., pupil transp. specialist Pa. Dept. Edn., Harrisburg, 1989-90, edn. adminstrn. specialist, coord. non pub. sch. svcs., 1990-93, basic edn. assoc., youth edn. and employment coord., 1993-97, basic edn. assoc., work-based learning coord., 1997—2005; pvt. practice Harrisburg, 2005—. Lobbyist for stamp commemorating adult edn.; educator for women's rights devel. and implementation of regis. apprenticeships for youth in Pa. Mem.: AARP, Fedn. State Cultural and Ednl. Profl. (founding mem. retirees local chpt. 2005), Apprenticeship Assn., Pa. Fedn. Tchrs., Eastern Seaboard Apprenticeship Conf., Nat. Assn. State and Territorial Apprenticeship Dirs., Alliance Ret. Ams. (charter, charter Pa. chpt.), Aux. to Pa. Ret. State Police. Roman Catholic. Avocations: reading, collecting antique prints, travel. Home and Office: 2412 Abbey Ln Harrisburg PA 17112 Personal E-mail: racb1228@aol.com.

BURNS, RED, academic administrator; 4 children. Joined, co-founder, interactive telecomms. program Tisch Sch. Arts NYU, 1979—, chair, interactive telecomms. program Tisch Sch. Arts, 1981—, Tokyo Broadcasting System Prof. Communications, 1997—. Bd. dirs. Media Lab Europe, The Visual Media Task Force, The Convergent Media Group; mem. adv. bd. The N.Y. Times Digital Company; juror On-Line Journalism Awards, Nat. Mag. Awards, Webby Awards; prin. investigator three on-going rsch. programs funded by Interval Rsch., Intel and Microsoft. Creator CD-ROM on chaos theory, Electronic Neighborhood. Bd. dirs. The Charles H. Revson Found.; ProBono.net; Ivrae Inst.; mentor The Ross Sch. Named one of 100 top leaders of N.Y.'s economy, Crain's N.Y., top 100 most influential women in bus., Top 25 Influential People on the Net, Newsweek's 50 for the Future, N.Y. Cyber Sixty, N.Y. Mag.; named to Silicon Alley's 100; recipient Matrix award, 1997, All-Star Educator award, Crain's, Award of Excellence in Sci. and Tech., Mayor of N.Y.C., Spl. Educator award, Art Dir. Club, Chrysler Design Award, 2002. Mem.: N.Y. New Media Assn. (founding mem.). Office: NYU Tisch Sch Arts 721 Broadway 4th Fl New York NY 10003-6807

BURNS, ROBIN, cosmetics company executive; Student, Syracuse U. Formerly with Bloomingdale's, N.Y.C., v.p.; pres. Calvin Klein Cosmetics; pres., CEO Estee Lauder USA, N.Y.C., 1990—. Office: Estee Lauder USA 767 5th Ave New York NY 10153-0003

BURNS, RUTH ANN MARY, television executive; b. New Brunswick, NJ, Nov. 7, 1944; d. Chester Patrick and Mary Francis (Norko) Shea; m. Carl William Burns, Sept. 6, 1965; children: Christopher Carl, Heather Shea. BA, Rutgers U., 1967, MA, 1976. War corr. AP, N.Am. Newspaper Alliance, Vietnam, 1967; editor News Tribune, Woodbridge, N.J., 1967-70; writer, cons. Star Ledger, N.Y. Times, Parade mag., 1970-76; sr. research and program assoc. Eagleton Inst. of Politics, New Brunswick, 1976-81; project dir. Ctr. for Am. Woman & Politics, New Brunswick, 1978-81; v.p. Sta. WNET, NYC, 1982-84, sr. v.p., 1984—88; pres. Burns Group, Manalapan, NJ; v.p. mktg and external affairs Georgian Court U., 2004—. Author: Women in Municipal Management, Choice, Challenge, Change, 1980 (HUD award); contbg. author: Women and the American City, 1981; also articles. V.p. Edison (N.J.) Bd. Edn., 1975-82; advisor Sch. Communications Rutgers U., 1985-87; trustee Rutgers U., 1987-; bd. dir., Found. for Child Dev. Recipient Nat. Writing award William Randolph Hearst Found., 1967, Achievement award Am. Soc. Pub. Adminstrn., 1981, Woman of Yr. award Raritan Valley Regional C. of C., 1982; named to Rutger's U. Hall Disting. Alumni and Douglass Society, NJ Woman of Achievement award. Mem. Nat. Assn. TV Arts and Scis., Am. Soc. Women in Radio and TV, Eastern Ednl. Network, Douglass Soc. Democrat. Roman Catholic. Office: VP Mktg & Ext Affairs Georgian Ct Univ 900 Lakewood Ave Lakewood NJ 08701 Office Phone: 732-987-2256. Business E-Mail: burnsr@georgian.edu.

BURNS, SARAH CHLOE, historian, educator; b. Owensboro, Ky., Nov. 24, 1949; d. Robert Louis and Eleanor Lucille Burns; children: Krista Lynn Denio, Deborah Ann Denio, Matthew Justin Denio. BA, Calif. State U., Bakersfield, 1994, MA, 1996. Tchg. intern Bakersfield Coll., 1995—96, prof. history, 1996—2002; instr. Porterville (Calif.) Coll., 1997; lectr. history dept. Calif. State U., Bakersvield, 2002—04; adj. faculty dept. history Coll. of the Canyons, Santa Clarita, Calif., 2005—. Lectr., presenter in field. Author: Daughters of Juno, Chronicle One; Matilda of Argyll, 2004; contbr. chapters to books, articles to profl. jours. Recipient Honorarium for book rev., Addison Wesley Longman Pubs., 1998. Mem.: AAUW (chmn. legal adv. fund 2000—01, v.p. ednl. found. 2001—02), Orgn. Am. Historians, Bodleian Libr., Phi Alpha Theta. Avocations: writing, piano, tennis, swimming, travel. Home: PO Box 20100 Bakersfield CA 93390-0100 Office Phone: 661-496-7114. Personal E-mail: scburns@bak.rr.com.

BURNS, SARAH ELLEN, law educator; b. Ponca City, Okla., June 13, 1949; d. John William and Sarah Elizabeth (Phillips) Burns BA magna cum laude, U. Okla., 1971, MA, 1972, Stanford U., 1976; JD, Yale U., 1979. Bar: DC 1979, NY 1989, US Supreme Ct., US Ct. Appeals DC, 4th, 10th, 11th Cirs., US Dist. Ct. DC, US Dist. Ct. So. and Ea. Dists. NY. Assoc. Covington & Burling, Washington, 1979-82, Patterson, Belknap, Webb & Tyler, Washington, 1982-83; coord. atty. ERA Legis. History Project, Washington, 1983; fellow Women's Law and Pub. Policy Program, Washington, 1983-84; asst. dir. sex discrimination clinic Georgetown U., Washington, 1984-86; legal dir. NOW Legal Def. and Edn. Fund, NYC, 1986-90; asst. prof. clin. law NYU Sch. Law, 1990—93, assoc. prof., 1993—96, prof., 1996—. Schefelman disting. lectr. U. Wash. Law Sch., 1990. Named Dyson Disting. Lectr. Pace U. Sch. Law, 1989. Mem. Phi Beta Kappa. Office: NYU Sch Law 245 Sullivan St 5th Fl New York NY 10012 Office Phone: 212-998-6464. E-mail: burns@juris.law.nyu.edu.

BURNS, SHIRLEY MACDONALD, artist, educator; b. Kingsport, Tenn., Oct. 1, 1934; d. Kenneth MacDonald and Louise Gwendolyn (Cox) Cross; m. Richard Carroll Burns, Dec. 15, 1960; children: Jay Bradford, Kurt MacDonald. BS, East Tenn. State U., Johnson City, 1957, postgrad., 1957-86. Cert. tchr., Tenn., Va., Wash. Tchr. 3d grade Kempsville Elem. Sch., Va., 1955-56; tchr. art Princess Anne H.S., Va., 1957-58, Mt. Vernon Elem. Sch., Alexandria, Va., 1959-60, Harrisburg Jr. H.S., Pa., 1961; tchr. 6th grade art and social studies Silverdale Elem. Sch., Wash., 1967-70; tchr. art North Kitsap H.S., Poulsbo, Wash., 1978-84. Drawing instr. Harrisburg YMCA, 1961, pvt. lessons, Hawaii, 1964-65; docent Hall of Indians/Mus. Natural History, Smithsonian Instn., Washington, 1970-71; ptnr. The Art Cellar, Silverdale, 1971-75; instr. adult craft classes Olympic Coll., Bremerton, 1975-77; instr. pottery Bainbridge Island Park and Recreation Dist., 1984-04, adult sculpture classes, 1995—; guide studio tour Bainbridge Island, Wash. Exhibited works in Bainbridge Arts and Crafts Gallery and Christmas Shows, 1991—, Studio Tour, Bainbridge Island, 1991-99, 03, 04, Bainbridge in Bloom, 1997-99; two-person show Collective Visions, 2001, 02; group show Collective Visions Gallery, Bremerton, Wash., 2001, Art Soup Gallery, Bainbridge Island, 2004; permanent display of sculptural works at Seattle Aquarium, 1995—. Fundraiser, Friends of the Libr., Bremerton, Wash. Recipient awards for art. Mem. AAUW, PEO, Bainbridge Island Music and Arts, The Clay People, Bainbridge Arts and Crafts, Bainbridge Island Arts and Humanities, Seattle Art Mus. Methodist. Avocations: music appreciation, tennis, reading. Home: 8270 NE Meadowmeer Rd Bainbridge Island WA 98110-1241 Personal E-mail: shrburns@aol.com.

BURNS, STEPHANIE A., chemicals executive; PhD in Organic Chemistry, Iowa State U.; post-doctoral student, U. Languedoc-Rousillon, France. Rschr. Dow Corning, Midland, Mich., 1983—87, prod. devel. mgr., electronics industry, 1987—94, dir. women's health, 1994—97, sci., tech. dir., Europe Brussels, 1997—99, industry dir. life scis., Europe to European elec. industry dir., 1999—2000, exec. v.p. Midland, Mich., 2000—03, pres., 2003—, COO, 2003—04, CEO, 2004—, chmn., 2006—. Bd. dirs. Dow Corning, 2000—, Manpower Inc., Chem. Bank Midland area, Mich. Molecular Inst. Adv. bd. Chem. & Engring. News. Bd. trustees Midland Cmty. Ctr. Named Mich. Woman Exec. of Yr., 2003; named one of 100 Most Powerful Women, Forbes Mag., 2005, 2006; recipient Vanguard award, Chem. Edn. Found., 2006. Mem.: Soc. Chem. Industry (mem. exec. com.), Am. Chem. Coun. (bd. dirs.), Am. Chem. Soc. Office: Dow Corning PO Box 994 Midland MI 48686-0994 Office Phone: 989-496-7881. Office Fax: 989-496-6731.*

BURNS, SUSAN KAY, music educator; b. Lafayette, Ind., Jan. 21, 1945; d. Ivan Luther and Rosemary Owings; m. Robert Eugene Burns, Dec. 21, 1943 (div.); children: Chad, Mandy, Monica. BS, Ind. State U., Terre Haute, 1967; MA, Valparaiso U., Ind., 1972. Tchr. music North Decatur Corp., Greensburg, Ind., 1967—68, North Newton Corp., Morocco, Ind., 1968—71; vocal instr. St. Joseph Coll., Rensselaer, Ind., 1971—72; tchr. music North White Corp., Monon, Ind., 1972—74, West Ctrl. Corp., Francesville, Ind., 1979, North White Corp, Monon, Ind., 2003—05; sub. tchr. Salesperson, spokesperson McMillan, McGraw-Hill Music Books, No. Ind., 2005. Choral dir. Pulaski County Choral Club. Mem.: Ind. Choral Dirs. Assn., Ind. Music Edn. Assn., Am. Choral Dirs. Assn., Sigma Alpha Iota (Sword of Honor), Alpha Sigma Alpha. Roman Catholic. Avocations: reading, travel, movies, concerts. Home: 1910 Rolling Meadows Ct Monticello IN 47960 E-mail: doramey@hotmail.com.

BURNS, TONI ANTHONY, artist; b. L.A., Sept. 6, 1937; d. Earle Francis and LaVerne Myrtle (Holmberg) Anthony; m. George Orin Burns, May 14, 1965; children: Robert Anthony, James Randolph. BFA, Calif. State U. Long Beach, 1959, postgrad., 1960. Cert. secondary tchr. Calif. Interior decorator Ruth Connor Interiors, Downey, Calif., 1960—62; tech. illustrator N.Am. Rockwell Corp., Downey, 1962—64, McDonnell-Douglas Aircraft, Long Beach, 1964—65; graphic layout artist Beckman Instruments, Fullerton, Calif., 1968—70; owner, creator Original Art Rock Owls, San Juan Capistrano, Calif., 1970—78; custom jewelry designer Jewelry by Toni Burns, San Juan Capistrano, 1979—98; jewelry designer, ptnr. SuperNatural Art, San Juan Capistrano, 1999—; prin., owner Silver Dolls, San Juan Capistrano, 2003—. Wholesale exhibitor L.A. Gift Show, 1971-78, Beckman Handcrafts, L.A., 1982. Juried shows include Village West Gallery, Laguna Beach, Calif., summers 1971-75, Art-A-Fair Festival, Laguna Beach, 1984-86, Downey Art Mus., 1992, Fine Arts Pavillion, 1993. Recipient 1st pl. San Clemente Art Gallery, 1984, 99. Mem. Am. Craft Coun., Metal Arts Soc. So. Calif. Avocations: family genealogy, travel, photography. Office Phone: 949-388-4309. Business E-Mail: sales@supernaturalart.com.

BURNS, URSULA M., printing company executive; b. NYC, Sept. 20, 1958; m. Lloyd Bean; children: Malcolm, Melissa. BS, Polytech. Inst., 1980; MS in Mech. Engring., Columbia U., 1981. Joined as mechanical engr., held several positions in engring., including product develop. and planning Xerox Corp, 1980; exec. asst. to chmn. & CEO Paul A. Allaire Xerox Corp., 1991, lead several bus. teams, 1992—2000, sr. v.p. corp. strategic svc., 2000—, pres. bus. group ops. Stamford, Conn., 2002—. Bd. dirs. Hunt Corp., Banta Corp., U. Rochester Med. Sch., Am. Express, Boston Scientific Corp., FIRST, Nat. Assn. Mfrs., PQ Corp., Rochester Bus. Alliance. Named one of 50 Most Powerful Women in Bus., Fortune mag., 2006. Mem.: Nat. Assn. Mfr. (bd. dirs.), Indsl. Mgmt. Coun. Rochester (bd. dirs.). Office: Xerox 800 Long Ridge Rd Stamford CT 06904*

BURNS, VIRGINIA, social worker; b. Boston, June 10, 1925; d. Thomas Patrick and Katherine Louise (Dempsey) Burns. AB in Sociology, Boston U., 1946, MSW, 1951; EdD honors, Wheelock Coll., 1994. Group work specialist Boston Children's Svc. Assn., 1951-58; group work cons. East London Family Svc. Units, 1958-59; assoc. exec. sec. group work coun. Welfare Fedn. Cleve., 1959-62; sr. staff mem. Office Juvenile Delinquency & Youth Devel. U.S. Dept. Health, Edn. and Welfare, Washington, 1962-67, asst. to asst. sec. cmty. svcs., 1967-69; sr. assoc. youth involvement study New Transcentury Found., Washington, 1969-70; assoc. prof., dir. social svc. project U. Chgo., Sch. Social Svc. Adminstrn., 1970-73; dir. cmty. svc., divsn. drug rehab. Dept. Mental Health, Boston, 1973-76; dir. cons. & edn. program Mass. Mental Health Ctr., Boston, 1976-82; lectr. mental health Harvard Med. Sch., Boston, 1978-82; dir. advocacy, Boston Children Svc. Assn. Mass. Soc. Prevention of Cruelty Children, Boston, 1983-94; instr. social welfare, coord. cmty. projects Smith Coll. Sch. Social Work, Northampton, Mass., 1994-99; instr. social welfare policy Salem (Mass.) State Coll. Sch. Social Work, 1993-99. Cons. in field. Contbr. articles to profl. jours., chpts. in books. Founding chair Children's Advocacy Network Mass., 1984—93, Latchkey Children's Coalition Mass., 1988—92; v.p. Mass. Human Svc. Coalition, 1984—99; legis. liaison Mass. Working Group on Women in Prison, 2000—; bd. dirs. Hispanic Office Planning and Evaluation, 1990—97, Here House, 1989—90, Parents Helping Parents, 2001—02, Inst. Health and Recovery, 2003—06; bd. advisors Aid to Incarcerated Mothers, 2002—06; active United Fair Economy, Boston, 1994—99, Tax Equity Alliance Mass., 1990—99; mem. adv. com. Wheelock Coll., 1999—2005. Named Alumna of Yr., Boston U. Sch. Social Work, 1968; scholar, Fulbright, 1958—58. Mem.: NASW (chair polit. action com. Mass. chpt. 1984—2006, award for greatest contbn. to social policy and change 1990, Lifetime Achievement award 2003—04), Boston U. Alumni Assn. (Disting.). Avocations: gardening, cooking, flower arranging, crossword puzzles. Home: 41A Cushing St Cambridge MA 02138-4581 Personal E-mail: Burns472@aol.com.

BURNS-BOWIE, MAUREEN ELIZABETH, sculptor; b. Wilmington, Del., Sept. 14, 1949; d. William John and Jean (Ribsam) Burns; m. Norman Ernest Bowie, Sept. 19, 1987; children: Brian Paul Bowie, Peter Mark Bowie. Student, U. Sorbonne, Paris, 1966, U. Del., 1968—73, studied under numerous ceramic masters, 1970—76. Exhibitions include St. Louis Artists Guild, 2000, Indpls. Mus. Art, Columbus, 2001, WPA Corcoran, Washington, 2002, Rockville Arts Pl., Md., 2003, Bienniale Internazionale Dell'Arte Contemporanea, Florence, Italy, 2003, Md. State Arts Coun., Balt., 2004, NH Inst. Art, Manchester, 2004, Acad. Mus., Easton, Md., 2005, NCECA Nat. Conf., Balt., 2005, numerous others. Co-founder, dir. Internat. Alliance Women in the Arts, 1993—98; v.p. Women's Art Registry of Minn., 1993—95. Mem.: Coll. Art Assn., Am. Crafts Coun. Women's Caucus for Art, Bioneers, Art and Healing Network, Art Culture Nature, Am. Ceramic Soc., Bklyn. Potters, Balt. Clayworks, Soc. N.Am. Goldsmiths, Internat. Scupture Ctr., Nat. Coun. Edn. in Ceramic Arts, Washington Sculpture Group, Am. Crafts Coun., Urban Glass. Green Party. Buddhist. Home: Innisfree PO Box 508 Trappe MD 21673

BURNSIDE, MARY ARDIS, psychologist; b. Milw., May 14, 1950; d. Glenn Grover and Edna Mae Chrystine (Mueller) B. B.A., Rice U., 1972; M.A., U. Houston, 1976, Ph.D., 1980. Lic. psychologist, Tex.; m. Bruce Edward Anderson, July 17, 1973; children: Aaron Hunter Anderson-Burnside, Andrew Chase Anderson-Burnside, Avery Elizabeth Anderson-Burnside. Clin. asst. prof. dept. psychiatry Baylor Coll. Medicine, Houston, 1980—; adj. faculty psychology dept. U. Houston, 1984—, Rice U., 1986—. Mem. Am. Psychol. Assn., Tex. Psychol. Assn., Houston Psychol. Assn., Phi Kappa Phi. Office Phone: 713-661-9767.

BURNSIDE, MARY BETH, biology professor, researcher; b. San Antonio, Apr. 23, 1943; d. Neil Delmont and Luella Nixon (Kenley) B. BA, U. Tex., 1965, MA, 1967, PhD in Zoology, 1968. Instr. med. sch. Harvard U., Boston, 1970-73; asst. prof. U. Pa., Phila., 1973-76, U. Calif., Berkeley, 1976-77, assoc. prof., 1977-82, prof., 1982—, dean biol. scis., 1984-90, chancellor prof., 1996-99, vice chancellor rsch., 2000—. Mem. nat. adv. eye coun. NIH, 1990-94; mem. sci. adv. bd. Lawrence Hall of Sci., Berkeley, 1983—, Whitney Labs., St. Augustine, Fla., 1993-97; mem. bd. sci. councillors Nat. Eye Inst., 1994—. Mem. editl. bd. Invest. Ophthalmol. Vis. Sci., 1992-94; contbr. numerous articles to profl. jours. Mem. sci. adv. bd. Mills Coll., Oakland, Calif., 1986-90; trustee Bermuda Biol. Sta., St. George's, 1978-83; dir. Miller Inst., Berkeley, Calif., 1995-98. Recipient Merit award NIH, 1989-99, Outstanding Alumna award U. Tex., 1999; rsch. grantee, NIH, 1972—, NSF. Fellow AAAS; mem. Am. Soc. Cell Biology (coun. 1980-84). Avocation: hiking. Office: U Calif MC # 3200 335 Life Scis Addn # 3200 Berkeley CA 94720-0001

BURNSIDE, WANDA JACQUELINE, elementary school educator; b. Highland Park, Mich., Mar. 9, 1950; d. Minor and Willie Lee (McCann) Palm; m. Simmie Lee Burnside, Jr., Nov. 4, 1972. BA in Humanities and Social Scis., U. Detroit. Clk. pers. dept. Blue Cross Blue Shield, Detroit, Mich., 1968-69; student asst. dir. libr. U. Detroit Edn. Libr., 1969-72; head clk NARO Fed. Project U.S. Atty.'s Office, Detroit, 1970; editor, office mgr. Detroit Ch. World, 1974-78; SDIP and IIE, ASIP Marygrove Coll., Detroit, 1979-81; elem. tchr. Martin L. King Jr. Ednl. Ctr., Detroit, 1981-88; sales rep. Five Stars Heating, Detroit, 1990-91; exec. sec. Second Ecclesiastical Ch. of God in Christ, Detroit, 1990—, office mgr., 1991—. Tchr. Head Start, Detroit, 1967; drama coach Martin L. King Jr. Ednl. Ctr., Detroit, 1980-88; monitor State of Mich. Nurse Lic. Dept., Detroit, 1980-81; tutor private home, Detroit, 1983-87; founder/pres. The Mother Willie Lee Palm Found., Write the Vision Min., 1995. Author: In My Neighborhood, 1972, Rejections-12 Steps To Recovery (Browning Internat. award), The Poetry Guide for Christian Writers. Mem. Joy of Jesus Ministries, 1975-76, So. Christian Leadership Coun., Detroit chpt., 1993. Recipe contest winner, Fayco Beverage Co., 1979, 2d, Thornapple Valley, 1988, 2d, Progresso Soups, 1989, 1st; cited for laity leadership Congress of Nat. Black Chs., Washington, 1990; Recipient Persistent Christian Writer of Yr., 1999, Am. Christian Writer Assn. Mem. Black Writers Guild, Christian Edn. for Handicapped, Christian Writers Inst., Am. Family Jour., The Called and Ready Writers (v.p.) Democrat. Avocations: writing devotional and poetry, cooking, crafts, reading, travel. Home: 8245 Mendota St Detroit MI 48204-3028 Office: Ch of God in Christ Hdqtrs SW Michigan 4439 E Nine MIle Rd Detroit MI 48091-2631 Personal E-mail: wtvision@hotmail.com.

BURNS-RIVIELLO, MICHAELA AILEEN, social studies educator; b. West Islip, NY, Dec. 23, 1974; d. Arthur Abercrombie and Maryanne Elizabeth Burns; m. Thomas Joseph Riviello, Dec. 3, 2005. BA in Social Sci. and Tchg. with honors, SUNY, Stony Brook, 1999, MA with honors, 2001. Cert. profl. development SUNY, 2001. Girls field hockey, volleyball & lacrosse athletic coach Babylon Sch., NY, 1994—2001; history tchr., chairperson Acad. St. Joseph's Sch., Brentwood, NY, 1999—2000; girls field hockey & lacrosse athletic coach Smithtown Schs., NY, 2000—05, social studies tchr., 2000—, instrnl. specialist. Mentor for new tchrs. Smithtown

Schs., Smithtown, 2001—03. Organizer, coord. Nat. Geog. Geography Bee, 2003—, Tsunami Fundraiser, 2004—05, Hurricane Katrina Relief & Aid; creator, organizer, coord. Letters to Soldiers Campaign, Washington, 2004—05; co-creator, co-organizer Salvation Army Food Dr., Smithtown, 1999—; creator, organizer, coord. Salvation Army Charity Dinner, 2002—04. Recipient Cmty. Svc. award, Salvation Army, 2004. Mem.: PTA, ASCD, Tchr. Web, LI Coun. Social Studies. Roman Catholic. Avocations: gardening, crafts, stained glass artwork. Office: Smithtown Schs Great Hollow MS 150 Southern Blvd Nesconset NY 11767 Office Phone: 631-382-2805. Office Fax: 631-382-2807. Business E-Mail: mriviello@smithtown.k12.ny.us.

BURRELL, KIMBERLY MEADOWS, assistant principal; d. Charles Ray and Donna Dodd Meadows; m. Robert Dean Burrell, May 24, 1997; 1 child, Andrew Whittington. BA in English, Harding U., Searcy, Ark., 1996; EdM in Leadership, Delta State U., Cleveland, Miss., 2003, EdS in Ednl. Leadership, 2006. H.S. English tchr. Wash. Sch., Greenville, Miss., 1996—99; English tchr. Olive Br. Mid. Sch., Miss., 1999—2002; asst. prin. DeSoto Ctrl. Mid. Sch., Southaven, Miss., 2003—. Mem. Church Of Christ. Office Phone: 662-349-6660.

BURRELL, LYNNE, credit manager; b. Westfield, Mass., Mar. 24, 1959; d. Douglas C. and Barbara Berggren; children: Jason Silverman, Thomas Silverman, Carolyn Silverman. BA, New Coll., 1979; MA in Art History, George Washington U., 1983; MBA, NYU, 1988; MA in English and Creative Writing, U. So. Fla., 2005. Gallery curator Xavier Fourcade Inc., NYU, 1982—86; mktg. asst. Smith Barney, NYU, 1987; exec. asst. dept. to commr. NYC Dept. Corrections, 1988—90; comml. credit analyst Fifth Third Bank, Sarasota, Fla., 2005—06; sr. credit analyst First Am. Bank, Osprey, Fla., 2005—. Editor, contbr.: jour. Sunscripts, 2003—04. Co-pres. Hendrick Hudson Edn. Found., Cortlandt Manor, NY, 2001—02; treas. Mother Connection, Montrose, NY, 1994; co-pres. Furnace Woods Elem. Sch., Cortlandt Manor, 2001—02, mem. health and safety com., 2001—02. Bus. fellow, GTE, 1986—88. Mem.: Manasota Track Club. Avocations: marathons, watercolors, writing, triathlons. Home: 4583 Country Manor Dr Sarasota FL 34233 Office Phone: 941-918-4073.

BURRELL, PAMELA, actress; b. Tacoma, Aug. 4, 1945; d. Donald A. and Mickey Rose (Curtiss) B.; m. Monty Silver, July 18, 1965 (div. 1978); children: Deirdre Paige, Emily Beth; m. Peter J. Gatto, Apr. 21, 1979. Studies with Sandy Miesner; student, San Francisco Ballet, N.Y.C. Ballet. Actress: (stage prodns.) Arms and the Man, 1967 (Theatre World award 1968), Where's Charley?, 1974, Berkeley Square, 1976, The Boss, 1976, Tatyana Repina, 1978, Biography, 1979, Strider, 1979, Sunday in the Park with George, 1985, also numerous regional stage appearances, 1967-86, (feature films) Da Duva, 1967, Popeye, 1980, (TV series) The Catlins, 1984-85, (TV episodes) Search for Tomorrow, Ryan's Hope, Spencer for Hire, 1986. Mem. Actors' Equity Assn., Screen Actors Guild, AFTRA.

BURRIS, HARRIET LOUISE, emergency physician; b. Alexandria Bay, N.Y., Apr. 7, 1949; d. Robert Barker and Harriet Louise (Dorman) Burtch; m. John Samuel Burris Jr., Nov. 30, 1974; children: Elizabeth Jane, Katherine Ann. SB, MIT, 1972; MD, SUNY, Syracuse, 1976. Diplomate Am. Bd. Family Practice, Am. Bd. Emergency Medicine, Nat. Bd. Med. Examiners; cert. added qualification in geriatrics. Resident in family practice St. Joseph's Hosp. Health Ctr., Syracuse, 1976-79; pvt. practice Cazenovia, N.Y., 1979-81; staff MD emergency dept. Middlesex Hosp., Middletown, Conn., 1982-83; staff MD family practice Cmty. Health Care Plan, Wallingford, Conn., 1983-84; staff MD emergency dept. Middlesex Med. Ctr.-Shoreline divsn. Middlesex Hosp., Essex, Conn., 1984—, acting med. dir., 1994. Fellow Am. Acad. Family Physicians; mem. Handweavers Guild Conn. (libr.). Avocations: knitting, handweaving, needle arts. Office: River Hosp 4 Fuller St Alexandria Bay NY 13607

BURRIS, KELLY L., lawyer; b. Mpls., Sept. 22, 1974; BA, U. Tex., Austin, 1997; JD, Tex. Tech U., 2000. Bar: Tex. 2000. Assoc. Godwin, Pappas, Langley & Ronquillo, L.L.P., Dallas. Assoc. editor: Tex. Tech Law Rev., 1998—99, articles editor:, 1999—2000. Mem. bd. barristers Tex. Tech U., 1998—2000. Named a Rising Star, Tex. Super Lawyers mag., 2006. Mem.: Dallas Assn. Young Lawyers (co-chair poker for playgrounds com. 2005, co-chair host com. Acad. Am. and Internat. Law 2004—), Tex. Young Lawyers Assn. (dist. 4 dir., state bd. 2002—03), ABA (mem. young lawyers divsn., mem. family lawyers divsn.), Dallas Bar Assn. (mem. family law sect.). Office: Godwin Pappas Langley Ronquillo LLP Renaissance Tower Ste 1700 1201 Elm St Dallas TX 75270 Office Phone: 214-939-4841. E-mail: kburris@godwinpappas.com.*

BURRIS-SCHNUR, CATHERINE, minister, pastoral psychotherapist, medical/surgical nurse, educator; b. Ft. Lee, Va., Nov. 22, 1961; d. Charlie Franklin and Geneva Mae (Melton) B. ADN, Eizabethtown C.C., 1981; BSN, U. Ky., 1984; postgrad., So. Bapt. Theol. Sem., 1986—90; MDiv, Garrett Evang. Theol. Sem., 1994; D of Ministry, Chgo. Theol. Sem., 2002. RN Ill., LCPC, 2005; ordained to ministry Am. Bapt. Ch., 1997; lic. clin. profl. profl. 2004. Staff nurse Ctrl. Bapt. Hosp., Lexington, Ky.; rehab. specialist Intacorp, Louisville; nurse mgr. St. Anthony Med. Ctr., Louisville, nurse mgr., med.-surg. educator, continuing edn. adminstr., dir. ednl. svcs., 1986—91; clin. fellow pastoral psychotherapy tng. program Ctr. for Religion and Psychotherapy, Chgo., 1994—97; assoc. dir. admissions Garrett Evang. Theol. Sem., Evanston, Ill., 1995—97; pastoral psychotherapist, co-dir. edn. Ctr. for Religion and Psychotherapy, Chgo., 1997—. Recipient various nursing scholarships; named to Outstanding Young Women of Am., 1991. Mem.: ANA, Ill. Counseling Assn., Ill. Mental Health Counselors Assn., Mins.' Coun.

BURRITT, BARBARA, artist; b. Meadville, Pa., Apr. 22, 1947; d. Robert Henry and Gertrude Leone (Kennedy) B.; children: Shane P. Jernigan, Erin A. Jernigan. AA, Ctr. Creative Studies, 1968; BFA, Mpls. Coll. Art & Design, 1980; postgrad., Royal Coll. Art, England, 1992. With K.T.C.A. TV, St. Paul, 1981; courtroom illustrator W.C.C.O. TV, Mpls., 1981-82; arts cons. Cir. Fine Arts Gallery, San Francisco, 1983-84; asst. dir. art Vorpal Art Gallery, San Francisco, 1984; coord. vis. svcs. Mpls. Inst. Arts, 1988-92; tutor art St. Paul, 1998—; artists, leather crafts White Raven Visual Arts, Portland, 1993—. Author: Arising from the Ashes, 1992, Eclipse of Fate, 2005. Art facilitator Wisdom Cirs., Minn., 1994-2001. Mem. Visionary Artists No. Calif. Avocation: renaissance festival artisan. Home: 909 Glendower St Ashland OR 97520 Office Phone: 541-488-5248. Personal E-mail: Graalqueen@yahoo.com.

BURROS, MARIAN FOX, writer; b. Waterbury, Conn. children: Michael, Ann. BA English lit., Wellesley. Food editor Washington Post, 1974—81; food reporter NY Times, 1981—83; food columnist NY Times Dining Sect., 1983—; syndicated columnist NY Times Syndicated Sales Corp. Consumer reporter WRC-TV, Washington DC (Emmy award, 1973), contbr. NBC Radio Network News, United Features, Washington Daily News, Washington Star; author: (cookbooks) Elegant but Easy, 1967, Freeze with Ease, 1968, Come for Cocktails, Stay for Supper, 1970, The Summertime Cookbook, 1972 (Tastemaker award), Pure & Simple, 1978 (Tastemaker award), Keep It Simple, 1981, You've Got It Made, 1984, The Best of De Gustibus, 1988, 20 Minute Menus, 1989, Eating Well is the Best Revenge, 1995, The Elegant but Easy Cookbook, 1995, The New Elegant but Easy Cookbook, 2003, Cooking for Comfort, 2003. Recipient Nat. Press Club award, 1988, Matrix Award, NY Women in Comm., 1990, Betty Furness Consumer Media Svc. award, Consumer Fedn. Am., 2000, Mass Media award (3-time winner), AAUW, Vesta award (3-time winner), Hearth & Home, Penney-Mo. award, James Beard award. Office: NY Times Dining Sect 229 W 43rd St New York NY 10036

BURROUGHS, JEANNETTE, elementary school educator; d. Harry and Mary Manning; m. Gary Burroughs; children: April, Mary Albert, Lavada Eggart, Tommy. BA, Fla. Atlantic U., 1977. Cert. Elem. Edn. grades 1-6 Fla., 1977, Middle grades English 5-9 Fla., 1989. 4th grade tchr. Ctrl. Elem. Sch., Clewiston, Fla., 2003—. Leadership team Ctrl. Elem. Sch., Clewiston, Fla., 2004—. Cmty. advisor Pahokee Fire Rescue Explorer Program, Fla., 2000—04; Sunday sch. tchr. Lakeside Bapt. Ch., Pahokee, Fla., 1992—2006; sec. Lakeside Condominium Assn., Pahokee, Fla., 2004—06. Recipient Tchr. of Month, Edn. Found. of Palm Beach County, 1988, 1998; grantee Edn. Grant, Citicorp, 2006. Mem.: Hendry County Edn. Assn. (assoc.; pres. 2006—). Baptist. Avocations: reading, travel, crocheting. Office: Ctrl Elem Sch 1000 Deane Duff Ave Clewiston FL 33440 Office Phone: 863-983-1550. Office Fax: 863-983-1558. Business E-Mail: burroughsj@hendry.k12.fl.us.

BURROUGHS, MARGARET TAYLOR GOSS, artist, former museum director; b. St. Rose, La., Nov. 1, 1917; d. Alexander and Octavia (Pierre) Taylor; m. Bernard Goss, 1937; 1 child, Gayle; m. Charles Burroughs, 1949; 1 adopted child, Paul. BA in Edn, Art Inst. Chgo., 1946, MA, 1948; LHD (hon.), Lewis U., 1972; DHL (hon.), Chgo. State U., 1983. Tchr. art Chgo. Public Schs., 1944-68; prof. humanities Kennedy King Coll., Chgo., 1969-79; exec. dir., founder DuSable Mus. African Am. History, Chgo., 1961-84, dir. emeritus, 1984—; group shows include: LA County Mus., 1976, Corcoran Gallery, 1980; mem. Chgo. Council Fine Arts, 1976-80, Nat. Commn. Negro History and Culture, 1981—; founder Nat. Conf. Artists, 1959. Fellow NEH, 1968. Office: DuSable Museum 740 E 56th Pl Chicago IL 60637-1495 Office Phone: 312-742-4737.

BURROUS, BETH A., lawyer; b. Kalamazoo, Mich., May 12, 1960; BS in nutritional biochemistry with honors, Cornell U., 1982; PhD in nutritional biochemistry, MIT, 1987; JD, Georgetown U. Law Ctr., 1993. Bar: D.C. 1993. Postdoctoral research fellow Nat. Inst. Health Lab. Devel. Biol. & Anomolies, Bethesda, Md., 1987—88; patent examiner U.S. Patent & Trademark Office, 1988—90; law clk. to Hon. Pauline Newman U.S. Ct. Appeals, Fed. Cir., 1993—95; ptnr. Foley & Lardner LLP, Washington, 1995—, chmn. biotech./pharm. practice group. Mem.: Sigma Chi Scientific Research Soc., Omicron Nu Honor Soc. Fluent in french. Office: Foley & Lardner LLP 3000 K St NW Ste 500 Washington DC 20007-5101 Office Phone: 202-672-5475. Business E-Mail: bburrous@foley.com.

BURROW, NANCY KAY, special education educator; b. Toledo, Ohio, Oct. 25, 1953; d. Richard Allen and Norma Jean Rader; m. Paul Irving Burrow, Sept. 8, 1979; children: Rachel, Timothy. BS in Spl. Edn., St. Cloud (Minn.) State U., 1975. Tchr. Shelby-Tennant Schs., Shelby, Iowa, 1975—76, Oskaloosa (Iowa) Sr. H.S., 1976—, dept. head, special education, 1995—. Contbr. articles to profl. jours. Mem.: Delta Kappa Gamma (chpt. pres. 1998—2000). United Methodist. Avocations: music, needlecrafts. Office: Oskaloosa Sr High Sch 1816 N 3d St Oskaloosa IA 52577-1898

BURROWS, BERTHA JEAN, retired academic administrator; b. Brush, Colo., June 15, 1930; d. John and Marie Pabst; m. Leslie R. Burrows, Sept. 2, 1951; children: Paul Eric, Amy Susan, Julie Diane, David Arthur. BA in Bus., U. Colo., 1952. Sec. Dental Found. Colo., Denver, 1969—70, John Boswick, MD, Denver, 1970—72; adminstrv. cons. dept. contg. edn. U. Colo. Sch. Dentistry, Denver, 1975—76; asst. dir. vol. svcs. U. Colo. Health Sci. Ctr., 1977—80; sec. Denver Neurosurg. Assn., Denver, 1981—83; ret., 1983. Bookkeeper Clark & Co., Denver, 1981—83; com. mem. U. Colo. Hosp., Denver, 1999—. Vol. U. Colo. Hosp., Denver, 1970—; treas., asst. mgr. U. Colo. Hosp. Gift Shop, 1997—, bd. mgrs., 1987—. Recipient Who Care award, Channel 9 TV Denver, 2005. Mem.: Colo. Assn. Healthcare Auxilians and Vols. (treas. 2000—01, chmn. gift shop 2002—03, pres.-elect 2003—04, pres. 2004—05), U. Colo. Srs. Assn. (pres. 2002—). Home: 6911 E Iliff Place Denver CO 80224

BURROWS, DORNA B., elementary school educator; b. Chgo., Dec. 5, 1947; d. Paul and Barbara Benzaquin; children: Robert Wilson, Paul Melville, Timothy Kemble. BA, Marietta Coll., Ohio, 1969; MS, U. Ariz., Tucson, Ariz., 1998. Cert. tchr. Ariz., 1984. Tchr. Tucson (Ariz.) Unified Sch. Dist., 1984—. Tchr. mentor Tucson (Ariz.) Unified Sch. Dist., 1990—2006, sci. facilitator, 1990—; instr. Internat. Inst. Americas, Tucson. Registrar Tangue Verde Little League, Tucson, 1988—95. Named Mid. Sch. Sci. Tchr. of Yr., Tucson (Ariz.) Unified Sch. Dist.; recipient Newmast award, NASA, 1984, Edn. award, Internat. Inst. Americas; grantee, NASA, 1992—98. Mem.: ASTD (assoc.). Home: 790 Wells Road Wethersfield CT 06109 Office: Tucson Unified School District 1010 E Tenth Tucson AZ 85719 Personal E-mail: dornabb@yahoo.com.

BURROWS, ELIZABETH MACDONALD, religious organization executive, educator; b. Portland, Oreg., Jan. 30, 1930; d. Leland R. and Ruth M. (Frew) MacDonald. Certificate, Chinmaya Trust Sandeepany, Bombay; PhD (hon.), Internat. U. Philosophy and Sci., 1975; ThD, Christian Coll. Universal Peace, 1992. Ordained to ministry First Christian Ch., 1976. Mgr. credit Home Utilities, Seattle, 1958, Montgomery Ward, Crescent City, Calif., 1963; supr. Oreg. dist. tng. West Coast Tele., Beaverton, 1965; pres. Christ Ch. of Universal Peace, Seattle, 1971—, prof. religion, also bd. dirs.; pres. Archives Internat., Seattle, 1971—; v.p. James Tyler Kent Inst. Homeopathy, 1984-95; sec. Louis Braille Inst. for the Blind, 1995—. Author: Crystal Planet, 1979, Pathway of the Immortal, 1980, Odyssey of the Apocalypse, 1981, Harp of Destiny, 1984, Commentary for Gospel of Peace of Jesus Christ According to John, 1986, Seasons of the Soul, 1995, Voyagers of the Sand, 1996, The Song of God, 1998, Hold the Anchovies, 1996, Pilgrim of the Shadow, 1998, Maya Sangh and the Valley of the White Ones, 2001, The Secret Jesus Scroll, 2002, Poetry Chapbook, 2002, Visions, 2002, Maya Sangh and the Valley of the White One, Eat to Heal, 2002, Mystic Voyage, 2004, Htrae, 2005, Psalms Solemnis, 2005. Recipient Pres. award for literary excellence CADER, 1994, 95, 97, Diamond Homer award Famous Poets Soc., 1998, Pub.'s Choice award Poets of the New Era, 2002. Mem. Internat. Speakers Platform, Internat. New Thought Alliance, Cousteau Soc., Internat. Order of Chivalry, The Planetary Soc. Home: 10529 Ashworth Ave N Seattle WA 98133-8937 Office Phone: 206-362-4134. Personal E-mail: starbase2001@earthlink.net.

BURROWS, SHANIA KAY, civilian military employee; b. Russellville, Ala., Mar. 21, 1967; d. J. W. Saint and Dorothea Patricia Melton; m. Kim Stewart Burrows, Mar. 31, 1999; children: Conor Stewart, Shandi Nicole. Student, John C. Calhoun State C.C., Decatur, Ala., 1996—98; BA in Psychology summa cum laude, Athens State U., Ala., 2000; MS in Mgmt. and Logistics Mgmt, Fla. Inst. Tech., Melbourne, 2004; grad. with honors, U.S. Army Logistics Leadership Ctr., 2001; grad. with distinction, US Army Logistics Mgmt. Coll., 2001. AMCOM Lean Six Sigma Green Belt US Army Aviation and Missile Command, Ala., 2005, cert. acquisition profl. level III Life Cycle Logistics Def. Acquisition U., 2004. Logistics mgmt. specialist and data analyst US Army Logistics Support Activity, Redstone Arsenal, Ala., 2001—04; logistics mgmt. specialist and item mgr. US AMCOM Utility Helicopter Directorate, 2004; assoc. dir. aviation staff US AMCOM Integrated Materiel Mgmt. Ctr., 2004—05; asset acquisition mgr. US Army AMCOM Utility Helicopter Directorate, 2005; continuous improvement facilitator US Army AMCOM Office Continuous Improvement, 2005—06; program integrator demilitarization US Army AMCOM G-3 Ops., 2006—. Retrograde distbn. managment integration product team US AMC LOGSA, Redstone Arsenal, Ala., 2003—04; mem. enterprise bd. AMCOM G-3 Ops., 2006—; designer demil integration product team PM Demilitarization, Picatinny Arsenal, NJ, 2006—, demilitarization R&D integration product team, 2006—, strategic planning integration product team, 2006—. Named Outstanding Psychology Grad., Athens State U., 2000—01; named to, Nat. Dean's List, 1997—98; scholar, Athens State U., 1996—98. Mem.: Nat. Def. Indsl. Assn., Mensa. Avocations: reading, puzzles, swimming, contining education, internet research. Home: 124 Greenwood Dr Madison AL 35758 Office: US Army Aviation and Missile Command G-3 Bldg 5308 Sparkman Cir Redstone Arsenal AL 35898 Office Phone: 256-876-6156. E-mail: shania.burrows@us.army.mil.

BURRY, JENNIFER WILBORN, medical/surgical nurse; b. Memphis, Aug. 16, 1961; d. Richard C. and Margaret A. (Boals) Montgomery; m. Allen Burry, Nov. 21, 1980; children: Matthew, Michele. LPN, Aurora Pub. Schs. Tech. Ctr., Colo., 1980; ADN, Community Coll. Denver, 1986; BSN, U. Colo., 1993. RN, Colo. Nurse's aide Swedish Med. Ctr., Englewood, Colo., 1978-81, LPN, 1981-86, RN, relief charge nurse, 1986-93; home health nurse, nursing supervisor Home Health One, Denver, 1993-98; RN, staff nurse neurosurgery/neuroscis. Swedish Med. Ctr., 1998—2005, First Choice Home Health Care, 2005—. Home: 4240 S Yukon Way Lakewood CO 80235-1932

BURRY-STOCK, JUDITH ANNE (ANNE BURRY), education educator; b. Cleve., July 19, 1942; d. Harry Alice (Baine) Mesnick; m. June 1, 1968 (div. Apr. 1977); children: Steven, Christine, Heidi; m. Carl William Stock, July 1993. BS in English and Elem. Edn., Bowling Green State U., 1964; EdM in Reading, SUNY, Buffalo, 1968; EdS in Ednl. Psychology, U. No. Colo., 1984, PhD in Applied Stats. and Rsch. Methods, 1984. Tchr. South Euclid-Lyndhurst Pub. Schs., Ohio, 1964-66, jr. high sch. reading cons. Ohio, 1966-67; instr. SUNY, Buffalo, 1967-68; ednl. cons., Buffalo, 1968-78; internship program U. No. Colo., Greeley, 1978-81, rsch. asst., 1981-84; asst. prof., rsch. assoc. U. Kans., Lawrence, 1984-88; prof. stats., measurement, evaluation/assessment U. Ala., Tuscaloosa, 1988—. Cons. on student and tchrs. assessment States of Colo., Kans., Fla., Iowa, Tenn., Ala., and internationally, also Ednl. Testing Svc.; conf. presenter, 1983—. Contbr. articles to profl. jours. Project dir. Ctr. for Rsch. on Ednl. Accountability and Tchr. Evaluation, 1990-95. Named NDEA fellowship, 1966; grantee tchr. evaluation Office of Edn. Rsch. and Improvement Kans. Dept. Edn., 1985-88, S.D. divsn. Edn., 1988, U. Ala. Coll. Edn., 1988, 89, 90, Dwight D. Eisenhower, 1993; recipient Capstone Coll. of Edn. Acad. Excellence award, 1993. Mem. APA, AAAS, Am. Ednl. Rsch. Assn., Am. Evaluation Assn. Am. Statis. Assn., Nat. Assn. Rsch. on Sci. Tchg., Nat. Coun. on Measurement in Edn., Mid-South Ednl. Rsch. Assn., Phi Delta Phi, Phi Delta Kappa, Phi Lambda Theta. Unitarian Universalist. Avocations: reading. exercising, hiking, music. Office: U Ala Profl Studies Behavioral Studies PO Box 870231 Tuscaloosa AL 35487-0154

BURSLEY-HAMILTON, SUSAN, secondary school educator; b. Redbank, N.J., May 6, 1955; d. Robert Kelly and Irene Magdolin (Connell) Bursley; m. Raymond Hamilton, June 20, 1981; 1 child, Robert. BA in Edn., No. Ariz. U., 1978, MA, 1988. Prin. La Senita Elem. Sch. Recipient Silver Beaver award Boy Scouts Am.; Order Eastern Star scholar. Office Phone: 928-757-4328.

BURSON-DYER, LORRAINE, library executive; b. Omaha, Dec. 20, 1925; d. Elmer Ivan and Marie Eleanor (Benedict) Eastman; m. Francis Mark Burson, Apr. 25, 1948 (wid.); children: Melanie Burson Daniel, Brent Donald, Brian Lee; m. Eldon A. Dyer, July 11, 2004. BA with honors, Portland State U., 1975. Cons. Congregational Libr., Portland, 1975—; libr. Peace Ch. of Brethren, Portland, 1948—55, Burlingame Bapt. Ch., Portland, 1961—88, Village Bapt. Ch., Beaverton, Oreg., 1987—93; exec. dir. Ch. and Synagogue Libr. Assn., Portland, 1987—2006; ret. Author: Recruiting and Training Volunteers for Church/Synagogue Libraries, 1986; contbr. articles to numerous mags. Named Outstanding Scholar, Portland State U., 1974. Mem. Pacific N.W. Assn. Ch. Librs. (pres. 1988-89), N.W. Assn. Christian Librs., Assn. Christian Librs., Nat. Ch. Libr. Coun., Congregational Librs. Assn. of B.C., Luth. Ch. Libr. Assn., Evangel. Ch. Libr. Assn. Baptist. Home: 10880 SW Davies Rd Apt 1014 Beaverton OR 97008-8007

BURSTEIN, SHARON ANN, corporate communications specialist, apparel designer; b. Schenectady, N.Y., July 18, 1952; d. Harold Edward and Lois Ida (Hesner) Rieck; m. Richard Lyle Burstein, Sept. 8, 1985; 1 child, Alexandra Blaire. BA, Nat. Lewis U., 1974; postgrad., Russell Sage Coll., 1974-78, Union Coll., 1980. Cert. tchr., N.Y. Elem. tchr. Saratoga Springs (N.Y.) Schs., 1974-80; ednl. cons. Whitcomb Assocs., Boston, 1980-81; ednl. mktg. specialist Monroe Sys. for Bus., Newington, Conn., 1981-83; nat. mktg. mgr. Victor Techs., Hartford, Conn., 1983, Exclusives, Boston, 1984-85; dir. pub. rels. Lawrence Group, Albany, NY, 1985-87, dir. corp. comm., 1987-88, v.p., 1988-89, v.p investors rels. N.Y.C., 1987-89; pres. S.A. Burstein & Assocs., Albany, 1989—; pres., designer women's tennis, golf and sports apparel Neswick Court, 1994-99. Adj. prof. Russell Sage Coll., Troy, N.Y., 1994-99; exec. prodr. Carmine's TV Show-NBC; cons. N.Y. Assn. Bus. Ofcls., 1982-83; trustee Nat. Lewis U., 2005—. Editor: Helpline newspaper, 1985, 87; co-prodr. Playing It Safe, 1986 (Nori award 1987), To Be As Independent As You Can be (Nori award 1989), Cookbook Capital Connoisseur (Nori award 1989), Camp Ever Young (Nori award 1993); acted in TV comml., 1981 (Addy award 1982); prodr. Carmine's Table TV Show (NBC); exec. prodr. A Place With a Heart, 2004 (Comm. award). Bd. dirs. Multiple Sclerosis Soc., Albany, 1986, Mohawk Pathways Girl Scouts U.S.; active N.Y. Spl. Olympics, 1987; v.p. bd. dirs. Capital Repertory Theater Guild, 1999—. Recipient Distinguished. Alumni award, Nat. Lewis U., 2004. Mem. Nat. Investor Rels. Inst., Am. Mgmt. Assn., Assn. Profl. Communicators, Nat. Assn. Investment Clubs, Tennis Industry Assn., Albany C. of C. (women's bus. coun.), Women's Press Club, Kappa Delta Pi. Democrat. Avocations: writing, tennis, golf, skiing, reading. Home: 4 Birch Hill Rd Loudonville NY 12211-2004

BURSTYN, ELLEN (EDNA RAE GILLOOLY), actress; b. Detroit, Dec. 7, 1932; m. William Anderson, 1950 (div. 1955); m. Paul Roberts, 1957 (div. 1959); m. Neil Burstyn, 1960 (div. 1971); 1 child, Jefferson. LHD (hon.), Dowling Coll.; DFA (hon.), Sch. Visual Arts. Artistic dir. The Actor's Studio, N.Y.C., 1982-88. Actress (films) Gunfight in Black Horse Canyon, 1961, Alex in Wonderland, 1970, Tropic of Cancer, 1970, The Last Picture Show, 1971, The King of Marvin Gardens, 1972, The Exorcist, 1973, Harry and Tonto, 1974, Alice Dosen't Live Here Anymore (Acad. award for Best Actress), 1974, Same Time, Next Year, 1978, Resurrection, 1980, Silence of the North, 1981, In Our Hands, 1984, The Ambassador, 1984, Twice in a Lifetime, 1985, Hanna's War, 1988, Grand Isle, 1991, Dying Young, 1991, The Cemetery Club, 1993, The Color of Evening, 1994, Choosing One's Way: Resistance in Auschwitz/Birkenau (narrator, presenter), 1994, When a Man Loves a Woman, 1994, Roommates, 1995, The Baby-Sitters Club, 1995, How to Make an American Quilt, 1995, The Spitfire Grill, 1996, Deceiver, 1997, You Can Thank Me Later, 1998, Playing by Heart, 1998, Walking Across Egypt, 1999, Requiem for a Dream, 1999, The Yards, 1999, Divine Secrets of the Ya-Ya Sisterhood, 2002, Distance, 2002, (voice only) Red Dragon, 2002, Down in the Valley, 2005, The Elephant King, 2006, The Wicker Man, 2006, 30 Days, 2006; (TV movies) Thursday's Game, 1974, The People vs. Jean Harris, 1981, Acting: Lee Strasberg and the Actos Studio, 1981, Surviving, 1985, Into Thin Air, 1985, Something in Common, 1986, Act of Vengeance, 1986, Hellow Actors Studio, 1987, (voice only) Dear America: Letters Home from Vietnam, 1987, Pack of Lies, 1987, When You Remember Me, 1990, Mrs. Lambers Remembers Love, 1991, Taking Back My Life: The Nacy Ziegenmeyer Story, 1992, Shattered Trust: The Shary Karney Story, 1993, Getting Out, 1994, Getting Gotti, 1994, Trick of the Eye, 1994, My Brother's Keeper, 1995, Follow the River, 1995, Timepiece, 1995, Our Son, The Matchmaker, 1996, Murder in the Mind, 1996, A Deadly Vision, 1997, Flash, 1998, The Patron Saint of Liars, 1998, Night Ride Home, 1999, Mermaid, 2000, Within These Walls, 2001, Dodson's Journey, 2001, Brush with Fate, 2003, The Madam's Family: The Truth About the Canal Street Brothel, 2004, The Five People You Meet in Heaven, 2004, Our Fathers, 2005, Mrs. Harris, 2005; (TV series) The Ellen Burstyn Show, 1986-87; (mini-series) A Will of Their Own, 1998; (TV appearances) Cheyenne, 1955, Gunsmoke, 1955, Maverick, 1957, The Big Valley, 1965, The Time Tunnel, 1966, The Bold Ones: The Lawyers, 1969; Author:(autobiography) Lessons in Becoming Myself, 2006 Mem. individual artists grants and policy overview panels Nat. Endowment for the Arts, Theater Adv. Council City of New York. Named to, The Mich. Women's Hall of Fame, 1997. Mem. Actors Equity Assn. (pres. 1982-85) Office: Creative Artists Agy care Steve Tellez 9830 Wilshire Blvd Beverly Hills CA 90212-1804*

BURT, GWEN BEHRENS, educational association administrator; b. Clinton, Ind., Nov. 6, 1946; d. Henry Milum Allbright and Marjorie Evelyn (Muir) Wiot; m. Kurt Fredric Behrens, Mar. 28, 1970 (div. June 1984); m. Gary

Orren Burt (dec. Sept. 1998), Sept. 5, 1996; 1 child, Amy Lynn. BS, Ind. State U., 1969, MS, 1974. Tchr. Center Grove Cmty. Schs., Greenwood, Ind., 1969-71; tchr. reading Vigo County Sch. Corp., Terre Haute, Ind., 1971-77; summer adminstr. Maercker Sch. Dist., Clarendon Hills, Ill., 1991-98, Title I dir., 1977-98; prin. Sauk Sch., Matteson (Ill.) Dist. 162, 1998—. Adj. lectr. Lewis U., Romeoville, Ill., 1996; presenter workshops and lectures, 1987—. Coord. single adult program, Grace United Meth. Ch., Naperville, Ill., 1992-95, coord. youth ministry program, 1985-87; vol. numerous charitable orgns. including Am. Cancer Soc., Am. Heart Assn., etc. Mem. NEA (various offices Ill. and Ind. chpts.), AAUW, Internat. Reading Assn. (various offices Ill. and Ind. chpts.), Nat. Assn. Elem. Schs. Prins., AAUW, ASCD, Ill. Prins. Assn., Ill. Reading Coun., Ill. Women Adminstr., Ill. Title I coords., Adminstrs. and Reading Spl. Interest Coun., Delta Kappa Gamma. Republican. Avocations: power boating, golf, antiques, genealogy, lighthouses. Office: Sauk Sch 4435 S Churchill Dr Richton Park IL 60471-1101 Home: PO Box 3338 Galveston TX 77552-0338 E-mail: gaboating1@cs.com, gburt@sd162.org.

BURT-MURRAY, ANGELA, editor-in-chief; m. Leonard Murray; 2 children. BS in Fin., Hampton U. Fashion and beauty features editor Essence mag., NYC, 1998—2001; exec. editor Honey mag., 2001—03; beauty dir. Teen People, NYC, 2001, features dir., asst. mng. editor then exec. editor, 2003—05; editor-in-chief Essence mag., NYC, 2005—. Articles appearing in Working Mother, Parenting, Heart & Soul, Atlanta CityMag, Black Elegance. Co-author (with Denene Millner and Mitzi Miller): (novels) The Angry Black Woman's Guide to Life; author The Vow. Mem.: Am. Soc. of Mag. Editors, Nat. Assn. of Black Journalists. Office: Essence 1500 Broadway 6th Fl New York NY 10036

BURTON, ANN MAPES, historian, retired academic administrator; b. Detroit, Mar. 4, 1933; d. Ralph James and Edith Blanch (Moore) B. BA in History, Duke U., Durham, N.C., 1954; MA in History, U. Mich., Ann Arbor, 1955; DPhil in History, Oxford U., 1960. Instr. Hunter Coll., CUNY, 1961-63; asst. prof. Bklyn. Coll., CUNY, 1964-71, assoc. prof., 1971-79, prof., 1979-84, prof. emeritus, 1984—; assoc. dean faculty arts & scis. N.Y.U., 1981-86, dean arts & sci. adminstrn., 1986-93; v.p. acad. affairs Swiss Hosp. Inst., Washington, 1994, pres., 1995—97. Mem. doctoral faculty in history CUNY Grad. Sch., 1975-84; sec. univ. faculty senate CUNY, 1975-76, chmn. com. on funding alternatives, 1975, vice-chmn. univ. faculty senate, 1976-78, chmn. univ. faculty senate, trustee, 1978-81; chmn. coll. com. on master planning and ednl. policy Bklyn. Coll., 1975-76, chmn. curriculum com., 1974-76, dep. chmn. dept. history, 1969-71, chmn. dept. history, 1976-80; screening com. in history, Fulbright Commn., 1974-75. Contbr. articles to profl. jours. Trustee Grace Opportunity Project, 1985-93, Grace Ch. Sch., 1980-86, Gunn Meml. Libr., 1993-96; chmn. music com. Grace Episcopal Ch., N.Y.C., 1979-89, treas., 1987-89, vestry mem., 1976-81; bd. dirs. N.Y. Chamber Soloists, 1980-92; altar guild St. John's Ch., Washington, Conn., 1989—, vestry mem., 1991-98, warden, 1994-98;1 chmn. Wash. Repub. Town Com., 2000-02; trustee After Sch. Arts Program, 2004-; chmn. grants, trustee Conn. Cmty. Found., v.p., bd. trustees, 2005-06, pres., 2006-. Mem. AAUW (fellow 1963-64), Am. Philos. Soc. (grantee 1963-64). Home: PO Box 1417 Washington CT 06793-0417

BURTON, BARBARA, marketing executive; b. Plainfield, N.J., May 29, 1953; d. Frank James and Helen Sellmyer Wolf; m. Allen Craig Burton, June 21, 1986; children: Matthew James, Abigail Elizabeth. BA, Northwestern U., 1975; MLS, Rutgers U., 1977. Indexer N.Y. Times Info. Svc., Parsippany, N.Y., 1977-78, customer svc. rep., 1979-81, nat. tng. mgr., 1981-83; online mktg. coord. Dun & Bradstreet, Parsippany, 1983-84; account exec. Dow Jones & Co., Princeton, N.J., 1984-88, account devel. mgr., 1988-97, infopro alliance mgr., 1997—. Mem. Spl. Librs. Assn., Westfield Hist. Soc., Friends of Westfield Libr., Beta Phi Mu. Home: 620 Lenox Ave Westfield NJ 07090-2161

BURTON, BARBARA ABLE, psychotherapist; b. Columbia, S.C. d. Eugene Walter Able and Mary Louise (Chadwick) Cantelou; 1 child, Stacia Louise. BA in Psychology, Ga. State U.; MSW, U. Ala., 1970. Diplomate Am. Bd. Examiners in Clin. Social Work, Internat. Acad. Behavioral Medicine, Counseling and Psychotherapy. Assoc. exec. dir. Positive Maturity, Inc., Birmingham, Ala., 1970—72; comm. orgn. planner Cmty. Svc. Coun., Inc., Birmingham, 1972—75; mem. adj. faculty U. Ala., Tuscaloosa, 1975—77; dir. Ensley Outpatient Drug Abuse Clinic, Birmingham, 1975—77; dir. Sch. Social Work, Miles Coll., Birmingham, 1977—78; program mgr. and clin. cons. Goodwill Industries Ala., Birmingham, 1977—81; pvt. practice New Orleans, 1983—. Cons. Omega Internat. Inst., New Orleans, 1988-94. Author: Love Me, Love Me Not, and Other Matters That Matter, 1990. Past chmn. policy and program com. Birmingham Urban League; mem. Ala. Adv. Com. on Social Svcs., Ala. Com. for Devel. Higher Ed., Ala. Conf. Social Work. NIMH fellow Inst. on Human Sexuality, U. Hawaii, 1976. Mem. NASW (diplomate in clin. social work), Am. Assn. Sex Educators, Counselors and Therapists, Pvt. Practitioners Unit of New Orleans, Acad. Cert. Social Workers, Internat. Platform Com., Psi Chi. Avocations: creative writing, reading, interior design. Office: 110 Country Club Dr Covington LA 70433 Personal E-mail: baburton@charter.net, bb251@bellsouth.net.

BURTON, BARBARA ANNE, plumbing and heating company executive; b. Flushing, NY, Nov. 28, 1948; d. Victor Arthur and Anne (Inglima) Schettini; m. Maurice John Burton, Mar. 10, 1973; children: Anthony John, Christopher Maurice. Diploma, Flushing H.S., 1966. Loan payers Household Fin. Corp., NYC, 1966-67; sec. P.F. Collier Inc., London, 1968-69, exec. sec., 1969-70; sec. Bill Lutz Assocs., NYC, 1970-72; exec. sec. merchandising Courtaulds N.Am., NYC, 1972-75; sec.-treas. M. Burton Plumbing & Heating Corp., NYC, 1975—. Republican. Roman Catholic. Avocations: decorating, travel, reading. Office: M Burton Plumbing & Heating 206-01 48th Ave Bayside NY 11364-1046 Office Phone: 718-224-0693.

BURTON, BETSEY (MARY ELIZABETH BURTON), retail executive; b. Richmond, Va., Dec. 18, 1951; d. Samuel Bayard and Dottie (Brown) Jeter. BA in Sociology, Coll. William and Mary, 1973; MBA, U. Chgo., 1975. Corp. trainee Jewel Cos., Chgo., 1975—82, mdse. mgr. Osco Drug div., 1980—82; pres. Bee Discount, Hillside, Ill., 1982—83, Victory Beauty Systems (parent of Bee Discount), Hillside, Ill., 1983—87; CEO Supercuts Inc., 1987—91, PIP Printing, 1991—92, BB Capital Inc., 1992; chmn., CEO The Cosmetic Centre, 1998—99; acting CEO Zale Corp., 2006, pres., CEO, 2006—. Bd. dirs. Zale Corp., Staples Inc., Rent-A-Center, Aeropostale Inc; past bd. dirs. Sports Authority. Mem. mental health task force United Methodist Ch., Naperville, Ill., 1982. Grantee, NSF, 1972, George Hay Brown Found., U. Chgo. Grad. Sch. Bus., 1975. Mem.: Com. of 200, U. Chgo. Women's Bus. Group. Republican. Avocations: aerobics, jogging. Office: Zale Corp 901 W Walnut Hill Ln Irving TX 75038*

BURTON, BETTY JANE (B.J. BURTON), playwright; d. Robert Ellis and Barbara Elizabeth (Williams) Burton. BA in Theater, U. Mo., Kansas City, 1973; postgrad., Am. Conservatory Theatre, 1978; grad. in Theater, Villanova U., Pa., 1997; MFA Creative Writing, Rosemont Coll., Pa., 2006. Author: (plays) Hunting Season, 1990, Buddy, 1992, Lunch on the Fifth, 1993, Lobelia Lodge, 1995, Pizza Again, 1996, Green Benches, 2000, Marjorie and Helen, 2000, Room For Love, 2002, Newsroom, 2004. Recipient Pa. Playwriting award, Theatre Assn. Pa., 1994; fellow, Pa. Coun. Arts, 1990, 2000. Mem.: AFTRA, SAG, Actors Equity Assn., The Dramatists Guild. Avocations: painting, photography. Office: PO Box 445 Wayne PA 19087 Personal E-mail: bj_burton@hotmail.com.

BURTON, BETTY JUNE, retired pastor; b. Muskegon, Mich., June 11, 1923; d. Bernard J. and Louise Ella (Weaver) Mulder; m. Harold Ver Berkmoes, June 4, 1943 (div. 1966); children: Suzanne (dec.), James, Michael, William, Judith, David (dec.); m. Eldon Franklin Burton, June 27, 1971 (dec. May 2003). Student of music, psychology and religion, Hope Coll., 1941-45; student, Garrett Evang. Theol. Sem., 1984-85. Ordained to ministry United Meth. Ch., 1986. Librarian Vassar Hosp. Sch. Nursing, Poughkeepsie, NY, 1958-60, Hackley Pub. Library, Muskegon, 1960-64, Boyne City (Mich.) Pub. Library, 1972-74; reporter Ludington (Mich.) Daily News, 1975-81; caseworker Aid to Dependent Children Mich. Dept. Social Services, Hart, 1974-78; pastor various Meth. Chs., Norwood, Barnard and Charlevoix, Mich., 1981-83, Mears (Mich.) United Meth. Ch., 1985, 86; assoc. pastor United Meth. Centenary, Pentwater, Mich., 1986-90; pastor First Congl. Ch. of Central Lake, Mich., 1990-92, Thompsonville (Mich.) Congl. Church, 1982—83. Guest preacher, spkr. various chs. Sec. Pentwater Planning Commn., 1985; vol. chaplain Grand Tranverse Pavilions Nursing Home. Mem. NAFE, Internat. Platform Assn., Am. Platform Assn., Am. Assn. Christian Counselors, Nat. Christian Counselors Assn., Nat. Trust Hist. Preservation, Am. Mus. Natural History, Nat. Audubon Soc., Am. Acad. Ministry, Hist. Soc. Mich., Oceana County Hist. Soc., Kappa Beta Phi (pres. 1943), Xi Gamma Beta (sec. 1970). Clubs: Women's of Pentwater (v.p. 1986—), Garden of Pentwater (pres. 1986—), Sierra. Republican. Avocations: writing, fishing, gardening, birding, travel. Home: 3950 Scenic Rdg Apt 108 Traverse City MI 49684-3904

BURTON, CHERYL, newscaster; b. Chgo. BS in Psychology and Biology, U. Ill., Champaign. Host Minority Bus. Report WGN-TV, Chgo., 1989; reporter WMBD-TV, Peoria, Ill., 1990; weekend anchor KWCH-TV, Wichita, Kans., 1990—92, host Viewpoint, 1990—92; weekend co-anchor and reporter WLS-TV, Chgo., 1992—2003, co-anchor and contbg. anchor 5 pm news, 2003—. Vol. Boys and Girls Club of Am., Rush-Presbyn./St. Luke's Fashion Show; motivational spkr. Chgo. Pub. Sch.; bd. mem. City Yr., Chgo. Recipient Kizzy Image and Achievement award, 1998, Phenomenal Woman award, Expo Today's Black Woman, 1997, Emmy award, 2002. Mem.: Nat. Assn. of Black Journalists, Chgo. Assn. of Black Journalists (now named Russ Ewing award 1996, 2003), Life with Lupus Guild, Delta Sigma Theta. Office: WLS-TV 190 N State St Chicago IL 60601*

BURTON, EVE B., lawyer; b. NYC, Oct. 16, 1958; BA, Hampshire Coll., 1982; JD, Columbia U., 1989. Bar: NY 1990, U.S. Dist. Ct. NY (ea. and so. dist.) 1993, U.S. Ct. Appeals (2nd cir.) 1996, U.S. Supreme Ct. 1997. Law clerk U.S. Dist. Ct. NY (so. dist.), 1985—86; internat. corp. fin. assoc. Milbank, Tweed, Hadley & McCloy, NY and Hong Kong, 1989—90; v.p., dep. gen. counsel Daily News, NYC, 1990—91; sr. litigation assoc. Weil, Gotshal & Manges, 1991—95; v.p., chief legal counsel CNN, NYC, 2000—01; v.p., gen. counsel Hearst Corp., NYC, 2002—. Mem. ethics com. CNN, 1995—2000; adj. prof. Columbia U., 1999—. Contbr. articles to profl. jours. Recipient First Amendment award, Nat. Press Club, 1998, NY Press Club, 1998, Soc. Profl. Journalists, 1999; Fulbright Rsch. Scholar, Thmmasat U., Thailand. Mem.: ABA, Assn. Bar. City of NY (mem. comm. com.). Office: Hearst 250 W 55th St New York NY 10019-5201 Office Phone: 212-649-2000. E-mail: eburton@hearst.com.

BURTON, JANET RUTH WISNER, music educator; b. Ft. Payne, Ala., Nov. 25, 1955; d. Robert Thurston and Mary Lou (Garrett) Wisner; m. David Lee Malone (div.); 1 child, Mara Ruth Malone; m. O.E. "Buddy" Burton, Oct. 18, 1991. AA in Music, Nat. Sch. Music, Roanoke, Ala., 1979; Assoc., N.E. State Jr. Coll., Rainsville, Ala., 1990; BSE, Athens State Coll., 1992; MusMA, Jacksonville State U., Ala., 2004. Cert. tchr. Ala., Tenn. Substitute tchr. Catawba County Schs., Maiden, NC, 1992—94; music dir. Cornerstone Ch., Maiden, NC, 1992—95; tchr. Lincolnton (NC) H.S., 1994—95; music dir. Gault Ave. Bapt. Ch., Ft. Payne, Ala., 1995—96; substitute tchr. Lake Travis Schs., Austin, Tex., 1995—99; tchr. Hilltop Acad., Cedar Park, Tex., 1997—99; program dir. Hilltop Bapt. Ch., Cedar Park, Tex., 1997—99; band interium Geraldine (Ala.) H.S., 1999—2000; music tchr. K-6 Plainview H.S., Rainsville, Ala., 2000—01, Huntland (Tenn.) H.S., 2004—05. Owner, prodr. (TV show) Gospel Music Time with Buddy & Janet Burton, 2002—05; composer: numerous songs, 1980—2000; author, instr. Do Re Mi's of Music. Named Miss Congeniality, DeKalb County Jr. Miss, Ft. Payne, 1974; recipient Ballroom Dance award, Fred Astaire Studios, 1985, Leadership award, Omicron Delta Kappa, 2003; grantee, Ala. Arts Coun., 1995. Mem.: Tenn. Tchrs. Edn. Assn., Nat. Assn. Music Educators, C.C. Rainsville. Avocations: painting, reading, nature walks, movies, musical instruments. Home: PO Box 8 Rainsville AL 35986 Office: Huntland HS 300 Gore St Huntland TN 37345 Office Phone: 256-638-6591. Personal E-mail: buddy@fumcscottsboro.org.

BURTON, JANIS ELAINE (JAN BURTON), retired writer, editor; b. Waitsburg, Wash., May 25, 1933; d. Carroll Everett and Hope Olive (Bolender) Fairbanks; m. Armond Sidney Burton Jr., June 14, 1953; children: Charity Ann Burton Burkhart, Armond Fairbanks. B, Phillips U., 1958; postgrad., U. Okla., 1973. Cert. tchr., Okla. Tchr. home econs. Madison Jr. High Sch., Bartlesville, Okla., 1960-67; proofreader The Norman (Okla.) Transcript, 1968-69, reporter, 1969-71, asst. wire editor, 1972-75; assoc. writer Media Info. U. Okla., Norman, 1975-77, writer Media Info., 1977-78, sr. writer Media Info., 1978-79, assoc. Sports Info., 1980-84, dir. Sports Publs., 1984-90; ret., 1990; cons. Athletic Novelties U. Okla., Norman, 1985-90; editor, Living section Norman Transcript, 1991—95; owner Jan Burton, Editing, Etc., Norman, 1992—2000. Former editor football programs and sports brochures. Recipient recieved numerous awards in writing and pubs. Mem. Football Writers Am., Okla. Coaches Wifes Assn., U. Okla. President's Ptnrs., assoc. mem. O Club, first woman inductee, Phillips U. Hall of Fame, 1988. Democrat. Mem. Christian Ch. Avocations: travel, collecting teddy bears.

BURTON, KATE, actress; b. Geneva, Sept. 10, 1957; arrived in NYC, 1961; d. Richard Burton and Sybil Christopher; m. Michael Ritchie, 1984; children: Morgan, Charlotte. BA in Russian Studies and European History, Brown U., 1979; grad., Yale Drama Sch., 1983. Actress (Broadway plays) Present Laughter, 1982 (Theatre World award, 1983), Alice in Wonderland, 1982 (Theatre World award, 1983), Doonesbury, 1983, Wild Honey, 1986, Some Americans Abroad, 1990, Jake's Women, 1992, Company, 1995, An American Daughter, 1997, The Beauty Queen of Leenane, 1998, Hedda Gabler, 2001 (Callaway award, 2002), The Elephant Man, 2002, The Constant Wife, 2005, (plays) Boston Marriage, (Off-Broadway) The Water's Edge, 2006, (plays) Three Sisters, Give Me Your Answer, Do!, Company, The Playboy of the Western World, Winners (Theatre World award, 1983), (films) Anne of the Thousand Days, 1969, Big Trouble in Little China, 1986, Life With Mikey, 1993, August, 1996, The First Wives Club, 1996, The Ice Storm, 1997, Celebrity, 1998, The Opportunists, 2000, Unfaithful, 2002, Swimfan, 2002, The Paper Mache Chase, 2003, Stay, 2005, Some Kind of Heaven, 2005, (TV miniseries) Ellis Island, 1984, Evergreen, 1985, Empire Falls, 2005, (TV series) Home Fires, 1992, Monty, 1994, (TV films) Uncle Tom's Cabin, 1987, Journey Into Genius, 1988, Notes for My Daughter, 1995, Mistrial, 1996, Ellen Foster, 1997, Obsessed, 2002, The Diary of Ellen Rimbauer, 2003, (guest appearance TV series) The West Wing, 2004, The Practice, Law & Order, 2004, Judging Amy, 2005, Grey's Anatomy, 2005. Bd. trustees Broadway Cares/Equity Fights AIDS. Mem.: Actor's Equity Assn.*

BURTON, KATHLEEN T., mental health services professional; b. Lynn, Mass., Jan. 29, 1962; d. Charles W. and Mary L. (Mayer) Burton. BA in Psychology/Comm., Notre Dame Coll., South Euclid, Ohio, 1985; MEd in Counseling, Cleve. State U., 1990, EdS in Counseling, 1991; PhD in Clin. Psychology, Saybrook Inst., San Francisco, 2006. Cert. rational marriage and family therapist, diplomate cognitive-behavioral therapy. Human rels. & devel. coord. Kaiser Permanent, Cleveland Heights, Ohio, 1984—87; counselor Cleve. Treatment Ctr., 1989—90; tchg. asst., counselor intern Cleve. State U., 1989—91; cmty. trainer Woodland (Calif.) Cmty. Options, 1991—95; mental health profl., psychologist intern Davis, Calif., 1992—95; pvt. practice mental health profl. Woodland, Calif., 1995—2001; undergrad. psychology instr. Computer Quest Ltd., 2003; personal growth coach and human rels. cons., 2004—. Group facilitator human sexuality course dept. psychiatry Davis Med. Sch., 1994—2001; group leader, facilitator anxiety, phobias and panic Woodland Sr. Ctr., 1993—99; mental health cons., creator Mental Health Matters, Pub. TV, 1995; founder Sr./Youth Fair, Woodland, 1995; mental health writer Davis Enterprise; lectr. anxiety, phobias, panic, drug addictions, Moscow, Kiev, 1994. Author: (poetry) Hold on Tight; contbr. articles to profl. jours. Recipient 1st pl., Nat. Future Design Competition, 1984. Mem.: ACA, Bus. Network Internat., Nat. Assn. Cognitive Behaviorial Therapists. Roman Catholic. Avocations: gardening, dance, camping, hiking. Office Phone: 216-227-9481.

BURTON, LUCY, enterostomal therapy nurse; b. Bradford, Pa., July 16, 1956; d. John H. and Mary ann (Chobody) B. BSN, Villa Maria Coll., 1978; postgrad., Roswell Park Meml. Inst., 1981, U. Ariz., 1985-86. Cert. enterostomal therapy nurse; cert. case mgr.; cert. pub. health nurse. Field nurse Home Health Svcs. of Erie County, Erie, Pa.; enterostomal therapy nurse St. Vincent Health Ctr., Erie; instr. Tucson Med. Ctr.; enterostomal therapy nurse Grossmont Hosp., La Mesa, Calif.; clin. instr. enterostomal therapy nurse edn. program Tucson Med. Ctr.; enterostomal therapy nurse cons. Ind. Contractor and Care Home Health, San Diego County, Calif., 1993—; enterostomal therapy nurse Long Beach Meml. Med. Ctr., Calif., 1995—2004. Nurse cons., expert witness elder abuse cases, L.A., 1999, 2000. Contbr. articles to profl. pubs. Ostomy visitor program coord. Am. Cancer Soc., 1983, coord. "I Can Cope," 1984-85, 88-90. Mem. Wound, Ostomy Continence Nurse Soc. (northeast region conf. chmn. 1984, chmn. San Diego chpt. 1990-92). Home: 4114 Elm Ave Apt 1 Long Beach CA 90807-2769 Office Phone: 562-981-3258.

BURTON, PEGGY, advertising and marketing executive; b. N.Y.C. BSBA, NYU, 1960. Freelance TV producer, N.Y.C., 1964-67; TV producer Young & Rubicam, N.Y.C., 1967-69; sr. acct. exec. Daniel & Charles, N.Y.C., 1969-74; ptnr., v.p. Bruderer Hartnett Advt. Agy., N.Y.C., 1974-76; dir. Comm. Am. Express Co., N.Y.C., 1976-83; pres. advt. Dreyfus Corp., N.Y.C., 1983-95; pres. Burton Commns. Multi Media, N.Y.C., 1995—. Vol. Met. Mus. Art; bd. dirs. Nat. Sch. Com. Econ. Edn., Mallon Fund. Mem. Internat. Advt. Assn., N.Y. New Media Assn., Fin. Women's Assn., Fgn. Policy Assn., Bus. Execs. for Nat. Security, NYU Gallatin Arts Com., N.Y. Athletic Club, Nat. Arts Club. Address: 220 Central Park S New York NY 10019-1417 Office Phone: 212-581-4592. E-mail: pegbur@aol.com.

BURTON, SHEILA BELLE, music educator; b. Springfield, Ill., July 20, 1945; d. James Eugene Gurnsey, Hazel Belle Gurnsey; m. Charles Arlie Burton. B in Music Edn., Bradley U., 1968. Music instr. Chandlerville Unit Dist., Ill., 1968—70, Beardstown Unit Dist. #15, Ill., 1970—75; unit vocal and band instr. VIT, Table Grove, Ill., 1984—93; band instr. Schuyler Unit Dist. #1, Rushville, Ill., 1993—2004; ret. Auxiliary/dance line dir. Schuyler Unit Dist. #1, Rushville, 1993—2004, girls golf coach, 1993—. Mem.: MENC - IMEA. Methodist. Avocations: golf, reading, gardening. Home: 80 Parkview Rd RR#2 Box 23 Rushville IL 62681 Office: Schuyler Dist #1 730 N Congress Rushville IL 62681 Office Fax: 217-322-2844. Personal E-mail: sburton@frontiernet.net. Business E-Mail: sburton@sid5.com.

BURTT, ANNE DAMPMAN, special education educator; b. Phila., Nov. 22, 1950; d. Elmer and Anne (Scott) Dampman; m. James Burtt, Aug. 5, 1972. BS in Edn. cum laude, Duquesne U., 1972; MEd, U. Pitts., 1976, Temple U., 1985. Cert. spl. edn., elem. tchr., reading specialist. Tchr. Pitts. Pub. Schs., 1972-77; tchr. Montgomery County (Pa.) Intermediate Unit, 1997—2000, Archdiocese of Phila. Schs., 2000—; archdiocese Phila. Schs., 2000—. Mem. PTO, 1972—, Chpt. Attention Deficit Disorders, 1989—, CHADD Bux-Mont. Divsn., Behavioral Disorders/Learning Disorders. Recipient Pius X award Archdiocese Phila., Most Successful Grad. 25th Yr. Reunion West Phila. Cath. Girls' H.S. Mem. Pa. State Edn. Assn., Coun. for Exceptional Children, Behavior Disorders and Learning Disabilities. Home: 131 Maple Ave Willow Grove PA 19090-2902

BURTT, LARICE ANNADEL ROSEMAN, artist; b. Phila., June 22, 1928; d. Milo A.J. Roseman and Anna Sterling; m. James C. Burtt, June 25, 1960; childen, James M., Kyleann S. BS in Biology, Bucknell U., 1950; MS in Nursing, Yale U., 1955; studied art with Dr. Selma Burke, studied with William A. Smith; cert., Katherine Gibbs Sec. Sch., 1951. Med. clinical instr. Jefferson Hosp., Phila., 1956-57; med. surgical instr. Rowan Meml. Hosp., Salisbury, NC, 1958-59. Workshop leader Yale, New Haven Hosp. Pain Mgmt. Ctrs., New Haven, Ct., 1996, Attleboro Nursing Home, Langhorne, Pa., Chandler Hall, Newtown, Pa.; demo instr. Delaware Valley Schs., Pa., 1979—; profl. demonstrator in field, 1977—. Painter (3 dimensional stone painting), many locations, 1976-99; one person shows include Phila. Art Mus. Gallery, 1985, Arnot Art Mus., Elmira, N.Y., 1987, Cannon Bldg., Washington, DC 1995, Yale Univ. Sch. Nursing, New Haven, Conn., 1996, Abington Art Ctr., Pa., Upstairs Gallery, Buckingham, Pa.; exhibited in group shows at Immaculata Coll., Accent and Images Gallery, Lahaska, Pa., Nova, 1990-2004, Jane Anthony Gallery, Newtown, Pa., 2000, Abington (Pa.) Art Ctr., Wilson Sch. Mt. Lakes Gallery Show, 2001-04, Galleria Veronese, New Orleans, La., 2005, many area group exhbns., 1977—; represented in permanent collection Grand Canyon Nat. Pk. Mus. Mem. AAUW, Northampton Hist. Soc., Middletown Grange, Bucks County Guild Craftsman (exhbn. at Franklin and Marshall Coll. 1979-96), James Michener Art Mus., Doylestown (Pa.), Doylestown Art League, Pa. Guild, Bucks County Arts and Culture Coun., Charchville Nature Ctr. Avocations: tennis, piano, visual/performing arts, community affairs, service art shows. Home: 31 Beth Dr Richboro PA 18954-1901 Personal E-mail: lariceburtt@aol.com.

BURWELL, EDITH BRODIE, retired elementary school educator; d. Nathaniel and Mary Brodie; m. Jamie L. Burwell, June 9, 1962. BS, Fayetteville State U., N.C. Second grade tchr. Eaton Johnson Elem., Henderson, NC, 1961—62; first and second grade tchr. Newark NJ Pub. Schs., 1963—65; first grade tchr. Rockaway Twp. Pub. Sch., NJ, 1965—2001; ret., 2001. Trainer for tchrs. Rockaway Twp. Schs., Bd. of Edn., NJ. Mem.: NEA, N.J. Edn. Assn., AKA Sorority (scholarship com. 1960—2006). Avocations: travel, reading, photography, exercise. Home: 60 Georgetown Woods Dr Youngsville NC 27596

BURYK, ALEXIS, advertising executive; b. 1953; Attended, Wagner Coll., Fordham U. With NY Times, NYC, 1977—, retail advt. dir., advt. sales mgr. retail, advt. sales mgr. spl. projects and direct response, sales mgr. free standing inserts, v.p. advt. dept., 1993—2000, group v.p. advt. sales, 2001—06, sr. v.p. advt., 2006—. Office: The NY Times Co 229 W 43rd St New York NY 10036*

BURZIK, CATHERINE M., pharmaceutical executive; B in Math., Canisius Coll.; M in Math., Univ. Buffalo. Software engr. to various mgmt. positions Eastman Kodak; mgmt. positions Critikon, Inc.; pres. Ortho-Clinical Diagnostics, Inc.; COO, exec. v.p. Applied Biosystems, Foster City, Calif., pres., 2004—; and sr. v.p. Applera Corp., Foster City, Calif., 2004—. Bd. trustees Canisius Coll. Office: Applied Biosystems 850 Lincoln Ctr Dr San Mateo CA 94404 Office Phone: 650-638-5800. Office Fax: 650-638-5884.

BURZYNSKI, SUSAN MARIE, newspaper editor; b. Jackson, Mich., Jan. 1, 1953; d. Leon Walter and Claudia (Kulpinski) B.; m. James W. Bush, May 22, 1976 (div. 1989); children: Lisa M., Kevin J.; m. George K. Bullard, Jr., Mar. 21, 1992. AA, Jackson C.C., 1972; BA, Mich. State, 1974. Reporter Saratogian, Saratoga Springs, N.Y., 1974, Gongwer News Svc., Lansing, Mich., 1975, The State Jour., Lansing, 1975-79; Metro editor Port Huron (Mich.) Times Herald, 1979-82, mng. editor, 1982-86; asst. city editor Detroit News, 1986-87, Sunday news editor, 1987, news editor, 1988-91, asst. mng. editor/news, 1991-96, asst. mng. editor, recruiting and tng., 1996-98, asst. mng. editor, adminstr., 1998-2000, assoc. editor, 2000—04, mng. editor, 2004—. Roman Catholic. Avocations: swimming, tennis, bicycling, knitting. Office: Detroit News 615 W Lafayette Blvd Detroit MI 48226-3197 Office Phone: 313-222-2772. Business E-Mail: sburzynski@detnews.com.

BUSBEA, VIRGINIA BETH, mathematics educator; d. Thomas L. and Deborah J. Busbea. BSE, Ark. State U., Jonesboro, 2000. Math tchr. Northland Christian Schools, Houston, 2001—03, Valley View H.S., Jonesboro, Ark., 2003—. Fin. adv. Delta Zeta Sorority, Jonesboro, Ark., 2003—06. Mem.: Ark. Coun. of Teachers of Math., Nat. Coun. of Teachers of Math., Am. Math. Soc., Kappa Delta Pi, Delta Zeta Sorority (life; fin. advisor 2003—06, Alumni of Yr. 2000).

BUSBIN, BRENDA C., public health nurse; b. Irwin County, Ga., Sept. 15, 1949; d. Richard E. and Lois (Williams) Wilder; m. Van V. Clark, Sept. 17, 1967 (dec. Sept. 4, 2003); children: Kim, Wendy, Kasey; m. Anthony D. Busbin, Jan. 24, 2004. AS, Abraham Baldwin Agrl. Coll., Tifton, Ga., 1984; EMT, Moultrie Area Tech. Sch., Tifton, Ga., 1987; LPN, Tifton Vocat. Sch., 1976. Part-time supr. Palemon Gaskins Nursing Home, Ocilla, Ga.; pub. health nurse, perinatal case mgmt. program Ben Hill County Health Dept. John Henry scholar. Home: 151 Sly Hill Rd Ocilla GA 31774-3639

BUSBY, BARBARA SUE HUGHES, geriatrics nurse; b. Cherokee County, Ala., June 14, 1939; d. Herman and Dorcas Irene (Palmer) Moats; m. Charles Lee Hughes, Feb. 18, 1956 (dec. 1992); children: Deborah Kay Bowman, Charles Lydell Hughes, Barry Todd Hughes; m. Winford Lee Busby, Oct. 6, 1995. LPN, Coosa Valley Vocat. Sch., Rome, Ga., 1979; ADN, Floyd Coll., 1989. RN, Ga. LPN in acute care Chattooga Med. Ctr., 1979-86, LPN in emergency rm., 1986-89, clin. coord. mental health unit, 1989-90, asst. DON, 1990-93, DON, 1993, RN mgr. nursing home residents, 1993-95, employee edn. coord., 1995-96, PRN, 1996—. V.p. Ch. of God Ladies Ministry, 1990-95, Sunday sch. tchr., 1993-95; vol. Hospice Cmty. Care Program, 1995. Mem. Bus. and Profl. Women's Orgn. (corr. sec. 1994-95, rec. sec. 1995—). Office: Chattooga Med Ctr/Long Term Care PO Box 449 1010 N Highland Ave Summerville GA 30747-1932

BUSBY, MARJEAN (MARJORIE JEAN BUSBY), retired journalist; b. Kansas City, Mo., Jan. 31, 1931; d. Vivian Eric and Stella Mae (Lindley) Phillips; m. Robert Jackson Busby, Apr. 11, 1969 (dec. Feb. 1989). B.J., U. Mo., 1952. With Kansas City Star Co., 1952-2000, editor women's news, 1969-73, assoc. Sunday editor, People Sect. editor, 1973-77, fashion editor, 1978-81, feature and home writer, 1981-2000; ret., 2000. Mem. Fashion Group (1st recipient Kansas City appreciation award 1978), LSV, Mortar Board, Soc. Profl. Journalists, Friends of Art, Belle of Am. Royal Orgn., Kappa Alpha Theta (pres. Alpha Mu chpt. 1951-52) Presbyterian. Home: 9804 Mercier St Kansas City MO 64114-3860

BUSBY, NITA JUNE, small business owner; b. Pitts., Aug. 28, 1932; d. William Frederich and Monica (Vinciunes) Guidotti; m. Michael Petrunio (div.); children: Michele, Donna, David, Elizabeth, William; m. Harry Leslie Busby BA in English, Calif. State U., Fullerton, 1973, MLS, 1976; cert. in Career Transition Coaching, Chapman U., 2005, cert. in Job Career Transition Coaching, 2004. Health sci. libr. Whittier Hosp., Calif., 1978-82; owner, gen. mgr. Resumés, Etc., Orange, 1982—. Sec. Orange County chpt. Calif. Staffing Profls., 2000—04. Founder porphyria support group, So. Calif., 2001—. Mem. Nat. Assn. Women Bus. Owners (pres. Orange county chpt. 1991-92), Women in Mgmt. (pres. Orange County chpt. 1984-85), Profl. Assn. Resumé Writers (author monthly book revs. 1992-93), Assn. Profl. Cons., Calif. State U. Libr. Sci. Alumni Assn. (pres. 1976-77, 89-90, 90-91) Republican. Roman Catholic. Avocations: reading, walking, vegetable gardening. Office: Resumés Etc 438 E Katella Ave Ste G Orange CA 92867-4857 Office Phone: 714-633-2783. Personal E-mail: resumes100@aol.com. Business E-Mail: nbusby@resumesetc.net.

BUSBY, REBECCA ANN, church musician, pianist; b. Traiguen, Chile, Dec. 26, 1953; d. Donald Wayne and Constance May Waddell (Stepmother); 1 child, Bryn Kathryn Tucker. BS in Edn. magna cum laude, Midwestern State U., Wichita Falls, Tex., 1977. Cert. tchr. Tex., 1977, Kodaly Level I, II, III tchr. Tex., 1985, elem. music tchr. Tex., 1977. Tchr. Bellevue Ind. Sch. Dist., Bellevue, Tex., 1983—84, NW Ind. Sch. Dist., Justin, Tex., 1984—90, Kemp Ind. Sch. Dist., Kemp, Tex., 1990—94; choir dir. First United Meth. Ch., Mabank, Tex., 1991—94; music specialist, gen. music, choirs, hand bells and chimes Denton Ind. Sch. Dist., Denton, Tex., 1994—; ch. musician Immaculate Conception Cath. Ch., Denton, 1995—. Dir. Bilingual Choir, Immaculate Conception Cath. Ch., Denton, Tex., 2006—. Prodr.(dir.): (cd) Shooting for the Stars with the Borman Astros. Grantee Impressionism in Sight and Sound, Denton Pub. Schools Found., Inc., 2002, Family Harmony: A Musical Model for Group Counseling, 2006. Mem.: Assn. of Tchrs.s and Profl. Educators (life). Independent. Avocations: travel, gardening, reading. Office Phone: 940-369-2571. Business E-Mail: rbusby@dentonisd.org.

BÜSCH, ANNEMARIE, retired mental health nurse; b. Ger. d. Jurgen Julius and Anna (Stark) B. RN, Anschar Sch. Nursing, Kiel, Fed. Republic Germany, 1954; student, Traverse City State Hosp., Mich., 1959, Wayne State U., 1962, Colby-Sawyer Coll., New London, N.H., 1981. Lic. nurse, N.H., Vt., Fed. Republic Germany. Asst. head nurse Univ. Eye Inst., Kiel, 1954-56; nurse aide, grad. nurse Ontario Hosp., London, Canada; staff nurse, charge nurse Grace Hosp., Receiving Hosp., Detroit, 1962-67; coll. health nurse Wayne St. U., Detroit, 1967-70; staff nurse Mary Hitchcock Meml. Hosp., Hanover, 1970-71, nurse mental health dept., 1978-82; charge nurse Dartmouth Coll. Health Svc., Hanover, NH, 1971-77; staff nurse, charge nurse Hanover Health Terrace; staff nurse Temporary Nurses, Inc., Hanover, Vis. Nurse Alliance of Vt. and N.H., White River Junction, Vt.; ret., 1997. Camp nurse Nat. Music Camp InterLochen, Mich.

BUSCH, ANNIE, library director; b. Joplin, Mo., Jan. 6, 1947; d. George Lee and Margaret Eleanor (Williams) Chancellor; 1 child, William Andrew Keller. BA, Mo. U., 1969, MA, 1976. Br. mgr. St. Charles (Mo.) City Coun. Libr., 1977-84, Springfield/Greene County (Mo.) Libr., 1985-89, exec. dir., 1989—. Exec. bd. Mo. Libr. Network Corp., St. Louis, 1991-96. Adv. bd. Springfield Pub. Sch. Found., 1992—94, St. John's Health Sys., Boys and Girls Town, Good Cmty. Task Force, 1999—2002; pres. Ozarks Regional Info. On-Line Network, Springfield, 1993—98; mem. Gov.'s Commn. on Informational Tech., Cmty. Task Force, Springfield, 1993—98, Cmty. Partnership of the Ozarks, 1998; exec. bd. Mo. Rsch. and Edn. Network, pres., 1996—97; task force Mo. Goals 2000, Mo. Census 2000 Complete Count Com., 1999—2000; coord. com. Springfield Vision 20/20; chair Sec. of State Adv. Coun., 2001—05; adv. com. S.W. Mo. State U. Coll. Humanities and Pub. Affairs; bd. dirs. Ozarks Pub. TV, 1994—2000, Every Kid Counts, Wilson's Creek Nat. Battlefield Found., Mayors Commn. for Children, 2005—; bd. trustees Forest Inst. Profl. Psychology. Mem.: Mo. Libr. Assn. (exec. bd. 1990—94, pres. 1993—94), Springfield Area C. of C. (bd. dirs.), Springfield Rotary (pres. 1998—99). Office: Springfield-Greene Cty Libr PO Box 760 Springfield MO 65801-0760 Office Phone: 417-847-8120 ext 5. E-mail: annie@mail.sgcl.org.

BUSCH, JOYCE IDA, small business owner; b. Madera, Calif., Jan. 24, 1934; d. Bruno Harry and Ella Fae (Absher) Toschi; m. Fred O. Busch, Dec. 14, 1956; children: Karen, Kathryn, Kurt. BA in Indsl. Arts & Interior Design, Calif. State U., Fresno, 1991. Cert. interior designer, Calif. Stewardess United Air Lines, San Francisco, 1955-57; prin. Art Coordinates, Fresno, 1982—, Busch Interior Design, Fresno, 1982—. Art cons. Fresno Community Hosp., 1981-83; docent Fresno Met. Mus., 1981-84. Treas. Valley Children's Hosp. Guidance Clinic, 1975-79, Lone Star PTA, 1965-84,; mem. Mothers Guild San Joaquin Mem. H.S., 1984-88. Mem. Am. Soc. Interior Designers. Republican. Roman Catholic. Avocations: gardening, art history. Office Phone: 559-260-3202. Personal E-mail: joyce.busch@sbcglobal.net.

BUSCH, SUSAN ELLEN, reading specialist; b. Tonawanda, NY, May 26, 1952; d. Joseph J. and Jessie (Wilk) Stromeyer; m. Wayne Paul Busch, Oct. 7, 1978; children: Brian C, Mark A. BSc, SUNY Brockport, 1970—74; M in edn., SUNY Buffalo. Cert. Reading Specialist NY, 1979, Public School Teacher 1999. Tchr. Gates-Chili Sch. Dist., Rochester, NY, 1975—78; reading tchr. Akron Ctrl. Sch., NJ, 1979—87; dir. religious edn. Our Lady Czestochowa Ch., No. Tonawanda, NY, 1987—99; reading tchr. Grand Is. Ctrl. Sch., NY, 1993—2000; adj. prof. Niagara U., NY, 1999—2001; reading tchr. Ken-Ton Sch. Dist., Kenmore, NY, 2000—. Bd. mem., outreach chmn. Niagara Frontier Reading Coun., Buffalo, 1995—; co-facilitator Kenton Family Literacy Com., 2005—. 2d lit., adminstrv. personnel Civil Air Patrol, Kenmore, NY, 2000—; mem. Chs. Creating Cmty., 2005—; folk group dir. Our Ldy of Czestochawa, 1970—. Mem.: Internat. Reading Assn., NY State Reading Assn., Niagara Frontier Reading Coun. Roman Cath. Avocations: reading, guitar, flute. Home: 144 Cleveland Dr Buffalo NY 14227 Office: Herbert Hoover Elem Sch Buffalo NY 14223 Office Phone: 716-874-8414. Personal E-mail: sbusch526@adelphia.net.

BUSCHKOPF, DEBORA J., court reporter; b. Elkhorn, Wis., Aug. 24, 1956; d. Clyde D. and Irma G. (Ryder) Buschkopf. Adminstrv. secretarial diploma, Bryant & Stratton Bus. Coll., Milw., 1975; AA, Gateway Tech. Inst., Kenosha, Wis., 1982. Cert.: (profl. reporter) 1985, registered: 1991. Freelance ct. reporter, Atlantic City, 1987—95; ofcl. ct. reporter State of Nebr., Chadron, 1995—; dental asst., 2001. Recipient Queen for a Day award, Chadron Christian Women's Club, 2000. Mem.: International Order of Job's Daughters (Numerous in the organization 1972—76), Friends of Pets, Ivy Leaf Chapter #60, Order of the Eastern Star (Numerous in the organization 1996—), Business and Professional Women (2d v.p. 2001—02, 1st v.p. 2002—03). Methodist. Avocation: working with animals and local youth groups. Office: Dawes County Courthouse P O Box 630 Chadron NE 69337 Office Phone: 308-432-0112. Personal E-mail: dawescountycourtreporter@yahoo.com.

BUSCH-VISHNIAC, ILENE JOY, mechanical engineering educator, researcher; b. Phila., Jan. 28, 1955; d. Leonard and Ruth (Rudnick) Busch; m. Ethan Tecumseh Vishniac, June 13, 1976; children: Cady Anne, Miriam Rachel. BA in Math. magna cum laude, U. Rochester, 1976, BS in Physics magna cum laude, 1976; MSME, MIT, 1978, PhD in Mech. Engring., 1981. Mem. tech. staff acoustics rsch. dept. Bell Labs., 1980-82; asst. prof. mech. engring. U. Tex., Austin, 1982-86, assoc. prof., 1986-91, prof., assoc. chmn. mech. engring. for acad. affairs, 1991-95, Harry H. Power prof., 1994-98; dean Whiting Sch. of Engring. Johns Hopkins U., 1998—2003; prof., mech. engring. John Hopkins U., 2003—. Cons. AT&T Bell Labs., 1982-84, Nat. Inst. Justice, 1988, Body, Vickers, Daniels, 1989-93, to Tex. atty. gen., 1989-95; also others; mem. vis. com. dept. mech. engring. MIT, 1993-99; presdl. young investigator NSF, 1985; numerous presentations to profl. soc. mtgs., workships, confs.; numerous invited lectures; chmn. session on micro-automation, sensing and hardware issues Internat. Symposium on Robotics and Mfg., 1992, mem. mfg. program com., 1994; numerous others. Author: Electromechanical Sensors and Actuators, 1999; contbg. author: Handbook of Acoustics, 1992; contbr. numerous articles to sci. jours. Program mentor YWCA, 1989; speaker Tex. Energy Sci. Symposium for H.S.'s, 1989, Austin Sci. Acad., 1989, 90; speaker, session chmn. Expanding Your Horizons Workshop, 1991. Recipient Curtis McGraw rsch. award Am. Soc. for Engring. Edn., 1994, best paper award in mfg. Internat. Symposium on Robotics and Mfg., 1994; fellow Fannie and John Hertz Found., MIT, 1976-80, GM Found. Centennial tchg. fellow in mech. engring., 1985; grantee NSF, 1983—, Univ. Rsch. Inst., 1983-85, U. Tex. Bur. Engring. Rsch., 1983-85, Office Naval Rsch., 1985-87, Bosque Found., 1986-88, Semicondr. Rsch. Corp., 1987-90, GM, 1988-89, Tex. Instruments, 1989, Tex. Dept. Transp., 1994—; others. Fellow Acoustical Soc. Am. (v.p. 1997-98, tech. com. on engring. acoustics 1982—, tech. com. on noise 1982—, exec. com. 1988-91, com. on status of women in the Soc. 1992—, chmn. Austin chpt. 1986, nominating com. 1989, Lindsay award 1987); mem. ASME (micro-mech. sys. panel dynamic sys. and control div. 1992—, Outstanding Mech. Engring. Faculty Advisor award 1983), Inst. Noise Control Engring. (assoc.), Soc. Women Engrs. (Achievement award 1997), AAUW, Golden Key, Phi Beta Kappa. Achievements include patent on electret transducer with a selectively metallized backplate, with a variably charged electret foil, with a variable electret foil thickness, with a variable effective air gap, with a variable actual air gap; integrated capacitive microphone, electret transducer for blood pressure monitoring, six degree-of-freedom optical sensor. Office: John Hopkins U 223 Latrobe Hall 3400 N Charles St Baltimore MD 21218 E-mail: ilenebv@jhu.edu.

BUSER, ROSE M., elementary school educator; b. Port Washington, Wis., Oct. 2, 1948; d. Arthur Leo and Louise Angela Buser; children: Hajira, Rabiah, Joshua. BS in Edn., U. Wis., Whitewater, 1971, MS in Tchg., 1973; postgrad., Ohio State U., 1978—81. Lic. tchr. Dept. of Pub. Instrn., Wis., 1999. Tchr. Abbott Acad., Santo Domingo, Dominican Republic, 1972; instr. Briam Instituto de Idiomas, Madrid, 1973—74; Spanish tchr. Yellow Springs (Ohio) Schs., 1978—81; instr. U. Houston, 1981—82; immersion tchr. Milw. Pub. Schs., 1990—91; bilingual tchr. Christian Day Sch., San Juan, PR, 1991—92; ESL tchr. Oshkosh Area Sch. Dist., Oshkosh, Wis., 1995—. Coord., family cmty. ctr. Oshkosh Area Sch. Dist., 1999—; pub. spkr, Bhopal, India, 1983; bd. dirs. EvenStart Program, Oshkosh, Wis., 2002—, Lao Hmong Assn., Oshkosh, Wis., 2003—; diversity chairperson AAUW, Oshkosh, Wis., 2001—; at risk restructuring bd. Oshkosh Area Sch. Dist., 2003—; cooperating tchr. U. of Wis., Oshkosh, 2001—; vol. tchr. Newman Club, Chimayo, N.Mex., 1967—69, Orphanage La Esperanza, Mexico City, 1970; bilingual sec. Agencia Antillana, Santo Domingo, Dominican Republic, 1972; adj. instr. social justice program U. Wis., Oshkosh. Bd. dirs. Tchrs. Against Prejudice, 2005—. Recipient Tchr. of the Yr. award, Target Found., 1998; Healthy Nurturing grantee, Aurora Found., 2003, Assisting Endangered Langs. grantee, Alce Cozzi Found., 2003. Mem.: AAUW (diversity chair 2001—), Lake Winnebago Area Mut. Assistance Assn. (bd. dirs. 2003—06), Tchrs. of English to Speakers of Other Langs. (assoc.), Wis. Tchrs. of English to Speakers of Other Languages (assoc.), Wis. Edn. Assn. (assoc.), Delta Pi. Democrat. Roman Catholic. Office: North High Sch 1100 Smith St Oshkosh WI 54901 Office Phone: 920-424-0460. E-mail: busers@mac.com.

BUSET, JOANNA LYNN, counselor; b. Belleville, N.J., Aug. 25, 1978; d. Bruno Jr. and Linda Ann Buset. BA in Psychology and minor art, Coll. St. Elizabeth, NJ, 2000; MA in Counseling, Montclair State U., NJ, 2005. Lic. Associate Counselor. Assisted living counselor developmentally disabled adults Cmty. Options, Boonton, NJ, 2000; behavioral health counselor St. Clares Hosp. Psychiatric Intensive Care Unit, Boonton, 2000—03; supportive housing counselor chronic mentally ill adults St. Clares Hosp. Residential Svcs., Denville, NJ, 2003—05, clinician residential svcs. program, 2005—. Mem.: ACA, Psychology Nat. Honor Soc., Psi Chi. Avocations: exercise, reading, travel. Office: St Clares Hosp 50 Morris Ave Denville NJ 07834 Home: 6 Hillside Ave Unit 2E Nutley NJ 07110 E-mail: bellajolynn@aol.com.

BUSEY, ROXANE C., lawyer; b. Chgo., June 15, 1949; BA cum laude, Miami U., 1970; MAT, Northwestern U., 1971, JD, 1975. Bar: Ill. 1975. Ptnr. Baker & McKenzie LLP, Chgo. Mem. ABA (chair health com., antitrust sect. 1989-92, antitrust sect. coun. 1992-95, officer 1995-03, chair antitrust sect. 2001-02, chmn. task force antitrust modernization 2004-), Ill. State Bar Assn. (chair antitrust coun. 1984-85), Chgo. Bar Assn. (chair antitrust sect. 1990-91). Office: Baker & McKenzie LLP 1 Prudential Plz 130 E Randolph Dr Ste 3500 Chicago IL 60601 Office Phone: 312-861-8281. Business E-Mail: roxane.c.busey@bakernet.com.

BUSH, BARBARA PIERCE, former First Lady of the United States, volunteer; b. Rye, NY, June 8, 1925; d. Marvin and Pauline (Robinson) Pierce; m. George Herbert Walker Bush, Jan. 6, 1945; children: George Walker, Pauline Robin (dec.), John Ellis, Neil Mallon, Marvin Pierce, Dorothy Walker. Student, Smith Coll., 1943-44; degree (hon.), Stritch Coll., Milw., 1981, Mt. Vernon Coll., Washington, 1981, Hood Coll., Frederick, Md., 1983, Howard U., Washington, 1987, Judson Coll., Marion, Ala., 1988, Bennett Coll., Greensboro, NC, 1989, Smith Coll., 1989, Morehouse Sch. Medicine, 1989. First Lady of the U.S., Washington, 1989—93; oper. & facilities div. Dept. Administration, Washington, 1992. Author: C. Fred Story, 1984, Millie's Book, 1990, Barbara Bush: A Memoir, 1994, Reflections: Life After the White House, 2003. Hon. chair adv. bd. Reading is Fundamental; hon. mem. Bus. Coun. for Effective Literacy; mem. adv. coun. Soc. of Meml. Sloan-Kettering Cancer Ctr.; hon. mem. bd. dirs. Children's Oncology Svcs. of Met. Washington, The Washington Home, The Kingsbury Ctr.; hon. chmn. nat. adv. coun. Literacy Vols. of Am., Nat. Sch. Vols. Program; sponsor Laubach Literacy Internat.; nat. hon. chmn. Leukemia Soc. of Am.; hon. mem. bd. trustees Morehouse Sch. of Medicine; hon. nat. chmn. Nat. Organ Donor Awareness Week, 1982-86; pres. Ladies of the Senate, 1981-88; mem. women's com. Smithsonian Assocs., Tex. Fedn. of Rep. Women, life mem., hon. mem.; hon. chairperson for the Nat. Com. on Literacy and Edn. United Way, Barbara Bush Found. for Family Literacy, 1989-, Washington Parent Group Fund, Girls Clubs of Am., 10th anniversay Harvest Nat. Food Bank Network; hon. chmn. Nat. Com. for the Prevention of Child Abuse and Childhelp U.S.A.; hon. pres. Girl Scouts U.S; hon. chair Nat. Com. for Adoption; mem. bd. trustees Mayo Clinic Found.; hon. chair Read Am., Boarder Baby Project; mem. bd. visitors M. D. Anderson Cancer Ctr.; hon. chair Leukemia Soc. Am., Children's Literacy Initiative; hon. mem. Reading is Fundamental; ambassador at large Americares; honorary mem. Barbara Bush Found. for Family Literacy. Recipient Nat. Outstanding Mother of Yr. award, 1984, Woman of Yr. award USO, 1986, Disting. Leadership award United Negro Coll. Fund 1986, Disting. Am. Woman award Mt. St. Joseph Coll., 1987, Free Spirit award Freedom Forum, 1995. Mem. Tex. Fedn. Rep. Women (life), Internat. II Club (Washington), Magic Circle Rep. Women's Club (Houston), YWCA. Episcopalian. Avocations: reading, gardening, needlepoint.*

BUSH, CHRISTINE GAY, dental hygienist; b. Toledo, Dec. 31, 1951; d. Jack G. and Virginia Aileen (Doyle) Tornga; m. John Howard Mosher, May 11, 1974 (div. July 1990); children: Heather Kristen, Andrew Jacob; m. Robert Milton Counts, July 5, 1991 (dec. Mar. 1993); m. Charles T. Bush II, June 16, 1998. BS in Dental Hygiene, U. Mich., 1974. Registered dental hygienist, Nat. Bd. Dental Examiners, Ind. State Bd. Dentistry, Fla. State Bd. Dentistry, Mich. State Bd. Dentistry. Asst. supr. dental hygiene Ind. U., South Bend, Ind., 1974-75; expanded functions hygienist South Bend Dental Ctr., 1975; periodontal hygienist Dr. John B. Lehman, South Bend, 1976-82, Dr. Cristene Maas, Longwood, Fla., 1983-84, Dr. Richard Altman, Orlando, Fla., 1984-85; dental hygienist Dr. H. Raymund Barcus, Winter Park, Fla., 1984—2000; periodontal hygienist Dr. Michael Abufaris, 2000—05. Adj. instr. So. Coll., Orlando, 1984. Med./dental mission Wekiva Presbyn. Ch., Honduras, 1987, 89, Diocese of Orlando, Dominican Republic, 1994, 95, Fla. Hosp. Found., Jamaica, 1997; deacon Presbyn. Ch., 1992; mem. Festival of Orchs. League. Mem.: Greater Orlando Dental Hygiene Assn. (sec. 1986—87), Messiah Soc., Shepherd's Hope (exec. bd. 2006—, bd. dirs. 2006—), U. Mich. Club Orlando (treas. 1998—2001), Alpha Chi Omega (chpt. pres. 1995—97, Lyre editor 1997—98, pres. Gamma Upsilon Gamma chpt. 1998—99, Lyre editor 2000—01, nat. scholarship com. 2006). Republican. Roman Catholic. Avocations: cross-stitch, playing piano, reading. Personal E-mail: ctbushx2@earthlink.net.

BUSH, DAWN MARIE, elementary school educator; b. Hammond, Ind., Mar. 13, 1979; d. Thomas Paul and Norene Carol DeBold; m. Eric Andrew Bush, Jan. 12, 2002; 1 child, Collin Andrew. B in Elem. Edn., No. Ill. U., DeKalb, 2001. Cert. elem. edn. Ill., 2001. Mid. sch. math tchr. Manteno Mid. Sch., Ill., 2002—. Active St. John's United Ch. Christ, Mokena, Ill., 2003—06. Office: Manteno Middle School 250 N Poplar Manteno IL 60950 Office Phone: 815-928-7188.

BUSH, DEBRA W., occupational health nurse; b. Salem, Ill., Dec. 22, 1952; d. Merle D. and Georgia Lee (Johnson) Anderson; m. Thomas E. Howarth, June 16, 1973 (div. Sept. 1979; 1 child, Michael T.; m. Gene Bush, Feb. 14, 2004. Diploma in Practical Nursing, Vo-Tech Teche Area, New Iberia, La., 1972; ADN, Miss. Delta Jr. Coll., Moorhead, 1975. LPN, La.; cert. occupl. health nurse. LPN in ICU Iberia Gen. Hosp., New Iberia, 1972-73, head nurse ICU, 1979-81; charge nurse infection control Bolivar County Hosp., Cleveland, Miss., 1973-79, dir. long-term care, 1981-89; sr. indsl. nurse Baxter Healthcare Corp., Cleveland, 1989-96, Tampa, Fla., 1996—. Mem.: Fla. Assn. Occupl. Health Nurses, Am. Assn. Occupl. Health Nurses. Republican. Baptist. Avocations: reading, singing, cross-stitch, exercise. Office: Baxter Healthcare Corp 7511 114th Ave Largo FL 33773-5129 Office Phone: 727-548-2770. Business E-Mail: debbie_bush@baxter.com.

BUSH, ELIZABETH OLNEY, marine lab technician; d. Robert Olney and Marcia Allen Bush. BS, Coll. William and Mary, 1977. Libr. asst. Coll. William and Mary, Williamsburg, Va., 1975—77; lab. technician Va. Rsch. Ctr. for Archaeology, Williamsburg, Va., 1978—81; lab. asst. Colonial Williamsburg Found., 1982, lead excavator, lab. analyst, 1982—84, lab. technician, 1984—86, conservation technician, 1986—88; lab. technician Va. Inst. Marine Sci., Gloucester Point, Va., 1988—89, lab. specialist, 1989—. Interpretive asst. War Meml. Mus. Va., Newport News, 1981, clk., mus. asst., 1981—82. Mem.: Am. Chem. Soc. Office: Va Inst Marine Sci 1208 Greate Rd Gloucester Point VA 23062 Office Phone: 804-684-7697. E-mail: ebush@vims.edu.

BUSH, JILL LOBDILL, artist; b. Grand Island, Nebr., May 11, 1942; d. Oran Russell and Sylvia Salome (Dobbs) Lobdill; m. William Richard Bush, Aug. 28, 1963; children: Jennifer Wynn, Beau Richard. B in Advt. Art and Design, Tex. Tech. U., 1964. Art juror Trinity Arts Guild, Ft. Worth, 1973, Gen. Dynamics Recreation Area, Ft. Worth, 1973, Eastside Creative Arts Club, Ft. Worth, 1977, Gregg Art Guild's Silver Anniv. Show, 1982, L&L Gallery, 1982, Mayfest, Ft. Worth, 1992, 93, 94, Tex. Coll. Osteopathic Medicine, Ft. Worth chpt. Composers, Authors and Artists Am., 1992; demonstrator, lectr., tchr. in field. One-woman shows include Latch String Gallery, Ft. Worth, 1975, Moulton Galleries, Ft. Smith, Ark., 1980, L&L Gallery, Longview, Tex., 1982, Southwestern Regional Ballet Festival, Evelyn Siegel Gallery, Ft. Worth, 1986; exhibited in group shows at Odyssey Gallery, Ft. Worth, 1972, L&L Gallery, 1974, 87, 89, 91, Latch String Gallery, Ft. Worth, 1976, Evelyn Siegel Gallery, 1984-85, 92, 1st Ann. Main St. Tex. Invitational Art Show, Ft. Worth, 1986, 3d Salon des Pastellists, Lille, France, 1987, Ashland (Ky.) Area Gallery, 1989; featured artist Moulton Galleries spring show, 1986, L&L Gallery 25th anniv. show, 1993; represented in permanent collection Duncanville (Tex.) H.S., St. Joseph's Hosp., Ft. Worth, So. La. State U., Holt Crock Clinic, Ft. Smith, Ft. Worth Women's Club, 1st Fed. Savs. Loan, Ft. Smith, Darby's Ranger's Mus., Ft. Smith, Cooper Clinic, Ft. Smith, Drawing Bd., Dallas, Carlton Card divsn. Am. Greeting Cards, Dallas, Tex. Christian U., Ft. Worth, Harris Meth. Hosp., Hurst-Euless-Bedford, Tex., St. Joseph's Hosp., Ft. Worth; contbr. paintings to books Pastel Interpretations, 1992, Still Life Techniques, 1993, The Art of Pastel Portraiture, 1996. Recipient 1st place Heritage Hall Competition, Ft. Worth, 1969, Circuit award Jurors' Choice award, citation award Tex. Fine Arts Assn., 1972, Schwann Weber award PSA 8th Ann. Competition N.Y., 1980, PSA award, San Marcus, 1980, Pastel Soc. Southwest 1st place & honorable mention, 1985, PSA Ann. N.Y. Pruchase award, 1994. Mem. Pastel Soc. Am. (signature, award, hon. mention 1979, Schwann Weber award, 1980), Nat. League Am. Pen Women, Pastel Soc. S.W. (1st place award, hon. mention 1985). Home: 6440 Curzon Ave Fort Worth TX 76116-4402

BUSH, KAREN LEE, lawyer; b. Denville, NJ, May 29, 1958; BA with honors in English, cum laude, Bucknell U., 1980; JD with honors, George Washington U., 1984. Bar: Calif. 1984, DC 1988, Md. 1996. Assoc. Rutan & Tucker, 1985—86; dep. city atty. Signal Hill & Laguna Beach, Calif., 1985—86; ptnr. Anderson Kill Orlick & Oshinsky LLP, Washington, 1986—, co-chmn. diversity com./quality of life com. Mem.: Md. State Bar Assn., DC Bar. Office: Dickstein Shapiro Morin & Oshinsky 1201 L St NW Washington DC 20037-1526 Office Phone: 202-955-6601. Office Fax: 202-887-0689. Business E-Mail: BushK@dsmo.com.

BUSH, LAURA WELCH, First Lady of United States; b. Midland, Tex., Nov. 4, 1946; d. Harold Bruch and Jenna Louise (Hawkins) Welch; m. George Walker Bush, Nov. 5, 1977; children: Jenna, Barbara. BS in Edn., So. Meth. U., 1968; MLS, U. Tex., Austin, 1973. Tchr. Longfellow Elem. Sch., Dallas, 1968—69, John F. Kennedy Elem. Sch., Houston, 1969—72; libr. Houston Pub. Lib., 1973—74, Dawson Elem. Sch., Austin, 1974—77; First Lady State of Tex., 1995—2001; First Lady of the U.S., 2001—. Established Adopt-A-Caseworker programs, Tex., Rainbow Rooms, Tex.; launched National Book

Festival, 2001; speaker Republican Nat. Convention, NYC, 2004. Vol. Hurricane Help for Schools. Named one of Most Powerful Women, Forbes mag., 2004, 2005. Republican. Address: The White House 1600 Pennsylvania Ave NW Washington DC 20500*

BUSH, LAUREN, model; b. 1984; d. Neil and Sharon. Student, Princeton U. Appeared in fashion mag. including Town and Country, Vogue; model Abercrombie & Fitch, Tommy Hilfiger clothing line, 2002—. Hon. spokesperson World Food Program, UN, 2004—. Office: Elite Modeling Agy 111 E 22nd St New York NY 10010

BUSH, LYNN JEANNE, federal judge; b. Little Rock, Dec. 30, 1948; d. John E. Bush III and Alice Saville B.; 1 child, Brian Bush Ferguson. BA, Antioch Coll., 1970; JD, Georgetown U., 1976. Assoc. Steptoe and Johnson, Washington, summer 1975; part-time law clk. Nat. Labor Rels. Bd., Washington, 1976; trial atty. comml. litigation br. US Dept. Justice, Washington, 1976-87; sr. trial atty. Naval Facilities Engring. Command, Dept. of Navy, Alexandria, Va., 1987-89, counsel engring. field activity, 1989-96; adminstr. judge Bd. of Contract Appeals US Dept. Housing & Urban Devel., Washington, 1996-98; judge US Ct. Fed. Claims, Washington, 1998—. Mem. Nat. Bar Assn., Nat. Assn. Women Judges, Bd. of Contract Appeals Judges Assn., Bd. of Contract Appeals Bar Assn., Sr. Exec. Assn.

BUSH, REBECCA R., psychologist; d. George T. Bush and Paula Saverino. BS, Tex. A&M U., Coll. Sta., Tex., 1991; MS, U. Houston, Clear Lake, Tex., 1995. Lic. ednl. psychologist. Psychologist Anaheim (Calif.) Union H.S. Dist., 1997—; pvt. practice L.A., 2004—. Author: Special Ed: Helping Students Feel Good About Being in Special Education, 2006. Mem.: Nat. Assn. Sch. Psychologists (cert.), Calif. Assn. Sch. Psychologists, Orange County Assn. Sch. Psychologists. Democrat. Avocations: interior decorating, running, kayaking, travel.

BUSH, SANDI TOKOA, elementary school educator; b. Albany, Ga., Aug. 1, 1953; d. Charlie and Beauty (Miller) Bush; 1 child, Allen. BS, Barry U., Miami, 1983; MS, Nova U., 1987; PhD, Union Inst. and U., U. Cin., 2001. Cert. tchr. Fla. Counselor Health and Rehab. Svcs., Miami, Fla., 1979-86; tchr. Dade County Pub. Schs., Miami, 1986—. Tchr., tutor Ind. Children's Group, Miami, 1987—; co-chmn. Hall of Fame Dade County Sch. Bd., 1986—, world difference, 1987—; Miami tchg. fellow Miami-Dade Sch. Sys. Author: (book) World of Poetry Anthology The Sun, 1991; co-author: Experiences with Discrimination: From Deep Within, 1998; contbr. articles to profl. jours.; author: Does the Infusion of Conflict Resolution Intervention Strategies Into a School's Curriculum Effectively Reduce or Extinguish Violent or Aggressive Behavior in At-Risk Students. Miami Tchg. fellow. Mem.: Nova U. Assocs., Nova U. Alumni Assn. (mem. recruitment com. 1987—88, Recognition award 1988), Smithsonian Assocs. (Recognition award 1988), Am. Mus. Natural History (assoc.). Avocations: reading, classical music, walking, jogging, tennis. E-mail: sbush33050@yahoo.com.

BUSH, SARAH LILLIAN, historian; b. Kansas City, Mo., Sept. 17, 1920; d. William Adam and Lettie Evelyn (Burrill) Lewis; m. Walter Nelson Bush, June 7, 1946 (dec.); children: William Read, Robert Nelson. AB, U. Kans., Lawrence, 1941; BS, U. Ill., Champaign-Urbana, 1943. Clk. circulation dept. Kansas City Pub. Library, 1941-42, asst. librarian Paseo br., 1943-44; librarian Kansas City Jr. Coll., 1944-46; substitute librarian San Mateo County Library, Woodside and Portola Valley, Calif., 1975-77; various temporary positions, 1979-87; owner Metriguide, Palo Alto, Calif., 1975-78. Author: Atherton Lands, 1979, rev. edition 1987. Editor: Atherton Recollections, 1973. Pres., v.p. Jr. Librarians, Kansas City, 1944-46; courtesy, yearbook & historian AAUW, Menlo- Atherton branch (Calif.) Br.; asst. Sunday sch. tchr., vol. Holy Trinity Ch., Menlo Park, 1955-78; v.p., membership com., libr. chairperson, English reading program, parent edn. chairperson Menlo Atherton High Sch. PTA, 1964-73; founder, bd. dirs. Friends of Atherton Community Library, 1967-2002, oral historian, 1968-2002, chair Bicentennial event, 1976; bd. dirs. Menlo Park Hist. Assn., 1979-82, oral historian, 1973-2002; bd. dirs. Civic Interest League, Atherton, 1978-81; mem. hist. county commn. Town of Atherton, 1980-87; vol. Allied Arts Palo Alto Aux. to Children's Hosp. at Stanford, 1967—, oral historian, 1978—, historian, 1980—; vol. United Crusade, Garfield Sch., Redwood City, 1957-61, 74-88, Encinal Sch., Menlo Park, Calif., 1961-73, program dir., chmn. summer recreation, historian, sec.; vol. Stanford Mothers Club, 1977-81, others; historian, awards chairperson Cub Scouts Boy Scouts Am.; founder Atherton Heritage Assn. 1989, bd. dirs., 1989-2004, dir., 1989-94; mem. Guild Gourmet, 1971—, Mid Peninsula History Consortium, 1993-95; oral historian St. Andrew's Ch., Saratoga, Calif., 2003—; vol. Los Gatos Meadows, Calif.; family hist. rschr. for writer. Recipient Good Neighbor award Atherton Civic Interest League, 1992. Mem. PTA (life). Episcopalian. Avocations: gourmet cooking, entertaining, reading.

BUSH, SOPHIA, actress; b. LA, July 8, 1982; d. Charles William and Maureen Bush; m. Chad Michael Murray, Apr. 16, 2005 (separated). Actor: (films) Van Wilder, 2002, Learning Curves, 2003, Supercross, 2005, Stay Alive, 2006, John Tucker Must Die, 2006; (TV films) Point of Origin, 2002; (TV series) One Tree Hill, 2003—; guest star Sabrina, the Teenage Witch, 2003, Nip/Tuck, 2003. Office: c/o United Talent Agency 9560 Wilshire Blvd, 5th Fl Beverly Hills CA 90212*

BUSH, YVONNE, writer, counselor; b. Madelia, Minn., Jan. 29, 1935; d. Guy Pearl and Frances Louise (Traver) Burk; m. William Clarence Bush; children: Donald, Steven, Billie Jean Vogel, Thomas Bush Lovelace, Tami li Robbins, Christopher Clark. AA Edn., Yavapai Coll., 1985; BA, Prescott Coll., 1989, MA, 1999. Cert. EMT 1987, St. Joseph's Med. Center/Newborn,Child Normal Devel. 1983, Feeding and Swallowing Disorders of Infancy; Assessment and Mgmt. 1991, Fetal Alcohol Syndrome/Instructor 1993, Parenting the Teen Years 1987, Understanding Aids 1987, Failure to Thrive, Infant Mental Health 1988, Breast Cancer Self examination/Instructor 1983. Office mgr. Allen's New Way Retail Grocery Store, Prescott, Ariz., 1980—82; head cashier K Mart, Prescott, 1982—83; case mgr. Cath. Social Services of Yavapai, Prescott, Ariz., 1987—90, Ariz. Dept. of Econ. Security, Prescott, 1990—98. Trust com. Acker Trust Bd., Prescott, 1983—85; organizer, co-leader Scholls Cmty. Orgn., Scholls, 1978—80; bd. dirs. Sierra Comm., Inc., Prescott; charter mem. Ariz. Pub. Svc. Project Voice, Phoenix; bd. dirs. Child Haven, Prescott Crisis Nursery; den mother Boy Scouts of Am., Rowland Heights, 1965—66; bd. dirs. Affordable Constrn., Inc. Prescott. Author: Bonding and Attachment, 2001, Beyond Tears, A Book To Encourage Women, 2002. Small claims hearing officer Prescott Justice Ct., 1998—2005; bd. dirs. Willow Creek Charter Sch., Prescott, 2004—; leader women's ministries Alliance Bible Ch, Prescott, 2002—04. Mem.: Prescott Pub. Library/Friends of the Libr. Conservative. Office Phone: 928-443-5218. Personal E-mail: bybush@cableone.net.

BUSHNELL, CANDACE, columnist, writer; b. Glastonbury, Conn., 1959; d. Calvin Camille Bushnell; m. Charles Askegard, July 4, 2002. Attended, Rice U., NYU. Writer Ladies' Home Journal, Good Housekeeping, Self, Mademoiselle, Cosmo Beauty and Fitness, Family Circle, GQ, Vogue; Sex and the City columnist New York Observer, 1994—96; host Candace Bushnell's Sex, Success, and Sensibility talk show, Sirius Stars Channel 102, 2006—. Author: (short stories) Four Blondes, 2000, (novels) Sex and the City, 1996, Trading Up, 2003, Lipstick Jungle, 2005. Recipient Matrix award for books, NY Women in Comm. Inc., 2006. Achievements include collection of columns for New York Observer, Sex and the City, was made into HBO series of same name, 1998-2004. Office: c/o Atlantic Monthly Press 841 Broadway New York NY 10003 Mailing: c/o Heather Schroder ICM 40 West 57th St New York NY 10019*

BUSHNELL, PRUDENCE, diplomat, former management consultant, trainer; b. Washington, Nov. 26, 1946; d. Gerald Sherman and Bernice Edna (Duflo) B.; m. Richard Alan Buckley, Oct. 26, 1979. BA, U. Md., 1969; MS, Russell Sage Coll., 1980. Bi-lingual sec. Embassy of Morocco, Washington, 1969-70; chief sec. U. Md., College Park, 1970-72; tng. mgr. Legal Svcs. Tng. Program, Washington, 1972-76; dir. Cultural Learning Concepts, Dallas, 1976-81; dep. adminstrv. ops. U.S. Consulate Bombay, U.S. Embassy, Dakar, 1982-86; dir. exec. devel. Fgn. Svc. Inst., Washington, 1986-89; dep. chief mission U.S. Embassy Dakar, Dept. State, Washington, 1989-92; dep. asst. sec. for African affairs Dept. State, Washington, 1993-96; U.S. amb. to Kenya Dept. of State, Nairobi, 1996-99, U.S. amb. to Guatemala, 1999—2002, dean Leadership and Mgmt. Sch., Fgn. Svc. Inst., 2002—. Avocations: gardening, walking, writing. Office: US Dept State 2201 C St NW Washington DC 20520

BUSHONG WHITEHEAD, PAT J., science educator, consultant; b. Tiffin, Ohio, July 24, 1955; d. Raymond Merrill Bushong and Vivian Josephine Hart Bushong Weinreber, George Martin Weinreber (Stepfather). AA in Humanities and Fine Arts, Niagara County C.C., N.Y., 1980, AAS in Mech. Engring. and Computer Programming, 1987; BS in Edn. and Math., SUNY Buffalo State Coll., 1990; MA in Liberal Studies and Physics, SUNY Empire State Coll., 2000. Cert. mfg. technologist, N.Y., 1986; tchr. math. K-12 N.Y., 1990, tchr. physics K-12 N.Y., 1990, tchr. earth scis. N.Y., 1990, tchr. gen. scis. N.Y., 1990. Tchr. sci. Niagara Wheatfield H.S., Sanborn, NY, 1997—2002, Wayne County H.S., Jesup, Ga., 2003—. Author & photographer (book) Breach Birth. Mem. Buffalo Geol. Soc., 1989—2001, Ont. Field Tripper's, Niagara Falls, Canada, 1994—2001; membership & retention chair Soc. Mfg. Engrs., Sanborn, 1985—87. Recipient Women's Assn. scholarship, SUNY Coll. at Buffalo, 1988; grantee, SUNY, 1988—90. Liberal. Avocations: environmental activist, animal rights activist, nature photography.

BUSKA, SHEILA MARY, controller, writer, columnist; b. Brewer, Maine, May 9, 1941; d. George William Sanderlin and Margaret Owenita Harrah; m. Roland Michael Buska, Nov. 28, 1959; children: Bryan Michael, Craig William, Christine Mary, Paul Kevin. AA, U. San Diego, 1959; BS in Acct. magna cum laude with distinction, San Diego State U., 1984. Cert. mgmt. acct., CPA Calif. Sr. acct. Peak Health Plan, San Diego, 1984-86; legal entity acct. M/A-COM Govt. Sys., San Diego, 1986-87; sr. acct. Lois A. Brozey, CPA, San Diego, 1987-89; controller Soco-Lynch Corp. dba Crown Chem. Corp., Chula Vista, Calif., 1989-98; fin. mgr. Dermagraft Joint Venture, 1998—99; controller Monarch Sch. Project, San Diego, 2003—; sec., treas. Monarch Café, Inc., 2005—. Author: (poems) Young America Sings, 1957, Sermons in Poetry, 1957, (non-fiction) Time Outs for Grown-Ups: 5 Minute Smile Breaks, 2003; columnist: newspapers, 1997—, www.smile-breaks.com, interim editor: The Columnist, 2005, web editor: Nat. Soc. Newspaper Columnists, 2005—. Mem.: Inst. Mgmt. Accts. (v.p. membership and mktg. 1985—86, dir. cert. mgmt. accts. 1989—90, dir. corp. devel. 1992—93, treas. 1993—94, dir. membership acquisition 1995—96, Most Valuable Mem. 1990—91), Hardhats Toastmasters (v.p. pub. rels., editor Hardhats Herald 1998, pres. 2000). Democrat. Roman Catholic. Avocations: travel, music, poetry, tennis, theater. Home: 509 Burgasia Path El Cajon CA 92019-2640 Office: Monarch School Project 808 W Cedar St San Diego CA 92101 Office Phone: 619-685-8242. Personal E-mail: sbuska@cox.net.

BUSKIRK, PHYLLIS RICHARDSON, retired economist; b. Queens, N.Y., July 19, 1930; d. William Edward and Amy A. Richardson; m. Allen V. Buskirk, Sept. 13, 1950; children: Leslie, William, Carol (dec.), Janet. AB cum laude, William Smith Coll., 1951. Rsch. asst. W.E. Upjohn Inst. for Employment Rsch., Kalamazoo, 1970-75, rsch. assoc., 1976-83, sr. staff economist, 1983-87; co-editor Bus. Conditions in the Kalamazoo Area, Quar. Rev., 1979-84; asst. editor Bus. Outlook for West Mich., 1984-87; mem. civil svc. bd. City of Kalamazoo, 1977-91, chmn., 1981-91; trustee First Presbyn. Ch., Kalamazoo, 1984-87, chmn., 1985, 86, mgr. adminstrn. and fin., 1987-92, co-chair 150th ann., 1997-98, chair 150th ann., 1999-2000. Trustee Sr. Citizens Fund, Kalamazoo, 1984-88, exec. bd. 1986-88; bd. dirs. Heritage Cmty. Kalamazoo, 1988-2004, chair 1995-96, exec. com., 1997; Kalamazoo County Futures Com., 1985-86, bd. dirs., 1987-89. Fellow Presbyn. Ch. Bus. Adminstrn. Assn.; mem. Nat. Assn. Ch. Bus. Adminstrn., P.E.O., Kalamazoo Network, YWCA; bd. dirs. Friends of Univ. Librs. Western Mich. U., 2000—. Mem.: Phi Beta Kappa. Home: 3324 Saint Antoine Ave Kalamazoo MI 49006-5522 E-mail: prb1769@cs.com.

BUSQUET, ANNE M., Internet company executive; BS in Hotel Adminstrn., Cornell U.; MBA, Columbia U. Mktg. mgr. Am. Express, 1978, sr. v.p., gen. mgr. Optima card divsn., 1988—92, sr. vp., gen. mgr. mdse. svcs. bus., 1992—93, exec. v.p. consumer card group, 1993—95, pres. relationship svcs. divsn., 1995—2000, pres. interactive svcs. and new bus. divsn., 2000—01; pres. AMB Advisors, LLC; sr. advisor InterActiveCorp, 2003—04, CEO local svcs., 2004—. Office: InterActive Corp 152 West 57th St 42nd Fl New York NY 10019

BUSS, EMILY, law educator; b. 1960; BA in English, Yale Univ., New Haven, Conn., 1982; JD, Yale Law Sch., New Haven, Conn., 1986. Bar: Pa. 1988, Md. 1989, Ill. 1997. Law clk. to Hon. Louis H. Pollack US Dist. Ct. Ea. Dist. Pa., 1986—87; law clk. to Justice Harry A. Blackmun US Supreme Ct., Washington, 1987—88; staff atty. child advocacy unit Legal Aid Bur., Inc., Balt., 1989—90; staff atty. Juvenile Law Ctr., Phila., 1990—93, dep. dir., 1993—96; asst. prof. law U. Chgo. Law Sch., 1996—2001, prof., 2001—, faculty dir. academic affairs, 2001—03, Kanter Dir. Chgo. Policy Initiatives. Mem. U. Chgo. Athletic Bd., Chgo., 1998—2001, Local Sch. Coun., Blair Early Childhood Ctr., Chgo., 1999—2000, pres., 2000—02; mem. Chgo. Bd. Student and Campus Life Subcommittee on Athletics, Chgo., 2001—02, chmn., 2002. Office: U Chgo Law Sch 1111 E 60 St Chicago IL 60637 Office Phone: 773-834-0007. E-mail: e-buss-doss@uchicago.edu.

BUSS, JEANIE, professional sports team executive; d. Jerry Buss; m. Steve Timmons, Feb. 14, 1990 (div. 1993). Grad., U. So. Calif. Owner, gen. mgr. L.A. Strings, 1981—93; owner, pres. L.A. Blades, 1994—97; pres. Sports Forum Inc.; pres., dir. booking Great Western Forum, L.A., 1995—99; exec. v.p. bus. ops. L.A. Lakers, 1999—. Bd. dirs. L.A. Sports Coun., 1995—. Office: LA Laker Great Western Foru 555 N Nash St El Segundo CA 90245-2818

BUSSABARGER, MARY LOUISE, retired mental health services professional; b. Chgo., Sept. 16, 1923; d. Joseph and Nellie Wheelen Sterling; m. Robert Franklin Bussabarger, May 11, 1946; children: Wendi Newell, David. BA, U. Mo., 1960, MA English Lit., 1963. Instr. English U. Mo., Columbia, 1960—82; mental health commr. State of Mo., Jefferson City, 2001—06; ret., 2006. Instr. English as a fgn. lang. Indo-Am. Soc., Calcutta, India, 1961—62, 1968—69, Seoul, South Korea, 1995—96; tchr. Yoga, 1969—2002; co-dir. Women's Place Agy., 1974—77; liaison officer Danforth Found., 1976—80. Mem. Nat. Alliance for the Mentally Ill, 1985—; commr. parks and recreation City of Columbia, 1975—77; mem. spkrs. bur. Internat. Women's Year, 1975—; mem. Planning Coun. for Devel. Disabilities, 1990—97, State Adv. Coun. for Psychiat. Svcs., 1985—90; mem. nat. steering com. Nat. Women's Polit. Caucus, 1974—75; pres. Columbia Women's Polit. Caucus, 1975—76; del. State Dem. Convs., 1968, 1972, alt., 1976; mem. state steering com. Mo. Women's Polit. Caucus, 1972—76. Mem.: MLA, AAUW, Delta Tau Kappa. Achievements include invitation and attendance to the John F. Kennedy School of Government at Harvard University for "Leadership for the 21st century", Oct. 2004. Office: Dept Mental Health 1706 E Elm St PO Box 677 Jefferson City MO

BUSSARD, JANICE WINGEIER, retired secondary school educator; b. Lowell, Mich., Mar. 2, 1925; d. Carl L. and E. May (Velzy) Wingeier; m. James W. Bussard, June 15, 1947; children: Jane, Jody, Jiselle, Jill. BS, Western Mich. U., 1946. Cert. secondary edn. tchr., Mich. Tchr. bus. edn. Spring Lake H.S., Mich., 1965—86; inventor Spring Lake, 1987—97. Achievements include 10 issued patents in U.S. and 1 in Canada in the field of holography. Mfr. holographic labels for security, authentication and decoration for applications to any substrate. Home: 201 N Fruitport Rd Spring Lake MI 49456-0193 Office Phone: 616-842-5626. Personal E-mail: hologirl25@hotmail.com.

BUSSE, EILEEN ELAINE, special education educator; b. Green Bay, Wis., Oct. 16, 1957; d. Ervin F. Dohl and Elaine I. (Behnke) Richmond; m. John F. Busse, July 5, 1980; children: Jessica Lynn, Jeremy John. BS in Elem. and Spl. Edn., U. Wis., Eau Claire, 1979; MS in Spl. Edn., U. Wis., Whitewater, 1985. Cert. tchr. elem. and spl. edn. Tchr. spl. edn.-mentally retarded Ithaca Pub. Schs., Wis., 1979-80; spl. edn. tchr. Walworth County CDEB, Whitewater, Wis., 1980—, Lakeview Elem. Sch., 1991-2000, Whitewater H.S., 2000—, transition specialist, 2004—. Coop. tchr. U. Wis., Whitewater, 1988—; summer sch. tchr. St. Thomas U., St. Paul, Minn., 2003-2005. Author: Student Owned Spelling, 1991, II, 1992, III, 1994. Mem. First English Luth. Ch. edn. com., Whitewater, 1990-95, 98-2005, chmn. edn. com., 1993-95, mem. ch. coun., 1993-94, 97-2005; active Girl Scouts U.S.A., 1992-2000; advisor sr. high youth 1st English Luth. Ch., 1998-2005. Recipient Excellence in Edn. award U.S. Dept. Edn., 1984-85, Recognized spl. educator, 1998. Mem. Coun. for Exceptional Children, Wis. Assn. Children with Behavioral Disorders, Delta Kappa Gamma. Avocations: reading, travel, gardening. Home: 455 Ventura Ln Whitewater WI 53190-1548 Office: Whitewater HS 534 S Elizabeth St Whitewater WI 53190 Personal E-mail: bussee@charter.net. E-mail: ebusse@wwusd.org.

BUSSINO, MELINDA HOLDEN, human services administrator; b. Boston, Apr. 20, 1946; d. Sharon Virtulan and Grace (Fitzgerald) Holden; m. Louis Logue Doyle, Feb. 14, 1974 (dec. Oct. 1980); children: Sarah, Joseph; m. Fred John Bussino, Sept. 22, 1998 (dec. Jan. 2000). BA in Psychology, U. N.H., 1968. Dir. outreach and tng. Stratford County Cmty. Action, Somersworth, NH, 1968—73; trainer, cons. New Eng. Regional Commn., Boston, 1971—73; office mgr. Beacon Banjo Co., Westminster, Vt., 1980—88; asst. to pastor United Meth. Ch., Brattleboro, Vt., 1985—89; exec. dir. Brattleboro Area Drop In Ctr., 1989—; cons. Putney, Vt., 1994—. Chmn. Brattleboro Human Resource Coun., 1990—; bd. dirs., past pres. Vt. Affordable Housing Coalition, 1990—, Vt. Campaign to End Child Hunger, 1991-99; vice chair Windham Regional Commn., Brattleboro, 1995—; organizer, bd. dirs. N.H. Low Income Advocacy Coun., 1972-73, Operation Low Income People, N.H., 1969-73; adv. coun., bd. dirs. Vt. Protection Advocacy, Montpelier, Vt., 1995-2001; vice chair Westminster (Vt.) Planning Commn., 2003—. Recipient Vt. Woman of Distinction award, 1996, Humanitarian award Brattleboro Pastoral Counseling Ctr., 2001. Democrat. Baptist. Avocations: gardening, cooking, skiing. Home: PO Box 387 Putney VT 05346-0387 Office: Brattleboro Area Drop In Ctr PO Box 175 Brattleboro VT 05302-0175 Office Phone: 800-852-4286 x103. Business E-Mail: badicmelinda@together.net.

BUSTEED, DIANA LYNN, speech educator, theatre director; d. Dana Lawrence and Elsie Elizabeth Morris; m. Wallace Bruce Busteed, June 9, 1987; children: Brian, Eric, Jesse Tarbutton, Amber Polk. BA, Pan Am. U., Edinburg, Tex.; MEd, U. North Tex., Denton, 1982. Cert. Tchr. Tex., 1982. Theatre dir., vocat. tchr. Corsicana H.S., Tex., 1979—84; theatre dir. Groesbeck H.S., Tex., 1985—90, New Caney H.S., Tex., 1990—92; theatre dir./speech tchr. Coldspring H.S., Tex., 1992—97, Shepherd H.S., Tex., 1997—. Sponsor Texas Thespian Troupe 6059, 1998—. Actor: (community theatre). Mem.: Assn. Tex. Profl. Educators, Tex. Tchrs. Assn., Tex. Fedn. Tchrs., Internat. Thespian Soc., Tex. Thespians (assoc.). Independent. Office: Shepherd High School 1401 South Byrd Ave Shepherd TX 77371 Office Phone: 936-628-7731. E-mail: dbusteed @shepherd.net.

BUSTLE, TRINA GAYLE, gifted and talented educator; b. Mt. Vernon, Ky., July 23, 1969; d. Earl Clinton Cummins and Sandra Gayle Eaton; m. Elbert Carl Bustle, June 11, 1988; 1 child, Alyssa Gayle. MS in Math., MA in Math. Edn., Ea. Ky. U., Richmond, 2002. Cert. secondary math. tchr., K-12 prin. Ky., 1991. Tchr. math. Rockcastle County H.S., Mt. Vernon, Ky., 1992—2004; coord. elem. gifted and talented Rockcastle County Schs., Mt. Vernon, Ky., 2004—. Math. Tchg. scholarship, Ky. Higher Edn. Assistance Authority, 1987-1991. Avocations: clogging, travel, crafts. Home: Rt 1 Box 473 Brodhead KY 40409-9179 Office: Brodhead Elem Sch Silver Street PO Box 187 Brodhead KY 40409 Office Phone: 606-758-8512. Business E-Mail: trina.bustle@rockcastle.kyschools.us.

BUSTREO, FLAVIA, epidemiologist; b. Padua, Italy, Aug. 17, 1961; d. Lino and Maria Bustreo. Grad. in Communicable Disease Epidemiology, London Sch. of Hygiene and Tropical Medicine, 1994; grad., CUAMM Coll., Padova, Italy, 1993; postgrad. in sports medicine & rehab., U. Padova, Italy, 1990, grad. in Medicine and Surgery with honors, 1987. Clinician Italian Assn. of Physicians, 1987. Clinician in internal medicine Inst. Gris, Treviso, Italy, 1990—91; sports medicine and rehab. physician Ctr. di Medicina Dello Sport, Venice, Italy, 1990—93; clinician rschr. Regional U. Ctr. of Sports Medicine, Padova, Italy, 1990—93; med. officer in the integrated program on communicable diseases WHO, Copenhagen, 1994—95, med. officer in the global tb program Geneva, 1995—97, med. officer in child health Khartoum, Sudan, 1997—99; sr. pub. health specialist World Bank Hdqs., Washington, 1999—; dep. dir. Child Survival Partnership, NYC, 2004—. Presenter in field. Contbr. articles to profl. jours. Sec. of Venice sect. Internat. Physicians forPrevention of Nuc. War, Venice, 1990—2005; vol. Italian NGOs, Padova, 1992—93, Rijeka, Croatia, 1991—93; mem. of del. to Iraq to assess the situation of children in the country after the war and the sanctions Internat. Physicians for the Prevention of Nuc. War, Italy, 1992. Recipient Bank award for Capacity Bldg. for Sr. WHO and World Bank Staff, World Bank, 2000, Bank award for Senegal Cmty. Nutrition Project, 2002, Bank award for Preparation of the Healthy Start in Life Conf., 2002; scholar 3 Yr. Scholarship For Postgrad. Med. Studies, Italian Ministry of Universities and Sci. Rsch., 1988-1990. Avocation: languages. Office Phone: 202-458-2175. Personal E-mail: fbustreo@worldbank.org.

BUSWELL, DEBRA SUE, small business owner, computer technician, financial analyst; b. Salt Lake City, Apr. 8, 1957; d. John Edward Ross and Marilyn Sue (Patterson) Potter; m. Randy James Buswell, Aug. 17, 1985; 1 child, Trevor Ryan. BA, U. Colo., Denver, 1978. Programmer, analyst Trail Blazer Systems, Palo Alto, Calif., 1980-83; data processing mgr. Innovative Concepts, Inc., San Jose, Calif., 1983-86; owner Egret Software, Milpitas, Calif., 1986—. Mem.: IEEE. Home and Office: 45701 Vineyard Ave Fremont CA 94539-4817 E-mail: dbuswell@ieee.org.

BUTCHER, DEBORAH, public relations and communications consultant; b. Balt., Apr. 23, 1954; d. Robert Cleveland and Mildred Lois Butcher; m. Darwin Scott Bull, May 4, 1985; 1 child, Margeaux Gabrielle Bull. BS, Towson (Md.) U., 1988. Pub. rels. coord. Farm Credit Banks, Sparks, Md., 1981-83, pub. rels. mgr., 1983-85; v.p. Curry Comms. Group, Timonium, Md., 1985-89; account exec. Blue Cross/Blue Shield Md., Owings Mills, 1989-90, mgr. DARE Found., 1991; sr. coord. comms. Nat. Rural Electric Coop. Assn., Arlington, Va., 1992-96; owner, founder, pres. Deborah Butcher Pub. Rels./Bus. Comms., Hillsborough, N.J., 1997—. Vol., Somerset County Dem. Com., Somerville, N.J., 1999. Recipient award of merit Internat. Assn. Bus. Communicators, 1992, 93, 94, Cert. of Excellence, Am. Soc. Assn. Execs., 1993. Mem. Somerset County C. of C. (pub. rels. com. 1998-2000, legis. com. 1998-99). Avocations: gardening, golf. Office: Deborah Butcher Pub Rels/Comms 200 Hockenbury Rd Hillsborough NJ 08844

BUTCHER, DIANE, chaplain, bereavement facilitator; b. Passaic, N.J., Aug. 25, 1944; d. Richard William and Marion Rosalyn Butcher; m. William R. Schweitzer, Aug. 1975 (div. Oct. 1978); 1 child, Noreen Rozsa. BA, William Paterson Coll., Wayne, N.J., 1966, MA in Nat. History, 1972; postgrad., Montclair (N.J.) State U., 1975. Tchr. elem. edn. Bd. Edn., Kearny, N.J., 1966-68, Hasbrouck Heights, N.J., 1970-97; bereavement facilitator Four Seasons Hospice, Hendersonville, NC, 1997—, dir. Watchman program, 2001—. Mem. steering com. Franciscan AIDS Hospitality House, Wallington, N.J., 1995-97. Named Vol. of Yr., Four Seasons Hospice, 1999. Mem. Assn. Profl. Chaplains, We. N.C. Aids Project, Asheville. Roman Catholic. Avocations: music, hiking, camping, pottery, watercolors. Home: 2121 Delaview Ave Wilmington DE 19810-4146

BUTCHER, KAREN A., lawyer; b. Dec. 30, 1966; BS, U. Va, 1988; JD, U. Va. Sch. Law, 1993. Bar: Va. 1993, D.C. 1994. Ptnr. Morgan, Lewis & Bockius LLP, Washington, asst. leader intellectual property trademark/copyright practice group. Mem.: Internat. Trademark Assn.-Info. Resources Com. Office: Morgan Lewis & Bockius 1111 Pennsylvania Ave NW Washington DC 20004 Office Phone: 202-739-5526. Office Fax: 202-739-3001. Business E-Mail: kbutcher@morganlewis.com.

BUTENIS, PATRICIA A., ambassador; b. NJ; BA in Anthropology, U. Pa.; MA in Internat. Rels., Columbia U. Vice consul US Dept. State, Karachi, 1980—82, vice consul and polit. officer San Salvador, El Salvador, 1982—85, desk officer, 1988—90, consul New Delhi, 1985—88, consul, chief Am. citizen svcs. Bogotá, Colombia, 1990—93, consul gen., 2001—04, field liaison Visa Office, 1994—97, consul gen. Warsaw, 1998—2001, dep. chief of mission Islamabad, Pakistan, 2004—06, US amb. to Bangladesh Dhaka, 2006—. Office: DOS Amb 2130 Dakar Pl Washington DC 20521-2130*

BUTERA, ANN MICHELE, consulting company executive; b. Bayside, N.Y., Apr. 27, 1958; d. Gaetano Thomas and Josephine (Inserro) B. BA, L.I. U., 1979; MBA, Adelphi U., 1982. Dept. mgr. Abraham & Straus Schs., Huntington, NY, 1978-80; mgmt. cons. Chase Manhattan Bank N.A., Lake Success, NY, 1980-83, Nat. Bankcard Corp., Melville, NY, 1983-84; pres. Whole Person Project, Inc., Elmont, NY, 1984—. Adv. bd. mem. LI Devel. Corp.; bd. dirs. Nassau County coun. Girl Scouts U.S., 1985—95. Recipient Bus. Achievement award Women on the Job, 1990. Mem. NAFE, ASTD, Fin. Women Internat., L.I. Networking Entrepreneurs (pres. 1984-91), Inst. Internal Auditors, Assn. Govt. Auditors, L.I. Ctr. for Bus. and Profl. Women, World Futurists Soc. Republican. Roman Catholic. Avocations: tennis, dance, gardening. Home and Office: Whole Person Project Inc 82 Cerenzia Blvd Elmont NY 11003-3631 Office Phone: 516-354-3551. E-mail: annbutera@cs.com.

BUTHOD, MARY CLARE, school administrator; b. Tulsa, Aug. 20, 1945; d. Arthur Paul and Mary Rudelle (Dougherty) B. MA in Teaching, Tulsa U., 1969; M Christian Spirituality, Creighton U., 1981. Joined Order of St. Benedict. Asst. tchr. HeadStart, Tulsa, 1966; tchr. Madalene Parish Sch., Tulsa, 1968-69, Monte Cassino Pvt. Sch., Tulsa, 1969-79; prin. Monte Cassino Elem. Sch., Tulsa, 1979-86; dir. Monte Cassino Sch., Tulsa, 1986—. Mem. convent coun. Benedictine Sisters, Tulsa, 1975-88, dir. formation programs, 1983—; examiner Okla. Quality Found., 2004. Active State Congl. Ednl. Com., Tulsa, 1989-90; co-chair for edn. and human devel. Tulsa Coalition Against Illegal Use of Drugs, 1990-91; adv. com. Okla. State Schs. Attuned, 2002—, Tulsa Pub. Sch. Quality Bd., 2005-06; adv. bd. Ret. Sr. Vol. Program, 2004— Recognized for Excellence in Edn. U.S. Dept. Edn., 1993-94. Mem. Tulsa Reading Coun. (sec. 1975-77), Nat. Cath. Edn. Assn., Delta Kappa Gamma. Home: 2200 S Lewis Tulsa OK 74114-3117 Office: Monte Cassino Sch 2206 S Lewis Ave Tulsa OK 74114-3109 Business E-Mail: smc@montecassino.org.

BUTLER, AQUETTA DENNIS, elementary school educator, social worker; b. Natchez, Miss., Feb. 18, 1963; d. Longino Dennis and Leonia Alberta Evans; m. Calvin Jeronemo Butler, Aug. 15, 1992; children: Darius S., Calvin Jeron. BSW, U. So. Miss., 1990; MS in Elem. Edn., Alcorn State U., Miss., 2003. LCSW. Mental health counselor S.W. Miss. Mental Health, Natchez, 1990—92; social worker Adams County Dept. Human Svcs., Natchez, 1992—98; classroom instr. Natchez Pub. Schs., 1998—. Rec. sec. Nat. Coalition 100 Black Women, Natchez, 1999—; parliamentarian Natchez H.S. Band Boosters, 2003—; sec. Natchez-McLaurin PTA, 2003—; 2d v.p. Natchez H.S. PTA, 2004—. Named Tchr. of Yr., McLaurin Elem. Sch., 2002—03, Natchez Pub. Sch. Sys., 2003, Adams County C. of C., 2003; ednl. grantee, Entergy, Natchez, 1992, ednl. sci. grantee, Bell South Pioneers, Natchez, 1993. Mem.: Adams County Assn. Edn. (treas. 1998—), Delta Sigma Theta (Natchez alumnae chptr.). Democrat. Baptist. Avocations: exercise, reading, cooking, gardening. Home: 23 Davis Ct Natchez MS 39120 Office: Natchez Adams Pub Schs 170 Sgt S Prentiss Dr Natchez MS 39120

BUTLER, BRETT, comedienne, actress; b. Montgomery, AL, 1958; d. Roland Decatur Anderson, Jr. and Carol; adoptive parent Bob Butler; m. Charles Wilson, 1978 (div. 1981); m. Ken Ziegler, 1987. Waitress, Houston, 1981-82; stand-up comedian, 1982—. Star, exec. prodr. TV series Grace Under Fire, 1993-98; appeared on TV in It's Just A Ride, 1994; in film Bruno, 1999; TV film It's Just a Ride, 1994.

BUTLER, CAROL ANN, psychotherapist, mediator; b. N.Y.C., Mar. 14, 1942; d. Anthony Aloysis and Madeline Gladys (Pearlmuter) Marino; B.A., Queens Coll., 1962; M.A., N.Y.U., 1967, Ph.D., 1970; cert. in psychoanalytic psychotherapy Washington Sq. Inst. for Psychotherapy and Mental Health, 1969, Nat. Accreditation Assn. for Psychoanalysis, 1976, Masters and Johnson Inst., 1975, The SATTI Group, 1994, Ctr. for Family and Divorce Mediation, 1994, lic. psychoanalyst N.Y., 2006; m. Adonis Carl Butler, Sept. 10, 1961; children— Adam, Aisha. Employment interviewer, correctional vocat. rehab. specialist N.Y. State Employment Service, 1963-65; counselor, supr. Springfield Coll. Guidance Center, 1965-67; adj. asst. prof. N.Y.U., 1970-72, 86—; pvt. practice psychotherapy, psychoanalysis, group psychotherapy, mediation, N.Y.C., 1967—; coordinator Women's Psychoanalytic Study Group, 1975-80; psychotherapist The SATTI Group, 1993-2003. Cons. co-author: The Divorce Mediation Answer Book, 1999; editor: Psychoanalytic Psychology, 1986-96. Recipient Founders Day award N.Y.U., 1970. Mem. APA, Assn. for Conflict Rersolution, Authors Guild, Nat. Accreditation Assn. Psychoanalysis, N.Y.C. Coun. Divorce Mediation, N.Y. Acad. Sci. Office: 60 W 13th St New York NY 10011-7959 Office Phone: 212-807-0008.

BUTLER, CAROL GREEN, music educator; b. Alamosa, Colo., July 29, 1953; d. Joseph Franklin and Janie (Stowell) Green; m. Harold Lamont Butler; children: Amanda, Randy. BA in Music, William Jewell Coll., Liberty, Mo., 1975; MusM, Baylor U., 1977. Pvt. instr. piano Carol Butler Piano Studio, Nashville, 1977—; pvt. and class piano instr., accompanist Free Will Bapt. Bible Coll., Nashville, 1993—. Piano accompanist for choirs and ann. broadway dinner theater First Bapt. Ch., Nashville, 1988—. Piano arranger: published in collection of arrangements Come Celebrate! Contemporary Piano Arrangements for Worship, 2000. Mem.: Nat. Guild of Piano Tchrs., Nashville Area Guild of Piano Tchrs. (pres. 1993—94, treas. 2002—05), Music Tchrs. Nat. Assn. (cert.), Tenn. Music Tchrs. Assn. (recording sec. 2001—03), Nashville Area Music Tchrs. Assn. (pres. 1997—99, treas. 2003—, Tchr. of Yr. 1997). Avocations: travel, videography. Home: 604 Darlington Pl Nashville TN 37211-5101

BUTLER, DEBRA YVONNE, special education educator, small business owner; b. Mobile, Ala., June 25, 1961; d. Percy and Lucille Tensley Butler; children: Jerrod Ferrilando Lindsey, Jerrico Dewon Lindsey. AA, S.D.Bishop State C.C., Mobile, Ala., 1989; BA, Mobile Coll., 1991; MEd, Ala. State U., Montgomery, 1997. Cert. Class A MA Special Edn. (047) grades p-12 Ala., 1977. Mental health technologist Albert P. Brewer Devel. Ctr., Mobile, 1980—84; med. sec. supr. Franklin Meml. Primary Health Ctr., Mobile/Prichard, 1984—88; news reporter intern Wala Action News-10, Mobile, 1988—90; news reporter/pub. affairs dir. WQLS Radio 101.3, Dothan, Ala., 1991—92; news reporter WDHN-TV-18, Dothan, 1991—93; alternative sch. tchr. Dothan City Sch., Ala., 1991—96; spl. educator Vivian B Adams Sch., Ozark, Ala., 1994—95; spl. educator/soccer coach Mobile County Sch., 1996—2000; spl. educator Columbus Edn. Orgn., Maui, Hawaii, 2000—04, Hawaii Dept. Edn., Wai'Anae, 2004—. Music entrepreneur Raw Talent Dx, Bklyn., 2004—; exec. protection specialist Maui Arts And Cultural Ctr., Kahului, Hawaii, 2000—04; talk show host Akaku - Maui Cmty. Tv Inc., Kahului, Hawaii, 2000—04; motivational spkr. Les Brown Inc., Potomac, Md., 1998—2003. Prodr.: (photography) Infinite Illusions (Internat. Libr. of Photography award, 2003), Visions Of The Soul; dir.: (video) Young People Our Hope Is In You (Black History award, 2000); contbr. articles pub. to profl. jour. Pres. READ(Reading Educates All Diversity) Found. INC., Honolulu, 2000; acting v.p. Oprah 'S Book Club, Maui, Hawaii, 2004; del. Ala. Edn. Assn., Mobile, Ala., 1996—2000; ea. star Order Of Ea. Star, Prichard/Dothan, Ala., 1977; bd. mem. Epileptic Found. Of Maui, Maui, Hawaii, 2000. Recipient Everyday Heroes Award, Pukalani Cmty. - Maui, Hi., 2003, Excellence In Services To Hawaii's Children With Disabilities, Columbus Edn. Orgn., 2000—04, Kingdom Of Hawaii Sovereign Nation Of God, King Akahi Nui And Cabinet, 2003—05, Wall Of Tolerance, Rosa Parks, 2000—02, Championship Award For Excellence In News Reporting, FAA, 1991; scholar Tchr. Edn., Dewitt Wallace - Reader's Digest Ctr., 1993—95, Ala. Assn. Of Women's Club, Inc. And Youth Affiliates, 1995—96. Mem.: Hawaii Assn. Of Sch. Psychology (assoc.), Nat. Assn. Of Sch. Psychology (assoc.), NEA (life; edn. policy and profl. practice commn. 1998—2003). Achievements include patents for Hair And Scalp Conditioner; invention of Breast Protection Shells For Female Boxers. Avocations: yoga, boxing, Tae Kwon Do, singing, dance. Office Phone: 808-685-3461. Home Fax: 808-685-1290; Office Fax: 808-697-7017. Business E-Mail: debrabutler1@aol.com.

BUTLER, DONNA MARCIA, mathematics educator; d. Donald Marshall and Delores Gladine Butler. BS in Math., So. Ill. U., Edwardsville, 1974. Cert. tchr. Ill. Math. tchr. Cahokia Sch. Dist., Ill., 1974—. Trustee Cahokia Pub. Libr. Dist., 1996—2005. Mem.: Math. Assn. Am. Lutheran. Avocations: genealogy, crafts. Office: Cahokia HS 800 Range Ln Cahokia IL 62206

BUTLER, ELIZABETH ROSANNE, music educator, director; d. Billie Joe Gambrell, Sr. and Betty Joy (Looney) Gambrell; 1 child, Leah Michelle. AA, East Miss. C.C., 1974; MusB in Edn., U. West Ala., 1977; MA, U. North Ala., 1981. Dir. band, instr. choral Lisman Jr. H.S. and East Choctaw Jr. H.S., Butler, Ala., 1978; dir. band Beulah Hubbard H.S., Little Rock, Miss., 1978—79, Colbert County H.S., Leighton, Ala., 1979—83, Clarkdale H.S., Meridian, Miss., 1983—86; tchr. music Meridian (Miss.) Pub. Schs., 1986—99; dir. band Choctaw County H.S., Butter, 1999—2000; tchr. band, music John Essex H.S., Demopolis, Ala., 2000—01; dir. band Olive Branch (Miss.) Mid. Sch., 2001—04; tchr. music Desoto Ctrl. Elem. Sch., Southaven, Miss., 2004—. Pvt. piano instr., Southaven, Miss. Mem.: Miss. Band Dirs. Assn., Music Educators Nat. Conv. Baptist. Avocations: crafts, sewing, gardening, pets. Office: Desoto Ctrl Elem Sch 2411 Central Pkwy Southaven MS 38672

BUTLER, GAYLE, editor-in-chief; m. Scott Butler; children: Sarah, Ellen. BA, Univ. Richmond. With Potomac Elec. Power Co.; joined Meredith Corp., 1983, assoc. editor, Better Homes & Gardens Mag. to sr.home editor, Better Homes & Gardens books, various positions Spl. Interest Pubs., editl. dir., Spl. Interest Pubs., 2004—06, editor-in-chief, Better Homes & Gardens Mag., 2006—. Bd. dir. Des Moines Libr. Found. Recipient Disting. Svc. award, Univ. Richmond Alumni Assn., 2005. Mem.: Phi Beta Kappa. Office: Better Homes & Gardens Meredith Corp 1716 Locust St Des Moines IA 50309 Office Phone: 515-284-3000.*

BUTLER, GLORIA SINGLETON, state legislator; children: Felicia, Leslie. AS in Bus. Adminstrn., Perimeter Coll. Fiscal acctg. asst. Health Scis. Ctr., Emory U., Atlanta; mem. Ga. State Senate, Atlanta, 1999—, sec. pub. safety com., mem. edn., retirement and transp. coms. Leg. asst. to U.S. Congresswoman Cynthia McKinney, Washington, 1992; mem. USIA Speaker program, South Africa, Zimbabwe, Swaziland, 1994; asst. to dir. AmeriCorps Team for Nat. Svc., 1996 Olympics and paralympics; dir. operation Big Vote, Coalition for Black Voter participation, 4th Congrl. Dist., DeKalb County, 1996; pub. rels. dir. Martin Luther King Jr. March com., 1997; mem. exec. staff, staff of intergovtl. rels. Office DeKalb County Sheriff. Mem. NOW, NAACP (exec. bd. DeKalb County chpt.), Nat. Coun. Negro Women, DeKalb Women's Polit. Caucus, Nat. Women's Polit. Caucus. Democrat. Office: Ste 420D State Capitol Atlanta GA 30334-9003

BUTLER, GRACE CAROLINE, medical researcher; b. Lima, Peru, Dec. 19, 1937; (parents Am. citizens); d. Everett Lyle and Mary Isabella (Sloatman) Gage; m. William Langdon Butler, Dec. 28, 1961; children: Mary Dyer, William Langdon Jr. AA, Stephens Coll., 1957; BS in Nursing, Columbia U., 1960; postgrad., Union County Coll., 1984. Head nurse N.Y. State Psychiat. Inst., N.Y.C., 1960-61; clin. instr. Columbia U., N.Y.C., 1960-61; staff nurse, educator Vis. Nurse Service, Summit, N.J., 1962-63; health adminstr. Eagle Island Girl Scout Camp, Tupper Lake, N.Y., 1964; evening supr. Ashbrook Nursing Home, Scotch Plains, N.J., 1968-72; teaching asst. Scotch Plains-Fanwood (N.J.) Sch. System, 1975-78; staff nurse Westfield (N.J.) Med. Group, 1980-82, head nurse, 1982-83, supr., 1983-84; office adminstr. Harris S. Vernick, MD, PA, Westfield, 1984-86, corp. v.p., office adminstr., 1986-88, Assocs. in Medicine, Westfield, 1988-90; pvt. researcher, 1990—. Diabetes instr. Boehringer Manneheim Diagnostics, 1984—, Eli Lilly and Co., Indpls., 1984—; microbiologist tester Med. Technol. Corp., Somerset, NJ, 1984—; computer advisor Cordis Corp., Miami, 1985—. Asst. leader Girl Scouts U.S., Fanwood, 1970—73; bd. dirs. PTA, Scotch Plains, Fanwood, 1973—79; religious instr. All Sts. Episcopal Ch., Scotch Plains, 1967—82, 1995—, mem. altar guild, 1994—, mem. vestry, 1999—2005, lay eucharistic min., 2001—. Mem.: Am. Soc. Notaries, League Ednl. Advancement RNs, Columbia U./Presbyn. Hosp. Sch. Nursing Alumni Assn. Republican. Episcopalian. Avocations: sewing, water sports, gardening, wood refinishing. Home: 125 Russell Rd Fanwood NJ 07023-1063

BUTLER, JANNETTE SUE, human resources professional; b. Eugene, Oreg., Mar. 15, 1960; d. Robert Eugene and Dorothy Marilyn (Irvin) Butler. BS in Hotel Adminstrn., U. Nev., Las Vegas, 1982. Cert. health promotion dir., sr. profl. in human resources. Pers. mgmt. trainee The Sheraton Corp., San Diego, 1982-83, dir. pers. Palm Coast, Fla., 1983-85, dir. human resources Dallas, 1985-89; corp. dir. human resources Hilton Reservations Worldwide, Carrollton, Tex., 1989-95; human resource cons. Symantec Corp., Eugene, Oreg., 1995-97; mgr. human resources Microsoft Corp., Redmond, Wash., 1997-99, sr. mgr. human resource, 1999—2000, group human resources mgr., 2000—01, human resource dir., 2001—. Mem., vol. Nat. Multiple Sclerosis Soc., Redmond Police Dept., 2001—; mem. steering com. Lane County Career Ctrs., 1995-97. Recipient Volunteerism award Lodging Industry Tng. Ctr., 1988. Mem. Soc. for Human Resource Mgmt., Northwest Human Resource Mgmt. Assn. (pres. elect 1997), Inst. for Internat. Human Resource Mgmt., Eugene C. of C. (edn. com.). Episcopalian. Avocations: boating, gardening, skiing. Office: Microsoft One Microsoft Way Redmond WA 98052

BUTLER, JESSIE D., community activist, retired educator, counselor; b. Conroe, Tex., Oct. 26, 1938; d. Floyd and Datchie (Walker) Davis; m. Franklin Delano Dismuke (div.); m. Lee Hayward Butler, Sr. (dec.). BA, Prairie View A&M U., 1962; MA, Atlanta U., 1969, postgrad. Caseworker Crockett (Tex.) State Sch. for Girls, 1962-63; substitute tchr. Houston Ind. Sch. Dist., 1963-64; tchr. Sealy (Tex.) Ind. Sch. Dist., 1964-65; tchr., counselor Jasper County Pub. Schs., Monticello, Ga., 1965-67; guidance counselor Harrisburg (Pa.) Sch. Dist., 1968-97. Recipient cmty. svc. plaques; recipient Diamond Life award NAACP. Mem. AAUW, NAACP (life, v.p. Pa. state 1991—, pres. Harrisburg 1991-96, Golden Heritage life mem., nat. bd. dirs. v.p. Pa. state 1991-2005), NEA, NOW, ACLU, Am. Assn. Ret. Persons, So. Christian Leadership Conf., Am. Bus. Womens Assn. (v.p. 1999—, pres. 2000-02), Pa. State Edn. Assn.- Coalition Trade Black, Prairie View A&M U. Alumni Assn. (life), Omnia Bona Inc. (co-founder, past pres. nat. sec.), Golden Heritage (life), Order Eastern Star, Phi Delta Kappa, Delta Sigma Theta (life, pres. Harrisburg alumni chpt. 2003-05). Democrat. Baptist. Avocations: travel, reading, volunteer work. Home: 3102 Schoolhouse Ln Harrisburg PA 17109-4628 Personal E-mail: jdb1026@verizion.net.

BUTLER, KARLA, psychologist, educator; b. Richmond, Calif., June 14, 1933; d. Clifford Thomas and Ethel Marie (Larson) B.; m. James P. Thomas, June 11, 1953 (div.); children: Rhys Clifford, Evan Charles. BA in Psychology, Stanford U., 1954; PhD, U. Calif.-Berkeley, 1963. Mem. faculty Calif. State U., Northridge, 1966—, prof. psychology, 1974—; enrolled agent tax practitioner Sherman Oaks, Calif., 1993—. Contbr. articles, book chpts. to profl. publs. NIMH grantee, 1969-73. Mem. Phi Beta Kappa, Sigma Xi. Office: Calif State U Dept Psychology 18111 Nordhoff St Northridge CA 91330-0001

BUTLER, KATHERINE ANN, elementary school educator; b. Yorktown, Va., Dec. 7, 1966; d. Charles Edward and Carol Ann Scott. BA in Edn., Christopher Newport U., 1989. Cert. tchr. Tchr. York County Pub. Schs., Yorktown, Va., 1989—91, Hampton City Pub. Schs., 1992—. Vol. ARC, 1987—. Baptist. Avocations: aerobics, crafts, reading, bowling, swimming, volleyball, jogging. Home: 134 Leslie Ln Yorktown VA 23693-4420 Office Phone: 757-728-6783. Business E-Mail: kbutler@sbo.hampton.k12.va.us.

BUTLER, KATHERINE E., lawyer; BA, Smith Coll; JD, Suffolk U.; LLM, Boston U. Bar: Mass. 1980. Lead legal counsel Software Internat. Corp., Andover, Mass.; atty. GE, 1981—98; lead counsel GE Info. Svcs. Europe; sr. counsel GE Info. Svcs., Rockville, Md.; sr. v.p., gen. counsel Software AG, Inc. (USA), Reston, Va., 1998—. Avocation: bicycling. Office: Software Ag Inc 11700 Plaza America Dr Ste 700 Reston VA 20190-4739

BUTLER, KATHLEEN A., education educator, consultant; b. Willimantic, Conn., July 26, 1946; d. William J. and Anastasia Desrosiers; m. Kerry B. Butler, Nov. 23, 1968; children: Erin Kathleen, Johanna Butler Cahill. BA, U. Conn., Storrs, 1968, MA, 1969, PhD, 1982. Lic. sch. adminstr. Conn. Pres. The Learner's Dimension, Columbia, Conn., 1982—2005; assoc. prof. edn. St. Joseph Coll., West Hartford, Conn., 2001—. Cons. Nat. Coll. Sch. Leadership, Nottingham, 2003—, Region 10 Ednl. Svc. Ctr., Prins.' Leadership Acad., Richardson, Tex., 1996—, Conn. Assn. Schs., Conn. Prins.' Ctr., Cheshire, Conn. Author, rschr.: ednl. material ViewPoints on Style; author: Performance Based Learning with Style. Choir mem. Ch. of the Holy Family, Hebron, Conn., 2002—05. Recipient Unification of Tchr. Prepartory Program grant, State of Conn., 2002—04; Tchr. Quality Preparation grantee, Conn. Dept. Higher Edn., 2005, 2006. Mem.: ASCD, Nat. Staff Devel. Coun., Phi Delta Kappa. Roman Catholic. Avocations: travel, gardening. Home: 7 Lakeview Dr Columbia CT 06237 Office: St Joseph Coll 1678 Asylum Ave West Hartford CT 06117 Office Phone: 860-231-5322.

BUTLER, KERRY, actress; Actor: (Broadway plays) Les Miserables, 1987—2003, Blood Brothers, 1993—95, Beauty and the Beast, 1994—95, Hairspray, 2002—03, Little Shop of Horrors, 2003— (nominated best actress Outer Critics Cir.), The Man in the White Suit, 2005, (regional stage shows) Prodigal, Le Passe Muraille, Bat Boy The Musical, The "I" Word, The Folsom Head, Bright Lights, Big City, Oklahoma, The Opposite of Sex, 2006. Office: Abrams Artists Agy 26th Fl 275 Seventh Ave New York NY 10001 Office Phone: 646-486-4600. Office Fax: 646-486-0100.*

BUTLER, LESLIE WHITE, epidemiologist; b. Huntington, N.Y., July 22, 1954; d. John B. and Inez M. (Montecalvo) W.; m. Thomas Butler, 1997. BS, Mary Washington Coll., 1976; MPH, Johns Hopkins U., 1990; postgrad., U. Md., 1993—95. Microbiologist II Am. Type Culture Collection, Rockville, Md., 1980—83; analyst InterAm. Assocs., Rockville, 1984—86; sr. assoc. Triton Corp., Washington, 1986—87; health analyst Row Scis., Inc., Rockville, 1987—88; rsch. analyst Nat. BioSys., Rockville, 1988—90; sr. assoc. Clement Internat., Fairfax, Va., 1990—92; project dir. epidemiology Consultants in Epidemiology and Occupl. Health, Washington, 1992—93, 1999—; dir. epidemiology Scis. Internat., Inc., Alexandria, Va., 1993—94; cancer epidemiologist Lombardi Cancer Ctr. Georgetown U., 1998—99; sr. epidemiologist, cons. in epidemiology and occupl. health Washington, 1999—2001. Pres. Epidemiology and Health Rsch., Inc., Bethesda, Md., 1994—2005; realtor Weichert Realtors, Potomac, Md., 1997—2004, Long and Foster, 2004—; epidemiologist Indexer Info. Venture, Phila., 2003—. Mem. APHA, U.S. Tennis Assn., Soc. Epidemiologic Rsch., Md. Assn. Realtors, Nat. Assn. Realtors, Greater Capitol Area Assn. Realtors, No. Va. Assn. Realtors, Bethesda Country Club. Avocations: tennis, ballet, reading, public health. Office: PO Box 6490 Woodbridge VA 22195-6490 Office Phone: 301-412-1137. Personal E-mail: lesliewbutler@comcast.net. Business E-Mail: leslie@lesliewbutler.com.

BUTLER, LINDA LOUISE, elementary educator; b. Harrisburg, Pa., Apr. 6, 1938; d. John Rippel and Louise (Windsor) Thompson; m. Rudolph Earl Butler Jr., May 14, 1966; children: Rudolph III, Heather J. BS in Edn., Bucknell U., 1959; MEd in Curriculum, Penn State U., 1983, postgrad., 1984. Cert. elem. educator, reading specialist. Tchr. Dept. of Def., Preswick, Scotland, 1961-62, Tripoli, Libya, 1962-64, Tokyo, Japan, 1964-65, Carmel (Calif.) Mid. Sch., 1965-66; reading specialist Harrisburg (Pa.) Sch. Dist., 1985—. Bd. dirs. Harrisburg Area Community Coll.; v.p., treas., pres. Susquehanna Twp. Sch. Bd., Harrisburg, 1975—. IDEA fellow. Fellow Assn. Secondary Curriculum Devel.; mem. Internat. Reading Assn., Keystone Reading Assn., Capitol Reading Council, Falcon Families.

BUTLER, MARGARET KAMPSCHAEFER, retired computer scientist; b. Evansville, Ind., Mar. 7, 1924; d. Otto Louis and Lou Etta (Rehsteiner) Kampschaefer; m. James W. Butler, Sept. 30, 1951; 1 child, Jay. AB, Ind. U., 1944; postgrad., U.S. Dept. Agr. Grad. Sch., 1945, U. Chgo., 1949, U. Minn., 1950. Statistician U.S. Bur. Labor Statistics, Washington, 1945-46, U.S. Air Forces in Europe, Erlangen and Wiesbaden, Germany, 1946-48, U.S. Bur. Labor Statistics, St. Paul, 1949-51; mathematician Argonne (Ill.) Nat. Lab., 1948-49, 51-80, sr. computer scientist, 1980-92; dir. Argonne Code Ctr. and Nat. Energy Software Ctr. Dept. Energy Computer Program Exch., 1960-91; spl. term appointee Argonne Nat. Lab., 1993—2006. Cons. AMF Corp., 1956—57, OECD, 1964, Poole Bros., 1967. Author: Careers for Women in Nuclear Science and Technology, 1992; editor Computer Physics Communications, 1969-80; contbr. (chpt.) The Application of Digital Computers to Problems in Reactor Physics, 1968, Advances in Nuclear Sci. and Technology, 1976; contbr. articles to profl. jours. Treas. Timberlake Civic Assn., 1958; rep. mem. nomination com. Hinsdale Caucus, Ill., 1961-62; coord. 6th dist. ERA, 1973-80; elected del. Rep. Nat. Conv., 1980; bd. mgr. DuPage dist. YWCA Met. Chgo., 1987-90; computer and info. sys. adv. bd. Coll. DuPage, 1987-95; industry adv. bd. computer sci. dept. Bradley U., 1988-91; vice chair Ill. Women's Polit. Caucus, 1987-90; chair voters svc. LWV, Burr-Ridge-Willowbrook, 1991-93; vol. Morton Arboretum, 1996—, Friends of Indian Prairie Pub. Libr., 2000-02; active LaGrange Park Friends Libr., 2002-; bd. dirs. Plymouth Place Residents Coun., 2003-05; treas. Plymouth Landing Gift Shoppe, 2004—, spl. fin. and program coms, 2005-06. Recipient cert. of leadership Met. YWCA, Chgo., 1985, Merit award Chgo. Assn. Technol. Socs., 1988; named to Fed. 100, 1991; named Outstanding Woman Leader of DuPage County Sci., Tech. and Health Care, 1992. Fellow Am. Nuclear Soc. (mem. publs. com. 1965-71, bd. dirs. 1976-79, exec. com. 1977-78, chmn. bylaws and rules com., 1979-82, profl. women in ANS com. 1991-93, reviewer for publs., spl. award math. and computer divsn. 1992); mem. Assn. Computing Machinery (exec. com., sec. Chgo. chpt. 1963-65, publs. chmn. nat. conf. 1968, reviewer for publs.), Assn. Women in Sci. (pres. Chgo. area chpt. 1982, nat. exec. bd. 1985-87), Nat. Computer Conf. (chmn. Pioneer Day com. 1985, tech. program chmn. 1987). Independent. Home: 107 Brewster Lane La Grange Park IL 60526-6003

BUTLER, MARY EDITH, academic administrator, school librarian; b. Jackson, Miss., Sept. 21, 1955; d. Russell Elliott and Audrea Jones Hobgood; m. Christopher Williams Butler, June 10, 1977. BS, Miss. Coll., Clinton, 1977; MLS, U. Miss., Oxford, 1980. Asst. prin. and tchr. United Meth. Children's Home, Tahleqdah, Okla., 1982—85; adj. instr. Northeastern Okla. State U., Tahleqdah, 1983—85; libr. dir. and tchr. Haileyville Pub. Sch., Okla., 1985—97; dir. of libr. and coord. of assessment Eastern Okla. State Coll., Wilburton, 1997—2006, asst. vice pres., media svcs., 2006—. Editor: Footsteps: A Choctaw's Jour., 2003. Com. chair Wilburton Main St., Okla., 2001—; bd.dirs., sec. CASA of Southeast Okla., Inc., McAlester, 2000—05; dist. officer and mem. Wilburton Lions Club, 1986—. Recipient Excellence in Edn. medal, Nat. Inst. for Staff and Org. Develop., 2006. Mem.: Okla.Assn.of

Cmty. Coll., Okla. Assn. of Instl. Rsch., Assn. for Inst. Rsch. Episc. Avocations: travel, cooking. Home: 1301 West Main Wilburton OK 74578 Office: Eastern Okla State Coll 1301 West Main Wilburton OK 74578

BUTLER, MARY K., prosecutor; b. 1956; AB, Vassar Coll.; JD, U. Wis. Bar: Fla. 1981. Atty. Hopkins and Sutter, Chgo.; asst. U.S. atty. (so. dist.) Fla. US Dept. Justice, Miami, 1987—99, chief corruption sect., 1997—98, atty. pub. integrity sect. Washington, 1999—. Spkr. in field. Office: US Dept Justice 950 Pennsylvania Ave NW Washington DC 20530*

BUTLER, NANCY TAYLOR, gender equity specialist, religious program administrator; b. Newport, RI, Oct. 31, 1942; d. Robert Lee and Roberta Claire (Brown) Taylor; m. Edward M. Butler, Aug. 22, 1964; children: Jeffrey, Gregory, Katherine. AB, Cornell U., 1964. Asst. dir. Career Equity Assistance Ctr. for Tng. Coll. of N.J., 1990-98; owner Equity Resources, Tinton Falls, N.J., 1993—. Mem. N.J. Dept. Edn. Gender Equity Adv. Comm., 1995—, sec., 1996-2000, chair, 2000-03. Editor Equity Exch., 1991-2003. Monmouth County dist. ethics com. Supreme Ct. N.J., 1987-91; pres. Vol. Ctr. Monmouth County, Red Bank, 1985-89; mem. Cornell U. Coun., Ithaca, N.Y., 1987-91, 1994-2004, 06—, adminstrv. bd., 1996-2003, vice-chair, 2001-03; dir. Cornell Assn. Class Officers, 1991-97; chair Cornell Alumni Trustee Nominating Com., 1994. Recipient Woman of Achievement award Commn. on Status of Women, 1988, Women's History Tribute NOW-N.J., 1995, Woman Leader award N.J. Assn. Women Bus. Owners, 1996, Frank H.T. Rhodes Exemplary Alumni Svc. award, 2004. Mem. AAUW (life; pres. N.J. chpt. 1988-90, Edn. Found. Named Gift 1982, 83, 84, 86, 87, 89, 91), Nat. Coalition for Sex Equity in Edn. Home: 20 Cedar Pl Tinton Falls NJ 07724-2807

BUTLER, NAOMI WITMER, librarian, educator; b. Boonsboro, Md., Aug. 25, 1934; d. Howard David and Lavina Lucy (Faulders) Witmer; m. Philip Anthony Butler, Sept. 7, 1962. AB, Shepherd Coll., 1957; MS in Libr. Sci., U. N.C., 1966; AGS, U. Md., 1988. Libr. media specialist Frederick (Md.) County Schs., 1957-67, 68-69; asst. prof. Shippensburg (Pa.) U., 1967-68, Shepherd Coll., Shepherdstown, W.Va., 1969-70; sch. outreach liaison Md. State Dept. Edn., Baltimore, 1970-95; coord. Educators Lit. Corps, Boonsboro, Md., 1995—; tng./advocacy coord. We. Md. Pub. Librs., 1996—. Mem. Delta Kappa Gamma. Avocations: reading, travel, water sports. Home and Office: 109 David Dr Boonsboro MD 21713-1055 Office Phone: 301-739-3250 x 142.

BUTLER, PATRICIA, protective services official; b. Salem, Mass., Aug. 13, 1958; d. Frank Arthur and Ruth Elizabeth (Bartlett) B. Paramedic degree, Davenport Coll., 1984, AA in Mgmt. of Emergency Med. Svcs., 1987; Mich. Law Enforcement Officers Tng. Coun. cert., Grand Valley State U., 1988; BA in MHR, Spring Arbor Coll., 1994. CEO Whispering Winds, Inc., L'Anse, Mich., 1985—; firefighter Grand Rapids (Mich.) Fire Dept., 1985; security, data entry clerk Lacks Industries, Grand Rapids, 1985-88; loss prevention officer Woodland Mall Security, Kentwood, Mich., 1988-89, Butterworth Hosp., Grand Rapids, 1989; police officer Lakeview Police Dept., 1989, Edmore (Mich.)-Home Mcpl. Police Dept., 1989-90, Coopersville (Mich.) Police Dept., 1989-90; chief police Lakeview Village Police Dept., 1990-94, Mich. State Police, 1994—. Mem. Mich. Paramedic, 1986-98. Mem. NAFE, Nat. Assn. Chiefs, Mich. Chief's Assn. (v.p. 1991-94), Internat. Assn. Women Police, Mich. Assn. Chief of Police, Women Police Mich. Avocation: freelance artist. Office: Mich State Police L'Anse Post 88 PO Box 100 Lanse MI 49946-0100

BUTLER, PATRICIA, mental health nurse, educator, consultant; b. Galesburg, Ill., Aug. 31, 1943; d. Allen Dale and Mary Lacky; m. Glen William Butler, Mar. 14, 1964 (div. Apr. 1974); children: Scott Lewis, Andrew William, Suzanne Elizabeth; m.Walter Sage Julio, April 8, 1980. AA in Nursing/Journalism, Sacramento City Coll., 1965; BS in Sociology/Psychology, SUNY, Albany, 1992. Cert. legal nurse cons., 2006. Clin. nurse Mercy Gen. Hosp., Sacramento, Sacramento Med. Ctr.; Davis (Calif.) Cmty. Hosp.; clin. nurse Woodland (Calif.) Meml. Hosp., 1965-74; dir. nurses Woodland Skilled Nursing, 1978-79; head nurse/psychiatry St. Croix Mental Health, Christiansted, U.S. V.I., 1974-79; clin. program mgr. Yolo County Mental Health, Woodland, 1980—2005, legal nurse, cons., 2006—. Instr. Yuba C.C., Marysville, Calif., 1988—. Author curriculum; mem. editl. adv. bd. Daily Democrat. Bd. dirs. Concilio of Yolo County, Woodland, 1984-87; mem. Red Cross Nat. Disaster Mental Health, 1996—. Recipient Bell award Mental Health Assn. Yolo County, 1993, Christine West award, 1999, Clara Barton award Yolo County Red Cross; NIMH grantee, 1989-90. Mem. LWV (recording sec. 1997, 98, co-pres. 1999—), Calif. Elected Women's Assn. Edn. & Rsch., Virgin Islands Nurses Assn., Forensic Mental Health Assn. Calif. (sec. 1991-93, conf. planning 1990-91, dir. edn. and tng. 1996-98), Rotary Internat. Independent. Roman Catholic. Avocations: diving, boating, travel, golf. Home: McKinney-Rubicon Rd Homewood CA 96141 Office: PO Box 436 Homewood CA 96141

BUTLER, PAULA KAY, elementary school educator; b. Oklahoma City, Apr. 13, 1957; d. Harry Van Buren and Betty Lou Shumard; m. Max D. Butler, May 28, 1977; children: Nathan Douglas, Cody Orin. BS in Home Econs., Okla. State U., Stillwater, 1979. Tchr. home econs. Cedarville High Sch., Ark., 1979—84; substitute tchr. Cedarville Schs., 1988—98; tchr. sci. Cedarville Mid Sch., 1998—. Mem., sec. Pers. Policy Com., Cedarville, 1998—. Youth leader, tchr. 1st Bapt. Ch., Cedarville, 1980—2005; youth worker, asst. sec., tchr. Cedarville Assembly God Ch., 2005—. Mem.: Nat. Sci. Tchrs. Assn. Avocations: swimming, boating, skiing. Home: 4251 Bronco Ct Natural Dam AR 72948

BUTLER, SALLY KATHRYN, history educator; b. Fort Wayne, Ind., Mar. 29, 1959; m. Neal Charles Butler, May 23, 1981. MS Edn., Ind. U., Ft. Wayne, 1988. Tchr. Geyer Mid. Sch., Ft. Wayne, 1985—95; tchr. U.S. history Meml. Park Mid. Sch., Ft. Wayne, 1996—. Bd. mem. Friends Lincoln Mus., Ft. Wayne, 2000—06. Avocations: travel, bicycling, tennis, reading, hiking. Office: Memorial Park Middle School 2200 Maumee Avenue Fort Wayne IN 46803

BUTLER, SHIRLEY ANN, social worker; b. New Orleans, Apr. 18, 1951; d. John and Will A. (Powell) Cain; children: Chander Lynn, Twann Gerald-Lynn. BSW, So. U. New Orleans, 1980, MSW, 1991. Lic. practical nurse; cert. phlebologist; qualified mental retardation profl. Social worker intern Comty. Svc. Ctr., New Orleans, 1979, VA Hosp. New Orleans, 1979-80; social worker Hope Haven/Madonna Manor, Marrero, La., 1980-81; tchr. Orleans Parish Sch. Bd., New Orleans, 1981-87; psychiat. technician River Oaks Mental Hosp., West Harahan, La., 1981-82; counselor Vols. of Am., New Orleans, 1985—89; mental retardation profl. Met. Developmental Ctr., Belle Chase, La., 1989-92; case mgr. No AIDS Task Force, New Orleans, 1992-93; nurse St. Anna Nursing Home, New Orleans, 1993-94, Meds Force, 1994-99, St. Charles Manor, 1994-98. Social worker intern Carrollton Hollgrove Comty. Ctr., New Orleans, 1977; invited to testify on renewal of The Family and Med. Act. of 1993, Women's Legal Def. Fund; spkr. Dept. Commerce. Contbr. rsch. articles to profl. jours. Active People's Inst. for Survival and Beyond, New Orleans, 1990—. Mem. NASW, Acad. Cert. Baccalaureate Social Workers. Democrat. Baptist. Home: 9412 Fig St New Orleans LA 70118-1723 Personal E-mail: sbutler27@cox.net.

BUTLER, SUSAN, writer; b. N.Y.C., June 29, 1932; d. Walter H. and Grace (Koehler) Liebman; m. Robert Bendheim, 1954 (div. 1977); children: Lynn, Kim; m. Allan Churchill Butler, 1982. BA, Bennington Coll., 1953; MA, Columbia U., 1973. Author: East to the Dawn, The Life of Amelia Earhart, 1997, My Dear Mr. Stalin. The Complete Correspondence of Franklin D. Roosevelt and Joseph V. Stalin, 2005. Bd. dirs. Planned Parenthood of the Mid Hudson Valley, 1993-2001; chair Conservation Adv. Coun., Town of Northeast, N.Y., 1991-93. Mem.: PEN Club, The Explorers Club. Avocations: sailing, golf, tennis. Home: 2300 N Scenic Hwy Lake Wales FL 33898-6626

BUTLER, SUSAN LOWELL, educational association executive, writer; b. Bklyn., Feb. 10, 1944; d. John William and Catherine (Mauro) Yost; m. Horace Hamilton Lowell (div. 1982); m. James Thomas Butler, Feb. 12, 1983; stepchildren: James, Kevin, Michael. BA, Lycoming Coll., 1965; postgrad., U. Pa., 1965-67. Tchr. English and Journalism Bristol Twp. Schs., Levittown, Pa., 1967-70; field rep. Nat. Edn. Assn., Washington, 1970-74, dir. comm., 1974-80, dir. western states region Austin (Tex.) and Denver, 1980-84; acct. supr. Dale Chrisman & Assocs., Austin, 1984-86; pvt. cons. Austin, 1986-88; exec. v.p. Women in Comm., Inc., Washington, 1988-91; nat. exec. dir. Nat. Women's Hall of Fame, Seneca Falls, NY, 1991-96; dir. Coalition For America's Children, Washington, 1996—97; managing partner Butler Pub. Affairs, 1998—; sr. dir. pub. edn. Nat. Mental Assn., 2000—; v.p. comms. and public affairs The Hospices of Nat. Capital Region, Fairfax, Va., 2000—. Mem. bd. The Media Inst., Washington, 1989-91, mem. family lodge steering com. NIG, 2000—. Author: National Education Association: A Special Mission, 1987, Handbook of Association Communications, 1987, Pressing Onward: The Women's Historical Biography of the National Education Association, 1996. V.p. pub. affairs Mental Health Assn. of Tex., Austin, 1987-88; bd. dirs. Nat. Women's Hall of Fame, Ovarian Cancer Nat. Alliance, 1997—; co-chair Ovarian Cancer Coalition Greater Washington, 1997—; dirs. consumer liaison group Nat. Cancer Inst. Dirs. Consumer Liaison Group, 1997—; adv. bd. Nat. Archives History Project, 1995-96; active Alexandria (Va.) Commn. for Women, 1996—, 250th Anniversary Commn., 1997—; bd. dirs. co-founder, v.p. Ovarian Cancer Nat. Alliance, 1997—. Mem. Am. Soc. Assn. Execs., Pub. Rels. Soc. Am. (accredited), Women in Comm. Inc. Episcopalian. Avocations: skiing, photography. Home and Office: Butler Pub Affairs 406 Skyhill Rd Alexandria VA 22314-4920

BUTLER, TAMMY J. WILEY, medical, surgical, and pediatric nurse; b. Emporia, Va., Oct. 9, 1967; d. Danny Thomas and Joan (Evans) Wiley; m. Lawrence Graham Butler, July 20, 1991; children: Lawrencia Joan, Laren Talane, Leiara Lane. BSN, Med. Coll. Va., 1990; postgrad., Va. Commonwealth U., 1997-2001. RN Va., cert. ACLS, PALS, MSW. Charge nurse med./surg. and pediatrics Greensville Meml. Hosp., Emporia, 1990—, clin. coord., 1991—, quality assurance coord., 1993—. Baptist. Avocations: walking, reading, skating, outdoor summer games. Home: 736 Reedy Creek Rd Freeman VA 23856-2318 Office: Greensville Memorial Hospital 727 N Main St Emporia VA 23847-1274

BUTLER-PURRY, KAREN L., electrical engineer, educator; BS in Elec. Engrng. (summa cum laude), Southern U., Baton Rouge, La., 1985; MS, U. Tex., Austin, 1987; PhD in Elec. Engring., Howard U., 1994. Registered profl. engr., La., Tex., Miss. Joined as vis. asst. prof. Tex. A&M Univ., 1994, assoc. prof., elec. engring. College Station, Tex., asst. dean grad. studies, Dwight Look Coll. Engring., asst. dir., Power System Automation Lab. Spkr. in field; dir., Coll. Engring. Undergraduate Rsch. program Tex. A&M Univ., initiated the engrng. grad. invitational. Contbr. articles in profl. jours. Recipient Faculty Career award, NSF, 1995, Young Investigator award, Office of Naval Rsch., 1999, 2005 AAAS Mentor award, 2006; secured grants from the US Dept. Homeland Security, Sloan Found. and NSF. Mem.: Soc. Women Engineers (faculty advisor, Tex. A&M Univ. chpt.), Nat. Soc. Black Engineers (faculty advisor, Tex. A&M Univ. chpt.), La. Engring. Soc., Am. Soc. for Engring. Edn., IEEE, Power Engring. Soc. Office: Elec and Computer Engring Dept Tex A&M Univ 3128 TAMUS Office #216G ZEC 216G Zachry Engineering Ctr College Station TX 77843-3128 Office Phone: 979-847-9048. Office Fax: 979-845-6259. Business E-Mail: klbutler@ee.tamu.edu.*

BUTLER YANK, LESLIE ANN, artist, writer, editor; b. Salem, Oreg., Nov. 19, 1945; d. Marlow Dole and Lala Ann (Erlandson) Butler; m. Howard Dennis Yank, July 4, 2001. Student, Lewis and Clark Coll., 1963-64; BS, U. Oreg., 1969; postgrad., Portland State U., 1972-73, Lewis and Clark Coll. 1991. Creative trainee Ketchum Advt., San Francisco, 1970-71; asst. advt. dir. Mktg. Systems, Inc., Portland, Oreg., 1971-74; prodn. mgr., art dir., copywriter Finzer-Smith, Portland, 1974-76; copywriter Gerber Advt., Portland, 1976-78; freelance copywriter Portland, 1983-84, 83-85; copywriter McCann-Erickson, Portland, 1980-81; copy chief Brookstone Co., Peterborough, NH, 1981-83; creative dir. Whitman Advt., Portland, 1984-87; prin. L.A. Advt., 1987—; portrait artist. Author: The Dream Road and Other Tales From Hidden Hills, 1997; editor (arts and antiques): Living mag.; designer of fence featured in Better Homes & Gardens, 2000; one-woman shows include Ocean Lodge, Cannon Beach Oreg., 2004, Fifth Ave. Stes., Porland, 2004, Lawrence Gallery, Portland, 2004, City Hall, 2005, one-man shows include Fifth Avenue Suites, 2006, exhibitions include Rhodes Stingfellow Gallery, Cannon Beach, Oreg., 2004—, Brodrick Gallery, Portland, 2004, Sikta Art Invitational, 2003, 2004, Associated Arts Regional Juried Fine Arts Show, Ocean Shores, Wash., 2005, Coos Art Mus., Richland, Wash., 2005, exhibited in group shows at Grants Pass Mus. Art, 2006, exhibitions include many others, Represented in permanent collections George and Barbara Bush, Houston, Rue McClanahan, Bevelry Hills, Michael Jackson, Hollywood, Gary Maffei and Marc Linter, Portland. Spokeswoman Nat. Alopecia Areata Found., San Rafeal, Calif., 2004; Co-founder, v.p., newsletter editor Animal Rescue and Care Fund, 1972—81; mem. Friends of the Performing Arts Ctr., Portland Art Mus., Oreg. Humane Soc.; pres. OMSI; bd. dirs. Portland Opera Assn., 2000—02, Oreg. Humane Soc., 2002—. Recipient Internat. Film and TV Festival N.Y. Finalist award, 1985, 86, 87, 88, Internat. Radio Festival of N.Y. award, 1984, 85, 88, Hollywood Radio and TV Soc. Internat. Broadcasting award, 1981, TV Comml. Festival Silver Telly award, 1985, TV Comml. Festival Bronze Telly, 1986, AVC Silver Cindy, 1986, Los Angeles Advt. Women LULU, 1986, 87, 88, 89 Ad Week What's New Portfolio, 1986, N.W. Addy award Seattle Advt. Fedn., 1984, Best in the West award, 1985, Portland Advt. Fedn. Rosey Finalist award, 1986, Nat. winner Silver Microphone award, 1987, 88, 89. Mem.: Portland Art Mus., Portland Inst, Contemporary Art, Nat. Oil and Acrylic Painters Soc., People for Ethical Treatment of Animals. E-mail: labartist@aol.com.

BUTO, KATHLEEN A., health products executive; BA, Rutgers U.; MPA, Harvard U. With Health Care Financing Adminstrn., 1982—2000; sr. health advisor Congl. Budget Office, 2000—02; v.p. for health policy, govt. affairs Johnson & Johnson, Washington, 2002—. Office: Johnson & Johnson 1350 Eye St NW #1210 Washington DC 20005 Office Phone: 202-589-1000.

BUTTA, DEENA CELESTE, librarian; b. Chgo., June 1, 1950; d. Joseph James and Michaline Ann (Pabisinski) Weglarz; m. William C. Hartray, Apr. 21, 1974 (div. 1983); m. Raymond Peter Butta, June 2, 1984; children: Alexander Michael, Maris Michael, Philip Adrian. BA, Northwestern U., 1972; MLS, Rosary Coll., River Forest, Ill., 1978. Mem. staff Evanston (Ill.) Pub. Libr., 1969-79; libr. Triton C.C., River Grove, Ill., 1981, Libr. of Health Scis., U. Ill., Chgo., 1982-85; family day care provider Starchild Daycare, Chgo., 1985—97; staff mem. Des Plaines (Ill.) Pub. Libr., 1995-97, Glenview (Ill.) Pub. Libr., 1997—. Counselor Bach Flower Soc., Lynbrook, N.Y., 1987—; mem. Day Care Action Coun., Chgo., 1985-97; past treas. Echo 33, Chgo.; Reiki III practitioner; co-founder Caretakers Priory, 1996; team leader geneology seciton Ill Click Wesite. Co-editor Isis-Seshat Jour., 2004—; panelist TV series Man's Ultimate Destiny, 1992; interviewed for A&E The Unexplained. Presenter Day of Prayer, Monastic Interreligious Dialogue, others; dancer Old Town Renaissance Consort, 1983—. Mem. Fellowship of Isis (priestess, del. representing fellowship to Parliament of the World's Religions), Eleusis of Chgo. (planning and facilitating com. FOI ann. convs.), Bach Flower Remedy Soc. Avocations: quilting, calligraphy, dance, anthropology, healing. Home: 3334 W Eastwood Ave Chicago IL 60625-5304

BUTTE, AMY S., brokerage house executive; b. Jan. 8, 1968; BA in Polit. Sci. and Psychology, Yale U.; MBA, Harvard U. Various positions Anderson Consulting, Merrin Fin., Bridge Trading Co., Inc., Merrill Lynch; sr. mng. dir. Bear Stearns, 1999—2002; CFO, chief strategist fin. svcs. divsn. Credit Suisse First Boston, 2002—03; exec. v.p. NY Stock Exch. Inc., NYC, 2004—06, CFO, 2004—06; CFO, global ops. Man Financial, Inc., Chgo., 2006—. Co-chair corp. adv. bd. NYC Ballet; participant World Econ. Forum's Young Global Leader Program. Mem.: Nat. Orgn. Investment Professionals, NY Women's Found. Office: Man Financial Inc 717 5th Ave New York NY 10022*

BUTTE, NORINE, marketing executive; d. Felix Charles Butte and Audrey Perry Hunt. AA, Lincoln U., Calif., 1977; MA, U. Calif., Berkeley, 1980, PhD in Philosophy, 1981. Dir. mktg. Hawthorn Suites Hotels, Dallas, 1993—95; area gen. mgr. Jackson Hewit Inc., Ft. Worth, 1994—99; corp. sales mgr. Sierra Springs Co., Grand Prairie, Tex., 1998—2000; nat. acct. mgr. All Dance Data Sys., Dallas, 2000—04, Mail Box, 2000—04; bus. devel. mgr. Jaldive Digital Image, Arlington, Tex., 2004—. Pres. Direct Mktg Assoc. Den, Dallas, 2001—; industry co-chair USPS Dallas Task Force, 2003—; v.p. Den Mailers Assn., 2005—. Author: (nat. newsletter) Nat. Assn. Christmas Icons, 1975. Workgroup mem. MTAC-USPS Headquarters, Washington, 2003—; mem. Major Mailers Assn., Dallas, 2003—; mem. bd. dirs. Dallas Postal Customer Connect, 2003—. Recipient MQCS award, USPS, 2000—02, MCP award, 2001, PCC leadership award, 2004. Mem.: Jr. League, Brookhaven Country Club. Avocations: golf, winemaking, gourmet cooking, theater. Office: Inline Digital Image 612 North graet Southwest Pkwy Arlington TX 76011

BUTTEL, STACEY JEANNE, social studies educator; d. Buttel and Penrod. BA, Ohio U., Athens, 1995; MA, Ohio State U., Columbus, 1997. Cert. in comprehensive social studies edn. Ohio. Tchr. social studies Southwestern City Schs., Grove City, Ohio, 1995—.

BUTTER, ANDREA, marketing executive, consultant; arrived in U.S., 1980; MA, Stanford U., 1985. Founder, prin. Vekia, Menlo Park, Calif., 2001—; v.p., mktg. U3, Redwood City, Calif., 2005—. Author: Piloting Palm. The Inside Story of Palm, Handspring, and the Birth of the Billion-Dollar Handheld Industry, 2002. Dir. mktg. Women in Consulting, San Jose, Calif., 2005. Mem.: Soc. for Advancement of Consulting. Office Phone: 650-854-4132.

BUTTERFIELD, ANDREA CHRISTINE, psychology educator, educational association administrator; Student study abroad program, U. Md., Munich, Germany, 1973; BA in Childhood Edn., U. Fla., 1975; MEd in Reading, Beaver Coll., 1977; postgrad. reading supr. cert. program, Millersville U., 1985; DEd in Adult Edn., Pa. State U., 1995. Cert. supervisory I supr. reading, instrnl. II reading specialist-elem., Pa., supervisory II, Shippensburg U., 2003. Reading specialist Lauderdale Lakes Middle Sch., Fla., 1977-78; coord., oper. individual title I Roman Cath. H.S. for Boys Sch. Dist. of Phila., 1978-85; supr. of reading specialist interns and grad. instr., clin. practicum reading clinic Millersville U., Pa., 1985-86; reading specialist Ebenezer Elementary Sch. and Cedar Crest Middle Sch., Cornwall-Lebanon Sch. Dist., Lebanon, Pa., 1985—. Adj. instr. Camden County Coll., N.J., 1980; cons. to ednl. orgns., 1994—; part-time faculty ednl. psychology Pa. State U., Harrisburg, 1995—. Speaker in field. Planning commr., bd. officer Derry Township, Hershey, Pa., 1992—, design rev. bd. mem., 1994—. Mem. ASCD, PASCD (pres. elect so. region, chmn. so. region spring conf. planning com.), Internat. Reading Assn., Phi Kappa Phi, Phi Kappa Delta. Home: 440 Leearden Rd Hershey PA 17033-2140 Personal E-mail: acbutterfield@yahoo.com.

BUTTERFIELD, DEBORAH KAY, sculptor; b. San Diego, May 7, 1949; m. John Buck; 2 children. BA, U. Calif., Davis, 1971, MFA, 1973; DFA (hon.), Mont. State U., 1998, Rocky Mountain Coll., Billings, Mont., 1997, Whitman Coll., Walla Walla, Wash., 2004. Asst. prof. sculpture U. Wis., Madison, 1975-76, Mont. State U., Bozeman, 1979-81, adj. prof., 1981-84. One-man shows include Lowe Mus. Art U. Miami, Coral Gables, Fla., 1992, San Diego Mus. Art, 1996, Yellowstone Art Mus., Billings, Mont., 2003-04, The Contemporary Mus. Art, Honolulu, 2004, Appleton Mus. Art, Ocala, Fla., 2004, U. Art Mus., U. La., Lafayette, 2005, Neuberger Art Mus., Purchase N.Y., 2005, Norton Mus. Art, West Palm Beach, Fla., 2005; exhibited in groups shows U. Mus. Berkeley, Calif., 1974, Whitney Mus. Am. Art, N.Y., 1979, Albright-Knox Gallery, Buffalo, 1979, Israel Mus., Jerusalem, 1980, Arco Ctr. Visual Art, 1981, Walker Art Ctr., Mpls., 1982, Dallas Mus. Fine Arts, 1982, Oakland, 1983, Chgo., 1985, Contemporary Art Ctr., Honolulu, 1986, Whitney Mus., 1988, Contemporary Art Mus., Honolulu, 1993, Seattle Mus. Art, 1994, The White House, Washington, Yale U., New Haven, 1997; represented in permanent collections Whitney Mus. Am. Art, N.Y., San Francisco Mus. Contemporary Art, Israel Mus., Jerusalem, Walker Art Ctr., Mpls., Met. Mus. Art, N.Y., Hirshhorn Mus., Washington, Seattle Art Mus., UCLA Sculpture Garden, L.A. Mus. Contemporary Art; commd. Copley Square, Boston, Portland (Oreg.) Airport, Denver Art Mus., Kansas City (Mo.) Zoo, White House, Washington, 2000, Monte Carlo, Monaco, 2000, Smithsonian Instn., Washington, San Francisco Internat. Airport. Nat. Endowment Arts grantee, 1977, 80, Guggenheim grantee, 1980; Commission Portland Internat. Airport.

BUTTERFIELD, KAREN, educational association administrator; EdD. Art tchr. Coconino H.S.; founder, dir. Flagstaff Arts and Leadership Acad., 1996—. Named State Tchr. Yr. Ariz., 1993, Disney Am. Tchr. award, 1993.

BUTTERLY, KATHY, sculptor; b. Amityville, NY, 1963; BFA, Moore Coll. Art, Phila., 1986; MFA, U. Calif., Davis, 1990. Exhibited in group shows at Fourth Concorso Nazionale della Ceramica d'Arte: Savona-Fortezza Primiar, Savona, Italy, 1990, Contemporary Ceramics, Bennington Coll. Gallery, Vt., 1992, Talentborse Handwerk, Munich, 1994, Forms and Transformations of Clay, Queens Borough Pub. Libr. Gallery, Jamaica, NY, 1997, Byron Cohen Gallery Contemporary Art, Kans. City, Mo., 2000, 2002, 15th Anniversary Exhbn., Franklin Parrasch Gallery, NYC, 2001, Kanazawa World Craft Forum, Japan, 2003, Very Familiar: Celebrating 50 Yrs. of Collecting Decorative Arts, Carnegie Mus. Art, 2003, Couples, Ctr. Maine Contemporary Art, Rockport, 2004, Carnegie Internat., Carnegie Mus. Art, Pitts., 2004—05, one-woman shows include Moore Coll. Art, Phila., 1992, Clay Studio, 1993, Franklin Parrasch Gallery, NYC, 1994, 1995, 1996, 1997, 1998, 1999, Bernard Toale Gallery, Boston, 2000, Tibor de Nagy Gallery, NYC, 2002, 2004, Shoshana Wayne Gallery, Santa Monica, Calif., 2003. Recipient Anonymous Was a Woman Grant award, 2002; grantee Evelyn Shapiro Found. grant, 1993, Empire State Crafts Alliance grant, 1995, NY Found. for the Arts grant, 1999. Mailing: c/o Tibor de Nagy Gallery 724 Fifth Ave New York NY 10019*

BUTTERS, DOROTHY GILMAN See GILMAN, DOROTHY

BUTTERWORTH, NONA ANGEL, artist, educator; b. Spartanburg, S.C., Jan. 28, 1929; d. James Oscar and Joyce (Beatty) Angel; m. James Ebert Butterworth, Jr., Dec. 18, 1954; children: James Ebert III, Alison Angel, Joy Evans. Student, Randolph Macon's Womans Coll., 1947—49, Ringling Sch. Art, 1949—50, Art Students League, N.Y.C., 1950—51. Jr. curator art Pack Meml. Libr., Asheville, NC, 1951—52; artist advt. dept. Ivey's Dept. Store, Asheville, 1952—53; comml. artist Ayer & Gillette Advt. Agy., Charlotte, NC, 1953—55; instr. watercolor Ctrl. Piedmont C.C., 1981—96, Charlotte-Mecklenburg Recreation Ctr., 1996—; tchr. art Mint Mus., Charlotte, 1973—75, Charlotte Country Day Sch., 1975—76, 1977. One-woman shows include Charlotte Country Club, 1972, Charlotte Country Day Sch., 1977, Copeland House Art Gallery, 1982, Christ Episcopal Ch., 1982, 1991, Ausable Club, St. Hubert's, N.Y., 1988, 1991, 1994, 1997, 2000, 2003, 2006, exhibitions include Charlotte Meml. Hosp., 1985, Ivey's Dept. Store, 1985, one-woman shows include Depot Theatre, Westport, NY, 2003, 2006, exhibited in group shows at First Union Bank, Charlotte, 1973, 1974, 1975, 1976, 1977, 1985, 1988, Wachovia Bank, 1975, WSOC-TV, 1975—78 (1st prize, 1978), Lincolnton City Hall, N.C., 1974, 1975, N.C. Nat. Bank, 1971, 1972, 1976—77, 1984, 1985, 1984, Charlotte Festival in the Park, 1972—86, Spl. Bicentennial Invitational Exhibit, Queens Coll., 1976, Mint Mus. Art Biennial Juried Show, 1977 (Purchase award, 1977), 1981, 1988, N.C. State Art Mus. Juried Show, 1977, 1978, N.C. Watercolor Juried Show, 1977 (Merit award, 1977), 1987 (Merit award, 1987), 1992 (Merit award, 1992), N.C. Watercolor Soc., 1985, High Point, 1978, Greenville, 1977, Fayetteville, 1986, 1989 (Merit award, 1989), Lexington, 1987, Carrboro, 1987, Davidson Coll., 1979, Shelby Nat. Juried Show, 1983—84, 1985, Elon Coll., 1986, Springs Traveling Show, N.C., S.C., Ala., 1988 (Merit award, 1988), Represented in permanent collections Phila., Charlotte, Asheville, Gastonia, Banker mag., 1988; author: Charlotte mag., 1981—84. Pres. Friends Mint Mus., 1972—73, 1976—77; v.p. Artists Guild, 1973—74; 2d v.p. Women's Aux Mint Mus., 1975—76, chmn. overseas tours, 1975—, mem. artist's adv. bd., 1977—; bd. dirs. Women's Assn. Charlotte Symphony; co-chmn. Charlotte Symphony Designer House, 1975; bd. dirs. Arts and Sci. Coun., 1978—81, Guild Charlotte Artists, 1984—85, Charlotte Writers Club, 1984—85; mem. Charlotte Little Theater, 1981, 1984, 1985, 1987, Piedmont C.C. Summer Theater, 1983; chmn. Christ Episcopal Ch. Fair, 1968. Named Best Supporting Actress, Charlotte Little Theater, 1987; recipient Merit award, Pa. State Hon. Soc., 1966, 1st prize, Guild Charlotte Artists, 1978, 1991, 2d prize, 1992, 3d prize, 1983, 2d prize, 2005, 3d prize, 2006, 1st prize, 1996, hon. mention, 1983, 1st prize, 2003, Bus. Beautification Grand prize, City of Charlotte, 1992, 3d prize, N.C. Watercolor Soc., Hickory, 1985. Mem.: Myers Park Homeowners Assn. (bd. dirs.), Ausable Club, Charlotte Writers Club (pres. 1982—84, 1st prize children's story contest 1981), N.C. Watercolor Soc., Arts and Sci. Coun. (sec. exec. com. 1977—80), Guild Charlotte Artists (pres. 1976—77, dir. 1983—84, sec. 1992), Jr. League Charlotte, Charlotte Country Club. Home (Summer): PO Box 742 Keene Valley NY 12943-0742

BUTTNER, JEAN BERNHARD, diversified financial services company executive; b. New Rochelle, NY, Nov. 3, 1934; d. Arnold and Janet (Kinghorn) Bernhard; m. Edgar Buttner, Sept. 13, 1958 (div.); 3 children. BA, Vassar Coll., 1957; cert. bus. adminstrn., Harvard-Radcliffe program, 1958; Montessori diploma, Coll. Notre Dame, Belmont, Calif., 1967; D Bus. Administrn. (hon.), U. Bridgeport, 1994. Past v.p. Buttner Cos., Oakland, Calif.; pres. Value Line Inc. (subs. Arnold Bernhard & Co., Inc.), N.Y.C., 1985; chmn., pres. Vanderbilt Advt., Inc., 1988—, Arnold Bernhard & Co., Inc., N.Y.C., 1988—, Compupower, 1988—, Value Line Securities, Inc., 1988—, Value Line Pub., Inc., 1990, Value Line Distbn. Ctr., Inc., 1999—. Chmn., pres. Value Line Mut. Funds. Editor-in-chief Value Line Investment Survey. Past trustee Skidmore Coll.; past pres. Piedmont Sch. Bd.; past dir. Berkeley Montessori Sch.; past mem. NYC Partnership, Com. of 200; past adv. coun. Stanford Bus. Sch.; past mem. Presdl. Roundtable; past vis. com. for bd. overseers Harvard Bus. Sch.; past bd. dirs. Harvard Bus. Sch. Club Greater N.Y.; past west coast admissions rep. Vassar Coll.; past trustee Radcliffe Coll., Williams Coll., Emma Willard Sch., Coll. Prep. Sch. Com. for Econ. Devel.; trustee Choate Rosemary Hall. Named one of NY's 75 Most Influential Women in Business, Crain's, 1996, One of NY's 100 Most Influential Women in Business, Crain's, 1999; recipient Alumni Achievement award, Harvard U. Grad. Sch. Bus. Adminstrn., 1995, Alumnae award Choate Rosemary Hall, Wallingford, Conn., 1995, Emma Lazarus award Associated Builders and Owners of NY, Inc., 1996; Life Achievement award Emma Willard Sch., 1998. Republican. Congregationalist. Avocations: reading, swimming, bicycling, tennis, skiing. Office: Value Line Inc 220 E 42nd St Fl 6 New York NY 10017-5891 E-mail: jbb@valueline.com.

BUTTON, KATY, professional athletics manager; BS Sch. Fgn. Svc., Georgetown U. Policy advisor Hillary Rodman Clinton, 1994—2000; gen. mgr. Washington Freedom Women's United Soccer Assn., Washington, 2000—. Office: Washington Freedom Soccer 9385 Gerwig Ln Ste A Columbia MD 21046-2894

BUTTON, RENA PRITSKER, public relations executive; b. Providence, Feb. 15, 1925; d. Isadore and Esther (Kay) Pritsker; m. Daniel E. Button, Aug. 16, 1969; children by previous marriage: Joshua, Bruce, David Posner. Student, Pembroke Coll., 1942—45; BS, Simmons Coll., 1948; postgrad., Union U., 1968—69. Spl. asst. to U.S. Rep., 1967-69; spl. projects coord. United Jewish Appeal, 1971-74; exec. dir. Nat. Coun. Jewish Women, Inc., N.Y.C., 1974-76; pres. Button Assos., N.Y.C., 1976—; exec. v.p. Catalyst, N.Y.C., 1980-82; pres. Button & Button, Albany, NY, 1982—. Adv. coun. N.Y. State Senate Minority, 1980—; exec. dir. N.Y. State Coun. on Alcoholism and Other Drug Addictions, 1990-93; pres., founder Two Together, A Pilot Reading Program for Young People, 1997-2003. Co-producer, moderator: TV pub. affairs program Speak For Yourself, Albany, N.Y., 1963-66. Chair pub. affairs com. Marymount Manhattan Coll.; past bd. dirs. Albany YWCA, Albany Coun. Chs. Devel. Corp., World Affairs Coun., Planned Parenthood Assn. Albany; trustee Jerusalem Women's Seminar, Citizens for Family Planning, N.Y. Com. Integrated Housing, Hist. Albany Found. Ctr. for Counseling, Town of Bethlehem Pub. Libr., 1999; pres. Sr. Svc. Ctr. Albany Area, Two Together, 1997; bd. dirs. Com. Modern Cts.; exec. dir. N.Y. Head Injury Assn., 1993-96; candidate N.Y. State Assembly 102d Dist., 1996; trustee Albany Symphony Orch., 2002—. Mem. Siasconset Casino Club, Univ. Club. Clubs: Siasconset Casino (Siasconset, Mass.), Univ. (Albany). Home and Office: 16 Spruce Ct Delmar NY 12054-2614 Personal E-mail: rbutton96@verizon.net.

BUTTS, CHERIE LAVAUGHN, biomedical researcher; b. Baton Rouge, Feb. 13, 1971; d. Harry LeVaughn Butts and Linda Marie Sublet; m. Daniel Harris, Nov. 13, 1992 (div. Sept. 1999); 1 child: Daniel A. Harris. BA, Johns Hopkins U., 1992, MS, 1997; PhD, U. Tex., Houston. Rsch. asst. Johns Hopkins U., Balt., 1991-92, Morgan State U., Balt., 1995-96, U. Md., Balt., 1996-98; grad. rsch. asst. U. Tex. M.D. Anderson Cancer Ctr., Houston, 1998—. Trainee rep. M.D. Anderson Assocs., Houston, 1999—. Inventor Foster speculum, 1996; contbr. articles to profl. jours. Travel fellow 6th Biennial Symposium on Cancer, Minorities and the Underserved, Houston, 1998; fellow Am. Physiol. Soc., Nat. Inst. Diabetes and Digestive Disorders, Washington, 1998; Cancer Rsch. Tng. fellow Nat. Cancer Inst., Bethesda, Md., 1999. Mem. Am. Assn. for Cancer Rsch. (assoc.). Methodist. Avocation: biking.

BUTZ, GENEVA MAE, pastor; b. Emmaus, Pa., May 11, 1944; d. Edwin F. and Arlene E. (Engler) B. BA, Hood Coll., 1966; MRE, Union Theol. Sem., 1968; D Divinity (hon.), Ursinus Coll., 1994. Ordained clergywoman United Ch. of Christ, 1972. Dir. Christian edn. United Ch. of Christ, Palos Verdes, Calif., 1968-72; mng. editor Youth mag., United Ch. Bd. for Homeland Ministries, Phila., 1972-75; affiliate rep. Ecumenical Community of Taizé, France, New Zealand, Australia, Indonesia, India and others, 1975-77; parish worker Temple Presbyn. Ch., Phila., 1978-83; pastor Old First Reformed Ch., United Ch. Christ, Phila., 1984—2003; assoc. conf. minister Pa. SE Conf. United Ch. Christ, 2003—. Bd. dirs. Met. Christian Coun. of Phila., 1985-96, 98—; chair Ch. and Ministry Com., Phila. Assn. United Ch. Christ, 1983-86; cons. Auburn Theol. Sem., N.Y., 1988-89; coord. 5-Day urban seminar for incoming students Lancaster Theol. Sem., 1986-93, The Small Ch. and Cultural Change, Bangor Theol. Sem., 1988; mem. adv. com. on evangelism and membership growth priority United Ch. Christ, 1989=90; team chair Toward the 21st Century, A Church-wide Planning Process for the United Ch. Christ, 1990-93; spkr. Faith Journey, consultation XVI in Parish Ministry for United Ch. Christ Clergy, Orlando, Fla., 1991; guest preacher Nat. Cathedral, Washington, 1993; commencement spkr. Lancaster Theol. Sem., 1996; sabbatical visitor to ch. in Indonesia through Common Global Mission Bd. (Disciples of Christ/United Ch. Christ), 2001. Author: Color Me Well, 1986, Christmas Comes Alive, 1988, Christmas in All Seasons, 1995; contbr. Women Pray, Karen Roller, Ed, 1986. Bd. dirs. Bethesda Project, Inc., Phila., 1986-98, Phila. Religious Leadership Devel. Fund, 1988-98, Maternity Care Coalition, Phila., 1999—; del. Gen. Synod-United Ch. Christ, Cleve., Ft. Worth, Providence, Kansas City, 1987-89, 99-2001; ecumenical del. Gen. Assembly Presbyn. Ch. (USA), 1989; adv. bd. Seamen's Ch. Inst., Phila., 1992-2003; trustee Lancaster Theol. Sem., 1992—; 2d v.p. Met. Christian Coun. Phila., 1998—. Named One of 85 People to Watch, Phila. Mag., 1985, One of 7 Clergy Leading U.S. Constl. Bicentennial Parade, 1987, Valiant Woman of Yr., Ch. Women United, 1991; recipient Human Rels. award, NCCJ, Phila., 1985; fellow Merrill fellow, Harvard Div. Sch., 1993. Mem. Nat. Orgn. of Women, Ch. Women United of Greater Phila., Old Phila. Clergy, Assn. United Arts and Religion, Phila. Assn. (ministrial standing). Democrat. Office: Pa SE Conf United Ch of Christ 505 S 2d St Collegeville PA 19426 E-mail: gbutz@psec.org.

BUYANOVSKY, SOPHIA, linguist, educator; b. Moscow, Nov. 17, 1956; d. Michael and Lubor Yakobishvili; m. Lev Buyanovsky, Aug. 27, 1977; children: Michael, Paul, Daniel. BA, MA, Moscow State U. Tchr. of Russian S.I. Tech. H.S., N.Y.C., 1989—. Home: 16850 Collins Ave #128 Sunny Isles Beach FL 33160-4238

BUYSE, LEONE KARENA, orchestral musician, educator; b. Oneida, N.Y, Feb. 7, 1947; d. Leonard Cornelius and Ione Esther (Hinman) B.; m. Michael Fanning Webster, Sept. 7, 1987. MusB, Eastman Sch. Music, Rochester, N.Y., 1968; MusM, Emporia (Kans.) State U., 1980; cert., Paris Conservatory, 1971. 2d flute and piccolo Rochester Philharm. Orch., 1971-78; asst. prin. flute San Francisco Symphony, 1978-83, Boston Symphony Orch., 1983-90, acting prin., 1990-93; prin. flute Boston Pops Orch., 1983-90; prof. flute U. Mich., Ann Arbor, 1993-97; prof. flute and chamber music Shepherd Sch. Music, Rice U., Houston, 1997—. Mem. faculty Boston U., 1983-93, Tanglewood Inst. of Boston U., Lenox, Mass., 1984-94, New Eng. Conservatory, 1988-93. Fulbright grantee, Paris, 1968-69. Mem. Nat. Flute Assn. (bd. dirs. 1985-86, conv. program chmn. 1987), Greater Boston Flute Assn. (founder, pres. 1992-93), Mu Phi Epsilon (winner internat. competition 1970), Pi Kappa Lambda. Avocations: physical fitness, gardening, vegetarian cuisine. Office: Rice University Shepherd Sch of Music PO Box 1892 Houston TX 77251-1892 E-mail: lbuyse@rice.edu.

BUYSE, MARYLOU, pediatrician, geneticist, medical association administrator; b. NYC, June 27, 1946; d. George J. and Barbara M. (Sauer) B.; m. Carl N. Edwards, Jan. 22, 1982. AB, Hunter Coll., 1966; MD, Med. Coll. Pa., 1970; MS in Med. Adminstrn., U. Wis., 1993. Diplomate Am. Bd. Med. Genetics. Intern U. Mich., 1970-71; resident in pediatrics L.A. County-U. So. Calif. Med. Ctr., 1971-73, fellow, 1973-75, U. So. Calif. Sch. Medicine, 1975-84, asst. prof. pediatrics, 1973—75, 2004—, Tufts U., 1976-84; coord. Myelodysplasia Clinic Tufts-New Eng. Med. Ctr., Boston, 1976-79; dir. Cystic Fibrosis Clinic, staff pediatrician Ctr. for Genetic Counseling and Birth Defects Evaluation, 1975-82; med. dir. Ctr. for Birth Defects Info. Service, 1978-82, dir. center, 1982-94; pres. Medx Ltd., 1985-94, Ctr. for Birth Defects Info. Scis., Inc., 1985-94; dir. clin. genetics Children's Hosp., Boston, 1985-86; mem. med. adv. bd. Mass. Cystic Fibrosis Found., 1977-79; med. dir. Fernald State Sch., 1988—94; assoc. med. dir. MassPRO, 1993-95; mem. Mass. Bd. Registration in Medicine, 1994-95; assoc. med. dir. Care Advantage Health Sys., Inc., med. dir., 1996-97, United Health Care of New England, 1997-98, consulting physician advisor, 1998-99, v.p. health affairs, 1999-2001; pres., CEO Mass. Assn. Health Plans, 2001—. Chair R.I. Folic Acid Coun., R.I. March of Dimes, 1999-2001; cons. in field. Assoc. editor Birth Defects Compendium, 2d edit., 1979; assoc. editor Syndrome Identification Jour., 1977-82, editor, 1982; editor Jour. Clin. Dysmorphology, 1982-86, Dysmorphology and Clinical Genetics, 1986-94; editor-in-chief Birth Defects Encyclopedia, 1990. Recipient Physicians Recognition award AMA, 1975, Alumni Achievement award Med. Coll. Pa., 1987; named to Alumni Hall of Fame, Hunter Coll., 1998. Fellow: Mass. Med. Soc. (asst. sec.-treas. 1991—94, trustee 1991—2000, sec.-treas. 1994—96, v.p. 1996—97, pres.-elect 1997—98, pres. 1998—99), Am. Acad. Pediat.; mem.: AAAS, Mass. Health Coun. (v.p. 2005—), Teratology Soc., Am. Coll. Physicians Execs., Soc. Craniofacial Genetics (pres. 1986), Am. Med. Writers Assn., Am. Soc. Human Genetics, Am. Mgmt. Assn., Am. Med. Women's Assn. (pres. Mass. br. 39 1986—91), Charles River Dist. Med. Soc. (pres. 1993—95), Alpha Omega Alpha. Office: Ctr Birth Defects Info Svcs Inc Box 1776 Dover MA 02030

BUZBEE, SALLY STREFF, news correspondent; b. Walla Walla, Wash. d. Eldyn and Monica Streff; m. John Buzbee; children: Margaret, Emma. BA in Journalism, U. Kans., 1988; IEMBA, Georgetown U., 1997. Joined AP, Topeka, 1988, bus. writer Kansas City, Kans., 1988—92, with L.A., 1992—93, correspondent in charge of San Diego bur., 1993—95, with Washington bur., 1995—2004, reporter, Washington bur., 1995—96, news editor, 1996, world svcs. supr., Washington bur., asst. chief, bur. for news, Washington bur., 2003—04, chief of Mid. East news Cairo, 2004—. Office: Associated Press 2021 K St NW 6th fl Washington DC 20006-1082

BUZZELL, MARGARET, association adminstrator; m. Jerry Buzzell; children: Joseph F., Gregory E. Exec. dir. Advancement for Commerce, Industry & Tech., Farmingdale, NY. Editor: (co. newspaper) Business Advance. Adv. bd. sch. bus. Adelphi Univ. Office: Advancement for Commerce Industry & Tech PO Box 151 Farmingdale NY 11735 E-mail: acitinc@msn.com.

BYARS, AMANDA, performing company executive, musician, educator; b. Spartanburg, S.C., Oct. 18, 1952; MusB, Converse Coll., 1974; MusM, So. Meth. U., 1977. Cert. tchr. piano. Piano tchr. Mountain View Coll., Dallas, 1975-80; asst. prof. So. Meth. U., Dallas, 1980-88; co-founder, dir. Dallas Music, 1988-92; ind. piano tchr. Dallas, 1992-98; dir. artist and educator rels. Steinway Hall, Dallas, 1998—. Piano adjudicator, 1985. Contbr. articles to profl. jours. Mem. Tex. Music Tchrs. Assn. (chmn. ind. music tchrs. 1997—), Dallas Music Tchrs. Assn. (pres. 1996-98, v.p. 1998—).

BYARS, BETSY CROMER, writer; b. Charlotte, Aug. 7, 1928; d. George Guy and Nan (Rugheimer) Cromer; m. Edward Ford Byars, June 24, 1950; children: Laurie, Betsy Ann, Nan, Guy. Author: Clementine, 1962, The Dancing Camel, 1965, Rama, the Gypsy Cat, 1966, The Groober, 1967, The Midnight Fox, 1968 (Am. Book of Yr. selection Child Study Assn. 1968, Lewis Carroll Shelf award 1970), Trouble River, 1969 (Am. Book of Yr. selection Child Study Assn. 1969), The Summer of the Swans, 1970 (Am. Book of Yr. selection Child Study Assn. 1970, John Newbery medal 1971), Go and Hush the Baby, 1971, The House of Wings, 1972 (Am. Book of Yr. selection Child Study Assn. 1972, Nat. Book award nomination 1973), The 18th Emergency, 1973 (Am. Book of Yr. selection Child Study Assn. 1973, New York Times Outstanding Book of Yr. 1973, Dorothy Canfield Fisher Meml. Book award Vt. Conress of Parents and Teachers 1975), The Winged Colt of Casa Mia, 1973 (Am. Book of Yr. selection Child Study Assn. 1973, New York Times Outstanding Book of Yr. 1973), After the Goat Man, 1974 (Am. Book of Yr. selection Child Study Assn. 1974), The Lace Snail, 1975 (Am. Book of Yr. selection Child Study Assn. 1975), The TV Kid, 1976 (Am. Book of Yr. selection Child Study Assn. 1976), The Pinballs, 1977 (Woodward Park School Annual Book award 1977, Child Study Children's Book award Child Study Children's Book Com. at Bank Street Coll. of Edn. 1977, Ga. Children's Book award 1979, Charlie May Simon Book award Ark. Elem. School Coun. 1980, Surrey School Book of Yr. award Surrey School Librs. of Surrey 1980, Mark Twain award Mo. Assn. of School Librs. 1980, William Allen White Children's Book award Emporia State Univ. 1980, Young Reader medal Calif. Reading Assn. 1980, Golden Archer award Dept. Libr. Sci. Univ. of Wis.-Oskosh 1982), The Cartoonist, 1978, Good-bye Chicken Little, 1979 (New York Times Outstanding Book of Yr. 1979), The Night Swimmers, 1980 (Am. Book of Yr. selection Child Study Assn. 1980, Best Book of Yr. School Libr. Jour. 1980, Am. Book award for Children's Fiction 1981), The Cybil War, 1981 (Tenn. Children's Choice Book award Tenn. Libr. Assn. 1983, Sequoyah Children's Book award 1984), The Animal, the Vegetable, and John D. Jones, 1982 (Parents' Choice award for Lit. Parents' Choice Found. 1982, Best Children's Book Sch. Libr. Jour. 1982, CRABbery award Oxon Hill Br. of Prince George's County Libr. 1983, Mark Twain award Mo. Assn. of School Librs. 1985), The Two-Thousand-Pound Goldfish, 1982 (New York Times Outstanding Book of Yr. 1982), The Glory Girl, 1983, The Computer Nut, 1984 (Charlie May Simon award 1987), Cracker Jackson, 1985 (S.C. Children's Book award 1988, Md. Children's Book award 1988), The Not-Just-Anybody Family, 1986, The Golly Sisters Go West, 1986, The Blossoms Meet the Vulture Lady, 1986, The Blossoms and the Green Phantom, 1987, A Blossom Promise, 1987, Beans on the Roof, 1988, The Burning Questions of Bingo Brown, 1988, Bingo Brown and the Language of Love, 1989, Hooray for the Golly Sisters, 1990, Bingo Brown, Gypsy Lover, 1990, Seven Treasure Hunts, 1991, Wanted.Mud Blossom, 1991, The Moon & I, 1992, Bingo Brown's Guide to Romance, 1992, McMummy, 1993, The Golly Sisters Ride Again, 1994, The Dark Stairs: A Herculeah Jones Mystery, 1994, Coast to Coast, 1994, My Brother, Ant., 1996, Tornado, 1996, Dead Letter: A Herculeah Jones Mystery, 1996; editor: Growing Up Stories, 1995, Death's Door, 1997, Ant plays Bear, 1997, Disappearing Acts, 1998. Recipient Regina medal Catholic Libr. Assn., 1987. Avocation: flying.

BYARS, LEISA, marketing professional, music company executive; b. Warren, Ohio, 1967; m. Delfon McSpadden. BA in Econs. and Govt., Oberlin Coll.; MA in Pub. Policy, U. Mich.; MBA in Mktg. and Fin., U. Pa. From mem. staff to group mgr. Innovative Mktg. Solutions Group Ford Motor Co., Dearborn, Mich., 1995—2000, group mgr. Innovative Mktg. Solutions Group, 2000, mgr., global media, agency, events and alliances; v.p. mktg. EMI Christian Music Group EMI, Tenn., 2005—. Recipient Outstanding Women in Mktg. and Comms. award, Ebony Mag., 2001. Office: EMI CMG PO Box 5010 Brentwood TN 37024-5010*

BYARS, MERLENE HUTTO, accountant, artist, writer; b. West Columbia, SC, Nov. 8, 1931; d. Gideon Thomas and Nettie (Fail) Hutto; m. Alvin Willard Byars, June 10, 1950 (dec.); children: Alvin Gregg, Robin Mark, Jay C., Blaine Derrick; m. Fred W. Klutzow, Dec. 10, 1999. Student, Palmer Coll., Midlands Tech., U. S.C., 1988—; diploma in Journalism, Internat. Corr. Sch., 1995, Longridge Writers Group, 1995. Acct. State of SC, 1964-93; ret., 1993; pres. Merlene Hutto Byars Enterprises, Cayce, 1993—. Designer Collegiate Licensing Co., US Trademark, 1989—; mem. Thinktank for Ret. Employees, U. SC Edn. Found., 1998—2003. Pub. Lintheads, 1986, Olympia-Pacific: The Way It was 1895-1970, 1981; Did Jesus Drive a Pickup Truck, 1993, Fate, Faith and Fortitude, 2003; The Plantation Era in South Carolina; pub., produr. (play) Lintheads and Hard Times, 1986; creator quilt which hung in SC State Capital for bicentennial celebration, 1988; designer Saxe Gotha Twp. Flag, 1993; author: The State of South Carolina Scrap Book, Orangeburg District, 1990, A Scrap Book of SC, Dutch Fork, Saxe Gotha, Lexington County, 1994, The Plantation Era of SC, 1996, Colonization, Plantations and More in South Carolina, 2004, A History of St. Luke's Lutheran Church within the Olympia-Pacific Community Columbia, South Carolina, 2004; exhibited art at Oxford (Eng.) U., 1997, Internat. Congress on Arts and Comm., 1997, Sonesta Hotel, New Orleans, 1998—; exhibited art and book From My Scrap Book of the State of SC; Xlibris publ. new book, 2003, Fate, Faith and Fortitude, Life of F.W. Klutzow, MD., Four Seasons, The Ritz, 1999—; exhibited genealogy and art work St. John's Coll., Cambridge U., 2001. Life mem. Women's Missionary Soc., United Luth. Ch., 1954—; mem. edn. found. U. SC, 1969-93; treas. Airport HS Booster Club, 1969-76; sec. Saxe Gotha Hist. Soc., Lexington County, 1994-96; mem. USC Edn. Found., Think-Tank for 2001 fundraising campaign/ret. faculty and staff, 1998-2001; rep. Cayce Hist. Com. at Am. Biographical Inst./Internat. Biographical Ctr. Congress, New Orleans, 1998. Recipient numerous awards for quilting SC State Fair, 1976—, Cert. for rose rsch. test panel Jackson and Perkins, 1982, Foremost Women in Comm. award, 1969-70, Cayce Amb. award, City of Cayce, 1994. Fellow Internat. Biog. Assn. (dep. dir. gen. 1999—), U.S.C. Caroliniana Soc., U. S.C. Thomas Cooper Libr. Soc.; mem. Cayce Mus. History (contbr. books, award for contribution 1987), SC State Mus., Town and Country Assn., Kiwanis Internat. Found. (disting. internat. sec. 2004-05), Kiwanis Club Cayce-West Columbia. Avocations: history, genealogy, reading, sewing, travel. Home: PO Box 3387 West Columbia SC 29171-3387 Office Phone: 803-794-6288. Personal E-mail: needle1@msn.com.

BYAS, TERESA ANN URANGA, customer service administrator, interior designer, consultant; b. Plainview, Tex., Mar. 20, 1955; d. Adam T. and Lucy (Sandoval) Uranga; m. Wesley W. Byas, Sept. 11, 1972 (div. 1992); children: Chad W., Christina Ann. Student, Tex. Wesleyan U., 1983—, Tarrant County Coll., Ft. Worth, various yrs., student, 95, 97, 99. Teller Allied Nat. Bank (now named 1st Interstate), Ft. Worth, 1985-87, Nowlin Savs. and Loans (now named Comerica), Ft. Worth, 1987-88; missionary United Meth. Ch. Global Bd. World Missions, Brazil, 1988-91; asst. mgr. Bag 'n Baggage, Ft. Worth, 1991-92, store mgr., 1992-93; med. record clerical coord. Total Home Health Svcs., Inc., Ft. Worth, 1993-94; nurses aide Total Home Svcs. In Med. Home Health, 1994-96, Nurture Care, Ft. Worth, 1995-96; customer svc. staff Home Depot Installation Svcs., Ft. Worth, 1996—2003, design cons. Arlington, Tex., 2000—03, Keller, Tex., 2003—. Mem. Women's Polit. Caucus, Ft. Worth, United Meth. Women's Group; hon. mem. Westcliff United Meth. Women's Group (chpt. named in her honor 1991); mem. Brother Sister Orgn., Ft. Worth. Mem. Am. Bus. Women's Assn. Democrat. Avocations: photography, reading, writing, languages. Office: Home Depot Installation Svcs 2800 Forest Ln Dallas TX 75234 Home: 2013 Hwy 377 Keller TX 76248 Office Phone: 972-402-3800.

BYATT, NANCY, psychiatrist; b. Sheffield, England, Feb. 25, 1976; d. Peter and Miranda Helen Black; m. Stephen James Byatt, June 16, 2001. BA with hons., Lehigh U., 1998; MBA, N.Y. Inst. Tech., 2003; DO, N.Y. Coll. Osteo. Medicine, 2003. Lic. physician Mass. Med. Bd., 2005. Resident psychiatrist U. Mass. Meml. Med. Ctr., Worcester, Mass., 2003—. Team capt. walk Nat. Alliance for the Mentally Ill, Woburn, Mass., 2004—05; mem. human rights com. Cmty. Health Link, Worcester, 2005—06. Recipient Stanley Scholar Award, L.I. (N.Y.) Jewish Hosp., 2002, Excellence in Behavioral Medicine award, N.Y. Coll. Osteo. Medicine, 2003, Team Capt. award, Nat. Alliance Mentally Ill, 2005, Emergency Psychiat. award, janssen Am. Assn., 2006; scholar, Lehigh U., 1998; Howard Hughes scholar, 1996. Mem.: Mass. Med. Soc., Am. Soc. Psychopharmacology, Am. Assn. Emergency Psychiat., Mass. Psychiat. Soc., Am. Psychiat. Assn. (mem. consultation-liaison emergency mental health interst group 2005—06, mem. pub. sector interest group 2005—06), Phi Eta Sigma. Democrat. Avocations: hiking, backpacking, skiing, tennis, mountain biking. Office: UMass Memorial Medical Center 361 Plantation St Worcester MA 01605 Office Phone: 508-856-8952.

BYBEE, DEBORAH ANN, director, educator; d. Edward Henry and Margaret Druga Jarecki; m. David Michael Bybee, May 8, 1993; children: Jared Ryan-Phillip, Aran Ross. MA, Slippery Rock U. Pa., 1992. Family therapist Cath. Charities Family Focus, Lebanon, Pa., 1994—99; faculty Harrisburg Area C.C., Lebanon, 1999—; behavior specialist, therapist Pa. Counseling Svcs., Lebanon, 1999—2004. Coord. disability svcs. Harrisburg Area C.C., Lebanon, 2003—. Actor: (plays) Barefoot in the Park (Best Supporting Female Actor award, 1991); dir., actor, singer: (musical comedy prodn.) Working; dir., choreographer Once Upon a Mattress. Recipient Outstanding Faculty award, Harrisburg Area C.C. Lebanon, 2000, 2001, 2002. Democrat. Byzantine Catholic. Avocations: performing/directing, 18th century living history, writing. Office: HACC Lebanon 735 Cumberland St Lebanon PA 17042 Office Phone: 717-270-6333.

BYER, DIANA, performing company executive; b. Trenton, NJ, Aug. 31, 1946; d. Fred and Norma (Handis) B. Student, Juilliard Sch., 1964—66. Soloist Manhattan Festival Ballet, N.Y.C., 1972, Les Grands Ballet Canadiens, Montreal, Can., 1975; dir. Ballet Sch. of N.Y., N.Y.C., 1978—, N.Y. Theatre Ballet, 1978—. Dir., founder Project LIFT scholarship program for children living N.Y.C. homeless shelters, 1989—. Helen Weiselberg scholar, Nat. Arts Club, 1988, 1990, 1993. Achievements include being subject of Lincoln Ctr. presentation Dreams on a Shoestring, 1992. Office: NY Theatre Ballet 30 E 31st St New York NY 10016-6825 Office Phone: 212-679-0401. Business E-mail: dianabyer@nytb.org.

BYERLEIN, ANNE P., human resources specialist, food products executive; Various positions PepsiCo., v.p. corp. human resources, 1988—96; v.p. human resources Yum Brands, Inc. (formerly Tricon Global Restaurants), Louisville, 1997—2002; chief people officer KFC, 2000—02, Yum Brands, Inc., Louisville, 2002—. Past pres. Leadership Palm Beach County. Office: Yum Brands Inc 1441 Gardiner Ln Louisville KY 40213 Office Phone: 502-874-8300. Office Fax: 502-874-8790.

BYERS, ELIZABETH, education educator; b. Cedar Rapids, Iowa, Mar. 22, 1964; d. Charles A. Byers and Mary Ann Hetherington-Byers. BA in Music, Coe Coll., 1986, BA in English and Speech, 1986; MA in Rhetorical Studies, U. Iowa, 1988, MA in English Edn., 2002. Tchg. asst. in pub. speaking U. Iowa, Iowa City, 1987—88, rsch. asst., 1987, tchg. asst. bus. and profl. speaking, 1987—88, art history teaching asst., 2000; English/speech instr. Kirkwood C.C., Iowa City, 1988—89; English and speech instr. Mt. Mercy Coll., Cedar Rapids, 1989—93; elem. edn. instr. Iowa Wesleyan Coll., Mt. Pleasant, 2001—. ESL tutor Kirkwood C.C., Iowa City, 1988—93, Mt. Mercy Coll., 1988—93; pub. speaking cons., Iowa City, 1988—93. Grad. student editor: Basil Blackwell Companion, 1989; editor: Communicating, 1992, author web page for postsecondary tchrs. Vol. Habitat for Humanity, Iowa City, 1999—2001, Cath. Worker House, Cedar Rapids, 1990—93. Mem.: DAR (Good Citizenship award 1982), Mu Phi Epsilon, Pi Lambda Theta (Teaching Excellence award 2001), Phi Beta Kappa. Home: PO Box 156 Morning Sun IA 52640-0156

BYERS, MERANDA FAITH, secondary school educator; b. Subic Bay, Philippines, Aug. 16, 1982; d. Zane Richard and Cynthia Jane Byers. Bachelors Degree, Coll. Notre Dame Md., Balt., 2003. Rsch. asst. NASA, Greenbelt, Md., 2002—04; sci. tchr. Annapolis (Md.) H.S., 2004—. Office: Annapolis High School 2700 Riva Rd Annapolis MD 21204

BYERS, NINA, physics professor; b. LA, Jan. 19, 1930; d. Irving M. and Eva (Gertzoff) B.; m. Arthur A. Milhaupt, Jr., Sept. 8, 1974 (dec.). BA in Physics with highest honors, U. Calif., Berkeley, 1950; MS in Physics, U. Chgo., 1953, PhD, 1956; MA, U. Oxford, Eng., 1967. Research fellow dept. math. physics U. Birmingham, Eng., 1956-58; research assoc., asst. prof. Inst. Theoretical Physics and dept. physics Stanford, 1958-61; asst. then assoc. prof. physics UCLA, 1961-67, prof. physics, 1967—. Mem. Sch. Math., Inst. Advanced Studies, Princeton, N.J., 1964-65; ofcl. fellow Somerville Coll., Oxford, 1967-68, Janet Watson vis. fellow, 1968-74; faculty lectr., mem. dept. theoretical physics Oxford U., 1967-74, sr. vis. scientist, 1973-74; official fellow and tutor in physics, Somerville Coll. John Simon Guggenheim Meml. fellow, 1964-65, Sci. Rsch. Coun. fellow Oxford U., 1978, 85. Fellow AAAS (mem-at-large physics sect., com. on freedom and responsibility 1983-86), Am. Phys. Soc. (councillor-at-large 1977-81, panel pub. affairs 1980-83, vice-chmn. forum on physics and soc. 1981-82, 2002--, chmn. 1982-83, vice-chmn. forum on history of physics 2002-03, chair-elect, 2003-04, chair 2004-05); mem. Fedn. Am. Scientists (nat. coun. 1972-76, 78-80, exec. com. 1974-76, 78-80). Achievements include research in theory of particle physics and superconductivity; history of physics; contributions of 20th century women to physics. Office: U Calif Dept Physics Los Angeles CA 90095-0001

BYERS-PEVITTS, BEVERLEY, college administrator, educator; b. Ohio County, Ky., Aug. 15, 1939; d. Stanley Beveridge and Vera Elizabeth (Amos) Byers; m. Robert Richard Pevitts, June 12, 1966; 1 child, Robert Stanley. BA, Ky. Wesleyan Coll., 1961; MA, So. Ill. U., 1967, PhD, 1980. Dir. theatre and faculty Dept. English, Speech, Drama Young Harris (Ga.) Coll., 1966-69; dir. theatre and asst. prof. speech and theatre arts Western Carolina U., Cullowhee, NC, 1969-71; coord. supplementary progr., asst. prof. Eng. and drama Pfeiffer Coll., Misenheimer, NC, 1972-74; dir. and prof. speech and theatre Ky. Wesleyan U., Owensboro, 1974-86; chair theatre arts U. Nev., Las Vegas, 1986-89, prof. and dir. grad. studies in theatre arts, 1986-90; dean coll. of humanities and fine arts, prof. U. No. Iowa, Cedar Falls, 1990-95; v.p. acad. affairs Tex. Woman's U., Denton, 1995—2001; pres. Park U., Parkville, Mo., 2001—. Lectr. in field; conductor workshops in field. Editor: Theatre Topics, 1990-93; contbr. articles to profl. jours.; author: (plays) Reflections in a Window, 1982, rev., 1983, Beauty and the Beast, 1982, Time and the Rock, 1981, Family Haven, 1979, Take Courage, Stand Beside Us, 1977, A Strange and Beautiful Light, 1976-77; co-author: Epilogue to Glory, 1966. Bd. dirs. Waterloo/Cedar Falls Symphony Orch., 1990-94, Iowa Citizens for the Arts, 1991-94; coord. spl. drama programs WeCan, Inc., Las Vegas, 1986; tchr. Elderhostel Program; program coord. NOW. NEH Seminar grantee U. Wis.-Milw., 1983, NYU, 1977; recipient Outstanding Alumni award Ky. Wesleyan Coll., 1983; named Disting. Woman Am. Theatre Assn., 1977; grantee Ford Found., Exxon Corp.; elected to Nat. Theatre Conf., 1992—. Mem. Assn. for Theatre in Higher Edn. (founding pres. 1986-87, bd. govs. 1986-89), Assn. for Communication Adminstrn. (exec. com. 1988-91), Univ. and Coll. Theatre Assn. of Am. Theatre Assn. (pres. 1985-86), League Profl. Theatre Women N.Y., Internat. Coun. of Fine Arts Deans, Coun. of Colls. of Arts and Scis., Order of Oak and Ivy, Alpha Psi Omega. Avocations: gourmet cooking, travel, collecting antiques. Office: Park Univ 8700 NW River Park Dr Kansas City MO 64152 E-mail: president@mail.park.edu.

BYKOVA, MARINA F., philosopher, educator; b. Rostov-on-Don, Russia, Oct. 22, 1960; d. Fedor E. Bykov and Rozalia A. Bykova; m. Andrey V. Kuznetsov, June 28, 1991; 1 child, Ivan A. Kuznetsov. MPhil, Rostov-on-Don State U., Russia, 1982; PhD, Russian Acad. Scis., Moscow, 1985, Dr. Habil., 1993. Prof. philosophy Inst. Philosophy Russian Acad. Scis., Moscow, 1993—2000; asst. prof. philosophy NC State U., Dept. Philosophy and Religion, Raleigh, 2000—04, assoc. prof. philosophy, 2004—. Mem. rsch. program bd. Internat. Ludwig Feuerbach-Soc., Germany, 2000. Fellow, Austrian Found. Sci. and Scholarly Exch., Vienna, 1977, Alexander von Humboldt Found., 1989—90, U. Zürich, Philos. Faculty, 1990; scholar, Ohio Sate U., Dept. Philosophy. Columbus, 1995; Lisa Meitner Rsch. fellow, Inst. Philosophy U. Vienna, 1996—96. Mem.: N.Am. Fichte Soc., N.Am. Hegel Soc., Internat. Fichte-Gesellschaft, Internat. Hegel-Gesellschaft, Am. Philos. Assn. Achievements include research in German classic philosophy, especially the philosophical systems of Kant, Fichte, and Hegel. Avocations: travel, swimming, snorkeling, diving, theater. Office: North Carolina State Univ Dept Philosophy and Religion 2301 Hillsborough St Box 8103 Raleigh NC 27695-8103 Office Phone: 919-515-6332. Office Fax: 919-513-4351. E-mail: mfbykova@unity.ncsu.edu.

BYMEL, SUZAN YVETTE, talent manager, film producer; b. Chgo. d. Howard Behr and Jacqueline Shirley (Richards) B. Student, U. Ill., Chgo. Exec. asst. Kenny Rogers Prodns., 1981; prodn. exec. Pinehurst Prodns., 1982; music mgmt. assoc. Frontline Mgmt., 1983; pres. Suzan Bymel & Assocs., 1985-94; oper. ptnr. Bymel/O'Neill Mgmt., 1995—, Meg Ryan Prodns. (a.k.a. Fandango Films), 1988-93, Bymel/O'Neill Mgmt., 1995-98; operating ptnr. Talent Entertainment Group, Beverly Hills, Calif., 1998—; founding ptnr. Management 360. Freelance screenwriter, actress. Mem. Hollywood Woman's Polit. Com., L.A. Office: Talent Entertainment 9111 Wilshire Blvd Beverly Hills CA 90210 Fax: 310-205-5385. E-mail: sbymel@mmbon.com.*

BYNES, AMANDA, actress; b. Thousand Oaks, Calif., Apr. 3, 1986; d. Rick and Lynn Bynes. Actor: (films) Big Fat Liar, 2002, What a Girl Wants, 2003, Lovewrecked, 2005, (voice) Robots, 2005, She's the Man, 2006; (TV series) All That, 1996—2000 (nominee Cable Ace award, 1997), The Amanda Show, 1999—2002, (voice) Rugrats, 2002—04, What I Like About You, 2002—06, (voice): (videos) Charlotte's Web 2: Wilbur's Great Adventure, 2003; appeared as herself/guest panelist (TV series) Figure It Out, 1997—2000. Recipient Favorite TV Actress, Kid's Choice Awards, 2001, 2002, 2003, Favorite Movie Actress, 2003. Achievements include discovered at age 10 at a kid's comedy showcase at the Laugh Factory, LA and signed immediately by Nickelodeon for TV series All That.*

BYNUM, GAYELA A., public information officer; b. Sulphur, Okla., Oct. 28, 1945; d. Martin Cleveland and Birdie Burnett Sparks Word; m. Ronald Orr Bynum, June 6, 1965 (div. Apr. 1983); children: William Blaine, Bradley Word; m. Robert F. Hannon, Oct. 28, 1995. Student, U. Okla., 1963-66; BA, U. Ark., 1969; postgrad., George Washington U., 1991-93. Lic. real estate agt., legal asst. Supr. NAS, Jacksonville, Fla., 1972-79; mgmt. analyst Chief Naval Ops., Washington, 1979-85; pres. Gayela Bynum & Assocs., Washington, 1985-88, The Carpet Bagger, Ltd., Oklahoma City, 1997—; pub. affairs advisor HUD, Washington, 1988—2003. Treas. Globint, LLC, Carefree, Ariz., 199-2002, Globe Car, Ltd., Wilmington, Del., 1998-2002; exec. v.p. Sea Spur, Ltd., Wilmington, 1997—; internat. cons. Mideast Presdl. Candidate, Washington, 1988. Vice chmn. The Opera Camerata, Washington, 2001—02; fundraiser various polit. campaigns, 1985—88; mem. Congl. Steering Com., Washington, 1985—88; bd. govs. Summer Opera Theater, Washington, 2003—. Mem.: DAR, Nat. Press Club (mem. spkrs. com. 1996—2000, newsmakers com. 2001—02, bd. govs. 2002—). Avocations: running, sailing, aerobics, music, painting, crafts. Home and Office: 5902 Mount Eagle Dr Apt 408 Alexandria VA 22303-2516

BYNUM, MAGNOLIA VIRGINIA WRIGHT, retired secondary school educator; b. Waynesboro, Ga., Jan. 10, 1934; d. George and Edith Arilee (Williams) Wright; m. Marvin Bynum, Sept. 17, 1955 (dec. Oct. 1977). BS in Bus. Edn., N.C. A&T State U., Greensboro, N.C., 1956; postgrad., NYU, 1964—65; MS in Edn., CUNY, Bklyn., 1985, Adv. Cert. Guidance & Counseling, 1986. Engring. adminstr. Radio Receptor Co., Bklyn., 1957—59; data processing staff NYU, N.Y.C., 1959—64; tchr., dean, counselor Lincoln H.S., Jersey City, 1964—92; ret., 1992. Adj. prof. CUNY, Bklyn., 1986—90; asst. to Congressman Edolphus Towns, 10th Congl. Dist., Bklyn., 1982—90; counselor incentive program dept. human resources Bklyn. Coll., 1992—93; cons. Parent Advocacy, Medgars Evers Coll., Bklyn., 1984—85. Editor-in-chief (newsletter) Cornerstone Torch, 1993—97. Mem. Cmty. Coalition for Edn., Greensboro, NC, NAACP; spearheaded Hard of Hearing campaign, Bklyn.; women's day chairperson New Zion Missionary Bapt. Ch., Greensboro, NC; chairperson bd. dirs. Chama Child Devel., Bklyn., 1983—91, Cornerstone Day Care Ctr., Bklyn., 1991—97. Named to Faculty Achievement Hall of Fame, Lincoln H.S., 1981; recipient Outstanding Cmty. Svc. award, Bklyn. Coll. Grad. Students, 1984, citations, Congl. Record, 1990, 1997; scholar Myers Jacob Guidance & Counseling scholar, 1984. Mem.: Alpha Kappa Alpha, Phi Delta Kappa, Kappa Delta Pi. Baptist. Avocations: reading, travel, singing. Home: 563 Summerwalk Rd Greensboro NC 27455

BYNUM, SARAH SHUN-LIEN, writer, educator; b. Feb. 14, 1972; married. BA, Brown U.; MS in Fiction Writing, Iowa Writers Workshop. Tchr. English & Am. Hist. Berkeley Carroll Sch., Bklyn.; v.p., sr. cons. Goodale Assocs., N.Y.C., 2000—. Author: Madeleine Is Sleeping (Nat. Book Award finalist, 2004); contbr. articles to profl. jours. Mem.: Phi Beta Kappa. Office: Goodale Assocs 509 Madison Ave Ste 1112 New York NY 10022

BYRD, BETTY RANTZE, writer; b. Oklahoma City, July 8, 1949; d. Rolande Brown and Mary Louise Haner; m. Bill Byrd, Sept. 16, 1995; 1 child from previous marriage, Elizabeth Chase Rantze. Student, Ariz. State U., Tempe, Ohio State U., Columbus; BA in Creative Writing and French, U. Ariz, Tucson, 1974; legal asst. cert., Capital U. Law Sch., Columbus, 1975. Editor The Spectator Newspapers, Columbus, 1974—75; mng. editor Ohio State U. Dental Newsletter, 1974—75; paralegal, pub. defender Lewisburg, Pa., 1976—77. Author: Trinity's Daughter, 2002; actor: appeared in numerous commls., films, and TV, 1978—93. Vol. Salvation Army, Meals-on-Wheels, San Diego, Spl. Olympics, San Diego, San Diego Family Recovery Ctr. Recipient Best Fiction Writer's Guild award, Santa Barbara Writer's Conf., 2004. Mem.: AFTRA, SAG, Nat. Charity League, Rancho Lit. Soc. Avocations: photography, golf, travel, walking, scrapbooks. Home and Office: PO Box 2593 Rancho Santa Fe CA 92067 E-mail: bettybyrd@sbcglobal.net.

BYRD, CAROL ANN, music educator; b. Hallsville, Tex., July 15, 1968; d. James R. and Joyce Jackson; m. Jeff B. Byrd, Mar. 7, 1999; 1 child, Jarod Ryan Jackson. MusB, East Tex. Bapt. U., Marshall, 1990. Cert. All-level Music Educator Tex., 1991. Tchr. music McClure Magnet Sch. Internat. Studies, Longview, Tex., 1991—. Accompanist Mulberry Springs Bapt. Ch., Hallsville, 2003—. Named Tchr. of Yr., McClure Magnet Sch., 2004. Avocations: showing quarter horses, reading. Home: 13480 FM Hallsville TX 75650 Office: McClure Magnet School 500 Melba Longview TX 75601 Personal E-mail: cbyrd@lisd.org.

BYRD, CHRISTINE WATERMAN SWENT, lawyer; b. Oakland, Calif., Apr. 11, 1951; d. Langan Waterman and Eleanor (Herz) Swent; m. Gary Lee Byrd, June 20, 1981; children: Amy, George. BA, Stanford U., 1972; JD, U. Va., 1975. Bar: Calif. 1976, U.S. Dist. Ct. (ctrl., so. no., ea. dists.) Calif., U.S. Ct. Appeals (9th cir.). Law clk. to Hon. William P. Gray U.S. Dist. Ct., L.A., 1975—76; assoc. Jones, Day, Reavis & Pogue, L.A., 1976—82, ptnr., 1987—96; asst. U.S. atty. criminal divsn. U.S. Atty.'s Office, Ctrl. Dist. Calif., L.A., 1982—87; ptnr. Irell & Manella, L.A., 1996—. Mem. Calif. Law Revision Commn., 1992-97. Author: The Future of the U.S. Multinational Corporation, 1975; contbr. articles to profl. jours. Fellow: Coll. Comml. Arbitrators, Am. Coll. Trial Lawyers; mem.: ABA (vice chmn. ADR Advocacy in Litig. 2003—05), Assn. Bus. Trial Lawyers (bd. govs. 1996—99), 9th Jud. Cir. Hist. Soc. (pres. 1997—2002, bd. dirs. 1986—), Century City Bar Assn. (bd. govs. 2001—05), Stanford Profl. Women L.A. County, Am. Arbitration Assn. (large and complex case panel 1992—, nat. energy panel 1998—, class action panel 2004—, bd. dirs. 1999—), Women Lawyers Assn. L.A. County, L.A. County Bar Assn., Calif. State Bar (com. fed. cts. 1985—88), Stanford U. Alumni Assn. Republican. Office: Irell & Manella LLP 1800 Ave Of Stars Ste 900 Los Angeles CA 90067-4276 Office Phone: 310-277-1010. Business E-Mail: cbyrd@irell.com.

BYRD, DEBORAH LEA, literature and language professor; b. Morgantown, W.Va., May 16, 1953; d. Leland Eugene Byrd and Elizabeth Louise Machen; 1 child, Derek. BA in English, Duke U., Durham, N.C., 1974; MA in English, Emory U., Atlanta, 1977, PhD in English, 1981. Assoc. prof. English and women's studies Lafayette Coll., Easton, Pa., 1981—. Founder Landis Outreach Ctr., Easton, 2006; mem. Third St. Alliance for Women and Children, Easton, 2006. Mem.: Phi Beta Kappa. Office: Lafayette Coll 316 Pardee Hall Easton PA 18042 Office Phone: 610-330-5238. Office Fax: 610-330-5606.

BYRD, DEBRA ANN, actor, theater producer, performing company executive; b. NYC, Oct. 26, 1965; d. Carlos Raymond Machicote and Marie Glenn; m. Nathan Robert Byrd, June 6, 1987 (div.); children: Martha Nicole Glenn, Joshua Alexander Glenn. BFA, Marymount Manhattan Coll., 2001. Cert. accounting clk., N.Y. Bilingual Inst., N.Y.C., 1986; arts leadership Tchr.'s Coll., Columbia U., 2004. Customer svc. rep. Banker's Trust Corp., N.Y.C., 1986—87; sr. svc. rep. Barclay's Bank Of NY, N.Y.C., 1987—89; sec. Phillips, Capiello, et al Esqs., N.Y.C., 1989—90, Barish & O'Brien, CPAs, N.Y.C., 1990—91; founder & chief exec. Take Wing And Soar Productions, Inc., N.Y.C., 1991—; asst. to the prodr. Nat. Black Theatre, Inc., N.Y.C., 2002—; assoc. prodr. 6-10 Productions, LLC, Kansas City, Mo., 2002—. Asst. to prodr. Am. Showcase Theatre, Bklyn., 1993—94; producing cons. Shining Star Productions, N.Y.C., 1996—98; prodn. stage mgr. New Fed. Theatre/Nat. Black Touring Circuit, N.Y.C., 2003. Actor: (theater) The Domestic, Brown Women Who Fly, Nzinga's Children, Love's Labor's Lost, For Colored Girls Who Have Considered Suicide, Antigone, Trifles, A Midsummer Night's Dream, Nobody Loves A Black Little Girl, The Importance Of Being Earnest, Aunt Vanya, Freedom Train, Say Yes To Jesus, Sweet Daddy & Amazing Grace, Looking For Love In Darkness, Once On This Island, The Bad Seed, You Shouldn't Have Told, (feature film) Harlem Aria; prodr.: (theater) Richard III, The Other Woman, The Women of Shakespeare, Coriolanus: The African Warrior, The TWAS Classical Lab Reading Series, The Darker Face of the Earth, Serenade.The Music and Words of Oscar Brown Jr.; prodr.'s asst. (theater) A Secret Lies Inside My Sister's Womb; make-up designer: (theater) The Making Of A Perfect Mate; editor: (the griffin year book 2001) Journey To Success; author: (research publication) JURIES: An MMC Actor Prepares (Marymount Manhattan Honors Colloquium award, 2001). Festival devel. dir. Harlem Health Festival, Inc., N.Y.C., 2002. Recipient Black Family Theatre award, In-A-Woman Productions, Inc., 1996, Women Of Excellence award, N.Y.C. Dist. Leader Hon. Theresa Freeman, 1997, Gold medal For Academic Excellence in Acting, Marymount Manhattan Coll., 2001, MMC Gold Cross award, 2001, Dorothy L. Stickney Theatre award, Zonta Womens Club of N.Y., 2001, Women's Forum Ednl. award, Women's Forum Inc., 2001, NY State Proclamation, NY State Senator David A. Paterson, 2003; Madeline Burns scholarship, Marymount Manhattan Coll., 1999, William T. Morris Found. scholarship, 2000, Mary Colquhoun Acting scholarship, Joseph Papp Pub. Theatre Shakespeare Lab, 2001, Arts Mgmt. Tng. scholarship, Arts Leadership Inst., 2004, Nancy Quinn Fund grant, Alliance of Resident Theatres N.Y., 2004—05. Mem.: Theatre Comm. Group, Harlem Arts Alliance, Alliance Of Resident Theatres NY, Arts & Bus. Coun., AUDELCO, Theatre Devel. Fund, N.Y. Coalition of Profl. Women in Arts & Media, League Profl. Theatre Women (life), Actor's Equity Assn. (life), Omicron Delta Kappa (life), Am. Scholars Nat. Honor Soc. (life). Presbyterian. Avocation: arts and culture researcher, dramaturgy. Office Phone: 212-696-6575. Business E-Mail: dabyrd@takewingandsoar.org. E-mail: info@takewingandsoar.org.

BYRD, EVA WILSON, communications executive; Dir. media Bates Health World, New York, NY, 1994—, v.p., dir. media. Office: Grey Health Butler & McDowell Fl 8 100 Ave of the Americas New York NY 10013-1687

BYRD, JOANN KATHLEEN, newswriter; b. Baker, Oreg., Jan. 5, 1943; d. Joe Bryant and Anne Bradford (Dickson) Green; m. James Douglas Byrd, Mar. 11, 1978 (dec. 1988); 1 child from previous marriage, Drew Joseph Gibbs. BS in Journalism, U. Oreg., 1964; MA in Philosophy, U. Wash., 1992. Student reporter East Oregonian, Pendleton, 1956—64; reporter Spokane (Wash.) Daily Chronicle, 1964—69, 1972—74, asst. city editor, 1974—78; city editor The Herald, Everett, Wash., 1978—81, mng. editor, 1981, exec. editor, 1981—92; ombudsman The Washington Post, 1992—95; profl.-in-residence U. Washington, 1995—96. Bd. dirs. New Directions for News, juror, 1988, 89, Pulitzer Prizes; bd. visitors John S. Knight Fellowships Stanford II, 1983—84, program com., 1984—95; continuing studies chmn. Wash. AP News Execs., 1984—85, v.p., 1986—87, pres., 1987—88; judge Ernie Pyle awards, 1984. Fellow, Gannett Ctr. for Media Studies Columbia U., 1989. Home: 6700 Roosevelt Way NE Seattle WA 98115-6637

BYRD, KATHRYN SUSAN, psychologist, educator; d. George Washington Byrd and Josie Beth Mayes. BA, Centenary Coll., Shreveport, La., 1974; MS, Northwestern State U., Natchitoches, La., 1977; PhD, U. Tex, Richardson, 1995. Cert. mediator Tex., 2004. Coord. of academic advising, communication arts & tech. divsn. Eastfield Coll., Mesquite, Tex., 2001—, adj. faculty, 2001—. Acad. adv. Eastfield Coll., Mesquite, Tex., 1999—; apptd. to district-wide ednl. improvement coun. Garland Ind. Sch. Dist., 2004—05. Mem. of class of 2002, Eastfield Coll. rep. Leadership Garland, Mesquite, Tex., 2002. Mem.: APA, Romance Writers Am., Bluebonnet Bebes Doll Collectors Club. Republican. Southern Baptist. Office: Eastfield College 3737 Motley Dr Mesquite TX 75150 Office Phone: 972-860-7671. Business E-Mail: ksb4323@dcccd.edu.

BYRD, LORELEE, state treasurer; b. Bassett, Nebr., Apr. 14, 1956; m. Scott Byrd, 1976 (div.); children: Amy, Ryan. Auditor Mut. Protective Ins. and Mut. Ins.; aide to state and fed. lawmakers; unclaimed property admin., 1995; dep. state treas. Nebr., 1995—2001; state treas. Nebr., 2001—. Past mem. Rep. State Ctrl. Com., Douglas County Rep. Ctrl. Com.; past pres. Metro Right to Life; past mem. bd. dirs. Nebr. Right to Life; aide to Senator Sharon Beck Omaha; aide to Owen Elmer Indianola; aide to U.S. rep. Doug Bereuter Nebr. Office: PO Box 94788 Lincoln NE 68509-4788 E-mail: lbyrd@treasurer.org.

BYRD, MELANIE SUE, history professor; d. Joseph Perry and Wilda Jean Byrd; m. John Patrick Dunn, July 26, 1992. MLS, Kent State U., Ohio, 1986; PhD, Fla. State U., Tallahassee, 1992. Prof. history Valdosta State U., Ga., 1993—. Spkr. in field. Co-author: Proceedings of the Consortium on Revolutionary Europe, 1750-1850. Fellow: Internat. Napoleonic Soc.; mem.: Am. Rsch. Ctr. in Egypt. Avocations: gardening, walking, films, classical music, crafts. Office: Valdosta State Univ N Patterson St Valdosta GA 31698 Office Phone: 229-333-5947.

BYRD, SHARON FAYE, medical/surgical nurse; b. Dumas, Ark., May 28, 1965; d. George Henry and Mabel Juanita Kerr; m. Billy Andrew Byrd, Aug. 17, 1991; children: Thomas C. Sexton, Andrea N., William C. Nursing lic., N.W. Vo-Tech, Springdale, Ark.; acctg. diploma, Am. Coll., Fayetteville, Ark. Evening charge nurse Barry County Care Ctr., Cassville, Mo., 1992—. Democrat. Baptist. Avocations: writing, reading, coin collecting/numismatics. Home: 1415 Townsend Ave Cassville MO 65625 Office: Barry County Care Ctr 1300 County Farm Rd Cassville MO 65625

BYRNE, JENNIE LOUISE, psychiatrist, researcher; b. York, Pa., Sept. 4, 1973; d. Michael Benton and Ellen Bers Johnson; m. Tom Edward Byrne, Oct. 15, 2005. MD, PhD, NYU, 1996—2004. Resident Mt. Sinai Med. Ctr., N.Y.C., 2004—. Presenter in field. Contbr. papers to profl. jours. and pubs. Grantee, NIH, 1998—2001, Mt. Sinai Sch. Medicine, 2005—06. Mem.: Am. Psychiatry Assn., Phi Beta Kappa. Independent. Office: Mt Sinai Dept Psychiatry One Gustave Levy Pl New York NY 10029 Office Phone: 646-549-9488. Business E-Mail: jennie.byrne@mssm.edu.

BYRNE, KELLEY ANNE, special education educator; b. Fitchburg, Mass., Sept. 20, 1962; d. Joseph Dominic and Linda Eileen Byrne; m. Patrick Wayne Irish, Aug. 13, 2005; children: Taryn Kelly Trafton, Caitlin September Trafton, Maria Aili Mitchell. MS Spl. Edn., Fitchburg State Coll., Mass., 1997. Cert. Profl. Tchr. K-12 Maine, 2001. Tchr. spl. edn. MSE/MHC, New Gloucester, Maine, 1998—2004, Lake Region Mid. Sch., Naples, Maine, 2004—06, Yarmouth Sch. Dist., Maine, 2006—. Advisor Student Assistance Team, Naples, 2005—06. Recipient Kappa Delta Pi, Nat. Honor Assn., 1988—91. Home: 53 Mill Rd North Yarmouth ME 04097 Office: Lake Region Middle School 204 Kansas Rd Naples ME 04055 Office Phone: 207-846-2499. Office Fax: 207-647-0991. Business E-Mail: k_irish@yarmouth.k12.me.us.

BYRNE, MARGARET ELLEN, voice educator; b. West Allis, Wis., May 14, 1971; d. Thomas Hubert and Ellen Jean Schmidt; m. Daniel Patrick Byrne, July 16, 1994; 1 child, Catherine Margaret. MusB, Bryn Mawr Coll., 1993; B in Music Edn., U. No. Iowa, 1994; MS in Edn., Western Ill. U., 2005. Cert. tchr. K-12 Music Iowa. Dir. choral activities Pleasant Valley (Iowa) HS, 1995—. Mem.: Am. Choral Dirs. Assn. D-Liberal. Roman Cath. Avocations: gardening, genealogy. Office: Pleasant Valley HS PO Box 332 Pleasant Valley IA 52767 Office Phone: 563-332-5151. Office Fax: 563-332-8525.

BYRNE, PATRICIA CURRAN, small business owner; b. Tannersville, N.Y., Mar. 17, 1915; d. Michael Edward and Catherine Mary (Keogh) Curran; m. Owen Perry Byrne, July 6, 1939 (dec. Sept. 3, 1970); children: Sharon Byrne Van Dyke, Maureen E., Kevin O., Brian H., Sean M. BA, Hunter Coll., 1936; MS in Edn., SUNY, New Paltz, 1975. Tchr. elem. sch. H.T. Ctrl. Sch., N.Y., 1937-41, 52-53; mgr., co-owner restaurant Curran's Tavern, Tannersville, N.Y., 1953-70, owner-operator, 1970—. Democrat. Roman Catholic. Avocations: skiing, walking, swimming, poetry. Address: PO Box 201 Tannersville NY 12485-0201

BYRNE, ROSEANNE, library director; d. Rosemary L. Schoch; m. David Edward Byrne, May 29, 1971; children: Matthew, William, Anne R. BA, Coll. of St. Catherine, 1971; MLS, No. Ill. U., 1974. Children's svcs. libr. Des Plaines (Ill.) Pub. Libr., 1971; libr. St. Paul Pub. Libr., 1972—73; reference libr. Hennepin County Libr., Edina, Minn., 1975—78, sr. libr., 1978—82, prin. libr. Minnetonka, Minn., 1982—94, pub. svcs. mgr., 1995—97, co-ord.libr. Edina, Minn., 1997—2000; dep. dir. Dakota County Libr., Eagan, Minn., 2000—. Pres., mem. exec. bd. Coll. of St. Catherine Friends of the Libr., St. Paul, 1998—. Exec. bd. Minn. chpt. Pan-Pacific and S.E. Asian Women's Assn., St. Paul, 1994—2005. Mem.: ALA (assoc.), Minn. Libr. Assn. (pub. libr. chair, mem. exec. bd. 1985—2005), Phi Beta Kappa, Kappa Gamma Pi, Beta Phi Mu. Avocations: skiing, tennis, yoga. Office: Dakota County Libr 1340 Wescott Rd Eagan MN 55123 Home: 669 Maple Park Dr Mendota Heights MN 55118 Office Phone: 651-450-2931. Office Fax: 651-450-2934. Business E-Mail: roseanne.byrne@co.dakota.mn.us.

BYRNE, SUSAN M., investment company executive; Asst. treas. GAF Corp.; founder, chmn., CEO Westwood Mgmt. Group, Dallas, 1983—. Investment advisor, pres. The Gabelli Westwood Funds; bd. mem. U. Tex.

Investment Mgmt. Co.; trustee City Dallas Employees Retirement Fund, Southwestern Med. Found.; chair investment com. First Presbyn. Ch. Dallas Found.; mem. Tex. Govs. Bus. Coun.; mem., former bd. mem. Com. of 200. Mem.: Dallas Soc. Securities Analysts, N.Y. Soc. Securities Analysts, Internat. Women's Forum (bd. mem. Dallas chpt.). Office: Westwood 200 Crescent Ct Ste 1200 Dallas TX 75201-1807

BYRNE-DEMPSEY, CECELIA (CECELIA DEMPSEY), journalist; b. L.A., Aug. 7, 1925; d. John Joseph and Margaret Agnes (Frakell) B.; m. John Dempsey, Mar. 25, 1951 (dec. June 1981); children: Margaret, Elizabeth, John, Cecelia, Cathrine, Patricia, Bridget, Charles, Mary Teresa. Student, Immaculate Heart Coll., 1944; BA in Psychology, Calif. State U., Northridge, 1975, BA in Journalism, 1978, MA in Mass Comm., 1992. Staff Lockheed Aircraft Corp., Burbank, Calif., 1943—, Office Naval Rsch., San Francisco, 1947—; with Sisters of Mercy, Burlingame, Calif., 1945—, Sisters of Presentation, San Francisco, 1949—; mem. staff Calif. State U., 1976—. Rschr., journalism historian early Am. newspapers, 1978—. Author: The Meaning Index: A Model for Early American Newspaper Indexing: a research guide, 1992. Mentor 4-H Club; past mem. Urban Corp., L.A Mem. Mensa, Kappa Gamma Delta. Republican. Jewish. Avocations: poetry, gardening, philosophical meditation.

BYRNES, CHRISTINE ANN, internist; b. Darby, Pa., Dec. 18, 1951; d. John Edward and Olga (Rebechi) B. BA, U. Del., Newark, 1974; MD, Jefferson Med. Coll., Phila., 1978. Diplomate Am. Bd. Internal Medicine. Resident internal medicine Thomas Jefferson U. Hosp., Phila., 1978-81; coord. internal medicine residency program U. Med. & Dentistry of N.J./Cooper Med. Ctr., Camden, 1981-82; attending physician Thomas Jefferson U. Hosp., 1982-87, instr. medicine, 1982-85, clin. asst. prof. medicine, 1985-87; assoc. dir. Merck Human Health, West Point, Pa., 1987-89, sr. assoc. dir., 1989-91, dir., 1991-92, sr. dir., 1992—. Mem. ACP, Soc. Gen. Internal Medicine, Am. Soc. Internal Medicine, Am. Geriatrics Soc. Home: 1305 Idaho Ave Cape May NJ 08204-2727

BYRNES, GAIL M., endoscopy nurse; b. Bronx, N.Y., Feb. 4, 1955; d. John J. Jr. and Fay Helen (Mirro) Franchi; m. Gilbert J. Byrnes III, Oct. 19, 1984; children: Tara N., Gilbert J. IV (Skip). ASN, U. Bridgeport, Conn., 1975; student, Trenton State Coll., 1980. RN, N.J. Asst. nursing arts lab. U. Bridgeport; staff nurse med./surg. unit, endoscopy nurse, preceptor, asst. nurse mgr. med. day stay, clin. nurse III Monmouth Med. Ctr., Long Branch, NJ, 1975—99; staff nurse, interim dir. nursing, initiator sick child day care unit Ctrl. Jersey Surgery Ctr., 1999—2003; asst. nurse mgr. Advanced Endoscopy & Surgery Ctr., 2003—. Mem. Soc. Gastrointestinal Nurses and Assts.

BYRNES, HEIDI, academic administrator, German language educator; b. Breslau, Germany, Mar. 13, 1944; came to U.S., 1964; d. Alfred and Elfriede (Herold) Simon; m. David F. Byrnes, Apr. 4, 1964 (div. Mar. 1988); children: Sabina Byrnes McMahan, Eric R. BS in Edn., U. Kans., 1967; MA in Modern Lang./Linguistics, Kans. State U., 1969; PhD in German/Linguistics, Georgetown U., 1979. Temp. instr. German Kans. State U., Manhattan, 1967-71; instr. overseas divsn. U. Md., Germany, 1973-74; contract translator Joint Publs. Rsch. State Dept., Washington, 1974-75; asst. prof. German Georgetown U., Washington, 1979-84, assoc. prof. German, 1984-91, prof. German, 1991—, chair German dept., 1987-93, chair reaccreditation self-study, 1991-93, assoc. v.p. acad. affairs, 1993—. Chair 1990 N.E. Conf. Teaching Fgn. Langs., 1989-90, vice chair, 1989, bd. mem., 1984-91; mem. adv. com. Coll. Bd. Fgn. Langs. 1991—, devel. com. German Advanced Placement test, 1986-89; cons. Calif. fgn. lang. competency Stanford U., 1991—, SAIC, McLean, Va., 1988-93, Ctr. Applied Linguistics, Washington, 1987-89, States of Va., Md., Calif. Author: (with Stefan R. Fink) Wendepunkt, 1987, (with Janet Swaffar and Katherine Arens) Reading for Meaning: An Integrated Approach to Language Learning, 1991; editor: Contemporary Perceptions of Languages: Interdisciplinary Dimensions, 1982, (with Michael Canale) Defining and Developing Proficiency: Guidelines, Implementations and Concepts, 1986, Languages for a Multicultural World in Transition, 1992. Recipient Stephen A. Freeman award, 1982; Alumni fellow Kans. State U., 1989, Andrew W. Mellon Found. fellow Nat. Fgn. Lang. Ctr., 1991. Mem. MLA (chair adv. com. fgn. langs. and literatures 1990-93, chair exec. com. teaching of lang. 1989-90), Am. Assn. Tchrs. German (program chair nat. conf. 1994, task force profl. standards 1990—, lehrerfortbildung planning com. 1988—, pres. met. Washington chpt. 1982-87, Outstanding Educator award 1989), Am. Coun. Teaching of Fgn. Langs. (selection com. Emma Marie Birkmaier award 1988-89, chair 1989-90, selection com. Paul Pimsleur award 1989-90, selection com. Florence Steiner award 1988-89, oral proficiency testing adv. com. 1989-92, contbg. editor Oral Proficiency Interview Tester Tng. Manual 1989). Roman Catholic. Avocations: music, art, textile crafts. Office: Georgetown U Office Of Exec Vp Washington DC 20057-0001

BYRNES, HOPE HUSKA, volunteer; b. N.Y.C., Sept. 17, 1939; d. Charles John and Irma Kapalla Huska; m. Paul Joseph Byrnes, July 20, 1968; children: Paul, Jr., Kate, Sean. BA in Polit. Sci., Stetson U., DeLand, Fla., 1961. Legis. asst. U.S. Ho. of Reps., Washington, 1961—64, press asst., 1964—65; asst. supt. U.S. Senate Radio and TV Gallery, Washington, 1965—68; adminstrv. asst. Am. Bankers Assn., Washington, 1968—70. Pres. Sarasota Opera Guild, Fla., 1990—92, Asolo Theatre Guild, Sarasota, Fla., 1992—94, Sarasota Sister Cities Assn., Fla., 1994—2001, Fla. West Coast Children's Chorus, 2003—; bd. mem. Jazz Club Sarasota, arts coun. cultural exec. com. rep.; charter mem. Bus. Women's Network, Madrid, 1986—88. Recipient Mayor's award for Outstanding Cmty. Svc., Outstanding Achievement award, Fla. Sisster Cities Assn. Mem.: All-Fla. News Media Exec. Roundtable, U.N. Assn., Sarasota County Openly Plans for Excellence, Am. Legion Aux. (Post 30). Achievements include chair, City of Sarasota 100th Anniversary Opening Dinner and founder, Asolo Theatre Guild Guilder Award for local HS that has done most to promote new and innovative theater; performer Sarasota Sr. Theater. Avocations: singing, volunteer work.

BYRON, BEVERLY BUTCHER, retired congresswoman; b. Balt., July 27, 1932; d. Harry C. and Ruth Butcher; m. Goodloe E. Byron, 1952 (dec.); children: Goodloe E. Jr., Barton Kimball, Mary McComas; m. B. Kirk Walsh, 1986. Student, Hood Coll., 1962-64. Mem. 96th-102nd Congresses from 6th Md. dist., 1979-93; Presdl. appt. to base closing and realignment commn., 1993. Bd. dirs. McDonnell Douglas, Constellation Energy Group, Blue Cross/Blue Shield, UNC Corp., Farm and Mech. Nat. Bank, LMI, Def. Adv. Commn. on Women in the Mil.; exec. panel Chief of Naval Ops.; adv. bd. NASA, A.F. Meml. Found. State treas. Md. Young Dems., 1962, 65; bd. assocs. Hood Coll.; bd. visitors USAF Acad., 1980-87; trustee Mt. St. Mary's Coll.; bd. dirs. Frederick County chpt. ARC; sec. Frederick Heart Assn., 1974-79; mem. Frederick Phys. Fitness Commn.; chmn. Md. Phys. Fitness Commn., 1979-89; mem. Frederick County Landmarks Found.; bd. dirs. Am. Hiking Soc.; bd. dirs. Adventure Sports Inst., 1992—; bd. advisors Internat. Studies Frostburg State U., 1990—, Am. Volkssport Assn., 1991—; mem. bd. vis. U.S. Naval Acad., 1995—, chair, 1997-2002; chair TedCo. Recipient Pres.'s medal John Hopkins U. Democrat. Episcopalian. Home: 306 Grove Blvd Frederick MD 21701-4813

BYRON, E. LEE, real estate broker; b. Gt. Falls, Mont., Oct. 1, 1945; d. Chase and Mary Lee (Evans) Kimball; m. H. Thomas Byron Jr., May 18, 1966 (dec. 2000); children: H. Thomas Byron III, Chase K. (dec. June 2002), Lee-Hayes. AB, Smith Coll., 1967; MA, Monterey Inst. Fgn. Studies, 1971; Montessori cert., St. Nicholas. Ctr., London, 1971. Lic. real estate broker, Fla. Lectr. Monterey (Calif.) Inst. Fgn. Studies, 1971-72; founder, dir., owner Children's Sch. and Summer Dynamics, Auburn, Ala., 1975-79; instr. Child Study Ctr. Auburn U., 1973-79; hosp. dir. Fruitville Vet. Clinic, Sarasota, Fla., 1980-93; broker assoc. Michael Saunders & Co., Sarsasota, 1993—. Founder, adv. bd. mem. Guaranty Bank, North Port, Fla., 1987-99; owner, ptnr. Lee Ventures Real Estate Partnership, Sarasota, 1984-99; presenter in field, organizer discussion panels. Co-author: Preschool Theme Lesson Plans, 1975. Bd. dirs. Jr. League, Sarasota, 1981-90; bd. dirs. Pine View Assn. PTA, 1981-90, chmn., 1984-85; bd. dirs. Teen Ct., Sarasota, 1990—, Fla. Sch. Bd. Assn., cert., 1993; bd. dirs. Taxpayers Assn. Sarasota County, 1995-99, pres., 1996-97; bd. dirs. Civic League Sarasota, 1995-2001, 2nd v.p., 1997-98, 1st v.p., 1998-99, pres., 1999-2000; chmn. Sarasota County Exceptional Student Edn. Sch. Adv. Bd., 1984-90; mem. Pine View Sch. Adv. Com., 1994-98, chmn., 1994-97; bd. dirs. Consortium for Children and Youth, Sarasota, 1986—, pres., 1993-97; vice chair Action Task Force Venice (Fla.) 20/20, 1995-97, Children and Youth Svcs. Adv. Com., 1993-2001, chair, 1996-98, vice chair, 1999-2000; bd. dirs. Sarasota County Human Svcs. Adv. Commn., 2002-; co-chmn. Pres.'s Spl. Com. Exceptional Edn. Fla. Sch. Bd. Assn., 1992-93; mem. Bishop's Com. Sexual Misconduct Cath. Diocese, Venice, 1994-95, Multi-Stakeholder's Group (Future Land Planning East Sarasota County), 1995-99; mem. adv. com. Fla. House Inst., 1998—; mem. Sarasota County Sch. Bd., 1990-94; sec. Big Bros./Big Sisters of the Suncoast Found., 2004-05, v.p., pres. 2005—; active Fla. Women's Alliance, 1994-2000, Sarasota Women's Alliance, 2001—; eucharistic minister St. Patrick's Ch., 1995—; elected mem. student bd. Rice Sch. Pastoral Ministry, 2004-06; mem. nominating com. Girl Scout Coun., 2005—, chmn., 2006—. Recipient Sustainer of Yr. award Sarasota Jr. League, 1993, Cmty. Svc. award, 1995; Women of Power award Nat. Coun. Jewish Women, 1997, Cmty. Svc. award Michael Saunders & Co., 2006; named one of 100 Vols. for 100th birthday, Internat. Assn. Jr. Leagues, 1996. Mem. Sarasota Assn. of Realtors (program com. 1995-99, govt. affairs com. 2001—), Nat. Assn. Realtors (Grad. Realtor Inst. 1996). Republican. Roman Catholic. Avocations: reading, swimming, skiing. Home: 653 Sinclair Dr Sarasota FL 34240-9367 Office: Michael Saunders & Co 5100 Ocean Blvd Sarasota FL 34242-1693 Office Phone: 941-349-3444. Personal E-mail: byron@sarasota.com.

BYRUM, EDITH WARD, retired music educator; d. Cecil Thomas Ward, Sr. and Nora Lee (Rountree) Ward; children: Steven Ward, Susan Yvonne. BS in Music Edn., Longwood Coll., 1960. Tchr. Deep Creek H.S., Chesapeake, Va., 1960—61, Rena B. Wright Elem., Chesapeake, 1967—70, G.W. Carver Elem., Chesapeake, 1970, Sparrow Rd. Elem., Chesapeake, 1971—77; tchr. music G.A. Treakle Elem., Chesapeake, 1977—86, Crestwood Elem., Chesapeake, 1986—97, Deep Creek Elem., Chesapeake, 1996—2004, Deep Creek Intermediate, Chesapeake, 2001—03, Grassfield Elem., Chesapeake, 2003—04, Hickory Mid., 2004; ret. Pianist, organizer New Horizon Gospel Quartet, Chesapeake, 1993—97; Sunday sch. tchr. Deep Creek Bapt. Ch., Chesapeake, 1972—83, pianist, organist, 1975—98, fin. com., 1966—67, 1975—76, sr. adult pianist. Mem.: Music Educators Nat. Conf., Va. Music Educators Assn., PTA (life), Sigma Alpha Iota. Avocations: cooking, gardening, travel. Home: 620 Brisa Ct Chesapeake VA 23322

BYSIEWICZ, SUSAN, state official; b. New Haven, Conn. m. David Donaldson; 3 children. BA magna cum laude, Yale Coll., 1983; JD, Duke U., 1986. Corp. atty. White & Case, N.Y., 1986-88, Robinson & Cole, Hartford, Conn., 1988-92; with law dept. Aetna Life and Casualty, 1992-94; state rep. 100th dist. judiciary com. State of Conn., 1993—99, chair govt. adminstrn. and elections com., 1995—99, sec. of state, 1999—. Author: Ella: A Biography of Governor Ella T. Grasso, 1984. Conn. Bar Assn., N.Y. Bar Assn. Democrat. Address: Rm 104 State Capitol Hartford CT 06106 Office Phone: 860-509-6200. Office Fax: 916-653-4620. E-mail: susan.bysiewicz@po.state.ct.us.

BYSTRITSKY, MARINA, psychologist; b. St. Petersburg, Russia, June 24, 1959; arrived in U.S., 1979; d. Rem Shmidt and Frida Slomovic; children: Rachel, Hannah. BA, NYU, 1982; PhD, UCLA, 1999. Clin. psychologist pvt. practice, L.A., 1998—2005, Matrix Addiction Clinic, L.A., 2005; program dir. Adolescent Clin. Svcs., Palo Alto, Calif., 2005—; clin. psychologist pvt. practice, Palo Alto, 2005—. Mem.: Anxiety Disorders Assn. Am., APA. Avocations: skiing, mountain biking, yoga, jewelry making. Office: 467 Hamilton Ave #21 Palo Alto CA 94301

BYTHER-SMITH, IDA W., social services administrator; d. Leroy and Josephine Wilson; children: James, Melissa, Lavinia, Branden Shirelle. BA in Edn., Gov. State U., Chgo., 1988. Renal technologist Renal Care Group, Chgo., 1984—2001; group counselor Alliance for Cmty. Empowerment, Chgo., 2002—05; founder, CEO Jo-Ray House, Inc., Chgo., 2003—. AIDS counselor Chgo. Women's AIDS Project, 2001—05. Co-author: A Woman's Story: Overcoming the Shame of HIV, 2002. Chair membership com. Planning Coun. for Mayor Chgo. Recipient Dr. Sherry E. Luck award, Alliance for Cmty. Empowerment, 2002, Gigi Nicks award, Let's Talk, Let's Test, 2004, Long Term Survivor award, Educate Adv. Support Empower Orgn., 2004. Office: Jo-Ray HOuse Inc 23 W 115th St Chicago IL 60628

BZDELL, SUSAN ROSENBLUM, archivist, educator; b. Huntsville, Ala., May 21, 1952; d. Fred O. and Valtena Gibbs Rosenblum; m. Stephen S. Bzdell, Jr., Aug. 13, 1988. BA, U. Ala., Huntsville, 1971—82; MA, Fla. State U., Tallahasse, 1987—89. Picture framer, artifact display, Huntsville, Ala., 1971—86; contractor, cons. Elkmont, Ala., 1988—91; asst. archivist Limestone County Commn., Athens, Ala., 1991—95; archivist Morgan County Commn., Decatur, Ala., 1995—. Cons. Athens State Archives, Ala., 1999—2001. Author: Heritage of Morgan County, 1998, South of the River, 2003. Bd. mem. Old State Bank, Decatur, Ala., 2002—05, Main St., Decatur, Ala., 2003—05. Mem.: Morgan County Hist. Soc., Morgan County Genealogical Soc., Nat. Assn. Govt. Activists and Record Adminstrs., Am. Assn. State and Local History, Assn. County Commns., Soc. Ala. Archivist. Avocations: reading, painting, sewing, crafts.

CABALLERO, SHARON, academic administrator; m. Roger Caballero. BS Journalism/English, San Diego State U., 1968; MA Secondary Edn., U.S. Internat. U., 1976, EdD Ednl. Leadership, 1980. Dir. pub. rels. & mktg. Southwestern Cmty. Coll., Chula Vista, Calif., 1984—85; assoc. exec. dir. Calif. Assn. Cmty. Colls. (now Cmty. Coll. League Calif.), 1985—87; dean, communs. & fine arts Grossmont Coll., El Cajon, Calif., 1988—91; asst. supt. & v.p. acad. svcs. Rio Hondo Cmty. Coll. Dist., 1991—97; pres. San Bernardino Valley Coll., 1997—2002, N.Mex. Highlands U., Las Vegas, N.Mex., 2002—. Mem. Arrowhead United Way, Bernardino Valley Coll. Found., Victor Valley Women's Club, KVCR-FM/TV Found.; San Bernardino C. of C.; chmn. journalism dept., instr. mass media, telecommunications coll. newspaper. Named Calif. Woman of Yr. 58th Dist., 1994. Mem. Cailf. Cmty. Colls. Exec. Bd. (CEO mem. bd. 1995—), Mgmt. Devel. Commn. Assn. of Calif. Cmty. Coll. Adminstrs. (chair 1989—), Am. Assn. Women in Cmty. & Junior Colls. (nat. v.p. for profl. devel. 1987—89, nat. pres. 1989—91), Rotary. Office: NMex Highlands U 701 S Mt Vernon Ave San Bernardino CA 92410

CABANISS, CHARLOTTE JONES, library services director; b. Jefferson County, Ala., Apr. 13, 1951; d. Laurens Whipple Sr. and Sally Riddell Jones; m. Thomas Willard Cabaniss, Sept. 14, 1971 (div. Nov. 1998); children: Lauren Cabaniss Sellers, Amanda May, Willard Matthew. BA, Auburn U., 1973. English tchr. Rogers (Ark.) City Schs., 1984-92; libr. svcs. dir. Bay Minette (Ala.) Pub. Libr., 1994—. Dir. North Baldwin Cmty. Concerts, Inc., Bay Minette, 1995-98; mem. Baldwin County United, 1996—; chmn. bd. North Baldwin Literacy Coun., Bay Minette, 1995—; mem. adv. bd. Family Finders, 2000-02, Cath. Social Svcs., 2001; pres. bd. dirs. Jumbo Shrimp Theatre, 2002--; bd. dirs. Baldwin Co. United, 2003—, Ala. Ctr. for the Book, 2001—mem. steering com. Mobile/Baldwin United Envision, 2002--; founding mem. Fairhope Ctr. for the Writing Arts; mem. grant selection com. Ala. Arts and Humanities; founder Ala. Athenaum Writers Series. Recipient Outstanding Svc. award Area Action Women's Group, 1998, Lynn Stuart Cmty. Svc. award, 2002; named among Women to Watch in South Ala., So. Cities mag., 2002. Mem. ALA, C. of C. (youth task force chair 1996-98, tourism com. chair, 1998), North Baldwin C. of C. (dir. 1996-99), Baldwin County Libr. Cooperative, Kappa Delta Pi, Phi Kappa Phi. Methodist. Avocations: reading, community volunteerism.

CABANISS, DALE, government agency administrator; BA, U. Georgia; JD, Columbus Sch. Law at Catholic U. Legislative asst. and dir. to Sen. Frank Murkowski; chief counsel Senate Govt. Affairs Subcommittee on Post Office and Civil Service; staff member Senate Appropriations Subcommittee; chmn. Federal Labor Relations Authority, 2001—. Office: FLRA 607 14th St NW Washington DC 20424

CABE, CRISTA RUTH, academic administrator; b. Waynesboro, Va., Sept. 3, 1960; d. Thomas Reid and Patricia Edna (Loughran) C. BA, Coll. William & Mary, 1982; MA, U. Chgo., 1983. Dir. audience devel. Ct. Theatre, Chgo., 1984-86; program dir. alumni rels. U. Chgo., 1986-88; from exec. dir. alumnae activities to dir. advancement Mary Baldwin Coll., Staunton, Va., 1988-97, assoc. v.p. comm., mktg. and pub. affairs, 1997—. Mem. Coun. Advancement and Support of Edn., Coll. Comms. Assn., Augusta Bird Club (pres.), Va. Soc. Ornithology (bd. dirs.). Avocation: birding. Office: Mary Baldwin Coll Staunton VA 24401

CABLE, DIANE LYNNE, marriage and family therapist, educator; d. Ronald James LeBansky and Shirley Ann Malvrek; m. Bruce A. Cable. BA in Secondary Edn. and English, Concordia Coll., Mequon, Wis., 1987; MA in Marriage and Family Therapy, Phillips Grad. Inst., Encino, Calif., 1998. Lic. secondary tchr. Wis., marriage and family therapist Calif., 2005. Mgr. McDonald's Corp., Milw. and Fox Point, Wis., 1983—87; tchr. Trinity Luth. Jr. H.S., Reseda, Calif., 1987—88, Canoga Park Luth. Sch., 1989—91; med. legal dept. Orthop. Med. Ctr., Reseda, 1991—95; therapist Luth. Social Svcs., Bakersfield, 1996; foster care social worker Refugro Para Niños, West Covina, 1997—2000; mental health therapist Coll. Cmty. Svcs., Rosamond, 2000—05; sound tech. Agua Dulce Living Springs Foursquare Ch., Calif., 2005—. Participant 12 Step Program. Recipient Moeller award (English), Concordia U., 1987. Mem.: Calif. Assn. Marriage and Family Therapists. Democrat. Mem. Foursquare Ch. Avocations: reading, writing, roller hockey, ATV's.

CABRASER, ELIZABETH JOAN, lawyer; b. Oakland, Calif., June 23, 1952; AB, U. Calif., Berkeley, 1975; JD, U. Calif., 1978. Bar: Calif. 1978, U.S. Dist. Ct. (no., ea., cen. and so. dists.) Calif. 1979, U.S. Ct. Appeals (2d, 3rd, 5th, 6th, 9th, 10th, and 11th cirs.) 1979, U.S. Tax Ct. 1979, U.S. Dist. Ct. Hawaii 1986, U.S. Dist. Ct. Ariz. 1990, U.S. Supreme Ct. 1996. Ptnr. Lieff, Cabraser, Heimann & Bernstein LLP, San Francisco, 1978—. Contbr., editor California Causes of Action, 1998, Moore's Federal Practice, 1999, editor-in-chief California Class Actions Practice and Procedures, 2003; contbr. articles to law jours. Named one of Top 100 U.S. Lawyers, 1997, 2000, Top 50 Women Lawyers, Nat. Law Jour., 1998, Top Ten Lawyers in Bay Area, San Francisco Chronicle, 2003; recipient Presdl. Award of Merit, Consumer Attys. Calif., 1998, Matthew O. Tobriner Public Service Award, Legal Aid Soc., 2000, Disting. Jurisprudence Award, Anti-Defamation League, 2002, U. Calif., Berkeley Sch. Law Citation Award, 2003. Mem. ABA (tort and ins. practice sect., sect. litig. com. on class action and derivative skills, chair subcom. on mass torts), ATLA, Coun. Am. Law Inst., Calif. Constn. Rev. Commn., Nat. Ctr. for State Cts. (mass tort conf. planning com.), Women Trial Lawyer Caucus, Consumer Attys. Calif., Calif. Women Lawyers, Assn. Bus. Trial Lawyers, Nat. Assn. Securities and Comml. Attys., Bay Area Lawyers for Individual Freedom, Bar Assn. San Francisco (v.p. securities litig., bd. dirs.). Office: Lieff Cabraser Heimann & Bernstein LLP Embarcadero Ctr W 30th Fl 275 Battery St San Francisco CA 94111-3305 E-mail: ecabraser@lchb.com.

CABROL, NATHALIE AGNES, research scientist; b. Bagneux, France, Aug. 30, 1963; d. Jean Cabrol and Michele Marcelle Quatre-Sols; m. Edmond Antoine Grin, Apr. 15, 2000. Masters in Planetary Sciences, U. Paris-Sorbonne and Obs. of Paris-Meudon, France, 1986, PhD in Planetary Sciences, 1991; Cert. on the list Maitre de Conferences in geology, Paris, France, 1995. Fellow NASA Ames Rsch. Ctr., Space Sci. Divsn., Moffett Field, Calif., 1996—98; prin. investigator SETI Inst., NASA Ames Rsch. Ctr., Space Sci. Divsn., Moffett Field, Calif., 1998—. Spkr. in field. Contbr. chapters to books, articles to profl. jours. Recipient Silver Medal for Rsch. Work, Obs. of Triel (France), 1992, Bronze Medal for Edn. and Pub. Outreach, Ecole des Mines de Douai (France), 1996, Silver Medal, Societe d'Encouragement au Progres, 1997, Gold medal Internat. Water and Sci. award, Unesco, European Parliament, 2000, Medal for Edn. and Pub. Outreach, City of Triel, France, 2000, ASIP, 2004, Women of Discovery: Air and Space Award, World Wings Quest, 2005; grantee Mars Exploration Rover Mission Participating Scientist, NASA, 2002—, NASA Ames Rsch. Ctr., 2002—03, NASA Astrobiology Inst., 2003—, NASA Astrobiology Sci. and Tech. for Exploring Planets, 2003—; Carey Fellow, Wings World Quest, 2005. Achievements include research in exploring the highest lakes on Earth as analogs to ancient Martian lakes in order to understand their potential for life inception and survival and study the limits of life on Earth; the Gusev crater as a landing site for the Mars Exploration Mission; first to free dive (without oxygen tanks) in high-altitude lakes (5, 916 m or 18, 500 ft) to study human physiological response and adaptation to high altitude; develop science exploration strategies for automated robotic vehicles (rovers) to search for habitable environments and life on Mars; being a member of the Mars Exploration Rover Science Team. Avocations: Climbing, hiking, diving, scientific high altitude mountaineering and free diving (without oxygen tanks), music, painting, visiting art galleries and mus. Office: SETI Inst 515 N Whisman Rd Mountain View CA 94043 also: NASA Ames Rsch Ctr Space Sci Divsn MS 245 3 Moffett Field CA 94035 Home Fax: 650-967-6981; Office Fax: 650-604-6779. Business E-Mail: ncabrol@mail.arc.nasa.gov.

CACCAMISE, GENEVRA LOUISE BALL (MRS. ALFRED E. CACCAMISE), retired librarian; b. July 22, 1934; d. Herbert Oscar and Genevra (Green) Ball; m. Alfred E. Caccamise, July 7, 1974. BA, Stetson U., 1956; MLS, Syracuse U., N.Y., 1967. Tchr. grammar sch., Sanford, Fla., 1956-57; tchr. elem. sch. Longwood, Fla., 1957-58; tchr., libr. Enterprise (Fla.) Sch., 1958-63; libr. media specialist Boston Ave. Sch., DeLand, Fla., 1963-83; head media specialist Blue Lake Sch., DeLand, 1983-87; ret., 1987. Author: Volusia County manual Instructing the Library Assistant, 1965, Echoes of Yesterday: A History of the DeLand Area Public Library, 1912-1995, 1995, A Quest for Beauty: A History of the Garden Club of DeLand, Florida, 1927-97, 1997, Index to Reflections: West Volusia County, 100 Years of Progress, 2002, (compilation) The Minutes and Memorials of the Old Settlers of DeLand, Fla., 1882-1926, 2003. Charter mem. West Volusia Meml. Hosp. Aux., DeLand, 1962—81; leader Girl Scouts US, 1955—56; area dir. Fla. Edn. Assn., Volusia County, 1963—65; bd. dirs. Alhambra Villas Home Owners Assn., 1972—75; trustee DeLand Pub. Libr., 1977—86, sec., 1978—80, v.p., 1980—82, pres., 1982—84; v.p. Friends of DeLand Pub. Libr., 1987—88, 1998—2005, bd. dirs., 1987—, pres., 1989—90, 1995—97, 2006—, newsletter editor, 1992—95, 1999—2005; charter mem. Guild of the DeLand Mus. Art, 1988—, v.p., 1990, pres., 1991—92, co-rec. sec., 1997—98, rec. sec., 2005—, mus. bd. dirs., 1991—95; co-orgn. chmn. Friends of DeLand Mus. Art, 1993. Recipient Woman's Club Lit. award for contbns. to arts in West Volusia County, 1995. Mem.: DAR (asst. chief page Continental Congress, Washington 1962—65, chpt. registrar 1969—80, Excellence in Cmty. Svc. award 1995), AAUW (rec. sec. 1961—65, 2d v.p. chpt. 1965—67, rec. sec. 1978—80, pres. 1980—82, parliamentarian 1982—84), Volusia County Ret. Educators Assn. (pres. Unit II 1988—90, scholarship chmn. 1992—95, corr. sec. 2003—), Volusia County Assn. Media in Edn. (treas. 1977), Fla. Libr. Assn., Assn. Childhood Edn. (corr. sec. 1963—65, 1st v.p. 1965—66), Roots and Brs. Geneal. Soc. of West Volusia County (corr. sec. 2006—), Nat. League Am. Pen Women (corr. sec. 1996—98, pres. 1998—2000, corr. sec. 2000—04), Magna Carta Dames, Stetson U. Alumni Assn. (class chmn. for ann. fund dr. 1968), Soc. Mayflower Descendants (lt. gov. Francis Cook Colony 1988—90), Pilgrim John Howland Soc., Colonial Dames XVII Century, Nat. Soc. New Eng. Women (v.p. Daytona Beach Colony 1990—91), Nat. Soc. US Daus. of 1812 (rec. sec. Peacock chpt. 1989—90), Fla. Hist. Soc., West Volusia Hist. Soc. (libr. 1993—, sec. 1996, v.p. 2000—02, pres. 2002—03, bd. dirs., Historian of Yr. 2002), Morning Glory Garden Cir., Hibiscus Garden Cir. (treas. 1988—89, v.p. 1990—93, 1996—97, pres. 1997—99, treas. 2001—03), DeLand Garden Club (corr. sec.

1993—95, editor newsletter 1993—95, v.p. 1997—99), Bus. and Profl. Women's Club (corr. sec. DeLand 1968—71, 2d v.p. 1969—70), Delta Kappa Gamma (pres. Beta Psi chpt. 1982—84). Address: PO Box 241 Deland FL 32721-0241

CACCIATORE, JOANNE, social worker; b. NYC, Nov. 16, 1965; d. John Louis and Josephine Cacciatore; children: Arman John Sadeghi, Cameron Michael, Stevie Jo, Joshua Cheyne, Cheyenne (Deceased). BS, Ariz. State U., Phoenix, 2001, MSW, 2004; PhD, U. Nebr., Lincoln, 2006. CEO MISS Found., Phoenix, 1996—; faculty Ariz. State U., 2005—. Dir. Elisabeth Kubler-Ross Found., Scottsdale, Ariz., 2004—. Author: (book) Dear Cheyenne, (manual/book) The Power of Compassion: A New Attitude in Healthcare; editor: (publication for agency) MISSing Angels; contbr. film by japanese public television, chapters to books. Vol. MISS Found., Glendale, 1996—2005; mem. Ariz. Domestic Violence Fatality Rev. Com., Phoenix, 2002—03; mem., past chair Ariz. Dept. Health Services, 1999—2006; founding mem. Elisabeth Kubler Ross Found., Scottsdale, Ariz., 2004—06, Internat. Stillbirth Alliance, Chgo., 2002—05; dir. Elisabeth Kubler Ross Found., 2004—; founder The Kindness Project, Peoria, 1997—2006. Recipient Laurel award, St. Luke's Charitable Health Trust; fellow, Assn. Death Edn. and Counseling; grantee, St. Luke's Charitable Health Trust; scholar, Ariz. State U., 2001, 2003, 2004. Mem.: Compassionate Friends, Unexplained Infant Death Adv. Coun., Internat. Stillbirth Alliance (assoc.), Psi Chi, Golden Key Internat. Honor Soc. (hon.). Libertarian. Achievements include first to successfully lobby the Arizona legislature to pass the first MISSing Angels Bill in the United States, later successsfully spearheaded the same bill's passage in 16 other states since; successfully lobbied the federal government for first-time funding on stillbirth and maternal health through the National Institutes of Health; successfully lobbied the Arizona legislature in the creation of the Unexpected Infant Death Advisory Council, a formal, multidisciplinary team charged with research and education of infant deaths; successfully lobbied the Az legislature to pass SB1003, a one-time tax exemption for families after an infant's death to help offset funeral and birth costs; successfully rallied a team to lobby the Congress to sign National Children's Memorial Day Act. Avocations: reading, hiking, surfing, rock climbing. Home: 3642 W Magellan Anthem AZ 85086 Office: Arizona State University/MISS Foundation CHS/Dept of SW 4701 W Thunderbird Glendale AZ 85306 Office Phone: 602-543-6659. Home Fax: 623-979-1001. Personal E-mail: joanne727@cox.net. E-mail: joanne.cacciatore@asu.edu.

CADWALLADER, FAY MARGARET, social worker; b. New Orleans, Jan. 2, 1964; d. Joseph Dale and Maria Natalie (Lovoi) C. Lic. in cosmetology, Glen Dow Acad. Hair Design, 1985; BA in Social Work, Southeastern La. U., 1988; M in Social Work, Walla Walla Coll., 1993. Recreation asst. Tamarack Ctr., Spokane, 1989-90, residential counselor, 1990-91, designated shift supr., 1990-91, admissions, discharge, aftercare coord., 1991-93; child and adolescent program mgr., social svcs. dir. River Crest Hosp., Lewiston, Idaho, 1993-94; psychiat. social worker Sacred Heart Hosp., Spokane, 1994—2001; self employed sex offender treatment provider Counselor Youth Force, Spokane, 2001—. Mem. Grace Harvest Fellowship. Mem. NASW, Profl. Svc. Orgn. Avocations: socializing, singing, canoeing, white water rafting, camping. Office: 539 W Sharp Ste 150 Spokane WA 99201 Personal E-mail: fay_youthforce@hotmail.com.

CADWALLADER, GWEN NATALIE, elementary school educator, music educator; b. New Orleans, Feb. 18, 1962; d. Joseph Dale Cadwallader and Maria Natalie Lovoi; 1 child, Johnathan Miles. B in Music Edn., Southeastern La. U., 1984; MEd, Whitworth Coll., 1990; degree in Orff-Schulwerk III, Seattle Pacific U., degree in Kodaly III. Cert. tchr. grades K-12 music, grades K-8 elem. edn. Wash., K-12 prin. Wash., kindermusik Kindermusik Internat. Elem. music specialist Ctrl. Valley Sch. Dist. #356, Spokane Valley, Wash., 1985—. Adj. faculty Whitworth Coll., Spokane, Wash., 1991—93; dir. Kindermusik with Gwen Cadwallader, Spokane, 1998—2002; presenter in field. Pres. Glenngill Ct. Homeowners Assn., Spokane Valley, 1999—2005. Mem.: NEA, Ctrl. Valley Edn. Assn., Wash. Edn. Assn., Wash. Assn. Sch. Prins., Wash. Music Educators Assn., Music Educators Nat. Conf., Kindermusik Educators Assn., N.W. Kodaly Educators, Orgn. Am. Kodaly Educators, Inland Empire Orff Chpt. (pres. 2001—03), Am. Off-Schulwerk Assn., Pi Lambda Theta, Delta Omicron (life). Republican. Avocations: music, swimming, reading, genealogy. Personal E-mail: gncad@icehouse.net.

CADWELL, COURTNEY BRADSHAW, elementary school educator; d. John and Judy Bradshaw; m. Kevin Cadwell, Jan. 7, 1995. BA, U. Tex., Austin, 1995; MA, Dallas Theol. Sem., 1999; MEd, Vanderbilt U., Nashville, 2002. Cert. tchr. Tex. Tchr. McCulloch Intermediate Sch., Dallas, 1995—99, 2001—. Recipient Profl. Achievement award, HPISD, 2005—06. Office Phone: 214-780-3500. Business E-Mail: cadwelc@hpisd.org.

CADY, SHERRY L., astrobiologist, educator; BA (with highest honors) in Geology, U. Calif. Berkeley, 1987, PhD in Geology, 1994. Office mgr., bus. products and supplies co., San Francisco, 1981—87; grad. student, dept. geology U. Calif. Berkeley, 1987—94; rsch. assoc., geomicrobiology NRC, NASA Ames Rsch. Ctr., Calif., 1994—96; prin. investigator, rsch. scientist SETI Inst., Menlo Park, Calif., 1996—98; asst. prof., dept. geology Portland State U., Oreg., 1998—2002, assoc. prof., dept. geology Oreg., 2002—. Mem. biosciences steering group NSF. Contbr. chapters to books, scientific papers, articles to profl. jours.; editor-in-chief Astrobiology, 2001—, mem. editl. bd. Geobiology. Mem.: Geological Soc. Am. (co-founder, vice chair geobiology and geomicrobiology divsn.), Environmental Biogeochemistry (mem. internat. com. 1999). Achievements include working on various projects connected to the search for life on Mars and the investigation of how microorganisms leave their biosignatures in extreme environments. Office: Dept Geology Portland State U PO Box 751 Portland OR 97207-0751 Address: Portland State U Dept Geology Rm 17 Cramer Hall 1721 SW Broadway Portland OR 97201 Office Phone: 503-725-3377. Office Fax: 503-725-3025. Business E-Mail: CadyS@pdx.edu.*

CAFARO, DEBRA A., real estate company executive; Bar: Ill., Pa. Founding mem. Barack Ferrazzano Kirschbaum Perlman & Nagelberg; pres., dir. Ambassador Apartments, Inc., 1997—98; pres., CEO Ventas. Inc., Louisville, 1999—, chmn. bd., 2003—. Adj. prof. law Northwestern U. Law Sch., 1988—92. Mem.: Nat. Assn. of Corp. Dirs., Nat. Assn. of Real Estate Investment Trusts (bd. dirs.). Office: Ventas, Inc Ste 300 10350 Ormsby Park Pl Louisville KY 40223

CAFFERATA, PATRICIA DILLON, state official; b. Albany, NY, Nov. 24, 1940; d. Kenneth P. and Barbara Vucanovich (Farrell) Dillon; m. H. Treat Cafferata, June 17, 1961; children: Elisa, Reynolds, Farrell. Student, Mills Coll., 1958—61; BA, Lewis and Clark Coll., 1963; JD, Southwestern Sch. Law, 1989—. Mem. Nev. Assembly, 1980—82; treas. State of Nev., Carson City, Nev., 1982—86; nominee Gov. of Nev., 1986; dist. atty. Lincoln County, Nev., 1992, Lander County, Nev., 1995—96, Esmeralda County, Nev., 2000—03; of counsel Jenkins Law Office, Reno, 2005—. Named Outstanding Freshman Legislator, Nev. State Med. Assn., 1981. Roman Catholic. Office: Jenkins Law Office 423 W Plumb Ln Reno NV 89509 Office Phone: 775-324-9970.

CAFFERTY, ANITA A., music educator; d. Anthony Frank and Jeanne Martha Biondolillo. BS, Hofstra U., 1965; MS, C.W. Post U., 1981. Music/chorus tchr. Sewanaka Sch. Dist., New Hyde Park, NY, 1965—66, Sachem CSD #5, Holbrook, NY, 1966—97. Pvt. piano and voice coach, L.I., NY, 1966—; adjudicator voice N.Y. State Sch. Music Assn., L.I., 1993—; music dir./condr. Sachem Sch. Dist., Holbrook, 1993—; guest condr. Sachem Festival, 1993, Suffolk County Music Educators Festival, 2004. Composer: Dare to Dream, 1986. Vol. piano performer various nursing homes, L.I., 1980—; Eucharistic min. Good Samaritan Hosp., West Islip, NY, 1998—. Recipient Nat. Meritorious award, Am. Fedn. Tchrs., 1971, PR Disting. Svc. award, Pilot Club Internat., 1982—90. Mem.: Music Educators Nat. Conf., Sweet Adelines (bass sect. leader 2000—), 99 Internat. Orgn. Women Pilots. Avocations: flying, boating, ballroom dancing, golf, animal rescue.

CAFFERTY, PASTORA SAN JUAN, education educator; b. Cienfuegos, Las Villas, Cuba, July 29, 1940; arrived in US, 1947; d. Jose Antonio and Hortensia (Horruitiner) San Juan; m. Michael Cafferty, Apr. 13, 1971 (dec. 1973); m. Henry P. Russe, Aug. 18, 1988 (dec. 1991). BA, St. Bernard Coll., 1967; MA, George Washington U., 1969, PhD, 1971; DHC, Columbia Coll., 1987. Instr. George Washington U., Washington, 1967-69; asst. to sec. U.S. Dept. Transp., Washington, 1969-70, U.S. HUD, Washington, 1970-71; asst. prof. U. Chgo., 1971-76, assoc. prof., 1976-83, prof., 1983—2005, prof. emeritas, 2005—. Bd. dir. Kimberly-Clark Corp., Dallas, Peoples' Energy Corp., Chgo., Waste Mgmt. Inc., Houston, Harris Fin. Corp., Chgo. Author: The Politics of Language: The Dilemma of Bilingual Education for Puerto Ricans, 1981, Backs Against The Wall, 1983, The Dilemma of American Immigration, 1983, Hispanics in the U.S.A., 1985, 2d edit., 1992, Hispanics: An Agenda for 21st Century, 1999, 2d edit., 2002. Bd. dirs. Lyric Opera Assn., Chgo., 1990—, Rush Univ. Med. Ctr., 1993— White House fellow U.S. Govt., 1969-70. Mem. Chgo. Yacht Club. Democrat. Roman Catholic. Office: U Chgo 969 E 60th St Chicago IL 60637-2677 Office Phone: 773-702-8959. E-mail: p_caffert@uchicago.edu.

CAFFEY, LINDA KAYE, elementary school educator; b. Taft, Calif., Dec. 31, 1946; d. Ellis E. and Eathel (West) Green; m. Henry Charles Eriksson, Oct. 25, 1975 (dec.); 1 child, David Keith; m. Jesse Randall Caffey, Sept. 20, 2000. AA in Edn., S.W. Bapt. Coll., 1966; BS in Edn., Ohio U., 1969; MEd, U. Mo., Columbia, 1990. Cert. elem. and reading tchr. 3d grade tchr. Athens (Ohio) City Schs., 1969-70; traffic contr., office mgr. U-Haul Co. of San Diego, 1970-75; substitute tchr. Tampa (Fla.) City Schs., 1977-83, Camdenton (Mo.) R-III Schs., 1985-86, Chpt. I tchr.'s aide, 1986-89; Chpt. I tchr. Birmingham (Ala.) Pub. Schs., 1991-95, Title I tchr., 1995—. Mem. com. Boy Scouts Am., Birmingham, 1992-96; mem. com. Hugh O'Brian Youth Found., Birmingham, 1995-2002, dir. jr. staff Ala. Youth Leadership Programs, Birmingham, 2002—, U. Ala., Birmingham, 2002—, lead tchr., tech. coord., chairperson of bldg. leadership team and honors and awards com., 2000—; tchr. children's ch. Bluff Pk. Bapt. Ch., 2002—; facilitator Wenonah Elem. Sch., 1998-99. Named Birmingham Pub. Schs. Tchr. of Yr., 1995-96. Mem. Internat. Reading Assn., Delta Kappa Gamma. Republican. Baptist. Avocation: square dancing (v.p. Square Dance Club 1993-94, pres. 1994-95). Home: 1363 Badham Dr Vestavia Hills AL 35216-2947 Office: Wenonah Elem Sch 3008 Wilson Rd SW Birmingham AL 35221-1717 Office Phone: 205-231-1800. Personal E-mail: lkcaffey@aol.com.

CAFFREY, PATRICIA, diversified financial services company executive; With JP Morgan Chase & Co., NYC, 1993—, mng. dir. global syndicated fin. group, mng. dir. restructuring group, regional mgr. Chase Bus. Credit, 2006—. Office: JP Morgan Chase & Co 270 Park Ave New York NY 10017 Office Phone: 212-270-6000. Office Fax: 212-270-1648.*

CAFIERO, JENNIFER ANNETTE, academic administrator, educator; b. Bklyn., Jan. 8, 1975; d. Pasquale and Annette Rosemary Cafiero. Master's degree, Pace U., 2001. Cert. tchr. N.Y. Exec. asst. Pace U., NYC, 1997—98, coord. enrollment rsch., 1998—2000, dir. enrollment planning and reporting, 2000—04, Rider U., 2004—. Adj. prof. math. Pace U., 2002—04, instr. mktg. rsch., 2006. Mem.: Assn. for Instl. Rsch., Am. Motorcyclist Assn. Avocations: motorcycling, home improvement, travel. Personal E-mail: jennifer_cafiero@yahoo.com.

CAFRITZ, PEGGY COOPER, communications executive; b. Mobile, Ala., Apr. 7, 1947; d. Algernon Johnson and G. Catherine (Mouton) C.; married; 2 children. BA in Polit. Sci., George Washington U., 1968, JD, 1971. Bar: DC 1972. Founder Workshops for Careers in Arts, Washington, 1968; developer, chmn. bd. Duke Ellington Sch. Arts., Washington, 1968-84; dir. Arrowstreet, Architects and Planners Inc., Cambridge, Mass., 1972-74, Washington, 1972-74; spl. asst. to pres. Post-Newsweek Stas. Inc., Washington, 1974-77; programming exec., producer documentary films Sta. WTOP-TV, Washington, 1974-77; pres. DC Bd. Edn., Washington, 2000—. Cultural arts critic (PBS TV show) Around Town, 1986—. Mem. exec. com. D.C. Commn. Arts and Humanities, 1970-75, chmn., 1979-87, chmn. emeritus, 1987—; trustee Am. Film Inst., 1972-74, Pratt Inst., 1991; bd. govs. Corcoran Gallery Art, Washington, 1972-74; exec. dir. gt. issure program D.C. Bicentennial Commn., 1974; bd. dirs. Washington Performing Arts Soc., 1983—, Kennedy Ctr. Performing Arts, 1986—, Women's Project, 1987—, Nat. Guild Community Schs. of Arts, 1976-80, Pennsylvania Ave. Devel. Corp., Washington, 1979-87, Atlanta U., 1983-86, Washington, Am. Place Theater, N.Y.C.; co-chmn. Mayor's Blue Ribbon Task Force on Cultural and Econ. Devel., 1988; mem. exec. bd. Nat. Assembly State Arts Agys., 1979-86, planning com., 1986-87; mem. conv. staff Dem. Nat. Com., 1972, 76; mem. steering com. Carter-Mondale, Washington, 1976; mem. nat. panel Arts, Edn. and Ams., 1975-79; mem. internat. com. UNICEF, 1976-79; chair Smithsonian Cultural Edn. Com., 1989—; co-chair Smithsonian Cultural Equity Com., 1988—; mem. adv. bd. W.E.B. DuBois Inst., Harvard U., 1992-; mem. African-Am. Instnl. study adv. com. Smithsonian Instn., 1990— pres., D.C. St. Bd. of Education, 2001-. Fellow Woodrow Wilson Internat. Ctr. for Scholars, 1971; recipient John D. Rockefeller III award, 1972, George F. Peabody award U. Ga., 1976, Emmy award, 1977, 27th Ann. Broadcast Media award, 1977, Zeta Phi Beta award for outstanding contbn. in the arts, 1974, N.Y. Black Film Festival award, 1976, Women's Achievement award Pub. TV, 1984, Brava award for Outstanding Contbn. to Arts in Washington, 1988, Mayor's Art award for excellence in svc. to arts, 1991, 20th Malcolm X DayAnniversary award Arts Advocacy, 1991, Ann. Cultural Alliance award, 1992; named Washingtonian of Yr. Washingtonian mag., 1972, Woman of Yr. Mademoiselle mag., 1973, and numerous other awards. Mem.: DC Bar Assn., ABA. Home and Office: 3030 Chain Bridge Rd NW Washington DC 20016-3410 Office: DC Board of Ed 825 North Capitol St NE Nineth Floor Washington DC 20002 E-mail: peggy.cafritz@k12.dc.us.

CAGE, ALLIE M., communications executive; b. Memphis, Feb. 2, 1953; d. Ernest Hampton Sr. and Robie Lee (Bynum) Cage. BS, Cornell U., 1975; MBA, Tenn. State U., 1986. Pres., owner Profl. Svc., Inc., Memphis, 1981-83; dir. tutorial ctr. Tenn. State U., Nashville, 1984-85; rsch. assoc. Inst. African Affairs, Nashville, 1986-88; ptnr. Cage, Smith & Assocs., Nashville, 1988-91; mktg. dir. So. Colour, Inc., Brentwood, Tenn., 1994—; owner, pres. Cage Comm. Co., Madison, Tenn., 1988—. Bd. dirs. So. Colour, Inc. Author: (weekly publ.) Rap Sheet, 1983—86; co-author: (pub., cassette rec.) Arbitration, 1975; freelance reporter various newspapers, 1986—. Bd. dirs. Rainbow Coalition Davidson County, Tenn., 1984—, Nat. Coalition to Save Black Colls., Nashville, 1986—; pres. Lit. Soc., 1991—; publicity coord., vol. coord. Unity Build Habitat for Humanity, project dir. Ecumenical Build 2002; publicity coord., vol. coord. Unity Build Bldg. Together for Christ, 1999—; min. in tng. St. Luke CME Ch., Nashville, min. Named to So. Women in Pub. Svc., Stennis Ctr. Pub. Svc. and Miss. U. for Women, 1992. Mem.: NAACP (life), Am. Mgmt. Assn., Nat. Hook-Up Black Women. Democrat. Avocations: travel, reading, tennis, volleyball, music. Office: 510 Heritage Dr Unit 25 Madison TN 37115-6001 E-mail: amcage@msn.com.

CAGER, CHEZIA THOMPSON, poet, literature educator; BA, Washington U., 1973, MA, 1975; DA, Carnegie-Mellon U., 1984. With St. Louis C.C., Forest Park, 1975—80; asst. prof. English Clarion State Coll., 1980—82; asst. prof. Afro-Am. studies U. Md. Balt. County, 1982—85; prof. theater/African-Am. studies Smith Coll., Mendenhall Ctr. for the Performing Arts, 1985—88; cons. African Am. Newspaper Archives and Rsch. Ctr., 1989—92, Balt. City Pub. Schs. Multicultural Initiative, 1992—94; prof. lang. and lit. Md. Inst. Coll. Art, 1994—, faculty advisor FIRE:MICA Student Poetry Jour., 1995—, dir. Spectrum of Poetic Fire Reading Series, 1999—. Freelance cultural reviewer various publs., 1969—2000; coord. reading and writing workshop St. Louis Pub. Libr., 1976; site reviewer Expansion Arts Program Nat. Endowment for the Arts, 1984; artist-in-residence Albany (Ga.) State Coll., 1994; artist-in-residence theater dept. U. Pa.; presenter in field. Author: Power Objects: A Message In A Bottle to My Daughter and Her Friends, 1996, The Presence of Things Unseen: Giant Talk, 1996, numerous poems; editor: When Divas Laugh, 2001, When Divas Dance, 2004; contbr. articles to profl. jours. Bd. dirs. Md. Art Place, 1991—2000, Balt. Writers' Alliance, 1999—2000. Finalist Naomi Madgett Long Poetry Competition, Lotus Press, 2002; recipient Individual Artist award in poetry, Md. State Arts Coun., 1999, 2001, Disting. Black Marylander award in the arts, Towson U., 2000, The Legacy award, People's Poetry awards, 2005; Washington U. Black Studies Program scholar, U. West Indies, 1974, Carnegie-Mellon U. doctoral fellow, 1976—80, assoc. fellow in poetry, Atlantic Ctr. for the Arts, 2002, Lucus grant in support of tchg. writing, MICA, 2000, Lucus grant in tchg. poetry, 2001, tuition grant in poetry, Bread Loaf, 2002. Mem.: MLA, Langston Hughes Soc., Poetry Soc. Am., Acad. Am. Poets, Nat. Coun. Tchrs. English. Office Phone: 410-225-2350.

CAGLE, GLENDA JOHNSTON, elementary school educator; d. Robert L. and Rosemary Johnston; m. Terry A. Cagle, Aug. 31, 1984; 1 child, Amanda Cagle Stewart. BA in Mid. Grades Edn., Brenau U., Gainesville, Ga., 1998; MA in Early Childhood Edn., Piedmont U., Demerost, Ga., 2001; postgrad., Lincoln Meml. U., Harrogate, Tenn., 2002—03. Cert. tchr. Ga. Med. clk. Hosp., Jasper, Ga., 1981—83, radiology transcriptionist Canton, Ga., 1983—84; loan officer asst. Bank, Canton, 1984—85, bank teller Jasper, Ga., 1985—86; radiology trascriptionist Hosp., Canton, 1986—98; substitute tchr. Sch., Jasper, Ga., 1997; studetn support coord. Jasper Mid. Sch., 2003—06, 6th grade tchr., 2005—, lang. arts sch. coord., 2005—06. Sectional leader So. Assn. Colleges and Schools Com., Jasper, Ga., 2003—06. Scholar, Reinhardt Coll., 1994—96. Home: 117 Cagle Rd Jasper GA 30143 Office: Jasper Mid Sch 339 West Church St Jasper GA 30143 Office Phone: 706-253-1760. Personal E-mail: gjc30143@yahoo.com.

CAGLE, KARIN KNOWLES, lawyer; b. San Antonio, Mar. 5, 1960; d. Walter Eaton Knowles, R. David (Stepfather) and Patty (McCollum) Broilas; m. Michael Glenn Cagle, Mar. 5, 1989; children: Grace Ann, Calvin McCollum. BS Basic Sci., New Mex. Inst. Mining and Tech., Socorro, N.Mex., 1984; MA Tchg., Tex. Wesleyan U., Ft. Worth, 1996; JD magna cum laude, Tex. Wesleyan U. Sch. Law, 2003. Bar: Tex. 2004, US Dist. Cts. (no. dist.) Tex. 2005, US Ct. Appeals (5th cir.) 2006. Analytical chemist Alcon Labs., Ft. Worth, 1985—89; tchr. sci. mid. sch. Ft. Worth Ind. Sch. Dist., 1996—99; legal asst. Law Offices David Broilas, Ft. Worth, 1999—2004, assoc., 2004—05; ptnr. Cagle & Broilas, Ft. Worth, 2006—. Legal adviser Save Our Parks, Ft. Worth, 2006. Mem.: ACLU (sec. 2004—, legal com. 2006—, bd. dirs. Ft. Worth chpt., legal panel chair 2006—). Office: Cagle & Broilas 100 N Forest Park Fort Worth TX 76102

CAGLE, MARGARET BROUGHTON, retired parochial school educator; b. Bay Minette, Ala., Mar. 7, 1941; d. Charles Edward and Alberta (Davis) Broughton; m. James Malcolm Cagle, Aug. 13, 1960 (dec. Sept. 1999); children: David Marshall, Darlene Marsha. Student, Bob Jones U., Greenville, S.C., 1959—60; AA, Pensacola Jr. Coll., Fla., 1966; BA in History, U. W. Fla., 1970. Tchr. George Stone Vo-Tech Sch., Pensacola, 1970—72, Daytona Beach (Fla.) Christian Sch., 1972—74, Trinity Christian Acad., Jacksonville, Fla., 1974—90, Heritage Christian Acad., Orange Park, Fla., 1990—2000; ret., 2002. Editor newsletter, head aerospace edn. Civil Air Patrol, Jacksonville, 1980—83. Baptist. Avocations: reading, writing, sewing, singing. Home: 11200 Ramhall Rd Jacksonville FL 32219

CAGLE, MELINDA REEVES, editor; d. Harry Tillman Reeves and Lillie Mae Dunn; m. Carrol Dean Cagle, June 2, 1968; children: Jeffrey, Thomas, Andrew, David, Sarah, Caroline, Anne, John. Student, Tex. Tech. U., 1967—68; BFA, U. Houston, 1975; postgrad., No. Ill. U., 1976—77. Mem. history coun. Bapt. Gen. Conv. Tex., Dallas, 2003—05. Editor: (history jour.) The Herald, 2003—. Historian, ch. coun. First Bapt. Ch., Woodlands, Tex., 1998—. Mem.: Jr. League Houston, Inc. (chmn. The Goldfarb Project 1988—90), Montgomery County Geneal. and Hist. Soc. (bd. mem. 2000—, Vol. of Yr. 2003). Avocations: piano, painting, genealogy. Home: 18 W Shaker Ct The Woodlands TX 77380

CAHALAN, AMY K., secondary school educator; d. Terry Allen and Judith Lynn Postmus; m. Gregg S. Cahalan, Aug. 20, 1994; 1 child, Johnathon; children: Caley McNamara, Megan McNamara. BA, Mich. State U., East Lansing, 1987; MA, Grand Valley State U., Allendale, Mich., 1994. Tchr. Lansing (Mich.) Pub. Schs., 1987—88, Grand Haven (Mich.) Area Pub. Schs., 1988—, mentor tchr. coord. and trainer, 2000—. Pathwise mentor trainer of trainers Edn. Testing Svcs., Phila., 2000—. Mem.: Mich. Sci. Tchrs. Assn., Grand Haven Edn. Assn. (v.p. 2004—06, pres. 2006—). Avocations: reading, gardening. Office: Grand Haven Area Pub Schs 900 S Cutler Grand Haven MI 49417

CAHAN, CORA, not-for-profit developer; m. Bernard Gersten. Dancer; co-founder, exec. dir. The Feld Ballet, N.Y.C.; co-founder, v.p. Joyce Theater, N.Y.C., 1979—98; pres., dir. The New 42nd St., Inc., N.Y.C., 1990—. Trustee emeritus Joyce Theatre. Recipient All-Star 2001 award, Crain's N.Y. Bus. mag., Ernie award, Dance/USA, 2002. Office: The New 42nd St Inc 10th Fl 229 West 42nd St New York NY 10036-7299

CAHILL, CATHERINE FRANCES, environmental scientist, educator; b. Woodland, Calif., July 30, 1968; d. Thomas Andrew and Virginia Arnoldy Cahill. BS in Applied Physics, U. Calif., 1990; MS in Atmospheric Scis., U. Wash., 1994; PhD in Atmospheric Scis., U. Nev., 1996. Fulbright fellow Univ. Coll. Galway, Ireland, 1996—97; vis. asst. rsch. prof. Desert Rsch. Inst., Reno, 1997—98; prof. U. Alaska, Fairbanks, 1998—. Program chair for atmospheric sci. program U. Alaska Fairbanks, Alaska, 2000—01. Contbr. articles pub. to profl. jour. Mem. U.S. China Polar Sci. Panel. Fellow Fulbright Fellowship, Coun. for the Internat. Exch. of Students, 1996-1997. Mem.: Am. Assn. Aerosol Rsch., Am. Geophys. Union, Am. Chem. Soc. (chair alaska sect. 2000—01), Sigma Pi Sigma, Sigma Xi. Democrat-Npl. Achievements include research in long-range transport of aerosols to the Arctic. Avocations: travel, reading. Office: Univ Alaska Fairbanks 900 Yukon Dr Rm 182 Fairbanks AK 99775 Office Phone: 907-474-6905. Office Fax: 907-474-5640. Business E-Mail: ffcfc@uaf.edu.

CAHILL, CATHERINE M., orchestra executive; m. William Bernhard. Gen. mgr. NY Philharmonic, NYC, 1994-98; exec. dir. Toronto Symphony, Canada, 1998—99; exec. dir. cancer rsch. fund Damon Runyon-Walter Winchell Found., NYC, 1999—2001; CEO Bklyn. Philharmonic Orch., 2001—. Office: Bklyn Philharmonic Orch 138A Court St Brooklyn NY 11201 Office Phone: 718-488-5902.

CAHILL, EILEEN MARY, secondary school educator; b. Norwich, N.Y., Nov. 3, 1950; d. Kevin Tracey and Martha Sue (Eckard) C. BA, D'Youville Coll., Buffalo, 1972; MA, U. Toronto, 1974; PhD, SUNY, Buffalo, 1987. Cert. tchr., N.Y. English tchr. North Collins (N.Y.) Ctrl. Sch., 1972-85; curator of lit. Rosenbach Mus. and Libr., Phila., 1988-89; instr. English Temple U., Phila., 1987-88, Bryn Mawr (Pa.) Coll., 1987-88; English tchr. Marlborough Sch., L.A., 1989-96; dir. studies Salem Acad., Winston-Salem, N.C., 1998—. Mem. Stanford (Calif.) Ctr. for Rsch. on Women, 1990-94. Author articles. Coun. for Basic Edn. Nat. fellow for ind. study in humanities, 1993. Mem. MLA, Am. Conf. for Irish Studies, Irish Am. Cultural Inst. Democrat. Avocations: writing, travel, photography. Home: 7825 Fair Oaks Dr Clemmons NC 27012-8407 Office: Salem Acad 500 E Salem Ave Winston Salem NC 27101-5386 Office Phone: 336-917-5506.

CAHILL, VERNA ELEANORE, writer; b. Nashua, N.H., Mar. 20, 1916; d. Edward Nazairre Dufault; m. Albert Pressey, Aug. 1936 (div. Oct. 1958); m. George Cahill (dec. Sept. 15, 1983). Student, Holy Cross Coll., 1973—79, U. N.H., 1958—60. Asst. editor Ins. mag., 1961—70. Editor: (poetry column) Sunday Union Leader; contbr. articles to numerous mags. and anthologies;

author: But To The Hungray Soul Grant from Mass, 1985; host Edit, Talk Show, 1986. Mem.: Poetry Soc. N.H. (v.p., rec. sec., editor soc. publ., historian, bd. dirs., pres. 1964—). Avocations: interior decorating, landscaping, classical music.

CAHILLY, KAREN L., quality assurance professional; b. Phila., Oct. 23, 1952; d. Frances Bedford and June Marilyn (Thompson) Beddall; m. Donald Hullings Cahilly II, June 21, 1975; children: Carolyn Anne, Melanie Susan. BSN cum laude, U. Del., 1976. Cert. Bd. Cert. Am. Bd. Quality Assurance Utilization Review Physicians, 1999; RN Tex. Case mgr. St. Luke's Episc. Hosp., 1995—97, med. staff quality mgr., 1997—. Developed Quality Assurance Tool analyzing infection rates of exit sites, incidence of peritonitis, incidence of catheter replacement. Served as community resource. Fellow: Am. Inst. Healthcare Quality; mem.: Nat. Assn. Healthcare Quality, Tex. Assn. for Health care Quality, Gulf Coast Assn. for Healthcare Quality. Home: 335 Swords Bnd Stafford TX 77477-6251 Office Phone: 832-355-2926. E-mail: kcahilly@sleh.com.

CAHINHINAN, NELIA AGBADA, retired public health nurse, health facility administrator; b. Laguna, Philippines, Sept. 20, 1939; d. Manuel Navarro and Milagros Agbay (Adea) Agbada; m. Rodolfo DeGuia Cahinhinan, Jan. 29, 1967; children: Rodney Paul, Roel James, Renee Ann, Nelie Rose. Diploma, U. Philippines, 1961; BSN, U. Guam, 1985. RN; cert. in nursing adminstrn. Pub. health nurse Dept. Health, Laguna, 1962-67, Dept. Pub. Health and Social Svc., Agana, Guam, 1967-73; pub. health nurse supr., home care Dept. PHSS, Mangilao, Guam, 1974-82; cmty. health nurse supr. Regional Pub. Health Ctr., Dept. PHSS, Tamuning, Guam, 1982-86; nursing and program supr. maternal child health Family Planning Program, Dept. PHSS, Mangilao, 1986-89; asst. nursing adminstr. Bur. Family Health and Nursing Svcs., Dept. PHSS, Mangilao, 1990-94. Mem. adv. coun. Coll. Nursing, U. Guam, Mangilao, 1994-95; mem. nursing asst. program adv. coun. Guam C.C., Mangilao, 1995-96; mem. profl. adv. bd. Clarke Home Nursing Svc., Tamuhning, 1995-97. Bd. dirs. Am. Cancer Soc., Agana, 1976—78; mem., sec., chair nursing and health svcs. com. ARC, 1980—83; chair membership com. So. Tagalog Assn., 1980—2006. Recipient Centennial Leadership award Nat. League of Nursing, 1993, Outstanding Woman of Yr. award Govt. of Guam, 1996; named Guam Top Ten Suprs., Gov. of Guam, 1990. Mem.: Laguna Assn. Guam (pres. 2000—01, advisor 2002—06), Cath. Daus. of Ams. (treas. 1999—2001, 2006—), Guam Meml. Hosp. Vol. Assn. (dir.-at-large 1999—2002), Guam Nurses Assn. (treas., dir. 1980, pres. 1994—95, vol. mems. hosp. 1999—2006, Svc. award 1983, Guam Nurse of Yr. 1985, Most Disting. Mem. award 1996), U. Philippines Alumni Assn. (pres. 1991—93, advisor 1994—2006, treas., dir., Outstanding Svc. award 1993, Oblation award Outstanding Alumni and Cmty. Svc. 2005). Roman Catholic. Avocations: decorating, gardening, flower arrangement. Home: PO Box 11234 Tamuning GU 96931-1234

CAHOON, SUSAN ALICE, lawyer; b. Jacksonville, Fla., Oct. 14, 1948; d. Robert Harold and Alice (Dubberly) C. BA in History, Econs. summa cum laude, Emory U., 1968; JD cum laude, Harvard U., 1971. Bar: Ga. 1971, US Dist. Ct. (no. dist.) Ga. 1971, US Dist. Ct. (no. & ea. dists.) Tex. 1977, US Dist. Ct. (mid. dist.) Ga. 1978, US Dist. Ct. (we. dist.) Wis. 1979, US Supreme Ct. 1979, US Ct. Appeals (4th cir.) 1980, US Dist. Ct. (so. dist.) Ga. 1981, U.S. Ct. Appeals (5th, 11th & D.C. cirs.) 1981, US Ct. Appeals (6th cir.) 1983. Assoc. Kilpatrick & Cody, Atlanta, 1971-76, ptnr., 1977—97; ptnr., chair Litig. Practice Kilpatrick Stockton LLP, Atlanta, 1997—, mem. exec. com. Contbr. articles to law revs., chpts. to books. Chmn. Stone Mountain Park Authority, Atlanta, 1984-93; v.p. Fulton County Divsn. Am. Heart Assn., Atlanta, 1992-93, pres., 1993-95; v.p. USO Coun. Ga., Inc., Atlanta, 1992—; bd. dirs. Atlanta Conv. & Visitors Bur., 1992—, vice chmn. 1996, Metro Atlanta Crime Commn., 1990-92, Fed. Defender PRogram, 1987-92; pres. Atlanta Area Alumni Club, 1975; mem. Leadership Atlanta, 1982, LeadershipGa., 1989. Fellow Am. Coll. Trial Lawyers, Am. Bar Found., Ga. Bar Found.; mem. ABA (litigation sect. com. chair 1986-88, com. chair 1995—), Ga. Bar Assn. (com. chair 1980-81), Atlanta Bar Assn. (bd. dirs. 1981-87, Leadership award 1991), D.C. Bar Assn., Am. Law Inst., Phi Beta Kappa, Omicron Delta Kappa, Lumpkin Inns of Ct. (master bencher). Baptist. Avocations: travel, piano. Office: Kilpatrick Stockton LLP Ste 2800 1100 Peachtree St NE Atlanta GA 30309-4530 Office Phone: 404-815-6325. Office Fax: 404-541-3145. E-mail: SCahoon@KilpatrickStockton.com.

CAHOUET, ANN P., lawyer; b. Annapolis, Md., Sept. 7, 1957; BA in comparative lit., Scripps Coll., 1980; JD, U. Pitts., 1991. Bar: Pa. 1991. Positions in book pub. and advt.; joined Reed Smith LLP, Pitts., 1991, named dir. pro bono and cmty. svc., 1996, now dir. cmty. support. Mentor Career Literacy for African Am. Youth program, Duquesne U. Recipient Children's Voice Award, Allegheny County Ct. Apptd. Spl. Advocates, 2002, Caritas Award for Pub. Svc., Cath. Charities of Pitts., 2003. Mem.: Allegheny County Bar Assn. (mem. adoption com.), Pa. Bar Assn., ABA. Office: Reed Smith LLP 435 Sixth Ave Pittsburgh PA 15219 Office Phone: 412-288-4198. Office Fax: 412-288-3063. Business E-Mail: acahouet@reedsmith.com.

CAI, MING ZHI, chemist, researcher, film producer; b. Changsha, China, Feb. 22, 1935; arrived in U.S., 1986; d. Xian Cai and Xian Jiao Du; m. Jing Yi Jin, Apr. 18, 1958; children: Ge Jin, Jun Jin. BS with hons. in Chemistry, Wu Han U., 1957. Tchr. polymer sci. U. Sci. and Tech. China, 1958—73; tchr. Raman spectroscopy Ctr. Instrumental Analysis Tsing Hua U., 1973—86; surface rschr. enhanced Raman spectroscopy UCLA, 1991—93. Rschr. Micro-Raman spectroscopy Sch. Chemistry Ga. Inst. Tech., Atlanta, 1986—89, rschr. Ultra Violet resonance Raman spectroscopy dept. chemistry, 1989—90. Prodr.: (video series for TV stas.) Local Conditions and Customs of America, 1998—; (films, TV stas.) The Stories of Chinese Americans, 2001—; (documentaries) Teacher of Ballet, 2003, Gymnastic Coaches, 2003, Mongolia Doctor in LA, 2003, World Basketball Invitational Tournament for Chinese, 2003, Joys of Spring, 2004, Paradise on the Sea, 2004, The Coast Cities of Mexico, 2004, I Love You China, 2004, Kentucky Derby, 2004, Magical Photographer, 2004, At Xmas Eve, 2004, Antique Cars, 2004, The Tournament of Roses Parade, 2005, Celebrate Lunar New Year, 2005, One Hundred Years of Las Vegas, 2005, Entrepreneur, 2006, Chinese Folk Dance, 2006, National Date Festival, 2006, Air Show, 2006, Hundred Years City - Whittier, 2006, Walk to L.A., 2006, Mission San Juan Capistrano, 2006, others, sci. and edn. films, —. Mem.: Internat. Artist Photographer Soc., Assn. Rsch. Vision and Opthalmology, Microbeam Analysis Soc., Internat. Soc. Eye Rsch., Sci. and Tech. Soc. China, Instrumental Measurement Soc. China, Chem. Soc. China, Nat. Mus. Women in Arts. Avocations: painting, photo design, film editing, travel, organic agriculture. Personal E-mail: mingzhicai@yahoo.com.

CAIN, COLEEN W., writer, educator; b. Birmingham, Iowa, Sept. 2, 1916; d. Marida Irwin Cain and Effie Levina Walters; m. James Cazort McClurkin, Feb. 5, 1937 (dec. Jan. 1938); m. James Robert Cazort, Dec. 24, 1942 (div. Oct. 1970); 1 child, Sidney Cain; m. Eugene Everett Bauer, Nov. 3, 1974 (div. Feb. 1983). BA in Journalism, U. Ark., 1938. Cert. real estate agt. Wash., 1946, Ark., 1948. Tech. writer Manpower, Inc., Huntsville, Ala., 1966—69; editor, arts reviews Huntsville Times, 1969—70; fgn. news corr. Beijing PRC Jour. Am., Bellevue, Wash., 1980—83; instr. Beijing Fgn. Langs. Inst., 1981—83; lectr. Continuing Edn. Bellevue & South Seattle C.C., 1983—88; pres., owner Cain-Lockhart Press, Issaquah, Wash., 1985; instr. Issaquah Cmty. Ctr., 1996, North Bellevue Cmty. Sr. Ctr., 1997—2006; pres., owner Grazel-Pierce Pubs., 2004. Spkr. in field. Author: 115 Jet Stories for Your Briefcase, 2001, 2d edit., 2003, Beth Bauer's Enjoy China More, 1985, Wild Blue, 1st of WWII Series, 2002, 2d edit., 2005, Glory After the War, 2d of WWII Series, 2005; editor: All At Once, 3d of WWII Trilogy, 2006. Singer Seattle Symphony Chorale, New Orleans Opera Soc., Cascadian Chorale, Huntsville Cmty. Chorus; mem. 41st dist. Democrats, Bellevue, 1972; alt. del. King County Democrats, Seattle, 1992; election judge Westlake Precinct, Issaquah, 1991—98; mezzo soloist in choirs, chorales. Recipient cert. of excellence, City of Bellevue Parks and Cmty. Svcs. Dept., 2001. Mem.: Seattle Free Lances (treas. 1997—98, adviser 2001), Pacific Northwest Writers Assn. (critique editor 1995—99, 3rd place nonfiction award 1976). Democrat. Presbyterian. Avocation: music. Home: 19510 S E 51st St Issaquah WA 98027-9327 Personal E-mail: cwcain@peoplepc.com.

CAIN, JUDITH SHARP, mathematics professor, consultant; d. Sturdy O. and Erna E. Sharp; children: Jason Charles, Crystal Heather, Jeffrey Ronald. MEd, U. La., Lafayette, 1989. Cert. tchr. 1-8, secondary math., mid. sch. math. La., supr. of instrn. La., adminstr. La., nat. bd. cert. EA/math tchr. 2005. Estimator Sellers, Dubroc & Assoc., Inc., Civil Engrs., Lafayette, La., 1972—81; tchr. mid. sch. math. Lafayette Parish Sch. Bd., Cathedral Carmel Sch., 1986—97; lead tchr., mid. sch. math. Lafayette Parish Sch. Bd., 1999—, presenter workshops and inservices, 1997—. Math. workshop cons./tchr. trainer various sch. districts, La., 1999—; mem. com. grade level expectations and textbook adoption, intern rev. LEAP range finding, iLEAP rev. com., LAA2 com., LEAP item rev. com. La. Dept. Edn., 2003—; adj. instr. U. La., Lafayette, 2004—. Author: An Evaluation of the Connected Math. Project. Active St. Anne's Cath. Ch., Youngsville, La. Named Outstanding Tchr., Diocese of Lafayette, 1993—94, Tchr. of Yr., Lafayette Parish, 2000. Mem.: NEA, ASCD, Nat. Coun. Suprs. Math., La. Tchrs. Math., Nat. Coun. Tchrs. Math. Office: Lafayette Parish Sch Bd PO Drawer 2158 Lafayette LA 70502 Office Phone: 337-501-7452. Personal E-mail: cain.judy@gmail.com.

CAIN, KAREN MIRINDA, musician, educator; b. Anna, Ill., Feb. 25, 1944; d. James Paul and Margaret Camilla (Sinks) C. MusB, So. Ill. U., 1966, MusM in Voice and Choral Conducting, 1967; postgrad., Trinity Coll., Washington, 1985. Cert. music tchr., Md. Choral music tchr., Prince George's County, Md., 1969-71; music tchr. class piano Montgomery County, Md., 1972-89; music tchr., founder of studio Rockville, Md., 1972—; co-founder, dir., arranger, profl. madrigal ensemble The Renaissance Revelers, 1985—. Choral music dir. and soloist various chs. and synagogues, Rockville, 1972-92; soprano soloist, sect. leader Grace Luth. Ch., Washington, 2000—; singer Paul Hill Chorale, Washington, 1982-90, mem. chorale staff, music theory instr., 1984-90; contbr. minstrel and history guilds, performer, mem., Md. Renaissance Festival, 1987—. Dir., editor: (CD) Renaissance Romance, 1994 (CD) Journey into Light, 2002; arranger choral works featured on Renaissance Romance, Journey Into Light; dir.: performances at The Lutheran Reformation Svc. held at The Washington Nat. Cathedral, 1995, The White House, Kennedy Ctr.; co-author (with John Sinks): Sinks: A Family History, 1980. Mem. AAUW, Md. Music Tchrs. Assn., Montgomery County Class Piano Tchrs. Assn., Mu Phi Epsilon. Home and Office: 862 College Pkwy # T-1 Rockville MD 20850-1938

CAIN, LINDA JOANNE, academic administrator; b. Oakland, Calif., Aug. 5, 1943; d. John Gunnar and Virginia Helen (Johnson) Lyle; m. Mark E. Cain, Mar. 15, 1985. A.B. in History, U. Calif., Berkeley, 1965; A.M.L.S., U. Mich., 1967. Supr. microform reading room, periodicals reading room, interlibrary loan unit at grad. libr. U. Mich., 1967-69, U. Calif., Berkeley, 1969-78, reference, coll. devel. librarian Moffitt Undergrad. Libr., 1969-72, coord. pub. svcs. Moffitt Undergrad. Library, 1972-75, adminstrv. asst. to assoc. univ. librarian for pub. svcs., 1977-78, instr. bibliography I, 1971, 74-75; head librarian reference svcs., acting asst. dir. pub. svcs. U. Tex., Austin, 1978-80, assoc. dir. pub. svcs., 1980-84, assoc. dir., 1984-87; dean and libr. U. Cin., 1987-90, assoc. provost, 1990—2004, orientation to learning instr., 2003-04; Mem. editl. bd. Jour. Acad. Librarianship, 1980-88; contbr. articles to profl. jours. Council Libr. Resources acad. library mgmt. intern, 1975-76. UCLA sr. fellow, 1985. Mem. ALA, ALAO, AHE, Educause. Office: U Cin Adminstrn PO Box 210097 Cincinnati OH 45221-0097 Business E-Mail: linda.cain@uc.edu.

CAIN, WANDA NEIL, secondary school educator; b. Palmer, Tex., Nov. 13, 1929; d. Johnnie Q. and Juanita I. Schwartz; m. Benton W. Cain, Mar. 30, 1956; 1 child, Candace A. Ahlfinger. EdM, U. NT and Howard Payne U., Denton and Brownwood Tex., 1962. Cert. tchr. and mid-mgmt. Tex., 1950. English tchr. Melvin H.S., Tex., 1960—68; English tchr., asst. prin. Waxahachie H.S., Tex., 1968—2006. Adj. prof. Southwestern Assembly of God U. Tchr. First Bapt. Ch., Waxahachie, 1968—2006. Recipient Tchr. of Year award, Waxahachie HS. Mem.: Assn. Tex. Profl. Educator. Office Phone: 214-236-5253. Business E-Mail: wcain@sagu.edu.

CAINE, EDYE, social studies educator; b. Houston, Tex., Apr. 13, 1961; d. Robert E. and Sunny W. Caine; children: Laura, Mark. MA in Elem. Edn., Mercy Coll., 1998; MA in Edn. Adminstrn. and Supervision, Fordham U., 2005. Spl. edn. tchr. Brewster H.S., 1998—99; social studies tchr., dept. chair Yorktown CSD, NY, 1999—2002; social studies supr. Eastchester UFSD, Eastchester, NY, 2002—. Presenter in field. Mem.: ASCD, Nat. Coun. for Social Studies. Democrat. Office: Eastchester UFSD 2 Stewart Pl Eastchester NY 10709

CAINE, VIRGINIA A., city health department administrator; BS, Gustavus Adolphus Coll., Minn., 1973; MD, N.Y. Upstate Med. Ctr., Syracuse. Resident U. Cin.; resident, infectious diseases U. Wash., Seattle; assoc. prof., medicine Ind. U. Sch. Medicine; dir. Marion Co. Health Dept., Indpls., 1993—. Mem., com. credentialing for pub. health workforce CDC, mem., bioterrorism and emergency preparedness com. Co-dir. Indpls. Campaign for Healthy Babies Initiative; bd. mem. Damien AIDS Ctr.; bd. mem., substance abuse Fairbanks Hosp.; bd. mem. Ind. AIDS Fund, Indpls. Alliance for Health Promotion, Ind. State Women's Health Com.; mem. Cmty. Drug Summit, Mayor's Commn. on Family Violence, City of Indpls. Mayor's Emergency Preparedness Task Force; mem. adv. bd. Women's Fund of Ctrl. Ind. Named one of Influential Women in Indpls., Indpls. Bus. Jour., The Ind. Lawyer; recipient Superstar award, Ind. AIDServe, 1998, Outstanding Svc. award, Indpls. Bus. Jour. Mem.: Ind. Pub. Health Assn., Nat. Med. Assn. (chair, infectious diseases, co-chair, AIDS sect., Internist of Yr. 1999), Nat. Assn. of County and City Health Officials, Am. Pub. Health Assn. (pres. 2004—, New Leadership award). Office: Marion Co Health Dept 3838 N Rural St Indianapolis IN 46205-2930*

CAINES, CHERYL LYNNE, supervisor; b. Phila., Pa., Apr. 4, 1958; d. William Edward and Vivian Joyce Bishop; m. H. Randolph Caines, June 5, 1993 (dec. July 2005). MA, Cabrini Coll., Radnor, Pa., 1993. Supervisory Pa., 2004. Dept. chair Allentown Sch. Dist., Allentown, Pa., 1997—2005; secondary supr. of spl. edn. Pleasant Valley Sch. Dist., Brodheadsville, Pa., 2002—. Ednl. cons. Children's Guidance Ctr., East Stroudsburg, Pa., 2001—04. Mem. African Am. Network, East Stroudsburg, Pa., 2003—04. Recipient Hilda Dolgin Outstanding Spl. Edn. Tchr. of the Yr., Phila. Sch. Dist., 1991. Mem.: Coun. of Exceptional Children, Kappa Gamma Pi. Bapt. Avocations: reading, travel. Office: Pleasant Valley Sch Dist 1 Sch Ln Rte 115 Brodheadsville PA 18322 Office Phone: 570-402-1000. Personal E-mail: ccaines@ptd.net. Business E-Mail: caines.cheryl@pvbears.org.

CAIRNS, ANNE MARIE, public relations executive; Pres. Cairns & Assocs., Inc., N.Y.C., 1982—.

CAIRNS, SARA ALBERTSON, retired physical education educator; b. Bloomsburg, Pa., July 18, 1939; d. Robert Wilson and Sara (Porter) Albertson; m. Thomas Cairns, Apr. 13, 1968. BS in Edn., Pa. State U., 1961; MS in Edn., West Chester U., 1965. Cert. tchr., Pa., Del., prin., Del.; adaptive p.e. specialist. Phys. edn. tchr., coach Cen. Columbia County High Sch., Bloomsburg, Pa., 1961-64; phys. edn. tchr. Christina Sch. Dist., Newark, Del., 1964—2006, coord. adult edn., 1998—2006; ret., 2006. Cons. U. Del., Newark, 1984—, coop. tchr., 1965—; area coord. New Castle (Del.) County Parks and Recreation, 1973—; presenter in field. Contbr. articles to profl. publs. Chair Leasure Elem. Sch. campaign United Fund, 1987-91. Recipient Outstanding Svc. award New Castle County Parks and Recreation, 1985, Svc. award, New Castle County, 2005; named Adaptive Phys. Edn. Tchr. of Yr., State of Del., 2005 Mem. NEA, AAUW, AAHPERD, Del. Assn. Health, Phys. Edn., Recreation and Dance (v.p. dance 1991-94, exec. bd.), Del. State Edn. Assn. Democrat. Presbyterian. Avocations: toy poodles, beach, walking. Home: 40 Vansant Rd Newark DE 19711-4839

CAJIAO SALAS, TERESA, language educator, educator; b. Iquique, Chile, May 16, 1927; came to U.S., 1963, naturalized, 1972; d. Ramon G. and Donatila L. (Amaya) C.; m. Alberto J. Salas, Nov. 27, 1952; children: Alberto J., Arturo C. Primary edn. degree, Escuela Normal Superior, Santiago, 1954; Profesora de Estado, Tech. U. Chile, 1957; M.Ed. (Fulbright fellow 1959-60), Kent State U., Ohio, 1960; MA, Western Res. U., 1965; PhD, Case Western Res. U., 1969. Tchr. Tech. U. Chile, 1948-63; instr. Kent State U., 1963-65; mem. faculty SUNY Coll. at Buffalo, 1965—, prof. Spanish, 1971—; dir. SUNY summer program U Salamanca, Spain, 1982, 84, 86, 88. Instr. Peace Corps tng. program U. Notre Dame, summers 1963, 64; dir. jr. semester abroad program U. Costa Rica, 1970; hon. consul of Chile in Buffalo, 1966-72 Author: Temas y símbolos en la obra de Luís Alberto Heiremans, 1969, El teatro de hoy en Costa Rica, 1973, Asedios a la poesía de Nicomedes Santa Cruz, 1982; also articles. Summer research grantee SUNY, Buffalo, 1980 Mem. MLA, Am. Assn. Tchrs. Spanish and Portuguese, Comparative Edn. Soc., Latin Am. Studies Assn., Sigma Delta Pi. Office: SUNY Dept Fgn Langs 1300 Elmwood Ave Dept Fgn Buffalo NY 14222-1004

CALABRESE, ELEANOR WALLACE, social worker; b. Rockville Centre, N.Y., Feb. 1, 1950; d. William Howard and Eleanor E. (DeBaun) Wallace; m. Alphonse F.X. Calabrese, July 13, 1980; children: William, Paul. BA, Molloy Coll., 1972; MSW, Adelphi U., 1979. Cert. Am. Bd. Examiners in Clin. Social Work. Clin. social worker Christian Inst. for Psychotherapy, Hicksville, NY, 1979—83; pvt. practice Ludlow, Vt., 1983—92; clin. social worker Vt. Cath. Charities, Rutland, 1992—. Pres. Black River Good Neighbor Svc., Ludlow, 1989-91; mem. parish coun. Holy Trinity Orthodox Ch., Springfield, Vt., 1999— Mem. NASW (diplomate clin. social work), Vt. Coalition Residential Programs Home: 73 Godfrey Rd Ludlow VT 05149-9509 Office: Vermont Catholic Charities 24 1/2 Center St Rutland VT 05701-4041

CALABRESE, KAREN ANN, artist, educator; b. NYC, May 27, 1952; d. Daniel Alexander and Janet Russell (Anderson) McKnight; m. Joseph Salvatore Calabrese, Apr. 27, 1974; children: Joseph S. Jr., Brian Patrick. Art cert., Ridgewood Sch. Art, 1973. Paste-up artist, designer Ridge Type Svc., Ridgewood, NJ, 1973—77; artist, prodn. mgr. Ea. Art, Garfield, NJ, 1977—81; various jobs, freelance artist, 1981—; art tchr. Highland Lakes, NJ, 1995—2002, Phoenix Sch. Art, Vernon, NJ, 1998—2005; pvt. art tchr., 2005—. Exhibited in group shows at Highland Lakes Country Club, 1994, 1995, 1999—2001 (1st Pl. award, 1995, Hon. mention, 1999, 2000), Pub. Gallery, 1995, 1998—2001, (Juried Show award), Lake Mohawk Country Club, Sparta, N.J., 1995 (Juried Show award), Skylands Assn., Ringwood, N.J., 1997 (Juried Show award), Drue Chryst Gallery, Sparta, N.J., 1999, Perona Farms, Andover, N.J., 1999, Sussex County C.C., 2001— (Juried Show award), Sussex-Warren Winter Show, Oxford, NJ, 2002—, exhibitions include Flying Pig Gallery, Sussex, NJ, 1999—, Ringwood Manor Assn. Arts, 2004 (1st Pl. award drawing, 2004). Recipient 1st Pl. award, Decorative Artist's Workbook Mag., 1998, 3d Pl. award, 22d Ann. Warwick Valley Telephone Directory Cover Competition. Avocations: photography, hiking, hunting, fishing, physical fitness.

CALABRESE, MARGARET HOYE, secondary school educator; b. Dallas, Oct. 13, 1959; m. John Anthony Calabrese; children: Timothy James Mathis, Emily Kathryn Mathis. BA, Tex. Woman's U., Denton, 1979—84. Cert. Secondary Tchr. Tex. Dept. Edn., 1982. Tchr. Apollo, Richardson, Tex., 1993—2002, Ryan HS, Denton, 2002—. Recipient Tchr. of Month, Ryan Renaissance, 2005. Home: 2525 Hillview Ct Denton TX 76209 Office: Ryan HS 5101 E McKinney Denton TX 76209 Office Phone: 940-369-3000.

CALABRESE, ROSALIE SUE, management consultant, writer; b. NYC, Feb. 17, 1938; d. Julius and Florence (Tuck) Hochman; m. Anthony J. Calabrese, June 15, 1960 (div.); 1 child, Christopher. BA in Journalism, CCNY, 1959. Asst. news editor Electronic News, N.Y.C., 1960; asst. to publicist Abner Klipstein, N.Y.C., 1963; asst. to producer Leonard Field, N.Y.C., 1964; mgr. Am. Composers Alliance, N.Y.C., 1969-85, exec. dir., gen. mgr., 1985-94; dir. Rosalie Calabrese Mgmt., N.Y.C., 1983—. Music advisor Phyllis Rose Dance Co., NYC, 1987—, also bd. dirs.; sec. bd. dirs. Am. Composers Orch., NYC, 1987-93; pres., bd. dirs. 1st Ave. Ensemble, 1993—, Golden Fleece Ltd., 1994—, sec. 1996-; bd. dirs. Friends Am. Composers, treas., 1991-94; adv. bd. Downtown Music Prodns., 1991—, Joan Miller's Dance Players, NYC, 1991-94, Copland House, 1996-97; mem. editl. adv. bd. New Music Connoisseur Mag., 2002-05; mem. music com., Estate Project for Artists with AIDS, 2001-03. Author, lyricist: (musicals) A Hell of An Angel, Simone, Not in Earnest, Murdering Macbeth, Pop Life, Does Anyone Here Speak Arabic?, Friends and Relations, Double-Play, C-R; assoc. prodr., treas. box office: (play) Courtyard, 1959, The Mime and Me; co-prodr.: various plays at White Lake (N.Y.) Playhouse, also packaged tours for Prodn. Assocs.; dir. The Bagel Baker's Daughter, 1999, night club acts for Florence Hayle; contbr. short stories and poetry to lit., nat. mags. and anthologies. Mem.: Poetry Soc. Am., Poets and Writers, Broadcast Music Inc., Dramatists Guild. Office: Rosalie Calabrese Mgmt PO Box 20580 New York NY 10025-1521

CALABRO, JOANNA JOAN SONDRA, artist; b. Waterbury, Conn., Dec. 2, 1938; d. Theodore Gruwien and Madeleine Elizabeth (Raynor) Reinhard; m. John Paul Calabro, Oct. 15, 1960; 1 child, Victor Theodore. Student, Paier Sch. Art, 1965-66, Mus. of Fine Arts Sch., 1976, Rice U., 1977; student of sculpture with, Bruno Lucchesi, Pietrasanta, Italy, 1982. Art instr. at gallery workshops, Houston, 1975-78; co-owner Archway Gallery, Houston, 1975-78, Fine Arts of Rockport, Mass., 1989—. One woman shows include Five Star Gallery, Houston, 1974-75, Roberts Gallery, Houston, 1977, Dayton (Ohio) Soc. of Painters, 1983, Wilmington (Ohio) Coll., 1983, Rockport Art Assn., 1989, 92; represented in permanent collections at Am. Embassy, Bratislava, Slovak Republic. Sculpture instr. for merit badge Sam Houston Area coun. Boy Scouts Am., Houston, 1978; juror for scholastic art shows, Tex., 1975, Ohio, 1982, numerous other art shows, Conn., Tex., Ohio, Mass., 1970—; mem. art coun. Bd. Selectmen, Rockport, 1994. Recipient numerous awards including 1st Place award Champions Art, 1974, Am. Pen & Brush Women, 1975, Conn. Classic Art, 1978, Martha Moore Meml. award, 1989, Richard Ricchia Meml. award, 1990, R.V. T. Steeves award, 1990, William N. Ryan award, 1991. Mem. Am. Artist Profl. League, Rockport Art Assn. (bd. dirs. 1992-93), Guild Boston Artists, The Copley Soc. of Boston, Am. Medallic Sculpture Assn., Federation Internat. de la Me'daille. Avocations: foreign travel, study of the arts. Home: 16011 Champion Dr Spring TX 77379-6706

CALAMAR, GLORIA, artist; b. NYC, Sept. 7, 1921; d. Louis B. and Dina (Cotter) Calamar; m. R.L. Redgate, Aug. 22, 1950 (div. 1972); children: Chris James, Steven Clay, Michael Cotter. Cert., Otis Art Inst., L.A., 1943; student, Art Students League, N.Y.C., 1944-45; BA in Art History, State Univ. Coll. N.Y. at New Paltz, 1970. Instr. art history and painting Orange County (N.Y.) Community Coll., 1964-69; instr. art history Mt. St. Mary Coll., Newburgh, NY, 1968-69; instr. painting Santa Barbara City Coll., 1975-80. Judge Hallmark Art Contest, N.Y., 1968; lectr. Woodstock (N.Y.) Sch. Art, 1994; color slide lectr. throughout world. Artist in water color, oil, pen and ink, 1946—; one woman shows include Georgetown U., 1974, Portland (Oreg.) C.C., 1973, Willamette U., 1972, U. Oreg., 1971-72, U. Calif. at Berkeley, 1969, Santa Barbara (Calif.) Mus. Art, 1950, Musée d'Art Moderne de la Ville de Paris, 1967, Galèrie de la Madeleine, Brussels, Belgium, 1964, Landau Gallery, Beverly Hills, Calif., 1953, Parnassus Sq., Woodstock, N.Y., 1978, Ibiza, Balearic Islands, Spain, 1978, Santorini, Greece, 1980, Beaux Arts Ctr., Tunis, Tunisia, 1981, Alkamal Gallery, Jerusalem, Israel, 1981, Jaisalmer, India, 1984, Women's Cmty. Bldg., Santa Barbara, 1986, Jewish Cmty. Ctr., San Francisco, 1986; group shows include Delgado Mus., New Orleans, 1950, San Francisco Art Assn., 1953, L.A. County Mus. Art, 1954, Bertrand Russell Centenary Invitational, London, 1972-73, Woodstock Art Assn., 1978, Faulkner Gallery Santa Barbara, 1992, 93; curated Santa Barbara Visual Artists League Exhbn., 1993, 94; book video Tar Pits Park Landmark Proposal, Portola Sycamore Tree Landmark Proposal, Carpinteria Airport Landmark Proposal, Juarez-Hosmer Adobe Landmark Proposal, Leaping Greyhound Bridge Landmark Proposal, Los Clavelitos Landmark Proposal,

Los Cruces Adobe Landmark Proposal, De la Cuesta Adobe Landmark Proposal; painted the facade of Wells Cathedral, 1999-00; producer video TV program; author: Traveling Artist, 1995; prodr. TV video series Traveling Artist; contbr. articles to publs; prodr. (video) The Traveling Artist, 1996—. Curator Visual Artists League Exhbn., Santa Barbara, 1992, 93, 94, 95; mem. Santa Barbara County Hist. Landmark Adv. Commn. Nat. Endowment for Arts grantee, 1980-81; recipient Calif. Gov.'s Historic Preservation award Santa Barbara County Hist. Landmark Adv. Commn., 1999. Mem. Woodstock (N.Y.) Art Assn. (life), Alumni Assn. Otis Art Inst. (L.A.), Art Students League N.Y. (life), Santa Barbara Visual Artists League.

CALAME, KATHRYN LEE, microbiologist, educator; b. Leavenworth, Kans., Apr. 23, 1940; d. Jay O. and Marjorie B.; m. Byron Edward Calame, June 9, 1962; children: Christine Lee, Jonathan David. BS, U. Mo., 1962; MS, George Washington U., 1965, PhD, 1975. Asst. prof. biol. chemisty UCLA, 1980-85, assoc. prof., 1985-88, prof., 1988; prof. microbiology Coll. Physicians and Surgeons Columbia U., N.Y.C., 1988—. Mem. sci. rev. bd. Howard Hughes Med. Inst., 2002—. Exec. editor: Nucleic Acids Rsch., 1992-98; mem. bd. rev. editors: Sci. Mag., 1988-2000; assoc. editor Jour. Clin. Investigation; contbr. articles to profl. jours. Trustee Leukemia Soc. Am., N.Y.C., 1992—2001, chair grant rev. com., 1992-96; mem. bd. sci. counselors Nat. Inst. Child Health and Devel., 1999—2004. Recipient Stohlman award Leukemia Soc. Am., 1989, Faculty Alumni award U. Mo., Columbia, 1996; disting. lecture in basic sci., Columbia Physicians and Surgeons, 1998. Fellow: AAAS, Am. Acad. Arts and Sci.; mem.: Am. Assn. Biochemistry and Molecular Biology (chair pub. com. 1992—93). Democrat. Avocations: cooking, gardening, reading, antiques. Office: Columbia U Dept Microbiology 701 W 168th St New York NY 10032-2704 Business E-Mail: klc1@columbia.edu.

CALDEIRA, CHARLENE A., lawyer; b. New Bedford, Mass., Jan. 31, 1971; BA in Psychology, cum laude, Bridgewater State U., 1994; JD cum laude, Suffolk U., 1998. Bar: Mass. 1998, US Dist. Ct. (Dist. Mass.) 2000, US Ct. Appeals (1st Cir.) 2000. Law clk. to Assoc. Justice Neil L. Lynch Supreme Judicial Ct., 1998, rsch. asst. to Assoc. Justice Joseph R. Nolan; assoc. Family and Probate Law Group Todd & Weld, LLP; assoc. Family and Probate Law, Criminal Law and Appellate Law Group Casner & Edwards LLP, Boston. Adj. prof. family law New England Sch. Law. Mem.: ABA, Mass. Bar Assn., Boston Bar Assn. Office: Casner & Edwards LLP 303 Congress St Boston MA 02210 Office Phone: 617-426-5900. Office Fax: 617-426-8810. E-mail: caldeira@casneredwards.com.*

CALDER, MARY ALBERTA, elementary education educator, consultant; b. Richford, Vt., Aug. 4, 1950; d. Glenn Wilfred and Mary Rosalind (Metz) C.; m. Ronald Joseph Simon, Dec. 19, 1990. BS in Edn., U. Vt., 1972, MEd, 1983. Tchr. Underhill (Vt.) Graded Sch., 1972-95. Math. instr. Ctr. for Innovation in Edn., Saratoga, Calif., 1985—; cons. in field, presenter in field. Contbr. articles to profl. jours. Recipient Outstanding Elem. Tchr. U. Vt., 1991, Presdl. award Excellence in Maths. and Sci. Tchg. NSF, 1992, 93. Mem. Nat. Edn. Assn., Coun. Presdl. Awardees in Math., Soc. Elem. Presdl. Awardees, Nat. Assn. Educators Young Children.

CALDERÓN, SILA MARIA, former governor; b. San Juan, Sept. 23, 1942; 3 children. B in Polit. Sci. with honors, Manhattanville Coll., degree (hon.); MPA, U. P.R.; degree (hon.), Boston U., New School U., Hunter Coll., Rutgers U., Manhattanville, Calif. Worked for Sec. of Labor; spl. asst. econ. devel. and labor for Gov. Hernández Colón, 1974; chief of staff Gov. Hernández Colón, 1985, sec. state, 1988; mayor City of San Juan, 1996—2000; gov. PR, San Juan, 2001—. Bd. dirs. Banco Popular P.R., P.R. Pub. Broadcasting Corp., Pueblo Supermarkets. Named Outstanding Woman of Yr., PR C. of C., 1975, 1985, 1987, Puerto Rican Products Assn., 1986, PR chpt. Am. Assn. Pub. Works, 1988; recipient Harvard Found. award, Golden Plate award, Acad. Achievement. Mem.: Sister Isolina Ferré Found. Achievements include becoming first woman elected to office of governor of Puerto Rico; spearheaded the Special Communities Project for disadvantaged residents of Puerto Rico. Office Phone: 787-753-8310.

CALDERONE, JEAN LESLIE, art educator, artist; b. Columbus, Ohio, Sept. 28, 1959; d. Thomas Leroy and Margaret Lyon Sixt; m. Paul Anthony Calderone, Oct. 3, 1956; children: Natalie Elizabeth, Lexy Katherine. BA in Art, U. Calif., Santa Barbara, 1983; MS in Edn., U. Dayton, Ohio, 1991. Instr. mid. sch. art Pickerington Local Schs., Ohio, 1988—. Avocations: artist, member in a dream study group. Office: Lakeview Junior High School 12445 Ault Rd Pickerington OH 43147 Office Phone: 614-830-2200. Personal E-mail: jcalart@yahoo.com. E-mail: jean_calderone@fc.pickerington.k12.oh.us.

CALDICOTT, HELEN, physician; b. Melbourne, Australia, Aug. 7, 1938; d. Philip and Mona (Coffey) Broinowski; m. William Caldicott; 3 children. MBBS, U. South Australia, 1962. Intern Royal Adelaide (Australia) Hosp., 1962-63; fellow in nutrition Children's Hosp. Med. Ctr., Boston, 1967-68; researcher Adelaide Children's Hosp., 1973-75; mem. faculty Harvard Med. Sch., 1975-80; pres. Physicians for Social Responsibility, 1978-83. Author: Nuclear Madness: What You Can Do!, 1979, Missile Envy: The Arms Race and Nuclear War, 1984. Fellow Royal Australian Coll. Physicians; mem. Women's Action for Nuclear Disarmament (founder).

CALDWELL, ALETHEA OTTI, health care systems executive; b. British Guyana, May 27, 1941; d. Charles Manoram BS, Pacific Union Coll., Angwin, Calif., 1961; MS, U. Calif.-Irvine, Orange, 1973. Asst. dir. to dir. Intercommunity Hosp., Covina, Calif., 1963-71; contracts officer Orange County, Santa Ana, Calif., 1972-73; assoc. hosp. adminstr. Cedars-Sinai Med. Ctr., L.A., 1974-77, assoc. adminstr., 1977-80; exec. assoc. dir. U. Calif.-Irvine Med. Ctr., Orange, 1980-84; CEO Univ. Med. Ctr., Tucson, 1984-87; pres., chief exec. officer Ancilla Systems Inc., Chgo., 1987-91; dir. Ariz. Dept. Health Svcs., Phoenix, 1991-94; former pres., COO Managed Health Network, Inc., L.A., 1994—. Heath care co. cons.; trustee Mercy Health System, 1988—; mem. health adv. com. Sch. Mgmt. Bringham Young U., 1988; bd. dirs. Health Alliance, 1988—; bd. dirs. Health Trust Inc., Nashville. Contbr. to profl. publs., newspapers Bd. dirs. Cath. Community Svcs., Tucson, 1984-85, United Way, Tucson, 1984-85; nat. bd. advisors U. Ariz. Coll. Bus. and Pub. Adminstrn.; bd. turstees mercy Health System, 1988—. Recipient Women in Business and Industry award YMCA, Orange County, Calif., 1983, Women on the Move award YMCA, Tucson, 1984; Yr. of Ariz. Women award Ariz. Press Women, 1985; named one of Top 25 Turnaround Execs., Healthweek. Fellow Am. Coll. Healthcare Execs.; mem. Health Insights (bd. dirs. 1984—), Health Alliance (bd. dirs. 1988—), U. Hosp. Consortium (bd. dirs. 1984-87), Coun. of Tech Hosps., Am. Hosp. Assn., Cath. Health Assn. (multi-instl. systems com. 1988-89). Avocation: dance. Office: Managed Health Network Po Box 14621 Lexington KY 40512-4621

CALDWELL, ANN WICKINS, academic administrator; b. Rochester, N.Y., Dec. 3, 1943; d. Ralph Everett and Constance Ann (McCoy) Wickins; m. Herbert Cline Caldwell, Sept. 17, 1966; children: Constance Haley Blacklow, Robert James. BA in English Lit., U. Mich., 1965. Reporter Democrat & Chronicle, Rochester, 1961-64; asst. to dean Harvard Grad. Sch. of Edn., Cambridge, Mass., 1965-70, editor alumni quarterly, 1968-71; freelance editor, writer Harvard U. and Radcliffe, Cambridge, 1971-73; assoc. sec. Philips Acad., Andover, Mass., 1973—80; v.p. for planning and resources Wheaton Coll., Norton, Mass., 1980-90; assoc. dir. Mus. Fine Arts, Boston, 1990—91; v.p. for devel. Brown U., Providence, 1991—97; pres. MGH Inst. Health Professions, Boston, 1997—. Chair bicentennial com. Newburyport, Mass., 1974—76; citizens adv. com. Pub. Sch., Newburyport, 1979—80; bd. dirs. Am. Laryngological Voice Rsch. & Edn. Found., 1999—2005; trustee Women's Edn. and Indsl. Union, Boston, 1988—91, John Hope Settlement Ho., Providence, 1997—, Jr. Achievement of Ea. Mass., 2004—05. Mem.: Am. Coun. Edn. (comm. status women in higher edn. 2005—, chair 2006—), Women in Devel. Boston (pres. 1984—86, founder), Coun. for Advancement and Support of Edn. (trustee, sec. dist. 1 1985—87, trustee, sec. nat. 1987—89), Boston Club, Chilton Club, Phi Delta Kappa. Avocations: sailing, skiing, travel, reading. Office: Charlestown Navy Yard 36 First Ave Boston MA 02129-4724 Office Phone: 617-726-8002. Business E-Mail: acaldwell@mghihp.edu.

CALDWELL, BETTYE MCDONALD, education educator, director; b. Smithville, Tex., Dec. 24, 1924; d. Thomas Milton and Juanita (Mayes) McDonald; m. Fred T. Caldwell, Jr., June 8, 1947 (dec. Apr. 2004); children: Paul Frederick, Elizabeth Lanier. BA, Baylor U., 1945; MA, U. Iowa, 1946; PhD, Washington U., St. Louis, 1951. Research assoc. Upstate Med. Ctr., Syracuse, N.Y., 1959-65; prof. edn. Syracuse U., 1965-69; prof. U. Ark., Little Rock, 1969-78, Disting. prof., 1978-93; prof. pediatrics U. Ark. Med. Sci., 1993—. Belding prof. Found. for Child Devel., 1987-88; bd. dirs. First Comml. Bank, Little Rock. Editor: Child Devel. Jour., 1968-72, Rev. Child Devel. Research, III, 1973, Infant Education, 1977; contbg. editor: Working Mother, 1984—. Bd. dirs. Ark. Advs., Little Rock, 1977-85; bd. dirs. Child Care Action Campaign, Ark. Early Childhood Commn. Recipient Woman of Yr. award Ladies Home Jour., 1976, Alumna of Yr. award Baylor U., 1980, Excellence award U. Ark., 1990, Disting. Svc. award Nat. Gov.'s Assn., 1990, Distinction award Ark. Profl. Women, 1991, Dolley Madison award for lifelong contbn. to devel. and well being of infants, 2001. Mem. Fellow Soc. Rsch. in Child Devel. (governing bd. 1977-81, Disting. Contbns. award 1993); mem. Nat. Assn. for Edn. Young Children (pres. 1982-84), Kappa Delta Pi (laureate chpt. 1977—). Democrat. Office: College of Education UALR 2801 S University Little Rock AR 72204 Home: 12780 Rivercrest Dr Little Rock AR 72212-1444 Business E-Mail: caldwellbettyem@uams.edu.

CALDWELL, CASSANDRA DENISE, education educator; d. Cassie Tucker and Dennis Napoleon Caldwell. BA, U. NC, Chapel Hill, 1993; MPA, NC Ctrl. U., Durham, 1998; PhD, Ohio State U., Columbus, 2005. Creative Traning Techniques NC State U., 1996, Continuous Quality Improvement NC State U., 1997, Human Subjects Research NIH, 2005, Life/Health Insurance Agent N.C. Dept. of Ins., 2000, Leadership Assessments Ctr. for Creative Leadership, 2001. Pres., ceo Caldwell and Assoc., Inc., Morrisville, NC, 1991—; 4-h youth devel. agt. NC State U., Raleigh, 1994—95, ext. asst., 1996—98; grad. rsch. assoc. Ohio State U., Columbus, 1998—2000; asst. prof. NC Ctrl. U., Durham, NC, 2003—. Founding mem. Next Generation of African-Am. Philanthropists, Durham, NC, 2004; bd. mem. Summit Ho. Raleigh, NC, 2005. Recipient Future Leader award, Am. Assn. for Higher Edn., 2000, Martin Luther King, Jr. Scholarship award, U. NC at Chapel Hill, 1992, Nat. Early Career award, Epsilon Sigma Phi, 1997; Grad. Rsch. assoc., Ohio State U., 1998. Mem.: U. NC at Chapel Hill Gen. Alumni Assn., Nat. Black M.B.A. Assn., Phi Beta Delta, Pi Alpha Alpha Nat. Hon. Soc. Missionary Baptist. Avocations: culinary arts, interior decorating, travel. Office Phone: 919-389-1549.

CALDWELL, COURTNEY LYNN, lawyer, real estate consultant; b. Washington, Mar. 5, 1948; d. Joseph Morton and Moselle (Smith) Caldwell. Attended, Duke Univ., 1966-68, U. Calif., Berkeley, 1967, 1968-69; BA, U. Calif., Santa Barbara, 1970, MA, 1975; JD (hon.), George Washington Univ., 1982. Bar: DC, Wash. 1986, Calif. 1989. Jud. clk. U.S. Ct. Appeals for 9th Cir., Seattle, 1982-83; assoc. Arnold and Porter, Washington, 1983-85, Perkins Coie, Seattle, 1985-88; dir. western ops. Edn. Real Estate Svc., Inc., Irvine, Calif., 1988-91, sr. v.p., 1991-98; ind. cons., Orange County, Calif., 1998—. Bd. dir. Univ. Town Ctr. Assn., 1994; bd. dir. Habitat for Humanity, Orange County, 1993-94, chair legal com., 1994. Named Nat. Law Ctr. Law Rev. scholar, 1981—82. Mem.: Calif. Bar Assn. Avocation: fgn. languages. Home and Office: 140 Cabrillo St 15 Costa Mesa CA 92627 Office Phone: 949-650-8170. Personal E-mail: clcaldwell@earthlink.net.

CALDWELL, ELEANOR, artist; b. Kansas City, Mo., May 1, 1927; d. Earl Kendrick and Etta (Clark) Caldwell. BS in Edn., Soutwest Mo. State U., 1948; MA, Columbia U. Tchrs. Coll., 1953, EdD, 1959. Tchr. art h.s. in Mo. and Iowa, 1948—52; instr. art Southwest Mo. State U., 1953—54; asst. prof. Ft. Hays State U., Kans., 1954—57; instr. Columbia U. Tchrs. Coll., N.Y.C., 1957—59; prof., chmn. art dept. N.W Mo. State Coll., Maryville, 1959—60; assoc. prof. Edinboro State Coll., Pa., 1960—62, Pa. State U., Collegeville, 1962—63, No. Ill. U., De Kalb, 1963—64, Fort Hays State U., Kans., 1964—67; prof. art No. Ill. U., De Kalb, 1967—83, prof. emeritus, 1983—. Supr. children's art carnival Mus. Modern Art, 1957—59; lectr. art edn. Queens Coll., Bklyn., 1957—59; dir. Oakbrook Inviational Craftes Exhbn., 1968—84; consulting tchr. Arrowmont Sch. Arts and Crafts, Gatlinburg, Tenn., 1974. Represented in permanent collections Denver Pub. Schs., Colo. Women's Coll., Ft. Hays State Coll., No. Ill. U., Sheldon Meml. Art Mus., Lincoln, Nebr., Arrowmont Sch. Arts and Crafts; editor: Contemporary Jewelry, 1970. Mem. Fine Arts bd. U. Ariz., 1999—; bd. trustees Tucson Mus. Art, Tucson, 1996—2002. Recipient Pub. Svc. award, Ill. Sesquicentennial Commn., 1968; grantee, No. Ill. U., 1968, 1970, 1974—80. Mem.: Ariz. Designer Craftsmen, Am. Crafts Coun., Soc. N. Am. Goldsmiths, Delta Kappa Gamma, Kappa Delta Pi, Pi Lambda Theta.

CALDWELL, GAIL, book critic; b. Amarillo, Tex., Jan. 20, 1951; d. Bill M. and Ruby C. BA, U. Tex., 1978, MA in Am. Studies, 1980. Instr. U. Tex., Austin, to 1981; staff writer, critic Boston Globe, 1985—, book editor, 1992—95. Judge Radcliffe Bunting Fiction Fellowship; nominator Irish-Times/Aer Lingus Internat. Fiction Prize; mem. Pulitzer jury fiction, 1991 (chmn. of jury 1995 & 1997). Recipient Pulitzer Prize for criticism, 2001. Mem. PEN New Eng. (bd. dirs.), Nat. Book Critics Circle. Office: The Boston Globe PO Box 55819 Boston MA 02205-5819

CALDWELL, JO LYNN, research psychologist; b. Opp, Ala., Dec. 5, 1958; d. Milton D. and Maxie Nell (Edgar) Woodard; m. John A. Caldwell, Jr., July 18, 1981 BA Social Work, U. Ala., Tuscaloosa, 1980; MA Psychology, U. So. Miss., 1983, PhD Psychology, 1989. Asst. psychiat. social work Eufaula Adolescent Ctr., Ala., 1980—81; assoc. psychologist Hudspeth Retardation Ctr., Whitfield, Miss., 1983—84; rsch. asst. Children's Hosp. Nat. Med. Ctr., Washington, 1984—85, coord. project, 1985—86; instr. psychology, rsch. asst. U. So. Miss., Hattiesburg, 1986—88; adj. prof. psychology Troy State U., Dothan, Ala., 1990—94; contract rsch. cons. various orgns., Jack, Ala., 1994—95; rsch. psychologist U.S. Army Aeromed. Rsch. Lab., Ft. Rucker, Ala., 1989—95; sleep specialist Sleep Disorders Ctr., Birmingham, Ala., 1995—98; rsch. psychologist U.S. Army Aeromed Rsch. Lab., 1998—2002; sr. rsch. psychologist USAF Rsch. Lab., Brooks City Base, Tex., 2002—05; vis. scholar USAF Acad., USAF Academy, Colo., 2005—. Cons. FAA, Oklahoma City, 1995; stats. cons. sci. rev. com. Army Aeromed. Rsch. Lab., Ft. Rucker, 1993-94 Contbr. articles to sci. jours Pianist St. Columba Cath. Ch., Dothan, 1998-2001, St. John's Cath. Ch., Enterprise, Ala., 1989-97; Christmas choir pianist Army Aeromed. Rsch. Lab., 1992-93; alto spl. choir LDS Ch., Enterprise, 1994 Recipient commendation for exceptional svc. Army Aeromed. Rsch. Lab., 1991-93 Mem. AAAS, Sleep Rsch. Soc., Am. Sleep Disorders Assn Republican. Achievements include conducting the first investigation of the effects of the hypnotic triazolam on sleep inertia and flight performance of helicopter pilots. Home: 4207 E Muledeer Dr Apt L Usaf Academy CO 80840-1147 Office: USAF Acad Dept Behavioral Sci and Leadership Fairchild Hall U S A F Academy CO 80840 Office Phone: 719-333-9544. E-mail: jo.caldwell@usafa.af.mil.

CALDWELL, JOAN MARIE, artist, educator; b. Lancaster, Pa., Dec. 17, 1927; d. George Joseph and Doris (Fay) Brouillette; m. Richard Holmes Caldwell, Dec. 24, 1970 (div. Jan. 8, 1987); children: Toni Lauren, Wendy Ann, Andrea Joy, Richard Blake, Spencer Edward. Diploma, Mus. Fine Arts Sch., Boston, 1949; BA magna cum laude, U. Calif., San Diego, 1988; MFA in Studio Painting, Calif. State U., Fullerton, 1993. Tchr. Sch. Organic Edn., Fairhope, Ala., 1950-52, Mobile (Ala.) H.S., 1952, Monteverde Sch., Costa Rica, 1955-60; instr. Calif. State U., Fullerton, 1993; artist, 1952—. Exhbns. include Orlando Gallery, Tarzana, Calif., 1993-, Downey Art Mus., 1995, Self Help Graphies, 1995, Miracosta Coll., 1996, San Diego (Calif.) Mus. Art, 1998, S.W. Coll., 1999, Oceanside Mus. Art, 2003. Avocations: writing, photography. Home: 4410 41st St San Diego CA 92116 Office Phone: 619-283-0154. E-mail: jocaldwell@mac.com.

CALDWELL, JUDITH, horticultural educator; Prof. Clemson U., S.C. Recipient Outstanding Undergrad. Educator award, 1992. Office: Dept of Horticulture Rm D136 Pool EGG Ctr Clemson U Clemson SC 29634-0375

CALDWELL, JUDY CAROL, advertising executive, consultant, writer; b. Nashville, Dec. 28, 1946; d. Thomas and Sarah Elizabeth Carter; 1 child, Jessica. BS, Wayne State U., 1969. Tchr. Bailey Mid. Sch., West Haven, Conn., 1969-72; editorial asst. Vanderbilt U., Nashville, 1973-74; editor, graphics designer, field researcher Urban Observatory of Met. Nashville, 1974-77; account exec. Holden and Co., Nashville, 1977-79; bus. tchr. Federated States of Micronesia, 1979-80; dir. advt. Am. Assn. for State and Local History, Nashville, 1980-81; dir. prodn. Mktg. Communications Co., Nashville, 1981-83; ptnr. Victory Images of Tenn., Inc., Nashville, 1990-92; sr. tech. advisor UN, 2002; owner, pres., writer, designer Ridge Hill Corp., Nashville, 1983—. E-mail: ridgehillcorp@comcast.net.

CALDWELL, L. SCOTT, actress; b. Chgo., Apr. 17, 1944; Mem. Milw. Repertory Theatre, 1981-82. Mem. Negro Ensemble Co. Appeared in The Daughters of the Mock, 1978, A Season to Unravel, 1979, Old Phantoms, 1979, Plays from Africa, 1979, Home, 1979, 80, Boesman and Lena, 1981, Colored People's Time, 1982, About Heaven and Earth, 1983; other theater appearances include A Raisin in the Sun, Buffalo, 1982, A Play of Giants, 1984, Come and Gone, New Haven, 1985, Boston, 1986, N.Y.C., 1988 (Antoinette Perry award for best featured actress in a play, 1988), Proposals, A Month of Sundays, N.Y.C., 1987, Going to St. Ives, 2005 (Obie award, Village Voice, 2005); appeared in films Without a Trace, 1983, Exterminator 2, 1984, Up Against the Wall, 1991, Dutch, 1991, The Fugitive, 1993, The Switch, 1993, Soweto Green, 1995, The Net, 1995, Devil in a Blue Dress, 1995, Graham's Diner, 1999, Mystery, Alaska, 1999, Dragonfly, 2002, Gridiron Gang, 2006; TV films: God Bless the Child, 1988, Dangerous Passion, 1990, Love, Lies and Murder, 1991, Baby of the Bride, 1991, Extreme Justice, 1993, Darkness Before Dawn, 1993, For the Love of My Child: The Anissa Ayala Story, 1993, Down Came a Blackbird, 1995. Twilight Man, 1996, Dying to Be Perfect: The Ellen Hart Pena Story, 1996, Weapons of Mass Distraction, 1997, Intimate Betrayal, 1999, The Last Man On Planet Earth, 1999; TV series The Outsiders, 1990, Queens Supreme, 2003, recurring role in Judging Amy. Mailing: c/o Primary Stages 59 East 59th St New York NY 10022*

CALDWELL, LESLIE RAGON, lawyer, former prosecutor; b. Pitts., Aug. 30, 1957; BA in economics summa cum laude, Pa. State U., 1979; JD with honors, George Washington U., 1982. Bar: NY 1983. Assoc. Cadwalader, Wickersham & Taft LLP, NYC, 1984—87; asst. US atty. US Atty.'s Office Ea. Dist. NY, Brooklyn, 1987—98, dep. chief Narcotics Sect., dep. chief General Crimes Sect., chief Violent Criminal Enterprises Sect., 1994—97, sr. trial counsel, 1997—98; asst. US atty. US Atty.'s Office No. Dist. Calif., San Francisco, 1998—2002, dep. chief Criminal Divsn., chief Econ. Crimes Unit, chief Securities & Fraud Sect., chief Criminal Divsn., 2001—02; ptnr. Morgan Lewis & Bockius LLP, NYC, 2004—. Dir. Enron Task Force, US Dept. Justice, 2002—04; adj. faculty NY Law Sch. Recipient Henry L. Stimson Medal, Assn. Bar City NY, 1994, John Marshall Award for Trial of Litig., Atty. Gen., Award for Fraud Prevention, Spl. Achievement Award, US Dept. Justice. Office: Morgan Lewis & Bockius LLP 101 Park Ave New York NY 10178-0060

CALDWELL, LINDA E., critical care nurse; b. Spencer, Iowa, June 23, 1954; d. George W. and Elaine Wava (Parks) D.; m. Bill Caldwell, June 25, 1988. ADN, Cumberland County Coll., 1984; EMT, Cumberland Adult Edn., 1986. RN; cert. EMT. Staff nurse Newcomb Med. Ctr., Vineland, NJ; head nurse Leesburg State Prison, Delmont, NJ; charge nurse, ICU South Jersey Hosp. Divsn., Millville, NJ, 1991—; co-owner P.S. & L. Emergency med. tech. Bridgeton Ambulance Svc. Mem. EOF (past pres.), AACN. Home: PO Box 976 Millville NJ 08332-0976 Office Phone: 877-724-6478. Personal E-mail: linda4847@aol.com. Business E-Mail: psl@painspray.com.

CALDWELL, LOUISE PHINNEY, historical researcher, community volunteer; b. Dallas, Sept. 19, 1938; d. Carl Lawrence and Louise (Snow) Phinney; m. Josef Caldwell, Sept. 8, 1962; children: Mattie Caldwell Roberts, Jane Barron Caldwell Jackson, Josef Caldwell Jr., Charles Phinney Caldwell. Grad., The Hockaday Sch., 1956; student, Sweet Briar Coll., 1956-57. Owner retail bus., Dallas, 1965-75; project chmn. Mus. of Dallas History, 1985—95; interim dir. Dallas Hist. Soc., 1990, chmn., 1991-93, pres., 1987-91, life trustee, 1991—, exec. com., 2005—; bd. Friends of the Dallas Publ. Libr., 2003. Membership chair trustee com. Tex. Assn. Mus., Austin, 1986-88; mem.-at-large Women's Coun. Dallas County, 1991—; adv. 36th Inf. Divsn. Mus. Com., Camp Mabry, Austin, Tex.; v.p., treas. Hist. Inquiry, Inc., 1992—. Author rsch. project 150 Years of Lone Star Cuisine, 1986. Mem. Dallas County Hist. Commn., 1989-90; chmn. Awards for Excellence in Cmty. Svc., Dallas, 1983-89; founding co-chmn. Jubilee Dallas! Celebrating 150 Years, 1990-91; mem. charter bd. dir. Friends of Fair Park, Dallas, 1985-91; mem. Crystal Charity Ball Com.; chmn. Festival Shakespeare, 1994. Recipient Heritage award Dallas County Heritage Soc., 1982. Fellow Dallas Hist. Soc. (chmn. Fellows 1982-84), Mayflower Soc., Nat. Soc. of Colonial Dames, Daus. of Republic of Tex. (chpt. v.p. 1991-92), Dallas Woman's Club, Dallas Garden club, Charter 100 Club, Belterling Found. Democrat. Episcopalian. Avocations: collects & catalogues, antique glass trade beads, folk art of Hispanic southwest.

CALDWELL, MARCIA DIANE, nurse; b. Turlock, Calif., June 12, 1947; d. Stanley Ellsworth Oie and Lydia Cornelia (Coey) Hammer; m. Gary Allen Caldwell, Dec. 21, 1968; children: David Alan, Michael Benjamin. BS in Bus., Fresno State U., 1969; AS in Nursing, Coll. Sequoias, 1985. RN; cert. inpatient obstetric nurse; cert. lactation educator; bd. cert. lactation cons. CNA-OB Visalia Cmty. Hosp., Calif., 1977-85, nurse II family birthing Calif., 1987-95; med.-surg. nurse Kaweah Delta Hosp., Visalia, Calif., 1985-87, nurse II Family Birthing Ctr., 1994-96, lactation specialist, 1996—; ret. Breastfeeding instr., prenatal classes Sierra Med. Group, 1979-85, others; lectr. La Leche League, Calif., 1995. Mem. Assn. Women's Health, Obstetric and Neonatal Nurses, Internat. Lactation Cons. Assn. (cert.). Home: 11971 Avenue 274 Visalia CA 93277-9301 Office: Kaweah Delta Hosp Family Birthing Ctr 400 W Mineral King Ave Visalia CA 93291-6263

CALDWELL, MARY ELLEN, language educator; b. El Paso, Ark., Aug. 6, 1908; d. Clay and Mabel Grace (Coe) Fulks; m. Robert Atchison Caldwell, Feb. 22, 1936; 1 child, Elizabeth. PhB, U. Chgo., 1931, MA, 1933. Instr. English U. Ark., Fayetteville, 1940-42, U. Toledo, 1946-48; from instr. to asst. prof. to assoc. prof. U. N.D., Grand Forks, 1952-79, assoc. prof. emeritus, 1979—, prof. ext. divsn., 1979-2000. Author: North Dakota Division of the American Association of University Women, 1930-63, A History, 1964; co-author: The North Dakota Division of the American Association of University Women, 1964-84, 2d vol., 1984; contbr. revs. and articles to scholarly jours. Sec. citizen's com. Grand Forks Symphony Assn., 1960-66. Mem. AAUW (life, N.D. state pres. 1968-70), P.E.O., MLA (life), Soc. for Study of Midwestern Lit. (bibliography staff 1973-2002, MidAm. award for disting. contbns. to study of midwstern lit. 2000), Linguistic Cir. of Man. and N.D. (pres. 1981), Melville Soc. Democrat. Episcopalian. Home: 3300 Cherry St #D138 Grand Forks ND 58201-7634

CALDWELL, NAOMI RACHEL, library and information scientist, educator, writer; b. Providence, Mar. 31, 1958; d. Atwood Alexander II and Juanita (Johnson) Caldwell; 1 child, William Earl Wood. BS, Clarion State Coll., 1980; MSLS, Clarion U. Pa., 1982; postgrad., Tex. A&M U., 1986—87, Providence Coll., 1990—92; PhD in Libr. and Info. Studies, U. Pitts., 2002. Cert. tchg. libr.; cert. libr. media specialist. Asst. dir., adult svcs. libr. Oil City (Pa.) Pub. Libr., 1984—85; microtext reference libr. Sterling C. Evans Libr., Tex. A&M U., College Station, 1985—87; libr. media specialist Nathan Bishop Mid. Sch., Providence, 1987—92; libr. sci. doctoral fellow dept. libr. sci. Sch. Libr. and Info. Sci. U. Pitts., 1992—94; sch. library media specialist Feinstein H.S. for Pub. Svc., Providence, 1994—99; asst. prof. U. R.I. Grad.

Sch. Libr. Info. Studies, 2002—. Mem. discovery award com. U.S. Bd. on Books for Young People, 1994; mem. com. R.I. Children's Book Award, 1990—92, R.I. Read-Aloud, 1990—92; participant Native Am. and Alaskan Native Pre-Conf. to White House Conf. on Librs. and Info. Scis., Washington, 1991, George Washington U. Nat. Indian Policy Ctr. Forum on Native Am. Librs. and Info. Svcs., Washington, 1991; participant, del., spkr. Internat. Indigenous Librs. Forum, Auckland, New Zealand, 1999, Santa Fe, 2003; hon. del. White House Conf. on Libr. and Info. Svcs., Washington, 1991; bd. dirs. Ocean State Freenet; mem. exec. bd. R.I. Ednl. Media Assn., 1996—97; cons. Am. Coll. Testing, 1995—; mem. exec. bd. Native Am. child literacy program If I Can Read, I Can Do Anything, 2001—; mem. Coalition Libr. Advocates, 2002—; del., spkr. Internat. Indigenous Libr. Forum, Santa Fe, 2003; presenter in field. Mem. editl. adv. bd., reviewer: Multicultural Rev., 1991—; mem. adv. bd. Native Ams. Info. Dir., 1992, OYATE, 1992—, Gale Ency. Multicultural Am., Native N.Am. Ref. Libr.; mem. exec. bd.: OYATE, 2001—05; reviewer Clarion Books, Greenwood Press, Random House, Harcourt Brace Trade Divsn., Browndeer Press, Oryx Press; contbr. articles to profl. jours. Mem. State of R.I. Libr. Bd., 1996-97, Spl. Presdl. Adv. Com. on Libr. of Congress, 1996-97; mem. nominating com. R.I. chpt. Girl Scouts of Am., 1998-99; enrolled mem. Ramapough Lenape Tribe; bd. dirs. Tomaquaq Indian Mus., 2005—. Mem.: ALA (councilor-at-large 1992—96, chmn. com. on status of women in librarianship 1995—97, nominating com. 1996—97, legis. assembly 1996—98, councilor-at-large 1996—2000, assembly on planning and budget 1998—99, presdl. task force spectrum program, com. on coms. 1999—2000, spectrum jury com. 2001—02, com. on diversity 2001—04, pres.'s adv. com. 2003—04), R.I. Coalition of Libr. Advs. (sec. 2003), Native Am. N.E. Librs., Worcraft Cir. Native Writers and Storytellers, Windwalker Coalition, Libr. Adminstrn. Mgmt. Assn., Spl. Librs. Assn., Am. Assn. Sch. Librs., Am. Indian Libr. Assn. (new mems. round table publicity com. 1986, new mems. round table minority recruitment com. 1986—88, OLOS libr. svcs. for Am. Indian people subcom. 1986—88, ALCTS micro-pub. com. 1988—90, OLOS libr. svcs. for Am. Indian people subcom. 1990—91, pres. 1990—94, mem. coun. com. on minority concerns 1991—92, chmn. 1992—94, sec. 1994—96, mem. coun. com. on minority concerns 1994—96, chair book award task force 2004, chair youth book award com. 2005—), Alpha Kappa Alpha Inc. Home: 475 Sowams Rd Barrington RI 02806-2745 Office: U RI Grad Sch Libr and Info Studies 11 Rodman Hall Kingston RI 02881 Office Phone: 401-874-2278. Personal E-mail: inpeacencw@aol.com.

CALDWELL, PATRICIA ANN, language educator; b. Mullins, W.Va., June 7, 1954; d. Eldon and Julia Mason Fox; m. Gary Caldwell, Mar. 2, 1974; children: Fred Scott, Julia Lynn. BS in Elem. Edn., Union Coll., 1993, MEd in English & Commn., 1997. Lic. prin. K-12 Ky. Tchr. Verda Elem., Ky., 1993—97; English tchr. Hall Elem., Grays Knob, Ky., 1997—, asst. prin., 2005—. First priority sponsor Hall Elem., 1999—; mem. dist. improvement team Harlan County Schs., Ky., 2002—04. Grantee, Dept. Agr., 1994—96, 1998, Harlan County Soil Conservation Dept., 2005. Mem.: NEA, Ky. Coun. Tchrs. English. Baptist. Avocations: reading, exercise.

CALDWELL, PAULETTE M., law educator; b. 1944; BS, Howard U., 1966, JD, 1969. Bar: NY 1972. Atty. Patterson, Belknap, Webb & Tyler, NYC, 1969-72, 1974-79; asst. counsel The Ford Found., NYC, 1972-74; asst. prof. NYU Sch. Law, 1979-80, assoc. prof., 1980-84, prof., 1984—. Office: NYU Sch Law Vanderbilt Hall Rm 318 40 Washington Sq S New York NY 10012-1099 Office Phone: 212-998-6192. E-mail: paulette.caldwell@nyu.edu.

CALDWELL, TONI MARIE, religious organization administrator; b. Winston-Salem, N.C., Aug. 19, 1951; 1 child, Christopher Bradley Bowman. BS in Commerce, Knoxville Coll., 1973; PhD in Bibl. Studies, St. Luke Evang. Sch. Bibl. Studies, 1999. Adminstr. R.J. Reynolds Tobacco Co., Winston-Salem, 1974—92; prin., owner A Gift of Love, 2003—; with Mary and Jesus Acad. Water to Wine Ministries. Served with U.S. Army, 1981. Democrat. Avocations: calligraphy, painting, crocheting, cake decorating, macramé. Office: A Gift of Love 1220 Argonne Blvd Winston Salem NC 27107 Office Phone: 336-251-8749.

CALDWELL, TRACY ELLEN, surface chemist, researcher; b. Arcadia, Calif., Aug. 14, 1969; d. James and Mary Ellen C. BS, Calif. State U., Fullerton, 1993; PhD, U. Calif., Davis, 1997. Journeyman electrician J.C. Electric Co., Cherry Valley, Calif., 1987-92; environ. lab. asst. Rsch. and Instrnl. Safety Office Calif. State U., Fullerton, 1990-93, rsch. asst. chemistry, 1991-93; tchg. asst. chemistry U. Calif., Davis, 1993-94, rsch. asst. chemistry, 1994-96, rsch. asst. physics, 1996-97, Camille and Henry Dreyfus postdoctoral fellow Irvine, 1997—; astronaut, 1998—. Contbr. articles to profl. jours. including Polyhedron, Jour. Am. Chem. Soc., Surface Sci., and Jour. Phys. Chemistry. Recipient NASA Superior Accomplishment Award, 2000, NASA Performance Award, 2001, 2003. Mem. Am. Chem. Soc., Am. Vacuum Soc. (Nellie Yeoh Whelton award 1996, Grad. Rsch. award 1996), Sigma Xi. Presbyterian. Achievements include mem. Russian Crusader Team, Office ISS Operations Branch, 1999; Crew Support Astronaut, 5th ISS Expedition crew, 2000. Office: NASA Johnson Space Ctr Astronaut Office Houston TX 77058

CALDWELL-COLBERT, A. TOY, academic administrator, psychology professor; b. Salina, Kans., Sept. 21, 1951; d. Robert Chester and Bessie (Ellis) Caldwell; m. Charles Cornelius Colbert, July 1, 1978; children: Joffre-Charles, Jordan; 1 stepchild, LaTatia. BA, Spelman Coll., Atlanta, 1973; MS, U. Ga., 1975; postgrad., Brown U., 1975-76; PhD, U. Ga., 1977. Lic. clin. psychologist, Kans., Ind., Ill. Grad. teaching asst. U. Ga., Athens, 1977; asst. prof. psychology U. Man., Winnipeg, 1977-78; lectr. psychology/student affairs Emporia (Kans.) State U., 1978-82, asst. prof. psychology, 1982-84, interim asst. v.p. acad. affairs, grad. studies, rsch., 1985-86, assoc. prof. and coord. indsl. psychology grad. program, 1984-88; spl. asst. to chancellor U. Kans., Lawrence, 1987-88; asst. v.p. acad. affairs, assoc. prof. psychology Ind. State U., Terre Haute, 1983-88, assoc. provost for acad. affairs, prof. psychology, 1993-94; assoc. v.p. acad. affairs U. Ill., Urbana, 1994—, prof. psychology and ednl. psychology, 1994—. Fellow Am. Coun. on Edn. Fellows Program, Washington, 1987-88; profl. assoc The Menninger Found., Topeka, Kans., 1987—; coord. N. Cen. Assn. self-study accreditation Ind. State U., 1988-90; cons. S.W. region Ind. Soc. Med. Tech., 1989—. Contbg. author: Minorities on Campus: A Handbook for Enhancing Diversity, 1989, Valuing Diversity. A Guide, 1996; sr. author: How to Recruit and Hire Ethnic Minority Faculty, 1996; contbr. articles to profl. jours.; editorial bd. Jour. Behavioral Assessment, 1981-85. Commn. mem. SOS Rape and Battered Women's Core Commn., Emporia, 1982-85; coun. mem. Kans. Arts Coun., Topeka, 1978-88; vice chair and bd. dirs. Emporia Human Rels. Commn., 1981-88; state bd. Kans. Children's Svc. League, Wichita, 1985-88; bd. dirs. Terre Haute Minorities Offering Direction Encouragement and Leadership Strategies, 1990; active Covered Bridge coun. Girl Scouts U.S., Terre Haute, 1992—; bd. mem. Devel. Svcs. Ctr., Champaign, 1995; mem. Head Start Found.-Champaign County, 1996; active Green Meadows Girl Scout Coun. Bd., Urbana, Ill., 1996. Recipient Disting. Kans. Citizen award Kans. Children's Svc. League, 1985, faculty award for profl. svc. Emporia State U., 1986; SIGNA grantee, 1987. Mem. APA (pres.-elect divsn. 12-sect. 6 1997, program mem. divsn. 35 1981-94, commn. for recruitment, retention and tng. of ethnic minority psychologists 1994-96), Assn. for Advancement Behavior Therapy (rep.-at-large 1978-80, chpt. pres. black spl. interest group 1979, 89, award of appreciation 1980), Midwestern Psychol. Assn., Links (pres. Normal-Champaign chpt., past pres. Ctrl. Ill. chpt., chmn. svcs. to youth and chmn. nominating com. ctrl. area), Ind. Coalition Blacks in Higher Edn., Ill. Com. on Black Concerns in Higher Edn. Democrat. Presbyterian. Avocations: gourmet cooking, travel, tennis, antiques. Office: U Ill 378 Henry Adminstrn Bldg 506 S Wright St Urbana IL 61801-3620 Home: 2703 Unicorn Ln Nw Washington DC 20015-2233

CALEGARI, MARIA, ballerina; b. NYC, Mar. 30, 1957; d. Richard A. and Marion (Gentile) C. Student, DuPons Dance Studio, Queens, 1960-66, Ballet Acad., 1966-71, Sch. Am. Ballet, 1971-74. Mem. corps de ballet N.Y.C. Ballet, 1974-81, soloist, 1981-83, prin., 1983-94; guest artist Richmond Ballet, 1996—; artistic dir. dance Conn. Conservatory of the Performing Arts, New Milford, 2002—; artistic dir. The Maria Calegari Schl of Ballet, New Milford, Conn., 2003—. Artist-in-residence Richmond Ballet, Richmond Ctr. for Dance, State Ballet of Va., 1997—98, Conn. Cons. of Performing Arts, New Milford, 1999—. Dancer in N.Y.C. Ballet's Balanchine Celebration, 1993, Celebrating Balanchine, Kennedy Ctr., 1995. Repétiteur George Balanchine Trust, Robbins Rights Trust. Recipient Alumni award, Profl. Children's Sch., 1986. E-mail: mcale50064@aol.com.

CALETTI, DEB L., writer; b. San Rafael, Calif., June 16, 1963; d. Paul Albert Caletti and Evelyn Ann Siler; m. Elliott Wolf, 2004 (div. July 1999); children: Samantha Bannon, Nicholas Bannon. BA in Journalism, U. Wash., 1985. Mem. adv. bd. Bellevue (Wash.) C.C. Ctr. for Liberal Arts; spkr. and lyricist. Author: The Queen of Everything, 2002, Honey, Baby, Sweetheart, 2003 (Nat. Book Award finalist, 2004, Pacific N.W. Booksellers award, 2005, Best Books of 2004 award, Calif. Young Reader medal finalist, 2005, Notable Children's Book award Internat. Reading Assn., 2005, Hon. Book awards Soc. Sch. Librs., award PEN, award State, Internat. Book awards), Wild Roses, 2005, The Nature of Jade, 2007. Literary fellow, Artist Trust-Wash. State Arts Commn., 2001. Mem.: PEN USA, Amnesty Internat. Avocations: painting, writing.

CALFEE, LAURA PICKETT, university administrator, photographer; b. Liberty, Tex., Oct. 30, 1952; d. Benjamin Ellis and Florence Ellen (Watson) Pickett; m. Gary Wayne Calfee, Dec. 21, 1981. BJ, U. Tex., 1979. Com. clk. Tex. Ho. of Reps., Austin, 1973-77; asst. to dir. Legis. Divsn. Ho. of Reps., Austin, 1977-83; com. coord. Tex. Ho. of Reps., Austin, 1983-87; spl. asst. for govtl. rels. Univ. Houston Sys., Austin, 1987-92, asst. vice chancellor, 1992—. Exec. prodr. Capitol Report, Sta. KUHT-TV, Houston, 1989—2004; moderator 1993. Co-author: (dance/theater) Chicken Tawk, performed at DIA Ctr. for Arts, N.Y.C., 1991; photographer: Gary's Best (hon. mention Best of Photography ann. 1992, 1st Pl. Lucie award 2006, 2d Pl. Lucie award 2006), Maria's Geese (hon. mention Best of Photography ann. 1994); permanent collections include Harry Ransom Humanities Rsch. Ctr. Photography Collection/U. Tex. at Austin, Tex. Midcontinent Oil and Gas Corp., Mus. Fine Art, Houston, Tex., Simon Gorsky Mus., Longview Mus. Art. Bd. dirs. Ctr. for Women and Their Work. Grantee: Tex. Hist. Commn., 1992-93; recipient Hon. Mention award Phoenix Gallery Ann. Juried Competition, 1994, State of the Art Nat. Juried Competition, 1994, State of the Art Nat. Juried Competition, Ithaca, N.Y., 1995, Grand award Govtl. Rels. Program, Coun. for Advancement and Support of Edn., Region IV, 1995, Santa Fe Workshops Project Competition, 1st pl./2d pl. Viewpoint 96 Bosque County Conservatory of Fine Art Competition, 1996, Best of Show award Gov.'s Exhbn., 1996, Hon. Mention, Golden Light awards, 2005. Mem.Tex. Photog. Soc. (bd. dirs.) Home: 19001 Fm 1826 Driftwood TX 78619-4201 Office: U Houston System 1005 Congress Ave Ste 820 Austin TX 78701-2487 E-mail: studio@lauracalfee.com.

CALHOUN, GLORIA LYNN, experimental psychologist; b. Mpls., Nov. 12, 1951; d. Robert Willard and Wilma Marie (Schmoock) Alrutz; m. Kevin Paul Calhoun, Apr. 20, 1974 (div.); children: Mark Allen, Brian Patrick. m. Dean Frank Kocian, Feb. 3, 1990; 1 child, Sara Lynn. BA, Coll. Wooster, 1974; MA, Wright State U., 1984. Document rsch. analyst Bunker Ramo Corp., Dayton, Ohio, 1974-75; human factors engr., Dayton, Ohio, 1975-81; rsch. psychologist Systems Rsch. Lab., Dayton, 1981-82; engring. rsch. psychologist AF Rsch. Lab., Dayton, 1982—. Contbr. articles to profl. publs. Wright State U. scholar, 1980; NSF grantee, 1973. Recipient Leach Meml. prize in psychology Coll. Wooster, 1974. Mem. Assn. Unmanned Vehicle Sys. Internat., Human Factors Soc., Sigma Xi (assoc.). Home: 218 Babington Ct Dayton OH 45440-3645 Office: AFRL/HECI Wright-Patterson AFB Dayton OH 45433

CALHOUN, RAMONA, human services administrator, academic administrator, consultant; b. Akron, Ohio, Sept. 2, 1950; d. Howell and Rebecca (Hammonds) C.; m. William J. Webb, Sept. 1969 (div. 1973); 1 child, Forrest J. Webb. BS, U. Akron, 1980; MS, SUNY, Oswego, 1988; PhD, Walden U., 2001. Sales corr./sec. Monsanto Co., Akron, Ohio, 1973-77; student instr./career guide U. Akron; instr. SUNY Delhi Coll., Delhi, 1980-82; Dept. chair-bus. SUNY Morrisville Edn. Opportunity Ctr., Syracuse, 1983-88; dir. program opns., Job Tng. Partnership Agy. City of Syracuse, 1988—91; dir., student svcs, grants Ivy Tech State Coll., 1991—95; acad. dir. Ctr. Ohio Tech Coll. Artist charcoal sketch Portrait in Bronze (Best of Show, 1990); writer-poet Rain Dance, 1979; contbr. poetry to African Am. Jour. Bd. dirs. YWCA of Syracuse and Onandaga, 1990-92, City/County Youth Bd., 1989-91; com. mem. N.Y. State Task Force on the Older Worker, Albany, 1990-91, N.Y. State Task Force for Career Pathways for Youth. Recipient Leadership award, SUNY Oswego, 1988. Mem. N.Y. Assn. Tng. and Employment Profls., Partnership for Employment and Tng. Avocations: reading, writing (short stories, poetry, novels), painting.

CALHOUN, SABRINA, communications executive; m. Bill Calhoun; 3 stepchildren. BS in Elec. Engring., MS in Elec. Engring., Univ. Ala., Birmingham; PhD, Univ. Ala., Tuscaloosa. Engr., network mechanization BellSouth, 1987, mgr., network planning integration, 1990; sr. engr. Cox Comm., 1997—2000, dir., ops. engring., 2000—. Rep., BellSouth Nat. Standings Com.; mem. bd. dir. Cable Telecom. Assn. Ga. Mem.: IEEE, Nat. Cable Telecom. Assn., Soc. Cable Telecom. Engrs. (Women in Tech. award 2001), Women in Cable TV. Office: Cox Comm 1400 Lake Hearn Dr Atlanta GA 30319*

CALI, MARY ANN, music educator; b. NYC, May 20, 1956; d. Raymond and Ana Cecilia Gonzalez; m. Charles T. Cali, July 19, 1980 (dec. Aug. 1998); children: Dina Marie, Michael Raymond. MS in Edn., LI U., Greenvale, NY, 1978, BFA in Music Edn., 1982. Instrumental music tchr. Garden City Sch. Dist., NY, 1978—79, Valley Stream Unified Sch. Dist., NY, 1979—. Musician (violinist): Nassau Pops Symphony Orch., Lawrence Phil. Orch. Recipient Josef Marx Alumni Music award, C.W. Post Orch., Lifetime award, Valley Stream Unified Sch. Dist. PTA. Mem.: Music Educators Nat'l. Conf., Nassau Music Educators Assn. Roman Catholic. Avocations: music, travel, sports. Home: 621 Wyngate Dr E Valley Stream NY 11580 Office: James A Dever Elem Sch 585 N Corona Ave Valley Stream NY 11580

CALINESCU, ADRIANA GABRIELA, curator, art historian; b. Bucharest, Romania, Dec. 30, 1941; came to U.S., 1973; d. Nicolae and Tamara Gane; m. Matei Alexe Calinescu, Apr. 29, 1963; children: Irena, Matthew. BA, Cen. Lyceé, Bucharest, 1959; MA in English, U. Bucharest, 1964; MLS, Ind. U., 1976, MA in Art History, 1983. Asst. prof. Inst. Theater and Cinema, Bucharest, 1967-73; rsch. assoc. Ind. U. Art Mus., Bloomington, 1979-83, Thomas T. Solley curator ancient art, assoc. scholar, 1992—. Vis. assoc. mem. Am. Sch. Classical Studies, Athens, Greece, 1984. Author: The Art of Ancient Jewelry, 1994, Egypt After Alexander, 2005; author, co-editor: Ancient Art from the V. G. Simkhovitch Collection, 1988; editor: Ancient Jewelry and Archaeology, 1996. NEA fellow, 1984; grantee Salzburg Seminar, 1970, NEA, 1987, 93, Kress Found., 1991, Internat. Rsch. and Exchanges Bd., 1991. Mem. Am. Inst. Archaeology, Classical Art Soc., Beta Phi Mu. Office: Ind U Art Mus E 7th St Bloomington IN 47405 Office Phone: 812-855-1033.

CALINOIU, ILEANA NIA, psychiatrist; b. Bucharest, Romania, Mar. 30, 1968; arrived in U.S., 1996; d. Sielian and Aurelia Beldescu; m. Silviu Calinoiu, Aug. 31, 2001. MD with honors, U. Medicine, Bucharest, 1994. Diplomate Am. Bd. Psychiatry and Neurology. Resident Albert Einstein Med. Ctr., Phila., 1999—2002; fellow child and adolescent psychiatry U. Wash., Seattle, 2002—04, chief resident, 2003—04; pvt. practice Bellevue, Wash., 2004—; attending psychiatrist Eating Disorders Clinic Children's Hosp. and Med. Ctr., Seattle, 2004—05; attending psychiatrist Caild Study and Treatment Ctr., Tacoma, 2006—. Mem. clin. faculty U. Wash., 2004—, clin. supr. Named Resident of Yr., Albert Einstein Med. Ctr., 2002. Mem.: APA, Wash. State Child and Adolescent Psychiatry Assn. (pres. advocacy issues 2004—06, pres.-elect 2006—). Avocations: photography, writing. Office: 1530 140th Ave NE 201 Bellevue WA 98005

CALISHER, HORTENSE (MRS. CURTIS HARNACK), writer; b. NYC, Dec. 20, 1911; d. Joseph Henry and Hedvig (Lichtstern) C.; m. Curtis Harnack, Mar. 23, 1959; children by previous marriage: Bennet Hughes, Peter Heffelfinger. AB, Barnard Coll., 1932; LittD (hon.), Skidmore Coll., 1980, Grinnell Coll., 1986; LittD, Adelphi U., 1988. Adj. prof. English Barnard Coll., N.Y.C., 1956-57. Vis. lectr. State U. Iowa, 1957, 59-60, Stanford U., 1958, Sarah Lawrence Coll., Bronxville, N.Y., 1962, 67; adj. prof. Columbia U., N.Y.C., 1968-70, CCNY, 1969; vis. prof. lit. SUNY, Purchase, 1971-72, Brandeis U., 1963-64, U. Pa., 1965; Regent's prof. U. Calif., 1976; vis. prof. Bennington Coll., 1978, Washington U., St. Louis, 1979, Brown U., spring 1986; lectr., Fed. Republic of Germany, Yugoslavia, Rumania, Hungary, 1978; guest lectr. U.S./China Arts Exch., Republic of China, 1986. Author: (novels) False Entry, 1961, Textures of Life, 1962, The New Yorkers, 1969, Journal from Ellipsia, 1965, Queenie, 1971, Standard Dreaming, 1972, Eagle Eye, 1973, On Keeping Women, 1977, Mysteries of Motion, 1984, The Bobby-Soxer, 1986 (Kafka prize U. Rochester 1987), Age, 1987, (under pseudonym Jack Fenno) The Small Bang, 1992, In the Palace of the Movie-King, 1994, In the Slammer with Carol Smith, 1997; (novellas) The Railway Police, 1966, The Last Trolley Ride, 1966; short stories include In The Absence of Angels, 1951, Tale for the Mirror, 1962, Extreme Magic, 1963, Collected Stories, 1975, Saratoga Hot, 1985; autobiography: Herself, 1972; memoir: Kissing Cousins, 1988; contbr. short stories, articles, revs. to Am. Scholar, N.Y. Times, Harpers, Yale Rev., New Criterion, others. Guggenheim fellow, 1952, 55; Dept. of State Am. Specialists's grantee to S.E. Asia, 1958; recipient Acad. of Arts and Letters award, 1967, Nat. Council Arts award, 1967, Lifetime Achievement award Nat. Endowment for the Arts, 1989. Mem. Am. Acad. Arts and Letters (pres. 1987-90), PEN (pres. 1986-87). Office: Marion Boyaris Pubc/o Fem Press 365 5th Ave #5406 New York NY 10016-4309

CALKINS, SUSAN W., state supreme court justice; Grad., U. Colo.; JD, U. Maine; M, U. Va. Sch. of Law. Staff atty., exec. dir. Pine Tree Legal Assistance; judge Maine Dist. Ct., 1980-90, chief judge, 1990—94; judge Maine Superior Ct., 1995—98; justice Maine Supreme Ct., 1998—. Ct. liaison Bd. of Bar Examiners, Jud. Ethics Com., Advisory Com. on Rules of Evidence. Fellow: Maine Bar Foundation; mem.: ABA (mem. Judges' Advisory Com. on Ethics & Professional Responsibility). Office: Maine Supreme Ct 142 Federal St PO Box 368 Portland ME 04112-0368*

CALKINS, SUSANNAH EBY, retired economist; b. Bucyrus, Ohio, Jan. 16, 1924; d. Samuel L. and Mae (McClure) Eby; m. G. Nathan Calkins, Nov. 19, 1949 (dec.); children: Helen E. (dec.), Margaret S. Van Auken, Sarah A. (dec.), Abigail Calkins Aguirre. AB, Goucher Coll., 1945; MS in Econs. (Univ. scholar 1946-47), U. Wis., 1947. Fiscal analyst U.S. Bur. Budget, 1945-50; economist U.S. Council Econ. Advisors, 1950-51, U.S. Office Price Stabilization, 1951-53, U.S. Bur. Budget, 1953-55; cons. U.S. Adv. Commn. on Intergovtl. Rels., Washington, 1972-73, 74-75, cons. on counter-cyclical aid programs, 1977-78, sr. analyst, 1979-87, exec. asst. to dir., 1987-89. Cons. revenue sharing Brookings Instn., Washington, 1973—74. Author (with R. Nathan and A. Manvel): Monitoring Revenue Sharing, 1975. Sponsor S.S. Goucher Victory, Balt., 1945; bd. dirs. Bread for the City, 1994—2002. Mem.: Am. Econs. Assn., George Towne Club (Washington), Cosmos Club (assoc.), Phi Beta Kappa. Presbyterian. Home: 6504 Dearborn Dr Falls Church VA 22044-1115

CALL, AMY LYNN, music educator, director, classical singer; b. Salem, Va., Nov. 19, 1976; d. Danny Hughes and Edith Jane Call. MusB, James Madison U., 1998; MusM, Ind. U., 2003; student, Shenandoah Conservatory, 2004—. Cert. vocal music tchr. grades pre-kindergarten through 12 Va., 1998. Music tchr., choral dir. Montgomery County Pub. Schs., Blacksburg, Va., 1998—2000, Warren County Pub. Schs., Front Royal, Va., 2003—. Bd. dirs. Choral Arts Support Team, Front Royal, 2003—; pvt. voice tchr., Front Royal, 2004. Ch. choir mem. Braddock St. United Meth., Winchester, Va., 2004—. Lucie M. Kohlmeier scholarship, Ind. U., Bloomington, 2001—03, Grad. fellowship, Shenandoah Conservatory, Winchester, Va., 2004—. Mem.: Nat. Assn. Music Edn., Sigma Alpha Iota (life Sword of Honor 1997). Democrat. Methodist. Avocations: travel, singing, flute, counted cross stitch, reading. Office: AS Rhodes Elementary Sch 224 W Strasburg Rd Front Royal VA 22630

CALL, DENISE HODGINS, curator, artist, freelance/self-employed writer; b. Philadelphia, Pa., Oct. 27, 1942; d. James Francis Hodgins and Catherine C. Whitney-Lear; m. Stephen M. Call, Jan. 22, 1994; m. Edward J. Gilhooly, July 16, 1966 (div.); children: Caitlyn Gilhooly Parker, Mairin Gilhooly Kuligowski, Edward J. Gilhooly, III, Bevin J. Gilhooly. BA in English with honors, Cabrini Coll., 1960—64; Grad. studies, University of Pa., 1964—66. Reader svc. editor Chilton Co./Food Engring., Philadelphia, Pa., 1960—66; tchr. English Marylawn of the Oranges, South Orange, NJ, 1978—80; jet fuel sales Exxon Co. Internat., Florham Park, NJ, 1980—97; v.p. of mktg. BA Internat., Morristown, NJ, 1984—86; artist and freelance writer DHC Enterprises, Morristown, NJ, 1998—; assoc. curator NJ. Ctr. for Visual Arts, Summit, NJ, 2000—05. Dir. Artemis Group, Morristown, NJ, 1990—98; cons. curator Visual Arts Ctr., NJ, 2006—. Mem.: Somerset Art Assn., Astrological Soc. of Princesses. Avocations: cross country skiing, hiking. Home: 20 Raven Dr Morristown NJ 07960 Office: Visual Arts Ctr New Jersey 68 Elm St Summit NJ 07901 Office Phone: 908-273-9121. Personal E-mail: dhcall@aol.com.

CALL, WHITNEY L., paralegal; b. Knoxville, Tenn., Mar. 12, 1979; AA, Pellissippi State Cmty. Coll., 2000. Paralegal The Davis Law Firm, Knoxville, 2000—05, Whelchel, May & Assoc., Knoxville, Tenn., 2005—. Mem.: Assn. of Trial Lawyers Am., Tenn. Trial Lawyers Assn.

CALLAGHAN, GEORGANN MARY, lawyer; b. Bklyn., June 25, 1944; d. George Louis and Jean (Russo) Carpenito; m. Matthew John Callaghan, June 7, 1969; children: Matthew, Michael, Christian. BS in Hist. Studies, SUNY Empire State Coll., 1994; JD, Pace U., 1999. Bar: Conn. 1999, N.Y. 2000, D.C. 2000. Adminstr. Wood & Scher, Scarsdale, 1986—99, atty., 1999—2001; assoc. Colucci & Umans, 2001—. Mem. environ. adv. coun. Scarsdale. Mem. ABA, N.Y. State Bar Assn., Westchester County Bar Assn., Conn. Bar Assn., D.C. Bar Assn., Westchester Women's Bar Assn., So. Poverty Law Ctr., Scarsdale Town and Village Club. Home: 49 Carman Rd Scarsdale NY 10583-6328 Office: Colucci & Umans 670 White Plains Rd Scarsdale NY 10583 E-mail: gmcallag@hotmail.com.

CALLAGHAN, MARJORIE SEYMOUR, music educator; b. Norwalk, Conn., Nov. 13, 1968; d. Robert Arthur and Marianne Sterling Seymour; m. Kevin William Callaghan, July 12, 1997; children: Rory William, Braeden Robert. BA, Gettysburg Coll., Pa., 1990; MMus, Hartt Sch. Music, Hartford, Conn., 1992; D in Musical Arts, Manhattan Sch. Music, NYC, 1998. Asst. prof. music Western Conn. State U., Danbury, 2000—06, assoc. prof. music, 2006—. French horn player Ridgefield Symphony Orch., Conn., 1993—; freelance musician (horn player). Author: The Horn Guide: A Reference For Solving Technical Problems, 2005. Mem. Long Ridge Handbell Choir, Danbury, 1993—; sec. Ch. Coun., Danbury, 1995—; chair Nurture Com., Danbury, 2005—. Mem.: Music Educators Nat. Conf., Internat. Horn Soc., Am. Fedn. Musicians. Office: Western Connecticut State University 181 White St Danbury CT 06810 Office Phone: 203-837-8351. Business E-Mail: callaghanm@wcsu.edu.

CALLAHAN, BARBARA ANN, librarian; b. Brockton, Mass., Nov. 3, 1953; d. Leo Francis and Betty Rose (Hayden) C.; m. Stephen Gary Jennings BA, Bridgewater State Coll., Mass., 1977; M.L.S., Simmons Coll., 1981. Library asst. Brockton Hosp., 1972-79; library asst. Mass. Coll. Pharmacy and Allied Health Scis., Boston, 1979-81; librarian combined libraries Gray

Herbarium and Arnold Arboretum, Harvard U., Cambridge, Mass., 1981—. Cons. Wasson Ethnomycological Library, Botanical Mus., Harvard U.; mem. preservation com. Harvard U. Library Council Mem. Council on Bot. and Hort. Libraries Avocations: field botany; photography; bicycling; stamp collecting. Home: 474 Broadway Cambridge MA 02138-3960 Office: Harvard U Herbaria 22 Divinity Ave Cambridge MA 02138-2020

CALLAHAN, CONNIE J., psychologist, educator; b. Kansas City, Mo. d. Joann Laney; children: Brent D., Mitzi L. MS in Psychology, Pittsburg State U., Kans., 1981; PhD in Counseling Psychology, U. of N.Mex, Albuquerque, 1991. Lic. profl. clin. counselor Ky. Bd. of Counseling, marriage and family therapist N.Mex Lic. Marriage and Family Therapy Bd. Owner Southwestern Counseling Svcs., Albuquerque, 1990—97; prof. of counseling & ednl. psychology Ea. Ky. U., Richmond, 1997—. Owner Callahan Cons., Lexington, Ky. Author: (book) Treatment of Depression in Children and Adolescents, The Way. Grant project dir. for elem. and secondary counseling grant U.S. Dept. of Edn. Office of Safe, Washington, 2003—06. Recipient 1.2 million dollar grant, U.S. Dept. of Edn., 2003—06, Commendation for svc. to families, schs., and comtys., Ho. of Reps., Commonwealth of Ky., 2000, Best Scholarly and Rsch. Jour. award, ACA, 2000, 2001, 2002, 2003, 2005, 2005, Spl. Merit Rsch. award, Edn. Jour., 2000. Fellow: Ky. Counseling Assn. (pres. 2005—06, Profl. Devel. award for Tng. Counselors 2004, Kearney Campbell award, Highest State award for Counselors 2003, Counselor Educator of Yr. 2000). Achievements include research in Special Merit Research Award. Education Journal. Awarded 2000. Avocation: photography. Office: Ea Ky Univ 406 Combs Richmond KY 40475 Office Phone: 859-622-1124. Business E-Mail: connie.callahan@eku.edu.

CALLAHAN, CONSUELO MARIA, federal judge; b. Palo Alto, Calif., June 9, 1950; married; 2 children. BA, Leland Stanford Jr. Univ., 1972; JD, McGeorge Sch. Law, Univ. Pacific, 1975; LLM, Univ. Va., 2004—. Bar: Calif. 1975. Dep. city atty. City of Stockton, Stockton, Calif., 1975—76; dep. dist. atty. Dist. Atty. Office, San Joaquin County, Calif., 1976—82, sup. dist. atty., 1982—86; ct. comm. Mcpl. Ct. of Stockton, Stockton, Calif., 1986—92; judge San Joaquin County Superior Ct., San Joaquin, Calif., 1992—96; Assoc. judge Ct. of Appeal, State of Calif., Calif., 1996—2003; judge, U.S. Court of Appeals (9th. cir.), 2003—. Recipient Award for Criminal Justice Programs, Gov., Susan B. Anthony Award for Women of Achievement, Stockton Peacemaker of the Yr., 1997, Mexican-Am. Hall of Fame, San Joaquin County, 1999. Achievements include first hispanic, first woman named to San Joaquin Co. Superior Ct. Office: US Ct Appeals 501 I St Sacramento CA 95814 Office Phone: 916-930-4160.*

CALLAHAN, DEBRA JEAN, political organization worker; b. Burbank, Calif., June 4, 1958; d. Robert Bascom and Betty Jean Callahan; m. Kenneth A. Cook. Student, Calif. State Poly. U., San Luis Obispo, 1976-79; BA magna cum laude, U. Calif., Santa Barbara, 1981. Legal asst. Loo, Merideth & McMillan, L.A., 1982-83; field staff Mondale for Pres., Washington, 1984; dep. state campaign mgr. Mondale-Ferraro Com., Kansas City, Mo., 1984; regional polit. dir. League of Conservation Voters, Portsmouth, NH, 1985-86; dep. campaign mgr. Kent Conrad for U.S. Senate, Bismarck, ND, 1986; exec. asst. to Senator Kent Conrad, Washington, 1986-87; dep. nat. polit. dir. Gore for Pres., Washington, 1987-88; exec. dir. Ams. for the Environment, Washington, 1988-90; campaign mgr. Re-election Rep. Howard Wolpe (D-Md.), 1990; policy cons. Nat. Toxics Campaign, 1991—; program dir. W. Alton Jones Found., 1992-95; exec. dir. Brainerd Found., Seattle, 1995-96; pres. League of Conservation Voters, Washington, 1996—2006. Polit. cons. League of Conservation Voters, 1988. Field dir. Hands Across Am., St. Louis, 1986; bd. dir. World Resources Inst., 1998—, Earth Day Network, 1999-2003. U. Calif. Dept. Environ. Studies scholar, Santa Barbara, 1981, Alumni award, 1998. Avocations: travel, reading, scuba diving, bicycling, music. Office: League of Conservation Voters 1920 L St NW Ste 800 Washington DC 20036-5045

CALLAHAN, JEAN M., personnel administrator; d. John Martin Hildebrandt and Catherine Mary Dore; m. Gerald Francis Callahan, July 11, 1969; 1 child, Christopher. BS, CUNY, 1967, MEd, 1969; MA in Labor studies, SUNY, 1981; MS in Spl. Edn., Adelphi U., N.Y., 1983; diploma in adminstrn., Long Island U. CW Post, N.Y., 1989. Cert. home and careers, elem. edn. and spl. edn. N.Y. Tchr. home and careers various schs., Long Island, NY, 1971—83; consumer tchr. Ea. Suffolk Bd. Cooperative Svcs. Edn., Long Island, NY, 1985; spl. edn. tchr. Miller (N.Y.) Pl. Union Free Sch. Dist., 1985—96, adminstr. pupil personnel adminstr., 1994—. Chairperson spl. edn. Miller (N.Y.) Pl. Union Free Sch. Dist., 1994—96; ednl. cons. ACCES Partnerships, Long Island, NY, 1993—96, N.Y. Dirs. Com., 2001—. Mem.: Coun. Exceptional Children, Coun. Adminstrs. Spl. Edn. (Long Island Chpt.) (treas. 2000—). Avocations: exercise, swimming, reading. Office: Miller Pl Union Free Sch Dist 275 Rte 25A Miller Place NY 11764 E-mail: jcallaha@millerplace.k12.ny.us.

CALLAHAN, PATRICIA R., bank executive; BSME, MIT, M in Mgmt. and Fin. Various mgmt. positions Crocker Nat. Bank, 1977—84, sr. v.p., mgr. corp. svcs., 1984—93; dir. human resources Wells Fargo & Co., 1993—97, exec. v.p. wholesale banking sys. fin. and ops., 1997—98, exec. v.p., dir. human resources, 1998—. Bd. dirs. United Way Bay Area; bd. trustees Dominican U. Calif. Office: Wells Fargo & Co 420 Montgomery St San Francisco CA 94163

CALLAHAN, SUSAN JANE WHITNEY, accountant; b. Salt Lake City, Dec. 2, 1950; d. Nathaniel R. Jr. and Mary Jeanette (Schroeder) Whitney. BS in Acctg. and Bus. Adminstrn., Black Hills State U., Spearfish, S.D., 1973. Agt. IRS, Rapid City, S.D., 1979—. Pres., bd. dirs. Black Hills Chamber Music Soc., Rapid City, 1992—; active First Presbyn. Ch. Rapid City. Named Civil Servant of Yr., Fed. Exec. Bd. Minn., 1999. Mem. AAUW. Avocations: music, skiing. Home: 4925 Raven Cir Rapid City SD 57702-9018

CALLAHAN, SUSAN LANE, mathematics professor; b. Kansas City, Aug. 27, 1956; d. Carter and Dora (Lane) Callahan. BS in Math., U. Mo.-Rolla, 1978, MS in Applied Math., 1980. Grad. tchg. asst. U. Mo., Rolla, 1978—80; faculty mem. math. Cottey Coll., Nevada, Mo., 1980—85, asst. prof. math., 1985—93, assoc. prof. math., 1993—. Recipient Gov.'s award for Excellence in Tchg., Coordinating Bd. Higher Edn., Mo., 2002. Mem.: Assn. Women in Math., Nat. Coun. Tchrs. Math., Am. Math. Assn. Two-Year Colls., Math. Assn. Am. (Mo. sect. sec./treas. 1998—2004), Soroptimist Internat. Club (treas., v.p., pres., dir. 1998—2004, Nevada, Mo.), Phi Kappa Phi. Avocations: horseback riding, playing clarinet, walking, hiking. Office: Cottey College 1000 W Austin Nevada MO 64772 Office Phone: 417-667-8181.

CALLAHAN, VIVIAN, broadcast executive; d. Albert Lewis Snyder and Gloria Elaine Snyder (nee, Gentry); m. Gregory James Callahan, June 1, 1996. Grad. H.S., Redondo Beach, Calif. Singer New Christy Minstrels, L.A., 1973, USO, L.A., 1973—74; writer/prodr. Ken Belsky Prodns., Studio City, Calif., 1981—82, CBS TV Network, L.A., 1983—88, assoc. dir., 1988—92; dir. Fox Broadcasting Co., L.A., 1992—96, exec. dir., 1996—. Mem., gold ribbon judge, presenter/spkr. PROMAX, Internat., L.A., 1993—97; mem. Mayor Riordan's Arts Adv. Com., L.A., 1996—97; pres., founding mem. Fox Talkz (Toastmasters), Century City, Calif., 1997—2000. Prodr., writer: 16-episode TV series Join The Group, TV spl. The Best Moments of 90210, The Rock and Roll Skating Special; prodr.: (TV spl.) Love Thy Neighbor: The Baddest and Best of Melrose Place. Founding mem. The Story Project, Culver City, Calif., 1996—2000; mem./mentor L.A. Maritime Inst., San Pedro, Calif., 2002—05; founding mem. Soc. Women Adventurers, 2005. Recipient Cert. of Merit, Internat. Film and TV Festival of N.Y., 1990, Hollywood Radio and TV Soc., 1990, award, Columbus Internat. Film and TV Festival, 1991, Mobius Advt. Com., 1991. Mem.: Acad. TV Arts and Scis., Soc. Women Adventurers (founding mem.). Avocations: sailing (transoceanic), travel, reading, creative writing, skiing. Office Phone: 310-369-4976. Business E-Mail: vivian.callahan@fox.com.

CALLAN, CLAIR MARIE, physician, laboratory director, educator; b. Sleaford, Lincolnshire, Eng., May 18, 1940; d. Joseph Edward and Margaret Mary (Hart) Mills; m. John Patrick Callan, Apr. 4, 1964; children: Eoin, Grainne, Colm, Maeve. M.B., B.Surgery, B. in Art of Obstetrics, Univ. Coll., Dublin, Ireland, 1963, MBA U. Phoenix, 1993. Intern Mater Hosp., Dublin, 1963-64, resident in anesthesia, 1964-65; staff physician State of Conn., Middletown, 1966-68; anesthesiologist St. Francis Hosp., Hartford, Conn., 1972-76; med. dir. Dept. of Income Maintenance, State of Conn., Hartford, 1978-84; v.p. med. and regulatory affairs, dir. med. affairs Abbott Labs., Abbott Park, Ill., 1985-92, venture head, 1992-93, v.p. med. and regulatory affairs and advanced rsch. hosp. products divsn., 1993—; clin. asst. prof. med., Chgo. Med. Sch./U. Health Scis., 1987—; CEO Callan Consulting, 2004—; sr. fellow Nat. Alliance for Health Info. Tech. Contbr. articles to profl. jours. Pres. PTA, Wethersfield, Conn., 1974, Capitol Region Assn. of Pvt. Swim Clubs, Hartford, 1978. Mem. Am. Med. Women's Assn. (pres. 1984-85, councillor 1981-83), AMA (pres. Conn. aux. 1979-81, v.p. sci. quality and pub. health 1999-2004, interim sr. v.p. profl. stds.), Am. Acad. Med. Dirs. Republican. Roman Catholic. Avocations: tennis; golf; needlework. Home: 1835 W North Pond Ln Lake Forest IL 60045-4819

CALLANAN, KATHLEEN JOAN, Internet company executive, retired electrical engineer; b. Detroit, Feb. 10, 1940; d. John Michael and Grace Marie (Kleehammer) C. BSE in Physics, U. Mich., 1963; postgrad., Northeastern U., 1963-65; MSEE, U. Hawaii, 1971; diploma in Japanese lang., St. Joseph Inst. Japanese, Tokyo, 1973; cert. in mgmt., Boeing MIl. Airplane Co., 1985. Religious missionary Maryknoll Sisters St. Dominic, 1966-79; vis. scholar Sophia U., Tokyo, 1976-79; elec.-eletronic components engr. Boeing Mil. Airplane Co. (later Boeing Def. and Space Group), Wichita, Kans., 1979-83, instrumentation design engr., 1983-85, strategic planner for tech., 1985-86, rsch. and engring. tech. supr., 1986-87, electromagnetic effects avionics mgr., 1987-89, elec. and electronics mgr., 1989, design tech. support mgr., 1990-92, engring. leader, 1992-95, ret., 1995; pres. KJC Web, Inc., 2003—04. Contbr. articles to profl. jours. Mem. Rose Hill Planning Commn., Kans., 1982-85; coord. Boeing Employees Amateur Radio Soc., Wichita, 1982-83, sec., 1991. Fellow Soc. Women Engrs. (sr. mem.; sect. rep. 1981-83, sec.-treas. 1985-86, regional bd. dirs. 1983-85, sect. pres. 1987-88); mem. Quarter Century Wireless Assn. (comms. com. 1985-86), Assn. Old Crows (bd. dirs. 1988-91, chpt. pres. 1991), Toastmasters (local pres. 1985-86, competent toastmaster 1985), Nat. Soc. DAR (officer Estero Island chpt. 2000—). Home: 473 Copenhagen St North Fort Myers FL 33903-2125 E-mail: kjcallanan@callanan.org, kjcallanan@torchlake.com.

CALLANDER, KAY EILEEN PAISLEY, business owner, retired education educator, writer; b. Coshocton, Ohio, Oct. 15, 1938; d. Dalton Olas and Dorothy Pauline (Davis) Paisley; m. Don Larry Callander, Nov. 18, 1977. BSE, Muskingum Coll., 1960; MA in Speech Edn., Ohio State U., 1964, postgrad., 1964-84. Cert. elem., gifted, drama, theater tchr., Ohio. Tchr. Columbus (Ohio) Pub. Schs., 1960-70, 80-88, drama specialist, 1970-80, classroom, gifted/talented tchr., 1986-90, ret., 1990; sole prop. The Ali Group, Kay Kards, 1992—. Coord. Artists-in-the Schs., 1977-88; ednl. cons. Innovation Alliance Youth Adv. Coun., 1992—; cons., presenter in field. Producer-dir., Shady Lane Music Festival, 1980-88; dir. tchr. (nat. distbr. video) The Trial of Gold E. Locks, 1983-84; rep., media pub. relations liason Sch. News., 1983-88; author, creator Trivia Game About Black Americans; presenter for workshop by Human Svc. Group and Creative Edn. Coop., Columbus, Ohio, 1989. Benefactor, Columbus Jazz Arts Group; v.p., bd. dirs. Neoteric Dance and Theater Co., Columbus, 1985-87; tchr., participant Future Stars sculpture exhibit, Ft. Hayes Ctr., Columbus Pub. Schs., 1988; tchr. advisor Columbus Coun. PTAs, 1983-86, co-chmn. reflections com., 1984-87; mem. Columbus Mus. Art, Citizens for Humane Action, Inc.; upt.'s adv. coun. Columbus Pub. Schs., 1967-68; presenter Young Author Seminar, Ohio Dept. Edn., 1988, Illustrating Methods for Young Authors' Books, 1986-87; cons. and workshop leader seminar/workshop Tchg. About the Constitution in Elem. Schs., Franklin County Ednl. Coun., 1988; sponsor Minority Youth Recognition Awards, 1994. Named Educator of Yr., Shady Lane PTA, 1982, Columbus Coun. PTAs, 1989, winner Colour Columbus Landscape Design Competition, 1990; Sch. Excellence grantee Columbus Pub. Schs.; Commendation Columbus Bd. Edn. and Ohio Ho. of Reps. for Child Assault Prevention project, 1986-87; first place winner statewide photo contest Ohio Vet. Assn., 1991; recipient Muskingum Coll. Alumni Disting. Svc. award, 1995. Mem. ASCD, AAUW, Assn. for Childhood Edn. Internat., Ohio Coun. for Social Studies, Franklin County Ret. Tchrs. Assn., Nat. Mus. Women in the Arts, Ohio State U. Alumni Assn., U.S. Army Officers Club, Navy League, Liturgical Art Guild Ohio, Columbus Jazz Arts Group, Columbus Mus. Art, Nat. Coun. for Social Studies, Columbus Art League, Columbus Maennerchor (Damen sect.). Republican. Avocations: painting, photography, swimming, golf, playing piano and organ. Home: 9131 Indian Mound Rd Pickerington OH 43147 Personal E-mail: paiscallander@earthlink.net.

CALLAWAY, LINDA MARIE, special education educator; b. Upland, Calif., June 21, 1940; d. Elwyn T. and Fladger Idell (Flake) Bice; m. David Barry Callaway, May, 1957 (div. sept. 1962); children: Tess Callaway Tyler, Darren Francis. B in English, Calif. State U., Fullerton, 1975; MEd Adminstrn., Calif. State U., L.A., 1991. Cert. tchr. L.A. County Office Edn., 1984—88; resource specialist spl. edn. Pomona (Calif.) Unified Sch. Dist., 1990—. Presenter U. St. Petersburg, Russia, 2002. Mem. Soc. Of Friends. Avocations: travel, jewelry making. Home: 2225 Brescia Ave Claremont CA 91711-1807 Office: Pomona HS Pomona Unified Sch Dist 475 Bangor St Pomona CA 91767-2449 Office Phone: 909-397-4498.

CALLENDER, NORMA ANNE, counselor, public relations executive; b. Huntsville, Tex., May 10, 1933; d. C.W. Carswell and Nell Ruth (Collard) Hughes Bost; m. B.G. Callender, 1951 (div. 1964); remarried 1967 (div. 1973); children: Teresa Elizabeth, Leslie Gemey, Shannah Hughes, Kelly Mari; m. E Purfurst, June 1965 (div. Aug. 1965). BS, U. Houston, 1969; MA, U. Houston, Clear Lake, 1977; postgrad., Tex. So. U., 1971, Lamar U., 1972-73, U. Houston-Clear Lake, 1979, 87, 89-93, postgrad., 1998, St. Thomas U., 1985, 86, Aerospace Inst., NASA, Johnson Space Ctr., 1986, San Jacinto Coll., 1988—99, postgrad., 2001—03; PhD, Cornerstone U., 1998. Cert. profl. reading specialist, Tex.; lic. profl. counselor. Tchr. Houston Ind. Schs., 1969-70; co-counselor, instr. Ellington AFB, Houston, 1971; tchr. Clear Creek Schs., League City, Tex., 1970-86; owner, dir. Bay Area Tutoring and Reading Clinic, Clear Lake City, Tex., 1970—, Bay Area Tng. Assocs., 1982-98, Bay Area Family Counseling, 1995—; cons., LPC intern Guidance Ctr., Pasadena (Tex.) Ind. Sch. Dist., 1993-95; prin., dir. pub. rels. Gateway Foods USA, 2005—. Instr. San Jacinto Coll., Pasadena, 1980-81, 91-93; adj. instr. U. Houston, Clear Lake, 1986-91; founder, editor BATA Books Pub., 1997—. Author: numerous poems. State advisor U.S. Congl. Adv. Bd., 1985-87; vol., bd. dirs. Family Outreach Ctr., 1989-92; vol. Bay Area Coun. on Drugs and Alcohol, Nassau Bay, Tex., 1993-94; bd. dirs. Ballet San Jacinto, 1985-87; adv. bd. Cmty. Ednl. TV, 1990-92; charter mem. Nat. Women's History Mus., Washington, 2005. Recipient Franklin award U. Houston, 1965-67; Delta Kappa Gamma/Beta Omicron scholar, 1967-68, PTA scholar, 1973, Berwin scholar, 1976, Mary Gibbs Jones scholar, 1976-77, Found. Econ. Edn. scholar, 1976, Insts. Achievement Human Potential scholar, Phila., 1987. Mem.: ACA, The NET: Bay Area Mental Health Providers Network, Clear Creek Educators Assn. (past, honorarium 1976, 1977, 1985), Sam Houston Chpt., Daughters of Am. Revolution, Houston Symphony League, Bay Area, Houston Symphony League of Bay Area, Leadership Clear Lake Alumni Assn. (charter, program and projects com. mem. 1986—87, edn. com. 1985), U. Houston Alumni Assn. (life), Phi Theta Kappa, Phi Delta Kappa, Kappa Delta Pi, Psi Chi (life), Phi Kappa Phi (life). Mem. Life Tabernacle Ch. Office: Ste R 1234 Bay Area Blvd Houston TX 77058-2538

CALLENTINE, KATHERINE NAOMI, elementary school educator; b. Twin Falls, Idaho, Dec. 3, 1947; d. William Eugene and Barbara Naomi (Warner) Kevan; m. James Larry Callentine; children: Brian Douglas, Brandon William. BA in History, Wash. State U., 1970; MEd, Calif. State U. Stanislaus, 1976. Cert. tchr. Calif., 1976. Tchr. Merced (Calif.) Union H.S. Dist., 1970—2005, Magic Valley Christian Sch., Twin Falls, Idaho, 2005—, counselor, 2005—. Mem. choir First Bapt. Ch., Merced, 1978—2005. Republican. Baptist. Avocations: quilting, reading, travel, sewing, interior decorating. Office: Magic Valley Christian School 1631 Grandview Drive North Twin Falls ID 83301 E-mail: kevan@highdesertlawn.myrf.net.

CALLESEN-GYORGAK, JAN ELAINE, special education educator; b. Manistee, Mich., Sept. 21, 1959; d. Carl Wayne and Patsy Arlene (Haglund) Callesen; m. Gregg Gyorgak, Oct. 27, 1990; children: Danielle Marie, Nathaniel Charles, Kristen Lynn, Wayne Anthony, Raymond Jacob. BS in Edn., Bowling Green State U., 1981; M in Curriculum and Instrn., Cleve. State U., 1988. Lic. elem. edn., spl. edn., libr. and media scis. Montessori tchr. Children's Home of Parma, Ohio, 1981-82; kindergarten tchr., coord. Murton's Child Devel. Ctr., Fairview Park, Ohio, 1983-85; spl. edn. tchr.-learning disabilities Cleve. Pub. Schs., 1985—. Advisor Safety Patrol, Cleve., 1986-99. Mem. Cleve. Tchrs. Union, Coun. for Exceptional Children (divsn. learning disabilities). Avocations: needlepoint, embroidery, collecting precious moments figurines, scrapbooks. Home: 6283 Surrey Dr North Olmsted OH 44070-4813 Office: Walton Elem Sch 3409 Walton Ave Cleveland OH 44113-4942

CALLEY, TRANQUIL HUDSON, travel consultant, educator; b. New Amsterdam, Guyana, Nov. 27, 1937; arrived in US, 1938; d. Adrian Wilfred Maurice Hudson and Nancy Hilda Turner; m. John Edward Calley, Sept. 17, 1971; stepchildren: John James, Griffyd Adams; m. Loren Rue Smith, June 17, 1957 (div. June 1970); children: Loren Adrian Smith, Kalyn David Smith-Tranquil'son(dec.). AA in Liberal Studies, West Valley C.C., Campbell, Calif., 1970; BA in English, Calif. State U., Fresno, 1976; MA in English Lit., U. Calif., Riverside, 1989. Tchg. credential Calif., cert. c.c. tchr. State of Calif., travel agt. Inst. of Cert. Travel Agts., destination specialist (Europe and Latin America) Inst. of Cert. Travel Agts. Fit travel cons. Travel Planners, San Jose, Calif., 1969—70; travel cons. Bashford Travel, Fresno, Calif., 1974—77; mgr. Giselle Travel, Fresno, Calif., 1977—78, Travel Network, Hemet, Calif., 1978—82; travel cons. Travel by George, Riverside, 1982—90; instr. Mt. San Jacinto (Calif.) Coll., 1989—92; travel agent outside sales Unique Vacations, Riverside, 1990—92; advisor, counselor dept. liberal studies U. Redlands, 1999—2002. ESL instr. Mt. San Jacinto C.C., Hemet, 1989—92; trainer sexual harassment in the workplace Riverside (Calif.) County Office Edn., 1996—99; spkr Lesbian Gay Bisexual Transgender Gala, A Mother's Journey over the Rainbow; adv. counselor U. Redland, 1999—2002; adj. prof. U. Redlands, 2002—. Editor: (books of poetry) Whispers in the Gale: An AIDS Journal; dramatist: (dramatic poetry performance piece) Whispers in the Gale: Living and Dying with AIDS. Vol. for AIDS awareness; rep. to Sacramento Riverside Alumni Advocacy Com., Riverside, 2000—05; mem. local spiritual assembly Baha'i Faith, Fresno, 1975—78, sec., 1975—78; dir. Advocates Sch. for Underperforming Students, Grand Terrace, Calif., 1997—2000; mem. scholarship com. U. Calif.-Riverside Alumni Assn., Riverside, 2004—05. Recipient Supporting U. Calif.-Riverside Lesbian Gay Bisexual Transgender students award, Chancellor's Adv. Com. Status of Lesbians, Gays, Bisexuals, Transgenders, June 3 2004. Mem.: U. Calif. Alumni Assn. (bd. dirs. 2005). Home: 23715 Coldwater Ct Moreno Valley CA 92557-2864 Personal E-mail: tcalley747@aol.com.

CALLIHAN, D. JEANNE, psychologist, educator; b. Belton, Tex., Mar. 16, 1930; d. Loyd Whitfield Galzener and Jewel Erline Moss; m. Milton Louis Callihan, Dec. 29, 1957; 1 child, Debra Ann. BS, U. Mary-Hardin Baylor, 1951; MS, Iowa State U., 1955; PhD, U. Ala., Tuscaloosa, 1966. Lic. psychologist Tex., cert. tchr. Tex., adminstr., supr. Tex. Home and consumer scis. tchr. Albin (Wyo.) H.S., 1951—54; instr. tchr. edn. dept. Miss. State Coll. for Women, Columbus, 1961—64; psychologist VA Psychiat. Hosp., Tuscaloosa, 1966—68; asst. prof. edn. U. Ala., Tuscaloosa, 1968—69; assoc. prof. edn. U. Houston, 1969—71; prof. edn. and psychology Trinity U., San Antonio, 1971—90; prof. early childhood edn. Taipei (Taiwan) Mcpl. Tchrs. Coll., 1990—91; vis. prof. divsn. edn. U. Tex., San Antonio, 1991—93; pvt. practice cons. psychol. svcs. San Antonio, 1993—. Established 1st tchr. tng. program in edn./early childhood edn. Am. Coll. for Girls, Am. U., Cairo, 1955—57; chmn. bd. dirs. Early Childhood Educators 15 Dist. Coalition, San Antonio, 1975—90; U.S. rep. Internat. Conf. on Early Childhood Edn., Melbourne, Australia, 1978. Author: Kindergarten Teacher Resource Guilde, 1970, 2d edit., 1975, Stories for Young Readers: Our Mexican Ancestors, Vols. I and II, 1981; contbr. rsch. papers to profl. publs. Mem. family focus bd. United Way Svc. for Distressed Families, San Antonio, 1966—98; mem. World Affairs Coun. of San Antonio, 2004—; vol. ARC. Grantee, Tex. Edn. Assn., 1986—88, Taiwan Ministry Edn., 1990—91, Ford Found./NSF, Egypt. Mem.: APA, Tex. Assn. Childhood Edn. (pres. 1990), Assn. Childhood Edn. Internat., Tex. Psychol. Assn., World Orgn. for Early Childhood Edn. (past regional dir.), Delta Kappa Gamma (pres. 1982, 1984, Woman of Yr. 1985—87). Republican. Achievements include established first college teacher tng. in early childhood education. Avocations: exercise, writing, reading. Home: 241 E Sunset Rd San Antonio TX 78209-2717 Office: Deer Oaks Mental Health Assocs 7272 Wurzback Ste 601 San Antonio TX 78240 Personal E-mail: DJCallihan@aol.com.

CALLINAN, PATRICIA ANN, legal secretary; b. Harrisburg, Pa., Dec. 29, 1943; d. Albert Frances and Gilda Mary (Cifani) Pugliese; 1 child, Tricia Ann Corder. Comml. diploma, Bishop McDevitt, 1961. Chief enforcement sec. Commonwealth of Pa., Harrisburg, 1961-66; supt. sec. Cape May (N.J.) County Vocat. Tech. Ctr., 1966-67; asst. br. mgr. Continental Title Ins., Wildwood, N.J., 1967-91; legal sec. Corino & Dwyer, Esqs., Wildwood, 1991—. Past. pres., treas. Cape May County Legal Sec., 1968-70, St. Ann's PTA, Wildwood, 1980-84; past pres. Wildwood Cath. Parent Guild, 1986-88; bd. sec. Wildwood Crest Tourism Commn., 1990-93. Mem. Cape May County Women's Rep. Club; apptd. commr. Cape May County Mcpl. Utilities Authority, 1999; sunshine chmn. Cape May County Rep. Orgn. Named Legal Sec. of Yr., Cape May County Legal Sec., 1970, 73. Mem. Victoria Village Homeowners (sec. 1994-96), Lower Township Rep. Club, Lower Township Rep. Orgn. (committeewoman 1994-96, 96—, mem. exec. com. rec. sec. 1994—), Cape May County Legal Secs. Assn. Roman Catholic. Avocations: walking, dance, reading, plays. Home: 36 Canterbury Way Cape May NJ 08204-4268 Office: Corino & Dwyer Esqs 9700 Pacific Ave Wildwood NJ 08260-3334

CALLIS, KAREN DENISE, elementary school educator; d. Beverly Vinson and Martha Ann (Griffin) Hughes; m. Charles Hunter Callis, June 13, 1998; 1 child, Colston Hunter. BS in Edn., U. Memphis, 1998. Cert. tchr. grades 1-8, gifted edn. tchr. Children's dir., asst. Bellevue Bapt. Ch., Cordova, Tenn., 1995—97; tchr. 4th grade St. Mary's Sch., Jackson, Tenn., 1998—. Tchr. Camp Invention, Jackson, 2003—04, St. Mary's After-Sch. Sci. Club, Jackson, 2004—05. Mem.: Nat. Cath. Educator's Assn.

CALLOWAY, CAROLYN, elementary school educator; b. Ft. Lauderdale, Fla., Jan. 19, 1953; d. Charlie and Marie (Dudley) Ross; m. Joseph Calloway, May 20, 1976; children: Vanessa, Tina, Joseph, Andrea. BA, Tenn. State U., 1974. 5th grade tchr. Myrtle Grove Elem. Sch., Opa Locka, Fla., 1974—, sci. resource tchr., 1990-99, science fair coord., 1990-95, 98-99; dist. science fair judge Dade County Sch., Miami, Fla., 1995-99; student coun. adv. Myrtle Grove Elem. Schs., 1990-94. Sec. sunday Bible sch. House of God Ch., Ft. Lauderdale, trustee, bd. mem., ordered deacon. Mem. Dade County Sci. Tchrs. Assn., Dade County Math Tchrs. Assn. Democrat. Home: 1589 NW 31st Way Fort Lauderdale FL 33311-4353

CALVANO, LINDA SUE LEY, insurance company executive; b. Franklin, Ind., Nov. 27, 1949; d. Jiles Rex and Naomi Katherine (Van Horn) Riggs; m. Thomas Alan Ley Calvano, Feb. 28, 1987. BS in Edn. with distinction, Ind. U.-Purdue U., 1971, MS in Edn. with highest distinction, 1975. Cert. paralegal; lic. life, accident, health, property and casualty ins. agt., Ind.; cert. total quality mgmt.; project mgmt. profl. designation. Elem. tchr. Indpls. Pub. Schs., 1972-74, Center Grove Community Schs., Greenwood, Ind., 1974-81; dir. adminstrn. Brougher Agy., Inc., Greenwood, 1981-84; mgr. claims/customer svc. The Associated Group, Inc., Indpls., 1984-89; v.p. team ops. Key Benefit Adminstrs., Inc., Indpls., 1989-92; regional mgr. ops. & rev. projects Anthem Blue Cross Blue Shield, Indpls., 1992-97, quality assurance dir., 1997—. Mem. cotillion com. Humane Soc. Indpls., 1991; vol. Riley Run for Children, Indpls., 1985-92. Recipient Good Girl Citizenship award Women's Aux. of Am. Legion, 1968. Mem. Am. Mgmt. Assn., Nat. Assn. Life Underwriters, Nat. Assn. Health Underwriters, Inst. Internal Auditors, Indpls. Paralegal Assn., Project Mgmt. Inst., Toastmasters Internat. Republican. Episcopalian. Home: 6358 Bluff Acres Dr Greenwood IN 46143-9037 Office: Anthem Blue Cross Blue Shield 220 Virginia Ave Indianapolis IN 46204 Office Phone: 317-287-8160.

CALVANO, PHYLLIS, publishing executive; BBA in Acctg., Iona Coll., 1978; MBA, NYU, 1986. CPA N.Y. From controller Times Books, WQXR and Edn. Enrichment Materials to v.p., controller The N.Y. Times The N.Y. Times Co., 1982—2004, v.p., 2004—, controller The N.Y. Times, 2004—. Office: The NY Times 229 W 43rd St New York NY 10036

CALVERT, SUSAN KADEY, music educator; b. Peoria, Ill., Oct. 7, 1962; d. Deane B. and Joan B. Ballard; m. Marc E. Calvert, Feb. 2, 1961; children: Hilary M., Tyler D., Abigail L., Daniel M., Charles W. BA in Voice/Piano Performance, Roberts Wesleyan Coll., Rochester, NY, 1984. Dir. Elmbrook Ctr. for the Arts, Brookfield, Wis., 1989—96; worship dir. Harvest Cmty. Ch., Oak Creek, Wis., 1996—99; tchr. The Classical Acad., Colorado Springs, Colo., 2001—. Home: 28 Saber Creek Dr Monument CO 80132 Office: The Classical Academy 975 Stout Rd Colorado Springs CO 80129 Office Phone: 719-484-0081. Personal E-mail: susankadey@adelphia.net.

CALVIN, DOROTHY VER STRATE, computer company executive; b. Dec. 22, 1929; d. Herman and Christina (Plakmyer) Ver Strate; m. Allen D. Calvin, Oct. 5, 1953; children: Jamie, Kris, Bufo, Scott. BS magna cum laude, Mich. State U., 1951; MA, U. San Francisco, 1988, EdD, 1991. Mgr. data processing Behavioral Rsch. Labs., Menlo Park, Calif., 1972-75; dir. Mgmt. Info. Sys. Inst. for Profl. Devel., San Jose, Calif., 1975-76; sys. analyst, programmer Pacific Bell Info. Sys., San Francisco, Calif., 1976-81, staff mgr., 1981-84; mgr. applications devel. Data Architects Inc., San Francisco, Calif., 1984-86; pres. Ver Strate Press, San Francisco, Calif., 1986—. Instr., Downtown C.C., San Francisco, 1980-84, Cañada C.C., 1986-92, Skyline Coll., 1988-92, City Coll. of San Francisco, 1992—; mem. computer curriculum adv. coun. San Francisco City Coll., 1982-84. V.p. LWV, Roanoke, Va., 1956-58. Pres. Bulliss Purissima Parents Group, Los Altos, Calif., 1962-64; bd. dirs. Vols. for Israel, 1986-87. Mem. IEEE Computer Soc., Assn. Sys. Mgmt., Assn. Women in Computing, Phi Delta Kappa. Democrat. Avocations: computing, gardening, jogging, reading. Office: Ver Strate Press 1645 15th Ave San Francisco CA 94122-3523 Personal E-mail: dcalvin2@aol.com.

CALVIN, JAMIE DUIF, retired interactive designer; b. Lansing, Mich., July 28, 1954; d. Allen David and Dorothy Viola Calvin; m. Craig Aaron Tovey, Mar. 23, 1980 (div. Oct. 1994); children: Kendl, David, Leo. BBA in Computer Info. Sys., Ga. State U., 1990. Pres. Strategy, Inc., Atlanta, 1982-94; sr. designer Jade River Designs, Atlanta, 1994-98; sr. tech. cons. interactive media IBM, Atlanta, 1998-99; v.p. global retail practice Scient, San Francisco, 1999—, ret. Author: 6 Myths of Web Marketing, 1996, Marketing Manager's Plain English Guide to the Internet, 1998; columnist Chess Life Mag., 1996-97. Mem. ACM, Assn. Internet Profls., HTML Writers Guild (governing bd. 1998), U.S. Chess Fedn. (publs. com. 1996-97, Top 50 U.S. Women Chessplayers). Avocation: chess.

CAMAC, MARGARET VICTORIA, construction company executive; b. Wellington, New Zealand, Mar. 26, 1946; came to U.S., 1981; d. Paul and Cavel (Durnett) Leonard; m. Barry John Camac, June 1, 1968; children: Bianca, Karla, Paula, Victoria. BA, U. Manitoba, Winnipeg, Manitoba, Can., 1977; MEd, U. Manitoba, Winnipeg, Can., 1978. Tchr., New Zealand, 1966-69, Can., 1969-76; vol. set up parent programs for handicapped children various bus., Rio Grande Valley, Tex., 1981-86; v.p. Wellington Constrn. Co., 1991-92; pres. Hadney 5 Design, 1992-2000; v.p. Concrete Pumping Co., 1998-2000. Child advocate. Vol. Ga. Coun. Child Abuse, Atlanta, 1990-91; developmental disabilities com. Atlanta Jewish Cmty. Ctr., 1998-2000. Mem. Jr. League Atlanta (named one of Twelve Outstanding Vols. in Atlanta, 1990-91, mem. fidelity trust 1991). Avocations: classical piano, flower judging and design, sewing, weaving, hiking. Home: 335 Mount Paran Rd NW Atlanta GA 30327-4605

CAMARDESE, AMY HOFFMAN, education educator; b. Massillon, Ohio, Sept. 5, 1950; d. Paul Wilbur and Anne Kelly Hoffman; m. Zachary Camardese, Dec. 22, 1973; children: Christina, Margaret, Stephanie. BS in Edn., Ohio U., 1972; MS in Edn., U. Pitts., 1975; PhD, Kent State U., 2002. Tchr. Keystone Oaks Sch., Pitts., 1972—75; tchr. spl. edn. Liberty Schs., Youngstown, Ohio, 1985—99; asst. prof. Geneva Coll., Beaver Falls, Pa., 1999—2001, Westminster Coll., New Wilmington, Pa., 2001—. Grant reviewer FIPSE, Washington, 2003; text reviewer Houghton-Mifflin Pub., 2003; mem. com. Notable Trade Books for Young People, Carter Woodson Book Award. Bd. dirs. Children's Internat. Summer Villages, 1994, Relay for Life, Am. Cancer Soc. Recipient Martin Luther King award, East Ohio Edison, 1995; Jennings scholar, Liberty Schs., 1995. Mem.: Coun. Exceptional Children, Delta Kappa Gamma, Phi Delta Kappa (sec. 2003). Methodist. Avocations: reading, walking, running. Home: 12 Redfern Dr Youngstown OH 44505

CAMBER, DIANE WOOLFE, museum director; b. Miami Beach, Fla. m. Isaac Camber. BA in Art History, Barnard Coll.; postgrad., Columbia U., Mass. Coll. Art; MEd in Arts Edn., Boston State Coll. Mus. lectr., pub. rels. specialist Albright-Knox Art Gallery, Buffalo, 1962—64; mus. educator De Cordova and Dana Mus., Lincoln, Mass., 1967—68; mus. lectr. Mus. Fine Arts, Boston, 1968—69; art specialist L.A. Pub. Schs., 1970—77; instr. Ft. Lauderdale (Fla.) Art Inst., 1978—79; assoc. dir. Miami (Fla.) Design Preservation League, 1978—80; acting dir. Bass Mus. Art, Miami, 1980—82, exec. dir., chief curator, 1982—. Co-author: Frank Lloyd Wright: Decorative Objects, Prints, Drawings, Florida Projects, 1984. Campaigned to place Miami's Art Deco Dist. on the Nat. Register of Historica Places; bd. dirs. Chaim Gross Found., NY. Recipient Chevalier des Arts et Lettres, French Govt., 1989. Mem.: Fla. Art Mus. Dirs. Assn. (v.p. 1984—86, pres. 1986—), Mus. Trustees Assn. (mem. adv. coun. dirs.), Am. Assn. Art Mus. Dirs. Office: Bass Mus Art 2121 Park Ave Miami Beach FL 33139

CAMBERN, ANDREA, newscaster, reporter; m. Brett Cambern. Student, Ariz. State U. With Sta. KTSP-TV, Phoenix, Sta. KVOA-TV, Tucson; owner pub. rels. firm; anchor, reporter Sta. WBNS-TV, Columbus, Ohio, 1991—. Named Female Anchor of Yr., Nat. Assn. Television Journalists; recipient Emmy awards (4). Office: WBNS-TV 770 Twin Rivers Dr Columbus OH 43215

CAMELO, DIANNE M., lawyer; b. Bronx, N.Y., Apr. 9, 1960; AB cum laude, Colgate U., 1982; JD, Fordham U., 1985. Bar: N.J., U.S. Dist. Ct., Dist. of N.J. 1985, N.Y., U.S. Dist. Ct., So. and Ea. Dists. of N.Y. 1986. Ptnr. Levy, Stopol & Camelo, LLP, Uniondale, NY; of counsel Audiovox Corp., Hauppauge. Mem.: N.Y. State Bar Assn., Nassau County Bar Assn. Office: Levy, Stopol & Camelo, LLP 1425 EAB Plaza Uniondale NY 11556-1425 Office Phone: 516-802-7007.

CAMER, MARY MARTHA, retired secretary; b. McAdoo, Pa., Oct. 30, 1932; d. John Fiolich and Elizabeth (Chomo) Sussick; m. Kenneth Camer, Feb. 10, 1952; children: Kenneth, Curtis, Marybeth. AA in Bus. Mgmt., Bucks County Community Coll., 1982. Sch. sec. Neshaminy Sch. Dist., Langhorne, Pa., 1959-61; NCR bookkeeper Gen. Doors Corp., Bristol, Pa., 1962-65; jr. acct., NCR bookkeeper Lower Bucks Hosp., Bristol, Pa., 1965-68; office mgr., bookkeeper Archdiocese of Phila., Blessed J. Neumann Nursing Home, 1968-78; payroll coord. Warner Lambert Co. Alphamedics Divsn., Levittown, Pa., 1979-81, human resouces pers. coord., 1978-86; sec. Rohm and Haas, DVI, Bristol, 1988-95. Election judge Middletown, Pa., 2001. Recipient Outstanding Adult award Pa. Assn. for Adult Continuing Edn., 1981. Democrat. Roman Catholic. Home: 94 Queen Lily Rd Levittown PA 19057-1914

CAMERON, ANN M., language educator; b. Fargo, N.D., Dec. 18, 1950; d. Edwin Frank and Helen Charlotte Baumler; m. G. Bruce Cameron, July 26, 1972; children: Caitlin E., Lily J. BA in Humanities, Mich. State U., 1971, MA in English, 1972; PhD in English, Purdue U., 2000. Instr. English, Ind. U., Kokomo, 1977—82, asst. prof., 1983—2000, assoc. prof., 2001—, chmn. Dept. Humanities, 2006—. Author: Sidekicks in American Literature, 2002. Mem.: MLA, Am. Lit. Soc. of MLA, Soc. Early Americanists, Phi Beta Kappa. Office: Ind U Kokomo 2300 S Washington PO Box 9003 Kokomo IN 46904-9003

CAMERON, BROOKE BULOVSKY, art educator, artist; b. Madison, Wis., Mar. 10, 1941; d. George Frank and Frances Lucille Bulovsky; m. Ben D. Cameron, July 22, 1967. BS in Art Edn. with honors, U. Wis., Madison, 1963; MA in Printmaking, U. Iowa, Iowa City, 1966. Instr. Menominee Pub. Schs., Mich., 1963—64, Tex. Christian U., Ft. Worth, 1966—67; prof. U. Mo., Columbia, 1967—. Chair art dept. U. Mo., 1979—81. Intaglio prints, nat. and internat. juried exhbns.; contbr. articles to profl. jours.; presenter in field. Donor Assistance League of Mo., Columbia, art donations to Flood Relief, New Orleans. Mem.: So. Graphics Coun., Coll. Art Assn. Avocation: travel. Home: 923 College Park Dr Columbia MO 65203 Office: Univ Mo Dept Art A126 FA Columbia MO 65211 Office Phone: 573-882-9449. Business E-Mail: cameronbb@missouri.edu.

CAMERON, DONNA, artist, art educator; b. Mishawaka, Ind., Apr. 7, 1951; d. Donald Peter Benjamin Cameron and Carmela Barbara Milo; m. Phillip Emil Sloan, Jan. 12, 1975; 1 child, Andrew Cameron Sloan. BFA in Film, Painting and Drawing, RISD, 1974; BFA in Film, Sch. of Art Inst. of Chgo., 1980; postgrad., Atelier Herbo, Paris, 1982—84. Fla. Keys corr. Miami (Fla.) Herald Newspaper, 1976—78; film artist Mus. Modern Art, N.Y.C., 1992—; sr. editor Manhattan Arts Internat. Mag., N.Y.C., 1995—. Adj. asst. prof. Tisch Sch. of Arts, N.Y.C., NY, 1994—. Author: more than 80 short films and videos; Fedn. Modern Sculptors and Painters, N.Y.C. Bd. dirs. NY Film and Video Coun., N.Y.C., 1998—; consw. mem. Univ. Coun. Arts Educators, N.Y.C., 1998—. Nominee Rockefeller fellowship, 2004; fellow, Art Students League NY, N.Y.C., 1984—86, Jerome Found., St. Paul, 1989, 1993, MacDowell Colony, Peterborough, NH, 1998, Macdowell Colony, Peterborough, NH, 1999, 2000. Achievements include patents for cinematic paper emulsion. Avocations: gardening, bicycling, hiking, animal rights advocacy, volunteer emergency medical squad worker. E-mail: papercam@aol.com.

CAMERON, FRANCES MARILYN, elementary school educator; b. Denison, Tex., July 19, 1936; d. Cornelius McLeod and Duressie Amelia Andersno; m. Leo Samuel Cameron, Apr. 6, 1963 (dec. Feb. 8, 1973); children: Reginald Eugene, Derrick Leon. BS, Prairie View A&M U., Tex., 1954—58, MEd, 1959—63. Cert. tchr., elem. & secondary edn. Tex. Dept Edn. 4th grade tchr. Floydada Pub. Schs., Tex., 1958—59; 3rd grade tchr. Denison Ind. Sch. Dist., 1959—62; tchr., 8th grade & typing Bonham Ind. Sch. Dist., 1962—64; 3rd grade tchr. Denison Ind. Sch. Dist., 1965—94; reading Edison-Sherman, Sherman, 1995—2000; remedial reading tchr. Sherman Ind. Sch. Dist., 2000—. Mem., rep. Texoma Coun. of GDU, Sherman, 1992—2002; sec., mem. Denison Ind. Sch. Dist. Bd., 1997—, Texoma Edn. Fed. Credit U., Sherman, 1997—. Mem. N. Town Shalom Corp., Denison, 1992, NAACP, Sherman & Dennison, 1999. Recipient State Retiree of Yr. award, Tex. Classroom Tchr. Assn., Austin, 1995, Dream Maker award, Tex. House of Rep., Denison, 1999, Edn. award, NAACP, Sherman, 1999. Mem.: Delta Kappa Gamma. Avocations: travel, working with youth, reading, stage plays. Home: 800 W Elm St Denison TX 75020

CAMERON, HEATHER ANNE, publishing executive; b. Montreal, Quebec, Can., Mar. 12, 1951; came to U.S., 1981; d. Douglas George and Jeanne Sutherland (Thompson) C.; m. Ward Eric Shaw, Dec. 20, 1980; 1 child, Geoffrey Cameron. BA, Queen's U., Kingston, Ont., Can., 1973; MLS, McGill U., Montreal, 1977. Head reference and bibliography sect. Nat. Libr. Can., Ottawa, 1977-80; head editl. dept. Librs. Unltd., Inc., Denver, 1981-86; v.p. acquisitions and editl. devel. ABC-CLIO, Inc., Santa Barbara, Calif., 1986-92, pres., pub. Santa Barbara, Denver and Eng., 1992-97; v.p., gen. mgr. Westgroup, San Francisco, 1997—. Bd. dirs. Friends of Librs. U.S.A., v.p., 1996, pres., 1997—. Mem. ALA (com. chair 1993—), Friends of Librs., USA (dir. 1994—, pres. 1997-2000), Amnesty Internat., Phi Beta Mu. Office: Thomson-West 425 Market St San Francisco CA 94105 Office Phone: 415-344-5010. Business E-Mail: heather.cameron@thomson.com.

CAMERON, JUDITH LYNNE, secondary school educator; b. Oakland, Calif., Apr. 29, 1945; d. Alfred Joseph and June Estelle (Faul) Moe; m. Richard Irwin Cameron, Dec. 17, 1967; 1 child, Kevin Dale. AA in Psychol., Sacramento City Coll., 1965; BA in Psychol., German, Calif. State U., 1967; MA in Reading Specialization, San Francisco State U., 1972; postgrad., Chapman Coll.; PhD, Am. Inst. Hypnotherapy, 1987; PhD in Parapsychology, St. John's U., 2005. Cert. tchr., Calif. Tchr. St. Vincent's Cath. Sch., San Jose, Calif., 1969-70, Fremont (Calif.) Elem. Sch., 1970-72, LeRoy Boys Home, LaVerne, Calif., 1972-73, Grace Miller Elem. Sch., LaVerne, Calif., 1973-80, resource specialist, 1980-84; owner, mgr. Pioneer Take-out Franchises, Alhambra and San Gabriel, Calif., 1979-85; resource specialist, dept. chmn. Bonita H.S., LaVerne, Calif., 1984; mentor tchr. in space sci. Bonita Unified Sch. Dist., 1988-99, rep. LVTV; owner, therapist So. Calif. Clin. Hypnotherapy, Claremont, Calif., 1988—. Bd. dirs., recommending tchr., asst. dir. Project Turnabout, Claremont, Calif.; Teacher-in-Space cons. Bonita Unified Sch. Dist., LaVerne, 1987-99; advisor Peer Counseling Program, Bonita High Sch., 1987—; advisor Air Explorers/Edwards Test Pilot Sch., LaVerne, 1987—; mem. Civil Air Patrol, Squadron 68, Aerospace Office, 1988-92; selected amb. U.S. Space Acad.-U.S. Space Camp Acad., Huntsville, Ala., 1990; named to national (now internat.) tchg.faculty challenger Ctr. for Space Edn., Alexandria, Va., 1990; regional coord. East San Gabiel Valley Future Scientists and Engrs. of Am.; amb. to U.S. Space Camp, 1990; mem. adj. faculty Challenger Learning Ctr. Calif. State U., Dominguez Hills, 1994, state sch. accreditation team, 2000, 03, 05, negotiating team, 1998-2003; rep. ceremony to honor astronauts Apollo 11, White House, 1994; exec. bd. Bonita Unfied tchrs. assoc., 1995—, negotiating team, 1998-2003; flight dir. mission control, Challenger Learning Ctr., Long Beach, Ca., 2002—; mem. WASC accrediting team, Calif. Vol. advisor Children's Home Soc., Santa Ana, 1980-81; dist. rep. LVTV Channel 29, 1991; regional coord. East San Gabriel Valley chpt. Future Scientists and Engrs. of Am., 1992; mem. internat. invesigation Commn. UFOs, 1991; field mem. Ctr. for Search for Extraterrestrial Intelligence, 1996; tchr., leader Ctr. for the Study Extraterrestrial Intelligence, 1997—. Recipient Tchr. of Yr., Bonita H.S., 1989, continuing svc. award, 1992; named Toyolaa Tchr. of Yr., 1994. Mem. NEA, AAUW, Internat. Investigations Com. on UFOs, Coun. Exceptional Children, Am. Psychol. Assn., Calif. Assn. Resource Specialists, Calif. Elem. Edn. Assn., Calif. Tchrs. Assn., Calif. Assn. Marriage and Family Therapists, Planetary Soc., Mutual UFO Network, Com. Sci. Investigation L5 Soc., Challenger Ctr. Space Edn., Calif. Challenger Ctr. Crew for Space Edn., Orange County Astronomers, Chinese Shar-Pei Am., Concord Club, Rare Breed Dog Club (L.A.), gardening club of Am., ctr. for the extraterrestrial intelligence, diplomat, 1997. Republican. Avocations: skiing, banjo, guitar, flying, astrophotography. Home: 3257 La Travesia Dr Fullerton CA 92835-1455 Office: Bonita High Sch 115 W Allen Ave San Dimas CA 91773-1437 Office Phone: 714-992-0360.

CAMERON, KAY, conductor, composer; b. Robbins, N.C. d. Joe and Gladys Cameron. MusB, U. N.C., 1972, MusM, 1973. Music dir. Kennedy Ctr. For the Performing Arts, Washington, 1994—; condr. Words and Music, Musicals in Concert; music supr. Sondheim Celebration. Tchr. Richmond Pub. Schs., Va., 1973-77; music dir., condr. broadway and nat. tours, N.Y., 1978-1996; arranger, orchestrator musicals and TV, 1979-1996; vis. lectr. U. N.C., Wilmington, 1997-98; condr. concert featuring Cy Coleman, Kennedy Ctr. Opera House Orch. Music dir., condr. State Fair, The Will Rogers Follies, Phantom, The King and I, On The 20th Century, Sugar Babies, Showboat, The Sound of Music, Salute To The Broadway Composer, The Sound Of Rodgers And Hammerstein, New Moon, La Cage Aux Folles (opera) Amelia Goes To The Ball, Candide, Die Fledermaus, Hansel and Gretel, The Medium, Madama Butterfly, The Telephone, others; arranger, orchestrator Show Boat on PBS, United Nations 40th Anniversary, Herman & Soundheim Together, (compositions) A Christmas Carol, Heroes, others. Mem. Am. Fedn. Musicians. Home: 121 Loder Ave Wilmington NC 28409 E-mail: kcameron@kennedy-center.org.

CAMERON, LUCILLE WILSON, retired dean; b. Nashua, N.H., Dec. 21, 1932; d. Hugh Alexander and Louise Perham (Baldwin) C.; m. James Robert Doris, Aug. 19, 1976; children: Glenn A. Browning, Gail W. Browning, Valerie B. Cruickshank. BA, U. R.I., 1964, MLS, 1972. Social case worker R.I. Dept. Pub. Assistance, Providence, 1964-70; asst. circulation libr. U. R.I. Libr., Kingston, 1970-72, reserve libr., 1972-73, reference/bibliographer, 1973-88, head reference unit, 1983-86, chair pub. svcs., 1988-89, interim dean, 1989-90, dean, 1990—, dean emerita. Bd. trustees North Scituate (R.I.) Pub. Libr., 1995, pres., 1996. Co-author: Labor and Industrial Relations Journals and Serials, 1989; contbr. articles to profl. jours. Bd. trustees North Scituate (R.I.) Pub. Libr., 1995—, pres., 1996—. Recipient Computerized Intergrated Libr. System award Champlin Founds., Providence, 1989, 90, 91, Coll. Tech. Libr. Program award U.S. Dept. Edn., Washington, 1990, Disting. Alumna award Grad. Sch. Libr. and Info. Studies, U. R.I., Kingston, 1991. Mem. ALA, Assn. Coll. and Rsch. Librs., Consortium R.I. Acad. and Rsch. Librs., Higher Edn. Libr. Info. Network (chair), Univ. Press New England (gov.), North Scituate (R.I.) Pub. Libr. Assn. (bd. trustees 1995—, pres. 1996—), Alpha Kappa Delta.

CAMERON, RITA GIOVANNETTI, writer, publishing executive; b. Washington; d. Joseph Angelo and Adeline Katherine (Fochett) C. BS with honors, U. Md., 1957; MEd, Am. U., Washington, 1962; DEd, Nova U., 1978. Tchr. D.C. pub. schs., Washington, 1959-64; prin. Prince George's County (Md.) Pub. Schs., 1964-73, 76-84; supr. instrn. K-12 Prince George's County pub. schs., 1973-76; free-lance writer ednl. materials Media, Materials Inc., Balt., 1965-75, Learning Well, Balt., 1995, World Class Learning Materials, Inc., Balt., 2000—; free-lance writer travel articles AAA, Washington, 1978-83; owner, pub. Sch. House Global Enterprises, Fort Washington, Md., 1980—. Presenter, cons. to sch. systems and ednl. orgns., 1985—. Author: Let's Learn About Maryland and Prince George's County, 1970, Let's Learn About Maryland, 1972, 95, Super Sub! Or How to Substitute Teach in Elementary School, 1974, AAA Travel articles and Traffic Safety Teacher Guide Grades 4-6, 1982, 83; author, pub.: The Master Teacher's Plan and Record Book, 1985, The School House Encyclopedia of Educational Programs and Activities, 1991; author, publisher and nat. marketer of 89 social studies and sci. ednl. materials for students grades 4-10; developer/owner School House Global Enterprises Pub. Co. Food preparer So Others Might Eat, Washington, 1985—, food preparer for Missions of Charity Home for AIDS Victims, Washington, 1992—, sponsor Christian Found. for Children and Aging, 1998—. Recipient Outstanding Citizenship award DAR, 1954, Nat. Tchr. award Expedition Nat. Tchr. Awards Program, 1960-61, Outstanding Tchr. Sci. award D.C. Coun. Engring. and Archtl. Soc. and Washington Acad. Scis., 1964, Outstanding Educator of Yr. award Prince George's County Bd. Edn., 1982-83, Am. Hist. award DAR, 1987, Outstanding Contbn. to Bicentennial Leadership Project award Couns. for Advancement of Citizenship, 1989. Mem.: Kennedy Ctr. Stars, Ford Theater, Smithsonian Assocs. (contbg. mem. Smithsonian), Phi Kappa Phi. Roman Catholic. Avocations: art, music, theater, antiques, travel. Office: Sch House Global Enterprises PO Box 441028 Fort Washington MD 20749-1028 Office Phone: 301-292-8877. Business E-Mail: dawn@schoolhouseglobalenterprises.com.

CAMERON, STACEY REBECCA, benefits compensation analyst; b. Hondo, Tex., Feb. 15, 1973; d. George William and Mary Lou Cameron. BA in English, Schreiner Coll., Kerrville, Tex., 1995. Med. transcriptionist Medina Cmty. Hosp., Hondon, Tex., 1995—98, Medquist, Inc., San Antonio, 1998—2001; tchr. First Bapt. Ch. Sch., Hondo, 2001—03; clk. Medina County, Hondo, 2003—05, benefits specialist, 2005—. Mem.: Tex.Assn. of Counties, Govt. Treasurers Org. of Tex., MENSA, Sigma Tau Delta Internat. Avocations: reading, writing, films, music.

CAMERON, VIRGINIA ANNE, music educator; b. Marion, Ohio, Dec. 16, 1947; d. Carl Paul and Wilma Genivieve Wasson; m. Ronald Wayne Cameron, Aug. 1973; children: Kirk Adam, Cara Elise, Scott P.H. BA Music Edn., Olivet Nazarene U., Bourbonais, Ill., 1969; MA Vocal Pedagogy, Ohio State U., Columbus, 1972; D, Inst. Worship Studies, Jacksonville, Fla., 2005. Therapist activity and music Richmond State Hosp., Ind., 1966—68; dir. choral music Bishop MacNamara H.S., Kankakee, Ill., 1968—69; rsch. asst. Ohio State U., 1970—72; voice instr. Cameron Voice Studio, Mount Vernon, Ohio, 1970—; prof. vocal, choral, church music Mount Vernon Nazarene U., 1970—. Dir. music, choral Linden Ch. Nazarene, Columbus, 1970—73; dir. fine arts and music ministry Lakeholm Ch. Nazarene, Mount Vernon, 1974—99; adj. voice instr. Kenyon Coll., Gambler, Ohio, 2005—. Composer (arranger): Incarnation, Great Day, Blessed Jesus, 1980—; editor (hymnal): A Collection of Wesleyan Communion Hymns for the 21st Century, 2005—; dir.: Operas, musicals, contatas, concerts. Named Outstanding Young Women Am., Outstanding Musicians of 20th Century, 2001; named to Who's Who Am. Colls. and Univs., 1969; recipient Pres.'s award Tchg. Excellence, Mount Vernon Nazarene Coll., 1973—74. Mem.: Ohio Choral Dirs. Assn., Nat. Assn. Tchrs. Singing. Republican. Avocations: bicycling, gardening, reading, bagpipes. Home: 7419 Sharp Rd Mount Vernon OH 43050 Office: Mount Vernon Nazarene Univ 800 Martinsburg Rd Mount Vernon OH 43050 E-mail: vcameron@mvnu.edu.

CAMERON-GODSEY, MELINDA A. BRANTLEY, artist; b. El Dorado, Ark., Jan. 3, 1954; d. Austin Van and Jamie Lou (Middleton) Brantley; m. James Stephen Cameron, Jan. 5, 1973 (div. Nov. 1985); children: Kelly Van Cameron, Courtney Y. Cameron; m. William Paul Godsey, Jan. 1, 1995. BFA, La. Tech. U., 1979. Registered interior designer Ark. One-woman shows include San Diego Internat. Exhbn., 1985 (Best of Show award), Southwestern Water Soc., Dallas, 1985 (2 awards), Watercolor Art Soc., Houston, 1985, 1987, Ariel Gallery, N.Y.C., 1986, Dishman Art Gallery, Beaumont, Tex., 1987, Hot Springs (Ark.) Art Ctr., 1988, South Ark. Art Ctr., El Dorado, 1988, 1991, 1995, Ark. River Valley Art Ctr., Russellville, 1989, Adirondacks Nat. Exhbn., N.Y., 1989, Riverside Art Gallery, Shreveport, 1990, Salmagundi Club, N.Y.C., 1999, others, U.S. Senator Blanche Lincoln, Washington D.C., 2003—; art work published in: Am. Artist's Ann. Publ., Watercolor 90, Crazyhorse, 1990, 1997, Poet's Market, others. Named Ark. Woman Artist, Russell State Bldg., Washington. Mem.: Southwestern Watercolor Soc., Mid-So. Watercolor Soc. (signature mem.), Knickerbockers Artists. Episcopalian. Home and Office: 1217 Cypress Dr El Dorado AR 71730-3668 Office Phone: 870-862-9693. E-mail: cameronmelinda@yahoo.com.

CAMHI, REBECCA ANN, librarian, writer; b. Montgomery, W.Va., Nov. 23, 1949; d. Shelborn W. and Margie F. (Woodson) Cale; m. Alan S. Camhi, July 3, 1977; children: Liza, Jonathan. BA, Marietta Coll., 1974; MLS, SUNY, Buffalo, 1978. Libr. City of Tonawanda Schs., NY, 1978-80, Lockport City Schs., NY, 1981-84, Newfane Schs., NY, 1985-86, Kenmore Tonawanda Schs., NY, 1987—. Presenter NY State Whole Lang. Conf. 1992. Writer novels and poetry. Mem. ALA, Conservatory of Am. Letters, Am. Libr. Assn., Conservatory Am. Letters, Phi Delta Kappa, Western NY Writing Project Canisius Coll. Home: 6 Foxcroft Ln Buffalo NY 14221-3202 Office: Kenmore Middle Sch 155 Delaware Rd Buffalo NY 14217

CAMMACK, ANN, librarian, secondary school educator; b. Akron, Ohio, Sept. 24, 1947; d. Matthew John and Anna (Maxim) Klinovsky; m. Robert Floyd Cammack, Sept. 27, 1969; children: Lisa Ann, Holly Ann, Noël Ann, Monica Ann. BA, Youngstown State U., Ohio, 1969; MLS, Tex. Woman's U., Denton, 1995, PhD, 2001. Cert. tchr. secondary sch. Ohio, elem. and secondary sch., Tex. English tchr. Struthers (Ohio) City Schs., 1969-83; asst.

cataloger Amon Carter Mus., Ft. Worth, 1997, 2000—01; libr. asst. spl. collections U. Tex., Arlington, 2005—. Life mem. Tex. Parent Tchrs. Assn., historian Arlington, 1991-92. Doctoral fellow Tex. Woman's U., 1996. Mem. AAUW, ALA, Ladies Aux. VFW, Tex. Libr. Assn., Youngstown State U. Alumni Assn., Beta Phi Mu. Avocation: golf. E-mail: acammack@sbcglobal.net.

CAMMARATA, JOAN FRANCES, Spanish language and literature educator; b. Bklyn., Dec. 22, 1950; d. John and Angelina Mary (Guarnera) Cammarata; m. Richard Montemarano, Aug. 9, 1975. BA summa cum laude, Fordham U., 1972; MA, Columbia U., 1974, MPhil, 1977, PhD, 1982. Preceptor Columbia Coll., N.Y.C., 1974—82; adj. instr. Fordham U., N.Y.C., 1980—81; adj. asst. prof. Iona Coll., New Rochelle, NY, 1982—84; asst. prof. Manhattan Coll., Riverdale, NY, 1982—90, assoc. prof., 1990—96, prof., 1996—. Author: Mythological Themes in the Works of Garcilaso de la Vega, 1983; editor: Women in the Discourse of Early Modern Spain, 2003; mem. editl. bd. Modern Lang. Studies; editl. reviewer D.C. Heath; contbr. articles and revs. to profl. jours. Fellow arts and sci. Columbia U., 1972-75; grantee Manhattan Coll., 1985, 91, NEH, 1987, 88, Spain's Min Edn. Culture, 1997—; Rsch. Fellowship grantee NYU Faculty Seminars, 1992, 94; named univ. assoc. Faculty Resources Network Program NYU, 1985—; Andrew Mellon Found. vis. scholar, 1990; scholar-in-residence NYU, 1991-92, 97-98. Mem.: MLA (del. assembly), N.Y. State Assn. Fgn. Lang. Tchrs., Am. Assn. Tchrs. Spanish and Portugese, Assn. Internat. de Hispanistas, Renaissance Soc. Am., Inst. Internat. de Lit. Iberoamericana, South Atlantic, South Ctrl. and Midwest MLA, N.E. MLA (rsch. fellow 1991, v.p. 1997—98, pres. 1998—), Am. Coun. Tchg. of Fgn. Langs, Cervantes Soc. Am., Hispanic Inst. Roman Catholic. Avocations: piano, gardening, writing, needlecrafts. Office: Manhattan Coll Bronx NY 10471 Business E-Mail: joan.cammarata@manhattan.edu.

CAMMERMEYER, MARGARETHE, retired medical/surgical nurse; b. Oslo, Mar. 24, 1942; arrived in U.S., 1951; d. Jan and Margrethe (Grimsgaard) Cammermeyer; m. Harvey H. Hawken, Aug. 1965 (div. 1980); children: Matthew Hawken, David Hawken, Andrew Hawken, Thomas Hawken; life ptnr. Diane Divelbess. BS, U. Md., 1963; MA, U. Wash., 1976, PhD, 1991. RN Wash. Staff nurse VA Hosp., Seattle, 1970-73, clin. nurse specialist in neurology, epilepsy, 1976-81; clin. nurse specialist in neuro-oncology VA Med. Ctr., San Francisco, 1981-86, clin. nurse specialist in neuroscis., nurse rschr. Tacoma, 1986-96; ret., 1996. Co-author: Neurological Assessment for Nursing Practice, 1984 (named Book of Yr. ANA), Serving in Silence, 1994; co-editor, contbg. author: Core Curriculum for Neuroscience Nursing, 1990, 1993; contbr. articles to profl. jours.; host radio-Internet talk show, 1999—2001. Hon. bd. Ctr. Study of Sexual Minorities in Mil., Svc. Mem.'s Legal Def. Network. Served to capt. U.S. Army, 1961—68, capt. to col. USAR, 1972—88, col. Wash. N.G. U.S. Army, 1988—97. Decorated Bronze Star; named Woman of the Yr., Woman's Army Corps Vets. Assn., 1984, Nurse of the Yr., VA, 1985; recipient Presdl. cert. for Outstanding Cmty. Achievement Vietnam Era Vets., 1979, Woman of Power award, NOW, 1993, 1998, Human Rights award, ANA, 1994, Disting. Alumna award, U. Wash. Nursing Assn., 1995. Mem.: Am. Vets. for Equal Rights. Home and Office: 4632 S Tompkins Rd Langley WA 98260-9695 Office Phone: 360-221-5882. Business E-Mail: grethe@cammermeyer.com.

CAMP, ALICE W., retired elementary education educator; b. Meriden, Conn., May 25, 1931; d. Anton H. and Esther M. (Jennison) Wiese; m. Robert H. Camp, Apr. 21, 1971 (wid. Dec. 1995). BS, Cen. Conn. State U., 1953. Elem. tchr. Bd. Edn., Meriden, Conn., 1953-89. Vol. sch. lectr. Meriden Sch. System, 1989-97. Mem. Washington Park Drum Corps, sec./aide 1960-97. Named Educator of Yr. Probus Club, Meriden, 1987. Mem.: Delta Kappa Gamma.

CAMP, ALIDA DIANE, mediator, arbitrator, law educator; b. Feb. 14, 1955; d. Seymour and Pearl (Aisen) C.; m. Roger Morris Arar, June 3, 1984. BA, SUNY, Binghamton, 1976; JD, Columbia U., 1980. Bar: N.Y. 1981, U.S. Dist. Ct. (so. and ea. dists.) N.Y. 1982, Calif. 1986, U.S. Dist. Ct. (cen. dist.) Calif. 1987. Student intern U.S. Atty.'s Office, N.Y.C., 1979—80; assoc. Kaye, Scholer, Fierman, Hays & Handler, N.Y.C., 1980—83; asst. prof. bus. law Grad. Sch. Bus. Adminstrn. U. Mich., Ann Arbor, 1983—86, sr. faculty adviser Mortarboard, 1983; cons. Treat Mgmt., L.A., 1986; gen. counsel, v.p. bus. and legal affairs Concorde-New Horizons Corp., L.A., 1987—90; ind. feature film prodr., 1990—96; ind. prodn. counsel, 1997—98. Mediator L.A. County Superior Ct., N.Y. State Supreme Ct., U.S. Dist. Ct. (ea. dist.) N.Y., Am. Arbitration Assn., U.S. EEO, Commn. Vol. Lawyers for the Arts, N.Y. Stock Exch., others, NASD. Contbr. articles to profl. jours. Mem. Met. Mus. Art, 1997—, Am. Mus. Natural History, N.Y.C., 1983—, Nature Conservancy, 1988—; alumni adviser Sch. Law Columbia U., 1985—; vol. atty. mediator-negotiator Calif. Lawyers for the Arts; vol. Lawyers for Arts, N.Y.C., 1982—83. Recipient Outstanding Vol. Lawyer, Vol. Lawyers for the Arts, 2004. Mem.: ABA (entertainment and sports law forum 2001, vice-chair entertainment law alternate dispute resolution com.), Assn. Conflict Resolution (greater N.Y. chpt. 2002—), Assn. of Bar of City of N.Y. (alternate dispute resolution com. 2000—03), Beverly Hills Bar Assn., Columbia U. Law Sch. Alumni Assn., Phi Beta Kappa. Jewish. Home and Office: 114 E 84th St New York NY 10028-0919 E-mail: alicamp@mindspring.com.

CAMP, HAZEL LEE BURT, artist; b. Gainesville, Ga., Nov. 28, 1922; d. William Ernest and Annie Mae (Ramsey) Burt; m. William Oliver Camp, Jan. 24, 1942; children: William Oliver, David Byron. Student, Md. Inst. Art, 1957-58, 62-63. Exhibitions include Miniature Painters, Sculptors and Gravers Soc. Washington, 1987—2003, Nat. League of Am. Pen Women Cork Gallery, Lincoln Ctr., N.Y.C., 1994, Suffolk Art League, 1994, 1996—2001, Town Hall Gallery, Epe, The Netherlands, 1999, Piedmont Art Assn, Martinsville, Va., 2000, Seaside Art Gallery, Nags Head, NC, 2001—03, Falk Gallery, Christopher Newport Univ., Va., 2003, Falk Gallery, Christopher Newport U., 2005, Rawls Gallery Art, Courtland, Va., 2004, Charles Taylor Gallery, Hampton, Va., 2004, Cristallo's Glass and Art Gallery, Williamsburg, Va., 2004, Sumner Sh. Mus., Washington, 2004, Studio 107, Norfolk, Va., one-woman shows include Ga. Mus. Art, Rockville Art Mus., Coll. Notre Dame (Balt.), U. Md., Balt. Vertical Gallery, Cleveland Meml. Gallery (Balt.), Unicorn Gallery, 1982, Hampton Ctr. for Arts and Humanities (Va.), 1985, Bendann Art Gallery, Balt., 1980, Cultural Art Ctr. on the Hill Gallery, 1995, 2000—03, Gallery on the York, 2003—04, Nansemond-Suffolk Acad., Suffolk, Va., 2006, others, exhibited in juried show, Peale Mus., Balt., Muscarelle Mus. of Art Coll. of William and Mary, Williamsburg, Va., 1998, Wilmington (Del.) Fine Arts Ctr., Smithsonian Inst., City Hall Gallery, Balt., 1982, Balt. Watercolor Soc., 1983, 1994, Arts Club, Washington, 1987—96, Strathmore Hall Arts Ctr., Md., 1997—2004, Fells Point Gallery, Balt., 2000, 2002, Hampton Bay Days Raddison Hotel Gallery, 1988, Twentieth Century Gallery, Williamsburg, Va., 1989—2004, 2005, 2006, D'Art Ctr., Norfolk, Va., 1989, Virginia Beach Ctr. for Arts, 1990, Verona, 1991, William King Regional Arts Ctr., Abingdon, Va., 1992, 2002, Lore A. Degenstein Gallery, 1994, 2004, Longwood Ctr. Visual Arts, Farmville, Va., 1995, Fine Arts Ctr., Lynchburg, Va., 1996, Va. Watercolor Soc., Martinsville, Va., 2000, Yorktown Cultural Arts Ctr., Va., 1991—2006, Furman U., 1992, Goucher Coll., Towson Md., Hermitage Found. Mus., Norfolk, 1994, 1998, 2000, Francis Land House Tidewater Artists Assn., Va. Beach, 1994, Salmagundi Club, NYC, 1995, The Nat. League of Am. Pen Women, Miniature Art Soc. Fla., 1999, 2001, St. Petersburg Mus. Fine Arts, 2000, Dunedin Fine Arts Ctr., 2002, Gulf Coast Mus. Art, Fla., 2003, Suffolk Art Mus., 2004, Hoyt Inst. Fine Arts, New Castle, Pa., So. Alleghenies Mus. Art, Loretto, Pa., 2005, Twentieth Century Gallery, Williamsburg, Va., 1989—2005, Augusta Art Ctr., Staunton, Va., 2006. Recipient 3d prize Nat. Biennial Exhibit, Tulsa, 1966, 1st prize Md. chpt. Artists' Equity, 1967, St. Mary's County Art Assn., 1964, 67, 1st prize still life Cape May, N.J., 1969, Catonsville (Md.) C.C., 1969, Nat. League Am. Pen Women Exhibit at St. John's Coll., 1969, Best in Show York (Pa.) Art Assn. Gallery, 1972, 2d award Md. Inst. Alumni Founding Chpt., Balt., 1976, Best in Show Three Arts Club, Balt., 1978, Adelia E. Chiswell 2nd award, 1996, Purchase award Old Point Nat. Bank, Hampton, Va., 1985, Merit award Hampton (Va.) City Hall, 1986, Juror's Choice award Twentieth Century Gallery, Williamsburg, Va., 1987, 1st prize 1999; Award of Excellence Md. State Biennial Eliminations of Nat. League Am. Pen Women at Essex C.C., 1989, Montgomery Coll., Rockville, Md., 1987, award Eagleton's Inc., 1996, 1st prize Virginia Heritage Exhibit, Yorktown Arts Found., 1998, Willows award Suffolk Art League, 1999, 2d prize Hist. Triangle exhibit Yorktown Arts Found., 2005, 2006. Mem. Nat. League Am. Pen Women (pres. Carroll branch 1968-70, editor The Quill 1975-76, Carroll br. 1982-83, rec. sec. nat. exec. bd. 1979-80, nat. nominating com. 1982, Md. art chmn. 1982, illustrator Nat. Roster 1990 and The Pen Woman mag. 1995, roster 2004-06), Rehoboth Art League (Adelia E. Chiswell 2d award 1996), Del. Hampton Arts League, Va. Watercolor Soc. (signature artist mem.), Pa. Watercolor Soc. (signature mem.), Balt. Watercolor Soc. (signature artist life mem., sec. 1978-80), Peninsula Fine Arts Ctr., This Century Gallery, Yorktown Cultural Arts Ctr., Tidewater Art Assn., Miniature Painters, Sculptors and Gravers Soc. of Washington, DC, Hampton (Va.) Arts League, Miniature Art Soc. Fla. Methodist. Home: 2 Bayberry Dr Newport News VA 23601-1006

CAMP, KIMBERLY N., museum administrator, artist; b. Camden, N.J., Sept. 11, 1956; d. Hubert E. and Marie (Dimery) C.; m. Seydou Coulibaly, Apr. 1997 (div. June 2006). BA, U. Pitts., 1978; MS, Drexel U., 1986. Dir. artistic design project City Camden, 1984-86; program dir. Pa. Coun. on Arts, Harrisburg, 1986-89; dir. exptl. gallery Smithsonian Instn., Washington, 1989-94; pres. Charles H. Wright Mus. African Am. History, Detroit, 1994-98; pres., CEO Barnes Found., Merion, Pa., 1998—2005. Evaluator Am. Assn. Mus., Washington, 1994—; panel chair Nat. Endowment for Arts, Washington, 1991-92; vice chair, bd. dirs. Assn. Am. Cultures, Washington, 1987-89. One-woman shows include Clifton Art Ctr., N.J., Glouchester County Coll., Deptford Township, N.J., Passaic Count C.C., Paterson, N.J., Diggs Gallery, Winston-Salem, N.C., Galerie Francois, Washington, Banneker Douglass Mus., Annapolis, Md., 3d Bienniel Nat. Black Arts Festival, Atlanta, Manchester Craftsmen's Guilde, Pitts., Caribbean Cultural Ctr., N.Y.C., Jr. Black Acad. Arts and Letters, Dallas, Walt Whitman Ctr. Arts and Humanities, Camden, Longwood Gardens, Kennett Square, Pa., Art Mus. Western Va., Raonoke, Harrison Mus. African Am. Culture, Roanoke, 1994; represented in permanent collections J.B Speed Art Mus., Manchester Craftsmen's Guild, Reader's Digest, Camden Hist. Soc.; mng. editor Nat. Conf. Artists Phila. Chpt. newsletter, 1980-84. Bd. dirs. Bus. Vols. for Arts, 1994-97. Recipient Nat. Svc. award Nat. Conf. Artists, 1984, Arts Achievement award City of Camden, 1984, Cmty. Svc. award Assn/ Negro Bus. and Profl. Women, 1985, Builders of Cmty. award Camden County Cultural and Heritage Commn., 1986, Purchase award J.B. Speed Art Mus., 1988, Spirit of Detroit award Detroit City Coun., 1994; Arts Internat. grantee Ctr. Internat. Exch. Scholars, 1994, Roger L. Stevens Nat. Arts award Carnegie Mellon U. H. John Heinz Sch. Mgmt., 1999; fellow Kellogg Nat. Leadership Program, 1997-2000. Mem. Assn. Am. Cultures (bd. dirs. 1989—91), Am. Assn. Museums (bd. dirs. 1995-97), Links, Inc., N.J. Coun. on Arts. Address: 1202 Yarmouth Rd Wynnewood PA 19096 Office Phone: 610-658-0944. Business E-Mail: kcamp911@msn.com.

CAMP, SHARON L., reproductive health organization administrator; B. with honors, Pomona Coll.; MA, PhD, Johns Hopkins U. Sr. v.p. Population Action Internat., 1975—93; coord. Internat. Consortium for Emergency Contraception, 1993—98; pres., CEO Women's Capital Corp., 1998—2003, Guttmacher Inst., NYC, 2003—. Sr. lectr. Columbia U. Mailman Sch. Pub. Health; former chair Family Health Internat., Nat. Coun. Internat. Health, Internat. Ctr. Rsch. on Women; founding chair Reproductive Health Technologies Project; former dir. Nat. Family Planning & Reproductive Health Assn., AVSC Internat. (name changed to EngenderHealth, 2001), Mgmt. Sciences for Health, Population Action Internat. Office: Guttmacher Inst 21st Fl 120 Wall St New York NY 10005 Office Phone: 800-355-0244.*

CAMPAGNA, DIANNA GWIN, real estate broker; b. Pueblo, Colo., Mar. 9, 1948; d. Everett Paul Gwin and Ava Mariea (Calvert) Johnson; m. Michael E. Campagna. Staff asst. The White House, Washington, 1971-77, exec. asst. to counsel, 1981-89; sales agt. Rand Real Estate, Alexandria, Va., 1977-79, Pagett Real Estate, Alexandria, 1979-81; assoc. broker WJD & Assocs., Alexandria, 1985-93; assoc. broker, asst. mgr. adminstrn. Long & Foster Realtors, 1993-96; prin. broker, v.p. Century 21 Campaigne, 1996-98; mng. broker Century 21 New Millennium, 1998-99; planner Mgmt. Bus. Planning Sys., Alexandria, 1999—2001; prin. dir., exec. secretariat Dept. HUD, Washington, 2001—03; mgr. ops. Nat. Commn. on Terrorist Attacks Upon the U.S., 2003—04. Exec. aide to chmn. Edward Lowe Industries, Inc., 1990—91. Del. Va. Rep. Conv., 1981, 1982, 1984. Roman Catholic. Home: 311 Park Rd Alexandria VA 22301-2737

CAMPAGNOLO, ANN-CASEY, retail executive; b. Newport, R.I., July 17, 1972; d. Eugene Louis and Kathleen Ellen (Laughlin) C. BS in Agr. and Resource Econs., U. Md., 1995. Asst. buyer petites Bloomingdale's, N.Y.C., 1995-96; asst. buyer Salon Z Saks Fifth Ave., N.Y.C., 1996-97, assoc. buyer sportswear, 1997-98, store planner casual, 1998-99, corp. planner ready-to-wear divsn., 1999-2001, dir. corp. merchandise planning, 2001—02, sr. dir. planning and allocation mens and cosmetics, 2002—03, sr. dir. planning and allocation designer, childrens and home, 2003—05, v.p. planning and allocation, outlet divsn., 2003—05; sr. cons. XRoads Solutions Group, 2006—. Bd. dirs., treas. Saks Fifth Ave. Employee Fed. Credit Union, 2002—. Mem. Jr. League N.Y. Mem.: Order of Omega (Outstanding Chpt. Pres. award 1994), Gamma Phi Beta (Province collegiate dir. 1996—2001, sec. alumnae N.Y.C. chpt. 1995—96, pres. Beta Beta chpt. 1993—94). Republican. Roman Catholic. Avocations: cooking, reading, travel. Office: XRoads Solutions Group 400 Madison Ave New York NY 10017

CAMPAGNOLO, MARY FRANCES, physician; b. Teaneck, N.J., 1956; MD, George Washington U., 1982. Diplomate with qualification in geriat. Am. Bd. Family Medicine. Intern Overlook Hosp., Summit, NJ, 1982—83, resident in family practice, 1983—85; staff physician Virtua-Meml. Hosp. of Burlington County, Mt. Holly, NJ, 1987—; chief dept. family practice Virtua-Meml. Hosp. Burlington County, 1993—. Named an Outstanding Woman of Burlington County, 2006; named one of Top Drs. 2003, N.J. Monthly Mag., Del. Valley Consumer, Top Drs. for Women, N.J. Living, Top Drs., Phila. Mag., 2004, South Jersey Mag., 2005, Top Doctors, 2006. Mem.: N.J. Acad. Family Physicians (Lifetime Achievement Chair award 2005). Office: Ashurst Family Physicians PA 1561 Rte 38 Ste 6 Lumberton NJ 08048 Office Phone: 609-267-2100. Business E-Mail: mcampagnolo@ashurstfp.com.

CAMPANELLA, YVETTE LYNN, cosmetics executive; b. Rockland County, N.Y., May 31, 1952; d. John Alfred and Marie Christine (Hill) Johnson; m. John Deloach Campanella, Sept. 22, 1978; 1 child, Jon Thomas. BA in Psychology, Vassar Coll., 1974. Operational analyses and controls sr. analyist Met. Life Ins. Co., N.Y.C., 1975—78; indsl. engr. Security Pacific Bank, LA, 1979; dir. mktg. rsch. and adminstrn. Max Factor & Co., Hollywood, Calif., 1979—. Mem.: Am. Mgmt. Assn., Am. Inst. Indsl. Engrs., Nat. Assn. Female Execs. Conglist. Office: 2049 Century Park E Ste 1400 Los Angeles CA 90067-3116

CAMPANY, KAY HUDKINS, biology educator, assistant principal; d. Roger Jay Hudkins and Edna Church Elrod; m. Donald Campany; children: Courtney Eugene, Stacy Nicole. BS in Biology, Piedmont Coll., Demorest, Ga., 1974; MA in Edn. and Biology, Western Carolina U., Cullowhee, NC, 1979; postgrad., Appalachian State U., Boone, NC, 2004—06. Nat. bd. cert. tchr. sci., adolescent - young adult Nat. Bd. for Profl. Tchg. Stds., 2003. Resident social worker therapist Youth Help Inc., Wilmington, NC, 1975—76; sci. tchr. Savannah H.S., Ga., 1979—80; environ. educator Oatland Island Edn. Ctr., Savannah, 1980; biology tchr. Fairmount H.S., Ga., 1981—83, Glynn Acad. H.S., Brunswick, Ga., 1983—86, Shelby H.S., NC, 1986—88, Avery County H.S., Newland, NC, 1990—, asst. prin. for curriculum, 2006—. Leader Girl Scouts Am., Boone, NC, 1991—2004. Named Grad. Rsch. award, Appalachian State U., 1990, Girl Scout Leader of Yr., Watauga Girl Scout Svc. Unit, 2000; Intel's Teach for Tomorrow grantee, Intel, 2003—06. Mem.: Nat. Assn. for Profl. Devel. Schs., NC Sci. Tchrs. Assn., NC Assn. for Rsch. in Edn., Appalachian State U. Pub. Sch. Partnership Coordinating Coun. (corr.), Sigma Xi, Phi Kappa Phi. Democrat. Baptist. Achievements include research in habitat preservation for an endangered plant, fringed gentian, in North Carolina. Home: 255 Northridge Dr Boone NC 28607 Office: Avery County High School 401 High School Rd Newland NC 28657 Office Phone: 828-733-0151. Business E-Mail: kaycampany@avery.k12.nc.us.

CAMPBELL, ALMA JACQUELINE PORTER, elementary school educator; b. Savannah, Ga., Jan. 5, 1948; d. William W. and Gladys B. Porter. BS in Elem. Edn., Savannah State Coll., 1969; MEd, SUNY, Brockport, 1971, cert. advanced study in adminstrn. magna cum laude, 1988. Cert. permanent elem. tchr., N.Y. Elem. tchr., Savannah, 1969-70, 71-74; tchr. intern project unique Rochester (N.Y.) City Sch. Dist., 1970-71, tchr., 1974-88, adminstrv. intern chpt. 1 office, 1988; mem. student progress task force, 1994; mem. coun. elem. leadership, mem. instrnl. com.; basic skills cadre Francis Parker Sch., Rochester, 1988—, lead tchr. mentor, 1991—; lead tchr., mentor tchr., basic skills cadre John Walton Spencer Elem. Sch. No. 16, 1992—; vice prin. Theodore Roosevelt Sch. # 43, 1993—94, prin., 1994—2003; dir. Newburn Fellowship Learning Ctr. Pre-Schoolers, 2006. Demonstration tchr., 1987-88; active Effective Parenting Info. and Children program, 1987-89; active coop. tchr. program Nazareth Coll. and Rochester City Sch. Dist., 1987; mem. policy bd. Rochester Tchr. Ctr., 1994, adminstrv. rep. to policy bd., 1995-97; adv. com. N.Y. State Systemic Iniative, 1994, sch. quality reviewer; coord., presenter ednl. workshops; apptd. mem. Student Progress Task Force, 1995; asst. WXXI Broadcasting Partnership and Sch. Number 43; coord. Sch. Quality Rev. Initiative, 1996-97; establisher partnership with Urban Schs. Inst. in conjunction with U. Rochester, 1996-97; mem. Supt. Janey's Profl. Devel. Focus Group, 1997; apptd. Profl. Devel. Acad. Adv. Bd., 1999, vis. practitioner Prin.'s Ctr. Harvard U., 2000; mem. Oxford Round Table, St. Anthony's Coll.; advisor F.C.D. Hall of Fame, Inc., Rochester. Author: (with McGriff) Quick Reference Manual for Teachers, 1989-90; co-author: A Quick Reference Manual for Teachers and Absolutely Jam-Packed With Super Teaching Tips, 1991-92. Mem. Martin Luther King Commn. on Edn., Rochester, 1988-89, Francis Parker Sch. PTA, 1988—; mental health asst. Curriculum Task Force, Rochester City Sch. Dist., 1991, coop. learning tchr., trainer, 1990, 91-92; asst. dir. Meml. A.M.E. Zion Ch., 1979-82, dir. summer camp, 1982-85, asst. sec. bd. Christian edn., 1987-89; bd. dirs. Hamm House, Jefferson Area Child Devel. Ctr., 1990-91, Save Our Sisters; bd. trustees Dr. William J. Knox, 2005—; active United Way; mem steering com. African Am. Devel. Program; exec. bd., Dem. Women's Leadership Coun Mem. ASCD (assoc.), NAFE (sub-adv. com. Strong Mus. sch. programs), Am. Assn. Sch. Adminstrs., Internat. Reading Assn., Rochester Coun. Elem. Leadership, Kiwanis Internat., Phi Delta Kappa (treas. 1996-97), Alpha Kappa Alpha (chair nominating com. 1988-89, Ivy Leaf reporter 1992—, Cert. of Achievement 1988). Democrat. Avocations: reading, travel, collecting mugs, visiting amusement parks. also: Meml AME Zion Ch Clarissa St Rochester NY 14604 also: Harvard U 536 Leverett House Mail Ctr 28 De Wolfe St Cambridge MA 02138 Home: Apt 225 270 Exchange Blvd Rochester NY 14608-2769 Office Phone: 585-342-5020, 585-342-7270. E-mail: ACampbel43@frontiernet.net.

CAMPBELL, BEBE MOORE, writer; b. Phila. m. Ellis Gordon Jr.; 2 children. BS in Elem. Edn., Univ. Pitts. Author: (memoir) Sweet Summer, Growing Up With and Without My Dad, 1989, (novels) Your Blues Ain't Like Mine, 1992 (NY Times Notable Book of Yr., NAACP Image award for Lit.), Brothers and Sisters, Singing in the Comeback Choir, 2000 (NY Times Bestseller list), What You Owe Me, 2001 (NY Times Bestseller list, LA Times Best Book, 2001), 72 Hour Hold, 2005, (non-fiction) Successful Women, Angry Men: Backlash in the Two-Career Marriage, 2000, (children's books) Sometimes My Mommy Gets Angry, 2003 (Nat. Alliance for Mentally Ill Outstanding Lit. award, 2003); contbr. articles to NY Times Mag., Washington Post, LA Times, Essense, Ebony, Black Enterprise, others; regular commentator on NPR's Morning Edition. Mem. Nat. Alliance for Mentally Ill (NAMI); founding mem. NAMI-Inglewood, Calif. Mailing: c/o Gordon/Barash Assoc Inc Ste 1501 3255 Wilshire Blvd Los Angeles CA 90010-1418*

CAMPBELL, BETH B., science educator; d. James H. and Sylvia H. Brown; m. Jason W. Campbell, Mar. 4, 2000; 1 child, Hayden S. MS, Miss. State U., Starkville, 1999. Cert. tchr. Miss., 1998. Instr. biology Itawamba C.C., Fulton, Miss., 1999—. Tchr. First Bapt. Ch., Fulton, 2003—, deacon's wife, 2004—. Recipient Lamplighter award, Miss. Cmty. Colls., 2002, Excellence Award, NISOD, 2006; fellow Colors of the North Country Project, Earthwatch, 2001, Save The Rainforest Expdn., Fundacion Neotropica, 2001. Mem.: Faculty Assn. (assoc.; v.p. 2005—06, pres. 2006—), NSTA (assoc.). Baptist. Office: Itawamba C C 602 W Hill St Fulton MS 38843 Office Phone: 662-862-8372. Business E-Mail: bacampbell@iccms.edu.

CAMPBELL, CHERYL GAY, history educator; b. Cin., Ohio, Aug. 10, 1964; d. William Thomas Campbell and Phyllis O'Cull-Campbell. BS in Edn., U. of Cin., 1988, MA in Ednl. Tech., 2000. Cert. U. of Cin., Dept. of Edn. of Ohio. History tchr. Amelia H.S., Batavia, Ohio, 1994—. Coord. internat. baccalaureate coord. and small sch. Amelia H.S., Batavia, 2002—05. Mem.: NEA. Office: Amelia H S 1351 Clough Pike Batavia OH 45103 Office Phone: 513-947-7400. Personal E-mail: cheryl.g.campbell@worldnet.att.net.

CAMPBELL, CLAIRE PATRICIA, nurse practitioner, educator; b. Jan. 10, 1933; d. Hugh Paul Campbell and Clara Louise Campbell. Student, So. Meth. U., 1956—57; BSN, U. Tex. Sch. Nursing, Galveston, 1959, FNP, 1979; MS in Nursing, Tex. Woman's U. Sch. Nursing, 1971. Cert. nurse Tex. Staff nurse Parkland Meml. Hosp., Dallas County Hosp Dist., 1955-70; head nurse gen. surgery, chest surgery, neurosurgery orthopedics and internal medicine, until 1970; instr. nursing Tex. Woman's U. Sch. Nursing, Dallas, 1971-72; rschr. nursing diagnosis Dallas, 1972-77; FNP Otis Engring. Health Svc., Dallas, 1979-86; nurse pracitioner pain mgmt. program Dallas Rehab. Inst., 1986-95, HealthSouth SubAcute Unit, Dallas, 1995-97, HeathSouth Med. Ctr.-Rehab., Dallas, 1997—2005. Adj. asst. prof. U. Tex. Sch. Nursing, Arlington, 1976-98; cons. nursing diagnosis. Author: Nursing Diagnosis and Intervention in Nursing Practice, 1st edit., 1978, 2d edit., 1984. Mem.: ANA, Tex. Nurses Assn. Roman Catholic.

CAMPBELL, CYNTHIA, retail executive; From regional v.p. Bus. Svcs. Group Southeast Region to exec. v.p. Delivery Sales N.Am. Office Depot, Inc., Delray Beach, Fla., 1995—2003, exec. v.p. Delivery Sales N.Am., 2003—; v.p., gen. mgr. Info. Svcs. GTE Corp., 1976—95. Office: Office Depot Inc 2200 Old Germantown Rd Delray Beach FL 33445

CAMPBELL, DELLA ANNE, nurse, researcher; b. Englewood, NJ, June 29, 1953; d. Joseph Michael and Dorothy Edna Campbell. Diploma in nursing, Clara Maass Sch. Nursing, Belleville, NJ, 1974; BSN, Coe Coll., Cedar Rapids, Iowa, 1976; MS, Wagner Coll., S.I., NY, 1985; postgrad., NJ Inst. Tech., U. Medicine and Dentistry NJ, Rutgers U., NJ, 2006. RN NJ, cert. advanced practice nurse, NJ, nurse adminstr., ANA. Coord. Elizabeth Gen. Hosp., NJ, 1979—85; dir. Kaiser Permanente, LA, 1985—88; advanced practice nurse Morristown Meml. Hosp., NJ, 1988—91; adminstr. women's svcs. St. Peter's U. Hosp., New Brunswick, NJ, 1991—99; chief nurse exec. Win, Inc., Harrison, NY, 1999—2002; asst. prof. Seton Hall U., South Orange, NJ, 2002—05; rsch. coord. U. Medicine and Dentistry NJ, 2003—. Cons., presenter in field. Contbr. articles to profl. publs. Mem.: APHA, ACOG, Nat. Perinatal Assn., Coun. Childbirth Edn. Specialists, Myasthenia Gravis Found., Assn. Women's Health, Obstetric and Neonatal Nurses, Sigma Theta Tau, Alpha Epsilon Lambda. Address: 757 Clark Ave Ridgefield NJ 07657-2607

CAMPBELL, EILEEN M., oil industry executive; married; 2 children. Bachelor's, U. Md. Lobbyist Gov. NJ; with Nat. Assn. Mfrs.; lobbyist United Gas Pipe Line Co.; mgr. govt. affairs Marathon Oil Corp., Houston, 1991—98, v.p. human resources, 2000—; dir. state govt. affairs USX, 1998—2000. Office: Marathon Oil Corp Corp Hdqrs 5555 San Felipe Rd Houston TX 77056-2723

CAMPBELL, FRANCES ALEXANDER, psychologist; b. Greensboro, N.C., Feb. 3, 1933; d. Norman and Nancy Miriam (Spoon) Alexander; m. Bobby Jack Campbell, Aug. 24, 1957; children: Carol Stuart, John William BA, U. N.C., Womans Coll., 1955; MA, U. N.C., 1958, PhD, 1963. Lic. psychologist, N.C. Asst. prof. Rosary Hill Coll., Williamsville, NY, 1964—65; asst. prof., rsch. assoc. U. N.C. Sch. Medicine, Chapel Hill, 1968—71; rsch. assoc. Child Devel. Inst. U. N.C., Chapel Hill, 1972—78, investigator, 1975—80, coord. psychol. assessment, 1980—90, sr. investigator, 1990—93, fellow, 1994—99, sr. scientist, 2000—. Chmn. Acad. Affairs Internal Rev. Bd. on Human Subjects U. N.C., 1993—97. Keynote spkr. Spearman Conf., Sydney, 2001; contbr. articles to profl. jours. Fellow Am. Orthopsychiat. Assm.; mem. APA, Soc. Rsch. Child Devel., Soc. Rsch. Adolescence Office: U NC Child Devel Ctr Cb # 8180 Chapel Hill NC 27599-0001

CAMPBELL, FRANCES HARVELL, real estate developer; b. Goldston, NC; d. George Henry and Evelyn (Meggs) Harvell. BS magna cum laude, U. Md., 1982; postgrad., Fla. State U., 1997—99. Asst. to Congressman Claude Pepper U.S. Ho. of Reps., 1966-80, staff dir., 1980-89; exec. dir. Claude Pepper Ctr., 1996—2004; pres. Claude Pepper Found., 1986—2004; mng. ptnr. CPC Affordable Homes, 2005—. Exec. dir. Franklin D. Roosevelt Meml. Commn., 1988-92; bd. dirs. Claude Pepper Found, 1985- Del. White House Conf. on Aging; v.p. Dem. Women of Capitol Hill, 1982—83; bd. dirs. Fla. State U. Found., 1995—2001, Nat. Com. to Preserve Social Security and Medicare, 1994—2004, v.p., 2004; bd. dirs. Econ. Club Fla., 1993—99, Fla. Assn. Non-profit Orgns., Zonta, 1998—2002, Killearn Homeowners Assn., 2001—03, League of Women Voters of Fla., 2002—. Mem. ACLU, AAUW, LWV (v.p. 2002-04), Tiger Bay Club, Zonta, Econ. Club of Fla., Phi Kappa Phi, Alpha Sigma Lambda. Avocations: orchid culture, reading, travel, the Arts. Home: 3943 Leane Dr Tallahassee FL 32309-2210 Personal E-mail: francescampbell6@aol.com.

CAMPBELL, HELEN R., gifted and talented educator; b. Fairfield, Calif., Dec. 21, 1956; d. John Wilson Rourk and Gussie Mae Davidson; m. Thomas George Campbell, June 12, 1954; children: Thomas Corey, Curtis Wilson. BS, Lander U., Greenwood, S.C, 1975—79; MEd, U. S.C., Aiken, 1981—83. Cert. Educator S.C. Bd. Edn., 1979. Tchr. 4th grade Gloverville Elem., SC, 1979—82; 4th/6th grade tchr. Summerfield Elem., North Augusta, 1982—85; 2nd/4th grade tchr. North Augusta Elem., 1985—90; kindergarten tchr. Grace Meth. Ch., North Augusta, 1990—93; sixth grade tchr. Paul Knox Mid. Sch., North Augusta, 1993—95, sci. tchr., 1996—2005, tchr. of gifted and talented, 2005—. Edn. learning ptnr. S.C. Aquarium, Charleston, 1999—2002; dir. learning smart Paul Knox Mid. Sch., 2001—03; mentor steering com. Aiken County Sch. Dist., 2004—. Sunday sch. tchr. Grace Meth. Ch., North Augusta, 1990—2006. Named Paul Knox Tchr. of Yr., 1999, 2004, Outstanding Coach, SC Sci. Olympiad, 2003, 2006; recipient Education's Unsung Hero, No. Life, 1998, DCAT Making a Difference, Nat. Sci. Tchr. Assn., 2003; grantee Kids in Need Teacher's grant, SHOPA Kids in Need Found., 2006. Mem.: Sch., Home and Office Products Assn., Drug, Chem. and Associated Techs., S.C. Sci. Assn. (assoc.), Nat. Sci. Tchr. Assn. (assoc.), SC. Edn. Assn. (assoc.), Delta Kappa Gamma. Methodist. Avocations: reading, travel, crossword puzzles, tennis. Home: 1005 Kingswood Ln North Augusta SC 29860 Office: Paul Knox Mid Sch 1804 Wells Rd North Augusta SC 29841 Office Phone: 803-442-6300.

CAMPBELL, JACQUELYN C., community health nurse; b. Camden, NJ, Aug. 2, 1946; d. Joseph and Dorothy (Cutler) Bowman; 1 child, Christina, Bradley. BSN, Duke U., 1968; MSN, Wright State U., 1980; PhD in Nursing, U. Rochester, 1986. RN, Mich. Instr. Sinclair Community Coll., Dayton, Ohio, 1976-79, Wayne State U. Coll. Nursing, Detroit, 1980-82, mem. faculty, 1984—, assoc. prof., 1988—; teaching asst. U. Rochester (N.Y.) Sch. Nursing, 1982-84; Anna D. Wolf Endowed Prof., Sch. Nursing Johns Hopkins U., associate dean for the Ph.D. program and res., Sch. Nursing. Bd. dirs. Family Violence Prevention Fund, House of Ruth; mem. violence rev. panel NIMH, Washington. Co-author: Nursing Care of Victims of Family Violence, 1984 (AJN Book of Yr.); author: To Have & To Fit, Cultural Perspectives on Wife Beating, 2d edit., 1999, Assessing Dangerousness: Violence by Sexual Offenders, Batterers and Child Abusers, 1994, Ending Domestic Violence: Changing Public Perceptions/Halting the Epidemic, 1997, Empowering Survivors of Abuse: Health Care for Battered Women and their Children, 1998, Family Violence and Nursing Practice, 2003, Nursing Care Survivors of Family Violence 2d edit., 1993; mem. editorial bd. to sci. jours.; contbr. articles to profl. jours. V.p., bd. dirs. Women's Justice Ctr., Ann Arbor, Mich., 1987—; pres. Coun. on the Status of Women, Detroit, 1988-92; support group facilitator My Sister's Place, Detroit, 1989-92; mem. adv. bd. Wayne County Adv. Bd. Interpersonal Violence, Detroit, 1991-92, adv. panel Robert Wood Johnson Found., Princeton, N.J., 1990-92; prin. investigator NIH, NCNR, 1990—; mem. Dept. Defense Task Force on Domestic Violence. Recipient First ward NIH, 1987-92; W.K. Kellogg Found., 1990-93. Mem. ANA (chair task force on violence 1991-92), APHA, Am. acad. Nursing, a.A.N. award 1988), Inst. Medicine, Midwest Nursing Rsch. Soc. (Helen Werley new investigator 1992), Nursing Rsch. Consortium on Violence and Abuse, Nursing Network on Violence Against Women. Democrat. Avocation: tennis. Office: Johns Hopkins Univ Sch Nursing 525 N Wolfe St Baltimore MD 21205-2110

CAMPBELL, JANE See GROBLEWSKI, JANE

CAMPBELL, JANE LOUISE, former mayor; b. May 19, 1953; d. Paul and Joan (Brown) C.; m. Hunter Morrison, Dec. 8, 1984; children: Jessica Elizabeth, Catherine Joanna. BA in History, U. Mich., 1974; MS in Urban Studies, Cleve. State U., 1980. Mem. State of Ohio Ho. of Reps. 11th dist., Columbus, 1984—92, majority whip, 1992—2000; mayor City of Cleve., 2001—05. Apptd. mem. Nat. Com. on Welfare Reform; mem. Cuyahoga County Plan Commn., Fin. and Appropriations Com., Ways and Means Com., Aging and Housing Com.; active Nat. Coun. State Legislators, vice-chair Human Svcs. Com., Children, Families and Youth Com., past pres. Women's Network, mem. Federal Budget and Taxation Com.; chair Abused, Neglected Children Oversight Com.; vice-chair Select Com. on Child Abuse and Juvenile Justice, 1989; mem. gov. task force on Adolescent Sexuality and Pregnancy, 1986, com. to Study Ohio's Sch. Found. Program Distribution of State Funds to Sch. Dists., 1991; exec. dir. Friends of Shaker Square, 1982-84; nat. field dir. ERAmerica, 1979-82; founding dir. Womenspace, 1975-79. Elder Heights Christian Ch. Recipient Legislative Leadership award Ohio Psychological Assn., 1986, Legislative award Ohio Hunger Task Force, 1987, Recognition award Ohio Primary Care Assn., 1987, Dean's Disting. Alumni award Cleve. State Univ., 1987, Hall of Fame award Nat. Senior Citizens, 1988, State Public Official of the Year award Ohio Chpt. Nat. Assn. of Social Workers, 1988, Found. award Ohio Chpt. ACLU, 1988, Legislative award Ohio Assn. of Counseling and Devel., 1989, Ohio Assn. of County Bds. of Mental Retardation/Developmental Disabilities award, 1989, Cancer Fighter award Ireland Cancer Ctr., 1990, Legislative award Ohio Human Svcs. Dirs. Assn., 1990, Hosephine Irwin award Womenspace, 1991, Spcl. Recognition award Providence House, 1991, Citizen award Ohio Assn. for the Edn. of Young Children, 1991, Legislator of the Year award Greater Cleve. Nurses Assn., 1991, Legislative award Nat. Assn. of Sch. Psychologists, 1992, Outstanding Svc. award Public Children's Svcs. Assn., 1992., numerous others. Democrat. Office: Cleveland City Hall 601 Lakeside Ave Rm 202 Cleveland OH 44114 Office Phone: 216-664-3990. Business E-Mail: mayorcampbell@city.cleveland.oh.us.

CAMPBELL, JANET CORAL, architect; b. Albuquerque, Nov. 24, 1953; d. Ovid Sylvester Campbell II and Evelyn Grace (Kistler) Campbell London; m. Rodney Lee Pope, June 12, 1977 (div. 1991). BS, Ga. Inst. Tech., Atlanta, 1975, MArch, 1977; MS in Real Estate, Ga. State U., Atlanta, 1989. Registered architect, Ga. Assoc. planner Metro Atlanta Rapid Transp. Authority, 1977-78; project designer Toombs, Amisano & Wells, Atlanta, 1978-80; project arch., designer Thompson, Ventulett & Steinback, Atlanta, 1980-84; project arch. Dimery, Corbet & West, Atlanta, 1984; arch., renderer Dan Harmon & Assocs., Atlanta, 1984-85; pres. Chantilly Properties, Inc., Atlanta, 1985-91; prin. Campbell Pope & Assocs., Atlanta, 1985-91; arch. J.D. & Assocs., Burlingame, Calif., 1991; sr. arch. U. Calif., San Francisco, 1991—99; prin. Campbell and Assoc., San Francisco, 1992—; arch. Skidmore, Owings & Merrill, 2002, Soga and Assoc., 2003—05. Exhibitions include High Mus., Atlanta, 1982. Elected mem. 12th dist. Rep. Party Ctrl. Com., San Francisco, 2005—06. Recipient Nat. Inst. for Arch. Edn. award, 1975. Mem. AIA (bd. dirs. Ga. chpt. 1989-91, Excellence of Studies award 1977). Mem. Plymouth Brethren Ch. Avocations: painting, reading. Home: 2 Parker Ave # 302 San Francisco CA 94118-2659 Office Phone: 415-261-2613.

CAMPBELL, JANET SCHWAGLER, biology educator; b. North Tonawanda, N.Y., Oct. 11, 1969; d. Martin Henry and Sandra Ellen Schwagler; m. Thomas Scott Campbell, Nov. 22, 1997; children: Martin William, Brady Patrick. BS, Syraucse U., N.Y., 2001; MS, LeMoyne Coll., Syracuse, 2003. Cert. tchr. N.Y., 2003. Biology tchr. Altmar-Parish-Williamstown H.S., Parish, NY, 1996—, sci. dept. chair, 2004—. Cub scout den leader Boy Scouts of Am., Chittanango, NY, 2006. Home: 141 West Genesee St Chittenango NY 13037 Office: Altmar-Parish-Williamstown High School County Rte 22 Parish NY 13131 Office Phone: 315-625-5220. Personal E-mail: jcampbell@apw.cnyric.org.

CAMPBELL, JOAN BROWN, religious organization executive; BA, MA, U. Mich.; DDiv (hon.), Bethany Coll., Coe Coll., Lynchburg Coll., Doane Coll. Ordained, Christian Ch., also Am. Bapt. Churches (USA). Assoc. exec. dir. Communited United Headstart, 1967-69; exec. sec. Welfare Action Coalition, Cleve., 1969-71; exec. dir. Coun. for Action in Pub. Edn., Ohio, 1971-73; program developer Roman Cath. Diocese, N.Y.C., Cleve., 1973; assoc. exec. dir. Greater Cleve. Interch. Coun., 1973-79; asst. gen. sec. Commn. Regional and Local Ecumenism, Nat. Coun. Chs., 1979-85; exec. dir. U.S. office World Coun. Chs., 1985-91; gen. sec. Nat. Coun. Chs. Christ in U.S.A., N.Y.C., from 1991; dir. dept. religion Chatuauqua Instn. Spkr. in field, chmn. Global Peace Initiative of Women Pub. articles in numerous publ. Founder, 1st pres. WomenSpace, Cleve. Women's Ctr., 1974-76; v.p. Cleve. Urban League, 1975-79; pres. Nat. Assn. Ecumenical Staff, 1976-78; mem. steering com. U.S. Ch. Leaders, 1989—; bd. dirs. Ind. Sector, 1993—, Union Theol. Sem., 1993—; mem. adv. com. Pew Global Stewardchip Initiative, 1993—; trustee Nat. Religious Partnership for Environment, 1993—. Named to Women of Achievement, YWCA, Leadership Cleve., Martin Luther King Jr. Bd. Preachers, Sponsors and Collegium of Scholars, Morehouse Coll. Mem. NAAPC (life, bd. dirs.), Coun. on Christian Unity, Christian Ch. (Disciples of Christ) (life), Mortar Bd., Phi Beta Kappa. Address: Chautauqua Institution Director Dept of Religion PO Box 28 Chautauqua NY 14722-0028

CAMPBELL, JOAN VIRGINIA LOWEKE, secondary school educator, language educator; b. Detroit, Nov. 8, 1942; d. George Paul and Lolamae (Weians) L.; m. James Bachelder Campbell, July 26, 1975; 1 child, James Bachelder Loweke. BA in German, French, Hope Coll., 1965; student, U. Cologne (Germany), 1964, U. Salzburg (Austria), 1968, U. Stuttgart (Germany), 1970-71, Sampere Inst., Madrid, 1982, Millersville (Pa.) State U., 1983, 84, 90, Va. Poly. Inst. and State U., 1976-77, 80-84, U. Va., 1996-97, 98-99. Cert. secondary tchr., Mich., Kans., Va. Tchr. French and German I, II Grand Haven (Mich.) Jr. H.S., 1965-69; asst. instr. elementary and intermediate German U. Kans., Lawrence, 1969-70, 71-72; tchr. German I, II Ctrl. Jr. H.S., Lawrence, Kans., 1972-74; tchr. French I, II, sr. English Oskaloosa (Kans.) H.S., 1974-75; tchr. German I-IV Highland Park H.S., Topeka, 1975-76; tchr. French I-V, Spanish I and II Blacksburg (Va.) H.S., 1977—. Tchr. French, Spanish YMCS, YMCA evening courses, Blacksburg, Va., 1976-80; mem. audio visual com. Montgomery County Fgn. Lang. Collaborative Group, Blacksburg, 1984-87; chaperone Am. Inst. Fgn. Study, Germany, France, Spain, 1968-82, area adminstr. summer and winter programs abroad, Western Mich., 1968-69; chaperone Ednl. Adventures, Quebec City, Montreal, 1984, 90-91, 93-94, 98, Montgomery County Schs.; presenter in field. Author: The Gothic Cathedral, 1995. Mem. Internat. Host Family Orgn. Va. Poly. Inst. and State U., Blacksburg, 1977— Fulbright exch. fellow U. Kans., 1970-71, Fulbright fellow Goethe Insts., 1976, Rockefeller fellow Rockefeller Assn. and Nat. Endowment Humanities, 1986, NDEA fellow, 1966; recognized as Va. Gov.'s Sch. Outstanding Educator, 1990. Mem. Am. Assn. Tchrs. French (state and region IV U.S. Recognition effort, dedication and high scores on nat. French exams, 1988, 96, 97, founder La Soc. Hon. de Français for Outstanding Students in French Blacksburg chpt. 1977, state com., dist. adminstr. Le Grand Concours-Nat. French Exams 1980—), Am. Assn. Tchrs. Spanish and Portuguese, Am. Assn. Tchrs. German (life, Va. exec. com. sec. 1977-83, co-chmn. nat. German exams Va. chpt. 1984-87, state nominating com. 1984-87, chmn. 1984-85, life), Nat. Assn. Edn. (Blacksburg H.S. rep. 1980-82), Va. Assn. Edn., Montgomery County Assn. Edn., Assn. Supervision and Curriculum Devel., Fgn. Lang. Assn. Va. (life) Republican. Presbyterian. Avocations: gardening, hiking, travel, classical music, art history. Home: 3003 Mclean Ct Blacksburg VA 24060-8110 Office: Blacksburg HS 520 Patrick Henry Dr Blacksburg VA 24060-3106 Personal E-mail: jayhawk@vt.edu.

CAMPBELL, JOANN CAVO, social worker; b. Cetara, Salerno, Italy, Dec. 2, 1950; BA, SUNY, Oneonta, 1972; MSW, Ariz. State U., 1977. LCSW N.Y. Family therapist Family Svcs. of Greater Utica, NY, 1977-84; case mgmt. supr. Cath. Charities of Utica-Rome, Utica, 1980-85, coord. clin. svcs., 1985-88, dir. social svcs., 1988-92; pvt. practitioner of social work Utica, 1992—; clin. program coord. Oneida County Alcohol and Substance Abuse Svcs., Utica, 1993-97; NY State trainer for mandated child abuse reporters Madison-Oneida BOCES, Verona, NY, 1990—; social worker New Hartford Ctrl Sch. Dist., NY, 1997-99, Whitesboro Ctrl. Sch. Dist., NY, 1999—. Vice chair social work adv. bd. Utica Coll., 1978-83; treas., co-chair, chair Mohawk Valley Com. for Prevention of Child Abuse and Neglect, Utica, 1977—; bd. dirs., treas., sect. NY State chpt. Nat. Com. for Prevention of Child Abuse, Albany, 1982-90. Chair program com. Hugh R. Jones Sch. PTA, Utica, 1991-94; active Oneida County Rep. Com., 2004—, Whitestown Rep. Com., 2004-06; bd. dirs. NY State Sch. Social Workers Assn., 2004-. Recipient Teddy Bear award NY state chpt. Nat. Com. for Prevention of Child Abuse, 1990, Outstanding and Dedicated Svc. award Cath. Charities, 1990. Republican. Roman Catholic. Office: 65 Oriskany Blvd Whitesboro NY 13492-1323

CAMPBELL, JUDITH E., retired insurance company executive; BA, Chestnut Hill Coll., 1969. With Chem. Bank, N.Y., sr. v.p. consumer sales and svc. delivery N.Y., head ops. and adminstrn. consumer banking NY, sr. v.p., 1991—92; with Consumer Banking, 1992—97; sr. v.p., chief info. officer, bd. dirs. N.Y. Life Ins. Co., NYC, 1997—. Bd. trustees Drew U. Office: NY Life Ins Co 51 Madison Ave New York NY 10010-1603

CAMPBELL, JUDY, medical/surgical nurse, educator; b. Kosciusko, Miss., Jan. 19, 1957; d. Wilbur Aaron and Linda Ann McGee; m. David Lee Campbell, Aug. 28, 1979; children: Jeremiah, Kari. AA, Holmes Jr. Coll., Goodman, Miss., 1977; BSN, U. So. Miss., Hattiesburg, 1979; MSN, U. Fla., Gainesville, 1995, postgrad., 2004—. RN, Fla., Nebr. Staff nurse Midlands Community Hosp., Papillion, Nebr., 1979-82; nurse supr., insvc., orientation coord. Titusville Nursing and Convalescent Ctr., Fla., 1983-85; staff nurse, ob-gyn unit Wuesthoff Meml. Hosp., Rockledge, Fla., 1985-88; asst. dir. nursing svc. Vista Manor Care Ctr., Titusville, 1988-90; staff nurse, orthopedic unit Wuesthoff Meml. Hosp., Rockledge, 1990-92; asst. prof. Brevard Cmty. Coll., Cocoa, Fla., 1990—2004. Assoc. degree nursing coord., 1999—2001; rsch. asst. U. Fla., 2004—. One-woman shows include NYU Contemporary Art Gallery, NYC, 1975, Marist Coll., Pughkeepsie, NY, 1979, Roko Gallery, NYC, 1950, 1961, 1963, 1967, 1970, 1975, Union Am. Hebrew Congregations, 1982, Pleiades Gallery, NYC, 1989, 1991, 1993, 1994, 1996, 1998, 1999, 2001, 2002, Embasy Austria, Washington, 1996, Denise Bibro Gallery, NYC, 2005, exhibited in group shows at Hudson Guild Gallery, 1984—2001, Elaine Benson Gallery, Brigehampton, NY, 1983, NYU Contemporary Art Gallery, Loeb Student Ctr., 1972, 1975, 1979, Whitney Mus. Art, NYC, 1948—49, Carnegie Inst., Georgetown Coll., Ky., Ball State U., Ind., Wesleyan Coll., Ga., Park Ave. Atrium, NYC, Nassau CC, LI, NY, Purdue U., Ind., Jessee Besser Mus., Mich., NYU Small Works Show, Represented in permanent collections Mus. City NY, NY Hist. Soc., Schomber Ctr. Rsch. Black Culture, NYC, Slater Meml. Mus., Norwich, Conn., Laura Masser Inst., Muscatine, Iowa, Yeshiva U. Mus., NYC, Cape Ann Hist. Assn., Goucester, Mass, NYC Transit Mus. Vol. nurse sch. clinic. Recipient ROTC scholarship, Brevard Commty. Coll. Peer Awd., Brevard Commty. Coll. Svc. Learning Awd.,Brevard Cmty. Coll., 2000; Disting. Ed. Finalist, BCC Vol. Incentive Performance Award, 2001 (College-wide) and 2003 (Div.); Bcc Nursing Program recieved US Dept. of Ed. Career & Tech. Consortium designation as an Exemplary program, 2001; BCC Leadership Challenge Award & Extended Profl. Leave, 1993-1995. Mem.: ANA, Sigma Phi Omega (gerontology honor soc. 2005—), Gerontol. Soc. Am., Fla. Nurses Assn. (Heather Scaglione Award 2001, Excellence in Tchg. award 2002), Sigma Theta Tau, Phi Theta Kappa. E-mail: elijah@cfl.rr.com.

CAMPBELL, KARI MELISSA, elementary school educator; Degree in secondary social sci. edn. with honors, U. Ctrl. Fla., Orlando, 2004. Horseback riding instr. Ace of Hearts Ranch, Cocoa, Fla., 2002—04; 7th grade world cultures tchr., cheerleading coach Space Coast Jr./Sr. HS, Cocoa, 2004—. Avocations: travel, reading, tutoring. Office: Space Coast Jr/Sr HS 6150 Banyan St Cocoa FL 32927 Office Phone: 321-638-0750.

CAMPBELL, KARLYN KOHRS, speech educator; b. Blomkest, Minn., Apr. 16, 1937; d. Meinhard and Dorothy (Siegers) Kohrs; m. Paul Newell Campbell, Sept. 16, 1967 (dec. Mar. 1999). BA, Macalester Coll., 1958; MA, U. Minn., 1959, PhD, 1968; LHD (hon.), Mich. State U., 2004. Asst. prof. SUNY, Brockport, 1959-63; with The Brit. Coll., Palermo, Italy, 1964; asst. prof. Calif. State U., L.A., 1966-71; assoc. prof. SUNY, Binghamton, 1971-72, CUNY, 1973-74; prof. comms. studies U. Kans., Lawrence, 1974-86, dir. women's studies, 1983-86; prof. comms. studies U. Minn., Mpls., 1986—, dept. chair, 1993—96, 1999—2005. Inaugural Gladys Borchers lectr. U. Wis., Madison, 1974; vis. prof Dokkyo U., Tokyo, 2005-. Author: Critiques of Contemporary Rhetoric, 1972, rev. edit., 1997, Form and Genre, 1978, The Rhetorical Act, 1982, rev. edit. 2002, The Interplay of Influence, 1983, rev. edit., 2005, Man Cannot Speak for Her, 2 Vols., 1989, Deeds Done in Words, 1990, editor: Women Public Speakers in the United States, 1800-1925: A Bio-Critical Sourcebook, 1993, Quar. Jour. Speech, 2001-04; co-editor: Guilford Revisioning Rhetoric series, 1995-2000; mem. editl. bd. Comm. Monographs, 1977-80, Quar. Jour. Speech, 1981-86, 92-94, editor, 2001—, Critical Studies in Mass Comm., 1993-99, Rhetoric and Pub. Affairs, 1997-2000, Philosophy and Rhetoric, 1988-93; contbr. articles to profl. jours. Recipient Woolbert Rsch. award, 1987, Winans-Wichelns Book award, 1990, Ehninger Rsch. award, 1991, Elizabeth Andersch award, U. Ohio, 2004; Tozer scholar Macalester Coll., 1958, Tozer fellow, 1959; fellow Shorenstein Barone Ctr., JFK Sch. of Govt., Harvard, 1992; Disting. Woman scholar U. Minn., 2002. Mem. Nat. Comm. Assn. (disting. scholar award 1992, Francine Merritt award for significant contbns. to the lives of women in comm. 1996 Women's Caucus), Ctrl. States Speech Comm. Assn., Rhetoric Soc. Am., Phi Beta Kappa, Pi Phi Epsilon. Office: U Minn Dept Comm Studies 225 Ford Hall 224 Church SE Minneapolis MN 55455 Business E-Mail: campb003@umn.edu.

CAMPBELL, KATHERINE LUCILLE, gifted and talented educator; b. Neodesha, Kans., Sept. 25, 1937; d. Dale L. Chisham and Dorothy M. Fulbright; m. Bobby D. Campbell, Sept. 27, 1957; children: Robert D., Janice M., William D., Tommy D., Augretta N.(dec.). BA, Southwestern, 1970; student, Pitts.State, 1983. Gifted tchr. Author: Missing Pieces, 1989, Alien Logic Problems, 1989. Mem.: Sons and Daughters of the Pilgrims (past state treas.), Continental Soc. Daughters of Indian Wars, Soc. New England Women (pres. Kans. colony), Daughters of Am. Colonists, DAR. Democrat. Bapt. Avocations: writing, music. Home: 11745 500 Rd Neodesha KS 66757

CAMPBELL, KATHERINE MARIE LANGREHR, elementary and secondary education educator; b. N.Y.C., Dec. 4, 1947; d. Anton A. and Katherine (Batky) Langrehr; m. Frederick Augustus Campbell, Nov. 4, 1967; children: Julie Ann, Alicyn Katherine. BA in History, U. Bridgeport, 1970; MS in Lang. Arts Edn., Ctrl. Conn. State U., 1992. Tchr. grades 3 and 5 Holy Rosary Parochial Sch., Bridgeport, Conn., 1968-71; outreach worker Migratory Children's Program Vernon (Conn.) Bd. Edn., 1980-81; sales rep. Procter & Gamble, Wilton, Conn., 1982-86; reading/math tutor Bennet Jr. H.S., Manchester, Conn., 1986-87; tchr. lang. arts Elisabeth M. Bennet Mid. Sch., Manchester, Conn., 1987-96, dept. head lang. arts, 1994-96; tchr. grade 5 Verplanck Elem. Sch., Manchester, 1996—2005; tchr. grade 4 Buckley Elem. Sch., Manchester, 2005—. Mem. content validation com. Nat. Bd. Profl. Teaching Stds., 1996; presenter in field. Mem. Gifted & Talented Bd. Vernon Bd. Edn., 1992-93; dir. Planning Bd. Emergency Shelter, Vernon, 1984-85; scout leader Girl Scouts Am., Vernon, 1979-80; treas., bd. dirs. PTO Vernon Elem. Sch., 1976-80. Recipient Celebration of Excellence award State of Conn., 1992; Conn. Writing Project fellow, 1989; nominee Heroes in Edn. award Readers Digest, 1992, Am. Tchrs. award Disney, 2001. Mem.: Internat. Reading Assn. Office: Buckley Elem Sch 250 Vernon St Manchester CT 06040

CAMPBELL, KAY NORDAN, nurse, health educator; b. Raleigh, N.C., Sept. 6, 1949; d. James Wilson and Annie Mitchell (Hogwood) Nordan; 1 child from a previous marriage, Kimberley Angelia Beaird; m. Jimmy Nelson Campbell, June 13, 1975; children: Stephanie Ann, Lisa Gray. Diploma, Rex Hosp. Sch. Nursing, 1970; BS in Health Occupations Edn., N.C. State U., Raleigh, 1987, MEd, 1992, EdD, 1997. RN, N.C.; cert. cmty. nurse, cert. occup. health nurse. Occupl. health nurse GlaxoSmithKline, Research Triangle Park, NC, 1984—90, mgr. occup. health svc., 1990—96, health adminstr., 1996, mgr. health and wellness resources, 1997—, U.S. employee health support and resilience mgr., 2000—. Cons. Healthy Directions, Cary, N.C., 1995; educator in field. Author and editor in field. Bd. dirs. Drug Action, Inc., 1992-94, Wake County Cancer Soc., Raleigh, 1977-88, Child Care Resource and Referral Agy., 1999-; mem. pub. edn. com. N.C. Cancer Soc., 1978-87. Recipient Great 100 award, N.C., 1989, others. Fellow: Am. Assn. Occupl. Health Nurses (bd. dirs. 1998—2002, sec. 2003—, jour. editor); mem.: ANA, Am. Assn. Pub. Health, N.C. Tarheel Assn. Occupl. Health Nurses (pres., chair rsch. com., edn. com., bd. dirs.), N.C. Nurses Assn., N.C. Assn. Occupl. Health Nurses (pres., chair edn. com., Occupl. Health Nurse of Yr. 1980), Kappa Delta Pi. Avocations: beaches, old english sheepdog. Office: GlaxoSmithKline S E 2483 Research Triangle Park NC 27709 E-mail: kay.n.campbell@gsk.com.

CAMPBELL, KRISTINE KOETTING, academic administrator; b. Arcadia, Wis., Feb. 22, 1952; d. John Joseph and Dorothy Ann (Vogel) Koetting; m. Douglas William Campbell, Feb. 1, 1980; children: Colin William, Ryan Joseph BSN, Viterbo Coll., La Crosse, Wis., 1974; MSN, Ohio State U., 1983; PhD, Oregon Health Scis. U., Portland, 2000; M Strategic Studies, Army War Coll., 2001. RN Oreg., Wash. Staff nurse Natal ICU Madigan Army Med. Ctr., Tacoma, 1974—76; head nurse nursery U.S. Army Hosp., Augsburg, Germany, 1976—79, head nurse pediat. Ft. Campbell, Ky., 1979—81; instr. pediat. and nursery nurses Columbus Tech. Inst., Ohio, 1983—84; instr. pediat. nursing Ohio State U., Columbus, 1984—87; grad. rsch. asst. Oreg. Health Scis. U., Portland, 1988—97; nursing supr. Landstuhl Army Med. Ctr., Germany, 1990—91; chief nurse 396th Combat Support Hosp., Vancouver, Wash., 1995—97, comdr. Bosnia-Herzegovina, 1997—98, 6250th U.S. Army Hosp., Ft. Lewis, Wash., 1998—99; asst. surgeon gen. force mgmt., mobilization & res. affairs Office Surgeon Gen., Falls Church, Va., 1999—2003; exec. dir. Oreg. Ctr. Nursing, Portland, 2004—. Child educator tng. adults in positive parenting, Longview, Wash., 1992-95 Co-author: (computer simulation) Lucy Web a four year old with Down's Syndrome undergoing a tonsillectomy Mem. PTO, Longview, 1988—. Capt. U.S. Army, 1974-81; brig. gen. USAR, ret. 2005 Recipient Instnl. Nat. Rsch. Svc. award, Oreg. Health Scis. U., 1990; Disting. Alumni award Sch. Nursing Ohio State U.; Disting. Alumni award Viterbo Coll. Mem. ANA, Nat. Coun. Family Rels., Res. Officers Assn., Assn. Mil. Surgeons U.S., Sigma Theta Tau Democrat. Avocations: jogging, reading. Home: 3 Country Club Dr Longview WA 98632-5424 Office Phone: 503-943-7184. E-mail: kkcinwa@aol.com.

CAMPBELL, MARIA BOUCHELLE, lawyer, consultant; b. Mullins, S.C., Jan. 23, 1944; d. Colin Reid and Margaret Minor (Perry) C. Student, Agnes Scott Coll., 1961-63; AB, U. Ga., 1965, JD, 1967. Bar: Ga. 1967, Fla. 1968, Ala. 1969. Pvt. practice law, Birmingham, Ala., 1968-94; law clk. U.S. Cir. Ct. Appeals, Miami, Fla., 1967-68; assoc. Cabaniss, Johnston and Gardner, 1968-73; sec., counsel Ala. Bancorp., Birmingham, 1973-79; sr. v.p., sec., gen. counsel AmSouth Bancorp., 1979-84, exec. v.p., gen. counsel, 1984-94, AmSouth Bank, 1984-94; exec. asst. to rector Parish of Trinity Ch., N.Y.C., 1994-99; lawyer, mediator Sirote & Permutt, 1999-2001; cabinet ofcl., supt. of banks State of Ala., Montgomery, 2001—03; chmn. fin. svcs. SC& B Strategic Solutions, Montgomery, 2003—; of counsel Steiner Crum & Byars, Montgomery, 2003—. Bd. trustees Ptnrship for Women's Health Columbia U., 1996-2000; bd. dirs. Leake and Watts Childrens Svcs., Inc., 1997-99; lectr. continuing legal edn. programs; cons. to charitable orgns. Exec. editor Ga. Law Rev, 1966-67. Bd. dirs. St. Anne's Home, Birmingham, 1969-74, chancellor, 1969-74; bd. dirs. Children's Aid Soc., Birmingham, 1970-94, 1st v.p., 1988-90, pres., 1990-92; trustee Canterbury Cathedral Trust in Am., 1992—, Discovery 2000 Children's Mus., 1991-94, Soc. for Propagation of Christian Knowledge, 1991-93; bd. dirs. NCCJ, 1985-94, 99-2002, state chair, 1990-93; bd. dirs. Positive Maturity, 1976-78, Mental Health Assn., 1978-81, YWCA, 1979-80, Op. New Birmingham, 1985-87, pers. com., 1987-90, v.p., 1990-94; bd. dirs. Soc. for the Fine Arts U. Ala., 1986-89, Baptist Hospital Found. of Birmingham Inc., 1994-95, Alliance for Downtown N.Y., 1995-99, chair affordable housing initiative region 2020, 2000-01, Habitat for Humanity of Birmingham, 2000-02; commr. Housing Authority, Birmingham Dist., 1980-85, Birmingham Partnership, 1985-86, Leadership Birmingham, 1986—, program com., 1989-90, co-chair program com., 1990-91, mem.'s coun., 1999-2002; mem. pres. adv. coun. Birmingham So. Coll, 1988-92, chair bd. overseers Masters Program, 1990-94; mem. pres.'s cabinet U. Ala., 1990-95; trustee Ala. Diocese Episcopal Ch., 1971-72, 74-75, mem. canonical revision com., 1973-75, 89-91, liturg. commn., 1976-78, treas., chmn. dept. fin., 1979-83, 2000-03; mem. coun., 1983-87, chancellor, 1987-91, cons. on stewardship edn., 1981-94, dep. to gen. conv., 1985, 88, 91; mem. Standing Commn. on Constn. and Canons, 1988-94, mem. investment com., 2000—, vice chmn., 2003—; vestryman St. Luke's Episcopal Ch., 1991-94; bd. advisors So. region of Am. Soc. Corp. Secs., pres., 1992-94; cmty. advisor Jr. League Birmingham, 1992-93; mem. adv. bd. Cahaba River Soc., 1991-94; trustee St. Andrew's Sewanee Sch., 1998—; commr. Ala. Securities Commn., 2001-03; bd. dirs. Ala. Agrl. Commn., 2001-03; bd. dirs. Ala. Housing Fin. Authority, 2001-03; bd. regents Univ. of the South, 2002—; bd. dirs. Housing Enterprise Ctrl. Ala., 2003—, Fin. Investors of South, 2003—04, Associated Long Term Care Ins. Co., 2004—. Named One of Top 10 Women in Birmingham, 1989, One of Top 5 Women in Bus., 1993. Mem. ABA, State Bar Ga., Fla. Bar, Ala. Bar Assn., Birmingham Bar Assn., Am. Corp. Counsel Assn. (bd. dirs. Ala. 1984-89), Assn. Bank Holding Cos. (chmn. lawyers com. 1986-87), Greater Birmingham C. of C. (bd. dirs. 1988-94, exec. com. 1992-94, vice chmn., gen. counsel 1993-94), Kiwanis, The Church Club N.Y., Order of St. John of Jerusalem, Summit Club. Office: PO Box 668 Montgomery AL 36101 Office Phone: 334-956-6800. Personal E-mail: mcampbell@scbstrategic.com.

CAMPBELL, MARTA SMITH, librarian; b. Buffalo, June 25, 1941; d. Frank Lawrence Jr. and Alice (Bement) Smith; m. Harry William Campbell Jr., 1964 (div. 1981); children: Marta Christine, Jennifer Leigh. BA in English Lit., Bucknell U., Lewisburg, Pa., 1963; MLS, So. Conn. State U., New Haven, 1983. Libr. and head of collection mgmt. Westport (Conn.) Pub. Libr., 1983—. Democrat. Congregational. Home: 10 Bauer Pl Westport CT 06880 Office: Westport Pub Libr Westport CT 06880 Office Phone: 203-291-4842. Business E-Mail: mcampbell@westportlibrary.org.

CAMPBELL, MARY SCHMIDT, dean; b. Phila., Oct. 21, 1947; d. Harvey Nathaniel and Elaine Juanita (Harris) S.; m. George Campbell, Jr., Aug. 24, 1968; children: Garikai, Sekou, Britt Jackson. BA in Eng. Lit., Swarthmore Coll., 1969; MA in Art Hist., Syracuse U., 1973, PhD Humanities, 1982; ArtsD (hon.), Pace U., 1991; DFA (hon.), CCNY, 1992; PhD (hon), Colgate U., 1994; PhD (hon.), Coll. of New Rochelle, 2001. Art editor Syracuse New Times, NY, 1973—77; guest curator, curator Everson mus., Syracuse, 1974—76; exec. dir. Studio Mus. in Harlem, N.Y.C., 1977—87; commr. cultural affairs City of N.Y., 1987—91; dean Tisch Sch. Arts, NYU, N.Y.C., 1991—. Bd. mgrs. Swarthmore (Pa.) Coll., 1987-99; mem. fine arts vis. com. bd. overseers, Harvard Coll., Harvard U., Cambridge, Mass., 1991-95; mem. Tony nominating com., 1996-98, 2000-2002. Co-author: Harlem Renaissance: Art of Black America, 1987, Memory & Metaphor, 1991; prodr. (film) Sembene: A Biography, 1994. Mem. N.Y.C. Mayor's Adv. Commn. on Culture, 1991-94; co-chmn. subcom. on culture Dem. Nat. Conf., N.Y.C., 1992; bd. dirs. N.Y. Shakespeare Festival, 1993—, Harlem Sch. Arts, 1997-2001; bd. trustees Am. Acad. in Rome, 1999—, Bklyn. Mus. Art, 1999-2002, mem. bd. trustees, United Nations Internat. Sch., 2001-. Recipient George Arents award Syracuse U., 1993, Project of Yr. award N.Y. Coun. on Humanities; Tisch Sch. fellow Am. Acad. Arts & Scis. Democrat. Baptist. Avocations: jogging, writing. Office: NYU Tisch Sch of the Arts 721 Broadway 12th Flr New York NY 10003-6862

CAMPBELL, MARY STINECIPHER, retired chemist; b. Chattanooga, Feb. 26, 1940; d. Jesse Franklin and Florence Gladys (Marshall) S.; m. John David Fowler Jr. (div. Mar. 1979); children: John Christopher, Jesse David; m. Billy M. Campbell (dec. 2006), Jan. 1995. BA, Earlham Coll., 1962; PhD, U. N.C., 1967. Cert. organic fruit grower. Postdoctoral researcher Research Triangle Inst., Research Triangle Park, NC, 1966-68, 74-76; staff Los Alamos (N.Mex.) Nat. Lab., 1976—2004; ret., 2004. Adj. prof. organic, inorganic and phys. chemistry U. N.Mex. Grad. Ctr., Los Alamos, 1989—, instr. chemistry lab., 1989; vis. scientist AFOSR (AFATL), Eglin AFB, Fla., 1980-81. Contbr. articles to profl. jours.; inventor ammonium nitrate explosive systems and other explosive salts. Commr. Acequia Sancochada Cmty. ditch; mem. Habitat for Humanity. Mem. Am. Chem. Soc., N.Mex. Network Women in Sci. and Engring. (v.p. 1985-86, pres. 1986-87, No. chpt. pres. 1999), Bio-Integral Rsch. Ctr., N.Mex. Apple Coun. Democrat. Unitarian Universalist. Avocations: skiing, dog training, hiking, singing, gardening. Personal E-mail: bmcampbell@newmexico.com.

CAMPBELL, MELISSA LYNNSIMMONS, music educator; d. Ralph Thorton and Barbara Fay Simmons; m. Donald James Dwight Campbell, Jan. 1, 1998. MusB in Edn., Susquehanna U., Selingsgrove, Pa., 1978; MEd, Cambridge Coll., Mass., 1990. Substitute tchr. Ctrl. Berkshire Regional Sch. Dist., Dalton, Mass., 1978—79, tchr. elem. gen. and instrumental music, dir. band, 1979—80, tchr. instrumental music, gifted and talented class Dalton Jr. H.S., 1980—81, tchr. music, dir. chorus, concert and marching band, drill and flag team, all classroom music classes Wahconah Regional H.S., 1981—84, tchr. all dist. elem. instrumental music, dir. band, 1984—. With cleaning and maintenance crew Camp Danbee, Peru, Mass., 1975—92, instr. horseback riding r., 1989—92. Designed and compiled (method book for each band instrument:) My Flute's Band-Aid, My Clarinet's Band-Aid, My Saxophone's Band-Aid, My Trumpet's Band-Aid, My Trombone's Band-Aid, My Drum's Band-Aid. Mem. United Meth. Ch. of Lenox, Mass., 2003; sustaining mem. Doris Day Animal League, Washington, 1998; sustaining mem./adopted animal guardian Farm Sanctuary, Watkins Glen, NY, 2000; sustaining mem. Physicians Com. For Responsible Medicine, Washington, 2000; percussionist Eagles Band, Pittsfield, Mass., 1978—83. Recipient William Manning award, Marion Manning, 1974; Orff Music Workshop grant, Berkshire Taconic Found., 2004. Mem.: Mass. Tchrs.' Assn., Music Educators Nat. Conf. Achievements include development of Horseback riding program at Camp Danbee; First full high school marching Color Guard and Drill Team in Berkshire County; Co-founded a music collaborative for professional development of area music and arts teachers. Avocation: veganism.

CAMPBELL, MILBREY ANNE, physical education educator; b. McKeesport, Pa., Sept. 17, 1952; d. Thomas William Bercik and Lillian Marie Poplin; m. Thomas Hendon Campbell, May 4, 1974; children: Thomas Marshall, Michael Brent. Med, Mid. Tenn. State U., Murfreesboro, Tenn., 1977. Milbrey Bercik Campbell Tenn. Dept. of Edn., 1977. Phys. edn. tchr. Rutherford County Schools, Murfreesboro, Tenn., 1975—. Recipient Tchr. of Yr., Rutherford County Bd. of Edn., 2003. Mem.: Delta Kappa Gamma (life; sec. 1994—98). Home: 1726 Haynes Dr Murfreesboro TN 37129 Office: Smyrna Primary Sch 200 Walnut St Smyrna TN 37167 Office Phone: 615-459-3161.

CAMPBELL, MILDRED CORUM, business owner, nurse; b. Warfield, Va., Feb. 24, 1934; d. Oliver Lee and Hazel King (Young) Corum; m. Hugh Stuart Campbell, Dec. 2, 1972. BSN, U. Va., 1956. Head nurse plastic surgery U. Va. Med. Ctr., Charlottesville, 1956-58, head nurse cardio-surg., 1958-61; staff nurse oper. rm. NIH Heart Inst., Bethesda, Md., 1961-62; supr. oper. and recovery rms. Med. Univ. of S.C., Charleston, 1962-64; head nurse cardio operating rms. Meth. Hosp., Tex. Med. Ctr., Houston, 1964-67; supr. oper. and recovery rms. Cedars of Lebanon Med. Ctr., L.A., 1967-68; product-nurse cons. Ethicon, Inc., Somerville, N.J., 1968-69; nurse cons. Johnson & Johnson, New Brunswick, N.J., 1969-70; gen. mgr. Ariz. Heart Inst., Phoenix, 1970-72; owner, pres., bd. dirs. Highland Packaging Labs., Inc., Somerville, 1983—2002; ret., 2002. Mem., moderator Nat. Ass. Operating Rm. Nurses, Denver, 1963-76; pres. Aux. Orgn., Muhlenberg Hosp., Plainfield, N.J., 1979-80; chmn. Assn. for Retarded Citizens Fund Raising Ball, Somerset County, N.J., 1982. Mem.: Inst. Packaging Profls. Home: 29 Lambert Dr Princeton NJ 08540-2304 Personal E-mail: hs.cam@verizon.net.

CAMPBELL, NANCY DUFF, lawyer; b. 1943; BA, Barnard Coll., 1965; JD, NYU, 1968. Bar: DC 1975, N.Y. 1968. Atty. Ctr. Social Welfare Policy and Law; prof. Cath. U. Sch. Law, Georgetown U. Law Ctr.; founder, co.-pres. Nat. Women's Law Ctr. Mem. US Commn. on Child and Family Welfare. Author: jour. articles on women's legal issues. Bd. adv. Community Tax Law Report, Alliance Nat. Def., Inst. Women's Policy Rsch.; mem. Nat. Conf. State Legis. Child Care Adv. Comm., Campaign Family Leave Income Adv. Comm.; bd. dirs. Low Income Investment Fund; adv. bd. Princeton U. Ctr. for Rsch. on Child Wellbeing. Named Woman of Genius, Trinity Coll.; named one of 25 Heroines, Working Woman mag.; recipient Lifetime Achievement award, US Dept. Health and Human Svcs., William J. Brennan award, D.C. Bar. Fellow: ABA. Office: Nat Womens Law Ctr Ste 800 11 DuPont Cir Washington DC 20036 Office Phone: 202-588-5180. E-mail: campbell@nwlc.org.

CAMPBELL, NANCY JEANNE, science educator; b. Warren, Mich., Oct. 6, 1950; d. John Atia and Donna Kirschner; m. James K. Campbell, Mar. 24, 1978; children: Matt, Colleen. BA, Mich. State U., East Lansing, 1971; MA, Saginaw Valley State U., Mich., 1976. Cert. Mich., 1976. Tchr. Warren Consol. Sch., 1971—. Leader Girls Scouts Am. Office: Grissom Mid Sch 35701 Ryan Rd Sterling Heights MI 48310 Office Phone: 586-825-2560. E-mail: campbell@mail.wcs.k12.mi.us.

CAMPBELL, NAOMI, model; b. London; d. Valerie Campbell. With Elite Model Mgmt., N.Y., 1987-93, Elite Premier, London, Ford Models, Inc., Paris, 1991—, N.Y., 1993—, Women Model Mgmt., N.Y.C. Appearances include (T.V. series) The Fresh Prince of Bel Air, The Cosby Show, (videos) George Michael's Freedom, Michael Jackson's In the Closet, (book) Madonna's Sex, 1992, (films) Ready to Wear, 1994, Miami Rhapsody, 1995, Unzipped, 1995, To Wong Foo, Thanks for Everything, Julie Newmar, 1995, Catwalk, 1995, Girl 6, 1996, Invasion of Privacy, 1996, An Alan Smithee Film: Burn Hollywood Burn, 1997, Beautopia, 1998, Trippin, 1999, Prisoner of Love, 1999, Destinazione Verna, 2000, (TV film) Naomi Conquers Africa, 1998; author: Swan, 1994; album: Love and Tears, 1994. Achievements include first black model to appear on the cover of French Vogue.

CAMPBELL, NELL, mayor; b. Walnut, Miss. d. Newton Alcy and Lula Elizabeth (Luker) Vinson; m. Robert Fred Campbell, May 24, 1946 (widowed, Oct. 3, 1976); children: Elizabeth Ann, Robert Fred Jr., Rose Marie. Student, Jackson State, 1978. Cert. flower arranging. Machine operator Corinth Mfg. Co., Miss., 1944-46, Adamsville Mfg., Tenn., 1953-64, Kimberly Clark Inc., Memphis, 1945-46; supr. H.I.S. Coro., Saltillo, Tenn., 1964-89; florist Enville, Tenn., 1989—; mayor Town of Enville, 1994—. City bd. mem. Town of Enville; bd. mem. C. of C. Ruritan Club. Democrat. Baptist. Avocations: quilting, sewing, gardening, travel, reading, crafts. Home: 6805 Main St Enville TN 38332-5205

CAMPBELL, NEVE, actress; b. Guelph, Ont., Can., Oct. 3, 1973; m. Jeffrey Colt, Apr. 1995 (div. 1997). Student, Nat. Ballet Sch. Can. Actress (films) Scream, 1996 (Saturn award for Best Actress, MTV Movie award nomination, MTV Movie award for Best Female Performance), The Craft, 1996, Scream 2, 1997 (Blockbuster Entertainment award for Favorite Actress-Horror, MTV Movie award for Best Female Performance), 54, 1998, Wild Things, 1998, Three to Tango, 1999, Scream 3, 2000, Drowning Mona, 2000, Hairshirt, 2001, Investigating Sex, 2001, Lost Junction, 2003, Blind Horizon, 2004; (theatre) Resurrection Blues, 2006; writer, actor (films): The Company, 2003. Named one of 50 Most Beautiful People, People mag., 1998. Office: Creative Artists Agy 9830 Wilshire Blvd Beverly Hills CA 90212-1825*

CAMPBELL, REGINA FARRELL, literature and language educator; b. Honesdale, Pa., Oct. 26, 1951; d. John W. and Anne C. Farrell; m. William F. Campbell, Jr., Aug. 9, 1975; children: Pat W., Katie E. BA, Marywood U., Scranton, Pa., 1973; MA, U. Scranton, 1979. Cert. Tchr. English 7-12 N.Y., 1973. Tchr. English 7-12 Eldred Ctrl. Sch. Dist., NY, 1973—. Coord. English Eldred Ctrl. Sch., 2003—; instr. English Sullivan County C.C., Loch Sheldrake, NY, 1989—. Vol. Am. Cancer Soc., Honesdale, Pa., 1975—85, Nat. Bone Marrow Donor Orgn., Honesdale, 1990—91; com. chair Cub Scouts of Am., Beach Lake, Pa., 1990—96; sec. Wayne Highlands Mid. Sch. Band Parents, Honesdale; vol. Wayne Highlands Track Parents, Honesdale, 2001—05, Wayne Highlands Golf Parents, Honesdale, 1998—2002. Recipient Educator of Excellence award, N.Y. State English Coun., 1999. Master: PTSO; mem.: PTA, Eldred Ctrl. Sch. Dist. Faculty Assn. (sec. 1998, v.p. 1980—82), Delta Kappa Gamma (chair membership com. 1980—83, pres. 1983—85, mem. state projects com. 1998—2000, Album of Distinction 2000, 2001). Roman Catholic. Achievements include Creation Of Educational Learning Tools. Avocations: reading, collecting costume jewelry, beach life, Penn State football games. Office: Eldred Central School PO Box 249 Eldred NY 12732 E-mail: rcampbell@eldredschools.org.

CAMPBELL, REGINNA GLADYS, medical/surgical nurse; b. Dover, N.J., Oct. 16, 1952; d. Reginal C. Steele and Ruth E. Stelle; m. Danny Kay Campbell, June 29, 1974 (div. Sept. 2004); children: Catherine, David. Diploma in nursing, St. Joseph Hosp. Sch. Nursing, 1977; BSN, Ind. Wesleyan U., 2006. Cert. post anesthesia nurse. Staff nurse, charge nurse ICU/critical care unit Cameron Hosp., Angola, Ind., 1977—84; staff nurse post anesthesia care unit Cmty. Health Ctr. Branch County, Coldwater, Mich., 1984—2005, dir. surg./pediat., 2005—. 1st lt. Nurse Corp Res. U.S. Army, 1991—2002, capt. Nurse Corp Res. U.S. Army, 2002—, Kuwait/Iraq. Mem.: Soc. Pediatric Nurse, Med. Surgical Assn., Ind. Soc. Perianesthesia Nurses (v.p 2000—01, pres.-elect 2001—02), Am. Soc. Perianesthesia Nurses (membership com. 2001—02), Res. Officer Assn., Boy Scouts Am. (charter rep. 1995—2003), Angola Bus. and Profl. Women. Republican. Methodist. Office Phone: 517-279-5339. Business E-Mail: rcamp@dmei.net.

CAMPBELL, SARAH, elementary school educator, special education educator; b. Altavista, Va., Jan. 4, 1940; d. Charlie and Emma Francis (Morgan) Dalton; m. James Campbell, June 12, 1961; children: Saunta, Sidra. AA, Altantic C.C., 1976; BA magna cum laude, Glassboro State Coll., 1978; nursery sch. cert., Rutgers U.; spl. edn. cert., Glassboro State Coll., 1986; grad., Garden State Bible Sch., Pleasantville, N.J., 1994. Cert. tchr., NJ; asst. chaplain, Bapt. Ch.; ordained to ministry Bapt. Ch., 1995. Tchr. Head Start program Atlantic Human Resources, Inc., Atlantic City; edn!. area supr. Head Start program Adriatic Day Care Ctr., Atlantic, N.J.; head tchr., mgr. Atlantic Human Resources, Ind./Adriatic Day Care Ctr., Atlantic. Edn. con. Pleasantville Day Care Ctr., N.J. Past pres. dist. 8 Second Bapt. Ch.; choir libr. Gt. Choir; co-dir. children's ministry; tchr. Bible studies Greater Exodus Missionary Bapt. Ch. Mem. ASCD, Nat. Assn. Edn. Young Children.

CAMPBELL, SELAURA JOY, lawyer; b. Oklahoma City, Mar. 25, 1944; d. John Moore III and Gyda (Hallum) C. AA, Stephens Coll., 1963; BA, U. Okla., 1965; MEd, Chapel Hill U., 1974; JD, N.C. Cen. U., 1978; postgrad. atty. mediation courses, South Tex. Sch. of Law, Houston, 1991, Atty. Mediators Inst./Dallas, Dallas, 1992. Bar: Ariz 1983; lic. real estate broker, N.C.; cert. tchr. N.C. With flight svc. dept. Pan Am. World Airways, N.Y.C., 1966-91; lawyer Am. Women's Legal Clinic, Phoenix, 1987. Charter mem. Sony Corp. Indsl. Mgmt. Seminar, 1981; guest del. Rep. Nat. Conv., Houston, 1992; judge all-law sch. mediation competition for Tex., South Tex. Sch. Law, Houston, 1994. Mem. N.C. Cen. U. Law Rev., 1977-78. People-to-People del. People's Republic of China, 1987; guest del. Rep. Nat. Conv., Houston, 1992. Mem. Ariz. Bar Assn., Humane Soc. U.S., Nat. Wildlife Fedn., People for the Ethical Treatment of Animals, Amnesty Internat., Phi Alpha Delta. Republican. Episcopalian. Avocations: mountain climbing, horseback riding, photography. Home: 206 Taft Ave Cleveland TX 77327-4539

CAMPBELL, STACEY LYNNE, music educator; b. Manchester, N.H., June 13, 1978; d. James Campbell and Nora Ellen Lyons. BS in Edn., U. Conn., Storrs, 2001, BA in Music, 2001; MEd in Edn., U. Phoenix, 2004. Cert. tchr. music pre-K-12 State of Conn., 2001. Tchr. Deben H.S., Felixstowe, England, 2001—02, Six to Six Interdistrict Magnet Sch., Bridgeport, Conn., 2002—. Curriculum writer Six to Six Interdistrict Magnet Sch., Bridgeport, Conn., 2004—05. Presdl. scholar, U. Conn., 1996—2000. Mem.: Conn. Arts Administrator's Assn., Am. Choral Director's Assn., Music Educator's Nat. Conf., Waterbury Chorale. Avocations: singing, technology, travel, fitness. Office: Six to Six Interdistrict Magnet Sch 601 Pearl Harbor St Bridgeport CT 06610 Office Phone: 203-330-6016. E-mail: campbels@ces.k12.ct.us.

CAMPBELL, SYLVIA JUNE, secondary school educator; b. Dyersburg, Tenn., Jan. 13, 1957; d. Ernest Martin and Shoko (Okuyama) Stanley; m. Paul Timothy Campbell, June 14, 1980; 1 child, Colin Blair. B Music Edn., Baylor U., 1979. Cert. tchr. instrumental music, Tex. Band dir. Edward H. White Mid. Sch., San Antonio, 1979-80, Richfield H.S., Waco, 1980-83, Midway Ind. Sch. Dist., 1987-88, Lake Air Mid. Sch., 1988-90, China Spring Ind. Sch. Dist., Tex., 1990-92, band dir. Mid. Sch., 1992—96; band dir. Waco HS, Tex., 1996—97, China Spring Mid. Sch., 1997—2006. Asst. condr. Waco Symphony Youth Orch. Exec. bd. prin. flutist/piccoloist Waco Cmty. Band, 1981-2006, charter mem., 2004-06. Mem. Tex. Music Educators Assn., Tex. Bandmasters Assn. United Methodist. United Methodist. Avocations: gardening, singing, outdoor activities, reading. Home: 615 Willow Way Wylie TX 75098

CAMPBELL, THERESA MARIE, mathematics educator; b. Port Jefferson Station, NY, Oct. 29, 1981; d. Michael Daniel and Carmela Theresa Campbell; m. Sergio Avgoustidis, July 17, 2004. BA in Math., SUNY, Geneseo, 2003; MA in Liberal Studies, SUNY, Stony Brook, 2006. Cert. tchr. 7-12. Math. tchr. Eastpoint-South Manor Ctrl. Jr./Sr. HS, Manorville, NY, 2003—. Pvt. math. tutor, Brookhaven, NY, 1999—. Mem.: Nat. Coun. Tchrs. Math. Democrat. Roman Catholic. Avocations: travel, jogging, yoga, reading.

CAMPBELL, VICKI F., counseling administrator, educator; d. Gus Harold and Clara Mae Frossard; m. James Russell Campbell, Oct. 23, 1976; children: Kathleen, James Reese. BSc in Edn., Abilene Christian Coll., 1971; MEd, Tarleton State U., 1995. Cert. elem. self-contained State Bd. for Educator Certification/Tex., 1971, elem. psychology State Bd. for Educator Certification/Tex., 1971, lang. and/or learining disabled State Bd. for Educator Certification/Tex., 1975, counselor State Bd. for Educator Certification/Tex., 1995, spl. edn. counselor State Bd. for Educator Certification/Tex., 1995. Elem. tchr. Big Spring Ind. Sch. Dist., Tex., 1971—76; v.p. Master Fl. Systems, Inc., Abilene, Tex., 1986—88; instrn. specialist Region XIV Edn. Svc. Ctr., Abilene, 1991—93; case coord. Ctrl. Tex. Mental Health Mental Retardation Ctr., Brownwood, 1996—97; sch. counselor Cross Plains Ind. Sch. Dist., Tex., 1998—2003; counselor, vocation Tex. State Tech. Coll. West Tex., Brownwood, 2003—. Profl. devel. course adv. subcommittee Tex. State Tech. Coll. West Tex., Sweetwater, Tex., 2004—; student engagement subcommittee Tex. State Tech. Coll. West Tex. Quality Enhancement Plan, Sweetwater, Tex., 2004—; evaluation and assessment subcommittee Tex. State Tech. Coll. Quality Enhancement Plan, Sweetwater, Tex., 2004—; student fees adv. com. Tex. State Tech. Coll. West Tex., Brownwood, Tex., 2003—; validation com. Region XIV Edn. Svc. Ctr., Abilene, Tex., 2002—02, program presenter, 1993—94. Editor: (cookbook) From the Kitchens of East Texas. Mem. campus planning com. Brownwood Mid. Sch., 1995—96; coord. ladies' activities Suez Shrine Ctr., San Angelo, Tex., 1978—2005; honors banquet coord. Tex. State Tech. Coll. West Tex., 2003—05, team leader state employee charitable campaign, 2003—04, sponsor Student Govt. Assn., 2003—05, planning com. Ann. Women's Conf. Sweetwater, 2004; mem. tng. coalition bd. Family Svcs. Ctr., Brownwood, 1996—98; treas. Brownwood Band Boosters Club, 1994—95; gen. chairperson Mother's Mar. of Dimes, Coleman City, Tex., 1977—78. Mem.: ACA. Avocations: travel, reading. Office: Tex State Tech Coll West Tex 305 Booker St Brownwood TX 76801 Office Fax: 325-641-9827. Business E-Mail: vicki.campbell@brownwood.tstc.edu.

CAMPBELL, VIRGINIA HOPPER, piano concert artist, composer, educator; b. Oklahoma City, Okla., June 3, 1930; d. James Robert and Emily (Hess) Hopper; m. Rev. Walter Erlin Campbell, Jr., June 3, 1950; children: Walter Erlin III, James Andrew, Mary Catherine, Anne Charlotte, Patricia. B Music in Piano Performance cum laude, Oklahoma City U., 1985, M Music, 1988; studied in Europe, with Jörg Demus. Adj. prof. Okla. City U., tchr. of piano to 30 students, 1945—; tchr. St. Luke's Meth. Sch. Cont. Edn.; empresaria, founder, pres. Piano Artist Series, Oklahoma City, 1984—. Performances and concerts in Austria, Germany, Mex., U.S., including Vienna, Salzburg, 1990—; primary ch. organist Episcopal Chs. in Okla. and Tex., 1978—; also performed at Hilton Hotel, Oklahoma City Golf and Country Club, Peroleum Club, Waterford Hotel; concerts in Oklahoma City, Norman, Edmond, Ponca City, Duncan, Durant and Guthrie, Okla.; pianist on CDs and cassettes including Virginia Live, 1993, Just Gershwin, 1998. Mem. Okla. Music Tchrs. Assn., Nat. Music Tchrs. Assn., Ladies Music Club (pres. composers divsn. 1990-99, program chair music appreciation 19977-99), Sigma Alpha Iota, Pi Kappa Lambda. Home: 1815 W Wilshire Blvd Oklahoma City OK 73116-4115

CAMPBELL, ZENITA A. D., environmental engineer, educator, safety engineer; b. Minot, N.D., Oct. 17, 1961; d. Ida Mae and Clayton Campbell; 1 child, James Dorris. AS in Fire Safety Engring. Tech., Ea. Ky. U., Richmond, 1997, BS in Occupl. Safety Engring., 1999, MS Loss Prevention and Safety, 2000. Cert. fire and explosive investigator 1998, fire and explosive instr. 1998. Maintenance planning tech. Kuparuk Maintenance Planning, Alaska, 1986—91; engr. Kuparuk Facility Engring., Anchorage, 1991—94; sr. safety specialist L-3 Commns., Lexington, Ky., 2000—. Adj. prof. Coll. Fire and Safety, Ea. Ky. U., Richmond, 1995—; supt. cert. Six Sigma Blackbelt Expert, Lexington, 2000—. Mem.: Nat. Assn. Fire Investigation, Nat. Safety Mgmt. Soc., Am. Soc. Safety Engrs. (student pres. 1998—99), Ky. Safety and Health Network, Inc. (labor cabinet, Robert V. Moyer award

1999), Alpha Phi Sigma. Home: 192 Plum Street Stanton KY 40380 Office: L-3 Communications 5749 Briar Hill Rd Lexington KY 40516 Personal E-mail: zenita.campbell@yahoo.com. Business E-Mail: Zenita.Campbell@SOFSA.mil.

CAMPBELL-DUCKWORTH, TERRI ELAINE, elementary school educator; b. Bay Springs, Miss., Sept. 2, 1974; d. Carnell and Helen Teresia Campbell; m. Shannon Romareo Duckworth, Aug. 8, 1998; 1 child, Torri Duckworth. Degree in Elem. Edn./ Adminstrn., Jackson State U./Miss. Coll., Jackson, Clinton, 1996. Cert. tchr. Nat. Bd. Profl. Tchg. Standards, 2005, math. Jackson State U., 1997, gifted cert. Mississippi Coll., 2004. Tchr. Duckey's Learning Ctr., Taylorsville, Miss., 1992—94; dir. Duckey's Daycare, Taylorsville, Miss., 1995—96; tchr. Bright Ideas Enrichment Ctr., Flowood, Miss., 1996—97, Power Academic Performing Complex Elem., Jackson, Miss., 1997—. Tutor, Jackson, Miss. Youth dir./tchr. Jerusalem M.B. Ch., Bay Springs. Recipient Metro Tchr. of Yr., 2004; grantee, Jr. League, Ednl. Found. Trust, Bell South, 1997, 1998, 2000, 2001, 2003, 2004, 2005. Mem.: Nat. Coun. Tchr. of Math. Office: Power Academic Performing Complex 1120 Riverside Dr Jackson MS 39202 Office Phone: 601-960-5387. Business E-Mail: tduckworth@jackson.k12.ms.us.

CAMPBELL-GROTHE, RUTH ANN, retired budget analyst; b. La Plata, Md., Aug. 25, 1948; d. Lawrence Gilbert Pilkerton and Eleanor Garretter (Swann) Pilkerton-Grimm; m. Joseph Harvey Campbell, May 22, 1970 (dec. Oct. 1989); children: Joseph Lawrence, Timothy Craig; m. William Smith Grothe Jr., Apr. 24, 2004. Clk.-stenographer Gen. Svcs. Adminstrn., Washington, 1966-68, sec., stenographer, 1968-70, program asst., 1970-71, adminstrv. asst. Mpls., 1971-72, Washington, 1974-75, program analyst, 1975-78, corr. specialist, 1978-79, program analyst, 1979, budget analyst, 1979—2004; ret., 2004. Sec. Fed. Women's Program/Gen. Svcs. Adminstrn., Washington, 1981—82, PTA, Waldorf, Md., 1981—83; treas. Cub Scout pack Boy Scouts Am., La Plata, Md., 1982—87, Athletic Boosters Club, 1993—94; sec. Warrior Stadium Steering Com.; team capt. Thursday Nite Mixed Bowling League, 1976—; mem. vestry Christ Ch., Wayside, 1990—94, 2000—04, treas. Woman's Guild, 1990—. Mem. Am. Assn. Budget and Program Analysis. Episcopalian. Avocations: bowling, camping, horseshoes, travel, reading. Home: 7305 Saint Marys Ave La Plata MD 20646-3968 Office: Gen Svcs Adminstrn Bldg 4 Rm 1105 Washington DC 20406-0001 Personal E-mail: no1nanie082548@verizon.net.

CAMPBELL-JACKSON, CARLA LANETTE, insurance company executive; d. Samuel L. and Rosa Marion Campbell; m. Kevin B. Jackson, Aug. 27, 1988; 1 child, Bradley Ross Jackson. B in Comm., Drake U., Des Moines, Iowa, 1987; MS, Ill. State U., Normal, 2002. CPCU assoc. in claims Ill., 1995, assoc. in gen. ins. Ill., 1996, assoc. in ins. svcs. Ill., 2005. Intern State Farm Ins. Co., Des Moines, 1986—88, claim rep. Chgo., 1988—93, pers. rep., 1993—95, mgr. Bloomington, 1995—. Contbr. articles to periodicals. Founder program Mentoring And Providing Scholarships, 2000—; bd. mem. Girl Scouts USA, 2003—, YWCA, 2004—. Named Woman of Distinction, YWCA, 2006; recipient NBC's 25 Women in Leadership award, WEEK-TV, 2003, Dr. Martin Luther King, Jr. award, Human Rights Commn., 2004, Congl. award, U. S. Congress, 2005, Spirit of State Farm award, State Farm Ins. Co., 2006. Mem.: NAACP (v.p. 1998—), Alpha Kappa Alpha Sorority, Inc. (assoc.; v.p. 2002—06, Sorority Sister of Yr. 2000, 2004). Baptist. Avocations: reading, gospel music, travel, poetry, public speaking. Office: State Farm Ins Co 2702 Ireland Grove Rd Bloomington IL 61702 Office Phone: 309-763-6609.

CAMPION, JANE, film director, screenwriter; b. Wellington, New Zealand; d. Richard and Edith Campion. BA in Anthropology, Victoria U., Wellington, 1975; Diploma of Fine Arts, Chelsea Sch. Arts, London, 1979; degree, Sydney Coll. Arts, 1979; Diploma in Direction, Australian Film and T.V. Sch., Sydney, 1984; DLitt (hon.), Victoria U., 1999. Adj. prof. Sydney Coll. Arts, 2000. Dir., screenwriter Peel: An Exercise in Discipline, 1982 (also editor, Palme d'Or short film category Cannes Internat. Film Festival 1986, Diploma of Merit Melbourne Film Festival, 1983, finalist Greater Union awards, Australian Film Inst. awards 1983-84), A Girl's Own Story, 1983 (with Gerard Lee, Rouben Mamoulian award 1984, Best overall short film Sydney Film Festival 1984, Unique Artist Merit Melbourne Film Festival 1984, Best Direction, Best Screenplay, Best Cinematography Australian Film Inst. 1984, First Prize Cinestud Amsterdam Film Festival, 1985, Best Film Cinestud 1985, First Prize Festival and Press prize), writer/dir. Mishaps of Seduction and Conquest, 1984-85, Passionless Moments (also prodr., dir., writer, with Gerard Lee and dir. photography, Unique Artist Merit Melbourne Film Festival 1984, Best Exptl. Film Australian Film Inst. 1984, Most Popular Short Film Sydney Film Festival 1985), screened at Cannes Un Certain Regard, 1986, After Hours, 1984 (XL Elders award Best Short Fiction, Best Short Fiction Melbourne Internat. Film Festival 1985), Dancing Daze (TV series), Two Friends (TV movie), 1986 (Golden Plaque TV category Chgo. Internat. Film Festival 1987, Best Dir., Best Telemovie, Best Screenplay Australian Film Inst. awards 1987, screened at Cannes in Un Certain Regard, 1986, Edinburgh Film Festival, Sydney and Melbourne Film Festival, 1986), Sweetie, co-writer, dir. 1988, (Georges Sadoul prize Best Fgn. Film, Best Dir., Best Actress, Best Film Australian Critics awards 1990, New Generation award L.A. Film Critics, 1990, Best Fgn. Film Spirit of Independence awards 1990), An Angel at my Table, 1990 (Byron Kennedy award Australian Cinema 1990, Spl. Jury prize, Elvira Notari award Best Woman Dir., Agia Scuola Italian Min. Culture, Best Film Si presci award Panel Internat. Critics, Best Film O.C.I.C. award Christian journalists, Best Film for Young Audiences Cinema e Ragazzi Italian film critics prize, Critics award Toronto Film Festival, Most popular film in the Forum, Otto Debelius prize Berlin Film Festival, Best Fgn. Film, Spirit of Independence Awards, Venice Film Festival, World Premiere, 1990); writer, dir. The Piano, 1993 (Palme d'Or Cannes Internat. Film Festival 1993, Academy Award Best Original Screenplay 1994, Best Picture, Best Dir., Best Cinematography nominations, Acad. Awards, Australian Film Inst. awards, Australia Film Critics, Southeastern Film Critics Assn., others, Best Fgn. Film Chgo. Film Critics, Caesar awards (2000 WIN award, Wimfemme Film Festival Women's Image Network); composer: Feel the Cold, 1983, (play) The Portrait of A Lady, 1996; co-writer, dir.: Holy Smoke, 1998-99 (Best Film Francesco Pasinetti award, pres. Internat. jury Mostra Internat. Art Cinematogrophy Festival Venice Film Festival, 1997, Nat. Union Film Journalists, nominated Best Costume Acad. awards 1997, nominated Best Supporting Actress Acad. awards 1997); dir. In the Cut, 2002-03, 8-The Water Diary, 2005. Office: HLA Mgmt Pty Ltd 87 Pitt St Redfern NSW 2016 Australia also: PO Box 1536 Strawberry Hills NSW 2012 Australia Office Phone: 612 9310 4948. E-mail: hla@hlamgt.com.au.

CAMPION, KATHLEEN FRANCIS, lawyer, gifted and talented educator; b. Middletown, NY, Dec. 13, 1952; d. William Aloysius Campion and Margaret Johanna Roll; m. Conard Morris Smith, Dec. 28, 1988; 1 child, Anthony Daniel Campion-Smith. JD, U. N.Mex, Albuquerque, 1991, MA, 2005. Bar: N.Mex 1991. Pvt. practice atty., Corrales, N.Mex., 1991—; tchr. Albuquerque Pub. Schs. Advanced placement coord. Eisenhower Sch., Albuquerque, 2003—, instrnl. com. Leader Boy Scouts, Corrales, N.Mex., 2001; com. mem. sr. affairs Village of Corrales. Mem.: N.Mex State Bar (mem. com. delivery legal svc. to mentally ill 1994—97), Golden Key. Democrat. Avocations: reading, debate, travel, gardening, travel. Home: PO Box 957 Corrales NM 87048

CAMPOS-ORREGO, NORA PATRICIA, lawyer, consultant; b. Lima, Peru, Sept. 3, 1959; d. Victor M. Campos and Ofelia A. Orrego. BA, Cath. U. Peru, 1979, LLB, 1983, Lawyer, 1984; JD magna cum laude, InterAm. U. P.R., San Juan, 1989. Bar: PR 1989, Peru 1984, U.S. Supreme Ct. 2003. Legal asst. women's affairs commn. P.R. Gov.'s Office, San Juan, 1988-89, lawyer women's affairs commn., 1989-93, P.R. Gov.'s Office/Immigration Law Practice, Miami, Fla., 1993-94; women's discrimination cons. San Juan, P.R., 1994-95; pvt. practice specializing in immigration law Miami, 1996—. Editor: Law Sch. Mag., 1988—89. All Am. scholar U. P.R., 1988-89. Mem. ABA, FBA, Am. Immigration Lawyers Assn., P.R. Bar Assn., Peru Bar Assn. Roman Catholic. Avocations: sightseeing, reading, dance, walking. Office: Apostolic Mission Christ 261 NE 23 St Miami FL 33137 Office Phone: 305-951-8737. Personal E-mail: nora2003@bellsouth.net.

CANADA, MARY WHITFIELD, retired librarian; b. Richmond, Va., June 13, 1919; d. Waverly Thomas and Ruth Bradshaw (Smith) C. BA magna cum laude, Emory and Henry Coll., 1940; MA in English, Duke U., 1942; BS in LS, U. NC, 1956. Asst. circulation dept. Duke U. Libr., 1942-45, undergrad. libr., 1945-55, reference libr., 1956-85, asst. head reference dept., 1967-79, head dept., 1979-85, ret., 1985. Contbr. articles to profl. jours. Mem. exec. com. Friends of Duke U. Libr. Duke U. grantee Can., 1979, 81. Mem. ALA (life; initiated performance evaluation discussion group), Southeastern Libr. Assn. (sec. coll. and univ. sect., chmn. nominating com. reference svcs. divsn., also chmn. divsn.), NC Libr. Assn. (chmn. nominating com., chmn. newspaper com., chmn. coll. and univ. sect.), Alumni Assn. Sch. Libr. Sci. U. NC (pres.), Va. Hist. Soc. (life), Va. Geneal. Soc., DAR (chpt. regent), Friends of Va. State Archives, Campus club (Duke U.), Planning Adv. Com. North Ctrl. Durham, Va. Mus. Beta Phi Mu. Methodist. Home: 1312 Lancaster St Durham NC 27701-1132

CANADY, ALEXA IRENE, pediatric neurosurgeon, educator; b. Lansing, Mich., Nov. 7, 1950; d. Clinton Jr. and Hortense (Golden) C.; m. George Davis, June 18, 1988. BS, U. Mich., 1971, MD cum laude, 1975; DHL (hon.), Marygrove Coll., 1994; DHL (hon.) (hon.), U. Detroit, 1997; DSc (hon.), Ctrl. Mich. U., 1999, U. So. Conn., 1999. Diplomate Am. Bd. Neurol. Surgery. Intern in surgery Yale U., New Haven, 1975-76; resident in neurosurgery U. Minn., Mpls., 1976-81; fellow in pediatric neurosurgery Children's Hosp. Pa., Phila., 1981-82; instr. neurosurgery U. Pa., Phila., 1981-82; staff neurosurgeon, instr. neurosurgery Henry Ford Hosp., Detroit, 1982-83; asst. dir. neurosurgery Children's Hosp. Mich., Detroit, 1986-87, chief of neurosurgery, 1987-97; assoc. prof. neurosurgery Wayne State U., Detroit, 1988-91, vice chmn. neurosurgery, 1991—2001; prof. neurosurgery Sacred Heart Hosp., Pensacola, Fla., 1997—2001, 2006—. Clin. instr. neurosurgery Wayne State U. Sch. Medicine, 1985, mem. internal rev. com. dept. anatomy, 1988, chmn. search com. dept. neurosurgery, 1989, internal rev. com. dept. neurology, 1991-92, 125th anniversary celebration com., 1992, internal rev. com. dept. pediat., 1993, chmn. search com. dept. ophthalmology, 1992-93, internal rev. com. dept. neurosurgery, 1994; chmn. neurobiol. devices panel, FDA, cons. neurol. devices panel Med. Devices Adv. Com., 1994—, chmn., 1998-2000, co-chair ctr. devices and regulatory health enhanced sci. rev., 2001; vis. prof. Med. Coll. S.C., 1990; mem. surg. com. Children's Hosp. Mich., chmn. operating room subcom. surg. com., intensive care unit com., med. record com., med. exec. com.; mem. med. staff Children's Hosp. Mich., William Beaumont Hosp, Royal Oak and Troy, Mich., Harper-Grace Hosps., Detroit, Hutzel Hosp., Detroit, Sinai Hosp., Detroit, Huron Valley Hosp., Milford, Mich., Crittenton Hosp., Rochester Hills, Mich., St. John Hosp. and Med. Ctr., Detroit; presenter various profl confs. in U.S. and internat. Contbr. chpts. to books. Mem. Mich. Head Injury Alliance, Mich. Myelodysplasia Assn.; bd. dirs. Inst. Am. Bus., 1986-88. Recipient citation Women's Med. Assn., 1975, Candace award Nat. Coalition 100 Black Women, N.Y., 1986, Golden Heritage award, 1989, Leonard F. Sain Esteemed Alumni award U. Mich., 1990, Disting. Alumni award Everett H.S., Pres.'s award Am. Med. Women's Assn., 1993, Variety Heart award for Med., Sci. and Tech. Variety Club, 1994, Shining Star award Colgate-Palmolive Co./Starlight Found., 1994, Golden Apple award Roeper Sch., 1995, Athena award Alumni Assn. U. Mich., 1995, Golden Apple Faculty Tchg. award U. Fla. Pediat. Residents, 2004, Chmn. Recognition award Fla. Bd. Medicine, 2005; named Outstanding Young Woman in Am., 1977, Top 100 Bus. & Profl. Women of Am., 1985, Woman of Yr. Detroit Club Nat. Assn. Negro Bus. & Profl. Women's Club, Inc., 1986; named to Mich. Woman's Hall of Fame, 1989; grantee Am. Cancer Soc., 1979, Minn. Med. Found., 1979, Am. Cancer Soc., 1981-82, Widman Found. Early Intervention Treatment and Follow-Up of Infants with Post-hemorrhagic Hydrocephalus, 1984-85, Neuropsychol. Recovery and Family Adaptation to CHI Children's Hosp. Mich., 1987-88, Hydrocephalus Induced Endocrinopathies: Morphologic Correlates Children's Hosp. Mich., 1989, 91; finalist Inst. Medicine African Am. Portrait Gallery, 2006; poster placed in Nat. Acad. Medicine Gallery African Am. Physicians, 2006. Mem. AMA, ACS, Am. Assn. Neurol. Surgeons, Congress Neurol. Surgeons, Am. Soc. Pediatric Neurosurgery, Nat. Med. Assn. Detroit Med. Soc., Mich. Assn. Neurol. Surgeons (sec. 1992-93, v.p. 1994-95, pres. 1995-96), Transplantation Soc. Mich. (adv. bd. 1993-94), Mich. State Med. Soc. (child abuse and neglect divsn. 1986), Southeastern Mich. Surg. Soc. (sec. 1986-87), Soc. Crit. Care Medicine, Wayne County Med. Soc. (ethics com., pub. affairs com., law com.), U. Mich. Med. Ctr. Alumni Soc., Delta Sigma Theta. Office: 6064 Forest Green Rd Pensacola FL 32505 Office Phone: 850-416-7101. Personal E-mail: alexacanady@aol.com.

CANALES, DENISE NILES, software company executive; b. San Antonio, Jan. 31, 1968; d. Dennis Wesley Niles and Sylvia Amend Batha; m. Roberto R. Canales Jr., Aug. 21, 1993; 1 child, Olivia Elise. Student, Tex. Luth. U., 1986—87; BA, U. Tex., 1992; MA, Trinity U., San Antonio, 1994. Sr. rsch. intern Psychol. Corp., San Antonio, 1993—94; sr. rsch. asst. U. Tex. Med. Sch., Houston, 1994—97; dir. compliance Baylor Coll. Medicine, Houston, 1997—2000, dir. rsch. informatics, 2000—02; dir. rsch. and ops. API, Lexington, Ky., 2002—04, pres., CEO, 2004—. Spkr. in field. Contbr. chpt. to book. Mem.: Applied Rsch. Ethics Nat. Assn. (regional rep. coun. 1998—2003). Republican. Baptist. Avocations: painting, gardening, golf, reading, writing. Office: API Inc 167 W Main St Ste 210 Lexington KY 40507 Office Phone: 859-233-2006.

CANALES, VIOLA, management consulting executive, writer; JD, Harvard Univ. Litig. atty. O'Melveny and Myers; regional adminstr. SBA, San Francisco, 1994—2001; now v.p. emerging mkts. TEC Internat., Inc., San Diego. Author: (short stories) Orange Candy Slices and Other Secret Tales, 2001, (children's books) Tequila Worm, 2005 (Am. Libr. Assn. Pura Belpre Author Medal, 2006). Bd. dir. Radio Bilingue. Served to Capt. U.S. Army. Office: TEC Internat Inc Ste 400 11452 El Camino Real San Diego CA 92130 Office Phone: 858-523-6800. Office Fax: 858-934-4540.*

CANARY, LEURA GARRETT, prosecutor; m. William J. Canary; children: William James, Margaret Garrett. Grad., Huntington Coll.; JD, U. Ala. Asst. atty. gen State of Ala., 1981—90; trial atty. civil divsn. US Dept. ustice, 1990—94; asst. U.S. atty. (mid. dist.) Ala. US Dept. Justice, 1994—2001, U.S. atty. (mid. dist.) Ala., 2001—. Office: US Attys Office One Ct Sq Ste 201 Montgomery AL 36104*

CANARY, NANCY HALLIDAY, lawyer; b. Cleve., Apr. 21, 1941; d. Robert Fraser and Nanna (Hall) Halliday; m. Sumner Canary, Dec. 1975 (dec. Jan. 1979). BA, Case Western Res. U., 1963; JD, Cleve. State U., 1968. Bar: Ohio 1968, Fla. 1972, US Dist. Ct. (no. dist.) Ohio 1975, US Supreme Ct. 1974, US Dist. Ct. (so. dist.) Fla. 1994. Law clk. to presiding judge Ohio Ct. Appeals, Cleve., 1968—69; ptnr. McDonald, Hopkins & Hardy, Cleve., 1969—83; ptnr. managing Palm Beach office Thompson, Hine, LLP, Cleve., 1984—2002; sole practitioner Palm Beach, Fla., 2003—. Trustee Beck Ctr. for Cultural Arts, Lakewood, Ohio, 1980—90, Ohio Motorists Assn., 1989—95, Ohio Chamber Orch.; trustee, mem. devel. adv. com. Fairview Gen. Hosp., Cleve., 1980—96; chairperson Sumner Canary Lectureship com. Case Western Res. U. Law Sch.; sec. bd. govs. Churchill Ctr., Washington, 2000—02; bd. dirs. Comerica Bank & Trust Co., F.S.B., 1993—2000. Mem. Ohio State Bar Assn., Cleve. Bar Assn., Palm Beach County Bar Assn., Estate Planning Coun. Cleve., Estate Planning Coun. Palm Beach County, Gulf Stream (Fla.) Golf Club, Westwood Country Club (Cleve.). Republican. Avocations: music, horseback riding, collecting Churchill books. Home: Unit 1806 12500 Edgewater Dr Cleveland OH 44107-1677 also: 200 N Ocean Blvd Delray Beach FL 33483-7126 Office: 125 Worth Ave # 117 Palm Beach FL 33480 Office Phone: 216-226-7466.

CANAVAN, CHRISTINE ESTELLE, state legislator; b. Dorchester, Mass., Jan. 25, 1950; m. Paul Canavan; 2 children. Grad., Massasoit C.C., 1983; BS summa cum laude, U. Mass., 1988. RN. Mem. Mass. Ho. of Reps., Boston, 1993—, chair second fl. divsn., spl. legis. com. on foster care. Mem. Brockton (Mass.) Sch. Com., 1990-94, vice chmn., 1992-2000, Brockton (Mass.) Libr. Found. Mem. Polish White Eagles, Brockton (Mass.) Hist. Soc. Democrat. Roman Catholic. Home: 29 Mystic St Brockton MA 02302-2825 Office: Mass Ho of Reps Mass State House Rm 122 Boston MA 02133 Office Phone: 617-722-2006. Business E-Mail: rep.christinecanavan@hou.state.ma.us.

CANCINO, NELLY, language educator, adult education educator; b. Chihuahua, Mex., Jan. 27, 1962; arrived in U.S., 1983; d. Gustavo Franco and Angela Gonzalez; m. Kevin Mobbs, Nov. 16, 2004; 1 child from previous marriage, Jesus Jr. BS in Mgmt. and Comm. Info. Sys., Park U., 2001. Instr. English as 2d lang. San Jacinte Adult Learning Ctr., El Paso, Tex., 2003—. Office: San Jacinto ALC 1216 Olive Ave El Paso TX 79901 Office Phone: 915-533-9072.

CANCIO, MARGARITA R., infectious disease physician; b. Pinar del Rio, Cuba, Sept. 29, 1959; d. Jose and Maria Cabrera; m. Derry H. Cancio, June 6, 1982. BS magna cum laude, U. South Fla., 1979; MD. Am. Bd. Internal Medicine, Infectious and Tropical Medicine. Clin. assoc. prof. dept. internal medicine USF Coll. Medicine, 2001—; chief of staff dept. internal medicine Tampa Gen. Hosp.; epidemiologist Town & Country Meml., Vencor, Tampa and Saint Petersburg. Served numerous med. staff coms. at area hosps.; lectr. in field. Founder, med. dir. Internat. Traveelr's Clinic, Infectious Disease Assocs. Tampa Bay, Kidcare; mem. comty. Hillsborough County AIDS Coordination Coun., Suncoast AIDS Network Fla., Shadow program coll. medicine students, USF and USF-HRS AIDS Patient Care Clinic. Named physician of Yr. Tampa Bay Latin Am. Med. Soc., 1997, Hispanic Woman of Yr., 1998. Fellow ACP; mem. AMA, Hillsborough County Med. Assn., Infectious Disease Soc. Am. (pres. 1989—), Soc. Hosp. Epidemiology, Am. Soc. Microbiology, Fla. Infectious Disease Soc., Fla. Health Sci. Bd. (trustee), USF (trustee), Alpha Omega Alpha. Office: Infectious Disease Assoc 4 Columbia Dr # 820 Tampa FL 33606 Fax: (813) 254-6414. Office Phone: 813-251-8444. Business E-Mail: cfalcon@travelerclinic.com.

CANDELA, VANESSA ENGLISH, lawyer; BS in Fin., Boston Coll., 1995; JD, Northeastern U. Law Sch., 2000. Bar: Mass. 2001. Mem.: Women's Bar Assn., Boston Bar Assn., ABA. Avocations: travel, golf. Office: Foley Hoag LLP Seaport World Trade Center West 155 Seaport Blvd Boston MA 02210-2600 Office Phone: 617-832-1720. Office Fax: 617-832-7000. E-mail: vcandela@foleyhoag.com.*

CANDELARIA, ANGIE MARY, special education educator; b. Durango, Colo., July 13, 1939; d. Angelo and Lucia (Mattevi) Dallabetta; m. David Candelaria, Sept 24, 1958 (div. Mar. 1964); children: David D., Craig D.; m. Richard James McMullen, July 3, 1982 (dec. Mar. 1999). BA, Ft. Lewis Coll., Durango, 1965; postgrad., U. North Colo., 1997-99. Cert. tchr. spl. edn., Colo. Tchr. Sch. Dist. R25, Loveland, Colo., 1967-68; tchr. spl. edn. Sch. Dist. 9R, Durango, 1968-98, mem. profl. devel. com., 1990-97; ret., 1998. Ind. rschr. Josten Integrated Computer Edn. Co. Colo. Dept. Edn. spl. edn. grantee, 1966, cross-cultural inst. grantee, 1972-74, Sch. Dist. 9R grantee, 1992. Mem. ASCD, NEA, Colo. Edn. Assn., Durango Edn. Assn., Internat. Reading Assn., VFW Aux. (life), Am. Legion Aux., Elks, Colombo Lodge. Republican. Roman Catholic. Avocations: computers, travel, reading, animals. Home: 16B 1741 Tustin Ave Apt 16B Costa Mesa CA 92627-3294 also: PO Box 472 Durango CO 81302-0472

CANDLIN, FRANCES ANN, psychotherapist, social worker, educator; b. Phila., July 18, 1945; d. Francis Townley and Wilma (David) C. BA magna cum laude, Loretto Heights Coll., 1967; MSW with honors, St. Louis U., 1971. Diplomate Am. Bd. Clin. Social Work; cert. social worker; lic. clin. social worker, Colo. Trainee recreational therapist Jewish Hosp., St. Louis, 1970—71; trainee social worker Jefferson Barracks VA Hosp., St. Louis, 1970—71; social worker Adams County Juvenile Probation, Brighton, Colo., 1972—74, Boulder County Social Svcs., Colo., 1974—75; sch. social worker Adams County Sch. Dist. #50, Westminster, Colo., 1975—80; workshop presenter Human Enrichment Cons., Denver, 1980—90; pvt. practice Denver, 1980—; dir. Madison St. Counseling Ctr., Denver, 1991—97; founder, dir. Women's Mysteries Tour Co., 1993, Enneagram Ctr. of Colo., 1997—. Cons. Mountain Plains Regional Ctr., Denver, 1981-85, Dept. Edn., Topeka, 1981-87, Dept. Spl. Edn., Nebr., Colo., Mo., N.Mex., Utah, 1982-86. Bd. dirs. Denver Sch. for Gifted, 1982-86, Weaver Found., 1985-86, St. Mary's Acad., Englewood, Colo., 1985-88. Recipient stipend NIMH, 1969, VA Social Work Trainee, 1970. Mem. NASW, NOW, Acad. Cert. Social Workers, Internat. Enneagram Assn., Assn. Transpersonal Psychology, Colo. Assn. Clin. Social Workers, Vajra Soc. (bd. dirs. 1990—). Avocations: world travel, women's issues, spiritual devel. Office: Enneagram Ctr Colo PO Box 933 Glenwood Springs CO 81602

CANDREIA, PEGGY JO, medical educator; b. Pawhuska, Okla., Aug. 23, 1944; d. Joseph Leonard and Wilma Jane (Brook) C. Student, U. Ozarks, 1965. Supr. credit and collections Credit Bur. Bartlesville, Okla., 1965-69; credit rep. Shell Oil Co., Tulsa, Okla., 1969-88; owner, mgr. Gorgeous Car Care, Tulsa, 1988-90; fin. analyst H.A. Chapman Inst., Children's Med. Ctr., Tulsa, 1990—2002, fin. coord. Children's Med. Network Telethon, 1994—2002; data coord. Hillcrest Healthcare Sys., Tulsa, 2002—03; asst. acctg. mgr. Preferred Pediat. Home Health Care, Tulsa, 2003—04; instr. med. office mgmt. Career Point Inst., 2005—. Founder local chpt. Parents and Friends of Lesbians and Gays, Tulsa, 1988-90; v.p. Tulsa Oklahomans for Human Rights, 1988-89; bd. dirs. Follies Rev., Tulsa, 1993-97, Broken Arrow Cmty. Playhouse, 1998-99; mem. steering com., sec., treas., Names Project, Tulsa, 1990—, co-chmn. ctrl. region logistics, Washington, 1996. Recipient Honor of Ky. Col. Republican. Roman Catholic. Avocations: designing homes, travel, skiing, fundraising, drawing. Home: 1525 N College Ave Tulsa OK 74110-2719 Personal E-mail: varican@worldnet.att.net.

CANDRIS, LAURA A., lawyer; b. Frankfort, Ky., Apr. 5, 1955; d. Charles M. and Dorothy (King) Sutton; m. Aris S. Candris, Dec. 22, 1974. AB with honors and distinction in polit. sci., Transylvania Coll., 1975; postgrad., U. Pitts., 1975-77, U. Fla., 1977-78; JD, U. Pitts., 1978. Bar: Fla. 1978, U.S. Dist. Ct. (mid. dist.) Fla. 1978, U.S. Ct. Appeals (4th cir.) 1980, Pa. 1981, U.S. Dist. Ct. (we. dist.) Pa. 1982, U.S. Ct. Appeals (3d cir.) 1983. Assoc. Coffman, Coleman, Andrews & Grogan, Jacksonville, Fla., 1978-80, Manion, Alder & Cohen, Pitts., 1981-85, Eckert, Seamans, Cherin & Mellott, Pitts., 1985-86, ptnr., 1987-96, vice chmn. labor and employment law dept, mem. practice mgmt. com., mem. strategic planning com.; ptnr. Meyer Unkovic & Scott, LLP, Pitts., 1996—, chair labor, employment law and employee benefits sect., mem. litigation and transactions depts. Contbr. over 30 articles to profl. jours. including Compensation and Benefits Rev., Forum Reporter, Employment Law Inst. manuals, Ref. Manual for the 34th Ann. Mid-West Labor Law Conf. Dynamic Bus. Mem. O'Hara Twp. Coun., 1986—90, O'Hara Twp. Planning Commn., 1990; bd. dirs. Tri-State Employers Assn., 1991—93, Parent and Child Guidance Ctr., 1991—2001, v.p., 1998—99, mem. exec. com., 1998—2001, pres., 1999—2000, sec., 2000—01; treas., mem. exec. com. SMC Bus. Couns., 1993—94, bd. dirs., 1993—96, Big Bros. and Big Sisters Greater Pitts., 1998—, v.p. planning, 2001—02, mem. exec. com., 2001—05, v.p. adminstrn., 2003—04, pres., 2004, 2005; bd. dirs. The Whale's Tale, 2000—01, Mediatio Coun. Western Pa., 2006—; bd. dirs., mem. exec. com. FamilyLinks, 2000—01. Nat. Merit Found. scholar 1972-75; named Ky. Col., 1974. Fellow: Allegheny County Bar Found.; mem.: ABA (EEO com., dispute resolution com.), Allegheny County Bar Assn. (coun. on professionalism 1990—2000, mem. coun. employment sect. fed. cts. sect. 2003—, coun. mem. 2003—, newsletter editor 2003—, vice chmn. 2004—05, chair 2006—, coun. mem. 2006—, women in the law div., hqrs. com. and pers. subcom.), Pa. Bar Assn. (employment sect.), Fla. Bar Assn. Republican. Avocations: skiing, travel, bicycling, reading. Office: Meyer Unkovic & Scott LLP 1300 Oliver Bldg Pittsburgh PA 15222 Office Phone: 412-456-2891. Business E-Mail: lac@muslaw.com.

CANE, SUSANNAH RICHARDS, music educator; b. Easton, Pa., Dec. 13, 1954; d. Linwood John and Helen Richards Pearson; m. Daniel Joseph Cane, Aug. 15, 1998; children: Phillip John Ansell children: Christopher Blair Ansell, Meredith Lora Ansell. BS in music edn., Mansfield U., Pa., 1975; MEd in elem. edn. (hon.), Millersville U., Pa., 1981. PA Dept of Ed Professional Certificate PA, 1980. Music tchr. W.I. Beahm Jr. HS, Mt. Joy, Pa., 1976—81; tchr. Montessori Children's Ho. of York, Pa., 1984—86; music tchr. Dallastown Area Sch. Dist., Pa., 1994—. Bus. enterprise: parent/child preschool music program Mostly Music, York, Pa., 1990—92. Author: (alliance for learning grant) Using Music to Enhance Reading Performance. Avocation: Karate (black belt). Office: Ore Valley Elem Sch Springwood Rd York PA 17402 Office Phone: 717-505-5051. Business E-Mail: susannah.cane@dallastown.net.

CANELAS, DALE BRUNELLE, library director; b. Chgo., Jan. 13, 1938; d. Ralph Everley and Margaret Barbara (Clark) Brunelle; m. L. Marcelo Canelas, June 17, 1961; 1 child, Cathryn Margaret. BS in Humanities, Loyola U., Chgo., 1960; MLS, Rosary Coll., 1966; cert. in mgmt., U. Md., 1971. Asst. dir. Palatine Pub. Libr., Ill., 1966-68; asst. dir. adminstrv. svcs. Northwestern U. Libr., Evanston, Ill., 1969-75; assoc. dir. Stanford U. Libr., 1975-84; dir., univ. libr. U. Fla. Librs., Gainesville, 1985—. Vice pres. Freedom to Read Found., Chgo., 1977-78. Mem. ALA (various coms. and offices), Libr. Adminstrn. and Mgmt. Assn. (pres. 1978-80), Assn. Rsch. Librs. (bd. dirs. 1992—, various coms. 1985—). Office: U Fla Librs 210 Library W Gainesville FL 32611-2048 Office Phone: 904-392-0342. E-mail: dcanelas@ufl.edu.*

CANELLI, JEANNE, early childhood educator; b. Framingham, Mass., June 9, 1948; d. Francis J. and Jeanne T. (Landry) Keefe; m. Gerard P. Canelli, Aug. 5, 1972; children: Gerry Jr., Jill, Jennifer. BS in Elem. Edn., Framingham State Coll., 1970; MS, Wheelock Coll., 1987; PhD, Lesley Coll., 1999. Cert. tchr. in elem. edn., moderate spl. needs, young children with spl. needs, Mass. Tchr. Holliston Pub. Schs., 1970—73, Bellingham Pub. Schs., Mass., 1980—81; dir., head tchr. ECDC Sherborn Pre sch., Mass., 1981—87; assoc. prof. dept. edn., dir. child devel. lab. Framingham State Coll., 1987—, chmn. Dept. Edn., 2005—. Validator Nat. Acad. Early Childhood Programs, 1993—; tchg. fellow Lesley Coll. Grantee Mass. Dept. Edn. Mem. Nat. Assn. Edn. Young Children (founder, pres. Framingham chpt.), Mass. Assn. Early Childhood Educators Office Phone: 508-626-4761. Personal E-mail: jccdl@comcast.net. Business E-Mail: jcanell@frc.mass.edu.

CANETTI, ALEXANDRA, psychiatrist; b. San Juan, PR, Aug. 28, 1975; d. Luis Francisco Canetti and Doris Rochet. BS in pre med. sci. (cum laude), U. Puerto Rico; MD, U. Ctrl. Caribe, Bayamón, Puerto Rico, 2002. Resident in psychiatry Cabrini Med. Ctr., NYC, 2002—; psychiatrist Realization Ctr., NYC, 2005—; fellow child and adolescent psychiatry St. Vincent's Hosp., N.Y.C., 2006—. Mem.: Am. Psychiat. Assn. Roman Catholic. Avocations: travel, yoga. Office: Cabrini Med Ctr 227 East 19th St New York NY 10003 Office Phone: (212)995-600.

CANFIELD, CINDY SUE, art educator; b. Farmington, Mo., June 22, 1960; d. Lee Roy and Dale Collins; m. John M. Canfield II, Aug. 2, 1987; children: Clara Seleena, Johnell Mckinlee, Macarthur. B in Art Edn., Coll. Ozarks, 1983; postgrad., Drury, 1984, U. Va., 1992, SW Mo. State U., 1996, SW Bapt. U., 2004, Lindenwood U., Mass., 2005, postgrad., 2006. Cert. tchg. Mo. Weaver Coll. Ozarks, Point Lookout, 1978—83; tchr H.S. art Steelville Pub. Schs., 1983—85, Miller Pub. Schs., 1985—86, Strafford Pub. Schs., 1986—92; educator elem. art Hollister Pub. Schs., Mo., 1992—. Arts basic program site coord. Hollister Pub. Schs., Taney County, 1992—, dir. cmty. art events, Hollister, 1992—, new sch. com. bond organizer, 1994—95; dir. pub. rels. Sch. Bond Issue, 1994—. Author: Southwest Arts Reference Directory, 1991, K-12 Sequential Art Curriculum Guide, 1991. Active Taney County Character Edn. Bldg. Team, 2005; participant Memory Walk for Alzheimers, 2001—, Relay for Life Cancer Fundraiser, 1999—; mem. PTO. Named Tchr. of the Month, 2006; recipient Nat. Tchr. Inst. Excellence award, Robert Rauschenburg, 1994, Conservation award, Soil Water Co., 2001, 2004; Arts Alliance grantee, Getty Found., 1992—94. Mem.: S.W. Dist. Art Tchrs. Assn., Nat. Art Educator's Assn. Avocations: reading, writing, painting, sculpting, swimming. Home: 295 Quincy Rd Kirbyville MO 65679 Office: Hollister Pub Schs 1798 State Hwy Hollister MO 65672 Office Phone: 417-336-2225. Business E-Mail: blcny922cancun@wmconnect.com.

CANFIELD, CONSTANCE DALE, retired accountant, retired medical/surgical nurse, retired military officer; b. Fairmont, W.Va., May 2, 1940; d. Robert Alman and Dorothy Jane (Motter) C. Flight nurse diploma, Sch. Aerospace Med., 1967; BS in Acctg., Rollins Coll., 1979; student, Stetson U., 1975-76, Fla. Inst. Tech., 1976-77; grad., Army Comd. Gen. Staff Coll., Ft. Levenworth Kans., 1991. RN Fla.; registered Nurse Fla. Prin. C. D. Canfield, Acct., Melbourne, Fla., 1979-90; acct. C.D. Canfield, Acct., Melbourne, Fla., 1991—2002; ret., 2002. Gov.'s appointee Women in Mil. for Am. Meml. Found., Washington, 1991; gov.'s escort Fla. Freedom Festival, Inc., Tallahassee, 1991; state coord. VietNam Women's Meml. Project, Inc., Washington, 1986—; adminstrv. bd. United Meth. Ch., Melbourne, 1987—; musician Melbourne Mcpl. Band, 1980-90, Space Coast Philharmonic Orch., 1986-87; vol. Habitat for Humanity. With USAF, 1963—70, with U.S. Army, 1970—75, lt. col. U.S. Army, 1989—2000. Decorated Air Force Commendation medal, Army Commendation medal, Fla. Meritorious Svc. medal, Order of Mil. Med. Merit. Mem. AACN, Nat. Soc. Tax Profls., Nat. Soc. Pub. Accts., Fla. Assn. Ind. Accts. (sec. space coast chpt. 1992-93), Internat. Biog. Assn. (life), VFW (life), Vietnam Vets. Am. (life), Vietnam Vets. of Brevard, Inc. (life), N.G. Officers Assn., Fla. Hist. Soc., U.S. C. of C., Internat. Lions Club (pres. local club), Order Mil. Med. Merit. Republican. Avocations: fishing, camping, music, boating, jet skiing.

CANFIELD, JUDY S., psychologist; b. NYC, May 15, 1947; d. Arthur and Ada (Werner) Ohlbaum; m. John T. Canfield (div.); children: Oran David, Kyle Danya. BA, Grinnell Coll., 1963; MA, New Sch. Social Rsch., 1967; PhD, U.S. Internat. U., 1970. Psychologist Mendocino State Hosp., Talmage, Calif., 1968-69, Douglas Coll., New Westminster, BC, Can., 1971-72, Family & Childrens Clinic, Burnaby, BC, Can., 1971-72; psychologist, trainer, cons. VA Hosp., Northampton, Mass., 1972-75; dir. New England Ctr., Amherst, Mass., 1972-76; dir., psychologist Gateways, Lansdale, Pa., 1977-78; asst. prof., psychologist Hahnemann Med. Ctr., Phila., 1978-84; pres., dir. Inst. Holistic Health, Phila., 1978-85; psychologist, cons. Berkeley, Calif., 1986—. Mem. task force, tng. com. Berkeley Dispute Resolution Svc., 1986-89; mem. measure H com. Berkeley United Sch. Dist., 1987-88. Mem. APA, Nat. Register Health Svc. Providers in Psychology, Nat. Assn. Advancement Gestalt Therapy (steering com. 1990), Calif. Psychol. Assn., Alameda County Psychol. Assn. (info.-referral svc. 1989—), Assn. Humanistic Psychology. Avocations: piano, horseback riding, ice skating. Office: 2031 Delaware St Berkeley CA 94709-2121

CANGEMI, LISA LYNNE, art director, graphics designer; b. Bklyn., May 20, 1963; d. Robert A. and Elizabeth J. (Kopter) C. BFA in Graphic Design with honors, Sch. Visual Arts, NYC, 1985. Owner C&C Graphic Design, 1985—; art dir. Amerchol, Associated Bus. Pub., AT&T Corp., Briarcliffe Coll., Cablevision, Cahners Pub., CMP Media, Condé Nast, CTB Pub., Deloitte, Touche & Tomatsu, Dover Pub., Earnshaw Pub., Famous Brands, Gattefossé, Grey Advt., 2004—, Miller Freeman, Nassimi Corp., New Phase Tech., NJ Savvy, Patchogue Theatre, LI Petrolite Corp., TalkAIDS, United-Guardian, VNU Pub., 2004—; Walker and Co. prof. graphic design Briarcliffe Coll., 2004—. Prof. Graphic Design Briarcliffe Coll., NY. One-woman shows include painting exhbns. NY galleries and librs., 1993—2006 (GD USA, Folio, Creativity, and Davey awards, over 3 dozen graphic design awards). Avocations: photography, painting, travel. Office: PO Box 782 Lynbrook NY 11563-0782 Office Phone: 516-295-0936. Personal E-mail: CCGraphics85@aol.com.

CANN, SHARON LEE, retired health science librarian; b. Ft. Riley, Kans., Aug. 14, 1935; d. Roman S. and Cora Elon (George) Foote; m. Donald Clair Cann, May 16, 1964. Student, Sophia U., Tokyo, 1955-57; BA, Calif. State U., Sacramento, 1959; MSLS, Atlanta U., 1977; EdD, U. Ga., 1995. Cert. health scis. libr. Recreation worker ARC, Korea, Morocco, France, 1960-64; shelflister Libr. Congress, Washington, 1967-69; tchr. Lang Ctr., Taipei, Taiwan, 1971-73; libr. tech. asst. Emory U., Atlanta, 1974-76; health sci. libr. Northside Hosp., Atlanta, 1977-85, libr. cons., 1985-86; libr. area health edn. ctr., learning resource ctr. Morehouse Sch. Medicine, 1985-86; edn. libr. Ga. State U., 1986-93; dir. libr. svcs. Ga. Bapt. Coll. Nursing, 1993-99, ret., 1999. Author: Life in a Fishbowl: A Call To serve, 2003; editor Update, publ. Ga. Health Scis. Libr. Assn., 1981; contbr. articles to profl. jours. Chmn. Calif. Christian Youth in Govt. Seminar, 1958. Named Miss Far East Air Force, 1956, Alumni Top Twenty, Calif. State U., Sacramento, 1959; recipient Miss Meiji Bowl Tokyo, 1956. Mem. ALA, Med. Libr. Assn. (hon. life; bookkeeper So. chpt. 1996-98, credentialing com. 1996-2000, 05, nursing and allied health sect. continuing edn. chair 1998-2000), Spl. Libr. Assn. (dir. South Atlantic chpt. 1985-87), Ga. Libr. Assn. (spl. libr. divsn. chmn. 1983-85), Ga. Health Scis. Libr. Assn. (hon. life, chmn. 1981-82), Atlanta Health Sci. Libr. (chmn. 1979, 95), Am. Numis. Assn., ARC Overseas Assn., Audubon Soc., Women in Mil. Svc. for Am., Suncity Hilton Head Computer Club (v.p. 2003). Home: 69 Plymouth Ln Bluffton SC 29909-5062 E-mail: sharoncann@aol.com.

CANNEZZARO, NIKKI ECKLAND, lawyer; b. St. Paul, June 18, 1975; d. Gary R. and Kathy J. Eckland; m. Chris J. Cannezzaro, May 19, 2001. BA, U. Kans., 1997; JD, U. Mo., Kansas City, 2000. Bar: Mo., Kans. Assoc. atty. Franke Schultz & Mullen, P.C, Kansas City, Mo., 2001—05; ptnr. Franke Schultz & Mullen, P.C., 2005—. Mem.: Lawyers Assn. Kans. City (bd. mem. 2001—04), Assn. Women Lawyers (bd. dirs. 2004—05), Kans. City Met. Bar Assn., Mo. Bar Assn., Kans. Bar Assn. Office: Franke Schultz and Mullen PC 8900 Ward Pky Kansas City MO 64114 Office Phone: 816-421-7100. Office Fax: 816-421-7915. Business E-Mail: ncannezzaro@fsmlawfirm.com.

CANNISTRACI, DIANE FRANCES, sales executive; b. Bronx, N.Y., Jan. 9, 1950; d. John and Dorothy (Romano) C. Student, Orlando (Fla.) Jr. Coll., 1968-70, Teiko Post Coll., 1991-92. Ea. regional sales mgr. Kierulff Airline/Internation Supply, 1979-86; western regional sales mgr. C & K Unimax, Wallingford, Conn., 1989-90; sales and mktg. rep. U.S. C. of C., 1990-91; store mgr. Petite Sophisticate, Manchester, Conn., 1991-92; internat. and airline mktg. Richey Cypress Electronics, Wallingford, 1992-96; sales account exec. Midway Indsl. Electronics, Plainview, NY, 1996—2000; Rep. coord. Suffolk County Bd. Election, 2000—. Fund raiser Am. Heart Assn., Rocky Hill, Conn., Am. Diabetes Assn.; vol. Hartford (Conn.) Hist. Soc., Hartford; committeewoman Rep. Party, Huntington, NY; dir. and treas. Fedn. Rep. Women of 10th Jud. Dist., 2006—; 2d v.p. Suffolk County Rep. Women, 2006. With USNG, 1981—86. Recipient All Around Womanhood award, Huntington Sta., N.Y. PTA, 1968. Mem.: Air Carrier Purchasing. Roman Catholic. Home: 345 Depot Rd Huntington Station NY 11746-3339

CANNISTRARO, CAROLYN MARIE, financial recruiter; b. Yonkers, N.Y., July 24, 1972; d. Philip Attilio and Diane Rose (Spinelli) C. BA in Psychology, Boston Coll., 1995. Fin. recruiter Robert Half Internat., White Plains, N.Y., 1996—; exec. recruiter Lindsey and Co., Inc., Darien, Conn., 1998—. Mgr. Millennium divsn. Millennium Staffing Accts. on Call; mktg. dir. human resources discipline, mktg. dir. fin. and acctg. divsn. Romac Internat.; self-expression coach Landmark Edn., N.Y. Classically trained opera singer. Mem. NAFE, Am. Soc. Women Accts. (mem. chair 1997-98, dir. membership, pub. rels. chair 1998—, High Profile Women of Month 1998), Women in Sales, Fairfield County Bus. Women's Network, Soc. for Human Resource Mgmt. Republican. Roman Catholic. Avocations: opera, racing cars.

CANNIZZARO, LINDA ANN, geneticist, researcher; b. S.I., N.Y., Aug. 4, 1953; BS, St. Peter's Coll., 1975; MS, Fordham U., 1977, PhD, 1981. Postdoctoral fellow Dartmouth U. Med. Sch., Hanover, N.H., 1981-83; fellow in human genetics Children's Hosp. Phila., 1983-84; co-dir. cytogenetics Milton S. Hershey (Pa.) Med. Ctr., 1984-86; dir. gene mapping S.W. Biomed. Rsch. Inst., Scottsdale, Ariz., 1986-89; asst. prof. Fels Inst. Temple U. Med. Sch., Phila., 1989-91; asst. prof. Jefferson Cancer Inst., Phila., 1991-93; assoc. prof. Albert Einstein Coll. Medicine, Bronx, NY, 1993—2001; dir. cancer and molecular cytogenetics Albert Einstein Coll. Medicine and Montefiore Hosp., Bronx, N.Y., 1993—; prof. pathology Albert Einstein Coll. Medicine, 2001—; prof. Montefiore Med. Ctr. and Albert Einstein Coll. Medicine, 2006—. Co-editor-in-chief Cytogenetics Cell Genetics, 1995—; contbr. articles to profl. jours. Grantee Am. Cancer Soc., 1989-90, 94-97; Kriser awardee in Lung Cancer Rsch., 1999-2001. Mem. AAAS, AAUW, Am. Soc. Human Genetics. Avocations: painting, hiking, reading, writing. Office Phone: 718-405-8103. E-mail: cannizza@earthlink.net.

CANNON, ALICE GRACE, counselor; b. Greenville, N.C., Nov. 3, 1949; d. Carl William Hannah and Lula Estelle Briley; children: Mary Alice Cannon Blankenship, Laren Jay. PhD, DD, Progressive Universal Life Ch., 2000. Commd. 2d lt. USAF, 1973, advanced through ranks to staff sgt., 1980, ret., 1993; clk. U.S. Postal Svc., Norfolk, Va., 1994—97, ret.; min. Progressive Universal Life Ch., Sacramento, 2000—, counseling practitioner, 2001—, min., 2000; counsoler practioner, 2001. Staff sgt. USAF, 1983, Greneda Invasion, staff sgt. USAF, 1991—92, Desert Storm. Mem.: AARP, Air Force Meml. Assn., Disabled Vets. Assn. Avocations: Black Belt in Tae Kwan Do, reading, museums, travel, music. Home: PO Box 10333 Goldsboro NC 27532-0333 E-mail: snowy777@msn.com.

CANNON, BARBARA SOMERS, secondary school educator; b. Charlotte, NC, Dec. 3, 1940; d. Ewell Porter and Ila May (Corry) Somers; m. James Edward Cannon, Sept. 1, 1961; children: Suzanne Corry, James Edward Jr. BS in edn., Winthrop U., 1962. Tchr. No. Myrtle Beach H.S., 1964—71, Olympic H.S., Charlotte, NC, 1978—2003; ret., 2003. Pres. NC Assn. Family and Consumer Sci., 1986; nat. exec. council adv. Family, Career, Cmty. Leaders of Am., Reston, Va., 2003—04. Bd. chmn. Betty Feezor Scholarship Found., Charlotte, 1987, 1997. Recipient Tchr. of Yr., Nat. Family and Consumer Sci., 2002. Democrat. Presbyn. Home: 2236 Lake Ridge Dr Belmont NC 28012

CANNON, CONSTANCE MARIE, literature and language educator; b. Burwell, Nebr., July 7, 1948; children: Hope Marie, Jeanne Marie, John Albert. BA in English, Stetson U., Deland, Fla., 1973, MAT in Am. Studies, 1977. Cert. mentor tchr. gifted edn. Nat. Bd. Tchr. Cert. Tchr. English Seabreeze H.S., Daytona Beach, Fla., 1973—79; tchr. DeKalb Christian Sch., Decatur, Ga., 1979—81; dept. chair, tchr. English Social Circle H.S., Ga., 1986—. Mem.: PAGE, Ga. Coun. English Tchrs. Methodist. Avocations: travel, reading, entertaining. Home: 174 Heritage Park Social Circle GA 30025 Office: Social Circle H S 154 Alexa Dr Social Circle GA 30025

CANNON, DANNIE PARKER, special education educator; b. Knoxville, Tenn., Sept. 19, 1951; d. Tommie Isaac and Mary (Halliburton) Parker; m. Robert Kyle Cannon Sr., Aug. 2, 1975; children: Thomas Parker, Jonathan Ray, Robert Kyle Jr., Daniel Cameron, Laura Lee. BS in Edn., U. Tenn., 1973, MS, 1975. Cert. tchr. emotionally disturbed, neurologically impaired, learning and behavior disorders. Tchr. 2d and 3d grade Farragut Primary, Knoxville, 1973-75; elem. resource tchr. Brown Sch., Louisville, 1975; spl. edn. resource tchr. Waggener High Sch., Louisville, 1975-95; tchr. 2nd and 3d grades St. Matthews Elem. Sch., Louisville, 1995—. Tchr. exptl. program U. Tenn., Knoxville, 1972-73; project tchr. CAEVEP-CSDC Project, Louisville, 1977-78. Sunday sch. tchr. Hurstbourne Bapt. Ch., Louisville, 1984-86, Pleasant Grove Bapt. Ch., Louisville, 1987-90. Recipient Amgen award, Jefferson County Ky. Program, 2000. Fellow NEA, Parents Tchrs. Students Assn., Ky. Edn. Assn., Jefferson County Tchrs. Assn., Southeast Christian Ch. Republican. Avocations: piano, doll collecting, antiques, genealogy, reading. Home: 10611 Kinross Ct Louisville KY 40243-1760 Office: St Matthews Elem Sch 601 Browns Ln Louisville KY 40207-4043 Office Phone: 502-485-8321. E-mail: fifthtenn@mindspring.com.

CANNON, DYAN, actress; b. Tacoma, Jan. 4, 1937; m. Cary Grant (div.); 1 dau., Jennifer; m. Stanley Fimberg, 1985 (div. 1990). Student, U. Wash.; studied with Sanford Meisner. Former model; TV appearances include Diane's Adventure, Harlequin's Diamond Girl, 1998; Broadway appearances include Ninety-Day Mistress; with road company How to Succeed in Business Without Really Trying; motion pictures include Bob and Carol and Ted and Alice, 1969 (Acad. award nomination), Le Casse, 1970, The Anderson Tapes, 1971, The Love Machine, 1971, Such Good Friends, 1971, Doctors' Wives, 1971, The Last of Sheila, 1973, Shamus, 1973, Child Under a Leaf, 1974, Revenge of the Pink Panther, 1978, Heaven Can Wait, 1978 (Golden Globe award Best Supporting Actress), Coast to Coast, 1980, Honeysuckle Rose, 1980, Author, Author, 1982, Deathtrap, 1982, Caddyshack II, 1988, The End of Innocence (also dir. and prod. screenwriter), 1990, The Pickle, 1993, One Point of View, That Darn Cat, 1997, Out to Sea, 1997, 8 Heads in a Duffel Bag, 1997, Drop Dead, 1998, Kiss of a Stranger, 1999, Kangaroo Jack, 2003; appeared in TV movies Virginia Hill Story, 1974, Lady of the House, 1978, Having It All, 1983, Master of the Game, 1984, Arthur the King, 1985, Jenny's War, 1985, Rock and Roll Mom, 1988, Jailbirds, 1991, Christmas in Connecticut, 1992, Based on an Untrue Story, 1993, A Perry Mason Mystery: The Case of the Jealous Jokester, 1995, The Rockford Files: If the Frame Fits., 1996, The Sender, 1997, Allie & Me, 1997, Beverly Hills Family Robinson, 1998, Diamond Girl, 1998, Black Jaq, 1998, My Mother, the Spy, 2000; appeared in TV series Ally McBeal, 1997, Three Sisters, 2001; dir., writer, prodr. short live action film Growing Pains: Number One, 1976 (Acad. award nomination). Named Best Actress of Yr., Nat. Assn. Theater Owners.

CANNON, ELIZABETH H., dress and clothing designer, artist; b. Lawrence, Kans., Aug. 30, 1951; d. John Thomas and Ann Ellison (Tuller) C. BFA, R.I. Sch. Design, Providence, 1973. Children's book illustrator and creator Pantheon Books, N.Y.C., 1976-79; dir. film L'Union Libre, N.Y.C., 1980-81; fashion editor Bomb mag., N.Y.C., 1988-91. Author, illustrator: A Cat Had a Fish about a Dream, 1976; illustrator: The Seed, 1975, Why Worry, 1979; exhibited works in shows at Gotham Bookmart, N.Y.C., 1974, 76, EM Donahue Gallery, N.Y.C., 1986, Tom Cugliani Gallery N.Y.C., 1994, Christine Rose Gallery, N.Y.C., 1995;, Lindsey Brown Gallery, N.Y.C., 2001, 02, fashion shows, N.Y.C., 1981—; costume designer Winterreise, Trisha Brown Dance Co., Lincoln Ctr., 2002, Paris Opera Ballet, 2004, Da Gelo, Schwetzingen Festival, 2006, others. Office: Design Salon 460 W 24th St Apt 1B New York NY 10011-1366 Office Phone: 212-929-8552.

CANNON, FAYE E., bank executive; b. Frederick, Md., 1949; m. Robert P. Cannon; 1 child, Jennifer Serenyi. BA, Shepherd Coll., 1971; postgrad., Frostburg State U. V.p. mktg. and bus. devel. F&M Nat. Bank, 1974—85; v.p. mktg. Hagerstown Trust Co., 1985—88; sr. ops. officer and v.p. First Bank Frederick, 1988—90; exec. v.p. retail banking F&M Bancorp., 1990—93, pres., CEO, 1993—. Bd. dirs. F&M Bancorp/F&M Nat Bank, 1993—, Home Fed. Savs. Bank, 1996—; vice-chair bd. trustees Hood Coll., 1996—97. Bd. mem. Christmas in April, Frederick County, 1994—96, The Jefferson Sch., Sheppard Pratt, 1996—97; chair pvt. industry coun. PIC-Frederick County, 1996—97; chair cmty. edn. coun. Frederick C.C., 1997—99. Named one of MD. Top 100 Women, Daily Record, 2001; named to Phenomenal Women Panel, Arthur Anderson; recipient Character Counts Support award, Frederick County YMCA, 1997, Youth Devel. award, F&M Bank Big Bros. and Big Sisters, 2000. Mem.: Md. Banking Assn. (chair Md. Banking Sch. 1997), Bank Mktg. Assn. (pres. 1997), Am. Bankers Assn. (chair govt. rels. coun. 1999—2000). Office: F&M Bancorp & Farmers and Mechanics Nat Bank 110 Thomas Johnson Dr Frederick MD 21702

CANNON, FRANK See MAYHAR, ARDATH

CANNON, GAYLE ELIZABETH, lawyer; b. Dallas, May 12, 1941; d. Harry Feldman and Rosalie Bertha (Fischl) Lack; m. Joe D. Goldstrich, Dec. 23, 1962 (div. July 1977); m. Charles B. Cannon, Oct. 29, 1978; children: Josh, Marc, Jeremy. Student, U. Tex., 1959-60; BA, So. Meth. U., 1961, JD, 1965. Bar: Tex. 1965. Asst. gen. counsel Pizza Inn Inc., Dallas, 1977-88, v.p., sec., gen. counsel, 1986-88; of counsel Thompson & Knight LLP, 1995—. Spkr. franchising seminars ABA Forum on Franchising, State Bar of Tex., Dallas Bar, Southwestern Legal Found., Internat. Franchising Assn. Bd. dirs. Shakespeare Festival of Dallas, past pres.; bd. dirs. Children's Cancer Fund. Named named in top 200 Dallas Lawyers Best Lawyers in America, Woodwar/White, Inc., 1998—2004, named Super Lawyer, Texas Monthly, 2002—05; named one of Best Lawyers in Dallas and Fort Worth, 1997—2005. Mem.: ABA. Democrat. Office Phone: 214-969-1700. E-mail: gayle.cannon@tklaw.com.

CANNON, GRACE BERT, retired immunologist; b. Chambersburg, Pa., Jan. 29, 1937; d. Charles Wesley and Gladys (Raff) Bert; m. W. Dilworth Cannon, June 3, 1961 (div. 1972); children: Michael Quayle Cannon, Susan Radcliffe Cannon Antolin, Peter Bert Cannon. AB, Goucher Coll., 1958; PhD, Washington U., St. Louis, 1962. Fellow Columbia U., N.Y.C., 1962—64, Columbia U. Coll. Physicians and Surgeons, N.Y.C., 1964—65; staff fellow Nat. Cancer Inst. NIH, Bethesda, Md., 1966—67; cell biologist Litton Bionetics, Inc., Kensington, Md., 1972—80, head immunology sect., 1980—85; dir. sci. ImmuQuest Labs., Inc., Rockville, Md., 1985—88; pres. Biomed. Analytics, Inc., Rockville, 1988—2001; mgr. ATLIS Fed. Svcs., Inc., Rockville, 1991—95, dir. Silver Spring, Md., 1995—97; sr. assoc. United Info. Sys., Inc., Bethesda, 1998—2000; ret., 2000. Mem. contract rev. coms. Nat. Cancer Inst., 1983-87 Contbr. articles to profl. jours Mem. Pub. Health Svcs. Club, Bethesda, 1984-2006, sec., 1990-2000. Grantee USPHS, 1959-65, NSF, 1959 Mem. AAAS, Am. Assn. Cancer Rsch., N.Y. Acad. Sci., Sigma Xi Home and Office: 1908 Nero Ct Walnut Creek CA 94598 Personal E-mail: gracecannon@astound.net.

CANNON, JENENE, music educator; b. Ft. Worth, Tex. m. Ken Cannon; children: Katie, Joel. B of Music Edn., East Tex. State U., Commerce, 1980. Cert. elem. tchr. East Tex. State U., Orff-Schulwerk East Tex. State U. Tchr. elem. music Springtown Ind. Sch. Dist., Tex., 1980—81; choir tchr. Paris Ind. Sch. Dist., Tex., 1981—85; tchr. elem. music North Lamar Ind. Sch. Dist., 1994—. Children's worship leader 1st Bapt. Ch., Paris, 2005—06; ch. organist. Named Bailey Intermediate Tchr. of Yr., North Lamar Ind. Sch. Dist., 1999—2000, Outstanding Young Women of Am., Bailey Yearbook Dedicatee, 2005—06. Mem.: Tex. Classroom Tchrs. Assn., Tex. Music Educators Assn. Baptist. Office: North Lamar Ind Sch Dist 3201 Lewis Ln Paris TX 75460 Office Phone: 903-737-7977.

CANNON, KATHLEEN, lawyer, educator; b. Monterey, Calif., Nov. 11, 1951; d. Jack Dempsey and Virginia Ann Cannon; m. Richard Eiden, May 26, 1979; children: Joncannon, Katrina. BS, Mich. State U., 1973; JD, Southwestern Law Sch., L.A., 1977. Bar: Calif. 1977. Paralegal VISTA/Peace Corps, Pacoima, Calif., 1973-74; prosecutor L.A. City Atty.'s Office, 1977-78; lawyer Los Angeles County Pub. Defender's Office, L.A., 1978-89, San Diego County Pub. Defender's Office, San Diego, 1989—. Instr. Nat. Inst. Trial Advocacy, 1992—; prof. Calif. Western Sch. Law, San Diego, 1993—, U. San Diego, 1995; spkr. Continuing Edn. Bar, San Diego, 1995-97. Bd. dirs., treas. North County Forum, Vista, Calif., 1997—. Mem. Calif. Pub. Defenders Assn. (bd. dirs. 1999—, spkr.). Avocations: hiking, travel. Office: San Diego County Pub Defender's Office 400 S Melrose Dr Ste 200 Vista CA 92083-6632

CANNON, LENA FERRARA (LEE), retired education educator; b. Morgantown, W.Va., Oct. 12, 1918; d. Emil and Philomena (Purificato) Ferrara; m. Robert Young Cannon, June 10, 1948; children: Emilie, Robert Y. Jr., Leigh. BS, W.Va. U., 1940, MS, 1944; postgrad., U. Wis., 1945-48. Tchr. Osage (W.Va.) Jr. High Sch., 1941-45; rsch. asst. U. Wis., Madison, 1945-48;

asst. prof. Auburn (Ala.) U., 1948-70, asst. producer, host Ala. Pub. TV, 1955-84, specialist in foods nutrition Ala. Extension Svc., 1970-84; ret., 1984. Weekly TV program PBS-TV, 1955-84, weekly columns Montgomery Adv., 1979-84, Columbus Enquirer, 1960-65; women's philanthropy bd. Auburn U. Author: Today's Home, Vols. 1-3, 1953-84, Southern Living's Quick and Easy Cookbook, 1979, Menu Celebrations; contbr. articles to profl. jours. Bd. dirs. Commn. Aging, Montgomery, Ala., 1981-83, Apobonna Commn. Aging, 1979-83, Am. Heart Assn.; adv. bd. Auburn U. Theatre; bounder Auburn Cotillion. Mem. Internat. Platform Assn., Am. Home Econs. Assn., Am. Women Radio TV, Women in Communications, Phi Upsilon Omicron. Roman Catholic. Avocations: cooking, dance, entertaining, bridge, reading.

CANNON, MARY ALICE, literature and language educator; d. Roy A. and Mary Eileen Jensen; m. Steven R. Cannon, Aug. 9, 1975; children: Scott Louis, Jason Roy, Steven Brian, Mary Michelle, Jeffrey Edward. A, Ricks Coll., Rexburg, Idaho, 1972—2002; BA, Brigham Young U., Provo, 2004. Cert. Nat. Bd. Profl. Tchg. Stds., 2000. English tchr. South Rich H.S., Randolph, Utah, 1974—75; Title I tchr. Springville (Utah) Mid. Sch., 1975—76; Title I aide Idaho Falls, Idaho, 1980—81; sec. Deseret Industries, Idaho Falls, Idaho, 1985—88; English tchr. North Bonneville Jr. High Sch. and Rocky Mountain Mid. Sch., Idaho Falls, 1989—; lang. arts profl. learning team chairperson Rocky Mountain Mid. Sch., Idaho Falls, 2000—05, 8th grade team leader, 2001—, site coord. SREB grant, 2005—. Reader, scorer state direct writing assessment Idaho State Dept. Edn., Boise, 1999—2004. Leader, tchr. Ch. of LDS, Idaho Falls, 1981—2006; vice chairperson Bonneville Edn. Found., Idaho Falls, 2004—. Named Tchr. of Month, Rocky Mountain Mid. Sch., 2001. Mem.: Bonneville Edn. Assn. (bldg. rep. 2000—04), Idaho Mid. Level Assn. (assoc.). Avocations: reading, travel, interior decorating. Office: Rocky Mountain Mid Sch 3443 N Ammon Rd Idaho Falls ID 83401 Office Phone: 208-525-4403.

CANNON, PATRICIA ALTHEN, librarian, writer; b. Granite City, Ill., Feb. 26, 1947; d. Eugene and Miriam (Knowles) Althen; m. Marvin E. Watson Jr., June 26, 1967 (div. 1975); m. Thomas Milton Cannon Jr., Dec. 24, 1982. BS in Psychology, West Tex. State U., 1976, MA in Jr. Coll. Teaching, 1978; MLS, Tex. Woman's U., 1982, PhD in Library Sci., 1988. Area office mgr. SSS, Dallas Naval Air Sta., Tex., 1979-84; vocat. evaluation program dir. Goodwill Rehab. Ctr., Amarillo, Tex., 1979-80; researcher pers. dept. City of Ft. Worth, 1981; br. reference librarian Amarillo Pub. Library, 1981-82, br. dir., 1983-85; asst. librarian office products div. Xerox Info. Svcs., Dallas, 1982; grad. teaching asst. Sch. Library and Info. Studies, Tex. Woman's U., Denton, 1985-87; asst. prof. dept. library and info. studies Northern Ill. U., DeKalb, 1987—94; freelance writer.

CANNON, SHERRY CLOUD, special education educator; b. Johnson City, Tenn., Mar. 27, 1980; d. Stephen Howard and Mary Elizabeth (Anderson) Cloud. BS in Spl. Edn., U. Ga., 2002, MEd, 2006. Summer camp counselor Roswell Parks and Rec, Roswell, Ga., 1996—2000; after sch. program counselor Clarke County Sch., Athens, Ga., 1999—2002; spl. edn. tchr. Fulton County Sch., Duluth, Ga., 2002—. Tutoring coord. Communiversity, Athens, Ga., 1999—2002. Big sister Communiversity, Athens, Ga., 1998—2002; vol. Habitat for Humanity, Athens, 1998—2002. Mem.: Coun. for Exceptional Children, Kappa Delta Epilson. Meth. Avocations: reading, aerobics. Home: 4785 Diggers Way Sugar Hill GA 30518 Office: Wilson Creek Elem 6115 Wilson Rd Duluth GA 30097

CANO, KRISTIN MARIA, lawyer; b. McKeesport, Pa., Oct. 27, 1951; d. John S. and Sally (Kavic) C. BS in Biochemistry, Pa. State U., 1973; MS in Forensic Sci., George Washington U., 1975; JD, Southwestern U., 1978; LLM in Securities Regulation, Georgetown U., 1984. Bar: Calif. 1978, U.S. Dist. Ct. (cen., no. and so. dists.) Calif. 1984, U.S. Dist. Ct. Ariz., 1988, U.S. Supreme Ct. 1988, U.S. Ct. Appeals (9th cir.) 1992. Assoc. Yusim, Cassidy, Stein & Hanger, Beverly Hills, Calif., 1979-81, Walker and Hartley, Newport Beach, Calif., 1981-82, Milberg, Weiss, Bershad, Spethrie & Lerach, San Diego, 1984; pvt. practice Newport Beach, 1984—. Bd. dirs., v.p. Sandcastle Community Assn., Corona del Mar, Calif., 1987-97; active Leadership Tomorrow Class of 1994. Mem. Orange County Bar Assn., Balboa Bay Club. Democrat. Roman Catholic. Avocations: ballet, ice skating, bicycling, photography, golf. Office: 1 Corporate Plaza Dr Ste 110 Newport Beach CA 92660-7924 Office Phone: 949-759-1505. Business E-Mail: cano@securities-law.com.

CANO, MARTA MENDENDEZ, securities company executive, financial consultant; b. Havana, Cuba, July 29, 1941; came to U.S., 1961; d. Jose F. and Maria C. (Llanio) Menendez; m. Peter J. Cano, Nov. 30, 1960 (div. Jan. 1982); children: Marta, Eileen, Marianne, Peter, Andres. BA in English cum laude, U. Havana, 1961; MEd, U. P.R., 1970. Lic. securities profl., mgmt., life and health ins., notary pub. Dir. ESOL program Colegio Rosa-Bel, Bayamon, P.R., 1966-75; v.p. import/export Distribuidora Delmar, Inc., Bayamon, 1975-79; advanced sales specialist Sun Life of Can., Morristown, N.J., 1980-87; sr. fin. cons. Smith Barney, West Palm Beach, Fla., 1987-94; v.p. investments Prudential Securities, Inc., North Palm Beach, Fla., 1995-97, Brinker Capital Securities, Inc., Coral Gables, Fla., 1997—. Speaker in field. Founder Hispanic Coalition, Palm Beach County; nominated bd. dirs. Pal, Beach County, 1994; participant Directions 94, 1994; bd. commrs. Palm Beach County Health Care Spl. Taxing Dist., 1993—, Housing Authorities, City of West Palm Beach, 1994—; bd. dirs. Citizens Adv. for Health and Human Svcs., Palm Beach County, 1993—, Palm Beach County Budget Task Force, 1991—; mem. St. Ignatius Cathedral Parish coun., 1989-91; mem. Healthy Start Coalition, 1991—, others. Mem. Internat. Businessmean's Assn. (v.p. 1989-93), Internat. Assn. Fin. Planners. Roman Catholic. Avocations: walking, reading, theater, charity. Fax: 561-691-9718. E-mail: martamcano@msn.com.

CANOBBIO, LINDA J., elementary school educator; d. William and Kathryn Means; m. Lewis Canobbio; children: Andrew, Alyssa. BS, Edinboro U., Pa., 1968—72; MS, U. Pitts., 1980—82. RN Pa., 1986, NJ, 1986. Tchr. Diocese Pitts., 1968—86; nurse Children's Hosp. Phila., 1986; tchr. LaSalle Coll. HS, Wyndmoor, Pa., 1986—92; don Genesis HealthCare, Kennett Square, Pa., 1992—99; adj. prof. Holy Family U., Phila., 1999—2002; tchr. Monroe Twp. Pub. Schs., Williamstown, NJ, 1999—; adj. prof. Gloucester County Coll., Sewell, NJ, 2000—. Recipient Tchr. of Yr., Walmart, 2000, 2001, Joint Legislative Resolution and Recognition for new Mars student imaging project, Jersey Senate & Gen. Assembly, Lead Tchr. award for Mars student imaging project, Williamstown Mid. Sch.

CANONERO, MILENA, costume designer; b. Turin, Italy; m. Marshall Bell. Costume designer: (films) A Clockwork Orange, 1971, (with Ulla-Britt Soderlund) Barry Lyndon, 1975 (Academy award best costume design 1975), Midnight Express, 1978, The Shining, 1980, Chariots of Fire, 1981 (Academy award best costume design 1981, British Academy award best costume design 1982), The Hunger, 1983, The Cotton Club, 1984, Give My Regards to Broad Street, 1984, Out of Africa, 1985 (Academy award nomination best costume design 1985, British Academy award nomination best costume design 1986), Haunted Summer, 1988, Tucker: The Man and His Dream, 1988 (Academy award nomination best costume design 1988), Dick Tracy, 1990 (Academy award nomination best costume design 1990), The Godfather, Part III, 1990, Damage, 1992, (with Elisabetta Beraldo) Camilla, 1993, The Life Aquatic, 2004, Oceans Twelve, 2004, (TV series) Miami Vice, 1986-89; costume designer, visual cons.: (films) Barfly, 1987; assoc. prodr.: (films) Good Morning Babylon, 1987, Mamba, 1988; costume design cons.: (films) Lost Angels, 1989, Reversal of Fortune, 1990. Recipient Coty Am. Fashion Critics' award 1984, Career Achievement award in Film from Costume Designers Guild, 2001. Office: care Marc H Glick Glick and Weintraub 1501 Broadway New York NY 10036-5601

CANONIZADO, GLORIA M., choreographer, educator; b. San Antonio, Mar. 23, 1940; d. Noberto Pobre and Primitiva Pablo (Madarang) Canonizado; m. Jose Honrado Villanueva, June 6, 1965 (annulled 1968); 1 child, Mary Josephine Villanueva Frijas. BS in Elem. Edn., Philippine Normal U., Manila, 1961; BS in Phys. Edn., Nat. Coll. Phys. Edn., Manila, 1962; MA in Edn., East Carolina U., Greenville, N.C., 1976. Cert. tchr. Tchr. phys. edn. Assumption Convent, Manila, 1961-71; tchr. Palma Elem. Sch., Manila, 1961-63; thcr. phys. edn. Quezon City H.S., Manila, 1963-66, U. of the East, Manila, 1966-69; tchr. Terrell County Schs., Columbia, N.C., 1972-75; instr. U. N.C., Pembroke, 1976-81, Southeastern C.C., Whiteville, N.C., 1985-87; tchr. Pub. Schs. of Robeson County, Pembroke, 1981-86, Yonkers (N.Y.) City Schs., 1987-89, Inst. Human Dynamics, Bronx, N.Y., 1987-89, Pub. Schs. of Robeson County, Maxton, N.C., 1989—. In-charge nurse aide Allen County Health Ctr., Ft. Wayne, Ind., 1971-72; aerobic instr. Lumberton Recreation Ctr., 1976-85, ballroom dance instr., 1976-85; dir., choreographer, aerobic instr. Maharlika Dance Troupe, 1977—. Mem. Human Rels. Commn., Lumberton, 1994-97; amb. of goodwill Baranggay Folk Dance Troupe, Manila, 1958-71; active Girl Scouts, 1961-72, Eagle Scouts, 1961-63; religious instr. St. Franics de Sales Cath. Ch., 1992—; com. chair Entertainment Internat. Festival, Fayetteville, N.C., 1996—. Recipient various awards, including Coach of the Yr., Carolina Conf. UNCP, 1978, Cert. of Appreciation, Ft. Bragg, Fayetteville, N.C., 2002, 25th Yr. Svc. award Maharlika Dance Troupe, 2003. Mem. Fgn. Lang. Assn. N.C., Philippine-Am. Club of Fayetteville, N.C. (life, Outstanding Svc. and Leadership award 2001). Democrat. Roman Catholic. Avocations: reading, travel to historical and exotic places, dance, swimming, visiting museums. Home: 517 E 14th St Lumberton NC 28358-4706 Office: Pub Schs Robeson County PO Box 2909 Lumberton NC 28359-2909 E-mail: gcanonizado@aol.com.

CANRIGHT, SARAH ANNE, artist, educator; b. Chgo., Aug. 20, 1941; d. William and Constance (Clark) C.; m. Edward C. Flood, Apr. 15, 1968 (div. 1979). B.F.A., Art Inst. Chgo., 1964. Vis. artist Sch. of Art Inst. Chgo., 1974, 82, Skowhegan Sch. Painting and Sculpture, Maine, 1980; instr. Princeton U., 1978-80, 83; lectr. Phila. Coll. Art, 1978, 80-81, Sch. Visual Arts, N.Y.C., 1981; sr. lectr. U. Tex., Austin, 1982—; instr. Princeton U., 1978-80, 83—. Artist: visual books Franklin Furnace, 1979; exhibited one-man shows, Phillis Kind Gallery, Chgo., 1974, 79, Pam Adler Gallery, N.Y.C., 1979, 81, 83, 84, Artemesia Gallery, 1986, Marvin Seline Gallery, 1987, Lyons Matrix Gallery, Austin, Tex., 1993, various group shows. Recipient Armstrong award Art Inst. Chgo., 1971; nat. Endowment for Arts grantee, 1975, 78, 85; N.Y. State Council for the Arts grantee, 1977, NEH grantee, 1985. Home: 161 Mulberry St New York NY 10013-3784 Office: Princeton Univ 185 Nassau St Princeton NJ 08544-2003

CANTOR, MIRA, artist, educator; b. N.Y.C., May 16, 1944; d. Milton and Sara (Hochhauser) C.; m. Otto Piene, July 18, 1976 (div. 1983); 1 child, Chloe. BFA, U. Buffalo, 1966; MFA, U. Ill., 1969. Instr. U. Hawaii, Honolulu, 1970-71; with Northeastern U., Boston, 1983—, lectr. art, 1987-88, asst. prof. to assoc. prof. to prof., 1988—. Represented in collections at Mus. Fine Arts, Boston, Rose Art Mus., Brandeis U., others. Ctr. for Advanced Visual Studies MIT fellow, 1978-80, Fulbright fellow, Egypt, 1994, Genovese/Sullivan Gallery, Boston, 1999, 2002, 2005. Office: Northeastern U 360 Huntington Ave Boston MA 02115-5000

CANTOR, NANCY, academic administrator; b. NYC; m. Steven Brechin; children: Maddy, Archie. AB, Sarah Lawrence Coll., 1974; PhD in Psychology, Stanford U., 1978. Faculty, chair dept. psychology Princeton (NJ) U., 1991—96; dean Horace H. Rackham Sch. Grad. Studies, vice provost for acad. affairs U. Mich., Ann Arbor, 1996—97, provost, exec. v.p. acad. affairs, 1997—2001; chancellor U. Ill.-Urbana-Champaign, 2001—04; chancellor, pres. Syracuse U., NY, 2004—, disting. prof. psychology and women's studies. Mem. adv. bd. NSF; mem. com. on nat. needs in biomed. and behavioral sci. rsch. NRC, mem. com. on women in sci. and engring. Co-author (or co-editor): 3 books; contbr. 50 articles to profl. jours., chpts. to books. Recipient Woman of Achievement award, Anti Defamation League. Fellow: Soc. for Personality and Social Psychology, APA (Disting. Sci. award for early career contbn. in psychology), Am. Psychol. Soc.; mem.: Am. Assn. for Higher Edn. (vice chair bd. dirs.), Am. Acad. Arts and Sci., Inst. of Medicine of NAS. Office: Syracuse U 300 Tolley Adminstrn Bldg Syracuse NY 13244-1100 E-mail: cancellor@syr.edu.*

CANTOR, PAMELA CORLISS, psychologist; b. NYC, Apr. 23, 1944; d. Alfred Joseph and Eleanor (Weschler) C.; m. Howard Feldman, Sept. 11, 1969; children: Lauren Jaye, Jeffrey Lee. BS cum laude, Syracuse U., 1965; MA, Columbia U., 1967, PhD, 1972; postgrad., Johns Hopkins U., 1969-70, Harvard U., Boston, 1973-74. Assoc. prof. psycholoyg Boston U., 1970-80; instr. Radcliffe Inst., Harvard U., 1977-78; pvt. practice clin. psychology, South Natick, Mass., 1980—. Mem. faculty Med. Sch., Harvard U.; lectr. in field, also TV and radio appearances Author: Understanding a Child's World—Readings in Infancy through Adolescence, 1977; cons. editor Suicide and Life-Threatening Behavior; columnist For Parents Only; contbr. articles to profl. jours., chpts. to hanbooks. Mem. statewide adv. bd. Mass. Gov.'s Office for Children, 1980—; mem. adv. bd. Samaritans of Boston; pres. Nat. Com. Youth Suicide Prevention; mem. Presdl. Task Force on Youth Suicide, HHS. Mem. APA, Am. Assn. Suicidology (pres. 1985-86, bd. dirs.), Am. Orthopsychiat. Assn., Mass. Psychol. Assn. Home: 6 Phillips Pond South Natick MA 01760 Office Phone: 508-545-2700. Personal E-mail: drpamcantor@comcast.net.

CANTOR, SUSAN, advertising executive; b. 1968; m. Ross C.; children: Emily, Lauren. BA, Univ. Mich., 1989. New bus. adv. assoc. Griffin Bacal Adv., 1989—91, acct. supervisor, 1991—94; head acct. mgmt. Lowe Worldwide, NYC, 1994—97; sr. v.p. Lowe New York, 1997, former exec. v.p., currently pres.

CANTRELL, CAROL HOWE, municipal administrator; b. Martins Ferry, Feb. 10, 1947; d. Ferd A. and Geraldine (Hayne) Howe; m. William O. Cantrell, Dec. 29, 1968 (div. Oct. 1997); children: David, Paul, Emily. BS in Acctg. magna cum laude, U. Rio Grande, Ohio, 1982. Formerly cost analyst Holzer Med. Ctr.; formerly tax adminstr. Rio Grande, Ohio; adminstr. mcpl. income tax and ins. Village of Middleport, Ohio, 1988—. Vol. in orgns. that supprot children and teenagers; mem. First united Presbyn. Ch., Gallipolis. Mem. Greater Ohio Assn. Tax Adminstrs. Presbyterian. Home: 662 4th Ave Gallipolis OH 45631-1231 Office: Tax Dept 237 Race St Middleport OH 45760-1054

CANTRELL, CAROL WHITAKER, educational administrator; b. Cin., July 25, 1951; d. James Ross and Edna M. Whitaker; m. David F. Justus, Jan. 23, 1970 (div. May 1981); 1 child, Holly; m. Pierce E. Cantrell Jr., May 24, 1986; 1 child, Janette. BS, postgrad., West Tex. A&M U., 1973, Tex. A&M U., 1974, 88. Dir. adminstrn. and budgets Tex. Engr. Experiment Sta., College Station, 1984-87, asst. agt. dir., 1987-97, assoc. agy. dir., 1997—; asst. vice chancellor Tex. A&M U. Sys., College Station, 1987—. Regents life fellow Tex. A&M U. System, 1998—; grantee USIA, 1998. Mem. Soc. Rsch. Adminstrs., Nat. Coun. Univ. Bus. Officers, Tex. Assn. Sr. State U. Bus. Officers, Exec. Women in Govt., Nat. Coun. Univ. Rsch. Adminstrs., Mu Phi Epsilon. Avocations: music, piano.

CANTRELL, GEORGIA ANN, realtor; b. Hall, Ky., May 26, 1950; d. Melvin Johnson and Liza Ann (Collins) Johnson; children: David Cantrell, Jr., Mary Elizabeth Cantrell Riley. Grad. h.s., Fedcreek, Ky. Cert. realtor Ky. Owner Cantrell Supply, Winchester, Ky., 1979—2000; realtor Coldwell Banker Mc Mahan, Winchester, Ky., 1995—. Recipient Leadership award, Winchester-Clark Co. C. of C., 1996. Mem.: Boonesboro Lions Club, Million Dollar Club (life). Baptist. Avocations: travel, reading, walking. Home: 330 Runnymeade Dr Winchester KY 40391 also: 125 S Main St Winchester KY 40391-2621 Personal E-mail: gcantrell@coldwellbanker.com.

CANTRELL, JOYCE ANN, mathematics educator; b. Paola, Kans., Jan. 1, 1973; d. Howard Rex and Ila May Gillogly; m. Timothy Victor Cantrell, May 25, 1996; children: Josiah Levi, Caleb Eli, Naomi Joy. BS, SW Bapt. U., Bolivar, Mo., 1995. Tchr. Archie R-5 Sch., Mo., 1995—. Sunday sch. tchr. Ch. on the Rock, Harrisonville, Mo., 2001—06. Mem.: Mo. State Tchrs. Assn. Office Phone: 816-293-5312.

CANTRELL, LANA, actress, lawyer, singer; b. Sydney, Australia, Aug. 7, 1943; d. Hubert Clarence and Dorothy Jean (Thistlethwaite) C. JD, Fordham Law Sch., 1993. Bar: N.Y. 1994. Former of counsel Ballon Stoll Bader & Adler, N.Y.C.; assoc. Sendroff & Assocs. PC, N.Y.C., 1996—. Singer supper clubs, TV programs, Australia, 1958-62; U.S. debut: TV show The Tonight Show, NBC, 1962; rec. artist RCA and Polydor Records, 1967— (Grammy award as Most Promising New Female Artist, Nat. Assn. Rec. Arts and Scis. 1967); recs. include Lana!, Act III, And Then There Was Lana, The Now of Then! Pres. Thrush, Inc.; U.S. rep. Internat. Song Festival, Poland, 1966, UN Internat. Women's Year Concert, Paris, France, 1975. Decorated Order of Australia, 2003; recipient 1st prize Internat. Song Festival Poland, 1966; 1st Internat. Woman of Yr. award Feminist Party, 1973 Office: 300 E 71st St New York NY 10021-5234

CANTRELL, LINDA MAXINE, counselor; b. Ann Arbor, Mich., June 20, 1938; d. Donald LaVerne and Lila Maxine (Crull) Katz; m. Douglas D. Cantrell, Dec. 28, 1963; children: Douglas David Jr., Warren Vincent, Bryan LaVerne BA, U. Mich., 1960, MA, 1963, postgrad., 1963—65. Cert. secondary tchr., Mich. Caseworker Cook County Dept. Pub. Aid, Chgo., 1960; psychometrist Evanston Schs., Ill., 1960—61; rsch. assoc. U. Mich., Ann Arbor, 1961—64; guidance counselor Radcliff Mid. Sch., Garden City, Mich., 1964—66; dir. guidance and counseling St. Mary Acad., Monroe, Mich., 1985—87; counselor, head counselor, instr. Ypsilanti Adult Edn. Ypsilanti Pub. Schs., Mich., 1987—. Tchr. young adult program Ypsilanti Pub. Schs., 1995—97. Rep. precinct leader Ann Arbor, 1971; clk., marker, rec. sec. Thrift Shop Ann Arbor, 1981—; bd. dirs. Ypsilanti Adult/Cmty. Edn. Adv. Com., 1990-95; treas. Burns Park Sch. PTO, Ann Arbor, 1978-79; rec. sec. Chapel of Love Ch., 1989-97; co-chmn. benefits Ann Arbor Chamber Orch., 1981-82; chmn. ann. benefit Rudolf Steiner Sch. Ann Arbor, 1984-85; vol. Greenhills Schs., 1978-81, St. Paul's Luth. Sch., 1972-73 Recipient Gil Bursley award Rep. Party, 1972; scholarship Chi Omega, 1957 Mem. AAUW (fellowship chmn. 1971-73), Mich. Assn. for Counseling and Devel. (membership chmn. Monroe County chpt. 1986-87), Ypsilanti Fedn. Tchrs. (rec. sec. 1989-91), Mich. Assn. for Acad. Advisors Cmty. Edn., Washtenaw Counselors Assn., Monroe County Counselors Assn. (membership chmn. 1985-87), Ann Arbor Women's City Club (membership com. 1985-87), Ea. Mich. U. Coll. Bus. Wives (program chmn. 1974, pres. 1975), Phi Kappa Phi, Pi Lambda Theta Avocations: dance, making jewelry, self-improvement, art, swimming, music. Office: Ypsilanti Adult Edn Ypsilanti Pub Schs 1055 Cornell Ypsilanti MI 48197

CANTRELL, SHARRON CAULK, principal; b. Columbia, Tenn., Oct. 2, 1947; d. Tom English and Beulah (Goodin) Caulk; m. William Terry Cantrell, Mar. 18, 1989; 1 child, Jordan; children from previous marriage: Christopher, George English, Steffenee Copley. BA, George Peabody Coll. Tchrs., 1970; MS, Vanderbilt U., 1980; EdS, Mid. Tenn. State U., 1986. Tchr. Ft. Campbell Jr. High Sch., Columbia, Tenn., 1970-71, Whitthorne Jr. High Sch., Columbia, Tenn., 1977-86, Spring Hill (Tenn.) High Sch., 1986—. Mem. NEA, AAUW (pres. Tenn. divsn. 1983-85), Maury County Edn. Assn. (pres. 1983-84), Tenn. Edn. Assn., Assn. Preservation Tenn. Antiquities, Maury Alliance, Friends of Children's Hosp., Rotary (bd. dirs.), Phi Delta Kappa. Mem. Ch. of Christ. Home: 5299 Main St Spring Hill TN 37174-2495 Office: Spring Hill High Sch 1 Raider Ln Columbia TN 38401-7346

CANTU, DELIA, training services executive; b. Anthony, N.Mex., Jan. 13, 1949; d. Jose Perea and Eusebia (Ostos) Montes; m. Theodore Oscar Almaguer, Jan. 4, 1969 (div. Apr. 1974); m. Robert V. Cantu, June 23, 1979; 1 child, Fernando. BA, N.Mex. State U., 1971, MA, 1973. Counselor coord. N.Mex. State U., Las Cruces, 1973-74, asst. dir., 1974-77, dir., 1977-79; mem. faculty U. Santa Clara, Ft. Knox, Ky., 1979; bus. owner Cantu Photography & Camera, Radvliff, Ky., 1979-88; fin. adminstr. Vogue Coll., Las Cruces, 1988-89; border ops. tng. coord. Johnson & Johnson Med., Inc., Juarez, Mex., 1989-93; regional staff svcs. officer Tex. Dept. Health, El Paso, 1993-96; tng. and orgnl. devel. coord. Eureka, El Paso, 1996—2001; mem. faculty U. Phoenix, Santa Teresa, N.Mex., 1995-99, faculty curriculum coord., 1997—. Co-author: Counseling the Mexican American Student, 1972. Mem. workforce adv. bd. El. Paso C.C.; bd. dirs. Ysleta Learning Ctr., El Paso; mem. faculty adv. bd. U. Phoenix; chair El Paso Mfrs. Tng. Consortium, 2001; mem. Adult Bilingual Curriculum Inst, 2001. Mem. ASTD.

CANTU, JENNIFER ST. JOHN, gifted and talented educator; b. Washington, June 21, 1969; d. James E. and Carolin M. G. St. John; m. Christopher G. Cantu, May 27, 2006. BA, U. Va., 1992, M in Tchg., 1992. Lic. tchr. Va. Classroom tchr. Fairfax County Pub. Schs., Centreville, Va., 1992—96, gifted and talented specialist Fairfax Station, Va., 1996—, web curator, 2004—. Mem.: NEA, ASCD, Fairfax Edn. Assn., Va. Edn. Assn., Nat. Assn. for Gifted Children, U. Va. Alumni Assn. (life), Kappa Delta Pi, Alpha Delta Pi (life; guard 1988—89). Roman Catholic. Office: Silverbrook Elem - FCPS 9350 Crosspointe Dr Fairfax Station VA 22039 Home: 6832 Austin Harbor Loop Sherwood AR 72120 Personal E-mail: jkstjohn@prodigy.net. E-mail: jennifer.st.john@fcps.edu.

CANTÚ, NORMA V., law educator, former federal official; b. Brownsville, Tex., Nov. 2, 1954; BS summa cum laude, Pan Am. U., 1973; JD, Harvard U., 1977. Bar: Tex. 1978, U.S. Dist. Ct. (so. dist.) Tex. 1979, U.S. Dist. Ct. (we. dist.) Tex. 1981, U.S. Ct. Appeals (5th and 11th cirs.) 1982, Calif. 1985, U.S. Ct. Appeals (10th cir.) 1986, U.S. Dist. Ct. (no. dist.) Tex. 1992. Tchr. English, Brownsville, 1974, San Antonio, 1979; intern Office of Atty. Gen. Tex., 1977-78; atty. Mex. Am. Legal Def. and Ednl. Fund, 1979—93, regional counsel, 1985-93; asst. sec. for civil rights Office for Civil Rights U.S. Dept. of Edn., Washington, 1993—2001; prof. law and edn. U. Tex., Austin, Tex., 2001—. U.S. rep. OAS Commn. on Children, 1999—2001. Officer Avance Parent Child Tng. Program, 1990; bd. dirs. Hispanic Health Policy Devel. Program, 1992, Leadership San Antonio, 1992—93, MALDEF, 2001—02, Mex. Am. Leadership Coun., 2002—. Named to San Antonio Women Hall of Fame, Women in Sports Edn. Hall of Fame. Office: U Tex at Austin Sch Law Townes Hall Rm 3118M 727 E Dean Keeton St Austin TX 78705 Home: 140 Twinleaf Ln San Antonio TX 78213 Office Phone: 512-232-7111. Business E-Mail: ncantu@law.utexas.edu.

CANTU, SANDRA LOU, special education educator; b. Searcy, Ark., June 19, 1962; d. Stewart Kenneth Smith and Bettye Lou (Hulsey) Ramsey; m. Dino Antonio Cantu, May 12, 1984; children: Derek Anthony, Dylan Alex, Deanna Antonia. BS in Edn., Ark. State U., 1984; MA in Tchg., Webster U., 1992. Cert. tchr., Mo. Spl. edn. tchr. Maynard Pub. Schs., Ark., 1988-89, North St. Francois County Schs., Bonne Terre, Mo., 1989-90, Ste. Genevieve R-II Sch., Mo., 1990—98, profl. devel. rep. Mo., 1990—98; tchr. Muncie Cmty. Sch., 1998—2004, Bullis Lab. Sch., 2004—. Author: Alarm: A Behavior Strategy, 1994. Mem. Found. for Restoration of St. Genevieve, 1993-98; mem. S.E. Mo. Regional Profl. Devel. Mem. Coun. for Exceptional Children, Mo. Subdivsn. Learning Disabilities (pres. 1994, chairperson dist. profl. devel. com.). Democrat. Avocation: piano. Home: 4609 W Sandpiper Dr Muncie IN 47304-2895 Office: Bullis Lab Sch Muncie IN 47306

CANTWELL, MARIA E., senator; b. Indpls., Oct. 13, 1958; d. Rose and Paul Cantwell. BA in Public Adminstrn., Miami U., Ohio, 1981. Public relations cons. Cantwell and Associates, 1981—87; state repr. Dist. 44 Wash., 1987—92; mem. 103rd Congress from 1st Wash. dist., Washington, 1993—95; v.p. mktg. Progressive Networks, Seattle, 1995—97; sr. v.p. consumer and e-commerce Real Networks (formerly Progressive Networks), Seattle, 1997—2000; US Senator from Wash., 2001—. Mem. com. commerce, sci. and transp. US Senate, com. energy and natural resources, com.

Indian affairs, com. small bus. and entrepreneurship. Bd. dirs. Wash. Econ. Develop. Fin. Authority. Named Woman of Yr., KING-TV Evening Mag., 2001; recipient Cyber Champion award, Bus. Software Alliance, 2003, Friend of Blues, Experience Music Project-Vulcan, Inc., 2003. Democrat. Roman Catholic. Office: US Senate 717 Hart Senate Bldg Washington DC 20510 also: District Office Ste 3206 915 Second Ave Seattle WA 98174-1011 Office Phone: 202-224-3441, 206-220-6400. Office Fax: 202-228-0514, 206-220-6404.*

CANTY, DAWN M., lawyer; b. Chgo., June 21, 1964; AB, U. Chgo., 1986; JD, U. Mich., 1989. Bar: Ill. 1989. Ptnr. Katten Muchin Zavis Rosenman, Chgo. Mem.: ABA, Am. Bar Assn., Trial Bar of No. Dist. of Ill. Office: Katten Muchin Zavis Rosenman 525 W Monroe St Chicago IL 60661 Office Phone: 312-902-5253. Office Fax: 312-577-8607. E-mail: dawn.canty@kmzr.com.

CAO, HUI, physics and astronomy professor; BS, Peking U., 1990; MA in Mech. and Aerospace Engring., Princeton U., 1992; PhD in Applied Physics, Stanford U., 1997. Asst. prof., physics and astronomy Northwestern U., 1997—2002, assoc. prof., physics and astronomy, 2002—. Contbr. articles to profl. publs., chapters to books; reviewer Nature, Science, Physical Review/Physical Review Letters, Applied Physics Letters, Journal of Optical Society of America, Optical Express, Optics Communications, Applied Optics, Photonics Technology Letters, IEEE, Journal of Selected Topics in Quantum Electronics, NSF, Am. Chem. Soc. Petroleum Rsch. Fund, US Civilian R&D Found., Rsch. Corp., Australian Rsch. Coun., and Sci. Found. Ireland. Recipient NSF Career award, 2001, Outstanding Young Researcher award, Overseas Chinese Physics Assn., 2004, Friedrich Bessel Rsch. award, Alexander von Humboldt Found., 2004; Guang-Hua Fellowship, 1989, Zonta Internat. Found. Amelia Earhart Fellowship, 1992, Karel Urbanek Grad. Fellowship, 1997, David and Lucille Packard Fellow, 1999, Alfred P. Sloan Fellow, 2000. Mem.: IEEE, Optical Soc. Am. (mem. Max Born prize com. 2005, vice-chair, technical group on waves in random and periodic media 2004—06), Am. Phys. Soc. (Maria Goeppert-Mayer award 2006). Office: Dept Physics and Astronomy Northwestern U 2145 Sheridan Rd Evanston IL 60208-3112 Office Phone: 847-467-5452. Office Fax: 847-491-9982. Business E-Mail: h-cao@northwestern.edu.

CAPALDI, ELIZABETH ANN DEUTSCH, psychological sciences professor; b. NYC, May 13, 1945; d. Frederick and Nettie (Tarasuck) Deutsch; m. Egidio J. Capaldi, Jan. 20, 1968 (div. May 1985) AB, U. Rochester, 1965; PhD, U. Tex., 1969. Asst. prof. dept. psychol. scis. Purdue U., West Lafayette, Ind., 1969-74, assoc. prof., 1974-78, prof., 1979-86, asst. dean Grad. Sch., 1982-86, head dept. psychol. scis., 1983-88, sec.-treas. council of grad. dept. psychology, 1986-88; prof. U. Fla., Gainesville, 1988-2000, provost, v.p. acad. affairs, 1996-99; provost SUNY, Buffalo, 2000—04; vice chancellor SUNY Albany, 2004—; chief of staff SUNY, 2004—. Spl. asst. to pres., U. Fla., 1991-96. Author: Psychology, 1989, 4th edit., 1996; cons. editor Jour. Exptl. Psychology, 1991-96; assoc. editor Psychonomic Bull. Rev., 1993-98; contbr. articles to profl. jours. NIMH grantee, 1984-94, NSF grantee, 1995-98. Fellow AAAS, APA, Am. Psychol. Soc. (mem. governing bd. 1991-96, pres. 1999); mem. Psychonomic Soc. (mem. governing bd. 1992-97), Midwestern Psychol. Assn. (sec.-treas. 1988-90, pres. 1991), Sigma Xi. Office: SUNY State University Plz T-12 Albany NY 12246 Office Phone: 518-443-5538. Business E-Mail: betty.capaldi@suny.edu.

CAPALDINI, LISA CLAIRE, physician, educator; b. Bluefield, W.Va., Dec. 19, 1955; MD, U. Calif. San Francisco, 1982; M in Pub. Health, U. Calif. Berkeley, 1983. Intern San Francisco Gen. Hosp. U. Calif., 1983—84, resident, 1983—86; assoc. clin. prof. medicine U. Calif. San Francisco, course dir. nursing sch., 1998—; pvt. practice internal medicine, 1998—. Contbr. articles to profl. jours. Office: 45 Castro St Ste 227 San Francisco CA 94114-1033 Office Phone: 415-861-3366.*

CAPEHART, BONNIE, language educator; d. Kenneth James and Marion June Hawkins; m. Donn Robert Holmer (div.); 1 child, Robert James Holmer; m. David Harold Capehart, Aug. 22, 1992. BA in Applied Arts and Scis. Art, San Diego State U., 1987; M in Tchg., U. San Diego, 2005. Cert. tchr. Calif. Avid coord. S.W. Mid. Sch., San Diego, 1999—2006, English tchr., 1999—2006; tchr. Bonita Vista Mid. Sch., Chula Vista, Calif., 2006—. Mem.: NEA, Calif. Tchrs. Assn., Nat. Coun. Tchrs. English. Avocations: genealogy, reading. Office: Bonita Vista Mid Sch Sweetwater Union HS Dist 650 Otay Lakes Rd Chula Vista CA 91910 Office Phone: 619-397-2200.

CAPELL, CYDNEY LYNN, editor; b. Jacksonville, Fla., Dec. 20, 1956; d. Ernest Clary and Alice Rae (McGinnis) C.; m. Garrick Philip Martin, July 16, 1983 (div. Jan. 1988). BA, Furman U., 1977. Mktg. rep. E.C. Capell & Assocs., Greenville, S.C., 1977-80; sales rep. Prentice-Hall Publs., Cin., 1980-81; sales, mktg. rep. Benjamin/Cummings, Houston, 1981-83; sales rep. McGraw-Hill Book Co., Houston, 1983-85, engring. editor N.Y.C., 1985-87; acctg. and infosys. editor Bus. Pubs., Inc., Plano, Tex., 1988-89; sr. editor Gorsuch Scarisbrick Pubs., Scottsdale, Ariz., 1989-90; editor-in-chief rsch. dept. Rauscher, Pierce, Refsnes Stock Brokers, 1990-94; editor-in-chief, dir. mktg. Marshall & Swift, L.A., 1994-98; sr. mng. editor Pearson Custom Pub., Tulsa, 2000—. Editor Talon mag., 1972; news editor Paladin newspaper, 1977. Named Rookie of Yr. McGraw-Hill Book Co., 1985. Mem. NOW, NAFE, Women in Pub., Women in Comm., Mensa. Republican. Avocations: tennis, ballet.

CAPELLE, ELAINE M., financial planner; b. Green Bay, Wis., June 29, 1941; d. Stanley E. and Lena J. (DeValk) Van De Hey; m. Ralph Unsin, Sept. 3, 1958 (div. Sept. 1960); m. John J. Capelle, July 28, 1962; children: Debra Ann, Laura Marie. William Arthur. Student, U. Wis., Green Bay, 1999—. A/p specialist Shopko Gen., Green Bay, Wis., 1964-74; fin. specialist U. Wis., Green Bay, 1974-99; bookkeeper Comml. Laundry Sales, 2002—. Bd. dirs. United Way, Green Bay, 1990-94; chair NWPC, Northeastern Wis., 1994-96; income tax asst. UWGB- Acctg., 1990—; family fin. counselor Brown County Extension, Green Bay, 1989-90. Mem. Nat. Fedn. Bus. & Profl. Women, Wis. Fedn. Bus. & Profl. Women (past state pres.), Green Bay-De Pere Bus. & Profl. Women (past local pres. and rec. sec.), AAUW, NWPC. Democrat. Roman Catholic. Avocations: reading, knitting. Home: 2032 Deckner Ave Green Bay WI 54302-3532 E-mail: emcapella@greenbaynet.com.

CAPELLE-FRANK, JACQUELINE AIMEE, writer; b. Fond du Lac, Wis., Dec. 23, 1935; d. Ira Richard and Aimee Cecilia (Dignin) Capelle; divorced; children: P. Malachi, Tamara, Daria Frank-Weber. AA, Edison C.C., Naples, Fla., 1986; cert., U. Cambridge, Eng., 1991, U. Oxford, 1992, Paris Am. Acad., 1992; BA, Fla. Internat. U., 1994. Part-time instr. Internat. Coll., 1999. Author: (children's book) What's a Library, 1974, (anthologies) Poetic Voices of America, 1996, 97. Mem. adv. bd. Greater Naples Leadership, Inc., 1999—. Mem. AAUW, DAR, Nat. Mus. Women, Collier County Hist. Soc. (bd. dirs. 1994-2002, pres. 1997-2001), Nat. Trust for Hist. Preservation, Mus. Trustee Assn., Soc. Mayflower Descendants, Antiques Automobile Club Am. Republican. Presbyterian. Avocations: reading, travel, country walks, gardening, swimming. Home: 143 4th Ave N Naples FL 34102-8421

CAPELLO, LINDA, artist; b. Bklyn., July 12, 1949; m. John Capello; 1 child, Joanna. AAS, Fashion Inst. Tech., N.Y.C., 1968. Art tchr. figure drawing; art tchr. Guild Hall's Young At Art Program; art tutor Empire State Coll.; art tchr., dept. head Bialik Sch., Bklyn., 1985-87; illustrator for children's newspaper The Waldo Tribune; artist Karl Mann studios, 1978-80; freelance fashion illustrator. Exhibited in group shows at ann. Guild Hall shows, East Hampton, ann. Goat Alley Gallery 725 shows, Sag Harbor, ann. Southampton Artists group shows, Adelphi U. Gallery, L.I., 1973, Belanthi Gallery, Bklyn., 1979-81, BACA Small Works show, Bklyn., 1986, AFA at Lever House, N.Y.C., 1989, Mark Humphries Gallery, Southampton, 1993, Goodman Deisgn Gallery, Southampton, 1993, Clayton-Libratore Gallery, Bridgehampton, N.Y., 1993, 51st Ann. Audubon Exhibit, N.Y.C., 1993, Ashwagh Hall, East Hampton, 1994, Catherine Lorillard Wolf Art Club ann. show, N.Y.C., 1994, Am. Pen Women show, Farmingville, N.Y., 1995, Sundance Gallery, Bridgehampton, 1995, EEAC Juried Show, Riverhead, N.Y., 1995, Jennifer Garrigues, Palm Beach, Fla., 2000, Hampton Rd. Gallery, Southampton, N.Y., 2003; oil paintings, drawings in pvt. collections; murals on pub. and pvt. walls. Mem. Southampton Artists, Artists Alliance East Hampton, Nat. Assn. Women Artists. Office Phone: 631-725-5851.

CAPERNA, LISA MARIA, lawyer; BA magna cum laude, Boston Coll., 1997; JD, Boston Coll. Law Sch., 2000. Bar: Mass. 2001, US Dist. Ct. (Dist. Mass.), US Ct. Appeals (1st Cir.). Assoc. Curley & Curley PC, Boston, 2001—. Mem.: Phi Beta Kappa. Office: Curley & Curley PC 27 School St Boston MA 02108-4391 Office Phone: 617-523-2990. Office Fax: 617-523-7602.*

CAPES, BONNIE HEATHER, music educator; b. Ottawa, Ont., Can., Aug. 9, 1979; d. Charles Henry and Lorna Diane Hoens; m. James Adam Capes, Aug. 26, 2002; 1 child, Autumn Olivia. BS in Music Edn., U. Pa., 2001; MA, Columbia U., 2004. Music tchr. Constable Elem. Sch., Kendall Park, NJ, 2001—02, Brooks Crossing Elem. Sch., Monmouth Junction, NJ, 2002—. Music dir. Playful Theater Co., Mercerville, NJ, 2002—; pvt. instr., NJ, 2001—. Musician: (musical) Fiddler on the Roof; dir.: (musical) Annie, Damn Yankees; musician: (musical) Oklahoma; dir.: (musical) The Secret Garden; musician: (musical) How To Succeed In Business Without Really Trying, Oliver, Seussical, Cats. Mem.: NEA (assoc.), N.J. Music Educators Assn. (assoc.), Music Educators Nat. Conf. (assoc.). Office Phone: 732-821-7478. Personal E-mail: bonniehcapes@comcast.net.

CAPETILLO, CHARLENE VERNELLE, music educator, special education educator; b. Streator, Ill., Sept. 18, 1944; d. Miles Bryan and Lillian Mae Baker; m. Benjamin Capetillo, July 20, 1963; children: Christiana, Matthew Bryan, Susannah Carlina. Photography cert., Woodland Hills Occupl. Ctr., 1979; student, Pierce Coll., 1985, student, 1987. Sales staff Avon, Pasadena, Calif., 1963—78; pvt. seamstress Calabasas, Calif., 1963—; piano and voice tchr. pvt. and pub. schs., Conejo and L.A., 1978—; dir. sales Neo-Life Diamite Health Products, 1985—; singer L.A. Opera, Opera Pacific, 1985—95, L.A. Camerata Orch., 1985—; owner, pres. Hollywood Angels Childrens' Photography, L.A., 1994—; spl. edn. tutor LA Unified Sch. Dist., 1999—. Performer: Carnegie Hall, 1999, 2001, 2003; performer: (soloist) China Tour, 2004; exhibitions include Chouinards Art Inst., LA, 1963—64; author: numerous poems. Vol. performer various retirement homes, L.A., 1992—; soloist numerous chs., L.A.; vol. charity fundraisers; choir mem. Grace Cmty. Ch., Sun Valley, Calif., 1994—96. Mem.: Phi Beta, Pi Alpha Theta. Republican. Avocations: travel, hiking, quilting, art. Home: 6519 W 87th Pl Westchester CA 90045 Personal E-mail: cmesinging@aol.com.

CAPITO, SHELLEY MOORE, congresswoman; b. Glen Dale, W.Va., Nov. 26, 1953; m. Charles L. Capito, Jr.; children: Charles, Moore, Shelley. BS in Zoology, Duke U., 1975; MEd, U. Va., 1976. Career counselor W.Va. State Coll.; dir. Ednl. Info. Ctr. W.Va. Bd. Regents; mem. W.Va. State Ho. Dels. from 30th Dist., 1996—2000, US Congress from 2nd W.Va. dist., 2001—, mem. rules com. Mem. YWCA (past pres.), Cmty. coun., Kanawha Valley, West Va. Interagency Coun. Early Intervention. Republican. Presbyterian. Office: US Ho Reps 1431 Longworth Ho Office Bldg Washington DC 20515-4802 Office Phone: 202-225-2711.*

CAPLAN, JESSICA MARIE, small business owner, artist; b. Cleve., Aug. 11, 1969; d. Harry Walter Caplan and Susan Elaine Klein. BFA, Carnegie Mellon U., 1991. Asst. mgr. Crystal Dragon Gallery, Madrid, N.Mex., 1992—94; owner, dir. Humana Gallery, Madrid, 1994—96; owner, tchr. Sun Studios, Santa Fe, 1996—97; owner, pres. Jezebel, Inc., Santa Fe, 1997—. Spkr. Arts Coun. U. Pa., 1990. Inventor glass slumping process. Office: Jezebel Gallery 236 Delgado St Santa Fe NM 87501

CAPLAN, KAREN B., food products executive; CEO, pres. Frieda's, Los Alamitos, Calif. Recipient awards in innovation and gen. excellence Working Woman mag. Office: Frieda's 4465 Corporate Center Dr Los Alamitos CA 90720-2561

CAPLES, LINDA GRIFFIN, retired secondary school educator; b. Tuscaloosa, Ala., Sept. 20, 1941; d. Melvin Mack and Inez (Watkins) Griffin; m. Thomas Ray Caples, Apr. 7, 1962; children: Thomas David, Gina Lynn Stegenga BA, U. Ala., 1962, MA, 1965; MS, So. Ill. U., 1975. Tchr. math. Tuscaloosa City Schs., 1962—64, Anniston City Schs., Ala., 1965—66, Demopolis City Schs., Ala., 1966—67, St. Charles Sch. Dist., Mo., 1969—70, 1974—97; ret., 1997. Spkr. profl. orgns Contbr. Active Calvary Evang. Free Ch. Mem. NEA, Nat. Coun. Tchrs. Math., Mo. Coun. Tchrs. Math., Mo. Edn. Assn., Math. Educators Greater St. Louis Avocations: travel, camping, bicycling. Home: 14 Wendy Ln Saint Peters MO 63376-2135 Personal E-mail: lcaples@charter.net.

CAPLIN, JO ANN, communications company executive; b. Indpls.; d. Irvin and Mildred Shirley (Brodsky) C. B.A., U. Mich.; M.A., Yale U., NYU. TV producer ABC News, N.Y.C., 1972-79, CBS News, N.Y.C. and Washington, 1979-85; pres. Caplin Communications, Inc., N.Y.C., 1986—; instr. New Sch. for Social Rsch., N.Y.C., 1980-81. Producer numerous TV shows, including: (documentary) Incest: The Best Kept Secret, 1979 (Emmy award 1980); (series) 30 Minutes, 1978-82 (Emmy award 1982), 20/20, CBS Mag., HBO Consumer Reports Spl., Adam Smith's Money World; exec. producer: The Bulletin. Mem. NATAS, NAFE, WGA East.

CAPLIN, OLGA YEROMINA, psychiatrist; b. Kamensk-Uralsky, Russia, July 6, 1967; d. Stanislav Alexandrovich Yeryomin and Ludmila Pavlovna Yeryomina; m. Herbert M Caplia, Feb. 24, 1996. MD, Blagovoschensk State Med. Inst., 1984—90. Psychiatry resident Acad. Physicians, 1992—94, fellow, 1994—95; psychiatry resident So. Ill. U. Psychiatry Dept., 2000—04. Mem.: Am. Psychiat. Soc. Avocations: painting, skiing, kayaking. Personal E-mail: caplin6@hotmail.com.

CAPLOE, ROBERTA, magazine editor; b. Framingham, Mass., Mar. 24, 1962; d. Robert Coleman and Jeanne Adele (Goldburg) Caploe. BA, Barnard Coll., 1984. Sr. prodr. Phone Programs Inc., N.Y.C., 1985—88; exec. editor Soap Opera Digest Presents, N.Y.C., 1988—89; West Coast editor Soap Opera Digest, L.A., 1989—95; exec. editor Seventeen mag., N.Y.C., 1997—2000; editor-in-chief Youth Entertainment Group, Primedia, 2000—03; exec. editor Ladies Home Jour., N.Y.C., 2003—. Co-author (with Jamie Caploe): Melrose Confidential. Assoc. mem. Acad. TV Arts and Scis. Avocation: tennis. Office: Ladies Home Jour 20th Fl 125 Park Ave New York NY 10017

CAPODILUPO, ELIZABETH JEANNE HATTON, public relations executive; b. McRae, Ga., May 3, 1940; d. Lewis Irby and Essee Elizabeth (Parker) Hatton; m. Raphael S. Capodilupo, Jan. 21, 1967. Grad., Dale Carnegie Inst., 1976. Sec. A.R. Clark Acct., Fernandina Beach, Fla., 1958-59; receptionist, girl Friday Sta. WNDT-TV, N.Y.C., 1960-62, Coy Hunt and Co., N.Y.C., 1962-69; clk. Woodlawn Cemetery, Bronx, N.Y., 1969-71, historian, cmty. affairs coord., 1971-84, editor newsletter, 1979—, asst. to pres., 1984-99, dir. pub. rels., 1984; grad. asst. Dale Carnegie Inst., 1977-78. Rschr. Woodlawn Cemetery's Hall of Fame; contbr. articles to Collier Encyclopedia, 1985; contbr. articles to profl. jours. Chmn. ann. Adm. Farragut Honor Ceremony, Bronx, 1976—; founder, chmn. Toys for Needy Children, 1983-97; bd. dirs. Bronx Mus. Arts, v.p., 1983-84; pres. Bronx Coun. Arts, 1987-90, Network Orgn. Bronx Women, 1997-98; adv. bd. Salvation Army, 1985, Bronx Arts Ensemble, 1985; bd. mgrs. Bronx YMCA, 1985, vice-chmn., 1989—; bd. dirs. Bronx Urban League, 1985, Bronx Coun. on Arts, 1985, pres. 1987-90; active Bronx Landmarks Task Force, 1994—. Recipient award citation VFW, 1976, Voice of Democracy Program judge's citation, 1980, Disting. Community Svc. award N.Y.C. Council, Il Leone di Sanmarco award Italian Heritage & Culture Com. Bronx, 1989, Lifetime Achievement Humanitarian award Bronx Coun. on Arts, 1999-2000; named Woman of Yr., YMCA, Bronx, 1986, Network Orgn. Bronx Women, 1986, Jeanne and Ray Capodilupo named as Mr. & Mrs. Bronx 1989-90 proclaimed by Borough Pres., named Pioneer of the Bronx, 1992, Citizen of Yr. Bronx Club, 1995; recipient cert. appreciation Dale Carnegie Inst., 1977, Outstanding Citizenship award Bronx N.E. Kiwanis Club, 1981, Service to Youth award YMCA of Bronx, 1983; recipient proclamation City Council of N.Y., Italian Heritage and Culture Com. of the Bronx, 1989; Outstanding Cemeterian award Am. Cemetery Assn., 1987-88; Citation of Merit Bronx Borough Pres.'s Office, 1988; Spl. Hons. for Outstanding Vol. Work Ladies Aux. Our Lady of Mercy Med. Ctr.; named Hon. Grand Marshall Bronx Columbus Day Parade, 1987-89, Bronx Meml. Day Parade, 1989; apptd. to commn. celebrating 350 yrs. of the Bronx by Borough Pres., recipient Pioneer award for Women's History Month for Outstanding Humanitarian Svcs., 1991, Lifetime Achievement award Bronx YMCA, 1999-2000, Role Model award Columbus Alliance, 2000; Jeanne Hatton Capodilupo Day proclaimed by Bronx Borough Presdl. Proclamation, 1999. Mem. Bronx County Hist. Soc., Network Orgn. Bronx Women (pres. 1997-99), Women in Communication, Bronx C. of C. (sec. 1988), YMCA (life mem.), N.Y. Press Club, Italian Big Sisters Club, Women's City Club, Order Eastern Star. Methodist. Office: 371 Scosdale Rd Yonkers NY 10707 Personal E-mail: smilerjean@aol.com.

CAPONE, MARYANN, financial planner; b. Bklyn., July 25, 1952; d. Pasquale and Dorothy (Rizzo) Capone; m. Donald Walter Huebner, June 7, 1975; 1 child, Melissa Lauren. BA, Queens (N.Y.) Coll., 1974; MBA, St. John's U., Queens, 1980. Cert. financial planner, enrolled agent for the IRS 2001. Asst. to head rsch. F. Eberstadt, N.Y.C., 1975-78; asst. v.p. Merrill Lynch, N.Y.C., 1978-81; v.p. Integrated Resources, N.Y.C., 1981-84, Mid-Island Equities, Wesbury, N.Y., 1984-85, Am. Savs. Bank, N.Y.C., 1985-86; 1st v.p. Greater N.Y. Savs. Bank, N.Y.C., 1986-97; prin. MCH Fin. Planning, Massapequa, N.Y., 1997—; enrolled agt. IRS. Adj. prof. acctg. Molloy Coll., Rockville Centre, 2003. Instr. religious edn. St. James Roman Cath. Ch., Seaford, N.Y., 1988—, mem. adv. bd. religious edn., 1996—; bd. dirs. Fin. Planning Assn. L.I., 2004—, Women Fin. Group, 2004; trustee Plainedge Sch. Bd. Edn., 2006. Roman Catholic. Home and Office: MCH Fin Planning & Tax Svc 433 N Atlanta Ave North Massapequa NY 11758 Office Phone: 516-752-4178. E-mail: mcapone7@optonline.net.

CAPONNETTO, MARIANNE, information technology executive; b. N.Y.C., June 29, 1951; married; 2 children. BA in English Lit., Romance Lang., U. Calif. Berkeley, 1972; student, NYU. Media rsch. asst. McCann-Erickson Worldwide; sr. v.p., dir. media svcs. Lord Einstein O'Neill & Ptnrs., 1975-89; dir. strategic mktg. then dir. corp. mktg. Dow Jones & Co., 1989—94; v.p., worldwide media and digital media IBM Corp., 1994, v.p., publishing, global media & entertainment; chief sales and mktg. officer DoubleClick, Inc., 2006—. Bd. dir. Audit Bur. Circulations (ABC), 1995—2001, chair, bd. dirs.; bd. dir. Ad Club NY, Bus. Publs. Assn., Assn. Nat. Advertisers CASIE Com.; mem. steering com. Fast Forward; spkr. in field. Bd. dir. Family Friendly Forum; mem. YWCA Acad. Women Achievers. Office: DoubleClick Inc 111 Eighth Ave 10th Fl New York NY 10011*

CAPOTORTO, ROSETTE, small business owner, printing company executive, writer; d. Philip Vito Capotorto and Mary Cuffari-Capotorto; 1 child, Sophia. BA summa cum laude, Hunter Coll., 1986. Co-owner Full House Printing, Hoboken, NJ, 1988—. Tchr./cons. Hoboken (N.J.) Charter Sch., 1998—2003; cons. Bklyn. (N.Y.) Children's Mus., 1998—2001; tchr. Elysan Charter Sch., 2004. Contbr.; co-author: Are Italians White: How Race is Made in America, 2003, Italian American Writers on New Jersey, 2003. Mem. Future Forum Program, Englewood, NJ, 1999. Recipient A. Ginsberg Poetry award, Paterson Lit. Rev., 2000; fellow, Edward F. Albee Found., 1988, 1994. Mem.: Italian Am. Writers Assn., Malia Collective Italian Am. Women, Phi Beta Kappa. Avocations: photography, painting, travel. Office: 303 First St Hoboken NJ 07030 Office Phone: 201-798-7073.

CAPOZZI, SUZANNE, literature and language educator; d. Michael and Kathleen Capozzi. BA, State U. of NY Coll. at Geneseo, 1999; MA, CW Post, Long Island, NY, 2003. 7-8 grade English tchr. and lead tchr. of teaming Commack Mid. Sch., Commack, NY, 2001—. Office: Commack Mid Sch Vanderbilt Pkwy Commack NY 11705 Office Phone: 631-912-2099 4126.

CAPPEL, CONSTANCE, educational consultant, writer; b. Dayton, Ohio, June 22, 1936; d. Adam Denison and Mary Louise (Henry) C.; m. R.A. Montgomery Jr., June 16, 1962 (div. Apr. 1980); children: Raymond A. Montgomery III, Anson Cappel Montgomery. Grad., The Masters Sch., Dobbs Ferry, NY, 1955; BA, Sarah Lawrence Coll., 1959; MA, Columbia U., N.Y.C., 1961; PhD, Union Inst. & Univ., Cin., 1991. Editor Newsweek, N.Y.C., 1961—63, Vogue, N.Y.C., 1964—66; mem. faculty Pine Manor Coll., Chestnut Hill, Mass., 1968—72, prof.; grad. prof. Goddard Coll., Plainfield, Vt., 1975—80; founder, CEO, pub. Vt. Crossroad Press, Waitsfield, 1972—82; comml. realtor Investmark, Dayton, 1983—85; prin., founder, CEO Cappel Cons., San Francisco, 1986—94; bus. advisor U.S. Peace Corps, Lodz, Poland, 1994—96; mgr. Price Waterhouse Real Estate, Warsaw, 1996—97; dir. devel. Conflict Resolution Catalysts, Montpelier, Vt., 1997; tchr. trainer U.S. Peace Corps., Kazakhstan, 1998; pres. Newport (N.H.) Earth Inst., 1999; faculty Norman Rockwell Mus., 2000—02. Adj. faculty PhD program Union Inst. and U., 2002—05. Author: Hemingway in Michigan, 1966, paperback 1977, 99, Vermont School Bus Ride, 1977, Utopian Colleges, 1999, Sweetgrass and Smoke, 2002, A Stairwell in Lodz, 2004, A Union of Voices: Accounts of the Union Institute & University, 2004; editor: Odawa Language and Legends: Andrew S. Blackbird and Raymond Kiogima, 2006. Founder Women's Rights Project/ACLU, Vt., 1973-74; grad. alumni/ae bd. The Union Inst. & Univ., 1992-94, 1999-2006, sec., 1993, pres., 2004-06; bd. dirs. Chief Andrew Blackbird Mus., 2002-2005, pres. 2004-2006; bd. trustees Harbor Springs Hist. Soc., 2002-05 McDowell Colony fellow, Peterborough, N.H., 1972, 1974. Mem.: Petoskey Audabon Soc., New Eng. Antiquities Rsch. Assn., Soc. Strang Studies (treas. 2005—06), Archaeol. Conservancy, Audubon Soc., Mich. Hemingway Soc., Ernest Hemingway Soc., Great Lakes Lighthouse Keepers Assn., PEN Am. Ctr. Democrat. Office: 524 Pine St Harbor Springs MI 49740

CAPPELLANO, ROSEMARIE ZACCONE, small business owner; b. Council Bluffs, Iowa, Apr. 1, 1952; d. Carl Paul and Marianna (Urbano) Zaccone; m. Al Cappellano, June 23, 1940; children: Marco, Mario. Degree in bus., U. Nebr., 1978. Owner Al's Angels and Gifts, Omaha, 1996—. Spkr. in field; exhibitor An Event With Angels. Named Columbus Day Queen, Sons of Italy, 1976. Mem.: Cath. Daus. Democrat. Roman Catholic. Avocations: travel, gourmet cooking, music, movies. Office: Al's Angels and Gifts 12105 W Center Rd # 132 Omaha NE 68144 Office Phone: 402-330-1333. Office Fax: 402-333-4325. E-mail: alsangels291@aol.com.

CAPPELLAZZO, AMY, art appraiser, writer; BA in Fine Arts, NYU; MA in Urban Design and City Planning, Pratt Inst., NYC. Dir. Rubell Family Collection & Found., Miami; internat. co-head, post-war and contemporary art dept. Christie's, NYC. Bd. dir. LA Contemporary Exhbns.; lectr. in field. Co-editor In Company: The Collaborations of Robert Creeley, 1999. Bd. dir. Miami Light Project. Named one of 40 Under 40, Crain's New York Bus. Journal, 2006. Office: Christie's/NY 20 Rockefeller Plz New York NY 10020 Office Phone: 212-636-4932. Office Fax: 212-636-4932. Business E-Mail: acappellazzo@christies.com.*

CAPPELLO, EVE, speaker, trainer, writer; b. Sydney, Australia; d. Nem and Ethel Shapira; children: Frances Soskins, Alan Kazdin. BA, Calif. State U., Dominguez Hills, 1974; MA, Pacific Western U., 1977, PhD, 1978. Singer, pianist, L.A., 1956—76; profl. devel. and mgmt. staff tng. Calif. Inst. Tech., 1977—; instr. Calif. State U., St. Mary's Coll., U. So. Calif., Loyola Marymount U.; founder, pres. A-C-T Internat.; founder WIN Internat. Invited speaker World Congress Behavior Therapy, Israel, Melbourne U., Australia; newspaper columnist, 1976—. Author: Let's Get Growing, 1979, The Professional Touch, 1988, 3d edit., 2000, Dr Eve's Garden, 1984, Act, Don't React, 4th edit. 2000, The Game of the Name, 1985, The Perfectionist

Syndrome, 1990, Why Aren't More Women Running the Show?, 1994, Great Sex After 50, 2d edit., More Great Sex After 50, 2003; contbr. articles to profl. jours. Named to Internat. Hall of Fame, Bus. and Profl. Women, 1994. Mem. Internat. Platform Assn. (bd. dirs., affirmative action com., bd. govs.), Toastmasters (pres.), DTM (area gov.), Alpha Gamma. Office Phone: 626-794-4076. Personal E-mail: dreve@earthlink.net.

CAPPELLO, LAURIE SUE, vocalist, educator; b. Spokane, Wash., May 20, 1957; d. Robert Joseph Cappello and Rosemary Dingillo; m. Kirk Lane Marcy, July 23, 1991; 1 child, Chiara Maria Marcy. AA, Spokane Falls CC, 1977; BA in Music Edn., Whitworth Coll., 1980; MEd, Gonzaga U., 1986; postgrad., U. Wash., 2005. Music dir. Sprague (Wash.)/Lamont Sch. Dist., 1981—83; vocal dir. Ctrl. Valley HS Ctrl. Valley Sch. Dist., Greenacres, Wash., 1988—90, vocal dir., Greenacres Jr. HS, 1983—90; vocal dir. Kenmore (Wash.) Jr. HS Northshore Sch. Dist., 1990—91; vocal dir. Evergreen Jr. HS Everett (Wash.) Sch. Dist., 1991—2002, vocal dir. Cascade HS, 2002—; co-dir. Soundsation Jazz Camp, Edmonds C.C., Lynnwood, Wash., 2002—. Guest music condr. Boise (Idaho) Sch. Dist., 1995; guest condr. Alaska all-state womens choir Alaska Activities Assn., Fairbanks. Composer: (choral arrangement) There's a Rainbow in the Rain, Blue and Green; contbr. articles to profl. jours. Recipient Outstanding Jr. High Vocal Jazz Soloist, Downbeat Mag., 2000, Outstanding Jr. High Vocal Jazz Choir, 2001—03, Outstanding HS Vocal Jazz Soloist, 2003. Mem.: NEA, Sno-King Music Assn. (pres. 1995—96), Music Educators Nat. Conf., Am. Choral Dirs. Assn. (Pacific N.W. divsn. repertoire and stds. chair Jr. HS/Mid. Sch. 2000—04, condr. ctrl. divsn. Jr. HS/Mid. Sch. honor choir 2006), Internat. Assn. Jazz Educators, Eastern Wash. Music Educator's Assn. (sec., treas. 1986—88). Office: Cascade HS 801 E Casino Rd Everett WA 98203

CAPPETTA, ANNA MARIA, art educator; b. New Haven, Feb. 14, 1949; d. Alfonso M. and Elvira (Bove) Cavaliere. BS in Art Edn., So. Conn. State U., 1971, MS in Spl. Edn., 1973, MS in Supervision/Adminstrn., 1980, MS in Art Edn., 1981. Sub. tchr. West Haven (Conn.) Sch. System, 1971; art educator/coord. North Haven (Conn.) Sch. System, 1971—; adj. prof. art So. Conn. State U., New Haven, 1984-92. Cons. Area Coop. Ednl. Svcs., Conn., 1987—. Co-author: (mag.) Art Education, 1990, School Arts, 1986—, Impace II Experienced Teachers Handbook, 1992; contbg. editor School Arts mag., 1991—. Recipient North Haven Tchr. of Yr. award, 1986, Conn. Celebration of Excellence award, 1987, 90, 92, Nat. Art Educator award, 1988, 89, Conn. Art Educator award, 1989, 95, North Haven Tchr. of Yr. award, 1989. Fellow Nat. Coun. Basic Edn.; mem. Nat. Art Edn. Assn. (nat. elem. dir. 1991-95, Nat. Art Educator award 1988, 89, advisory 1994, Briefing Paper Series 1993), Conn. Art Edn. Assn. (Conn. Art Educator award 1989, 95), Nat. Women's Art Caucus, Phi Delta Kappa (co-editor newsletter 1987-89), Delta Kappa Gamma. Home: PO Box 1399 19 Johnson Ln Madison CT 06443-2212

CAPPIELLO, MIMI, elementary school educator; b. Atella, Potenza, Italy, Feb. 3, 1952; d. Giovanni Turro and Rosa Maria Palese; m. Gerard Cappiello; children: Jessica, Vera, Andrew John. Degree in bus. mgmt., Eckerd Coll., St. Petersburg, Fla., 2000. Cert. grade sch. tchr. Tchr. Scoula Elem. Statale, Atella, Italy, 1972—74; bus. mgr. All-Ifemcare Ob-Gyn Ctr., Clearwater, Fla., 1983—96; sch tchr. Elem. Sch., 1992—. Mem.: Holy Sepulchre (Lady Commander 1992—2002). Roman Catholic. Avocations: gardening, painting, gourmet cooking, archaeology. Home: 1965 Lynnwood Ct Dunedin FL 34698 Personal E-mail: Anjeve @aol.com.

CAPPS, LOIS RAGNHILD GRIMSRUD, congresswoman, former school nurse; b. Ladysmith, Wis., Jan. 10, 1938; d. Jurgen Milton and Solveig Magdalene (Gullixson) Grimsrud; m. Walter Holden Capps, Aug. 21, 1960 (dec.); children: Lisa Margaret, Todd Holden, Laura Karolina. BSN with honors, Pacific Luth. U., 1959; MA in Religion, Yale U., 1964; MA in Edn., U. Calif., Santa Barbara, 1990. RN, Calif.; cert. sch. nurse, Calif.; jr. coll. instr., Calif. Asst. instr. Emanuel Hosp. Sch. Nursing, Portland, Oreg., 1959-60; surgery flr. nurse Yale/New Haven Hosp., 1960-62, head nurse, out patient, 1962-63; staff nurse Vis. Nurse Assn., Hamden, Ct., 1963-64; sch. nurse Santa Barbara Sch. Dists., Calif., 1968-70, 77-98; dir. teenage pregnancy and parenting project Santa Barbara, 1985-86; mem. U.S. Congress from 23rd Calif. dist., Washington, 1998—; mem. Budget com. and Energy and Commerce com. Mem. commerce com., former mem. sci. com., internat. rels. com; mem U.S. Congress, campaign finance reform task force, budget task force, Calif. ISTEA task force, congrl. caucus women's issues, congrl. task force tobacco and health, diabetes caucus, congrl. caucus on the arts, House com. on the budget; instr. Santa Barbara City Coll., 1990—. Bd. dirs. Am. Heart Assn., Santa Barbara, 1989—, The Adoption Ctr., Santa Barbara, 1986-90, Family Svc. Agy., Santa Barbara, 1994—, Stop AIDS Now, Santa Barbara, 1994—, Santa Barbara Women's Polit. Com., 1991—; instr. CPR, first aid, ARC, Santa Barbara, 1985—; bd. dirs. Pacific Luth. Theol. Sem. Democrat. Lutheran. Office: US House of Reps 1707 Longworth Ho Office Bldg Washington DC 20515-0523 Home: 1216 State Street Suite 403 Santa Barbara CA 93101 Fax: 202-225-5632. E-mail: lois.capps@mail.house.gov.

CAPRA, LINDA ANN, elementary education educator; b. Bklyn., Mar. 23, 1948; d. John Khoury and Sadie (Nobile) Grayeb; m. Joseph Vincent Capra, June 25, 1971; children: Lauren, Alena. BA cum laude, CUNY, 1969, MS in Early Childhood Edn. cum laude, 1972. Cert. tchr. N-6 and Reading, N.Y. Grade 1 tchr. N.Y.C. Bd. Edn., Bklyn., 1979-74, Headstart tchr., 1972, Title I tchr. strengthening early edn., 1974-79, chpt. I math. specialist, 1979-84, chpt. I math./computer staff developer, 1984-94, grade 1 tchr. Bayside, N.Y., 1994-97, computer software reviewer Bklyn., 1984—; tchr. pre-K Bayside Bd. Edn., NY, 1998—2005, tchr. kindergarten, 2005—06, tchr. grades k-5 math., 2006—. Chpt. leader United Fedn. Tchrs., N.Y.C., 1988-94, 96—; various coms., N.Y.C. Bd. Edn. Recipient Newsday Good Health grant, L.I., N.Y., 1994. Mem. Nat. Coun. Tchrs. Math., Kappa Delta Pi. Avocations: walking, bicycling, painting. Office: PS 213 Queens 23102 67th Ave Flushing NY 11364-2706 Office Phone: 718-423-8747.

CAPRIATI, JENNIFER MARIA, professional tennis player; b. NYC, Mar. 29, 1976; d. Stefano and Denise (Deamicis) Capriati. Profl. tennis player, 1990—. Mem. U.S. Wightman Cup Team, 1989, U.S. Fed Cup Team, 1990—91, 1996, 2000. Winner: (jr. singles) French Open, 1989, U.S. Open, 1989, (jr. doubles, with McGrath) Italian Open, 1989, Wimbledon, 1989, Championships: Roland Garros, 2001, Australian Open, 2001, 02, Gold medal, U.S. Women's Singles, Barcelona Olympic Games, 1992, Espy award as Comback Athlete of Yr., 2002; named Comback Player of Yr., WTA, 1996, Female Athlete of Yr., AP, 2001, Singles Champion of Yr., Internat. Tennis Fedn., 2001, Sportswoman of the Year by US Olympic Comm., 2001. Avocations: dance, swimming, reading, music, golf. Address: Ste 1500 One Progress Plaza Saint Petersburg FL 33701 Office: International Management Group 420 W 45th St New York NY 10036-3503

CAPRONI, VALERIE E., lawyer, federal agency administrator; BA in Psychology magna cum laude, Tulane U., New Orleans, 1976; JD summa cum laude, U. Ga., 1979. Clk. Hon. Phyllis Kravitch, U.S. Ct. Appeals, 11th cir., 1979—80; assoc. litigation dept. Cravath, Swaine & Moore, N.Y.C., 1980—85; asst. U.S. atty. Criminal divsn. U.S. Atty.'s Office, Ea. Dist. N.Y., 1985—89; gen. counsel N.Y. State Urban Devel. Corp., 1989—92; chief of spl. prosecutions, chief organized crime and racketeering sect. U.S. Atty.'s Office, 1992—94, chief criminal divsn., 1994—98; regional dir. Pacific Regional office SEC, L.A. and San Francisco, 1998—2001; counsel Simpson Thacher & Bartlett, N.Y.C., 2001—03; gen. counsel Office of Gen. Counsel, FBI, Washington, 2003—. Office: FBI J Edgar Hoover Bldg 935 Pennsylvania Ave NW Washington DC 20535-0001

CAPSHAW, KATE (KATHY SUE NAIL), actress; b. Ft. Worth, Nov. 3, 1953; m. John Capshaw (div.); 1 child: Jessica; m. Steven Spielberg, Oct. 12, 1991; children: Theo, Sasha, Sawyer, Mikaela, Destry. MA in Learning Disabilities, U. Mo. Actress: (feature films) A Little Sex, 1982, Indiana Jones and the Temple of Doom, 1984, Best Defense, 1984, Dreamscape, 1984, Windy City, 1984, Power, 1986, Spacecamp, 1986, Ti Presento un'Amica, 1988, Black Rain, 1989, Love at Large, 1990, My Heroes Have Always Been Cowboys, 1991, Love Affair, 1994, Just Cause, 1995, How to Make an American Quilt, 1995, Duke of Groove, 1995, The Locusts, 1997, Life During Wartime, 1997, No Dogs Allowed, 1996; (TV series) The Edge of Night, Black Tie Affair, 1993, (TV movies) Missing Children: A Mother's Story, 1982, The Quick and the Dead, 1987, Her Secret Life, 1987, Internal Affairs, 1988, Next Door, 1994, Due East, 2002; (TV miniseries) A Girl Thing, 2001; actress, prodr.: The Love Letter, 1999. Mem. Screen Actors Guild, AFTRA. Office: Creative Artists Agy care Kevin Huvane 9830 Wilshire Blvd Beverly Hills CA 90212-1804

CAPSTICK, MICHELLE, special education educator; b. Medina, NY, June 27, 1969; d. Donald Kennedy and Virginia Davis, Patricia Kennedy (Stepmother) and Raymond Davis (Stepfather); children: Casey Alexis, Kevin Neil. BS in Edn., SUNY, Fredonia, 1991; MS in Edn., SUNY, Brockport, 1998. Cert. tchr. spl. edn. NY, 2003, tchr. elem. edn. NY, 1991. Asst. camp dir. ARC of Orleans, Albion, NY, 1991; spl. edn. tchr. mid. sch. Medina (NY) Ctrl. Sch., 1992, spl. edn. tchr. kindergarten, first grade, 1996—. Spl. edn. team leader Medina Ctrl. Sch., 2003—, new tchr. mentor, 2004—. Office Phone: 585-798-4011.

CAPUTE, COURTNEY G., lawyer; b. Granville, Ohio, Sept. 20, 1954; BA, Ohio Wesleyan U., 1977; JD, U. Md., 1986. Bar: Md. 1987. Ptnr., Real Estate Dept, Comm. Dept. Venable LLP, Balt., compensation com., assoc. evaluation com., chiar, partnership selection com. Notes & comments editor Md. Law Rev., 1985—86. Pres. Turnaround Inc., Balt., 2002—06; pro bono counsel Manna House, Balt. Mem.: ABA, Md. State Bar Assn., Bar Assn. Balt. City. Office: Venable LLP 1800 Mercantile Bank & Trust Bldg 2 Hopkins Plz Baltimore MD 21201 Office Phone: 410-244-7531. Office Fax: 410-244-7742. Business E-Mail: cgcapute@venable.com.

CAPUTO, ANNE SPENCER, knowledge and learning programs director; b. Eugene, Oreg., Jan. 14, 1947; d. Richard J. and Adelaide Bernice (Marsh) Spencer; m. Richard Philip Caputo, July 15, 1977 (dec. Sept. 1997); 1 child: Christopher Spencer Caputo. BA in History, Lewis and Clark Coll., Portland, Oreg., 1969; MA, U. Oreg., 1971; MALS, San Jose State U., 1976. Librarian San Jose State U., Calif., 1972-76; online instr. DIALOG Info. Svcs., Palo Alto, Calif., 1976-77, chief info. scientist Washington, 1977-85, mgr. classroom instrn. program, 1986-89, dir. acad. programs, 1990-96; sr. dir. prof. devel. Knight-Ridder Info., Arlington, Va., 1996-97; sr. dir. acad. and profl. market devel. The Dialog Corp., Arlington, 1998; dir. info. pro and acad. programs Factiva, Washington, 1998—. Asst. prof. info. sci. Cath. U. Am., Washington, 1978—2000; online cons. Nat. Com. Library-Info. Sci., Washington, 1980—82; adj. prof. U. Md. Coll. Info. Studies, 2000—. Author: Brief Guide to DIALOG Searching, 1979; contbr. articles to profl. jours. Named Info. Sci. Tchr. of Yr. Catholic U. Am., 1983; recipient Rose Vormelker award, 2004. Mem.: ALA, Am. Assn. Sch. Librarians, D.C. Library Assn., Am. Soc. for Info. Sci. (chair Potomac Valley chpt. 1985—86, officer), Spl. Library Assn. (pres. 2002, bd. dirs. 2005—, Rose Vormalker award 2004). Episcopalian. Avocation: photographing architectural details on national trust buildings. Home: 4113 Orleans Pl Alexandria VA 22304-1618 Office: Factiva Ste 300 1600 K St NW Washington DC 20006 E-mail: anne.caputo@factiva.com.

CAPUTO, KATHRYN MARY, paralegal; b. Bklyn., June 29, 1948; d. Fortunato and Agnes (Iovino) Villacci; m. Joseph John Caputo, Apr. 4, 1976. AS in Bus. Adminstrn., Nassau C.C., Garden City, N.Y., 1989. Legal asst. Jacob Jacobson, Oceanside, NY, 1973—77; legal asst., office mgr. Joseph Kaldor, P.C., Franklin Square, 1978—82, William H. George, Valley Stream, 1983—89; exec. legal asst., office adminstr. Katz & Bernstein, Westbury, 1990—93; sr. paralegal and office adminstr. Blaustein & Weinick, Garden City, NY, 1993—2004, Mark R. Blaustein, P.C., 2004—. Instr. adult continuing edn. legal sec. procedures Lawrence (N.Y.) H.S., 1992—. Spl. events coord. Bklyn.-Queens Marriage Encounter, 1981, 82, 83, 85, 86; mem. Lynbrook Civic Assn., St. Raymond's R.C. Ch. Pastoral Coun., 1999-2002, sec. 2000-02, Renew 2000, mem. rev. bd.; mem. St. Vincent DePaul Soc., sec., 2001—. Mem. L.I. Paralegal Assn. Avocations: travel, reading, theater, gardening. Office: Mark R Blaustein PC 1325 Franklin Ave Garden City NY 11530-1629 Personal E-mail: kacapbwparalgl@hotmail.com. Business E-Mail: kcaputo@mrbpclaw.com.

CAPUTO, LISA M., finance company executive; b. Wilkes-Barre, Pa. d. A. Richard and Rosemary (Shea) C. BA in French and Polit. Sci. magna cum laude, Brown U., 1986; MS in Journalism with highest honors, Northwestern U., 1987. Press sec., fed. grants coord. U.S. Rep. Bob Traxler, Washington, 1987-89; press sec. nat. issues Dukakis-Bentsen Campaign, Boston, 1988; press sec. U.S. Senator Tim Wirth, Washington, 1989-92; dir. vice presdl. media ops. Dem. Nat. Conv., N.Y.C., 1992; press sec. to Hillary Rodham Clinton Clinton-Gore Campaign and Presdl. Transition, Little Rock, 1992; dep. asst. to Pres., press sec. to First Lady The White House, Washington, 1993-96; v.p. corporate comm. CBS, 1996—98; v.p., global comm. and synergy Disney Pub. Worldwide, 1998—99; pres., CEO, Women and Co. Citigroup Inc., 2000—, mng. dir., bus. ops. and planning, global consumer div., 2003—05; sr. mng. dir. bus. ops. and planning Globe Consumer Group, 2005—. Contbg. editor George Mag., 1997—2000; co-host, Crossfire CNN; co-host, Equal Time CNBC, MSNBC; mem. Coun. Foreign Relations, Fin. Women's Assn. Office: Citigroup Inc 399 Park Ave New York NY 10022

CARABILLO, VIRGINIA ANNE (TONI CARABILLO), writer, editor, graphic designer; b. Bklyn., Mar. 26, 1926; d. Anthony S. and Anne Virginia (Woods) C. AB cum laude, Middlebury Coll., 1948; MA, Columbia U., 1949; postgrad., UCLA, 1960-61. Dir. pub. relations Vassar Coll., Poughkeepsie, N.Y., 1949-51; pub. relations and publs. editor Daystrom Electric Corp, 1952-54, Daystrom Western Indsl. div., 1954-59; mng. editor Empire Mag., Los Angeles, 1959; adminstrv. asst. System Devel. Corp., Santa Monica, Calif., 1959-61, employee publs. editor, 1961-62, head corp. publs. office, 1962-66, asst. mgr. corp. communications, 1966-70, head corp. publs., 1966-68, head graphic design, 1968-70, editorial cons., 1964-70; pres. Graphic Communications Cons., Los Angeles, 1971—; editor Nat. NOW Times, Washington and Los Angeles, 1977-85; assoc. editor Eleanor Smeal Report, Washington and Los Angeles, 1985-91. Author: Poetry of Personhood, 1971, (with Eleanor Smeal) Why and How Women Will Elect the Next President, 1984, (with Judith Meuli) A Passion For The Possible, 1985, The Feminization of Power, 1988, A Guide to the Videotape, Abortion: For Survival, 1989 (with Meuli and June Bundy Csida) The Feminist Chronicles, 1953-1993, 1993; contbr. articles to profl. jours; designer, writer almanac, calendar; exec. producer: (videotape) Abortion: For Survival, 1989; co-producer, writer: (videotape) Abortion Denied: Shattering Young Women's Lives, 1990. Founding mem. Calif. chpt. NOW, 1966, pres. L.A. chpt., 1968-70, 80-82, v.p. L.A. chpt., 1988—, nat. bd. dirs. 1968-77, nat. v.p., 1971-74, chmn. Nat. Adv. Com., 1975-77; dir. Nat. ERA Countdown Campaign Office, L.A., 1982; del. Dem. Conv., 1984; v.p. The Fund for the Feminist Majority, 1987—. Recipient multiple awards Internat. Indsl. Editors Assn., 1960-70 Leadership awards NOW, 1982, 94. Mem. Feminist Found. (v.p.). Democrat. Roman Catholic. Office: 11816 Kling St Valley Village CA 91607-4010

CARAM, EVE LA SALLE, language educator, writer; b. Hot Springs, Ark., May 11, 1934; d. Raymond Briggs and Lois Elizabeth (Merritt) La Salle; m. Richard George Caram, Apr. 19, 1965 (div. Apr. 1978); 1 child, Bethel Eve. BA, Bard Coll., 1956; MA, U. Mo., 1977. English instr. Stephens Coll., Columbia, Mo., 1974,79-82; fiction writing grad. instr. Sch. Profl. Writing U. So. Calif., L.A., 1982-87; English lit. and writing instr. Calif. State U., Northridge, 1983—; sr. fiction writing instr. The Writers' Program UCLA, 1983—. Fiction contest judge Calif. State U., Long Beach, 1992, 94, writer's conf. spkr., 1985-87, 94; spkr., mem. panel Tex. Am. Studies Assn., Wichita Falls, 1998. Author: Dear Corpus Christi, 1991, 2d edit., 2001, Wintershine, 1994, Rena, A Late Journey, 2000, The Blue Geography, 2005; editor: Palm Readings, Stories from Southern California, 1998; fiction editor West/Word, 1991. Mem.: AAUP, Assn. Calif. State Profs., Nat. Assn. Tchrs. English, Poets and Writers, PEN Ctr. U.S.A. West, Inst. Noetic Scis., Greenpeace. Democrat. Avocations: swimming, beach walks, outdoors. Home: 3400 Ben Lomond Pl Apt 121 Los Angeles CA 90027-2952 Office: UCLA Ext The Writers' Program 10995 Le Conte Ave Los Angeles CA 90095-3001 also: Calif State U English Dept 1811 Nordoff Northridge CA 91330-0001 E-mail: ecaram1@earthlink.net.

CARAMICO, LYDIA FRANCES, meeting planner; b. NYC, Dec. 2, 1957; d. John and Angie (Bizzios) Janow; m. Gerard F. Caramico, May 2, 2004. BA cum laude, CCNY, 1978; grad., CBS Div. Publ., 1984. Cert. meeting planner. Exec. sec. Family Weekly Mag., N.Y.C., 1978-81, asst. mdse. mgr., 1981-83; spl. events mgr. Family Weekly/USA Weekend, N.Y.C., 1983-86; mgr. meetings & events Mag. Pubs. Assn., N.Y.C., 1986-88; conv. svcs. mgr., sales & catering mgr. Sheraton Heights Hotel, Hasbrouck Heights, N.J., 1989-91; conf. mgr. Aviation Week Group McGraw Hill Inc., N.Y.C., 1991-93, dir. tradeshows and confs., 1993—. Editor: Newsletter Heights Hotel, 1991; contbr. articles to profl. jours. Camp counselor, Hellenic-Am. Neighborhood Action Com., N.Y.C., 1974-78; tchr., Sunday sch., St. Spyridon Ch., N.Y.C., 1974-80. Mem. Internat. Assn. Exhibit Mgrs., Meeting Planners Internat., Assn. Trade Show Exhibitors, Internation Assn. for Exposition Mgmt., Exhibit Mgrs. and Conf. Organizers. Greek Orthodox. Avocations: photography, sports, reading. Home: 8 Gallagher Ct #B Bergenfield NJ 07621-1216 Office Phone: 212-904-3225. Personal E-mail: ljanow@aviationnow.com.

CARANGELO, LORI, writer, not-for-profit developer, volunteer; b. New Haven, Apr. 3, 1945; 1 son. Student, Santa Barbara City Coll., Coll. of the Desert. Adminstrv. asst. Pvt. Industry Coun., Santa Barbara, Calif.; founder, pres. Americans for Open Records, Palm Desert, Calif., 1989. Author: The Ultimate Search Book, 1997, 7th edit. 2005, Chosen Children: Billion Dollar Babies in America's Foster Care, Adoption and Prison Systems, 2002, Italian Tonight!, 2003; contbr. articles to profl. jours. Data reporting source Rights of the Child project UN, Hague Intercountry Adoption/Abduction Treaty Confs.; leader internat. adoption open records and anti-adoption movements. Mem. Lit. Guild of Palm Springs, Open Records Movement. Office: AmFOR PO Box 401 Palm Desert CA 92261-0401 E-mail: accesspress@yahoo.com.

CARBO, TONI (TONI CARBO BEARMAN), information scientist, educator; b. Middletown, Conn., Nov. 14, 1942; d. Anthony Joseph and Theresa (Bauer) Carbo; m. David A. Bearman, Nov. 14, 1970 (div. Nov. 1995); 1 child, Amanda Carole Bearman Rochon; m. Clark Coolidge, July 7, 1962 (div. Oct. 1966). AB, Brown U., 1969; MS, Drexel U., 1973, PhD, 1977. Bibliog. asst. Am. Math. Soc., Math. Revs., 1962-63; supr. Brown U. Phys. Scis. Library, Providence, 1963-66, 67-71; subject specialist U. Wash. Engring. Library, Seattle, 1966-67; teaching and research asst. Drexel U., Phila., 1971-74; exec. dir. Nat. Fedn. Abstracting and Info. Svcs., Phila., 1974-79; cons. for strategic planning and new product devel. Instn. Elec. Engrs., London, 1979-80; exec. dir. U.S. Nat. Commn. on Libraries and Info. Sci., Washington, 1980-86; prof. U. Pitts. Sch. Info. Sci., 1986—, dean, 1986—2002. Adv. com. U.S. Dept. Commerce, Patent and Trademark Office, 1987—90; Lazerow lectr. U. Ind., 1984, U. Toronto, 1999; Schwing lectr. La. State U., 1988; Cunningham lectr. Vanderbilt U., 2002; Sigma chpt. lectr. Drexel U., Phila.; numerous other lectureships; bd. dirs. Pa. Info. Hwy. Consortium; chair jury Senator John Heinz Award for Technology, the Economy and Employment, 2001. Co-editor: Internat. Info. and Libr. Rev., 1989—92; editor, 1993—; mem. editl. bds. profl. jours.:; contbr. articles to profl. jours. Mem. presdl. adv. com. Carnegie Libr. Pitts.; mem. adv. coun. Women and Girls Found. Western Pa., 2004—; chair Bd. Policy Archive, 2004—; bd. dirs. Greater Pitts. Literacy Coun. Named Disting. Dau. Pa., Gov. Penn. Edward Rendell, 2004; recipient Disting. Alumni award, Drexel U. Coll. Info. Studies, 1984, 100 Most Disting. Alumni award, 1992, 100th Anniversary medal, Drexel U., 1992, Silver Anniversary award, U.S. Nat. Commn. Librs. & Info. Sci., 1996, Leadership award in Sci. and Tech., YWCA Greater Pitts., 2000, Innovation in Sci. award, Women and Girls Found. Western Pa., 2005; fellow Madison Coun., Libr. Congress, 2002—03. Fellow: AAAS (chmn. sect. T 1992—93, coun. 1997—99), Spl. Librs. Assn. (rsch. com. 1987—92, internat. rels. com. 1991), Inst. Info. Scientists, Nat. Fedn. Abstracting and Info. Svcs. (hon.); mem.: ALA (coun. 1988—92, 50th Anniversary Honor Roll 1996), Internat. Women's Forum Western Pa., Assn. Libr. and Info. Sci. Edn. (bd. dirs. 1996—2000, pres. 1997—98, chair conf. planning com. 1997—98, 1999—2000, governance com. 2005, Profl. Contbn. to Libr. and Info. Sci. Edn. award 2002, 2005), Internat. Fedn. Info. and Documentation (co-chair U.S. nat. com. 1990—2000, chair global info. infrastructure and superhighways taskforce 1993—96, mem. coun., chair info. structures and policies com. 1997—2000), Nat. Info. Stds. Orgns. (bd. dirs. 1987—90), Pa. Libr. Assn. (Disting. Svc. award 1996), Am. Soc. Info. Sci. and Tech. (chmn. networking com., chmn. 50th ann. conf., pres. 1989—90, chmn. planning and nominations com. 1990—91, Watson Davis award 1983), 3 Rivers Connect (bd. dirs., exec. com. 1998—2004, vice chair 1999—2004), Ctr. Democracy and Tech. (bd. dirs. 1996—2007, chair 1999—2002, chmn. audit com. 2006—07), Laurel Initiative (bd. dirs. 1990—93). Home: 263 Maple Ave Pittsburgh PA 15218-1523 Office: 135 N Bellefield Ave Pittsburgh PA 15213-2609 Office Phone: 412-624-9310. Business E-Mail: tcarbo@mail.sis.pitt.edu.

CARBONE, CASSANDRA A., theater educator; b. Fullerton, Calif., Mar. 29, 1980; d. Earl A and Mary A Carbone. BA in Theatre, Calif. State U., Fullerton, 2003. Cert. tchr. Calif., 2004. Theatre dir. Named Hon. Thespian, Internat. Thespian Soc. Mem.: Drama Tchrs. Assn. of So. Calif. (assoc.). Independent-Republican. Christian.

CARBONE, DIANE M., psychologist, consultant; b. Jersey City, Apr. 16, 1957; d. Daniel Joseph and Lillian Lydia Napolitano; m. John V. Carbone, Sept. 15, 1990; children: Darren John, Nicole Diane, Gianna Michelle. BA cum laude, Fordham Univ., Bronx, N.Y., 1979; MA cum laude, Fairleigh Dickinson Univ., Teaneck, N.J., 1988, PhD, 1990. Lic. psychologist Bd. Psychol. Examiners, N.J. Intern NYU Med. Ctr. Rusk Inst., 1989—90; clin. dir. employee asst. program So. Ocean County Hosp., Manahawkin, NJ, 1990—92; pvt. practice, cons. Wall Twp., Lakewood, NJ, 1990—. Den leader Boy Scouts Am., Monmouth County, NJ, 2000—01; mem. PTO Allenwood Elem Sch., Allenwood, NJ, 1997—2005. Mem.: APA, Nat. Acad. Neuropsychology, Monmouth Ocean County Psychol. Assn., NJ Psychol. Assn. Home: PO Box 497 Allenwood NJ 08720

CARBONELL, JOSEFINA G., federal agency administrator; b. Cuba; 1 child, Alfredo. Grad., Fla. Internat. U. With Little Havana Activities and Nutrition Centers, Dade County, Fla., 1972—2001, pres., CEO, 1982—2001; asst. sec. for aging HHS, Washington, 2001—. Named one of the Most Influential Hispanic Women, Hispanic Bus., 2003; recipient Citizen of Yr. award, Miami, 1992, Charles Whited Spirit of Excellence award, Miami Herald, 1993, Cmty. Svc. award, Nat. Alliance for Hispanic Health, 1995, Monsignor Bryan Walsh Outstanding Human Svc. award, United Way, 1997, Commrs. Team award, Social Security Adminstrn., 1997, Claude Pepper Cmty. Svc. award, 2001; Kellogg Fellowship in Health Mgmt., John F. Kennedy Sch. Govt., Harvard U. Office: HHS Adminstrn Aging 1 Massachusetts Ave NW Washington DC 20201*

CARCICH, MICHELE LEIGH, biology educator; b. Hackensack, NJ, Aug. 10, 1978; d. Robert Eugene and Lorin Ellen Carcich. MA in Edn., Montclair State U., NJ, 2006; BS in Biol. Sci., Rowan U., Glassboro, NJ, 2001. Biology tchr. River Dell H.S., Oradell, NJ, 2001—. Head coach soccer, winter track, spring track River Dell H.S., Oradell, 2001—. Office: River Dell Regional High School 55 Pyle St Oradell NJ 07649 Office Phone: 201-599-7200 ext. 5030. Office Fax: 201-599-2294. Business E-Mail: carcm@riverdell.k12.nj.us.

CARDANEO, DONNA MARIE, music educator, director; b. South Amboy, N.J., Oct. 30, 1964; d. Walter Michael and Constance Regina Kawalec; m. James Peter Cardaneo, Dec. 16, 1989. BA, Trenton State Coll., Ewing, N.J.,

1986, MA in Conducting, 1995. Asst. marching dir. South Brunswick H.S., Monmouth Junction, NJ, 1986—96, assoc. dir. band, 2005—; dir. band Sayreville (N.J.) H.S., 1988, Notre Dame H.S., Lawrenceville, NJ, 1988—92; assoc. dir. South Brunswick Mid. Sch., Monmouth Junction, 1995—97; dir. band Immaculata H.S., Somerville, NJ, 1997—2005. Home: 3 English Ln Princeton NJ 08540 E-mail: dcardaneo@msn.com.

CARDARELLI, LISA MONICA, school system administrator; b. Akron, Ohio, Aug. 18, 1978; d. William Joseph and Filomena McIntyre; m. Nick Anthony Cardarelli. BS in Secondary Edn., Kent State U., 1999, MA in Curriculum and Instrn., 2003. Lic. prin., tchg. Ohio. Tchr. English Ravenna City Schs., Ohio, 2000—04, dean of students Ohio, 2004—. Profl. devel. leader Ravenna City Schs., 2004—. Author: (article) Prin. Mag., 2005. Mem.: Ohio Assn. Secondary Sch. Prins., Assn. Supervision and Curriculum Devel., Nat. Coun. Tchrs. of English. E-mail: lcardarelli@neo.rr.com.

CARDENAS, NORMA ALICIA, music educator; b. Edinburg, Tex., May 1, 1952; d. Jesus Maria and Rose Mary (Hon) C. BA, Pan American U., 1974. Orch. dir. North Jr. High Sch., Edinburg, 1974-80, Edinburg Jr. High Sch., 1980-85, South Jr. High Sch., Edinburg, 1985-99; music dept. head South Mid. Sch., 1999—. Violist, violinist Valley Symphony Orch., Edinburg, 1965—, South Tex. Chamber Orch., Edinburg, 1980-, Valley Sinfonette, Edinburg, 1990—, South Tex. Festival orch., Harlingen, 1994-; mem., mgr. The Silken Strings, Edinburg, 1974—; SBDM coun. sec. South Jr. High Sch., 1996-98; mem. SBDM, South Mid. Sch., 2000-01, music dept. head, 2000-. Mem. South Tex. Symphony Assn., Edinburg, 1976—. Mem. Nat. Sch. Orch. Assn., Tex. Music Educators Assn. (treas. 1982-86, 94-98), Tex. Orch. Dirs. Assn., Am. Strings Tchrs. Assn., Tex. Classroom Tchrs. Assn., Mu Phi Epsilon (sec. 1978-82). Democrat. Roman Catholic. Avocations: performing in numerous musical groups, arranging music, reading. Home: 10105 N 12th St Mcallen TX 78504-3281 Office: South Mid Sch 601 W Freddy Gonzalez Dr Edinburg TX 78539-6133 Office Phone: 956-316-7767. Personal E-mail: normeecar@aol.com.

CARDER-THOMPSON, ELIZABETH B., lawyer; BA magna cum laude, Brown Univ., 1975; JD, Coll. William & Mary, 1978. Bar: DC 1979, US Ct. Appeals (DC cir.). Assoc. to ptnr., health care practice Reed Smith LLP, Washington, 1978—. Editor (notes & comments): William & Mary Law Rev. Mem.: Am. Health Lawyers Assn. (bd. dir., past chair fraud & compliance forum, chair Pharmaceutical & Device Inst.), Women's Bar Assn. (past chair health law forum), Women in Govt. Rels., Phi Beta Kappa. Office: Reed Smith LLP Ste1100 E Tower 1301 K St NW Washington DC 20005 Office Phone: 202-414-9213. Office Fax: 202-414-9299. Business E-Mail: ecarder@reedsmith.com.

CARDINAL-COX, SHIRLEY MAE, education educator; b. Morann, Pa., May 6, 1944; d. Thomas Joseph and Mary Louise (Nemish) Giza; BS, Lock Haven U., 1966; MEd, Pa. State U., 1970. Mentor cert. Ind. State, 2006. Tchr. Bald Eagle Nittany Corp., Mill Hall, Pa., 1966-68; tchr., supr. Pa. State U., University Park, 1968-76; tchr., chairperson State Coll. (Pa.) Area Schs., 1968-76; primetime educator Oregon-Davis Corp., Hamlet, Ind., 1984—. Instr., cons. Dept. Edn., Indpls., 1979—, cons. energy edn., 1980—85, educator linker, 1981—, rep. prime time, 1987—; prof. Ancilla Coll., Donaldson, Inc., 1976—; chair for evaluation North Ctrl. Accreditation Assn., 1988—89, mem. leadership team, 1996, North Ctrl. Regional Lab., 1991—92, 1993—, mem. steering com., 1996—97; mem. leadership team Fermi Nat. Accelerator Lab., 1994—. Author: Energy Activities with Learning Skills, 1980. Chmn. publicity com. Rep. Orgn. Plymouth, Ind., 1983—; mem. Teacher Talk, Ind. Gov.'s Com., 1988-89; usher capt. dept. athletics Notre Dame U., 1997—. Named Outstanding Supervising Tchr. in Ind., 2004; recipient Mankind and Edn. award, U.S. Jaycees and Ind. Jaycees, 1981, Tchr. of Yr. award, Ind.'s Educator Outstanding Coop., 2004. Mem. Ind. State Tchr. Assn., Marshall County Reading Assn., Pa. State U. Club, Proficiency Bd. Accreditation (chairperson 1996), Phi Delta Kappa (v.p. programs South Bend chpt. 1992-93, v.p. membership 1994-95), Pi Lambda Theta, Sigma Kappa (chmn. Parent Club), Tri Kappa. Roman Catholic. Avocations: reading, aerobics, jogging, biking, tennis. Home: 10101 Turf Ct Plymouth IN 46563-9494

CARDINALE, KATHLEEN CARMEL, retired health facility administrator; b. Donegal, Ireland, July 13, 1933; came to U.S., 1958, naturalized, 1966; d. Denis and May (Cannon) O'Boyle; m. Anthony Cardinale, Aug. 28, 1965. BA, Jersey City State Coll., 1971, MA, 1973. RN, N.Y., U.K.; cert. nursing adminstr. advanced; nat. managed care cert., 1996. Nurse Walton Hosp., Liverpool, Eng., 1955; staff nurse, acting-in-charge Manhattan Gen. Hosp., N.Y.C., 1958-59; charge nurse, acting-in-charge Met. Hosp., N.Y.C., 1959-60; charge nurse, relief supr. Manhattan Gen. Hosp., N.Y.C., 1960-64, asst. dir. nursing, 1964-68, staffing coord., 1968-70; acting assoc. dir. nursing Bernstein Inst., N.Y.C., 1970; clin. supr., clin. specialist Beth Israel Med. Ctr., N.Y.C., 1971-73; asst. dir. nursing Cabrini Med. Ctr., N.Y.C., 1974-77, assoc. DON, 1977-78, v.p. nursing svcs., 1978-94, sr. v.p. nursing svcs., 1994-2000; ret., 2000. Mem. ANA, Greater N.Y. Hosp. Assn. (mental hygiene com.), Am. Hosp. Assn., Am. Orgn. Nurse Execs., Dean and Dirs., N.Y.C. Inc. (sec. 1993-94), Am. Coll. Health Care Execs. (assoc.). Home: 545 E 14th St New York NY 10009-3020 Personal E-mail: nungie0713@yahoo.com.

CARDINALE, LORETTA ANN, educator; b. Erie, Pa., Mar. 29, 1954; BS in Biology/Microbiology, Gannon U., 1976, MEd in Natural Sci., 1986; PhD in Curriculum and Instrn., Pa. State U., 1990. Cert. gen. sci., biology and chemistry tchr., Pa. Biology tchr. Villa Maria Acad., Erie, Pa., 1985-87; instrnl. team tchr. dept. curriculum and instrn. Pa. State U., 1988-90, instr. SAT math rev. course Office Continuing Edn., 1988-90, supplemental instrn. supr. Learning Assistance Ctr., 1989-90; asst. prof., grad. advisor Old Dominion U., 1990-93; project coord. Acad. Alliance for Higher Edn., Eisenhower Program, 1992-93, Va. Space Grant Consortium, 1992; employee trainer Norfolk (Va.) Pub. Schs., 1992-93; asst. prof. SUNY at New Paltz, 1993—. Instr. Equal Opportunity Programs, Gannon U., Erie, 1985-87; chemistry instr. Jamestown (N.Y.) C.C., 1987; external reviewer Simon Fraser U., B.C., 1992; presenter in field. Contbr. articles to profl. jours. Recipient Alumni Soc. Rsch. award Pa. State U., 1989-90; NASA fellow Pa. State U., 1988-89; Faculty grantee Old Dominion U., 1991, NSF grantee Biotechnology Inst., 1993-94. Mem. Internat. Assn. for Computer Info. Systems.

CARDINALI, NOREEN SADLER, state agency administrator; b. Bklyn., May 7, 1955; d. John William and Mary Agnes (Henry) Sadler; m. Louis Joseph Cardinali, July 30, 1983 (div. Jan. 1998). BA, Fordham U., 1977. Mgr. Employer Trip Reduction program N.J. Dept. Transp., Trenton, 1994-97, chief mobility measures sect., 1997—. Mem. Assn. Commuter Transp. (v.p. 1984-85). Roman Catholic. Avocations: gardening, collecting antiques. Home: 28 Windingbrook Rd Bordentown NJ 08505-3150 Office: NJ Dept Transp PO Box 600 1035 Parkway Ave Trenton NJ 08625

CARDO, MARIANNE, lawyer; b. North Valley Stream, NY, Oct. 26, 1977; d. Vito Anthony Cardo, Jr. and Alice W. Cardo. BA, Sacred Heart U., Fairfield, Conn., 1999; JD, Union U., Albany, NY, 2002. Bar: NY 2003. Atty. Thomas A. Toscano, P.C., Mineola, NY, 2003—06. Mem.: ABA, Am. Trial Lawyer's Assn., Nassau County Bar Assn., Women's Bar Assn. State NY, NY State Bar Assn. Roman Catholic. Office: Thomas A Toscano PC 200 Old Country Road Suite 100 Mineola NY 11501 Office Phone: 516-741-9300.

CARDONE, BONNIE JEAN, freelance/self-employed photojournalist; b. Chgo., Feb. 21, 1942; d. Frederick Paul and Beverly Jean Rittschof; m. David Frederick Cardone, June 9, 1963 (div. 1978); children: Pamela Susan, Michael David. BA, Mich. State U., 1963. Editorial asst. Mich. State Dental Assn. Jour., Lansing, 1963-64; asst. editor Nursing Home Adminstr. mag., Chgo., 1964-65, Skin Diver Mag., L.A., 1976-77, sr. editor, 1977-81, photographer, 1981—, exec. editor, 1981-97, editor, 1997-99; mystery novelist, 1999—. Author: Fireside Diver, 1993; co-author: Shipwrecks of Southern California, 1989. Named Woman Diver of Yr. Women's Scuba Assn., 1999; recipient Calif. Scuba Svc. award St. Brendan Corp., 1999; named to Women Diver's Hall of Fame, 2000, Women's Scuba Assn. Mem. Calif. Wreck Divers Club (Wreck Divers Hall of Fame, 2003), Hist. Diving Soc. (bd. dirs. 1997-2001). E-mail: bjcardone@hotmail.com.

CARDOZO, ARLENE ROSSEN, writer; b. Mpls., Jan. 12, 1938; d. Ralph and Beatrice (Cohen) Rossen; m. Richard Nunez Cardozo, June 29, 1959; children: Miriam, Rachel (déc.), Rebecca. B.A., U. Minn., 1958, M.A., 1982, PhD, 1990. Founder, dir. Writers Unlimited, Mpls., 1972-76, Woman at Home Workshops, Mpls., 1976-81; lectr. U. Minn. Summer Arts Study Ctr., 1981-85; artist-in-residence Split Rock Arts Ctr., Duluth, Minn., 1984-85, Dept. Mass Communications U. Minn., 1990-97, Augsburg Coll., 1994-96, St. Cloud State U., 1994, U. Miami, 1998-2000; cons. Sequencing Mothers, 1986—, manuscript and pub. industry. Author: The Liberated Cookbook, 1972, Woman at Home, 1976, Jewish Family Celebrations, 1982, Sequencing, 1986, 89, 96; editor, pub. The Read-Aloud Rev.; contbr. essays, articles, reviews to Chgo. Sun Times, Mpls. Star/Tribune, Cleve. Plain Dealer, Newsday; L.I. Journalism Quar.; prodr., narrator (radio) Once Upon a Time; guest lectr. Harvard-Radcliffe U., 1982; others; guest appearances Today Show, Phil Donahue Show, Dr. Ruth Show, CBS News Nightwatch, Attitudes, radio and TV, U.S. and Can.; featured in NY Times, Washington Post, Mpls. Star Tribune, Redbook Mag. Founder, Harvard Neighbors, Cambridge, 1963-64; vol. Mpls. pub. schs., 1972-82; pres. Rachel Liba Cardozo Children's Found., 1992-; dir. Brownstone Distbg., 1991-. Mem. Authors Guild, Authors League Am., Nat. Press Club, Nat. Book Critics Circle (charter), Hadassah (life). Jewish. Home: 202A Sunrise Dr Key Biscayne FL 33149 also: 1007 Pine Tree Trl Stillwater MN 55082 E-mail: arcardozo@worldnet.att.net.

CARDUCCI, JUDITH WEEKS BARKER, artist, retired social worker; b. Norwood, Mass., Feb. 25, 1935; d. Harold O. and Catherine E. (Stone) Barker; m. Dewey J. Carducci, June 22, 1961; 1 child, David E.B. BA, U. Maine, 1956; MS, Columbia U., 1958. Coor. psychiatry and social work programs Cleve. VA Med. Ctr., Brecksville, Ohio, 1964-94; now artist, 1994—. Instr. art workshops, Cuyahoga Valley Art Ctr., Cuyahoga Falls, Ohio; mem. faculty Portrait Soc. Am. Mag., Am. Artists Mag., 1997, 2001, Artist's Mag., 1998, 2000, book, The Best of Portrait Painting, 1998, Internat. Artist, 1999, 2000, Pastel Artist Internat., 1999, 2001, mag., 2003, Pastel Jour., 2003, 1999, book, Beautiful Things, 2000, Paint! Figure & Portrait, 2000, juried art shows include, State Tchrs. Retirement Sys., 1997, 1998 (Purchase award, 1997), Pastel Soc. Am., Nat. Arts Club, Am. Artists Profl. League, Salmagundi Club, Hilton Head Art League, Grand Exhbn., Akron, Portrait Soc. Am., Reston, Va., Degas Pastel Soc., New Orleans, Pastel Soc. of the West Coast, Calif., Butler Inst. Am. Art, Youngstown, Ohio, KLH Fine Art Competition, Bennington (Vt.) Ctr. Fine Art, Cahoon Mus. Am. Art, Mass., Lexington (Ky.) Art League (Best of Show), Cin. Art Club (3d prize, 2003), one-woman shows include Gallery 732, Akron Women's City Club, 1997, Hudson (Ohio) Galleries, 1997, Akron Jewish Cmty. Ctr., 1997, Moos Gallery, Western Res. Acad., Ohio, exhibited in group shows at Churski Gallery, Bath, Ohio, 1996—, Veerhoff Gallery, Georgetown, Va., exhibitions include Butler Inst. Am. Art, Youngstown, Ohio, Spaces Gallery, Cleve., Summit Art Space, Akron, Ohio, Represented in permanent collections Ohio Edn. Assn., State Tchrs. Retirement Sys., Rep. Sav. Bank, Hudson Libr. and Hist. Soc., Cuyahoga Valley Youth Ballet, Hudson C. of C., City of Hudson, Case-Barlow Hist. Farm, Cleve. State U., Hosp. for Spl. Surgery., N.Y.C., U. Maine Mus. Art; author: (represented in book) How Did You Paint That--100 Ways to Paint People, 2004 (Internat. Artist award); co-author: (book) The Caring Classroom-A Guide for Teachers Troubled by the Difficult Student & Classroom Discription, 1984; Exhibited in group shows at Cin. Art Club Nat. Show, 2003. Recipient Best of Show nat. pastel competition LaFond Galleries, Portrait Soc. Am. Internat. Competition, Best of Show, 2005. Mem.: Hudson Soc. Artists (pres. 1996—97), Am. Artists Profl. League, Portrait Soc. Am. (charter, bd., faculty), Akron Soc. Artists (Best of Show award), Degas Pastel Soc. (award of Excellence 1998, Patrons Purchase award 2001, Daler-Rowney award 2001, Award of Merit 2002), Pastel Soc. Am. (Art Times award, David B. Korostoff Purchase award, Silberman Purchase award 2005), Cin. Art Club, Salmagundi Club, Phi Kappa Phi, Phi Beta Kappa. Home: 197 Sunset Dr Hudson OH 44236-3347 Office Phone: 330-650-4069. E-mail: djcarducci@aol.com.

CARDWELL, NANCY LEE, editor, writer; b. Norfolk, Va., Apr. 2, 1947; d. Joseph Thomas Cardwell and Martha (Bailey) Underwood BA in Econs., Duke U., 1969; MS in Journalism, Columbia U., 1971. Copy editor Wall Street Jour., N.Y.C., 1971-73, reporter, 1973-76, editor fgn. dept. and Washington bur., 1977-80, night news editor, 1981-83, nat. news editor, 1983-87, asst. mng. editor, 1987-89; sr. editor Bus. Week mag., N.Y.C., 1989-91; editor Habitat World, Habitat for Humanity Internat., Americus, Ga., 1991-94; freelance editor/writer, 1994—. Episcopalian.

CARDWELL, NINA FERN, special education educator; b. Queens, Aug. 25, 1960; d. Lazarus and Elizabeth Ann Cardwell. BA, Bennett Coll., 1982. Tchr. Durham County, Durham, NC, Conway (SC) Horry County Sch. Sys., Poughkeepsie City Sch. Dist., NY, Cumberland County, Fayette, NC. Mem.: ASCD, PTA, NEA, Delta Sigma Theta (sec. 1990). Home: 980 S Hardin Southern Pines NC 28387 Office Phone: 910-690-6462. E-mail: nina4321@earthlink.net.

CARDWELL, SANDRA GAYLE BAVIDO, engineering company executive; b. Vinita, Okla., July 14, 1943; d. Amos Calvin Wilkins and Gretta Odell (Pool) Wilkins Kudlemyer; m. Phillip Patrick Bavido, Nov. 26, 1964 (div. Dec. 1973); 1 child, Phillip Patrick Bavido Jr.; m. Max Loyd Cardwell, Jan. 18, 1979 (div. Apr. 1992). AA, Tulsa Jr. Coll., Okla., 1973; BS cum laude, U. Tulsa, 1975. Sec. with various cos., 1966—69; sec. U.S. Dept. Fgn. Langs., West Point, NY, 1969—70; dep. ct. clk. civil divsn. Tulsa County Dist. Ct., 1975—76, dep. ct. clk. U.S. Passport Office, 1976—77; broker-assoc. Gordona Duca, Inc., Realtors, Tulsa, 1977—91; mem. admissions staff St. Francis Hosp., Tulsa, 1997—2000; admissions prof. Oral Roberts U., Tulsa, 2000—01; with MPW Engring., LLC, Tulsa, Okla., 2005—. Vol. children's rights and child abuse legis. and statutes.; bd. of trustees Asbury United Meth. Ch., 2003—05. Mem. AAUW, Tulsa Met. Bd. Realtors, Okla. Bd. Realtors, Tulsa Christian Women's Club (contact advisor 1988-89), Stonecroft Ministries (life publs. 1987-88), United Meth. Women (bd. dirs. 1986-87), Phi Theta Kappa (pres.), Pi Sigma Alpha (treas. 1974). Republican. Methodist. Avocations: piano, boating, gardening, reading, walking. Home: 3908 S St Louis Tulsa OK 74105-3317 Office: MPW Engring LLC 111 W 5th Ste 900 Tulsa OK 74103

CARDWELL, SUE WEBB, psychology professor; d. Frank Elbert Webb and Susie Josephine Rankin Webb; m. Walter Douglas Cardwell, May 15, 1938; children: Walter Jr., Janet Sue, Mary-Ann, David Webb, Elbert Hugh. MS, Butler U., 1962, EdS, 1965; STM with spl. distinction, Christian Theol. Sem., Indpls., 1970; Phd, Ind. U., 1978. Cert. psychology pvt. practice Ind. State Bd. Psychology, lic. psychologist Ind., health svc. provider in psychology Ind. State Psychology Bd.; ordained missionary United Christian Missionary Soc. Missionary, Indpls. and the Congo, 1945—57; psychometrist, adminstrv. asst. Christian Theol. Sem., Indpls., 1962—76, psychologist, rsch. assoc., 1976—79, assoc. then dir. I Pastoral Counseling Svc., 1981—88, asst. prof. psychology and counseling, 1979—84, assoc. prof. psychology and counseling, 1984—88, prof. psychology and counseling emerita, 1988—. Mem. theol. sch. inventory com. Ministry Inventories, Dallas, 1971—98; mem. adv. coun. Buchanan Counseling Ctr., Indpls., 1981—2001, interim dir., 2000—01; mem. editl. com. Jour. Pastoral Care, 1990—; cons., mem. Commn. on Ministry, Christian Ch., Indpls., 1967—80; mem. planning com. Ann. Conf. on Ministry with Aging, Zionsville, Ind., 1996—2005. Author: (manual) Guide to Interpreting the TSI, 1991; contbr. articles to profl. jours. Fellow: Am. Assn. Pastoral Counselors (diplomate, v.p., pres. 1984—88); mem.: APA (life), Ind. Psychol. Assn., Commn. on Ministry, Christian Ch., Ind. Depressive and Manic-Depression Assn. (bd. dirs. 1999—2001), Theta Phi. Disciples Of Christ. Home: Apt 265 5354 W 62d St Indianapolis IN 46268

CARETHERS, ANDREA, pharmacist; b. Detroit, June 11, 1968; d. Frank H. Jr. and Genevieve Jackson; m. Paul Anthony Carethers, Aug. 26, 1994; children: Paul Anthony, Jordan Alexander, Alexander Michael. BS in Pharmacy, Wayne State U., 1995. Lic. pharmacist, Mich. Pharmacist intern Perry Drug Store, Detroit, 1992-95; pharmacist Arbor/CVS Drug, Detroit, 1995—. Founder, pres. T.M.G. Investment Club, 1999. Mem. Am. Pharm. Assn. Avocations: gardening, reading. Home: 34937 Drake Heights Dr Farmington MI 48335-3301 Office: Arbor/CVS One CVS Dr Woonsocket RI 02895

CARETTI, ANN M., school system administrator; d. Anthony S. Caretti and L. Caretti Cristina. BA, U. RI, 1976; MEd, RI Coll., 1981; PhD, Capella U., 2005. Cert. spl. edn. adminstr. Mass., dir. spl. edn. RI. Spl. edn. resource tchr. Pawtucket (RI) Sch. Dept., 1986—96, asst. dir. spl. edn., 1994—95; dir. spl. edn. East Providence (RI) Sch. Dept., 1997—2000; dir. spl. svcs. Beacon Edn. Mgmt., Westboro, Mass., 2000—01; dir. student svcs. Nauset Pub. Schs., Orleans, Mass., 2001—. Adj. instr. Providence Coll., 1991—. Mem. Lower Cape Coalition, Eastham, Mass., 2001—02; bd.dirs. Conservation Commn., Bristol, RI, 1994—97, Nat. Alliance for Mentally Ill Cape Cod, Hyannis, Mass., 2002—05. Mem.: ASCD, Coun. Exceptional Children, Assn. Spl. Edn. Dirs. Mass. Avocations: photography, tennis, gardening. Home: 3 Glenwood Dr Harwich MA 02645 Personal E-mail: acaretti@earthlink.net.

CAREY, CATHERINE ANITA, artist, educator; b. Washington, Sept. 27, 1960; d. Charles William Carey and Geraldine Elizabeth Sheil; m. Brian Elliot Sinofsky. Student, Corcoran Sch. Art, 1976—78; BFA, Va. Commonwealth U., 1982. Fine art painter, Escondido, 1982—; graphic artist Circuit City Stores, Inc., Richmond, Va., 1985—87, Circuit City stores, Inc., Walnut, Calif., 1987—89; art dir. W. Coast Cmty. Newspapers, Encinitas, Calif., 1989—91; freelance art dir. Elements Graphic Design, Escondido, 1991—; tchr. Art Methods and Materials Show, Pasadena, Calif., 1998—; workshop leader Golden Door, Escondido, 2001—; tchr., owner The Glass House Art Studio, Escondido, 2001—; tchr. Artists' Materials Expo, Santa Fe, 2004. Workshop leader Daler-Rowney Art Mfr., 1998—; workshop demonstration artist Savoir Faire, San Diego, 2000—. One-woman shows include, Escondido Artists Gallery, 2003, La Costa, Calif., 2005, exhibitions include, La Jolla, Calif., 2000, Escondido, Calif., 2001, San Diego, 2002, Escondido, Calif., 2003, Art Studio Tour, 2004, Art Walk, San Diego, 2005, Rick Blound Gallery, Calif.; author: The Philosophy of Color, 2004. Organizer art shows for children, Encinitas, 1990—91, San Diego, 1999—2000, 2000—01. Recipient Blue Ribbon, San Dieguito Art Club, 1990, Honorable Mention, San Diego Watercolor Soc., 2000, Escondido Art Assn., 2001, Blue Ribbon, 2003. Master: Scripps Ranch Art Club (pres. 2000—01, founder 2000). Avocations: hiking, photography, swing dancing, gardening, cooking. Office: Glass House Studio 2048 Ridgecrest Pl Escondido CA 92029 Office Phone: 760-489-9109. Business E-Mail: element@abac.com.

CAREY, ELLEN, artist; b. NYC, June 18, 1952; BFA, Kansas City Art Inst., 1976; MFA, SUNY, Buffalo, 1978. Assoc. prof. of photography Hartford Art School, U. of Hartford, Hartford, CT. One woman shows include Concord Gallery, N.Y.C., 1985, Zone, Springfield, Mass., 1986, Real Art Ways, Hartford, Conn., 1986, Art City, N.Y.C., 1986, Simon Cerigo, N.Y.C., 1987, Internat. Ctr. of Photography, N.Y., 1987, John Good Gallery, N.Y.C., 1989, Schnider-Bluhm-Loeb Gallery, Chgo., 1990, Nat. Acad. of Scis., Washington, 1992, Jayne H. Baum Gallery, N.Y.C., 1992, 94, Gallery 954, Chgo., 1994, Nina Freudenheim Gallery, Buffalo, N.Y., 1995, Mus. Contemporary Photography, Chgo., 2002; exhibited in numerous group shows including Dayton (Ohio) Art Inst., 1993, The Dallas Mus. of Natural History, 1993, Rochester Mus. of Sci. Ctr., Rochester, 1993, L.A. Mus. of Natural History, Charles and Emma Frye Art Mus., Omniplex Sci. Ctr., Seattle, 1993, Fernback Mus. of Natural History, Atlanta, 1993, Calif. Acad. of Scis., 1993, Cleve. Mus. of Natural History, 1993, Tatischeff Gallery, N.Y.C., 1993, Mus. of Modern Art, 1994, U. N.C., Greensboro, 1993-94, Herter Gallery, U. Mass., Amherst, Mass., 1993-94, Palazoo de Exhbns., Rome, 1993-94, Art Inst. of Chgo., 1994, Caldwell (N.J.) Coll., Artspace, New Haven, Conn., 1994, Akron Art Mus., 1994, Ansel Adams Ctr. for Photography, San Francisco, 1994, Park Avenue Atrium, N.Y.C., 1994, Charter Oak Cultural Ctr., Hartford, 1995, Kingsborough Cmty. Coll. Art Gallery, Bklyn., 1995; represented in permanent collections Albright-Knox Art Gallery, Art Inst. of Chgo., Bell Atlantic, Bklyn. Mus. of Art, Chase Manhattan Bank, Coca Cola Corp., First Bank of Mpls., Fogg Mus., Harvard U., Internat. Ctr. of Photography, Mus. of Fine Arts, many others; contbr. articles to profl. jours. Office: Hartfrod Art School U of Hartford 200 Bloomfield Ave Hartford CT 06117-1545 Home: 155 Kenyon St Hartford CT 06105

CAREY, FRANCES JANE, elementary school educator; b. Radford, Va., Aug. 31, 1944; d. Alfred Nicholas and Frances Jane (Kennedy) Hoffmann; m. Wayne John Carey, Apr. 1, 1972; 1 child, Michael Steven. BS, U. Del., 1969, MEd, 1972. Cert. elem. tchr. Tchr. Brandywine Sch. Dist., Wilmington, Del., 1969—; adj. faculty mem. Wilmington Coll., Wilmington, 1991—. Mem. Del. State Sch. adv. bd., Dover, Del., 1989—, Delmarva Power & Light Energy Edn. adv. bd., 1989-91, Del. Sci. Frameworks Commn. adv. bd., 1992—. Contbr. articles to profl. jours. Recipient Du Pont grants, 1986, 87, 93, Sci. Alliance Recognition Excellence award, 1990, U. Del. Commitment to Edn. award, 1993, Presdl. award for Sci. & Math. Teaching, 1994. Mem. NEA, Nat. Sci. Tchrs. Assn., Nat. Coun. Tchrs. of Math, Sci. Alliance, Delta Kappa. Avocations: golf, sewing, gardening. Office: Lancashire Elem Sch 2000 Naamans Rd Wilmington DE 19810-2655

CAREY, JACQUELINE CARTER, retired elementary school educator; b. Norfolk, Va., Mar. 13, 1944; d. James William and Cornelia Francis (Graves) Andrews; m. Linwood G. Robinson, Nov. 24, 1965 (div. 1990), m. William J. Carey, July 1, 2001; children: John Allen, Elizabeth Anne BS, Longwood Coll., 1966; MS, SUNY, New Paltz, 1973. Cert. Tchr. Elem. N.Y. Tchr. Fishkill Plains-Wappingers Ctrl. Sch. Dist., NY, 1967—73, Krieger-Poughkeepsie Sch. Dist., NY, 1987—2002; chmn. bd. dirs. New Hackensack Nursery Sch., Wappingers, 1973—79; substitute tchr. Wappingers Sch. Dist., 1986—87; ret., 2002. Vol. Meals on Wheels, Wappingers Falls, N.Y., 1981-87, Habitat for Humanity, Guiding Eyes for the Blind; leader Boy Scouts Am., Poughkeepsie, 1981-83, Girl Scouts U.S.A., Poughkeepsie, 1986-88; Sunday sch. tchr. New Hackensack Reformed Ch., Wappingers Falls, 1972-89, deacon, elder, 1986-89, 2001- Recipient Tchr. of Yr. award New Hackensack Reformed Ch Mem. Mid-Hudson Reading Coun., Am. Fedn. Tchrs., N.Y. State Tchrs. Assn., Poughkeepsie Tchrs. Assn., United Tchr. Assn., AAUW, Hudson Valley Ice Boat Club Home: 11 Innsbruck Blvd Hopewell Junction NY 12533-8315 E-mail: jacarey1@aol.com.

CAREY, JANA HOWARD, lawyer; b. Huntsville, Ala., Apr. 20, 1945; d. Ernest Randall and Mary Regna (Baites) Howard; m. James Johnston Hale Carey, Jan. 15, 1983. BS in Home Econs., Auburn U., 1967; MS in Audiovisual Communications, Towson State U., 1973; JD, U. Balt., 1976. Bar: (U.S. Ct. Appeals (4th cir.)) 1977, (U.S. Dist. Ct. (Md. dist.)) 1978, (U.S. Ct. Appeals (3d cir.)) 1994, (U.S. Supreme Ct.) 1995, (U.S. Ct. Appeals (Md. cir.)) 1996. Tchr. Hampton High Sch., Melbourne, Australia, 1967; home economist U. Ga., Athens, 1967-70, devel. specialist state youth program, 1970-72, U. Md., College Park, 1972-73; clk. appellate div. Pub. Defender's Office, Balt., 1974; assoc. Venable, Baetjer & Howard, Balt., 1975, 76-84, ptnr., 1994—2003, past chair labor and employment group, 1995-97. Spkr in field. Co-author: (book) Legal Aspects of the Employment Relationship: An Introduction for the General Practitioner, 1978; mem ed bd: Employment Testing Law and Policy Reporter, Nat Employment Law Inst Adv Bd, Am Employment Law Coun Adv Bd; contbr. articles to profl jours. Chair dean's adv coun U. Balt. Law Sch.; pres. U. Balt. Edn. Found., U. Balt. Bd. Visitors; past mem pres adv coun St Mary's Col, Pension Oversight Comn Anne Arundel County. Named Top 100 Women for Outstanding Achievement, Daily Record, 1997, 2000, 2002; recipient Circle of Excellence, 2002, Univ. Baltimore Alumnae of Yr., 1999, Distinguished Alumnae Award, 2004. Mem.: ABA (past chair sect. coun. labor and employment law sect., past mgt. co-chair insts. and meetings com., EEOC liaison com. sects. com. equal employment opportunity law, mem. standing com. CLE, dep. chair labor & employment law com. sect. pub utility, comm, transp, health law forum, commn. on women in the profession), Univ. Baltimore Women's Bar Assn., Nat Asn Women Lawyers (past mem. gender bias com.), Am Col Labor and Employment Lawyers, Nat Labor Lawyers Adv Comt CUE. Personal E-mail: janahowardcarey@comcast.net.

CAREY, KATHRYN ANN, retired foundation administrator, editor, consultant; b. LA, Oct. 18, 1949; d. Frank Randall and Evelyn Mae (Walmsley) Carey; m. Richard Kenneth Sundt, Dec. 28, 1980. BA in Am. Studies with honors, Calif. State U., L.A., 1971; postgrad., Georgetown U., Washington, D.C., Boston Coll. Cert. comml. pilot instrument rated, advanced cert. corp. cmty. rels. Tutor Calif. Dept. Vocat. Rehab., L.A., 1970; tchg. asst. U. So. Calif., L.A., 1974-75, UCLA, 1974-75; claims adjuster Auto Club So. Calif., San Gabriel, 1971-73; corp. pub. rels. cons. Carnation Co., L.A., 1973-78; cons., adminstr. Carnation Cmty. Svc. Award Program, 1973-78; pub. rels. cons. Vivitar Corp., 1978; sr. advt. asst. Am. Honda Motor Co., Torrance, Calif., 1978-84; exec. dir. Am. Honda Found., 1984—2006, Honda Philanthropy, Office of the Ams., 1996—2006. Adminstr. Honda Involvement Program; mgr. Honda Dealer Advt. Assns., 1978—84; cons. in field. Asst. editor: Friskies Rsch. Digest, 1973—78; editor: Vivitar Voice, 1978, Honda Views, 1978—84, Found. Focus, 1984—, Instrument Pilots' Survival Manual (Rod Machado), 1991; contbg. editor: Newsbriefs and Momentum, 1978—. Dir. devel. The Spencer Theater, 2006—. Recipient Silver award, Wilmer Shields Rich award, Coun. Founds. Excellence in Comm., 1995, 2003, Gold award, 1997, 2001, Bronze award, 2005, award of Excellence, Soc. Tech. Comm., 1995, Merit award, 1996, 1997, 1999, 2001, Apex award, Excellence in Comm., 1997—2001, 2003, Bronze award, 2004; scholar, Calif. Life Scholarship Found., 1967. Mem.: Affinity Group on Japanese Philanthropy (pres.), Coun. on Founds., So. Calif. Assn. Philanthropy, Pub. Rels. Soc. Am., Advt. Club L.A., Elsa Wild Animal Appeal, Humane Soc. U.S., Am. Humane Assn., Ocicats Internat., Greenpeace, L.A. Soc. Prevention of Cruelty to Animals, Aircraft Owners and Pilots Assn., Am. Quarter Horse Assn., Ninety-Nines. Office Phone: 505-336-0015. E-mail: kcarey@spencertheater.com.

CAREY, LEVENIA MARIE, counselor; d. Easy Mae Evans; m. Robert William Carey, June 15, 1991; children: Danielle LaTrice, Shontrice Nicole, Robert William Carey, II. EdM, East Ctrl. U., Ada, Okla., 1998. Lic. profl. counselor Okla. State Dept. Mental Health, 2001. Pvt. lic. profl. counselor, McAlester, 2001—; project dir. campus violence prevention project Ea. Okla. State Coll., Wilburton, 2005—. Cons., trainer, educator Dept. Def., McAlester, 2001—. Bd. mem. Pittsburg County Child Abuse Response Effort, McAlester, 2005. Recipient Okla. Collegiate State Champion Informative Speaking award, East Ctrl. U., 1996, Outstanding Pub. Spkr. award, 1995, 1996. Mem.: ACA (assoc.). Republican. Mem. Church Of Christ. Avocations: church youth activities, mentoring, travel. Office: Eastern Oklahoma State College 1301 West Main Wilburton OK 74578 Office Phone: 918-465-1757. Office Fax: 918-465-4436. Business E-Mail: lcarey@eosc.edu.

CAREY, LOIS J., psychotherapist; b. Pitts., Aug. 7, 1927; d. Robert Gray Doeblin and Thelma (Pettit) Harris; m. David Carey, June 22, 1947; children: David, Norman, Arlene Keiser. BS, Columbia U., 1973, MS, 1974. Diplomate Am. Bd. Examiners, Am. Bd. Clin. Social Work. Pvt. practice, specializing in sand play therapy, Upper Grandview, N.Y., 1980—; dir. Ctr. for Sandplay Studies, East Coast Sandplay Assn. Workshop leader in U.S., Can., South Africa, Greece, Holland, Ireland; adj. prof. play therapy Hofstra Univ., 2003—. Author: Sandplay Therapy with Children and Families, 1999; co-editor: School-Based Play Therapy, Family Play Therapy; editor, contbr.: Expressive and Creative Arts Methods for Trauma Survivors, 2006; contbr. articles to profl. jours. Recipient Lifetime Achievement award N.Y. Assn. Marriage and Family Therapy, 1999. Mem. NASW, Am. Assn. Marriage and Family Therapy (past pres. West/Mid-Hudson), Assn. for Play Therapy (past pres. N.Y. br.). Avocations: clay, writing. Home: 254 S Boulevard Nyack NY 10960-4125 Personal E-mail: ljcarey@optonline.net.

CAREY, MARIAH, vocalist, songwriter; b. Huntington, NY, Mar. 27, 1970; d. Alfred Roy and Patricia Carey; m. Thomas Mottola, June 5, 1993 (div. Mar. 5, 1998). Back up vocalist with Brenda K. Starr. Launched own jewelry line Glamorized by Mariah Carey, 2006. Albums: Mariah Carey, 1990, Emotions, 1991, Mariah Carey MTV Unplugged, 1992, Music Box, 1993 (Grammy nomination, Best Pop Female Vocal for Dreamlover), Merry Christmas, 1994, Daydream, 1995, Butterfly, 1997, #1's, 1998, Rainbow, 1999, Charmbracelet, 2002, Through the Rain, 2003, Emancipation of Mimi, 2005 (Album of Yr., Vibe awards, 2005, Grammy award, Best Contemporary R&B Album, 2006, Outstanding Album, NAACP Image award, 2006); appeared in movies All That Glitters, 1998, The Bachelor, 1999, (mini series) Motown 40: The Music Is Forever. Recipient Best New Artist, Grammy Awards, 1990, Best Pop Vocal Performance by Female, 1990, Best Female R&B Vocal Performance for We Belong Together, 2006, Best R&B Song for We Belong Together, 2006, Artist of Yr., Vibe Awards, 2005, R&B Voice of Yr., 2005, Best R&B Song, We Belong Together, 2005, Favorite Female R&B Artist, Am. Music Awards, 2005, Female R&B/Hip-Hop Artist of Yr., Billboard Music awards, 2005, Female Billboard 200 Album Artist of Yr., 2005, Hot 100 Song of Yr., Rhythmic Top 40 Title of Yr and Hot 100 Airplay of Yr. for the song We Belong Together, 2005, Song of Yr. for We Belong Together, Radio Music Awards, 2005, Best-Selling Pop Female Artist, World Music Awards, 2005, Best-Selling R&B Artist, 2005, Female Entertainer of Yr., 2005.*

CAREY, REIKO MARIE, music educator; b. Wheeling, W.Va., Oct. 25, 1972; d. Richard Wayne and Hisako Mangiopane; m. David Joseph Carey, June 4, 1999; 1 child, Maxwell Richard. MusB, Kent State U., Ohio, 1996. Tchr. k-8 music Holy Family Sch., Stow, Ohio, 1996—97; dir. vocal music Euclid City Schs., 1999—2003, South Euclid Lyndhurst Schs., 2003—06. Mem.: Ohio Music Educators Assn. Home: 533 North Rocky River Drive Berea OH 44017 Office: South Euclid Lyndhurst Schools 4875 Glenlyn Road Lyndhurst OH 44124 Office Phone: 216-691-2088. Office Fax: 216-691-2064. Personal E-mail: reikomarie@yahoo.com.

CAREY, SARAH COLLINS, lawyer; b. NYC, Aug. 12, 1938; d. Jerome Joseph and Susan (Atlee) Collins; m. James J. Carey, Aug. 28, 1962 (div. 1977); 1 child, Sasha; m. John D. Reilly, Jan. 27, 1979; children: Sarah Reilly, Katherine Reilly. BA, Radcliffe Coll., 1960; LLB, Georgetown U., 1965. Bar: D.C. 1966, U.S. Supreme Ct. 1977. Soviet specialist USIA/U.S. Dept. State, 1961-65; assoc. Arnold & Porter, Washington, 1965-68; asst. dir. Lawyers Com. for Civil Rights, Washington, 1968-73; ptnr. Heron, Burchette, Ruckert & Rothwell/predecessor firms, Washington, 1973-90; chair CIS Practice Steptoe and Johnson, Washington, 1990-99; chair CIS Practice, sr. ptnr. internat. Squire, Sanders & Dempsey, Washington, 1999—. Cons. Ford Found., 1975—83; bd. dirs. Yukos Oil Co., 2001—05, Akbars Bank, 2006—. Bd. dirs. Acad. for Ednl. Devel., 2004—; chair bd. dirs. Eurasia Found., 1994—; bd. dirs. Russia-Am. Enterprise Fund, 1993—95, Def. Enterprise Fund, 1994—2001, Georgetown U. Sch. Law Inst. Pub. Representation, 1971—85, Am. Arbitration Assn., 1975—82. Mem.: Internat. Women's Forum, Atlantic Coun., Coun. Fgn. Rels. Democrat. Office: 1201 Pennsylvania Ave NW Washington DC 20004-2401 Business E-Mail: scarey@ssd.com.

CAREY, SHIRLEY ANNE, nursing consultant; b. Syracuse, N.Y., Sept. 27, 1939; d. John Crothy and Eva Mae (Pratt) Walsh; m. John Paul Carey, July 23, 1966; children: Jason Leo, Jonathan Paul, Jennifer Anne. BSN, Nazareth Coll., 1961. RN Calif. Charge nurse surg. svcs. L.A. County Hosp., 1962-64; instr. nursing L.A. County-U. So. Calif. Med. Ctr. Sch. Nursing, 1964-70; rschr., developer nursing edn. films Concept Media, Irvine, Calif., 1971—; cmty. health educator Huntington Beach Hosp. and Med. Ctr., Calif., 1983—2005; dir. staff devel. Columbia Huntington Beach, 1995-99, Columbia San Clemente Hosp. and Med. Ctr., San Clemente, Calif., 1995-99; nursing cons., health educator, writer Huntington Beach, 1988—; prodn. and sales coord. Concept Media, Irvine, Calif., 1999—. Bd. trustees Huntington Beach City Sch. Dist., 1990—, clk., 1993, 97, 2001, pres., 1993, 98, 2002, 03. Author (ednl. video): Impaired Mobility, 1993, Basic Patient Care, 1994, Infection Control, 1995, Elder Issues: Nutrition, Falls and Abuse, 2002; author: Infection in Elderly, 2003; prodn. coord.: (films) Human Development: Conception to Neonate, 1992; Human Development: First 21/2 Years, 1992; coord. The Vulnerable Child, 2000; Birth to 2 1/2, 2001; Young Children With Developmental Challenges (Autism, ADHD), 2001; Nutrition in Young Child, 2002; Nutrition in Infant, 2002; coord. (films) Diabetes, 2004. Mem., past officer Orange County Adoptive Parents, Calif., 1975—80; active Girl Scouts Am., Costa Mesa, Calif., 1984—98, PTA, Huntington Beach, 1976—; bd. dirs. West Orange County Consortium Spl. Edn., Huntington Beach, 1991—92, clk., 1992; active Huntington Coalition Against Substance Abuse, 1999—2000, Orange County Com. on Sch. Dist. Orgn., 1994—, v.p., 1997, pres., 1998—; pres., bd. dirs. Harry W. Montague Basketball Meml. Scholarship Com., Huntington Beach, 1989—2004; sec., bd. dirs. Huntington Beach Sister City Assn., 1993—95; commr. Huntington Beach Cmty. Svcs. Commn., 1994—2000, v.p., 1996—97; active Huntington Beach Children's Needs Task Force, 1995—, chmn., 2000—02, 2006; active Huntington Beach Collaboration, 1997—2001; exec. bd. dirs. Huntington Beach PRIDE Found., 1995—; v.p. Huntington Beach PRIDE/DARE Found., 1998, 2002, chair, 2000—01; founder, coord. Substance Abuse and Violence Edn. Task Force, 2001—. Finalist, AMA Internat. Film Festival, 1996; nominee Clara Barton Spectrum award, ARC, 2001; recipient Hon. Svc. award, PTA, 1988, 2d Pl. award, Am. Jour. Nursing Film Festival, 1994, 1996, Gold Svc. award, Orange Svc. Ctr. Coun., 1994, Marian Bergeson award, Orange County Sch. Bd. Assn., 2004, Freddie award for Diabetes, 2004. Mem.: AAUW (exec. bd. dirs. Huntington Beach chpt. 1996—2001, co-pres. 1997—98, Calif. pub. policy com. 1998—2000, Eleanor Roosevelt Fund honoree Huntington Beach br. 1998), Calif. Sch. Bd. Assn. (legis. network 1990—, del. assembly 1993—, nomination com. 1999, ann. conf. planning comm. 2004—05), Nat. Sch. Bd. Assn. (fed. rels. network 1993—97), Orange County Sch. Bds. Assn. (v.p. 2001, pres. 2002), AHA (bd. dirs. Huntington Valley divsn. 1996—98). Avocations: travel, music, working with children and teenagers. Home and Office: 21142 Brookhurst St Huntington Beach CA 92646-7407 Office Phone: 714-968-7287. Personal E-mail: scarey5000@aol.com.

CAREY, SUSAN M., psychologist; b. Chgo., Sept. 29, 1942; d. Malcolm Hall MacLeod and Elizabeth Frances Bailey; m. James Patrick Carey, Aug. 21, 1965 (div. May 1976); children: Kevin, Tim, Brian, Colleen. AB in English, French Edn., Marquette U., 1964; MS in Ednl. Psychology and Counseling, U. Wis., 1967; MA in Theology, MA in Clin. Psychology, Fuller Seminary, 1991, PhD in Clin. Psychology, 1999. Registered counselor, Wash. Tchr. 3d grade Milw. Schs., 1964-66; Montessori remedial Mary Linsmeier, Inc., Milw., 1967-71; tchr. presch. and Montessori Kinderkamp, Mansfield, Ohio, 1971-72; rschr. Mansfield Schs., 1973; tchr. presch. and Montessori Country Village Day Sch., Mercer Island, Wash., 1974-76; substitute, asst. gymnastics coach Mercer Island Schs., 1976-80; assessment specialist ESD 123, Wallawalla, Wash., 1980-81; tchr. French, English, and typing Lake Washington Jr. H.S., Kirkland, Wash., 1981-82; tchr. bus. edn. Quinault (Wash.) H.S., 1982; tchr. French and English Dallas Schs., 1982-83; sch. psychologist Peninsula Schs., Gig Harbor, Wash., 1983-85, Bremerton, Wash., 1985-86, Seattle Schs., 1986; pvt. practice psychology Seattle, 1997—. Author: (game) Hamunculus; author rsch. papers. Singer Folk Choir, Mercer Island, 1982-99; founding mem., bd. dirs. You Theater, Mercer Island, 1989; Eucharistic min. St. Monica's Ch., Mercer Island, 1982-88. Mem. APA, Nat. Assn. Sch. Psychologists, Wash. Assn. Sch. Psychologists (ethics com., writer ethics manual 1985-86), Wash. Edn. Assn. (Seattle Edn. Assn., Christian Assn. Psychol. Svcs., Coun. Exceptional Children. Avocations: dance, drama, skiing, tennis, writing. Home: 2500 81st Ave SE Apt 101 Mercer Island WA 98040-2244 E-mail: SMC7388@aol.com.

CAREY-SHULER, BARBARA, county commissioner; BA in Speech, Fla. A&M U., 1961; M in Comms. and Speech, Ohio State U., 1962; M in Guidance, U. Miami, 1969; EdD in Edn., U. Fla., 1978. County commr. dist. 3 Miami Dade County, Fla., 1979—; chair Miami Dade County Commn., Fla., 2002—04; exec. dir. office of multicultural programs Dade County Pub. Schs., 1990-92, asst. supt., 1992-96. Office: 111 NW 1st St Miami FL 33128-1902 Office Phone: 305-375-5393. Business E-Mail: district3@miamidade.gov.

CARGILL, JENNIFER S., librarian, dean, educator; MLS, La. State U. Dean librs., prof. libr. and info. scis. La. State U. Contbr. articles to profl. jours. Mem.: ALA (adv. com. American Libraries online 2006—), Assn. Southeastern Rsch. Librs. (bd. dirs.). Office: LSU Librs Baton Rouge LA 70803 Office Phone: 225-578-2217. E-mail: cargill@lsu.edu.*

CARIELLO, KRISTINE, music educator; b. Flushing, N.Y., Aug. 29, 1976; d. Karen Faulkner. MusB, Boston Conservatory Music, 1998; MA, NYU, N.Y.C., 2001. Cert. tchr. grades K-12 NY, 2001, Vt., 2002. Clarinet instr. N.Y. Pops Ednl. Program, N.Y.C., 1999—2000; chamber music coach Horace Mann Sch., Riverdale, 2001; instrumental music/band dir. Kingston City Schs., 2002—. Music rsch. asst. Marlboro Music Schs. and Festivals, N.Y.C., 1999—2001; adj. clarinet faculty NYU, N.Y.C., 1999—2001, Plattsburgh (N.Y.) State Coll., 2002; woodwind chamber ensemble coach Vt. Youth Orch., Colchester, 2002—03; clarinet faculty Hotchkiss Sch., Lakeville, Conn., 2004—. Musician (clarinetist): The Newton Symphony, The Longy Chamber Orchestra; author: (poetry) Long Island (2nd Pl. Walt Whitman LI Poetry Contest, 1994). Active Team in Tng./Leukemia Lymphoma Soc., Albany, NY, 2004—05. Attilo Poto Clarinet scholar, Boston Conservatory Music, 1994—97, Dorothy Morse Clarinet scholar, NYU, 1999, J E & B Collins Music scholar, 2000. Mem.: NY State United Tchr., NY State Sch. Music Assn., Nat. Assn. for Music Edn. Office: ER Crosby School 767 Neighborhood Rd Lake Katrine NY 12449 Office Phone: 845-382-2633. Personal E-mail: kcariello@kingstoncityschools.org.

CARINI, KAREN MICHELLE, elementary school educator; b. Richlands, Va., Aug. 31, 1970; d. Garren W. and Linda Faye McGlothlin; m. Robert Michael Carini; children: Cole, Neil, Russ BA in Interdisciplinary Studies, U. S.C., 1992; MEd, Ind. Wesleyan U., 1996. Chpt. I tchr. John P. Thomas Elem. Sch., Columbia, S.C., 1993, tchr. 2d grade, 1993-94; tchr. 1st grade New Palestine (Ind.) Elem. Sch., 1994-95; multiage tchr. grades 1-2 South Hancock County Sch. Corp., New Palestine, 1995-98; tchr. grade 6 Monroe County Cmty. Sch. Corp., Bloomington, Ind., 1998-99, tchr. grade 1, 1999—2002, tchr. grade 2, 2002—03; tchr. grade 2-3 Bullitt County Sch. Corp., Shepherdsville, Ky., 2003—05; tchr. grade 3-4 Roby Elem., Shepherdsville, 2005—06, kindergarten tchr., 2006—. Mem. Coll. of Edn. steering com. U.S.C., Columbia, 1991-92. U. S.C. scholar, 1991-92. Mem. NEA, Ind. State Tchrs. Assn., Internat. Reading Assn., Golden Key, Gamma Beta Phi, Phi Delta Kappa. Southern Baptist. Avocations: aerobics instructing, travel, reading, photography. Office: Roby Elem Hwy 44 E Shepherdsville KY 40165 Home: 757 Helmwood Cir Mount Washington KY 40047-6787 Business E-Mail: michelle.carini@bullitt.kyschools.us.

CARINO, AURORA LAO, psychiatrist, health facility administrator; b. Angeles, Philippines, Jan. 11, 1940; arrived in U.S., 1967; d. Pedro Samson and Hilaria Sanchez (Paras) Lao; m. Rosalito Aldecoa Carino, Dec. 2, 1967; children: Robert, Edwin, Antoinette. AA, U. of the East, Manila, 1961; degree in Medicine, U. of the East, Quezon City, Philippines, 1966. Lic. psychiatrist NY, Va., Conn., Fla.; cert. Am. Bd. Psychiatry and Neurology. Resident in pediat. U. of the East-R.M. Meml. Hosp., Quezon City, 1966-67; rotating intern Stamford Hosp., Conn., 1967-68; resident in psychiatry Norwich Hosp., Conn., 1968-71, staff psychiatrist, 1971-75; staff psychiatrist, unit chief, acting clin. dir. Harlem Valley Psychiat. Ctr., Wingdale, NY, 1975-80; svc. chief Fla. State Hosp., Chattahoochee, 1982-83; unit chief Hudson River Psychiat. Ctr., Poughkeepsie, NY, 1983-89, dep. med. dir., acting clin. dir., 1989-90, asst. to clin. dir., 1990-93, dep. med. dir.-admissions, 1993-97. Cons. Dept. Mental Hygiene, Dutchess County, Poughkeepsie, 1976—. Mem.: Am. Psychiat. Assn. Republican. Roman Catholic. Avocations: gardening, country music, recording/listening to spiritual enhancement. Home: 10 Millbank Rd Poughkeepsie NY 12603-5112 Office Phone: 845-486-3700.

CARINO, LINDA SUSAN, business consultant; b. San Diego, Nov. 4, 1954; d. DeVona (Clarke) Dungan. Student, San Diego Mesa Coll., 1972—74, student, 1989—90. With Calif. Can. Bank, San Diego, 1974-77, from ops. supr. to ops. mgr., 1977-82; asst. v.p. ops. mgr. First Comml. Bank (formerly Calif. Can. Bank), 1982-84; v.p. data processing mgr. First Nat. Bank, 1984-91; v.p. conversion adminstr. Item Processing Ctr. Svc. Corp., Denver, 1991-92; mgr. computer ops. FIserv, Inc., Van Nuys, Calif., 1992-93; v.p., data processing mgr. So. Calif. Bank, La Mirada, 1993-94, v.p. tech. support mgr., 1994-96; cons. First Nat. Bank of Ctrl. Calif., Salinas, 1996-97; project mgr. EDS Corp., Burbank, 1997-98, customer group mgr. Charlotte, NC, 1998-99, bus. svcs. rep., 1999-2000, project mgr., 2000—02; installation project mgr. Jack Henry & Assocs., Inc., Charlotte, 2003—. Democrat. Avocations: swimming, bicycling, camping, knitting, sewing. Home: PO Box 481084 Charlotte NC 28269 Office Phone: 704-357-0298. E-mail: lcarino@carolina.rr.com.

CARISTO-VERRILL, JANET ROSE, international management consultant; b. Quincy, Mass., Jan. 30, 1945; d. John J. and Adelaide Caristo; m. Richard M. Verrill, Mar. 31, 1984 (dec. Feb. 1995). BS, Boston U., 1968; diploma in social anthropology, Lady Margaret Hall, Oxford, Eng., 1974; MBA in Internat. Mgmt. and Fin., Am. Grad. Sch. Internat. Mgmt., 1982. Social studies tchr. Boston, Pembroke & Cohasset Schs., Mass., 1969-81; summer planner, reunions MIT Alumni Office, Cambridge, 1973-76; pres. Macro Projects Internat., Wayland, Mass., 1984—. Advisor Govt. Can., 1985, Nepal, 1986, Nizhny Novgorod, 1994, Algeria, 1994, Bosnia, 1996, 97, Ctr. for Religious Dialogue, Sarajevo, 1999-2001, Montenegro, 2000, Kosovo, 2002, Habitat for Humanity, Belfast Unltd., 1994-96; guest spkr. energy conf. Govt. Turkey, Ankara, 1997; NGO del. UN Sci. & Tech. Commn., N.Y.C., 1993; mem. adv. bd. Ctr. for Macro Projects and Diplomacy, Roger Williams U., R.I., 2003—; anthropology lectr., U3A Adult Edn., Golden Bay, New Zealand, 2006-. Author: Civilian Military Cons. Corps, 1992,96; contbr. Macro Problems and World Projects, 1998. Filmmaker, vol Mother Theresa's Hosps., Calcutta, India, 1980; vol. U.S. Peace Corps., Nigeria, 1964—66, U.S./China People's Friendship, Cambridge, 1982—83; treas. Internat. Sunsat Energy Coun., 1986—; adv. com. MIT Dewey Libr., Cambridge, 1993—2000; mem. dispute resolution forum Harvard Law Sch., 2000—; guest White House Conf. Trade & Devel. No. Ireland, 1995; participant Friends Raoul Wallenberg Conf., Stockholm, 1997. Mem.: World Boston, English Spkg. Union, World Citizens Orgn. (dir. 2000—), Macro Engring. (pres. Boston chpt. 1985—), Internat. Assn. Macro-Engring. Soc. (dir. 1996—, anthropology lectr. adult edn. Golden Bay, New Zealand 2006—), Brookline Bird Club, Oxford & Cambridge Club New Eng., United Oxford & Cambridge U. Club (London). Avocations: poetry, birdwatching, gardening, music, art. Office: Macro Projects Internat Inc 174 Pelham Island Rd Wayland MA 01778-2513 E-mail: passingpeace@comcast.net.

CARL, SUSAN MARIE, photographer, photojournalist; b. Ft. Hancock, N.J., Oct. 2, 1966; d. William Paul and Dolores Ruth Carl. BA, Coll.William and Mary, Williamsburg, VA, 1994; MA, U. Ga., Athens, 1997. Photojournalist U.S. Navy, Norfolk, Va., 1984—92; photojournalist U.S. Naval Reserves, Washington, 1992—2001; asst. archeologist U. Ga., Carthage, Tunisia, 1992—97; undergrad. asst. Coll. William and Mary, Williamsburg, 1992—94; grad. asst. U. Ga., Athens, 1995—97; photographer European Stars and Stripes, Darmstadt, DC, Germany, 1996—96. Action Press, Sarajevo, Bosnia-Herzegovina, 1997—98; programme mgr. Ind. Bur. for Humanitarian Issues, Islamabad, Pakistan, 1998; photo editor The European & Pacific Stars and Stripes, Washington D.C., DC, 1999—2001; vol. U.S. Peace Corps Island Hospice, Harare, Mashonalan, Zimbabwe, 2001; graphics designer Ft. Wainwright Morale, Welfare and Recreation, Fairbanks, Alaska, 2002—05; fgn. svc. officer, 2005—. Consulting Photographer Internat. Com. Red Cross, Sarajevo, 1998—98. Petty Officer 1st Class U.S. Navy, 1984—92, Norfolk, VA. Named Military Photographer of Yr., U.S. Military and Nat. Press Photographers Assn., 1996. Avocation: travel. Personal E-mail: SCARL49932@hotmail.com.

CARLETON, PATRICIA ANN, librarian; b. Long Beach, Calif., Oct. 30, 1952; d. Russell and Alice Spencer Carleton; children: Daniel Elliot Shown, Spencer Maxwell. AA in Child Devel., Santa Rosa Jr. Coll., Calif., 1975; BA in Liberal Studies, Calif. State U., Sacramento, 1985; MS in Libr. Sci., U. N.C., Chapel Hill, 1989. Provider family day care, Roseville, 1979—83; libr. asst. Roseville Pub. Libr., 1983—87; asst. mgr. Carpenter br. St. Louis Pub. Libr., 1989—91, mgr. Divoll br., 1991—93, mgr. cen. youth svcs. outreach and programs, 1994—2000, assoc. dir. youth svcs., 2000—04, dir. youth svcs., 2004—. Mem. adv. bd. Lerner Books, Mpls., 2005—; sec. Coretta Scott King Award Jury and Task Force, 2004—. Author: (monthly column) Savvy Family Mag., 2004—. Fundraiser Wellness Comty. St. Louis, 2002. Mem.: ALA, Assn. Libr. Svc. for Children (mem. Newbery Award com. 2003). Bahai. Avocations: interior decorating, antiques, gardening. Office: St Louis Pub Libr 1301 Olive St Saint Louis MO 63103

CARLEY, TAMATHA LYNN, music educator; b. Manitowoc, Wis., May 9, 1972; d. Donald Joseph and Donna Mary Kapinos; m. Toby Jeff Carley, June 3, 2000; children: Molly Tamatha, Maggie Lorraine. BA, U. Wis., Eau Claire, 1995. Cert. gen. and instrumental music instrn. grades 5-12 Wis., 1998. Tchr. instrumental music grades 5-12 Frederic Sch. Dist., Wis., 1998—2001; tchr. instrumental and gen. music grades 6-8 Barron Sch. Dist., Wis., 2001—. Office: Barron Sch Dist 135 West River Ave Barron WI 54812 Home: 1095 11th Ave Cumberland WI 54829 Office Phone: 715-537-5641 x514.

CARLILE, JANET LOUISE, artist, educator; b. Denver, Apr. 28, 1942; d. Jessie Crawford and Alice Essie (Williams) Carlile. BFA, Cooper Union, 1966; MFA, Pratt Inst., 1971. Prof. Bklyn. Coll., CUNY, 1971—; prin., owner, dir. Red Mountain Gallery, Ouray, Colo., 2001—. Founder Incline Village (Nev.) Fine Arts Ctr., 1966—68; instr. Sch. Visual Arts, N.Y.C., 1968—70, Printmaking Workshop, N.Y.C., 1971, Scarsdale (N.Y.) Studio Workshop, 1971—73, SUNY-Stony Brook, L.I., 1976, Bard Winter Coll., Rhinebeck, NY, 1980; head printmaking, asst. dir. Bklyn. Mus. Art Sch., 1971—77; dir. Bklyn. Coll. Press, 1977—2003; cons. Woodstock (N.Y.) Sch. Art, 1980—84; judge Alpine Artists Show, Ouray, Colo., 1989; judge Landscape Painting Show Woodstock Art Assn., 1995; owner, dir. virtual gallery www.artinouray.com, 2003—. One-woman shows include Blue Mountain Gallery, N.Y.C., 1980, Stetson U., Deland, Fla., 1995, Fairleigh Dickinson Coll., Teaneck, N.J., 1995, exhibited in group shows at Associated Am. Artists Gallery, N.Y., 1971—81, Bklyn. Mus., 1976, Ulster County Artists Show, N.Y. State Coun. Show, 1984, Alpine Artists Show Ouray County, 1987, IRT Bklyn. Mus. Sta., work appears in, Libr. of Congress Collection, Washington. Sec. San Juan Vista Landowners Assn., Ridgway, Colo., 1980—86. Recipient Hirshorn Purchase prize, Soc. Am. Graphic Artists, 1969, Best of Show award, Alpine Artists Show Ouray County, 1987, Creative Incentive award, Rsch. Found., CUNY, 1992—2004, Pollack/Krasner Found. award, 2002—03; fellow, Pratt Inst., Bklyn., 1971; grantee NEA workshop, Colo. Coun. Arts; full scholarship, Cooper Union, N.Y.C., 1962—66. Mem.: Ouray County Arts Assn. (pres. 1991—93). Avocation: Avocations: hiking, backpacking, skiing, yoga, rock climbing. Office: Brooklyn Coll Art Dept Bedford at Ave H Brooklyn NY 11210 Office Phone: 970-325-4668.

CARLIN, CATY C., artist, director; d. James N. Carlin and Mary C. Lowery. Cert., Meyer Sch. of Design, N.Y.C., 1976; Hon. diploma, U. N.C., Charlotte, 1983; student, Penland Sch. of Crafts, N.C., 1984. Cert. School For Body Mind Centering Berkeley Calif., 1995. Self employed studio artist, Burnsville, NC, 1980—2006; dir. Theatre and Soul, Fla., 2003—06. Textiles, pub. figurative fabric sculpture, Barcelona Show, one-woman shows include puppets Mus. of York County, Rockhill, S.C., fiber show, textile doll show, Renwick Mus., Wash., DC, 1992, fiber competition, Spirit Square Ctr. for the Arts, 1987, fantasy furniture and silk mural, Charlotte Pub. Libr., 1992, figurative wall sculpture, pedat. group, Austin. Bd. mem. Hands in Outreach, Penland, NC, 1987—94. Recipient First Pl., Sausalito Art Show, 1994, 1995. Mem.: Noetics. Avocations: nature, travel. Home: 302 W Howry Ave Deland

FL 32720 Office: Theater of the Soul 302 W Howry Ave Deland FL 32720 Office Phone: 386-736-8817. Personal E-mail: catycarlin@earthlink.net. Business E-Mail: into@theaterofthesoul.net.

CARLIN, MARIAN P., secondary school educator; b. NYC, July 7, 1949; d. Gerard Richard and Wanda Priscilla (Duglin) Preville; m. Howard Sandy Carlin, Aug. 9, 1969; children: Jonathan, Jason, Jennifer, Jillian. BS History, Mercy Coll., 1985; MSED, LI U., 1993. Profl. diploma ednl. adminstrn. Long Island U., 2000. Tchr. Lakeland High Sch., Shrub Oak, NY, 1991—2001, CW Stanford Mid. Sch., Hillsborough, NC, 2002—. Tutor Lakeland Sch. Dist., Scrub Oak, 1991—99, pvt. practice, Mohegan Lake, 1991—97. Editor: Substitute Teacher's Handbook, 1997. Mem.: NCMSA, NCAE, NSTA, ASCD. Avocations: mentoring, travel, reading, music, exercise.

CARLIN, SYDNEY, state representative; b. Wichita, Kans., Nov. 20, 1944; m. John Carlin; 4 children. BS in Social Sci. City commr. City of Manhattan, Kans., 1993—96, mayor, 1996—97; state rep. Dist. 66, Kans., 2003—. Democrat. Roman Catholic. Office: 521-W State Capitol 300 SW 10th Ave Topeka KS 66612 Office Phone: 785-296-7665. Business E-Mail: carlin@house.state.ks.us.

CARLINI, PAT, newscaster; married; 3 children. Grad., Ohio State U. With Sta. WVAH-TV, W.Va.; anchor, reporter Sta. WCHS-TV, Charleston; with the Bob and Tom Show morning team Q-95 Radio, 1988—; anchor Sta. WTHR-TV, Indpls., 1988—. Office: WTHR-TV 1000 N Meridian St Indianapolis IN 46204

CARLISLE, DARLA JEAN, elementary school educator, consultant; b. Nampa, Idaho, Apr. 5, 1949; d. William Eugene and Bonnie Levaughn Robison; m. David Eugene Carlisle, Nov. 22, 1974; children: Natalie Jean Dodson, Richard Brian. BA in Edn. with honors, Ea. Wash. U., Cheney, 1974. Cert. ednl. kinesiologist Calif. Edu-K. Elem. tchr. Apache Junction Schs., Ariz., 1985—88, Le Jardin Acad., Kailua, Hawaii, 1988—. Brain gym instr. Edu-K, Ventura, Calif., 1990—. Young women's pres. LDS Ch., Kaneohe, Hawaii, 2004—. Republican. Avocations: travel, basketball. Home: 44-361-4 Nilu St Kaneohe HI 96744 Office: Le Jardin Acad 917 Kanlanioneole Hwy Kailua HI 96734 Office Phone: 808-261-0707. E-mail: dcarlisle@lejardinacademy.com.

CARLISLE, LINDA ELIZABETH, lawyer; b. San Antonio, Dec. 17, 1948; d. Charles and Elizabeth (Chalkley) Herrera; m. Charles Larry Carlisle, Aug. 22, 1969; 1 child, Zachary Charles. BA in Biology, U. Tex., 1970; JD, Cath. U., 1980; MLT, Georgetown U., 1984. Bar: D.C. 1980, U.S. Ct. Appeals (D.C. cir.) 1980, U.S. Tax Ct. 1981, N.Y. 1990. Assoc. Cadwalader, Wickersham & Taft, Washington, 1980-84, ptnr., 1987-91; atty., adv. office tax legislation Dept. Treas., Washington, 1984-85, spl. asst. to asst. sec. tax policy, 1985-87; shareholder McClure, Trotter & Mentz, Washington, 1991-95; ptnr. White & Case, Washington, 1995—. Mem. bd. contbrs. Jour. of Taxation of Investment. Mem. ABA (sect. taxation, fin. transactions com.), Fed. Bar Assn., Am. Law Inst., Bar Assn. Dist. Columbia (tax sect., chair fin. products com.), N.Y. State Bar Assn. (sec. taxation and fin. instruments com.), Internat. Fiscal Assn. Republican. Home: 3215 Newark St NW Washington DC 20008-3346 Office: White & Case LLP 701 13th St NW Washington DC 20005 Office Phone: 202-626-3666.

CARLISLE, PEGGY JANE, elementary school educator; b. Jackson, Miss., Feb. 17, 1951; d. William Estes and Minnie Mae (Hawkins) Wood; m. York Anthony Carlisle, July 17, 1976; children: Jennifer, Emily. BS, U. So. Miss., 1973; MEd, Miss. Coll., 1975. First grade tchr. Rankin County Sch. Dist., Brandon, Miss., 1973—84; third grade instr. Poindexter Elem. Sch., Jackson, Miss., 1993—2001; EXCEL instr. Pecan Pk. Elem. Sch., Jackson, 2001—. Author: (book) Clean, Green and Healthy Schools, 2003. Mem. cmty. adv. coun. Miss. Children's Mus., Jackson, 2005—. Recipient Presdl. award, Nat. Sci. Found., 1999, Butler-Cooley Excellence in Edn. award, Turnaround Mgmt. Assn., 2005. Mem.: Nat. Acad. Sci (mem. tchr. adv. coun. 2002—, com. preschool and elem. sci. edn. 2006—), Soc. Elem. Presdl. Awardees, Miss. Sci. Tchrs. Assn. (Outstanding Elem. Sci. Educator), Nat. Sci. Tchrs. Assn. (sci. screen report award 2005, Tchr. of Yr. 2002). Avocations: sailing, gardening, restoring furniture. Office: Pecan Pk Elem Sch 415 Claiborne Ave Jackson MS 39209

CARLISLE, SHEILA A., judge; b. Michigan CIty, Ind., Jan. 16, 1963; d. Andrew Thomas Gembala and Beverly Kay Gregory; m. William A. Rogers, Mar. 26, 2004; children: Alexander, Kelsey. BS in Criminal Justice, Ind. U., Bloomington, 1985, JD, 1987. Intern Marion County Prosecutor, Indpls., 1987—88, dep. prosecutor, 1988—90; chief dep. prosecutor Johnson County Prosecutor, Franklin, 1991—95; felony chief prosecutor Marion County Prosecutor, 1996—97, chief trial dep., 1997—2000; judge domestic violence divsn. Marion Superior Ct., 2001—03, judge criminal divsn., 2004—. Bd. trustees Ind. Criminal Justice Inst., Indpls., 2005—06; mem. jury com. Supreme Ct. Adminstrn., 2001—. Mem. adv. bd. Protective Order Project, 2002—; mem. bd. Christian edn. St. Johns United Ch. Christ, Indpls., 2005—06. Recipient Trial Process award, Lawyers Coop. Pub. Co., Bloomington, 1987, Lugar Excellence in Pub. Svc. Series Grad., 2006. Fellow: Ind. Bar Found.; mem.: Indpls. Bar Assn., Nat. Assn. Women Judges. Republican. Office: Marion Superior Ct Criminal Rm #3 W242 City County Bldg Indianapolis IN 46204

CARLISLE-FRANK, PAMELA L., writer, researcher, consultant; d. James E. and Barbara Carlisle; m. Joshua M. Frank, Mar. 13, 1988. BA with honors, U. Chgo., 1985, MA, 1986; PhD, U. Calif., Irvine, 1991. Rschr. The Hardiness Inst., Chgo., 1983-86, U. Chgo., 1983-86, U. Calif., Irvine, 1987-91, Eastern N.Mex. U., Portales, 1991-92; rsch. cons. Rsch. Inst. on Addictions, Buffalo, 1992; co-founder, pres. Found. Interdisciplinary Rsch./Edn. Promoting Animal Welfare, (FIREPAW), 1992—; self employed rsch. cons. San Francisco, NY, 1992—98; prof. Ea. N.Mex. U. Cons. Crisis Ctr., Clovis, N.Mex., 1991-92, Mental Health Resources, Clovis, 1992-93; adj. instr. Coll. San Mateo, Calif., 1997-98, Russell Sage Coll., Troy, N.Y., 1999; prof. Green Mountain Environ. Coll., 2000-01. Author, playwright: (stageplay) Subway Vision, 2006; co-author: Addictive Behaviors in Women, 1994, Silent Victims: Recognizing and Stopping Abuse of the Family Pet, 2006; contbr. articles to newspapers, mags., profl. jours. Vol. Homeless Teens, San Francisco, 1995—98. Regents fellow, 1998; U. Calif. Irvine rsch. fellow, 1990. Mem.: APA, Internat. Soc. Anthrozoology, Psychologists for Ethical Treatment of Animals, Am. Sociol. Assn. (sect. animals and soc.). Avocations: writing novels, hiking, painting. Office Phone: 713-493-2585. Business E-Mail: drpfrank@firepaw.org.

CARLOCK, REBECCA GAIL, biology educator, chemistry educator; b. Dallas, Dec. 15, 1971; d. Clarence John and Nellie Gray Haak; m. Brian Keith Carlock, Aug. 20, 1994; children: Braxton Keith, Haden Brice. BBA, U. Tex., Arlington, 1994; MS in Secondary Edn., Tex. A&M U., Commerce, 2005. Tchr. sci. Vines H.S., Plano, Tex., 2002—04, Centennial H.S., Frisco, 2004—. Mem.: TSTA. Office: Centennial High School 6901 Coit Rd Frisco TX 75035 Office Phone: 469-633-2891.

CARLOCK, SANDRA LYNN, musician, educator; b. Oklahoma City, Nov. 5, 1944; d. Kenneth Lynn Carlock and Edith Ruth Lavers. MusB, Oberlin Coll. Conservatory, Ohio, 1965; MusM, SUNY, Stony Brook, 1971; postgrad. study, Juilliard Sch. Music, 1965—66. Arthur Judson Disting. Faculty Chair in piano, tchr. by spl. arrangement Settlement Music Sch., Phila., 1970—. Internat. concert pianist, 1989—; lectr., recitalist specializing in piano music of Clara Schumann and Edward MacDowell. Musician: (recs.) Sandra Carlock in Recital, 1999, Piano Music by Edward MacDowell, 2005 (Classical CD of the Week Pick, London Evening Std., 2005, Pianist Recommended Stamp of Approval, Pianist Mag., 2005). Recipient prize, 1st Internat. Emma Feldman Meml. Competition, Phila., 1967, exclusive concert mgmt., Nat. Music League, NYC, 1967. Mem.: Music Tchrs. Nat. Assn., Pi Kappa Lambda. Avocations: reading, photography, travel. Personal E-mail: carlock@voicenet.com.

CARLS, ALICE CATHERINE, history professor; b. Mulhouse, France, June 14, 1950; came to U.S., 1977; d. Victor Adrien Clement and Lise Simone (Ebersolt) Maire; m. Stephen Douglas, June 25, 1977; children: Philip, Elizabeth, Paul. BA, Sorbonne U., Paris, 1970, MA, 1972, PhD, 1976. Asst. prof., polit. sci. Lambuth Coll., Jackson, 1985-88, asst. prof., history, polit. sci., 1988-92; asst. prof. history U. Tenn., Martin, 1992-96, chmn. dept. history, 1997-2000, assoc. prof. history, 1996-2001, prof. history, 2001—05, Tom Elam Disting. prof. history, 2005—, chmn. civil rights conf., 2001—. Ea. European corr. Ctr. Pub. Justice, Washington, 1981—97, mem. editl. bd., 1998—, World History Connected, 2005—, Poésie Première, 2005—. Author: La Ville Libre de Dantzig en crise ouverte, 1938-1939, 1982; translator (Wladyslaw Grzedzielski): Le Cavalier Polonais, 1991; translator: (Jan Kochanowski) La Vie qu'il faut choisir, 1992; translator: (Jozef Wittlin) La saga du patient fantassin, 2000; translator: (Stephen D. Carls) Louis Loucheur, ingénieur, homme d'Etat, modernisateur de la France 1872-1931, 2003; translator: (Anna Frajlich) Le Vent, à nouveau me cherche, 2003; contbr. articles to profl. jours. Mem. Bicentennial Com., Ad-hoc Bicentennial Com., Jackson, 1987; alt. dir. Ad-hoc Com. Memories Life Bemis Jackson, 1991-92; dir. Ad-hoc Com. Polish Week, Sterling, Kans., 1982. Grantee Herbert Hoover Instn. for War, Revolution and Peace, 1984, Herbert Hoover Pub. Libr. 1979, Deutscher Akademischer Austausch Dienst 1975, French Ministry Fgn. Affairs 1973-75; recipient Internat. Scholar award U. Tenn., Martin, 1999. Cunningham award U. Tenn., Martin, 2002; featured scholar U. Tenn., Martin, 1999, Legacy award U. Tenn., 2004. Mem.: Am. Hist. Assn., Ctr. for Pub. Justice, So. Hist. Assn. (Simpson and Smith awards com. of the European history sect. 2001—, sec.-treas. European history sect. 2002—), Polish Inst. Arts and Sci., Am. Assn. for Advancement of Slavic Studies, Polish-Am. Hist. Assn. (exec. com. 1989—91, mem. editl. bd. 1991—93), UN Assn.-USA, Am. Hist. Assn., Phi Alpha Theta, Pi Delta Phi, Phi Kappa Phi. Presbyterian. E-mail: accarls@utm.edu.

CARLSEN, MARY BAIRD, clinical psychologist; b. Salt Lake City, Utah, Aug. 31, 1928; d. Jesse Hays and Susannah Amanda (Bragstad) Baird; m. James C. Carlsen, May 1, 1949; children: Philip, Douglas, Susan, Kristine. Student, St. Olaf Coll., 1946-47; BA, Whitworth Coll., 1950; MA, U. Conn., 1967; PhD, U. Wash., 1973. Profl. organist, piano tchr., Wash., Oreg., Ill., Conn., 1949-68; staff counselor Presbyn. Counseling Svc., Seattle, 1976-79; pvt. practice clin. psychologist, marriage therapist, cognitive, devel. psychology, career devel. Seattle, 1978-95; cons. creative aging Walla Walla, 1996—. Chmn. sr. adult adv. coun. Seattle Parks Dept., 1975-76; adv. bd. Northwest Ctr. for Creative Aging, 1995-98; mem. steering com. Quest Learning Inst., Walla Walla, Wash., 1997-2001, mem. faculty, 1997—; mem. nat. adv. bd. Ctr. for Creative Retirement, Asheville, N.C., 1998-2001. Author: Meaning-Making: Therapeutic Processes in Adult Development, 1988, Creative Aging: A Meaning-Making Perspective, 1991, 2d edit., 1996, Transformational Meaning-Making and the Practices of Career Counseling, 1991; contbr. chpts. to books and articles to profl. jours. Grantee PEO Rsch., 1972, U. Wash. Women's Guidance Ctr., 1972. Mem. AAUW, APA, Am. Soc. Aging, Nat. Coun. on Aging.

CARLSON, ALYSSA, literature and language educator; BA in English Lit. and Creative Writing, Loyola U., Chgo., 2002. Cert. tchr. English Ill. State Bd. Edn., 2002, Minn. State Bd. Edn., 2004. English tchr. Prosser Career Acad., Chgo., 2002—04, Pk. Ctr. H.S., Brooklyn Park, Minn., 2004—. Prep. instr. ACT/SAT Advantage Prep. Ednl. Svcs., 2004—; produced and assessed writing prompts Ill. Writing Test, 2003—04; profl. learning communities sch. facilitator Park Ctr. H.S., Brooklyn Park, Minn., 2005—06. Breast cancer fundraiser Pk. Ctr. H.S., Brooklyn Park, Minn., 2005. Recipient Tchg. award, Suave Corp. Orgn., 2002, Golden Apple Tchg. award, 2003. Office Phone: 763-569-7688. Personal E-mail: alyssamcarlson@yahoo.com.

CARLSON, CATHERINE KOSSAN, secondary school educator; b. Freeport, Pa., Oct. 26, 1933; d. Joseph Bill Kossan and Edith Thelma (Robinson) Hill; m. Leonard Merton Carlson, July 2, 1955; children: Sue Ann Carlson Fucilla, Richard Eugene, Laura Jean Carlson Bieritz. BS in Biology, Chemistry, English, Marion Coll., Ind., 1956. Cert. tchr. Ind., Mich., Tex., Conn. Tchr. Roseburg (Ind.) Elem. Sch., 1957—60, Litchfield (Mich.) Cmty. HS, 1962—63, Hillsdale (Mich.) Jr. HS, 1964—67, Bethel (Conn.) Mid. Sch., 1967—70, Naperville (Ill.) Ctrl. HS, 1972—79, Richardson (Tex.) Jr. HS, 1979—82, Parkhill Jr. HS, Dallas, 1982—2005; tchr., secondary sci. specialist Richardson Ind. Sch. Dist., 2005—. Presenter in field. Co-author: Holt Science Plus Blue Version, 1987. Leader Girl Scouts U.S.; life mem. PTA; mem. ch. coun., sec. Luth. Ch. Sci. Curriculum fellow, ASCD, 1992—95. Mem.: NEA, Tex. Assn. Biology Tchrs., Richardson Edn. Assn., Sci. Tchrs. Assn. Tex. (pres.), Nat. Sci. Tchrs. Assn. Republican. Avocation: travel. Home: 192 Belmont Ln Van Alstyne TX 75495 Office: Richardson Ind Sch Dist Richardson TX 75080 Personal E-mail: lmckcarl@earthlink.net.

CARLSON, CHERYL ANN, literature and language educator; d. James Robert and Sarah Louise Bybee; m. David Carlson, Aug. 7, 1976; children: James, Katherine Seifert. AA, Iowa Ctrl. C.C., Fort Dodge, 1976; BA Edn., Westmar Coll., LeMars, Iowa, 1976; MA Edn., U. St. Mary's, Mpls., 1995. Dir. curriculum Ind. Sch. Dist. #518, Worthington, 1990—95, tchr. secondary edn., 1977—. Author: Biography of Dr. Seuss, Biography of Charles Scultz. Mem. PEO, Worthington, 1972—2006. Finalist Tchr. of Yr., Worthington H.S., 2006; Mentor grant, Improving Instrn., Stds. Implementation, Minn. Dept Edn., 1990—95. Mem.: ASCD, Nat. Coun. Tchrs. English. Dfl. Lutheran. Avocations: travel, reading, writing, interior decorating, photography.

CARLSON, CYNTHIA JOANNE, artist, educator; b. Chgo. d. Ivan Morris and Ruth (Holmes) Carlson. BFA, Sch. Art Inst., Chgo., 1965; MFA, Pratt Inst., Bklyn., 1967. Instr. Phila. Coll. Art., 1967-72, U. Colo., Boulder, 1972-73; asst. prof. painting Phila. Coll. Art., 1973; assoc. prof. Phila Coll. Art., 1979-82; prof. Phila. Coll. Art., 1982-87, Queens Coll., CUNY, 1987—. One-woman shows include Allen Meml. Art Mus., Oberlin, Ohio, 1980, Milw. Art Mus., 1982, Pam Adler Gallery, N.Y.C., 1983, Albright-Knox Art Gallery, Buffalo, 1985, Queens Mus., Flushing, N.Y., 1990, Charles More Gallery, Phila., 1990—96, AIR Gallery, N.Y.C., 1992, Neuberger Mus., Purchase, N.Y., 1999, exhibited in group shows at Contemporary Art Ctr., Cin., 1980, Whitney Mus. Art, N.Y.C., 1980, Hayden Art Gallery, MIT, Cambridge, 1981, Jacksonville (Fla.) Art Mus., 1982, Represented in permanent collections Guggenheim Mus., N.Y.C., Bklyn. Mus. Art, Phila. Mus. Art, Richmond (Va.) Mus. Fine Arts, Denver Art Mus., Allen Meml. Art Mus., commn., L.A. Metro Rail Sys., 1992—93, Criminal Justice Ctr., Phila., Dept. Arts and Culture, 1995. Grantee, NEA, 1975, 1978, 1981, 1987, Creative Artists Pub. Svc., 1978. Home: 139 W 19th St New York NY 10011-4105 Office: CUNY Queens Coll Art Dept Klapper # 172 Flushing NY 11367-0904 Personal E-mail: ccarlson607@yahoo.com. Business E-Mail: ccynccyn@earthlink.net.

CARLSON, DALE BICK, writer; b. N.Y.C., May 24, 1935; d. Edgar M. and Estelle (Cohen) Bick; children: Daniel, Hannah. BA, Wellesley Coll., 1957. Lic. wildlife rehabilitator. Founder, pres. Bick Pub. House, 1993—. Founder, pres. Bick Pub. House, 1993—. Author young adult books, adult books, Perkins the Brain, 1964, The House of Perkins, 1965, Miss Maloo, 1966, The Brainstormers, 1966, Dracula, 1967, Frankenstein, 1968, The Electronic Teabowl, 1969, Warlord of the Genji, 1970, The Beggar King of China, 1971, The Mountain of Truth, 1972 (Spring Festival Honor book, named Am. Libr. Assn. Notable Book), Good Morning Danny, 1972, Hannah, 1972, The Human Apes, 1973 (named ALA Notable Book), Girls Are Equal Too, 1973;: 2d edit., 2000 (named ALA Notable Book), Baby Needs Shoes, 1974, Triple Boy, 1976, Where's Your Head?, 1971 (Christopher award), The Plant People, 1977, The Wild Heart, 1977, The Shinning Pool, 1979, Lovingsex for Both Sexes, 1979, Boys Have Feelings Too, 1980, Call Me Amanda, 1981, Manners That Matter, 1982, The Frog People, 1982, Charlie the Hero, 1983—85, The Jenny Dean Science Fiction Mysteries, The Mystery of the Shining Children, The Mystery of the Hidden Trap, The Secret of the Third Eye, The James Budd Mysteries, The Mystery of Galaxy Games, The Mystery of Operation Brain, 1985, Miss Mary's Husbands, 1988, Basic Manuals in Wildlife Rehabilitation, 6 vols., 1993—94, Basic Manuals for Friends of the Disabled Series, 1995—96, Living With Disabilities, 1997, Wildlife Care for Birds and Mammals, 1997, Stop the Pain: Mediations for Teenagers, 1998 (N.Y. Pub. Libr. Best Books, 2000), Confessions of a Brain-Impaired Writer: A Memoir, 1998; Stop the Pain: Adult Meditations, 2000; editor: What Are You Doing With Your Life, 2001, In and Out of Your Mind: Teen Science, Human Bites, 2002 (named Best Book, N.Y. Pub. Libr., 2003), Who Said What? Philosophy Quotes for Teens, 2003 (Voya Honor award, 2003), The Teen Brain Book, 2004 (Book of Yr. Bronze award Foreword Mag., 2004), Talk, Teen Art of Communication, 2006. Mem. Authors League Am., Authors Guild. Address: 307 Neck Rd Madison CT 06443-2755 Office: Agent Hagenbach-Bender 20 Gutenbergstrasse Bern Switzerland Business E-Mail: bickpubhse@aol.com.

CARLSON, DESIREE ANICE, pathologist; b. Clinton, Iowa, June 10, 1950; d. Donald Richard and Bernice Elfriede (Jacobs) C. MD, Duke U., 1975. Diplomate in anat. and clin. pathology, blood banking and cytopathology Am. Bd. Pathology. Resident in pathology U. Wash., Seattle, 1975-76, N.E. Deaconess Hosp., Boston, 1976-77, Peter Bent Brigham Hosp., Boston, 1977-79; pathologist W. Roxbury VA Med. Ctr., Boston, 1979-82; med. dir. blood bank Univ. Hosp., Boston, 1982-90; assoc. chief pathology N.E. Meml. Hosp., Stoneham, Mass., 1990-93; chief pathology Brockton (Mass.) Hosp., 1993—, sec., treas. med. staff, 2001—02, v.p. med. staff, 2003—04, pres. med. staff, 2005—. Asst. prof. pathology Boston U. Sch. Med., 1983—; cons. pathology Brigham and Women's Hosp., Boston, 1984-95; mem. adv. bd. ARC, Dedham, 1982-96. Contbr. chapters to books, articles to profl. jours. Recipient Outstanding Contbd. Article award Med. Lab. Observer, 1988. Mem. Coll. Am. Pathologists (N.E. regional commr. 1991—), Am. Med. Women's Assn., Am. Assn. Blood Banks, Mass. Med. Soc. (coms.), Mass. Pathology Soc., N.E. Pathology Soc. (sec. 1996-98, treas. 1998-2000, pres.-elect 2000-01, pres. 2001-02, joint sponsored activities coord. 2002-04). Republican. Presbyterian. Avocations: dance, aerobics. Office: Brockton Hosp 680 Centre St Brockton MA 02302-3395 Office Phone: 508-941-7321. Business E-Mail: dcarlson@brocktonhospital.org.

CARLSON, EILENE THERESA, counseling administrator; b. Jamestown, N.D., Feb. 21, 1948; d. Leonard Earl Ellis and Helen Elizabeth Ellis (Ness); m. C. Mauritz Carlson; children: Theresa Jenny (Carlson) Howatt, Erik Joshua. BS, ND State U., 1970; MS in Edn., No. State U., Aberdeen, SD, 2000. Cert. profl. school counselor State of ND Dept. of Edn., 2000. Substitute post master US Postal Svc., Sheyenne, ND, 1986—91; ins. agt./customer svc. Cmty. Credit Union, New Rockford, ND, 1991—98; counselor Four Winds Cmty. HS, Fort Totten, ND, 1998—. Recorder Career Tech. Edn. Adv. Bd., Fort Totten, ND, 1999. Vice chmn. Grace Luth. Ch., Sheyenne, ND, 1990—96. Mem.: ND Sch. Counseling Assn. Home: 2991 71st Ave NE Sheyenne ND 58374 Office: Four Winds Cmty HS PO Box 239 Fort Totten ND 58335 Office Phone: 701-766-1474. Home Fax: 701-766-1475.

CARLSON, ELIZABETH BORDEN, historian, educator; b. Fall River, Mass., Oct. 5, 1937; d. Richard and Elizabeth McGinley Borden; m. William C. Badger, Sept. 14, 1957 (div. July 1974); children: Christopher C. Badger, Lisa A. Badger; m. Robert F. Carlson, May 5, 1985. Student, Radcliffe Coll., Cambridge, Mass., 1955—57; BA cum laude, Harvard U., 1975; MA with honors, U. Calif., Santa Barbara, 1983, PhD with honors, 1988. Assoc. and contbg. editor The Carlisle Gazette, Mass., 1975—80; head pub. relations Gregory Fossella Assocs., Boston, 1978—80; tchr. Westmont Coll., Santa Barbara, Calif., 1986—90; pres. The Ednl. Design Found., Norwich, Vt., 1991—. Active Master Planning Com., Carlisle, Mass., 1974—78; Carlisle rep. Master Planning Com. of Greater Boston, 1978—80; bd. trustees Westmont Coll. Found., 2005—; pres. PTA, Carlisle, 1967—69; bd. dirs. The Fenn Sch., Concord, Mass., 1969—73. Mem.: Soc. of Archtl. Historians. Avocations: reading, birdwatching, tennis, swimming, skiing. Home: 502 Plaza Rubio Santa Barbara CA 93103 Office: The Ednl Design Found PO Box 25 66 Old Coach Rd Norwich VT 05055

CARLSON, HELEN LOUISE, educator; b. Duluth, Minn., Oct. 20, 1940; d. Erling Emil and Ethel Florence (Lindberg) Nelson; BS summa cum laude, U. Minn., 1961, MA, 1975; PhD, U. Minn., 1981; m. Gordon Jerome Carlson, Aug. 4, 1961; children: David J., Amy L., John D. Elem. tchr., pub. schs., Brockton, Mass., St. Paul and La Mesa, Calif., 1961-66; tchr. early child care provider, 1970-75; rsch. asst. U. Minn., Duluth, 1975-77, instr., 1977-81, asst. prof. profl. edn., 1981—, head dept. child and family devel., 1984-89, assoc. prof. child and family devel., 1986—, prof. dept. edn., 1991—; cons. St. Mary's Child Care Center, 1981-82, Midwest Regional Trainer Communication Model, 1982; bd. dir. Duluth Early Childhood Consortium, 1981-82; mem. adv. bd. Duluth Cmty. Schs. Parent and Family Life Programs, 1980-82, U. Minn. Duluth Child Care Center, 1980-82; mem. edn. adv. bd. Duluth Head Start, 1979-80; adv. bd. Dean's Grant, U.S. Office Edn., Nat. Coun. Social Studies, Early Childhood, State history curriculum devel. project; nat. grant peer reviewer, 1999—; presenter in field. Contbr. articles to profl. jours. and books. Grantee Ednl. Devel. Program, 1981-82, 82-87, 85-87, U. Minn., 1986-87, Northwest Area Found., Minn. Hist. Soc., 1989-90, Bush Found., 1990, Tech. in Edn., 2000-03. Instr. designer, interactive videodisc edn. core curriculum, 1985—. Mem. World Orgn. Early Childhood Edn., Nat. Assn. Edn. Young Children, Nat. Council Social Studies (nat. rsch. bd.), Internat. Coun. Edn. Tchrs., Minn. Assn. Edn. Young Children (sec. 2000-02), Phi Delta Kappa (research grantee 1978; treas. chpt. 1978-81, v.p. chpt. 1981-82), Alpha Delta Kappa (historian 2004-06). Office: U Minn 228 Montague Hall Duluth MN 55812 Home: 6615 Lake Shore Dr South 917 Richfield MN 55423 Business E-Mail: hcarlson@d.umn.edu.

CARLSON, JACQUELINE ANN, elementary school educator; b. Passaic, NJ, Dec. 4, 1943; d. Martha Elizabeth and Gerald Raymond Zeek; m. Steven Hilmer Carlson, Nov. 27, 1965; children: Kurt Erik, Kristofer David. BA, U. R.I., Kingston, 1965; MEd, R.I. Coll., Providence, 1992. Cert. elem. tchr. RI. 4th grade tchr. Quidnick-Anthony Sch., Coventry, RI, 1965—66, North Elem. Sch., Winston-Salem, NC, 1966—69; children's libr. N.Smithfield Pub. Libr., RI, 1986—92; 8th grade English tchr. N.Cumberland Mid. Sch., RI, 1994—. Pres. Friends of N.Smithfield Libr., 1987—95, Burrillville H.S. Band Boosters, RI, 1998—2001. Independent. Avocations: music, dance, reading, gardening, theater. Home: PO Box 223 27 Waterfront Cir Glendale RI 02826 Office Phone: 401-333-6306.

CARLSON, JANET FRANCES, psychologist, educator; b. Newport, RI, Oct. 3, 1957; d. Robert Carl and Alice Marion (Orina) Carlson; m. Kurt Francis Geisinger, Sept. 22, 1984. BS summa cum laude, Union Coll., Schenectady, 1979; MA in Clin. Psychology, Fordham U., 1982, PhD in Clin. Psychology, 1987. Lic. psychologist NY and Tex., cert. sch. psychologist NY. Clin. psychology intern Conn. Valley Hosp., Middletown, Conn., 1983-84; rsch. fellow Schering-Plough Found., Bronx, NY, 1984-85; psychologist I Creedmoor Psychiat. Ctr., Queens Village, NY, 1985-86; psychologist Hallen Sch., Mamaroneck, NY, 1986-88; asst. prof. psychology Fordham U., Bronx, NY, 1988-89; asst. prof. sch. and applied psychology Fairfield (Conn.) U., 1989-93, dir. sch. and applied psychology programs, 1989-90; from asst. prof. counseling and psychol. svcs. to prof. SUNY, Oswego, 1993—2002, assoc. dean Sch. Edn., 1998-2001; prof. psychology, head dept. gen. academics Tex. A&M U., Galveston, 2002—06. Cons. N.Y.C. Bd. Edn. Office Rsch., Evaluation and Assessment, 1988—92; vis. asst. prof. psychol. LeMoyne Coll., Syracuse, NY, 1992—93; dir. Office Tchg. Resources in Psychol., 2001—; vis. prof. ednl. psychology and psychology U. Nebr., Lincoln, 2006—. Recipient Sugarfree scholarship, 1984—85; grantee Sigma Xi, 1984—85. Fellow: APA; mem.: NASP, N.Y. Assn. Sch. Psychologists, Northeastern Ednl. Rsch. Assn. (ed newsletter 1988—91, bd dirs. 1990—93, pres. 1995—96), N.Y. State Psychol. Assn., Eastern Psychol. Assn., Am. Ednl. Rsch. Assn., Sigma Xi, Psi Chi, Phi Kappa Phi (pres. 1995—96). Avocations: wildlife preservation, conservation issues.

CARLSON, JEANNIE ANN, writer; b. Bklyn., Jan. 13, 1955; d. Lloyd Arthur and Ruth Frances (Riley) C.; m. Kenneth D. Williams, May 15, 1976 (div. 1981); 1 child, Carl Philip; m. H. Daniel Hopkins, Dec. 16, 1987 (div. 1994); m. Timothy R. Burns, Mar. 21, 1998. BA, Randolph-Macon Woman's Coll., 1977. Mktg./editing rep. Harris Pub., White Plains, NY, 1982; adminstrv. asst. Ray Fried Assocs., Inc., Eastchester, NY, 1980—84; proofreader Nat. Pennysaver, Elmsford, NY, 1983—84; chief writer Profl. Resume and Writing Svc., St. Petersburg, Fla., 1984—87; exec. writer, pres. Viking Comm., Inc., 1987—98; v.p. comm. Technifax Svcs. Inc., St. Petersburg, 1998—2001, exec. v.p., 2001—04; dir. comm. Nat. Risk Svcs. Inc., St. Petersburg, 2004—. Staff corr. Tampa Bay Newpapers Inc., Largo, 1998—; feature writer Asbury News, Crestwood, N.Y., 1983-84; editl. asst. Children's Rights Am., Largo, 1984; pub. rels. coord. The Renaissance Cultural Ctr., Clearwater, Fla., 1985; com. mem. work area on commn. Pasadena Cmty. Ch., St. Petersburg, 1986-88, 2000—, Christian edn. bd. Our Savior Luth. Ch., St. Petersburg, 1991-93; editl. advisor Grief Recovery Ctrs., Fla., 1992; columnist Believer's Bay Online mag., St. Petersburg, 2000-02 Recipient Golden Poet award World of Poetry, 1985, 88, 89, 91, 92, Silver Poet award, 1986, 90, Merit award, 1983 (2), 85, 87, 88 (2). 91, 92, Recognition award Nat. Soc. Poets, 1979, poetry awards Internat. Publs., 1976-77, Editor's Choice award Nat. Libr. Poetry, 1994, Woman of Yr. award ABI, 1995, 96, 97 Mem. Nat. League Am. Pen Women, Profl. Assn. Resume Writers, Phi Beta Gamma Methodist. Avocations: theater, culinary arts, music. Office: Nat Risk Svcs Inc 6170 Central Ave Ste 100 Saint Petersburg FL 33707

CARLSON, JENNIE PEASLACK, bank executive; b. Ft. Thomas, Ky., June 11, 1960; d. Roland A. and Shirley (Willen) Peaslack; m. Charles I. Michaels, Aug. 13, 1983 (div. May 1989); m. Richard A. Carlson, May 2, 1992. BA in English, Centre Coll., 1982; JD, Vanderbilt U., 1985. Bar: Ohio 1985, Minn. 2002. Atty. Taft, Stettinius & Hollister, Cin., 1985-91; sr. v.p., dep. gen. counsel Star Banc Corp., Cin., 1991—95; gen. counsel Star Bank Corp., Firstar Corp, 1995—2001; dep. gen. counsel U.S. Bancorp, 2001, exec. v.p., human resources Mpls., 2002—. Office: US Bancorp US Bancorp Ctr 800 Nicollet Mall Minneapolis MN 55402 Office Phone: 612-303-7699. E-mail: jennie.carlson@usbank.com.

CARLSON, JO ANNE, nurse; b. Emmetsburg, Iowa, July 23, 1932; d. Joseph Michael and Mary Victoria (Roper) McN. BSN, Briar Cliff Coll., 1956; MA, U. Redlands, Calif., 1979. Registered nurse. Pediatric supr. St. Joseph Mercy Hosp., Sioux City, Iowa, 1955-57; staff nurse Good Samaritan Hosp., West Palm Beach, Fla., 1957-58; psychiat. supr. Glenwood Hills Hosp., Mpls., 1958-61; surg. staff nurse VA Hosp., Mpls., 1961-62; pediatric nurse Mt. Sinai Hosp., Los Angeles, 1963-64, instr. inservice, 1964-69; instr. nursing Los Angeles Unified Sch., 1970-74; edn. coordinator Century City Hosp., Los Angeles, 1975-85; coordinator quality assurance Temple Community Hosp., L.A., 1986-91, dir. edn., 1986-91; sch. nurse L.A. Unified Schs., 1991—; ret., 2001. Mem.: Nat. Assn. Sch. Nurses, Philanthropist Ednl. Organization, L.A. Coun. Sch. Nurses, Calif. Sch. Nurse Orgn., Spina Bifida Assn., Calif. Sch. Nurse Assn. Democrat. Roman Catholic. Avocations: piano, golf, stamps, plates, poetry. Home: 15241 Via De Las Olas Pacific Palisades CA 90272 Office: La Unified School District PO Box 513307 Los Angeles CA 90051-1307

CARLSON, KATHLEEN BUSSART, law librarian; b. Charlotte, N.C., June 25, 1956; d. Dean Allyn and Joan (Parlette) Bussart; m. Gerald Mark Carlson, Aug. 15, 1987. BA in Polit. Sci., Ohio State U., 1977; JD, Capital U., 1980; MA in Libr. and Info. Sci., U. Iowa, 1986. Bar: Ohio (inactive) 1980. Editor Lawyers Coop. Pub. Co., Rochester, NY, 1980-83; asst. state law libr. State of Wyo., Cheyenne, 1987-88, state law libr., 1988—. 2d v.p., bd. dirs. Wyo. coun. Girl Scouts U.S., Casper, 1990—92, 1st v.p., bd. dirs., 1993—96; mem. bd. adjustment City of Cheyenne, 2001—, chair, 2006—. Mem.: Bibliog. Ctr. Rsch. (trustee 1991—95), Wyo. Libr. Assn. (sec. acad. and spl. librs. sect. 1990—92, pres. 1994—95), Western Pacific Assn. Law Librs. (pres. 1996—97, 2003—04), Am. Assn. Law Librs. (mem. edn. com. state and county librs. sect. 1991—92, sec.-treas. 1992—95, mem. indexing legal periodical lit. adv. com. 1993—96, chair 1994—96, mem. scholarship com. 1996—98, chair grants com. 1997—98, mem. nominating com. 1998—99, mem. citatition format com. 1998—2000, co-chair membership com., chair edn. com. 2000—01, mem. fair bus. practices com. 2000—04, mem. citatition format com. 2002—03, exec. bd. 2003—06), Zonta (pres. local club 2002—03), Beta Phi Mu, Kappa Delta. Avocations: arts and crafts, baking, travel. Home: 911 E 18th St Cheyenne WY 82001-4722 Office: State Law Libr 2301 Capitol Ave Cheyenne WY 82002-0001 Office Phone: 307-777-7509. Business E-Mail: kcarlson@courts.state.wy.us.

CARLSON, KAYE LILIEN, retired music educator; b. Mpls., Minn., July 23, 1947; d. Herbert Richard and Hilma Emma Hermann; m. Jerry Dale Carlson; children: Richard Dale, Sharon Kristine. BA, Augsburg Coll., Mpls., 1969; MusM, Mankato State U., 1980. Band dir. Anoka-Hennepin Ind. #11, Anoka, Minn., 1969—70, Fridley Mid. Sch., Fridley, Minn., 1970—, ret., 2003. Supr. student tchrs. Fridley Mid. Sch., 1970—, music dept. chairperson, 1987—94; chair. nat. rsch. com. Band Lit. List. Facilitator of after care groups St. Mary's Rehab. Ctr., Mpls., 1989—92; facilitator of student support groups Fridley Mid. Sch., Fridley, Minn., 1985—90. Mem.: NEA, Fridley Edn. Assn., Edn. Minn., Minn. Band Dirs. Assn., Music Educator's Nat. Conf., Am. Sch. Band Dirs. Assn. (past sec. of Minn. chpt., past state chair, panel moderator 1985). Avocations: reading, travel. Home: 1690 Canyon Ln New Brighton MN 55112 Personal E-mail: jerrykaye@hotmail.com.

CARLSON, LINDA MARIE, language arts educator, consultant; BS in English and Polit. Sci., U. Minn., Duluth, 1973, MEd in Rhetorical Theory, 1979; MBA, U. St. Thomas, 1987; postgrad., Rensselaer Poly. Inst., 1992—. Cert. Myers-Briggs Type Indicator adminstrn., cert. tchr., Minn. Tchr. English, curriculum leader Ind. Sch. Dist. 13, Columbia Heights, Minn., 1973-76, publs. advisor, coach, 1974-76; exec. asst. to provost Univ. Minn., Duluth, 1977-80; tech. editor EG and G (U.S. Dept. Energy), Idaho Falls, Idaho, 1980; tchr. English, gifted and talented Ind. Sch. Dist. 11, Coon Rapids, Minn., 1980—, lang. arts curriculum developer, 1981—, publs. advisor, 1982-84, learning styles cons., 1986—, assessment cons., 1989—. Performance assessment cons. Minn. State Dept. Edn., St. Paul, 1990-98; writing assessment cons. Minn. State Graduation Rule Pilot Site, St. Paul, 1994-98; lang. arts cons., curriculum design cons., multicultural cons. pvt. and pub. schs. Minn., 1987—. Mem. Minn. Arthritis Found., St. Paul, 1981-90, Commn. on Health and Healing, Mpls., 1984-86. Recipient Golden Apple Teaching award Ashland Oil Co., 1994; All-Univ. scholar Rensselaer Poly. Inst., 1992. Mem. NEA, ASCD, Am. Ednl. Rsch. Assn., Nat. Coun. for Tchrs. of English, Anoka-Hennepin Edn. Assn. (pub. rels. com. 1980-85). Avocations: jewelry making, hiking, white-water rafting, travel. Home: 11117 Cottonwood St NW Coon Rapids MN 55448-3385

CARLSON, LIZABETH LEN, nursing educator, dean; b. Pocahontas, Ark., Dec. 22, 1953; d. Jerry Stephen and Hermena Jewell Manes; m. Cyril A. Bishop, May 4, 1972 (dec. July 12, 1983); 1 child, Stephen Robert Bishop; m. Terry Carlson, Feb. 14, 1986. ADN, Mo. State U., 1985, BSN, 1989; MSN, U. Ala., 1994; Dr. in Nursing Sci., La. State U., 2003. LPN, South Cen. VoTech Ctr., 1981, RN inpatient OB, Miss., Nurses Credentialing Corp., 1985. Staff nurse Baxter Med. Ctr., Mountain Home, Ark., 1986—87; office nurse Gen. Med. Ctr., Springfield, Mo., 1988—89; nurse officer, capt. USAF, Keesler Air Force Base, Miss., 1989—95; staff nurse Ozark Med. Ctr., West Plains, Mo., 1992—96; instr. nursing U. So. Miss., Hattiesburg, 1995—95, Copiah Lincoln C.C., Wesson, 1995—98; asst. prof. nursing Delta State U., Cleveland, Miss., 1998—2003, assoc. prof. nursing, 2003—04, dean nursing, 2004—. Cons. Hurst Rev. Svcs., Brookhaven, Miss., 1998—99; presenter various profl. confs. Author: (OB review questions) Davis's Q & A for the NCLEX-RN, 1998; contbr. articles to profl. jours., chapters to books. Capt. Air Force USAF, 1989—95. Named 2nd Counsel Nursing Honor Soc., Delta State U. Sch. Nursing, 1999—2000, Dean of Yr., Miss. Student Nurses Assn., 2005—06; named to Nursing Honor Soc., Delta State U. Sch. Nursing, 1999—2000; recipient Innovations In Health Regional award, SW Mo. State U., 1989, recognition for contbns. to women's health, Keesler AFB Health Promotion Com., 1993, Student Advocacy award, Delta State U. Sr. Nursing Class, 2000. Mem.: Mo. Nurses Assn., Miss. Nurses Assn., Miss. Perinatal Assn., Assn. for Women's Health, Obstetric and Neonatal Nursing, Nightengale Soc. (hon.), Phi Beta Kappa, Sigma Theta Tau (pres.-elect 2000—02, pres. 2002—04, Pi Xi chpt.). Liberal. Methodist. Achievements include design of fabric pregnancy and postpartum model. Avocations: reading, gardening. Office: Delta State U Sch Nursing 1003 W Sunflower Rd Cleveland MS 38733 Office Phone: 662-846-4268. Business E-Mail: lcarlson@deltastate.edu.

CARLSON, MARIAN BILLE, geneticist, researcher, educator; b. Princeton, N.J., Oct. 19, 1952; d. B.C. and L.W. Carlson; m. Stephen P. Goff, Oct. 15, 1977; children: Sarah Carlson, Thomas Carlson. BA summa cum laude, Harvard U., 1973; PhD with distinction, Stanford U., 1978. Asst. prof. genetics Columbia U., N.Y.C., 1981-87, assoc. prof., 1987-88, prof., 1988—, prof. microbiology, 1991—, sr. assoc. dean for rsch., 2005. Mem. genetic basis of disease rev. com. NIH, 1991-95; mem. sci. adv. com. Damon Runyan-Walter Winchell Cancer Rsch. Fund, 1992-96. Assoc. editor Genetics. 1988-95, 97-99; mem. editl. bd. Molecular and Cellular Biology, 1987-2004, Cell Metabolsim, 2005, Current Opinion in Genetics and Devel., 1991—, editor, 97-2003, Microbiol. and Molecular Biol. Rev.; contbr. chpts. to books, articles to profl. jours. Mem. basic sci. adv. com. March of Dimes, 1993-95, mem. sci. adv. coun., 1996—; coun. mem. Harvey Soc., 1998-2001. NSF fellow, 1973-76, Jane Coffin Childs fellow, 1976-81; recipient Irma T. Hirschl Career Sci. award, 1982-87, Lamport award for basic rsch. Columbia U., 1987, Faculty Rsch. award Am. Cancer Soc., 1988-92, NIH Merit award, 1996. Fellow AAAS, Am. Acad. Microbiology, Am. Acad. Arts & Sci.; mem. Genetics Soc. Am. (bd. dirs. 1994-96, v.p. 2000, pres. 2001), Am. Soc. Microbiology (lectr. ASM Found. for Microbiology 1990-91), Phi Beta Kappa, Sigma Xi. Office: Columbia U 701 W 168th St New York NY 10032-2704 Office Phone: 212-305-6314. Business E-Mail: mbc1@columbia.edu.

CARLSON, NATALIE TRAYLOR, publisher; b. St. Paul, Feb. 15, 1938; d. Howard Ripley and Maxine Smith; m. James S. Carlson, Oct. 6, 1990; children: Drew Michael, Dacia Lyn, Dana Ann. BA with honors, Jacksonville (Ala.) State U., 1975. Dir. Madison County Assn. of Mental Health, Huntsville, Ala., 1966-67; campaign mgr. U.S. Senatorial Race, No. Ala., 1968; pub. rels. Anniston Acad., 1970-76; journalist The Anniston Star, 1970-74, The Birmingham News, 1972-76; dir. Ala. affiliate, Am. Heart Assn., Birmingham, 1976-77; mgr. San Vincent New Home div., San Diego County Estates Realty, 1978-79; dir. sales Blake Pub. Co., San Diego, 1980-86; CEO, owner Century Publ., San Diego, 1986—. Alternate del. at large Rep. Nat. Conv., San Francisco, 1964; fin. chmn. Madison County Rep. Exec. Com., Huntsville, Ala., 1966-69; pres. Madison County Rep. Women, Huntsville, 1967, 68; Diocesan Conv. del. Grace Episcopal Ch., Ala., 1975; active Nat. Rep. Party, 1962—; mem. St. James Episcopal Ch., Newport Beach, 1990—, mem. scholarship com., mem. welcomer's com.; mem. Nat. Rep. Pres.'s Club, 1996-97, 2000, 2001, 04. Recipient 1st Pl. AP Newswriting award, 1971, 72, 73, 1st place So. Heart Assn. Profl. Staff award for profl. paper Am. Heart Assn., 1977; nominee Outstanding Woman of Yr., Huntsville Area Jaycees, 1967. Mem. Am. C. of C. (47 Comm. Excellence awards, 2000-06), Long Beach Area C. of C., Palm Springs C. of C. (Spl. Svc. plaque), Glendale C. of C., Huntington Beach C. of C. (Nat. Athena award 2004), Redding C. of C., Santa Clarita Valley C. of C., Santa Rosa C. of C., Walnut Creek C. of C., Newport Beach C. of C., Yuma County C. of C., Ariz, Soroptimist Internat. (rec. sec. Huntington Beach 2001, co-chair charity holiday gala, 1998), Kappa Kappa Gamma. Avocations: boating, reading, travel.

CARLSON, NORA, elementary school educator; b. Pasadena, Calif., Apr. 5, 1956; d. Charles T. and Geraldine (Wood) C. BA, Wash. State U., 1978; MEd, Eastern Wash. U., 1981. Cert. elem. edn., spl. edn., Wash. Elem. tchr. Marysville (Wash.) Sch. Dist., 1978—99, Edmonds Sch. Dist., 1999—2000, Northshore Sch. Dist., 2000—. Recipient Golden Acorn award, PTSA. Mem. Alpha Delta Kappa. Personal E-mail: ndcarlson.56@hotmail.com.

CARLSON, STACY C., former motion picture association executive; b. Burbank, Calif., Sept. 6, 1960; BA in Econ., Calif. State U., 1982; MBA, Stanford U., 1988. Legis. asst. to Rep. Bill Thomas, 1982-84; chief of staff Kern County Bd. Suprs., 1984-86; various positions including sr. v.p. strategic planning and spl. projects Silicon Valley Bank, Santa Clara, Calif., 1989-93; minority staff dir. Com. House Adminstrn., 1993-94; staff dir. Com. House Oversight, 1995—97; mng. dir. emerging growth divsn. Imperial Bank (now Comerica), 1997—99; sr. advisor for pub. law & policy Akin, Gump, Strauss, Hauer & Feld, LLP, 1999—2004; dir. Washington DC office Office Gov. Calif., 2004; exec. v.p. govt. affairs Motion Picture Assn. Am., Encino, Calif., 2005.

CARLSON, SUZANNE OLIVE, architect; b. Worcester, Mass., Aug. 20, 1939; d. Sigfrid and Helga (Larson) C. BS, RI Sch. Design, 1963. Jr. ptnr. Dingnam-Fauteux & Ptnrs., Worcester, 1969-70; ptnr. Richard Lamoureux Assoc., Worcester, 1970-75, Herron & Carlson (AIA), Worcester, 1975-96; arch. Edgecomb, Maine, 1997—. Guest lectr. Holy Cross Coll., 1969-70. Chmn. Worcester Hist. Commn., 1976-88; trustee Worcester Heritage Soc., 1982-88, Park Spirit of Worcester Inc., 1987—, Friends of Ft. Edgecomb, 2005-; v.p. Lincoln County Hist. Assn., 2001—; trustee Worcester Girls Inc. of Worcester, pres. 1989-92, 95-2002, sec. 1994-95; trustee Performing Arts Sch. Worcester, 1977-86, v.p. 1980-85; trustee Cultural Assembly Greater Worcester, 1981-86, v.p., 1982-83; pres. Edgecomb Hist. Soc., 1997—. Recipient European Honors Program grant Rome, Italy, 1961-62; recipient AIA School medal for excellence, 1963. Mem. AIA (exec. bd. Ctrl. Mass. chpt. 1969-71, sec.-treas. 1970-71, v.p. 1971-72, pres. 1972-73), Mass. Soc. Archs. (exec. bd. 1972-74, v.p. 1975, pres. 1976), New Eng. Regional Coun. Archs. (pres. 1977), New Eng. Antiquities Rsch. Assn. (membership chair 1982-84, 90-94, resource devel. chair 1994—, graphics dir. jours. 1982—, publs. chair 1995—, trustee 1990—). Home and Office: Suzanne O Carlson Architect 94 Cross Point Rd Edgecomb ME 04556-3208 Office Phone: 207-882-8155. E-mail: krosspt@lincoln.midcoast.com.

CARLSON-JUKES, HOLLY ANN, social studies educator; b. Kansas City, Mo., Dec. 31, 1970; d. Ronald Dean Carlson and Patricia Ann Brady; m. James Jukes, Aug. 23, 1996. AA, Johnson County C.C., Cleveland Park, 1995; BA in History, BA in History, U. Mo. Kansas City, 2000. 9th grade tchr. Imagine Sch., Kansas City, 2003—05; 7th grade tchr. Raytown Sch. Dist., Mo., 2005—. Sec. Frank Rushton Neighborhood Assn., 2005—. Mem.: Greater Kansas City Coun. for the Social Studies, U. Mo. Alumni Assn. Avocations: gardening, reading. Home: 2610 W. 45th Ave Kansas City KS 66103

(CARLSON)RENO, ARLETTA LOU, administrative assistant; b. Columbus, Ohio, June 21, 1943; d. William Louis Carlson, Sr. and Gladys Arletta (Syverud)Carlson; m. Glen Edward Reno, Sr., Oct. 21, 1961 (dec. May 22, 1999); children: Susan Gayle Reno, Glen Edward Reno, Jr., Tara Lynn (Reno)Riordan. Cert. Flight Attendant, McConnell Airline Sch., Mpls., 1961. Clk. Crop & Shop, Metuchen, NJ, 2004—; sec. St. Peter's Episc.l Ch., Perth Amboy, NJ, 2005—. Employment cons. Gene Rogers Assocs., Metuchen, NJ, 1976—79. Keywoman NJ Jaycee-ettes, Metuchen, NJ, 1965—77. Recipient Keywomen aAward, NJ Jaycee-ettes, 1977. Episcopalian. Home: 13 Monaghan Rd Edison NJ 08817-4121 Office: St Peter's Episcopal Church 183 Rector St Perth Amboy NJ 08861 Office Phone: 732-826-1594.

CARLSON-RUKAVINA, PATRICIA ANN, small business owner; b. St. Paul, Minn., Oct. 9, 1945; d. Frank Ludomil and Bertha Mahala (Patterson) Loss; m. Thomas Arnold Carlson (div.); children: Christina Marie Carlson Shadwick, Erick Michael Carlson; m. Carl Robert Rukavina, Sept. 6, 1980. BA, Sch. of Associated Arts, 1978. Lic. cosmetology Oliver Thein Beauty Sch., 1970, diploma Mind Control Inst. Inc., 1972, cert. honorary Rufus Hays cert. Acad. of Hairdressing, 1970, lic. life insur. Minn. State Bd. Insurance agent Western Fraternal Life Assoc., Cedar Rapid, Iowa, 1984—87; sales assoc. Host Internat., Mpls./St Paul, Minn., 1987—88; owner 1st Impressions Photography, St. Paul, 1989—91; sales Avon, 1987—91, Herbalife Internat., Los Angeles, Calif., 2001—03; sales assoc. Silver Gallery, Colo., 1980—2004; owner, artist Lone Bird Studio, St. Paul, 1991—. Asst. dir. Minn. State Fine Arts Bd., St. Paul, 1979; art tchr. Guadalupe Primary Sch., Puerto Vallarta, Mexico, 1978. Exhibitions include visual arts Just for the Season Gallery, 2004—05, Represented in permanent collections Minn. Mus. Art. Disaster response team Am. Red Cross, St. Paul, 1998; fund raiser Naomi House Woman's Shelter, St. Paul, 1991; fund raiser, trade ambassador Minn. World Trade Ctr., St. Paul, 1986; fundraiser, participant Minn. Leukemia Soc. Marathon, 1996; deaconess Park Baptist Ch., St. Paul, 1980. Mem.: Mpls. Inst. Art, Minn. Inst. Art, Sokol Minn. (delegate 1995—), ZCBJ Lodge #69 Orel-Western Fraternal Life (treas. 1994—). Baptist. Avocations: reading, gardening, travel, sports, religion.

CARLSON-SWEET, KIM LYNETTE, dermatologist; b. Loma Linda, Calif., Sept. 3, 1967; d. Loren Edward and Joanne Carolyn Carlson; m. Clifford Franklin Sweet, III, June 4, 1993; children: Fiona Caroline Sweet, Oliver Martin Sweet. MD, Loma Linda U. Sch. Medicine, Calif., 1993. Diplomate Am. Bd. Dermatology, 2004. Fellow dermatology clin. rsch. U. Okla., Okla. City, 1998—2000, clin. instr. dermatology, 2000—01, resident dermatology, 2001—04; dermatologist Permanente Med. Group, Santa Rosa, Calif., 2006—. Author: (book chpt.) Textbook of Dermatapathology, 2004. Vol. physician No. Calif. Flood Relief Actions, Sacramento, 1997, Bapt. Med. Ctr. Free Clinic, Okla. City, 1999—; tuition support for children in Ctrl. Am. Project Share, 1992—. Maj. USAF, 1993—98, Tex., Calif. Recipient Humanitarian award, USAF, Sacramento, 1998. Fellow: Am. Acad. Dermatology; mem.: AMA. Democrat. Seventh-Day Adventist. Avocations: cooking, interior decorating, hiking. Office: Kaiser Permanente 401 Bicentennial Way Santa Rosa CA 95403

CARLTON, HEIDI LEE, pianist, music educator; b. Fresh Meadows, N.Y., Aug. 10, 1951; d. Alan J. and Elizabeth B. Lee; m. Edmund Everett Carlton, Sept. 9, 1979; children: Vanessa, Gwendolyn, Edmund. Student, Hofstra U., 1971, Fairleigh Dickinson, 1973; BA, Ramapo Coll., 1974. Pianist, educator Heidi Lee Carlton Sch. Music, Shohola, Pa., 1976—; music tchr. Homestead Sch., Glen Spey, N.Y., 1993—. Mem. Milford Garden Club. Office: Heidi Lee Carlton Sch Music 140 Maple Dr Shohola PA 18458-4111 Home: RR 1 Box 1330 Maple Dr Shohola PA 18458

CARLTON, ROBBIN BRILEY, elementary school educator; b. South Boston, Va., Jan. 22, 1973; d. David Clifton and Gwen Godwin Briley; m. Daniel Ray Carlton, June 26, 1999; children: Dillon Ray, Madison Lynn. BS in Elem. Edn., E.Carolina U., Greenville, NC, 1997, MEd in Instrnl. Tech., 2004. Tchr. 6th grade lang. arts & math / 7th grade sci. S.W. Snowden Elem. Sch., Beaufort County Schs., Aurora, NC, 1997—99; tchr. 5th grade North Rowan Elem. Sch., Rowan-Salisbury Schs., Spencer, NC, 1999—2002; tchr. 7th / 8th grade math and sci. Extended Day Sch., Davidson County Schs., Lexington, NC, 2002—. Named North Rowan Elem. Tchr. of Yr., Rowan-Salsibury Sch. Sys., 2001—02, Extended Day Sch. Tchr. of Yr., Davidson County Schs., 2004—05; Mini-Grant Winner Ecosystems in Our Own Backyard, Title VI, 2001—02, Project Based Learning Grant Team, Davidson County Schs. / Buck Inst., 2002—03. Mem.: NSTA (assoc.), Nat. Coun. Tchrs. Math. (assoc.), N.C. Assn. Educators (assoc.). Methodist. Achievements include Middle School Conference Committee Member - Current; Chair, Project Wild 1998-1999; Assistant Coach, Girls Volleyball Team 1997-1999; Yearbook Committee 1998-1999; Mentor / Lead Mentor - Extended Day School - Current; Technology Leadership Team - Extended Day School - Current; NCETC Technology Showcase Presenter - 2000-2001, Representing Rowan-Salsibury Schools; Grade Level Chairperson 2000-2002; Point of Contact for the National Science Education Standards K-5 1999-2002; Science Fair Committee 1997-2002; Chair, School Climate Committee (SACS) 1998-1999; Chair, Science Olympiad 1997-1999. Avocations: arts & crafts, photography, web page design, reading, cooking. Home: 163 O'Farrell Street Winston Salem NC 27107 Office: Extended Day School 2065 E Holly Grove Road Lexington NC 27292 Office Phone: 336-242-1459. Office Fax: 336-242-1456. E-mail: rcarlton@davidson.k12.nc.us.

CARLUCCI, MARIE ANN, nursing administrator, consultant; b. N.Y.C., Apr. 22, 1953; d. Clarence Hugh and Anna Rebecca (Mills) McNamee; m. Paul Pasquale Carlucci, Aug. 18, 1973; children: Christine, Patricia. Diploma in nursing, Mt. Vernon Hosp. Sch. Nursing, N.Y., 1974; BS in Behavioral Sci. summa cum laude, Mercy Coll., 1991; MPH, N.Y. Med. Coll., 1997. Cert. emergency nurse; cert. nurse adminstr.; lic. healthcare risk mgr.; cert. legal cons. Staff nurse Mt. Vernon (N.Y.) Hosp., 1974-82, Lawrence Hosp., Bronxville, N.Y., 1982-84, No. Westchester Hosp., Mt. Kisco, N.Y., 1984-91, asst. dir. nursing, mem. nurse mgmt. and ethics coms., 1991-94; asst. DON svcs. Ferncliff Manor, Yonkers, N.Y., 1994-95, dir. nursing svcs., 1995-97; dep. dir. nursing svcs. Taylor Care Ctr., Westchester, N.Y., 1997-2000; dir. residential svcs. Hillsborough (Fla.) Assn. for Retarded Citizens, 2000; dir. nursing Am. Retirement Corp., Sun City Center, Fla., 2000—01; med.-legal nurse cons., 2001—. Religious edn. tchr. St. John and St. Mary's Ch., Chappagua, N.Y., 1984-99; campaign mgr. Com. to Elect Paul P. Carlucci, Chappagua, 1990; mem. Surrogate Decision Making Com., N.Y. Commn. Quality Care for Mentally Disabled; mem. bd. trustees Field Home-Holy Comforter, 1995-99; guardian ad litem 13th Judical Cir., Tampa, Fla., 2000—; bd. adv. Hillsborough County Children's Svcs., 2002-. Mem.: Phi Gamma Mu, Psi Chi. Roman Catholic. Home: 3916 Appletree Dr Valrico FL 33594-4315

CARLYLE, BOBBIE KRISTINE, sculptor; b. Idaho, 1948; d. Howard and Ethel Seelos Carlyle; children: K. Justin Lawyer, Jennifer Crosby, Jared Lawyer, Jessika Tora, Joshua Lawyer, Jacob Lawyer, Jonas Lawyer. BFA, Brigham Young U., Provo, Utah, 1989. Sculptor Bobbie Carlyle Sculpture Studios, Loveland, Colo., 1967—. Sculptor (bronze sculpture) Diadems, Buffalo Soldier, Day's Catch, Chief's Daughter, For Love of the Game, Endeavor, Yield Curve, Balance and Harmony, Espirit de Corps, The Fabric of Her Soul, Stretch the Limits, Descent Into Night, Hard to Leave, Hunter, In Progress, Jennifer, Lorelei, Moses, Mounting Relief, On the Brink of Tomorrow, One Point Landing, Pace the Wind, Phoenix Rising, Priority Mail, Puppy Dog Tales, Reeds, Self Made Woman, Storyteller, Sunriser, Self Made Man, Upper Limits, La Vendemia, Aviator, Puppy Dog Tales, #1 Handicap, A State of Grace, Ariel, At The Well. Recipient Ettel Grant award, Allied Artists of Am., 1990. Mem.: Nat. Sculpture Soc. Office Phone: 970-622-0213. Personal E-mail: bobbiecarlyle@att.net.

CARMACK, MILDRED JEAN, retired lawyer; b. Folsom, Calif., Sept. 3, 1938; d. Kermit Leroy Brown and Elsie Imogene (Johnston) Walker; m. Allan W. Carmack, 1957 (div. 1979); 1 child, Kerry Jean Carmack Garrett. Student, Linfield Coll., 1955-58; BA, U. Oreg., 1967, JD, 1969. Bar: Oreg. 1969, U.S. Dist. Ct. Oreg. 1980, U.S. Ct. Appeals (9th and fed. cirs.) 1980, U. S. Claims Ct. 1987. Law clk. to Hon. William McAllister Oreg. Supreme Ct., Salem, 1969-73, asst. to ct., 1976-80; asst. prof. U. Oreg. Law Sch., Eugene, 1973-76; assoc. Schwabe, Williamson & Wyatt, Portland, Oreg., 1980-83, ptnr., 1984-96, ret., 1996. Writer, lectr., legal educator, Oreg., 1969—; mem. exec. bd. Appellate sect. Oreg. State Bar, 1993-95. Contbr. articles to Oreg. Law Rev., 1967-70. Mem. citizen adv. com. State Coastal Planning Commn., Oreg., 1974-76, State Senate Judiciary Com., Oreg., 1984; mem. bd. visitors Law Sch. U. Oreg., 1992-95; mem. Oreg. Law Commn. Working Group on Conflict of Laws, 2000. Mem. Oreg. State Bar Assn., Order of Coif.

CARMACK, MONA, library administrator; b. Deadwood, SD, May 10, 1940; d. Clarence Olen and Alice Etta (Merow) Mooney; divorced; children: Cheryl Swanson, Ann Bremer, Sara Heath. BSc, No. State U., 1962; MLS,

Western Mich. U., 1969. Head libr. Brookings Pub. Libr., SD, 1969—75; dir. Ames Pub. Libr., Iowa, 1975—80, Gt. River Regional Libr., St. Cloud, Minn., 1980—88; county libr. Johnson County Libr., Overland Park, Kans., 1988—. Pres. SD Libr. Assn., 1973, Minn. Libr. Assn., 1988. Mem.: ALA (coun. mem.), Mountain Plains Libr. Assn. (Disting. Svc. award 2003), Kans. Libr. Assn. (chair legis. com. 2001—03, Presdl. award 2003), Overland Pk. Rotary Found. (sec. 2004—, Paul Harris fellow). Avocations: photography, travel, history. Office: Johnson County Libr 9875 W 87th St Overland Park KS 66201 Business E-Mail: carmackm@jocolibrary.org.

CARMAN, KAM, announcer; b. Phoenix; m. David Kramer; children: Kellan Charles Kramer, Jacquelyn Casey Kramer 1 stepchild, Courtlandt Kramer. Grad., No. Ariz. U. News/weather anchor KNAZ-TV, Flagstaff, Ariz.; on-camer, meteorologist Weather Channel, Atlanta; meteorologist Jim Harper and The Breakfast Club, WNIC-FM Radio, Detroit; weathercaster WJBK-TV, Detroit, co-anchor New Morning, 2000—01, morning weathercaster, 2001—02, co-anchor New Morning 5am, 2002—, co-anchor News at Noon. Office: WJBK Fox 2 PO Box 2000 Southfield MI 48037-2000

CARMAN, MARY ANN, retired special education educator; b. Kerrville, Tex., July 12, 1941; d. William Earl and Virginia (Tracy) Gregg; m. Douglas Gary Carman, July 20, 1968; 1 child, Christina Tracy. BA in Psychology, So. Meth. U., 1959-63; MS in Spl. Edn., East Tex. State U., 1971. Cert. spl. edn. tchr., Iowa; teaching credential, Tex. Salesperson James K. Wilson Clothing Store, Dallas, 1963; sec. psychology dept. So. Meth. U., Dallas, 1964; EEG technician Dr. Paul Levin, Neurologist, Dallas, 1965-68; sec. geography dept. E. Tex. State U., Commerce, 1968-70; tchr. pilot program early childhood edn. Farmers Br. (Tex.) Sch. Dist., 1971; chair dept. spl. edn. U. Dubuque, Iowa, 1972-75; tchr.'s aide Crockett Elem. Sch., San Marcos, Tex., 1978, 79; spl. edn. tchr. Travis Elem. Sch., San Marcos, 1980—2000, ropes course facilitator campus improvemnt team, 1994-95, tchr. class-within-a-class 2d and 3d gr. levels, presenter project math 2d gr. campus improvement team, ropes course facilitator, 1995-96, tchr. total inclusion class within a class, 1997—2000; ret., 2000. Mem. dist. ednl. improvement coun. San Marcos Consol. Ind. Sch. Dist., 1991, participant strategic planning workshop, 1991, learning styles tng. course, 1992, chmn. sight based mgmt. team, 1991; facilitator ROPES course, 1993. Winant vol. Epsicopal Ch., E. India Dock, London, 1963; coach state meet Spl. Olympics team San Marcos Consol. Ind. Sch. Dist., 1981, ofcl. at state games, 1988; facilitator exptl. edn. TRUST (Teamwork, Responsibility, Understanding for Students and Tchrs.), cert. ropes course facilitator Highs, Lows, and Handicapped, 1993; key vol. Spl. Olympics, 2003, 04. Recipient 1st place Bill Gray award Tex. Assn. Bus., The Spl. Kid's Co., 1991, Teaching Excellence award Lions Club San Marcos, 1991. Mem. ASCD, Phi Delta Kappa. Home: 817 Willow Creek Cir San Marcos TX 78666-5061

CARMAN, MARY ANN, realtor, writer, retired medical/surgical nurse; b. Wichita, Kans., Jan. 5, 1953; d. Herbert William and Alberdine Esther Kumba; m. Randy Paul Carman, Apr. 8, 1972 (div. Sept. 27, 1990); children: Chad William, Kenneth Franklin. AA, San Bernadino Valley Coll., 1980; AS in Nursing, SUNY, 1993. Lic. practical nurse, Calif., 1980; Realtor 2003. Disaster team mgr. ARC / BSA Explorer Post, Albuquerque, 1982—84; nurse Veterans Med. Ctr., Tucson, 1990—2001; fiction author self employed, 1998—; REALTOR Long Realty Co., 2003—04; realtor Real Estate Mktg. Profls., Tucson, 2004—. Author: Never To Love. Mem. Nat. Writers Union, Tucson, 2002—03. Mem.: Women's Coun. REALTORS Tech., Tucson Assn. REALTORS (fair & affordable housing com. 2003—04), Ariz. Assn. REALTORS, Nat. Assn. REALTORS, Ariz. Author's Assn., Soc. Southwestern Author's, Romance Writers Am. Avocations: writing, reading, travel. Office: Real Estate Mktg Profls Tucson 2462-1 N Pantano Rd Tucson AZ 85715 Personal E-mail: maryann@maryanncarman.com. E-mail: maryann@mywordsworth.com.

CARMAN, SUSAN HUFERT, nurse coordinator; b. Detroit, Oct. 2, 1940; d. Theodore Louis and Margaret L. (O'Connor) Hufert; children: Amy E., Holly C., John T. BSN, Johns Hopkins U., 1964; MEd, Northeastern U., 1975; MS in Health Care Adminstrn., Simmons Coll., 1988. Instr. psychiat. nursing Salem (Mass.) Hosp. Sch. Nursing, 1975-78, Curry Coll., Milton, Mass., 1978-80; editor Beacon Comm. Corp., Acton, Mass., 1980-84; writer health promotion Honeywell Inc., Waltham, Mass., 1984-85; mgr. mental health unit Heritage Hosp., Somerville, Mass., 1986-87; specialist adult psychiatry Mass. Dept. Mental Health, Boston, 1987-93; clinician intensive clin. svcs. MHMA, Boston, 1994-96; dir. Arbour Counseling Svcs. Boston, 1996—. With SHC Assocs., Boston, 1993—; bd. dirs. Com. to End Elder Homelessness, Boston, Mass., 1993-99; bd. dirs. Dept. Social Svcs., Lowell, sec., 1982-92. Chair health planning com. Jamaica Plain (Mass.) Tree of Life/Arbol da Vida, 1994—2003; docent Arnold Arboretum, Boston, 1989—2000; founding mem. Boston Coalition for Promotion of Child and Adolescent Mental Health, 2000—; bd. dirs. First Steps/Health Families, Jamaica Plain, 1998—2002, Match-Up Interfaith, Boston, 2001—; chmn. Jamaic Plain Domestic Violence Provider Network, 2001. Mem. ANA. Avocations: travel, reading, walking, classical music.

CARMICHAEL, SALLY W., volunteer; b. Jackson, Ms., Jan. 14, 1925; d. Benton McMillin and Adele Rhodes Wakefield; m. Charles Ellis Carmichael; children: Chris, Charles E. Jr. Student, Hollins U., Roanoke, Va., 1942—44; BA in Sociology, U. Ga., Athens, 1946. With Ms. Sch. Supply Co.; radio commentator. Advisor Miss. Childrens Mus., 2004—06; pres. Miss. Symphony Found., 1986, sec., 1990—2005; bd. govs. Miss. Symphony Orch., 1974—83, 1985—2001, sec., 1976, search com., 2000; pres. Jackson Symphony League, 1974, bd. dirs., 1974—2005; exec. v.p. Miss. Assn. Symphony Orchs., 1979—83; pres. nat. vol. coun. Am. Symphony Orch. League, 1982—83, mem. exec. com., 1982—83, nat. coun. panelist, 1979—86, 1990, vol. cons., 1986—91, chair S.Ea. regional conf. Jackson, 1981, newsheet editor nat. vol. coun., 1976—80; sec. of bd. Arts Alliance, 1987—88, mem. exec. com., 1988—91; pres. Gallery Guild Miss. Mus. Art, 1982, mem. aux. bd., 1989—97; mem. exec. com. Miss. Friends of the Arts, 1980—86; mem. adv. coun. Jackson Pub. Sch. Dist. Acad. and Peforming Arts Complex, 1991—2000; commr. Miss. Arts Ctr./Planetarium, 1983—91; docent Govs. Mansion, 1989—; panelist S.Ea. Mus. Conf., 1991; bd. dirs. Miss. Meth. Rehab. Ctr., 1990—2006; pres. and bd. advisor So. Christian Svcs. for Children and Youth, 1990—2006; sec., bd. dirs., advisor Jr. League Jackson, 1956—66; active Wilson Found. Bd., 2000—06; past pres. Jackson chpt. Goodwill Industries Vol. Svcs., v.p. nat. chpt. Named Vol. of Yr., Goodwill Industries, 1993, Ms. Mus. Art, 1993; recipient Nat. Cmty. Arts award for first concert at a rehab. hosp., 1979, Miss. Govs. award for the arts, 2002. Mem.: Nat. Mus. Women in Arts (Miss. State Com.). Home: 4730 Old Canton Rd Jackson MS 39211 Personal E-mail: ccarmic525@aol.com.

CARMODY, CAROL JONES, transportation executive, former federal agency administrator; BA, U.of Oklahoma; M in Public Administration, American U. Aviation staff member Senate Commerce Comm., 1988—94; U.S. rep. to the Council Internat. Civil Aviation Org., Montreal, 1994—99; mem. Nat. Transportation Safety Bd. (NTSB), Washington, DC, 2000—05, vice chmn., 2001—02; dir. transp. initiatives Nat. Acad. Pub. Adminstrn., 2005—. Office: Nat Acad Pub Adminstrn Ste 1090 E 1100 New York Ave, NW Washington DC 20005-3934 Office Phone: 202-204-3666. E-mail: ccarmody@napwash.org.

CARMODY, MARGARET JEAN, retired social worker; b. Wauwatosa, Wis., Aug. 5, 1924; d. Peter and Gertrude Francelia (Brown) Galijas; m. James Matthew Carmody, Apr. 3, 1971 (dec. May 2005). BA, Marquette U., 1945; MA, U. Chgo., 1949. Social worker Denver Gen. Hosp., 1950-51; Fulbright fellow France, 1951-52; med. social work cons. U. Ill., Chgo., 1954-60; health scientist, adminstr. USPHS, Washington, 1960-96; ret., 1996. Mem. Acad. Cert. Social Workers. Democrat. Roman Catholic. Home: 40 Riverside Ave # 6 I Red Bank NJ 07701 Personal E-mail: gertrude8@verizon.net.

CARNAHAN, ELLEN, venture capitalist; BBA magna cum laude, Univ. Notre Dame; MBA with highest honors, Univ. Chgo. CPA Ill. With Price Waterhouse & Co.; mgr., fin. planning & analysis Trailer Train Co.; v.p. mktg. & planning SPSS Inc.; with William Blair Capital Ptnrs. LLC, Chgo., 1988—, now mng. dir., head tech. investing. Bd. dir. CPRi, Inc., Vericept, Chgo. Software Assn., WPS Resources Corp., 2003—. Bd. dir. Chgo. Communities in the Schools, Chgo. Network. Named one of 100 Most Influential Women, Crain's Chicago Business, 2004; recipient Luminary award, Girl Scouts of Chgo., 2003. Mem.: Ill. Venture Capital. Assn. (bd. dir., Fellowship award 2003), Women Corp. Directors, Ill. Info. Tech. Assn. (bd. dir.), Chgo. Software Assn. Office: Wm Blair Capital Ptnrs 222 W Adams St Chicago IL 60606 Office Phone: 312-364-8250. Office Fax: 312-236-5728.

CARNAHAN, JEAN, former senator; m. Mel Carnahan (former governor) (dec. 2000); children: Randy(dec.), Russ, Robin, Tom. BA in Bus. and Pub. Admin., George Washington U. First lady of Mo., 1993—2000; U.S. senator Mo., 2001—02. Mem. armed svcs. com, small bus. and entrepreneurship com., gov. affairs com., commerce, sci. and transportation com., special com. aging, State of Mo.; co-founder Children in the Workplace; spkr. for domestic violence, cancer, osteoporosis, mental health, drug problems. Author: If Walls Could Talk, 1998, Christmas at the Mansion: Its Memories and Menus, 1999, Don't Let the Fire Go Out, 2004; contbr.: Vital Speeches of the Day, 1999, Will You Say a Few Words, 2000. Recipient Robert C. Goshorn award for pub. svc., State of Mo. Martin Luther King, Jr. Special Achievement award, Child Adv. of Yr. award, Boys' and Girls' Town Mo., 1995, Citizen of Yr., March of Dimes, 1997, Woman of Yr., St. Louis Zonta Clubs Internat., 1999. Bd. mem. William Woods U. Democrat. Achievements include representing her husband's posthumously won seat in the U.S. Senate from 2001 to 2002 after he and their son, Randy, tragically died in a plane crash.

CARNAHAN, ROBIN, state official; b. Mo. d. Mel and Jean Carnahan. BA in Economics with honors, William Jewell Coll., Liberty, Mo.; JD, U. Va. Sch. Law, 1986. Atty., corp. & bus. law Thompson & Mitchell, St. Louis; spl. asst. to chmn. Export-Import Bank of US; sec. of state State of Mo., 2004—. Mem. Nat. Dem. Inst. Democrat. Office: Office Sec of State 208 State Capitol Jefferson City MO 65101 Fax: 573-751-2490. Office Phone: 573-751-4936. Business E-Mail: sosmain@sos.mo.gov.*

CARNELL, TERESA BURT, lawyer; b. Phila., Sept. 15, 1964; BA cum laude, U. Del., 1986; JD, U. Md., 1992. CPA; bar: Md. 1992, U.S. Ct. Appeals, Fourth Cir., U.S. Dist. Ct. (Dist. Md.). Legis. counsel Md. Gen. Assembly's Dept. Legis. Svcs.; assoc. Ballard Spahr Andrews & Ingersoll, LLP; of counsel Venable LLP, Baltimore, 2004—. Mem. Econ. Matters Com.; lectr. in field. Contbr. Named one of Baltimore's Top Lawyers: The Next Generation, Baltimore Mag., 2003; recipient Cunningham Award. Mem.: ABA, Md. State Bar Assn. (co-chair Com. Corp. Laws, formerly, Bus. Law Sect.), Omicron Delta Kappa, Pi Sigma Alpha. Office: Venable LLP 1800 Mercantile Bank & Trust Bldg 2 Hopkins Plaza Baltimore MD 21201 Office Phone: 410-244-7526. Office Fax: 410-244-7742. E-mail: tcarnell@venable.com.

CARNES, JULIE ELIZABETH, judge; m. Stephen S. Cowen. AB summa cum laude, U. Ga., 1972, JD magna cum laude, 1975. Bar: Ga. 1975. Law clk. to Hon. Lewis R. Morgan U.S. Ct. Appeals (5th cir.), 1975-77; spl. counsel U.S. Sentencing Commn., 1989, commr., appellate chief, 1990-96; asst. U.S. Atty. U.S. Dist. Ct. (no. dist.) Ga., Atlanta, 1978-90, judge, 1992—. Office: US Courthouse 75 Spring St SW Ste 2167 Atlanta GA 30303-3309

CARNES, LA ZETTA, retired secondary school educator; b. Dallas, Dec. 1, 1933; d. Clint Leo and Jimmie Lee Rosser C. BA, U. Dallas, 1969; MEd, East Tex. State U., 1978; postgrad., Richmond Coll., London, 1984, Tex. A&M U., 2000. Tchr. Mineral Wells (Tex.) Ind. Sch. Dist., 1969-71, St. Mary's, Sherman, Tex., 1972-73, Grayson County Jr. Coll., Sherman, Tex., 1986, Whitewright (Tex.) Ind. Sch. Dist., 1973-80, Bells (Tex.) Ind. Sch. Dist., 1973-95, Sherman Ind. Sch. Dist., 1998—2001, ret., 2001. Author of poems. Mem. AAUW, United Daus. Confederacy, Tex. Ret. Assn., Grayson County Retired Sch. Personnel. Home: 1508 N Highland Ave Sherman TX 75092-3500

CARNES, TARA LEA BARKER, music educator; d. Blaine Byers and Arlene Quesillon Barker; m. Thomas Paul Carnes, May 23, 1987 (div. Sept. 15, 1995); 1 child, Emma Louise. Student, Bartlesville Wesleyan U., Okla., 1981—82; MusB, U. S.D., Vermillion, 1982—85; MA in Musicology, U. N.Tex., Denton, 1986—91. Cert. tchr. Tex. Dept. Edn. Pianist, choir dir., organist Krum UMC, Tex., 1987—88; organist St. Paul UMC, Hurst, Tex., 1988—89; music tchr. Holy Family Sch., Ft. Worth, 1988—89; music tchr., band dir. Fonville Mid. Sch., Houston, 1989—92; music tchr. Holy Spirit Episcopal Sch., Houston, 1992—94, Duchesne Acad. of the Sacred Heart, Houston, 1994—, chair, fine arts dept. Pvt. music instr., Pierre, SD, 1985; presenter in field. Organist, choir dir. Bethel Ch., Houston, 1989—, chair, choir robe come., 1995, mem., pastoral search com., 2000, chair, hymnal com., 2004. Mem.: Chorusters Guild, Am. Guild Organists, Tex. Choral Dir.'s Assn. Roman Catholic. Avocations: piano, reading, gardening, composing. Office: Duchesne Acad of the Sacred Heart 10202 Memorial Dr Houston TX 77024 Business E-Mail: tara.carnes@duchesne.org.

CARNEY, ANN VINCENT, retired secondary school educator; b. Slippery Rock, Pa., Feb. 17, 1933; d. Arthur Porter and Leila Felicia (Watson) Vincent; m. Charles Lucien Carney Jr., Dec. 15, 1954 (div. 1974); children: Adrienne Ann, Stephen Vincent. BS, Drexel Inst. Tech., 1955; MEd, U. Pitts., 1972. Cert. tchr., reading specialist, Pa. Tchr. English Allegheny Valley Sch. Dist., Springdale, Pa., 1957-62; reading specialist Gateway Sch. Dist., Monroeville, Pa., 1972-98. Mem. AAUW, Internat. Reading Assn., Keystone State Reading Assn., Three Rivers Reading Coun., Phi Kappa Phi, Omicron Nu. Republican. Avocations: reading, travel, needlecrafts, cooking, gardening. Home: 4013 Impala Dr Pittsburgh PA 15239-2705

CARNEY, JANE W., lawyer; BA, U. Calif., Riverside; JD, U. Calif., Davis. Founding ptnr. Carney & Delany LLP, 1994—. Gov. bd. mem. S. Coast Air Quality Mgmt. Dist.; chair Citizens U. Com.; trustee Riverside Cmty. Coll.; vice chair Econ. Devel.; chair Mayor's Strategic Action Team for Good Jobs; bd. mem. James Irvine Found. Recipient Citizen of the Yr., Greater Riverside Chamber of Commerce, Woman of Achievement award, Black Voice News, Woman of the Yr. award, Calif. State Senate. Mem.: Riverside County Bar Assn. (former pres., former chair ad-hoc courts com., Krieger Meritorious Svc. award). Office: Carney & Delany LLP Ste 750 3801 University Ave Riverside CA 92501*

CARNEY, JEAN KATHRYN, psychologist; b. Ft. Dodge, Iowa, Nov. 10, 1948; d. Eugene James and Lucy (Devlin) C.; m. Mark Krupnick, Jan. 1, 1977 (dec. Mar. 2003); 1 child, Joseph Carney Krupnick. BA, Marquette U., 1970; MA, U. Chgo., 1984, PhD, 1986. Registered clin. psychologist, Ill. Reporter Milw. Jour., 1971-76, editorial writer, 1976-79; asst. prof. psychology St. Xavier Coll., Chgo., 1985-86; dir. Lincoln Park Clinic, Chgo., 1986-87; pvt. practice psychotherapist Chgo., 1987—. Sci. staff Michael Reese Hosp. Med. Ctr., Chgo., 1987-2002; instr. Northwestern U. Med. Sch., 1991-95; clin. asst. prof. U. Ill. Coll. Medicine, 1993—. Editor: Self Regulation: Attention and Attachment, Psychoanalytic Inquiry, 2002, Jewish Writing and the Deep Places of the Imagination, 2005, (article in) Psychoanalytical Inquiry, vol. 22, no. 3. Recipient Best Series Articles, 1975, Best Editorial, 1978, Milw. Press Club, William Allen White Nat. Award for Editorial Writing, 1978, Robert Kahn Meml. Award for Research on Aging, Univ. Chgo., 1985. Mem. APA, Ill. Psychol. Assn., Chgo. Assn. Psychoanalytic Psychology. Office: 55 E Washington St Chicago IL 60602-2115 E-mail: jkcarney@usa.net.

CARNEY, MICHELLE CATHERINE, assistant principal; b. Atlantic City, N.J., Feb. 22, 1971; d. James Arthur and Jacqueline Elenor Carney. BA, The Coll. of William and Mary, Williamsburg, Va., 1989—93; MS in Edn., Old Dominion U., Norfolk, Va., 1994—96; MEd, Widener U., Chester, Pa., 2004—05. Tchr. of Handicapped Va. Dept. Edn., 1996, N.J. Dept. Edn., 1997, Learning Disability Tvhr./Cons. N.J. Dept. Edn., 2001, cert. Prin. N.J. Dept. Edn., 2005. Tchr. of the handicapped SECEP, Norfolk, Va., 1995—97; tchr. of handicapped Brigantine Pub. Schools, NJ, 1997—2002; learning disability tchr./cons. Galloway Twp. Pub. Schools, 2002—05; asst. prin. Egg Harbor Twp. Mid. Sch., 2005—; asst. coach-varsity Holy Spirit HS. Absecon, 2001—04; asst. coach-varisty The Richard Stockton Coll. of NJ., Pomona, 2004—05. Recipient Golden Key Nat. Honor Soc., Old Dominion U., 1996. Mem.: Nat. Assn. Secondary Sch. Principals, ASCD, Phi Delta Kappa. Democrat. Roman Catholic. Avocations: singing, music, travel, basketball/crew/working out, dance. Office: Egg Harbor Twp Mid Sch 4034 Fernwood Ave Egg Harbor Township NJ 08234 Office Phone: 609-383-3355 1503. Business E-Mail: carneym@eht.k12.nj.us.

CARNEY, RITA J., educational association administrator; b. Hoboken, NJ, July 17, 1941; BA, Beaver Coll., Glenside, Pa., 1962; MA, Seton Hall U., South Orange, N.J., 1965; EdD, Columbia U., 1977; MA, Princeton Theol. Sem., 1980. Tchr. Latin and English, Phillipsburg (N.J.) Pub. Schs., 1962-65; guidance counselor Jefferson Twp. Pub. Schs., Oak Ridge, NJ, 1965-67; admin. asst. Supt./H.S. prin. Madison Twp. Pub. Schs., Old Bridge, NJ, 1967—70; program devel. N.J. Dept. Edn., Trenton, 1970—75; county supt. schs. Middlesex County, NJ, 1975—80; N.J. asst. commr. for rsch., planning and evaluation; assoc. v.p. for acad. adminstrn. Temple U., Phila.; asst. to pres., v.p. for acad. and student affairs Georgian Ct. Coll., Lakewood, NJ, 1990—2001. Lectr, presenter profl and ch related orgns; consult planning and orgn analysis. Pres. Diocesan Pastoral Coun., Trenton, Blessed Sacrament Parish Coun., Trenton, NJ, Hiltonia Civic Assn., Trenton; chmn. exec. com. Mercy Higher Edn. Colloquium, 1994—2000. Mem.: Soc Col and Univ Planning (state rep 1996—2000). Home: 32 N Avon Dr Jackson NJ 08527-3975 E-mail: ritacarney@care2.com.

CARNEY, SHANNON MAUREEN, small business owner, educator; b. Lansdale, Pa., Oct. 29, 1975; d. James Patrick and Patricia Dorothy (Somers) Gillespie; m. Kevin Patrick Carney, July 27. BA, DeSales U., Allentown, Pa., 1998. Dance instr. Buckingham Dance, Pa., 1998—2001, Conservatory of Music and Dance, Harleysville, Pa., 1998—2006, asst. choreographer, 1998—2006; owner, instr. Shannon Carney Dance Acad., Silverdale, Pa., 2005—. Office: Shannon Carney Dance Academy PO Box 370 Silverdale PA 18962 Office Phone: 215-257-2292.

CARNEY, TERYL DAWN, physician assistant; b. Kettering, Ohio, June 2, 1967; d. Terry R. and Helen C. (Ruark) Carney; m. Brian M. Cifarelli, July 6, 1996 (div.). BA in English, U. Fla., 1989; BS in Health Scis., Hahneman U., 1995, physician asst. cert., 1995. Physician asst. A. Kagan Orthopedics, Ft. Meyers, Fla., 1995-98, Internal Medicine Assocs., Ft. Meyers, 1998—. Vol. physican asst. Boston Red Sox, Fort Myers, Fla., 1995-97. Mem. Am. Acad. Physician Assts., Fla. Physician Asst. Assn., U. Fla. Alumnia Assn. Republican. Avocations: tennis, scuba diving, travel, music, working out. Office: Internal Med Assocs 2675 Winkler Ave Ste 300 Fort Myers FL 33901-9329

CAROFF, PHYLLIS M., social work educator; b. Bklyn., Feb. 22, 1924; d. Harry and Irene (Lesser) Friedman; m. Joseph Caroff, May 16, 1943; children: Michael, Peter. BA, Douglass Coll., 1944; MSW, N.Y. Sch. Social Work, 1947; DSW, Columbia U., 1969; DHL (hon.), Hunter Coll, CUNY, 1995. Caseworker ARC, 1944-45; caseworker, student supr. Community Service Soc., N.Y.C., 1956-61; from lectr. to assoc. prof. Hunter Coll. Sch. Social Work, N.Y.C., 1961-76, prof., 1976-87; dir. Postmasters Program in Advanced Clin. Social Work, 1977-87; pvt. practice psychotherapy N.Y.C., 1964—. Cons. VA Hosp., N.Y.C., 1977-85, USPHS Hosp., S.I., 1974—; mem. adv. bd. Found. Thanatology, 1976—; mem. profl. adv. com. Grad. Program in Social Work, Inst. Health Professions, Mass. Gen. Hosp., 1980-86. Author: (with others) Before Addiction, 1973; editorial bd. Clin. Social Work Jour., 1972-, Jour. Gerontol. Social Work, 1978-; editor: (with others) Social Work in Health Services: An Academic Practice Partnership, 1980, A New Model in Academic/Practice Partnership, 1985, Psychosocial Advances in Clinical Social Work, 1985. Mem. exec. com. of bd. Planned Parenthood N.Y.C., 1974-79, chmn. rsch. and evaluation com., 1974-77, bd. dirs., 1971-86. Named Disting. Practitioner, Nat. Acad. Practice in Social Work, 1983; NIMH fellow, 1964-65; various grants. Fellow Am. Orthopsychiat. Assn., N.Y. Acad. Medicine; mem. AAUP, Nat. Assn. Social Workers (chmn. clin. council 1981-84, mem. peer rev. adv. com. 1982-84), N.Y. State Soc. Clin. Social Work Psychotherapists, The Douglass Soc. Home: 15 W 81st St New York NY 10024-6022

CAROLEO, LINN E., mathematician, writer; b. Oslo, Dec. 6, 1968; d. Lawrence S. Damon and Barbra M. Enger; m. Wayne A. Caroleo, May 5, 2001. BA, U. Calif., San Diego, 1997; MS, Calif. State U., San Marcos, 1999; EdD, U. West Fla., Pensacola, 2005. Master Farrier Am. Horseshoeing Assn., 1988. Math. prof. Calif. State U., San Marcos, 1997—2001; adj. prof. Northeastern U., Boston, 2001—02; math. prof. Emmanuel Coll., Boston, 2001—02; adj. math. prof. U. West Fla., Pensacola, 2002—04; spl. projects reporter The Sun, Yuma, Ariz., 2004—05; regulatory scientist Gowan Co., Yuma, Ariz., 2005—06. Grad. and tchg. asst. Office of Juvenile Studies, Pensacola, 2003—04. Author (reporter): (newspaper articles) Blue Heaven (Second Pl., Ariz. Newspaper Assn., 2005). With USN, 1989—93. Mem.: Sons of Norway (assoc.; asst. to pres. 2004—05).

CAROLIN, KIRSTIN KERRY, secondary school educator; b. Detroit, July 6, 1970; d. Ralph Russell and Jacqueline Faith Romer; m. Sean Joseph Romer, June 7, 2003. BS, Wayne State U., Detroit, 1999; MA in Tchg., Marygrove Coll., Detroit, 2004. Cert. profl. tchr. Mich., 2004, provisional tchr. Mich., 1999. Tchr. Malow Jr. High, Shelby Township, Mich., 1999—; co-dir. Eisenhower forensics Eisenhower H.S., Shelby Township, 1999—2006. Precinct del. Macomb Rep. Party, Sterling Heights, Mich., 1996. Mem.: Mich. Interscholastic Forensics Assn., Mich. Speech Coaches, Inc. (sec. 1997—2003, pres.-elect 2003—04, pres. 2004—05, past pres. 2006—, pres.-elect 2006—), Golden Key (life). Republican. Lutheran. Office Phone: 586-797-3518. Personal E-mail: kirstin.carolin@gmail.com.

CAROOMPAS, CAROLE JEAN, artist, educator; b. Oregon City, Oreg., Nov. 14, 1946; d. John Thomas and Dorothy Lietta (Dirks) C. BA, Calif. State U., Fullerton, 1968; MFA in Painting, U. So. Calif., 1971. Instr. El Camino Coll., Torrance, Calif., 1971—72; vis. artist Calif. State U., Northridge, 1972—75; instr. Immaculate Heart Coll., L.A., 1973—76; vis. artist Calif. State U., Fullerton, 1976—78; instr. U. Calif., Irvine, 1976—80, Claremont (Calif.) Grad. Sch., 1976—79, Art Ctr. Coll. of Design, Pasadena, Calif., 1978—86, UCLA Ext., 1984—93; prof. fine arts Otis Coll. Art and Design, L.A., 1981—. Vis. artist Anderson Ranch Art Ctr., Aspen, Colo., 1996, 98, 2005. One-woman shows include Jan Baum Art Gallery, L.A., 1978-82, Karl Bornstein Gallery, L.A., 1985, L.A. Contemporary Exhbns., 1989, U. Calif., Irvine, 1990, Sue Spaid Fine Art, L.A., 1992, 94, P.P.O.W., N.Y.C., 1994, Otis Coll. of Art and Design Art Gallery, 1997-98, Mark Moore Gallery, Santa Monica, 1997, 99, 2000, Western Project, Culver City, Calif., 2004; exhibited in group shows at Pasadena Mus. Art, 1972, Whitney Mus. of Art, 1978, Mus. Modern Art, N.Y.C., 1976, L.A. County Mus., 1982, Corcoran Gallery of Art, 43rd Biennial Exhbn. of Contemporary Am. Painting, Washington, 1993, Under Contstrn. Armory Ctr. for Arts, Pasadena, 1995, UCLA Hammer Mus. of Art, L.A., 1996, L.A. County Mus. Art, 1996, Beaver Coll., 1996, L.A. Mcpl. Art Gallery, 1997, UCLA Hammer Mus. Art, 2000, Calif. State U., Fullerton, 2001, San Jose Mus., 2002, Rosamund Felson Gallery, Santa Monica, Calif., 2003, Lewis and Clark Coll., Portland, Oreg., 2003, San Luis Obispo Art Ctr., 2003, In-A-Gadda-Da-Vida, Baby, Western Project, Culver City, 2004, Western Project, Culver City, 2006, The Lab, San Francisco, 2006; also a vocalist; recs. include 2 individual albums and inclusion in The Record: 13 Vocal Artists; featured in book L.A.-Artland, 2005; contbr. articles to Paris Rev., Dreamworks, Whitewalls. Grantee, NEA, 1987, 1993, Visual Arts Funding Initiative, Calif. Cmty. Found., 2005, Peter S. Reed Found., 2006; Faculty Devel. grantee, New Sch. Social Rsch., 1989, Support grantee, Esther and Adolph Gottlieb Found., 1993, Guggenheim Meml. fellow, 1995,

Individual Artist's fellow, City of L.A. Cultural Affairs Dept., 2000, Peter S. Reed Found. grantee, 2006. Office: Otis Coll Art and Design 9045 Lincoln Blvd Los Angeles CA 90045-3505 Office Phone: 310-838-0609.

CARPENTER, ANGIE M., small business owner, editor, county legislator; b. Bay Shore, N.Y., Sept. 30, 1943; d. Joseph and Ida (Gullo) Linarello; m. Joe David Carpenter, Apr. 13, 1964; children: Richard, Robert. Student, Nassau C.C., 1962-63. Office mgr., graphic designer, typographer Merrick (N.Y.) Typographers and Maverick Pubs., 1966-76; founder, v.p. AC Typesetters and Printing, Inc., West Islip, NY, 1976-93; dep. presiding officer Suffolk County Legislature. Editor, pub., co-founder West Islip Record, 1986-91; columnist The Graphic, The Beacon, 1985-87. Chmn. publicity com., trustee Babylon/West Islip Windmill Com., Inc., Babylon, N.Y., 1986—, ASK US, 1987-98; trustee West Islip After-Sch.-Care program, 1987-97, Our Lady of Consolation Geriatric Care Ctr.; chmn. West Islip Youth Enrichment Svcs., 1986-87; mem. govt. action coun. L.I. Assn., 1987; mem. recycling panel Town of Islip, 1987; chairperson TOI Blue Ribbon Com. on Recycling, 1987-88; trustee Suffolk County Vanderbilt Mus., 1990-93; vice chair Salvation Army adv. bd., Suffolk County, mem. legis., 1993-05, dep. presiding officer, chmn. pub. safety com., vice chmn. budget and fin., county treas., 2005-. Mem. West Islip C. of C. (v.p., mchts. dir. 1982-84, pres. 1985, 86, 87, 88), Govt. Fin. Officer's Assn. Republican. Roman Catholic. Office: 330 Center Dr Riverhead NY 11901-3311 Office Phone: 631-852-1500. Personal E-mail: angiecarp930@aol.com. Business E-Mail: angie.carpenter@co.suffolk.ny.us.

CARPENTER, BETTY O., writer; b. Montreal, June 1, 1926; d. Harry and Dorothy (Schacher) Shmerling; m. David G. Ostroff, Apr. 6, 1946 (div. 1972); children: Jack Ostroff, Lucy Ostroff Harrow; m. Russell William Carpenter, Jr., Oct. 2, 1976 (dec.); stepchildren: Annette Marie Carpenter Freedman, Cynthia Carpenter Jefferson, Lori Carpenter Bembry. BA in Edn., Bklyn. Coll., 1947, MA in Edn., 1953; PhD in Adminstrn., NYU, 1973. Cert. sch. supt., prin., N.J., guidance counselor, elem. tchr., N.Y. Tchr. elem. grades N.Y.C. Pub. Schs. 54 and 139, Bklyn., 1946-54, 62; asst. prin. Pub. Sch. 139, Bklyn., 1962-67; pres. asst. prin. assoc. Ctrl. Office Bd. of Edn., N.Y.C., 1967-68, v.p. coun. suprs. and adminstrs., 1968-69, adminstrv. asst. pers., 1968-70; asst. supt. Plainfield (N.J.) Pub. Schs., 1970-74; supt. schs. Glen Rock (N.J.) Pub. Schs., 1974-84; ret. Author: Curriculum Handbook for Parents and Teachers, 1991, Tutoring for Pay, 1991, Musing, 1994, (book of poetry) The Brosh (Bionic Replacement of Species Humanoid), 1998, Lady of the Lake, 1999, Inherit the Rainbow, 2000, Art and Craftiness, 2001, Crystal Slopes, 2002, A Style of Their Own, 2002, Make Way for Pugsley, 2002. Trustee Glen Rock Libr. Bd., 1974-80, United Fund Bd., Glen Rock, 1975-77; vice chmn. Iredell County Bd. of Adjustment N.C., 1990-95; fellow mem. Lake Owners Gathered in Concern, N.C., 1985-88. Recipient Founders Day award NYU, 1973, Adminstrv. Leadership award NACEL, 1984. Mem. Soc. Children's Book Writers and Illustrators, Romance Writers Am., Nat. Writers Assn., Bergen County Supts. Assn. (pres.-elect), Nat. Scrabble Assn., Am. Contract Bridge League, Ariz. Writers Assn. Avocations: sculpture, golf, water aerobics, computers, bridge. Home: 11730 N 91 Pl Scottsdale AZ 85260-6866 Personal E-mail: bcbcarp@cox.net.

CARPENTER, BOGDANA MARIA MAGDALENA, language educator; b. Czestochowa, Poland, June 2, 1941; came to U.S., 1965; d. Jozef Konrad and Maria (Gordon) Chetkowska; m. John Randell Carpenter, Apr. 15, 1963; children: Michael, Magdalena. MA, Warsaw U., 1963; PhD, U. Calif., Berkeley, 1974. Asst. prof. U. Wash., Seattle, 1974-83, U. Mich., Ann Arbor, 1983-85, assoc. prof., 1985-91, prof., 1991—, chmn. dept. Slavic lit. and langs., 1991—. Adv. coun. Wilson Ctr. East European Program, Washington, 1985-90; selection com. Internat. Rsch. and Exch., Princeton, N.J., 1987-88; discipline adv. com. Coun. for Internat. Exch. Scholars, Washington, 1989-90. Author: Poetic Avantgarde in Poland, 1918-1939, 1983, Monumenta Polonica, 1989 (1st prize Am. Coun. of Polish Cultural Clubs 1991); translator: Selected Poems of Zbigniew Herbert, 1977 (Poetry Soc. Am. prize 1979), Z. Herbert's Report from the Besieged City, 1987, Still Life with a Bridle, 1991 (Columbia U. Translation Ctr. Merit award 1992), Mr. Cogito, 1993; assoc. editor: Cross Currents, 1987—; contbr. articles and revs. to profl. jours. Fulbright-Hays grantee, 1976, IREX grantee, 1976, NEH grantee, 1987-88, ACLS grantee, 1990-91. Mem. Am. Assn. for Advancement Slavic Studies (exec. bd. Midwest chpt. 1989—), Am. Assn. Tchrs. Slavic and East European Langs. Office: U Mich Dept Slavic Lit & Langs 3040 Mlb Ann Arbor MI 48109

CARPENTER, CANDICE, writer, former media executive; m. Peter Olson, 2001; children: Michaela, Ellie. BS in Biology, Stanford U.; MBA, Harvard U. V.p. consumer mktg. Am. Express Co., N.Y.C.; pres. Time Life Video & Television (Time Warner), N.Y.C., 1989-93, QVC, Inc. (Q2 shopping channel), 1993-94; co-founder, CEO iVillage, N.Y.C., 1995—2000, chair, 2000—01. Author: Chapters: Create a Life of Exhilaration and Accomplishment in the Face of Change, 2001. Dir. Breakthrough Found. E-mail: candicec123@aol.com.

CARPENTER, CAROL DENISE, writer, educator; b. Artesia, N.Mex. d. Shirley Kay and Thomas Elwood Carpenter. M in Profl. Writing, U. So. Calif., L.A., 1998. Program dir. Coll. Santa Fe, 2003—05, faculty creative writing program, 2003—, assoc. dir. co-curricular programs, 2005—. Prodr.: (play) The Arisen. Mem. Madrid (N.Mex.) Landowner's Assn. and Water Co-Op, 2003—06. Recipient Ed Moses Fiction prize, U. So. Calif., 1998, Presdl. award, Coll. Santa Fe. Mem.: Investigative Reporters and Editors (assoc.). Green Party. Avocations: theater, horseback riding, literature, dance. Office: Coll Santa Fe 1600 St Michael's Dr Santa Fe NM 97505 Office Phone: 505-473-6282. Office Fax: 505-473-6282.

CARPENTER, DOROTHY SCHENCK, retired special education educator; b. Tewksbury, Mass., Feb. 17, 1942; d. William Edmond and Grace (Scott) Schenck; m. Booker Stephen Carpenter, Sept. 12, 1964; children: B. Stephen II, Sean D., Dreux S., Seth B. BA, George Washington U., 1987; MS, Johns Hopkins U., 1996. Cert. tchr., sch. counselor, Md. Spl. edn. instr. asst. Montgomery County, Md. Pub. Schs., Gaithersburg, 1980-87, spl. edn. tchr. Rockville, 1987—2003. Recipient Perry Botwin award, 1987; grantee, Montgomery Coll., 1979—80, Bd. Trustees George Washington U., 1986; Columbia Women's scholar, 1986. Mem. Coun. Exceptional Children, Pi Lambda Theta (sec. 1989-90). Home: 12200 Greenridge Dr Boyds MD 20841-9032

CARPENTER, ELIZABETH JANE, mediator; b. Cleve., Mar. 29, 1949; d. Robert E. and Joan Jaffe. BA, Western Coll., Oxford, Ohio, 1970. Pub. rels. asst. Lennen & Newell/Pacific, Honolulu, 1970-73; account exec. Marschalk Advt., Cleve., 1973-76; cons. Carpenter Advt. & Pub. Rels., Cleve., 1976-80; internat. pub. rels. mgr. Wang Labs., Inc., Boston, 1980-82, advt. mgr., 1982-87; mgr. worldwide comm. CSS Digital Equipment Corp., Merrimack, N.H., 1987-92, advt. mgr. U.S. Svcs. group, 1992-99; mktg. mgr. Logic Divsn. Avanti Corp., North Billerica, Mass., 2000—02; owner J. Carpenter Mediation and Group Facilitation. Assoc. producer Am. Treasure, TV spl., 1986, The Entrepreneurs, TV spl., 1986-87. Home: 9 Secret Cive Ln Boothbay Harbor ME 04538-1746

CARPENTER, HEATHER L., athletic trainer; b. Pitts., Feb. 4, 1976; d. Michael Joseph McElvenny and Susan Lee Zulka; m. Russell David Carpenter, Oct. 23, 2004. BS, California U. of Pa., 1999. Cert. athletic trainer, EMT, Pa. Athletic trainer NovaCare Rehab., Bentworth Sch. Dist., Bentleyville, Pa., 2001—. Home: 625 Speers Ave Charleroi PA 15022-1073

CARPENTER, JANELLA ANN, retired librarian; b. Knoxville, Tenn., Sept. 20, 1936; d. J. Beecher Carpenter, M. Janella Hooper. BS, U. Tenn., 1958; MA, George Peabody Coll. Tchrs., 1963. Cert. tchg. cert. N.C., 1958. Libr. Elizabeth Elem. Sch., Charlotte, NC, 1958—63, Merry Oaks Elem. Sch., Charlotte, NC, 1963—64; libr., media specialist Rama Rd. Elem. Sch., Charlotte, NC, 1964—88; ret., 1988. Sch. area rep., tchrs. adv. coun. Charlotte-Mecklenburg Schs., Charlotte, NC, 1983—88. Bd. dirs. Newport/Cocke County Mus., Newport; mem. Newport Regional Planning Commn., Newport, 1995—, Newport/Cocke County Tourism Coun., Newport, 1995—2002; mem. coordinating com. for growth planning Newport/Cocke County, Newport, 1998—2002; newsletter editor Dead Pigeon River Coun., Newport, 1989—93. Named Carpenter Ctr., Rama Rd. Elem. Sch., 1988. Mem.: ALA, DAR, Classroom Tchrs. Assn. (pres. 1975—76), Profl. Educators N.C. (life; 1st pres. 1979—82), Newport Garden Club, Alpha Omicron Pi, Beta Sigma Phi, Delta Kappa Gamma. Republican. Baptist. Avocations: amateur desktop printing, painting, genealogy, gardening, football. Personal E-mail: janella@planetc.com.

CARPENTER, JENNA PRICE, mathematics professor, academic administrator; d. Birtrum Mason and Stella Virginia Price; m. George Walter Jr. Carpenter, Aug. 26, 1983; children: George Walter III, Emma Claire. BS in Math., La. Tech U., Ruston, 1983; MS in Math., La. State U., Baton Rouge, 1986; PhD in Math., La. State U., 1989. Assoc. prof. La. Tech U., Ruston, La., 1997—, acad. dir., 1998—2006, prof., 2006—. Mem. WEPAN, 1997—2006. Mem.: Am. Soc. of Engring. Edn. (dir., ednl. rsch. methods divsn. 2005—, chair, math. divsn. 2005—06, Disting. Educator and Svc. award 2006), WEPAN (bd. dirs. 2006—), Math. Assn. of Am. (chair, La. and Miss. sect. 2005—06). Southern Baptist. Office: Louisiana Tech University PO Box 10348 Ruston LA 71272 Office Phone: 318-257-2101.

CARPENTER, LIZ (ELIZABETH SUTHERLAND CARPENTER), journalist, writer, equal rights leader, lecturer; b. Salado, Tex., Sept. 1, 1920; d. Thomas Shelton and Mary Elizabeth (Robertson) Sutherland; m. Leslie Carpenter, June 17, 1944 (dec.); children: Scott Sutherland, Christy. BJ, U. Tex., 1942; PhD (hon.), Mt. Vernon Coll., Austin Coll. Reporter UP, Phila., 1944-45; propr. with husband of news bur. representing nat. newspapers Washington, 1945-61; exec. asst. to V.P. Lyndon B. Johnson, 1961-63; pres. sec., staff dir. to Mrs. Johnson, 1963-69; v.p. Hill & Knowlton, Inc., Washington, 1972-76; cons. LBJ Library, Austin, Tex.; asst. sec. Dept. Edn., 1980-81; with White House Com. on Aging, 1998—; now sr. cons. Hill and Knowlton. Co-chmn. ERAmerica, 1976-81; dir. Nat. Wildflower Rsch. Ctr. Author: Ruffles and Flourishes, 1970, Getting Better All the Time, 1987, Unplanned Parenthood, 1994, Start with a Laugh. An Insider's Guide To Making Speeches, Roasts, and Eulogies, 2000. Recipient Woman Year award in field of politics and pub. affairs Ladies Home Jour., 1977, Disting. Alumnae award U. Tex., 1974-75; named to Tex. Women's Hall Fame, 1985. Mem. Nat. Women's Polit. Caucus (founding mem. 1971), Women's Nat. Press (pres. 1954-55), Alpha Phi, Theta Sigma Phi (Nat. Headliners award 1962), Press Club (Washington), Headliners Club (Headliner award), Univ. Club (Austin).

CARPENTER, MARLENE, retired philosopher, educator; arrived in U.S., 1936; d. Charles and Anne Selner. BA, Hunter Coll., NYC, 1962; MA, Georgetown U., Washington, 1967; PhD, Walden U., Tampa, Fla., 1979. Instr. philosophy Prince George's CC, Largo, Md., 1967—69, asst. prof. philosophy, 1969—71, assoc. prof., 1971—73, prof., chmn. philosophy dept., 1973—2006, prof. emeritus dept. philosophy, 2006—. Home: 2718 Yeomans Lantern Ct Annapolis MD 21401-7805

CARPENTER, NANCY J., health science association administrator; Assoc. dir. H.A. Chapman Inst. Med. Genetics, Tulsa, Okla.; pres. Am. Bd. Med. Genetics, 2001—. Adj. prof. biochemistry Okla. State U. Office: H A Chapman Inst Med Genetics 4502 E 41st St Tulsa OK 74135-2553 Business E-Mail: ncarpenter@hillcrest.com.*

CARPENTER, ROSALIE T., education educator, consultant; b. Braddock, Pa., Apr. 6, 1954; d. Frank William and Clara Zezzo Tigano; m. Stephen G. Carpenter, Jan. 7, 1978; children: Claire Elizabeth, George Wilson II. BA, Wesleyan U., 1976; MA, Marshall U., 1983; EdD, W.Va. U., 1994. Asst. prof. Fairmont (W.Va.) State Coll., 1995—96, Waynesburg (Pa.) Coll., 1996—2000; assoc. prof. Washington & Jefferson Coll., Washington, Pa., 2000—, dir. elem. edn. Cons. Ednl. Futures, Morgantown, W.Va., 1990—. Mem.: Coun. Exceptional Children, Nat. Assn. Edn. Young Children, Kappa Delta Epsilon (counselor). Avocations: walking, strength training, exercise. E-mail: rcarpenter@washjeff.edu.

CARPENTER, SHEILA JANE, lawyer; b. Kyoto, Oct. 16, 1950; d. Chester Elwin and Betty (Boulger) C.; m. William Joseph McCarthy, May 26, 1973; 1 child, Diana Elizabeth. BA, Purdue U., 1972; JD, Yale U., 1975. Bar: Md. 1975, U.S. Dist. Ct. Md. 1976, D.C. 1977, U.S. Dist. Ct. D.C. 1978, U.S. Supreme Ct. 1980, U.S. Dist. Ct. (no. dist.) Ohio 1980, U.S. Claims Ct. 1982, U.S. Ct. Appeals (D.C. cir.) 1983, U.S. Ct. Appeals (4th and Fed. cirs.) 1984, U.S. Ct. Appeals (8th cir.) 2000, U.S. Ct. Appeals (5th cir.) 2004. Assoc. Weinberg & Green, Balt., 1975-77, Sutherland, Asbill & Brennan, Washington, 1977-82, ptnr., 1982-96, Jorden Burt LLP, Washington, 1996—. Pub. svc. com. Sutherland, Asbill & Brennan, 1990-94, chair, 1990-92, chair litigation group Washington office, 1991-93; web chair life, health and disability com. Def. Rsch. Inst., 2000-04. Contbr. articles to profl. jours. Fellow Am. Bar Found.; mem. ABA (mem. excess surplus lines and reins. com. TIPS sect., vice chmn. 1992-94, chair 1995-96, vice chair pub. regulation ins. commn. TIPS sect. 1995-00, mem. life ins. com. TIPS sect., vice chair 2004-), Am. Arbitration Assn. (arbitrator large complex case panel), Md. Bar Assn., Phi Beta Kappa. Office: Jorden Burt LLP Ste 400E 1025 Thomas Jefferson St NW Washington DC 20007-5208 Office Phone: 202-965-8165. E-mail: sjc@jordenusa.com.

CARPENTER, STACY, secondary school educator; b. Troy, Ala., Jan. 24, 1973; d. Joe and Sherry Lane Carpenter; m. Christopher Adam Dykes, Dec. 3, 2004. BS in English and Biology Edn., Troy State U., Ala., 1994, MS in Biology Edn., 1999, MS in Sch. Counseling, 2004. Cert. profl. educator Ala. State Dept. Edn., 1994. Tchr. sci. Pike County H.S., Brundidge, Ala., 1995—98, Clayton H.S., Ala., 1998—2000, Charles Henderson H.S., Troy, 2000—. Recipient Outstanding Grad. Student award, Troy State U., 2004. Mem.: NEA (assoc.), Troy Edn. Assn. (assoc.), Ala. Edn. Assn. (assoc.), Chi Sigma Iota (hon.). Presbyn. Avocations: gardening, travel. Office: Charles Henderson High School 150 George Wallace Drive Troy AL 36081 Business E-Mail: carpenters@troyschools.net.

CARPENTER, SUSAN KAREN, defender; b. New Orleans, May 6, 1951; d. Donald Jack and Elise Ann (Diehl) C. BA magna cum laude with honors in English, Smith Coll., 1973; JD, Ind. U., 1976. Bar: Ind. 1976. Dep. pub. defender of Ind. State of Ind., Indpls., 1976-81, pub. defender of Ind., 1981—; chief pub. defender Wayne County, Richmond, Ind., 1981. Bd. dirs. Ind. Pub. Defender Coun., Indpls., 1981—; Ind. Lawyers Comm., Indpls., 1984-89; trustee Ind. Criminal Justice Inst., Indpls., 1983—. Mem. Criminal Code Study Commn., Indpls., 1981—, Supreme Ct. Records Mgmt. Com., Indpls., 1983—, Ind. Pub. Defender Commn., 1989—, Ind. Supreme Ct. Commn. on Race and Gender Fairness, 2000—. Mem. Ind. State Bar Assn. (criminal justice sect.), Nat. Legal Aid and Defender Assn., Nat. Assn. Defense Lawyers, Phi Beta Kappa. Office Phone: 317-232-2475. Business E-Mail: scarpenter@iquest.net.

CARPENTER-MASON, BEVERLY NADINE, quality assurance professional, medical/surgical nurse, pediatric nurse practitioner, consultant, writer; d. Frank Carpenter and Thelma Deresa (Williams) Carpenter Smith; m. Sherman Robert Robinson Jr., Dec. 26, 1953 (div. Jan. 1959); 1 child, Keith Michael Robinson; m. David Solomon Mason Jr., Sept. 10, 1960; 1 child, Tamara Nadina Mason. Grad., Shadyside Hosp. Sch. Nursing, Pitts.; BS, St. Joseph Coll., North Windham, ME, 1979; MS, So. Ill. U., 1981; PhD, Columbia Pacific U., 1995. RN Pa., DC, Fla., cert. PNP; state ombusman long term care North Pinellas Pasco County Long Term Care Ombudsman Coun., parish nurse 2004, lay spkr. 1999, lay del. Fla. Conf. United Meth. Ch., 1998. Staff nurse med. surgery, ob-gyn neonatology and pediat. Pa., NY, Wyo., Colo. and Washington, 1954—68; mr. clinician dermatol. svcs. Malcolm Grow Med. Ctr., Camp Spring, Md., 1968—71; PNP Dept. Human Resources, Washington, 1971—73; asst. DON Glenn Dale Hosp., Md., 1973—81; nursing coord. medicaid divsn. Forest Haven Ctr., Laurel, Md., 1981—83, spl. asst. to supr. for med. svcs., 1983—84; spl. asst. to supt. for quality assurance Bur. Habilitation Svcs., Laurel, 1984—89; exec. asst. quality assurance coord. Mental Retardation Devel. Disabilities Adminstrn., Washington, 1989—91, also bd. dirs.; owner, prin. BCM Assocs., 1992—; coord. quality assurance health svcs. divsn. UPARC, Clearwater, Fla., 1993—94. Mem. exec. com. Am. Found. Edn. Healthcare Quality, 1995—97; bd. dirs. Dist. V, Fla. Dept. HHS, 1997—2002; cons., lectr. in field. Author: (book) Quality Assurance: Toward a Paradigm of Universality, 1995; mem. editl. bd., case study editor: Am. Jour. Quality Assurance, 1985—; contbr. articles to profl. jours. Mem., star donor ARC Blood Dr., Washington, 1975—91; mem. health and human svcs. bd. Fla. Dept. Children and Families, 1997—2000, cons. Dist. XI, 1998; bd. dirs. Pinellas County (Fla.) Coun., Pinellas County WAGES Coalition, 1999; mem. Parish Nurse Assn., 2004—; vol. chief cons. Am. Bd. Med. Quality 2005 Cert. Examination Devel., 2005—; vol. curriculum specialist cons. Accreditation Coun. for Edn. and Tng., 2001—; lay del. United Meth. Ch. Fla. Conf., 1998—; bd. ordained ministry apptd. by the bishop of United Meth. Ch., 2004—; bd. dirs. North Pinellas divsn. Am. Cancer Soc., 2002—04; bd. trustees, dir. Upper Pinellas Assn. Retarded Citizens Bd./Found., 2002—; chair nominations com. Prince Georges Nat. Coun. Negro Women, Md., 1984—85; exec. sec. Pipers Meadow Home Owners Assn., 1993—2001; mem. Long Term Care Fla. State Ombudsman Coun., 2000—. Named Woman of the Yr., 1990—96; recipient awards, Dept. Air Force and DC Govt., 1966—92, Della Robbia Gold medallion, Am. Acad. Pediat., 1972, John P. Lamb Jr. Meml. Lectureship award, E. Tenn. State U., 1988, Outstanding Svc. award, U.S. Congress Adv. Bd. Svc., 1991. Fellow: Am. Coll. Med. Quality (Disting., case study editor, mem. jour. editl. bd. 1985—2004, chmn. publs. com. 1987—2003, asst. treas. 1988—93, Svc. award 1999); mem.: NAFE, Internat. Platform Assn., Healthcare Quality Inst., Assn. Retarded Citizens, Am. Bd. Quality Assurance and Utilization Rev. Physicians (asst. treas. 1988—94, chair exam. com. 1990—93, chief proctor exam. com. 1995—97, Chmn. of the Yr. award 1992, presdl. citation, Calvin R. Openshaw Svc. award 1993), Am. Assn. Mental Retardation (conf. lectr. 1988), Top Ladies Distinction (1st v.p. 1986—91), World Cir. Lang. Club (1st v.p. 2003—05), Soroptimists Internat. (sec. Pinellas chpt. 1999, Achievement in Healthcare award 1997), Order Ea. Star (Achievement award Deborah chpt. 1991). Democrat. Avocations: studying languages, travel, reading, writing, collecting antiques. Personal E-mail: drbevearpmason@aol.com.

CARPENTIERI, CAROL ELLEN, artist, educator; b. Bklyn., Nov. 3, 1941; d. Nicholas Francis and Marie Ann Mecchella; m. Frank Dominick Carpentieri, Oct. 20, 1962; children: Diane P. Michaeli, Frank N., Marc J. AB, Westchester Bus. Sch., 1960; student, Fashion Inst. Tech., 1986. Tchr. art West Patent Elem. Sch., Bedford Hills, NY, 1972—82. Author: A November Walk, 2004, Winter in South Salem, 2005; exhibitions include West Side Art Coalition, 2004, Katonah Mus., 2005, Cork Gallery, Avery Fisher Hall, Licnoln Ctr. Plaza, 2005, Licht Blick Studios Gallery, 2005, Armonk United Meth. Ch., 2005, 96th St. Gallery, 2005. Vol. kitchen help God's Love We Deliver, N.Y.C., 1993—99. Recipient Tri State Art Competition award, Katonah Art Mus., 2005, Hon. Mention award, Westchester Land Trust, 2006. Mem.: Katonah Mus. Artist Assn., West Side Arts Coalition, Nat. Mus. Women in Arts, Lewisboro Garden Club. Democrat. Avocations: horseback riding, kayaking, gardening, yoga, knitting. Home: 29 Hoyt St South Salem NY 10590

CARPENTIERI, SARAH C., neuropsychologist, researcher, clinical psychologist; b. Naples, Italy, Aug. 30, 1967; m. James F. Asbury. BBA/BA, U. Notre Dame, 1989; MS, U. Memphis, 1991, PhD, 1994. Lic. psychologist, neuropsychologist. Rschr. St. Jude Children's Hosp., Memphis, 1990—94; psychology intern Harvard Med. Sch. /Children's Hosp., Boston, 1994—95; neuropsychology post-doctoral fellow Harvard Med. Sch., 1995—97; instr., asst. psychology and neuropsychologist Harvard Med. Sch., Boston, 1997—; assoc. rsch. and neuropsychologist Children's Hosp., Boston, 1997—. Lead investigator pediatric brain tumor rsch. program Children's Hosp., Boston, 1998—; cons. Dana Farber Cancer Inst., Boston, 2001—. Contbr. articles to profl. jours. Fellow VanVleet, U. Memphis, 1993—94; grantee Rsch., Pitino Found., 1999—2000, Murphy Child's Trust, 1999—2000, S&S Found., 1997—2003. Mem.: APA, Nat. Acad. Neuropsychology, Internat. Neuropsychology Soc. Personal E-mail: sarah.carpentieri@carpenburymed.com.

CARPER, BARBARA ANNE, nursing educator; BSN, Tex. Women's U., 1959; clin. cert. in anesthesia, U. Mich., 1962; MEd, Columbia U., 1966, EdD, 1975. Instr. U. N.Mex. Coll. Nursing, Alburquerque, 1966-69; assoc. prof. Tex. Women's U. Coll. Nursing, Denton, 1976-80, prof., coord. doctoral program, 1980-82; prof. grad. program U. So. Maine Sch. Nursing, Portland, 1982-84; prof., chairperson dept. nursing Colby-Sawyer Coll., New London, N.H., 1984-88; prof. Regents Coll., SUNY, Albany, 1985-89; assoc. prof., coord. undergrad. program U. N.C. Coll. Nursing, Charlotte, 1989-91, interim dean, 1991-92, prof., assoc. dean for acad. affairs, 1992—99, prof., 1994—99, prof. emeritus. Vis. scholar Harvard U., 1981-82; mem. Nursing Theory Think Tank, 1982; mem. exec. bd., chmn. project com. New Eng. Orgn. Nursing, 1986-88; vis. prof. Marion A. Buckley Sch. Nursing, Adelphi U., 1989-90; Green Chair honor prof. Harris Coll. Nursing, Tex. Christian U., 1980-81; Margaret D. McLean lectr. Meml. U. Nfld., Can., 1990; numerous consultations, workshops, lectures, seminars and speeches in field. Mem. editorial bd. Jour. Advances in Nursing Sci., 1978-99, Asian Jour. Nursing Studies, 1993-95; contbr. articles to profl. jours. Bd. dirs., mem. exec. com., mem. patient and cmty. svcs. com. Nat. Kidney Found. N.H., 1987-89; bd. dirs. Hospice at Charlotte, 1991-97, co-chairperson ethics adv. com., 1995-97, vice chair at large 1996-97; bd. dirs. Cmty. Health Svcs., 1991-94. Fellow Am. Acad. Nursing (co-chair ethics/legal adv. com. 1983-86, mem. planning com. 1988, Ann. Sci. Sessions of Acad., mem. expert panel on ethics 1991—); mem. ANA (coun. nurse rschrs.), N.C. State Nursing Assn., Sigma Theta Tau (Disting. lectr. 1994-95), Phi Kappa Phi.

CARPER, FERN GAYLE, small business owner, writer; b. Pitts., Jan. 28, 1934; d. Phillip Jack and Jean Edith (Epstein) Whitman; m. Robert S. Carper, Aug. 3, 1958; children: Pamela Hope, Bruce Alan. Diploma, Taylor Alderdice H.S., 1952. Exe. sec. J.J. Gumberg & Co., Pitts., 1952—58; author, owner Pete The Toad Enterprises, Potomac, Md., 2000—. Author: Pete The Toad and Friends, 2002. Democrat. Achievements include development of line of Pete The Toad stuffed animals and tee shirts. Avocations: oil and acrylic artist, still life painting, singing. Home: 9203 Gatewater Terr Potomac MD 20854 Office: Pete The Toad Enterprises 9203 Gatewater Terr Potomac MD 20854 Office Phone: 301-279-0926.

CARPER, GERTRUDE ESTHER, small business owner, real estate developer; b. Jamestown, N.Y., Apr. 13, 1921; d. Zenas Mills and Virgie (Lytton) Hanks; m. J. Dennis Carper, Apr. 5, 1942; children: David Hanks, John Michael Dennis, Michelle Kristen. Student violinist, Nat. Acad. Mus., 1931-41; diploma fine arts, Md. Inst. of Art, 1950; voice student, Frazier Gange, Peabody Inst. Music, 1952-55. Interior decorator O'Neill's (Importers), Balt., 1942-44; auditor Citizens Nat. Bank, Covington, Va., 1945-46; owner, developer Essex Yacht Harbour Marina, Balt., 1955—, owner, developer St. Michael's Sanctuary wildlife preserve, 1965—. Jewelry designer, 1987—; portrait artist, 1947—; exhibited one-woman shows Ferdinand Roten Gallery, Balt., 1963, Highfield Salon, Balt., 1967, Le Salon des Nations a Paris, 1985, Ducks and Geese of North Am., 1986, Series of Lighthouses, 1991; exhibited group shows Md. Inst. Alumni Show, 1964, Essex Libr., 1981, Hist. Preservation of Am., Hall of Fame, 1989, others; works included in collections including Prestige de la Peinture d'Aujourd'hos dans le Monde, 1990, Artists and Masters of the Twentieth Century, 1991; author: Expressions for Children, 1985, Fidere, 1993, Mentation, 1993; contbr. articles and poetry to ch. publs. and newspapers. Vol. tchr. of retarded persons, 1942—; leader Women's Circle at local Presbyn. chs., 1952-87, mem. 40 yrs. of choir svc. Mem. Md. Inst. Art Alumni Assn. (life), Grand Coun. World Parliament of Chivalry (Nobless of Humanity citation), Nat.

Mus. Women in the Arts (charter, Washington). Avocations: raising orchids, reading, writing essays and poetry. Office: Essex Yacht Harbour Marina 500 Sandalwood Rd Baltimore MD 21221-5830

CARPI, JANICE E., lawyer; b. Whittier, Calif., June 15, 1952; d. Leonard William and Elizabeth Louise (Severns) Carpi; m. Garland M. Harwood III, July 3, 1993; 1 child, Sarah Elizabeth. BA in Internat. Affairs, George Washington U., 1975; JD, So. Meth. U., 1978. Bar: Nev. 1978, Tex. 1979, Va. 1994. Assoc. Wesner Wylie & Pleasant, Dallas, 1979—80; underwriting atty. Chgo. Title Ins. Corp., Dallas, 1980—83; underwriting counsel Lawyers Title Ins. Co., Dallas, 1983—86, v.p., sr. underwriting counsel Richmond, Va., 1986—98, Land Am. Fin., Richmond, 1998—. Spkr. Practicing Law Inst., N.Y.C., 1998—. Contbr. chpts. in books. Vol. Jr. League Dallas, 1983—85, Habitat for Humanity, Richmond, 1996—; eucharistic min. St. Martin's Episc. Ch., Richmond, 2001—. Fellow: Am. Coll. Real Estate Lawyers (chair meetings com. 2001—); mem.: ABA (chair Title Ins. com. 2001—), Coll. of State Bar Tex., Phi Delta Phi. Avocation: travel. Office: Land America Fin Group 101 Gateway Centre Pkwy Richmond VA 23235

CARR, ANNE ELIZABETH, theology studies educator; b. Chgo., Nov. 11, 1934; d. Frank James and Dorothy Margaret (Graber) C. AB, Mundelein Coll., 1956; AM, Marquette U., 1963, U. Chgo., 1968, PhD, 1971; DDiv (hon.), Jesuit Sch. Theology, 1983; LHD (hon.), Loyola U., 1995; ThD (hon.), Cath. Theol. Union, 2000. Instr. Mundelein Coll., Chgo., 1963-66, asst. prof., 1966-71, Ind. U., Bloomington, 1972-74; asst. prof., asst. dean U. Chgo. Divinity Sch., 1975-78, assoc. prof., assoc. dean, 1978-88, prof., 1988—. Donnelan vis. prof. Trinity Coll., Dublin, Ireland, 1983. Author: Theological Method of K. Rahner, 1977, Transforming Grace, 1988, Search for Wisdom and Spirit, 1988; editor: (with E.S. Florenza) Women, Work and Poverty, 1987, Motherhood: Experience, Institution, Theologu, 1989, Women's Special Nature?, 1991; bd. cons. Jour. of Religion, 1975-86, co-editor, 1987-94; assoc. editor Horizons, 1974—; editorial bd. Concilium, 1985-91. Trustee Mundelein Coll., Chgo., 1977-91. Postdoctoral fellow Harvard Divinity Sch., 1983-84, John Courtney Murry award, 1997. Mem. Am. Acad. Religion (program com. 1978-80), Cath. Theol. Soc. Am., Coll. Theology Soc. Roman Catholic. Office: U Chgo Divinity Sch 1025 E 58th St Chicago IL 60637-1509

CARR, BESSIE, retired middle school educator; b. Nathalie, Va., Oct. 10, 1920; d. Henry C. and Sirlena (Ewell) C. BS, Elizabeth City Coll., N.C., 1942; MA, Columbia U. Tchrs. Coll., 1948, PhD, 1950, EdD, 1952. Cert. adminstr., supr., tchr. Prin. pub. sch., Halifax, Va., 1942-47, Nathalie-Halifax County, Va., 1947-51; prof. edn. So. U., Baton Rouge, 1952-53; supr. schs. Lackland Schs., Cin., 1953-54; prof. edn. Wilberforce U., Ohio, 1954-55; tchr. Leland Sch., Pittsfield, Mass., 1956-60; chair math. dept., tchr. Lakeland Mid. Sch., N.Y., 1961-83. Founder, organizer, sponsor 1st Math Bowl and Math Forum in area, 1970-76; founder Dr. Bessie Carr award Halifax County Sr. High Sch., 1962. Mem. Nat. Women's Hall of Fame. Mem. AAUW (auditor 1970-85), Delta Kappa Gamma (auditor internat. 1970-76), Assn. Suprs. of Math. (chair coordinating council 1976-80), Ret. Tchrs. Assn., Black Women Bus. and Profl. Assn. (charter mem. Senegal, Africa chpt.). Democrat. Avocations: travel, photography, souvenirs.

CARR, CAROL ELAINE, biology professor; BA, Hampton (Va.) U., 1990, MA, 1993. Instr. biology John Tyler C.C., Chester, Va., 1995—. Faculty senator Faculty Senate of Va., Richmond, 2006. Campus coord. BRIDGES to Baccalaureate, Chester, 2005. Office: John Tyler CC 13101 Jefferson Davis Hwy Chester VA 23831 Office Phone: 804-706-5091. E-mail: ccarr@jtcc.edu.

CARR, CAROLYN KINDER, art gallery director; b. Providence, R(I; BA in Art History, Smith Coll.; MA in Art History, Oberlin Coll.; PhD in Art History, Case Western Reserve U. Instr. art history Kent (Ohio) State Univ., 1963-65, 67-68; art critic Akron (Ohio) Beacon Jour., 1968-73; chief curator Akron Art Mus., 1978—83; asst. dir. for collections Nat. Portrait Gallery, Washington, 1984-90, dep. dir., chief curator, 1991—. Vis. lectr. Akron U., Spring 1975, '76; organizer numerous art exhbns. Akron Art Mus., 1978—83, Nat. Portrait Gallery, 1984—. Contbr. articles to art publs. including Nat. Portrait Gallery, The Dictionary of Art, Am. Art, The Am. Art Jour., Dialogue, Currier Gallery of Art Bull.; author: art catalogs for exhibitions at Akron Art Mus., Chrysler Mus. of Art, Nat. Portrait Gallery and Smithsonian Instn. Office: Nat Portrait Gallery 750 9th St NW Box 37012 Washington DC 20013-7012 Office Phone: 202-275-1867. Business E-Mail: carrc@si.edu.

CARR, CLAUDIA, art gallery director, artist, art gallery owner; b. NYC, June 7, 1948; d. Charles Robert and Geraldine Carr; m. Jacques Marcel Levy, Apr. 27, 1980; children: Maya, Julien. BA, Adelphi U., 1970; MA, SUNY, Buffalo, 1976. Artist, curator 22 Wooster Art Gallery, N.Y.C., 1977-84; assoc. dir. Sindin Gallery, N.Y.C., 1991-92; instr. art history Colgate U., Hamilton, N.Y., 1992-93, 94-95, asst. curator collections Picker Art Gallery, 1993-94; owner, dir. Claudia Carr Gallery, N.Y.C., 1996—; curator Jenny Okun at Show Walls, the Durst Orgn., 2002. Curator Architectonics, Durst Orgn., 2002. Painting exhbns. include 22 Wooster Gallery, 1978, 80, Provincetown Art Assn., 1984; author: (essay) Towards Abstraction, 1975, (catalogues) Harold Wallin: Anchorage Mus., 1999, Jason Stewart Spirals, 1999. Pres. Shuttleworth Artists Corp., NY, 1978—81. Recipient Regents award N.Y. State, 1966, 5 Towns Music and Art Sculpture award 5 Towns L.I., 1968. Mem. Soho Alliance. Office: Claudia Carr Gallery 478 W Broadway New York NY 10012-3168 Office Phone: 212-673-5518. E-mail: claudiacarr@nyc.rr.com.

CARR, E. BARBARA, librarian; d. George Albert Jr. and Ella Mae (Carter) Buckner; m. Richard Lenard Carr, Feb. 12; children: Richard Lenard Jr., Eric Antonio, Lakelsha Reneé(dec.). BS in Food and Nutrition, Lincoln U., Jefferson City, Mo., 1966. Cert. libr. Mo., home economist Mo. Caseworker Mo. Divsn. Family Svc., St. Louis, 1966—73; tchr. St. Louis Pub. Schs., 1986—88, libr., 1988—. Sec. Sherman Cmty. Sch. Edn. Bd., St. Louis. Editor, designer: AKA Souvenir Fashionetta, 1993. Sec., v.p. St. Charles U. Extension, Mo., 1980—85; mem. St. Peters Betterment Coun., Mo., 1980—86, St. Peters Planning and Zoning Commn., 1980—85. Mem.: AAUW, One Hundred Black Women, Alpha Kappa Alpha. Episcopalian. Avocations: crafts, knitting, computer design, piano, sewing.

CARR, GLADYS JUSTIN, publishing executive, consultant, editor, writer; b. N.Y.C. d. Jack and Mollie (Marmor) Carr. BA, MA, Smith Coll.; postgrad., Cornell U. Sr. editor Prentice-Hall, Inc., Englewood Cliffs, NJ, 1969; exec. editor Cowles Comm., Inc., N.Y.C., 1969-71; editl. dir., editor-in-chief Am. Heritage Press, N.Y.C., 1971-75; sr. editor McGraw-Hill, Inc., N.Y.C., 1975-81, editor in chief, editorial dir., chmn. editorial bd., 1981-89, v.p., pub., 1988-89, HarperCollins Pubs., Inc., N.Y.C., 1989-2000; mng. dir. GJ Carr Assocs., N.Y.C., 2000—. Contbr. articles, fiction and poetry to literary and profl. jours. Marjorie Hope Nicholson trustee fellow, Smith Coll., Ford Found., Walter Francis Wilcox fellow, Cornell U. Mem. PEN Am. Ctr., Women's Media Group, Acad. Am. Poets, Poetry Soc. Am., Nat. Arts Club, Exec. and Chemists Club, Smith Coll. Club (N.Y.C.), Phi Beta Kappa. Home and Office: 920 Park Ave New York NY 10028-0208 also: 1 Boulder Ln East Hampton NY 11937-1047

CARR, LISA DIANE, lawyer; b. 1975; BA, Smith Coll., 1997; JD, Boston Coll. Law Sch., 2002. Bar: Mass. 2002. Assoc. Real Estate Practice Group Goulston & Storrs PC, Boston. Mem.: Boston Bar Assn., Mass. Bar Assn., ABA. Office: Goulston & Storrs PC 400 Atlantic Ave Boston MA 02110-3333 Office Phone: 617-574-4006. Office Fax: 617-574-7556. E-mail: lcarr@goulstonstorrs.com.*

CARR, MARGARET, elementary school educator; b. St. Louis, Mar. 13, 1947; d. John William Henry and Dorothy Eugene Ryan Long; m. Douglas A. Ries Jr., June 7, 1969 (div. July 1979); children: Colleen Margaret, Kathryn Anne; m. Daniel Francis Carr, Sept. 25, 1982. AB cum laude, St. Louis U., 1969; MA in Tchg., Webster U., 1979. Life cert. tchr., Mo. Tchr. St. Timothy's, St. Louis, 1970-71, St. Peter's, St. Charles, 1972-73, Immocolata, St. Louis, 1971-72, 76-77; tchr., home tutor Spl. Sch. Dist., St. Louis, 1977-80; tchr. Our Lady of Sorrow Sch., St. Louis, 1980-84, United Ch. of Christ Sch., St. Louis, 1984-86, Mary Queen of Peace Sch., Webster Groves, Mo., 1987—. Author: Fort San Carlos, May 26, 1780, 1997, History of Mary Queen of Peace School, 1999. Recipient award and medal Am. citizenship VFW, 1998; named Tchr. of Yr., VFW, 2001. Mem. Mo. State Soc. U.S. Daus. of 1812 (state pres. 1998—, pres. St. Louis pioneer chpt. 1995-98), DAR Mo., Continental Soc. Daus. of Indian Wars (gov. Mo. soc. 1994-98, hon. gov. 1998—), New Eng. Women (state pres. 199—), Colonial Dames of the 17th Century (vice regen Margaret Allyn Wyatt chpt.), Colonial Dames of Am., Descs. of the Founders of Hartford, Sons and Daus. of the Pilgrims, Daus. of Union Vets., Delta Kappa Gamma (Beta Theta chpt. 1996—). Avocations: collection sewing tapes, antique costume jewelry, angels. Home: 17 S Maple Ave Webster Groves MO 63119-3021 Office: Mary Queen of Peace Sch 680 W Lockwood Ave Webster Groves MO 63119-3598 E-mail: margcarr@swbell.net.

CARR, MARIE PINAK, book distribution company executive, publishing executive; b. Buffalo, June 17, 1954; d. Henry and Hildegard (Poech) Pinak; m. Richard Wallace Carr, Oct. 18, 1980; children: Katharine Marie, Ann Louise, Elizabeth Ashby. BS, Syracuse U., 1976. Cancer microbiologist Nat. Cancer Inst., Rockville, Md., 1976-78; mktg. specialist Precision Sci., Washington, 1978-80; art importer Dicmar Trading Co., Inc., Washington, 1981-83, book dist. Silver Spring, Md., 1983—. Co-author: The Willard Hotel, 1986. Bd. dirs. Salvation Army Women's Aux., Washington, 1982—, pres., 1990-91; bd. dirs. Am. Cancer Soc., Washington, 1988-90; co-chmn. Nat. Cancer Ball, 1989, 90; active Jr. League Washington, 1987-90; bd. dirs. Achievement Rewards for College Students, 2000—; mem. exec. bd. CARE USA. Mem.: Chevy Chase Club, Washington Club. Republican. Roman Catholic. Avocations: gardening, collecting textiles, tennis, travel. Office: Dicmar Trading Co Inc 4057 Highwood Ct NW Washington DC 20007-2131

CARR, MARSHA HAMBLEN, elementary school principal; b. Dunlap, Tenn., Nov. 28, 1961; d. Jackie Robert and Molly Ann (Johnson) Hamblen; m. Lonnie Gerron Carr, Feb. 26, 1980; 1 child, Gerra Sheree. BS in Spl. Edn. magna cum laude, Tenn. Tech. U., 1989, MA in Supervision of Instrn., 1992, ednl. specialist degree Edn. Leadership, 1997. Resource tchr. Sequatchie County Bd. Edn., Dunlap, 1989-90; early childhood spl. edn. tchr. Project CHILD Sequatchie County Bd. Edn., Dunlap, 1990-91, coord., 1991-97; principal Griffith Elem. Sch., Dunlap, Tenn., 1997—. Presenter Tenn. Young Children Assn., Chattanooga, 1992—; mem. adv. bd. Tenn. Early Intervention System, Chattanooga, 1990—; behavior mgmt. cons., Dunlap, 1990—; presenter Am. Edn. Rsch. Assn., San Diego. Active First Bapt. Ch. of Dunlap; Title I Sch. Support Svc. Facilitator. Mem. NEA, Tenn. Edn. Assn., Sequatchie County Edn. Assn., Assn. Supervision and Curriculum, Internat. Plastform Assn., Phi Kappa Phi, Delta Kappa Gamma (1st v.p., Internat. Xi state mem. chair), Pi Lambda Theta, Kappa Delta Pi. Democrat. Baptist. Avocations: reading, painting, travel, old movies. Home: 1043 Tram Trl Dunlap TN 37327-4446 Office: Griffith Elem Sch PO Box 819 Dunlap TN 37327-0819 Fax: (423) 949-6872.

CARR, PAMELA, librarian; b. Ogden, Utah, Jan. 19, 1945; d. Raymond Virgil and Jane Fox Cohrt; m. Robert Winston Carr (div.); children: David Robert, Steven Anthony, Andrea Carol. Student, Carretos Jr. Coll., Cypress Jr. Coll. Legal sec. Dist. Atty.'s Office, Southgate, Calif., 1962—63; mem. staff Rancho Amigo Hosp., Downey, 1963—64, LA County Fire Dept., LA, 1964—66, Orange County Juvenile Probation Dept., Orange, Calif., 1978—81; med. claims adjuster Found. Med. Care, Orange, 1981—82; sec. 3 County Office Edn., Downey, 1982—85; libr. asst. adminstr. Office of LA County Libr., Downey, 1988—98; libr. asst. Hemet (Calif.) Libr., 2005—. Mem. affirmative action com. LA County Libr., Downey, 1988—98. Contbr. poems to lit. publs. Sunday sch. Mormon Ch., Cerritos, Calif., 1972—74, music leader Buena Park and La Habra, Calif., 1995—98. Democrat. Avocations: singing, piano, dance, reading. Home: 628 S Santa Fe # 4 Hemet CA 92543 Office: 300 E Latham Hemet CA 92544

CARR, PATRICIA WARREN, adult education educator; b. Mobile, Ala., Mar. 24, 1947; d. Bedford Forrest and Mary Catherine (Warren) Slaughter; m. John Lyle Carr, Sept. 26, 1970; children: Caroline Elise, Joshua Bedford. BS in Edn., Auburn U., 1968, MEd, 1971. Tchr. DeKalb County Schs., Atlanta, 1969-70; counselor Dept. Defense Schs., Okinawa, Japan, 1972-75; tchr. Jefferson County Schs., Jefferson, Ga., 1975-76; counselor Clarke County Schs., Athens, Ga., 1976-78; tchr. Fairfax County Schs., Adult and Community Edn., Fairfax, Va., 1980—. Instrnl. supr. Vol. Learning Program; coord. Enrichment for Srs. Program Fairfax Area Agy. on Aging and Adult and Cmty. Edn., 1985-89; cons. State Va. Dept. Edn., 1984—, Va. Assn. Adult and Cmty. Edn., 1987, Commn. on Adult Basic Edn., 1988; instr. George Mason U., Fairfax, 1985. Tchr. Met. Meml. United Meth. Ch., Washington, 1981—; co-leader McClean, Va. troop Girl Scouts U.S., 1985-88. Mem. Am. Assn. Adult and Community Edn., Smithsonian Nat. Assocs., No. Va. Assn. Vol. Adminstrs., Va. Assn. Adult and Community Edn., Greater Washington Reading Coun. Methodist. Avocations: tennis, horseback riding. Office: Fairfax County Adult & Community Edn Woodson Adult Ctr 9525 Main St Fairfax VA 22031-4006 Business E-Mail: patricia.carr@fcps.edu.

CARR, RUTH MARGARET, plastic surgeon; b. Waco, Tex., July 2, 1951; MD, U. Okla., 1977. Intern U. Okla. Med. Sch., Oklahoma City, 1977-78; resident U. Okla. Health Sci. Ctr., Oklahoma City, 1978-81, UCLA, 1981-83; plastic surgeon St. John's Hosp., 1989—. Clin. asst. prof. UCLA, 1983—, U. So. Calif., 1984-. Mem.: Bay Surgical Soc. (pres. 2004), Calif. Soc. Plastic Surgeons (parliamentarian 2004—05), Am. Soc. Plastic Surgeons. Office: 1301 20th St Ste 470 Santa Monica CA 90404-2082 Office Phone: 310-315-0222. Business E-Mail: rcarr@ucla.edu.

CARR, THERESA, mathematics educator; d. James and Philomena Raftery; m. Joseph Carr, Mar. 25, 1984. BA, St. John's U., Jamica, N.Y., 1979, MS, 1987. Cert. permanent tchr. math grades 7-12 N.Y.S. Dept. Edn., 1987. Math. tchr. Christ the King Regional H.S., Middle Village, NY, 1979—81, Nazareth Regional H.S., Bklyn., 1981—87, Riverhead H.S., NY, 1987—, math. team advisor, 1997—, tchr. math to ESL students, 1997—98. Named Secondary Tchr. of Yr., L.I. U. Office: Riverhead High Sch 700 Harrison Ave Riverhead NY 11901 Office Phone: 631-369-9486. Office Fax: 631-369-9486. E-mail: theresa.carr@riverhead.net.

CARR, WINIFRED WALKER, artist, historian; b. Shanghai, June 8, 1925; d. Lawrence Henry Schultz and Ann Winifred Walker; m. Walter James Carr, Mar. 21, 1953; children: James Lawrence, Robert David. BFA, Carnegie Mellon U., 1948. Lectr. AAUW, Pitts., 1960—. One-woman shows include (Alumna of Yr. award, 1992). Vol. schs., YWCA, galleries, mus., Pitts., 1953—2000; arranger polit. awareness programs AAUW, Pitts., 1994—2004. Mem.: AAUW (pres. 2004—06). Democrat. Unitarian. Home: 1460 Jefferson Heights Rd Pittsburgh PA 15235 E-mail: wjamescarrjr@att.net.

CARRAHER, MARY LOU CARTER, art educator; b. Cin., Mar. 9, 1927; d. John Paul and Martha Leona (Williams) Carter; m. Emmett Carraher, Nov. 6, 1943 (div. July 1970); children: Candace Lou Holsenbeck-Smith, Michael Emmett, Cathleen C. Kruska. Student, U. Cin., 1946-48, Calif. State U., 1973-74. Lifetime credential in adult edn.: art, ceramics, crafts, Calif. Substitute tchr. Cobb County Schs., Smyrna, Ga., 1961-63; art tchr. pvt. lessons Canyon Country, Calif., 1968-72; adult edn. art tchr. Wm. S. Hart H.S. Dist., Santa Clarita, Calif., 1973-97; children's art and calligraphy cmty. svcs. Coll. of the Canyons, Santa Clarita, Calif., 1976-96. Fine arts coord. Santa Clarita Sr. Ctr., 1998—; founder, bd. dirs. Santa Clarita Art Guild, 1972-80; art dir. European tours Continental Club, Canyon Country, 1977-81; art tour guide and travel cons. Northridge (Calif.) Travel, 1981-91; vol. art tchr. stroke patients Henry Newhall Meml. Hosp., Valencia, Calif., 1993-96; craft tchr. for respite care program, Newhall, Calif., 1995-96, Respite Care Ctr., Santa Clarita Valley Sr. Ctr., 1995-96; art tour guide, Andulusia, Spain, 1997, 99. Artist, author History of Moreland School District, San Jose, California, 1965; prin. works include Paintings for each season of Church Year, 1970's, Baptismal painting, 1988, Sr. Ctr. Watercolors Ctr. Scenes, 1993, Watercolors of Christmas Charity Home Tour, 1993, Henry Mayo Newhall Meml. Hosp., 1997, 1999, 2001, 2002, 2003, 2004, murals painted for Christian Ch. and Sr. Ctr., 1997—99, mall st. painting for charity, 2000, exhibitions include Art Walk, Arts Coun., 2002—. Tchr., mem. Santa Clarita United Meth. Ch., 1966-96; judge for art contests and exhibits, Santa Clarita, 1973-96; mem. Santa Clarita Valley Hist. Soc., 1989-96; mem. Alumni Assn., Norwood (Ohio) City Schs., 1993-96; leader art tours to Spain, 1997, 99, 2002, Italy, 2001, Portugal, 2002, Australia, New Zealand and Fiji, 2003; designer certs, with scenes of Sr. Ctr., Cir. of Friends certs; leader art tour Rhine River Cruise, France, 2003-2004, Rhone River Tour, 2003, 04. Recipient Bravo award nomination for Outstanding Achievement in Art, 1995, Sr. of Yr. Santa Clarita Valley Sr. Ctr. and Svc. Newspaper "The Signal", 1995, Christian Svc. award Santa Clarita United Meth. Ch., 1988; invited by Citizen Amb. Program of People to People Internat. to join U.S. del. to assess bus. and trade opportunities of the craft industry in China. Mem. Santa Clarita Valley Arts Coun., Hosp. Home Tour League, Nat. Women in the Arts (charter, Washington). Republican. Methodist. Avocations: travel, crafts, reading.

CARRANZA, JOVITA, delivery service executive; b. Chgo., June 29, 1949; m. Joel Roque; 1 child, Klaudene. Undergraduate, U. Miami, Calif. State U., LA; MBA for exec., U. Miami. Night-shift hub clerk UPS, LA, 1976; supr. UPS, Metro LA Hub Oper., 1976—79; human resources supr. UPS, Metro LA, 1979—85, workforce planning mgr., 1985—87, bus. mgr., 1987; dist. human resources mgr. UPS, Cent. Tex., 1987—90, UPS, Ill., 1990—91, divsn. mgr. hub, packer, and feeder opers. Ill., 1991—93, ctrl. Fla. dist. mgr., 1993—96, divsn. mgr. hub, packer, and feeder opers. Wis., 1996—99, mgr. Am. regions (including Mexico, PR, Dominican Rep., Virgin Islands), 1999—2000, region mgr. internat. opers. Miami, 2000—03, v.p. air opers. Louisville, 2003—. Vol. Habitat for Humanity; bd. mem. Libr. Found., Louisville. Named Woman Yr., Hispanic Bus. Mag., 2004; named one of 50 Most Important Hispanics in Tech. & Bus., Hispanic Engr. & Info. Tech. mag., 2005. Mem.: Nat. Coun. La Raza. Achievements include first female internat. region pres. in UPS history; highest ranking Hispanic female at UPS; expanded UPS in Latin Am. Office: UPS 2245 Hikes Ln Louisville KY 40218 Office Phone: 502-459-8788.*

CARRASQUILLO, KATRINA BEAUFORT, secondary school educator, consultant; d. Benjamin Franklin and Virginia Dare Beaufort; m. Gerardo Carrasquillo, July 8, 1978 (dec. Jan. 15, 1993); 1 child, Karmen Zenobia. BA, Lincoln U., Oxfor, Pa., 1976; MS in Lang. Arts, Fayetteville State U., NC, 1993. Cert. advanced tech., on-line tchg. Fayetteville Tech. C.C., 1996; critical thinking Ctr. Cognitive Coaching, 1999, cognitive coaching Ctr. Cognitive Coaching, 2001. Tchr. Reading Sch. Dist., Pa., 1972—76; reading tchr. Cumberland County Schs., Fayetteville, 1976—78; ESL, reading, English tchr. DODDS, Clark Air Base, Philippines, 1978—83; Chpt. I tchr. Cumberland County Schs., Fayetteville, 1983—95; tchr. 71st Elem., Fayetteville, 1990—95; comm. skills tchr. Douglass Byrd Mid., Fayetteville, 1995—2000; English/freshman seminar tchr. 71st High, Fayetteville, 2000—. Active United Order Tents, Fayetteville, 1984; tutorial coord. Williams Chapel FWB Ch., Spring Lake, NC, 2005—06; mem. EE Smith Nat. Alumni Assn., Fayetteville, 2000; publicity chairperson Delta Sigma Theta Sorority, Inc., Fayetteville, 2000—06. Named Tchr. of Yr., 71st Elem., 1989; NC Writing fellow, U. NC Pembroke, 1996. Mem.: NCAE. Democrat. Baptist. Avocations: interior decorating, reading, writing, singing, travel. Home: 5247 Foxfire Rd Fayetteville NC 28303 Office: Seventy-First High School 6764 Raeford Rd Fayetteville NC 28304-2771 Office Phone: 910-867-3116.

CARR-CAROTHERS, MARCELLA IRENE, medical surgical nurse; b. McCook, Nebr., Oct. 9, 1938; d. Carl Oscar and Ruby Marcella (Miller) Peterson; m. Robert Connell Carr, Aug. 20, 1957; children: Brenda Irene Barela, Robert Carl Carr, David Alan Carr., m. Charles Douglas Carothers, April 27, 2001. LPN diploma, Mid Plains C.C., 1977; ADN, Dakota Wesleyan U., 1985; BS, U. Nebr., 1987. RN, Kans., Nebr., Fla.; cert. BLS, Am. Heart Assn. Stenographer, clk. Frontier County Welfare Office, Curtis, Nebr., 1956-66; office asst. Charles E. Hranac, M.D., Cozad, Nebr., 1967-75; staff nurse Cozad (Nebr.) Community Hosp., 1977-87; staff nurse part-time Richard Young Hosp., Kearney, Nebr., 1989-93; pool nurse Great Plains Health Alliance, Phillipsburg, Kans., 1985—93; home health nurse Cozad (Nebr.) Cmty. Hosp., 1993-94; house supr. Southview Manor Care Ctr., Cozad, 1994-96; supr. Hilltop Estates, Gothenburg, Nebr., 1996—98; ret., 1998. Mem. ANA, Nat. League Nursing, Kans. Nurses Assn., Nebr. Nurses Assn., Am. Assn. Ret. Persons, Royal Neighbors Am. (oracle 1964-66), Maccabees, Psi Chi. Republican. Mem. Ch. of Christ. Avocations: motorcycle riding, gardening, crafts, reading, hiking. Home: 1418 Avenida Sierra North Fort Myers FL 33903-1326 Personal E-mail: mcarothers@gmail.com.

CARR-DERAMUS, DENISE, mental health counselor; b. Boston, Dec. 15, 1951; d. Gilman and Blanche (Francis) Carr. BA, Boston State Coll., 1981; MEd, U. Mass., 1983, CAGS, 1988, postgrad., 1988—. Lic. mental health counselor; addictions specialist, clin. mental health counselor, approved supr. Rehab. counselor Quincy (Mass.) Mental Health Ctr.; staff psychologist Wrentham (Mass.) State Sch.; psychologist III Mass. Treatment Ctr., Bridgewater, Pocasset MNC, Ala., 2004—, Ala. Dept. Corrections, Montgomery, 2004—. Mem. Ala. Multicultural Counseling and Devel., Ala. Mental Health Counselors Assn., Ala. Assn. Addiction and Offenders Counselors, Internat. Assn. Corrections and Forensic Psychologists, Vietnam Vets. Am.

CARREL, MARIANNE EILEEN, music educator; b. Greenville, Pa., Aug. 28, 1957; d. Francis Raymond Cremi, Betty Hutton Cremi; m. Marion Lee Carrel. Student, Clarion U. Pa., 1975—76; BS, Edinboro U., 1979, MEd, 1985. Cert. elem. tchr. Ohio. Substitute tchr. Greenville and Reynolds Sch. Dists., Greenville, Pa., 1979—80; tchr. music Webster County Schs., Cowen, W.Va., 1980—84; grad. asst. Edinboro U., Edinboro, Pa., 1984—85; tchr. music Madison Local Schs., Madison, Ohio, 1985—86; tchr. music Geneva Area City Schs., Geneva, Ohio, 1986—. Sec. All-Am. Judges Assn., Ohio, 1989—. Named Assoc. of Yr., Am. Bus. Women's Assn., 2000-2001. Mem.: NEA, Internat. Double Reed Soc., Music Educators Nat. Conf., Ohio Edn. Assn., Kappa Delta Pi, Sigma Alpha Iota (life). Home: 4850 Boughner Rd Rock Creek OH 44084 Office: Geneva Area Schs 839 Sherman St Geneva OH 44041 Office Phone: 440-466-6651. Personal E-mail: mandmcarrel@direcway.com.

CARRELL, JENNIFER LEE, writer; d. William Dayton and Melinda Carrell; m. Johnny N. Helenbolt. BA, Stanford U., 1984; MA, Oxford U., 1987; PhD, Harvard U., 1994. Classical music, opera, dance critic Ariz. Daily Star, Tucson, 1999—2001; lectr., preceptor Harvard U., Cambridge, 1994—98. Author: (non-fiction book) The Speckled Monster: A Historical Tale of Battling Smallpox.

CARRICK, KATHLEEN MICHELE, law librarian; b. Cleve., June 11, 1950; d. Michael James and Genevieve (Wenger) C. BA, Duquesne U., Pitts., 1972; MLS, U. Pitts., 1973; JD, Cleve.-Marshall U., 1977. Bar: Ohio 1977, U.S. Ct. Internat. Trade 1983. Rsch. asst. The Plain Dealer, Cleve., 1973-75; head reference SUNY, Buffalo, 1977-78, assoc. dir., 1978-80, dir., asst. prof., 1980-83; dir., assoc. prof. law Case Western Res. U., Cleve., 1983—. Cons. Mead Data Central, Dayton, Ohio, 1987-91. Author: Lexis: A Research Manual, 1989, From Litchfield to Lexis: A Bibliography of American Legal Education, 2004; contbr. articles to profl. jours. Fellow Am. Bar Found.; mem. ABA, Am. Law Inst., Am. Assn. Law Librs., Assn. Am. Law Schs., Scribes. Home: 1317 Burlington Rd Cleveland OH 44118-1212 Office: Case Western Res U 11075 East Blvd Cleveland OH 44106-5409 Office Phone: 216-368-6357. Business E-Mail: kxc4@case.edu.

CARRIER, RACHEL ESTHER, music educator, director; b. Dayton, Ohio, Dec. 22, 1949; d. Robert Richard Folkerth and Amber Mae Spitler; m. Harold Gene Carrier, Jan. 27, 1968; children: Bryan Patrick, Alan Brent. BA in Performing Arts, Wittenberg Univ., 1975; student, Sinclair Coll., 1986—87,

Wright State U., 1987—90; studied with, Douglas MacCash, 1964—84, D. Maddafore, 1968—73, Joan Swank. Cert. dental asst. nat., 1980. Orthodontic asst. Drs. King, Mayerson, Pope, Dayton, 1968—73; dental forensic asst. Wm. Bernard Weaver, D.M.D, Dayton, 1978—93; vocal instr. Northmont H.S., Clayton, Ohio, 1994—. Music cons. Bel Canto Young Singers Music Club, Dayton, 1997—; dir. children's drama and show choir Miami-Montage Children's Theater, Vandalia, Ohio, 1996—98; dir. children's choir Concord United Meth. Ch., Englewood, Ohio, 1973—74, asst. dir. music, youth dir., 1977—92; youth choir dir. Englewood (Ohio) United Meth. Ch., 1989—91; dir. music Vandalia (Ohio) United Meth. Ch., 1993—98; dir. music ministries and drama and Christian edn. Shiloh Ch., Dayton, 1998—, dir. christian edn., 1998—2001; vocal judge Regional Star Search, Cincinnati-Dayton, Ohio, 2004; dir. Music Ministries and Drama. Singer: George Washington Episc. Ch., Dayton (Ohio) Opera. Dir. Dayton (Ohio) Performing Arts Programs, 1998—2003. Named Woman of the Yr., Am. Biog. Assoc., 2001. Mem.: Dayton Music Club (corr.; cons. to the jr. music club 1998—2003), The Fellowship/Music and Worship Arts (corr.), Ohio Fedn. of Music Clubs (state festival chmn. 1998—), Ohio Ea. Star (past matron 1979—80, State of Ohio Vocalist 1978, 1979, 1980, 1982, 1984). Republican. Protestant. Avocations: breeding english springer spaniels, swimming, acting, gardening, directing handbells. Home: 4339 Gorman Ave Englewood OH 45322 Office: Shiloh Church UCC 5300 Philadelphia Dr Dayton OH 45415 Office Phone: 937-277-8953. Personal E-mail: rachcar898@aol.com. E-mail: rachelcarrier@shiloh.org.

CARRIER, TERRIRUTH, industrial engineer; d. Joseph Ernest and Maryruth Carrier; m. Douglas Paul Fenster, May 19, 1979; children: Kristen Mae Carrierfenster, Kellyn Lindsay Carrierfenster. BS in Indsl. Engring. and Ops. Rsch., Syracuse U., 1979, MS in Engring. Adminstrn., 1987. Preplan engr. Packard Electric divsn. GM, Warren, Ohio, 1979—80; corp. info. and mgmt. dir. Anaren, Syracuse, 1980—93; info. sys. and tech. dir. Joseph J. Pietrafesa LLP, Syracuse, 1993—96; br. mgr., network integration dir. Interim Tech., Syracuse, 1996—97; project mgr., bus. analyst Tech. Design Group, Inc., Syracuse, 1997—. Mem. impact team on preventing violence United Way, Syracuse, 2003. Recipient Lumen Christi award, Bishop Ludden HS, 2001. Mem.: Inst. Indsl. Engring., Mensa. Avocation: web site development for small companies. Office: Technology Design Group Inc 4854 Pembridge Cir Syracuse NY 13215 Business E-Mail: carrier@tdgrp.com.

CARRILLO, JUANITA, gerontological services consultant; b. Passaic, N.J., June 5, 1937; d. William and Channie (Fortney) Pitts; m. Manuel Carrillo, Jan. 1, 1961 (div. Sept. 1992); children: Manuel Jr., Karen. BMusEd magna cum laude, Howard U., 1959; MSW, Fordham U., 1977, PhD of Social Work, 2002. LCSW N.Y. Dept. Edn., 1978. Caseworker, supr. Bur. Pub. Assistance N.Y.C. Human Resources Adminstrn., 1961—80, dir. programs for homeless individuals and families Crisis Intervention Svcs., 1980—86, supr. profl. social workers Medicaid/Disability Rev. Divsn., 1986—90, dir. through Regional Adminstr. Home Care Svcs. Program, 1990—2001; cons. gerontology Fordham U., N.Y.C., 2002—. Consortium mem. through project coord. Pilot Program for Professionalism in Elder Care Forham U., N.Y.C., 2002—; UN rep. Internat. Assn. Gerontology, 2004. Pub. policy com. mem. N.Y. State Soc. on Aging, Albany, 2002—; bd. dirs. SonRise CDC First Bapt. Ch., Englewood, NJ. Mem.: NASW, AAUW (co-v.p. Northern Valley chpt. 2003—), Nat. Assn. Black Social Workers, Gerontol. Soc. Am., Alpha Kappa Alpha Sorority (life). Avocations: music, home decorating.

CARRILLO, LINDA MARIE, counselor; b. Fukuoka, Kyushu, Japan, Dec. 29, 1955; came to U.S., 1958; d. Julio and Tomiko (Yamamoto) C.; m. Gillard Gunshi Matsumiya, June 1, 1975 (div. 1981); 1 child, Sibyl Matsumiya; m. Carl Russell Nelson, Feb. 14, 1982 (div. 1990); 1 child, Christina; m. Carl Russell Nelson, Dec. 25, 1994. BA in Psychology, U. Hawaii-Manoa, Honolulu, 1977; MA in Communication, U. Hawaii, 1980; MEd in Counseling and Guidance, U. Hawaii-Manoa, 1990. Realtor Horita Realty, Inc., Kalihi, Hawaii, 1978-93; counselor Dept. of Edn., 1990—. Pres. Am. Field Service, Wahiawa, Hawaii, 1972-73. Mem. AACD, ASCD, Hawaii State Tchrs. Assn. (v.p. 1992-93), Hawaii Mental Health Counselors Assn., Hawaii Sch. Counselor Assn., Pi Lambda Theta. Home: 95-066 Hokuiwa St Apt 116 Mililani HI 96789-1502 E-mail: linda.carrillo@gmail.com.

CARRIM, RHONDA LYNNE, theology studies educator, priest; b. Emmett, Idaho, Apr. 11, 1964; d. Robert Leon and Glennea Sherie Gibson; m. Rosman Errol Carrim, May 26, 1990; 1 child, Kimberly Roslynne. BA, NW Nazarene U., Nampa, Idaho, 1986; MDiv, Nazarene Theol. Sem., Kansas City, Mo., 1990; DMin, Asbury Theol. Sem., Wilmore, Ky., 2000; postgrad., Nazarene Theol. Coll., Manchester, Eng., 2000. Ordained elder Ch. of the Nazarene, 1994. Co-pastor Ch. of the Nazarene, Felicity, Trinidad and Tobago, 1990—96; faculty Caribbean Nazarene Theol. Coll., Cantaro, 1990—2000, dir. admissions, 1992—96, acad. dean, 1996—99; adj. faculty Nazarene Theol. Coll., Manchester, 2001—04; pastor Didsbury Ch. of the Nazarene, Manchester, 2002—04; faculty NW Nazarene U., Nampa, 2004—. Recipient Leon Doane Young Alumnus award, NW Nazarene U., 2000. Mem.: Soc. for the Study of Christian Spirituality, Wesleyan Theol. Soc., Wesleyan Hist. Soc. Mem. Ch. Of The Nazarene. Avocations: camping, fishing, travel. Office: Northwest Nazarene Univ 623 Holly St Nampa ID 83686 Office Phone: 1-208-467-8349. Office Fax: 1-208-467-8252. Business E-Mail: rlcarrim@nnu.edu.

CARRINGTON, MARIAN DENISE, academic administrator, counselor, motivational speaker; b. Smithfield, N.C., Aug. 12, 1960; d. James A. Stevens and Marian Louise (Revels) Whitley; children: Wynnona Alexis, Crystal Elizabeth. BS, Old Dominion U., 1982; MA, Hampton U., 1991; doctoral student in Am. Studies, Coll. William and Mary. Coord. cooperative edn. and internships Hampton (Va.) U., 1982-90; corporate recruitment coord. Christopher Newport U., Newport News, Va., 1990-91, dir. multicultural student affairs, 1991—. Grantwriter The Lighthouse Found., Bethel Temple, Hampton, Va., 2000—; founder MARVEL M. Presentations, Hampton, 1990—, The Coun. for Humanity, Urban Renewal and Cmty. Wholeness, 1994—; founder, dir. New Beginnings for God's Women, Hampton, 1994—; cons. U. Ala., Tuscaloosa, 1985. Mem. exec. bd. YWCA Phyllis Wheatley Br., Newport News, 1992—, Hampton Coalition for Youth, Hampton, 1993—, Machen Elem. Sch. PTA, Hampton, 1994-95, Colonial Coast Girl Scout Coun., Norfolk, Va., 1994; bd. mem. Menchville House Ministries, Inc., 1998—. Grantee U.S. Dept. Edn., 1983-90, State Coun. Higher Edn., 1990-94, 93-96. Mem. Va. Assn. Black Faculty and Adminstrs., Va. Counselor's Assn., Vocat. Edn. Adv. Coun. Avocations: singing, volleyball, reading suspense novels, poetry. Office: The Lighthouse Found 1705 Todds Ln Hampton VA 23666-3122

CARRINGTON, VIRGINIA GAIL (VEE CARRINGTON), marketing professional, consultant; b. Dodge City, Kans., Apr. 20, 1949; d. Virgel Troy and Betty Lou (Rynerson) Fakes; Lynn Nugent Friesner, Aug. 4, 1971 (div. Feb. 1985); m. Paul Henry Carrington, Apr. 4, 1987. BA, Kans. Wesleyan, 1971; MS, U. Ill., 1972; MA, Kans. State U., 1978. Sci. cataloger Kans. State U. Libr., Manhattan, 1972-74, humanities bibliographer, 1974-78; dir. libr. devel. State Libr. Kans., Topeka, 1978-84; libr. network dir. Kans. Libr. Network, Topeka, 1982-84; edn. officer Pub. Libr. Assn. ALA, Chgo., 1984-86; pres. Carrington Cons., Waterbury, Conn., 1986-97; promotion coord. Assn. Coll. and Rsch. Libr. ALA, Middletown, Conn., 1997-01; pres. Carrington Cons. Assocs., Waterbury, 2001—; mgr., analyst The Carrington Co., Southington, Conn., 2001—. Mgr. mem. svcs. Mattatuck Mus., Waterbury, 1992-97. Asst. editor: Guide to Reference Books, 11th edit., 1994; asst. to editor: Guide to Reference Books Supplement to 10th ed., 1990; contr. articles to profl. jours. Mem. ALA (Continuing Libr. Edn. Network and Exch. Roundtable, Ind. Librs. Exch. Roundtable, chair membership com. 2004-05), Am. Mktg. Assn., Mountain Plains Libr. Assn., New Haven Postal Customer Coun. (exec. bd. 2002-, industry co-chair 2005—, vendor show workshop com. 2005-). Democrat. Methodist. Avocations: travel, reading. Home: 130 Melbourne Ter Waterbury CT 06704-1843 Office: Carrington Co PO Box 392 Southington CT 06489 Personal E-mail: veegeecee@yahoo.com.

CARROLL, BARBARA, musician, composer, singer; b. Worcester, Mass., Jan. 25, 1925; d. David Louis and Lillian Rose (Lavine) Coppersmith; m. Joseph Shulman, Sept. 20, 1954 (dec. Aug. 2, 1957); m. Bertram Joseph Block, Oct. 7, 1960 (dec. July 9, 1986); 1 child, Suzanne Elizabeth. Student, New Eng. Conservatory of Music, 1943-44; D in Music (hon.), Pine Manor Coll., 1980. Leader Barbara Carroll Trio, 1951-60. Appearances for 3 months Bemelmans Bar, The Carlyle, N.Y.C., spring and fall; Broadway appearances in Me and Juliet; TV appearances include All My Children, 1983, Today Show, Tonight Show, CBS Sunday Morning, 1995; (albums) Have You Met Miss Carroll, It's a Wonderful World, (CDs) Live At the Carlyle, This Heart of Mine, Everything I Love, Old Friends. Bd. mem. Duke Ellington Meml. Fund. Mem. ASCAP, Songwriter's Guild, Friars Club. Avocations: gardening, entertaining, cooking.

CARROLL, BETTY JEAN, retired application developer; b. San Antonio, Tex., Dec. 5, 1930; d. Jesse Irvin Casbeer and Nelda Martha Blum; m. John D. Kissack, Oct. 5, 1957 (div. Oct. 0, 1963); m. Richard Andrew Carroll, Oct. 3, 1946 (div. Mar. 0, 1954); children: Peggy Jean Choka, Martha Ann Scott, Betty Jacquelyn, Richard Andrew, Michael Neil. AA, San Antonio Coll., Tex., 1956; BA in Liberal Arts, Wright State U., Dayton, Ohio, 1976. Office mgr. and acct. Civilian Bldg. and Supply, Ft. Wayne, Ind., 1963—66; staff acct. Rignanese, Shannon & Horn CPA, 1966—67; cost acct. Air Flow Heating and Air Conditioning, 1967—70; computer specialist/programmer Wright-Patterson AFB, Dayton, Ohio, 1970—95; office mgr. and acct. So. Ohio Growth Partnership, Portsmouth, 1995—98; computer programmer STAR Fin. Bank, Ft. Wayne, Ind., 2000—03. Author: The Foothill Spirits-Book One: Frontier Life & the Shawnees, 2001, rev., 2005, The Foothill Spirits-Book Two: Shawnees & Runaway Slaves, 2006, The Mystery of the Red-Brick House, 2002. Sec.-treas. Gingerbread Ho. Day Care, Fort Wayne, Ind., 1999—2003; mem. speaker's collective and women's ctr. task force Dayton Women's Liberation, Ohio, 1970—75; v.p. Women's Internat. League Peace and Freedom, 1974—75, Miami Valley Freedom of Choice, 1979—80; co-chair Women Racial & Econ. Equality, 1987—91; bd. mem. Midway Day Care Ctr., 1969—70; charter mem. Federally Employed Women, Fairborn, 1973; sec.-treas. AFGE Coun. 214, Dayton, 1980—82; charter mem. Coalition of Labor Union Women, Fairborn, 1985; pres. Am. Fedn. Govt. Employees AFL-CIO Local 1138, Dayton, 1991—95. Mem.: The Scribes. Unitarian-Universalist. Avocations: reading, book discussion groups, writer's group mentor, history, book collecting. Home: 7109 Lower Huntington Rd Fort Wayne IN 46809-9615 E-mail: betty-casbear-carroll@foothill-spirits.com.

CARROLL, CONSTANCE MARIE, pianist, educator; b. Hartford, Conn., May 6, 1945; d. Joseph Deglan and Elizabeth Tracy Carroll; 1 child, Jackson William Blossom. MusB magna cum laude, U. Hartford, 1968; MusM, Manhattan Sch. Music, 1980; postgrad., Ind. U., 1981—84. Pvt. tchr. piano, Conn. and NY, 1965—. Ch. organist, music dir. Ridgebury Congl. Ch., Ridgebury, Conn., 2002—; accompanist Lubeck Ballet and Musical Theatre, Germany, 1992—93, Luzern Ballet, Switzerland, 1993—94, Basel Ballet, Switzerland, 1994—96. Scholar, NY State PTA, 1983. Mem.: Am. Guild Organists, Music Tchrs. Nat. Assn., Conn. State Music Tchrs.' Assn. Home and Office: 35C Sky Hollow Ct Oakville CT 06779 Office Phone: 860-274-4198.

CARROLL, CORLIS FAITH, artist, educator; b. Troy, N.Y., Oct. 11, 1950; d. Thomas Francis and Dorothy May (Sellingham) C.; children: Heather Elise Hewitt, Heidi Carroll Hewitt. BA summa cum laude, U. Albany, 1994. Artist, 1983—. Represented in private collections. Mediator Matrimonial and Cmty. Dispute Resolution. Mem. Phi Beta Kappa. Home: 20 Beldale Rd Slingerlands NY 12159

CARROLL, CYNTHIA B., mining executive; b. Phila., Pa. married; 4 children. BS in Geology, Skidmore Coll., 1978; MS, U. Kansas, 1982; MBA, Harvard U., 1989. Geologist Amoco, 1982—87; bus. analyst, asst. to the pres. Alcan Inc., 1988, bus. analyst rolled products group, 1989—91, v.p., gen. mgr. US foil products, 1991—95, mng. dir. Aughinish Alumina subs. Ireland, 1996—98, pres. bauxite, Alcan's alumina and specialty chemicals group, 1998—2001, pres., CEO primary metal group, 2002—06; CEO elect Anglo American plc, 2007—, also bd. dirs., 2007—. Bd. dirs. Sara Lee Corp., 2006—. Mem.: Internat. Aluminum Inst. (bd. dirs.), Am. Aluminum Assn. (bd. dirs.). Office: Anglo American plc 20 Carlton House Terr London SW1Y 5AN England*

CARROLL, DIAHANN, actress, singer; b. N.Y.C., July 17, 1935; d. John and Mabel (Faulk) Johnson; m. Monte Kay (div.); m. Fredde Glusman (div.); m. Robert DeLean, 1975 (dec. 1977); m. Vic Damone, 1987. Student, N.Y. U. Began career as model; actress: (motion pictures) Claudine (Nominated for Acad. award as best actress by the Acad. Motion Picture Arts and Scis. 1974), Carmen Jones, 1954, Porgy and Bess, 1959, Paris Blues, 1961, Hurry Sundown, 1967, The Split, 1968, The Five Heartbeats, 1991, Eve's Bayou, 1997; (On Broadway) No Strings, House of Flowers; appeared in: play Same Time, Next Year; (TV series) Dynasty, 1984-87, The Colbys, 1986, Lonesome Dove, 1994-95; (TV movies) Death Scream, 1975, I Know Why the Caged Bird Sings, 1979, Sister, Sister, 1982, Murder in Black and White, 1990, Sunday in Paris, 1991, A Perry Mason Mystery: The Case of the Lethal Lifestyle, 1994, The Sweetest Gift, 1998, Motown 40: The Music is Forever, 1998, Having Our Say: The Delany Sisters' First 100 Years, 1999; (TV miniseries) Roots: The Next Generations, 1979, Motown 40: The Music is Forever, 1998, Jackie's Back!, 1999, The Courage to Love, 2000, Sally Hemmings: An American Scandal, 2000, Livin' for Love: the Natalie Cole Story, 2000; guest appearances Julia, 1970, 1971, Different World, 1991, 1992, 1993, Evening Shade, 1994, Touched By An Angel, 1995, Strong Medicine, 2003, Whoopi, 2003, Soul Food, 2004, The 4th Annual TV Land Awards: A Celebration of Classic TV, 2006 and others; host Diahann Carroll Show, 1976.*

CARROLL, DONNA M., academic administrator; MA, U. Cin., 1977, PhD in Edn., 1981. Program dir. U. Cin.; dean of students Fairleigh Dickenson U., Madison, NJ, Mt. Vernon Coll., Washington, v.p. devel.; sec. Fordham U., 1991—94, exec. sec. Bd. Trustees, 1991—94; pres. Dominican U., River Forest, Ill., 1994—. Recipient Chief Exec. Leadership award, Coun. Advancement and Support of Edn., 2004. Office: Dominican U 7900 W Division River Forest IL 60305

CARROLL, JANE HAMMOND, artist, writer, poet; b. Greenville, SC, May 15, 1946; d. Charles Kirby and Margaret (Cooper) Hammond; m. Robert Lindsay Carroll Jr., Feb. 3, 1968; children: Jane-Gower, Robert Lindsay III. BA, U. SC, 1968. Tchr. A.C. Flora High Sch., Columbia, S.C., 1968-70; exec. field dir. N.E. Ga. Girl Scout Coun., Athens, 1970-71; asst. dir. AID-Vol. Greenville, 1971-73; author, artist Winston Derek Pubs., Nashville, 1985—. Author: Grace, 1987 (Gov.'s Collection 1988), Intimate Moments, 1987 (Gov.'s Collection), Dayspring, 1989; one-woman shows include Williams Salon, Atlanta, 1989, 92-95, 99-2000, 05, 06, Galerie Timothy Tew, Jenny Pruitt Realty, 1989, Ariel Gallery, Atlanta, 1996, Revis Lewis Gallery, Greenville, 2002; group shows include Fine Art Mus. of the South, Mobile, Beyond the Wall, 1990, Sumner Mus. Archives, Washington, 1992, Internat. Pastel Show, Ga., 1991, 95, Savannah Nat. (1st pl. award in drawing), Telfare Mus. Savannah, 1995, 2000, 02, 04, Telfare Art Fair, Ariel Gallery, 1995-99, Calloway Garden, 1998, Cathedral of St. Philips, Atlanta, 2000, Nat. Art Exhbn. South Cobb Alliance, 2000, 02-03, Ga. Nat. Fair, Perry, (Drawing prize, Merit award), Holly Mitchell Fine Art, Greenville, 2004, Portrait Soc., Atlanta, juried shows, 2005, 06; permanent collections represented Greenville Meml. Hosp., SC, Embassy Suites, Ill., Macan Motor Cars, Ga., Jenny Pruitt Reality, Ga., others; commns. include Landscape, Portraits, family, others; pub. and pvt. collections; author numerous poems. Bd. mgr. Greenville Jr. League, 1971-73; artist for fundraiser Rehab. Edn. for Handicapped Adults and Children, Atlanta, 1992-95; vol. artist Arts in the Atlanta Project, 1993, Symphony of Greenville Art Sale fundraiser, 2002. Mem. Nat. League Am. Pen Women (chair art's program 1984-2000, Achievement award 1987, 89, 93-98), Atlanta Artist Club (v.p. 1984-85, Merit mem.). Presbyterian. Achievements include master artist workshops with Nelson Shanks, Phila. 2001-06. Avocations: travel, reading, outdoor activities, yoga. Home and Office: 2979 Majestic Cir Avondale Estates GA 30002-1611 Office Phone: 404-294-8167. Business E-Mail: janescapeltd@cs.com.

CARROLL, JEAN GRAY, mathematics educator; b. Louisville, Ky., May 27, 1939; d. McDonald and Jean Dawson Gray; m. John Gillespie Carroll, Sept. 7, 1963; children: Lewis McDonald, Stephen Gillespie, Elizabeth Carroll Ovelman. BS, U.Ky., Lexington, Ky., 1961; MAT, Spalding U., Louisville, Ky., 1980. Cert. tchg. Ky. State Dept. of Edn., 1980. Computer programmer and sr. systems analyst Commonwealth Life Ins. Co., Louisville, 1961—70; real estate agt. and broker Bass and Weisberg Real Estate, Louisville, 1975—79; substitute tchr. Jefferson County Pub. Schs., Louisville, 1979—80, math and computer tchr., 1980—. Adj. math faculty Jefferson CC, Louisville, 1987—95. Fund raiser Actors' Theater of Louisville, Louisville, 1965—66; vol. Red Cross Blood Bank, Louisville, 1956—59; mem. Jr. League of Louisville, 1963—87, chmn. horse show program, 1971; by laws com., choir, Christian edn. tchr., treas. women of the ch. St. Lukes Episcopal Ch., Anchorage, Ky. Mem.: Nat. Coun. of Tchrs. of Math. (assoc.). Democrat. Episcopalian. Avocations: animals, reading, travel, bridge. Home: 3520 Foxglove Ln Louisville KY 40241 Office: Ballard HSH 6000 Brownsboro Rd Louisville KY 40222 Office Phone: 502-485-8206. Personal E-mail: gmomc@bellsouth.net. Business E-Mail: jean.carrol2@jefferson.kyschools.us.

CARROLL, JILL, freelance journalist; b. Ann Arbor, Mich., 1977; d. Jim and Mary Beth Carroll. BA in Journalism, Univ. Mass., Amherst, 1999. Reporter covering Wash., DC Wall Street Journal; network commentator MSNBC; freelance contbr. Boston Globe; journalist States News Svc., Christian Science Monitor. Released 82 days after being kidnapped by Iraqi Insurgency group, Brigades of Vengeance, 2006; US Marines arrested four Iraqi men for participating in the kidnapping in August, 2006. Feature for the 11 part series Hostage: The Jill Carroll Story, Christian Science Monitor, 2006; contbr. articles to numerous profl. jours. Office: The Christian Sci Monitor One Norway St Boston MA 02115 Office Phone: 617-450-2000.*

CARROLL, KAREN COLLEEN, pathologist, epidemiologist; b. Balt., Nov. 7, 1953; d. Charles Edward and Ida May (Simms) C.; m. Bruce Cameron Marshall, Feb. 13, 1982; children: Kevin Charles Marshall, Brian Thomas Marshall. BA, Coll. Notre Dame of Md., 1975; MD, U. Md., 1979. Diplomate Am. Bd. Internal Medicine, Am. Bd. Infectious Diseases, Am. Bd. Pathology. Intern U. Md., 1979-80, U. Rochester, AHP, 1980-82, chief med. resident in internal medicine, 1982-83; fellow infectious diseases U. Mass., 1984-86; fellow med. microbiology Health Scis. Ctr. U. Utah, 1989-90; asst. prof. pathology U. Utah Med. Ctr., Salt Lake City, 1990-97, adj. asst. prof. infectious diseases, 1990-97, assoc. prof. pathology, adj. assoc. prof. infectious disease, 1997—; dir. microbiology lab. Associated Regional and Univ. Pathologists, Inc., Salt Lake City, 1990—. Contbr. articles to profl. jours. Fellow Am. Acad. Microbiology, Coll. Am. Pathologists; mem. Am. Soc. for Microbiology, Infectious Diseases Soc. Am. Avocations: skiing, hiking, reading. Office: U Utah Med Ctr Dept Pathology 50 N Medical Dr Salt Lake City UT 84132-0001 E-mail: carrolkc@aruplab.com.

CARROLL, KIM MARIE, nurse; b. Ottawa, Ill., Feb. 13, 1958; d. John J. and Charin E. (Reilley) Marmion; m. Thomas Christopher Carroll, Aug. 25, 1979; children: Christopher John, Meaghan Elizabeth, Sean Reilley. BSN, U. Denver, 1983; diploma, Copley Meml. Hosp. Sch. Nursing, Aurora, Ill., 1979. RN, Ill., Ind., Colo., Calif.; critical care practitioner. Staff nurse Penrose Hosp., Colorado Springs, Colo., 1979-83, asst. head nurse cardiac floor, 1983-84; asst. dir. nurses Big Meadows Nursing Home, Savanna, Ill., 1985-86, dir. nurses, 1986-88; clin. dir. Ind. Heart Physicians, Inc., Beech Grove, Ind., 1989-95; ambulatory care adminstr. The Gates Clinic, Denver, 1995-98; clin. mgr. Aurora Denver Cardiology Assoc., 1998—2002; triage nurse McKesson Health Solutions, Englewood, Colo., 2002—04; clin. mgr. nursing program C.C. Denver-Ctr. Health Svcs.-Lowry, 2004—06; clin. nurse educator Denver Health Med. Ctr., 2006—. Mem. Sigma Theta Tau. Roman Catholic. Avocation: skiing. Home: 5293 S Cathay Way Centennial CO 80015-4859 Office: Denver Health Med Ctr 777 BAnnock St MC 8300 Denver CO 80204-4507 Office Phone: 303-436-6832. Personal E-mail: tom.kim.carroll@prodigy.net. Business E-Mail: kim.carroll@dhha.org.

CARROLL, LUCY ELLEN, theater director, educator; b. NYC, Oct. 11; d. Edward Joseph and Lucy Sophie (Czapszys) C. B in Music Edn., Temple U., 1968; MA, Trenton State Coll., 1973; D in Musical Arts, Combs Coll. Music, Phila., 1982. Cert. tchr. music, N.J., Pa., Nat. Cert., 1991. Tchr. music Log Coll. Jr. High Sch., Pa., 1968-72, Ind. (Pa.) High Sch., 1972-73, William Tennent High Sch., Warminster, Pa., 1973-98, dir. mus. theater, 1973-98; choir dir. St. John Bosco Parish Choir, 1999—2001; organist, dir. Carmelite Monastery, Phila., 1996—. Music coord. Centennial Schs., 1991-98; founder, dir. Madrigal Singers, Warminster, Pa., 1971-98; choral dir. Cabrini Coll., Radnor, Pa., 1974-77, First Day Singers, Phila., 1979-83, Combs Coll. Music, Phila., 1981-84, 87-88; choral adjudicator various Music festivals, 1973-98; theatre dir., Villa Joseph Marie (Holland), 1998-99; del. Internat. Arts Conf., Cambridge, Eng., 1992; adj. assoc. prof. Westminster Choir Coll., Princeton, 2002—; lectr. in field. Singer (operas Ambler Festival): Street Scene, 1970, Death of Bishop of Brindisi (premiere); (Robin Hood Dell) La Boheme; dir. (jazz theater piece N.Y.C.): Murder of Agamemnon, 1980, (drama) Power of Love (1705), 1986, (outdoor music theater) Vorspiel (Pa. Historic Commn. 1989); editor: The Monastery Hymnal, 2002, Music of the Ephrata Cloister, 2003; columnist: Polyphony mag., Adoremus Bulletin, 2002—; creator: Churchmouse Squeaks cartoons, Monastery Mice cartoons; author: The Music of EPHRATA, 2003, The Bastet Worry-Stone and Other Tales, 2004, Monastery Mice: Life in the Loft, 2006; contbr. articles to profl. jours. and mags. Dir. Monastery Choir, Phila., 2001—. Recipient awards Writers of Future, 1985, 87, Andrew Ferraro award Combs Coll. Music, 1989, plaque for svc. to music Bucks County Commr., 1991, Disting. Citizen medal Southampton Twp., 1994, Harmony award Country Gentlemen Nat. Soc. for Preservation and Encouragement Barbershop Quartet Singing in Am., 1994; Scholar-In-Residence, Pa. Hist. and Museum Commn.; named Humanities Spkr. for 2000, Pa. Humanities Coun. Mem. Am. Choral Dirs. Assn., Sci. Fiction Fantasy Writers of Am., Am. Musicol. Soc., Am. Guild Organists, Organ Hist. Soc., Latin Liturgy Assn., Del. Valley Composers (choral cons. 1988-90), Hist. Soc. Pa., Smithsonian Assocs., Musical Fund Soc. of Phila., Soc. for Am. Music, Pa. Music Educators Assn. (adv. bd. 1986-87, contbg. writer Spotlight on Tchg. Chorus 2003), Nat. Assn. State Tchrs. of the Yr., Ephrata Cloister Assocs., Kelpius Soc. (editor newsletter 2004—, v.p., chair rsch. publs. 2005—), Sigma Alpha Iota. Republican. Roman Catholic. Avocation: travel. Home: 712 High Ave Hatboro PA 19040-2418 Personal E-mail: LucyCarroll@att.net.

CARROLL, MARGARET KELLY, education educator; b. Chgo., Sept. 6, 1956; d. Walter John and Eva Mary (Staudenmeyer) Kelly; children: Daniel Patrick, Hannah Margaret, Timothy Andrew. BS, U. Ill., 1977; postgrad., Ill. State U., 1977-78; MS, Chgo. state U., 1981; EdD, Loyola U., Chgo., 1985, St. Xavier U. Cert. tchr., Ill. Tchr. Normal (Ill.) Community High Sch., 1977-79, Schrum Jr. High Sch., Calumet City, Ill., 1979-82; asst. prof. Chgo. State U., 1981-83; tchr. Forkosh Meml. Hosp., Chgo., 1983; asst. dir. tchr. edn. Loyola U., Chgo., 1983-84; project dir. Archdiocese of Chgo., 1984-85; assoc. prof. to prof. tchr. edn. St. Xavier U., Chgo., 1985—. Cons. Inst. Ednl. Rsch., Glen Ellyn, Ill., 1985-86, Ill. State Bd. Edn., Springfield, 1985-86, U.S. Forestry Svc., Washington, 1985-86, Silver-Burdett-Ginn, N.J., 1987; cons., author Blue Cap Sch. Developmentally Disabled, Blue Island, Ill., 1985—; author for Blue Island Devel. Commn., 1989-98. Author: The Home as Learning Center: The Family as Educator, 1990, Around the World in Metropolitan Chicago: A School Field Trip Guide to Ethnic Museums and Restaurants, 1991, What Did You Do at School Today? A Guide to Schooling and School Sucess, 1998; contbr. articles to edn. publs. Con. Field Mus. Natural History, Chgo., 1988. Mem. Coun. Exceptional Children (chpt.

faculty moderator 1988—), Alpha Sigma Nu, Phi Delta Kappa. Avocations: sign language, historic home restoration, children's literature. Office: Saint Xavier Univ 3700 W 103rd St Chicago IL 60655-3105

CARROLL, M(ARGARET) LIZBETH CARR, art educator, graphics designer, photographer; b. Washington, Feb. 9, 1936; d. J. Franklin and Dorothy Mae (Colborn) Carr; m. Eugene R. Carroll, Jr., June 2, 1979 (div. May 2000); children: Kyung Soo Kim, Whan Kim. BFA in Studio Art, U. DC, 1979; MFA in Visual Comm. & Photography, George Washington U., 1984; postgrad., Union Inst. and U., 2004—. Visual info. specialist U.S. Fed. Govt., Washington, 1966—84; graphics designer Office of the Comptr. of the Currency, Dept. of the Treasury, Washington, 1984—94, sr. graphics designer, 1994—99; adj. prof. fine arts U. D.C., Washington, 1989—; asst. prof. lectr. in art George Washington U., Washington, 2001—06. Adv. for Native Am. artists/pvt. cons. ArtDirections, Washington, 1994—. Author, photographer: Native Peoples Mag., 1995, Piecework Mag., 1998, Am. Rivers, Pres.'s Coun. Environ. Quality, U.S. Congl. Record, Friends of the Earth, U.S. Nat. Pk. Svc., Nat. Pks. Conservation Assn., Sierra Club, Wilderness Soc. in support of conservation and wilderness legis.; Represented in permanent collections U.S. Dept. Interior, Grand Canyon Nat. Pk., exhibitions include Gallery 42, U. D.C., 2003, exhibited in group shows at Martin Luther King, Jr. Libr., Washington, 2003, U. D.C., 1976—79, Cath. U. Am., 1979; photographer Dimock Gallery, Washington, D.C., 1984. Home: 3313 Runnymede Pl NW Washington DC 20015-2415 Office: Univ DC Dept Mass Media Visual & Performing Arts 4200 Connecticut Ave NW Washington DC 20008

CARROLL, MARIE-JEAN GREVE, retired art educator, artist; b. Paterson, N.J., Dec. 19, 1930; d. William John and Charlotte Marie (Kranich) McGill; m. Theodore R. Greve, 1950 (div. 1979, dec. 2005); 3 children; m. William P. Carroll, 1981 (dec. 2002). BA in Art Edn., William Paterson Coll., 1971, MA in Visual Art, 1976. Cert. art tchr., N.J. Tchr. art Ramapo HS, Franklin Lakes, NJ, 1986—2000; ret., 2000. Juried shows NW Bergen Art Ctr., 2005. Works exhibited at shows in Fla. galleries, 1983, Longboat Key Art Gallery, 1983-84, Manatee Art Gallery, 1984, Pike County Art Show, Milford, Pa., 1994-96, NJ Printmakers Coun., Sommerville, Paterson Pub. Libr., 1998, Mommouth County Mus., 2004, Bergen Sr. Art Exhibit, 2005. Recipient art awards. Mem. NEA, Bergen County Edn. Assn., NJ Edn. Assn., Nat. Art Edn. Assn., Watercolor Soc. NJ (assoc.), Chaucer Guild NJ Poetry Group. Avocations: poetry, swimming laps, golf.

CARROLL, MARY PATRICIA, writer; b. Chgo., June 28, 1938; d. Anthony Bernard Carroll and Marie Cecilia Delaney. Student in writing, Columbia Coll., U. Fla.; BS in Humanities magna cum laude, Loyola U., Chgo., 1961, MSW, 1965; DSW, Smith Coll., 1970. Caseworker II Cook County Dept. Pub. Assistance, Chgo., 1961—64; sr. psychiat. social svc. worker Chgo. Bd. Health, Lower North Cmty. Mental Health Ctr., 1964—66; sch. social worker Sch. Dist. #81, Schiller Park, Ill., 1966—68; dist. dir. Family Svc. Assn. Greater Boston, 1970—73; program rep. United Cerebral Palsy Assns., N.Y.C., 1973—75; assoc. prof. George Williams Coll., 1975—77, Ind. U.-Purdue U., Indpls., 1977—81; assoc. prof., chmn. social work dept. U. Alaska, Anchorage, 1981—85; writer Mary P. Caroll Enterprises, 1985—. Contbr. articles, essays, short stories, poems to profl. and lit. publs. Recipient Hon. Mention award for fiction Writers Digest, 1987, for poetry, 1999, 2003; fellow VA Pub. Health, 1963-65, NIMH, 1968-70. Mem. Poetry Soc. of Va., Live Poets Soc., Amnesty Internat., Acad. Am. Poets, Nat. Com. to Preserve Social Security and Medicare, Friends of Libr of Alexandria Va. Duncan Br., Humane Soc. of U.S., Sierra Club. Democrat. Roman Catholic. Avocation: outdoor activities. E-mail: wnm4444@aol.com.

CARROLL, SUSAN VICTORIA, lawyer; b. Naples, Fla., Sept. 26, 1957; d. George Elwood Carroll and Mary Louise Simpson. BA in History, Fla. State U., Tallahassee, 1987, JD, 1990; BTh, Christian Life Sch. Theology, Panama City, 2001. Bar: Fla., (U.S. Dist. Ct., Mid. Dist. Fla), (U.S. Dist. Ct., No. Dist. Fla). Assoc. Bush & Derr, Tallahassee, 1990—92, 1993, Bruce L. Scheiner & Assoc., Ft. Myers, 1992—93, Mark E. Frederick, P.A., Destin, 1994—95; pvt. practice Panama City, 1996—. Republican. Office: 309 Harrison Av Panama City FL 32401

CARROLL, TERESA FISKE, mathematics educator; b. Leesburg, Va., June 26, 1960; d. John William and Rose Helton Fiske; m. Thomas Michael Carroll, June 21, 1991 (div. Jan. 1999); 1 child, Taylor Faith. BS in Elem. Edn., George Mason U., Fairfax, Va., 1983, MEd in Curriculum and Instrn., 2003. Cert. tchr. State Dept. of Va. Tchr. mid. sch. math. and pre-algebra Loudoun County Pub. Schs., 1983—. Subject area lead tchr. Smart's Mill Mid. Sch. Loudoun County Pub. Schs., Leesburg. Mem.: NEA, Nat. Coun. Tchrs. of Math. Democrat. Spiritual. Avocations: touring historical sites, walking, book club, browsing antique stores, resistance exercise. Home: 212 Connery Terrace SW Leesburg VA 20175 Office Phone: 703-669-1480. Personal E-mail: halfull44@aol.com.

CARROLL, YVETTE, voice educator; d. Rodolfo and Virginia Gonzales; m. Neish Carroll, June 17, 1989. MusB, U. Tex., El Paso, 1992. Choral dir. El Paso Ind. Sch. Dist., 1992—93, Austin Ind. Sch. Dist., 1993—. Choral libr. St. Mary's Schola Cantorum, Austin, 1998—2006, choir mem., 1993—2006. Mem.: Tex. Music Educator's Assn. (assoc.). Roman Catholic. Avocations: singing, travel. Office: Webb Middle School 601 E St Johns Austin TX 78752 Office Phone: 512-414-4397. E-mail: ycarroll@austinisd.org.

CARROTHERS, CAROL ANN, special education services professional, educator; b. Seattle, Dec. 26, 1955; d. Murray Everett and Ann Cumming; m. David Wayne Carrothers, June 30, 1984; children: Erick David, Ryan David. BS in Spl. Edn., Ctrl. Wash. U., 1977; MS in Deaf Edn., We. Oreg. U., 1980. Tchr. spl. edn. Elm Lake Sch. Dist., Kirkland, Wash., 1978—79; tchr. deaf edn. North Thurston Sch. Dist., Olympia, Wash., 1980—82; asst. prof. Ctrl. Wash. U., Ellensburg, 1984—2000; state coord. deaf svc. Wash. Sensory Disabilities Svc., Ellensburg, 2000—. Deaf edn. specialist Ellensburg Sch. Dist., 1997—2000; bd. dirs. Coun. Am. Instrn. of Deaf, 2003—. Bd. dirs. Ellensburg Christian Sch., 1990—96; dir. family retreat Lazy F. Camp and Retreat, Ellensburg, 2001—; bd. dirs. Young Life, Ellensburg, 2003—. Mem.: Coun. Exceptional Childen, Nat. Registry Interpreters of Deaf, Nat. Assn. Deaf (cert. sign lang. interpreter). Avocations: knitting, horseback riding, fly fishing. Office: Wash Sensory Disabilities Svc/CWU 7409 400 E University Ave Ellensburg WA 98926

CARSON, DENISE WILKINSON, gifted and talented educator; b. Providence, R.I., Dec. 29, 1946; d. Thaddeus Archiebald and Helen Gautier Wilkinson; m. Keith Robert Carson, Sept. 9, 1967; children: Jeanne-Marie, Corwin Keith. BS in Math. & Govt., Fla. State U., Tallahassee, 1967—69; MAEd, Coll. of William & Mary, Williamsburg, Va., 1988—89. Am. Montessori Soc. Montessori Tchr. Edn. Ctr., Mich., 1980, Gifted Cert. Shenandoah U., Va., 1998. Statistician Fla. Bd. Regents, Tallahassee, 1969—70; mathematician RCA, Alexandria, Va., 1971—72; budget officer Arlington Sch. Sys., Va., 1972—74; tchr. of students & tchrs. Troy Montessori/Montessori Tchr. Ed Ctr., Troy/West Bloomfield, Mich., 1978—83; tchr./adminstr. It's A Small World Sch., Tacoma, Wash., 1984—85; tchr. St. Patrick's Cath. Sch., Tacoma, 1985—87; elem. tchr. Armstrong Fundamental Sch., Hampton, Va., 1990—2001; tchr. of gifted South Morrison Elem., Newport News, Va., 2001—. Chmn. Gifted Adv. Bd., Tacoma, 1985—86. Author (compiler): (student books used in school) Jamestown/Early American History, Government, Explorers & Simple Machines; co-author (academic units for gifted) Maps Skills; Ancient Greece & Ancient Rome. Grantee Va. Art grant, Va. Art Coun., 1992—93. Mem.: Nat. Sci. Tchr. Assn., Va. State Reading Assn., Nat. Math. Tchr. Assn., Daughters of Am. Revolution, Beta Sigma Phi (life; chpt. pres. 1999—2000, pres. peninsula coun. 2000—02, chpt. pres. 2006—, Woman of Yr. 1991—92, 1994—95, 1999—2000, Peninsula Woman of Yr. 2001—02). Roman Catholic. Avocations: travel, reading, needlecrafts. Office: South Morrison NNPS 746 Adams Dr Newport News VA 23601-2626

CARSON, DORA A., secondary school educator; b. Dayton, Ohio, Nov. 3, 1945; d. Neely C. and Mary A. (Whitelow) Sampson; m. Alfred N. Carson, Mar. 18, 1967; 1 child, Tyra Lynne. BS, Wright State U., 1972, MS, 1978. Prin. Meadowdale High Sch., Dayton, Ohio, 1969—. NFL Teacher of the Year, 1992. Mem. Dayton Adminstrs. Assn. Home: 1233 Sunnyview Ave Dayton OH 45406-1927 Office: Meadowdale HS for Internat Studies 4417 Williamson Dr Dayton OH 45416 Office Phone: 937-542-7030. Business E-Mail: dcarson@dps.k12.oh.us.

CARSON, ELLEN GODBEY, lawyer; b. Kingsport, Tenn., Apr. 30, 1955; d. Lewis Anderson and Doris Louise (Dempsey) C.; m. Robert Carson Godbey, June 2, 1979. BA summa cum laude, U. Tenn., Knoxville, 1976; JD cum laude, Harvard U., 1980. Consumer complaint specialist FTC, Boston, 1980; atty. civil rights divsn. HHS, Washington, 1980-81; assoc. Landis, Cohen, Rauh & Zelenko, Washington, 1981-87, Paul Johnson Alston & Hunt, Honolulu, 1987-91; ptnr., dir. Alston Hunt Floyd & Ing, Honolulu, 1991—. Mem. disciplinary bd. Hawaii Supreme Ct., 1990-95. Former pres., dir. D.C. Rape Crisis Ctr., Washington, Sex Abuse Treatment Ctr., Honolulu, Hale Kipa Youth Svcs., Honolulu; pres., trustee Ctrl. Union Ch., 1998-2002; past dir. Aloha United Way, Hawaii Women's Legal Found. Named Outstanding Woman Profl., YWCA, 1990; recipient Outstanding Svc. award Hawaii Women Lawyers, 1991, ABA Margaret Brent Women Lawyers of Achievement award, 2006; named one of Best Lawyers in Am., 2005—. Mem. Hawaii State Bar Assn. (pres., dir. 1995-1996, Pro Bono award 1989), Hawaii Women Lawyers (pres., dir. 1989-90, Women Lawyer of Yr. 1992, Disting. Svc. award 2000), Hawaii Justice Found. (v.p., dir. 1996-2002), Inst. Human Svcs. (pres., dir. 1996-2002). Avocations: scuba, quilting. Office: Alston Hunt Floyd & Ing 18th Fl ASB Tower 1001 Bishop St Ste 1800 Honolulu HI 96813-3689 Office Phone: 808-524-1800. E-mail: ecarson@ahfi.com.

CARSON, ELLEN KATHLEEN, biology professor; b. Lewisburg, Tenn., July 16, 1952; d. Howard Ray and Sue Ellen Holman; m. Donald Reid Carson, June 26, 1945. BS in Biology, Mid. Tenn. State U., Murfreesboro, 1974, MS in Tchg. (Biology), 1977; PhD in Environ. Sci. and Pub. Policy, George Mason U., Fairfax, Va., 2005. Postgrad. profl. tchg. lic. Va., 1999, profl. tchg. lic. Tenn., 1974. Commd. officer USN, 1979, advanced through grades to comdr., 1994, lt. comdr. ADP plans br. chief U.S. Comdr. in Chief of the Pacific Forces Camp H. M. Smith, Hawaii, 1988—92, lt. comdr., officer in charge Pers. Support Detachment Patuxent River, Md., 1992—94, comdr., dep. comdr. Navy Recruiting Dist. Chgo., 1994—96, comdr., spl. asst. for women's policy Sec. of the Navy Washington, 1996—99, ret., 1999; adj. faculty George Mason U., Fairfax, Va., 2000—05; prof. Fla. C.C., Jacksonville, 2005—. Decorated Nat. Def. Svc. medal Sec. of the Navy, Navy Achievement medal, Meritorious Svc. medal, Navy Commendation medal, Navy Recruiting ribbon Comdr. Navy Recruiting Command, Washington, Def. Meritorious Svc. medal Sec. of Def.; Field Rsch. grantee, Wash. Biologists' Field Club, 2002—04, Grad. fellow, George Mason U., 2002—04. Mem.: Ret. Officer Assn., Charles Darwin Found., Inc., Orgn. for Tropical Studies, Soc. for the Study of Amphibians and Reptiles, Soc. for Conservation Biology. Avocations: travel, camping, kayaking. Office: Florida Community College Jacksonville 4501 Capper Rd Jacksonville FL 32218 Office Phone: 904-766-6741. Personal E-mail: ecarson@fccj.edu.

CARSON, JENIFFER A.P., lawyer; b. Boston, Mar. 8, 1974; BS in Legal Argument Communication, Suffolk U., 1992—96; JD, Suffolk U. Law Sch., 1997—99. Bar: Mass. 1999, US Dist. Ct. (Dist. Mass.) 2003. Intern Arakelian Real Estate Inc., Billerica, Mass., 1994—99; assoc. lobbyist Armenian Assembly Am., Washington, 1995; fgn. and domestic embassy liaison World Jurist Assn., Washington, 1995; law clk. Law Office of Chester A. Darling, Boston, 1996—98; contract adv., acting assoc. dir. Suffolk Corp. Training and Edn., Boston, 1995—97; law clk. Latronic & Whitestone, Boston, 1998; arbitration atty. John Hancock Mutual Life Ins. Co., Boston, 1999—2000; assoc. Governo Law Firm LLC, Boston, 2000—. Mem. parish coun. St. James Armenian Ch., Watertown, Mass., 2002—06, mem. strategic plan steering com., 2003—, chair fundraising com., 2003—05. Office: Governo Law Firm LLC 15th Floor 260 Franklin St Boston MA 02110 Office Phone: 617-737-9045. Office Fax: 617-737-9046.*

CARSON, JOANNE, art educator, artist; BA, U. Ill.; MFA, U. Chgo. Prof. & chairperson art dept. U. at Albany, SUNY. One-woman shows include, Bklyn. Mus., 2002, Plus Ultra Gallery, Bklyn., 2001, Sylvia Schmidt Gallery, New Orleans, 1994, Ruth Siegel Gallery, N.Y.C., 1990, Options, Mus. Contemporary Art, Chgo., 1985, exhibited in group shows at Spring Exhibit, AAAL, 2002, New Works on Wood, Fleming Mus., Burlington Vt., 2001, Frederick Weisman Collection, New Orleans Mus., 1997, Whitney Biennial, Whitney Mus. Am. Art, N.Y.C., 1985. Recipient Purchase Prize Sculpture, AAAL, 2002; Rome Prize Fellowship Painting, Am. Acad. Rome, Artists Fellowship, Nat. Endowment Arts. Office: University at Albany, SUNY Art Dept 1400 Washington Ave FA 216 Albany NY 12222 Office Phone: 518-442-4020. Office Fax: 518-442-4807.

CARSON, JULIA M., congresswoman; b. Louisville, July 8, 1938; 2 children. Student, Ind. U., 1960-62, St. Mary the Woods, 1976-78. Mem. Ind. Ho. of Reps., Indpls., 1972-76, Ind. Senate, 1976-90, U.S. Congress from 7th Ind. dist. (formerly 10th), 1997—. Mem. fin. svcs. com., 1997—, Vets. Affairs com., 1997—. V.p. Greater Indpls. Prog. Com.; nat. Dem. committeewoman; trustee YMCA; bd. didrs. Pub. Svc. Acad. Recipient Woman of Yr. Ind. award, 1974, Outstanding Leadership award AKA, Humanitarian award Christian Theol. Sem.; named one of Most Influential Black Americans, Ebony mag., 2006. Mem. NAACP, Urban League, Nat. Coun. Negro Women. Democrat. Baptist. Office: US Ho Reps 1535 Longworth Ho Office Bldg Washington DC 20515-1410 Office Phone: 202-225-4011. Office Fax: 202-225-5633.*

CARSON, LINDA MARIE, elementary school educator; b. La Salle, Ill., Aug. 3, 1947; d. Francis Harold and Dorothy Groleau; m. Randolph William Carson, Aug. 20, 1971; children: Sean, Kevin, Bethany. BS in Edn., No. Ill. U., 1969, MS in Edn., 1978. Cert. elem. tchr., Ill. Elem. tchr. Dist. 300, Dundee, Ill., 1969-85; instr. ESL, Elgin (Ill.) Community Coll., 1986; tchr. Dist. 15, McHenry, Ill., 1986—. Instr. ACT rev. McHenry County Coll., Crystal Lake, Ill., 1991. Co-pres. Eastview Sch. PTO, Algonquin, Ill., 1981-82; pres. Algonquin Women's Club, 1987-89. Home: 631 Webster St Algonquin IL 60102-2869 Office: Valley View Sch 6515 W State Route 120 Mchenry IL 60050-7450

CARSON, MARGARET, human services administrator; d. Chief and Lena Mae Carson. Cert. dietian cooking Vigo County Health Dept., Ind., nurses tng. Vigo County Health Dept., Ind., CPR Vigo County Health Dept., Ind., home health Vigo County Health Dept., Ind.; RN Vigo County Sch. of Nursing, 1965. Home health nurse numerous; organizer variuos cmty. svc. projects with the sole purpose of ending hunger and poverty. Mem. regional bd. Los Angeles County Food Bank, Calif., 1998—2003; music dir., mem. choir 54th St. Seventh Day Adventist Ch., L.A., 1999—2002, dir. cmty. svcs. program. Recipient Cmty. Services Dir. of the Yr., L.A. City Cmty. Svc. Dept., 2001, Excellence in Serving Your Cmty., L.A. City Mayor's Office, 2002, Fighting Hunger Giving Hope award, L.A. Regional Food Bank, 2006, award, So. Calif. Seventh Day Adventists, 2006. Democrat. Seventh-Day. Avocations: serving her community, singing, fundrasing, interior decorating, catering for the less fortunate. Office: SDA Ch Cmty Svcs 1973 W 54th Street Los Angeles CA 90062-2610 Office Phone: 323-292-2762. Business E-Mail: office@54thstreetsda.org.

CARSON, REBECCA ANN, performing arts association administrator; b. Chgo., July 15, 1974; d. Douglas Lee and Mary Ann Carson. BA, U. Wis., Eau Claire, 1996; MFA, U. Md., College Park, 1999. Office mgr. pub. rels. U. Md., 1997—98, acting theatre mgr., 1999; mgr. prodns. and ops. Ctr. Creative Arts, St. Louis, 1999—2003, dir. performing arts, 2003—. Mentor Arts Midwest, Indpls., 2005. Recipient semifinalist, Nat. Forensics Assn., 1995, 1996, Emerging Leadership award, Assn. Performing Arts Presenters, 2002. Mem.: Theatre Comm. Group, Internat. Performing Arts for Youth. Office: Ctr for Creative Arts 524 Trinity Ave Saint Louis MO 63130 Business E-Mail: rcarson@cocastl.org.

CARSON, REGINA E., healthcare administrator, pharmacist, educator, geriatric specialist; b. Washington; BS in Pharmacy, Howard U.; MBA in Mktg., Loyola Coll., Balt., 1987, MBA in Health Care Adminstrn., 1987. Asst. prof., asst. dir. pharmacy U. Md., Balt., 1986-88; asst. prof., coord. profl. practice Howard U., Washington, 1988-95; prin. Marrell Cons., Randallstown, Md., prin., mng. ptnr., 1993—; exec. dir. Sunrise Assisted Living, Fairfax, Va., 1997-99. Drug utilization rev. cons. Md. Pharmacy Assn., Balt., 1986—90; cons. pharmacist Balt. County Adv. Coun. Drug Abuse, Towson, Md., 1984—86; edn. cons. Assn. Black Women in Higher Edn., Accra, Ghana, 2000; program evaluator Train Pharm., U. Medicine and Pharmacy Cluj, Romania, 1999—2002; master gardener U. Md., College Park, 2001—. Bd. dirs. N.W. Hosp. Ctr. Aux., Randallstown, Joshua Johnson Coun., Balt. Mus. Art, Alzheimers Assn. Ctrl. Md.; trustee C.C. of Baltimore County, 1997—. Named Outstanding Alumni, Howard U. Coll. Pharmacy, 1992; recipient Grigore T. Popa medal, U. Medicine and Pharmacy, Iasi, Romania, 2000. Fellow: Am. Soc. Cons. Pharmacists; mem.: Nat. Assn. Retail Druggists (adv. com., long-term care com.), Nat. Pharm. Assn. (life, Outstanding Women in Pharmacy 1984), Am. Assn. Colls. Pharmacy, Nat. Assn. Health Svc. Execs. Avocations: pharmacognosy, gardening, American art.

CARSON, TERESA CATHERINE, pediatrician; b. Carbondale, Pa., Oct. 19, 1958; d. Tony and Rose Marie Carson. BS, Marywood Coll., Scranton, Pa., 1980; MS, Fordham U., Bronx, N.Y., 1982; MD, Jefferson U., Phila., 1987. Diplomate Am. Bd. Pediats. Resident Children's Hosp. Buffalo, 1987—89, Med. Coll. Pa., Phila., 1989—90; pediatrician Kantor Curley Pediats., Phila., 1990—91, Dekalb Pediats., Norristown, Pa., 1991—96, Sacred Heart Health Sys., Allentown, Pa., 1996—98, Jefferson Faculty Pediats., Phila., 1998—2000, Dawgert and Zukoski Pediats., Dickson City, Pa., 2000—02, New Windsor (N.Y.) Pediats., 2002—. Fellow: Am. Acad. Pediats. Democrat. Avocations: reading, travel, cultural events, dance, interior decorating. Office: New Windsor Pediatrics 448 Temple Hill Rd New Windsor NY 12553 Office Phone: 845-502-2191. Business E-Mail: nwpeds@hvc.rr.com. E-mail: TCarson@newlandspediatrics.com.

CARSON, VIRGINIA GOTTSCHALL, academic administrator, biology educator; b. Pitts. d. Walter Carl and Rosalie (Paulin) Gottschall; m. John Richard Carson (div.); children: Margaret Rosalie, Kenneth Robert. BA in Math., Calif. State U., L.A., 1960, MA in Psychology, 1965; PhD in Physiology, UCLA, 1970. Asst. prof. dept. biology Chapman U., Orange, Calif., 1971-77, pre-med. advisor, 1974—, assoc. prof. dept. biology, 1977-83, chmn. div. natural sci., 1983-91, prof. dept. biology, 1983—, chmn. dept. biology, 1993—98; dean Wilkinson Coll. Letters and Scis., 1998—2002. Asst. rsch. pharmacologist U. Calif., Irvine, 1972-81, assoc. rsch. pharmacologist, 1981-83, 91-2000; assoc. prof. So. Calif. Coll. Optometry, Fullerton, 1979-83. Contbr. numerous articles to profl. jours. Elder First Presbyn. Ch. Orange, 1989-92, 2004-05, chmn. faculty Chapman U., 1987-88, 97-98. NIH fellow UCLA, 1972-74. Fellow AAAS; mem. Orange County Sci. Edn. (assn. (bd. dirs. 1989—, chmn. 1993-94), Grad. Women in Sci. (chpt. sec. 1989-93, pres. 1993-95, nat. pres. 1999-2000). Republican. Home: 717 S Yorba St Orange CA 92869-5043 Office: Chapman Univ 1 Univ Dr Orange CA 92866-1099

CARSTAIRS, SHARON, legislator; b. Halifax, N.S., Can., Apr. 26, 1942; d. Vivian and Harold Connolly; m. John Esdale Carstairs, 1966; children: Catherine, Jennifer. BA in Polit. Sci. and History, Dalhousie U., 1962; MA in Tchg. of History, Smith Coll., 1963; postgrad., Georgetown U., 1964, U. Calgary, 1968; LLD (hon.), Brandon U., 2003. Tchr. Dana Hall Sch. for Girls, Wellesley, Mass., 1963-65, Calgary (Alta.) Separate Sch. Bd., 1965-71; chmn. bd. referees Unemployment Ins. Commn., 1973-77; tchr. St. John's Ravenscourt Sch., Winnipeg, Man., 1978-81, St. Norbert (Man.) Collegiate, 1982-84; elected leader Liberal Party in Man., 1984; elected mem. Man. Legis. Assembly, River Heights, 1986—; elected leader Ofcl. Opposition, 1988-90; apptd. to Senate, 1994—; apptd. dep. leader of the govt. in the Senate, 1997-99; leader of the govt. in the Senate, 2001—03; minister with spl. responsibility for palliative care, 2001—03. Scriptwriter, narrator Calgary and Region Ednl. TV, 1967-69. Brownie leader, Halifax and Winnipeg; mem. Parks and Recreation Bd., City of Calgary; fund-raiser Manitoba Heart Found.; canvasser Can. Cancer Soc., Alta., Man., Alta. Soc. for the Mentally Retarded; vol. Man. Mus. of Man and Nature; bd. mem. Women and the Arts, Nursing Coun. Man.; campaign worker provincial elections, Nova Scotia, 1948, 52, 56, 60; exec. positions Dalhousie U. Liberal Club, Nova Scotia, 1958-62; nat. exec. Univ. Liberals, Nova Scotia, 1960-62, others; poll capt. Fed. elections, Alta. 1965, 68, 72, 74; exec. Alta. Women's Liberal Assn., 1965-68; sec. Liberal Party, Alta., 1968-70, v.p., 1972-74, pres., 1975-77, nat. exec. 1975-77; Calgary Regional v.p., Liberal Party Alta., 1970-72; mem. Fed. Campaign com., Alta. 1972, 74, Man. 1983—; candidate Provincial Liberal, Alta. 1975; poll worker Ft. Rouge Provincial constituency, Man., 1977, Ft. Garry Fed. constituency, Man., 1979-80; office mgr, Tuxedo Provincial constituency, Man., 1981; exec., River Heights Provincial constituency, Man., 1983—; mem. Man. Legislative Assembly 1986—; elected leader Official Opposition, Man., 1988-90. Recipient Dalhousie U. Entrance scholarship, Dalhousie U. scholarship, Smith Coll. Grad. fellowship. Mem. Winnipeg C. of C. Liberal Party Can.

CARSTEN, ARLENE DESMET, financial executive; b. Paterson, N.J., Dec. 5, 1937; d. Albert F. and Ann (Greutert) Desmet; m. Alfred John Carsten, Feb. 11, 1956; children: Christopher Dale, Jonathan Glenn. Student, Alfred U., 1955-56. Exec. dir. Inst. Burn Medicine, San Diego, 1972-81, adv. bd. mem., 1981-92; founding trustee Nat. Burn Fedn., 1975-83; CFO A.J. Carsten Co., Inc., San Diego, 1981-91, A.J. Carsten Co., Ltd., Powell River, B.C., Canada, 1992—96; pres. Raven View Holdings Ltd., 1997—2003. Contbr. articles to profl. jours. Organizer, mem. numerous cmty. groups; chmn. San Diego County Mental Health Adv. Bd., 1972-74, mem., 1971-75; chmn. cmty. rels. subcom., mem. exec. com. Emergency Med. Care Com., San Diego, Riverside and Imperial Counties, 1973-75; pub. mem. psychology exam. com. Calif. State Bd. Med. Quality Assurance, 1976-80, chmn., 1977; mem. rep. to Health Svcs. Agy. San Diego County Govt., 1980; mem. Calif. Dem. Ctrl. Com., 1968-74, exec. com., 1971-72, 73-74; treas. San Diego Dem. County Ctrl. Com., 1972-74; chmn. edn. legis. com. women's divsn. So. Calif. Dem. Com., 1972; dir. Muskie for Pres. Campaign, San Diego, 1972; organizer, dir. numerous local campaigns; chair Rep. for Casady for Mayor San Diego, 1981; councilwoman City of Del Mar, Calif., 1982-86, mayor, 1985-86; bd. dirs. Gentry-Watts Planned Indsl. Devel. Assn., 1986-90, pres., 1987-90; v.p. Okeover Rate Payers Assn., 1996-97, pres., 1997-2003, bd. dirs., 1996—2003; sec. Powell River Hosp. Found. Millenium Celebration Com., 1998-99; mem. Alliance for Responsible Shellfish Farming, 2000—, chair, 2000-04; mem. adv. bd. Malaspina Complex Integrated Action Plan, 2002—04; commencement spkr. Alfred U., 1984. Recipient Key Woman award Dem. Party, 1968, 72, 1st Ann. Cmty. award Belles for Mental Health, Mental Health Assn., San Diego, 1974, citation Alfred U. Alumni Assn., 1979. Home: RR 2 Malaspina Rd C-68 Powell River BC Canada V8A 4Z3 E-mail: carsten@armourtech.com.

CARSTENS, CHARLENE B., composer, music educator; b. Chgo., Dec. 11, 1932; d. Sidney and Anne Dunner Gross; m. Jay M. Brown, June 28, 1953 (div. Apr. 1976); children: Sharon Brown, Julie Brown; m. H. Paul Carstens, Oct. 17, 1986. BMus, Roosevelt U., Chgo., 1969; MMus, Roosevelt U., 1978. Mgr. R & D grad. program libr. Northwestern U., Evanston, Ill., 1971—73; editor books, reports, papers Joan Masters, Inc., Chgo., 1976—77; founder, dir. The Music Sch., Springfield, Ill., 1978—81; faculty St. Martha's Sch., Sarasota, Fla., 1981—85, Manatee C.C., Sarasota, 1986—88; tchr. piano The Music Sch., Springfield, 1970—89; pvt. piano tchr. Chgo., Sarasota, 1970—89. Concert pianist various civic, music and ch. groups, various locations; lectr. in field; judge various piano competitions; rschr., dir. program of rare Am. civil war music City of Springfield, 1979; radio commentator

Sunday Song, WSSR pub. radio, Springfield, 1978—80. Composer: Sing Along with Grandma Char, vols. I and II, 1991—92; author: Remembrances: Growing Up in Hollywood Park (Chicago, Ill.), 2002. Music dir. La Traviata Roman Cultural Soc., Springfield, 1981; chmn. Lincolnfest, Celebrity Corner City of Springfield, 1981; dir.75th anniversary show Sarasota Power Squadron, 1989; bd. dirs. Fla. West Coast Symphony Music Festival, Sarasota, 1987—89. Mem.: Sarasota Music Tchrs. Assn., Music Tchrs. Nat. Assn., Coll. Music Soc. Home: 7777 Calle Facil Sarasota FL 34238

CARSTENS, CYNDY LOUISE, artist; b. St. Paul, Minn., June 8, 1955; d. John and Dolores Alexander; m. Douglas Carstens, Apr. 30, 1988; children: Angela Yarnell, Tiffanie, Jonathan Yarnell, Robynn Yarnell. Student, Pitts. State U., 1974—75, Kans. State U., 1975—76, Wichita State U., 1976—77, Ariz. State U., 2003—. Owner/creative dir. Olaf & Yarnell, Inc., Wichita, 1978—88; illustrator/owner Autograph Collection Ltd., Glendale, Ariz., 1986—; art dir. Brinton Advt., Scottsdale, Ariz., 1986—; artist/owner Carstens Fine Art Studio, Glendale, Ariz., 1988—. Dir. Gallery Nineteen Artist Coop, Phoenix, 1994—96; juried mem. Ariz. Artist Guild, 1990—, bd. dirs., Mar. of Dimes Birth Defects Found., Wichita; mem. Ariz. Watercolor Assn., 1990—2004; mem.-at-large Women In Comm., Inc., Phoenix, NAFE, Phoenix; bd. dirs. Nat. Kidney Found., Wichita. Mem. Nat. Mus. Women in Arts, 2000—; vocalist St. Joan of Arc Ch., Phoenix, 1989—2002, 1989—99; mem./fund raising chair Mar. of Dimes Birth Defects Found.; mem./spl. events Nat. Kidney Found.; coop dir./dir. of devel. Ariz. Artist Guild. Recipient West Award of Excellence in Design, BC&MA West awards, 1990, Award for Design Excellence, Assn. of Art Directors, Wichita, KS, 1985, 1987, 1989, 1990. Mem.: Ariz. Artist Guild (dir. of artist coop, bd. dirs. 1994—97). Avocations: travel, skiing, music. Home: 5423 West Greenbriar Dr Glendale AZ 85308 Office Phone: 602-298-1404.

CARSTENSEN, MARIA ELENA, academic administrator; b. San Francisco, Aug. 31, 1956; d. Juan and Helen (Fowler) O'Gorman; children: Genevieve, Thomas; m. Larry E. Carstensen, Nov. 22, 1996. BA, Trinity U., 1978; MA, U. Tex., San Antonio, 1984; MEd, Trinity U., 2002. Cert. counselor Tex., 1986, prin. Tex. State Bd. Edn., 2002. Tchr., counselor Northside Ind. Sch. Dist., San Antonio; lead tchr. Northside Alt. Elem., San Antonio. Mem.: NAESP, ASCD, PDK Internat. Home: 7402 Louisa Allen Ct San Antonio TX 78240-3612 Business E-Mail: mariacarstensen@nisd.net.

CARSWELL, JANE TRIPLETT, retired family physician; b. Raeford, N.C., Feb. 26, 1932; d. Arthur Dula and Madeline Mapp (Warburton) C. Student, Flora Macdonald Coll., 1950-52; AB in Chemistry, U. N.C., 1954; MD, Med. Coll. Va., 1958. Diplomate Am. Bd. Family Practice. Resident Med. Coll. Va., Richmond, 1958-61; practice medicine specializing in family medicine Harlan, Ky., 1961-62, Lenoir, NC, 1962—. Chmn. Lenoir Human Relations Com., N.C., 1962-64; vice-chmn. Caldwell County Council Status of Women, Lenoir, 1976-78 Mem. Caldwell County Med. Soc. (pres. 1965), N.C. Acad. Family Physicians (N.C. Family Physician of Yr. award 1983), N.C. Med. Soc., Am. Acad. Family Practice (Nat. Family Dr. of Yr. award 1984) Presbyterian. Avocations: hiking, backpacking, skiing, photography.

CARSWELL, LINDA GAIL, language educator, department chairman; b. Houston, May 15, 1948; d. Robert Bryant and Helen Meeker Stamps; m. Jerry L. Carswell, Jan. 30, 1971; children: Jordan Daniel, Robert Justin. BA in English and Comm., Baylor U., Waco, Tex., 1970. Tchr. English and debate coach Booker T. Wash. HS, Houston, 1970—71, Granbury HS, 1977—79; tchr. and chair English dept. Mayde Creek Jr. HS, Houston, 1979—81; gifted & talented program specialist Katy Ind. Sch. Dist., 1981—84; tchr. and coord. English Tomball HS, 1984—85; tchr. gifted and talented, honors English West Meml. Jr. HS, Katy, 1985—97; tchr. gifted and talented, advanced placement English Mayde Creek HS, Houston, 1997—2000; tchr. and chair English dept. Cinco Ranch HS, Katy, 2000—. Advisor Nat. Honor Soc. chpt. Katy Ind. Sch. Dist., Tex., 1985—2000; cons. and exam reader Coll. Bd., Princeton, NJ, 2003—. Organizer Katy Parents Gifted and Talented, Tex., 1980—84, pres., 1980—82. Named Secondary Tchr. of Yr., Katy Ind. Sch. Dist., 2000, Tchr. of Yr., Mayde Creek H.S., 2000; recipient Mayor's Tchr. Excellence award, City of Houston, 2000. Mem.: Sigma Tau Delta, Delta Kappa Gamma (v.p. 1983—85), Mortar Bd. (life). Achievements include development of Gifted and Talented curriculum; Advanced Placement curriculum.

CARSWELL, LOIS MALAKOFF, botanical garden executive, consultant; b. NYC, Mar. 2, 1932; d. Arthur and Dora (Krechevsky) Malakoff; m. Donald Carswell, Oct. 12, 1957; children: Anne Carswell Tang, Alexander, Robert Ian. AB magna cum laude, Radcliffe Coll., 1953; cert. in bus. adminstrn., Harvard U. and Radcliffe Coll., 1954. Editor Dell Pub. Co., N.Y.C., 1954-56; publicist Ruth E. Pepper Co., N.Y.C., 1957-58; vol. Bklyn. Botanic Garden, 1964—, co-chmn. plant sales, 1967—, co-chmn. capital campaign, 1984-88, chmn. bd. dirs., 1989-98, chmn. emeritus, 1998—. Chmn. Coalition Living Mus. N.Y. State, N.Y.C., 1980—; cons. N.Y. State Natural Heritage Trust, 1982—. Office: Bklyn Botanic Garden 1000 Washington Ave Brooklyn NY 11225-1008 Office Phone: 718-623-7225. E-mail: loiscarswell@bbg.org.

CARSWELL, MELISSA J., counselor, director; b. Warsaw, N.Y., Sept. 5, 1975; d. Rhonda G. Clark; m. Charles S. Carswell, May 29, 2005. B in Religion, Practical Bible Coll., 2000; MA, Liberty U., 2004. Counselor Cath. Charities, Endicott, NY, 2001—03; dir./minister New Life Free Meth. Ctr., Endicott, 2003—04; founder/dir. True Hope Counseling Ctr., Endicott, 2004—. Cons. chs./schs. Broome County, 2003—; spkr. various chs./orgns., 2003—. Mem.: Am. Counseling Assn., Am. Assn. Christian Counseling. Christian. Avocations: writing, reading, music, painting. Office: True Hope Counseling 201 Hill Ave Endicott NY 13760 Business E-Mail: info@truehopecounseling.com.

CARTAINO, CAROL ANN, editor; b. NYC, Dec. 7, 1944; d. Pietro Michael and Ann Wanda (Scotch) C.; 1 child, Clayton Collier-Cartaino. BA, Rutgers U., 1966; postgrad., NYU, 1967-68. Cert. English tchr., N.J. Prodn. editor trade book Prentice-Hall, Inc., Englewood Cliffs, N.J., 1966-68, from asst. to assoc. editor trade book, 1968-72, editor trade book, 1972-77; editor-in-chief Writer's Digest Books, Cin., 1978-86, freelance editor and collaborator, 1986—; editl. dir. Don Aslett, Inc., Pocatello, Idaho, 1987-93, Marsh Creek Press, Pocatello, Idaho, 1993—; assoc. Collier Assoc. Literary Agy., Seaman, Ohio, 1987-94; proprietor freelance editing and book cons. svc. White Oak Edits., 1987—; proprietor Carol Cartaino, Lit. Agt., 1994—. Speaker in field; instr. in writing So. State C.C., Hillsboro and Wilmington, Ohio, 1989—. Author: Keeping Work Simple, 1997, Get Organized, Get Published!, 2001. Vol. nurses aide Hackensack (N.J.) Hosp. State of N.J. scholar, 1962-66, Emerson (N.J.) PTA scholar, 1962. Roman Catholic. Avocations: hiking, photography, gardening, nature study. Home and Office: 2000 Flat Run Rd Seaman OH 45679-9412 Office Phone: 937-764-1303. E-mail: cartaino@aol.com.

CARTEE, KAREN JOHNSON, education educator, consultant; b. Bluefield, W.Va., July 31, 1956; d. Easel Endel Johnson and Betty Jane Maddox; m. Michael Jackson Cartee, July 18, 1987. BA in Govt., Coll. William and Mary, Williamsburg, Va., 1978; MS in Comm., U. Tenn., Knoxville, 1979, PhD in Polit. Sci., 1984. Temporary asst. prof. WAB, 1982; asst. prof. U. Ala., 1983, co-dir. Capstone Poll, 1987—88, assoc. prof., 1989, assoc. dean, 1991, prof., 1996—. Co-author (with G.A. Copeland): Negative Political Advertising: Coming of Age, 1991, Inside Political Campaigns: Theory and Practice, 1997, Manipulation of the American Voter, 1997, Strategic Political Communication: Rethinking Social Influence, Persuasion, and Propaganda, 2004; author: News Narratives and News Framing: Constructing Political Reality, 2005, numerous articles, book chpts., and book revs. Grantee, Coll. Comm. Rsch. and Svc Com., 1988. Office: Univ Ala Coll Comm and Info Svcs Box 870172 Tuscaloosa AL 35487-0172 Business E-Mail: cartee@apr.ua.edu.

CARTER, ANNA DEAN, volunteer; b. Lafayette, Tenn., June 21, 1935; d. Virgil Heston and Elsie Irene (Law) King; m. Billy Wilson Carter, Nov. 3, 1954; children: Billy Jr., Gerald, Debra. Grad. high sch., Lafayette, Tenn. Waitress Walgreen Drug, Lafayette, Tenn., 1951-54; factory Formfit Rogers, Lafayette, Tenn., 1955-56; substitute tchr. Macon County Schs., Lafayette, Tenn., 1958-59; factory True Loom Mfg. Co., Lafayette, Tenn., 1959-67; sch. sec. Macon County Schs., Lafayette, Tenn., 1968; bookkeeper Macon-Trousdale Coop., Lafayette, Tenn., 1968-98; retired, 1998. County commn. Macon County Govt., 1990—; E911 bd. dirs. Macon County, 1994—; mem. Tenn. Rural Health, Cookeville, 1998; sec. Macon County Health Coun., 1996—2001; v.p. Upper Culberland Health, 1998—2000; mem. Macon County Fair Bd., 1996—; active Macon County Job Svc., 1997—2002; mem. Macon Edn. Found., 1997—; bd. dirs. Tenn. Families First, 1998—, Cordell Hull Echomanic Opportunity Cooperation, 1998—2003. Named to, Board-Macon County Sports Hall of Fame, 2000. Mem.: Am. Assn. Retired People, Macon Sch. Health Advisory Bd., Macon County C. of C. (bd. dirs. 1998—2001, pres. 1999—2000), Sr. Citizens Orgn. (bd. dirs. 1999—), Historic Preservation Soc. (pres. 1996—). Baptist. Avocations: reading, needlecrafts, photography, writing, walking. Home: 209 Donoho Ave Lafayette TN 37083-1404

CARTER, ANNETTE WHEELER, state legislator; b. May 24, 1941; divorced. Grad., Ala. State Coll. Mem. Conn. Ho. of Reps., Hartford, 1988—, mem. pub. safety, cmty. and exportation coms., vice chmn. appropriations com., asst. majority leader, mem. black caucus; assembly dist. 7 rep. Conn. House of Reps., Hartford; housing advisor Capitol Region Conf. Chs. Spkr. in field. Recipient Outstanding Accomplishments award Hope SDA Ch., 1990, Crispus A. Tucks award, 1991, Conn. State Black Dem. award, 1992. Mem. NAACP (award 1993), Greater Hartford Black Dem. Club. Democrat. Episcopalian. Home: 207 Branford St Hartford CT 06112-1406 Office: Conn Ho of Reps Legislative Office Bldg Hartford CT 06106

CARTER, AUDREY E., secondary school educator; b. Model, Tenn., Aug. 29, 1955; d. James Alvin and Edna Carlene Cathey; m. Jack Ellis Carter II, Oct. 21, 1990; children: Jake Ellis III, Carlene Elizabeth. BS in Health, Phys. Edn. and Sci., Austin Peay State U., Clarksville, Tenn., 1978. Cert. tchr. Fla., 1984, fitness instr. Aerobics and Fitness Assn. Am., Fla., 1985. Tchr. West Orange H.S., Winter Garden, 1985—. Pvt. fitness instr., Orlando, Fla., 1984—. Methodist. Avocations: exercise, scrapbooks, reading. Home: 170 Temple Grove Dr Winter Garden FL 34787 Office: West Orange HS 1625 S Beulah Rd Winter Garden FL 34787 Office Phone: 407-905-2400. E-mail: acarter997@aol.com.

CARTER, BARBARA DALE, musician, educator, clinical counselor; b. Boulder, Colo., Jan. 15, 1932; m. Frank Pierce Carter, Aug. 25, 1952; children: Frank Pierce Jr., Roseann Marie, Michael Gene. AA, Stephens Coll., 1952, BA, 1989; MA, Washington U., 1995, postgrad., 1993—. Nat. cert. in piano, theory, music therapy. Performer concerts and piano presentations, 1936-99; ind. piano tchr., 1948-99. Participant Van Cliburn Piano Competition, 1984; owner pvt. counseling svc., 1990-99. Den mother coach Boy Scouts Am., 1958; mem. Calif. bd. Campfire Girls Am., 1968; pres. Children's Theatre, Savannah, Ga., 1963; dir. Mental Health Assn., Savannah, 1964-65, Mental Health Assn., San Bernardino, Calif., 1969; creator Design for Living program. Recipient Most Outstanding Air Force Wife cert. Hunter AFB, 1966. Mem. Nat. Music Tchrs. Assn., Am. Assn. Women Deans, Am. Pen Women (poetry awards 1984), Ill. State Music Tchrs. Assn. (chair music therapy 1980-81, mem. state bd. certification 1981), Metro-East Music Tchrs. Assn. (pres. 1979-81). Avocations: raising old english sheepdogs, collectibles, fashion. E-mail: fpcarter3@netscape.net.

CARTER, BETSY L., editor, writer; b. NYC, June 9, 1945; d. Rudy and Gerda Cohn; m. Gary Hoenig. BA, U. Mich., 1967. Editorial asst. McGraw Hill, 1967—68; editor co. mag. Am. Security and Trust Co., 1968—69; editorial asst. Atlantic Monthly, 1969—70; researcher Newsweek, N.Y.C., 1971—73, asst. editor, 1973—75, assoc. editor, 1975—80; sr. editor Esquire Mag., N.Y.C., 1980—81, exec. editor, 1981—82, sr. exec. editor, 1982—83, editorial dir., 1983—85; creator, editor-in-chief New York Woman, N.Y.C., 1988; editor-in-chief New Woman mag., N.Y.C., 1994—97; founding editor-in-chief AARP's My Generation, 1999—2003. Author: Nothing to Fall Back On, 2002, (novels) Orange Blossom Special, 2005; contbr. articles to popular mags. including Atlantic, Washington Post, Glamour, Oprah, NY Mag. Mem.: Am. Soc. Mag. Editors (exec. com. 1988—91, v.p. 1997—). E-mail: bcarter@nyc.rr.com.

CARTER, CARMEN M., elementary education educator, consultant; b. Louisville, Ky., Jan. 14, 1950; d. Michael S. and Bernice F. (Vessels) Anastasio; m. Gordon E. Carter; children: Michelle M. Luckett, Todd S. Luckett. BS in Elem. Edn. summa cum laude, U. Louisville, 1990, MEd, 1993. Cert. elem. tchr. Tchr. Bardstown (Ky.) Elem. Sch., 1990—. Cons. Ky. Coun. Econ. Edn., Louisville, 1990—; speaker various convs.; with Mid-South Japan in the Schs. project, N.Y.C., 1992. Author: Economics Unit, 1991 (Internat. Paper Co. award); co-author: Pocketwise. Fulbright-Hayes scholar. Mem. ASCD, Phi Kappa Phi. Avocations: reading, crafts, travel. Home: 2116 Lauderdale Rd Louisville KY 40205-1536 Office: Bardstown Elem Sch Bardstown KY 40004

CARTER, CAROLYN HOUCHIN, advertising agency executive; b. Louisville, Nov. 2, 1952; d. Paul Clayton and Georgia (Houchin) C.; m. Jeffrey Starr, Dec. 8, 1988. BS in Journalism, Northwestern U., 1974, MS in Journalism, 1975. Asst. account exec. SSC&B Advt., Inc., N.Y.C., 1975-76, account exec., 1976-77, Grey Advt., Inc., N.Y.C., 1977-79, account supr., 1979-82, v.p., 1981-82, v.p., mgmt. supr., 1982-87, v.p., group mgmt. supr., 1985-87, sr. v.p., 1987-92, exec. v.p., 1992—2000; pres. Grey Worldwide Europe, Mid. East and Africa, 2000—02, Grey Global Group Europe, Mid. East, Africa, 2002—04; pres., CEO Greyglobal Group Europe, Mid. East, Africa, 2004—. Mem. Nat. Advt. Rev. Bd., 1983-87; mem. adv. bd. advt. history Smithsonian Nat. Mus. Am. History, 1988-94. Chmn. media advt. coun. March of Dimes, 1981-86; mem. U.S. coun. World Comm. Yr., 1983; active YMCA Acad. Women Achievers, 1992. Recipient Clairol Mentor award Clairol, Inc., 1991. Mem. Women in Comm. (pres. N.Y. chpt. 1982-83, N.Y. Matrix award in advt. 1988, Nat. Headliner award 1991), Internat. Women's Forum (bd. dirs. N.Y. chpt. 1994), Advt. Women N.Y. (bd. dirs. 1987-88). Office: Grey Global Group 777 3d Ave New York NY 10017-1401

CARTER, CATHERINE LOUISE, retired elementary school educator; b. Oakland, Calif., Mar. 31, 1947; d. Robert Collidge and Mae (Riedy) Carter. BA, Ohio Wesleyan U., 1969. Tchr. Barclay Elem. Sch., Cherry Hill, NJ, 1969-72, Malberg Elem. Sch., Cherry Hill, 1972-80, Beck Mid. Sch., Cherry Hill, 1980-89, 94-95, Carusi Jr. HS, Cherry Hill, 1989—94, 1995—2002; ret., 2002. Coord. Nat. Women's History Month Cherry Hill Jr. Schs., 1993—2002. Advisor Mother Earth and Friends Environ. Club, 1989—2000; mem. dist. Recycling Program Cherry Hill Pub. Schs., 1990—94, Nat. Women's History Mus., Nat. Mus. Women Arts, Women's Philharm.; sponsor Childreach; mem. dist. Womyn and Religion Unitarian Universalist Ch., Cherry Hill. Mem.: NOW, Population Comm. Internat., Freedom from Hunger, Seeking Edn. Equity and Diversity (mem. study group 1994), Alice Paul Centenial Found., Planned Parenthood, Global Fund Women, World Wildlife Fedn., Cherry Hill Ret. Tchr. Edn. Assn., Camden County Ret. Tchr. Edn. Assn., N.J. Ret. Tchr. Edn. Assn., Nat. Ret. Tchr. Educators Assn. Avocations: foreign travel, foreign films, arts, nature, jazz. Home: 10 Brookwood Dr Voorhees NJ 08043-4757

CARTER, CHARLENE ANN, psychologist; b. Marshall, Mich., Apr. 7, 1941; d. Charles V. F. and Eva L. (Hesling) Hampton.; m. Ross E. Carter, Jan. 15, 1966; children: Laura, Paul. BA in Psychology and Sociology, Albion Coll., 1962; MA in Clin. Psychology, Mich. State U., 1964, PhD in Clin. Psychology, 1968. Lic. psychologist, Wis. Clin. intern VA Hosp., Battle Creek, Mich., 1963-65, Psychol. Clinic Mich. State U., East Lansing, 1965—66, Counseling Ctr. Mich. State U., 1966—68, asst. prof., 1968—69; pvt. practice Bangor, Maine, 1971, Media, Pa., 1974-75; assoc. clin.prof. dept. psychiatry Med. Coll. Wis., Milw., 1983—; pvt. practice, 1988—. Dir. clin. tng. Wis. Sch. for Girls, Oregon, Wis., 1969—70; staff psychologist The Counseling Ctr., Cmty. Mental Health Ctr., Bangor, Maine, 1971; mem. staff Aurora Psychiat. Hosp., 1992—, Rogers Hosp., 2001—; psychologist cons. Office of Hearing and Appeals, Social Security Adminstrn., Milw., 1986—91; lectr. in field. Contbr. articles to profl. jours. USPHS fellow, 1962, 65, 66. Mem. APA. Office: Mayfair North Tower 2600 N Mayfair Rd Ste 320 Milwaukee WI 53226-1313 Office Phone: 414-258-9984.

CARTER, CHRISTINE, retired assistant principal; b. Macon, Miss., Aug. 3, 1948; d. Dan and Letha Bridges; children: Angelica Latrice, Letha LeAnn Carter-Clark. BS, Jackson State U., Miss., 1970; MA, Roosevelt U., Chgo., 1990. Tchr. Chgo. Pub. Schs., 1971—96, asst. prin., 1996—2004; ret., 2004. Mem.: NAACP, Zeta Phi Beta. Home: 34 E 126th St Chicago IL 60628-7327

CARTER, CYNTHIA (CINDY) LYNN, writer; m. Thomas Kenneth Carter, June 5, 1993. BA in Radio, TV & Film, U. Md., College Park, MD, 1989—93; MA in Film and Video, Am. U., Washington, DC, 1993—95. Film reviewer Creative Screenwriting Mag., Los Angeles, Calif., 1995—2001, bd. script reviewers, 1998—2001; freelance writer Millsboro, Del., 2002—; screenplay writing cons. ScriptFix, Kensington, Md., 1999—2001. Author: (screenplays) Home (Hon. Mention Writer's Digest Writing Contest, 1995), The Willing Prey (aka The Cult) (Quarter Finalist Quantum Quest Screenplay Search, 1998, Semi-Finalist Lone Star Screenplay Competition, 1996, Quarter Finalist The Writer's Network Screenplay & Fiction Competition, 1997), The Actor (Quarter Finalist Lone Star Screenplay Competition, 1997, Semi-Finalist America's Best Screenplay Competition, 1997), (short stories) Lists. Named a Semi-Finalist, Nat. Merit Scholars, 1978. Mem.: Golden Key Nat. Honor Soc. (life). Personal E-mail: cindylynncarter@aol.com.

CARTER, DIXIE, actress; b. McLemoresville, Tenn. m. Hal Holbrook, May 27, 1984. Student, U. Tenn., Southwestern U., Memphis; B in English, Memphis State U. Actress: The Winter's Tale, Oklahoma!, Kiss Me Kate, Carousel, The King and I; broadway: Sextet, 1974, Pal Joey, 1976, The Master Class, 1997, Thoroughly Modern Millie, 2004; off broadway Fathers and Sons, (Drama Desk nomination), Jesse and the Bandit Queen (Theatre World award), A Coupla White Chicks Sitting Around Talking, Buried Inside Extra (TV series) One Life to Live, 1974, The Edge of Night, 1974-76, On Our Own, 1977-78, Out of the Blue, 1979, Filthy Rich, 1982-83, Diff'rent Strokes, 1984-85, Designing Women, 1986-93, Ladies Man, 1999, Family Law, 1999-2002; (films) The Killing of Randy Webster, (TV films) Gambler V: Playing for Keeps, 1994, Dazzle, 1994, Judith Krantz's Dazzle, 1995, Gone in the Night, 1996, Comfort and Joy, 2003; (instructional video) Dixie Carter's Unworkout, 1993; author: Trying to get to Heaven: Opinions of a Tennessee Talker, 1996. Avocations: family, singing.

CARTER, EDITH HOUSTON, statistician, educator; b. Charlotte, NC, Oct. 12, 1936; d. Z. and Ellie (Hartsell) Houston; m. Fletcher F. Carter, Apr. 2, 1961. BS, Appalachian State U., 1959, MA, 1960; PhD, Va. Poly. Inst. and State U., 1976. Transcript analyst Fla. Dept. Edn., Tallahassee, 1961-65; instr. Radford U., 1969-70, 91-94, asst. prof., 1994—. Prof. New River C.C., Dublin, Va., 1970-83, dir. instl. research, 1974-78, asst. dean Coll. Arts and Scis., 1978-79, statistician, 1979-83. Editor Community Coll. Jour. Research and Planning, 1981-93, Am. Assn. Community Colls. Jour. (rsch. review editor 1991-95), Newsletter Southeastern Assn. C.C. Research, 1972—; mem. editl. bd. C.C. Rev., 1990-93. Violist New River Valley Symphony, Va. Poly. Inst. and State U. Orch., Radford U. Orch., S.W. Va. Opera Soc. Orch., summer mus. Enterprise ORch., 1999—; sec./treas. Radford New River Valley chpt. Am. Sewing Guild, 1991-94, pres., 1994-96. Mem. Am. Ednl. Rsch. Assn., State and Regional Ednl. Rsch. Assn. (sec./treas. 1989-93, pres. 1993-95, svc. chmn. 1995-97, database chair 2003—, Leadership award 1995, 2002-03), Assn. Instl. Rsch. (exec. bd. 1976-78), Southeastern Assn. C.C. Rsch. (exec. bd. 1976-78, Outstanding Svc. award, Disting. Svc. award 1981, Edith Carter Svc. award 1998), Nat. Coun. Rsch. and Planning (Outstanding Svc. award 1992, James R. Montgomery Svc. award, 2001), Coll. Music Soc., Am. String Tchrs. Assn., Va. Ednl. Rsch. Assn. (pres. 1997, corr. sec. 2002-04), Va. Fedn. Women's Clubs (dir. 1968-70), Va. Tech. U. Alumni (pres. New River Valley chpt. 1982-83), So. Assn. for Instnl. Rsch., Radford Jr. Woman's Club (pres. 1967-68), Phi Delta Kappa (pres. New River Valley chpt. 1997-99, newsletter editor, 2003-06). Presbyterian. Home: 6924 Radford Univ Radford VA 24142 Office: Radford U Peters Hall Radford VA 24142 Office Phone: 540-831-5510, 540-639-1263. Business E-Mail: ecarter@radford.edu.

CARTER, ELEANOR ELIZABETH, account executive; b. Durham, N.C., July 16, 1954; d. Joseph William Jr. and Sheila Dale (Swartz) C. BS in Social Work, N.C. State U., 1977. Field worker family planning Wake County Health Dept., Raleigh, N.C., 1975-76; sales rep. Bristol-Myers Products, N.C., 1977-80, regional adminstn. asst. Dallas, Tex., 1980, regional trainer Washington, N.C., Va., 1980, sales adminstrn. mgr. corp. hdqrs. N.Y.C., 1980-81, dist. supr. Cin., 1981-82; account rep. Fuji Photo Film U.S.A., Inc., Cin., 1982-83, spl. account mgr. Chgo., 1983-90; nat. account mgr. Fuji Photo Film U.S.A., Itasca, Ill., 1991-97, v.p. nat. accounts, 1997—. Mem. NAFE, Alpha Kappa Delta. Presbyterian. Avocations: jogging, horseback riding, travel, dance. Office: 850 Central Ave Hanover Park IL 60133-5422 Office Phone: 800-869-8600 x5807. Business E-Mail: lcarter@fujifilm.com.

CARTER, EMILY ANN, physical chemist, researcher, educator; b. Los Gatos, Calif., Nov. 28, 1960; d. David and Rebecca (Blumberg) C.; m. Bruce E. Koel, 1994; children; Adam, Brent (step), Jacqueline (step). BS in Chemistry, U. Calif., Berkeley, 1982; PhD in Chemistry, Calif. Inst. Tech., 1987. Postdoctoral rsch. assoc. U. Colo., Boulder, 1987—88; asst. prof., physical chemistry UCLA, 1988—92, assoc. prof., 1992—94, prof., 1994—2002, prof. chemistry and materials sci. and engring., 2002—04, Arthur W. Marks prof. mech. engring. and applied math., 2006—. Mem. Def. Sci. Study Group, 1996-97; vis. scholar in physics Harvard U., 1999; cons. Inst. for Def. Analysis, 1998-, Los Alamos Nat. Lab., 2000-2005; mem. theoretical divsn. rev. com., 2000-05, DOE-BES coun. chem. sci., 2006-; vis. scholar in aeronautics Calif. Inst. Tech., 2001; UCLA dir. modeling and simulation Calif. Nano Systems Inst., 2000-04; McDowell lectr. U. B.C., 2002, Merck-Frosst lectr., Concordia U., 2005. Mem. editl. bd. Jour. Phys. Chemistry, 1995-00, Surface Sci., 1994-99, Ency. Chem. Physics and Phys. Chemistry 1996-01, Chem. Phys. Letters, 1998-, Phys. Chem. Comm., 1998-2002, Chem. Phys. Chem., 2000-, Jour. Chem. Phys., 2000-02, Modeling and Simulation in Materials Sci. and Engring., 2001-, SIAM Multiscale Modeling and Simulation Jour., 2001-; guest editor Jour. Phys. Chem., 1999-00; contbr. numerous articles to tech. jours; given over 275 invited lectures. Mem. MPS Theory Steering Com., 2004—05; chmn. APS, Divsn. Chem. Physics, 2004—05, Am. Conf. Theoretical Chemistry, 2005. Recipient rsch. innovation recognition awards Union Carbide Co., 1990, 91, New Faculty award Camille and Henry Dreyfus Found., 1988, others; NSF Presdl. Young Investigator award, 1988, Dreyfus Tchr. Scholar award, 1992, Alfred P. Sloan fellow, 1993, Internat. Acad. of Quantum Molecular Sci. medal, 1993, Exxon faculty fellow, 1993, Glen T. Seaborg Rsch. award, 1993, Herbert Newby McCoy Rsch. award, 1993, Peter Mark Meml. award Am Vacuum Soc., 1995, Dr. Lee vis. rsch. fellow Oxford U., 1996, UCLA Hanson-Dow award, 1998, UCLA Dean's Recognition award for rsch., 2002. Fellow AAAS, Am. Vacuum Soc., Am. Phys. Soc., Inst. of Physics; mem. Am. Chem. Soc., Material Rsch. Soc., MInerals, Metals, Materials Soc., Sigma Xi, Phi Beta Kappa. Avocations: theater, films, cooking, reading, tennis. Office: Princeton U Dept MAE E Quad Rm D404A Princeton NJ 08544-5263 Office Phone: 609-258-5391. Business E-Mail: eac@princeton.edu.

CARTER, ETHEL ILENE, secondary school educator; b. Colorado Springs, Aug. 2, 1947; d. Delbert William and Vera Lauretta Lacy; m. James Dale Carter, Dec. 27, 1969 (div. Dec. 9, 1996); children: James Dale Jr., Heidi Jo. BS in Secondary Edn., Olivet Nazarene U., Ill., 1970; MA in Ednl. Theatre, NYU, 1999. Cert. Tchg. Type 09 Ill., 1970. Tchr. home econs. St. Anne Cmty. HS, Ill., 1970—73, Ill. Valley Ctrl. HS, Chillicothe, 1981—84;

owner, mgr. Monical's Pizza, Canton, Ill., 1984—96; tchr. coop. vocat. edn., English, family and consumer sci. Canton HS, Ill., 1990—2000; tchr. theatre and family and consumer sci. Kaneland HS, Maple Park, Ill., 2000—. Dept. head home econs. St. Anne HS, Ill., 1970—73; judge-speech team Canton HS, Ill., 1991—97, tech prep-bus. ptnrs. in edn. com., 1991—2000, sponsor-nat. hon. soc., 1994—97, asst. coach-speech team, Maple Park, Ill., 1996—97, play dir., 1996—2000; play dir., thespian sponsor Kaneland HS, Maple Park, Ill., 2001—, speech team coach, 2004—, discipline com., 2004—, curriculum com., 2005—. Dir.: (over 35 sch. and cmty. plays, musicals, and children's theatre); co-dir.: (prodn. Creative Arts Team) Youth Theatre Co., 1998. Contemporary worship svc. com. First Christian Ch., Canton, Ill.; children's ch. dir., Snday sch. tchr., vacation bible sch. tchr., christian edn. com. Ch. of the Nazarene, Peoria, Ill.; bible sch. dir., play dir. Evang. Free Ch., Canton, Ill.; mem. Fulton County Playhouse, Canton, Ill., 1993—95; com. mem. Kaneland Found. Fine Arts Festival, Maple Park, Ill., 2004—06. Mem.: Ednl. Theatre Assn. Office: Kaneland Unit Sch Dist 47W326 Keslinger Rd Maple Park IL 60151 Office Phone: 630-365-5100 320. Business E-Mail: icarter@kaneland.org.

CARTER, EVELYN, retired elementary school educator; d. James Kyle and Mable Kuykendall; m. Willie James Carter (dec.). BS, Prairie View Coll., Tex., 1939, MEd, 1952. Tchr., Tex., 1939—76; ret., 1976. Musician, vol. Bapt. Ch., Nacogdoches, Tex., 2006—. Named to Hall of Fame, Asberry HS, Yoakum, Tex., 1992; recipient Silver Fawn award, Boy Scouts Am., 1973. Mem.: AAUW (historian 2000—06), Nacogdoches Ret. Tchrs., Tex. Ret. Tchrs. Baptist. Avocations: reading, piano, dance, singing. Home: 2533 Woden Rd Nacogdoches TX 75961

CARTER, FRANCES ANN, secondary school educator; d. Bill and Hazel Francis Combs; m. Danny Dale Carter, Nov. 24, 1978. AA, Somerset C.C., Ky., 1976; BS, Ea. Ky. U., Richmond, 1985, MA, 1988. Provisional tchr. cert. Ky., 1988. Lab technician Harard Hosp., Ky., 1976—77, Ft. Logan Clinic, Stanford, Ky., 1977—80; DHIA technician U. Ky. Ext., Lexington, 1980—81; tchr. Casey County H.S., Liberty, Ky., 1985—93, Southwestern H.S., Somerset, 1993—. Sponsor and dir. Southwestern H.S. Conservation Club and Raptor Ctr., Somerset, 1993—. Founder Raptor Rehab. Ctr.; bd. dirs. Ky. Environ. Edn. Coun., Frankfort, Ky., 1993—2006. Named Outstanding Biology Tchr., NABT, 1999, H.S. Tchr. of Yr., Pulaski Coun., 2005; Toyota Tapestry grantee, Toyota, 1998. Mem.: IWRA (assoc.), NWRA (assoc.), KSTA (assoc.), KAEE (assoc.). Democrat. Office: Southwestern High School 1765 WTLO Rd Somerset KY 42503 Office Phone: 606-679-6980. Office Fax: 606-678-9277. Business E-Mail: frances.carter@pulaski.kyschools.us.

CARTER, FRANCES MOORE, secondary school educator, personnel director, writer, foundation administrator; b. Washington; d. Joel Presley and Ora Emma Moore; m. Richard Dunn Carter, July 2, 1949 (dec. 1992); children: Karen Anne, Marcia Lee, Richard Dunn Jr. BA in English, Coll. William and Mary, 1947; MA in Arts and Humanities, West Chester U., 1972; EdD in Edn. and Adminstrn., U. Pa., 1978. Cert. elem. and secondary tchr., secondary prin., curriculum and instrn. supr., supt., Pa. Tchr. elem. Chester-Upland Sch. Dist., Chester, Pa., 1968—69; tchr. English and humanities Marple Newtown Sch. Dist., Newtown Square, Pa., 1969—78; adj. prof., English and edn. Villanova U., Pa., 1978—79; adj. prof. English and edn. St. Joseph's U., Phila., 1978—79; dir. career edn. Del. County Intermediate Unit, Media, Pa., 1979—83; dir. industry-edn. Del. County Partnership for Econ. Devel., Media, 1979—83; exec. dir. Chester Edn. Found., Pa., 1989—90; assoc. Career Solutions Planning Group, Paoli, Pa., 1990—93; pres. Micro-Graph, Inc., Broomall, Pa., 1993—95, Drexel U. Founds., Phila., 1999—. Commr. Accrediting Commn. for Career Schs. and Colls. of Tech., Washington, 1990-94; bd. mem., exec. com., chair rev. com. Pa. State Bd. Pvt. Licensed Schs., Harrisburg, 1987-95; mem. Phila. Regional Labor Task Force, 1989-92; writer Drexel U. Found. Author: (curriculum series) Employability and Life Skills Training, 1982, (book) Delaware County Job Planning Guide, 1982, Delaware County Training Resource Guide, 1983, Meeting the Challenge of Change, 1988; scriptwriter Cable TV series Solving the Job Puzzle, 1983; writer Drexel U. Found. Charter Schs., 1999—. Chmn. bus./industry com. Partnership for Econ. Devel., Media, 1988-90; founder, dir. Clearinghouse for Edn./Industry, Delaware County, Pa., 1983-89; bd. mem., mem. exec. com., Resource Ctr. for Human Svc., Phila., 1986-92, Leadership, Inc., Phila., Class of 1986-87; elder Presbyn. Ch. (USA), 1968—; bd. dir. Girl Scouts of Del. County, Media, 1985-90, Girls Coalition S.E. Pa., sec., pres., 1983—; clk. of session Swarthmore (Pa.) Presbyn. Ch., 1993—elder, 1968—; mem. adv. bd. Pa. State U. (Lima campus), 1988—. Recipient Athena award Del. County C. of C., 1990, Educator of Yr. award, Nat. Assn. for Industry/Edn. Cooperation, 1989, Woman of Distinction award, Del. County Women's Commn., 1989, Disting. Svc. award, Del. County Coun., Media, 1988, Exemplary Achievement award Del. County Coun., 1984. Mem. Del. County Press Club (bd. dirs., chair comm. day 1987—), Phi Delta Kappa, Pi Lambda Theta, Mortarboard, Pi Beta Phi. Presbyterian. Avocations: reading, piano, theater, sailing, travel. Home and Office: 77 S Rolling Rd Springfield PA 19064-2415

CARTER, FRANCES TUNNELL (FRAN CARTER), fraternal organization administrator; b. Springville, Miss. d. David Atmond and Mary Annie (McCutcheon) Tunnell; m. John T. Carter; children: Wayne, Nell Branum. BS, U. So. Miss., 1946; MS, U. Tenn., 1948; EdD, U. Ill., 1954. Tchr. elem. sch., Thaxton, Miss., 1942—43, Cumberland, Miss., 1943—44; tchr. h.s. home econs. Randolph, Miss., 1944—45, Maben, Miss., 1946—47; instr. Wood Coll., Mathiston, Miss., 1947—48, East Ctrl. Jr. Coll., Decatur, Miss., 1948—49; prof. home econs. Clarke Coll., Newton, Miss., 1950—56; prof. Samford U., Birmingham, Ala., 1956—84; editor, children and youth products and resources Woman's Missionary Union, Birmingham, 1983—85; pres. CarterCraft, Inc., Birmingham, 1985—89; nat. exec. dir. Kappa Delta Epsilon, Birmingham, 1987—2003. Vis. prof. Hong Kong Bapt. U., 1965-66, Anhui Normal U., People's Republic of China, 1987; medical/dental mission team mem. Honduras, Mex., 1983, 84, 89, 1994; tchr. workshops in China, 1988, 90, 92, 95, 97, 2000; tchr. workshops in Indonesia, 1993; lectr. in symposium at invitation of Russian Edn. Ministry, Moscow, 1994, U. Nanjing, People's Republic of China, 1997; curriculum writer Bapt. Brotherhood Commn., 1986-90; writer N.Am. Mission Bd., 1995-98. Author: Sammy in the Country, 1960, Tween-Age Ambassador, 1970, Ching Fu and Jim, 1978; co-author: Sharing Times Seven, 1977, also short stories, articles; feature writer: Crusader Mag., 1986-95, The Current, 1987-2003; editor 103 Rosie Stories, 2001. Tchr. Sunday sch. Bapt. Ch., Birmingham, 1980—; mem., lt. col. CAP, 1968—1996, bd. dirs. Aerospace Edn. Ala. Wing, 1991-94, dir. pub. affairs regional S.E., 1994-95; v.p. Women's Civic Club of Birmingham, 1997-98, 2002-03; placement officer ESL Sch., 1995-98, pres., 1982-83, Test of English as a Fgn. Lang. tchr., 1998-. Recipient Career Achievement award Profl. Fraternity Assn., 1988, Outstanding Alumnae award Wood Coll., 1992, Outstanding award Kappa Delta Pi, 1992, Brewer award for Aerospace Edn. Southeast region CAP, 1994, Vol. of Yr. award Nat. Profl. Fraternity Assn., 1999, Lillian K. Keil award WWII Vets. Com., Washington, DC, 2004; named Birmingham's Woman of Yr., 1977, Birmingham's Vol. of Yr., 1980, Silver rep. Dist. 6 Ala. Nat. Silver Haired Congress, 1991-96, Ala. Silver Haired Legislator Dist. 55 Jefferson County, 1996—, cert. Rosie the Riveter reunion, Little White House, Warm Springs, Ga., 1997; named to Sr. Citizen Hall of Fame, 2002. Mem. AARP (local pres. 1988-89, asst. state dir. 1989-93, Nat. Cmty. award 1992), Birmingham's Women C. of C. (pres. 1975-76, 2003-04), Nat. League Am. Pen Women (3rd v.p. 1988-90, nat. pres. 1994-96), Ala. League Pen Women (pres. 1970-72), Birmingham League Am. Pen Women (pres. 1968-70, 76-78), Ala. Writers Conclave (pres. 1978-79), Ala. State Poetry Soc. (pres. 1979-82), Ala. Federated Women's Clubs (dist. dir. 1988-90, Outstanding Woman of Ala. Club award 1988), Freedoms Found. Valley Forge (pres. Birmingham area chpt. 1990-91), Nat. Fellowship Bapt. Educators (sec. 1987-93), Birmingham Bus. and Profl. Club (pres. 1986-87), Am. Rosie the Riveter Assn. Inc. (founder, pres. 1998-2003, nat. exec. dir. 2003—), Kappa Delta Epsilon (nat. pres. 1980-85, exec. dir. 1987-2003, co-dir. ESL Sch. 1994-98), Alpha Delta Kappa, Delta Kappa Gamma, Phi Delta Kappa (Nat. Profl. Fraternity Assn. award 1999, cert. emeritus 2000), Birmingham Civic Club (v.p. 2003-04), Birmingham Women's C. of C. (pres. 2003-04), Samford U. Retired Faculty Assn. (pres. 2004-) Home and Office: 3470 Loch Ridge Dr Birmingham AL 35216 Office Phone: 205-822-4106. E-mail: fran.carter@juno.com.

CARTER, GAIL RAE, history educator; b. Presque Isle, Maine, Aug. 25, 1938; d. Ray Horace Carter and Mavis Evelyn Farnham; children: Mark Carter Harvey, Sarah Helen Harvey. BA, U. Maine, Orono, 1960. Cert. secondary edn. educator Maine. History tchr. Greely H.S., Cumberland, Maine, 1987—. Dir. restoration Downtown Gardiner; mem. Maine State Mus. Commn., 1976—90, chmn., 1990; mem. city coun. City of Gardiner, Maine, 1979—81. Mem.: DAR, United Empire Loyalists, Mayflower Soc. (life). Republican. Episcopalian. Achievements include research in early Maine revolutionary history. Home: 305 Commercial St Portland ME 04101 Office: MSAD #51 Main St Cumberland ME 04021 Office Phone: 207-829-4805 225. Personal E-mail: gail-carter@msad51.org.

CARTER, GEORGIAN L., minister; b. St. Mary's, Ga., July 3, 1939; d. Leroy Sr. and Abbie (Myers) Logan; m. Calvin L. Carter, Mar. 26, 1956; children: Janice Carter Slocumb, Arlette Carter Fletcher, Eric. AA, Prince Georges Community Coll., Largo, Md., 1973; cert., Dale Carnegie Sch., 1980. Ordained to ministry Deliverance Ch. of Christ, 1983. Clk., trustee Deliverance Ch. of Christ, Seat Pleasant, Md., 1968-87, Bible class tchr., 1983-89; sec., sick and shut-in ministry Full Gospel A.M.E. Zion Ch., Temple Hills, Md., 1989-92; mem. Live Oak Ch. of God, Hinesville, 1992, Sunday sch. tchr. of adult class, 1993—. With HUD, Washington, 1967-89; tchr. noon-time Bible study U.S. State Dept. Fellowship, 1989-91; lay min.; sunday sch. tchr. adult classes Live Oak Ch. of God, 1993-. Asst. dir. Glenarden (Md.) Housing Authority, 1973-75. Democrat. Home: 909 Byrum Dr Hinesville GA 31313-5752 Personal E-mail: gcarter@coastalnow.net.

CARTER, IRIS BROWN, pre-school educator; b. New Orleans, Jan. 14, 1952; d. Birthena Hawkins; children: Norman Butler, Nia Jovan Butler. AS, Delgado CC, New Orleans, 2002. Tchr. headstart Thibodaux Head Start, La., 2003—; tchr. early heastart St. Charles Parish Headstart, Hahnville, La.; substitute tchr. St Charles Parish Sch. Bd., Hahnville; tchr. preschool First Meth. Ch., New Orleans, Victory Fellowship Day Care, Metairie, La. Bd. mem., spokesperson La. Bucket Brigade, Norco, La., 2000; vol. Children's Outreach Ministry Harvest Cathedral, Houma, La. D-Liberal. Achievements include development of Started Homeless Ministry at Victory Fellowship Church in Metairie, LA 1989. Avocations: travel, cooking, bowling. Office: Thibodaux Head Start Veterans Hwy Thibodaux LA 70301 Office Phone: 985-447-3521. Personal E-mail: convertible_lane@yahoo.com.

CARTER, JAINE M(ARIE), human resources specialist, director; b. Chgo., Oct. 29, 1946; m. James Dudley Carter, Apr. 8, 1970; children: Paul, Todd. BS, Northwestern U., 1968; PhD, Walden U., 1988. Mgmt. cons. to bus., 1969; chmn. bd. Pers. Devel., Inc., Palatine, Ill., 1969—; dir. women's divsn. Lake Forest Coll. Advanced Mgmt. Inst., Ill., 1970—. Writer, lectr., tchr., cons. mgmt. devel. programs; faculty AMA; speaker weekly cable TV series Life Skills; pres. bd. dirs. Family Renewal Inst., 1991—96. Author: How to Train for Supervisors, 1969, Career Planning Workshop for Women, 1975, Training Techniques That Bring About Positive Behavioral Change, 1976, Assertive Management Role Plays, 1976, Understanding the Female Employee, 1976, Rx for Women in Business, 1976, New Directions Needed in Management Training Programs, 1980, The Burnout of Retirement, 1983, Successfully Working with People, 1984, Assertiveness Training for Supervisors, 1985, Successfully Managing People, 1986, The New Success, 1986, Employee Assistance Program Handbook, 1988, Stay Out of Your Own Way-And Get the Job You Want, 1989, He Works/She Works-Successful Strategies for Working Couples, 1996; columnist: Scripps- Howard News Svc., Balancing Work and Family, 1996—2004; columnist Scripps-Howard News Svc. He Works/She Works, 1996—2004; moderator, content expert (TV spl.) Commitment to Quality, Nat. Tech. U., 1989; author: (TV series) Executive Communications, 1988 prodr.: (TV series) Relationships, 1992; creator, prodr., host (TV series) Choices, 1992, 1993, host (radio talk show), 1992—96, co-host Your Own Business!, 1993—97. Mem.: Pres.'s Forum (exec. dir. 1998—).

CARTER, JANE FOSTER, agricultural industry executive; b. Stockton, Calif., Jan. 14, 1927; d. Chester William and Bertha Emily Foster; m. Robert Buffington Carter, Feb. 25, 1952 (dec. Dec. 1994); children: Ann Claire Carter Palmer, Benjamin Foster; m. Frank Anthony Bauman, Aug. 15, 1998 (div. Aug. 2003). BA, Stanford U., 1948; MS, NYU, 1949. Pres. Colusa (Calif.) Properties, Inc., 1953—; owner Carter Land and Livestock, Colusa, 1965—; pres. Sartain Mut. Water Co., Inc., 1992—2003, Carter Mut. Water Co. Inc., 2003—, J&B Rice Farms, Inc., Colusa, 1996—. Sec./treas. Carter Farms, Inc., Colusa, 1975—94, pres., 1994—2002; bd. dirs. Colusa Bean Growers, Inc., 1996—2002, sec., 1998—2002. Author: If the Walls Could Talk, Colusa's Architectural Heritage, 1988; author, editor: Colusa County Survey and Plan for the Arts, 1981—83, Implementing the Colusa County Arts Plan, 1984—86. Adv. mem. Calif. Gov.'s Commn. Agr., Sacramento, 1979—82; trustee Calif. Hist. Soc., 1979—89, regional v.p., 1984—89; mem. Calif. Reclamation Bd., 1982—96, sec., 1986—96; mem. Calif. Hist. Resources Commn., 1994—2001, vice chair, 1996—97, chair, 1997—99; mem. Colusa Heritage Preservation Com., 1976—2000, chmn., 1977—83, vice chmn., 1983—91, sec., 1997—2000; bd. dirs. Colusa Cmty. Theatre Found., 1980—99; trustee Calif. Preservation Found., 1989—95; del. Rep. Nat. Conv., Kans. City, Mo., 1976, Detroit, 1980, Dallas, 1984; mem. Calif. Rep. Ctrl. Com., 1976—94; bd. dirs. English-Spkg. Union U.S., N.Y.C., 1995—2001, English-Spkg. Union, San Francisco, 1992—, pres., 1993—95, v.p., 1995—; bd. dirs. Leland Stanford Mansion Found., Sacramento, 1992—; bd. dirs. Colusa County br. Am. Cancer Soc., 1960—86, chmn., 1964—86; mem. exec. com. Sacramento River Water Contractors' Assn., 1974—2003, sec., 1992—2003. Recipient award of Merit for Hist. Preservation, Calif. Hist. Soc., 1989, Design award, Calif. Preservation Found., 1990, Pres.'s award, 2001, Citizens award, English-Speaking Union U.S., 2002, Congl. Order Merit, Nat. Rep. Congl. Com., 2003. Mem.: Francisca Club (San Francisco), Kappa Alpha Theta. Episcopalian. Avocations: travel, the arts, historic preservation. Home and Office: 4746 River Rd Colusa CA 95932-4200

CARTER, JEAN GORDON, lawyer; b. Fort Belvoir, Va., July 30, 1955; d. Thomas Laney and Cleone (Hunter) Gordon; m. Michael L. Carter, Sept. 17, 1977; children: Christina Jean, William Gordon. BS in Accountancy magna cum laude with honors, Wake Forest U., 1977; JD with high honors, Duke U., 1983. Bar: N.C. 1983; CPA; bd. cert. specialist in estates. Acct. Arthur Andersen & Co., Charlotte, NC, 1977-80; atty. Moore & Van Allen, Raleigh, NC, 1983-90; ptnr. Hunton & Williams, Raleigh, NC, 1990—. Mem. Am. Coll. Trusts and Estates Coun., N.C. Bar Assn., Wake County Estate Coun. (pres. 1991-92), Order of Coif, Phi Beta Kappa. Democrat. Presbyterian. Avocation: reading. Home: 3913 Stratford Ct Raleigh NC 27609-6351 Office: Hunton & Williams One Bank of America Plz Raleigh NC 27601-2947 Office Phone: 919-899-3088. Business E-Mail: jcarter@hunton.com.

CARTER, JEANIE, performing company executive; b. Decatur, Ill., May 16, 1950; children: James L. Cook, Abigail G. Cook, Sarah E. Mason;. B in music, Millikin U., 1972. Cons. Hewitt Assoc., Lincolnshire, Ill., 1989—2000; vocal instr. Willow Creek Arts Ctr., South Barrington, Ill., 2002—03; pres., artistic dir. Bel Canto Studios, Barrington, Ill., 2001—. Voice lessons Clare Kittner, Northbrook, Ill., 1972—85, Willow Creek Arts Ctr., South Barrington, 2002—03; mem. Willow Creek, McHenry County vocal team, 2005. Composer: Footprints, 2002. Soprano soloist 1st Presbyn. Ch., Libertyville, Ill., 1972—92; vocal ministry Willow Creek Cmty. Ch., South Barrington, 2002—03. Mem.: Nat. Assn. Tchr.'s Singing, Music Tchr.'s Nat. Assn. Office: 217 Park Ave Barrington IL 60010 Office Phone: 847-382-2560, 847-682-9601. Business E-Mail: jeaniecarter@belcantostudios.com.

CARTER, JEANNE WILMOT, lawyer, publishing executive; b. Iowa City, Iowa, Oct. 25, 1950; d. John Robert and Adelaide Wilmot (Briggs) Carter; m. Daniel Halpern, Dec. 31, 1982; 1 child, Lily Wilmot. BA cum laude, Barnard Coll., N.Y.C., 1973; MFA, Columbia U., 1977; JD, Yeshiva U., N.Y.C., 1986. Bar: N.Y. 1987. Assoc. Raoul Lionel Felder, P.C., N.Y.C., 1986—; pres., co-owner, dir. Ecco Press, Hopewell, NJ, 1992—. Author: Dirt Angel, 1997, Tales from the Rain Forest, 1997; editor: On Music, 1994; contbr. articles to profl. jours. and books including Reading the Fights, N.Am. Rev., O'Henry Prize Stories 1986, Antaeus, Antioch Rev., Arts and Entertainment Law Jour., Ont. Rev., Denver Quar., Jour. Blacks in Higher Edn., others. Bd. dirs. Nat. Poetry Series, 1981—, AIDS Helping Hand, N.Y.C., 1987-95, Planned Parenthood of Mercer County, 1998—; vol. litigator Womanspace, Princeton, N.J., 1994; mem. Jr. League of N.Y.C., 1980-91; chmn. Princeton Alcohol and Drug Alliance, 2000—; pres. bd. Corner House Found., 2004—. N.Y. Found. of the Arts fellow, 1989. Mem. ABA, N.Y. State Bar Assn.

CARTER, JOANN MARTIN, retired education educator; b. Seminole, Okla., Sept. 29, 1932; d. George Light and Bess (Hill) Martin; m. Darold W. Carter, June 10, 1951; children: Christine Smith, M. Andrew, Matthew. BS, N. Tex. U., 1965; MA, George Peabody Coll., 1966; MEd, So. Meth. U., 1969; EdD, U. Mo., St. Louis, 1980. Tchr. Lincoln Pub. Schs., Lincoln, Nebr., 1966-69; tchr. St. Louis Pub. Schs., 1969-70, Univ. City Pub. Schs., St. Louis, 1970-71, Spl. Sch. Dist. St. Louis County, St. Louis, 1971-80; asst. prof. Carson-Newman Coll., Jefferson City, Tenn., 1980-82; coord. student teaching, prof. U. Sci. and Arts Okla., Chickasha, 1982-95, prof. emeritus, 1995—. Bd. dirs., program chmn. Okla. Lupus Assn.; bd. dirs. St. Louis Ovarian Cancer Awareness, 2003—, Barnes Jewish St. Peters Hosp. Aux., 2003. Mem. Okla. Reading Assn. (bd. dirs. 1988-96, pres.-elect 1990-92, pres. 1992), Internat. Reading Assn. Avocation: sailing.

CARTER, JOY T., science educator; d. Judith and John Cappello; m. Ron Carter, Aug. 20, 1994; children: Gabrielle Teresa, Jacob Lee. BS oin Sci. Edn., Trenton State Coll., Ewing, N.J., 1991; M in Adminstrn./Supervision, Jersey City State U., N.J., 2002. Tchr. sci. High Point Regional H.S., Sussex, NJ, 1991—. Office: High Point Regional HS 299 Pidgeon Hill Rd Sussex NJ 07461 Office Phone: 973-875-3101. Personal E-mail: jcarter@hpregional.org.

CARTER, JULIA MARIE, secondary school educator; b. Topeka, May 2, 1958; d. Jack Earnest and Bonita Aileen (Hatfield) Estes; m. Dan W. Carter; children: John-Thomas, Jessica Raye. BA, Ouachita Bapt. U., 1982; MBA, U. Phoenix, 2003; PhD candidate, Capella U. Cert. tchr. K-12, Ark., Fla., Md., Va., Pa., Mich., Ohio, Iowa. Tchr. French Dunbar Jr. High, Little Rock, 1989-91; tchr. Mt. Vernon (Ark.) Schs., 1991; tchr. French Cathedral Sch., Little Rock, 1991-92; tchr. St. Mark's Episcopal Sch., Oakland Park, Fla., 1992-93; tchr. French Miramar (Fla.) High Sch., 1993-96, Benjamin Franklin Sch., 1996—98, West Village Acad., 1999—2000, Detroit Public Sch., 2000—01, Bettendorf (Iowa) Pub. Schs., 2001—, Davenport (Iowa) Pub. Schs., 2003—. Owner Carter's Ednl. Svcs.; author, presenter in field. Vol. Chicot Elem., Little Rock, 1989-90, Silver Lake Mid. Sch., North Lauderdale, Fla., 1992-93, Miramar High Sch., 1993-95; mem. Ednl. Materials Equality Com., Little Rock, 1990-91. Fullbright scholar, 1989. Mem. Am. Assn. Tchrs. French (Prof. du Laureat 1989, 92), Am. Fedn. Tchrs. Democrat. Methodist. Avocations: travel, historic research, writing. Home: 3946 Madison St Dearborn Heights MI 48125-2156

CARTER, KAREN ZEPP, music educator, elementary school educator; b. Medford, Mass., Sept. 12, 1957; d. Ira Gilbert and Mary Dodd Zepp; 1 child, Rachael Elizabeth. MusB in Edn., Shenandoah Conservatory of Music, Winchester, Va., 1979; MusM, U. of Md., College Park, 1982. Tchg. Md. State Dept. Edn. Tchr.'s aide Montessori Sch., Westminster, Md., 1994—96; substitute tchr. Carroll County Pub. Schs., Wesminster, Md., 1996—98, tchr. instrumental music Westminster, Md., 1998—2003, Bryant Woods Elem. Sch., Columbia, Md., 2003—. Chairperson cultural arts com. LFES, Columbia, 2000—01; sch. rep. Howard County Parents for Sch. Music, Columbia, 2000—02; adjudicator Md. State Band, Balt., 2004—, Howard County Elem. Band, Columbia, 2004—, Balt. County Solo and Ensemble Festival, Balt., 2006—. Musician: Chamber Music on the Hill Concert Series, Carroll County Concert Band Sousa Series, McDaniel College Flute Choir. Recipient Homer Ulrich award, U. of Md., 1982, Music Educator of the Yr. nomination2006, Howard County Parents for Sch. Music, 2006, Outstanding Tchr. nomination, Carroll County Chamber of Commerce, 2003. Mem.: NEA, Music Educators Nat. Conf. Democrat. Methodist. Avocations: reading, performing, entertainment news. Office: Bryant Woods Elem Sch 5450 Blue Heron Ln Columbia MD 21044 Home: 5632 Vantage Point Rd Columbia MD 21044 Office Phone: 410-313-6859. Office Fax: 410-313-6864. Personal E-mail: k12rdygo@comcast.net. Business E-Mail: sean_martin@hcpss.org.

CARTER, KATHRYN GIBSON, education educator, consultant; b. Mullins, SC, Sept. 20, 1950; d. Mathew Brunson and Viola Faile Gibson; m. Harry Carlisle Carter, Apr. 4, 1982. Student, Winthrop U., 1968—70; BA, U. SC, 1972, MEd, 1976, MEd, 1978, EdD, 1995. Cert. tchr./prin. S.C., 1972. Tchr. Lexington Dist. Four, Swansea, SC, 1972—77; cmty. sch. dir. Florence (SC) Sch. Dist. One, 1977—78; coord. Richland Sch. Dist. One, Hopkins, 1978—92; cmty. edn. coord. SC. Dept. Edn., Columbia, 1992—98; exec. dir. S.C. Commn. Nat. & Cmty. Svc., Columbia, 1998—2005; CEO Carter's Leasing and Cons., LLC, Columbia, 2005—. Adj. faculty U. S.C., Columbia, 1999—2002. Editor: (spl. issue on svc. learning) Nat. Cmty. Edn. Jour.; author: (book) Hooking Out of School Youth Through Service Learning; co-author: Powerful Allies: Afterschool Programs, Service Learning and Community Education; dir.: (30 minute video for TV) Serving to Learn. Bd. mem. Nat. Cmty. Edn., Alexandria, Va., 1986—89, Family Shelter, Columbia, SC, 1992—96; mem. /bd. mem. Leadership Columbia Alumni Assn., 1989—2005; bd. mem. Capital Sr. Ctr., 2005—. Recipient Palmetto Pride award, Palmetto Project, 1995, Frank Manley Lectr., Nat. Cmty. Edn. Assn., 1997, Lamplighter award, Youth Svc. Charleston, 1997, Disting. Svc./Lifetime Membership award, S.C. Assn. Cmty. Edn., 1998, Disting. Alumni award, U. SC Coll. Edn., 2005;, Delta Kappa Gamma Internat. scholar, 1995, Paul Harris fellow, Rotary Internat., 1997, Internat. Cmty. Edn. Conf. Nairobi, Kenya scholarship, Pendell Pub. Co., 1987. Mem.: AAUW (bd. dirs. 2006), Low County Women in Philanthropy, Delta Kappa Gamma (past pres. 1990—92, Alpha Delta chpt.), Phi Delta Kappa (past bd. mem. 1998—99). Baptist And Presbyterian. Achievements include development of. Avocations: reading, travel, golf, college football, politics. Home: 100 Steeplechase S Columbia SC 29209 Office: Carters Leasing and Cons LLC 412 Vets Rd Ste K Columbia SC 29209 Office Phone: 803-776-7161. Office Fax: 803-734-4825. Personal E-mail: kathycarter@earthlink.net. Business E-Mail: kgibson@sde.state.sc.us.

CARTER, KIMBERLY, obstetrician, gynecologist; d. Jerry and Betty Jean Carter; m. Paul Carter. BA, Southwestern U., Georgetown, Tex., 1990; MPP, U. Chgo., 1994; MD, Baylor Coll. Medicine, Houston, 1998. Diplomate Am. Bd. Ob-Gyn., 2005. Mem. staff Austin Ob-Gyn. Assocs., Tex. Mem.: Austin Physicians for Social Responsibility (bd. dirs. 2004—), Tex. Med. Assn. (mem. maternal and perinatal health com., bd. dirs. Ins. Trust), Alpha Omega Alpha. Office: Austin Ob/Gyn Associates 2911 Medical Arts Sq Ste 3 Austin TX 78705 Office Phone: 512-474-0017.

CARTER, LA RAE DUNN, music educator; b. Salt Lake City, Oct. 17, 1932; d. Charles Oscar Dunn and Gretta Smith Haslam-Dunn; m. Ronald G. Carter, Aug. 7, 1956; children: Gary, Eric, Thomas, Jeffrey, John, Kristen, Karen, Shannon, Joseph. BA, Brigham Young U., 1954, MA, 1955; D in Musical Arts, Claremont U., 1996; cert. in tchr. edn., Boise State U., 1982. Music tchr. Boise Sch. Dist., 1954—56; vocal instr. Brigham Young U., Provo, Utah, 1956—57; music tchr. Nebo Sch. Dist., Springville, Utah, 1982—86; choral instr. Claremont (Calif.) Sch. Dist., 1987—99, chair fine arts depts., 1989—98; dir. choral activities Park City (Utah) H.S., 1999—, chair fine arts dept., 2001—. Dist. music team leader Park City Sch. Dist., 2001—03; adj. prof. music So. Va. U., 2004—06, vis. asst. prof., music dept., program coord., music dept., mus. dir., mus. theatre. Recipient Bravo award for the Arts, L.A. Music Ctr., 1996—97. Mem.: Utah Music Educators Assn.,

Music Educators Nat. Conf., Am. Choral Dirs. Assn., Utah Sch. Activities Assn. (region choral chmn. 1999—). Republican. Mem. Lds Church. Office Phone: 540-261-8400. Personal E-mail: ldcarter@adelphia.net.

CARTER, LINDA ANN, music educator; b. Kenmore, NY, Aug. 14, 1969; d. Ronald Joseph and Loretta Ann Sarafin; m. Gary James Carter, July 19, 1997; children: Ashley, Jason. MusB in Edn. with Performing Arts, Syracuse U., NY, 1991; MusM, Morehead State U., Ky., 1992. Lic. tchr. NY. HS band dir. Vernon-Verona-Sherrill Schs., NY, 1992—, co-tchr. leader music dept., 2002—. Mem.: NY State Sch. Music Assn. (all-state selection com., adjudicator), Phi Kappa Phi, Pi Lambda Theta. Avocations: scrapbooks, gardening, cooking, pets, golf. Office: Vernon Verona Sherrill HS 5275 State Rte 31 Verona NY 13478

CARTER, LINDA WHITEHEAD, oncological nurse, educator; b. Bluefield, W.Va., Dec. 20, 1941; d. Lee Joseph and Kathleen (Witherspoon) Whitehead; m. J. Stephen Carter, Mar. 11, 1961; children: Paul Scott, Kristin Hope. Student, Westmoreland Coll., Youngwood, Pa., 1980-83, St. Vincent Coll., Latrobe, Pa., 1984-85; BSN, Carlow Coll., Pitts., 1986; MSN, U. Pitts., 1992. RN Pa., cert. advanced oncology nurse, clin. nurse specialist. Oncology staff nurse Westmoreland Hosp., Greensburg, Pa., 1986-93, facilitator support group, 1988-93, oncology educator, 1990-93; clin. nurse specialist Magee Women's Hosp., Pitts., 1993-94; homecare nurse, 1996—; home care nurse U. Pitts. Med. Ctr. Home Care, 1996—98, case mgr., 1998—2005. Faculty Carlow Coll. Divsn. Nursing, Pitts., 1993-97; grad. asst. Pitts. Cancer Inst., 1990; grad. clin. nurse specialist Allegheny Gen. Hosp., Pitts., 1991-92; nurse of hope Am. Cancer Soc., 1987, mem. pub. edn. com. Westmoreland Unit, 1987-88, mem. nursing edn. com., 1987-94, mem. profl. edn. com., 1990-93, bd. dirs., 1989-92. Mem. editl. rev. bd. Oncology Nursing Forum, 1994-98. Named Vol. of Yr., Am. Cancer Soc., 1988, Pa. Div. scholar, 1987, Nat. scholar, 1989-91. Mem. ANA, Pa. Nurses Assn., Nat. League for Nursing, Oncology Nursing Soc. (nominating com. Greater Pitts. chpt. 1990-91, newsletter com. 1992-93, chair awards com. 1997-2001, Found. liaison com. chair), Internat. Soc. Nurses in Cancer Care, Sigma Theta Tau. Home: 2922 Bryer Ridge Ct Export PA 15632-9393 E-mail: lincarter@adelphia.net, lincarter101@yahoo.com.

CARTER, LYNDA, actress, entertainer; b. Phoenix, July 24, 1951; m. Ron Samuels May 28, 1977 (div. 1982); m. Robert Altman Jan. 29, 1984; 2 children. Student, U. Ariz. Beauty and fashion dir. Maybelline Cosmetics; profl. motivational spkr. Actor: (TV series) Wonder Woman, 1976-79, Partners in Crime, 1984, Hawkeye, 1994, (TV films) The New Original Wonder Woman, 1975, A Matter of Wife.and Death, 1976, The Last Song, 1980, Born to Be Sold, 1981, Hotline, 1982, Rita Hayworth: The Love Goddess, 1983, Stillwatch (also exec. prodr.), 1987, Mike Hammer: Murder Takes All, 1989, Daddy, 1991, Posing: Inspired by Three Real Stories, 1991, When Friendship Kills, 1996, She Woke Up Pregnant, 1996, Family Blessings, 1996, A Prayer in the Dark, 1997, Someone to Love Me: A Moment of Truth Movie, 1998, Terror Peak, 2003, (films) Bobbie Jo and the Outlaw, 1976, Lightning in a Bottle, 1993, Super Troopers, 2001, The Creature of the Sunny Side Up Trailer Park, 2004, Sky High, 2005, The Dukes of Hazzard, 2005; singer: (album) Portrait, 1978. Hon. crusade chmn. Am. Cancer Soc., 1985-86; hon. chairperson Exceptional Children Found., 1987-88. Named Miss World-USA, 1972; recipient Hispanic Woman of Yr. award, 1983, Golden Eagle award, 1986. Office: William Morris Agy 151 S El Camino Dr Beverly Hills CA 90212-2775

CARTER, MAE RIEDY, retired academic official, consultant; b. Berkeley, Calif., May 20, 1921; d. Carl Joseph and Avis Blanche (Rodehaver) Riedy; m. Robert C. Carter, Aug. 19, 1944; children: Catherine, Christin Ann. BS, U. Calif., Berkeley, 1943. Ednl. adviser, then program specialist div. continuing edn. U. Del., Newark, 1968-78; asst. provost women's affairs, exec. dir. status of women Office Women's Affairs, U. Del., 1978-86; mem. adv. bd. Rockefeller Family Grant Project, 1979-83. Regional v.p. Del. PTA, 1960-62; pres. Friends Newark Free Library, 1968-69; mem. fiscal planning com. Newark Spl. Sch. Dist., 1972. Author: Research on Seeing and Evaluating People, 1982, (with Geis and Butler) Seeing and Evaluating People, 1982, revised, 1986, (with Haslett and Geis) The Organizational Woman: Power and Paradox, 1992, also papers and reports in field. Recipient Outstanding Svc. award Women's Coordinating Coun., 1977, 79, Spl. Recognition award Nat. U. Extension Assn., 1977, award for credit programs, 1971, Creative Programming award, 1971, medal of distinction U. Del., 1998; AAUW grantee, 1968; Fulbright grantee, 1976; annual award named for returning Adult Students, 1988—, named to Del. Women Hall of Fame, 1995, professorship named for, in Women's Studies, 2003. Mem. AAUW (past br. pres.), LWV, NOW, Legal Momentum, Nat. Women's Polit. Caucus, Global Fund Women, Planned Parenthood, Freedom From Hunger, Population Comm. Internat. Democrat. Home: 604 Dallam Rd Newark DE 19711-3110

CARTER, MAJORA, urban planner; b. Bronx, NY; BA, Wesleyan U., 1988; MFA, NYU, 1997. Project dir. The Point Cmty. Develop. Corp., 1997—98, assoc. dir. cmty. develop., 1998—2001; founder and exec. dir. Sustainable South Bronx (SSB), NY, 2001—. Open Soc. Inst. Cmty. Fellow, 2002, Drum Major Inst. Fellow, 2005, MacArthur Fellow, John D. and Catherine T. MacArthur Found., 2005. Office: Sustainable South Bronx 890 Garrison Ave 4th Floor Bronx NY 10474

CARTER, MARGARET L., legislator; b. La., Dec. 29, 1935; d. Emma Carter; 9 children. BA, Portland State U., 1972; MEd, Oreg. State U., 1973; postgrad., Washington State U. Community organizer, asst. dir. Community Action Agy., Shreveport, La.; tchr. Albina Youth Opportunity Sch., Portland; counselor Portland Community Coll.; mem. Oreg. Ho. of Reps., Salem, 1984-98, Oreg. Senate from 22nd dist., Salem, 2001—. Mem. Joint Com. on Ways & Means, 2003, Spl. Senate Com. on Budget, 2003, Spl. Senate Com. on Oreg. Health Plan, 2003, Ways & Means Subcom. on Transp. & Econ. Devel., 2003; co-chair Human Resources com., 1985, vice chair, 87, Edn. com., 1985, 87, 89, Conf. com. on Dr. Martin Luther King State Holiday, co-chair, 1985, Joint Health Care com. 1986. Founder, mus. dir. Joyful Sound Singers Piedmont Ch. Christ; vol. counselor various juvenile detention ctrs. and women's prisons, voter registration drives in Portland's black neighborhoods, Project Pride; organizer Oreg. chpt. of Sickle Cell Anemia Found.; founder Oreg. Black Leadership Conf.; mem. Oreg. State Commn. on Post Secondary Edn. and the Oreg. Alliance for Black Sch. Educators, Spl. Commn. for the Parole Bd. on the Matrix System; mem. Gov.'s Task Force on Pregnancy and Substance Abuse, 1989—, Coun. on Alcohol and Drugs, 1989—, bd. dirs. ARC, Emanuel Med. Ctr. Found. Recipient Jeanette Rankin Award Oreg. Women's Polit. Caucus, 1985. Mem. Nat. Organ. Black Legis. Elected Women (v.p. 1985), Nat. Black Caucus (exec. com.), Blacks in Gov. (regional pres.), Alpha Kappa Alpha. Democrat. Home: 2948 NE 10th Ave Portland OR 97212-3240 Office: Oreg State Senate State Capitol S310 Salem OR 97301

CARTER, MARJORIE JACKSON, special education educator, consultant; b. Moulton, Ala., Dec. 2, 1946; d. Johnnie Henry Stover and Marie Edith McDaniel; m. Youncy Pippin Carter, June 27; 1 child, Coreen Marie Diaz. BS in Edn., Slippery Rock U., Pa., 1968; MEd in Spl. Edn., U. Pitts., 1974. Cert. tchr. Pa., tchr. spl. edn., social studies, learning disabilities, mental retardation Fla. Spl. edn. tchr. Pitts. Bd. Edn., 1974—79; program specialist Fla. Atlantic U., Boca Raton, 1981—82; program dir. Ann Storck Ctr. for the Disabled, Ft. Lauderdale, Fla., 1982—83; tchr. spl. edn. Broward County Schs., Ft. Lauderdale, 1982—. Mem. com. Cmty. Action Plan, Ft. Lauderdale, 2000—; bd. dirs. Wiggins-Henry Found., Pembroke Pines, Fla., 2001—. Democrat. Baptist. Avocations: real estate investment, tutoring, aerobics. Office: Dillard HS 2501 NW 11th St Fort Lauderdale FL 33311

CARTER, MARY ANDREWS, paralegal; b. Greenville, S.C., Sept. 27, 1958; d. Harold M. Andrews and Mary Nancy Dollar; m. Donald P. Carter, Aug. 1, 1982 (div. Sept. 27, 1986); children: Christina Marie, Jason Paul. Diploma in paralegal, Greenville Tech., 1988. Paralegal Alan. O Campbell, P.E., Inc., Sullivan's Island, SC, 1995—99; pvt. practice, 1999—2001; paralegal Campbell, Schneider & Assocs., John's Island, SC, 2001—. Mem. adv. coun. Clark Acad., Charleston, 1998—2000; guardian ad litem State of S.C., Charleston, 1999—. Office: Campbell Schneider and Assocs 3690 Bohicket Rd Ste 1D Johns Island SC 29455

CARTER, MELVA JEAN, retired medical technician; b. Pitts., Aug. 24, 1942; d. William Skinner and Gladys Gaines; m. Samuel Edward Carter, June 15, 1965; 1 child, Daphne Denise. Bus. cert., Detroit Inst. Comms., 1962; AS, Wayne County C.C., 1979; postgrad., Wayne State U., 1982. Cert. med. lab. technician bd. eligible. Teletype oper. N.Y. Telephone Co., N.Y.C., 1963—65; credit cons. Creditors Svc., Detroit, 1965—68; med. lab. technician Profl. Labs., Detroit, 1977—80; exec. office mgr. ARC, Detroit, 1969—77, med. lab. technician II, 1980—2004. Taught first aid various pub. schs.; pvt. tchr. music and voice. Observer search and rescue CAP-Aux. USAF, Selfridge AFB, Mich.; vol. neighborhood watch Mayor's Anti-Arson Com., Detroit, 2001—; neighborhood canvasser Dept. Elections, Detroit; manned several first aid stas.; poll counter Mich. Dept. Elections, Detroit, 1983; dir. bibl. plays at various chs. Recipient Name placed on Wall of Tolerance, Montgomery, Ala., Spirit of Detroit award, City Coun. Detroit, 1989, Cmty. Svc. cert., Mayor's Com., 2004, Cert. Recognition, House of Miracles, 2004. Mem.: So. Poverty Law Ctr., Murray Hill Block Club (block patrol 2000—). Democrat. Pentacostal. Avocations: bowling, drawing, music, reading, coin collecting/numismatics.

CARTER, NANETTE CAROLYN, artist; b. Columbus, Ohio, Jan. 30, 1954; d. Matthew Gameliel and Frances (Hill) C. BA, Oberlin Coll., 1976; MFA, Pratt Inst. of Art, 1978. Tchr. art Dwight Englewood Prep Sch., Englewood, NJ, 1978-87; profl. artist, 1987-92, CCNY, 1992-93; vis. lectr. Pratt Inst. of Art, Bklyn., 2001—. Artist-in-residence Triangle Workshop, Pine Plains, NYC, 1991. One-woman shows include Ericson Gallery, NYC, 1983, G.R. N'Namdi Gallery, Detroit, 1984, 86, 92-2002, Birmingham, Mich., 1989, 92, 96, 99, Chgo., 1999-2002, Cinque Gallery, NYC, 1985, Montclair (NJ) Art Mus., 1988, Jersey City (NJ) Mus., 1990, June Kelly Gallery, NYC, 1990, 94, 97, 2000, 04, Southampton (NY) Coll., 1991, Franklin Marshall Coll., Lancaster, Pa., 1992, Kebede Fine Arts, LA, 1992, Sande Webster Gallery, Phila., 1993, 95, 97, 99, 2001, 03, Alitash Kebete, LA, 1995, Hodges-Taylor Gallery, Charlotte, NC, 1997, Noel Gallery, Charlotte, N.C., 2004; exhibited in group shows at Bklyn. Mus., 1981, Newark Mus., 1985, Pa. Acad. Fine Arts, Phila., 1986, Clocktower Gallery, NYC, 1986, Associated Am. Artists Gallery, NYC, 1986, Wennigger Gallery Boston, 1987, Kenkelaba Gallery, NYC, 1987, Fashion Moda Gallery, Bronx, NY, 1988, Studio Mus. in Harlem, NY, 1988, Louisa McIntosh Gallery, Atlanta, 1990, Sande Webster Gallery, 1990, East Hampton Ctr. for Contemporary Art, NY, 1990, Space Gallery, Cleve., 1991, Mary Ryan Gallery, NYC, 1991, New Visions Gallery, Ithaca, NY, 1991, Bennington (Vt.) Coll., 1991, The Rifle Gallery, Columbus, Ohio, 1991, Bristol-Myers Squibb Co., Princeton, NJ, 1992, The Nat. Mus. of Woman in the Arts, Washington, 1992, The Paine Webber Art Gallery, NYC, 1993, Mus. Art, R.I. Sch. of Design, Providence, 1994, 98, Pratt's Inst.'s Manhattan Ctr., NYC, 1995, Skoto Gallery, NYC, 1995, Phila. Mus. Art, 1996, Wayne State U., Detroit, 1996, Pitts. Ctr. for Arts, 1996, W.Va. Wesleyan Coll., Buckhannon, 1996, Yale U. Art Gallery, New Haven, 1996, Spelman Coll. Mus. Fine Art, Atlanta, 1996, Rush Art, NYC, 1997, The Schomburg Ctr., NYC, 1998, Louis Ross Gallery, NYC, 1998, Nabisco, East Hanover, NJ, 1998, The Parish Art Mus., Southampton, NY, 1998, Elise Goodheart Gallery, Sea Harbor, NY, 1998, RI Sch. Design, Providence, 1998, Arlene Bujese Gallery, East Hampton, NY, 1999, Nat. Arts Club, NYC, 1999, Concordia Coll., Ann Arbor, Mich., 2000, Ark. Arts Ctr., Little Rock, 2000, Lambert Gallery, Atlanta, 2004, Rongio Gallery, Bklyn., 2004, and numerous others; represented in permanent collections Planned Parenthood, NYC, Jane Zimmerli Art Mus., Rutgers U., New Brunswick, NJ, Jersey City Mus., Libr. of Congress, Washington, ARCO, Phila., Reader's Digest, Pleasantville, NY, Schomburg Libr., NYC, Salomon Bros., NYC, Newark Mus., Herbert Johnson Mu., Art, Cornell U., Ithaca, NY, Studio Mus. Harlem, NY, MCI Telecomm., Chgo., Times Mirror, NYC, AT&T, NJ, IBM, Stamford, Conn., Lang Comm., Randolph, Vt., Merck Pharm. Co., Phila., Johnson & Johnson, Inc., New Brunswick, Pepsi-Cola, NYC, Motown Corp., L.P., LA, Am. Express, Mpls., Mus. Art RI Sch. Design, Providence, Yale Gallery of Art, New Haven, Conn., USA Assurance, San Antonio, Tex., Nextel Corp., LA, GE, Fairfield, Conn., Cochran Found., La Grange, Ga., Rutgers Grad. Sch. Mgmt., Newark, ARCO, Phila., Magic Johnson Enterprises, LA, Nissho Iwai Am. Corp., NYC, Pa. Acad. Fine Arts, Phila., Lucent Tech., Basking Ridge, NJ, Butler Inst. Am. Art, Youngstown, Ohio, Conkling Gallery, Minn. State Univ., Mankato, MN, 2002; Group shows: Jacktilton Gallery, NYC; Exhibit A Gallery, NYC; Pfizer Incorp., NYC, 2002; and numerous others. Grantee Nat. Endowment for Arts, 1981, The Jerome Found., 1981, NJ Coun. on Arts, 1985, NY Found. for Arts, 1990, The Pollock-Krasner Found., 1994, Wheeler Found., NYC, 1996, Fellowship, Lower East Side Printshop, NYC, 1997, Fellowship, Brandywine Workshop, Philadelphia, 1999

CARTER, PAMELA JEAN, elementary school educator; b. L.A., Apr. 9, 1949; d. Wallace Everett and Gordena (Olmstead) Lane; m. Clarence Calvin Carter Jr., July 8, 1970 (dec. Oct. 28, 2003); children: Marianne Ellen, Patricia Ann. BA in Edn. with honors, Ea. Wash. State Coll., 1970. Cert. elem. edn. tchr., Wash. Substitute tchr. Tukwila Sch. Dist., Wash., 1986—, Highline Sch. Dist., Burien, 1986—2003. Pres. Adv. Coun. Tukwila Schs., 1991-95, chair sch. levy and bond campaign, 1992-98. Mem. site coun. Foster H.S., 1994—; city councilmember City of Tukwila, 1995—; mem. exec. bd. Airport Communities Coalition, King County, Wash., 1996; chair South County Area Transp. Bd., King County, 1999, 2006; bd. dir. Assn. Wash. Cities., 2001-, pres., 2005-06; vice chair first tier suburbs coun. Nat. League of Cities, 2006; mem. Wash. Traffic Safety Commn., 2006—. Recipient Cmty. Recognition award Wash. Assn. Sch. Adminstrs., 1992. Mem.: NEA. Office: 6200 Southcenter Blvd Tukwila WA 98188-2544 E-mail: pcarter@ci.tukwila.wa.us.

CARTER, PAMELA LYNN, former state attorney general; b. South Haven, Mich., Aug. 20, 1949; d. Roscoe Hollis and Dorothy Elizabeth (Hadley) Fanning; m. Michael Anthony Carter, Aug. 26, 1971; children: Michael Anthony Jr., Marcya Alicia. BA cum laude, U. Detroit, 1971; MSW, U. Mich., 1973; JD, Ind. U., 1984. Bar: Ind. 1984, U.S. Dist. Ct. (no. dist.) Ind. 1984, U.S. Dist. Ct. (so. dist.) Ind. 1984. Rsch. analyst, treatment dir. U. Mich. Sch. Pub. Health and UAW, Detroit, 1973—75; exec. dir. Mental Health Ctr. for Women and Children, Detroit, 1975—77; consumer litigation atty. UAW-Gen. Motors Legal Svcs., Indpls., 1983—87; securities atty. Sec. of State, Indpls., 1987—89; Gov.'s exec. asst. for health and human svcs. Gov.'s Office, Indpls., 1989—91, dep. chief of staff to Gov., 1991—92; with Baker & Daniels, 1992—93; atty. gen. State of Ind., Indpls., 1993—96; ptnr. Johnson & Smith, 1996—97; v.p., gen. mgr. Europe, Mid. East & Africa Cummins Engine Co., Inc., Columbus, Ind., 1998—. Author (numerous poems). Active Jr. League, Indpls., Dem. Precinct, Indpls., Cath. Social Svcs., Indpls. Named Breakthrough Woman of the Year, 1989; named one of Outstanding Young Woman of America, 1977; recipient Outstanding Svc. award, Ind. Perinatal Assn., 1991, Cmty. Svc. Coun. Ctrl. Ind., 1991, Non-profl. Healthcare award, Family Health Conf. Bd. Dirs., 1991, award for excellence, Women of the Rainbow, 1991. Mem.: Ind. Bar Assn., Nat. Bar Assn., Coalition of 100 Black Women. Democrat. Avocations: gardening, hiking, travel, reading. Office: VP, Global Sales & Marketing Cummins Engine Co Inc 500 Jackson St Columbus IN 47201

CARTER, REBECCA GAIL, critical care nurse; b. Fayetteville, N.C., May 28, 1961; d. Edward Delano and Katharina Maria (Scheder) Comer; m. Ted Lee Carter, Jr., Apr. 19, 1980; children: Christopher Allen, Rachael Lauren. ADN, Fayetteville Tech. Inst., 1984; BSN, Fayetteville State U., 1998; MSN, East Caroline U., 2006. Cert. CPR instr. Nursing asst. Highland House Nursing Home, Fayetteville, NC, 1972-80; staff nurse Good Hope Hosp., Erwin, N.C., 1984-85; from staff nurse to clin. dir. Highsmith-Rainey Meml. Hosp., Fayetteville, 1987—96; clin. dir. open heart surgery/ICU Cape Fear Valley Hosp., Fayetteville, 1996. Documentation chmn. Highsmith Hosp., 1989—, mem. bioethics com., 1990, mgr. nurse adminstrn. computer system, 1992. Mem.: Am. Assn. Critical Care Nurses, Sigma Theta Tau. Avocations: drawing, gardening, needlepoint.

CARTER, REGINA, jazz violinist; b. Detroit, 1962; d. Grace Louise Carter. Violin performance student, New Eng. Conservatory Music; BA, Oakland U., Rochester, Mich., 1985. Musician: (albums) Regina Carter, 1995, Something for Grace, 1997, Rhythms of the Heart, 1998, Motor City Moments, 2000, Freefall, 2001, Paganini: After a Dream, 2003, I'll Be Seeing You: A Sentimental Journey, 2006, (with Straight Ahead) Look Straight Ahead, 1991, Body & Soul, 1993, (with String Trio of NY) Octagon, 1992, Blues.?, 1993, Live au Petit Faucheux, 1993, (with Mary J. Blige) My Life, 1994, (with Patti LaBelle) Flame, 1997, (with Cassandra Wilson) Traveling Miles, 1999, (with Danilo Perez) Motherland, 2000, (films) I Shot Andy Warhol, 1996, (documentaries) Jazz, 2001, (Operas) Wynton Marsalis' Blood on the Fields. MacArthur fellow, John D. & Catherine T. MacArthur Found., 2006. Office: c/o Michelle Taylor NIA Entertainment Ltd 90 Amsterdam Ave Teaneck NJ 07666 Office Phone: 201-837-0596. Office Fax: 201-837-0597.*

CARTER, ROBERTA ECCLESTON, counseling administrator; b. Pitts. d. Robert E. and Emily B. (Bucar) Carter; divorced; children: David Michael Kiewlich, Daniel Michael Kiewlich. Student, Edinboro State U., 1962-63; BS, California State U. Pa., 1966; MEd, U. Pitts., 1969; MA, Rosebridge Grad. Sch., 1987. Tchr. Bethel Park Sch. Dist., Pa., 1966-69; writer, media asst. Field Ednl. Pub., San Francisco, 1969-70; educator, counselor, specialist Alameda Unified Sch. Dist., Calif., 1970—. Master trainer Calif. State Dept. Edn., Sacramento, 1984—; personal growth cons., Alameda, 1983—. Author: People, Places and Products, 1970, Teaching/Learning Units, 1969; co-author: Teacher's Manual Let's Read, 1968. Mem. AAUW, NEA, Calif. Fedn. Bus. and Profl. Women (legis. chair Alameda br. 1984-85, membership chair 1985), Calif. Edn. Assn., Alameda Edn. Assn., Charter Planetary Soc., Oakland Mus., Exploratorium, Big Bros of East Bay, Alameda C. of C. (svc. award 1985). Avocations: gardening, travel. Home: 1516 Eastshore Dr Alameda CA 94501-3118 Office Phone: 510-522-7981.

CARTER, ROSALYNN SMITH (ELEANOR ROSALYNN CARTER), former First Lady of the United States; b. Plains, Ga., Aug. 18, 1927; d. Edgar and Allie (Murray) Smith; m. James Earl Carter, Jr., July 7, 1946; children: John William, James Earl III, Donnel Jeffrey, Amy Lynn. Attended, Ga. Southwestern Coll., 1944—46; DHL (hon.), Morehouse Coll., 1980; LLD (hon.), U. Notre Dame, 1987. First Lady of U.S., Washington, 1977—81; disting. centennial lectr. Agnes Scott Coll., Decatur, Ga., 1988—92; disting. fellow, Women's Studies Dept. Emory U., Atlanta, 1990—. Author: First Lady from Plains, 1984; co-author (with Jimmy Carter) Everything to Gain: Making the Most of the Rest of Your Life, 1987, (with Susan Golant) Helping Yourself Help Others: A Book for Caregivers, 1994, (with Susan Golant) Helping Someone With Mental Illness: A Compassionate Guide for Family, Friends and Caregivers, 1998. Co-founder Every Child by Two Campaign for Early Immunization; co-founder (with Jimmy Carter) The Carter Ctr., 1982, trustee, creator and chair Mental Health Task Force; ann. host Rosalynn Carter Symposium on Mental Health Policy; founder Rosalynn Carter Fellowships for Mental Health Journalism, 1996; chair Internat. Com. of Women Leaders for Mental Health; adv. bd. mem. Habitat for Humanity; mem. Ga. Gov.'s Commn. to Improve Svcs. for Mentally and Emotionally Handicapped, 1971; pres. bd. dir., Rosalynn Carter Inst. for Caregiving Ga. Southwestern State U.; hon. chair Pres.'s Commn. on Mental Health, 1977—78. Recipient Vol. of Decade award Nat. Mental Health Assn., 1980, Presdl. Citation APA, 1982, Nathan S. Kline medal of merit Internat. Com. Against Mental Illness, 1984, Disting. Alumnus award Am. Assn. State Colls. and Univs., 1987, Dorothea Dix award Mental Illness Found., 1988, Dean's award Columbia U. Coll. Physicians and Surgeons, 1991, Notre Dame award for internat. humanitarian svc., 1992, Eleanor Roosevelt Living World award Peace Links, 1992, Nat. Caring award The Caring Inst., 1995, Kiwanis World Svc. medal Kiwanis Internat. Found., 1995, Jefferson award Am. Inst. for Pub. Svc., 1996, Presdl. Medal of Freedom, 1999; named to Nat. Women's Hall of Fame, 2001. Fellow: Am. Psychiat. Assn. (hon.). Democrat. Avocations: fly fishing, birdwatching, swimming, bicycling. Office Phone: 404-331-3900.

CARTER, SARALEE LESSMAN, immunologist, microbiologist; b. Chgo., Feb. 19, 1951; d. Julius A. and Ida (Oiring) Lessman; B.A., National Coll., 1971; m. John B. Carter, Oct. 7, 1979; children: Robert Oiring, Mollie. Supr. lab. immunology Weiss Meml. Hosp., Chgo., 1973-80; lab. immunology supr. Henrotin Hosp., Chgo., 1980-84; tech. dir. Lexington Med. Labs., West Columbia, S.C., 1984—; mem. nat. workshop faculty Am. Soc. Clin. Pathologists; clin. instr. faculty Med. U. S.C. Mem. Am. Soc. Clin. Pathologists (subspecialty cert. in microbiology and immunology, cert. med. technologist). Researcher Legionnaires Disease and mycoplasma pneumonia World Soc. Pathologists, Jerusalem, Israel, 1980. Contbr. articles to profl. jours.; Mem. Rep. Senoritorial Inner Circle, co-chmn. S.C. Young Profls. for George Bush. Office: 110 Medical Ln E Ste 100 West Columbia SC 29169-4817

CARTER, SYLVIA, journalist; b. Keokuk, Iowa; d. Charles Sylvester and Frances Elizabeth (Smith) C. B of Journalism, U. Mo., 1968. Intern Quincy (Ill.) Herald-Whig, 1966, Detroit Free Press, 1967; reporter The N.Y. Daily News, 1968-70; successively gen. assignment reporter, edn. reporter, food writer, restaurant critic, food columnist Newsday, Melville, NY, 1970—; food writer, restaurant critic N.Y. Newsday, N.Y.C., 1985-95; founder, editor Kidsday Newsday, Melville, columnist, 2005—. Author: Eats: The Best Little Restaurants in New York, 1988, Eats N.Y.C.: A Guide to the Best, Cheapest, Most Interesting Restaurants in Brooklyn, Queens and Manhattan, 1995; contbr. to Family Circle and other publs. Trustee Anne O'Hare McCormick Scholarship Fund, N.Y.C., 1988—; bd. dirs. Art Inst. N.Y., 2003-05. Recipient Feature Writing award U. Mo., 2000; nominee James Beard Journalism awards, 2001. Mem. Newswomen's Club N.Y. (pres. 1990-92, bd. dirs., Front Page award 1982). Democrat. Presbyterian. Avocations: reading, collectibles, hiking, music, cooking. Home: 46 Crescent Bow Ridge NY 11961-2915 Office Phone: 631-775-9534. E-mail: sylviacarter@optonline.net.

CARTER, TONYA M., science educator; b. Cleveland, Miss., Dec. 21, 1969; d. Clarence and Earlene (Jackson) Davis, David Henry and Jacquelyn (Wallace) Carter (Stepmother), Ruthie Jean Carter. BS, Alcorn State U., Lorman, Miss., 1993; MS Natural Scis., Delta State U., Cleveland, 1996. Tchr., dept. head Greenville Pub. Schs., Miss., 1995—. Aux. dir. Greenville Weston Band, 2001—; sponsor Nat. Beta Club Greenville Weston H.S., 2002—, acad. tutor, 1999—; coord. Small Learning Cmty. Greenville Pub. Sch., 2001—05. Leader Youth Dept. Poplar Grove Ch., Shaw, Miss., 2002. Named, Who's Who Among H.S. Tchrs., 2003—04, 2005—06, Outstanding Sci. Tchr., Delta Sci. Tchrs., 1999—2000, Tchr. of Month-Aug., Greenville Weston H.S., 2005, Tchr. of Month-Dec., 2004, Tchr. of Month-Apr., 2003; recipient Biology Inst. award, Millsaps Coll., 1999. Mem.: Miss.Sci. Tchrs. Assn., Miss. Assn. Biology Educators, Order Ea. Stars, Alpha Kappa Alpha, Tau Beta Sigma (v.p. 1990—92, Outstanding Svc. award). Baptist. Avocations: travel, reading. Home: 250 Cypress Ln Apt 14D Greenville MS 38701 Office: Greenville Pub Schs 901 Archer St Greenville MS 38701 Home Fax: 662-334-7091; Office Fax: 662-334-7081. E-mail: tmcarteraka@hotmail.com, tcarter@gville.112.ms.us.

CARTER, YVONNE PICKERING, art educator; b. Washington, Feb. 6, 1939; d. Irving Lorenzo and Esther (Robinson) P.; m. Joseph Payne Carter, Feb. 11, 1964 (div. 1985); 1 child, Cornelia Malisia. AB, Howard U., 1962, MFA, 1968. Library asst. Coll. Fine Arts Howard U., Washington, 1963-71; from instr. to prof. art U. D.C. (formerly Federal City Coll.), 1971—, chmn. dept., prof., 1986-90; commonwealth prof. George Mason U., 1990-92; chair dept. mass media, visual and performing arts U. D.C., 1995—. Visual arts panelist D.C. Commn. on Arts and Humanities, 1985-87. Exhibited in group shows at Butler Inst., Ohio, 1983, Corcoran Gallery Art, 1986, Main Library Miami-Dade Cultural Ctr., 1986, Black Women in the Visual Arts, 1986,

Kenkeleba Gallery, N.Y.C.; represented in pub. collections Fed. Res. Bank, Raleigh, N.C., Gibbes Art Gallery, Charleston, S.C. D.C. Commn. on Arts and Humanities grantee, 1981, 82, 95. Mem. Coll. Art Assn., Women's Caucus for Arts, Artists Equity, AAUP. Democrat. Roman Catholic.

CARTER-JOHNSON, JEAN EVELYN, management consultant; b. Front Royal, Va., Sept. 22, 1956; d. William Robert Carter and Hilda Mae Jett; m. Ronald Malcolm Johnson, Sept. 27, 1985; 1 child, Sherard Akeem Johnson. Dental Assistance Cert., Montgomery Jr. Coll., Takoma Park, Md., 1977, AA, 1978; BSBA, Southeastern U., Washington, 1990; MBA, U. Md., Coll. Pk., 2006. Licensing info. asst. Nuc. Regulatory Commn., Silver Spring, Md., 1982—86; freedom info. act/privacy act specialist U.S. Info. Agy., Washington, 1986—88; paralegal Fed. Trade Commn., Washington, 1988—2001; mgmt. analyst Dept. Commerce, Silver Spring, Md., 2001—. Freedom info. act/privacy act program mgr. Nat. Oceanic and Atmospheric Adminstrn., Silver Spring, Md., 2001—. Songwriter: CD America, 2005, In The Beginning, 2006. Mentor Young Adult Orgn., 2004. Fellow: Md. State Bd. Dental Examiners (lic. 1977). Avocations: reading, writing, cooking, piano, coin collecting/numismatics. Home: 7510 Somerset Terr Frederick MD 21702 Office: Dept Commerce 1315 Eastwest Hwy Silver Spring MD 20901 Personal E-mail: jeancj@adelphia.net.

CARTER-MILLER, JOCELYN, retail executive; BSc in Acctg., U. Ill., Urbana-Champaign; MBA in Mktg. and Fin., U. Chgo. CPA. Various sr. level positions Mattel, Inc., 1984—91; corp. v.p., chief mktg. officer Motorola, Inc., 1992—2002; exec. v.p. Office Depot, Inc., Delray Beach, Fla., 2002—, chief mktg. officer, 2002—. Bd. dir. Principal Fin. Group, Inc. Author (with Melissa Giovagnoli): Networlding: Building Relationships and Opportunities for Success, 1998. Office: Office Depot Inc 2200 Old Germantown Rd Delray Beach FL 33445

CARTER PEREIRA, CLAUDINE RENEE, forensic specialist; d. Ronald Kallip and Joy Rita Carter; m. Rodrigo Miranda Batista Pereira, Oct. 12, 2002; 1 child, Arianna Lillie Pereira. BS, Loyola Coll., Balt., Md., 1995; MS, Va. Commonwealth U., Richmond, Va., 1997. Cert. latent print examiner Internat. Assn. Identification, 2000, tchr. Dance Educators Am., 2001. Technician crime lab. Balt. (Md.) City Police Dept., 1997—99; examiner latent prints Broward Sheriff's Office, Ft. Lauderdale, Fla., 1999—2000, sr. examiner latent prints, 2000—04, supr. latent prints, 2004—. Asst. dance instr. Lois Seiler Acad. Dance, Freeport, Bahamas, 1988—89; dance instr. Anna Appicella Sch. Dance, Balt., 1992—95; asst. artistic dir. Jubilee Dance Theatre, Inc, Ft. Lauderdale, 2003—. Dancer Don Quixote, 2000, 2003, The Nutcracker, 2000—02, Cinderella, 2001, Peter and the Wolf/Sleeping Beauty, 2004, MLK Gala Awards, 2004, dancer, asst. artistic dir. Out of The Box, 2003, dancer, artistic dir. NBC 6 South Fla. Today Show, 2004, dancer, asst. artistic dir. No Boundaries, 2004, asst. artistic dir. Pan African Bookfest, 2005, Arts Express, 2005, dancer, asst. artistic dir. Sounds of Freedom, 2006, Louder Than Words, 2006. Tchr. adult ballet classes African Am. Rsch. LIbr. and Cultural Ctr., Jubilee Dance Theatre, Inc., 2004—; ballet instr. Morton St. Dance Ctr., Balt., 1997—99, Regency Dance Acad., Richmond, Va., 1995—97, St. Frances HS, Balt., 1992—93. Mem.: Internat. Assn. Identification (assoc.), Alpha Phi Sigma. Avocation: dance. Office: Broward Sheriff's Office Crime Lab 201 SE 6th Street N Wing Rm 1799 Fort Lauderdale FL 33301 Office Phone: 954-831-3578. Business E-Mail: claudine_pereira@sheriff.org.

CARTON, LONNIE CAMING, educational psychologist; b. Balt. d. Daniel and Shirley (Cooper) Caming; m. Edwin B. Carton; children: Evan, Deborah, Paula. BS, Johns Hopkins U.; MS, U. Md.; PhD, Pa. State U. Tchr. Laurel (Md.) H.S.; instr. Pa. State U., State College, Temple U., Phila.; newspaper columnist Delaware County Times, Chester, Pa.; instr., then asst. prof. Tufts U., Medford, Mass., 1964—80; learning sys. cons. Tufts New Eng. Med. Ctr., Boston, 1968—73. Broadcast journalist CBS Radio, N.Y.C., 1974—; family support sys. cons. Boston Ptnrs. in Edn., 1985—; ind. cons., lectr., workshop leader in field; guest appearances of various radio and TV shows; family lit. cons. Mass. Dept. Edn., 2001—; v.p., dir. teen and family resources Warm 2 Kids, Inc., 2003—; adv. panel SeaWorld Entertainment. Author: Mommies, 1960, Daddies, 1963, Raise Your Kids Right, 1980, No is a Love Word, 1992, (cassette tapes) Parenting Preschoolers from the Park Bench, 1999; sr. editor Edn. Today, Boston, 1992-98; broadcast journalist Voice of Am., 1995-98; contbr. articles to profl. publs. Grantee Gannet Found., U.S. Dept. Edn., Mass. Dept. Edn., U.S. Dept. Hwy. Safety, Mass. Gov.'s Alliance Against Drugs; recipient Nat. Media award APA, 1978, 80, San Francisco State Broadcast Media award, 1983, Contbn. to Lives of Children award UNICEF, Margaret Sanger Soc. award Planned Parenthood, 1985, Don Bosco Friend of Youth award Salesian Soc., awards from Mass. Psychol. Assn., Nat. Commn. Against Drunk Driving, Gabriel Broadcaster's and Allied Communicators, Mass. Soc. Against Cruelty to Children, 1988; named to One Hundred Most Remarkable Women in Mass., Boston Woman's Mag., 1989, Freedoms Found., George Washington medal for pub. comms., 1998. Avocations: tennis, spectator football, reading. Personal E-mail: ebclcc@aol.com.

CARTWRIGHT, CAROL ANN, retired academic administrator; b. Sioux City, Iowa, June 19, 1941; d. Carl Anton and Kathryn Marie (Weishapple) Becker; m. G. Phillip Cartwright, June 11, 1966; children: Catherine E., Stephen R., Susan D. BS in Early Childhood Edn., U. Wis., Whitewater, 1962; MEd in Spl. Edn., U. Pitts., 1965, PhD in Spl. Edn., Ednl. Rsch., 1968. From instr. to assoc. prof. Coll. Edn. Pa. State U., University Park, 1968-72, from assoc. prof. to prof., 1972-79, dean acad. affairs, 1981-84, dean undergrad. program, vice provost, 1984-88; vice chancellor acad. affairs U. Calif., Davis, 1988-91, prof. human devel., 1988-91; pres. Kent State U., Ohio, 1991—2006. Bd. dirs. First Energy Corp. (formerly Ohio Edison), Akron, 1992—, KeyCorp., Cleve., PolyOne Corp., The Davey Tree Expert Co., Kent; exec. bd. Nat. Coun. for Accreditation Tchr. Edn., 2002—; chair NCAA Exec. Com.; mem. N.E. Ohio Coun. Higher Edn., Knight Commn. Intercollegiate Athletics, 2000. Editorial bd. Topics in Early Childhood Special Education, 1982-88, Exceptional Education Quarterly, 1982-88. Pres., bd. dirs. Child Devel. Coun. of Center County, Title XX Day Care Contractor, 1977-80; bd. dirs. Center County United Way, State College, Pa., 1984-88, Urban League of Greater Cleve., 1997—; bd. mem. Davis (Calif.) Art Ctr., 1988-91, Davis Sci. Ctr., 1989-91; bd. dirs. Ohio divsn. Am. Cancer Soc., 1993-2000, nat. bd. dirs., 1993—; mem. nat. bd. First Ladies Libr.; bd. trustees Woodrow Wilson Internat. Ctr. for Scholars, 1999—; bd. dirs. Ctr. for Rsch. Libs., 2002—. Named to Ohio Women's Hall of Fame; recipient Disting. Alumni award, U. Wis.-Whitewater, U. Pittsburgh Sch. Edn., Clairol Mentor award, Women of Achievement award, YWCA of Greater Cleve., Franklin Delano Roosevelt award for Excellence, March of Dimes. Mem. AAUW, Am. Coun. Edn. (Commn. on Women in Higher Edn., 2003-), Am. Ednl. Rsch. Assn., Am. Assn. for Higher Edn., Nat. Assn. State Univs. and Land-Grant Colls., Coun. for Exceptional Children, the Greater Akron Chamber, Cleve. Tomorrow. Roman Catholic. Avocations: walking, reading, travel. Home: 1703 Woodway Rd Kent OH 44240-5917 E-mail: carol.cartwright@kent.edu.*

CARTWRIGHT, KATHARINE AILEEN, geologist; d. Martha Leigh Giles and Gerald Dale Cartwright; m. Dan Eliot Verrillo, Aug. 3, 1993; 1 child, Van Keith Herridge Jr. BA, Coll. Charleston, 1991; MS, Syracuse U., 1995. Fellow Syracuse U., NY, 1991—95; lectr. Skidmore Coll., Saratoga Springs, NY, 1995—. One-woman shows include The Wine Series. Founder, pres. Foster Parents Assn. Talbot County, Md., 1978—80; pres. Colonie (N.Y.) Art League, Inc., 2002—03. Recipient Edward Emerson Towell Sci. award, Coll. Charleston, 1991, Estwing award, 1991, Marjorie T. Hooker award, Syracuse U., 1994, Parker W. Dodge award, Colonie Art League, Inc., 2001; grantee, Geol. Soc. Am., 1993; Lettie Pate Whitehead scholar, Coll. Charleston, 1990. Mem.: North East Watercolor Soc., The Colonie Art League, Phi Kappa Phi (Outstanding Rsch. award 1991). Independent. Achievements include research in geological investigation of the paleoenvironmental changes associated with the Triassic-Jurassic mass extinction event, 200 million years ago; geologic investigation into the antecendent topographical controls of the migration of the barrier island system at Folly Beach, S.C. Avocation: sailing. Office Phone: 518-580-5193. Business E-Mail: kcartwri@skidmore.edu.

CARTWRIGHT, LILLIAN, psychologist, researcher, artist; b. NYC, Apr. 27, 1933; d. Louis and Tabitha Kaufman; divorced; children: David, Derrick, Caitlin, Rosannah. BA in Psychology summa cum laude, Queens Coll., 1950; MA in Psychology, U. Ill., 1955; PhD in Psychology, U. Calif., 1970. Dir. curriculum evaluation U. Calif. Sch. Medicine, 1971—75; rsch. faculty U. Calif., Berkeley, San Francisco; prof. Calif. Sch. Profl. Psychology, Calif., dean academic affairs. One-woman shows include U. Calif., San Francisco, 1999, U. Club, 1999, Mindful Body, 2000, Coleman Advs., San Francisco, 2000, exhibited in group shows at Ardency Gallery, Oakland, 2002, Oakland Group Show of Leading Painters, Oakland Galleries, 2003, Jewett Gallery, San Francisco Pub. Libr., 2003, Biannual Figure Drawing Collective, Mendocino, Calif., 2004, exhibitions include SomArts Main Gallery, 2004, Scharfenberger Cellars, 2005, Macromedia, 2005; contbr. articles on women's adult devel. to profl. jours. in field.

CARTWRIGHT, NANCY, actress, television producer; b. Kettering, Ohio, Oct. 25, 1957; d. Frank and Miriam Cartwright; m. Warren Murphy, Dec. 24, 1988; children: Lucy Mae, Jackson. Student, Ohio U., 1976—77; BA in theatre, UCLA, 1981. Founder Cartwright Entertainment Inc. Author: (biography) My Life as a 10-Year-Old Boy, 2000; prodr.: (animated internet series) The Kellys, 2001—; actor(voice): (TV series) The Richie Rich/Scooby-Doo Hour, 1980, Richie Rich, 1981, Monchichis, 1983, Saturday Supercade, 1983, Alvin & the Chipmunks, 1983, The Shirt Tales, 1983—85, The Snorks, 1984, Galaxy High School, 1986, My Little Pony and Friends, 1986, Pound Puppies, 1986, Popeye and Son, 1987, (voice of Bart Simpson) The Tracy Ullman Show, 1987—89, (voice) Fantastic Max, 1988, (voice, Bart Simpson/Nelson/Todd Flanders/Ralph Wiggum/others) The Simpsons, 1989— (Emmy award outstanding voice-over performance, 1992), (voice) Dink, the Little Dinosaur, 1989, Goof Troop, 1992, Raw Toonage, 1992, Bonkers, 1993, Animaniacs, 1993 (Daytime Emmy awards honors for contbg., 1996), Problem Child, 1993, The Pink Panther, 1993, Aladdin, 1993, 2 Stupid Dogs, 1993, The Critic, 1994, Timon and Pumbaa, 1995, The Twisted Adventures of Felix the Cat, 1995, Toonsylvania, 1998, Pinky, Elmyra & the Brian, 1998 (Daytime Emmy awards honors for contbg., 1999), Mike, Lu & Og, 1999, Big Guy and Rusty the Boy Robot, 1999—, God, the Devil and Bob, 2000, (voice of Chuckie) Rugrats, 2001—04, (voice of Rufus) Kim Possible, 2002, (voice of Chuckie) All Grown Up, 2003, (voice): (videos) The Land Before Time VI: The Secret of Saurus Rock, 1998, Wakko's Wish, 1999, Timberwolf, 2002, Kim Possible: The Secret Files, 2003; (TV films) Kim Possible: A Stitch in Time, 2003; (films) The Chipmunk Adventure, 1987, The Little Mermaid, 1989, Petal to the Metal, 1992, Rugrats Go Wild!, 2003,: (TV films) Marian Rose White, 1982, The Rules of Marriage, 1982, Deadly Lessons, 1983, Not My Kid, 1985, Yellow Pages, 1988, On Hollywood Blvd., 1988, Precious Victims, 1993, Vows of Deception, 1996, Suddenly, 1996; (films) Twilight Zone: The Movie, 1983, Flesh & Blood, 1985, Godzilla, 1998; (plays) The Transgressor, 1980, Guys and Dolls, 1984, Coming Attractions, 1985, In Search of Fellini, 1995 (DramaLogue award best performance one-person show, 1996), Cat's Meow, 1998. Cofounder Neko Tech Learning Ctr., Ghana, W. Africa, 2000; mem., commr. Citizens Commn. on Human Rights, 1996—; active with Famous Fone Friends, The World Literacy Crusade, Make A Wish Foundation, The Way to Happiness Internat. Recipient Am. Libr. Assn. award, 1992, Elizabeth Andersch award, 1992, County of LA Pub. Libr. award, 1994, Annie award for outstanding individual achievement for voice acting field of animation, Internat. Animated Soc., 1995, PMA Star Power award, 2000. Mem.: Screen Actors Guild. Office: Cartwright Entertainment Inc 9420 Reseda Blvd #572 Northridge CA 91324

CARTWRIGHT, TALULA ELIZABETH, management consultant, educator; b. Asheville, NC, Oct. 25, 1947; d. Ralph and Sarah Helen (Medford) C.; m. Edwin Byram Crabtree, May 23, 1976 (div. Sept. 1984); children: Charity, Baxter; m. Richard Thomas England, Apr. 27, 1986; 1 child, Isaac. BA, U. N.C., 1971, MEd, 1974, EdD, 1988. Instr. McDowell Tech. Inst., Marion, NC, 1972-73, Guilford Tech. CC, Jamestown, NC, 1973-89, Guilford Coll., Greensboro, NC, 1982-87, U. NC-Greensboro, 1982-87; instr. leadership NC A&T State U., Greensboro, 1984-85. With Communication Assocs., Lenoir, Shelby, Asheboro, Greensboro, 1981—; dean continuing edn. Caldwell C.C., Lenoir, N.C., 1989-92; v.p. acad. programs Cleve. C.C., 1992-95; sr. faculty and program mgr. Ctr. for Creative Leadership, Greensboro, N.C., 1996—; chmn. bd. dirs. Cleve. Abuse Prevention Coun., 1993-95. Bd. dirs. Family Crisis Ctr., 2003—. Tchr. of Yr. award Guilford Tech. C.C. Edn. Assn., 1982, Edn. Honor Roll award 1989; winner Human Rights Writing Contest, 1988, 89. Mem. NCAE (pres. local unit 1988-89, chmn. higher edn. commn. 1989-90, 92-95), Am. Assn. Women in C.C., Women's Adminstrs. in N.C. (exec. bd. 1995). Office Phone: 336-286-4509.

CARTY, VICTORIA LOUISE, sociologist, educator; BA in Sociology, U. Calif., Santa Cruz, 1990; PhD, U. N.Mex, Albuquerque, 1999. Prof. sociology, activist Niagara U., Niagara Falls, NY, 2001—06; prof. sociology Chapman U., Orange, Calif., 2006—. Grantee, Niagara U., 2003, 2004. Home: 1201 E Fairhaven Santa Ana CA 92705 Office: Chapman University Dept Sociology 1 University Dr Orange CA 92866 Office Phone: 714-997-6763. Business E-Mail: carty@chapman.edu.

CARUNCHIO, FLORENCE REGINA, financial planner; b. Jersey City, July 30, 1952; d. Alfred Peter and Florence Concetta (Pirozzi) Carunchio. BA summa cum laude, Montclair State U., 1975. CFP; lic. ins. provider N.J., N.Y., Va., Fla., Pa.; tchr. psychology and social studies K-12 N.J. Tchr. social studies St. Michael's Acad., Palisades Park, NJ, 1975—79; coord. film libr. and youth programs World Vision, Midland Park, 1981—82; owner Gifts of the Magi, Westwood, 1982—84; exec. asst. to CEO, Biomatrix, Inc., Ridgefield, 1985—94; assets mgr. Balden Assoc., Ridgefield, 1985—94; personal fin. advisor Am. Express Fin. Advisors, Paramus, 1995, advanced advisor, 1996—2002, sr. fin. advisor, 1999—2002. Advisor of record pension plan, I.U.O.E. Am. Express Fin. Advisors, Paramus, 2000—06, Ameriprise Fin. Svcs. Inc., Washington Twp., NJ, 2005—; spkr. in field. Avocations: music, literature, Bible translation and distribution.

CARUSO, ADRIENNE IORIO, retired language educator; b. Saratoga Springs, N.Y., May 30, 1926; d. Andrew and Josephine Pompay Iorio; m. Carl Thomas Caruso, June 27, 1953 (dec. Feb. 2, 2001). BA, N.Y. State Coll. Tchrs., Albany, 1948, MA, 1951. Cert. tchr. N.Y. Dept. Edn. Tchr. English, French, art and libr. Oppenheim Ephratah Ctrl. Sch., NY, 1948—50; tchr. English Corinth H.S., 1951—52, Saratoga Springs Secondary Sch. Complex, 1952—82. Practice tchr. supr. Saratoga Springs City Sch. Dist.; faculty advisor Nat. Honor Soc.; faculty advisor yearbook, book club, others Saratoga Springs Secondary Complex. Permanent mem. Saratoga Performing Arts Ctr.; donor U. at Albany Found., NY; v.p. Saratoga Springs Ret. Tchrs. Assn., 1985—97; pres. Ladies Aux. BPOE Lodge 161, 1985—86; past bd. mem. and treas. LWV. Mem.: AAUW (life; pres. Saratoga Springs br. 1983—85, 1990—91), Catholic Daughters of Am., N.Y. State Retired Tchrs. Assn. (life; pres. Ea. zone 1995—98, honoree 1990), Hist. Soc. Saratoga Springs, Friends Saratoga Springs Pub. Libr., U. Albany Alumni Assn. (life; bd. dirs. 2000—). Republican. Roman Catholic. Avocations: art, dance, music, photography, travel. Home: 280 Lake Ave Saratoga Springs NY 12866-3735

CARUSO, AILEEN SMITH, managed care consultant; b. Albany, N.Y., July 25, 1949; d. Robert Vincent and Mary (Prince) Smith; 1 child, Patrick Michael. AAS in nursing, Russell Sage Jr. Coll., Albany, 1970; BSBA cum laude, Coll. St. Rose, 1994. Cert. case mgr., adminstr. Physician Practice Mgmt. (CAPPM); RN N.Y. Staff nurse neuro and thoracic surgery units VA Hosp., 1970-71; staff nurse family practice Milton F. Gipstein, MD, Schenctady, N.Y., 1971-74; psychiat. nurse Peter F. Andrus, MD, Albany, 1977-81; coll. health nurse State U. N.Y., Albany, 1979-82; orthopedic staff nurse Rosa Road Orthopedics, Schenectady, 1980-82; coll. health nurse Union Coll., Schenectady, 1982-87; customer svc. rep. Empire Blue Cross, Albany, 1987-88; fin. planner N.Y. Life Ins., Albany, 1988-89; sr. mgr. Corp. Health Demensions, Troy, N.Y., 1989-94, dir. implementation and tng., 1994-96, dir. implementation and corp. case mgmt., 1996, v.p. implementation, 1997, v.p. ops., 1998-99; dir. clin. ops. U.S. Oncology Network, 1999—2004; dir. cancer care program St. Peters Hosp., Albany, NY, 2004—. Mem. adv. bd. Amgen, MGI Pharma, CTI Pharm., 2004; advisor Gen. Elec. Corp. R&D Safety Com., Schenectady, 1992-94; chmn. profl. devel. Northeast N.Y. Health Promotion, Albany, 1994-99; com. chair Schenectady Health Coalition, 1993-95; edn. and by laws com., com. chair govt. affairs Am. Occupational Health Nurses, Albany, 1994-99; cert. adminstr. physician practice mgmt.; chmn. N.Y. state sect. Patient Advocate Found., N.Y., 2000—; cons. in field. Co-author: Occupational Health Services Administrative/Patient Management Manual. Pres. Ch. Women, St. George's Episcopal Ch., 1994-97, mem. exec. bd. dir., 1989-97, sr. vestry, 2004—, mem. exec. search com., 1998-99, also lector, sr. vestry, 2004—; chmn. worksite program N.E. N.Y. Tobacco-Free Coalition, 1993-94; co-mgr. The Bookshop at St. Georges, 1993-95; mem. Futures Charity Golf Tournament; mem. USON Exec. Leadership/Clin. Leadership Coun., mem. exec. bd., 2002—; co-chair Cancer Survivors Day, 2001-02; mem. reimbursement com. Uson Clin. Leadership Coun.; mem. Nat. Patient Advocate Found., 2001-06, state policy liaison, 2006; co-chair N.Y. state task force Patient Advocate Found., 2005—, N.Y. State Policy Liaison; mem. Am. Cancer Soc. Making Strides Work. Recipient Rector's Recognition award St. George's Ch., 1991, U.S. Oncology Excellence award, 2004, Outstanding Leadership and Advocacy award Nat. Patient Advocate Found., 2004. Mem. Am. Assn. Occupl. Health Nurses (chair govtl. affairs com., 1989-99), Capital Dist. Occupl. Health Nurses (nominating com.), Schenectady County Health Promotion Consortium, Health Promotion Coun. of N.E. N.Y., Oncology Nurses Soc., Soc. Radiation Oncology Adminstrs., Am. Soc. Therapeutic Radiation Oncologist, Am. Soc. Radiation Oncology, Hospice and Palliative Care Assn. N.Y., Capital Dist. Case Mgmt. Assn. (nominating com.), Am. Acad. Physician Practice Mgmt., Schenectady County Bus. and Profl. Women, Alpha Sigma Lambda. Avocations: travel, reading, golf. Home: 1156 Spearhead Dr Scotia NY 12302-3122 Office: St Peters Hosp Ste 160 317 S Manning Blvd Albany NY 12208 Office Phone: 518-525-5947. E-mail: asmith-caruso@stpetershealthcare.org.

CARUSO, ANN S., fashion editor, stylist; b. Worcester, Mass., Feb. 6, 1966; d. John Stephen and Helene Patricia Caruso. BS, Bentley Coll., 1989. Design asst. Ralph Lauren, N.Y.C., 1989-91; Vogue fashion editor Vogue Mag. Conde Nast, N.Y.C., 1991-96; fashion editor Quest Mag., N.Y.C., 1999-2001; contbg. fashion editor Tatler Mag., London, 2001—. Stylist for VH1 Fashion Awards show, 1996; stylist for advt. campaigns, including Nautica, St. Regis Hotel, Weight Watchers, Am. Express, Neiman Marcus, London Fog, Susan Lazar, Douglas Hannant, Tommy Hilfiger, Ralph Lauren, among others; freelance cons. various mags., including Tatler, Vanity Fair, InStyle, Marie Claire, Esquire, N.Y. Mag., others. Chmn. Kids N' U Found., N.Y.C., 1993-98; mem. Bot. Gardens, 1998-2001, Nat. Hist. Mus., 1992-2000, Henry St. Settlement, 1999-2000, N.Y. Acad. Art, 1994-98, Group for the South Fork, 1997-2000, Chances for Children, 1999, Parrish Art Mus., 2001, ASPCA, 2000, 01. Home: 141 E 56th St Apt 8h New York NY 10022-2716

CARUSO, CAROL BEVERLY, physical education educator; b. Kenosha, Wis., Apr. 15, 1965; d. Martha Lou and Wade Richard Beverly; m. Mark Anthony Caruso, May 11, 1985; children: Beverly Lee Ann, Gabriele Maria, Sarah Theresia. BS in History, Fayetteville State U., N.C., 1994—96; MSS, U.S. Sports Acad., Daphne, Ala., 2001—04. CPR, First Aid Red Cross, 2005. Intern Christopher Newport U., Newport News, Va., 2003, La. State U., Baton Rouge, 2003—04, rsch. fitness specialist, 2004. Election ofcl. City of Norton, Va., 2005—; com. mem. Best Friend Festival, Norton, 2006; mem. Pro Art, Wise, Va., 2005. Recipient All Am. scholar, 1995. Mem.: NIRSA, AAHPERD, NASSM (assoc.). Home: 557 Oak Ave Norton VA 24273 Personal E-mail: cbcaruso@verizon.net.

CARUSO, JOANNE E., lawyer; BA magna cum laude, Boston Coll., 1982, JD cum laude, 1986. Bar: State Bar Conn. 1986, DC Bar 1987, State Bar Calif. 1996, registered: US Supreme Ct. 1993, Supreme Ct. Calif. 1996, US Ct. Appeals, fifth cir. 1999, US Ct. Appeals, seventh cir. 1992, US Ct. Appeals, ninth cir. 1999, Calif. Dist. Ct., Ctrl. Dist. 1996, Calif. Dist. Ct., No. Dist. 1999, Calif. Dist. Ct., Ea. Dist. 1999, Calif. Dist. Ct., So. Dist. 1999, Tex. Dist. Ct., No. Dist. 1997, Md. Dist. Ct. 1988, DC Dist. Ct. 1988. Ptnr., mem. exec. com. Howrey Simon Arnold & White LLP, LA, 1986—. Author: (article) Are You The Court Reporter? Deposition Practice from a Woman's Perspective, 1998, Successful Partnering Between Inside & Outside Counsel, 2002. Bd. dir., treas. St. Vincent de Paul Soc. Named one of So. Calif. Super Lawyers - bus. litig., LA mag., 2005. Mem.: Women Lawyers Assn. LA (bd. gov. 2002—), LA County Bar Assn., DC Bar Assn., Calif. State Bar Assn., Assn. Bus. Trial Lawyers (LA Chpt., membership chmn., bd. gov.), ABA (mem., litig. & antitrust sect.). Office: Howrey Simon Arnold & White LLP 550 South Hope St Ste 1100 Los Angeles CA 90071 Office Phone: 213-892-1853. Office Fax: 213-892-2300. Business E-Mail: CarusoJ@howrey.com.

CARUTHERS, TARA M., physics educator; b. Arlington Heights, Ill., May 28, 1974; d. P. Reid and Christine M. Caruthers. BA, U. Tex., Austin, 1997. Tchr. integrated physics and chemistry Mesquite H.S., Tex., 1997—2001, tchr. physics, 2001—; counselor BIOS Sch. on Wheels, Orange, 2001—; instr. sci. superstars Stark Found., Shangrila Bot. Gardens, DuPont, and Invista, Orange, 2004—06. Chmn. staff devel. Mesquite H.S., 1999—, mentor cadre new tchr. mentor, 1999—, mem. Lighthouse award steering com., 2004—, tchr. leadership com., 1998—2002. Recipient Tchr. of Yr., Mesquite H.S., 2005. Mem.: Mesquite Edn. Assn., Parent, Tchr., Student Assn., Assn. Tex. Profl. Educators, Sci. Tchr. Assn. Tex., U. Tex. Execs. (life). Office: Mesquite High School 300 E Davis Mesquite TX 75149 Office Phone: 972-882-7800. E-mail: tcaruthers@mesquiteisd.org.

CARVALHO, JULIE ANN, psychologist; b. Washington, Apr. 11, 1940; d. Daniel Henry and Elizabeth Cecilia (Gardiner) Schmidt; children: Alan R., Dennis M., Melanie D., Celeste A., Joshua E. BA with high honors, U. Md., 1962, postgrad., 1962-63, 68-73; MA, George Washington U., 1966; postgrad., Va. Poly. Inst., 1979-88; Dal studies in curriculum and instrn., Argosy U., 2003—04. Social sci. rsch. analyst Mental Health Study Ctr., NIMH, Adelphi, Md., 1963-67; edn. and tng. analyst Computer Applications, Inc., Silver Spring, Md., 1967-68; edn. program specialist, program analyst Nat. Ctr. for Ednl. R&D, U.S. Office of Edn., Washington, 1969-73; equal opportunity specialist Office of Sec., HEW, Washington, 1973-77; legis. program, civil rights analyst Office for Civil Rights Dept. Health and Human Svcs., Washington, 1977-85; ind. cons. Adj. lectr. No. Va. C.C., George Mason U., Montgomery Coll., Strayer U., Park U., Shepherd Coll., Germanna Coll., U. Md. U. Coll., Va. Internat. U., Prince William Hosp., Fairfax County Pub. Schs., Fairfax County Dept. Social Svcs., all Washington area, 1986—; proposal evaluator HUD, HHS, 1989—; presenter in field. Contbr. articles to profl. jours. Bd. dirs. Child Care Ctrs., 1970—76, HEW Employees Assn., 1973—78; steering com. Alliance for Child Care, 1975—80. Mem.: ASPA (condr. panels 1975, 1991), APA (panel condr. 1969—75, editor Bull. of Peace Psychology 1991—97, divsn. 48), Unitarian Universalists for Social Justice (bd. dirs. Balt.-Washington region 2003—), Federally Employed Women (nat. editor 1975—79, chair, action com. on the status of women), Psychologists Soc. Responsibility (cons., chair action com. on status of women, chair action com. status women), Capitol Area Social Psychologists Assn. (conf. chmn. 1985, 1993), Fairfax County Assn. for the Gifted (pres. 1980), Phi Alpha Theta, Psi Chi, Alpha Sigma Lambda (hon.). Address: 4931 Americana Dr #203 Annandale VA 22003 Office Phone: 703-453-9119, 703-354-0838.

CARVER, DOROTHY LEE ESKEW (MRS. JOHN JAMES CARVER), retired secondary school educator; b. Brady, Tex., July 10, 1926; d. Clyde Albert and A. Maurine (Meadows) Eskew; m. John James Carver, Feb. 26, 1944; children: John James, Sheila Carver Bentley, Chuck, David. Student,

So. Oreg. Coll., 1942-43, Coll. Eastern Utah, 1965-67; BA, U. Utah, Hayward, 1968; MA, Cal. State Coll. at Hayward, 1970; postgrad., Mills Col., 1971. Instr. Rutherford Bus. Coll., Dallas, 1944-45; sec. Adolph Coors Co., Golden, Colo., 1945-47; instr. English Coll. Eastern Utah, Price, 1968-69; instr. speech Modesto (Calif.) Jr. Coll., 1970-71; instr. personal devel. men and women Heald Bus. Colls., Oakland, Calif., 1972-74, dean curricula Walnut Creek, Calif., 1974-86; instr. Diablo Valley Coll., Pleasant Hill, Calif., 1986-87, Contra Costa Christian H.S., 50 1992; ret., 1992. Communications cons. Oakland Army Base, Crocker Bank, U.S. Steel, I. Magnin, Artec Internat.; presenter in field. Author: Developing Listening Skills. Mem. Gov.'s Conf. on Higher Edn. in Utah, 1968; mem. finance com. Coll. Eastern Utah, 1967-69; active various cmty. drives; bd. dirs. Opportunity Ctr., Symphony of the Mountain; pres. adv. bd. Walnut Creek Srs., 1998—. Mem. AAUW, Bus. and Profl. Womens Club, Nat. Assn. Deans and Women Adminstrs., Delta Kappa Gamma. Episcopalian (supt. Sunday Sch. 1967-69). Clubs: Soroptimist Internat. (pres. Walnut Creek 1979-80, sec., founder region 1978-80); Order Eastern Star. Home: 20 Coronado Ct Walnut Creek CA 94596-5801

CARVER, JUANITA ASH, inventor; b. Apr. 8, 1929; d. Willard H. and Golda M. Ashe; children: Daniel Charles, Robin Lewis, Scott Alan. Student, Ariz. State U., Tempe, 1948, student, 1972, Mira Mar Coll., San Diego, Calif., 1994. Pres. Carver Corp., Phoenix, 1977—. Author series of children's stories. Republican. Methodist. Achievements include patents for latch hook Yarner; Pressure Lift.

CARVER, JULIA, retired physical education educator; b. Salt Lake City, Utah, Sept. 1, 1923; d. William George Carver and Julia Augusta Sabina. BA, Brigham Young U., 1952; MA, NY U., 1954; PhD, U. Oreg., 1964. Tchr. Brigham Young U., Provo, Utah, 1952, Allegheny Coll., Meadville, Pa.; assoc. prof. Montclair State Coll., NJ, U. Oreg., Ch.Coll. of Hawaii, Brigham Young U., N.Mex. State Coll.; ret., 1990. Home: 109 South Temple Apt 6F Salt Lake City UT 84111

CARVER, RITA, not-for-profit fundraiser, consultant; b. Minden, Nebr. d. Jess Albert and Marguerite Florence Ford; children: David Christopher, Heather Michelle; m. Kris E. White, Apr. 30, 2004. BS in Comm., Dallas Bapt. U., 1976; MA in human scis., Our Lady of the Lake, 2000. Freelance writer, 1976—82; account exec. Walvoord, Killian, McCabe, Dallas, 1982—86; sr. v.p. Resource Devel., Inc., Plano, Tex., 1986—2001; pres. R-Designs Inc., Plano, 2001—. Instr. Resource Inst., Springfield, Mo., 1986-99. Creative dir.: Portraits of Hope, 1996; editor: He Leadeth Me, 1999. Vol. Collin County Children's Adv. Ctr., Plano, 1999—. Named Outstanding Young Women of Am., 1980, Most Stressed Out Bus. Traveler, Rosewood Hotel and Resorts, 1994. Mem. AAUW, NAFE, Sierra Club, Plano C. of C. Methodist. Avocations: scuba diving, writing, dance, travel. Office: R-Designs Inc 752 Nicklaus Dr Plano TX 75025 Office Phone: 972-527-2265. Personal E-mail: rmcrdi@aol.com.

CARY, ALICE SHEPARD, retired physician; b. Gaziantep, Turkey, June 2, 1920; parents U.S. citizens; d. Lorrin Andrews and Virginia (Moffat) Shepard; m. Otis Cary, Dec. 9, 1944; children: Beth D., Ann B., Frank B., Ellen Cary Bearn. BA, Wellesley Coll., 1942; MD, Yale U., 1945. Intern, resident New Haven Hosp., 1945-47; physician Doshisha U. Health Ctr., Kyoto, Japan, 1947-50, Japan Bapt. Hosp., Kyoto, 1955-95; dir. Aoibashi Family Clinic Counseling Ctr., Kyoto, 1981-91; ret., 1996. Assoc. missionary United Ch. Bd. World Ministries, N.Y.C., 1947-96. Mem. adv. com. on women's issues UN Women's Decade, Prime Min.'s Office, Tokyo, 1970—75; trustee Piedmont (Calif.) Cmty. Ch. Recipient 40th Anniversary award Coll. Women's Assn. Japan, 1989, internat. contbn. award City of Kyoto, 1992. Mem.: East Bay Chpt. UN Assn., U.S.A. Democrat. Mem. United Ch. of Christ. Home: 33 Linda Ave Apt 1601 Oakland CA 94611-4817

CARY, EMILY PRITCHARD, columnist; b. Pitts., Sept. 6, 1931; d. Ernest Markwood Pritchard and Adelaide Elizabeth Stuart; m. Boyd Balford Cary, Jr., Sept. 28, 1953; children: Matthew Roger, Roland Mylles. BA, U. Pa., 1952; MA, Kean Coll., 1975; postgrad., U. Md., Rutgers U., U. Rochester, George Mason U., U. Ariz. Lic. specialist in tchg. gifted/talented Va. State Dept. Edn. Music tchr. Pittsford (N.Y.) Pub. Schs., 1967—71; tchr. Millburn (N.J.)-Short Hills Schs., 1971—79, Fairfax (Va.) County Pub. Schs., 1979—95; entertainment columnist Jour. Newspapers of Washington (now DC Examiner), Alexandria, Va., 1981—; music cons., reviewer Tchr. Mag., Greenwich, Conn., 1971—79. Alpha Delta Kappa rep. WCOTP Assembly of Dels., Stockholm, 1993. Author: My High Love Calling, 1977, Ghost of Whitaker Mountain, 1979, Ghost of Whitaker Mountain, reissue, 2002, Duet, 1991; contbr. articles to profl. jours. and mags. Recipient scholarship for grad. studies, Greater N.Y.C. Area Panhellenic, 1975. Mem.: DAR, Alpha Delta Kappa (scholarship for grad. studies 1985), Alpha Chi Omega. Avocations: music, genealogy, travel, archaeology.

CARY, LORENE EMILY, writer; b. Phila., Nov. 29, 1956; d. John William and Carole Joan (Hamilton) C.; m. Robert C. Smith, Aug. 27, 1983; children: Laura Hagans, Zoe Drayton; 1 stepchild, Geoffrey. BA, MA in English, U. Pa., 1978; MA in Victorian Lit., U. Sussex, 1980; LittD (hon.), Colby Coll., 1992; LittD, Keene State Coll., 1998, Chestnut Hill Coll., 1998. Apprentice writer Time, 1980; assoc. editor TV Guide, 1980-82; tchr. St. Paul's Sch., Concord, N.H., 1982-83; contbg. editor Newsweek, 1993-94; lectr. U. Pa. Dept. English, Phila., 1995—. Founder Art Sanctuary, 1998; guest lectr. in field. Author: Black Ice, 1991, The Price of a Child, 1995, Pride, 1998, FREE!, 2006; contbr. essays to mags. Trustee St. Paul's Sch., Concord, N.H., 1987-91. Fellow, Pew Found. fellow Arts, 1995—96. Mem.: PEN, Authors Guild, Union Benevolent Assn. (pres. 2006—, Phila. award 2003). Office: U Pa Dept English 34th and Walnut Sts Philadelphia PA 19104

CASADA, HILAREE A., lawyer; b. Nov. 29, 1971; BA cum laude in Broadcast Journalism, So. Meth. U., 1993; JD magna cum laude, So. Meth. U. Sch. Law, 2000. Bar: Tex., US Dist. Ct. (ea., no. and so. dists. Tex.), 5th, 9th and 11th Cir. Ct. Appeals, US Supreme Ct. Sr. assoc. Hermes, Sargent & Bates, L.L.P., Dallas. Named a Rising Star, Tex. Super Lawyers mag., 2006. Mem.: Dallas Bar Assn. (mem. appellate sect., mem. judiciary com.), State Bar Tex. (mem. appellate sect.), Dallas Assn. Young Lawyers (co-chair women in the law com., named a Rising Star 2004). Office: Hermes Sargent Bates LLP 901 Main St Ste 5200 Dallas TX 75202 Office Phone: 214-749-6512. E-mail: hilaree.casada@hsblaw.com.*

CASAL, EILEEN, lawyer; V.p., gen. counsel, clerk Stratus Computer, Inc., 1986—99; v.p., gen. counsel, asst. clerk Teradyne Inc., 1999—2000, v.p., gen. counsel, clerk, 2003—; v.p., gen. counsel, corp. sec. Adero, Inc., 2000—01, GSI Lumonics, Inc., 2001—03. Office: Teradyne Inc 321 Harrison Ave Boston MA 02118

CASAL, LAURA C., literature educator, consultant; b. Youngstown, Ohio, June 12, 1953; d. Thomas R. Ciarniello and Celia Casal-Ciarniello. MA, George Wash. U., Washington, 1986; student, George Mason U., Fairfax, Va., 1999—. Asst. prof. English No. Va. C.C., Manassas, Va., 1986—. Ednl. facilitator Casal Aveda Inst., Youngstown, 1999—; adj. prof. George Mason U., Fairfax, Va., 1995—; coord. faculty No. Va. C.C., 1995—2006. Author: Nobel Madness. Recipient Tchr. Excellence Award, 2006. Democrat. Avocations: writing, book collecting, gardening, reading, writing. Office: Northern Virginia Community College 6901 Sudley Road Manassas VA 20109 Office Phone: 703-257-6692. E-mail: lcasal@nvcc.edu.

CASALE, HELEN E., lawyer; BA, Lynchburg Coll., Va., 1990; JD, Rutgers U. Sch. Law, Camden, NJ, 1994. Bar: NJ, Pa. 1991, US Dist. Ct. Ea. NJ 1994, US Supreme Ct. 2004. Clk. Superior Ct. NJ, Family Divsn., 1994—95; atty. Wolf, Block, Schorr & Solis-Cohen LLP Family Law Practice Group, Phila., ptnr., 2006—. Named one of Lawyers on the Fast Track, Am. Lawyer Media-Pa., 2005; recipient Nat. Assn. Women Lawyers award, Rutgers U. Sch. Law - Camden, 1994, 40 Under 40 award, Phila. Bus. Jour., 2006. Mem.: ABA, Doris Jonas Freed Am. Inn of Ct., Camden County Bar. Assn., Montgomery Bar Assn., NJ Bar Assn., Pa. Bar Assn. (vice-chmn. Com. on the Legal Rights of Gay Men & Lesbians). Office: WolfBlock Family Law Practice Group Ste 500 1 W Main St Norristown PA 19401 also: WolfBlock Family Law Practice Group Ste 200 1940 Rt 70 E Cherry Hill NJ 08003 Office Phone: 610-278-1523. Office Fax: 610-272-6976. E-mail: hcasale@wolfblock.com.*

CASALS, ROSIE, retired professional tennis player; b. San Francisco, Sept. 16, 1948; Profl. tennis player, 1968—; nat. championships and major tournaments include U.S. Open singles (finalist), 1970, 71, U.S. Open doubles, 1967, 71, 74, 82, U.S. Open mixed doubles, 1975, Wimbledon doubles, 1967, 68, 70, 71, 73, Wimbledon mixed doubles, 1971, 73, finalist with Dick Stockton, 1976, Italian doubles, 1967, 70, Family Circle Cup (winner), 1973, Wightman Cup, 1967, 76-81, Bridgeston doubles championships (finalist), 1975, Spalding mixed doubles, 1976, 77, U.S. Tennis Assn. Atlanta doubles, 1976, Fedn. Cup, 1967, 76-81; winner 1st Virginia Slims tournament, 1970; 3d place Virginia Slims Championships, 1976, 4th place, 1977, 78; winner Murjani-WTA championship, 1980; Fla. Fed. Open doubles, 1980; pres. sports promotion co. Sportswoman, Inc., Sausalito, Calif., 1981—; Virginia Slims Legends Tour, 1995—. Mem. Los Angeles Strings team, World Team Tennis, 1975-77; founder Women's Sports Legends Inc. Virginia Slims Event tennis winner, 1986, doubles winner (with Martina Navratilova), 1988, 89; inducted in to Marin Women's Hall of Fame, 1995, Internat. Tennis Hall of Fame, Newport, R.I., 1996, Bay Area Sports Hall of Fame, 2000, African Am. and Ethnic Hall of Fame, 2005. Mem. Women's Internat. Tennis Assn. (bd. dirs.). Office: PO Box 537 Sausalito CA 94966-0537 Office Phone: 760-772-9411. E-mail: sportswomn@aol.com.

CASAS, LAURIE ANN, plastic surgeon; b. May 26, 1956; married; 2 children. BS, BA, U. Ill., Champaign/Urbana, 1974—78; MD, Northwestern U. Med. Sch., Chgo., 1978—82. Diplomate Am. Bd. Plastic Surgery. Resident, gen. surgery Northwestern U. Med. Ctr., Chgo., 1982—85, resident, plastic surgery, 1985—88; microsurgery rsch. fellow So. Ill. U., Springfield, 1988; aesthetic plastic surgery fellow NYU, N.Y.C., 1989; breast reconstruction fellow St. Joseph Hosp., Atlanta, 1989; clin. instr., surgery Northwestern U. Med. Sch., Chgo., 1987—88, asst. prof., surgery, 1990—2001, assoc. prof., surgery, 2001—; adj. staff, asst. attending in plastic/reconstructive surgery Evanston Hosp., Ill., 1990, assoc. attending in plastic/reconstructive surgery, 1992, attending in plastic/reconstructive surgery, 1996; co-dir., ctr. for plastic and aesthetic surgery Glenbrook Hosp., Glenview, Ill., 1990—95, adj. staff, asst. attending in plastic/reconstructive surgery, 1990, assoc. attending in plastic/reconstructive surgery, 1992, attending in plastic/reconstructive surgery, 1996; acting head, divsn. plastic surgery Evanston Hosp. Corp., Ill., 1993—96; head, divsn. plastic surgery Evanston Northwestern Healthcare, Glenbrook Hosp., Glenview, Ill., 1996—. Mem. editl. bd. Plastic Surgery Today, 2000, Guide to Aesthetic Plastic Surgery, 2000, Your Image, 2002—03, editor-in-chief Aesthetic Soc. News, 2000—; editor: Aesthetic Surgery Jour., 2005—. Bd. dirs. Plastic Surgery Edn. Found. Fellow: Am. Coll. Surgeons; mem.: AMA, Ill. Med. Soc., Plastic Surgery Rsch. Coun., Internat. Soc. Aesthetic Plastic Surgery, Midwestern Assn. Plastic Surgeons, The Rhinoplasty Soc., Chgo. Med. Soc., Chgo. Plastic Surgery Soc., Am. Soc. Plastic Surgery, Am. Soc. Aesthetic Plastic Surgery (bd. dirs. 2003—). Office: 2050 Pfingsten Ste 270 Glenview IL 60026 Office Phone: 847-657-5884. Business E-Mail: lcasas@enh.org.

CASAS, MARTHA, education educator; b. Huntington Pk, Calif. d. Roberto Rubio and Enriqueta Garcia Casas. BS in Edn., U. Tex., El Paso, 1978; MA in edn., U. Tex. at El Paslo, 1991; EdD, Harvard Grad Sch. of Edn., 1997. Elem. sch. tchr. El Paso Ind. Sch. Dist., 1978—91; doctoral student Harvard Grad. Sch. Edn., 1991—95; curriculum specialist El Paso Ind. Sch. Dist., 1993—99; asst. prof. in tchr. edn. U. Tex. at Permian Basin, Odessa, 1999—2001, U. Tex., El Paso, 2001—. Author: (book) Grolier's Encyclopedia Latina, 2003. Grant, Hervey Found., 2003, Univ. Tex. at El Paso, 2004. Mem.: Assn. Edn. Rsch. Assoc., Assoc. for Supervision of Curriculum Develop., Phi Delta Kappa Internat. Avocations: dance, gardening, swimming, travel. Home: 1213 Cambria Cove El Paso TX 79912 Office: Univ Tex at El Paso 500 W University El Paso TX 79968 Office Phone: 915-747-7616. Business E-Mail: mcasas@utep.edu.

CASASANTA, MARY FRANCES, medical/surgical nurse; b. Ft. Jay, N.Y., June 17, 1962; d. John Joseph and Marlene Ann (Maiwald) C. BSN, West Tex. State U., 1984. RN, Tex. Nurse St. Anthony's Hosp., Amarillo, Tex.; nurse orthopedics unit Spohn Hosp., Corpus Christi, Tex.; autotransfusionist/perfusion asst. Harbor Perfusion, Inc., Corpus Christi, Tex.; orthopedics nurse Bay Area Med. Ctr.; coastal infusion therapist Bayside Home Health, Prin. Health Care; per diem PACU RN Sequoia Surg. Pavillion, 2003—; per diem RN Reproductive Sci. Ctr., 2005—; PACU RN Valley Care Med. Ctr., 2006—.

CASAZZA, MONICA KATHRYN, art educator; d. Albert J. and Mary Vitelli Berti; m. Christopher F Casazza, Mar. 26, 1994; children: Christine, Jack. MA, NYU, 1990; BFA, Alfred U., 1986. Tchr. art Gt. Neck Pub. Sch., NY, 1987—. Author: (arts and activities) Painterly Pools and Self-Portraits with a Twist. Personal E-mail: m.casazza@att.net.

CASE, ELIZABETH JOY, psychology and educational assessment director; b. Phila., Oct. 12, 1948; d. Edward N. and Helene (LeBlanc) C. BS in Edn./Spl. Edn., Ashland Coll., 1970; MA in Spl. Edn., Fairfield U., 1975; PhD, U. N.Mex., 1985. Cert. tchr. spl. edn. K-12, regular edn. K-12, adminstr. Tchr. second grade Mansfield (Ohio) Pub. Schs., 1969-70; supr., tchr. spl. edn. Greenwich (Conn.) Pub. Schs., 1970-78; cons. Nat. Learning Disabilities Assistance Project, Washington, 1976-78; instr. Fairfield (Conn.) U., 1975-79; grad. asst., fellow U. N.Mex., Albuquerque, 1978-81, instr., 1980-85; cons. IBM, White Plains and Arwork, N.Y., 1976-81; asst. prin. Albuquerque Pub. Schs., 1981-82, coord. spl. edn., 1989—93; with Minn. Dept. Edn., 1993—97; dir. rsch. Harcourt Assessment, Inc., 1997—. Cons. Office of Spl. Edn., U.S. Dept. Edn., Washington, 1980—; dir. regional large sch. testing programs, mid-continent Harcourt Edn. Measurement, 1999—, grants and devel. Minn. Dept. Children, Families, and Learning, Minn. Assessment Project, Rsch. on Spl. Populations Harcourt Assessment, Inc./The Psychol. Corp.; presenter in field. Contbr. articles to profl. jours./publs. Chmn. Gov.'s Com. on the Concerns of the Handicapped, Santa Fe, N.Mex., 1988-92; pres. Civitan/Sierra Vista, Albuquerque, 1989, Albuquerque Wheelchair Tennis Assn., 1985; pres., CEO World Inst. on Disabilities, 1997-98; adv. bd. Protection and Advocacy, Albuquerque, 1988-90; vice-chmn. N.Mex. Vols. for the Outdoors, Albuquerque, 1988-91; bd. dirs. Very Spl. Arts, 1984—, Easter Seal Fundraiser, 1976—, Spl. Olympics, 1986—. Named Vol. of the Yr., N.Mex. Vols. for the Outdoors, 1988, Nat. Woman's Single Champion/Nat. Wheelchair Tennis Assn., Irvine, Calif., 1985, Most Inspirational Tennis Player, 1985, Outstanding Leader in Elem. Edn., Ashland, Ohio, 1976, Conn. Outstanding Young Woman, Hartford, 1976. Mem. N.Mex. Coun. Exceptional Children (treas. 1990-92), Am. Ednl. Rsch. Assn., Phi Delta Kappa (pres. local chpt. 1990-91). Office: Harcourt Assessment Inc 19500 Bulverde Rd San Antonio TX 78259 Business E-Mail: betsy_case@harcourt.com.

CASE, JANICE CHANG, naturopathic physician, psychologist, lawyer; b. Loma Linda, Calif., May 24, 1970; d. Belden Shiu-Wah and Sylvia (Tan) Chang; m. Steven Lewis Case, Sept. 12, 2004. BA, Calif. State U., San Bernardino, 1990, cert. paralegal studies, 1990, cert. creative writing, 1991; JD, LaSalle U., 1993; D in Naturopathy, Clayton Sch. Natural Healing, 1993; DFA in Creative Writing: Poetry, Am. Internat. U., 1999; MD in Alternative Medicines, Open Internat. U., 2001; D of Psychology, Calif. Coast U., 2002; LLM in Taxation, Wash. Sch. Law, 2006. Bd. cert. alternative med. practitioner, registered naturopath; cert. loan signing agt., notary pub. Calif., lic. real estate salesperson Calif. Victim/witness contact clk.-paralegal Dist. Atty.'s Office Victim/Witness Assistance Program, San Bernardino, Calif., 1990; gen. counsel JMC Enterprises, Inc., Riverside, Calif., 1993—; adj. law prof. LaSalle U., Mandeville, La., 1994-97; corp. counsel, CFO JDS Assocs., Inc., Loma Linda, 1998-99, DJS, L.P., Loma Linda, 1998-99; trust officer/trust svcs. Southeastern Calif. Conf. Seventh-Day Adventists, Riverside, 1998—; CFO/mgr. Stanberden Properties, LLC, 2001—; CFO, gen. counsel SJD Enterprises, LLC, 2005—. Contbr. poetry to anthologies, including Am. Poetry Anthology, 1987-90, The Pacific Rev., 1991, The Piquant, 1991, River of Dreams, 1994, Reflections of Light, 1994, Musings, 1994 (Honorable Mention award 1994), Treasured Poems of America, 1994, Windows of the Soul, 1995, Best Poems of 1995 (Celebrating Excellence award 1995, Inspirations award 1995), Am. Poetry Annual, 1996, 99, Best New Poems of 1996, Interludes, 1996, Meditations, 1996, Perspectives, 1996 (Honorable Mention award 1996), Keepsakes, 1997 (Honorable Mention award 1997), Best Poems of 1997, Poetic Voices of America, 1997, The Isle of View, 1997, The Other Side of Midnight, 1997, Treasures, 1998, Best Poems of 1998, Writingscapes: Insights & Approaches to Creative Writing, 1998, Mirrors, 1999 (Pres.'s Lit. Excellence award), Pieces of the Heart, 2000, The Silence Within, 2001, Nature's Echoes, 2001, The Best Poems and Poets of 2001, The Best Poems and Poets of 2002; contbr. to Internat. Libr. Photography: Tapestry of Dreams, 1999, Mystical Seasons, 1999, Candid Captures, 2001, The Mirror's Reflection, 2003. Vol. Health Fair Expo La Sierra U., 1988, 1989, Path of the Just Tree Project, 1998; vol. first aid, CPR, other classes ARC, 1994—; sponsor Student Employment Recognition Banquet La Sierra U., Riverside, Calif., 1999—2003. Recipient Poet of Merit award, Am. Poetry Assn., San Francisco, 1989, Golden Poet award, World of Poetry, Washington, 1989, Publisher's Choice award, Watermark Press, 1990, Pres.'s award for lit. excellence, Iliad Press, 1995—99. Fellow Am. Coll. Internat. Physicians; mem. ABA, ATLA, Am. Coll. Legal Medicine, Nat. Notary Assn., Brit. Guild Drugless Practitioners (life). Republican. Seventh-Day Adventist. Avocations: poetry writing, photography, music, drama, literature, coin collecting/numismatics. Home: 1025 Crestbrook Dr Riverside CA 92506-5662 Office: Southeastern Calif Conf 7th-Day Adventists PO Box 8050 11330 Pierce St Riverside CA 92515-8050 Office Phone: 951-509-2229. E-mail: casejm@secc-sda.org.

CASE, KAREN ANN, lawyer; b. Milw., Apr. 7, 1944; d. Alfred F. and Hilda M. (Tomich) Case. BS, Marquette U., 1963, JD, 1966; LLM, NYU, 1973. Bar: Wis. 1966, U.S. Ct. Claims 1973, U.S. Tax Ct. 1973. Ptnr. Meldman, Case & Weine, Milw., 1973-85, Meldman, Case & Weine divsn. Mulcahy & Wherry, S.C., 1985-87; Sec. of Revenue State of Wis., 1987-88; ptnr. Case & Drinka, S.C., Milw., 1989-91, Case, Drinka & Diel, S.C., Milw., 1991-97, CoVac, 1997—. Lectr. U. Wis., Milw., 1974-78; guest lectr. Marquette U. Law Sch., 1975-78; dir. WBBC, 1998—. Contbr. articles to legal jours. Mem. gov.'s Commn. on Taliesin, 1988, gov.'s Econ. Adv. Commn., 1989-91, pres.'s coun. Alverno Coll., 1988-94, nat. coun., 1998-2000; bd. dirs. WBCC, 1998—. Fellow Wis. Bar Found. (dir. 1977-90, treas. 1980-90); mem. ABA, Milw. Assn. Women Lawyers (founding mem., bd. dirs. 1975-78, 81-82), Milw. Bar Assn. (bd. dirs. 1985-87, law office mgmt. chair 1992-93), State Bar Wis. (bd. govs. 1981-85, 87-90, dir. taxation sect. 1981-87, vice chmn. 1986-87, 90-91, chmn. 1991-92), Am. Acad. Matrimonial Lawyers (bd. dirs. 1988-90), Nat. Assn. Women Lawyers (Wis. del. 1982-83), Milw. Rose Soc. (pres. 1981, dir. 1981-83), Friends of Boerner Bot. Gardens (founding mem., pres. 1984-90), Profl. Dimensions Club (dir. 1985-87), Tempo Club (sec. 1984-85). Office: CoVac 9803 W Meadow Park Dr Hales Corners WI 53130-2261 Office Phone: 414-425-5672.

CASE, KAREN ELIZABETH, theater educator; b. Diboll, Tex., May 29, 1974; d. James Maron and Beatrice Elizabeth Furgurson; m. Joseph Mann Case; 1 child, Kamryn Elizabeth. BA in Edn., SW Tex. State U., San Marcos, 1997. Theatre arts and speech tchr. Austin (Tex.) Ind. Sch. Dist., 1997—. Workshop presenter Ctr. for Educator Devel. in Fine Arts, Austin. Faith team mem. Gt. Hills Bapt. Ch., Austin. Named Rookie Tchr. of Yr., Murchison Mid. Sch., 1997—98, Tchr. of Yr., 2003—04; Academic scholar, Temple Inland Found., 1992. Mem.: Tex. Ednl. Theatre Assn. (Mid. Sch. Tchr. of Yr. nominee 2005—06). Office: Murchison Mid Sch 3700 North Hills Dr Austin TX 78731 Office Phone: 512-414-3254. Office Fax: 512-343-1710.

CASE, MARY ANNE, law educator; b. 1957; BA magna cum laude, Yale U., 1979; grad. study, Ludwig Maximilians U., Munich, 1979—80; JD cum laude, Harvard U., 1985. Bar: NY 1986. Litig. assoc. Paul, Weiss, Rifkind, Wharton & Garrison, NYC, 1986—90; assoc. prof. law U. Va. Sch. Law, 1990—95, prof., 1995—96, Class of 1996 prof. law, 1996—99; prof. U. Chgo. Law Sch., 1999—2003, Arnold I. Shure prof. law, 2003—. Vis. prof. law NYU Sch. Law, 1996—97, 1999, U. Chgo. Law Sch., 1998; Bosch pub. policy fellow Am. Acad. Berlin, 2004. Office: U Chgo Law Sch 1111 E 60th St Chicago IL 60637 Office Phone: 773-834-3867. E-mail: macase@law.uchicago.edu.

CASE, NAN BARKIN, psychologist; b. Brookline, Mass., Nov. 30, 1936; d. David and Libby (Hershon) Barkin; m. Robert B. Case, Nov. 9, 1973; 1 child, R. Miles Robert. BA, Radcliffe/Hunter Coll., 1959; MA, Columbia U., 1969, PhD, 1973. Psychology intern, clin. fellow Westchester div. N.Y. Hosp., White Plains, 1969-73; sr. psychologist NYC Dept. Health Employee Counseling Svcs., 1973-74; sr psychologist North Shore U. Hosp., Manhasset, NY, 1974—; clin. asst. prof. psychology in psychiatry Cornell U. Med. Coll., NYC, 1990-95; asst. prof. psychology in psychiatry NYU Med. Coll., 1995—. Mem. Am. Psychol. Assn. Home: 130 E 75th St New York NY 10021-3277

CASE, RACHEL, elementary school educator; d. Cecilia and David Escajeda; m. Kevin Dewane Case, Aug. 2, 1996. BS in Edn., Baylor U., Tex., 1999; MEd in Sci., Tex. Wesleyan U., 2004. Cert. Esl Tex., 1999. Tchr. Mary Louise Phillips Elem., Ft. Worth, 1999—. Grade level chair Mary Louise Phillips Elem., Ft. Worth, steps-spl. edn. adv. com., campus events and calendar com., campus hospitality com. Mem.: United Educators Assn., Phi Delta Kappa Profl. Frat. in Edn., Alpha Chi Nat. Coll. Honor Soc., Golden Key Nat. Honor Soc., Kappa Delta Pi Internat. Honor Soc. in Edn. Office: Mary Louise Phillips Elem 3020 Bigham Blvd Fort Worth TX 76116 Office Phone: 817-377-7270.

CASE, ROSALIND See AVRETT, ROZ

CASE, TAMMY, bank executive; BBA magna cum laude, Upsala Coll., 1995; grad. with honors, U. Del., 1998. Platform asst. to asst. br. mgr. Nat. Bank Sussex County, 1977—81, adminstrv. asst. to asst. cashier, 1981—86, asst. v.p., compliance officer, 1986—89, v.p., 1989—93; sr. loan officer Newton (NJ) Trust Co., 1993—, sr. v.p. bus. banking svcs., 2001—. Chair Sussex County C. of C., past chair govt. legis. com.; past chair ARC; trustee Patriots Path Boy Scout Coun., Ct. Appointed Spl. Advocates; past chair found. bd. SCARD; mem. interfaith hosp. network Sparta Presbyn. Ch.; bd. dirs. Sussex County Econ. Devel. Ptnrship. Named one of 25 Women to Watch, US Banker Mag., 2003; recipient Vol. of Yr. award, Sussex County C. of C., 2001, Women of Yr. award, Patriot's Path Boy Scout Coun., 2001. Office: Newton Trust Co 29 Trinity St Newton NJ 07860

CASEI, NEDDA, mezzo soprano; b. Balt. d. Howard Thomas and Lyda Marie (Graupman) Casey; m. John A. Wiles, Jr., 1971 (div. 1979); m. Samuel Strasbourger, 1983 (dec. 1987). Cert., Mozarteum, Salzburg, Austria, 1959; B in Performing Arts Adminstrn. magna cum laude, Fordham U., 1982; studied voice with, William P. Herman, N.Y.C., Vittorio Piccinini, Milan, Italy, Loretta Corelli, N.Y.C.; also student piano, langs., modern dance, pilates, ballet. Tchr. master classes, lectr. univs. and festivals. Judge vocal competitions for Met. Opera, Fulbright Scholarship, Rosa Ponselle Internat. Competition, Savannah Festival, George London Found. Competition, First Internat. Vocal Competition, Baku, Azerbaijan, Nagakute Internat. Coval Competition, and others; vis. prof. Aichi Prefectural U. Fine Arts and Music, Nagoya, Japan, 1993-95, 2003—; guest prof. Flaine Festival/Paris Conservatory, Haut Savoie, France, Mannes Coll. Music, New Sch. Social Rsch., N.Y.C., Internat. Vocal Arts Inst., Tel Aviv; pvt. tchr. Operatic debut Theatre Royal de la Monnaie, Brussels, 1960, with La Scala, Milan, Met. Opera, N.Y.C., 1964; operatic performances at Met. Opera, 1964-86, Basel Stadttheater, Gran

Liceo, Barcelona, Teatro Carlo Fenice, Genova, San Remo Festival, Trieste Opera, Opera du Rhin, Strasbourg, Salzburg Festspielhaus, Teatro San Carlo, Naples, Chgo. Lyric Opera, Bogota Opera, Caracas Opera, Pitts. Opera, Vancouver Opera, Cape Town Opera, Brno Opera, Bratislava Opera, Kosice Opera, Prague Opera, Miami Opera, Houston Opera, San Diego Opera, Hartford Opera, Phila. Opera, Toledo Opera, Dayton Opera, Memphis Opera, Mobile Opera, Los Angeles Opera, Boston Opera, N.J. Opera, Taipei Opera, Opera of Mexico City; performances in numerous mus. festivals, concerts, recitals and operatic guest appearances in Europe, South Africa, Cen. Am., S.Am., Can., U.S., Far East, Middle East and Australia, including Detroit Symphony, Cin. Orch., Toronto Symphony, Liepzig Gewandhaus Philharm., Phila. Orch., Brussels Philharm., NY Philharm.; performed on radio and TV in Holland, Belgium, Leipzig, Japan, U.S., German Dem. Republic, Fed. Republic of Germany, Hong Kong, Manila, Singapore; performed at White House, Washington; made various recs. Supraphon, Everest, Nonesuch, Concert Hall, Vanguard, CETRA, VAI, others; contbr. articles to profl. jours.; guest editor Opera Quar. Coord. mus. events and benefits for Internat. Ctr. for Disabled, Morningside Home, Aging in Am. Gerontol. Acad.; mem. adv. bd. Fordham U at Lincoln Ctr., 1984—; bd. dirs. Theatre for a New Audience, Am. Coun. for Arts, Nat. Cultural Alliance, Songs of Love; mem. Career Transition for Dancers Nat. Adv. Bd. Recipient Outstanding Young Singers award, 1959, Martha Baird Rockefeller Found. award, 1962, 1963, 1964, Woman of Achievement award, 1969, Cmty. Leaders and Noteworthy Americans, 1975—76, Outstanding Achievement award on behalf of Arts and Edn., Opera Music Theater Internat. and Children's Emergency Med. Fund, 2000, Outstanding Lifetime Achievement award, Licia Albanese/Puccini Found., 2001, Extraordinary Women award, 2000, honors at, 100 Year Verdi Celebration by Met. Opera, Mozart Celebration at Met Opera, 2006. Mem. AFTRA, Actors Equity, Am. Guild Mus. Artists (nat. pres. 1983-93. chmn. Emergency Relief Fund 1983-94), Nat. Assn. Tchrs. Singing (bd. govs.), N.Y. Singing Tchrs. Assn., The Players, James Beard Found. Personal E-mail: neddanewyork@nyc.rr.com. Business E-Mail: neddanagoya@guitar.ocn.ne.jp.

CASEIRAS, JO ANN STRIGA, artist, educator; b. Bklyn., Dec. 17, 1950; d. Michael Striga and Stella Mary Lango; m. Frank Caseiras, May 21, 1983; children: Michael Allen, Kevin Frank, Amanda Beth, Robert Anthony. BFA, St. John's U., Jamaica, N.Y., 1972; MFA, SUNY, New Paltz, 1975. Tchr. continuing edn. SUNY, New Paltz, 1974-75, prof. Buffalo, 1976-78; tchr. Marlboro (N.Y.) Elem. Continuing Edn., 1980-82; parent advocate Rondout Valley Ctrl. Sch. Dist., Accord, N.Y., 1992-97, tchr. program for the handicapped, 1999—. Exhibited in shows at Reavin Gallery, New Paltz, N.Y., 1976, Benjamin's Works of Art, Buffalo, 1977, Art Zone 208, New Paltz, 1979, Mamaroneck Artists Guild, White Plains, N.Y., 1979, Womanart Gallery, N.Y.C., Schenectady (N.Y.) Mus., 1980, New Rochelle (N.Y.) Art Assn., 1994, Heritage Art Gallery, Poughkeepsie, N.Y., 1995, St. John's U., Jamaica, N.Y., 1996, Heritage Gallery, Rhinebeck, N.Y., 1997, Highland (N.Y.) Cultural Art Ctr., 1996-98, Coffey Gallery, Kingston, N.Y., 1998, Woodstock (N.Y.) Art Assn., 1995—, First Union Bank, New Paltz, 2000, Marbletown Arts Assn., 2002, Marbletown Tricentennial Exhbn., 2003. Recipient Mortimer L. Medrich Meml. award, 1979. Mem.: Woodstock Art Assn., Art Soc. Kingston, Downs Syndrome Assn. Democrat. Roman Catholic. Avocations: sports, swimming, piano, photography. Personal E-mail: jstrigacaseiras@aol.com.

CASELLA, MARGARET MARY, artist; b. Bklyn. d. John August and Ann Elizabeth (Krajci) Butkovsky; m. Anthony Joseph Casella, Nov. 23, 1961; children: Paul Joseph, David John, Gregory Anthony. Cert. in Merchandising, Tobe-Coburn Sch., N.Y.C., 1961; BFA, L.I. U., 1982, MFA, 1984. Lectr. in field. Photographer: (book) Garbage or Art?, 1990 (Gold award Photo Design Mag. 1990); exhbns. at Midtown Y Photography Gallery, N.Y.C., 1991, Grand Ctrl. Terminal, N.Y.C., 1991, Ctr. for Photography at Woodstock, N.Y., 2000, Hort. Soc. N.Y./Webster Gallery, 2000, Elaine Benson Gallery, Bridgehampton, N.Y., others; group shows include Samuel Dursky Mus. Art, New Paltz, N.Y., U. Tex. at Arlington, Deutser Art Gallery, Houston, Heckscher Mus., Huntington, N.Y., Konica Plz., Tokyo, Firehouse Gallery, Garden City, N.Y., The Visual Club, N.Y.C., Hillwood Art Mus., Greenvale, N.Y.; works in permanent collections of Mus. for Photography, Branschweig, Germany, Yergeau Musee Internat. d'Art, Montreal, Fine Art Mus. of L.I., Hempstead, N.Y., Houston fotofest Permanent Archives, Houston. Founder, dir. Art Upstairs Gallery, East Williston, 1983-91; mem. adv. bd. C.W. Post Campus Sch. of Visual and Performing Arts. Named to Women's Roll of Honor, Town of North Hempstead, NY, 2003. Avocation: gardening. Studio: Casella Photography 889 Broadway New York NY 10003-1212 E-mail: nyctwoonetwo@aol.com.

CASERIA, CAROL SHULER, elementary school educator, researcher; b. Marion, Kans., Dec. 25, 1919; d. Harry Elston and Edith May (Mosher) Shuler; m. Armando Caseria, Feb. 20, 1943; children: Priscilla, Philip, Jeffrey. BA, Wichita State U., 1941; MA, U. of Redlands, 1966. Cert. elem. edn., standard supervision. Tchr. English, history Nortonville (Kans.) High Sch., 1941; file clk. Dept. of Agr., Lincoln, Nebr., 1942; clk. typist Air Transport Command, Gravelly Point, Va., 1942-43; prin., tchr. Nursery-Kindergarten, Ft. Myer, Va., 1947-51; kindergarten tchr. Weisbaden (Fed. Republic Germany) Am. Nursery Kindergarten, 1953-55; prin. tchr. St. Michael's Kindergarten, Arlington, Va., 1956-60; tchr. kindergarten Edison Elem. Sch., Redondo Beach, Calif., 1960-63; tchr. kindergarten, 1st-2nd grades Grand Terrace (Calif.) Elem., 1963-65; intern supr. Liason Calif. State U., Colton, 1965, 66, 68; tchr. Colton Joint Unified Sch. Dist., 1965—95; ret. Aide-participant White House Golden Ann. Conf. on Children and Youth, Washington, 1960. Mem. NEA, Calif. Tchrs. Assn., Am. Colton Educators (rep.), AAUW, Panhellenic, San Bernardino Women's Club, Arrowhead Garden Club, San Bernardino Rep. Women Federated, Beta Sigma Phi, Alpha Phi. Avocations: travel, reading. Home: 26037 Holly Vista Blvd San Bernardino CA 92404-3516 Office: Lincoln Elem Sch 444 E Olive St Colton CA 92324-2717 Office Phone: 909.

CASERIO, REBECCA JOANN, dermatologist, educator; b. Pa., Aug. 2, 1949; d. James Joseph and Jolanda Marie (Denale) C.; m. Chris Max Allen, Apr. 15, 1978. BS summa cum laude, U. Pitts., 1971, MD cum laude, 1975. Intern Montefiore Hosp., Pitts., 1975—76, resident in internal medicine, 1976—78, chief resident, 1978; staff internist Penn Group Health Plan, Pitts., 1978—80; resident in dermatology U. Pitts., 1981—83, chief resident in dermatology, 1983; dir. hair clinic Falk Clinic, Pitts., 1984—87, clin. asst. prof. dermatology, 1985—92, clin. assoc. prof. dermatology, 1992—2001. Mem. Pa. Med. Soc., Pitts. Acad. Dermatology, Pa. Acad. Dermatology, Am. Acad. Dermatology, Am. Soc. Dermatol. Surgeons, Allegheny County Med. Soc., Am. Contact Dermatitis Soc., Internat. Soc. Cosmetic & Laser Surgery, Am. Soc. Photodynamic Therapy, Phi Beta Kappa, Kappa Kappa Gamma, Alpha Omega, Alpha, Beta Beta Beta, Alpha Epsilon Delta. Roman Catholic. Home: 4142 Bigelow Blvd Pittsburgh PA 15213-1408 Office Phone: 412-784-1606.

CASERTA, JENNIFER, communications executive; b. 1971; Mktg. positions Radio Advt. Bur., Westwood One, Oxygen Media, The Food Network; v.p., ad sales mktg. Court TV; sr. v.p. mktg. Ind. Film Channel, NYC, 2004—. Named one of 40 Executives Under 40, Multichannel News, 2006. Office: Independent Film Channel 323 6th Ave New York NY 10014*

CASE-SCHMIDT, MARY E., pathologist, educator; b. Jefferson City, Mo., Feb. 27, 1943; BA, U. Mo., 1965; MD, St. Louis U. Sch. Medicine, 1969. Resident in pathology St. Louis U. Sch. Medicine, St. Louis, 1969—71, asst. in pathology, 1969—73; postdoctoral fellow Nat. Inst. Neurol. Disease and Stroke, St. Louis, 1971—72; resident in neuropathology St. Louis U. Sch. Medicine, 1972—73; instr. in pathology, 1973—75; vis. asst. prof. neuropathology U. Mo., Sch. Medicine, Columbia, Mo., 1975—77; asst. prof. pathology St. Louis U. Sch. Medicine, 1975—81; cons. neuropathology St. Luke's Hosp., East and West, 1973—77; asst. med. examiner St. Louis County, 1975—88, City of St. Louis, 1977—80; assoc. prof. pathology St. Louis U. Sch. Medicine, 1981—99; dep. chief med. examiner City of St. Louis, 1980—85; cons. neuropathology St. John's Mercy Hosp., St. Louis, 1973—88; spl. projects, divsn. forensic and environ. pathology St. Louis U. Sch. Medicine, 1985—; chief med. examiner St. Charles County, 1986—, St. Louis County, 1988—, Jefferson County, 1992—, Franklin County, 1993—; prof. pathology St. Louis U. Health Scis. Ctr., 1999—, co-dir., divsn. forensic pathology, 1996—. Dean's adv. bd. St. Louis U., 2000—; bd. dirs. Greater St. Louis Region Critical Incident Stress Mgmt. Team, 1995—; mem. Nat. Medicolegal Rev. Panel for Devel. Guidelines for Death Invest. for Nat. Inst. Justice, 1996—. Recipient Spl. Leadership award for Professions, Meto. St. Louis YWCA, 1990, Norman Westbrook "Hall of Fame" award, Mo. Police Juvenile Officers Assn., 1992, Recognition award "Teen Drinking and Driving", St. Louis Metro. Med. Soc., 2001, Spl. Recognition award, St. Charles Crime Stoppers, 2002. Fellow: Am. Acad. Forensic Sci. (ethics com. 2001—), Am. Soc. Clin. Pathology, Coll. Am. Pathologists; mem.: AMA, Nat. Assn. Med. Examiner (bd. dir. 2000—, exec. com. 2001—), Am. Assn. Neuropathologists, Internat. Acad. Pathology, St. Louis Path. Soc., St. Louis Metro. Med. Soc., Am. Profl. Soc. on Abuse of Children, Mo. State Med. Assn., Mo. Network of Cert. Pathologists for Child Death Autopsies (chmn. 1996—), Am. Journal Forensic Medicine and Pathology. Office: St Louis U Sch Medicine Dept Pathology 1402 S Grand Saint Louis MO 63104-1004

CASEY, BARETTA A., physician, educator; BA, Pikeville Coll.; MD, U. Ky. Former pvt. practice physician, Pikeville, Ky.; dir. E. Ky. Family Practice Residency Program, U. Ky., Hazard, 2002—, Ctr. for Rural Health, Hazard, 2005—. Prof. U. Ky. Coll. Medicine, vice chair Dept. Family and Cmty. Medicine. Mem.: AMA (mem. Coun. Med. Edn.), Ky. Med. Assn. (pres. elect 2005, past v.p., Ednl. Achievement Award). Office: Chandler Med Ctr 800 Rose St (MN-150) Lexington KY 40536 Office Phone: 606-439-3557. Office Fax: 606-439-1131. E-mail: bcase2@email.uky.edu.*

CASEY, BETH MENTELLE, music educator; b. Houston, Miss., June 30, 1959; d. Robert Paul and Evelyn Baldwin; m. Brian Casey, Nov. 19, 1981; children: Sean Baker, Clay Colman. B in Music Edn., San Houston State U., Huntsville, Tex., 1982, MusM, 1984. Choir dir. h.s. Spring Branch Ind. Sch. Dist., Houston, 1984—85; choir, orch. dir. Brakesport H.S., Freeport, Tex., 1985—90, Coral Springs (Fla.) H.S., 1990—91; piano tchr. Hammocks Mid. Sch., Miami, Fla., 1991—92; voice, theory tchr. Branosport Jr. Coll., Lake Jackson, Tex., 1992—94; supr. choral music, choir dir. h.s. Angleton (Tex.) Ind. Sch. Dist., 1994—. Adj. UIL, Austin, Tex., 1994—2006; voice coach Lamar U., 1998—2006. Singer: Houston Symphony Chorus, 1999. Named Outstanding Tchr., Angleton H.S., 2005. Mem.: Tex. Music Educators Assn., Tex. Choral Dir. Assn., Am. Choral Dir. Assn. Methodist. Office: Angleton High Sch 1201 Henderson Angleton TX 77515 Office Phone: 979-848-0625. Business E-Mail: bcasey@angletonisd.net.

CASEY, BONNIE MAE, artist, educator; b. Chgo., Aug. 1, 1932; d. Edward Frances Kusch, Bessie Elaine (Moulding) Kusch; m. George Daniel Casey, Feb. 21, 1953; children: Cheryl Ann, Stuart Evan, Charles Alan. Student, Am. Acad. Art, Chgo., Harper Jr. Coll., Schamburg, Ill. Instr. Village Art Sch., Skokie, Ill., 1965—80, Art Barn, Elk Grove Village, Ill., 1978—83, Mountain Artists Guild, Prescott, Ariz., 1985—2000, Pima Coll., Green Valley, Ariz. Bd. dirs. Southwestern Artists Assn.; mem. visual arts com. Prescott Fine Arts Assn., 1995—2003; bd. dirs. Prescott Arts and Humanities, 1986—99; tchr. Vaison la Romaine, France, San Mignel del Allende, Mexico; instr. in field; organizer, arts curator Open Space Alliance, 2001. Contbr. articles to Fine Art Collector mag., Wine and Dine mag.; prin. works include painting 9-11-01, 2001, logo design, Arts and Humanities Coun., Prescott, Town of Chino Valley, Ariz., mural design, History of Chino Valley, one-woman shows include Mitchell Mus., Trinidad, Colo., 1992, 50 Yr. Art Retrospective, 2003, exhibited in group shows at Phippen Mus. Named Curator of Yr., Prescott Fine Arts Assn.; recipient Grumbacher Gold medal, 1992, 1996, Gov.'s award nominee, Ariz. Commn. on Arts; featured artist 50 Yrs. of Art Retrospective, Prescott Fine Arts Gallery, 2003. Mem.: Southwestern Artists Assn., Western Acad. Women Artists (historian), Oil Painters Am., Phippen Western Art Mus., Prescott Art Docents (docent auditor 1996—2003). Avocation: travel. Home: 3380 N Yuma Dr Chino Valley AZ 86323 E-mail: geocasey@northlink.com.

CASEY, DARLA DIANN, elementary school educator; b. West Linn, Oreg., Mar. 21, 1940; d. Karl F. and Lucille Iona (Wilson) Lettenmaier; m. Charles Emerson Casey, July 30, 1965; children: John, Michael, Kim. BSEd, U. Wis., Milw., 1965; MEd, postgrad., Oreg. State U., U. Oreg., West State, Port State. Cert. tchr. grades K-9, basic art grades 1-12. Tchr., grade 3, swimming instr., grades 4-6 Lakeside (Oreg.) Elem.; tchr., readiness rm. K-1 Siuslaw Elem., Florence, Oreg.; tchr., grades K and 1st, spl. reading, art Washington Elem., Canon City, Colo.; tchr., grade 1 Sam Case Elem. Sch., Lincoln County Sch. Dist., Newport, Oreg. Mentor tchr. N.W. Sci. Survey Com.; aerospace sci. tchr. 3d through 5th and 4H Young Astronauts 3d through 5th NASA's Space Down to Earth Program, 1998; speaker in field. Contbr. articles to profl. jours. Named Oreg. Elem. Sci. Tchr. of Yr. Am. Electronics Assn. and Dept. Edn., 1989; NASA scholar (Nasa ednl. workshop for elem. sci. tchrs. program), 1992, 95, Oreg. Cadre for All tchrs. of Sci. scholar, 1993, NASA Flight Opportunities for Sci. Tchr. Enrichment Project scholar, 1995, Am. Astron. Soc. Tchr. Resource Agt., 1996, ASTRA scholar U. Tex. and McDonald Observatory, 1996. Mem. Oreg. Sci. Tchrs. Assn., Oreg. Reading Assn., Oreg. Seacoast Reading Coun. (past pres.), Oreg. Math. Tchrs. Assn., Phi Delta Kappa. Home: PO Box 527 Lincoln City OR 97367-0527 E-mail: dasey1@harborside.com.

CASEY, JOAN MAUREEN, secondary school educator; b. Georgetown, Guyana, June 7, 1953; d. Herbert Elias and Genevieve Lucia Casey; children: Chaka M.A., Roscoe A.K. BA in Geography, U. Guyana, 1977; Diploma in Internat. Rels., U. W.I. St. Augustine, Trinidad, 1983; MA in Edn., Bklyn. Coll., 1988. Head dept. geography Wismar Govt. Secondary Sch., Guyana, 1977—82; tchr., head dept. social studies St. Mark's Day Sch., Bklyn., 1986—90; tchr. IS320, Bklyn., 1990—93, MS61, Bklyn., 1993—2005, FDA IV, Bklyn., 2005—. Curriculum cons. St. Mark's Day Sch., Bklyn., camp dir., after-sch. dir. Named Most Dedicated Tchr., MS61, 2002—04, Outstanding Social Studies Tchr., 2003. Mem.: ASCD. Avocations: yoga, tennis, jogging, body-building. Home: 592 Linden Blvd Brooklyn NY 11203-3116

CASEY, KATHLEEN L., commissioner; b. Tripoli, Libya; BA in Internat. Politics, Penn State U., 1988; JD, George Mason U., 1993. Bar: DC, Va. Staff dir. Subcom. on Fin. Institutions and Regulatory Relief U.S. Senate Banking Com. US Senate, 1994—96, legis. asst. to Senator Richard Shelby, 1993—94, legis. dir., chief of staff, 1996—2003, staff dir., counsel, Banking, Housing, and Urban Affairs Com., 2003—06; commr. SEC, 2006—. Mem.: Va State Bar Assn., DC Bar Assn. Office: SEC Hdqs 100 F St NE Washington DC 20549 Office Phone: 202-551-6551.*

CASEY, LINDA SUSAN, school system administrator; d. Walter Carl and Ruth C. (Dockery) Schmidt; m. Michael John Casey, May 12, 1973; children: Kerry, Kevin, Michael, John. BS in Edn., Chgo. State U., 1972; MA in Edn., St. Xavier U., Chgo., 1996; MA in Edn. Adminstrn., Dominican U., River Forest, Ill., 2000. Tchr. computer lab., dean Queen of Peace H.S., Burbank, Ill., 1973, 1987—2001; tchr. bus. Lourdes H.S., Chgo., 1978; tchr. 4th grade St. Michael, Chgo., 1984—85; assoc. prin. Resurrection H.S., 3. Trainer Criss, Chgo., 2005—. Mem.: ASCD. Roman Catholic. Office: Maria H S 6727 S California Chicago IL 60629

CASEY, MARGARET ELLEN, elementary school educator, real estate agent; b. New Brunswick, N.J., Sept. 23, 1951; d. Patrick T. and Eleanor G. (Crosson) C. BA, Georgian Ct. Coll., 1973; MS in Edn., Monmouth U., 1977. Elem. tchr. Toms River Regional Schs., NJ, 1973-78, elem. guidance counselor, 1978-89, supr. instrn., 1989—2005, ret., 2005; real estate sales profl. Coldwell Banker Rivera Reality, 1986—. Cons. in field. Mem. ASCD, Nat. Coun. Tchrs. Math., Nat. Alliance Mentally Ill (N.J. chpt.), N.J. Realtors, Nat. Assn. Realors, N.J. Prins. & Suprs. Assn. Roman Catholic. Home: 891 Royal Ln Toms River NJ 08753-5667 Office: Coldwell Banker Riverra Realty 1310 Hooper Ave Toms River NJ 08753

CASEY, PAULA JEAN, former prosecutor; b. Charleston, Ark., Feb. 16, 1951; d. Arthur Clinton and Mildred Aleene (Underwood) C.; m. Gilbert Louis Glover II, Mar. 13, 1981. BA, Ea. Cen. U., Okla., 1973; JD, U. Ark., 1977. Staff atty. Ctrl. Ark. Legal Services, Hot Springs, Ark., 1977-79; dep. pub. defender 6th Jud. Dist. Pub. Defender, Little Rock, 1979; clinic supr. U. Ark. at Little Rock Law Sch., 1979-81, asst. prof., 1981-84, assoc. prof., 1984-92, prof., 1992-93, assoc. dean, 1986-90; legis. dir., chief counsel U.S. Senator Dale Bumpers, 1990-92; lobbyist Ark. Bar Assn., 1993; U.S. atty. Ea. Dist. Ark., 1993—2001; prof. law U. Ark. at Little Rock Law Sch., 2001—. Cons. for juvenile affairs 6th Jud. Dist. Judges, Ark., 1987; mem. trust com. Ark. Bar Found., 2004—; repprter Ark. Supreme Ct. Com. Jury Instrns.-Criminal, 2005—. Author, editor: Poverty Law Practice Manual, 1985. Sec. Pulaski County Dem. Com., Little Rock, 1984-89; mem. Ark. Dem. Com., 1984-89; mem. Juvenile Adv. Group, Little Rock, 1985-89; mem. Gov.'s Task Force on Juvenile Cts., Ark., 1987; chmn. Ark. Dem. Jud. Com., 1987; bd. dirs. Ctrl. Ark. Legal Svcs., Little Rock, 1986-89. Named One of Top 100 Women in Ark., Ark. Bus. Pubs., 1996, 98, 99; recipient Gale Pettus Pontz award U. Ark.-Fayetteville Law Sch. Women Students Assn., 1994, award of merit Organized Crime Drug Enforcement Task Force, 1997. Fellow Ark. Bar Found. (bd. dirs.); mem. Ark. Bar Assn. (del. 1986-90), Am. Inns Ct., Overton Am. Inns of Ct., Henry Woods Am. Inn of Ct., 8th Cir. Ct. Appeals (fed. adv. comm. 2001-05). Democrat. Office: U Ark at Little Rock Sch Law 1201 McMath Blvd Little Rock AR 72202 E-mail: pjcasey@ualr.edu.

CASEY, SUE (SUZANNE MARGUERITE PHILIPS), actress, real estate broker; b. LA, Apr. 8, 1926; d. Burke Dewey and Mildred Louise (Hansen) Philips; children: Colleen O'Shaughnessy, John Joseph Durant III, Christopher Kent Durant, Diane M. Kelly; m. Jack Hoffmann (div.); stepchildren: Joy Hoffmann Molloy, Kristen Hoffmann Blutman. Student, UCLA Extension, 1972-75. Lic. real estate broker and saleswoman, Calif. With Coldwell Banker, Beverly Hills, Calif. Appeared in numerous movies, including swimming in 5 Esther Williams films, singing and dancing in over 20 films, Goldwyn Girl, 1945-47; Star Is Born, Surf Terror, 1965, Catalina Caper, 1967, Happy Ending, Secrets of Monte Carlo, The Family Jewels, Marriage Young Stockbroker, The Big Circus, The Errand Boy, Two Weeks in Another Town, Paint Your Wagon, Camelot, Evil Speak, 1981, Swamp Country, Ladies Man, Lucky Lady, Annie Get Your Gun, Show Boat, Carpetbaggers, Rear Window, Breakfast at Tiffany's, The Scarf, Main Event, Brady Bunch Sequel, 1996, American Beauty, 1999; appeared in TV shows, including Hunter, Hotel, Hart to Hart, White Shadow, Sunny Valley, Lucy, Gunsmoke, Arnie, Marcus Welby, Sky Terror, Dallas, Days of Our Lives, Unsolved Mysteries, Rosie O'Neill, Haggerty, Emergency, California Fever, I Love Lucy, Farmer's Daughter, Beverly Hillbillies, Delta House, Bodies of Evidence, The Faculty, Divorce Court, Colgate Comedy Shows, Carol Burnett Shows, Red Skelton Show, Roy Bolger Show, All Star Revues, Bob Hope Specials, Ann Southern Show, Family Medical Center, Red Shoe Diaries, What Love Sees, Boy Meets World, 1997, Diagnosis Murder, 1999; has appeared in over 200 TV commls.; stage appearances include Picnic, Goodnight Ladies. Ball chmn. The Footlighters, Inc., 1971-73, 93-94, press chmn., 1972-73, pres., 1982-83, 98-99, parliamentarian, 1983-94, 99-00,02-03, hospitality chmn., 1992-93. Named Ms. Sr. Am. of L.A., 1993. Mem. AFTRA, SAG, Actors Equity Assn. Office: Coldwell Banker 301 N Canon Dr Beverly Hills CA 90210-4722 Office Phone: 310-777-6344. E-mail: suecaseyla@yahoo.com.

CASEY, THERESA L., science educator; b. Evansville, Ind., Aug. 25, 1955; d. Richard Elliott and Henrietta Juanita Leighton; m. Barry Alan Casey, Apr. 12, 1980; children: Christopher Ryan, Ashley Erin, Brennan Shawn, Kyle Evan. BS in food sci., Purdue U., 1974—77. Secondary Education Unified Science Mo., 1990. Quality control supr. Pet, Inc., Wayland, Mich., 1978—80; quality control mgr. Holland Am. Wafer, Grand Rapids, Mich., 1980—82; tchr. presch. Trinity Episcopal Ch., 1992—95; substitute tchr. Ralls County Schs., 1995—98; h.s. sci. tchr. Ralls R-II Schools, Center, Mo., 1999—. Girl scout leader Becky Thatcher Girl Scout Coun., Hannibal, Mo., 1991—98; deacon First Christian Ch., Hannibal, 2000—05. Recipient Conservation Tchr. of the Yr., Soil and Water Conservation Dist. of Mo., 2004, Environ. Educator of the Yr., Mo. Forestry Coun., 2004, Outstanding Beginning Tchr., Mo. Colleges of Edn., 2001; Conservation Grant for Outdoor Classroom, Mo. Dept. of Conservation, 2003, Environ. grant, Walmart, 2003. Mem.: Ralls County Teachers Assn. (v.p. 2002—05), Mo. Environ. Edn. Assn., Sci. Teachers of Mo., Mo. State Teachers Assn., Nat. Assn. of Sci. Teachers, Nat. Assn. of Biology Teachers. Avocations: gardening, sewing, crafts, reading. Home: 54897 Hwy M New London MO 63459 Office: Ralls County R-II Schools 21622 Hwy 19 Center MO 63436 Office Phone: 573-267-3397. E-mail: theresa_casey@hotmail.com.

CASH, CAMILLE GENEVA, physician; b. Balt., Oct. 8, 1969; d. William Henry, III and Cheryl (Griffin) Cash; m. Roderick Delano Lowe, June 3, 1995; children: Lauren Shelby Lowe, Kennedy Camille Lowe, Christopher Delano Lowe. BS, Howard U., 1991; MD, Baylor U., 1995. Diplomate Am. Bd. Surgery, 2002, Am. Bd. Plastic Surgery, 2004. Intern in gen. surgery Christus St. Joseph Hosp., Houston, 1995—96, resident in gen. surgery, 1996—2002, fellow in plastic surgery, 2002—. Mem.: ACS, Houston Soc. Plastic Surgery, Harris County Med. Soc., Tex. Soc. Plastic Surgery, Tex. Med. Assn. Roman Catholic. Office: 1315 St Joseph Pkway Ste 1305 Houston TX 77002 Home: 3747 Maroncal Houston TX 77025 Office Phone: 713-571-0600. Personal E-mail: cashmd@hotmail.com. E-mail: info@camillecashmd.com.

CASH, DEANNA GAIL, retired nursing educator; b. Coatesville, Pa., Nov. 28, 1940; Diploma, Jackson Meml. Hosp., 1961; BS, Fla. State U., 1964; MN, UCLA, 1968; EdD, Nova U., Ft. Lauderdale, Fla., 1983. Staff and relief charge nurse Naples (Fla.) Comty. Hosp., 1961-62; staff nurse Glendale (Calif.) Comty. Hosp., 1964-65; instr. Knapp Coll. Nursing, Santa Barbara, Calif., 1965-66; staff nurse, team leader Kaiser Found. Hosp., Bellflower, Calif., 1968-69; prof. nursing El Camino Coll., Torrance, Calif., 1969-96, ret., 1996. Coord., instr. Internat. RN Rev. course, L.A., 1974-76; mentor statewide nursing program, Long Beach, Calif., 1981-88; clin. performance in nursing exam. evaluator Western Performance Assessment Ctr., Long Beach, 1981-96.

CASH, JEANIE MARITTA, educational association administrator; b. Nashville, Ark., Dec. 18, 1948; d. Roy M. and Doris M. Reed; m. Ronald David Cadh, Apr. 17, 1971; children: Brandon Reed, Kristofer Robert. BA, Whittier Coll., 1971; MA, U. La Verne, 1985. Cert. adminstr. Calif., 1985, nat. curriculum auditor Calif., 2000. Prin. Bellflower Unified Sch. Dist., Calif., 1985—99, Los Alamitos, Calif., 1995—99; assoc. supt. Chino Unified Sch. Dist., Calif., 1999—2005; asst. supt. Placentia-Yorba Linda Unified Sch. Dist., Calif., 2005—. Com. of practitioners State Dept. Edn., Sacramento. Contbr. articles to profl. jours. Curriculum writer Am. Bapt. Assn., Texarkana, Tex., 1980—2005. Mem.: State Dept of Edn., Assn. Calif. Sch. Adminstrs. (pres., curriculum coun. 2005), Delta Kappa Gamma, Phi Delta Kappa (assoc.). Republican. Baptist. Avocations: music, rollerblading, travel. Home: 9352 Julie Beth Cypress CA 90630 Office: Placentia-Yorba Linda Unified Sch Dist 1301 E Orangethorpe Placentia CA 92870 Office Phone: 714-985-8650. Office Fax: 714-577-8104. Business E-Mail: jcash@pylusd.org.

CASH, KRISTY RAE, language educator; b. Decatur, Ill., Mar. 18, 1962; d. Ray R. Willan and Sheila D. Hepworth, Miriam H. Willan (Stepmother); m. Kenneth J. Cash, Sept. 28, 1985; children: Michaela Lauren, Alexander Joseph. BA, Loretto Heights Coll., Denver, 1986. Cert. Montessori Educator CMTE, 1999. Tchr., erdkinder program devel. Compass Montessori, Golden, Colo., 1999—2003; tchr. English, dir. program Compass Montessori H.S., Golden, 2003—. Dir.: (play) The Search for Signs of Intelligent Life in the Universe, The Laramie Project. Achievements include first to Design, develop, implement first Montessori secondary charter school in the U.S. Office: Compass Montessori High School 4441 Salvia Street Golden CO 80403 Personal E-mail: kcash@jeffco.k12.co.us.

CASH, LAVERNE (CYNTHIA CASH), physicist; b. Statesville, NC, Oct. 7, 1956; d. William J. and Martha Lee (Stroud) C. BS, Appalachian State U., 1979; MS, Clemson U., 1982; AA, Mitchell C.C., 1976; PhD, Johns Hopkins U., 1999. Physicist U.S. Army Material Systems Analysis Activity, Aberdeen Proving Ground, Md., 1984-88; rsch. physicist U.S. Army Edgewood Chem. and Biol. Ctr., Aberdeen Proving Ground, 1988—. Contbr. articles to profl. jours.; author: New Beginnings: A Hogan's Heros Story, 2004. Mem. Oak Grove Bapt. Ch, Bel Air, Md., singer in choir, sound engr., numerous others. Mem. Am. Phys. Soc., Sigma Phi Sigma, Pi Mu Epsilon, Phi Theta Kappa, Gamma Beta Phi. Baptist. Home: 100 Drexel Dr Bel Air MD 21014-2002 Office Phone: 410-436-1763. Personal E-mail: lavernecash@yahoo.com.

CASH, MARY FRANCES, minister, retired civilian military employee; d. Hugh Lester and Myrtle Victoria (Byrd) Flucas; m. William Hadley Cash, May 7, 1966; children: Aleta Grace Pearson, William Anthony, Antonio Hadley. Diploma, Atlantic Bus. Coll., 1961; Assoc. in Religious Edn., Washington Saturday Coll., 1996; Masters Degree in religious edn., Bethel Bible Coll./Seminary, 2003. Ordained elder African Meth. Episcopal Ch., 1999. Sec., stenographer Dept. Human Resources, Washington, 1964—77; adminstr. Flu-Bea Enterprises, Landover, Md., 1977—80; substitute tchr. Pineview Elem. Sch., Valdosta, Ga., 1980—81; sec. Moody AFB, Valdosta, 1981—82, Andrews AFB, Camp Spring, Md., 1982—92, Dept. Def., Va., 1992—94; pastor Cmty. African Meth. Episcopal Ch., Whitehall, Ark., 1998—. Dean bd. examiners East Northeast Ark. Conf., sec. annual conf., trustee ann. conf. Leader, trainer Girl Scout Coun. Am., Washington, 1971—79, Valdosta, Ga., 1980—82, Washington, 1982—96; mem. adv. bd. Duke Ellington Sch. Art, Washington, 1986; instr. Summer Tchg. Program for Children, Jonesboro, 1996—2000; dir. Saturday Sch. Brown Meml. African Meth. Episcopal Ch., Washington, 1990—96. Named Mother of the Yr., Brown Meml. African Meth. Episcopal Ch., 1988; recipient Spl. Svc. award, Girl Scout Coun. Nations Capitol, 1994, Superior award, Young and Adult Missionary Soc., 1996. Mem.: East No. Ark. Annual Conf. of the 12th Episcopal Dist. (Sec. 2002—).

CASH, ROSANNE, singer, songwriter; b. May 1955; d. John R. Cash and Vivian (Liberto) Distin; m. Rodnay J. Crowell, Apr. 7, 1979 (div. 1992); children: Caitlin Rivers, Chelsea Jane, Carrie Kathleen; m. John Leventhal, Apr. 30, 1995; 1 child: Jakob William. Student, Vol. State C.C., 1974, Vanderbilt U., 1976, Lee Strasberg Theatre Inst., 1977. Rec. artist Ariola Records, Europe, 1978-84, CBS Records, worldwide, 1979—95; chair Earth Comm. Office, 1989—91; rec. artist Capitol Records, 1995—. Songwriter Blue Moon with Heartache, 1979, Seven Year Ache, 1980 (Gold Record award Rec. Industry Assn. Am. 1981), I Don't Know Why You Don't Want Me, 1984, (Grammy award 1985), Hold On (Robert J. Burton award 1987), others; Albums: Right Or Wrong, 1979, Seven Year Ache, 1980, Somewhere in the Stars, 1982, Rhythm & Romance, 1985, King's Record Shop, 1987, Hits 1979-89, 1989, Interiors, 1990, The Wheel, 1993, 10 Song Demo, 1996, Retrospective, 1997, What Kinda Girl Live, 1999, Rules of Travel, 2003, Black Cadillac, 2006; composer (films) Mariners & Musicians, 2006. Bd. advisors Nashvillians for Nuclear Arms Freeze, 1987-90; mem. PAX, 2001-. Mem. AFTRA, Nat. Acad. Rec. Arts and Scis. (Grammy award 1985), Am. Fedn. Musicians, Screen Actors Guild, Broadcast Music, Inc. (Spl. Achievement awards), Nashville Songwriters Assn. Internat., Pen Am. Democrat. Mailing: c/o Danny Kahn Cross Road Mgmt 45 West 11th St Ste 7B New York NY 10011

CASH, STEFANIE LYNN, music educator, director; b. Ironton, Ohio, Mar. 10, 1973; d. Robert Elmer and Linda Lee Kersey; m. Courtney Sean Cash, Sept. 28, 2002. MusB in Edn., Morehead State U., Ky., 1995; MusM, U. Ky., Lexington, 2002. Choral dir. Conkright Mid. Sch., Winchester, Ky., 1996—99, North Cobb HS, Kennesaw, Ga., 2002—. Performer Atlanta Symphony Chorus, 2006—. Mem.: Music Educators Nat. Conf., Am. Choral Dirs. Assn. Baptist. Office: North Cobb HS 3400 Hwy 293 North Kennesaw GA 30101

CASH, SUSAN W., career planning administrator; d. Blanche Watts; m. Troy Cash, Apr. 6, 1996; children: Hunter, Mackenzie. BS in Psychol. and Spl. Edn., James Madison U., Harrisonburg, Va., 1993; MEd in Sch. Counseling, Lynchburg Coll., Va., 2001. Tchr. sped Fairfax County Schs., Centerville, Va., 1993—94; tchr. sped-ld/ed Amherst County Schs., Amherst, 1994—2001; career counselor Lynchburg City Schs., 2001—. Recipient Creating Excellence award, Va. Dept. Edn., 2006. Mem.: Va. Career Counselor Assn., Va. Counselor Assn., Optimist Club. Office: Heritage High School 3020 Wards Fery Rd Lynchburg VA 24502 Office Phone: 434-582-1147. Business E-Mail: cashsw@lcsedu.net.

CASH, SWIN (SWINTAYLA MARIE CASH), professional basketball player; b. McKeesport, Pa., Sept. 22, 1979; d. Kevin Menifee (Stepfather) and Cynthia Cash. Grad., U. Conn., 2002. Basketball player McKeesport High Sch., McKeesport, Pa., U. Conn., 1998—2002; basketball player, forward Detroit Shock, WNBA, 2002—; founder Swin Cash LLC. Mem. USA Basketball Women's Senior Nat. Team, 2004. Named Parade Magazine, USA Today and Street & Smith All-Am. first team, 1998, Gatorade Pa. Player of the Yr., 1998, Kodak/WBCA All-District I, 2002, Final Four Most Outstanding Player, 2002; named to All-Big East third team, 2000, All-Big East second team, 2001, All-Big East first team, 2002, AP All-American second team, 2001, Kodak/WBCA & US Basketball Writers Assn. All-Am. first team, 2002, WNBA All-Star Team, 2003, all-WNBA second team, 2003. Achievements include mem. NCAA Divsn. 1 Nat. Championship Team, U. Conn., 2000, 2002; mem. WNBA Championship Team, Detroit Shock, 2003; mem. US Women's Basketball Team, Athens Olympic Games, 2004. Office: USA Basketball 5465 Mark Dabling Blvd Colorado Springs CO 80918-3842

CASHIN, MAURA DENNEHY, psychologist, music educator; b. Chester, N.Y., Mar. 15, 1974; d. Edward James Dennehy and Mary Elizabeth Brady; m. Brian Terence Cashin, Aug. 18, 2000; 1 child, Maeve. BA, Boston Coll., 1996; MEd, Columbia U., 2000. Cert. sch. psychologist N.Y., 2003. Pvt. practice tchr. piano, NY, 1992—; tchr. Princeton Rev., Westchester, NY, 1998—2000; psychologist North Mermek (N.Y.) Union Free Schs., 2000—. Mem.: Nat. Assn. Sch. Psychologists, Mensa. Roman Cath. Home: 11 Bluebell Ct Garden City NY 11530-1710

CASHION, ANN, food service executive; b. Jackson, Miss. B, Harvard U., 1976; postgrad., Stanford U., 1976—78. With Oh-la-la!, San Francisco, 1982; chef Restaurant Nora, Washington, Dakota; head chef Austin Grill, Washington, 1988; exec. chef Jaleo, Washington, 1993—95; chef, owner Cashion's Eat Pl., Washington, 1995—; ptnr. Johnny's Half Shell, 1999—. Named Chef of Yr., Restaurant Assn. Met. Washington, 1997, Am. Express Best Chef Mid-Atlantic, James Beard Found., 2004. Mem.: So. Foodnays Alliance. Office: Cahions Eat Pl 1819 Columbia Rd NW Washington DC 20009-2005 Office Phone: 202-797-1819.

CASHMAN, BEVERLY J., music educator; b. Winona, Minn., Jan. 8, 1952; d. Hugh R. Shaw and Mary E. Norton; children: Brianna, Kelsey, Michael, Deven, Maeve. BA in Music Edn., Coll. St. Teresa, 1974. Tchr. vocal Marian St. Mary's, Owatonna, Minn., 1974—75, Bethlehem Acad., Faribault, Minn., 1975—79; tchr. choir Owatonna (Minn.) Pub. Schs., 1982—83; tchr. vocal music St. Mary's Sch., Owatonna, 1986—98, Medford (Minn.) Pub. Sch., 1998—. Pres. Edn. Minn., Medford, 2005—; artistic dir. annual musicals Medford (Minn.) H.S. Actor: Little Theater Owatonna. Pres. Owatonna (Minn.) Human Rights Commn., 2000—; bd. dirs. Steele County Food Shelf, Owatonna, 1996—2000. Recipient Woman of Achievement award, Bus. and Profl. Women, 2000; grantee, Blandin Found., 1998. Mem.: Music Educators Nat. Conf., Am. Choral Dirs. Assn. Avocations: walking, reading. Home: 628 E Academy St Owatonna MN 55060 Office: Medford Pub Sch 750 2nd Ave SE Medford MN 55049

CASHMAN, SUZANNE BOYER, health services administrator, educator; b. Phila., Apr. 14, 1947; d. Vincent Saul and Ethel (Wolf) Boyer; m. Daniel Cashman, Jan. 16, 1971; children: Adam, Rebecca, David. BA, Tufts U., 1969; MS, Cornell U., 1973; ScD, Harvard U., 1980. Sr. analyst Urban Sys. Rsch., Cambridge, Mass., 1979-82; cons. Mass. Dept. Pub. Health, Boston, 1982-83; spl. asst. to v.p. Brigham and Women's Hosp., Boston, 1983-85; assoc. dir. rsch. Boston U. Office Spl. Projects, 1985-89; asst. prof. Boston U. Sch. Pub. Health, 1985-96; evaluator Cmty. Oriented Primary Care, Boston, 1989-91; assoc. dir. Ctr. for Cmty. Responsive Care, Boston, 1991-97; pub. health cons. U. Mass. Med. Ctr., Worcester, 1998; assoc. prof. dept. family medicine, cmty. health, dir. cmty. health Med. Sch. U. Mass., Worcester, 1999—, asst. dir. preventive medicine residency, 1999—. Cons. Acad. Health Ctrs., Derby, Conn., Columbia, SC, Atlanta, Balt., 1995—97; conf. planner New. Eng. Rural Health Roundtable. Co-editor: Community Oriented Primary Care, 1998; contbr. articles to profl. jours. Mem. leadership tng. program., sec. alumni orgn. com. NCCJ, Boston, 1995—2002; sec. bd. exec. com., conf. planner Cmty.-Campus Partnerships for Health and New England Rural Health Roundtable; task force Healthy People 2010 Curriculum; leadership support team Common Pathways; bd. dirs. Cmty. Ptnrs., Inc. Mem. APHA, Assn. for Prevention Tchg. and Rsch. (conf. planner, bd. dirs., exec. com.), Mass. Pub. Health Assn. Avocations: ballet dancing, sewing, cooking, jogging, gardening. Home: 17 Calvin Rd Newtonville MA 02460-2104 Office: U Mass Med Ctr Dept Family Medicine 55 Lake Ave N Worcester MA 01655-0002 Office Phone: 508-856-2930. Business E-Mail: suzanne.cashman@umassmed.edu.

CASIANO, KIMBERLY, publishing executive; b. NY; m. Juan Woodroffe; children: Natalia, Juan Antonio. BA in politics and Latin Am. studies, Princeton U.; MBA, Harvard. Founded Caribbean Mktg. Overseas Corp., 1981—88; v.p. Casiano Comm., 1988—94, pres., CEO, 1994—. Bd. mem. Ford Motor Co., 2003—, mem. fin. bd. com., mem. nom. com., mem. corp. governance com., mem. environ. and pub. policy com. Mem. Access Am. Com. US C. of C.; bd. trustees Hispanic Coll. Fund; mem. bd. dirs. Young Pres. Orgn. (YPO) PR chpt., Mutual of Am. Named one of Elite Women, Hispanic Bus. mag., 2004. Achievements include apptd. to US Savings Bond Nat. Com. by US Treas. Sec. Office: Casiano Comm 1700 Ave Fernandez Juncos San Juan PR 00909-2938 Office Phone: 787-728-3000. Office Fax: 787-268-1216.

CASINI, JANE SLOAN, wholesale distribution executive; b. Richmond, Va., Sept. 22, 1947; d. James Turner and Jane Patrick (Coleman) Sloan; m. Mauro Casini (div.). Student, Villa Mercede, Florence, Italy. Owner, Richmond and Washington; retailer; leather salesman Florence. Bd. dirs. Va. Home for Boys, Richmond, 1991. Office: Jane Casini 5407 Lakeside Ave Richmond VA 23228

CASKEY, BETHANY ANNE, artist; b. San Diego, Dec. 29, 1950; d. Bruce and Phyllis Margarite (Forst) C.; m. Russell Austin Kness, Apr. 1, 1988 (div.); 1 child, Echo Caskey Kness. BA in Art, Graceland Coll., 1974. Studio artist, Albia, Iowa, 1977—; v.p., co-founder and performer Vintage Show Co., Albia, 1985—; internet provider, web page designer, 1997—. Founder CKNET, 1997—. Artist: (painting) Cottontail/Iowa Habitat Print, 1985; illustrator for Equine mags., 1990—; designer USET Endurance team logo; mng. editor Trail Blazer Mag.; contbr. articles to profl. jours. Mem. Am. Acad. Equine Art, Soc. Animal Artists. Avocations: competitive trail riding, photography, writing. Office: Caskey Gallery PO Box 263 Albia IA 52531-0263

CASKEY, CAROLINE T., lab administrator; b. 1967; m. Sam Goodner. BA, Duke U.; MBA, Rice U., Houston, 1993. V.p. Laboratories for Genetic Svcs.; founder, pres., CEO Identigene Corp., Houston, 1993—. Bd. dir. Tex. Lyceum. TV appearances Dateline NBC, NBC Nightly News, Today Show. Mem.: Young Entrepreneur's Orgn. Office: Identigene Corp 5615 Kirby Ste 800 Houston TX 77005*

CASON, MARILYNN JEAN, academic administrator, lawyer; b. Denver, May 18, 1943; d. Eugene Martin and Evelyn Lucille (Clark) C.; married. BA in Polit. Sci., Stanford U., 1965; JD, U. Mich., 1969; MBA, Roosevelt U., 1977. Bar: Colo. 1969, Ill. 1973. Assoc. Dawson, Nagel, Sherman & Howard, Denver, 1969-73; atty. Kraft, Inc., Glenview, Ill., 1973-75; corp. counsel Johnson Products Co., Inc., Chgo., 1975-86, v.p., 1977-86, mng. dir. Lagos, Nigeria, 1980-83, v.p. internat. Chgo., 1986-88; v.p., gen. counsel DeVry, Inc., Chgo., 1989-96, sr. v.p. gen. counsel, corp. sec., 1996—. Trustee Arthritis Found., Atlanta, 1993—96, Chgo. Symphony Orch., 1997—2003; bd. dirs. Ill. chpt. Arthritis Found., Chgo., 1979—, chmn., 1991—93; bd. dirs. Internat. House, Chgo., 1986—92, Interfaith House, Chgo., 1996—2002, Ill. Humanities Coun., Chgo., 1987—96, chmn., 1993—96; bd. dirs. Lit. for All of Us, 1997—, chmn., 2002—. Mem. ABA, Nat. Bar Assn., Cook County Bar Assn. (pres. cmty. law project 1986-88), Stanford Club (Chgo., pres. 1985-87). Office: DeVry Inc 1 Tower Ln Ste 1000 Oakbrook Terrace IL 60181-4663 Home: 2333 Central St Apt 405 Evanston IL 60201-1475 Office Phone: 630-574-1901. Business E-Mail: mcason@devry.com.

CASON, NICA VIRGINIA, nursing educator; b. Edna, Tex. 1 child, Cynthia Diane. Diploma, Lillie Jolly Sch. Nursing, 1965; BSN, U. Tex. Med. Br., Galveston, 1967; MSN, U. So. Miss., 1981. RN Miss. Pub. health nurse Miss. State Dept. Health, Pascagoula, 1978; nursing instr. Miss. Gulf Coast Community Coll.-Jackson County Campus, Gautier, 1981-84, chair ADN program, 1984—2004, ADN divsn. chair, 2004—. Col. USAFR, ret. Mem. NOADN, Nat. League Nursing, Sigma Theta Tau, Phi Kappa Phi.

CASPER, BERNADETTE MARIE, critical care nurse; b. Buffalo, Jan. 13, 1961; d. Frank David and Mary Ann (Zmozynski) C. BSN, D'Youville Coll., 1983, MS. Cert. BLS and ACLS instr./provider, critical care instr., N.Y. Staff/charge nurse, preceptor, clin. instr. faculty Millard Fillmore Hosp., Buffalo, 1983—. Bd. dirs. Villa Maria Acad., Buffalo. Mem. AACCN, AACN (legis. com. dist. 1), N.Y. Nurses Assn., Profl. Nurses Assn. (we. N.Y. dist. 1), Sigma Theta Tau (sec. Zeta Nu chpt.) Avocations: crafts, dance, reading, travel, sports. Home: 5121 William St Lancaster NY 14086-9465 Office: Millard Fillmore Hosp 3 Gates Cir Buffalo NY 14209-1194

CASPER, PEGGY WIEDMAN, court reporter; b. Kiowa, Kans., Aug. 31, 1927; d. Charles August Wiedman and Artie Acenith Burkey; children: Diana Lynette Doyle, Brenda Sue Petersen, Nancy Jane Powell. Grad., Clarendon Jr. Coll., Tex., 1945, Baylor U. Nursing Sch., 1946, Wichita Bus. Coll., 1947. Court reporter Probate and Juvenile Ct., Wichita, Kans., US Dist. Ct., Cape Girardeau, Mo., 1962—63, State Dist. Ct., Omaha, 1965—70, US Dist. Ct., 1970—95. Con. antique dolls We. Heritage Mus., Omaha; expert witness patent lawsuit, Newport Beach, Calif. Author: Fashionable Terri Lee Dolls, 1988, Terri Lee Identification and Price Guide, 2001; contbr. articles to profl. mags. Displayer antique dolls City Libr., Cape Girandeau, Mo., 1962; appraiser of antique dolls Durham We. Heritage Mus., Omaha, 2004. Cadet nurse Baylor Hosp., 1946. Mem.: PTA (pres. 1962), United Fedn. Doll Clubs. Republican. Methodist. Avocations: stamp collecting/philately, doll collecting. Home: 4401 South 153rd St Omaha NE 68137

CASPILLO, CAROL A., secondary school educator; b. Newark, Ohio, Dec. 12, 1945; d. Edmond L. and Hilda G. Bonham; m. Maurice F. Caspillo, June 18, 1972; children: Carrice N., Eric J. BS in Edn., Ohio State U., 1967; MA in Adminstrn. and Curriculum, Gonzaga, U., 1999. Cert. novice data modeling and SQL instr., Java instr. Oracle Internet Acad., Java Instructor Oracle Internet Acad., 2004, cert. internet and computing Certiport. Math. educator Lincoln Jr. HS, Newark, 1968—72, Kapa'a (Hawaii) HS, 1978—. Mem.: ASCD (assoc.), NEA (assoc.), Hawaii State Tchrs. Assn., Nat. Coun. Tchrs. Math. (assoc.), Phi Delta Kappa (assoc.). Avocations: exercise, reading. Home: PO Box 181 Kilauea HI 96754 Office: Kapa'a HS 4695 Mailihuna Rd Kapaa HI 96746 Office Phone: 808-821-4400. Home Fax: 808-826-6313. Business E-Mail: ccaspill@notes.k12.hi.us. E-mail: ccaspillo@hawaiiantel.net.

CASS, MARY LOUISE, librarian; b. Jersey City, May 27, 1956; d. Eugene Louis and Catherine (Reynolds) Cass; m. Edward John Skillin, Dec. 2, 2000. BA History, Rutgers U., 1978, MLS, 1979. Cataloguer Fairleigh Dickinson U., Madison, NJ, 1979—81; mgr. Montclair Pub. Libr., NJ, 1982—96, br. dir., 1996—2005, acting dir., 2006—. Bibliographer (book) Suicide, 1991. Treas. Upper Mountain Gardens Bd., Montclair, 1998-2003. Mem. ALA (pres. cmty. info. sect. 1991-92). Democrat. Roman Catholic. Home: 29 Upper Mountain Ave Montclair NJ 07042-1919 Office: Montclair Pub Libr 50 S Fullerton Ave Montclair NJ 07042 Office Phone: 973-744-0500. Business E-Mail: mlskillin@montlib.org.

CASSEL, CHRISTINE KAREN, physician; b. Mpls., Sept. 14, 1945; d. Charles Moore and Virginia Julia (Anderson) Cassel. BA, U. Chgo., 1967; MD, U. Mass., 1979. Diplomate Am. Bd. Internal Medicine (chmn. 1998-99). Intern, resident in internal medicine Children's Hosp., San Francisco, 1976—78; fellow in bioethics Inst. Health Policy Studies, U. Calif., San Francisco, 1978—79; fellow geriatrics Portland (Oreg.) VA Hosp., 1979—81; asst. prof. medicine and public health U. Oreg. Health Scis. U., 1981—83; asst. prof. geriatrics and medicine Mt. Sinai Med. Ctr., N.Y.C., 1983—84; prof. medicine, prof. pub. policy U. Chgo., 1989—95, chief gen. internal medicine, 1985—95; chmn. and prof. geriatrics and medicine Mt. Sinai, 1995—2002; dean sch. of medicine Oreg. Heatlh and Sci. U., 2002—03; pres., CEO Am. Bd. Internal Medicine and ABIM Found., 2003—. Adj. prof. medicine U. Pa., 2004—. Author: Ethical Dimensions in the Health Professions, 1981, 2nd edit., 1993, Geriatric Medicine: Principles and Practice, 1984, 4th edit., 2003, Nuclear Weapons and Nuclear War: A Sourcebook for Health Professionals, 1984, Geriatric Medicine, A Practical Guide to Aging, 1997, Medicine Matters: What Geriatric Medicine Can Teach American Health Care, 2005. Bd. dirs. Greenwall Found., 1999—2004, chmn., 1999—2004. Henry J. Kaiser Family Found. faculty scholar, 1982—85, Hastings Ctr. fellow. Master: ACP (regent 1989—98, pres. 1996—97); fellow: Am. Geriatrics Soc.; mem.: Am. Soc. Law and Medicine (bd. dirs. 1988—94), Soc. Health and Human Values (pres. 1986), Physicians for Social Responsibility (dir. 1983—86, pres. 1988—89), Inst. of Medicine (coun. 2002—). Office: Am Bd Internal Medicine Ste 1700 510 Walnut St Philadelphia PA 19106-3699 Business E-Mail: ccassel@abim.org.

CASSELL, KAY ANN, librarian; b. Van Wert, Ohio, Sept. 24, 1941; d. Kenneth Miller and Pauline (Zimmerman) C. BA, Carnegie-Mellon U., 1963; M.L.S., Rutgers U., 1965; MA, Bklyn. Coll., 1969. Reference librarian Bklyn. Coll. Library, 1965-68; adult svcs. cons. NJ State Libr., Trenton, 1968-71; libr. cons.-vol. Peace Corps, Rabat, Morocco, 1971-73; adult svcs. cons. Westchester Libr. System, White Plains, NY, 1973-75; dir. Bethlehem Pub. Libr., Delmar, NY, 1975-81, Huntington (N.Y.) Pub. Libr., 1982-85; exec. dir. Coordinating Coun. Lit. Mags., NYC, 1985-87; univ. libr. New Sch. Social Rsch., 1987-88; assoc. dir. collections and svcs. br. librs. NY Pub. Libr., 1989—2006; asst. prof. Sch. Communication, Info., and Libr. Studies, Rutgers U., 2006—. Adj. faculty Grad. Sch. Libr. Sci., SUNY, Albany, 1976-78, Palmer Sch. Libr. and Info. Scis., L.I. U., 1986-90, Grad. Sch. Info. and Libr. Sci., Pratt Inst., 1994—; chmn. cmty. adv. com. Capital Dist. Humanities Program, Albany, 1980-81; bd. dirs. Literacy Vols. of Suffolk, Bellport, N.Y., 1981-85; chmn. N.Y.C. Sch. Libr. Sys. Coun., 1991-94; treas. Libr. Pub. Rels. Coun., 1993-98, pres., 1999-2000. Mem. ALA (pres. reference and adult svcs. divsn. 1983-84, chair membership com. 1991-95, coun. 1992—, chair pub. com. 1999-01, chair human resources com., 2003-04), Freedom to Read Found., NY Libr. Assn. (pres. reference and adult svcs. sect. 1975-76), Feminist Press (bd. dirs.), Beta Phi Mu.

CASSELLE, CORENE, elementary school educator; b. Chgo., Jan. 26, 1943; d. Lawrence Edward Walker and Dorothy Monterie Sims; married; children: Lawrence Walter Kwakou, Anika Fani Foreman, Omowale Khalfani, Adjovi Abeeku Austin. BS, No. Ill. U., 1964; MEd, U. Ill., Urbana-Champaign, 1970; EdD, U. Nev., Las Vegas, 1977. Cert. std. spl. tchr./reading Ill., gen. adminstrn./supervision Ill. Reading specialist, adminstr. Sch. Dist. #299, Chgo., 1992—. Curator BENIZRT, Justice, Ill., 1986—. Author: Country of the Black People. Achievements include invention of peppermill filler. Home: 8651 S 87th Ave Ste 201 Justice IL 60458-2020 Office Phone: 708-475-0200. E-mail: ccasselle@yahoo.com.

CASSENS, SUSAN FORGET, artist; b. Ft. Pierce, Fla., May 11, 1956; m. Steven Dale Cassens, Mar. 4, 1979; children: Christopher, Michael, Scott. AA, U. Fla., 1976; BA in Edn. with honors, Fla. Atlantic U., 1978. Tchr. Garden City Elem., Ft. Pierce, 1978-79; owner Brush Strokes Art Gallery, Ft. Pierce, 1993-95; co-owner Indian River Crafters Guild, Ft. Pierce, 1995; pub., mfr. Somerset Greetings USA, 1998. Bd. mem. St. Lucie County Cultural Affairs Coun., Ft. Pierce, 1993-97, chmn., 1996-97. Cover artist: Cracker Cuisine, 1993; exhbns. include A.E. Backus Gallery and Mus., Ft. Pierce, Treasure Coast Art Gallery, Ft. Pierce. Chpt. sec. P.E.O. chpt. R., Ft. Pierce, 1987, chpt. pres., 1989; bd. dir. A.E. Backus Art Gallery and Mus., Mainstreet (Ft. Pierce) Inc., St. Lucie Hist. Soc.; chair St. Lucie Mural Soc., Ft. Pierce, 1994. Mem. Nat. Mus. Women in Arts (charter), Heathcote Bot. Gardens (charter), Nat. Mus. Am. Indians, Nat. Trust Hist. Preservation. Presbyterian. Avocations: antiques, travel, art. Office: PO Box 593 Fort Pierce FL 34954-0593 Business E-Mail: susieart@aol.com.

CASSIDAY, KAREN LYNN, psychologist; b. Salina, Kans., Mar. 18, 1960; d. Donald Marion and Rosalie Jean (Yeoman) Cassiday; m. John Edward Calamari, May 26, 1989. BA, Wheaton Coll., 1982; PhD, Chgo. Med. Sch., 1990. Staff psychotherapist The Anxiety Clinic, Chgo., 1990-91; instr. dept. clin. psychology Chgo. Med. Sch., North Chicago, Ill., 1991—; program dir. Behavior Med, Inc., Lake Bluff, Ill., 1991-92; co-dir. Cognitive Behavioral Treatment Ctr., Arlington Heights, Ill., 1992-95; dir., owner Anxiety and Agoraphobia Treatment Ctr., Kenosha, Wis., 1995—. Cons. Deborah's Pl., Chgo., 1987—88; clin. asst/ prof. Rosalind Franklin U., 1992—; clin. instr. Rush Med. Sch., 1995—. Contbr. articles to profl. jours.; author various manuals. Chair scientific adv. bd. Obsessive Compulsive Found., Chgo., 1992—; bd. mem. clin. adv. bd. Anxiety Disorders Assn. Am., 2006—. Mem. Psi Chi. Episcopalian. Avocations: cross country skiing, bicycling, running, white water canoeing. Home: 9810 14th St Kenosha WI 53144-7771 Office: Anxiety & Agoraphobia Treatment Ctr 10400 75th St # 311 Kenosha WI 53142-7884

CASSIDY, CINDY JANE, secondary school educator; b. Putnam, Conn., Dec. 28, 1972; d. John Allen and Susan Jane Cochran; m. Christopher Michael Cassidy, July 4, 2002; children: Kiera Erin McCarthy, Katherine Mae. BS, Ea. Conn. State U., Willimantic, 1994; MEd, Sacred Heart U., Fairfield, Conn., 1995. Edn. specialist NE Utilities, Waterford, Conn., 1996—99; sch. to career coord. Waterford Pub. Schs., 1999—2002; social studies tchr. Stonington Bd. Edn., Pawcatuck, Conn., 2002—. Democrat. Home: 1501 Rt 85 Oakdale CT 06370 Office: Stonington Bd Edn North Stonington Rd Old Mystic CT 06372

CASSIDY, DOROTHY ANN, special education educator; b. Burke County, N.C., July 1, 1947; d. Roscoe and Mary Etta Junie Pruitt; m. Kenneth Howard Cassidy, Dec. 21, 1970 (div. Dec. 1981); 1 child, Kenneth Wayne. BA in Polit. Sci., U.N.C., 1970; MEd in Spl. Edn., U. Va., 1982; postgrad., U.S.C., 1986—. Homebound tchr. Pittsylvania County Schs., Chatham, Va., 1975-79, learning disabilities, resource tchr., 1979-82; county resource tchr. Brunswick County Schs., Southport, N.C., 1982-85; tchr. learning disabilities and visually impaired Horry County Schs., Conway, S.C., 1985—, self-contained exptl. tchr., 1994-99, h.s. tutorial resource tchr., 1999—2004; tchr. adult edn., spl. edn., 2004—. Spkr. in field on ADHD and ADD; seminar presenter. Recipient awards tchr. incentive program S.C. Bd. Edn., 1988-90; scholar Rotary Club, Myrtle Beach, S.C., 1991. Mem. NEA, Internat. Ctr. for the

Study of Psychiatry and Psychology, S.C. Edn. Assn., Horry county Edn. Assn., Meher Spiritual Ctr. Independent. Methodist. Avocations: reading, spiritual books, fitness. Home: 2406 Bert Dr North Myrtle Beach SC 29582-4322 Office Phone: 843-272-3432. E-mail: dorothycas@aol.com.

CASSIDY, ESTHER CHRISTMAS, retired government official; b. Upper Marlboro, Md., Aug. 5, 1933; d. Donelson and Esther Christmas; divorced; children: William Keeling, Carroll Cassidy Drewyer, Daniel Clark. BA, Manhattanville Coll., 1955. Phys. scientist, R&D Nat. Bur. Standards, Gaithersburg, Md., 1955-73; sci. advisor U.S. Congressman Teno Roncalio, Washington, 1973-74; asst. dir. congl. affairs Energy R&D Adminstrn. Dept. Energy, Washington, 1974-78; dir. congl. and legis. affairs Nat. Inst. Stds. and Tech., Gaithersburg, 1978-98; ret., 1998. Contbr. articles to profl. jours. Mem. IEEE (sr.). Avocations: horse racing, golf.

CASSIDY, KATHERINE, energy executive; V.p., treas. Gen. Electric. Mem. bd. dir. Wilton Edn. Found. Office: Gen Electric 3135 Easton Tpk Fairfield CT 06828-0001 Office Phone: 203-373-2211. Office Fax: 203-373-3131.*

CASSIDY, SUKHINDER SINGH, information technology executive; Grad., U. Western Ontario. With British Sky Broadcasting, Merrill Lynch, NYC, London, Amazon.com, Junglee Corp.; co-founder, sr. v.p. bus. devel. Yodlee.com Inc., 1999—2003; v.p. Asia-Pacific and Latin America ops. Google Inc., Mountain View, Calif., 2003—. Bd. advisors Bus. Signatures. Office: Google Inc 1600 Amphitheatre Pkwy Mountain View CA 94043 Office Phone: 650-253-0000. Office Fax: 650-253-0001.*

CASSO, REBECCA LYNN, music educator; d. Richard Waldron and Dorothy Zhanel Brainerd; m. Carlos Gilberto Casso, Aug. 14, 1993; children: Michelle Elise, Daniel Ryan. MusB Edn., West Tex. State U., Canyon, 1981. Cert. All Level Music Educator Tex. State Bd. Edn., 1981, Tchr. Elem. Self-Contained Grades 1-8 Tex. State Bd. Edn., 1995. Dir. mid. sch. band Borger Mid. Sch., Tex., 1981—83; asst. dir. band Klein Intermediate Sch., Tex., 1983—84, head dir. band, 1984—90; asst. dir. band Randall H.S., Canyon, 1990—95; specialist elem. music Crestview Elem., Canyon, 1995—. Presenter fall tchr. acad. Canyon Ind. Sch. Dist., 2005—, mem. dist. tech. com., 2002—, mem. dist. grading com., 2002—04; mem. music ec-12 std. setting com. Nat. Evaluation Sys.; mem. music frameworks and item rev. com. Tex. State Bd. of Educator Certification, Austin, 2001—03; mem. ctr. for educator devel. in fine arts leadership team Tex. Edn. Agy., Fine Arts Divsn., Austin, 1998—2000; mentor student tchr. Coll. Edn., West Tex. A & M U., Canyon, 1997—. Symphonic musician Amarillo Symphony, Tex., 1990—2006, Amarillo Opera, 1997—2006, Chamber Music Amarillo, 1998—2006; orch. com. Amarillo Symphony, 2005—. Named Educator of Yr., Tex. Region 16 Svc. Ctr., 2004. Mem.: Tex. Music Educators Assn. (assoc.). Avocation: French horn. Home: 8000 Fouts Pl Amarillo TX 79121 Office: Crestview Elementary 80 Hunsley Rd Canyon TX 79015 Personal E-mail: 4casso@amaonline.com.

CASSON MADDEN, CHRIS, entrepreneur, interior designer; m. J. Kevin Madden; children: Patrick, Nick. Student, Fashion Inst. Tech. Founder, CEO Chris Madden Inc., Rye, NY, 1995—; photographer Sports Illustrated; with Random House, G.P. Putnam & Sons, Farrar, Straus & Giroux. Design expert Today Show, Good Morning Am., Oprah, CBS Sunday Morning, CNN; nat. spokesperson JC Penny Home Collection, 2003—. Author: The Complete Lemon, 1979, The Summer House Cookbook, 1979, Baby Hints Handbook, 1982, Baby's First Helpings: Super-Healthy Meals for Super-Healthy Kids, 1984, Kitchens: Information and Inspiration for Making the Kitchen the Heart of the Home, 1993, Bathrooms: Inspiring Ideas and Practical Solutions for Creating a Beautiful Bathroom, 1996, Chris Madden's Guide to Personalizing Your Home: Simple, Beautiful Ideas for Every Room, 1997, A Room of Her Own: Women's Personal Spaces, Clarkson Potter, 1997, Getaways: Carefree Retreats for All Seasons, 2000, Bedrooms: Creating the Stylish Comfortable Room of Your Dreams, 2001, Chris Casson Madden's New American Living Rooms, 2003; co-author: Interior Visions: Great American Designers and the Showcase House, 1988, Rooms With a View: Two Decades of Outstanding American Interior Design from the Kips Bay Decorator Show Houses, 1995, Interior Details: The Designers' Style, 1996; columnist: Interiors by Design; host (TV series) Interiors By Design, HGTV, 1995—.

CASSULLO, JOANNE LEONHARDT, foundation administrator; b. Glen Cove, NY, Dec. 2, 1955; d. John Louis and Dorothea Louise (Leonhardt) C. BA in English, Elementary Ed., & Fine Arts, Roanoke Coll., Salem, Va., 1978; MFA, So. Meth. U., 1982. Cert. tchr. elem. edn., Va. Dir. counseling and edn. PCI, Inc., Ft. Worth, 1978-80; gallery asst. Washburn Gallery, Inc., NYC, 1983-86; pres. Dorothea L. Leonhardt Found., NYC, 1988—. Contbr. articles to profl. jours. Trustee Whitney Mus. Am. Art, NYC, 1985—, v.p.; bd. dirs. Phoenix House Found., Inc., NYC, 1982—, Bklyn. Acad. Music, 1989—, Children of Alcoholics Found., NYC, 1990—, RxART, Children's Advocacy Ctr. of Manhattan, Housing Enterprises for Less Privileged (HELP USA). Helena Rubinstein fellow in Mus. Studies, Whitney Mus. Am. Art, 1982-83. Mailing: c/o Whitney Mus Am Art 945 Madison Ave New York NY 10021

CAST, ANITA HURSH, small business owner; b. Columbus, Ohio, July 11, 1939; d. Charles Walter and Hulda Marie (Ramsey) Hursh; m. William R. Cast, Apr. 1, 1961; children: Jennifer, Carter, Meghan. BA, DePauw U., 1961. Ptnr. Cast Hursh and Assocs., Ft. Wayne, Ind., 1982—; pianist Words and Music, Ft. Wayne, 1983—; owner Anita Cast's Wearable Art, Ft. Wayne, 1986—. Bd. dirs. Fort Wayne Philharm., Indpls. Internat. Violin Competition; past pres. Ind. U. Friends of Music, Ind. Endowment for the Arts; mem. adv. bd. Leadership Ft. Wayne; mem. nat. adv. bd. IV Jacobs Sch. Music. Author: (arts chpt.) New History of Fort Wayne, New History of Fort Wayne/Allen County. Advisory bd., pres. Am. Symphony Orch. League, vol., v.p., 1985—86; commr. Ind. Gov.'s Mansion Commn., 1987, Ind. Arts Commn., 1979—87; bd. dirs. Ft. Wayne Philharm., pres., 1977—79; mem. Mayor's Bicentennial Exec. Bd., 1989—94, Ind. Cultural Congress Hon. Com.; active Ft. Wayne's Celebrate 2000 Com.; bd. dirs. WBNI Nat. Pub. Radio, Ft. Wayne; chmn. bd. dirs. Fine Arts Found., Ft. Wayne, 1988; pres. bd. dirs. Ind. Endowment Arts; chmn. bd. dirs. Arts United Greater Ft. Wayne, 1988—90; bd. dirs. Arts United; pres., bd. dirs. Ind. U. Friends Music, 1995—97, past pres. exec. com.; v.p. adv. bd. Leadership Ft. Wayne; pres. Met. YMCA, Ft. Wayne, 1986—; bd. mem. Internat. Violin Competition, Ind. Named Miss Ind.; recipient Sagamore of the Wabash awards (2); Lily Endowment Leadership fellow. Mem.: Quest Club (pres.), Duodecimo Club (hon.). Republican. Episcopalian. Avocations: music, cooking, golf, hiking, reading. Home and Office: Anita Cast Wearable Art 4401 Taylor St Fort Wayne IN 46804-1913 Personal E-mail: anitatune@yahoo.com.

CASTAGNA, VANESSA J., retail executive; b. Muncie, Ind., 1949; m. Neil Castagna. BS in psychology and speech comm., Purdue U., 1971. With Lazarus most recently as sr. v.p. and gen. mgr., 1972—85; v.p. merchandising - women's Target Stores, 1985—92; sr. v.p., gen. merchandising mgr. - women's and jr.'s Marshall's Stores, Mass., 1992—94; sr. v.p., gen. mdse. mgr. - home decor, furniture, crafts, children's apparel Wal-Mart Stores, Bentonville, Ark., 1994—96, sr. v.p., gen. mdse. mgr. - women's and children's accessories and apparel, 1996—99; exec. v.p. J.C. Penney Co., Inc., Plano, Tex., 1999—2004; COO JC Penney Stores, Merchandising, & Catalog, 1999—2001; pres., COO J.C. Penney Stores, Catalog, & Internet, 2001—03; chmn., CEO JC Penney Stores, Catalog, & Internet, 2003—04; chmn. Mervyns, 2005—; with Cerberus Capital Management LP, 2005—. Chair Women's Leadership Coun. United Way of Met. Dallas; bd. dirs. JC Penney Afterschool Fund, Nat. Minority Supplier Devel. Coun., Cox Sch. Bus. So. Methodist U. Named one of most powerful women, Forbes mag., 2001—05; recipient AMY award, Young Menswear Assn., 2006. Office: Cerberus Capital Mgmt 299 Park Ave New York NY 10171*

CASTEEL, CAMILLE, school system administrator; EdD, Nova Southeastern U. Fischler Grad. Sch. of Edn. and Human Svcs., 1991. 1st grade tchr. to supt. Chandler (Ariz.) Unified Sch. Dist., 1971—91, supt., 1991—. Named Ariz. Nat. Supt. of Yr., 2002; recipient Excellence award, Ariz. Sch. Pub. Rels. Assn., Achievement award, Ariz. Year Round Edn. Assn. Office: Chandler Unified Sch Dist 1525 W Frey Rd Chandler AZ 85224

CASTEEL, DIANN BROWN, education educator; b. Greeneville, Tenn., Dec. 16, 1953; d. Harold James Brown and Clara Ruth (Phillips) Johnston; m. Everette Kenneth Casteel, Oct. 7, 1972; children: Trisha DiAnn, Mary Camille, Cheyenne James. BS, East Tenn. State U., 1973, MA, 1976, EdD, 1994. Cert. tchr., Tenn. Tchr. Greene County Bd. Edn., Greeneville, 1973-90; dir. Project Choice, Greeneville-Greene County Ctr. for Tech., 1990-91; tchr. Doak Sch., Tusculum Sta., Tenn., 1992-2000; asst. prin. Chuckey (Tenn.) Elem. Sch., Greene County Bd. Edn., 2001—03, Mohawk, Tenn., 2000—01; asst. prof. edn. Tusculum Coll., 2004—; asst. prin. Doak Elem. Sch., Greeneville, 2003—04; ret., 2004. Founder Iowa-Tenn. Student Exch. Program, Dayton and Greeneville, 1986—87; asst. prof. edn. Tusculum Coll., Greenville, Guidance and Assessment for Single Parent/Displaced Homemaker Program, 1989—90. Founder Hay Relief Program, Tenn., 1986-87; leader 4-H Club, Baileyton Elem. Sch., 1985-88; mem. Ottway United Meth. Ch., Greenville, 1985-92; v.p. Ottway United Meth. Women, Greeneville, pres., 1976; mem. women's group study exch. to India, Rotary Internat., 1989; mem. 1st Christian Ch., Greenville, Tenn., 1992—. Recipient Horse of Yr. award Appalachian Horse Show Assn., 1967, Outstanding Citizen award Ruritan Nat., 1986, 4-H Emerald Club Leader award, 1987, DIANA award Epsilon Sigma Alpha, 1990, Book of Golden Deeds award Greeneville (Tenn.) Exchange Club, 1992. Mem. NEA, Greene County Edn. Assn., East Tenn. Edn. Assn., Tenn. Edn. Assn., Internat. Platform Assn., U.S.S. Greenville, Inc., Andrew Johnson Women's Club, Kappa Delta Pi, Phi Delta Kappa. Republican. Avocations: cooking, reading, swimming. Home: 2545 Flatwoods Rd Greeneville TN 37745-8582 Office: Tusculum Coll 60 Shiloh Rd Greeneville TN 37743 Office Phone: 423-636-7300 ext. 5126. Business E-Mail: dcasteel@tusculum.edu.

CASTELEIRO DE GOIZUETA, OLGA See GOIZUETA, OLGA

CASTELGRANT, ELIZABETH ANN SAYLOR, physical education educator, consultant; b. Neshanic Station, N.J., Jan. 9, 1951; d. Clement Joseph and Dorothy Ann (Wargo) Saylor; m. Daniel Peter Castelgrant, Apr. 20, 1991. BS, East Stroudsburg U., 1972. Phys. edn. tchr. West Amwell Sch., Lambertville, N.J., 1972-87, Lebanon (N.J.) Borough Sch., 1978-88, Flemington (N.J.) Raritan Schs., 1987—. Steering com. Juvenile Task Force, Flemington, 1980-83; mem. task force Sch. Health and Edn. Resource Ctr., Flemington, 1983-85; cons. North Hunterdon In-Svc. Day, Clinton, N.J., 1983; mem. EIC Tchr. Adv. Bd., Morristown, 1983-86; training cons. N.J. Edn. Assn., 1993—; in-svc. cons. Hunterdan County, 1999. Editor: Hunterdon County Edn. Assn. Bulletin, 1976-97. Publicity chair Hunterdon County Spl. Olympics, 1973-77; chair Camp Isabel Internat. Food Festival, Flemington, 1979, Tchrs. to Re-elect Meyner, Florio, McConnel, Foran, Weidel, 1976-90, South County Sr. Citizen's Program, Hunterdon County, 1978-82; vol. LVW, Hunterdon County, 1980-85, local bicentennial com., Lambertville, 1976, Deborah Hosp. Fund Drive, Flemington, 1984-86, Big Bros./Sisters, Flemington, 1983-86; mem. Flemington Tenants' Orgn., 1984-86, Hunterdon/Somerset Bus. and Edn. Partnership Adv. Coun., 1990—, Hunterdon County Dental Health Commn., 1989—, chair, 1995—; steering com. Hunterdon County Staff Devel. Coop., 1996—, paradigm pioneer com., 1993—; decision making com. Flemington Raritan Participatory, 1996—. Mem. AAUW, NEA, AAHPERD, N.J. Edn. Assn. (mem.'s rights com. 1972—, chair 1975—, chair Be Heard Campaign, 1980, mem. fair play com. 1983—, del. assembly 1978-83, 90-92, 98—), Hunterdon County Edn. Assn. (pres. 1978-82, 90-92, v.p. 1992—), Flemington-Raritan Edn. Assn. (v.p.-at-large 1987—, shared decision making com. 1993—), Hunterdon-Somerset County Bus. and Edn. Partnership (adv. bd., steering com. 2001/SCANS project 1991-97), Delta Kappa Gamma (1st v.p. Rho chpt.), Alpha Omicron Pi. Avocations: helping others, reading, quiet times. Home: 223 Longview Rd Bridgewater NJ 08807-2091 Office: Desmares Sch 16 Old Clinton Rd Flemington NJ 08822-5700 also: Njea 27 Minneakoning Rd Flemington NJ 08822-5726

CASTELLANO, CHRISTINE MARIE, lawyer; b. Jacksonville, Fla., Jan. 10, 1966; d. James Todd and Constance Marie (Wallis) Drylie; m. Ralph Castellano, Sept. 15, 1997. BA summa cum laude, U. Colo., 1987; JD cum laude, U. Mich., 1990. Bar: Colo. 1990, Ill. 1991, U.S. Dist. Ct. Colo. 1991, U.S. Dist. Ct. (no. dist.) Ill. 1991, U.S. Dist. Ct. (ctrl. dist.) Ill. 1994, U.S. Ct. Appeals (10th cir.) 1991, U.S. Ct. Appeals (7th cir.) 1993, U.S. Supreme Ct. 1995. Clk. to chief judge Sherman G. Finesilver U.S. Dist. Ct. Colo., Denver, 1990-91; income ptnr. McDermott, Will & Emery, Chgo., 1991-96; ops. atty. Corn Products divsn. of CPC Internat. Inc., Summit-Argo, Ill., 1996-97; atty. Corn Products Internat., Inc., 1998—2002, counsel, U.S. and Can., 2002—04, assoc. gen. internat. counsel, 2004—. Adminstr. Family Law Project, Ann Arbor, Mich., 1988-91; judge Julius H. Miner Moot Ct., Northwestern U. Sch. Law, 1993-95, Northwestern U. Sch. Law Negotiation Competition, 1992-94. Writer newspaper The Res Gestae, 1987-90; editor yearbook The Quadrangle, 1988-90; contbg. editor Jour. of Law Reform, 1988-90. Vol. Lincoln Park Homeless Shelter, Chgo., 1991-92, Chgo. Cares, 1993-96; co. coord. Youth Motivation Program, 1991-96. Recipient Negligence Sect. award Mich. Bar Assn., 1990; Carl B. Gussin Meml. prize U. Mich., 1991; scholar Elk's, 1983-84, faculty U. Colo., 1983-84; U. Colo. grantee, 1987. Mem. ABA, Colo. Bar Assn., Ill. Bar Assn., Denver Bar Assn. (vol. teen ct. 1991), Chgo. Bar Assn., Chgo. Coun. Laywers, Women Law Students Assn., U. Colo. Alumni Assn., U. Mich. Alumni Assn., Moot Ct., Mortar Bd., Phi Beta Kappa, Pi Sigma Alpha. Avocations: photography, ice skating, camping, hiking. Office: Corn Products Internat 5 Westbrook Corporate Ctr Westchester IL 60154

CASTELLANO, JOSEPHINE MASSARO, medical records specialist; d. Ignazio and Maria Massaro Castellano. BS in Med. Tech., Fla. State U., 1952; tchrs. cert., U. Tampa, 1955; MA, Columbia U., 1961. Med. technologist St. Joseph's Hosp., Tampa, Fla., 1952—55; tchr. Hillsborough County Sch. Bd., Tampa, 1955—85; med. records specialist Robert Martinez, M.D., Tampa, 1985—95, David L. Castellano, DDS, Tampa, 1996—, Domenic M. Castellano, DDS, Tampa, 1996—. Mem.: AAUW (mem. adv. bd. 1999—2002), Christian Med. Found. (mem. adv. bd. 1996—2003), Kappa Delta Pi (mem. adv. bd. 2000—02). Roman Catholic. Avocations: reading, horseback riding, tennis, gardening, bowling. Home: 305 N Hesperides St Tampa FL 33609-2020 Office: David L and Domenic M Castellano DDS 8365 W Hillsborough Ave Tampa FL 33615-3899

CASTELLANOS, JOSEPHINE FALCON, insurance agent, composer; b. Havana, Cuba, 1933; arrived in U.S., 1962; d. Manuel Falcon and Rita Maria dela Portilla; m. Hector Manuel Castellanos, Apr. 9, 1955 (dec. 2002); 1 child, Josefina. Degree, Ins. Sch., Miami, Fla.; student, Normal Sch. Kindergarten Tchrs., Havana, Cuba. Tchr. kindergarten, Havana, Cuba; customer rep. First Federal and Fin. Fed. Savings and Loan Assn., Miami; ins. agent Fortis Ins., Miami; freelance songwriter, composer Miami; with Hilltop Records, Hollywood, Calif. Songwriter Come Back to Me, 2005, Hazme Vibrar, 2005, Devuelve Mi Alma, 2006, songwriter, composer Certified Love Letter, 2006, Blue Mountain, 2006, Aun te Quiero, 2006, Mi Barca, 2006. Mem.: Third Order Discalced Carmelites. Republican. Roman Cath. Avocations: reading, knitting, country music, concerts, opera. Office Phone: 305-383-3174.

CASTELLINI, MARY MERCER, author; b. Portland, Oreg., Apr. 4, 1923; d. Reuben Howard and Alma Evangeline (Holmes) Mercer; m. Edgar Aldo Castellini, Aug. 25, 1946 (dec. Febr. 1983); children: Edgar M., Anita M. BA in Am. Civilization, Dominican Coll., 1974. Bot. rschr. at Herbarium Calif. Acad. Scis., San Francisco, 1984-87. Author: A Victorian Heritage in Old Cow Hollow, 1977, Herbarium Messages from California Flora, 1978, Herbarium: A Noetic Herbal Expedition, 1979; contbr.: An Anthology of American Women Writers, 1979; exhibitor, lectr., artist San Francisco Pub. Libr., 1977, Marin (Calif.) Pub. Libr./Marin Civic Ctr., 1977, Tiburon Pub. Libr., 1991, Golden Gate Theol. Sem., Mill Valley, Calif., 1992—. Den leader Boy Scouts Am., Stuart Hall Sch. for Boys, San Francisco, 1955-57; leader Girl Scouts U.S., Convent of the Sacred Heart, San Francisco, 1957-59; mem. Mothers' March on Polio, Polio Soc., San Francisco, 1955; freshman YWCA pres. U. Wash., Seattle, 1943; mem. chorus Emeritus Coll. of Marin. Named Outstanding Californian, Rare Books and Calif. History, The Bancroft Libr., U. Calif. Berkeley, 1993—. Mem. Ina Coolbrith Cir. (life), AAUW (Washington, life, Individual grant Ednl. Found. 1977-78, 78-79), Calif. Bot. Soc., Alpha Chi Omega. Avocations: writing, studying, vol. work, swimming, hiking. Home and Office: 212 Mountain View Dr Healdsburg CA 95448-4315

CASTELLON, CHRISTINE NEW, information systems specialist, real estate agent; b. Pittsfield, Mass., June 22, 1957; d. Edward Francis Jr. and Helen Patricia (Cordes) New; m. John Arthur Castellon, Oct. 1, 1988. BS in Elec. and Computer Engring., U. Mass., 1979; MBA, Northea. U., 1986. Engr. microwave radio system design New England Tel. Co., Framingham, Mass., 1979-82, mgr. minicomputer support group Dorchester, Mass., 1982-85; mgr. current sys. planning/network svcs. NYNEX Svc. Co., Boston, 1985-87; mem. tech. staff computing environs. Bellcore, Piscataway, N.J., 1987-90; assoc. dir. info. sys. provisioning NYNEX Telesector Resources Group, N.Y.C., 1990-93; sales assoc. Weidel Realtors, Flemington, N.J., 1994—. Spkr. Careers-In-Engring. program New England Tel., 1980-82. Leader 2nd violin sect. Ctrl. Jersey Symphony Orch., Raritan Valley C.C., N.J., 1988—; prin. 1st violinist New England Conservatory Extension Divsn., Boston, 1979-87; violinist Civic Symphony Orch., Boston, 1982-87; active coll./industry adv. com. U. Mass. Named Monument Mountain H.S. valedictorian, 1975; recipient Arion Music award Monument Mountain H.S., 1975, cert. Applied Music and Theory Pittsfield Cmty. Music Sch., 1975. Mem. N.E. U. MBA Alumni Assn. Roman Catholic. Home: 622 Old York Rd Neshanic Station NJ 08853-3600

CASTELLUCCIO, CHRISTIA MARIE, elementary school educator; b. Pitts., Nov. 9, 1975; d. Prospero and Debra Carol Castelluccio. BS in elem. edn., Edinboro U., Pa., 2000. Cert. elem. tchr. Pa., 2000. Elem. tchr., 2000—06. Mem.: Zeta Tau Alpha. Democrat. Roman Catholic. Home: 1209 Kenzie Dr Pittsburgh PA 15205

CASTILLO, CARMEN, staffing company executive; b. Mallorca, Spain; Founder, pres., CEO Superior Design Internat., 1992—. Bd. mem. Fla. Regional Minority Bus. Coun. Named Minority Supplier Yr. (for Superior Design Internat.), Nat. Minority Supplier Devel. Coun. (NMSDC), 2002, 34th Largest Hispanic Bus. in US, Hispanic Fortune mag., 2002, Class III Supplier Yr., Ga. Minority Supplier Devel. Coun., 2002, NY/NJ Minority Purchasing Coun., 2002; named to Top 200 Fla. Pvt. Co., Fla. Trend, 2000; recipient Corporate Plus award, Nat. Minority Supplier Devel. Coun. (NMSDC), 1997. Achievements include featured in Women's Enterprise mag., 2003. Office: 6365 NW 6th Way Ste 360 Fort Lauderdale FL 33309 Office Phone: 954-938-5400. Office Fax: 953-772-5061.

CASTILLO, CHRISTINE LYNN, pediatric neuropsychologist; d. James Robert and Sharon Joy French. BA summa cum laude, Pacific Christian Coll. of Hope Internat. U., Fullerton, Calif., 1998; PhD, Tex. A&M U., College Station, 2003. Cert. in sch. psychology NASP, 2003, sch. psychologist Md. State Dept. Edn., 2004, lic. psychologist Tex., specialist in sch. psychology Tex. Predoctoral neuropsychology intern Lewisville Ind. Sch. Dist., Tex., 2002—03; pediat. neuropsychology postdoctoral fellow Mt. Washington Pediat. Hosp., Balt., 2003—05; pediat. neuropsychologist Children's Med. Ctr., Dallas, 2005—. Clin. supr. Loyola Coll. in Md., Balt., 2005; lectr. Mt. Washington Pediatric Hosp., Balt., 2003—05; guest lectr. U. Md. Sch. Medicine, Balt., 2004—05; mem ADHD adv. coun. Md. State Dept. Edn., Balt., 2004—05; guest lectr. Tex. A&M U., College Station, 2001; tchg. asst. Pacific Christian Coll. of Hope Internat. U., Fullerton, Calif., 1998; adj. prof. Hope Internat. U., Fullerton, Calif., 2005. Contbr. articles and revs. to profl. jours., chapters to books. HEEP fellow, Tex. A&M U., 1998—2001, Alumni Assn. scholar, Pacific Christian Coll. of Hope Internat. U., 1997, Christian Svc. and Leadership scholar, 1994—98, Presdl. scholar, 1994—98, Calif. Scholarship Fedn. scholar, 1994. Mem.: APA, Tex. Psychol. Assn., Nat. Assn. Sch. Psychologists, Nat. Acad. Neuropsychology, Internat. Neuropsychol. Soc. Office: Childrens Med Ctr Dallas 1935 Motor St Dallas TX 75235 Business E-Mail: christine.castillo@childrens.com.

CASTILLO, FLORA M., health plan administrator, transportation executive; b. El Salvador; arrived in US, 1981; B. in Pub. Adminstrn., Mktg. & Acctg., Long Island U. Cert. Healthcare Ins. Exec., 2005. Assoc. v.p. pub. affairs & mktg. Keystone Mercy Health Plan, Phila., 2000—, leader Health Ministry Program for Women. Bd. dir. NJ Transit, 1999—, chmn. customer svc. & adminstrn. coms.; founder NJ ch. Conf. Minority Transp. Officials, 2002, mem. nat. bd., 2002—; mem. Latino adv. bd. N. Phila. Health System; mem. adv. bd. Congreso's Women Wellness Ctr.; mem. Del. Region Consortium for Latino Health. Named Emerging Leader of Yr., Conf. Minority Transp. Officials, 2003; recipient Martin Luther King, Jr. Commemorative Commn. Triumph award, NJ Dept. State, 2001, Woman of Yr. award, Women's Transp. Seminar, 2003, El Diario La Prensa Latinas Destacada award, 2003, 40 Under 40 award, Atlantic County, 2004, Phila. Bus. Jour., 2006; Exec. Leadership Fellow, Am. Health Ins. Plans, 2005. Mem.: Hispanic Alliance of Atlantic County (1st v.p., mem. Latin Am. Festival com.). Office: Keystone Mercy Health Plan 200 Stevens Dr Philadelphia PA 19113*

CASTILLO, KATHERINE LYNN, writer, translator, business owner; b. Columbus, Ohio, Aug. 30, 1970; d. Dana Leslie and Judith Lynn Jordan; m. Pedro Castillo, Dec. 28, 1999; children: Dana Pedro, Andrew Patrick. BS in Edn., Kent State U., 1994; MA in Distance Edn., 2003, PhD in Distance Edn., 2004. Cert. tchr. K-12 Spanish Ohio, 1994, ATA translations Ohio, 1995. Translator, interpreter Spanish, English pvt. practice, Stow, Ohio, 1991—2005; lead tchr. Spanish Kent State U. Upward Bounds Program, 1998—2002; tchr., translator Berlitz Lang. Sch., Akron, 1998—2003; tchr. K-8 Spanish, music St. Matthew's Parish Sch., 1999—2002; activity coord. Alzheimer's patients Maison Aine, Stow, 1999—2002; online fgn. lang. tchr. Ohio Distance and Electronic Learning Acad., Akron, 2002—05; fgn. lang. tchr. Euclid HS, 2006—. Author: (children's novel) Say Hello to the World; translator: Go Get Benjamin. Precious parent mem. Akron Children's Hosp., 2001—05; hand bell choir Stow United Meth. Ch., Stow, 2002—05, sec., 2002—03, mission team, 2003—04, sec. United Meth. women, 2002—04, mission team mem., translator, 2003—04. Recipient Outstanding Am. Tchr. award, 2006; scholar, Ravenna Profl. Bus. Women, 1989, Stow Teachers, 1989. Mem.: Am. Translators Assn. Democrat. Methodist. Achievements include research in Research in Foreign Language Online Education; development of Online Spanish for Law Enforcement Program; first to Online Education K-12. Avocations: travel, reading, computers, course design, crafts. Home: 3421 Sanford Ave Stow OH 44224 Personal E-mail: kathycastillo830@yahoo.com. Business E-Mail: kcastillo@euclid.k12.oh.us.

CASTILLO, SUSAN, school system administrator; b. LA, Aug. 14, 1951; m. Paul Machu. BA, Oreg. State U., 1981. Mem. staff Oreg. Pub. Broadcasting Radio, 1979-82; journalist, reporter legis. sessions Sta. KVAL-TV, Salem, 1991, 93, 95, journalist, reporter Eugene, 1982-97; mem. Oreg. State Senate, Salem, 1997—2002, vice chair edn. com., mem. health and human svcs. com., mem. transp. com., asst. Dem. leader legis. sessions, 1999, 2001; supt. pub. instrn. State of Oreg., Salem, 2003—. Leader Oreg. Women's Health & Wellness Alliance. Mem. Gov.'s Task Force on DUII, 1997, Gov.'s Task Force on Cmty. Right to Know; bd. dirs. Oreg. Commn. on Hispanic Affairs, 1997, Birth to Three, Oreg. Environ. Coun.; mem. adv. com. Oreg. Passenger Rail Adv. Coun.; mem. Labor Comm.'s Adv. Com. on Agrl. Labor; vice-chair Farm Worker Housing Task Force. Democrat. Achievements include being the first Hispanic woman to serve in Oregon legislature. Office: Oregon Dept Education 255 Capitol St NE Salem OR 97301-0203

CASTLE, NANCY MARGARET TIMMA, accountant, banker; b. Seattle, June 16, 1945; d. Guy Church and Nancy L. (Fraser) B.; m. George L. Wittenburg (div. May 1972); 1 child, Guy Charles; m. Geoffrey Baird Castle, Dec. 12, 1992. Student, Stephens Coll., 1963-64. Legal adminstr. Mullen, McCaughey & Henzell, Santa Barbara, Calif., 1965-67; trust adminstr. First Interstate Bank of Calif., Santa Barbara, 1974-84; pres., owner, acct. N.T.B. Profl. Bus. Svc., Santa Barbara, 1984—. Owner Castle Enterprises, Ltd., Castle Catering Co., 1992—; mem. Continuing Edn. Bar. Mem. Am. Inst. Banking, Nat. Assn. Female Execs, Nat. Fedn. Ind. Bus. Clubs: Santa Barbara Assocs., University (Santa Barbara), Santa Barbara Yacht Club, Cottage Assocs., Santa Barbara Cottage Hosp. Republican. Episcopalian. Avocation: tennis.

CASTLEBERRY, VIVIAN LOU ANDERSON (MRS. CURTIS WALES CASTLEBERRY), free-lance writer, consultant, former newspaper editor; b. Lindale, Tex., Apr. 8, 1922; d. William Clarence and Jessie Lee (Henderson) Anderson; m. Curtis Wales Castleberry, May 4, 1946; children: Carol Janet (Mrs. Michael Lynn Tate), Chanda Elaine (Mrs. George Philip Robertson), Keeta Shawn (Mrs. Ingo Rodolfo Rupp), Kimberley Diana (Mrs. Mark Anthony Saucedo), Catherine Ann (Mrs. Ian Denison Tracy). BS, So. Meth. U., 1944. Editorial asst. Petroleum Engr. Pub. Co., 1944-45; editorial asst. Cousins Pub. Co., 1945-46; women's editor Tex. A. and M. Bn., 1948-51; home editor Dallas Times Herald, 1954-56, women's editor, 1957-84, editorial bd., 1974-86. Cons. Mgmt. Seminar for Women Execs., 1963—. Mem. women's group Dallas Council World Affairs, 1964—, Dallas Internat. Cultural and Social Circle, 1965—; convener Global Peace: An Internat. Conf., 1987-88; bd. dirs. Women's Ctr., Planned Parenthood, Dallas Women's Found., Women's Issues Network. Recipient awards for women's news reporting U.P.I., 1963, 65, 77; Katie awards Dallas Press Club, 1968, 70, 72; J.B. Marryat Meml. award, 1980; Outstanding Woman award So. Meth. U., 1970; Headliners Club award, 1970; Southwestern Journalism Forum award, 1971; Extra Mile award Bus. and Profl. Women's Club, 1975; Women Helping Women award Soroptomist Club, 1977; Women Helping Women award Women's Center, Dallas, 1978; Vivian Castleberry award Assn. of Women Journalists, 1992; named to Tex. Women's Hall of Fame, 1984; Laurel award AAUW, 1986; named Dallas Peacemaker of Yr., 1988, Les Femmes du Monde's, 1990, Dallas Sr. Citizen Hall of Fame, 1990. Home: 11311 Buchanan Dr Dallas TX 75228-1939

CASTLEMAN, PAMELA ANN, assistant principal; d. James and Shirley Castleman; m. Paul Silven (div.). BA in Liberal Arts, Stephen F. Austin State U., Nacagdoches, Tex., 1996; MEd in Ednl. Adminstrn., Tex. A&M U., Commerce, 2001. Cert. tchg. composite social studies Tex., prin. Calif., Tex. Tchr. psychology, sociology, govt., geography, cheerleaders' coach Mesquite Ind. Sch. Dist.-Mesquite H.S., Tex., 1996—2001; asst. prin. Simi Valley Unified Sch. Dist.-Royal H.S., Calif., 2001—. Mem. curriculum coun. Simi Valley Unified Sch. Dist., 2001—, mem. student attendance rev. bd., 2001—, mem. safety task force, 2003; prin. summer sch. Simi Valley H.S., 2004, 05. Mem.: Assn. Calif. Sch. Adminstrn., Assn. Supervision and Curriculum Devel. Republican. Southern Baptist. Avocations: gardening, antiques, travel.

CASTNER, CATHERINE S., information technology administrator; b. L.A., Apr. 14, 1968; d. Stanley Vernon Castner and Ursula Philomena McCaffrey. BS, Calif. Poly. State U., 1991; MBA, Belmont U., 2000. Participant svc. rep. Bankers Trust, L.A., 1992-94, interactive voice response analyst Nashville, 1994-97; tech. project mgr., dir. MetLife, Nashville, 1998-2000; tech. project mgr. Coval Bus. Solutions, Nashville, 2000—. Avocations: international travel, mystery novels, counted cross stitch, photography, cooking. Home: 3500 Glenfalls Dr Hermitage TN 37076-4446

CASTO, BARBARA L., counselor; b. Sarahsville, Ohio, June 9, 1949; adopted d. Goldie M. and Charles H. Laughlin; 1 child, Rachel Rodene Doak. BA, Spring Arbor U., 1973. Lic. Social Worker State of Ohio Counselor and Social Work Bd., 1989; Chem. Dependency Counselor III Internat. Certification & Reciprocity Consortium/Alcohol and Other, 2005. Tchr. Sarahsville Elem. Sch. Noble Local Sch. Dist., Ohio, 1970—71; field rep. Girl Scouts U.S.A., Jackson, Mich., 1973—74; social worker Cambridge Psychiat. Hosp., Ohio, 1975—96; specialist corrections program Noble Correctional Instn., Caldwell, Ohio, 1996—98, coord. corrections program, 1998—. Trainer Cambridge Psychiat. Hosp., 1977—78, mem. quality assurance com., 1995—96, facilitator quality improvement team, 1995—96. Mem. Noble County Hist. Soc., Caldwell, 2006; officer Noble County Gideons Aux., Caldwell, 1993—2002, Ohio Gideons Aux., 2000—02; mem., leader Free Meth. Ch., Caldwell, 1992—2006; mem. Mensa, Columbus, Ohio, 1992—2006. Avocations: needlecrafts, genealogy, puzzles, gardening. Office: Noble Correctional Institution 15708 McConnellsville Road Caldwell OH 43724 Personal E-mail: barbara_casto2000@yahoo.com.

CASTON, JANE PEARS, school nurse practitioner; arrived in U.S., 1969; d. Thomas Pears and Hilda Joyce (Pears) Dimmick; m. Paul Gerard Caston, June 6, 1981; 1 child, Genevieve Paulette. RN, Royal Alexandra Hosp., Brighton, Eng., 1969. RN Eng. Tutor San Diego Sch. Nursing, 1970—72; operating rm. nurse, asst. Plastic Surg. Inst., San Diego, 1972—75, 1977—83; matron Sampford Pl. Children's Home, Melksham, England, 1975—77; part-time staff nurse pediat. and neonatal ICU's St. Michael's Hosp., Bristol, England, 1984—89, Royal Alexandra Hosp., Bath, 1984—89; sch. nurse Stonar Girls Sch., Atworth, 1986—89, Royal Sch. Bath, Bath, 1991—98; surg. nurse Dr. R.O. Gregory Celebration Inst. Aesthetic Surgery, Fla., 2000—02; sch. nurse Pk. Maitland (Fla.) Sch., 2002—. Health edn. cons. Stonar Sch., England, 1986—89, Royal Sch., Bath, England, 1991—98; summer camp nurse Girls Camp Glen Arden, NC, 2005—06. Vol. nurse internat. mission work in Mex., Brazil and Honduras various orgns., 1979—2002; vol. instr. first aid, adult and child care. Mem.: Fla. Assn. Sch. Nurse, Nat. Assn. Sch. Nurse. Anglican. Avocations: travel, music, art. Office: Park Maitland Sch 1450 S Orlando Ave Maitland FL 32751 Office Phone: 407-647-3038 112.

CASTORO, ROSEMARIE, sculptor; b. Bklyn., Mar. 1, 1939; d. Michael Peter and Camille C. Student in painting, Mus. Modern Art, N.Y.C., 1955-56; BFA cum laude, Pratt Inst., Bklyn., 1963. Tchr. Sch. Visual Arts, N.Y.C., 1971, Hunter Coll., N.Y.C., 1972, Calif. State U., Fresno, 1973, Syracuse (N.Y.) U., 1975, U. Colo., Boulder, 1977, Stockton State U., NJ, 1983, Boston Mus. Sch., 1983, Am. U., Corciano, Italy, 2000. Lectr. art Boston Mus. Sch. Art, 1971, 80, New Sch. Social Rsch., N.Y.C., 1972, 73, Phila. Coll. Art, 1974, Atlanta Coll. Art, 1974, Rome Art Assn., N.Y. State, 1975, Syracuse (N.Y.) U., 1975, U. Calif., Berkeley, 1976, Suzuki-Walker, Sausalito, Calif., 1976, Art Inst. Sch., Chgo., 1980, Pratt Inst., N.Y.C., 1982, 95, C.W. Post, L.I., N.Y., 1984, San Jose (Calif.) U., 1984, 85, N.J. Ctr. for Visual Arts, Summit, 1989, Ecole Nat. Superieure des Beaux-Arts, Paris, 1995. One-woman shows include Tibor de Nagy Gallery, N.Y.C., 1971, 1972, 1973, 1975, 1976, 1978, 1981, 1983, 1985, 1989, Hal Bromm Gallery, 1976, 1978, 1979, 1980, 1983, 1987, 1991—92, 1997, 2002, Julian Pretto, 1978, 1979, Marion Deson, Chgo., 1981, Am. Ctr., Paris, 1983, Eaton/Shoen Gallery, San Francisco, 1984, 1986, Newark Mus., 1991, Arnaud Lefebvre Gallery, Paris, 1993, 1995, 1997, 1998, 1999, 2003, 2004, Stella R Graphics, Paris, 1993, Eaton Fine Arts, West Palm Beach, Fla., 2000, 2004, exhibited in group shows at Bklyn. Mus., 1963, Tibor de Nagy Gallery, 1966, Stable Gallery, 1966, Dwan Gallery, N.Y.C., 1968, 1969, Richard Feigen Gallery, 1968, Paula Cooper Gallery, 1969, 1971, Vancouver (B.C., Can.) Art Gallery, 1970, Stadtische Kunsthalle, Dusseldorf, Germany, 1970, Allen Art Mus., Oberlin, Ohio, 1970, Hundred Acres Gallery, N.Y.C., 1970, 112 Greene St Gallery, 1971, 1972, Richard Gray Gallery, Chgo., 1972, Storm King Art Gallery, Mountainville, N.Y., 1972, 1974, 1975, Grapestake Gallery, San Francisco, 1975—76, Moore Coll. Art, Phila., 1977, John Weber Gallery, N.Y.C., 1977, Hal Bromm Gallery, 1977, 1981—82, 1985—87, 2006, Indpls. Mus. Art, 1978, Whitney Mus. Am. Art, N.Y.C., 1978, Nancy Lurie Gallery, Chgo., 1978, Smithsonian Instn., Washington, 1980, Hunter Mus. Art, Chattanooga, Tenn., 1980, Banco Gallery, Brescia, Italy, 1980, Hirshhorn Mus. and Sculpture Garden, Washington, 1981, Pratt Inst. Art Gallery, Bklyn., 1981, Eaton/Shoen Gallery, 1982, 2003, 2006, Maier Mus. Art, Lynchburg, Va., 1983, 1990, Laguna Gloria Art Mus., Austin, Tex., 1985, Mus. Modern Art, N.Y.C., 1985, Newark Mus., 1987, Marvin Seline Gallery, Houston, 1990, Jan Baum Gallery, LA, 1990, Stellar Graphics, Paris, 1992, Galerie Arnaud Lefebvre, 1993, 1995—96, 2001, 2003, 2004, 2006, Henry St. Settlement, N.Y.C., 1993, Athenaeum Music & Arts Libr., La Jolla, Calif., 1995, Beaumanoir, Le Leslay, France, 1995, 2004, PS #1, N.Y.C., 2004, many others, commns. include, Battery Park City, N.Y.C., 1978, GSA, Topeka, Kans., 1979, Am. Ctr., Paris, 1983, Athena Found., L.I., N.Y., 1986, Woodstock '94, Saurgerties, N.Y., 1994, Millbrook, N.Y., 2005, Represented in permanent collections Allen Art Mus., Oberlin, Ohio, Boca Raton (Fla.) Mus., Bank of Am., Calif., Chase Manhattan Bank, N.A., GSA, Washington, Mus. Modern Art, N.Y.C., Newark Mus., Fonds Nat. d'Art Contemporain, Paris, Univ. Art Mus., U. Calif., Berkeley, U. Mass., Woodward Found., Washington. Treas. HIV-Arts, N.Y.C., 1994—2006. Guggenheim fellow, 1971; grantee Woodward Found., 1970, CAPS, 1972, 74, NEA, 1974-75, 84-85, Tiffany Found., 1977, Pollock-Krasner Found., 1989-90, 97-98. Home: 151 Spring St # 6 New York NY 10012-3850 Office Phone: 212-966-4637. E-mail: rcastoro@earthlink.net.

CASTRO, CHRISTINE, Internet company executive; BA in Journalism, Univ. So. Calif., MA in Comm. Mgmt. Mgr. employee comm. program Rockwell Internat., Milwaukee, Wis., 1991—95; dir. corp. comm. SunAmerica, Inc., L.A., 1995—99; dir. and v.p., corp. comm. Walt Disney Co., Burbank, Calif., 1999—2002; sr. v.p., chief comm. officer Yahoo!, Inc., Sunnyvale, Calif., 2002—. Mem. bd. dir. Tomas Rivera Policy Inst. Office: Yahoo! Inc 701 First Ave Sunnyvale CA 94089 Office Phone: 408-349-3300. Office Fax: 408-349-3301.

CASTRO, JAN GARDEN, writer, art educator, consultant; b. St. Louis, June 8, 1945; d. Harold and Estelle (Fischer) Garden; 1 child, Jomo Jemal. Student, Cornell U., 1963—65; BA, U. Wis., 1967; pub. cert., Radcliffe Coll., 1967; MA in Tchg., Washington U., St. Louis, 1974, MA, 1994. Life cert. tchr. secondary English, speech, drama and social studies, Mo. Tchr., writer, St. Louis, 1970—; dir. Big River Assn., St. Louis, 1975-85; adj. prof. humanities Lindenwood Coll., 1980—. Co-founder, dir. Duff's Poetry Series, St. Louis, 1975-81; founder, dir. River Styx P.M. Series, St. Louis, 1981-83; arts cons. Harris-Stowe State Coll., 1986-87; vis. scholar Am. Acad. in Rome, summer 2000. Contbg. author: rev. books San Francisco Rev. Books, 1982—85, Am. Book Rev., 1990—93, Mo. Rev., 1991, New Letters, 1993, 1996, Tampa Rev., 1994—2000, The Nation, Am. Poetry Rev., Sculpture Mag., 1997—; author: (poetry) Mandala of the Five Senses, 1975, The Art and Life of Georgia O'Keeffe, 1985, 1995, Memories and Memoirs.Contemporary Missouri Authors, 2000, (poetry) The Last Frontier, 2001—, Sonia DeLaunay: La Moderne, 2002—; editor: (jours.) River Styx mag., 1975—86; co-editor: (essays) Margaret Atwood: Vision and Forms, 1988; co-prodr.(TV host, co-prodr.): (shows) The Writers Cir., Double Helix, 1987—89; contbg. editor: (jours.) Sculpture Mag. Seeking St. Louis, Voices from a River City, 1670—2000. Mem. University City Arts and Letters Commn., Mo., 1983-84. NEH fellow UCLA, 1988, Johns Hopkins U., 1991, Camargo Found. fellow (Cassis, France), 1996; recipient Arts and Letters award St. Louis Mag., 1985, Editor's award and editor during G.E. Younger Writers award to River Styx Mag., Coord. Coun. for Lit. Mags., 1986, Arts award Mandrake Soc. Charity Ball, 1988, Leadership award YWCA St. Louis, 1988. Mem. MLA, CAA, PEN Am. Ctr., Nat. Coalition Ind. Scholars, Margaret Atwood Soc. (founder). Home: PO Box 486 New York NY 10159-0486 Office Phone: 212-684-5851. E-mail: jan_g_castro@mail.com.

CASTRO, MARIA GRACIELA, medical educator, geneticist, researcher; b. Buenos Aires, Mar. 2, 1955; d. Nestor Antonio Castro and Maria Esther Rodriquez; m. Pedro Ricardo Lowenstein, Jan. 12, 1988; 1 child, Elijah David Lowenstein. BSc 1st class in Chemistry, Nat. U. La Plata, Argentina, 1979, MSc in Biochemistry, 1981, PhD in Biochemistry, 1986. Fogarty postdoctoral fellow Lab. Neurochemistry and Neuroimmunology NICHHD/NIH, Bethesda, Md., 1986-88; sr. rsch. fellow Lab. Molecular Endocrinology, dept. biochemistry and physiology U. Reading, England, 1988-90; lectr. dept. molecular and life scis. U. Abertay, Dundee, Scotland, 1991-92; lectr. in neurosci., dept. physiology U. Wales Coll., Cardiff, 1991-95; sr. lectr. medicine Sch. Medicine U. Manchester, England, 1995-98, prof. molecular medicine, 1998—, dir. molecular medicine and gene therapy unit, 1996—. Expert Women in Sci. Tech., Sheffield, England, 1996—; neurosci. panel Wellcome Trust, England, 1999—; co-dir. dept. molecular medicine Cedar-Sinai Med. Ctr., 2001—; co-dir. bd. govs. Gene Therapeutics Rsch. Inst., Cedars Sinai Med. Ctr., 2001—; prof. medicine UCLA, 2002—, prof. molecular and med. pharmacology, 2004—. Mem. editl. bd.: Jour. Endocrinology, Jour. Molecular Endocrinology, Current Gene Therapy, Gene Therapy, Pituitary, 2000, Neuro Molecular Medicine, 2001—; contbr. articles to profl. jours. Rsch. grantee, Brit. Heart Found., 1997, Med. Rsch. Coun., 1998, Biotech. and Biol. Rsch. Coun., 1999—2000, Wellcome Trust, 1999, NIH, 2003—. Mem.: Nat. Inst. Neurol. Disorders and Stroke, Internat. Soc. Nerovirology (founding mem.), Soc. Neurosci., Endocrine Soc., Am. Gene Therapy Assn. Achievements include patents in field; research in program development of gene therapy for chronic neurological diseases and brain cancer. Business E-Mail: castromg@cshs.org.

CASTRO, ROSA, drug counselor; b. N.Y.C., Mar. 4, 1960; BA in Psychology, Fordham U., 1985; postgrad., Hunter Coll., 1992—. Cert. addictions counselor, N.Y.; cert. psychotherapist, APA. Tchr. asst. Herbert Birch Childhood Ctr., Bronx, N.Y., 1985; clin. counselor Gramercy Park Med. Ctr., N.Y.C., 1986-89; student asst. counselor Operation Survival, N.Y.C., Bklyn., 1989; drug rehab. counselor Stuyvesant Sq., N.Y.C., 1990-93; alcohol counselor Greenwich House, N.Y.C., 1993-94; shop owner, tchr., psychic Mystic Earth, N.Y.C., 1994—; caseworker Bowery Residence Committer, N.Y.C., 1998; clin. therapist Metro. Ctr. Mental Health, 2005—. Psychic, tchr. Inst. of Intuitive Svcs., N.Y.C., 1992—; Reiki master Usui Shiki Ryoho, N.Y.C., 1993—; workshop leader; lectr. in field; psychic, tarot, and astrology cons. Author: Magical Guide, 1992, (manual) Reiki Reference Manual, 1993, Healing Words for Women, 1996, Meditation Basics, 1996, Intuitive Notebook, 1996, The Chakrabook Workbook, 1996, Pastlives Workbook, 1997, Channeling Workbook, 1997; co-author: Reiki Journals, 1995; editor-in-chief Mystic Earth newsletter, 1995. Founder Manhatten Psychic Club (pres. 1995—). Avocations: teach intuitive classes, aromatherapy, reiki healing, poetry, watercolor painting. Home: 535 W 155th St Apt 22 New York NY 10032-7851

CASTRO, TERESA JACIRA, small business owner; b. Chgo., July 18, 1956; d. Jene Paul and June Edith (Aleff) Harper; m. Oscar Armando Rodriguez (div. 1981); 1 child, Avelina; m. Jorge Castro (div. 1993); 1 child, Pablo. AA in Opera, Fleming Coll., Florence, Italy, 1975; BA in Spanish and Portuguese cum laude, U. N.Mex., Albuquerque, 1979; MS in Info. Tech., Am. Intercontinental U., Ft. Lauderdale, 2001. Owner, founder, pres. Access Word Processing, San Francisco and Viña del Mar, Chile, 1983-95; pers. banker Chase Manhattan Bank, Santiago, 1993-94; pres. SalsaPower.com, Inc., 2000—; freelance computer and systems analyst. Tech. translator and simultaneous interpreter specializing in engring., fin. and legal matters, Ft. Lauderdale, Fla., 1995—; owner, Accent Translations, 1995—; founder/dir. Absolute Salsa Dance Studio, 1999—. Vol. notary pub. People With AIDS/ARC, 1985-91, The AIDS Found./Shanti Project, San Francisco, 1986-90; chairperson bilingual adv. bd. Buena Vista Sch., San Francisco, 1986; bd. dirs. Escola Nova de Samba, San Francisco, 1987; vol. working on reunification searches for adoptees and birth parents, Calif., N.Y., Latin Am.; tchr. Spanish law enforcement pers. San Francisco Police Acad., 1988-89, Spanish for med. pers. Kaiser Permanente Med. Ctr., San Francisco, 1988-89. Mem. NAFE, Nat. Assn. Photoshop Profls., Toastmasters Internat. Avocations: dancing samba, salsa, teaching children's dance classes.

CASTRO-KLAREN, SARA, Latin American literature professor; b. Arequipa, Sabandia, Peru, June 9, 1942; d. José Andrés and Zoila Rosa (Rivas) Castro-Valdivia; m. Peter F. Klaren, Sept. 3, 1962; 1 child, Alexandra. BA, UCLA, 1962, MA, 1965, PhD, 1968. Asst. prof. Dartmouth Coll., No. Hampshire, NH, 1970-84; chief Hispanic div. Lib. of Congress Fed. Govt., Washington, 1984-86; prof. Latin Am. lit. Johns Hopkins U., Balt., 1986—. Dir. program Latin Am. Studies, JHU. Author: El Mundo Magico de J.M. Arquedas, Lima, 1973, Mario Vargas Llosa, Analisis Introductorio, Lima, 1988, Escritura Sujeto y Transgresión, Mex., 1989, Understanding Mario Vargas Llosa, U.S.C., 1990; editor: Women's Writing in Latin America, 1991, Latin American Women's Narrative: Practices and Theoretical Perspectives, 2003, Beyond Imagined Communities: Reading and Writing the Nation in Nineteenth Century Latin America, 2003. Fellow Woodrow Wilson Ctr. for Scholars, Washington, 1977-78. Mem. MLA, AAUP, Latin Am. Studies Assn. Avocation: gardening. Home: 9438 Rabbit Hill Road Great Falls VA 22066

CASTRONOVO, BERNADINE MARRO, music educator; b. Peekskill, NY, Oct. 17, 1949; d. Joseph A. and Mary L. Marro; m. Charles Castronovo, Aug. 14, 1982. BS in Music Edn., We. Conn. U., 1971, MS in Music Edn., 1975. Music tchr./chorus dir. Austin Rd. Elem., Mahopac, NY, 1971—75, Mahopac H.S., Mahopac, 1975—86, Mahopac Falls Elem., Mahopac, 1975—77, Lakeview Elem., Mahopac, 1977—80, Mahopac Jr. H.S., Mahopac, 1980—86, Mahopac Mid. Sch., Mahopac, 1986—92, Lakeview Elem., Mahopac, 1992—. Choral dir./Mahopac H.S. in performance at Carnegie Hall, N.Y.C., 1982. Recipient Ruth DeVilla Franca Music award, We. Conn. U., 1971, Cert. Recognition award, Nat. Assn. Music Edn. Mem.: Nat. Assn. Music Edn., We. Conn. Univ. Alumni Assn., N.Y. State Sch. Music Assn., N.Y. State United Tchrs., Music Educators Nat. Conf. Avocation: animals, swimming, cooking, singing. Home: 453 Austin Rd Mahopac NY 10541 Office: Lakeview Elem Lakeview Drive Mahopac NY 10541

CASTRO-POZO, TALÍA, dancer, educator; b. Lima, Peru, Oct. 2, 1975; came to U.S., 1995; d. Jose and Renée Castro. Profl. preformer degree in Ballet and Modern Dance, Nat. Ballet Sch., Lima, Peru, 1992; studied with Sergei Radchenko, Mabel Silvera Studio, Buenos Aires, 1992; studied in Profl. Actor Program with Program William Esper Studios, N.Y.C., 2003—05; student, Sch. Am. Ballet, 1995-96. Soloist Nat. Ballet, 1992-95; co-dir., performer, tchr. ballroom dancing Stepping Out Studios, 1999—; dir., mgr. profl. actor program William Esper Studios, N.Y.C., 2003—. Rep. Internat. Ballet Competition, U.S.A., 1994, World Ballet Competition, Osaka, Japan, 1995, 30th Course of Ballet and Modern, Varna, Bulgaria. Featured dancer in film Summer of Sam; choreographer in ind. film Angela, 1999. Dancer/choreographer Korean Army Festivities, Lima, 1992; dancer First Festival for Children's Rights, Lima, 1995. Recipient 1st Place award Latin Am. competition, 1989; Best Dancer of Yr. award Peruvian Press, 1991. Mem. Nat. Assn. Writers and Artists, Internat. Dance Coun. Personal E-mail: taliacpc@yahoo.com.

CASWELL, DOROTHY ANN COTTRELL, performing arts association administrator; b. N.Y.C., Dec. 18, 1938; d. Donald Peery and Eleanor Hildaborg (Westberg) Cottrell; m. Allen Edward Caswell, Oct. 24, 1959; children: David Alan, Bruce Leland. Student, Carleton Coll., Northfield, MN., 1956-59; AB in Psych., George Wash. U., 1960-61; postgrad. in vocal performance, SUNY, Oneonta, 1971-76. Sec. U.S. Fgn. Service, Tunis, Tunisia, 1959-61; mng. dir. Glimmerglass Opera, Inc., Cooperstown, NY, 1975-78; exec. dir. Upper Catskill Community Council on the Arts, Oneonta, NY, 1978-80; devel. officer Catskill Arts Consortium, Oneonta, 1981-83; devel. cons. Otsego Urban Rural Self-Devel. Assocs., Inc., Oneonta, 1982-83; co-founder, pres. Catskill Choral Soc., 1970-76, 81-84; assoc. producer Orpheus Theatre, Inc., Oneonta, 1984-91; voice tchr. Oneonta, 1984—; ptnr., co-owner OnStage Prodn. Svcs., 1991—. Cons., arts adminstrv. Dorothy Caswell Assocs., Oneonta, 1981—; past pres., mem. sub-area coun. Health Sys. Agy. NE, NY, mem. planning adv. group, rev. adv. Singer/actress: Orpheus Theatre, 1984—; actor(film series Susquehanna Stories): WSKG-TV Pub. TV, 1990—. Mem. chorus Glimmerglass Opera, Cooperstown, 1974—; mem. mil. acad. selection com. Congressman Sherwood Boehlert, NY, 1993—; mem. Otsego County Health Planning Adv. Coun. Otsego Publ Health Partnership; bd. dirs. Otsego County Tourism Bur., 1987—90, Oneonta Downtown Coalition, 1982—84. Recipient Honored for Outstanding Performance and Svcs. to Cmty., SUNY, 1975. Democrat. Avocations: painting, performing arts, gardening, swimming.

CASWELL, FRANCES PRATT, retired language educator; b. Brunswick, Maine, June 25, 1929; m. Forrest Wilbur Caswell, June 30, 1956; children: Lucy Caswell Hilburn, Helen Caswell Watts, Harold F. BA, U. Maine, 1951; MA, U. Mich., 1955. Tchr. English, Bridgton (Maine) High Sch., 1951-54, Grosse Point (Mich.) High Sch., 1955-56; instr. South Maine Tech. Coll., South Portland, 1968-84, chmn. dept., 1984-93. Bd. dirs. Maine Vocat. Region 10, 1993-2003. Author: Growing Through Faith, A History of the Brunswick United Methodist Church, 1821-1996, 1996; contbg. author: Brunswick, Maine, 250 Years A Town, 1989. Pres. United Pejepscot Housing Inc., Brunswick, 1987-93. Mem. AAUW, Casco Bay Art League. Methodist. Avocations: painting, gardening.

CATALANO, JANE DONNA, lawyer; b. Schenectady, N.Y., Feb. 21, 1957; d. Alfred and Joan (Futscher) Martini; m. Peter Catalano, June 18, 1988. BA, SUNY, Plattsburgh, 1979; JD, Albany Law Sch., 1982. Bar: N.Y. 1983, U.S. Dist. Ct. 1983. Atty. Pentak, Brown & Tobin, Albany, NY, 1982-87, Niagara Mohawk Power Corp., Albany, 1987—. Mem. N.Y. State Bar Assn., Albany County Bar Assn. Home: 7 Blackburn Way Latham NY 12110-1943 Office Phone: 518-433-5257. Business E-Mail: jane.catalano@us.ngrid.com.

CATALFO, BETTY MARIE, health service executive, nutritionist; b. N.Y.C., Nov. 2, 1942; d. Lawrence Santo and Gemma (Patrone) Lorefice; children— Anthony, Lawrence, Donna Marie. Grad. Newtown High Sch., Elmhurst, N.Y., 1958. Sec., clk. ABC-TV, N.Y.C., 1957-60; founder, lectr., nutritionist Weight Watchers, Manhasset, N.Y., 1964-75; founder, pres. Every-Bodys Diet, Inc. dba Stay Slim, Queens, N.Y., 1976—; dir. in-home program N.Y. State Dept. Health, N.Y.C., 1985—; founder, pres. Delitegul Diet Foods, Inc., 1988—; lectr. in field. Author: 101 Stay-Slim Recipes, 1983, Get Slim and Stay Slim Diet Cook Book, rev. ed., 1987, Diet Revolution, 1991, Holiday Cookbook, 1992, Fat Counts in Fast Food Spots, 1992, Choose to Loose!, 1993, You Are Not Alone, 1993, Eating Out, 1994, Change or Select, 1994, Calories Do Count!, 1994, Fat Free Receipes, 1994; author, dir., producer: (video) Dancersize for Overweight, 1986, Get Slim and Stay Slim Diet Cook Book, Eating Right for Your Life, Hello It's Me and I'm Slim, (videos) Stay Slim Line Dancing, 1989, Stay Slim Food Facts, 1989, Help Me Before I Give In, 1990, A New Year A New You!, 1991, Relax and Meditate, 1991, Come Shop with Me, 1991, Change or Accept, 1993, The Bag Lady, 1993, Sneak Eater, 1993, Sins That Every Dieter Makes, 1994, Stay Slim from Start to Finish, 1994, Here's Some Helpful Diet Tips, 1994, What Every Smart Dieter Knows, 1994, Mirror Mirror on the Wall, 1994, Weight Management Techniques, 1995; author, editor: (video) Eating Right For Life, 1985, Isometric Techniques for Weight Reduction, Dance Your Calories A-Weigh; author, producer: (video) Eating Habits, 1986—; (video) Isometric Techniques for Weight Reduction, 1986, Patience Is a Virtue When Weight Loss is the Goal, 1986, Slow Down You Eat to Fast, 1994, Always Giving Never Receiving, 1994, Relax and Don't You Worry, 1994; producer, dir.: (video) Positive and Negative Diet Forces, 1987, (video) Hello It's Me and I'm Thin, 1987, (video) Dance Your Calories A-Weigh, 1987, (video) Positive and Negative Diet Forces, 1987. Sponsor, lectr. St. Pauls Ctr., Bklyn., 1981—, Throgs Neck Assn. Retarded Children, Bronx, 1985—; active ARC, LWV, Am. Italian Assn., United Way Greenwich, Council Chs. and Synagogues, Heart Assn., N.Y. Meals on Wheels, 1985—, Health Assn. Fairfield County, Food Svcs. for Homeless People, 1993, 94, 95; chairperson, sponsor Battered Women, 1994—. Named Woman of Yr., Bayside Womens Club, N.Y., 1983, O, PK Woman of Yr., 1986—, Woman of Yr. Richmond Boys Club, 1987, Woman of Yr. Bronx Press Club Assn., 1987; recipient Merit award for Svc. Cath. Archdiocese of Bklyn., 1985, Merit award Svcs. Cath. Archdioces of Bklyn. and Queens, 1992, 93, 94, Community Service award Sr. Citizens Sacred Heart League Bklyn./Queens Archdiocese. N.Y. State Nutritional Guidance for Children Nat. Assn. Scis. Mem. Nat. C. of C. for Women (Woman of Yr. 1987, 90), Pres.'s Coun. on Nutrition, Roundtable for Women in Food Service, Bus. and Profl. Women's Club, Pres. Council for Phys. Fitness, Nat. Assn. Female Execs., Assn. for Fitness in Bus. Inc., Nat. Assn.

Female Bus. Owners. Democrat. Roman Catholic. Club: Mothers Sacred Heart Sch. (chairperson 1979-82). Avocations: reading; travel, golf, family. Home: 21422 27th Ave Flushing NY 11360-2608 also: 58 Riverview Ct Greenwich CT 06831-4127 Office: 10005 101st Ave Ozone Park NY 11416-2601

CATANESE, KATHLEEN SMITH, secondary school educator; b. Trenton, N.J., Apr. 21, 1949; d. Peter Joseph and Mabel Marie (Smith) C.; m. Frank John Bitetto, Dec. 27, 1975; children: Mary Anne, Tricia Megan. BS, Trenton State Coll., 1972. Cert. K-12 art tchr., K-8 elem. tchr., N.J. Asst. dir. young printmakers workshop Trenton State Coll., 1972-73; tchr. art Summit (N.J.) Bd. Edn., 1972-75, Union Twp. Bd. Edn., Union, N.J., 1975-76, Hamilton Twp. Bd. Edn., Hamilton Square, N.J., 1978-84, 88—. Chmn. Am. Edn. Week Com., Hamilton Twp., 1992-94. Author, illustrator: The Sun Sent Streaks, 1991 (N.J. Bell award 1991), Angel in the House, 1994, Quiet Joy, 1996. Organizer Active Citens for Environ., East Amwell, N.J., 1992—. Recipient gov.'s tchr. recognition award State of N.J., 1992; grantee Geraldine R. Dogge Found., 1993. Mem. NEA, N.J. Edn. Assn., Nat. Art Edn. Assn., Art Educators N.J. (exec. bd. 1994-95, asst. youth art month 1993-95, corr. sec., publicity chmn. 1994), Seminar for Rsch. in Art Edn., Ctr. for Book Arts, Printmaking Coun. N.J. Avocations: book arts, publishing, printmaking, painting, writing. Home: PO Box 387 Ringoes NJ 08551-0387 Office: Hamilton Twp Bd Edn 90 Park Ave Trenton NJ 08690-2024

CATCHINGS, TAMIKA DEVONNE, professional basketball player; b. Stratford, NJ, July 21, 1979; d. Harvey Catchings and Wanda Cathings. Grad., U. Tenn., 2001. Basketball player U. Tenn., 1997—2001; profl. basketball player Ind. Fever, WNBA, 2001—. Mem. USA Basketball Women's Sr. Nat. Team, 2004. Host Catch the Fever basketball camp, 2002, 2003, Catch the Fitness clinic, 2003. Named Naismith Player of Yr., 2000, AP Player of Yr., 2000, US Basketball Writers Assn. Player of Yr., 2000, Kodak/WBCA Player of Yr., 2000, Coll. Women's Basketball Player of Yr., ESPY Awards, 2001, WNBA Rookie of the Yr., 2002; named to WNBA All-Star Team, 2002, 2003, First Team All-WNBA, 2002, 2003; recipient Reynolds Soc. Achievement Award, Mass. Eye and Ear Infirmary, Off-Season WNBA Cmty. Assist Award, 2002, 2003. Achievements include mem. US Women's Basketball FIBA Jr. World Championship Gold Medal Team, 1997; mem. US Women's Basketball FIBA World Championship Gold Medal Team, 2002; mem. US Women's Basketball Team, Athens Olympics, 2004. Office: 125 S Pennsylvania St Indianapolis IN 46204

CATE, JAN HARRIS, lawyer; b. NYC, Jan. 9, 1964; BA with honors, Univ. Calif., San Diego, 1986; JD, Boston Univ., 1989. Bar: Calif. 1989. Ptnr., leader Bank Fin. practice Pillsbury Winthrop Shaw Pittman, LA. Contbr. articles to profl. jours. Mem.: LA County Bar Assn. Office: Pillsbury Winthrop Shaw Pittman Suite 2800 725 S Figueroa St Los Angeles CA 90017 Office Phone: 213-488-7539. Office Fax: 213-629-1033. Business E-Mail: jan.cate@pillsburylaw.com.

CATERINO, LINDA CLAIRE, psychologist; b. N.Y.C., June 25, 1949; d. Carl Peter and Marie Veronica (Dughi) Caterino; m. Raymond William Kulhavy, July 17, 1977, (dec.); children: Nicole Dawn Marie Siqueiros, Kathryn Elisabeth Dawn. BA, Fordham U., 1971; MA, Ariz. State U., 1975, PhD, 1977. Lic. psychologist Ariz., 1977, Calif., 2002. Head psychologist Kyrene Sch. Dist., Tempe, Ariz., 1977-84; pvt. practice Mesa/Chandler, Ariz., 1977—; tng. dir. sch. psychology program Ariz. State U. Contbr. articles to profl. jours., chpts. to books. Co-leader Girl Scouts U.S., Mesa, 1989-91; vol. Mesa Sch. Dist., 1986-94, Queen of Peace Sch., Mesa, 1992-95. Fellow Am. Acad. Sch. Psychology; mem. APA (v.p. div. 16 profl. affairs), Nat. Assn. Sch. Psychologists, Am. Bd. Sch. Psychology (treas. 1994-96), Nat. Acad. Neuropsychology. Avocations: travel, art history. Office: 5410 S Lakeshore Dr Ste 102 Tempe AZ 85283 Personal E-mail: lindapsych@aol.com.

CATES, JO ANN, library director; b. Ft. Worth, June 25, 1958; d. Charles Kimbrough and Lydia Joe (Sachse) C.; children: Jacob Abraham Frank, Mabel Rose Frank. BS in Journalism, Boston U., 1980; MLS, Simmons Coll., 1984. Advt. asst. Boston Phoenix, 1978-79; med. serials asst. Mass. Gen. Hosp., Boston, 1979-80; editorial asst. Exceptional Parent Mag., Boston, 1980-81; libr. reference asst. Lesley Coll., Cambridge, Mass., 1981-84; head reference libr. Lamont Libr., Harvard U., Cambridge, Mass., 1984-85; chief libr. Poynter Inst. for Media Studies, St. Petersburg, Fla., 1985-91; head transp. libr. Northwestern U., Evanston, Ill., 1991-94; regional rsch. mgr. Ctr. for Bus. Knowledge Ernst & Young, 1997—2001; libr. dir. Columbia Coll., Chgo., 2001—04, dean of the libr., 2004—, assoc. v.p. acad. rsch., 2005—. Tchr. News Libr. and Newsroom Seminars Poynter Inst., 1990-91; mem. Harvard Com. on Instrn. Libr. Use, 1984, mem. adv. com. on book and serial budgets, 1991-94; mem. Acad. Affairs Commn., 2001—; book reviewer Libr. Jour., Choice, 1985-2000, Am. Reference Book Annual, 1993-2000; knowledge mgmt. column editor B&F Divsn. Bull., 1999-2000. Author: Journalism: A Guide to the Reference Literature, 1990, 3d edit., 2004; editor Transp. Divsn. Bull., 1992-94; mem. editorial bd. Footnotes, 1991-94; contbr. articles to profl. jours. Mem. Transp. Rsch. Bd. Info. Svcs. Com., 1991-94; media intern Dem. Nat. Com., Boston, 1979-80. Scholar Women in Comm., 1976-78; Trustee scholar Boston U., 1978-80; Simmons Coll. grantee, 1982-84. Mem. Spl. Librs. Assn., Assn. for Edn. in Journalism and Mass Comm., Suncoast Info. Specialists (pres. 1990-91). Am. Libr. Assoc. Home: 540 Hinman Ave Apt 4 Evanston IL 60202-3081

CATES, SUE SADLER, special education counselor; b. Ft. Worth, Aug. 7, 1947; d. Randall and Mary Jo (Merkt) Sadler; m. Dennis Lynn Cates, Aug. 9, 1975. BA, Baylor U., 1970; MEd, Sul Ross State U., 1977. Cert. tchr., counselor, ednl. diagnostician, Tex. Tchr. spl. edn. Eagle Pass (Tex.) Ind. Sch. Dist., 1974-76, Beeville (Tex.) Ind. Sch. Dist., 1976-80; supr., ednl. diagnostician Sinton (Tex.) Ind. Sch. Dist., 1980-81; counselor, diagnostician Snyder (Tex.) Ind. Sch. Dist., 1981-86; ednl. diagnostician Pampa (Tex.) Ind. Sch. Dist., 1987-89; elem. counselor Richland County Sch. Dist., Columbia, SC, 1989-95; ednl. diagnostician Wichita Falls (Tex.) Ind. Sch. Dist., 1995-97, Graham (Tex.) Ind. Sch. Dist., 1997-98, Carrollton-Farmers Branch (Tex.) Ind. Sch. Dist., 1998-2000, Cedar Hill Ind. Sch. Dist., 2000-01, Arlington (Tex.) Ind. Sch. Dist., 2001—02, Ft. Worth (Tex.) Can! Acad. Charter Sch., 2002—, Ft. Worth Can! Acad. Charter Sch., 2002, Van Zandt/Rains County SSA-Edgewood Ind. Sch. Dist., 2003—04, Rains Ind. Sch. Dist., Emory, 2004—06, Pittsburg Ind. Sch. Dist., 2006—. Bd. dir. Scurry County Sheltered Workshop, 1981-85, Tex. Assn. Children with Learning Disabilities, 1976-77, 81-83; coach Tex. Spl. Olympics, Beeville, amd Sinton, 1978-81; mem. sanctuary choir Floral Heights United Meth. Ch., Wichita Falls, 1995-98, Stephen Ministry, 1992-2005, Stephen Ministry L.T.C., 2005—, tchr. Sunday sch., youth coord. Mem. NEA, AAUW, Tex. Ednl. Diagnosticians' Assn., Coun. Exceptional Children, Coun. Edn. Diagnosticians, Assn. Supervision and Devel., Nat. Assn. Workshop Dirs., Tex. State Tchrs. Assn., Tex. Classroom Tchrs. Assn., Am. Assn. Counseling and Devel., Tex. Assn. Counseling and Devel., Tex. Ednl. Diagnosticians Assn., Phi Delta Kappa, Zeta Phi Eta. Avocations: swimming, coin collecting/numismatics, travel, singing, jewelry. Home: PO Box 234 Detroit TX 75436 Office Phone: 903-856-1142. Personal E-mail: bu70@prodigy.net.

CATHCART, LINDA, art historian; b. Oct. 20, 1947; BA in Fine Arts, Calif. State U., Fullerton, 1969; MA in Art History, CUNY, 1972. Exhbns. asst. Met. Mus. Art, NYC, 1970; asst. curator Whitney Mus. Art, NYC, 1971; Fulbright fellow Courtauld Art Inst., 1973-74; curator Albright-Knox Art Gallery, Buffalo, 1975-79; dir. Contemporary Arts Mus., Houston, 1979-87, Ctr. Study Mexican Popular Arts, Santa Barbara, Calif., 1998—; prin. Linda Cathcart Gallery, Santa Barbara, Calif. Organizer exhbns. in field, 1989-95; prof. art history UCLA, 1996, U. Tex., Austin, 1997. Office: Casa Dolores 1023 Bath St Santa Barbara CA 93101

CATHCART, SHEILA K., athletic trainer; d. Larry T. and Joan M. (Durham) Ferrer; m. Chad D. Cathcart, Aug. 15, 1998; 1 child, Carmen Faith. BS, Charleston So. U., 1998; MA, Regent U., Va. Beach, 2003. Cert. athletic trainer 1999, lic. cert. athletic trainer S.C., 2002. Exercise leader in cardiac rehab. Piedmont Med. Ctr., Rockhill, SC, 1998; indsl. athletic trainer West Rehab. Svcs., Inc., Hinesville, Ga., 1999; guidance counselor, aide, test examiner U.S. Army Edn. Ctr., Schweinfurt, Germany, 2000—02; cert. athletic trainer Sports Plus Physical Therapy, Aiken, SC, 2002—. Clinical instr. U. S.C., Aiken, 2004—. Instr. ARC, Aiken, SC, 2003—, bd. dirs., 2003—04. Decorated Family Readiness Group Co-leader Appreciation award Inf. Battalion. Mem.: S.C. Athletics Trainer's Assn., Nat. Athletic Trainers Assn. Baptist. Avocations: reading, crafts, sports.

CATHEY, GERTRUDE BROWN, retired medical/surgical nurse; b. NYC, Sept. 1, 1933; d. William Robert Brown and Helen Elizabeth Dobrovich-Brown; m. Delter Dalton Cathey, Apr. 20, 1960; children: William, Colleen, Eileen, Christopher. Diploma in nursing, Bellevue Hosp., 1954; BS in Edn., Hunter Coll., 1961; MPA, John Jay Coll., 1984. Staff nurse, head nurst Bellevue Hosp., N.Y.C., NY, 1954—58, supr., 1965—88, asst. dir. nursing, 1988—92; staff nurse, head nurse St. Mary's Hosp., Passaic, NJ, 1958—59; office nurse Dr. Harold Cole, Rutherford, NJ, 1959—65. Facilitator support group Alzheimer's Assn., Rutherford, 1995—. Vol. Kip Ctr., Rutherford, 1992—, Star Fish, Rutherford; mem. social concerns com. St. Mary Ch., Rutherford, 1992—, extraordinary min. of Holy Communion, 2002—. Named Vol. of Yr., Kip Ctr., 2002. Mem.: AARP (sec. Rutherford chpt. 1995—2000), ANA. Home: 35 Union Ave East Rutherford NJ 07073

CATHEY, MARY ELLEN JACKSON, religious studies educator; b. Florence, S.C., Jan. 12, 1926; d. John William and Mary Ellen (Heinrich) Jackson; m. Henry Marcellus Cathey, May 31, 1958; children: Mary Emily Cathey Ewell, Henry Marcellus Jr. AB, Winthrop Coll., 1947; MRE, Presbyn. Sch. Christian Edn., Richmond, Va., 1953. Cert. Christian educator. Tchr. English, drama Jenkins Jr. High Sch., Spartanburg, S.C., 1947-51; dir. Christian edn. First Presbyn. Ch., Anderson, S.C., 1953-56, Bethesda (Md.) Presbyn. Ch., 1956-59; organizer, dir. Co-op Nursery Sch., Bethesda Presbyn. Ch., 1967-70; dir. Christian edn. Potomac Presbyn. Ch., Potomac, Md., 1977-83, Bethesda Presbyn. Ch., 1983-85, Nat. Presbyn. Ch., Washington, 1985-88; freelance cons. and educator Nat. Capital Presbytery, Washington, 1988—. Edn. cons. Covenant Presbyn. Ch., Arlington, Va., 1987, First Presbyn. Ch., Arlington, 1989-91, Lewinsville Presbyn. Ch., McLean, 1990; elder Nat. Presbyn. Ch., 1990—; elder commr. Gen. Assy., Presbyn. Ch., Milw., 1992. Author hymn text: God Almighty, God Eternal, 1956, others, numerous poems; co-author: Confirmation Guidebook, 1988, The Circle of Wholeness, 1991. Mem. Nat. Leadership Ctr., Washington, 1999—2000; mem. pres.;s adv. coun. Union Sem.-Presbyn. Sch. Christian Edn., Richmond, Va.; pub. trustee Washington Theol. Consortium; elder Presbyn. Ch. USA, copmmr. gen. assembly, 1992. Recipient Sparkler Award Presbyn. Sch. of Christian Edn. Alumni/ae Coun., 1991. Mem. Hymn Soc. U.S. and Can., Presbyn. Writers' Guild, Presbyn. Assn. Musicians, Assn. Presbyn. Ch. Educators, Nat. Capital Presbytery Educators. Avocations: travel, theater, music, dance, writing. Home: 400 Avinger Ln Apt 209 Davidson NC 28036-9705

CATHEY, PATRICE ANTOINETTE, secondary school educator, director; b. Buffalo, Oct. 13, 1954; d. Eulis Merle and Ruth Houston Cathey; children: Jonathan Eulis Barr, Patrick Jason Barr, Stephan James Barr. BA, Canisius Coll., 1995—98, EdM, 2000—02; PhD, Walden U., 2002—. Cert. of Interior Design J.R. Powers Sch., 1982. Founder/dir. Poetically Speaking Poetry Workshops For Children, Buffalo, 1995—, Ethics and Etiquette, Buffalo, 1996—; writers in edn. instr. Just Buffalo Lit. Ctr., 1996—2000; tchr. St. John Christian Acad., Buffalo, 1997—2000; academic coord. Upward Bound of Buffalo State Coll., 2000—01; dir. Liberty Partnerships Program, Buffalo, 2001—. Comm. coord. B.E.A.M.-Buffalo-Area Engring. Awareness for Minorities, 1996—; founder/pub. Onya Pub., Buffalo, 1998—; dir. of mentoring/tutoring Liberty Partnerships Program, Buffalo, 2001—. Actor: (performance poetry) A Woman of Her Words; author: (cd) Perhaps Virginia, When Poems Take Wings.Life Poems, 2003, numerous poems. Mem. Cmty. Sch. #53, Buffalo, 2001—02; vol. Darwin Martin Ho., Buffalo, 2002, Albright Knox Art Gallery, Buffalo. Recipient Distinguished Alumni Award, The Buffalo Sem., 2002, Uncrowned Queens, African Am. Women Cmty. Builders of Western N.Y., 2001; scholar Academic Scholarship, Women's Bus. Soc. of Amherst, 1997. Mem.: Internat. Soc. of Poets (award 2000), Poetry Soc. of Am., The Acad. of Am. Poets, Women in Higher Edn., Nat. Assn. of U. Women, Nat. Assn. of Black Sch. Educators, AEEE, The Jr. League of Buffalo, Alpha Kappa Alpha Sorority. Office: Liberty Partnerships Program 1300 Elmwood Avenue-CLL-E103 Buffalo NY 14222 Personal E-mail: patricecathey@yahoo.com. E-mail: catheypc@buffalostate.edu.

CATHEY-GIBSON, SHARON SUE RINN, principal, academic administrator; b. Reed City, Mich., June 11, 1940; d. Sherwood and Ellen (Hutson) Rinn.; children: Joel A. Cathey, Julie A. Maez, Sharon Sue Rinn Cathey-Gibson, Aug. 27, 1996; m. Warren Gibson. BA in Edn., San Francisco State U., 1962; postgrad., U. Mich., 1972-74, U. Calif., 1975-77; MA in Edn., U. Nev., 1988, EdD in Curriculum and Instrn., 1991. Tchr. Laguna Salada Union Sch. Dist., Pacifica, Calif., 1962-64, Redwood City (Calif.) Sch. Dist., 1964-66, Lapeer (Mich.) Sch. Dist., 1970-74; tchr., choral dir. Pine Middle Sch., Reno, 1978-84; tchr. Washoe County Sch. Dist., Reno, 1985—, adminstrv. elem. edn. cons., 1991-92; adminstrv. cons. Nev. State Dept. Elem. Edn., Carson City, 1990—; prin. Anderson Elem. Sch., Reno, 1992—, Elizabeth Lenz Elem. Sch., 1994, Libby Booth Sch., Reno, 1994-97; prof., adminstr. Sierra Nev. Coll., 1994—2002, adminstr., 1997—2002, ret., 2002; asst. prof. U. Nev., Reno, 2002—, cons. for literacy, 2001—05; cons., ptnr., editl. staff Superior Edn. and Leadership Inc.; interim dir. Ctr. Learning & Literacy, U. Nev., Reno, 2004—05. Statewide exec. dir. tchr. edn. Thompson Learning Ctr., Reno, 1987—89, diagnostician, 1987—89; asst. U. Nev., Reno, 1988—90; adminstr., prof. and coord. sch. based programs, dir. tchr. edn. dept. Sierra Nev. Coll.; ct. apptd. spl. adv. worker; cons., editor Superior Learning & Leadership Corp.; ptnr. Superior Learning Co.; cons., presenter in field. Adminstr., founder, and pres. Sierra Advocates for Family Equity. Recipient Celebrate Literacy award, Internat. Reading Assn., 2003; grantee, Nev. ESSA, 1977. Mem.: AAUW (pres. 1976—2005), Nev. Assn. Coll. Tchrs. Edn., Nat. Coun. Tchrs. English, Nat. Reading Assn., Internat. Reading Assn. (state pres. 1992, local pres. 1993—94, Literacy award 1995, Celebrate Literacy award 2003), Washoe County Tchrs. Assn., Kiwanis (Reno Sunrisers chpt. sec. 1995—98, pres. 2001—02, Kiwanian of Yr. 2003, Disting. Club Pres. 2003), Kappa Delta Epsilon (adviser), Delta Kappa Gamma (state pres. 1989—91, chptr. pres. 2004—, chair nominating com.), Phi Kappa Phi, Golden Key (hon.; ct. appted spl. advocate 2002—05). Republican. Episcopalian. Avocations: music, art, swimming. Home: 2550 Comstock Dr Reno NV 89512-1347 E-mail: sharons@gbis.com.

CATHOU, RENATA EGONE, chemist, consultant; b. Milan, June 21, 1935; d. Egon and Stella Mary Egone; m. Pierre-Yves Cathou, June 21, 1959. BS, MIT, Cambridge, 1957; PhD, MIT, 1963. Fellow, rsch. assoc. in chemistry MIT, Cambridge, 1962-65; rsch. assoc. Harvard U. Med. Sch., Cambridge, 1965-69, instr., 1969-70; rsch. assoc. Mass. Gen. Hosp., 1965-69, instr., 1969-70; asst. prof. dept. biochemistry Sch. Medicine, Tufts U., 1970-73, assoc. prof., 1973-78, prof., 1978-81; pres. Tech. Evaluations, Lexington, Mass., 1983-2000; sr. cons. SRC Assocs., Park Ridge, NJ, 1984-93. Sr. investigator Arthritis Found., 1970-75; vis. prof. dept. chemistry UCLA, 1976-77; mem. adv. panel NSF, 1974-75; mem. bd. sci. counselors Nat. Cancer Inst., 1979-83; ind. cons. and writer. Mem. editl. bd. Immunochemistry, 1972-75; contbr. chpts. to books and articles to profl. jours. MIT Company Founders citation, 1989; NIH predoctoral fellow, 1958-62; grantee Am. Heart Assn., 1969-81, USPHS, 1970-81. Mem. AAAS, Am. Soc. for Biochemistry and Molecular Biology, Am. Assn. Immunologists, Circumnavigators Club. Avocations: photography, opera, fine arts. Personal E-mail: rcathou@aol.com.

CATLEY-CARLSON, MARGARET, not-for-profit executive; b. Nelson, B.C., Oct. 6, 1942; d. George Lorne and Helen Margaret Catley; m. Stanley F. Carlson, Oct. 30, 1970. BA with honors, U. B.C., 1966, LLD (hon.), 1994; postgrad., Inst. Internat. Rels., U. W.I., St. Augustine, Trinidad and Tobago, 1970; LLD (hon.), U. Regina, 1985; LittD (hon.), St. Mary's U., 1985; LLD (hon.), Concordia U., 1989, Mt. St. Vincent U., 1990, Carleton U., 1994, U. Calgary, 1994. Joined Dept. External Affairs, Canada, 1966, with, 1970-74, asst. under-sec., 1981-82; 2d sec. Can. High Commn., Colombo, Sri Lanka, 1968, econ. counsellor London, 1975-77; v.p. Can. Internat. Devel. Agy., 1978, sr. v.p., acting pres., 1979-80, pres., 1983-89; asst. sec. gen. UN; dep. exec. dir. ops. UNICEF, 1981—83; fellow Ryerson Poly. U., 1986; dep. min. Health and Welfare Country Can., 1989—92; pres. Population Coun., NYC, 1993—99. Chmn. Global Water Partnership; chmn. water resource adv. com. Group Suez, Paris; chmn. change devel. and mgmt. team CGIAR, Washington, 2001; vice-chair Internat. Devel. Rsch. Ctr., Ottawa; chmn. Ctr. Agr. Rsch. Dry Areas, Syria; mem. 2020 vision policy, global food policy Internat. Food Policy Rsch. Inst., Washington; with Libr. Alexandria, Egypt, Inter-Am. Dialogue, Washington; clin. prof. Tulane U., New Orleans. Home: 249 E 48th St Apt 8A New York NY 10017

CATO, GLORIA MAXINE, retired secondary school educator; b. Covington, La., Mar. 22, 1942; d. Dan and Roxieana (Washington) Smith; widowed; 1 child, Mark. BS, Southern U., 1965; MS, Pepperdine U., 1974. Tchr. Los Angeles Unified Sch. Dist., 1965-81, counselor, magnet program coordinator, 1981—, PUSH for Excellence program coordinator, 1978-80, student activities coordinator, 1982-84, coll. advisor, 1984-85, personnel specialist, tchr. advisor, 1986-87, asst. prin., 1992—99; ret., 1999. Edn./counselor cons. L.A. Unified Sch. Dist. Trustee L.A. Ednl. Allance Restructuring Now. Recipient Community-Sch. Service award City of Los Angeles, 1978; named to Top Ladies of Distinction, 1992. Charter mem. NEA, Nat. Assn. Biology Tchrs. (finalist Tchrs. award 1978), Magnet Coordinator Assn., Los Angeles Counselors Assn.; mem. United Tchrs. Los Angeles, Associated Adminstrs. L.A., Assn. Calif. Sch. Adminstrs., Asst. Prin. Secondary Counseling Svcs. Orgn., Phi Delta Kappa, Alpha Kappa Alpha (Mu Beta Omega chpt.). Democrat. Baptist. Home: 3661 Kensley Dr Inglewood CA 90305-2230

CATOE, BETTE LORRINA, pediatrician, educator; b. Apr. 7, 1926; d. John Booker and Laura Beola (Adams) C.; m. Warren J. Strudwick, Sept. 17, 1949; children: Laura Christina, Warren J., William J. BS cum laude, Howard U., 1948, MD, 1951. Intern Freedmen's Hosp., Washington, 1951-52; pediat. resident Howard U./Freedman's Hosp., 1952-55, practice medicine specializing in pediatrics Washington, 1956—2003; cons. Govt. of DC Income Maintenance Adminstrn., Washington, 2003—; instr. bacteriology Howard U., 1955-57; mem. staff Providence Hosp., Columbia Hosp., Howard U. Hosp., Wash., Hosp. Ctr.; sch. health officer Dept. Health, Washington, 1960-64; clin. instr. Howard U., 1956-58; health cons., 2003—; cons. income maint. admin. Govt. DC, 2003—. Mem. DC Health Planning Adv. Coun., 1967-77, chmn. 1973-77; chmn. DC Devel. Disabilities Adv. Coun., 1970-74; mem. DC Mayor's Commn. on Food and Nutrition, 1971-72, Mayor's Commn. on Maternal and Child Health, 1978-84, appt. vice chmn. Pub. Benefit Corp., 1997-2001; mem. DC Commn. Jud. Tenure and Disabilities, 1977-2001, chmn. Bd. Public Benefit Corp. of DC, 1998-2001; bd. govs. St. Alban's Sch., 1978-84; bd. dirs. DC Health and Welfare Coun., 1968-73, pres., 1973-74; del. Democratic Nat. Conv., 1976; bd. dirs. Met. Washington Health and Welfare Coun., 1970-72, Parent Coun. of Washington, 1974-75, Met. Med. Founds., Inc., Silver Spring YMCA, 1977-80, Kingsburg Ctr., 1997-99; mem., chair emergency med. com. Mayor's Health Policy Coun., 1998-2001; cons. income maintenance adminstrn. Govt. of DC Dept. Human Svcs., 2003—. Mem.: NAACP, AMA, Women's Aux. Medico-Chirurg. Soc., Assn. Comprehensive Health Planners (dir. 1975—77), Urban League, Am. Med. Women's Assn., Nat. Med. Assn. (chmn. pediat. sect. 1981—83), D.C. Chirurg. Soc. (trustee 1996—99, nominating com. 2000—03, jud. legis. com. 2001—03), Women's Nat. Dem., Jack and Jill Am., Carrousels Club (nat. v.p. 1986—88, nat. pres. 1988—90), Links Club, Century Club of Nat. Assn. Negro Bus. and Profl. Women's Clubs (pres. 1985—89), Alpha Kappa Alpha. Home and Office: 1748 Sycamore St NW Washington DC 20012-1031 Office Phone: 202-882-2406. Personal E-mail: bcatoemd@aol.com.

CATOLINE-ACKERMAN, PAULINE DESSIE, small business owner; b. Ft. Worth, Dec. 17, 1937; d. Byron Hillis and Dessie Elizabeth (Plumlee) Doggett; children: Sherry Lou, Brenda Lynn; m. Donald Ralph Ackerman, Feb. 19, 1993. BA in Bus. Mgmt. (labor rels. specialty), Hiram Coll., 1989. Sec. Gen. Am. Life Ins. Co., Ft. Worth, 1956—57, Kelly Girl Svcs., Youngstown, Ohio, 1965—69; legal sec. Burgstaller, Schwartz & Moore, Youngstown, 1962—65, Green, Schiavoni, Murphy & Haines, Youngstown, 1969—71, Flask & Policy, Youngstown, 1971—83; sec. We. Res. Care Sys., Youngstown, 1983—87, exec. sec., 1987—90; owner, mgr. Pauline's Place, Youngstown, 1990—; legal sec. Henderson, Covington, Stein, Donchess & Messenger Law Firm, 1993—94; exec. adminstrv. asst. to pres. CEO, sr. v.p. Internat. Renaissance Developers, Youngstown, 1994—96; adminstrv. asst. to v.p. and client svc. mgr. Bank One Investment Mgmt. & Trust Group, Youngstown, 1996—2000; admin. assoc. regional divsn. Am. Heart Assn., Youngstown, 2000—01; owner, mgr. Paulines Pl., 2001—; staff Kelly Svcs., Youngstown, 2001—. Sub. tchr. K-12 Austintown Sch. Sys., 2001. Pres. PTA, Cottage Hills, Ill., 1968-69, brownie and scout leader Girl Scouts U.S.A., 1968-69 Mem. Mahoning County Legal Secs. Assn. (v.p. 1973-74, editor monthly booklet 1974-75), Exec. Link, Missionary Group Club. Democrat. Methodist. Avocations: painting, reading poetry, tennis, swimming, horseback riding. Home: 3961 Cannon Rd Youngstown OH 44515-4604 Office Phone: 330-793-4265.

CATTANEO, JACQUELYN ANNETTE KAMMERER, artist, educator; b. Gallup, N.Mex., June 1, 1944; d. Ralph John and Gladys Agnes (O'Sullivan) Kammerer; m. John Leo Cattaneo, Apr. 25, 1964; children: John Auro, Paul Anthony. Student, Tex. Woman's U., 1962-64. Portrait artist, tchr., Gallup, N.Mex., 1972. Coord. Works Progress Adminstrn. art project renovation McKinley County, Gallup, Octavia Fellin Performing Arts wing dedication, Gallup Pub. Libr.; formation com. mem. Multi-Modal/Multi-Cultural Ctr. for Gallup; exch. with Soviet Women's Com. USSR Women Artists del., Moscow, Kiev, Leningrad, 1990; Women Artists del. and exch., Jerusalem, Tel Aviv, Cairo, Israel; mem. Artists Del. to Prague, Vienna and Budapest; mem. Women Artists Del. to Egypt, Israel and Italy, 1992, artist del., Brazil, 1994, Greece, Crete, Turkey, Spain, 1996, N.S. and Ont., N.B., PEI, Can., 2000. One-woman shows include Gallup Pub. Libr., 1963, 66, 77, 78, 81, 87, Gallup Lovelace Med. Clinic, Santa Fe Sta. Open House, 1981, Gallery 20, Farmington, N.Mex., 1985—, Red Mesa Art Gallery, 1989, Soviet Retrospect Carol's Art & Antiques Gallery, Liverpool, N.Y., 1992, 97, N.Mex. State Capitol Bldg., Santa Fe, 1992, Lt. Govt. Casey Luna-Office Complex, Women Artists N.Mex. Mus. Fine Arts, Carlsbad, 1992, Rio Rancho Country Club, N.Mex., 1995; exhibited in group shows including Navajo Nation Libr. Invitational, 1978, Santa Fe Festival of the Arts Invitational, 1979, N.Mex. State Fair, 1978, 79, 80, Catharine Lorrilard Wolfe, N.Y.C., 1980, 81, 84, 85, 86, 87, 88, 89, 90, 91, 92, 2004, 2005, 4th ann. exhbn. Salmagundi Club, 1984, 90, 98, 3d ann. Palm Beach Internat., New Orleans, 1984, Fine Arts Ctr., Taos, 1984, The Best and the Brightest O'Brien's Art Emporium, Scottsdale, Ariz., 1986, Gov.'s Gallery, 1989, N.Mex. State Capitol, Santa Fe, 1987, Pastel Soc. West Coast Ann. Exhbn., Sacramento Ctr. for Arts, Calif., 1986-90, gov.'s invitational Magnifico Fest. of the Arts, Albuquerque, 1991, Assn. pour la Promotion du Patrimone Artistique Française, Paris Nat. Mus. of the Arts for Women, Washington, 1991, Artists of N.Mex., Internat. Nexus '92 Fine Art Exhbn., Trammell Corw Pavillion, Dallas, Carlsbad (N.Mex.) Mus. Fine Art; represented in permanent collections Zuni Arts and Crafts Ednl. Bldg., U. N.Mex., C.J. Wiemar Collection, McKinley Manor, Gov.'s Office, State Capitol Bldg., Santa Fe, Hist. El Rancho Hotel, Gallup, Sunwest Bank, Fine Arts Ctr., Taos, Armand Hammer Pvt. Collection, Wilcox Canyon Collections, Sadona, Ariz., Galaria Impi, Netherlands, Woods Art and Antiques, Liverpool, N.Y., Stewarts Fine Art, Taos, N.Mex., Rehoboth McKinley Christian Hosp. & Sacred Heart Cathedral, Gallup, NM, 2005. Mem. Dora Cox del. to Soviet Union-U.S. Exch., 1990. Recipient Cert. of Recognition for Contbn. and Participation Assn. pour la Patrimone du Artistique Français, 1991, N.Mex. State Senate 14th Legislature Session Meml. # 101 for Artistic Achievements award, 1992, Award of Merit, Pastel Soc. West Coast Ann. Membership Exhbn., 1998, Disting. Mem. Juried Exhbn., 2006, award N.Mex. State Ho. Reps. for Artistic Achievement, 2001,

Holbein award for excellence in painting Pastel Soc. West Coast Internat. Juried Exhbn., Award of Merit Pastel Soc. S.W. Ann. Signature and Disting. Pastelists Juried Exhbns., 2006; honored for preservation of WPA Dept. Edn. N.Mex. State Ho. of Reps., 2001. Mem. Internat. Fine Arts Guild, Am. Portrait Soc. (cert.), Oil Painters of Am., Pastel Soc. Am. (signature, Award of Merit 2004), Pastel Soc. of West Coast (cert., signature, Hobein award, award of excellence mem.'s show 1999), Mus. N.Mex. Found., N.Mex. Archtl. Found., Mus. Women in the Arts, Fechin Inst., Artists' Co-op (co-chair), Gallup C. of C., Gallup Area Arts and Crafts Coun. (nat. and internat. artist of distinction award 1997), Catharine Lorillard Wolfe Art Club of N.Y.C. (Pastel Soc. of Am. award for Excellence, 2004, oil and pastel juried membership, 1st Pl. Pastel Membership Exhbn. award 2004, 2d Pl. Pastel Membership Exhbn. award 2005), Oil Painters of Am., Pastel Soc. N.Mex. (participant artist's presentation Australia chpt. 2006), Soroptomists (Internat. Woman of Distinction 1990), Salmagundi Art Club. Address: 210 E Green St Gallup NM 87301-6130 Office Phone: 505-722-4090. Business E-Mail: cattaneo@cnetco.com.

CATTERLIN, CINDY LOU, music educator, language educator; b. Linton, Ind., Nov. 20, 1958; d. Ralph Lloyd and Betty Lou Miller; m. Davey Lee Catterlin Jr., July 3, 1982; children: Davey Lee III, Melissa Joy. BS summa cum laude, Ind. State U., 1980, MS, 1981. Cert. advanced profl. tchr. Music tchr. Kossouth St. Bapt. Sch., Lafayette, Ind., 1981-82; pvt. instrumental music instr. Beckley, W.Va., 1986-94; bd. dir. Raleigh County Bd. Edn., Beckley, 1994-95; tchr. music and English Heritage Christian Acad., Englewood, Fla., 1997—, fine arts dir., 2001—, also bd. dirs., choir dir. Pianist Calvary Bapt. Ch., Englewood, 1995—, boys and girls Awana dir., 1995—2003. Named Tchr. of Yr., Heritage Christian Acad., 2005. Mem. Am. Assn. Christian Schs., North Port Concert Band, North Port Band Chorale. Avocations: sewing, music. Office: Heritage Christian Acad 75 Pine St Englewood FL 34223-3925 Home: 12148 Wellington Port Charlotte FL 33981 Personal E-mail: ccatterlin@yahoo.com.

CATTERTON, MARIANNE ROSE, occupational therapist; b. St. Paul, Feb. 3, 1922; d. Melvin Joseph and Katherine Marion (Bole) Maas; m. Elmer John Wood, Jan. 16, 1943 (dec.); m. Robert Lee Catterton, Nov. 20, 1951 (div. 1981); children: Jenifer Ann Dawson, Cynthia Lea Uthus. Student, Carleton Coll., 1939—41, U. Md., 1941—42; BA in English, U. Wis., 1944; MA in Counseling Psychology, Bowie State Coll., 1980; postgrad., No. Ariz. U., 1987—91. Registered occupl. therapist, Occupl. Therapy Cert. Bd. Occupl. therapist VA, NYC, 1946—50; cons. occupl. therapist Fondo del Seguro del Estado, PR, 1950—51; dir. rehab. therapies Spring Grove State Hosp., Catonsville, Md., 1953—56; occupl. therapist Anne Arundel County Health Dept., Annapolis, Md., 1967—78; dir. occupl. therapy Ea. Shore Hosp. Ctr., Cambridge, Md., 1979—85; cons. occupl. therapist Kachina Point Health Ctr., Sedona, Ariz., 1986. Regional chmn. Conf. on revising Psychiat. Occupl. Therapy Edn., 1958-59; instr. report writing Anne Arundel C.C., Annapolis, 1974-78. Editor: Am. Jour. Occupl. Therapy, 1962—67. Active Md. Mental Health Assn., 1959—60; mem. task force on occupl. therapy edn. Md. Dept. Health, 1971—72; chmn. Anne Arundel Gov. Com. on Employment of Handicapped, 1959—63; gov.'s com. to study vocat. rehab. Md., 1960; com. mem. Annapolis Youth Ctr., 1976—78; curator Dorchester County Heritage Mus., Cambridge, 1982—83; citizen interviewer Sedona Acad. Forum, 1993, 1994; vol. Respite Care, 1994—98, Verde Valley Caregivers, 1993—; ministerial search com. Unitarian Ch. Anne Arundel County, 1962; v.p., officer Unitarian-Universalist Fellowship Flagstaff, 1988—93, v.p., 1993—97; co-moderator, founder Unitarian-Universalist Fellowship Sedona, 1994—96, pres., 1997—98, co-pres., 2001—03. Mem.: Dorchester County Mental Health Assn. (pres. 1981—84), Md. Occupl. Therapy Assn. (del. 1953—59), Am. Occupl. Therapy Assn. (chmn. history com. 1958—61), PR Occupl. Therapy Assn. (co-founder 1950), Sedona Muses, Population Connection, Ret. Officers Assn., Pathfinder Internat., Air Force Assn. (sec. Barry Goldwater chpt. 1991—92, 1994—2006), Toastmasters, Internat. Club (chmn. publicity Annapolis chpt. 1966), Severn Town Club (treas. 1965, sec. 1971—72, 1994—95), Delta Delta Delta. Republican. Home: 415 Windsong Dr Sedona AZ 86336-3745

CATTRALL, KIM, actress; b. Liverpool, Eng., Aug. 21, 1956; d. Dennis and Shane Cattrall; m. Larry Davis, 1975 (div.); m. Andre J. Lyson, 1982 (div. 1989); m. Mark Levinson, Sept. 4, 1998. Student, London Acad. Music and Dramatic Art, Banff Sch. Fine Arts, Alta., Can.; grad., Am. Acad. Dramatic Arts, N.Y.C. Actor: (films) Rosebud, 1975, Tribute, 1980, Ticket to Heaven, 1981, Porky's, 1982, Police Academy, 1984, Turk 182!, 1985, City Limits, 1985, Hold-Up, 1985, Big Trouble in Little China, 1986, Mannequin, 1987, Masquerade, 1988, Palais Royale, 1988, Midnight Crossing, 1988, The Return of the Musketeers, 1989, La Famiglia Buonanotte, 1989, Honeymoon Academy, 1990, Bonfire of the Vanities, 1990, Star Trek VI: The Undiscovered Country, 1991, Split Second, 1992, Breaking Point, 1993, Live Nude Girls, 1995, Above Suspicion, 1995, Where Truth Lies, 1996, Unforgettable, 1996, Exception to the Rule, 1997, Modern Vampires, 1998, Baby Geniuses, 1999, The Devil and Daniel Webster, 2001, 15 Minutes, 2001, Crossroads, 2002, Ice Princess, 2005, others; (TV films) Sins of the Past, 1984, Miracle in the Wilderness, 1992, Double Vision, 1992, Two Golden Balls, 1994, Running Delilah, 1994, OP Center, 1995, The Heidi Chronicles, 1995, Every Woman's Dream, 1996, Invasion, 1997, Creature, 1998, 36 Hours to Die, 1999, Sex and the Matrix, 2000; (TV series) Angel Falls, 1993, Sex and the City, 1998—2004 (SAG award, 2001, Golden Globe award, 2002, Women in Film Lucy award, 1999), Him and Us, 2006—; (TV miniseries) Wild Palms, 1993, (various TV guest appearances); (plays) Whose Life Is It Anyway?, 2005; co-author (with Mark Levinson): Satisfaction, 2002; author: Sexual Intelligence, 2005. Office: c/o Jeffrey Witjas William Morris Agy 151 El Camino Dr Beverly Hills CA 90212

CATZ, SAFRA, computer software company executive; b. Israel; married; 2 children. BA, U. Pa., 1983, JD, 1986. Various investment banking positions Donaldson, Lufkin & Jenrette, 1986—94, sr. v.p., 1994—97, mng. dir., 1997—99; sr. v.p. Oracle Corp., Redwood City, Calif., 1999, exec. v.p., 1999—2004, co-pres., 2004—, interim CFO, 2005—. Bd. dirs. Oracle Corp., 2001—. Named one of 100 Most Powerful Women, Forbes mag., 2005—06, 50 Women to Watch, Wall Street Journal, 2005. Office: Oracle Corp 500 Oracle Pkwy Redwood City CA 94085 Address: PeopleSoft Inc 4460 Hacienda Dr Pleasanton CA 94588-8618*

CAUCIA, LOUISA B., retired elementary school educator; b. San Francisco, Aug. 9, 1946; d. Louis and Blanca Caucia. BA in Journalism, Calstate U., Hayward, 1969. Cert. Elem. Calif, English secondary tchr. Calif. Elem. tchr. San Francisco Unified Sch. Dist., 1970—77; mid. sch. tchr. Berryessa Unified Sch. Dist., San Jose, 1976—87, LA Unified Sch. Dist., 1987—2006; ret., 2006. Mid. sch. commr. Nat. Journalism Edn. Assn., 1999—2000. Mem. Latino Children's Action Coun., L.A., 1995, Glendale Dem. Club, 2001—06. Mem.: Hispanic Ams. for Fairness in Media. Democrat. Avocations: films, hiking, travel, reading.

CAUDLE, LETHA GRACE, secondary school educator; b. Bristow, Okla., June 21, 1949; d. William Frederick and Effie Dorothy Caudle. BS, Okla. State U., Stillwater, 1971; MA, Okla. State U., 1977. Tchr. Bristow Pub. Schs., 1973—. Contbr. articles to publs. Pres. Faculty Club, Bristow, 1985—86, Bus. Profl. Women's Club, Bristow, 1989—90, Am. Legion Aux., Bristow, 1991—93, Okla. State History Day Tchrs. Adv. Coun., Oklahoma City, 1996—, Bristow Edn. Assn., 1999—2003; mem. Tulsa (Okla.) Oratorio Chorus, Tulsa Vocal Arts Ensemble. Named Tchr. of Yr., Dist. 6 History Day, Okla., 1999, 2000, 2002; recipient cert. of appreciation Voice of Democracy, Bristow VFW and Aux., annually, 1973—85, cert. of appreciation, Nat. Geog. Soc., 1993, 1994, 1995. Mem.: Okla. Hist. Soc., Okla. Coun. Tchrs. Social Studies, Okla. Coun. History Tchrs. (bd. dirs. 2005—, sec. 2006), Nat. Coun. Social Studies. Baptist. Avocations: reading, piano, singing, writing. Home: PO Box 177 Bristow OK 74010 Office: Bristow Mid Sch Bristow Pub Schs 10 Weatherwood Way Bristow OK 74010 Office Phone: 918-367-3551. Office Fax: 918-367-1362. Business E-Mail: lcaudle@bristow.k12.ok.us.

CAULFIELD, CAREEN ANNE, secondary school educator, biologist; b. Abington, Pa., Jan. 28, 1972; d. George and Kathleen Marie Bulka; m. Patrick Michael Caulfield, June 26, 1999; children: Ryan Patrick, Matthew Connor. BA in Secondary Edn., Bloomsburg U., Pa., 1994; MEd, Pa. State U., 1999. Tchr. biology Tri-Valley H.S., Hegins, Pa., 1996—. Organizer charity North Schuylkill Lady Spartans Basketball, Ashland, Pa., 1999—2006. Home: 526 Airport Road Ashland PA 17921 Office: Tri-Valley High School 155 East Main Street Hegins PA 17938 Office Phone: 570-682-3125.

CAULFIELD, CARLOTA, education educator, researcher, poet; b. Havana, Cuba, Jan. 16, 1953; came to U.S., 1981; d. Francis and Ada (Robaina) C.; 1 child, Franco Caulfield Gonzalez. BA, U. Havana, 1979; MA, San Francisco State U., 1986; PhD, Tulane U., 1992. Lectr. San Francisco State U., 1985-86; publ., editor Literary Gazette/El Gato Tuerto, San Francisco, 1984-88; from teaching asst. to rsch. asst. Tulane U., New Orleans, 1988-92; prof. Spanish & Spanish Am. studies Mills Coll., Oakland, Calif., 1992—. Free-lance acquisitions editor Mercury House, San Francisco, 1988-90; free-lance copy editor John Wiley & Sons, Inc., N.Y.C., 1988; vis. fellow Inst. Romance Studies, U. London, 2002, 06; vis. prof. U. Coll. London, 2006. Author: Visual Games for Words and Sounds, 1993, (poems) Angel Dust, 1990, Oscurita Divina, 1990, 34th Street, 1987, A las Puertas del Papel Con Amoroso Fuego, 1996, the Book of Giulio Camillo, 2003, Quincunce/Quincunx, 2004, Ticket To Ride. Essays and Poems, 2005 Recipient Internat. Poetry prize Ultimo Novecento, 1988, hon. mention Premio Plural, Mex., 1993, hon. mention poetry prize Federico Garcia Lorca, 1994, Italy poetry prize Riccardo Machi-Torre di Calafuria, 1995, hon. mention poetry prize Latin Am. Writers Inst., 1998, First Internat. Poetry prize 2002; Cintas fellow, 1988, 96, Quigley fellow Mills Coll., 1994, 97, 98, 2005, 06; Nat. Hispanic scholar, 1991; Mellon Summer Rsch. grantee Tulane U., 1990. Mem. MLA, Latin Am. Jewish Studies Assn., Philol. Assn. the Pacific Coast, PEN Internat., Gruppo Internat. Lettura (hon., pres. U.S. chpt. 1988—), Libera Acad. Galileo Galilei (hon.). Avocations: gardening, cats, theater, travel. Office: Mills Coll 5000 Macarthur Blvd Oakland CA 94613-1301 Office Phone: 510-430-2356.

CAULFIELD, JOAN, director, educator; b. St. Joseph, Mo., July 17, 1943; d. Joseph A. and Jane (Lisenby) Caulfield; m. Alan Warne, Sept. 7, 1996. BS in Edn. cum laude, U. Mo., 1963, MA in Spanish, 1965, PhD, 1978; postgrad. (Mexican Govt. scholar), Nat. U. Mexico, 1962-63. TV tchr. Spanish Kansas City (Mo.) pub. schs., 1963-68; tchr. Spanish, French Bingham Jr. High Schs., Kansas City, 1968-78; asst. prin. S.E. High Sch., Kansas City, 1984; prin. Nowlin Jr. High Sch., Independence, Mo., 1984-86, Lincoln Coll. Preparatory Acad., Kansas City, Mo., 1986-88; asst. supt. Kansas City, 1988-89; part-time instr. U. Mo.-Kansas City; dir. English Inst. Rockhurst Coll., summers 1972-75; coord. sch. coll. rels. Rockhurst U., 1989-2001, chmn. edn. dept.; adj. prof. St. Louis U.; pres., CEO The Brain Inc., 2001—. Mem. nat. steering com. Brain-Based Learning Network, facilitator; assessor dept. elem. and secondary edn. State Mo.; mem. women's coun. bd. U. Mo.-Kansas City, 1994-98, pres. 1998-; pres., CEO The Brain Inc.; vis. social scientist Midwest Rsch. Inst.; adj. prof. Baker U. Co-author: Inciting Learning: a Guide to Brain Compatible Instr., Bridging the Learning/Assessment Gap: Showcase Teaching, The Adolescent Brain, 2006 (Hon. Alumni award U. Mo. Coll. Edn., 2006); contbr. articles to profl. jours. Active Sister City Commn., Kansas City, 1980—, Kans.' Quality Performance Assessment Team, Metro-Vision Task Force; ofcl. translator to mayor on trip to Seville, Spain, 1969; bd. dirs. Kansas City chpt. NCCJ, Expo '92 World's Fair, Seville, transl., 1992, St. Theresa's Acad., 1991-94, Kansas City Acad. of Learning; selected leadership training Greater Mo.; trainer Harmony in a World of Difference, 1989-93; task force C. of C. bd. dirs.; edn. alumni bd. U. Mo., Kansas City; del. leader Spain People to People Internat., 1997; trustee Kansas City Pub. Libr., treas. bd.; mem. mayor's commn. on race, Kansas City; mem. adv. bd. NCCJ, 2002—; mem. humanitarian project to Ukraine Rotary Club, 2006. Named Outstanding Secondary Educator, 1973, Disting. Alumnus, U. Mo.-Columbia, 2006. Mem.: MLA (contbr. jour.), ASCD, Mo. Mid. Sch. Assn. (contbr. jour.), Am. Assn. Tchrs. Spanish and Portuguese, Nat. Assn. Secondary Sch. Prins., Magnet Schs. Am. (contbr. jour.), Friends of Art, Friends of Seville, Sigma Delta Pi, Phi Kappa Phi, Delta Kappa Gamma (state scholar 1977—78, contbr. jour. Bull.), Phi Delta Kappa, Phi Sigma Iota, Kappa Delta Pi. Presbyterian. Home: 431 W 70th St Kansas City MO 64113-2022 Office Phone: 816-361-6192. Personal E-mail: joancaulfield@prodigy.net.

CAULFIELD, KATHLEEN MARIE, medical health information administrator, geriatrics nurse; b. Albany, N.Y., Aug. 4, 1956; d. Frederick A. Caulfield and Mary G. Graver; 1 child, Jean Marie. BS in Med. Record Adminstrn., SUNY Coll. of Tech., Utica, 1983. RN N.Y., 1976; registered health info. mgmt. adminstr. RN St. Clare's Hosp., Schenectady, NY, 1976—79, New Eng. Deaconess Hosp., Boston, 1979—81, Teresian Ho., Albany, NY, 1981—83; nursing supr. Oneida City Hosp., NY, 1983—87; dir. of med. records N.Y. State Dept. of Corrections, Albany, 1987—2001; supervising med. record adminstr., psychiat. nurse Bronx Psychiat. Facility, NY, 2002—03; mgr. in health info. dept. U. Conn. Health Ctr., 2003—. Religion mentor St. Brigid's Cath. Ch. Mem.: Conn. Health Info. Mgrs. Assn., Am. Health Info. Mgr. Assn., Health Info. Adminstr. (registered), Toastmasters (sec.). Roman Catholic. Avocations: exercise, bicycling, quilting, feng shui cons., dog grooming. Office Phone: 860-674-3464.

CAUSEY, LINDA, secondary school educator; MEd, U. La., Monroe, 1976. Cert. educator La., Tex. Chemistry tchr. Ouachita HS, Monroe, 1987—2002; AP and pre-AP chemistry tchr. Coppell (Tex.) HS, 2001—. Office Phone: 214-496-6369.

CAUTHEN, CARMEN WIMBERLEY, legislative staff member, jewelry designer; b. Raleigh, N.C., Aug. 4, 1959; d. William Peele and Cliffornia (Grady) Wimberley; m. Ricky Leon Cauthen, May 26, 1990; 1 child, Kena Elizabeth. Student, Ga. Inst. Tech., 1977-78; BA in Polit. Sci., N.C. State U., Raleigh, 1986. Asst. sgt.-at-arms N.C. Ho. of Reps., Raleigh, 1981, 82, computer calendar clk.; owner, jewelry designer Accessories and Things, Raleigh, 1984—; sec. Coll. Humanities/Social Sci. N.C. State U., Raleigh, 1989-91; owner bookkeeping/typing svc. CTYPE, Raleigh, 1990—; jour. clk. N.C. Ho. of Reps., Raleigh, 1992-94, adminstrv. clk., 1992—. Mem. Am. Soc. Legis. Clks. and Secs. Democrat. Christian. Avocations: reading, furniture refinishing, cross-stitch, sewing. Home: 703 Latta St Raleigh NC 27607-7203 Office: NC Gen Assembly House Prin Clks Office Legis Bldg Jones St Raleigh NC 27603-5924

CAUTHORNE-BURNETTE, TAMERA DIANNE, family practice nurse practitioner, consultant; b. Richmond, Va., Apr. 13, 1961; d. Robert Francis Cauthorne and Lois Avery (Lloyd) Cumashot; m. William Nichols Burnette, Dec. 3, 1983. BSN, U. Va., 1983; postgrad., Med. U. S.C., 1988; MSN, Old Dominion U., 1993, grad. cert. in women's studies, 1994; postgrad., Univ. Coll., Oxford (Eng.) U., 1996. RN, Va.; family nurse practitioner. Staff nurse, charge nurse gynecology-oncology unit U. Va. Med. Ctr., Charlottesville, 1983, staff nurse, charge nurse high-risk labor and delivery, ICU, 1984-85; staff nurse, charge nurse, preceptor med. ICU Med. U. S.C., 1985-87, staff nurse ICU, 1988; staff nurse, charge nurse med.-surg. ICU, progressive care Stuart Cir. Hosp., Richmond, Va., 1988-90; staff nurse pediat. and neonatal ICU Childrens' Hosp. of the King's Dau., Norfolk, Va., 1990, staff nurse, team leader neonatal ICU, 1990-91; pvt. health care cons., 1993—; with Delmar Pub., 1994—; pres. The Foxmont Co., LLC, 1995—; with Sussex Ctrl. Health Ctr., 1995; men's responsibility clinic coord. Planned Parenthood, 1996; chief nurse practitioner med. svcs. Va. League Planned Parenthood, 1997-99; pvt. practice Air Park Med., Ashland, Va., 1999-2001; with James Jones and Assocs. Ob-gyn., 2001. Cons. Old Dominion U. Coll. Health Sci., Sch. Nursing, 1993—, undergrad. clin. facility, 1994—; condr. analysis of Russian and Ukrainian health care system; breast self-exam instr. Am. Cancer Soc., 1982—; presenter at profl. confs.; mng. mem. The Foxmont Co., L.L.C.; mem. adj. faculty Sch. Nursing U. Va., 1996; primary med. provider Va. League Planned Parenthood, 1997; mem. clin. faculty sch. of nursing Va. Commonwealth U., 1999, assoc. prof., 2001. Contbg. author A Quick Reference for Health Assessment, 1997, Clin. Companion to Health Assessment and Physical Examination, 1998; contbr. articles to profl. jours. Vol. Ronald McDonald House, 1980-83; docent Spoleto Festival USA, 1984-92, MacArthur Meml. Mus., 1991; vol. receptionist info. ctr. Gibbes Art Gallery, 1987-89; vol. ARC Blood Donation Ctr., 1986-92; mem. coun. U. Va. Coll. of Health Scis.; mem. adv. coun. U. Va. Sch. Nursing, 1997—; chmn. Va. Nurses PAC, 2002. Named Vol. of Yr., U. Va. Sch. Nursing. Fellow Internat. Pedagogical Acad./Moswoc. Order of Omega Nat. Honor Soc., Raven Honor Soc. U. Va., Sorenson Inst. Polit. Leadership U. Va.; mem. AACN, DAR, AAUW, Va. Coalition for Nurse Practitioners, U. Va. Sch. Nursing Alumnae Assn. (pres., CEO 1994—, adv. coun. 1997—), Jr. League Va. (chair state pub. affairs com.), Virginians Patient Choice Coalition, Jr. League Norfolk and Virginia Beach (state pub. affairs vice chmn./lobbyist 1995), Daus. of Confederacy, Carolina Art Assn., S.C. Hist. Soc., Confederate Meml. Lit. Soc., U. Va. Coll. Health Scis. Coun., Alpha Delta Pi (chmn. nat. panhellenic rels. com., nat. by-laws and resolutions com.), Sigma Theta Tau. Avocations: riding, raising and showing thoroughbred racing horses, collecting sporting art, foxhunting.

CAUTHRON, ROBIN J., federal judge; b. Edmond, Okla., July 14, 1950; d. Austin W. and Mary Louise (Adamson) Johnson. BA, U. Okla., 1970, JD, 1977; MEd, Cen. State U., Edmond, Okla., 1974. Bar: Okla. 1977. Law clk to Hon. Ralph G. Thompson US Dist. Ct. (We. Dist.) Okla., 1977-81; staff atty. Legal Svcs. Ea. Okla., 1981-82; pvt. practice law, 1982-83; spl. judge 17th Jud. Dist. State Okla., 1983-86; magistrate US Dist. Ct. (We. Dist.) Okla., Oklahoma City, 1986-91, judge, 1991—, chief judge. Editor Okla. Law Rev. Bd. dirs. Juvenile Diabetes Found. Internat., 1989-92; mem. nominating com. Frontier Coun. Boy Scouts Am., 1987, Edmond Ednl. Endowment; trustee, sec. First United Meth. Ch., 1988-90. Mem. ABA, Okla. Bar Assn., Okla. County Bar Assn. (bd. dirs. 1990— bench and bar com.), McCurtain County Bar Assn. (pres. 1986), Am. Judicature Soc., Nat. Assn. Women Judges, Fed. Bar Assn., Nat. Coun. Women Magistrates (bd. dirs. 1990-91), Okla. Jud. Conf. (v.p. 1985), Am. Inns of Ct. (pres. 1991-92), Order of Coif, Phi Delta Phi. Office: US Courthouse 200 NW 4th St Ste 3108 Oklahoma City OK 73102-3029

CAVALIER, GINA M., lawyer; b. Long Beach, Calif., Jan. 19, 1971; BA in Internat. Rels., summa cum laude, Boston U., 1993; JD cum laude, Georgetown U., 1996. Bar: NY 1997, DC 2000. Atty. Atty. Gen.'s Honors Program, US Dept. Justice; law clk. to Hon. Mary Ellen Bittner Drug Enforcement Adminstrn.; assoc., health care group Reed Smith; assoc., health law group Shaw Pittman; assoc., health care practice group Sonnenschein Nath & Rosenthal LLP, Washington, 2003—04, ptnr., 2004—. Mem.: Health Care Compliance Assn., Healthcare Businesswomen's Assn., DC Bar Assn., Am. Health Lawyers Assn. Office: Sonnenschein Nath & Rosenthal LLP Ste 600, E Tower 1301 K St NW Washington DC 20005 Office Phone: 202-408-9156. Office Fax: 202-408-6399. Business E-Mail: gcavalier@sonnenschein.com.

CAVALLARO, JUDITH, secondary school educator; b. Weirton, W.Va., May 6, 1959; d. Cavallaro Louis and Cavallaro Florine. M, Nat. U., 1989. Tchr. Perris Union H.S. Dist., Calif., 1985—. Mem.: Perris Secondary Edn. Assn. (pres. 2005—). Home: 1209 Osprey St San Jacinto CA 92583 Office: Perris Lake High School 418 Ellis Ave Perris CA 92570 Personal E-mail: cav6@earthlink.net. E-mail: jcavallaro@puhsd.org.

CAVALLO, JO ANN, language educator; b. Summit, NJ, May 21, 1959; d. Joseph Anthony and Jacqueline Amelia (Toth) C.; children: Maria Cristina, Alberto Joseph. Student, U. Florence, Italy, 1979-80, U. Valencia, Spain, 1980; BA, Rutgers U., 1981; student, Inst. French Studies, Avignon, 1982; MA, Yale U., 1984, PhD, 1987. Instr. dept. Italian Yale U., New Haven, 1983-86, instr. dept. Spanish, 1986-87, instr. Sch. Music, 1986-87; asst. prof. U. Wash., Seattle, 1987-88; assoc. prof. of Italian Columbia U., N.Y.C., 1988—. Mem. sci. com. Boiardo Quincentennial Celebration, Italy, 1993-94; founder and program dir. Columbia U. Summer Program in Scandiano, Italy, 1995-2001. Author: Boiardo's Orlando Innamorato: An Ethics of Desire, 1993; co-editor: Fortune and Romance: Boiardo in America, 1998; adapter: Orlando Innamorato for young readers, 2001; author: Il Maggio Epico Emiliano: ricordi, riflessioni, brani, 2003, The Romance Epics of Boiardo, Aristo, and Tasso: From Public Duty to Private Pleasure, 2004. Recipient scholarship Nat. Italian Am. Found., Washington, 1986, fellowship grant Columbia U. Coun. for Rsch. in the Humanities, 1989, 90. Mem. Am. Assn. for Tchrs. of Italian, Am. Assn. of Italian Studies, Renaissance Soc. Am., Am Folklore Soc., Phi Beta Kappa. Roman Catholic. Home: 733 Buchanan St Toms River NJ 08753-7207 Office: Columbia Univ Italian Dept 1130 Amsterdam Ave Hamilton Hall Rm 514 New York NY 10027 Office Phone: 212-854-4982. Business E-Mail: jac3@columbia.edu.

CAVALLO-BEST, MARIA ISOLINA, language educator; d. Joseph Anthony and Maria Isolina Cavallo; m. George Anthony Best, Apr. 12, 2003. BS in Elem. Edn., St. John's U., Staten Island, NY, 1992; MA in Urban Edn./English Second Lang., Jersey City State Coll., 1997; postgrad., Coll. SI, 2002—04. Tchr. elem. sch. NYC Dept. Edn., Staten Island, 1992—94, tchr. bilingual eucation, 1994—94, tchr. english as 2d lang., 1994—2004, bilingual edn. evaluator, 1997—2004, dual lang./english lang. learner instrnl. support specialist, 2004—. Mem.: Coun. Sch. Suprs. and Adminstrs., Am. Com. Italian Migration (assoc.), Delta Kappa Gamma. Office Phone: 718-420-5689. Office Fax: 718-420-5689. E-mail: mcavall4@nycboe.net.

CAVANAGH, CAITLIN, music educator; d. William and Joanne Cavanagh. BS in Music Edn., West Chester U., Pa., 2000; MA in Conducting, Am. Band Coll., Ashland, Oreg., 2004. Tchr. music Dulaney H.S., Timonium, Md., 2000—. Tchr. jazz band Dulaney H.S., Timonium, Md., 2002—; adv. Savin' the Music, Timonium, 2004—. Sect. leader Chesapeake Concert Band, Timonium, 2001—06. Named one of Outstanding Am. Tchrs., Nat. Honor Roll, 2006. Mem.: Music Educators Nat. Conf., Sigma Alpha Iota (sgt. at arms 1998—2000, musical dir. 1998—2000). Office Phone: 410-887-7640.

CAVANAH, SARAH E., music educator; b. Chillicothe, Mo., Apr. 10, 1974; d. Martens; m. Brad R. Cavanah, July 27, 1996; children: Macy Elizabeth, Lauren Camille. MusB in Edn., Ctrl. Meth. Coll., 1996. Dir. bands Nev. (Mo.) Pub. Schs., 1997—2000, Marshall (Mo.) Pub. Schs., 2001—. Mem.: Mo. Educators Nat. Conv., Mo. Bandmasters Assn., Mo. Music Educators Assn. Methodist. Office Phone: 660-886-2244.

CAVANAUGH, JANIS LYNN, protective services official, educator; b. Montebello, Calif., Feb. 15, 1952; d. William Franklin Cavanaugh and Anne Mildred Dederick; life ptnr. Jeanne Lynn Renner, Aug. 14, 1992. AS in Police Sci., Rio Hondo Coll., Whittier, Calif., 1973; BS in Criminal Justice, Calif. State U., L.A., 1995; MPA, U. of La Verne, Calif., 2000. Police officer El Monte Police Dept., Calif., 1972—77, Amtrak R.R. Police, L.A., 1977—84; asst. rangemaster Rio Hondo Police Acad., Whittier, 1977—96; prof. adminstrn. of justice and forensic sci. Rio Hondo C.C., Whittier, 1996—; coord. forensic sci. program & acad. La Puente Valley Regional Occupl. Program, City of Industry, Calif., 2003—, pub. safety coord., 1992—2000, instr., 2002—, supr., coord., 2000—02, supr., 2002—. Cons. Tri-Cities Regional Occupl. Program, Whittier, 2000—, East San Gabriel Valley Regional Occupl. Program, West Covina, Calif., 2002—, SE Regional Occupl. Program, Cerritos, Calif., 1995. Mem. Whittier Conservancy, 1984—; vol. ARC, Whittier, 1984—. Recipient Women of Yr. award, Soroptimist Orgn., 1996; Vocat. Ednl. Equipment grantee, State of Calif., 2001, Vocat. Ednl. grantee, 2003. Mem.: Am. Acad. Forensic Sci., Crim. Justice Educators, Forensic Sci. Club (advisor 2000—), Nat. Assn. Pub. Adminstrn. (assoc.), Rio Hondo Faculty Assn. (assoc.; sec. 1996—98), Calif. Assn. Criminal Justice Educators (assoc.; sec. 1994—96), Internat. Assn. Identification (assoc.), So. Calif. Assn. Fingerprint Officers (assoc.), Kiwanis Greater Whittier, NRA (life), Calif. Police Pistol Assn. (life), Alpha Gamma Sigma (assoc.; advisor 1996—2003, v.p. 2002—03). Presbyterian. Achievements include patents pending for forensic identification logo; forensic science curriculum. Avocations: combat shooting, hiking, photography. Home: 11743 North Circle Dr

Whittier CA 90601 Office: La Puente Valley ROP 18501 E Gale Ave City Of Industry CA 91748 Office Phone: 562-699-6704. Personal E-mail: cavarenn@aol.com. E-mail: msforensics@janiscavanaugh.com.

CAVANAUGH, LUCILLE J., oil industry executive; b. Phila. Bachelor's, Immaculata Coll. With Exxon Mobil Corp., 1977—; former head Asia Divsn.; gen. mgr. supply and engring. Exxon Mobil Corp., pres. credit corp., gen. mgr. west coast refining and mktg., v.p. global supply and distbn., v.p. human resources, 2002—. Bd. dirs. United Way Met. Dallas. Office: Exxon Mobil Corp 5959 Las Colinas Blvd Irving TX 75039-2298 Office Phone: 972-444-1000. Office Fax: 972-444-1198.*

CAVANAUGH, MARGARET, aide; d. Freda Margaret Berg and William Francis Prindle. Student, Tex. Tech, Lubock, 1962—63. CPCU Am. Soc. Chartered Property and Casualty Underwriters, 1986. Prin. aide Hennepin County, Mpls., 1994—95; constituent svcs. dir. Jim Ramstad, Mem. of Congress, Minnetonka, Minn., 2000—. Third congl. dist. rep. co-chair Rep. Party, Edina, Minn., 1993—. Chair Human Rights Commn., Bloomington, Minn., 1985—92; nat. del. Rep. Party, Minn., 1996—2004, state and congl. del. Minn., 1982—2006, state party exec. com. mem. St. Paul, 1995—2006. Named Vol. of Yr., 2000; recipient Lincoln-Reagan Outstanding Party Svc. award. R-Consevative. Baptist. Avocations: reading, fitness, crocheting, knitting. Home: 1005 W 104th St Bloomington MN 55431 Office: Jim Ramstad Member of Congress 1809 Plymouth Rd Minnetonka MN 55305 Office Phone: 952-738-8200. Personal E-mail: mcavana677@aol.com.

CAVANAUGH, MARIANNE, secondary educator; BA, St. Joseph Coll., 1974; MA, Ctrl. Conn. State U., 1980; postgrad., U. Hartford, 1997—. Lectr. U. Conn., 1998—; head tchr., math K-12, 1992—; secondary math tchr., 1975—. Presenter in field. Named Conn. Tchr. of Yr., 998, Middle Sch. Tchr. of Yr. Conn. Assn. of Schs., 1997. Mem. Nat. Coun. for Suprs. of Math., Assn. for Tchrs. of Math. in Conn., Nat. Coun. for Tchrs. of Math., Conn. Coun. for Leaders in Math., Nat. State Tchrs. of Yr. Office: Glastonbury High Sch Hubbard St Glastonbury CT 06033 E-mail: awecav@aol.com.

CAVANAUGH, MAXINE CORNELL, clinical psychologist; b. Phila., Mar. 18, 1931; d. David and Jeanette (Willensky) Cornell; m. David K. Cavanaugh, Feb. 8, 1953; children: David Charles, Carolyn Jeanne Claire. BS, Pa. State U., 1952, MS, 1953; PhD, U. Buffalo, 1958. Lic. psychologist N.Y. Intake supr. U. Buffalo Psychiat. Clinic, 1958; part-time staff psychologist Buffalo Psychiat. Ctr., 1958; chief psychologist Psychiat. Clinic, Jewish Family Svc., Buffalo, 1958-61; pvt. practice Tonawanda, N.Y., 1961—. Cons. Office of Vocat. Rehab., Buffalo and Albny, 1972-85; instr. U. Buffalo, 1958-67; panelist TV show AM-Buffalo, 1979—; mem. Office Profl. Discipline N.Y. State Bd. Regents (psychology), 1997-. Mem. APA, Psychol. Assn. Western N.Y. (chmn. ethics com. 1982—, Disting. Achievement in Psychology award 1989). Home and Office: 161 Sweetbriar Rd Tonawanda NY 14150-7511 E-mail: mcavanaugh@aol.com.

CAVANAUGH, REBECCA JO, medical nurse; b. Cameron, Tex., Jan. 30, 1950; d. Steve and Sylvia Mae (Rayford) Taplin; m. Lorace Cavanaugh, Jr., July 12, 1971; 1 child, Michael Lorace. A. Bus., Temple (Tex.) Comml. Coll., 1969; Diploma in Vocat. Nursing, Temple Jr. Coll., 1980. LVN II, BLS. Sch. sec., adult edn. tchr. Bethune Elem. Sch./Temple Ind. Sch. Dist., 1969-72; with Am. Mayflower Moving & Storage, Temple, 1973-74; sch. sec., adult edn. tchr. Wheatley Elem. Sch./Temple Ind. Sch. Dist., 1974-79; lic. vocat. nurse II Scott & White Hosp., Temple, 1980—. Vol. East Bell County Free Clinic, Temple, 1993-94;/ mem. Temple 4C, 1976-77. Recipient Star award, Scott & White Focus Svc., 2005. Mem. Tex. Lawman (assoc.), Tex. League Vocat. Nursing (Bell County chpt. pres. 1992-93), Scott & White LVN Group (sec., pres.). Baptist. Avocations: sewing, gardening, fishing, reading. Home: PO Box 4388 Temple TX 76505-4388

CAVE, YVONNE S., retired librarian; m. Richard K. Cave, Oct. 27, 1951 (dec.). Student, Fenn Coll. (now Cleve. State), Ohio, 1943—44; BS in Edn., Bowling Green State U., Ky., 1944—48; student, The Coll. of Wooster, Ohio, 1950; MA, Union Theol. Seminary, Tchrs. Coll.-Columbia U., 1950—51. HS libr., Willoughby, Ohio, 1948—50; mission rsch. libr. Union Theol. Seminary, N.Y.C., 1950—51; libr., children's rm./reference Bentley Pub. Libr., Columbus, Ohio, 1955—57; libr. Kent State U., North Canton; part-time libr., law libr. Stark County Libr., Alliance, 1967—68. Active Panel Am. Women, Canton, Human Rels. Coun. Greater Canton. Mem.: AAUW. Independent. Presbyterian. Avocations: reading, gardening, stamp collecting/philately, history, biography. Home: 7822 Peachment Ave NW #G-2 Canton OH 44720

CAVENDER, REBECCA ANN, music educator; b. Ft. Belvoir, Va., Jan. 8, 1962; m. Lowell Cavender, June 28, 1980; children: Clay Andrew, Ever Chastian. MusB in Edn., U. Cen. Ark., Conway, 1988. Cert. instrumental music K-12, vocal music K-12 Ark. Dir. bands, woodwind specialist Bob Courtway Mid. Sch., Conway, 1997—2005; head band dir. Ctrl. Jr. H.S. Band, Springdale, Ark., 2005—. Dir. Conway High Mus. Theater, 1995—2005. Assoc. mem. Dixie Band Camp, Conway, 2003—05. Recipient Disting. Svc. award for 15 yrs., 2003. Mem.: Ark. Sch. Band and Orch. Assn. D-Conservative. Baptist.

CAVENDISH, ELIZABETH A. (BETSY CAVENDISH), lawyer; married; 2 children. BA summa cum laude, Yale U., 1982, JD, 1988. Asst. prof. U. Ill. Coll. Law; office of legal counsel US Dept. Justice; legal dir. NARAL, 1998—2003; interim pres. NARAL Pro Choice Am., 2004. Office: NARAL Pro Choice Am Ste 700 1156 15th St NW Washington DC 20005

CAVENDISH, KIM L. MAHER, museum administrator; b. Washington, Feb. 25, 1946; d. Joseph Wilson and Helen Elizabeth (Bell) Leverton; m. William Fredrick Maher, June 12, 1965 (div. 1980); 1 child, Lauren Robinson; m. Daryl Kent Cavendish, Feb. 26, 2000. Student, Duke U., 1963-65, George Washington U., 1966; BA in English, U. Fla., 1969. Social worker Fla. Health and Rehab. Svc., Gainesville, 1969-71, Delray Beach, 1972-74, fraud unit supr. West Palm Beach, 1974-76, direct svc. supr., 1977-78; ctr. dir. Palm Beach County Employment and Tng. Adminstrn., West Palm Beach, 1979-81; exec. dir. Discovery Ctyr., Inc., Ft. Lauderdale, Fla., 1981-92, Mus. Discovery & Sci., Ft. Lauderdale, 1992-94; CEO Va. Air and Space Ctr., Hampton, 1995-99; pres. Orlando Sci. Ctr., 2000—02, Mus. Discovery & Sci., Ft. Lauderdale, 2002—. Bd. dirs. Singing Pines Mus., Boca Raton, Fla., 1984-88, Broward Art Guild, Ft. Lauderdale, 1985-91, Va. Space Grant Consortium, Va. Aerospace Bus. Roundtable, Hampton, 1995—2000, Assn. Sci./Tech. Ctrs., 2002—, Giant Screen Theater Assn., 2005—; mem. Leadership Broward II, Ft. Lauderdale, 1983-84; mem. faculty Inst. New Sci. Ctrs., 1992; mem. Cultural Execs. Coun. Broward County. Recipient Cultural Arts award Broward Cultural Arts Found., 1985, Woman of Yr. award Women in Comm., 1990, Woman of Distinction award So. Fla. Mag., 1993; namedOutstanding Fundraiser, Fla. Assn. Nonprofit Orgns., 1994. Mem. Am. Assn. Mus., Assn. Sci. and Tech. Ctrs., Southeastern Mus. Conf., Va. Assn. Mus. (bd. dirs. 1999—), Fla. Sci. Tchrs. Assn. (bd. dirs.), Fla. Assn. Mus. (bd. dirs. 1989—, pres. 1993-95), Leadership Broward Alumnae (curriculum com. 1984—), Ft. Lauderdale Downtown Coun. (bd. dirs. 1992—), Women's Exec. Club, Phi Kappa Phi. Democrat. Methodist. Avocations: scuba diving, piano, creative writing, collecting art and antiques, painting. Office: Mus Discovery & Sci 401 SW 2nd St Fort Lauderdale FL 33311

CAVIN, JACINDA ANN, music educator; b. Murray, Ky., May 9, 1978; d. Gerald Wayne and Jennifer Kaye McGuire; m. Paul Edward Cavin, Apr. 17, 2004. MusB, Lambuth U., Jackson, Tenn., 2002. Lic. tchr. Tenn. Adolescent day treatment specialist Carey Counseling, Paris, Tenn., 2002—04; elem. music tchr. Henry County Schs., Paris, 2004—. Mem.: NEA, Nat. Assn. for Music Edn., Henry County Edn. Assn., Tenn. Music Edn. Assn., Tenn. Edn. Assn. Democrat. Methodist.

CAVIN, KRISTINE SMITH, lawyer; b. Decatur, Ga., Mar. 26, 1969; d. Richard Theodore and Sherri (Nash) Smith; m. James Michael Cavin, May 13, 1995. BA, Furman U., 1991; JD, Calif. Western Sch. Law, 1995. Bar: Ga. 1995. Legal asst. Smith & Jenkins, P.C., Atlanta, 1991-92; intern child abuse and domestic violence unit San Diego City Atty.'s Office, 1995; ptnr. Smith, Ronick & Corbin, LLC, Atlanta, 1995—. Mem. ABA, Nat. Assn. Women Lawyers, Nat. Assn. Profl. Mortgage Women, Mortgage Bankers Assn. (assoc.), Ga. Bar Assn., Ga. Assn. Women Lawyers, Ga. Real Estate Closing Attys. Assn. (sec. 1997-2004, v.p. 2004—2006, pres. 2006-), Atlanta Bar Assn. Avocations: gourmet cooking, wine, gardening. Office: Smith Ronick & Corbin LLC 750 Hammond Dr NE Bldg 11 Atlanta GA 30328-5532 Office Phone: 404-256-9000. Business E-Mail: kristinecavin@closingattorney.com.

CAVIN, SUSAN ELIZABETH, sociologist, writer; b. Trion, Ga., Mar. 18, 1948; d. John Charles and Mary (Risk) C.; 1 child, Julian Samuel Cavin-Zeidenstein. BA, Vanderbilt U., 1970; MA, Rutgers U., 1973, PhD, 1978. Teaching asst., sociology Rutgers U., Newark, N.J., 1970-75; typesetter SoHo News, N.Y.C., 1976; asst. prof. sociology Green Mountain Coll., Poultney, Vt., 1979-83; lectr. women's studies Rutger's U., New Brunswick, 1984-91, asst. dir. women's studies, 1988-91; project dir. women in engring. sci. tech. program, 1991-97; rsch. scientist N.Y.C. Dept. Health, 1999; lectr. women's studies Rutgers U., Newark, 1999—2000; dir. evaluation Annenberg Grant, 2002—05. Cons. Gov.'s Study Commn. on Discrimination, Trenton, NJ, 1992; adj. asst. prof. sociology NYU, 1990—97, assoc. prof., 1998—; regional technician N.Y. Regional Census Ctr., Census 2000, 2000. Author: Lesbian Origins, 1985, poetry book, 1973, (cd-rom) Alice in Techiland, 1997; founding editor: (newspapers) Radical Chick, 1992-95, Big Apple Dyke News (B.A.D. News), 1981-88, Green Mountain Dyke News, 1980, (jour.) Tribad, 1977-79. Named Outstanding Tchr. of Yr., Green Mountain Coll., Poultney, 1982-83; Declamation award Ga. High Sch. Assn., 1965, 66, Fiction prize N.Y.C. Gay Ctr. Ann. Writing Contest, 2002-03, award for tchg. excellence NYU-SCPS, 2006; N.Y.C. Tchg. fellow Bd. Edn., 2000-06. Mem. Nat. Writers Union, Am. Sociol. Assn., Nat. Women's Studies Assn., N.Y. Acad. Scis. Democrat. Avocations: writing, poetry. Business E-Mail: susan.cavin@nyu.edu.

CAVITT, REBECCA LYNN, secondary school educator; b. Sweetwater, Tex., Nov. 5, 1971; d. Lester Morris Cavitt and Annealia Ruth Glasgow-Cavitt; 1 child, Casey. BS Biology, W. Tex. A&M U., Canyon, 1995. Tchr. Copperas Cove Ind. Sch. Dist., Tex., 1996—98; tchr., coach Arlington Ind. Sch. Dist., Tex., 1998—99, Klein Ind. Sch. Dist., Houston, 1999—. Emergency med. tech. Cypress Creek Emergency Med. Svcs., Houston, 2001—05. Mem.: Am. Fedn. Tchrs. Avocations: sports, music, museums. Office: Klein Ind Sch Dist 11800 Misty Valley Houston TX 77066

CAVNAR, MARGARET MARY (PEGGY CAVNAR), researcher, retired state legislator; b. Buffalo, July 29, 1945; d. James John and Margaret Mary Nightengale; m. Samuel M. Cavnar, 1977 (div. 2000); children: Heather Anne Hicks, Heide Lynn Gibson. BSN, D'Youville Coll., 1967; MBA, Nat. U., 1991. Utilization rev. coord. South Nev. Meml. Hosp., Las Vegas, 1975-77. Pres. PS Computer Svc., Las Vegas, 1978—86; bd. mem. Nev. Eye Bank, 1987—89, exec. dir., 1990—91; dir. health fairs Centel & Ch13TV, 1991—94; pres. Bridge Counseling Assocs., 1994—95; healing touch practitioner, 1994—; 1st v.p. bd. dirs. Nev. Alternative Medicine Assocs., 1997—2000; clin. rsch. coord. dept. psychiatry and neurology U. Nev. Sch. Medicine, 2000—04; care mgr. Family Home Hospice, 2005—. Mem. Clark County Rep. Ctrl. Com., 1977-87, Nev. Rep. Ctrl. Com., 1978-80; mem. Nev. Assembly, 1979-81; Rep. nominee for Nev. Senate, 1980, for Congress from Nev. 1st dist., 1982, 84; bd. dirs., treas. Nev. Med. Fed. Credit Union; v.p. Cmty. Youth Activities Found., Inc., Civic Assn. Am.; mem. utilization rev. bd. Easter Seals; trustee Nev. Sch. Arts, 1980-87; nat. advisor Project Prayer, 1978-2000; co-chmn. PRIDE com., 1983-2000, tax limitation com., 1983, personal property tax elimination com., 1979-82, self-help against food tax elimination denial com., 1980; mem. nat. bd. dirs., co-chmn. Nev. Pres. Reagan's Citizens for Tax Reform Com., 1985-88; mem. Nev. Profl. Stds. Rev. Orgn., 1984; co-chmn. People Against Tax Hikes, 1983-84; bd. dirs. Nev. Eye Bank, 1988-90. Mem. Nev. Order Women Legislators (charter, parliamentarian 1980—), Cosmopolitanly Hers Info. (pres.), Sigma Theta Tau. Home: 9736 Derbyhill Cir Las Vegas NV 89117-6681

CAVNER, NADIA, investment company executive; BS, Tex. Wesleyan U.; MBA, Tex. Christian U. Sr. v.p., sr. fin. cons. US Bancorp Investments, Springfield, Mo.; exec. v.p., head brokerage div. Signature Bank, Springfield, Mo., 2005—, head Nadia Cavner Group; bd. mem. City Bancorp Inc. Mem. Mo. Health and Edn. Facilities Authority. Mem.: Am. Bible Soc. (fin. com.), Springfield Cmty. Found. (fin. com. adv. bd.). Office: Signature Bank PO Box 4023 Springfield MO 65808-4023

CAWLEY, MAUREEN E., pharmacist; b. Apr. 10, 1966; Pharm D, U. Pacific, Stockton, Calif., 1993; BS in biochemistry, San Francisco State U., 1990. Clin. pharmacist Stanford Hosp. and Clins., Calif., 1993-2000; assoc. med. commn. scientist Genentech, Inc., South San Francisco, Calif., 2000—. Author: (book) Advances in Pharmacology, 1998. Mem.: Calif. Soc. Health Systems Pharmacists (sec.). E-mail: mcawley@gene.com, maureencawley@yahoo.com.

CAWLEY, PATRICIA BLONTS, secondary school educator; d. Edward Conrad and Donna Branch Blonts; m. Daniel Joseph Cawley, Mar. 12, 1994; 1 child, Seamus Patrick. BA, Old Dominion U., Norfolk, Va., 1993, MS, 2003. English tchr. Chesapeake (Va.) Pub. Sch. Communication dir. Women's Polit. Caucus, Norfolk, Va., 1992—99. Mem.: NEA (assoc.), Chesapeake Edn. Assn. (assoc.; comm. dir. 1997—99), Va. Edn. Assn. (assoc.), Va. Reading Coun. (assoc.), Southeastern Va. Assn. of Tchr. of English (assoc.), Va. Assn. of Tchr. of English (assoc.), Nat. Coun. of Tchr. of English (assoc.), Phi Kappa Phi. Democrat-Npl. Episc. Avocations: family, travel, literature.

CAWOOD, ELIZABETH JEAN, public relations executive; b. Santa Maria, Calif., Jan. 6, 1947; d. John Stephen and Gertrude Margaret (Shelton) Dille; m. Neil F. Cawood, Jan. 4, 1975; 1 child, Nathan Patrick. BA, Whitworth Coll., 1964-68. Dir. pub. info. Inland Empire Goodwill, Spokane, Wash., 1967-72; adminstrv. asst. N.W. Assn. Rehab. Industries, Seattle, 1973-74; pres., counselor Cawood, Eugene, Oreg., 1974—. Pres. Women in Comm., Inc., 1981-83; stragegy bd. Benton Lane Lincoln Linn Region, 1993-99, chair, 1993-94; bd. dirs. AAA Oreg./Idaho Editor: Dictionary of Rehabilitation Acronyms, (newsletters) INTERCOM, Family Communicator, Oreg. Focus, (dictionary) Work-Oriented Rehabilitation Dictionary and Synonyms, 1st and 2nd edits. Bd. dirs. Laurel Hill Ctr., 1993—, v.p., 2001, pres. 2002-2004; bd. dirs. Lane County Boy Scouts Am., 1986-2001, Eugene Action Forum, 1981-86, Birth-to-Three, 1982-85, Lane County chpt. ARC, 1982-83, 84-89, Lane County chpt. Am. Cancer Soc., 1984-87, Eugene Opera, 1985-88, Joint Com. Econ. Diversification, 1985-89, 91-93, Lane County United Way, 1987-93, campaign cabinet, 2002-04, chair leadership, 2001-2003, Lane Econ. Com., vice chmn., 1990-95, chair, 1996-2001; bd. dirs. So. Willamette Pvt. Industry Coun., 1985-88, pres., 1988; chmn. Eugene Pvt. Industries Coun., 1981-83, vice chmn., 1983-84; chmn. Bus. Owners Network, Eugene, 1980-81; advisor Eugene Jr. League; trustee Nature Conservancy, Oreg., 1999—, exec. com., 2005—; advisor Sustainable Advantage Conf., U. Oreg., 2004—; mem. educator quality task force Chalkboard Project, 2005-06. Recipient Hunger Buster award, Oreg. Food Bank, 2006. Mem. LWV (bd. dirs. 1979), Pub Rels. Soc. Am. (bd. dirs. Columbia River chpt. 1987-88, advisor U. Oreg. chpt. 1987-91, pres. Greater Oreg. chpt. 1991-92, bd. dirs. 1991-93), Oreg. Nat. Rehab. Assn. (pres. 1980-81), Profl. Women's Network (bd. dirs. Oreg. chpt. 1982), Eugene C. of C. (bd. dirs. 1980-87, 92-97, local govt. affairs coun. 1999-2002, econs. devel. coun. 2002-2004, chmn. econ. devel. 1982-83, bd. dirs. exec. com. 1984-87, v.p. 1987, 93, chmn. edn. com., pres.-elect 1994, pres. 1995), Mid-Oreg. Advt. Club (bd. dirs. 1985-87), Oreg. Sales and Mktg. Execs. (bd. dirs. 1985-87), Eugene/Springfield Assn. Quality and Performance (chmn. 1991-93, bd. dirs. 1991-94), Internat. Assn. Sports and Human Performance (bd. dirs. 1993), Rotary (Eugene pub. rels. chair 2000-2004), Eugene City Club (bd. dirs. 1992-98, pres.-elect 1995, pres. 1996) Office: Cawood 1200 High St Ste 200 Eugene OR 97401-3266 Office Phone: 541-484-7052. Business E-Mail: liz@cawood.com.

CAWS, MARY ANN, literature and language professor; b. Wilmington, NC, Sept. 10, 1933; d. Harmon Chadbourn and Margaret Devereux (Lippitt) Rorison; m. Peter Caws, June 2, 1956 (div. 1987); children: Hilary, Matthew. BA, Bryn Mawr Coll., 1954; MA, Yale U., 1956; PhD, U. Kans., 1962; DHL (hon.), Union Coll., 1983. Asst. instr. Romance langs. U. Kans., Lawrence, 1957-62, asst. editor Univ. press, 1957-58, vis. asst. prof., spring 1963; lectr. Barnard Coll. Columbia U., NYC, 1962-63; mem. faculty Sarah Lawrence Coll., Bronxville, NY, 1963-64, Hunter Coll. CUNY, NYC, 1966-88; prof. Grad. Sch. CUNY, NYC, 1969-88, exec. officer comparative lit. program Grad. Sch., 1977-79, exec. officer French program Grad. Sch., 1979-86, Disting. prof. French and comparative lit. Grad. Sch., 1983—, prof. English, 1985—, Disting. prof. French, comparative lit., English Grad. Sch., 1987—. Phi Beta Kappa vis. scholar, 1982-83; dir. NIH summer seminars for coll. tchrs., 1978, 85; mem. faculty Sch. of Criticism and Theory, Dartmouth U., 1988, Sch. Visual Arts, 1993; professeur associé Université de Paris VII, 1993-94; co-chair Henri Peyre Inst. for the Humanities, 1980-1996, French Inst., 1997-2002; lectr. NY Coun. for Humanities, 1992-96. Author: Surrealism and the Literary Imagination, 1966, The Poetry of Dada and Surrealism, 1970, The Inner Theatre of Recent French Poetry, 1972, The Presence of René Char, 1976, René Char, 1977, The Surrealist Voice of Robert Desnos, 1977, La Main de Pierre Reverdy, 1979, The Eye in the Text, Essays on Perception, Mannerist to Modern, 1981, André Breton, 1982, 96, The Metapoetics of the Passage, Architextures in Surrealism and After, 1982, Yves Bonnefoy, 1984, Reading Frames in Modern Fiction, 1988, Edmond Jabès, 1988, The Art of Interference: Stressed Readings in Visual and Verbal Texts, 1989, Women of Bloomsbury, 1991, Robert Motherwell: What Art Holds, 1996, Carrington and Lytton: Alone Together, 1996, The Surrealist Look: An Erotics of Encounter, 1997, Picasso's Weeping Woman: The Life and Art of Dora Maar, 2000, Virginia Woolf: Illustrated Life, 2002, Robert Motherwell with Pen and Brush, 2003, Marcel Proust: Illustrated Life, 2003, To the Boathouse: A Memoir, 2004, Pablo Picasso, 2005, Henry James, 2006, Surprised in Translation, 2006; co-author: Bloomsbury and France: Art and Friends, 1999; editor: Dada-Surrealism, 1972, co-editor, 1980-2002, Le Siècle éclaté, 1974-78, About French Poetry from Dada to Tel Quel, 1974, Selected Poetry Prose of Stéphane Mallarmé, 1982, Selected Poems of St.-John Perse, 1983, Writing in a Modern Temper, 1984, Textual Analysis, 1986, Perspectives on Perception: Philosophy, Art, and Literature, 1989, City Images, 1992, Joseph Cornell's Theater of the Mind: Selected Diaries, Letters and Files, 1994, Manifesto: A Century of Isms, 2001, Mallarme in Prose, 2001, Surrealist Painters and Poets, 2001, Surrealist Love Poems, 2002, Vita Sackville-West: Selected Writings, 2002, Surrealism, 2004, Yale Anthology of Twentieth-Century French Poetry, 2004, Maria Jolas: Woman of Action, 2004; co-editor: Selected Poems of René Char, 1992, Contre-Courants: Les femmes s'écrivent à travers les siècles, 1994, Écritures de femmes: Nouvelles Cartographies, 1996; translator: Poems of René Char, 1976, Approximate Man and other Writings of Tristan Tzara, 1975, Mad Love, 1987, The Secret Art of Antonin Artaud, 1998, Ostinato, 2002; co-translator: Poems of André Breton, 1984, Communicating Vessels, 1990, Break of Day, 1999; chief editor Harper Collins World Reader, 1994, Manifesto: A Century of isms, 2001, Surrealist Painters and Poets, 2001, Mallarmé in Prose, 2001, Yale Anthology of Twentieth-Century French Poetry, 2004; contbr. articles to profl. jours. Decorated officier Palmes Académiques, France; fellow Guggenheim Found., 1972-73 NEH, 1979-80, Fulbright traveling fellow, 1972-73, Rockefeller Found. fellow at Bellagio, 1994, 2005; Getty scholar, 1990. Mem. MLA (exec. coun. 1973-77, v.p. 1982-83, pres. 1983-84), Am. Assn. Tchrs. French, Assn. for Study Dada and Surrealism (pres. 1982-86), Internat. Assn. Philosophy and Lit. (exec. bd. 1982—, chmn. 1984), Acad. Lit. Studies (pres. 1985), Am. Comparative Lit. Assn. (exec. com. 1981, v.p. 1986—, pres. 1989-91). Home: 140 E 81st St New York NY 10028-1805 Office: CUNY Grad Ctr 365 Fifth Ave New York NY 10016 Office Phone: 212-817-8371. E-mail: cawsma@aol.com.

CAZABON, REBECCA MARIA, lawyer; BA, Wellesley Coll., 1994; JD, George Washington U. Law Ctr., 1998. Bar: Mass. Atty. Foley Hoag LLP, Boston, dir. Domestic Violence Prevention Project. Co-chair Domestic Violence Coun. Inc.; mem. Boston Law Firm Pro Bono Roundtable; student mentor Citizens Schools Eigth Grade Acad. Program; vol. choir mem. St. Paul's Ch., Brookline; mem. Cambridge Cmty. Chorus. Mem.: Women's Bar Assn., ABA, Mass. Bar Assn. Office: Foley Hoag LLP Seaport World Trade Ctr West 155 Seaport Blvd Boston MA 02210-2600 Office Phone: 617-832-1755. Office Fax: 617-832-7000. E-mail: rcazabon@foleyhoag.com.*

CAZALAS, MARY REBECCA WILLIAMS, lawyer, nurse; b. Atlanta, Nov. 11, 1927; d. George Edgar and Mary Annie (Slappey) Williams; m. Albert Joseph Cazalas (dec.). BS in Pre-medicine, Oglethorpe U., Atlanta, 1954; MS in Anatomy, Emory U., 1960; JD, Loyola U., 1967, Loyola U., New Orleans, 1967. RN, Ga.; Bar: La. 1967, U.S. Dist. Ct. (ea. dist.) La. 1967, U.S. Ct. Appeals (5th cir.) 1972, U.S. Supreme Ct. 1975, U.S. Ct. Appeals (fed. cir.) 1999. Gen. duty nurse, 1948-68; instr. maternity nursing St. Josephs Infirmary Sch. Nursing, Atlanta, 1954-59; med. rschr. in urology Tulane U. Sch. Medicine, New Orleans, 1961-65; legal rschr. for presiding judge La. Ct. Appeals (4th cir.), New Orleans, 1965-71; pvt. practice New Orleans, 1967-71; asst. U.S. atty., 1971-79; sr. trial atty. Equal Employment Opportunity Commn., New Orleans, 1979-84; owner Cazalas Apts., New Orleans, 1962—. Lectr. in field. Contbr. articles to profl. jours. Bd. advisors Loyola U. Sch. Law, New Orleans, 1974, v.p. adv. bd., 1975; active New Orleans Drug Abuse Adv. Com., 1976-80; task force Area Agy. on Aging, 1976-80, pres. coun. Loyola U., 1978—; adv. bd. Odyssey House, Inc., New Orleans, 1973; chmn. womens com. Fed. Exec. Bd., 1974; bd. dirs. Bethlehem House of Bread, 1975-79. Named Hon. La. State Senator, 1974; recipient Superior Performance award U.S. Dept. Justice, 1974, Cert. Appreciation Fed. Exec. Bd., 1975-78, Rev. E.A. Doyle award, 1976, Commendation for tchg. Guam Legislature, 1977, Career Achievement award Mt. de Sales Acad., 1995. Mem. Am. Judicature Soc., La. Sate Bar Assn., Fed. Bus. Assn. (v.p. 1976—, pres. 1976-78, bd. dirs. 1972-75), Fed. Bar Assn. (1st v.p. 1973, pres. New Orleans chpt. 1974-75, nat. coun. 1974-79), Assn. Women Lawyers, Nat. Health Lawyers Assn., DAR, Bus. and Profl. Womens Club, Am. Heart Assn., Emory Alumni Assn., Oglethorpe U. Alumni Assn., Loyola U. Alumni Assn. (bd. dirs. 1974-75, 77, v.p. 1976), Jefferson Parish Hist. Soc., Sierra Club, Zonta, Leconte Hon. Sci. Soc., Phi Delta Delta (merged with Phi Alpha Delta pres. 1970-72, bd. dirs., vice justice 1974-75), Alpha Epsilon Delta, Phi Sigma. Democrat.

CAZAN, SYLVIA MARIE BUDAY (MRS. MATTHEW JOHN CAZAN), retired real estate executive; b. Youngstown, Ohio, Nov. 17, 1915; d. John J. and Sylvia (Grama) Buday; m. Matthew John Cazan, July 14, 1935; 1 child, Matthew John G. Student, U. Bucharest, Romania, 1933—35, Youngstown Coll., 1936—38, Georgetown U. Inst. Langs. and Linguistics, 1950. Adminstrv. asst. statistics US Dept. Def., 1941—52; spl employee Dept. Justice, 1956—58; mgr. James L. Dixon & Co. Realtors, Falls Church, Va., 1959—70, Lewis & Silverman, Inc., Chevy Chase, Md., 1970—2006; ret. Mem. bd. examiners Georgetown U., 1950. Bd. dirs. Magnolia Internat. Debutante Ball; mem. Rumanian Orthodox Ch. Recipient Commendation and Meritorious award, Dept. Justice, 1958. Mem.: Washington No. Va. Real Estate Bds., Md. Bd. Realtors, Interscholastic Debating Soc., Gen. Fedn. Women's Clubs (pres. 1955—56). Home: 6369 Lakeview Dr Lake Barcroft Estates Falls Church VA 22041

CAZDEN, COURTNEY B(ORDEN), education educator; b. Chgo., Nov. 30, 1925; d. John and Courtney (Letts) Borden; m. Norman Cazden (div. 1971); children: Elizabeth, Joanna. BA, Radcliffe Coll., 1946; MEd, U. Ill., 1953; EdD, Harvard U., 1965. Elem. tchr. pub. schs., N.Y., Conn., Calif., 1947-49, 54-61, 74-75; asst. prof. edn. Harvard U., Cambridge, Mass., 1965-68, assoc. prof., 1968-71, prof., 1971-95, Charles William Eliot prof. emerita, 1996—. Vis. prof. U. N.Mex. summer 1980, U. Alaska, Fairbanks, summer 1982, U. Auckland, N.Z., spring 1983, Bread Loaf Sch. of English, Vt., 1986—; chairperson bd. trustees Ctr. Applied Linguistics, Washington, 1981-85. Author: Child Language and Education, 1972, Classroom Discourse: The Language of Teaching and Learning, 2d edit., 2001, Whole Language plus Essays on Literacy in the US and New Zealand, 1992; co-editor: Functions of Language in the Classroom, 1972, English Plus: Issues in Bilingual Education, 1990; editor: Language in Early Childhood Education, rev. edit., 1981. Trustee Highland Ednl. and Rsch. Ctr., New Market, Tenn., 1982-84; bd. dirs. Feminist Press, Old Westbury, N.Y., 1982-84; clk. New Eng. regional office Am. Friends Svc. Com., Cambridge, 1989-92. Recipient Alumna Recognition award Radcliffe Coll., 1988; fellow Ctr. Advanced Study in Behavioral Scis., Stanford, Calif., 1978-79; Fulbright research fellow, New Zealand, 1987. Mem. Nat. Acad. Edn., Coun. on Anthropology and Edn. (pres. 1981, George & Louise Spindler award 1994), Am. Assn. Applied Linguistics (pres. 1985), Nat. Conf. on Rsch. in English (pres. 1993-94), Am. Ednl. Rsch. Assn. (exec. com. 1981-84, award for disting. contbns. to ednl. rsch. 1986). Mem. Soc. Of Friends. Office: Harvard U Grad Sch Edn Appian Way Cambridge MA 02138

CAZEAUX, ISABELLE ANNE MARIE, retired music educator; b. N.Y.C., Feb. 24, 1926; d. François and Marie-Anne (Fort) C. BA magna cum laude, Hunter Coll., 1945; MA in Musicology, Smith Coll., 1946; MS in Libr. Sci., Columbia U., 1959, PhD in Musicology, 1961. Licence d'Enseignement, Ecole Normale de Musique, Paris, 1950; Première Médaille, Conservatoire Nat. de Musique, Paris, 1950. Sr. music cataloguer, head sect. music and phonorecords cataloguing N.Y. Pub. Libr., N.Y.C., 1957-63; mem. faculty Manhattan Sch. Music, N.Y.C., 1969-82, Bryn Mawr Coll., Pa., 1963-92, chmn. dept., 1978-92, prof., 1972-92, Alice Carter Dickerman prof. emeritus music, 1992—. Vis. prof. Douglass Coll. Rutgers U., New Brunswick, N.J., 1978. Author: French Music in the 15th and 16th Centuries, 1975; editor: The Chansons of Claudin de Sermisy, 1974; translator: The Memoirs of Philippe de Commynes, 1969, 2d vol., 1973; contbr. articles to profl. jours. Recipient Libby van Arsdale prize Hunter Coll., 1945; fellow Smith Coll., 1945-46, Inst. Internat. Edn., 1948-50; Martha Baird Rockefeller Fund grantee, 1971-72, Herman Goldman Found. grantee, 1980. Mem. Am. Musicol. Soc. (coun. 1968-70, com. on status of women 1974-76), Music Libr. Assn., Soc. Française de Musicologie, Internat. Musicol. Soc. Roman Catholic. Avocations: opera, concerts. Home: 415 E 72nd St Apt 5FE New York NY 10021-4412

CEBULA, MARY ANN ANTIONETTE, special education educator, speech correctionist; b. Orange, N.J., Oct. 20, 1950; d. Dominic and Frances (Romano) Cianci; m. Charles Michael Cebula, July 28, 1973; 1 child, Jessica Ann. BA, Kean State Coll., Union, N.J., 1972; MA, Georgian Ct. Coll., Lakewood, N.J., 1991. Cert. nursery sch. tchr. handicapped, learning disability tchr. cons. Resource room and speech tchr., reading recovery specialist St. Anthony's Sch., Belleville, NJ, 1972-73, mid. sch. tchr., 1973-78; elem. tchr. Our Lady of Mt. Carmel Sch., Orange, N.J., 1982-86, Holy Family Sch., Lakewood, 1986-88; tchr. spl. edn. Stafford Twp. Sch., Manahawkin, N.J., 1988—. Asst., helper Tournament of Champions, Toms River, 1991. Co-author curriculum for multiply handicapped students, 1991. Asst., helper Spl. Olympics, Toms River, 1988—. Mem. N.J. Edn. Assn., Learning Disabled Assn., N.J. Coun. Learning Disabled, Stafford Twp. Edn. Assn. Roman Catholic. Avocations: reading, crafts. Home: 123 Oak Hill Dr Toms River NJ 08753-1729

CEBULSKI, KATHERINE K., elementary school educator; b. Chgo., May 10, 1965; d. Lawrence VanHooser and Barbara Janine Schoeps; m. Robert H. Cebulski, Jr., Oct. 4, 1986; children: Erin M., Kelly K. AA, Harper Coll., Palatine, Ill., 1988; postgrad., Northeastern Ill. U., Chgo., 1994; MA in Ednl. Leadership, Aurora U., Ill., 2001. Sales assoc. Ednl. Resources, Elgin, Ill., 1988—91; sci. educator Cicero Sch., Ill., 1994—97, Canton Mid. Sch., Streamwood, Ill., 1997—2004, Kenyon Woods Mid. Sch., South Elgin, Ill., 2004—. Mem.: NEA, ASCD, Ill. Edn. Assn. Republican. Roman Catholic. Avocations: golf, tennis, gardening, travel. Home: 1427 Ashwood Dr Elgin IL 60123 Office: Kenyon Woods Mid Sch 1515 Raymond St South Elgin IL 60177

CECCHINI, SONIA NATHALIE, speech and drama educator; b. Cholet, Maine et Loire, France, Nov. 4, 1976; d. Jean-Claude and Joelle Le Gay; m. Israel George Cecchini, May 31, 2002; children: Savannah Oceane, Emma Marine. M in Comm., Okla. U., Oklahoma, 2003. Alternative tchg. cert. Okla., 2004. French and Spanish tchr. Ruston Pub. Schs., La., 1999—2001; Spanish tchr. Seeworth Acad., Oklahoma City, 2003—04; speech and drama tchr. Norman Pub. Schs., Okla., 2004—.

CECERE, CAROL, secondary school educator; b. Johnstown, Pa., Apr. 5, 1967; d. Richard D. and Martha J. Fatula; m. Ralph J. Cecere, Jr., July 6, 1996; children: Courtney, Adam, Madeline. BS in Art Edn., Indiana U. of Pa., 1990. Tchr. art Forest Hills H.S., Sidman, Pa., 1990—, basketball coach, 1990—. Mem.: NEA. Democrat. Roman Catholic. Avocations: art, sports. Office: Forest Hills High Sch 489 Locust St Sidman PA 15955

CECIL, ELIZABETH JEAN, writer; b. Biloxi, Miss., Apr. 13, 1938; d. Dudley Charles and Margaret Jean (Gilchrist) Andrews; m. Anthony Francis Cieslewicz (Cecil), Nov. 22, 1962; children: Stephen Charles, Sarah Jean. BA, Colo. State Coll., 1959; MA, Stanford U., 1963. Cert. speech and lang. pathologist, Wis. Speech-lang. pathologist Racine Unified Sch. Dist., Wis., 1985—95, ret., 1995. Author: (booklet essays) Jean's Stuff, 1993; author series of pictorial geneal. books. Office Vocat. Rehab. fellow Stanford U. Mem.: ASCD. Presbyterian. Personal E-mail: writeshop@wi-net.com.

CEDARBAUM, MIRIAM GOLDMAN, federal judge; b. NYC, 1929; d. Louis Albert and Sarah (Shapiro) Goldman; married; 2 children. BA, Barnard Coll., 1950; LLB, Columbia U., 1953. Bar: N.Y. 1954, U.S. Dist. Ct. (so. dist.) N.Y. 1956, U.S. Ct. Appeals (2d cir.) 1956, U.S. Ct. Claims 1958, U.S. Supreme Ct. 1958, U.S. Dist. Ct. (ea. dist.) N.Y. 1980, U.S. Ct. Appeals (5th and 11th cirs.) 1981. Law clk. to judge Edward Jordan Dimock U.S. Dist. Ct. (so. dist.) N.Y., 1953-54, asst. U.S. atty., 1954-57; atty. Dept. Justice, Washington, 1958-59; part-time cons. to law firms in litig. matters, 1959-62; 1st asst. counsel N.Y. State Moreland Act Commn., 1963-64; assoc. counsel Mus. Modern Art, N.Y.C., 1965-79; assoc. litig. dept. Davis Polk & Wardwell, N.Y.C., 1979-83, sr. atty., 1983-86; acting village justice Village of Scarsdale, NY, 1978—82, village justice, 1982-86; judge U.S. Dist. Ct. (so. dist.) N.Y., 1986-98, sr. judge, 1998—. Trustee emerita Barnard Coll.; com. defender svcs. Jud. Conf. U.S., 1993—99; mem. emerita bd. visitors Columbia Law Sch., chmn. NY state selection com. for Rhodes scholar, 2003, 04. Mem. bd. revising editors Columbia Law Rev.; contbr. articles to profl. jours. James Kent scholar; recipient Medal of Distinction Barnard Coll., 1991, Jane Marx Murphy prize Columbia Law Sch. Mem. ABA (chmn. com. on pictorial graphic sculptural and choreographic works 1979-81, copyright com. fed. practice and procedure 1983-84), Am. Law Inst., Fed. Bar Coun., Copyright Soc. U.S.A. (trustee, exec. com. 1979-82), Supreme Ct. Hist. Soc., Am. Judicature Soc Jewish. Office: US Dist Ct US Courthouse 500 Pearl St Rm 1330 New York NY 10007-1312

CEDEL, MELINDA IRENE, music educator, violinist; b. Ft. Worth, July 31, 1957; d. Albert and Emilia Florence (Sylvester) C. Student, N.C. Sch. Arts, 1974-77; MusB Edn., U. S.C., 1979. Cert. tchr., S.C. Tchr. music Charleston (S.C.) County Pub. Schs., 1979—92. Pvt. tchr. music, 1983—, part-time violin tchr. Glynn County Pub. Schs.; concertmaster Brunswick (Ga.) Civic Orch., 1993-97, pers. mgr., 1995-96 Performed with Florence Symphony, Columbia Philharm., S.C. Chamber Orch., Augusta Symphony, Jacksonville Symphony Orch., Savannah (Ga.) Symphony, Hilton Head (S.C.) Symphony, Jacksonville Summer Symphonetta, Valdosta (Ga.) Symphony Orch.; musician Charleston Symphony, 1979-92, Charleston Symphony Chamber Orch., Long Bay (S.C.) Symphony; musician, mgr. Charlestowne String Quartet, 1983-92; condr. Charleston County Prep. Orch., 1983-84; performer Piccolo Spoleto, 1980-91; co-dir. Charleston County Strolling Strings. Bd. dirs. Brunswick Cmty. Concert Assn. Mem. Am. String Tchrs. Assn., Mensa, Kappa Phi Kappa. Avocations: sailing, water sports, reading, travel, tennis. Home: 220 Five Pounds Rd Saint Simons Island GA 31522-1903

CEDERING, SIV, poet, writer; b. Overkalix, Sweden, Feb. 5, 1939; came to U.S., 1953, naturalized, 1958; d. Hilding and Elvy (Wikstrom) C.; children: Lisa, Lora, David. Artist Elaine Benson Gallery, Bridgehampton, NY, 1991—98, Loveland Mus., Loveland, Colo., 1992, East End Arts Coun. Gallery, Riverhead, NY, 1992, Clayton-Liberatori Gallery, Bridgehampton, NY, 1991, Guild Hall Mus., East Hampton, NY, 2001, Hutchin Gallery, Green Vale, NY, 1993, Peconic Gallery, Riverhead, NY, 1993, East. New Mex. Univ., Portales, N.Mex., 1992, Nordic History Mus., 1998. Lectr. U. Mass., Amherst, 1973; cons. Coordinating Council Lit. Mags., 1972-75 Author: (poems and photographs) Cup of Cold Water, 1973, Letters from the Island, 1973; (poems) Letters from Helge, 1974, Two Swedish Poets, Gost Friberg and Goran Palm (transl. from Swedish), 1974, Mother Is, 1975, The Juggler, 1977, How to Eat a Fortune Cookie, 1977, Color Poems, 1978, Letters From the Floating World: New and Selected Poems, 1984, The Blue Horse, 1979; (children's poems) Leken i Grishuset, 1980 (books transl. into Japanese, Swedish); Oxen, 1981, Letters From an Observatory, 1998, Poetry Paintings, 2003, Adirondack Notebook, 2004; editor, translator: Det Blommande Trädet (The Flowering Tree, collection Am. Indian and Eskimo lyrics), 1973, You and I and the World, Poems by Werner Aspenström, 1980, Letters From The Observatory New and Selected Poem 1973-1998, 1998, Painting Poems, 2003, Adirondack Notebook, 2004; poems and prose published in several periodicals, including, Harper's, New Republic, Partisan Rev., Paris Rev., Quar. Rev. Lit., others, exhibited photography, Modernage Galleries, NYC, 1973. Recipient William Marion Reedy award Poetry Soc. Am., 1970, John Masefield Narrative Poetry award, 1969; Annapolis Fine Arts Festival poetry prize Md. Fine Arts Council, 1968; Photography prize Sat. Rev., 1970; Borestone Mountain Poetry award, 1974; Pushcart prize, 1977; Emily Dickinson award, 1978; NY State Council on Arts fellow, 1974; Swedish Writers Union stipend, 1979; grantee Swedish Writers Found., 1995-2000. Mem. Poetry Soc. Am. Home: 93 Merchants Path PO Box 1300 Sagaponack NY 11962-1300

CEHELSKA, OLGA M., music educator, flight instructor; b. Austria, Apr. 6, 1946; d. George Michael and Veronica Bronislava (Drozdowska) C. BMus magna cum laude, Temple U., 1968; MusM, U. Miami, 1978; MSc, Am. Coll. Holistic Health, 1995; PhD holistic nutrition, Clayton Coll. Natural Health, 1999. Cert. music educator, N.J.; cert. flight instr., FAA; cert. music therapist Nat. Assn. Music Therapy. Tchr. music Phila. Pub. Sch. System, 1967-71; flight instr. Tamiami Airport, Homestead Airport, Homestead, Fla., 1973-74, Fulton County Airport, Atlanta, 1974-75; intern activity therapy Ga. Mental Health Inst., Atlanta, 1974; dir. activity therapy Met. Psychiat. Ctr., Atlanta, 1974-75; coord. adult psychiat. day treatment North Dekalb Cmty. Mental Health Ctr., 1975-80; piano instr., 1962—; CEO Cehelska Piano Studio, 1991—; flight instr. Norfolk Airport, Va., 2000—. Musician Young Audiences of Va., Norfolk, 1990-95, cons. Dekalb County Day Program, 1975-80, Nutritional Wellness, Vairginia Beach, 2000—. Contbr. articles to profl. jours. Mem. Ukrainian Women's League of Am., Ukrainian Scouting, Ukrainian Dancers of Miami, Ukrainian Am. Club of Miami, Nat. Assn. Music Therapy, Aircraft Owners and Pilots Assn., Nat. Assn. Flight Instr., Sigma Alpha Iota Alumni, Tidewater Music Tchrs. Forum, Music Tchrs. Nat. Assn., Va. Music Tchrs. Assn. Ukrainian Catholic. Avocation: traditional Ukrainian music on bandura. Office: Cehelska Piano Studio/Nutr Wellness 2313 Beach Haven Dr Unit 103 Virginia Beach VA 23451-1263 Personal E-mail: OMCstudio@msn.com.

CEHELSKY, MARTA, scientific organization executive; BA, Barnard Coll., 1964; MA in Polit. Sci., Columbia U., 1968, PhD in Polit. Sci., 1974. News editor Latin Am. Rsch. Rev., 1970-71; vis. sr. rsch. assoc. U. Houston Inst. Urban Studies, 1974; asst. prof. dept. polit. sci. Bklyn. Coll., CUNY, 1971-76; pub. policy cons., 1967-68, 77-79; policy analyst Lyndon B. Johnson Space Ctr., 1977-79, NASA Hdqrs., 1979-80; spl. asst. Senator Ernest F. Hollings, Washington, 1983-84; from polit. analyst to exec. officer Nat. Sci. Bd. NSF, Washington, 1980—2002; sr. adv. sci. and tech., dept. sustainable devel. InterAm. Devel. Bank, 2002—06; sr. advisor Office. of Dirs., NSF, 2006—. Author: Land Reform in Brazil: The Management of Social Change, 1979, Guatamala Election Factbook, 1966; contbr. chpts. to books, articles to profl. jours.; presenter in field. Charter mem. The Washington Group (bd. dirs.). Fulbright fellow, 1964, Fulbright Hays fellow, 1965, Ford Fgn. Area fellowp, LEGIS Exec. fellow, Nat. Def. Fgn. Lang. fellow Barnard Soc. Proctors. Fellow AAAS; mem. AIAA, Exec. Women in Govt., Sr. Execs. Assn., Ukranian Phys. Soc., Am. Astronautical Soc., Am. Polit. Sci. Assn. Office: NSF 4201 Wilson Blvd Arlington VA 22230 Office Phone: 703-292-8003. Business E-Mail: mcehelsk@nsf.gov.

CEKO, THERESA C., law educator, lawyer; BA, Univ. Chgo., 1981; JD, DePaul Univ., 1984. Clin. prof. Loyola Univ., Chgo., 1987—, dir. Cmty. Law Ctr., 1999—. Contbr. articles to Ill. Ct. publ. Office: Loyola University Chicago School of Law 25 E Pearson Ste 1400 Chicago IL 60611

CELELLA, KAREN ANN, music educator, writer; b. Altoona, Pa., Aug. 16, 1954; d. Alfred Richard and Anna Irene (Harpster) Gerhard; m. Philip Gregory Celella, Sept. 6, 1976 (div.); m. Kelly Ann, Philip Richard. AA, Nassau C.C., Uniondale, N.Y., 1972-74; BA, L.I. U., Brookville, N.Y., 1974-76. Nat. cert. musician. Sales Brandells, Garden City, N.Y., 1972-74, Wordsworth Books, Garden City, 1974-77; ind. music tchr. piano, organ, keyboard, theory, Suffolk County, N.Y., 1972—; tchr. Erol Piano Studio, Coram, 1976-79, Frank & Camille's Studio, Port Jefferson, N.Y., 1982-84, K.C. Studio, Coram, 1979—. Adjudicator Music Educators Nat. Conf., 1993—, Am. Coll. Musicians, Nat. Guild Piano Tchrs., 1998—. Author: KAC Music Assignment Journal, 1995—, also articles; presenter workshops. With USCG auxilliary. Named to Piano Guild Hall of Fame, 2001, Nat. Honor Roll, Nat. Piano Playing Auditions, 1988—. Mem. Suffolk Piano Tchrs. Forum (treas. 1990-96, pres. 1996-2000, v.p. 2000-02, bd. dir., 2002—), Am. Coll. Musicians (cert. tchr.), Music Educators Nat. Conf., Music Tchrs. Nat. Assn., U.S. Coast Guard Aux. Avocations: art (cut mat board designs), flying, computers. Home: 20 Summercress Ln Coram NY 11727-2617 Office: KC Studio 20 Summercress Ln Coram NY 11727-2617 Personal E-mail: KCelella2@aol.com. Business E-Mail: KCStudio1@aol.com.

CELENTANO, SUZANNE, movement educator; b. Pitts., Nov. 4, 1967; d. Patrick Earl and Dixie Lea Carmack; m. Ronald Joseph Celentano, June 19, 1993; children: Christopher, Brandon, Sophia. BA in Comm. Arts and Theater, Allegheny Coll., 1989; MFA in Theater, U. Ala., 1991. Cert. instr. group fitness, pilates and yoga. Actor, dir., choreographer, 1992—; professorial lectr. dept. performing arts Am. U., Washington, 2003. Adj. instr. theater Coll. Charleston, SC, 1992—95, St. Louis U., 1996—99; arts mgmt. cons., 1992—; spkr., presenter in field, 1992—. Dancer Am. Coll. Dance Festival Nat. Gala and Southeastern Gala, 1990; co-author: (book) Theatre Management: A Successful Guide to Producing Plays on Commercial and Nonprofit Stages, 1998; performer (actor, dancer): (films, TV and theater) April Is My Religion, 2001 (award); co. mem., dancer: Kathy Harty Gray Dance Theatre, 2003—06; author: (plays) Phoenix Theatre, 2004; actor: Wilma Theatre, Ala. Shakespeare Festival, Walt Disney World; choreographer Lorton Arts Found. Theater coord. Piccolo Spoleto Festival, Charleston, 1994; bd. dirs. Lorton Arts Found., Va., 2002—05; 1st v.p. Lorton Sta. Elem. Sch. PTA, 2003—04. Scholar, Internat. Thespian Soc., 1985, Bolling AFB and Ft. Belvoir Officer's Wives Club, 2006. Mem.: Dance Critics Assn., Southeastern Theatre Conf., Pilates Method Alliance (cert. instr. and master trainer of mat and apparatus), Officers Wives Clubs (scholarship coord. 1994—95, 2000—01), Officers Spouses Club (pres. 2001—02), Alpha Chi Omega Found. Democrat. Roman Catholic. Avocations: distance running, community activist, yoga. Home: 8710 Bitterroot Ct Lorton VA 22079 Office Phone: 703-298-6934. Personal E-mail: scelentano@aol.com.

CELESTINO-ARGUINZONI, WILMA, academic administrator; b. Bklyn., Aug. 3, 1952; d. Ramon and Julia Arguinzoni; children: Myriam Berrios, Angelisse Pepin. AS, Bunker Hill C.C., Boston, 1989; BA, Suffolk U., 1991, MEd, 1998. Asst. dir. multicultural affairs Suffolk U., Boston, 1990—. Notary pub., Boston; justice peace, Chelsea, Mass. Recipient Hispanic Heritage award Gov. Michael Dukakis, 1984, Yes You Can award Nat. Puerta Rican Forum, 1997; Truman scholar Harry S. Truman Found., 1989. Mem. Justic Peace Assn., Nat. Puerto Rican Coalition, Centro Latino (bd. dirs., v.p., 1998). Office: Suffolk U 8 Ashburton Pl Boston MA 02108-2770

CELL, GILLIAN TOWNSEND, retired historian, educator; b. Birkenhead, Cheshire, Eng., June 5, 1937; arrived in US, 1962; d. Thomas Edmund and Doris Abigail (Clark) Townsend; m. John Whitson Cell, Oct. 19, 1962 (dec.); children: Thomas K., Katherine A., John D. BA, U. Liverpool, Eng., 1959, PhD, 1964. Instr. U. N.C., Chapel Hill, 1965-66, asst. prof., 1966-70, assoc. prof., 1970-78, prof., 1978-91, affirmative action officer, 1981-83, chmn. dept. history, 1983-85, dean Coll. Arts and Scis., 1985-91; provost Lafayette Coll., 1991-93, Coll. of William and Mary, 1993—2003; ret., 2003. Author: English Enterprise in Newfoundland; 1577-1660, 1969; editor: Newfoundland Discovered, 1982. Home: 1152 Fearrington Post Fearrington Village NC 27312-5014 E-mail: gtcell@wm.edu.

CELMER, VIRGINIA, psychologist; b. Detroit, June 26, 1945; d. Charles and Stella (Kopicko) C. BA in English, Marygrove Coll., 1968; MA in Theol. Studies, St. Louis U., 1977; PhD in Counseling Psychology, Tex. Tech. U., 1986. Lic. psychologist; lic. chem. dependency counselor; cert. diplomate in managed mental health care; bd. cert. alcohol and drug counselor level III diplomate; internat. cert. alcoholism and drug abuse counselor; cert. group psychotherapist; cert. sex addiction therapist level II. Chaplain Mercy Ctr. for Health Care Svcs., Aurora, Ill., 1977-81; grad. asst. counselor U. Counseling Ctr., Tex. Tech. U., Lubbock, 1982-86, pre-doctoral intern in counseling psychology, 1985-86; post-doctoral intern Consultation Ctr., San Antonio, 1986-89, staff psychologist, 1989-90; pvt. practice psychologist San Antonio, 1989—. Instr. dept. psychology Tex. Tech. U., Lubbock, 1981-85, Oblate Sch. Theology, San Antonio, 1989-90. Contbr. articles to profl. jours. Mem. APA, Tex. Psychol. Assn., Bexar County Psychol. Assn., Am. Group Psychotherapy Assn., San Antonio Group Psychotherapy Assn., Nat. Assn. Alcoholism and Drug Abuse Counselors, Tex. Assn. Alcoholism and Drug Abuse Counselors. Office: 5440 Babcock Rd Ste 110 San Antonio TX 78240-3946 Office Phone: 210-641-7400.

CELOTTA, BEVERLY KAY, psychologist; b. Monroe, La., June 16, 1944; d. Morton and Geraldine (Hermalin) Lauter; m. Robert James Celotta; children: Jennifer Ann, Daniel Wayne. BA in Psychology, Queens Coll., 1965; MS, Bkyln. Coll., 1967; PhD in Ednl. Psychology, U. Colo., 1971. Lic. psychologist, Md. Research asst. Inst. for Devel. Studies, NYU, 1967; sch. psychologist Bur. of Child Guidance, N.Y.C., 1967-69, Head Start Program, N.Y.C., 1968-69, Montgomery County Pub. Schs., Rockville, Md., 1973-74, ednl. researcher, 1976-77; sch. psychologist Fairfax (Va.) County Pub. Schs., 1975-76; asst. prof. counseling and personnel services dept. U. Md., College Park, 1977-83, asst. chair, 1982-83; pres. Celotta, Jacobs & Assocs., Inc., Darnestown, Md., 1983-91; pvt. practice Darnestown, 1991—. Lectr. psychology Montgomery Coll, Rockville, 1975-76; faculty assoc. Johns Hopkins U., Balt., 1993-97; cons. Treatment and Learning Ctrs., 1993—, Family Support Ctr., 1992-2000; spkr. in field. Contbr. articles to profl. jours. Mem. APA (editorial bd. div. cons. psychology 1989-99), Assn. for Measurement and Evaluation in Counseling and Devel. (chmn. membership and program coms., mem. editorial bd. 1989-91). Home and Office: 13517 Haddonfield Ln Gaithersburg MD 20878-3622

CENDALI, DALE MARGARET, lawyer; b. NYC, Feb. 11, 1959; d. John Amos and Eleanor M. (Avocato) C.; m. John Francis Fitzpatrick, Sept. 12, 1987. BA summa cum laude, Yale U., 1981; JD, Harvard U., 1984. Bar: N.Y. 1985, U.S. Dist. Ct. (so. and ea. dists.) N.Y. 1985, U.S. Dist. Ct. (ea. dist.) Mich. 1988, U.S. Dist. Ct. (no. dist.) Calif. 2001, U.S. Ct. Appeals (2d cir.) 1989, U.S. Ct. Appeals (Fed. cir.) 1990, U.S. Ct. Appeals (9th cir.) 2001, U.S. Supreme Ct. 2002. Assoc. Fried, Frank, Harris Shriver & Jacobson, NYC, 1984-91, O'Melveny & Myers, NYC, 1991—. Editor-in-chief Harvard Jour. Legis. 1983-84; contbr. numerous articles to profl. jours. Named one of Am. Top 50 Women Litigators, Nat. Law Jour., The Magnificent 7 - IP's Best Young Trial Lawyers, IP Worldwide Mag., Nifty 50 - Harvard Law Sch. Women Alumnae, Harvard Law Bulletin. Mem. ABA (chair intellectual property com. litig. sect., programming co-chair 1993 litig. sect. ann. meeting), N.Y. State Bar Assn. (chair work for hire subcom. intellectual properties com. fed. and comml. sects.), Assn. of Bar of City of N.Y. (copyright and literary property com., media law com., chair trademark com.); Phi Beta Kappa. Avocations: theater, books collector, sailing, comic book collecting. Office: O'Melveny & Myers LLP Times Sq Tower 7 Times Sq New York NY 10036 Office Phone: 212-326-2051. Business E-Mail: dcendali@omm.com.

CENTENO-DAINTY, SONIA MARGARITA, artist; b. Arecibo, P.R., Mar. 4, 1948; arrived in U.S., 1960; d. Eugenio Centeno Faria and Carmen Maria Valencia Franco; m. James Albert Dainty, Jan. 17, 1970; 1 child, James William Dainty. Student journalism and art schs. Educator Boys & Girls Club, N.Y.C.; real estate realtor N.Y.C.; owner constrn. co. Produced portraits and landscapes for pvt. collections. Republican. Roman Catholic. Avocations: gardening, travel, sewing, photography. Home: 348 Old Dutch Hollow Rd Monroe NY 10950

CENTOFANTI, DEENA, announcer; m. Keith Stironek; 1 child, Casey Stironek. BS in Mass Comm., Miami U., Oxford, Ohio. Anchor WSYZ-TV, Ohio; prodr. WBNS-TV, Ohio; anchor/reporter WTOV-TV, Ohio; anchor WWHO-TV, Columbus, Ohio, 1994—97; co-anchor morning news WJBK-TV, Detroit, 1997, co-anchor Fox 2 News Weekend, 1997—, health reporter. Recipient Emmy award, 1999, award for gen. excellence in reporting, Mich. AP. Office: WJBK Fox 2 Po Box 2000 Southfield MI 48037-2000

CENTRELLO, GINA, publishing executive; Joined as copy editor Pocket Books, Simon & Schuster, 1981, exec. v.p. pub., 1993—94, pres. pub., 1994—99, Ballantine Books, 1999—2003, Random House Pub. Group, 2003—. Office: Random House Pub Group 1745 Broadway New York NY 10019

CEPIELIK, ELIZABETH LINDBERG, elementary school educator; b. Syracuse, N.Y., Sept. 18, 1941; d. Herman Elroy and Kathryn Emily (Karl) Lindberg; m. Michael A. Zemel, Apr. 22, 1967 (div. Jan. 1973); 1 child, Molly; m. Martin Joseph Cepielik, Mar. 10, 1973; children: Jeffrey, Kristina, Julie. AA, Stephens Coll., Columbia, Mo., 1961; BA, San Jose State Coll., 1963; postgrad., Calif. State U., L.A., 1963-67. Tchr. Humphreys Ave. Sch., L.A., 1963-71; math. specialist Non-Pub. Schs. Program, L.A., 1971-84; tchr. Sheridan Street Sch., L.A., 1984—2003; receptionist Weight Watchers, Arcadia, Calif., 1987—. Editor News of Polonia. Vol. Sta. KPCC, Pasadena, Calif., 1988-94. Mem.: DAR (sec 2004—), Swedish Am. Ctrl. Assn. (auditor 1987—90, sec. 1989—), Polish Nat. Alliance (sec. lodge 1980—, sec. coun. 1983—93, treas. Woman's divsn. 1992—93), Polish Am. Congress (sec. 1990—93, auditor 2001—), Skandia (auditor, sec. Pasadena lodge 1983—), Stephens Coll. Alumnae Club (pres. Pasadena chpt. 1967—68), Swedish Am. Women's Club (sec. 2004—). Republican. Presbyterian. Address: Ste 104/177 2245 E Colorado Blvd Pasadena CA 91107-3651 Personal E-mail: polishnews@earthlink.net.

CEREN, SANDRA LEVY, psychologist, writer; b. N.Y.C., June 27, 1936; d. Samuel and Claire Irene (Abramson) Levy; m. Mal Ceren, Dec. 22, 1960 (div. 1975); children: Daniel Keith, Pamela Jane; m. Ely Levinsky, May 18, 1986. BA, Bklyn. Coll.; MS, CUNY, 1959; PhD, U.S. Internat. U., San Diego, 1975. Lic. psychologist, Calif.; diplomate Am. Bd. Family Psychology. Psychologist N.Y.C. Bur. Child Guidance, 1959-63, Hackensack (N.J.) Schs., 1968-70, White Plains (N.Y.) Psychiat. Ctr., 1970-73, N.J. Ctr. Psychotherapy, Englewood, 1968-70, Westchester Community Mental Health Bd., Yonkers, N.Y., 1963-66; pvt. practice Tenafly, 1968-73, San Diego, 1975—. Mem. Am. Bd. Family Psychology, 1986-88, sec., 1985-87; mem. coun. Nat. Register Health Svc. Providers in Psychology; oral commr. Calif. Bd. Psychology. Mem. APA. Democrat. Jewish. Avocations: theater, film, dance. Home: 15023 Tierra Alta Del Mar CA 92014-3928 Office Phone: 858-755-0088.

CERFOLIO, NINA ESTELLE, psychiatrist, educator; b. Paterson, NJ, Feb. 15, 1960; d. Robert David and LaVerne Estelle Cerfolio. BA, Grinnell Coll., 1986; MD, Chgo. Med. Sch./U. Health Scis., 1991. Cons., liaison fellow Meml. Sloan Kettering, NYC, 1991—94; human sexuality fellow Cornell U. Med. Ctr., NYC, 1992—93; cons. liaison attending psychiatrist NYU, NYC, 1993—94; chief psychiat. emergency room and walk-in clinic St. Vincent's Hosp., NYC, 1995—98; attending psychiatrist NYU Med. Ctr., NYC, 1998—, clin. asst. prof. psychiatry, 1999—; clin. asst. prof. ob/gyn. NYU Downtown Hosp., NYC, 1998—. Contbr. articles to profl. publs. Founding mem. Grief Relief Network, 2001; pregnancy expert E Pregnancy Mag., 2002; bd. advisors Achilles Track Club, Disabled Iraqi Vets., 2004—; bd. dirs. Tri-State Cmty. Adv. Bd. Edn. Broadcasting, 2003—. Oncology fellow, Am. Cancer Soc., 1992—93. Fellow: Am. Psychiat. Assn. (founding mem. early career psychiatry exec. coun. 1996—98, corr. mem. com. on women, coun. on nat. affairs 1998—99, chmn. com. on women NY County dist. br. 2002—03, mem. exec. coun. NY County dist. br. 2002—06, disting., Woman of Yr. 2006); mem.: Morgagni Med. Soc. (mem. exec. com. 1997—99). Avocations: ironman competitions, tennis, ultra-marathons, triathlons. Home: 20 E 9th St 4J New York NY 10003 Office 2: 2 Fifth Ave # 5 New York NY 10011 Office Phone: 212-414-0531. Business E-Mail: ninacerf@nyc.rr.com.

CERNEY, ANGELA DAWN, athletic trainer, health facility administrator; b. Marion, Ill., Sept. 22, 1969; d. Margie and Delbert Craig (Stepfather); m. Randy Cerney, Apr. 21, 1990; children: Bradley, Brandon. Degree in phys. edn. & athletic tng., So. Ill. U., Carbondale, 1999—2002. Cert. athletic trainer Ill., 2002. Cert. athletic trainer Rehab Unlimited, Carbondale, Ill., 2002—; cmty. health & wellness coord. So. Seven Health Dept., Ullin, Ill., 2004—. Mem.: Nat. Athletic Trainer Assn.

CERNYAK-SPATZ, SUSAN E., retired language educator; b. Vienna, July 27, 1922; arrived in U.S., 1946; m. Hardy Spatz (dec.); m. Bernard Fishman (dec.); children: Jackie Fishman, Todd Fishman, Wendy Fishman. BA cum laude, U. Mo., Springfield, 1967; MA, U. Kans., Lawrence, PhD, 1972. Prof. fgn. langs. U. NC, Charlotte, 1972—92, prof. emerita, 1992—. Lectr. in field. Author: German Holocaust Literature, 1985, 2d edit., 1989; translator: Theresienstadt: Hitler's 'Gift' to the Jews, 1991, paperback edit., 2004; editor: Language and Culture: A Transcending Bond: Vienna and Exile, 1938-1988, 1993; author: Protective Custody: Prisoner 34042, 2005; contbr. articles to profl. publs. Founding mem. NC Coun. Holocaust, Raleigh, NC. Fellow, Woodrow Wilson Found., 1968—72; grantee, Fulbright Found., 1981, 1993. Mem.: Kans. U. Alumni Assn., Woodrow Wilson Found. Achievements include prisoner Auschwitz-Birkenau, 1942-1945. Home: 3516A Colony Rd Charlotte NC 28211

CERRA, WENDY, psychotherapist; BS in Clin. Psychology, Marywood Coll., 1997; MA in Clin. Psychology, Marywood U., 2000; MS in Clin. Psychology, Phila Coll., 2004; postgrad., Phila. Coll., 2004—. Clin. intern Scranton (Pa.) Counseling Ctr., 1997; social worker Jewish Home Ea. Pa., Scranton, 1997—2000; mobile therapist, behavior specialist, cons. Family Enrichment Ctr. Profl. Corp., Scranton, 2000—03; intern VA Med. Ctr., Wilkes-Barre, Pa., 2003, First Hosp., Kingston, Pa., 2004. Jerome F. Gaudenzi scholar, IHM scholar. Mem.: APA, Assn. Advancement of Behavior Therapy, Pa. Psychol. Assn., Delta Epsilon Sigma, Psi Chi.

CERVANTEZ, MICHELLE, marketing professional; b. 1965; BS in Bus., Univ. So. Calif.; MBA, Univ. Notre Dame. Intern J. Walter Thompson; customer rels. rep. Ford Motor Co., 1988—92; group leader, supr. Ford Customer Assistance Ctr., 1992—94; Asia Pacific product planner Ford Motor Co., 1994—95, mktg. comm. specialist, Lincoln Mercury, 1997—2000, brand devel. mgr. Lincoln Mercury, 1997—2000, v.p. N. Am. mktg. Jaguar, 2000—03; v.p. mktg. Mercedes-Benz USA, Montvale, NJ, 2003—. Named one of the Women to Watch, Ad Age mag., 100 Leading Women in the N. Am. Auto Industry, Automotive News, 50 Most Important Hispanics in Tech. & Bus., Hispanic Engr. & Info. Tech. mag., 2005.*

CESARE, CHRISTINE B., lawyer; BA magna cum laude, Conn. Coll., 1981; JD, Fordham U., 1984. Bar: NY 1985, Conn. 1986. Ptnr. comml. litig., mem. oper. group Bryan Cave LLP, NYC. Office: Bryan Cave LLP 1290 Ave of the Americas New York NY 10104 Office Phone: 212-541-1228. E-mail: cbcesare@bryancave.com.

CÉSPEDES, MELINDA BROWN, elementary school educator, dancer; b. San Jose, Calif., Sept. 9, 1942; d. Oren Able and Mildred Virginia (Bayless) Tolliver; m. Luis Pascual Céspedes, Dec. 3, 1981 (div. Sept. 1991); 1 child, Cara Thäis Brown. BS, Calif. State Poly., San Luis Obispo, 1964; std. elem. credential, U. Calif., Berkeley, 1967, adminstrv. svcs. credential, 1986; studies in belly dancing with, Bert Balladine, Sonya Ivanovna, Sabah, Najia, Amina; studied acting with John Parkinson. Cert. tchr. English Lang. Devel., Calif. Tchr. kindergarten Orinda (Calif.) Union Sch. Dist., 1968-76; tchr. 3rd grade Oakland (Calif.) Unified Sch. Dist., 1983-85, tchr. kindergarten, 1985-89; tchr. 1st grade Hayward (Calif.) Unified Sch. Dist., 1989-90, program coord., 1990-92, tchr. Charquin program, tchr. 2nd and 3rd grades, 1992-93, tchr. 1st grade English lang. devel., 1993-94, tchr. 1st and 2nd grades English lang. devel., 1994—. Chairperson faculty adv. coun. Webster Sch., Oakland Unified Sch. Dist., 1984-86, chairperson sch. site coun., 1984-87, circuit chairperson, 1985-86, 87-88, certification trainer, 1986-87, acting asst. prin., 1986, coord. Gifted and Talented Edn. program, 1988-89, coord. collaborative self-study, 1987-89, asst. prin. adminstrv. intern-fine arts summer sch., 1988, implementer cognitive coaching model, 1995; coord. Gifted and Talented Edn. program Burbank Sch., Hayward Unified Sch. Dist., 1990-92, dir. Markham Variety Show, 1993, mem. bilingual advisor-leadership team Markham Elem. Sch., 1994-95, conflict mgmt. trainer, 1992-95, curriculum coun. rep., 1995-96; performer, instr. Middle Ea. dance Ibiza, Spain, Berkeley, Sausalito, Larkspur and Corte Madera. Author: Common Ground, 1996; dir. Troupe Latifa, Ibiza, Veiled Threats, Sausalito, Dancers of DeNile, 1991-96, Larkspur and Sausalito; past mem. Sabah Ensemble, Berkeley; performed at Club Vasilas, Athens, Greece, BAzouki Club, Kos, Greece; regular featured performer at El Morocco, concord, Grapeleaf, San Francisco, El Mansour, San Francisco, Cleopatra, San Francisco, Cairo Cafe, Mill Valley, Mykonos, Berkeley, Powell Station, San FranciscoGreek Taverna, San Francisco, Bagdad, San Francisco, various clubs in Ibiza, Tenerife, Marbella, and Madrid, various dance festivals. Marcus Foster grantee for kindergarten marine biology program, Oakland, 1987. Mem. Calif. Tchrs. Assn., Common Cause, Amnesty Internat., Global Exchg., Phi Delta Kappa (v.p. programs 1988-90, editor newsletter 1987-88). Personal E-mail: latifa_1@hotmail.com.

CESSNA, JANICE LYNN, systems administrator, information technology manager; d. Alexander Carl and Camilla Dorothy Wagenfohr; 1 child, Christopher Alexander. AS data processing, Pasco-Hernando C.C., New Port Richey, Fla., 1982—84, AA, 1995—97; BS in Computer Info. Systems, St. Leo U., St. Leo, Fla., 1998—2000; MS computer info. tech., Regis U., Denver, Colo., 2001—05. Info. processing mgr. Pasco-Hernando C.C., New Port Richey, Fla., 1985—90, programmer/analyst, 1990—96, systems mgr., 1996—98, dir. mgmt. info. services, 1998—. Chair/mem., tech. adv. Fla. Cmty. Coll. Computer Consortium, Pensacola, Fla., 1994—; mem., MISAT-FOR Fla. Cmty. Coll. Sys., Tallahassee, 1998—; mem. - CIO com. Fla. Cmty. Coll. Sys., Tallahassee, 1998—. Mem.: N.Am. UNISYS User Assn. (assoc.), The Fla. Assn. Ednl. Data Systems (assoc.), The Rotary Club (v.p.). Independent Thinkers. Luth. Avocations: exercise, travel, gardening, cooking, reading. Office: Pasco-Hernando Cmity Coll 10230 Ridge Road New Port Richey FL 34654 Business E-Mail: cessnaj@phcc.edu.

CEULEMANS, SOPHIA, biochemist; d. Ceulemans and Mumm. Student in Biochemistry and Molecular Biology, Marquette U., Milw., Wis., 2003—. Tchg. asst. Marquette U. Biology Dept., Milw., 2005—. Sci. judge Milw. Regional Sci. and Engring. Fair, 2005—06; adv. Sexual Assault Treatment Ctr., Milw., 2005—; peer educator Violence Opposition in Cmty. Edn. Liason Marquette U. and healthcare sys. V-Day Planning Com., Milw., 2006—. Ignatius scholarship, Marquette U., 2003—. Mem.: Nat. Soc. Genetic Counseling (counselor 2003—), Genetic Alliance. Achievements include research in exploring a gene sequence in S. Cerevisiae via complementary gene testing.

CEYER, SYLVIA T., chemistry professor, department chairman; Grad. summa cum laude, Hope Coll., Holland, Mich.; PhD, U. Calif., Berkeley. Postdoctoral fellow Nat. Bur. Standards; faculty mem. dept. chemistry MIT, Cambridge, Mass., 1981—, J.C. Sheehan prof. chemistry, assoc. dept. chmn. Recipient Recognition award for young scholars AAUW Ednl. Found., 1988, Nobel Laureate Signature award for Grad. Edn. in Chemistry, Am. Chem. Soc., 1993. Fellow AAAS, NAS (chmn. chemistry sect.), Am. Phys. Soc., Am. Acad. Arts and Scis. Office: MIT 6-217 Dept Chemistry 77 Mass Ave Dept Cambridge MA 02139-4307 Business E-Mail: stceyer@mit.edu.

CHACON, DELIA C., secondary school educator; d. Raymond Francis and Marie Theresa Collins; m. Fernando Chacon, Mar. 20, 1982 (div. Dec. 28, 1993); children: Danielle Marie Snelling, Stephanie Martha; m. David Trent Lipscomb, Dec. 27, 1998. AA in Liberal Arts, No. Essex C.C., Haverhill, Mass., 1979; BA in Am. Studies and Elem. Edn., U. Lowell, Mass., 1981. Cert. tchr. social studies-history/early adolescence Nat. Bd. Profl. Tchg. Stdds., profl. educator Fla., profl. clear multiple subject tchg. credential Calif., cert. lifetime elem. educator Mass. Bilingual elem. tchr. Mark Twain Elem., Lynwood, Calif., 1987—94; drama tchr. Hosler Jr. HS, Lynwood, 1994—98; tchr. mid. sch. social studies/lang. arts Windy Ridge K-8 Sch., Orlando, Fla., 1998—2003; tchr. AP Am. govt., AP macroeconomics, Am. history/leadership Oak Ridge HS, Orlando, 2003—. Dept. chair Windy Ridge K-12, 1999—2003. Sch. coord. Red Cross Blood Bank, Orlando, 2003—06; schoolwide coord. Pasta for Pennies Campaign, Leukemia and Lymphoma Soc., Orlando, 2003—06; sponsorship chair Relay for Life, Ctrl. Fla. Am. Cancer Soc., Orlando, 2003—06. Named Mid. Sch. Social Studies Tchr. of Yr., Ctrl. Fla. Regional History Ctr. and Orange County Pub. Schs., 2002, Tchr. of Yr., Lynwood Unified Sch. Dist., 1990. Mem.: ACLU, ASCD, Internat. Ctr. Leadership in Edn., Nat. Tchrs. Assn., Classroom Tchrs. Assn., Nat. Coun. Social Studies, Fla. Coun. Social Studies (Tchr. of Yr. 2002), Orange County Coun. ocial Studies (pres. 2004—06), Kappa Upsilon. Office: Oak Ridge HS 6000 S Winegard Rd Orlando FL 32809 Office Phone: 407-852-3200 ext 2284. Office Fax: 407-850-5152. Personal E-mail: shakesmom@earthlink.net. E-mail: chacond@ocps.net.

CHACON, MARIA, government agency administrator; 2 children. B in Mgmt. Various NASA Dryden Flight Rsch. Ctr., Edwards, Calif., dep. chief info. officer. Avocations: watersports, travel. Office: NASA Dryden Flight Rsch Ctr PO Box 273 MS 4838 Edwards CA 93523-0273 Business E-Mail: maria.chacon@mail.dfrc.nasa.gov.

CHADHA, GURINDER, film director; b. Kenya; m. Paul Mayeda Berges. Reporter BBC Radio, London; documentary dir. BBC; founder Umbi Film Prodn., 1990—. Dir., writer (TV films) I'm British But, 1990; dir.: (films) Acting Our Age, 1992; dir., writer: Bhaji on the Beach, 1993; Nice Arrangement, 1994; dir., prodr. What Do You Call an Indian Woman Who's Funny, 1994; dir., writer, prodr. Bend It Like Beckham, 2002; What's Cooking, 2000; Bride and Prejudice, 2004.

CHAFEL, JUDITH ANN, education educator; b. Rochester, N.Y., Apr. 8, 1945; d. James Arthur and Florence Joan (Santangelo) Chafel. AB, Vassar Coll., 1967; MSEd, Wheelock Coll, 1971; PhD, U. Ill., 1979. Cert. elem. tchr., Mass., N.J., N.Y. Tchr. Spruce St. Sch., Lakewood, NJ, 1972-74, Sodus (N.Y.) Primary Sch., 1974-76; grad. research and teaching asst. U. Ill., Urbana, 1976-79; vis. asst. prof. U. Tex., Austin, 1979-80; asst. prof. dept. curriculum and instrn. Ind. U., Bloomington, 1980-86, assoc. prof., 1986—2001, prof., 2001—; mem. profl. staff U.S. Ho. Reps., Washington, 1989-90. Adj. assoc. prof. philanthropic studies Ctr. on Philanthropy, 1991-2001; reviewer Hist. Publs. and Records Commn., Nat. Archives, Washington, 1979, Little, Brown and Co., Boston, 1982-84, Office for Ednl. Rsch. and Improvement, U.S. Dept. Edn., 1991, 93. Mem. editl. adv. bd. Early Child Devel. and Care, 1985—, Youth and Soc., 1995-2005, cons. editor Early Childhood Rsch. Quar., 1988-91, 92-95, 2005—; contbr. editor Am. Jour. of Orthopsychiatry, 2000—; reviewer, book editor; contbr. articles to profl. jours.; contbr. chapts. to books. Proffitt Endowment grantee, Ind. U., 1982, 88, 1998, Ctr. on Philanthropy grantee, 1991, Spencer Found. grantee, 1985, 98; Congl. Sci. fellow Soc. Rsch. in Child Devel., 1989. Mem. Soc. Rsch. in Child Devel. (program com. 1986, 92), Am. Ednl. Rsch. Assn. (program com. various yrs., nominations com. 1986, 88, chair 1993-95, mem.-at-large spl. interest group on early edn. and child devel. 1991-93), Nat. Assn. Edn. Young Children (reviewer 1980—), Assn. Childhood Edn. Internat. (pub. com. 1982-84, bull. and pamphlets rev. editor jour. 1982-84, rsch. com. 1984-88), Nat. Soc. for the Study of Edn. E-mail: chafel@indiana.edu.

CHAFFEE, MONICA WEAVER, primary school educator; b. St. Louis, Mar. 18, 1969; d. Bernard Miller and Ida Dean Weaver; m. Stephen Clark Chaffee, June 27, 1998; children: Eva Victoria Weaver, Sarah Madeline Weaver. BS, James Madison U., Harrisonburg, Va., 1991; MS, Shenandoah U., Winchester, Va., 2002. Cert. reading specialist Va. Kindergarten tchr., reading specialist Culpeper County Sch., Va., 1992—2003; kindergarten tchr. St. Luke's Luth. Sch., Culpeper, 2004—. Cons. in field. Mem.: Va. State Reading Assn. Republican. Methodist. Avocations: walking, reading, cooking. Home: 1154 Old Rixeyville Rd Culpeper VA 22701 Office: St Luke's Luth Sch 1200 Old Rixeyville Rd Culpeper VA 22701 Office Phone: 540-825-8890. E-mail: mchaffee@stlukes-school.org.

CHAFFIN, LAVERNE, music educator; d. Eddie and Ruby Chaffin. BS, Albany State U., Ga.; MS, ednl. specialist, Troy State U., Ala. Tchr. Randolph County schs., Clay County Elem. Sch. Mem.: Ga. Coun. Arts (coord.), Ga. Assn. Edn., Music Edn. Nat. Conf., Delta Sigma Theta. Avocation: coaching. Home: PO Box 413 Fort Gaines GA 39851

CHAFKIN, RITA M., retired dermatologist; b. N.Y.C., Apr. 11, 1929; d. Joseph and Dora (Winslow) Melnick; m. Samuel Chafkin, June 29, 1952; children: Elise Ceil Perkins, Marc David Chafkin (dec.). BA, NYU, 1949; MD, NYU Med. Sch., 1953; cert. in dermatology, NYU Postgrad. Med. Sch., 1957. Diplomate Am. Acad. Dermatology, 1959. Intern in internal medicine Kings County Hosp., Bklyn., 1953-54; dermatology resident Bellevue Hosp., N.Y.C., 1954-55; postgrad. trainee NYU Postgrad. Med. Sch., 1955-56, fellow in dermatology, 1956-57; precepteeship with Dr. Marion Sulzberger; pvt. practice dermatology Modesto, Calif., 1958—94; ret., 1994; assoc. clin. prof. dermatology U. Calif., Davis, 1975-97. Clinic dir. dermatology Stanislavs County Med. Ctr., Modesto, 1958-97. Artist in mixed media. Bd. dirs. Stanislaus County Med. Ctr. Found., 1982-97, pres. 1984-85. Recipient Tchr. of the Yr. award Stanislaus County Med. Ctr., Modesto, 1988, Founder's Dinner honoree, 1992. Fellow Am. Acad. Dermatology; mem. AMA, Calif. Med. Soc., San Francisco Dermatology Soc., Stanislaus County Med. Soc. (pres. 1983-84), Pacific Dermatology Assn. (fin. com. 1959—). Jewish.

CHAGNON, LUCILLE TESSIER, literacy acceleration consultant; b. Gardner, Mass., June 1, 1936; d. Fred G. Tessier and Alfreda C. (Ross) Noel; m. Richard J. Chagnon, Sept. 16, 1978; children: Daniel, David. BMus, Rivier Coll., Nashua, N.H.; cert. in human resource mgmt. and cmty. devel., Inst. Cultural Affairs, Chgo., 1969; MEd, Boston Coll., 1972. Educator, N.H., 1960-73; internat. cons. Inst. Cultural Affairs, Chgo., 1973-79; staff tng. dir. CO-MHAR, Inc., Phila., 1979-81; pres., owner Chagnon Assocs., Collingswood, N.J., 1981-86; prin. Sacred Heart Sch., Camden, N.J., 1986-87; founder, dir. Lifeline Literacy Project, 1988-94; literacy and developmental learning specialist Rutgers U., Camden, 1989-99; coord. work readiness, Workforce Devel. Inst. Drexel U., Phila., 1999-2000. Adj. grad. faculty dept. counseling psychology Temple U. Sch. Edn., Phila., 1984—89; project cons. Right Mgmt. Cons., Phila., 1982—91, 2001—03. Author (with Richard J. Chagnon): The Best is Yet to Be: A Pre-Retirement Program, 1985; author: Easy Reader, Learner, Writer, 1994, Voice Hidden, Voice Heard: A Reading and Writing Anthology, 1998, You, Yes YOU, Can Teach Someone to Read: A Step by Step How-To Book, 2005. Bd. dirs. Camden County Literacy Vols. of Am., 1987—91, Handicapped Advocates for Ind. Living, 1987—; mem. Collingswood (N.J.) Bd. Edn., 1985—89. Mem.: Nat. Coun. Tchrs. English, Internat. Reading Assn., Internat. Alliance for Learning, Inst. Cultural Affairs, Brain-Based Edn. Network. Home and Office: 408 River Rd Wilmington DE 19809-2731 Office Phone: 302-762-0282. E-mail: chagnon@comcast.net.

CHAGNON, MARJORIE MARIE, retired elementary school educator; b. Ft. Wayne, Ind., Aug. 26, 1936; d. Leo Joseph and Marquerite Marie (Yingling) Walters. BS in Elem. Edn., Ball State U., 1958; MS in Elem. Edn., St. Francis Coll., Ft. Wayne, 1965. Cert. elem. tchr., reading specialist, Ind., elem. tchr., N.Y., Mich. Tchr. 1st grade East Allen County Schs., New Haven, Ind., 1958-69, Bemus Point (N.Y.) Ctrl. Schs., 1969-80; substitute tchr. Monroe County Schs., Bloomington, Ind., 1980-86; tchr. 3d and 5th grades St. Mary's Sch., Avilla, Ind., 1986—2001; ret., 2001. Mem. Internat. Reading Assn., Nat. Cath. Ednl. Assn. Home: PO Box 3 Auburn IN 46706-0003

CHAGNONI, KATHLEEN, energy executive; BA with honors, Stanford U., 1981; JD, Columbia U., 1985. Assoc. O'Melveny & Myers, Washington, 1985—89, Hogan & Harlson, Balt., 1989—94; asst. v.p., assoc. group counsel USF&G Corp., 1996—98; v.p., corp. group gen. counsel St. Paul Cos., Inc., 1999—2003; v.p., gen. counsel, corp. sec. Constellation Energy, Balt., 2002—. Office: Constellation Energy Group 750 E Pratt St Baltimore MD 21202

CHAIR, LISA, science educator; d. Jack and Lillian McLemore; m. Perry Chair, 1981; children: Amanda, Skye. BS in Sci. Edn., Northeastern State U., Tahlequah, Okla., 1988. Tchr. Cave Springs HS, Stillwell, 1989—94, Gore (Okla.) HS, 1994—. Mem. emergency procedure com. Gore HS, mem. discipline com. Named 4-H Leader of the Yr., 1997, Tchr. of the Yr., Gore Sch. Dist., 2004—05. Mem.: Nat. Earth Sci. Tchr. Assn., Nat. Sci. Tchr. Assn., Gore Tchrs. Assn. Democrat. Bapt. Avocations: antiques, cooking, sewing, reading. Office: Gore HS PO Box 580 Gore OK 74435

CHAIRSELL, CHRISTINE, academic administrator; children: T., Tyler. EdD, U. Nev. Las Vegas, MA in polit. sci., BA in polit. sci., U. Nev. Las Vegas. Acting pres. Nev. State Coll., 2002; assoc. vice chancellor U. & CC Sys. Nev.; assoc. vice pres. Computing Svc.; dean spl. programs CC So. Nev.; dir. environ. edn. U. Nev. Las Vegas, faculty polit. sci. dept. Pres. Aqua Vision, 1992—94; mem. Leadership Las Vegas Class, 1993. Recipient women of achievement edn., Las Vegas Chamber Commerce, 1993.

CHAIT, FAY KLEIN, health administrator; b. Chgo., Jan. 12, 1929; d. Victor and Rose (Begun) Magid; m. Jerome G. Klein, June 27, 1948 (div. 1970); children: Leslie Susan Janik, Debra Lynne Maslov; m. Manuel Chait, Aug. 28, 1994. BA in English, UCLA, 1961; MA in Pub. Adminstrn., U. So. Calif., 1971. Cert. health adminstrn. Supr. social workers L.A. County, 1961-65; program specialist Econ. and Youth Opportunity Agy., L.A., 1965-69; sr. health planner Model Cities, L.A., 1971-72; dir. prepaid health plan Westland Health Svcs., L.A., 1972-74; exec. dir. Coastal Region Health Consortium, L.A., 1974-76; grants and legis. cons. Jewish Fed. Council of L.A., 1976-79; planning coun. Jewish Fed. Coun. of So. Fla., Palm Beach to Miami, 1979-82; adminstrv. dir. program in kidney diseases Dept. Medicine UCLA, 1982-84; exec. dir. west coast Israel Cancer Rsch. Fund, L.A., 1984-94; cons. to non-profit orgns. Santa Monica, 1994—. Cons. Arthritis Found., L.A., 1984, Bus. Action Ctr., L.A., 1982, Vis. Nurses Assn., L.A., 1982. Charter mem. L.A. County Mus. of Art, Mus. of Contemporary Art; cons. L.A. Mcpl. Art Gallery, 1979; mem. UCLA/Armand Hammer Mus. Fellow U.S. Pub. Health, U. So. Calif., 1970-71. Mem. APHA, UCLA Alumni Assn. (life), U. So. Calif. Alumni Assn. (life). Office Phone: 310-393-1644.

CHAITMAN, HELEN DAVIS, lawyer; b. NYC, July 5, 1941; d. Philip and Miriam (Pfeffer) D.; m. Edmund Chaitman, Feb. 29, 1964 (div. 1978); children: Jennifer, Alison; m. George B. Gelman, Oct. 21, 1979. AB cum laude, Bryn Mawr Coll., 1963; JD, Rutgers U., 1976. Bar: N.J., 1976, N.Y. 1978, U.S. Dist. Ct. N.J. 1976, U.S. Dist. Ct. (so. and ea. dists.) 1978, U.S. Supreme Ct. 1981, Ct. Fed. Claims 2001, U.S. Ct. Appeals (8th cir.) 2002. Assoc. Paul, Weiss, Rifkind, Wharton & Garrison, N.Y.C., 1977-82; ptnr. Wilentz, Goldman & Spitzer, Woodbridge, NJ, 1983-87, Ross & Hardies, Somerset, NJ, 1987-99, Wolf Haldenstein Adler Freeman & Herz LLP, N.Y.C., 1999—2002, Phillips Nizer LLP, NYC, 2002—. Author: The Law of Lender Liability, 1990; contbg. author: Commercial Damages, 1985; editor Emerging Theories of Lender Liability, 1985-87, Lender Liability Law Report, 1987— Mem.: ABA (chmn. comml. fin. svcs. com. 1994—97, sect. bus. law), Am. Law Inst. (sustaining mem. 1992—2006). Home: The Farm 115 Fairview Rd Frenchtown NJ 08825-3013 Office: Phillips Nizer LLP 666 Fifth Ave New York NY 10103-0084 also: 45 Essex St Hackensack NJ 07601 Office Phone: 212-841-1320. Business E-Mail: hchaitman@phillipsnizer.com.

CHALCRAFT, ELENA MARIE, actress, singer; b. Bklyn., Oct. 14, 1959; d. James Abdou and Vivian (Trovato) Edwards; m. Rory Charles Chalcraft, Aug. 1, 1992; 1 child, Christopher Aston. BA in Speech, English and Theater Arts, Shippensburg State Coll., 1981; MFA in Acting, Va. Commonwealth U., 1984. Human resources analyst APA, Washington, 1985-98; music dir. Our Lady Queen of Peace Ch., Arlington, Va., 1992-98; soprano Philomusica Chamber Choir, 1999—2006; ind. kitchen cons. The Pampered Chef, 1999—; soprano St. Bartholomew Choir, 2000—01; substitute tchr. South River Elem. Sch. and Corpus Christi Sch., South River, NJ, 2005—. Substitute tchr. South River Elem. Sch., 2005—, Corpus Christi Sch., 2005—. Actor, singer (plays): Man of La Mancha, 1988, Ben, 1989-90, Maryland Renaissance Festival, 1987-91, Ziggy, 1992, The Snow Queen, 1994; actor: (play) Broadway Bound, 1993, (tng. film) GAO, 1990; dramaturg (play) Ballets Russes and Drood, 1993. Mem. liturgy com. Our Lady Queen of Peace Ch., 1995—98. Roman Catholic. Avocations: reading, writing children's books, piano, cross-stitch, crosswords. E-mail: emcrcc@worldnet.att.net.

CHALFANT-ALLEN, LINDA KAY, retired Spanish language educator; b. New Kensington, Pa., Oct. 9, 1943; d. Fred and Evelyn V. (Peters) C.; m. Charles V. Utley, Sr., Jan. 26, 1963 (div.); children: Charles V. Utley, Yvette Melissa Utley; m. Simon Allen, Feb. 13, 1998. BA in Child Study, Vassar Coll., 1965; MS in Spanish and Linguistics, Georgetown U., 1971. Cert. tchr., N.Y., D.C. Bilingual rsch. asst. Georgetown U., Washington, 1966-71; curriculum writer D.C. Pub. Schs., 1969-70, 91; asst. prof., rsch. assoc. U. D.C., 1982-85; asst. to dir. Latin for Modern Sch., McLean, Va., 1968-94; tchr. D.C. Pub. Schs., 1965-95, ret., 1995; freelance cons., editor, 1961—; bilingual legal sec. Wilkinson, Barker, Knauer & Quinn, Washington, 1996-97; legal sec. Thelen Reid & Priest, 1998-2000. Proposal review panelist Nat. Endowment for Humanities, Washington, 1984, 87, 89, U.S. Dept. Edn., Washington, 1986. Founder, 1st pres. Fgn. Lang. Action Group, Washington, 1978-79; Sunday sch. tchr., Washington, 1972-93. Recipient Grad. Study fellowship King Juan Carlos Found., Spain, 1994, Travel grant Spain '92 Found., 1994. Roman Catholic. Avocations: travel, reading, bowling, baking, exercise, crochet.

CHALIF, RONNIE, medical association administrator, artist; b. NYC, Apr. 14, 1933; d. Norman and Ruth London Stern; m. Seymour Chalif, June 13, 1954; children: John Lewis, Peter Adley. Grad. with honors, Parson Sch. Design, 1953; BS in Art Edn., NYU, 1954. Buyer I. Magnin & Co., NYC, 1954—59; founder, dir. Neuropathy Assn., NYC, 1995—2006, pres., 2005—. Author, illustrator: Exercising with Neuropathy, 2001; one-woman shows include Guild Hall Mus., East Hampton, NY, Benson Gallery, Bridghampton,

NY, 1972, 1975, Fed. Court House, NYC, 1984—85, Marymount Manhattan Coll. Gallery, 1986, Jackb K. Javits Fed. Bldg., 1986, Gayle Willson Gallery, 2000, 2003, Garrison Arts Ctr., NY, 1989, Benton Gallery, Southampton, NY, 1989, Arlene Bujese Gallery, 1996, 2001, exhibited in group shows at GE Co., Farifield, Conn., 1983, Benson Gallery, 2000—02, Atelier 14, NYC, 2000, Ashwagh Hall, East Hampton, NY, 1987—2005, Guild Hall Mus., 1992—93, Arlene Bujese Gallery, 1995—2006, others. Represented in permanent collections Guild Hall Mus., Continental Telephone Co., Washington, McGraw-Hill, Inc., Cadillac-Fairview, Dallas, GE Internat. Hdprs., Fairfield, Grey Advt. Inc., NYC, US Home Corp., Houston, Zimmerli Art Mus., New Brunswick, NJ, World Trade Ctr. Mem.: Women's Caucus for Art, Women in Arts Found., Nat. Assn. Women Artists, Artists Craftsmen NY, NY Soc. Women Artists. Studio: 204 Upper Seven Ponds Rd PO Box 20 Water Mill NY 11976 E-mail: schalif@kayescholer.com.

CHALIFOUX, ALICE ELLEN, harpist, educator; b. Birmingham, Ala., Jan. 22, 1908; d. Oliver and Alice (Hallé) C.; m. John Gordon Rideout, Apr. 27, 1937 (dec.); 1 child, Alyce. MusB, Curtis Inst., 1931; DFA (hon.), Bowdoin Coll., 1991. First harp Cleve. Orch., 1931-74; tchr. of harp Cleve. Inst. Music, 1931—, Oberlin (Ohio) Conservatory Music, 1931—, Baldwin-Wallace Conservatory, Berea, Ohio, 1970—. Dir. Summer Harp Colony, Camden, Maine, 1961—. Republican. Episcopal. Home: 35428 Appalachian Trail Rd Round Hill VA 20141-2300

CHALIFOUX, THELMA, Canadian senator; b. Calgary, AB, Can., Feb. 8, 1929; children: Robert, Scott, Clifford, Deborah, Orleane(dec.), Sharon, Paul. Student, Chgo. Sch. Interior Design, So. Alta. Inst. Tech., Lethbridge C.C. Field staff cmty. devel. Co. Young Can., 1973—75; land claims negotiator, 1979—82, 1996—98; panel mem. Alta. Family and Social Svcs., 1989—98; senator The Senate of Can., Ottawa, 1997—. Cons. Chalifoux & Assocs., 1996—98; cons., senator Metis Nation of Alta. Assn., 1990—95. Recipient Nat. Aboriginal Achievement award, 1995. Liberal.

CHALK, BARBARA ANN, retired medical/surgical nurse; b. Watertown, NY, May 1, 1936; d. Herbert Graham Chalk and Julia Rosemead Donaldson. Diploma in nursing, House of Good Samaritan Hosp., Watertown, 1957. Staff nurse oper. rm. Ho. of Good Samaritan Hosp., 1957—59; head nurse neurosurgery oper. rm. U. Va. Hosp., Charlottesville, 1959—75; clin. coord. neurosurgery oper. rm. Norfolk Gen. Hosp., Va., 1975—2000; ret., 2000. Vol. Heart Hosp., Norfolk Gen. Hosp., 2000—, Parkinson Support Group, 2000—; bd. dirs. Parkinson Disease Assn., Virginia Beach, Va., 2003—. Recipient Cert. of Merit, Parkinsons Disease Assn., Va., 2001. Avocations: needlepoint, ceramics. Home: 444 Adelphia Rd Virginia Beach VA 23464

CHALK, ROSEMARY ANNE, health science association administrator; b. Cin., May 25, 1948; d. John Henry and Virginia R. (Kamphaus) Chalk; m. Michael Anthony Stoto, June 28, 1986; children: Anna Murilius, Benjamin John. BA, U. Cin., 1970; postgrad., George Washington U., 1970-72. Policy analyst Libr. of Congress, Washington, 1972-75; rsch. fellow MIT, Cambridge, Mass., 1982-83; program dir. AAAS, Washington, 1976-86; cons. Harvard Sch. Pub. Health, Boston, 1986-87; study dir. Inst. of Med., Washington, 1987-89, Nat. Acad. Sci., Washington, 1989—; dir. Bd. on Children, Youth, and Families, Inst. of Med., Washington, 2000—. Cons. The Field Found., N.Y.C., 1986-87, The Acadia Inst., Bar Harbor, Maine, 1988-91; adv. com. on ethics and values studies NSF, 1984-87. Editor: Science, Technology and Society: Emerging Relationships, 1988; contbr. articles to profl. jours. Fellow AAAS (coun. and section officer 1987—), Fedn. Am. Scientists (coun. mem. 1982-90), Student Pugwash USA (bd. dirs. 1988—). Roman Catholic. Office: Inst Medicine NAS 500 Fifth Street NW Washington DC 20001

CHALKLEY, JACQUELINE ANN, retail company executive; b. Benson, Minn., Jan. 3, 1946; d. Vincent Otto and Dorothy Mildred (Alsaker) Kaehler; m. C. Wayne Callaway. BA in Art History cum laude, Brown U., 1967; MA, Columbia U., 1968; postgrad. in Contemporary Art, New Sch. for Social Rsch., NYC, 1968—70; postgrad. in Ceramics, U. Md., 1970—72. Art tchr. Summit (NJ) HS, 1968-70, Rockville (Md.) HS, 1970-74; adj. prof. ceramics Montgomery Coll., Rockville, 1974-78; owner Jackie Chalkley at Foxhall Sq., Washington, 1978-99, Jackie Chalkley at Willard Collection, Washington, 1986-99, Jackie Chalkley at Chevy Chase Plz., Washington, 1989-99; retail and product devel. cons., 1999—. Juror Rhinebeck Craft Fair, 1981, New Eng. Buyers Market, Boston, 1982, Craft Art 1982, Richmond, Va. Craft Show, 1983, Smithsonian Crafts Exhbn. 1983, Smithsonian Instn. Women's Com. Craft Show, 1984, Annie Albers fashion show at Renwick Gallery, 1984, Morristown Craft Fair, 1984, Washington Craft Show, 1986, Potomac Craftsmen's Guild Show, 1987, Harrisburg Arts Festival, 1987, Ceramic Guild Washington, 1987, Washington Guild Goldsmiths, 1987, 18th Bienniel Exhbn. Creative Crafts Coun., 1988, Art Balt., 2003-04, Torpedo Factory Art Ctr., 2006, others; appointee screening com. Piedmont Craftsman's Guild, Winston-Salem, NC, 1983-86, DC Commn. Arts, 1983-85; hon. com. Brandeis Art Exhbn., 1984, Textile Mus., 1984-86. Featured in Ceramics Monthly, 1994, Women's Wear Daily, 1995. Hon. com. 34th St. Art Fair, John Eaton Sch., 1985; benefit com. Washington Charitable Fund, 1989; hon. bd. trustees DC chpt. Design Industries Found. for AIDS, 1989-90; auction benefit com. Washington Project for Arts, 1989, 90; benefit com. Source Theater, 1993, Corcoran Mus. Jazz Evening, 1993, Living Stage & Arena Theatre, 1997-99; hon. com. Lab Sch. Wash., 1992, Aid to Artisans DC, Cambodian Embassy, 2003; hon. benefit com. Arena Stage Living Theater, 1997-98; sponsor Wearable Art Fashion Show, Renwick Mus., 1993; juried Smithsonian Craft Show, 1994; hon. chair Friends of the Corcoran Mus. Benefit, 1999-2000, exec. com., 2001-02; chair Craft Leaders Caucus Day 2000; nat. resource bd. James Renwick Alliance of Renwick Mus., 2000-03, gala exec. com. Rincones Dance Theater, 2001—; fundraising chair Aid to Artisans Benefit, DC, 2005 Appeared on cover of Forecast Mag., 1978; recipient Best Taste in Washington award Washingtonian Mag., 1982, 1st Ann. Outstanding Accessories Merchandising award Accessories Mag., 1985; named one of 23 People to Watch in 1983, Washingtonian Mag., 1982; her apt. chosen as Residential Interior of Yr., Am. Soc. Interior Designers, 1985, 92; her store named 1986 Comml. Interior of Yr., Am. Soc. Interior Designers; nat. award for logo Am. Corp. Identity, 1988, 91 Mem. Am. Craft Coun., Washington Fashion Group, James Renwick Craft Leaders Caucus, Chmns. Guild of the Corcoran Gallery of Art, Washington Performing Arts Soc. (impresario coun. 2001-), Nat. Gallery Art and Hishorn Mus. (cir. mem.). Avocations: travel, dance, visual arts, swimming. Office: Jackie Chalkley 2130 Cathedral Ave NW Washington DC 20008-1502

CHALLENGER, VICKI LEE, elementary school educator; b. Parkersburg, W.Va., Jan. 5, 1962; d. Harold Leroy and Lois Jeanette Rush; 1 child, Vincent Lance. M in Adminstrn., Cleve. State U., 1993. Cert. tchr. Ohio, 1993. Tchr. art Sunbeam Elem. Sch., Cleve., 1993—94; tchr. Monticello Mid. Sch., 1994—. Dem. precinct ward capt., Olmsted Township, Ohio, 2006, 2006. Avocation: golf. Home: 27012 Oakwood Dr Apt#102 Olmsted Falls OH 44138 Office: Monticello Middle School 3665 Monticello Blvd Cleveland Heights OH 44118 Office Phone: 216-320-4999. Personal E-mail: vlcgolf@yahoo.com.

CHAMBERLAIN, BARBARA KAYE, small business owner, communications executive; b. Lewiston, Idaho, Nov. 6, 1962; d. William Arthur and Gladys Marie (Humphrey) Greene; m. Dean Andrew Chamberlain, Sept. 13, 1986 (div.); children: Kathleen Marie, Laura Kaye; m. Daniel Eric Pocklington, Apr. 11, 1998 (div.). BA in English cum laude, BA in Linguistics cum laude, Wash. State U., 1984; MPA, Ea. Wash. U., 2002. Temp. sec. various svcs., Spokane, Wash., 1984-86; office mgr. Futurepast, Spokane, 1986-87; dir. mktg. and prodn. Futurepast: The History Co., Melior Publs., Spokane, 1987-88, v.p., 1988-89; founder, owner PageWorksInk, 1989—; mem. dist. 2 Idaho State Ho. of Reps., 1990-92; mem. Idaho State Senate, 1992-94; dir. comm. and pub. affairs Wash. State U., Spokane, 1998—. Adj. faculty North Idaho Coll., 1995, trustee, 1996-2001, bd. chair, 1999-2001. Author North Idaho's Centennial, 1990; editor Washington Songs and Lore, 1988. Bd. dirs. Mus. North Idaho Coeur d'Alene, 1990-91, Ct. Apptd. Spl. advocates, 1993-96; bd. dirs. Spokane Pub. Rels. Coun., 1999-2004, pres., 2002-03; bd. dirs. Friends of the Falls, 2005—; co-chair Citizens for Spokane Schs., 2005-06. Named Child Advocate Legislator of Yr., Idaho Alliance for Children, Youth and Families, 1993. Democrat. Office: Academic Ctr PO Box 1495 Spokane WA 99210-1495

CHAMBERLAIN, CANDACE SUE, music educator; b. Modesto, Calif., Aug. 8, 1953; d. Earl Edwin and Lois Mary Chamberlain. BA, Calif. Stat U. Stanislaus, Turlock, 1977. Cert. tchr. K-12 single subject-music Calif. Tchr. music Delhi Unified Sch. Dist., Calif., 1979—86, Ceres Unifed Sch. Dist., Calif., 1986—2005, tchr. music/drama Calif., 2005—. Mentor tchr. Ceres Unified Sch. Dist., 1992—98; master tchr. Calif. State U. Stanislaus, 1978—2004. Pres./CEO Expression Children's Choir, Ceres, 2005—. Named Woman of Distinction, Soroptomist Internat., 1999, Mid. Sch. Educator of Yr., CLMS, 1998. Mem.: Stanislaus County Music Educators Assn. (pres. 1985—), Am. Choral Dirs. Assn., Calif. Educators Assn. Avocations: musical theater, interior decorating, reading, travel. Home: 3208 Rhone Dr Ceres CA 95307 Office: Ctrl Valley H S PO Box 307 Ctrl and Svc Rd Ceres CA 95307 Personal E-mail: mewbgr8@sbcglobal.net. Business E-Mail: cchamberlain@ceres.k12.ca.us.

CHAMBERLAIN, DIANE, psychotherapist, writer, social worker; b. Plainfield, N.J., Mar. 18, 1950; d. John and Anna Delores (Chamberlain) Lopresti; m. Richard David Chmielewski, Apr. 14, 1973 (div. 1993); m. David Earl Heagy, June 8, 1996. BSW, San Diego State U., 1975, MSW, 1978. Clin. social worker Social Advocates for Youth, San Diego, 1978-80; clin. social worker Sharp Meml. Hosp., San Diego, 1980-83, Children's Hosp. and Nat. Health Ctr., Washington, 1983-85; pvt. practice psychotherapy Alexandria, Va., 1985-92. Author: (novels) Private Relations, 1989, Lovers and Strangers, 1990, Secret Lives, 1991, Keeper of the Light, 1992, Fire and Rain, 1993, Brass Ring, 1994, Reflection, 1996, The Escape Artist, 1997, Breaking the Silence, 1999, Summer's Child 2000, The Courage Tree, 2001, Kiss River, 2003, In Her Mother's Shadow, 2004, Bay at Midnight, 2005, The Secret Life of CeeCee Wilkes, 2006; contbr. nonfiction articles to profl. jours. Mem. Novelists Inc. Democrat. Personal E-mail: diane@dianechamberlain.com.

CHAMBERLAIN, ELIZABETH SIMMONS, retired English language educator; b. St. Louis, June 15, 1929; d. George Edwin and Myrtle Coline (Smith) Simmons; m. Barnwell Rhett Chamberlain Jr., Aug. 11, 1956; 1 child, Edwin Rhett. AB, Wellesley Coll., Mass., 1951; AM, U. Mich., Ann Arbor, 1955; PhD, U. N.C., Chapel Hill, 1979. Tchr. English and Bible history, adminstr. Kingswood Sch. Cranbrook, Bloomfield Hills, Mich., 1951-55, Ashley Hall, Charleston, S.C., 1955-56; tchr. English and social studies Charlotte (N.C.) Country Day Sch., 1956-58; instr. English Meredith Coll., Raleigh, N.C., 1962-68; asst. prof. English N.C. Ctrl. U., Durham, 1981-95; ret., 1995. Active Human Rels. Com., Durham, 1983-88, 91-94, chair, 1986-88, 93-94; active Civic Ctr. Authority, Durham, 1988-91, merger com. City and County Planning Depts., Durham, 1983-84, Nursing Home Adv. Com., Durham, 1982-85, exec. com. Dem. Party N.C., 2000—; chmn. precinct com. Buncombe County Dem. Party, 2003—; mem. platform resolutions com. N.C. Dem. Party, 2006. Mem. Common Cause (dist. bd. 1996-2002), DAR, Today's Book Club (sec. 1996-98, v.p. 1999-2001) Democrat. United Methodist. Avocations: politics, reading. Home: 340 Blackberry Inn Rd Weaverville NC 28787-9766

CHAMBERLAIN, JEAN NASH, consultant, former county government department director; b. Chgo., Oct. 14, 1934; d. William Edmund and Virginia Jean (La Fon) Nash; m. James Staffeld Chamberlain, Dec. 29, 1953; children: James W., William S., Caren T., Martha J. Student, U. S.C., Columbia, 1951-53. Dept. dir. Oakland County, Mich., 1982—2003; polit. dir. Tribune/United Cablevision, Huntington Woods, Mich., 1982; orgn. dir. polit. campaign, Oakland, Mich., 1983-84; dir. fin. Dan Murphy for Gov., Mich., 1985-86; exec. mgr. Greater Royal Oak (Mich.)/Oak Park C. of C., 1986-93; bus. and polit. cons. Royal Oak, Mich.; pres. JNC Consulting LLC. Bd. dir. Mich. Trust Bank. Chair Oak Park Bus. and Edn. Alliance; sec.-treas. Woodward Ave. Action Assn.; vice chair Rep. com., Oakland County, Mich., 1971—73; chair Rep. 18th congl. dist., 1973—77; del. Rep. Nat. Conv., Kansas City, Mo., 1976; bd. dir. Oakland County Mental Health Bd., Mich., 1976—93, chair, 1983—86; bd. dir. Nat. Heritage Route, Give A Christmas Yr. Around, Grand Nat., 8 Mile Blvd. Assn. Named among top thirty Outstanding Women State Mich., Mich's. Womens Commn., 1998. Mem. Mich. State C. of C., Harnack Firefighters Scholarship Fund (bd. dirs.), Woodward Dream Cruise (bd. chair). Roman Catholic. Avocations: tennis, bridge, sports, cooking. Office Phone: 248-821-0665. E-mail: jean@jncconsulting.com.

CHAMBERLAIN, KATHRYN BURNS BROWNING, retired military officer; b. Rapid City, S.D., Jan. 17, 1951; d. George Alfred III and Mildred Doty Browning; m. Thomas Richard Masker, Apr. 19, 1975 (widowed Sept. 1978); m. Guy Caldwell Chamberlain III, Mar. 25, 1980 (div. Oct. 1988); children: Burns Doty, Anne Caldwell. BA, La. Tech. U., 1973; postgrad., Naval Postgrad. Sch., Monteray, Calif., 1978-79; MA, Auburn U., 1984; postgrad., U. Ill., 1994-96, Govs. State U., 1995-96. Ensign USN, 1974, lt. jg., 1976, lt., 1978, advanced through grades to comdr., 1983, surface warfare designation, 1980, joint staff officer, 1986, comdg. officer Mil. Sealift Command Office Alaska, 1986-88; comdr., exec. officer USNAVFAC, Nfld., 1991-94; planner City of Montgomery, 1998—. Mem. Am. Inst. Cert. Planners, Am. Planning Assn., Urban and Regional Info. Sys. Assn. Home and Office: 364 Felder Ave Montgomery AL 36104-5616 Office Phone: 334-241-2699. Business E-Mail: kchamberlain@ci.montgomery.al.us. E-mail: kchamberlai1@earthlink.net.

CHAMBERLAIN, PATRICIA ANN, retired land use planner, farmer; b. Tex. d. James Franklin and Roberta Marie; m. Herbert F. Chamberlain, July 20, 1962 (div. Oct. 1967); children: Norma, Catherine; m. Clayton C. Wright, Mar. 5, 1994 (dec. May 2000). AA, Odessa (Tex.) Jr. Coll., 1970; BS in Secondary Edn., Tex. Tech. U., 1971, PhD in Land Use Planning, Mgmt. & Design, 1984. Cert. wildlife biologist. Lab. and x-ray tech. Med. Ctr. Hosp. and Drs. offices, Odessa, 1964-68; supr. urban wildlife program Tex. Rodent & Predatory Animal Control Svc., San Antonio, 1972-80; rsch. wildlife biologist USDA U.S. Forest Svc., Lubbock, Tex., 1981-84; community planner USAF San Antonio Real Property Maintenance Agy., 1985-87; environ. engr. USAF SARPMA, San Antonio, 1987-88; br. chief USAF Environ. Br., Brooks AFB, Tex., 1988-91; community planner USAF Ctr. Environ. Excellence, San Antonio, Brooks AFB, 1991-94, natural resources specialist, 1994-98; freelance writer, farmer, 1998—. Mem. USAF Graphics Working Group, Washington, 1987-91. Mem. Target '90 Goals for San Antonio, 1986-87. With U.S. Army, 1960-62. Caesar Kleberg Wildlife Rsch. Found. grantee, 1980-84; named to San Antonio Women's Hall of Fame, 1992. Mem. Am. Planning Assn. (regional treas. 1986-87), Soc. Am. Mil. Engrs., Wildlife Soc. (nat. urban wildlife and regional planning com. 1980-82), Phi Kappa Phi, Sigma Tau Delta, Beta Beta Beta. Avocations: photography, art (oils and acrylics), fishing, hunting.

CHAMBERLAIN HAYMAN, SUSAN DENISE, psychotherapist, physical therapist; b. Platte, S.D., Feb. 18, 1954; d. Oran Lee and Lola Marion Chamberlain; m. Paul William Hayman, Dec. 17, 1984; children: Tiffany Cheré, Prairie Rose. BS, Black Hills State U., 1983; MS, S.D. State U., 1997. Lic. profl. counselor, S.D. Dir., owner Life Without Boundaries, Rapid City, S.D.; pain mgmt. therapist Rapid City Regional Hosp.; mental health therapist Luth. Social Svcs., Rapid City. Mem. Polit. Incident Stress Debriefing Team Katharsis, Rapid City, 1999—. Advisor, Parent Alliance Concerning Teen Support, Rapid City, 1998. E-4, U.S. Army. Mem. AAUW, Am. Counseling Assn., Am. Rehab. Counselors Assn., S.D. Counseling Assn. Avocation: bassist. Home: 3405 Leland Ln Rapid City SD 57702 Office: Life Without Boundaries 3202 W Main St Rapid City SD 57702 E-mail: hayman@rapidnet.com.

CHAMBERS, ANNE COX, publishing executive, former diplomat; b. Dayton, Ohio; Student, Finch Coll., N.Y.C.; D in Pub. Svc. (hon.), Wesleyan Coll., 1982; DHL (hon.), Spelman Coll., 1983; LLD (hon.), Oglethorpe U., 1983; DHL (hon.), Brenau Coll., 1989; LLD (hon.), Clark Atlanta U., 1989. Chmn. bd. Atlanta Jour.-Constn.; Am. amb. to Belgium, 1977-81. Bd. dirs. Cox Enterprises, Inc. Bd. dirs. Atlanta Arts Alliance, High Mus. Art, Cmtys. in Schs., MacDowell Colony, Forward Arts Found., Emory Mus. Art and Archaeology, N.Y. Bot. Garden, Coun. Am. Ambs., Chmn.'s Coun., Met. Mus. Art, Fr.-Am. Found.; trustee Mus. Modern Art, Carter Ctr.; mem. internat. coun. Mus. Modern Art; mem. nat. com. Whitney Mus. Am. Art. Decorated Legion of Hon. (France); named one of Forbes Richest Americans, 2006. Mem. Coun. Fgn. Rels. Office: 6205 Peachtree Dunwoody Rd Atlanta GA 30328

CHAMBERS, CLYTIA MONTLLOR, retired public relations consultant; b. Rochester, NY, Oct. 23, 1922; d. Anthony and Marie (Bambace) Capraro; m. Joseph John Montllor, July 2, 1941 (div. 1958); children: Michele, Thomas, Clytia; m. Robert Chambers, May 28, 1965. BA, Barnard Coll., N.Y.C., 1942; Licence en droit, Faculte de Droit, U. Lyon, France, 1948; MA, Howard U., Washington, 1958. Assoc. dir. dept. rsch. Coun. for Fin. Aid to Edn., N.Y.C., 1958-60; asst. to v.p. indsl. rels. Sinclair Oil Corp., N.Y.C., 1961-65; writer pub. rels. dept. Am. Oil Co., Chgo., 1965-67; dir. editorial svcs., v.p. Hill & Knowlton Inc., N.Y.C., 1967-77, sr. v.p., dir. spl. svcs. L.A., 1977-90, sr. cons., 1990—. Cons. and trustee Children's Inst. Internat., L.A., 1988-93. Co-author: The News Twisters, 1971; editor: Critical Issues in Public Relations, 1975. Mem.: Calif. Rare Fruit Growers (editor Fruit Gardener 1979—2000, editor emerita 2000—). Home: 11439 Laurelcrest Dr Studio City CA 91604-3872 Personal E-mail: clytia@sbcglobal.net.

CHAMBERS, DENNING JESSYCA, middle school educator; b. Westport, Conn., Feb. 15, 1952; d. James Peter and Iva Fay (Owens) McCleery; m. Thomas Neil Chambers (div.); 1 child, Melanie. BS in Mus. Edn. cum laude, U. Bridgeport, Conn., 1992; M in Mus. Edn., SUNY, Fredonia, 1998. Cert. tchr. NY. Vocal and music tchr. various elem. schs. and East Mid. Sch., West Seneca, NY, 1993—. Panelist Arts in Edn. Inst.; presenter, lectr. in field. Musician (soloist): Orchard Park Symphony. Pianist, vocalist Our Lady of Sacred Heart Ch., Colden, NY, 2002—04. Named Best Performer of Music Sch., U. Bridgeport, 1990; Dana scholar, 1990. Mem.: NY State Music Educators Assn., Erie County Music Educators Assn. Independent. Avocation: horseback riding. Home: 60 Tarn Tr Glenwood NY 14069

CHAMBERS, ELENORA STRASEL, artist; b. Strassel, Oreg. d. Augustine George and Frieda Rose (Westermann) Strasel; m. Edward Lucas Chambers, Oct. 9, 1954; children: Robert, Margaret L. BA, Marylhurst (Oreg.) Univ., 1942; student, Portland Art Mus. Sch., U. Miami, Fla., Fla. Internat. U. One person shows include Mirell Gallery, Coconut grove, Fla., 1961, Miami Mus. Modern Art, 1965, 80 Washington Sq. E., N.Y.C., 1983; Kendall Campus Art Gall., Miami, 1992, group exhbns. include Ringling Mus. Sarasota, Fla., 1956, Norton Gallery, West Palm Beach, 1956, Lowe Art Mus., Miami (award winner), 1957, 1976, Soc. of Four Arts, Palm Beach, 1958, 61, 62, 65, 67, 72, 74, 77, 81, Ft. Lauderdale Mus. Arts (award winner), 1964, 65, Profl. Women Artists, Lowe Art Mus., Miami, 1976, Mus. of Arts and Scis., Daytona Beach, Fla., 1979, Met. Dade County Coun. of Arts and scis., Miami, 1979, Lowe Levinson Gallery, Miami Beach, 1981, North Miami Mus. and Art Ctr., 1987, Metro-Dade Cultural Ctr., Miami, 1990, Mus. Contemporary Art, 1995, House Art Gallery, N.Y., 1996, Ambrosino Gallery, Miami, 1997, Ambrosino Gallery, Miami, 1998, Robert Hittel, Ft. Lauderdale, 1998, Dorsch Gallery, Miami, 1999, Kendall Campus Art Gallery, Miami, 2000, Snitzer Gallery, Miami, 2002; works in permanent collections Miami Mus. Modern Art, Hopkins-Easton Assocs., Omni Internat., many pvt. collections. Recipient Beaux Art award Lowe Art Mus., 1957, Hortt Meml. award Ft. Lauderdale Mus. Arts, 1964, Atwater Kent award 29th Ann. Exhbn. Contemporary Am. Paintings, Soc. Four Arts, 1967, 39th Ann. exhbn., 1977. Home: 5790 SW 51st Ter Miami FL 33155-6324

CHAMBERS, IMOGENE KLUTTS, school system administrator, financial consultant; b. Paden, Okla., Aug. 6, 1928; d. Odes and Lillie (Southard) Klutts; m. Richard Lee Chambers, May 27, 1949. BA, East Ctrl. State U., 1948; MS, Okla. State U., 1974, EdD, 1980. High sch. math. tchr. Marlow (Okla.) Sch. Dist., 1948-49; with Bartlesville (Okla.) Sch. Dist., 1950-94; asst. supt. bus. affairs, treas. Ind. Sch. Dist. 30, 1977-87, treas., 1985-94; fin. acctg. cons. Okla. State Dept. Edn., 1987-92; dir. Plz. Bank, Bartlesville, 1984-93. Adv. dir. Bank Okla., 1994-96. Treas. Okla. Schs. Ins. Assn., 1982—97, adminstr., 1993—97; bd. dirs. Mutual Girls Club, 1981—. Mem. Okla. Assn. Sch. Bus. Ofcls., Assn. Sch. Bus. Ofcls. Internat., Okla. Ret. Educators Assn., Washington County Ret. Educators Assn., Okla. State U. Alumni Assn., East Ctrl. U. Alumni Assn. (bd. dirs. 1994-96). Democrat. Methodist. Home: 911 SE Greystone Pl Bartlesville OK 74006-5141 Personal E-mail: ikcgene@bartnet.net.

CHAMBERS, JOAN LOUISE, retired librarian, retired dean; b. Denver, Mar. 22, 1937; d. Joseph Harvey and Clara Elizabeth (Carleton) Baker; m. Donald Ray Chambers, Aug. 17, 1958 BA in English Lit., U. No. Colo., Greeley, 1958; MS in L.S., U. Calif.-Berkeley, 1970; MS in Systems Mgmt., U. So. Calif., 1985; cert., Coll. for Fin. Planning, 1989. Libr. U. Nev., Reno, 1970-79; asst. univ. libr. U. Calif., San Diego, 1979-81, univ. libr. Riverside, 1981—85; dean librs., prof. Colo. State U., Ft. Collins, 1985-97, emeritus dean and prof., 1997—. Mgmt. intern Duke U. Libr., Durham, N.C., 1978-79; sr. fellow UCLA Summer, 1982; cons. tng. program Assn. of Rsch. Libraries, Washington, 1981; libr. cons. Calif. State U., Sacramento, 1982-83, U. Wyo., 1985-86, 94-95, U. Nebr., 1991-92, Calif. State U. System, 1993-94, Univ. No. Ariz., 1994-95. Contbr. articles to profl. jours., chpts. to books. Bd. dirs. Consumers Union, 1996—. U. Calif. instl. improvement grantee, 1980-81; State of Nev. grantee, 1976, ARL grantee, 1983-84. Mem.: PEO, Colo. Mountain Club, Phi Kappa Phi, Kappa Delta Phi, Phi Lambda Theta, Beta Phi Mu. Avocations: hiking, snow shoeing, skiing, bicycling, tennis. Home and Office: PO Box 1477 Edwards CO 81632-1477 E-mail: chambers@vail.net.

CHAMBERS, KRISTA RUTH, mathematics educator; m. William Chambers; children: Shauna, Cara. MS Secondary Edn., Math., SUNY Brockport, Brockport, NY, 1993—96. Cert. secondary math. tchr. N.Y., 1993. Math. tchr. Medina H.S., NY, 1993—. Office: Medina High School 1 Mustang Dr Medina NY 14103 Office Phone: 585-798-2710.

CHAMBERS, LINDA DIANNE THOMPSON, social worker; b. Mexia, Tex., Apr. 21, 1953; d. Lee and Essie Mae (Hopes) Thompson; m. George Edward Chambers, Nov. 30, 1978; 1 child, Brandon. AS cum laude, Navarro Coll., 1974; B in Social Work magna cum laude, Tex. Women's U., 1976; cert. gerontology and Human Svcs. Mgmt., Sam Houston U., 1982; M in Social Work, U. Tex., Arlington, 1990. Lic. marriage and family therapist, social worker-advanced practitioner; cert. family life educator; registered sex offender treatment provider. Mem. social work staff Dept. Human Res., Ft. Worth, 1975, Children's Med. Ctr., Dallas, 1976, Mexia State Sch., Tex., 1976-93, Methodist Home, Waco, Tex., 1993-96, Tex. Dept. Health, Waco, Tex., 1996—, Parkview Regional Hosp., 1996—; mem. social work staff geripsychiatric program Limestone Med. Ctr., 2001—. Pres. Raven Exquisites, Mexia, 1983-84, sec.-treas., 1984-85; pres., bd. dirs., Limestone County Child Welfare Bd., Hospice, Inc., Limestone County unit Am. Cancer Soc. Bd. dirs. Gibbs Meml. Libr., Teen Pregnancy Prevention Coun., Childcare Mgmt. Svcs.; vol. McLennan County Pub. Health Dist. AIDS Clinic, Ctr. for Action Against Sexual Assault, Family Abuse Ctr.; coord. founder Limestone County Teen Parent Program; co-founder Limestone County Parenting Coalition; co-founder Limestone County Youth Adv. Com, Limestone County Parenting Coalition; PTO sec. Ctrl. Tex. Literacy Coalition, 1992—; active Tex. Hist. Found., Nat. Mus. Women in the Arts, 1985—. Recipient awards for scholarship and profl. excellence. Fellow Internat. Biog. Assn. (dep. bd. gov., life); mem. NAFE, AAUW, Am. Sociol. Soc. (sec. 1975-76), Tex. Dem. Women, Univ. Women's Assn., Am. Childhood Edn. Internat., Nat. Assn. Social Workers, Am. Assn. Mental Retardation, Nat. Assn. Future Women, Am. Soc. Profl. and Exec. Women, Nat. Assn. Negro Bus. and Profl. Women's

Clubs, Tex. Woman's U. Nat. Alumni Assn., Mortar Bd. Honor Soc. (sec.-treas. 1975-76), Tex. Soc. Clin. Social Workers, Internat. Platform Assn., Internat. Assn. Bus. and Profl. Women, Am. Biog. Assn. (dep. bd. govs.), Nat. Mus. Women Arts, Los Amigos, Phi Theta Kappa, Alpha Kappa Delta, Alpha Delta Mu, Young Dems. Avocations: reading, gardening, gourmet cooking. Home: 102 Harding Mexia TX 76667 Personal E-mail: chambers3686@glade.net.

CHAMBERS, MARJORIE BELL, historian; b. N.Y.C., Mar. 11, 1923; d. Kenneth Carter and Katherine (Totman) Bell; m. William Hyland Chambers, Aug. 8, 1945; children: Lee Chambers-Schiller, William Bell, Leslie Chambers Trujillo, Kenneth Carter. AB cum laude, Mt. Holyoke Coll., South Hadley, Mass., 1943; MA, Cornell U., 1948; PhD, U. N.Mex., 1974; LLD honoris causa, Ctrl. Mich. U., 1977; LHD (hon.), Wilson Coll., 1980, Northern Michigan U., 1982. Staff asst. Am. Assn. UN, League of Nations Assn., N.Y.C., 1944-45; program specialist dept. rural sociology Cornell U., Ithaca, NY, 1945-46, rsch. asst. dept. speech and drama, 1946-48; substitute tchr. Los Alamos (N.Mex.) Pub. Schs., 1962-65; project historian U.S. AEC, Los Alamos, 1965-69; adj. prof. U. N.Mex., Los Alamos, 1970-76, 84-85; pres. Colo. Women's Coll., Denver, 1976-78; dean Union Inst. and U. Grad. Sch. Interdisciplinary Arts and Scis., Cin., 1979—82, mem. core faculty Grad. Sch., 1979—; interim pres. Colby-Sawyer Coll., New London, NH, 1985-86. Vis. prof. Cameron U., Lawton, Okla., 1974; commr., vice-chair N.Mex. Commn. on Higher Edn., Santa Fe, 1987-91; dir. N.Mex. Endowment for Humanities, 1995-2002, sec.-treas. 2001-2002; mem. bd. dirs. Coun. Ind. Colls. and Univs., Santa Fe, 1991-2001; rep. Los Alamos County Labor Mgmt. Bd.; lectr. U. N.Mex., Albuquerque, 1986. Contbr. articles to profl. jours. Coun. treas. Sangre de Cristo Girl Scouts Am., 2002; chair Los Alamos County Coun., 1976, councilor, 1975-76, 79; Rep.candidate N.Mex. 3d Congl. Dist., 1982, lt. gov. N.Mex., 1986; chair Sec. of Navy's Advisor Bd. on Edn. and Tng., Washington and Pensacola, Fla., 1981-89; chair Citizen Bd. of U.S. Army Command and Gen. Staff Coll., Fort Leavenworth, Kans., 1989-1992; acting chair, vice-chair adminstrn. Pres. Carter's Com. for Women, Washington, 1977-80; chair Pres. Ford's Nat. Adv. Bd. on Women's Ednl. Programs, Washington, Los Alamos County Pers. Bd., 1985-90, mem. bd., 1983-90; mem. nat. adv. coun. U.S. SBA, 1990-92; mem. Los Alamos and N.Mex. Rep. Ctrl. com., 1982—; trustee Colby-Sawyer Coll., New London, N.H., 1980-89; pub. mem. U.S. Dept. State Fgn. Svc. selection bd., 1978; mem. U.S. del. UN Conf. Women, Copenhagen, 1980; bd. dirs. N.Mex. Endowment for the Humanities, 1997—. Recipient Teresa d'Avila award Coll. St. Teresa, Winona, Minn., 1978, Disting. Woman award U. N.Mex. Alumni Assn., Albuquerque, 1990, N.Mex. Disting. Pub. Svc. award Gov. and Awards Coun., Albuquerque, 1991, Zia award U. N.Mex. Alumni Assn., 2001; named Outstanding N.Mex. Woman Gov. and Com. on Status of Women, Albuquerque, 1988, 89, Lifetime Achievement award, 2003. Mem. AAUW (life, U.S. rep. coun. 1973-75, nat. pres. 1975-79, pres. Edn. Found.), DAR, Bus. and Profl. Women (Los Alamos parliamentarian and dist. parliamentarian 1991-93), Nat. Women's Polit. Caucus (gov. bd. conv., keynoter, vice-chair Rep. caucus 1971-89), Internat. Women's Forum (founding mem. Colo. forum), N.Mex. Hist. Soc. (pres.), Los Alamos Hist. Soc. (pres., Sangre de Cristo Girl Scouts "Woman of Distinction" 1996). Presbyterian. Avocations: figure skating, skiing, swimming, painting, public speaking.

CHAMBERS, RUTH COE, writer; d. Walter Homer Coe and Ruth Lucille Johnson; m. Jack Allen Chambers, Aug. 24, 1957; children: Melissa Ann, Wendy Colleen. BA, Calif. State U., 1981. Coord. of info. services projects U. of Pitts., Pittsburgh, Pa., 1986—89; grad. coord. biol. sci. U. of Md., Baltimore, Md., 1989—91; adminstrv. asst. Fla. C.C., Jacksonville, Fla., 1991—2001. Editl. readers bd. Kalliope A Jour. of Women's Lit. and Art, Jacksonville, Fla., 1994—; planning com. Fla. First Coast Writers' Festival, Jacksonville, Fla., 2001—. Author: (novel) The Chinaberry Album, (short story) Uncle Henry, Friends; contbr. articles to mags.; author: (plays) Changing Places (1st place, Fla. First Coast Writers Festival, 2005). Mem.: Phi Kappa Phi. Democrat-Npl. Home: 2028 Marye Brant Loop N Neptune Beach FL 32266 Personal E-mail: ruthcchambers@aol.com.

CHAMBERS, SUSAN (M. SUSAN CHAMBERS), retail executive; B. in systems and data processing, William Jewell Coll., Liberty, Mo. With Amoco Oil Corp.; dir. applications devel. Hallmark Cards Inc.; joined Wal-Mart Stores Inc., 1999, store, club mgr., 1999, v.p. applications devel. merchandising, Info. Systems Divsn., sr. v.p. CMI benefits and ins. adminstrn., 2002—03, exec. v.p. risk mgmt. benefits adminstrn., 2004—06, exec. v.p. Human Resources Divsn., 2006—. Mem. bus. advisory bd. Kansas State U.; advisory coun. Women Impacting Public Policy Advisory Coun. Office: Wal-Mart Stores Inc Bentonville AR 72716-8611*

CHAMBERS-ROSS, CHARLOTTE BOYD, social worker, artist; b. Ashland, NH, May 19, 1922; d. Earl George and Angie Prudence Boyington; life ptnr. Reece M. Ross, Apr. 24, 1974; m. Charlyn Dicta Chambers; 1 child, Franklyn Dean Chambers (dec.); 1 child, Charlyn Chambers. Degree in fashion design, Copley Fashion, 1940; MA in Theater Arts, Tufts Coll., 1944; BA in Sociology Art, U. Calif., 1952. Window decorator Jordan Marsh Co., Boston, 1942—45; freelance interior decorator San Bernardino, Calif., 1955—65; store decorator Harris Co., San Bernardino, Calif., 1955—65; artist Spirit Gallery, Charleston, W.Va., 1985—2005. Teen dir. YMCA, San Bernardino, Calif., 1946—55; correctional adv. C.I.W. Prison, Frontera, Calif., 1962—80. Contbr. poems to jours.; Represented in permanent collections Bank One, W. Va., one-woman shows include, 1970—2002, pvt.collections including dr.'s offices, hosps., and bus. offices; past mem. Palm Springs Primary Art Gallery. Charter mem. Nat. Women in Arts, Washington, 1987; art donator for battered women and girls YWCA, 1990—2002; charter mem. Nat. Mus. Am. Indian, Washington, 2002, Watercolor West. Recipient many prizes, nat. juried art shows, 1965—2005. Avocations: walking, reading, writing, travel, sculpting. Home and Office: Singing Spirit Gallery 57 Co Co Hollow Rd Elkview WV 25071

CHAMBERS TUCKER, JOHNNIE L., elementary school educator, rancher; b. Crocket County, Tex., Sept. 28, 1929; d. Robert Leo and Lois K. (Slaughter) Tucker; m. R. Boyd Chambers; children: Theresa A., Glyn Robert, Boyd James, John Trox. EdB, Sul Ross State U., Alpine, Tex., 1971. Tchr. 1st and 2d grades Candelaria Elem. Sch., Tex., 1971-73; head tchr. K-8 Ruidosa Elem. Sch., Tex., 1973-77, Candelaria Elem. Sch., 1977—91, tchr. 2d and 3d grades, 1991—93, tchr. pre-kindergarten, kindergarten and 1st grade, 1993—98; acting prin. Candelaria Elem. and Jr. High, 1995—98, head tchr. pre-K to 8th grades, 1996—98, tchr. pre-K, kindergarten, 1st and 2d grades, 1996—99; tchr. pre-K-6 Redford Elem. Sch., Tex., 2001, tchr., 2001—. Mem. sight-base decision making, Presidio, 1991-94; mem. Chihuahuan Desert Rsch. Inst., Alpine, 1982-94. Leader Boy Scouts Am., Ruidosa and Candelaria, 1973-91, Cub Scout leader, 1973-91; chpt. mem. Sheriffs Assn. Tex., Austin, 1980; bd. dirs. Big Bend Regional Hosp. Dist., 2001—, Family Crisis Ctr. Big Bend Inc., 2006; mem. Ctr. for Big Bend Studies. Recipient awards Boy Scouts Am., 1969, 83, Litter Gitter award, 1994-95. Mem. Tex. State Tchrs. Assn., Tex. Fedn. Rep. Women, The Archaeol. Conservancy, Phi Alpha Theta. Avocations: hiking, camping, anthropology, cave exploring, cooking. Home: 99 Retirement Cir Marfa TX 79843 Personal E-mail: johnnieltc@yahoo.net. Business E-Mail: johnnieltc@brooksdata.net.

CHAMBLESS, DIANNE L., psychology professor; BA, Tulane U., 1969; MA in Psychology, Temple U., 1972, PhD in Clin. Psychology, 1979. Prof. Dept. Psychology U. Pa., Phila., dir. clin. tng. Dept. Pscyhology. Fellow: Acad. Cognitive Therapy. Office: Dept Psychology Univ Pa 3815 Walnut St Philadelphia PA 19104-6196 Office Phone: 215-898-5030. Office Fax: 215-898-7301. E-mail: chambless@psych.upenn.edu.*

CHAMBLESS, LORI K., secondary school educator; b. Texarkana, Ark., Oct. 27, 1964; d. Kennith Wright and Marjorie Ann Keith; m. Jerry Paul Chambless, July 23, 1988; children: Julia Kay, Christi Ann, Lexie Beth. BS in Edn., So. Ark. U., Magnolia, 1988; M in Edn. Adminstrn., Tex. A&M U., Texarkana, 2006. Math. tchr. Texarkana (Ark.) Ind. Sch. Dist., 1988—91, Spring Hill Sch. Dist., Hope, Ark., 1991—. Tchr. Hope Ch. of Christ, 1988—2006. Daryl Crouch scholar, Tex. A&M U., Texarkana, 2004—05, Ednl. Asst. scholar, 2004—06, Women's scholar, 2005—06. Mem.: NEA (assoc.), Nat. Coun. Tchrs. Math. (assoc.), Ark. Coun. Tchrs. Math. (assoc.), Ark. Edn. Assn. (assoc.). Office: Spring Hill Sch Dist 633 Hwy 355 W Hope AR 71801 Office Phone: 870-722-7430. Business E-Mail: lchambless@springhill.k12.ar.us.

CHAMBLISS, LINDA R., obstetrician, consultant; b. Summit, N.J., Feb. 13, 1951; d. Robert E. and Alice (Dunne) C. BSN, Duke U., 1973; MD, Mich. State U., 1980; MPH, Johns Hopkins U., 2004. Diplomate with spl. certification in maternal-fetal medicine Am. Bd. Ob-Gyn. Pediat. intern U. Chgo., 1980—81; resident in ob-gyn. Cook County Hosp., Chgo., 1981—85; fellow in maternal-fetal medicine U. So. Calif.-LA County Hosp., LA, 1988—90; chief obstetrics Indian Health Svcs., Tuba City, Ariz., 1985-88; clin. prof. ob-gyn. U. Ariz., 2001—06; prof. ob-gyn. St. Louis U., 2006—, med. dir. labor and delivery, 2006—. Comdr. USPHS, 1985—. Recipient Alumna Excellence award Mich. State U., 1996, Nat. Faculty Excellence award Coun. on Resident Edn. in Ob-Gyn., 1995. Fellow ACOG; mem. AMA (cons.), AAUW, Soc. Maternal Fetal Medicine, Am. Women's Med. Assn., Ariz. Western Riding Club (mem. exec. bd.). Democrat. Office: St Lous Univ 6420 Clayton Rd Saint Louis MO 63117 Personal E-mail: olddoctor@excite.com.

CHAMMAS, JUDITH ANN, diplomat; m. Labib Chammas; 1 child, Isabelle. Grad., Gustavus Adolphus Coll., 1971. With Minn. Internat. Ctr., Inst. of Internat. Edn., Washington, US Dept. State, 1984—, mgmt. officer Syria, Iraq, Yemen, Sri Lanka, and Tunisia, assignments officer, dep. exec. dir. Bur. of Human Resources, charge d'affaires to Bangladesh, 2005—. Avocations: needlepoint, reading, theater. Office: US Embassy in Bangladesh 6120 Dhaka Pl Washington DC 20521-6120

CHAMPE, PAMELA CHAMBERS, biochemistry professor, writer; b. Oakland, Calif., Aug. 29, 1945; d. Robert Leroy and Leah June (Musser) Chambers; m. Sewell Preston Champe, June 28, 1969 (dec.); stepchildren: Mark Adrian, Sewell Peter. BA, Stanford U., 1967; MS, Purdue U., 1969; PhD, Rutgers U., 1974. Instr. Rutgers Med. Sch., Piscataway, N.J., 1974-76; asst. prof. Robert Wood Johnson Med. Sch. U. Medicine and Dentistry N.J., Piscataway, 1977-84, assoc. prof. Robert Wood Johnson Med. Sch., 1984-96; prof. emeritus Robert Wood Johnson Med. Sch., 1996—. Lectr. several med. schs. and tng. programs. Co-editor: Gene Families of Collagen and Other Proteins, 1980; co-author: Biochemistry (Lippincott's Illus. Revs.), 1987, 3d edit., 2004; Pharmacology (Lippincott's Illus. Revs.), 3d edit., 2006. Health and Human Svcs. grantee, 1988-94; recipient Nat. award Basic Med. Sci. Educator of the Yr., 1995. Mem. AAAS, Assn. Am. Med. Colls., N.Y. Acad. Scis., Alpha Omega Alpha. Avocation: malachology. Office: U Medicine and Dentistry NJ Robert Wood Johnson Med Sch 675 Hoes Ln Piscataway NJ 08854-5627

CHAMPEY, ELAINE, science foundation director; b. Amityville, N.Y., Sept. 1, 1950; d. Chris Strum-Arden and Celia Strum; m. Michael Champey, June 20, 1976; children: Christine Anne, Michael Edward, Lauren Marie. BA in Polit. Sci., St. John's U., 1971, postgrad., 1974-76; M in Liberal Scis., SUNY, Stony Brook, 1993. Permanent cert. in chemistry, biology, gen. sci. Rsch. technician dept. pharmacology SUNY, Stonybrook, 1977-80; pvt. piano instr. Smithtown, N.Y., 1980-96; substitute tchr. St. Anthony's H.S. Smithtown Sch. Dist., 1991-96, tchr., 1996—; adj. prof SUNY, Albany, 1999—. Cons. Dept. Edn. Grant, 1999; technician tissue culture Procs. of NAS, 1978, technician biochem. assays, 1980; mentor finalists Siemens-Westinghouse Sci. Competition, 1999, 2000, 02. Named Tchr. of Merit, Intel Sci. Talent Search, 1998-2002; recipient Commendation for finalist Internat. Sci. and Engrng. Fair, 2000, Recognition award N.Y. Sci. Talent Search, 1998, 99, 2000, 2001, 2002; First Robotic Advisor, 2001-2003; Recognition award Jr. Scis. and Humanities Symposium, 2001. Mem. N.Y. State Tchr. Union, Smithtown Parent Tchr. Assn., Smithtown Sch. Dist. Tchr. Ctr. (vice chair 1996-2001, mini-grantee 1998), Smithtown H.S. Industry Adv. Bd. (exec. bd., com. chair 1996-2003), Suffolk County Sci. Tchrs. Assn. (historian 1999-2000). Avocations: playing piano, singing. E-mail: echampey@juno.com.

CHAMPION, CHERYL, educator; b. Waverly, NY, Dec. 6, 1947; d. Max Elliott and Frances (Henton) Coleman; children: Mark Elliott Schamel, Kendra Anne; m. Robert L.; stepchildren: Erin, Christopher. BS, SUNY, Geneseo, 1969; MS, SUNY, Buffalo, 1975. Cert. permanent tchr., N.Y. Tchr. Penfield (N.Y.) Cen. Schs., 1969-71, Akron (N.Y.) Cen. Schs., 1971-73, Williamsville (N.Y.) Cen. Schs., 1976-84; instr. edn. Johnson County Community Coll., Overland Park, Kans., 1987-89; tchr. Union Endicott Schs., N.Y., 1989—. Democrat. Methodist.

CHAMPION, CRYSTAL, literature and language educator; d. Jeffrey and Paula Champion. BS in Secondary English Edn., Mo. State U., Springfield, 2000—04. English/reading tchr. Hillcrest H.S., Springfield, Mo., 2004—. Mem.: NEA.

CHAMPION, KATHLEEN ANN, mathematics professor; d. Richard J and Patricia A Schreier. BA, Coll. of St. Catherine; MS in edn., U. of Minn., 1994; PhD, U. of ND, 2004. Cert. Math. Tchg. grades 7-12 Edn. Standards & Practice Bd., 2002, Sci. Tchg., grades 5-12 MN Dept. of Edn., 1990, Math Tchg., grades 7-12 MN Dept. of Edn., 1990. Sci., math. tchr. Anoka-Hennepin Sch. Dist. ISD 11, Coon Rapids, Minn., 1990—97; asst. prof. of math. edn. Mayville State U., Mayville, ND, 2000—. Contbr. presentation. Sch. bd. mem. Finley- Sharon Sch., Finley, ND, 2001—04. Mem.: NCTM (corr.), NDCTM (corr.). Avocations: sewing, swimming, gardening. Office: Mayville State U 330 Third St NE Mayville ND 58257 Office Phone: 800-437-4104. Business E-Mail: k_champion@mayvillestate.edu.

CHAMPION, MARGE (MARJORIE CELESTE CHAMPION), actress, choreographer, dancer; b. LA, Sept. 2, 1919; d. Ernest and Gladys (Basquette) Belcher; m. Art Babbitt (div.); m. Gower Champion, Oct. 5, 1947 (div. 1973); children: Blake (dec.), Gregg; m. Boris Sagal, Jan. 1, 1977 (dec. 1981). Student pub. schs., Los Angeles. Stage debut L.A. Civic Opera, 1936; movie debut (under name Marjorie Bell) in The Castles, 1938; live action model for cartoon heroines in: Walt Disney prodns. Blue Fairy in Pinocchio, 1938, Snow White, 1937, Hippo and Storks in Fantasia; appeared on Broadway musicals Dark of the Moon, 1945, Beggar's Holiday, 1946; first profl. appearance with Gower Champion as Gower and Bell Normandie Roof, Montreal, Que., Can., 1947; N.Y. debut as Marge and Gower Champion at Hotel Plaza, 1947; weekly show Admiral Broadway Review, Dumont and NBC TV Network, 1949, Marge and Gower Champion Show, 1957; with husband staged dances for revues: Lend an Ear, 1949, Make A Wish, Small Wonder; movies include: Showboat, 1951, Lovely to Look At, 1952, Everything I Have is Yours, 1952, Give A Girl a Break, 1953, Three for the Show, 1955, Jupiter's Darling, 1955, The Swimmer, 1968, The Party, 1968, The Cockeyed Cowboy of Calico County, 1970, That's Entertainment, Part 2, 1976; various TV appearances, including TV show Toast of the Town, 1953; Three for Tonight, 1955, Shower of Stars, 1956, GE Theatre, 1957, Dinah Shore Show, 1958, Telephone Hour, 1960; acting debut Hemingway and All Those People, Indpls., 1958; title role: Sabrina Fair, 1960; choreographer: Queen of the Stardust Ballroom, 1975 (Emmy award), 1992, Day of the Locust, 1975; author: (with Marilee Zdenek) Catch the New Wind, 1972, God is a Verb, 1974; dialogue coach and choreographer: The Awakening Land, NBC-TV, 1978, Masada, ABC-TV, 1979, Diary of Anne Frank, NBC-TV, 1980, When the Circus Comes to Town, CBS-TV, 1980; appeared: TV series Fame, 1982; dir., choreography: TV prodn. I Do, I Do, 1983, Stepping Out, Berkshire Theatre Festival, 1988, 89, Lute Song, 1989, She Loves Me, 1990; dancer: 5-6-7-8, Dance!, Radio City Music Hall, 1983, No No Nanette, St. Louis Muny Opera, 1990, Follies, 2000. Recipient Legend of Dance award, 1991. Office: Tanya Bickley Entertainment PO Box 1656 New Canaan CT 06840-1656

CHAMPION, NORMA JEAN, communications educator, state legislator; b. Oklahoma City, Jan. 21, 1933; d. Aubra Dell (dec.) and Beuleah Beatrice (Flanagan) Black; m. Richard Gordon Champion, Oct. 3, 1953 (dec.); children: Jeffrey Bruce, Ashley Brooke. BA in Religious Edn., Cen. Bible Coll., Springfield, Mo., 1971; MA in Comm., Mo. State U., 1978; PhD in Tech., U. Okla., 1986. Producer, hostess The Children's Hour, Sta. KYTV-TV, NBC, Springfield, 1957-86; asst. prof. Cen. Bible Coll., 1968-84; prof. broadcasting Evangel U., Springfield, 1978—; mem. Springfield City Coun., 1987-92, Mo. Ho. of Reps., Jefferson City, 1993—2002, Mo. Senate, 2003—, chair aging and health com., appropriations, edn. Adj. faculty Assemblies of God Theol. Sem., Springfield, 1987—, pres. coun.; bd. dirs. Global U.; mem. Commn. on Higher Edn., Assemblies of God, 1998—; spkr. Internat. Pentecostal Press Assn. World Conf., Singapore, 1989. Mem. bd. Mo. Access to Higher Edn. Trust, 2003-, pain mgmt. bd., 2004-, Boys & Girls Town of Mo.; adv. coun. pain mgmt.; judge Springfield (Mo.) City Schs. Recipient commendation resolution Mo. Ho. of Reps., 1988; numerous awards for The Children's Hour; Aunt Norma Day named in her honor City of Springfield, 1976; named 20 Most Influential Women in Ozarks, Springfield Bus. Jour., 2005. Mem. Nat. Broadcast Edn. Assn., Mo. Broadcast Edn. Assn., Nat. League Cities, Mo. Mcpl. League (human resource com. 1989, intergovtl. rels. com. 1990), Nat. Assn. Telecom. Officers and Advisors, PTA (life). Republican. Mem. Assemblies of God Ch. Avocations: gardening, reading, yoga. Home: 3609 S Broadway Ave Springfield MO 65807-4505 Office: Evangel Univ 1111 N Glenstone Ave Springfield MO 65802-2125 Office Phone: 573-751-2583. Business E-Mail: normachampion@senate.mo.gov.

CHAMPION, SARA STEWART, lawyer; d. William Julius Champion and Mary Cunningham; m. Wayne L. Kinsey, Dec. 12, 1964 (div. Feb. 1971); m. John Q. Adams, Apr. 25, 1998 (div. Oct. 2000). BA, Duke U., 1963; MA, U. Calif., Davis, 1974; JD cum laude, N.Y. Law Sch., 1992. Bar: N.Y. 1992, Conn. 1992. Rsch. analyst Nat. Security Agy., Ft. Meade, Md., 1963-65; instr. Russian Def. Lang. Inst., Monterey, Calif., 1970-72; claims rep. Social Security Adminstrn., San Francisco, 1974-78, claims rep., ops. supr. N.Y.C., 1978-87; office adminstr. Bachelder Law Offices, N.Y.C., 1987-97, assoc., 1992-97, ptnr., 1997—2002; ptnr., shareholder, head NY exec. compensation practice Vedder, Price, Kaufman and Kammholz, N.Y.C., 2002—. Mem.: DAR (1st vice regent NYC chpt.), New Eng. Soc. (steward), Soc. Mayflower Descs. (bd. assts.), Colonial Dames Am., Silver Spring Country Club (Ridgefield, Conn.), Univ. Club, Wianno Yacht Club (Osterville, Mass.). Avocation: genealogy. Office: Vedder Price Kaufman & Kammholz 805 3d Ave New York NY 10022 Office Phone: 212-407-7785. Business E-Mail: schampion@vedderprice.com.

CHAMSON, SANDRA POTKORONY, psychologist; b. N.Y.C., Nov. 6, 1933; d. Daniel and Rose (Sukenik) Potkorony; m. Allan Chamson, Dec. 25, 1954 (div. 1978); children: Eugene. BA in Psychology, NYU, 1955; MS in Sch. Psychology, CCNY, 1957; PhD in Psychology, Fla. Inst. Tech., Melbourne, 1983. Lic. psychologist, N.Y.; clin. psychologist, N.Y. Psychologist Anne Arundel County Schs., Anapolis, Md., 1957-58, Bur. Child Guidance, N.Y.C., 1960-64, Region VI Dist., Bergen County, N.J., 1965-84; sole practice psychology N.Y.C., 1985—. Psychol. cons. Ramaz Sch., N.Y.C., 1974-81. Mem. APA, N.Y. Acad. Sci., Am. Orthopsychiat. Assn. Address: 200 W 86th St Apt 18E New York NY 10024-3379

CHAN, ASHELY MICHELLE, lawyer; b. Camden, NJ, 1971; BA, Rutgers U., 1993, JD with honors, 1996. Bar: NJ 1997, Pa. 1997, US Dist. Ct. (ea. dist.) Pa. 1998. Law clk. to Hon. Gloria M. Burns US Bankruptcy Ct., Dist. NJ, 1996—97; ptnr. Hangley Aronchick Segal & Pudlin, P.C., Phila., 2001—. Mem.: ABA, Pa. Bar Assn., Phila. Bar Assn. Office: Hangley Aronchick Segal & Pudlin One Logan Sq 18th & Cherry Streets, 27 Fl Philadelphia PA 19103-6933 Office Phone: 215-496-7050. Office Fax: 215-568-0300. E-mail: achan@hangley.com.*

CHAN, ELAINE ELIZABETH, elementary school educator; d. Tommy and Mary Chan. BS, No. Ariz. U., 1983; MS in Computer Application, Nova U., Phoenix, 1993. Cert. in Edn. Adminstrn. Ottawa U., Phoenix, 2002, in Edn. Intervention Ottawa U., Phoenix, 2002; lic. tchr. basic elem. K-8 Ariz., reading specialist endorsement K-12 Ariz., cert. prin. Ariz. Tchr. 1st and 4th grade Paradise Valley Sch. Dist., Phoenix, 1984—94, tchr. 4th grade, 1984—, Title I math. specialist, 1995—2003; assessment coord. Ariz. Literacy and Leaning Ctr., Phoenix, 2004—05. Grantee, Marion Found., 1993, Wells Fargo, 2000. Mem.: Paradise Valley Edn. Assn. Office Phone: 602-493-6360.

CHAN, HENG CHEE, ambassador; b. Singapore, Apr. 19, 1942; Degree, U. Singapore, Cornell U.; DHL (hon.), U. Newcastle, Australia, 1994, U. Buckingham, England, 1998. Lectr. Nat. U. Singapore, 1967—75, sr. lectr., 1976—80, assoc. prof. of polit. sci., 1981—, Head Dept. Polit. Sci., 1985—88, prof., 1990; dir. Inst. Policy Studies, 1988; amb. to Mexico, 1989—91; high comdr. in Canada, 1989—91; permanent rep. from Singapore UN, NYC, 1989—91; dir. Inst. S.E. Asian Studies, 1993; exec. dir. Singapore Internat. Found., 1991—96; ambassador to U.S. Embassy of Singapore, Washington, 1996—. Mem. Internat. Coun. of Asia Soc., NYC, 1991; mem. coun. Internat. Inst. for Strategic Studies, London, 1993—; mem. Nat. Com. Security Cooperation in the Asia-Pacific, Singapore, 1993—; mem. internat. adv. bd. Coun. on Fgn. Rels., NY, 1995—; mem coun. Internat. Inst. for Strategic Studies, Hong Kong, 1995—. Author: The Dynamics of One Party Dominance: The PAP at the Grassroots, 1978 (Nat. Book award), A Sensation of Independence: A Political Biography of David Marshall, 1984 (Nat. Book award, 1986), The Prophetic and the Political, 1987. Named Singapore's Woman of Yr., 1991; recipient Inaugural Internat. Woman of Yr. award, Orgn. Chinese Am. Women, 1998. Office: Singapore Embassy in US 3501 International Pl NW Washington DC 20008 also: Singapore Internat Found 111 Somerset Rd 11-07 Devonshire Wing DC 238164 Singapore Office Phone: 202-537-3100. Office Fax: 202-537-0876. Business E-Mail: singemb@verizon.net.*

CHAN, JANET, editorial director; children: Jack, Laura. Sr. editor Glamour Mag., NYC; exec. editor Redbook, NYC, 1991—94, Good Housekeeping, NYC, 1994—96; editor-in-chief Parenting Mag., NYC, 1996—; and editl. dir. The Parenting Group, NYC, 1996—. Editl. dir. Time Inc.'s Parenting Group including Mom-to-Be Babytalk, and Parenting mags. Office: The Parenting Group 3d Fl 135 W 50th St New York NY 10020 Office Phone: 212-522-9808. Office Fax: 212-522-8750.*

CHAN, PATTY G., librarian; b. Richmond, Calif., 1951; BS in Health Sci., Calif. State U., San Francisco, 1973; MS in Libr. Sci., U. Calif., Berkeley, 1974. Sr. br. libr. Contra Costa County Libr., Antioch, Calif., 1975—; libr. Los Medanos Coll., Pittsburgh, Calif., 1976—; libr. I. Alameda County Libr., Fremont, Calif., 1985—. Treas. Antioch, Chichibu Sister City Orgn., 1981—; mem. bd. dir. Give Always to Others, Antioch, Calif., 1990—. Recipient Antioch Citizen Yr. award, Antioch C. of C., 2001, Employee award, Contra Costa County Libr., 2002. Mem.: AAUW (v.p. 1988—), Calif. Libr. Assn. (assoc.), Kiwanis Club, Lion's Club, Woman's Club Antioch (assoc.), Friends of Antioch Libr. (life). Office: Contra Costa County Libr Antioch 501 West 18th St Antioch CA 94509 Personal E-mail: pattychan@hotmail.com. Business E-Mail: pchan@ccclib.org.

CHAN, SIU-WAI, materials science educator; m. Kung Yip Cheung; children: L.Y., K.Y. BS, Columbia U., 1980; ScD, MIT, 1985. Mem. tech. staff Bellcore, Murray Hill, NJ, 1985-86, Red Bank, NJ, 1986-90; assoc. prof. materials sci. Columbia U., N.Y.C., 1990—2002, prof., 2002—. Presdl. Faculty fellow, NSF, 1993, Guggenheim fellow, 2003—04. Office: Columbia U Sch Engring & Applied Sci 200 Mudd Bldg MC 4701 500 W 120th St New York NY 10027-8031 Business E-Mail: sc174@columbia.edu.

CHAN, SUSAN S., music educator; b. Hong Kong, Feb. 16, 1964; d. Kin Man Chan and Hung Ying Liu. BA with 1st class honors, U. Hong Kong, 1986, MPhil in Music, 1988; MusD, Ind. U., Bloomington, 1994. Cert. music tchr.chrs. Music Tchrs. Nat. Assn., 2000. Assoc. instr. Ind. U. Sch. of Music,

Bloomington, Ind., 1989—92; asst. prof. of music Heidelberg Coll., Tiffin, Ohio, 1993—94; asst. prof. of music, assoc. prof. of music Wash. State U., Pullman, Wash., 1994—2004; asst. prof. of music Portland State U., Oreg., 2004—. Adjudicator Music Tchrs. Nat. Assn., Cin., 1995—. Musician: (piano concerto performances) Hong Kong Chamber Orch., (piano concerto competition) Mozart piano concerto competition (Winner), (piano competition) Indipls. Matinee Musicale Piano Competition (First prize), (guest pianist in summer music festival) Dartington Internat. Summer Sch., Devon, UK, (service-learning (community outreach) Music Svc.-Learning: A Powerful Tool of Transformation (Civic Engagement Award, Portland State U., 2006), (piano recital) Carnegie Hall, (piano concerto performance) Hong Kong Sinfonietta, (cd recording of chamber music) Bevelander and Bassett, Intuition, (cd recording of piano music) Pièces Parisiennes, East West Encounter, (chamber music competition) Hong Kong Young Musicians Award Competition (First prize). Recipient Acad. Enrichment award, Wash. State U., 2000, The Provost's PSU Found. Faculty Devel. award, Portland State U., Faculty Enhancement award, 2006—; scholar Sir Man Kam Lo/Jardine scholar, U. of Hong Kong, 1984—86, Rayson Huang scholar, 1987—88, S.L. Pao Found. scholar, Hong Kong, 1988—90. Mem.: Music Tchrs. Nat. Assn., Coll. Music Soc., Pi Kappa Lambda. Avocations: travel, exercise and fitness of the mind, body and spirit. Office: Portland State University Music Dept PO Box 971 Portland OR 97207-0751 Office Phone: 503-725-3119.

CHAN, WILMA, state legislator; b. Boston; 2 children. BA, Wellesley Coll.; M. in Edn. Policy, Stanford U. Mem. Oakland (Calif.) Bd. Edn., 1990—94, Alameda County Bd. Suprs., Oakland, 1994—2000, Calif. State Assembly, Dist. 16, 2000—, majority leader, 2002—04, chair JALAC, 2004, chair edn. budget com., 2004, chair assembly health com., 2005, mem. transp., budget/edn., labor/employment coms., 2005. Mem. com. on health, aging & long term care, com. on jobs, economic develop. and economy, com. on govt. organization, com. on banking and fin. Calif. State Assembly, chair, select com. on Calif. children's sch. readiness and health, co-chair, select com. on language access to state svcs., vice chair, Asian-Pacific Islander legislative caucus, mem. legislative women's caucus, mem. environmental caucus, mem. internet caucus, mem. smart growth caucus. Office Phone: 510-286-1670. Business E-Mail: assemblymember.chan@assembly.ca.gov.

CHANATRY-HOWELL, LORRAINE MARIE, artist, educator; b. Utica, N.Y., Aug. 6, 1934; d. Elias and Catherine (Esso) Chanatry; m. James Burt Howell, III, Feb. 18, 1995. BFA, Syracuse U., 1955; MA, Cath. U. Am., 1958; postgrad., Temple U., 1963, U. San Francisco-Guadalajara, Mex., 1965; EdD, U. South Fla., 1966; postgrad., U. Valencia, Spain, 1966, Am. U. Beirut, 1968. Cert. art tchr. Art supr./tchr. New Hartford (N.Y.) Ctrl. Sch., 1955-56; guidance counselor Washington-Lee H.S., Arlington, Va., 1959-60; interior designer B. Altman & Co., N.Y.C., 1960-61; chmn. art depts. Maitland (Fla.) Jr. H.S., 1962-64; chmn. art dept. Mid-Fla. Tech. Inst., Orlando, 1964-70, Liverpool (N.Y.) H.S., 1970-72; owner, dir. Lorraine Marie Art Ctr., Liverpool, 1972-73, Utica, N.Y., 1973-94; freelance artist and designer, cons., 1994—. Cultural amb., Egypt, Syria, Lebanon, Jordan, 1961; adj. prof. fine arts Mohawk Valley C.C., Utica, 1988-94, Utica Coll., 1976-77. One-woman shows include Syracuse U., 2005, St. Francis Peace Garden, Cath. Ctr., Syracuse U., 2005, numerous exhbns. and permanent collections in U.S., Can., Europe, Middle East, Mex., S.Am. Bd. govs. Cath. U. Am., Washington, 1995—. Mem. Syracuse U. Alumni Assn. (pres. 1964-70, sec. 1980-88, class '55 reunion com., co-chmn. class gift and class favor com.), Alpha Omicron Pi (charter 2d Century Soc., v.p. alumni chpt. Orlando 1966-69, pres. Syracuse 1970-72, found. amb., 2000—) Greek Melchite Catholic. Avocations: art, music, theater, photography, genealogy. Home: 23 Shadow Brooke Dr Bridgeton NJ 08302-3616 Home (Winter): 429 San Jose Winter Haven FL 33884-1742

CHANCELLOR, ELIZABETH ANN, music educator; b. Warner Robins, Ga., May 6, 1968; d. Zebbie Lomus Chancellor Jr. and Connie Lyons Chancellor; 1 child, Ashley Michelle Burke. B of Music Edn., Ga. So. U., 1993. T-4 Ga. Profl. Stds. Commn., 1993. Band dir. and chorus dir. Dodge County Mid. Sch., Eastman, Ga., 1993—99; band dir. Byron Mid. Sch., Byron, Ga., 1999—. Clinician, instr. Ga. Coll. & State U. Symphonic Band Camp, Milledgeville, Ga., 2000—. Dir.: (performance) Georgia Music Educators Assn. Large Group Performance Evaluation. Mem. Magna Charta Dames, Phila., 1999—2005, DAR, Jackson, Ga., 2003—05, US Soc. Daughters of 1812, Macon, Ga. Mem.: United Dau. of Confederacy, Nat. Flute Assn., Music Educators Nat. Conf., Women Band Dirs. Internat., Nat. Band Assn., Ga. Music Educators Assn., PA of Ga. Educators. Methodist. Avocations: swimming, music, website design. Home: 104 Windsor Dr Warner Robins GA 31088 Office: Byron Mid Sch 201 Linda Dr Byron GA 31008 E-mail: echancellor@peachschools.org, echance@cox.net, echancellor@gmail.com.

CHANCE-REAY, MICHAELINE K., educator, psychotherapist; b. Gary, Ind. m. Neville William Reay III. BS in English and Social Studies, Ball State U., 1966, MA in English and Social Studies, 1967; PhD in Humanities Edn., Ohio State U., 1984, MSW in Mental Health and Women's Studies, 1994. Tchr. Bolsa Grande H.S., Garden Grove, Calif., 1967-70; rsch. asst. U. Kans., 1970-73; tutor, substitute tchr. L.A. City Schs., 1973-74; tchr., co-chairperson dept. reading and language arts Morgan Mid. Sch., Yellow Springs, Ohio, 1975-78; tchg. assoc., acad. counselor, supr. humanities edn. Ohio State U., 1978-85; asst. prof. edn., asst. dir. reading and study ctr. Otterbein Coll., Ohio, 1987-90; adj. faculty women studies and secondary edn. Kansas State U., Manhattan, 1995—. Adj. faculty Columbus State C.C., Ohio, 1986-94. Author Lacd Grant Ladies: Kansas State University Presidential Wives; contbr. articles to profl. jours.; presentor in field. Dissertation Rsch. grantee Ohio State U., 1981, Spl. Rsch. grantee U. Rsch. Assn. Mem. NASW, Am. Culture Assn. Office: Kans State U 447 Bluemont Hall Manhattan KS 66506-5300

CHANDLER, ALICE, retired academic administrator, educational consultant; b. Bklyn., May 29, 1931; d. Samuel and Jenny (Meller) Kogan; m. Horace Chandler, June 10, 1954; children: Seth, Donald, Barnard C. AB, Columbia U., 1951, MA, 1953, PhD, 1960; LHD, Kean U., 1997, Ramapo Coll., 2001. Instr. Skidmore Coll., 1953-54; lectr. Columbia U. Barnard Coll., 1954-55, Hunter Coll., CUNY, 1956-57; from instr. to prof. CCNY, 1961-76, v.p. instl. advancement, 1974-76, v.p. acad. affairs, 1974-76, provost, 1976-79, acting pres., 1979-80; pres. SUNY, New Paltz, 1980-96; interim pres. Ramapo Coll., 2000-2001; ret., 2001. Cons. in higher edn., 1996—. Author: The Prose Spectrum: A Rhetoric and Reader, 1968, The Theme of War, 1969, A Dream of Order, 1970, The Rationale of Rhetoric, 1970, The Rationale of the Essay, 1971, From Smollett to James, 1980, Foreign Student Policy: England, France, and West Germany, 1985, Obligation or Opportunity: Foreign Student Policy in Six Major Receiving Countries, 1989, Access, Inclusion and Equity: Imperatives for America's Campuses, 1997, Public Higher Education and the Public Good: Public Policy at the Crossroads, 1998, Paying the Bill for International Education: Programs, Purposes and Possibilities at the Millenium, 1999. Bd. dirs. Mohonk Mountain House, NJ Coun. Humanities, chair. Lizette Fisher fellow. Mem.: Lotos, Phi Beta Kappa. E-mail: hchand5066@aol.com.

CHANDLER, ANN ROGERS TOMLINSON, music educator, director; b. Florence, S.C., May 5, 1953; d. Rodgers Wallace and Carolyn Purvis (Jones) Tomlinson; m. William Henry Chandler, July 31, 1982; children: J.W. Nelson, Martha E.H., Ann Paisley S. MusB, Converse Coll., Spartanburg, S.C., 1975, MusM, 1980. Organist Lake City First Bapt. Ch., Lake City, SC, 1968—79; pvt. piano tchr. Hemingway, SC, 1975—; instr. Converse Coll., 1979—82; organist Indian Presbyn. Ch., Hemingway, 1982—97; dir. music First Presbyn. Ch., Florence, SC, 1998—, organist, 1998—. Bd. visitors Converse Coll., 2003—06; mem. parent's coun. Hollins Coll., Spartanburg, 1995—99, Wofford Coll., Spartanburg, 2003—06. Musician: Truluck/Tomlinson Duo, 1975—81, Florence Symphony, 1979, 2006. Mem. music com. New Harmony Presbytery, Florence, 2005—, mem. worship com., 2005—. Mem.: DAR, Nat. Assn. Music Tchrs. Presbyn. Avocations: travel, music. Home: 1949 Henry Rd Hemingway SC 29554 Office: First Presbyn Church 700 Park Ave Florence SC 29501

CHANDLER, AUSTIN GRACE, psychologist; BA in Psychology with honors, Columbia U., 1970, MA, 1972; PhD, Fordham U., 1982; postgrad. in Bus., U. N.C., Greensboro, 1990. Lic., clin. psychologist. Corp. cons. Farr Assocs., 1983-85; mem. adj. faculty, founder, dir. coll. counseling ctr. Greensboro Coll., 1985-92; founder, pres. Allied Counseling and Consulting Enterprises, 1992—; chief psychologist Evergreens Sr. Health Care Facilities, NC, 1997—2001; psychology cons. Therapeutic Alternatives, Inc., NC, 2002—03; dir. psychology Guilford Child Health, Inc., NC, 2003—. Mem. adj. faculty U. N.C., Greensboro; bd. dirs. Ashley Industries. Author: (with Jack Bornstein) Food is Killing You, 1997; contbr. articles to profl. jours. Bd. dirs. N.C. Aging and Mental Health Coalition. Recipient Psychologist of Yr. award N.C. Chiropractic Assn. Mem. APA, N.C. Psychol. Assn., Prescription Privileges for Psychologists Register (charter), Sigma Xi. Avocations: painting, writing, following the stock market, skiing. Office: Allied Counseling & Consulting Enterprises 8200 Crows Nest Ln Greensboro NC 27455-9294 Office Phone: 336-272-1050. Office Fax: 336-643-6850. Business E-Mail: austin_chandler@bellsouth.net.

CHANDLER, FAY MARTIN, artist; b. Norfolk, Va., Sept. 15, 1922; d. Howard Gresham and Alpine Douglas (Gatling) Martin; m. Alfred Dupont Chandler Jr., Jan. 8, 1944; children: Alpine C. Bird, Mary C. Watt, Alfred D. III, Howard Martin. BA, Sweetbriar Coll., 1943; MFA, Md. Inst. Coll. Art, Balt., 1967. Coord., dir. Fell's Point Gallery Md. Inst. Coll. Art, 1968-73; fellow Va. Ctr. Creative Arts, Sweetbriar, 1993. Hon. bd. dirs. Mass. Vol. Lawyers Arts; founder, bd. dirs. The Art Connection, Boston; arts in edn. adv. coun. Harvard Grad. Sch. Edn.; mem. Coun. Arts at MIT; adv. bd. Boston Landmarks Orch. One-woman shows include Kenneth Taylor Little Gallery, Nantucket, 1973, 76, Fells Point Gallery, Balt., 1974, 76, Mills Gallery, Boston, 1974-88, Main St. Gallery, Nantucket, 1977, Ensign-Sibley Gallery, Nantuckett, 1978, Sibley Gallery, Nantucket, 1980-85, Billiard Room Gallery, Cambridge, Mass., 1980, Helen Shlien Gallery, Boston, 1980, Bodley Gallery, NYC, 1980, St. Botolph Club, Boston, 1982, Stebbins Gallery, Cambridge, Mass., 1987, Bentley Coll., Waltham, Mass., 1987, Columbia (Md.) Ctr. for the Arts, 1987, Babcock Gallery Sweet Briar Coll., Va., 1993, Wenham (Mass.) Mus., 1993, Nantucket Island Sch. Design Gallery, 1994, Boston Ctr. For the Arts, 1995, Children's Mus., Boston, 1996, Decker Gallery/Md. Inst. Art, 1997, Steinbaum Krauss Gallery, NYC, 1997, Sacramento St. Gallery, Cambridge, Mass., 2002, Revolving Mus., Lowell, Mass., 2003, Boston Ctr. for the Arts, 2005; exhibited in group shows. Papers and slides chosen to be preserved Schlesinger Libr., Radcliffe Coll., Cambridge, Mass. Mem. Cambridge Art Assn Avocations: mystery books, philosophy. Home: 1010 Memorial Dr Apt 17E Cambridge MA 02138-4857 Studio: Engine House Studios 444 Western Ave Boston MA 02135-1016 Business E-Mail: fay@dougwatt.com.

CHANDLER, HARRIETTE LEVY, state legislator, management consultant, educator; b. Balt., Dec. 20, 1937; d. S. Lester and Reba K. Levy; m. Burton Chandler, July 12, 1959; children: Frank Levy, Victoria Jane, Edward Lee. BA, Wellesley Coll., 1959; MA, Clark U., 1963, PhD, 1973; MBA, Simmons Coll., 1983; PhD in Pub. Adminstrn. (hon.), Worcester State Coll., 1998. HS history tchr. Worcester (Mass.) Pub. Schs., 1959-61; polit. sci. prof. Clark U., Worcester, 1973-77; prof. polit. sci. Tufts U., Medford, Mass., 1977-78; exec. dir. nat women's com. Brandeis U., Waltham, Mass., 1978-81; cons. Prime Computer, Natick, Mass., 1983-84; mgr. documentation tng. Adelie Corp., Cambridge, Mass., 1984-85, mgr. mktg. svcs., 1985-87, prin., 1987-89; dir. communication Open Software Found., Cambridge, 1989; mgmt. cons. Chandler Assocs., 1990—. Author: U.S. Soviet Relations During World War II, 1982. Chmn. com. on shareholder responsibility Clark U., 1982—86; founding mem. Worcester Women's Polit. Caucus, 1985; chmn. bd. trustees Worcester Meml. Auditorium, 1987—89; com. mem. Worcester Sch., 1992—94, vice-chmn., 1994, Mass. Comm. on Common Core of Learning, 1994, Transp. Com., Worcester Com. Fgn. Rels.; incorporator YWCA, Greater Worcester Cmty. Found., Worcester Art Mus.; past pres. Jewish Healthcare Ctr.; chair Joint Com. Comty. Devel. and Small Bus.; state rep. 13th Worcester Dist., Mass. Legislature, 1995—2000; mem. Dem. State Com., 1999—; state sen. 13th Worcester Dist., Mass. Legislature, 2001—; mem. steering com. Reforming States Group, 1996—; various coms. Ctrl. Mass. Legis. Caucus, 1991—, co-chair, 2001—02, co-chair women's legis. caucus, 2006, co-chair oral health com. Mem.: Worcester Econs. Club. Jewish. Avocations: walking, swimming, cooking, reading. Home: 97 Aylesbury Rd Worcester MA 01609-1314 Office: State House Rm 312D Boston MA 02133 Business E-Mail: hchandle@senate.state.ma.us.

CHANDLER, JULIE LIGHT, secondary school educator; b. Indpls., Dec. 8, 1949; d. Edward Carl and Genneve Elder Light; m. Felix Chandler Jr. (dec. Dec. 30, 1991); 1 child, Scott Andrew. BS in Edn., Ind. U., Bloomington/Indpls., 1984, MS, 1984. Tchr. Cathedral HS, Indpls., 1981—84; h.s. tchr. Indpls. Pub. Schs., 1984—. Recipient Scholastic Achievement award, Sigma Pi Alpha, 1981. Home: 353 E Clear Lake Ln Westfield IN 46074 Office: Broad Ripple HS 1115 Broad Ripple Ave Indianapolis IN 46220 Office Phone: 317-693-5700. Personal E-mail: chandlerj@insightbb.com.

CHANDLER, KATHLEEN, retired executive secretary; b. Clayton, Wis., Oct. 13, 1927; d. William Henry and Evelyn Jean (Vassau) Olson; m. Calvin Hewitt Chandler, Dec. 21, 1954; children: Sarah Kay, Blake Hewitt. BA in Bus./Psychology summa cum laude, Briar Cliff Coll., Sioux City, Iowa, 1991. Lic. realtor, Mass. Sec. to pres. Union State Bank, Amery, Wis., 1948-51; sec. to mgr. Social Security Adminstrn., Mpls., 1951-52; sec. to asst. contr. N.W. Banco, Mpls., 1952-54; sec. to v.p. Celanese Corp., Charlotte, N.C., 1954-55, Monsanto Chem. Co., St. Louis, 1955-58; exec. sec. AC Rochester divsn. Gen. Motors Corp., Sioux City, 1981-92. Editor GM plant newspaper Throttle Body Lines, 1982-92. Mem Welcom Wagon Club of Sun City West, Ariz., pres., 1997—. Mem. AAUW, PEO Sisterhood (treas. DQ chpt. 1995—), Sun City West Iowa Club (pres. 1995—). Presbyterian. Avocations: bridge, reading, art.

CHANDLER, KIMBERLEY LYNN, educational association administrator; b. Waynesboro, Va., Sept. 28, 1961; d. Alden Hugh and Cecille Frances (Brooks) C. BA in Elem. Edn., Coll. William and Mary, 1984, MA in Gifted Edn., 1992, PhD in Ednl. Policy, Planning and Leadership, 2004. Lic. educator, Va. Tchr. Fredericksburg (Va.) Pub. Schs., 1984-87, Henrico County Pub. Schs., Richmond, Va., 1987-98; gifted edn. resource specialist Hanover County Pub. Schs., Richmond, Va., 1998-2000; supr. enrichment programs, coord. of sci. K-12 Amherst County Pub. Schs., Va., 2000—03; cert. curriculum cons. Ctr. for Gifted Edn., 2002—; panel reviewer Jacob K. Javits Grant Program, U.S. Dept. Edn., 2002; postdoctoral fellow Ctr. for Gifted Edn. Coll. of William and Mary, Williamsburg, Va., 2003, curriculum dir., 2003—; acad. rev. team leader Va. Dept. Edn., 2004—. Summer sch. coord. Henrico County Pub. Schs., 1996, 97, staff devel. presenter, 1996, 97; curriculum cons. Coll. of William and Mary, Williamsburg, Va., 1996; presenter in field.; mem. gifted edn. staff devel. talent bank, mem. tchr. stds. com. Va. Dept. Edn.; mem. peer coaching program, Prin.'s Acad.; sch. renewal planning team facilitator Hanover County Pub. Schs.; mem. adj. faculty U. Va. Sch. Continuing and Profl. Studies, 2001—; instr. Casenex, Inc.; participant David L. Clark Grad. Student Seminar, 2003. Author: (curriculum unit) Literary Reflections, 1992; author: (with others) Aiming for Excellence-Gifted Program Standards: Annotations to the NAGC Pre-K-Grade 12 Gifted Program Standards, ERIC Research Report, 2002, (book review) Gifted and Talented International; editor (newsletter): Va. Assn. for the Gifted, 1999—. Vol. Hanover Humane Soc., 1994—, Habitat for Humanity Global Village Program, Nicaragua Disaster Relief Mission Team, 1999, Brazil VBS Mission Team, 2000; mem. Habitat for Humanity Global Village Team to South Africa, 2001. Recipient Doctoral Student award Nat. Assn. for Gifted Children, 2002, Hollingworth Rsch. award, 2003; grantee Henrico Edn. Found., 1997, Henrico Gifted Adv. Coun., 1997, Pntrs. in Arts grantee Richmond Arts Coun., 1996, Hanover Edn. Found., 1999, Coll. William and Mary, 2003; postdoctoral fellow Ctr. Gifted Edn., Coll. William and Mary, 2003—. Mem.: Va. Assn. for the Gifted (ex officio bd. dirs.), Va. Soc. for Tech. in Edn., Hanover County Prins. Acad., Nat. Assn. for Gifted Children (sec./treas. technol. divsn. 1997—99, sec./treas. profl. devel. divsn. 1997—99, chair profl. devel. divsn. 2003—, Harry Passow Classroom Tchr. scholarship 1997, Outstanding Curriculum award 2000, Doctoral Student award 2002, Hollingworth award 2003), Delta Kappa Gamma, Kappa Delta Pi (chpt. sec.). Home: 11444 New Farrington Ct Glen Allen VA 23059-1629 Office: Coll William and Mary Ctr for Gifted Edn PO Box 8795 Williamsburg VA 23187-8795 Personal E-mail: kchan11444@aol.com. Business E-Mail: klchan@wm.edu.

CHANDLER, MARCIA SHAW BARNARD, farmer; b. Arlington, Mass., Aug. 22, 1934; d. John Alden and Grace Winifred (Copeland) Barnard; m. Samuel Butler Chandler, Aug. 31, 1952 (dec. 1986); children: Shawn Chandler Seddinger, Mark Thurmond, Matthew Butler. BA, Francis Marion Univ., Florence, S.C., 1976; MEd, U. S.C., 1985. Resource person United Cerebral Palsy of S.C., Dillon, 1976-79; instr. English Horry-Georgetown Tech. Coll., Conway, S.C., 1980-81; farm owner, mgr. Dillon; drama critic Dillon (S.C.) Herald, 1986—. Author: (with others) Best of Old Farmer's Almanac, First 200 Years, 1991, A Primer for the New Millennium, 1999; cover artist So. Bell Telephone Directory, 1988; artist Dillon County Lib., 1998. Nat. poetry judge DAR, 1982; pres. Dillon Area Arts Coun., 1980—85, Jr. Charity League of Dillon, 1960—75; Dunbar libr. com. Dillon County, 1998—; bd. dirs., publicist, artist Dillon County Theatre, Inc., 1985—, MacArthur Ave. Players, Dillon, 1990—; bd. dirs. Friends of Francis Marion U., 1985—95. Recipient Honorable Commendation for civic involvement S.C. Ho. Reps., 1990, Vol. Yr., Dillon County C. of C., 2005. Mem. Ctr. Environ. Edn., Internat. Fund Animal Welfare, Nature Conservancy, Sea Shepherd Conservation Soc., Humane Soc. U.S., Ocean Conservancy, Nat. Wildlife Fund, Animal Protection Inst., Nat. Humane Edn. Soc., Dillon county C. of C. (amb. 1995—). Avocations: snorkeling, theater, travel. Home: 309 E Reaves Ave Dillon SC 29536-1919 Personal E-mail: marciacani@aol.com.

CHANDLER, MARGUERITE NELLA, real estate company executive; b. New Brunswick, N.J., May 16, 1943; d. Edward A. and Marguerite (Moore) Chandler; m. Ronald Wilson, May 30, 1964 (div. Nov. 1973); children: Mark Wilson, Adam Wilson; m. Richmond Shreve, Nov. 22, 1979; 1 child, Laura Shreve. BS in Acctg., Syracuse U., 1964; MS in Polit. Mgmt., George Washington U., 1968. Tax acct. Peat Marwick Mitchell, Providence, 1964; grant adminstr., psychology dept. Brown U., Providence, 1965; intern in devel. cons. Washington, 1973-75; prin., tng. cons. M. Chandler Assocs., 1975-76; mgmt. cons. Edmar Corp., Bound Brook, NJ, 1976-78, pres., chief exec. officer, 1978-90, pres., 1991—. Vol. Peace Corps, 1966—68, Somerset Cmty. Action Program, 1969—71; treas. Somerset County Day Care Assn., 1969—71; established Food Bank Network Somerset County, 1982, pres., 1982—85; established Worldworks Found., Inc., 1983; founder PeopleCare Ctr., 1984, pres., 1984—86; bd. dirs. United Way Somerset Valley, 1984—91, gen. campaign mgr., 1985—86; recorder Blue Ribbon Com. Ending Hunger in N.J., 1984—86; bd. dirs. N.J. Coun. Arts, 1986—87; mem. N.J. Gov.'s Task Force Pub./Pvt. Sector Initiatives, NJ, 1986—91; mem. adv. bd. US-USSR Youth Exch., Ptnrs. in Peacemaking, Giraffe Project; chmn. bd. dirs. Friends Retirement Inc., 1996—2002; Dem. candidate U.S. Congress Dist. 12, 1990; vol. Missionaries Charity, Calcutta, India, 1981; pres. bd. trustees N.J. Coun. Chs., 1985—90. Named Woman of the Yr., Women's Resource Ctr. Somerset County, 1983, Citizen of the Yr., N.J. chpt. Nat. Assn. Soc. Workers, 1986, Bus. and Profl. Women's Club, 1987, Person of the Decade, Courier-News, 1989, Bus. Person of the Yr., Bus. Ctrl. N.J. mag., 1993; recipient People's Champaion award, Somerset Family Planning Svc., 1985, Disting. Svc. award, N.J. Speech-Lang.-Hearing Assn., 1986, N.J. Women of Achievement award, Douglass Coll. and N.J. Fedn. Women's Clubs, 1986, Brotherhood award, Ctrl. Jersey chpt. Nat. Conf. Christians and Jews, 1986, Presdl. End Hunger award, Presdl. End Hunger award, 1987, Somerset Alliance for the Future Quality of Life award, 1996. Mem.: Celebrate N.J. (founder, coord. 2005—), World Bus. Acad. (bd. dirs. 1988—89), Assn. N.J. Recyclers (pres. 1991—93), Regional Plan Assn. (bd. dirs. 1994—96), Somerset C. of C. (chmn. bd. dirs. 1989—90, chmn. strategic planning cultural and heritage com., tourism coun., Citizen of the Yr. 1985), Crossroads Am. Revolution Assn. (founder, pres. 2001—05), Heritage Trail Assn. Somerset County (founder, pres. 1994—99), Rotary (pres. Bound Brook-Middlesex 1993—94). Quaker. Avocation: quilting. Home: PO Box 250 Cape May Point NJ 08212 Office: PO Box 246 Cape May Point NJ 08212 Office Phone: 732-469-9950.

CHANDLER, MARSHA, academic administrator, educator; BA, CCNY, 1965; PhD, UNC Chapel Hill, 1972; grad. in advanced Mgmt. Program, Harvard Bus. Sch., 2004. Prof. political econ. Univ. Toronto, 1977-96, dean arts and sci., 1990-97; sr. vice chancellor U. Calif., San Diego, 1996—. Vis. scholar Harvard U., 1995-96, 2004-05. Co-author: Trade and Transmissions, 1990, The Political Economy of Business Bailouts, 2 vols., 1986, The Politics of Canadian Public Policy, 1983, Public Policy and Provincial Politics, 1979, Adjusting to Trade: A Comparative Perspective, 1988; contbr. articles to profl. jours. Fellow, Royal Soc. of Canada, mem.dirs. San Diego Opera, Mingei Mus. Internatl. Folk Art (bd. dir.), UCSD Found. Bd. and the Charter 100, adv. com. on Fed. Judicial Appts., Canadian Inst. for Adv. Rsch.; trustee (bd. mem.), Art Gall. of Ontario, Mt. SInai Hosp., Huntsman Marine Sci. Ctr., Ontario Lightwave, Laser Rsch. Ctr. Office: U Calif 9500 Gilman Dr La Jolla CA 92093-5004

CHANDLER, NETTIE JOHNSON, artist; b. Christian County, Ky., Nov. 15, 1912; d. Sol James and Georgia Bell (Davis) Johnson; m. Percy Scott Chandler, Oct. 14, 1944. Student, Watkins Inst., Nashville, 1937—45, Watkins Inst., 1953—56, Harris Sch. Art, Nashville, 1937, Oklahoma City U., 1952, Coll. William and Mary, 1957—58; AS cum laude, Thomas Nelson C.C., 1983. Bookkeeper Keach Furniture Co., Hopkinsville, Ky., 1929—32; office sec., bookkeeper Baus Mfg. Co., Hopkinsville, 1933—35; bookkeeper Castner Knott Co., Nashville, 1936—39; sec., artist, editor Young South page Baptist & Reflector, Nashville, 1939—45; real estate saleswoman Grinnell Realty, Nashville, 1950—51; typist Griffiss AFB, Rome, NY, 1952—53; sec., artist Tenn. State Libr., Nashville, 1953—56; tech. illustrator NASA, Hampton, 1956—72. Comml. artist to 1972, fine arts painter, 1973—. Represented in permanent collections Va. Air and Space Mus. Vol. ARC, Nashville, 1985—86. Recipient awards for art including 2d pl. Watkins Inst., 1955, 1st place Parthenon, Nashville, 1956, 1st place Watkins Inst., 1956, 1st place (3 times) Tenn. State Fair, 1985-96, Best of Show, Watkins Inst., 1986, 3d pl. Watkins Inst., 1987, 2d pl. for miniatures Tenn. Art League (3 times), 1988-92, 3d pl. Tenn. Art League, 1989, Best of Show, 1990, 2d pl. for graphics, 1996, 2d pl. oils, 2005, Best of Show, Gallery Eight WDCN TV, 1997, Daily Press Newport News, Va. Snapshot award, 1983. Mem. Tenn. Art League (leader Monday Painters 1984-98). Republican. Baptist. Avocations: writing, reading, painting, computer designing and printing, knitting. Home: 404 Deer Lake Dr Nashville TN 37221-2108 Office Phone: 615-646-7163. Personal E-mail: nettie.chandler@comcast.net.

CHANDLER, PATRICIA ANN, retired special education educator; b. Stow, Maine, May 25, 1929; d. Herbert Raymond and Tressia May (Walker) Harmon; m. Robert Leslie Chandler, Mar. 25, 1949 (dec. June 1991); children: Rose Ann Chandler Savage, Alexander Michael. BS, U. Maine, Portland, 1965; MEd, U. So. Maine, 1978. Tchg. prin. Annie Heald Sch., Lovell, Maine, 1954—70, New Suncook Sch., Lovell, Maine, 1970, Sadie Adams Sch., North Fryeburg, Maine, New Suncook Sch., Lovell, Maine; ret., 1983. Contbr. articles to profl. jours. Mem.: Cumberland County Alumni Chpt., Maine Assn. of Retirees, Inc. (licentiate). Republican. United Ch. Of Christ Congl. Avocations: cooking, travel, writing, painting.

CHANDLER, ROBIN MARY, artist, educator, writer; b. Boston, Apr. 3, 1950; d. Byron G. and Frances A. (Freeman) Chandler; m. Leonard D. Smith, Aug. 1971 (div. June 1979); 1 child, Nuri G. Chandler-Smith. BA in Studio Art/Art History, U. Mass., 1974, MEd, 1977; PhD in Sociology, Northeastern U., 1992. Founding editor Drum Mag., Amherst, Mass., 1969-71; founding dir. Peace Doors Project, 1993—; instr. Commonwealth Sch., Boston, 1988-89; artist-in-residence divsn. fine arts Northeastern U., Boston, 1978—, asst. prof. dept. African Am. studies, 1992—99, assoc. prof., 1999—, dept. chair, 2001—02, dir. women's studies African Am. studies, 2002—04. Founding dir. Caravan for Internat. Culture, Inc., 1980—; cons. Mass. Coun. on Arts and Humanities, Artists Found., Danforth Mus., Boston Pub. Schs., Cambridge Pub. Schs., Lynn (Mass.) Pub. Schs.; guest host 'Basic Black' WGBH/TV Boston, 2005-, lectr. in field. One-woman shows include Northeastern U. AAMARP Galleries, 1984, Simmons Coll., Boston, 1986, Lois Mailou Jones Studio Gallery, Edgartown, Mass., 1988, 91, Western Md. Coll., 1992, Mills Gallery, Boston, 1995, U.S. State Dept. Arts in Embassies Program., Internat. Tour Am. Embassies, 1996-, BAT Ctr., Durban, South Africa, 1996, Purdue U., 1997, Johannesburg Art Gallery, 1997, Parish Gallery, Washington, 1998, Gallery @ Piano Factory, 2002, Boston City Hall Chambers Councilman Arroyo, 2003; exhibited in group shows at Isobel Neal Gallery, Chgo., M.L. King Ctr. for Performing Arts, Ohio, Harriet Tubman House Gallery, Copley Soc. Gallery, Boston, Wellesley Coll., U. Mass., Boston, Arts Festival of Atlanta, Noho Gallery, N.Y.C., Mus. Sci. and Industry, Chgo., Howard U. Gallery, DC, 1999, U. Mass. Amherst Hampden Gallery, 2001, Darious Gallery, Atlanta, 2002, Gallery; poet: featured in numerous articles, books; contbr. articles to profl. jours. Artists Found. grantee, 1985, Northeastern U. Faculty Travel grantee, Brazil, 1989, 90, Australia, 1999, China, 2006, NEA-Pyramid Atlantic grantee, 1993, Northeastern U. Faculty Travel grantee, 1993-94, 97, NSF grantee, 2001-04; Fulbright scholar South Africa, 1995-96. Mem. Coll. Art Assn., African Studies Assn., Internat. Soc. Ford Edn. Through Art, Nat. Ethnic Studies Assn. (bd. mem.), Inst. for Race and Justice, Northeastern U., Phi Kappa Phi, Alpha Phi Gamma. Office: Northeastern U 132 Nightingale Hall Boston MA 02115 Office Phone: 617-373-5681. Business E-Mail: r.chandler@neu.edu.

CHANDLER, SHERRY, writer, editor; b. Owenton, Ky., Feb. 15, 1945; d. Howard Kenneth and Katherine Botts (Keith) C.; m. Thomas Robert Williams, Aug. 9, 1972; children: Morgan Steele, Thomas Chandler. BA, Georgetown (Ky.) Coll., 1970; MA, U. Ky., 1972. Consumer affairs specialist William Wrigley Jr. Co., Chgo., 1973-77, consumer affairs supr., 1977-79; freelance writer Paris, Ky., 1979—; staff asst. U. Ky. Hosp., Lexington, 1988-90; data coord. U. Ky. Coll. Medicine, Lexington, 1990-92, editl. assoc., 1992-96; staff assoc. Sanders-Brown Ctr. on Aging, U. Ky., Lexington, 1996-99, sr. staff assoc., 1999—. Workshop leader Am. Med. Writers Assn., Rockville, Md., 1993-95. Author/performer: (radio commentary) Early World on WRVG Radio, 1999; peer reviewer (book) Biomedical Communications, 1997; author of poetry and short fiction, (poetry book) Dance the Black-Eyed Girl, 2003, My Will and Testament is on the Desk, 2003. Mem. fourth Friday com. Lexington Art League, 1999-2000, site based com. Paris H.S., 1995-97; mem. strategic planning com. Paris Ind. schs., 1995-97; bd. dirs. Paris H.S. Band Boosters, 1994-96; mem. Ky. Coalition Against the Death Penalty, 1999-2000. Profl. Devel. grantee Ky. Arts Coun., 1989, 2005. Mem. Am. Med. Writers Assn. (subchpt. pres. 1993-01), Bd. of Editors in the Life Scis., Ky. Writers Coalition, Ky. State Poetry Soc. (pres. 2006), Green River Writers, Inc. (bd. chair 2003—). Office: Sanders-Brown Ctr on Aging Univ of Ky 101 Sanders Brown Bldg Ky Lexington KY 40536-0001 E-mail: sherry@sherrychandler.com.

CHANDLER, VICTORIA JANE, elementary school educator, writer; b. Chestnut Hill, Pa., Oct. 27, 1954; d. Roland Jay and Elisabeth Ann (Renton) Turner; m. Howard Steven Chandler, June 24, 1978; children: Christopher, Robert. BS, Kutztown State U., 1976; postgrad., Loyola Coll., Towson, Md., 1977, 79; MEd, Beaver Coll., Glenside, Pa., 1991. Cert. tchr., Pa. Tchr. spl. edn. Md. Sch. for Blind, Balt., 1976-80; tchr. 2nd grade Lehigh Christian Acad., Phila., 1986-91; tchr. vision support Montgomery County IU #23, Norristown, Pa., 1991-92; tchr. instructional support team Sch. Dist. of Springfield Twp./Montgomery County, Oreland, Pa., 1992-94; spl. edn. tchr. Council Rock Sch. Dist., 1994-95; dir. instrn., elem. prin. Calvary Christian Acad., Phila., 1995—2000, tchr. 2d grade, 2001—. Asst. dir. Mustard Seed Farm Camp for Handicapped, Spring City, Pa., 1980-85. Author: Journey From Insanity to Sanity--A Mother's Journey With Her Son, 2000. Active Ch. Sunday Sch. Calvary Chapel, Feasterville, Pa., 1992—. Active Ch. Sun. sch. Berachah, Cheltenham, Pa., 1982-90. Avocations: photography, educational board games. Home: 509 Brook Ln Warminster PA 18974-2719

CHANEY, ELIZABETH MONCRIEF, state agency administrator; d. James Ernest and Nellie Louise Moncrief; children: Catrina Elaine Lassiter, Roland A'mar Lassiter. BBA in Acctg., Davenport U., Dearborn, Mich., 1988; MS in Project Mgmt., George Washington U., Washington, D.C., 2002; MBA in Tech. Mgmt., U. Phoenix, Grand Rapids, Mich., 2004. Clk. gen. calculations Mich. Dept. Labor, Detroit, 1975—77; coord. cost data Mich. Dept. Mental Health, Detroit, 1978—88; from tax auditor to officer Mich. Dept. Treasury, Lansing, Mich., 1988—2002, officer tax disclosure, 2002—. Treas. Palestine Missionary Bapt. Ch., Detroit, 1984—85; mgr. cmty. project Williams St. Ch. of God in Christ, Detroit, 1998—2000. Mem.: Project Mgmt. Inst. (newsletter editor cap. area chpt. 1999—2005), Am. Bus. Women's Inst., Carrier Creek Condominum Assn. (treas. 1997—2000), Nat. Assn. Negro Bus. and Profl. Women's Clubs, Inc. (tech. chmn. north ctrl. dist. 2004—06). Office: Michigan Department of Treasury 430 West Allegan Street Lansing MI 48922 Office Phone: 517-335-0629. Home Fax: 517-622-3085.

CHANG, ANNETTE M., research scientist; MD, MS, U. Mich., Ann Arbor. Asst. prof. internal medicine U. Mich. Med. Sch., Ann Arbor, 2004—. Recipient Individual Nat. Rsch. Svc. award, NIH/NIA, 2002—04, Rsch. Career Devel. award, Dept. Veterans Affairs, 2004—. Mem.: Am. Diabetes Assn. (Young Investigator Innovation award Geriatric Endocrinology 2003—05). Office: University of Michigan 5570 MSRB II 1150 W Medical Center Dr Ann Arbor MI 48109-0678 Office Phone: 734-763-3056.

CHANG, BARBARA KAREN, medical educator; b. Milltown, Ind., Jan. 6, 1946; m. M.F. Joseph Chang-Wai-Ling, Oct. 6, 1967; children: Carla Marie Yvonnette, Nolanne Arlette. BA, Ind. U., 1968; MA, Brandeis U., 1970; MD, Albert Einstein Coll. Medicine, 1973. Diplomate Am. Bd. Internal Medicine, Am. Bd. Med. Oncology, Am. Bd. Hematology. Resident in internal medicine Montefiore Med. Ctr., Bronx, NY, 1973-75; fellow in hematology/oncology Duke U. Med. Ctr., Durham, NC, 1975-78; staff physician VA Med. Ctr., Augusta, Ga., 1978-95, chief hematology/oncology, 1980-89, assoc. chief of staff edn., 1990-95, chief of staff, chief med. officer Albuquerque, 1995—2002; prof. medicine Med. Coll. Ga., Augusta, 1978-95; assoc. dean U. N.Mex. Sch. Medicine, Albuquerque, 1995—2002; cons. Capital Assets Realignment for Enhanced Svcs. Program VA Ctrl. Office, Washington, 2002—03, dir. program evaluation Office Academic Affiliations, 2003—. Mem. Sci. Adv. Bd., Washington, 1983-88; mem. expert panels computer applications Dept. Vets. Affairs, Washington, 1988-95. Contbr. numerous articles on cancer rsch. to profl. jours. Youth coord. Am. Hemerocallis Soc., Augusta, 1993-95, pres. local chpt. 1997, Albuquerque, garden judge 1997-03, region 6 youth liaison, 2000-01, exhbn. judge, 2001—, nat. youth liaison com., 2003-06. Grantee Nat. Cancer Inst., Am. Cancer Soc., 1978-93; David M. Worthen award Acad. Excellence Dept. Vet. Affairs, 2000. Fellow ACP, Am. Soc. Clin. Oncology, Bioelectromagnetic Soc. (bd. dirs. 1983-86). Office: Dept Vets Affairs Med Ctr 1501 San Pedro Dr SE Albuquerque NM 87108-5153 Business E-Mail: barbara.chang@med.va.gov.

CHANG, CARMEN, lawyer; b. Nanjing, China, 1948; BA, Sarah Lawrence Coll., 1970; MA, Stanford U., 1973, JD with distinction, 1993. Bar: Calif. 1994, U.S. Ct. Appeals (9th cir.) 1994. Ptnr. Shearman & Sterling, LLP, Menlo Park, Calif., 2003—05; ptnr., leader China practice Wilson Sonsini Goodrich Rosati, Palo Alto, Calif., 2005—. Spkr. in field; mem. adv. bd. Stanford Project Regions of Innovation and Entrepreneurship Asia-Pacific Rsch. Ctr. Stanford U., Stanford, Calif. Contbr. articles to profl. jours. Fluent in English, Mandarin, Cantonese, Japanese. Office: Wilson Sonsini Goodrich & Rosati 650 Page Mill Rd Palo Alto CA 94304 Business E-Mail: cchang@wsgr.com.

CHANG, DEBBIE I-JU, health programs and research executive, director; BS in Chem. Engring., MIT, 1984; MPH, U. Mich., 1987. Presdl. mgmt. intern Health Care Fin. Adminstrn. Office Legislation and Policy, 1987-89; sr. health policy advisor Senator Donald W. Riegle Jr., 1989-94; dir. office legis. and intergovt. affairs Health Care Fin. Adminstrn., Washington, 1994-98; dir. State Children's Health Ins. Program Health Care Fin. Adminstrn., Dept. HHS, 1997-99; dir. Medicaid coverage benefits and payments Health Care Fin. Adminstrn., Balt., 1998; dep. sec. health care financing Medicaid Md. Dept. Health and Mental Hygiene, Balt., 1999—2003; sr. v.p., exec. dir. Nemours Divsn. Child Health and Prevention Svcs., Del., 2004—. Contbr. articles to profl. jours. Office Phone: 302-444-9127. Personal E-mail: dchang@nemours.org.

CHANG, HELEN T., municipal official; BA, Nat. Chung Hsing U.; MBA, Auburn U., Ala. Former instructor Inst. of Bus. Administration, Taiwan; former rsch. statistician U. Washington, Seattle; former admin. assoc. Baylor Coll. of Med., Houston; news anchor So. Chinese TV, 1988—91; former mem. advisory council on ed. statistics US Dept. of Ed., Washington; former mem. Tex. Statewide Hlth. Coord. Council, 1990—93; exec. asst. Off. of Mayor, Houston, 1992—, and dir. Internat. Affairs & Econ. Develop. Mem. Internat. Trade Com. of Greater Houston Partnership, Org. of Women in Internat. Trade-Houston, E.B. Cape Ctr. Sr. Professional Develop. Com., Houston Com. on Foreign Relations; founder & chair US Asian Bus. Partnership; chair Asian-Am. Heritage Assn. of Houston; pres. Chinese Women's Bus. Assn., Asian-Am. Voters' Coalition. Named Honorary Citizen, City of Dalian, China, 1997. Office: City of Houston 901 Bagby 4th Fl Houston TX 77002 Office Phone: 713-247-3595. Business E-Mail: helen.chang@cityofhouston.net.

CHANG, HEMMIE, lawyer; b. Mar. 19, 1960; AB, Princeton Univ., 1981; JD, Harvard Univ., 1984. Bar: Mass. 1985. Law clk. Judge David S. Nelson, US Dist Ct. (Mass.); assoc. Ropes & Gray, Boston, 1985—93, ptnr. corp. dept., 1993—, head energy & utilities practice group. Bd. mem. South Cove Nursing Home; bd. mem. Cambridge Ctr for Adult Edn.; bd. mem. Commonwealth Sch. Mem.: Women's Corp. Counsel Network, Boston Law Firm Group. Office: Ropes & Gray 1 International Pl Boston MA 02110-2624 Office Phone: 617-951-7317. Office Fax: 617-951-7050. Business E-Mail: h.chang@ropesgray.com.

CHANG, HSUEH-LUN SHELLEY, historian, researcher, writer; b. Nanning, China, Sept. 18, 1934; d. Chun-su Loh and Chien-Yun Huang; m. Chun-shu Chang, Sept. 26, 1959; children: Chien-ju Jean, I-Ju Deborah, Wei-chung Victor. BA in History, Nat. Taiwan U., 1956; MA in History, Boston U., 1961. Rsch. assoc. Ctr. Chinese Study, Ann Arbor, Mich., 1984—. Vis. lectr. Chinese U. Hong Kong, 1983—85, U. Lan-chou China, 1984; vis. assoc. prof. U. Mich., Ann Arbor, 1987, 94, v.p. women's rsch. club, 91. Author: Windmills: A Collection of Essays, 1970, History and Legend, 1990; co-author: Crisis and Transformation in 17th-Century China, 1992, Redefining History, 1998. Mem.: Assn. Asian Studies, Am. Hist. Assn. Home: 3236 Bluett Dr Ann Arbor MI 48105

CHANG, JANE P., chemical engineering educator; BS, Nat. Taiwan U., 1993; MS, MIT, 1995, PhD, 1998. Engring. intern Merck and Co., Inc., Lansdale, Pa., 1994, Dow Chem. Co., Midland, Mich., 1994; postdoctoral mem. tech. staff Bell Labs, Lucent Technologies, Murray Hill, NJ, 1998—99; asst. prof. chem. engring. UCLA, 1999—2003, assoc. prof. chem. engring., 2003—. Vice chair com. undergrad. admission and rels. with schools UCLA, 2004—05. Contbr. articles to profl. jours. Named Prof. of Yr., UCLA, 2003—04; recipient Chancellor's Career Devel. award, 2000—02, Career award, Nat. Sci. Found., 2002, TRW Excellence in Tchg. award, TRW, 2002, Young Investigator award, Office of Naval Rsch., 2003, Hugo Schuck Best Paper award, Am. Automatic Control Coun., 2004; Rumbel Practice School Fellowship, MIT, 1993. Mem.: Material Rsch. Soc., Am. Vacuum Soc. (Coburn and Winters award 1996), Am. Inst. Chem. Engrs., Am. Physics Soc., Electrochem. Soc., Am. Chem. Soc., Phi Tau Phi. Office: UCLA Chem Engring Dept BH 5532-D 420 Westwood Plz Los Angeles CA 90095

CHANG, LAN SAMANTHA, writer, educator; b. Appleton, Wis., Jan. 18, 1965; d. Nai Lin and Helen Chung-Hung (Hsiang) Chang. BA, Yale U., 1987; MPA, Harvard U., 1991; MFA, U. Iowa, 1993. Tchg., writing fellow U. Iowa, Iowa City, 1991—93; Stegner fellow Stanford U., Calif., 1993—95, Jones lectr., 1995—98; Hodder fellow Princeton U., NJ, 1999—2000; Radcliffe fellow Harvard U., Cambridge, Mass., 2000—01, Briggs-Copeland lectr., 2002; vis. assoc. prof. U. Iowa, Iowa City, 2001—02, prof. creative writing, 2006—; dir. Iowa Writers' Workshop, U. Iowa, Iowa City, 2006—. MFA faculty Warren Wilson Coll., Asheville, NC, 2000—. Author: Hunger: A Novella and Stories, 1998, Inheritance: A Novel, 2004. Recipient Calif. Book award silver medal, Bay Area Book award, James-Michener-Copernicus award; Nat Endowment for the Arts grantee, 1998. Office: Grad Program in Creative Writing Univ Iowa 102 Dey House Iowa City IA 52242-1408*

CHANG, LENG KAR, interior designer; b. Ipoh, Perak, Malaysia, Aug. 31, 1973; arrived in U.S., 1997; MA, Savannah Coll. Art and Design, 1999; cert., Visionary Designing, 2001. Interior designer Innervision Design Cons., Kuala Lumpur, Malaysia, 1994—96, Winsonart Design and Contracts, Paya Lebah, Singapore, 1997—98, Ai Group, Atlanta, 2000—. Contbr. (design) Residential Product and Interior Design, Home Max, 1997. Named Monroe Curus Propes fellow, Savannah Coll. Art and Design, 1998, Internat. and Regional winner, Interior Design Educators Coun. Student Design Competition, 1999; scholar, Savannah Coll. Art and Design, 1998. Home: PO Box 190802 Atlanta GA 31119-0802 Office: Ai Group 3424 Peachtree Rd NE Ste 1600 Atlanta GA 30326 Personal E-mail: lengkar@hotmail.com. Business E-Mail: lchang@aigroupdesign.com.

CHANG, LYDIA LIANG-HWA, social worker, educator; b. Wuhan, Hubei, China, Sept. 25, 1929; came to U.S., 1960; d. Shu-Tze Yu-Rou and Jian-Bung (Young) C.; m. Norman Stock, Aug. 20, 1998; children: Elizabeth Shu-Mei L. Ip, George Shu-Ang Lee. Diploma in Spanish and Lit., U. Sorbonne, Paris, 1959; MSW, NYU, 1963; cert. in advanced social work, Columbia U., N.Y.C., 1977, PhD in Social Work, 1980. Cert. social worker, cert. sch. bilingual social worker, N.Y.; LCSW; LMSW. Supr. Cath. Charities, N.Y.C., 1969-71; dir. mental health cons. ctr. Univ. Settlement, N.Y.C., 1971-73; psychotherapist Luth. Med. Ctr., Bklyn., 1974-78; assoc. prof. U. Cin., 1978-80; asst. prof. Borough of Manhattan C.C., N.Y.C., 1983-86; bilingual sch. social worker N.Y.C. Bd. Edn., 1987-98, instr. for staff devel. program, 1991-98; psychotherapist Western Queens (N.Y.) Consultation Ctr., 1998—2004; pvt. practice psychotherapy, 2005—. Govt. ofcl.; cmem. mty. sch. bd. Dist. 30 N.Y.C. Bd. Edn., 1999-2004; cons. Cath. Social Svc. Bur., Cin., 1978-80; faculty advisor Borough of Manhattan C.C., 1983-86. Author: numerous poems; contbr. articles to profl. jours. Adv. bd. Pub. Sys. of Schs., Cin., 1978-80, Orange County Asian Am. orgn., Goshen, NY, 1980-82; founder of the Shu-Tze Chang and Jian-Bung Young Chang Ednl. scholarship fund, China, 1996. Mem. NASW, Nat. Assn. Sch. Social Workers, Columbia Alumni Assn., Nankai Alumni Assn. (v.p. 1991-94), Am. Voters Assn., Asian-Am. Dem. Assn. Episcopalian. Avocations: flute, tai chi, swimming, reading. Home: 77-11 35th Ave Apt 2P Jackson Heights NY 11372 E-mail: stockchang@mac.com.

CHANG, MARIAN S., filmmaker, composer; b. Atlanta, Aug. 19, 1958; d. C. H. Joseph and C. S. (Chun) Chang. MusB, Harvard U., Cambridge, Mass., 1981; MFA in Film Making, Columbia U., N.Y.C., 1994. Composer, dir., choreographer Exptl. Theatre, Dance, Boston, 1981-88; composer for modern dance co. Performing Arts Ensemble, Boston, 1986-88; co-dir., choreographer, performer Theatre S., Boston, 1987-88; prodr., dir., writer, sound designer, composer N.Y.C., 1991—. Founder, prodr. Shy Artists Prodns., Boston, N.Y.C., 1988—94. Recipient 1st prize, Kansas City Music Scholarship Competition, 1976, Nino Cerruti Film award, 1995; fellow, Mass. Artists' Fellowship Program in Choreography, 1987, Mass. Artists' Fellowship Program in Music Composition, 1988; grantee, N.Y. Coun. Humanities, 1998. Achievements include first artist in Mass. Artists' Fellowship Program to receive awards in both music and choreography. Home: 220 E 27th St Apt 7 New York NY 10016-9234

CHANG, MONA MEI-HSUAN, computer programmer, analyst; b. NYC, Sept. 7, 1962; d. Meng-Hsiu and Lydia Chia-Hwa (Chu) C. BA in Computer Sci. and Biochemistry, Columbia U., 1985, MA in Med. Informatics, 1997, MPhil in Med. Informatics, 1999. Data mgr. NY Hosp., Cornell U. Med. Ctr., NYC, 1990—92, computer programmer analyst, 1992—96; trainee in med. informatics Nat. Libr. Medicine, Columbia U., NYC, 1999—2001; rsch. data coord. Meml. Sloan-Kettering Cancer Ctr., NYC, 2002—. Mem. Cancer and Leukemia Group B (chmn. computer com. for data mgrs. 1990-92), Iota Sigma Pi. Avocations: chinese butterfly harp, chinese watercolor painting, tennis. Home: 549 W 123rd St Apt 19F New York NY 10027-5041 E-mail: changm@mskcc.org.

CHANG, NANCY T., pharmaceutical executive; b. Taiwan; PhD in Biological Chemistry, Harvard Med. Sch. Dir. rsch. Molecular Biology Group Centocor Inc., 1981—86; founder Tanox Inc., 1986, pres., 1986—, CEO, 1990—, chmn. bd. dir., 1986—2003; with Roche Inst. of Molecular Biology, 1980—81. Assoc. prof. molecular virology Baylor Coll. Medicine; bd. dir. Biotechnology Industry Orgn., Houston Tech. Ctr., BioHouston, Greater Houston Partnership. Contbr. articles to profl. jour. Named Houston Entrepreneur of Yr.; named one of Top 20 Houston Women in Tech.; named to Tex. Sci. Hall of Fame, 2001. Office: Tanox Inc 10555 Stella Link Houston TX 77025-5631

CHANG, PATTI, foundation administrator; b. Hawaii; BA in Internat. Rels., Stanford U., JD. Pres., CEO Women's Found., San Francisco, 1993—2003, Women's Found. Calif., San Francisco, 2003—. Past commr. San Francisco Commn. on the Environment. Mem.: Women's Inst. for Leadership Devel. for Human Rights (mem. adv. bd.), San Francisco Commn. on the Status of Women (past pres.), Nat. Com. for Responsible Philanthropy (nat. adv. bd.), GenderPAC (nat. adv. bd.), Women's Leadership Alliance, Asian Pacific Am. Women's Leadership Inst. (bd. mem.), Women's Funding network (chair bd. dirs., bd. mem.). Office: Womens Found Calif Ste 302 340 Pine St San Francisco CA 94014

CHANG, SOPHIA HO YING C., pediatrician; b. Shanghai, Mar. 21, 1923; arrived in U.S., 1948; d. Zia Pieu Chien and Shu Jean Li; m. Charles Chi Chang, Dec. 16, 1950 (dec.); children: Betty W., Nancy C. Amberson. BS, St. John's Univ., Shanghai, 1945, MD, 1948; postgrad. in Pediat., Harvard Med. Sch., Boston, 1950. Intern Washington County Hosp., Hagerstown, Md., 1948—49; resident in pediat. New Eng. Hosp. for Women and Children, Boston, 1949—50; sr. pediat. resident St. Paul's Hosp., Dallas, 1951—52; resident in contagious diseases Willard Parker Hosp., NYC, 1952—54; rsch. fellow in virology, instr. pediat. NYU-Bellevue Med. Ctr., NYC, 1955—56; asst. prof. pediat. Downstate Med. Coll., Bklyn., 1956—99. Pres. Bklyn. Acad. Pediat., 1978. Recipient scholarship, AAUW, 1950. Fellow: Am. Assn. Pediat.

CHANG, SUN-YUNG ALICE, mathematics professor; b. Ci-an, China, Mar. 24, 1948; came to U.S., 1970; d. Fann Chang and Li-Ching Chen; m. Paul Chien-Ping Yang, Mar. 24, 1973; children: Ray Yang, Lusann Yang. BS, Nat. Taiwan U., 1970; PhD, U. Calif., Berkeley, 1974. Asst. prof. math. U. Md., College Park, 1977-79; prof. UCLA, 1981—, Princeton U., 1998—. Speaker Internat. Congress of Math., 1986, 2002. Sloan Found. fellow, 1977, 78; Guggenheim fellow, 1999. Mem. Am. Math. Soc. (v.p. 1989, 90, Ruth Lyttle Satter prize 1995), Am. Women in Math. Office: Princeton Univ/Dept Math Fine Hall Washington Rd Princeton NJ 08544-1000 Office Phone: 609-258-5114. Business E-Mail: chang@math.princeton.edu.

CHANG, SYLVIA TAN, health facility administrator, educator; b. Bandung, Indonesia, Dec. 18, 1940; came to U.S., 1963. d. Philip Harry and Lydia Shui-Yu (Ou) Tan; m. Belden Shiu-Wah Chang, Aug. 30, 1964 (dec. Aug. 1997); children: Donald Steven, Janice May. Diploma in nursing, Rumah Sakit Advent Indonesia, 1960; BS, Philippine Union Coll., 1962; MS, Loma Linda U., 1967; PhD, Columbia Pacific U., 1987. Cert. RN, PHN, ACLS, BLS instr., cmty. first aid instr., IV, TPN, blood withdrawal. Head nurse Rumah Sakit Advent, Bandung, Indonesia, 1960—61; critical care, spl. duty and medicine nurse, team leader White Meml. Med. Ctr., L.A., 1963—64; nursing coord. Loma Linda U. Med. Ctr., 1964—68; team leader, critical care nurse, relief head nurse Pomona Valley Hosp. Med. Ctr., Calif., 1966—67; evening supr. Loma Linda U. Med. Ctr., 1967—69, night supr., 1969—79, adminstrv. supr., 1979—94; sr. faculty Columbia Pacific U., San Rafael, Calif., 1986—94; dir. health svc. La Sierra U., Riverside, Calif., 1988—. Site coord. Health Fair Expo La Sierra U., 1988-89; adv. coun. Family Planning Clinic, Riverside, 1988-94; blood and bone marrow drive coord. La Sierra U., 1988—. Counselor Pathfinder Club Campus Hill Ch., Loma Linda, 1979-85, crafts instr., 1979-85, music dir., 1979-85; asst. organist U. Ch., 1982-88. Named one of Women of Achievement YWCA, Greater Riverside C. of C., The Press Enterprise, 1991, 2000, Safety Coord. of Yr. La Sierra U., 1995. Mem. Am. Coll. Health Assn., Pacific Coast Coll. Health Assn., Adventist Student Pers. Assn., Sigma Theta Tau. Republican. Seventh-day Adventist. Avocations: music, travel, collecting coins, shells and jade carvings. Home: 1025 Crestbrook Dr Riverside CA 92506-5662 Office: 4500 Riverwalk Pkwy Riverside CA 92515-8247 Office Phone: 951-785-2200. Business E-Mail: schang@lasierra.edu.

CHANG, VIVIAN K., orthopedist, surgeon; b. N.Y.C., June 25, 1959; d. Victor C.L. Chang and Eun Sook Kim. Cert. Am. Bd. Orthop. Surgery. Chief divsn. orthop. surgery Tuba City Regional Health Care Corp., Ariz., 2001—. Office: Tuba City Regional Health Care Corp 101 N Main PO Box 600 Tuba City AZ 86045-0600 Office Phone: 928-283-2400.

CHANG, YUAN, neuropathologist, researcher, educator; m. Patrick S. Moore, 1989. MD, U. Utah. Neuropathologist, rschr. Columbia U., NY, 1992, prof. pathology, 1992; prof. dept. pathology U. Pitts. Sch. Medicine, 2002—. Mem. editl. bd.: Am. Jour. Pathology, Jour. Human Virology; contbr. articles and reviews in medical literature with Patrick S. Moore. Recipient Meyenburg Found. award Cancer Rsch., Robert Koch Prize, NYC Mayor's award for Excellence in Sci. and Tech., Paul A. Marks Prize, Meml. Sloan-Kettering Cancer Ctr., 2003, Charles S. Mott prize, GM Cancer Rsch. Found., 2003. Achievements include discovery of causative agent of Kaposi's Sarcoma-associated Herpes virus or human herpes virus 8; research in disorders that involve a compromised immune system.*

CHANG-ROBBINS, JOYCE, diversified financial services company executive; b. Knoxville, Iowa, May 22, 1965; m. David I. Robbins; children: Matthew, Isabel. Degree, Columbia U., 1986; M in Pub. Affairs, Princeton U., Woodrow Wilson Sch. Pub. and Internat. Affairs, 1990. Intern Ms. Magazine; cons. US AID, Manila, Philippines, Amman, Jordan, New Delhi; emerging mktg. strategist Saloman Brothers, 1990—96; mng. dir., global head of internat. emerging markets rsch. Merrill Lynch, 1996—99; mng. dir., global head fgn. exchange, emerging markets and commodities rsch. group JP Morgan Chase & Co., NY, 1999—. Named Number One Emerging Markets Strategists, Institutional Investor, Euromoney, 2004; named one of 50 Women to Watch, Wall Street Journal, 2005. Office: JP Morgan Chase & Co 270 Park Ave New York NY 10017-2014*

CHANNELL, LINDA GUYNES, education educator; d. Cecil George and Mae Nell Guynes; m. Ronnie Lee Channell, Dec. 15, 1951; children: Jennifer Leigh, Preston Truett. M Elem. Edn., Miss. Coll., 1995; M Reading Edn., Jackson State U., 1996, D Early Childhood Edn., 2000. Tchr. Capiah County

Schs., Crystal Springs, Miss., 1990—99, Jackson (Miss.) Pub. Schs., 1999—2001; asst. prof. Jackson State U., 2001—. Cons. Edn. and Cmty. Connections Cons., Jackson, 2005—. Assoc. mem. Crystal Springs Jr. Aux., 1990—. Recipient Light House Svc. Learning award, 2004. Mem.: ASCD, Reading First Tchr. Edn. Network (nat. evaluator, cons.), Internat. Reading Assn. Baptist. Office: Jackson State U 1400 Jr Lynch St Jackson MS 39217

CHANNING, STOCKARD (SUSAN ANTONIA WILLIAMS STOCKARD), actress; b. NYC, Feb. 13, 1944; d. Lester Napier and Mary Alice Stockard; m. Walter Channing, Jr., 1963 (div. 1967); m. Paul Schmidt, 1970 (div. 1976); m. David Debin, 1976 (div. 1980); m. David Rawle, 1982 (div. 1988). Attended, Radcliffe Coll.; BA in History and Lit., Harvard U. Actress movies include Up the Sandbox, 1972, The Fortune, 1975, The Big Bus, 1976, Sweet Revenge, 1977, The Cheap Detective, 1978, Grease, 1978, A Different Approach, 1978, The Fish That Saved Pittsburgh, 1979, Safari 3000, 1982, Without a Trace, 1983, The Men's Club, 1986, Heartburn, 1986, A Time of Destiny, 1988, Staying Together, 1989, Meet the Applegates, 1991, Married To It, 1991, Lunes de Fiel, 1992, Six Degrees of Separation (Acad. award nomination Best Actress), 1993, To Wong Foo, Thanks for Everything! Julie Newmar, 1995, Smoke, 1995, The First Wives Club, 1996, Up Close and Personal, 1996, Moll Flanders, 1996, Edie and Pen, 1997, Twilight, 1998, Lulu on the Bridge (voice), 1998, Practical Magic, 1998, The Venice Project, 1999, Other Voices, 2000, Isn't She Great, 2000, Where the Heart Is, 2000, The Business of Strangers, 2001, Life or Something Like It, 2002, Behind the Red Door, 2002, Bright Young Things, 2003, Le Divorce, 2003, Anything Else, 2003, Must Love Dogs, 2005; TV movies include Girl Most Likely to., 1973, Lucan, 1977, Silent Victory: The Kitty O'Neill Story, 1979, Table Settings, 1984, Not My Kid, 1985, The Room Upstairs, 1987, Echoes in the Darkness, 1987, Tidy Endings, 1988, Perfect Witness, 1989, Lincoln, 1992, David's Mother, 1994, Mr. Willowby's Christmas Tree, 1995, An Unexpected Family, 1996, Lily Dale, 1996, The Prosecutors, 1996, An Unexpected Family, 1996, An Unexpected Life, 1998, The Baby Dance, 1998, The Truth About Jane, 2000, Confessions of an Ugly Stepsister, 2002, The Matthew Shepard Story, 2002 (Emmy Outstanding Supporting Actress in a Miniseries or a Movie, SAG award), Hitler: The Rise of Evil, 2003, The Piano Man's Daughter, 2003, Jack, 2004 (Outstadning Performer in a Children's Spl., Daytime Emmy award, Acad. TV Arts & Scis., 2005); TV series include Sesame Street, 1969, The Stockard Channing Show, 1980, Road to Avonlea, King of the Hill (voice), Batman Beyond (voice), 1999, The West Wing, 2001-06 (Emmy Outstanding Supporting Actress in a Drama Series 2002), Out of Practice, 2005-; actress (plays) A Day in the Death of Joe Egg, 1985 (Tony Actress in a Play, 1985), House of Blue Leaves, Four Baboons Adoring the Sun, The Little Foxes, Hapgood, Women In Mind, The Rink, The Golden Age, The Lion in Winter, They're Playing Our Song, Love Letters; TV mini series A Girl Thing, 2001. Office: ICM c/o Andrea Eastman 40 W 57th St Fl 16 New York NY 10019-4098*

CHANYUNGCO, DELLY YANGCO, dean; b. Sept. 25, 1945; BS in Elem. Edn., Philippine Normal Coll., MA in Guidance and Counseling, 1982; PhD in Counseling Psychology, De La Salle U., U. Philippines, 1986. Vocat. placement coord./chief career guidance & placement svcs. Dept. Edn., Culture & Sports, Manila, 1979-86; student svcs. divsn. supr. Marikina Inst. Sci. and Tech., Philippines, 1986—90; internat. student advisor/coord. Truman Coll., Chgo., 1991—96; chief non-immigrant sect. Azulay & Azulay, P.C., 1996—2000; admin. and human resource dir. Azulay, Horn & Seiden, LLC, 2003—05; dean student affairs and employment Northwestern Inst. Health and Tech., Chgo., 2005—. Cons. in field. Vol. leader self-help programs Ravenswood Hosp. and Med. Ctr., Chgo.; vol. counselor APNA GHAR Inc., Chgo.; intake counselor DARE Found. Philippines; vol. cons. ASEAN Regional and Nat. Coun. Welfare and Disabled Persons. Named Outstanding Trainer, Tarlaac Divsn. Pub. Schs., Outstanding SNLP Coord., Dept. Edn., Culture and Sports; recipient Plaque of Recognition, Malaysia Vocational Guidance Assn., Kuala Lumpur, 1982, Plaque of Appreciation, Commonwealth Schs. Commn., Canberra, Australia, 1986, President's award of Recognition, Truman Coll., 1996, Pub. Svc. Merit award, Marikina Dist. Teacher's Club. Mem.: Assn. Am. Women Cmty. Colls., Nat. Notary Assn., Assn. Internat. Educators. Office: Northwestern Inst Health and Tech 4641 N Ashland Chicago IL 60640 E-mail: dchanyungco@sbcglobla.net.

CHAO, ELAINE LAN (HSIAO LAN CHAO), secretary of labor; b. Taipei, Taiwan, Mar. 26, 1953; d. James S.C. and Ruth M.L. (Chu) C.; m. Mitch McConnell, Feb. 6, 1993. AB, Mt. Holyoke Coll., 1975; MBA, Harvard U., 1979; LLD (hon.), Villanova U., 1989, St. John's U., 1991, Sacred Heart U., 1991, U. Notre Dame, 1998, St. Marys Coll., 2002, Fu-Jen Cath. U., 2003, Cath. U. Am., 2004; DHL (hon.), Niagara U., 1992, Bellarmine Coll., 1995, U. Toledo, 1995, Goucher Coll., 1996, U. Louisville, 1996, U. S.C., 2001, No. Ala. U., 2003, Centre Coll., 2003, Wingate U., 2004; DHum (hon.), Drexel U., 1992, Thomas More Coll., 1994, Ky. Wesleyan Coll., 1998; D Arts and Letters (hon.), Miami-Dade C.C., 2001; DPA (hon.), Campbellsville U., 2002, No. Ky. U., 2004; D Pub. Svcs. (hon.), DePauw U., 2002; D in Orgnl. Leadership (hon.), Regent U., 2003. Assoc. Gulf Oil Corp., Pitts., summer 1978; sr. lending officer Citicorp, NA, N.Y.C., 1979-83; v.p. capital markets group BankAmerica, San Francisco, 1984-86; dep. maritime adminstr. U.S. Dept. Transp., Washington, 1986-88; chmn. Fed. Maritime Commn., Washington, 1988; dep. sec. U.S. Dept. Transp., Washington, 1989-91; pres. United Way Am., Alexandria, Va., 1992-96; sr. editor, disting. fellow The Heritage Found., Washington; sec. U.S. Dept. Labor, Washington, 2001—. White House fellow, 1983-84; adj. asst. prof. Grad. Sch. Bus. Adminstrn., St. John's U., 1984; dir. Peace Corps., 1991-92. Recipient Young Achiever award Nat. Coun. Women U.S., Inc., 1986; Eisenhower Fellow Assn. fellow, 1984; named. one of 10 Outstanding Women of Am., 1988. Mem. Coun. on Fgn. Rels., Inc., Am. Coun. Young Polit. Leaders (bd. dirs. 1989), Harvard Bus. Sch. (vis. com. 1989, Outstanding Alumni award 1993), Harvard Club. Republican. Office: US Dept Labor Office of Sec 200 Constitution Ave NW Washington DC 20210*

CHAO, YU CHEN, cellist, educator; b. Fengshan, Taiwan, Feb. 26, 1961; came to U.S., 1987; d. Kun-Ho and Kuei-Lan (Ma) C. BA, Taung-Hai U., Taichung, Taiwan, 1985; MMus in Performance, Manahttan Sch. Music, 1990, MMus in Orch. Performance, 1994. Assoc. prin. N.Y. Chamber Sinfonia, N.Y.C., 1992-94; substitute Albany (N.Y.) Symphony Orch., 1995; assoc. prin. N.Y. Asiana Orch., N.Y.C., 1995-97. Solo recitalist St. Peter's Ch., N.Y.C., 1998, Riverside Ch., N.Y.C., 1998, Carnegie Hall/Weill Recital Hall, N.Y.C., 1998; music dir. Cello Allegro, Inc., N.Y.C., 1996—; founder, tchr. Harlem Cello Sch. Program, N.Y.C., 1999. Recipient Laura R. Conover Pedagogy award Cecilian Music Club, 1998, Schlarship award Elan Internat. Music Festival, 1998; winner Artist Internat. Competition, 1998, Alumni winner, 1999; Victoria Summer Festival scholar, 1992, Waterloo Summer Festival fellow, 1990; participating hon. 104th Congress at the White House, 1995. Avocations: gardening, photography, travel, checkers, charity works. Home: 302 W 107th St Apt 3B New York NY 10025-2716

CHAPELLE, SUZANNE ELLERY GREENE, history professor; b. Phila., Sept. 21, 1942; d. John Channing and Jessie Horn (Myers) Ellery; m. Michael Thomas Greene, Sept. 15, 1972 (dec. 1973); 1 child, Jennifer; m. Francis Oberlin Chapelle, Apr. 14, 1984 (dec. 1999). BA, Harvard U., 1964; MA, Johns Hopkins U., 1966, PhD, 1970. Asst. prof. Am. history Towson State U., Balt., 1969-71; assoc. prof. Am. history Morgan State U., Balt., 1971-75, prof., 1975—, coord., environ. studies program. Author: Books for Pleasure, 1976, Baltimore: An Illustrated History, 1980, 2d rev. edit., 2000; sr. author: Maryland: A History of its People, 1986; revisions author: A Child's History of the World, 1994, African American Leaders of Maryland, 2000, The Maryland Adventure, 2001; mem. publs. bd. Md. Hist. Soc. Bd. dir. Md. Interfaith Coalition for the Environment, 1997-2001, v.p., 1999-2001; bd. dirs. Md. Conservation Coun., 1999-2000; bd. trustees Irvine Nature Ctr., 2001—; mem. water quality adv. coun. Md., 2004-06; mem. Md. State Dept. Edn. Social Studies Task Force, 2004—. Mem. Am. Hist. Assn., Am. Studies Assn. (mem. exec. bd. Chesapeake chpt. 1988-90), Popular Culture Assn. (bd. dirs. 1980-82), Orgn. Am. Historians, Md. Hist. Soc. (publs. com. 1998—), Mid-Atlantic Popular Culture Assn. (pres. 1977-80), Balt. County League Environ. Voters (exec. bd. 1992-96), Episcopal Diocese of Md. Com. on the Environ. (sec. 1994-2003), Ruxton-Riderwood Assn. (bd. govs. 1987-91), The Johns Hopkins Club, The Harvard-Radcliffe Club Md. Episcopalian. Home: 6021 Lakeview Rd Baltimore MD 21210-1033 Office: Morgan State U Hist Dept Baltimore MD 21251-0001 Office Phone: 443-885-3190. Personal E-mail: suechapelle@yahoo.com.

CHAPLIN, PEGGY LOUIE, lawyer; b. Guantanamo Bay Naval Base, Cuba, Nov. 22, 1940; d. Raymond Gerard Fannon and Joan Marie (Carguil) Boyce. BS, Johns Hopkins U., 1971; JD, U. Md., 1973; LLM in Internat. Comml. Law, Georgetown U., 1983. Bar: Md. 1973, U.S. Dist. Ct. Md. 1973, U.S. Ct. Internat. Trade 1975, U.S. Ct. Appeals (fed. cir.) 1986, (D.C. cir.) 1988, U.S. Supreme Ct. 2003. V.p. Vanguard Shipping & Import, Balt., 1972-77, F.W. Myers & Co., Inc., Balt., 1977-84; assoc. Ober, Kaler, Grimes & Shriver, Balt., 1984-91, ptnr., 1992-97, Sandler, Travis & Rosenberg, P.A., Balt., 1997—. Chair Johns Hopkins U. Inst. of Policy Studies com. Logistics and the Economy, 1996-99. Contbr. articles to bar jours. Mem. Gov.'s Commn. World Trade Efforts, 1984, Balt. City Wage Commn., 1986-90, Md. Trade Policy Com., 1986; chair 2d Ann. Md. Internat. Trade Conf.; chair air cargo devel. com. BWI Econ. Devel. Coun., 1993-96. Mem.: NAFTA (chpt. 19 roster), Assn. Transp. Law Profls. (newsletter editor Import/Export Regulation), Am. Assn. Exporters and Importers, Am. Arbitration Assn. (panelist), Md. Internat. Trade Assn. (pres. 1984—86), Women's Bar Assn. Md. (pres. 1977—78), Md. State Bar Assn. (chair internat. comml. law sect. 1991—92), Md. C. of C. (chmn. internat. trade com. 1984—97). Office: Sandler Travis & Rosenberg PA 111 S Calvert St Ste 2700 Baltimore MD 21202-6143 Office Phone: 410-385-5208. E-mail: pchaplin@strtrade.com.

CHAPMAN, AMY L., religious studies educator; Bachelor, Boston Coll., 2004, Master, 2005. Cert. secondary history tchr. Mass. Tchr. Nativity Prep. Mid. Sch., Jamaica Plain, Mass., 2004—05, Natick H.S., Mass., 2005—. Dir. religious edn. St. Ignatius Ch., Mass., 2004—06. Recipient Henry P. Wittenberg, S.J. award, Boston Coll., 2004. Roman Cath. Avocations: travel, reading.

CHAPMAN, ANGELA MARIE, science educator; b. Wayne, Mich., Aug. 7, 1964; d. Hugh Richard and Sarah Treva Norris; m. Joseph Alfred Chapman, Jan. 5, 1985. BS in Zoology, Mich. State U., 1990; MS in Biology, U. Ky., 1994. Cert. profl. educator Fla. Tchg. asst. U. Ky., Lexington, 1991—93; adj. faculty Midway (Ky.) Coll., 1993; instr. Baker Coll., Flint, Mich., 1994—99; rsch. asst. Mich. State U., East Lansing, 1994—2000; prof., instr. Lansing (Mich.) C.C., 1999—2002, Polk C.C., Lakeland, Fla., 2003—; tchr. Polk County Schs., Lakeland, 2004—. Pres. C & S Works, Holt, Mich., 1995—2001; grad. student coun. Mich. State U., 1995—99, dean's student adv. coun., 1996—97; chairperson metric olympics com. Sleepy Hill Mid. Sch., Lakeland, 2003—, curriculum com. mem., 2005—; chairperson, textbook adoption, curriculum devel. Polk County Schs., Bartow, Fla., 2005—; co-director Polk Regional Sci. Fair, Bartow, 2005—; exec. dir., founder Sci. Explores Examines Discovers, Lakeland, 2006—. Author: Fundamentals of Neuroanatomy; contbr. articles various profl. jours. Named Tchr. of Yr., Sleepy Hill Mid. Sch., 2005; recipient Tchr. Hon., Disney, 2006; Summer fellowship, U. Ky., 1992, 1993, Rsch. fellowship, Mich. State U., 1995, Tchr. to Tchr. Developer grant, Polk Edn. Found., 2005, Classroom grant, Fla. Assn. Sci. Tchrs., 2005. Mem.: AAAS, AAUW, NEA, NSTA (point of light rep. 2004—06), Fla. Assn. Sci. Tchrs. Avocations: reading, travel, bicycling, photography. Office: Sleepy Hill Mid Sch 2215 Sleepy Hill Rd Lakeland FL 33810 Office Phone: 863-815-6577.

CHAPMAN, CAROLYN, broadcasting director; b. Portsmouth, Ohio, Feb. 4, 1933; d. Roger Donald and Flowery Alice (Callaway) Carr; diploma Portsmouth Interstate Bus. Coll., 1954, S. Ohio Manpower Tng. Ctr., 1965; m. Edward J. Chapman, May 13, 1966; children— Cheryl, Roger, Lisa, Mark, Edmond, Sean. Dep. probation officer Scioto County Juvenile Ct., Portsmouth, 1960-63: coder II, Aid for Aged, Ohio Dept. Pub. Welfare, Columbus, 1964; clk. typist II, Bur. Vital Stats., Dept. Health, Columbus, 1964, clk.-stenographer II, CD Div., 1966; clk.-stenographer ABC, Los Angeles, 1967, ops. coordinator, 1968-72, assoc. dir., on-air dir., 1972—; cons. in video tape and TV prodn.; mem. negotiating com. Teamsters Union, Los Angeles, 1970. Ch. sec. Findlay St. Meth. Ch., Portsmouth, 1959-63, chmn. women's day program, 1962, chmn. commn. on missions, 1959-62, del. ann. conf., Cleve., 1963, sec. ofcl. bd., 1959-62; pres. local chpt. Ohio Republican Council, 1959-62, mem. state bd., 1962, del. from Scioto County to State Rep. Conv., Ohio, 1962; mem. film editing com. Social Health and Hygiene Assn., 1961-62; tribute com. for Tribute to Dorothy Arzner, 1975; Los Angeles Jr. C. of C., 1977. Mem. ABC Employees Assn. (pres. Hollywood branch, 1971-73), Dirs. Guild Am. (council 1981-83). Address: PO Box 43025 Los Angeles CA 90043-0025

CHAPMAN, CYNTHIA B., lawyer; b. Bronxville, New York, July 7, 1965; BA in Art History, U. of Calif., San Diego, 1988; JD, U. of San Diego Law School, 1992. Bar: Texas, California. Assoc. English & Gloven, LLP, Seltzer, Caplan, Wilkens, and McMahon; partner Caddell & Chapman. Named one of top 50 Litigators, Nat. Law Journal, 2001, top 40 under 40 most successful litigators, 2002, Houston's 200 Best Lawyers, H Tex. Mag., 2005. Mem.: Houston Bar Assoc., Assoc. of Trial Lawyers of Am., Trial Lawyers for Public Justice. Office: Caddell & Chapman The Park in Houston Center 1331 Lamar Houston TX 77010

CHAPMAN, DALAINE, music educator; b. Syracuse, NY, Nov. 15, 1960; d. Harold Leonard and Ann Naum Chapman. AA, Brevard CC, Cocoa, Fla., 1980; B in Music Edn., Fla. State U., 1983, M in Music Edn., 2002. Cert. music tchr. (kindergarten through twelfth grade) Fla. Band dir. Bartow HS, Fla., 1984—88, S.W. Jr. High, Palm Bay, Fla., 1988—98, Bayside HS, Palm Bay, Fla., 1998—2001, Titusville HS, 2002—03; supr. music Brevard Pub. Schs., 2003—. Named Tchr. of Yr., S.W. Jr. High, 1994, Bayside HS, 1998; recipient 5 Yr. Superior award, 1993, 1998. Mem.: Music Educators Nat. Conf., Fla. Music Suprs. Assn. (sec.), Fla. Music Educators Assn., Nat. Band Assn., Fla. Bandmasters Assn. (7th and 8th grade chairperson, mid. sch., jr. high rep. 1996—98, all state band condr., clinician 1999, Benevolence com. chair 2000—, adjudicator 2002—, 5 Yr. Superior award 1993, 1998), Phi Beta Mu. Home: 2411 Windchaser Ct West Melbourne FL 32904

CHAPMAN, DELORES, elementary school educator; b. Chgo., June 22, 1945; d. John Calvin and Julia (Frazier) C. AA, Kennedy-King Coll., 1966; BA, Northeastern Ill. U., 1968, MA, 1979. Tchr. Chgo. Bd. Edn., 1968—; v.p. Chapman's Security Systems, Inc., Country Club Hills, Ill., 1990—. Chpt. I reading tchr. Fed. Govt./Chgo. Bd. Edn., Chgo. Archdiocese, 1982-85; mem. profl. poers. adv. com. Carver Primary Sch., Chgo., 1990—, chmn. sci. fair, 1987-91. Vice chmn. Emmanuel Christian Sch. Bd., Chgo., 1992-96, chmn., 1996-2002; dir. Emmanual Bapt. Ch. Children's Choir, 1973-2003. Chgo. Found. for Edn. grantee, 1992. Mem. NAACP, ASCD, Nat. Sci. Tchrs. Assn., Ill. Sci. Tchrs. Assn., Northeastern Ill. U. Alumni Assn., Ill. Coun. Tchrs. Math. Avocations: playing the piano, reading. Home: 936 Garden Ln Homewood IL 60430-2046

CHAPMAN, ELIZABETH NINA, counselor; b. Canton, N.Y., July 5, 1947; d. Kenneth Wallace and Kathryne Mary (Moulton) Loucks; children: Scott, Brian, Lori, Katie. RN, Hepburn Sch. Nursing, Ogdensburg, NY, 1968; BS in Profl. Arts, St. Joseph's Coll., North Windham, Maine, 1981; M in Counseling, Internat. Sem., Plymouth, Fla., 1991. RN, N.Y.; bd. cert. faith-based therapist; lic. min. Counselor, speaker, writer Restoration Svcs., DeKalb Jct., NY. Author: Patchwork, 1987. Mem. Nat. Right to Life. Mem.: Internat. Inst. Faith (bd. counseling 2004—), Am. Assn. Christian Counselors.

CHAPMAN, FAY L., lawyer; b. San Jose, Calif., Dec. 17, 1946; BA, UCLA, 1968; JD, NYU, 1972. Bar: N.Y. 1973, Wash. 1975. Atty. Foster Pepper & Shefelman, Seattle, 1979—97; exec. v.p., gen. counsel Washington Mutual, Inc., Seattle, 1997—99; sr. exec. v.p., gen. counsel Washington Mutual Inc, Seattle, 1999—. Mem. Amer Bar Assn., Wash. Bankers Assn., Wash. Savs. League. Office: Washington Mutual Inc 1301 2nd Ave Ste 3301 Seattle WA 98101

CHAPMAN, GENEVA JOYCE, entrepreneur, educator, writer; b. Calvert, Tex., Sept. 23, 1951; d. John Henry and Deborah Betty Chapman. BA, Cameron U., 1973; MEd, Wichita State U., 1976; EdSp in early intervention edn., U. Toledo, 1997. Cert. tchr., Ohio. Tchr.'s aide Newton Pub. Schs., Kans., 1973—74; classroom tchr. Wichita Pub. Schs., 1976—83; ednl. cons. Ginn and Co., Columbus, Ohio, 1984—86; vol. coord. Friends of Homeless Shelter, Columbus, 1986—88; family life educator Pilot Program, Toledo, 1988—89; journalist Toledo Jour., 1989—91; behavior mgmt. specialist Lucas County Bd. Mental Retardation/Devel. Disabilities, Toledo, 1991—98, tchr. spl. edn., 1998—99, habilitation specialist, 1999—; CEO TALMAR, Toledo, 1993—. Dir. Showcase Prodns. divsn. TALMAR. Newspaper columnist Chit-Chat, 1989-1995; reporter The Sojourner's Truth Newspaper, 2002; editor The Holland Herald, 2002; author (musical comedy) The Race, 1975, (musical): A Marvel, A Miracle, America, 1982, (drama) B.R.AIDS, 1990; founder a Capella duo Two Voices Only, 1991; mem. Spectrum, women's music group, 1989-95; creator Ms. Hipps comic strip, 1984; featured playwright Chgo. Dramatist Workshops, 1993-94; writer, dir., prodr. original musical drama: Juneteenth, 1990. Founder Toledo Blackstage Theatre Co., 1990, playwright-in-residence; founder For Colored Girls Repertory Co., 1994; mem. Da' Coloured Gurlz Collective, 1995—; U.S. del. World AIDS Conf., Paris, 1990 Recipient Community Svc. Fine Arts award Save Our Children, 1993. Mem. NEA (bldg. supr. 1974-79), NAFE, Am. Fedn. Tchrs., Nat. Assn. to Advance Fat Acceptance (Toledo kwanzaa com. 1992—, bd. trustees 2004—) Avocations: acting, writing and directing plays, singing. Office Phone: 419-243-0007. E-mail: gjcinc@yahoo.com.

CHAPMAN, HOPE HORAN, psychologist; b. Chgo., Feb. 13, 1954; d. Theodore George and Idelle (Poll) H.; m. Stuart G. Chapman, Dec. 4, 1983. BS, U. Ill., Champaign-Urbana, 1976; MA, No. Ill. U., DeKalb, 1979; cert. lawyer's asst. program, Roosevelt U., Chgo., 1996, 97; student, Ballet Russe Sch., 1999—2002. Lic. pharmacy technician, Ill.; diplomate Am. Bd. Disability Analysts. Psychologist Glenwood State Hosp. Sch., Iowa, 1979-83, Gov. Samuel H. Shapiro Devel. Ctr., Kankakee, Ill., 1985-86, dir. staff tng. and devel. Glenkirk, 1988-90; clin. assoc. Bennett & Assocs., 1990-91; psychologist Singer Mental Health & Devel. Ctr., Rockford, Ill., 1992-93; forensic psychologist Elgin Mental Health Ctr., Ill., 1993-94. Contbr. articles to profl. jours., papers to confs. Active Omaha Symphonic Chorus, 1981-83; mem. Omaha Pub. Schs. Citizens Adv. Com., 1980-81; mem. edn. com. Anti-Defamation League, 1980-85, chmn. com. anti-Semitism and Jewish youth, 1983; commr. youth commn. Village of Hoffman Estates, Ill., 1988-94; vice chmn. oversight com. Vogelei Teen Ctr., 1988-94; commr. Environ. Commn., Village of Hoffman Estates, 1994-2000, chmn. Schaumburg Twp. Mental Health Bd., 1993-94; election judge Cook County, 1992—; judge's asst. Cook County Cir. Ct., 1996-2004, membership chmn. Chicagoland chpt. U.S. Amateur Ballroom Dancers Assn. 2003; mem. coun. Roosevelt U. Alumni Bd., Robin campus, 2004-05; counselor Life Span Crisis Line, 2005—. State of Ill. scholar. Fellow Am. Coll. Forensic Examiners; mem. APA, Am. Bd. Disability Analysts, Ill. Paralegal Assn. (Pro Bono Svc. award 2004, 05, 06), Salt Creek Ballet Guild, Phi Kappa Phi, Psi Chi. Jewish. Personal E-mail: Hopehcmail@cs.com.

CHAPMAN, JACQUELYN SULLIVAN, retired elementary school educator; b. Chgo., June 6, 1928; d. Harold Patrick and Alyce Cecilia (Hagan) Sullivan; m. James H. Chapman, June 23, 1951; children: Kevin, Brian, Mark. BA, Clark Coll., Dubuque, Iowa, 1949; MusM, DePaul U., 1951; student, U. Galney, 1980, Coll. New Rochelle. Tchr. music various jr. high and high schs., spl. edn. educator, cons. Chgo. Bd. Edn., 1950-93; ret., 1993. Vol. Park Ridge (Ill.) Garden Club, 1972—, 20th Century Club, Park Ridge, 1993—, Park Ridge Women's Club, 1993—; active Found. Internat. Rels., Chgo., 1993—. Mem.: Clarke Coll. Alumnae Assn. (pres. 1960—65), Delta Kappa Gamma (pres. Kappa chpt. 1990—92, chmn. sect. music 1974—90). Roman Catholic. Avocations: travel, piano, literature, European antiques, opera. Home: 1604 S Western Ave Park Ridge IL 60068-5066

CHAPMAN, JUDITH GRIFFIN, psychologist, educator, academic administrator; b. Kane, Pa., Oct. 22, 1949; d. Leon B. and Shirley J. (Winslow) Griffin; m. Robert J. Chapman, Jan. 16, 1971; children: Jessica Lynn, Joshua Griffin. BA cum laude, St. Bonaventure, N.Y., 1971, MA, 1975; PhD with distinction, Syracuse (N.Y.) U., 1987. Instr. psychology U. Pitts., Bradford, 1972-74, Empire State Coll., Buffalo Regional Learning Ctr., 1976-77; instr. psychology Jamestown C.C., Olean, N.Y., 1975-83; cons. Syracuse Rsch. Corp., 1984-85; lectr. SUNY, Oneonta, 1987-88; assoc. prof. psychology St. Joseph's U., Phila., 1988—, prof., 2000—, dean Coll. Arts and Scis., 1996—2002, assoc. provost, 2005—. Contbr. articles to profl. jours. PHEA acad. scholar, 1967-71 Mem. Am. Psychol. Soc. (charter), Ea. Psychol. Assn., Soc. for Personality and Social Psychology, Soc. for Advancement Social Psychology, Sigma Xi, Psi Chi. Office: St Josephs U 5600 City Ave Philadelphia PA 19131-1308

CHAPMAN, KARINA M., elementary school educator; d. Clemente and Maria A. Cantu; m. Kenton W. Chapman, Nov. 24, 1990; 1 child, Madalyn R. BA, Calif. State U., Sacramento, 1989. K-8 profl. tchg. credential Calif., 1992, K-8 tchg. credential Maine, 1995. Columnist, freelance photographer, writer Eureka Times-Standard Newspaper, Calif., 1984—86; clerical asst. dean's office health and human svcs. Calif. State U., Sacramento, 1986—89, clerical asst. tchr. preparation offices Sch. Edn., 1989—91; sec. tax dept. KPMG Peat Marwick LLP, Sacramento, 1993—95; tchr. grade 5 Maine Sch. Adminstrn. Dist. #60, Lebanon Elem. Sch., 1996—2003; sci. tchr. grade 8 Maine Sch. Adminstrn. Dist. #60 - Noble Mid. Sch., Berwick, Maine, 2003—. Cohort 2 fellow Maine Govs. Acad. for Sci. and Math. Edn. Leadership Maine Math and Sci. Alliance, Augusta, 2003—05; sci. and conceptual change collaborative grant tchr. leader level 1 MSAD #60 / Maine Math and Sci. Alliance, Berwick, 2005—06. Exhibitions include Chevron Photography Competition (first prize, 1985). Publicist Lebanon Elem. Online Auction Fundraiser Lebanon Elem. Sch., 1999—2002. Nominee Disney Creative Tchr. award, 2005—06. Mem.: Nat. Sci. Tchrs. Assn. Avocations: travel, writing, photography, reading, scrapbooks. Office: Noble Mid Sch 46 Cranberry Meadow Rd Kennebunkport ME 04046 Personal E-mail: chapmanx3@verizon.net.

CHAPMAN, LAURA HILL, art education consultant; b. Miami, Fla., Apr. 24, 1935; d. Rob Kelly and Flora Margaret (Cochrane) C. BS cum laude, Fla. State U., 1957; MA, NYU, 1960; PhD, Ohio State U., 1966. Art tchr. Cin. Pub. Schs., 1970-71, Dade County Schs., Miami, Fla., 1957-59; instr. art edn. Ind. U., Bloomington, 1957-59, Ohio State U., Columbus, 1962-64, asst. prof. art edn., 1966-70, Univ. Ill., Champaign-Urbana, 1964-66; assoc. prof. art edn. U. Cin., 1971-73, prof. art edn., 1973-78; cons., writer art edn. pvt. practice, Cin., 1978—. Cons. Nat. Instructional TV, Bloomington, Ind., 1966-68, 72-79, Ohio State Dept. Edn., Columbus, 1969-73, 74-75, Nat. Assessment of Ednl. Progress, Denver, 1976-79, 80-81, NEA, Washington, 1986-87, J. Paul Getty Trust Programs on Edn. in Art, L.A., 1982-87; mem. editorial bd. 7 jours., 1975-87. Author: Approaches to Art in Education, 1978, Instant Art, Instant Culture: The Unspoken Policy for American Schools, 1982, Discover Art 1-6, 1985, Teaching Art 1-6, 1988, Art: Images and Ideas, 1991, A World of Images, 1991, Maken is De Kunst, 1992, Adventures in Art, 1993, Didaktike tes Technes, 1993; contbr. numerous articles to profl. jours. Program coord. Nat. Sculpture Conf., Cin., 1986-87; evaluator art curriculum Tex. State Dept. Edn., 1988-90, tchr. edn. in art, U.S. Dept. Defense Dependent Schs., Atlantic Region and Germany, 1991 Recipient Vis. Faculty fellowship Western Australia Inst. Tech., Perth, 1980, Corbett award Cin. Post and Corbett Found., 1988, Hon. award Mid Am. Coll. Art Assn., 1989, Gov.'s award in the arts Ohio Arts Coun., 1994. Mem. Nat. Art Edn. Assn. (sr. editor Studies in Art Edn. 1977-79, lectr. 1984, McFee award 1978, Disting. fellow,

1985, Nat. Art Educator of Yr. 1997, Disting. Svc. award, 2005, Zeigleld award, 2005, Barkan award, 2006), Ohio Art Edn. Assn. (Art Educator of Yr. 1987), Am. Ednl. Rsch. Assn. Office: Brighton Pl Office 2159 Colerain Ave Cincinnati OH 45214

CHAPMAN, LINDA LEE, computer company executive, consultant; b. Omaha, Apr. 27, 1965; d. Olin Parks Chapman and Phyllis May Chapman-Wakefield; m. Chris Barkley; children: Lea Lee Noell, Phillip Wayne Noell, Cameron David Barkley, Jasmine Lauren Barkley. Grad., Centennial H.S., Utica, Nebr., 1983. MCSE, MCP Microsoft, cert. product specialist NT 4.0 Enterprise Microsoft, product Ssecialist NT 4.0 Workstation Microsoft, product specialist NT 4.0 Server Microsoft, product specialist IIS 3.0 and Index Server Microsoft. LAN mgr. and programmer Wiig-Codr Underwriters, Omaha, 1986—93; sr. IT engr. MCI Consumer Markets, Austin, Tex., 1993—94; sr. migration cons. Levi-Strauss & Co., San Fransisco, 1994—95, Advanced Micro Devices (AMD), Austin, 1995—96; sr. migration cons., tech. project mgr. Continental Airlines, Houston, 1996—97; sr. migration cons., global arch. Dell Computer Corp., Round Rock, Tex., 1997—99, sr. product mgr., 1999—2000; pres., CEO, founder Migration Specialists Inc., Round Rock, 2001—. Recipient Outstanding Tech. Article award, 2000. E-mail: linda@migrationspecialists.com.

CHAPMAN, MARGARET ELIZABETH, elementary school educator; b. Haverstraw, N.Y., Aug. 12, 1946; d. William David Sr. and Pauline Ann (Newell) C.; divorced June 1978; 1 child, Jennifer. Student, Rockland Community Coll., 1964-67; BS in Edn., St. Thomas Aquinas Coll., 1975; postgrad., Fairfield U., 1977. Cert. elem. tchr., counselor, N.Y. Elem. tchr. Immaculate Conception Sch., Stony Point, NY, 1967-72; elem. tchr. Haverstraw-Stony Point Sch. Dist., Garnerville, NY, 1975—. Counselor Haverstraw-Stony Point Sch. Dist., Garnerville, 1988—; tchr. liason, PTA, 1999—; student coun. advisor, 2000—; mem. health adv. coun., mid. sch. adv. coun; bd. dirs. Rockland Tchrs. Ctr. Bd. dirs. Rockland Coun. on Alcoholism, Nyack, N.Y., 1989—; developer Impact II, 1987, adaptor, 1989; com. mem. Am. Cancer Soc. Relay for Life Kids Walk. AIDS Mini grantee Regional Health Ctr., Yorktown Heights, N.Y., 1989, Bus. Week grantee Bus. Week Mag., 1990. Mem. Rockland Tchrs.' Ctr. (bldg. rep., co-chairperson 1986-88), Assn. for Supervision and Curriculum Devel. Roman Catholic. Avocations: travel, tutoring, counseling, curriculum writing. Home: 44 Blauvelt Ave West Haverstraw NY 10993-1307 Office: Haverstraw Stony Point Cen Sch Dist 65 Chapel St Garnerville NY 10923-1238 Office Phone: 845-942-3200. Personal E-mail: mchap2@aol.com.

CHAPMAN, MARY KATHRYN, elementary school educator; b. Birmingham, Ala., May 31, 1958; d. Vincent and Mary Helen (Treadwell) York; m. Jere Clark Chapman, Dec. 18, 1982; children: Lacy Dawn, John Luke. BS in Edn., Auburn U., 1980, MS, 1982. Cert. tchr., Ala., Tex. Tchr. elem. Fews Elem Sch., Montgomery, 1980—83; tchr. elem., computer rep. Morningview Elem. Sch., Montgomery, 1988—91; tchr. phys. edn. Jackson Elem. Sch., Abilene, Tex., 1983—85, Austin Elem. Sch., Abilene, 1986—87; tchr. W.L. Radney Elem. Sch., Alexander City, Ala., 1991—98, tchr. drama, 1991—94, mem. bldg. leadership team, 1994—95; tchr. Alexander City Mid. Sch., 1998—. Workshop presenter Montgomery Schs., 1990. Sunday sch. and Bible sch. tchr. Alexander City Ch. of Christ, 1991—; adult leader Girl Scouts U.S.A., Alexander City, 1992—; sponsor Alexander City Cheerleaders, 1992. Named Tchr. of Yr., Alexander City Sch., 1993, Alexander City C. of C., 1993; recipient Class Act award Sta. WSFA-TV, Montgomery, 1994. Mem. NEA, Ala. Edn. Assn. Avocations: gymnastics, swimming, reading, sewing, jogging. Home: 1953 Morningside Dr Alexander City AL 35010-3154 Office: Alexander City Mid Sch 359 State St Alexander City AL 35010 Business E-Mail: kchapman@alex.k12.al.us.

CHAPMAN, ROBYN LEMON, music educator; b. Ogden, Utah, Jan. 17, 1974; d. Kent Lowell Lemon and Joanette Avonne Emery, Steven George Piccoli (Stepfather) and Cathy S. Lemon (Stepmother), Rick Alden Emery (Stepfather); m. Christopher Carl Chapman, Apr. 8, 2001. MusB, U. Nev. Las Vegas, 1998. License for Educational Personnel Nev., 1998, Residential Education Certificate Wash. Supt. of Pub. Instrn., 2002. Long term substitute Mike O'Callaghan Mid. Sch., Las Vegas, 1998, band dir., 1998—2001, Theron Swainston Mid. Sch., North Las Vegas, 2001—02; music specialist Totem Falls Elem. Sch., Snohomish, Wash., 2002—05. Camp adminstr. U. of Nev., Las Vegas Bands, 1993—2002; mid. sch. honor band chair Clark County Sch. Dist., Las Vegas, 2000—02. Recipient New Tchr. of the Yr., Clark County Sch. Dist., 1998—99. Mem.: Women Band Dirs. Internat., Wash. Music Educators Assn., Nat. Band Assn., Music Educators Nat. Conf. D-Conservative. Mem. Lds Ch. Avocations: reading, bicycling, bowling. E-mail: robyn_chapman@msn.com.

CHAPMAN, SALLY, chemistry professor; b. Phila., July 28, 1946; d. Robert Francis and Gwen (Jenkins) C. AB summa cum laude, Smith Coll., 1968; PhD, Yale U., 1973. Asst. prof. Barnard Coll., N.Y.C., 1975-80, assoc. prof., 1980-86, prof. of chemistry, 1986—; chair dept., 1986-89, 91-94; Ann Whitney Olin prof., 97—, Barnard Coll., N.Y.C., 1990-95. Mem. chem. div. adv. bd. NSF, Washington, 1986-89. Mem. Am. Chem. Soc. (com. on profl. tng. 1991—, chair 1994-96, petroleum rsch. fund adv. bd. 1991-95, petroleum rsch. fund adv. bd. 1996—), Am. Phys. Soc., Assn. Women in Sci., Phi Beta Kappa, Sigma Xi. Democrat. Mem. Soc. Of Friends. Office: Barnard Coll Dept Chemistry 3009 Broadway New York NY 10027-6501 E-mail: schapman@barnard.edu.

CHAPMAN COLLINS, JANICE, school system administrator; b. L.A. d. William and Milrene Hooks; m. Michael Dean Collins; children: Arshaun, Ashley. BA in Liberal Arts, Pepperdine U., 1979, EdM, 1985, MS in Sch. Mgmt. & Adminstrn., 1989, MA in Edn., 1985. Ryan Multiple Subject Credential Calif. Commn. Tchr. Credentialing, 1979, Sylvan Program Instr. Sylan Learning Ctr., 1998, Adminstrv. Svcs. Credential Calif Commn. Tchr. Credentialing, 2000, Cert. Profl. Devel. Trainer L.A. Unified Sch. Dist.-Calif., 2002. Elem. tchr. L.A. Unified Sch. Dist., 1979—92, instrnl. coord., 1992—94, advisor, 1994—96, mid. sch. tchr., 1996—99, adminstr., mentor tchr. program, 1999—2000, adminstr., mid. sch. programs, 2000—. Mentor tchr. L.A. Unified Sch. Dist., 1986—92, drop out prevention coord., Seventy-Fifth St. Sch., 1986—88, adult sch. tchr., 1987—89, program quality rev. team mem., 1990, ldpass/aemp facilitator, 1996—99, sylvan program instr., 1998—99, adminstrv. facilitator, phys. edn. focus group, 2000—, social studies adv. bd. mem., 2001—, mem.- secondary redesign com., 2003—, mem. Calif. phys. edn. content standards devel. com., 2004; cons. USC: Calif. writing project Calif. Subject Matter Projects, L.A., 1987—; mem. social studies adv. bd. Pearson Prentice Hall Pub., L.A., 2003—; mem. phys. content standards devel. com. Calif. Dept. Edn., mem. com. phys. edn. model content standards. Contbr. ednl. handbook, Successful Strategies Handbook, curriculum guide, History-Social Sci. Guidelines for Instrn.; co-author: America History For Our Nation, 2005. Founding mem. Nat. Campaign for Tolerance, Montgomery, Ala., 2005—; adminstrv. liasion L.A. Unified Sch. Dist. Nat. Campaign To Stop Violence, Washington, 2000—. Recipient Do the Write Thing Challenge 2003, Nat. Campaign to Stop Violence, 2003, 2004. Mem.: ASCD, Associated Adminstrs. L.A., Calif. Assn. Health Phys. Edn., Recreation and Dance, Orgn. Mgmt. Adminstrs., Calif. League Mid. Schools, Coun. Black Adminstrs. (profl. devel. com. 1998), Nat. Women's History Mus. (charter mem.), Pepperdine Alumni Assn., Phi Delta Kappa. Baptist. Avocations: travel, art collector, creative writing, theater. Office: LA Unified Sch Dist 333 S Beaudry Ave 25th Floor Los Angeles CA 90017 Office Phone: 213-241-4134. Business E-Mail: janice.collins@lausd.net.

CHAPMAN HOLLEY, SHAWN SNIDER, lawyer; b. LA, Apr. 11, 1962; d. Henry Stewart and Freddi (Snider) King; m. Michael J. Chapman, Sept. 12, 1992. BA in English, UCLA, 1984; JD, Southwestern U., 1988. Bar: Calif. 1988, U.S. Dist. Ct. (ctrl. dist.) Calif. 1989. Deputy pub. defender L.A. County Pub. Defenders Office, 1988-94; mng. ptnr. The Cochran Firm (formerly Law Offices of Johnnie L. Cochran Jr.), L.A., 1994—. Commr. of community affairs Southwestern U. Sch. of Law, L.A., 1987. Mem. Black Pub. Defenders Assn., Black Women Lawyers, Langston Bar Assn. Democrat. Office: The Cochran Firm 4929 Wilshire Blvd Ste 1010 Los Angeles CA 90010-3825 E-mail: sholley@cochranfirm.com.

CHAPON, EUNICE KIM, lawyer; b. 1969; BA, Tufts U., 1996; JD, William and Mary Sch. Law, 1999. Bar: Mass. 1999, US Dist. Ct. (Dist. Mass.). Ptnr. Corp. Dept. Choate, Hall & Stewart LLP, Boston. Mem.: Boston Bar Assn., Asian Am. Lawyers Assn. Mass. (v.p.), ABA. Office: Choate Hall & Stewart LLP Two International Pl Boston MA 02110 Office Phone: 617-248-5256. Office Fax: 617-248-5000. E-mail: echapon@choate.com.*

CHAPPELL, ANNETTE M., educational consultant, minister; b. Washington, Oct. 31, 1939; d. Joseph John and Annette B. (Harley) C.; m. Brian Thomas Flower, Sept. 3, 1960 (div. Mar. 1983); m. Frank Joseph Sanders, Apr. 8, 1985 (dec. Dec. 1995). BA in English, U. Md., 1962, MA, 1964, PhD, 1970; MDiv, Gen. Theol. Sem., 2003. Lectr. European div. U. Md., Eng., 1965-66, instr. English College Park, 1966-69; asst. prof. English Towson (Md.) U., 1969-72, assoc. prof., 1972-79, prof., 1979—99, spl. asst. to pres., affirmative action officer, 1974-77; dean humanistic, social and managerial studies Towson (Md.) State U., 1977-82, dean Coll. Liberal Arts, 1982-95, assoc. v.p. acad. affairs, 1995-99; ind. cons., 1999—; rector Ch. of the Redemption, Balt., 2003—. Contbr. articles to profl. jours. and book revs. to Ms Mag., Balt. Sun. Lay reader, chalicist All Saints Episcopal Ch., Reisterstown, Md., 1973-2003; pres. Baltimore County Commn. for Women, 1977-79; bd. dirs. Baltimore County Sexual Assault and Domestic Violence Center, 1978-83, pres., 1980-82. Mem. AAUP, MLA, Am. Assn. Higher Edn., Council Colls. Arts and Scis. (bd. dirs. 1984-86), Exec. Women's Council Md. (1st v.p. 1980, pres. 1981) Business E-Mail: achappell@towson.edu.

CHAPPELL, ANNIE-DEAR, retired business manager; b. Riverside, Calif., Oct. 24, 1947; BSBA, Kensington U., 1985. Bus. mgr. Santa Clara Valley Ear, Nose and Throat Clinic, Sunnyvale, Calif., 1983-93; dir. adminstrv. svcs. NCA Computer Products, Sunnyvale, Calif., 1994-96; mgr. adminstrn. Datatools/BMC Software, Sunnyvale, Calif., 1996-97; br. adminstr. Bay Alarm Co., Santa Clara, 1997-99; tech. mgr. IBM bus. unit Analysts Internat., San Jose, Calif., 1999—2001; owner A.C.T., 2001—04; ret., 2003. Vol. Hugh O'Brian Youth Leadership High Sch. Sophomores. Recipient Hoby Outstanding Recruitment award, 2004—05, Vol. of Yr., Hoby Oreg., 2005. Mem.: Cherokee Nat. Hist. Soc. Avocation: women's self defense. Home: 1334 Zinfandel Ct Mcminnville OR 97128-2492

CHAPPELL, BARBARA KELLY, retired child welfare consultant; b. Oct. 17, 1940; d. Arthur Lee and Katherine (Martin) Kelly; 1 child, Kelly Katherine. BA in English and Edn., U. S.C., 1962, MSW, 1974. Tchr. English Dept. Edn., Honolulu, 1962-65, Alamo Heights HS, San Antonio, 1965-67; caseworker Dept. Social Svcs., Columbia, SC, 1969-70; supr. Juvenile Placement and Aftercare, Columbia, 1970-72; child welfare cons. Edna McConnell Clark Found., N.Y.C., 1974-75; dir. Children's Foster Care Rev. Bd. Sys., Columbia, 1975-85, child welfare cons., 1985-89; adminstr. Dept. Human Resources and Juvenile Svcs., Balt., 1989-92; exec. dir. New Pathways, Inc., Balt., 1992-97; accreditation coord./social worker IV Dept. Mental Health, Columbia, 1997—2004, ret., 2004. Lectr. in field. Contbr. articles to profl. jours. Coord. Child's Rights to Parents, Columbia, 1970—75. Episcopalian. Home and Office: 3215 Girardeau Ave Columbia SC 29204-3314

CHAPPELL, ELIZABETH IRENE, special education educator; b. Macon, Ga., Nov. 11, 1973; d. Rodney Lewis and Colleen Nova Chappell. BS in spl. edn., Bob Jones U., Greenville, S.C., 1995; MA in curriculum and instrn., Nat. Louis U., Evanston, Ill., 2001. Cert. tchr. in mental disabilities, emotional disorders, learning disabilities Ill. Mid. sch. spl. edn. instr. Kankakee Spl. Edn. Coop., Manteno, Ill., 1995—96; HS spl. Edn. instr. Plainfield Sch. Dist. 202, Plainfield, Ill., 1996—2001; alternative HS spl. edn. instr. Indian Prairie Sch. Dist. 204, Naperville, Ill., 2001—02, HS spl. edn. instr., 2002—. Activities coord. Greenville (S.C.) County Spl. Olympics, 1995; athlete asst. Spl. Olympics, Chgo., 2000—. Pub. rels. Shadow Lakes Assn., Wilmington, Ill., 2000—01; organist Phelan Acres Bible Ch., Wilmington, Ill., 1988—, bible sch., Sunday sch. tchr., 1991—. Grantee Academic Scholarship, Lion's Club, 1991—95. Mem.: NEA (union rep. 1997—2001), Coun. for Exceptional Children. Mem. Independent Bible Ch. Avocations: swimming, reading, exercise, softball, volleyball. Home: 177 Smallmouth Ln Wilmington IL 60481 Personal E-mail: wildwave27@hotmail.com.

CHAPPELL, REBECCA A., music educator; b. Big Spring, Tex., May 15, 1954; d. Robert O. and Wanda Jewette James; m. Stephen A. Pinkerton, Dec. 23, 1995; children: Jason S., Angela R. Maxwell, Andrew J., Tiffany N. BA, Anderson U., Ind., 1976; MusM, Oklahoma City U., 1978; ArtsD, Ball State U., Muncie, Ind., 1991. Prof. music Anderson U., 1979—. Condr. Feast of Tabernacles celebration Internat. Christian Embassy, Jesusalem, 2001. Mem.: Music and Entertainment Industry Educators Assn. (pres. 2003—), Am. Fedn. Musicians. Home: 716 Northwood Dr Anderson IN 46011 Office: Anderson U 1100 E 5th St Anderson IN 46012-3495 Fax: 765-641-3809. Office Phone: 765-641-4461. E-mail: rachappell@anderson.edu.

CHAPPELL, VALERIE, educational consultant; d. William and Kathie Karr. BS, U. NH, 2002; MEd in Spl. Edn., Plymouth State U., NH, 2005; EdD in Spl. Edn., Columbia U., 2005. Cert. gen. spl. educator N.H., 2004. Spl. edn. tchr. Milford Sch. Dist., Milford, NH, 2002—05; spl. advisor Brown Lloyd James, N.Y., 2006—, coord. internat. forum Shafallah Ctr., 2006—. Coord. confs.; coord. global initiative Abilities!, N.Y., 2006—; cons. in field. Coord. program Milford (N.H.) Pks. and Recreation Dept., 2002—04. Named Recreation Mgmt. and Policy Student of Yr., U. N.H., 2002; scholar, Tchrs. Coll., 2006. Mem.: Am. Assn. Mental Retardation (assoc.), Coucil Exceptional Children (assoc.; v.p. chpt. 45 2005). Achievements include research in teacher understanding of IDEA 04' requirements in regards to grading students with disabilities. Personal E-mail: chapp2@msn.com.

CHAPPELLE, LOU JO, physical therapist assistant; b. Watertown, N.Y., Mar. 7, 1952; d. Harold Joseph and Alice Jean (Marcellus) Getman; m. Richard George Tobey, Aug. 14, 1982 (div.); m. Gerald E. Chappelle, Sept. 14, 1996; stepson, Scott C. AA, Hudson Valley Community Coll., 1972; BSE, State U. Coll., Cortland, N.Y., 1974; AAS, St. Philips Coll., 1981. Cert. elem. and secondary tchr., N.Y. Educator phys. edn., coach Gilbertsville (N.Y.) Central Sch., 1974-79, 1000 Islands Jr.-Sr. High Sch., Sand Bay-Clayton, N.Y., 1980-82; phys. therapist asst. II N.Y. State Veteran's Home, Oxford, 1982-91; phys. therapy asst. F.F. Thompson Health Sys., Inc., Canandaigua, N.Y., 1992-98, SunDance Rehab Corp, Ontario County Health Facility, 1998, Finger Lakes Vis. Nurse Svc., 1999—. EMT Gilbertsville (N.Y.) Emergency Squad, 1983-89. Capt. USAR, 1977-96. Decorated Army Achievement medal. Home: 4313 Deep Run Cv Canandaigua NY 14424-9777

CHAPPER, BARBARA MAE, retired pediatrician; b. Detroit, Mich., May 22, 1925; d. Frank Edward and Rose Caroline Chapper; m. Harold M. White, Mar. 12, 1970 (dec. 1984); 4 stepchildren. BS, U. Detroit, 1947; MD, Wayne State Med. Sch., 1953. Intern Providence Hosp., Detroit, 1953—54; resident Children's Hosp., Detroit, 1954—56; dr. St. Joseph Hosp., Ghana, 1956—57; pvt. practice pediats. Detroit, 1987—90; ret., 1990. Mem.: Am. Acad. Pediats., Wayne State Med. Soc., Mich. State Med. Soc. Home: 20404 Old Colony Dearborn Heights MI 48127

CHAR, PATRICIA HELEN, lawyer; b. Honolulu, Mar. 23, 1952; d. Lincoln S. and Daisy Char; m. Thomas W. Bingham, Mar. 20, 1982; children: Matthew Thomas Bingham, James Nathan Bingham. BA, Northwestern U., 1974; JD, Georgetown U., 1977. Bar: Wash. 1977, U.S. Dist. Ct. (we. dist.) Wash. 1977, U.S. Dist. Ct. (ea. dist.) Wash. 1982, U.S. Ct. Appeals (9th cir.) 1981, U.S. Supreme Ct. 1984. Assoc. Bogle & Gates, Seattle, 1977-84; ptnr., mem. Bogle & Gates PLLC, Seattle, 1984-99; of counsel Garvey, Schubert & Barer, Seattle, 1999-2000; ptnr. Preston Gates & Ellis LLP, Seattle, 2000—. Author: Ownership By a Fiduciary, 1997. Trustee YWCA, Seattle-King County-Snohomish County, 1997-2005, United Way King County, 2004—, Childrens Hosp. and Regional Med. Ctr., Seattle; vol. King County Big Sisters, United Way of King County, Seattle, 1987-90, Guardian Ad Litem Program, Seattle, 1987-93 Fellow Am. Coll. Trust and Estate Counsel; mem. ABA, Wash. State Bar Assn. (co-author chpts. 3 and 4 Wash. Civil Procedure Deskbook 1992). Office: Preston Gates & Ellis LLP 925 4th Ave #2900 Seattle WA 98104-1158 Office Phone: 206-623-7580. Business E-Mail: pchar@prestongates.com.

CHAREN, MONA, columnist; b. NYC, Feb. 25, 1957; d. George and Claire (Rosenfeld) C.; m. Robert P. Parker. BA, Columbia U., 1979; JD, George Wash. U., 1984. Editorial assoc. Nat. Review Mag., N.Y.C., 1979-81; speechwriter White House, Washington, 1984, assoc. dir., office of pub. liaison, 1985-86; speechwriter Jack Kemp for Pres., Washington, 1986; syndicated columnist Creators Syndicate, L.A., 1987—. Panelist The Capital Gang CNN, Washington. Contbr. articles profl. mags. and publs.; author: Useful Idiots, 2003, Do-Gooders, 2005. Republican. Jewish. Office: Creators Syndicate 5777 W Century Blvd Ste 700 Los Angeles CA 90045-5675 Personal E-mail: charenmail@cox.net.

CHARETTE, CECILE M., music educator; b. Lowell, Mass., Oct. 15, 1920; d. Arthur Joseph and Eva Marie (Croteau) C. MusB, U. Montreal, 1956, MusM, 1962; postgrad., Boston U., 1965-67. Joined Order of Holy Cross, 1939. Prof. music Basile Moreau Coll., St. Laurent, Que., Canada, 1946—62, Notre Dame Coll., Manchester, NH, 1962—2002; pvt. music instr. Goffstown, NH. Choir dir., dir. operas, 1974-78. Mem. Nat. Assn. Tchrs. Singing (N.H. gov. 1978-84), Metro. Opera Guild. Roman Catholic. E-mail: cecilecha@aol.com.

CHARETTE, SHARON JULIETTE, library administrator; b. Woonsocket, RI, Apr. 24, 1956; d. Roland Alfred Lionel and Juliette Cecile (Lavoie) C. BA in French and English, R.I. Coll., 1978; MLS, U. R.I., 1981; cert. in computer info. systems, Bryant Coll., 1989; student, RISD, 1989—91. Asst. serials Wheaton Coll., Norton, Mass., 1978—79, catalog asst., 1979—82, libr. acquisitions, 1982—86; dir. libr. and instnl. rsch. New Eng. Inst. Tech., Warwick, RI, 1986—. Seamstress, designer, craftsman, 1976—; webmaster, publicist for Greg Bonin, 2002—; webmaster Charlie Hall's Ocean State Follies, 2005— Chair Franco Am. com. R.I. Heritage Commn., Providence, 1987-90, treas., 1982-87; costume designer Kaleidoscope Theatre, 2003—. Mem. ALA, New England Libr. Assn., R.I. Libr. Assn., No. R.I. Coun. of Arts, Theatre Works (costume designer 2001-05, web mgr. 2002-05), Mensa, TechACCESS of R.I. (bd. dirs., sec. 1992-98, 2003—, chair 1998-2003, web mgr. 2002—04). Avocations: music, theater, costume design, website design, jewelry design. Home: 147 Greenville Rd North Smithfield RI 02896-7422 Office: New Eng Inst Tech 2500 Post Rd Warwick RI 02886-2244 E-mail: scharette3@cox.net.

CHARGOIS, DEBORAH MAJEAU, psychology professor, researcher; b. New Orleans, Nov. 8, 1940; d. John Ashton and Marie Barbot Majeau; m. Ashton Joseph Chargois, Sept. 6, 1969. BA, U. Notre Dame, South Bend, Ind., 1963; MS, La. State U., New Orleans, 1967; PhD, La. State U., 1969, MD, 1983. Lic. physician Calif., Fla. Rsch. assoc. in otorhinolaryngology La. State U. Med. Ctr., New Orleans, 1965—67, instr. in otorhinolaryngology and physiology, 1967—70, liason officer to NASA, 1967—74, asst. prof. otorhinolaryngology and physiology, assoc. mem. grad. faculty, 1970—74, asst. prof. physiology, mem. grad. faculty, 1974—77, dir. dental physiology programs, 1975—79; postdoctoral fellow in clin. chemistry and toxicology La. State U. Med. Ctr. and VA Hosp., New Orleans, 1979—81, resident in psychiatry, 1983—87; sr. rschr. sonic boom studies Miss. Test Facility, 1967—69; sr. rschr. high voltage elec. field studies Hebert Rsch. Facility, 1980—84; rsch. assoc. in elec. engring. Tulane U., New Orleans, 1980—82, adj. asst. prof. elec. engring., mem. grad. faculty, 1982—84; clin. toxicologist River Oaks Hosp., New Orleans, 1987—91; adj. prof. psychology, mem. grad. faculty Jacksonville (Ala.) State U., 1998—. Spl. lectr. divsn. engring. rsch. La. State U., Baton Rouge, 1969—71; vis. scientist Charity Hosp. of La. at New Orleans, 1969—71, 1981—83; moderator panel on schizophrenia Am. Psychiat. Assn. Ann. Conv., Dallas, 1985; advisor Inst. Rev. Bd. Jacksonville State U., 2005—. Contbr. articles to profl. jours. Contbr. Am. Nat. Red Cross, Washington, 2001—, Magen David Adom, Jerusalem, 2001—; mem. Dem. Nat. Com., Washington, 2000—, Ala. Dem. Party, Birmingham, 2002—. Lt. comdr. USN, 1982. Recipient 1st pl. award for presentation, Am. Speech and Hearing Assn., 1969, 2d pl. award for sci. merit, 1969; fellow Medicine in the Tropics, Bur. Medicine and Surgery, USN and Gorgas Meml. Lab., Panama, 1982; predoctoral fellow in physiology, NIH, 1966—67, postdoctoral fellow in tropical medicine, 1973, Bio-Space Tech. Tng. Program fellow, 1969, postdoctoral fellow in clin. chemistry and toxicology, 1979—81. Mem.: AMA, APA, So. Med. Assn., Am. Psychol. Soc., Am. Psychiat. Assn., Mensa, Psi Chi, Sigma Xi. Jewish. Avocations: stamp collecting/philately, coin collecting/numismatics, amateur radio, history, sailing. Home: 2040 Highland Ave # 804 Birmingham AL 35205 Office: Jacksonville State U 700 Pelham Rd N Jacksonville AL 36265 Office Phone: 256-782-5402. Office Fax: 256-782-5637. Personal E-mail: chargois2@aol.com.

CHARIS, BARBARA, nutritionist, consultant, medical researcher; b. Pitts., Feb. 26, 1934; d. Robert Edward and Clara L. Wakefield; m. Roger S. Markle, May 19, 1956 (div. July 1980); children: Mitchell, Tarri, Heidi, David. Student, Pa. State U., 1951-53, U. Pitts., 1954, Harbor Coll., Wilmington, Calif., 1966; M. in Holistic Health Sci., Columbia Pacific U., San Rafael, Calif., 1982. Dir., cons. Charis Holistic Ctr., North Hollywood, Calif., 1982—. Host (radio show) The Health Beat, L.A., 1988-89; producer (TV show) Sharing from the Heart, L.A., 1996-97; author: Sharing from the Heart, 1995. Mem. Nat. Health Fedn., Vegetarian Soc. (v.p. 1982-83), Book Publicists So. Calif. Avocations: poetry, songwriting, lecturing, spiritual counseling, running (L.A. Marathon 1994, 99, 2004). Home and Office: Charis Holistic Ctr 6227 Morse Ave 304 North Hollywood CA 91606-2948 Office Phone: 818-506-8768. Personal E-mail: barbaracharis@aol.com.

CHARLES, LAURA JO, mathematics educator; b. Milw., Nov. 26, 1979; d. Rick Allen and Brenda Jo Charles. BS in Secondary Math. Edn., Okla. State U., 2002, MS in Math. Edn., 2004. Cert. tchr. Okla. State Dept. Edn. Grad. tchg. asst. Okla. State U., Stillwater, 2002—04; math. tchr. Ponca H.S., Ponca City, Okla., 2004—. Mem.: Math. Assn. Am., Pi Mu Epsilon.

CHARLES, MARILYN KAY, secondary school educator; b. Rock Springs, Wyo., Oct. 16, 1947; d. Walter Harvey and Mariam Louise (Tanner) Banks; m. Clinton Robert Charles, Jan. 30, 1975; stepchildren: Coralynn, Shane. AA, Western Wyo. Coll., Rock Springs, 1967; BA, Brigham Young U., Provo, Utah, 1971. Cert. secondary edn. tchr. Wyo. Typist/sec. dept. med. records Wyo. State Hosp., Evanston, 1972—73; instr. English, phys. edn. Evanston Jr. H.S., 1973—75; sec. Lyman H.S., 1978—86, instr. English, health, 1986—88, instr. English, 1988—2006. Drill team advisor Evanston H.S., Wyo., 1974—75; class advisor Lyman H.S., Wyo., 1986—, drill team advisor, 1987—89, yearbook advisor, 1992—98. Author: Roadshow Prodn. (LDS Ch. Stake award). Mem.: Wyo. Edn. Assn., Lyman Edn. Assn. Avocations: rock-hound, creative writing, crocheting, gardening, art work.

CHARLES, NANCY DUFRESNE, reading educator, consultant; arrived in U.S., 1967; m. Johnny F. Charles (div.); 1 child, Catherine Alexander. BS in Mktg., Fashion Inst. Tech., N.Y.C., 1984; student, U. Hawaii, Honlulu, 1990—92. Tchr., French U. Hawaii, 1991—93; tchr., English Iwakuri, Japan, 1993—96; tchr, life mgmt. Grove Counseling Ctr., Longwood, Fla., 1997—99; tchr., social studies Excel Alternatives, Orlando, 1999—2001, acad. specialist, 2001—02; student advocate, parent liaison Orange County Pub. Schs., Orlando, 2002—05, reading coach, 2005—. Pres. Haitian Am. Consulting, Altamonte Springs, 2004—; assoc. Mium & Assoc., Ft. Lauderdale, 2004—. Vol., 1st & 2d ann. fundraiser First Haitian Cmty Ctrl. Fla., Orlando, 2004—; vol., fundraiser Water for Haiti Rosen Hotel Resorts, Orlando, 2005; art & culture promoter Haitian Am. Mus. Art & Culture, Orlando, 2005—06; mem. Orange County Reading Coun., 2005—; bd. mem.

First Haitian Cmty. Ctr. Ctrl. Fla., 2002—, edn. chair, 2005; bd. mem., pub. rels. Haitian Am. Mus. Art, 2004—. Grantee Family Lit. mini-grant, Gov.'s Office, Tallahassee, Fla., 2005—06. Roman Catholic. Avocations: reading, camping, travel, music, exercise. Office: Orange County Pub Schs 1445 W Amelia St Orlando FL 32801

CHARLES, SALLY ALLEN, financial analyst; b. Atlanta, Jan. 9, 1950; d. Thomas Roach Jr. and Lucille (Blake) Allen; m. Darrell Charles, Dec. 28, 1974; children: Carey Robert, Jane Allen. BA in Speech Comm., Auburn U., 1972; MBA, Kennesaw State U., 1989; cert. in small bus. mgmt., U. Ga., 1995, cert. in govtl. acctg., 2004. Cons. Small Bus. Devel. Ctr. Kennesaw (Ga.) State U., 1990-96, dir. Small Bus. Inst., 1992-96; purchasing agt. Portal Tech., CD Rom Tng. Voice Overs, Mgmt. Com., 1997—99; exec. asst., v.p. fin. Johnson Controls, 2000—02; registered bus. analyst, fellow Am. Acad. Fin. Mgmt., 2004—. Mem. adj. faculty dept. mgmt. and entrepreneurship Kennesaw State U., 1991-94; mem. small bus. adv. coun. Apple Computers, Napa Valley, Calif., 1994, mem. Assn. Fin. Profl., 2005-; mem. Ga. Fiscal Mgmt. Coun., 2005-; mentor AMEN, Inc., 2004—. Contbr. cover quote, reviewer: Market Planning Guide (Andy Bangs), 1998. Press credentials chair Woodstock (Ga.) Welcome for Pres. and Mrs. George Bush, 1992; instr. annual tng. Ga. Soc. CPA's, Atlanta, 1993; advisor facilities Kappa Alpha Theta, Emory U., Atlanta, 1994-2003, chmn. recruitment reference bd., 2004—. Recipient Outstanding Young Citizen award, Woodstock (Ga.) Jaycees, 1985; recipient Small Bus. Inst. Cases of the Yr. award Ga.-U.S. Small Bus. Adminstrn., Atlanta, 1992, 93, 95; Small Bus. Inst. grantee U.S. Small Bus. Adminstrn., Washington and Atlanta, 1991-95. Fellow Am. Acad. Fin. Mgmt.; mem. Small Bus. Inst. Dirs. Assn. (mem. adv. com. 1994-96, reviewer 1996-99, newsletter editor 1995-97, track chair 1998, coord. new dir. tng. 1995, v.p. 1996, Showcase award 1994). Republican. Baptist. Office: State of Ga Road and Tollway Authority 101 Marietta St 2500 Atlanta GA 30303 Home: 5830 Raventree Ct Atlanta GA 30349-1684 Office Phone: 404-893-6136. Business E-Mail: sallycharles@comcast.net.

CHARLETON, MARGARET ANN, child care administrator, consultant; b. Orange, Calif., Aug. 3, 1947; d. Arthur Mitchell and Isabelle Margaret (Esser) Charleton; m. Terrence Joseph Marecic, July 21, 2001. AA in Liberal Arts, Orange Coast Coll., 1968; BA in Psychology, Chapman U., 1984. Head tchr. Presbyn. Ch. of the Master, Mission Viejo, Calif., 1977-81; child care program adminstr. Crystal Stairs, Inc., L.A., 1981—2001. Mem. adv. bd. Children's Home Soc., Santa Ana, Calif., 1982-83; cons. Calif. Sch. Age Consortium, Costa Mesa, 1987, Calif. State Dept. of Edn., 1988; trainer preschool edn. program Sesame Street PBS, 1994-96; lectr. in field; presenter Western Regional Child Care Food Program Conf., San Francisco, 1997, Save the Children Conf., Atlanta, Ga., 1998, 10th Ann. Child Care Food Program Sponsor's Conf., 2001. Contbr. articles to profl. jours. Mem. South Orange County Community Svc., Mission Viejo, 1983—; liaison Family Svcs.-Marine Base, El Toro, Calif., 1989—; mem. adv. bd. Dept. Social Svc., 1997—. Recipient Plaque of Recognition, Vietnamese Community of Orange County, 1984. Mem. NAFE. Roman Catholic. Avocations: sailing, skiing, travel, wine. Office: Child Nutrition Program So Calif 7777 Alvarado Rd Ste 700 La Mesa CA 91941

CHARLTON, SHIRLEY MARIE, educational consultant; b. Nashville, Nov. 20, 1934; d. Ottis Ruby and Irene Lenoir (Cabler) C.; children: David Matthew Christian Sironen, Charlton Gwynn Cabler Sironen. BS, George Peabody Coll. Tchrs., 1954; MA in Ednl. Adminstrn. and Supervision, U. Tenn., Chattanooga, 1970. Cert. supr., Tenn. Classroom tchr. Albany (Ga.) Pub. Schs., 1954-55, 56-57, Orlando (Fla.) Pub. Schs., 1960-61, Grand Forks (N.D.) Pub. Schs., 1962-65; TV and resource tchr. Chattanooga Publ Schs., 1965-67, supr., 1967-97; cons., 1997-99. Mem. NEA, Tenn. Edn. Assn., Chattanooga Edn. Assn. (charter mem. negotiating team 1979-81), Alpha Delta Kappa (v.p. 1981-83). Episcopalian. Avocations: history, genealogy, acting, art, music.

CHARNEY, LENA LONDON, property manager, historian, poet; b. Simyatycze, Poland, Jan. 26, 1919; d. Moysei Isaakovitch and Emma (London) Barengolts; m. Roy L. Charney, Nov. 10, 1955 (dec. 1972); 1 child, Craig Russell. BA cum laude, Hunter Coll., 1941; MA, Clark U., 1942; postgrad., Columbia U. Cert. tchr., adminstr. N.Y. Owner, mgr. London's Studio Apts., 1959—. Millinery designer Sanjour Studio, 1937, 1939—41, Lenblac Millinery, 1938; sec. to mgr. N.Y.C. Office Ins. Field, 1945; saleswoman Bonwit-Teller, Lane Bryant, Arnold Constable, 1947—49; tchr., prin. St. Basil's Acad. Garisson, NY, 1968—73; substitute tchr. various sch. dists., NY, 1974—82. Featured poet Evening of Poetry, Mt. Pleasant Libr., Pleasantville, N.Y.; contbr. to profl. jours., revs. and mags.; asst. editor: Ins. Weekly, 1946. Charter mem., rec. sec., bd. dirs., Sunday sch. tchr. Lakeland Jewish Ctr., Mohegan Lake; tchr. Sunday sch. Temple Betham, Yorktown Heights; dir., tchr. Workmen's Cir. Yiddish Sch., Shrub Oak, NY; active Hudson Valley Hosp. Ctr. Aux., U.S. Holocaust Mus., Greenpeace, Amnesty Internat., Am. Found. Blind, Gen. Israel Orphans Home Girls, Mohegan Lake Vol. Fire Assn., Mohegan Lake Vol. Ambulance Corps, Nat. Yiddish Book Ctr., Lighthouse, Rec. for Blind, Jewish Braille Inst., Am. Printing Ho. for Blind, Eye Bank Sight Restoration, Glaucoma Rsch.; mem. Westchester Arts Coun.; active United Jewish Appeal-Fedn. Telethon; chmn. eye rsch. project, chmn. Am. affairs, chmn. Zionist affairs, v.p. edn., pres. Aviva chpt. Hadassah; active World Jewish Congress, Union Couns. Soviet Jews; rec. sec. Mohegan Lake Resort Owners Assn., NY; v.p. Mohegan Lake Improvement Corp.; v.p. publicity Brandeis U. Named Women's Com. Outstanding Sr. of Yr., Compound Sr. Citizens Club, Woman of Yr., Aviva Hadassah. Mem.: ACLU, Poetry Soc. Am., Acad. Am. Poets, Hudson Valley Writers Ctr., Nat. Writers Union, Acad. Polit. Sci., Am. Hist. Assn., Anti-Defamation League. Avocations: swimming, walking, dance, movies, travel. Home: PO Box 145 Mohegan Lake NY 10547-0145

CHARNIN, JADE HOBSON, magazine executive; b. N.Y.C., Mar. 12, 1945; d. John Louis Campo and Elizabeth (Anne) Stanton); m. David Alan Hobson,Dec. 30 (div. 1972); m. Martin Charnin, Dec. 18, 1984. BA, NYU, 1967. Asst. editor Glamour mag., N.Y.C., 1970; accessory editor Vogue mag., N.Y.C., 1970-78, fashion editor, 1978-81, fashion dir., 1981-86, creative dir. fashion, 1987-88; v.p., dir. creative svcs for fashion and design group Revlon Inc., 1988; exec. creative dir. Mirabella Mag., 1988-94; fashion dir. N.Y. Mag., 1994-98; freelance journalist, 1999—. Pres. and landscape designer Growing Things, Inc., Wilton, Conn., 2002—; cons. editor Self mag., N.Y.C., 1979—81. Costume coord. for off-Broadways shows Upstairs at Oneals, 1981, Laughing Matters, 1989, Martin Charnin, the Hits and the M.S.'s, 1990. Mem.: ASPCA, Am. Assn. Landscape Archs., Hort. Soc. N.Y., Am. Hort. Soc., Assn. Profl. Landscape Designers, Humane Soc. N.Y. (bd. dirs.), Wilton Garden Club (bd. dirs.). Avocations: opera, ballet, theater, skiing. Personal E-mail: jadehobson@aol.com.

CHARNLEY, CRISTEN MARIE, secondary school educator; b. Tunkhannock, Pa., Sept. 21, 1979; d. Charles Alfred and Mary Ann Place; m. James Alberts Charnley, Sept. 25, 2004. BS in Chem. Engring., Lafayette Coll., 2002; MS in Edn., U. Pa., 2004. Cert. tchr. Pa., 2004. Tchr. Easton (Pa.) Area H.S., 2004—. Marquis scholar, Lafayette Coll., 1998—2002. Mem.: Nat. Coun. Tchrs. Math., NSTA, Alpha Gamma Delta. Avocations: photography, travel. Office Phone: 610-250-2481.

CHARNVEJA, PAT S., civic leader, former oil and gas industry executive; b. Bangkok; came to US, 1961; m. Kitipot Charnveja; 3 children. Attended, W. Tex. A&M, Canyon, Tex., U. Houston. Various positions in oil and gas industry, 1976—98; mng. dir. PSKC Internat. LLC. Liaison Royal Thai Embassy & Royal Thai Consulate Gen. Founder & pres. Thai Am. Chamber of Commerce; pres. Thai Arts and Culture of Houston; former pres. Thai Assn. of Greater Houston; mem. bd. dirs. & former pres. Asian/Pacific Am. Heritage Assn.; mem. Focus Group for Leadership Ed. for Asian Pacifics, Inc.; mem. cultural diversity com. Holocaust Museum Houston; treasurer Asian Am. Voters' Coalition; adv. bd. mem. Asia Soc. Tex. Ctr.; mem. Chinese Cmty. Ctr., VN Teamwork. Office: Thai Am Chamber Commerce PO Box 681277 Houston TX 77268-1277 Office Phone: 281-477-8803. E-mail: prapatip@sbcglobal.net.

CHARO, ROBIN ALTA, law educator; b. Bklyn., June 6, 1958; d. Jon and Ethel (Munach) C. AB in Biology (cum laude), Harvard-Radcliffe Coll., 1979; JD, Columbia U. Sch. Law, 1982. Bar: N.Y. 1983. Asst. dir. Legis. Drafting Rsch. Fund, Columbia U., NYC, 1982—83, assoc. dir., 1983—85; lectr. Columbia Law Sch., NYC, 1983-85; Fulbright Jr. lectr. in Am. Law, assoc. prof. U. Paris, Pantheon-Sorbonne, 1985-86; legal analyst, biol. applications program Congl. Office of Tech. Assessment, Washington, 1986-88; AAAS Diplomacy fellow, policy develop. divsn. of office of population U.S. Agy. for Internat. Devel., Washington, 1988-89; asst. prof., law & bioethics, dept. med. history & bioethics U. Wis. Law Sch., U. Wis. Med. Sch., Madison, 1989—95; assoc. prof. law U. Wis. Law Sch., Madison, 1995—98, Warren P. Knowles prof. law & bioethics, 1998—2003, Elisabeth S. Wilson prof., 2003—. Cons. N.J. Bioethics Comm., Draft Legsi. on Living Wills, 1988, Congl. Office of Tech. Assessment, 1988-92, U.S. AID, Office of Population 1988-91, Can. Law Reform Commn., Ottawa, Can., 1989-90, Comm. on Uniform Laws, Draft Legislation on Surrogacy, 1989, NIH office Protection from Rsch. Risks; mem. NIH Human Embryo Rsch. Panel, 1993-94, Presdl. Nat. Bioethics Adv. Comm., 1996-2001, ethics standard working group, Calif. Inst. for Regenerative Medicine, 2005-; vis. lectr. and professorships Fachbereich Rechtswissenschaft, Justus-Liebig-Univ., Giessen, Germany, 1992, Centre de Droit de la Famille, Université de Lyon, France, 1992, Escuela Latinoamericana de la Bioetica, La Plata, Argentina, 1992, Instituto Superior de la Medicina, Santiago, Cuba, 1996, Nova Law Sch., Ft. Lauderdale, Fla., 2001, Facultad Latinoamericana de Ciencias Sociales, Buenos Aires, Argentina, 2003, U. Va. Law Sch., Charlottesville, Virginia), 2004, vis. prof. law, U. Calif. Berkeley Law Sch., 2006-; mem. bioethics adv. bd., Howard Hughes Med. Inst., 2004-, Internat. Soc. for Stem Cell Rsch., 2004-; mem. adv. bd., project on reproductive genetics, Ctr. for Genetics and Pub. Policy, John Hopkins U., 2004-; current mem. com. to review the FDA and U.S. nat. system for assurance of drug safety. Contbr. articles to profl. jours.; mem. editl. bd. Cloning: Science and Policy, 98-, Monash Bioethics Review, 99-, Am. Jour. Bioethics, 2000-01, Public Library of Science, 2003-; policy review editor Journal of Law, Medicine, Healthcare, and Ethics, 1993-. Active U. Wis. Human Subjects Com., Madison, U. Wis. Hosp. Ethics Com., Madison, Abortion Strategy Group, Madison; cons. Rural South Cen. Wis. Perinatal Substance Abuse Project, 1989-; mem. Univ. Bioethics Adv. Com., U. Wis., 1998-, mem. stem cell rsch. program, 2003-; bd. dir. Alan Guttmacher Inst., 1991-96, 98-2000, 2002-,Found. for Genetic Medicine, 1997-Nat. Med. Com. Planned Parenthood Fedn. Am., 2004-; mem. scientific adv. bd. CuresNow, 2002-, Juvenile Diabetes Rsch. Found., WiCell, 2002-, Wis. Stem Cell Rsch. Program, 2004-. Fulbright grantee, 1985-86. Fellow AAAS, Wis. Acad. Sciences, Arts and Letters, Inst. Soc., Ethics & Life Sciences; mem. Internat. Bioethics Assn., Am. Soc. Law and Medicine, NAS(cons.; mem. bd, on life sciences, 2001-, mem.comm. on preventing destructive applications of biotechnology, 2002-03), Inst. Medicine (cons.; mem. com. on smallpox vaccination program implementation, 2002-05, mem. comm. on HIVNET 012 HIV Perinatal Transmission Trials, 2004-, mem. assess the drug safety system in the US, 2005-; (in conjunction with NRC) BLS liaison, comm. on embryonic stem cell rsch guidelines, 2004-, mem. adv. com. human embryonic stem cell rsch., 2006-), Soc. for the Advancement of Women's Health, 1998-2000, Am. Assn. Bioethics (bd. dir.), Open Soc. Inst. Program on Reproductive Health & Rights, 1999-. Democrat. Jewish. Avocations: travel, folk and salsa music, foreign languages, poker, reading, rollercoaster riding, home renovation. Office: U Wis Law Sch Law Bldg 975 Bascom Mall Rm 5211C Madison WI 53706-1399 Office Phone: 608-262-5015. Office Fax: 608-262-5485. Business E-Mail: racharo@wisc.edu.*

CHAROENWONGSE, CHINDARAT, pianist, music educator; b. Bangkok, Aug. 18, 1968; d. Vivat and Yuwadee Charoenwongse; m. George Grover Shaw, Sept. 25, 1999. BFA, Chulalongkorn U., Bangkok, 1989; M of Music Edn., U. Rochester, 1993; D of Musical Arts in Piano Performance, and Pedagogy, U. Okla., 1998. Instr. piano Chulalongkorn U., Bangkok, 1989-90; instr, lectr. piano Kasetsart U., Bangkok, 1990-91; exec. sec., adminstrv. asst. Johnson Electric Indsl. (Thailand) ltd., Bangkok, 1989-91; dir. piano dept. Chintakarn Music Inst., Bangkok, 1997-98; pianist, instr., dir. In Tune Music Co. Inc., Oklahoma City, 1999—; asst. prof. piano, divsn. head U. Ctrl. Okla., 2000—. Clinician, workshop presenter and cons., Alfred Publs., Bangkok, 1998, 2004-, Chintakarn Music Inst., 1993, 97-98, 2000—, Hal Leonard Publs., Bangkok, 2000—; guest lectr. Chulalongkorn U., Bangkok, 1998, 2000—, Srinakharinwirot U., Prasanmitr Campus, 2000-, Mahidol U., 2004-, Rangsit U., 2005-. Contbr. articles to profl. jours. Pianist Outreach Mission Com., Norman, Okla., 1996-97, 1999, St. John's Episcopal Ch., Norman, 1996-97. Fulbright scholar, 1991-93, Marjorie Martin Caylor scholar, U. Okla., Norman, 1994-96, Martha Boucher scholar, U. Okla., Norman, 1996-97; rsch. grantee U. Okla., Norman, 1997, Dean's fellow Coll. Arts, Media and Design, U. Ctrl. Okla., 2005 Mem. Music Tchrs. Nat. Assn., Okla. Music Tchrs. Assn. (v.p. local assn. and coll. chpt. 2005-06, collegiate chpt. chair 2006—), Ctrl. Okla. Music tchrs. Assn. (co-chmn. notification com. 1998-2003), Phi Kappa Phi, Sigma Alpha Iota (sec. corr. com. 1996-97). Avocations: travel, reading, musical performances, theater, opera. Office: U Ctrl Okla Sch Music 100 N Univ Dr Edmond OK 73034

CHARRIERE, SUZANNE, architectural firm executive; Mng. ptnr. Corgan Assocs., Dallas. Rep. for firm Dallas (Tex.) Citizen's Coun. Pres. Friends of Dallas (Tex.) Police Assn.; adv. bd. Women's Mus., Dallas; bd. dir. Goodwill Industries, Dallas, Dallas (Tex.) Pks. and Trees Found. Mem.: Nat. Assn. Women Bus. Owners (Louise Razzio Pathfinder award 2004), Internat. Women's Forum (v.p.), Greater Dallas (Tex.) C. of C. (bd. dir.). Office: Corgan Associates Inc 501 Elm St Dallas TX 75202

CHARRINGTON, KAREN HILLARY, lawyer, consultant; b. Bklyn., Sept. 03; d. George William and Sadie Evadne Charrington; m. Jerry Charrington, Aug. 13, 2000. BA, NYU, 1996; JD, CUNY, 2001. Bar: N.Y. 2000, U.S. Dist. Ct. (so. dist.) N.Y. 2002. Asst. dist. atty. Bronx (N.Y.) Dist. atty., 1999—2004; sr. trial atty. Bozeman, Trott and Savage, LLP, Mount Vernon, NY, 2004—06, of counsel atty., 2006—; civil and criminal litigator Charrington Medard, P.C., Rosedale, NY, 2005—. Spkr. in field. Earl Warren scholar, NAACP Legal Def. Fund, 1996—99. Mem.: ATLA (assoc.). Office: Charrington Medard PC One Cross Island Plaza Rosedale NY 11422 Office Phone: 718-528-4422. Office Fax: 718-528-4420. Business E-Mail: khc230@aol.com.

CHARRON, HELENE KAY SHETLER, retired nursing educator; b. West Bloomfield, NY, Nov. 17, 1937; d. Ellis John and Helene Esther (Moore) Shetler; m. Ronald W. Charron, July 1964; children: Michele Gefell, Andrea Hagen. Diploma, Rochester State Hosp. Sch., N.Y., 1958; BS in Nursing, U. Rochester, 1964, MS in Nursing Edn., 1965. Staff nurse Strong Meml. Hosp., Rochester, 1958-60; head nurse Monroe Community Hosp., Rochester, 1961-63; coord. psychiat. nursing Monroe CC, 1965—87; mental hygiene staff devel. specialist Rochester Psychiat. Ctr., 1982-83; chair dept. nursing Monroe CC, Rochester, 1987—96; ptnr. Initiatives in Nursing Edn., West Bloomfield, N.Y., 1995—. Writer numerous instructional computer programs, ancillaries, test banks, videotapes and games in field. Office: 9148 Dugway Rd West Bloomfield NY 14585-0196

CHARTERIS, FRANCES A., art educator, artist; b. Paris, Oct. 16, 1950; arrived in U.S., 1977; d. Hugo Guy Francis Charteris and Virginia Mary Forbes Adam; m. Albert U. Chong (div.); children: Ayinde Netifnet, Chinwe Amelia Chances. BA, U. York, Heslington, Eng., 1970; BFA with honors, Sch. Visual Arts, N.Y.C., 1979; MFA, U. San Diego, Calif., 1992. Freelance photographer, 1969—72; with Inroads Performance Troupe, 1970—72; photographer Sotheby and Parke Bernet, London, 1973—75; tchr. Kingston Coll., Jamaica, 1975—77; illustrator's agent Bettman Archives, Bronx, 1980—83; photo printer UN, N.Y.C., 1984—87; tchg. asst. U. Calif., San Diego, 1988—92; sr. instr. U. Colo., Boulder, 1993—, dir. Paris study abroad, 2005—. Dir., founder Farouche Performance Troop, 2006—; prof. art history NYU, Paris, 1999—2001. Exhibitions include Tucuman, Argentina, 2006. Builder, vol. Habitat for Humanity, Boulder, 1995—96; vol. homeless shelter, Boulder, 1995—97. Mem.: Women's Caucus for Art, Jung Study Group, Coll. Art Assn., Boulder Faculty Assembly. Democrat. Avocations: dance, hiking, travel, African and Jungian studies, healing. Office: Univ Colo Dept Art and Art History Boulder CO 80304 Office Phone: 303-492-3580. Business E-Mail: frances.charteris@colorado.edu.

CHARTERS, ANN, literature educator; b. Bridgeport, Conn., Nov. 10, 1936; d. Nathan and Kate Danberg; m. Samuel B. Charters, Mar. 14, 1959; children: Mallay, Nora Lili. AB, U. Calif.-Berkeley, 1957; MA, Columbia U., 1960, PhD, 1965. Mem. faculty Colby Jr. Coll., New London, NH, 1961—63; lectr. Columbia U., 1965—66; asst. prof. Am. lit. N.Y.C. Community Coll., 1967-70; assoc. dean of the coll. Brown U., 1989-90; prof. Am. lit. U. Conn., Storrs, 1974—. Author: Nobody—Life and Times of Bert Williams, 1967, Kerouac, 1973, 2d edit., 1986, I Love—Story of Vladimir Mayakovsky and Lili Brik, 1979, The Story and Its Writer, 7th edit., 2006, The Beats: Literary Bohemians in Post-War America, 1983, Beats and Company: A Portrait of a Literary Generation, 1986, The Viking Portable Beat Reader, 1992, Major Writers of Short Fiction, 1993, The Viking Portable Jack Kerouac Reader, 1995, Selected Letters of Jack Kerouac, 1995, (with Samuel Charters) Literature and Its Writers, 1997; author intro. Penguin Classic edit. Three Lives and Q.E.D. (Gertrude Stein), On the Road (Jack Kerouac), Selected Letters of Jack Kerouac, vol. 2, 1999, The American Short Story and Its Writer, 1999, (with Samuel Charters) Blues Faces, 2000, Beat Down to Your Soul, 2000, The Portable Sixties Reader, 2003. Office: U Conn Dept English PO Box U-25 Storrs Mansfield CT 06269-0001 Office Phone: 860-486-2141. Business E-Mail: acharters@uconn.edu.

CHARTERS, CYNTHIA GRACE, artist, educator; b. Fort Bragg, Calif., Sept. 14, 1949; d. Morris James and Virignia Lola (Davis) C.; m. William Terrance Foley, Aug. 30, 1970 (div. 1983); m. Peter Vladimir Tkacheff, Jan. 31, 1987; 1 child, Alexandra Petrovna. BA in Art, U. Calif., Davis, 1972, BS in Design, 1972, MA, 1981. Curator, registrar R.L. Nelson Gallery, U. Calif., Davis, 1982-85; lectr. art Calif. State U.-Stanislaus, Turlock, 1985-87, art lectr., dir. univ. art gallery, 1988-91; art instr. Cosumnes River Coll., Sacramento, 1997—2006. Guest lectr., panelist, cons. for numerous civic and pvt. orgns. including Sacramento Met. Arts Commn., Sacramento City Coll., Inst. Design and Exptl. Art, Sacramento; juror art exhbns.; artist in residence Yosemite Nat. Pk., Calif., 1988; art instr. Menaocino Art Ctr., 2004-05. One-woman shows include U. Calif., Davis, 2006, Menadocino Art Ctr., 2006, Represented in permanent collections numerous. Arts commr. City of Turlock, 1989-90. Mem. Am. Assn. Museums, Assn. Coll. and Univ. Museums and Galleries, Coll. Art Assn.

CHARTERS, KAREN ANN ELLIOTT, critical care nurse, health facility administrator; b. Chelsea, Mass., Apr. 3, 1946; d. Albert Charles and Hazelle Marie (Kraus) Elliott; m. Byron James Charters, Feb. 4, 1972. Diploma, Grace New Haven Sch. Nursing, New Haven, Conn., 1967; student, So. Conn. State Coll., 1968, U. New Haven, 1974; BS in Healthcare Adminstrn., St. Leo Coll., 1999. CCRN. Asst. head nurse Yale New Haven (Conn.) Hosp., 1972-76; staff nurse critical care unit Hosp. Corp. Am., 1982—; relief clin. coord. Cmty. Hosp. of New Port Richey, Fla., 1987—, nursing supr. Fla., 1997—. Mem. AACN (bd. dirs. Gulf Coast chpt. 1990-91, 96-97, treas. 1991-93), Am. Heart Assn. (past bd. dirs.). Home: 7519 Clanton Trail Hudson FL 34667 Office: Cmty Hosp New Port Richey 5637 Marine Pkwy New Port Richey FL 34652

CHARTIER, MARY EILEEN, music educator; b. Alpena, Mich., Aug. 19, 1935; d. John Chester Brunette and Eileen Rosemond Woods; m. Duane Edward Chartier, Apr. 15, 1983; children: Joseph John Bonk, Julie Anne Bonk. AA, Delta Coll. Cert. Music Tchr. Mich. Music Tchrs. Assn., 1965. Sec. to mgr. Social Security Adminstrn., Bay City, Mich., 1954—57; pvt. music tchr. Mich., 1965—. Various positions Saginaw Tuesday Musicale, 1970—. Mem.: Music Tchrs. Bay County (cmty. outreach chmn. 1996—), Music Tchrs. Assn. (scholarship chmn. 1996—), Mich. Music Tchrs. Assn. (state bd. 2000—, Tchr. of Yr. award Saginaw chpt. 1991, Emeritus cert. 1990), Saginaw Tuesday Musicale (past pres.). Home and Studio: 3252 Pinehurst Dr Gladwin MI 48624-9738

CHARYTAN, LYNN R., lawyer; b. Oct. 29, 1965; BA summa cum laude, Columbia Univ.; JD magna cum laude, Harvard Univ., 1990. Bar: DC 1991, NY 1991. Law clk. Judge Stanley Sporkin, US Dist Ct. (DC dist.), 1990—91; in-house counsel Washington Post, 1991—93; ptnr., vice chmn. Comm. & E-Commerce dept. Wilmer Cutler Pickering Hale & Dorr, Washington. Mem.: ABA, Fed. Comm. Bar Assn., Phi Beta Kappa. Office: Wilmer Cutler Pickering Hale & Dorr 1801 Pennsylvania Ave NW Washington DC 20006 Mailing: Wilmer Cutler Pickering Hale & Dorr 2445 M St NW Washington DC 20037 Office Phone: 202-663-6455. Office Fax: 202-663-6363. Business E-Mail: lynn.charytan@wilmerhale.com.

CHASE, ALEXANDRA NIN, psychologist, writer; b. Panama City, Panama, June 19, 1958; arrived in U.S., 1963; d. Paul Thorvald and Derith Alexander Chase; life ptnr. Richard Allen Frustere. BA in Sociology, San Francisco State U., 1981; MA in Creative Writing, San Francisco State U., 1985; PhD in Psychology, Calif. Inst. Integral Studies, 2001. Lic. psychologist Calif. Bd. Psychology, 2002. Instr. creative writing San Francisco (Calif.) State U., 1985—91, City Coll. San Francisco, 1989—94; rsch. assoc. Kaiser Permanente, Oakland, Calif., 1996—2000; counselor mental health Pyramid Alternatives, Pacifica, Calif., 2000—01; clin. psychologist Westside Cmty. Mental Health, San Francisco, 2001—; geriatric psychologist Vericare Sr. Svcs., San Diego, 2003—05; pvt. practice Pacifica, Calif., 2005—. Editor: Five Fingers Rev., 1987—91; author: The Beginning of Difficulty, 1989 (nomination L.A. Times Book prize, 1989); contbr. poetry to jours. Vol. instr. sr. writing workshop Raphael House Sr. Program, San Francisco, 1986—87; v.p. Light Up the Sky Fourth of July Fireworks Prodn., Half Moon Bay, Calif., 2005. Mem.: APA. Avocations: dogs, dance, dream work, collage. Office: Westside Community Mental Health 1663 Mission 310 San Francisco CA 94103 Address: 80 Eureka Sq 213 Pacifica CA 94044 Personal E-mail: alekac@comcast.net.

CHASE, BEVERLY FANGER, lawyer; b. 1949; AB magna cum laude, Radcliff Coll., 1970; JD cum laude, Fordham U., 1974. Bar: N.Y. 1975, registered: U.S. Dist Ct. So. Dist. N.Y. 1975, U.S. Ct. Appeals, second cir. 1975, U.S. Tax Ct. 1987. Law clk. to judge of U.S. Dist. Ct., so. dist., N.Y., 1974—76; assoc. Davis, Polk & Wardwell, N.Y., 1976—85, ptnr., 1985—, head trusts & estates practice group. Mem.: Am. Bar City N.Y. (Com. Trusts, Estates & Surrogate's Cts. 1987—90, 1999—2001), N.Y. State Bar Assn. (co-chmn. Com. Estates & Trusts Tax Sect. 1990—91), ABA. Office: Davis Polk & Wardwell 450 Lexington Ave New York NY 10017 Office Phone: 212-450-4383. Office Fax: 212-450-3383. Business E-Mail: beverly.chase@dpw.com.

CHASE, CAROL JOHNSON, mathematics educator; b. New London, Conn., Nov. 21, 1954; m. Graham R. Chase, June 5, 1976; children: Molly C.W., Samuel J.V. BS in Math., Ctrl. Conn. State U., New Britain, 1972, MS, cert. in supervision and Adminstrn., 1988. Lic. Conn., 1976. Math. tchr. West Hartford (Conn.) Bd. Edn., 1976—. Named Tchr. of Yr., West Hartford, 1997—98. Mem.: West Hartford Edn. Assn. (mem. exec. bd. 1979—2006). Home: 1596 Boulevard West Hartford CT 06107-2501 Office: Sedgwick Mid Sch 128 Sedgwick Rd West Hartford CT 06107 Office Phone: 860-570-6500.

CHASE, CHRISTA JOY, music educator; b. Washington, Aug. 21, 1955; d. Norman and Eva Mae Chase. MusM, U. Cin., 2000. Music tchr. Dalton Pub. Sch., Ga., 1977—83; asst. dir. Creative Arts Guild, Dalton, 1983—86; music tchr. Whitfield County Sch., Dalton, 1986—90, Cobb County Schs., Marietta, Ga., 1990—98, 2003—, Cin. Hills Christian Acad., 2000—03. Elem. chairperson Ga. Music Educators, Atlanta, 1995—97. Children's choir dir. St. Peter and St. Paul Episcopal Ch., Marietta, 2003—. Mem.: Music Educators Nat. Conf., Kodaly Educators of Ga. (bd. mem. 2006—). Republican. Episcopalian. Avocations: travel, singing. Home: 4545 River Pky # 7G Atlanta GA 30339 Office: Cobb County Schs Marietta GA Personal E-mail: cjchase2@excite.com.

CHASE, DAWN EILEEN, language educator; b. Oak Park, Ill., Apr. 30, 1941; d. Ralph A. and Alice M. (Nischwitz) Eggert; m. Rowland K. Chase. BA, Knox Coll., 1966; MA, San Jose State U., 1975. Cert. secondary tchr., Calif. Tchr. English Campbell (Calif.) Union H.S. Dist., 1967-96, chair English dept., 1975-95; adj. English instr. San Jose (Calif.) State U., 1997-2000; univ. supr. tchr. edn. program Stanford (Calif.) U., 2001—. Tchr./cons. San Jose Area Writing Project, 1978—, mem. adv. bd., 1979-81, 95-97; presenter workshops on English edn., No. Calif., 1979—. Author, editor: (anthology) Looking Back, Moving Forward, 1992. Del. UN Conf. on Women, Beijing, 1995. Mem. Nat. Coun. Tchrs. of English, Calif. Assn. Tchrs. of English. Democrat. Avocations: reading, writing, travel.

CHASE, DORIS TOTTEN, sculptor, educator, filmmaker; b. Seattle, 1923; d. William Phelps and Helen (Feeney) Totten; m. Elmo Chase, Oct. 20, 1943 (div. 1972); children: Gregary Totten, Randall Jarvis Totten. Student, U. Wash., 1941-43. Lectr. tours for USIA in S.Am., 1975, Europe, 1978, India, 1972, Australia, 1986, Eastern Europe, 1987, Ireland, England, France; vis. lectr., presenter U. Colo., Boulder, Mary Mount Coll., N.Y., the Kitchen Ctr. for Film & Video, Nat. Film Bd. of Can., Toronto, N.Y. Grad. Sch.; artist-in-residence Pilchuck Glass Sch., 1999. One-woman shows include Ruth White Gallery, N.Y.C., 1967, 69, 70, Fountain Gallery, Portland, Oreg., 1970, U. Wash. Henry Gallery, 1971, 77, 98, Wadsworth Athenum, Hartford, Conn., 1973, Hirshhorn Mus., Washington, 1974, 77, Anthology Film Archives, N.Y.C., 1975, 80, 83, Donnell Libr., N.Y.C., 1976, 79, 83, 92, Performing Arts Mus. at Lincoln Ctr., 1976, Mus. Modern Art, N.Y.C., 1978, 80, 87, 93, 98, High Mus., Atlanta, 1978, Herbert Johnson Mus., 1982, A.I.R. Gallery, N.Y.C., 1983-85, Art in Embassies, USIS, 1984-88, Inst. Contemporary Art, London, 1989, Woodside/Braseth Gallery, 1990, 92, 94, John F. Kennedy Ctr., 1990, Seattle Arts Mus., 1990, 92, 95, 99, 2002, Mus. N.W. Art La Conner Wash., 1995; circulating exhibit Western Mus. Assn., 1970-71, Am. Inst. Archs., Seattle, 1994, Friesen Gallery, Seattle, 1997, 98, 99, 2001, 04; represented in permanent collections Finch Coll. Mus., N.Y.C., Mus. Modern Art, N.Y.C., Seattle Art Mus., Ashai Shimbum, Tokyo, Georges Pompidou Ctr., Paris, Battelle Inst., Mus. Fine Arts Boston, Milw. Art Inst., Art Inst. Chgo., Mus. Fine Arts Houston, Frye Art Mus., Seattle, Nat. Collection Fine Arts, Smithsonian Instn., Washington, Wadsworth Athenum, N.C. Mus. Art, Raleigh, Mus. Modern Art, Kobe, Japan, Pa. Acad. Art, Phila., Portland Art Mus., Vancouver (B.C.) Art Gallery, Montgomery (Ala.) Mus. Fine Art, Hudson River Mus., N.Y.C., Tacoma Art Mus.; works represented in archival collections Ctr. for Film and Theatre Rsch., U. Wis., Madison, U. Wash., Seattle, UCLA Film Archives, Lincoln Ctr. Performing Arts Libr., N.Y.C., Pompideau, Paris, Archieves of Am. Art Smithsonian Instn., Washington; executed monumental kinetic sculpture Kerry Park, Seattle, Lake Park, 1976, Anderson, Ind., Expo '70, Osaka, Japan, Sculpture Park, Atlanta, Met. Mus. Art, N.Y.C., Montgomery Mus. Fine Arts, monumental bronze sculpture installed, Seattle Ctr., 1999; multi-media sculpture for 4 ballets, Opera Assn. Seattle; included in Sculpture in Park program N.Y.C., Playground of Tomorrow ABC-TV, L.A.; prodr., dir. (film and video) Doris Chase Dance Series, 1971-80, Concept Series, 1980-85, By Herself Series: Table for One (with Geraldine Page), 1985; prodr. (with Jennie Ventris) Glass Curtain, 1984(with Anne Jackson) Dear Papa, 1986, (with Luise Rainer) A Dancer, 1987, (with Priscilla Pointer) Still Frame, 1988, (with Joan Plowright) Sophie, 1989, The Chelsea, 1994, Danse de colour, 2002; prin. works include U. Wash., Seattle, 2005. Recipient honors and awards at numerous festivals in U.S. and fgn. countries; grantee Nat. Endowment for Arts, Am. Film Inst., 1988, N.Y. State Coun. for Arts, Mich. Arts Coun., Seattle Art Commn., 1992, Jerusalem Film Festival, 1987, Berlin Film Festival, 1985, 87, Athens Film Festival, 1995, London Film Festival, 1986, Am. Film Inst. Festival, 1987, 94, Retirement Rsch. Found., 1994, Lockwood Found., Herzman Family Found., Seattle Center Found., NEA, N.Y. State Coun. for Arts; subject of documentary Doris Chase: Portrait of the Artist, PBS, 1985; subject of book and video: Artist in Motion, 1993; subject of documentary Doris Chase: Circle at the Center, PBS, 1999; Doris Chase Day proclaimed by Mayor and City Coun. Seattle; recipient Wash. Gov.'s Art award, 1992; honored at N.Y. Pub. Libr. and N.Y. Film Video Coun., 2003. Mem. Actors Studio (writer, dirs. wing 1986). Achievements include all work in film and video being in collection and archives of Museum Modern Art, NYC; established Doris Totten Chase art scholarship fund University of Washington, 2002, 04, 05. Office Phone: 206-382-3649.

CHASE, JACLYN BOSWORTH, secondary school educator; b. Lemonister, Mass., Apr. 25, 1978; d. Edward Joseph and Suzanne Claire Chase. BS in Phys. Edn. and Health, Frostburg State U., Md., 2001; MS in Curriculum and Instrn., McDaniel Coll., Westminster, Md., 2005. Tchr. phys. edn. Joppatowne H.S., Joppa, Md., 2001—. Head coach lacrosse Joppatowne H.S., 2001—. Office: Joppatowne High School 555 Joppa Farm Rd Joppa MD 21085 Office Phone: 410-612-1510.

CHASE, JACQUELYN VERONICA, marketing professional; b. Balt., Jan. 25, 1965; AA in Applied Sci. & Bus. Mktg., Balt. City CC, 1997; BSBA in Mktg., Towson U., 2005. Sales mgr. Ann Taylor, Inc., Balt., 1990—2004; rsch. analyst Towson U., Md., 2001—. Amb. Towson U., 2000—02; pres. Am. Mktg. Assn., Towson, 2002—03. Evangelist missionary Friendship Bapt. Ch., Balt., 1998—2005. Office: Towson U 8000 York Rd Towson MD 21252-0001 Office Phone: 410-935-3460. Business E-Mail: jchase2@towson.edu.

CHASE, JENNY WEI-LANG KAO, singer, music educator; b. Quan Ming, China, June 15, 1941; arrived in U.S., 1964; d. Pun-Fei and Shu Kao; m. Robert Chase, June 28, 1969; 1 child, Wayne Hwa. BA, Judson Coll., 1966; MusM cum laude, U. Miss, 1968; studied with Dolf Swing, Juilliard Sch., 1969—72; cert. adminstr., U. Bridgeport, 1986. Music tchr. Yonkers Bd. Edn., 1969—99; voice tchr. Music Conservatory of Westchester, White Plains, NY, 1982—2002; prin., founder Chinese Sch. So. Westchester, Scarsdale, NY, 1981—95, pres. bd. dirs., 1981—99, hon. pres., prin., 1998—. Soprano soloist Mt. Vernon Cmty. Ch., 1974—79, Ch. in the Highlands, 1979—92, Carnegie Hall, NYC, 1981; concert (soprano) recitalist Lincoln Ctr., NYC, 1983—85. Soprano: CD Memory, 1997, Phoenix Rising, 2004; one-woman shows include Spring Hill Br., Merchants Nat. Bank, 1965, U. Miss., 1966, Mus. Oxford, Miss., 1967, Pen Women's Assn., Bronxville Pub. Libr., NY, 1984. Founder Evergreen Club Westchester, 2000; pres. Westchester Chinese Assn., 1997—99. Named Outstanding Alumna, Nat. Taiwan Coll. Arts, 2000; recipient Outstanding Leadership award, Westchester Chinese Assn., 1996, Dynamic Achiever award, Orgn. Chinese Americans, 1989, Art Achievement award, Chinese Am. Arts Coun., 1999. Mem.: Yonkers Fedn. Tchrs., Westchester Musicians Guild, Delta Omicron (life Cert. of Honor 1982). Mem. United Ch. Of Christ. Home: 17 Morgan Pl White Plains NY 10605 Personal E-mail: rac02rac@yahoo.com.

CHASE, KAREN HUMPHREY, elementary school educator; b. New Bedford, Mass., Nov. 17, 1948; d. Clifton Humphrey and Alice (Duffy) C. BA in Sociology, Stonehill Coll., 1970; MA in Edn., Lesley U., 2003. Cert. tchr. K-8, Mass. Elem. tchr. Minot (Maine) Consol. Sch., 1970-72; tchr. social studies George R. Austin Mid. Sch., Lakeville, Mass., 1972—2002, co-coord. students as mediators program, 1996—98; tchr. social studies Freetown-Lakeville Mid. Sch., 2002—. Dept. leader social studies, Austin Mid. Sch., Lakeville, 1976-80; supt. search team Freetown-Lakeville Sch. Dist., 1995. Actor/dir.: Your Theatre, Inc. New Bedford, Mass., 1985—; mem. Marion Arts Ctr., 1973—; 2nd v.p. Educators Assn. Freetown-Lakeville, 1991-93, 1st v.p., 1993-2003. Named Young Careerist of Yr., Bus. and Profl. Women, Wareham, Mass., 1979. Mem. Plymouth County Educators Assn. (Significant Svc. Honor award 1995), Mass. Tchrs. Assn., NEA, Nat. Coun. for Social Studies. Avocations: travel, reading, hiking, gardening, yoga. Home: 196 Clapp Rd Rochester MA 02770-4000 Office: Freetown-Lakeville Mid Sch 96 Howland Rd Lakeville MA 02347

CHASE, KAREN SUSAN, English literature educator; b. St. Louis, Oct. 16, 1952; d. Stanley Martin and Judith C.; m. Michael H. Levenson, Dec. 30, 1984; children: Alexander Nathan, Sarah Sophie. BA, UCLA, 1974; MA, Stanford U., 1977, PhD, 1980. Asst. prof. U. Va., Charlottesville, 1979-85, assoc. prof., 1985-91, prof., 1992—. Author: Eros and Psyche, 1984, George Eliot's Middlemarch, 1990; co-author: The Spectacle of Intimacy: A Public Life For The Victorian Family, 2000, Middlemarch in the Twenty-First Century, 2005. Office: Univ Va English Dept 219 Bryan Hall Charlottesville VA 22903

CHASE, LINDA (LINA CHASE), social worker, psychotherapist; b. Bklyn., Sept. 25, 1943; d. Albert A. and Frances (Rosenstein) Lessner; m. Alan Chase, Sept. 14, 1968 (div. June 1976); children: Nicole Shana, Isaac Lessner. BA in Sociology, SUNY, Buffalo, 1965; MS in Criminal Justice, U. New Haven, 1976; MSW, U. Conn., 1983. Cert. ind. social worker; lic. clin. social worker. Caseworker Suffolk County Child Welfare, Bayshore, N.Y., 1966-67; social worker Montefiore Hosp., Bronx, N.Y., 1967-68, Dept. Child Welfare, New Haven, 1968-70, Dept. Children and Youth Svcs., New Haven, 1976-77; supr. parent-aides Coord. Coun. for Children in Crisis, New Haven, 1978-84; dir. bereavement svcs. Conn. Hospice, Branford, 1984-92, social worker, 1985-88; pvt. practice, Orange, Conn., 1985-97, Branford, 1990—2003; social worker Yale New Haven Hosp., 2005—. Reiki master/practitioner, Branford, Conn., 1993—2003, New Haven, 2005—. Avocations: yoga, reading, dance. Home: 78 Olive St New Haven CT 06511-6981 Office Phone: 203-688-3254. E-mail: linachase@sbcglobal.net.

CHASE, LINDA, curator, writer; d. Sidney and Helen (Ganges) Chase; m. Timothy Knox (div.); 1 child, Leila Knox; m. Tom Blackwell, June 6, 1969. BA, Sarah Lawrence Coll., 1963; MA, U. Pitts., 1965. Dir., curator Tokyo Met. Mus., Tokyo, 1974, Rothman's Pall Mall Can., Ltd, Toronto, Canada, 1976, Naples Mus. of Art, Fla., 2002; curator The Currier Gallery of Art, Manchester, NH, 1982, Roxbury Arts Ctr., NY, 1999; freelance writer. Guest spkr. Pace Coll., New York, 1995, Des Moines Art Ctr., 1996, Zimmerli Art Mus., Rutgers U., East Brunswick, NJ, 2004; lectr., moderator Naples Mus. of Art, Fla., 2002; lectr., instr. Writers in Mountains, Roxbury, 2004. Author: (art book) Hyperrealism, 1975, Ralph Goings, 1987, Hollywood on Main Street: The Movie House Paintings of Davis Cone, 1988, Duos: Alice Neel's Double Portraits, 2002, (novel) Perfect Cover, 1994, (television drama) For Art's Sake, Alfred Hitchcock Presents, 1988; co-author: (art book) Photo Realism at the Millennium, 2002; contbr. critical anthology. Founder, chmn. New Kingston Valley Assn., NY, 1989. Grantee Individual Artist's Grant award, NY State Coun. of Arts, 1995, 1996, 2003; Non-Fiction Lit. fellow, NY Found. for Arts, 1999. Mem.: Authors Guild. Home: PO Box 374 New Kingston NY 12459 Business E-Mail: linda.chase@earthlink.net.

CHASE, NAOMI FEIGELSON, poet; b. Pitts., May 26, 1932; d. Henry and Rachel Savage Ellenbogen; m. Eugene Feigelson (div.); children: Elizabeth Feigelson, Jonathan Feigelson; m. Gordon Chase (dec. July 1971). BA magna cum laude, Radcliffe U., 1954; MA, Brandeis U., 1956. Program and policy staff Gov. Frank Sargent, Boston, 1974—75; cons. media publs. Mass. Coun. on Arts and Humanities, Boston, 1975—77; cons. to commr. on media Mass. Dept. Social Svcs., Boston, 1980—82; mktg. dir. Met. Transp. Authority, N.Y.C., 1982—83; dir. comm. John F. Kennedy Sch. Govt., Harvard U., Cambridge, Mass., 1986—87; asst. dir. news office Mass. Inst. Tech., Cambridge, 1988—92; pub. affairs mktg. Naomi F. Chase, Inc., Boston and N.Y.C., 1991—93. Author: (poetry) Listening for Water, 1980, The Judge's Daughter, 1996, Waiting for the Messiah in Somerville, Mass., 1983, Stacked, 2000, The One Blue Thread, 2003, Gittel, the Would-Be Messiah, 2005, (non-fiction) The Underground Revolution: Hippies, Yippies and Others, 1970, A Child is Being Beaten, 1975; reporter: Village Voice, 1964—74. Grantee writer's fellow, Yaddo, 1992; acad. fellow, Brandeis U., 1957—58, Columbia U., 1968, writer's fellow, MacDowell Colony, 1979, 1981, 1983, Yaddo, 1990, Banff Ctr. for the Arts, 1991. Democrat. Jewish. Avocation: painting. Home: PO Box 1231 Truro MA 02666

CHASE, SANDRA LEE, clinical pharmacist, consultant; b. Oak Park, Ill., July 31, 1959; d. William Warren and Charlene Lois (Johnson) Chase; m. Christopher Paul Bloch, Sept. 8, 1984; children: Kyle Thaddeus Bloch, Matthew William Bloch. Student, Mich. State U., 1977-80; BS in Pharmacy, U. Mich., 1983, PharmD, 1984. Lic. pharmacist Del., Mich., Pa.; cert. leader arthritis found. YMCA Aquatic Program. Rsch. asst. U. Mich., Ann Arbor, 1980-81; pharmacy intern Three Rivers (Mich.) Hosp., 1981, Cmty. Pharmacy, Ann Arbor, 1980-83; pharmacy intern, grad. intern St. Francis Hosp., Wilmington, Del., 1982-83; resident in hosp. pharmacy Thomas Jefferson U. Hosp., Phila., 1984-85, clin. pharmacist in cardiopulmonary medicine, 1985-89; sr. med. info. coord. ICI Pharms. Group, Wilmington, Del., 1989-92; clin. pharmacist Thomas Jefferson U. Hosp., Phila., 1989-93, clin. pharmacist drug use policy and clin. svcs., 1993-98; clin. pharmacy specialist Spectrum Health, Grand Rapids, Mich., 1999—. Adj. asst. prof. clin. pharmacy Temple U. Coll. Pharmacy, 1990—98, Ferris State U. Coll. Pharmacy, 1999—; clin. instr. in pharmacy practice Phila. Coll. Pharmacy and Sci., 1985—87, clin. asst. prof., 1987—88, clin. assoc. prof., 1988—98; instr. clin. care cardiopulmonary medicine in nursing Episcopal Hosp., Phila., 1986—88, Thomas Jefferson U. Hosp., Phila., 1985—91, Our Lady of Lourdes Med. Ctr., Camden, NJ, 1988—91; coord., prof. pharmacology and drug therapeutic for advanced nursing practice course Sch. Nursing Ctr. Profl. Devel., U. Pa., Phila., 1994—2001; mem. Pa. Osteporosis Soc. Bd., 1996—98; presenter in field. Mem. editl. bd.: RN, referee:; contbg. editor; mem. editl. bd.: Med. Econs., referee: AHFS Drug Info., Am. Druggist, Am. Jour. Hosp. Pharmacy, Nursing 96 Drug Handbook, Nursing 97 Drug Handbook, Pharmacotherapy, Annals of Pharmacotherapy, U. Hosp. Consortium Monographs; contbr. articles to profl. jours. Mem. adv. bd. Nursing Mothers Network; cert. leader aquatic program Arthritis Found. YMCA, 2000—; chmn. Coll. Pharmacy Alumni Soc., 2000—04; mem. women's heart advantage steering com. Spectrum Health, 2003—05; mem. alumni bd. govs. U. Mich. Coll. Pharmacy, 1991—97, 1998—2004, chair bd. govs., 2000—03; mem. Heartbeat Gala com. Am. Heart Assn., 2004—; mem. State of Mich. Task Force for Cardiovasc. Health, 2002—03; bd. dirs. U. Mich Alumni Soc., 2004—; chair edn. com. Mich. Soc. Health Sys. Pharmacists, 2001—; bd. dirs. Corey Lake Assn., 2003—. Recipient Alumni Svc. award, U. Mich. Coll. Pharmacy, 2006; fellow, Mich. Pharmacists Assn., 2001. Mem.: Am. Heart Assn., Aerobics and Fitness Assn. Am., Western Mich. Soc. Health-Sys. Pharmacists (bd. dirs. 1998—2000), Pediat. and Adult Asthma Network West Mich., Mich. Soc. Health Sys. Pharmacists (chair edn. com. 2000—, Pharmacist of Yr. 2005), Mich. Pharm. Assn. (mem. exec. bd. 2002—, pres.elect 2005, pres. 2006), Del. Pharm. Soc. (conv. com. 1990—94, ACPE com. 1990—94), Nat. Headache Found., Am. Diabetes Assn., Am. Pharm. Assn., Am. Soc. Health Sys. Pharmacists, Am. Coll. Clin. Pharmacy, U. Mich. Alumni Assn. (bd. dirs. 2004—), Rho Chi Pharm. Soc. Republican. Lutheran. Avocations: aerobics, waterskiing, cross country skiing, gardening. Office: Spectrum Health Dept Pharmacy 1840 Wealthy St SE Grand Rapids MI 49506 Office Phone: 616-774-5264. Business E-Mail: Sandra.Chase@spectrum-health.org.

CHASE-BRAND, JULIA, psychiatrist, researcher; d. John Waddell and Rosemary Morrisson Chase; m. George Howard Brand, July 9; children: Gretchen Ross, Jonathan Brand. BA, Smith Coll., Northampton, Mass., 1965; PhD, Ind. U., Bloomington, 1972; MD, Albert Einstein Coll. Medicine, Bronx, 1996. Asst. prof. biology Rutgers U., New Brunswick, NJ, 1971—76; assoc. prof. biology Barnard Coll., Columbia U., NYC, 1976—90; intern, 1990—2006; child psychiatrist Hackensack Hosp., NJ, 2001—04; psychiatrist pvt. practice, Englewood Cliffs, 2004—. Contbr. articles to profl. jours., chapters to books. Mem.: Animal Behavior Soc., Am. Psychiat. Assn. Home: 187 Crescent Ave Leonia NJ 07605 Office: 510 Sylvania Ave Englewood Cliffs NJ 07632

CHASSIER, JANICE, elementary school educator, art educator; b. New Brunswick, NJ, June 25, 1955; d. Robert J. and Dorothy Rose Cook; m. Raymond Chassier, Mar. 1, 1980; children: Jacqueline Helene, Kimberly Rose. BA (hon.), Kean Coll. NJ, Union, 1977. Driver United Parcel Svc., Vineland, NJ, 1975—83; tchr. 2nd grade, 4th grade, art Pittsgrove Twp. Bd. Edn., 1993—. Mem.: Art Educators NJ (assoc.; v.p. 2005—06). Office: Olivet School 235 Sheep Pen Rd Pittsgrove NJ 08318 Office Phone: 856-358-2081. Personal E-mail: chassier4@comcast.net.

CHAST, ROZ, cartoonist; b. Bklyn., Nov. 26, 1954; d. George and Elizabeth (Buchman) C.; m. William Franzen, Sept. 22, 1984; children: Ian, Nina. BFA, RISD, 1977. Contract artist The New Yorker Mag., N.Y.C., 1979—; cartoonist The Scis. Mag. Author: (cartoon collections) Unscientific Americans, 1982, Parallel Universes, 1984, Mondo Boxo: Cartoon Stories, 1987, The Four Elements, 1988, Proof of Life on Earth, 1991, The Party, After You Left: Collected Cartoons 1995-2003, 2004; illustrator of various books including The Joy of Being Single, 1992, Meet My Staff, 1998, Now I Will Never Leave the Dinner Table, 1999, Rationalizations to Live By, 2000, The New Yorker Book of Kids Cartoons, 2001, Weird and Wonderful Words, 2002, You're an Animal, Viskovitz!, 2003; work has been featured in Scientific American, N.Y. Times Mag., Rolling Stone, Nat. Lampoon.

CHASTAIN, BRANDI DENISE, professional soccer player; b. San Jose, Calif., July 21, 1968; m. Jerry Smith; 1 stepchild. Student, U. Calif., Berkeley, 1986—88; BA in TV Comm., Santa Clara U., 1991. Mem. U.S. Women's Soccer Team, 1996—; asst. coach women's soccer team Santa Clara U.; profl. soccer player San Jose CyberRays, 2001—03. Mem. Shiroke Serena, Japan, 1993, U.S. Olympic Soccer Team, Athens, 2004. Named World Cup Champion, 1999; recipient Gold medal, Atlanta Olympic Games, 1996, Gold Medal, Athens Olympic Games, 2004, Silver medal, Sydney Olympic Games, 2000. Achievements include mem. championship team U.S. Olympic Festival; CONCACAF Championship, N.Y., 1993. Office: c/o Santa Clara U Athletics Dept 500 El Camino Real Santa Clara CA 95050-4345 also: US Soccer Fedn 1801 S Prairie Ave # 1811 Chicago IL 60616-1319

CHATFIELD, MARY VAN ABSHOVEN, librarian; b. Bay Shore, NY; d. Cornelius and Elma Elizabeth (Sumner) van Abshoven; m. Robert W. Chatfield, June 22, 1963 (div. 1981); 1 child, Robert Warner Jr.; m. Alexander Watts, Jan. 6, 1996 (div. 2000). AB, Radcliffe Coll., 1958; SM, Columbia U., 1961; MBA, Harvard U., 1972. With library system Harvard U., Cambridge, Mass., 1961-92, librarian Bus. Sch., 1963-78, head libr., 1978-92; acting head libr. Countway Libr. Harvard Med. Sch., 1988-89; head libr. Angelo State U., San Angelo, Tex., 1992-95; collections care mgr. Fosterfields, Morristown, NJ, 1996-97; mgr. libr. svcs. Montclair (N.J.) Art Mus., 1997; exec. dir. Mendham (N.J.) Free Pub. Libr., 1997-99; coord. pub. and tech. svcs. Tom Green County Libr., San Angelo, Tex., 1999—2004; Concho Valley Master Gardener, docent, rschr. San Angelo Mus. Fine Arts, 2004—; ind rschr.; v.p. mktg. rsch. Xurex Nano-Coatings Corp., 2005—. Rschr., tutor Adult Literacy Coun.; bd. dirs. Historic San Angelo; pres. Friends Tom Green County Libr. Episcopalian. Avocations: reading, embroidery, collecting, museum studies, public art. Home: 115 N Jackson St San Angelo TX 76901-3215 Personal E-mail: marychat@wcc.net.

CHATFIELD-TAYLOR, ADELE, historic site director; b. Jan. 29, 1945; d. Hobart and Mary Owen (Lyon) C-T; m. John Guare, May 20, 1981. BA, Manhattanville Coll., 1966; MS in Hist. Preservation, Columbia U., 1974; postgrad., Harvard U., 1978-79; ArtsD (hon.), Lake Forest Coll., 1995. Archtl. historian Hist. Am. Bldg. Survey, Washington, 1967; co-founder, dir. Urban Deadline Archs., Inc., 1968-73; with N.Y.C. Landmarks Preservation Commn., 1973-80; founder, exec. dir. N.Y. Landmarks Preservation Found., 1980-84; dir. design arts program Nat. Endowment for Arts, 1984-88; pres. Am. Acad. in Rome, N.Y.C., 1988—. Adj. prof. hist. preservation program Grad. Sch. Arch. and Planning, Columbia U., 1976-84; guest lectr. Harvard U., MIT, Columbia U., NYU, U. Va. Contbr. articles to profl. jours. Mem. Thomas Jefferson Found. for Monticello, 2001—; bd. dir. Preservation ACTION, 1976—84, Internat. Design Conf., Aspen, 1986—90, Nat. Bldg. Mus., 1989—95; trustee Ctr. for Bldg. Conservation, 1978—84, Tiber Island History Mus., 1983—, Nat. Trust for Hist. Preservation, 1999—; mem. U.S. del. to China Women in Arch., 1977, 1980, Hist. Preservationists, 1982; mem. exec. com. U.S./Internat. Coun.on Monuments and Sites, 1979—84; vice chmn. design arts policy panel U.S./Internat. Coun. on Monuments and Sites, 1978—82; mem. commn. Fine Arts, 1990—94; mem. restoration com. South St. Seaport Mus., 1975—84; mem. adv. bd. Jeffersonian Restoration, 1989—; bd. dir. Greenwich Village Trust for Hist. Preservation, 1983—84; trustee Inst. Classical Architecture and Classical Am., 2002—; mem. lawn adv. bd. U. Va., 1982—86. Recipient Rome prize Am. Acad. in Rome, 1983-84, Merit award AIA N.Y. chpt., 2003; Loeb fellow Harvard U, 1978-79; named to Grand Office Ordine al Meito Pres. Italian Republic, 2002; fellow N.Y. Inst. Humanities, 1983-89. Fellow Am. Acad. Arts & Scis.; mem. Nat. Trust Hist. Preservation, Friends of Cast Iron Arch., Met. Mus. Art, Century Assn., Pug Dog Club of Greater N.Y. Office: Am Acad in Rome 7 E 60th St New York NY 10022-1001 E-mail: a.chatfield-taylor@aarome.org.

CHATMAN, DANA (POKEY CHATMAN), women's college basketball coach; b. Ama, La., June 18, 1969; BA, LSU, 1992. Student asst. LSU, 1992—93, asst. coach, 1993—99, assoc. coach, 2000—03, head coach. Named Kodak All-American, 1991; named to Freshman All-SEC Team, 1988, All-SEC Team, 1989—91. Achievements include coaching SEC Tournament Champions, 2006. Office: LSU Athletics Dept PO Box 25095 Baton Rouge LA 70894-5095*

CHATTERJI, ANGANA P., anthropologist; b. Calcutta, India, Nov. 17, 1966; d. Bhola and Anubha (Sengupta) C.; m. Richard Murray Shapiro, May 10, 1998. MA, U. Delhi, 1989; PhD, Calif. Inst. Integral Studies, San Francisco, 1999. Cons. Planning Com. India, New Delhi, 1990-92; dir. rsch. Asia forest network program Ctr. South Asia Studies U. Calif., Berkeley, 1992—. Asst. adj. prof. Calif. Inst. Integral Studies, 1997—; cons. Swed Forest Internat., Stockholm, 1997—; cons. in field Author: In Search of Reality, 1984. Ford Found. grantee, 1993. Mem. Am. Anthropol. Assn. Avocations: gliding, reading, computers, travel, symphony.

CHATTOPADHYAY, COLLETTE ADELE, art historian, critic; d. James Gordon and Jean Marie (Miller) Diller; m. Shubroto Chattopadhyay; 1 child, Jacqueline. BA in Fine Arts (hon.), Wheaton Coll., Ill.; MFA (hon.), U. Chgo. Assoc. faculty Saddleback Coll., Mission Viejo, Calif., 1996—, dept. chair, 2004—. Guest curator Pacific Asia Mus., Pasadena, Calif., 2002—03; guest lectr. L.A. County Mus. Art, 2005, AAUW, Mission Viejo, 2004, Laguna Art History, Laguna Beach, Calif., 2002. Contbg. editor: Artweek, 1990—, Sculpture Mag., 1996—; contbr. chapters to books, articles. Mem.: Internat. Assn. Word and Image Studies, Am. Com. S. Asian Art, Internat. Assn. Art Critics. Avocations: reading, travel, cooking. Home: PO Box 50128 Irvine CA 92619 Office: Saddleback Coll 28000 Marguerite Pkwy Mission Viejo CA 92692 Office Phone: 949-348-6031. Office Fax: 714-838-5666. E-mail: collete.chatto@cox.net.

CHAU, PIN PIN, bank executive; b. Hong Kong; d. Waihing Wong; m. Raymond Chau; 1 child, Christine. BA, Coe Coll., 1965; MA in Asian hist., Yale U., 1967; grad., Rutgers U. With Nat. Westminster Bank (now Fleet), 1970—87; chief lending officer United Orient Bank, N.Y.C., 1987—88, COO, 1988—89, pres., CEO, 1989—93, The Summit Nat. Bank, Atlanta, 1993—; CEO Summit Bank Corp., Atlanta, 1999—. Bd. dirs. Consumer Credit Counseling Service; exec. com. Ga. Dept. Industry, Trade and Tourism, 1999—. Bd. dirs. Atlanta Coll. Arts; bd. councilors Carter Ctr. Mem.: Internat. Women's Forum, Soc. Internat. Bus. Fellows (assoc.). Avocation: painting. Office: Summit Bank Corp 4360 Chamblee-Dunwoody Rd Atlanta GA 30341

CHAUDERLOT, FABIENNE-SOPHIE, foreign language educator; b. Marseilles, France, Aug. 11, 1960; came to U.S., 1985; d. Michel Hubert and Georgia Kalafatides. Maitrise English Lit., U. Scis. Humaines, Aix-en-

Provence, France, 1982; MBA in Internat. Adminstrn., Puyricard, France, 1985; PhD, U. Calif., San Diego, 1995. Lectr. U. Calif., Riverside, 1995-96; asst. prof. U. P.R., Mayaguez, 1996-97, Wayne State U., Detroit, 1997-2000; with Veritas Software Internat. Strategies, 2000—. V.p. Alliance Francaise, San Diego, 1990-93; founder, pres. Femmes Francaises du Sud Calif., San Diego, 1989-93. Rsch. grantee Humanities Ctr., Detroit, 1997-98. Avocations: painting, piano, cats, aerobics, photography. Office: Wayne State U 487 Manoogian Hall Detroit MI 48202 E-mail: f.chauderlot@Wayne.edu.

CHAUDHRY, MARIE-LAURENCE, elementary school educator; b. France, July 18, 1947; came to U.S., 1963; d. Gerard Leopold and Gisèle Delienne Dominique; children: Aisha Khan, Daud, Sara, Sadia. Student, Northwestern U., 1964-68; M of Applied Tchg. in Reading, Northeastern Ill. U., 1975; Cert. of Advanced Studies in Ednl. Leadership and Adminstrn., Nat. Louis U., 1993. Lab. technician Evanston (Ill.) Hosp., 1968-69; chemist libr. Velsicol Chem., Chgo., 1969-70; tech. libr. C-E Refractories, Chgo., 1970; tchr. Chgo. Pub. Schs.-Schiller Sch., 1970-80, Hilel Sch., Chgo., 1980-82; tchr. elem. edn. Hammond Sch., Chgo., 1982—, staff devel. facilitator, 1993—; adminstr. Melrose Pk. Sch., Sch. Dist. 89, Chgo., 2000. Owner, mgr. apt. bldgs., Melrose Park, Ill., 1994—, several shopping centers and malls; ins. prodr., 1998—; pres. MLC Enterprises, Inc. Organizer Ednl. Confs. for Hammond Schs., 1991-99; regional pres. ladies aux. Ahmadiyya Movement in Islam, 1990-93, pres. local chpt., 1988-93; regional sec. Children's Aux. Orgn., 2001—; vol. DuPage Convalescent Ctr., Wheaton, 1993-95; spkr. Women in Islam, various univs. Moslem. Home: PO Box 1236 Wayne IL 60184-1236

CHAUDOIR, JEAN HAMILTON (JEAN HAMILTON), secondary school educator; b. Lake Charles, La., July 31, 1945; d. John Gardiner and Nora (Alford) Hamilton; divorced; 1 child, Elizabeth Jean. BS, La. State U., 1967, MEd, 1986, postgrad., 2002. Tchr. 3d grade St. Pius X Sch., Baton Rouge, 1967-69; tchr. 2d grade St. Francis Cabrini Sch., Alexandria, La., 1969-75; tchr. 3d grade St. Theresa Sch., Shreveport, La., 1975-76; tchr. 4th grade Sacred Heart Sch., Baton Rouge, 1976-79, West Baton Rouge Parish, Brusly, La., 1979-80; tutor Ed-U-Care, Baton Rouge, 1987-88; with summer program East Baton Rouge Parish, Baton Rouge, 1990-91, tchr. Chpt. 1 summer sch., 1993, 94; part time tchr. Modern Curriculum Press, Baton Rouge, 1995—; tchr. for instrnl. support Lanier Elem. Sch., Baton Rouge, 1997—2002, chair improvement team. Chair Adopt-A-Sch. at Park Forest Elem., Baton Rouge, 1986-94; chair mktg. com. Park Forest Elem. Sch., Baton Rouge, La., 1986-94, mem. adv. coun., 1993-94, chair monitoring com., 1993-94; mem. Title 1 Sch. Wide Com., 1995. Sustaining mem. Jr. League Baton Rouge, 1985—2001. Mem.: Delta Kappa Gamma (pres.). E-mail: jchaudoir@ebrpss.k12.la.us.

CHAUNDRA, GALE BUCKELS, nursing administrator, writer; b. Euclid, Ohio, Apr. 28, 1980; d. Tamara Dea (Boyer) and William Burke; children: Tristan Edward Davis-Buckels, Sydney Leigh Buckels, Braden Walter Grady Buckels. Diploma, Hondros Coll., Independence, Oh, 2001, Willoughby-Eastlake Sch. Nursing, Ohio, 2003. Charge nurse Rae-ann Geneva, Ohio, 2004—. Mem.: Internat. High IQ Soc. (life). Home: 6901 Claymoor Ave Madison OH 44057 Office: Rae-Ann Geneva 839 W Main St Geneva OH 44066 Office Phone: 440-417-0995. Personal E-mail: invweb_cb@yahoo.com.

CHAUVIN, CALLY HEBERT, science educator, educational consultant; d. Albert J. Jr. and Sherry Hebert; m. Donald Chauvin, Nov. 18, 1994; children: Logan J. Callahan, Amber M. Callahan, Jennifer M., Jeffrey B. Degree in elem. edn., Nicholas State U., Thibodaux, La., 1984; MEd, Am. InterContinental U, Hoffman Estates, Ill., 2006. Tchr. St. Charles Parish Sch. Bd., Luling, La., 1989—2000; sci. tchr. Lafourche Parish Sch. Bd., Thibodaux, 2000—. Ednl. cons. Barataria-Terrebonne Nat. Estuary, Thibodaux, 1998—. Editor: (activity book) When the Salt Water Came; author: (ednl. resource) Lafourche Parish: From the Beginning, (laminiated flip cards) Invasive Species of Bayou Lafourche. Eucharistic min., lector, commentator St.Hilary Cath. Ch., Mathews, La., 1992—2006. Named Lafourche Parish Mid. Sch. Tchr. of Yr., Lafouche Parish Educators Assn., 2005, Educator of Yr., Chamber Lafourche and Bayou Region, 2005, Citizenship Edn. Tchr. of Yr., Henry Robertson Am Legion, 2005—06; grantee, Gov.'s Office Environ. Edn., 2000; LEARN grantee, La. Dept. Edn., 1998—2000, Quality Sci. and Math. grantee, La. State Tchrs. Assn., 1998—99, 2002—04, Am. History grantee, La. Dept. Edn., 2002. Mem.: La. Assn. Sci. Leaders (assoc.; sec. 2005—06). Democrat. Office: Cally's Ed & Cons Svcs 6150 Hwy 56 Chauvin LA 70344 Office Phone: 985-532-2597.

CHAVE, CAROL, arbitrator, retired lawyer; b. Chgo., Jan. 30, 1948; d. Grant Carruthers and Priscilla Morrison (Shaw) C.; m. Robert Edmund Hand; children: Joshua, Chloe, Robert, Grant. BA, U. Chgo., 1970; MAT, Oakland U., 1971; JD, Loyola U., Chgo., 1976. Bar: Ill. 1976, N.Y. 1980. Tchr. corps intern Pontiac (Mich.) Pub. Schs., 1970-71; sec., receptionist Grad. Sch. Bus., U. Chgo., 1971; counselor Sonia Shankman Orthogenic Sch., Chgo., 1972; pvt. practice Chgo., 1976-78; asst. v.p., assoc. counsel Bank of Tokyo, N.Y.C., 1978-85; substitute tchr. N.Y.C. Pub. Schs., 1986-88; with Breckenridge Law Offices, 1986-88; sr. v.p., counsel, mgr. human resources Tokai Bank, N.Y.C., 1988-97; dir., counsel Deutsche Bank, N.Y.C., 1997-99; arbitrator Internat. Ctr. for Dispute Resolution, N.Y.C., 2001—. Arbitrator Am. Arbitration Assn., N.Y.C., 1986—. Vol. lawyer Chgo. Vol. Legal Svcs., 1977-78; designer playground PS 41 Parent Assn., Greenwich Village, N.Y., 1987. Avocations: weaving, dance. Personal E-mail: chavec@gmail.com.

CHAVERS, BLANCHE MARIE, pediatrician, educator, researcher; b. Clarksdale, Miss., Aug. 2, 1949; d. Andrew and Mildred Louise C.; m. Gubare Mpambara, May 21, 1982; 1 child, Kaita. BS in Zoology, U. Wash., 1971, MD, 1975. Diplomate Am. Bd. Pediats. Intern U. Wash., Seattle, 1975-76, resident in pediatrics, 1976-78; instr. U. Minn., Mpls., 1982, asst. prof. pediatrics, 1983-90, assoc. prof. pediatrics, 1990-99, prof. pediatrics, 1999—. Attending physician dept. pediatrics, U. Minn. Sch. Medicine, Mpls., 1982. Co-editor: Am. Jour. Kidney Diseases, 2001—; contbr. articles to profl. jours. Recipient Clin. Investigator award NIH, 1982; Pediatric Nephrology fellow U. Minn., 1978-81. Mem. Am. Soc. Nephrology, Am. Soc. Pediatric Nephrology, Internat. Soc. Nephrology, Internat. Soc. Pediatric Nephrology, Am. Soc. Transplantation, Internat. Pediatric Transplant Assn. Democrat. Methodist. Avocations: tennis, reading, collecting African artifacts, art. Office: Univ Minn MMC 491 420 Delaware St SE Minneapolis MN 55455-0348

CHAVERT, GEORGIA, nutritionist, educator; b. Atlanta, Ga., July 9, 1953; m. James L. Morgan, Oct. 16, 1982; children: Richard, Eliott. BS, U. N.H., Durham, 1975; MS, Columbia U., N.Y.C., 1979. Registered dietitian. Dietetic intern Med. Coll. Va., Richmond, 1976, therapeutic dietitian, 1976—78; sys. and tng. clin. dietitian Meml. Sloan-Kettering Cancer Ctr., N.Y.C., 1979—81; nutritionist Vis. Nurse Assn., Allegheny County, Pa., 1982; chief clin. dietitian Hosp. St. Raphael, New Haven, 1982—88, asst. dir. food sci. dept., 1988—93. Cons. in field; mem. adv. bd. Yale-New Haven Hosp., 1997—. Contbr. papers to profl. publs. Bd. dirs. Woodbridge (Conn.) Park Assn., 2005—; commr. Woodbridge Libr., 1997—2001. Mem.: Soc. for Nutrition Edn., Conn. Dietetic Assn. (chair edn. com. 2000—04), Am. Dietetic Assn. Democrat. Avocations: fitness, Alpine skiing, gospel choir, scuba diving. Office: U New Haven 300 Boston Post Rd West Haven CT 06516

CHAVEZ, FAITH COOTS, medical nurse; b. Cindad Bolivar, Venezuela, June 22, 1956; d. David L. and Joan A. (Maxwell) Coots; 1 child, Marisol Barbara. BSN, Biola U., 1979. RN, Calif.; cert. critical care nurse, ACLS. Clinician IV med. surg. fl., aide New Born Nursery; staff nurse SICU Meth. Hosp. So. Calif., Arcadia; staff nurse ICU Desert Samaritan Med. Ctr., Mesa, Ariz. Mem. AACN, Am. Assn. Critical Care Nursing. Home: 3930 W Monterey St Unit 134 Chandler AZ 85226-2256

CHAVEZ, JEANETTE, editor; BS in Journalism, U. Colo., 1973. Mem. staff Office of U.S. Rep. Spark Matsunaga, Washington; reporter Colorado Springs (Colo.) Sun, 1973—74; reporter, copy desk chief, city editor, news editor Ft. Collins (Colo.) Coloradoan, 1974—81; copy editor Daily Herald, Arlington Heights, Ill., 1981—82; copy editor, then news editor bus. sect. Chgo. Sun Times, 1982—84; dep. news editor Denver Post, 1984—86, news editor, 1987—88, asst. mng. editor, 1988—91, assoc. editor features, 1991—97, mng. editor, 1997—. Office: Denver Post 1560 Broadway Denver CO 80202-1577

CHAVEZ, LINDA, civil rights organization executive; b. Albuquerque, June 17, 1947; m. Christopher Gersten Chavez; 3 children. BA, U. Colo., 1970; postgrad., UCLA, 1970-72, U. Md., 1974-75. Mem. staff House Judiciary Subcom. on Civil and Constl. Rights, Washington, 1972-74; asst. dir. legis. Am. Fedn. Tchrs., 1975—77; cons. civil rights sect. Office Mgmt. and Budget, Washington, 1977; editor Am. Educator mag., 1977-83; asst. to pres. Am. Fedn. Teachers, 1982—83; staff dir. U.S. Commn. on Civil Rights, 1983-85; dep. asst. to pres. and dir. Office Pub. Liaison Exec. Office of Pres., 1985-86; US Senate candidate Md., 1986; chmn. Nat. Commn. Migrant Edn., 1988—92; mem. UN Subcommission on prevention of discrimination and protection of minorities, 1992—96; founder, pres. Ctr. for Equal Opportunity, Washington, 1995—, Stop Union Polit. Abuse, 2001—; founder, chmn. Rep. Issues Campaign, 2003—. Bd. dirs. ABM Industries, Inc.; polit. analyst FOX News Channel; Pres. George Bush's nominee for Sec. Labor until she withdrew her name from consideration, 2001. Author: Out of the Barrio: Toward a New Politics of Hispanic Assimilation, 1991, An Unlikely Conservative: The Transformation of an Ex-Liberal, 2002; syndicated weekly columnist Chgo. Tribune; freelance columnist Wall St. Jour., Washington Post, The New Republic, Commentary, Crisis; appeared on To the Contrary, CNN & Co., Equal Time, The McNeil-Lehrer News Hour; host (radio show) Linda Chavez Show. Bd. dirs. Campaign to Prevent Teen Pregnancy. Recipient Living Legend award, Libr. of Congress, 2000. Mem.: Coun. Fgn. Rels. (co-chair com. on diversity 1998—2000). Office: Ctr for Equal Opportunity 14 Pidgeon Hill Dr Ste 500 Sterling VA 20165-6151

CHAVEZ, MARIA LUCINDA, band director, educator; b. Albuquerque, Aug. 30, 1971; d. Edward Jerry and Donna Louise Chavez. B in Music Edn., U. N.Mex, Albuquerque, 1996; postgrad., No. Ariz. U., Flagstaff, 2001—04. Lic. tchr. Asst. band dir. Santa Fe H.S., 1996—97; band dir. Ortiz Mid. Sch., Santa Fe, 1996—97, Capshaw Mid. Sch., Santa Fe, 1997—2001; asst. band dir. Capital H.S., Santa Fe, 1997—98; band clinician Hummingbird Music Camp, Jemez Springs, N.Mex., 1998; grad. asst. No. Ariz. U. Bands, Flagstaff, 2001—. Head band instrument purchasing com. Mill Levy for Santa Fe Pub. Schs., Santa Fe, 2000—01; mid. sch. band rep. Music Educator's Task Force for Santa Fe Pub. Schs., Santa Fe, 2000—01; treas. North Cen. N.Mex Music Educator's Assn., Santa Fe, 1999—2001; band dir. Pojoaque Valley Intermediate and Mid. Sch., 2004—. Clarinetist NAU Wind Symphony and Cmty. Band/Orch. Recipient Grad. Assistantship, No. Ariz. U. Bands, 2000—01; scholar Full Out-of-State Tuition scholar, No. Ariz. U. Grad. Coll., 2002—03, Activity scholar, U. of N.Mex Bands, 1989—92. Mem.: Nat. Educator's Assn., N.Mex Music Educator's Nat. Assn. (treas. 1999—2001), Sigma Alpha Iota (founding mem. U. N.Mex. Coll. chpt., pres. 1990—96, Coll. Leadership award 1994, Sword of Honor 1993). Liberal. Avocations: playing jazz alto saxophone, hiking in the mountains, reading, chess. Office: Pojoaque Valley Schs PO Box 3684 Santa Fe NM 87501 Personal E-mail: mariasmusical1st@aol.com. Business E-Mail: mlc47@pvs.k12.nm.us.

CHAVEZ, MARY ANN, osteopathic family physician; b. York, Pa., Dec. 6, 1942; d. Henry David Gross and Mary Ellen (Ness) Rhoads; m. Richard L. Ziegler, Dec. 24, 1965 (div. Jan. 1983); children: Richard L. Ziegler Jr., Mara L. Tammaro, Brian L. Ziegler. BS, Alvernia Coll., 1983; DO, Coll. Osteo. Medicine, Phila., 1992. Legal sec. Louis Sager, Esquire, Pottstown, Pa., 1962-67; homemaker, tailor in pvt. practice Pottstown, 1967-85; intern Riverside Hosp., Wilmington, Del., 1992-93, resident in family practice, 1993-95; pvt. practice Spring Grove, Pa., 1995-97, Lancaster, Pa., 1997-999, Chillicothe, Ohio, 1999-2000, Sullivan, Ind., 2001—. Pell grantee, Beog grantee Alvernia Coll., 1979-83. Mem. AMA, Am. Osteo. Assn., Am. Coll. Osteo. Family Physicians, Am. Acad. Osteopathy, Ind. State Med. Assn., Ind. Osteopathic Assn., Sullivan Rotary Club, Sullivan Bus. and Profl. Women's Club. Avocations: painting, piano, tailoring, gardening. Home: 204 W Giles St PO Box 450 Sullivan IN 47882-0450 Office: Sullivan Med Clinic 222 W Beech St Sullivan IN 47882 E-mail: maryann.chavez@verizon.net.

CHAVEZ, MARY ROSE, counselor, educator; b. Agujita, Coahuila, Mexico, Oct. 7, 1954; arrived in U.S., 1959; d. Ignacio Chavez and Josefina Villa; m. Pedro Pablo Tijerina, Mar. 18, 1978; children: Pablo Esteban Tijerina, Daniel Ignacio Tijerina. MD, U. Monterrey, Mexico, 1984; MA, Tex. A&M Internat. U., Laredo, 2004. Med. license Mex., 1984. Physician Plan Integral de Salud, Monterrey, 1984—99; qualified mental health profl. Border Region Mental Health and Mental Retardation, Laredo, 2000—01; adj. faculty Tex. A&M Internat. U., Laredo, 2001—, counselor, 2005—, assoc. dir. career svcs., 2001—04. Dir. edn. Tex. Careers, Laredo, 2004—05. Scholar, Dominican Coll., 1972. Mem.: APA (assoc.), Neuvo Laredo Assn. Female Physicians, Am. Coll. Counseling Assn. Democrat. Roman Catholic. Avocations: reading, dance, swimming, knitting, painting. Home: 9903 Crystal Ct #117 Laredo TX 78045 Office: Texas A&M International University 5201 University Blvd Laredo TX 78041 Office Phone: 956-326-2762. Office Fax: 956-326-2231. Personal E-mail: chavezmd2000@yahoo.com. Business E-Mail: mchavez@tamiu.edu.

CHAVEZ, NELBA R., state agency administrator, former federal agency administrator; b. Mar. 9, 1940; BA in Sociology and Psychology, U. Ariz.; MSW, UCLA; PhD in Philosophy, U. Denver; student sr. exec. program in state and local govt., Harvard U. From therapist to exec. dir., CEO, COO La Frontera Ctr., Tuscon, 1971-89; prin. Chavez and Assocs., 1989-91; dir. juvenile probation svcs. City and County of San Francisco, 1991-94; adminstr. Substance Abuse and Mental Health Svcs. Adminstrn., U.S. Dept. Health and Human Svcs., Washington, 1994-2000; dep. dir. Ariz. Rehab. Svcs. Dept. Econ. Security, Phoenix, 2003—. Bd. dirs. nat. coalition of Hispanic Health and Human Svc. Organs.; mem. U.S. Senate Hispanic Adv. Com., Pres. Nat. Coun. on Handicapped, White House Prevention Com. on Drug-Free Am. Mem. Tucson Mayor's Task Force on Children. Recipient Outstanding Leadership award Ariz. State U., 1985, Dedication and Commitment award Tenth Ann. Chicano Conf., 1989, Disting. Svc. award Nat. Assn. Profl. Asian Am. Women, 1995, Mujer 95 award League United L.Am. Citizens, 1995, Rafael Tavares, MD, Meml. award Assn. Hispanic Mental Health Profls., 1995, Nat. Health Leadership award Nat. Coalition Hispanic Health and Human Svcs., 1997, Leadership award Fedn. Families for Children's Mental Health, 1997, Nat. Coun. on Aging award for Leadership in Health Promotion, 2000; named to Honor Roll Latino Behavioral Health Inst., 1998. Office: Ariz Rehab Svcs Dept Econ Security 1789 W Jefferson 2NW PO Box 6123 Phoenix AZ 85007

CHAVEZ, VIRGINIA, counselor; b. Fontana, Calif., June 22, 1958; d. Jose Frausto Chavez, Jr. and Ruth Saldaña. AA, Chafty Coll., Altaloma, Calif., 1978; BA, U. LaVerne, Calif., 1983; MA, Calif. State U., San Bernardino, 2003. Cert. nursing asst.; counseling credential U. Redlands, Calif. Rschr. Ariz. State U., Tempe, 1991—97; job coach Cole Vocational, Moreno Valley, Calif., 1997—98; counselor intern Moreno Valley Unified Sch. Dist., 2005—06; employment program rep. Employment Devel. Dept., Riverside; counselor Fresh Start Ministries, Ontario, 2006—. Vol. D.D. Men's Group Home, Moreno Valley, Calif., 2001—. Contbr. chapters to books, scientific papers to profl. meetings and seminars, articles to profl. jours. Sgt. USAR, 1986—, sgt. nat. guard U.S. Army, 1978—2006. Fellow, Baylor Coll., 1992. Mem.: ACA, Am. Rehab. Assn., Am. Sociol. Assn., Calif. Assn. Sch. Counselors. Office: Fresh Start Ministry and Cmty Svcs Inc 610 A N Euclid Ave Ontario CA 91762 Home: 12952 Douglas St Yucaipa CA 92399

CHAVEZ-HILL, TAMMY LYNN, elementary school educator; b. Selma, Calif., Jan. 26, 1965; d. Roy C. and Flodell M. Brewer; m. Gary E. Hill, Nov. 15, 2005; children: Abbie L. Chavez, Bailely A. Chavez. Masters Degree, Avila U., Kansas City, Mo., 2000, Southeastern Okla. State U., Durant, 2002; postgrad., U. Phoenix, 2006—. Cert. elem. edn. Okla., 1987, early chilhood edn. Okla., 1987. Tchr. Dekalb Co. Schs., Atlanta, 1987—91, Memphis City Schs., 1991—96, Kansas City (Mo.) Sch. Dist., 1996—2001, Ft. Worth Ind. Sch., 2000—01, Colbert (Okla.) Pub. Schs., 2001—. Mem. sch. adminstr. rev. com. SOSU. Named Tchr. of Yr., Colbert Sch., 2006. Democrat. Baptist. Home: 1406 Greenbrier Sherman TX 75092 Office Phone: 580-296-2626. Personal E-mail: tchillout@yahoo.com.

CHAVEZ-THOMPSON, LINDA, labor union administrator; b. Lubbock, Tex., Aug. 3, 1944; m. Robert Thompson (dec.); 2 children. Union sec. Am. Fedn. State, County & Mcpl. Employees, 1967-71, internat. rep., 1971-73, asst. bus. mgr., bus. mgr., exec. dir. local 2399, 1973-95, exec. dir. coun. 42, 1977-95, nat. v.p. labor coun. L.Am. Advancement, 1986-96, internat. v.p., 1988-96, exec. dir. Tex. Coun. 42, 1977-95; v.p. AFL-CIO, Washington, 1993-95, exec. v.p., 1995—. Office: AFL-CIO 815 16th St NW Washington DC 20006-4145

CHAVIS, GENEVA BOONE, retired dean; d. John L. and Flossie M. (Anderson) Boone; m. Kanawha Zeblon Chavis, Apr. 18, 1952; children: Doneva, Kanawha Z., Jo Jr., Arlin Teresa, Karan Geneva. BS, Shaw U., Raleigh, NC, 1951; MLS, NC Ctrl. U., Durham, 1971; EdD, Nova U., Ft. Lauderdale, Fla., 1979. Tchr. Mecklenburg County, Charlotte, NC, 1951—53; tchr., libr. Nash County, Nashville, NC, 1959—74; libr. Nash Tech. Inst., Rocky Mount, NC, 1974—79, dean, v.p., 1979—80; dean Nash C.C., Rocky Mount, 1980—93. Pres. NC Learning Resources Assn., 1978—79. Mem., sec. bd. trustees Shaw U., 1983—; founding mem. Twin County Edn. Found., Rocky Mount; founding mem. com. Black Issues Forum, U. NC Pub. TV, Chapel Hill; mem. Red Oak precinct Nash County Dem. Party; mem. parish coun. Immaculate Conception Ch., 1958—. Named Disting. Alumna, Shaw U., 1989, Nat. Assn. Equal Opportunity Higher Edn.; recipient Johnnie R. Clark award for excellence in c.c. adminstrn., Am. Assn. Jr. and Cmty. Colls., Educator, Humanitarian award, Silhouettes of Kappa Alpha Psi, Rocky Mount, 1992, St. Monica, Mother Teresa awards, African Am. Ministry Evangelization Network, KC, Raleigh, 2004. Mem.: Shaw U. Nat. Alumni Assn. (Elijah Shaw Meritorious Svc. award 1990), African Ancestry Ministry Evangelization Network. Roman Catholic. Avocations: gardening, piano, organ, reading, genealogy.

CHAVOOSHIAN, MARGE, artist, educator; b. NYC, Jan. 8, 1925; d. Harry Mesrob and Anna (Tashjian) Kurkjian; m. Barkev Budd Chavooshian, Aug. 11, 1946; children: J. Dean, Nora Ann. Student, Art Students League, 1941, Reginald Marsh, NYC, 1943, Mario Cooper, 1977. Designer Needlework Arts Co., N.Y.C., 1943-44; illustrator John David Men's Store, N.Y.C., 1944-45; illustrator, layout artist Fawcett Publs., N.Y.C., 1945-47; designer, illustrator Pa. State U., University Park, 1947-49; art tchr. Trenton Pub. Sch., N.J., 1958-68, art cons. Title One Program N.J., 1968-74; painting instr. Princeton Art Assn., N.J., 1974-77, 96, Jewish Cmty. Ctr., Ewing, N.J., 1974-85, Comtemporary Club, Trenton, 1974-85, YMCA, YWCA, Trent Ctr., Trenton, 1974—, various watercolor workshops, N.J., 1990—. Artist-at-large Alliance For Arts Edn., NJ, 1979—80; adj. asst. prof. art instr. Mercer County Coll., West Windsor, NJ, 1985—93; tchr. watercolor workshops Chalfonte, Cape May, NJ, 2001—05, H. Leech Studio, Sarasota, Fla., 1998—99, Art Ctr., Sarasota, 2001—03. One-woman shows include Rider U., 1974, 2000, Jersey City Mus., 1980, N.J. State Mus., 1981, Trenton City Mus., 1984, 1987, Arts Club, Washington, 1991, Magnolia Rm., Cape May, 1993—2004, Coryell Gallery, Lambertville, NJ, 1993—2006 (award, 2004), 2006, Louisa Melrose Gallery, 2002, exhibited in group shows at Douglas Coll., N.J., 1977, Bergen Mus., Paramus, NJ, 1980—82, Hunterdon Art Ctr., Clinton, N.J., 1982, 1995, Morris Mus., Morristown, N.J., 1984, Allied Artists of Am., 1984, 1986, 1989, 1991—2006, Salmagundi Club, N.Y.C., 1988, 1991—92, 1994—2004, one-woman shows include, N.Y.C., 2006, exhibited in group shows at Barron Art Ctr., Woodbridge, NJ, Ridgewood (N.J.) Art Inst., 2004—05 (Kent Art Assn. award, 2004), Art Works of Princeton and Trenton, 1995, Hunterdon County Cultural and Heritage Commn. Show, Clinton, N.J., 1995, N.J. State Mus., 2001, Trenton City Mus., 2001, 2002, 2003, 2004, 2005, others, Represented in permanent collections Mercer County Cultural and Heritage Commn., Arts Club of Washington, N.J. State Mus., Jersey City Mus., Morris Mus., Rider U., Art Mus. San Lazarre, Italy, Bristol Myers Squibb, Johnson and Johnson, Schering Plough Corp., Pub. Svc. Electric and Gas Co., U.S. Trust, N.J. Blue Cross and Blue Shield, Eden Inst., Princeton, N.J., Ellarslie, Trenton City Mus., NJ, Zimmerli Mus., Rutgers U., New Brunswick, others. Recipient numerous awards Union Coll., E. Jane Given Meml. award, 1996, Pres. award, 1996, Rockport Pubs. Mass. Pub. Inclusion: Best of Watercolor, 1995, Watercolor Places, 1996, Graphic-Sha Pub. Co., The Best of Watercolor, Tokyo, 1996, Landscape Inspirations, 1997, Best of Sketching & Painting, 1998, The Artistic Touch 3, Creative Art Press, 1999, Mercer County Cultural and Heritage Commn. purchase award, 1999, Phillips Mill, Walter E. Martin Meml. award 1992, Patrons award for watercolor 1994, Phila Watercolor Club, Ligorno and Solansky award Hunterdon County Cultural and Heritage Commn., 1991, Cynthia Goodgal Meml. award, Moshe Bahire award Ridgewood Art Inst., 1992, 99, Kent Art Assn. award, 2004, Ruth Ratay award Cmty. Arts Assn. Mid Atlantic Show, 1994, Elliot Liskin Meml. award Salmagundi Open Show, 1995, 96, Thomas Moran Meml. award Salmagundi Open Show, 1999, 2006, Mus. award Trenton City Mus., 2000, D. Rodney and DaVinci Paint award Garden State Watercolor Soc., 2000, Dale Meyers medal, Salmagundi Club, NY, 2002, Pen & Brush Club award Salmagundi Club, 2004, Niece Lumber award, Coryell Gallery, Lambertville, 2003, Kent Art Assoc. award, 2004, Am. Artists Profl. League N.J. Herb-Chris Carbone award, 2004, Coryell Gallery award, Lambertville, 2004, Cynthia Goodgal Meml. award Ocean County Coll., N.J., 2004, Winsor Newton Watercolor award Ridgewood Art Inst., 2005, Friedlander award Adarondacks Exhbn., Am. Watercolors, Old Forge, NY, Phillips Mill 75th Anniversary Publ. award, New Hope, Pa., 2005, Ken McCann Meml. award Garden State Watercolor Soc., 2005, Trenton Artists Workshop Assn., 2005, A. Waldron award N.J.-Am. Artists Profl. League, 2005, Thomas Moran Meml. award for Watercolor, Salmagundi Club, N.Y., 2006, Ida Wells and Clara Stroud award, 2006; named Woman of Month Woman's Newspaper of Princeton, 1984, NJ State Coun. Arts fellow, 1979. Fellow Am. Artists Profl. League (Am. Arts Coun. award 1973, Winsor Newton award 1980, Gold medal, Barron Art Ctr. award 1991, 93, Merit award 1993, Am. Artists Profl. League award 1994, Best in Show award, Best in Watercolor award 1995, others, representational painting award 1995); mem. Nat. Assn. Women Artists (two yr. nat. travel award 1985, Jeffrey Childs Willis Meml. award 1999), S. Winston Meml. award 1988, (two yr. travel award 1996—), Catherine Lorillard Wolfe Art Club (Bee Paper Co. award 1977, Anna Hyatt Huntington bronze medal, 2000, Cynthia Goodgall Meml. award 1995, 2004, Mary Hill Meml. award, 2004), Allied Artists Am. (elected mem., Henry Gasser Meml. award 1992), NJ Watercolor Soc. (Newton Art Ctr. award 1972, Helen K. Bermel award 1984, Howard Savs. Bank award 1986-87, Forbes Mag. award 1997, Lambertville Hist. Soc. award Coryell Gallery, 1995, 2001-04, Judi Rae Meml. award 2005), Painters and Sculptors Soc. (Medal of Honor, Digby Chandler medal, others), Garden State Watercolor Soc. (Triangle Art Ctr. award 1976, 89, 94, Grumbacher Silver medal 1981, Merit award 1982, Trust Co. award 1987, Triangle award 1994, Art Express award, 1995, Rider U. Gallery award 1995, Cranbury Sta. Art Gallery award 1997, Daler Rowney and Da Vinci paint award 2000, Ken McCann Meml. award 2005), Midwest Watercolor Soc., Nat. Arts Club (John Elliott award 1988), Phila. Watercolor Club (Village Art award 1991), Nat. Watercolor Soc. (signature), Am. Watercolor Soc. (signature). Democrat. Mem. Apostolic Ch. Armenia. Home: 222 Morningside Dr Trenton NJ 08618-4914

CHAWNER, LUCIA MARTHA, language educator; b. Ithaca, N.Y., Dec. 2, 1933; d. Lowell Jenkins and Lucia Mary (Soule) Chawner; m. Movses Guichen Andreassian, Mar. 18, 1967 (div. June 1971). Student, Earlham Coll., 1951-53; BA, U. Colo., 1956; MA, So. Meth. U., 1975. Provisional cert. elem., secondary and talented and gifted Tex., profl. cert. reading specialist

Tex. Tchr. grade 7 lang. arts and social studies Stonewall Jackson, Dallas Ind. Sch. Dist., 1959-63; reading clinician Reinhardt, Dallas Ind. Sch. Dist., 1963-66; Reading Resource Pilot Project Lakewood, Dallas Ind. Sch. Dist., 1972-74; devel. curriculum specialist El Centro Coll., Dallas County C.C. Dist., Dallas, 1977-78; English tchr. Health Magnet, Dallas Ind. Sch. Dist., 1979-95; univ. supervising tchr. U. Tex. Dallas, Richardson, 1996—. Part-time instr. El Centro & Richland Colls., Dallas, 1978—88, Brookhaven Coll., Farmers Branch, Tex., 1996—98; mem. English lit. textbook adoption com. Dallas Ind. Sch. Dist., 1988—89, chmn. English dept. Health Magnet, 1989—94, mgr. innovative grant, 1994—95. Region 7 chmn., nat. bd. dirs. English-Speaking Union, 1996—2000; co-leader child and youth study U. Md., Dallas, 1967—69; pres. English-Speaking Union, Dallas, 1992—96, mem. nat. edn. com., 1996—; mem. Leadership Arts Dallas Bus. Com. Arts, 1994—95; mem. World Affairs Coun. Greater Dallas. Named Tchr. of the Yr., Health Magnet, 1991, Rotary Tchr. of the Yr., 1993; recipient Nat. Merit award, English-Speaking Union, 2000; Advanced Study grantee, Dallas Ind. Sch. Dist., 1973, Instrnl. grantee, Richland Coll., 1980. Mem.: Brit. Am. Bus. Coun., Assemblage (pres. 1987—88), Friends SMU Librs. (bd. dirs. 1995—98), Dallas Mus. Art League (bd. dirs. 1997—2004), New Conservatory Dallas (bd. dirs. 1999—, sec. 2002—), Dallas Knife and Fork Club (bd. dirs. 2003—), Soc. Mayflower Descs., Dau. Brit. Empire (sec. 2003—), Pi Lambda Theta (chpt. pres. 2002—), Phi Delta Kappa, Delta Delta Delta. Avocations: sculpture, needlepoint, fitness exercise, travel. Office: PO Box 141179 Dallas TX 75214-1179 Office Phone: 972-883-2730.

CHEADLE, LOUISE, music educator, musician; b. Donora, Pa., July 4, 1935; d. Max Raphael and Helen Louise Busto; m. William George Cheadle, Feb. 12, 1959 (dec. Dec. 1993); children: William Robert, Amy Louise Fleming. BMusic, The Juilliard Sch., 1959. Founder, dir. Westminster Conservatory of Music/Rider U., Princeton, NJ, 1972—82; head piano dept. Amherst Summer Music Ctr., Raymond, Maine, 1971—72; adj. instr. music Bucks County C.C., Newtown, Pa., 1982-85; nationwide concert tours and workshops, various mgmts. and agys., throughout U.S., 1980s; nat. adjudicator Nat. Guild Piano Tchrs., Austin, Tex., 1999—; freelance recitals, workshops and pvt. tchg. includes Lincoln Ctr., Carnegie Hall, N.Y.C., 1980—. Debut recital with Pitts. Concert Soc., 1954; contbg. author: Teaching Piano, 1981; CD release Virtuoso Piano Music by Cecile Chaminate and Fanny Mendelssohn-Hensel, 2002. Bd. dirs., chair Cmty. Outreach. Juilliard Sch. scholar, 1956-59. Mem. Music Tchrs. Nat. Assn., N.J. Music Educators Assn. (bd. dirs., v.p.), N.J. Music Tchrs. Assn. (chair Young Artist Competition 1999, 2000, chair Master Class Competition 1999, 2000), Rossmoor (N.J.) Music Assn. (bd. dirs.), Piano Tchrs. Congress N.Y., Music Club of Princeton. Avocations: writing, reading, cooking, cultural events. E-mail: chealou@aol.com.

CHEATHAM, WANDA M., music educator; b. Memphis, June 29, 1952; d. Roy Bennett Cheatham, Billie Jewel Cheatham. BS in Music Edn., U. Memphis, 1974, MEd in Music, 1983; student fgn. study program, Univ. of So. Miss., Vienna, Austria, 1991, Glasgow (Scotland) U., 1995; student, Univ. of Miss., 1997. Elem. music tchr. Memphis City Schs., 1975—81; h.s. choral dir. Evangelical Christian Sch., Cordova, Tenn., 1981—. Audition and rehearsal pianist Theatre Memphis, 1998, 2001. Organist Ctrl. Ch., Memphis, 1972—83, First Evangelical Ch., Memphis, 1984—2001; organist/music dir. St. Andrews Presbyn. Ch., Cordova, 2001—. Named a Outstanding Young Woman of Am., 1983; recipient, 1985, Outstanding Tchr. award, Tenn. Gov.'s Sch. for Arts, 1993, 1997, 1999. Mem.: Tenn. Music Educators Assn., Music Educators Nat. Conf., Am. Choral Dir. Assn. Presbyterian. Avocations: antiques, travel, reading, walking, gardening. Office: Evangelical Christian PO Box 1030 7600 Macon Rd Cordova TN 38088 Office Phone: 901-754-7217. Office Fax: 901-754-8123. Personal E-mail: wcheatham@ecseagles.com.

CHECCONE, IOLE CARLESIMO, foreign language educator; b. Frosinone, Lazio, Italy, Dec. 7, 1943; d. Alfredo Tullio and Caterina (Morelli) Carlesimo; m. Albert Checcone, June 14, 1969; children: Emidio Albert, Mark Anthony, Anne Marie. BA, Marygrove Coll., Detroit, 1965; MA, Wayne State U., 1968; PhD in French Lit., U. Pitts., 1995. Cert. tchr., Mich., Ohio. Grad. tchg. asst. Wayne State U., Detroit, 1965-67; French tchr. Oak Park (Mich.) Local Schs., 1966-68, Grosse Pointe (Mich.) Local Schs., 1968-70; tchg. fellow U. Pitts., 1987-90; asst. prof. French lit. Youngstown (Ohio) State U., 1999—. Mem. adv. com. for gifted children Canfield (Ohio) Local Schs., 1979. Democrat. Roman Catholic. Avocations: singing, reading, sewing, quilting. Office: Youngstown State U Dept Fgn Langs One University Plz Youngstown OH 44555-3461

CHECINSKA, BOZENA TERESA, media specialist; d. Tadeusz Jerzy Swinecki and Wanda Rawicz-Kosinska; 1 child, Aurika Hays. M in Musical Arts, Acad. Music, Lodz, Poland, 1968; M in Sociology, U. Lodz, 1971; MEd, Columbia U., NYC, 1981, EdD, 1990. Adminstr. Columbia U., 1979—87; libr. corp. records, supr., mgr. Ednl. Broadcasting Corp., NYC, 1992—. Contbr. articles to profl. jours. Mem.: Archivists Round Table Met. N.Y., ARMA Internat., Polish Inst. Arts and Scis. Am. Avocations: travel, music, video/photography. Office Phone: 212-560-3181.

CHEE, ANN-PING, music educator; b. July 26; came to U.S., 1964; d. To-Khiem Thi and Thanh-Phuc Dong; m. Anthony N.C. Chee, Dec. 27, 1969; children: Andrew, Lawrence. BA in Music cum laude, Conn. Coll., 1970. Tchr. piano, music theory, Houston, 1972—. Named to Piano Guild Hall of Fame, Austin, Tex., 1997. Mem. Nat. Guild Piano Tchrs. (cert.), Music Tchrs. Nat. Assn. (cert.), Tex. Music Tchrs. Assn., Houston Music Tchrs. Assn., Houston Fedn. Music Clubs, Forum Music Tchrs. Assn., Associated Bd. Royal Schs. Music London.

CHEEK, NORMA JEAN, retired secondary school educator; b. Ada, Okla., Feb. 7, 1928; d. John Herbert and Jewell Esther (Hobbs) Winters; m. George A. Cheek, Dec. 5, 1947; children: George Allen III, Michael Kirby. AA, Conners Jr. Coll., 1948; BS, Ctrl. State Coll., Edmond, Okla., 1961, MEd, 1964. Tchr. Mid-Del Schs., Midwest City, Okla., 1961-89, coach, 1978-87. Salesman vol. YMCA, 1970—; bldg. rep. Midwest City Assn. Classroom Tchrs., 1980. Mem. AAUW, Alpha Delta Kappa (various positions including v.p. 1980). Democrat. Baptist. Home: 604 Traub Pl Midwest City OK 73110-2738 Personal E-mail: normacheek@yahoo.com.

CHEESEBORO, MARGRIT, retired economics educator; b. Zurich, Switzerland; BA of Bus. Mgmt., U. Redlands, 1980; MSEd, U. So. Calif., 1981; MA in Ednl. Adminstrn., Calif. State U., L.A., 1982; postgrad, UCLA, 1990. Cert. tchr. and adminstr. Sch. office adminstr. Mid-City Alternative Sch., LA, 1973—80; tchr. econ., govt., US and world history Crenshaw HS, LA, 1982—2006; ret., 2006. Bd. dirs. Baldwin Village Cmty. in Action, 1998—; sec., treas. Baldwin Village Apt. Owners Assn., 2004—. Mem. United Tchrs. L.A. (chpt. chmn. 1991-98), Kappa Delta Pi. Home: 3525 S Bronson Ave Los Angeles CA 90018-3636

CHEEVER, SUSAN, writer; b. N.Y.C., July 31, 1943; d. John and Mary Watson (Winternitz) C.; m. Robert Cowley, May, 1967 (div. 1975); m. Calvin Tomkins, II, Oct. 1, 1982; m. Warren James Hinckle III, June 10, 1989; children: Sarah Liley Cheever Tomkins, Warren James Hinckle IV. BA, Brown U., 1965. Tchr., Colo. Rocky Mountain Sch., Colo., 1965-67, Scarborough Sch., N.Y., 1968-69; writer Westchester-Rockland Newspapers, N.Y., 1970-72; editor, writer Newsweek Mag., N.Y., 1974-78; free lance writer, N.Y., 1978—; council mem. Authors Guild. Author: Looking for Work, 1980, A Handsome Man, 1981, The Cage, 1982, Home Before Dark, 1984, Doctors and Women, 1987, Elizabeth Cole, 1989, Treetops: A Famiy Memoir, 1991, A Woman's Life, 1994, Note Found In A Bottle, 1999, As Good As I Could Be, 2001, My Name is Bill, Bill Wilson's Life, 2004. Recipient Associated Press award, 1970; Guggenheim Found. fellow, 1984, nominee Nat. Book Critics Circle, 1984. Mem. Pen/Am. Ctr., Authors League. Democrat. Episcopalian E-mail: susancheever@aol.com.

CHELARIU, ANA RADU, library director; b. Bucharest, Romania, Nov. 19, 1946; m. Serban H. Chelariu; 1 child, Andrea. MA, U. Bucharest, 1972; MLS, Rutgers U., 1981. Indexer H. W. Wilson Co., N.Y.C., 1981-85; dir. Palisades Pk. (N.J.) Pub. Libr., 1981—99, Cliffside Park (N.J.) Pub. Libr., 1999—. Mem. Soc. Romanian Studies, N.J. Libr. Assn. Christian Orthodox. Office: Cliffside Park Pub Libr 505 Palisade Ave Cliffside Park NJ 07010 Office Phone: 201-945-2867. E-mail: chelariu@bccls.org.

CHELL, BEVERLY C., lawyer; b. Phila., Aug. 12, 1942; d. Max M. and Cecelia (Portney) C.; m. Robert M. Chell, June 21, 1964. BA, U. Pa., 1964; JD, N.Y. Law Sch., 1967; LLM, NYU, 1973. Bar: N.Y. 1967. Assoc. Polur & Polur, N.Y.C., 1967-68, Thomas V. Kingham Esq., N.Y.C., 1968-69; v.p., sec., asst. gen. counsel, dir. Athlone Industries Inc., Parsippany, N.J., 1969-81; asst. v.p., asst. sec., assoc. gen. counsel Macmillan Inc., N.Y.C., 1981-85, v.p., sec., gen. counsel, 1985-90; vice chmn., gen. counsel K-III Holdings, N.Y.C., 1990-92; vice chmn., gen. counsel, sec. Primedia Inc. (formerly K-III Comm. Corp.), N.Y.C., 1992—. Adv. bd. U. Pa. Athletic Dept. Mem. Assn. of Bar of City of N.Y., Am. Soc. Corp. Secs. Home: 1050 5th Ave New York NY 10028-0110 Office: Primedia Inc 745 5th Ave Fl 23 New York NY 10151-0099

CHELSTROM, MARILYN ANN, political science educator, consultant; b. Mpls., Dec. 05; d. Arthur Rudolph and Signe (Johnson) Chelstrom. BA, U. Minn., 1950; LHD, Oklahoma City U., 1981. Staff asst. Mpls. Citizens Com. Pub. Edn., 1950—57; coord. policies and procedures Lithium Corp. Am., Inc., Mpls. and N.Y.C., 1957—62; dir. The Robert A. Taft Inst. Govt., N.Y.C., 1962—77, exec. v.p., 1977—78, pres., 1978—89, pres. emeritus, 1990—; polit. edn. cons., 1990—; pres. Chelstrom Connection, 1992—. Compiler (book) Tribute to Outstanding Minnesota Women, 2001. Home: 9600 Portland Ave Minneapolis MN 55420-4564 Office: 155 E 38th St New York NY 10016-2660

CHELTE, JUDITH SEGZDOWICZ, secondary school educator; b. Springfield, Mass., Aug. 23, 1951; d. Stanley (dec.) and Stella Margaret Segzdowicz; m. Raymond J. Chelte, Sr., July 31, 1982. BA in English/Secondary Edn., Westfield State Coll., 1973; MAT in English and Secondary Edn., Smith Coll., 1974; PhD in English, U. Mass., 1994. Cert. in adolescence young adulthood English and lang. arts Nat. Bd. for Profl. Tchg. Stds., 1999. Tchr. English Chicopee (Mass.) Pub. Schs., 1974—. Mentor Chicopee Comprehensive H.S., 2000—. Contbr. articles to profl. jours.; website creator New Eng. Adolescent Rsch. Inst., 2000. Sec. Friends of the Chicopee Pub. Libr., Inc., 1995-97, newsletter editor, 1997-99. Named Intel Master Tchr., 2001; grantee Mass. Dept. Edn., Malden, 1997, 98-99; finalist Mass. Tchr. of Yr., 2001. Mem. MLA, NEA, Mass. Tchrs. Assn., Chicopee Edn. Assn. Democrat. Roman Catholic. Avocations: reading, cross country skiing. Home: 63 Davenport St Chicopee MA 01013-2808 Office: Chicopee Comprehensive HS 617 Montgomery St Chicopee MA 01020-1634

CHEMBERLIN, PEG, minister, religious organization administrator; b. York, Nebr., Sept. 27, 1949; d. Charles Norman and Donna May (Chemberlin) Bean. BA cum laude, U. Wis., Parkside; grad., United Theol. Sem. Twin Cities, 1982. Ordained deacon Moravian Ch. Am., 1982, consecrated presbyter Moravian Ch. Am., 1986. Formerly dir. campus ministries, tchr., youth min.; also outreach min., parish intern pastor; exec. dir. Minn. Coun. Chs., 1995—. Former pres., former program chmn. Nat. Assn. Ecumenical and Interfaith Staff, 1992, 97; hon. campaign chair Minn. Food Share, 2003. Recipient Women of Excellence award Minn. Gov., 1994, NOVA Peace and Justice award, 1985; Angel of Reconciliation award, 2003. Mem.: Nat. Coun. of Ch. (exec. bd. 2003). Office: Minn Coun Chs 122 W Franklin Ave Minneapolis MN 55404-2447

CHEMIDLIN, MICHELE LYNN, athletic trainer, consultant; b. Vineland, NJ, Jan. 31, 1975; d. Dennis Joey and Joyce Ann Swawola; m. Andrew Chemidlin. BA in Phys. Edn., Kean U., Union, NJ, 2000, BA in psychology, 2000. Cert. instr. ARC. Asst. athletic trainer NJ City U., Kessler Inst., Jersey City, 2000—02; athletic trainer Montclair H.S., 2002—. Athletic trainer USA Field Hockey Assn.- Futures Program, Montclair, NJ, 2002—; cons. Essex County Coll. Police Acad., Cedar Grove, 2006—. Active ARC, NJ, 1993, Am. Inst. Cancer Rsch., 1993, Mar. Dimes, 2000, Susan G. Komen Breast Cancer Fund, 1999. Recipient Acad. All-Am., Ea. Collegiate Athletic Assn., 1994, 1996, Field Hockey Defensive Player Yr., 1996. Mem.: NJ Edn. Assn., Athletic Trainer's Soc. NJ, Nat. Athletic Trainer's Assn. Avocations: travel, scrapbooks, camping, canoeing, athletic activities. Office: Montclair High School 100 Chestnut Street Montclair NJ 07042 Office Phone: 973-509-4100 3920. E-mail: mchemidlin@montclair.k12.nj.us.

CHEN, CHING-CHIH, information science educator, consultant; b. Foochow, Fukien, China, Sept. 3, 1937; came to U.S, 1959; d. Han-chia and May-ying (Liu) Liu; m. Sow-Hsin Chen, Aug. 19, 1961; children: Anne, Catherine, John. BA, Nat. Taiwan U., Taipei, 1959; MLS, U. Mich., 1961; PhD, Case Western Res. U., 1974. Asst. Sch. Libr. Sci. U. Mich., Ann Arbor, 1960-61, svc. libr., 1961-62; sci. reference libr. McMaster U., Hamilton, Ont., Canada, 1962-63, head sci. libr., 1963-64; sr. sci. libr. U. Waterloo, Ont., Canada, 1964-65, head engring., math. and sci. libr., 1965-68; assoc. sci. libr. MIT, Cambridge, Mass., 1968-71; asst. prof. Grad. Sch. Libr. and Info. Sci. Simmons Coll., Boston, 1971-76, asst. dean for acad. affairs, 1977-79, assoc. dean, prof., 1979-96, prof., 1979—. Cons. Am. Soc. Info. Sci./Cath. U. Am., 1976-77, Chung-Shan Inst. Sci. Rsch., Taiwan, 1977-87, Abt Assocs., Inc., 1980-82, Sci. and Tech. Info. Ctr. Nat. Sci. Coun., Taiwan, 1973-77, S.E. Asia Region WHO, 1980, 81, Engring. Info. Inc., 1982, UNESCO, Paris, 1984, Nat. Geog. Soc., 1985, Norman Bethuen U. Med. Scis. Libr., 1986, Getty Trust, 1988, USIA, 1988, Ont. Coun. Gradual Studies, 1989, FID, 1989, World Bank, 1990, UNESCO, 1991, DataConsult, Mex., 1991, Soros Found., 1992-93, USIA, 1993-95, UN Devel. Program, 1997, Tsinghua U., Taiwan, 1997, Nat. Sci. Coun., Taiwan, 1998—2001, OCLC Global Digital Initiative, 2005—; mem. US President's Info. Tech. Adv. Com., 1997-2002; guest prof. Tsinghua U., Beijing, 1999-2002; U. prof. U. Hainan, China, 2004, cons. Chinese Acad. Sci. Libr., 2002—. Author, editor 36 books including Biomedical, Scientific and Technical Book Reviewing, 1976, Sourcebook on Health Sciences Librarianship, 1977, Quantitative Measurement and Dynamic Library Service, 1978, Scientific & Technical Information Sources, 2nd edit., 1987, (with others) Numeric Databases, 1984, HyperSource on Hypermdia/Multimedia Technologies, 1989, HyperSource on Optical Technologies, 1989, Optical Technologies in Libraries; Use & Trends, 1991, Planning Global Information Infrastructure, 1995, Consortium of Electronic Resources, 1999, IT and Global Digital Library Development, 1999, Global Digital Library Development in the New Millennium, 2001; editor-in-chief: Microcomputers for Information Management, 1983-96; mem. editl. bd.: Electronic Library, 1990-; also editor numerous conf. procs.; contbr. over 150 articles to profl. jours. Barbour scholar U. Mich., 1959-61, Case Western Res. U. fellow, 1973-74, NATO fellow, 1975, AAAS fellow, 1985; Emily Hollowell Rsch. grantee, 1972—, Simmons Coll. Fund Rsch. grantee, 1972-81, co-principal investigator NSF US-China Million Book Digital Libr. Grant Project, 2001-; recipient Disting. Svc. award Chinese-Am. Librs. Assn., 1982, Cert. of Appreciation, Asian-Pacific-Am. Librs. Assn., 1983, Disting. Alumni award U. Mich., 1983, Outstanding Svc. award Nat. Cen. Libr., 1986, Disting. Svc. award Asian-Am. Libr. Assn, 1992, Cindy award Assn. Visual Comm., 1992, Grazella Shepherd Meml. award for Excellence in Edn., Case Western Reserve U. Educator's Forum, 1999, NSF Internat. Digital Libr. Program award Chinese Memory Net: U.S.-Sino Collaborative Rsch., 1999-2003, NSF Internat. Digital Libr. Program award, 2000—, Ernest A. Lynton award Am. Assn. Higher Edn., 2001, NSF IDLP Project, Global Memory Net, 2002—. Fellow AAAS; mem. ALA (disting. svc. award 1989, Humphrey award 1996), AAUP, Am. Soc. Info. Sci. (best Info. Sci. Tchr. award 1983), Assn. Am. Libr. Schs., Assn. Coll. and Rsch. Librs., Libr. Info. Tech. Assn. (Gaylord Libr. and Info. Tech. Achievement award 1990, Outstanding Achievement Libr. Hi Tech. award 1994, Frederick Kilgous award 2006), New Eng. Libr. Assn. (Emerson Greenaway award 1994), Assn. Libr. and Info. Sci. Edn. (1st ALISE Pratt-Severn Nat. Faculty award 1997). Avocations: travel, stamp collecting/philately. Home: 1400 Commonwealth Ave Newton MA 02465-2830 Office: Simmons Coll 300 Fenway Boston MA 02115-5820 Business E-Mail: chen@simmons.edu.

CHEN, DEL-MIN AMY, lawyer; b. Balt. d. Chung-Hsien and Show-Fen Chen. BA, U. Tex., Austin, 1993; MPA, JD, Rutgers U., Camden, NJ, 1998. Law clk. Superior Ct. NJ, 1998—99; presdl. mgmt. intern, 1998—2000; with US Dept. Labor, Washington, 1999—. Pro bono atty., guardian ad litem Lawyers for Children Am., 2003—. Cmty. affairs com. chair Labor's Effective Advocates Devel. (L.E.A.D.), 2005—. Mem.: DC Bar. Avocations: reading, volunteering, baking, entertaining, floor hockey.

CHEN, JOIE, news correspondent; b. Chgo., Aug. 28, 1961; married; 1 child. B in Journalism, M in Journalism, Northwestern U. Reporter Sta. WCIV-TV, Charleston, SC, 1983—85; from reporter to anchor Sta. WXIA-TV, Atlanta, 1985—91; host CNNI World News, Atlanta, 1991—94; news anchor CNN, 1994—2001; former co-host CNN Saturday Morning News and CNN Sunday Morning News, Atlanta, 1994-96; former co-anchor The World Today, CNN; news corr. CBS News, Washington, 2002—. Office: CBS News 2020 M St NW Washington DC 20036

CH'EN, LI-LI, literature and language educator, writer; b. Beijing, Apr. 6, 1934; came to U.S., 1951, naturalized, 1963; d. Shujen and Yu-wu (Kuan) C. BA magna cum laude, Wilson Coll., 1957, Litt.D., 1980; MA, Radcliffe Coll., 1958; PhD (Harvard-Yenching Inst. fellow, Ford Found. fellow), Harvard U., 1969. Prof. Chinese lang., lit. and comparative lit., dir. Chinese program Tufts U., Medford, Mass., 1972—94, prof. emerita, 1994—. Translator: Master Tung's Western Chamber Romance, 1977 (Nat. Book Award for Transl.); Contbr. articles to profl. jours. Am. Council Learned Socs. grantee, 1976-77; MacDowell Colony fellow, 1980; Michael Karolyi Found. fellow, 1980; Recipient Nat. Mag. Award for Fiction, Criticism, and Belles Lettres for short story Peking! Peking!, 1977 Mem. Phi Beta Kappa. Home: 186 Upland Rd Cambridge MA 02140-3624 Office: Tufts U Olin Hall Medford MA 02155

CHEN, LIYA, chemist; b. Taishun, Zhejiang, China, Jan. 12, 1956; came to U.S., 1994; d. Jinde Chen and Cailian Pan; m. Ronghui Lin, Jan. 24, 1987; 1 child, Cindy (Xinyue) Lin. BS, Hangzhou (China) U., 1982, MS, 1986, So. Ill. U., 1997. Technician Taishun (China) Chem. Co., 1982-83; lectr. Zhejian Med. U., Hangzhou, 1986-93; rsch. assoc. So. Ill. U., Carbondale, 1995-97, Chiron Corp., Emeryville, Calif., 1997-98; chemist Merck & Co., Inc., Rahway, NJ, 1998—. Contbr. articles to profl. jours.; patentee in field. Recipient excellent paper award Zhejiang Soc. Sci. and Tech., 1991. Mem. Am. Chem. Soc. Avocations: cooking, sewing, dance, singing. Home: 23 Bearsley Dr East Brunswick NJ 08816-2041 Office: Merck & Co Inc PO Box 2000 RY 800-B309 Rahway NJ 07065-0900

CHEN, LORIS JEAN, science educator; b. Hamilton, Ohio, May 20, 1953; d. Marvin and Dorothy Johnston; m. James Chen, Apr. 22, 1978; children: Jason Suez, Tiffany Belle. BSin Biology, Rensselaer Poly. Inst., Troy, N.Y., 1975; MBA with distinction, Pace U., N.Y.C., 1984. Cert. tchr. sci. N.J. Dept. Edn., 1993, elem. tchr. N.J. Dept. Edn., 1993. Tchr. sci. North Arlington Mid. Sch./H.S., NJ, 1992—2002; tchr. sci. grade 8 Eisenhower Mid. Sch., Wyckoff, NJ, 2002—. Tchr. cons. Mid-Atlantic Ctr. for Ocean Sci. Edn. Excellence, NJ; tchr. cons. edn. videos Nat. Geog. Soc.; featured educator video series Thirteen/WNET Nat. Tchr. Tng. Inst., NJ. Author: (curriculum guide) Where are the Gardens in the Garden State? Middle School Lessons on Sustainable Agriculture and Farmland Preservation; contbr. curriculum guide, curriculum module, curriculum guide; author: (article) Green Tchr. Mag. Trustee Fair Lawn Bd. Edn., NJ, 1990—93; officer Am. Acad. Figure Skating Club, Hackensack, NJ, 1997—2002, N.J. Coun. of Figure Skating Clubs, Montclair, 2000—06; parents com. mem. U.S. Figure Skating, Colorado Springs, 2005—. Finalist Shell Sci. Tchg. award, NSTA, 2005; named Outstanding Environ. Educator, Alliance for N.J. Environ. Edn., 1995; recipient Environ. Quality award, EPA, 1997, Vol. award, Bergen County, N.J., 1997, award for Excellence in Environ. Edn., N.J. Audubon Soc., 1998, Presdl. award for Excellence in Math. and Sci. Tchg., US Govt., 2002, Tchr. of Yr., N.J. Agrl. Soc., 2002, award, A+ for Kids Found., 1995, 1996, 1998; fellow, Govt. of Japan, 2006; grantee, various cos. Mem.: Alliance for N.J. Environ. Edn., NJ Edn. Assn., NEA, NSTA, N.J. Sci. Tchrs. Assn., US Figure Skating. Office: Eisenhower Mid Sch 344 Calvin Ct Wyckoff NJ 07481 Office Phone: 201-848-5750. Business E-Mail: lchen@wyckoffschools.org.

CHEN, LU, figure skater; b. Changchun, Jilin, China, Nov. 24, 1976; Figure skater, China, 1981—. Mem. Chinese Nat. Figure Skating Team, 1988—. Recipient Bronze medal Olympic Games, Nagano, 1998, 7 time Chinese Nat. Champion and 2 time Olympic Bronze medalist. Avocations: reading, music, dance.

CHEN, LU, neurobiologist, biology professor; BS, U. Sci. and Tech., China, 1993; PhD, U. So. Calif., 1998. Postdoctoral fellow U. So. Calif., 1998—99, U. Calif., San Francisco, 1999—2002, asst. prof. neurobiology Berkeley, 2003—, mem., Helen Wills Neuroscience Inst. Author: (articles) published in journals such as Nature, Jour. of Neuroscience, and Proceedings of the Nat. Acad. of Sciences USA. Named an Disting. Young Scholars in Med. Rsch., W.M. Keck Found., 2005; MacArthur Fellow, John D. and Catherine T. MacArthur Found., 2005. Office: Univ Calif Berkeley Dept Molecular & Cell Biology 124 Life Sciences Addition # 3200 Berkeley CA 94720-3200 Office Phone: 510-643-8163. Office Fax: 510-643-6791. E-mail: luchen@berkeley.edu.

CHEN, LYNN, actress; b. NYC, Dec. 24, 1976; m. Abe Forman-Greenwald. BA in Music and Women's Studie, Wesleyan U. Performer in band with husband YPOK2. Actor: (films) Up to the Roof, 2002, Fortune, 2002, Saving Face, 2004 (Outstanding Newcomer, Asian Excellence Awards, 2006), Fly Me Home, 2005, Little Manhattan, 2005; guest appearances Law & Order, 2001, Law & Order: Special Victims Unit, 2001, All My Children (11 episodes), 2003, Law & Order: Trial By Jury, 2005, Numb3rs, 2005. Address: c/o Schachter Entertainment 1157 S Beverly Dr Los Angeles CA 90035*

CHEN, XINGZHI MARA, science educator; b. Hubei, China, 1963; d. Binling Chen and Jiming Zhou; m. C. Sean Sun; children: Charles Sun, Christy Sun. B of Engring., China U. Geosci., 1983, MS, 1986; PhD, U. Iowa, 1992. Instr. China U. Geosci., Wuhan, Hubei, 1986—87; asst. prof. Salisbury U., Md., 1994—2000, assoc. prof. remote sensing and environ. geology, 2000—. Contbr. articles to profl. jours. Parent adv. bd. Fruitland Primary, Md., 2005; cons. Somerset County Health Dept, Md., 2002. Grantee, NSF, 1998; scholar, China Edn. Commn., 1987, U. Ky., Lexington, 1993—94. Mem.: Chinese Profl. Geog. Info. Systems (newsletter editor-in-chief 1999—2000), Assn. Am. Geographers. Office: Salisbury U 1101 Camden Ave Salisbury MD 21801 Office Phone: 410-543-6460. E-mail: mxchen@salisbury.edu.

CHEN, YVONNE, economics professor; d. Hsing-Chu Chen and Mei Chang; m. Brigido Subiaur; 1 child, Sofie Subiaur. Peace cert., U. Wis., Milw., 1990; BA in Econs. and Math., MA in Econs.; PhD, U. Wis., Milw., 1998. Lectr. econs. U. Wis.-Whitewater, 1998—99; asst. prof. Ming-Hsin Inst. Tech., Hsing Fong, Hsing-Chu, Taiwan, 1999—2001; vis. asst. prof. DePaul U., Chgo., 2000—04; asst. prof. Shenandoah U., Winchester, Va., 2004—. Global economy cons. ComOpt, Arlington, Va., 2003—04. Contbr. articles to profl. jours. Campaign asst. Dem. Party, Milw., 1991—92. Grantee, NSC of Taiwan, 2000. Mem.: Soc. Actuarial Sci., Nat. Soc. Collegial Scholars (life; disting. mem.). Office: Shenandoah Univ Harry E Byrd Jr Sch Bus 1460 University Dr Winchester VA 22601 Office Phone: 540-665-1285. Office Fax: 540-665-5437.

CHENAULT, SHERYL ANN, elementary school educator; b. Springfield, Mo., May 16, 1953; d. Melvin James and Helenkay (Peterson) Catt; m. Daniel Alden Chenault, June 7, 1975. BS, East Tex. State U., Commerce, 1975; MEd, U. North Tex., Denton, 1987. Resource tchr. Brentfield Elem.,

Richardson, Tex., 1975-83, Liberty Jr. High Sch., Richardson, 1983-86, Jess Harben Elem., Richardson, 1986-88; tchr. 3rd grade, resource spl. edn., 4th grade Risd Acad., Richardson, 1988-95; tchr. 4th grade Classical Magnet Sch., Richardson, 1995—2000; tchr. 6th grade Richland Elem., Richardson, 2000—02; instrnl. specialist Dover Elem., Richardson, 2002—. Demonstration tchr. reading tchrs., Richardson, 1990; facilitator sch.-based mgmt., Richardson, 1990. Mem. ASCD, Internat. Reading Assn., Tex. Assn. Children and Adults with Learning Disabilities, Assn. Tex. Profl. Educators, Richardson Edn. Assn., Phi Delta Kappa, Kappa Delta Pi Alumnae Assn. (cert. of honor for outstanding svc. 1983), Alpha Delta Pi. Home: 1622 Tynes Dr Garland TX 75042-4701

CHENAULT MINOT, MARILYN, legal executive; b. Mt. Vernon, Ill., Oct. 21, 1949; d. Nathan Bullock and Marguerite (Woodberry) Chenault; m. Tom Dee McFall, Aug. 29, 1969; children: Shannon, Nathan; m. Troy David Phillips, Aug. 14, 1981; stepchildren: Todd, Brittany; m. Winthrop Gardner Minot, June 6, 1998; stepchildren: Hilary, Amory, Constance. BS with honors, Okla. State U., 1970. Retail analyst Opticks, Inc. divsn. G. D. Searle, Dallas, 1977-78; dir. of adminstrn. Glast, Phillips and Murray, Dallas, 1978-81; exec. dir. Haynes and Boone L.L.P., Dallas, 1981-94; prin. Chenault and Co., 1994-95; exec. dir. Wolf, Greenfield & Sacks, P.C., 1995-96; COO Legalink Corp., 1997-98, Wolf, Greenfield & Sacks, P.C., Boston, 1999—2000, Hill & Barlow, 2000—01; founder, pres., CEO Disbursement Mgmt. Assocs., LLC, 2001—. Adj. prof. So. Meth. U. Sch. Law, Dallas, 1981-94; instr. paralegal program So. Meth. U., 1981-85; legal adv. coun. Wang Labs., 1985-91, Pitney Bowes, 1991-96; mem. Tech. Task Force, 1989-93; chair Practicing Law Profitability Conf., 1984, Large Law Firm Tech. Conf., 1990; co-chair Law Net Inc. Conf., 1988. Contbr. articles to Nat. Law Jour., PC Week. Lou Wentz scholar Coll. Bus., Okla. State U., Stillwater, 1969-70, also C.V. Richardson scholar, 1969-70; named Outstanding Coll. Bus. Grad., 1970. Mem. NAFE, State Bar Tex. (law office mgmt. com. 1991-94), Dallas Bar Assn. (strategic planning com. 1990-94, chair mktg. subcom.), Tex. Lawyer Law Tech. Planning Com. 1992, Nat. Assn. Legal Adminstrs. (dir. of adminstrn. sect. 1979-85, large firm adminstrn. sect. 1985-91, com. mem. 1986-88, vice-chmn. 1989-90, chmn., 1990-91, chair in-house tng. task force, 1990-91, communication/governance/structure issues task force 1988-89, instr. law office adminstrn. course 1984, 87, pres. Dallas chpt. 1985-86, prin. adminstrs. team 1992-96, nat. nominating com. 1992-93, nat. certification task force 1996-97, vice-chair intellectual property affinity group 2000—), Inst. Assoc. Devel. Home: 42 Nichols Rd Cohasset MA 02025-1166 E-mail: marilyn_minot@dmalaw.com

CHENEY, ANNA MARIE JANGULA, retired medical/surgical nurse; b. Wishek, N.D., Nov. 27, 1935; d. Jacob Jangula and Eva Wald; m. Edwin J. Cheney, Feb. 6, 1965; children: Alan, Deborah, Darrell. Diploma, Sisters of St. Joseph Sch. Nursing, Grand Forks, N.D., 1957; BSN, St. Louis U., 1960; MSN, UCLA, 1965. Oper. rm. instr. Sisters of St. Joseph, Grand Forks, 1957-58; staff nurse Cardinal Glennon Meml. Hosp., St. Louis, 1958-60, VA Med. Ctr., St. Louis and L.A., 1960-62, head nurse West L.A., 1963-64; staff nurse UCLA Med. Ctr., 1964-65; head nurse Meml. Hosp., Culver City and L.A., 1965-66; staff nurse West Pk. Hosp., Canoga Park, Calif., 1980-84, VA Med. Ctr., Sepulveda, Calif., 1984-89, clin. nurse specialist med./surg., 1989—94, clin. nurse specialist ambulatory care, 1994; charge nurse ambulatory care West L.A. Med. Ctr., Calif., 1996—97, ret. Calif., 1997. Instr. CPR Am. Heart Assn., L.A., 1991-94; facilitator stop smoking Am. Cancer Soc., L.A., 1991—, instr. breast self exams, 1991—. Contbr. articles to profl. jours. Vol. mem. spkr. bur. Am. Cancer Soc., 1997—. Named Outstanding Pub. Spkr., Am. Cancer Soc., 1993; recipient Outstanding Spkrs. award, 1998, Project Team Leadership award, 1999, 1st place age group, Am. Heart Assn. 5K Run, 1996, 1998, Mission Delivery Person Vol. of the Yr., Am. Cancer Soc., 2004—05; grantee, UCLA, 1963—64. Mem. Toastmaster Internat. (v.p. edn. 1991-92, pres. 1992-93, Cert. of Appreciation 1992, competent toastmaster, Toastmaster Leadership Excellence award 1995, Bronze award 1998). Democrat. Roman Catholic. Avocations: horticulture, singing, tennis, jogging, reading. Home: 23741 Highlander Rd West Hills CA 91307-1825

CHENEY, DENISE KAY, music educator; d. Dennis John and Roberta Louise Schibonski; m. Daniel Sean Cheney, Apr. 27, 1991; children: Brett Howard, Aaron Zack, Danica Robin. BS in Music Edn., U. Minn., Mpls., 1986—90. Music tchr. Waverly Elem. Sch., Minn., 1990—91; music dir. Bison Sch. Dist., SD, 1991—94; band & choir dir. Upsala Area Schs., Minn., 1994—. Student coun. advisor Upsala Area Schs., 1998—. Dir. of music Gethsemane Luth. Ch., Upsala, 1995—2006. Mem.: Minn. Band Dirs. Assn. (assoc.), Music Educators Nat. Conf. (assoc.), Minn. Music Educators Assn. (assoc.). Lutheran. Avocations: singing, piano. Office: Upsala Area Schs 415 S Main St Upsala MN 56384 Personal E-mail: dcheney@upsala.k12.mn.us.

CHENEY, ELEANORA LOUISE, retired secondary school educator; b. Seneca Falls, NY, June 3, 1923; d. Guy Darrell and Alice Augusta (McCoy) Stevenson; m. John C. Dinsmore, Jan. 13, 1941 (div. 1953); children: Patricia Walter, Nancy Dinsmore, Jon Dinsmore (dec.); m. Daniel Lavern Cheney, Aug. 8, 1959. BA, Rutgers U., 1966; MA, U. Glassboro, 1971. Account clk. GE, Auburn, N.Y., 1953-58; supr. accounts payable Sylvania Electric, Camillus, N.Y., 1958-60; cost acctg. clk. RCA, Cherry Hill, N.J., 1960-64; honors English tchr. Lenape Regional High Sch., Medford, N.J., 1966-74; guidance counselor Shawnee High Sch., 1974—84; owner Another World of Travel, Marlton, N.J., 1984-86; co-founder, trustee, sec. Danellie Found., 1991—. Travel agt., 1986— Counselor Contact Ministries, Moorestown, NJ, 1976-99; fin. com., nominating com. Haddonfield (NJ) United Meth. Ch., 1987-92, supr. ch. sch., 1980-82; bd. dirs. Fellowship House, Camden, NJ, 1994—, Robins' Nest, Glassboro, NJ, 1995-2000; adminstrv. coun. Haddonfield United Meth. Ch., 1996-99, leader small group, 1990—, adminstrv. coun., 2003—; established Jon W. Dinsmore Meml. Math. Scholarship Cherry Hill West, NJ, 1997—,vol. Interfaith Caregivers, Haddonfield, NJ, 2006-. Named to Nat. Woman's Hall of Fame, 1994. Mem. AAUW. Republican. Methodist. Avocations: reading, knitting, gardening. Home: 5 Periwinkle Pl Marlton NJ 08053-5556

CHENEY, LYNNE VINCENT, humanities educator, writer; b. Casper, Wyo., Aug. 14, 1941; d. Wayne and Edna (Lybyer) Vincent; m. Richard Bruce Cheney, Aug. 29, 1964; children: Elizabeth, Mary. BA with highest honors, Colo. Coll., 1963; MA, U. Colo., 1964; PhD in 19th century Brit. lit., U. Wis., 1970. Freelance writer, 1970-83; lectr. No. Va. CC, 1968—71, George Washington U., Washington, 1972-77, U. Wyo., Casper, 1977-78; researcher, writer Md. Pub. Broadcasting, Owings Mills, 1982-83; sr. editor Washingtonian mag., Washington, 1983-86; chmn. NEH, Washington, 1986-93; W.J. Brady Jr. fellow Am. Enterprise Inst., Washington, 1993-95, sr. fellow, 1996—. Commr. U.S. Constitution Bicentennial Commn., Washington, 1985-87. Author: Executive Privilege, 1978, Sisters, 1981, Telling the Truth, 1995; (with others) Kings of the Hill, 1983, 96, (with Victor Gold) The Body Politic, 1988, (report) American Memory: A Report on the Humanities in the Nation's Public Schools, 1988, (essay) Academic Freedom, 1992; (children's books) America: A Patriotic Primer, 2002, A Is for Abigail: An Almanac of Amazing American Women, 2003, When Washington Crossed the Delaware: A Wintertime Story for Young Patriots, 2004, A Time For Freedom: What Happened When in America, 2005; contbr. articles to profl. jours. Mem. Women's Forum, Washington. Mem.: Congl. Club, Kappa Alpha Theta, Phi Beta Kappa. Republican. Methodist. Office: Am Enterprise Inst 1150 17th St NW Ste 1100 Washington DC 20036-4603

CHENEY, MARY CLAIRE, Internet company executive; b. June 14, 1969; d. Dick and Lynne Cheney; life ptnr. Heather Poe. BA in History, Colo. Coll., Colo. Springs, 1991; MBA, U. Denver, 2002. With promotions dept. Colo. Rockies baseball team, 1993—94; pub. relations mgr. Coors Brewing Co., 1994—2000; position with audience bus. dept. Am. Online, Inc., Dulles, Va., 2005—06, chief of staff, 2006—. Author: Now It's My Turn: A Daughter's Chronicle of a Political Life, 2006. Mem. Bush-Cheney Campaign, 2000; mem. adv. bd. Rep. Unity Coalition, 2002—03; dir. v.p. ops. Bush-Cheney 2004 Presdl. re-election campaign, 2003.*

CHENG, AMY, artist; b. Gaoshiung, Taiwan, Dec. 8, 1956; came to U.S., 1967; d. Nai Ling and Chai-Ying (Lai) C. BFA, U. Tex., 1978; MFA, Hunter Coll., 1982. Lectr. Hunter Coll., N.Y.C., 1985-86, Princeton (NJ) U., 1989-90; asst. prof. studio art Bard Coll., Annandale-Hudson, NY, 1990-97; assoc. prof. art SUNY, New Paltz, NY, 0997—. Travel grantee Arts Internat., 1994; grantee Ford Found., 1977-78, N.Y. Found. for the Arts fellow, 1990, 96. Home: 27 Rte 299 New Paltz NY 12561 Office: SUNY 75 S Manheim Blvd Ste 1 New Paltz NY 12561-2499 Office Phone: 845-257-3840. Business E-Mail: chena@newpaltz.edu.

CHENG, GRACE ZHENG-YING, music educator; arrived in U.S., 1982; d. Chang Cheng and Guan-Zhi Fang. B Music, Shanghai Conservatory Music, China, 1980; M Music, U. Nebr., 1985. Tchg. asst. Shanghai Conservatory Music, China, 1976—82, U. Nebr., Lincoln, 1983—85; piano tchr. Freehold (N.J.) Music Ctr., 1985—. Piano soloist Arts in the Aisles, Lincoln, Nebr., 1984, Cecilian Music Club, Monmouth County, NJ, 1986—92; pianist, NJ, 1985—. Recipient Laura R. Conover Pedagogy award Outstanding Tchg., Carnegie Hall, N.Y.C., 1998, 5th Yr. Tchr.'s award, Cecilian Music Club, 1997. Mem.: ASPCA, Nat. Guild Piano Tchrs. (piano adj. 1994—), N.J. Music Tchrs. Assn. (piano adj. 1998), Nat. Music Tchrs. Assn. (piano adj. 1993), Sierra Club. Avocations: internet, travel, photography, gardening. Home: 1 Swallow Ln Howell NJ 07731 Office: Freehold Music Ctr 3681 Unit 4 Rte 9 Freehold NJ 07728 Personal E-mail: gchennj@aol.com.

CHENG, MEI-FANG, psychobiology educator, neuroscientist; b. Kee Lung, Taiwan, Republic of China, Nov. 24, 1938; came to U.S., 1959; d. Chao-Chin Hsieh and Ai Tsu; m. Wen-Kwei Cheng; m. June 7, 1963; children: Suzanne, Po-Yuan, Julie. BS summa cum laude, Nat. Taiwan U., Taipei, 1958; PhD, Bryn Mawr Coll., 1965. Postdoctoral fellow U. Pa., Phila., 1965-68; asst. rsch. prof. Inst. Animal Behavior Rutgers U., Newark, 1969-73, assoc. prof., 1973-79, prof., 1979, acting dir. Inst. Animal Behavior, 1989—91, dir., 1991-95. Cons. NIMH, mem. neurosci. study sect., 1991-95; cons., mem. behavioral neurobiology br. NSF; mem. NIH Reviewers Res., 1995—; cons. numerous granting agys. Author: Advance in the Study of Behavior, 1979; co-editor: Reproduction: A Behavioral and Neuroscientific Perspective, 1986; assoc. editor Hormones and Behavior, 1986-96; cons. Brain Rsch., Sci., others; contbr. articles to profl. jours. Fulbright scholar, 1959; recipient Rsch. Scientist Devel. award NIMH, 1974-79, 79-84, Johnson & Johnson Discovery award, 1989, Hoechst-Celanese Innovative award, 1993, award of excellence in rsch. Rutgers Bd. Trustees, 1998. Mem. Internat. Conf. Neuroethology, Neurosci. Achievements include discovery that a bird's own songs stimulate the endocrine changes; demonstration of the vocal-auditory-endocrine pathways involved in voice and sound mediation of endocrine change, and provide anatomical basis for emotion-based motor theory of acoustic communication; discovery of cell loss can trigger neurogenesis in the adult brain and may be harnessed for brain repair and functional recovery. Office: Rutgers U Dept Psychology 101 Warren St Newark NJ 07102-1811 Office Phone: 973-353-5440 x 226. Business E-Mail: mcheng@axon.rutgers.edu.

CHENG, PAULINE SHYH-YI, mathematics educator; d. Robert and Jeanne Cheng. BS, Keene State Coll., NH, 1990; MS, U. North Tex., Denton, 1997. Tchr. secondary math. Denton H.S., 1997—2004, Wylie H.S., 2004—. Mem. Denton Bible Ch., Tex., 1995—2006. Scholar, Keene State Coll., 1986—90. Mem.: Am. Fedn. Tchrs. Office: Wylie High School 2550 W Fm 544 Wylie TX 75098 Office Phone: 972-429-3100. E-mail: pauline.cheng@wylieisd.net.

CHENOWETH, KRISTIN, actress; b. Broken Arrow, Okla., July 24, 1968; MA in Opera, Oklahoma City U. Actor: (Broadway plays) Steel Pier, 1999 (Theatre World award), You're a Good Man, Charlie Brown, 1999 (Tony award Best Featured Actress, 1999, Drama Desk award, 1999, Clarence Derwent award, 1999, Outer Critics Circle award, 1999), Epic Proportions, 1999—2000, Funny Girl, 2002, Wicked, 2003—04 (Tony award nominee, Best Actress in a Musical, 2004); (plays) A New Brain, Scapin, The Fantasticks, Dames at Sea, Strike Up the Band, 1998, The Apple Tree, 2005; (TV series) LateLine, 1998, Frasier, 1993, Kristin, 2001, Baby Bob, 2002, Sesame Street, 2003—, The West Wing, 2005—06; (TV miniseries) Paramour, 1999; (TV films) Annie, 1999, The Music Man, 2003; (films) Topa Topa Bluffs, 2002, Bewitched, 2005, The Pink Panther, 2006; guest soloist: West Side Story Suite of Dances; singer: (albums) Let Yourself Go, 2001, As I Am, 2005. Metropolitan Opera award. Performed leading roles at Goodspeed Opera House, Guthrie Theatre, Paper Mill Playhouse, North Shore Music Theatre; guest soloist with National Symphony Orchestra, New York Philharmonic, London's Divas at Donmar series, Carnegie Hall, Lincoln Center and the Kennedy Center, and has performed with Placido Domingo, Paul Newman, Joshua Bell and Harvey Fierstein. Office: c/o SAG 360 Madison Ave #12 New York NY 10017-7111*

CHER, (CHERILYN SARKISIAN), singer, actress; b. El Centro, Calif., May 20, 1946; d. Gilbert and Georgia LaPiere; m. Sonny Bono, Oct. 27, 1964 (div. June 26, 1975); 1 child, Chastity; m. Gregg Allman, June 30, 1975 (div. Jan. 16, 1979); 1 child, Elijah Blue. Student drama coach, Jeff Corey. Singer with husband as team, Sonny and Cher, 1964-74; star TV shows: Cher, 1975-76, The Sonny and Cher Show, 1976-77; concert appearances with husband, 1977, numerous recs., TV, concert and benefit appearances with Sonny Bono; TV appearances, ABC-TV, 1978, appearance with Sonny Bono in motion pictures, Good Times, 1966, Chastity, 1969; film appearances include Come Back to the Five and Dime, Jimmy Dean, Jimmy Dean, 1982, Silkwood, 1983, Mask, 1985 (Best Actress, Cannes Internat. Film Festival), The Witches of Eastwick, 1987, Suspect, 1987, Moonstruck (Golden Globe award 1988, Acad. award for best actress 1988), 1987, Mermaids, 1990, The Player, 1992, Pret-a-Porter, 1994, Faithful, 1996, Tea With Mussolini, 1999; TV movies Club Rhino, 1990, If These Walls Could Talk, 1996, Happy Birthday Elizabeth: A Celebration of Life, 1997, AFI's 100 Years.100 Movies, 1998; helped form rock band, Black Rose, 1979; recorded albums include Black Rose, 1980, Cher, 1988, Heart of Stone, 1989 (Double Platinum and 3 Gold Singles), Love Hurts, 1991, It's A Man's World, 1996, The Casablanca Years, 1996, Believe, 1998 (Grammy award best dance recording 1999), Not Commercial, 2000, Living Proof, 2002; exec. prodr. Sonny & Me: Cher Remembers, 1998. also: Reprise Records 3000 Warner Blvd Burbank CA 19010-4694

CHEREM, BARBARA BROWN, education educator; b. Detroit, May 4, 1946; d. Max Frederick and Dorothy Catherine (Bender) Brown; m. Gabriel Jerome Cherem, May 26, 1973; children: Mariah, Max. BA in English and Secondary Tchg., U. Mich., 1968; MA Ed. in Spl. Edn., Mich. State U., 1975; postgrad., Ea. Mich. U., 1984-86; PhD in Edn., Mich. State U., 1991, postgrad. Tchr. Romulus (Mich.) H.S., 1970-71; tchr. spl. edn. Hawthorn Children's Psychiat. Sch., Northville, Mich., 1971-73; program dir. Homme Home for Boys, Wittenberg, Wis., 1973-74; tchr. Wittenberg (Wis.)-Birnamwood H.S., 1973—74; pres., owner Learning Shop, Columbus, Ohio, 1974-77; tchr. cons. Jackson (Mich.) Pub. Schs., 1977-79; rsch. project dir. Ea. Mich. U., Mich. Evaluation Resource Ctr., 1979-81; rsch. and curriculum devel. grantee Ea. Mich. U., Ypsilanti, 1979-83; cmty. resource specialist Interpretation Ctr., Ann Arbor, Mich., 1981-83; acad. coord. adult mgmt. program Spring Arbor (Mich.) Coll., 1983-87, cons., with affiliate colls., 1984-90, dir. R&D, 1987-89, dir. R&D adult and continuing edn., 1989-91, assoc. prof. edn., 1991-93, prof., 1993—, prof., dir. instnl. assessment, 1994—. V.p. Interp Ctrl., Chelsea, Mich., 1979-89; presenter to 14 nat. confs., 1986-90; mem. bd. advs. Adult Faith Resources pls., 1988-91; cons. Mich. Dept. Social Svcs., Lansing and Detroit, 1989. Contbg. author, editor: Securing Occupational Achievement Through Readiness Sls, 1981, Parents in Parenting, 1993; contbr. articles to profl. jours. Trustee Chelsea (Mich.) Pub. Sch. Bd., 1986-90; mem. adminstrv. bd. First United Meth. Ch., Chelsea, 1983-85. Mich. State U. Scholars' fellow, 1988-89. Mem. AAUW, Am. Assn. Adult Continuing Edn. (trustee 1993—), Am. Assn. Sch. Adminstrs., Mich. Assn. Sch. Bds., Mich. Assn. Cmty. Adult Edn., Mich. Assn. Adult and Continuing Edn. (editl. bd. Options 1991-92, bd. dirs. 1993—), U. Mich Alumni club, Phi Delta Kappa, Alpha Delta Pi (philanthropy chair 1967). Avocations: reading, travel, internet, exercise, cooking. Office: Assessment Farmington PS 33000 Thomas St Farmington MI 48336-2347

CHERMAYEFF, ALEXANDRA SASHA, artist; b. N.Y.C., Feb. 17, 1960; d. Ivan and Sara Anne (Duffy) C.; m. Philip W. Howie, May 10, 1992; children: Phineas Alexander, Olivia Isabel BA, U. Vt., 1982; postgrad., N.Y. Studio Sch., 1983—86. Cert. appraiser N.Y. U. Sch. Appraisal Studies. Cons. Alexandra Chermayeff Artist Svcs., N.Y.C., 1987—91; asst. to chmn., bd. dirs. Andy Warhol Found., N.Y.C., 1991—93; collection mgr., curator Frederick Hughes, N.Y.C., 1991—2000; dir. exhbns. Thomas Cole Hist. Site Gallery, 2001—04. Exhibited Bowery Gallery, N.Y., 1992, Addison Gallery, Andover, Mass., 1993, Parrish Art Mus., N.Y., 1994 (award 1994), N.Y. Studio Sch. Gallery, 1995, Carrie Haddad Gallery (award), Hudson, N.Y., 2000, Global Art Source, Zurich, 2001, 02, A.D.D. Gallery, 2005, Sideshow Gallery, N.Y.C., 2005, 2006. Recipient Allied Artist award Nat. Arts Club, 1985; Ellen Battell Stoeckel fellow Yale U., 1985 Mem. Friends of Hudson, Riverkeeper Avocations: birdwatching, fossils. E-mail: philandsasha@verizon.net.

CHERNOFF, DEBORAH SHELLEY, art educator; b. Phila., Jan. 10, 1951; d. Bernard and Helene Chernoff. AA, Atlantic Cape C.C., Mays Landing, N.J., 1973; BS, Moore Coll. Art and Design, 1974; MA, Rowan U., 1980. Cert. Nat. Bd. Profl. Tchg. Stds., Nat. Bd. Profl. Tchg. Standards 2002. Instr. art Atlantic City H.S., 1988—93; instr. comml. and fine arts Mainland Regional H.S., Linwood, NJ, 1975—. Bd. dirs. edn. Jewish Fedn. Atlantic County; mem. So. Regional Inst. Stockton State Coll., Pomona, NJ, 2002—. Represented in permanent collections Congregation Beth Judah Sch., Atlantic Cape C.C.; artist, illustrated Haggadah Beth Judah's 75th Anniversary. Bd. dirs. Atlantic City Concerts Assn. Mem.: NEA, Art Educator's N.J., Phila. Calligrapher's Soc., N.J. Edn. Assn., Nat. Art Edn. Assn. (presenter conv.), Shaloma Hadassah (life), Phi Delta Kappa. Home: 208 N Newark Ave Ventnor City NJ 08406 Office: Mainland Regional HS 1301 Oak Ave Linwood NJ 08221 Office Phone: 609-927-4151.

CHERNOW, ANN LEVY, artist, educator; b. N.Y.C., Feb. 1, 1936; d. Edward P. and Mollie (Citrin) Levy; m. Philip Chenok, Aug. 11, 1957 (div. Jan. 1969); children: David Charles Chenok, Daniel Joshua Chenok; m. Burt Chernow, Dec. 11, 1970. MA, NYU, 1969. Instr. Mus. Modern Art, N.Y.C., 1966-71; prof., head art dept. Norwalk (Conn.) Cmty. Tech. Coll., 1974-96. Guest lectr., instr. studio and art history Silvermine Sch. Arts Silvermine Coll., 1968—80; vis. artist, lectr. Housatonic C.C., Conn., 1975—80; guest lectr. Am. Coll. in Paris, 1985, Salem State Coll., 1993, 94, Yale U., 1995, Westport Hist. Soc., 1994, Fairfield U., 1993; vis. artist CAP program Wesleyan U., 1979; coord. Bicentennial Exhbn. Norwalk C.C., 1976, Yale U. Art Gallery, 1996; master drawing class The Nat. Acad., N.Y.C., 2000—, N.Y.C., 2001; vis. artist and lectr. Bryn Mawr U., 2003, Ind. U., 2003; vis. artist Pa. Acad. Fine Arts, 2004, U. Ind., 2002. One-woman shows include Queens Coll., N.Y.C., 2000, Erlich Gallery, Marblehead, Mass., 2002, Uptown Gallery, N.Y.C., 2002, 2004, Raclin Gallery Ind. U., 2003, Print Ctr., Phila., 2003, Dorothy Rogers Fine Art, Santa Fe, N.Mex., 2003, Silvermine Guild, Conn., 2005, Uptown Gallery, N.Y.C., 2006, Amity Art Found., Conn., 2006, numerous others, exhibited in group shows at Millennium Portfolio of Time and Place, 1999—2001, Americas, 2000, Bklyn. Mus., 2001, Nat. Acad., 2001, NY Soc. Etchers, 2002, Nat Arts Club, NYC, 2002, Mus. City of NY, 2002, Salle des Fetes, Paris, 2003, Trois Rivieres, Can., 2003, Lessedra Gallery, Sophia, Bulgaria, 2004, Black Ch. Gallery, Dublin, 2004, Westport Arts Ctr., Conn., 2004, Housatonic Mus. Art, 2005, NAD, N.Y.C., 2005, numerous others, Nat. Arts Club, NYC, 2005, Uptown Gallery, 2006, Represented in permanent collections Met. Mus. Art, Rose Art Mus., Brandeis U., Nat. Mus. Women in Arts, Washington, William Benton Mus. Art, Storrs, Conn., Mus. of City of N.Y., UN, Westport, Achenbach Found., San Francisco, New Britain Mus. Am. Art, Conn., Neuberger Mus., Purchase, N.Y., Housatonic Mus. Art Yale U., Mattatauk Mus., Lehigh U. Art Collection, Pa., Utah Mus. Fine Arts, U. Ariz. Art Collection, Lyman Allyn Mus., Conn., Bruce Mus., Butler Inst. Am. Art, Ohio, Rutgers U., Hofstra U., Elvejhem Mus., Wis., N.Y. Pub. Libr., Duxbury Mus. Mass., USO of Met. N.Y., Amity Art Found., Conn., Reading (Pa.) Pub. Mus., Portland (Oreg.) Art Mus., De Cordova Mus., Lincoln, Mass., Yale U. Art Gallery, Utah Mus. Fine Arts, Ohio Wesleyan U., Worcester Mus. Art, Mass., Oakland Mus., Calif., U.S.O. Greater Met. N.Y., Reading Pub. Mus., Pa., Transit Mus., N.Y.C., Bklyn. Mus., Libr. Congress, Nat. U. Coalition Taiwan, San Diego Mus. Art, Nat. Acad. N.Y.C., San Diego (Calif.) Mus., Sacred Heart U., Conn., Fairfield U., Toledo Mus. Art;, author numerous poems; contbr. articles to profl. jours.; artistic dir.: (documentaries) A Gathering of Glory; Years in the Making. Active Westport Arts Adv. Com., Westport Schs. Permanent Art Collection Com. Named Conn. Woman of Decade in Arts, UN Assn., 1987, U.S.A. rep., Agart World Print Festival, Ljubljana, Slovenia, 1999, UN Artist of Yr., 2002; recipient Purchase award, Delta Internat. Prints, 1996, Etching award, L.A. Printmaking Soc., 1997, Painting award, Manhattan Arts Internat., 1997, Etching award, Audubon artists, 1997, Print Biennial Silvermine Guild of Art, Conn., 1998, Four winners award, Stamford Mus. & Nature Ctr., Conn., 1998, Eisner Found. award, 1998, Richard Florsheim award, 1998, Exhbn. award/Boston Printmakers and Delta Internat. awards, Print Club, 2001, Purchase award, Delta Internat. Prints, 2001, Trustees Merit award, Housatonic C.C., 2003, Legion of Honor award, Achenbach Found., San Francisco, Catalog Raisonée Graphics award, Amity Art Found., 2003, Lifetime Honors award, Silvermine Guild, Conn., 2004; fellow Yale Mellon, 1993—94; grantee Yale/Mellon, 1995; scholar Conn. Humanities Coun., 1980—. Mem.: N.Y. Etchers Soc., Print Club Albany, Print Club Phila., L.A. Print Soc., Boston Printmakers, Calif. Soc. Printmakers, Nat. Acad. Art, Nat. Acad. Art (elected Academician Graphics), Soc. Am. Graphic Artists (past coun.). Studio: 2 Gorham Ave Westport CT 06880-2531 Office Phone: 203-227-8016. Personal E-mail: ctfinearts@sbcglobal.net.

CHERRI, MONA Y., computer scientist, educator, computer scientist, consultant; d. Mitri Ibrahim Abo Chedid and Yvonne Gerges Madi; m. Youssef Ali Cherri, Nov. 1, 1952; children: Mike Youssef, John Youssef, David Youssef, Jacob Youssef. MS in Math., Okla. State U., Stillwater, 1982, PhD in Math., 1985; PhD in Computer Sci., U. North Tex., Denton, 1996. Assoc. prof. computer sci. Tex. Woman's U., Denton, 1989—98; info. specialist EDS, Plano, Tex., 1998—99; cons. Excel Comm., Carrolton, Tex., 1999; data translation staff engr. Ericsson Inc., Richardson, Tex., 1999—2001, EXI Parsons, Richardson, 2001—03; cons. Plexon, Inc, Richardson, Tex., 2003—04; mem. computer info. sci. faculty North Lake Coll., Irving, Tex., 2004—. Contbr. articles to profl. jours. Recipient Maclachlan award, Okla. Sate U., 1982; grantee, NIH, 1994—98. Mem.: IEEE (assoc.), Upsilon Pi Upsilon (life), Pi Mu Epsilon (life). Mem. Lds Ch. Home: 4437 Avebury Dr Plano TX 75024 Office: North Lake College 5001 N Mac Arthur Blvd Irving TX 75038 Office Phone: 972-273-3472. Home Fax: 972-273-3472; Office Fax: 972-273-3471. Personal E-mail: jcherri@flash.net. Business E-Mail: mcherri@dcccd.edu.

CHERRINGTON, PAMELA JO, special education educator; b. Binghamton, NY, Mar. 15, 1957; d. William and Marian Baldwin Timson; m. James W. Cherrington, July 7, 1979; children: Ian James, Kellie Marie. AA, Broome CC, 1976; BA in Edn., SUNY, Cortland, 1978; MA in Edn., Nat. U., 1986; student, Azusa Pacific U. Cert. Resource Specialist U. Calif., Riverside, Elem. Edn. Tchr. SUNY, Cortland, in Spl. Edn. Nat. U. Elem. tchr. St. Thomas Aquinas, Binghamton, NY, 1978—79, Broward County Sch. Dist., Coral Springs, Fla., 1979—80; pvt. tutor Broward County, 1980—82; pre-sch. dir., kindergarten tchr. Country Day Sch., Coral Springs, 1982—84; substitute tchr. Escondido Elem. Sch. Dist., Calif., 1984—86; spl. day class tchr. Temecula Valley, Calif., 1986—93; resource specialist United Sch. Dist., Temecula, 1993—. Mem.: Calif. Assn. Resource Specialists, Calif. Assn. Sch. Psychologists (student mem.). Republican. Presbyterian. Avocations: travel, gardening, interior decorating. Home: 34105 Milat St Temecula CA 92592

CHERRY, KELLEY, secondary school educator; d. Al (Stepfather) and Sheila Matson; m. Johnathan Aaron Cherry, June 12, 2004. Bachelor (hon.), U. North Tex., Denton, 2002. Cert. tchr. Tex., 2005. Retirement specialist Fidelity Investments, Westlake, Tex., 2002—04; dance, drill team, and pom squad dir. So. Belles of Lee H.S., Tyler, Tex., 2004—. Corp. trainer Fidelity Investments, Westlake, Tex., 1999—2004, Red Lobster, Lewisville, Tex.,

1999—2004. Dancer (jazz, modern, ballet, tap). Bbible study leader, evangelist, & mission work Denton Bible Ch. & Grace, Denton & Tyler, Tex., 2000—06. Scholar Bus. scholarship, U. North Tex., 3; Dance scholarship, Kilgore Coll., 1 yr. Mem.: ATPE (assoc.). Achievements include research in effects of physical activity on student achievement. Avocations: running, reading, cooking, gardening, volunteer work. Office Phone: 903-262-2694.

CHERRY, SANDRA OSBURN, mathematics educator; b. Balt., Nov. 7, 1942; d. Robert Dudley and Doris Douglas (Jones) Osburn; m. Charles S. Cherry (div.); children: Cassandra Cherry Brosvik, Michael. BA, U. Md., College Park, 1963; MA, U. Ky., Lexington, 1969; postgrad., Western Ky. U., Bowling Green, 1975. Tchr. Prince George's County Pub. Schs., Md., 1964—65, Jefferson County Schs., Louisville, 1967—2000; substitute tchr. pvt. and pub. schs. Louisville, 2000—. Named Outstanding Math Tchr., Greater Coun. Tchrs. Math., 1996, 2000. Mem.: Mensa, MacDowell Music Club, Delta Kappa Gamma. Democrat. Episcopalian. Avocation: music. Home: 901 Lake Forest Pkwy Louisville KY 40245

CHERRY, SANDRA WILSON, lawyer; b. Dec. 31, 1941; d. Berlin Alexander and Renna Glen (Barnes) Wilson; m. John Sandefur Cherry, Sept. 24, 1976; 1 child, Jane Wilson. BA, U. Ark., 1962, JD, 1975. Bar: Ark. 75, U.S. Dist. Ct. (ea. dist.) Ark. 79, U.S. Supreme Ct. 79, U.S. Ct. Appeals (8th cir.) 79. Tchr. social studies Little Rock Sch. Dist., 1966—70; chmn. social studies dept. Horace Mann Jr. H.S., Little Rock, 1970—72; asst. U.S. atty. Dept. Justice, Little Rock, 1975—81, 1983—, 1st asst. U.S. atty., 2002—; commr. Ark. Pub. Svc. Commn., Little Rock, 1981—83. Adj. instr. U. Ark. Sch. Law, Little Rock, 1980; mem. 8th cir. gender fairness task force, Ark. dist. ct. magistrate selection panel, 2001. Contbr. case note to Ark. Law Rev., 1975. Pres. bd. dirs. Gaines House, Inc.; pres. U. Ark. at Little Rock Law Sch. Assn., 1980—81, bd. dirs., 1982, Jr. League Little Rock, 1974, Ark. Cmty. Found., 1997—, Gov.'s Mansion Assn., 1998—2004, Good Shepherd Ecumenical Ctr., 2004—. Recipient Gayle Pettus Pontz award, U. Ark. Law Sch. Women Lawyers Assn., 1990. Mem.: Ark. Women's Forum, Little Rock C. of C., Ark. Bar Assn. (com. on the status of women and minorities), Ark. Women Lawyers Assn., Pulaski County Bar Assn. (bd. dirs. 1989—90, 1991—92, pres.-elect 1993—94, pres. 1994—), Ark. Bar Assn. (Ho. of Dels. 1984—86, sec.-treas. 1986—89, 8th cir. Gender Fairness Task Force 1989—94, Ho. of Dels. 1989—, tenured del. 1994, exec. coun. chair 1995—96, pres. 2001—02, Golden Gavel award 1992), Met. Coun., Phi Beta Phi. Republican. Presbyterian. Home: 1 River Bend Little Rock AR 72202 Office: US Atty's Office PO Box 1229 Little Rock AR 72203-1229 Business E-Mail: sandra.cherry@usdoj.gov.

CHERRY, SARAH KATHRYN, lawyer; BA in Comm., U. British Columbia, 1998; JD, U. Toronto Law Sch., 2001. Bar: Mass. Assoc. Proskauer Rose LLP, Boston. Office: Proskauer Rose LLP One International Pl Boston MA 02110-2660 Office Phone: 617-526-9769. Office Fax: 617-526-9899. E-mail: scherry@proskauer.com.*

CHERRYH, C. J., writer; b. St. Louis, Sept. 1, 1942; d. Basil L. and Lois Ruth (Van Deventer) C. BA in Latin, U. Okla., 1964; MA in Classics, Johns Hopkins U., 1965. Cert. tchr., Okla. Tchr. Oklahoma City Pub. Schs., 1965-77. Lectr. in field Author: (novels) Gate of Ivrel, 1976, Well of Shiuan, 1978, Brothers of Earth, 1976, Hunter of Worlds, 1976, The Faded Sun: Kesrith, 1977, The Faded Sun: Shon'Jir, 1978, Fires of Azeroth, 1979, The Faded Sun: Kutath, 1979, Hestia, 1979, Sunfall, 1981, Downbelow Station, 1981 (Hugo award for best novel 1982), Wave Without a Shore, 1981, The Pride of Chanur, 1982, Merchanter's Luck, 1982, Port Eternity, 1982, Forty Thousand in Gehenna, 1983, The Dreamstone, 1983, The Tree of Swords and Jewels, 1983, Chanur's Venture, 1984, Cuckoo's Egg, 1985, Visible Light, 1985, The Kif Strike Back, 1985, Angel with the Sword, 1985, Chanur's Homecoming, 1986, Exile's Gate, 1988, Cyteen, 1988 (Hugo award 1988, 89), Smuggler's Gold, 1988, Rimrunners, 1989, Rusalka, 1989, Chernevog, 1990, Yvgenie, 1991, Heavy Time, 1991, Rumrunners, 1991, Hellburner, 1992, Chanur's Legacy, 1992, Goblin Mirror, 1993, Faery in Shadow, 1993, Tripoint, 1994, Foreigner, 1994, Rider at the Gate, 1995, Invader, 1995, Fortress in the Eye of Time, 1995, Inheritor, 1996, Cloud's Rider, 1996, Lois & Clark, 1996, Finity's End, 1997, Fortress of Eagles, 1998, Precursor, 1999, Hammerfall, 2001, Forge of Heaven, 2004, Collected Short Fiction of C.J. Cherryh, 2004, Destroyer, 2005; editor: Flood Tide, 1990; translator: Stellar Crusade by Pierre Barbet, 1980, The Green Gods by Nathalie & Charles Henneberg, 1980, The Book of Shai by Daniel Walther, 1982; contbr. short stories to numerous mags. Woodrow Wilson fellow, 1965; recipient John W. Campbell award for best new writer, 1977, Hugo award for short story, 1979, for novel, 1982, 89, Locus award for best sci. fiction novel, 1988. Mem. Sci. Fiction Writers Assn., Alpha Lambda Delta, Phi beta Kappa. Avocations: galactic mapping, guitar and music composition, travel. Office: c/o Matt Bialer Sanford J Greenburger Assoc 55 Fifth Ave New York NY 10003

CHESAK, KRISTEN, performing company executive; d. Harold James and Cynthia Jane Chesak. BA in Theater, Kalamazoo Coll., Mich., 1994; MFA in Performing Arts Adminstrn., Western Mich. U., Kalamazoo, 2006. Design intern Kalamazoo Civic Theatre, 1994—97, master carpenter, 1997—98, light/sound designer, 1998—2005, prodn. mgr., 2001—05, mng. dir., 2005—. Mem.: Am. Assn. Cmty. Theater, Rotary. Avocation: golf. Office: Kalamazoo Civic Theatre 329 S Park St Kalamazoo MI 49007

CHESBRO, KAREN E. HENISE, nurse; b. York, Pa., Oct. 2, 1960; d. Lamar and Bonnie (Palmer) Henise; children: Ashley B., Samuel T. BSN, West Chester (Pa.) U., 1982. RN, Pa.; cert. CPR instr.; cert. first aid instr. Primary care staff nurse Phoenixville (Pa.) Hosp., 1982-84, Brandywine Hosp., Coatesville, Pa., 1984-89; telemetry nurse Community Hosp. of Lancaster, Pa., 1989-95; staff nurse Kimberly Quality Care of Lancaster (Pa.), 1990-92; charge nurse Dauphin County Nursing Home, 1992-94; staff nurse Pinnacle Health Home Care, 1995-2000; nursing supr. Masonic Village Health Care Ctr., Elizabethtown, Pa., 2000—; staff nurse Ctrl. Penn Nursing Care, Inc., 2003—. Home: 9 Foxbury Dr Elizabethtown PA 17022-1760

CHESELSKI, PENNY LYNN, special education educator; b. Superior, Wis., Aug. 29, 1976; d. Gary Frank and Janice Kathryn Cheselski; 1 child, Tristan David. BS, U. Wis., 1999, MS in Edn., 2000. Spl. edn. dir. intern Unity H.S., Duluth, Minn., 2000—02; spl edn. tchr. Lake Superior H.S., Duluth, 2002—05. Mem.: Coun. Exceptional Children. Democrat. Home: 1306 Broadway St Superior WI 54880 Office: Denfeld High School 4405 W 4th St Superior WI 54880 Office Phone: 218-628-4863 ext. 308. Personal E-mail: lynn_54880@yahoo.com.

CHESLER, GAIL, arts organization development executive; b. Phila., May 22; d. Leon William and Sylvia (Spiegel) C.; m. Richard Allen Lippe (div. May 1989); children; Wendy Ann, David Allen. BA in History, Beaver Coll.; MA in Performing Arts Adminstrn., NYU, 1988. Outreach coord. North Shore Cmty. Arts Ctr., Gt. Neck, NY, 1976-79; pub. rels. cons. Gt. Neck, 1979-85; dir. of devel. and mktg. ART/New York, N.Y.C., 1987-88; exec. dir. Jennifer Muller/The Works, N.Y.C., 1989; dir. of devel. Temple Beth-El, Gt. Neck, 1989-92; nat. dir. planned giving and endowments Women's Am. ORT, N.Y.C., 1993-96; planned giving officer N.Y. Presbyn. Hosp./Weill Med. Coll. of Cornell U., N.Y.C., 1996-2000; dir. planned and spl. gifts The Met. Opera, N.Y.C., 2000—. Co-founder, bd. dirs. Teen to Teen, Carle Place, N.Y., 1985-88. Mem. Planned Giving Group of Greater N.Y. (past pres. 1999—, pres. 1998-99, v.p. 1997-98, treas. 1996-97). Avocations: opera, travel, theater. Home: 128 Central Park S # 3B New York NY 10019-1565 Office: The Metropolitan Opera Lincoln Ctr New York NY 10023

CHESNEY, MARGARET A., medical educator, medical researcher; BA in Psychology and Sociology, Whitman Coll., Walla Walla, Wash., 1971; MA in Psychology, Colo. State U., 1973, PhD in Psychology, 1975. Postdoctoral fellow dept. psychiatry Temple U., Phila., 1975—76; dir. and sr. health psychologist dept. behavioral medicine SRI Internat., 1976—87; assoc. prof. prevention scis. group, dept. epidemiology U. Calif., San Francisco, 1987—89, prof. prevention scis. group, 1989—, co-dir. Ctr. for AIDS Prevention Studies, 1994—; dir. behavioral core AIDS Clin. Trials Group San Francisco Gen. Hosp., 1994—. Sci. cons. behavioral medicine Stanford U. Med. Ctr., 1978—; chair working group on psychosocial factors in AIDS clin. trials and vaccine trials NIMH, 1993—; chair working group for women's health initiative clin. trial NIH, 1993—; co-chair recruitment, adherence, retention com. AIDS Clin. Trials Group, 1995—; mem. HIV vaccine working group NIAID, 1994—95; mem. data safety and monitoring bd. Women's Health Initiative NIH, 1993—; mem. panel on AIDS interventions and rsch. NAS, 1988—90; mem. AIDS adv. com. Nat. Heart, Lung and Blood Inst., 1987—93. Contbr. numerous articles to profl. jours.; co-author (with Ray Rosenman): Anger and Hostility in Cardiovascular and Behavioral Disorders. Mem.: APA (pres. health psychology divsn. 1990—91, Ann. Award for Outstanding Contbn. to Health Psychology 1982), Am. Psychosomatic Soc. (pres.-elect 1996, Ann. Award for Outstanding Contbn. to Health Psychology 1985), Inst. Medicine of NAS, Phi Beta Kappa, Sigma Xi.

CHESNEY, SUSAN TALMADGE, writer, educational association administrator; b. NYC, Aug. 12, 1943; d. Morton and Tillie (Talmadge) Chesney; m. Donald Lewis Freitas, Sept. 17, 1967 (div. May 1976); m. Robert Martin Rosenblatt, Apr. 9, 1980. AB, U. Calif., Berkeley, 1967. Placement interviewer U. Calif., Berkeley, 1972-74, program coord., 1974-79; pers. adminstr. Hewlett-Packard Co., Santa Rosa, Calif., 1982-84; pres. Mgmt. Resources, Santa Rosa, 1984-97; human resources mgr. BioBottoms Inc., Petaluna, Calif., 1990-91; human resources adminstr. Parker Compumotor, Rohnert Park, Calif., 1991-93; writer, developer The E-Myth Acad., Santa Rosa, 1997-98. Cons. Kensington Electronics Group, Healdsburg, Calif., 1984-85, Behavioral Medicine Assocs., Santa Rosa, 1985-86, M.C.A.I., Santa Rosa, 1986-87, Bowdon Designs, Santa Rosa, 1987-88, Bass & Ingram, Santa Rosa, 1988-96, Eason Tech., Inc., Healdsburg, 1995-96, Interim Svcs., Inc., Santa Rosa, 1995-98, Flex Products, Inc., Santa Rosa, 1996-97, Nev. Prodn. Co., 1998-99. Avocations: cooking, gardening, music. Personal E-mail: schesney@sonic.net.

CHESNUTT, JANE, publishing executive; b. Kenedy, Tex., Oct. 10, 1950; m. W. Mallory Rintoul. BJ, U. Tex., 1973. With Environment Information Ctr., NY, 1973; editorial asst. Am. Jour. Nursing, NYC, 1975-78; asst. editor Woman's Day mag., NYC, 1978—83, health editor, 1983—89, beauty, health, fashion editor, 1989-91, editor-in-chief, 1991—, sr. v.p., group editl. dir., 2002—. Sr. v.p. & group editl. dir. Transplant Am. Nat. Kidney Found. Mem. bus. adv. coun. Washington Irving H.S., N.Y.C. Named one of Editor of Yrl, Adweek, 1992, Top Players, Min Mag., 2000; recipient Editor of Yr., Adweek, 1992. Mem. Am. Soc. Mag. Editors, Women in Comms., Inc. (Clarion award 1985, Headliner award 1996), YWCA Acad. of Achievers. Office: Woman's Day Mag Hachette Filipacchi Mags Inc 1633 Broadway New York NY 10019-6708 Office Phone: 212-767-6250. Office Fax: 212-767-5610.*

CHESS, SONIA MARY, retired language educator; b. Ashton, Lancashire, Eng., Apr. 14, 1930; came to U.S., 1951, naturalized, 1963; d. Arthur and Sarah Ann (Hulme) Bradburn; m. Joseph Campbell Chess, Nov. 17, 1950; children: Denise Ann, Tanya Marie, Michele Elise, Luana Jo. BA in English Lit., U. Hawaii, Honolulu, 1970, MA, 1973, MA in Am. Studies, 1989, PhD in Am. Studies, 1996. Prof. English U. Hawaii/Honolulu Community Coll., 1971-93, chmn. English dept., 1980-84, div. chairperson lang. arts, 1989-91, ret. Tchr. cons. Hawaii Writing Project, Honolulu, 1983—; tchr. summer sch. Regent, Sandwich Isle chpt. Daus. of Brit. Empire, Honolulu, 1978-80. Recipient Excellence in Teaching medal, U. Hawaii Bd. Regents, 1983; Dickens fellow, Nat. Endowment for Humanities, 1985, Hawaii Writing Project fellow, U. Hawaii Found., 1983. Mem. Hawaii Council Tchrs. English, Assn. Women in Jr. Colls., Humanities Assn. Episcopalian. Avocations: writing, knitting, reading, swimming, travel, gardening.

CHESSHIRE, MARY CLAIRE, lawyer; b. Balt., 1962; BS, Johns Hopkins U., 1989; JD, U. Balt., 1993. Bar: Md. 1993. Ptnr. Whiteford, Taylor & Preston LLP. Lectr. Villa Julie Coll. Paralegal Prog.; trainer Md. Assn. Non Profit Orgns. Mem. exec. com. Villa Julie Coll. Bd. Trustees. Mem.: ABA, Baltimore City Bar Assn., Nat. Assn. Pub. Pension Attys., Md. State Bar Assn. Office: Whiteford, Taylor & Preston LLP 7 Saint Paul St Baltimore MD 21202-1626 Office Fax: 410-347-9465. E-mail: mchesshire@wtplaw.com.

CHESSIN, CATHY E., lawyer; b. Erie, Pa., 1955; BA, U. NC, 1977; JD summa cum laude, Tulane Law Sch., 1980. Bar: NC 1980, La. 1982. Sr. v.p., corp. coun. Hibernia Nat. Bank Corp. Mng. editor Tulane Law Rev., 1979—80. Fellow: La. Bar Found.; mem.: Assn. Women Atty., La. Bankers Assn. (Bank Counsel Sect.), ABA, La. State Bar Assn., Phi Beta Kappa, Order of Coif. Office: Hibernia Nat Bank Corp 313 Carondelet St New Orleans LA 70161 Office Phone: 504-533-3299. Office Fax: 504-533-2367.

CHESTER, LYNNE, foundation administrator, artist; b. Fargo, N.D., May 29, 1942; BA in Music, Hillsdale Coll., 1964; MA in Guidance Counseling, Mich. State U., 1965; PhD in Psychology, U. Mich., 1971. Tchr. Warren (Mich.) Consol. Schs., 1965-70; curriculum advisor Royal Oak (Mich.) Pub. Schs., 1974-75; co-founder, exec. dir. Peace Rsch. Found., Carmel, Calif., 1993-98. Assoc. Hillsdale Coll., 1989—; guest lectr. ceramics James Milliken U., Decatur, Ill., 1991; guest lectr. creative covergence Carl Cherry Ctr. for Art, Carmel, 1991, Compton lectr., Monterey, Calif., 1996—; mem. Nat. Assn. Fund Raising Execs., 1991-96; co-founder, bd. dirs. Monterey Peninsula Coll. Art Gallery, 1991—; guest juror Monterey County Essay Contest, 1997; cons. Monterey Mus. of Art; guest lectr. Hillsdale (Mich.) Coll., 1997; juror Monterey County Poetry Contest, 1993—; juror photographic show Beauty at the Heart of Things, Carl Cherry Ctr. for Arts, Carmel, 1999. Artist of multiple commd. sculptures for pvt. collections; also ceramics, sculpture and photographs in pvt. and corp. collections; represented in permanent collection at Krammert Art Mus., Champaign, Ill., Fresno (Calif.) Mus. Art; juried show Ctr. for Photographic Art, Carmel, Calif., 1996; art represented at Who's Who in Art, Monterey, 1989-96, Christmas Miniatures/Invitational Ctr. for Photographic Art, Carmel, 1996, Holiday Print Show Ctr. for Photographic Art, Carmel, 1996 (Dir.'s Choice 1996); author of poetry; juror essay contest Personal Heroes Monterey County K-12, 1997; juror poetry contest Monterey County 9-12 grades, Carl Cherry Ctr. for the Arts, 1993-2001; exhibited in photography show at Asilomer Conf. Ctr., Monterey Peninsula Airport, Pacific Grove Art Ctr., Carl Chevry Ctr., Seaside City Hall, Pacific Grove Mus. Natural History, 1995-98, Hillsdale Coll., 1997, Monterey Peninsula Airport, 1998, Calif. State U., Monterey Bay, 1998, Pacific Grove (Calif.) Art Ctr., 1998, Carl Cherry Ctr. for Arts, Carmel, Calif., 1998, Pacific Grove Mus. Nat. History, 1998, Salinas (Calif.) Courthouse, 1998, Asilomar Conf. Ctr., Pacific Grove, 1998, Prints Charming Gallery, Carmel, 1998, Triton Mus. Art, 1998, Pre-auction show KTEH, 1998, 2000, Triton Mus., 1998; one-woman show Prints Charming Gallery, Carmel, Calif., 2000; represented by Prints Charming Gallery and Carmel Express Internat. Co-founder Southfield (Mich.) Symphony, 1972, World Rhythms Festival, Carmel, 1994; mem. citizens adv. bd. City of Royal Oak, 1978-83; co-founder, bd. dirs. Monterey Bay Artists Day, Sta. KAZU-FM, 1987-89; pres., bd. dirs. Carl Cherry Ctr. for Arts, Carmel, 1988-94, 95, 97; bd. dirs. Monterey Peninsula Mus. Art, 1991-94, Carmel Pub. Libr. Found., 1991-94, Monterey Inst. for Rsch. in Astronomy, 1985-95, Cultural Coun. for Monterey County, 1993-98; fundraiser Student Art Gallery, Monterey Peninsula Coll., 1990-97, mem. mentors program Women Helping Women, 1998—. Recipient Citizens Adv. Coun. award City of Royal Oak, 1983, Best of Show award for monoprint Monterey Peninsula Coll., 1990, Poetry prizes Carl Cherry Ctr. for Arts, 1990-94, Benefactor of Arts award Monterey County Cultural Coun., 1992, 93, 94, Soccer Mgr./Coach of Yr. 1976-81, 1st pl. award photography contest Monterey Regional Park Dist. Celebration of Open Space, 1998; artist-in-residence Naubinway, Mich., 1997. Mem. AAUW, Internat. Platform Assn., Internat. Sculpture Ctr., Nat. Soc. Fund Raising Execs., Nat. Mus. Women in Art (charter mem.), Am. Crafts Coun., Sigma Alpha Iota (Ruby Sword of Honor 1963). Avocations: reading, playing piano, composing, hiking, photography. Home: 9645 Sandbur Pl Salinas CA 93907-1031

CHESTERMAN, MELANY SUE, lawyer; b. Sioux City, Iowa, July 16, 1966; d. Richard Dean and Connie Pauline Lanagan; m. William Blake Chesterman, Sept. 2, 1989; children: Stevie, Carly. BS, U. Nebr., Lincoln, 1989; JD, Creighton U., Omaha, 1993. Law clk., atty. Cassem, Tiernap, Omaha, 1991—95; in-house counsel Berkshire Hathaway/Nat. Indemnity, Omaha, 1995—99; ptnr., shareholder Ferguson, Chesterman & Arierno, Omaha, 1999—2004; atty. Hauptman O'Brien Wolf & Lathrop, Omaha, 2004—. Mem. Jud. Nominating Com., Omaha, 2005—. Mem. Omaha Charter Study Conv., 2003; candidate lt. gov. Nebr., 2002. Recipient David A. Svoboda Trial award, Creighton Law Sch., 1993; fellow, Nebr. State Bar Found., 2002. Mem.: ABA, Nebr. Bar Assn., Omaha Bar Assn. (mem. exec. coun.), Nebr. State Bar (mem. ho. dels. 2005—), Nebr. Women's Bar Assn. (pres. 2002—04). Office: Hauptman OBrien Wolf and Lathrop 1005 S 107th Ave # 200 Omaha NE 68114

CHESTNUT, COLETTE, broadcast executive; BS, Bucknell U. CPA. Sr. mgr. Price Waterhouse; controller Chiat/Day/Mojo (merger TWBA), NYC, 1992—95; Americas CFO TBWA Worldwide, NYC, 1995—2000; N.Am. CFO J. Walter Thompson Co. (JWT), NYC, 2000—06; exec. v.p., CFO MTV Networks, NYC, 2006—. Office: MTV Networks 1260 Ave of the Americas New York NY 10020 Office Phone: 212-397-6030.*

CHESTON, SHEILA CAROL, lawyer; b. Washington, Nov. 5, 1958; d. Theodore C. and Gabrielle Joan (Hellings) C. BA, Dartmouth Coll., 1980; JD, Columbia U., 1984. Bar: N.Y. 1986, D.C. 1986, U.S. Dist. Ct. D.C. 1987, U.S. Ct. Appeals (D.C. cir.) 1987, U.S. Dist. Ct. (so. and ea. dists.) N.Y. 1989, U.S. Ct. Appeals (2d cir.), U.S. Supreme Ct. 1989. Law clk. to judge U.S. Ct. Appeals for 9th Cir., L.A., 1984-85; assoc. Wilmer, Cutler & Pickering, Washington, 1985-92, ptnr., 1992-93; gen. counsel Def. Base Closure and Realignment Commn., 1993; spl. assoc. counsel to Pres. of U.S., 1994; dep. gen. counsel Dept. Air Force, 1993-95, gen. counsel, 1995-98; ptnr. Wilmer, Cutler & Pickering, Washington, 1998—2002; sr. v.p., gen. counsel, sec. BAE Systems, Inc., Rockville, Md., 2002—. Adj. prof. in internat. litig. Georgetown Law Sch., 1991—2003. Mem. ABA, D.C. Bar Assn., Women's Bar Assn., Am. Bar Found., Am. Soc. Internat. Law, Coun. on Fgn. Rels. Democrat. Episcopalian. Office: BAE Systems Inc 1601 Research Blvd Rockville MD 20850-3173 E-mail: sheila.cheston@baesystems.com.

CHETIN, HELEN CAMPBELL, writer; b. Chgo., July 6, 1922; d. Guy Edward Campbell and Helen May Collins; m. Adnan K. Chetin, May 1945 (div. 1980); children: Timur Claude, Sara Ruth. BS, U. Tex., 1945. Author: Tales From an African Drum, 1970, Perhans Promise, 1973, 1992, How Far is Berkeley?, 1977, Lady of Strawberries, 1978, Angel Island Prisoner, 1982, Chambers of the Heart, 1990, Handles to an Ax, 1999; editor: New Seed Press, 1972—97, The Wild Iris, 1973—79. Mem.: Calif. Writers Assn., U. Calif. Berkeley Alumni, Turkish Edn. Found. Independent. Home: 1663 Euclid Ave Berkeley CA 94709-1213

CHETKOVICH, CAROL, public policy educator; m. Glen Tepke. AB, Stanford U., Palo Alto, Calif., 1970; PhD, U. Calif., Berkeley, 1994. Program dir., v.p. Family Planning Alternatives, Sunnyvale, Calif., 1972—85; sr. analyst Berkeley Planning Assocs., 1987—89; asst., assoc. prof. Harvard U., Cambridge, Mass., 1997—2005; assoc. prof., program dir., pub. policy Mills Coll., Oakland, Calif., 2005—. Author: (book) Real Heat: Gender and Race in the Urban Fire Service (Choice's Outstanding Academic Book Award, 1998); co-author: From the Ground Up: Grassroots Organizations Making Social Change. Grantee, NSF, 1993. Office: Mills College 5000 MacArthur Blvd Oakland CA 94613 Office Phone: 510-430-3370. E-mail: cchetkov@mills.edu.

CHETTA, HOLLY ANN, transportation executive; b. New Orleans, Aug. 18, 1945; d. Henry John and Ernestine Rose (Blaise) C. BS, Tulane U., 1967, MS, 1970, MPH, 1977. Assoc. realtor Latter & Blum, New Orleans, 1978-83; adminstr. loan svc. First Fin. Bank, New Orleans, 1981-83; adminstr. USDA, New Orleans, 1982-84; pers. evaluator U.S. Dept. Transp., USCG, New Orleans, 1984-91, regional maritime pers. examiner, 1991—. Author: (poems) Toward the Twenty-First Century, 1985, New Year's Eve, 1984. Mem. Internat. Platform Assn. Republican. Roman Catholic. Avocations: pet training, poetry. Office: US Dept Transp US Coast Guard Exam Ctr 1615 Poydras St New Orleans LA 70112-1254 Home: 118 Wood Ave Metairie LA 70005-4206

CHEUNG, JUDY HARDIN, retired special education educator; b. Santa Rosa, Calif., Feb. 3, 1945; d. Robert and Edna Hardin BA, Calif. State U. Sonoma, Rohnert Park, 1966; MA, U. San Francisco, 1981. Tchr. St. Thomas Dept. Edn., V.I., 1967—71; spl. edn. tchr., basic functional and ednl. skills to disabled adults Sonoma Devel. Ctr., Eldridge, Calif., 1971—2001; co-adminstr. Redwood Empire Chinese Assn. Sch., 1996—2001, ret., 2001. Co-chair Ednl. Svcs. Profl. Practice Group, Eldridge, Calif., 1989-90, 93-94; pres. Poets of the Vineyard, 1998— Author, pub.: Acorn to Embers, 1987, Welcome to the Inside, 1984; author, photographer, pub. Captions, 1986 Recipient Silver Pegasus, 1983, Poets of Vineyard, 1986, 87, 2000, 01, award Ark. Writers Conf., 1988 Mem. Calif. Fedn. Chaparral Poets (pres. 1989-91, 93-95), Ina Coolbrith Cir. (pres. 1988-90), Calif. Writers Club (treas. Redwood writers br. 1985-86), Artists Embassy Internat. (v.p. 2003—, Amb. of Arts award 1992, 2001), World Congress of Cultures and Poetry (internat. bd. dirs. 1993-2000, Grand Cultures medal 1993, Cert. of merit 2000, Poetic Achievement 2000), Redwood Empire Chinese Assn. (sec., Appreciation award for svc. 2000), United Poets Laureate Internat. (sec.-treas. 2004—, Gold Crown and title Laureate Women of Letters, 2004, Poetic Achievement medal 2005) Avocations: photography, reading. Home and Office: 704 Brigham Ave Santa Rosa CA 95404-5245 E-mail: jhcheung@aol.com.

CHEUNG, SHERI T., lawyer; b. Gardena, Calif., Jan. 28, 1973; BA, Smith Coll., 1994; JD, Univ. So. Calif., 1997. Bar: Calif. 1997, US Dist. Ct. Ctrl. Calif., US Dist. Ct. So. Calif., US Ct. Appeals Ninth Cir. Assoc., intellectual property, labor & employment litigation Hogan & Hartson LLP, LA. Named a Rising Star, So. Calif. Super Lawyers, 2005—06. Office: Hogan & Hartson LLP Ste 1400 1199 Ave of the Stars Los Angeles CA 90067 Office Phone: 310-785-4600. Office Fax: 310-785-4601. Business E-Mail: stcheung@hhlaw.com.*

CHEVALIER, DENISE ANN, director; b. Houston, May 4, 1978; d. James Donald and Adline Ann Chevalier. BA in Acctg., U. Miss., University, 2000; BBA in Mgmt., U. Houston Downtown, 2003; MS in Edn., Capella U., Mpls., 2004, post grad. in Edn., 2005—. Fin. aid advisor, Houston, 2001—03, C.C., Kingwood, 2003—04; dir. of fin. aid Proprietary Sch., Houston, 2004—05, tchr., 2005—. Mem.: NAACP, Am. Women In Univs., Tex. Assn. Fin. Aid Adminstrs., So. Poverty Law Ctr., Delta Sigma Theta. Roman Catholic. Home: 19515 Shinwood Humble TX 77346 Personal E-mail: denise1913@hotmail.com.

CHEVALIER, JUDITH A., economics professor, finance professor; BA Distinction in the major Economics (summa cum laude), Yale U., 1989; PhD in Economics, MIT, 1993. Asst. prof. economics, dept. economics Harvard U., 1993—94; asst. prof. economics, grad. sch. bus. U. Chgo., 1994—97, assoc. prof. economics, grad. sch. bus., 1997—99, prof. economics, grad. sch. bus., 1999—2001; prof. economics and finance Yale Sch. Mgmt., 2001—. Faculty rsch. fellow Nat. Bur. Econ. Rsch., 1993—99, rsch. assoc., 1999—; bd. mem., com. on the Status of Women in Economics Profession Am. Econ. Assn., 2002—04; fellow, Davenport Coll. Yale U., 2002—. Assoc. editor Rand Journal of Economics, 1996—2004, Journal of Industrial Economics, 1997—2004, Review of Financial Studies, 1999—2002, Quarterly Journal of Economics, 1999—2003, Journal of Economic Perspectives, 1999—2003, Journal Finance, 2000—04 (Smith Breeden Disting. Paper prize, 1995, nominated paper, Smith Breeden prize, 1999), Review of Financial Studies, 1999—2002, adv. bd. Quantitative Marketing and Economics, 2002—, adv. editor, 2003—; editor: The B.E. Journals in Econ. Analysis and Policy, 2003—04; assoc. editor American Economic Review, 2001—02, co-editor,

2004—; contbr. articles to profl. jours. Recipient Elaine Bennett prize, Am. Econ. Assn., 1999; Sloan Rsch. Fellow, Alfred P. Sloan Found., 1997—99, NSF Grad. Fellowship, 1989—92, NSF rsch. grant, 1994—96. Fellow: Am. Acad. Arts & Sciences. Office: Yale Sch Mgmt 135 Prospect St New Haven CT 06520 also: Horchow Hall 55 Hillhouse Ave New Haven CT 06520 Office Phone: 203-432-3122. Business E-Mail: judith.chevalier@yale.edu.*

CHEVES, VERA LOUISA, retired librarian; b. Rockport, Mass., Nov. 13, 1908; d. Andrew Gustaf and Olga Amanda (Silen) Cederstrom; m. Robert Cheves, dec.; children: Robert (dec.), Constance. BS in Edn., Boston U., 1930; MLS, Simmons Coll., 1963. Libr. asst. Sawyer Free Libr., Gloucester, Mass., 1932-33; libr. Boston Pub. Libr., 1950-73; med. libr. Addison Gilbert Hosp., Gloucester, Mass., 1984-92. Organist Lanesville Congl. Ch., Gloucester, 1972—93. Home: 6 Hickory St Gloucester MA 01930-1112

CHEVIS, CHERYL ANN, lawyer; b. Ann Arbor, Mich., Nov. 9, 1947; d. Peter Paul and Antoinette (Slapinski) C.; m. Edwin Mahaffey Gerow, Nov. 18, 1976. BA, U. Wash., 1969, MA, 1974; postgrad. in Sanskrit, U. Chgo., 1974-77, JD, 1980. Bar: Ill. 1980, U.S. Dist. Ct. (no. dist.) Ill. 1980, U.S. Ct. Appeals (7th cir.) 1982, U.S. Tax Ct. 1982, Oreg. 1986. Tax assoc. Sidley and Austin, Chgo., 1979-80, Mayer Brown and Platt, Chgo., 1981-85; sr. tax atty. Perkins Coie, Portland, 1985-87, tax ptnr., 1987-99; assoc. gen. counsel Portland Gen. Electric, 1999—. Mem. faculty Ill. Continuing Legal Edn., Chgo., 1982; vis. lectr. U. B.C., Vancouver, Can., 1983; lectr. Chgo. Tax Club, 1983, Oreg. Securities Lawyers Bar, Bend, 1986, Internat. Employers Seminar, Portland, 1991. Contbr. articles to Jour. Taxation. Vol. atty. Com. Civil Rights Under Law, Chgo., 1982-85; exec. com., chair devel. com. Portland State U. Found.; exec. com., treas. Friends of Chamber Music; coun. mem. Oreg. Coun. for the Humanities. Grantee, Smithsonian Inst., 1981. Mem. ABA (tax sect., com. capital recovery and leasing), Oreg. State Bar (sister-bar com. with Lithuanian Lawyers Assn. 1997—). Avocations: music, theater, outdoor sports. Office: Portland Gen Electric 121 SW Salmon St Portland OR 97204-3713 Home: Apt 2504 1414 SW 3rd Ave Portland OR 97201-6625 Office Phone: 503-464-7193.

CHEW, LYNDA CASBEER, elementary school educator; b. Corpus Christi, Tex., Oct. 1, 1947; d. Joseph Olen and Ethel Jean (Milam) Casbeer; m. Jack H. Chew, Aug. 28, 1976; children: Doise Elizabeth, Charlotte Lee. BA, U. Tex., 1974; MA, S.W. Bapt. Sem., 1975; MEd, U. Tex., El Paso, 1988. Elem. tchr. Sierra Blanca (Tex.) Ind. Sch. Dist., 1979-80, Orange Grove (Tex.) Ind. Sch. Dist., 1987—88, Socorro Ind. Sch. Dist., El Paso, 1988—94, Leander (Tex.) Ind. Sch. Dist., 1994-95, Monor (Tex.) Ind. Sch. Dist., 1995—98, Marfo Ind. Sch. Dist., 1998—2000, Natalia (Tex.) Ind. Sch. Dist., 2000—. Pres. Horizon Heights PTA, El Paso, 1989-90; v.p. Hueco PTO, El Paso, 1990-91, chmn. Dist. PTO/PTA Counc., El Paso, 1989-91; mem. TEA stds. com. 5th grade sci. talks. Recipient 4 Regional Ctr. for Minorities sci. grants. Mem. Assn. Tex. Profl. Educators (bldg. rep., adv. com. 1990-92), Assn. for Compensatory Educators Tex., Sci. Tchrs. Assn. Tex., Elem. Sci. Tchrs., U. Tex. Alumni Assn. Baptist. Avocations: writing, softball, fishing, camping. Office: Natalia Ind Sch Dist PO Box 548 Natalia TX 78059 Home: 170 Bailee Cir Poteet TX 78065-4220

CHEW, PAMELA CHRISTINE, language educator; b. Nevada, Mo., Feb. 10, 1953; d. Harry and Delores (Trimmer) C. AA, Cottey Coll., 1973; BA in French, U. Mo., 1975, MA in French Lit., 1977; cert. art criticism, Univ. Internat. dell 'Arte, Florence, Italy, 1981. Admissions counselor Cottey Coll., Nevada, 1976-77; internat. publicist Jim Halsey Co., Tulsa, 1978-79; with archival dept. U. Tulsa, 1980, 81-82; English as second lang. instr. Cath. Social Services, Tulsa, 1981-87. Italian instr. Berlitz Sch. Langs., Tulsa, 1985, U. Tulsa, 1987-90; asst. prof. fgn. lang./ESL Tulsa C.C., 1985—; Italian adj. prof. Oral Roberts U., Tulsa, 2001, ITV Italian Northeastern State U., Broken Arrow, Okla., 2002—, Okla. State U., Stillwater, Okla.; leader middle sch. students to Utsunomiya Japan on Sister City Exch., Tulsa Global Alliance, 2001, 02; Rotary prof. Suva, Fiji, 2003—; presenter, spkr. in field. Drawings pub. Nimrod Internat. Jour. Prose and Poetry, 1996, Outside the Lines, 2000, 01, 02. Vol. Internat. Council Tulsa, 1985—, Gilcrease Mus. Am. Art & History, Tulsa, 1977-78, Okla. Territory Speaker, 2004-2005 Grantee Mimi Atwater Meml. Found., France, 1973-74, Rotary, 1980-81, 2003—, Tomorrow's Tchrs., Tomorrow's Tech., 1999, Rotary scholar, Florence, Italy, 1980-81, U. South Pacific, Fiji, 2003—; recipient cash awards for poetry, 1979, 86, essay, 1981, Excellence in Tchg. award, 1996, Paul Harris fellow, 2005; named ESL Profl. of Yr., State of Okla., 2004-05 Mem. TESOL, Am. Coun. Tchrs. Fgn. Langs., Okla. Tchrs. English as Second Lang., South Cen. MLA (sec. Italian sect. 1986-87), Okla. Fgn. Lang. Assn. (Breck Woman of 90's 1989), Am. Coun. Tchrs. Fgn. Langs., Tchrs. English to Speakers of Other Langs. Home: PO Box 4193 Tulsa OK 74159-0193 Office: Tulsa CC 3727 E Apache St Tulsa OK 74115-3150 Office Phone: 918-595-7442. E-mail: pchew@tulsacc.edu.

CHEWNING, RANGELEY BAILEY, lawyer; b. Dillon, SC, Mar. 10, 1977; d. D.L. and Diana (Hawkins) Bailey; m. Lawrence R. Chewning III, June 10, 2000; children: Lawson Chenwing, Elizabeth Anne Chenwing. BA, Columbia Coll., SC, 1998; JD, U. SC, Columbia, 2001. Jud. clk. Hon. John M. Milling, Darlington, SC, 2001—02; assoc. Willcox, Buyck & Williams, Florence, SC, 2002—03, Jebaily Law Firm, PA, Florence, 2003—. Address: PO Box 1871 Florence SC 29503-1871

CHI, LOIS WANG, retired biology professor, research scientist; b. Fuchow, China, May 12, 1921; came to U.S., 1941; d. Leland and Ada (Pang) Wang; m. Henry Chi; children: Lanie, David, Joycelyn. BS, Wheaton Coll., 1945; MS, U. So. Calif., 1947, PhD, 1954. Rsch. fellow Loma Linda (Calif.) U., 1954-57; instr. to assoc. prof. biology Immaculate Heart Coll., L.A., 1957-66; assoc. prof. to prof. biology Calif. State U., Dominguez Hills, 1966-91, rsch. dir., 1979-86, prof. emeritus. Mem. NIH Nat. Adv. Allergy and Infectious Disease Coun., 1973-74; dir. Minority Biomed. Rsch. Program Calif. State U., Dominguez Hills, 1979-86, Minority Honor Program, 1982-86. Contbr. more than 30 articles to profl. jours. Co-founder, pres. and v.p. Chinese Am. Faculty Assocs. So. Calif., Chinese Am. Engrs. and Scientists Assocs. So. Calif. Home: 2839 El Oeste Hermosa Beach CA 90254-2234

CHIANG, ALEXIS S., orthopedist, surgeon; BA, Princeton U.; MD. Resident NYU, Hosp. for Joint Diseases, NYC, 2002—.

CHIANG, YUAN JEN, mathematics professor; b. Hsinchu, Taiwan, Aug. 8, 1956; d. Sheng Lin Chiang. PhD, Johns Hopkins U., Balt., 1989. Prof. math. U. Mary Washington, Fredericksburg, Va., 2003—. Author: (annals of global analysis and geometry) Harmonic Maps of V-Manifolds. Home: 9809 Cannonball Ct Fredericksburg VA 22408 Office: Univ Mary Washington 1301 College Avenue Fredericksburg VA 22401 Office Phone: 540-654-1326. Office Fax: 540-654-2445. Business E-Mail: ychiang@umw.edu.

CHIAO, CHRISTINE LYNN, psychiatrist; d. J.W. and Marie Chiao. BA, Bowdoin Coll., Brunswick, Maine, 1998; DO, N.Y. Coll. Osteo. Medicine, Old Westbury, N.Y., 2005. Rsch. asst. N.Y. Presbyn.-Weil Cornell Med. Ctr., White Plains, 1998—2000; resident in psychiatry North Shore U. Hosp./NYU, Manhasset, 2005—. Fellow Stanley Grant Rsch. fellow, L.I.-Jewish Hosp., 2005. Mem.: AMA, Am. Osteo. Assn., Am. Psychiat. Assn. Avocations: tennis, skiing, kayaking, pottery.

CHIARA, MARGARET M., prosecutor, lawyer; BA, Fordham U.; MA Pace U.; JD, Rutgers U. Assoc. French and Lawrence, Cassopolis, Mich., 1979—82; prosecuting atty. Cass County Prosecutor's Office, 1982—96; adminstr. Trial Ct. Assessment Commn., 1997—98; policy and planning dir. Office of Chief Justice of Mich. Supreme Ct., 1999—2001; US atty. (we. dist.) Mich. US Dept. Justice, 2001—. Office: US Attys Office PO Box 208 Grand Rapids MI 49501 Office Phone: 616-456-2404.*

CHIAVARIO, NANCY ANNE, business and community relations executive; b. Centralia, Ill., Aug. 17, 1947; d. Victor Jr. and Alma Maria (Arsenault) C. Asst. mgr. rent supplement B.C. Housing Mgmt. Commn., Vancouver, 1975-81, adminstrv. asst., 1981-84, mgr. tenants and ops. svc., 1985-86, adminstrv. asst., 1986-87; commr., vice chmn. Vancouver Park Bd., 1986-90, chair, 1991-93; trustee Vancouver Pub. Libr., 1987-93; city councillor Vancouver, 1993-99; dir. Greater Vancouver Regional Dist., 1996-99; v.p. Greater Vancouver Housing Corp., 1994-99; NAC vol. cons., 1986—. Bd. dirs. B.C. Recreation and Parks Assn., 1986-91, pres. 1989-90; exec. dir. B.C. Sport and Fitness Coun. for the Disabled, 1989-90; dir. B.C. Wheelchair Sports Assn., 1991-92, Tree Can. Found., 1995—; mem. Non-Partisan Assn., 1986-99; vice chair Lower Mainland (Aboriginal) Treaty Adv. Com., 1994-96, chair, 1997-99; bd. dirs. Can. Oceans Blue Found., 1996—2000 (treas.), pres. Brewery Creek Hist. Soc., 1993—, Vancouver Police Hist. Soc. and Mus., 2000-, Columbia Housing Adv. Assn., 2000-; housing mgr. Downtown Eastside Residents' Assn., 2000-2001; founder, candidate Vancouver Civic Action Team, 2002 (bd. dirs. 2003-), B.C. Non- Profit Housing Assn. (Vancouver bd. dirs. 2001-), exec. dir., West End Sr. Network, 2003-, founding bd. mem., Network of East Vancouver Cmty. Org., 2003-, Vancouver Olympics, Inner City Bid Com., 2001-2003. Mem. Inst. Housing Mgmt. (cert. adminstr. 1983, cert. finance 1985), West End Commn. Ctr. Assn. (pres. 1985-86), Mt. Pleasant Commn. Ctr. Assn. (pres. 1981-83, dir. 2000-), Stanley Park Ecology Soc. (life; founder). Democrat. Avocation: journalism.

CHICAGO, JUDY, artist; b. Chgo., July 20, 1939; d. Arthur M. and May (Levenson) Cohen. BA, UCLA, 1962, MA, 1964; doctorate (hon.), Russell Sage Coll., 1992, Lehigh U., 2000, Smith Coll., 2000, Duke U., 2003. Co-founder Feminist Studio Workshop, L.A., 1973, Through the Flower Corp., 1977; prof.-inresidence We. Ky. U., 2001; vis. artist Ind. U., 1999, Duke U., 2000, U. N.C., 2000, Calif. Poly. Inst., Pomona, 2003. Author: Through the Flower: My Struggle as a Woman Artist, 1975, The Dinner Party: A Symbol of Our Heritage, 1979, Embroidering Our Heritage: The Dinner Party Needlework, 1980, The Birth Project, 1985, Holocaust Project: From Darkness Into Light, 1993, Beyond the Flower: The Autobiography of a Feminist Artist, 1996, The Dinner Party, 1996, Women and Art: Contested Territory, 1999, Fragments from the Delta of Venus, 2004, Kitty City: A Feline Book of Hours, 2005; one-woman shows include, Pasadena (Calif.) Mus. Art, 1969, Jack Glenn Gallery, Corona del Mar, Calif., 1972, JPL Fine Arts, London, 1975, Quay Ceramics, San Francisco, 1976, San Francisco Mus. Modern Art, 1979, Bklyn. Mus., 1980, 2002, Parco Galleries, Japan, 1980, Fine Arts Gallery, Irvine, Calif., 1981, Musee d'Art Contemporain, Montreal, 1982, ACA Galleries, N.Y.C., 1984, 85, 86, 2004, 05, Nat. Mus. of Women in the Arts, 2002; group exhbns. include Jewish Mus., N.Y.C., 1966, 67, Whitney Mus., 1972, Winnipeg Art Gallery, 1975; represented in permanent collections Bklyn. Mus., San Francisco Mus. Modern Art, Oakland Mus. Art, Pa. Acad. Fine Arts, L.A. County Mus. Art, also numerous pvt. collections. Office: Through the Flower 107 Becker Ave Belen NM 87002 E-mail: throughtheflower@judychicago.com.

CHICHESTER, FAITH CHRISTINE, elementary school educator; b. Grand Rapids, Mich., Nov. 6, 1975; d. Patricia A. and Michael A. Chichester. BS, Grand Valley State U., Allendale, Mich., 1998, EdM Ednl. Leadership, 2002, EdM in Sch. Counseling, 2004. Tchr. 8th grade math. Mona Shores Pub. Schs., Norton Shores, Mich., 1999—. Math-a-thon coord. St. Jude Childrens Rsch. Hosp. Mona Shores Mid. Sch., Norton Shores, 2000—, math counts advisor, 2001—, student congress advisor, 2003—, mentor tchr., 2003—; MEAP content adv. com. Mich. Dept. Edn., Lansing, 2004—, grade level content expectations clarification document grade span chair, 2006—; team mem. Mich. Math. Leadership Acad., Muskegon, 2004—. Grantee, DTE Energy, 2005, West Mich. Chpt., Soc. Metals, 2006. Mem.: ASCD, Mona Shores Tchrs. Edn. Assn. (v.p. 2006—), Am. Sch. Counselor Assn., Mich. Coun. Tchrs. Math. Roman Catholic. Avocations: designing jewelry, travel, exercise. Office: Mona Shores Public Schools 1700 Woodside Norton Shores MI 49441 Office Phone: 231-759-8506.

CHICHILNISKY, GRACIELA, mathematician, educator, economist, writer; b. Buenos Aires, Mar. 27, 1946; arrived in U.S., 1968, naturalized, 1992; d. Salomon Chichilnisky and Raquel Gavensky; children: Eduardo Jose, Natasha Sable. Student, MIT, 1967—68; MA, U. Calif., Berkeley, 1970, PhD in Math., 1971, PhD in Econs., 1976. Postdoctoral fellow Harvard U., 1974, lectr. dept. econs., 1975, fellow Harvard Inst. Internat. Devel., 1978; assoc. prof. Columbia U., N.Y.C., 1977—79, prof., 1980—, dir. Program on Info. and Resources, 1994—, prof. stats., 1996—, dir. Columbia Ctr. for Risk Mgmt., 1998—, UNESCO prof. math. and econs., 1995—99. CEO Cross Border Exch. Corp., 1999-2003, chmn. 2003-05; co-chmn. UN Latin Am. Econ. Forum, N.Y., 2006; spl. advisor World Fedn., UN Assns., 2006; sr. adviser to pres., U. Ariz., 2004—; architect global market for emissions trading The Kyoto Protocol of the UN, 1995-2003; mem. presdl. cabinet Banco Ctrl. Republica Argentina, 1971-74; co-prin. investigator Urban Inst., Washington, 1975-77; vis. scholar Internat. Inst. Applied Sys, Analysis Laxenburg, Austria, 1975-77; prin. investigator U.S. Dept. Labor, 1977-78, Rockefeller Found. Project Internat. Rels., 1981-83; project dir. UN Inst. Tng. and Rsch., N.Y., 1979-83; chaired prof. econs. U. Essex, 1980-81; vis. prof. inst. math and its applications U. Minn., 1983-84, U. Siena, Italy, summers, 1991-93, 2002; vis. prof. Stanford Inst. Theoretical Econs., Stanford U., summers, 1991-93, dept. econs., Inst. Internat. Studies, 1993—, vis. prof. depts., econ. and ops. rsch. Stanford U., 1993-94; prof. missionaire U. des Antilles et de la Guyane, spring 1984-85; NSF prof. dept. math. U. Calif., Berkeley, 1985-86; CEO, chmn. FITEL Ltd., 1985-89; exec. dir. Sci. Internat. Ltd., 1989-90; vis. prof. U. Cath. Buenos Aires, Aug. 1993; cons. in field; UNESCO chair in math. and econs., Columbia U., 1995—; Salinbemi chair U. Siena, Italy, 1994-95; spl. adv. World Fedn. UN Assns., 2006; mng. dir. Bizmakers, N.Y., 2006. Co-author: Catastrophe or New Society? A Latin American World Model, 1976; author: (with G. Heal) The Evolving International Economy, 1986, Oil in the International Economy, 1991, Sustainability: Dynamics and Uncertainty, 1998, Mathematical Economics, 1998, Topology and Markets, 1998, Markets, Information and Uncertainty, 1998, Environmental Markets: Equity and Efficiency, 1999; assoc. editor Jour. Devel. Econs., 1976-86, Advances in Mathematics, 1985, Risk Decision and Policy; mem. various editl. bds.; contbr. articles to profl. jours. Mem. coun. Social Health and Welfare Soc.; bd. trustees Nat. Resources Def. Coun., 1994—. Recipient Internat. Rels. award Rockefeller Found., 1983-84; named Most Disting. Woman Economist, Newcombe Found. and Omega Delta Epsilon, 1991, Leif Johansen award U. Oslo, Norway, 1995; grantee NSF, 1974—; fellow Ford Found., 1967-69, Banco Ctrl. Republica Argentina, 1972-74, spl. fellow UN Inst. Tng. and Rsch., 1977-76. Office: Columbia U Stats Dept 1255 Amsterdam Ave 10th Fl New York NY 10027 Mailing: 335 Riverside Dr New York NY 10025 Office Phone: 212-678-1148. Business E-Mail: gc9@columbia.edu.

CHICKLIS, BARBARA KAREN BURAK, retired data processing executive; b. Woonsocket, RI, July 1, 1942; d. Steven and Stella Burak; m. William A. Gianopoulos, Apr. 3, 1981; children: Karen Barbara, Paul Steven. BS in Math., Suffolk U., 1964; MSEE in Computer Sci., Northeastern U., 1974. Sys. programmer Raytheon Corp., Lexington, Mass., 1965—68, ITEK Corp., 1968—71; project and staff leader Computation Ctr. Northeastern U., Boston, 1971—74; staff cons. Control Data Corp., Waltham, 1974—2005, ret., 2005. Recipient Internat. Profl. Svcs. Analyst Symposium award, 1977. Mem.: Assn. Computing Machinery. Republican.

CHICKVARY, KARIN ELIZABETH, literature educator; b. N.Y.C., July 27, 1963; d. Verne Roger and Jayne Elizabeth Bowman; m. Jon Charles Chickvary, Aug. 22, 1990; children: Jeffrey, Lila, Fred. BA English, U. Mass., Amherst; MS Edn., U. Bridgeport. Cert. tchr. S.C. Tchr. 6th grade Washington Ave. Christian Sch., Greenville, SC, 1990—91; substitute tchr. Greenville County Sch. Dist., 1991—92, tchr. aide, 1992—95, tchr. 1st grade, 1998—2000; tchr. lit., lang. devel. tutor, dir. admissions and transitions Camperdown Acad., Greenville, 2000—. Tutor Orton-Gillingham, Greenville, 1998—. Mem.: Internat. Dyslexia Assn. (pres. bd. S.C. br. 2004—, v.p. bd., chair conf. S.C. br. 2003—04, bd. dirs. S.C. br. 2002). Roman Catholic. Avocations: horseback riding, gardening, yoga, reading, travel. Office: Camperdown Academy 501 Howell Rd Greenville SC 29615

CHIECHI, CAROLYN PHYLLIS, federal judge; b. Newark, Dec. 6, 1943; BS magna cum laude, Georgetown U., 1965, JD, 1969, LLM in Taxation, 1971, LLD honoris causa, 2000. Bar: DC 1969, U.S. Dist. Ct. DC, U.S. Ct. Fed. Claims, U.S. Tax Ct., U.S. Ct. Appeals (5th, 6th, 9th, DC, and fed. cirs.), U.S. Supreme Ct. Atty. advisor to Hon. Leo H. Irwin U.S. Tax Ct., Washington, 1969-71; assoc. Sutherland, Asbill & Brennan, Washington, 1971—76, ptnr., 1976—92; judge U.S. Tax Ct., Washington, 1992—. Mem. bd. regents Georgetown U., Washington, 1988—2001, mem. nat. law alumni bd., 1986—93; mem. bd. govs. Georgetown U. Alumni Assn., 1994—2000; bd. dirs. Stuart Stiller Meml. Found., 1986—99; prin. Coun. for Excellence in Govt., 1990—92. Dept. editor: Jour. Taxation, 1986—92; contbr. articles to profl. jours. Recipient Law Alumni award, Georgetown U., 1994, Alumnae Achievement award, Georgetown U. Law Ctr., 1998. Fellow: Am. Coll. Tax Counsel, Am. Bar Found.; mem.: Am. Judicature Soc., Women's Bar Assn., DC Bar Assn., Fed. Bar Assn. Office: US Tax Ct 400 2nd St NW Washington DC 20217-0002

CHIEF EAGLE, JOAN, secondary school educator; b. Pine Ridge, June 27, 1952; d. Eugene J. Chief Eagle, Alice V. Weasel Bear/Chief Eagle; children: Leslee M. McMath, Joelle M., Lorena L., Danielle J. McCane. AA, Standing Rock Coll., Ft. Yales, N.D., 1989; BA, Minot State U., N.D., 1991. Native Am. artist Five Nations Arts, Mandan, ND, 1987—; tchg. asst. Ft. Yates Pub. Sch. #4, Ft. Yates, 1993—97, fgn. lang. tchr., 1998—. Cons. for Native Am. lang. and art Ft. Yates Pub. Sch. #4, 1994—. With U.S. Army, 1970—71. Avocations: reading, sewing, culinary arts. Home: 179 Box 500 Sioux Village Fort Yates ND 58538 Office: Fort Yates Public Sch #4 105 Agency Ave Fort Yates ND 58538

CHIEGER, KATHRYN JEAN, recreational facility executive; b. Detroit, July 13, 1948; BA, Purdue U., 1970; MA, U. Mich., 1974; MBA, U. Denver, 1983. Libr. U. Mich., Ann Arbor, 1970-74; staff aide U.S. Sen. Gary Hart, Denver, 1974-79; dir. fin. rels. Petro-Lewis Corp., Denver, 1979-86; dir. investor rels. Kraft Inc., Glenview, Ill., 1987-89; v.p. corp. affairs Gaylor Container Corp., Deerfield, Ill., 1989-96; v.p. corp. and investor rels. Brunswick Corp., Lake Forest, Ill., 1996—. Mem. Nat. Investor Rels. Inst. (chpt. bd. dirs. 1979-84, v.p. mem. 1982-83, pres. 1983-84, nat. bd. dirs. 1984-88), Chgo. Execs. Club, Investor Rels. Assn. (vice chmn. membership), Chgo. Coun. Fgn. Rels., Sr. Investor Rels. Roundtable (mem. steering com.). Office: Brunswick Corp 1 N Field Ct Lake Forest IL 60045-4811 E-mail: kathryn.chieger@brunswick.com.

CHIERCHIA, MADELINE CARMELLA, management consulting company executive; b. Bklyn., Jan. 30, 1943; d. Lawrence Cataldo Carrozzo and Victoria Angel (torchio) Carrozzo Petrisic; m. Jerry Chierchia, Oct. 3, 1959 (div. July 1975); children: Gertrude Chierchia Kraljic Teleisha, Geraldine Rosalie Gorga. Student parochial schs., Bklyn. Pres. mgr. Argyle Pers. Agy., N.Y.C., 1976-77; clk. typist Atlantic Mut. Ins. Co., N.Y.C., 1977-78; sec. ARC, N.Y.C., 1978-82; mgr. D.F. King & Co. Inc., N.Y.C., 1982-89, asst. v.p., 1989-90, v.p., 1990—; ret. Mem. NAFE, Securities Industry Assn. (proxy div., exec. bd. 1990—), Southwest Securities Transfer Assn., Reorganization Securities Industry Assn., Am. Soc. for Profl. and Exec. Women. Corp. Transfer Agts. Assn. Democrat. Roman Catholic. Avocations: bowling, chess, reading, old movies. Office: DF King & Co 48 Wall St New York NY 10005

CHILD, ABIGAIL, filmmaker, educator; b. Newark, Jan. 1, 1949; d. Albert L. Natelson and Ruth (Robinson) Natelson Pollack; m. Jonathan Child, 1969 (div. 1977). B.A. in History and Lit. magna cum laude, Radcliffe Coll., 1968; M.F.A. in Graphics and Film with honors, Yale U., 1970. Vis. prof. film SUNY-Purchase, 1979; adj. prof. film & TV NYU, Sch. Arts, N.Y.C., 1980-85; asst. prof. film Mass. Coll. Art, Boston, 1985, vis. prof. film, San Francisco Art Inst., 1989, adj. prof., intro to film/video, Sch. of Visual Arts, N.Y., 1989-90, assoc. prof., humanities and art, Hampshire Coll., 1990-91, prof., film/video in studio arts, Sarah Lawrence Coll., 1991-99, chair, film/animation area, program design, sr. faculty, Sch. of the Museum of Fine Arts, Boston, 2001-. Film programmer 80 Langton St., San Francisco, 1979; lectr. Inst. Policy Studies, Washington, 1981; judge Creative Artist Pub. Service Grants, N.Y.C., 1982; curator Corcoran Gallery, Washington, 1982; reader, performer, and spkr. in field; Filmmaker-dir., prodr., editor documentaries, including: Except the People, 1970, Game, 1972; Between Times, 1976, Mothe Movie, 1973, Tar Garden, 1975, Peripeteia I, 1977, Peripeteia II, 1978, Ornamentals, 1979, Perils, 1986, Mayhem, 1987, Swamp, 1990, 8 Million, 1992, Through the Looking Lass, 1993, B/side, 1996, Her Thirteenth Year, 1998, Below the New, 1999, Surface Noise, 2000, Subtalk, 2002, The Milky Way, 2003, Cake and Steak, 2004, The Future Is Behind You, 2004, The Party, 2004; filmmaker-dir. prodr., editor exptl. films, including: Mutiny, 1982-83; Prefaces, 1981, Covert Action, 1984, Both, 1988, Mercy, 1989, Dark Dark, 2001; Author: From Solids, 1983; Climate/Plus, 1986, A Motive for Mayhem, 1989, Mob, 1994, Scatter Matrix, 1996, This Is Called Moving: A Critical Poetics of Film, 2005; also articles. Vice pres. 303 E. 8th St. Project, N.Y.C., 1982—; artist (collages) The Magician, 1986, New Modern Times, 1987. Films are in permanent collections of the Mus. of Modern Art, N.Y., Centre Pompidou, Paris, Univ. Calif., Berkeley, Harvard Univ. Film Archive and several others. Recipient Playlist Artist award, 2003, Harvestworks Residency award, 2004, Fulbright Fellowship to St. Petersburg, 1992-93, John Simon Guggenheim Fellowships in Film, 1995-96, and several others; grantee Am. Film Inst., 1972, Creative Artist Pub. Service, 1980, MacDowell Colony, 1983, 86, N.Y. Cultural Found., 1985, Electronic TV Ctr. Media Grant, 1990, 1992, 1998, 1999, 2003, 2004, LEF Found. Film Production Grant, 2003, 2004 and several others. Mem. Canyon Cinema Coop., 1978-, The San Francisco Cinematheque, 1978-, AIVF, 1985-, N.Y. Filmakers Coop., 1980-, N.Y.Cinewomen 1998-, Avocation: swimming. E-mail: achild@mindspring.com.

CHILDEARS, LINDA, foundation administrator; b. Council Bluffs, Iowa, Jan. 25, 1950; d. Nolan Glen and Mary Lucile (Dunken) Jackson. Grad., U. Wis., Am. Inst. Banking; student, U. Colo., U. Denver. Various positions First Nat. Bank Bear Valley (formerly Norwest Bank Bear Valley), Colo., 1969-79; v.p. adminstrn. First Nat. Bancorp., 1979-83; pres., CEO, Equitable Bank of Littleton, 1983—87; founder The Fin. Consortium; pres., CEO, Young Ams. Bank, Denver, 1987—2005, also vice-chmn. bd. dirs.; pres., CEO Daniels Fund, 2005—. Pres., CEO, vice chmn. Young Ams. Edn. Found. Contbr. articles to Time and Newsweek. Bd. dirs. Cherry Creek Art Festival, Denver, 1989-96, Jr. Achievement, Mile High United Way, Cherry Creek Bus. Improvement Dist., U. Denver Bridge Project; mem. adv. bd., nat. past pres. Camp Fire Coun. Colo., Daniels Coll. of Bus.; bd. mem. Cableland Home Found. Named hon. life mem. Nat. CampFire, past chmn., numerous other awards Camp Fire Inc. Mem. Am. Bankers Assn. (past chmn. Edn. Found.), Found. Tchg. Econs. (trustee), Colo. Bankers Assn., Metro C. of C. Republican. Office: Daniels Fund 101 Monroe St Denver CO 80206*

CHILDERS, MARGARET ANNE, science educator; d. Florence and Charles Allen Campbell; m. Phil Craig Childers, Dec. 9, 1983; children: Aaron Craig, Scott Kenneth. MA, Colo. Christian U., 2000. Lic. secondary edn. Colo. Dept. Edn., 2005. Sci. tchr. Nampa Sr. H.S., Idaho, 1978—96, Grand Junction H.S., Colo., 1996—2006. Office: Grand Junction HS 1400 N 5th Grand Junction CO 81501 Office Phone: 970-254-6921. Business E-Mail: childers@mesa.k12.co.us.

CHILDERS, MARTHA PATTON, librarian; b. St. Joseph, Mo., Oct. 22, 1948; d. Thelbert E. and Louise Burns (Patton) C. Student, U. London, 1968; BA, Tarkio Coll., 1970; MS, U. Ill., 1981; postgrad., Univ. de Lausanne, Switzerland, 1982-84, Harvard U., 1985-87, U. Mo., Kansas City, 1999—. Libr. asst. Tarkio (Mo.) Coll., 1966-71, computer asst., 1971-72; data processing clk. Salzburger Landesdatenverarbeitung, Austria, 1972-73; pvt. English tutor Kyoto, Japan, 1973-76; prof. English Imperial Iranian Navy,

Padegan Mil. Acad., 1977-78; grad. asst. U. Ill., 1979-81; head cataloging dept. Swiss Inst. Comparative Law, Lausanne, 1981-84; cataloger Romance lang. Harvard U. Law Libr., Cambridge, Mass., 1984-88; head cataloging San Diego County Law Libr. San Diego County Law Libr., 1988-94; assoc. libr. for tech. svcs. Nelson-Atkins Mus. of Art, Kansas City, Mo., 1994—. Contbr. numerous articles to libr. publs., profl. jours. Mem. ALA, Art Librs. Assn., Calif. Libr. Assn., Am. Assn. Law Librs., So. Calif. Law Librs., Kansas Libr. Assn., Govt. Documents Roundtable. Democrat. Home: Ste 305M 4730 Terrace St Kansas City MO 64112-1128 Office: Johnson County Libr 9875 West 87th St Overland Park KS 66212

CHILDERS, REGINA WORTMAN, counseling administrator; b. Brevard, N.C., Nov. 22, 1962; d. J.P. and Lois Garver Wortman; m. Richard Steven Childers, June 24, 1989; 1 child, Rachel. AA, Brevard Coll., 1983; BA, Mars Hill Coll., 1985; MA in Edn., Western Carolina U., 1986, Clemson U., 2003. Cert. tchr. S.C., secondary English and guidance and counseling grades K-12 S.C. Youth dir. Carr's Hill Bapt. Ch., Brevard, NC, 1981—83; English tchr. Laurens (S.C.) H.S., 1986—2002; sch. counselor Sanders Middle Sch., Laurens, 2002—. Site coord. Making Middle Grades Work Sanders Mid. Sch., Laurens, 2004—, co-advisor Nat. Jr. Honor Soc., 2004—; adj. instr. Piedmont Tech. Coll., Greenwood, SC, 1991—95. Newsletter editor Gateway Cmty. Ch., Laurens, 1999—, youth dir., 2002—, chmn. bd. trustees, 2002—; mem. S.C. Disaster Relief S.C. Bapt. Conv., Columbia, 2000—. Mem.: NEA, S.C. Sch. Counselors Assn., S.C. Edn. Assn. Avocations: music, hiking. Office: Sanders Middle Sch 609 Green St Laurens SC 29360

CHILD-OLMSTED, GISÈLE ALEXANDRA, retired language educator; b. Port-au-Prince, Haiti, Dec. 27, 1946; (parents Am. citizens); d. Daniel McGuire Child and Alice Dejean Child; m. Hans George Bickel, Sept. 1967 (div. Apr. 1984); children: Anna Kristina Villemez, Maia Selena Deubert; m. Jerauld Lockwood Olmsted, June 17, 1988. BA in French with honors, U. Md., 1970; MA in French, Johns Hopkins U., 1978, PhD in Romance Langs., 1981; cert. in translation, Georgetown U. Vis. instr. U. Md., College Park, 1980-81; instr. Johns Hopkins U., Balt., 1981-82; lang. instr. Holton-Arms Sch., Bethesda, Md., 1982-83; asst. prof. dept. modern langs. and lit. Loyola Coll., Balt., 1983-89, assoc. prof., 1989-98, chair dept. modern lang. langs. and lit., 1989-94, prof., 1998—2003; ret., 2003. V.p. faculty coun. Loyola Coll., 1998—2000, mem. steering com. Ctr. for Humanities, 1989—94; organizer, dir. Colloquia on Lang., Lit. and Soc., Balt., 1990, Balt., 95, Balt., 99, Balt., 2002. Author: Jean Genet: Criminalité et Transcendance, 1987; contbr. articles to profl. jours. Faculty Rsch. grant Loyola Coll., 1984, 89, Study grant French Embassy, 1986, 89; Gillman fellow, 1970-73, 79-80; visitor's scholar U. Cape Town, South Africa, 1995. Mem. MLA (del. Mid-Atlantic region 1992-94, 96-98), Am. Assn. Tchrs. French, Soc. Prof. Français et Francophones d'Amérique, Les Amis de Stendhal, Phi Beta Kappa. Avocations: painting, golf, antiques, classical music, flamenco dancing. Home: 7735 Arrowood Ct Bethesda MD 20817-2821

CHILDRESS, SUSAN LYNETTE, retired elementary school educator; b. Abilene, Tex., May 4, 1951; d. Curtis Townly and Bonnie Jean (Constance) Hall; m. Dwain Pinson Childress, Aug. 7, 1971 (div.); children: Marc Dwain, Randy Wayne. BS in Health & Phys. Edn., Angelo State U., 1972, MA in Teaching Mentally Retarded, 1974. Tchr. aide Belaire Elem., San Angelo, Tex., 1972-73; spl. edn. tchr. Wall Ind. Sch. Dist.-Grape Creek Campus, San Angelo, 1973-77; phys. edn. tchr., coach Grape Creek-Pulliam Ind. Sch. Dist., San Angelo, 1977—2001; ret., 2001. Baptist. Home: 7637 Sandpiper Way San Angelo TX 76901-6645

CHILDS, CHRISTINE MANZO, language arts educator; m. David Law Childs, July 23, 2005. BA, Southeastern La. U., Hammond, 1995; ESL Endorsement, Regis U., Denver, 2005. Cert. secondary English tchr. Colo. Dept of Edn., 1999. Lang. arts tchr. Aurora Pub. Schs., Colo., 1999—2001; lang. arts/ reading/lit. tchr. Adams County Sch. Dist. 50, Denver, 2001—. Fellow: Denver Writing Project (life).

CHILDS, DONNA, finance company executive; b. 1966; BS in Molecular Biophysics and Biochemistry, Yale Univ., 1988; MA in Internat. Econ. Fin., Brandeis Univ., Boston, Mass.; MBA, Columbia Univ. Bus. Sch., NYC. Founder, CEO Childs Capital, LLC, NYC. Mem. bd. examiners Malcolm Baldridge Nat. Quality Prog. Named one of Forty Under 40, Crain's NY Bus., 2004. Mem.: Owner Pres. Mgmt. Program Class. Office: Childs Capital 82 Wall St New York NY 10005

CHILDS, ERIN C., lawyer; b. Chgo., 1977; BA, St. Louis U., 1998; JD, U. Cin., 2002. Bar: Ohio 2002, US Dist. Ct. Southern Dist. Ohio 2002, US Ct. of Appeals Sixth Cir. 2004. Assoc. Thompson Hine LLP, Cin. Ct. apptd. special adv. ProKids. Named one of Ohio's Rising Stars, Super Lawyers, 2006. Mem.: Ohio State Assn., ABA, Cin. Bar Assn. (sec., Young Lawyers Divsn.). Office: Thompson Hine LLP 312 Walnut St 14th Fl Cincinnati OH 45202-4089 Office Phone: 513-352-6756. Office Fax: 513-241-4771.*

CHILDS, ERIN THERESE, psychotherapist; b. Redlands, Calif., Apr. 2, 1958; d. C. Russell and Maryann (Carpenter) C. BA in Psychology cum laude, Loyola Marymount U., LA, 1979, MA magna cum laude in Counseling Psychology, 1980; postgrad. in behavioral medicine, Calif. Grad. Inst., 1982-84. Lic. marriage, family and child therapist, 1982, Calif. Youth counselor II, Chino Youth Svcs., Calif., 1979-80; counselor chem. dependency Behavioral Health Svcs., Gardena, Calif., 1981-83; pvt. practice psychotherapy, LA, 1986—; vis., adjunct faculty Phillips Grad. Inst., Grad. Sch. Psychology, 1997-2000; instr. Human Svcs. program U. Phoenix, 2000-; psychotherapist, cons. Thomas Aquinas Psychotherapy Clinic, Encino, Calif., 1981-83; clin. dir. Emergency Crisis Counseling, West LA, 1983; counselor, unit supr. Southbay Outpatient Unit, Behavioral Health Svcs., Gardena, Calif., 1980-82, dir. driving under the influence program, 1984-86; clin. treatment coord. New Beginnings, Century City Hosp., LA, 1985-86, staff psychotherapist, cons. immune supressed unit, 1987-93; instr. cmty. svcs. Pierce Jr. Coll., Woodland Hills, Calif., 1983, Santa Monica City Coll., Calif., 1984, West LA CC., Culver City, Calif., 1984, mental health clinician, Addiction Medicine Dept. Cedar Sinai Med. Ctr., LA, 1997-2000; facilitator Cancer Support Group H.O.P.E. Found., 2001-05; oral examiner Calif. State Bd. Behavioral Sci. Examiners for Marriage Family Therapists; presenter in field. Mem., bd. dirs. Wilton House, 2002-; pres. St. Matthews Luth. Ch., North Hollywood, Calif., 2002-03, coun. mem. 2003-04, v.p. 2005-06; participant Honolulu Marathon, 2001, Vancouver Marathon, 2003, San Francisco Marathon, 2005, as fundraising for the Nat. AIDS marathon. Mem. Calif. Assn. Marriage and Family Therapists, Psi Chi, Alpha Sigma Nu. Democrat. Lutheran. Office: 11650 Riverside Dr Ste 7 Studio City CA 91602 E-mail: etchilds@sbcglobal.net.

CHILDS, MATTIE SUE, mathematics educator; b. Americus, Ga., Oct. 16, 1960; d. Jesse Cooper and Eleanor H. Mays; m. Claude W. Childs, Feb. 14, 1997; 1 child, Victoria Brittany Okpala. BS in Math., Ga. Southwestern U., Ga., MEd in Math., 1985. Tchr. math. Crisp County Jr. H.S., Cordele, Ga., 1982—85, Lithonia H.S., 1985—95; tchr. math, head coach girls basketball Cross Keys H.S., Atlanta, 1995—2000; tchr. math., coach Lithonia H.S., 2000—. Presenter in field. Author: Lesson Helpers. Mem. Greater Faith Bapt. Ch., Stone Mountain, Ga., 2000. Recipient Outstanding Am. Tchr., Nat. Honor Roll, 2005—06. Mem.: GAE. Home: 6283 Dogwood Trail Lithonia GA 30058 Office: Lithonia High School 2440 Phillips Road Lithonia GA 30058 Office Phone: 678-676-2902. Home Fax: 770-484-5631. Personal E-mail: mch4618769@aol.com.

CHILDS, WENETTA GRYBAS, artist; b. Chgo. d. Joseph and Hattie Zilewicz Grybas; widowed; children: Carol, April Childs Kerr. Student, U. Chgo., 1933—35, Chgo. Art Inst., 1933—35. Exhibitions include San Diego (Calif.) County Fair (Best of Sculpture award San Diego County Fair, 1981), San Diego (Calif.) Mus. Contemporary Art, Represented in permanent collections Sun Sculpture, Solana Beach Plaza, Calif. Lead numerous coms. to beautify Solana Beach, Calif., 1953—80; including redesign and landscape of Solana Beach Plaza, 1966—68; established landscaped median strips on Hwy. 101, 1974—75; established maintenance dists., 1974—75; created bike trail on Hwy. 101, 1974—75; mem. Solana Beach Civic & Hist. Soc., Calif., 1953—, chair billboard removal Calif., 1955—65, pres. Calif., 1970—71; dir. Solana Beach C. of C., Calif., 1973—76, mem. Sun Festival Calif., 1976; mem. citizens' com. rev. cultural arts ctr. feasibility Solana Beach, 1988—89. Co-recipient Hist. monument dedicated to her and Senator Bill Craven, Solana Beach Civic and Hist. Soc., 2003; named Solana Beach Citizen of Yr., Blade Tribune, Oceanside, Calif., 1977; named one of Outstanding Women of North County, Assn. Retarded Citizens, County of San Diego, 1984; recipient Grand prize, Holy Cross Luth. Ch. Festival, Claremont, Calif., 1968. Avocations: classical music, reading, travel.

CHILES, CAROL S., architectural firm executive; Assoc. prin. Tsoi/Kobus & Assoc. Inc., Cambridge, Mass., 1998—2002, prin., v.p., 2002—. Office: Tsoi/Kobus & Assoc Inc One Brattle Sq PO Box 9114 Cambridge MA 02238-9114

CHILES, MARY JANE, secondary school educator; b. Hampton, Iowa, Apr. 26, 1950; d. Thomas Donald and Grace Hermina (Bouvink) Stark; m. Stephen Eugene Chiles, July 8, 1972; 1 child, Samantha Kathryn Chiles Graef. BA, U. Iowa, 1972; postgrad., Morningside Coll., Sioux City, Iowa, 1974, Okla. State U., Stillwater, 1979—82. Tchr. 7th and 8th grade English Woodbury Ctrl. Sch., Moville, Iowa, 1974—75; tchr. 5-8th grade English Anderson Mid. Sch., Sand Springs, Okla., 1979—80; tchr. 6th grade Anderson Elem. Sch., Sand Springs, 1980—81; tchr. 9th and 10th grade English Moore West Mid. H.S., Okla., 1981—88; tchr. 9th grade English Moore West Jr. H.S., 1988—2005, Moore Ctrl. Jr. H.S., 2005—. Mem. Supt.'s Adv. Coun., Moore, 1997—, Supt.'s Patron Adv. Coun., Moore, 1997—, chair profl. devel. com., 1998-2000; field tester book Elements of Writing, 1993 Mem. steering com. Educators Moore PAC, 1983—90. Mem.: NEA (del. assembly 1985—, Western regional conf. 1990—, mem. elections com. 2003, 2005, 2006), Moore Assn. Classroom Tchrs. (profl. negotiations team 1982—2004, exec. com. 1985—86, sec. 1986—88, exec. com. 1988—, chair constn. com. 1989—90, chair resolutions com. 1992—94, v.p. 1996—98, chair constn. com. 1998—99, treas. 1999—, chmn. constn. com. 2005—06, treas. 2006—), Okla. Edn. Assn. (del. assembly 1983—, sec. resolutions com. 1984—97, standing rules com. 1997—98, resolutions com. 1998—2002, mem. ESP com. 2003—06, bd. dirs. 2003—06), Moore C. of C. (edn. com. 1997—). Democrat. Avocations: travel, swimming. Home: 3201 Willow Lane Moore OK 73170-7912 Office: Moore Ctrl 400 N Broadway Moore OK 73160 Business E-Mail: maryjanechiles@mooreschools.com.

CHILLINGWORTH, LORI, bank executive; Grad., Pacific Coast Banking Sch., U. Wash. Sr. v.p., mgr. women's financial group Zions Bank (subsidiary of Zions Bancorporation), Salt Lake City, 1997—. Bd. mem. Family Counseling Ctr., Pete Sauzo Bus. Ctr., Salt Lake Community Coll. Found., Utah Micro-Enterprise Loan Fund; mem., credit com. Salt Lake County Revolving Loan Fund. Named one of 25 Women to Watch, US Banker mag., 2005. Office: Zions Bank One S Main St Salt Lake City UT 84111*

CHILMAN, CATHERINE EARLES STREET, social welfare educator, author; b. Cleve., Sept. 20, 1914; d. Elwood Vickers and Augusta (Jewitt) Street; m. C. William Chilman, Sept. 27, 1936 (dec. 1977); children: Margaret Chilman Carpenter, Jeanne Chilman Klovdahl, Catherine Chilman Brown. AB, Oberlin Coll., 1935; MA, U. Chgo., 1938; PhD, U. Syracuse, 1958. Caseworker United Charities Chgo., 1937-39, Family Svcs., Roanoke, Va., 1939-40; psychiat. cons. ARC, Syracuse, N.Y., 1943-44; tchr. dept. child devel., family rels. Syracuse U., 1947-49, instr., 1949-57, asst. prof., 1957-61; sr. social worker N.Y. State Mental Health Rsch. Unit, Syracuse, 1955-57; parent edn. specialist Children's Bur. HEW, Washington, 1961-64; rsch. adminstr. U.S. Welfare Adminstrn., 1964-69; dean faculty Hood Coll., Frederick, Md., 1969-71; curriculum dir. Internat. Population Planning and Social Work Edn. Project, U. Mich., Ann Arbor, 1971-72; prof. Sch. Social Welfare, U. Wis., Milw., 1972-86, prof. emerita, 1986—; pres. Nat. Groves Conf. on the Family, 1975-78. Speaker, cons. on rsch., family life, pub. policy to univs., fed. govt. and profl. orgns. Author: Your Child: 6 to 12, 1966, Moving into Adolescence, 1966, Growing Up Poor, 1967, Adolescent Sexuality in a Changing American Society, 1983, Families in Trouble, 5 vols., 1988, (with others) Mental Health Crisis and the Nation's Children, 1972, Programs and Policies of National Family Organizations, 1997; mem. edit. bd. Jour. Marriage and Family, 1963-69; contb. articles to profl. jours., chpts. to books. U.S. Office Edn. grantee, 1960-62; Wis. State grantee, 1973-75; Nat. Inst. Child Devel. grantee, 1976-77; recipient Hon. Alumni award Sch. Social Svcs. Adminstrn., U. Chgo., 1978, Honored Scholar award Groves Conf. Marriage and the Family, 1989. Fellow APA; mem. Nat. Coun. on Family Rels. (bd. dirs. 1991-93, sec. 1992-93), Groves Conf. on Marriage and Family (hon. life, bd. dirs., nat. workshop dir. 1992). Home: Cluster 3110 10450 Lottsford Rd Mitchellville MD 20721-2734

CHILTON, ELIZABETH EASLEY EARLY, newspaper executive; b. Williamson, W.Va., Dec. 9, 1928; d. Carl Brooks and Susie Mason (Easley) Early; m. William Edwin Chilton III, Apr. 5, 1952 (dec. Feb. 1987); 1 child, Susan Carroll Chilton Shumate Student, Hollins Coll., Va., 1946—48; AA Primary Edn., Marjorie Webster Coll., Washington, 1950; LLD (hon.), W.Va. State U., 2004; D (hon.), U. W.Va., 2004. Pub. rels. staff Charleston Gazette, W.Va., 1952—87; v.p., treas. Daily Gazette Co., Charleston, 1987—91, pres., 1991—, pub., 2004—, also dir., chmn. bd. dirs., 1994—. Mgmt. com. The Charleston Newspapers, 1991-99; adv. bd. Eberly Coll. Arts and Scis., 1996 Mem. editl. bd. The Charleston Gazette, 1987— Chmn. W.Va. Gov.'s Mansion Preservation Found., Charleston, 1989—; bd. trustees U. Charleston, 1989-98, Marshall U.-Yeager Scholars, Huntington, W.Va., 1990-96, W.Va. State Coll. Found., 1988-96, WSWP-TV Pub. Broadcasting, 1980-94, Faculty Merit Scholars, 1991—, W.Va. Humanities Coun., 1994-00; bd. dirs. BIDCO, 1996-98, Advantage Valley, Charleston, 1996-98, Greater Kanawha Valley Found., 1980-86, adv. bd., 1986—; bd. dirs. W.Va. U., Sulgrave Manor Found., 2001, Childrens Express, Charleston Renaissance, Washington, Gunston Hall Plantation, 1977-92, pres., 1989-92; bd. dirs. Clay Ctr. Arts and Scis., Nat. Youth Sci. Found., 1998, Kid's Count; bd. dirs. Worth Bingham Prize Found., exec. com. 1987—; sec. bd. govs. W.Va. U., 2004—. Recipient John Marshall medal for civic responsibility, Marshall U., 1997, Pres. Disting. Svc. award, W.Va. U., 2000, Second Century award for excellence in leadership, W.Va. State Coll., 2003. Mem. So. Newspaper Pubs. (journalism edn. com. 1992-94, minority affairs com. 1994—), Nat. Soc. Colonial Dames W.Va. (pres.), Internat. Press Inst. (dir. Am. com. 1994—), Newspaper Assn. Am. (com. 1987—), Nat. Trust for Historic Preservation, Garden Club Am. (chmn. libr., bd. dirs. 1989-92), Jr. League Charleston, Edgewood Country Club Charleston, Yale Club N.Y.C., Sulgrave Club Washington, Briar Hills Garden Club, Kanawha Garden Club, Sea Pines Country Club Hilton Head Democrat. Presbyterian. Avocations: travel, reading, gardening. Home: 806 Cedar Rd Charleston WV 25314-1206 Office: The Charleston Gazette 1001 Virginia St E Charleston WV 25301-2895

CHILTON, MARY-DELL MATCHETT, chemical company executive; b. Indpls., Feb. 2, 1939; d. William Elliot and Mary Dell (Hayes) Matchett; m. William Scott Chilton, July 9, 1966; children— Andrew Scott, Mark Hayes BS in Chemistry, U. Ill., 1960, PhD in Chemistry, 1967; Dr. honoris causa, U. Louvain, Belgium, 1983. Research asst. prof. U. Wash., Seattle, 1972-77, research assoc. prof., 1977-79; assoc. prof. Washington U., St. Louis, 1979-83; exec. dir. agrl. biotech CIBA-Geigy Corp., Research Triangle Park, N.C., 1983-91, v.p. agrl. biotech, 1991—; disting. sci. fellow, prin. sci. II Syngenta Biotech. Inc. Adj. prof. genetics N.C. State U., Raleigh, 1983—; adj. prof. biology Washington U., 1983—; Gov. appointee N.C. Bd. Sci. and Tech. Mem. editorial bd. Proceedings of the NAS; author: over 100 sci. publs. Recipient of Rank Prize for Nutrition, 1987, Hendricks Medal, Am. Chem. Soc., 1987, John Scott award, 2002, Benjamin Franklin Medal in Life Scis., 2002; named to Hall of Fame, Women in Tech. Internat., 2004. Fellow Am. Acad. Scis., Am. Acad. Arts and Scis. Am. Acad. Microbiology; mem. NAS (coun. 1988—). Achievements include research in improving technology for introducing new genes into plants. Office: Syngenta Crop Protection PO Box 18300 Greensboro NC 27419

CHILTON, SHIRLEY R., state agency administrator; Sec. State and Consumer Svcs. Agy., State of Calif. Office: State & Consumer Svcs Agy 915 Capitol Mall Ste 200 Sacramento CA 95814-4801

CHIN, BEVERLY ANN, language educator; b. Balt. BA in English, Fla. State U., 1970, MA in English Edn., 1971; PhD in Curriculum and Instrn., U. Oreg., 1975. Cert. lifetime tchg. secondary English Fla., Ariz., reading endorsement Fla. CC, Fla., Ariz. English tchr., adult edn. instr. Melbourne HS, Fla., 1971—73; dep. dir. field experience program Alt. Sch. Tchr. Edn. Program, Coll Edn., U. Mass., Amherst, 1972; grad. tchg. fellow U. Oreg. Coll. Edn., Eugene, 1973—75; asst. prof. elem. and secondary edn. U. New Orleans, 1976—77; asst. prof. English Ariz. State U., Tempe, 1977—78; adj. asst. prof. English Pinal CC, Mesa, Ariz., 1977—78; vis. asst. prof. edn. U. Oreg., Eugene, 1978; asst. prof. edn. U. Ctrl. Fla., Orlando, 1978—81; prof. English U. Mont., Missoula, 1981—. Chair Jt. Com. K-16 Composition Stds., 1999—2000; sr. advisor Mont. U. Sys., Writing Proficiency Admissions Stds.; cons. in field. Author: On Your Own: Writing Process, 1990, On Your Own: Grammar, 1991; editor: Chinese-American Literature, 1992, Dictionary of Characters in Children's Literature, 2001, How to Study for Success, How To Write a Great Research Paper, How to Ace Any Test, How to Build a Super Vocabulary, 2004; advisor Expanding the Canon: Teaching Multicultural Literature in High School, expert commentator, web writer, 2004, advisor Teaching Multicultural Literature: A Workshop for the Middle Grades, expert commentator, web writer, 2005, cons. Grammar for Writing, Grades 9-12, 2000, Glencoe Literature: The Reader's Choice, 2000; contbr. articles to profl. jours. Named Outstanding Young Women Am., 1980, Disting. Tchr., U. Mont., 1990, U. Disting. Alumni Coll. Edn., Fla. State U., 1995, Disting. Educator, Mont. Assn. Tchrs. English Lang. Arts, 2001. Mem.: ASCD, Conf. English Leadership (mem. at large 2003—), Conf. English Edn., Internat. Reading Assn., N.W. Regional Ednl. Lab. Assessment Adv. Coun., Nat. Coun. Tchrs. English (pres. 1995—96), Mont. Project Excellence (chair 1988—89), Mont. Assn. Tchrs. English Lang. Arts. (pres. 1984—85), Nat. Bd. Profl. Tchg. Stds. (mem. bd. 1995—2003), Phi Kappa Phi, Phi Delta Kappa, Kappa Delta Pi, Phi Beta Kappa. Office: U Mont Dept English Liberal Arts 133 Missoula MT 59812 Office Phone: 406-243-2463. Office Fax: 406-243-5130. Business E-Mail: beverly.chin@umontana.edu.

CHIN, CECILIA HUI-HSIN, librarian; b. Tientsin, China; came to U.S., 1961; d. Yu-lin and Ti-yu (Fan) C. BA, Nat. Taiwan U., Taipei, 1961; MSL.S., U. Ill., 1963. Cataloger, reference librarian Roosevelt U., Chgo., 1963; reference librarian, indexer Ryerson & Burnham Libraries, Art Inst. Chgo., 1963-70, head reference dept. indexer, 1970-75; acting dir. libraries Art Inst. Chgo., 1976-77, assoc. librarian, head reference dept., 1975-82; chief librarian Smithsonian Am. Art Mus. and Nat. Portrait Gallery, Smithsonian Inst., Washington, 1982—. Compiler: The Art Institute of Chicago Index to Art Periodicals, 1975 Recipient awards, Nat. Portrait Gallery, Smithsonian Instn., 1984, 1989, Smithsonian Instn. Libr., 2001. Mem. Art Librs. Soc., D.C. Libr. Assn., Washington Rare Book Group. Office: 750 9th St # 2100 Washington DC 20560-0975 Office Fax: 202-275-1929. Business E-Mail: chinc@si.edu.

CHIN, JANET SAU-YING, data processing executive, consultant; b. Hong Kong, July 27, 1949; came to U.S., 1959; d. Arthur Quock-Ming and Jenny (Loo) C. BS in Math, U. Ill., Chgo., 1970; MS in Computer Sci., U. Ill., Urbana, 1973. Sys. programmer Lawrence Livermore (Calif.) Lab., 1972-79; sect. mgr. Tymshare Inc., Cupertino, Calif., 1979-83, Fortune Systems, Redwood City, Calif., 1983-85; div. mgr. Impell Corp, Berkeley, Calif., 1985; pres. Chin Assocs., Oakland, Calif., 1985-88; bus. devel. mgr. Sun Microsystems, Mountain View, Calif., 1988-92; engring. dir. Cadence Design Systems, San Jose, Calif., 1992-94; quality dir. Cadence Design Sys., San Jose, Calif., 1994-95; asst. to CEO, Avant! Corp., Fremont, Calif., 1995-99; provost World Inst. Tech., Fremont, Calif., 1996-98; cons. Second Resource, Oakland, 2000—. Vice-chmn. Am. Nat. Standards Inst. X3H3, N.Y.C., 1979-82, internat. rep. X3H3, 1982-88. Co-author: The Computer Graphics Interface, 1991; contbr. tech. papers to profl. publs. Mem. Assn. Computing Machinery, Sigma Xi. Avocations: Karate, iaido, science fiction/fantasy, piano. E-mail: janetchin2003@yahoo.com.

CHIN, KATHERINE MOY, nutritionist, consultant; b. Washington, Apr. 13; d. David Chee Nie and Mary Ng Jue Hie Moy; m. Calvin Chin, Oct. 7, 1951; 1 child, Stephanie Anne Chung. BS, U. Md., College Park, 1951. Registered dietitian Md., lic. nutritionist Md. Clin. dietitian Johns Hopkins Hosp., Balt., 1954; instr. nutrition, dietetics Sch. Nursing Johns Hopkins Hosp., Balt., 1955—68; owner Chinese Gourmet Restaurant, Balt., 1980—83; nutrition edn. and tng. specialist Balt. County Pub. Sch., Md., 1983—98; partnership specialist Bur. Census Dept. Commerce, Balt., 1999—2000. Bi-lingual interpreter for Cantonese speaking students Balt. County Pub. Schs., 1983—; commr. Asian-Pacific Am. Adv. Coun., Md., 1997—; instr. chinese cooking sch. The Internat. Gourmet Ctr., 1969—79; mem. Osteoporosis Prevention and Edn. Task Force Md. Dept. Health & Mental Hygiene, 2002—; chmn. health med. com. Balt. Xiamen Sister City, 2006—. Coord., fundraiser Asian Cmty., Balt., 1960; lay reader ch. Mem.: Towson U. Asian Arts/Culture Ctr., Balt. Asian Trade Coun. (chairperson 1968—), Am. Dietetic Assn., AAUW, Md. Sch. Food Svc. Assn. (pres. 1984—86), Md. Dietetic Assn. (pres. 1968—70). Democrat. Episcopalian. Avocations: travel, reading, music, volunteering. Home: Unit 208 4100 N Charles St Baltimore MD 21218 Office: Balt Asian Trade Coun 4100 N Charles St Unit 208 Baltimore MD 21218

CHIN, MAY LIN, anesthesiologist; b. Penang, Malaysia, 1952; MD, U. Melbourne, Australia, 1975. Diplomate Am. Bd. Anesthesiology. Internist Royal Melbourne Hosp., 1976; res. anesthesiology George Washington Hosp., D.C., 1979-81; fellow anesthesiology and critical care medicine Nat. Med. Ctr., Children's Hosp., D.C., 1982. Assoc. prof. George Washington U. Mem. DCMS, Am. Soc. Anesthesiologists, Internat. Anesthesiologists Rsch. Soc. Office: 2201 Goldentree Way Vienna VA 22182-5173

CHIN, SUE SOONE MARIAN (SUCHIN CHIN), artist, photojournalist; b. San Francisco; d. William W. and Soo-Up (Swebe) C. Grad., Calif. Coll. Art, Mpls. Arts Inst.; scholar, Schaeffer Design Ctr.; student, Yasuo Kuniyoshi, Louis Hamon, Rico LeBrun. Photojournalist All Together Now Show, 1973, East-West News, Third World Newscasting, 1975-78, Sta. KNBC Sunday Show, L.A., 1975, 76, Live on 4, 1981, Bay Area Scene, 1981. Chmn. Full Moon Products; pres., bd. dirs. Aumni Oracle Inc. Graphics printer, exhbns. include: Kaiser Ctr., Zellerbach Pla., Chinese Culture Ctr. Galleries, Capricorn Asunder Art Commn. Gallery (all San Francisco), Newspace Galleries, New Coll. of Calif., L.A. County Mus. Art, Peace Pla. Japan Ctr., Congress Arts Comm., Washington, 1989; SFWA Galleries, Inner Focus Show, 1989—, Calif. Mus. Sci. and Industry, Lucien Labaudt Gallery, Salon de Medici, Madrid, Salon Renacimento, Madrid, 1995, Life is a Circus, SFWA Gallery, 1991, 94, UN/50 Exhibit, Bayfront Galleries, 1995, Somar Galleries, 1997, 2003 (Merit award 2003), Sacramento State Fair, 2000, Star Child, Women thru the Ages - Somarts Gallery, 2000, Kings Gallery, San Francisco, 2004, AFL-CIO Labor Studies Ctr., Washington, Asian Women Artists (1st prize for conceptual painting, 1st prize photography), 1978, Yerba Buena Arts Ctr. for the Arts Festival, 1994; represented in permanent collections L.A. County Fedn. Labor, Calif. Mus. Sci. and Industry, AFL-CIO Labor Studies Ctr., Australian Trades Coun., Hazeland and Co., also pvt. collections; author: (poetry) Yuri and Malcolm, The Desert Sun, 1994 (Editors Choice award 1993-94). Del. nat., state convs. Nat. Women's Polit. Caucus, 1977-83, San Francisco chpt. affirmative action chairperson, 1978-82, nat. conv. del., 1978-81, Calif. del., 1976-81. Recipient Honorarium AFL-CIO Labor Studies Ctr., Washington, 1975-76, Bicentennial award 1976; award Centro Studi Ricerche delle Nazioni, Italy, 1985; bd. advisors Psycho Neurology Found. Bicentennial award LA County Mus. Art, 1976, 77, 78, Mandalay Merit award Som Arts Gallery, 2003. Mem. Asian Women Artists (founding v.p., award 1978-79, 1st award in photography of Orient 1978-79, Merit award 2003), Calif. Chinese Artists (sec.-treas. 1978-81), Japanese Am. Art Coun. (chairperson 1978-84, dir.), San Francisco Women Artists, San Francisco Graphics Guild, Pacific/Asian Women Coalition Bay Area, Chinatown Coun. Performing and Visual Arts. Address: PO Box 421415 San Francisco CA 94142-1415

CHIN, SYLVIA FUNG, lawyer; b. NYC, June 27, 1949; d. Thomas and Constance (Yao) Fung; m. Edward G.H. Chin, July 10, 1971; children: Arthur F., Benjamin F. BA, NYU, 1971; JD, Fordham U., 1977. Bar: NY 1978, US Dist. Ct. (so. and ea. dists.) NY 1979, US Supreme Ct. 1990. Law clk. to dist. judge US Dist. Ct. (so. dist.), NYC, 1977-79; assoc. White & Case, NYC, 1979-86, ptnr., 1986—. Adj. assoc. prof. law Fordham U., NYC, 1979-81. Mem. editl. bd.: Bus. Law Today, 1996—2002. Mem.: ABA, Am. Bar Found., Am. Law Inst., Am. Coll. Comml. Fin. Lawyers, Am. Coll. Investment Counsel (bd. dirs. 1999—2005, pres. 2002—03), Nat. Asian Pacific ABA (treas. 1997—98, pres. law found. 2005—06), Women's World Banking (bd. dirs.), Asian Am. Bar Assn. (bd. dirs. 1991—97, pres. 1994—96), NY County Lawyers Assn. (bd. dirs. 2004—), Assn. Bar City NY, Asian Am. Law Fund NY (bd. dirs.), Fordham Law Alumni Assn. (bd. dirs.). Office: White & Case LLP 1155 Ave of Americas New York NY 10036-2711 Office Phone: 212-819-8200. Business E-Mail: schin@whitecase.com.

CHING, HO, surgeon; b. Kaoshung, Taiwan, Feb. 20, 1950; arrived in U.S., 1970; d. Feng Chih and Ai Hua Yin Ho; m. Stephen Jay Keller; children: Lisa, Michele. BS, Nat. U. Taiwan, Taipei, 1970; PhD, U. Cin., 1975, MD, 1984. Rsch. fellow Roche Molecular Biol. Inst., Nutley, NJ, 1975—76; Fogarty fellow Nat. Cancer Inst., NIH, Bethesda, Md., 1976—78; rsch. assoc. U. Cin., 1978—80; surg. resident Jewish Hosp., Cin., 1989, surgeon, 1989—91, Donna Stahl Assocs., Cin., 1991—2000; pvt. practice surgery Cin., 2000—. Assoc. dir. surg. resident program Jewish Hosp., 1992, mem. exec. com., 2001—03; chmn. women in medicine Acad. Medicine, Cin., 1998; co-chair dept. surg. Bethesda North Hosp., Cin., 2005—06. Named one of Top Drs., Cin. Mag., 2001, 2003. Fellow: ACS; mem.: Am. Soc. Microbiology, Cama Cinti (pres. 2005—06), Am. Soc. Cell Biology. Avocations: yoga, travel. Office: Ching Ho MD Inc 4760 E Galbraith Rd Cincinnati OH 45236 Office Phone: 513-891-1200. E-mail: drho@fuse.net.

CHINNI, ROSEMARIE CATHERINE, science educator; b. Hazleton, Pa., Mar. 14, 1976; d. Joseph Anthony and Roseann Chinni. BS, King's Coll., Wilkes-Barre, Pa., 1998; PhD, U. of S.C., Columbia, 2002. Rsch. coord. II Savannah River Ecology Lab., Aiken, SC, 2002—04; asst. prof. Alvernia Coll., Reading, Pa., 2004—. Cons. Applied Rsch. Assocs., Albuquerque, 2006. Contbr. articles to profl. jours. Mem.: Soc. for Applied Spectroscopy, Beta Kappa Chi. Office: Alvernia Coll 400 St Bernardine St Reading PA 19607 Office Phone: 610-568-1492. Business E-Mail: rosemarie.chinni@alvernia.edu.

CHINTELLA, MARILYNN ANITA, elementary school educator, department chairman; b. Ballard, Wash., June 29, 1949; d. John Burnett and Elinor Anita Brydges; m. Mark Bartholomew Chintella, Apr. 19, 1974; children: Blair Bartholomew, Angela Alicia, Chelsea Anita. AAS, Shoreline CC, Wash., 1969; EdB, Ctrl. Wash. U., Ellensburg, 1971. Std. tchg. cert. Office Supt. Pub. Instrn. Sci. tchr. US Peace Corps, Moyamba, Sierra Leone, 1971—73; phys. sci. tchr. Gwynn Pk. Jr. HS, Brandywine, Md., 1974—75; biology tchr. Toledo (Wash.) HS, 1976—78; 7th and 8th grade sci. tchr. Toledo Mid. Sch., 1989—, sci. dept. chair, 1995—. Sci. olympiad coach Toledo Mid. Sch., 1990—2000; mem. Acad. Learning Improvement Team, 1995—97; mem. curriculum com. Toledo Sch. Dist., 1999—2000. Charter pres. PTO/PTA, Chehalis, Wash., 1984—85; pre-walk chairperson Puget Sound Walk to Emmaus, Lake Stevens, Wash. Fellow, Internat. Inst. Edn., 2001; grantee, Nat. Sci. Found./U. Hawaii, Hilo, 1995, Bill and Melinda Gates Found., 2001—03. Mem.: NEA (assoc.), Wash. Edn. Assn. (assoc.), Toledo Edn. Assn. (assoc.), Nat. Sci. Tchrs. Assn. (assoc.), Wash. Sci. Tchrs. Assn. (assoc.), Delta Kappa Gamma (assoc.). Avocations: flying kites, bicycling. Office Phone: 360-864-2395.

CHIPMAN, DEBORAH J., elementary school educator; d. Harry P. and Elizabeth C. Gray; m. J. Scott Chipman, Dec. 27, 1976; children: Trevor, Blake. BS in Elem. Edn., Ft. Hays State U., Kans., 1974, MS in Elem. Adminstrn., 1996. Tchr. 2d grade Beeson Elem. Sch., Dodge City, Kans., 1974—. Home: 1808 Debray Dr Dodge City KS 67801 Office: Beeson Elem Sch 1700 W Beeson Rd Dodge City KS 67801

CHIPMAN, DEBRA DECKER, title insurance executive; b. Oneonta, N.Y., Sept. 21, 1959; d. Leon Hannibal and Patricia Elizabeth (Ainsworth) Decker; m. Michael A. Chipman, May 24, 1980 (div. Sept. 1990); 1 child, Amanda Michelle. Student, Robert Morris Coll., 1988—94. Sec., receptionist Power Engring. Corp., Binghamton, NY, 1977—78; accts. payable clk. Old Dominion U. Rsch. Found., Norfolk, Va., 1978—80; adminstrv. asst. U. Pitts., 1980—81; paralegal Papernick & Gefsky, Attys. at Law, Pitts., 1981—93; mgr. Preferred Settlement Svcs., Inc., Pitts., 1993—97; asst. v.p., agy. rep. First Am. Title Ins. Co., Pitts., 1997—2000; v.p., mgr. We. Pa. agy. Fidelity Nat. Title Ins. Co., 2000—. Recipient award Otsego County Bankers Assn., 1977. Mem.: Pa. Land Title Assn. (chair 2002—, we. Pa. chpt. sec.), Pa. Assn. Notaries, Pitts. Paralegal Assn. (co-chair fundraising com. 1990). Methodist. Avocations: golf, skiing. Home: 2593 Hunters Point Ct S Wexford PA 15090-7986 Office: Fidelity Nat Title Ins Co Grant Building Ste 1412 Pittsburgh PA 15219-2203 E-mail: dchipman@fnf.com.

CHIRA, SUSAN, editor; married; 2 children. BA in History and East Asian Studies, Harvard U., 1980. Reporter The NY Times, 1982—84, Tokyo corr., 1984—89, dep. fgn. editor, 2004—. Author: A Mother's Place, 1998. Office: The New York Times 229 W 43rd St New York NY 10036-3959

CHIRCO, JENNIFER B., special education educator; b. Natick, Mass., Oct. 13, 1974; d. Charles A. Woodward and Deborah B. Paredes; m. Christopher A. Chirco, Oct. 11, 2003. BS, Springfield Coll., Mass., 1996; MS in Edn., Simmons Coll., Boston, 2001. Cert. intensive spl. needs K-12 tchr. Level I tchr. NECC, Southboro, Mass., 1998—99, level II tchr., 1999—2000, head classroom tchr., 2000—01; self-contained classroom tchr. City of Methuen Schs., Mass., 2001—. Cons. ABA, LLC, Framingham, Mass., 2002—03. Avocations: hiking, scrapbooks, surfing, mountain biking, camping.

CHIRICHELLA, DEBRA, publishing executive; BA, Princeton Univ., 1985; MBA, Harvard Univ., 1990. Dir., strategic devel. Primedia, NYC, 1993—95, v.p., corp. operations, planning, 1995—96, v.p., corp. devel., 1996—97, CFO, mag. group, 1997—2000, COO, Enthusiast publications, 2000, exec. v.p., bus.-to-bus. group, 2000; sr. v.p., fin. Conde Nast Publications, NYC, CFO, 2005—. Office: CFO Conde Nast Publications 4 Times Sq New York NY 10036

CHIRICO-ELKINS, URSULA, retired librarian; arrived in Can., 1958, arrived in U.S., 1961; d. Friedrich Winter and Gertrud Naake; m. John H. Elkins (dec.); children: Amadeus, Naomi, George, Tabitha; m. Francesco Chirico, 2003. Student, Mercer County C.C., N.J.; diploma, Inst. Children's Lit., 1980, diploma, 1990. Libr. asst. Princeton U., NJ, 1978—81, libr. asst. David Sarnoff Rsch. Ctr., 1981—87, sr. libr. asst. David Sarnoff Rsch. Ctr., 1983—87; prin. asst. Rider U., Lawrenceville, NJ, 1987—89, 1990—93; ret., 1993. Author: A Celebration of Poets, 1998, Michelangelo's Creation of Adam, 1998, Falling Snow, 1998, Unending Love, 1999, Omnipotence, 1999, Universal Truth, 2000, Springtime, 2003, Freedom of Spirit, 2004, Let Not Your Heart Be Troubled, 2004, (anthology) Great Poems of the Western World, 2004. Vol. libr. Calvary Ch., Pemberton, NJ, 2000; literacy vol. Toms River, NJ, 1993—; vol. Samaritan Hospice, Moorestown, NJ, 1995—; mem. edn. coun. Indian Nations, Albuquerque, 2004. Mem.: Am. Indian Edn. Found. (bd. dirs., coun. 2003—), Internat. Soc. Poets (Disting. Mem.). Avocations: painting, classical music, literature, embroidery. Personal E-mail: whiteswan@netzero.com.

CHISHOLM, MARGARET ELIZABETH, retired library director; b. Grey Eagle, Minn., July 25, 1921; d. Henry D. and Alice (Thomas) Bergman; children: Nancy Diane, Janice Marie Lane. BA, U. Washington, 1957, MLS, 1958, PhD, 1966. Libr. Everett (Wash.) C.C., 1961-63; from asst. to assoc. prof. edn. U. Oreg., Eugene, 1963-67; assoc. prof. edn. U. N.Mex., Albuquerque, 1967-69; prof., dean U. Md. Coll. Libr. and Info. Svcs., College Park, 1969-75; v.p. univ. rels. and devel. U. Washington, Seattle, 1975-81; dir., prof. Grad. Sch. Libr. and Info. Sci., U. Wash., Seattle, 1981-92; ret., 1992. Adv. com. White House Conf. on Libr. and Info. Sci., 1989-91, Pub. Broadcasting Svc. Archive; commr. Western Interstate Commn. Higher Edn., Colo., 1981-85. Author: Information Technology: Design and Applications (with Nancy Lane), 1990. Mem. USIA del. to Mexican-Am. Commn. on Cultural Coop., 1990. Civilian aide U.S. Army, 1978-88. Recipient Ruth Worden award U. Wash., Seattle, 1957, Disting. Alumni award St. Cloud (Minn.) U., 1977, Disting. Alumni award U. Wash., 1979, John Brubaker award Cath. Libr. Assn., 1987, Pres.'s award Wash. Libr. Assn., 1991. Mem. ALA (exec. bd. 1989-90, pres. 1988-89, v.p. 1986-87), Assn. Pub. TV Stas. (trustee 1975-84, 87-93), White House Conf. on Libr. and Info. Svcs. (adv. com. 1989-91), U. Wash. Retirement Assn. (v.p. 1995-96, pres. 1996-98). Home: 20900 Big Basin Way Saratoga CA 95070-5750

CHISHOLM, MARTHA MARIA, dietitian; b. Havana, Cuba, Nov. 27, 1958; arrived in U.S., 1961; d. Robert Lester and Martha Clara (Latour) C. BS in Dietetics and Nutrition, Fla. Internat. U., 1983, MS in Dietetics and Nutrition magna cum laude, 1995. Lic. dietitian, Fla. Pediatric clin. dietitian Miami (Fla.) Children's Hosp., 1983-86, 92-96, pediatric gastroenterology dietitian, 1986-92, dietitian Ketogenic Diet Ctr., 1994-96, pediatric clin. dietitian, staff relief, 1997; dietitian Pediatric Cystic Fibrosis Ctr., 1993-96, dietitian feeding and swallowing disorder team, 1994-96; clin. dietitian Oncology and Hospice Mercy Cath. Hosp., 1997—2005, So. Miami Hosp., Miami, Fla., 2005—. Cons. United Cerebral Palsy Assn. Miami, 1989-94, Roche Labs., Miami, 1991-95, Children's Rehab. Network, Miami, 1990-95. Mem. Homeless Ministry, St. Louis Cath. Ch., Miami, 1991-94, Eucharistic min., 1993-96, young adult ministry co-leader, 1994-96; mem. fgn. mission ministry Amor En Accion, 1995-2000. Mem. Am. Dietetic Assn. (registered dietician), Fla. Dietetic Assn. (Disting. Dietitian 1997), Miami Dietetic Assn. (sec. 1988-89, Recognized Young Dietitian award 1988, Hurricane Andrew Relief Fund chair 1992-93, mem. nominating com. 1993-94, Disting. Dietitian 1996), Sierra Club (Miami chpt. cert. outings leader 1998-2000), Phi Kappa Phi. Republican. Roman Catholic. Avocations: dog shows, backpacking, bicycling, photography, canoeing, rowing. Home: 5935 Turin St Coral Gables FL 33146-3245 Office: S Miami Hosp Bapt Health Sys 6200 SW 73d St Miami FL 33143-4989 Office Phone: 786-662-4952.

CHISHOLM, SALLIE WATSON, biological oceanography educator, researcher; b. Marquette, Mich., Nov. 5, 1947; BA, Skidmore Coll., 1969; PhD in biology, SUNY, 1974. Postdoctoral researcher biol. oceanography Scripps Instn. Oceanography, 1974-76; vis. scientist, biology dept. Woods Hole Oceanog. Instn., 1978—; prof., dept. civil and environ. engring. MIT, Cambridge, 1976—, Edgerton asst. prof., 1977—78, Doherty prof. ocean utilization, 1980—82, prof. dept. biology, 1993—, McAfee prof. engring. (endowed chair), 1995—2000, Lee & Geraldine Martin prof. environ. studies, co-dir., Earth Sys. Initiative, 2002—, co-dir., Terrascope, 2003—, Gordon and Betty Moore Found. investigator in marine sci., 2004—. MIT dir. MIT-Woods Hole Joint Program in Oceanography, 1988-95; steering com. U.S. Joint Global Flux Study, 1989-92; mem. ocean studies bd. NRC, 1990-93, com. on molecular biology, 1991-92; corp. mem. Bermuda Biological Station, 1992-96; vis. com. oceanography, Brookhaven Nat. Labs., 1995-98; mem. sci. adv. bd. Joint Genome Inst., Dept. Energy, 2000-, mem. policy bd., 2003; mem. adv. com. Carnegie Instn. Dept. Global Ecology, 2003-; mem. bd. trustees Inst. Ecosystem Studies, 2003-. Assoc. editor Jour. Phycology, 1983-87; mem. editorial bd. Jour. Marine Molecular Biology and Biotech., 1991—, Marine Ecology Progress Series, 1992—, Oceanus Mag., 1991-93, Environmental Microbiology, 1998-; subject editor Aquatic Microbiol Ecology, 1995-99; contbr. articles to profl. jours. Recipient Rosenstiel Award in Ocean Sciences, 1991; fellow, Am. Acad. of Arts and Sciences, 1992; Guggenheim fellow, 1997—98, Resident Scholar, Bellagio Ctr., Italy, 1998, elected, NAS, 2003. Mem.: Internat. Ecology Inst., Soc. of Analytical Cytology, AAAS, Ecological Soc. of Am., The Oceanography Soc., Am. Geophysical Union (fellow 1996), Phycological Soc. of Am., Am. Soc. Microbiology (fellow 1993), Am. Soc. Limnology and Oceanography, Sigma XI. Office: MIT 48-419 15 Vassar St Cambridge MA 02139

CHISNELL, DEBRA JEAN, special education educator; b. Burlington, Wis., Oct. 11, 1967; d. Donald Francis and Judith Ann Morrow; m. Jerry Clinton Chisnell, June 22, 1991; children: Dylan Donald, Abigail Lee. BS, Silver Lake Coll., Manitowoc, Wis., 1990; MA, Marian Coll., Fond du lac, Wis., 2003. Cert. elem. edn. K-8, spl. edn. K-8, prin. K-12, dir. instrn., spl. edn. Profl. aide Markesan (Wis.) Schs., 1997—98, spl. edn. tchr., 1998—, summer sch. coord., 2002—. Chair dept. Markesan Schs., 1999—, ins. liason, 1999—, tech. process coord., 2004—. Trustee Markesan Pub. Libr., 1999—2005; mem. religious edn. com. St. Joseph's Ch., Markesan, 2000—. Mem.: Coun. for Exceptional Children, Assn. for Supervision and Curriculum Devel. Avocation: reading. Office: Markesan Elem Sch PO Box 248 Markesan WI 53946

CHISTENSON, ROSE MARY, elementary school educator; d. Harold George and Charlotte Irene Pankratz; m. James Milford Christenson, July 6, 1971; children: Nicole Christenson-Keisacher, Karrie Christenson, Christenson Erika. BS in Family Consumer Sci., S.D. State U., Brookings, 1971, MS in Math., 1996. Tchr. elem. sch. Douglas Sch. Dist., Ellsworth AFB, SD, 1972—74; prin., owner Small World Preschool, Brandon, SD, 1978—87; tchr. Garretson (S.D.) Sch. Dist., 1987—94, Brandon (S.D.) Valley Mid. Sch., 1994—. With S.D. Sci. Edn., Pierre, SD, 2004—06, S.D. Dept. Edn., Pierre, 2004—06; adv., coord. Brandon (S.D.) Valley Mid. Sch., team leader mid. sch.; freelance tutor. Named Brandon (S.D.) Valley Tchr. of Yr., Brandon (S.D.) Sch. Dist., 2001. Mem.: NEA, S.D. Edn. Assn., Nat. Sci. Tchrs. Assn., S.D. Sci. Tchrs. Assn. Roman Cath. Avocations: baking, candy making, sewing, running, gardening. Office: Brandon Valley Mid Sch 700 E Holly Blvd Brandon SD 57005 Personal E-mail: rosem600@alliancecom.net.

CHITTICK, ELIZABETH LANCASTER, advocate; b. Bangor, Pa., Nov. 11, 1908; d. George and Flora Mae (Mann) Lancaster. Student, Columbia U., 1944—45, N.Y. Inst. Fin., 1950—51, Hunter Coll., 1952—56, Upper Iowa U., Fayette, 1976. Adminstrv. asst., chief clk U.S. Naval Air Stas., Seattle and Banana River, Fla., 1941—45; v.p., treas. W.A. Chittick & Co., Manila, 1945—52; real estate salesperson La Jolla, Calif., 1949; registered rep. Bache & Co., N.Y. Stock Exch., N.Y.C., 1950—62, Shearson & Hamil, 1962—63, investment adviser, 1962—65; revenue officer IRS, N.Y.C., 1965—72; pres. Nat. Woman's Party, Washington, 1971—89, Woman's Party Corp., 1978—91; commr. Washington Commn. on Status of Women, 1982—86; pres., adminstr. Sewall-Belmont House. Bd. dirs. Wexita Corp., N.Y.C., Pan Am. Liason Com. of Women's Orgns. Inc.; 1st v.p., bd. dirs. Nat. Coun. Women U.S. Lectr., TV and radio commentator on Equal Rights Amendment; author: Answers to Questions About the Equal Rights Amendment, 1973, 76. Mem. Coalition for Women in Internat. Devel., Internat. Women's Yr. Continuing Com., 1978-81, Women's Campaign Fund, Washington, 1975-80, Women's Nat. Rep. Club, N.Y.C., Women Govt. Rels., Washington; mem. U.S. com. of cooperation to Inter-Am. Commn. of Women, OAS, 1974-80; del. U.S. World Conf. of Internat. Women's Yr., Mexico City, 1975; mem. women's history ctr. task force Am. Revolution Bicentennial Adminstrn., 1973-76; mem. adv. com. U.S. Ctr. for Internat. Women's Yr., 1973-76; vice convenor com. on law and status of women Internat. Coun. of Women; chmn. UN Drive for war orphans and widows, Manila, 1949 Mem. Greater Washington Soc. Assn. Execs., Internat. Coun. Women (Paris), Nat. Fedn. Bus. and Profl. Women's Clubs, Gen. Fedn. Women's Clubs, Women's Press Club (N.Y.C.), Am. Newswomen's Club, Nat. Press Club, Order Eastern Star. Home and Office: 4046 5th Ave Lake Worth FL 33462-2012

CHITTISTER, JOAN DAUGHERTY, writer, educator; b. Dubois, Pa., Apr. 26, 1936; d. Harold C. and Loretta (Cuneo) C. BA, Mercyhurst Coll., 1962; MA, U. Notre Dame, 1968; PhD, Pa. State U., 1971; LLD (hon.), Chestnut Hill Coll., 1986, Villa Maria Coll., 1988, Loyola U., Chgo., 1989, St. Leo (Fla.) Coll., 1990, Loyola U., New Orleans, 1990, Santa Clara U., 1994, St. John's U., 1997; HHD (hon.), St. Mary's Coll., Notre Dame, Ind., 1989, Barry U., 1999; HMD (hon.), Cath. Theol. Union, 2001; DHL (hon.), St. Michael Coll., 2002. Tchr. elem. sch. Diocese of Erie (Pa.), 1955-59, tchr. secondary sch., 1959-74; pres. Fedn. St. Scholastica Benedictine Sisters, 1971-78, Conf. Am. Benedictine Prioresses, 1974-90; prioress Benedictine Sisters of Erie, 1978-90; exec. dir. Benetvision, Erie, 1990—. Author: Women, Church and Ministry, 1983, Winds of Change: Women Challenge Church, 1986, Wisdom Distilled from the Daily, 1990, Job's Daughters: Women & Power, 1990, Womanstrength, 1990, Rule of Benedict: Insights for the Ages, 1992, The Fire in these Ashes, 1995, There is a Season, 1995, In a High Spiritual Season, 1995, A Passion for Life: Fragments of the Face of God, 1996, Beyond Beijing: The Next Step for Women, 1996, The Psalms: Meditations for Each Day of the Year, 1996, Songs of Joy: New Meditations on the Psalms, 1997, Heart of Flesh: A Feminist Spirituality for Women and Men, 1998, Light in the Darkness: New Reflections on the Psalms, 1998, In Search of Belief, 1999, Gospel Days: Reflections for Every Day of the Year, 1999, Living Well: Scriptual Reflections for Every Day, 2000, The Story of Ruth, 2000, The Illuminated Life, 2000, Seeing With Our Souls, 2002, New Designs, 2002, Scarred by Struggle, Transformed by Hope, 2003, Twelve Steps to Inner Freedom, 2003, Listen With the Heart, 2003, Called to Question, 2004, In the Heart of the Temple, 2004, Becoming Fully Human, 2005, The Way We Were, 2005, The Friendship of Women: The Hidden Tradition of the Bible, 2006; co-author: Faith and Ferment: Study of Christian Beliefs and Practices, 1983, The Tent of Abraham, 2006; co-author, editor: Climb Along the Cutting Edge, 1977; web columnist Nat. Cath. Reporter, 2003—; contbr. articles to profl. jours. Bd. dirs. Emmaus Ministries, Inc., Erie, 1990—, Nat. Cath. Reporter, Kansas City, 1983-2000; bd. corporators St. Vincent Health Ctr., Erie, 1986-2000; bd. trustees Erie Cmty. Found., 1993-2002, Global Edn. Assn., N.Y., 1981-93; mem. exec. bd. Ecumenical/Cultural Rsch. Ctr., Collegeville, Minn., 1976-96; mem. internat. com. Peace Coun., 1995—; co-chair Global Peace Initiative of Women, 2002—, Tikkun Cmty., 2005-; active Niwano Peace Found., 2003—. Recipient U.S. Cath. award U.S. Cath. mag., 1992, St. Catherine of Sienna award Dominican Sisters, Springfield, Ill., 1992, Book award Cath. Press Assn., 1996, 97, 2001, 04, 05, Thomas Merton award, 2001; named Disting. Pennsylvanian Gannon U., Erie, 1984, Disting. Alumna of Yr. Mercyhurst Coll., Erie, 1986, Woman of Yr. The Erie 80 Club, 1989, Disting. Daughter Pa., Harrisburg, 1991, Pope Paul VI Tchr. of Peace Pax Christi USA, 1990. Mem. Speech Communication Assn. Roman Catholic. Avocations: music, reading, computers. Home: 355 E 9th St Erie PA 16503-1107 Office Phone: 814-459-0314. Business E-Mail: office@benetvision.org.

CHITTUM, HEATHER, chef; m. Anthony Chittum. B in Govt. and Internat. Rels., Clark U., 1994; attended Fundamental of Pastry Arts prog., L'Academie de Cuisine, 2001. Worked for former NY Senator Daniel Patrick Moynihan, Share Our Strength; cook Equinox restaurant; pastry chef Circle Bistro, 2004, Dish, 2004—, Notti Bianche, 2005—, Michel Richard Citronelle. Named one of Washington DC's Rising Stars, StarChefs.com, 2006. Office: Notti Bianche 824 New Hampshire Ave NW Washington DC 20037 Office Phone: 202-298-8085.*

CHITWOOD, SHARON CARMICAL, elementary school educator; d. Marion Theodore and Juanita Martin Carmical; m. Philip Ray Chitwood, June 14, 1969; children: Philip Brent, Kristin Joann Lester. BA, Union Coll., Barbourville, Ky., 1982; MA, Union Coll., Barbourville, 1985; Reading Specialist Endorsement, Union Coll., Barbourville, Ky, 1985; Charter Mem. Ky. Reading Project, Ea. Ky. U., Richmond, Ky., 1999. Cert. tchr. Ky. Primary tchr. Harlan Ind. Sch., Harlan, Ky., 1982—. Mem. 3 terms Harlan Elem. Site Based Coun., Harlan, Ky., 2002; dist. facilities com. Harlan Ind. Sch., Harlan, Ky., 2004. Recipient Excellence in Tchg. Award, Campbellville U., 2002. Mem.: NEA, Ky. Reading Assn., Ky. Edn. Assn. Ch. Of Christ. Avocations: reading, gardening, travel. Office: Harlan Ind Sch Ctrl St Harlan KY 40831 Office Phone: 606-573-8700.

CHIU, BELLA CHAO, astrophysicist, writer; b. Beijing, May 24, 1931; came to U.S., 1938; d. Yuen Ren and Buwei (Yang) Chao; m. Hong-Yee Chiu, June 25, 1960 (div. 1966); 1 child, Lihu Mason Chiu. BA, U. Calif., Berkeley, 1953; MS, Cornell U., 1956. Rsch. staff MIT, Cambridge, 1971-81; tchr. ESL Ctrl. S. U. Tech., Changsha, China, 1982-83; fgn. expert Qinghua U., Beijing, 1986-87; writer Arlington, Mass., 1987-97; rschr., 1997—. English editor Nat. Assn. Chinese Ams., 1984-86. Grantee NSF, 1972, 75, 79. Mem. Am. Astron. Soc. (hist. divsn.), Archeol. Inst. Am., Women's Health Initiative. Achievements include research in role of solar eclipses in El Nino and La Nina storms. Personal E-mail: bellacchiu@aol.com.

CHIU, DOROTHY, retired pediatrician; b. Hong Kong, Aug. 8, 1917; came to U.S., 1946; d. Yan Tse Chiu and Connie Kwai-Ching Wan; m. Kitman Au; children: Katherine, Margo, Doris, James, Richard. BS, Lingnan U., 1939; MD, Nat. Shanghai Med. Coll., 1945. Diplomate Am. Bd. Pediats. Sch. physician L.A. Sch. Dist., 1954-55; pvt. practice Burbank, Calif., 1955—56, San Fernando, Calif., 1956—2000. Staff pediatrician Holy Cross Med. Ctr., Mission Hills, Calif., 1961-2000. Bd. dirs. Burbank Cmty. Concert, 1970-80. Fellow Am. Acad. Pediats.; mem. Calif. Med. Assn., L.A. County Med. Assn. Republican. Avocations: handicrafts, music, travel, reading, photography.

CHIULLI, E. ANTOINETTE, lawyer; b. Pescara, Italy, Oct. 30, 1950; arrived in U.S., 1955; d. Nino and Maria (Mezzanotte) C.; children: Christopher J., Jason A. BA, Marymount Coll., 1972; JD, Rutgers U., 1976. Legal asst. Judge Manuel Greenberg, Atlantic City, N.J., 1976-77; pvt. practice Somerdale, N.J., 1978-86. Econ. analyst Nat. Econ. Research Assocs., N.Y.C., 1972-73; panelist Matrimonial Settlement Program, 1985—. Cons., Alternatives for Women Now, Camden, 1978-80, Women's Counseling Ctr., 1981-83, Glassboro (N.J.) Coll. Together Program, Jaycettes of Camden County; trustee, Haddonfield Child Care, 1989—. Mem. N.J. State Bar Assn., Camden County Bar Assn. (family law com., scholarship com.), Burlington Co. Bar Assn. Office: 100 Grove St Haddonfield NJ 08033 Office Phone: 856-795-4900. Personal E-mail: echiulli@aol.com.

CHIVERTON, PATRICIA ANN, dean, nursing educator; b. Rochester, N.Y., Nov. 21, 1947; d. Paul and Eleanor (Buyck) Gilmore; 1 child, Laura. BS, Ctrl. Mo. State U., 1970; MS, U. Rochester, 1980, EdD, 1990. Exec. dir. Alzheimer's Assn., Rochester, NY, 1987-89; clin. assoc. U. Rochester, 1987-89, clin. chief psychiat. mental health nursing, 1990-97, asst. prof. clin. nursing, 1994-95, interim chair health care sys. divsn., 1994-95, assoc. prof. clin. clin. nursing, 1996—99, CEO cmty. nursing ctr., 1996—, assoc. dean clin. affairs Sch. Nursing and Med. Ctr., 1998—99, interim dean Sch. Nursing and Med. Ctr., 1999—2000, dean Sch. Nursing and Med. Ctr., 2000—. Judge Book of the Yr., Am. Jour. Nursing, 1999, reviewer, 1998—; cons. F.f. Thompson Continuing Care Facility, Canadaigua, N.Y., 1997-99. Contbr. chpts. to books. in field. Rep. N.Y. State Alzheimer's Assn., 1985-88; bd. dirs. Health and Wellness Ctr., Livingston County, N.Y., Monroe County Long Term Care Agy., Rochester, 1997—. Mem. Am. Psychiat. Nurses Assn. (pres. Northwestern chpt. 1995-97, Excellence in Leadership award 1994), Ea. Nursing Rsch. Soc., Nat. Acads. Practice (Disting. Practitioner), Sigma Theta Tau. Office: U Rochester Sch Nursing 601 Elmwood Ave Rochester NY 14642-0001 E-mail: patricia_chiverton@urmc.rochester.edu.*

CHLANDA, SUZANNE LEA, secondary school educator; b. St. Louis, Feb. 6, 1969; d. Herbert Walter and Gail Lea Jacobus; m. William Todd Chlanda, Oct. 16, 1993; 1 child, William Cody. BS in Secondary Edn., SW Mo. State

U., Springfield, 1993. Cert. fire svc. instr. Mo. Divsn. Fire Safety, 2002. 8th grade sci. tchr. Meml. Mid. Sch., Joplin, Mo., 1994—2004. 8th grade girls' basketball coach Joplin Jr. High, 1993—95. Vol. firefighter Redings Mill Fire Dept., Joplin, 1999—2006. Mem.: Mo. State Tchrs. Assn. Office: Memorial Middle School 310 W 8th St Joplin MO 64801

CHMELYNSKI, DONNA, elementary school educator; d. George Sommer and Pearl Clark; m. Paul Chmelynski, Oct. 25, 1980; 1 child, Adam. BS in Edn., Calif. State Coll., 1974; MEd, U. Pitts., 1976. Cert. tchr. Pa. Dept. Edn., 1977. Tchr. Meml. Elem. Sch. Bethel Pk. (Pa.) Sch. Dist., 1974—. Avocations: reading, gardening, hiking. Office: Memorial Elem Sch 3301 South Park Rd Bethel Park PA 15102

CHOATE, MELODY LYNN, mathematics professor; b. Newton, Kans., Nov. 13, 1964; d. Bruce R. and Phyllis C. Southard. MA, U. Kans., Lawrence, 1987—90. Math instr. Rockhurst Coll., Kansas City, 1990—91, Butler CC, El Dorado, Kans., 1991—. Mem.: Kans. NEA. D-Liberal. United Methodist. Avocation: reading. Home: 809 Fredrick Dr El Dorado KS 67042 Office: Butler CC 901 S Haverhill Rd El Dorado KS 67042 Personal E-mail: mchoate@butlercc.edu.

CHODOROFF, NANCY ARLENE, elementary school educator; m. Arthur David Chodoroff, June 21, 1970; children: Joel Daniel, Joshua Adam. BE, Temple U., Phila., 1972, MEd, 1987. Cert. elem. edn. tchr. Dept. Edn., Pa., 1973, reading specialist Dept. Edn., Pa., 1987, elem. tchr. Dept. Edn., NJ, 1987, K-12 reading tchr. Dept. Edn., NJ, 1987. Tchr. Sch. Dist. Phila., 1972—74, Bensalem Twp. Schs., Pa., 1982—86, Ewing Twp. Schs., NJ, 1987—; adj. prof. Rider U., Lawrenceville, NJ, 2000—. Presenter in field. Mem.: NJ Coun. Social Studies, NJ. Mid. Sch. Assn., Nat. Mid. Sch. Assn., Nat. Assn. Secondary Sch. Prins. (assoc.; mem. nat. task force on mid. level leadership 2006—). Avocations: reading, music, clarinet. Office: GJ Fisher Mid Sch 1321 Lower Ferry Rd Ewing NJ 08618

CHODOROW, NANCY JULIA, psychotherapist, educator; b. NYC, Jan. 20, 1944; d. Marvin and Leah (Turitz) C.; children: Rachel Esther Chodorow-Reich, Gabriel Issac Chodorow-Reich. BA, Radcliffe Coll., 1966; PhD, Brandeis U., 1975; grad., San Francisco Psychoanalytic, 1993. Cert. in adult psychoanalysis Am. Psychoanalytic Assn., 1993. From lectr. to assoc. prof. U. Calif., Santa Cruz, 1974-86, from assoc. prof. sociology to prof. Berkeley, 1986—2005, clin. faculty dept. psychology, 1999—, prof. emeritus, 2005. Faculty Psychoanalytic Inst. New Eng., East, San Francisco Psychoanalytic Inst., 1994—, Psychoanalytic Inst. New England, East, 2005—, Boston Psychonalytic Inst., 2005—, Mass. Inst. Psychoanalysis; vis. prof. psychiatry Harvard Med. Sch., 2005-06. Author: The Reproduction of Mothering, 1978 (Jessie Bernard award Sociologists for Women in Soc. 1979, named one of Ten Most Influential Books of Past 25 Years, Contemporary Sociology 1996), 2nd edit., 1999, Feminism and Psychoanalytic Theory, 1989, Femininities, Masculinities, Sexualities, 1994, The Power of Feelings: Personal Meaning in Psychoanalysis, Gender, and Culture, 1999 (L. Bryce Boyer prize Soc. for Psychol. Anthropology 2000); contbr. articles to profl. jours. Fellow Russell Sage Found., NEH, Ctr. Advanced Study Behavioral Scis., ACLS, Guggenheim Found., Radcliffe Inst. for Advanced Study; recipient Contbn. to Women and Psychoanalysis award APA, L. Bryce Boyer prize Soc. for Psychol. Anthropology, 2000. Mem. Internat. Psychoanalytic Assn., Am. Psychoanalytic Assn., San Francisco Psychoanalytic Soc., Boston Psychoanalytic Inst., Psychoanalytic Inst. New Eng. East, Mass. Inst. Psychoanalysis. Office: 75 Richdale Ave #4 Cambridge MA 02140 Office Phone: 617-354-1200. Business E-Mail: nancy_chodorow@hms.harvard.edu.

CHOHLIS, DANA MARIE, school system administrator, theater director; b. San Francisco, Dec. 8, 1957; d. Francis P. and Irene Marion (Edwards) Severn; children: Alyssa Katrina, Christina Alexis. BA, Calif. State U., Hayward, 1992, MA, 2000. Cert. English tchr. Tchr. San Leandro (Calif.) Unified Sch. Dist., 1992—2005; instr. pub. spkg. Peralta C.C., Oakland, Calif., 2000—; asst. prin. Lafayette (Calif.) Sch. Dist., 2005—. Dir. A Midsummer Night's Dream, 1999, Bridge to Terabithia, 1998, Circus in the Wind, 1997, A Case for Two Detectives, 1996, Electra, 2001; performer: Cypress, Taming of the Shrew, Edinburgh Fringe Festival, 2002. Tech. grantee San Leandro Bus. Assn., 1997, 98, 99, 2004, Long's Drugs Adopt-a-Class grantee, 2001. Mem. San Leandro Tchrs. Assn. (sec.), No. Calif. Edn. Theatre Assn. (rep. mem. English/lang. arts stds. com., master tchr., retention program coord.), Alameda YAcht Club (sec. exec. bd. 2002-2004). Avocations: sailing, yacht racing, acting, dance, hiking. Home: 1448 Church Ave San Leandro CA 94579-1523 Office Phone: 510-895-7985. E-mail: argumentationclass@yahoo.com, danabegood@yahoo.com.

CHOI, NAMHONG LEE, retired psychologist; b. Fushun, China, Oct. 28, 1934; arrived in U.S., 1968; m. Hyosup Choi, Mar. 27, 1956; 3 children. MA in Psychology, Rowan U., 1972. Cert. clin. psychologist, sch. psychologist NJ. Staff clin. psychologist Vineland (NJ) Devel. Ctr., 1969—75, Graystone (NJ) Psychiat. Hosp., 1975—77, Woodbridge (NJ) Devel. Ctr., 1977—2003; ret. Founder, exec. dir. Korean Assn. Retarded Children, Seoul, 1967; interviewer Clergy Candidate Assessment, NJ, 1985—2002; advisor NJ Protection and Advocacy, 0993—. Mem.: APA. Methodist. Avocation: art. Home: 361 Elkwood Terr Englewood NJ 07631

CHOI, NAMOK, education educator; arrived in US, 1990; d. Chuntack and Bockran (Lee) Choi; m. Robert Roy Eagle, July 20, 2002. BA, Sungshin Womens U., Seoul, 1983; MS, Okla. State U., 1993, PhD, 1997. Tchr. Dept. Edn., Kwangwon, Republic of Korea, 1983—90; from rsch. asst. to tchg. asst. Okla. State U., Stillwater, 1991—97; asst. prof. Ga. So. U., Statesboro, 1997—2000, U. Louisville, 2000—04, assoc. prof., 2004—. Mem. editl. bd.: Jour. Social Psychology, 1999—, Jour. Counseling and Devel., 2004—, reviewer: Jour. Ednl. Psychology, 2003—; contbr. articles to profl. jours. Vol. St. John Homeless Ctr., Louisville, 2001—03; bd. dirs. Louisville Korean Sch., 2004—. Mem.: Am. Ednl. Rsch. Assn. (proposal reviewer 1998—, session chair 1999, newsletter editor 2001—03, session chair 2004, textbook reviewer 2004, co-chair jur. faculty mentoring 2005, newsletter editor 2005, program co-chair Divsn. E counseling sect. 2006). Democrat. Presbyterian. Avocations: literature, reading, gardening, tennis. Office: Univ Louisvile Coll Edn and Human Devel Louisville KY 40292 Business E-Mail: namok@louisville.edu.

CHOI, SYLVIA SEUNG-YUN, pediatrician, educator; d. Tai-Soon and Yong-ui Choi; m. Thomas Michael Chalifoux, Dec. 1, 2001. MD, Boston U., 1994. Pediat. residency U. Pitts. Children's Hosp., 1994—97; pediat. chief resident U. Pitts. Sch. Medicine, 1997—98, clin. instr. pediat., 1998—2001, asst. prof. pediat., 2001—. Med. dir. ltd. stay unit Children's Hosp. Pitts., 1998—. Bd. dirs. Healthy Homes Resources, Pitts., 2004—06. Named one of Best Drs. in Am., 2001—06; named to Guide to America's Top Pediatricians, Consumers' Rsch. Coun. Am., 2006; recipient Health Care Hero award, Pitts. Bus. Times, 2002, Cmty. Champion, Jefferson Awards, 2002, Faculty Recognition award, U. Pitts. Sch. Medicine, 2003, 2005, Patient Satisfaction award, Children's Hosp. Pitts., 2004. Fellow: Am. Acad. Pediat. Office: Children's Hosp Pitts 3705 Fifth Ave Pittsburgh PA 15213 Office Phone: 412-692-5135.

CHOICE, PRISCILLA KATHRYN MEANS (PENNY CHOICE), retired educational association administrator; b. Rockford, Ill., Nov. 8, 1939; d. John Z. and Margaret A. (Haines) Means; m. Jack R. Choice, Nov. 14, 1964; children: William Kenneth, Margaret Meta. BA, U. Wis., 1963; MEd, Nat.-Louis U., 1990; MA, N.E. Ill. U., 1995. Field rsch. dir. Tatham-Laird and Kudner Advt., Chgo., 1964-69; drama specialist Children's Theatre Western Springs (Ill.), 1969-81; gifted teaching asst. Sch. Dist. 181, Hinsdale, Ill., 1980-84; tchr. Sch. Dist. 99, Cicero, Ill., 1984-85; gifted edn. program coord. Cmty. Consolidated Sch. Dist. 93, Carol Stream, Ill., 1985-99; coord. gifted edn. and fine arts Ednl. Svcs. Divsn., Lake County Regional Office Edn., Grayslake, Ill., 1999—2004; retired, 2004—. Drama specialist, cons. Choice Dramatics, Hinsdale and Clarendon Hills, Ill., 1976-2004; producing dir. Mirror Image Youth Theatre, Hinsdale, 1986-88; adj. prof. Coll. DuPage, Glen Ellyn, Ill., 1990-92, Nat.-Louis U., Evanston, Ill., 1991—, Aurora (Ill.) U., 1995—, Govs. State U., University Park, Ill., 1992-93; internat. cons. in gifted edn. and drama-in-edn., 1989—; co-chair advocacy com. Ill. Assn. Gifted Children, 2002-05, co-chair underserved populations, 05—; trustee Friends of the Lake Co. Discovery Mus., 2003—; chair arts divsn. Nat. Assn. for Gifted Children, 2003-05, sec., treas. global awareness divsn., 2005—; tchr. First Folio Shakespeare Festival, 2005— Contbg. author Gifted/Arts Resource Guide, 1990; contbg. editor Ill. Theatre Assn., Followspot News, 1992-95. 96-2002. Mem. gifted adv. com. Ednl. Svc. Ctr., Wheaton, Ill., 1987—90, 1992—95, Regional Office of Edn., Wheaton, 1995—99, Northeastern Ill. U.1993-95., Chgo., 1993—95; co-chair advocacy Com. Ill. Assn. for Gifted Children, 2002—05, ch-chair underserved populations com., 2005—; bd. dirs. Ill. Theatre Assn., Chgo., 1983—87. Recipient Ill. State Bd. Edn. gifted edn. fellowship, 1988, AAUW continuing edn. scholarship, 1986, 90, Excellence award Ill. Theatre Assn., 1991, Excellence award Ill. Math. and Sci. Acad., 1990, 98, Recognition of Excellence, No. Ill. Planning Commn. Gifted Edn., 1990, Award of Excellence Ill. and Math. Sci. Acad., 1998. Mem. ASCD, World Coun. on Gifted Edn., Nat. Assn. Gifted Children, Ill. Assn. Gifted Children (membership chmn. 1992-94, advocacy com. 1995—, co-chair advocacy com. 2002-05, co-chair underserved populations 2005—), Ill. Coun. Gifted, Am. Assn. Theatre in Edn., Ill. Theatre Assn. (bd. dirs. 1983-87, Outstanding Achievement award 1991), Inst. for Global Ethics, Ill. Alliance Arts Edn., Theatre Western Springs, Phi Delta Kappa. Avocations: swimming, walking, reading. Home and Office: 113 S Prospect Ave Clarendon Hills IL 60514-1422 Office Phone: 630-452-6675. E-mail: pennychoice@comcast.net.

CHOKSI, MARY, investment company executive; BA in French, U. Minn.; MA in Internat. Rels., John Hopkins U.; MPA, U. Minn. With pension devel. divsn. World Bank, sr. program officer South and S.E. Asia; mng. dir. Strategic Investment Ptnrs. Inc. and Emerging Markets Investors Corp., Arlington, Va., 1987—. Bd. mem. Emerging Markets South Asia Fund, Emerging Markets Quantitative Portfolio, HJ Heinz Co. Trustee Nat. Mus. Women in the Arts; bd. dirs. Beauvoir-The Nat. Cathedral Elem. Sch. Office: Strategic Investment Group 16th Fl 1001 19th St N Arlington VA 22209-1722

CHOLDENKO, GENNIFER, writer; married; 2 children. BA cum laude with honors, Brandeis Univ.; BFA in Illustration, RI Sch. Design. Author: (children's books) Moonstruck: The True Story of the Cow Who Jumped Over the Moon, 1997, Notes From a Liar and Her Dog, 2001, Al Capone Does My Shirts, 2004 (Newbery Honor Book, 2005, Am. Libr. Assn. Notable Book, 2005, Best Children's Book of Yr, Publisher's Weekly), Tales of a Second-Grade Giant, 2005. Mailing: c/o Penguin Group Putnam Publicity 345 Hudson St New York NY 10014

CHOLDIN, MARIANNA TAX, librarian, educator; b. Chgo., Feb. 26, 1942; d. Sol and Gertrude (Katz) Tax; m. Harvey Myron Choldin, Aug. 28, 1962; children: Kate and Mary (twins). BA, U. Chgo., 1962, MA, 1967, PhD, 1979. Slavic bibliographer Mich. State U., East Lansing, 1967—69; Slavic bibliographer, instr. U. Ill., Urbana, 1969—73, Slavic bibliographer, asst. prof., 1973—76, Slavic bibliographer, assoc. prof., 1976—84, head Slavic and East European Libr., 1982—89, head, prof., 1984—2002, dir. Russian and East European Ctr., 1987—89, C. Walter and Gerda B. Mortenson Disting. prof., 1989—2002, dir. Mortenson Ctr. for Internat. Libr. Programs, 1991—2002, prof. emerita, 2003—. Author: Fence Around the Empire: Russian Censorship, 1985; editor: Red Pencil: Artists, Scholars and Censors in the USSR, 1989, Books, Libraries and Information in Slavic and East European Studies, 1986. Chair Soros Found. Network Libr. Program Bd., 1997—2000; pres. coun. Rudomino Libr., 2005—. Recipient Pushkin gold medal for contbns. to culture, Russian Presdl. Coun. on Culture, 2000. Mem. ALA (John Ames Humphry/OCLC/Forest Press award 2005, Internat. Librarianship award 2005), Am. Assn. for Advancement of Slavic Studies (pres. 1995), Phi Beta Kappa. Jewish. Home: 888 S Michigan Ave #403 Chicago IL 60605 Personal E-mail: mcholdin@ameritech.net.

CHOLEWKA, PATRICIA ANNE, health facility administrator; m. Michael A. Cholewka; children: Maureen, Kathleen. Diploma in Nursing, Bellevue Sch. Nursing, 1967; BSN magna cum laude, Castleton State Coll., 1979; MPA in Pub. and Nonprofit Mgmt. Policy, NYU, 1987; EdD in internat. Edn. Devel., Columbia U., 1999; MA in Healthcare Informatics, NYU, 2005. RN; cert. nursing adminstrn. ANA; cert. Nat. Assn. Healthcare Quality. Mgr. med.-surg. clin. svcs. in acute and managed care orgns., 1967-95; asst. prof. dept. nursing NY Coll. Tech., CUNY, N.Y.C., 1995—; rschr. healthcare policy and econ. mgmt., 1993—. Healthcare orgn. devel. cons. Razgrad Hosp., Bulgaria, 1993, Kaunas Med. Acad. Hosp., Lithuania, 1996-98, Lviv (Ukraine) Mcpl. Health Dept., 1998; reviewer curriculum med. quality mgmt., Am. Coll. Med. Quality, 2005; asst. prof. Dept. Nursing, Coll. Tech. CUNY, 2006—. Author: Comparative Analysis of Two Post-Soviet Healthcare Organizations in Lithuania and Ukraine: Implications for Continuous Quality Improvement, 1999, Factors Affecting Sustainable Health Care Management Programs in Post-Soviet Transitional Economics; editor Jour. Healthcare Quality; guest editor Internat. Jour. Econ. Devel.; mem editl. bd Nursing Outlook, Jour. Nursing Scholarship, Jour. Transcultural Nursing. Mem. citizen emergency response team, Bay Ridge, 2004—; mem. cmty. coun., 2003—. Recipient Disting. Rsch. award, Columbia U., 1999, Fed. Nurse Traineeship award, NYU, 2003. Mem. Phi Delta Kappa, Sigma Theta Tau. Republican. Roman Catholic. Personal E-mail: pacholewka@verizon.net.

CHONMAITREE, TASNEE, pediatrician, educator, epidemiologist; b. Bangkok, Dec. 9, 1949; came to U.S., 1975; d. Surajit and Arporn (Maitong) C.; m. Somkiat Laungthaleong Pong, June 27, 1981; children: Ann L. Pong, Dan L. Pong. BS, Mahidol U., 1971; MD, Siriraj Med. Sch., 1973. Diplomate Am. Bd. Pediat., Am. Bd. Pediat. Infectious Diseases. Rotating intern Siriraj Hosp., Bangkok, 1973—74, resident in pediat., 1974—75, Lloyd Noland Hosp., U. Ala., Birmingham, 1975—78; fellow infectious disease U. Rochester, NY, 1978—81; asst. prof. pediat. U. Tex. Med. Br., Galveston, 1981—87, asst. prof. pathology, 1985—87, assoc. prof. pediat. and pathology, 1987—94; prof. pediat. and pathology, 1994—. Assoc. dir. clin. virology lab. U. Tex. Med. Br., Galveston, 1985-92, dir. divsn. pediat. infectious disease, 1985-92. Contbr. 65 articles to profl. jours. Grantee NIH, 1993—. Fellow Am. Acad. Pediat., Pediat. Infectious Diseases Soc., Infectious Diseases Soc. Am.; mem. Soc. Pediat. Rsch., European Soc. for Pediat. Rsch., Tex. Infectious Disease Soc. Buddhist. Avocation: classical music. Home: 1906 Cherrytree Park Cir Houston TX 77062-2327 Office: U Tex Dept Pediat Med Br Ninth St & Market Galveston TX 77555-0001 Office Phone: 409-772-2798. Business E-Mail: tchonmai@utmb.edu.

CHOPP, REBECCA S., academic administrator; m. Frederick H. Thibodeau; 3 children. BA, Kans. Wesleyan U., 1974; MDiv, St. Paul Sch. Theology, 1977; PhD, U. Chgo., 1983; DD (hon.), Lehigh U. Asst. prof. theology U. Chgo. Div. Sch., 1982—86; asst. prof. Candler Sch. and Grad. Divsn. Religion Emory U., Atlanta, 1986—89, assoc. faculty Inst. Liberal Arts, 1987, assoc. faculty Inst. for Women's Studies, 1987, dean of faculty and acad. affairs Candler Sch. of Theology, 1993—97, prof. theology Candler Sch. and Grad. Divsn. Religion, 1993, Charles Howard Chandler prof. theology Grad. Divsn., 1996, interim provost, v.p. acad. affairs, 1997—98, provost, exec. v.p. for acad. affairs, 1998—2001, dir. grad. studies Inst. for Women's Studies; dean, Titus Street prof. theology and culture Yale U. Div. Sch., 2001—02; pres., prof. philosophy and religion Colgate U., 2002—. Bd. dirs. Scholars Press; trustee Carnegie Found. Author: The Praxis of Suffering: An Interpretation of Liberation and Political Theologies, 1986, The Power to Speak: Feminism, Language, God, 1989, Saving Work: Feminist Practices of Theological Education, 1995; Co-editor: Differing Horizons: Feminist Theory and Theology, 1997, Reconstructing Christian Theology, 1999; theology editor Religious Studies Rev., 1989-93; editor-at-large Christian Century, 1989-95; editor Quar. Rev., 1998-; editl. bd. Emory Theol. Studies, Religion and Ideology, Jour. of Religion, Word and World, Internat. Jour. of Practical Theology; contbr. articles to profl. publs. Recipient Alumna Achievement award Kans. Wesleyan U., 1990, Disting. Alumna award St. Paul Sch. of Theology, 1991, Founder's Day award Baker U., 1995, Alumna of Yr. award U. Chgo. Divinity Sch., 1997. Mem. Am. Acad. of Religion (pres. southeastern divsn.), Am. Theol. Soc. (chair women in leadership project). Office: Colgate U 301 James B Colgate Hall Hamilton NY 13346 Office Phone: 315-228-7444. Office Fax: 315-228-6010. E-mail: rchopp@mail.colgate.edu.*

CHOPRA-SUKUMARAN, PRATIBHA, secondary school educator; d. Harbans Lal and Vimla Chopra; m. Dinesh Kumar Sukumaran, Aug. 8, 1987; 1 child, Divya Leela Sukumaran. PhD, U. Buffalo SUNY, 1990. Lectr. Buffalo State Coll., SUNY, 2001—04; pps aide Williamsville (NY) Sch. Dist., 2004—. Sec. Hindi Samaj Buffalo, 1996—2006; cultural sec. India Assn. Buffalo, Williamsville, 1996—2005; tchr. Chinmaya Mission, Buffalo, 2000—06; sec. Asian Am. Womens Assn., Buffalo, 2000—06; mem. Amherst (NY) Youth Bd., 2005—06. Named Person of Yr., India Assn. Buffalo, 2005; scholar, Govt. of India, 1992; Nat. Sci. Talent scholar, 1970—82, Postdoctoral fellow, Assn. U. Women, 1991. Mem.: Nat. Sci. Tchrs. Assn. (assoc.). Home: 297 Sausalito Dr East Amherst NY 14051 Office: Williamsville S HS 5950 Main St Buffalo NY 14221 Office Phone: 716-626-8200. Personal E-mail: pratibhac@adelphia.net.

CHORAZY, ANNA JULIA LYJAK, retired pediatrician; b. Braddock, Pa., Feb. 25, 1936; d. Walter Lyjak and Cecilia Swiatkowski; m. Chorazy Chester John, May 6, 1961; children: Paula Ann, Mary Ellen, Mark Edward. BS, Waynesburg Coll., Pa., 1958; MD, Woman's Med. Coll. Pa., Phila., 1960. Gen. intern St. Francis Gen. Hosp., Pitts., 1960—61; resident in pediats., tchg. fellow Children's Hosp. Pa., Pitts., 1961—63, pediatrician devel. clinic, 1966—75; house physician, pediatrician Western Pa. Hosp., Pitts., 1963—66; med. dir. Home for Crippled Children, Pitts., 1975—90, Rehab. Inst., Pitts., 1990—98, Children's Inst., Pitts., 1975—2001, interim med. dir., 2002—03; clin. asst. prof. pediats. Children's Hosp. Pitts., U. Pa. Sch. Medicine, 1971—94, clin. assoc. prof. pediats., 1994—2001; ret. Pediat. cons. Children's Home Pitts., 1985—2001; lectr., spkr., presenter, cons. in field. Contbr. articles to profl. publs. Co-chmn. Ea. Allegheny County Health Corp., Pitts., 1980—85; med. cons. United Cerebral Palsy, Pitts., 1972—74; mem. adv. con. 10th Nat. Conf. Child Abuse and Neglect, Pitts., 1993. Recipient Miracle Maker award, Children's Miracle Network, 1995, Disting. Alumna award, Waynesburg Coll., 2002. Mem.: Allegheny County Med. Soc., Pa. Med. Soc., Am. Acad. Pediats. Avocations: comedy, theater, music, opera, reading. Home: 131 Washington Rd Pittsburgh PA 15221 Office: Children's Inst 1405 Shady Ave Pittsburgh PA 15217 Office Phone: 412-420-2268.

CHOTIN, ELIZABETH ETTLINGER, science foundation director; b. Chgo., Apr. 11, 1946; d. Ralph Jr. and Margery (Helm) Ettlinger; m. Arthur David Chotin, Apr. 5, 1970; children: Matthew, David. BA, Boston U., 1968. Mem. staff civil rights divsn. U.S. Dept. Justice, Washington, 1968-72; mem. nat. staff McGovern Presdl. Campaign, Washington, 1972; lexis supr. Mead Data Ctrl., N.Y.C., 1973-77; dir. Nat. Abortion Rights Action League Polit. Action Com., Washington, 1978-79; internat. affairs officer Carter Adminstrn., Washington, 1979-81; exec. dir. Fund for Integrative Biomed. Rsch., Washington, 1982-83; corp. and found. officer NAS, Washington, 1988-90; dir. devel. Washington Lawyers' Com. for Civil Rights, 1991-94; dir. Washington office Weizmann Inst. Sci., 1994—. Cons. infield, 1983-88. Campaign vol. Dem. Party; vol., officer Washington elem., jr. high and high schs.; active religious and polit. orgns., Washington. Democrat. Jewish. Avocation: sailing. Office: Am Com for Weizmann Inst Sci 1730 Rhode Island Ave NW Washington DC 20036-3101

CHOU, CHARISSA J., staff scientist; d. Si-Ying and Chung Yi Kao. BA in Acctg., Nat. Taiwan U., 1966; PhD in Stats., Kans. State U., 1972. CPA Pa., 1981. Statistician Kans. State U., Manhattan, Kans., 1972—73; asst. prof. Villanova U., Pa., 1974—81, assoc. prof., 1981—85; sys. analyst Rockwell Hanford Operations, Richland, Wash., 1985—88; principal scientist Westinghouse Hanford Co., Richland, 1988—93, prin. scientist, 1993—96; staff scientist V PAcific Northwest Nat. Lab., Richland, 1996—. Edtl. bd. Jour. of Environ. Monitoring and Assessment, Dordrecht, Netherlands, 2004—. Contbr. articles various profl. jours. and cptrs. in books. Recipient Outstanding Performance Svc. award, Pacific Northwest Nat. Lab., 2000, 2001, 2003, 2004, Women's Hist. Month Cert. of Honor award, 1998. Mem.: Nat. Rep. Com., Tri-Cities Chinese/Am. Assn. Achievements include development of liquid effluent monitoring program at the U.S. Dept. of Energy Hanford site. Avocations: gardening, travel, hiking. Office: Pacific Northwest Nat Lab K6-75 PO Box 999 Battelle Blvd Richland WA 99354 Office Phone: 509-372-3804. Office Fax: 509-376-2210. Business E-Mail: charissa.chou@pnl.gov.

CHOU, RUBY, finance educator, real estate broker, consultant; Adj. prof. U. La Verne, Calif., 2000—.

CHOUINARD, KAREN REIKO, elementary school educator; b. Honolulu, June 13, 1947; d. Rex Shinzen and Ruth Fujiko (Arakawa) Ishiara; m. Jerry Thomas Pardue, Oct. 21, 1978 (dec. Sept. 1994); 1 child, Holly; m. Nicholas Lambiase, Mar. 17, 1998 (div. July 1999)., m. John J. Chouinard, March, 19, 2005 BS, Western Ill. U., 1969; MA, U. No. Colo., 1971, 72. Tchr. home econs. Galesburg (Ill.) H.S., 1969-70; tchr. spl. edn. Jefferson County Pub. Schs., Golden, Colo., 1973-85, 87-94; tchr. 2d and 3d grade Englewood (Colo.) Christian Sch., 1985-86; tchr. 2d grade Jefferson County Pub. Schs., 1994—. Adj. instr. Colo. Christian U., Lakewood, 1989—; mem. recommended basic list com. Jefferson County Pub. Schs., 1993-95. Grantee Colo. Dept. Edn., 1976, Jefferson Found. Venture, 1988. Mem. ASCD, Colo. Coun. Learning Disabilities, Jefferson County Ednl. Assn., Jefferson County Internat. Reading Assn., Delta Kappa Gamma (rec. sec. 1988-89, pres. 1990-92, treas. 1994-96, Values award for exemplary performance 2001-2002). Avocations: reading, sewing. Home: 15771 Allendale Ln Golden CO 80403

CHOW, AMY, gymnast, Olympic athlete; b. San Jose, Calif., May 15, 1978; Student, Stanford U. Mem. USA Team, Hamamatsu, Japan, 1993, World Championships Team, Dortmund, Germany, 1994, Pan Am. Games Team, Mar del Plata, Argentina, 1995, U.S. Olympic Team, Atlanta, 1996. Placed 1st vault U.S. Gymnastics Championships, Ohio, 1992, 1st all around, vault, uneven bars, balance beam, 2d floor exercise, Mex. Olympic Festival, 1992, 3rd all around, vault, 1st floor exercise, USA/Japan Competition, Hamamatsu, Japan, 1993, 3rd vault Coca-Cola Nat. Championships, Nashville, Tenn., 1994, 1st vault, 2d uneven bars, 3rd all around Pan Am. Games, Mar del Plata, Argentina, 1995; recipient Gold medal Women's Gymnastics Team competition and Silver medal uneven bars, Olympic Games, Atlanta, 1996. Mem., U.S. Olympic Team, Sydney, 2000. Address: Octagon 2 Union St #300 Portland ME 04101-4295

CHOW, IRENE A., biopharmaceutical company executive; b. 1939; Pres. biopharm. divsn. Genelabs Techs., Inc., Redwood city, Calif., 1993-95, dir., 1993, pres., 1995-99, COO, 1995, pres., CEO, 1995—99, chmn., 1999—, CEO, 2001—04. Office: Genelabs Techs Inc 505 Penobscot Dr Redwood City CA 94063-4737 Fax: 650-368-0709. E-mail: investorinfo@genelabs.com.

CHOW, RITA KATHLEEN, nursing consultant; b. San Francisco, Aug. 19, 1926; d. Peter and May (Chan) Chow. BS, Stanford U., 1950, nursing diploma, 1950; MS, Case Western Res. U., 1955; profl. diploma in nursing edn. adminstrn, Columbia U., 1961, EdD, 1968; B of Individualized Studies, George Mason U., 1983. Asst. in teaching Stanford U., Calif., 1951—52; instr., dir. student health Fresno Gen. Hosp. Sch. Nursing, Calif., 1952—54; instr. Wayne State U. Coll. Nursing, Detroit, 1957—58; rsch. assoc., project dir. cardiovasc. nursing rsch. Ohio State U., Columbus, 1965—68; commd. officer USPHS, 1968, advanced through grades to nurse dir. (capt.), 1974; spl. asst. to dep. dir. Nat. Ctr. Health Svcs. Rsch., Health Svcs. and Mental Health Adminstrn., HEW, Rockville, Md., 1969—73, dep. dir. manpower utilization br., 1970—73; dep. dir. Office Long Term Care; dep. chief nurse officer USPHS, Rockville, 1973—77; chief quality assurance br. div. long-term care Office Stds. and Certification, Health Standards and Quality Bur., Health Care

Fin. Adminstrn., HHS, 1977—82; supervisory clin. nurse and spl. asst. to health systems adminstr. USPHS Indian Hosp., HRSA, HHS, Rosebud, SD, 1982—83; dir. patient edn., asst. dir. nursing G. W. Long Hansen's Disease Ctr., USPHS, Carville, La., 1984—89; dir. nursing Fed. Med. Ctr., Ft. Worth, 1989—95; pvt. cons., 1995—98; dir. Nat. Interfaith Coalition on Aging, Natl. Coun. on Aging, Washington, 1998—. Author: (book) Identifying Nursing Action with the Care of Cardiovascular Patients, 1967, Cardiosurgical Nursing Care: Understandings, Concepts and Principles for Practice, 1975; mem. editl. bd. Nursing and Health Care, 1983—95; contbr. articles to profl. jours. With Nurse Corps U.S. Army, 1954—57, with USAR, 1957—68. Recipient Nursing Svc. award, Assn. Mil. Surgeons U.S., 1969, Commendation medal, USPHS, 1972, Meritorious Svc. medal, 1977, Disting. Svc. medal, 1987, citation for outstanding contbn. to cardiovascular nursing, Am. Heart Assn., 1972—79, award for disting. achievement in nursing rsch., Nursing Edn. Alumni Assn., Columbia U. Tchrs. Coll., 1973, Disting. Alumnus award, Case Western Res. U. Sch. Nursing, 1979, Women's Honors in Pub. Svcs. award, ANA, 1988, USPHS Commendable Svc. medal, U.S. Dept. Justice, Bur. Prisons, 1995, Holistic Nurse of the Yr. award, Am. Holistic Nurses Assn., 2001, Artist of Life First prize, Internat. Womens Writing Guild, 1987, Chief Nurse Officer award, USPHS, 2003; grantee, Sigma Theta Tau, 1966. Fellow: Am. Assn. Advancement Sci., Am. Acad. Nursing, Gerontological Soc. Am., Nat. Gerontological Nursing Assn., Am. Assn. of Integrative Medicine (diplomate Coll. of Nursing 2003).

CHOY, JUDY, secondary school educator; children: Joshua Tam, Joseph Tam, Jeremy Tam. Tchr. Palo Alto H.S., Calif., 2000—. Office: Palo Alto HS 50 Embarcadero Rd Palo Alto CA 94301 Personal E-mail: jchoy1021@sbcglobal.net. E-mail: jchoy@pausd.org.

CHOYKE, PHYLLIS MAY FORD (MRS. ARTHUR DAVIS CHOYKE JR.), management executive, editor, poet; b. Buffalo, Oct. 25, 1921; d. Thomas Cecil and Vera (Buchanan) Ford; m. Arthur Davis Choyke Jr., Aug. 18, 1945; children: Christopher Ford, Tyler Van. BS summa cum laude, Northwestern U., 1942. Reporter City News Bur., Chgo., 1942-43, Met. sect. Chgo. Tribune, Chgo., 1943-44; feature writer OWI, N.Y.C., 1944-45; sec. corp. Artcrest Products Co., Inc., Chgo., 1958-88, v.p., 1964-88; pres. The Partford Corp., Chgo., 1988-90. Founder, dir. Harper Sq. Press div., 1966-90. Author: (under name Phyllis Ford) (with others) (poetry) Apertures to Anywhere, 1979; editor: Gallery Series One, Poets, 1967, Gallery Series Two, Poets—Poems of the Inner World, 1968, Gallery Series Three Poets: Levitations and Observations, 1970, Gallery Series Four, Poets, I am Talking About Revolution, 1973, Gallery Series Five/Poets—To An Aging Nation (with occult overtones), 1977; (manuscripts and papers in Brown U. Library). Bonbright scholar, 1942. Mem.: DAR (corr. sec. Gen. Henry Dearborn chpt. 1991—92, treas. 1992—2003, regent 2003—06), Acad. Am. Poets (NYC), Poetry Soc. Am. (NYC), Chgo. Press Vets. Assn., Soc. Midland Authors (bd. dirs. 1987—, treas. 1988—93, pres. 1993—95, membership dir. 1997—98, corr. sec. 1999—), Mystery Writers Am. (assoc.), John Evans Club (Northwestern U.), Arts Club Chgo. Home: 23 Windsor Dr Elmhurst IL 60126-3971

CHRETIEN, CAROL ANN, chemical engineer; b. Biddeford, Maine, Oct. 1, 1967; d. Roval Raymond and Yvonne Deodati C. BS in Chem. Engring., U. Maine, 1990, cert. advanced study, 1990. Chem. engr. Brown and Root, Houston, 1990-93, 95-96, Internat. Tech., Houston, 1994-95, Asea Brown Boveri, Houston, 1997—99, Fluor Corp., 2001—. Pulp and Paper Found. scholar, 1986-90. Mem. AICHE, Technical Assn. Pulp and Paper Industry (treas. student sect. 1989). E-mail: Chret@hotmail.com, CChretien@aol.com.

CHRETIEN, JANE HENKEL, internist; b. Jersey City, Mar. 24, 1941; m. Paul B. Chretien, Apr. 11, 1970; children: Jean Paul, Yves. AB, Barnard Coll., 1962; MD, N.J. Coll. Medicine, 1966; MPH, Harvard U., 1970. Diplomate Am. Bd. Internal Medicine, Am. Bd. Infectious Disease. Intern Cornell U. Med. Divsn-Bellevue Hosp. Ctr., N.Y.C., 1966-67; resident Meml. Hosp. Sloan Kettering Inst. Med. Ctr., N.Y.C., 1967-69; fellow Georgetown U. Hosp., Washington, 1970-72, clin. instr., staff physician student health svc., 1972-75, asst. dir. student health svc., 1975-87, med. dir., 1987-94, clin. asst. prof., 1975-79, clin. assoc. prof., 1979-94; assoc. prof. George Washington U., 1994-98, clin. assoc. prof., 1998—. Fellow ACP; mem. Internat. Soc. Travel Medicine. Office Phone: 301-656-4010.

CHRISMAN, NANCY CAROL, city manager, director, small business owner; b. Walnut Ridge, Ark., Mar. 22, 1943; d. Williford Ray and Syble Oleeta (Atkinson) Cooksey; m. Herbert Dale Chrisman, June 4, 1961; children: Stanley Ray, Eric Dale. Student, Ark. State U., 1963. Payroll clk. GE, Jonesboro, Ark., 1965-66, 68; sec., bookkeeper 1st Christian Ctr., Jonesboro, 1969-76; payroll clk. GE, Jonesboro, 1976-77; office mgr. Barrett, Wheatley, Smith and Deacon, Jonesboro, 1977-88; adminstrv. asst. Richard Stevenson, M.D., P.A., Jonesboro, 1988-89; adminstr. N.E. Ark. Women's Clinic, P.A., Jonesboro, 1989-98; exec. dir. Jonesboro Ctrl. Planning Assn., 1999—2003; co-owner La Boutique Panache, Jonesboro, 2003—. Dir. Mid South Bank, Jonesboro, 1995—; mem. Widowed Persons Adv. Bd., Jonesboro, 1990-98. Charter bd. dirs., past sec., past chmn. Crime Stoppers, Jonesboro, 1991-95; pres. Showtime divsn. Found. Arts, Jonesboro, 1992; chmn. leadership coun. Jonesboro Cmty. Oriented Policing, 1998-99; dir. Cmty. Policing Inst., Knoxville, 1999—. Recipient Good Neighbor Spotlight award Sta. KAIT-TV, 1993. Mem. Med. Group Mgmt. Assn., Univ. Rotary Club (Paul Harris fellow 1995, dir. 1998-01), Jonesboro C. of C. (dir. 1994-99, treas. 1997, chmn. 1997-98, Leadership Jonesboro 1993), Pi Omega Pi Democrat. Baptist. Avocations: needlepoint, reading. Office: Jonesboro Ctrl Planning Assn 407 Union St Jonesboro AR 72403-9246

CHRIST, CAROL TECLA, academic administrator; b. NYC, May 21, 1944; d. John George and Tecia (Bobrick) Christ; m. Larry Sklute, Aug. 15, 1975 (div. Dec. 1983); children: Jonathan Sklute, Elizabeth Sklute. BA, Douglas Coll., 1966; M.Ph., Yale U., 1969, PhD, 1970. Asst. prof. English U. Calif., Berkeley, 1970-76, assoc. prof., 1976-83, prof., 1983—89, dean dept. English, 1985-88, dean dept. humanities, 1988, acting provost, dean, 1989-90, provost, dean Coll. Letters and Sci., 1990-94, vice chancellor, provost, 1994-2000; pres. Smith Coll., Northampton, Mass., 2002—. Fomer dir. summer seminars secondary and coll. tchrs. NEH; former tchr. Bread Loaf Sch. English; invited lectr. Am. Assn. Univs., Am. Coun. Edn. Author: The Finer Optic: The Aesthetic of Particularity in Victorian Poetry, 1975, Victorian and Modern Poetics, 1984; mem. editl. bd. Victorian Literature, The Victorian Visual Imagination, The Norton Anthology of English Literature; contbr. articles to profl. jours. Fellow: Am. Acad. Arts & Sci.; mem.: MLA. Office: Smith Coll College Hall 20 Northampton MA 01063

CHRIST, ROXANNE E., lawyer; BA, UCLA, 1982; JD, Loyola Law Sch., 1985. Bar: Calif. 1985. With Paul, Hastings, Janofsky & Walker, Latham & Watkins L.A., ptnr., 2001—. Office: Latham and Watkins LLC 633 W Fifth St Ste 4000 Los Angeles CA 90071

CHRISTENBURY, LEILA, education educator; BA English, Hollins Coll., 1972; MA English, U. Va., 1973; EdD English Edn., Va. Tech., 1980. Tchr. English Roanoke Cath. High Sch., Va., 1973—75, William Fleming High Sch., 1975—78; asst. prof. dept. English lang. and lit. U. No. Iowa, Cedar Falls, 1979—80; asst. prof. English dept. James Madison U., Harrisonburg, Va., 1982—86; asst. prof., assoc. prof. Sch. Edn. Va. Commonwealth U., Richmond, 1968—95, prof. Sch. Edn., 1996—. Contbr. articles to profl. jours. Scholar, Va. Commonwealth U. Sch. Edn., 1993. Mem.: Va. Writers' Club, Va. Conf. English Educators, Va. Assn. Tchrs. English (treas., Frances Wimer award 2001), Assembly Women in Lit., Assembly Appalachian Lit., Assembly Lit. Adolescents, Nat. Conf. Rsch. Lang. and Lit., Nat. Coun. Tchrs. English (pres., Rewey Belle Inglis award Outstanding Women in English Edn. 1997), Omicron Delta Kappa, Phi Beta Kappa, Phi Kappa Phi, Phi Delta Kappa. Office: Va Commonwealth U Sch Edn PO Box 842020 Richmond VA 23284-2020

CHRISTENSEN, CYNTHIA L., music educator; b. Kittery, Maine, Dec. 16, 1970; d. Randall M. and Gloria D. Mills; m. Erik L. Christensen, June 21, 1997; 1 child, Ella L. B in Music Edn., U. Colo., Boulder, 1994. Instrumental dir. Ft. Morgan (Colo.) Mid. Sch., 1994—. Trustee United Meth. Ch., Ft. Morgan. Recipient Crystal Apple Tchg. award, Ft. Morgan Times Newspaper, 2006. Office: Ft Morgan Mid Sch 300 Deuel St Fort Morgan CO 80701 Office Phone: 970-867-8253.

CHRISTENSEN, DORIS ANN, antique dealer, researcher, writer; b. Safford, Ariz., Dec. 31, 1938; d. Joseph Solomon Welson and Bernice Beatrice (Blasius) Van Order; m. Donald Edward Christensen, Apr. 22, 1967. Student, Eastern Ariz. Coll., 1961-66. Sec. to dean of admissions Eastern Ariz. Coll., Thatcher, 1963-67; sec. to pres. United Homes Corp., Federal Way, Wash., 1969-89; office mgr. Heller Co. Realtors, Federal Way, Wash., 1990-94; antique dealer All That & Everything, Graham, Wash., 1995—. Author: Violin Bottles, Banjos, Guitars and Other Novelty Glass, 1995, Road to Rhyme in the U.S.A., 2006. Recipient Good Citizen's cert., DAR, 1957, Oustanding Citizenship award, Am. Legion, Safford, 1957. Mem.: Violin Bottle Collectors Assn. (editor newsletter U.S. and Can. 1995—98). Avocations: collectibles, writing. Office: All That & Everything 9908-196th St E Graham WA 98338-8460

CHRISTENSEN, GLORIA JEAN, secondary school educator; b. Stevens Point, Wis., Oct. 23, 1947; d. Raymond and Eleanore Mikich; m. Roland A. Christensen, June 22, 1968; children: Tara, Dana. BS, U. Wis., Stevens Point, 1970. Math. tchr. Argyle H.S., Wis., 1970—74, sci. tchr. Wis., 1974—76, Phelps H.S., Wis., 1979—. Curriculum biotech cadre CESA @9, Tomahawk, Wis., 1993; curriculum starlab cadre CESA #9, Wis., 1995; Selected to HS Leaderhip conf., Washington, 2004. Pres. St. Peter's Bd. Edn., Eagle River, Wis., 1988—90. Mem.: Wis. Edn. Assn. (v.p. Phelps chpt. 2003—), Wis. Soc. Sci. Tchrs., Nat. Sci. Tchrs. Assn. Avocations: gardening, golf, travel, water sports. Home: PO Box 1716 Eagle River WI 54521 Office: Phelps HS 4451 Old School Rd Phelps WI 54554 Office Phone: 715-545-2724. E-mail: gchristensen@phelps.k12.wi.us.

CHRISTENSEN, IONE, Canadian senator; b. Oct. 10, 1933; m. Arthur Christensen; children: Paul, Philip. BSBA, Coll. San Mateo. With Govt. Yukon Territory, 1958—67; justice of peace, juvenile ct. judge, chair City of Whitehorse, 1971—75, mayor, 1975—79; commr. Yukon Territory, 1979; pres. Hospitality North Ltd., 1980—86; with Energy, Mines and Resources Can. office City of Whitehorse, 1984—89; chair adv. com. on waste mgmt. Govt. of Yukon, 1989—94; ptnr. Cameras North, 1994—99; senator The Senate of Can., Ottawa, 1999—. Chair Assn. Yukon Municipalities, 1975—79; bd. dirs. Fedn. Can. Muncipalities, Petro-Can., Panarctic Oil Ltd.; chair Yukon Placer Mining Guidelines Rev. Com., 1980—86; vice-chair Yukon Econ. Coun., 1984—89; exec. dir. Crossroads Alcohol and Drug Treatment Ctr., 1989—94; bd. dirs. Nat. Assn. Can. Land Surveyors. Office: 552-N Centre Block The Senate of Canada Ottawa ON Canada K1A 0A4

CHRISTENSEN, JILL RENEE, mathematics educator; b. Sioux Falls, SD, Nov. 21, 1960; d. Robert Lowell and Carol Ann Smidt; m. Doyle Shawn Christensen, July 26, 1980; children: April, Derek. BA in Math., Northwestern Coll., Orange City, Iowa, 1983. Math. tchr. Parker Ind. Sch. Dist., SD, 1983—. Sec., treas. Profl. Educators Parker, 1995—. Adv. bd. nat. girls and women sports SD HS Activities Assn., 2004—; vol. song leader, piano player children's group Lennox, SD, 1978—; Sunday sch. tchr., youth group leader II Ref. Ch. Named to Athletic Hall of Fame, Northwestern Coll., 1990. Mem.: SD Coun. Math. Tchrs., SD Volleyball Coaches Assn., SD HS Coaches Assn. (SD Volleyball Coach of the Yr. 1990). Avocations: reading, sports, running. Home: 45931 279th St Parker SD 57053 Office: Parker Sch Dist 60-4 PO Box 517 Parker SD 57053

CHRISTENSEN, KAREN KAY, lawyer; b. Ann Arbor, Mich., Mar. 9, 1947; d. Jack Edward and Evangeline (Pitsch) Christensen; m. Kenneth Robert Kay, Sept. 2, 1977; children: Jeffrey Smithson, Braden Kay, Bergen Kay. BS, U. Mich., 1969; JD, U. Denver, 1975. Bar: Colo. 1975, DC 1976, U.S. Supreme Ct. 1979. Atty., advisor office of dep. atty. gen. U.S. Dept. of Justice, Washington, 1975-76, trial atty. civil rights div., 1976-79; legis. counsel ACLU, Washington, 1979-80; staff atty. DC Pub. Defender Svc., Washington, 1980-85; asst. gen. counsel Nat. Pub. Radio, Washington, 1985-93; gen. counsel Nat. Endowment Arts, Washington, 1993-98, acting dep. chmn. for grants and partnership, 1997-98, dep. chmn. grants and awards, 1998—2001; arts cons., 2002—. Mem. DC Bd. Profl. Responsibility, 1990—98, chair, 1996—98. Bd. dirs. Corcoran Art Mus., 2001—03, Liz Lerman Dance Exch., 2002—05, Tucson Pima Arts Coun. Pub. Art Com., 2005—; vice chair bd. Mus. Contemporary Art, Tucson, 2005—; mem. pub. adv. com. KUAT-KUAZ (Pub. Radio/TV Com. Group), 2005—. Mem.: NCA/ACLU (mem. exec. bd. 1986—93, chair 1993), DC Bar Assn., Phi Beta Kappa. Personal E-mail: chriskk2@earthlink.net.

CHRISTENSEN, KATHARINE ELEANOR, retired education educator; b. Camden, N.J., Sept. 20, 1929; d. Werner Paul and Agatha Ruth (Raisbeck) Meyer; m. John Paul Christensen, July 5, 1952; 1 child, Carrie Joan. BA, Mich. State U., 1951, MA, 1958; PhD, U. Del., 1972. Tchr. various pub. sch. systems, Mich., 1951-62; dir. pvt. kindergarten, nursery sch. Newark, Del., 1965-67; dir. tutoring program for early readers, 1967-70; supr. student tchrs. U. Del., Newark, 1971-72; assoc. prof. West Chester (Pa.) U., 1972-90, prof. edn., 1990-94, asst. chair, grad. coord., 1980-93, ret., 1994. Cons. in field; presenter at profl. confs. Contbr. articles on reading to ednl. publs. Grantee Commonwealth of Pa., 1987. Mem. Internan. Readin Assn., Keystone State Reading Assn., Phi Delta Kappa, Delta Kappa Gamma, Alpha Upsilon Alpha. Avocation: travel.

CHRISTENSEN, SONYA MARIE, school librarian; b. Ithaca, N.Y., Mar. 14, 1947; d. Raymond Hruschka and Marie Georgianna Poitras; m. Carl William Christensen, Sept. 22, 1968; children: Candace, Benjamin, Michael, Sally. BA, Antioch Coll., Yellow Springs, Ohio, 1969; MLS, SUNY, Buffalo, 1989. Cert. permanant tchg. cert. N.Y., publ. librarian N.Y., 1989. Librarian U.S. Peace Corps, Jamaica, 1969—71, S.W. Oreg. CC, Coos Bay, Oreg., 1971—85, librarian, acting dir., 1983—84; med. librarian Vet. Med. Ctr., Portland, 1981—82; children's librarian Coos Bay (Oreg.) Publ. Libr., 1985—87; sch. librarian Rochester (N.Y.) City Sch. Dist., 1989—91, Pittsford Ctrl. Sch. Dist., Rochester, NY, 1991—2003. Treas. Greater Rochester (N.Y.) Area Sch. Librs., 1992—95; tech. coord. Pittsford Mid. Sch., Rochester, NY, 1993—98; tchr. trainer Pittsford Ctrl. Schs., 1995—2003; mentor Rochester (N.Y.) Area Librarians, 1998—2003. State bd. mem. League of Women Voters, Coos Bay, Oreg., 1975—76, pres., 1976—77; organizer start library Sch. #56, Rochester, NY, 1990, Grabow, South Africa, 2002, Jamaica, 1970, Pittsford Mid. Sch., 1993; tax preparer CASH/United Way, Rochester, NY, 2004—; organizer, gardener St. Paul Pocket Park, Rochester, NY, 2004—. Recipient Woman of Yr., Coos Bay Area Jaycees, 1974—75; grantee Melchor scholarship, Am. Library Assn., 1988. Mem.: Hope Found., St. Paul Pocket Park Neighborhood Assn., Iroquois Garden Club (horticulturalist 2004—). Democrat. Roman Catholic. Avocations: gardening, travel. Home: 218 Navarre Rd Rochester NY 14621

CHRISTENSEN, VICKIE J., secondary school educator; b. Idaho Falls, Apr. 14, 1958; d. Shirley Guymon; m. Neil Christensen, Aug. 7, 1976; children: Ryan, Tyson. BA in English, Idaho State U., Pocatello, 1980, MEd, 2006. Tchr. Skyline High Sch., Idaho Falls, 1980—2006. Achievements include research in education; writing. Office Phone: 208-525-7770. E-mail: chrivick2d91.k12.id.us.

CHRISTENSON, EILEEN ESTHER, geriatrics nurse; b. Fosston, Minn., July 26, 1950; d. Arthur L. and Gertrude E. (Jaworsky) Maruska; m. Leonard Dale Christenson, Mar. 16, 1968; children: Kristy, Dale, Melissa, Alicia. Grad., Thief River Fall Tech. Inst., Minn., 1967. LPN, Ill., N.Mex., Minn. Staff nurse Beltram (Minn.) Nursing Home, 1990—, Clearwater County Meml. Hosp., Bagley, Minn. Troop leader Land O'Lakes coun. Girl Scouts U.S., 1974-89. 1st lt. USAF, 1968-76, Vietnam. Decorated Purple Heart, Silver Cross, Bronze Star with bronze oak leaf cluster. Mem. VFW, Am. Legion, Eagles 351. Home: 8161 Hillcrest Dr NE Bemidji MN 56601-8531

CHRISTIAN, BETTY JO, lawyer; b. Temple, Tex., July 27, 1936; d. Joe and Mattie Manor (Brown) Wiest; m. Ernest S. Christian, Jr., Dec. 24, 1960. BA summa cum laude, U. Tex., 1957, LL.B. summa cum laude, 1960. Bar: Tex. 1961, U.S. Supreme Ct. 1964, D.C. 1980. Law clk. Supreme Ct. Tex., 1960-61; atty. ICC, 1961-68, asst. gen. counsel Washington, 1970-72, assoc. gen. counsel, 1972-76, commr., 1976-79; ptnr. Steptoe & Johnson, Washington, 1980—. Atty. Labor Dept., Dallas, 1968-70 Fellow Am. Bar Found., Tex. Bar Found.; mem. ABA, FBA (Younger Fed. Lawyer award 1964), Tex. Bar Assn., Am. Law Inst., Am. Acad Appellate Lawyers, Adminstrv. Conf. US. Office: 1330 Connecticut Ave NW Washington DC 20036-1704 Office Phone: 202-429-8113. Business E-Mail: bchristi@steptoe.com.

CHRISTIAN, CAROLE ANN, psychologist, academic administrator; d. James Clifford and Jean LaBoyteaux Christian; m. Christopher Henry Hayden, Oct. 17, 1999; children: Jennifer, Kimberly, John, Jeff. BA in Psychology, Gettysburg Coll., Pa., 1965; MEd in Edn., Goucher Coll., 1966; MA in Counseling, Rider U., 1984; D in Psychology, Rutgers U., 1992. Cert. sch. psychologist NJ, 1984, profl. mediator Lemmen Inst., 1987, hypnotherapist Rankin, 1998, Gatekeeper Instr. QPR Suicide Prevention, 2006. Tchr. Cheltenham Schs., Wyncote, Pa., 1966—68, Riverside Sch., Princeton, NJ, 1968—69; tchr. spl. edn. Princeton (N.J.) Regional Schs., 1969—73, 1977—90; counselor Rider U., Lawrenceville, NJ, 1987—92, dir. counseling Westminster Choir Coll., 1992—, dir. counseling svcs., 1994—. Mem. dean's multi-cultural coun. Rutgers U., Piscataway, NJ, 1995—2000, mem. focus on diversity group, 2001—, coord. ednl. program Prayers for Bobby, 1996; lectr. in field. Pres. bd. edn. Pennington (N.J.) Nursery Sch., 1980—83. Recipient Ednl. Opportunity Program award, Westminster Choir Coll., 1998. Mem.: NEA, APA, Assn. U. and Coll. Counseling Ctr. Dirs. Office: Rider Univ and Westminster Choir Coll 101 Walnut Lane Princeton NJ 08540

CHRISTIAN, CLAUDETTE MARIE, lawyer; b. St. Thomas, V.I., June 1, 1954; d. Claude Victor and Elva Barbara (Daniel) C. BA magna cum laude, U. Pa., 1976; JD, Havard U., 1979. Bar: DC 1980. Counsel Export-Import Bank, Washington, 1979-84; assoc. Arent, Fox, Kinter, Plotkin & Kahn, Washington, 1984—; ptnr. Hogan & Hartson LLP, Washington, 1994—. Named one of Am.'s Top Black Lawyers, Black Enterprise Mag., 2003. Mem. Am. Bar Assn., Harvard Club, Phi Beta Kappa. Democrat. Home: 3001 Veazey Ter NW Washington DC 20008-5454 Office: Hogan & Hartson LLP 555 13th St NW Washington DC 20004-1109

CHRISTIAN, CORA L.E, health facility administrator, physician; b. St. Thomas, VI, Sept. 11, 1947; d. Alphonso Augustine and Ruth Christian; m. Simon B. Jones-Hendrickson, Oct. 23, 1976; children: Nesha Christian-Hendrickson, Marcus Christian-Hendrickson. BS in Biology, Marquette U., 1967; MPH, Johns Hopkins U., 1975; MD, Jefferson Med. Coll., Phila., 1971. Diplomate Am. Coll. Forensic Examiners, Am. Bd. Quality Assurance and Utilization Rev., Am. Acad. Family Practice. Pvt. family-based practice, Frederiksted, VI, 1975—; asst. commr. Dept. Health, St. Croix, VI, 1977—91; educator, CEO, now med. dir. VI Med. Inst., Inc, St. Croix, 1978—; dir., prin. investigator US VI Household Survey, St. Croix, VI, 1988; chief med. cons., med. dir. Hovensa, LLC, St. Croix, 1990—; cons. VI AIDS Edn. and Tng., NYC, 1992—2005. Pres. Caribbean Studies Assn., 2000—01; pres., exec. sec., treas. VI Med. Soc., St. Croix, 1995—. Contbr. articles to profl. jours., chapters to books. Bd. dirs. Am. Cancer Soc., St. Croix, 1991—2005. Named to Trail Blazers for Women's History, Women's Bus. Ctr., 2000; Paul Harris fellow, Rotary, 1997. Mem.: AARP (nat. bd. dirs. 2004—), Am. Acad. Family Physicians (com. mem. 1996—2005, pres. VI chpt. 1976—). Sgi/Buddhist. Avocation: dance. Home: PO Box 1338 Frederiksted VI 00841 Office: VI Med Inst Inc PO Box 5989 Christiansted VI 00823-5989 Office Phone: 340-712-2400. Office Fax: 340-712-2449. Personal E-mail: cchrisitian@aarp.org. E-mail: cchristi@viqio.sdps.org.

CHRISTIAN, MARY JO DINAN, educational administrator, educator; b. Denver, May 7, 1941; d. Joseph Timothy and Margaret Rose Dinan; m. Ralph Poinsett Christian, Aug. 27, 1966. BA, Regis U., Denver, 1964; MA, George Washington U., 1983. Cert. English educator, adminstrn. and supervision secondary edn. English tchr. Denver Pub. Schs., 1964-67, Prince George's County Pub. Sch., Md., 1967-81; vice-prin. Prince George's County High Sch., Md., 1981-97; program dir. Tchr. Equity Equals Achievement, 1997—99, tchr., mentor, 2002—. Presenter tchr. equity and student achievement Nat. Conf.; Generating Expectations for Student Achievement equity assurance coord. instrs. in-svc. and adminstrs., 1997—99; tchr. mentor, 2002; pres. Tchr. Equity Equals Student Achievement Inc.; owner Independence House Bed and Breakfast, Washington, 2000—. Columnist: WomenSpeak, 1981-91. Rep. Prince George's County Commn. Women UN Fourth World Conf. Women Forum, Beijing, 1995. Md. Ho. of Dels. recognition. Mem. ASCD, NEA (chair adminstrs. caucus 1991-93, adminstr.-at-large resolutions com. 1986-92, polit. action com. 1984-86, coord.-at-large women's caucus 1981-91, Creative Leadership award 1989, Human and Civil Rights award 1989), Md. State Tchrs. Assn. (state coord. Sen. Sarbane campaign 1982, state voter registration coord. 1984, issue coord. Tom McMillen campaign 1986, Women's Rights award 1988), Phi Delta Kappa, Alpha Delta Kappa. Home: 504 Independence Ave SE Washington DC 20003-1143

CHRISTIAN, MICHAELE CHAMBLEE, internist, oncologist; b. 1948; MD, Georgetown U., Washington, 1980. Diplomate Am. Bd. Internal Medicine. Assoc. dir. CTEP, NCI, Bethesda, Md. Mem.: Am. Assn. Cancer Rsch. (bd. dirs.). Office: National Cancer Inst Executive Plz N Rm 742 6130 Executive Blvd Bethesda MD 20892

CHRISTIAN, MILDRED STOEHR, health products executive; b. Phila., July 7, 1942; d. Harvey Edward and Alice Emily Stoehr. BS, Pa. State U., 1963, MS, 1965; PhD, Thomas Jefferson U., 1979. Sr. scientist McNiel Laboratories, a J and J Co., Fort Washington, Pa., 1965—79; pres. Argus Rsch. Laboratories, Horsham, 1979—89, Argus Internat., Inc., 1980—; sr. advisor sci. and compliance CRL - Argus Rsch., 1989—2003; chmn. and CEO Argus Health Products, LLC, 2004—. Dir. Pro-Pharmaceuticals, Inc., Newton, Mass., 2003—; founding editor, editor in chief Jour. Am. Coll. Toxicology, Washington, 1981—. Initiated hist. restoration of lamposts Franklin Lamposts, La., 2003—05; pres. Hist. Preservation Soc. - Restored 200 yr. old bldg., Phila., 2000—04; pres., bd. trustees Kensington M.E. Ch. (Old Brick), 1980—; donated children's libr. (Stoehr libr.) to Girard coll. Girard Coll., 2002—04. Recipient Lifetime Achievement award, ACT, 2004, Distinguished Scientists award, Genzyme Transgenics Corp., 2000, Outstanding Graduate award, Thomas Jefferson U., 1995. Mem.: Acad. Toxicologic Scientists (pres. 1999—2000), Teratology Soc. (pres. 1989—90), European Teratology Soc. (councilor 2002—), Am. Coll. Toxicology (pres. 1992—93), Soc. Quality Assurance (hon.), Plimsoll Club (state sec. 2000—), Patriotic Order Sons Am., Thomas Jefferson Alumni Soc. (pres. 1992—93). Conservative. Methodist. Avocations: piano, opera, travel. Office: Argus Health Products 933 Horsham Rd Horsham PA 19044 Office Phone: 215-672-8867.

CHRISTIAN, PEARL C., musician; b. N.Y.C., July 18, 1927; d. Joseph Obadiah and Clotilda Cecelia Clifton; m. Lloyd Micah Christian, Jan. 28, 1948; children: Peter Lloyd, Donna Laverne, Lawrence Micah. Piano instr. Queens Village Sch. of Music, N.Y., 1989—91, pvt. studio, N.Y., 1991—. Performer: (Concert) Bklyn. Queens Conservatory Music, 2000—05. E-mail: pcpianos1@aol.com.

CHRISTIAN, SHIRLEY ANN, journalist, author; b. Jan. 16, 1938; d. Herbert Walsh and Minnie Lucille (Acker) C. BA, Pittsburg State U., Kans., 1960; MA, Ohio State U., 1966. UN corr. AP, 1970-73, copy editor fgn. desk N.Y.C., 1974-77, chief of bur. Santiago, Chile, 1977-79; Latin Am. corr. Miami (Fla.) Herald, 1979-84; fgn. affairs reporter N.Y. Times, Washington, 1985-86, bur. chief Buenos Aires, 1986-91, bur. chief Ctrl. Am., 1991-93;

pres. Hemisphere Bus. Books, 1994-97; publ. editor, sr. writer Stowers Inst. for Med. Rsch., Kansas City, Mo., 1998—2003. Adj. prof. journalism Columbia U., 1977. Author: Nicaragua: Revolution in the Family, 1985, Before Lewis and Clark: The Story of the Chouteaus, The French Dynasty that Ruled America's Frontier, 2004. Nieman fellow Harvard U., 1973-74; recipient Pulitzer prize for internat. reporting, 1981, George Polk Meml. award for fgn. reporting, 1981. Home and Office: 6836 Glenwood St Overland Park KS 66204-1453 Personal E-mail: schristian@everestkc.net.

CHRISTIAN, SUZANNE HALL, financial planner; b. Hollywood, Calif., Apr. 28, 1935; d. Peirson M. and Gertrude (Engel) Hall; children: Colleen, Carolyn, Claudia, Cynthia. BA, UCLA, 1956; MA, Redlands U., 1979. CFP. Instr. L.A. City Schs., 1958-59, Claremont (Calif.) Unified Schs., 1972-84, dept. chair, 1981-84; fin. planner Waddell & Reed, Upland, Calif., 1982-96, sr. acct. exec., 1986; br. mgr. Hornor, Townsend & Kent, Claremont, 1996—2002, Linsco Pvt. Ledger Fin. Svcs., 2002—. Past corp. mem. Pilgrim Place Found., Claremont; lectr. in field. Author: Strands in Composition, 1979; TV cable host Money Talks with Suzanne Christian, 1993—. Legal and estate planning com. Am. Cancer Soc., 1988-95; profl. adv. com. YWCA-Inland Empire, 1987; treas. Fine Arts Scripps Coll., 1993-94; bd. dirs. Casa Colina Hosp., 1994-2003; past bd. dirs. Galelio Soc. Harvey Mudd Coll. Recipient Athena Internat. Businesswoman of Yr. award, 1997. Mem. Fin. Planning Assn., Estate Planning Coun. Pomona Valley (pres. 2001-2002, bd. dirs. 2000—), Claremont C. of C. (pres., bd. dirs. 1994-95), Curtain Raisers Club Garrison (pres. 1972-75), Circle of Champions (pres.'s coun. 1994-95, Silver Crest award 1985-87, 94-95, HTK top ten leader 1996-2003), Harvey Mudd Coll. Galileo Soc. (bd. dirs. 1997-98), Patriots Club (Chmns. award), Chairman's Club, Kappa Kappa Gamma (pres. 1970-74). Avocations: tennis, gardening, archaeology. Home: PO Box 1237 Claremont CA 91711-1237 Office: Linsco Pvt Ledger 419 Yale Ave Claremont CA 91711-4340 Fax: 909-625-3661.

CHRISTIAN-BROUGHAM, RUBY ROSALIE, education educator; d. Frank and Sylvia Arangure Brougham; m. William Steptoe Christian, IV, Dec. 20, 1996. PhD, U. So. Calif., L.A., 1998. Postdoctoral rschr. Nat. Inst. of Aging U. So. Calif., L.A., 1998—2000; asst. prof. Chapman U., Orange, Calif., 2000—. Curriculum devel. for criminal justice com. Nat. Alliance for the Mentally ill, Pasadena, Calif., 2005—. Author: (jour. article) Current Psychology, Internat. Jour. Aging & Human Development. Mem. Latino Orgn., Orange, 2006—, Human Soc., Pasadena, 2002—. Fellow Ruth L. Kirschstein Nat. Rsch. Svc. award, Nat. Inst. Aging, 1992—95. Mem.: Gerontol. Soc. Am. (assoc.), Western Psychol. Assn. (assoc.), Assn. Psychol. Sci. (assoc.). Office: Chapman Univ One University Dr Orange CA 92866 Office Phone: 714-744-7640.

CHRISTIAN-CHRISTENSEN, DONNA MARIE, congresswoman; b. Teaneck, NJ, Sept. 19, 1945; d. Almeric L. Christian and Virginia Sterling; children: Rabiah Green, Karida Green; m. Chris Christensen; stepchildren: Lisa, Esther, Bryan, David. BS, St. Mary's Coll., Ind., 1966; MD, George Washington U., 1970; LLD (hon.), Moravian Coll. Pvt. medical practice, 1973—74; cmty. health physician U.S. V.I. Dept. Health; med. dir. Gov. Juan F. Luis Hosp., St. Croix; vice chairperson U.S. V.I. Dem. Territorial Com., 1980; mem. U.S. V.I. Bd. Edn., 1984; committeewoman Nat. Dem., 1984; apptd. U.S. V.I. Status Commn., 1988-92; del. Dem. Nat. Conv.; at large repr. US Congress from VI, 1997—; chair Congl. Black Caucus Health Braintrust, 1999—. Mem. Resources Com., Small Bus. Com.; mem. Select Com. Homeland Security; mem. Congl. Caucus Women's Issues; mem. Steering Com. Congl. Travel and Tourism Caucus; mem. Congl. Rural Caucus, Congl. Nat. Guard and Res. Caucus. Trustee, founding mem. Caribbean Youth Orgn. Named an Most Influential Black Americans, Ebony mag., 2006; recipient Disting. Alumni award, George Washington U., Disting. Svc. award, Howard U. Sch. Medicine. Mem. Nat. Med. Assn. (trustee), Caribbean Studies Assn., V.I. Med. Inst., V.I. Med. Soc. (pres., sec.), Women's Coalition St. Croix, St. Croix Environ. Assn. Democrat. Achievements include first to be the female delegate from U.S. Virgin Islands. Office: 1510 Longworth Ho Office Bldg Washington DC 20515-0001 also: Dist Office Nisky Ctr Ste 207 St Thomas VI 00802 Office Phone: 202-225-1790. Office Fax: 202-225-5517. E-mail: donna.christensen@mail.house.gov.*

CHRISTIANSEN, BERNYCE LEEANN, librarian; b. St. Louis, Apr. 9, 1943; d. Elmer Ernst and Bernice (Kuehne) Wesling; m. Lawrence Lee, July 18, 1964; children: Kevin Lawrence, Karie Lynn, Kolleen Marie. BS, St. Louis U., 1965; MA in Libr. Sci., U. Mo., 1979. Cert. tchr., libr., adminstr., Mo. Tchr. Orchard View HS, Muskegon, Mich., 1966-68, Cath. Ctr. HS, Muskegon, 1968-69; libr. Webster Groves (Mo.) Pub. Libr., 1971-82; tchr. St. John the Baptist, St. Louis, 1982-83; libr. Ursuline Acad., St. Louis, 1983—; libr. cons., coord. Mo. Tech., 2005—. Treas. St. Louis Regional Libr. Network, 1984-86, sec., 1986-87, coord., 1987—. Author, editor: Directory of Libraries in St. Louis Area, biannual 1991-; editor St. Louis Librs. NETnews, 1987—. Voter registration vol. St. Louis County Bd. Election, 1975—. Recipient Career Devel. scholarship U. Mo., 1979. Mem. Am. Libr. Assn., Mo. Libr. Assn., Cath. Libr. Assn., Cath. Edn. Assn., Sch. Libr. Assn. Roman Catholic. Avocations: reading, walking, sports. Home: 9425 Big Bend Blvd Webster Groves MO 63119-3924 Office: Ursuline Acad 341 S Sappington Rd Saint Louis MO 63122-6397 Office Phone: 314-395-1305. Business E-Mail: bchristiansen@ursulinestl.org.

CHRISTIANSEN, MARGARET LOUISE, law librarian, lawyer; d. James Birch and Elizabeth P. Dempsey; m. Phillip Edward Christiansen, June 1, 1996. BSBA in Econs., William Woods Coll., 1980; JD, Regent U., 1994; MS in Info. Sci., Fla. State U., Tallahassee, Florida, 2005. Bar: Va. 1996. Lectr. internat. trade Jiangsu Poly. Inst., Zhenjiang, China, 1990, Qingdao U., Shangdong, China, 1991; dir. career svcs. Regent U. Sch. Law, Virginia Beach, Va., 1994—95; faculty liaison Regent U. Law Libr., 1995—98, asst. libr., 1998—99, asst. dir., 1999—. Contbr. articles to profl. publs. Kids ch. leader Coastlands Cmty. Ch., Chesapeake, Va., 2004—05. Recipient Am. Jurisprudence award in Real Property, Lawyers Coop. Pub. Co. and Regent U., 1991. Mem.: Va. Assn. Law Librs. (co-editor newsletter 2002—04, chair membership com. 2005—), Southeastern Chpt. Am. Assn. Law Librs. (mem. scholarship com. 2005—), Am. Soc. for Info. Sci. and Tech., Focus on Christian Law Librarianship, Am. Assn. Law Librs. (centennial celebration com. 2004—), Va. Bar Assn. Conservative. Avocations: camping, backpacking, canoeing, travel. Office: Regent Univ Law Libr 1000 Regent Univ Dr Virginia Beach VA 23464 Office Fax: 757-226-4451. E-mail: margchr@regent.edu.

CHRISTIANSEN, WENDY LYNNE, music educator; b. Clear Lake, S.D., Dec. 28, 1966; d. Lorrell Glen and Eleanore Ruth Allen; m. Kyle Thad Christiansen, July 19, 1986; children: Tyler Lucas, Courtney Adaire. MusB, U. S.D., 1990. Tchr. Viborg Pub. Sch. 60-5, SD, 1990—. Named Outstanding Young Educator, Jaycees, 1992. Mem.: Viborg Ministerial Assn. (chmn. music 1993—99), S.D. H.S. AA (mem. region I choral com. 1998—), S.D. Music Educators Assn., Nat. Fedn. Music Assn., Am. Choral Dirs. Assn. Avocations: scrapbooks, water-skiing, golf, reading, gardening. Business E-Mail: wendy-christiansen@k12.sd.us.

CHRISTIE, CHERYL ANN, athletic trainer and physical therapist; b. Bay Shore, N.Y., June 8, 1964; d. Bernard James and Lena (Guccione) C BA, SUNY, Stony Brook, 1986; MS, Ill. State U., 1989; BS, Downstate Med. Ctr., 1993. Cert. strength and conditioning specialist 2003, athletic trainer N.Y., lic. phys. therapist N.Y. Athletic trainer Bay Shore H.S., 1989—91, with South Sports Medicine and Orthop. Rehab. Ctr., Bay Shore, 1989—93; with Sports Medicine Resource, Stony Brook, 1993—94, Plainview Phys. Therapy, NY, 1994—97; athletic trainer, phys. therapist Paragon Phys. Therapy and Fitness Tng., Deer Park, 2006—. Office Phone: 631-242-9200. E-mail: paragonpt@getonline.net.

CHRISTIE, JACQUELINE ANN, nurse; d. Alexander Michael and Dorothy Agnes (Schneider) Hefter; m. Paul John Christie, Sept. 10, 1994; 1 child, Holly. Student, U. Wis., 1980—82; diploma in nursing, Moraine Park, 1985; diploma in writing, Inst. Children's Lit., 2004. LPN, Wis., 1985. CNA St. Francis Home, Fond du Lac, Wis., 1980—82; LPN Care Ctr., Fond du Lac, Wis., 1987—91, Fond du Lac (Wis.) County, 1991—2005. Author: The Shepherd's Bell Sheep, 2005, Roger's Big Adventure, 2005; prodr.: (CD) Sacrifice of Praise. Small group leader Taycheedah Correctional, Fond du lac, Wis., 1985—2003, praise and worship leader, 1985—2003; missions chair person Fond du lac Assembly of God, Fond du lac, Wis., 2003—05. Nominee Poet of Yr. award, Am. Poets Soc., 2005. Mem.: Fond du lac Assembly of God (missions chair 2003—), Gospel Music Assn. Republican. Avocations: singing, poetry, guitar, piano. Home and Office: 186 E 10th St Fond Du Lac WI 54935

CHRISTIE, PAMELA SUE, music educator; b. North Tonawanda, N.Y., May 14, 1953; d. William Edward and Martha Lee (Lancet) Fishback; m. Harold C. Christie, Oct. 11, 1986; 1 child, Michael Joseph. MusB in Edn., Grove City Coll., Pa., 1975; student, U. Buffalo, 1976—80. Tchr. music East Aurora (N.Y.) Pub. Schs., 1975—85, Kenmore (N.Y.) Town Tonawanda Union Free Sch. Dist., 1985—. Bd. dirs. Greater Buffalo (N.Y.) Youth Orch., 2000—03. Named String Music Educator of Yr., ECCMC/BPO, 2005. Methodist. Avocations: travel, string quartets. Business E-Mail: pamela_christie@kenton.k12.ny.us.

CHRISTINA, SONJA (ALISA MORRIS), writer, poet; b. Dec. 21, 1925; m. Desmond Halton Morris, June 17, 1950; 1 child, Belinda. Owner La Esmeralda Club and Restaurant, London, 1947—50; owner art gallery Domani, N.Y.C., 1968. Model for painter Sir Augustus John, London, 1941-43; dancer Phillis Dixy Prodns., London, 1943-45. Author: (poetry) Emotions, 1973, If, 2002, The Secret to Her Heart, 2002, Ground Zero, 2002; prodr. (play) The Future Was Yesterday, 1952; poem displayed at Mus. of Tolerance. Recipient 10 Merit awards World of Poetry, Outstanding Poetry award Am. Poetry Assn., 1986, Golden Poet award World of Poetry, 1985, 86, 88, 90, 91, 1st prize in short story Globe Contest, 1984, Editors Choice award Internat. Libr. Poetry, 1999, Recognition award Famous Poets Soc., 1999, Poets Fantasy award, 2000, Outstanding Achivement award Drury's Publs., 2002, nominated Poet of Yr. Internat. Soc. Poetry, 2005, others; world record holder (for personal jours.-293) Guinness Book of World Records, Editor's Choice award, Poetry Com. Internat. Libr. Poets, 2005. Mem. Internat. Soc. Poets (charter mem., Poet of Yr. 2005). Home: PO Box 142 Lenox Hill New York NY 10021-0012

CHRISTISON, MURIEL BRANHAM, retired museum director, art history educator; b. Mpls. d. Harold D. and Helen (Ferguson) Branham; children: Evelyn, Carolyn. BA, U. Minn., 1933, MA, 1940; diploma, U. Paris, 1936, U. Brussels, 1938. Grad. asst. dept. fine arts U. Minn., Mpls., 1933-36; curatorial rsch. asst. Mpls. Inst. Arts, Mpls., 1936-42, head edn., 1944-47; assoc. dir. Va. Mus. Fine Arts, Richmond, 1948-61; oper. and assoc. dir. Krannert Art Mus. U. Ill., Champaign, 1962-74, dir. Krannert Art Mus., 1975-82; ret., 1982; interim dir. Muscarelle Mus. Coll. William and Mary, Williamsburg, Va., 1984-85, 94-96, mem. vis. com., 1982-96, vis. prof. fine arts, 1983-98. Head grad. program mus. studies U. Ill., 1974—82; cons. U. Tex., Austin, Washington U., St. Louis, 1972—78, Ill. Arts Coun., 1968—82; v.p. Midwest Mus. Conf. Am. Assn. Mus., regional rep., 1972—82; examiner S.C. Arts Coun., 1984, 86, Ohio Arts Coun., 1986, Nat. Endowment for the Arts, 1973, 83, NEH, 1980. Author: numerous exhbn. catalogs; contbr. articles to profl. jours. Carnegie scholar Inst. Internat. Edn., 1936; CRB fellow Beligan-Am. Edn. Found., 1938; recipient Disting. Svc. award Midwest Mus. Conf., 1982 Mem.: Colonial Williamsburg Fund, William and Mary Found., Coun. Va. Mus. Fine Arts, Assn. Preservation Va. Antiquities, Am. Assn. Museums (regional rep. 1972—82, coun. 1972—82, surveyor, examiner 1982—), Assn. Art Mus. Dirs. (emerita 1982, hon. 1982—). Home: Apt 125 5700 Williamsburg Landing Dr Williamsburg VA 23185-5555 Personal E-mail: mbchri@aol.com.

CHRISTMAN, JOLLEY BRUCE, educational research executive, educator; b. Greenville, S.C., Aug. 30, 1947; d. James McDuffie and Mamie (Jolley) Bruce; children: Andrew, Kate, Sarah. BA, Randolph-Macon Woman's Coll., 1969; MS in Edn., U. Pa., 1971, PhD, 1987. Cert. secondary English and social studies tchr., Pa.; cert. prin., Pa. Tchr. Phila. Sch. Dist., 1970-75; lectr., cons. Grad. Sch. Edn. U. Pa., Phila., 1975-84; rsch. assoc. Phila. Sch. Dist., 1985-90, cons., 1990-92; pres. Rsch. for Action, Phila., 1992—. Bd. dirs. Coun. on Anthropology and Edn. Author: Anthropology and Education Quarterly, 1987, (chpt.) Speaking the Language of Power, 1993. Bd. dirs. Community Edn. Ctr., Phila., 1993—, Grad. Sch. Edn. Alumni Assn., U. Pa., Phila., 1990—. Recipient Ethnographic Evaluation award Am. Anthrop. Assn., 1992. Democrat. Episcopalian. Office: Rsch for Action 3701 Chestnut St Philadelphia PA 19104

CHRISTMAN, LESLIE ERIN, music educator; b. Reading, Pa., July 30, 1982; d. Martin Frank and Crystal Kay Miller; m. Jared Daniel Christman, June 26, 2004. MusB summa cum laude, Temple U., 2001—04. Music tchr. Ocean Springs H.S., Miss., 2004—; pvt. voice and piano tchr. Ocean Springs, Miss., 2005—. Worship team mem. The Harvest, Slidell, La., 2004—05. Grantee Presdl. scholar, Temple U., 2004, Dr. Millard Gladfelter scholarship, 2004. Mem.: Music Educator's Nat. Conf., Am. Choral Dir.'s Assn., Sigma Alpha Iota (editor 2002—03). Avocations: travel, reading, piano. Home: 7213 Bayou Landing Dr Ocean Springs MS 39564

CHRISTMAS, BOBBIE JAYE, freelance.self-employed editor and writer; b. Columbia, S.C., Sept. 18, 1944; d. Michael M. and Bernice (Mild) Rothberg; divorced, July 1983; 1 child, Sanford Lee Christmus. Student, U. S.C., 1962-64. Comm. specialist graphics dept. J.A. Jones Construction, Charlotte, N.C., 1974-76; editor Focus News, Greenville, S.C., 1976-78; account exec. Sta. WHYZ-AM, Greenville, 1978-83; supr. audio-visual dept. Leigh Mktg. Group, Greenville, 1983-84; coord. corp. comm. dept. Fluor Daniel, Greenville, 1984-87, asst. editor, reporter employee publs. dept., 1987-89, supr., editor employee publs. and media rels. dept., 1989-93; writer, editor, owner Zebra Comm., Atlanta, 1992—. V.p., dir. SC Writers Workshop, Columbia, 1991-92; founder Roswell (Ga.) Writers Workshop, 1994, Tri-County Writers Workshop, Worldwide Orgn., The Writers Network. Author: Write in Style: Using Your Word Processor and Other Techniques to Improve Your Writing, 2004; co-author The Legend of Codfish and Potatoes, 1999; contbr. articles, photography to local publs.; editor Heartbeat newsletter Greenville Cen. Area Partnership, 1988-91 Recipient 1st Pl. Writing award United Way Greenville County, 1992, 1st Pl. Nonfiction award Reader's Digest Workshop, 1991, Sandhills Writers' Conf., 1989, 1st Pl. Color award Greenville Mag., 2d Pl. Black and White award Travelors Advisory newspaper, 1981, 2 Runners-up awards Greenville C. of C., 1989, others; named One of Upstate's Most Interesting People, Greenville Mag., 1986 Mem. Quest Soc. (dir. pub., rec. sec. 1989-92), Ga. Writers Inc. (bd. dirs. 1996-2004), Women's Nat. Book Assn., Ga. Freelance Writers Assn., Ga. Writers Assn. (past pres., 2d mem. adv. bd., Ga. Author Yr. award, 2005.), Fla. Writers Assn., South Carolina Writers Workshop. Office: 230 Deerchase Dr Ste B Woodstock GA 30188-4438 Office Phone: 770-924-0528. E-mail: bobbie@zebraeditor.com.

CHRISTODOULOU, MARILENA, investment banker, finance company executive; b. Athens, Greece, Feb. 7, 1951; arrived in U.S., 1972; d. Demere and Theodora (Kasapoglou) Lyratzakis; m. Aris Christodoulou, Aug. 23, 1975; 1 child, Peter. License es scis. economiques with honors, U. Lausanne, Switzerland, 1972; MBA, U. Pa., 1974. With lending dept. Am. Express Internat. Banking Corp., NYC, 1974—75; corp. fin. assoc. Kuhn Loeb & Co., NYC, 1975—78, Lehman Bros., NYC, 1978—79; v.p. Worms & Co., Inc., NYC, 1979—86; exec. v.p. W. R. Assocs., Inc., NYC, 1984—86; dir. Mayfair Ptnrs., Inc., NYC, 1986—2000; dir. fin. and devel. Rubin Mus. Art, NYC, 2003—. Dir. Woodway Realty Corp., NYC, 1982—86. Bd. dirs. Greek Archdiocesan Cathedral, NY, trustee, v.p. NY; bd. dirs. 9/11 Environ. Action, Healthy Schs. Network, Inc.; chmn. bd. dirs. The Cathedral Sch. Mem.: Am. Assn. Mus., Wharton Club (N.Y.C.). Home: 137 E 66th St New York NY 10021-6150 Office: Rubin Mus Art 150 W 17th St New York NY 10011 Office Phone: 212-620-5000. Personal E-mail: marilenach@yahoo.com. Business E-Mail: mchristodoulou@rmanyc.org.

CHRISTOFFEL, KATHERINE KAUFER, pediatrician, epidemiologist, educator; b. N.Y.C., June 28, 1948; d. George and Sonya (Firstenberg) Kaufer; children: Kevin, Kimberly. BA, Radcliffe Coll., 1969; MD, Tufts U., 1973; MPH, Northwestern U., 1981. Diplomate Am. Bd. Pediat., Nat. Bd. Med. Examiners. Intern Columbus (Ohio) Childrens' Hosp., 1972-73; resident then fellow Children's Meml. Hosp., Chgo., 1973-76; asst. prof. Sch. Medicine U. Chgo., 1976-79; asst. prof., then assoc. prof. Northwestern U. Med. Sch., Chgo., 1979-91, prof., 1991—; dir. Nutrition Evaluation Clinic Children's Meml. Hosp., Chgo., 1982-2000; med. dir. violent injury prevention ctr. Children's Meml. Med. Ctr., Chgo., 1993—2000, interim dir. Mary Ann and J. Milburn Smith Child Health Rsch. Program, 2000—03, interim co-dir. Children's Meml. Inst. for Edn. and Rsch., 2001—03, med. and rsch. dir. Consortium to Lower Obesity in Chgo. Children, 2003—, dir. Ctr. on Obesity Mgmt. and Prevention, 2004—. Dir. then assoc. dir. Pediatric Practice Rsch. Group, Chgo., 1984-97; dir. statis. scis. and epidemiology program Children's Meml. Inst. for Edn. and Rsch., 1994-2000; chmn. steering com. HELP Network, Chgo., 1993-99, pres. bd. dirs., 1999—2006. Contbr. numerous articles to med. jours. Named one of 10 Most Powerful Women in Medicine in Chgo., Chgo. Sun Times, 2004; recipient M. Fay Spencer Disting. Woman Physician Scientist award, Nat. Bd. Hahnemann Med. Sch., 1997. Fellow Am. Acad. Pediat. (spokesperson on firearms 1985—, injury com. 1985-93, coun. on pediatric rsch. 1996-2000, chair adolescent violence task force 1994, 1st Injury Control award 1992); mem. APHA (Disting. Career award 1991), Am. Coll. Epidemiology, Soc. for Pediatric Rsch., Am. Pediat. Soc., Ambulatory Pediatric Assn. (bd. dirs. 2000-2003, Rsch. award 2000). Avocations: hiking, walking, creative writing, photography. Office: Childrens Meml Hosp 2300 N Childrens Plz #157 Chicago IL 60614-3394

CHRISTOPH, FRANCES, painter; b. Bronxville, N.Y., Mar. 27, 1931; d. Charles DeGuire and Reba (Skipwith) Christoph; m. Charles Robert Salerno, Apr. 4, 1952; 1 stepchild, Franklin Robert Salerno; children: Lucia Salerno Lilien, Christoph Robert Salerno. Student, Art Students League, 1945-49, Adelphia Coll., 1948, Temple U., 1949-50, State U. Iowa, 1950-51, U. Paris Sorbonne, 1951-52, Acad. de la Grande Chaumiere, Paris, 1951-52. One-man show South Mainland Libr., Micco, Fla., 2003; exhibited in shows at Am. Students and Artists Ctr., Paris, Pietrantonio Galleries, N.Y.C., S.I. Mus., Richmond Art Gallery, S.I., Internat. Art Exhbn., Mojacar, Spain, others; writer, editor: Salerno Sculpture, 1965. Mem. The Brevard (Fla.) Rare Fruit Coun., 2006—; pres. Homeowners Assn., Micco, 2005, sec., 2006; mem. Interfaith Alliance, South Mainland Libr. Bd., Fla. Mem.: Royal Scottish Country Dance Soc., Nat. Mus. Women in the Arts (Fla. coun.), Strawbridge Art League, Brevard Watercolor Soc., Archives Nat. Mus. Women in Arts, Art Students League (life), Micco Home Owner's Assn. (sec. 2006). Democrat. Episcopalian. Avocation: gardening. Home: 5828 Lindsay Rd Micco FL 32976-2604 E-mail: fansale@aol.com.

CHRISTOPHER, DORIS K., consumer products company executive; m. Jay Christopher, 1967; children: Julie, Kelley. BS in Home Econs., U. Ill., 1967. Cert. in family and consumer svcs. H.S. home econs. tchr.; with U. Ill. Coop. Extension Svc.; founder, chmn. The Pampered Chef Ltd. (acquired by Berkshire Hathaway, 2002), Addison, Ill., 1980—. Appeared on various TV programs including Oprah Winfrey Show, NBC Weekend Today, CNBC, CNN. Author: Come to the Table: A Celebration of Family Life, 1999, The Pampered Chef: The Story of One of America's Most Beloved Companies, 2005. Recipient Torch award Marketplace Ethics, Better Bus. Bureau, Chgo. & No. Ill., 1998. Mem.: Direct Selling Assn. (bd. dirs. 1992—, past chairperson), Am. Assn. Family and Consumer Scis., America's Second Harvest, Com. of 200. Office: The Pampered Chef 1 Pampered Chef Lane Addison IL 60101-5630 Office Fax: 630-261-8522.

CHRISTOPHER, IRENE, librarian, consultant; b. Greece, Nov. 17, 1922; arrived in US, 1923; d. George and Helen (Stephens) Christopher. AB, Boston U., 1944; BLS, Simmons Coll., 1945. Gen. asst. Robbins Pub. Libr., Arlington, Mass., 1945-46, Boston U. Chenery Libr., 1946-47, head circulation dept., 1947-48, head reference dept., 1948-62; dir. libr. Emerson Coll., Boston, 1962-68; dir. Gordon McKay libr. Harvard U., Cambridge, Mass., 1968-70; chief libr. Boston U. Med. Ctr., 1970-92. Mem. AAUW, ALA (various coms. 1962-82, coun. 1970-74), Spl. Librs. Assn. (various coms. Boston chpt. 1952-75), Am. Soc. Info. Sci., Women's Nat. Book Assn., North Atlantic Health Scis. Librs., Med. Libr. Assn., New Eng. Online Users Group, Inc., Mass. Libr. Assn., Boston U. Women's Coun. Home: 790 Boylston St Apt 11C Boston MA 02199-7911

CHRISTOPHER, KATHY LYNN, secondary school educator; b. Pontiac, Mich., Oct. 13, 1950; d. Donn and Lura Thompson; m. James Christopher; children: Jennifer Mlutkowski, James. BA, U. Mich., Ann Arbor; MA, Wayne State U., Detroit. Tchr. Anchor Bay HS, Fair Haven, Mich., 1986—. Home: 46409 Plum Grove Macomb MI 48044

CHRISTOPHER, MAURINE BROOKS, foundation administrator, writer, editor; b. Three Springs, Tenn. d. John Davis and Zula (Pangle) Brooks; m. Milbourne Christopher, June 25, 1949. BA, Tusculum Coll., Greenville, Tenn., 1941; LittD (hon.), St. John's U., 1984. Reporter, feature writer Balt. Sun, 1943-45; TV radio editor Advt. Age, 1947-51, sr. editor, head broadcast dept., 1951-77, dep. exec. editor N.Y.C., 1977-84; producer-moderator Adbeat, 1970-78; roving editor, mem. editorial bd. Advt. Age, 1984-91; chmn. Milbourne Christopher Found., 1991—. Author: America's Black Congressmen, 1971, Black Americans in Congress, 1976; co-author: The Milbourne Christopher Library, 1589-1900, The Illustrated History of Magic, 1996, 3d edit., 2006, The Milbourne Christopher Library II, 1901-1996, 1998; editor: Howard Thurston's Illusion Show Workbook II, 1992, Houdini's A Magician Among the Spirits-The Original Manuscript, 1996, Milbourne Christopher's Favorite Routines, 2000 Mem.: Internat. Brotherhood Magicians, Soc. Am. Magicians. Home: 333 Central Park W Apt 25 New York NY 10025-7104 Office Phone: 212-663-0200. Personal E-mail: mcfdtn@aol.com.

CHRISTOPHERSON, ELIZABETH GOOD, broadcast executive; b. Cin. d. Walter R. and Jean S. Good; m. Paul C. Christopherson; 1 child, Katherine. BA, Wellesley Coll. Chmn., CEO NJ State Coun. Arts, 1989—91; exec. dir. NJ Pub. TV and Radio, Trenton, 1994—; pres. NJN Found., 1994—. Bd. dirs. PNC Bank N.J., PBS, Liberty Sci. Ctr., Wellesley Coll. Bus. Leadership Coun., NJ State Coun. Arts. Pres., bd. dirs. Leadership Am. Assn., Alexandria, Va., 1991—92; bd. dirs. N.J. Tech. Coun. Mem.: Internat. Woman's Forum (past pres. N.J. chpt.). Office: NJ Network PO Box 777 Trenton NJ 08625-0777

CHRISTY, CINDY, telecommunications industry executive; m. Randy Christy; 4 children. BBA, Am. U. Joined AT&T Network Sys., 1988, various mgmt. positions in market rsch., market mgmt., sales, product planning, project mgmt. and product mgmt.; dir. CDMA/PCS Project Mgmt. Lucent Techs., Murray Hill, NJ, 1995—98, v.p. AMPS/PCS product mgmt. and mktg., 1998—2000, COO wireless networks group, 2001, COO mobility solutions group, 2002—03, pres. mobility solutions group, 2004—. Mem.: Cellular Telecom. Industry Assn. (bd. dirs., mem. exec. com.). Office: Lucent Techs 600 Mountain Ave Murray Hill NJ 07974

CHROMOW, SHERI P., lawyer; b. NYC, Aug. 27, 1946; d. Abe and Sara L. Pinsky. BA, Barnard Coll., N.Y.C., 1968; JD, NYU, 1971. Ptnr. Shearman & Sterling, N.Y.C., 1979—2001, Katten, Muchin, Rosenman LLP, N.Y.C., 2001—. Lectr. Practising Law Inst., N.Y. County Bar Assn., Urban Land Inst.; mem. exec. com. N.Y. dist. coun. U. L.I.; mem. adv. bd. Furman Real Estate Inst. NYU Law Sch.; mem. adv. bd. Ticor Title Ins. Co; award judge Real Estate Bd. N.Y., 2003, 04; bd. experts The Internat. Real Estate Trade Orgn. Bd. dirs. Bklyn. Philharm. Orch. Mem. Urban Land Inst. (former gen.

counsel), Assn. Fgn. Investors in Real Estate. Office: Katten Muchin Rosenman LLP 575 Madison Ave New York NY 10022 Office Phone: 212-940-8529. Business E-Mail: sheri.chromow@kattenlaw.com.

CHRZANOWSKI, ROSE-ANN CANNIZZO, art educator; b. Bklyn., Mar. 13, 1952; d. Francis Salvatore and Vincenza Pilaro Cannizzo; m. Raymond David Chrzanowski; 1 child, Karen Kuczenski. BA, CUNY, Bklyn., 1974; MS, Fordham U., 1977; postgrad., So. Conn. State U., 1990. Cert. in elem. edn. N.Y., Conn., nat. bd. cert., cert. in art. 3d grade tchr. St. Michael Sch., Bklyn., 1974—78; art tchr. Naugatuck Elem. Schs., Naugatuck, Conn., 1978—90; tchr. City Hill Mid. Sch., Naugatuck, 1990—2000, Naugatuck H.S., 2000—; adj. prof. Quinnipiac U., 2003—. Tchr., tutor supr. Naugatuck Youth Svcs., 1978—84; edn. program coord. Human Resources Devel. Agy., Naugatuck, 1985—87; adj. prof. Teikyo Post U., Waterbury, Conn., 1996; mem. adv. coun. Celebration Excellence, New Haven, 1998—. Contbg. author: Doing What's Right in the Middle, Promising Practices of Schools with Middle Grades, 1999. Chmn. Naugatuck Arts Commn., 1996—98; nat. tchr. forum rep. State Dept. Edn., 2001. Recipient Emeritus award, Celebration Excellence, 1999, Celebration of Excellence Developer award, 1998. Mem.: NEA, Conn. Art Edn. Assn., Nat. Art Edn. Assn., Phi Delta Kappa. Office: Naugatuck HS 543 Rubber Ave Naugatuck CT 06770 Personal E-mail: rayrochrz@earthlink.net.

CHU, ELLIN RESNICK, librarian, consultant; b. Bklyn., Nov. 23, 1932; d. David and Isobel (Janowitch) Resnick; m. Wallace Chu, Aug. 29, 1960 (div. Sept. 1979); children: Steven, Joshua, Amanda. BA in Modern European Hist. with honors, Ind. U., 1954, MA in Libr. Sci., 1956; postgrad., Columbia U., 1956-57. Young adult libr. Donnell br. N.Y. Pub. Libr., 1956-57; order libr. Nat. Indsl. Conf. Bd., 1957-58; reference libr. Columbia U. Reference Libr., 1958-59; libr. dir. Hillside Hosp., 1959-61, L.I. Jewish-Hillside Med. Ctr., 1972—; adult/young adult libr. Glen Cove (N.Y.) Pub. Libr., 1973-77; young adult cons. Rochester (N.Y.) Pub. Libr. Monroe County Libr. Sys., 1977-93, mgr. lit., religion and philosophy divsn., 1993-98, ret., 1998. Mem. nomination com. Glen Cove Interagy. Coun., 1976, chair youth recreation com., 1974-75, chair pre-screening com., info. and referral adv. bd. Nassau Libr. Sys., 1977; mem. libr. planning com. Rochester Sesquicentennial, 1984; mem. cen. libr. planning com. Rochester Pub. Libr., 1985-86; sec. Rochester Area Youth Dirs. Coun., 1980-81, mem. nominating com., 1987, profl. improvement com., 1987-89; presenter programming and svcs. for young adults Mid-Hudson Libr. Sys., Albany, N.Y., 1989-90; mem. On-line pub. catalog planning com. Monroe County Libr. Sys., 1986-92; libr. programming presenter and resource team mem. Learning Odyssey/SUNY Albany and New York State Divsn. Libr. Devel., 1989; active Brighton Cable Commn., 1980-93. Co-author: (chpt. to book) Our Family, Our Friends, Our World: An Annotated Guide to Significant Multicultural Books for Children and Teenagers, 1991; contbr. articles to profl. jours. Recipient 1st prize N.Y. Libr. Ad Hoc Com. on Women's Concerns, 1975; grantee Young Adult Libr. Instrn. Project, 1982-84; scholar Robert Flaherty Film Seminar, 1976, Lyman Langdon scholar Audubon Ecology Workshop, 1977. Mem. ALA (young adult svcs. divsn., chair high interest/low literacy level materials evaluation com. 1979-81, pub. liaison com. 1988-90, Margaret A. Edwards Author Award com. 1991-93), Ednl. Film Libr. Assn. (juror Am. Film Festival 1976-78, jury chair 1979-88), N.Y. Libr. Assn. (pres. youth svcs. sect. 1984, founding mem./sec. film/video roundtable 1977), Nassau County Libr. Assn. (founding mem. young adult sect. 1976).

CHU, JUDY MAY, assemblywoman; b. LA, July 7, 1955; d. Judson and May C.; m. Michael Eng, Aug. 8, 1978. BA in Math., UCLA, 1974; MA in Clin. Psychology, Calif. Sch. Profl. Psychology, 1977, PhD, 1979. Lectr. UCLA, 1980-86; assoc. prof. L.A. City Coll., 1981-88; prof. East L.A. Coll., Monterey Park, 1988—2001; mem. Monterey Park City Council, 1988—2001, Calif. State Assembly, 2001—. Chair, select com. on hate crimes Calif. State Assembly, mem. select com. on language access, mem. rules, labor and employment com., environ. safety and toxic materials com., human svcs. com. & transportation com. Author, editor: Linking Our Lives: Chinese American Women in Los Angeles, 1984; contbr. articles profl. jours. Mem. city coun. City of Monterey Park, 1988—, mayor, 1990-91, 94-95; bd. dirs. Garvey Sch. Dist., 1985-88; chair Comm. for Sex Equity, L.A. Unified Sch. Dist., 1984-85; bd. dirs. Rebuild L.A.; mem. adv. com. U.S. Census Bur., 1994—; Bd. dirs. Gabriel Valley chpt. ARC; bd. dirs. Asian Youth Ctr., San Gabriel Valley United Way, West San Gabriel Valley Juvenile Diversion Project. Named One of 88 Leaders for 1988, L.A. Times, 1988, Dem. of Yr., 59th Assembly Dist. Dem. Com., 1989, Vol. of Yr. San Gabriel Valley chpt. United Way, 1989, L.A. Outstanding Founder, 1995; recipient Achievement award Asian Pacific Family Ctr., 1980, Pub. Svc. award Asian Pacific Legal Ctr., 1989, award for Excellence in Pub. Svc., UCLA Alumni, 1991, Leadership award West San Gabriel Valley chpt. ARC. Mem. Soroptimists. Office: Calif State Assembly PO Box 942849 Sacramento CA 94249 Business E-Mail: assemblymember.chu@asm.ca.gov.

CHU, LILI, jewelry designer, consultant; b. Hong Kong, Aug. 14, 1960; d. Woon Charn and Wai (Sau) C.; 1 child, Cassandra Chu Currens. BFA in Illustration, Parsons Sch. Design, 1984. Jewelry designer Carvin French, Inc., N.Y.C., 1987-89; design dir. Omar Torres, Inc., N.Y.C., 1992-94; jewelry designer Avon Products, Inc., N.Y.C., 1994-96; design dir. Mikimoto, N.Y.C., 1996—. Designer of collection for Mikimoto Internat., Walt Disney Art Classics: Fantasia 2000, Burbank, Calif.; cons. for Avons Products, Smithsonian Instn. Product Devel., Washington, 1994-96. Recipient 26th ann. Internat. Pearl Design contest Japan Pearl Promotion Soc., 1998, Jewelry Hons. with Josie Natori Asia Soc., 1998. Avocations: tennis, bird watching, photography, painting, motherhood.

CHU, MARGARET S.Y., former federal agency administrator; b. Jan. 10, 1946; BS in Chemistry, Purdue U., 1967; PhD in Phys. Chemistry, U. Minn., 1973. Mem. tech. staff Sandia Nat. Labs., Albuquerque, 1980-86, disting. mem. tech. staff, 1986-91, tech. mgr., 1991-97, sr. mgr. nuclear waste mgmt., 1997-99, dir. nuclear waste mgmt., 1999—2002; dir. Civilian Radioactive Waste Mgmt. US Dept Energy, Washington, 2002—05. Contbr. numerous articles to sci. and profl. jours. Founding faculty mem. Albuquerque Chinese Sch., 1980. Mem. Am. Chem. Soc., N.M. Chinese Assn., Chinese Inst. Engrs. (bd. dirs., officer N.Mex. chpt. 1997-98).

CHU, SYLVIA, lawyer; b. Boston, Mar. 1972; BA in Psychology, cum laude, U. Pa., 1994; JD, Boston Coll. Law Sch., 1997. Bar: Mass. 1997, NY 1998, US Dist. Ct. (Dist. Mass.) 1999. Atty. The McCormack Firm LLC, Boston. Mem.: Mass. Bar Assn. Office: The McCormack Firm LLC 7th Floor One International Pl Boston MA 02110 Office Fax: 617-951-2929, 617-951-2672. E-mail: schu@mccormackfirm.com.*

CHUA, AMY, law educator; AB magna cum laude, Harvard U., 1984, JD cum laude, 1987. Law clk. to Hon. Patricia M. Wald US Ct. Appeals, DC Cir., 1987—88; assoc. Cleary, Gottlieb, Steen & Hamilton, 1988—93; assoc. prof. law Duke U., 1994—99, prof. law, 1999—2001; John M. Duff, Jr. prof. law Yale U., New Haven, 2001—. Vis. prof. law Columbia U., 1999, Stanford U., 2000, NYU, 2000. Author: World on Fire: How Exporting Free Market Democracy Breeds Ethnic Hatred and Global Instability, 2003; contbr. articles to law jours. Grantee Internat. Affairs Fellowship, Coun. Foreign Relations, 1998—99. Mem.: NY State Bar. Office: Yale Law Sch PO Box 208215 New Haven CT 06520 E-mail: amy.chua@yale.edu.

CHUBBUCK, LINDA J., music educator, singer; d. Ralph and Jeanne Marie Chubbuck; children: Jessica L. Johnson, Adam C. Johnson, August M. Johnson. MusB in Edn., Washburn U., 1970. Cert. K-12 vocal music tchr. Kans. Dept. of Edn., 1970, music practitioner Music for Healing and Transition Program, 2002. Stained glass artist, tchr. Country Glass Works (self-employed), Concordia, Kans., 1981—95; freelance writer Concordia, Kans., 1992—95; vocal music instr. Tescott (Kans.) Sch., 2002—. Owner, operator Chubbuck Grain Co., Concordia, 1981—2001; musical dir. Unitarian Universalist Fellowship, Salina, 2001—03; pvt. instr. voice and piano, Salina, 2001—; musical dir., mem. Key of Three A Cappella Trio, Salina, 2004—. Singer (songwriter): (albums) Diamonds & Moose; singer: (songwriter, arranger) A Taste of A Cappella. Founding mem. Wellspring Artists' Coop., Concordia, 1996—98; facilitator Artist's Way Class, Concordia, 1995—2001; founder, facilitator Circles of Song, Salina, 2001—05. Scholar, Rotary Internat. and Concordia Rotary Club, 1998; Horizons Developing Artist grant, Salina Arts and Humanities Commn., 2004. Mem.: Kans. Music Educator's Assn., Music Educator's Nat. Conf., Sierra. Avocations: gardening, travel, yoga, reading. Personal E-mail: songs@lindachubbuck.com.

CHUDNOV, MARLENE MYRA, elementary school educator, educational consultant; b. Chgo., Nov. 9, 1939; d. Bernard and Bernice Waxman; children: Judith Solomon, David, Daniel. BA in Elem. Edn., Roosevelt U., Chgo., 1961; MS in Reading Specialization, Butler U., Indpls., 1982. Cert. gifted and talented Purdue U., 1982. Fifth and sixth grade tchr. Chgo. Pub. Sch., 1961—63; chap. one reading tchr. Indpls. Pub. Sch., 1982—85; third and fifth grade tchr. Washington Township, Indpls., 1985—87; third and fourth grade tchr. Hillel Day Sch., Farmington Hills, Mich., 1987—89; reading clinician Southfield Pub. Sch., Southfield, Mich., 1989—2005. Lectr. in edn. Butler U., Indpls., 1982—93; reading dept. chair Southfield Pub. Sch., Mich., 1997—2000. Contbg. author: Comprehensive Curriculum for Gifted Learners, 1988. Active Temple Israel, West Bloomfield, Mich. Recipient Outstanding Tchr., Sch. 67, 1985, Nora Sch., 1987, Outstanding Svc. award Founders Day, Southfield Pub. Sch., 2003. Mem.: NEA, Southfield Edn. Assn., Mich. Reading Assn., Hadassah. Avocations: walking, knitting, reading, music. Office: Stevenson Elem Sch 27777 Lahser Rd Southfield MI 48034

CHUGHTAI, RAANA LYNN, psychiatric nurse practitioner; d. Arshad Iqbal and Lynnette Janet Chughtai. BSN, U. Pitts., 2000. RN Pa., 2001. Crisis clinician Mercy Behavioral Health, Pitts., 2000—02, nurse/therapist Wexford, Pa., 2002—. Rsch. asst. U. Pitts., 1999—2000. Mem.: Grad. Nursing Student Orgn., Am. Psychiat. Nurses Assn., Three Rivers Rowing Assn., Golden Key.

CHUMLEY, SHANNON JACKSON, elementary school educator; b. Hackensack, N.J., Jan. 12, 1977; d. Thomas J. Jackson and Donna M. James; m. Nick A. Chumley, Mar. 2, 2002; children: Jackson H., Pearson H. BS in Elem. Edn., Coll. Charleston, S.C., 2000; M in Curriculum and Instrn., Nova Southeastern U., Ft. Lauderdale, Fla., 2006. Cert. tchr. SC., 2000. Tchr. Frierson Elem., Wadmalaw Island, SC, 2000—01, Rawlinson Rd. Mid. Sch., Rock Hill, SC, 2001—. Tchr. Sunday sch. Oakland Ave. Presbyn., Rock Hill, SC, 2005—. Office Phone: 803-981-1500. E-mail: schumley@rock-hill.k12.sc.us.

CHUN, A. MARISA, lawyer; BA summa cum laude, Yale Univ., 1987; JD cum laude, Harvard Law Sch., 1991. Bar: Calif. 1992, DC 1995, US Dist. Ct. (no. dist.) Calif., US Dist. Ct. (so. dist.) Tex., US Ct. Appeals (9th cir.), US Supreme Ct. Law clk. Hon. Robert Boochever US Ct. Appeals (9th cir.), 1991—92; trial atty. to sr. trial atty., civil rights divsn. US Dept. Justice, Washington, 1992—96; reporter, legal commentator KREM-TV (CBS), Spokane, Wash.; ptnr. Coblentz, Patch, Duffy & Bass LLP, San Francisco, 2003—. Mediation panel US Dist. Ct. (no. dist.) Calif. Develop. editor Harvard Law Rev., 1990—91; contbr. articles profl. journals. Named one of Best Lawyers Under 40, Nat. Asian Pacific Am. Bar Assn., 2004, No. Calif. Super Lawyers, San Francisco mag., 2005; grantee Coro Public Affairs Fellow, LA. Mem.: ABA, State Bar Calif. (chairperson, com. on Fed. Cts. 2004—05), Bar Assn. San Francisco (exec. com., litig. sect.), Korean Am. Bar Assn., No. Calif. (pres. 2001—02). Office: Coblentz Patch Duffy & Bass LLP St 200 One Ferry Bldg San Francisco CA 94111-4213 Office Fax: 415-989-1663. Business E-Mail: amchun@coblentzlaw.com.

CHUN, CHERYL, music educator; b. Honolulu; d. George and Patsy Chun. B in Secondary Edn., U. Hawaii, Honolulu, 1985. Cert. tchr. Hawaii. Band tchr. Lahaina (Hawaii) Intermediate Sch., 1988—92, Aiea (Hawaii) Intermediate Sch., 1992—. Guest condr. Maui Intermediate Music Festival Mass Band. Mem.: Oahu Band Dirs. Assn., Music Educators Nat. Conf., Honolulu Cmty. Concert Band. Office: Aiea Intermediate School 99-600 Kulawea St Aiea HI 96701 Office Phone: 808-483-7230. Office Fax: 808-483-7235. Business E-Mail: cheryl_chun/aieai/hidoe@notes.k12.hi.us.

CHUN, JACQUELINE CLIBBETT, artist, educator; d. Sydney H. and Hilda C. Moore; m. Edward W.C. Chun, Dec. 1967; children: Christine, Diana, David. Student, London Coll. Music, 1956—58; BA summa cum laude, U. Hawaii Manoa, 1992, MFA, 1997. Freelance musician, singer, songwriter, 1960—; pres. JCM Prodns., Honolulu, 1978—; lectr. painting Kapiolani C.C., Honolulu, 1999; faculty Kaimuki Cmty. Sch. Adults, Honolulu, 1988—; lectr. U. Hawaii Manoa, Honolulu, 1996—. Courtroom sketch artist KGMB TV, KHNL TV, Honolulu, 2000—; founder, dir. Girl Scout Band and Choir, 1987; poetry editor Hawaii Rev., 1992—93, asst. mng. editor, 1993—94, nonfiction editor, 1994—95; vice chair publs. bd. U. Hawaii at Manoa, 1988—89; mem. art adv. bd. Kapiolani C.C., U. Hawaii. Author: (plays) By the Hand of a Woman, 1992; co-author (illustrator, editor): Moiliili, The Life of a Community, 2005; editor: The Touch of God, 1999, The Science of Happiness, 2000; composer: (songs) (ofcl. sch. song) Ala Wai Elem. Sch., 1978, (ofcl. theme song) Girl Scout Coun. 75th Anniversary, Girl Scouts, 1988; contbr. articles to profl. jours. Band dir., choir dir. Girl Scout Coun. Pacific, Honolulu. Recipient Acquisition award, State Found. Culture and Arts, All USA Coll. Acad. First Team, USA Today, 1990, House Reps Resolution Ednl. Contribution award, State of Hawaii, Spirit award, Hawaii Rev., 1992, Gold award, 16th Ann. Shizuoka Friendship Postcard Art Contest, Japan, 2004, 1st pl., Nat. Arts Program, Honolulu Hale, 2006. Mem.: ASCAP, Am. Fedn. Musicians, Acad. Am. Poets, Portrait Soc. Am., Nat. Music Pub. Assn., Musician's Assn. Hawaii, Phi Beta Kappa. Avocations: swimming, gardening, travel.

CHUN, JENNIFER, communications executive; b. 1971; Law degree, Berkeley Sch. Law, U. Calif. Assoc. Pillsbury Madison & Sutro; v.p. bus. and legal affairs Fox Cable Networks, 2000, sr. v.p. bus. and legal affairs. Named one of 40 Executives Under 40, Multichannel News, 2006. Office: Fox Cable Networks Corporate Headquarters 2121 Fox Plz Los Angeles CA 90067 Office Phone: 310-369-1000.*

CHUN, SHINAE, federal agency administrator; m. Kyong Chul Chun; 2 children. BA, Ewha Women's U., Seoul, Korea; MA in Edu. and Social Policy, Northwestern U.; fellowship, Harvard U. John F. Kennedy Sch. of Govt. Project dir. Title IX Multiethnic Training, Assistance and Dissemination Project; founding mem. Asian Am. Advisory Council to Gov. James R. Thompson State of Ill., 1982—84, special asst. on Asian Am. affairs to gov., 1984—87; dir. Dept. of Fin. Institutions, Chgo., 1988—90, Labor Dept., Chgo., 1991—99; dir. women's bur. US Dept. of Labor, Washington, 2001—. Author: From the Mountains of Masan to the Land of Lincoln, 1996, Korean Culture: A Passage Through Hermit Kingdom, 1980. Recipient Special Achievement for Leadership award, Bus. Women's Network, 2004. Office: US Dept Labor Women's Bur 200 Constitution Ave NW Washington DC 20210

CHUNG, AMY TERESA, lawyer, property manager; b. San Francisco, Sept. 1, 1953; d. Burk Him and Mary Angeline (Lin) C.; children: Adrian Thomas, Alison Nicole. AB in Psychology, U. Calif., Berkeley, 1975; JD, U. Calif., Hastings Coll. of Law, San Francisco, 1978. Bar: Calif. Legal counsel M & B Assocs., San Francisco, 1978—; v.p. Anza Parking Corp., Burlingame, Calif., 1993—. Mem. adv. com. U. Calif., San Francisco, 1992—; v.p. Castle Peak Homeowners Assn., West Hills, Calif., 1987-89; v.p. Chinatown Stockton St. Mchts. Assn., San Francisco, 1994-1999; chair Chinese Cmty. Housing Corp., San Francisco, 1991-1999; project area com. Mid-Market, San Francisco, 1996—. Mem. Calif. Bar Assn. Avocations: piano, singing, ballet, swimming. Office: M & B Assocs 835 Washington St San Francisco CA 94108-1211

CHUNG, CAROLINE, marketing professional; b. Washington, Apr. 27, 1970; d. Jae Wan and Soojun Chung. BS, U. Wis., 1992; MBA, Vanderbilt U., 1997. Cert. Mad Dogg Spinning Instr., Aerobics and Fitness Assn. Am., Group Excercise Instr.; cert. Pilates instr. Mgr. ops. rsch. and statis. analysis Continental Airlines, 1997—99; mgr. product devel. US Airways, 1999—2001; ops. rsch. cons. Warden Assocs., 2001—03; fgn. svc. officer, 2d sec. U.S. Dept. State, 2003—05; sr. dir. mktg. MAXjet Airways, Inc., 2005—. Roman Catholic. Avocations: health and fitness, travel, reading, world maps, music. Personal E-mail: carolinechung@hotmail.com.

CHUNG, CHRISTINA, lawyer; BA, Stanford Univ., 1992; JD, Univ. Mich., 1996. Staff atty., project. dir. Asian Pacific Am. Legal Ctr., LA. Named one of Best Lawyers Under 40, Nat. Asian Pacific Am. Bar Assn., 2004. Office: Asian Pacific Am Legal Ctr 2nd fl 1145 Wilshire Blvd Los Angeles CA 90017 Office Phone: 213-977-7500 ext 239.

CHUNG, CONNIE (CONSTANCE YU-HWA CHUNG), broadcast journalist; b. Wash., Aug. 20, 1946; d. William Ling and Margaret Chung; m. Maurice Richard Povich. BS, U. Md., 1969; DJ (hon.), Providence Coll., 1988; LHD (hon.), Brown U., 1987; LLD (hon.), Wheaton Coll., 1989. News copyperson, writer, reporter Sta. WTTG-TV, Metromedia, Washington, 1969—71; corr. CBS News, Washington, 1971—76; TV news anchor Sta. KNXT-TV, CBS, L.A., 1976—83; anchor NBC News, NBC News at Sunrise, NBC Nightly News (Saturday), NBC News Digests, NBC News Mag. 1986, NBC News Spls., N.Y.C., 1983—89, Saturday Night with Connie Chung, CBS-TV, 1989—90, CBS Evening News (Sunday edit.), 1989—93, Face to Face, 1990—91, Eye to Eye, 1993—95; co-anchor CBS Evening News, 1993—95; anchor, corres. 20/20 ABC, N.Y.C., 1997—2002; anchor CNN, New York, NY, 2002—03; co-host Weekends with Maury & Connie, 2006. Recipient Achievement Cert. for series of broadcasts, U.S. Humane Soc., 1969, Metro Area Mass Media award, AAUW, 1971, Outstanding Young Women of Am. award, 1971, Atlanta chpt. Nat. Assn. Media Women award, 1973, Outstanding Excellence in News Reporting and Pub. Svc. award, Chinese-Am. Citizens Alliance, 1973, Hon. award for news reporting, Chinese YMCA, Boston, 1974, Woman of Distinction award, Golden Slipper Club, Phila., 1975, Best TV Reporting award, Sta. KNXT-TV and L.A. Press Club, 1977, Outstanding TV Broadcasting award, Valley Press Club, 1977, Golden Mike award for best documentary, 1978, Emmy award for individual achievement, L.A. chpt. NATAS, 1978, 1980, Mark Twain trophy, Calif. AP TV and Radio Assn., 1979, Best News Broadcast 4:30 p.m., 1980, Women in Comm. award, Calif. State U. at L.A., 1979, George Foster Peabody award for programs on environ., Md. Ctr. Pub. Broadcasting, 1980, Portraits of Excellence award, Pacific S.W. region B'nai B'rith, 1980, Newscaster of Yr. award, Temple Emanuel Brotherhood, 1981, First Amendment award, Anti-Defamation League of B'nai B'rith, 1981, Best Newscast 6:00 p.m. award, AP, 1981, Calif. AP TV and Radio Assn. award, 1981, Golden Mike award for best news broadcast, 1981, Disting. Contbns. in area of Comm. Media award, L.A. Basin Equal Opportunity League, 1983, Women in Bus. award, 1983, L.A. Press Club award for 4:30 p.m. boradcast, 1983, L.A. Press Club award for 6:00 p.m. broadcast, 1983, Emmy award, 1986, Emmy award for outstanding interview, 1989, 1990, Silver Gavel award, ABA, 1991, Ohio State of Achievement of Merit award, 1991, Nat. Headliner award, NCCJ, 1991, Clarion award, Women in Comm., 1991, Commendation award for AIDS and rape stories, Am. Women in Radio and TV, Commendation award for best implant stories, 1991, Godl Apple award, Nat. Media Network Film and Video Competition, 1999, Edward R. Murrow award for best news documentary, Nat. Assn. Radio and TV News Dirs., 1999, Cine Golden Eagle award, 1999, East Seals EDI award, 1999, Comm. award, Crystal award of Excellence, 1999, plaque award, Nat. Network for Youth, 2000, Gold Camera award, U.S. Internat. Film and Video Festival, 2000, 1999 award, Chgo. Internat. TV Competition, 2000, Media Spotlight award, Amnesty Internat., 2000, Salute to Excellence award, Nat. Assn. Black Journalists, 2000.

CHUNG, CYNTHIA NORTON, communications specialist; b. Milton, Mass., Apr. 14, 1955; d. Ralph Arnold and Mary Elizabeth (McDonald) N.; m. Chinsoo Chung; children: Sara Jane, Steven Joonmok. BFA in Archtl. and Graphic Design, U. Mass., 1977. Graphic designer Garber Travel, Inc., Brookline, Mass., 1977-78; graphic and exhibit designer Rust Craft, Inc., Dedham, Mass., 1978-80; corp. advt. artist Morse, Inc., Canton, Mass., 1980-83; pvt. practice designer Boston, 1983-84; asst. art dir. Cahners Pub. Co., Newton, Mass., 1984-86, art dir., 1986-87, Knapp, Inc., Brockton, Mass., 1987-89; customer svc. rep. TWA, Boston, 1990; communications specialist Boston Fin., Quincy, Mass., 1992—. Designer graphs and charts for Vols. I and II State Budget Commonwealth of Mass., 1982; art dir. Mini Micro Systems, 1984-87. Mem. Kappa Kappa Gamma (Pres. 1975-76). Avocations: photography, real estate, travel. Home: 134 Samoset Ave Quincy MA 02169-2452 Office: Boston Financial 2000 Crown Colony Dr Quincy MA 02169

CHUNG, LINDA H., obstetrician, gynecologist; b. Seoul, Republic of Korea, Apr. 27, 1972; d. Young S. and Moon S. Chung; m. Moses Kim, May 9, 1998; children: Wesley Kim, Nathaniel Kim. BA, Stanford U., Palo Alto, Calif., 1994; MD, U. Calif., San Francisco, 1998. Staff physician Ob-gyn. Assocs., Houston, 2003—06. Fellow: Am. Coll. Ob-gyn.; mem.: Harris County Med. Soc., Phi Beta Kappa. Home: 1606 White Willow Ln Pearland TX 77581 Office: OGA Bay Area 3203 W Broadway St Pearland TX 77588

CHUNG, SUE FAWN, educator, researcher; b. L.A., Mar. 11, 1944; d. Walter K. and Jane Beverly (Chan) C.; m. Alan Moss Solomon, Apr. 17, 1980; children: Walter Moss, Alexander Moss. BA, UCLA, 1965; AM, Harvard U., 1967; PhD, U. Calif., Berkeley, 1975. Lectr. San Francisco State U., 1971-73; asst. prof. U. Nev., Las Vegas, 1975-79, assoc. prof., 1979—, dir. internat. programs, 1985-87, chmn. dept. history, 1994—96. Mem. media panel NEH, 1992; dir. Asia and Nev. project Nev. Humanities Com., 1992-94. Bd. dirs. Preserve Nev., 2001-, mem. Nev. Bd. Mus. and History, 2001-. Recipient Excellence in Edn. award Las Vegas C. of C., 1996, Lion's Club, 2005, Asian Chamber, 2005; fellow ACLS, 1977, U. Calif., 1968-70; grantee U. Nev., 1976, 81. Mem. Am. Hist. Assn., Assn. for Asian Studies, Soc. for Qing Studies, U.S.-China Friendship Assn. (co-founder Las Vegas chpt. 1975), Harvard U. Alumni Assn. (bd. dirs. 1994—), Phi Kappa Phi (v.p. Las Vegas chpt. 1986-88), Nat. Trust for Historic Preservation (bd. adv., diversity coun., 2000-). Democrat. Avocations: swimming, hiking, horseback riding, sewing, cooking. Office: U Nev 4505 S Md Pky Las Vegas NV 89154-5020 Office Phone: 702-895-3351. Business E-Mail: suefawn.chung@unlv.edu.

CHUNIAS, JENNIFER LYNN, lawyer; BA, U. Va., 1993; JD, Northeastern U. Law Sch., 1999. Lectr. Harvard Law Sch., Climenko/Thayer lectr. law, 2004—05; assoc. Litig. Practice Group Testa, Hurwitz & Thibeault, LLP, Boston; assoc. Litig. Dept. Goodwin Procter LP, Boston. Adj. prof. Northeastern U. Sch. Law. Bd. trustees New England Innocence Project. Mem.: ABA, Mass. Bar Assn., Boston Bar Assn. Office: Goodwin Procter LLP Exchange Place 53 State St Boston MA 02109 Office Phone: 617-570-8239. Office Fax: 617-523-1231. E-mail: jchunias@goodwinprocter.com.*

CHUN OAKLAND, SUZANNE NYUK JUN, state legislator; b. Honolulu, June 27, 1961; d. Philip Sing and Mei-Chih (Chung) Chun; m. Michael Sands Chun Oakland, June 11, 1994; children: Mailene Nohea Pua Oakland, Christopher Michael Sing Kamakaku Oakland, Lauren Suzanne LeRong Kemelenohea Oakland. BA in Psychology and Comms., U. Hawaii, 1983. Adminstrv. asst. Au's Plumbing and Metal Works, Hawaii, 1979-90; community svc. specialist Senator Anthony Chang, Hawaii, 1984; adminstrv. asst. Smolenski and Woodell, Hawaii, 1984-86; rsch. asst., office mgr. City Coun. Mem. Gary Gill, Hawaii, 1987-90; mem. Hawaii Ho. of Reps., 1990-96, Hawaii Senate, Dist. 14, Honolulu, 1996—; chair com. health and human svcs. Hawaii Senate, 1999—, co-chair com. human resources, 1997—; mem. coms. health and environ., consumer protection; commerce and info. tech., 1997—. Past chair, mem. several coms. Hawaii State Senate; mem. Sterile Needle Exch. Oversight Com., 1992—; apptd. pres. Kalihi-Palama Svc. Area Bd. on Mental Health and Substance Abuse, gov. Hawaii, 1985-89. Mem. adv. bd. Lanakila Multi-Purpose Sr. Ctr., 1991—, Sex Abuse Treatment Ctr.,

1993—, Teen Line, 1993, Hawaii Cmty. Found. Children's Trust Fund, 1995—, Habitat for Humanity, 1998—; mem. Grow For It Program, 1996—, Hawaii Early Childhood Alliance, 1995-96, Families Together Initiative Core Team, 1993-95; coun. mem. Hawaii Even Start Family Literact Program, 1993-94; mem. coord. coun. Hawaii Early Intervention, 1993—, Early Childhood Edn. and Care, 1992-96; mem. adv. coun. Children's Trust Fund, 1993—; mem. adv. com. West Honolulu Pub. Health Nursing Sect., 1992—, Honolulu divsn. Casey Family Program, 1994—, Early Childhood Sys. Cost/Implementation, 1992-94; chair Liliha/Kalapama Neighborhood Bd., 1984-90; mem. project steering com. Hawaii Summit 2011, 1996—; mem. Healthy Mothers, Healthy Babies Coalition, 1992; convenor Elder Abuse and Neglect Task Force, 1995—; mem. task force Blueprint for Change, Child Protective Svcs., 1994-96, Hawaii Assistive Tech. Tng. and Svcs. Project Cmty., 1995—; mem. coun. Hawaii Kids Count, 1994—; bd. dirs. Honolulu Neighborhood Housing Svcs., 1986-88, 89—, pres., 1987-88, 92-93, 93-94; bd. dirs. McKinley H.S. Found, 1989—; Catholic Immigration Ctr., 1991-97, Hawaii Dem. Movement, 1991-97, Hawaii Cmty. Svcs. Coun., 1993-97, Hawaii Cmty. Edn. Assn., 1984-98, Hawaii Lawyers Care, 1994—, Susannah Wesley Cmty. Ctr., 1994—, Hawaii Housing Devel. Corp., 1993—, YWCA, 1994—, ARC, 1998—, Breakthroughs for Youth at Risk, 1998—, Providing Awareness Referrals Edn. Nurturing Therapy Support, 1999—; precinct pres. Hawaii Dem. Party, 1990. Named Legis. of Yr. Hawaii Long Term Care Assn., 1993, 98, Healthcare Assn. Hawaii, 1993, 95, Hawaii Psychiat. Med. Assn., 1994, Autism Soc. Hawaii, 1994, Mental Health Assn. Hawaii, 1996, Aloha State Assn. of Deaf, 1999; recipient cert. of appreciation YMCA, 1985, Hawaii Assn. for Edn. of Young Children, 1992, Winners at Work, 1993, Am. Box Car Racing Internat., 1996, Congress of Visayan Orgn., 1996, Pack 201 Boys Scouts Am., 1997, Partners in Policymaking Hawaii, 1998, Excellence award Honolulu Neighborhood Housing Svcs. Inc., 1988, mini internship program cert. Honolulu County Med. Soc., 1993, Friend of Social Workers award NASW, 1995, Outstanding Govt. Svc. award Hawaii Pacific Gerontol. Soc., 1996, Outstanding Legislator award Hawaii Med. Assn., 1996, Na Lima Kokua Ma Waema O Makua award Pacific Gerontol. Soc., 1996, Friend of the Family award Hawaii Assn. for Marriage and Family Therapy, 1998. Mem. Liliha/Palama Bus. Assn. (bd. dirs. 1994—), Hawaii Women's Legal Found., Good Beginnings Alliance, Kalihi-Palama Culture and Arts Soc., Chung Wah Chung Kung Hui, Hawaii Chinese Civic Assn., Hawaii State Youth Vol. Bd. (past pres.), Ma'ema'e Sch. SCBM, Legis. Women's Caucus, Small Bus. Caucus, Keiki Caucus (co-chair 1991—), Chinese C. of C., McKinley Alumni Assn. (bd. dirs. 1989—). Democrat. Episcopalian. Avocations: raising animals, gardening, swimming. Office: State Senate 415 S Beretania St Rm 228 Honolulu HI 96813-2407 Office Phone: 808-586-6130. E-mail: senchunoakland@capitol.hawaii.gov.

CHURCH, KATRINA J., pharmaceutical executive; AB magna cum laude, Duke University; JD, N.Y.U. Sch. Law. With law firm Hopkins & Carley; v.p., gen. counsel, sec. VISX, Inc., 1991—98; v.p. legal affairs and corp. counsel Connetics, 1998—2000, sr. v.p., gen. counsel, corp. sec., 2000—. Recipient Arthur T. Vanderbilt medal, N.Y.U. Sch. Law. Office: Connetics Corporation 3160 Porter Dr Palo Alto CA 94304-1212

CHURCH, LILLIAN HAZEL See BROOKS, LILLIAN

CHURCH, MARTHA ELEANOR, retired academic administrator; b. Pitts., Nov. 17, 1930; d. Walter Seward and Eleanor (Boyer) Church. BA, Wellesley Coll., 1952; MA, U. Pitts., 1954; PhD, U. Chgo., 1960; DSc (hon.), Lake Erie Coll., 1975; LittD (hon.), Houghton Coll., 1980; LHD (hon.), Queens Coll., 1981, Ursinus Coll., 1981, St. Joseph Coll., 1982, Towson State U., 1983, Dickinson Coll., 1987, Coll. Notre Dame Md., 1995; LLD (hon.), Hood Coll., 1995; LHD (hon.), Ill. Coll., 2003. Instr. geography Mt. Holyoke Coll., South Hadley, Mass., 1953-57; lectr. geography Ind. U. Gary Ctr., 1958; instr., then asst. prof. geography Wellesley Coll., 1958—65; dean coll., prof. geography Wilson Coll., 1965-71; assoc. exec. sec. Commn. Higher Edn., Mid. States Assn. Coll. and Secondary Sch., 1971-75; pres. Hood Coll., Frederick, Md., 1975-95, pres. emerita, 1995—; sr. scholar Carnegie Found. for Advancement of Tchg., Princeton, 1995—97; interim pres. Ill. Coll., 2002—03; interim v.p. acad. affairs Holy Names U., Oakland, Calif., 2005—06. Bd. dirs. Farmers and Mechanics Nat. Bank, 1982—2000, dir. emerita, 2000—; cons. Choice: Books for Coll. Librs.; co-chmn. nat. adv. panel Nat. Ctr. for Rsch. to Improve Postsecondary Tchg. and Learning, U. Mich., 1985—90; mem. bd. visitors Def. Intelligence Coll., 1988—91; mem. adv. bd. dirs. Automobile Club Md., 1991—2002; bd. dirs. AAA Mid-Atlantic, 1997—2002; mem. adv. bd. The Boyer Ctr. Messiah Coll., Grantham, Pa., 1997—2005. Author: The Spatial Organization of Electric Power Territories in Massachusetts, 1960; Co-editor: A Basic Geographical Library: A Selected and Annotated Book List for Am. Colls, 1966; cons. editor, Change mag., 1980-01. Bd. dirs. Coun. for Internat. Exch. of Scholars, 1979-80, Japan Internat. Christian U. Found., 1977-91, Nat. Ctr. for Higher Edn. Mgmt. Sys., 1980-83; bd. dirs. Am. Coun. on Edn., 1976-79, vice chmn., 1978-79, mem. nat. identification panel, 1977-95, Nat. Rsch. Com., 1993-96; bd. advisors Fund for Improvement of Postsecondary Edn., HEW, 1976-79; mem. Sec. of Navy's Adv. Bd. on Edn. and Tng., 1976-80; chmn. Md. Commn. on Civil Rights, 1981-82; trustee Bradford Coll., Mass., 1982-87, Peddie Sch., N.J., 1982-98, chair acad. affairs com., 1987, 96-97, adv. trustee, 1998—, trustee; trustee Carnegie Found. for the Advancement of Tchg., 1986-96, vice chair, 1990-92, chair, 1992-94; trustee Nat. Geog. Soc., 1989—, mem. com. for rsch. and exploration, 1998-2006, chair audit rev. com., 1993-98, chair membership, medals and awards com., 2000—, mem. exec., audit and compensation coms., mission coms.; trustee Nat. Geog. Soc. Edn. Found., 1989-96, 99—; chmn. bd. dirs. Medici Found., Princeton, N.J., 1985-05; trustee United Bd. for Christian Higher Edn. in Asia, 1995-04, sec. bd. trustees, 1998-2003, chmn. com. on trustees, 1997-04, chmn. East and Intra-Asia program subcom., 1996-97, exec. com., 1998-04; mem. Md. Humanities Coun., 1985-86, Md. Jud. Disabilities Commn., 1985-94; commr. Edn. Commn. States, Md., 1981-99; exec. com. Campus Compact: Project for Pub. and Cmty. Svc., 1986-89; trustee Internat. Partnership for Svc. Learning, 1999-02. Mem. AAUW, Am. Assn. Advancement of Humanities (bd. dirs. 1979-81), Am. Assn. Higher Edn. (chmn. 1980-81, bd. dirs. 1979-83), Assn. Am. Geographers, Nat. Assn. Ind. Colls. and Univs. (bd. dirs. 1983-86), Md. Ind. Colls. and Univs. Assn. (pres. 1979-81, mem. exec. com. 1988-92), Assn. Am. Colls. and Univs. (mem. adv. com. project on status and edn. of women 1980-85), Women's Coll. Coalition (mem. exec. com. 1976-80, 87-89), Am. Conf. Acad. Deans (sec., editor 1969-71), Coun. Protestant Colls. and Univs. (bd. dirs. 1969-71), Soc. Coll. and Univ. Planning (mem. editl. bd. 1979-95), Cosmos Club (mem. jour. editl. bd. 1990-94), Inst. Ednl. Leadership (bd. dirs. 1982-87), Sigma Delta Epsilon, Delta Kappa Gamma (hon.). Home: 3124 Chartwell Crescent Ln Adamstown MD 21710-9643 Office Phone: 301-644-1441. Personal E-mail: marthachurch@edurostream.com.

CHURCH, PAMELA T., lawyer; b. Columbia, SC, Sept. 5, 1956; BA cum laude, Yale Univ., 1978; postgraduate, Univ. Bonn, Germany, 1978—79; JD, NYU, 1982. Bar: NY 1983. Ptnr., Global Mergers & Acquisition practice Coudert Bros. LLP, NYC, former mem. exec. bd. Contbr. articles to profl. jours. Mem.: ABA, Assn. Bar City of NY. Office: Coudert Bros LLP 1114 Ave of the Americas New York NY 10036 Office Phone: 212-626-4976. Office Fax: 212-626-4120. Business E-Mail: churchp@coudert.com.

CHURCH, SONIA JANE SHUTTER, librarian; b. York, Pa., Dec. 15, 1940; d. Robert Benjamin and Eva Alverta (Horn) Shutter; m. Ernest Layton Church, May 20, 1966; children: Robert Bruce, Jennifer Grace. BS in Edn., Millersville Coll., 1962; MLS, U. Pitts., 1978. Playground supr. York City Sch. Dist., Pa., 1961; children's libr. Prunedale br. Monterey County Libr., Calif., 1978-79, youth svcs. coord., 1979-83, 85-88, head libr. Prunedale br., 1983-85; children's svc. mgr. Ventura (Calif.) County Libr., 1988-94; youth svcs. coord. Chattanooga Hamilton County Bicentennial Libr., 1994-95; head Children's Learning Ctr. Pub. Libr. Cin. and Hamilton County, 1995—. Writer Book Beat column for Fortnighter Newspaper, Salinas, 1983-85, Book Corner column, Warm 98 Family Mag., 1997—. Editor pamphlet: What Will We Do with the Baby?, A Collection of Nursery Rhymes and Finger Plays, 1977. Mem. Deferred Comp. Task Force, Monterey County, 1983-88, Mgmt. Coun., Monterey County, 1983-88; chmn. adminstrv. com. Social Svcs. Commn., Monterey County, 1983-85, chmn. ad hoc com., 1983-88; coord. com. Boy Scouts Am., Salinas, 1983-85; mem. Children's Svcs. Mgmt. Consortium, 1986-87; tchr. Sun Sch., Luth. Ch. Good Shepherd, Salinas, 1982-88; chmn. latchkey com. Child Care Task Force, Ventura County; chmn. children's com. Black Gold Libr. Sys., Calif., 1991; mem. children's coord. coun. Ventura County, 1993-94; asst. coord. S.W. chpt., Ohio Libr. Coun., 1998-99, coord., 1999-2000. Capt. USMC, 1962-66. Recipient Celebrate Literacy award Internat. Reading Assn., Margaret Lynch Exemplary Svc. award Calif. Reading Assn.; Sico scholar, 1958-62. Mem. ALA, Assn. Libr. Svc. to Children (liaison with nat. orgns. serving child com.), Calif. Libr. Assn. (pres. children's svcs. chpt. 1989-90, Beatty award com. 1990-92, chair Beatty com. 1993-95, children's svcs. mgmt. chpt., assembly 1991-95, planning com. 1992-95), Ohio Libr. Coun., Assn. Children's Librs. No. Calif., Sch. and Pub. Librs. Assn. Monterey Bay Area (pres. 1979-80, 85-86), Assn. Childhood Edn. Internat., Nat. Story League (co-founder Ventura County storytellers group), Calif. Reading Assn., Internat. Reading Assn. (pres. 1991-92), Ventura County Lit. Coun., So. Calif. Coun. Lit. for Children and Young People, Soc. Children's Book Writers, Am. Legion (comdr. 1984-85), Women's Internat. Bowling Congress, Women's Bowling Assn., U. Pitts. Alumni Assn., Millersville U. Alumni Assn., Beta Phi Mu, Beta Sigma Phi. Democrat. Lutheran. Office: Pub Library 800 Vine St Cincinnati OH 45202-2071 E-mail: childrenhead@plch.lib.oh.us.

CHURCHILL, MAIR ELISA ANNABELLE, medical educator; b. Liverpool, Eng., Nov. 28, 1959; BA in Chemistry, Swarthmore (Pa.) Coll., 1981; PhD in Chemistry, Johns Hopkins U., 1987. Lab. asst. Swarthmore Coll., 1979-81; teaching asst. Johns Hopkins U., Balt., 1981-83; non-clin. sci. staff grade I MRC Lab. Molecular Biology, Cambridge, Eng., 1987-93; asst. prof. biophysics U. Ill., Urbana, 1993-98; assoc. prof. biophysics U. Colo., Denver, 1998—. Contbr. numerous articles to profl. jours. Am. Cancer Soc. fellow, 1987-89, Cambridge U. fellow, 1988-91. Mem. Am. Chem. Soc., Sigma Xi (assoc.). Office: U Colo Health Scis Dept Pharm PO Box 6511 MS8303 Aurora CO 80045

CHUTE, DEANNA, mathematics educator; Math tchr. The Brearley Sch., N.Y.C., 1993—99, Palo Alto H.S., Palo Alto, Calif., 2000—. Office: Palo Alto High School 50 Embarcadero Rd Palo Alto CA 94040 Office Phone: 650-329-3845. E-mail: dchute@pausd.org.

CHUTE, MARY L., library director; BA in art history, U. Mich.; MA in art history, Boston U.; MLS, Simmons Coll. With Mass. Libr. Sys.; pub. libr. cons. divsn. of devel. Md. State Dept. Edn., 1997—99; dir. and state libr. Del. Divsn. Libr./State Libr., 1999—2002; dep. dir. libr. services The Inst. Mus. & Library Services, Washington, 2002—, acting dir., 2005—06. Office: Inst Mus & Library Services 1800 M St NW 9th Fl Washington DC 20036*

CHU-ZHU, JANICE GAIL, social worker; b. NYC, Aug. 13, 1958; d. Lamtin Adam and Jane Yuk (Leung) C.; m. Xiang Zhu, May 29, 1994. BA, Binghamton State U., 1981; MSW, Fordham U., 1990. LCSW NY. Tchr. English Berlitz Sch. of Languages, Madrid, 1980-82, Leo Burnett, S.A., Madrid, 1982-84; caseworker-foster care Sheltering Arms Children's Svc., NYC, 1984-87; social worker-family ct.- PINS mediation & diversion Children's Aid Soc., NYC, 1987-89, social worker-foster care, 1989-91; pluralism strategy cons. Girl Scouts USA, NYC, 1991-95, quality recognition specialist, 1995-98, mgr., 1998-2001; sr. cmtys. sch. cons. Children's Aid Soc. Nat. Tech. Assistance Ctr. for Cmty. Schs., NYC, 2001—. Bd. dirs. Fordham U. Grad. Sch. Svc. Alumni Bd., N.Y.C., 1990-94. Mem. Nat. Assn. Social Workers. Democrat. Roman Catholic. Avocations: travel, reading, swimming, bowling. Home: 19 Liberty St Ossining NY 10562-5924 Office: Children's Aid Soc Nat Tech Assistance Ctr 4600 Broadway New York NY 10040- Fax: 212-544-7609. E-mail: janicec@childrensaidsociety.org.

CHVANY, CATHERINE VAKAR, foreign language educator; b. Paris, Apr. 26, 1927; m. 1948; 3 children. BA, Radcliffe Coll., 1963; PhD, Harvard U., 1970. Instr. Russian Wellesley Coll., 1966-67; instr. MIT, 1967-70, lectr., 1970-71, asst. prof., 1971-74, assoc. prof. Russian, 1974-83, prof., 1983-94, emerita, 1994—. Fellow Harvard Russian Rsch. Ctr., 1979—83; vis. prof. U. de Paris 7, 1991; vis. lectr. Harvard U., 1995; Lindholm vis. prof. U. Oreg., 1999. Author: On the Syntax of BE-Sentences in Russian, 1975, Selected Essays, 1997; co-editor: Slavic Transformational Syntax, 1974, Morphosyntax in Slavic, 1980, Gertruda Vakar. Stikhotvorenija, 1984; New Studies in Russian Language and Literature, 1987; mem. editl. adv. bd. Essays in Poetics, Syntax; contbr. more than 100 articles on linguistics, poetics, Russian and Bulgarian langs. to profl. jours. Lilly postdoctoral teaching award fellow MIT, 1975-76; recipient Phi Beta Kappa, 1963; Disting. Scholarly Career award Assn. Tchrs. Slavic and East European Langs, 1991, Best Book prize 1997. Mem. Bulgarian Studies Assn. Office: MIT 77 Massachusetts Ave Rm 14n305 Cambridge MA 02139-4307 Business E-Mail: cvchvany@mit.edu.

CHWALEK, CONSTANCE, real estate broker, mortgage broker; b. N.Y.C., Nov. 1, 1928; d. Sylvester James Maguire and Justine Rita Nigra; m. Raymond McVey, Feb. 27, 1949 (div. Oct. 1959); 1 child, Deidre McVey; m. Frank Charles Chwalek, Aug. 15, 1975. Student, Empire State Coll. Bookkeeper/adminstr. various cos., N.Y.C., 1953-75; real estate broker, mortgage broker Century 21 Fortune Realty, N.Y.C., 1975—. Mem. L.I. Bd. Realtors, Howard Beach Civic Assn. Republican. Roman Catholic. Avocations: golf, tennis, skiing, art, dance. Home: 15535 Huron St Howard Beach NY 11414-2854

CHWAT, ANNE, food service executive; JD, NYU, 1987. Assoc. Clearly Gottlieb Steen & Hamilton, 1987—95; assoc. corp. counsel Joseph E. Seagram & Sons, Inc., 1995—2000; v.p. legal and bus. affairs BMG Music, N.Y.C., 2000—03, gen. counsel, sr. v.p. legal and bus. affairs, 2003—04, chief ethics and compliance officer; exec. v.p., gen. counsel Burger King Corp. Office: 5505 Blue Lagoon Dr Miami FL 33126 Office Phone: 305-378-7913. Business E-Mail: achwat@whopper.com.

CHWATSKY, ANN, photographer, educator; b. Phila., Jan. 11, 1942; BS in Art Edn., Hofstra U., 1965, MS, 1971; postgrad., L.I. U., 1973—74. Cert. tchr. Photography editor L.I. Mag., 1976-80; instr. Internat. Ctr. Photography, N.Y.C., 1979-80, Parrish Art Mus., Southampton, N.Y., 1984—. Mem. art faculty NYU, 1991—. Author, photographer: The Man in the Street, 1989; photographer The Four Seasons of Shaker life; photographs featured in Time, Newsweek, Newsday, Manchete, N.Y. Times, MD Med. Times; one person shows include Lincoln Ctr., Buenos Aires, 1983, Photographers Gallery, London, 1985, shakers, Nassau County Mus. Fine Arts, 1987, Greater Lafayette (Ind.) Mus. Art, 1988, Bklyn. Coll., 1990, Kiev, USSR Exhbn. Hall, 1991, Bklyn. Coll., Carrie Haddad Gallery, Hudson, N.Y., 2001, N.Y. Faculty show, 2003, Digital Artist, 2005, Little Rock, 2004, Puck Bldg., NYC, 2005, Hampshire Coll. Gallery, Amherst, Mass., 2005; group shows include The Other, Houston Ctr. Photography, 1988, L.I. Fine Arts Mus., 1984, Women's Interart Ctr., N.Y.C., 1976, 80, Parrish Art Mus., Southampton, 1979, Internat. Ctr. Photography, N.Y.C., 1980, 82, Nassau County Mus. Fine Arts, 1983, Soho 20 Gallery, N.Y.C., 1984, New Orleans World's Fair, 1984, Southampton Gallery, 1988, 89, Lizan Tops Gallery, L.I., 1994, Apex Art, N.Y.C., 1995, Am. Mus., Prague, 1997, First Seoul Internat. Tribunal, 1998, Carrie Haddad Gallery, Hudson NY, 2002, Hampshire Coll. Garden, 2005, Puck Bldg. N.Y.C., 2006; represented in permanent collections Bass Mus. Art, Fla., Forbes N.Y.C., Midtown YWCA, Nassau County Mus. Fine Arts, Susan Rothenberg, others. Recipient Estabrook Disting. Alumni award Hofstra U., 1984; Kodak Profl. Photographers award, 1984; Eastman Found. grantee, 1981-82, Poloroid grantee, 1980. Mem. Assn. Am. Mag. Profls., Picture Profls. Am., Profl. Women Photographers N.Y.C. Studio: 29 E 22nd St Apt 3N New York NY 10010-5305 Personal E-mail: annphotog@aol.com.

CIABARRA, LOUISE, secondary school educator, medical/surgical nurse; b. Phila., Jan. 28, 1940; d. Nick and Lillian Caruso; m. Mario Ciabarra, Sept. 25, 1965; children: Mimi, Anthony, Lilliana, Nicole, Christopher, Mario. BA, Temple U., 1965; MS, Villanova U., 1975. LPN, Pa.; tchr. chemistry and biology, Pa. Part-time nurse Holy Redeemer Hosp., Pa., 1981—92; tchr. H.S. Phila. Parochial Sch., 1966—. Camp nurse Phila. Diocesan Camp, Jamison, Pa., summers 1988-95, pvt. travel camp, Blue Bell, Pa., summers 1996-2005. Sunday sch. tchr. St. Raymond's Parish, 1976—. Named Tchr. of Yr., Diocesan Sch., Phila., 1987-88, Tchr. of Quarter, 2003; recognized by award "Hero in Edn." by Aktion Club, sponsored by Jenkintown & Glenside Kiwanis Clubs on May 6, 2003. Roman Catholic. Office: Archbishop Wood HS 655 York Rd Warminster PA 18974-2001 Office Phone: 215-672-5050. Business E-Mail: kiabarraabw@yahoo.com.

CIAMBRONE, CHERYL C., mathematics educator; d. Robert Leroy and Sylvia Jane Coursen; children: Patrick, Anthony, Margaret. BS in Secondary Edn., Pa. State U., University Park, 1983; MEd in Secondary Sch. Adminstrn., East Stroudsburg U., Pa., 1989. Cert. secondary edn. level II, secondary adminstr. Math. tchr. Stroudsburg HS, 1984—90, Easton (Pa.) HS, 2001—. Mem.: MAA, Nat. Coun. Tchrs. Math. Office: Easton Area HS 2601 William Penn Hwy Easton PA 18045

CIANCIO, MARILYN, television producer; b. Jamestown, NY, June 4, 1943; d. James S. and Casima M. (Lisciandro) Bonfiglio; m. Sebastian G. Ciancio, Nov. 16, 1963; children: Michele Ann, Sebastian James. BA, SUNY, Buffalo, 1973, MA, 1978. Cert. tchr. NY. Elem. tchr. St. Peter and Paul Sch, Jamestown, 1963—65, St. Benedict Sch., Buffalo, 1963—65; lectr. in leadership and volunteerism various local and nat. orgns., 1979—; alt. host Reggie Keaton Show Adelphia TV, Buffalo, 1984—94, prodr., host Artscope, 1994—, arts corr. Crossroads, 2001—. Mem. spkrs.' bur. World U. Games, Buffalo, 1993; mem. spl. studies faculty Chautauqua (NY) Instn., 1993; collaborative prodr. Video Arts Coun., Buffalo, 2003—04; adv. coun. Ctr. Arts U. Buffalo. Contbg. editor: handbook Here's Buffalo, 1984; co-editor: (theatrical cookbook) Women of Studio Arena Theatre - Edible Entertainment, 1985—87; prodr.: (documentary) Women's Pavilion PanAm, 2001. Bd. dirs. Arts Coun. Buffalo and Erie County, 1999—; bd. mgrs. Women's Pavilion PanAm 2001, Buffalo, 2000—02; mem. adv. bd. Cir. of Daus., Buffalo, 2002—; co-founder, bd. dirs. Chautauqua Dental Congress, 1980—; trustee, sec. Studio Arena Theatre, Buffalo, 1987—89; pres. Women's Dental Guild, 1974, Women of Studio Arena, 1985—87, U. Buffalo Women's Club, 1994. Named Women of Distinction, NY State Senate, 2005; recipient Artie Theatre award, Artvoice, Buffalo, 2001, Bronze Telly award, Nat. Telly Awards, Cin., 2003, 2004, Zodiaque Dance Co. Dir.'s award, U. Buffalo, 2003, spl. citation, Town of Amherst, 2004, Outstanding Supporter and Adv. for the Arts award, Arts Coun. in Buffalo and Erie County, 2006. Avocations: organ, needlepoint, travel, art, art advocacy.

CIANCIOLO-CARNEY, ROSSANA, investigative analyst; b. Knoxville, Tenn., July 4, 1964; d. Salvatore and Mariluz Cianciolo; m. Patrick Michael Carney, Jan. 8, 1961. BA in Polit. Sci./Fgn. Langs., Stephens Coll., 1986. Intelligence rsch. specialist Nat. Drug Intelligence Ctr., Johnstown, Pa., 1994-95; investigative analyst FBI, San Diego, Calif., 1995—. Informal resolution program counselor Nat. Drug Intelligence Ctr., Johnstown, 1995. Spkr. Cmty. Outreach, 1995—, participant/San Diego Elder Abuse Fraud Task Force, 1998—; wish grantor Make-a-Wish, San Diego, 1997—; bd. dirs. Women in Bus. Aiding the Cmty., 1996—. Republican. Roman Catholic. Avocations: running, swimming, reading, travel. Home: 369 Park Street NE Vienna VA 22180 Office: FBI 7799 Leesburg Pike Falls Church VA 22037 Office Phone: 412-432-4461. Business E-Mail: rossanacarney@usa.net.

CIANI, JUDITH ELAINE, retired lawyer; b. Medford, Mass., July 24, 1943; d. A. Walter and Ruth Alice (Bowman) C.; m. Marion M. Smith, Sept. 29, 1982. Grad., Thayer Acad., Braintree, Mass., 1961; MA, Mt. Holyoke Coll., 1965; JD, Boston Coll., 1970. Bar: Calif. 1971, U.S. Dist. Ct. (no. dist.) Calif. 1971, U.S. Ct. Appeals (9th cir.) 1971. Aide/press sec. Rep. James A. Burke, Washington, 1965-67; atty. Pillsbury, Madison & Sutro, San Francisco, 1970-78, ptnr., 1978-90; ret., 1990. Del. Calif. Bar Conv., San Francisco, 1973-78, 83-85. Mem. San Francisco Police Commn., 1976-80, Juvenile Justice Task Force, San Francisco, 1981-83; bd. dirs. Bernard Osher Found., San Francisco, 1977—; pres. Common Fund for Legal Svcs., San Francisco, 1985—, Sinfonia San Francisco, 1985-86. Fellow Am. Bar Found.; mem. Bar Assn. San Francisco (bd. dirs., pres. Found. 1978—, bd. dirs. 1981-83, treas. 1987). Home: PO Box 960 Inverness CA 94937-0960 E-mail: jeciani@svn.net.

CIANNELLA, JOEEN MOORE, small business owner; b. Warren, Ohio, Mar. 20, 1948; d. Joseph Alvie and Elizabeth Dorthea Moore; m. Christopher M. Ciannella, July 31, 1976 (div. Jan. 1987); children: Bryce C., Tara E. BA in French, Denison U., 1970. Profl. staff US Senate Rep. Policy Com., Washington, 1971-75; owner Jo Moore-Sophisticated Country, Park Ridge, NJ, 1984—; dist. dir. Congresswoman Marge Roukema US Ho. Reps., Ridgewood, NJ, 1985—2002; exec. dir. Hermitage Mus., Hohokus, NJ, 2003—04; dir. devel. Helen Hayes Theatre Co., Nyack, NY, 2004—05; dir. external affairs Greater North Jersey chpt. Nat. Multiple Sclerosis Soc., Paramus, NJ, 2005; pres. JTB Enterprises, LLC, Park Ridge, NJ. Mem. Nat. coun. Boy Scouts Am., 1995—98; trustee Greater Roles and Opportunities for Women NJ GOP, 1997—2002; mem. Park Ridge Bd. Health, 1984—86; founding mem. Pioneer Women Bergen County, 1992—; mem. exec. bd. Bergen coun. Boy Scouts Am., 1991—98, co-chair Pascak Valley Dist. Luncheree, 1991—92, chair spl. events fin., 1993—94, mem. exec. com., 1993—98, vice chmn. fin., 1995—98, mem. exec. bd. No. NJ coun., 1999—, vice chair fin., 2000—02; mem. exec. bd. Ramapo Coll. Found., 1991—, theme chairperson fundraiser, 1991—94, disting. citizen dinner com., 1991—, mem. bus. network com., 1994—97, chmn. pub. rels. and mktg. com., 1996—2000, mem. exec. com., 1996—, chmn. mktg./instl. rels., 2000—; com. mem. NJ Network Found. Gala, 2000—02; bd. dirs. Helen Hayes Theater Co., Nyack, NY, 2001—, mem. devel. com. spl. events, 2002—, Day in the Garden, 2003; chairperson spl. effects West Bergen Mental Health 40th Anniversary Ruby Ball, 2003; founding mem. W. Bergen Mental Health Found., 2003—; active Bush for Pres. Campaign, 1988, 1992, Dole for Pres. Campaign, 1996; elected mem. Park Ridge County Com., 1983—, mcpl. chairperson, 1986—96; active Bergen County Rep. Com., 1983—, Park Ridge Rep. Orgn., 1983—, v.p., 1988—89; active NE Rep. Orgn. Dist. 39, NJ, 1984—, sec. NJ, 1990—91, treas. NJ, 1991—92, chairperson NJ, 1992—93; ofcl. com. mem. NJ GOP Conv., 1991; charter mem. Women Leadership Summit Rep. Network to Elect Women, 1996—97. Recipient Mission award, Ramapo Coll. Found., 1999, Silver Beaver award, Boy Scouts Am., 1999. Mem.: Jr. League Bergen County (com. mem. Festival of Trees 1988), Ridgewood Unit Rep. Women, Bergen County Women's Rep. Club, NJ Fedn. Rep. Women, Rep. Women of 90's State NJ, Rotary (mem. com. annual auction Park Ridge chpt. 1990—, chairperson holiday party 1991—). Avocations: gardening, antiques, sports, travel. Home: 34 Spring Valley Rd Park Ridge NJ 07656-1860 Office: JTB Enterprises LLC 34 Spring Valley Rd Park Ridge NJ 07656 Personal E-mail: jciannella@optonline.net.

CICCOLO, ANGELA, lawyer; b. Indpls., Aug. 12, 1961; BSFS, Georgetown U., 1983, JD, 1992. Bar: DC 1992, admitted to practice: US Dist. Ct. (DC) 1993. Asst. gen. counsel NAACP, interim gen. counsel, 2005—. Staff mem. Georgetown Internat. Environ. Law Rev., 1990—91, Writing Program Editor, 1991—92. Mem.: Women's Bar Assn., DC Trial Lawyers Assn., Bar Assn. DC. Democrat. Office: NAACP 4805 Mt Hope Dr Fifth Floor Baltimore MD 21215 Office Phone: 410-580-5792.

CICCONE, AMY NAVRATIL, art librarian; b. Detroit, Sept. 19, 1950; d. Gerald R. and Ruth C. (Kauer) Navratil. BA, Wayne State U., 1972; AM in Library Sci., U. Mich., 1973. Rsch. libr. Norton Simon Mus., Pasadena, Calif., 1974-81; chief libr. Chrysler Mus., Norfolk, Va., 1981-88; head libr. Architecture and Fine Arts Libr. U. So. Calif., L.A., 1988-97, acting asst. univ. libr. pub. svcs., 1993-95, ref. libr., 1997—2004, assoc. coord. collection devel., 2004—. Contbr. articles to profl. jours. and chpts to books; cons. editor Art Reference Svcs., 1990-98. Mem. Art Libraries Soc. N.Am. (moderator Decorative Arts Roundtable, 1991-93, facilities standards com. 1986-91, chmn. strategic planning task force 1994-96, vice-chmn. So. Calif. chpt.

1989, chmn. 1990, chmn. 2001 conf.), Rsch. Librs. Group, Art & Architecture Group (steering com. 1992-94). Office: U So Calif Libr Los Angeles CA 90089-0187 Office Phone: 213-740-1958. Business E-Mail: aciccone@usc.edu.

CICCONE, MADONNA LOUISE VERONICA See MADONNA

CICERCHI, ELEANOR ANN TOMB, not-for-profit fundraiser; b. Sayre, Pa., Dec. 11, 1944; d. William Horton and Brinton Elizabeth (Cauffiel) Tomb; m. Robert A. Weskerna, Nov. 19, 1966 (div. Feb. 1981); children: Amy Marie, Robert Campbell; m. Philip J. Cicerchi, July 1982. AB with great distinction, Mt. Holyoke Coll., 1966; MS, New Sch. Social Rsch., 1992. Cert. fundraising exec. Sr. mktg. rep. Group Health Plan, Guttenberg, NJ, 1976-79; dir. comty. rels. Burke Rehab. Ctr., White Plains, NY, 1979-84; exec. dir. Bergen comty. Coll. Fedn., Paramus, NJ, 1984-86; campaign counsel Brakeley John Price Jones, Inc., Stanford, Conn., 1986-88; v.p. instnl. advancement Marymount Coll., Tarrytown, NY, 1988-93; dir. maj. gifts Am. Found. for AIDS Rsch., N.Y.C., 1993-95, chief devel. officer, 1995-96; v.p. devel. and external affairs ORBIS Internat., Inc., N.Y.C., 1996-2000; assoc. v.p. devel. Save the Children, Westport, Conn., 2000—02; dir. devel. The Corning Mus. of Glass, 2002—. Faculty mem. Fundraising Sch., Ctr. Philanthropy, Ind. U., Indpls., 1989—; adj. grad. faculty mem. NYU, N.Y.C., 1990-97, New Sch. for Social Rsch., N.Y.C., 1995—, chmn. PR Group for Vision 2000: The Right to Sight, Geneva, 1998-99; bd. dirs. AMD Alliance, 1999-01; devel. and marching com. Am. Assn. Mus., vice chair devel. and membership com., 2005-. Author: Raid!, 1978, Anonymous Giving, 1991; co-author: The Earth Shook and the Sky Was Red, 1976, The Flower of the Virginian, 1980; editor: The Architecture of Bergen County, 1991. Bd. dirs., past chmn. Philharmonia Virtuosi, Dobbs Ferry, NY, 1985—2002; v.p. Orch. of the Finger Lakes, 2003—05, pres., 2005—, Dem. Club, River Vale, NJ, 1978—81; bd. dirs., sec. Am. Anorexia-Bulimia Assn., N.Y.C., 1984—99; bd. dirs. Planned Parenthood of the So. Finger Lakes, 2003—. Woodrow Wilson fellow, 1966; Sarah Williston scholar, 1964, Mt. Holyoke scholar, 1963. Mem. Am. Assn. Fundraising Profls. (Greater N.Y. chpt. v.p. 1993-95, Finger Lakes chpt. v.p. 2005—, Finger Lakes chpt. Philanthropist of Yr. 2004), Assn. of Fundraising Profls. (Profl. Fundraiser of Yr., Finger Lakes chpt. 2004), Assn. for Rsch. on Nonprofit Orgns. and Voluntary Action, Phi Beta Kappa. Office: The Corning Museum of Glass One Museum Way Corning NY 14830 Office Phone: 607-974-5683. Business E-Mail: cicerchiet@cmog.org.

CICERO, DIANNE, special education educator; BS, Nazareth Coll. Rochester, 1975; MS, SUNY, Geneseo, 1977. Cert. (permanent) spl. edn., speech and hearing handicapped. PSEN resource rm. tchr. Mt. Morris (N.Y.) Ctrl. Sch., 1978—87; tchr. Steuben-Allegany BOCES, Hornell, NY, 1987—96, Livingston-Wyoming Arc, Geneseo, NY, 1998—.

CIELINSKI-KESSLER, AUDREY ANN, writer, publishing executive, small business owner; b. Cleve., Sept. 10, 1957; d. Joseph and Dorothy Antoinette (Hanna) Cielinski. BJ with high honors, U. Tex., 1979. Reporter, writer Med. World News mag., N.Y.C., 1979, asst. copy chief Houston, 1983—84; free-lance writer, editor, 1984—; editl. asst. Jour. Health and Social Behavior, Houston, 1980—81; sec. dept. psychiatry Baylor Coll. Medicine, Houston, 1980—81; procedures analyst, tech. writer, tech. libr. Harris County Data Processing Dept., Houston, 1981—83; comm. specialist III, Wang sys. adminstr. Office Planning and Rsch. Houston Police Dept.; tchr. tech. writing class, 1985—89; tech. writer Chevron Exploration and Prodn. Svcs. Co., Houston, 1990—92; freelance tech. writer, 1992—; owner Write Hand Ohio, Kent, 1992—. Editor: (newsletter) At the Siammut, Signals, CEPS Synergy, PCLIBtm Letter, Insights, Steps & Specs., The Voter, LPC Portage County Leader, Kent Environ. Coun.; contbr. stories and articles to newspapers and mags. Vol. editor newsletters Greater Houston area Am. Cancer Soc., VGS, Inc., W. Knoll News; mem. bd. zoning appeals City of Kent, 1996—2003, vice chair, 1998, 2004—05, chair, 1999—2002, mem. shade tree commn., 1996—, chair, 1999—2002, mem. assessment equalization bd., 1998—2003, mem. fair housing bd., 1998—, mem. environ. commn., 1999, mem. cmty. reinvestment area housing coun.; mem. transp. study citizen involvement com. Akron Met. Area, 1999—, vice chair, 2000, chair, 2001—02; mem. Leadership Portage County, 1999; bd. dirs. Keep Kent Beautiful, vice chair, 2002—05; mem. Portage County Flood Variance Bd., 2005—, Geauga Ashtabule Portage Partnership Area 19 Workforce Investment Bd., 2005—; bd. dirs. Kent Environ. Coun., newsletter editor; vol. writer, graphic designer office religious edn. St. Ambrose Roman Cath. Ch., Houston, 1983—92; trustee Cath. Charities Portage County, v.p., 2002, 2005, pres., 2003—04; mem. bd. bldg. appeals Portage County. Recipient Commendation award, Chief of Police, Houston, Chief's Command Employee of Month award, 1989. Mem.: NAFE, Soc. Tech. Comm. (mgr. policies and procedures spl. interest group, Disting Spl. Interest Group Svc. award), Am. Med. Writers Assn., Nat. Assn. Desktop Pubs., Women in Comm., Soc. Children's Book Writers (assoc.), Kent Area C. of C., Women's Network, Alpha Lamda Delta, Phi Kappa Phi, Sigma Delta Chi. Home and Office: 1638 S Lincoln St Kent OH 44240-4449 Office Phone: 330-677-8598. Personal E-mail: audck@neo.rr.com.

CIENCIALA, ANNA MARIA, history educator; b. Gdansk, Poland, Nov. 8, 1929; d. Andrew M. and Wanda M. (Waissmann) C.; came to U.S., 1965, naturalized, 1970; B.A., U. Liverpool, 1952; M.A., McGill U., 1955; Ph.D., Ind. U., 1962. Lectr. European history U. Ottawa, 1960-61, U. Toronto (Ont., Can.), 1961-65; asst. prof. history U. Kans., Lawrence, 1965-67, assoc. prof., 1967-71, prof. history and Soviet and Eastern European area studies, 1971-2002, ret., 2002. Recipient prize Pilsudski Inst. Am., 1968; Ford Found. fellow, 1958-60; Can. Council grantee, 1963; Fulbright-Hays fellow, 1968-69; U. Kans. gen. research grantee, 1965-75, 80-81; Am. Council Learned Socs. grantee, 1980, 83; Irex fellow, Poland, 1979-80, Russia 1993-94; NFH Poland 1993. Mem. AAUP, AAUW, Am. Assn. Advancement Slavic Studies, Am. Hist. Assn., Kosciuszko Found., PAU, Pilsudski Inst. Am., Polish-Am. Inst. Arts and Scis., Polish-Am. Hist. Assn., Hist. Preservation. Author: Poland and the Western Powers, 1938-39, 1968; From Versailles to Locarno, Keys to Polish Foreign Policy, 1919-25; editor: (with A. Headlam-Morley and R. Bryant) A Memoir of the Paris Peace Conference 1919, 1972; Jozef Beck Polska Polityka Zagraniczna, 1926-39, 1990; contbr. articles to profl. jours. Home: 3045 Steven Dr Lawrence KS 66049-3025 Personal E-mail: hanka@ku.edu.

CIERPIOT, CONNIE, former state legislator; b. Kansas City, June 6, 1953; m. Charles Michael Cierpiot; 2 children. Mem. from dist. 52 Mo. Ho. of Reps., Jefferson City, 1994—2002. Mem.: bd. Truman Neurological Center, bd. Jackson County United Way, Concerned Women for Amer., Santa Fe Trails Women's Republican Club, Jackson County Republican Comm. Republican.

CIESNIEWSKI, ANN MARIE, marriage and family therapist; b. Joliet, Ill., July 29, 1949; d. James Edward and Angela Loretta (Pirc) Riley; m. Anthony Richard Ciesniewski, Apr. 10, 1977 (div. Aug. 1995); children: Lisa Ann, Reneé Marie. MA in Marriage and Family Therapy, Pacific Oaks U., 1999. Computer operator Moore Bus. Forms, Glenview, Ill., 1976-77; family day care provider La Canada, Calif., 1980-87; sales rep., orthopedic fitter Self Care Products, Montrose, Calif., 1987-88; alcohol and drug counselor Phoenix House, Lakeview Terrace, Calif., 1994-99, case mgr., intern therapist, 1999—2001; clinician The Sycamores, Pasadena, 2001—02, lead clinician, lic. family therapist, 2002—. Alcohol and drug counselor Salvation Army, Pasadena, 1992-96. Chair social ministry com. Luth. Ch. in the Foothills, La Canada, 1986-88. Profl. Ednl. Orgn. scholar, 1996. Mem. Calif. Assn. Marriage and Family Therapists, Calif. Assn. Alcohol and Drug Counselors, Calif. Assn. Alcohol and Drug Educators. Avocations: jet skiing, swimming, hiking. Home: PO Box 133 La Canada Flintridge CA 91012-0133

CIESZEWSKI, SANDRA JOSEPHINE, artist, retired manufacturing company manager; b. Cleve., June 7, 1941; d. Chester L. and Cecilia (Laska) C. BA in Chemistry, Ursuline Coll., 1962; BA in Art History, Cleve. State U., 1981; Exec. MBA, Baldwin Wallace Coll., 1989; postgrad., U. N.C., Greensboro, 2005—. Chemist Harshaw Chem. Co., Cleve., 1962-65, Union Carbide Corp., Parma, Ohio, 1965-79; project mgr. Gould, Inc., Eastlake, Ohio, 1979-91; product engrng. mgr.- lithium Duracell Global Bus. Mgmt. Group, Lexington, NC, 1992-2001; interim exhbns. coord. Davidson County C.C., 2003—04. Mem. Cleve. Garden Ctr., Cleve. Mus. Art, sec., 2006—; master gardener vol. Davidson County, 2004— Mem.: Muddy River Art Assn., High Point Art Guild, Soc. Women Engrs., Electrochem. Soc. (treas. 1980), Soc. Applied Spectroscopy, Am. Chem. Soc., Winston-Salem Cinema Soc. (programming chmn. 1997—98, bd. dirs. 1997—2004, treas. 1998—2002), Assoc. Artists of Winston-Salem (bd. dirs. 1998—2004, sec. 1999—2002, interim exec. dir. 2002, pres. 2002—03), Women's Club (sec. Walton Hills chpt. 1985, treas. 1991). Avocations: gardening, skiing, bicycling. Home: 1494 Hickory Tree Rd Winston Salem NC 27127-9142 E-mail: scies@aol.com.

CIEZADLO, JANINA A., art critic, educator; MFA in Printmaking, Ind. U., Bloomington, MA in Comparative Lit. Adj. prof., dept. liberal edn. Columbia Coll.; adj. asst. prof., dept. art and design U. Ill. at Chgo. Published (reviews, scholarly monographs, articles, poetry, exhibited art work), art critic Chgo. Reader, Afterimage, Jour. of Media Arts and Cultural Criticism. Mem.: Chgo. Art Critics Assn. Address: 7200 West Oak 4NE River Forest IL 60305 Office: U Ill at Chgo 106 Jefferson Hall MC036 Chicago IL 60612 Office Phone: 312-996-3337. Business E-Mail: janina@uic.edu.

CIFOLELLI, ALBERTA CARMELLA, artist, educator; b. Erie, Pa., Aug. 19, 1931; d. Charles and Adeline (Tonti) C.; m. Charles Perry Lamb, Jr., July 9, 1955; children: Mark Charles, John Jamison, Todd Vincent. Diploma in Painting, Cleve. Inst. Art, 1953; BS in Art Edn., Kent State U., 1955; MA in Communications, Fairfield U., 1975. Chmn. art Laurel Sch., Shaker Heights, Ohio, 1964-67; instr. painting and drawing Cleve. Inst. Art, 1967—70; arts adminstr. Conn. Commn. on Arts, Bridgeport, 1972—76; visual arts tchr. Interarts, 1972—76; assoc. prof. art Sacred Heart U., 1977—. Prof. art Grad. Sch., Coll. New Rochelle, N.Y., 1985—; co-dir. 31st Art of the N.E., Silvermine Guild Ctr. for Arts, Conn., 1982; keynote spkr. Pa. Art Educators Confs., 1999; co-curator About Paint Westport Arts Ctr. Conn., 2005; keynote spkr. Pa. Art Educators, 1999; curator About Paint Exhbn., Westport Arts Ctr., 2005. One woman shows Housatonic Mus. Art, 2002, Silvermine Guild Ctr. Arts, New Canaan, Conn., 1978, Noho Gallery, N.Y.C., 1982, Artist's Signature Gallery, New Haven, 1982, Kaber Gallery, N.Y.C., 1983, Captiva Gallery, Fla., 1984, 1999 (Retrospective), Stamford Mus., Stamford, Conn., 1988, Conn. Gallery, Marlborough, 1988, Harmon-Meek Gallery, Naples, Fla., 1992, 93, 95, Reece Gallery, N.Y.C., Sacred Heart U., 1998, Art Place, 2001 (Artist of Yr.), Housatonic Mus. Art, 2003 (dir.'s choice), Silvermine Guild, 2003, White Gallery, Lakeville, Conn., 2004, 06; exhibited in group shows at Alice Nash Gallery, N.Y.C., Cleve. Inst. Art, 1967-69, Slater Meml. Mus., Norwich, Conn., 1977, Lyman Allyn Mus., Aldrich Mus. Contemporary Art, New London, Conn., 1983, Armstrong Gallery, N.Y.C., 1984, Aldrich Mus. Contemporary Art, Ridgefield, Conn., 1988, Portland (Maine) Mus. Art, 2002, Nat. Mus. Women i Arts, Washington, 1990, Bruce Mus., Greench, Conn.; residency to live and work at Djerassi Found., Woodside, Calif., May-June 1986; represented in permanent collections Nat. Mus. Women in the Arts, Reagan Libr., Simi Valley, Calif., Butler Inst. Am. Art, Youngtown, Ohio, Francis Lehman Loeb Arts Ctr., Vassar Coll., Poughkeepsie, N.Y., UN, N.Y., Stamford Ct. House; represented in Archives of Am. Art and over 100 pub. collections. Co-campaign mgr., 1st selectman Democratic Orgn., Westport, Conn., 1977; mem. Westport Democrat Town Com., 1978-79. Recipient Best in Show award Ind. Artists, John Herron Art Mus., Indpls., 1959, Doris Kriendler award NAD, 1974, Salute to Women award Fairfield County YWCA, 1988; Conn. Commn. on Arts grantee, 1973-77; Outstanding Conn. Women award, 2003. Mem. Visual Art Steering Com. Westport Arts Ctr., Inst. Visual Arts (chairwoman 1988-89). Achievements include papers listed in Archives of American Art. E-mail: artistac@aol.com.

CIGARROA, JOSIE A., psychiatrist; b. Laredo, Tex., Feb. 25, 1952; d. Marco and Rebeca Cigarroa Uribe; children: Kacy, Jessica, Robert, Tifini. Student, So. Meth. U., Dallas, 1969—73; MD, Tex. Tech. U., Lubbock, 1977. Bd. cert. neurology and psychiatry. Psychiatrist pvt. practice, Laredo, Tex., 1982—85, 1990—2003, Tex. MHMR, Laredo, 1985—89, Camino Real MHMR, Lytle, Tex., 2003—. Alt. del. Tex. Med. Assn., San Antonio, 2005—06. Vol. walker Alcoholics Anonymous, Breast Cancer Awareness. Recipient Award of Excellence, Tex. Tech. Sch., 1977. Mem.: Bexar County Psychiat. Soc., Bexar County Med. Soc., Am. Psychiat. Assn. Roman Catholic. Avocations: jogging, needlepoint. Home: # 813 250 Freeline Pk San Antonio TX 78209 Office: Camino Real MHMR 19965 FM 3175 N Lytle TX 78052

CILELLA, MARY WINIFRED, director; b. Oak Park, Ill., Aug. 24, 1943; d. Charles William Sr. and Theresa Mary (Gilligan) Broucek; m. Salvatore G. Cilella Jr., Aug. 29, 1970; children: Salvatore George III, Peter Dominic. BA, Dominican U., 1965; MAT, U. Notre Dame, 1966; grad. The Prin.'s Inst., Harvard U., 1993; postgrad., U. S.C., 1994-97. Tchr. Miner Jr. H.S., Arlington Heights, Ill., 1966-67; sec. White House, Washington, 1969-70; devel. officer Textile Mus., Washington, 1982-83; dir. meetings and continuing edn. Am. Assn. Mus., Washington, 1983-87; interim lower sch. head, lower sch. head Heathwood Hall Episc. Sch., Columbia, S.C., 1989-94, dir. acad. adminstrn., 1994-95, dir. fin. and adminstrn., 1995-96, asst. head, 1996-98, assoc. head fin. and ops., 1998—2001; cons. Park Tudor Sch., Indpls., 2001—02, dir. Russel and Mary Williams Learning Project, 2002—05; head The Howard Sch., Atlanta, 2005—. Mem. profl. edn. unit adv. com. U. S.C., 1996-2001; mem. U.S. Dept. of Edn.'s Blue Ribbon Schs. Planning Group, 1996; examiner Malcolm Baldrige Nat. Quality award bd. U.S. Dept. Commerce and Nat. Inst. Stds. and Tech., 1999, 2000; adv. coun. Office Ministry Persons with Disabilities, Archdiocese Atlanta, 2006—. Mem. ASCD, Internat. Dyslexia Assn. (bd. Ga. br. 2006—), Phi Delta Kappa. Roman Catholic. Avocations: gardening, antiques, music. Home: 767 Springlake Ln NW Atlanta GA 30318 Office: Howard Sch 1192 Foster St Atlanta GA 30318 Office Phone: 404-377-7436. Business E-Mail: mcilella@howardschool.org.

CILIBERTI, AVA CAROL, artist; b. Reading, Pa., Jan. 21, 1949; d. Nicholas R. Ciliberti and Edith Jean Sabol; m. Stephen Craig Eckhardt, Apr. 19, 1980 (div. Sept. 1985); children: Nicholas Clayton, Camille Alexandra. BFA, Temple U., 1971; MFA, SUNY, Brockport, 1996. Cert. Permanent tchr. art K-12, N.Y., Fla., Pa., Calif. Art instr. U. Calif. San Diego, La Jolla, 1972—75; art prof. Manatee C.C., Bradenton, Fla., 1983—88; tenured art faculty Rochester Sch. dist., N.Y.C., 1991—2002; mem. art faculty Paradise Valley Unified Sch. Dist., 2004—; art faculty North HS, Phoenix, 2005—06. Prof. art Wells Coll., Aurora, NY, 2002—04. E-mail: avaciliberti@earthlink.net.

CIMA, CHERYL ANN, medical/surgical nurse; b. St. Charles, Mo., Jan. 29, 1965; d. Harry H. and Margaret Mary (Schuette) C. Diploma in nursing with honors, St. Luke's Sch. Nursing, St. Louis, 1986; BSN magna cum laude, U. Mo., St. Louis, 1988. RN, Mo. Staff nurse cardiothoracic stepdown unit Barnes Hosp., St. Louis, 1986-93, staff nurse interventional and vascular radiology, 1993-99; staff nurse, acute dialysis unit Barnes Jewish Hosp., 1999—2004; clin. rsch. nurse coord. Dept. Surgery Washington U., St. Louis, 2003—04; nurse coord. musculoskeletal sect. radiology Barnes Jewish Hosp., St. Louis, 2004—. John Sullivan Waggoner scholar, St. Luke's Merit scholar, Bridgeton Kiwanis scholar. Mem. U. Mo.-St. Louis Nursing Honor Soc., Sigma Theta Tau. Home: 12480 Larkwood Dr Saint Louis MO 63146-4634 Office Phone: 314-362-2825. Business E-Mail: cimach@mir.wustl.edu.

CIMINO, ANN MARY, education educator; b. Easton, Pa. d. John and Melina (Castelluzzo) C. BS, Pa. State U., 1955, MEd, 1958; student cert., Lehigh U. Cert. reading specialist. Instr. Sonoma State U., Santa Rosa, Calif., 1958-59, U. Md., 1959-60; asst. prof. Muhlenberg Coll., Allentown, Pa., 1960-69, Towson (Md.) State U., 1967-68; assoc. prof. Kutztown (Pa.) U., 1996-2001; menter L.V. adv. bd. Pa. State U., 2001—. Bd. dirs. Alumni Coun., Coll. Edn.-Pa. State U., mem. Lehigh Valley adv. bd.

CIMINO, CYNTHIA R., neuropsychologist, education educator; b. Marshfield, Mass., May 11, 1958; d. Benjamin E and Lila V Rodrigues; m. Patrick T Cimino, Aug. 13, 1983; 1 child, Anthony S. BS, U. Fla., 1981, PhD, 1988. Licensed Psychologist State of Fla., 1991. Assoc. prof. U. of South Fla., Tampa, 1989—. Edn. adv. com. APA Divsn. 40 Neuropsychology, Washington; chair, data monitoring bd. VA Coop. Study CS#029, Palo Alto, Calif., 1998—2000; conf. del. Houston Conf. for Splty. Tng. in Neuropsychology, 1997; post doctoral fellowship Brown U., 1988. Mem. editl. bd. (jour.) Neuropsychology, 1996—, Archives of Clin. Neuropsychology, 2004—. Mem. Hyde Pk. Preservation, Tampa, Fla.; v.p. of projects Hyde Pk. Garden Club, Tampa, 2003—05. Recipient U. So. Fla. Tchg. award, 1995, Faculty Devel. award, U. of South Fla., 1998, Faculty Internat. Travel award, 2000; Rsch. and Creative Scholarship grant, 1990, 1993, Aging Pilot arant, Inst. on Aging USF, 1998, Rsch. and Creative Scholarship grant, U. of South Fla., 1999. Mem.: APA (ednl. adv. com.), Assn. for Edn. in Clin. Neuropsychology (sec. 1997—2001), Assn. for Doctoral Edn. in Clin. Neuropsychology (pres. 2002—04), Am. Psychol. Soc., Internat. Neuropsychological Soc., Sigma Xi. D-Liberal. Catholic. Avocations: reading, travel. Office: Psychology Dept Univ of South Florida 4202 E Fowler Ave PCD4118 Tampa FL 33620 Office Phone: 813-974-0385. Office Fax: 813-974-4617. E-mail: cimino@mail.cas.usf.edu.

CINCIOTTA, LINDA ANN, lawyer; b. Washington, May 18, 1943; d. Nicholas Joseph and Laverne Cinciotta; m. John P. Olguin, Aug. 4, 1979. BS, Georgetown U., 1965; JD with highest honors, George Washington U., 1970; grad. Sr. Managers in Govt. Program, Kennedy Sch. of Govt., Harvard U., 1991. Bar: DC 1970. Assoc. Arent, Fox, Kinter, Plotkin & Kahn, Washington, 1970-77, ptnr., 1978-83; dir. Office Atty. Recruitment and Mgmt. Dept. Justice, Washington, 1983—2002, dir. Office Dispute Resolution, 2002—, sr. counsel for alternative dispute resolution, 2002—. Pres. DC chpt. Women in Radio and TV, 1980—81; bd. dirs. Nat. Assn. for Law Placement, 1988—90, liaison to ABA commn. on women in the profession, 1992—95. Recipient US Law Week award, George Washington U. Nat. Law Ctr., 1970. Mem. ABA, Fed. Comm. Bar Assn. (pres. 1980-81, ABA del. 1977-79), DC Bar Assn., Order of Coif. Office: US Dept Justice Office Dispute Resolution 950 Pennsylvania Ave NW Washington DC 20530-0001

CINELLI, BETHANN, school health educator; b. Norristown, Pa., Apr. 23, 1958; d. Anthony and Donna (George) C. BS, Ind. U. of Pa., 1980; MEd, Temple U., 1982; EdD, Pa. State U., 1986. Cert. health edn. specialist. Health edn. instr. Pa. State U., State College, 1982-86; asst. prof. health edn. West Chester (Pa.) U., 1987—. Pres. Healthcor Assoc., Exton, Pa., 1989—. Contbr. articles to profl. jours. Com. HIV/AIDS Edn. Pa. Acad. Profession of Teaching, Harrisburg, 1990, comprehensive sch. health Pa. Dept. Health, Harrisburg, 1990. Mem. Am. Sch. Health Assn. (bd. dirs. 1989-90), Pa. Sch. Health Assn. (pres. 1990). Office: West Chester U Dept Health West Chester PA 19383-0001

CINO, MARIA, federal agency administrator; b. Buffalo, Apr. 19, 1957; d. Richard J. and Lucy M. (Tripi) C. BA in Polit. Sci., St. John Fisher Coll. Project supr. Rep. Nat. Com., 1981-82, dir. local programs, 1983-84, exec. asst. field dir., 1985-86, dep. chmn. polit. and congl. rels., 2000—01, dep. chmn., 2003—05; rsch. analyst Am. Viewpoint, Inc., 1986-88; adminstrv. asst. Rep. L. William Paxon, 1989-93; exec. dir. Nat. Rep. Congl. Com., 1993—97; sr. advisor Wiley, Rein & Fielding, 1997—99; nat. polit. dir. Bush for Pres., 1999—2000; asst. sec. & dir. general, U.S. comml. svc. US Dept. Commerce, Washington, 2001—03; dep. sec. US Dept. Transport., Washington, 2005—, acting sec., 2006. Mem. Ho. Adminstrv. Assts. Assn. Republican. Avocations: antiques, travel, golf. Office: US Dept Transport 400 7th St SW Rm 10200 Washington DC 20590

CIOCAN, EUGENIA, physicist, educator; arrived in U.S., 1998; d. Nicolae and Georgeta Lazaroniu; m. Razvan M. Ciocan, July 2, 1988; 1 child, Mihai. BS, Al. I. Cuza U., 1985; MS, Bucuresti U., 1986; PhD, Al. I. Cuza U., 1998; M.S., Case We. Res. U., 2002. Rsch. scientist Inst. Nuc. Rsch., Pitesti, Romania, 1986—98; rsch. and tchg. asst. Case We. Res. U., Cleve., 1998—2002; lectr. Clemson (S.C.) U., 2004—. Contbr. articles to profl. jours. Scholar, Case We. Res. U., 1998—99. Business E-Mail: eciocan@clemson.edu.

CIOCHINA, DEBRA A., secondary school educator; d. Raymond Charles and Neara Achzet Freeman; m. Garry A. Ciochina, July 28, 1979; children: Lindsey, Carey, Nicholas. BS, Ball State U., Muncie, Ind., 1979; MS, Purdue U., Hammond, Ind., 1986. Tchr. Lowell H.S., Ind., 1979—89, Crown Point H.S., Ind., 1989—91, 1996—. Asst. dir. drama theater Crown Point H.S., 1997—. Editor: Crown Point Language Project, 2000—. Bd. dirs. Crown Point Cmty. Theatre, 2000—. Recipient Crystal Apple award, 2000. Mem.: NEA. Office: Crown Point High Sch 1500 S Main St Crown Point IN 46307

CIOCIOLA, CECILIA MARY, not-for-profit developer; b. Chester, Pa., Feb. 9, 1946; d. Donato Francis Pasqual and Mary Theresa (Dugan) C. BA, Immaculata Coll., 1975; MA, West Chester U., 1984. Tchr. Archdiocese of Phila., 1964-72, Harrisburg Diocese, Pa., 1972-74, Camden Diocese, NJ, 1974-76; tchr., elem. sci. chairperson Archdiocese of Phila., 1976-86; ednl. cons. Macmillan Pub. Co., Delran, NJ, 1986-88; program officer PATHS/PRISM, Phila., 1988-90; mgr. spl. programs minority engring., math., sci. program Prime, Inc., Phila., 1988-99; dir. partnership and cmty. devel. FOUNDATIONS, Inc., 1999-2001; grants adminstr. Chester Cmty. Charter Sch., Pa., 2001—04; grant writer Jewish Fedn. So. NJ, Cherry Hill, 2005—. Tchr. cert. adv. com. U. the Scis., Phila.; cons. Delaware County Intermediate Unit, Media, Pa.; chair elem. (grades 1-8), sci. com. Phila. Archdiocese, 1985-86; coord. Chester County Cath. Schs.: Computer Edn., Pa., 1982-84, Fed. Nutrition Program, St. Agnes Sch., West Chester, Pa., 1982-84, Justice Edn. Teaching Strategies, St. Agnes Sch., West Chester, 1983-84; mem. Mayor's Telecom. Policy Adv. Com., Phila., 1998-2000, Phila. 4-H Program Devel. Com., 1998-2000. Author, editor: (curriculum) Elementary Life and Earth Science, 1984. Mem. adv. com. environ. edn. program Fairmount Pk. Commn., 1998. NSF grantee Operation Primary Phys. Sci., La. State U., 1997-2000, Project GLOBE, 1997-2000. Mem. ASCD, Exceptional Needs Found (bd. dirs., 2003—). Avocations: poetry, country music, reading, photography, exercise. Office: 1301 Springdale Rd Ste 200 Cherry Hill NJ 08003-2761 Office Phone: 856-751-9500. Personal E-mail: ceilciociola@comcast.net. Business E-Mail: cciociola@jfedsnj.org.

CIOFALO, CAROL ELLEN, obstetrician, gynecologist; b. N.Y.C., Aug. 30, 1951; MD, Georgetown U., 1978. Diplomate Am. Bd. Ob-Gyn. Intern Georgetown U., Washington, 1978-79, resident, 1979-82, clin. instr., 1982—; obstetrician Alexandria (Va.) Hosp., 1982—. Mem. AMA, Am. Coll. Ob-Gyn., Va. State Med. Soc., Arlington County Med. Soc. Office: Alexandria WomenCare Ltd 4660 Kenmore Ave Ste 902 Alexandria VA 22304-1310

CIOTOLA, LINDA ANN MILLER, lifestyle counselor; b. Balt., Sept. 17, 1947; d. Lawrence Andrew and Virginia Arnetta (Wertley) Miller; m. Joseph A. Ciotola, July 26, 1969; children: Joseph John, Alyson Marie. BA, Mt. St. Agnes Coll., Balt., 1969; MEd, Loyola Coll., Balt., 1975. Cert. health edn. specialist; cert. personal trainer and fitness instr. Am. Coun. on Exercise; gold cert. lifestyle and weight mgmt. cons.; cert. post rehab. fitness specialist; cert clin. practitioner psychodrama, sociometry and group psychotherapy. Tchr. The Cath. HS of Balt., Md., 1969-73, Alholton HS, Columbia, Md., 1975-76; instr. Broadcasting Inst. Md., Balt., 1976-77; dir. student activities Villa Julie Coll., Stevenson, Md., 1976-79; nutritionist, personal trainer, fitness instr. The Fitness Movement, 1982—; instr. Villa Julie Coll., Stevenson, 1987-91; outreach coord. Mercy Ctr. for Eating Disorders, Balt., 1991-93; lifestyle counselor The Fitness Movement, Md., 1993—. Regional mgr. Speaking of Fitness of Durango, Colo., 1990-92, cons., 1990-92 Author: (manual) Action of Methods for Treatment of Eating Disorders: Beyond The Silence & Fury; contbg. writer (book and tapes) Think Light, 1991. Mem. Am. Coll. Sports Medicine, IDEA-The Assn. Fitness Profls., Am. Soc. Group Psychotherapists and Psychodramatists, Eating Disorders Resource Network (founder), Internat. Assn. Eating Disorder Profls., Sigma Phi Sigma. Avocations: piano, reading, writing, exercise. Office: 4 Bateau Lndg Grasonville MD 21638-9660 Office Phone: 410-827-8324.

CIPARICK, CARMEN BEAUCHAMP, state appeals court judge; b. NYC, 1942; m. Joseph Damian Ciparick; 1 child. Grad., Hunter Coll., 1963; JD, St. John's U., 1967. Staff atty. Legal Aid Soc., NYC, 1967—69; asst. counsel Office of Jud. Conf. State of NY, 1969—72; chief law asst. NYC Criminal Ct., 1972—74; counsel Office of NYCAdminstrv. Judge, 1974—78; judge NYC Criminal Ct., 1978—82, NYC Supreme Ct, 1982—94; assoc. judge NY State Ct. Appeals, NYC, 1994—. Former mem. N.Y. State Commn. Jud. Conduct. Trustee Boricua Coll.; bd. dirs. St. John's U. Sch. of Law Alumni Assn. Named to Hunter Coll. Hall of Fame, 1991. Office: NY State Ct Appeals 122 E 42nd St New York NY 10168-0002 Address: State NY Court of Appeals 20 Eagle St Albany NY 12207-1095*

CIPLIJAUSKAITE, BIRUTE, humanities educator; b. Kaunas, Lithuania, Apr. 11, 1929; came to U.S., 1957; d. Juozas and Elena (Stelmokaite) C. BA, Lycée Lithuanien Tubingen, 1947; MA, U. Montreal, 1956; PhD, Bryn Mawr Coll., 1960. Permanent mem. Inst. Rsch. in Humanities U. Wis., Madison, 1974, asst. prof., 1961-65, assoc. prof., 1965-68, prof., 1968-73, John Bascom prof., 1973—. Author: Solitude and Spanish Contemporary Poetry, 1962, Poetry and the Poet, 1966, Baroja, a style, 1972, Plenitude as Commitment: The Poetry of Jorge Guillén, 1973, The Generation of 1898 and History, 1981, The Unsatisfied Woman: Adultery in Realist Novel, 1984, Contemporary Women's Novel (1970-85), 1988, Literary Sketches, 1992, Of Signs and Significations. I: Games of the Avant-Garde, 1999, Carmen Martín Gaite, 2000, Guilleniana, 2002, Construction of the Feminine I in Literature, 2004; editor: (Luis de Góngora), Complete Sonnets, 1969, 75, 79, 81, 85, 99, critical edit., 1989, Jorge Guillén, 1975, (with C. Maurer) The Will to Humanism. Homage to Juan Marichal, 1990, Novísimos, postnovísimos, clásicos: Poetry of the 80s in Spain, 1991; translator: (Juan Ramón Jiménez), Platero and I, 1982, (María Victoria Atencia), Trances of the Holy Virgin, 1989, Voices Within Silence: Contemporary Lithuanian Poetry, 1991, Birute Pukeleviciute, Lament, 1994, (with Nicole Laurent-Catrice) Twenty Lithuanian Poets of Today, 1997, (Vidmante Jasukaityte), The Miraculous Grass Along the Fence, 2002, (J. Degutytė and B. Pukelevičiute) Between the Sun and Dispossession, 2002, (Mercè Rodoreda) The Girl of the Doves, 2002, (Nijole Miliauskaitė) Forbidden Room, 2003, (with Emilio Coco) That Rustle of Nordic Herbs. Anthology of Lithuanic Contemporary Poetry, 2006, others. Guggenheim fellow, 1968 Mem. Assn. For Advancement Baltic Studies (v.p. 1981), Asociación Internacional de Hispanistas, Order Alfonso X elSabio (named commdr. Spain, 2003) Office: U Wis Inst Rsch in Humanities 1401 Observatory Dr Madison WI 53706-1209

CIPRIANI, REBECCA MICHELE, elementary school educator; b. Norwich, Conn., Mar. 11, 1978; d. Paul Cipriani, Jr. and Janet Helen (Panciera) Cipriani. BS, U. Conn., Storrs, 1996—99, MA, 1999—2000, student, 2004—. Cert. Tchr. k-6 Conn. Dept. Edn. 6th grade tchr. Chaplin Elem. Sch., Conn., 2000—01, Sayles Sch., Sprague, 2001—03, 5th grade tchr., 2003—. Enrichment club adv. Sayles Sch., 2001—02, sci. com., 2002—, beginning educator support tng. mentor, 2003—06. Summer reading program dir. Sprague Pub. Libr., 1994—; summer rec. program dir. Town of Sprague, 2005—. Mem.: NEA, NSTA, Conn. Sci. Tchrs. Assn. Avocations: horseback riding, reading, crafts, needlecrafts. Home: 55 Salt Rock Rd Baltic CT 06330 Office: Sayles Sch 25 Scotland Rd Baltic CT 06330

CIPRICH, PAULA MARIE, lawyer, gas industry executive; BA, U. Dallas1982; JD, SUNY, Buffalo, 1985. Bar: NY 1986. Assoc. Jaeckle, Fleischmann & Mugel, 1985—88; atty. Nat. Fuel Gas Co., Williamsville, NY, 1988—91, sr. atty., 1991—92, asst. gen. mgr., 1992—94, gen. mgr., 1994—97, gen. counsel, asst. sec., 1997—. Office: Nat Fuel Gas Co 6363 Main St Williamsville NY 14221 Office Phone: 716-857-7048. E-mail: ciprichp@natfuel.com.

CIRILO, AMELIA MEDINA, educational consultant; b. Parks, Tex., May 23, 1925; d. Constancio and Guadalupe (Guerra) Cirilo; m. Arturo Medina, May 31, 1953 (div. June 1979); children: Dennis Glenn, Keith Allen, Sheryl Amelia, Jacqueline Kim. BS in Chemistry, U. North Tex., 1950; MEd, U. Houston, 1954; PhD in Edn. and Nuc. Engring., Tex. A&M U., 1975; cert. in radioisotope tech., Tex. Woman's U., Denton, 1962; cert. in pub. speaking, Dale Carnegie, 1993. Cert. in supervision, bilingual Spanish Tex., permanent profl. tchr. Tex. Tchr. sci. dept. Starr County Schs., Rio Grande City, Tex., 1950—53; elem. tchr. San Benito-Brownsville, Tex., 1953—54, Kingsville (Tex.) Schs., 1954—56; tchr. sci. dept. head chem. physics LaJoya (Tex.) Pub. Schs., 1956—70; tchg. asst. Tex. A&M U., College Station, 1970—74; instr. fire chemistry Del Mar Jr. Coll., Corpus Christi, Tex., 1974—75; exec. dir. Hispanic Ednl. Rsch. Mgmt. Analysis Nat. Assn., Inc., Corpus Christi, 1975—79; head dept. chem. physics San Isidro (Tex.) HS, 1979—82; tchr. chemistry W.H. Adamson HS, Dallas, 1982—84; ednl. cons. Skyline HS, 1992—, tchr. high intensity lang. sci., 1984—86, chmn. faculty adv. com., 1983—84, chemistry tchr., 1986—92. Mem. core faculty Union Grad. Coll., Cin., P.R., Ft. Lauderdale and San Diego, 1975—79; mathematician Well Instrument Devel. Co., Houston, 1950—85; panelist, program evaluator Dept. of Edn., Washington, 1977—79; program evaluator, Robstown, Tex., 1975—79; tchr., trainer Edn. 20 and 2 Region Ctrs., Corpus Christi and San Antonio, 1975—79; rschr., writer Coll. Edn. and Urban Studies Harvard U., Cambridge, Mass., 1978—80; vis. prof. bilingual dept. East Tex. State Coll., Commerce, 1978; ednl. cons. and supr. Adult Basic Edn. Dallas Pub. Schs., 1994—99, kindergarten tchr., 1999—2000, tchr. elem. sci. and math., 2000—02, newcomers ESL tchr., 2002—; conf. presenter program evaluation, 1977—79. Author, rschr. Comparative Evaluation of Bilingual Programs, 1978 (named one of best US books), (poetry) Reflections, 1983; contbr. chapters to books. Mem. Srs. Active in Life adv. com. Dallas City Parks and Recreation; Brazos County advisor Tex. Constl. Revision Commn., 1973—74; sec. Goals for Corpus Christi Com. of 100; Corpus Christi rep. Southwestern Ednl. Authority, Edinburg, Tex., 1977—79; pres. Elem. PTA, 1972—75; mem. Women's Polit. Caucus, Mex. Am. Dems.; exec. bd. Nat. Com. Domestic Violence, 1978—80; bd. trustees Sci. Cluster Skyline HS, 1994—; bd. dirs. Meth. Home for Elderly, Weslaco, Tex., 1968, Am. Cancer Soc. fund drive, College Station, 1971—74; co-founder, bd. dirs. Women's Shelter, Corpus Christi, 1977—78. Named Educator of Yr., Literary Couns. of Greater Dallas, 1997—98; recipient Sr. Salute award for achievements in edn., City of Dallas and NYL Care, 1996; grantee, NSF, The Women's U., 1963—65. Mem.: AAUW, NEA, Metroplex Educators Sci. Assn., Rocky Mountain Sociol. Assn., So. Sociol. Assn., Chem. Soc., Tex. Assn. Bilingual Educators, Tex. Tchrs. Assn., League United Latin Am. Citizens (pres. College Station 1973—74, past dist. dir. Corpus Christi), Pan Am. Round Table, Fiesta Bilingual Toastmasters. Avocations: ballroom dancing, comedy. Home and Office: 5005 Oak Trl Dallas TX 75232-1643

CIROCCO, ANGELA V., adult education educator; b. N.Y.C., Mar. 8, 1944; d. Felix and Regina Decline; m. Joseph Cirocco; children: Theresa, Nicholas, Anthony, Joseph. AS, Moorpark Coll., Calif., 1982; BA, Calif. State U., Northridge, 1986, ESL adult credential, 1989; MA, Calif. State U., 2000. Classroom aide Simi Valley (Calif.) Unified Sch. Dist., 1988—90, ESL tchr., 1990—. Author: (poetry collection) Bridges, 2000; contbr. poems to lit. mags. Vol. Simi Valley Hosp., Simi Adventist; vol. Elem. Sch. S.V. Sch. Dist. Mem.: Calif. Coun. Adult Edn. (scholar 1996—97). Avocations: hiking, reading, walking along the beach, wildflowers. Office: Simi Valley Adult Sch 3192 E Los Angeles Ave Simi Valley CA 93065

CIRONA, JANE CALLAHAN, investment company executive; b. Detroit, Feb. 23, 1949; d. Earl J. and Madeline Katherine (Freihaut) Callahan; children from previous marriage: Christopher Randall, Elisabeth Anne; m. James M. Cirona, Aug. 29, 1992. BA, Albion Coll., 1970; postgrad., Aquinas Coll., 1989—. Asst. mgr. Nat. Bank of Detroit, 1971-75; program coord. Muskegon (Mich.) C.C., 1978-79; services coord. Muskegon (Mich.) County Cmty. Mental Health, 1979-81; supr. engring. services Teledyne Continental Motors, Muskegon; v.p. investment UBS Fin Svcs., Muskegon, 1982—. Dir. Muskegon Econ. Growth Alliance, 1987—, Every Woman's Place, Muskegon, 1979-86; mem. Albion Coll. Planned Giving Adv. Bd., 1989—; mem. Commn. on Growth and Devel. Episcopal Diocese of Western Mich., 1985-88, Consumers Power Citizen Adv. Panel, Muskegon, 1983-84; bd. dirs. Mercy Hosp., Muskegon. Mem.: Zonta Internat. Avocation: travel. Office: UBS Fin Svcs Inc 945 W Norton Ave Muskegon MI 49441-4105 Office Phone: 231-739-9802. E-mail: jane.cirona@ubs.com.

CISAR, MARGARET, special education educator; b. Chgo., Oct. 13, 1951; d. William Miser and Winifred (Stevens) F.; m. Thomas Joseph Cisar, Jan. 14, 1977; children: Winifred Catherine, William George. BS in Edn., U. Ariz., 1973; postgrad., U. of the South, 1992-96; MA in Ednl. Leadership, Aurora U., 2001. Cert. tchr. Ill.; cert. in learning disabilities, behavior disorders, trainable mentally handicapped, educable mentally handicapped, exceptional needs; nat. bd. cert. tchr./exceptional needs specialist. Grad. asst. No. Ill. U., DeKalb, 1974-75; tchr. Project Adv., Aurora, Ill., 1975-78; Christian edn. dir. Grace Episcopal Ch., Hinsdale, Ill., 1990-96; tchg. asst. Hinsdale South High Sch., Darien, Ill., 1997; spl. edn. tchr. Waubonsie Valley High Sch., Aurora, Ill., 1997—, spl. edn. dept. liaison, 2001—. Co-chair social comms. com. Vocat. Alliance Autism Project, 2002—03. Vol. humane edn. Hinsdale Humane Soc., 1981—, vol. pet therapy, 1989-90; vol. coord. Lyons Twp. HS, LaGrange, Ill., 1997-98. Mem.: Coun. Exceptional Children (sec. Ill. divsn. on devel. disabilities), Assn. Supervision and Curriculum, Delta Delta Delta (1st v.p. 2003—). Office: Waubonsie Valley High Sch 2590 Ogden Ave Aurora IL 60504-5999

CISLER, THERESA ANN, osteopath; b. Tucson, Dec. 20, 1951; d. William George and Lucille (Seeber) Cisler; 1 child, Daniel Luttrell. BSN, U. Ariz., 1974; DO, Kirksville Coll. Osteopathy, 1983. Diplomate Am. Bd. Osteopathic Manipulative Medicine. Operating room technician St. Joseph's Hosp., Tucson, 1973-74, operating room nurse, 1974-78, operating room inservice coordinator, 1978-79; intern Tucson Gen. Hosp., 1983-84; family practice and manipulation Assoc. Jane J. Beregi, D.O., Tucson, 1984-87; practice medicine specializing in osteo. manipulation Tucson, 1987—. Active med. staff Tucson Gen. Hosp., 1984—91, med. records chmn., 1986—87; part-time med. staff Westcenter Drug & Rehab., Tucson, 1984—88; vol. med. staff St. Elizabeth Hungary Clinic, 1984—87; mem. substance abuse com. Westcenter-Tucson Gen. Hosp., 1986—88, mem. osteo. concepts com., osteo. manipulative cons., 1986—91. Chair Ariz.-S. Nev. Jr. Civitan, 2001—; eucharistic min. St. Pius X Ch., Tucson, 1984—86, eucharistic min. coord., 1087—1990. Mem.: Cranial Acad. (bd. dirs. 1997—2003, pres. 2003—05), Ariz. Osteo. Med. Assn. (at-large ho. of dels. 1985—93), Am. Acad. Osteopathy (chair med. econs. com. 1994—99, bd. govs. 1997—2005), Am. Osteo. Assn., Kirksville Coll. Osteopathy-Century Club, Roadrunner Civitan (pres. 2000—01). Roman Catholic. Avocations: sewing, country dancing. Home and Office: 800 N Swan Rd Ste 128 Tucson AZ 85711-1276 Office Phone: 520-795-3772.

CISNEROS, DEBORAH KATHLEEN, technology educator; d. Joseph Milton Adams and Betty Jo Reeb; children: Christian Lee, Joseph Luis Edward, Matthew Alan. AAS, Tex. State Tech. Coll., Waco, 1997. Security + CompTia, Ill., 2005, cert. profl. Microsoft, 2002. Computer operator Dept. Human Svcs., Austin, Tex., 1984—95, LAN adminstr., 1998—2000; customer networks staff GTE, Austin, 1997—98; instr. Tex. State Tech. Coll., Waco, 2000—. Faculty senate sec. Tex. State Tech. Coll., Waco, 2000—03. Mem. Keep Waco Beautiful, 2006—. Mem.: Phi Theta Kappa (Paragon award 2006, Advisor Hall of Honor 2006). Office: Texas State Technical College Waco 3801 Campus Dr Waco TX 76705 Office Phone: 254-867-2277. Personal E-mail: debi.cisneros@tstc.edu. Business E-Mail: dcisneros@cns.tstc.edu.

CISZKOWSKI, GRACE MARIE, art educator; b. Buffalo, Sept. 15, 1962; d. Edward Anthony and Clara Helen (Weibel) Strozyk; m. David A. Ciszkowski, July 19, 1986; children: David Edward, Kristina Marie. BS in Art Edn., SUNY, Buffalo, 1984, MS in Art Edn., 1990. Cert. tchr. art, N.Y. Tchr. art St. Mary's Elem. Sch., Lancaster, N.Y., 1986-91, SS Peter & Paul Elem. Sch., Depew, N.Y., 1988-89; freelance artist Phila., 1991—. Founder Sch. Art Gallery, Lancaster, 1989; mem. com. Textbook Com., Buffalo, 1989-90; chair subcom. Art Curriculum Com., Buffalo, 1989-90. Cub scout leader Boy Scouts Am., 1998—; pres. Jr. Explorers Club. Homeschoolers, 2002—; founder Christian Homeschool Fellowship Club, 2004—. Mem. Nat. Art Edn. Assn. Avocations: camping, travel, gardening, reading, child care. Home: 1128 Arrott St Philadelphia PA 19124-3139

CITRANO-CUMMISKEY, DEBRA MOIRA, chemist, network technician; b. Glen Cove, NY, Feb. 23, 1957; d. Helen Marie and Roy Maurice Citrano; 1 child, Nikki Marie Cummiskey. Student, Hofstra U.; BS in Edn., Almeda U., 2004, BS in Chemistry, 2004. A+ Certification Computer Career Ctr., 2002. Raw materials auditor Hi-Tech Pharm., Amityville, NY, 2003—; qc raw materials chemist Kos Pharmaceuticals, Edison, NJ, 2003—03. Corp. reference std. coord. DuPont Pharmaceuticals, Garden City, NY, 1978—2001. Mem.: Am. Chem. Soc. American Independent. Roman Catholic. Avocations: dance, swimming. Office: Hi-Tech Pharmacal Co Inc 369 Bayview Avenue Amityville NY 11701 Personal E-mail: corporatewoman@msn.com.

CITRO, JANET, elementary school educator, coach, secondary school educator; d. Anthony and Irene Citro. BS, Concord Coll., Athens, W.Va., 1975. Cert. tchr. W.Va., N.J., 1975. Tchr. Hazlet Twp. Sch. Dist., NJ, 1976—. Coach softball and field hockey Hazlet Twp. Sch. Dist., 1976—. Named Coach of Yr. Field Hockey, Hazlet Twp. Sch. Dist., 1995, Coach of Yr. Softball, 2004; recipient Tchr. of Yr., 1995—96. Office: Raritan HS 419 Middle Rd Hazlet NJ 07730 Office Phone: 732-264-8411 1034. Office Fax: 732-264-2825. Business E-Mail: jcitro@mail.hazlet.org.

CITRON, BEATRICE SALLY, law librarian, lawyer, educator; b. Phila., May 19, 1929; d. Morris Meyer and Frances (Teplitsky) Levinson; m. Joel P. Citron, Aug. 7, 1955 (dec. Sept. 1977); children: Deborah Ann, Victor Ephraim. BA in Econs. with honors, U. Pa., 1950; MLS, Our Lady of the Lake U., 1978; JD, U. Tex., 1984. Bar: Tex. 1985; cert. sch. libr., tchr. Tex. Claims examiner Social Security Adminstrn., Pa., Fla. and N.C., 1951-59; head libr. St. Mary's Hall, San Antonio, 1979-80; media, reference and rare book libr., asst. and assoc. prof. St. Mary's U. Law Libr., San Antonio, 1984-89; asst. dir. St. Thomas U. Law Libr., Miami, Fla., 1989-96, assoc. dir./head pub. svc., 1996-99, acting dir., 1997-98. Law libr. cons., 2000—. Mem.: ABA, South Fla. Assn. Law Librs. (treas. 1992—94, v.p. 1994—95, pres. 1995—96), S.E. Assn. Law Librs. (newsletter, program and edn. coms. 1991—98), S.W. Assn. Law Librs. (continuing edn. com. 1986—88, chmn. local arrangements 1987—88), Am. Assn. Law Librs. (publs. com. 1987—88, com. on rels. with info. vendors 1991—93, bylaws com. 1994—96).

CITRON, DIANE, lawyer; b. Cin., Oct. 9, 1953; d. Carl and Georgia (Reid) C. BA, Franklin and Mareshall Coll., 1975; JD, Case Western Res. U., 1978. Bar: D.C. 1978, Calif. 1985. Assoc. Wasserman, Orlow, Ginsberg & Rubin, Washington, 1978-80; staff atty. SEC, Washington, 1980-83; sr. counsel Freddie Mac, Washington, 1983-84; assoc. Orrick, Herrington & Sutcliffe, San Francisco, 1984-85, Brown & Wood, San Francisco, 1985-87; spl. counsel Skadden, Arps, Slate, Meagher & Flom, San Francisco, 1987-92; ptnr. Mayer, Brown Rowe & Maw LLP, N.Y.C., 1992—; gen. counsel, chief compliance officer Carrington Capital Mgmt. LLC, Greenwich, Conn. Adj. prof. law real estate LLM program John Marshall Law Sch. Real Estate, Chgo, 1995—. Mem. ABA (subcom. securitization real property sect.), FBA, Women's Art Assn. D.C., Bar Assn. D.C., Pi Gamma Mu. Democrat. Jewish.

CIURCZAK, ALEXIS, librarian; b. Long Island, NY, Feb. 13, 1950; d. Alexander Daniel and Catherine Ann (Frangipane) C. BA Art History magna cum laude, U. Calif., L.A., 1971; MA Libr. Sci., San Jose State U., 1975; cert. tchr. ESL, U. Calif., Irvine, 1985. Intern IBM Rsch. Libr., San Jose, Calif., 1974-75; tech. asst. San Bernardino Valley Coll. Libr., Calif., 1975; tech. svcs. librarian Palomar Coll., San Marcos, Calif., 1975-78, pub. svcs. librarian, 1978-81, libr. dir., 1981-86, pub. svcs. librarian, 1987—, instr. Libr. Technology Cert. Program, 1975—; exchange librarian Fulham Pub. Libr., London, 1986-87; coord. San Diego C.C. Consortium Semester-in-London Am. Inst. Fgn. Study, 1988-89. Fulbright fellow, 2d Air Divsn. Meml. Libr., Norwich, Eng., 2004—05. Mem. ALA, San Diego Libr. Svcs. com., Calif. Libr. Media Educators Assn., Patronato por Niños, Kosciuszko Found., So. Calif. Tech. Processes Group, Pacific Coast Coun. Latin Am. Studies, Libros, Reforma, Libr. Assn. (British), Calif. Libr. Assn., Calif. Tchrs. Assn., Phi Beta Kappa, Beta Phi Mu. Office: Palomar CC 1140 W Mission Rd San Marcos CA 92069-1415 also: Meml Libr Forum Millennium Plain Norwich NR2 1AW Norfolk England Office Phone: 760-744-1150. E-mail: alexis.ciurczak@palomar.edu.

CIVISH, GAYLE ANN, psychologist; b. Lynnwood, Calif., Sept. 29, 1948; d. Leland and Arline (Frazer) Civish; children: Nathan Morrow, Shane Morrow. BA, U. Nev., Reno, 1970; MA, U. Colo., 1973; PhD, U. Colo., Boulder, 1983; student in Theology, U. Denver, 2001—. Lic. psychologist Colo., Pa., cert. sch. psychologist Colo. Sch. psychologist Jefferson County Schs., Colo., 1983-89; psychologist in pvt. practice Lakewood, Colo., 1983-99, Boulder, Colo., 1999—. Cons. charter schs. integrated spl. edn., 1998. Contbr. articles to profl. jours. and books. Mem.: APA (editor newsletter regional divsn.), Assn. Women Psychology, Feminist Therapy Inst. (mem. steering com. 1994—99), Am. Soc. Clin. Hypnosis, Colo. Women Psychologists (past external liaison), Pa. Psychol. Assn., Colo. Psychol. Assn. (bd. dirs. 1990—93), Phi Delta Kappa, Phi Kappa Phi. Democrat. Office: 10200 W 44th Ave #210-B Wheat Ridge CO 80033 Office Phone: 303-443-9570.

CLABEAUX-FECHTER, BARBARA JEAN, artist, educator; b. Buffalo, Sept. 3, 1937; d. George Gregory Clabeaux and Guistina Irvira Puleo; m. Ronald W. Fechter, Jan. 5, 1957 (div.); children: Michael, Peter, Julianne, Ronald. Student, State Tchrs. Coll., 1955, U. Buffalo, 1961—80, Villa Maria Coll., 1980; student in Advt. Design, Boces Coll., 1987—89. Tchr. St. Francis of Assisi Sch., Buffalo, 1957—58, St. Gregory the Great Sch., Williamsville, NY, 1958—59; advt. artist Roizen Advt., Buffalo, 1959—60, BVM Advt., Buffalo, 1960—61. Author: My Poetry, 2004; children's books, medical books. Scholar, Buffalo Found., 1955—. Mem.: Cheektowaga Artist Guild, Williamsville Art Soc. (mem. hospitality 2002—03). Avocations: classical music, flowers, gardening.

CLAES, GAYLA CHRISTINE, writer, editor, consultant; b. L.A., Oct. 17, 1946; d. Henry George and Glorya Desiree Blasdel; m. Daniel John Claes, Jan. 19, 1974. AB magna cum laude, Harvard U., 1968; postgrad., Oxford (Eng.) U., 1971; MA, McGill U., Montreal, 1975. Adminstrv. asst. U. So. Calif., L.A., 1968-70; teaching asst. English lit. McGill U., Montreal, 1970-71; editorial dir. Internat. Cons. Group, L.A., 1972-78; v.p. Gaylee Corp., L.A., 1978-81, CEO, 1981-88; writer, cons. L.A. and Paris, 1988—. Dir. pub. rels. Ctr. Internat. for the Performing Arts, Paris and L.A., 1991—2000. Author: (play) Berta of Hungary, 1972, (novel) Christopher Derring, 1990; contbr. articles to lit. and sci. jours. Co-founder White Swan Awards, ann. benefit for Crippled Children's Soc. dba AbilityFirst, 1999. Mem. Harvard-Radcliffe Club of So. Calif., Royal Commonwealth Soc. (London).

CLAFLIN, JANIS ANN, psychotherapist, management consultant; b. Fort Worth, Oct. 24, 1939; d. Claybourne Guy and Thalia Lee (Brown) Davenport; m. Roger Dale Armstrong, June 17, 1960 (div. 1978); children: Allen Glenn, David Lynn, Joy Elizabeth; m. David Claflin, Aug. 16, 1980. BA in English, Ga. Peabody Coll. for Tchrs., 1961; MA in Religion, Yale Div. Sch., 1964. Conf. dir. Continuing Edn. Ctr. at Yale, New Haven, 1966-69; exec. dir. Lanier Found., Houston, 1972-73; asst. dir. Child Care Coun. Greater Houston, 1974-75; founder, exec. dir. Childrens Resource and Info. Svc., Houston, 1975-79; pvt. practice orgnl. cons. psychotherapist Austin, 1974—; pres., owner Claflin and Assocs., Austin, 1985—. Vis. instr. Univ. Tex. Sch. Pub. Health, Univ. Houston, Baylor Coll. Medicine, San Jacinto Jr. Coll., Univ. Tex. Sch. Nursing; mgmt. cons. John E. Fetzer Found., Kalamazoo, Mich., 1987—, N.C. Nat. Bank, Tex., 1988, Am. Banker's Assn., Washington, 1988, Tex. Bankers Assn., Hills Med. Group, Austin, The Health Connection, Total Health Environments, Sachem Fund, New Haven, Moody Found., Linfield Design Inc., and others. Author: (values clarification curriculum) Reflections for Living, 1978. Founder Austin (Tex.) Ctr. for Attitudinal Healing, 1981, Houston (Tex.) Ctr. for Attitudinal Healing, 1983; trustee John E. Fetzer Inst., Kalamazoo, 1987—; bd. dirs. Dispute Resolution Ctr., Austin, 1991. Mem. ASTD, Inst. Noetic Scis., Orgn. Devel. Network. Avocations: golf, reading, travel, writing, walking. Office: Claflin and Assocs 1301 Capital of Tex Hwy PO Box 128 Austin TX 78767-0128 Office Phone: 512-327-4726. Personal E-mail: jcforpeace@aol.com.

CLAFLIN, TRACIE NADINE, private school educator; b. Rapid City, S.D., June 28, 1970; d. Ron H. Williams and Patricia Claflin; BFA, Ringling Sch. Art and Design, Sarasota, Fla., 1993. Freelance artist; art tchr., 1999—; tchr. Prew Acad., Sarasota, 1994—; field trip supt., art tchr. YMCA, Sarasota, 1994—; art tchr. Divine Mercy and Our Lady of Lourdes, Brevard County, Fla. Home: 221 Miami Ave Indialantic FL 32903-3518

CLAGETT, DIANA WHARTON SINKLER, museum docent; b. Phila., Aug. 24, 1943; d. James Mauran Rhodes and Sarah Brinton (Wentz) Sinkler; m. Peter John Knop, Nov. 23, 1966 (div.); children: Alexandra Brinton, Peter Rhodes Quast, William James Wharton; m. Brice McAdoo Clagett, July 26, 1987. BA, George Wash. U., 1966. Rsch. asst. Nat. Investigations Com. on Aerial Phenomena, Washington, 1966—69; docent Asia Hall Smithsonian Instn., Washington, 1982—83, docent Sackler Gallery, 1989—, docent Freer Gallery, 1993—; propr. Georgian Antiques and Decorative Arts, Washington, 1983—; docent Anderson House, Washington, 2004—. Bd. dirs. Sinkler Corp., Wentz Corp.; mem. Smithsonian Ednl. Vol. Adv. Bd., 1990-93. Mem. bd. devel. Hosp. for Sick Children, Washington, 1980—, vice chmn. bd. devel., 1985-86, co-chmn. flower and garden festival, 1988-90; mem. bd. devel. Children's Hearing and Speech Ctr., Washington, 1988—; mem. women's com. Phila. Acad. Fine Arts, 1980—; mem. alumni bd. Foxcroft Sch., Middleburg, Va., 1983-86; trustee The McLean Sch., 1993-96; mem. The Founders Washington Com. for Historic Mt. Vernon, 2001—; trustee, Tudor Place Found., 2003—, chmn. collections com., 2004— Mem. City Tavern Club (bd. govs. 1990-98), Radnor Hunt Club (racing com.), Acorn Club, Evermay Club Georgetown, New Scotland Garden Club (pres. 1993-94), Sulgrave Club. Avocations: gardening, Asian art. Home: Holly Hill PO Box 86 Friendship MD 20758 also: 3331 O St NW Washington DC 20007-2814

CLAGETT, VIRGINIA PARKER, state official; b. Washington, July 18, 1943; d. William Merrick and Virginia (Lawrence) Parker; m. Brice McAdoo, Sept. 18, 1965; children: John Brice, Ann Brooke. Student, U. Geneva, 1963-64; BA, Smith Coll., 1965. Asst. reporter Triangle Stas., Phila., 1966-68; county councilwoman County of Anne Arundel, Annapolis, Md., 1974-94, council chmn., 1984-91; mem. Md. Gen. Assembly Ho. of Dels., 1994—. Vice chmn. Balt. Regional Planning Coun., 1984—; trustee Hammond-Harwood Ho., 1978—, Chesapeake EPA, 1976—; mem. Alcohol and Drug Abuse Adv. Com., 1985—; mem. Anne Arundel County Agrl. Adv. Com., 1978—; bd. dirs. Historic Annapolis, Inc. Mem. Am. Bus. Womens Assn., Md. Assn. Counties (legis. com.). Democrat. Episcopalian. Avocations: tennis, gardening, horseback riding. Home: PO Box 1 West River MD 20778-0001 Office: Ho of Dels Md Gen Assembly 212 Lowe Office Bldg 84 College Ave Annapolis MD 21401 Office Phone: 410-841-3216. E-mail: virginia_clagett@house.state.md.us.

CLAIBORNE, LIZ (ELISABETH CLAIBORNE ORTENBERG), fashion designer; b. Brussels, Mar. 31, 1929; came to U.S., 1939; d. Omer Villere and Louise Carol (Fenner) C.; m. Arthur Ortenberg, July 5, 1954; 1 son by previous marriage, Alexander G. Schultz. Student, Art Sch., Brussels, 1948-49, Academie, Nice, France, 1950; DFA, R.I. Sch. Design, 1991. Asst. Tina Lesser, N.Y.C., 1951-52, Omar Khayam, Ben Reig, Inc., N.Y.C., 1953;

designer Juniorite, N.Y.C., 1954-60, Dan Keller, N.Y.C., 1960-76, Youth Guild Inc., N.Y.C., 1976-89; designer, pres., chmn. Liz Claiborne Inc., N.Y.C., 1985-89, pres., 1976-89, chmn., chief oper. officer, until 1989; chmn. Liz Claiborne Cosmetics, 1985-89, cons. Guest lectr. Fashion Inst. Tech., Parsons Sch. Design; bd. dirs. Coun. of Am. Fashion Designers, Fire Island Lighthouse Restoration Com. Recipient Designer of Yr. award Palciode Hierro, Mexico City, 1976, Designer of Yr. award Dayton Co., Mpls., 1978, Ann. Disting. in Design award Marshall Field's, 1985, One Co. Makes a Difference award Fashion Inst. Tech., 1985, award Coun. Fashion Designers, 1986, Gordon Grand Fellowship award Yale U., 1989, Jr. Achievement award Nat. Bus. Hall of Fame, 1990, Frederick A.P. Barnard award Barnard Coll., 1991, Hon. Doctorate, R.I. Sch. of Design, 1991; named to Nat. Sales Hall of Fame, 1991. Mem. Fashion Group. Roman Catholic.

CLAMAR, APHRODITE J., psychologist; b. Hartford, Conn. d. James John and Georgia (Panas) Clamar; m. Richard Cohen, June 24, 1973. BA, CCNY, 1953; MA, Columbia U., 1955; PhD, NYU, 1978; student, S. Adler Conservatory Acting, 1987-91. Mgmt. cons., psychologist Milla Alihan Assocs., N.Y.C., 1957-62; rsch. psychologist coord. Inst. Devel. Studies N.Y. Med. Coll., N.Y.C., 1964; intern psychologist Bellevue Psychiat. Hosp., N.Y.C., 1964-66; assoc. prof. Fashion Inst. Tech., N.Y.C., 1966-69; supervising psychologist Lifeline Ctr. Child Devel., N.Y.C., 1966-67; chief psychologist I Spy Health Program Beth Israel Med. Ctr., N.Y.C., 1967-70; dir. community-sch. mental health programs Soundview Community Svcs., Albert Einstein Coll. Medicine Yeshiva U., N.Y.C., 1970-73; dir. treatment program court-related children, dept. child psychiatry Harlem Hosp.; mem. faculty dept. psychiatry Coll. Physicians and Surgeons Columbia U., N.Y.C., 1973-76; pvt. practice psychotherapy, N.Y.C., 1976—; co-founder, pres. Richard Cohen Assocs. Pub. Rels. Agy., N.Y.C., 1979—99; prof. John Jay Coll., CUNY, 2000—. Cons. to pub. health and mental health agys., N.Y.C., 1976-91; mem. faculty Lenox Hill Hosp. Psychoanalytic Psychotherapy Tng. Program, 1982-88; theater producer, artistic dir. Tom Cat Cohen Prodns., Inc., 1990—. Author: (with Budd Hopkins) Missing Time, 1981; contbr. articles to profl. jours. Fellow: AAAS; mem.: APA, Authors Guild. Democrat. Greek Orthodox. Home: 155 W 68th St Apt 1618 New York NY 10023-5829 Office Phone: 212-724-1091.

CLANCEY, JEANNE KATHERINE, neurosurgical nurse; b. Erie, Pa., Dec. 31, 1948; d. Albert E. and Ruth A. (Gillespie) C. Diploma, St. Vincent Hosp. Sch. Nursing, 1969; BSN, Pa. State U., State College, 1983; MSN, U. Pitts., 1987. RN, Pa., W.Va.; cert. neurosci. nurse. Staff nurse med./surg. unit St. Vincent Hosp., Erie, 1969—71; staff nurse neurosurgery unit Presbyn. U. Hosp., Pitts., 1971—77, staff nurse recovery rm., 1977—78; coord. neurosurg. clin. Montefiore Hosp., Pitts., 1978—90; clin. nurse specialist neurosurgery West Penn Neuro-surgery and West Penn Hosp., Pitts., 1990—2005; educator, devel. specialist West Penn Hosp., 2005—. Bd. dirs. Oncology Nursing Certification Corp. Mem. Am. Assn. Neurosci. Nurses (bd. dirs. 1987-89, pres.-elect 1990, pres. 1991). Home: 622 Whitney Ave # 5 Pittsburgh PA 15221-3353 Office: 4800 Friendship Ave Pittsburgh PA 15224-1722 Office Phone: 412-578-5456. Personal E-mail: jkclancey@aol.com. Business E-Mail: jclancey@wpahs.org.

CLANCY, CAROLYN M., internist, federal agency administrator; m. Bill Clancy. BS in math and chemistry, magna cum laude, Boston Coll., 1975; MD, U. Mass., 1979. Henry J. Kaiser Family Found. fellow U. Pa., 1982—84; asst. prof. medicine, dir. med. clinic Med. Coll. Va., 1984—90; with Agy. Healthcare Rsch. and Quality, HHS, 1990—, dir. Ctr. Primary Care Rsch., dir. Ctr. Outcomes and Effectiveness Rsch., 1997—2002, acting dir., 2002—03, dir., 2003—. Clin. assoc. prof. dept. medicine George Washington U.; sr. assoc. editor Health Services Rsch.; mem. editl. bd. Annals of Family Medicine, Am. Journal Med. Quality, Med. Care Rsch. and Rev. Recipient award, APHA Women's Caucus. Master: Am. Coll. Physicians; mem.: Inst. Medicine. Office: Agy Healthcare Rsch and Quality John M Eisenberg Bldg 540 Gaither Rd Rockville MD 20850 Office Phone: 301-427-1200. Office Fax: 301-427-1201. E-mail: cclancy@ahrq.gov.*

CLANCY, DENYSE FINN, lawyer; BA magna cum laude, Yale U., 1989; MA in English, Columbia U., 1992; JD summa cum laude, So. Meth. U. 1999. Bar: Tex. 1999. Atty. Baron & Budd, P.C., Dallas. Editor: So. Meth. U. Sch. Law Rev. Named a Rising Star, Tex. Super Lawyers mag., 2006. Mem.: Tex. Trial Lawyers Assn., Assn. Trial Lawyers of Am. Office: Baron & Budd PC 3102 Oak Lawn Ave Ste 1100 Dallas TX 75219 Office Phone: 214-521-3605. E-mail: dclancy@baronbudd.com.*

CLANCY, PATRICIA, state representative; b. Cin., Aug. 10, 1952; BS, U. Cin. State rep. dist. 29 Ohio Ho. of Reps., Columbus, 1996—2004, mem. fin. and appropriations, rules and reference, and state govt. coms., mem. agr. and devel., and ethics and elections subcoms., majority fl. leader; state senator Ohio Senate Dist. 8, Columbus, 2005—, mem. fin. and fin. instns. com., mem. health, human svcs. and aging com., mem. hwys. and transp. com., mem. ins., commerce and labor com., vice chair judiciary and criminal justice com. Mem. Hamilton County Solid Waste Dist. Task Force, Colerain Ave. Task Force; past pres., trustee Colerain Twp. Mem.: Hamilton County Twp. Assn. (sec.-treas.), Colerain Twp. Hist. Soc., Colerain Twp. Rep. Club (sec.), Hamilton County Rep. Club. Republican. Office: Ohio Senate Statehouse Rm 143 Columbus OH 43215

CLANTON, KAYE REAMES, secondary school educator; d. Julian T. and Lucille Greene Reames; m. Dan W. Clanton, July 27, 1968; children: Dan W. Jr., Kristin K. Ferryman, Jeff T., Kara L. BS, U. Ctrl. Ark., 1970, MSE, 1976. Tchr. Conway H.S. West, Conway, Ark., 1983—; instr. U. of Ctrl. Ark., Conway, Ark., 2001—. Mem.: Am. Meteorol. Soc., Nat. Earth Sci. Teachers Assn., Ark. Sci. Teachers Assn., NSTA. Meth. Avocations: gardening, sewing. Office: Conway HS - West 2300 Prince Conway AR 72034 Office Phone: 501-450-4880.

CLANTON HARPINE, ELAINE, educational consultant, educator; b. Dallas, Apr. 30, 1952; d. Ellen Irene and Jesse Doyle Clanton; m. William Douglas Harpine, Dec. 24, 1977; children: David William Harpine, Virginia Elaine Harpine, Christina April Harpine. BS in Edn., S.W. Tex. State U., 1974; MA, Tex. Tech U., 1975; PhD, U. Ill., 1982. Spl. programs instr. Coll. William and Mary, Williamsburg, Va., 1980—82; dir. Motivational Inner-City Summer Workshop Children, Chgo., 2002; inner-city reading clinic Open-M Neighbor Ctr., Akron, Ohio, 2002—04; dir., founder summer reading program Summer Inner-City Reading Clinic, Bronx, 2003—04; designer ednl. program ALMS, Dare to Care Program Sierra Leone, Africa, NYC, 2004—05. Seminar instr. U. Ill. Exec. Devel. Ctr., Urbana, 1978; program cons. Abingdon, Nashville, 2000; with reading clinic inner-city children United Meth. Ch. Mission Sch., Tampa, Fla., 2001; adj. prof. Kent State U. Geagua, Burton, Ohio, 2002—05; coord. svc. learning project Open-M Neighborhood Ctr., Akron, 2004; tng. cons. tchrs. ALMS, Dare to Care Program Sierra Leone, Africa, NYC, 2004—; adj. prof. U. SC Students Coop. Assn., Aiken, 2005—06; with reading clinic Trinity River Mission, Dallas, 2005—06, Boys and Girls Club of Aiken (S.C.), 2006. Author: Youth-Led Meetings, 1989, No Experience Necessary!, 1992 (Excellence award, 1995), The Christmen Tree vol. 1, 1994, vol. 2, 1998, vol. 3, 2004, Come Follow Me! vol. 1 and 2, 2001. Girl scout leader Western Res. Girl Scouts, Akron, 1989—2004; organizer children's clowning program Children's Hosp., Akron, coord. children's clowning program, 1991—2002; vol. to fight world hunger Heifer Project Internat., Cuyahoga Falls, Ohio, 1994—2004; coord. children's ann. project Make a Difference Day, Cuyahoga Falls, 1996—2004; spkr. drug prevention with youth Kent State U., 2003. Mem.: APA, Southwestern Psychol. Assn., Phi Kappa Phi, Alpha Lambda Delta. Methodist. Avocations: writing, cooking, sewing. Home: 450 Crystal Peak Rd Graniteville SC 29829-3753 Office: U SC U Students Coop Assn 471 Univ Pkwy Aiken SC 29801 Office Phone: 440-834-4187. Business E-Mail: elaineh@usca.edu.

CLAPP, AMANDA GRACE, elementary school educator; b. Norwood, Mass., Nov. 21, 1976; d. David and Carol Clapp; m. Rene Uhalde, Aug. 21, 2004. BA in Anthropology, U. Mass., Amherst, 1999, BS in Natural Resource Studies, 1999; MA in Phys. Anthropology, U. Tex., Austin, 2004. Cert. tchr. NC, 2004. Rsch. asst. SUNY Stony Brook, Antananarivo, Madagascar, 2001; tchg. asst. U. Tex., Austin, 2002—03; sci. tchr. mid. grades Cullowhee Valley Sch., NC, 2004—. Active Watershed Assn. Tuckaseegee River, Bryson City, NC. Grantee Learning Links Grants for Curriculum Devel., Cmty. Found. Western NC, 2005—06; GK-12 fellow, NSF, 2003—04, Profl. Devel. grantee Tech Team GEMS, ETV, 2006—. Mem.: NSTA, NEA. Avocations: natural history study, evolutionary theory/human evolution, hiking, travel. Home: 252 Tulip Dr Sylva NC 28779 Personal E-mail: clapp@mchsi.com.

CLAPP, MEGAN ELIZABETH, art educator; b. New Haven, Oct. 14, 1975; d. John and Patricia Rechi; m. Steven Robert Clapp. BA in Studio Art, Moravian Coll., 1997; MS in Ednl. Tech., Ea. Conn. State U., 2006. Cert. tchr. Conn. Office mgr., graphic designer Triton Environ., Inc., New Haven, 1998—2000; grade K-8 art tchr. St. Andrew Sch., Bridgeport, Conn., 2000—02; art tchr., grade k-4 Bishop Woods Sch., New Haven, 2002—03; grades 8-12 art and graphic design tchr. High Rd. Sch., Hamden, Conn., 2002—03; grade 5-8 graphic design tchr. Sheridan Comm. and Tech. Magnet Sch., New Haven, 2003—. Freelance graphic designer, Hamden, 1997—. Democrat. Avocations: hiking, backpacking, cross country skiing. Office: Sheridan Comm and Tech Mid Sch 191 Fountain St New Haven CT 06515 Office Phone: 203-946-8828.

CLAPP, MILLICENT EVANS, real estate broker; b. Enfield, N.H., Sept. 1, 1923; d. Walter Edgar and Georgianna M. (Bourdeau) Evans; m. Michael Sabal, Apr. 5, 1943; 1 child, Kerry Eileen. Student, Travelers Ins. Co. Group Agency, Hartford, Conn., 1941-43, Am. Inst. Banking, 1960, U. N.H., 1972, Vt. Real Estate Inst., 1973. Radio broadcaster Sta. WTSL, Hanover, N.H., 1952-55, Sta. WOTW, Nashua, N.H., 1952-55; dir. publicity and pub. rels. N.H. Children's Aid Soc., Nashua, 1956-57; asst. to execs. Soc. for Savs., Hartford, Conn., 1957-62; customer svc. rep. Hallmark Cards, Kansas City, Mo., 1966-68; make-up artist Max Factor, Hollywood, Calif., 1968; real estate broker Mass., N.H., Vt. and Fla., 1984—, Mackle Bros., Fla., 1969; with U.S. Census 2000 Bureau. Owner Milly's Antiques and Collectibles, 1990—. Vice chmn. Ellington (Conn.) Rep. Party, 1961-68; chmn. Enfield Bicentennial Com., 1975-77. Recipient Disting. Svc. award Deltona Corp., 1969. Mem. Nat. Assn. Realtors, Abenaki Nation of N.H. Lutheran. Avocations: travel, antiques, photography, writing children's stories. Home: RR 1 Box 1186 Kingfield ME 04947-9801

CLAPPER, MARIE ANNE, magazine publisher; b. Chgo., Nov. 21, 1942; d. Chester William and Hazel Alice (Gilso) Reinke; m. William Neil Petersen, Aug. 17, 1963 (div. 1975); children: Elaine Myrtice Petersen, Edward William Petersen; m. Lyle N. Clapper, Jan. 1, 1980; children: Jeffrey Leland, Anne Reinke stepchildren: John Scott, Susan Louise Clapper Kashmier. Student, Augustana Coll., Rock Island, Ill., 1960-63; EdB, Northeastern U., 1964. Writer Pack-o-Fun mag., Park Ridge, Ill., 1976-77, editor Des Plaines, Ill., 1977-78, pub., 1990—; asst. to pub., circulation dir. Crafts 'n Things mag., Des Plaines, Ill., 1978-82, pub., 1982—, Decorative Arts Painting mag., Des Plaines, 1990—, The Cross Stitcher mag., Des Plaines, 1991—, 101 Bridal Ideas mag., Des Plaines, 1991—; pub., pres. Clapper pub., 2005—. Host TV show The Crafts 'n Things Show, 1984-86, Crafting for the 90s, 1990-94; author: EveryDay Matters, 1996. Mem. TEC, Mag. Pubs. Am. (bd. dirs.), Hobby Industry Am. (bd. dirs., treas. 1998-99). Office: Crafts 'n Things 2400 E Devon Ave Ste 375 Des Plaines IL 60018-4618

CLAPSADDLE, PATRICIA LEE, art educator; b. Cleve., Dec. 13, 1950; d. George Thomas and Jean (Sweet) Fuller; m. William Harold Clapsaddle, Apr. 13, 1974; children: Sarah Aubrey, Eben Weston. BFA, U. Cin., 1973; MFA, Kent State U., 1990. Art educator Ipswich (Mass.) Sch. Dist., 1973-77, West Geauga Sch. Dist., Chesterland, Ohio, 1979-82, Chardon (Ohio) Sch. Dist., 1982—. Adj. prof. Lake Erie Coll., Painesville, Ohio; lead mentor Chardon Sch. Dist., 2002—05. Mem. N.E. Ohio Edn. Assn., Ohio Art Edn. Assn., Nat. Art Edn. Assn. Avocations: pottery, running, travel. Office: Chardon HS 151 Chardon Ave Chardon OH 44024-1097 Office Phone: 440-285-4057.

CLAREY, PATRICIA T., health insurance company executive, former state official; BS, Union Coll., Schenectady, NY, 1975; MPA, Harvard U. John F. Kennedy Sch. of Govt., Cambridge, Mass., 1983. Govt. affairs rep. Chevron Corp., San Francisco; govt. rels. position Ashland Oil, Inc.; dep. dir. legis. affairs Nat. Park Svc., Washington; congl. liaison US Dept. Interior, Washington, 1986—89; dep. chief of staff to Gov. State of Calif., Sacramento; v.p. public affairs Transamerica Corp., San Francisco, 1999—2001; pres. Transamerica Found., San Francisco, 1998; v.p. govt. rels. Health Net, Inc. (formerly known as Foundation Health Sys., Inc.), LA, 2001—03; ran primary campaign for Gov.-elect Arnold Schwarzenegger; chief of staff to Gov. State of Calif., Sacramento, 2003—06; COO Health Net of Calif., Inc., Woodland Hills, 2006—. Former bd. dir. Calif. Found. on the Environ. and the Economy; mem. joint pub. adv. com. Commn. for Environ. Cooperation of N.Am., 2003—. Office: Health Net of Calif Inc 21281 Burbank Blvd Woodland Hills CA 91367*

CLARIZIO, JOSEPHINE DELORES, retired foundation administrator, retired manufacturing executive, retired engineering company executive; b. Montclair, NJ, Dec. 15, 1922; d. Thomas and Raffaela (Caruso) D'Andrea; m. N. Robert Clarizio, June 3, 1951. Cert., Katharine Gibbs Sch., 1942; BS, Seton Hall U., 1947; postgrad., Fordham U. Sch. Law, 1947-48, N.Y. Inst. Fin., 1964. Registered rep. Drexel, Burnham & Co., N.Y.C., 1965-70; asst. to pres. Wheelabrator-Frye Inc., Hampton, NH, 1970-78, corp. sec., 1981-83. Pres. Wheelabrator Found. Inc., Hampton, 1978-83; cons. Signal Cos. Inc., N.Y.C., N.H., 1983-85. Mem. Am. Assn. Ret. Persons, Seton Hall U. Alumni Assn. Republican. Roman Catholic.

CLARIZIO, LYNDA M., advertising executive, lawyer; b. Newark, Aug. 19, 1960; d. Attavio and Yolanda Clarizio; m. Mark Foulon, July 8, 1988. AB summa cum laude, Princeton U., 1982; JD, Harvard U., 1985. Bar: D.C. 1985. Ptnr. Arnold & Porter LLP, Washington, 1992—99; exec. v.p. Audience Bus. Am. Online LLC, 1999—2006; pres. Advertising.com, Balt., 2006—. Bd. dirs. Network Live, Human Rights First. Articles editor Harvard Internat. Law Jour., 1984-85. Mem. Phi Beta Kappa. Office: Advertising com 1020 Hull St Ivory Bldg Baltimore MD 21230*

CLARK, ALICIA GARCIA, political party official; b. Vera Cruz, Mex. arrived in US, 1970; d. Rafael Garcia Aully and Maria Luisa (Cobos) Garcia; m. Edward E. Clark, Oct. 20, 1970; 1 child, Edward E. MSChemE, Nat. U. Mex., Mexico City, 1951. Chemist Celanese Mexicana, Mexico City, 1951—53, lab. mgr., 1953—60, sales promotion mgr., 1960—65, sales promotion and advt. mgr., 1965—70; nat. chmn. Libertarian Party, Houston, 1981—83, coord. coun. state chairs, 1987—95. Pres. San Marino (Calif.) Guild of Huntington Hosps., 1981-82, chmn. Celebrity Series, 1989-91; mem. Mex. Olympic Com., 1968. Pres. bd. dirs. LA Opera League, 1990-96; founder, co-chair Hispanics for LA Opera, 1991-99; bd. dirs. Guild Opera Co., 1994-96, Club 100, 1996-99; mng. dir. L.A. Opera, 1995—; opera panel Nat. Endowment for Arts, 1997; active Redcat Theater Coun. Recipient award La Mujer de Hoy mag., 1969, Heroes LA award Hispanic Traditions and Heritage Coun., 1995, Star of Our Culture award Mex. Cultural Inst. LA, 1998, Placido Domingo award, 2000, Zachary Soc. Ann. award, 2001, Life Achievement award, Hypenics for L.A. Opera, 2006. Mem. Fashion Group (treas. 1969-70, award 1970). Home Fax: 626-796-3485.

CLARK, BABAA RITAH ANNETTE, massage therapist; b. Columbus, Ohio, Mar. 4, 1949; d. Calvin Owen and Willa Beatrice Clark; children: Michelle Renee', Lauren Elaine. Grad., Ctrl. Ohio Sch. Massage, Columbus, 1979. Cert. massage therapist Ohio. Massage therapist, owner Health Choices Massage Clinic, Columbus, 1983—. Part-time massage therapist YMCA, 1979—83, Jewish Ctr., 1979—83; tchr. drumming Health Rhythms Workshop, 2004—; mem. profl. drum groups Sisger Ngoma, Columbus, Ibu Ayan, Cleve. Coord. dance and drumming activities Palaver Hut in Village, Howard Recreation Ctr.; leader drum troupe AKWAABA. Address: 84 N 20th St Columbus OH 43203-1967

CLARK, BARBARA JUNE, elementary school educator; b. Leoti, Kans., May 29, 1934; d. Robert Carter and Adlee Belle (Wilson) C. BS in Edn., Ft. Hays State U., 1958, MS in Edn., 1967. 4th grade tchr. McKinley Elem., Liberal, Kans., 1954—56, Lincoln Elem., Liberal, 1958—61, 1961—62, 5th grade tchr., 1962—2001. Mathfest chmn. Unified Sch. Dist. 480, Liberal, 1987-88, grade level chmn., 1988-89, social studies textbook selection com., 1990-92, intensive assistance team, 89-91, Lincoln Sch. site coun., 1993-94, Lincoln preassessment team, 1992-98, Lincoln strategic action com., 1994-98, reading textbook selection com., 1995-96, others; quality performance accreditation chmn. math team, 1998-2001; with Ft. Hay State U. travel study tours, Hawaii, 1960, Europe, 1962. Editor: Wilson History, 1970—; author Lincoln School History, 1978. Vol. Lincoln Elem., 2002—05; singer Meth. Chancel Choir; treas. Meth. Wesleyan Svc. Guild, 1960—62, v.p., 1962—63, pres., 1963—66, rec. sec. Dodge City Dist., 1965—68; sponsor, bus. mgr. Meth. Ctrl. Kans. Conf. Mission Edn. Tour, 1975—78; rec. sec. United Meth. Ch. Circle 9, 1986—88, v.p., 1995—99, United Meth. Ch. Circle 8, 1999—. Recipient Representative Young Tchr. award Jr. C. of C., Liberal, 1962, PTA Life Membership, Lincoln Elem., Liberal, 1962, Morale Enhancement award, 2001, Elem. Tchr. of Yr., 2001. Mem. NEA, Kans. Edn. Assn., Liberal Edn. Assn.(Master Tchr. award 1989), Bus. and Profl. Women's Club (pres. 1979-80, treas. 1989-90, 94—, v.p. 1991-94, fin. chair 1992—, Woman of Yr. award 1974), Beta Sigma Phi (Laureate Pi chpt. treas. 1981-91, pres. 1991-06, Silver Circle award 1992, Order of Rose award 1974), Delta Kappa Gamma (Phi state conv. registration chmn. 1974, 95, rec. sec. 1986-88, music chmn. 1992-94, pres. 1999-2002, state mem. com. 2001-03, state rsch. com. 2003—), Santa Fe Trail Assn. (charter life), Seward County Retired Tchrs.Assn.(historian, 2003-06). Avocations: genealogy, history.

CLARK, BETTY SUSAN, elementary school educator; d. W. D. Davis and Gertrude Davis (Ross); children: Krystie L. Smith, Eric S., Steve S. Faupel. MSE, Ark. State U., Jonesboro. 2nd grade tchr. Vanndale (Ark.) Elem. Sch., 1987—94, 5th grade tchr., 1995—. Named Tchr. of the Yr. for Ark., DARE, 2004. Office: Vanndale Elementary School Hwy 1B Vanndale AR 72387 Office Phone: 870-238-8521. Office Fax: 870-238-0188.

CLARK, BEVERLY ANN, retired lawyer; b. Davenport, Iowa, Dec. 9, 1944; d. F. Henry and Arlene F. (Meyer) C.; m. Richard Floss; children: Amy and Barry (twins); stepchildren: Heather, Gretchan. Student, Mich. State U., 1963—65; BA, Calif. State U., Fullerton, 1967; MSW, U. Iowa, 1975, JD, 1980; grad., Iowa Massage Inst., 1999. Bar: Iowa 1980; lic. social worker, Iowa; nat. cert. lic. massage therapist. Probation officer County of San Bernardino, San Bernardino, Calif., 1968, County of Riverside, Riverside, Calif., 1968-69; social worker Skiff Hosp., Newton, Iowa, 1971-73, State of Iowa, Mitchellville, 1973-74, planner Des Moines, 1976-77, law clk., 1980-81; corp. counsel Pioneer Hi-Bred Internat., Inc., Des Moines, 1981-2000; atty. Jasper County Legal Aid, 2002—03; pvt. practice, 2000—06; ret., 2006. Instr. Des Moines Area C.C., Ankeny, Iowa, 1974—75, 2000—; adj. prof. Drake Law Sch., 1993—96, Buena Vista U., 2002—; pub. Sweet Annie Press; past owner Annie's Place, The B&B Connection Gift Catalog. Editor: Proceedings: Bicentennial Symposium on New Directions in Juvenile Justice, 1975; author monthly column Wellfem-In-Law; contbr. articles to prof. jours. Founder Mother of Twins Club, Newton, 1971; co-chmn. Juvenile Justice Symposium, Des Moines, 1974-75; mem. Juvenile Justice Com., Des Moines, 1974-75; mem. Nat. Offender Based State Corrections Info. Sys. Com., Iowa rep., 1976-78; incorporator, dir. Iowa Dance Theatre, Des Moines, 1981; mem. Pesticide User's Adv. Com., Fort Collins, Colo., 1981-88; co-developer Iowa Migrant Ombudsmen Project, Pioneer, Inc. and Proteus, Inc. Recipient Disting. Alumni award U. Iowa, 1990, Nat. award Ctr. for Pub. Resources. Mem.: DAR, ABA (termination-at-will subcom. 1982—2000, subcom. on devel. individual rights in work place), Iowa Bar Assn., Iowa Orgn. Women Attys. (bd. dirs., sec. 2001). E-mail: clarklaw@pcpartner.net.

CLARK, BONNIE A., small business owner, real estate agent; b. June 2, 1944; Student, Pierce Coll., Phila., 1965-68. Pres. Old Town Travel Agy., Alexandria, Va., 1980-86; dir. mktg. and pub. rels. Inst. Cert. Travel Agts., Wellesley, Mass., 1986-88; dist. mgr. Classic Hawaii Tours, Phila., 1988-90; exec. v.p. A Better Courier, Westville, N.J., 1990—; realtor Century 21 Mary Allen Realty, Inc., Ship Bottom, NJ, 2004—. Artist: (mural) Tree of Learning 1998. Troop leader Ocean County Girl Scouts, 1998—; supt. Sunday Sch. Holy Trinity Luth. Ch., 1999. Mem. Greater Phila. C. of C., Air Transport Assn. (pub. mgr., outstanding achievement 1979). Office: 2909 Long Beach Blvd Ship Bottom NJ 08008 Office Phone: 609-494-0700 216. Personal E-mail: lbiclark@gmail.com.

CLARK, CANDY, actress; b. Norman, Okla., June 20, 1947; d. Thomas Prest and Ella Lee C. Student public schs., Ft. Worth. Appeared in movies Fat City, 1971, American Graffiti, 1973 (nominated for best supporting actress), The Man Who Fell to Earth, 1975, I Will, I Will.for Now, 1976, Citizens Band, 1976, The Big Sleep, 1977, When Ya' Coming Back Red Ryder, 1978, More American Graffiti, 1978, National Lampoon Goes to the Movies, 1981, Q, 1982, Blue Thunder, 1983, Amityville 3-D, 1983, Stephen King's Cat's Eye, 1984, Hambone and Hillie, 1984, At Close Range, 1986, The Blob, 1988, Blind Curve, 1988, Cool-As-Ice, 1991, Buffy the Vampire Slayer, 1992, Original Intent, 1992, Deuce Coupe, 1992, Radioland Murders, 1994, Niagara, Niagara, 1996, Cherry Falls, 1999, The Month of August, 2002, appeared in TV movies James Dean, 1976, Amateur Night at the Dixie Bar and Grill, 1978, Circus of the Stars #4, 1979, Where The Ladies Go, 1980, Rodeo Girl, 1980, Cocaine and Blue Eyes, 1983, Popeye Doyle, 1986, Plan of Attack, 1992; TV Appearances: Banacek, 1973, Faerie Tale Theatre, 1982, Magnum P.I., 1985, Simon & Simon, 1986, Starman, 1986, Hunter, 1986, The Hitchhiker, 1987, Matlock, 1987, St. Elsewhere, 1988, Father Dowling Mysteries, 1989, Baywatch Nights, 1995. appeared in off-Broadway show A Coupla White Chicks Sitting Around Talking, 1981, (play) It's Raining on Hope Street, 1988, Loose Lips, 1995.

CLARK, CAROLYN CHAMBERS, nurse, educator, publishing executive; b. Superior, Wis., Mar. 25, 1941; d. John and Phyllis (Olsen) Stark. BS, U. Wis., 1964; MS, Rutgers U., Newark, 1966; EdD, Columbia U., 1976. RN, Fla.; cert. advanced registered nurse practitioner, Fla.; diplomate Am. Bd. Forensic Nursing. Instr. Bergen C.C., Paramus, N.J., 1972-74; pvt. practice wellness nursing, 1972—. Found. dir. The Wellness Inst., Sloatsburg, 1979-84; assoc. prof. Pace U., Pleasantville, N.Y., 1983-84; prof., wellness coord. U. Tampa, Fla., 1984-85; cons. VA Med. Ctr., Bay Pines, Fla., 1988-89, provider continuing programs for nurses, 1990—; nurse practitioner/cons. Bay Area Psychol. Svcs., 1994—; dir. Women's Wellness Ctr. of the Resource Ctr. for Women, 1994—; mem. grad. faculty Walden U., 1999—, Schiller Internat. U., 1998—, mem. doctoral faculty, 1998—. Author: Nursing Concepts and Processes, 1977, The Nurse as Group Leader, 1977, 3rd edit., 1994 (also pub. in Swedish, German), Mental Health Aspects of Community Health Nursing, 1978, Classroom Skills for Nurse Educators, 1978, Assertive Skills for Nurses, 1978, Management in Nursing, 1979, The Nurse as Continuing Educator, 1979, Enhancing Wellness: A Guide for Self-Care, 1981, Wellness Nursing: Concepts, Theory, Research and Practice, 1986, Deadlier than Death, 1993, Dangerous Alibis, Cast Into The Fire, 1994, Wellness Practitioner, 1996, Creating a Climate for Power Learning, 1997, Integrating Complementary Procedure Into Practice, 2000; editor, pub. The Wellness Newsletter, 1980-94; editor Alternative Health Practitioner: The Jour. of Complementary and Natural Care, 1995-99; pres. Wellness Resources, 1992—; editor-in-chief Ency. Complementary Health Practice, 1999; contbr. articles to profl. jours.; mem. editl. bd. Am. Jour. Holistic Nursing, 1985-88, Women's Health Care Internat., 1985—. Recipient award Fla. Free Lance Writers Assn., 1988, 92, comm. and media award Fla. Nurses Assn., 1997, Book of the Yr. awards, 1996, 99. Fellow Am. Acad. Nursing. Office: 1817 Bridge St Englewood FL 34223-1522

CLARK, CAROLYN COCHRAN, lawyer; b. Kansas City, Mo., Oct. 30, 1941; d. John Rogers and Betty Charleton (Holmes) Cochran; m. L. David Clark, Jr., Dec. 29, 1967; children: Gregory David, Timothy Rogers. BA, U. Mo., 1963; LLB, Harvard U., 1968. Bar: N.Y. 1968, Fla. 1979. Assoc. Milbank, Tweed, Hadley & McCloy, N.Y.C., 1968-76, ptnr., 1977—2001, cons. ptnr., 2002—. Mem. deferred giving com., former regional chmn. major gifts com. Harvard Law Sch. Fund; mem. vis. com. Harvard Law Sch., 1982-88; mem. com. on trust and estate gift plans Rockefeller U.; trustee Madison Ave. Presbyn. Ch., 1984-86, N.Y. Bot. Garden, 1993-96, Vis. Nurse Assn. N.Y. and Vis. Nurse Health Care, 1991-96, Riverdale Country Sch., 1994-98, Milbank Meml. Fund, 1996—, The Woodlawn Cemetery, 1999—; del. John D. Rockefeller Conf. Philanthropy in the 21st Century, N.Y., 1989; bd. advisors NYU program Philanthropy and the Law; chmn. program taxation exempt orgns. NYU Tax Inst. Recipient Disting. Alumna award U. Mo., 1989. Fellow Am. Coll. Trust and Estate Counsel (ind. regent, chmn. com. on charitable giving and exempt orgns.), N.Y. Bar Found., Am. Bar Found.; mem. ABA (chmn. subcom. income taxation of charitable trusts 1976-78, chmn. com. charitable instns. 1989-94), Assn. Bar City of N.Y. (chmn. com. on non-profit orgns. 1986-89, sec. com. philanthropic orgns. 1976-82, mem. com. trusts, estates and surrogates cts. 1977-80, 85-86), N.Y. State Bar Assn. (com. estate planning, trusts and estates sect. 1978-89), Am. Law Inst., Practising Law Inst. (lectr.), Harvard U. Law Sch., Assn. Greater N.Y. (trustee 1978-80, v.p. 1980-81, pres. 1981-82), NYU Tax Inst. (chmn. conf. tax planning charitable orgns. 1993-95), Nat. Harvard Law Sch. Alumni Assn. (exec. com. 1978-80, v.p. 1986-90, pres. 1990-92), Soc. Colonial Dames Am. in Mo., Maidstone Club. Home: 161 E 79th St New York NY 10021-0480 Office: Milbank Tweed Hadley Et Al 46th Fl 1 Chase Manhattan Plz New York NY 10005-1401 E-mail: cclark@milbank.com.

CLARK, CATHY SUE, special education educator; b. Pleasanton, Calif., Jan. 7, 1953; d. William Edward and Bettie Jo (Bragg) Wheeler; m. Ronald Dwayne Clark, June 7, 1980; children: Bradley, Brian. BS in Edn., U. Cin., 1976; MEd in Adminstrn., U. Dayton, 1988. Cert. spl. edn. tchr., Ohio. Tchr. West Clermont Local Schs., Amelia, Ohio, 1977-80; ednl. specialist Cook-DuPage County Schs., Chgo., 1980-82; tchr. spl. edn. Western Brown Local Schs., Mt. Orab, Ohio, 1982—97; tchr. spl. edn., intervention specialist West Clermont Local Schs., Glen Este, Ohio, 1997—. Pee wee cheerleading coach Western Brown Youth Football Assn., 1992; varsity cheerleader sponsor Western Brown High Sch., 1983-97. Mem.: NEA, Internat. Dyslexia Assn., U. Dayton Alumni Assn., Ohio Ed. Assn., Glen Este PSTO. Avocations: sports, reading, walking. Home: 4237 Wilson s Lndg Batavia OH 45103-1961 Office: Glen Este H S Cincinnati OH 45245 Office Phone: 513-947-7624. Business E-Mail: clark_c@westcler.org.

CLARK, CHRISTINE W., elementary school educator; d. George Lester Jr. and Waleria Cowart; m. Delmas Eric Clark, Oct. 3, 1971; children: Steven, Erin. M in Elem. Edn., Ga. So. U., Statesboro, 1976. Tchr. Reidsville (Ga.) Elem. Sch., 1971—. Pres. Beta Sigma Phi, Reidsville, 1996. Named Outstanding Dist. Sci. Tchr., Ga. Sci. Tchrs. Assn., 1986—87. Methodist. Avocations: reading, gardening.

CLARK, CLAUDIA ANN, business development manager; b. Sharon, Pa., Sept. 15, 1954; d. Harry Malin Shilling and Betty Ann Harper Shilling; m. Charles Irving Shaffer, Jan. 8, 1973 (div. Apr. 1979); 1 child, Clover Shaffer. BS in Environ. Sci., Westminster Coll., 1982; M in Environ. Pollution Control, Pa. State U., 1988. Sci. educator Bellefonte (Pa.) Sch. Dist., 1984, Harrisburg (Pa.) Sch. Dist., 1985—86; account exec. Wadsworth/Alert, Canton, Ohio, 1986—88; regional sales mgr. Roy F. Weston, University Park, Ill., 1988—94; bus. devel. mgr. Paragon Analytics, Ft. Collins, Colo., 1994—. Mem.: Soc. Am. Mil. Engrs. Avocations: skiing, horseback riding. Office: Paragon Analytics Inc 225 Commerce Dr Fort Collins CO 80524

CLARK, COLLEEN ROMICK, academic administrator; b. Marietta, Ohio, Mar. 29, 1962; d. Lawrence Henry and Delores Doline (Jones) Romick; m. Carl W. Clark Jr., Dec. 30, 2000. AB, Ohio U., 1984; MA, Ohio State U., Columbus, 1987. Grad. teaching assoc. English dept. Ohio State U., 1986-88, grad. rsch. asst. English dept., 1988-89, grad. teaching assoc., 1989—. Ohio State U. fellow, 1985-86. Mem. Phi Beta Kappa (Thomas M. Wolfe award 1984), Phi Kappa Phi. Democrat. Methodist. Office: Ohio State U Denney Hall 164 W 17th Ave Columbus OH 43210-1326

CLARK, CYNTHIA ZANG FACER, federal agency administrator; b. Sterling, Colo., Apr. 1, 1942; d. Joseph Elmer and Flora Burnell Zang; m. Glenn Willett Clark, Aug. 20, 1963; children: Randall, Drew, Ariel Silver, Allison, Timothy, Emily BA in Math., Mills Coll., Oakland, Calif., 1963; MS in Math., U. Denver, 1964; MS in Stats., Iowa State U., 1973, PhD in Stats., 1977. Instr. dept. maths. U. Denver, 1963-66, Drake U., Des Moines, 1971-72; mathematical statistician Statistical Rsch. Divsn. Bur. Census, 1977-79; econ. statistician Office Fed. Statistical Policy and Standards Dept. Commerce, 1979-81; statistical policy analyst Statistical Policy Office Office Info. and Regulatory Affairs Office Mgmt. & Budget, 1981-83; asst. divsn. chief for rsch. & methodology Agriculture Divsn Bur. Census, 1983-90, dir. rsch. and applications divsn., 1990-92; dir. survey mgmt. divsn. Nat. Agrl. Statistics Svc. Dept. Agriculture, 1992-96; assoc. dir. methodology and standards Bur. Census Dept. Commerce, Washington, 1996—2004; dir. methodology Office of Nat. Stats. U.K., London, 2004—. Contbr. articles to profl. jours. Recipient Sr. Exec. Svc. bonus award, 1994, 1995, 1997—2003. Fellow Am. Statis. Assn. (mem. InterCASIC 1996 conf. planning com., past pres. sect. govt. statistics, bd. dir.); mem. Am. Assn. Pub. Opinion Rsch., Washington Statis. Soc. (past pres.), Internat. Assn. Survey Stats., Sr. Exec. Assn. (Dept. Agr. chpt. pres. 1993-95), Caucus for Women in Stats. (past pres.), Natural Resource Conservation Svc. (blue ribbon panel on info. and data mgmt. 1996), Internat. Stats. Inst. (chair com. on women in stats. 2003—), Internat. Assn. Survey Statisticians (former bd. mem.). Mem. Ch. of Jesus Christ of Latter Day Saints. Avocations: genealogy, ice skating, cultural activities, travel. Office: Office for National Statistics 1 Drummond Gate London SW1V 2QQ England Home: Hugh St 32 Royal Belgrave House London SW1V 1RR England Office Phone: 4420 7533 6151. Business E-Mail: cynthia.clark@ons.gov.uk.

CLARK, DAWN A., architect; BArch in Environ. Design, U. Colo. From arch. to prin. Callison Architecture Inc., Seattle, 1987—2001, prin., 2001—. Presenter in field. Office: Callison Architecture Inc 1420 Fifth Ave Ste 2400 Seattle WA 98101-2343

CLARK, DEANNA DEE, volunteer; b. Cedar Rapids, Iowa, June 1, 1944; d. Cyrus Dean and Isabelle Esther Thomas; m. Glen Edward Clark, July 16, 1966; children: Andrew Curtis, Carissa Jane. AA, Coll. of the Desert, 1964; BA, Coe Coll., 1966. Fund devel. chmn. Nat. Assistance League, 1992—94; resource devel. writer and trainer, 1992—2002; convenor U.S. Internat. Youth Exch. Initiative Cmty. Network, Utah, 1984—94; human svcs. subcom. child advocacy project, social justice and peacemaking min. unit Presbyn. Ch. U.S.A., 1992—93; sustaining mem. Jr. League Salt Lake City, 1976—, Assistance League Salt Lake City, 1986—; bd. dirs. Friends of Libr., U. Utah, 1991—94; numerous civic coms. and found. Utah, 1992—; pres. Provo-Jordan River Pkwy. Found., 1993—95; moderator, nominating com. Synod of the Rocky Mountains, 1999—2002; sec., vice-chmn. City of Holladay Interfaith Coun., 1999—2006; pres. bd. Neighborhood House Assn., 2006—; info practices com. Utah Legislature, 1990; exec. com. of Gen. Assembly Coun., Presbyn. Ch. (U.S.A.), 1993—97; elder Presbyn. Ch., 1983—; mem. coun. Presbytery of Utah, 1985—2001, moderator, 2000—01. Mem. LWV (Utah pres. 1981-83), P.E.O. (historian Utah chpt. 1992-95, chpt. H pres. 1995-97, Utah chmn. Gump and Ayers Scholarship Com. 1998-99). Home: PO Box 711098 Salt Lake City UT 84171-1098

CLARK, DEBORAH J., nursing administrator, educator; b. Chgo., Jan. 15, 1958; d. Edward Carl and Marlene Evelyn (Lester) Otto; m. Larry Edward Clark, Aug. 2, 1980; 1 child, Zachary Edward. ADN, Parkland Jr. Coll., Champaign, Ill., 1981; BS in Nursing, Ga. Coll. & State U., Milledgeville, 1992, MSN in Nursing Admin., 1994, PhD in Nursing, 2003. Cert. critical care RN. Clin. coord. Cole Hosp., Champaign; staff RN, ISUC Mercy Hosp., Urbana, Ill.; dir. of nursing, utilization rev.-quality assurance coord. Cole Hosp., Champaign, 1985—88; staff nurse, asst. nurs mgr, nurs mgr., charge nurse, nurse educator Med. Ctr. of Central Ga., Macon, 1988—95; asst. prof. of nursing Gordon Coll., Barnesville, Ga., 1995—98; asst. prof of nursing, dept. of adult & gerontological nursing Ga. Coll. & State U., Milledgeville, 1998—99, asst. prof of nursing, dept. of healthcare sys. & informatics, 1999—; assoc. dean nursing, assoc. prof. nursing Dept. Nursing Clayton Coll. & State U., Morrow, Ga., 2004—. Mem.: Assn. of Critical Care Nurses, Assn. of Internet Rschrs., Sigma Theta Tau Internat. Soc. of Nursing. Office: Clayton Coll & State Univ Bus & Health Scis Bldg 61E, 5900 N Lee St Morrow GA 30260-0285 Office Phone: 770-961-3481. Office Fax: 770-961-3639. E-mail: deborahclark@mail.clayton.edu.

CLARK, DEBRA ELIZABETH, music educator; b. Seymour, Ind., Jan. 15, 1956; d. Emil Ray and Elizabeth Ellen (Ray) Clark. AB in Edn. & Music, Ky. Christian Coll., Grayson, 1978; BS in Elem. Edn., Morehead State U., Ky., 1979; M in Elem. Edn., DePauw U., Greencastle, Ind., 1986. 1st grade tchr. Kingsway Christian Sch., Avon, Ind., 1979—81; 2nd & 3rd grade tchr. Brentwood Elem. Sch., Plainfield, 1982—97, music tchr., 1997—. Children's choir dir. Plainfield Christian Ch., 1985—. Republican. Mem. Christian Ch. Avocations: singing, piano, drawing, cooking. Office: Brentwood Elem Sch 1630 Oliver Plainfield IN 46168 Office Phone: 317-839-4802.

CLARK, DIANNE ELIZABETH, religious studies and reading educator; b. Vinton, Iowa, Apr. 20, 1951; d. Edward J. and Bernadine H. (Potthoff) Rhinehart; m. John T. Clark, Oct. 31, 1999; children: Daniel, Craig, Andrea Fullerton. BS/LTD, Concordia Tchr.'s Coll., 1972; MA, U. Iowa, 1986; specialist degree in Christian edn., Concordia Coll., Seward, Nebr., 1991. Cert. classroom tchr. K-9, reading clinician K-12. Dir. Christian edn. Peace Luth. Ch., Hastings, Nebr., 1991—; tchr., reading curriculum com. chair Columbus Community Schs., Columbus Junction, Iowa; tchr. Sylvan Learning Ctr., Coralville, Iowa; substitute tchr. Iowa City Public Schs., Iowa City. Ednl. adv. com. Iowa Wesleyan Coll.; mem. Our Redeemer Preschool Bd.; presenter in field. Mem. NEA, Internat. Reading Assn., Iowa Edn. Assn., Tri-area Reading Assn., Columbus Edn. Assn., Autism Soc. Am., Luth. Edn. Assn. Home: 69 Modern Way Iowa City IA 52240-3068

CLARK, DONNA M., retired elementary school educator; b. Roseville, Mich., Sept. 15, 1939; d. Granville Raymond Jewel and Evelyn Marie Steiger-Jewel; m. Buddy Lee Clark, Dec. 30, 1979; children: Thomas, Douglas Lee Jewel, Nancy Gruber, Barbara Merkle. BS in Elem. Edn., Olivet U., 1962; M in Elem. Edn., St. Francis Coll., 1970. First grade tchr. VanDyke Pub. Sch., Warren, Mich., 1969; upper elem. tchr. DeKalb County Ea. Cmty. Sch. Dist., Butler, Ind., 1969—2005; ret., 2005. Upper elem. dept. chair DeKalb County Ea., Riverdale Elem., Saint Joe, Ind., 1984—2005; summer sch. coord. DeKalb County Ea. Cmty. Sch. Dist., 1980—82. State field rep. Ind. Jr. Hist. Soc., Indpls., 1971—79; county pres. DeKalb County Hist. Soc., Auburn, Ind., 1977—78. Mem.: Delta Dappa Kamma (assoc.; v.p. 1980—82), DAR (assoc.; chmn. radio, tv and movie com. 1990—93, state libr. 1994—97, state chaplain 1997—2000, corr. sec. 2006—, chpt. historian 2006—). Home: 7093 County Rd 59A Spencerville IN 46788

CLARK, ELOISE ELIZABETH, biologist, educator; b. Grundy, Va., Jan. 20, 1931; d. J. Francis Emmett and Ava Clayton (Harris) C. BA, Mary Washington Coll., 1951; PhD Zoology, U. N.C., 1958; DSc, King Coll., 1976; postdoctoral rsch., Washington U., St. Louis, 1957—58, U. Calif. Berkeley, 1958—59. Rsch. asst., then instr. U. N.C., 1952—55; from instr. to asst. prof. Columbia U., 1959—65, assoc. prof. biol. sci., 1966—69; with NSF, Washington, 1969—71, head molecular biology, 1971—73, divsn. dir. biol. and med. scis., 1973—75, dep. asst. dir. biol., behavioral and social scis., 1975—76, asst. dir. biol., behavioral and social scis., 1976-83; prof. biol. sci. to trustee prof. emeritus Bowling Green State U., Ohio, 1983—2002, trustee prof. emeritus, 2002—. Instr. Marine Biol. Lab., Woods Hole, Mass., 1958—62; v.p. acad. affairs Bowling Green State U., Ohio, 1983—96. Contbr. articles to profl. jours. and congl. hearings. Mem. alumnae bd. Mary Washington Coll., U. Va., 1967—70; bd. regents Nat. Libr. Medicine, 1973—83; mem. policy group competitive grants program U.S. Dept. Agr.; mem. White House Interdepartmental Task Force on Women, 1978—80, Task Force for Conf. on Families, 1980, Com. on Health and Medicine, 1976—80; vice chmn. Com. on Food and Renewable Resources, 1977—80; mem. selective excellence task force Ohio Bd. Regents, 1984—85; mem. Ohio Adv. Coun., Coll. Prep. Edn., 1983—84, Ohio Inter-Univ. Coun. for Provosts, 1983—96, chmn., 1984—85, 1995—96; nat. adv. rsch. resources coun. NIH, 1987—89; mem. informal sci. edn. panel NSF, 1986—88, adv. com., social, behavioral and econ. scis., 1997—2000; program adv. coun. sci., tech. and pub. policy Harvard U., 1988—90, mem. editl. bd. Forum, 1997—2001; mem. governing bd. OhioLink, 1990—96, vice chair, 1992, chair, 1993—94. Named Disting. Alumnus Mary Washington Coll., 1975; Wilson scholar, 1956; E.C. Drew scholar, 1956; USPHS postdoctoral fellow, 1957-59; recipient Disting. Svc. award NSF, 1978 Mem. AAAS (coun. 1969-71, bd. dirs. 1978-82, pres.-elect, 1992, pres., 1993, chmn. bd. 1994), Soc. Gen. Physiology (sec. 1965-67, coun. 1969-71), Biophys. Soc. (coun. 1975-76), Am. Soc. Cell Biology (coun. 1972-75), Am. Inst. Biol. Scientists, Marine Biol. Lab. (trustee 1993), NASULGC (higher edn. and tech. com. 1988-93, com. info. tech. 1994-96), Consortium Social Sci. Assn. (bd. dirs. 1993-96), Ohio Coun. Rsch. and Econ. Devel., Assn. Women Sci. (bd. dirs. 1998-2001), Phi Beta Kappa (com. qualifications 1985-2006, chair 1998-2004, senate 1996-2006, exec. com. 1997-2003), Sigma Xi, Omicron Delta Kappa Home: 1222 Brownwood Dr Bowling Green OH 43402-3503 Office: Bowling Green State U Dept Biol Scis Bowling Green OH 43403-0001 Office Phone: 419-372-9390.

CLARK, ELSA MYRIAM, artist; b. Boyaca, Colombia, Jan. 24, 1941; arrived in U.S., 1982; d. Guillermo Torres and Ana Elvia Sanchez; m. Victor Manuel Contreras (div.); children: Vivian Contreras, Liz Contreras, Francoise Contreras, David Contreras; m. George Bryan Clark, Jan. 16, 1983. Apprenticeship in Painting with Teresa Manrique; apprenticeship with David Manzur, Acad. of Art; apprenticeship with Pepe Garcia; degree, U. New Orleans. Interviewee Sta. 3-TV; appearance on TV show Primitive Portrait, Channel 5, 2005. Exhibitions include BCH Gallery, Bogota (Best in Show award), Heritage Gallery, Lafayette, La., Live Oak Gallery, Zigler Mus., Jennings, La., Nat. Art Appreciation Soc. (Blue Ribbon), Palm Beach Gallery, Fla., Herman Gallery, New Orleans, Deicas Gallery, LA Mus. Art, Avianca Gallery, Bogota, Colombia, internat. showings in Venezuela, Peru, Germany, Netherlands, Spain, Italy, France, and Romania. Home: 802 Dulles Dr Lafayette LA 70506 Office Phone: 337-993-9793. Personal E-mail: elsamyriam@hotmail.com.

CLARK, ETHELANN P., elementary school educator; b. Marysville, Calif., Feb. 1, 1948; d. Harmon D. and Luella Atkinson Pierson; m. Paul O. Wight (dec.); children: Tyler Wight(dec.), Jill M. Wight; m. Hugh L. Clark, Oct. 24, 1984. BS, Utah State U., Logan, 1996; Master in Elem. Edn., Utah State U., 2000. Tchr., aide Bear River Mid. Sch., Barland, Utah, 1982—92; tchr. Harris Intermediate, Tremonton, Utah, 1996—. Bd. mem. People with Disabilities, Brigham, 1996—98; area rep. Box Elder Edn. Assn., Brigham, Utah, 1996—2006, exec. bd., 2001—04. CEO, pres. Mae Found., Tremonton, 2004—; mem. M and E Yearbook Found.; campaign mgr. Citizens Party for Mayor, Tremonton, 2005. Recipient Nucor Ednl. award, Nucor Steel, 1998, Nucor Enviorn. award, 1999. Mem.: Nat. Sci. Tchr. Assn., Utah Mid-Level Assn. Home: 554 Wrightway Dr Tremonton UT 84337 Office Phone: 435-257-2560. Business E-Mail: epclark@frontiernet.net.

CLARK, EUGENIE, zoologist, educator; b. NYC, May 4, 1922; m. Hideo Umaki, 1942; m. Ilias Konstantinou, 1949; 4 children; m. Chandler Brossard, 1966; m. Igor Klatzo, 1969; m. Henry Yoshinobu Kon, 1997. BA, Hunter Coll., 1942; MA, NYU, 1946, PhD, 1950; DSc (hon.), U. Mass., Dartmouth, 1990, U. Guelph, 1995, U. South Hampton, 1995. Rsch. asst. ichthyology Scripps Instn. Oceanography, 1946-47; with NY Zool. Soc., 1947-48; rsch. asst. animal behavior Am. Mus. Nat. Hist., NYC, 1948-49, rsch. assoc., 1950-80; instr. Hunter Coll., 1954; exec. dir. Cape Haze Marine Lab., Sarasota, Fla., 1955-67; assoc. prof. biology CUNY, 1966-67; assoc. prof. zoology U. Md., 1968-73, prof. zoology, 1973-92, prof. emerita, sr. rsch. scientist, 1992—. Vis. prof. Hebrew U., 1972; sr. rsch. scientist, dir. emerita Mote Marine Lab., Sarasota, Fla., 1999—. Author: Lady with a Spear, 1953, The Lady and the Sharks, 1969, Desert Beneath the Sea, 1991; subject of biographies Shark Lady (Ann McGovern), 1978, Adventures of the Shark Lady (Ann McGovern), 1998, Eugenie Clark, Adventures of a Shark Scientist (Ellen R. Butts, Joyce R. Schwartz), 2000, Fish Watching with Eugenie Clark (Michael E. Ross), 2000, America's Shark Lady (Ann McGovern), 2004, Eugenie Clark, Marine Biologist (Ronald A. Reis) 2005, Dr. Eugenie Clark Swimming with Sharks (Lisa Rao), 2006. Recipient Myrtle Wreath award in sci. Hadassah, 1964, Nogi award in art Underwater Soc. Am., 1965, Dugan award in aquatic sci. Am. Littoral Soc., 1969, Diver of Yr. award Boston Sea Rovers, 1978, David Stone medal, 1984, Stoneman Conservation award, 1982, Gov. of S. Sinai medal, 1985, Lowell Thomas award Explorers Club, 1986, Wildscreen Internat. Film Festival award, 1986, medal Gov. Red Sea, Egypt, 1988, Nogi award in Sci., 1988, Women's Hall of Fame award State of Md., 1989, Women Educators award, 1990, Alumnae award, Franklin Burr award Nat. Geog. Soc., 1993, Wyland Icon award, 2005, Henry Luce III Lifetime Achievement award, Wings WorldQuest Women of Discovery Awards, 2006; named to Hunter Coll. Hall of Fame, 1990, Diver's Equipment Mfg. Assn. Hall of Fame, 1993, Bermuda Underwater Explorers Inst. Hall of Fame, 2004; Fellow AEC, 1950; Saxton fellow, 1952; Breadloaf Writer's fellow; Fulbright scholar Egypt, 1951. Fellow: AAAS; mem.: Am. Elasmobranch Soc. (disting. fellow 1999), Am. Littoral Soc. (v.p. 1970—89), Nat. Pks. and Conservation Assn. (vice chmn. 1976), Internat. Soc. Profl. Diving Scientists, Soc. Woman Geographers (Gold medal 1975, U. Md. Pres.'s medal 1993), Israeli Zool. Soc. (hon.), Am. Soc. Ichthyology and Herpetology (life). Achievements include research in ecology and behavior of tropical sand and coral reef fishes; morphology and taxonomy marine fish; isolating mechanisms of poecillid fish; behavior of deep sea sharks. Office: Ctr Shark Rsch Mote Marine Lab 1600 Ken Thompson Pkwy Sarasota FL 34236 Office Phone: 941-388-4441. Business E-Mail: yoppe@mote.org.

CLARK, EVE VIVIENNE, linguist, educator; b. Camberley, U.K., July 26, 1942; arrived in U.S., 1967; d. Desmond Charles and Nancy (Aitken) Curme; m. Herbert H. Clark, July 21, 1967; 1 child, Damon Alistair. MA with honors, U. Edinburgh, Scotland, 1965, PhD, 1969. Rsch. assoc. Stanford (Calif.) U., 1969-71, from asst. prof. to assoc. prof., 1971-83, prof., 1983—. Author: Ontogenesis of Meaning, 1979, Acquisition of Romance, 1985, The Lexicon in Acquisition, 1993, First Language Acquisition, 2003; co-author: Psychology and Language, 1977. Fellow Ctr. for Advanced Study in the Behavioral Scis., 1979-80, Guggenheim Found., 1983-84. Mem. Dutch Acad. Scis. (fgn.). Business E-Mail: eclark@psych.stanford.edu.

CLARK, EVELYN JEAN, artist, educator; b. New Brighton, Pa., Jan. 9, 1951; d. Chester Willis and Rhoda Marjorie (Duff) Clark; m. Jacob Wayne Rhyne, June 26, 1975 (div. 1986); 1 child, Tessa Gretel. BA, Slippery Rock U., 1973; MFA, U. S.C., 1985. Cert. art educator Pa. Art and craft specialist U.S. Army, Ft. Jackson, SC, 1975—76; program dir. Dept. Def., Republic of Korea, 1979; from studio asst. to tchg. asst. U. SC, Columbia, 1981—85, adj. faculty, 1985—88; prin., owner Clark Clay Art, Pa., 1986—; art tchr. Seneca Valley Sch. Dist., Harmony, Pa., 1995—2002. Artist-in-residence S.C. Arts Commn., 1986—89, Pa. Coun. on Arts, 1990—95, 2005—, Grazier, Clark's Dairy Farm, Inc., Brodnax, Va., 2002—03. Exhibitions include numerous galleries, 1973—94, Represented in permanent collections S.C. State Art Collection (Purchase award). Vol. Pa. Herpetological Atlas Project, Indiana, Pa., 1998—2002. Recipient Innovative Tchg. award, Pa. State Edn. Assn., 1997; Artist-in-Edn. grantee, Pa. Coun. on Arts, 2000, 2001. Avocations: herpetology, eco-agriculture.

CLARK, FAYE LOUISE, retired drama and speech educator; b. La., Oct. 9, 1936; m. Warren James Clark, Aug. 8, 1969; children: Roy, Kay Natalie. Student, Centenary Coll., 1954-55; BA with honors, U. Southwestern La., 1962; MA, U. Ga., 1966; PhD, Ga. State U., 1992. Tchr. Nova Exptl. Schs., Ft. Lauderdale, Fla., 1963—65; faculty dept. drama and speech Ga. Perimeter Coll. (formerly DeKalb Coll.), Atlanta, 1967—2003, chmn. dept., 1977—81, prof. emerita, 2004—. Pres. Hawthorne Sch. PTA, 1983-84. Mem.: High Mus. Art, Ga. Comm. Assn., Ga. Psychol. Assn., Ga. Theatre Conf. (sec. 1968—69, rep. to Southeastern Theatre Conf. 1969), Nat. Comm. Assn., Atlanta Hist. Soc., Thalian-Blackfriars, Friends of Atlanta Opera, Atlanta Press Club, Atlanta Artists Club (sec. 1981—83, dir. 1983—89), Kappa Delta Pi, Sigma Delta Pi, Pi Kappa Delta, Phi Kappa Phi. Home: 2521 Melinda Dr NE Atlanta GA 30345-1918

CLARK, GLORIA A., music educator; b. Indpls., Feb. 7, 1937; d. Franklin T. and Jean Agnes Gamage; m. Robert A. Mead, Dec. 5, 1957 (div. Dec. 1959); 1 child, Allison M. Szabo; m. William H. Clark, Jan. 25, 1981. BS in Sociology, Regents Coll., Albany, N.Y., 1989; MA in Philosophy, Calif. State U. Dominguez Hills, 1992. Svc. rep. United Telephone; prof. philosophy S. Fla. C.C.; tchr. Butte Ctrl. Cath. Schs. Performing musician; mural artist; organist, pianist Aldersgate United Meth. Ch., Butte, Mont.; pvt. piano tchr., Butte. Virginia City (Mont.) Art Festival, one-woman shows include Uptown Cafe, 2006. Bd. dirs. Cmty. Concerts, Butte; vol. cellist Butte Symphony, 1991—2001; pianist Grant Kohrs Nat. Park. Recipient Butte City Artist award, Butte Silver Bow County, 1991—97; grantee Music Edn. grant, Cmty. Concerts, Butte, 1996—2006. Mem.: Nat. Accredited Music Tchrs. Assn. Avocations: crocheting, theater, walking, cribbage, crossword puzzles. Home: 239 Mammoth Dr Butte MT 59701 Office Phone: 406-782-4500.

CLARK, JANET EILEEN, political science professor; b. Kansas City, Kans., June 5, 1940; d. Edward Francis and Mildred Lois (Mack) Morrissey; m. Caleb M. Clark, Sept. 28, 1968; children: Emily Claire, Grace Ellen, Evelyn Adair. AA, Kansas City Jr. Coll., 1960; AB, George Washington U., 1962, MA, 1964; PhD, U. Ill., 1973. Staff US Dept. Labor, Washington, 1962-64; instr. social sci. Kans. City Jr. Coll., Kans., 1964-67; instr. polit. sci. Parkland Coll., 1970-71; asst. prof. govt. N.Mex. State U., Las Cruces, 1971-77, assoc. prof., 1977-80; assoc. prof. polit. sci. U. Wyo., 1981-84, prof., 1984-94; prof. polit. sci., head dept. U. West Ga., Carrollton, 1994—2006; ret., 2006. Co-author: Women, Elections and Representation, 1987, The Equality State, 1988, Women in Taiwan Politics: Overcoming Barriers to Women's Participation in a Modernizing Society, 1990; editor Women and Politics, 1991-2000; contbr. articles to profl. jours. Wolcott fellow, 1963-64, NDEA Title IV fellow, 1967-69. Mem. Internat. Soc. Polit. Psychology (gov. coun., 1987-89), NEA (pres. chpt. 1978-79), Am. Polit. Sci. Assn., We. Polit. Sci. Assn. (exec. coun. 1984-87), Western Social Sci. Assn. (exec. coun. 1978-81, v.p. 1982, pres. 1985), Women's Caucus for Polit. Sci. (treas. 1982, pres. 1987), LWV (exec. bd. 1980-83, 2002-2003, treas. 1986-90, pres. 1991-93, 2004-06), Women's Polit. Caucus, Beta Sigma Phi (v.p. chpt. 1978-79, sec. 1987-88, treas. 1988-89, v.p. 1989-90, pres. 1990-91), Phi Beta Kappa Chi Omega (prize 1962), Phi Kappa Phi. Home: 2507 Waterford Rd Auburn AL 36832-4113

CLARK, JANET F., corporate financial executive; b. New Orleans; BA, Harvard Univ., 1977; MBA, Univ. Pa., 1982. CFO Santa Fe Energy Resources, 1997—98, sr. v.p., CFO, 1998—99; exec. v.p. corp. develop. & adminstrn. Santa Fe Energy Resources / Snyder Oil, 1999—2001; sr. v.p., CFO Nuevo Energy, 2001—04, Marathon Oil, Houston, 2004—. Bd. dir. Universal Compression Holdings. Bd. dir. New Hope Housing; trustee Joy Sch. Office: Marathon Oil 5555 San Felipe Rd Houston TX 77056-2723*

CLARK, JANET KAYE, music educator; b. Oklahoma City, May 8, 1950; d. Fae Wells; m. Stephen Lee Clark, Aug. 8, 1968; children: Julie Ann, James Scott. B of Music Edn. with honors, U. Cen. Okla., 1977; postgrad., Tenn. Tech. U., 1984-85; MA in Edn. with honors, Austin Peay State U., 1990. Cert. gen. music 1-8, instrumental music K-12, elem. edn. Band tchr. grades 7-8 Highland West Mid. Sch., Moore, Okla., 1977-81; woodwind specialist grades 7-12 Moore Pub. Schs., 1981-83; music tchr. grades 1-12 The

Clarksville Acad., Tenn., 1987-88; tchr. 2d grade Minglewood Elem. Sch., Clarksville, 1988-92; music tchr. grades K-5 Barksdale Elem. Sch., Clarksville, 1992—, team leader for specialists, 1994-95. Chmn. music profl. devel. Clarksville, Montgomery County Schs., 1995; reporter Adopt-A-Sch. Newspaper, 1993-2003. Author: The Star Program, 1993. Asst. den leader Boy Scouts Am., 1993-95; musician Mus. Meth. Handbell Choir, Clarksville, 1993-95; clarinetist Austin Peay State U., Cmty. Orch., 1985—, Austin Peay State U. Clarinet Choir, 1985-95; soloist Sch. Bd. Dinner at Minglewood, 1992. Mem. NEA, Tenn. Edn. Assn., Tenn. Music Edn. Assn., Mid. Tenn. Music Edn. Assn., Clarksville-Montgomery County Edn. Assn. (rep. 2004-06, Disting. Classroom Tchr. 1993-94, 96-97, Clarksville-Montgomery County Tchr. of Yr. Grades Prekindergarten-4 1997), Music Educators Nat. Conf. Avocation: reading. Home: 415 Kimberly Dr Clarksville TN 37043-6048 Office: Barksdale Elem Sch 1920 Madison St Clarksville TN 37043-5065

CLARK, JOAN HARDY, retired journalist; b. Toronto, Ont., Can., Apr. 17, 1934; came to the U.S., 1960; d. Henry Robert Hardy and Irene Elsie Stevens; children: Lisa Anne Hanson, Anthony David Stuart Hanson. BA, Carleton U., Ottawa, Can., 1954; postgrad., Sarah Lawrence Coll., 1973-75. Co-chmn. internat. coun. World Monuments Fund, 2004—; bd. dirs. N.Y. Pub. Libr., N.Y.C., 1996—, chmn. coun. conservators, 1986—2001, hon. chmn., 2001—; mem. exec. com. Whitney Nat. Com., 2003—; bd. dirs. Whitney Mus., N.Y.C., 1984—2003. Mem. Cosmopolitan Club. Home: 1 Gracie Sq New York NY 10028-8001 also: Deer Meadow Farm Andover VT 05143

CLARK, JODI D., theater director, educator; b. Bridgeport, Conn., Mar. 5, 1973; d. Jeffrey M. and Diane S. Clark; life ptnr. Jenny V. Karstad, Aug. 19, 2000. BA in Anthropology and Theater, Marlboro Coll., 1995; MA in Theater Edn., Emerson Coll., 1998. Adminstr. Sandglass Theater, Putney, Vt., 1999—2002; theatrical dir./co-founder Vt. Renaissance Festival, Brattleboro, 2000—; program dir. ActingOut of Monadnock Family Svcs., Keene, NH, 2006—. Assoc. dir. Conn. Renaissance Faire, Durham, Conn., 2002—; fight dir. New Eng. Youth Theater, Brattleboro, 2003—04; fencing tchr. Marlboro (Vt.) Coll., 1999—. Dir.: (play) Twelfth Night, (performance) Vermont Renaissance Festival. Avocations: gardening, historical recreation/reenactment, historical fencing. Office: Vt Renaissance Festival 122 Westminster St Bellows Falls VT 05101 Office Phone: 802-463-3783.

CLARK, JOYCE NAOMI JOHNSON, nurse, counselor; b. Corpus Christi, Tex., Oct. 4, 1936; d. Chester Fletcher and Ermal Olita (Bailey) Johnson; m. William Boyd Clark, Jan. 4, 1958; (div. 1967); 1 child, Sherene Joyce. Student, Corpus Christi State U., 1975-77. RN. Staff nurse Van Nuys (Calif.) Cmty. Hosp., 1963-64, U.S. Naval Hosp., Corpus Christi, 1964-68; patient care coord. Spohn Meml. Hosp. (formerly Meml. Med. Ctr.), Corpus Christi, 1968—2002; counselor Christus Spohn Wellness Program, 1999—; vol. nurse ARC Disaster Response Team; nurse cons. adult day care Portlant, 2004—; mem. disaster action and disaster health svcs. team ARC. Author: (novels) Katie, 2005. Vol. nurse, mem. DAT team ARC; leader Paisano coun. Girl Scouts U.S.A., Corpus Christi, 1968-74; vol. transporting those in need; disaster response team and disaster health svcs. ARC; tchr. CPR and First Aid; past comdr. 3rd group USAF Aux., CAP Air Search and Rescue, wing chief check pilot, ret. lt. col. 1993. Recipient Paul E. Garber award CAP, 1986, cert. of appreciation in recognition of Support Child Guard Missing Children Edn. Program Nat. Assn. Chiefs of Police, Washington, 1987, Charles E. Yeager Aerospace Edn. Achievement award, 1985, Grover Loening Aerospace award, 1986, Cert. of World Leadership Internat. Biographical Ctr., Cambridge, Eng., 1987, Gill Robb Wilson award, 1988, Merit award Drug Free Am. Through Enforcement, Edn., Intelligence Nat. Assn. Chiefs of Police, Sr. Mem. of Yr. USAF Aux., CAP Air Search and Rescue, 1986, Art Roberts Disaster Svcs. award ARC, 2005. Mem. USAF Aux. Avocation: flying. Home: 2802 Cimmaron Blvd Apt 221 Corpus Christi TX 78414-3455 Personal E-mail: pangyau@grandecom.net.

CLARK, JOYCE T., piano teacher, church organist; d. Richard LeVake Tonk and Louise (Fambrough) Richards; m. Jon Perryman Clark, July 17, 1982. BS in Elem. Edn., U. Calif., Santa Barbara, 1961; BA in Music, U. So. Maine, 2001. Lic. elem. edn. tchr. Calif., nat. cert. tchr. music. Elem. sch. tchr. Hudson Sch. Dist., LaPuente, Calif., 1961—62, Glendale (Calif.) Unified Sch. Dist., 1962—69; church organist Christian Sci. Soc., Boothbay Harbor, Maine, 1974—76; adminstrv. asst. David Wendell Assocs., Edgecomb, Maine, 1981—94; pvt. practice piano tchr. Woolwich, Maine, 1974—; church organist First Ch. of Christ, Scientist, Brunswick, Maine, 1976—; piano tchr. Portland Conservatory of Music, 2002—. Freelance accompanist various soloists and choruses, Maine, 1970—. Mem.: Am. Guild of Organists-Portland, Maine Music Tchrs. Assn. (treas. 1994—95, 2002—). Avocations: kayaking, knitting, canoeing, snowshoeing, quilting. Home: 255 Montsweag Rd Woolwich ME 04579 Personal E-mail: jjclark@gwi.net.

CLARK, JUDY ANN, elementary school educator; d. Leland Jack and Virginia Carol Satterlee; m. Arthur C. Clark; children: James Arthur, Chad Michael. AA with hons., Corning CC, N.Y., 1969; BA in Edn. magna cum laude, Elmira Coll., NY, 1972, MS in Edn., 1975, postgrad., 1988—2003. Tchr. Elem. Sch. Waverly Sch. Dist., NY, 1972—89, Horseheads Sch. Dist., NY, 1989—. Chmn. dist. grade level Horseheads Sch. Dist., 2001—; mentor tchr. student tchrs. SUNY, Cortland, 1989, 93, 97, 98, 2001, Mansfield U. Pa., 1995, 2002, 2005—, 2006—, SUNY, Geneseo, 2000, Elmira Coll., various dates; ednl. cons. student nurse cmty. edn. program Robert Packer Hosp. of Pa., 1982—89; ednl. dir. Adopt a Sr.-Citizen program, 1986—87; dist. rep to regional sci. com. Schuyler, Chemung and Tioga Counties BOCES, 1986—89, curriculum developer N.Y. State sci. syllabus, 1986—87; ednl. cons. NY State Electric and Gas (NYSEG) Energy Ctr. Task Force, 1989—91; ednl. facilitator Lang. Arts Curriculum Pub. Forum, 1995; elem. resource educator Career Devel. Coun., Inc., 1996—97. Author: Symbols Around The World, 2001. Mem.: Am. Fedn. Tchrs., NY State United Tchrs., Chemung Area Reading Coun., Horseheads Tchr. Assn. (exec. coun. 2003—05), DAR (chpt. chair nat. com. Good Citizen award 1986—87), Alpha Delta Kappa (N.Y. altruistic chairperson), Kappa Sorority for Women Educators (past pres., historian, sec., treas.). Avocation: photography. Office: Center Street Elementary Sch 812 Center St Horseheads NY 14845

CLARK, JULIA L. AKINS, labor union administrator, lawyer; BA summa cum laude in Polit. Sci., Okla. Baptist Univ., 1977; JD, Am. Univ., 1980. Honors program trial atty., antitrust divsn US Dept. Justice, Washington, 1980—85; pvt. practice, antitrust Washington, 1985—87; counsel Nat. Coalition for Homeless, Nat. Union of Homeless, Washington, 1987—88; atty. to gen. counsel Internat. Fedn. Profl. Technical Engrs., AFL-CIO, Silver Spring, 1988—. Office: Internat Fedn Profl Tech Engrs Ste 400 8630 Fenton St Silver Spring MD 20910 Office Phone: 301-565-9016. Office Fax: 301-565-0018. Business E-Mail: jclark@ifpte.org.

CLARK, JULIE, consumer products company executive; married; 2 children. English teacher; founder The Baby Einstein Co., 1997—2001; founder, CEO Aigner Clark Creative, The Safe Side (affiliated co.), 2002—. Recipient Entrepreneur of the Yr. award, Ernst & Young, Entrepreneur of the Yr. award: Most Philanthropic Co., Most Innovative Bus. and Best Small Co., Working Mother's, Disting. Alumni award, Mich. State U., 2003. Achievements include appearances on The Oprah Winfrey Show, Entertainment Tonight, Live! With Regis and Kelly, The View and The John Walsh Show; feature articles in USA Today, The New York Times, The Washington Post, The Wall Street Journal, Los Angeles Times, Time Magazine, People Magazine, Redbook, Elle, Entrepreneur, Parenting Magazine, Child Magazine, Baby Talk and Working Mother. Office: The Safe Side 9285 Teddy Ln Ste 215 Littleton CO 80124 Office Phone: 303-649-9374, 866-723-3022. Office Fax: 303-706-9799.*

CLARK, KAREN HEATH, lawyer; b. Pasadena, Calif., Dec. 17, 1944; d. Wesley Pelton and Lois (Ellenberger) Heath; m. Bruce Robert Clark, Dec. 30, 1967; children: Adam Heath, Andrea Pelton. Student, Pomona Coll., Claremont, Calif., 1962—64; BA, Stanford U., 1966; MA in History, U. Wash., 1968; JD, U. Mich., 1977. Bar: Calif. 1978. Instr. Henry Ford C.C., Dearborn, Mich., 1968-72; assoc. Gibson, Dunn & Crutcher LLP, Irvine, Calif., 1977-86, ptnr., 1986—2003, adv. counsel, 2004—. Bd. dirs. Dem. Found. Orange County, 1989-91, 94—, Planned Parenthood Orange County, Santa Ana, Calif., 1979-82, New Directions for Women, Newport Beach, 1986-91, Human Options, 2001-03, Erin Gruwell Edn. Project, 2004—, Women in Leadership, chair, 1995-99; trustee Newport Beach Pub. Libr., 2001—, vice chair, 2006-; mem. deans adv. coun. Sch. Humanities, U. Calif., Irvine. Recipient Choice award Planned Parenthood of Orange & San Bernardino Counties, 1996. Mem. Women in Leadership (founder 1993). E-mail: kclark@gibsondunn.com.

CLARK, KATHLEEN JULIA, mathematics educator; d. John Patrick and Elaine May Vallely; m. Peter David Clark; children: Patrick, Colleen, Kelley. BS, SUNY, Brockport, 1973. Cert. tchr. NY. Math tchr. Spencerport Ctrl. Sch., NY, 1973—. Recipient Certificate of Excellence, Commn. on Presdl. Scholars, 1983. Mem.: AMTNYS. Avocations: swimming, sewing, travel, drawing, painting. Home: 86 Walbert Dr Rochester NY 14624 Office: Spencerport Ctrl Sch Dist 2707 Spencerport Rd Spencerport NY 14559 Office Phone: 585-349-5200.

CLARK, KATHLEEN VERNON, special education educator; b. Nashville, Apr. 16, 1939; d. Walter Newton Jr. and E. Ruth (Mason) Vernon; m. Stanley Prentiss Clark, Apr. 16, 1962; children: Stanley Martin, Jennifer Clark Larsen. BA, So. Meth. U., Dallas, 1961; postgrad., George Peabody Coll., 1975; MA, U. Ala., Tuscaloosa, 1977; EdS, Jacksonville State U., Ala., 1986; EdD, U. Ala., Tuscaloosa, 1991. Cert. spl. edn. tchr., Ala. Tchr., spl. olympics coach Piedmont City Schs., Ala., 1975-86, testing coord. Ala., 1982-86; tchr. Tuscaloosa City Schs., 1986—90, continuing edn. presenter, 1989, chair dept. spl. edn., 1987—89; tchr. Lauderdale County Schs., Florence, Ala., 1990-97. Mem. grad. adv. coun. area of spl. edn. U. Ala., Tuscaloosa, 1989-90; adj. prof. spl. edn. U. No. Ala., 1991-96; spl. edn. tchr. Etowah County Schs., 1997-2001; mem. steering com. So. Assn. Colls. and Schs., sponsor Leo Club. Dir. Meth. Elem. Camps, Sumatanga, Ala., Southeastern Meth. Assembly Grounds; bd. dirs. Lake Junaluska, N.C., 1988-96; pres. Ch. Women United, Decatur, Ala., 1971-72; v.p. United Meth. Women, Northport, Ala., 1988-90; mem. Meth. Commn. on Status and Role of Women, Birmingham, Ala., 1990-92; mem. N. Ala. Meth. Bd. Social Concerns; chair comm. Ctrl. United Meth. Ch., Decatur, Ala., 2003—, lay leadership com., 2004-06; sec. Junaluska Assocs. bd. dirs. Southeastern Jurisdiction of the United Meth. Ch., 2004—; chair vision team Northwood United Meth. Ch., 1992-97, Ctr. First United Meth. Ch., 1997-2001. Recipient Most Outstanding Grad. Spl. Edn. Adminstrn. award, U. Ala., 1990, 1991. Mem. NEA, Coun. for Exceptional Children (Tchr. of Yr. 1978), Assn. for Retarded Citizens, Ala. Edn. Assn. (rep. 1988-90, 1999-2001), Kappa Delta Pi, Phi Kappa Phi, Psi Chi. Avocations: reading, travel. Home: 1001 Clarkview St SW Decatur AL 35601-6203

CLARK, KATHRYN, government agency administrator; m. Robert Ike. MA, PhD, U. Mich. Faculty dept. anatomy and cell biology U. Mich., 1993; dep. dir. NASA Comml. Space Ctr., 1996—98; space sta. chief scientist NASA Office Space Flight, Washington, 1998—. Grantee, NIH, Nat. Inst. Aging, Am. Fedn. for Aging Rsch., NSF, NASA. Mem.: Internat. Soc. Women Pilots, Internat. Soc. for Gravitational and Space Biology, Am. Soc. for Gravitational and Space Biology, Soc. for Neurosci., Am. Coll. Sports Medicine. Avocations: bicycling, swimming, skiing. Office: NASA Hdqs Bldg HQ Rm 4022 Washington DC 20546-0001

CLARK, KATHYRN A., elementary school educator; b. Framingham, Mass., Apr. 1, 1968; d. Gregory James and Edna Gertude (Glenna) Polanik; m. James W. Clark, Aug. 13, 1994; children: Andrew James, Matthew Joseph. BS in Elem. Edn., Fitchburg State Coll., Fitchburg, Mass., 1990; MEd in Special Edn., Fitchburg State Coll., 1996. Cert. Elem. Tchr. Mass., Special Edn. Mass., Social Studies tchr. 5-9 Mass., level 1 reading. Jr. high tchr. Lody Isle Sch., Portsmouth, NH, 1992—93; counselor, tchr. Riverside Residential Sch., Lowell, Mass., 1993—94; special edn. tchr. Robinson Mid. Sch., 1994—98; 4th grade tchr. Varnum Elem. Sch., 1998—. Cons. Ind. Edn. Cons., Lowell, 2006—; com. mem. Carter G. Woodson Book award, 2006—; social studies cons. Lady Isle Sch., 2001—. Familiy activity coord. Pawtucketville PTO, Lowell, 2005—, sec., 2003—05. Grantee Innovative Tchg. Mini grant, U. Mass., 2001—02. Mem.: Mass. Reading Assn., Nat. Coun. Social Studies. Office: Varnum Sch 116 Sixth St Lowell MA 01850

CLARK, LAVERNE HARRELL, writer; b. Smithville, Tex., June 6, 1929; d. James Boyce and Belle Bunte Harrell; m. L.D. Clark, Sept. 15, 1951. BA, Tex. Women's U., 1950; student, Columbia U., 1951-54; MA, U. Ariz., 1962, MFA, 1992. Reporter, libr., photographer Ft. Worth Press, 1950-51; with sales and advt. depts. Columbia U. Press, N.Y.C., 1951-53; asst. promotion-news Episcopal Diocese Bull., N.Y.C., 1958-59; founding dir. U. Ariz. Poetry Ctr., Tucson, 1962-66, photographer, 1966-99. Author, photographer: They Sang for Horses, 1966 (award U. Chgo. 1967), rev. edit., 2001, Revisiting the Plains Indian Country of Mari Sandoz, 1977, Focus 101, 1979, The Deadly Swarm and Other Stories, 1985, 87, Keepers of the Earth, 1997, 2d edit., 2002 (Best 1st Novel award Western Writers of Am. 1998), Mari Sandoz's Native Nebraska, 2000; editor, photographer: The Face of Poetry, 1976, 2d edit., 1979; photographer with 500 informal portraits of contemporary writers, 1962—. Recipient 19 awards Nat. League Am. Pen Women, 1967-96, Disting. Alumna award Tex. Woman's U., Denton, 1973; grantee Am. Philos. Soc., 1967, 69. Mem. PEN, Western Writers of Am., Westerners Internat., Women Writing the West, Sandoz Heritage Soc. (hon. mem. adv. bd. 1989-2002), Tex. Inst. Letters. Democrat. Episcopalian. Avocations: travel, bicycling, showing slides. Home: 604 Main St Smithville TX 78957 Office Phone: 512-237-2796. Personal E-mail: lhldclark@aol.com.

CLARK, LINDA MARIE, music educator; b. Evansville, Ind., Dec. 5, 1944; d. Pearlis Edgar Roy and Mary Minnette Miller; m. James Hugh Clark, Nov. 26, 1965; children: Jane Marie Brunk, Jill Lea Moore, Jacquelin Elise. BS, Oakland City U., Ind., 1966; MA, U. Evansville, 1972. Cert. Orff level I, II Purdue U. Gen. music tchr. Warrick County Sch. Corp., Boonville, Ind., 1967—; jr. choir dir. St. John's UCC, Boonville, 1990—97; choir dir. Baker Chapel Meth. Ch., Boonville, 1998—2001; pit orch. dir. Boonville H.S., 1998—2004. Adj. prof. U. So. Ind., 1996—2005. Mem.: NEA, Warrick County Tchrs. Assn., Ind. State Tchrs. Assn., Am. Orff Soc., Ind. Gen. Music Educators Assn., Ind. Music Educators Assn., Music Educators Nat. Conf., Delta Kappa Gamma. Office: Oakdale Elem Sch 802 S Eighth St Boonville IN 47601 Office Phone: 812-897-3710. Personal E-mail: lmcmusick6@aol.com.

CLARK, MARGARET ANN-CYNTHIA, television producer, writer; b. New Orleans, Aug. 20, 1964; d. Joseph Christian and Elizabeth Rose Muller; m. Samuel Varnell, Oct. 5, 1991 (div. Aug. 1997); m. Kenneth Clark, Sept. 12, 2000. Diploma, St. Mary's Dominican Coll., 1984; AS in Nursing, U. NY, 1990; BA in Journalism, 1999; postgrad., Harvard U., 2002; MS in internat. health, Touro U., 2005. Pediatric, neonatal therapist Charity Hosp., New Orleans, 1984-86; therapist/nurse Touro Infirmary, New Orleans, 1986-91; therapist St. John's Mercy Hosp., St. Louis, 1991-92; nurse Grady Meml. Hosp., Atlanta, 1992-95; dir. pulmonary rehab. Touro Infirmary, 1995-98; writer prodr. WYES-TV, New Orleans, 1996-00; contbr. The Shakespeare Bulletin, Easton, Pa., 1996-01; corr. Advance News Mags., King of Prussia, Pa., 1990—; clin. coord. pulmonary medicine Boston U., 2001—; writer Ga. Med. Care Found., 2003; program dir. Medscape/Webmd, 2004. Author: Inspiration, 1998, Write for You, 2000, Dinner with Francis, 2001, Irish New Orleans, 2005; editor: Medscape, 2001—; contbr. articles to profl. jours.; writer, producer (TV series) By Louisiana Hands, 1999, Steppin Out, 1996-99; 1st alto Jefferson Performing Arts Soc., 1996-98 Bd. dir. Shakespeare Festival, Tulane U., New Orleans, 1996—; pres. Officer's Wives Club, Ft. Gillen, Ga., 1993-95, Am. Med. Writers Assn., 2005; mem. La. Cols., New Orleans, 1997— Recipient Bird Lifetime Achievement award Am. Assn. Respiratory Care, 1996. Mem. Am. Assn. Respiratory Care, Am. Med. Writers Assn., Am. Coll. Chest Physicians, Nat. Acad. TV Arts & Sci. Roman Catholic. E-mail: maraisells@aol.com.

CLARK, MARIAN WILSON, writer; b. Hereford, Tex., Sept. 8, 1934; d. Robert Lee and Mabel Faulkner Wilson; m. Kenneth K. Clark, Dec. 29, 1963; children: Rebecca, Kevin. BS in Vocat. Home Econs. Edn., Tex. Tech. U., 1957. Home svc. advisor Tex. Elec., Ft. Worth, 1958—59; tchr. McCamey (Tex.) Pub. Schs., 1959—61, Odessa (Tex.) Pub. Schs., 1961—63. Writer Rt. 66 Mag. and Rt. 66 Fedn. Newsletter, 1993—; spkr. in field. Author: Southwestern Heritage Cookbook, 1989, Route 66 Cookbook, 1993, 2000, Main Street of America, 1997, Hogs on 66: Best Food for Road Trips on Route 66, 2004. Pres., bd. dirs. Camp Fire Girls, Tulsa, Okla., 1981—82; host family Am. Field Svc., 1984—86. Recipient Gulick award, Camp Fire Girls, Tulsa, 1983. Mem.: Green Country Home Economists (pres.), Mortar Bd., United Meth. Women (pres.), Salvation Army Aux., Phi Upsilon Omicron. Methodist. Avocations: travel, aerobics. Home: 3019 S Madison Ave Tulsa OK 74114 Personal E-mail: mclark66@sbcglobal.net.

CLARK, MARIE, secondary school educator; d. James Blackburn and Ruth Prescott Atlee; m. Danny Clark; children: Russell Atlee, Bryan Andrew, Bradley James. BA in History and English, Southwestern U., Georgetown, Tex., 1970. Cert. tchr. Tex. Edn. Agy. Tchr. Temple Ind. Sch. Dist., Tex., 1971—76, tchr. 7th grade, 1991—. Avocations: hiking, camping, travel, reading.

CLARK, MARY ELIZABETH, medical/surgical nurse, diabetes specialist; b. Kingsport, Tenn., Oct. 9, 1961; d. George and Mary C. BSN, Vanderbilt U., 1984. Assoc. clin. nurse Crawford Long Hosp., Atlanta, 1984-86, clin. nurse, 1986-88, nursing unit leader, 1988-90, nursing unit coord., 1990-99, diabetes educator, 1999—. Avocations: tennis, cooking, dance. Home: 213 Ridley Ln Decatur GA 30030-2912 Office: Crawford Long Hosp 550 Peachtree St NE Atlanta GA 30308-2225

CLARK, MARY ETTA, science writing consultant; b. Wilmington, Del., Mar. 15, 1961; d. Albert Ridge and Mary E. (Bendler) C. BA, U. Del., 1983; M in Tech. and Sci. Comm., Miami U., Oxford, Ohio, 1984; PhD, N.C. State U., 1997. Tchg. asst. U. Del., Newark, 1982-83, Miami U., 1983-84; med. writer ICI Pharms., Wilmington, Del., 1984-89; sci. writing cons. Wilmington, N.C., 1995—. Part-time faculty mem. U. N.C., Wilmington, 1998—; editl. cons. U. Del., 1986-87; substitute instr. N.C. State U., Raleigh, 1992-94. Vol. Meals on Wheels, Raleigh, 1989-97, Kairos Prision Ministry, Raleigh, 1998—. Grad. fellow N.C. State U. Alumni Assn., 1989, rsch. fellow Smithsonian Instn., 1993; rsch. grantee Am. Mus. Natural History, 1991. Mem. Am. Med. Writers Assn., Am. soc. Limnology and Oceanography, Sierra Club (publicity chair Del. chpt. 1986-88). Achievements include publishing first study to telemeter agonistic activity in a free-ranging marine invertebrate. E-mail: m_clark@mediwriter.com.

CLARK, MARY HIGGINS, writer, communications executive; b. NYC, Dec. 24, 1929; d. Luke J. and Nora C. (Durkin) Higgins; m. Warren Clark, Dec. 26, 1949 (dec. Sept. 1964); children: Marilyn, Warren, David, Carol, Patricia; m. John J. Coheeney, Nov. 3, 1996. BA, Fordham U., 1979; doctorate (hon.), Villanova U., 1983, Rider Coll., 1986, Stonehill Coll., 1992, Marymount Manhattan Coll., 1992, Chestnut Hill, 1993, Manhattan Coll., 1993, St. Peter's Coll., 1993. Advt. asst. Remington Rand, 1946; stewardess Pan Am., 1949-50; radio scriptwriter, prodr. Robert G. Jennings, 1965-70; v.p., ptnr., creative dir., prodr. radio programming Aerial Communications, N.Y.C., 1970-80; chmn. bd., creative dir. D. J. Clark Enterprises, N.Y.C., 1980—. Author: Silent Night, Aspire to the Heavens, A Biography of George Washington, 1969 (NJ Author award 1969), Where Are the Children?, 1976 (NJ Author award 1977), A Stranger Is Watching, 1978 (N.J. Author award 1978), The Cradle Will Fall, 1980, A Cry in the Night, 1982, Stillwatch, 1984, Weep No More, My Lady, 1987, While My Pretty One Sleeps, 1989, The Anastasia Syndrome and Other Stories, 1989, Loves Music, Loves to Dance, 1991, All Around the Town, 1992, I'll Be Seeing You, 1993, Remember Me, 1994, The Lottery Winner, 1994, Bad Behavior, 1995, Let Me Call You Sweetheart, 1995, Moonlight Becomes You, 1996, Pretend You Don't See Her, 1997, The Plot Thickens, 1997, You Belong to Me, 1998, All Through the Night, 1998, We'll Meet Again, 1999, Before I Say Good-Bye, 2000, Deck the Halls, 2000, Daddy's Little Girl, 2002, Silent Night/All Through the Night, 2002, On the Street Where You Live, 2002, Kitchen Privileges, 2002, The Second Time Around, 2003, Nighttime is My Time, 2004 (Publishers Weekly paperback bestseller list, 2005), No Place Like Home, 2005 (NY Times Bestseller list, Publishers Weekly Bestseller list), Two Little Girls in Blue, 2006; (with Thomas Chastain and others) Murder in Manhattan, 1986; editor: Murder on the Aisle: The 1987 Mystery Writers Anthology, 1987. Recipient Grand Prix de Litterature Policiere, France, 1980, Horatio Alger award, 1997, Gold Medal of Honor, Irish-Am. Hist. Soc., Spirit of Achievement award, Albert Einstein Coll. of Med., Yoshiva Univ., Nat. Arts Club Gold Medal in Edn., Grand Master award, Mystery Writers of Am., 2000. Mem. Mystery Writers Am. (pres. 1987, dir.), Authors League, Am. Soc. Journalists and Authors, Acad. Arts and Scis. Republican. Roman Catholic.

CLARK, MARY W., biology educator; b. Danbury, Conn., Jan. 10, 1962; d. William M. and Katherine J. Kearns; m. Raymond J. Clark, July 27, 1991; children: Laura A., Katherine M., Emily J. B, St. Anselm Coll., Manchester, N.H., 1984; MS, We. Conn. State U., Danbury, 1990; degree in sci. edn., So. Conn. State U., New Haven, 2000, degree in ednl. leadership, 2003. Sci. tchr. Shelton Bd. Edn., Conn., 1984—. Table leader, scorer State of Conn., Dept. Edn., Hartford, 2005—. Mem.: NEA. Office: Shelton High Sch 120 Meadow St Shelton CT 06484 Office Phone: 203-924-8739. E-mail: mclark@sheltonpublicschools.org.

CLARK, MARYLIZ M., retired minister; b. Orange, N.J., Aug. 12, 1935; d. James Alexander Milling and Fernanda DeAngelis; m. Robert E. Hales (div.); m. Wendell J. Clark (div.); children: Teresa, Gregory, Lynn, Kristen, Amy, Robert. BA in English, Ind. U., 1957; MDiv, Andover-Newton Theol. Sch., 1979. Cert.: Harris Bus. Sch. (paralegal); tchr. N.J. Tchr. Indpls. Pub. Schs., 1957—59, Lenola Sch., Moorestown, NJ, 1962—64; bedside tchr. and substitute Mass. Hosp. Sch., Canton, 1974—76; assoc. pastor High St. Congl. Ch., Auburn, Maine, 1979—83, First Congl. United Ch. of Christ, East Hartford, Conn., 1983—86; interim and supply pastor United Ch. of Christ churches, Phila., 1988—98; ret., 1998. Pres. Hartford East Assn., East Hartford, Conn., 1984—86; mem. Lewiston-Auburn Ministerium, Maine, 1979—83, Phila. Ministerium, 1987—. Author: The Rainbow Bible Curriculum, 1976, Web of Love & Lies, 2005; contbr. meditations and articles to periodicals. Bd. mem. United Way, East Hartford, 1984—85. Avocations: writing, reading, gardening, crafts. Home: 18 Mindy Dr Moorestown NJ 08057-3024

CLARK, MAURA J., oil and gas industry executive; CFO Clark Refining & Mktg. Inc.(now Premcor), Glen Ellyn, Ill., 1995—2000; v.p., fin. No. Am. Life Assurance Co.; sr. v.p., strategy and M&A Direct Energy, Toronto, Canada. Office: Direct Energy Atria III 4th Fl 2225 Sheppard Ave E Toronto ON M2J 5C2 Canada

CLARK, MAXINE, retail executive; b. Miami, Fla., Mar. 6, 1949; d. Kenneth and Anne (Lerch) Kasselman; m. Robert Fox, Sept. 1984. B.A. in Journalism, U. Ga., 1971. Exec. trainee Hecht Co., Washington, 1971, hosiery buyer, 1971-72, misses sportswear buyer, 1972-76; mgr. mdse. planning and research May Dept. Stores Co., St. Louis, 1976-78, dir. mdse. devel., 1978-80, v.p. mktg. and sales promotion Venture Stores div., 1980-81, sr. v.p. mktg. and sales promotion Venture Stores div., 1981-83, exec. v.p. mktg. and softlines, 1983-85; exec. v.p. apparel Famous-Barr, St. Louis, 1985-86; v.p. mdsing. Lerner Shops div. Limited Inc., N.Y.C., 1986-88; exec. v.p. Venture Stores, St. Louis, 1988-92; pres. Payless ShoeSource, Topeka, 1992-96; founder, CEO Smart Stuff, Inc. children's retail concept devel. firm and the Build-A-Bear Workshop, 1996—; bd. dirs. Earthgrains Co., Tandy Brands Accessories Co., Wave Techs., Inc., Dept. 56, J.C. Penney Co., Inc., 2003-. Sec., Lafayette Sq. Restoration Com., 1978-79; mem. Com. 200 Nat. Coun.

Coll. Arts and Scis. Washington U., St. Louis; trustee U. Ga. Found., 1995—; mem. nat. adv. coun. Girl Scouts U.S.A., 1995-97. Office: Build A Bear Workshop 1960 Innerbelt Business Center Overland MO 63114-5760

CLARK, MAYREE CARROLL, investment banking executive; b. Norman, Okla., Mar. 9, 1957; d. Benton C. Clark and Joan M. (Harris) Richards; m. Jeffrey P. Williams, Apr. 28, 1984; two children. BS, U. So. Calif., 1976; MBA, Stanford U., 1981. Econ. analyst Nat. Econ. Rsch., LA, 1976-79; assoc. Morgan Stanley, NYC, 1981-84, v.p., 1985-87, prin., 1987-89, mng. dir., 1990—, global rsch. dir., 1994—2001, head newly merged (Internat. Private Client Group and its Private Wealth Mgmt. bus.) private wealth businesses for wealthy individuals, 2002—03, head internat. individual investor businesses, 2003—05. Adj. prof. Columbia U., N.Y.C., 1988-89. Chmn. Student Sponsor Partnership, N.Y.C., 1996-99. Republican. Office: Morgan Stanley and Co 1585 Broadway Fl 14 New York NY 10036-8200

CLARK, MIZZELL PHILLIPS (MITZI CLARK), school librarian; b. Kansas City, Mo., May 15, 1925; d. Mizzell and Genevieve Dugey Phillips; m. Champ Clark, Feb. 2, 1949; children: Genevieve, Jane Bennett, Champ, Julie. Student, Washington U., 1942—43, Kansas City Jr. Coll., 1944—45, Piedmont Va. C.C., Charlottesville, 1980—90. Reporter city desk Kansas City Star, 1944—50; pub. rels. dir. Glenview (Ill.) Elem. Schs., Glenview, 1970—74; radio reporter news Sta. WJMA, Orange, Va., 1976—82; pub. rels. dir. Orange Phys. Therapy, 1992—95; spl. collections rschr. Alderman Libr. U. Va., Charlottesville, 1998—. Mem. First Ladies' adv. com. Susan Allen, Wife of Former Va. Gov. George Allen, 1995—96; del. Rep. Nat. Conv., Dallas, 1984; regional vice chmn. # 7 Dist. Rep. Com., Va., 1997—2001. Avocations: hiking, singing, reading, sports. Home: 3152 Gracefield Rd Apt 101 Silver Spring MD 20904 Personal E-mail: mitziclark@aol.com.

CLARK, NANCY LUCINDA BROWN, retired music educator; b. Akron, Ohio, Dec. 11, 1946; d. Gardner Lane Brown and Ruth Marie Thomas; m. Eugene Ernest Zielinski, Aug. 1968 (div. Mar. 1989); children: Ruth Karlotte Zielinski Hansen, Jennifer Jane Zielinski Webber; m. Douglas Napier Clark, Mar. 11, 1989. Student, Kent State U., 1964-66; BS in Mus. Edn., U. Ill., 1968; postgrad., Nazareth Coll., 1981-82. Music tchr. pre-kindergarten and kindergarten Diocese of Rochester, NY, 1970s; tchr., supr. Muzak Cranford (N.J.) Mid. Sch., 1982-87; asst. music dir. First Presbyn. Ch., Maplewood, NJ, 1984-89; music min. Salem Bapt. Ch., Lexington, Ga., 1990-96, ret., 1996. Cons. Nat. Postal Mus., 2004—06. Author: (book chpt.) Nantucket Postmarks to 1890, 1989, Philatelic Congress Book Maine Fancy Cancels, 2000; host (internet radio program) APS Stamp Talk with Nancy Clark; contbr. articles to profl. jours. Pres. Olymphilex 96, Atlanta, 1992—96; mem. Barnstable County Hist. Pres. Commn., 2001—; juror, team leader Juvalux 98, Luxembourg, 1998, Bangkok, 2000, Olymphilex, Greece, 2004; chmn. 1st Nat. Youth in Philately Symposium, 2002; v.p. Barnstable County Hist. Pres. Commn., 2002—03, chair, 2003—; dir. edn. Stamp Camp USA, 2003—04, co-chair, 2003—04; bd. dirs. Oglethorpe County Libr., Lexington, 1989—98, Athens-Clarke County Regional Libr., 1992—98. Recipient Internat. Gold award ROCPEX Taipei, China, 1981, Polska, 1997, Grand Stamporee award, Palm Beach, Fla., 1996, Rowland Hill award Southeastern Fed. Stamp Clubs, 2005. Mem.: Mass. Postal Rsch. Soc. (bd. dirs. 2003—, sec. 2006—), Mobile Post Office Soc. (bd. dirs. 2004—), Aux. Markings Club (pres. 2003—), Cape Cod Area Philatelic Group (bd. dirs. 2001—03, pres. 2004), Am. Assn. Philatelic Exhibitors, Boston Philatelic Group (sec.-treas. 2004—), Collectors Club N.Y., Am. Philatelic Soc. (Ernest Kehr award 2006). Personal E-mail: stampsintheclass@yahoo.com.

CLARK, NOREEN MORRISON, behavioral science educator, researcher; b. Glasgow, Scotland, Jan. 12, 1943; arrived in US, 1948; d. Angus Watt and Anne (Murphy) Morrison; m. George Robert Pitt, Dec. 3, 1982; 1 child, Alexander Robert. BS, U. Utah, 1965; MA, Columbia U., 1972, MPhil, 1975, PhD, 1976. Rsch. coord. World Edn. Inc., N.Y.C., 1972-73; asst. prof. Sch. Pub. Health Columbia U., N.Y.C., 1973-80, assoc. prof., 1980-81, Sch. Pub. Health U. Mich., Ann Arbor, 1981-85, prof., chmn. dept. health behavior and health edn., 1985-95, Marshall H. Becker prof. of pub. health, 1995—2005, dean, 1995—2005, dir. ctr. mng. chronic disease, 2005—; prof. pediatrics and com. diseases U. Mich. Medical Sch., Ann Arbor, 2003—. Adj. prof. health adminstrn. Sch. Pub. Health Columbia U., 1988—; prin. investigator NIH, 1977—; adv. com. pulmonary diseases Nat. Heart, Lung & Blood Inst., Rockville, Md., 1983-87, adv. com. for prevention, edn. and control, 1987-91, coord. com. Nat. Asthma Edn. Program, 1991—; assoc. Synergos Inst., NYC, 1987-99; nat. adv. environ. health scis. coun. NIH, 1999-2002; task force on preventive cmty. svc. CDC, 2002-05 Co-author: Evaluation of Health Promotion, 1984; editor Health Edn. and Behavior, 1985-97; assoc. editor Ann. Rev. of Pub. Health, 2002-05; mem. editl. bd. Women in Health, Advances in Health Edn. and Promotion, Home Health Care Services Quar.; contbr. articles to profl. jours. Bd. dirs., adv. Aaron Diamond Found., 1989-96, Family Care Internat., NYC, 1987—, Internat. Asthma Coun., 1996-2000, Am. Lung Assn., NYC, 1988—, World Edn., Inc., 1998-. Mem. Soc. Pub. Health Edn. (pres. 1985-86, Disting. Fellow award 1987), APHA (chair health edn. sect. 1982-83, Derryberry award in behavioral sci. 1985, Disting. Career award 1994), Am. Thoracic Soc. (Health Edn. Rsch. award Nat. Asthma Edn. Program 1992, Healthtrac Found. Health Edn. award, 1997), Internat. Union Health Edn., Soc. Behavioral Medicine, Coun. Fgn. Rels., Inst. Medicine of NAS, Pi Sigma Alpha. Office: U Mich Sch Pub Health 109 Observatory St Ann Arbor MI 48109-2029

CLARK, PATRICIA SHERBERT, secondary school educator; b. Spartanburg, S.C., Apr. 19, 1948; d. Brooks Boyd and Mary Christine Sherbert; m. Lewis Clary Clark, Sept. 6, 1969; children: Scott Douglas, Bradley Ryan, Shannon Clark Davis, Gregory Lewis. BA in Secondary Edn. magna cum laude, U. S.C., Aiken, 1990; M of Secondary Edn., English, U. S.C., Columbia, 1993. RN 1969. RN, Margaret Weston Health Care Ctr., Langley, SC, 1973—79, Edgefield County Health Dept., SC, 1969—71; tchr. Wardlaw Acad., Johnston, SC, 1990—95; tchr. English Strom Thurmond HS, Johnston, 1995—2006. Mem. Sch. to Work com. Piedmont Tech. Coll., Greenwood, SC, 1998—2000. Mem. chancel choir 1st Bapt. Ch., Johnston, SC, 1960—2006. Recipient Outstanding Yearbook Advisor, Delmar Publs.

CLARK, PATSY VEDDER, retired educator and staff developer; b. Forsyth, Ga., Mar. 28, 1944; d. Roland Roger and Nolia Ernestine (Piland) Vedder; m. James Edwin Clark, Aug. 10, 1965; children: Elizabeth Ellen, James Kenneth. BS in Edn., Tift Coll., 1966; MS in Edn., SUNY, Buffalo, 1976, degree in Specialist in Ednl. Adminstrn., 1989. Cert. elem. educator in social studies; cert. specialist in ednl. adminstrn. Tchr., adminstr. Niagara Falls (N.Y.) City Sch. Dist., 1966-99, staff developer, mentor tchr., 1985-87, asst. adminstr., 1990-92, 96-99. Ednl. cons. N.Y. State United Tchrs., Albany, 1988—. Mem. adv. bd. Friends of the Libr., Niagara Falls, 1999—; founder West Lincoln Cmty. Care, Smithville, Ont., Can., 1985; mem. Friends of Local History, Niagara Falls, 1999—. Mem. Nat. Coun. Tchrs. English (sec.), Delta Kappa Gamma (pres. 1988—, past v.p.), Phi Delta Kappa. Mennonite Brethren. Avocations: reading, travel.

CLARK, PAULA IRENE, elementary school educator, consultant; d. Phillip and Julie Clark. BS in Elem. Edn., U. South Fla., 1993; MS in Reading Edn., Fla. State U., 1999; EdD, Regent U., 2005. Cert. elem. tchr., primary tchr., ednl. specialist Fla. Tchr. Hernando County Sch. Dist., Brooksville, Fla., 1996—, reading specialist, 2001—; tng. evaluator Ednl. Testing Svc., Tampa, Fla., 2003—. Online faculty U. Phoenix, 2004. Treas. Pine Grove Elem. PTA, Brooksville, 1996—2002. Named Golden Poet, 1992, Nat. Disting. Faculty, US Dept. Edn., 1997, Person of the Yr., Hernando County PTA, 2001; Congressional scholar, Nat. Young Leaders Conf., 1988, Doane scholar, U. South Fla., 1993. Mem.: ASCD, Hernando County Acad. Tchrs., Fla. Reading Assn., Internat. Reading Assn. (manuscript reviewer 2001—), Kappa Delta Pi, Phi Delta Kappa. Republican. Personal E-mail: paula_27860@msn.com.

CLARK, RANJANA B., bank executive; arrived in U.S., 1987; BA in Econs., MA in Mktg. and Sales. With Deutsche Bank, Bombay, 1982; joined Wachovia Bank as product mgr. capital markets divsn. Charlotte, NC, 1989; sr. v.p. - group exec. Treas. Svcs. Divsn., 1999—2001; exec. v.p., head Treas. Svcs. Divsn. Charlotte, NC, 2001—. Named One of Most Powerful Women in Banking, U.S. Banker Mag., 2003. Office: Wachovia Bank 301 South College St Charlotte NC 28288-0570*

CLARK, ROSE ANN, chemist, educator; b. Akron, Ohio, Nov. 30, 1967; d. Allen Eugene and Abbie Jean Clark; m. Edward Paul Zovinka, May 28, 1994; children: Edward Alan Zovinka, Shane Paul Zovinka. BS in Chemistry, U. N.C., Wilmington, 1990; PhD in Chemistry, N.C. State U., 1995. NSF postdoctoral fellow Pa. State U., State College, 1995-97; assoc. prof. chemistry St. Francis U., Loretto, Pa., 1997—. Author (with others): (book) Electrochemistry in Neuronal Microenviroments, 1998; contbr. articles to profl. jours. Presenter Rural Outreach Chemistry for Kids, Loretto, 1997—2002. Fellow Electronic Materials, Dept. of Edn., 1992—95; grantee Tchg. Incentive, GE, 1990—91, Rsch., NSF, 1998, Soc. Analytical Chemists of Pitts., 2001, SACP, 2002. Mem.: AAAS, Coun. Undergrad. Rsch., Soc. Electroanalytical Chemists, Am. Chem. Soc., Iota Sigma Pi (Centennial award 2004), Sigma Xi. Avocations: golf, bicycling. Office: St Francis U PO Box 600 Loretto PA 15940-0600 Fax: 814-472-2773. Business E-Mail: rclark@francis.edu.

CLARK, ROSE SHARON, elementary school educator; b. Winslow, Ind., Oct. 31, 1942; d. William Noel Fettinger and Mary Emaline Jones; m. Charles Edgar Clark, June 2, 1968; children: Mary Elizabeth, Christopher Edgar. BS, Oakkland City (Ind.) U., 1964; MS, Ind. U., 1968. Elem. edn. tchr. Hendricks Twp. Sch., Shelbyville, Ind., 1964—67, Thomas A. Hendricks, Shelbyville, Ind., 1967—74, 1984—. Mem. bd. First Ch. of the Nazarene, Shelbyville, 1994—, First Ch. of God, Shelbyville, 1969—90; bd. dirs. Bright Star Pre-Sch., Shelbyville, 2001—. Mem.: AAUW (v.p.-treas. 1972—2000), Alpha Delta Kappa. Home: 2466 N Richard Dr Shelbyville IN 46176 Office: Thomas A Hendricks Sch 1111 St Joseph St Shelbyville IN 46176

CLARK, RUTH MAE, music educator; b. Ft. Meade, Md., Nov. 30, 1956; d. James Lee and Janet May Culver; m. Charles Andrew Clark, June 23, 1979; children: Jennifer Mae, Christopher Andrew. MusB in Edn., Sam Houston State U., Huntsville, Tex., 1978. Cert. Tex. Edn. Agy., 1978. Mid. sch. choir, elem. sch. tchr. Victoria (Tex.) Cmty. Ind. Sch. Dist., 1978—79; adminstrv. asst. to vp ops. Colonial Food Stores, Inc., San Angelo, Tex., 1980—85; legal sec. Rollert & McNeal, Traverse City, Mich., 1986—87; legal sec., paralegal Tudzin & Tobor Law Firm, Houston, 1987—90; music tchr. Ft. Bend Ind. Sch. Dist., Sugar Land, Tex., 1993—2006. Treas. GymMasters, Inc., Houston, 1998—2003; flutist Mo. City Pops Band, Missouri City, Tex., 2005—. Named Tchr. of Yr., Quail Valley Elem. Sch., Ft. Bend Ind. Sch. Dist., 2003; recipient Share the Hope award, Am. Sings. Mem.: Austin H.S. Athletic Booster Club (assoc.; sec. 2006—). R-Consevative. Methodist. Avocations: crafts, travel, music, theater. Home: 510 Scarlet Maple Dr Sugar Land TX 77479 Office: Oakland Elem Sch 4455 Watersides Dr Richmond TX 77469 Office Phone: 281-787-2438.

CLARK, SANDRA MARIE, school administrator; b. Hanover, Pa., Feb. 17, 1942; d. Charles Raymond Clark and Mary Josephine (Snyder) Clark Wierman. BS in Elem. Edn., Chestnut Hill Coll., 1980; MS in Child Care Adminstrn., Nova U., 1985; MS in Ednl. Adminstrn., Western Md. Coll., 1992. Cert. elem. tchr., elem. prin., Pa. Tchr. various elem. schs., Pa., 1962-75; asst. vocation directress Mt. St. Joseph Motherhouse, Chestnut Hill, Pa., 1975-76; tchr. St. Catharine's Sch., Spring Lake, N.J., 1976-77; asst. mgr. Jim's Truck Stop, New Oxford, Pa., 1977-81; adminstr. Little People Day Care Sch., Hanover, 1981-88, sec., treas. bd. dirs., 1985-86; coord. regional resource Magic Yrs. Child Care & Learning Ctrs., Inc., Hanover, 1987-88; prin. St. Vincent de Paul Sch., Hanover, Pa., 1988—. Presenter Hanover Area Seminar for Day Care Employees, 1983-86. Coord. sch. safety patrols St. Vincent's Sch., Hanover, 1969-75, vice-chmn. bd., 1982-84; multi-media instr. first aid ARC, Hanover, 1983-86, bd. dirs., 1984-88; exec. sec. of bd. of dirs. ARC, Hanover, 1988; 1st v.p. Hanover Area Coun. of Chs., 1988, pres., 1989; validator accredidation program Nat. Acad. Early Childhood Programs, Washington, 1987—; bd. dirs. Life Skills Unltd. Handicapped Adults, 1988—; facilitator Harrisburg Diocesan Synod, Hanover, 1985-88, parish del., 1988. Pa. Dept. Pub. Welfare tng. grantee, 1986. Mem. NAFE, Nat. Cath. Ednl. Assn. Clubs: Internat. Assn. Turtles (London). Democrat. Roman Catholic. Avocations: swimming, reading, writing children's stories. Home: 348 Barberry Dr Hanover PA 17331-1302 Office: St Vincent De Paul Sch Hanover PA 17331 Office Phone: 717-637-5190. Personal E-mail: smclark@netrax.net.

CLARK, SHARI JILL, literature and language professor; d. Barbara Faye Howard and Harley Jackson Ragland; m. Thomas Henry Malcik, May 16, 2003. BA in English, U. Tex., Arlington, 1990, MA in English; PhD, Tex. Tech U., Lubbock, 2001. Adj. asst. prof. English, Tarrant County Coll., South Campus, Tex., 1998—2002, Tex. Woman's U., Denton, 1999—2002, Tex. Wesleyan U., Ft. Worth, 1999—99; instr. English, U. Ala., Tuscaloosa, 2001; adj. asst. prof. English, U. of North Tex., Denton, 2001—03; asst. prof. Brit. lit. Fisk U., Nashville, 2003—. Contbr. articles to profl. jours. Vol. Rutherford County Dem. Party, Smyrna, Tenn., 2004—05. Mem.: MLA, S.C. MLA, Joseph Conrad Soc. of Am., Soc. for Lit., Sci., and Arts, Delta Phi Alpha, Sigma Tau Delta (sec. Theta Mu chpt. 1989, v.p. Theta Mu chpt. 1990). Avocations: water aerobics and swimming, films. Office: Fisk Univ 1000 17th Ave N Nashville TN 37208 Office Phone: 615-329-8695.

CLARK, SHARON ANN, educational consultant, music educator; b. Lowell, Mass., Aug. 3, 1961; d. William K. and Dorothy A. (McNamara) Clark; m. Eric J. Mortenson, July 11, 1998. MusB, U. of Mass. at Lowell, Lowell, MA, 1983; MED, Fitchburg State Coll., Fitchburg, MA, 1988; EdD, Nova Southeastern U., Ft. Lauderdale, Florida, 2003. Cert. tchr. Mass., 1983. Ednl. cons. Edn. Performance Systems, Inc., Woburn, Mass., 2000; instrnl. specialist Lowell Pub. Schools, Mass., 2001—. Music specialist Lowell Pub. Schs., Mass., 1998—2005. Choir mem. St. Margaret Ch., Lowell, Mass., 1997—. Vis. scholar Comprehensive Sch. Reform grant, Mass. Dept. of Edn., 2002; Lighthouse Tech. grant, 1999, Jordan Fundamentals grant, Michael Jordan Found. - NIKE, 2001, Creative Schools grant, Mass. Cultural Coun., 2002. Mem.: Lowell Sch. Adminstrs. Assn., Am. Fedn. Tchrs., Music Educators Nat. Conf., Nat. Staff Devel. Coun. Avocations: biking, painting, travel. Home: 18 Crestwood Dr Hudson NH 03051 Office: BFButler Mid Sch Tech 1140 Gorham St Lowell MA 01852 Office Phone: 978-970-5494. Personal E-mail: shadotclark@earthlink.net. E-mail: sharonclark@lowell.k12.ma.us.

CLARK, SHELIA ROXANNE, sports association executive, legislative analyst; b. June 28, 1959; d. Milton Cornell and Mable Juanita (Grubb) C. BS in Polit. Sci., Radford U., 1983; MPA, James Madison U., Harrisonburg, Va., 1987. Dir. Black Teenage World Scholarship Program, Va., 1977-88; intern Field Found., New River Valley, Va., 1984-85, Rep. Rick Boucher, Washington, 1987; adminstrv. asst. OMB Watch, Washington, 1988; legis. asst. Nat. Community Action Found., Washington, 1988-93; exec. dir. Gary Clark's Sports Camp, 1990—; interim dir. talent search program Va. Tech. U., Blacksburg, 1997-98, athletic acad. advisor/lectr., 1998—, asst. coord.-student athletic Office of Acad. Enrichment, 1998—. Project coord. Student Coalition Against Tobacco, 1994-95; cons., asst. Nat. Children's Day Found., Washington, 1991-93; advisor Soc. of African Am. Scholars, Alpha Kappa Mu, Va. Tech. U., Blacksburg; cons. Profl. Athletes Svcs. Success, 2002-. Program dir. Project Unity, Va., 1984; bd. mem. VA Action, 1985, Grassroots Leadership Project, N.C., 1987; campaign worker Clinton Presdl. Campaign/Transition, Washington, 1992. Internship The Field Found., 1984-85, Congressman Rick Boucher, Washington, 1987. Mem. Nat. Coun. Negro Women. Office: Gary Clarks Sports Camp PO Box 202 Dublin VA 24084-0202 E-mail: clarkclark80@aol.com.

CLARK, SHERYL DIANE, physician; b. Cleve., May 8, 1952; d. Crandall and Martha Jayne (McNeilly) C.; children: Milan, Gabriel. BA, Beloit Coll., 1974; postgrad., Hampstead Clinic Child Analysis and U. London, 1976-77; MD, Case Western Res. U., 1982. Diplomate Am. Bd. Dermatology. Intern Mt. Sinai Med. Ctr., Cleve., 1982-83; rsch. fellow Case Western Res. U., Kenya, Kenya, Africa, 1983-84, Washington U., St. Louis, 1984-88; resident in dermatology Barnes Hosp., St. Louis, 1985-88; vis. assoc. physician Rockefeller U. Hosp., N.Y.C., 1990-91; asst. attending physician N.Y. Presbyterian Hosp., N.Y.C., 1988—; asst. clin. prof. medicine Cornell Med. Ctr., N.Y.C., 1991—; pres. Sheryl Clark Enterprises, N.Y.C., 1991—. Cons. Rodale Press, N.Y.C., 1995—; speaker in field. Co-editor: Jour. of Biomed. Engrng. and Technology, 1977-78; contbr. articles to profl. jours. Rep. rape task force N.Y. Hosp., 1988-90; crisis intervention vol. Crisis Intervention Hotline, Beloit, Wis., 1973-74. Fellow N.Y. Acad. Medicine, Am. Acad. Dermatology; mem. AMA (cons. scientific advisory coun. 1992), Am. Soc. Lasers Medicine and Surgery, Am. Med. Women's Assn., Caribbean Med. & Edn. Found. (bd. dirs.), Soc. Investigative Dermatology, Internat. Soc. for Androgenic Disorders, Med. Soc. State of N.Y., N.Y. County Med. Soc., Phi Beta Kappa, Alpha Omega Alpha. Avocations: painting, scuba, skiing, sailing. Office: 109 E 61st St New York NY 10021-8101

CLARK, STEPHANI MICHELLE CALLAHAN, elementary school educator; d. Karin G. and Franklin Delano Callahan (Stepfather), Joe Denby Miles; m. Andrew William Clark; 1 child, Lacey Janae; m. Mitchell Andrew Featherston (div. Dec. 1990). AA Math. and Sci., Coll. Sequoias, Visalia, Calif., 1978; BS Animal Sci., U. Calif. Davis, 1982; MA Edn. Tech. Emphasis, Fresno Pacific U., Calif., 2006. Profl. Clear Tchg. Credential Calif. Commn. on Tchr. Credentialing, 1987, cert. Ann. First Aid & CPR Red Cross Calif., 1987. Park technician, mem. helitack crew Sequoia Nat. Park, Three Rivers, Calif., 1978—80; animal technician Pet Prevent A Care, Santa Rosa, Calif., 1983—84; rsch. asst. Davis Tchg. and Rsch. Facility U. Calif., Tulare, 1985—87; math, sci. & phys. edn. tchr. Orosi Unified Sch. Dist., Orosi, Calif., 1987—90; tchr. math, sci. & phys. edn. Three Rivers Elem. Sch., Calif., 1990—93; tchr. sci. and chair dept. Divisadero Mid. Sch. Visalia Unified Sch. Dist., Calif., 1993—. Coach profl. ski racing Sierra Summit Ski Team, Fresno, 1985—; coach volleyball Divisadero Mid. Sch., Visalia, 1994—; advisor Friday Night Live Club Divsiadero Mid. Sch., Visalia, 1993—, Three Rivers Elem. Sch., 1990—93, El Monte Mid. Sch., Orosi, 1987—90; animal packer Mineral King Pack Sta., Horse Corral Pack Sta., Three Rivers, 1983—94. Mem.: Stds. Based Report Card Com. (site rep. 2002—05), U.S. Ski and Snowboard Assn. (tech. del. candidate 1990—2006, cert. profl. coach and referee), Smithsonian Instn., Calif. Cattlemen's Assn., Calif. Scholarship Fedn. (life). R-Consevative. Achievements include research in Milk Quality Lab Techniques guide to bovine udder health. Avocations: horseback riding, managing cattle, sewing, travel, fishing.

CLARK, SUSAN (NORA GOULDING), actress; b. Sarnia, Ont., Can., Mar. 8, 1940; d. George Raymond and Eleanor Almond (McNaughton) Clark; m. Alex Karras; 1 child, Katie Karras. Student, Toronto Children's Players, Ont., 1956-59; student (Acad. scholar), Royal Acad. Dramatic Art, London. Ptnr. Georgian Bay Prodns. Actor: (stage prodn.) Appearances to the Contrary, 2000, Glass Menagerie, 2002, Sisters Rosensweig, 2002, BiCoastal Woman, 2003, Dancing at Lughnasa, 2003, Importance of Being Earnest, 2004, The Body, 2004, Triptych, 2006; (TV series) Webster, 1983, Emily of New Moon, 1998; (films) Nobody's Perfekt, 1981, Porky's, 1981, Butterbox Babies, 1995; (TV films) Babe, 1975 (Emmy for oustanding lead actress in a drama, 1975), Sherlock Holmes: The Strange Case of Alice Faulkner, 1981, The Choice, 1981, Maid in America, 1982, Tonya & Nancy: The Inside Story, 1994, Snowbound: The Jim and Jennifer Stolpa Story, 1994. Mem. ACLU, Am. Film Inst. Office: Ste 308 13400 Riverside Dr Sherman Oaks CA 91423-2541

CLARK, TERESA WATKINS, psychotherapist, clinical counselor; b. Hobart, Okla., Dec. 18, 1953; d. Aaron Jack Watkins and Patricia Ann (Flurry) Greer and Ralph Gordon Greer; m. Philip Winston Clark, Dec. 29, 1979; children: Philip Aaron, Alisa Lauren. BA in Psychology, U. N.Mex., 1979, MA in Counseling and Family Studies, 1989. Lic. profl. clin. counselor, N.Mex.; nat. cert. counselor. Child care worker social svcs. divsn. Family Resource Ctr., Albuquerque, 1978-79; head tchr., asst. dir. Kinder Care Learning Ctr., Albuquerque, 1979-80; psychiat. asst. Vista Sandia Psychiat. Hosp., Albuquerque, 1980-87; psychotherapist outpatient clinic Bernalillo County Mental Health Ctr.-Heights, 1989-91; therapist adult and adolescent program Charter/Heights Behavioral Health Sys., Albuquerque, 1991-2000; clin. therapist, clin. supr. New Day Youth and Family Svcs., Albuquerque, 2001—. Vol. coordr. Disaster Mental Health Svcs. ARC. Mem. ACA, Am. Assn. Multicultural Counseling and Devel., Nat. Bd. Cert. Counselors, N.Mex. Health Counselors Assn. (former cen. regional rep., ethics chair, bd. dirs.), Mental Health Councelor's Assn., Billy The Kid Outlaw Gang Hist. Soc. Democrat. Avocations: music, camping, horseback riding, reading. Office: New Day Youth and Family Svcs 1330 San Pedro Ne Ste 201B Albuquerque NM 87110

CLARK, TERRI, country singer; b. Montreal, Can., Aug. 5, 1968; d. Les Sauson and Linda Clark. Previous jobs include work at restaurants, Gilley's, the Wax Mus., Nashville. Albums: Terri Clark, 1995, Just the Same, 1996, How I Feel, 1998, Fearless, 2000, Pain to Kill, 2003. Named Top New Female Country Artist Billboard mag., 1995; recipient Album of Yr. award Country Music Assn., 1996, Song of Yr., 1996, Vista Rising Star award, 1996, Canadian County Music Assoc. best single, 2003.

CLARK, TRUDY H., career officer; BA in sociology with honors, U. Md., 1972; student, Comm. Electronics Officer Sch., 1973—74; MS in guidance and counseling, Troy State U., 1987; disting. grad., Squadron Officer Sch., Maxwell AFB, 1980, Air Command and Staff Coll., 1987, Armed Forces Staff Coll., 1992, Air War Coll., Maxwell AFB, 1993. Second lt. USAF, 1973, first lt., 1975, cptn., 1977, major, 1985, lt. col., 1989, col., 1994, brigadier gen., 1999, maj. general, 2003; dir. command, control, comm. and computer sys. US Strategic Command, Offutt AFB, Nebr., 1999—2001; deputy dir. Defense Threat Reduction Agency (DTRA), Ft. Belvoir, Va., 2003—; chief tel. installations 392nd Comm. Group, Vandenberg AFB, Calif., 1974—76; chief programs mgmt. div. 2006th Comm. Group, Incirlik AFB, Turkey, 1976—79; chief comm. branch Joint Studies Group, Nellis AFB, Nev., 1979—81; chief threat analysis 4440th Tactical Fighter Training Group, Red Flag, Nellis AFB, Nev.; chief facilities operation branch 2146th Comm. Group, Osan AB, Republic of Korea, 1981—82; chief telecom. div. Langley AFB, Va., exec. officer, Hdqs. Tactical Comm. Div. Va., 1982—84; comdr. 1880th Info. Systems Squadron, Tonopah Test Range, Nev., 1984—86; chief tactical command and control comm. sys. Hdqs. USAF, Washington, directorate, programs and evaluation, exec. officer for dep. dir. of programs and evaluation, 1987—89; comdr. staff support unit White House Comm. Agy., Washington, presdl. comm. officer, 1989—92; comdr. 60th comm. group Hdqs. 15th Air Force, Travis AFB, Calif., chief comm. div., 1993—94. Office: 8725 John J Kingman Rd MSC 6201 Fort Belvoir VA 22060-6201

CLARK, VICTORIA, actress; b. Dallas, Oct. 10, 1959; 1 child. B in Music, Yale Univ. Actor: (Broadway plays) Sunday in the Park With George, 1985, Guys and Dolls, 1992—93, A Grand Night for Singing, 1993—94, Titanic, 1997—99, Cabaret, 1999—2000, Urinetown, 2003, Bye Bye Birdie, 2004, The Light in the Piazza, 2005 (Tony award for best performance by a leading actress in a musical, 2005, Drama Desk award, outstanding actress in a musical, 2005, Outer Critics Circle award, outstanding actress in a musical, 2005, Joseph Jefferson award, 2005); (films) Cradle Will Rock, 1999; (TV series) Law and Order, 1998, Law and Order: SVU, 2003, (TV spl.) Sweeney Todd: The Demon Barber of Fleet Street in Concert, 2002; dir.: (numerous operas); tchr. (voice). Mailing: c/o Vivian Beaumont Theatre Lincoln Ctr 150 W 65th St New York NY 10003

CLARK-BOURNE, KATHRYN ORPHA, consul; b. Ft. Collins, Colo., Oct. 15, 1924; d. Andrew Giles and Orpha Mae (Spielman) Clark; m. Kenneth Barnes Bourne, Jr. (div.). BA cum laude, U. Wash., 1947; MA, U. Minn.,

1951; postgrad., George Wash. U., 1951—52. Draftsman Boeing Aircraft Co., Seattle, 1942—44; editor West Seattle Herald, 1947; intelligence analyst Dept. of Army, Tokyo, 1947—49; bookkeeper Panama Canal Co., Wash., 1951—52; editor, intelligence rsch. specialist Dept. State, Wash., 1952—56; polit. asst. U.S. Embassy, Teheran, Iran, 1956—58; consulate officer U.S. Consul Gen., Rotterdam, Netherlands, 1959—61, consulate & polit. officer Bombay, 1962—67; supr. comm. Coopers & Lybrand, N.Y.C., 1969—74; comm. cons. George R. Block Actuaries, N.Y.C., 1974—75; dep. dir. Office of Fisheries Affairs Dept. State, Wash., 1975—77; counselor for polit. affairs Am. Embassy, Lagos, Nigeria, 1977—80; dep. dir. Office of West Africa Dept. State, Wash., 1980—82; dep. chief of mission Am. Embassy, Canakey, Guinea, 1982—85; consulate officer Consul Gen., Doula, Cameroon, 1985—87; insp. Office Insp. Gen. Dept. State, Wash., 1988—89, sr. insp. Office Insp. Gen., 1990—93, hist. declassification Newington, Va., 1993—. Lectr. Nat. War Coll., Georgetown U., Emory U.; alternate del. Conf. on Least-Developed Countries in Hague; chair North Pacific SEAL Negotiations with Can., Japan and U.S.S.R. Recipient Meritorious Honor award, Dept. of State, 1995. Mem.: World Affairs Coun., Am. Fgn. Svc. Assn. (bd. mem. 1993—97), Asia Soc., Diplomatic Consular Officers, Ret. (bd. mem. 2000—04). Home: 2230 Calif St NW Apt 6BE Washington DC 20008 Office: Dept of State State Annex 4 Newington VA 22122

CLARKE, BETTY ANN, librarian, minister; b. Townsend, Va., Nov. 9, 1947; d. Joshua Samuel and Queenie Victoria (Morris) Spady; m. Kenneth Clarke, June 30, 1972; 1 stepchild, Cynthia Clarke Rhinehart. BA in Polit. Sci., Norfolk State U., 1970; postgrad., N.J. Conf. Ministerial INst., 1979—84; MA, Rowan U., 1995. Cert. libr. N.J. Sr. libr. Atlantic County, Mays Landing, NJ, 1978—; pastor St. Mark African Meth. Episcopal Ch., Lindenwold, NJ, 1987—. Chaplain trauma unit Cooper Hosp., Camden, NJ, 1990—98. Recipient Jarena Lee award, Harrisburg Dist. African Meth. Episcopal Ch., 1992, African Am. Women's Network Bronze Star, Delaware Valley Humanity Field Health, 1996, Woman Making A Difference award, Bethel African Meth. Episcopal Ch., 2002. Democrat. Avocations: reading, travel, writing, bowling. Home: 14 Jefferson Ave Browns Mills NJ 08021 Office: St Mark AME Ch 929 Walnut & Taylor Aves Lindenwold NJ 08021 Office Phone: 609-625-2776 ext. 6328.

CLARKE, CHERYL CRIDER, music educator; b. Tuscaloosa, Ala., May 31, 1956; d. Byron and Gloria Hall Crider; m. John Eugene (Gene) Clarke, July 8, 1978; children: Amy Elizabeth, Emily Dyan. BS in music edn., U. Ala., 1974—77. Band dir. Wilson Hall Mid. Sch., Grove Hill, Ala., 1977—; choir dir. Grove Hill United Meth. Ch., 1990—. Team mem. Clarke County Edn. Tech., Grove Hill, 1981—; state spl. talent coord. Ala. Jr. Beta Club, Montgomery, 1998—. Named Tchr. of Yr., Walmart, 1995; named one of Outstanding Young Women in Am., 1988—89. Mem.: Ala. Edn. Assn., Ala. Bandmasters Assn. Republican. Meth. Avocations: computers, theater, travel, books. Home: 143 Foscue Ave Grove Hill AL 36451 Office: Wilson Hall Mid Sch 401 Carter Dr Grove Hill AL 36451 Personal E-mail: cherclarke@aol.com.

CLARKE, CORDELIA KAY KNIGHT MAZUY, management consultant, artist; b. Springfield, Mo., Nov. 22, 1938; d. William Horace and Charline (Bentley) Knight; m. Logan Clarke, Jr., July 22, 1978; children by previous marriage— Katharine Michelle Mazuy, Christopher Knight Mazuy. AB in English with honors, U. N.C., 1960; MS in Stats., N.C. State U., 1962; BFA in Painting, Lyme Acad. Coll. Fine Arts, 2005; student in Visual Arts, Mass. Coll. Art, 2006—. Statistician Research Triangle Inst., Durham, NC, 1960—63; statis. cons. Arthur D. Little, Inc., Cambridge, Mass., 1963—67; dir. mktg. planning and analysis Polaroid Corp., Cambridge, 1967—70; dir. mktg. and bus. planning Transaction Tech. Inc., Cambridge, 1970—72; pres. Mazuy Assos., Boston, 1972—73; v.p. Nat. Shawmut Bank, Boston, 1973—74; sr. v.p., dir. mktg. Shawmut Corp., 1974—78; sr. v.p., dir. retail banking Shawmut Bank, 1976—78; v.p. corp. devel. Arthur D. Little, Inc., 1978—79; v.p. Conn. Gen. Life Ins. Co., 1979—85; pres. CIGNA Securities, 1983—85; exec. v.p. McGraw-Hill Inc., 1988-90; chmn. Templeton, Inc., 1985—92, 1995—; pres. micromarketing divsn. ADVO, 1990—95. Faculty Williams Sch. Banking; adv. com. Bur. of Census, 1978-84; bd. dirs. Guardian Life Ins. Co., Berkshire Life Ins., Providence Jour. Co.; tchr. Amos Tuck Grad. Sch. Bus., Dartmouth Coll., 1964-65, exec.-in-residence, 1978, 80; bd. overseers, 1979-85; exec.-in-residence Wheaton Coll., 1978; vis. prof. Simmons Grad. Sch. Mgmt., 1978; mem. schs. adv. coun. Bank Mktg. Assn., 1976-78; mem. corp. adv. bd. Hartford Nat. Bank & Trust Co., 1980-87. Columnist Am. Banker, 1976-78. Mem. Mass. Gov.'s Commn. on Status of Women, 1977-79; bd. corporators Babson Coll., 1977-80; adv. bd. Boston Mayor's Office Cultural Affairs, 1977-79; bd. dirs. McGraw-Hill, Inc., 1976-88, Blue Shield of Mass., 1976-79, Greater Hartford Arts Coun., 1979-93, Cybex Internat. Inc., 1996-2000; trustee Children's Mus. Hartford, 1980-82; corporator Inst. of Living, 1981-92; regent U. Hartford, 1982—; bd. dirs. Hartford Art Sch., 1982-94, Hartford Stage Co., 1985-99, Manhattan Theatre Club, 1988-91, Inst. for Future, 1988-92, N.Y. Internat. Festival of Arts, 1988-91, Goodspeed Opera, 1990—, Inst. Design, 1990-98, Aeroflex Found., 1972—. Mem. Artists Assn. Nantucket (elected), Conn. Women Artists (elected), Lyme Art Assn. (assoc.), Essex Art Assn. (assoc.), Provincetown Art Assn., Internat. Womens Forum, Power 10, Phi Beta Kappa, Phi Kappa Phi, Kappa Alpha Theta. Home and Office: 89 River Rd East Haddam CT 06423-1462 Office Phone: 860-526-3368.

CLARKE, CYNTHIA THERESE See HARRISS, CYNTHIA

CLARKE, FLORENCE DOROTHY, minister, educator; b. Charleston, SC, Feb. 21, 1941; d. Peter Glover and Janie Etta (Gilliard) Oliver; children: Stephanye R., Jamie J. BS, S.C. State U., 1963. Tchr. bus. Williams Meml. Sch., St. George, SC, 1963—65, Charles A. Brown H.S., Charleston, SC, 1965—68; sr. adminstrv. aide, sr. analyst Electric Boat Corp., Groton, Conn., 1968—96; assoc. min. African Meth. Episcopal Zion Ch., New London, Conn., 1975—98, supply pastor Cambridge, Mass., 1996—97, pastor Waterford, Conn., 1998—. Christian edn. dir. New Haven Dist., 1993—2004; chaplain Conn. Coll., New London, 2002—04; spkr. in field. Contbr. articles to mags. Bd. dirs. Noank (Conn.) Bapt. Group Homes, Inc., 1995—99. Named Outstanding Christian Educator, Walls Temple African Meth. Episcopal Zion Ch., 1997. Mem.: AAUW, NAACP (exec. bd., edn. commn.), Am. Correctional Chaplains Assn., Am. Correctional Chaplains Assn., Christian Edn. (dist. dir. 1990—2005), Nat. Coun. Negro Women (1st v.p. 1996—99, Outstanding Svc. award 1996). Methodist. Avocations: singing, reading, public speaking. Home: 11 Lodus Ct New London CT 06320-4328 Office Phone: 860-443-7561.

CLARKE, GRAY B., psychiatrist; b. Chapel Hill, N.C., June 15, 1967; d. Charles Lee and Karen Lee Clarke; 1 child, Benjamin C. Leyba. BS, U. N.Mex., Albuquerque, 1987—92, MD, 1993—98. Cert. Am. Bd. Psychiatry and Neurology, 2004. Asst. prof. U. N.Mex., Albuquerque, 2003—; med. dir., u. hosp. psychiatry consultation/liaison svc. U. N.Mex, Albuquerque, 2003—; attending psychiatrist, dept. psychiatry U. N.Mex., Albuquerque, 2003—. Contbr. chapters to books, papers to profl. jours. and pubs. Mem.: Assn. Academic Psychiatry, Acad. Psychosomatic Medicine, Am. Psychiat. Assn. Office: Univ New Mex Dept Psychiatry 2400 Tucker NE 4th fl FPC Albuquerque NM 87131 Office Phone: 505-272-4763. Business E-Mail: gclarke@salud.unm.edu.

CLARKE, HUGHETTE NAOMI, elementary school educator; b. Flushing, N.Y., Jan. 20, 1951; d. Hugh Calvin and Naomi L. Clarke. BA, Queens Coll., Flushing, 1973, MSc, 1977; EdD, Tchrs. Coll. Columbia U., N.Y.C., 2004. Cert. tchr. K-6 N.Y. State Dept. Edn., SPS N.Y. State Dept. Edn. Tchr. pre-K various schs., N.Y., 1974—2002; tchr. math. Longwood Mid. Sch., Mid. Island, NY, 2002—. Mem.: L.I. Black Educators, The Links, Inc., Alpha Kappa Alpha (pres. Sigma Psi Omega chpt. 2002—06). Avocations: skiing, reading. Office: Longwood Mid Sch 43 Mid Island-Yaphank Rd Middle Island NY 11953 E-mail: hughette@erols.com.

CLARKE, JANET MORRISON, marketing executive; d. Morton and Shirley (Harkinson) Morrison, m. Frederick G.E. Clarke, Oct. 4, 1980. BA in Architecture, Princeton U., 1976. Sales rep. Sci. Press, Ephrata, Pa., 1977-78, R.R. Donnelley & Sons Co., Chgo., 1978, various positions including sr. v.p. Information Technol. and dir. venture capital fund, 1978—97; mng. dir., global database mktg. Citibank, 1997—2000; chmn., CEO KnowledgeBase Marketing, Inc., 2000—01; exec. v.p. Young & Rubicam, Inc, 2000—01; chief mktg. officer DealerTrack, Inc., 2002—03; founder Clarke Littlefield LLC, 2001—, pres., 2001—02, 2003—. Bd. dirs. Cox Communications, 1995—, Asbury Automotive Group, ExpressJet Holdings Inc., 2002—, eFunds Corp., 2000—, Forbes.com Inc., Gateway Computers, 2005—; mem. sch. bd. Harvard Bus. Sch. Charter trustee, Princeton U.; bd. dirs. YWCA, Westbrook, Conn., 1984—; mem., regional chmn. Nat. Ann. Giving Com. Princeton (N.J.) U., 1985—. Mem.: Princeton (N.Y.C.); Landmark (Stamford, Conn.). Republican.

CLARKE, JEAN ALDERMAN, orchestra director; b. Memphis, May 15, 1949; d. Allison M. and Ruth Edwards Alderman; m. William Trantham Clarke, Nov. 19, 1977; 1 child, William Alderman Trantham. AB magna cum laude, Duke U., 1971; MS in Music Edn., U. Ill., 1972. Cert. tchr. S.C. Orch. dir. Charleston (S.C.) Sch. Dist., 1972—74, Sch. Dist. of Greenville County, SC, 1974—89, SC, 1996—97, Beech Springs Intermediate Sch., Duncan, SC, 1997—2005, Berry Shoals Internmediate Sch., Duncan, 2001—05; program coord., strings instr. Stone Acad. Comm. Arts, Greenville, SC, 2005—. Trustee bd. dirs. Greenville Symphony Assn., 1998—. Mem.: Music Educators Nat. Conf., Am. String Tchrs. Assn., Am. Viola Soc. (S.C. chpt. treas. 2001—), S.C. Music Educators Assn. (pres. orch. divsn. 1989—91, bd. dirs. 1987—93). Baptist. Avocations: running, tennis, sailing, swimming. Home: 9 Phillips Trl Greenville SC 29609-6421 Office: Stone Acad Comm Arts 115 Randall St Greenville SC 29609 Office Phone: 864-355-8400. Office Fax: 864-355-8455. Business E-Mail: jcclarke@greenville.k12.sc.us.

CLARKE, JUDY, lawyer; b. Asheville, N.C., 1953; m. Speedy Rice. B in Psychology, Furman U., 1974; JD, U. S.C., 1977. Trial atty. Fed. Defenders San Diego, Inc., exec. dir., 1983—91; pvt. practice, 1991-92; exec. dir. Fed. Defenders of Ea. Washington & Idaho. Mem. faculty Nat. Criminal Def. Coll., Macon, Ga., bd. regents, 1985—, pres. Nat. Assn. Criminal Def. Lawyers, 1996-97 Author: Federal Sentencing Manual; contbr. articles to profl. jours. Mem. NACDL (pres. 1996-97). Office: Fed Pub Defenders Office 10 N Post St Ste 700 Spokane WA 99201-0705

CLARKE, KATHLEEN BURTON, federal agency administrator; b. Bountiful, Utah; BA in Polit. Sci., UT State U. From dir. constituent svcs. to exec. dir. Office of Congressman James V. Hansen, 1987—93; dep. dir. Utah Dept. Natural Resources, 1993—98, exec. dir., 1998—2001; dir. Bur. Land Mgmt. U.S. Dept. Interior, Washington, 2001—. Office: US Dept Interior Bur Land Mgmt 1849 C St NW Washington DC 20240

CLARKE, KIT HANSEN, radiologist; b. Louisville, May 24, 1944; d. Hans Peter and Katie (Bird) Hansen; m. John M. Clarke, Feb. 14, 1976; children: Brett Bonnett, Blair Hansen, Brandon Chamberlain; stepchildren: Gray Campbell, Jeffrey William John M. AB, Randolph-Macon Woman's Coll., 1966; MD, U. Louisville, 1969. Diplomate Am. Bd. Radiology. Intern Louisville Gen. Hosp., 1969—70; resident in internal medicine and radiology U. Tenn., Knoxville, 1970—73; resident in radiology U.S. Fla., Tampa, 1973—74; staff radiologist Palms of Pasadena, St. Petersburg, Fla., 1974—, chmn. radiology dept., 1992—. Active Fla. Competitive Swim Assn. of Amateur Athletics Union. Fellow Am. Coll. Radiology; mem. AMA, Fla. West Coast Radiology Soc., Radiol. Soc. N.Am., Fla. Med. Assn., Pinellas County Med. Soc., Fla. Radiology Soc., Am. Horse Show Assn. (hunter, jumber divsn.). Episcopalian. Home: 7171 9th St S Saint Petersburg FL 33705-6218 also: PO Box 47948 Saint Petersburg FL 33743-7948 Office Phone: 727-341-7552. E-mail: khclarke@tampabay.rr.com.

CLARKE, LINDA DIANE, mental health services professional, psychotherapist; d. Robert Francis and Elaine Clarke. BS in Biology, Emporia State U., Kans., 1976, MS in Biology, 1982, MS in Counseling, 1985; postgrad., Clayton Coll. Natural Health, Birmingham, Ala., 2005. Lic. clin. profl. counselor Kans.; cert. job specialist Kans. Real estate agt. Farm & Home Real Estate, 1985—88; adj. instr. speech Allen County CC, 1987; instr., tchr.'s aide Flint Hills Area Vocat. Tech. Sch., 1987—88; mental health counselor Resource Ctr. Butler CC, El Dorado, Kans., 1988—90, adj. instr. biology, 1989—90, outreach advisor, adj. instr. psychology and speech, 1989—90; vocat.-rehab. counselor Profl. Rehab. Mgmt., Olathe, Kans., 1990—93; adj. instr. Emporia State U., Kans., 1989—90; family therapist The Farm, Inc., Emporia, 2002—. Presenter in field. Author: (guide) Signs of Satanism, 1984. Pres. Kans. Fedn. Humane Socs., Flint Hills Humane Soc., Emporia; team mem. Cmty. Emergency Response Team, El Dorado; mem. HIV Cmty. Planning Bd., Kans., 1997—99; Kans. Animal Health Adv. Bd., 1989—95; bd. dirs. El Dorado Safehouse, 1994—2004, Walnut Valley Area Coalition, El Dorado, 1996—. Named Outstanding Faculty Mem., Butler CC, 2001—04; recipient Disting. Svc. award, 2003. Mem.: ACA, Kans. Mental Health Assn., Kans. Assn. Counselors, Registrars and Advisors, Kans. Coll. Counseling Assn. (pres./treas.), Kans. Counseling Assn. Democrat. Avocations: cryptozoology research, reading, painting, gardening. Office: Butler CC W Dorm # 317 901 S Haverhill Rd El Dorado KS 67042

CLARKE, LOUISE RIGDON, gifted student program administrator, principal; b. Kansas City, Mo., July 23, 1936; d. Raymond Harrison and Margret (Britt) Rigdon; children: Michael Terrell, Steven Harrison. BA, Agnes Scott Coll., 1954-58; postgrad., U. Va.; M in Adminstrn. and Supervision, Radford U., 1986; CAGS in Adminstrv. Leadership, Va. Tech., 1994. Cert. middle sch. supr., prin. Arborvirus serologist Ctr. for Disease Control, Atlanta, 1958-64; English tchr. Chinese Middle Sch., Taipei, Taiwan, 1965-67; dir. Navy Relief Soc. for Marine Base Camp LeJeune, Jacksonville, N.C., 1975-76; sci. tchr. jr. high sch., 1980-84; hons. resource tchr. jr. high programs for gifted, 1984-86; coord. programs for gifted, talented and highly motivated Roanoke (Va.) City Pub. Schs., 1986-99, supr. sci. K-8, 1986-99; prin. Ctrl. Elem. Sch., South Williamsport, Pa., 1999—. Adj. faculty Hollins (Va.) Coll., 1989-98; past pres. Roanoke Regional Coun. Edn. of the Gifted. Mem. ASCD, Va. Assn. Supervision and Curriculum Devel., Nat. Assn. Gifted Children (pres.), Va. Assn. for Edn. Gifted, Am. Ednl. Rsch. Assn., Phi Dela Kappa. Avocations: tennis, bird watching, hiking. Office: South Williamsport Sch Dist 515 W Central Ave Williamsport PA 17702-7206 Home: 24 Upland Rd Williamsport PA 17701-1849

CLARKE, PAMELA JONES, headmaster; b. Boston, Jan. 11, 1945; d. Gilbert Edward and Jean (Morse) Jones; children: Jean, Henry David. BA in Ancient Greek, Vassar Coll., 1966; MA in Classics, Yale U., 1967; MEd in Counseling and Consulting Psych., Harvard U., 1979. Dir. curriculum Groton (Mass.) Sch., 1972-90; head of sch. The Masters Sch., Dobbs Ferry, NY, 1990—2000, St. Paul Acad. & Summit Sch., St. Paul, 2000—05, Trevor Day School, NYC, 2005—. Cons. The Mead Sch., Greenwich, Conn., 1970-72; site dir. CTY Johns Hopkins, Balt. and Carlisle, Pa., 1988, 89; tchr. winter term, Lenk, Switzerland, 1989; alumnae trustee Coll. Yr. in Athens, 1966-70. Contbr. articles to jours., newspaper. Treas. Town Soccer Bd., Groton, 1985-89; mng. Adult Ice Hockey Program, Groton, 1986-90; fund raiser The Shipley Sch., Vassar Coll. Mem. Coun. for Women in Ind. Schs. (mem. task force 1984-90). Democrat. Episcopalian. Avocations: travel, tennis, reading, skiing. Office: Trevor Day Sch 11 E 89th St New York NY 10128

CLARKE, PAULA KATHERINE, anthropologist, researcher, social studies educator; b. Berkeley, Gloucestershire, Eng., July 27, 1946; d. Percy George and Grace Anne C.; m. Warren Ted Hamilton. BA, U. Calif., Berkeley, 1982; PhD, U. Calif., San Francisco, 1991. Prof. anthropology and sociology Columbia Coll., Sonora, Calif., 1997—. Invited participant Oxford Round Table Diversity in Sce., 2006; invited spkr. in field. Contbr.: Men and Masculinities: A Social, Cultural, and Historical Encyclopedia, 2003; contbr. articles to ednl. jours. (Nominated-Kathleen Gregory Klein Award by Women's Caucus/Popular and Am. Culture Assn. for best unpublished article on feminism and popular culture, 1999). Creator Future Promise Award scholarship Columbia Coll., Sonora, 2001. Recipient Excellence in Tchg. award, Tuolumne County Bd. Edn., 2002. Office: Columbia Coll 11600 Columbia College Dr Sonora CA 95370 Office Phone: 209-588-5356. Business E-Mail: clarkep@yosemite.cc.ca.us.

CLARKE, SHARON ELIZABETH BORGES, music educator; d. Albert Anthony and Elizabeth Jane Borges; m. William Thomas Clarke, 1982; children: Brian, Andrew. A, Shenandoah Conservatory of Music, Winchester, Va., 1980; BA in Music Edn. K-12, Glassboro State Coll., NJ, 1982. Cert. tchr. music K- 12 NJ. Music tchr. Bernardsville Twp., NJ, 1982—84; music tchr., band dir. Voorhees Twp. Schs., NJ, 1989—. Contemporary youth choir dir. St. Marks United Meth. Ch., Hamilton, NJ, 2005—. Office: Voorhees Twp Schs Northgate Dr Voorhees NJ 08043 Business E-Mail: clarke@voorhees.k12.nj.us.

CLARKE, VICTORIA C. (TORIE CLARKE), former federal agency administrator; b. Pitts., Mar. 1959; m. Brian Graham; children: Colin, Charlie, Devan. BA, George Washington U., 1982. Editl asst., photographer, graphics editor Washington Star newspaper, 1979—82; press asst. to v.p. The White House, 1982; press sec. to Congressman, then Sen. John McCain, 1983—89; asst. U.S. Trade Rep. Exec. Office of the Pres., 1989—92; press sec. for reelection campaign Pres. George Bush, 1992; v.p. for pub. affairs and strategic counsel Nat. Cable TV Assn., 1993—98; pres. Bozell Eskew Advt.; gen. mgr. Hill and Knowlton, Washington; asst. sec. for pub. affairs U.S. Dept. Def., Washington, 2001—03; sr. advisor for comm. & govt. affairs Comcast Corp., Washington, 2003—; analyst CNN. Author: Lipstick on a Pig: Winning in the No-Spin Era by Someone Who Knows the Game, 2006. E-mail: torie@torieclarke.com.*

CLARKE-HALL, DEBORAH RENAY, elementary school educator; b. Washington, D.C., Aug. 15, 1954; d. Charlie and Claudelia Sweat Barnes; m. McLavern Hall, July 24, 1999. BS in Elem. Edn., Va. Union U., Richmond, 1979. Cert. tchr. Md. Bd. Edn., advanced profl. Md. Bd. Edn., 1982. Science educator Charles County, Md. Pub. Sch. Sys., Waldorf, 1979—95, 1995—. Mem. NAACP, Westmoreland County, Va.; served on numerous Democratic campaigns in Va. Named Outstanding Elem. Sci. Tchr., Md. Assn. Sci. Tchrs., 2002, Charles County Pub. Schs., 2006, So. Md. Elec. Co., 2006; recipient recognition as outstanding sci. educator, Millennium Chems., Frederick, Md., 2002. Mem.: NSTA (elem. sci. com. 2003—05, judge, Explora Vision awards 2004—06, judge, Craftsman Young Inventors 2005), Va. Assn. Sci. Tchrs., Com. on Elem. Sci. Internat., The Girl Friends, Inc. (Richmond chpt.). Democrat. Baptist. Avocations: birdwatching, antiques, tracking hurricanes using online data. Home: 8201 Eva Dr Port Royal VA 22535 E-mail: sweatclarke@hotmail.com.

CLARK-HARLEY, MARY DORCAS, retired radiologist; b. Hopwood, Pa., Oct. 31, 1921; d. Guy Moser Clark and Nell Mildred Gates; m. John Barker Harley (dec. 1995); children: John, Joanne Lynn, Tom, Mary Shearon. BS, W.Va. U., Morgantown, 1942; MD, U. Md., Balt., 1945. Intern, internal medicine resident U. Md. Hosp., Balt., 1945—47; radiology resident W.Va. Univ. Hosp., Morgantown, 1964—67, radiology fellow, 1967—68; physician health svcs. W.Va. U., Morgantown, 1947—48; physician pub. health svcs. Gallager Hosp., Washington, 1950—57; pvt. practice in internal medicine Terra Alta Preston Meml. Hosp., W.Va., 1950—57, W.Va. U. Med. Sch., 1957—64; asst. prof. W.Va. U. Med. Sch. and Hosp., 1972—80; radiologist Dakota Clinic, Fargo, ND, 1972—80, Indiana Hosp., Indiana, Pa., 1980—96; ret. Elder Grayston Presbyn. Ch., Indiana, 1997—2003. Named a Notable Woman, AAUW, 1996; named Civic Leader of Yr., Indiana County Svc. Club, 1988, Women's Imaging Ctr. in Her Honor, Bd. Mems., Ind. Regional Med. Ctr., 2005; recipient Athena award, Indiana C. of C., 1993. Mem.: AMA, Pa. Med. Soc., N.D. Med. Soc. Republican. Presbyterian. Avocations: sailing, skiing, wildlife preservation, quilting, dance. Home: 125 Oriole Ave Indiana PA 15701

CLARK-JOHNSON, SUSAN, publishing executive; b. Mount Kisco, NY, Feb. 21, 1947; d. Emile Schurmacher and Elizabeth Woolf; m. Samuel Brooks Johnson. BA in history, SUNY, Binghamton, 1967. With Niagara Gazette, NY, 1970—83; pub. Binghamton Press & Sun-Bulletin, 1983—84; v.p. N.E. region Gannett Co. Inc., 1984—85; pres., pub. Reno Gazette-Jour., 1985—2000; pres. Gannett West Gannett Co. Inc., 1985—94, sr. group pres. Pacific Newspaper Group, 1994—2005; chmn. & CEO Phoenix Newspapers, 2000—05; pub. Ariz. Republic, 2000—05; pres. Gannett Co. newspaper divsn., McLean, Va., 2005—. Bd. dirs. Harrah's Entertainment, Inc.; bd. visitors John S. Knight Fellowships for Profl. Journalists, Stanford U. Office: Gannett Co Newspaper Divsn 7950 Jones Branch Drive Mc Lean VA 22101*

CLARK-LANGAGER, SARAH ANN, curator, academic administrator; b. Lynchburg, Va., May 14, 1943; m. Craig T. Langager, 1979. BA in Art History, Randolph-Macon Woman's Coll., 1965; postgrad., U. Md., 1968; MA in Art History, U. Wash., 1970; PhD in Art History, CUNY, 1988. Assoc. edn. dept., lectr. Yale U. Art Gallery, New Haven, 1965-67, Albright-Knox Art Gallery, Buffalo, 1967-68; asst. to dir. Richard White Gallery, Seattle, 1969-70; curatorial asst. to curators painting and sculpture San Francisco Mus. Modern Art, 1970; assoc. edn. dept., lectr. Seattle Art Mus., 1971-73, 74-75; asst. curator, and then assoc. curator modern art, lectr. Seattle Art Mus., 1975-79; curator 20th century art, lectr. Munson-Williams-Proctor Inst., Utica, NY, 1981-86; asst. prof. art history, dir. Univ. Art Gallery, U. North Tex., Denton, 1986-88; dir. Western Gallery, curator outdoor sculpture collection Western Wash. U., Bellingham, 1988—, mem. adj. faculty, 1988—. Lectr., cons. in edn. NY Cultural Ctr., NYC, 1973-74; editl. asst. October, MIT Press, NYC, 1980; lectr. art history South Seattle C.C., 1975; lectr. 20th century art Cornish Inst. Fine Arts, Seattle, 1977-78; sole rep. for N.Y. State, Art Mus. Assn. Am., 1984-86; bd. dirs. Wash. Art Consortium, v.p., 1989-90, pres., 1990-93, acting pres., 1996, pres. 1990-93, 1999-2001, v.p. 1989-90, 2001-2003; cons. State of Wash. Save Outdoor Sculpture, 1994-2000, others. Contbr. articles to profl. jours.; curator exhbns., 1970—, including Rodney Ripps traveling exhbn., 1983, Sculpture Space: Recent Trends, 1984, Order and Enigma: American Art Between the Two Ward, 1984, Stars over Texas: Top of the Triangle, 1988, Public Art/Private Visions, 1989, Drawing Power, 1990, Focus on Figure, 1992, Chairs: Embodied Objects, 1993, Northwest Native American and First Nations People's Art, 1993, New Acquisitions, 1995, Stars and Stripes: American Prints and Drawings, 1995, Photographs from America, 1996, NW Artists' Books, 1999, Decades of Giving: Virginia Wright and Sculpture at Western, 1999, Surface Tension, 2003, A Sofa and., 2003, Noguchi & Dance, 2005, The Alt Vera Lesse Collection, W.Va., 2006, others; author: Master Works of American Art from the Munson-Williams-Proctor Institute, 1989, Audiophone Tour for Sculpture Collection-20 Interviews, 1991, The Outdoor Sculpture Collection: The Development of Public Art at Western, 2000, The Italian Period in Susan Bennerstoom, 2000, Sculpture in Place: A Campus as Site, 2002, Isamu Noguchi: Beyond Red Square, 2004. Recipient Woman of Merit in Arts award Mohawk Valley C.C. and YWCA, Utica, 1985; Kress Found. fellow U. Wash., 1970; Helena Rubenstein Found. scholar CUNY Grad. Ctr., 1980. Office: Western Wash U Western Gallery Fine Arts Complex Bellingham WA 98225-9068 Office Phone: 360-650-3963. Business E-Mail: sarah.clarklangager@wwu.edu.

CLARKSON, ADRIENNE, former Governor General of Canada; b. Hong Kong, 1939; m. John Ralston Saul. BA with honours, U. Toronto, MA in English Lit.; postgrad., Sorbonne, Paris. Host, writer, prodr. CBC TV, 1965-82; first agt.-gen. for Ont. Paris, 1982-87; pres, pub. McClelland & Stewart, 1987-88; exec. prodr., host, writer Adrienne Clarkson's Summer Festival, Adrienne Clarkson Presents, 1988-98; gov. gen. Govt. of Can., 1999—2005. Chair, bd. trustees Can. Museum of Civilization, Hull, Que.; pres. exec. bd. IMZ, Vienna; active numerous arts and charitable orgns. Exec. prodr., host CBC TV program Something Special, others; writer, dir. several films, Can. Named Officer of the Order of Can., 1992, Chancellor and Prin. Companion of the Order of Can., 1999. Office: 12A Admiral Rd Toronto ON Canada M5R 2L5 Office Phone: 416-964-2313. E-mail: ahouse12@rogers.com.

CLARKSON, ELISABETH ANN HUDNUT, volunteer; b. Youngstown, Ohio, Apr. 20, 1925; d. Herbert Beecher and Edith (Schaaf) Hadnut; m. William M. E. Clarkson, Sept. 23, 1950; children: Alison H., David B., Andrew E. AB, Wilson Coll., 1947, LHD, 1985; MA, SUNY, 1973, postgrad. With J. L. Hudson Co., Detroit, 1947-50; writer Minute Parade daily Sta. WGR, Detroit, 1948-50. Author: (book) You Can Always Tell a Freshman, 1949, An Adirondack Archive: The Trail to Windover, 1993; contbr. articles to profl. jours. Trustee Wilson Coll., Chambersburg, Pa., 1970—83, chmn. bd. trustees, 1979—82; collector, curator Graphic Controls Corp. art collection, 1976—83; active N.Y. State Mus., 1985—90; past chmn. jr. group Albright Knox Art Gallery; mem. Buffalo Art Commn., 1983—, chmn., 1990—96; sustainer Jr. League, 1983—; mem. exec. bd. arts adv. coun. SUNY, Buffalo, 1985—95; mem. cmty. adv. panel Niagara Frontier Transp. Authority, 1991—94; trustee Clarkson Ctr. Human Svcs., 1995—2000, Irish Classical Theatre Co., 1998—2004; mem. adv. bd. Tannery Pond Cmty. Ctr., North Creek, NY, 2002—; mem. Trinity Episcopal Ch., 1950—, Trinity Vestry, 1996—99, mem. cultural leadership group, 1994—96, 1998—2000; mem. racism commn. Episcopal Diocese of Western N.Y., 1989—92; mem. Companion of the Holy Cross, 1971—, companion-in-charge soc., 1985—90; bd. dirs. Buffalo Mus. Sci., 1972—87, 1990—96, Bischoff Clarkson Hudnut Corp., North Creek, NY, 1973—83, Windover Corp., 1997—, pres., 1998—2001; bd. dirs. N.Y. State Mus. Assn., Albany, 1985—90; adv. bd. dirs. North Creek R.R. Mus., 2003—. Recipient Trustee award for disting. svc., Wilson Coll., 1983, award in the arts, NCCJ, 1998. Mem.: Buffalo Club (art and archives com. 2004—), Sloane Club (London), Buffalo Tennis and Squash Club, Garret Club (bd. dirs. 2000—03, pres. 2001—02). Home: 156 Bryant St Buffalo NY 14222-2003: Log house Windover North Creek NY 12853

CLARKSON, KELLY BRIANNE, singer; b. Burleson, Tex., Apr. 24, 1982; d. Steve Clarkson, Jeanne and Jimmy Taylor (Stepfather). Winner inaugural Am. Idol contest, 2002; 2d place World Idol contest, 2004. Singer: (albums) Thankful, 2003 (Reached #1 on the Billboard Charts, 2004), Breakaway, 2004, (songs) Before Your Love/A Moment Like This, 2002 (Billboard best selling single of yr.), Because of You, 2004 (MTV Video Music award for Best Female Video, 2006); actor: (films) Issues 101, 2002, From Justin to Kelly, 2003; singer: (films) Love Actually, 2003, Ella Enchanted, 2004, The Princess Diaries 2: Royal Engagement, 2004. Co-recipient Song Writer award for Miss Independent (with Rhett Lawrence), ASCAP, 2004; recipient Best Female Video and Best Pop Video for Since U Been Gone, MTV Video Music Awards, 2005, Favorite Adult Contemporary Artist, Am. Music Awards, 2005, Favorite Female Performer, People's Choice Awards, 2006, Best Pop Vocal Album, Grammy awards, 2006, Best Female Pop Vocal Performance, 2006, Choice Music: Female Artist, Teen Choice Awards, 2006. Office: RCA Records 1540 Broadway New York NY 10036*

CLARKSON, PATRICIA, actress; b. New Orleans, Dec. 29, 1959; d. Buzz and Jackie Clarkson. Student, La. State U.; B in Theatre Arts, Fordham U., 1982; MFA, Yale U. Actor: (films) The Untouchables, 1987, The Dead Pool, 1988, Rocket Gibraltar, 1988, Everybody's All-American, 1988, Tune in Tomorrow, 1990, Jumanji, 1995, Pharaoh's Army, 1995, High Art, 1998, Playing by Heart, 1998, Simply Irresistable, 1999, Wayward Son, 1999, The Green Mile, 1999, Joe Gould's Secret, 2000, Falling Like This, 2000, The Pledge, 2001, Wendigo, 2001, The Safety of Objects, 2001, Welcome to Collinwood, 2002, Far from Heaven, 2002, Heartbreak Hospital, 2002, The Baroness and the Pig, 2002, Pieces of April, 2003 (Acad. award nomination for best supporting actress, 2004), All the Real Girls, 2003, The Station Agent, 2003, Dogville, 2003, Miracle, 2004, The Woods, 2005, The Dying Gaul, 2005, Good Night, and Good Luck, 2005, The Woods, 2006, All the King's Men, 2006; (TV films) The Old Man and the Sea, 1990, Legacy of Lies, 1992, An American Story, 1992, Four Eyes and Six-Guns, 1992, Blind Man's Bluff, 1992, Caught in the Act, 1993, She Led Two Lives, 1994, London Suite, 1996, Wonderland, 2002, Carrie, 2002; (TV series) Davis Rules, 1991, Murder One, 1995—96; (TV miniseries) Queen, 1993, (TV guest appearance) Six Feet Under, 2001—05 (Emmy for outstanding guest actress in a drama series, 2002), Frasier, 2001, (stage appearances) A Cheever Evening, 1993, Raised in Captivity, 1995, Three Days of Rain, 1997, The Maiden's Prayer, 1998, Streetcar Named Desire, 2004.*

CLARY, INEZ HARRIS, music educator; b. Portsmouth, Va., June 3, 1918; d. Ambrose Edward and Annie Eula Harris; m. Salone Clary, Oct. 18, 1936; children: Salone T., Margaret Elizabeth Clary Gray. BS in Music Edn., Norfolk State U., 1962; MS in Music Edn., Va. State U., 1973. Organist, choir dir. Bank St. Bapt. Ch., Norfolk, 1945—84; instr. piano Norfolk State U., 1954—64; tchr. music Norfolk Pub. Schs., Va., 1962—82. Mem. exec. bd. Choir Dirs./Organist Guild Hampton Univ. Mins. Conf. Mem.: Music Educators Nat. Conf., Order of Ea. Star (mem. Mt. Hermon chpt. #19), Alpha Kappa Alpha. Democrat. Baptist. Home: 2 Vaughn Ct Portsmouth VA 23701

CLARY, ROSALIE BRANDON STANTON, timber farm executive, civic worker; b. Evanston, Ill., Aug. 3, 1928; d. Frederick Charles Hite-Smith and Rose Cecile (Liebich) Stanton; m. Virgil Vincent Clary, Oct. 17, 1959; children: Rosalie Marian Hawley, Frederick Stanton, Virgil Vincent, Katheleen Clary Gorman. BS, Northwestern U., 1950, MA, 1954. Tchr. Chgo. Pub. Schs., 1951-61; faculty Loyola U., Chgo., 1963; v.p. Stanton Enterprises, Inc., Adams County, Miss., 1971-89; timber farmer, trustee Adams County, Miss., 1975—. Author Family History Record, geneaology record book, Kenilworth, Ill., 1977—. Lectr. Girl Scouts U.S., Winnetka, Ill., 1969-71, 78-86, Cub Scouts, 1972-77; badge counselor Boy Scouts Am., 1978-87; election judge Rep. Com., 1977—; vol. Winnetka Libr. Geneaology Projects Com., 1995—. Mem. Nat. Soc. DAR (Ill. rec. sec. 1979-81, nat. vice chmn. program com. 1980-83, state vice regent 1986-88, state regent 1989-91, rec. sec. gen. 1992-95, state parliamentarian 1999—), Am. Forestry Assn., Forest Farmers Assn., North Suburban Geneal. Soc. (governing bd. 1979-86, 99—, pres. 1997-99), WInnetka Hist. Soc. (governing bd. 1978-90, 95—), Internat. Platform Assn., Delta Gamma (mem. nat. cabinet 1985-89). Roman Catholic. Home: 509 Elder Ln Winnetka IL 60093-4122 Office: PO Box 401 Kenilworth IL 60043-0401

CLARY, WENDY ANNE, principal; b. St. Louis, Aug. 20, 1952; d. Paul Joseph and Carol Mae Wiesler; m. Dale Allan Clary; children: Jason, Benjamin. BA with high honors, U. Ill., Champaign, 1970—73; MA with high honors, Bradley U., Peoria, Ill., 1993. Phys. edn. tchr. Peoria Heights HS, Ill., 1974—77; perm. sub. tchr. Peoria Dist. #150, Ill., 1980—88; tchr. Father Sweeney Gifted Sch., Peoria, Ill., 1988—94; asst. prin. Mossville Sch., Ill., 1994—96, prin., 1996—. Gifted coord. Ill. Valley Sch. Dist., Chillicothe, 1994—; basketball coach Peoria Heights HS, Ill., 1974—77; tnr. for gifted edn. Ill. State Bd. Edn., Springfield, 1999—. Chmn. Race for the Cure, Peoria, Ill.; bd. dirs. Jr. League Peoria, Ill.; pres. U. Ill. Mother's Assn., Champaign, 1996—2003. Recipient 25 Women in Leadership Award, Peoria C. of C., 2000, Oustanding Tchr. Award, Woodruff HS, 1994. Mem.: Ill. Prin. Assn., Ill. Assn. Gifted Children, Phi Kappa Phi, Phi Lambda Theta. Office: Mossville Elem Sch 12207 N Old Galena Rd Mossville IL 61552

CLASTER, JILL NADELL, academic administrator, history educator; d. Harry K. and Edith Lillian Nadell; m. Millard L. Midonick, May 24, 1979; 1 child from previous marriage, Elizabeth Claster (dec.). BA, NYU, 1952, MA, 1954; PhD, U. Pa., 1959. Instr. history U. Pa., 1956-58; instr. ancient and medieval history U. Ky., Lexington, 1959-61, asst. prof., 1961-64; adj. asst. prof. classics NYU, N.Y.C., 1964-65, asst. prof. history, 1965-68, assoc. prof., 1968-84, prof., 1984—, acting undergrad. chmn. history, 1972-73, dir. M.A. in liberal studies program, 1976-78; assoc. dean Washington Sq. and Univ. Coll., 1978, acting dean, 1978-79, dean, 1979-86; dir. Hagop Kevorkian Ctr. for Near Eastern Studies, NYU, 1991-96. Appointee N.Y.C. Commn. on Status of Women. Author: Athenian Democracy: Triumph or Travesty, 1967, The Medieval Experience, 1982; Contbr. articles to profl. jours. Danforth grantee, 1966-68; Fulbright grantee, 1958-59 Mem. Am. Hist. Assn., Medieval Acad. Am. Home: 161 W 15th St New York NY 10011-6720 Office: NYU Dept History 53 Washington Sq S Dept History New York NY 10012-1098 Office Phone: 212-243-4445. Business E-Mail: jill.claster@nyu.edu.

CLAUS, CAROL JEAN, small business owner; b. Uniondale, N.Y., Dec. 17, 1959; d. Charles Joseph and Frances Meta (Fichter) C.; m. Armand Joseph Gasperetti, Jr., July 7, 1985. Student pub. schs., Uniondale. Asst. mgr. Record World, L.I., NY, 1977-82; mgr. Info. Builders Inc., N.Y.C., 1982-92; pres. Carol's Creations, Belen, N.Mex., 1994—2002, Friendly Vending, 2002—; adminstrv. asst. III U. N.Mex., Valencia, 2001—. Sec. bd. dirs. Tierra Grande Improvement Assn., 2001—. Mem. NAFE, NOW. Democrat. Office Phone: 505-925-8921. E-mail: cclaus@unm.edu.

CLAUSELL, DEBORAH DELORIS, artist; b. Mobile, Ala., July 16, 1951; d. Stephen Joseph and Estell Abney Clausell. BA in Sociology, U. Mobile, Ala., 1976; cert., Barbizon Modeling Sch., 1984. Movie extra Century Casting, Santa Monica, Calif., 1984—85; libr. Mobile Pub. Libr., 1996-97. Exhibited in group shows Greater Gulf State Fair, Mobile, 1990, 96 (3d, 2d and 1st prize ribbons), 1997 (3rd prize ribbon), 1999, 2005 (3d prize), Mercy Med. Gallery, Daphne, Ala., 1993, Mus. of City of Mobile, 1993, Fine Art Mus. of the South, Mobile, 1993, Spring Hill Art, Mobile, 1993, Greater Gulf State Fair Exhibit Fine Arts, 1999, Monticello-Thomas Jefferson Meml., 1993; pvt. collection The White House, Heritage Hall, 2000 and Art Auction, Energen Corp. Artpark Exbhn., 2001, Greater Gulf State Fair (Fine Art 3d prize), 2005 Mem. Smithsonian Inst., 2001, USS Constn. Mus., 2002, U.S. Border Control, 2003. 2d lt. USAF, res. Recipient Gold Eagles and Stars Letters from U.S. Pres. Bush, 2001, 3d prize fine art dept., Greater Gulf State Fair, 2005. Mem. VFW, Internat. Platform Assn., Nat. D-Day Mus., U.S. Naval Inst., Libr. Congress Assn., Nat. Trust for Hist. Preservation, Civil War Trust, Mt. Vernon Ladies Assn., Navel League, Preservation Alliance. Democrat. Roman Catholic. Avocations: classic guitarist, harmonica, swimming, vocal singing, reading. Home: 5859 Reams Dr N Mobile AL 36608-3652

CLAUSEN, JEANNE LORRAINE, musician; b. LA, Oct. 16, 1944; BA, Sarah Lawrence Coll., 1967; MA in Music, Cleve. Inst. Music, 1972. Mem. Calif. New Music Ensemble, L.A., 1975—78; mem. trio in residence Claremont Grad. Sch., Calif., 1976—79; concert mistress Ensemble Concerto, dir. Roberto Gini, Milan, 1983—86; mem. Amsterdam Baroque Orch., dir. Ton Koopman, Netherlands, 1986—87; founder, 1st violin La Cetra, San Francisco, 1982—2002. Author: Something Has Been Lost In the Passage of Time, (video) The Rhapsodic Art Of The Ancients. Esoteric Christian. Achievements include research on 16th century stringed instrument lira da braccia. Avocations: hiking, swimming, reading, good conversation, enjoying the mystical beauty of nature. Home: PO Box 2603 Nevada City CA 95959 Personal E-mail: jeannelc@earthlink.net.

CLAUSER, SUZANNE PHILLIPS, author, screenwriter; b. New Rochelle, N.Y., Aug. 25, 1929; d. Leonard Stanley and Elizabeth Louise (Jones) Phillips; m. Charles Edward Clauser, Aug. 28, 1951. BA, Ind. U., 1951. Research asst. econs. dept. Ind. U., Bloomington, 1951-57; freelance writer fiction and TV, 1963—2002. Author: (novel, TV movie) A Girl Named Sooner, 1972, (TV spls. mini-series) Little Women, 1978, Pride of Jesse Hallam, 1981 (Writers Guild award 1981), Calamity Jane, 1983 (Western Heritage award Cowboy Hall of Fame 1983), Christmas Snow, 1985 (San Francisco Internat. Film Festival award). Recipient Christopher award, 1978, 81. Mem. ACLU, People for the Am. Way.

CLAUSS-EHLERS, CAROLINE S., psychologist, educator, journalist; b. Manhasset, NY, July 17, 1967; d. Harold Wilson and Carole (Page) Clauss; m. Julian Charles Edward Clauss-Ehlers; children: Isabel S., Sabrina S. BA with honors, Oberlin Coll., 1989; MA, Columbia U., 1992, EdM, 1993, PhD, 1999. Bilingual clinician Henry St. Settlement, Cmty. Consultation Ctr., N.Y.C., 1992-96; clin. interviewer N.Y. State Psychiat. Inst., N.Y.C., 1995-98; predoctoral intern in clin. psychology NYU Med. Ctr./Bellevue Hosp., N.Y.C., 1996-97; columnist HOY, 2002—; psychologist pvt. practice, 2000—. Adj. asst. prof. psychology and edn. Tchr. Coll., Columbia U., 1998—2001; asst. prof. counseling psychology Rutgers U. Grad. Sch. Edn., 2001—; guest correspondent Univision, 2002—; cons. in field. Author: Diversity Training for Classroom Teaching: A Manual for Students and Educators, 2006; co-editor: Community Planning to Foster Resilience in Children, 2004; contbr. articles to profl. jours. Oberlin Alumni scholar, 1992; Tchrs. Coll. scholar, 1994-96; Leopold Schepp Found. fellow, 1994-97; Rosalynn Carter fellow for mental health journalism, 2004-05. Mem. APA, N.Y. State Psychol. Assn., Assn. Hispanic Mental Health Profls. Office: Rutgers U 10 Seminary Pl New Brunswick NJ 08901 Office Phone: 732-932-7496 ext 8312. Business E-Mail: csce@rci.rutgers.edu.

CLAUSSEN, EILEEN BARBARA, environmental services administrator, former federal agency administrator; b. N.Y.C., June 9, 1945; d. Louis and Elsie (Young) Lerner; children: Hillary Anne, Geoffrey David. BA, George Washington U., 1966; MA, U. Va., 1967. Systems analyst USN, Washington, 1967-68; cons. Booz, Allen & Hamilton, Inc., Washington, 1968-69; asst. dir. ctr. for comml. devel. Boise Cascade Corp., Washington, 1969-72; various mgmt. positions Office of Solid Waste U.S. EPA, Washington, 1972-83, dir. characterization and assessment div., 1984-87, dir. atmospheric & indoor air programs, 1987-93, acting dep. asst. adminstr. air & radiation, 1988-89, dep. asst. adminstr. Office Air & Radiation, 1990—91; spl. asst. to Pres., sr. dir. global environ. affairs NSC, Washington, 1993—96; asst. sec. oceans, internat. environment & science affairs US Dept. State, Washington, 1996—98; pres. Pew Ctr. on Global Climate Change, Arlington, Va., 1998—. Bd. dirs. Environ. Law Inst., Coun. Fgn. Rels., China Coun. for Internat. Cooperation on Environ. & Devel.; commr. Pew Ocean Commn. Recipient Career Achievement award, US Dept. State, Meritorious Exec. award for Sustained Superior Accomplishment, Disting. Exec. award for Sustained Extraordinary Accomplishment, Fitzhugh Green award for Outstanding Contributions to Internat. Environ. Protection. Office: Pew Ctr on Global Climate Change 2101 Wilson Blvd Ste 550 Arlington VA 22201

CLAWSON, AMY K., music educator; b. Mount Vernon, Ohio, Sept. 11, 1974; d. Edward Miles and Kayla Sue Clawson. BA, Mt. Vernon Nazarene Coll., Ohio, 1996. Cert. educator Ohio Bd. Edn., 1996. Music educator South Ctrl. Schs., Greenwich, Ohio, 1997—98; elem. music educator North Fork Local Schs., Utica, 1998—. Music dir. and prodn. worker Mt. Vernon Players, Inc., Ohio, v.p., 2005—06. Mem.: Ohio Music Educators Assn., Ohio Educators Assn.

CLAWSON, JUDITH LOUISE, middle school educator; b. Cleve., Nov. 24, 1938; d. Frank Anthony and Bettie (Cerny) Lisy; m. Robert Wayne Clawson, June 25, 1961; children: Deborah Marie, Gregory Scott. BS in Edn. magna cum laude, Bowling Green State U., 1960; postgrad., UCLA, 1961-65, Kent State U., 1976-80. Cert. secondary sch. math. tchr. Elem. tchr. Long Beach (Calif.) Unified Sch. Dist., 1960-61, L.A. Unified Sch. Dist., 1961-65, Stow (Ohio) City Schs., 1969-78, middle sch. math. tchr., 1978—97; ret., 1997. Cons., presenter in field. Recipient Cert. of Recognition, Martha Holden Jennings Foudn., 1987. Mem. ASCD, AAUW, NEA, LWV, Nat. Coun. Tchrs. of Math., Stow Tchrs. Assn., Ohio Edn. Assn., Ohio Coun. Tchrs. of Math., Delta Gamma (fin. advisor Kent State U. chpt. 1978-90, pres. alumnae chpt. 1987-89, 91-93, Pres.'s award 1987, housing dir. at-large nat. coun. 1997-2001), Kappa Delta Pi. Republican. Methodist. Avocations: golf, tennis, skiing, scuba diving, reading. Home: 7336 Westview Rd Kent OH 44240-5912

CLAXTON, HARRIETT MAROY JONES, language educator; b. Dublin, Ga., Aug. 27, 1930; d. Paul Jackson and Maroy Athalia (Chappell) Jones; m. Edward B. Claxton, Jr., May 27, 1953; children: E. B. III, Paula Jones. AA with honors, Bethel Woman's Coll., 1949; AB magna cum laude, Mercer U., Macon, Ga., 1951; MEd, Ga. Coll., 1965. Social worker Laurens County Welfare Bd., Dublin, 1951-56; HS tchr. Dublin, 1961-66; instr. Mid. Ga. Coll., Cochran, 1966-71, asst. prof. English, lit. and speech, 1971-85, assoc. prof., 1985-86, adj. prof., 1987—; rsch. tchr. Trinity Christian Sch., 1986, 92, sr. English tchr., 1986-87; ret., 1987. Instr. Ga. Coll., 1987, E. Ga. Coll., 1988—99; weekly columnist Dublin Courier Herald, 1995—. Author: (book) History of Laurens Superior Court; editor: Laurens County History, II, 1987; contbr. articles to profl. jours. and newspapers; anchor Dublin Poetry Club TV 35, 1990—. Pres., chmn. bd. Mensea/Laurens unit Am. Cancer Soc., 1995—; sec. Am. Assn. Ret. Persons, 1987—90; v.p. Dublin Cmty. Concert, 1991—98; mem. preservation com. Hardy Smith House, 1998—2000; chmn. Dublin Historic Rev. Bd., 1986—; bd. dirs. Friends Vets., Heart Ga. Altamaha Regional Devel. Ctr., 1998, sec., 2002—; bd. dir. Laurens County Libr., Dublin-Laurens Arts Coun., 2001—. Named Woman of the Yr., St. Patrick's Festival, Dublin, 1979, Most Popular Tchr., Dublin Ctr., 1985, Olympic Torch Bearer, 1996; recipient Outstanding Svc. award, Cancer Soc., Dublin, 1985, 1993, 1998, Outstanding Alumni award for cmty. svc., Ga. Coll., 1996. Mem.: UDC (chaplain 1999—), DAR (regent, vice regent, historian, state, dist., nat. awards), Ga. Press Assn., Dublin Assn. Fine Arts (pres. bd. 1974—76, 1982—84, 1990—98, 2001—03), Dublin Hist. Soc. (pres. 1976—78, 1995—98, bd. dirs. 1998—), Continental Soc. Daus. Indian Wars, Erin Garden Club (pres.), Woman's Study Club (pres.), U.S. Daus. of 1812, Daus. Colonial Wars (sec. 2004—), Daus. Am. Colonists (sec. 2004—), Delta Kappa Gamma, Chi Delta Phi (sec.), Phi Theta Kappa (treas.), Alpha Delta Pi (Middle Ga. alumni chpt. 1999—, scholarship plaque 1950), Sigma Mu. Democrat. Baptist. Home: 101 Rosewood Dr Dublin GA 31021-4129

CLAY, CAROL ANN, family nurse practitioner; BSN, Radford U., 1990; MSN, Old Dominion U., 1995. RN Va., cert. clin. specialist, Am. Nurse's Credentialing Ctr., family nurse practitioner, Am. Acad. Nurse Practitioners. RN charge nurse Southside Regional Med. Ctr., Petersburg, Va., 1990; RN staff nurse Culpeper (Va.) Meml. Hosp., 1990-91; RN charge nurse W.S. Hundley Annex, South Hill, Va., 1991; charge nurse, house supr. Brian's Ctr., Lawrenceville, Va., 1991-92; PN, NA instr. Southside Va. C.C., Alberta, 1991-95, 97-98; RN PRN pool Cmty. Meml. Health Ctr., South Hill, 1993-97, family nurse practitioner urgent care, 1997-98, family nurse practitioner occupl. health svcs., 1998—. Mem.: APHA, Am. Acad. Nurse Practitioners. Avocations: reading, rescuing abandoned animals. Home: 19491 Highway One Brodnax VA 23920-2247 Office: Cmty Meml Health Ctr 412 Bracey Ln South Hill VA 23970-1431 Office Phone: 434-774-2541. E-mail: cclay@cmh-sh.org.

CLAY, CYNTHIA JOYCE, writer, editor-in-chief; b. Cedar Falls, Iowa, Aug. 4, 1957; d. James Hubert and Delight Clay; m. Guillermo Jose Ramon, Jan. 7, 1987. Attended, Nat. Theater Inst., 1978; BA cum laude, Brandeis U., 1979; MFA, U. Ga., 1979. Editor-in-chief Oestara Pub. LLC, Key Biscayne, Fla., 2004—. Author: Vector Theory and the Plot Structures of Literature and Drama, (novels) Zollocco: A Novel of Another Universe (Eppie Sci. Fiction finalist, 2001), The Romance of the Unicorn, (short stories) New Myths of the Feminine Divine; editor: The Oestara Anthology of Pagan Poetry, 2006 (Eppie winner best poetry, 2006); actor: The First Loebner Prize Competition Touring Test, Lulu, Marriage of Figaro, Has Washington Got Legs?. Mem.: Electronically Pub. Internet Connection. Democrat. Avocations: travel, swimming, reading. Home: 575 Sabal Palm Dr Key Biscayne FL 33149 Personal E-mail: cynthia@oestarapublishing.com.

CLAYBURGH, JILL, actress; b. NYC, Apr. 30, 1944; d. Albert Henry and Julia (Door) C.; m. David Rabe, Mar., 1979; 2 children. BA, Sarah Lawrence Coll., 1966. Former mem., Charles Playhouse, Boston; Broadway plays include A Naked Girl on the Appian Way, 2005; Off-Broadway plays include The Nest; Broadway debut in The Rothschilds, 1970; stage appearances include In the Boom Boom Room (David Rabe), Design for Living (Noel Coward), Barefoot in the Park, 2006, The Busy World Is Hushed, 2006; film appearances include The Wedding Party, 1969, The Telephone Book, 1971, Portnoy's Complaint, 1972, The Thief Who Came to Dinner, 1973, The Terminal Man, 1974, Gable and Lombard, 1976, Silver Streak, 1976, Semi-Tough, 1977, An Unmarried Woman, 1978, Luna, 1979, Starting Over, 1979, It's My Turn, 1980, First Monday in October, 1981, I'm Dancing as Fast as I Can, 1982, Hannah K, 1983, In Our Hands, 1984, Where Are The Children, 1986, Shy People, 1987, Beyond the Ocean, 1990, Whispers in the Dark, 1992, Le Grand Pardon II, 1992, Rich in Love, 1993, Naked in New York, 1994, Fools Rush In, 1997, Going All the Way, 1997, Never Again, 2001, Vallen, 2001, Running with Scissors, 2006; appeared in TV films Snoop Sisters, 1972, The Art of Crime, 1975, Hustling, 1975, Griffin and Phoenix, 1976, Miles to Go., 1986, Who Gets the Friends?, 1988, Fear Stalk, 1989, Unspeakable Acts, 1990, Reason for Living: the Jill Ireland Story, 1991, Trial: The Price of Passion, 1993, Firestorm: A Catastrophe in Oakland, 1993, For the Love of Nancy, 1994, Honor Thy Father and Mother: The True Story of the Menendez Brothers, 1994, The Face on the Milk Carton, 1995, When Innocence is Lost, 1997, Sins of the Mind, 1997, Crowned and Dangerous, 1998, My Little Assassin, 1999, Phenomenon II, 2003; TV documentary: Ask Me Anything: How to Talk to Kids About Sex, 1989; TV series: Frasier, 1993, Ally McBeal, 1997, Trinity, 1998, Everything's Relative, 1999, Leap of Faith, 2002. Recipient Best Actress award for An Unmarried Woman, Cannes Film Festival; Golden Apple award for best film actress in An Unmarried Woman. Office: 12424 Wilshire Blvd Ste 1000 Los Angeles CA 90025-1071*

CLAYPOOL, NANCY, social worker; b. Monterey, Calif., Aug. 6, 1957; d. Harold Herbert and Nancy Jeanne (Klohe) C.; 1 child, James Paul. BA in Social Welfare cum laude, San Francisco State U., 1980; M Social Work, U. Calif., Berkeley, 1985. Lic. ind. social worker. Program developer Women's Found., San Francisco, 1984-85; foster care coord., house supr. Charila Svcs. for Girls, San Francisco, 1985-87; therapist Sierra Clinic, San Francisco, 1987-88; clin. social worker Youth Homes, Inc., Walnut Creek, Calif., 1988-90; homebased early childhood devel. tchr. Thurgood Marshall Family Resource Ctr., Oakland, Calif., 1990-92; psychiat. social worker Eden Med. Ctr., Castro Valley, Calif., 1992-94; chief clinician, primary therapist Transitions Geropsychiatry Alameda (Calif.) Hosp., 1994-96; program dir. transitions geopsychiatry Alameda (Calif) Hosp., 1996-97; cons. to orgns. serving sr. citizens-clin. social workers Washington Twp. Hosp., Fremont, Calif., 1997-98; spl. edn. social worker and therapist Deming (N.Mex.) Pub. Schs., 1998—. Contbr. articles to profl. publs. Mem. Alameda County Mental Health Bd., 1992-95, chair, 1993-94, vice chair, 1994-95. Named Regional Clinician of Yr., Horizon Mental Health Svcs., 1994; Health-Social Networking grantee, 1984. Mem. Nat. Assn. Social Workers, Internat. Platform Assn. (appointee 1995).

CLAYSON, CAROL ANNE, meteorologist, educator; m. Tristan Johnson; children: Johann Johnson, Anders Johnson. BS, Brigham Young U., 1988; MS, U. Colo., 1990, PhD, 1995. Asst. prof. earth and atmospheric scis. dept. Purdue U., West Lafayette, Ind., 1995—2001, assoc. prof., 2001—02; assoc. prof. meteorology Fla. State U., Tallahassee, 2002—, dir. Geophys. Fluid Dynamics Inst., 2003—. Mem. Bd. Atmospheric Scis. and Climate NRC, Washington, 2005—, mem. panel on water cycle and water, 2005—; chmn. SEAFLUX project Global Energy and Water Cycle Experiment, Silver Spring, Md., 2005—. Author: Small Scale Processes in Geophysical Fluid Flows, 2000, Numerical Modeling of Oceans, 2000. Recipient Career award, NSF, 1996, Presdl. Early Career award for scientists and engrs., Pres. Clinton, Nat. Sci. and Tech. Coun., 2000, Young Investigator award, Office Naval Rsch., 2000. Mem.: Am. Meteorol. Soc. (com. on interaction of the sea and atmosphere 2000—05). Office: Fla State U Dept Meteorology 404 Love Building Tallahassee FL 32306-4520 Office Phone: 850-644-0922. Office Fax: 850-644-9642.

CLAYTON, CAROL A., lawyer; b. Aug. 11, 1958; BA, Univ. Utah, 1979; JD, Univ. Va., 1982. Bar: DC 1982. Ptnr., environ. law practice Wilmer Cutler Pickering Hale & Dorr, Washington, asst. mng. ptnr., mem. mgmt. com. Editor (articles): Va. Jour. Natural Resources Law; contbr. chapters to books;

co-author: Environ. Auditing Handbook. Office: Wilmer Cutler Pickering Hale & Dorr 2445 M St NW Washington DC 20037 Office Phone: 202-663-6650. Office Fax: 202-663-6363. Business E-Mail: carol.clayton@wilmerhale.com.

CLAYTON, DIANE, education educator; b. Denver, May 4, 1950; d. William Alexander and Barbara Jean (Kimber) C.; m. Stephen Vincent Metz. BA in History, Macalester Coll., 1973; MA in South Asian Studies, U. Wis., 1978, MA in Libr. Sci., 1978. Prof., co-dir. Bush libr. Hamline U., St. Paul, 1978—. Mem. AAUP, Assn. Asian Scholars. Democrat. Office: Hamline University 1536 Hewitt Ave Saint Paul MN 55104-1284

CLAYTON, HEATHER LYNN, language educator; b. Lake Wales, Fla., Mar. 3, 1978; d. James Joseph Clayton and Kelly Sue Crain. BA in Elem. Edn., Anderson U., Ind., 2000. Cert. elem./secondary tchr. Ohio, Ind. Missionary Ch. of God, Quito, Ecuador, 2000—01; outdoor edn. tchr. Sky Ranches, Inc., Van, Tex., 2001—03; Spanish tchr. Greenon Local Schs., Springfield, Ohio, 2003—. Office Phone: 937-325-7343. Business E-Mail: hclayton@greenon.k12.oh.us.

CLAYTON, KATHERINE GAYLE, elementary school educator; b. Spokane, Wash., May 18, 1953; d. Mitchel Hollis Blackwood and Margaret Rasmussen; m. Melvin Edward Clayton; children: Kevin Edward, Kindra Gayle. BA in Edn., Ea. Wash. U., Cheney, Washington, 1974; MA in Sch. Adminstrn., U. Wash., Seattle, 1991. K-12 Education Certificate Wash. State, 1974. K-4 tchr. Ctrl. Valley Sch. Dist., Spokane, Wash., 1976—86; kindergarten tchr. Kennewick Sch. Dist., Kennewick, Wash., 1986; k-6 tchr. reading specialist Northshore Sch. Dist., Bothell, Wash., 1987—94; elem. prin. Monroe Sch. Dist., Monroe, Wash., 1994—98, Northshore Sch. Dist., Bothell, 1998—99, Cheney Pub. Schools, Wash., 1999—2006; exec. dir. Wash. State ASCD, Spokane, 2006—. Adj. faculty Seattle Pacific U., 1988—93. Recipient NEESPAW Disting. Prin. of the Yr., Assn. of Wash. Sch. Principals, 2004. Mem.: ASCD, NE Elem. Sch. Principals of Wash. (pres. and sec. 2000—04), Assn. Wash. Sch. Principals, Internat. Reading Assn. Home: 2825 S Chapman Rd Spokane WA 99016 Office: Washington State ASCD 2825 S Chapman Rd Spokane WA 99016 Office Phone: 509-893-2907. Personal E-mail: kclaytonwsascd@aol.com. E-mail: kclaytonwsascd@cheneysd.org.

CLAYTON, MARLA COOPER, speech pathology/audiology services professional; b. Roanoke Rapids, NC, May 1, 1973; d. Lawrence Gibson and Martha Solomon Cooper; m. Sean Decatur Clayton, June 18, 2005. BA, NC Ctrl. U., Durham, NC, 1995; MEd, NC Ctrl. U., 2000. Lic. Speech Pathology NC. Speech pathologist Durham Pub. Sch., Durham, NC, Alamance-Burlington Sch., Burlington, NC, Halifax County Schs., Halifax, NC, Operation Breakthrough/Durham Head Start, Durham, NC; legal asst. Glaxo Smith Kline, Inc., Rsch. Triangle Pk., NC. Mem.: NC Assn. Speech Pathologist, Delta Sigma Theta. Avocations: travel, exercise, rollerskating. Office: Durham Pub Sch PO Box 30002 Durham NC 27702

CLAYTON, PAMELA SANDERS, special education educator; b. Sulphur Springs, Tex., Feb. 8, 1952; d. Carl Louis Sanders, Jr. and Beatrice Coletha Sanders; children: Chad, Cicely. BS, East Tex. State U., 1974, MEd, 1991. Kindergarten cert., mental retardation cert. Tchr. Saltillo ISD, 1976—77, resource specialist, tchr., 1977—80, Lamar Elem. Sch., Sulphur Springs, 1980—98, Sulphur Springs H.S., 1998—. Dir. student coun., uil prose & poetry dir., taas tutorial coach Sulphur Springs H.S., 1999—2002. Actor: (plays) A Christmas Carol, 1997 (Best Supporting Actress, 1998); singer: (concert) N.E. Tex. Choral Soc., 1998. Mem. allocation com. Hopkins County United Way, Sulphur Springs, 2000—01; bd. dirs. Lakes Regional MHMR, Terrell, Tex., 1997—, Sulphur Springs Pub. Libr., 1994—96. Mem.: Tex. Classroom Tchrs., Delta Kappa Gamma. Methodist. Avocations: poetry, rollercoaster riding, reading, piano. Home: 404 Lamar St Sulphur Springs TX 75482 Office: Sulphur Springs ISD 1200 Connally St Sulphur Springs TX 75482 Office Fax: (903)439-6116. Personal E-mail: pclayton@ssisd.net.

CLAYTON, VERNA LEWIS, retired state legislator; b. Hamden, Ohio, Feb. 28, 1937; d. Matthews L. and Yail (Miller) Lewis; m. Frank R. Clayton, Feb. 4, 1956; children: children: Valerie S., Barry L. Office mgr. Village of Buffalo Grove, Ill., 1972-78, village clk., 1971-79, village pres., 1979-91; mem. Ill. Ho. of Reps., Springfield, 1993-99. Bd. dirs. Savannah Lakes Property Owners Assn., 2000, pres., 2004. Mem. Lake County Solid Waste Planning Agy., chmn. tech. com., chmn. agy., Nat. League of Cities, chmn. transp. and comms. steering com.; bd. govs. SC Patients Compensation Fund, 2005—; mem. Rep. Com. McCormick County; dist. legis. officer U.S. Power Squadrons. Recipient Disting. Svc. award Amvets, 1981; named Libr. Legislator of the Yr. 1997. Mem. N.W. Mcpl. Conf. (pres. 1983-84), Chgo. Area Transp. Study Coun. Mayors (vice chmn. 1981-83, chmn. 1985-91), Mcpl. Clks. Ill. (treas. 1978-79), Mcpl. Clks. Lake County (pres. 1977-78), Ill. Mcpl. League (bd. dirs., v.p. 1985-90, pres. 1989-90), Buffalo Grove Rotary Club (hon. mem.), Buffalo Grove C. of C. (bd. dirs.). Republican. Methodist. Home: 11 Overlook Pt Mc Cormick SC 29835-2850 E-mail: vclayton@wctel.net.

CLAYTON, XERNONA, media executive; b. Muskogee, Okla., Aug. 30, 1930; d. James Brewster; m. Paul L. Brady. BS with honors, Tenn. State U., 1952; postgrad., U. Chgo. Cert. tchr. Ill., Calif. Tchr. pub. schs., Chgo., Los Angeles; with So. Christian Leadership Conf., Atlanta; host Sta. WAGA-TV, Atlanta, 1967-79; with Sta. WTBS-TV, Atlanta, 1979—, host, producer, 1981-82, coordinator of minority affairs, 1982—, corp. v.p. of urban affairs; corp. v.p., cons. Turner Broadcasting Sys. Inc. Guest lectr. Harvard U.; appointed Motion Picture and TV Commn., Ga., commr. Bd. Review, Appellate Bd. of unemployment compensation. Author: (with Ed Clayton) The Peaceful Warrior. Coordinated Doctors' Com. for Implementation, Atlanta; bd. trustees Martin Luther King, Jr. Ctr.; bd. dirs Nat. Assn. Advancement Colored People, Multiple Sclerosis Soc., Sci. and Tech. Mus. Atlanta, Nat Assn Sickle Cell Disease; mem. Nat. Issues Forum of Jimmy Carter Presidential Library. U. Chgo. scholar; recipient numerous awards including Bronze Woman of the Year, 1969, President's award Nat. Conf. Mayors, 1983, Communications Woman of Achievement award Am. Women in Radio and TV, 1984-85, The Kizzy award, 1979, Humanitarian award, Hillside Internat. Truth Ctr., 1986, Acad. Women Achievers, YWCA, 1986, American Spirit award USAF Recruiting Service, 1987; Xernona Clayton Scholarship named in her honor by the Am. Intercultural Student Exchange, 1987-90; featured on cover of The New York Time Mag.; cited for her accomplishments by Ebony, Town & Country, Georgia Mags. Mem. Nat. Assn. Media Women (pres.), Alpha Kappa Alpha. Baptist. Office: Turner Broadcasting One CNN Center Atlanta GA 30303

CLAYTON-DODD, VALERA JO, health facility administrator; b. Anthony, Kans., Dec. 29, 1943; d. Garnett George and Pauline E. (Fowler) Clayton; m. R.M. Hardesty, July 2, 1965 (div. May 1987); children: Andrew Jay, Stacey Renee; m. Marvin Dodd, Aug. 8, 1991. BSN, Kans. U., 1965; MS in Adminstrn., Ctrl. Mich. U., 1990. RN, Kans., La. Supr. Wichita (Kans.)-Sedg County Health Dept., 1965-68; staff RN Grant County Health Dept., Ulysses, Kans., 1973-75; team leader Hutchinson (Kans.) Clinic, PA, 1979-89; dir. oncology Mt. Carmel Med. Ctr., Pittsburg, Kans., 1989-92; oncology program coord. St. Francis Med. Ctr., Cape Girardeau, Mo., 1992-93, dir. oncology Monroe, La., 1993-95; COO St. Francis Specialty Hosp., Monroe, 1995—. Bd. dirs. Am. Cancer Soc., Monroe, 1989-98. Mem. ANA (dist. bd. mem. 1997—), Am. Coll. Healthcare Execs. (cert. health care exec.), Oncology Nursing Soc. (cert. oncology nurse), La. Assn. Nurse Execs., Sigma Theta Tau. Republican. Episcopalian. Avocations: quilting, reading, working with team building using myers briggs type inventory (mbti). Office: St Francis Specialty Hosp Box 1532 309 Jackson St Monroe LA 71201-7407

CLAZIE, MELISSA A, literature and language educator; b. Caldwell, Idaho, Feb. 1, 1959; d. Juanita Y. and DeArmon D. Jones (Stepfather); m. Thomas P. Clazie, Aug. 8, 2003; children: Jason E. Fisher, Valerie J. Fisher. AA, Mesa CC, Ariz., 1993; BA in Secondary Edn. English, Ariz. State U., 1995; MA in Tchg., Nat. U., 2003. 8th grade lang. arts tchr. Sanders Mid. Sch., Sanders, Ariz., 1996—97; English tchr. Coachella Valley H.S., Thermal, Calif., 1997—2000; English and AP English tchr. La Sierra HS, Riverside, Calif., 2000—. Office: La Sierra HS 4145 La Sierra Ave Riverside CA 92505 Office Phone: 951-351-9235. Business E-Mail: crazieclazie@yahoo.com.

CLEAGE, PEARL MICHELLE, writer, playwright, journalist; b. Springfield, Mass., Dec. 7, 1948; d. Albert B. Clege Jr. and Doris (Graham) C.; m. Michael Lomax, 1969 (div. 1979); 1 child, Deignan Njeri Lomax; m. Zaron W. Burnett Jr., 1994. Student, Howard Univ., Washington, DC; BA in Drama, Spelman Coll., Atlanta, 1971. Faculty Spelman Coll.; press secy. speechwriter Mayor Maynard Jackson, Atlanta. Contbr. articles to Atlanta Jour. Constitution, Atlanta Tribune; co-founder, editor Catalyst, literary journ.; author (self-published vol.): Mad at Miles: A Blackwoman's Guide to Truth, 1990; author: The Brass Bed, 1991, (collection of essays) Deals with the Devil and Other Reasons to Riot, 1993, (novels) What Looks Like Crazy on an Ordinary Day, 1997 (NY Times Bestseller list, Oprah Book Club selection, 1998, BCALA Lit. award), I Wish I Had a Red Dress, 2001, Some Things I Thought I'd Never Do, 2003, Babylon Sisters, 2005, Baby Brother's Blues, 2006, (plays) Blues for an Alabama Sky, 1995, Flyin' West, 1992, Bourbon at the Border, 1997. Recipient Bronze Jubilee award for lit., 1983, Outstanding Columnist award, Atlanta Assn. Black Journalists, 1991. Office: Spelman College 350 Spelman Ln SW Atlanta GA 30314*

CLEARO, KELLIE ANNE, internist, pharmacist, psychiatrist; b. Syracuse, NY, Nov. 10, 1969; d. Albert Martin Clearo and Carmen Delia Vazquez. BS in Pharmacy, U. Fla., Gainesville, 1993; MD, U. Wash., Seattle, 2000. Pharmacist Rite-Aid, Seattle, 1994—2000; resident in internal medicine and psychiatry SUNY, Bklyn., 2000—02, Duke U., Durham, NC, 2002—05; physician Emory Hosp., Atlanta, 2005—. Mem.: Am. Coll. Physicians, Am. Psychiat. Assn., Am. Pharmacist Assn. Office: Emory U Hosp Clifton Rd Atlanta GA 30307 Business E-Mail: kellie.clearo@emoryhealthcare.org.

CLEARWATER, YVONNE A., psychologist; BA in Psychology summa cum laude, Calif. State U., Long Beach; PhD in Psychology, U. Calif., Davis. Sr. prin. investigator, rsch. psychologist NASA Ames Rsch. Ctr., Moffett Field, Calif., testbed devel. mgr., govt. industry liaison, info. designer, project mgr. Human Exploration Demonstration Project, design rsch. psychologist. Mem. panels Internat. Conf. Environ. Sys.; mem. sci. adv. com. Nat. Space Soc.; NASA rep. to Broad Alliance for Multimedia Tech. and Applications; lectr. Stanford U., U. Calif.; lectr. in field. Exec. prodr. SAE Human Modeling Tech. Standards Com.; contbr. articles to profl. jours. Recipient Nat. Human Environ. award Am. Soc. Interior Designers, 1989. Mem. Nat. Acad. TV Arts and Scis. (bd. govs. No. Calif. chpt.). Avocation: painting. Office: NASA Ames Rsch Ctr MS 269-1 Moffett Field CA 94035 Business E-Mail: yclearwater@mail.arc.nasa.gov.

CLEARY, BEVERLY ATLEE (MRS. CLARENCE T. CLEARY), writer; b. McMinnville, Oreg., Apr. 12, 1916; d. Chester Lloyd and Mable (Atlee) Bunn; m. Clarence T. Cleary, Oct. 6, 1940; children: Marianne Elisabeth, Malcolm James. BA, U. Calif., 1938; BA in Librarianship, U. Wash., 1939; LHD (hon.), Cornell Coll., 1993. Children's librarian Pub. Libr., Yakima, Wash., 1939-40; post librarian U.S. Army Regional Hosp., Oakland, Calif., 1942-45. Author: Henry Huggins, 1950, Ellen Tebbits, 1951, Henry and Beezus, 1952, Otis Spofford, 1953, Henry and Ribsy, 1954, Beezus and Ramona, 1955, Fifteen, 1956, Henry and the Paper Route, 1957, The Luckiest Girl, 1958, Jean and Johnny, 1959, The Real Hole, 1960, Hullabaloo ABC, 1960, 98, Two Dog Biscuits, 1961, Emily's Runaway Imagination, 1961, Henry and the Clubhouse, 1962, Sister of the Bride, 1963, Ribsy, 1964, The Mouse and the Motorcycle, 1965, Mitch and Amy, 1967, Ramona the Pest, 1968, Runaway Ralph, 1970, Socks, 1973, (play) The Sausage at the End of the Nose, 1974, Ramona the Brave, 1975, Ramona and Her Father, 1977 (Newbery Honor Book award ALA 1978), Ramona and Her Mother, 1979, Ramona Quimby, Age 8, 1981 (Newbery Honor Book award ALA 1982), Ralph S. Mouse, 1982, Dear Mr. Henshaw, 1983 (ALA Notable Book citation 1984, John Newbery medal 1984), Ramona Forever, 1984, Lucky Chuck, 1984, The Ramona Quimby Diary, 1984, Beezus and Ramona Diary, 1986, Janet's Thingamajigs, 1987, The Growing Up Feet, 1987, A Girl from Yamhill: A Memoir, 1988, Muggie Maggie, 1990, Strider, 1991, Petey's Bedtime Story, 1993, My Own Two Feet: A Memoir, 1995, Ramona's World, 1999. Recipient Disting. Alumna award U. Wash., 1975, Laura Ingalls Wilder award ALA, 1975, Regina medal Cath. Libr. Assn., 1980, De Grummond award U. Miss., 1982, U. So. Miss. medallion, 1982, Hans Christian Andersen medal nominee, 1984, Nat. Medal of the Arts, 2003, Libr. of Congress Living Legent medal, 2003. Mem. Authors Guild of Authors League Am. Office: c/o Harper Collins Children's Books 1350 Sixth Ave New York NY 10019-4702

CLEARY, MANON CATHERINE, artist, retired art educator; d. Frank and Crystal (Maret) C. Attended, U. Valencia, Spain, Cocoran Sch. Art; BFA, Washington U., St. Louis, 1964; MFA, Temple U., 1968. Instr. fine arts SUNY, Oswego, 1968-70; from instr. to assoc. prof. D.C. Tchrs. Coll., Washington, 1970-78; from assoc. prof. to prof. art U. DC, Washington, 1978—2004, 2005, ret., 2005. One woman shows include Mus. Modern Art Gulbenkian Found., Lisbon, Portugal, 1985, Iolas/Jackson Gallery, NYC, 1982, Osuna Gallery, Washington, 1974, 77, 80, 84, 89, Univ. D.C., 1987, Tyler Gallery SUNY at Oswego, 1987, J. Rosenthal Fine Arts, Washington, 1991, Addison/Ripley Gallery, Washington, 1994, 99, Md. Arts Pl., 1997, Kramer Book Afterwords, 1998, Pass Gallery, Washington, 2000, others; group exhibits include Twentieth Century Am. Drawings: The Figure in Context, Traveled Nat. Acad. Design, 1984-85, Butler Inst. Am. Art, Youngstown, Ohio, 1987, Art Inst. Chgo., 1999-00, Huntsville (Ala.) Mus., 1987, Boca Raton (Fla.) Mus. Art, 1987, Corcoran Gallery Art, Washington, 1987, 96, Dimock Gallery, Washington, 1987, Tretyakov Gallery, Moscow, 1990, Nohra Haime Gallery, N.Y.C., 1994, Holter Mus., Helena, Mont., 1996, Gallery Stendahl, NYC, 1996, Alt. Mus., NYC, 1996, Kasteyev Mus., Almaty, Kazakstan, 1996, Alouan Gallery, Almaty, 1997, Art Inst. Chgo., 1999-2000, RAP, Rockville, Md., 2000-01, Nat. Mus. Women in the Arts, Washington, 2000, Wadell Gallery, Sterling, Va., 2005, Corcoran Arthe Warehouse Gallery, Washington, C.C., 2005, Nat. Drawing Invitational Travelling Show, 2005—, others; artist-in-residence Herning Hojskole, Denmark, 1980, Ucross Found., Wyo., 1984, Bridge Assn., Creative Lab. Project, Almaty, 1996, 97. Recipient Mayor's 14th ann. award for excellence in an artistic discipline, 1998; individual artist grantee D.C. Commn. on the Arts, 2000-01. Mem. Coll. Art Assn., Pi Beta Phi. Office Phone: 202-297-5072. Personal E-mail: manonart@aol.com.

CLEAVE, MARY L., environmental engineer, former astronaut; b. Southampton, N.Y., Feb. 5, 1947; BS in Biol. Scis., Colo. State U., 1969; MS in Microbiol. Ecology, Utah State U., 1975, PhD in Civil and Environ. Engring., 1979. Mem. rsch. staff Utah State U., 1971-80; astronaut NASA, Lyndon B. Johnson Space Ctr., Houston, 1980-90, mission specialist STS 61-B, 1985, mission specialist STS-30, 1989; now dep. project mgr. NASA Ocean Color Satellite Program, Greenbelt, Md. Mem. Tex. Soc. Profl. Engrs., Water Pollution Control Fedn., Sigma Xi, Tau Beta Pi. Office: NASA Headquarters 300 E St SW Washington DC 20024-3202

CLEAVINGER, LAURIE A., science educator; d. Lyle Arthur and Sharon Lee Metz; m. John K. Cleavinger, Aug. 12, 1978; children: Sheryl, Catherine, Karl. BS, St. Mary Coll., Leavenworth, Kans., 1978; MA, U. Kans., Lawrence, 1984; ABD, Kans. State U., Manhattan, 2006. Cert. tchr. Kans. Sci. tchr. Unified Sch. Dist. #342, McLouth, Kans., 1978—. Adj. faculty St. Mary Coll, Leavenworth, 1989—91, Highland C.C., Highland, Kans., 1985; QuarkNet lead tchr. Kans. State U., 2003—06; conf. presenter in field. Project leader 4-H, Leavenworth County, 1980—99; music minister Sacred Heart Ch., Tonganoxie, Kans., 1980—2006. Named Employee of the Yr., Unified Sch. Dist. 342, 1997, Dist. Tchr. of the Yr., 2005. Mem.: NSTA, NEA (local bldg. rep. 2005—06), Kans. Assn. Tchrs. Sci. (bd. dirs. 2006), Phi Kappa Phi. Office: McLouth HS 217 Summit Mc Louth KS 66054 Office Phone: 913-796-6122. E-mail: cleavingerl@mclouth.org.

CLEGG, CYNDIA SUSAN, literature educator; d. Wayne Daniel and Virginia May Clegg; m. Michael McClave Wheeler, Dec. 17, 1977; 1 child, Caitlin Wheeler. PhD, UCLA, 1976, AB, MA. Disting. prof. English Pepperdine U., Malibu, Calif., 1978—. Author: (scholarly monograph) Press Censorship in Eliabethan England, (cultural history) Press Censorship in Jacobean England; editor: (facsimile edition) Peaceable and Prosperous Regiment of our Blessed Queen Elizabeth; contbr. articles to profl. jours. Sec. Friends of the Huntington Libr., San Marino, Calif., 1996—2000. Scholars Exch. fellow, Brit. Acad., 1996, 2003, Rsch. fellow, Bibliographical Soc. Am., 2002. Mem.: Pacific Ancient and MLA (assoc.; pres. 2004—05, exec. dir. 1990—2000), Shakespeare Assn. Am. (assoc.). Office: Pepperdine University 24255 Pacific Coast Hwy Malibu CA 91105 Office Phone: 310-506-4225. Business E-Mail: cclegg@pepperdine.edu.

CLEGG, DIXIE STALLINGS, art educator, studio owner; d. Hart Leon and Miriam Thurston Stallings; m. Charles Richard Clegg, Mar. 21, 1966; children: Marty, Brian, Heidi, Andrea, Jeremy, Melanie, Kimberly. BFA in Ballet, U. Utah, Salt Lake City. Owner, dir. Dixie Stallings Sch. of Ballet, Salt Lake City, 1961—72; showroom model NYC, 1964; tchg. assoc. in ballet U. Utah, Salt Lake City, 1967—68; dancer Jimmy Durante Variety Show, Utah and Calif., 1968, 1969; dancer, singer LA Civic Light Opera, 1969, The Dean Martin TV Show (NBC), Burbank, Calif., 1969; mem. Handshake Tour USO, Vietnam, 1969; instr. dance aerobics Aerobic Acad. and The Dance Co., Salt Lake City, 1979—93; owner, dir. The Dance Co., 1982—. Choir dir. LDS Ch., Salt Lake City, 1999—2006; vocalist Stallings Sisters Trio, Salt Lake City. Dancer Utah Civic Ballet, 1961—65. Named one of 10 Best Dressed, U. Utah, 1964—65. Mem.: AGVA, AFTRA, Actors Equity. Office: The Dance Co 2121 E 2100 S Salt Lake City UT 84109 Office Phone: 801-486-4933. Fax: 801-583-1111. E-mail: dixieclegg@hotmail.com.

CLEGG, KAREN KOHLER, lawyer; b. Junction City, Kans., Jan. 7, 1949; d. John Emil and Delores Maxine (Letkeman) Kohler; m. Stephen J. Clegg Jr., Mar. 28, 1970. BS, Emporia State U., 1970; JD, U. Kans., 1975; MBA, Rockhurst Coll., 1989. Bar: Kans. 1975, U.S. Dist. Ct. Kans. 1975, Mo. 1977, U.S. Dist. Ct. (we. dist.) Mo. 1977. Asst. atty. gen. State of Kans., Topeka, 1975-77; atty. The Bendix Corp., Kansas City, Mo., 1977-81, sr. atty., 1981-84; counsel Allied Corp. (now Allied Signal, Inc.), Kansas City, 1984-90, v.p. adminstrn., 1990—93, v.p. field svcs. Columbus, Md., 1994—95, v.p. ops. Kansas City, 1995—2001; pres. Honeywell Fed. Mfg. and Technologies Honeywell Internat., 2001—02, v.p. def. and space programs, Honeywell Aerospace; ret. Mem. council human resources mgmt. adv. bd. Commerce Clearing House, Chgo., 1985-88. Sec. Assn. Greater Devel. Coll. Blvd., Shawnee Mission, Kans., 1986-87; bd. dirs. adv. council Avila Coll. Bus., Kansas City, 1984—, Dimension's Unltd., Kansas City, 1985-86. Mem. ABA, Mo. Bar Assn., Am. Soc. Personnel Adminstrn. (v.p., bd. dirs. EEO 1985, profl. services 1986-87), Greater Kansas City C. of C. (centurian leadership program). Avocations: music, theater, art, reading, travel. Office: Honeywell 2000 E 95th St Kansas City MO 64131-3030 Home: 6909 Burnt Sienna Cir Naples FL 34109-7828

CLELAND, GLADYS LEE, academic administrator, adult education educator; b. Schenectady, Feb. 27, 1959; d. Anthony John and Anna Mae (Feight) Campana; m. Michael Joseph Cleland, Aug. 4, 1984. BA in Communications and Edn. cum laude, SUNY, Plattsburgh, 1981; MA summa cum laude, U. Fla., 1986; MS summa cum laude, Syracuse U., 1994. Asst. instr. communications SUNY, Plattsburgh, 1982-83, admissions/media rels. advisor, 1987-88; asst. instr. communications U. Fla., Gainesville, 1985-86; instr. English and communications Clinton Community Coll., Plattsburgh, 1986-87; news cons., acad. liaison Sta. WCFE-TV, Plattsburgh, 1987-88; pub. info. dir. Syracuse (N.Y.) U., 1989-93, pub. rels. coord., 1993-94; spl. projects mgr. SUNY Health Sci. Ctr., Syracuse, 1994-96. News. cons. Sta. WCFE-TV 57, Plattsburgh, 1987-88; producer, rschr. CVPH Med. Ctr., Plattsburgh, 1982-87; freelance talent Sta. WIXT-TV 9, Syracuse, 1988—; press steward Winter Olympic Games, lake Placid, N.Y., 1980; radio announcer, news reporter, sales rep. Sta. WIRY-AM, Plattsburgh, 1980-83; freelance producer, news reporter Sta. WPBT-TV, Miami, Fla., 1983-84. Author: Satellite News Gathering, 1986. Recipient broadcast awards N.Y. State Broadcast Assn., Plattsburgh, 1982-84, Outstanding Talent award Internat. TV Assn., Gainesville, 1986. Mem. Women in Comms. (Woman of Yr. award, 1994), Broadcast Educators Assn., Coll. Media Advisors, RTNDA, Pub. Rels. Soc. Am., Syracuse Press Club, Omicron Delta Kappa, Phi Kappa Chi. Roman Catholic. Avocations: gardening, boating, reading. Home: 4239 Mill Run Rd Liverpool NY 13090-1813 Office: SUNY 103 Charleton Hall Morrisville NY 13408

CLEM, KATHY, artist; b. San Francisco, Apr. 30, 1950; d. David Azael and Olga (Butter) Vallejo; m. Lee Clem, June 25, 1972. AS in Chemistry, Canton Agrl.-Tech. Coll., 1971; BS in Chemistry, Rochester Inst. Tech., 1977, MFA in Painting, 1988. Analytical chemist Eastman Kodak Co., Rochester, N.Y., 1971-77, rsch. chemist, 1977-79; grad. asst. in painting Rochester Inst. Tech., 1986-88. Bd. dirs. Pyramid Arts Ctr., Rochester, 1990— One-woman shows include Strasenburgh Planetarium, Rochester Mus. and Sci. Ctr., 1990, The Link Gallery, Rochester, 1993, Adams Gallery, Dunkirk, N.Y., 1991, City Ctr. Gallery, Rochester Inst. Tech., 1992; retrospective Wilson Arts Ctr., Rochester, 1993, Kathy Clem Studio and Gallery, Rochester, 2005; exhibited in group shows Multi Media Arts Gallery, N.Y.C., 1994, Shirley Fitterman Gallery, N.Y.C., 1995, Rochester Inst. Technology, 2002, NTID Dyer Arts Ctr. Rochester Inst. Tech., 2006; represented in permanent collections Rochester Mus. & Sci. Ctr., ARC, Rochester, Spectrum Color Labs, Rochester, Nazareth Coll., Rochester. Recipient President's Purchase award Nazareth Coll., Rochester, 1985. Mmem. Above and Below (founder, pres. 1991-93), Artist Breakfast Group, Arts for Greater Rochester, Phi Theta Kappa. Home: 8 Ten Eyke Cir Pittsford NY 14534-3140 Studio: 250 Goodman St N Rochester NY 14607-1100

CLEM, SARAH LYNN, special education educator; b. Houston, Oct. 5, 1971; d. Russell Clark Sutton and Dina Jemison Smith; m. Chris Turner Clem, Dec. 16, 1995; children: Seth Turner, Amy Elyse. BSc, Sam Houston State U., 1995; MA, Western N.Mex U., 2005. Cert. Elem., Spl. Edn., English (grades 1-8) State Dept. Tex., 1995, Elem., and Spl. Edn. Pub. Edn. Dept. N.Mex, 1996, Early Childhood Edn. State Dept., Tex., 2001. Presch. tchr. Lordsburg Mcpl. Schs., N.Mex., 1996—99, spl. edn. tchr., 2002—03, lead spl. edn. tchr., 2003—04, spl. edn. coord., 2004—05, iep facilitator, 1998—99, prin. adv. com., 1998—99, Christmas play dir., 2002, positive behavior support team, 2002—04, student asst. team coord., 2002—05, girl power facilitator, 2004—05, adminstrv. team, 2004—, elem. prin., spl. edn. dir., 2005—06; coord. sect. 504 Sierra Blanca Schs., Lordsburg Mcpl. Schs., 2003—; tchr. Sierra Blanca Schs., Tex., 2000—02, one act play dir., 2001, supt. adv. com., 2001—02; prin. R.V. Traylor Elem., 2005—. Leader Girl Scouts Am., Lordsburg, 1997—99; vacation bible sch. tchr. United Meth. Ch., Sierra Blanca, Tex. and Lordsburg, N.Mex, 1998—2004, vacation bible sch. dir., 1998—2004; co-chmn. Adminstrn. Bd., Lordsburg, 2003—05, edn. chmn., 2003—05. Olive Marlowe Smithson scholarship, Western N.Mex U., 2003, Preschool Inclusion grant, Pub. Edn. Dept., 2004, Least Restrictive Environment grant, Pub. Edn. Dept., NM, 2004, Least Restrictive Environment/Positive Behaviro Support grant, 2005—06. Mem.: Delta Kappa Gamma (second v.p. 2003—04, scholarship 2003), Zeta Tau Alpha (treas., rush chmn., jud. chmn., house mgr. 1992—95, White Rose nominee 1995), Beta Sigma Phi (treas., pres. 1997—2000, Woman of Yr. 2000, 2002). R-Consevative. Methodist. Avocations: exercise, reading. Office: Lordsburg Municipal Schs PO Box 430 Lordsburg NM 88045 Office Phone: 505-542-3252. Business E-Mail: sclem@lmsed.org.

CLEMENCE, CHERYL LYNN, systems administrator; d. Robert H. and Carolyn Marie Clemence. BS, Mt. Union Coll., Alliance, Ohio, 1987; MPH, U. Miami, Fla., 1990; MBA, U. Miami, 1993. Sr. rsch. assoc. dept. psychiatry and behavioral scis. U. Miami, 1990—94, sr. database tech. specialist, 1994—2000; mgmt. info. sys. and quality improvement dir. U. Miami Behavioral Health, 2000—. Contbr. articles to profl. jours. Mem.: Mensa,

Beta Gamma Sigma. Democrat. Methodist. Avocations: travel, music, reading, computers. Office: U Miami Behavioral Health PO Box 016960 (M-861) Miami FL 33101 Office Phone: 305-243-3169. Office Fax: 305-243-3098.

CLEMENS, BRENDA, medical/surgical nurse, educator; b. Zanesville, Ohio, Aug. 7, 1962; d. Philip and Darliss (Barr) M. BSN, Ohio State U., 1985, MS, 1992; postgrad., U. St. Francis, 2003. Cert. FNP-C, Am. Acad. Nurse Practitioners, 2003; endocrinology nurse practiitioner Ind. Med. Assocs. Diabetes nurse specialist Luth. Diabetes Treatment Ctr., Fort Wayne, Ind., 1993—2000; pediat. diabetes nurse specialist Luth. Children's Hosp., Fort Wayne, 2000—04; nurse practitioner endocrinology dept. Ind. Med. Assocs., Fort Wayne, 2005—. Clin. asst. prof. pediat. dept. nursing Ind. U.-Purdue U., Fort Wayne, 2004—06. Mem. Am. Diabetes Assn., Am. Assn. Diabetes Educators, Ind. Three Rivers Assn. Diabetes Educators, Juvenile Diabetes Assn., Coalition Advanced Practice Nurses Ind. E-mail: clem003@comcast.net, brendaclemens@verizon.net.

CLEMENS, ROSEMARY A., health facility administrator, foundation administrator; m. Mitchel Greenfield Garren, Aug. 30, 1985. BA, St. John's U., 1966; MA, NYU, 1968, PhD, 1973. Assoc. prof. Fordham U. Sch. Social Work and Edn., N.Y.C., 1973—83; dir. strategic planning and mktg. NY Hosp., N.Y.C., 1983—88; clin. instr. Cornell Med. Coll., Dept. Pub. Health, N.Y.C., 1983—88; dir. AIDS and adolscent awareness project Women's City Club, N.Y.C., 1988—92; dep. dir. NY State Inst. Basic Rsch. Devel. Disabilities, S.I., 1992—96; devel. and program dir. Skin Cancer Found., N.Y.C., 1996—98; pres., CEO N.Y. divsn. Prevent Blindness Am., N.Y.C., 1998—2001; CEO N.Y.Children's Vision Coalition, N.Y.C., 2001—. Author: (book) Lessons to be Learned - Adolescents and AIDS (Cmty. Achievement Award - NYS Optometric Assn, 2004). Bd. mem. Cmty. Bd. #1, Women's City Club, UN Assn., NYC, 1975—2005; rsch. assoc. Gov. Nelson A. Rockefeller Presdl. Campaign, 1968—69, Mayor John Lindsay's Adminstrn., N.Y.C., 1973—75; dir. decentralization studies State Sen. Roy M. Goodman Commn. on N.Y.C. Governance, 1975—77; rsch. asst. Ford Found., 1968. Mem.: Cosmopolitan Club of NY (pub. affairs com. 1997—99). Avocations: travel, reading, gardening, theater, interior decorating. Home: 7 Lexington Ave New York NY 10010 Office: NY Children's Vision Coalition 33 West 42nd St New York NY 10036 Home: 110 Atlantic Ave Palm Beach FL 33480 Office Phone: 212-997-3550. Personal E-mail: rosemaryclemens@aol.com.

CLEMENT, BETTY WAIDLICH, retired literacy educator, consultant; b. Honolulu, Aug. 1, 1937; d. William G. Waidlich and Audrey Antoinette (Roberson) Malone; m. Tom Morris, Jan. 16, 1982; 1 child, Karen A. Brattesani. BA in Elem. Edn., Sacramento State U., 1960; MA in Elem. Reading, U. No. Colo., 1973, MA in Adminstrn., EdD in Edn. & Reading, 1980. Elem. sch. tchr. pub schs., Colo., Calif., 1960-66; reading specialist, title I European area U.S. Dependent Schs., various locations, 1966-75; grad. practicum supr. U. No. Colo. Reading Clinic, Greeley, 1976-77; grant cons. Colo. Dept. Edn., Denver, 1978-81; adult edn. tutor, cons. various orgns., Boulder, Colo., 1983-87; student tchr. supr. U. San Diego, 1989-90; adult literacy trainer for vols. San Diego Coun. on Literacy, 1988—2002; ret., 2002. Adj. prof. U. Colo., Denver, 1981-82, U. San Diego, 1994-1999; adj. prof. comm. arts Southwestern Coll., Chula Vista, Calif., 1990-99; presenter various confs. Co-author, editor: Adult Literacy Tutor Training Handbook, 1990, author rev. edit., 1998. Grantee Fed. Right-to-Read Office Colo. Dept. Edn., 1979, curriculum writing Southwestern Coll., 1992. Fellow San Diego Coun. on Literacy (chair coop. tutor tng. com. 1991-93); mem. Whole Lang. Coun. San Diego, Calif. Reading Assn. Avocation: psychology. E-mail: baclement@cox.net.

CLEMENT, EDITH BROWN, federal judge; b. Birmingham, Ala., Apr. 29, 1948; d. Erskine John and Edith (Burrus) Brown; m. Rutledge Carter Clement Jr., Sept. 3, 1972; children: Rutledge Carter III, Catherine Lanier. BA, U. Ala., 1969; JD, Tulane U., 1972. Bar: La. 1973. Law clk. to Hon. Herbert W. Christenberry U.S. Dist. Ct., New Orleans, 1973-75; ptnr. Jones, Walker, Waechter, Poitevent, Carrere & Denegre, New Orleans, 1975-91; judge U.S. Dist. Ct. (ea. dist.) La., New Orleans, 1991—2001, U.S. Ct Appeals (5th cir.), New Orleans, 2001—. Fellow La. Bar Found. (life); mem. Am. Law Inst., La. Bar Assn., Federalist Soc. Advisory Bd. Louisiana Chpt., Maritime Law Assn. U.S., Fed. Bar Assn., Am Inn Ct., Com. Admin. Office of the Judicial Conference of the U.S., 5th Cir. Judicial Coun, Tulane Law Sch. Inn of Ct. Office: US Ct Appeals 5th Cir 600 Camp Street Rm 200 New Orleans LA 70130-3313*

CLEMENT, EVELYN GEER, librarian, educator; b. Springfield, Mass., Sept. 1, 1926; d. Elihu and Helen (Schenck) Geer; m. J.R. Clement, Sept. 9, 1946 (div. 1972); children: James Randall, Timothy B., Susan Henson, Marc W., Audrey Ethriedge. BA with honors, U. Tulsa, 1965; MLS, U. Okla., 1966; PhD, Ind. U., Bloomington, 1975. Libr. Tulsa City-County Libr., 1960—66; learning resources libr. Oral Roberts U., Tulsa, 1966—68; spl. instr. U. Okla., Norman, 1966—70; prof., chmn. libr. sci. Memphis State U., 1972—85, dir. Ctr. for Instructional Svc. and Rsch., 1985—95, chmn. acad. senate, 1979—80, mem. faculty tenure and promotion appeals com., 1980—82, mem. standing univ. com. on libr., 1975—80, 1986—87, chmn. women's task force, 1984—85; ret., 1995. Regional trustee Geer Family Assn.; dir. media consortium Tenn. Regents, 1993—95. Editor: Bibliographic Control of Nonprint Media, 1972; contbr. articles to profl. jours. Treas. bd. adminstrn. Harvard Pk. Village Neighborhood Assn., 2005—. Doctoral fellow, U.S. Office Edn., Title II-B, Ind. U., 1968—71. Mem.: ALA, Afghanistan Perceivers, Pi Gamma Mu, Beta Phi Mu, Phi Alpha Theta. Republican. Avocations: microcomputers, needlepoint, exercise, reading. Home: 5206 S Harvard Ave #336 Tulsa OK 74135-3591 Personal E-mail: erren@aol.com.

CLEMENT, HOPE ELIZABETH ANNA, retired librarian; b. North Sydney, N.S., Can., Dec. 29, 1930; d. Harry Wells and Lana (Perkins) Clement. BA, U. King's Coll., 1951, D of Civil Law (hon.), 1992; MA, Dalhousie U., 1953; BLS, U. Toronto, 1955. With Nat. Library of Can., Ottawa, Ont., 1955-92, chief nat. bibliography div., 1966-70, asst. dir. research and planning br., 1970-73, dir. research and planning br., 1973-77, assoc. nat. librarian, 1977-92; ret., 1992. Editor: Canadiana, 1966—69. (Outstanding Svc. to Librarianship award 1992), Internat. Fedn. Libr. Assns. (medal 1991).

CLEMENTS, JANICE, science educator; PhD, U. Md. Prof. Johns Hopkins U. Sch. Medicine, Balt. Contbr. articles to profl. jours. Achievements include research on molecular basis of viral diseases - SIV model for AIDS. Office: Johns Hopkins U Sch Medicine Traylor G-60 720 Rutland Ave Baltimore MD 21205-2109 Fax: 510-955-9823. E-mail: jclement@bs.jhmi.edu.

CLEMENTS, LYNNE FLEMING, marriage and family therapist, application developer; b. Bklyn., Aug. 8, 1945; d. Daniel Gillies and Dorothy Frances (Zitzmann) Fleming; m. Louis Myrick Clements, Feb. 19, 1972; children: Ryan Louis, Glenn Fleming. BA in Sociology, Bradley Univ., 1967; MSW, Fordham Univ., 1973; post grad. studies, Columbia Univ., 1970-71; cert. in family therapy, Inst. for Mental Health Edn., 1990. LCSW NJ, cert. social work mgr. Computer programmer Employer's Comml. Union Group Ins. Co., Boston, 1967-69, Harvard Bus. Sch., Cambridge, Mass., 1969-70, Volkswagon of Am., Englewood Cliffs, NJ, 1971; psychiat. social worker Associated Cath. Charities Family and Children's Svc., Paramus, NJ, 1973-74, Christian Health Ctr., Wyckoff, NJ, 1976; owner, mgr. Wicker Wagon, Bergenfield, NJ, 1977-85; psychotherapist The Psychotherapy Counseling Ctr., Bergenfield, NJ, 1982-89; programmer analyst Atlas Computing Svc., Secaucus, NJ, 1984-86; program coord., family therapist Divsn. Family Guidance, Hackensack, NJ, 1986-91; pres. Corp. Family Resources, Ridgewood, NJ, 1989—; family therapist cons. Family Recovery of Valley View, White Plains, NY, 1992-94, Furman Clinic, Fair Lawn, NJ, 1995-96, Van Ost Inst. for Family Living, Englewood, NJ, 1996—; cert. social work mgr., 1997—. Part time family therapist NJ Ctr. Psychotherapy Inc., Ridgefield Pk., NJ, 1990. Chmn. curriculum enhancement com. Bergen County Acad. Advancement Sci. and Tech., NJ, 1992—96; chmn. entertainment Bergen County Children's Festival, 1993; founder, chmn. Bergenfield Coun. of the Arts, 1993; chmn., designer Bergenfield Coun. Arts, 1993—99, chmn. author and poet program, 1996—, Bergenfield Coun. of the Arts, 1996—; mem. fundraising com., arts programming chmn. Bergenfield Cmty. Ctr., 2000—; co-chmn. Bergenfield Film Festival, 2004—; co-chmn., designer Bergenfield A Taste of the Arts Festival, 2003—; sec. Mayor's Beautify Bergenfield Com., NJ, 1991—95; chmn. bd. cmty. play ctr. All Saints Ch., 1977—78, Sunday sch. tchr., 1982—89; mem. Twin Boro Youth Ministry Coun., 1989—. Recipient First and Second Pl. awards, Bergenfield Art Contest, 1980, Best Practice Award for Author/Poet Program, N.J. Dept. Edn., 2003; grantee NIMH, 1973. Mem.: NASW, AAUW, N.J. Coalition Mental Health Profl., N.J. Soc. Clin. Social Workers (bd. dir., chmn. mktg. and vendor 1999—2003, membership chmn. 2003—), N.J. Commerce and Indsl. Assn. (child care com. 1990—, human resources com. 1990—), Fordham U. Alumni Assn., Am. Orthopsychiatric Assn., Acad. Cert. Social Workers, Gifted Child Soc. (parent workshop coord. 1989—, bd dir.), Women of Accomplishments (founder, pres. 1990—, chmn. women's coalition conf. 1993—), Zonta (Amelia Earhart chmn. 1987—88, chmn. status women com. 1993—94, lit. com. 1995—). Episcopalian. Avocations: walking, art, music, crafts, boating, acting. Home: 148 Harcourt Ave Bergenfield NJ 07621-1917 Office: Corp Family Resources 15 Godwin Ave Ste 1 Ridgewood NJ 07450-3739 Office Phone: 201-670-0269. Personal E-mail: lynne.clements@att.net.

CLEMETSON, CHERYL PRICE, minister, consultant; b. Des Moines, Wash, Aug. 31, 1958; d. Herman B. and Vivian P. Price; children: Alexander Sekou, Sierra Christiana. BA, Am. U., Washington, 1980; MDiv, Colgate Rochester Div. Sch., 1985; PhD, Sch. Theology, Claremont, Calif., 1992. Ordained to ministry Bapt. Ch., 1985. Dir. edn. and outreach Christ Luth. Ch., Rochester, NY, 1985-87; devel. coord. Inst. Religion & Wholeness, Claremont, 1987-88; cons. 2d Bapt. Ch., LA, 1988; dir. christian edn. and youth 1st United Meth. Ch., Ontario, Calif., 1988-89; nat. black pastors fellow AAAS & Congress Nat. Black Ch., Washington, 1989-90; mgr. tech. svc. and comm. Congress Nat. Black Ch., Washington, 1990-92; min. discipleship Met. Bapt. Ch., Washington, 1992-99; co-founder, christian edn. cons. New Cmty. Bapt. Ch., Washington, 1992-99; project mgr. Interaction Action Com., Capitol Heights, Md., 1999; asst. to pastor and min. of Christian Ed. Mt. Zion Bapt. Ch., Seattle, 2000—. Instr. Sch. Divinity Howard U., Washington, 1993, 99. Contbr. articles to profl. jour. Vol. Jewels Ann Pvt. Day Sch., Washington, 1996-97, Woodmore Elem. Sch., 1999; mem. Mayor's Com. Teeanage Pregnancy, Washington, 1997—. Mem. Am. Acad. Religion, Alpha Kappa Alpha. Avocations: reading, writing short stories, developing educational material, travel, swimming.

CLEMONS, BARBARA GAIL, history educator; b. Bastrop, Tex., Mar. 27, 1956; d. Robert Simpson and Hattie Aldridge; m. Robert Clemons, Apr. 25, 1986; 1 child, Cheree; 1 child, Monique Duvall. Bachelors, Bishop Coll., 1977; Masters, Tex. State U., San Marcos, 1980. Cert. prin. Prairie View U., 2005. Tchr. Bastrop ISD, 1977—, team leader, 1981—91, dept. head, 1991—. Resdient BEAT Team Bastrop Intermediate Sch., 2004—05. V.p. Mission F Ch. Macedonia Bapt., Bastrop, 2000—04. Named Tchr. of Yr., Bastrop Intermediate, 1998, Walmart Tchr. of Yr., 2001, Cmty. Tchr. of Yr., 2002. Mem.: ATPE. Democrat. Baptist. Avocations: gardening, travel, camping. Home: 2013 Pecan St Bastrop TX 78602 Office: Bastrop ISD Intermediate Sch 509 Old Austin Hwy Bastrop TX 78602 Business E-Mail: bclemons@bastrop.isd.tenet.edu.

CLEMONS, JANE ANDREA, state legislator; b. Poughkeepsie, N.Y., Apr. 2, 1946; d. Mary (Longendyke) Martin; m. Michael R. Clemons, Oct. 15, 1966; children: Bret, Nick, Benjamin. Student, Moore Gen. Hosp., Grasmere, N.H., 1966. Nurse various orgns., Nashua, N.H., 1967-89; mem. N.H. Ho. of Reps., Dist. 31, Nashua, 1990—, dep. Dem. House leader, 2005; dep. Dem. leader N.H. Ho. of Reps.; 2nd vice chair N.H. Dem. State Party, 2005—; ranking dem. election law com. N.H. Ho. of Reps Sponsor Sr. Citizen Computer Health Care Program, Nashua, 1983-84; ward chair Dem. City Com., Nashua, 1988; del. Dem. State Conv., Nashua, 1988; vol. Merrimack (N.H.) Friars Club, 1990-92; del. State Dem. Pary, 1993, Dem. Nat. Conv., 2004; chmn. Nashua Dem. City Com. Greek Orthodox. Avocations: gardening, reading, camping. Home: 177 Kinsley St Nashua NH 03060-3649 Office: NH House Reps State House Concord NH 03301 E-mail: JCSR119@aol.com.

CLEMONS, JULIE PAYNE, telephone company manager; b. Attleboro, Mass., June 13, 1948; d. John Gordon and Claire (Paquin) P.; m. W. Richard Johnson, Oct. 10, 1970 (div. Oct. 1980); m. E.L. Clemons, Apr. 23, 1988; adopted son, Jason Corey. BS, U. RI, 1970. Svc. rep. New Eng. Tel., East Greenwich, RI, 1970-71, So. Bell, Jacksonville, Fla., 1971-73, bus. office supr., 1973-77, bus. office mgr., 1978-84, staff mgr. assessment, 1984-86, mgr. assessment ctr., 1987-89; dir. human resource assessment State of Fla., Jacksonville, 1987-89, Customer Svcs. Revenue Recovery Ctr., 1989-93, mgr. small bus. sales and svc., 1994-95, br. mgr. small bus. No. Fla., 1995-97; product support mgr. Small Bus. Mktg., 1997-98, sr. product support mgr., 1998-2000, project mgr. network and transport svcs., 2000-01, ISDN product mgr., 2001—02; ret., 2002. Substitute tchr. Gwinnett County Sch. Bd., 2003—04, Ga. Med. Inst., 2003—04; bus. mgr. Dr. Kenneth J. Sobel, MD, 2004—. Vol. Learn to Read; bd. dirs. Duval Assn. Retarded Citizens, Jacksonville, 1981-86, treas., 1983-84; Boy Scouts den leader, Pack 569, 2002-06; mem. Leadership Jacksonville, Class of '97; with Career Network Ctr. Adminstrn. St. Lawrence Ch., 2003-04. Mem. NAFE, Am. Mgmt. Assn., Pioneers of Am., Jacksonville C. of C. Roman Catholic. Avocations: gardening, water and snow skiing. Office Phone: 770-513-8686. Personal E-mail: jpc@bellsouth.net. Business E-Mail: julie@ksobelmd.com.

CLENDENNING, BONNIE RYON, college administrator; b. Quincy, Mass., Dec. 30, 1945; d. Edward George and Mildred Audrey (Raynor) Bottenus; m. Philip Hamlin Clendenning, May 18, 1968 (div. Dec. 1988); 1 child, Max Hamlin. BA, Smith Coll., Northampton, Mass., 1967; cert. degré supérieur, U. Paris, 1973; MA, Tufts U., 1986; JD, New Eng. Sch. of Law, 2000. Bar: Mass. 2001. Tchr. English as fgn. lang. Keyhan Sch. Journalism, Tehran, Iran, 1968-69; bookseller Oriental and African dept. Heffer's, Cambridge, Eng., 1969-72; documentalist Internat. Coun. Museums, UNESCO, Paris, 1972-73; head info. svcs. World Fedn. of Friends of Museums, Brussels, 1976-79; asst. dir. Fletcher Sch. Law and Diplomacy, Tufts U., Medford, Mass., 1980-83, dir. external rels., 1983-85, Tufts U. Sch. of Medicine, Boston, 1985-88, Boston U. Sch. Law, 1988-89; v.p. Univ. Hosp., Boston, 1989-92; v.p. coll. rels. Radcliffe Coll., Cambridge, Mass., 1993—, dean external rels., 1999—2001; v.p. ops. The Edn. Alliance, 2001—03; exec. dir. Archaeological Inst. of Am., 2004—. Mem. alumni coun. Tufts U.; bd. dirs. New Repertory Theatre, 2006—, Fuller Craft Mus., 2006—. Mem. Boston Club. Home: 23 Blake St Newtonville MA 02460-2005 Office: 656 Beacon St Boston MA 02215

CLEVELAND, BEVERLY K., art educator, realtor; b. Salina, Kans., Mar. 6, 1960; d. Larry Laverne and Ethel Harriet Knox; m. Blaine Eugene Cleveland, July 4, 1983; children: Dustin, Josh. BA in Art Edn., Marymount Coll, 1983; BA Elem. Edn., Marymount Coll., 1987; MA in Edn. Adminstrn., Kans. State Coll., 2004. ESL tchr. Unified Sch. Dist. #305, Salina, Kans., 1991—92, art tchr., 1992—; realtor Prudential Brokers Realty, Salina, 2000—02, Realty Assoc, Salina, 2003—04. Mem.: Soc. Decorative Painters, Kans. Nat. Edn. Assn. Republican. Avocations: painting, sewing, reading. Home: 4277 N Sandy Ave Salina KS 67401 Office: Unified Sch Dist 305 1511 Gypsum Salina KS 67401 Personal E-mail: justasec@ksbroadband.net.

CLEVELAND, MARY LOUISE, librarian, media specialist; b. Clarksdale, Miss., Dec. 4, 1922; d. George Washington and Beatrice (Orange) Jones; m. Chester Lloyd Cleveland, June 5, 1950 (div. 1973); 1 child, Ann. BS, Ala. State U., 1947; MLS, Case-Western Res. U., 1957; EdD, East Tex. State Coll., 1991. Asst. prof. libr. edn. Ala. State U., Montgomery, 1957-65; head libr. Talladaga (Ala.) Coll., 1965-66; asst. prof. Atlanta U., 1966-71; head libr. Wiley Coll., Marshall, Tex., 1971-77; assoc. prof. Ala. A&M U., Huntsville, 1977-83; dir. libr. Tex. Coll., Tyler, 1985—. So. Edn. Found. fellow, 1963, East Tex. State U. fellow, 1982-83. Democrat. Methodist. Avocations: writing, preparation of audio-visual materials. Home: 2508 Fieldcrest Dr NW Huntsville AL 35810-2122 Office: Tex Coll 2404 N Grand Ave Tyler TX 75702-1962 E-mail: marylcleveland@dell.com.

CLEVELAND, PEGGY ROSE RICHEY, cytotechnologist; b. Cannelton, Ind., Dec. 9, 1929; d. "Pat" Clarence Francis and Alice Marie (Hall) Richey; m. Peter Leslie Cleveland, Nov. 25, 1948 (dec. 1973); children: Pamela Cleveland Litch, Paula Cleveland Bertloff, Peter L. Cert., U. Louisville, 1956, B in Health Sci., 1984. Cytotechnologist cancer survey project NIH, Louisville, 1956-59; chief cytotechnologist Parker Cytology Lab., Inc., Louisville, 1959-75; mgr. cytology dept. Am. Biomed. Corp., 1976-78, Nat. Health Labs., Inc., Louisville, 1978-89; with various hosps. and labs., 1990—. Leader cytotechnologist del. to China, 1986; clin. instr. cytology Sch. Allied Health, U. Louisville, 1989; ptnr. Sham Star Stable thoroughbred horse breeding and racing. Mem. Am. Soc. Clin. Pathologist (cert. cytotechnologist), Internat. Acad. Cytology (cert. cytotechnologist), Am. Soc. Cytology (del.-person to person cytology delegation, amb. USSR 1990), Kentuckiana Cytology Soc., Cytology Soc. Ind., Horseman's Benevolent and Protective Assn. Democrat. Roman Catholic. Home: 8774 Lieber Hausz Rd NE Lanesville IN 47136-8522

CLEVELAND, STEPHANIE MCDOWELL, secondary school educator; b. Long Branch, NJ, Oct. 27, 1978; d. James and Margo Cowan; m. Marcus Antonio Cleveland, Feb. 8, 2003; 1 child, Mackenzie Jayden. Bachelors Degree, U. Houston, 2001. Cert. tchr. Tex., 2003. Tchr. Stephen F. Austin H.S., Sugar Land, Tex., 2001—. Office: Stephen F Austin High School 3434 Pheasent Creek Dr Sugar Land TX 77478 Office Phone: 281-634-2000. Office Fax: 281-634-2074. Personal E-mail: stephanie.cleveland@fortbend.k12.tx.us.

CLEVELAND, SUSAN ELIZABETH, library administrator, researcher; b. Plainfield, N.J., Mar. 14, 1946; d. Robert Astbury and Grace Ann (Long) Williamson; m. Stuart Craig Cleveland, Aug. 21, 1971; children: Heather Elizabeth, Catherine Elisa. BA, Rutgers U., 1968, MLS, 1969. Acquisitions libr. Jefferson U., Phila., 1970-71; biomed. libr. VA Hosp., Hines, Ill., 1972; med. cataloger U. Ariz., Tucson, 1973-74; dir. U. Pa. Hosp. Libr., Phila., 1974-87; exec. dir. Cleveland, Lamb, Urban Assocs., 1987-89; libr. dir. Mt. Sinai Hosp., Phila., 1989, West Jersey Health System (now Virtua Health Sys.), Voorhees, NJ, 1990—2002, Our Lady of Lourdes Med. Ctr., Camden, NJ, 2002—. Cons. in field, Phila. USPHS fellow, Detroit, 1969-70; recipient Chapel of 4 Chaplains Legion of Honor. Mem. Med. Libr. Assn. (Phila. chpt.), Spl. Libr. Assn., Basic Health Sci. Libr. Consortium, So. N.J. Consortium for Health Info. Svcs., Health Scis. Libr. Assn. N.J., Acad. Health Info. Profls., Caravan Club. Home: 9 Sylvan Ct Laurel Springs NJ 08021 Office Phone: 856-757-3548. Business E-Mail: clevelands@lourdesnet.org.

CLEVEN, CAROL CHAPMAN, retired state legislator; b. Hanover, Ill., Nov. 2, 1928; d. Edward William and Vivian (Strasser) Chapman; m. Walter Arnold Cleven; children: Kern W., Jeffrey P. BS, U. Ill., 1950, postgrad., 1950-56. Elem. sch. tchr. Derinda Ctr., Ill., 1946-47; with rsch. staff U. Ill., Urbana, 1950-56; exec. dir. Crittenton Hasting House, Brighton, Mass., 1975-86; mem. Mass. Ho. of Reps., Boston, 1987—2003; ret., 2003. Mem. edn. com., mem. human svcs. com., mem. election laws com. Mass. Ho. of Reps., Boston; mem. Rep. Task Force Pediatric AIDS, Mass. Caucus Women Legislators, Gov.'s Adolescent Health Adv. Coun., Spl. Commn. Pub. Assistance, Spl. Com. Women and Criminal Justice; co-chair Legis. Caucus Older Citizen's Concerns, Dept. Social Svcs. Working Group; mem. steering com. Mass. Legis. Children's Caucuse. Mem. Chelmsford (Mass.) Sch. Com., 1969—87, mem. elem. needs com., 1969—71, mem. sch. bldg. com., 1971—76; bd. dirs. Camp Paul Exceptional Children, 1987—; past pres. Lowell (Mass.) YWCA, Lowell Coll. Club; mem. Merrimack River Watershed Coun., Mass. Coalition Pregnant and Parenting Teens, Alliance Young Families; treas. Boston Ctr. Blind Children; bd. dirs. Chelmsford Ednl. Found., Greater Lowell Alzeimers Assn., Eastern Mass. Alzheimers Assn.; mem. spl. adv. bd. Cmty. Teamwork, Inc. Mem.: Mass. Assn. Sch. Coms. (life), Florence Crittenton League Lowell, Chelmsford LWV, Chelmsford Hist. Soc., Friends of Libr., Sigma Delta Epsilon, Phi Sigma. Congregationalist. Home: 4 Arbutus Ave Chelmsford MA 01824-1113 E-mail: wcleven@comcast.net.

CLEVENGER, SARAH, botanist, consultant; b. Indpls., Dec. 19, 1926; d. Cyrus Raymond and Mary Beth (Stevens) C. AB, Miami U., 1947; PhD, Ind. U., 1957. Tchr sci. Radford Sch., El Paso, Tex., 1949-51, Hillsdale Sch., Cin., 1951-52; asst. prof. Berea (Ky.) Coll., 1957-59, 61-63, Wittenberg U., Springfield, Ohio, 1959-60, Eastern Ill. U., 1960-61, Ind. State U., Terre Haute, 1963-66, assoc. prof., 1966-78, prof., 1978-85, prof. emerita, 1985—. Mem. Am. Inst. Biol. Sci., Am. Soc. Plant Taxonomists, Bot. Soc. Am., Internat. Assn. Plant Taxonomy, Phytochem. Soc. N.Am. (past sec.). Home: 717 S Henderson St Bloomington IN 47401-4838 Personal E-mail: sclevenger@iquest.net.

CLEVER, LINDA HAWES, physician; b. Seattle; d. Nathan Harrison and Evelyn Lorraine (Johnson) Hawes; m. James Alexander Clever, Aug. 20, 1960; 1 child, Sarah Lou. AB with distinction, Stanford U., 1962, MD, 1965. Diplomate Am. Bd. Internal Medicine, Am. Bd. Preventive Medicine in Occupl. Medicine. Intern Stanford U. Hosp., Palo Alto, Calif., 1965—66, resident, 1966—67, fellow in infectious disease, 1967—68; fellow in cmty. medicine U. Calif., San Francisco, 1968—69, resident, 1969—70; med. dir. Sister Mary Philippa Diagonostic and Treatment Ctr. St. Mary's Hosp., San Francisco, 1970—77; chmn. dept. occupl. health Calif. Pacific Med. Ctr., San Francisco, 1977—. Clin. prof. medicine U. Calif. Med. Sch., San Francisco; NIIH rsch. fellow Sch. Medicine, Stanford U., 1967—68; mem. nat. adv. panel Inst. Rsch. on Women and Gender, 1990—, chair panel, 1998—2000; mem. San Francisco Comprehensive Health Planning Coun., 1971—76; bd. dirs., mem. Calif.-OSHA Adv. Com. on Hazard Evaluation Sys. and Info. Svc., 1979—85, Calif. Statewide Profl. Stds. Rev. Coun., 1977—81, San Francisco Regional Commn. on White House Fellows, 1979—81, 1983—89, 1992, 95, chmn., 1977—81, 2001—02; bd. sci. counselors Nat. Inst. Occupl. Safety and Health, 1995—. Editor We. Jour. Medicine, 1990—98; contbr. articles to profl. jours. Trustee Stanford U., 1972—76, 1981—91, v.p., 1985—91; pres. RENEW, 2000—; bd. dirs. Sta. KQED, 1976—83, chmn., 1979—81; bd. dirs. Ind. Sector, 1980—86, vice chmn., 1985—86; bd. dirs. San Francisco U. H.S., 1983—90, chmn., 1987—88; active Womens Forum West, 1980—, bd. dirs., 1992—93; mem. Lucile Packard Children's Hosp. Bd., 1993—97; Lucile Packard Found. Children, 1997—99; mem. policy adv. com. U. Calif. Berkeley Sch. Pub. Health, 1995—, chair, 1995—2000; bd. dirs. The Redwoods Retirement Cmty., 1996—2001, Buck Inst. for Rsch. in Aging, 2000—; bd. govs. Stanford Med. Alumni Assn., 1997—2002, 2003—, pres., 2003—05; bd. dirs. No. Calif. Presbyn. Homes and Svcs., 2000—. Master: ACP (gov. No. Calif. region 1984—89, chmn. bd. govs. 1989—90, regent 1990—96, vice chair bd. regents 1994—95); fellow: Am. Coll. Occupl. and Environ. Medicine; mem.: APHA, We. Assn. Physicians (pres. 2003), We. Occupl. Medicine Assn., Calif. Acad. Medicine, Calif. Med. Assn., Inst. Medicine NAS, Stanford U. Women's Club (bd. dirs. 1971—80), Chi Omega. Office: 2300 California St Ste 304 San Francisco CA 94115-1931 Office Phone: 415-600-3321. Business E-Mail: linda.clever@itsa.ucsf.edu.

CLICK, CARRIE, public relations executive; b. 1970; Degree in Humanities, Pepperdine U., degree in Spanish, M in Pub. Policy. Cert. Internat. Bus. Protocol Cons. Protocol Sch. of Washington, DC, profl. certification Susan Peterson Productions, Inc., Comm. Ctr. Intern rsch. Heritage Found., Washington; dep. assoc. dir. for Outreach Office of Faith-Based Cmty. Initiatives, The White House; dir., founder Click on.Etiquette. Mem. Southern Ariz. Ctr. Against Sexual Assault, New Parents Network, South of 45; bd. dirs. El Rio Found. Named one of 40 Under 40, Tucson Bus. Edge, 2006. Office: Click on.Etiquette 6719 E Camino Principal Tucson AZ 85715 Office Phone: 800-377-3132. Office Fax: 800-377-3135.*

CLIFF, JOHNNIE MARIE, mathematics and chemistry professor; b. Lamkin, Miss., May 10, 1935; d. John and Modest Alma (Lewis) Walton; m. William Henry Cliff, Apr. 1, 1961 (dec. 1983); 1 child, Karen Marie. BA in Chemistry, Math., U. Indpls., 1956; postgrad., NSF Inst., Butler U., 1960; MA in Chemistry, Ind. U., 1964; MS in Math., U. Notre Dame, 1980; postgrad., Martin U., 2000. Cert. tchr. Ind. Rsch. chemist Ind. U. Med. Ctr., Indpls., 1956-59; tchr. sci. and math. Indpls. Pub. Schs., 1960-88; tchr. chemistry, math. Martin U., Indpls., 1989—, chmn. math. dept., 1990—, divsn. chmn. depts. sci. and math., 1993—. Adj. instr. math. U. Indpls., 1991, Ivy Tech State Coll., Indpls., 2002. Contbr. scientific papers. Grantee NSF, 1961-64, 73-76, 78-79, Woodrow Wilson Found., 1987-88; scholarship U. Indpls., 1952-56, NSF Inst. Reed Coll., 1961, C. of C., 1963. Mem. AAUW, NAACP, NEA, Assn. Women in Sci., Urban League, NY Acad. Scis., Am. Chem. Soc., Nat. Coun. Math. Tchrs., Am. Assn. Physics Tchrs., Nat. Sci. Tchrs. Assn., Am. Statis. Assn., Am. Assn. Ret. Persons, Neal-Marshall-Ind. U. Alumni Assn., U. Indpls. Alumni Assn., U. Notre Dame Alumni Assn., Ind. U. Chemist Assn., Notre Dame Club Indpls., Kappa Delta Pi, Delta Sigma Theta. Democrat. Baptist. Avocations: gardening, sewing. Home: 405 Golf Ln Indianapolis IN 46260-4108 Office: Martin U 2171 Avondale Pl Indianapolis IN 46218-3878 Office Phone: 317-543-3235.

CLIFF, KARISSA, consumer researcher, recruiter; b. Lancaster, Calif., Dec. 15, 1965; d. John Oliver and Frances Kay (Spencer) Cliff; m. Kevin Kenneth Ross, Apr. 14, 1984 (div. June 1988); children: Kevin Kenneth Ross, II, Serenity Angeline Ross; m. Ira C. Baxter, 1998 (div. Feb. 2003); children: Madeline Elizabeth, Rosalyn Andrea Regina. BBA magna cum laude, Belmont U., 1995; MBA, Vanderbilt U., 1997. Mgr., liaison Mercantile Stores, Nashville, 1983-87; researcher Ericson Mktg. Comm., Nashville, 1994-95; marketer Armor All, Charleston, S.C., 1996; consumer rschr. Procter & Gamble, Nashville, 1997-2000; sr. analyst Clorox, Nashville, 2000—03; forecaster Gen. Mills, 2003—04; global researcher Mead Johnson, Evansville, Ind., 2004—. Cons. Am. Beauty Cosmetics, Gallatin, Tenn., 1995. Founder Homeless Day Labor, Nashville, 1996-97; chair 100% Owen Svc. Orgn., Nashville, 1996-97; vol. soup kitchen Union Rescue Mission, Nashville, 1995-97; vol. Refugee Relocation, Nashville, 1995-97. Wendell scholar for Mktg. Studies, Belmont U., 1994-95, Morris scholar Vanderbilt U., 1995-97. Fellow Ctr. for Transition and Orgnl. Design; mem. MENSA, Delta Gamma Beta. Democrat. Avocation: flute. Home: 2420 E Gum St Evansville IN 47714 Office Phone: 812-429-5268. E-mail: karissacliff@yahoo.com.

CLIFFORD, CAROLYN, news correspondent, reporter; b. Detroit; married; 3 children. Grad., Mich. State U. Anchor 10 pm news WLFL-TV, Raleigh, NC; anchor 10 pm newscast WPGH-TV, Pitts.; co-anchor Action News This Morning and Noon WXYZ-TV, Southfield, Mich., 1998—. Spkr. in field. Recipient Heroes award for media, Karmanos Cancer Inst., 1999, Emmy award for best news anchor, 2003. Office: WXYZ-TV 20777 W Ten Mile Rd Southfield MI 48037 Office Phone: 248-827-7777. E-mail: wxyzcarolyn@yahoo.com.

CLIFFORD, DOROTHY RING, journalist; b. Kingsport, Tenn., Jan. 13, 1930; d. Wiley Everett Ring and Mary Lee Barton; m. Gordon Henry, Jr. Clifford, May 11, 1957 (dec.); children: Wiley Howard, Elizabeth Clifford Simmons, Mary Gordon Clifford Cunningham. Diploma, Agnes Scott Coll., Ga., 1950, U. Tenn., 1952. Women's editor, reporter Kingsport Times News, Tex., 1948—57; reporter, editor Savannah News Press, 1957—58, women's editor, 1958—59; assoc. women's editor, women's editor Tallahassee Democrat, 1959—62, acting women's editor, 1970—72, assoc. editor, 1972—73, people's editor and food editor, 1973—84, features reporter, writer, 1985—2001, freelance writer, 2002—. Bd. mem. Fla. Press Club; bd. dirs. Le Mayne Art Found.; pres. Jr. League, 1968—69; bd. dirs. Murat House Mus., Tallahassee, 1970—73; founding pres. Fla. State U., Friends of Dance, Tallahassee, 1987—90. Recipient 1st Pl. in journalism, J.C. Penney and U. Mo., 1961, Dallas Market Ctr., 1982. Mem.: Tallahassee Lit. Club. Republican. Episcopalian. Home: 5353 Tewkesbury Trace Tallahassee FL 32309

CLIFFORD, GERALDINE JONCICH (MRS. WILLIAM F. CLIFFORD), retired education educator; b. San Pedro, Calif., Apr. 17, 1931; d. Marion and Geraldine Joncich; m. William F. Clifford, July 12, 1969 (dec. 1993). AB, UCLA, 1954, M.Ed., 1957; Ed.D., Columbia U., 1961. Tchr., San Lorenzo, Calif., 1954-56, Maracaibo, Venezuela, 1957-58; researcher Inst. Lang. Arts, Tchrs. Coll., Columbia, 1958-61; asst. prof. edn. U. Calif., Berkeley, 1962-67, asso. prof., 1967-74, prof., 1974-94, assoc. dean, 1976-78, chmn. dept. edn., 1978-81, acting dean Sch. Edn., 1980-81, 82-83, dir. edn. abroad program, 1988, 89, prof. grad. sch. Berkeley, 1994—97, prof. emerita, 1994. Author: The Sane Positivist: A Biography of Edward L. Thorndike, 1968, The Shape of American Education, 1975, Ed Sch: A Brief for Professional Education, 1988, Lone Voyagers: Academic Women in Coeducational Universities, 1870-1937, 1989, Equally in View: The University of California, Its Women, and The Schools, 1995. Macmillan fellow, 1958-59, Guggenheim fellow, 1965-66, Rockefeller fellow, 1977-78; recipient Willystine Goodsell award for Contbns. to Women in Edn. Mem. History Edn. Soc., Am. Ednl. Rsch. Assn., Phi Beta Kappa, Pi Lambda Theta. Home: Apt 733 1661 Pine St San Francisco CA 94109-0420 E-mail: gclifford@barkeley.edu.

CLIFFORD, LISA MARY, marketing and sales professional; b. Albany, NY, Nov. 23, 1969; d. John Rocco and Kathleen Mary Fedele; m. Timothy Stephen Clifford, Sept. 16, 1995; children: Christian Gerard, John Anthony. BS in Fin., St. John Fisher Coll., Rochester, N.Y., 1991. Pension consulting assoc. First Albany Corp., 1992—94; assoc. v.p. mktg. First Albany Asset Mgmt., 1994—2000; v.p., dir., mktg. and bus. devel. Curran Investment Mgmt., Albany, 2000—. Mem. profl. adv. com. The Cmty. Found. of Capital Region, 2006—. V.p. Wildwood Found., Albany, 2002—; mem. Capital Leadership Class 2004 Albany-Colonie C. of C., 2006. Recipient 40 Under Forty award, Albany Bus. Rev., 2004. Mem.: NAFE, Investment Mgmt. Cons. Assn. Office: Curran Investment Mgmt 30 S Pearl St Albany NY 12207 Office Phone: 518-391-4292. Business E-Mail: lclifford@curranllc.com.

CLIFFORD, LORI BEVIS, anesthesiologist; b. Charleston, S.C., Feb. 4, 1964; d. James Frederick and Melverie Del (Kops) Bevis; m. Albert James Clifford, June 4, 1994; children: Blake, Grant. BS, Oral Roberts U., Tulsa, 1986; MD, Med. U. S.C., 1991. Diplomate Am. Bd. Anesthesiology with subspecialty in pain mgmt. Resident in anesthesiology Med. U. S.C., Charleston, 1991-95; anesthesiologist/pain mgmt. physician Dallas-Ft. Worth Anesthesia, Irving, Tex., 1995—, dir. Obstetrics anesthesia, 1997. F.A. Petrik Scholarship award, 1982; Oral Roberts U. Acad. scholar, 1983-86. Mem. Am. Soc. Anesthesiologists, S.C. Soc. Anesthesiologists, Am. Soc. Regional Anesthesia, Tex. Med. Assn., Soc. for Ambulatory. Republican. Avocations: racquetball, school sports, bichon frise dogs, running, biking. Home: 2905 Pacific Ct Irving TX 75062-4690

CLIFFORD, MARYANNE THERESA, economics professor, researcher; d. James Edward Clifford and Mary Anne Monica Lord-Clifford. BA, Smith Coll., Northampton, Mass., 1990; MS, U. Ky., Lexington, 1995, PhD, 2000. Vis. asst. prof. U. ND, Grand Forks, 1998—2001; asst. prof. Ea. Conn. State U., Willimantic, 2001—06, assoc. prof., 2006—. Presenter in field. Author textbook supplements. Mem. alumni bd. Notre Dame Acad., Hingham, Conn., 2006—; vol. dog walker North East Conn. Coun. Govts., Dayville, 2005—06. Mem.: Mo. Valley Econ. Assn., Internat. Atlantic Econ. Assn., So. Econ. Assn., Am. Econ. Assn., Ea. Econ. Assn. Office: Ea Conn State U Econs Dept 83 Windham St Willimantic CT 06226 Office Phone: 860-465-5512. Office Fax: 860-465-4469. Business E-Mail: cliffordm@easternct.edu.

CLIFT, ELEANOR, news correspondent, writer; b. Bklyn., July 7, 1940; d. Erk and Inna Roeloffs; m. William Brooks Clift Jr., 1964 (div. 1981); children: Edward, Woodbury, Robert; m. Tom Brazaitis, Sept. 30, 1989 (dec. Mar. 30, 2005). Student, Hofstra U., Hunter Coll. Former sec. to nat. affairs editor Newsweek, NYC, former reporter Atlanta bur., former White House corr., named dep. Washington bur. chief, 1992, contbg. editor, 1994—; with Washington bur. LA Times, 1985—86. Regular panelist The McLaughlin Group, 1983—; polit. analyst Fox News Network; column Capitol Letter appears weekly on Newsweek-MSNBC website; co-chair bd. dirs. Internat. Women's Media Found. Co-author (with Tom Brazaitis): War Without Bloodshed: The Art of Politics, 1996, Madam President: Shattering the Last Glass Ceiling, 2000; author: Founding Sisters and the 19th Amendment, 2003. Office: Newsweek Washington Bur 1750 Pennsylvania Ave NW Washington DC 20006-4502 E-mail: eclift@newsweek.com, eclift@aol.com.

CLIFTON, ANNE RUTENBER, psychotherapist, educator; b. New Haven, Dec. 11, 1938; d. Ralph Dudley and Cleminette (Downing) Rutenber; 1 child, Dawn Anne. BA, Smith Coll., 1960, MSW, 1962. Lic. clin. social worker, Mass.; diplomate Clin. Social Work. Psychiat. case worker adult psychiatry unit Tufts-New Eng. Med. Ctr., Boston, 1962-68, supr. students, 1967-68; pvt. practice psychotherapy, Cambridge and Newton, Mass., 1966—. Supr. med. students, staff social workers out-patient psychiatry Tufts New Eng. Med. Ctr., 1973—, also mem. exec. bd. Women's Resource Ctr., interim co-dir., 1986-88; asst. clin. prof. psychiatry Tufts U. Med. Sch., 1974—, research dept. psychiatry, 1966-68, 73, 77—. Contbr. articles to profl. jours. Mem.: NASW, Acad. Cert. Social Workers, Cambridge Tennis Club, Mt. Auburn Tennis Club, Phi Beta Kappa, Sigma Xi. Home: 126 Homer St Newton MA 02459-1518 Office: 59 Church St Ste 4 Cambridge MA 02138-3724 Office Phone: 617-492-1927. Personal E-mail: AnneRClifton@aol.com.

CLIFTON, LUCILLE THELMA, author; b. Depew, N.Y., June 27, 1936; d. Samuel Louis and Thelma (Moore) Sayles; m. Fred James Clifton, May 10, 1958 (dec. Nov. 1984); children: Sidney, Fredrica (dec. 2000), Channing (dec. 2004), Gillian, Graham, Alexia. Student, Howard U., 1953-55, Fredonia State Tchrs. Coll., NY, 1955; DL (hon.), Dartmouth Coll., 2005. Prof. literature and creative writing U. Calif., Santa Cruz, 1985-90; dist. prof. humanities St. Mary's Coll. Md., 1990—, Hilda C. Landers endowed chair in liberal arts, 2000—. Poet-in-residence, Coppin State Coll., Balt., 1972-76, Jenny Moore vis. writer, George Washington U., 1982-83. Author: Good Times, 1969, Good News About The Earth, 1972, An Ordinary Woman, 1974, Generations, 1976, Two-Headed Woman, 1980, Sonora Beautiful, 1981, Next, 1987, Good Woman, 1987, Quilting, 1991, The Book of Light, 1993, Blessing the Boats, 2000 (Nat. Book award); Everett Anderson books and other books for children; co-author: Free to Be You and Me, 1974 (Emmy award), Free To Be A Family. Named Poet Laureate, State of Md., 1979; recipient Discovery award Poetry Center, 1969, winner Nat. Book Award, 2000; YMHA grantee, 1969; Nat. Endowment Arts grantee, 1970, 72 Fellow Am. Acad. Arts and Scis.; mem. Authors League, Author Guild, P.E.N., Acad. Am. Poets (chancellor), Poetry Soc. Am. (bd. dirs., Lila Wallace/Reader's Digest award 1999). Office: St Marys Coll of Maryland Divsn Arts and Letters Montgomery Hall 126 Saint Marys City MD 20686

CLIFTON, NELIDA, social worker; b. Buenos Aires, Aug. 16, 1944; arrived in U.S., 1968; d. Juan Antonio and Zaira Elizabeth (Vera) Tovar; m. Mark Earl Jolls, Nov. 8, 1968 (div. July 1984); children: Patricia Elizabeth, Michael Thomas, Diana Marie Kathleen; m. Anthony Gene Clifton, June 19, 1993. BA in Bus. Adminstrn., Nat. Sch. Commerce, Tucuman, Argentina; BA in Psychology magna cum laude, Fairleigh Dickinson U., 1986; postgrad., William Paterson Coll., 1988—89. Cert. diplomate Am. Psychotherapy Assn.; lic. cert. social worker Bd. Social Work Examiners, N.J.; cert. bilingual. Social worker Bergen County Bd. Social Svcs., Rochelle Park, NJ, 1987—. Crisis intervention counselor; phone counselor; cmty. resources referral profl. Mem. APA, NASW, Am. Assn. Christian Counselors, Phi Zeta Kappa, Phi Omega Epsilon, Psi Chi Nat. Honor Socs. Republican. Avocations: reading, chess, tennis, gardening. Home and Office: 25 Platt Ave Saddle Brook NJ 07663

CLIJSTERS, KIM, professional tennis player; b. Bilzen, Belgium, June 8, 1983; Profl. tennis player WTA, 1999—. Winner 30 singles, 11 doubles tennis tournaments including Luxembourg, 1999, Hobart, Leipzig, 2000, Stanford, Leipzig, Luxembourg, 2001, Hamburg, Filderstadt, Luxembourg, 2002, Sydney, Indian Wells, Rome, Rosmalen, Stanford, Los Angeles, Filderstadt, Luxembourg, 2003, Paris, Antwerp, 2004, Indian Wells, Miami, Eastbourne, Stanford, Los Angeles, Toronto, 2005, US Open, 2005, J&S Cup, 2006, Bank of the West Classic, 2006; finalist Bratislava, 1999, Filderstadt, 2000, Roland Garros, Indian Well's, Hertogenbosch, 2001. Office: Ste 1500 1 Prospect Plaza Saint Petersburg FL 33701-1500*

CLINE, ANN, artist, designer; b. Greensboro, N.C., Apr. 7, 1933; d. Grady Alton and Mae Josephine (Karsten) Merriman; scholar Cooper Union, N.Y.C., 1954, Fashion Inst. Tech., 1957, Arts Students League, 1961-62, Fine Arts Acad., 1962-63, Joachim Simon Atelier, Tel Aviv, 1962; A.B., N.E. La. U., Monroe, 1971; m. S.C. Johananoff, Mar. 9, 1959 (div. 1973); 1 child, Pamela; m. Francis X. Cline, Feb. 14, 1973. Asst. designer Adele Simpson Couture, 1959; pres. Johananoff Designs, 1967-70, Ann Cline Art Objects, Monroe, La., 1975—; pres. 165 North Properties; artist; works exhibited in group shows Haifa Mus., 1961, Am. Watercolor Soc., 1962; one person shows include: Barzansky Gallery, 1962, La. Polytech. U. Art Gallery, 1967, Mittel's Art Gallery, 1969, N.E. La. U., 1973, 71, Am. Consulate, Tel Aviv, 1962, Contemporary Gallery, Dallas, 1970, Brooks Gallery, Memphis, 1971, 14th Ann. Delta Art Exhbn. Nat. Found. Arts, 1971, Jackson Arts Ctr. Ann. Exhbn., Miss., (prize award 1971), 22d Ann. Delta Exhbn., Ark. Arts Ctr., 1972, 79, Mayor's Show, Monroe, 1979, Wesley Found. Award Show, 1979, 80, 81, Roundtree Gallery, Monroe, 1985-87, others. Bd. dirs. La. Council Performing Arts, 1974; rep. Gov.'s Conf. Arts; bd. adjustments Monroe Zoning Commn.; trustee Masur Mus., 1974-75; bd. dirs. Little Theater of Monroe, 1975-76; bd. dirs. Women of the Ch., Episcopal Ch., 1977-78, mem. Daus. of the King, 1979-82, chmn. meml. com. Recipient Young Designer competition award Fontana of Rome, 1957, 1st prize Fashion Inst. Tech., 1957, Young Designer's award Women's Wear Daily, 1960, 1st prize, Arts Students League, 1961, 2d prize, 1963, 2d prize Fine Arts Acad., 1962, 1st prize, Woodstock Gallery, 1962, 1st prize, La. Folk Art Festival, 1966, 68, 72, prize awards Temple Emmanuel Ann., Dallas, 1969, 71, 74. Mem. Internat. Butler Soc., Bayou Desiard Country Club, Little Rock Country Club, Lotus Club. Illustrator: Jessie Strikes Louisiana Gold, 1969, Rhet, the Egret.

CLINE, LYNN F.H., federal agency administrator; BA, East Carolina U., 1976; MA, U. Calif., Santa Barbara, 1979. Various mgmt. positions NASA internat. office, 1975—90; dept. dir. Internat. Rels. NASA, Washington, 1990—93, dir. space flight divsn., 1993—97, dep. assoc. adminstr. external rels., 1997—2003, dep. assoc. adminstr. space ops., 2003—. Recipient Aeronautics and Astronautics Internat. Coop. award, 1998, Presdl. Rank Meritorious Exec., 1997, 2004, NASA Exceptional Performance award, 1997, NASA Exceptional Svc. medal, 1988, 1993, Women in Aerospace Internat Space Yr. award, 1992, Fed. Rep. Germany Friendship award, 1983. Fellow: AIAA (assoc.), Am. Astronautical Soc.; mem.: Internat. Acad. Astronautics (corr.). Office: NASA Hqtrs Mail Ste 7P39 300 E St SW Washington DC 20546

CLINE, NANCY M., librarian, department chairman; b. Chambersburg, Pa., Sept. 21, 1946; d. Gerald E. and Mary Jane (Koons) C.; m. Laurence Hettich, Dec. 28, 1983; 1 child, Jennifer. AB in English, U. Calif., Berkeley, 1968, MLS in Librarianship, 1970. Pa. documents libr. Pa. State U., University Park, 1970-71, head govt. documents sect., 1971-80, chief bibliographic resources dept., 1980-84, asst. dean, head bibliographic resources and svcs. div., 1984-88, dean univ. librs., 1988—. Mem. ALA (Document to the People award 1983), Pa. Libr. Assn., Golden Key Hon. Soc. (hon.), Assn. Rsch. Librs. (task force on govt. info. in electronic format 1986-88, chair task force on telecom. 1989-91, info. policy com. 1990-93, rep. nat. steering com. coalition for networked info. 1990-94, bd. dirs. 1992-94, pres.-elect 1994-95), Rsch. Librs. Group (bd. govs. 1988-92, chair fin. and adminstrn. com. 1991-92). Office: Penn State Univ Librs 505E Pattee Library University Park PA 16802-1805

CLINE, RUTH ELEANOR HARWOOD, translator, historian; b. Middletown, Conn., Oct. 31, 1946; d. Burton Henry and Eleanor May (Cash) Harwood; A.B., Smith Coll., 1968; M.A., Rutgers U., 1969; Ph.D., Georgetown U., 2000; cert. translation from French, Georgetown U., 1978; m. William R. Cline, June 10, 1967; children: Alison, Marian. Reviewer, U.S. Dept. State, Washington, 1979-94. Former v.p. Smith Coll. Class of 1968; rsch. assoc. dept. history Georgetown U., 2002-. Mem. Am. Translators Assn. (cert. in French, Spanish and Portuguese), MLA, Internat. Arthurian Soc. Episcopalian. Translator English verse: Yvain; or the Knight with the Lion (Chretien de Troyes), 1975; Perceval; or the Story of the Grail (Chretien de Troyes), 1983, Lancelot or the Knight of the Cart (Chretien de Troyes), 1990 (Lewis Galantiere Prize 1992), Erec and Enide (Chretien de Troyes), 2000, Cliges (Chretien de Troyes), 2000. Home: 5315 Oakland Rd Chevy Chase MD 20815-6638

CLINE, STARR, elementary school educator; b. Bklyn., Feb. 27, 1937; d. Albert and Any (Barocas) Funess; B.A. magna cum laude, Molloy Coll., 1974; postgrad. Hofstra U., 1977; Ed.D., Columbia U., 1985; m. Jerome Z. Cline, Apr. 27, 1957; children— Adam, Larry. Tchr., Oceanside (N.Y.) Public Schls., 1974-81, tchr. gifted elem. program, Herricks Public Schs., 1981—; coordinator Inst. on Gifted and Talented, Columbia U. for Three Village Sch. Dist., Setauket, L.I., 1978, asst. coordinator summer inst., 1978; field reader U.S. Dept. HEW, 1978; adj. instr. Molloy Coll., Hofstra U., C.W. Post Coll., Adelphi U.; regional coordinator Advocacy for Gifted and Talented Edn., 1984, state coordinator, 1985; leader delegation U.S. Amb. Program to Moscow and Siberia, 1991; lectr., cons. in field. Pres., Ocean Lea Civic Assn., 1977; adv. com. N.Y.C. Gifted Ed., 1979. Winner 1st, 3d prizes Creative Problem Solving Inst., Buffalo, 1979; Pub. Service TV Tri-State award, N.Y., N.J., Conn., 1980, others. Mem. Advocacy Gifted and Talented Edn. (dir., treas., pres.), World Council Gifted and Talented Children, Nat. Assn. Gifted Children, Nat. Alliance State Assns. for Gifted Edn. (chair 1993), L.I. Soc. Gifted and Talented, Assn. for Supervision and Curriculum Devel. Clubs: Kiwanettes (trustee 1982, pres. 1985). Author: Independent Study, 1980, Teaching for Talent, 1984, The Independent Learner, 1986, What Would Happen If I Said Yes?, 1989; contbr. articles to profl. jours. Home: 14 Saint James Pl Lynbrook NY 11563-2618

CLINE, STEPHANIE E., food service executive; 2 children. V.p. sys. devel. Jack in the Box Inc., San Diego, 1994—2000, v.p., chief info. officer, 2000—. Named IT Operator of Yr., Hospitality Tech. mag., 2001. Office: Jack in the Box Inc 9330 Balboa Ave San Diego CA 92123

CLINE, VIVIAN MELINDA, lawyer; b. Seneca, S.C., Oct. 6, 1953; d. Kenneth H. and Wanda F. (Simmons) Fuller; m. Terry S. Cline, June 15, 1974 (div. Oct. 1986); 1 child, Alicia C. BSBA, Calif. State U., Northridge, 1974; JD, Southwestern U., L.A., 1983. Bar: Calif. 1983, Tex., 1990. Paralegal Internat. House Pancakes, North Hollywood, Calif., 1976-78; assoc. Tuohey & Prasse, Santa Ana, Calif., 1983-85; paralegal Smith Internat., inc., Newport Beach, Calif., 1978-83, sr. corp. counsel Houston, 1985—2005; gen. counsel bus. unit Smith Internat., Inc., 2005—06, sr. asst. gen. counsel contracts, 2006—. Bus. cons. Jr. Achievement, Houston, 1992—94, 1997—99. Mem. Exec. Women's Network (sec. 1993, pres. 1994, dir. programs 1995, sec. 1996, 2000, treas. 1998-2001), Soc. Corp. Secs. and Governance Profls.(sec. Houston chpt. 1995-96, treas. 1996-97, v.p., program dir. 1997-98, pres. 1998-99). Republican. Presbyterian. Office: Smith Internat Inc 16740 Hardy Rd Houston TX 77032-1125 Business E-Mail: vcline@smith.com.

CLINGAN, WANDA JACQUELINE, minister; b. Hunnewell, Kans., Oct. 29, 1928; d. Claude Charles Stephenson and Leta Nette (Davison) Phillips; m. Donald F. Clingan, Aug. 26, 1952; children: Stephen F., Jane Ellen Clingan Reynolds. BA, Phillips U., 1950. Lic. minister, 1973. State youth and children's worker Christian Ch. in Kans., Topeka, 1950-52; asst. to registrar Tex. Christian U., Fort Worth, 1952-55; dir. children's ministries and family life Downey Ave. Christian Ch., Indpls., 1967-73; mgr. Bethany Bookstore, Indpls., 1973-79; ministry dir. Ministry on Ch. Response to Family Violence Ill. Conf. Chs., Springfield, 1986-92, ret., 1992. Contbr. articles to profl. jours. Registered lobbyist Christian InnerCity Assn., Indpls., 1966; sec. to bd. dirs. Broadway Christian Ctr., Indpls., 1967; precinct committeewoman Dem. Cen. Com., Indpls., 1973-75. Mem. AAUW (chair cultural arts 1987-88, chair study group 1986-87), Nat. Assn. Ecumenical Staff. Home: 41 Westwood Ter Springfield IL 62702-4610

CLINTON, BARBARA MARIE, director, social worker; b. Bklyn., May 21, 1947; d. Lawrence Joseph and Kathleen Byrne C.; m. James Edward Selin, Sept. 12, 1981; children: Greta Maureen, Caitlin Carol. Auditor's cert., U. Tunis, Tunisia, 1968; BS, State U. Coll., Buffalo, 1971; student, SUNY, Buffalo, 1970-71; MSW, U. Ga., 1979. Child care worker Gateway United Meth. Youth Ctr., Williamsville, N.Y., 1970; caseworker Erie County Dept. Social Svcs., Buffalo, 1975-76; social worker Orchard Park (N.Y.) Nursing Home, 1976-77; group counselor Erie Med. Ctr., Buffalo, 1976-77; therapist Buffalo Children's Hosp., 1977-78; intern N.E. Ga. Community Mental Health Ctr., Athens, 1980-81; assoc. dir. ctr. health svcs. Vanderbilt U., Nashville, 1981-87, acting dir. ctr. health svcs., 1987-88, dir. ctr. health svcs., 1988—. Lectr. sch. medicine SUNY, Buffalo, 1977-78; gov.'s intern State of Ga., 1978, 79; dir. Maternal Infant Health Outreach Worker Project, 1982-90; adj. lectr. community health sch. nursing Vanderbilt U., 1986—; expert panelist Nat. Resource Ctr. Children Poverty Columbia U., 1987-89, Save The Children Fedn., Westport, Conn., 1992-93, cons.; evaluation advisor Tenn. Commn. Aging, 1991-92; mem. adv. bd. Vanderbilt U. Women's Ctr., 1992-94; presenter in field. Author: (with Mary Porter) Postnatal Home Visit Guide: The Second Year of Life, 1986, (with Toby Barnett) The Emotional Development of Infants: A Discussion Guide for Outreach Workers, 1987; contbr. articles to profl. jours. Active Bring Urban Recycling Nashville Today, Woodbine Community Orgn.; mem. steering com. S.E. Women's Employment Coalition, Lexington, Ky., 1988-91, bd. dirs., 1989-91; bd. dirs. Tenn. Coalition Def. Battered Women, 1990—, Vanderbilt Women's Ctr., 1992—, U. Ky. Coalition on Cancer, Lexington, 1992—. Regents scholar State of N.Y., 1965, 66, 68, 69; grantee Ford Found., 1982-88, J.C. Penny Found., 1983, Robert Wood Johnson Found., 1983-89, van Leer Found., 1986-93, Pub. Welfare Found., 1989-93, Unitarian Universalist Veatch Fund, 1988-93. Mem. APHA, NASW, Nat. Women's Health Network, Internat. Childbirth Edn. Assn., Tenn. Primary Care Assn., Acad. Cert. Social Workers. Home: 313 Peachtree St Nashville TN 37210-4925 Office: Vanderbilt U Ctr Health Svcs Sta 17 Nashville TN 37232-0001

CLINTON, BIRDEAN R., elementary school educator; b. Bronx, NYC, Jan. 21, 1962; d. Thomas Robinson and Dorothy Clinton. AAS, Elizabeth Seton Coll., 1984; BS in Bus. Admistrn., Marymount Coll., 1985; MS in Elem. Edn., 1996. Cert. elem. tchr. NY State, NJ, 1999. Tchr. All Saints Parochial Sch., NYC, 1993—95, NYC Bd. Edn., 1995—2000, Plainfield Pub. Schools, NJ, 2000—01, lit. coach, 2001—03, NJ Dept. Edn., Trenton, NJ, 2003—04; design coach Plainfield Pub. Schools, 2004—05; dir. instrn. Marian P. Thomas Charter Sch., Newark, 2005—. State, reading coach NJ Dept. Edn., Trenton, 2003—04; lit. cons. Hillside Bd. Edn., NJ, 2004, 05. Mem. Mt. Carmel Bapt. Ch., Bronx, NY, 1962—; D'Zert Club Phila., 2005—. Recipient Apple for Tchg. Recognition award, Iota Phi Lambda Soc., 2005. Mem.: ASCD, Internat. Reading Assn. Avocations: reading, music, travel, cooking, theater. Home: 957 East Front St #D Plainfield NJ 07062 Personal E-mail: brc121@msn.com.

CLINTON, CHELSEA VICTORIA, financial consultant, former first daughter; b. Little Rock, Ark., Feb. 27, 1980; d. William Jefferson and Hillary Rodham Clinton. BA in Hist., Stanford U., 2001; MA in Internat. Rels., Oxford U., 2003. Cons. McKinsey & Co., 2003—06; joined Ave. Capital Grp., NYC, 2006—. Office: Avenue Capital Group 535 Madison Ave 15th Fl New York NY 10022*

CLINTON, HILLARY (HILLARY DIANE RODHAM CLINTON), senator, lawyer, former First Lady of United States; b. Chgo., Oct. 26, 1947; d. Hugh Ellsworth and Dorothy (Howell) Rodham; m. William J. Clinton, Oct. 11, 1975; 1 child, Chelsea Victoria. BA in Polit. Sci., with high honors, Wellesley Coll., 1969; JD, Yale U., 1973; LLD (hon.), U. Ark., Little Rock, 1985, Ark. Coll., 1988, Hendrix Coll., 1992, U. Sunderland, 1993, U. Pa., 1993, U. Mich., 1993, U. Ill., 1994, U. Minn., 1995, San Francisco State U., 1995, U. Ulster, 2004; LLD, Marymount Manhattan Coll., 2005, Rensselaer Poly. Inst., 2005; D Pub. Svc. (hon.), George Washington U., 1994, U. Md., College Park, 1996; DHL (hon.), Drew U., 1996, Ohio U., 1997, Pace Univ., 2003, Manhattanville College, 2004. Bar: Ark. 1973, admitted to practice: US Dist. Ct. (Ea. Dist.) Ark. 1973, US Dist. Ct. (We. Dist.) Ark. 1973, US Ct. Appeals (8th Cir.) 1973, US Supreme Ct. 1975. Atty. Children's Def. Fund, Cambridge, Mass. and Washington, 1973-74; legal cons. Carnegie Coun. on Children, New Haven, 1973-74; counsel, impeachment inquiry staff Judiciary Com. US Ho. of Reps., Washington, 1974; asst. prof. law, dir. Legal Aid Clinic U. Ark. Sch. Law, Fayetteville, 1974-77, asst. prof. law Little Rock, 1979-80; ptnr. Rose Law Firm, Little Rock, 1977-92; First Lady of the US, 1993—2001; chair Presdl. Task Force on Nat. Health Care Reform, 1993; US Senator from NY, 2001—. Com. security and cooperation in Europe US Senate, com. armed forces, com. environ. and public works, com. health, edn., labor and pensions, spl. com. on aging. Author: Handbook on Legal Rights for Arkansas Women, 1977, 87, It Takes a Village: And Other Lessons Children Teach Us, 1996, Dear Socks, Dear Buddy: Kids' Letters to the First Pets, 1998, An Invitation to the White House, 2000, Living History, 2003; syndicated columnist Talking It Over, 1995-2000; contbr. articles to profl. journals. Bd. dirs. Childrens Def. Fund, Washington, 1976-92, chair, 1986-91, Legal Svcs. Corp., Washington, 1977-81, chair, 1978-80; founder, pres., bd. dirs. Ark. Advs. for Children and Families, 1977-84; bd. dirs. Wal-Mart Stores, Inc., 1986-92, TCBY, 1986-92, Child Care Action Campaign, 1986-92, Nat. Ctr. on Edn. and the Economy, 1987-92, Ark. Children's Hosp., 1988-92, Franklin and Eleanor Roosevelt Inst., 1988-92, Children's TV Workshop, 1989-92, Public/Private Ventures, 1990-92; chmn. Ark. Edn. Stds. Com., 1983-84; mem. commn. on quality edn. So. Regional Edn. Bd., 1984-92; chair ABA Commn. on Women in the Profession, 1987-91; former hon. pres. Girl Scouts of Am.; mem. adv. bd. HIPPY, 1988-92, bd. dirs.; former hon. chair Pres.' Com. on the Arts and Humanities, US Del., UN Fourth World Conf. on Women, 1995; hon. mem. The Pen and Brush, 1996—; hon. chair, NY Acad. Sciences Gala, 2005. Named Outstanding Layman of Yr. Phi Delta Kappa, 1984, Health Educator of Yr., Ryan White Found., 1995; recipient Lewis Hine award Nat. Child Labor Law Com., 1993, Albert Schweitzer Leadership award Hugh O'Brian Youth Found., 1993, Iris Cantor Humanitarian award UCLA Med. Ctr., 1993, Friend of Family award Am. Home Econs. Assn., 1993, Charles Wilson Lee Citizen Svc. award Com. for Edn. Funding, 1993, Claude D. Pepper award Nat. Assn. for Home Care, 1993, Commitment to Life award AIDS Project LA, 1994, Disting. Svc., Health Edn. and Prevention award Nat. Ctr. for Health Edn., 1994, First Ann. Eleanor Roosevelt Freedom Fighter award, 1994, Brandeis award U. Louisville Sch. of Law, 1994, Social Justice award United Auto Workers, 1994, Ernie Banks Positivism trophy Emil Verban Meml. Soc., 1994, Humanitarian award Alzheimer's Assn., 1994, Elie Wiesel Found., 1994, Internat. Broadcasting award Hollywood Radio and TV Soc., 1994, Ellen Browning Scripps medal Scripps Coll., 1994, Disting. Pro Bono Svc. award San Diego Vol. Lawyer Program, 1994, HIPPY USA award, 1994, C. Everett Koop medal Am. Diabetes Assn., 1994, Women's Legal Def. Fund award, 1994, Martin Luther King, Jr. award Progressive Nat. Bapt. Conv., 1994, 30th Anniversary Women at Work award in Pub. Policy, Nat. Commn. on Working Women, 1994, Greater Washington Urban League award, 1995, Servant of Justice award NY Legal Aid Soc., 1995, Presdl. award Bklyn. Coll., 1995, Outstanding Mother award Nat. Mother's Day Com., 1995, Dedication, Annual Survey Am. Law, NYU, 1995, Nat. Breast Cancer Coalition Leadership award, 1995, Faith in Humanity award Nat. Coun. Jewish Women, 1996, NICHE Humanitarian award, 1996, Nat. Assn. Elem. Sch. Prins. Dist. Svc. award, 1996, Grammy award, 1997, Bully Pulpit award Nat. Coun. for Adoption, 1997, Nat. Family Advocate award Parents' Plus Newspaper, 1997, Disting. Svc. to Edn. award Coll. Bd., 1997, Disting. Svc. award Columbia U. Ctr. of Addiction and Substance Abuse, 1997, Commitment to Children award The Elizabeth Glaser Pediat. AIDS Found., 1997, Eleanor Roosevelt Living World award Peace Links, 1997, Humanitarian award Am. Found. Suicide Prevention, 1999, Lifetime Humanitarian Achievement award Children of Chernobyl Relief Fund and Ukrainian Inst. Am., 1999, Mother Teresa award, Govt. Albania, 1999, Shalom Chaver award internat. leadership, Yitzhak Rabin Ctr. Israel Studies, 1999, Disting. Am. award John F. Kennedy Libr. Found., 2004, Woman of Yr. award Met. Coun. on Jewish Poverty, NY, 2004, Health Quality award Nat. Com. Quality Assurance, 2005, Intrepid Freedom award Intrepid Sea, Air and Space Mus., 2005, President's Vision and Voice award Am. Med. Women's Assn., 2005; Paul Harris fellow Rotary Found., 1996; named one of Most Powerful Women, Forbes mag., 2005, 100 Most Influential People, Time Mag., 2006; named to Nat. Women's Hall of Fame, NY, 2005; honored with life-sized figure, Madame Tussauds' wax museum, Times Square, NYC, 2006. Fellow: Am. Bar Found.; mem.: ABA (chair, commn. on women in the profession), Assn. Trial Lawyers Am., Pulaski County Bar Assn., Ark. Women Lawyers Assn., Ark. Trial Lawyers Assn., Ark. Bar Assn. Democrat. Meth. First First Lady elected to the US Senate and the first woman elected statewide in NY. Office: US Senate 476 Russell Senate Office Bldg Washington DC 20510 also: District Office Ste 2601 780 Third Ave New York NY 10017-2154 Office Phone: 202-224-4451, 212-688-6262. Office Fax: 202-228-0282, 212-688-7444.*

CLINTON, KISHA, elementary school educator; d. Erskine and Rosaura Clinton. Degree in secondary edn., Mercy Coll., Bronx, N.Y., 1984; degree in English lang. arts, Va. Union U., Richmond, 1994. Tchr. 4th grade St. Catherine of Sienna, Queens, NY, 1996—99, tchr. 7th and 8th grades, 1999—2000; tchr. 6th grade Abraham Lincoln Intermediate Sch., Bklyn., 2000—04, literacy coach, 2004—. Treas. Sch. Leadership Com., Bklyn., 2002—; sch. treas., Bklyn., 2005—. Recipient Outstanding Student Leadership award, Va. Union U., 1994. Mem.: ASCD, Internat. Reading Assn., Phi Delta Kappa, Delta Sigma Theta. Avocations: writing, poetry, photography. Home: Apt 2G 164-20 Highland Ave Jamaica NY 11432 Office: NY Dept Edn 528 Ridgewood Ave Brooklyn NY 11208

CLINTON, LOTTIE DRY EDWARDS, retired state agency administrator; b. Wilmington, N.C., July 26, 1937; d. King Solomon Dry and Bessie Theresa Mouzon; m. Edmund Russell Edwards III, Aug. 30, 1954 (dec. Aug. 29, 1969); children: Desireé, Vickie, Edmonia, Cheryl, Michele, Kevin; m. Robert Clinton, June 24, 1993. AAS in Bus. Adminstrn., Cape Fear Cmty. Coll., 1972; student, U. N.C., Wilmington, 1974—75, Ctrl. Piedmont Coll., 1984. Cert. Notary Pub. N.C. From acctg. clk. to supr. shipping and receiving N.C. State Port Authority, Wilmington, 1976—80, supr. open dock, 1980, adminstrv. supr., 1980—83, 1985—98, adminstr. supr. Charlotte Intermodal Terminal, 1983—85; ret., 1998. Apptd. 1898 Wilimgton Race Riot commn. State of N.C., 2002—. Chmn. Svc. to Disabled, Wilmington, 1970—80, Com. on African Am. History, Wilmington, 1980—90; bd. dirs. New Hanover Cmty. Health Ctr., Wilmington, 1997—. Named Woman of Yr. N.C. liberty light chpt., ABWA, 1979; named an Outstanding Citizen, Winston-Salem Alumni Assn., 1995. Democrat. African Methodist Episcopal Zionite. Achievements include appointed mem. of 1898 Wilmington Race Riot Commn. State of NC. Avocations: reading, sewing, gardening, music, beach. Home: 127 Blount Dr Wilmington NC 28411 Personal E-mail: loddec@aol.com.

CLINTON, MARIANN HANCOCK, educational association administrator; b. Dyersburg, Tenn., Dec. 7, 1933; d. John Bowen and Nell Maurine (Johnson) Hancock; m. Harry Everett Clinton, Aug. 25, 1956; children—Carol, John Everett. BMus, Cin. Conservatory Music, 1956; BS, U. Cin., 1956; MMus, Miami U., Oxford, Ohio, 1971. Tchr. music public schs., Hamilton County, Ohio, 1956-57; tchr. voice and piano Butler County, Ohio, 1964—; instr. music Miami U., 1972-75; exec. dir. Music Tchrs. Nat. Assn., Cin., 1977-86. Mng. dir. Am. Music Tchr., 1977-86. Mem. adminstrv. bd. Middletown (Ohio) 1st United Methodist Ch., 1968-72; bd. dirs. Friends of the Sorg Opera House; concert presenter Friends of Music of Charlotte County (Fla.). Mem. Music Educators Nat. Conf., Am. Ednl. Research Assn., Am. Soc. Assn. Execs., Nat. Fedn. Music Clubs, Pi Kappa Lambda, Kappa Delta Pi, Mu Phi Epsilon, Phi Mu. Republican. Home: 714 Macedonia Dr Punta Gorda FL 33950-8013

CLIPSHAM, JACQUELINE ANN, artist; b. Hertfordshire, Eng., July 27, 1936; (parents Am. citizens), July 27, 1936; d. George Frederick and Helene Lucille (Lees) C. BA, Carleton Coll., 1958; postgrad., Universita per Stranieri, Perugia, Italy, 1959; MA, Western Res. U., 1962. Mem. Clay Art Center, Port Chester, N.Y., 1963-66; dir. ceramics program and art workshop CORE Community Center, Sumter, S.C., 1965; mem. faculty Bklyn. Mus. Art Sch., 1968-79, Essex. County Coll., Newark, 1979-80. Mem. Atlantic Gallery, N.Y.C., 1974-83; mem. crafts task force Nat. Endowment for Arts, 1980; Culpeper Found. project coordinator, dept. community edn. Met. Mus. Art, N.Y.C., 1981-82; mem. grants panel for crafts N.J. State Council Arts, 1982; visiting artist, Dayton Hudson, 1987; instr. Carleton Coll., N. Field, Minn., 1987. One-woman show: Willoughby (Ohio) Fine Arts Ctr., 1982, Hunterdon Mus. Art, 2001; works exhibited: Mid-Atlantic States Arts Found., 1987, Schwab Rehabilitation Inst., Chgo., 1987, Cleve. Mus., Bklyn. Mus., Mus. Contemporary Crafts, N.Y.C., Butler Inst. Art, Youngstown, Ohio, Hunterdon Mus. Art, Clinton, N.J., Greenwich House Pottery, N.Y.C., Pratt Inst., Bklyn., Atlantic Gallery, N.Y.C., 1980, Webster Coll., St. Louis, 1981, Clay Art Ctr., Sound Shore Gallery, Port Chester, N.Y., 1983, Gemans Van Eck Gallery, N.Y.C., 1983, Thorpe Intermedia Gallery, Sparkill, N.Y., 1984, N.Y. Pub. Library, 1984, Fellowship Recipients, 2000; work loaned to Dept. Acad. Affairs, Met. Mus. Art, 1978; cons. dept. Am. art Met. Mus. Art, N.Y.C.; represented in permanent collections: Cleve. Mus. Art, Johnson & Johnson Corp. Collection, New Brunswick, N.J., Mus. Modern Art., N.Y.C., N.Y., Carnegie Mus., Pitts., Pa., N.J. State Mus., Trenton, N.J., Zimmerli Mus., Rutgers U., New Brunswick, N.J., Newark (N.J.) Pub. Libr., Hunterdon Mus., Clinton, N.J., Noyes Mus., Oceanville, N.J., Inst. for Jazz Studies Libr. Rutgers U., Newark, N.J., Alexander Libr., Rutgers U., New Brunswick, N.J. Featured in Women Artists' Book, Women's Caucus for Art Exhbn., 1982, Artists' Books, From the Traditional to the Avant Garde, 1982, Hunterdon County Notable Women, 2006, also govt. publ. on employment of disabled; reviewer NEA accessibility guidelines; artist in residence Balt. (Md.) Clayworks. Fellowship Rutgers Ctr., 2000; Recipient awards for ceramics and sculpture Butler Inst. Am. Art, 1963, 64, 65, nat. merit award for ceramics Mus. Contemporary Crafts, 1966; N.Y. State Council Arts grantee, 1982-83. Mem. Coll. Art Assn., Am. Crafts Council, Women's Caucus for Art (chair panel Nat. Conf.), Images of Disabled People in Western Art), Alumni Assn. Cleve. Inst. Art. Home and Studio: PO Box 387 Califon NJ 07830-0387 Office Phone: 908-832-2473.

CLOER, JANE, language educator; b. Copperhill, Tenn., Mar. 15, 1953; d. William Howard and Ruby Lee Cloer; m. Patrick Emmitt Elgan (div.); children: Mandy Lee Elgan, Erin Lynn Elgan. BS in edn. and English, Tenn. Tech. U., Cookeville, 1991; MEd in English, U. Tech., Chattanooga, 2000. Lic. profl. tchr. Tenn. English and lang. arts tchr. Mary Wheeler Elem., Pikeville, Tenn., 1991—92; English and journalism tchr. Bledsoe Co. HS, Pikeville, Tenn., 1992—96; GED tchr. Chattanooga State, 1996—2000; English and life skills tchr. Cumberland Hall, Chattanooga, 2000—01; English, reading and journalism tchr. Richard Hardy Meml. Sch., South Pittsburg, Tenn., 2001—. Office: Richard Hardy Meml Sch 1620 Hamilton Ave South Pittsburg TN 37380-1699

CLOGG, KATYE NARISE, music educator; b. Bellefonte, Pa., Jan. 25, 1979; d. Clifford and Judy (Ellenberger) Clogg. BS in Music Edn., Pa. State U., State College, 1997—2002. Elem. band tchr. E. Stroudsburg Area Sch. Dist., Pa., 2002—. Pvt. music instr., Stroudsburg, 2002—; musical pit orch. condr., East Stroudsburg, 2004—. Music accompanist, East Stroudsburg, Pa., 2004—06. Mem.: Nat. Band Assn., Assn. Music Edn. Home: 86 Broad St Stroudsburg PA 18360

CLOHAN, DEXANNE BOWERS, physical medical rehabilitation physician; b. Montgomery, Ala., Nov. 26, 1959; BA in Social Sciences, U. Colo.; postgraduate med. edn. in phys. medicine and rehabilitation, U. Calif., Irvine; MS in Adminstrn., George Washinton U., 1976; MD, George Washington U. Sch. Medicine, 1991. Diplomate Am. Bd. Phys. Med. Rehab. Intern U. Calif., Irvine, 1991-92, resident in phys. med. rehab., 1992-95; mem. staff Long Beach Meml. Med. Ctr., Calif., 1995—, Lakewood Regional Med. Ctr., Calif., 1995—; practiced medicine Rehabilitation Associates Med. Group; former med. dir. Meml. Independent Practice Assn., Meridian Health Care Mgmt., Thousand Oaks, Calif.; former nat. accounts med. dir. Aetna Inc., Santa Ana, Calif.; chief med. officer HealthSouth Corp., Birmingham, Ala., 2006—. Served on Am. Acad. Phys. Medicine and Rehabilitation Task Force on Medicare Inpatient Rehabilitation Criteria, Policy Adv. Panel to the JOINTS (Joint Replacement Outcomes in IRFs and Nursing Treatment Sites). Bd. dir. Calif. Health Decisions, 2003—06. Nat. Merit Scholar. Mem. AMA (mem. coun. on ethical and judicial affairs; dir. congl.affairs), Calif. Med. Assn-.(mem. coun. ethical affairs), Am. Assn. Phys. Medicine and Rehab., Calif. Soc. Phys. Medicine and Rehab., Phi Beta Kappa Office: HealthSouth Corp One HealthSouth Pkwy Birmingham AL 35243*

CLOSE, BETSY L., state representative; b. Shelton, Wash., May 4, 1950; m. Chris Close; 4 children. BA, Wash. State U., 1972, Ctrl. Wash. U., 1974; MS, Oreg. State U., 1978. Tchr. Wash. State Pub. Schs., 1974—76; grad. tchg. asst. Oreg. State U., Corvallis, 1976—78; instr., job devel. Benton County, 1978—79; tchr. Albany Pub. Schs., 1979—81; mem. Oreg. Ho. of Reps., 1998—. Chair Benton County Rep. Party, 1996—98; bd. dirs. Palestine Rural Fire, 1997—. Republican. Office: 900 Court St North East H-493 Salem OR 97301

CLOSE, CAROLE LYNNE, education educator, consultant; b. Coshocton, Ohio, Dec. 27, 1943; d. Robert Linn and Ruth Ann Close; m. Douglas Fabish, Aug. 27, 1977 (div. Dec. 30, 1982); 1 child, Coriana Lynne. BS in Edn., Bowling Green State U., 1966; MEd in Post-Secondary Edn. Adminstrn., Cleve. State U., 1979. Mediator Cmty. Youth Mediation Program, 1983. Advisor, coord. Winning Against Violent Environments (W.A.V.E.) Conflict Resolution Program, Cleve., 1983—; cons. and trainer Ohio Commn. on Dispute Resolution and Conflict Mgmt., Columbus, 1994—. Co-chair, mediation com. of the labor mgmt. coun. Cleve. Teachers Union, 1997—2004; ind. edn. and conflict resolution cons., 1983—; social studies tchr. Cleve. Pub. Schools, 1966—93. Edn. com. Assn. Conflict Resolution, Washington, D.C., 2002—02; civil rights and peace and justice activist Ohio, 1964—; mem. Hate Crime Com., Cleve., 1997—2004; steering com. mem. People Empowered Against Child Endangerment (PEACE), 1992—96; advisor Gov.'s Commn. Peace and Conflict Mgmt., Columbus, 1988—88. Named to Cleve. Mcpl. Sch. Dist. Educators and Alumni Hall of Fame, Grads Net, 2001; recipient The Global Peace award, Twenty-first Congl. Dist. Caucus, 1986, Leadership award, Cleve. Teachers Union, 1988, 1990, Governor's Spl. Recognition award for Outstanding Achievements in Mediation Edn., Gov. of Ohio, 1989, The Ghandi-King Peace award, Cath. Ch., 1989, Margaret Herrman Founder's award, Nat. Conf. on Peacemaking and Conflict Resolution, 1997, Liberty Bell Law Week award, Cleve. and Cuyahoga Bar Assn., 2001, Peace Works award, Strategies Against Violence Everywhere, 2003, Outstanding Tchr. award, Jr. Ahievement and the P.T.A. Mem.: Mediation Assn. No. Ohio, Women's Speakout for Peace and Justice. Achievements include development of school district-wide comprehensive peer mediation program. Avocations: reading, movies, travel. Home: 2184 Briarwood Rd Cleveland Heights OH 44118 Personal E-mail: cclose@aol.com.

CLOSE, GLENN, actress; b. Greenwich, Conn., Mar. 19, 1947; d. William and Bettine Close; m. Cabot Wade 1969 (div. 1971); m. James Marlas, 1984 (div. 1987); 1 child, Annie Maude Starke; m. David Shaw, Feb. 3, 2006. BA in drama and anthropology, Coll. William and Mary, 1974. Joined New Phoenix Repertory Co., 1974. Co-owner The Leaf and Bean Coffee House, Bozeman, Montana, 1993-94. Actor: (Broadway debut) Love for Love, 1974; (Broadway plays) The Rules of the Game, 1974, The Member of the Wedding, 1975, Rex, 1976, Barnum, 1980—81 (Tony award nomination for best featured actress in a musical, 1980), The Real Thing, 1984—85 (Tony award for best actress in a play, 1984), Benefactors, 1985—86, Death and the Maiden, 1992 (Tony award for best actress in a play, 1992), Sunset Boulevard, 1994—95 (Tony award for best actress in a musical, 1995), (other theatre appearances include) Uncommon Women and Others, The Singular Life of Albert Nobbs, 1982, Childhood, 1985, Joan of Arc at the Stake, 1985, Sunset Boulevard (LA), 1993—94, The Vagina Monologues, 1998; (films) The World According to Garp, 1982, The Big Chill, 1983, Greystoke: The Legend of Tarzan, Lord of the Apes (voice), The Natural, 1984, The Stone Boy, 1984, Jagged Edge, 1985, Maxie, 1985, Fatal Attraction, 1987, (voice) Gandahar, 1988, Dangerous Liaisons, 1988, Immediate Family, 1989, Reversal of Fortune, 1990, Hamlet, 1990, Meeting Venus, 1991, Hook, 1991, The House of the Spirits, 1993, The Paper, 1994, Mary Reilly, 1996, 101 Dalmations, 1996, Mars Attacks!, 1996, Paradise Road, 1997, Air Force One, 1997, Cookie's Fortune, 1999, (voice) Tarzan, 1999, Things You Can't Tell Just by Looking at Her, 2000, 102 Dalmations, 2000, The Safety of Objects, 2001, (voice) Pinocchio, 2002, Le Divorce, 2003, The Stepford Wives, 2004, Nine Lives, 2005, Heights, 2005, The Chumscrubber, 2005, (voice) Hoodwinked, 2005,: (TV films) The Rules of the Game, 1975, Too Far to Go, 1979, Orphan Train, 1979, The Elephant Man, 1982, Something About Amelia, 1984, Stones for Ibarra, 1988, She'll Take Romance, 1990, In the Gloaming, 1997, The Lion in Winter, 2003 (Golden Globe Award for best actress in a mini-series or TV movie, 2005, Screen Actors Guild Award for best actress in a TV movie or miniseries, 2005), Strip Search, 2004; (TV series) The Shield, 2005; actor, exec. prodr. (TV films) Sarah, Plain and Tall, 1991, Skylark, 1993, Serving in Silence: The Margarethe Cammermeyer Story, 1995 (Emmy award for best actress in a miniseries or special, 1995), Sarah, Plain and Tall: Winter's End, 1999, Baby, 2000, The Ballad of Lucy Whipple, 2001, South Pacific, 2001; exec. prodr.: (TV films) Journey, 1995. Recipient Woman of Yr. Award Hasty Pudding Theatricals, Harvard U., 1990, Dartmouth Film Award, 1990. Mem. Phi Beta Kappa. Office: Creative Artists Agy 9830 Wilshire Blvd Beverly Hills CA 90212-1804*

CLOUD, GARY LYNN, food and nutrition services administrator; b. Knoxville, Tenn., July 14, 1945; d. Henry Kelso Cloud. BS in Home Econs., Food and Nutrition, U. Tenn., 1966; MPH, U. N.C., 1972; postgrad., SUNY, Albany, 1988—. Lic. dietitian and pub. health nutritionist, Tenn.; registered Am. Dietetic Assn. Dietetic technician Fort Sander's Presbyn. Hosp., Knoxville, Tenn., 1966; dietetic internship N.Y. State Dept. Mental Hygiene Hudson River State Hosp., Poughkeepsie, N.Y., 1966-67; svc. systems corp. Del Monte, Inc., Bennington, Vt., 1967-70; sr. nutritionist, apprentice nutrition svc. cons. to nutrition svcs. cons. N.Y. State Dept. Health, 1970-73; assoc. nutritionist N.Y. State Bd. Social Welfare, Albany, 1973-76; playground supr. Knox County Dept. Recreation, Knoxville, 1980; chief clin. dietitian II, asst. dietary dept. dir. N.C. Dept. Human Resources, O'Berry Ctr., Goldsboro, N.C., 1980-82; nursing asst. Hillcrest North Nursing Home, Knox County, Tenn., 1988; libr. asst. U. Tenn. Libr.-Reserve Book Rm., 1990; shared facility registered dietitian Hillhaven Corp., Loudon Health Care, Tenn., 1990; auditor RQA Inc. Nat. Retail Quality Evaluators, Darion, Ill., 1994—. Regional supervising dietitian Svc. Sys. Corp., Del Monte Inc., 1967-70; dir. Bur. Nutrition Svcs. Mem. Am. Dietetic Assn., Tenn. Dietetic Assn., Knoxville Dist. Dietetic Assn., Knoxville Nutrition Coun.

CLOUD, LINDA BEAL, retired secondary school educator; b. Jay, Fla., Dec. 4, 1937; d. Charles Rockwood and Agnes (Diamond) Beal; m. Robert Vincent Cloud, Aug. 15, 1959 (dec. 1985). BA, Miss. Coll., 1959; MEd, U. So. Fla., 1976; EdS, Nova U., 1982; postgrad., Walden U., 1983. Cert. tchr. Fla. Tchr. Ft. Meade (Fla.) Jr.-Sr. HS, 1959-67, 80-89, Lake Wales (Fla.) H.S., 1967—80, drama coach vocal music dir., conversational Spanish composition, creative writing, English lit.; pres. Cloud Aero Svcs., Inc., Babson Park, Fla., 1992—; owner Diamond Firefox Peruvians. Part-time tchr. adults Spanish, English Polk County Schs., 1960—76; cons. Fla. Assn. Student Couns. Workshops, 1968—81; instr. Spanish Warner So. Coll., Lake Wales, 1974; instr. vocal music, drama, composition Webber Coll., Babson Park; pvt. tutor in field; writer, dir. numerous pageants for schs.; judge beauty pageants, theatre casting; cons. theatre workshops; guest reader local schs., 2002—03. Contbr. articles to profl. jours. and equine publs., poetry to The Color of Thought. Dir. Imogene Theatre, Milton, Fla., 2001; judge various beauty pageants and talent shows; soloist Babson Park Cmty. Ch., 1970—99, First Bapt. Ch., Jay, 1999—; charter mem., bd. dirs. Lake Wales Little Theatre, Inc., 1976; dir. Four Sq. swing choir; entertainer various orgns.; ring announcer Peruvian and Paso Fino Horse Shows, Naples, Fla. State Fair, 1987—88; mem. Defenders Crooked Lake; vol., dir. candy stripers Lakes Wales Hosp., 1973—79; dir. variety show Jokers Wild Imogene Theatre, Milton, Fla. Recipient Best Actress award, Lakes Wales Little Theatre, Inc., 1978—79. Mem.: AAUW, Fla. Ret. Tchrs. Assn., Fla./Santa Rosa County Ret. Educators Assn., Polk Fgn. Lang. Assn., Polk Coun. Tchrs. English, Fla. Coun. Tchrs. English, Nat. Coun. Tchrs. English, Jay Mural Soc. (bd. dirs.), Jay Hist. Soc., Sassy Singers, Babson Park Womans Club, Southeastern Peruvian Horse Club (life). Republican. Avocations: singing, acting, costume design, horseback riding. Home (Winter): 12174 Angell Rd Silver Creek NY 14136-9666 Home: Millers Landing 7332 Bent Grass Dr Winter Haven FL 33884

CLOUSE, BONNIDELL, psychology educator; b. San Jose, Costa Rica, July 5, 1928; came to U.S., 1930; d. Ranselaer and Lela (Freeland) Barrows; m. Robert Gordon Clouse, June 17, 1955; children: Gary, Kenneth. BA, Wheaton Coll., 1950; MA, Boston U., 1953; PhD, Ind. U., 1968. Psychiat. aide Inst. of Living, Hartford, Conn., 1950-52; asst. prof. edn. and psychology Bryan Coll., Dayton, Tenn., 1953-55; elem. tchr. Marion Twp. Schs., Marion, Iowa, 1958-63; teaching assoc. Ind. U., Bloomington, 1965-67; prof. ednl. and sch. psychology Ind. State U., Terre Haute, 1967—. Author: Moral Development: Perspectives in Psychology and Christian Belief, 1985, Teaching for Moral Growth, 1993; editor: Women in Ministry: Four Views, 1989; contbg. editor jours. Psychology and Theology, 1976—, Christian Parenting Today, 1988-91; contbr. articles to profl. jours. Sunday sch. tchr. First Brethren Ch., Clay City, Ind., 1964—; bd. dirs. YWCA, Terre Haute, Ind., 1976-79. Mem. Am. Psychol. Assn., Christian Assn. Psychol. Studies, Phi Kappa Phi. Democrat. Brethren. Avocation: needlecrafts. Home: 2122 S 21st St Terre Haute IN 47802-2634 Office: Sch Edn Ind State U Terre Haute IN 47809-0001

CLOUSE, NAN, elementary school educator, musician; b. Noel, Mo., Dec. 20, 1952; d. Bernard and Josephine McAbee. Bin Music Edn., John Brown U., Siloam Springs, Ark., 1974; M in Curriculum & Instrn., Northeastern State U., Tahlequah, Okla., 1995. Cert. tchr., adminstr. Okla. and Ark. Tchr. Pocola Pub. Schs., Okla., 2004—. Mem.: Music Educators Nat. Conf. (assoc.). Office: Pocola HS 603 E Pryor Ave Pocola OK Office Phone: 918-436-2424. Business E-Mail: nclouse@pocola.k12.ok.us.

CLOWNEY, MARY L., educational media specialist, librarian; b. Spartanburg, S.C., Aug. 20; d. Albert Clyde and Louise (Farr) Goode; m. Morris E. Clowney; children: Treva Marie, Shaun Edward. BS in LS, S.C. State U., Orangeburg, 1966; MA in Edn., Seton Hall U., 1987. Cert. pub. libr., sch. libr. Libr. Charleston St. Elem. Sch. Libr., Newark, 1966-67; children's libr. Newark Pub. Libr., 1967-68; libr. Peshine Ave. Sch., Newark, 1968-71, George Washington Carver Sch., Newark, 1971-91, East Side H.S., Newark, 1991-93; head libr. Malcolm X Shabazz H.S., Newark, 1993—. Mem. deaconess bd. Greater Abyssinian Bapt. Ch., also sec.; mem. Christian Advocates for Pub. Edn. Mem. Newark Sch. Libr. Assn. (pres.), Order Eastern Star, Tau Gamma Delta. Democrat. Baptist. Home: 1725 Cedarwood Dr Piscataway NJ 08854-2020 Office: Malcolm X Shabazz HS 80 Johnson Ave Newark NJ 07108-2729

CLOYDE, JAN R., bank executive; BA, MA, Okla. State U. V.p. Crocker Bank, 1980—84; sr. exec., mem. adminstrv. com. First Interstate Bancorp., 1984—96; mgmt. com. First Interstate Bank of Calif.; exec. v.p., dir. banking svcs. Home Savings of Am.; joined City Nat. Bank, Beverly Hills, 1998, exec. v.p., dir. banking svcs., mem. Strategy and Planning Com. Bd. mem. United

Way of Greater LA; bd. trustees U. Redlands'; bd. dirs. People Assisting the Homeless; founding mem., exec. women's com. Iris Cantor-UCLA Women's Health Ctr. Mem.: National Breast Cancer Coalition (mem. Pres. Coun.), Susan G. Komen Breast Cancer Found. (founding bd. mem., LA Chap.), Big Brothers/Big Sisters of Greater LA. Office: City Nat Corp City Nat Ctr 400 N Roxbury Dr Beverly Hills CA 90210

CLUGSTON, BONNIE IRENE, nurse; b. St. Louis, Aug. 9, 1954; d. William Ezra and Irene Alice Ditch; m. David Lee Clugston, Aug. 20, 1977 (dec. Aug. 1995); 1 child, Jennifer Ashley. AA in Nursing, Southeast Mo. State U., 1974, BSN, 1975. RN. Charge nurse St. Francis Hosp., Cape Girardeau, Mo., 1974-76; nurse ICU St. John's Mercy Hosp., St. Louis, 1976-77; asst. med. coord. St. Francis Hosp., 1977-78; group home parent Juneau (Alaska) Teen Homes, 1978-79; dir. nurses Harborview Devel. Ctr., Valdez, Alaska, 1980-91; program coord., acting dir. Seminole Cmty. Mental Healht Crisis Unit, Sanford, Fla., 1991-95; dir. med. svcs. AdvoServ, Mt. Dora, Fla., 1995—. Cons. in field. Named Top Ten Alumni, S.E. Mo. State U., 1998, 1999, 2000, 2002. Baptist. Avocations: skiing, water-skiing, horseback riding, travel, reading.

CLUNE, JOANN GUARDALIBENE, retired nurse; b. Lockport, NY, July 22, 1936; d. Joseph and Anna Guardalibene; m. Robert James Clune, Mar. 13, 1975; children: Elizabeth Ann, Christopher VanDeMark, Julie Crawford, Patricia Stein, Margaret Shaw, Megan McCormack, Allan VanDeMark, John. BSN magna cum laude, Niagara U., 1958; postgrad., Elmira Coll., 1982; postgrad, SUNY, Cortland, 1983. RN NY, 1958. Staff nurse, cardiology Vets. Hosp., Buffalo, 1958—59, head nurse oncology, 1959—60; staff nurse Lansing, Mich., 1960—61; sch. nurse Ithaca City Sch. Dist., NY, 1987—93, supr. nurses, 1994—99, sch. nurse, 2000—01; ret., 2001. Mem. NY Gov.'s Adv. Coun. on Transitional Care, Albany, 1995—98; exec. com. mem. NY State Rehab. Coun., Albany, 1998—; sec. adv. panel for students with disabilities NY State Commr. Edn., Albany, 1990—97, chair adv. panel, 1997—98. Instr. CPR for profl. rescuers Red Cross Health and Safety Svcs., Ithaca, 1997—2005, instr. health and safety tng. for child care providers, 1997—2005, instr. babysitter tng., first aid and CPR, 1997—2005; mem. coun., chair planning com. Alcohol and Drug Coun. Tompkins County, Inc., Ithaca, 2003—05; trustee Mountainview Hosp., Lockport, NY, 1970—73. Recipient Beta Chi Nu Purse award, Niagara U., 1958, NY State Nursing Assn. Gold Key award, 1958. Mem.: Sigma Theta Tau, Delta Kappa Gamma (treas. 2004—05). Home: 211 Christopher Ln Ithaca NY 14850

CLYDESDALE, PEGGY, artist, medical/surgical nurse; b. Spring Valley, Ill., Mar. 4, 1974; d. Arnold L. and Shirley F. Yunker; m. Jason Clydesdale, May 23, 2001. AAS, Ill. Vocat. C.C., Oglesby, 1995. RN, Ill. State Bd. Nursing, 1995, Nev. State Bd. Nursing, 2005, cert. Ill. Trauma Nurse Specialist, 2004, ACLS, Am. Heart Assn., 2006, Trained Nurse Critical Care, Nev., 2006. Mem., stuckist movement, White Trash Art/ Reno Stuckists, mixed media artwork, Senior Portfolio (Ill. Vocat. C.C. Art Scholarship Winner, 1992); editor: (periodical) Neva Mind. Mem.: Mensa. Personal E-mail: peg@ghosttraveller.com.

CLYMER, JANIS E., physics professor; d. Farrand A. and Betty J. Peterson; m. Paul D. Clymer, Jan. 28, 1948; children: Chris A., Traci M. BS in Physics and Math., Youngstown State U., Ohio, 1972; MS in Physics, Ohio State U., Columbus, 1975, PhD in Physics, 1983. Tchg. assoc., part time faculty Ohio State U., Columbus, 1972—87; part time faculty Franklin U., 1984—85, Columbus State U., 1989—92, Kent State U., Champion, 1994—95, Youngstown State U., 1997—. Coord. gen edn. physics sects. Youngstown State U. Panelist, workshop organizer Women Sci. & Engring., Youngstown, 1997—2006; judge Youngstown State U. Physics Olympics. Mem.: Am. Assn. Physics Tchrs., Am. Phys. Soc., Sigma Pi Sigma. Independent. Office: Youngstown State University - Physics One University Plaza Youngstown OH 44555 Office Phone: 330-941-2735. Personal E-mail: jeclymer@ysu.edu.

CLYNES, CAROLANN ELIZABETH, realtor; b. Hoboken, N.J., June 30, 1944; d. Merwin Cecil and Marie Dolores Beck; m. Patrick Robert Clynes, June 10, 1967 (div. Oct. 1986); m. Robert Bradford Bourne, Oct. 8, 1988; stepchildren: Jonathan Bourne, Christopher Bourne, Mark Kirkpatrick, Sarah Bourne, Susan Bourne, Molly Bourne. Student, Seton Hall U., 1964; BA in History and French, Georgian Ct. Coll., 1965; student, The Sorbonne, Paris, 1966; student in real estate courses, NYU Adult Edn., 1984; student, Inst. Residential Mktg., 1990. Cert. appraiser Nat. Realtors Appraisal Inst., 1987. Sales assoc. Helen Fisher Realty, 1970—72, Peter Farley Realtor, 1972—76; broker, sales assoc. Burgdorff Realtors, 1976—88; dir. sales Lois Schneider Realtor, 1988—94, Murray Hill Farm, 1988—94; broker, mgr., v.p. Summit office Burgdorff Realtors, Summit, NJ, 1994—96, v.p. corp. bus. devel. Murray Hill, NJ, 1996—, broker, sales assoc., 1997—. Mem. Summit Hist. Preservation Commn., 1995—2003, chair, 1995—2000, 2003; mem. planning com. Summit Downtown, Inc., 1994—96; mem. capital cabinet Nat. Interfaith Hospitality Network, 1997—; chmn. grants and loans com. NJ Hist. Trust, 2004, vice chmn. trust, 2005. Recipient award, Jr. League of Summit, N.J., 1997, appointment to N.J. Historic Trust, Gov. McGreevey, 2002. Mem.: Real Estate Brokerage Mgrs. Coun. (cert. 1995), N.J. Assn. Realtors Disting. Sales Club. Democrat. Episcopalian. Avocations: historic preservation, choral music, opera, French, antiques, reading. Home: 130 Pine Grove Ave Summit NJ 07901 Office: Burgdorff Realtors 401 Springfield Ave Summit NJ 07901 Office Phone: 908-522-3003. E-mail: carolann-clynes@burgdorff.com.

CMAR, JANICE BUTKO, home economist, educator; b. Pitts., Nov. 10, 1954; d. Edward Michael and Ruth Lillian (Pickard) Butko; m. Dennis Paul Cmar, children: Michael, Nicole. BS, Mansfield U., 1976; MS, Duquesne U., 1990. Home econ. tchr. Duquesne (Pa.) Sch. Dist., 1978-83; special edn. tchr. Allegheny Intermediate Unit, Pitts., 1985-95; home econs. tchr. Peters Twp. Sch. Dist., McMurray, Pa., 1995—. Sponsor Duquesne High Sch., Y-Teens and Future Homemakers Am., 1979-83, Pathfinder Student Coun., Bethel Park, Pa., Mon-Valley Secondary Sch. Yearbook and Prom, Jefferson, Pa. Vol. Allegheny County Dept. Cmty. Svcs., Pitts., 1986—97; mem. com. Allegheny County Dem. Orgn.; elected Borough Jefferson Hills Coun., 1997, 2001—03, coun. v.p., 2000, 2002; mem. cmty. adv. panel Hercules Corp., 2000; bd. dirs. South Hills Coun. Govts., 2000. Mem. Am. Fedn. Tchrs., Am. Assn. Family and Consumer Scis., State Assn. Family and Consumer Scis., Allegheny County Assn. Family and Consumer Scis. (pres. 1991-92), Phi Delta Kappa, Alpha Sigma Tau. Democrat. Home: 918 Old Hickory Ln Jefferson Hills PA 15025-3437 Office: 625 E Mcmurray Rd Mc Murray PA 15317-3497

COADY, MARY LUZ K., pediatrician; b. Dallas, June 5, 1933; d. Leo Dean Coady and Marie Guillen; m. Joseph Harlan Calhoun (div.); children: Julia Luz Calhoun, Lia Ann Reinholt; m. Henry Clay Baldwin III, May 25, 1991 (dec.). BA, U. Pa., Phila., 1955; MD, Woman's Med. Coll. Pa., Phila., 1962. Diplomate Am. Bd. Pediat. Resident Children's Hosp. Phila., 1963, San Francisco Children's Hosp., 1965—66, St. Christopher's Hosp., Phila., 1966—67; pediatrician Bryn Mawr, Pa., 1967—99; ret., 1999. Pediat. staff Byrn Mawr Hosp., 1967—99, dir. pediat. dept., 1984—90; pediat. staff St. Christopher's Hosp., 1968—99; bd. dirs. Child Guidance Clinic Children's Hosp. Phila., 1975—80. Mem.: Am. Acad. Pediat. Avocations: gardening, needlecrafts.

COAKLEY, DEIRDRE, columnist, writer; b. Detroit, Aug. 10, 1927; d. Cecil Francis and Elizabeth Kearney Coakley. Grad., Hollywood (Calif.) H.S., 1944. Mem. editl. staff L.A. Examiner, 1943-46; mem. editl. staff various other newspapers L.A., to 1954; advt. exec., mag. editor Las Vegas (Nev.) Sun, 1954-66, Sunday mag. editor, 1977-85; freelance advt. and pub. rels. exec. Las Vegas, 1966-68; pub. rels. exec. Jimmy Snyder Info. Unltd. Tropicana Hotel, Las Vegas, 1968-74; pub. rels. dir. Desert Springs Hosp., Las Vegas, 1974-77; writer, columnist Gadsden (Ala.) Times, 1985—. Editor: The Way it Was: Diary of a Pioneer Woman, 1979-80; author: The MGM Grand Hotel Fire, 1982, Portrait of a City: An Informal History of Gadsden, Alabama 1846-1996, 1996; writer, curator Voices and Images of World War II. Publicist United Way of Etowah County, Gadsden, 1994—; bd. dirs. Metro. Arts Coun., 1988-95, Gadsden Symphony Orch., 1990-96; mem. Gadsden Ctr. Cultural Arts. Mem. Gadsden Art Assn., Etowah Hist. Soc. Democrat. Roman Catholic. Avocation: genealogy. Home: 739 Church Rd Gadsden AL 35904-3143 E-mail: dcoakley@internetpro.net.

COAN, PATRICIA A., judge; b. NYC, July 21, 1945; 2 children. BSN, Georgetown U., 1967; JD, U. Denver, 1981. Bar: Colo. 1982; RN N.Y., Conn., Mont. Pvt. practice, Denver, Colo., 1982-96; magistrate judge U.S. Dist. Ct. for Dist. Colo., Denver, 1996—. Bd. dirs. Colo. Lawyers Health Program. Mem. Women's Bar Assn., Colo. Bar Assn., Denver Bar Assn., Sigma Theta Tau, Alpha Sigma Nu. Office: 901 19th St Denver CO 80294-1929 Office Phone: 303-844-4892.

COAN, RACHEL B., lawyer; AB, Smith Coll., 1977; JD, Rutgers U., 1984. Bar: NY 1985. Ptnr., co-chmn. pro bono com. LeBoeuf, Lamb, Greene & MacRae, NYC. Mem.: Assn. Bar City NY, ABA-Bus. Law Sect. (structured fin. sub-com., fed. regulation of securities com.). Office: LeBoeuf Lamb Greene & MacRae LLP 125 W 55th St New York NY 10019-5715 Office Phone: 212-424-8106. Office Fax: 212-424-8500. Business E-Mail: rbcoan@llgm.com.

COATES, DEBORAH PHILLIPS, visual arts educator; b. Savannah, Ga., Apr. 9, 1956; d. Edward and Joyce Trellis (Zittrouer) Phillips; m. Everett Lacy Coates, July 1, 1978; children: Heather Elizabeth, Emily Grace. BA in Art and Religion, Meredith Coll., Raleigh, N.C., 1978; MA in Art Edn., E. Carolina U., Greenville, 1980. Cert. tchr., N.C.; nat. bd. cert. early adolscence to young adulthood art. Course programmer Martin C.C., Williamston, N.C., 1978-80; tchr. Perquimans County High Sch., Hertford, N.C., 1981-87, Clayton Mid. Sch., Clayton, N.C., 1987—; lead tchr. art Johnston County Schs., Smithfield, 1991-94. Grassroots chmn. Johnston County Arts Coun., Smithfield, 1988-95; yearbook sponsor Clayton Mid. Sch., 1988—, art club sponsor, 1991-94; exploration chairperson and quality coun. rep. Clayton Mid. Sch., 2002-06; participant NCTAN seminar on East Asia, 2005. Exhibited in group shows at N.C. State Fair, 1988 (selected exhibitor), 11th Annual Juried Art Show, 1990 (selected exhibitor), 1st Annual Adult Art Show, 1991 (honorable mention), (juried exhbn.) Art from Triangle Pub. Schs.: Educators as Artist, 2004; selected quilter for N.C. Ctr. Advancement for Teaching dedication quilt, 1991. Named N.C. Mid. Sch. Art Tchr. of Yr., 1993, Vol. of Yr., Johnston County Arts Coun., 1995; grantee Johnston County Edn. Found., 1991, 92, 93, 95, 96, 97, 98, 2001, Boyette grantee, 1992, 97, 99, 2001, 02, 03; recipient Gov.'s award for Excellence in Edn., 1987. Mem. N.C. Art Edn. Assn. (presenter 1988, 95), Profl. Educators of N.C. Avocations: photography, acrylic and watercolor painting, papermaking. Home: 1011 Mulberry Rd Clayton NC 27520-2131 Office: Clayton Mid Sch 409 Guy Rd Clayton NC 27520-7204

COATES, SHIRLEY JEAN, finance educator, secondary school educator; b. Nashville, Tenn., Oct. 9, 1944; d. Jerry Baxter Springer and Cora Louise Green; m. Arthur Andrew Coates; children: Andrea, John. BS, Mid. Tenn. State U., 1968; MS, Brigham Young U., 1971. Lic. profl. tchr., cert. tchr. Tenn. career level III. Instr. Young Harris Coll., Young Harris, Ga., 1968—70, U. of Miss., Oxford, Miss., 1971—72; tchr. Dickson County Jr. H.S., Dickson, Tenn., 1972—73, Hickman County H.S., Centerville, Tenn., 1973—. Bus. dept. chmn. Hickman County H.S., Centerville, Tenn., 1994—. Sponsor, Hickman County - Tenn. type-a-thon Leukemia Soc. of Am., BPA Chpt., Nashville, 1989—99; sec. Hickman County H.S. Band Boosters, Centerville, Tenn., 1988—94, Hickman County H.S. Athletic Booster Club, Centerville, Tenn., 1995—96; pageant chmn. Hickman County 4-H Vol. Leaders, Centerville, Tenn., 1990—94; project dir. (head start book dr.) South Ctrl. Human Resources Agy., Centerville, Tenn., 1988—89. Named Tchr. of Yr., Hickman County HS Bd. of Edn., 1990, Bus. Dept. Tchr. of Yr., Hickman County H.S., 2000, Most Disting. H.S. Tchr., Hickman County Tenn. Edn. Assn., 2002; recipient, 2003. Mem.: Bus. Profls. Am. (honor adv. 1991, star advisor 1992), Assn. for Career and Tech. Edn., Daughters of Am. Revolution (asst. registrar, treas. 1998—2002).

COATS, KATHY LYNN, biology educator; b. Martinsville, Va., Dec. 9, 1975; BS, Va. Commonwealth U., Richmond, 1997; MAT, Va. Commonwealth U., 1999. Cert. Tchr. Adolescence and Young Adulthood Sci. Nat. Bd. For Profl. Tchg. Stds., 2005. Tchr. life sci. Henrico County Pub. Schs., Richmond, 1999—2000; tchr. biology Chesterfield County Pub. Schs., Midlothian, Va., 2000—. Coach cheerleading Clover Hill H.S., Midlothian, Va., 2000—. Mem.: NSTA, Chesterfield Edn. Assn., Va. Sci. Tchrs. Assn. Office: Clover Hill High School 13900 Hull Street Road Midlothian VA 23112 Office Fax: 804-739-6239. Business E-Mail: kathy_coats@ccpsnet.net.

COBA-LOH, CLAUDINE JEAN, psychology professor; b. Bridgeport, Conn., 1969; d. Josephine Grace Coba; m. Andrew J. Loh, June 15, 2002; children: Jason Andrew, Joshua Richard. BSc, Sacred Heart U., Fairfield, Conn., 1991; MSc, So. Conn. State U., New Haven, Conn., 1994. Mem. mental health staff Hall-Brooke Hosp., Westport, Conn., 1990—93; counselor battered women The Umbrella, Ansonia, Conn., 1993—94; counselor intake Families In Recovery, Stamford, Conn., 1994—96; counselor supported edn. Dept. Mental Health and Addiction Svcs., Trumbull, Conn., 1996—98; prof. Housatonic C.C., Bridgeport, Conn., 1998—. Cons. in field; adv. behavior healthcare cert. program Housatonic C.C., 1998—. Recipient Devel. Excellence award, Nat. Inst. Staff and Orgns., 2001. Mem.: APA, Am. Counseling Assn., Psi Beta. Home: 33 Sylvan Dr Shelton CT 06484 Office: Housatonic Cmty Coll 900 Lafayette Blvd Bridgeport CT 06604 E-mail: profcobaloh@aol.com.

COBB, CECELIA ANNETTE, retired counselor; b. Dayton, Ohio, June 22, 1944; d. Fred E. and Margaret Laverne (Ogle) C.; m. Robert A. Fackler, June 25, 1966 (div. Mar. 1981); m. James A. McCluskey, June 18, 1983; 1 child, James Christian; m. Charles H. Cole, Oct. 4, 2003. BS, Ohio U., Athens, 1967; MA in Teaching, Saginaw Valley State U., University Ctr., Mich., 1978; MA in Counseling, Oakland U., Rochester, Mich., 1993. Lic. profl. counselor, Mich.; cert. tchr., Mich. Tchr. L'Anse Creuse Pub. Schs., Mt. Clemens, Mich., 1966-91, counselor, 1993—2001. Cons. Establishment Crisis Ctr., Mt. Clemens, 1968-70; supr. tchr. Mich. State U., Lansing, 1970-72; leader pilot project Quest Inc., Findlay, Ohio, 1982-83. Provider shelter for homeless, Mt. Clemens, 1983-99. Mem. NEA, Am. Sch. Counseling Assn., Mich. Edn. Assn., Mich. Sch. Counseling Assn., Macomb County Assn. Counseling and Devel., Chi Sigma Iota. Democrat. Avocations: needlecrafts, golf, reading. Home: 7130 Fallen Oak Trce Dayton OH 45459-4844 Personal E-mail: ccobblpc@aol.com.

COBB, DELORES MASSEY, science educator; d. Gerald Rudolph and Dorothy Jackson Massey; m. Charles Cobb, May 19, 1994; children: Ryan Scott Lane, Jonathan Mark Lane. BS in Biology with honors, Atlantic Christian Coll. (now Barton), NC, 1973; MA in Edn.- Sci. Edn., East Carolina U., Greenville, N.C., 1990. Cert. tchr. Nat. Bd. Tchg. Profls., 2000. Sci. tchr. Goldsboro H.S., NC, 1974—92, Cary H.S., 1992—. Mem.: N.C. Sci. Tchrs. Assn., N.C. Assn. Educators. Methodist. Office Phone: 919-469-3549.

COBB, JANE OVERTON, government official; b. Charleston, S.C., July 23, 1962; d. Dolphin Dunnaha and Sue (Hagood) Overton; m. Robert Watson Cobb, July 15, 1989; children: Robert Watson, Jr., Johnson Hagood, Calvin Hayes. BA, Vanderbilt U., 1984, MEd, 1985. Cert. secondary tchr., Ga. Tchr. English Columbia High Sch., Atlanta, 1985-86; tchr. ESL Hangzhou, China, 1986-87; govt. affairs asst. Hewlett Packard Co., Washington, 1987-89; mem. congrl. staff U.S. Ho. Reps., Washington, 1989-2001; dir. congl. affairs Fed. Emergency Mgmt. Agy., Washington, 2000—02; dir. office legis. affairs SEC, Washington, 2002—. Office: SEC Office of Legis Affairs 100 F St NE Washington DC 20549 Office Phone: 202-551-2010.

COBB, JUDY LYNN, elementary school educator; b. Fresno, Calif., July 31, 1940; d. V.W. and Ruth (Benight) Keim; m. Jeffrey, Jay. BA, Calif. State U., Fresno, 1962. Tchr. Fresno (Calif.) Unified Sch. Dist., 1963-68, Lodi (Calif.) Unified Sch. Dist., 1976—2002, chpt. I ESL resource tchr., 1981-87. Designer, implementor curriculum for elem. students, using literature, oral and written language, and art to teach reading, social studies, science and multi-cultural activities; nat. grant participant Program Academic Excellence, 1984-87; mem. Lodi Dist. Yr. Round Sch. Com., Art Task Force; speaker, presenter in field. Contbg. author: Language Literature Approach to English as a Second Language; Represented in permanent collections Lodi Unified Sch. Dist. Named Mentor Tchr., 1986-88 Mem. San Joaquin Reading Assn., Calif. Reading Assn., Internat. Reading Assn. (artist dist. activities, Lodi dist. yr. round sch. com. and art task force). Home: 9531 Springfield Way Stockton CA 95212-2016 Personal E-mail: judylcobb@aol.com.

COBB, KAY BEEVERS, state supreme court justice, retired state senator; b. Quitman County, Miss., Feb. 28, 1942; m. Larry Cobb. BS, Miss. U. for Women; JD, U. Miss. Atty. priv. practice, Oxford, Miss., 1978—84; dir. prosecutors prog. U. Miss. Law Sch.; atty. Miss. Bur. of Narcotics, 1984—88; various positions including coord. SWEEPS anti-drug prog. Office of Miss. Atty. Gen., 1988—92; senator State of Miss., 1992—96; atty. priv. practice, Oxford, 1996—99; assoc. justice Miss. Supreme Ct., 1999—, presiding justice, 2004—. Former mem. President's Commn. on US Model State Drug Laws, Nat. Alliance for Model State Drug Laws. Mem. Miss. Bar Assn. (Chief Justice award 2003), Vets. Aux., C. of C. Baptist. Office: Miss Supreme Ct PO Box 117 450 High St Jackson MS 39205 Office Phone: 601-359-2099.

COBB, ROWENA NOELANI BLAKE, real estate broker; b. Kauai, Hawaii, May 1, 1939; d. Bernard K. Blake and Hattie Kanui Yuen; m. James Jackson Cobb, Dec. 22, 1962; children: Shelly Ranelle Noelani, Bret Kimo Jackson. BS in Edn., Bob Jones U., 1961; broker's lic., Vitousek Sch. Real Estate, Honolulu, 1981. Lic. real estate broker, Honolulu; cert. residential specialist, 1995-. Med. supr. Hawaii Med. Svc. Assn., 1964-65, 66-68; bus. mgr. Micronesian Occupl. Ctr., Koror Palau, 1968-70; prin. broker Cobb Realty, Lihue, Hawaii, 1983—; sec. Neighbor Island MLS Svc., Honolulu, 1985-87, vice chmn., 1987-88; chmn. MLS Hawaii, Inc., Honolulu, 1988-90. Assoc. editor Jour. Entymology, 1965-66. Sec. Koloa Cmty. Assn., 1981—98, pres., 1989, bd. dir., 2002—04, dir., 2005—; mem. Hoi'Ke Pub. TV, 1998—, treas., 1999, v.p., 2002, pres., 2000—02, 2003—04; vice chair Kauai Schs. Adv. Coun., 1995—98, pres., 2000; mem. adv. bd. KKCR Radio, 2000; chmn. Kauai Ctr. Arts, Edn. and Tech., 2003, 2004, 2005; bd. dir. Kekahu Found., 1999—2001, Kauai United Way, 2003—04, 2005—06. Mem.: Kauai C. of C., Kauai Bd. Realtors (v.p. 1984, pres. 1985, bd. dir. 1995—97, treas. 1999, 2007—, Realtor Assoc. of Yr. award 1983, Realtor of Yr. award 1986), Hawaii Assn. Realtors (state bd. dir. 1984, v.p. 1985, dir. 1995—96, 2004—06, cert. tchr.), Nat. Assn. Realtors (grad. Realtors Inst., cert. residential specialist), Soroptimists (bd. dir. Lihue chpt. 1986—89, treas. 1989). Avocations: reading, music, travel. Office: PO Box 157 Koloa HI 96756-0157 Office Phone: 808-742-9497. Business E-Mail: ro@jrcobb.net.

COBB, SHIRLEY ANN DODSON, public relations consultant, journalist; b. Oklahoma City, Jan. 1, 1936; d. William Ray and Irene Dodson; m. Roy Lampkin Cobb, Jr., June 21, 1958; children: Kendra Leigh, Cary William, Paul Alan. BA in Journalism with distinction, U. Okla., 1958, postgrad., 1972, Jacksonville U., 1962. Info. specialist Pacific Missile Test Ctr., Point Mugu, Calif., 1975-76; reporter, spltv. editor Religion and Fashion News Chronicle, 1977-81; cons. pub. rels., cable TV, telecom. Camarillo, Calif., 1977—; media mgr. pub. info. cable TV and telecom. City of Thousand Oaks, Calif., 1983-99. Contbr. articles to profl. jours. Pres. Point Mugu Officers' Wives Club, 1975-76; trustee Ocean View Sch. Bd., 1976-79; bd. dir. Camarillo Hospice, 1983-85, Long Term Care of Ventura County, Inc., 2001-03; sec. Ednl. TV for Conejo, 1997-98, pres., 1998-2000, bd. dir., 1997-2002; vice chair Greater Thousand Oaks Telecmty., 1999-2000; treas. Thousand Oaks Rep. Women Federated, 2001-03, pres., 2004; with Ventura County Leadership Acad., 1999-2002; bd. dir. LWV Ventura County, 1999-2003, v.p., comm. dir., 2002-03, Calif. Luth. Univ. Cmty. Leaders Assn., 1987-. Recipient Spot News award San Fernando Valley Press Club, 1979, First Pl. spl. program Calif. Assn. Pub. Info. Ofcls., 1985, Helen Putnam award League of Calif. Cities, 1989, Telecom. Proj. award, League of Calif. Cities Telecom., 1998, 1st pl. award Best Practice award Govt., Bus., Edn. Tech. Expo '98. Mem. Pub. Rels. Soc. Am. (LA chpt. liaison 1991), Calif. Assn. Pub. Info. Ofcls. (pres. 1989-90, Paul Clark Lifetime Achievement award 1993), Conejo Valley Hist. Soc. (sec. 1993-96, co-chmn. oral history com. 2001-, chair 2003-, bd. dir. 2003-), Las Posas Country Club, Spanish Hills Country Club, Town Hall of Calif. Club, Phi Beta Kappa, Chi Omega (v.p. 1957-58, mem. mortar bd.). Republican. Home: 2481 Brookhill Dr Camarillo CA 93010-2112 Personal E-mail: cobbweb@aol.com.

COBB, SUE MCCOURT, state official, former ambassador; b. Aug. 18, 1937; d. Benjamin Arnold and Ruth (Griffin) McCourt; m. Charles E. Cobb Jr., Feb. 28, 1959; children: Christian McCourt, Tobin Templeton. BA, Stanford U., 1959; JD, U. Miami, 1978. Bar: US Supreme Ct., Fla. 1978, Colo., DC 1989. Tchr. Crystal Springs Sch. for Girls, Hillsborough, Calif., 1960—68; CEO Fla. Dept. Lottery; founding ptnr. pub. fin. dept. Greenberg-Traurig Law Firm; US amb. to Jamaica US Dept. State, Kingston, 2001—05; ptnr. Cobb Ptnrs., Ltd., Coral Gables, Fla.; sec. state State of Fla., Tallahassee, 2005—. Chmn. bd. Fed. Res. Bank, Miami br., 1984, 1986, 1988; chmn. Dade County Super Bowl Authority, 1982—87; bd. dirs. Ransom-Everglades Sch., 1976—86; dir. United Way, Dade County; founder, sponsor US Dept. State's Cobb Award for Initiative and Success in Trade Devel. Recipient Order of the Falcon, Grand Cross Knight, Iceland, Humanitarian of Yr. award, Red Cross, Silver Medallion award, Nat. Conf. Christians and Jews. Achievements include being the first female US Chief of Mission at Embassy Kingston. Avocations: scuba diving, skiing, tennis. Office: Office Sec State RA Gray Bldg 500 S Bronough Tallahassee FL 32399 Office Phone: 305-441-1700.*

COBB, VANESSA WYNVETTE, elementary school educator; b. Sanford, NC, May 27, 1953; d. Ernest and Frances Olivia Cobb. BS, Hampton U., Va., 1976; MA, Mich. State U., East Lansing, 1977. Tchr. basic skills improvement East Orange Sch. Dist., NJ, 1977—94, tchr. math, soc. studies, 1994—95, tchr. 2nd grade, 1995—96, tchr. 5th grade sci., 1996—97, tchr. 1st, 2nd grade, 1995—96, tchr. 1st grade, 1998—2000, tchr. pre-K, 2000—02, 2003—05, tchr. 5th grade, 2002—03, tchr., kindergarten, 1st grade, 2005—. Mem. Newark Mus.; contbg. mem. UNICEF. Mem.: NEA, Am. Counseling Assn., NJ Sch. Counselor Assn., Am. Sch. Counselor Assn., Essex County Edn. Assn., NJ Edn. Assn., East Orange Edn. Assn., Gordon Parks Acad. Sunshine Club. Avocations: photography, ballet, reading, music, theater. Home: 9 Mill Rd Burlington NJ 08016

COBB, VIRGINIA HORTON, artist, educator; b. Oklahoma City, Nov. 23, 1933; d. Wayne and Ruth (Goodale) Horton; m. Bruce L. Cobb, Dec. 30, 1951 (div. 1985); children: Bruce Wayne, Juliann, William Stuart, M. Jerrold Friedman, 1988. Student, U. Colo., 1966-67, Community Coll., Denver, 1967; student of, William Schimmel, Ariz., 1965-66, Edgar Whitney, N.Y.C., 1966, Chen Chi, 1974. Comml. artist and designer Ruth Horton Studios, Oklahoma City, 1954-63; instr. seminars, 1974—, N.Mex. Watercolor Soc., Albuquerque, 1976, Okla. Mus. Art, Oklahoma City, 1976, Upstairs Gallery Workshops, Arlington, Tex., 1977, 78, 79, 80, St. Louis Art Guild, 1980, Alaska Water Color Soc., Anchorage, 1981, Needham (Mass.) Art Center, 1981, N.C. Watercolor Soc., Charlotte, 1981, San Diego Watercolor Soc., 1981, S.C. Water Color Soc., Florence, 1981, Hawaii Water Color Soc., 1989, Trillium Workshops, Toronto, 1989, 90, Baffin Island, 1992, Maui, Hawaii, 1993, Vancouver Island, 1990, 91. Guest instr. Crafton Hills Coll. Master Seminars, Yucaipa, Calif., 1979, 80, 81, U. Alaska, Anchorage, 1981, Master Class/Santa Fe Painting Workshops/Friedman Cobb Studios, 1989—; guest lectr. Watermedia 2000, Houston; lectr. Sta. KRDO-TV, 1977, Francis Marion Coll., Florence, 1981, Sta. KAKM, Anchorage, 1981; guest spkr. Watermedia, Houston, 2003. Author: Discovering The Inner Eye, 1988; author (with Jerrold Friedman) Alice.on bristol, 1996, (with Polly Hammett) Designsense, 2003; contbr. articles to art publs.; one-woman shows of watercolor paintings, Jack Meier Galleries, Houston, 1979-81, 83-85, One Artist: San Juan Coll., 1995, Art Resources, St. Paul, 1988, Sturh Mus., Grand Island, Nebr., 1982; group shows include recent acquisitions of the Nat. Acad., 1982, layering, an art of time and space, 1985, NAD, N.Y.C., 1978, 79-81, San Bernardino (Calif.) County Mus., 1978, Nat. Watercolor Invitational, Rochester, N.Y., 1981, Rocky Mountain Nat. Watermedia Exhbt., Golden, Colo., 1978, 79, 81, Albuquerque Mus. Art, 1985, Am. Watercolor Soc., 1985; invitational exhbns. include Internat. Waters: A Touring Exhibit, Canada, 1991, USA, 1992, Great Britain, 1992, Scotland, 1993; represented in permanent collections, NAD, Jefferson County (Colo.) Public Library, Foothills Art Center, Golden, Colo., St. Lawrence U., Canton, N.Y., N.Mex. Watercolor Soc., Albuquerque, Santa Fe Mus. Fine Arts. Recipient Foothills Art Ctr. award, 1976, Edgar Fox award Watercolor U.S.A., 1973, Denver award Rocky Mountain Nat. Exhbn., 1981, Am. Artist Achievement award, 1994. Mem. NAD (Walter Biggs Meml. award 1978, 81), Nat. Watercolor Soc. (Strathmore Paper Co. award 1975), Am. Watercolor Soc. (Paul B. Remmey Meml. award 1974,. Arches Paper Co. award 1977, Edgar Whitney award 1978, Mary Pleishner Meml. award 1980, High Winds medal 1981, Silver medal of Honor 1983, guest demonstrator 1980, nat. juror 1981, Dolphin fellow 1982, juror Watercolor West 1990, Juror award 1999), N.Mex. Watercolor Soc. (hon.), Rocky Mountain Watermedia Soc. Personal E-mail: veacobb@yahoo.com.

COBBINAH, INGENUE F., obstetrician, gynecologist; 1 child, Ysabelle. BS, Xavier U., New Orleans, 1988; MD, U. Pa., Phila., 1993. Diplomate Am. Bd. Ob-Gyn., 2000. Ptnr. Assoc. Women's Care Physicians, Lees Summit, Mo., 1999—. Med. dir. St. Mary's Med. Ctr. Blue Springs, Mo., 2001—. Office: 3450 NE Ralph Powell Rd Lees Summit MO 64064 Office Phone: 816-246-7200.

COBERLY, MARGARET, psychologist, educator; d. Charles Wheeler Coberly and Elizabeth Chandler Stephens; m. Harry Martin Eichelberger, III, Sept. 9, 1968 (div. 1981); children: Ariana Eichelberger, Ian Eichelberger. RN, St. Francis Sch. Nursing, San Francisco, 1965; BS, SUNY, Albany, 1989; MA, U. Hawaii, 1992, PhD, 1996. RN Calif., Hawaii. Staff and charge nurse Met. Hosp. Trauma Ctr., N.Y.C., 1978—81, Calif. Hosp. Med. Ctr., L.A., 1981—84; case mgr. Hospice Hawaii, Honolulu, 1989—93, dir. rsch., 1997—2001; dir. nurses, v.p., co-owner Respite Care Hawaii, Honolulu, 1993—96; psychology prof. U. Hawaii Windward, Kaneohe, 1999—. Bd. dirs. Jamyang Found., Honolulu; cons., tchr. in field. Author: Sacred Passage: How to Provide Fearless, Compassionate Care for the Dying, 2002, 2003; contbr. chapters to books, articles to profl. jours. Sec.-treas. Internat. Found. Transpersonal Studies, Honolulu, 1998—. Mem.: APA, Sakyadhita Assn. Buddhist Women (treas. 1991—). Achievements include development of unique system of tracking the stages of dying by using the ancient Tibetan Buddhist teachings about death. Avocation: writing. Office: Univ Hawaii Windward 45-720 Kea ahala Rd Kaneohe HI 96744 Home: 1221 Victoria St Apt 602 Honolulu HI 96814-1431

COBE-ROSS, LORI, casting director; b. N.Y.C., Jan. 20, 1967; d. Sandy Cobe and Marianne (Findler) Bobick. Office, personnel mgr. Calif. Mag., L.A., 1979-85; dir. bus. affairs, casting dir. Intercontinental Releasing, L.A., 1985-87; ind. casting dir. Lori Cobe Casting, Los Angeles, 1987—. Producer: (feature film) Nicky and the Kack, (play) Rocket to the Moon by Clifford Odets; casting dir. (films) Open House, The Jigsaw Murders, Eyewitness to Murder, Black Snow, Riding the Edge, Down and Dirty, Last Call, The Arrival, Lady's Choice, Total Exposure, Night Eyes, Night Eyes 2, Two-gether, Secret Games, Sexual Response, The Other Woman, The Pamela Principle, Night Rhythms, Animal Instincts, (TV) Divorce Court, Wake Rattle and Roll (PBS TV series) On Common Ground, 1999, Madison Heights, 2002, others. Recipient L.A. Dramalogue award for prodn. Rocket to the Moon, 1988; nominee Outstanding Daytime Casting, Casting Soc. Am. Mem. Women in Film, Casting Soc. Am., Acad. tV Arts and Scis., Ind. Feature Project West. Office: Lori Cobe-Ross Casting 2005 Palo Verde Ave PMB #306 Long Beach CA 90815

COBEY, VIRGINIA BRANUM, artist, collector, civic leader; b. Chgo.; d. Albert Marshall and Hope (Engelhard) B.; m. James Alexander Cobey, Aug. 1, 1942; children: Hope Cobey Batey (dec.), Christopher Earle Cobey, Lisa Cobey Kelland. AFA, Stephens Coll., 1939; BFA in Drama, U. Iowa, 1941. Hostess, Stage Door Canteen, NYC, 1942-43; mem. Am. Theatre Wing, NYC, 1942-43; actress Little Theater of the Rockies, 1939-40; model I. Magnin, LA, 1943-44; stylist Macy's, NYC, 1945; curator, Pacific Asia Mus., 1970; importer Va. Cobey Art/Antiques, Pasadena, Calif., 1978—. Bd. dirs. Women's Council KCET-PBS, LA, 1968; v.p. Pasadena Art Alliance, 1971-73; chmn., bd. dirs. Friends of Occidental Coll., LA, 1975-76; bd. dirs. Costume Council LA County Mus. Art, 1981-82, Friends of Vielles Maisons Françaises, LA, 1986; bd. dirs. Internat. Student Ctr., UCLA, 1985—; founder, chmn. Southwestern Affiliates Southwestern Sch. Law, 1983-85, named Outstanding Friend, 1985. Ford Found. grantee Tamarind lithography, 1971. Mem. League Women Voters (founder 1956), Hosp. Assistance League (founder 1958), Legis. Wives (pres. 1964), Mother's Club (bd. mem.), Beta Sigma Phi, Pi Beta Phi. Episcopalian. Clubs: Valley Hunt (Pasadena), Smoke Tree Ranch.

COBLE, ALICIA SHARON, retired elementary school educator, retired secondary school educator; b. De Land, Fla., July 4, 1948; d. Paul W. and Helen (Brown) C. BA, U. South Fla., 1969; MAT, Stetson U., 1971. Cert. tchr. elem.; elem. and jr. coll. level English and music; secondary level humanities. Tchr. secondary level English, music Volusia County Sch. Bd., DeLand; elem. tchr. Lighthouse Christian Acad., Deland; tchr. Deland H.S., Seabreeze H.S.; ret. Home: 920 Westridge Dr Debary FL 32713-2109 Personal E-mail: aliciascoble@yahoo.com.

COBLE, MARY GLORIA, protective services official, rancher; d. Alexander John Dennis, Jr. and Lillian Gloria (Plataunos Dennis) Stevens, George B. Stevens (Stepfather); m. Thomas Marrion Coble, July 9, 1977. Degree in Bookkeeping and Acctg., United Coll. Bus., 1983; grad. in Police Acad., Mo. So. Coll., 1993. Laborer Emmerson Electric, Rogers, Ark., 1976—79, Local Factories, Mo., 1979—80; cook Ponderosa Trail, Anderson, Mo., 1980—82; prin., owner B.U. Petal, Calif., 1982—83; truck driver CFI Ins., Joplin, Mo., 1989—90, Greens Farm, Pierce City, Mo., 1990—91; sheriff dep. McDonald County Sheriff Dept., Pineville, Mo., 1991—. Contbr. poetry to books. With U.S. Army, 1974—76. Republican. Avocations: writing, painting, native american healing. Home: 954 Town Hollow Rd Anderson MO 64831

COBURN, DEBORAH ANN, elementary school educator; b. Derby, Conn., June 26, 1955; d. William Lee and Trudie Wilson; m. Robert Albert Wilson, June 22, 1986. AAS, Dutchess C.C., Poughkeepsie, N.Y., 1976; BS, Plymouth State U., N.H., 1999. Cert. tchr. N.H., 1999. Vet. tech Russel Animal Hosp., Concord, NH, 1999—2000; 7th grade tchr. Pembroke Sch. Dist., NH, 2000—. Lab dir. North Am. Labs, Brewster, NY, 1996—98. Mississippi Taxpayers.

COBURN, MARJORIE FOSTER, psychologist, educator; b. Salt Lake City, Feb. 28, 1939; d. Harlan A. and Alma (Ballinger) Polk; m. Robert Byron Coburn, July 2, 1977; children: Robert Scott, Kelly Anne; children: Polly Klea Foster, Matthew Ryan Foster. BA in Sociology, UCLA, 1960; Montessori Internat. Diploma with honors, Washington Montessori Inst., 1968; MA in Psychology, U. No. Colo., 1979; PhD in Counseling Psychology, U. Denver, 1983. Lic. clin. psychologist. Probation officer Alameda County, Oakland, Calif., 1960—62; dir. Friendship Club, Orlando, Fla., 1963—65; probation officer Contra Costa County, El Cerrito, Calif., 1966, Fairfax County, Va., 1967; tchr. Va. Montessori Sch., Fairfax, 1968—70; spl. edn. tchr. Leary Sch., Falls Church, Va., 1970—72, sch. administr., 1973—76; tchr. Aseltine Sch., San Diego, 1976—77, Coburn Montessori Sch., Colorado Springs, 1977—79; pvt. practice psychotherapy Colorado Springs, 1979—82, San Diego, 1982—. Cons. in field. Author (with R.C. Orem): Montessori: Prescription for Children with Learning Disabilities, 1977; contbr. articles to profl. jours. Mem.: APA, Mensa, The Charter 100, San Diego Psychol. Assn., Calif. Psychol. Assn., Coun. Exceptional Children, Phobia Soc., Am. Orthopsychiat. Assn., Rotary. Episcopalian. Office: 836 Prospect St Ste 101 La Jolla CA 92037-4206 Office Phone: 858-456-5065.

COCCHIARELLI, MARIA, artist, educator; b. Bklyn., Apr. 10, 1956; d. Joseph Paul and Mary Jannace Cocchiarelli. BA in Art History, Syracuse U., 1978; BA in Art, CUNY, 1983, MS in Art Edn., 1985, MFA, 2004. Lic. art tchr. grades K-12, N.Y. Instr., curator Queens Coll. Ctr. for Improvement of Edn., NY, 1983—84, 1988—89; instr. Museum's Collaborative and N.Y.C. Youth Bur., Queens, 1984—85; mus. educator Queens Mus., 1985—87; journalist Cover Arts Jour., N.Y.C., 1986—88; curator Mission Graphics Support Gallery, N.Y.C., 1987—88; artist, tchr. Inst. for Contemporary Arts/P.S.1 Mus., L.I. City, 1989—91; artist in residence Children's Mus. Manhattan, N.Y.C., 1989—93, N.Y. Found. for Arts, N.Y.C., 1989—93; edn. dir. Socrates Sculpture Park, L.I. City, 1991—93; edn. curator U. Wyo. Art Mus., Laramie, 1993—96; dir. edn. Kemper Mus. Contemporary Art & Design, Kansas City, Mo., 1996—97; dir. programs Grand Arts, Kansas City, Mo., 1997—98; instr. watercolor summer H.S. residency program Kansas City Art Inst., 1999—2002; residence Mo. Arts Coun., 1999—2001; garden artist, project developer Gem Theater and Linwood YWCA Youth Arts Garden, Kansas City, 1999—2002; tchr. art K-5 and H.S. Kansas City Sch. Dist., Mo., 2000—, exhbn. planner, 2001; artist in residence Pub. Sch. #6, Manhattan, 2003—; prof. art Kean U., 2004—05; curator of collection Italian Am. Mus., Manhattan, 2004—. Pub. arts commns. for NYC Pub. Sch. Commn. One Percent for the Arts, Sci. City Union Sta., Kans. City; curator collections Italian Am. Mus., NY, 2004—. Assn. Queens Artists, 1994, one-woman shows include The Skyline, L.I. City, 1987, Nancy Bratton Gallery, N.Y.C., 1989, YWCA, Bklyn., 1993, Coal Creek, Laramie, Wyo., 1996, Prospero, Kansas City, 1999, Blue Bird, 1999, Commerce Bankshares, 1999, Muddy's, 1999, First Bank, Warrenton, Mo., 1999, State of the Art, 2000, Kansas City, Mo., 2000, Digital Sandbox Gallery, N.Y.C., 2004—05, exhibited in group shows at Clocktower Mus., 1991, Gallery 72, Omaha, 1991—96, Tribeca 148 Gallery, N.Y.C., 1993, Wyo. Arts Coun., 1994—95, U. Wyo. Art Mus., Laramie, 1994, Urban Ctr. Mcpl. Art Soc., N.Y.C., 1994, Yale U. Art Gallery, New Haven, 1995, Bennington (Vt.) Ctr. for the Arts, 1995, Nicyolaysen Art Mus., Casper, Wyo., 1996, Late Show Gallery, Kansas City, 1998, Manelyst, Oslo, 1999, Leedy Volkos Art Ctr., Kansas City, 1999, State of the Arts, 1999—2000, Museo Internazionale dell'Immagine Postale, Comune di Belvedere Ostrense, Italy, 2001, Coll. of Art, Seoul, 2001, Represented in permanent collections Nebr. Arts Coun., Omaha, Hallmark Cards Inc., Kansas City, Wyo. State Mus., Cheyenne, Omaha Children's Mus. Exhbn. planner UN World Habitat, N.Y.C., 1988; instr., organizer Environ. Arts, Laramie, Wyo., 1996; lectr., cons. J. Paul Getty Conf., Omaha, 1996; mem. steering com. Cmty. Anti-Violence Initiative, Kansas City, Mo., 1996-2001. Mem. NOW, Am. Assn. Mus., Nat. Orgn. Italian-Am. Women. Avocations: swimming, writing, singin. Studio: 184-36 Avon R Jamaica NY 11432 Office Phone: 212-642-2022. E-mail: mariacocch@yahoo.com.

COCCIA, JOANN, music educator, musician; d. Joseph and Sue Coccia. BA in Music Edn., Trenton State Coll. (now The Coll. NJ), MA in Music Performance. Cert. music tchr. N.J., tchr. pre-sch. - 8 N.J., music tchr. Pa., std. supr. N.J. String specialist., educator Coun. Rock Sch. Dist., Richboro, Pa., 1979—81; music educator Hamilton Twp. Sch. Dist., Hamilton Square, NJ, 1981—. Mem. core curriculum stds. framework com. arts State of N.J. Dept. Edn., 1997; facilitator Mercer County Arts Initiative; presenter in field. Musician: Greater Trenton Symphony, Del. Valley Philharmonic, Newton Chamber Orch., Boheme Opera, NJ, Carnegie Hall, Santandar Festival Tour, 2000. Recipient Govs. Tchr. award, State of NJ, 1988, Master Tchr. Collaborative, N.J. Symphony Orch., 1996—99. Fellow: AAUW; mem.: NEA, Mercer County Edn. Assn., N.J. Music Educators Assn., Music Educators Nat. Conf., Am. Fedn. Musicians, Am. String Tchrs. Assn., Hamilton Twp. Edn. Assn., N.J. Edn. Assn., Kappa Delta Pi, Delta Omicron (life). Roman Catholic. Avocation: arts and crafts. Office: McGalliard Elem Sch 1600 Arena Dr Hamilton NJ 08610 Office Phone: 609-631-4158.

COCCO, MARIE ELIZABETH, journalist; b. Malden, Mass., Jan. 15, 1956; d. Morris Alfred and Dorothy Anne (Colameta) C.; m. Thomas Neal Burrows, Sept. 4, 1982; children: Matthew C. Burrows, Michael C. Burrows. BA, Tufts U., 1978; MS, Columbia U., 1979. Journalist Daily Register, Shrewsbury, N.J., 1979-80, Newsday, L.I., N.Y., 1980—. Nat. syndication through The Washington Post Writers Group, 2002. Recipient Nat. Reporting award Sigma Delta Chi, 1991, Excellence in Editorial Writing award N.Y. State Pubs. Assn., 1992, N.Y. State AP award, 1997, 99. Mem. White House Corrs. Assn. (Barnet Nover award 1991), Nat. Press Club (Washington Corr. award 1991). Office: Newsday Washington Bur 1730 Pennsylvania Ave NW Washington DC 20006-4706

COCH, DORRIT ARIA, obstetrician, gynecologist; b. Ramat-Gan, Israel, Sept. 27, 1939; arrived in U.S., 1968; d. Aba and Ilse Scherzer; m. Alexander Coch, Aug. 26, 1962; children: Liora Lerner, Elizabeth Benstock, Michelle Klein. MD, U. Vienna, Austria, 1966. Diplomate Am. Bd. Ob-Gyn. Intern Maimonides Hosp., Bklyn., 1969—70, resident in ob-gyn, 1970—74; clin. instr. Down State U. Med. Sch., Bklyn., 1974—; pvt. practice ob-gyn. Bklyn., 1974—. Mem.: ACS, ACOG. Home: 4815 14th Ave Brooklyn NY 11219-3119

COCHÉ, JUDITH, psychologist, educator; b. Phila., Sept. 2, 1942; d. Louis and Miriam (Nerenberg) Milner; m. Erich Coché, Oct. 16, 1966 (dec. 1991); 1 child, Juliette Laura; m. John Anderson, Jan. 1, 1994. BA, Colby Coll., 1964; MA, Temple U., 1966; PhD, Bryn Mawr Coll., 1975. Diplomate Am. Bd. Profl. Psychology, lic. psychologist Pa., Md., N.J., Fla., cert. in group psychotherapy Nat. Registry Group Psychotherapists. Rsch. asst. Jefferson Med. Coll., 1965-66; diagnostician Law Ct., Aachen, Germany, 1967-68; staff psychologist N.E. Community Mental Health Ctr., Phila., 1969-74; family clinician Inst. Pa. Hosp., 1974-76; instr. psychology Drexel U., 1976-77; lectr. Med. Coll. Pa., 1977-78; asst. clin. prof. Hahnemann Med. Coll., Phila., 1979—; pvt. practice Phila., 1974—, N.J., 1985—; assoc. prof. psychiatry U. Pa., 1985—, clin. coord. Psychology, 1999—; assoc. clin. prof. psychology in psychiatry U. Pa. Med. Coll., 1986—; mem. faculty Family Inst. of Phila., 1990—; sr. cons. Phila. Child Guidance Clinic, 1992-96; assoc. clin. prof. psychology in psychiatry U. Pa. Med. Coll., 1986—. Clin. cons. Hilltop Prep Sch., 1977—86; clin. supr. Am. Assn. Marriage and Family Therapy. Co-author: Couples Group Psychotherapy, A Clinical Practice Model, 1990, Powerful Wisdom: Voices of Distinguished Women Psychotherapists, 1993; contbr. chapters to books, articles to profl. jours. Bd. dirs. Whitemarsh Art Ctr., 1977-78, Please Touch Museum, 1982-89; mem. prof. adv. bd. Parents Without Ptnrs., 1977-86; mem. adv. com. Pa. Ballet/Shirley Rock. Named Women of Distinction, Phila. Bus. Jour., 2004; grantee, Del. Children's Bur. Bryn Mawr Coll., 1974—75, Pa. Hosp., 1975—77. Fellow Am. Group Psychotherapy Assn.; mem. APA, Am. Assn. Marriage and Family Therapy (approved supr.), Am. Family Therapy Assn., Phila. Soc. Clin. Psychologists (pres. 1980-81), Family Inst. Phila., Pa. Psychol. Assn. (chmn. legis. com. 1982), Soc. Rsch. in Psychotherapy, Women's Exec. Forum (Phila.). Address: Acad House 1420 Locust St Ste 410 Philadelphia PA 19102-4202 also: Price Waterworks Bldg Ste 3023 359 96th St Stone Harbor NJ 08247 Office Phone: 215-735-1908.

COCHRAN, BETH, gifted and talented educator; b. New Orleans, La., Nov. 2, 1951; d. Hugh Greene Smith, Kathryn Ann Smith; m. Cole Cochran; children: Michael, Steven. B in Music Edn., Ctrl. Mo. State U., 1973; MEd, U. Kans., 1999. Cert. Vocal Music Edn., K-12 1973, Gifted Edn. 2001. Tchr. vocal music Lexington Sch. Dist., Lexigton, Mo., 1973—75; tchr. elem. music North Kansas City Schs., Kansas City, Mo., 1975—77; dir. edn. Tokyo Bapt. Ch., Tokyo, 1984—90; dir. choral music Piper Sch. Dist., Kansas City, Kans., 1990—2000; tchr. vocal music Appleton City Schools, Appleton City, Mo., 2000—02; gifted resource tchr. Appleton City Schs., Appleton City, Mo., 2001—02, Butler Schs., Butler, Mo., 2002—04, No. Kans. City Schools, Mo., 2004—. Min. music First Bapt. Ch., Adrian, Mo., 2001—04. Mem.: Gifted Assn. Mo. Baptist. Office: Butler R-5 Schs 4 South High St Butler MO 64730 Personal E-mail: cbcochran3@yahoo.com. E-mail: cbcochran@osagevalley.net.

COCHRAN, GLORIA GRIMES, retired pediatrician; b. Washington, June 24, 1924; d. Paul DeWitt and Muriel Ann (Quackenbush) Grimes; m. Winston Earle Cochran, June 10, 1950 (dec. June 19, 2003); children: Edith Ann, Winston Earle, Jr., Donald Lee, Robert Edward. BS in Zoology, Duke U., 1945; MD, 1949; MPH, Johns Hopkins Sch. Hygiene, Balt., 1979. Diplomate Nat. Bd. Med. Examiners, 1950, Am. Bd. Pediatrics, 1958. Asst. resident Pathology Boston Children's Hosp., Boston, 1949—50, asst. resident Pediatrics, 1950—51; chief resident Pediatrics Charlotte Memorial Hosp., Charlotte, NC, 1952—53; clinic pediatrician, sch. med. advisor health dept. Montgomery County, Md., 1955—65; fellow in pediat. habilitation St. Christopher Hosp. for Children, Phila., 1965-66; assoc. dir. Child Development Clinic Baylor Med. Sch., Tex. Children's Hosp., 1966-72; dir. Northern Va. Child Devel. Field Svcs. Bur. Child Health State Health Dept. Commonwealth Va., 1972-76; coord. Handicapped Svcs. Children's Hosp. Nat. Med. Ctr., Washington, 1976-78; acting chief Divsn. of Svcs. to Children with Spl. Needs Bur. Sch. Health Svcs., Washington, 1982-89; retired, 1989. Cons. Head Start Program, Md., Va., Tex., Pa., D.C., 1965-89; bd. mem. Ctrs. for Handicapped, Silver Spring, Md., 1982-89; Child Health com. Med. Soc. D.C., Washington, 1976-91. Producer, editor: (teaching film) Challenge for Habilitation: The Child with Congenital Rubella Syndrome, 1976. Steering com. Rock Days Inter-Church Camp, Washington, 1978-82; bd. mem. Open Door Cmty. Ctr., Columbus, Ga., 1993-94; co-chair curriculum com. Columbus Coll. Acad. of Life Long Learning, Columbus, 1994. Mem. Am. Assn. Mental Retardation, Am. Med. Women's Assn., Assn. for Retarded Citizens, Am. Acad. Cerebral Palsy, Am. Acad. Pediatrics, Phi Beta Kappa, Delta Omega. Democrat. Methodist. Avocations: travel, gardening. Home: 750 Canadian Trls Dr Apt 218 Norman OK 73072-7646 Office Phone: 405-447-8207.

COCHRAN, JUDY ANNE, psychiatric nurse practitioner; b. Springfield, Mass., Aug. 18, 1954; d. John and Marie Theresa (Roy) Cochran. RN Clin. Psychiatry, Bay State Med. Ctr. Sch. Nursing, Springfield, 1980. RN N.Y. State Edn. Dept. Profl. Licensing Svcs. divsn. Nurse psychiatry Inst. Living, Hartford, Conn., 1980—81, NYU Hosp., 1982—83; nurse psychiatry, coord. Longmont United Hosp., Colo., 1983—85; nurse psychiat. clinic Columbine Psychiat. Hosp., Highlands Ranch, Colo., 1987—93; nurse psychiatry West Pines Psychiat. Hosp., Wheat Ridge, Colo., 1993—97, Porter Hosp., Denver, 1997—2001. Nurse psychiatry Gilliam Juvenile Detention Ctr., Denver, 1995—97. Author (screenplay): Graven Images, 2000, The Garden, 2002; author: (teleplay) Twin Forks, 2003, For Heaven's Sake, 2000. Mem.: Women in Film, TV, Video (v.p. 1996, charter), Mensa. Avocations: fencing, art, horseback riding, dogs. Office: PO Box 625 Orient NY 11957

COCHRAN, KATHY HOLCOMBE, music educator, conductor; d. Bobby Neal and Louise Bryant Holcombe; m. Alan Randolph Cochran, June 14, 1975. AA, North Greenville Coll., 1973; MusB, Furman U., 1975; M in Music Edn., U. S.C., 1978; postgrad., Clemson U., 1997—. Cert. tchr. pub. sch. choral music K-12 S.C., elem. sch. educator S.C. Gen. and choral music specialist grades 6-8 Lexington (S.C.) Intermediate Sch., 1975—76; elem. music specialist K-2 Pierce Ter. Elem. Sch., Ft. Jackson, SC, 1976—78; elem. music specialist grades 1-5 Greenville County Schs., 1978—90, lead tchr. for choral dirs., 1996—97; choral dir. Berea H.S., Greenville, 1991—97, fine arts dept. chair, 1995—97; tchg. intern, asst. Clemson (S.C.) U., 1999—2000; tchr. choral music edn. Furman U., Greenville, 2001—. Dir. Young Artists Piano Competition Greenville Symphony Orch., 1990—91; sec. choral divsn. S.C. Music Educators Assn., 1996—97, pres.-elect, 1997—98. Author, composer Music for All Ages, 1985. Mem. Greenville County Legal Aux., 1978—; trustee North Greenville Coll., Tigerville, SC, 1996—2001, bd. advisors, 1994—96. Named Outstanding Young Educator, Greenville Jaycees, 1987, Wade Hampton Jaycees, Taylors, S.C., 1980. Mem.: Internat. Soc. for Music Edn., Choristers Guild, SC Music Educators Assn., NY Acad. Scis., Am. Choral Dirs. Assn., Assn. for Supr. and Curriculum Devel., Nat. Reading Conf., Internat. Reading Assn., Music Educators Nat. Conf. (S.C. Music in Our Schs. coord. 1980), Pi Kappa Lambda, Kappa Delta Pi, Phi Delta Kappa. Avocations: reading, cooking, boating.

COCHRAN, LINDA THORNTHWAITE, psychotherapist, social worker, consultant; b. Huntsville, Ala., Nov. 3, 1946; d. W.L. and Mildred (Bridges) Thornthwaite; m. Phillip O. Cochran, July 1, 1966; children: Jeremy, Amanda. BA in Psychology, U. N.C., Asheville, 1984; MSW, geriatric cert., U. S.C., 1986. LCSW. Dir. Coun. on Aging, Hendersonville, N.C., 1986; child protection svc. worker Transylvania County Dept. Social Svcs., Brevard, N.C., 1986-88; clin. social worker mental health unit Pardee Hosp., Hendersonville, 1988-93; wellness coord. for MOMS program Blue Ridge Health Ctr., Hendersonville, 1993-95; psychotherapist Hendersonville Psychol. Assocs., 1995-97, Alpha Ctr. for Solution Therapy, 1997—. Cons., Hendersonville, 1988—. Sec. Widowed Persons Svc., Hendersonville, 1989-97. Mem.: NASW, Assn. Cert. Social Workers. Democrat. Mem. Ch. of Christ. Avocations: reading, water color painting. Mailing: PO Box 483 Hendersonville NC 28793 Home: 1840-E Howard Gap Hendersonville NC 28792 Office: Alpha Ctr for Solution Therapy 223 Duncan Hill Rd Hendersonville NC 28792

COCHRAN, MYRTIS, librarian; b. Langdale, Ala., Jan. 14, 1953; d. George and Nan Cochran. BA, Ala. State U., 1974; MS, Purdue U., 1975; AMLS, U. Mich., 1981. Tech. asst. Purdue U., West Layfayette, Ind., 1974-80; asst. librarian Tex. A&M U., College Station, 1981-83, U. Calif., Berkeley, 1984—. Contbg. auhor (microfiche) Curriculum Collection Index, 1981, Afro-Americans: A Research Guide, 1984; contbr. articles to profl. jours. Mem. ALA, Alpha Kappa Delta. Avocations: singing, dance, reading, walking, yoga. Office: U Calif Doe Libr Rm 212 Rsch and Collections Berkeley CA 94720-6000

COCHRAN, SUSAN MILLS, research librarian; b. Grinnell, Iowa, Nov. 21, 1949; d. Lawrence Omen and Louise Jane (Morgan) Mills; m. Stephen E. Cochran, July 1, 1972; children: Bryan, Jeremy. Libr. Iowa Geneal. Soc., Des Moines, 1987-96; rsch. libr. Royal Gorge Regional Mus. & History Ctr. (formerly Local History Ctr., Canon City Pub. Libr.), Colo., 1997—. Editor: Mingo, Iowa 1884-1984, 1984; contbr. articles to profl. jours. Past mem. Jasper County Cemetery Commn., Newton; mem. Jasper County His. Soc.; past bd. dirs. Jasper County Libr., Newton, Iowa. Mem. Iowa Geneal. Soc., Jasper County Geneal. Soc., State Assn. for the Preservation of Iowa Cemeteries (charter), Fremont County Geneal. Group (coord.), Colo. Coun. Geneal. Socs. Avocations: genealogy, history, birding. Office: Royal Gorge Regional Mus & History Ctr 612 Royal Gorge Blvd Canon City CO 81212 Address: PO Box 1460 Canon City CO 81215 Office Phone: 719-269-9036. E-mail: historycenter@canoncity.org.

COCHRANE, BETSY LANE, former state senator; b. Asheboro, NC; d. William Jennings and Bobbie (Campbell) Lane; m. Joe Kenneth Cochrane, 1958; children: Lisa, Craig. BA cum laude, Meredith Coll., 1958. Tchr. Winston-Salem (NC) Sch. Sys., Highland Presbyn. Ch. Sch.; mem. NC Ho. of Reps., Raleigh, 1980-88, house minority leader, 1985-88; mem. NC Senate, Raleigh, 1988-2001, chmn. Commn. on Aging, 1989-99, vice chmn. higher edn. com., 1991-92, senate minority whip, 1993-94, senate minority leader, 1995-96, vice chmn. senate appropriations, 1995—2000, vice chmn. senate commerce commn., 1995—2000, ranking minority mem. senate agr., 1995—2000. Mem. Nat. Rep. Platform Com., Order of LongLeaf Pine, 1992, Joint Legis. Ethics Com., 1989—2000, chmn., 1989—90; mem. NC Parks Commn., 1989—96, Retail Mchts. Adv. Bd., 1989—2000, Govtl. Ops., 1989—97, Select Com. on Redistricting, 1991, 92, 94, Revenue Law, 1992—2000, Environ. Rev. Com., 1997—2001, Utility Rev. Com., 1997—2000, Gov.'s Advocacy Coun. on Children and Youth, 1990—2000, Gov.'s Blue Ribbon Task Force Environ. Indicators, 1989—91; spkr. in field. Trustee Davie County Hosp.; bd. advisors Z. Smith Reynolds Found., 1996—99, Meredith Coll., chmn. pres.'s adv. coun., 1999—2001, govs. adv. budget com., 1989—93, pub. sch. forum, 1985—99, mem. Meredith Challenge Bd., 2005—; mem. Davie County Schs. Task Force on Facilities, 2001—02, So. Regional Edn. Bd., 1987—2001; del. GOP Nat. Conv., 1976, 1988, 1992, 1996; trustee CUMC, 2006—; mem. Bible Study Fellowship, discussion leader, 2003—; mem. Faith Works Task Force, 2005—; bd. dir.

Davie County Sch. Mebane Challenge, 2004—, Forks of the Yadkin Mus., 2002—, vice chmn., 2004—. Named Disting. Citizen of Yr., N.C. Libr. Dirs., 1991, Legislator of Yr., N.C. Divsn. Aging, 1991, N.C. Assn. for Home Care, 1992, N.C. Health Facilities Assn., 1993, N.C. Wildlife Fedn., 1995, Autism Found., 1995, Disting. Alumnae of the Yr., Meredith Coll., 1996; named one of 10 Outstanding Legislators in Nation, 1987; named to N.C. GOP Hall of Fame, 2001, GOP Hall of Fame, Davie County, 2003; recipient Woman in Govt. award, N.C. Jaycees, 1985, Myers-Honeycutt award for excellence in pub. svc., 1996, Dr. Ewald W. Busse award, Aging Advocates of N.C., 1997, Women Achievement award, FWC N.C., 2002. Baptist. Home and Office: 331 Orchard Pk Dr Advance NC 27006-9582 Personal E-mail: betsycochrane@triad.rr.com. Business E-Mail: betsyc@ncleg.net.

COCHRUM, ELLEN JOAN, language educator; b. Tianjin, China, Jan. 19, 1929; arrived in U.S., 1947; d. Ivan Trofimovich Lukashik and Eleonore Elizabeth Mirksch; m. John Cochrum, Aug. 13, 1947 (dec.); children: Julie A. Bauer-Cook, J. Paul, Jeane M. Cabral, James R. BA in Fgn. Langs., Calif. State U., Fullerton, 1966; MA in Russian Lang. and Lit., Middlebury Coll., 1968; PhD in Russian Lang. and Lit., Mich. State U., 1977; AA in Exercise Sci., Santa Ana Coll., 2003. Instr. Russian Berlitz Sch. Langs., Santa Ana, Calif., 1959—60, Oceanside-Carlsbad Coll., Calif., 1960—61, Chapman U., Orange, Calif., 1961—62; instr. German and Russian Calif. State U., Fullerton, 1962—69, assoc. prof. German and Russian, 1985—91; instr. Russian Mich. State U., East Lansing, 1969—77, asst. prof. Russian, 1977—79; assoc. prof. Russian Calif. State U., Long Beach, 1979; lectr. Russian U. Calif., Irvine, 1980, UCLA, 1980—81. Chmn. Russian sect. Modern and Classical Langs. So. Calif., 1965—69; rsch., lang. specialist computer translation of sci. Russian texts, 1965—69; asst. prof. Russian Middlebury Coll., Vt., 1973, 74, 75, 76, 79, 80, 81, 82; sec.-treas. Mich. chpt. Am. Assn. Tchrs. Slavic and East European Langs., 1974—77. Translator: Ministry to the Hospitalized, 1980; author: (monograph) The Modern Teaching of Russian, 1963, (bibliography) A Bibliography of Works by and about Jurij Nagibin 1940-1978, 1979. Recipient Disting. Tchg. award, Calif. State U., Fullerton, 1967—68, Alumni Achievement award, Santa Ana Coll., 1997. Mem.: Tau Sigma, Phi Kappa Phi (life). Avocations: aqua aerobics, hiking, gardening, church secretarial work. Address: Apt 3 13641 Fairview St Garden Grove CA 92843-4225

COCKERHAM, SHERRY L., secondary school educator; b. Richmond, Ky., Nov. 10, 1969; m. Steve Cockerham, June 4, 1994. BSc, Ea. Ky. U., Richmond, 1991; MSc, East Tenn. State U., Johnson City, 1997. Tchr. Sci. Hill H.S., Johnson City, Tenn. Mem. Sierra Club, Johnson City, 1994—. Recipient Dist. Tchr. of Yr., Johnson City Schs., 2006. Mem.: Nat. Coun. Tchrs. of Math. Office Phone: 423-232-2192.

COCKRAM, SUZANNE M., elementary school educator; d. Joseph and Kathleen Rabedeaw; m. Donald R. Cockram, June 13, 1981; children: Joshua, Jason. BS, Ea. Mich. U., 1977, M in Reading, 1982. Cert. in reading recovery Mich. Tchr. Hillsdale (Mich.) Cmty. Schs., 1977—, reading recovery tchr., 1996—2001; tchr. literacy tng. Hillsdale Ind. Sch. Dist., 2002—. Den leader Boy Scouts Am., Hillsdale, coun. mem.

COCKRELL-FLEMING, SHELIA YVETTE, public health nurse; b. Houston, July 20, 1961; d. Morgan O. and Alma (Wheeler) Cockrell; m. Wesley T. Fleming, May 25, 1991; 1 child, Khelli E. BSN, U. Tex. Health Sci. Ctr., Houston, 1983. RN; cert. pub. health nurse. Asst. head nurse Harris County Hosp. Dist., Houston, 1988-89; perinatal nurse HealthMark, Houston, 1989-90, Meml. N.W. Hosp., Houston, 1990-91, Lompoc (Calif.) Hosp. Dist., 1991-92; pub. health nurse Santa Barbara County, Lompoc, 1992-94; perinatal nurse Spectrum Health Care, Vendenberg AFB, Calif., 1994-96; dir. health promotion/disease prevention Am. Indian Health and Svcs., Santa Barbara, Calif., 1996-99; pres., CEO Sojourner Nurse Cons., Lompoc, Calif., 1999—. Mem. adv. bd. Healthy Start, Lompoc, 1992-93; mem. cmty. adv. bd. Santa Barbara Health Initiative, 1997—; mem. Breast Cancer Early Detection Partnership Santa Barbara County, 1996—. Author poems. CPR, first aid instr. ARC. 1st lt. USAF, 1985-88. Mem. Nat. Coun. Nurse Adminstrs., Am. Diabetes Assn. Baptist. Avocations: reading, writing.

COCLANES, JACQUELINE ANN FIKES, elementary school educator; b. Waukegan, Ill., Jan. 15, 1978; d. Hiram Sanders Fikes IV, John Olino (Stepfather) and Victoria Mary Fikes-Olino; m. William John Coclanes Jr., July 1, 2005; children: Vincent John, Angelina Victoria. BS Elem. Edn., U. Iowa; MA Sch. Guidance and Counseling, Lewis U. Tchr. elem. Indian Prairie Dist. 204, Naperville, Ill., 2000—. Roman Catholic. Avocations: exercise, movies, scrapbooks. Home: 325 Aster Dr Minooka IL 60447

COCO, DONNA A. W., elementary school educator; d. Willard W. and Evelyn A. J. Winter; m. Russell L. Coco, Dec. 26, 1981; children: Russell W., Nicholas A., Jeremy L. M in Mid. Grades Edn., U. N.C., Greensboro, 2003. Tchr. Northeastern Randolph Mid. Sch., Liberty, NC, 2000—. Boy scout leader Boy Scouts Am., Ramseur, NC, 1988—2005, merit badge counselor Staley, 1995—2006, leader trainer, 1995—2003; tchr. Sunday sch. First United Meth. Ch., Liberty, 1988—2006, handbell choir dir., choir mem., chairperson nurture com., 1997—2006. Recipient Silver Beaver, Boy Scouts Am., 2000, Lay Person of Yr., First United Meth. Ch., 2004, Disting. Educator of Yr., Northeastern Randolph Mid. Sch., 2005—06. Mem.: NEA, N.C. Assn. Educators, Inc. Methodist. Home: 6068 Whites Chapel Rd Staley NC 27355 Office: Northeastern Randolph Mid Sch 3493 Ramseur Julian Rd Liberty NC 27298 Office Phone: 336-622-5808.

COCOVES, ANITA PETZOLD, psychotherapist; b. Princeton, N.J., June 2, 1957; d. Charles Bernard and Kathleen Marie (McDonald) Petzold; m. Nicholas John Cocoves, Oct. 11, 1997; 1 child, Nicholas Euthymius. AS in Bus., Indian River C.C., Fla., 1986; BS in Liberal Studies, Barry U., 1988; MS in Human Svcs. Adminstrn., Nova U., 1989, postgrad., 1989—91; PhD in Human Svcs. Adminstrn., LaSalle U., 1994. Lic. mental health counselor, Fla.; cert. addictions prevention profl.; internat. cert. alcohol and drug abuse counselor; nat. cert. counselor; cert. employee assistance counselor; nat. cert. clin. mental health counselor; nat. cert. addictions counselor; cert. DUI instr.; cert. family and county ct. mediator. Admissions coord. Palm Beach Inst., West Palm Beach, Fla., 1985—86; dir. admissions Heritage Health Corp., Jensen Beach, Fla., 1986—89; coord. rug abuse strategy Martin County Bd. of County Commrs., Stuart, Fla., 1989—2001; adminstr. health and human svcs. Martin County Bd. of County Commr., Stuart, 2001—. Mem. Drug Resource Team for the 12th Congl. Dist., Fla., 1990—, Juvenile Justice Assn. of the 19th Jud. Ct., Fla., 1993—, vice chmn. 1999—; grant writer in field. Vol. Hist. Soc. Martin County, Stuart, 1986—; mem. United Way Martin County, Stuart, 1993; mem. bd. dirs. Cmty. AIDS Adv. Project, Stuart, 1993; chmn. treatment com. Martin County Task Force on Substance Abused Children, Stuart, 1993; chmn. Legis. Subcom. Martin County Juvenile Justice Com., 1998—. Recipient Outstanding Cmty. Svc. award United Way Martin County, Stuart, 1993. Mem. NASW, Am. Mental Health Counselors Assn., Nat. Criminal Justice Assn., Nat. Assn. Alcoholism and Drug Abuse Counselors, Nat. Consortium Treatment Alternatives to St. Crime Programs, Am. Coll. Addiction Treatment Adminstrs., Am. Labor-Mgmt. Adminstrs., Fla. Alcohol and Drug Abuse Assn. Republican. Roman Catholic. Avocations: walking, reading. Home: 38 SE Ocean Blvd Stuart FL 34994-2215 Office Phone: 772-288-5785, 772-463-2868. Business E-Mail: acocoves@martin.fl.us.

CODE, AUDREY B., art educator; b. Pitts., Pa., Oct. 6, 1937; d. Martin Code and Adele Torchia; m. Alan Kleiman, Feb. 9, 1963; 1 child, Andrea Kristin Kleiman. BFA, Carnegie-Mellon U., Pitts., 1959; Master's equivalent, U. Pitts., 1961. Cert. tchr. N.Y.C., Pa. Art tchr. Pitts. Pub. Schs., 1959—61; art tchr., lectr. Stuyvesant Adult Ctr., N.Y.C., 1979—98; art tchr. San Francisco Art Inst., N.Y.C. Pub. Schs., 1963—77. Painter, pres. Grand St. Artists Coop., N.Y.C., 1975—85. A Hatched Resume; author: Eggplants and Other Murders, 1979; one-woman shows include Area Gallery, N.Y.C., 1964, Hansen Gallery, 1975, Frank Marino Gallery, 1979, Esta Robinson Gallery, 1987, Celebrity Ctr., 1989, La Nicola Gallery, L.A., 1990, Dactyl Found., N.Y.C., 1997, exhibited in group shows at Rabbitt Gallery, New Brunswick, N.J., 1989, Blondie Gallery, 1993—95, Puffin Rm. Gallery, 1996, Robert Steele Gallery, 1998, Howe Fine Arts Gallery, Keane, N.J., 1998, Atlantic Gallery, N.Y.C., 2000—05, Miller Gallery, Carnegie-Mellon U., Pitts., 2006. Avocations: travel, cooking, theater.

CODERRE, NANCY ADELE, financial analyst; b. Cleve., Aug. 21, 1962; d. Richard Alfred and Julia (Viedt) C. BA, U. Colo., 1984; MBA with high honors, Babson Coll., 1986. Cert. mgmt. acct. Sr. cost acct. M/A Com., Omni Spectra, Waltham, Mass., 1987-88; fin. analyst Analogic Corp., Peabody, Mass., 1988-93, Carrier Corp., Syracuse, N.Y., 1994-95; product specialist SAS Inst., Cary, NC, 1995—. Mem. Inst. Mgmt. Accts., Beta Gamma Sigma. Avocations: swimming, chess. Home: 205 Livingstone Drive Cary NC 27513 E-mail: ncoderre@nc.rr.com.

CODO, CHRISTINA, securities executive; b. Evanston, Ill., Jan. 13, 1960; d. Norman Fredric and Charlotte Jean (Bailey) Codo; m. Patrick Joseph Maloney; children: Beatrice Grace Codo Maloney, Daniel Patrick Codo Maloney. BA in Econs., Northwestern U., 1980; MBA, Yale U., 1987. Exec. officer in lending Lloyds Bank Internat. Inc., Miami, Fla., 1982-85; exec. officer high yield capital markets Salomon Inc., N.Y.C., 1987-89; with instnl. sales Whitehill Capital Inc., N.Y.C., 1989, v.p. instnl. sales, 1989-91; mem. instnl. adv. staff Euromobiliare, SpA, Milan, 1991-92; assoc. fgn. securities group JP Morgan, N.Y.C., 1992-93, v.p. Emerging Markets, 1993-94, Chgo., 1994-98; assoc., controller's divsn. Continental Ill. Bank and Trust Co. Inc., 1999—. Fin. dir. Jr. League of Evanston-North Shore, Winnetka, 1999—2001, co-chmn. fundraising com., 1997—98; mem. exec. bd. Ronald Knox Montessori Sch., chair fundraising com., 2001—02, pres. bd. dirs., 2003—04; vice chair New Trier Township Youth Com., 2000—. Mem.: Chgo. Coun. Fgn. Rels. Avocations: opera, golf, tennis, internat. travel.

CODOGNI, IWONA M., scientific information analyst, chemist; b. Ketrzyn, Poland, May 26, 1959; came to U.S., 1991; d. Tadeusz and Marianna Wyzlic; m. Zdzislaw Antoni Codogni, Dec. 26, 1997; 1 child, Christopher Thadeusz. MSc in Chemistry, Nicolaus Copernicus U., Torun, Poland, 1982, PhD, 1991. Rsch. assoc. Nicolaus Copernicus U., 1983-91; postdoctoral fellow Ohio State U., Columbus, 1991-93, rsch. assoc., 1993-95; asst. sci. info. analyst Chem. Abstracts Svc., Columbus, 1995-98, assoc. sci. info. analyst, 1998—. Contbr. articles to profl. jours.; patentee in field. Mem. Am. Chem. Soc. Office: Chem Abstracts Svc 2540 Olentangy River Rd Columbus OH 43202-1505

CODONER, SHEILA DOWDS, psychologist; b. Newark, Dec. 28, 1948; d. Peter Joseph, Jr. and Lois Marie Dowds; m. Manuel Joseph Codoner, III, June 21, 1987; 1 child, Benjamin Joseph. MA in Psychology cum laude, Fairleigh Dickinson U., Teaneck, N.J., 1972; MA in Edn. Adminstrn., San Francisco State U., 1983; BA magna cum laude, U. Charleston, W.Va., 1970. Cert. sch. psychologist, edn. amdinstrn. Calif., lic. ednl. psychologist Calif. Sch. psychologist Delware County Intermediate Unit, Media, Pa., 1973—79, Ravenswood Sch. Dist., East Palo Alto, Calif., 1979—83, Petaluma (Calif.) City Schs., 1983—. Scholar, U. Charleston; Rsch. fellow, Fairleigh Dickinson U. Mem.: Sonoma County Assn. Sch. Psychologists, Nat. Assn. Sch. Psychologists. Democrat. Buddhist. Home: 10 Fabian Ct Novato CA 94947

CODY, JUDITH, composer, writer; Student, U. Calif., Berkeley, 1977, Foothill Coll., Los Altos Hills, Calif., 1972—75; pvt. student in Japanese culture and music, 1966—68. Editor: Resource Guide on Women in Music, 1981; author: Vivian Fine: A Bio-Bibliography, 2001; (poems) Eight Frames Eight, 2002; author numerous poems; composer: Trio for flute, classical guitar and poem, 1974, Firelights: Variations for classical guitar, 1976-77, City and Country Themes in G, 1976, Dances, opus 8, 1977, Nocturne, opus 9, 1977, classical guitar Seven Concert Etudes, opus 7, 10, 11, 13, 14, 15 & 18, 1977, classical guitar, Christmas Theme, opus 17, 1977, Opus 16, flute & guitar, 1977, Trio, opus 21, two flutes and guitar, 1978, Three Songs of Middle English, opus 26, voice and guitar, 1978, Sonata, opus 22, flute and guitar, 1978, Theme and Variations, opus 27, piano, 1978, Three Patterns, opus 29, piano, 1978, Two Patterns, opus 30, piano, 1978, Flute Poems, opus 19, 1978, Meditation for Four Hands, duet, steel string and classical guitars, 1983, Rain on the Face of Buddha at Kamakura, classical guitar, 1984, Three Haiku Love Songs, piano and soprano, 1986, Danger Dance, piano and soprano, 1986, Whales' Song, piano, 1986, Swan River, piano, 1986, Looking Under Footprints, voice and classical guitar, 1986, Two Songs, piano, 1999, Heart-Blood-Heart, piano, 1999, Death of a Small Animal, piano, 1999, Earth of Ukraine, piano, 1999, Song Cycle: Updated History of the Universe, classical guitar, flute ensemble, voice, 2003. Founder steering com., mem. 1st Bay Area Congress on Women in Music, San Francisco State U., 1980—81. Recipient 1st Prize poem Amelia Mag., 1993, music composition winner New Times Concerts, La. State U., 1979, winner Atlantic Monthly Poetry Contest, 1973, Hon. Mention Emily Dickinson Poetry award, 2003; poetry in permanent collection Smithsonian Instn., Washington, 1978. Mem. PEN, Am. Music Ctr., Poets and Writers, Inc. Achievements include First to discover and document composer's creative explosions in youth and old age, 2001; first woman engineering drafter in city and county of San Francisco Power and Utilities Engineering Bureau. Avocations: soprano in opera chorus, classical guitar. Personal E-mail: poeticsethics-whoswho@yahoo.com.

COE, DIANA WARD (DINA COE), poet, writer; b. Balt., Mar. 30, 1943; d. Ward Baldwin, Jr. and Diana Chittenden Coe; m. Gregory James McGrath, Feb. 14, 1998; m. David Keller, Sept. 1, 1981 (div. Nov. 5, 1990). BA, Hollins Coll., Va., 1965; MA in Creative Writing, C.C. CUNY, N.Y.C., 1989. Flight attendant Pan Am. World Airways, Jamaica, NY, 1965—85; adj. prof. CCNY, N.Y.C., 1989—95, Rider Coll., Lawrenceville, NJ, 1996—97. Dodge poet Geraldine R. Dodge Found., Madison, NJ, 1986—2002; poet in the schs. N.J. State Coun. on the Arts, Trenton, 1988—2002. Author: numerous poems, —. Recipient Grolier prize, Grolier Bookstore, Boston, 1984; Fellowship in Poetry, N.J. State Coun. on the Arts, 1981, 1987, 1994, Bread Loaf Scholar, Bread Loaf (Vt.) Writer's Conf., 1989. Democrat. Avocations: gardening, hiking, belly dancing, vegetarian cooking. Home: 742 Canns Neck Way Great Cacapon WV 25422

COE, JILL, director, educator; d. Paul Daniel and Millie Middleton Coe; 1 child, Brooke Leigh. Instr. SW Tex. Jr. Coll., Uvalde, 1990—, dir. profl. devel., 2005—. Office Phone: 830-591-7334.

COE, JUDITH ANNE, music educator, composer, performer; b. Denver, June 11, 1955; d. James Arnold and Sonya Diane (Regnier) Hall; m. Loren R. Coe, June 14, 1975 (div. Dec. 1993); children: Jared, Joshua, Jessica. BM, Colo. State U., 1981, MM, 1983; DMA, U. Colo., 1991. Rsch. intern Denver Ctr. for Performing Arts Voice Lab., 1984-91; vis. artist Denver Sch. of Arts, 1991-92; vocal coach, vis. artist Denver Ctr. Theatre Co., 1991-92; instr. Front Range C.C., Ft. Collins, Colo., 1988-91; designer Vestige Pub. Co., Ft. Collins, 1994-96; asst. prof. dept. music Miss. U. for Women, Columbus, 1996-2001; asst. prof. music & entertainment industry studies and dir. comml. voice program U. Colo., Denver, 2001—, dir. comml. voice program, 2001—. Adj. prof. Colo. State U., Ft. Collins, 1990-94. Author: Report on the Status of Women in College Music, 2000; assoc. editor: (ency.) Women Musicians in America, 2000; author/compiler: (webliography) Cyberspace Music Resources, 1999. Performing arts roster Miss. Arts Coun., 1999—; cmty. outreach affiliate Columbus Arts Coun., 1999—. Miss. U. for Women Faculty Devel. grantee, 1996, 97, 98, 99, 00, Nat. Inst. for Deafness and Other Comm. Disorders grantee, 1990, 91, Columbus Arts Coun. grantee, 1999, 00, Blas Internat. Sch. Traditional Irish Music and Dance grantee, 1999; Vis. scholar Irish Music Archives, Boston Coll., 2006; Fulbright US Scholar's award U. Limerick, Ireland, 2006-. Mem. AAUW (Leadership award 1999), NOW, Internat. Alliance for Women in Music (coord. of pub. advocacy 1999—, bd. dirs. 1996—), Am. Soc. Composers, Authors and Pubs., Coll. Music Soc. (co-chair com. on music, women and gender 1999—, profl. devel. com./ann. planning com. 1999—), Acad. and Rec. Industry Alliances (team organizer 2000, bd. mem. for performance 2004—), Nat. Assn. Tchrs. Singing (v.p., adjudications chair 1983-85), Southeastern Composers League, Internat. Assn. for Study of Popular Music. Democrat. Avocations: web design and development, photography, architecture, popular culture, travel. Office: U Colo Arts Bldg 288H Campus Box 162 PO Box 173364 Denver CO Office Phone: 303-556-6013. Business E-Mail: judith.coe@cudenver.edu.

COE, JUDITH LYNN, retired automobile manufacturing company administrator; b. Washington, Oct. 4, 1945; d. Raymond G. and Lynn (Pulliam) Coe. BA in Math., Converse Coll., 1967; Exec. Sec. cert., Washington Sch. for Secs., 1968. Sec. to v.p. and sec. Nonprescription Drug Mfrs. Assn., Washington, 1968-72; sec. to regional mgr. Electro-Motive div. GM Corp., Atlanta, 1972-83; sec. to asst. zone mgrs. Pontiac div. GM Corp., Atlanta, 1983-87, zone mgr.'s sec. Washington, 1987-95; ret., 1995. Bd. dirs. Lynn Properties, Washington, 1989-99. Active Met. Meml. United Meth. Ch. Mem. Holton-Arms Sch. and Converse Coll. Alumnae Assn., The Washington Club (admissions com. 1998-2004, bd. govs. 1999-2002), Congl. Country Club. Republican. Home: 4802 Jamestown Rd Bethesda MD 20816-2711

COE, LAURIE LYNNE BARKER, photojournalist, artist; b. Miami, Fla., Nov. 26, 1954; d. George Felton Barker and Dorita Maria Comas; m. James Woodrift Coe, Sept. 29, 1980 (div. Apr. 2005); children: Blake Alexander, Alexandra Noelle. Profl. photography, N.Y. Inst. Photography, 1994; grad., Ringling Sch. Art & Design, 2004. Cert. in digital filmmaking, specializing in documentaries. Photographer Marie Selby Botanical Gardens, Sarasota, Fla., 1997—99; corr. North Port Rev., Englewood, Fla., 1997—99; pres. Artistic Endeavours, North Port, Fla., 1998—, Earthly Visions Photography, 2004—. Author: In The Beauty of the Morning, 2001; photographer to profl. mags., calendars, postcards, books, Sarasota, A Photographic Portrait, 2000, Greater Miami, a Photographic Portrait, 2002, (3 music videos) The Boswell Project, 2004, (documentaries) River People, the Peruvian Amazon, 2005, Masai, Under African Skies, 2005, (One Woman Exhibit) Masai Under African Skies, A Photographic Portrait, Sarasota Arts Coun. Photographer Sun Coast Humane Soc., Sarasota, 1998, North Port, 2000—01; bd. mem. Arts and Culture Alliance, Sarasota, 2002—. Recipient Muses award, Arts and Cultural Alliance, 2003, Wall of Tolerance, 2003. Mem.: N.Am. Nature Photographer Assn., North Port Area Art Guild (chairwoman all shows 1998—2001, chair ways and means 1998—2001, v.p. 1999—2001, photographic tchr. childrens summer workshop 2000—01). Achievements include recognition in Cambridge, England Living Legends. Avocations: mentor fo high schools, natural healing, gardening, music. Home and Studio: 2651 Colonade Ln North Port FL 34286 Office Phone: 941-626-1928. E-mail: earthlyvisionsphotography@yahoo.com.

COE, LINDA MARLENE WOLFE, retired marketing professional, freelance photographer; b. Logan, Ohio, Apr. 5, 1941; d. Kenneth William and Mary Martha (Eddy) Wolfe; m. Frederic Morrow Coe, Sept. 15, 1962; children: Christopher, Jennifer, Peter, Michael. BFA, Columbus Coll. of Art and Design, 1978. Freelance photographer, Columbus, 1978—; sec., receptionist Plaza Dental, Columbus, 1983; sec. Worthington (Ohio) Dental Group, 1983-85; mktg. and devel. adminstr. Custom Corp. Gift Svc., Worthington, 1985-92, Grandparents Living Theatre, 1993, Premiums & Promotions, Inc., 1995-96; ret., 1996. Trustees Met. Women's Ctr., Columbus, 1986-87. Docent trainee Columbus Mus. Art, 1982-83; mem. Worthington Arts Coun., 1982, 83, 85, 87, 89-93, 94. Mem. Zephyrus League, Phoenix Soc. (mem. exec. bd.), Nat. Soc. Fund Raising Execs., Women's Bus. Bd., Columbus Bus. and Profl. Women, Columbus C. of C., Columbus Coll. Art and Design Alumni Assn. Republican. Roman Catholic. Avocations: photography, reading, gardening, sailing. Home: Heron Bay 15240 Shoreline Dr Thornville OH 43076-8855

COE, MARGARET LOUISE SHAW, community service volunteer; b. Cody, Wyo., Dec. 25, 1917; d. Ernest Francis and Effie Victoria (Abrahamson) Shaw; m. Henry Huttleston Rogers Coe, Oct. 8, 1943 (dec. Aug. 1966); children: Anne Rogers Hayes, Henry H.R., Jr., Robert Douglas II. AA, Stephens Coll., 1937; BA, U. Wyo., 1939. Asst. to editor The Cody Enterprise, 1939-42, editor, 1968-71. Bd. trustees Buffalo Bill Historical Ctr., 1966—, chmn., 1974-98, chmn. emeritus, 1998—; trustee emeritus Ctrl. City Opera House Assn., Millicent Rogers Found.; commr. Wyo. Centenniel Commn., Cheyenne, 1986-91. Recipient The Westerner award Old West Trails Found., 1980, Gold Medallion award Nat. Assn. Sec. of State, 1982, disting alumni award U. Wyo., 1984, exemplary alumni award, 1994, Gov.'s award for arts, 1988; inducted Nat. Cowgirl Hall of Fame, 1983. Mem. P.E.O., Delta Delta Delta. Republican. Episcopalian. Avocation: duplicate bridge. Home: 1400 11th St Cody WY 82414-4206

COE, SUE, artist, journalist; b. Tamworth, England, 1951; Grad., Royal Coll. Art, London, 1973. Illustrator Time Magazine, N.Y. Times. Exhibitions include Thumb Gallery, 1979, Moira Kelly Fine Art, London, 1982, P.P.O.W. Gallery, 1982, 1985, Contemporary Art Ctr., 1986, Phyllis Kind Gallery, 1986, Anderson Gallery, Commonwealth U., Knight Gallery, Portland Art Mus., Wesleyan U., Contemporary Arts Mus., Ohio State U., San Francisco Art Inst., 1987, City Gallery of Contemporary Art, 1988, Mus. Modern Art, 1989, Oxford, Eng., 1989, Cornerhouse, Manchester, Eng., 1989, Orchard Gallery, Derry, Ireland, 1989, Herbert Art Gallery, Coventry, Eng., 1989, Galerie St. Etienne, 1989, Joan Whitney Payson Gallery of Art, Portland, Maine, 1990—91, Ind. U. Fine Arts, 1990—91, U. Mo., 1990—91, Wash. State U., 1990—91, Inter Am. Art Gallery, 1990—91, Miami Dade CC, 1990—91, Ga. State U. Art Gallery, 1990—91, Santa Monica Mus. Art, 1990—91, Brody's Gallery, 1990, 1994, Md. Art Place, 1993, Hirschhorn Mus., 1994, Galerie St. Etienne, 1992, 1994, 1996, 1999, 2000—01, NYC, 2005, Mead Art Mus., Amherst Coll., Mass., 1993, Mesa Coll. Gallery, 1995, Salt Lake City Art Ctr., 1996, Nelson Fine Arts Ctr., Ariz. State U. Art Mus., 1996—99, U. Ill., 1996—99, Guilfort Coll. Art Gallery, 1996—99, Tacoma Art Mus., 1996—99, Lewis and Clark U., William Benton Mus. Art, 2000—01, Tyler Art Gallery, 2002, David Winton Bell Gallery, 2002, Ctr. Contemporary Art, 2003, Fairbanks Gallery, Oreg., 2004, Overtones Gallery, Calif., 2004, exhibited in group shows at Am. Inst. Graphic Arts, 1977, Georges Pompidou Ctr., 1978, U.N. HQ, 1980, P.S.1, LI, 1984, Avery Arts Ctr., 1984, San Francisco Mus. Art, 1984, Holly Solomon Gallery, 1985, Mus. Modern Art, Italy, 1985, Art Inst. Chgo., 1986, LA County Mus. Art, 1987, Mus. Modern Art, NYC, 1988, Duke U., 1991, Drawing Ctr., NYC, 1992, Katonah Mus., 1992, Hood Mus., 1992, Montgomery Mus. Fine Art, 1992, Walker Art Ctr., 1993, Inst. Contemporary Art, 1993, Valentine Mus., 1993, Anacostia Mus., 1993, Nexus Contemporary Art Ctr., 1993, Ctr. Arts Yerba Buena, 1993, Md. Art Pl., 1993, Meud Art Mus., Amheart Coll., Mass., 1993, Mus. Modern Art, NYC, 1996, 1997, 2001, Represented in permanent collections Galerie St. Etienne; author: (books) How to Commit Suicide in South Africa, 1983, Paintings and Drawings, 1985, X (The Life and Times of Malcom X), 1986, Dead Meat, 1996, Pits Letter, 2000, Bully: Master of the Global Merry-Go-Round, 2004, Sheep of Fools.A Song Cycle for 5 Voices, 2005, (exhbn. catalogue) Police State, 1987. Named National Academician, 1994. Office: Galerie St Etienne 24 West 57th Street New York NY 10019

COEL, MARGARET SPEAS, writer; b. Denver, Oct. 11, 1937; d. Samuel Francis and Margaret Mary (McCloskey) Speas; m. George William Coel, July 22, 1961; children: William (dec.), Kristin Coel Henderson, Lisa Coel Harrison. BA, Marquette U., 1960. Newspaper reporter Westminister (Colo.) Jour., 1960-61; freelance journalist Boulder, Colo., 1972-90. Writing tchr. cmty. colls., Denver, 1985-90, U. Colo, Boulder, 1985-90. Author: (biography) Chief Left Hand, 1981 (Best Non-Fiction Book award 1981), Goin' Railroading, 1986 (Colo. Authors award 1986), The Eagle Catcher, 1995, The Ghost Walker, 1996, The Dream Stalker, 1997, The Story Teller, 1998, The Lost Bird, 1999, The Spirit Woman, 2000 (Colo. Book award), The Thunder Keeper, 2001, The Shadow Dancer, 2002 (Colo. Book award), Killing Raven, 2003, Wife of Moon, 2004 (Colo. Book award), Eye of the Wolf, 2005, The Drowning Man, 2006; contbr. articles to profl. jours., short stories to anthologies. Assoc. fellow Ctr. for Studies of Great Plains, U. Nebr. Mem. Colo. Authors League (pres. 1990-91; Best Non-Fiction Articles award 1991,

Best Novel award 1996, 97), Mystery Writers Am., Denver Women's Press Club. Democrat. Roman Catholic. Avocations: competitive tennis, skiing. Home: 3155 Lafayette Dr Boulder CO 80305-7112

COELING, HARRIET VAN ESS, nursing educator, editor; b. Grand Rapids, Mich., Dec. 3, 1943; d. Louis and Helen Angeline (DeGraff) Van Ess; m. Kenneth J. Coeling, June 27, 1970; children: Valerie Coeling Nandor, Beverly Coeling Corder. BSN, U. Mich., 1966, MS, 1968; PhD, Bowling Green State U., 1987. RN, Ohio; clin. nurse specialist. Head nurse, clin. specialist Presbyn. Univ. Hosp., Pitts., 1968-70; instr. U. Pitts. Sch. Nursing, 1970-72; staff devel. instr. Braddock (Pa.) Hosp., 1976-78, Med. Coll. Ohio, Toledo, 1978-83; asst. prof. U. Mich. Sch. Nursing, Ann Arbor, 1987-88, Kent (Ohio) State U. Coll. Nursing, 1988-93, asoc. prof., 1994—2004, prof., 2004—. Editor, Online Jour. Issues in Nursing, ANA/Kent State U., 1998—; contbr. articles to profl. jours. Vol. St. Malachi Healthcare Clinic, Cleve., 1993-98. Tchr. and Nonsvc. fellow Bowling Green State U., 1983-87; Nursing Practice award, ANA. Mem. Nat. Assn. Clin. Specialists, Ohio Assn. Advanced Practice Nurses, Ohio Nurses Assn. (chair human rights com. 1998—2002), Greater Cleve. Nurses Assn., Midwest Nursing Rsch. Assn., Christian Assn. Psychol. Studies, Sigma Theta Tau (Excellence in Use of Tehc. award 1997). Christian. Avocations: travel, swimming. Office: Kent State U 1743 Settlers Reserve Westlake OH 44145 Business E-Mail: hcoeling@kent.edu.

COEN, ADRI STECKLING See ADRI

COEN, JESSICA, blog writer, editor; Grad., U. Mich., 2002. Tchr. South LA HS, Teach for America; exec. asst. major TV studio; editor Gawker.com, Gawker Media, NY, 2004—. Blog writer (personal blog site) jessicacoen-.com, freelance writer NY Times, NY Observer, NY Post, ELLE, guest appearances Today Show, Topic A with Tina Brown. Named one of 100 Media People You Need to Know for 2005, Media Mag. Office: Gawker Media 81 Spring St New York NY 10012*

COETZER, AMANDA, professional tennis player; b. Hoopstad, South Africa, Oct. 22, 1971; Profl. tennis player, 1996—; winner tournament title WTA Tour Family Circle Championship, 1998; winner Budapest Ladies Open, 1997; mem. South African Fed Cup Team, 1992—93, 1995—97, South African Olympic Team, 1992, 1996, 2000. Named Most Improved Player and recipient Diamond ACES award and Karen Krantzcke Sportsmanship award, 1997; title holder Benelux Open, 2000. Office: WTA Tour 1 Progress Plz Ste 1500 Saint Petersburg FL 33701-4335

COEYMAN, EMILY NOLLIE ROGERS, civic worker; b. Waynesboro, Miss., Jan. 10, 1921; d. Olin Deauward and Ethel Louise (Finkbohner) Rogers; m. William Henry Coeyman, Apr. 5, 1941 (div. June 1952); children: Louis Brooke Roger, Louise Edna Coeyman Thomas. Student, Tomlinson Vocat. Inst., St. Petersburg, Fla., 1951, LaSalle Ext. Law U., 1957-59, St. Petersburg Jr. Coll., 1970-75, 85. Sec. Shorthand Reporter-Ct. Reporter, Washington, D.C., 1939-40, Colonial Decorating Co., Washington, D.C., 1940-41; clk-typist fin. and transp. dept. War Dept., Washington, D.C., 1941-43; clk. carrier U.S. P.O., Washington, D.C., 1943-44, ry. and postal clk. ry. mail svc., 1944; mdse. control clk. Hecht Co. Dept. Store, Washington, 1945-46; transcribing machine oprtor, clk.-typist REA, Washington, 1946; clk.-stenographer Glenn Dale (Md.) TB Sanitorium, 1946-48; clk.-cashier, admitting clk. Mound Park Hosp., St. Petersburg, 1948-51; clk.-typist VA, Pass-A-Grille, Fla., 1951-52; med. sec. to chief physiatrist Gallinger Hosp. (name now D.C. Gen. Hosp., Washington, 1955-60; ret., 1960. First woman mail carrier, Washington, D.C. (WWII), 1944. Bd.-dirs.-at-large, mem. citizens adv. com. Met. Planning Orgn., Pinellas County, Fla., 1984—; St. Petersburg rep. Tampa Bay Regional Planning Coun. Area Agy. on Aging, Pinellas County, 1981-90; bd. dirs.-at-large, mem. citizens adv. com. Pinellas Suncoast Transit Authority, Pinellas County, 1988-94, Fast Speed and High Speed Monorail, Pinellas, Hillsborough Counties Joint Com.-Citizens Adv., 1993—; active participant numerous city and county govt. meetings, including Environ. Devel. Commn., Bd. Adjustment, Pinellas County Sch. Bd., Pinellas Suncoast Transit authority, Juvenile Welfare Bd., Com. Neighborhood Assn. Named to Hon. Sr. Hall of Fame, City of St. Petersburg, 1987, Sr. Hall of Fame, 1988; recipient hon. proclamation as a vol. Pinellas County Commrs., 1991, hon. proclamation Pinellas Sports Authority, 1992. Mem. Nat. Assn. Ret. Fed. Employees, Am. Assn. Ret. Persons, Pinellas Geneal. Soc., Sr. Citizens Sunshine Ctr. Club, St. Petersburg Stamp Club, Suncoast Tiger Bay Club, Women of Moose, St. Petersburg Rock, Gem and Mineral Soc., UDC (assoc.). Republican. Baptist. Avocations: stamp and rock collecting, genealogy, volunteering. Home: 6936 40th Ave N Saint Petersburg FL 33709-4610

COFFEY, KIMBERLY E., secondary school educator; d. Jeffrey J. and Edith M. Morelock; m. Robert G. Coffey. BA in Math., Hartwick Coll., Oneonta, N.Y., 1995; MA in Math. Edn., Columbia U., 1997; postgrad., N.Y. Inst. Tech. Cert. permanent cert. in secondary math. N.Y. Tchr. math. Clarkstown Ctrl. Sch. Dist., New City, NY, 1997—. Pvt. tutor math., 1997—; curriculum devel. com. Felix Festa Mid. Sch., West Nyack, NY, 1997—. Mem.: Assn. of Math. Tchrs. of N.Y. State (Mem. Scholarship award 1998—), Nat. Coun. Tchrs. Math., Kappa Delta Pi. Office: Felix festa Mid Sch 30 Parot Rd West Nyack NY 10994

COFFEY, KITTY R., dietician, healthcare educator; PhD, U. Tenn. Registered dietitian, cert. LDN. Prof. and dean divsn. family and consumer sci. Carson-Newman Coll., Jefferson City, Tenn. Mem.: Am. Dietetic Assn. (Medallion award 2001). Office: Carson-Newman Coll Box 71881 Jefferson City TN 37760

COFFEY, LAURIANN GANT, elementary school educator; b. Marquette, Mich., Nov. 27, 1932; d. Luther Oeyvand and Gladys Esther (Hoff) Gant; m. Charles Edmund Coffey, July 11, 1957; children: Stephen Luther, David Charles. BS, No. Mich. U., 1954; MA, U. Mich., 1955. Cert. elem. tchr. Kindergarten tchr. Allen Park (Mich.) Pub. Schs., 1955-58; tchr. grade 1 Lincoln Consol. Schs., Ypsilanti, Mich., 1958-59; kindergarten tchr. Mellen Twp. Schs., Wallace, Mich., 1959-61, John D. Pierce Sch./No. Mich. U., Marquette, summer 1960; tchr. kindergarten, presch./1st grade Liverpool (N.Y.) Ctrl. Schs., 1967-72; tchr. grade 1 Marquette Area Pub. Schs., 1977—, mem. elem. math. com., 1990—. Mem. sch. improvement team Vandenboom Sch., Marquette, 1984-93. Chmn. City Election Counting Bd., Marquette, 1979—. Recipient Presdl. Award for Excellence in Elem. Math. Teaching, NSF, 1993, State Award for Excellence in Elem. Math. Teaching, Mich. Coun. Tchrs. Math./State Dept. Edn., 1991. Mem. AAUW, Coun. of Presdl. Awardees in Math., Nat. Coun. Tchrs. Math., Mich. Coun. Tchrs. Math., Upper Peninsula Reading Assn. (treas.), Mich. Reading Assn., Deleta Kappa Gamma. Presbyterian. Avocations: piano, knitting, reading, outdoor activities. Home: 1020 N Front St Marquette MI 49855-3514 Office: Vandenboom Elementary Sch 2000 Erie Ave Marquette MI 49855-1309

COFFEY, MARILYN JUNE, writer, educator; b. Alma, Nebr., July 22, 1937; d. June Thomas and Zelma Theola Coffey; m. John Raymond Powell, III (div.); m. Tom Henshaw (div.); 1 child, Ian Michael Henshaw. BA in Journalism, U. Nebr., Lincoln, 1959; MFA in Creative Writing, Bklyn. Coll., N.Y., 1981. Journalist Lincoln Evening Jour., Nebr., 1959—60, Good Housekeeping, N.Y.C., 1960—61, Home Furnishings Daily, N.Y.C., 1964—66; asst. prof. Boston U., 1969—71; tenured prof. Pratt Inst., Bklyn., 1966—69, 1973—90; co-founder Woman's Salon, NYC, 1975—85, Paris, 1975—85; comm. instr. St. Mary's Coll., Lincoln, 1990—92; tenured prof. creative writing Ft. Hays State U., Hays, Kans., 1992—2000; ret., 2000. Literature artist Kans. Arts Commn., Topeka, 1990—92, Nebr. Arts Coun., Lincoln, 1990—91; creative writer-in-residence Lawrence (Kans.) Arts Ctr., 1991. Author: Marcella: A Novel, 1973, 1976, Great Plains Patchwork: A Memoir, 1989, (book-length poem) A Cretan Cycle: Fragments Unearthed from Knossos, 1991. Co-founder The Women's Salon, 1977—85. Named Listed Writer, Poets and Writers, 1973—, Admiral Nebr. Navy, Nebr. gov., 1977, Marilyn Coffey Collection, U. Nebr.-Lincoln Librs. Archives and Spl. Collections, 1987—; recipient Pushcart prize, Pushcart Press, 1976; grantee rsch. grantee, Ludwig Vogelstein Found., 1985—87, Mellon Funds through Pratt Inst., 1987—88. Avocations: Hatha yoga, walking, music, confabulating, computer games. E-mail: marilyncoffey@cox.net.

COFFEY, NANCY, real estate broker; b. Palm Springs, Calif. d. Arthur Johnson and Joan (Hunter) Coffey. BA, Stanford U., 1967, MS in Engring., 1977. Comml. broker Coldwell Banker, San Francisco, 1980-87, Cushman & Wakefield, NYC, 1987—90; model Gilla Roos, NYC, 1991—96; real estate broker, 1990-96; comml. real estate broker Rolfe Group, NYC, 1997—98, Cushman & Wakefield, Inc., NYC, 1998—2000, Halstead Property, NYC, 2001—. Active Jr. League, San Francisco, 1981—87, N.Y.C., 1987—2000, sustainer, 1999—2000, Palo Alto Jr. League, 2000—01, N.Y. Jr. League, 2001—; mem. exec. com. spl. projects bd., vice chair thrift shop com. Meml. Sloan Kettering Cancer Ctr., N.Y.C., docents com., 2006—; vice chair membership com., vice chair Thrift Shop, Soc. Meml. Sloan Kettering, 1999—2000, mem. adminstrv. bd., 2002—; v.p. Class of 1967 Stanford U.; parish life com. mem. St. James Ch., 1997—2000. Mem.: River Club NY, Rockaway Hunting Club. Achievements include first female industrial real estate broker in Houston. Home: Smoke Tree Ranch Palm Springs CA 92264 Office Phone: 212-381-3355.

COFFEY, ROSEMARY KLINEBERG, educator; b. N.Y.C., Jan. 5, 1937; d. Otto and Selma Ruth (Gintzler) Klineberg; m. Joseph I. Coffey, June 28, 1963 (div. 1977); children: Megan Forbes, Susan Fox, James Odell; m. Zigmund L. Dermer, Apr. 7, 1990. BA, Vassar Coll., Poughkeepsie, N.Y., 1953-57; MA, Tufts U., Medford, Mass., 1958-59. Clk. typist United Nations Secretariat, N.Y.C., 1956, 1957; asst. editor, assoc. editor World Peace Found., Boston, 1959-61; research asst., assoc. Inst. for Defense Analyses, Washington, D.C., 1961-63; researcher Ctr. for Research on Conflict Resol, U. Mich., Ann Arbor, Mich., 1963-64; tchr. Pitts. Bd. Pub. Edn., 1975-78, tchr., editor, 1979-91; researcher, writer Brandegee Assocs., Pitts., 1978-79; sr. editor Coalition to Improve Mgmt. in State and Local Govt., 1991-93. Co-chair joint Bd. Union Coms. on Profl. Edn., Pitts., 1987, 1989. Author: The Story of Pittsburgh, 1986, co-author: America as Story, 2d edit., 1997 Com. chair, officer Pitts. Friends Meeting, 1978—, sec. Renaissance and Baroque Soc., 1983-85, Renaissance City Wind Music Soc., Pitts., 1987-90, class pres. Vassar Coll., Class, 1957, Poughkeepsie, 1987-92. Mem. Pitts. Vassar Club (treas., newsletter editor), World Federalist Assn. of Pitts. (bd. dirs. 1990—, pres. global solutions edn. fund Pitts. chpt. 2004—) Democrat. Avocations: reading, writing, community service. Home: 916 Bellefonte St Pittsburgh PA 15232-2204 Personal E-mail: rosemarycoffey@aol.com.

COFFEY, SHARON MARIE, music educator; d. Billy Bolan and Audra LaVerne Hale; m. Loy Clark Coffey, Aug. 14, 1992; children: Richard Clark, Michael Bolan, Rachael Marie. B.Mus.Edn., Baylor U., Waco, Tex., 1987. Cert. txhr. Tex., 1987. Choir tchr. Garland Independent Sch. Dist., Tex., 1987—88, Irving Independent Sch. Dist., Tex., 1988—94, Navasota Independent Sch. Dist., Tex., 2004—. Pvt. voice instr., Navasota, 1994—2004; music minister New Hope Cmty. Ch., Navasota, 2005—. Social chairperson Jaycees, Navasota, Tex., 1994—99; music dir. New Hope Cmty. Ch., Navasota, 2005—06. Grantee Sound Sys. of Music grantee, Navasot Edn. Found., 2005. Mem.: Tex. Choral Dirs. Assn., Tex. Music Educator's Assn. (assoc.). D-Conservative. Baptist. Avocations: pianist, singer, travel, movies, cooking. Office: Navasota ISD PO Box 511 Navasota TX 77868 Office Phone: 936-825-4225.

COFFEY, SHARON THORNTON, chemistry educator; b. New Orleans, Dec. 24, 1947; d. Daniel Raymond and June O'Donald Thornton; children: Cathryn Renee, Ann Michelle. BS in Biology and Phys. Therapy, Baylor U., Waco, Tex., 1970; MS in Biology, Tex. Womans U., Denton, 1994. Lic. phys. therapist, cert. tchr. Tex. Phys. therapist All Saints Hosp., Ft. Worth, 1970—72, Peter Smith Hosp., Ft. Worth, 1972—74, Harris Meth. Hosp., Ft. Worth, 1974—83, weekend rehab. phys. therapist, 1995—; tchr. sci. Trinity H.S., Euless, Tex., 1984—. Chemistry curriculum writer, 2004. Named Tchr. of the Yr., Trinity H.S., 2006; grantee, Hurst Euless Bedford Found., 1994—2006. Mem.: Assn. Tex. Ednl. Profls. Baptist. Avocations: reading, singing, gardening.

COFFEY, SUSANNA JEAN, art educator, artist; b. New London, Conn. d. Edwin Raymond and Magel C. (Willingham) C. BFA magna cum laude, U. Conn., 1977; MFA, Yale U., 1982. Tchg. asst. Yale U., 1982—; F.H. Sellers prof. painting Sch. of the Art Inst. of Chgo., Oxbow, Mich., 1985—. Vis. artist various schs., 1983—; adj. assoc. prof. U. Ill, 1983; vis. critic Royal Coll. Art, London, 1995, Vt. Studio Ctr., 1994; panel mem. Harvard Ctr. for Religious Studies, 2001. Illustrator: The H Hymn to Demeter, 1989, Monovassia (Eleni Fourtouni), 1979; one-woman shows include The Cultural Ctr. of the Chgo. Pub. Libr., 1986, Weatherspoon Gallery, Greensboro, N.C., 1993, Alpha Gallery 1995, 2001, 04, Galeria Alejandro Sales, Barcelona, 1995, Tibor De Nagy Gallery, 1996-97, 2001, 2003, others; represented in permanent collections Northwestern U., Evanston, Ill., Art Inst. Chgo., Mpls. Mus. Art, Bryn Mawr (Pa.) Coll., Boston Mus. Fine Arts, Weatherspoon Gallery, and pvt. collections. Individual Artists grant Conn. Commn. on the Arts, 1980, Chgo. Artists Abroad grant, 1990, Ill./Arts Coun. grant, 1985, 92, Studio Program grant Marie Walsh Sharpe Found., 1992, Nat. Endowment for the Arts grant, 1993; Guggenheim fellow, 1996; recipient Louis Comfort Tiffany Found. award, 1993, Acad. award in art Am. Acad. of Arts and Letters, 1995; named to Nat. Acad. Design, 2001. Office: Sch of the Art Inst of Chgo 37 S Wabash Ave Chicago IL 60603-3002

COFFIELD, SHIRLEY ANN, lawyer, educator; b. Portland, Oreg., Mar. 31, 1945; BA, Willamette U., 1967; MA, U. Wisc.-Madison, 1969; JD, George Washington U., 1974. Bar: D.C. 1975. Clk. Stitt, Hemmendinger and Kennedy, Washington, 1973-74; asst. gen. counsel Office U.S. Trade Rep., Washington, 1975-79; ptnr. Reaves & Coffield, Washington, 1979-82; sr. counsel to dep. asst. sect. textiles and apparel U.S. Dept. Commerce, Washington, 1982-85; spl. counsel Skadden, Arps, Slate, Meagher and Flom, Washington, 1985-87; ptnr. Piper & Marbury, Washington and Balt., 1987-90, Baker & Hostetler, Washington, 1990-94, Keller and Heckman, L.L.P., Washington, 1994-98, Duane, Morris & Heckscher, 1998-2000, Coffield Law, Washington, 2000—. Adj. prof. internat. econ. law Georgetown U. Law Sch., 1982—. Mem. Fed. Bar Assn., Am. Soc. Internat. Law, D.C. Bar, Pi Gamma Mu, Phi Delta Phi. Office: Coffield Law Ste 315 666 11th St NW Washington DC 20001-4530 Office Phone: 202-331-3097. Personal E-mail: coffieldlaw@yahoo.com.

COFFIN, BERTHA LOUISE, retired telecommunications industry executive; b. Atlanta, Aug. 19, 1919; d. William Wesley and Bertha Louise (Marsh) Mendenhall; m. J. Donald Coffin, Feb. 14, 1943 (dec. Sept. 1978). BA, U. Kans., 1940. Med. technologist Midwest Rsch. Lab., Emporia, Kans., 1940—43; ins. agt. Coffin Ins. Agy., Council Grove, Kans., 1943—99, sole owner, mgr., 1978—82; treas. Council Grove Tel. Co., 1947—50, sec.-treas., 1950—78, pres., chmn. bd., 1978—98, gen. mgr., 1978—99. Del. legis. confs. Nat. Tel. Coop. Assn., 1986, 88, 91-92, 94, 97, comem. comml. co. com., 1987-91, mem. govt. affairs com., 1991-98, exec. com., 1996-98; founder, pres., chmn. bd. Kans. Personal Comm. Svcs. Ltd., 1995-2005; officer Cities Unltd., Inc., 1999-2006. Copy preparation for book The Story of the Santa Fe Trail, 1982; author: History of Council Grove Telephone Company, 1991; ann. civic sects. tel. directory. Pres. various lit. clubs, Council Grove, 1945-72; speaker various civic, polit. and religious groups, 1962—; mem. adv. coun. Manhattan Christian Coll., 1983-86, trustee, 1986-92, 93-99, 2000-2006, chmn., 1991-92. Mem. Kans. Telecomm. Assn. (bd. dirs. 1992-95), Ind. Tel. Pioneers (dir. 1984-92). Avocations: travel, church related activities.

COFFIN, JOAN M., neuroscience educator; d. Charles E. and Mildred Anna (Vogt) Barry; m. Edward F. Coffin (dec.); 1 child, Lora. BS in Psychiatry, Gwynedd-Mercy Coll., Gwynedd, Pa., 1988; MA in Psychiatry, Temple U., Phila., 1991, PhD in Experimental Psychiatry, 1993. Asst. prof. psychiatry Phila. Coll. Textiles/Sci., 1993—94, King's Coll., Wilkes-Barre, Pa., 1994—2000, assoc. prof. neurosci., 2001—. Contbr. book chpt. to Neurobiology of Developmental Disorders, 2005. Named Fr. Frank O'Hara Disting. Svc. Profl. of Natural Sci., King's Coll., 2005—10. Mem.: IDA, SFN, Am. Psychiat. Soc. Office: King's Coll 133 N River St Wilkes Barre PA 18711

COFFINAS, ELENI, lawyer; b. Bklyn., Jan. 12, 1961; BA, Bklyn. Coll., 1982, JD, 1985. BAr: N.Y. 1985. Assoc. Sullivan & Liapakis, P.C., N.Y.C., 1986-93; ptnr. Sullivan, Papain, Block, McGrath & Cannavo, N.Y.C., 1993—, ptnr., supr. med. malpractice dept., 1994—. Mem. ATLA, Assn. Bar City N.Y. (med. malpractice com. 1996—), N.Y. State Trial Lawyers Assn. (bd. dirs. 1997—). Greek Orthodox.

COFFMAN, ELIZABETH THOMPSON, retired language educator; b. Biloxi, Miss., Mar. 8, 1933; d. William Carl and Elizabeth Burton Thompson; children: Philip H. Young Jr., Gage A. Bounds. BS, MA, U. South Ala., Mobile; PhD, U. So. Miss., Hattiesburg. Spl. edn. tchr. Bienville Sch., Mobile, Ala., 1963—65; English tchr. Vigor HS, Prichard, 1967—68; asst. adminstr., gorup counselor Am. Sch. Found. Mid. Sch., Mexico City, 1969; adult advisor U. South Ala., Mobile, 1969—70; adminstr., coord., counselor, instr. English remediation Reed's Chapel Sch., McIntosh, Ala., 1969—70; adminstrv. asst. Inst. Behavioral Objectives, U. South Ala., Mobile, 1970—71; English tchr. McGill-Toolen HS, Mobile, 1970—72; tchr. comm. skills and reading Brazier Elem. Sch., Mobile, 1973—75; instr. English Faulkner U., Mobile, 1976—77, James H. Faulkner State CC, Bay Minette, Ala., 1977—94; ret., 1994. Textbook editor Houghton Mifflin Co., NYC, 1980—94; grad. intern Am. Sch. Found., Mexico City; grad. instr. pub. edn. adminstrn. and supervision Ala. State U., 1975; adj. faculty Faulkner State CC, Fairhope, Ala. Co-author: Memorabilieia, 1993; contbr. poetry, revs., critiques to lit. publs. Mem.: Ea. Shore Rep. Women's Club, Ea. Shore Newcomers Discussion Group, Ea. Shore Creative Writers, Federated Women's Club. Avocations: dance, reading, classical music. Home: PO Box 269 Montrose AL 36559

COFFMAN, JENNIFER BURCHAM, judge; b. 1948; BA, U. Ky., 1969, MA, 1971, JD, 1978. Ref. libr. Newport News (Va.) Pub. Libr., 1972-74, U. Ky. Libr., 1974-76; atty. Law Offices Arthur L. Brooks., Lexington, Ky., 1978-82; ptnr. Brooks, Coffman and Fitzpatrick, Lexington, 1982-92, Newberry, Hargrove & Rambicure, Lexington, 1992-93; judge U.S. Dist. Ct. (ea. dist. and we. dist.) Ky., 1993—. Adj. prof. Coll. Law, U. Ky., 1979-81. Bd. dirs. YWCA Lexington, 1986—92, Shepherd Ctr., 2000—05. Mem. Ky. Bar Assn., Fayette County Bar Assn., U. Ky. Law Sch. Alumni Assn. Office: 136 US Courthouse 101 Barr St Lexington KY 40507-1313 Office Phone: 859-233-2453.

COFFMAN, SANDRA JEANNE, psychologist; b. San Antonio, May 31, 1945; d. Frederick and Dorothy Jane (Rothenbach) C.; children: Kevin, Sean. BA in English and French, Purdue U., 1967; MA in Internat. Studies, Am. U., 1969; PhD in Ednl. Psychology, U. Wash., 1978. Lic. psychologist, Wash. Postdoctoral intern U. Wash. Counseling Ctr., Seattle, 1982; clin. supr., psychologist U. Wash. and NIMH, Seattle, 1984—87, 1997—2002; clin. assoc. prof. dept. psychology U. Wash., Seattle, 1988—. Clin. cons. Eastside Domestic Violence Project, Bellevue, Wash., 1987-99, Group Health Behavioral Health, 2005-; co-dir. Women's Counseling Group, Seattle, 1981-90. Co-author: Talking It Out, 1984, You Don't Have To Take It!, 1993. Mem. steering com. Feminist Therapy Inst., 1997-2000. Mortarboard scholar Purdue U., 1967; scholar U. Wash., 1973; travel fellow U. Wash., 1976. Mem. APA; founding fellow Assn. Behavioral Cognitive Therapy. Office: 2003 Western Ave Ste 340 Seattle WA 98121-2162

COFIELD, VIRGINIA RILEY, elementary school educator, piano teacher; b. Columbia, S.C., Aug. 26, 1937; d. Harry and Viola Wilson Riley; m. Layton Cofield; children: Dwayne E., D'Jaris L. Cofield Holman. BA, Benedict Coll., 1959; MEd, U. SC, 1974. Cert. nat. literacy tutor. Music tchr. Elizabeth Heights H.S., Great Falls, SC, 1959—61, Webber Elem. Sch., Eastover, SC, 1961—65, Richland Sch. Dist. 1, Columbia, SC, 1965—90; part time music tchr. V.V. Reid Elem. Sch., Columbia, 1990—95. Pvt. piano tchr., 1954—. Chmn. Christian edn. Union Baptist Ch., Columbia, 1990—95, supt. Sunday Sch., 2000—, ch. musician, 1960—2001, v.p. missionary soc., 2000—. Recipient Tchr. of Yr., South Kilbourne Elem. Sch., 1986—87, Women's Day award, Union Baptist Ch., Cert. Recognition, State Dept. Edn., Recognition award for outstanding svc. to Richland County Sch. Dist. & State of S.C., Cert. of Svc., S.C. Ho. of Reps., 1990. Mem.: NEA, Richland County Edn. Assn., S.C. Edn. Assn., Red Hats Soc., Altruist Federated Club, Delta Sigma Theta (sgt. at arms Columbia chpt. 1982—84). Democrat. Bapt. Avocations: writing, collecting art, music paraphanelia, religious books, reading. Home: 51 Madera Dr Columbia SC 29203

COFRANCESCO, ANGELA, insurance agent, coach; b. New Haven, June 4, 1981; d. Eugene and Paula Cofrancesco. Degree in acctg., U. Conn., Storrs, 2003. Lic. CLCS Hartford Conn., 2004. Ins. broker North Haven Ins. Group, North Haven, Conn., 2003—, acct., bookkeeper, 2005—; basketball coach Amity H.S., Woodbridge, Conn., 2004—. Mem. New Haven Young Professionals, New Haven. Mem.: Conn. H.S. Coaches Assn. Home: 27 North Humiston Dr Bethany CT 06524 Office: North Haven Ins Group 193 State St North Haven CT 06473 Office Phone: 203-288-8429. Personal E-mail: angco25@aol.com.

COGAN, EVA, education educator; m. Stanley Cogan; children: Deena, Joshua. BS, Bklyn. Coll., 1970; PhD, Polytech. U., Bklyn., 1975. Asst. prof. Bklyn. Coll., 1984—. Author: articles in profl. jours. Mem.: Soc. Exact Philosophy, Assn. Computing Machinery. Avocations: needlecrafts, puzzles, plants. Office: Bklyn Coll 2900 Bedford Ave Brooklyn NY 11210 Business E-Mail: cogan@sci.brooklyn.cuny.edu.

COGAN, KAREN DIANE, psychologist educator; b. Redondo Beach, Calif., Sept. 20, 1963; d. William Dean and Betsy Alice (Rosselot) C.; m. Trent Anthony Petrie, Sept. 2, 1989 (div. 2002); children: Kyla, Braeden. BA in Psychology, UCLA, 1985, MS in Kinesiology, 1987; PhD in Psychology, Ohio State U., 1991. Lic. psychologist, Tex. Intern psychology U. Calif., San Diego, 1990-91; psychologist So. Meth. Univ., Dallas, 1991-92; prof., psychologist U. North Tex., Denton, 1992—; pvt. practice Denton, 1992—. Cons. sport psychology U. North Tex. and other univs., 1988—; sport psychology cons. to U.S. Ski Team; faculty mem. Ctr. Sport Psychology U. North Tex. Mem. APA (counseling divsn., sport psychology divsn., women divsn.), Assn. for Advancement of Applied Sport Psychology (cert. cons.). Avocations: exercise, movies, reading, wine tasting, triathalons. Office: Univ North Tex Counseling Ctr PO Box 310968 Denton TX 76203-0968 Home: 909 Chasewood Ln Denton TX 76205-8203 Office Phone: 940-565-4798. Business E-Mail: cogan@unt.edu.

COGAN, MARY HART, community activist, educator; b. Hyannis, Mass., Aug. 2, 1928; d. Walter Vincent and Marie Margaret (Welch) Hart; m. John F. Cogan, Jr., May 1, 1951 (div. Mar. 1989); children: Peter, Pamela, Jonathan, Gregory. BS in Edn., Bridgewater State Coll., 1951, D in Pub. Svc. (hon.), 1999. Tchr. Lexington (Mass.) Pub. Schs., 1951-58; health ins. cons. Mass. Businessman's Assn., Braintree, Mass., 1980-85. Elderly vote coord. Sen. Paul Tsongas, Mass., 1972; del. Dem. Nat. Conv., N.Y.C., 1974, 78; field dir. Mass. Carter Campaign, 1980; mem. fin. com. Dem. Nat. Com., 1988-92; pres. Boston U. Hops. Aux., 1985, Brigham and Women's Hosp. Aux., Boston, 1990; bd. dirs. Friends Monomoy Theater, Chatham, Mass., 1995-98, Acad. Performing Arts, Orleans, Mass., 1997—; trustee Boston Ballet, 1994—, Bridgewater Coll. Found., 1994—, Bridgewater State Coll., 1999—, Cape Mus. Art, 2000—, Heritage Gardens and Mus., 2004—. Mem. Stage Harbor Yacht Club, Bridgewater State Coll. Alumni Assn. (exec. bd. 1999—). Avocations: figure skating, biking, tennis, choral music, watercolor/pastel painting. Home: 77 Tisquantum Rd Chatham MA 02633-2573

COGDELL, PAULA L., secondary school educator, real estate agent; d. Billy Bob and Sandra L. Pierson; m. Blake I. Cogdell, Nov. 2, 1985; children: Kelsey L., Cameron B. BS, U. North Tex., Denton, Tex., 1983. Lic. tchr. Tex. State Bd. Edn., 1986. Cons. health Las Colinas Preventive Medicine Ctr., Irving, Tex., 1983—86; tchr. biology Coppell (Tex.) Ind. Sch. Dist., 1986—87; prin., owner All Am. Cheerleading & Gymnastics, The Woodlands, Tex., 1989—96; tchr. biology Montgomery (Tex.) Ind. Sch. Dist., 1997—2000, Magnolia (Tex.) H.S., 2000—; real estate agt. Keller Williams, Conroe, Tex. Dir. wellness Coppell (Tex.) Ind. Sch. Dist., 1986—87. Author: The Classroom Cell Project (Christa McAuliffe Tchg. Excellence award, 2005, Unsung Hero award ING, 2005). Vol.grade level advisor Nat. Charity League, Montgomery, 2002—04; chmn. Montgomery County Fair, Conroe, 2003—05. Mem.: Nat. Assn. Realtors, Assn. Tex. Profl. Educators (pres. local chpt. 1999—2006). Methodist. Avocations: horseback riding, exercise, reading, writing, travel. Home: PO Box 1345 Montgomery TX 77356 Office: Keller Williams 3500 W Davis Conroe TX 77304 Office Phone: 936-441-8000. Business E-Mail: pcogdell@kw.com.

COGEN, ROBERTA, retired nursing administrator, medical/surgical nurse; b. Bklyn., Feb. 2, 1929; d. Dewey and Sarah (Taylor) Gottlieb; m. Sanford Cogen, Nov. 14, 1949; children: Ellen, Jerald, Richard. Diploma in nursing, Jewish Hosp. and Med. Ctr., Bklyn., 1950. RN, N.Y. Staff nurse, instr. Sch. Nursing, Jewish Hosp. Bklyn., 1950-51; staff nurse surg. unit L.I. Jewish Med. Ctr., New Hyde Park, N.Y., 1966-69; coord. nursing care adult cardiology L.I. Jewish-Hillside Med. Ctr., New Hyde Park, 1969-94, ret., 1993. Guest lectr. Adelphi U.; clin. instr. SUNY, Stony Brook; presenter 10th World Congress Cardiology, Washington, 1986. Contbr. articles and book rev. to nursing jours.

COGGAN, PATRICIA CONNER, elementary school educator; d. Leslie Lynn and Grace Hartnell Conner; m. Leland Latrill Coggan, Jr., July 26, 1958; children: Robert Leslie, Sharon Coggan McBride. BS, U. Okla., 1958; M in Humanities, U. Dallas, 1983. Life tchg. cert. Tex., std. tchg. cert. Okla. 1st grade tchr. Dallas Ind. Sch., 1958—60; elem. tchr. The Hockaday Sch., Dallas, 1976—. Devel. tester Gesell Inst., New Haven, 1978—; trained tchr. Met. Opera-Creating Original Opera, N.Y.C., 1996—; trained evaluator All Kinds of Minds, Raleigh, NC, 1999—. Dallas host com. Rep. Conv., 1984; Presbyn. Women pres. Highland Pk. Presbyn. Ch., 1974; pres. Kappa Alpha Theta Alumnae, Dallas, 1970—71. Named hon. life mem., Presbyn. Women, 1974, hon. alumnae, Hockaday Alumnae Assn., 2003; Curriculum Writing grantee, Hockaday Bd. Trustees, 2002. Mem.: Nat. Coun. for Social Studies, Ela Hockaday Cum Laude Soc. (past pres. 1976—), Michael Stoner DAR (charter), Dallas Craft Guild, Tex. Old Missions and Forts Restoration Assn. Avocations: gardening, book binding, book reviewer. Office: The Hockaday Sch 11600 Welch Rd Dallas TX 75229

COGGER, CASSIA ZAMECKI, painter; d. Walter Zamecki and Debra Derrington; m. Stephen Cogger. Degree in Art Hist. and Studio Arts, U. Colo., Boulder; student, Art Students League, NYC. V.p. Art Students League NY, treas., 2006. One-woman shows include Nemick and Thompson Gallery, 2002, exhibited in group shows at 181st Ann. Invitational Exhbn. of Contemporary Am. Painters, Nat. Acad. Mus., NYC, 2006. Mailing: c/o Art Students League 215 W 57th St New York NY 10019*

COGGIN, CHARLOTTE JOAN, cardiologist, educator; b. Takoma Park, Md., Aug. 6, 1928; d. Benjamin and Nanette (McDonald) C. BA, Columbia Union Coll., 1948; MD, Loma Linda U., 1952, MPH, 1987; DSc (hon.), Andrews U., 1994. Diplomate Am. Bd. Pediatrics. Intern L.A. County Gen. Hosp., 1952-53, resident in medicine, 1953-55; fellow in cardiology Children's Hosp., L.A., 1955-56, White Meml. Hosp., L.A., 1955-56; rsch. assoc. in cardiology, house physician Hammersmith Hosp., London, 1956-57; resident in pediatrics and pediatric cardiology Hosp. for Sick Children, Toronto, Ont., Canada, 1965-67; cardiologist, asst. prof. medicine, co-dir. heart surgery team Loma Linda (Calif.) U., 1961-73, assoc. prof., 1973-91, prof. medicine, 1991—. Asst. dean. Sch. Medicine Internat. Program, 1973—75; v.p. for global outreach Loma Linda U. Health Scis. Ctr., 1998—; assoc. dean. Sch. Medicine Internat. Program, 1975—, spl. asst. to univ. pres. for interat. affairs, 1991; co-dir., cardiologist heart surgery team missions to, Pakistan and Asia, 63, Greece, 67, Greece, 69, Saigon, Vietnam, 1974—75, Saudi Arabia, 1976—87, China, 1984, China, 1989—91, Hong Kong, 1985, Zimbabwe, 88, Zimbabwe, 93, Kenya, 88, Nepal, 92, China, 92, Myanmar, 95, North Korea, 96. Author: Atrial Septal Defects, motion picture (Golden Eagle Cine award and 1st prize Venice Film Festival 1964); contbr. articles to med. jours. Recipient award for service to people of Pakistan City of Karachi, 1963, Medallion award Evangelismos Hosp., Athens, Greece, 1967, Gold medal of health South Vietnam Ministry of Health, 1974, Charles Elliott Weinger award for excellence, 1976, Wall Street Jour. Achievement award, 1987, Disting. Univ. Svc. award Loma Linda U., 1990; named Honored Alumnus Loma Linda U. Sch. Medicine, 1973, Outstanding Women in Gen. Conf. Seventh-day Adventists, 1975, Alumnus of Yr., Columbia Union Coll., 1984, Outstanding Achievement in Edn., Adventist Alumni Achievement award, 1999. Mem. AAUP, AAUW, Am. Coll. Cardiology, AMA (physicians adv. com. 1969—), Calif. Med. Assn. (com. on med. schs., com. on member svcs.), San Bernardino County Med. Soc. (chmn. comm. com. 1975-77, mem. comm. com, 1987-88, editor bull., 1975-76, William L. Cover, M.D. Outstanding Contbn. to Medicine award 1995), Am. Heart Assn., Med. Rsch. Assn. Calif., Calif. Heart Assn., Am. Acad. Pediatrics, World Affairs Coun., Internat. Platform Assn., Calif. Museum Sci. and Industry MUSES (Outstanding Woman of Yr. in Sci. 1969), Am. Med. Women's Assn., Loma Linda Sch. Medicine Alumni Assn. (pres. 1978), Alpha Omega Alpha, Delta Omega. Democrat. Home: 25052 Crestview Dr Loma Linda CA 92354-3415 Personal E-mail: jcoggin@verizon.net.

COGGINS, EILEEN M., lawyer; b. 1964; BA, West Chester U., 1987; JD, Widener U., 1992. In house counsel Keystone Care Group, Media, Pa.; asst. gen. counsel to gen. counsel, sr. v.p. Genesis Health Ventures, Kennett Square, Pa., 1998—2003; gen. counsel, sr. v.p. corp. compliance Genesis HealthCare, Kennett Square, Pa., 2003—. Mem.: Del. County Bar Assn., Am. Health Lawyers Assn., Pa Bar Assn., Guy G. deFuria Inn of Ct. Office: Genesis HealthCare 101 E State St Kennett Square PA 19348

COGNETTO, ANNA M., social worker; b. Herkimer, N.Y., May 25, 1957; d. Anthony N. and Margaret J. (Williams) C. AS with honors, Herkimer County C.C., 1977; BS with honors, Cornell U., 1979; MSW, Syracuse U., 1981. Lic. clin. social worker, N.Y.; cognitive behavioral therapist; diplomate in clin. social work. Social worker The Ctr. for Youth Svcs., Rochester, N.Y., 1981-82; psychiat. social worker Rockland Children's Psychiat. Ctr., Newburgh, N.Y., 1982-88; pvt. practice Poughkeepsie, N.Y., 1983—; social worker CHP Alcohol Clinic, Poughkeepsie, 1988-90; social worker II Dutchess City Dept. Mental Hygiene Alcohol Clin., Poughkeepsie, 1990-92, Cognetive Cons. Sanctuary, 2005—. Adj. lectr. Dutchess C.C., Poughkeepsie, 1985—; full-time instr. Dutchess C.C. dept. behavioral scis., Poughkeepsie; social worker, evaluator N.Y. State DWI Program, Poughkeepsie, 1991—; guest lectr. Sanctuary/N.Y. State Spl. Edn. Tng. Resource Ctr., Poughkeepsie, 1993—; cons. Hudson Valley Counseling, Poughkeepsie, 1993—. Mem. ARC, NASW (N.Y. State chpt., mem. gay and lesbian issues com., Hudson Valley Divsn. steering com., chair various coms., divsn. rep., chair, 1997-99, 99-2001), Am. Bd. Clin. Social Workers (diplomate), Internat. Coalition of Addiciton Studies Educators; life mem. Bd. of State Contact Recruitment Liason (curriculum com., 2002-). Avocations: reading, gardening.

COHANE, HEATHER CHRISTINA, publishing executive, editor; b. Camberley, Surrey, Eng. came to US, 1982; d. William Willoughby and Naomi Mary (Winder) Fausset; m. John Philip Cohane, May 13, 1961 (dec. Dec. 1981); children: Alexander, Candida, Ondine; m. Ossian Kare Berga, Nov. 2, 1985. (dec. Oct. 2000). Student pvt. schs., Isle of Wight, Eng. and Neuchatel, Switzerland. Founding editor, pub. Quest mag., NYC, 1987—; exec. v.p. Gotham Mag., NYC, 1999—2001; editor-at-large Avenue Mag., 2002—04; contbg. editor NY Dog, 2004—. Office Phone: 212-249-7872. Personal E-mail: hcohane@aol.com.

COHEN, ABBY JOSEPH, investment company executive; b. NYC, Feb. 29, 1952; d. Raymond and Shirley (Silverstein) Joseph; m. David M. Cohen. AB in Econs., Cornell U., 1973; MA in Econs., George Washington U., Washington, 1976. CFA. Economist Fed. Res. Bd., Washington, 1973-76; economist/analyst T. Rowe Price Assocs., Balt., 1976-83; investment strategist Drexel Burnham Lambert, NYC, 1983-90, Goldman, Sachs & Co., NYC, 1990—, mng. ptnr., 1998—. Trustee/fellow Cornell U.; bd. overseers Cornell Med. Sch. Named one of Most Powerful Women, Fortune Mag., 1998, Most Powervul, Smart Money Mag., 1998—2002, Most Powerful People, Forbes mag., 2005; named to top 50 in Global Fin., 1996; recipient Woman Achiever (Woman of Yr.), YWCA, NYC, 1989, Wall St. Week Hall of Fame, 1998. Mem. Nat. Assn. Bus. Economists, Inst. Chartered Fin. Analysts (chair), N.Y. Soc. Security Analysts (mem. bd. govs.), Nat. Economists Club (bd. govs.), Assn. for Investment Mgmt. and Rsch. (chair bd. govs. 1997-98), Coun. on Fgn. Rels., Coun. on Excellence in Govts. (bd. dirs.). Office: Goldman Sachs & Co 85 Broad St New York NY 10004-2456*

COHEN, ALICE, hematologist; b. 1954; MD, Univ. Health Scis.-Chgo. Med. Sch., 1981. Resident in internal medicine NYU-Manhattan VA Med. Ctr., N.Y.C., 1982—84; fellow in hematology and oncology George Washington U. Med. Ctr., 1984—86, Columbia Presbyn. Med. Ctr., N.Y.C., 1986—87; chief of hematology St. Michael's Med. Ctr., Newark, 1993—98; dir. hemophilia treatment ctr. Newark Beth Israel Med. Ctr., 1998—, dir. hematology/oncology fellowship tng. program, 1998—. Clin. asst. prof. medicine U. Medicine and Dentistry-N.J. Med. Sch.; assoc. clin. prof. medicine Columbia U. Coll. Physicians and Surgeons; mem. med. adv. bd. Hemophilia Assn. N.J.; mem. sickle cell adv. bd. N.J. Dept. Health, co-chair com for devel. emergency rm. guidelines and sickle cell disease, co-chair women with bleeding disorders subcom. Named one of Top Drs. in N.Y. Metro Area, Castle Connolly, Top Drs. 2003, N.J. Monthly Mag. Avocation: skiing. Office: Newark Beth Israel Med Ctr 201 Lyons Ave # E2 Newark NJ 07112-2094

COHEN, BARBARA ANN, artist; b. Milw., Feb. 18, 1953; d. Joseph and Irene Marion (Brown) C. BS in Art, U. Wis., 1975. One-woman shows include 1st Wis. Nat. Bank, 1981; exhibited in group shows at San Francisco State, 1975-76, Comprehensive Employment Tng. Act, Milw., 1979, San Dieguito Art Guild, 1981, Imperial Valley Art Show, 1982, La Jolla Light Photo Contest, 1986, Clairemont Art Guild, 1989-95. Recipient 1st place award for oil painting Imperial Valley Art Show. Democrat. Jewish. Home: 8627 Via Mallorca Apt D La Jolla CA 92037-9021

COHEN, BETSY Z., bank executive; m. Edward C. Cohen; children: Daniel, Jonathan, Abigail. BA cum laude, Bryn Mawr Coll.; JD cum laude, U. Pa. Law clk. hon. John Biggs chief judge U.S. Ct. Appeals 3rd Cir.; law prof. Rutgers U. Law Sch.; co-founder Spector, Cohen, Gadon & Rosen, Phila.; dir. First Union Corp. of Va., Dominion Bancshares, Inc., 1985—93; founder, chmn., CEO Jefferson Bank, Downingtown, Pa., 1974—; founder Jefferson Bank NJ, 1987; chmn., CEO JeffBanks, Inc., 1993—; founder, chmn., CEO, trustee RAIT Investment Trust, 1997—; dir. Hudson United Bancorp, 1999—2000; CEO Bancorp Bank, 2000—, chmn., 2003—; CEO Bancorp Inc., 2000—, dir., 2000—. Bd. dirs. Aetna US Healthcare, The Opera Co. Phila., WHYY-TV; trustee Phila. Mus. Art, Jewish Theol. Sem.; vice chair Bryn Mawr Coll., chair fin. com.; chair Phila. Mus. Art Corp. Ptnrs. Article editor The Law Rev. Recipient Paradigm award Greater Phila. C. of C., 1997, Elizabeth Dole Glass Ceiling award Southeastern Pa. ARC, 1998; named Delaware Valley Master Entrepreneur of the Yr., 1994, one to Top 50 Bus. Women in Commonwealth of Pa., 1996, one of 50 Leading Female Entrepreneurs of the World, Nat. Found. for Women Bus. Owners, 1997, A Woman of Distinction, Cmty. Women's Edn. Project, 1998; ranked 103 Working Woman Mags. Top 500 Bus. Women, 1998. Mem. Order of the Coif. Office: The Bancorp Bank 405 Silverside Rd Wilmington DE 19809 E-mail: bcohen@jeffbanks.com.*

COHEN, BETTY L., broadcast executive; b. Racine, Wis. BA in Comm., Stanford U., 1977. Broadcast prodr. Pub. Media Ctr., San Francisco, 1977; mgr. sr. prodr. on-air promotion Lifetime Television Services; writer-prodr. on-air promotion Cable Health Network; dir. on-air promotion and interstitial programming Nickelodeon/Nick at Nite, 1984—88; sr. v.p. & gen. mgr. Turner Network Television, 1988—92; founder, exec. v.p. Cartoon Network Worldwide, 1992—2001, pres., 1994—2001; with AOL Time Warner Inc., 2001—02; pres. Betty Cohen Media Consulting; pres., CEO Lifetime Entertainment Services, 2005—. Bd. trustees AOL Time Warner Found.; exec. com. Cable in the Classroom Nat. Cable Television Assn. Bd. dir. Anti-Defamation League; mentor Teach for Am.; bd. adv. Atlanta Girls' Sch., Roadtrip Nation. Named PROMAX Internat. Marketer of Yr., 1997; named one of Top 100 Marketers, Advertising Age, 1999, 50 Most Powerful Women in Bus., Fortune mag., 2000; recipient Vanguard award, NCTA, 2000, Pinnacle award, PROMAX/BDA, 2001, Global Programming award, Multichannel News, 2001. Mem.: Phi Beta Kappa. Office: Lifetime Entertainment Services World Wide Plz 309 West 49th St New York NY 10019 Office Phone: 212-424-7000. Office Fax: 212-957-4447.*

COHEN, BONNIE R., government official; b. Brockton, Mass., Dec. 11, 1942; d. Harold I. and Irma (Sims) Rubenstein; m. Louis R. Cohen, Sept. 29, 1965; children: Amanda, Eli. BA, Smith Coll., 1964; EdM, Harvard U., 1965; MBA, Harvard Bus. Sch., 1967. Analyst RMC, Inc., Washington, 1967-71; asst. to vice supt. Washington Pub. Schs., 1971-72; sr. cons. Levin & Assocs., Washington, 1972-76; treas. UMWA Funds, Washington, 1976-81; advisor Stanford U. Treas., Palo Alto, Calif., 1981; sr. v.p. Nat. Trust for Historic Preservation, Washington, 1981-93; asst. sec. of interior Dept. Iterior, Washington, 1993-97; undersec. for mgmt. Dept. State, Washington, 1997-2001; pres. B.R. Cohen and Assoc., Washington. Trustee ARC Retirement System, Washington, 1986-89; investment chair DC Retirement System, 1984-87; mem. bd. dir. Global Heritage Fund. Bd. dirs. Beauvoir Sch., Washington, 1985-88, Nat. Cathedral Sch., Washington, 1985-88, Environ. Defense Fund, Washington, 1982-86, Ctr. for Marine Conservation, Washington, 1987-93. Mem. Cosmos Club. Democrat. Avocations: sports, antiques, basketball refereeing. Office: BR Cohen and Assoc 1824 Phelps Pl NW # 1810 Washington DC 20008-1850

COHEN, CAROLYN A., healthcare educator; BS, Boston U., 1965; postgrad., Boston State Coll., U. Mass., 1978, Boston Leadership Acad., 1989, Boston Leadership Inst., 1997. Tchr., coach health and phys. edn. coord. girls athletics Roslindale H.S., Boston, 1965—76; tchr., coach health and phys. edn. coord. athletics West Roxbury H.S., Boston, 1976—87; asst. dir. health phys. edn. athletics Madison Park Campus, Boston, 1979—87; health educator dept. phys. edn./athletics West Roxbury H.S., Boston, 1989—90, 1990—, lead tchr., 1995—2000; commr. girls' basketball Boston Pub. Schs., 1979—. Cheerleading judge various orgns., 1963, 64, 65, 70, 74, 80, 69-74; coach recreational programs N.E. Deaconess Hosp. Sch. Nursing, 1962-64, Beth Israel Hosp. Sch. Nursing, 1961-64; basketball ofcl. Bay State League, Pvt. Sch. League, Cath. H.S., 1961-80; coach phys. edn. dept. Boston U., 1962-65, 65-68, programming guild chmn., 2005-; ofcl. Boston Park and Recreation Dept., 1962-75, summer playgrounds instr., 1961-65; instr. garening, athletic specialist agr. dept. Boston Schs., 1965-76. Trustee Adaptic Environ. Ctr., Boston, 1986—, treas., mem. exec. bd., 1990—; trustee Friends of Boston Harbor Islands, Inc.; instr. ARC, 1965—; rep. Office Children-Area IV, Roslindale, Boston, 1974—76; liaison West Roxbury H.S. and Cmty. Sch. New Move Unlimited Theatre, Boston, 1981—84; liaison spl. arts project West Roxbury H.S., 1993—94. Named to Boston U. Scarlet Key Soc., 1998, N.E. New Agenda Hall of Fame, 2003; recipient Spl. Citation, Boston U. Sargent Coll. Alumni Assn., 1980, Cert. of Appreciation, ARC Mass. Bay, 1986, New Agenda award, Boston Salute to Women in Sport, 1993, Disting. Svc. to Alma Mater award, Boston U., 1994, Citation, Mass. Celebration Women in Sports Day, 2002, citation, Mil. Order of World Wars, 2002, Youth Patriotic & Leadership, 2002, Patrick Henry award, YPAL Program of Officier's of World Wars, 2004. Mem.: Sargent Coll. Alumni Assn. (class sec., editor class newsletter 1965—, Spl. Citation 1980, Black Gold award 1995), Boston U. Nat. Alumni Coun., Boston U. Alumni Assn. (v.p. 1980—82, 1987—89, v.p. cmty. 1995—97, sec. 1997—, named to North East New Agenda Hall Fame 2003), Mass. Assn. Health, Phys. Edn., Recreation and Dance (state and exec. com. 1969—74, coord. registration ann. state conv. 1975—94, treas. 1981—94, Honor award recognition 1978, Presdl. Citation 1988, Joseph McKenney award 2002), AAHPERD (bud. mgr. nat. conv. 1988—89), Boston U. Women's Grad. Club (v.p. for scholarship 1981—83, 2005—).

COHEN, CLAIRE GORHAM, investment company executive; b. St. Johnsbury, Vt., May 9, 1934; d. John David and Muriel (Somers) Gorham; m. Richard D. Cohen, Nov. 26, 1959; 1 son, James H. Student, U. Vt., 1953—54; BA, Radcliffe Coll., 1956. Proofreader Dun & Bradstreet, Inc., 1956, mcpl. bond analyst, 1957-64, sr. state analyst, 1965-66, sr. analyst, 1970-71, Moody's Investors Svc. Inc., N.Y.C., 1971-75; v.p., assoc. dir. rsch. Mcpl. Bond Rsch. Divsn., N.Y.C., 1975-86, v.p. mng. dir. state ratings, 1986-89; exec. mng. dir. govtl. fin. Fitch Investors Svc., Inc., N.Y.C., 1989-91, exec. v.p., 1991-94, vice chmn., 1994-97, Fitch IBCA, N.Y.C., 1997—2004; cons., 2005—. Mem. Govt. Acctg. Stds. Adv. Bd., 1999-2002; mem. Fed. Acctg. Stds. Adv. Bd., 2002—; mem. Task Force on N.Y. State Pub. Authorities, 1974-75. Mem. N.Y. Harvard-Radcliffe Schs. Com.; 1952 class agt. St. Johnsbury Acad., 1981-86; 1956 class agt. Radcliffe Coll., 1981-86. Recipient Disting. Svc. award State Debt Mgmt. Network, 1999. Mem. Mcpl. Forum N.Y. (Career Svc. award 2002), Mcpl. Analysts Group N.Y. (treas. 1983-84, chmn. 1984-85, Career Achievement award 2004), Nat. Fedn. Mcpl. Analysts (bd. govs. 1984-86, chmn. awards com. 1984-85, Career Achievement award 1991), Soc. Mcpl. Analysts, India House Club (bd. govs. 2003—). Office: Fitch IBCA One State St Plz New York NY 10004-2614 Office Phone: 212-908-0552.

COHEN, CLAUDIA, journalist, television reporter; b. Englewood, NJ, Dec. 16, 1950; d. Robert B. and Harriet (Brandwein) C.; 1 child, Samantha. BA, U. Pa., 1972. Mng. editor The Daily Pennsylvanian; with More Mag., N.Y.C., 1973-76; mng. editor, 1976-77; reporter N.Y. Post, N.Y.C., 1977-78; editor, author Page Six column, 1978-80; daily columnist I, Claudia N.Y. Daily News, N.Y.C., 1980-81; tv entertainment reporter Live with Regis and Kathie Lee, 1983—; reporter Eyewitness News WABC, 1984—89. Bd. overseers Sch. Arts and Scis. U. Pa.; mem. adv. bd. N.Y. Hosp. Cornell Med. Ctr.; adv. coun. AIDS Cmty. Rsch. Initiative Am. Honoree Sarah Herzog Meml. Hosp. Centennial, 1995, Rita Hayworth Gala Benefit for Alzheimers, 2000; named Police Athletic League Woman of Year, 2006. Office: Sta WABC 7 Lincoln Sq New York NY 10023-5900

COHEN, CORA, artist; b. NYC, Oct. 19, 1943; d. George and Anne (Lenarsky) C. BA, Bennington Coll., 1964, MA, 1972. Vis. artist U. Pa., 1969-70, U. Chgo., 1983-95, Art Inst. Sch. Chgo., 1983-85, 97, Boston Mus. Sch. Fine Arts, 1994-95, U. Minn., 1996, Kunsthögskolan, Stockholm, 1996, Corcoran Mus. Sch. Art, 2000, Washington U., St. Louis, 2003; vis. prof. Art Inst. Sch. Chgo., 1992-93; adj. faculty NYU, 1990-2000, Rutgers U., Newark, 2004, Md. Inst. Coll. Art, 2005-06; assoc. prof. art U. N.C., Greensboro, 1998-2003, Vt. Studio Ctr., 1999-2002, 06; nat. focus artist Emory and Henry Coll., Emory, Va., 2003-04; guest lectr. New Sch., 2004; 4th yr. adviser Md. Inst. Coll. Art, 2005, 06. One-person shows include Everson Mus. Art, Syracuse, N.Y., 1974, Max Hutchinson Gallery, N.Y.C., 1979-80, 84, Wolff Gallery, 1988, Holly Solomon Gallery, 1990, New Arts Program, Kutztown, Pa., 1993, Jason McCoy Gallery, N.Y.C., 1993-94, David Beitzel Gallery, N.Y.C., 1994, Sarah Moody Gallery Art, Tuscaloosa, Ala., 1996, Joslyn Art Mus., Omaha, 1996, Hering Raum, Bonn, Germany, 1997-98, Rena Bransten Gallery, San Francisco, 1997, Jason McCoy Gallery, N.Y.C., 1997, Belvedere Strasse, 1999, Bentley Gallery, Scottsdale, Ariz., 1999, 2002, 05, Stefanie Hering, Berlin, 2000, McCoy Chelsea, 2001, Emory (Va.) and Henry Coll., 2003-04, Jason McCoy Inc., N.Y.C., 2004, Abaton Garage, Jersey City, 2005; exhibited in group shows at Baxter Art Gallery, Pasadena, Calif., 1985, Am. Acad. and Inst. Arts and Letters, N.Y.C., 1987, Barbara Krakow Gallery, Boston, 1987, Pamela Auchincloss Gallery, Contemporary Surfaces, N.Y.C., 1992, A/C Project Room, An Esemplastic Shift, N.Y.C., 1992, Sandra Gering Gallery, 1992, Piccolo Spoleto Festival, Charleston, S.C., 1992, The Fetish of Knowledge, A/C Project Room, N.Y.C., 1992, Daniel Weinberg Gallery, L.A., 1989, Wolff Gallery, N.Y.C., 1991, Feigen Gallery, 1991, Sytsema Galleries, Baarn, Holland, 1992, Jason McCoy Gallery, N.Y.C., 1993, The Painting Ctr., N.Y.C., 1993, White Columns, N.Y.C., 1993, Bill Maynes Contemporary Art, N.Y.C., 1994, Penine Hart Gallery, N.Y., 1994, Trans Hudson Gallery, Jersey City, Out of the Blue Gallery, Edinburgh, Scotland, 1994, Cepa Gallery, Buffalo, 1995, 2000, the Smart Fair, Stockholm, 1995, NYU, N.Y.C., 1995, Newhouse Ctr. Contemporary Art, S.I., N.Y., 1997, Galleri Mariann Ahnlund Umea, Sweden, 1996, Accrochage, Hering Raum, Bonn, 1996, Galerie Brigitte Schenk, Köln, Germany, Köln Art Fair, 1997, Cepa Gallery, Buffalo, Galleri Mariann Ahnlund, Stockholm, Stalke Out of Space, Copenhagen, Barbara Davis Gallery, Houston, 1998, Oppenhoff & Rädler, Leipzig, Stockholm Art Fair, Hunter Coll., Times Square Gallery, N.Y., The Art Fair, The 69th Regiment Armory, N.Y., 1999, 2002, 04, 06, McCoy, Kansas City, 2000, Open Studio to Benefit the Coalition for the Homeless, N.Y., 2000, U. Ariz. Mus. Art, Tucson, 2001, The Five and Dime Series, Jan Van de Donk, NY, 2001, Cynthia Broan Gallery, N.Y., 2002, Painting Painting N3 Project Space, Williamsburg, Brooklyn, N.Y., 2003, Sheldon Art Galleries, St. Louis, 2003, Stalke Collection Gallery, Gallery Kirke, Sonnerup, Denmark, 2006; photgrapher: Cohen, Cora: The Record, The Death, The Surprise, 1999. Recipient N.Y. Found. Arts Gottlieb Found. award, 1990, 2006, Pollock Krasner award, 1998, Kohler Fund award U. NC, 1999, Adolph and Esther Gottlieb Found. award, 2006; Painting fellow Nat. Endowment for the Arts, 1987; Yaddo Residence grantee, 1982, 95, New Faculty grantee U. N.C., 1999. Mem. Simon Wiesenthal Ctr., Coll. Art Assn. Jewish. Home: 287 Broadway New York NY 10007-2004 Office Phone: 212-267-9430. E-mail: ccohen287@earthlink.net.

COHEN, CYNTHIA MARYLYN, lawyer; b. Bklyn., Sept. 5, 1945; AB, Cornell U., 1967; JD cum laude, NYU, 1970. Bar: N.Y. 1971, U.S. Ct. Appeals (2nd cir.) 1972, U.S. Dist. Ct. (so. and ea. dists.) N.Y. 1972, U.S. Supreme Ct. 1975, U.S. Dist. Ct. (ctrl. and no. dists.) Calif. 1980, U.S. Ct. Appeals (9th cir.) 1980, U.S. Dist. Ct. (so. dist.) Calif. 1981, U.S. Dist. Ct. (ea. dist.) Calif. 1986. With Paul, Hastings, Janofsky & Walker LLP, L.A., N.Y.C. Bd. dirs. N.Y. chpt. Am. Cancer Soc., 1977-80; active Pres.'s Coun. Cornell Women; lawyer rep. Ninth Cir. Jud. Conf. Recipient Am. Jurisprudence award for evidence, torts and legal instns., 1968-69; John Norton Pomeroy scholar NYU, 1968-70, Founders Day Cert., 1969. Mem. ABA, Assn. Bar City N.Y. (trade regulation com. 1976-79), Assn. Bus. Trial Lawyers, Fin. Lawyers Conf., N.Y. State Bar Assn. (chmn. class-action com. 1979), State Bar Calif., Los Angeles County Bar Assn., Order of Coif, Delta Gamma. Avocations: tennis, bridge, rare books, wines. Home: 4531 Dundee Dr Los Angeles CA 90027-1213 Office: Paul Hastings Janofsky & Walker LLP 515 S Flower St 25th Fl Los Angeles CA 90071 Office Phone: 213-683-6000. Business E-Mail: cynthiacohen@paulhastings.com.

COHEN, DIANA LOUISE, psychologist, educator, consultant; b. Phila., Apr. 8, 1942; d. Nathan and Dorothy (Rubin) Blasberg; 1 child, Jennifer. BA, Temple U., 1964, MEd, 1969, PhD, 1996. Lic. psychologist, Pa., N.J.; lic. profl. counselor, N.J.; cert. mental health counselor. Caseworker Phila. Gen. Hosp., 1964-69, staff psychologist, 1969-70, Atlantic Mental Health Ctr., McKee City, N.J., 1970-80, unit dir., 1980-87, v.p. profl. svcs., 1987-91; pvt. practice Pa., N.J., 1991—. Adj. faculty Glassboro (N.J.) State Coll., 1988—; cmty. and family mediator Cmty. Justice Inst., Atlantic County, N.J., 1990—. Com. chmn. Atlantic County Commn. for Missing and Abused Children, 1984—89; co-project dir. Employee Assistance Program, 1994—. Grantee N.J. Dept. Edn., 1988-89, N.J. Job Tng. Partnership Act, 1990. Mem. APA (assoc.), N.J. Counseling Assn., N.J. Mental Health Counselors Assn. (pres.-elect 1996, pres. 1997), South Shore Region Mental Health Counselors Assn. (sec. 1994-97). Avocations: painting, tennis, cross country skiing. Home: 2 Dee Dr Linwood NJ 08221-1910 Office: 2106 New Rd Ste E1 Linwood NJ 08221-1052 Office Phone: 609-916-8777.

COHEN, DIANE A., rabbi; b. Boston, Dec. 1, 1945; d. Louis Hyman and Mary Aronson; m. Roy Cohen, June 18, 1967 (div. July 18, 1990); children: Scott David, Joshua Daniel, Charles Lawrence. BA in English, UCLA, 1967; MA in Edn., B of Hebrew Letters, U. of Judaism, L.A., 1989. Ordained rabbi Jewish Theol. Sem. of Am., 1993. Rabbi Temple Ohev Shalom, Colonia, NJ, 1995—2003, Temple Bnai Israel, Willimantic, Conn.; adj. rabbi Congregation Neve Shalom, Metuchen, NJ, 2003—. Author: (book chpt.) Women's Bible Commentary; contbr. articles to profl. jours. Mem. Middlesex County Human Rels. Commn., Middlesex County, NJ, 1997—2000; sec. Woodbridge (N.J.) Interfaith Clergy Coun. Recipient Woman of Excellence award, Middlesex County Comm. on the Status of Women, 1999. Mem.: Rabbinical Assembly N.J. Region (v.p., treas. 1999—2003), Rabbinical Assembly. Jewish. Avocations: reading, cooking, photography, grandchildren. Home: 7075 Vineyard Way Germantown TN 38138-1401 Personal E-mail: ravdina@aol.com.

COHEN, ELAINE HELENA, pediatrician, cardiologist, educator; b. Boston, Oct. 14, 1941; d. Samuel Clive and Lillian (Stocklan) C.; m. Marvin Leon Gale, May 7, 1972; 1 child, Pamela Beth Gale. AB, Conn. Coll., 1963; postgrad., Tufts U., 1963—64; MD, Woman's Med. Coll. Pa., 1969. Diplomate Am. Bd. Pediat. Pediat. intern Children's Hosp. of L.A., 1969-70, resident in pediat., 1970-71; fellow in pediat. cardiology UCLA Ctr. Health Scis., 1971-72, L.A. County/U. So. Calif. Med. Ctr., LA, 1972-74; pediatrician Children's Med. Group of South Bay, Chula Vista, Calif., 1974—. Clin. instr. dept. pediat. UCLA Sch. Medicine, 1971-72, U. So. Calif., L.A., 1972-74; asst. clin. prof. dept. pediat. U. Calif., Calif. Sch. Medicine, San Diego, 1974-98, preceptor dept. pediat., 1992—, assoc. clin. prof. dept. pediat., 1998—. Fellow Am. Acad. Pediat.; mem. Calif. Med. Assn., San Diego County Med. Soc. Avocations: sketching, design. Office: Children's Med Group South Bay 280 E St Chula Vista CA 91910-2945 Office Phone: 619-425-3951. Personal E-mail: leongalemarvin@msn.com.

COHEN, FERN K., music educator; b. Hartford, Conn., Jan. 24, 1944; d. Anne L. Kent-Wald and Felix Wald (Stepfather); m. Joel S. Cohen, June 19, 1966; children: Michael H., Rachel S. Cohen-Rodney, Naomi R. BA in Music Edn., Johns Hopkins U., 1966; MS in Music Edn., Ctrl. Conn. State U., 1991, postgrad., 2001. Cert. K-12 music tech. State Dept. Edn., Conn., 1966. Music tchr. k-8 Hartford (Conn.) Pub. Schools, 1966—69; music tchr. Plainville (Conn.) Pub. Schs., 1983—84, Newington (Conn.) Pub. Schs., 1984—, program leader music dept., 1996—. Dir. summer music program Newington (Conn.) Pub. Schs., 1999. Nominee Tchr. of Yr., Newington, 2004, Excellence in Music Tchg. award, New Haven Symphony Orch., 2005; recipient Tchr. of Yr., Martin Kellogg Mid. Sch., 1985; grantee, Music Academy, 2001. Mem.: Conn. Music Edn. Assn. (assoc.; region dir., chairperson No. region orch., No. region dir., adjudicator all-state and region festivals), MENC (assoc.), Am. String Tchrs. Assn. (assoc.; mem. at large, past pres.), Ctrl. Conn. U. Alummni (assoc.), Johns Hopkins Alumni (assoc.), Mu Phiu Epsilon (assoc.), Alpha Delta Kappa (assoc.). Independent. Jewish. Avocations: swimming, knitting, music. Home: 22 Jeffrey Ln Newington CT 06111 Office: Newington Pub Sch 131 Cedar St Newington CT 06111 Office Phone: 860-667-5888. Personal E-mail: stringteacher@cox.net. Business E-Mail: fcohen@newington-schools.org.

COHEN, GLORIA ERNESTINE, elementary school educator; b. Bklyn., July 6, 1942; d. Victor George and Marion Theodosia (Roberts) C. BS in Edn., Wilberforce U., 1965; MA in Elem. Edn., Adelphi U., 1975; Profl. Diploma in Ednl. Adminstrn., L.I. U., 1984; MS in Edn., Bklyn. Coll., 1986. Tchr. Bd. Edn., Bklyn., 1965—; case worker Dept. Welfare, Bklyn., 1965—. Mem. comprehensive sch. improvement program Pub. Sch. 149, 1990—91, mem. open corridor planning com., 1990—91, mem. consultation com., 1990—; tchr. in charge of after sch. reading and math. tutorial program, 1995—96; dean grades 4-6, 1996—98; supr. Sat. Acad.; tchr. in charge of Read Extended Day program, 1997—98; cons. tchr. for 4th grade class, 1999; tchr. in charge of food and nutrition distbn. Maxwell H.S., Bklyn., 1999, P.S. 64 Dist. 27, Queens, 2000; tutorial tchr. Pub. Sch. 149, 2001—02; tutorial reading tchr. P.S. 149, Bklyn., 2004; tchr. in charge of food and nutrition distbn. P.S. 174 Dist. 19, Bklyn., 2001—04, Dist. 27, Pub. Sch. 60, Queens, 2005—06. Mem.: U.S. Tennis Assn., Hempstead Lake Tennis Club, Rockville Racquet Club, Kappa Delta Pi, Zeta Phi Beta. Democrat. Roman Catholic. Avocation: tennis.

COHEN, IDA BOGIN (MRS. SAVIN COHEN), import/export company executive; b. Bklyn. d. Joseph and Yetta (Harris) Bogin; m. Barnet Gaster, June 26, 1941 (div. May 1955); m. 2d Savin Cohen, Aug. 30, 1964. Student, St. John's U., Bklyn.; BS, NYU, NYC. Sec.-treas. J. Gerber & Co., Inc., N.Y.C., 1942-54, v.p., dir., 1954-73. Pres., dir. Austracan U.S.A., Inc., N.Y.C., 1960-73; v.p. Parts Warehouse, Inc., Woodside, N.Y., 1970-72, sec.-treas., 1972-83; also engaged in pvt. investments. Contbr. articles to South African Outspan, newspapers. Home: 12 Shorewood Dr Sands Point NY 11050-1909

COHEN, JUDITH W., academic administrator; b. N.Y.C., May 14, 1937; d. Meyer F. and Edith Beatrice (Elman) Wiles; BA, Bklyn. Coll., 1957, MA, 1960; cert. advanced studies Hofstra U., 1978; MA Columbia U., 1986, postgrad. 1986—. m. Joseph Cohen, Oct. 19, 1957; children: Amy Beth (dec.), Lisa Carrie, Adam Scott Frank, Elyssa Lily. Tchr. N.Y.C. Pub. Schs., Bklyn., 1957-60; tchr. Mid. Country Sch. Dist., Centereach, N.Y., 1970-93, retired 1993; prof. psychology 5 Towns Coll., Dix Hills, N.Y., 1994—. prof. edn. Dowling Coll., Oakdale, N.Y., Title IX compliance officer, 1980-86, team leader 1987-91; dir. Long Island U. Summer Adventure Program, 1994—. Bus. adv. Women's Equal Rights Congress, Suffolk County Human Rights; chmn. bd. edn., Temple Beth David, trustee, 1975-79; pres. CHUMS, 1979-82; Tchr. of Gifted Post-L.I. U. Saturday Program, 1985—; L.I. Writing Project fellow, Dowling Coll., 1979—; cert. sch. dist. adminstr., supr., adminstr., N.Y. State; adj. prof. Five Towns Coll., 1994—; adj. prof. edn. Dowling Coll., Oakdale, N.Y., 1997—. Mem. Nassau Suffolk Coun. Adminstrv. Women in Edn. (prds. 1979-81), Assn. for Supervision and Curriculum Devel., Assn. Gifted/Talented Edn., Women's Equal Rights Congress Com. (exec. bd.), Suffolk County Coordinating Council Gifted and Talented, Phi Delta Kappa, Delta Kappa Pi. Author: Arts in Education Curriculum in Social Studies and Language Arts, 1981. Home: 35 Gaymor Ln Commack NY 11725-1305

COHEN, KATHLEEN FRANCIS, librarian; b. Boston, June 2, 1947; d. Alfred John and Ruth Kelleher Francis; m. Allan A. Cohen, Aug. 5, 1973; children: Joseph, Crista. BA in History, Fla. State U., 1969, MS in Libr. Sci., 1970; MA in History, U. Fla., 1986. Libr. Jacksonville Pub. Libr., Fla., 1970—73; libr. govt. docs. U. North Fla., 1973—77, head ref. dept., 1975—90, asst. dir. librs., 1989—2003, interim dir. libr.s, 2003—03, asst. dir. librs., 2006—. Pres. faculty assn. U. North Fla., 2000—02; pres. bd. dirs. Northeast Fla. Libr. Info. Network, 1993—97. Mem.: ALA, Assn. Coll. & Rsch. Librs., Phi Beta Kappa, Phi Kappa Phi. Home: 221 Woody Creek Dr Ponte Vedra Beach FL 32082 Office: U North Fla 4567 St Johns Bluff Rd S Jacksonville FL 32224

COHEN, LISA JANET, psychologist, educator; b. Chgo., Dec. 27, 1961; d. Morrel Herman and Sylvia Pauline (Zwein) C. AB, BFA, U. Mich., 1985; MA, CUNY, 1989, MPhil, 1991, PhD, 1992. Lic. psychologist, N.Y. Supervising psychologist Beth Israel Med. Ctr., N.Y.C., NY, 1996—; asst. prof. psychiatry Albert Einstein Coll. Medicine, 1996—2001, assoc. prof., 2001—. Pvt. practice psychology, N.Y.C., 1994—; asst. prof. psychology in psychiatry Mount Sinai Sch. of Medicine, 1993-96. Contbr. chapters to books, articles to profl. jours. Mem.: APA, N.Y. State Psychol. Assn. Office: Dept Psychiatry Beth Israel Med Ctr 1st Ave and 16th St New York NY 10003 Office Phone: 212-420-2316. E-mail: lcohen@chpnet.org.

COHEN, LOIS JEAN, developmental psychologist, retired; b. Grand Rapids, Mich., Feb. 12, 1924; d. Francis Canfield Carl and Violet Morine (McCurdy) Ford; m. H. George Cohen, June 30, 1952 (dec.); children; Marla Jean, Sarah Rachel. BA, U. Mich., 1944; MA, State U. of Iowa, 1947; PhD, State U. Iowa, 1949. Instr. in psychology Smith Coll., Northampton, Mass., 1949-54, asst. prof., 1955-57, researcher, 1963-66, class dean, 1966-81, rsch. assoc., 1981-84. Co-grantee NIMH, 1963, NSF, 1966. Mem.: LWV, APA, Sigma Xi. Personal E-mail: loisjean.c@hotmail.com.

COHEN, LOIS RUTH KUSHNER, health research consultant; b. Phila., May 31, 1938; d. Joseph George and Doris (Bronstein) Kushner. Tchr.'s diploma, Gratz Coll., Phila., 1957; BA, U. Pa., 1960; MS, Purdue U., 1961, PhD, 1963, LittD (hon.), 1989. Rsch. coord. dept. sociology Purdue U., 1963-64; social sci. analyst div. dental health USPHS, Washington, 1964-70; chief applied behavioral studies div. dental health USPHS, NIH, Bethesda, Md., 1970-71; chief Office Social and Behavioral Analysis, 1971-74; spl. asst. to dir. Div. Dentistry, 1974-76, Nat. Inst. Dental Rsch., 1976-83, chief Office Planning, Evaluation and Comms., 1983-89, dir. div. extramural rsch., 1989-98; assoc. dir. internat. health Nat. Inst. Dental and Craniofacial Rsch., 1998—2006. Vis. lectr. Howard U., spring 1964, health policy and social medicine Harvard U., 1981-88; Percy T. Phillips vis. prof. Columbia U. Sch. Dental and Oral Surgery, N.Y.C., 1988; cons. WHO, 1970, 74, 75, dental health unit WHO, 1970—, Inst. Medicine Nat. Acad. Sci., 1977-80; co-dir. Internat. Collaborative Study Dental Manpower Systems in Relation to Oral Health Status, 1970-84; sr. exec. Svc. Performance Award, 1992, 98, Fed. Dental Internat. Merit Award, 1995. Co-editor: Toward a Sociology of Dentistry, 1971, Social Sciences and Dentistry, Vol. I, 1971, Vol. II, 1984, Disease Prevention and Oral Health Promotion, 1995; editorial reviewer Social Sci. and Medicine, 1975—, Jour. Preventive Dentistry, 1973—, Scandinavian Jour. Dental Rsch., 1973—, Com. Dental Oral Epidemiology, 1999—; mem. editl. bd. Oral Diseases, 2000—05, Jour. Am. Dental Assn., 2005-, African Jour. Oral Health, 2005—; contbr. numerous articles to profl. jours., books. Recipient Phila. High Sch. for Girls Rowen stipend, 1956, Superior Svc. awards Pub. Health Svc., 1988, 93; Senatorial scholar U. Pa., 1960; David Ross Fellow NSF, 1963. Fellow AAAS (gov. coun. 1971), Am. Coll. Dentists (hon.), Internat. Coll. Dentists (hon.); mem. APHA, ADA (hon.), Am. Sociol. Assn., Behavioral Scientists in Dental Rsch. (founder, pres. 1971-72), Federation Dentaire Internationale (cons.), Internat. Assn. Dental Rsch. (dir. 1976-77, chmn. internat. rels. com. 1979-83, disting. sr. scientist award 1987, 96), Am. Assn. Dental Rsch. (dir. 1980-81), Alpha Omega. Address: NIDCR NIH Room 4B62 Bldg 31 Center Dr Bethesda MD 20892-2290 Office Phone: 301-594-2613. Business E-Mail: lois.cohen@nih.gov.

COHEN, LORI G., lawyer; b. Boston, May 18, 1965; BA cum laude, Duke U., 1987; JD with distinction, Emory U., 1990. Bar: Georgia, Am. Bar Assoc. Ptnr., products liability, medical malpractice def. litig. Alston & Bird LLP, Atlanta, 1990—2005; ptnr., litig. products liability, life sciences Greenberg Traurig LLP, Atlanta. Editor Medical Malpractice & Strategy, Product Liability Law & Strategy, Pharmaceutical and Medical Device Law Bulletin. Recipient Top Defense Wins Award, Top 10 Under 40, Nat. Law Journal, 1999—2000. Mem.: Product Liability Advisory Council, Defense Research Institute. Office: Greenberg Traurig LLP Ste 400 The Forum 3290 Northside Pkwy Atlanta GA 30327 Office Phone: 678-553-2385. Office Fax: 678-553-2386. Business E-Mail: cohenl@gtlaw.com.

COHEN, MADELEINE L., library and information scientist; b. N.Y. BA, Excelsior Coll., N.Y., 1978; MLS, Queens Coll. CUNY, N.Y.C., 1984; MA, Grad. Sch. CUNY, N.Y.C., 2004. Public libr. N.Y. State. Libr. iv N.Y. Pub. Libr. Sci. & Tech. Rsch. Ctr., N.Y.C., 1988—94; head of tech. processing N.Y. Pub. Libr. Sci., Industry and Bus. Libr., 1995—98, head info. svcs., 1998—2000, asst. dir. electronic resources, 2000—. Mem.: ALA. Office: NY Pub Libr Sci Industry and Bus Libr 188 Madison Avenue New York NY 10016-4314 E-mail: mcohen@nypl.org.

COHEN, MARCIA FRIEDLANDER, writer, editor-in-chief, journalist; b. Spring Valley, Pa. d. Morris and Belle Podolin Friedlander; m. Laurance Resnick Cohen, Jan. 10, 1953; children: Elizabeth Marion, Jesse Laurance. BA cum laude, Harvard U., 1952. Reporter/editor Sun-Bull., Binghamton, NY, 1968—72; exec. editor Hearst, N.Y.C., 1975—77; reporter/editor N.Y. Daily News, 1979—83; sr. corr. Earth Summit Times, N.Y.C., 1990; founding editor-in-chief Her N.Y., 1993. Author: The Sisterhood, 1988; co-author: The Parents' Pediatric Companion; contbr. articles to numerous mags. and newspapers. Dir. N.Mex. com. Nat. Mus. of Women in the Arts, Santa Fe; mem. Santa Fe Coun. on Internat. Rels.; mem., facilitator Nat. Urban League, Binghamton. Mem.: PEN Internat., Authors Guild, Vet. Feminists Am. Avocations: painting, travel, hiking, gardening.

COHEN, MARGARET ANN, artist, consultant; b. Ridgewood, N.J., Nov. 13, 1953; d. Ralph B. and Madeline Tompkins; m. Ian Phillip Cohen, Apr. 28, 1985; children: Andrew Michael, Matthew Scott. Student, U. Tours, France, 1975; BA in Studio Art, Rutgers U., 1976. Libr. asst. Rutgers U., New Brunswick, N.J., 1977-78; asst. art buyer Brentano's, N.Y.C., 1978-80, West Coast regional mgr. Beverly Hills, Calif., 1980-81; saleswoman Wally Findlay Galleries, Beverly Hills, 1981-82; corp. art cons. dir. Creative Galleries, L.A., 1983-90, 93-99; sole proprietor Artwork by Peggy Cohen, 2001—. Art cons. Verizon Calif. Hdqrs., Thousand Oaks, 1986-88, Transam. Ins. Hdqrs., L.A., 1987-89, Princess Cruises, L.A., 1988-90, Little Co. of Mary Hosp., Torrance, Calif., 2001-03, Northrop Grumman, El Segundo, Calif., 2001-03, Palomar Ventures, Santa Monica, Calif., 2001-06. Group shows include Gallery C., Hermosa Beach, Calif., 2004; represented in collections of Creative Galleries, L.A., Dion Gallery & Lisa's Gallery, Manhattan Beach, Calif., Point Vicente Interpretive Ctr., Rancho Palos Verdes, Calif. Mem. adv. coun. Middlesex County (N.J.) Cultural and Heritage Commn., 1977, fundraiser for Heal the Bay, 1992. Mem. Los Angeles County Mus. Art, Heal the Bay, Manhattan Beach C. of C. (amb.). Avocations: painting, printmaking, photography, swimming, biking.

COHEN, MARLENE LOIS, pharmacologist; b. New Haven, May 5, 1945; d. Abraham David and Jeanette (Bader) C.; m. Jerome H. Fleisch, Aug. 8, 1976; children: Abby Fleisch, Sheryl Fleisch. BS, U. Conn., 1968; PhD, U. Calif., San Francisco, 1973. Registered pharmacist, Calif., Conn. Postdoctoral fellow Roche Inst. of Molecular Biology, Nutley, NJ, 1973-75; sr. pharmacologist Eli Lilly & Co., Indpls., 1975-80, rsch. scientist, 1980-85, sr. rsch. scientist, 1985-89, rsch. advisor, 1989-94, disting. rsch. fellow, 1994—2002; co-founder Creative Pharmacol. Solutions LLC, Carmel, Ind., 2002—. Adj. asst. prof. dept. pharmacology and toxicology Ind. U. Sch. Medicine, Indpls., 1976-82, adj. assoc. prof., 1982-86, adj. prof., 1987—; rsch. asst. Pfizer Labs., Groton, Conn., 1967; cons. Drug Dependence Inst., Yale U., New Haven, 1974. Mem. editl. bd. Jour. Clin. and Exptl. Hypertension, 1978—99, Procs. of the Soc. for Exptl. Biology and Medicine, 1979-84, Life Sci., 1984—, Jour. Pharmacology and Exptl. Therapeutics, 1987—, Current Drugs: Serotonin 1992-2000, Current Topics in Pharmacology, 1994-2000; mem. Molecular Interventions Adv. Bd., 1999-2005; ad hoc reviewer for profl. jours.; author: (with others) Principles of Medicinal Chemistry, 1974, 3d edit., 1989, New Antihypertensive Drugs, 1976, The Serotonin Receptors, 1988, The Peripheral Actions of 5-Hydroxytryptamine, 1989, Central and Peripheral 5-HT3 Receptors, 1992; contbr. articles to profl. jours. Recipient Disting. Alumni award, U. Conn. Sch. Pharmacy, 2002. Mem. Soc. for Exptl. Biology and Medicine, Am. Soc. for Pharmacology and Exptl. Therapeutics (chair subcom. on women in pharmacology 1984-89, chairperson nominating com. 1984, com. on profl. affairs 1984-89, membership com. 1989-92, bd. publs. trustees 1989—95, pres. 2001), Serotonin Club (councilor 1987-90, nomenclature com. 1988—2000), Alpha Lambda Delta, Phi Kappa Phi, Rho Chi. Office: Creative Pharmacol Solutions LLC 10532 Coppergate Ste 101 Carmel IN 46032 Office Phone: 317-571-9878. E-mail: marlenelcohen@aol.com.

COHEN, MARSHA R., former diversified financial services company executive; BA in Math., Wheaton Coll., MBA. With Pricewaterhouse Coopers, Boston, 1976-84, ptnr., 1984-91, U.S. liason ptnr. London, 1991-95, ptnr. Boston, 1995-97, vice-chmn., CFO, 1997—98. Office: Pricewaterhouse Coopers 1301 6th Ave New York NY 10019

COHEN, MARY ANN, federal judge; b. Albuquerque, July 16, 1943; d. Gus R. and Mary Carolyn (Avriette) C. BS, UCLA, 1964; JD, U. So. Calif., 1967. Bar: Calif. 1967. Ptnr. Abbott & Cohen, P.C. and predecessors, L.A., 1967-82; judge U.S. Tax Ct., Washington, 1982—, chief judge, 1996-2000. Mem. ABA (sect. taxation), Legion Lex. Republican. Office: US Tax Ct 400 2nd St NW Washington DC 20217-0002 Office Phone: 202-521-0655.

COHEN, MELANIE ROVNER, lawyer; b. Chgo., Aug. 9, 1944; d. Millard Jack and Sheila (Fox) Rovner; m. Arthur Wieber Cohen, Feb. 17, 1968; children: Mitchell Jay, Stephanie Tomasky, Jennifer Sue, Jason Canel. AB, Brandeis U., 1965; JD, DePaul U., 1977. Bar: Ill. 1977, U.S. Dist. Ct. (no. dist.) Ill., U.S. Ct. Appeals (7th cir.). Law clk. to Justice F.J. Hertz U.S. Bankruptcy Ct., 1976-77; ptnr. Antonow & Fink, Chgo., 1977-89, Altheimer & Gray, Chgo., 1989—2003, Quarles & Brady, Chgo., 2003—. Mem. Supreme Ct. Ill. Atty. Registration and Disciplinary Commn. Inquiry Bd., 1982-86, Hearing Bd., 1986-94; instr. secured and consumer transactions creditor-debtor law DePaul U., Chgo., 1980-90; bd. dirs. Bankruptcy Arbitration and Mediation Svcs., 1994-96; instr. real estate and bankruptcy law John Marshall Law Sch. LLM program, Chgo., 1996-98, 2004-06. Contbr. articles to profl. jours. Panelist, spkr., bd. dirs., v.p. Brandeis U. Nat. Alumni Assn., 1981-90; life mem. Brandeis Nat. Women's Com., 1975—, pres. Chgo. chpt., 1975-82; mem. Glencoe (Ill.) Caucus, 1977-80; chair lawyers com. Ravinia Festival, 1990-91, chmn. sustaining com., 1991, mem. annual fund, 1991—. Fellow, Brandeis U. Fellow: Am. Coll. Bankruptcy; mem.: ABA (co-chair com. on enforcement of creditors' rights and bankruptcy), Leading Lawyer's Network, Internat. Women's Insolvency and Restructuring Confederation, Internat. Fedn. Insolvency Profls., Internat. Insolvency Inst., Turnaround Mgmt. Assn. (pres. Chgo./midwest chpt. 1990—92, internat. bd. dirs. 1990—2004, mem. mgmt. com. 1995—2003, pres. internat. bd. dirs. 1999—2000, chmn. internat. bd. dirs. 2000—01, Leading Lawyer 2004—), Comml. Fin. Assn. Edn. Found. (bd. govs.), Ill. Trial Lawyers Assn., Comml. Law League, Chgo. Bar Assn. (chmn. bankruptcy reorgn. com. 1983—85, Super Lawyer 2005—), Ill. State Bar Assn. Home: 167 Park Ave Glencoe IL 60022-1351 Office: Quarles & Brady 500 W Madison Ave Ste 3700 Chicago IL 60661 Office Phone: 312-715-5050. Business E-Mail: mcohen@quarles.com.

COHEN, MIRIAM, writer, educator; b. N.Y.C., Oct. 14, 1926; d. Jacob and Bessie (Gilman) Echelman; m. Sid Grossman, Mar. 31, 1949 (dec. 1955); 1 child, Adam; m. Monroe D. Cohen, May 31, 1959; children: Gabriel, Jem. Grad., Newburgh Free Acad., N.Y., 1943. Tchr. writing Queens Coll., Writer's Voice, N.Y.C., 1990-94. Author 24 books for children and young adults. Recipient 10 Best Books of 1985 award Parents Choice, 1985. Mem. Soc. Children's Books Writers, Author's Guild. Avocations: dancing, snorkeling, walking in N.Y.C.

COHEN, RACHEL RUTSTEIN, financial planner; b. Phila., June 10, 1968; d. Charles Lawrence and Ronna (Newman) Rutstein (Stepmother), Susan Ellen (Yokel) Sansweet; m. Kipp B. Cohen, Nov. 22, 1995; children: Brandon Erik, Ryan Cameron. BS in Bus. Adminstrn., Pa. State U., 1990; student, U. Tel Aviv, 1989; MBA in Fin., Temple U., 1997. CFP; cert. wealth mgmt. advisor. V.p. Merrill Lynch, Bala Cynwyd, Pa., 1990—. Author: Creating Workplace Community, 2004. V.p. bd. dirs. Phila. chpt. Shaare Zedek Hosp.Charity, 1992-96, co-chair Phone-A-Thon, 1993; active Childrens Hosp. Found., 2004, Merrill Lynch Make a Wish Fundraiser; co-chmn. playground campaign Or Ami Mem.: Phila. Fin. Assn. (co-chair dinner com.), Phila. C. of C. (diplomate 1991—95, nursery sch. com. 2003—, co-chmn. playground campaign 2004—), Green Valley Country Club. Republican. Avocations: golf, tennis, travel, language (spanish), reading. Office: Merrill Lynch 2 Bala Plz Bala Cynwyd PA 19004 Personal E-mail: kicohen@comcast.net. Business E-Mail: rachel_cohen@ml.com.

COHEN, RACHELLE SHARON, journalist; b. Phila., Oct. 21, 1946; d. Hyman and Diane Doris (Schultz) Goldberg; m. Stanley Martin Cohen, June 22, 1968; 1 child, Avril Heather. BS, Temple U., 1968. Editor Somerville (Mass.) Jour., 1968—70; reporter Lowell (Mass.) Sun, 1970—72, AP, Boston, 1972—79; state house bur. chief Boston Herald Am., 1979—80, editl. page editor, 1980—82; editl. page editor, columnist Boston Herald, 1982—. Mem.: Mass. Assn. Mental Health (bd. dirs. 1993—), Mass. Bar Assn. (bench, bar, press com.). Office: Boston Herald 1 Herald St Boston MA 02118-2200 Office Phone: 617-619-6492.

COHEN, ROBERTA JANE, think-tank associate; b. NYC, Feb. 5, 1940; d. George H. and Ethel (Israel) Cohen; m. David A. Korn, Apr. 8, 1981; stepchildren: Marie Korn, David Korn, Philip Korn, Stephen Korn. BA, Barnard Coll., 1960; MA, Johns Hopkins U., 1963; Doctorate (hon.), U. Bern, Switzerland, 2005. Exec. dir. Internat. League for Human Rights, N.Y.C., 1971-78; sr. adviser to U.S. del. to UN and human rights officer Dept. of State, Washington, 1978-80, dep. asst. sec. state for human rights, 1980-81; head pub. affairs office U.S. Embassy, Addis Ababa, 1982-85; hon. sec. Parliamentary Human Rights Group, London, 1985-86; sr. advisor to refugee policy group Washington, 1989-96; sr. advisor NAS Com. on Human Rights, Washington, 1991-95; sr. advisor on internally displaced to rep. UN Sec.-Gen., 1994—; co-dir. project on internal displacement Brookings Instn., Washington, 1994—, sr. fellow, 2001—. Cons. World Bank, various govt. and non-govt. orgns., 1991—94; chmn. task force on human rights UN Assn., Washington, 1993—94; chair task force on China Internat. Human Rights Law Group, Washington, 1997—99, vice chair, 1992—96; bd. dirs. Jacob Blaustein Inst. for Advancement Human Rights; mem. adv. com. Human Rights Watch/Africa, RFK Meml. on Human Rights, Internat. League Human Rights, Acad. on Human Rights and Humanitarian Law, Am. Univ. Washington Coll. Law, Trinity Coll. Human Rights Program; mem. Coun. Fgn. Rels., Women's Fgn. Policy Group; commr. Women's Commn. on Refugee Women & Children. Author: People's Republic of China: The Human Rights Exception, 1987; co-author (with Francis Deng): Masses in Flight: The Global Crisis of Internal Displacement, 1998; co-editor: The Forsaken People, 1998; co-editor: The Guiding Principles on Internal Displacement and the Law of the South Caucasus: Georgia, Armenia and Azerbaijan, 2003; mem. adv. com. Jour. Refugee Studies, adv. com. Forced Migration Rev. Pub. mem. U.S. del. UN Commn. on Human Rights, 1998, Orgn. for Security and Cooperation in Europe, 2003. Co-recipient The Grawemeyer award for Ideas Improving World Order, U. Louisville, 2005; recipient Superior Honor award, USIA, Addis Abada, 1985, Human Rights award, UN Assn., 1994, Fiftieth Ann. award for Exemplary Writing on Fgn. Affairs and Diplomacy, Diplomats and Consular Officers Ret., 2002, Disting. Alumna award, Barnard Coll., 2005, Social Scis. award, Washington Acad. Scis., 2005. Mem.: Cosmos Club. Office Phone: 202-797-6031. Personal E-mail: rcidp@msn.com.

COHEN, ROBIN L., lawyer; b. Phila., Oct. 27, 1961; BA magna cum laude, U. Pa., 1983, JD, 1986. Bar: Pa. 1986, NJ 1989, NY 1989. Ptnr. Anderson, Kill, Olick & Oshinsky, P.C., N.Y.C., Dickstein Saphiro Morin Oshinsky LLP, NYC, 1996, mem. exec. com., mng. ptnr. NY office. Office: Dickstein Shapiro Morin & Oshinsky LLP 1177 Avenue of the Americas New York NY 10036-2714 Office Phone: 212-835-1440. Office Fax: 212-997-9880. Business E-Mail: cohenr@dsmo.com.

COHEN, SASHA (ALEXANDRA PAULINE COHEN), ice skater; b. Westwood, Calif., Oct. 26, 1984; d. Roger and Galina Cohen. Achievements include Recipient Gardena Winter Trophy, 1999; winner, Junior Grand Prix, Stockholm, Sweden, 1999; 2nd place, U.S. Championships, 2000; winner, Pacific Coast Sectional, 2000; Finlandia Trophy, 2001; 3rd place, Trophee Lalique, 2001; Silver medalist, U.S. Nats. Championship, 2001-2002; 2nd place, U.S. Championships, 2002; 4th place, World Championships, 2002; 4th place, Olympic Winter Games, 2002; 2nd place, Hersheys Kisses Challenge, 2002; 4th place, Campbells Classic, 2002; 1st place, Skate Can., 2002; 1st place, Trophee Lalique, 2002; 2nd place, Cup of Russia, 2002; 1st place, Crest White Strips Challenge, 2002; bronze medalist, U.S. Nats., 2003; 4th place, Worlds, 2003; champion, Grand Prix Finals, 2003; 1st place, Trophee Lalique, 2004; 1st place, Skate Can., 2004; 1st place, Skate Am., 2004; 1st place, Campbells Soup, 2004; silver medallist, World Championships, 2004-

2005; 1st Place, U.S. Nats., 2006; silver medallist, Torino Olympics, Italy, 2006. Avocations: art, jewelry making, reading, designing costumes. Office: 9 Journey c/o Ice Palace Aliso Viejo CA 92656*

COHEN, SELMA, librarian, researcher; b. NYC, Mar. 14, 1930; d. George and Rose (Cohen) Unger; m. Irwin H. Cohen, Nov. 19, 1950; children: Barbara Katzeff, Joel. Asst. bookkeeper acctg. dept. Severud, Perrone et al, N.Y.C., 1970—75, Russell Reynolds Assoc., Inc., 1976—77, rsch. asst., 1977—, reference libr., 1985—. Chair Scott Tower Property Improvement Com., Bronx, N.Y., 2006— Home: 3400 Paul Ave 10H Bronx NY 10468-1042 Office: Russell Reynolds Assocs 200 Park Ave New York NY 10166-0005 Office Phone: 212-351-2032.

COHEN, SHARLEEN COOPER, interior designer, writer; b. L.A., June 11, 1940; d. Sam and Claretta (Ellis) White; m. R. Gary Cooper, Dec. 18, 1960 (dec. Feb., 1971); m. Martin L. Cohen, M.D., Aug. 27, 1972; children: Cami Gordon, Dalisa Cooper Cohen. Student, U. Calif., Berkeley, 1957-58, UCLA, 1958-60, L.A. Valley Film Sch., 1976-78. Owner, mgr. Designs on You, L.A., 1965-77; writer L.A., 1977—. Prodr. Jewish Repertory Theatre, N.Y.C., 1996. Author: The Day After Tomorrow, 1979, Regina's Song, 1980, The Ladies of Beverly Hills, 1983, Marital Affairs, 1985, Love, Sex and Money, 1988, Lives of Value, 1991, Innocent Gestures, 1994, (play) Solomon and Sheba, 1990, (musical) Sheba, 1996; assoc. prodr.: Broadway Street Corner Symphony; prodr.: Cookin' At The Cookery, The Best of Times, Bingo; assoc. prodr.: Duet; writer: Stormy Weather, 1999, Blackout, 2000. Mem. exec. com. Women of Distinction United Jewish Appeal, 1990-95; chair L.A. chpt. Nat. Gaucher Found., 1991-95; bd. dirs., mem. com. chair Calif. Coun. for the Humanities, San Francisco, 1992-98; bd. dirs. Amas Mus. Theatre; mem. acquisitions com. Modern Contemporary Art Coun., L.A. County Mus. Art. Recipient Hon. Mention, Santa Barbara Writers Conf., 1978, Writer's Digest Writing Competition, 2000, 04. Mem.: PEN, League of Profl. Theatre Women, The Drama League, Theatre Guild, Dramatists Guild, Writers Guild Am. E-mail: SccInc1@aol.com.

COHEN, SUSAN LOIS, writer; b. Chgo., Mar. 27, 1938; d. Martin and Ida Handler; m. Daniel E. Cohen, Feb. 2, 1958; 1 child, Theodora (dec.). BA, New Sch. for Social Rsch., 1960; MA in Social Work, Adelphi U., 1962. Social worker, N.Y.C., 1962-67; various social work positions in N.Y.C., 1962-68. Author: The Liberated Couple, 1969, reassued under title Liberated Marriage, 1973; author: (under name Elizabeth St. Clair) Stonehaven, 1974; author: The Singing Harp, 1975, Secret of the Locket, 1975, Provenance House, 1976, Mansion in Miniature, 1977, Dewitt Manor, 1977, The Jeweled Secret, 1978, Murder in the Act, 1978, Sandcastle Murder, 1979, Trek or Treat, 1980, Sealed with a Kiss, 1981; author: (with Daniel Cohen) The Kids' Guide to Home Computers, 1983; author: The Kids' Guide to Home Video, 1984, Teenage STress, 1984, Screen Goddesses, 1984, Rock Video Superstars, 1985, Wrestling Superstars, Vol. 1, 1985, Vol. 2, 1986, Hollywood Hunks and Heroes, 1985, Heroes of the Challenger, 1986, A Six-Pack and a Fake ID, 1986, The Encyclopedia of Movie Stars, 1986, A History of the Oscars, 1986, Teenage Competition: A Survival Guide, 1987, Young and Famous: Hollywood's Newest Superstars, 1987, Going for the Gold, 1987, What You Can Believe about Drugs, 1988, What Kind of Dog is That, 1989, When Someone You Know is Gay, 1989, Zoo Superstars, 1989, Zoos, 1992, Where to Find Dinosaurs Today, 1992, Going for the Gold: Medal Hopefuls for Winter '92, 1992, Gold Medal Glow: The Story of America's Women's Gymnastic Team, 1996, Pan Am 103, 2000, rev. edit., 2001, Hauntings and Horrors, 2002. Mem.: Wodehouse Soc. (pres.), Watson's Erroneous Deductions, Chapter One, The Capers of Sherlock Holmes, Clumber Spaniel Club of Am. Avocation: cats. Address: 877 W Hand Ave Cape May Court House NJ 08210-1865 Personal E-mail: BldgsCast@aol.com.

COHEN-DEMARCO, GALE MAUREEN, pharmaceutical executive; b. Rochester, NY, June 4, 1947; d. Maurice Cohen and Florence Michaels; m. David Earl McCarty, June 16, 1975 (div. Nov. 1979); 1 child, Brock Adam; m. Peter Francis DeMarco, Aug. 3, 1984. BA, U. Rochester, 1969; MA, SUNY, Buffalo, 1971. Various pharm. cos.; hosp. rep., dist. mgr., med. liaison Glaxo Pharms., 1987—97; regional bus. mgr. Axcan Pharma, 1997—2003, sr. regional account mgr., 2003—. Grantee, NIH, 1969; scholar, N.Y. State Regents, 1964. Democrat. Jewish. Avocations: environmental activities, charity organizations. Home: 27621 W Lakeview Dr N Wauconda IL 60084-2362 Office: Axcan Pharma 22 Inverness Ctr Pkwy Ste 310 Birmingham AL 35242 Office Phone: 847-987-6603. Personal E-mail: jap19472002@yahoo.com.

COHEN-STRONG, ELAYNE BARBARA, director, educator; b. Detroit, Jan. 29, 1952; d. Lawrence Cohen and Rae Sarah Saulles; m. Leroy Strong, Jr., May 16, 1987; 1 child, Kacie Leah Strong. BA, Mich. State U., 1974; student, Oakland C.C., Farmington Hills, Mich., 1969—71, Calif. State U., Long Beach, 1995. Cert. assistive tech. applications Calif. State U. Northridge, multi-subject tchg. credential Calif., Clear credential in spl. edn.-visually handicapped Calif. Med. technician Henry Ford Hosp., Detroit, 1975—85; adminstrv. asst. Hosp. Homecare of Orange County, Santa Ana, Calif., 1985—87; pvt. billing office asst. Doctors and Nurses, Newport Beach, Calif., 1987—91; dir. youth outreach dept. and tech., tchr. for the visually impaired Blind Children's Learning Ctr., Santa Ana, 1991—. Contbr. mag. Individuals with Disabilities News, newspaper In Focus, L.A. Times. Named Tchr. of the Yr., Wal-Mart, 1996. Mem.: PTA (assoc.; historian 2002—03), CEC (assoc.), Assn. for the Edn. and Rehab. of the Visually Impaired (assoc.), Calif. Transcribers and Educators of the Visually Impaired (assoc.). Avocations: swimming, travel, ceramics. Home: 6478 New Gate Way Yorba Linda CA 92886 Office: Blind Children's Learning Ctr 18542-B Vanderlip Santa Ana CA 92705 Office Phone: 714-573-8888. Personal E-mail: teachem45@pacbell.net. Business E-Mail: elayne.strong@blindkids.org.

COHEN-VADER, CHERYL DENISE, municipal official; b. Ft. Bragg, N.C., Mar. 23, 1955; BA, Princeton U., 1977; MBA, Columbia U., 1983. Treas. internat. divsn. commodity import-export financing Bank of N.Y., N.Y.C., 1977-81; v.p. Citicorp Securities Markets, Inc. Citicorp, N.Y.C., 1983-90; v.p. Weldon, Sullivan, Carmichael & Co., 1990-92; asst. v.p. Kirkpatrick Pattis, 1993-95; mgr. revenue dept. City of Denver, 1996—, dep. mayor, 2003—04. Mem. Mcpl. Securities Rulemaking Bd., 1998-2001. Bd. dirs. Mile High chpt. ARC, Colo. Episcopal Found., 1998-2001; bd. dirs. Black Ch. Intitiatives, 1998—. Recipient Consortium of Grad. Mgmt. Edn. fellowship, 1981-83, Recognition of Achievement award Five Points Bus. Assn., Inc., 1995, Leadership Denver award Denver C. of C., 1994; honored in Living Portraits of African-Am. Women Nat. Coun. Negro Women, 1997. Mem. Govt. Finance Officers Assn. Office: City Denver Revenue Dept McNichols Bldg Rm 300 144 W Colfax Ave Denver CO 80202-5391

COHN, JANE SHAPIRO, public relations executive; b. NYC, May 19, 1935; d. Harry I. and Ann (Safanie) Shapiro; m. Albert M. Cohn, June 30, 1957 (div. 1972); children: Theodore David, William Alan. BA, Brandeis U., 1956; postgrad., Coll. of New Rochelle, 1974-76; student, Harvard U., 1985. Dir. pub. rels. Hudson River Mus., Yonkers, N.Y., 1976-79; account exec. Dudley-Anderson Yutzy Pub. Rels. Agy. subs. Ogilvy Mather, N.Y.C., 1979-81; dir. communications Haines Lundberg Waehler, N.Y.C., 1981-91; prin. Jane Cohn Pub. Rels., Sherman, Conn., 1991—. Cons. to various firms in architecture, engring., and constrn. industry, 1983; spkr., mktg. promotion strategies conf., 1989, AIA N.Y. Chpt., panelist So. New England Chpt.; organizer, co-spkr.Interplan Conv.; organizer and moderator Soc. Mktg. Profl. Svcs. N.Y. Chpt., 1996; spkr. Soc. Mktg. Profl. Svcs. Nat. Conf., 1997; panelist AIA Nat. Conv., 1998. Contbr. articles to profl. jours., chpts. to books. Fellow Soc. Mktg. Profl. Svcs. (cert.; bd. dirs. N.Y. chpt. 1988-89, 92-95, spkr. ann. convs., Gold Medal award 1994); mem. AIA (assoc. 1988, 98, panelist nat. conv. 1998, spkr. ann. conv.), Am. Mktg. Assn. (panelist ann. conv. 1987, moderator profl. services sect. ann. conv. 1988, exec. mem.), Practice Mgmt. Assn. (spkr. promotion strategies conf. 1989) Democrat. Jewish. Avocations: art, sculpture, gardening. Office: Jane Cohn Pub Rels 31 Spring Lake Rd Sherman CT 06784-1201

COHN, MARIANNE WINTER MILLER, civic activist; b. Denver, Jan. 15, 1928; d. Henry Abraham II and Esther (Sheflan) Winter; m. Benjamin K. Miller, Dec. 29, 1948 (dec. Dec. 1972); children: Judy Ellen, Philip Henry (dec. 1996); m. Isidore Cohn Jr., Jan. 3, 1976; stepchildren: Ian Jeffrey Cohn, Lauren Kerry Cohn Fouros. Student, Colo. U., 1946-47. Women's bd. dirs. Nat. Jewish Hosp. at Denver, 1951—60, pres. women's divsn., 1960—61, mem., sec. gov. bd., 1972—76; mem. nat. bd. Nat. Jewish Ctr., 1976—; mem. exec. bd. Greater New Orleans Tourist and Conv. Commn., 1985; chmn. spouse program arrangements ACS, La., 1985; mem. exec. bd. NCCJ, New Orleans, 1987—96, sec., 1991—92, treas., 1993—94, nat. bd. dirs., 1993; bd. dirs. Jewish Endowment Found., New Orleans, 1987—88, La. ArtWorks of Arts Coun. of New Orleans, 2000; mem. Arts Coun. of New Orleans, 1988—, v.p. devel., 1991—92, v.p. grants, exec. bd., 1995—96, pres., 1997—98, chmn. bd., 1999, v.p. grants, 2001; chmn. Exhibit Sunking, Louis XIV La. State Mus., 1984, bd. dirs., 1994—2001, mem. governing bd., 1992—2005; pres. La. Mus. Found., 1989—90; bd. dirs. New Orleans Symphony Aux., 1980; chmn. Odyssey Ball of New Orleans Mus. Art, 1992—; bd. dirs. La. Coun. for Music and Performing Arts, 1991—92; regional vice chmn. Nat. Jewish Ctr., 1999—; mem. Sisterhood of Temple Emanuel Denver, pres., 1957—60. Recipient Edgar L. Feinberg Meml. award James D. Rives Surg. Soc., 1988, Woman of Fashion award Men of Fashion, 1989, Humanitarian award Nat. Jewish Ctr. Immunology and Respiratory Medicine, 1995, role model award Young Leadership Coun. New Orleans, 1998—, Nat. Jewish Ctr. Chmn.'s award, 1999, Robert S. Daniels M.D. Alumni Svc. award, La. State U. Sch. Medicine, 2006. Republican. Avocations: travel, cooking. Personal E-mail: sunkingmc@aol.com.

COHN, MARJORIE F., law educator, legal association administrator; b. Pomona, Calif., Nov. 1, 1948; d. Leonard L. and Florence Cohn; m. Pedro López children: Victor, Nicolas; m. Jerome P. Wallingford. BA, Stanford U., 1970; JD, Santa Clara U., 1975. Bar: Calif. 1975, U.S. Dist. Ct. (so. dist.) Calif. 1982, U.S. Dist. Ct. (no. dist.) Calif. 1983. Staff atty. Nat. Lawyers Guild, San Francisco, 1975-76, Agrl. Labor Rels. Bd., Sacramento, 1976-78, Appellate Defenders, Inc., San Diego, 1987-91; dep. pub. defender Fresno County Pub. Defender's Office, Fresno, Calif., 1978-80; pvt. practice Monterey and San Diego Counties, San Diego, 1981-87; prof. law Thomas Jefferson Sch. Law, San Diego, 1991—. Legal analyst on TV, radio and in print media. Co-author: Cameras in the Courtroom: Television and the Pursuit of Justice, 1998; editor-in-chief Guild Practitioner, 1994-2003. Recipient Golden Apple award, Student Bar Assn., Thomas Jefferson Sch. Law, 1995—98, Svc. to Legal Edn. award, San Diego County Bar Assn., 2005, Top Attys. award, San Diego, 2006. Mem. Nat. Lawyers Guild (nat. exec. com. 1996-2006, exec. v.p., pres. 2006-), Calif. Attys. for Criminal Justice. Office: Thomas Jefferson Sch Law 2121 San Diego Ave San Diego CA 92110-2986 Office Phone: 619-374-6923. Business E-Mail: marjorie@tjsl.edu.

COHN, MILDRED, retired biochemist, retired educator; b. NYC, July 12, 1913; d. Isidore M. and Bertha (Klein) Cohn; m. Henry Primakoff, May 30, 1938; children: Nina, Paul, Laura. BA, Hunter Coll., 1931, DSc (hon.), 1984; MA, Columbia U., 1932, PhD, 1937; DSc (hon.), Women's Med. Coll., 1975, Radcliffe Coll., 1978, Washington U., St. Louis, 1981, Brandeis U., 1984, U. Pa., Phila., 1984, U. N.C., 1985; PhD (hon.), Weizmann Inst. Sci., 1988; DSc (hon.), U. Miami, 1990. Rsch. asst. biochemistry George Washington U. Sch. Medicine, 1937—38; rsch. assoc. Cornell Med. Coll., 1938—46, Washington U. Sch. Medicine, 1946—58; assoc. prof. biol. chemistry Washington U., 1958—60; assoc. prof. biophysics and phys. biochemistry U. Pa. Med. Sch., 1960—61, prof., 1961—71, prof. biochemistry and biophysics, 1971—82, Benjamin Rush prof. physiol. chemistry, 1978—82, prof. emerita, 1982—; sr. mem. Inst. Cancer Rsch., Phila., 1982—85; chancellor's vis. prof. biophysics U. Calif., Berkeley, 1982; vis. prof. biol. chemistry Johns Hopkins U. Med. Sch., 1985—91. Rsch. assoc. Harvard U. Med. Sch., 1950—51; established investigator Am. Heart Assn., 1953—59; career investigator, 1964—78; vis. prof. chemistry Yale U., 1973. Mem. editl. bd. Jour. Biol. Chemistry, 1958—63, 1967—72. Recipient Hall of Fame award, Hunter Coll., 1973, Disting. Alumni award, 1975, Cresson medal, Franklin Inst., award, Internat. Assn. Women Biochemists, 1979, Humboldt award, Germany, 1980, 1982, Nat. Medal Sci., 1983, award, Am. Acad. Achievement, 1984, Mack award, Ohio State U., 1985, Chandler medal, Columbia U., 1986, Women in Sci. award, N.Y. Acad. Sci., 1992, Gov.'s award for excellence in sci., Pa., 1993, Founders medal, Magnetic Resonance in Biology, 1994, Stein-Moore award, Protein Soc., 1997. Mem.: NAS, Inst. de Biologie Physico-Chimique, Coll. Physicians of Phila. (Disting. Svc. award 1987), Am. Biophys. Soc., Am. Soc. Biochemistry and Molecular Biology (pres. 1978—79), Harvey Soc., Am. Chem. Soc. (chmn. divsn. biol. chemistry 1975—76, Garvan medal 1963, Remsen award Md. sect. 1988, Cinn. sect. Oesper award 2000), Am. Philos. Soc. (v.p. 1994—2000, sec. 2005—), Am. Acad. Arts and Scis., Iota Sigma Pi (hon. nat. mem. 1988), Sigma Xi, Phi Beta Kappa. Office: U Pa Med Sch 242 Anat Chem Bldg Dept Biochemistry & Biophys Philadelphia PA 19104-6059 Business E-Mail: cohn@mail.med.upenn.edu.

COHORST, LISA MOSELEY, elementary school educator; d. Francis Lawrence and Donna Brooks Moseley; m. Gary Lee Cohorst, Jr., June 29, 1991; children: Adam Lawrence, Christopher Lee. BA in History, Mercer U., Macon, Ga., 1989; M in Social Sci. Edn., U. Ga., Athens, 1995. Cert. elem. tchr. Ga. Tchr. Lilburn Mid. Sch., Ga., 1994—2001, Trickum Mid. Sch., Lilburn, Ga., 2001—. Scout leader Boy Scouts of Am., Lilburn, Ga., 2002—05; co-capt. Am. Cancer Soc.: Relay for Life, Lilburn, Ga., 2004—06; missions tchr./Vacation Bible Sch. tchr. Mountain Pk. First Bapt. Ch., Lilburn, Ga., 2003—06. Mem.: NAE. Home: 3867 Cynthia Way Lilburn GA 30047

COINER, MARYROSE C., psychologist; b. Newark, Dec. 14, 1949; d. William J. and Margaret (Queenan) Carew; m. H. Michael Coiner, Mar. 8, 1975; children: John P., Thomas M. BS, St. Peter's Coll., Jersey City, N.J., 1971; PhD, Yale U., 1978. Lic. psychologist, Mass. Asst. prof. psychology Millersville State U., Pa., 1978-80; staff psychologist Framingham Union Hosp., Mass., 1980-90; pvt. practice Marlboro and Framingham, Mass., 1981—. Bd. dirs. Together Inc., Marlboro, 1983-91, Advocates Inc., Framingham, 1991—. NSF fellow, 1971-74. Mem. APA, Mass. Psychol. Assn. Office: 14 Vernon St Ste 206 Framingham MA 01701-4733 Office Phone: 508-620-9948. E-mail: m.coiner@verizon.net.

COIROLO, CHRISTINA, writer, author representative; arrived in US, 1964, naturalized, 1972; d. Jose M. Coirolo and Ilia Barrios; m. Mikel Goodwin (div.); children: Lucy Abdo, Paulette Maloney, Mikel Goodwin, Christine Goodwin, Richard Goodwin. BA, Utah State U., Logan, 1971, MEd, 1972. Cert. interpreter Lang. Line Svc., Monterey, Calif. Mng. dir. Britannia Rds., Lansing, Mich., 1982—2000, The Writing Clinic, Charlotte, Mich., 2004—; author rep. Outskirts Press, Parker, Colo., 2006—. Cons. CNC Consulting, Lansing, 2001—. Author: Old Sins Cast Long Shadows, 2005, A Nice and Quiet Place, 2006, Roots of Evil, 2006, (manuals) Tour Management, 2000, Guide to Hispanics in the US, 2004, The Writing Clinic, 2004. Mem.: ACLU, Am. Assn. Univ. Women. Democrat. Avocations: writing, reading, interior decorating. Home: 1420 Jack Henry Dr Charlotte MI 48813 Fax: 517-541-0439. E-mail: criscoi@juno.com.

COJUANGCO, SAMANTHA CABALLES, elementary school educator; b. NYC, Apr. 25, 1983; d. Necito G. and Leila Caballes Cojuangco. BS in Biology, Coll. Mt. St. Vincent, Riverdale, NY, 2005. Cert. tchr. NY. Tchr. Green Sch., NY Bot. Gardens, Bronx, NY, 2003—05; resident asst. Coll. Mt. St. Vincent, 2003—05. Cantor Our Lady of Lourdes Ch., Massapequa, NY, 1991—2006. Erasmus scholar, Coll. Mt. St. Vincent, 2001—05. Mem.: Nat. Sci. Tchr. Assn. (assoc.), Kappa Delta Pi. Roman Catholic. Office: Pablo Neruda Acad 1980 Lafayette Ave Rm 497 Bronx NY 10473 Office Phone: 718-824-1682. Personal E-mail: abu2u2@aol.com.

COKER, MARY SHANNON, perinatal and perioperative nurse; b. Pasadena, Tex., May 30, 1947; d. James Edward and Ruby Dee (Langford) Shannon; m. Sherman Leigh Coker, Jan. 25, 1987; children: John Lynn Brinkley, Jamie Leigh Brinkley Kelley, Amanda Renee Coker, Roy Leigh Coker. ADN, Lee Coll., Baytown, Tex., 1990; BSN, U. Tex., Galveston, 1998, MSN, 2002. Insulator Daniel Constrn., Greenville, S.C., 1985-87; patient care attendant Humana Hosp., Baytown, 1988; staff perioperative nurse Meth. Hosp., Houston, 1989-91, Bay Coast Med. Ctr., Baytown, Tex., 1991-98; staff labor and delivery nurse Lyndon Baines Johnson Hosp., 1999—2003, East Houston Regional Med. Ctr., 2003—. Mem.: Consortium Tex. Cert. Nurse Midwives, Tex. Advanced Practice Nurses, Tex. Nurse Practitioners Assn., Gulf Coast Advanced Practice Nurses, U. Tex. Med. Branch Student Nurse Midwives, Am. Coll. Nurse Midwives, Sigma Theta Tau, Phi Theta Kappa.

COKER, MELINDA LOUISE, counselor; b. Springfield, Mo., Apr. 28, 1946; d. Joe H. and Margaret L. (Owens) Bull; m. Richard H. Coker, Aug. 12, 1967; children: Shay, Candace, Logan. BA, Baylor U., 1968; MS, East Tex. State U., 1994. Nat. cert. counselor Nat. Bd. Counselor Cert.; lic. profl. counselor, Tex. Tchr. Houston Ind. Sch. Dist., 1968-71; owner, mgr. Greenleaves, Tyler, Tex., 1978-84; realtor Coldwell Banker, Tyler, 1989-91; counselor intern Hunt County Mental Health Mental Retardation, Greenville, Tex., 1993, Andrews Ctr., Tyler, 1994; career counselor intern Tyler Jr. Coll., Tex., 1994-95, spl. populations counselor, 1995—2003, dir. career planning and placement svcs., 2005—; internet cons. Advanced Internet Cons., LLC, 2005—. Recipient Counselor of Yr. award, Piney Woods Counseling Assn., 2004. Mem. ACA, Nat. Career Devel. Assn., Chi Sigma Iota. Avocations: tennis, swimming. Home: 6701 Lacosta Dr Tyler TX 75703-5753

COKER, SYBIL JANE THOMAS, counseling administrator; b. Elizabeth, La., Aug. 16; d. Andrew J. and Lillye M. Thomas; m. Charles Mitchell Dolo Coker (dec. Apr. 13, 1983). AA, L.A. City Coll., 1952; BA, Calif. State U., L.A., 1955, Pepperdine U., 1957; MS, Mt. St. Mary's Coll., 1980. Tchr. Barton Hill Sch., 1957—58, 96th St. Sch., 1958—63; tng. tchr., reading specialist Hooper Ave. Sch., 1963—65, tng. tchr., 1980—87; reading specialist dept. chair Vermont Ave. Sch., 1965—68; head start tchr. L.A. Urban League, 1966—68; tng. tchr., tchr. of gifted clusters, grades 4,5,6 Angeles Mesa Sch., 1970—87; Eng. tchr., speech coach Horace Mann Jr. High Mid. Sch., 1987—88, speech coach, 1988—90, bilingual coord./ESL, career, coll. and chap. 1 counselor, 1988—92, 8th grade counselor, career counselor, 1992—94, counselor 8th grade ctr., 1994; counselor David Starr Jordan HS, L.A., 1995—2005. Pres., founder Charles Dolo Coker Jazz Scholarship Found., Inc., L.A., 1983—; freelance wedding coord., cons., 1960—; freelance writer, 1983—; sponsor Motivating Our Students Through Experience Horace Mann Jr. High Mid. Sch., sponsor Young Black Profls., sponsor USC Med Core, UCLA Partnership. Contbr. columns in newspapers. Founder, dir. 2d Bapt. Ch. Drama Guild, 1957—67. Named Media Woman of Yr., 1977; recipient Unsung Heroine in Edn. award, Top Ladies of Distinction, 1992, Dist. Svc. award, 2d Bapt. Ch., 1991, Trailblazer award for outstanding contbns. in field of music, Delta Mothers and Sponsors Club, 2002. Mem.: NEA, PTA (life), NAACP (life; past bd. mem. L.A. br., Joan J. Willis award Women in NAACP 2000), The Soc., Inc. (LA chpt. chaplain), Internat. Assn. Jazz Educators, Counselor's Assn., Black Women's Forum, L.A. Press Club, Soc. Profl. Journalists, Top Ladies of Distinction (LA chpt., area VI), Nat. Assn. Media Women (nat. recording sec., charter mem. Beverly Hills/Hollywood chap., past pres.), Pol. Action Com. of Educators, United Tchrs. of L.A., Nat. Coun. Negro Women (life Black Women Cmty. Leaders of Yr. NCNW and Aunt Jemima brands 1997), Santa Barbara Jazz Soc., LA Jazz Soc. (Teri Merrill-Aarons Educator award 2006), Internat. Assn. Jazz Appreciation, Emanon Birthday and Social Club (charter mem., pres.), Order of the Ea. Star, Phi Delta Kappa, Delta Sigma Theta (life; Century City alumnae chap., L.A. alumnae chap., Delta Choraliers, charter mem., past chpt. journalist). Democrat. Baptist. Avocations: creative writing, knitting, singing with the Delta Choraliers, studying piano, interior decorating. Home and Office: 5336 Highlight Pl Los Angeles CA 90016 Office Phone: 323-935-1374. Personal E-mail: sybilcoker@aol.com.

COLAGE, BEATRICE ELVIRA, education educator; b. Cleveland, Ohio, Aug. 13, 1958; BS in Edn., Bowling Green State U., 1980; M of Curriculum, Cleveland State U., 1985. Spanish tchr. Cleveland (Ohio) City Schs., 1980—84, Mayfield (Ohio) City Schs., 1984—85, Solon (Ohio) City Schs., 1985—86, Orange (Ohio) City Schs., 1986—; adult edn. tchr. Mayfield (Ohio) City Schs. Lectr. Italian, Spanish and English. Author: book of 101 poems, 2003. Humanitarian and supporter of arts, civic, social and cultural instns. Mem.: NEA, Il Cenacolo Cleve., Ohio Fgn. Lang. Assoc., Ohio Edn. Assn., Am. Assn. Tchrs. of Spanish and Portuguese.

COLALUCA, BETH, pediatric neurpsychologist; b. Dayton, Ohio, June 1, 1969; d. Mario Anthony and Janet Mae Colaluca; m. Michael R. Hooper, Oct. 19, 2002. BS, Tex. A&M U., 1991; MS, U.North Tex., Denton, 1996; PhD, U. North Tex., Denton, 1998. Lic. psychologist Tex. State Bd. of Examiners of Psychologists, registered nat. register health svc. provider Coun. for Nat. Register of Health Svc. Providers in Psychology. Pediat. psychologist Tex. Scottish Rite Hosp. for Children, Dallas, 2000—02; pediat. neuropsychologist Cook Children's Med. Ctr., Ft. Worth, 2002—. Mgr, hematology/oncology Cook Children's Med. Ctr., Ft. Worth, 2002—. Recipient rsch. grant, North Tex. Cancer Rsch. Found., 2003. Mem.: APA, Dallas Psychol. Assn., Tex. Psychol. Assn., Internat. Neuropsychology Soc., Nat. Acad. of Neuropsychology. Office: Cook Children's Med Ctr 1516 Cooper St Fort Worth TX 76104 Office Phone: 682-885-1480. Office Fax: 682-885-3600. Business E-Mail: bethc@cookchildrens.org.

COLAMARINO, KATRIN BELENKY, lawyer; b. N.Y.C., Apr. 29, 1951; d. Allen Abram and Selma (Burwasser) Belenky Lang;; m. Barry E. Brenner, June 1, 1974 (div. June 1979); 1 child, Richard Erin; m. Leonard J. Colamarino, Mar. 20, 1982 BA, Vassar Coll., Poughkeepsie, N.Y., 1972; JD, U. Richmond, Va., 1976. Bar: Ohio 1976, U.S. Ct. Appeals (fed. cir.) 1982. Staff atty. AM Internat., Inc., Cleve., 1977-79; atty. Lipkowitz & Plaut, N.Y.C., 1980-81, Docutel Olivetti Corp., Tarrytown, N.Y., 1981-84, NYNEX Bus. Info. Sys., White Plains, N.Y., 1984-85; corp. counsel, sec. Logica Data Architects, Inc., N.Y.C., 1986-90; corp. counsel SEER Technologies, Inc., N.Y.C., 1990-91; v.p. chief tech. counsel global relationship bank Citibank N.A., N.Y.C., 1991-97; v.p. asst. gen. counsel, mgr. technology and supplier contracts group JPMorgan Chase Bank, N.Y.C., 1997—2004; prin. Nicholas Consulting Co., 2005—. Lectr. CLE Computer Law Assn., Cyberspace Camp Conf., San Jose, Calif., 1997, Milbank Tweed Law Firm Global Tech. Transactions Conf., N.Y.C., 1999, Consumer Bankers Assn., 2000, N.Y. County Lawyers Assn., 2001. Exec. bd. Ethical Fieldston Sch. Alumni Assn., 1992—95, 1980—90, v.p., 1987—90; alumnae coun. rep. Vassar Coll., 1982—86, class corr. Vassar Quar., 1992—97, mem. Alumni/Alumnae of Vassar Coll. fund adv. bd., 1997—2000, dir.-at-large Alumni/Alumnae of Vassar Coll. Bd., 2000—04; bd. dirs. U. Richmond Law Sch. Alumni Assn., 1999—2002; pres.-elect Rotary Club, Templeton, Calif.; bd. dirs. Atascadero Performing Arts Ctr. Com., Calif., 2005—; bd. dirs., pub. chair Cuesta Master Chorale, San Luis Obispo, Calif., 2005—. Address: 8231 Los Osos Rd Atascadero CA 93422 Office Phone: 805-286-7480. E-mail: katrinc@nicholasconsulting.net.

COLBERG, LINDA, physical education educator; d. Harold Colberg and Jeanne Woudenberg. BS in Edn., Ea. Ill. U., Charleston, 1974; MEd, U. Ill., Champaign, 1992. Cert. personal trainer Am. Coun. Exercise. Instr. phys. edn. and health Wauconda Schs. # 118, 1974—77; sales rep. Maybelline Co., Chgo., 1979—80; instr. phys. edn. and life skills Glenview Schs. # 34, 1980—94; instr. phys. edn. Schaumburg Schs. # 54, 1994—2006, field leader elem. phys. edn., 2006—. Fitness supr., personal trainer Rolling Meadows Fitness Ctr., 2002; tchr. English Family Camp, Czech Republic, 2006. Editor articles for health and fitness pubs. Named Sales Rep. of Yr. for Midwestern U.S., Maybelline Corp., 1979; recipient Florence McAfee scholarship, Ea. Ill. U., 1972. Mem.: AAHPERD, Am. Assn. for Health Edn., Am. Assn. for Active Lifestyles and Fitness, Ill. Assn. Health, Phys. Edn. and Recreation. Home: 1339 S Parkside Dr Palatine IL 60067 Office: Schaumburg Sch Dist 54 524 Schaumburg Rd Schaumburg IL 60194 E-mail: LColberg710@comcast.net.

COLBERT, DEBORA A., director; d. Neil R. Montgomery; m. Jonathan L. Colbert; children: Robert N., Kathryn L., Curtis L. M in Mgmt., Regis U., 1999; PhD in Ednl. Leadership, Colo. State U., 2003. Cert. program planner LERN, 2002, program planner cert. programs LERN, 2004. Cmty. edn. coord. Nat. Technol. U., Fort Collins, Colo., 1996—2000; dir. distance degrees Colo. State U. Continuing Edn., Fort Collins, 2000—. Mem. Leadership Ft. Collins, 2004—05. Mem.: U. Continuing Edn. Assn., Nat. U. Degree Consortium (v.p. 2004—05). Office: Colorado State Univ Continuing Edn Spruce Hall Campus Delivery 1040 Fort Collins CO 80523-1040 Office Phone: 970-491-2645. Business E-Mail: dcolbert@learn.colostate.edu.

COLBERT-CORMIER, PATRICIA A., secondary school educator; b. Lake Charles, La., Nov. 12, 1943; 4 children. BS in Biology, U. La., 1965, MS in Microbiology, 1975. Edn. specialist cert. in reading 1978. Tchr. biology dept. Lafayette (La.) H.S., 1975—, mem. health acad. com., 2003—; lead sci. tchr. H.S. 802 Lafayette Parish. Mem. editl. adv. panel Cold Spring Harbor Labs. DNA Learning Ctr. Mem. Nat. Academics Tchrs. Adv. Group; past bd. dirs. Nat. Bd. Profl. Tchg. Stds. Finalist, Nat. Tchr. Hall Fame; DuPont fellow, 1994, Albert Einstein fellow, NASA, Washington, 2000—01, Disney Ch. Am. Tchr. and Tandy Tech. scholar, 1996. Office: Lafayette HS Biology Dept 3000 W Congress St Lafayette LA 70506 Office Phone: 337-984-5284. Personal E-mail: p53colbert@aol.com.

COLBURN, MARTHA, animator, filmmaker, artist; b. 1979; BA in Art, Md. Inst. Coll. Art, Balt., 1994; MA equivalent, Rijksakademie Van Beeldende Kunst (Royal Acad. Art), Holland, 2002. Several presentations and lectures in many fine art schools and art groups in the U.S.A., 2001; vis. prof. animation San Francisco Art Inst., 2001; Filmwerkplaats, Basics of Subversive and Traditional Animation, Rotterdam, Netherlands, 02; vis. artists, lecture Kunstakademie of Bergen, Norway, 2003, Statenskunst Akademie, Norway, 2003; vis. tutor Dutch Art Inst., Enschede, Netherlands, 2003; lectr., animation workshop Nanjing Art Inst., China, 2004; vis. artist, prof. Calif. Inst. Arts, 2004; vis. artist MIT, Mass., 2005, Sch. Mus. Fine Arts, Boston, 2005. Mus./archive/gallery film screenings Anthology Fim Archive, NY, Film Series, 1997, MoMA, NY Five Films Screened in Big As Life: An American History of 8 mm Films, 1998, Whitney Mus., NY, 2001, Pacific Film Archive, Calif., 2002, Mus. Contemporary Art, Lyon, France, 2002, Art Space, Auckland, New Zealand, 2004, and several others; solo visual exhibitions, De Kabinetten of De Vleeshal, Middelburg, Netherlands, INSE(X)CTS Major Art Fair, Amsterdam, Netherlands, 2002, Frankfurter Kunstverein, Young and Upcoming, Frankfurt, Germany., 2003, W.I.N.D.O.W. gallery, Walter Van Beirendonk Fashion shop, Antwerp, Belgium, 2003, group visual art exhbns., Courthouse Gallery, Anthology Film Archive, NYC, 2000, Las Palmas, Transmission: Emerging Artists living around the North Sea, Rotterdam, Netherlands, 2001, Outline Gallery, Haunted House Of Art, Amsterdam, Netherlands, 2002, Group Show, Diana Stigter Gallery, Amsterdam, 2003, Site Specific, Deiska, Amsterdam, Netherlands, 2003, Luggage Nanjing Art Institute Gallery, Nanjing, China, 2004, Vixens, Diana Stigter Gallery, Amsterdam, Netherlands, 2004, Liste Art Fair, Diana Stigter Gallery, Basel, Switzerland, 2004, Sideshow Gallery, Williamsburg, NY. US. group show with Jonas Mekas, 2004, and several others; film screenings Women in Film Series, Washington, DC, 1996, Oberlin Coll., Independent Film Series, Ohio, 1996, Halcyon Gallery, Balt., 1997, Layers in Time, Cin(E) Poetry Film Festival, San Francisco, 1997, NY Women's Film Festival, 1998, Contemporary Issues Film Festival, Portugal, 1999, NY and Chgo. Underground Film Festivals, 1999, Sundance Film Festival, Utah, 2000, MIX Film Festival (NY and Brazil), 2001, Traditional and Subversive Animation, Worm Cinema, Rotterdam, Netherlands, 2002, MIX Gay and Lesbian Film Festival, NY, 2002, Rhodes Coll., Memphis, Tenn., 2003, Phila. Film Festival, 2003, Netherlands Film Festival, 2004, LA Film Festival, Egyptian Theater, Calif., 2004, Utah Arts Festival, 2004, Super 8 Special 2004, Basel, Switzerland, 2004, Rotterdam Internat. Film Festival, Netherlands, 2005, DUTCH OPEN, Amsterdam, 2005, Brampton Indie Arts Festival, Calif., 2005, and several others; watercolors, films and large photgraphic works toured Norway with Nat. Touring Exhbns., 2001—05, commissions, Channel Four, GB, Titles for Animation Babylon, 1998, Park TV, Amsterdam, Berlin, NY, Two one hour programs, 2001, collections, BBC TV, One Film Purchased, 1999, Dibendetto Collection, private, video, 2000, private collection, Jonas Mekas, US, 2001; filmaker, animator Acrophobic Babies, 1994, First Film In X-tro, 1994, Feature Presentation, 1994, Alcohol, 1995, Asthma, 1995, Live Frazz, 1995, Zig Zag, 1995, Caroline Kraabel Solo, 1995, Caffine Jam, 1995, Improvisation, 1995, Killer Tunes, 1996, Kiwi and Wally, 1996, Who Knows?, 1996, My Secret Shame, 1996, I'm Gonna, 1996, Uberfail: Pee Poo and Flies, 1996, Hey Tiger, 1996, Dog Chow, 1996, Cholesterol, 1996, Persecution in Paradise, 1997, I Can't Keep Up, 1997, Ode to a Busdriver, 1997, Evil of Dracula, 1997, What's On?, There's a Pervert in our Pool!, 1998, A Totally Soleful Feeture Pedsintation, 1998, Lift Off, 1999, Spiders In Love: An Arachnogasmic Musical, 2000, Skelehellavision, 2001, Cats Amore, 2002, Groscher Lansangriff: Big Bug Attack, 2002, Secrets of Mexuality, 2003 (Dutch Film Fund completion grant, 2004), XXX Amsterdam, 2004, A Little Dutch Thrill, 2004, Cosmetic Emergency, 2005 (Dutch Film Fund production grant, 2004), several compact disc recordings; Whitney Biennial: Day for Night, Whitney Mus. Am. Art, NYC, 2006. Recipient Kenneth Patchen award, Nat. Poetry Film Festival, 1997, Juries Choice award, Super Super 8 Film Festival, 1997, Juries Choice award for no budget film making, Hamburg Short Festival, Del., 1998, Best Animated Film, NY Underground Film Festival, 1999, 2003, Chgo. Underground Film Festival, 1999, Sarah Lawrence Coll. Film award, 2002; Md. State Arts Grant, 1997, Filmcore Grant, NY Underground Film Festival, 1998, Chgo. Underground Film Festival Grant, 2000, Thaw Film Festival Grant, 2000, Rockefeller Grant Nominee, 2001, Dutch Ministry Edn., Culture and Sci., 2000—02, Stadsdeel de Baarsjes Grant Project: xxx Amsterdam, 2004. Address: c/o Diana Stigter Gallery Elandsstraat 90 1016 SH Amsterdam Netherlands Mailing: c/o Stux Gallery 530 W 25th St New York NY 10001 E-mail: info@marthacolburn.com, spidersinlove@hotmail.com.*

COLBURN, NANCY DOUGLAS, social worker, educator; d. Cleaveland Fisher Colburn and Virginia Bahrs. BA, Rutgers U., 1963; MSW, U. Ill., Chgo., 1971; MDiv, McCormick Theol. Sem., 1971; MPA, San Diego State U., 1997. LCSW Calif.; Ordained to ministry Vineyard Christian Fellowship 1990, cert. tchr./adminstr. child devel. programs Calif. Social worker Dept. Social Svcs. County of San Diego, 1979—92; social worker Family Advocacy, USN, San Diego, 1992—97.

COLBURN, NANCY HALL, medical researcher; b. Wilmington, Del., May 15, 1941; d. Robert Turner and Alice (Edwards) Hall; m. Willis S. Colburn, Aug. 29, 1964 (div. 1976); children: Carolyn Churchill, Christine Hall; m. Thomas D. Gindhart, May 30, 1981 (dec. 1985); m. John P. Farrell, Nov. 14, 1999. BA in Chemistry, Swarthmore (Pa.) Coll., 1963; PhD in Biochemistry, McArdle Lab., U. Wis., 1967. Asst. prof. dept. biol. sci. U. Del., Newark, 1968-72; NIH spl. rsch. fellow dept. dermatology U. Mich., Ann Arbor, 1972-74, asst. prof. depts. dermatology and biol. chemistry, 1974-75; expert lab. exptl. pathology DCCP, Nat. Cancer Inst., Bethesda, Md., 1976-79; chief cell biology sect. Lab. Viral Carcinogenesis, BCP, DCE, Nat. Cancer Inst., NIH, Frederick, Md., 1979-84; chief gene regulation sect. of Lab. Biochemical Physiology Nat. Cancer Inst., NIH, Frederick, Md., 1996—99, joined Basic Rsch. Lab, 1999, chief Lab. Cancer Prevention, Ctr. Cancer Rsch., 2003—; chair NCI Cancer Prevention FAculty, 2001—. Vis. scientist and cons. dept. environ. and indsl. health U. Mich., 1975-76; cons., chair Site Visit Teams for NIH Grants, Bethesda, 1985—; cons. Am. Cancer Soc. Study Sect., Atlanta, 1990-93, coun., 1996—; cons., sci. adv. bd. Eppley Inst. for Cancer Rsch., Omaha, 1991—, Mich. State U. Cancer Ctr., 1991—, Genetics Inst. Yonsei U. Medical Sch., Seoul, Koea; adj. prof. genetics George Washington U., pathology U. Md; chair Internat. Union Against Cancer Fellowships Commn., 1990-99. Editor, author: Growth Factors, Tumor Promoters and Cancer Genes, 1988, Genes and Signal Transduction Multistage Carcinogenesis, 1989; mem. editorial bd. Teratogenesis, Carcinogenesis and Mutagenesis, 1980-89, Internat. Jour. Cancer, 1984—, Molecular Carcinogenesis, 1986—, Oncology Rsch., 1988—, Cancer Rch., 1989—, Jour. Cancer Rsch. and Clin. Oncology, 1990, Biochem. Biophys. acta, 1998—; contbr. articles to profl. jours. Mem. vestry Episcopal Ch., Braddock Hts., Md., 1986-88. NIH grantee, 1972, 76, 79; Conte Inst. for Environ. Studies fellow. Mem AAAS, NOW, N.Y. Acad. Sci., Am. Assn. Cancer Rsch. (bd. dirs. 1990-93), Am. Soc. Biochem. and Molecular Biology, Common Cause, Sierra Club, Sigma Xi. Democrat. Avocations: hiking, backpacking, running, skiing, singing. Office: Nat Cancer Inst Bldg 576 Rm 101 Frederick MD 21702-1201 Office Phone: 301-846-1342. Office Fax: 301-846-6907. E-mail: colburn@ncifcrf.gov.

COLBY, ANN JULIA, history educator; b. Watertown, NY, Mar. 17, 1965; d. Henry Masters and Marie Anita Colby. BA in History, St. John Fisher Coll., Rochester, NY, 1987; MA in Internat. U.S. Rels., Coll. of St. Rose, Albany, 1992. Legis. rep. asst. L.O.B. Assemblyman Robert Nortz, Albany, 1990—92; history educator St. Patrick's Sch., Watertown, 1996—2000, Belleville Henderson Sch., Belleville, 2000—. Varsity volleyball/soccer coach Frontier League, Belleville, 1994—2006; dept. chmn. history Belleville Henderson, Belleville, 2004—06, cirrculm coun., 2004—06. Pres. Improvement Club, Pierrepont Manor, NY, 2000—03; com. woman Rep. Party, Ellisburg, NY, 1991—2006. Named one of Faces of the Crowd, Sports Illustrated, 1983. Mem.: Delta Kappa Gamma, Phi Alpha Theta. Avocations: photography, painting, travel, reading, sports. Office: Belleville Henderson Ctrl Sch PO Box 158 Belleville NY 13611

COLBY, JOY HAKANSON, critic; b. Detroit; d. Alva Hilliard and Eleanor (Radtke) Hakanson; m. Raymond L. Colby, Apr. 11, 1953; children: Sarah, Katherine, Lisa. Student, Detroit Soc. Arts and Crafts, 1945; BFA, Wayne State U., 1946; DFA (hon.), Coll. for Creative Studies, 1998. Art critic Detroit News, 1947—; originator exhibit Arts and Crafts in Detroit, 1906-1976; with Detroit Inst. Arts, 1976. Author: (book) Art and A City, 1956; contbr. articles to art periodicals. Mem. visual arts adv. panel Mich. Coun. Arts, 1974—79; mayor's appointment Detroit Coun. for the Arts, 1974; mem. Bloomfield Hills Arts Coun., 1974. Recipient Alumni award, Wayne State U., 1967, Art Achievement award, 1983, Headliner award, 1984, award arts reporting, Detroit Press Club, 1984, Art Leadership award, Coll. for Creative Studies, 1989. Office: 615 W Lafayette Blvd Detroit MI 48226-3124 Office Phone: 313-222-2276. Business E-Mail: jcolby@detnews.com.

COLBY, KAREN LYNN See WEINER, KAREN

COLBY, MARVELLE SEITMAN, retired business management educator, administrator; b. NYC, Oct. 31, 1932; d. Charles Edward and Lily (Zimmerman) Seitman; m. Robert S. Colby, Apr. 11, 1954 (div. Apr. 1979); children: Lisa, Eric; m. Selig J. Alkon, Dec. 6, 1986. BA, Hunter Coll., N.Y.C., 1954; MA, U. N.Colo., Greeley, 1973; PhD in Pub. Adminstrn., Nova U., Ft. Lauderdale, Fla., 1977; cert., Harvard Grad. Sch. Bus., 1979. V.p. SE Region URC Mgmt. Services Corp., Washington, 1972-77; dir. devel. Hunter Coll. Woman's Ctr. Community Leadership, N.Y.C., 1977-78; dir. tng. and career devel. Girl Scouts U.S., N.Y.C., 1978-79; dir. Overseas Tour Ops. Am. Jewish Congress, N.Y.C., 1979-81; chief exec. officer Girl Scout Council Greater N.Y.C., 1981-82; prof. bus. mgmt. Marymount Manhattan Coll., N.Y.C., 1982—2003, chmn. bus. mgmt. and acctg. div., 1982-89, 93-99, prof. emeritus, 2003—. Adj. prof. NYU, 1986-92; mem. exec. com. Assn. Recreation Mgmt., N.Y.C., 1982; cons. Rockport Mgmt., Washington, 1974-78. Author: Test Your Management IQ, 1984; co-author: Lovejoy's Four Year College Guide for the Learning Disabled, 1985, Introduction to Business, 1991; contbr. articles to profl. jours. Chmn. Met. Dade County Commn. Status Women, Miami, 1975-77; chief planner Met. Dade County U.S. SBA 1st annual conf. Future Women Bus., 1977. Named to Hunter Coll. Hall of Fame, 1986. Mem. Acad. Mgmt., Hunter Coll. Alumni Assn. (bd. dirs. 1978-79), Phi Delta Kappa. Clubs: Lotos (mem. literary com. 1983-89). Business E-Mail: mcolby@mmm.edu.

COLBY-HALL, ALICE MARY, language educator; b. Portland, Maine, Feb. 25, 1932; d. Frederick Eugene and Angie Fraser (Drown) C.; m. Robert A. Hall, Jr., May 8, 1976 (dec. 1997); stepchildren: Philip, Diana Hall Goodall, Carol Hall Erickson. BA, Colby Coll., 1953; MA, Middlebury Coll., 1954; PhD, Columbia U., 1962. Tchr. French, Latin Orono (Maine) HS, 1954-55; tchr. French Gould Acad., Bethel, Maine, 1955-57; lectr. French Columbia U., 1959-60; instr. Romance lit. Cornell U., Ithaca, NY, 1962-63, asst. prof., 1963-66, assoc. prof., 1966-75, prof. Romance studies, 1975-97, prof. emerita, 1997—, chmn. Romance studies, 1990-96. Author: The Portrait in Twelfth Century French Literature: An Example of the Stylistic Originality of Chrétien de Troyes, 1965; mem. editl. bd. Speculum, 1976-79, Olifant, 1974—. Fulbright grantee, 1953-54; NEH fellow, 1984-85; recipient Médaille des Amis d'Orange, 1985; decorated chevalier de l'Ordre des Arts et Lettres, 1997. Mem. Modern Lang. Assn., Medieval Acad. Am. (councillor 1983-86), Internat. Arthurian Soc., Société Rencesvals, Académie de Vaucluse, Phi Beta Kappa. Republican. Congregationalist. Home: 308 Cayuga Heights Rd Ithaca NY 14850-2107 Office: Cornell U Dept Romance Studies Ithaca NY 14853 Business E-Mail: amc12@cornell.edu.

COLE, ANGELA P., psychologist, educator; BS, Howard U., 1994; PhD, Stanford U., 1999. Postdoctoral fellow U. Mich., Ann Arbor, 1999—2001; asst. prof. Howard U., Washington, 2001—. Contbr. articles to profl. jours. Recipient Centennial Tchg. Asst. award, Stanford U., 1999; grantee, NSF, 2004—06; Summer Faculty and Student Rsch. Award Program fellow, Dept. Homeland Security, 2005, Atlantic Coast Social, Behavioral and Econ. Scis. grantee, NSF, 2005—. Mem.: APA (Minority Fellowship Program Dissertation grantee 1998—99, Minority Fellowship Program award 1994—97), Assn. Psychol. Sci., Golden Key Nat. Honor Soc., Psi Chi, Beta Kappa Chi. Office: Howard U Department Of Psychology Washington DC 20059 Office Phone: 202-806-9448.

COLE, ANN HARRIET, psychologist, consultant; b. Phila., Feb. 27, 1949; d. Albert and Deborah (Mann) Brawerman; m. Stephen Cole, June 4, 1969 (div. June 18, 1987); children: Richard David, Robert Walter; m. Allan J. Besbris, Aug. 4, 1998. BA, SUNY, Stony Brook, 1971, MA, 1975. Dir. field rsch. Opinion Rsch. Assocs., 1974-76; v.p. Social Data Analysts, Inc., 1976-86; rsch. assoc. Jay Schulman, Inc., N.Y.C., 1986-87; cons. Litigation Scis., Inc., N.Y.C., 1988-90, Stanley S. Arkin, P.C., N.Y.C., 1990, Chadbourne & Parke, N.Y.C., 1990-91; pres. Ann Cole Opinion Rsch. and Analysis, 1991—. CBS news cons., 1994-95. Mem. Am. Soc. Trial Cons. (bd. dirs. 1994-99, v.p. 1996-97, pres. 1997-99), Qualitative Rsch. Cons. Am. Office: 8913 Pennystone Ave Las Vegas NV 89134 also: Ann Cole Opinion Rsch and Analysis 860 Crow Hill Rd Arlington VT 05250-9043 Office Phone: 212-302-1650, 702-363-0390. E-mail: ahcole@acoraweb.com.

COLE, ANNA MOORE, chemistry educator; d. John Whitt and Elaine Marie Moore; m. David Wayne Cole, Dec. 16, 1988; children: Kaylee Michelle, Megan Renee, Ethan Wayne. BS, Nicholls State U., Thibodaux, 1990. Tchr. chemistry Ctrl. La Fourche H.S., Raceland, La., 1990—. Named Tchr. of Yr., Walmart, 2004; recipient Making a Difference award, Nicholls State U., 2001, Making a Difference Award, 2005. Office: Central La Fourche High School 4820 Hwy 1 Raceland LA 70394

COLE, CAROLYN, photojournalist; b. Boulder, Colo., Apr. 24, 1961; BA in Photojournalism, U. Tex., 1983. Staff photographer El Paso Herald Post, 1986—88, San Francisco Examiner, 1988—90; freelance photographer Mexico City, 1990—92; staff photographer Sacramento Bee, 1992—94, L.A. Times, 1994—. Contbr. (photographs) Holy Lands, Life Books, Time Inc., The American Spirit, Life--The Year in Pictures, 2002. Recipient Pictures of the Year, newspaper portrait/personality award of excellence, U. Mo., 1986, first place, feature pictures story for "Cadet McKeag: Wentworth Academy's Only Female", Calif. Press Photographers Assn., 1993, Mark Twain Award, first place picture story for "Haiti: Crisis in the Caribbean", AP News Execs. Coun., 1994, best spot news photo or photographic series for "Haiti: Crisis in the Caribbean", LA Times Editl. Award, 1994, best feature photo or photographic series for "Health Crisis in Russia", LA Time Editl. Award, 1995, first place, newspaper feature picture & newspaper feature story award of excellence, Pictures of the Year, U. Mo., 1994, issue reporting picture story award of excellence for "California's Fragile Future", 1996, third place issue reporting, 1998, Journalist of the Year Award, Times Mirror Corp., 1998, Pulitzer Prize, breaking news for LA Times team coverage of the North Hollywood shootout, 1998, newspaper feature story, second place for "In the Shadow of War", Pictures of the Year, U. Mo., 1999, global news picture story, award of excellence for "No Winners in War, 1999, general news picture award of excellence for "Face of Conviction", 2000, newspaper photographer of the year, Nat. Press Photographers Assn., 2002, Mark Twain Award for best of show, AP News Execs. Coun., 2002, first place, people in the news for "Church of the Nativity", World Press Photo, 2003, first place, mag. news story editing & second place, feature picture story for "Church of the Nativity", Pictures of the Year, U. Mo., 2003, Robert Capa Award for courage in photography for covering the siege at the Church of the Nativity, Bethlehem, Overseas Press Club, 2003, Newspaper Photographer of Yr., U. Mo., 2003, Nat. Press Photographers Assn., 2003, award for news photography for church of the nativity, Sigma Delta Chi, 2003, Pulitzer Prize for feature photography, 2004, George Polk award for photojournalism, 2004, Robert Capa award for courage in photography for Iraq war and civil conflict in Liberia, 2004, award for news photography Iraq war, Sigma Delta Chi, 2004, 2d pl. people in the news Iraq War, 3d pl. for civil conflict in Liberia, World Press Photo, 2004, 2d pl. natural disaster story, Hurricane Katrina, Pictures of the Yr., U. Mo., 2005, award of excellence for "Exhausted, But Alive"., 2005.

COLE, CAROLYN JO, brokerage house executive; b. Carmel, Calif. d. Joseph Michael Jr. and Dorothea Wagner (James) C. AB, Vassar Coll., 1965. Sr. v.p. UBS Painewebber, Inc., N.Y.C., 1975—95; exec. v.p. Tucker Anthony, Inc., Boston, 1995—97; chmn. Inst. Econ. & Fin., Inc., N.Y.C., 1997—98; mng. dir. Citigroup, N.Y.C., 1998—. Guest lectr. Harvard U. Bus. Sch.; lectr. Securities Industry Inst., Wharton Sch. U. Pa.; past chmn. bd. dirs. N.Y. Women's Bldg.; bd. dirs. Women's Venture Fund. Named to YWCA Acad. Women Achievers. Mem. NOW, DAR, N.Y. Soc. Security Analysts (past bd. dirs.), The CFA Inst., Soc. Fgn. Analysts, Aspen Inst. Humanistic Studies, Fin. Women's Assn., Women's Econ. Roundtable, Econ. Club N.Y., Women in Need (past bd. dirs.), Vassar Club, Univ. Club. Democrat. Office: Citigroup Private Equity 388 Greenwich St New York NY 10013-2339 Office Phone: 212-816-4766. Business E-Mail: cali.cole@citigroup.com.

COLE, DONNA KAY, elementary school educator, science educator; b. Roanoke, Va., May 31, 1963; d. Don Martin and Sherry Ann Schmidt; m. Larry Cole, Apr. 9, 1988; children: Spencer, Taggart. BEd, Concordia Coll., Portland, Oreg., 1985; MEd in Sci. and Natural Sci. Edn., We. Wash. U., Bellingham, Wash., 1992. Dir. program Camp Luthenwood, Bellingham, 1985—88; tchr. math. mid. sch. West View Burlington Edison (Wash.) Sch. Dists., 1989—90; tchr. Allen Burlington Edison (Wash.) Sch. Dists., 1990—92; tchr. sci. Edison Burlington (Wash.) Edison Sch. Dists., 1992—. Tchr. leadership project Burlington (Wash.) Sch. Dist., 1997—. Firefighter Whatcom County Fire Dept., 1988—2000, EMT, 1988—2000, fire commr., 2000—05. Recipient award, Coun. for Elem. Sci. Internat., 1994, ACE Intel, 2000, Earthwatch Brazil, 2003. Mem.: Nat. Sci. Tchrs. Assn. (named Sci. Tchr. of Yr. Wash. State chpt. 1992). Home: 691 Rainbow Dr Sedro Woolley WA 98284 Office: Edison Sch 5801 Main Ave Bow WA 98232

COLE, ELAINE ANN, marriage and family therapist, educator; b. L.A., Mar. 25, 1946; d. Louis Leo and Sadie Levanson; m. Paul B. Cole, Oct. 20, 1968; children: Jordan, Rebecca Sides. BA, U. Calif., L.A., 1987; MA, Calif. Grad. Inst., L.A., 1990. Co-administrator Stanley H. Kaplan Ednl. Ctr., L.A., 1990—; pvt. practice therapist Culver City, Calif., 1994—. Tchr. U. Judaism, L.A., 1987—; spkr. in field. Contbr. articles to profl. jours. Mem.: Bruin Profls., Calif. Assn. Marriage and Family Therapists, U. Calif. Alumni Assn. (life), Rotary. Avocations: skiing, tennis, reading, hiking. Office: Clinical Private Practice 5800A Hannum Ave 215 Culver City CA 90230

COLE, ELEANOR OPHELIA, retired medical/surgical nurse; b. Cuero, Tex., Sept. 28, 1926; d. Hubert and Beulah M. (Ritchie) Harryman; m. Thomas H. Cole, May 30, 1949; children: Richard Thomas, Ronald Walton. Grad., Baylor U. Sch. Nursing, 1947; student, Baylor U., 1947-49. Staff RN, supr. M.D. Anderson Hosp., Houston; staff RN Boothe Hosp., Covington, Ky., Ky. Bapt. Hosp., Louisville; head nurse M.D. Anderson Hosp., Houston; ret., 1992. Recipient Outstanding Nurse Oncologist award The Brown Found., Inc., 1985. Home: 11907 Rampart St Houston TX 77035-4216

COLE, ELMA PHILLIPSON (MRS. JOHN STRICKLER COLE), social welfare executive; b. Piqua, Ohio, Aug. 9, 1909; d. Brice Leroy and Mabel (Gale) Phillipson; m. John Strickler Cole, Oct. 3, 1959. AB, Berea Coll., 1930; MA, U. Chgo., 1938. Social work staff, 1930-42; dir. dept. social svc. Children's Hosp. D.C., Washington, 1942-49; cons. pub. coop. Midcentury White House Conf. on Children and Youth, Washington, 1949-51; exec. sec. Nat. Midcentury Com. on Children and Youth, N.Y.C., 1951-53; cons. recruitment Am. Assn. Med. Social Workers, 1953; assoc. dir. Nat. Legal Aid and Defender Assn., 1953-56; exec. sec. Marshall Field Awards, Inc., 1956-57; dir. assoc. orgns. Nat. Assembly Social Policy and Devel., 1957-73; assoc. exec. dir. Nat. Assembly Nat. Vol. Health and Social Welfare Orgns., 1974; dir. edn. parenthood project Salvation Army, 1974-76, asst. sec. dept. women's and children's social svcs., 1976-78, dir. rsch. project devel. bur., 1978-92, ind. cons., 1993—. Mem. Manhattan adv. bd., 1975—, sec., 1984—; cons. nat. orgns. Golden Anniversary White House Conf. on Children and Youth, 1959-60; mem. adv. coun. pub. svc. Nat. Assn. Life Underwriters and Inst. Life Ins.; judges com. Louis I. Dublin Pub. Svc. awards, 1961-74; v.p. Blue Ridge Inst. So. Cmty. Svc. Execs., 1977-79, exec. com., 1979-81; mem. awards jury Girls Clubs Am., 1981-93; adv. bd. Nat. Family Life Edn. Network, 1982-97. Com. pub. rels. and fundraising Am. Found. for Blind Commn. on Accreditation, 1964-67; task force on vol. accreditation Coun. Nat. Orgns. for Adult Edn., 1974-78; adv. bd. sexuality edn. project Ctr. for Population Options, 1977-86; bd. dirs., sec. James Lenox House, 1985-89, pres., 1989-94, treas., 1994-98; bd. dirs., sec. James Lenox House Assn., 1985-89, pres., 1989-94, sec., 1994-98; bd. dirs. Values and Human Sexuality Inst., 1980-85, Presbyterian Sr. Svcs., N.Y., 1998, Sexuality Info. and Edn. Coun. of U.S., 1993, exec. com. Mem. Pub. Rels. Soc. Am. (cert.), Nat. Assn. Social Workers (cert.), Nat. Conf. Social Welfare (mem. pub. rels. com. 1961-66, 69-82, chair adminstrn. sect. 1966-67), Soc. Sci. Study Sexuality, Jr. League N.Y., Women's Club of N.Y., Pi Gamma Mu, Phi Kappa Phi. Home: 420 Lexington Ave Rm 626 New York NY 10170-0626

COLE, ELSA KIRCHER, lawyer; b. Dec. 5, 1949; d. Paul and Hester Marie (Pellegrom) Kircher; m. Roland J. Cole, Aug. 16, 1975; children: Isabel Ashley, Madeline Aldis. AB in History with distinction, Stanford U., 1971; JD, Boston U., 1974. Bar: Wash. 1974, U.S. Supreme Ct. 1980, Mich. 1989, Kans. 1997, Ind. 1999. Asst. atty gen., rep. dept. motor vehicles State of Wash., Seattle, 1974-75, asst. atty. gen., rep. dept. social and health svcs., 1975-76, asst. atty. gen., rep. U. Wash., 1976-89; gen. counsel U. Mich., Ann Arbor, 1989-97, NCAA, Indpls., 1997—. Presenter ednl. issues various confs. and workshops. Contbr. articles to profl. jours. Fellow: Nat. Assn. Coll. and Univs. Attys. (mem. nominations com., mem. site selection com. 1987—88, co-chair student affairs sect. 1987—88, program 1988—89, mem. fin. com., articles com., by-laws com. 1988—89, co-chair student affairs sect. 1988—89, bd. dirs. 1988—91, program 1989—90, chair profl. devel. com. 1990—91, program 1991—92, honors and awards, ethics com. 1991—92, program 1992—93, bd. ops. 1992—93, mem. nominations com., mem. site selection com. 1995—96, CLE com. 1995—96, program 1995—96, CLE com. 1996—97, pub. com. 1996—97, CLE com. 2000—02, honors and awards com. 2002—03, named NACUA fellow 1998); mem.: Nat. Sports Law Inst. (bd. advisors 2001—), Sports Lawyers Assn. (bd. dirs. 2001—), Indpls. Bar Assn. (sports and entertainment sect. bd. dirs. 2001—), Seattle-King County Bar Assn., Wash. Women Lawyers (pres. Seattle-King County chpt. 1986, state chair candidate endorsement com. 1987, v.p. membership, state bd. dirs. 1987—88, state chair candidate endorsement com. 1988), Wash. State Bar Assn. (chair law sch. liaison com. 1988—89). Office: Ncaa Travel Serivce 111 Water St New Haven CT 06511-5759 E-mail: ecole@ncaa.org.

COLE, HEATHER ELLEN, librarian; b. Rochester, N.Y., Nov. 7, 1942; d. Donald M. and Muriel Agnes (Kimball) Cole; m. Stratis Haviaras; 1 child, Elektra Maria Muriel. BA, Cornell U., 1964; MS, Simmons Coll., 1973. Mgr. Brentano's, Boston, 1968-70; intern Harvard Coll. Libr., Cambridge, Mass., 1970-73, reference libr., 1973-77, libr., 1977—, Hilles Libr., 1977—2005, The Lamont Libr., 1977—. Mem.: AAUW, ALA, Am. Soc. Info. Sci. (New Eng. chpt.), Assn. Coll. Rsch. Librs. Democrat. Episcopalian. Avocation: gardening. Home: 19 Clinton St Cambridge MA 02139-2303 Office: Harvard Coll Lamont Library Cambridge MA 02138 Office Phone: 617-495-2455. Business E-Mail: hcole@eas.harvard.edu.

COLE, JANICE MCKENZIE, former prosecutor; b. Feb. 16, 1947; m. James Carlton Cole. BA summa cum laude, John Jay Coll Criminal Justice, 1975, MPA, 1978; JD, Fordham U., 1979. Bar: N.Y. 1980, N.C. 1983. Asst. U.S. atty. Eastern Dist. N.Y., 1979-83; sole practitioner, 1983-89; with firm Cole & Cole, 1989-90; dist. ct. judge First Jud. Dist. N.C., 1990-94; U.S. atty. N.C. Eastern Dist., 1994—2001; sole practitioner, 2001—. Office: Ste 106 1072 Harvey Point Rd Hertford NC 27944-1461

COLE, JEAN ANNE, artist; b. Greeley, Colo., Jan. 30, 1947; d. Philip Owen and Rose Margaret (Maser) Dahl; m. Nelson Bruce Cole, June 22, 1968; children: Ashley Paige, Travis Allyn. BA in Interior Design, U. Calif., Berkeley, 1968. Interior designer K.S. Wilshire Design, L.A., 1969-70, Milton Swimmer Planning & Design, Beverly Hills, Calif., 1970-73, Denver, 1973-75. Tchr. watercolor workshops, 1991—. Exhibited in numerous shows at Foothills Art Ctr., Golden, Colo., 1989, 91, 93, 94, 96, 98, 99, 2002, Brea (Calif.) Civic and Cultural Ctr., 1989, 90, Nevile Pub. Mus., Green Bay, Wis., 1990, 93, Nat. Watercolor Soc., 1991, Denver Mus. Natural History, 1991, Pikes Peak Ctr. Performing Arts, Colorado Springs, Colo., 1992, Colo. History Mus., 1992-98, Kneeland Gallery, Las Vegas, Nev., 1993, 94, 95, 97, Salmagundi Club, N.Y.C., 1994, 97, 99, Met. State Coll. Ctr. for Visual Arts, Denver, 1994, U. So. Colo., 1997, Wichita Art Mus., 1997, Colorado Springs Fine Art Ctr., 1998, Acad. of Art Gallery, San Francisco, Onewest Art Ctr., Ft. Collins, Colo., Wyo. Brennial, Wash. State Conv. and Trade Ctr., N.W. Watercolor Soc., Seattle, Arvada Ctr. Arts Humanities, 2002; work represented in various publs.; contbr. articles to mags.; artist greetings cards Leanin'Tree. Recipient 2d pl. watercolor award Art Zone Regional Show, 1988, 1st pl. watercolor award Colo. ARtists Convention, 1989, 1st pl., hon. mention People's Choice awards Denver Allied Artists, 1989, Best of Show award Pikes Peak Watercolor Invitational, 1992, Quaintance award Rocky Mountain Nat. Watermedia Exhibit, 1993, 1994, 1996, 2002, Best Show award Rocky Mountain Nat. Watermedia Exhibit, 1998, Paul Schwartz Meml. award Am. Watercolor Soc., 1994, Founder's award Watercolor West XXVI Ann. Nat. Transparent Watercolor Exhbn., Calif., 1994. Mem.: Am. Watercolor Soc., Rocky Mt. Nat. Watermedia Soc., Colo. Watercolor Soc. (pres., treas., award of merit 1993), Nat. Watercolor Soc. Republican. Avocations: hiking, skiing, gardening, photography, horseback riding.

COLE, JESSIE MAE, nursing assistant, freelance/self-employed writer; b. McGehee, Ark., Nov. 19, 1925; d. Alonso Smith and Estelle Hursey; m. Amos Burns, May 15, 1942; children: Bobbie D., Joyce R.; m. Mose Eddie Cole (div. Nov. 1972). AA, Fresno City Coll, 1985; BA, Charter Oak State Coll., 1999. Cert. tchr. Calif., 1979. Beautician Beauty Culture, Chgo., 1956—76; nursing asst. Hope Manor Facility, Fresno, Calif., 1983—. Pvt. piano tchr., Fresno, 1981—. Author: (website) How to Read Sheet Music, 1997; contbr. articles. Mem. Wall of Tolerance Nat. Campaign for Tolerance, 2002—03; bible study instr. Coll. Ch. of Christ, Fresno, 1975—. Recipient Employee of Year, Calif. Assn. Health Facilities. Mem.: Nat. Assn. Black Journalists. Home: 284 N Logsdon Pky Radcliff KY 40160

COLE, JOAN HAYS, social worker, clinical psychologist; b. Pitts., Sept. 4, 1929; d. Frank L. Wertheimer and Edith H. Einstein; m. Robert M. Wendlinger, June, 1984; children: Geoffrey F., Douglas R., Peter Hays. BA, Western Res. U., 1951; MSSA in Social Work, Case Western Res. U., 1962; PhD, Wright Inst., 1975. Cert. clin. social worker; diplomate Am. Bd. Orthopsychiat. Social group worker Alta House Settlement House, Cleve., 1958-59; housing dir. Cleve. Urban League, 1961-62; dir. Citizens for Safe Housing, Cleve., 1963; housing dir. United Planning Orgn., Washington, 1963-68; asst. prof. cmty. orgn. U. Md. Sch. Social Work and Cmty. Planning, Balt., 1968—72; assoc. prof. Lone Mountain Coll., San Francisco, 1975-78; psychotherapist, supr., orgnl. cons., Berkeley, Calif., 1977—. Cons. various pub. and vol. social welfare, health and housing agys., 1969—; mem. adj. faculty Union Grad. Sch. and Antioch West Coll., 1978-80; lectr. U. Calif. Sch. Social Welfare, Berkeley, 1980-84; mem. faculty Berkeley Psychotherapy Inst., 1981—, pres., 1983-85; clin. faculty Inst. Clin. Social Work, Berkeley, 2004—. Grantee NIMH, 1971-72, Sr. Social Work Career Devel. grantee, 1973-75. Fellow Soc. Clin. Social Work (diplomate), Am. Orthopsychiat. Assn.; mem. NASW, ACLU, Soc. for Study Social Issues, Acad. Cert. Social Workers, Nat. Conf. on Social Welfare and Psychotherapists for Social Responsibility. Office: 6239 College Ave Oakland CA 94618-1384 Office Phone: 510-654-5151. Personal E-mail: jhcole@earthlink.net.

COLE, JOHNNETTA BETSCH, academic administrator, educator; b. Jacksonville, Fla., Oct. 19, 1936; d. John Thomas and Mary Frances (Lewis) Betsch; m. Robert Eugene Cole (div. 1982); children: David, Aaron, Ethan; m. Arthur J. Robinson, Jr. (div. 2002). Student, Fisk U., 1953; BA in Sociology, Oberlin Coll., 1957; MA in Anthropology, Northwestern U., Evanston, Ill., 1959, PhD, 1967. Instr. UCLA, 1964; dir. black studies Wash. State U., Pullman, 1969-70; prof. anthropology U. Mass., Amherst, 1970-83, assoc. provost undergrad. edn., 1981-83; vis. prof. Hunter Coll., NYC, 1983-84, prof. anthropology, 1983-87, dir. Inter-Am. Affairs Program, 1984-87; pres. Spelman Coll., Atlanta, 1987-97, pres. emeritus, 1997—; pres. Bennett Coll. for Women, Greensboro, NC, 2002—. Corp. bd. dirs. Merck & Co., Inc.; presdl. disting. prof. anthropology, women's studies and Afro-Am. studies Emory U., 1998-2001. Author, editor: Anthropology for the Eighties, 1982, All American Women, 1986, Anthropology for the Nineties, 1988, Conversations: Straight Talk with America's Sister President, 1993, Dream the Boldest Dreams, 1998; author: (with Beverly Guy-Sheftall) Gender Talk: The Struggle for Women's Equality in African American Communities, 2003; mem. editl. bd. The Black Scholar. Immediate past chair bd. trustees United Way. Am. Recipient numerous hon. degrees. Fellow Am. Anthrop. Assn.; mem. Am. Acad. Arts and Scis., Assn. Black Anthropologists (past pres.). United Methodist. Office: Bennett Coll for Women 900 E Washignton St Greensboro NC 27401 Office Phone: 336-517-2225. Business E-Mail: jcole@bennett.edu.

COLE, KATHLEEN ANN, advertising executive, social worker; b. Nov. 22, 1946; d. James Scott and Kathryn Gertrude (Borisch) Cole; m. Brian Brandt, Mar. 21, 1970. BA, Miami U., 1968; MSW, U. Mich., 1972; MM, Northwestern U., 1978. Social worker Hamilton County Welfare Dept., Cin., 1969—70, Lucas County Children Svcs. Bd., Toledo, 1970—74, East Maine Sch. Dist., Niles, Ill., 1974—77; account supr. Leo Burnett Advt. Agy., Chgo., 1978—93; primary therapist Lifeline, Chgo., 1994—95; acct. dir. Green-House Comm., 1995—2001; program coord. North Shore Sr. Ctr., 2004—. Field instr. Loyola U., Chgo., 1976—77. Mem. North Shore United Meth. Congregation. Mem.: NASW (chair pub. rels. task force), Kellogg Alumni Assn., Northwestern U. Prof. Women's Assn., Miami U. Alumni Assn. (dir. 1976—78), Acad. Cert. Social Workers. Home: 414 Kelling Ln Glencoe IL 60022-1113 Office: 1779 Winnetka Rd Winnetka IL 60093 Personal E-mail: colemarketing@comcast.net.

COLE, K.C., journalist, writer; BA, Barnard Coll. Writer, editor Saturday Rev., San Francisco; editor Newsday; sci. commentator Pasadena Pub. Radio (KPCC); sci. writer L.A. Times, 1994—. Adj. prof. UCLA; tchr. sci. writing Yale U., Wesleyan U.; mem. Jour. Women Symposium; dir. PEN West; vis. prof. U. So. Calif. Annenberg, 2006—. Author: (book) The Hole in the Universe: How Scientists Peered Over the Edge of Emptiness and Found Everything, The Universe and the Teacup: The Mathematics of Truth and Beauty, First You Build a Cloud: Reflections on Phyics as a Way of Life, Mind Over Matter: Conversations with the Cosmos, 2003; contbg. writer: The New Yorker, The New York Times, Washington Post, Newsday, Esquire, Newsweek, others. Recipient Writing prize, Am. Inst. Physics, Edward R. Murrow award, Skeptics Soc., Elizabeth A. Wood Sci. Writing award, Am. Crystallographic Assn., 2001; fellow Math. Sci. Rsch. Inst., Exploratorium. Office: LA Times 202 W First St Los Angeles CA 90012 Office Phone: 213-237-7354. Office Fax: 213-237-4712. Business E-Mail: kc.cole@latimes.com.*

COLE, KIMBERLY REE, music educator, musician; b. Sacramento, Aug. 22, 1957; d. Thurston Olaf and Wynona Lois (Clayton) Cole. AA, Sacramento City Coll., 1976; MusB, Calif. State U., Sacramento, 1980; MA in Music, Long Beach State U., Calif., 1986. Tchg. credential Calif. Music tchr. San Juan Unified Sch. Dist., Sacramento, 1986—87, Sacramento City Unified, 1987—88, Davis Joint Unified, Calif., 1988—. Mem.: Calif. Tchrs. Assn., Calif. Music Educator's Assn. (state orch. rep. 2004—, capital sect. orch. rep. 1996—99, Outstanding Orch. Dir. award 2003), Am. String Tchrs. Assn. (state sec. 2000—04). Avocations: scrapbooks, travel, cooking, shopping, pets. Office: Davis Joint Unified Sch Dist 526 B St Davis CA 95616

COLE, LUANNA CHERRY, literature and language educator, theater educator; b. Baton Rouge, La., Dec. 29, 1950; d. Francis Edward and Hazel Marian Abernethy; m. Charles Eugene Cole, Feb. 8, 1975; children: Edward Maxwell, Leslie Marian. BFA, Stephen F. Austin State U., Nacogdoches, Tex., 1973. Cert. Provisional Tchg. Tex. Dept. of Edn., 1973. 7th, 8th, & 9th grade English tchr. W. H. Gaston Mid. Sch., Dallas, 1975—76; H S English i tchr. Woodrow Wilson H.S., Dallas, 1976—82; 7th & 8th grade English tchr. J.L. Long Mid. Sch., Dallas, 1981—86; English II and theater arts tchr. Garrison ISD, Garrison, 1989—. Mem.: Delta Kappa Gamma (sec. 2004—06). Independent. Methodist. Achievements include Taught and inspired future leaders. Avocations: swimming, fishing, travel. Office: Garrison HS 459 N US Hwy 59 Garrison TX 75946 Office Fax: 936-347-2529. Personal E-mail: luannacole@netdot.com. E-mail: cole@garrisonisd.com.

COLE, LYN P., tap dance instructor; d. Angie Richmond; m. Stacey Cole, Apr. 22, 1995. BA, U. of Ill. at Chgo., 1988. Tap dance instr. Old Town Sch. of Folk Music, Chgo., 2000—. Founder Rhythm of the St. Dancers, 2003. Dancer (tap dance prodn.) Virtual Insanity, dancer, tchr. Unsquare Dance, Road Song. Treas. Calumet Pk. Pub. Libr., Calumet Park, Ill., 1992. Mem.: Internat. Tap Assn. Office Phone: 630-291-2248. Personal E-mail: lcole@rhythmofthestreet.org.

COLE, MARY F., music educator; d. James W. and Mary B. Flick; m. Harold E. Cole, Oct. 13, 1984; children: Theresa L, Jonathon M, Matthew P, Nicholas A. M in Music Edn., SUNY, Fredonia, 1987. Music tchr. Letchworth Ctrl. Sch., Gainesville, NY, 1982—85, Avon (N.Y.) Ctrl. Sch., 1985—. Adjudicator N.Y. State Sch. Music Assn.-Music Educators Nat. Conf., 1992—. Mem.: Music Educators Nat. Conf. Home: 81 River St Avon NY 14414 Office: Avon Ctrl Schs 191 Clinton St Avon NY 14414 Office Phone: 585-226-2455. E-mail: mcole@avoncsd.org.

COLE, MAX, artist; b. Hodgeman County, Kans., Feb. 14, 1937; BA, Fort Hays State U., 1961; MFA, U. Ariz., 1964. One-man shows include Louver Gallery, LA, 1978, 80, Sidney Janis Gallery, NYC, 1977, 80, Zabriskie Gallery, NY, 1987, Haines Gallery, San Francisco, 1988, 93, 96, 98, Galerie Schlegl, Zurich, 1990, 96, 99-2000, Mus. Folkwang, Essen, Germany, 1993, Kunstraum Kassel (Germany), 1992, Roswell (N.Mex.) Mus. and Art Ctr., 1996, Stark Gallery, NY, Galerie Michael Strum, Stuttgart, 1997, 99, Mus. Modern Art, Otterndorf, Germany, 1998, Haus Konstructive und Konkrete Kunst, Zurich, 2001, Walter Storms Gallery, Munich, 2002, Kunstverein, Aschaffenberg, Germany, 2002, Diozesan Museum, Cologne, 2004; exhibited in group shows including LA County Mus. Art, 1976, Corcoran Gallery Art, Washington, 1977, La Jolla Mus., 1980, Santa Barbara Mus., 1980, Mus. Fine Arts of N.Mex., 1984, Neuberger Mus., Purchase, NY, 1984, Marilyn Pearl Gallery, NYC, 1985, Pratt Manhattan Ctr. Gallery, 1985, UCLA, 1988, Nat. Gallery Modern Art, New Delhi, 1988, Panza Found., Verese, Italy, 1995, Aagauer Kunsthaus, Aarau, Switzerland, 1995, Trento (Italy) Mus., 1996, Galerie Schlegl, Zurich, 1996, Manif, 1997, Internat. Art Forum, Seoul, 1997, Mus. Modern Art, Otterndorf, Germany, 1998, Haines Gallery, San Francisco, 1998; represented in permanent collections LA County Mus. Art, Newport Harbor Mus. Art, La Jolla Mus. Contemporary Art, Mus. N.Mex., Dallas Mus. Art, Santa Barbara Mus., Everson Mus., Tel Aviv Mus., La. Mus., Van Der Heyt Mus., Wuppertal, Germany, Denmark, Panza Collection, Italy, Diozesan Mus., Cologne, Chiat Found., NY, Panza Collection, Italy, Lembach Haus, Munich, Ingolstaadt Mus., Germany. Address: PO Box 56 Ruby NY 12475

COLE, NATALIE MARIA, singer; b. LA, Feb. 6, 1950; d. Nathaniel Adam and Maria (Harkins) Cole; m. Marvin J. Yancy, July 31, 1976 (div. 1980); 1 child, Robert Adam; m. Andre Fischer, Sept. 16, 1989 (div. 1995); m. Rev. Kenneth Dupress, Oct. 12, 2001 (div. 2004). BA in Child Psychology, U. Mass., 1972. Rec. singles and albums, 1975—; albums include Dangerous, 1985, Everlasting, 1987, The Natalie Cole Collection, 1987, Inseparable, Thankful, Good To Be Back, 1989, Unforgettable, 1991 (4 grammys, 3 grammys 1992), Too Much Weekend, 1992, I'm Ready, 1992, I've Got Love On My Mind, 1992, Take A Look, 1993 (Grammy award nominee best jazz vocal 1994), Holly and Ivy, 1994, Stardust (2 Grammy awards), Magic of Christmas, 1999, Snowfall on the Sahara, 1999, Greatest Hits, 2000, Ask a Woman Who Knows, 2002; television appearances include Big Break (host), 1990, Lily in Winter, 1994; appeared in TV movies The Wizard of Oz in Concert (as Glinda), 1995, Always Outnumbered, 1998, Freak City, 1999; co-author: Angel on My Shoulder, 2000; composer Easter Egg Escapade, 2005. Recipient Grammy award for best new artist, 1975, best Rhythm and Blues female vocalist 1976; recipient 1 gold single, 3 gold albums; recipient 2 Image awards NAACP 1976, 77; Am. Music award 1978, other awards. Mem.: Nat. Assn. Rec. Arts & Scis., AFTRA, Delta Sigma Delta. Baptist. Home: 700 N San Vicente Blvd Ste G910 West Hollywood CA 90069-5061

COLE, RACHEL P., science educator; b. McKenney, Va., Sept. 24, 1942; d. Alex Luther and Fannie Wynn Parham; m. Moses Cole, Sept. 20, 1969; 1 child, Marsha Lynn. BS in Biology, Va. State U., Petersburg, 1964; BA in Biology, NYU, 2002. CLU; ChFC, cert. Notary Pub. Sci. tchr. Franklin City Schs., Va., 1964—66; pension cons. Equitable Life, N.Y.C., 1966—91; sub. tchr. Bd. of Edn., N.Y.C., 1992—98; tchr. Aux. Svc. High Schs., N.Y.C., 1998—. Pres. Black Tchrs. Who Care, N.Y.C., 2000—; chairperson Scholarship Commn., N.Y.C., NY, 1993—; pres. Wynn's Family Reunion; treas. Fitts, Parham, Walker Family Reunion. Mem.: NAUW (fin. sec., Women of Yr. 2005—06, named Woman of Yr.), Va. State U. Alumni Assn. Democrat. Baptist. Avocations: reading, watching basketball, tennis.

COLE, SALLY J. (SARAH JEWELL COLE), archaeologist, researcher; b. Murfreesboro, Tenn., Apr. 8, 1942; d. John Jennnings and Sarah Hays Jewell; m. Charles Robert Cole, June 13, 1964. BA, Vanderbilt U., 1964, Mesa State Coll., 1981; MA, Norwich U., 1989. Ind. profl. photographer, various locations, 1968-82; ind. profl. archaeologist, 1981—. Profl. archaeologist-rsch. assoc. Utah Mus. Natural History, U. Utah, Salt Lake City, 1992—; cons. Mesa Verde Nat. Park, Colo., 1996—, U.S. Bur. Land Mgmt., Ariz., Colo., Utah; adj. dept. anthropology Ft. Lewis Coll., Durango, Colo. Author: Legacy on Stone: Rock Art of the Colorado Plateau and Four Corners Region, 1990, Katsina Iconography in Homol'ovi Rock Art, Middle Little Colorado River, Arizona, 1992, New Dimensions in Rock Art Studies, 2004, The Mesa Verde World, 2006; contbr. articles to profl. jours. Trustee Mus. Western Colo., Grand Junction, 1986-92. Grantee rsch. and publ. grantee, Colo. Endowment for the Humanities, 1988—89, 2000—01, field rsch. grantee, Ctr. for Field Rsch.-Earthwatch, 1993—2001, rsch. grantee, Colo. Hist. Soc., 1996—97, Colo. Hist. Soc. and Mesa Verde Nat. Pk. Mus. Assn., 1999—, Colo. Hist. Soc. and Ft. Lewis Coll., 2002—. Mem. Soc. for Am. Archaeology, Colo. Archaeol. Soc. (adv. bd. mem. 1986-92), Colo. Coun. Profl. Archaeologists (sec. 1985-86). Avocations: backpacking, hiking, wildlife watching, rafting, canoeing. Office: Utah Mus Natural History Univ Utah Pres Cir Salt Lake City UT 84112 also: Ft Lewis Coll Dept Anthropology 1000 Rim Dr Durango CO 81301

COLE, SANDRA SUE, healthcare educator; d. Bennie Frank and Ruby Pearl Cole. AA, Tyler Jr. Coll., Tex., 1964; BS, Stephen F. Austin State U., Nacodoches, Tex., 1967, MEd, 1969; D Phys. Edn., Ind. U., Bloomington, 1978. Asst. instr. Tarleton State U., Stephenville, Tex., 1967—68; grad. asst. Stephen F. Austin State U., 1968—69, instr., 1969—74, asst. prof., 1974—81, assoc. prof., 1981—89, prof. kinesiology and health sci., 1989—. Named to, Tex. Hall of Fame, 1995; Lucille Norton scholar, Stephen F. Austin State U., 1966, faculty rsch. mini-grantee, 1994, NDEA fellow, Ind. U., 1972—73. Mem.: NEA, AAHPERD, Tex. Assn. Health, Phys. Edn., Recreation and Dance (sec. measurement and evaluation sect. 1981—82, region VII rep. bd. dirs. 1986—89, sec. tech. sec. 2000, chmn.-elect tech. sect. 2001, chmn. tech. sect. 2002, past chmn. tech. sect. 2003), Tex. Faculty Assn., Tex. State Tchrs. Assn., Delta Psi Kappa, Phi Delta Kappa (sec. Stephen E. Austin State U. chpt. 1996—98), Delta Kappa (pres. Sigma chpt. 1986—88). Home: 629 County Rd 8201 Nacogdoches TX 75964-2129

COLE, SUSAN A., academic administrator, language educator; m. David Cole, two children. BA in English and Am. Lit., Columbia U., 1962; MA in English and Am. Lit., Brandeis U., 1964, PhD in English and Am. Lit., 1972. Tchg. asst. Clark U., 1964-65; assoc. prof. CCUNY-N.Y.C. Tech. Coll., 1968-77; assoc. dean for acad. affairs Antioch U., 1977-80; v.p. for univ. adminstrn. and pers. Rutgers U., New Brunswick, N.J., 1980-92; pres., prof. English Met. State U., Mpls. and St. Paul, 1993-98; pres. Montclair State U., Upper Montclair, N.J., 1998—. Guest adj. assoc. prof. Pace U., fall 1977; vis. sr. fellow in acad. adminstrn. Office Acad. Affairs, CUNY, 1991-93; bd. dirs. Western State Bank; presenter in field. Contbr. articles to profl. jours. Chmn. edn. resolutions sessions, coord. edn. panels N.Y. State meeting Internat. Women's Year, Albany, 1977; agy. mem. N.J. Gov.'s Mgmt. Improvement Program, 1982; v.p., bd. dirs. Bklyn. Ecumenical Coops., 1988-90; mem. cmty. health care policy task force Robert Wood Johnson Univ. Hosp., New Brunswick, 1991; mem. blue ribon task force Mpls. Pub. Libr., 1994-95; mem. steering com. Greater St. Paul Tomorrow, 1994—; trustee Twin Cities Pub. TV, 1994—, Sci. Mus. Minn., 1994; bd. dirs., mem. exec. com. St. Paul Riverfront Corp., 1994—; v.p., founding bd. dirs. St. Paul Pub. Schs. Found., 1995—; bd. dirs. St. Paul Found., 1995—. Mem. Am. Assn. State Colls. and Univs. (urban and met. steering com. 1993—), Am. Coun. on Edn. (Commn. on Women in Higher Edn. 1993—), Greater Mpls. C. of C. (enterprise devel. task force 1994—). Office: Montclair State U Office of Pres 1 Normal Ave Montclair NJ 07043-1624

COLE, SUSAN STOCKBRIDGE, retired theater educator; b. San Francisco, Jan. 26, 1939; d. Elmer Leroy Stockbridge and Martha Louise Rosenauer; m. John Michael Day, June 28, 1965 (div. May 1968); m. Willie Robert Cole, June 12, 1976. AB, Stanford (Calif.) U., 1960, MA, 1961; PhD, U. Oreg., 1972. Asst. prof. theatre Bakersfield (Calif.) Coll., 1962-69; grad. tchg. fellow U. Oreg., Eugene, 1969-72; asst. prof. theatre Keuka Coll., Keuka Park, NY, 1972-75; prof. Appalachian State U., Boone, NC, 1975—2005, dept. chair theatre and dance, 1989—2005; ret., 2005. Cons. Dept. Pub. Instrn., Raleigh, N.C., 1980—2005, N.C. Arts Coun., Raleigh, 1989-93. Author: American National Biography, 1999, Notable Women in American Theatre, 1990; designer more than 100 play prodns., 1962—; dir. more than 60 play prodns. Recipient Outstanding Svc. award, Coll. Fine and Applied Arts, Appalachian State U., 2005. Mem.: Am. Soc. for Theatre Rsch., Assn. for Theatre in Higher Edn., N.C. Theatre Conf. (pres. 1991—92, Svc. award 1997, Disting. Career award 2005), Southeastern Theatre Conf. (pres. 1998—99, Suzanne Davis award 2002), Lions Club Internat. (dist. officer 1997—, treas. 1999—2004, past pres.), Alpha Psi Omega (pres. 1997—2002). Democrat. Episcopalian. Avocation: reading. Home: PO Box 220 Todd NC 28684-0220 Personal E-mail: coless@appstate.edu.

COLEGATE, CAROL ANN, elementary school educator; b. Hamilton, Ohio, Aug. 26, 1950; d. Byron Lee Knollman and Alma Dean Haas; m. Gary D. Colegate, Sept. 20, 1949; children: Kevin Dean, Eric Bryan. BS, Miami U., Oxford, Ohio, 1971, MS, 1981. Tchr. S.W. Local, Harrison, Ohio, Ross Local, Hamilton, Ohio. Cons. in field. Contbr. articles to mags. Named Conservation Tchr. of Yr., Ohio, 2002; recipient Tchg. Excellence award, State Farm, 2002, Ross, 2004. Mem.: Nat. Sci. Tchrs. Assn., Butler County Sheep Assn. (sec. 2004—, treas. 2004—). Home: 2934 Morgan Ross Rd Hamilton OH 45013

COLELLA, CATHLEEN, waste management administrator; Pres. Hazardous Elimination Corp., Farmingdale, NY. Rep. Women Pres.'s Edn. Orgn., NY. Office: Hazardous Elimination Corp 195 H Central Ave Farmingdale NY 11735

COLEMAN, ARLENE FLORENCE, retired pediatrics nurse; b. Braham, Minn., Apr. 8, 1926; d. William and Christine (Judin) C.; m. John Dunkerken, May 30, 1987. Diploma in nursing, U. Minn., 1947, BS, 1953; MPH, Loma Linda U., 1974. RN, Calif. Operating room scrub nurse Calif. Luth. Hosp., L.A., 1947-48; indsl. staff nurse Good Samaritan Hosp., L.A., 1948-49; staff nurse Passavant Hosp., Chgo., 1950-51; student health nurse Moody Bible Inst., Chgo., 1950-51; staff nurse St. Andrews Hosp., Mpls., 1951-53; pub. health nurse Bapt. Gen. Conf. Bd. of World Missions, Ethiopia, Africa, 1954-66; staff pub. health nurse County of San Bernadino, Calif., 1966-68, sr. pub. health nurse Calif., 1968-73, pediatric nurse practitioner Calif., 1973—. Contbr. articles to profl. jours. Mem. bd. dist. missions Bapt. Gen. Conf., Calif., 1978-84; mem. adv. coun. Kaiser Hosp., Fontana, Calif., 1969-85, Bethel Sem. West, San Diego, 1987—; bd. dirs. Casa Verdugo Retirement Home, Hemet, Calif., 1985—; active Calvary Bapt. Ch., Redlands, Calif., 1974—; mem. S.W. Bapt. Conf. Social Ministries, 1993—. With Cadet Nurse Corps USPHS, 1944-47. Calif. State Dept. Health grantee, 1973. Fellow Nat. Assn. Pediatric Nurse Assocs. and Practitioners; mem. Calif. Nurses Assn. (state nursing coun. 1974-76). Democrat. Avocations: gardening, travel, reading. Home: 622 Esther Way Redlands CA 92373-5822

COLEMAN, BARBARA MCREYNOLDS, artist; b. Omaha, May 5, 1956; d. Zachariah Aycock and Mary Barbara (McCulloh) McR.; m. Stephen Dale Dent, Mar. 12, 1983 (div. Dec. 20, 1992); children: Madeleine Victoria, Matthew Stephen; m. Ross Coleman, Oct. 16, 1993; 1 child, Mia Jeanne Coleman. Student, U. N.Mex., 1979, MA in Cmty. and Regional Planning, 1984. Lectr. U. N.Mex. Sch. Arch., Albuquerque, 1979—82, 1991—2000; assoc. planner, urban designer planning divsn. City of Albuquerque, 1982-84, city planner, urban designer N.Mex. redevel. divsn., 1984-88; v.p. Hydra Aquatic, Inc., Albuquerque, 1997—. Cons. City of Albuquerque Redevel. Dept., 1987-88; urban design cons. Southwest Land Rsch., Albuquerque, 1991, instr. at Ctr. for Action and Contemplation, Albuquerque, NM, 1999—. Columnist: Kids and Art, 1990-92; author: Coors Corridor Plan (Albuquerque Conservation Assn. Urban Design award 1984), Electric Facilities Plan, Downtown Core Revitalization Strategy and Sector Development Plan; contbr. articles to profl. jours. and mags.; chpts. to books; exhibited at Dartmouth St. Gallery, Albuquerque, 1992—, Chimayo (N.Mex.) Trade and Mercantile, JoAnne Chappel Gallery, San Francisco, Southwest Arts Festival, Albuquerque, Act I Gallery, Taos, N.Mex., Nat. Arts Club, NYC, Hermitage Mus., Norfolk, Va., Schimmel Ctr. for the Arts, Pace U., NYC, Musée Granet, Aix-en-Provence, France, Fine Arts Gallery, Albuquerque, 1999 (1st pl.), Paragon Gallery, Albuquerque, Florence Biennial, 2005. Vol. art tchr. A. Montoya Elem. Sch., Roosevelt Mid. Sch., Albuquerque, 1989—. Recipient First Pl. for pastels N.Mex. Art League, 1991, Merit award Pastel Soc. of S.W., 1989, 1st pl. award N.Mex. State Fair Fine Arts Gallery, Albuquerque, 1999; finalist Nat. Cath. Reporter Jesus 2000 contest. Mem. Pastel Soc. of Am. (signature mem.), Pastel Soc. N.Mex. (pres. 1991-92, Best of Show 1990 award, 4th pl. Am. Artist Mag. award 1999). Democrat. Episcopalian. Avocations: hiking, skiing, running. Office: U NMex Sch Architecture Albuquerque NM 87131-0001

COLEMAN, BOBBIE RUTH, literature and language educator; b. Nashville, Ark., Sept. 17, 1949; d. Joe A. and Mary Ruth Sharp; m. Tom R. Coleman, July 26, 1980; children: Luke T., Leah Jo. BA English, Harding U., Searcy, Ark., 1971; MEd, Harding U., 1980. Tchr. Searcy H.S., 1976—. Named Searcy Tchr. of Yr., Ark. Journalism Advisor of Yr.; named to Hall of Honor, Searcy Edn. Found. Office: Searcy High School 301 N Ella Searcy AR 72143

COLEMAN, CAROLYN QUILLOIN, association executive; b. Savannah, Ga. 1 child. BS in History, Savannah State Coll.; MS in Adult Edn. and C.C. Adminstrn., N.C. A&T State U. Nat. staff mem. NAACP, N.C. state exec. dir., so. voter edn. dir., dir. voter registration/voter edn./voter turnout campaign in the South, 1989—92, coord. voter registration Ga., 1990, La., 1991, mem. nat. bd. dirs.; dir. James B. Hunt Jr. campaign for gov., 1992; spl. asst. for cmty. affairs to Gov. James B. Hunt Jr., 1993—. Mem.: Nat. Assn. Negro Bus. and Profl. Women, Greensboro Br. NAACP, Wildacres Leadership Initiative, Women's Polit. Forum, Delta Sigma Theta (Greensboro Alumnae chpt.). Baptist. Office: NAACP 4805 Mt Hope Dr Baltimore MD 21215

COLEMAN, CLAIRE KOHN, public relations executive; b. New Castle, Pa., Nov. 19, 1924; d. Louis and Florence (Frank) Kohn; m. Frederick H. Coleman, Mar. 10, 1957; children: Franklin, Elliot. BA, Pa. State U., 1945. Market editor Fairchild Publs., N.Y.C., 1945—48; asst. home editor N.Y. Times, 1949—50; pub. rels. dir. United Wallpaper, Chgo., 1950—53, Assoc. Am. Artists, N.Y.C., 1953—54; dir. Wallpaper Info. Bur., N.Y.C., 1954; dept. head Roy Bernard, Inc., N.Y.C., 1955—58; pub. rels. dir. Siesel Co., N.Y.C., 1972—, sr. v.p., 1988; pres. Tisch Trask Comm. Resources Pub. Rels. Group, 1988—89; sr. v.p. Anthony M. Franco, N.Y.C., 1989—90; pres. Coleman Comm., N.Y.C., 1990—. Ctrl. steering com. Sch. Dist. Critical Assessments, New Rochelle, NY, 1969—71; active Mayor's Adv. Coun. on Aging, 1966, Mayor's Adv. Coun. on Bd. Edn. Appts., 1969; v.p. Coun. of PTAs, 1969—70; chmn. women's divsn. United Jewish Appeal, New Rochelle, 1971; v.p. Found. Women Execs. Pub. Rels., 1992—93, pres., 1993—94, bd. dirs., 1998—; bd. dirs., v.p. Beechmont Assn., 1969—74, adv. bd., 1990—. Fellow: Internat. Furnishings and Design Assn. (formerly Home Fashions League) (founder 1947, exec. chmn. 1947, pres. 1947, v.p. 1948—50, v.p. Chgo. chpt. 1950—53, nat. treas. 1977—78, nat. pres. 1980—81, v.p. N.Y. chpt. 1994, nat. v.p. mktg. 1998—2000, v.p. NY chpt. 2006, Cir. of Excellence award 1994, Internat. Hon. Recognition award 1998); mem.: Women Execs. Pub. Rels. (bd. dirs. 1983—84, sec. 1986—87, pres.-elect 1994—95, pres. 1996—97). Fax: 914-576-6885. Office Phone: 914-633-6914. E-mail: ckcpr@aol.com.

COLEMAN, DEBBIE L., music educator; d. Elroy and Katie Purcell Fowler; m. Edward E. Coleman, Apr. 8, 1995. MusB in Edn., U. Ga., 1981; MusM in Edn., Valdosta State U., Ga., 1989; specialist in Ednl. Leadership, Ga. Coll. and State U., 2005. Cert. tchr. music P-12 Ga., ednl. leadership Ga. Gen. music tchr. Bacon County Elem. Sch., Alma, Ga., 1982—84; choral music tchr. Vidalia (Ga.)City Schs., 1984—86; gen. music/choral tchr. Waycross (Ga.) City Schs., 1986—91; choral music tchr. Houston County Schs., Perry, Ga., 1991—. Exploratory team leader Houston County Schs., 1992—99. Mem.: PAGE (assoc.), Am. Choral Dirs. Assn. (assoc.), Music Educator's Nat. Conf. (assoc.), Ga. Music Educators Assn. (assoc.; dist. choral chair 1995—2001, clinician 1998, all-state statewide audition organizer 1998—2000, Dist. 11 honor choirs organizer 1998—2003, all-state testing selector 1999—2004, vice-president of all-state activities 2001—03, state choral chmn. 2005—, cert. choral adjudicator). Baptist. Achievements include development of a system for legally blind students, using a modified braille system, to easily participate in choral sight-reading activities, including auditions and all-state choirs. Avocations: travel, sewing, motorcycling, singing. Home: 240 Kimbrell Dr Macon GA 31217 Office: Huntington Mid Sch 206 Wellborn Rd Warner Robins GA 31088 Office Phone: 478-542-2240. E-mail: dcoleman@hcbe.net.

COLEMAN, DEBRA LYNN, electrical engineer; b. Mobile, Ala., Apr. 7, 1966; d. Fred and Mattie Lois (Carter) C. BSEE, Boston U., 1988; MSEE, U. Wash., Seattle, 2002. Test engr. Raytheon Corp., Andover, Mass., 1987-88; liaison design engr. Boeing Co., Everett, Wash., 1988-89, software engr. Seattle, 1989-90, avionics engr. Renton, Wash., 1990-95, sr. payloads engr. Everett, Wash., 1995—98, acct. mgr., 1998—2001, sr. elec. engr., 2001—05; CEO Woof Studios, 2005—; lead sys. engr. Mooy Inc., Seattle, 2005—. Avocations: writing, reading, history. Home: 3020 21st Ave S Seattle WA 98144-5906 Personal E-mail: coolcandy@msn.com.

COLEMAN, DOROTHY CHARMAYNE, nurse; b. July 13, 1958; BS in Nursing, Mich. State U., 1981; MS in Nursing, Wayne State U., Detroit, 1988. RN. Obstet. high risk staff nurse Hutzel Hosp., Detroit, 1983—; ob-gyn. nurse practitioner The Wellness Plan, Detroit, 1991-98; clin. nursing instr. Wayne State U., Detroit, 1994, 95, 99. Named Nurse of Yr., Hutzel Hosp., 2001. Home: 20801 Kipling St Oak Park MI 48237-2747

COLEMAN, ELIZABETH, college president; b. NYC, Nov. 23, 1937; d. Lewis and Sophie (Brantman) Ginsburg; m. Aaron Coleman, June 14, 1959; children: Daniel, David. BA, U. Chgo., 1958; MA, Cornell U., 1959; PhD, Columbia U., 1965; Doctorate (hon.), Hofstra U.; LLD (hon.), U. Vt. Instr. humanities SUNY, N.Y.C., 1960-65; assoc. dean faculty New Sch. Social Research, N.Y.C., 1966-76, dean Coll. Arts and Scis., 1977-84, prof. literature and humanities, 1984-87; pres. Bennington (Vt.) Coll., 1987—. Vis. lectr. Hebrew U., 1972, SUNY-Stony Brook, 1975; curriculum cons. Howard U., 1973; chmn. outside evaluating com. CUNY, 1976 Contbr. articles to profl. pubs. Mem. nat. adv. coun. Woodrow Wilson Found., 1990; bd. dirs. Ctrl. Vt. Pub. Svc. Corp., 1990-96; bd. trustees Inst. Ecosystem Studies, 1994. Fellow Ford Found., 1954-58; Woodrow Wilson fellow, 1958-59; F.J.E. Woodbridge fellow Columbia U., 1963-64; Pres.'s fellow Columbia U., 1964-65 Mem. MLA, Am. Assn. Colls. Home and Office: Bennington Coll Office of Pres Rte 67A Bennington VT 05201

COLEMAN, FAY, literature and language educator, director; b. Detroit, May 8, 1949; d. Hiter Carrington and Etta Jewel (Roberts) Coleman. BS in English and History, Ea. Mich. U., 1971, MA in English Lit. and Langs., 1972. Tchr. adult edn. Melvindale High Sch., Mich., 1973—84; substitute tchr. Taylor Pub. Schs., Mich., 1974—77; tchr. English, history Taylor Ctr. HS, 1977—80, tchr. English, yearbook advisor, 1993—97; tchr. English, history West Jr. HS, Taylor, 1984—85, Brake Jr. HS, Taylor, 1985—93; tchr. English, dept. chair John F. Kennedy HS, Taylor, 1997—. Social chair Brake Jr. High Sch., 1985—92, union rep., 1991—92. Baptist. Avocations: travel, gardening, sewing. Home: 21609 Bayside Saint Clair Shores MI 48081 Office: John F Kennedy High Sch 13505 Kennedy Dr Taylor MI 48180

COLEMAN, JEAN BLACK, nurse, physician assistant; b. Sharon, Pa., Jan. 11, 1925; d. Charles B. and Sue E. (Dougherty) Black; m. Donald A. Coleman, July 3, 1946; children: Sue Ann Lopez, Donald Ashley. Grad., Spencer Hosp. Sch. Nursing, Meadville, Pa., 1945; student, Vanderbilt U., 1952-54. RN, Ga. Nurse, dir. nursing Bulloch Meml. Hosp., Statesboro, Ga, 1948-51, nurse supr. surgery, 1954-67, dir. nursing, 1967-71; physician's asst., nurse anesthetist Office Dr. Robert H. Swint, Statesboro, 1971-96; physician asst. Office Dr. Earl L. Alderman, Statesboro, 1996-98, Dr. Swaroop Reddy, Statesboro, 1998—. Mem. physician's asst. adv. com. Ga. Med. Bd., 1989-97; mem. physician assts. adv. com. Ga. Bd. Med. Examiners, 1987-97, ex-officio mem., 1994-95. Recipient Dean Day Smith Svc. to Mankind award, 1995; named Woman of Yr. in med. field Bus. and Profl. Women, 1980; Paul Harris fellow Rotary Club. Mem. ANA, Am. Acad. Physician Assts., Ga. Nurses Assn., Ga. Assn. Physician Assts. (bd. dirs. 1975-79, v.p. 1979-80, pres. 1980-81). Republican. Roman Catholic.

COLEMAN, JO-ANN S.E., social worker; d. Joseph B. Edwards and Annie M. Pimble-Edwards. A in Theology, Ch. of Christ Bible Inst., 1951; B in Religious En., Cmty. Bible Inst., 1957, M in Christian Counseling; DD, Wayne Theol. Sem., 2005. Ordained minister, cert. chaplain. Clerical Health and Hosp. Corp., N.Y.C., 1981—89; caseworker Dept. Homeless Svcs., N.Y.C., 1989—2002, supr., 2002—. Assoc. pastor White Rock Bible Ch., Inc., N.Y.C., 1972. Singer: Timoth Wright's Concert Choir. Mem. concert choir N.Y. Fellowship Mass Choir; mem. James Cleveland Gospel Mus. Workshop Am., Women of Substance, Bereavement Consortium Ctrl. Harlem, Inc. Baptist. Avocations: reading, singing, bowling, travel. Office: NYC DHS/Yale Holel 316 W 97th St New York NY 10025

COLEMAN, KATHRYN ANNE, lawyer; b. July 19, 1959; BA magna cum laude, Pomona Coll., 1980; JD, Univ. Calif., Berkeley, 1983. Bar: Calif. 1983. Law clk. Judge Martin Pence US Dist. Ct. Dist of Hawaii, 1983—84; joined Gibson Dunn & Crutcher LLP, San Francisco, 1986—, now ptnr. bus. restructuring and reorganization practice group, and ptnr.-in-charge Palo Alto office. Assoc. editor Calif. Law Rev., 1981—82, sr. articles editor, 1982—83. Mem.: Calif. State Bar Assn. (past mem. Uniform Comml. Code Com.), Phi Beta Kappa, Order of Coif. Office: Gibson Dunn & Crutcher LLP Ste 3100 One Montgomery St San Francisco CA 94104 Office Phone: 415-393-8265. Office Fax: 415-374-8417. Business E-Mail: kcoleman@gibsondunn.com.

COLEMAN, MARSHIA ADAMS, social sciences educator; b. Conway, Ark., Oct. 22, 1956; d. Marshall and Lucille Wolford Adams; m. George Coleman Jr., July 22, 1996; 1 child, Adam Joseph McClung. BS in Edn., U. Ctrl. Ark., 1988, MS in Edn., 1991. Cert. tchr. Ark. Tchr. Sacred Heart Sch., Morrilton, Ark., 1988—90, Little Rock (Ark.) Sch. Dist., 1990—. Tchr. Park U. Little Rock (Ark.) AFB, Jacksonville, 2000—; writer curriculum Little Rock (Ark.) Sch. Dist., 1990—; creater, writer Holocaust curriculum Park U.; Holocaust rschr. Charles U., Prague, Czech Republic, Jagiellonian U., Krakow, Poland; field rschr. U. Western Cape, Cape Town, South Africa; spkr. in field. Co-author: Celebrating Arkansas, 1997, 2002. Mem. PTA, Forest Heights Mid. Sch., mem. Ark. coun. social studies; mem. food team Bethlehem House St. Peter's Episc. Ch., Conway, Ark.; pres. bd. Knowing Our Past Found. Recipient Stephens Outstanding Tchr. award, City Edn. Trust, 2004. Fellow: Delta Tchr. Acad.; mem.: APA, NEA, Little Rock Classroom Tchrs. Assn., Ark. Edn. Assn., U.S. Holocaust Meml. Mus. Republican. Episcopalian. Avocations: horseback riding, reading, writing, music, walking. Home: 109 Cedar Valley Dr El Paso AR 72045 Office: McClellan High Sch 9417 Geyer Springs Rd Little Rock AR 72209 Office Phone: 501-447-2755. Business E-Mail: marshia.coleman@lrsd.org.

COLEMAN, MARY H., state legislator; b. Noxapater, Miss., July 25, 1946; m. Cayle Coleman, children Marcus, Crystal, Arqullas. Student, L.A. Trade-Tech. Coll., Tougaloo Coll. Mem. Miss. Ho. of Reps., 1987—; mem. edn., ins., pub. bldgs., pub. health coms.; mem. ways and means com. Exec. asst. to State Auditor, 1987-92; pres. Nat. Black Caucus of State Legislators. Recipient 100 Most Influential Black Americans, Ebony mag., 2006. Mem. NAACP, NOW, SCLC, Women in Govt., Alpha Kappa Alpha (Beta Delta Omega chpt.). Democrat. Baptist. Home: 308 Lynwood Ln Jackson MS 39206-3931 Office: State Capitol Bldg PO Box 1018 Jackson MS 39215-1018 Office Phone: 601-359-3360. E-mail: mcoleman@mail.house.state.ms.us.*

COLEMAN, MARY SUE, academic administrator; b. Richmond, Ky, Oct. 2, 1943; m. Kenneth Coleman; 1 child, Jonathan. BA, Grinnell Coll., 1965; PhD, U. N.C., 1969; DSc (hon.), Dartmouth Coll., 2005. NIH postdoctoral fellow U. N.C., Chapel Hill, 1969—70, U. Ky., 1971—72, instr., rsch. assoc. depts. biochemistry and medicine, 1972—75, asst. prof. dept. biochemistry, 1975—80, assoc. prof. dept. biochemistry, 1980—85, prof. dept. biochemistry, 1985—90; prof. dept. biochemistry and biophysics U. N.C., Chapel Hill, 1990—93; provost, v.p. for academic affairs, prof. biochemistry U. N.Mex., 1993—95; pres., prof. biochemistry, prof. biol. scis. U. Iowa, Iowa City, 1995—2002; pres. U. Mich., Ann Arbor, 2002—. NSF summer trainee Grinnell Coll., 1962; acting dir. basir rsch. U. Ky. Cancer Ctr., 1980—83; scientific cons. Abbott Labs., 1981—85, Collaborative Rsch., 1983—88; assoc. dir. rsch. L.P. Markey Cancer Ctr. U. Ky., 1983—90, dir. grad. studies biochem., 1984—87, trustee, 1987—90; assoc. provost, dean rsch. U. N.C., 1990—92; scientific cons. Life Techs., Inc., 1992; vice chancellor grad students and rsch. U. N.C., 1992—93; pres. Iowa Health Sys., 1995—2002; mem. Big Ten Coun. Pres.'s, 1995—2002; chair undergrad. edn. com. Am. Assn. Univs., 1997—; bd. trustees Univs. Rsch. Assn., 1998—; mem. task force on tchrs. edn. Am. Coun. Edn., 1998—; mem. Gov.'s Strategic Planning Coun., 1998—2000, Imagining Am. Pres.'s Coun., 1999—, Bus.-Higher Edn. Froum, 1999—; mem. rsch. accountability task force Am. Assn. Univs., 2000—; mem. stds. success adv. bd. Am. Assn. Univs. and he Pew Charitable Trusts, 2000—; co-chair Inst. Medicine Com. on Consequences of Uninsurance, 2000—; mem. Knight Commn., 2000—01; mem. exec. com. Am. Assn. Univs., 2001—; mem. bd. dirs. Johnson & Johnson, 2003—; bd. dirs. Meredith Corp., Am. Coun. Edn.; presenter in field. Mem. editl. bd.: Jour. Biol. Chemistry, 1989—93; contbr. articles to profl. jours. Trustee Crinnell Coll., 1996—; mem. bd. govs. Warren G. Magnuson Clin. Ctr., NIH, 1996—2000, State of Iowa Gov.'s ACCESS Edn. Commn., 1997; bd. dirs. United Way, Albuquerque, 1995; trustee John S. and James L. Knight Found., 2005—. Fellow postdoctral fellow, Clayton Found. Biochem. Inst., U. Tex., 1970—71. Fellow: AAAS, Am. Acad. Arts and Scis.; mem.: Nat. Coll. Athletic Assn. (bd. dirs. 2002—), Nat. Assn. State Univs. ans Land Grant Colls. Coun. Cchief Acad. Officers (exec. com. 1993—95), Am. Soc. Biochem. and Molecular Biology, Am. Assn. Cancer Rsch.*

COLEMAN, PATSY ANN, secondary school educator; b. Boyce, La., Jan. 20, 1946; d. Eugene Clark Watkins and Sibyl Melissa Miller; m. James Roy Coleman, May 31, 1968; children: James Eugene, William Travis. BS, Northwestern State U., Natchitoches, La., 1966, MS, postgrad., Northwestern State U., Natchitoches, La. Tchr. Buckeye HS, La., 1966—69, Menard HS, Alexandria, La., 1970—94, Northwood HS, Lena, La., 1994—. Named Outstanding Young Tchr., 1976, Tchr. of Yr. award, Walmart, 2004, Advisor of Yr. award, La. Assn. Student Coun.; recipient, So. Assn. Student Coun., 1980, Warren Schull award, Nat. Assn. Secondary Sch. Prin., La., 2003. Methodist. Office Phone: 318-793-8021. Office Fax: 318-793-8503.

COLEMAN, PHYLLIS, law educator; b. Bronx; d. Harvey and Amy Davis Gallub. BS in Journalism, U. Fla., 1970, MEd, 1975, JD, 1978. Bar: Fla. 1978, Fla. Supreme Ct. 1978. Reporter, news editor Gwinnett Daily News, Lawrenceville, Ga., 1972—73; assoc. Broad & Cassel, Bay Harbor, Fla., 1978—79; from asst. to full prof. law Nova Southeastern U., Fort Lauderdale, Fla., 1979—. Editor: Family Law: Text and Commentary (annual), 1997—; co-author: (casebook) Sports Law: Cases and Materials, 1999, Bush v. Gore: The Fight for Florida's Vote, 2001; contbr. articles to profl. jours., chapters to books. Mem. Broward County Managed Care Ombudsman Com., Fort Lauderdale, 2002; selection com. Hall of Fame Ind. Fla. Alligator, Gainesville, Fla., 2003—05; founding mem. animal law com. Fla. Bar, 2003—05. Named Outstanding Faculty Mem., Black Law Students, Nova Southeastern U., 1994, Prof. of Yr., Student Bar Assn., Nova Southeastern U., 2004—05; named to Hall of Fame, U. Fla., 1971, Alligator Hall of Fame, Ind. Fla. Alligator, 1999. Liberal. Jewish. Avocation: scuba diving. Office: Nova Southeastern U 3305 College Ave Fort Lauderdale FL 33314-7721 Office Phone: 954-262-6166. Office Fax: 954-262-3835. E-mail: colemanp@nsu.law.nova.edu.

COLEMAN, SANDRA SLOAN, librarian, academic dean; b. Summit, N.J., Mar. 20, 1943; d. John Whitfield and Dorothy May (Laux) S.; m. William F. Coleman, Aug. 11, 1965. BA, Eckerd Coll., 1966; M.L.S., Indiana U., Bloomington, 1970; M. Mgmt., U. N.Mex., 1981. Govt. documents librarian Ind. U. Library, Bloomington, 1968-70; cataloger, head tech. services, assoc. for public services, acting law librarian U. N.Mex. Law Sch. Library, Albuquerque, 1971-76; head reference dept., asst. prof., acting asst. dean for pub. services U. N.Mex. Gen. Library, Albuquerque, 1976-81; dep. law librarian Harvard Law Sch., Cambridge, Mass., 1982-89, sr. devel. officer, 1989-90, adminstrv. dean, 1990—. Coun. on Library Resources Acad. Library Mgmt. intern Stanford U., Calif., 1978-79; vis. prof. Sch. of Library Sci. Tex. Woman's U., Denton, 1981; mem. adv. com. The Arthur and Elizabeth Schlesinger Library on the History of Women in Am., Radcliffe Coll., 1983-87; vis. lectr. Simmons Coll. Sch. Library Sci., Boston, 1986; lectr. U. Calif.-Berkeley Grad. Sch. Libr. and Info. Studies, 1989; mem. adv. bd. Wellesley ABC, 1989—. Keyperson, United Way Campaign, Harvard U., Cambridge, 1983; mem. N.Mex. Gov.'s Adv. Council on Libraries, Santa Fe, 1974-75. HEA fellow Southwestern Library Assn., La. State U. Grad. Library Sch., 1975. Mem. Coun. for Advancement and Support Edn., Am. Assn. of Law Schools, Am. Assn. Law Libraries (cert. law librarian, chmn. acad. libraries sect. 1985-86, chmn. spl. interests sec. council, 1986-87), ALA, Assn. Coll. and Research Libraries (various coms.), Library Adminstrn. and Mgmt. Assn. (mem. various coms.) Democrat. Office: Harvard Law Sch Griswold Hall # 107 Cambridge MA 02138

COLEMAN, SHARON W., elementary school educator; d. James C. and Myrtis E. Worsham; children: Warren, Jared. BS, Miss. U. for Women, Columbus, 1971, MEd, 1974. Tchr. Cherokee County Schs., Woodstock, Ga., 1979—, Holly Springs Elem., Woodstock, Ga., 1999—. Chmn. dist. advancement Boy Scouts Am., Atlanta, 2006. Baptist. Home: 506 Arden Close Woodstock GA 30188-7891 Office: Holly Springs Elem 1965 Hickory Rd Canton GA 30115-4354 Office Phone: 770-345-5035. E-mail: rash71@bellsouth.net.

COLEMAN, WINIFRED ELLEN, academic administrator; b. Syracuse, NY, Oct. 3, 1932; d. Peter Andrew and Josephine (Fahey) C. BA, Le Moyne Coll., Syracuse, N.Y., 1954; MA, Marquette U., 1956; DHL (hon.), Le Moyne Coll., 1993. Dean of students Cazenovia (N.Y.) Coll., 1957-70, Trinity Coll., Washington, 1970-80; exec. dir. Nat. Coun. Catholic Women, Washington, 1980-85; pres. Cashel House, Ltd., Syracuse, NY, 1985—, St. Joseph Coll., West Hartford, Conn., 1991—. Trustee LeMoyne Coll., Syracuse, 1995—, The Mark Twain House, Hartford; trustee emerita Loretto Geriatric Ctr., Syracuse, N.Y.; pres. Assn. Mercy Coll. Presidents, 1993-97, Hartford Consortium for Higher Edn., 1993-97; bd. dirs. Conn. Higher Edn. Student Loan Adminstrn., Hartford Mutual Funds. Bd. dirs. St. Francis Hosp. and Med. Ctr. Hon. membership Trinity Coll. Alumnae, Washington, 1978, Cazenovia (N.Y.) Coll. Alumnae, 1961, Naming of Winifred E. Coleman Student Union, Cazenovia Coll., 1963; recipient Chantal Award, Catholic Woman of the Yr., 1965. Mem.: Nat. Jesuit Honor Soc. for Women, Gamma Pi Epsilon. Roman Catholic. Avocations: reading, composing lyrics. Home: 6010 Bay Hill Cir Jamesville NY 13078 Office: St Joseph Coll 1678 Asylum Ave West Hartford CT 06117-2764

COLEMAN-PERKINS, CAROLYN, retired medical/surgical nurse; b. Kansas City, Kans., Nov. 15, 1947; d. Samuel Coleman and Theorist Vernice Osborne-Coleman; m. Carl Edward Mitchell, June 1968 (div. Oct. 1973); 1 child, Vicki Lynn Mitchell; m. Charles Talmadge Perkins, July 20, 1977; 1 child, Cynthia Perkins. Diploma in nursing, 1966. Sales clk. J.C. Penney Dept. Store, Kansas City, Mo., 1964—65; nurse Bapt. Meml. Hosp., 1966—68, San Francisco Blood Bank, 1968—71, Kaiser Permanente Med. Ctr., 1972—2006, ret., 2006. V.p. Local 250 SEIU - United Healthcare Workers West, Oakland, Calif., 1988—. Democrat. Baptist. Avocations: football, walking. Home: 2208 89th Ave Oakland CA 94605-3928

COLEMAN SMITH, SALAAM, communications executive; b. 1970; m. Christopher Smith; 1 child, Asa. BS in Indsl. Engring., Stanford U. Mgmt. cons.; v.p., Programming Nickelodeaon/Nick at Nite; programming and creative exec. MTV Networks; sr. v.p., Programming E! Networks, 2003—06; sr. v.p. Style Network, E! Entertainment, Inc., 2006, exec. v.p., 2006—. Prin. mem. strategic planning team, Nickelodeon Networks. Named one of Top 35 Executives Under 35, Hollywood Reporter, 2003, 40 Executives Under 40, Multichannel News, 2006; Walter Kaitz Found. Cable TV Industry fellowship. Office: E! Entertainment Television Inc 5750 Wilshire Blvd Los Angeles CA 90036*

COLES, ANNA LOUISE BAILEY, retired dean, nurse; b. Kansas City, Kans., Jan. 16, 1925; d. Gordon Alonzo and Lillie Mai (Buchanan) Bailey; children: Margot, Michelle, Gina. Diploma, Freedmen's Hosp. Sch. Nursing, 1948; BSN, Avila Coll., Kansas City, Mo., 1958; MSN, Cath. U. Am., 1960, PhD in Higher Edn., 1967. Instr. VA Hosp., Topeka, 1950—52, supr. Kansas City, Mo., 1952—58; asst. dir. in-service edn. Freedmen's Hosp., Washington, 1960—61, adminstrv. asst. to DON, 1961—66, assoc. dir. nursing services, 1966—67, DON, 1967—69; dean Howard U. Coll. Nursing, Washington, 1968—86, dean emeritus, 1986—; pvt. practice Kansas City, Kans.; dir. minority devel. U. Kans., 1991—95. Pres. Nurses Examining Bd., 1967—68; cons. Gen. Rsch. Support Program, NIH, 1972—76; mem. Inst. Medicine, NAS, 1974—; cons. VA Ctrl. Office continuing edn. com., 1976—; mem. D.C. Health Planning Adv. Com., 1967—68, Tri-State Regional Planning Com. for Nursing Edn., 1969, Health Adv. Coun., Nat. Urban Coalition, 1971—73; bd. dirs. Hilton Grand Vacation CLub Seaworkd Internat. Ctr. Contbr. articles to profl. jours. Trustee Cmty. Group Health Found., 1976—77, cons., 1977—; bd. regents State Univ. Sys. Fla., 1977; adv. bd. Am. Assn. Med. Vols., 1970—72; bd. dirs. Iona Whipper Home for Unwed Mothers, 1970—72, Nursing Edn. Opportunities, 1970—72. Recipient Sustained Superior Performance award, HEW, 1962, Meritorious Pub. Svc. award, Govt. of D.C., 1968, medal of honor, Avila Coll., 1969, Disting. Alumni award, Howard U. Nat. Assn. for Equal Opportunity in Higher Edn., 1990, Cmty. Svc. award, Black Profl. Nurses Kansas City, 1991, Lifetime Achievement award, Assn. Black Nursing Faculty in Higher Edn., 1993, Svc. award, Midwest Regional Conf. on Black Families and Children, 1994. Mem.: ANA, Am. Assn. Colls. Nursing (sec. 1975—76), Am. Congress Rehab. Medicine, Nat. League Nursing, Societas Docta (charter, pres. 1996—99), Freedmen's Hosp. Nursing Alumni Assn., Alpha Kappa Alpha, Sigma Theta Tau. Home: 15107 Interlachen Dr Apt 315 Silver Spring MD 20906-5627

COLES, JOANNA, magazine editor-in-chief; BA in British & Am. Lit., U. East Anglia. With The Daily Telegraph, BBC2 TV, BBC Radio, The Guardian; NY bur. chief The Times of London, 1998—2001; articles and features editor New York mag., 2001—04; exec. editor More, 2004—06; editor-in-chief Marie Claire, NYC, 2006—. Co-host on XM Radio's Take Five channel. Mem.: Am. Friends of Royal Ct. Theater (founding mem.). Office: Marie Claire 1790 Broadway, 3rd Fl New York NY 10019 Office Phone: 212-649-5000. Office Fax: 212-649-5050.*

COLE-SCHIRALDI, MARILYN BUSH, occupational therapist, educator; b. NYC, Jan. 29, 1945; d. George Lyman and Theis (Maurer) Bush; m. Carl E. Cole, Aug. 31, 1968 (div. June 1981); children: Charlot E. Sleeper, Bradley Eric Cole; m. Martin M. Schiraldi Sr., July 3, 1982. BA, U. Conn., 1966; grad. cert., U. Pa., 1969; MS, U. Bridgeport, 1982. Registered occupl. therapist, Conn. Staff occupational therapy Ea. Pa. Psychiat. Inst., Phila., 1968-69; dir. occupational therapy Middlesex Meml. Hosp., Middletown, Conn., 1973-76; supervising occupational therapist Lawrence & Meml. Hosps. Day Treatment Ctr., New London, Conn., 1976-79; staff occupational therapist Newington Children's Hosp., Newington, Conn., 1980-82; asst. prof. occupational therapy Quinnipiac Coll., Hamden, Conn., 1982-95, assoc. prof., tenured, 1995—. Vis. faculty fellow Yale U., 1999-2001; cons. psychiat. svcs. VA Med. Ctr., West Haven, Conn., 1983-91; cons. Fairfield Hills Hosp., Newtown, Conn., 1989-91. Author: (textbook) Group Dynamics in Occupational Therapy, 1993, 3d edit., 2005; co-author Structured Group Experiences, 1982, Applied Theories in Occupational Therapy, 2006; contbr. chpts. to books, articles to profl. jours. Grantee Quinnipiac Coll, 1986, 2004, 2005; recipient Best Seller award Slack, Inc., 1999. Fellow: Am. Occupl. Therapy Assn. (Comms. award 1976, Svc. awards 1998, cert.); mem.: AAUW (cultural chair 1972, publicity chair 1973—76, edn. chair 1989—91, nominations 1993—96, membership treas. 1998—2001, fin. com. 2004—), Ctr. Study Sensory Integrative Dysfunction (cert. 1979), World Fedn. Occupl. Therapists, Conn. Occupl. Therapy Assn. (sec. 1978, nominations chair 1982—89, state mental health chair spl. interest sect. 1999—2005), Nat. League Am. Pen Women, U.S. Sailing Assn., Sigma Xi. Republican. Episcopalian. Office: Quinnipiac U Dept Occupl Therapy 275 Mount Carmel Ave Hamden CT 06518-1961 Business E-Mail: marli.cole@quinnipiac.edu.

COLETTA, ANDRIA, lawyer; b. Providence, Jan. 30, 1973; BA cum laude, Union Coll., 1994; JD, Georgetown U. Law Ctr., 1997. Bar: Mass. 1997, RI 1998, US Dist. Ct. (Dist. Mass.) 1998, US Dist. Ct. (Dist. RI) 1999. Assoc. Taylor, Duane, Barton & Gilman LLP, Boston & Providence. Mem.: Def. Rsch. Inst., ABA (tort and ins. practice divsn.), Am. Inns Ct., Mass. Bar Assn., RI Bar Assn. Office: Taylor Duane Barton & Gilman LLP 10 Dorrance St Providence RI 02903 also: Taylor Duane Barton & Gilman LLP 160 Federal St Boston MA 02110 Office Phone: 401-273-7171, 617-654-8200. Office Fax: 401-273-2904, 617-482-5350. E-mail: acoletta@taylorduane.com.*

COLEY, BRENDA ANN, elementary school educator; b. Indpls., Sept. 17, 1958; d. Jack Louis Mullis and Margaret Ann (Crites) Farris; m. Keith Alan Coley, Feb. 17, 1978; children: Amy Michelle, Jared Wesley, Adam Jacob. B Music Edn., Ind. U., 1981; MS in Music Edn., Ind. State U., 1987. Tchr. music Clay Community Sch. Corp., Staunton, Ind., 1981-84; choral dir. Spencer (Ind.)-Owen Community Sch. Corp., 1984-90, tchr. music, 1990—2000; asst. prin. McCormick's Creek Elem. Sch., Spencer, Ind., 2000—. Composer children's musical: Up! Up to the Moon!!, 1992; composer gospel music., founder "Jubilation in Christ", gospel singing group, 1997-. Choir dir. 1st Christian Ch., Spencer. Mem. NEA, Music Educators Nat. Conf., Ind. Music Educators Assn., Spencer-Owen Edn. Assn., Order Ea. Star, Kappa Kappa Kappa, Pi Lambda Theta, Delta Theta Tau. Democrat. Avocations: singing, sports, bowling. Home: 40 Mozart Ln Spencer IN 47460-9344 Office: McCormick's Creek Elem Sch 1601 Flatwoods Rd Spencer IN 47460-1499

COLEY, DONNA S., secondary school educator; d. Eugene Doyle and Kathryn Bowlan Coley; 1 child, Michael Jonathan. Bachelors, U. Tenn., Nashville, 1979; Masters, U. Memphis, 1984. Tchr. Temple Bapt. Sch., Southaven, Miss., 1979—95, Lausanne Collegiate Sch., Memphis, 1995—2001, Frisco H.S., Tex., 2001—. Office: Frisco High School 6401 Parkwood Dr Frisco TX 75034 Office Phone: 469-633-5500.

COLEY, JAN BRUMBACK, biology educator; d. Clifton and Violet Brumback; m. Bob Coley, June 23, 1979; children: Kimberly, Chad. MS, Auburn U., Ala., 1973. Tchr. biology, chmn. sci. dept. Jefferson County H.S., Dandridge, Tenn., 1986—. Recipient Disting. Sci. Tchg. award, Tenn. Acad. Sci., 2004. Office: Jefferson County High School 115 West Dumplin Valley Road Dandridge TN 37725 Office Phone: 865-397-3182. Office Fax: 865-397-4121. Personal E-mail: coleyj@k12tn.net.

COLEY, JOAN DEVELIN, education educator, academic administrator; b. Phila., Nov. 12, 1944; d. Paul Kennedy Develin and Lillian Marian Stiles; 1 child, David Kennedy. AB, Albright Coll., Reading, Pa., 1966; MEd, U. Md., 1970, PhD, 1973. Reading specialist Prince George's County (Md.), 1966-70, dir. secondary sch. vol. program, 1970-71; adj. prof. Univ. Coll., U. Md., College Park, 1971-73; prof., chair edn. dept., dean grad. programs, provost McDaniel Coll. (formerly Western Md. Coll.), Westminster, 1973—2000, pres., 2001—. Reading cons. Simon & Schuster Pub., 1986—. Editor: Reading: Issues and Practices, 1984-88; editorial adv. bd. Reading Rsch. and Instrn., 1977-81; author programmed reading vocabulary for tchrs. Mem. Internat. Reading Assn. (pres. Carroll County 1979-81, Tchr. Educator of Yr. 1989, Outstanding Educator in Reading 1982), Coll. Reading Assn. (bd. dirs. 1980-83), Nat. Reading Conf., Md. Higher Edn. Reading Assn. (pres. 1975-76). Home: 2 College Hill Westminster MD 21157-4450 E-mail: jcoley@mcdaniel.edu.

COLGATE, DORIS ELEANOR, sailing school owner, administrator; b. Washington, May 12, 1941; d. Bernard Leonard and Frances Lillian (Goldstein) Horecker; m. Richard G. Buchanan, Sept. 6, 1959 (div. Aug. 1967); m. Stephen Colgate, Dec. 17, 1969. Student, Antioch Coll., 1958-60, NYU, 1960-62. Rsch. supr. Geyer Moyer Ballard, N.Y.C., 1962-64; administrv. asst. Yachting Mag., N.Y.C., 1964-68; v.p. Offshore Sailing Sch. Ltd., Inc., N.Y.C., 1968-78, pres. Ft. Myers, Fla., 1978—2001; pres., CEO On and Offshore, Inc., Ft. Myers, 1984-2001; v.p. Offshore Travel, Inc., City Island, 1978-88; pres., CEO Offshore Sailing Sch. Ltd., Inc., Ft. Myers, 2001—. Pres. bd. dirs. Women's Sailing Found., 1998-2000, chmn. 2000-02, adv. coun., 2002—; chair US Sailing Comml. Sailing Schs., 2005—. Author: The Bareboat Gourmet, 1983, Sailing: A Woman's Guide, 1999; co-author: Fast Track to Cruising, 2004; contbr. articles to profl. jours. Bd. dirs. Fla. Repertory Theatre. Recipient Betty Cook Meml. Lifetime Achievement award, 1994, Sail Industry Leadership award, 1996, Timothea Larr award, U.S. Sailing, 2003. Mem. Royal Ocean Racing Club (London chpt.), Nat. Women's Sailing Assn. (founder, chair nat. women's adv. bd. 1990-94, pres. 1994-2000, chair 2000-02, Leadership in Women's Sailing award, 2004), Am. Women's Econ. Devel. Corp. (adv. bd. 1980-86), Boat U.S. (nat. adv. coun. 1995—), Sail Am. (bd. dirs. 2000—, chmn. comml. sailing com.), Internat. Sailing Summit (exec. com. 2000-, chair mktg. com. U.S. Sailing 2005—). Avocations: piano, sailing, photography, writing, cooking. Office: Offshore Inc 16731 McGregor Blvd Fort Myers FL 33908-3843 Office Phone: 239-985-7511. Business E-Mail: doris@offshoresailing.com.

COLIGAN, NERISSA, secondary school educator; b. Pasadena, Tex., Jan. 2, 1964; d. Tommie Floyd Dill and Patsy LaRue Beatty; m. Casey Christopher Coligan, Nov. 5, 1988. BS in Econs., U. Houston, 1987. Cert. tchr. English lang. arts and social studies Tex., 2004. English lang. arts tchr. Gary Ind. Sch. Dist., Tex., 2004—; theatre dir. Gary ISD, Tex., 2004—. Dir.: (theatre) The Magician's Nephew (Advancing Play for Zone One Act Play Compition, 2006). Independent. Roman Catholic. Office: Gary High School 1 Bobcat Dr Gary TX 75643 Office Phone: 903-685-2291.

COLIP, OLGA SHEARIN, retired home economist, volunteer; b. Van Alstyne, Tex., Mar. 7, 1920; d. Thester Hiram (N.) Shearin and Myrtle Kizzie (Parks) Hammack; m. William Leonard Colip, Feb. 10, 1946 (dec.); children: Gregory Russell, Tia Catherine, Terry Allen. BS in Home Econs., Tex. State Coll. Women, 1943, postgrad., 1963, Tex. Christian U., 1965. Dietitian N.Am. U., Grand Prairie, Tex., 1943, Orange (Tex.) Pub. Schs., 1944—45; tchr. U.S. Army Schs., Ponce, PR, 1946; civic vol. Grand Prairie, Tex., 1948—. Spl. svcs. hostess U.S. Army Camp Gruber, Muskogee, Okla., 1945—46. Bd. dirs. YMCA, Grand Prairie, 1998—, chmn. landscape, 1980; chmn. clean-up dr. Men's and Women's C. of C., Grand Prairie, 1980; organizer, sponsor Future Nurses Clubs at area high schs.; sponsor Get Acquainted with Am.; bd. dirs. Grand Prairie Libr., 1970—81. Recipient Hon. Mention award, Clean-up Dr. Washington, State Sears Roebuck award for YMCA landscaping. Mem.: Grand Prairie Woman's Club (charter mem.), Resebian Book Club (pres. 1958, charter mem.). Methodist. Avocations: needlecrafts, gardening, travel, architecture, art.

COLISH, MARCIA LILLIAN, history professor; b. Bklyn., July 27, 1937; d. Samuel and Daisy (Karch) Colish. BA magna cum laude, Smith Coll., 1958; MA, Yale U., 1959, PhD, 1965; DHL (hon.), Grinnell Coll., 1999. Instr. history Skidmore Coll., Saratoga Springs, NY, 1962-63; instr. Oberlin Coll., Ohio, 1963-65, asst. prof., 1965-69, assoc. prof., 1969-75, prof. history, 1975-2001, Frederick B. Artz prof. history, 1985-2001, chmn. dept. history, 1973-74, 78-81, 85-86; vis. fellow Yale U., 2001—, lectr. in history, 2004—05. Vis. prof. history and religious studies Yale U., 2002—03; lectr. history Case Western Res. U., Cleve., 1966—67; vis. scholar Am. Acad. Rome, 1968—69; editl. cons. W. W. Norton & Co., 1973, John Wiley & Sons, Inc., 1981, SUNY Press, 1983, 85, U. Chgo. Press, 1988, U. Calif. Press, 1988, Princeton U. Press, 1988, 96, 98, U. Notre Dame Press, 1991, 92, 94, 2005, U. Ill. Press, 1995, U. Pa. Press, 1995, 97, 99, Yale U. Press, 1997, 98, Oxford U. Press, 1998, 2001, 05, Blackwell's, 1998, Liturgical Press, 1999, Cambridge U. Press, 2002, 05, E. J. Brill, 2003, 04, Palgrave Macmillan, 2003, 05; cons. dept. history Grinnell Coll., 1974, Knox Coll., 1981, St. John's U., 1981, Whitman Coll., 1982, Hope Coll., 1995, Kenyon Coll., 1996; mem. exec. bd. Ohio Program Humanities, 1976—81, 1978—81, vice chmn., 1979—81; writing residency Villa Serbelloni, Bellagio, 1995; mem. Sch. Hist. Studies, Inst. Advanced Study, Princeton, 1986—87. Author: The Mirror of Language: A Study in the Medieval Theory of Knowledge, 2d rev. edit., 1983, paperback edit., 2004, The Stoic Tradition from Antiquity to the Early Middle Ages, 1985, enlarged paperback edit., 1990, Peter Lombard, 1994, Medieval Foundations of the Western Intellectual Traidtion, 400-1400, 1997, 2d printing, 1998, paperback edit., 1999, La Cultura del Medioevo, 2001, Ambrose's Patriarchs: Ethics for the Common Man, 2005, Studies in Scholasticism, 2006. Mem. exec. bd. Oberlin ACLU, 1970—74, chmn., 1972—74, rec. sec., 1976—77, vice chmn., 1979—80; mem. exec. bd. Oberlin YWCA, 1966—70. Named Etienne Gilson lectr., Pontifical Inst. Mediaeval Studies, Toronto, 2000; recipient Wilbur Cross medal, Yale Grad. Sch. Alumni Assn., 1993, Marianist award, U. Dayton, 2000; Samuel S. Fels fellow, Yale U., 1961—62, Younger Scholar fellow, Inst. Rsch. Humanities, U. Wis., 1974—75, Nat. Humanities Ctr. fellow, 1981—82, Guggenheim fellow, 1989—90, Woodrow Wilson Ctr. fellow, 1994—95, NEH fellow, 1968—69, 1981—82, NEH Summer grantee, U. Calif., 1993. Fellow: Medieval Acad. Am. (coun. 1987—89, 2d v.p. 1989—90, 1st v.p. 1990—91, pres. 1991—92, Haskins medal 1998); mem.: Internat. Soc. Intellectual History, Internat. Soc. Classical Tradition, Soc. Internat. pour Etude Philosophie Medievale, Ctrl. Renaissance Conf., Renaissance Soc. Am., Midwest Medieval Conf. (pres. 1978—79), Medieval Assn. Midwest (coun. 1978—81), Am. Hist. Assn., Phi Beta Kappa (vis. scholar 2006—07, vis. scholar 2006—). Home: 80 Seaview Terr #29 Guilford CT 06437 E-mail: marcia.colish@yale.edu.

COLLAMER, BARBARA ELLEN, social sciences educator; b. Salem, Ohio, Dec. 11, 1943; d. Charles Augustus Rohrer; m. Alfred William Farrand, Sept. 6, 2002. PhD, Ariz. State U., Tempe, Ariz., 1992. Faculty Maricopa C.C., Phoenix, 1987—89, We. Wash. U., Bellingham, Wash., 1989—. Spkr. in field. Author: The Ecology of Gender. Home: 25 N West Street Columbiana OH 44408 Office: Western Washington University 516 High Street MS 9089 Bellingham WA 98225 Office Phone: 360-650-3518. Business E-Mail: collamer@wwu.edu.

COLLARINI SCHLOSSBERG, ANTOINETTE MARIE, psychologist; b. N.Y.C., Apr. 12, 1950; d. Attilio and Ann (Pecoraro) Collarini; m. Harvey Schlossberg. BA, Fordham U., 1972; MS, Hunter Coll., 1974; M of Philosophy, Columbia U., 1982, PhD, 1982. Lic. psychologist, N.Y. Rsch. assoc. City of Yonkers, N.Y., 1972-74; rsch. dir. City of Mt. Vernon, N.Y., 1974-76; program adminstr. Westchester County Youth Bur., White Plains, N.Y., 1976-88, exec. dir., 1988-96; pvt. practice psychology Forest Hills, N.Y., 1983—. Research and orgnl. cons., N.Y.C., Westchester County, 1976—; assoc. prof. criminal justice and legal studies St. John's U., Queens, NY, 2002—; trainee NIMH, 1972-1974, 1979-1980. Recipient Craig Collins Excellence in Tchg. award, St. Johns U. Criminal Justice Student Assn., 2006. Mem. APA, NAFE, N.Y. State Psychol. Assn., Am. Soc. for Pub. Adminstrn. (chpt. v.p. 1986-87, pres. 1987-89).

COLLEDGE, DEBORAH GAIL, gifted and talented elementary educator; b. Altoona, Pa., Aug. 9, 1956; d. Charles E. Sr. and Shirley J. (Bragonier) C. BS, Clarion (Pa.) State, 1977; MEd, Pa. State U., 1981, EdD, 1993; prins. cert., 1983. Cert. elem. and middle sch. tchr., prin., adminstr., reading specialist, tchr. gifted. Elem. tchr. gifted Altoona Area Sch. Dist., 1978-85; tchr. Tuscarora Intermediate 11, McVeytown, Pa., 1983—85; tchr. gifted grades 3-6 Mesa (Ariz.) Pub. Schs., 1985—. Numerous grants. Mem. Assn. for Supervision and Curriculum Devel., Nat. Assn. for Gifted Children, Phi Delta Kappa, Kappa Delta Pi. Office: Mesa Pub Schs 63 E Main St 101 Mesa AZ 85201-7422 Home: 2212 11th Ave Altoona PA 16601

COLLETTE, FRANCES MADELYN, retired tax specialist, lawyer, consultant, advocate; b. Yonkers, N.Y., Aug. 5, 1947; d. Morris Aaron and Esther (Gang) Volbert; m. Roger Warren Collette, Dec. 25, 1971; children: Darren Roger, Bonnie Frances. BEd summa cum laude, SUNY, Buffalo, 1969; JD cum laude, U. Miami, 1980. Bar: Fla. 1980. Employment counselor Fla. Bur. Employment Security, Miami, Fla., 1969-73; unemployment claims adjudicator Fla. Bur. Unemployment, Miami, 1973-77; owner Unemployment Svcs. Fla., Inc., Miami, 1977-93. Cons. Fla. unemployment tax and personnel; lectr. in field. Mem. ad hoc comm. students with Asperger's Syndrome Dade County Pub. Schs., 1998-2000; vol. child advocate Exceptional Student Edn., 1993-; 1st v.p. BBB South Fla., 1980-81, bd. govs., 2d vice chair, 1990-91; mem. Supt.'s Dist. Adv. Panel for Students with Disabilities, Miami-Dade County Pub. Schs., 2003-; mem. adv. panel Fla. Diagnostic and Learning Resources System/South. Jewish.

COLLETTE, TONI, actress; b. Sydney, Australia, Nov. 1, 1972; m. Dave Galafassi, Jan. 11, 2003. Appeared in films: Efficiency Expert, 1991, Spotswood, 1992, This Marching Girl Thing, 1994, Muriel's Wedding, 1994, Lilian's Story, 1995, Arabian Knight, 1995 (as voice of nurse/good witch), Cosi, 1996, The Pallbearer, 1996, Emma, 1996, The Boys, 1997, Clockwatchers, 1997, The James Gang, 1997, Diana & Me, 1997, Velvet Goldmine, 1998, Hotel Sordide, 1999, Dead by Monday, 1999, 8 1/2 Women, 1999, The Sixth Sense, 1999, Shaft Returns, 2000, Changing Lanes, 2002, About a Boy, 2002, Hotel Splendide, 2000, Dirty Deeds, 2002, The Hours, 2002, Japanese Story, 2003, The Last Shot, 2004, In Her Shoes, 2005, The Night Listener, 2006, Little Miss Sunshine, 2006; TV appearances include The panel, 1998, Frontline, 1994, Dinner With Friends, 2001. Office: United Talent Agy care Adam Isaacs 9560 Wilshire Blvd Ste 500 Beverly Hills CA 90212-2427*

COLLIE, PAULA RENEA, secondary school educator; b. Gonzales, Tex., Dec. 23, 1971; d. Paul Jr. and Kathy (Maulding) C. BA in Geography and Polit. Sci., SW Tex. State U., 1994. Clk. City of Gonzales, 1989-90; salesperson Laurel Ridge Antiques, Gonzales, 1990; subs. tchr. Gonzales Ind. Sch. Dist., 1990—94; with Gonzales County Archives, Gonzales Hist. Commn., 1993-94; geography tchr. Luling (Tex.) H.S., 1994—, social studies dept. head, 1995—, student coun. sponsor, 1996—, summer sch. tchr., 2000—. Participant All State Tex. Alliance Conf., Clear Lake, 1994, Nat. Conf. for Geographic Edn., Lexington, Ky., 1994. Mem. Nat. Geographic Soc., Nat. Coun. for Geographic Edn., Tex. Alliance for Geographic Edn., NEA, Tex. Student Edn. Assn. Avocations: genealogy, fishing. Home: 1611 Gardien St Gonzales TX 78629-4318 Office: Luling Ind Sch Dist 218 E Travis Luling TX 78648

COLLIER, ALICE ELIZABETH BECKER, retired social services administrator; b. Akron, Ohio, June 09; d. Christian and Virginia (Schulmeister) Becker; m. John Robert Fenwick, Aug. 28, 1954 (dec. 1980); 1 child, Beth Alice; m. Thomas Collier, Mar. 8, 1980. BA in Edn., Heidelberg Coll., Tiffin, Ohio, 1949; MA in Edn1. Adminstrn., U. Akron, 1968. Cert. tchr., ednl. adminstr., Ohio. Tchr. Air Force Dependent Schs., Fed. Republic Germany and Eng., 1960-64, Akron Pub. Schs., 1964-68, adminstr., 1968-80; dep. mayor City of Akron, 1980-84; pres. Collier Pub. Rels./Mktg., Akron, 1984-86; gen. mgr., broker Coldwell Banker Real Estate, Akron, 1986-90; dir. comms. Area Agy. on Aging, Akron, 1990-94; v.p. Mktg. and Creative Solutions, 1994-97; ret., 1997. Author, editor: (Manual) Visual-Motor Training for the Developmentally Disabled Child, 1972, Different Strokes for Little Folks, 1974. Chmn. adv. coun. U. Akron, 1977-88; mem. Akron Health Commn., 1978-80, Akron Sr. Citizens Commn., 1980—94, Nat. Adv. Coun. on Aging, Bethesda, Md., 1982-84; pres. Tri-County Employee Assistance Program, Summit, Medina and Portage, 1985-97; charter rev. commn. Summit County, 1991; mem. women's adv. coun. Summa Health Sys., 1994—2003; v.p. Women's Network, Akron, 1987-88; trustee Cmty. Health Rsch. Group, Inc., 1980—2002, Cuyahoga Falls Gen. Hosp. Found., 1992-2005; pub. rels. chmn. State of Ohio Atty. Gen. Health Info. Com.; trustee No. Ohio Golf Charities Found., Firestone Country Club, 1999—2004, World Series of Golf, Firestone County Club, 1983—2000; vol. World Golf Championships, 2001—04. Recipient Svc. to Elderly award Am. Gerontol. Soc., 1982, Excellence in Comm. award Nat. Assn. Area Agys. on Aging, 1991. Mem.: AAUW, Akron Bd. Realtors (Salesperson of Yr. award 1988, Hall of Fame award 1988), Ohio Assn. Realtors (trustee 1988—90), Am. Mktg. Assn. (pres. Akron-Canton chpt. 1988—89, Spl. Merit award 1990), Woman's Golf Assn. (treas. Mission Valley 2002—04, v.p. Mission Valley chpt. 2005—), Akron Women's City Club, Heidelberg Coll. Alumni Assn., Medina Country Club, Mission Valley Country Club, Phi Lambda Theta (founding, charter). Republican. Avocations: church organist, golf, tennis, collecting hummel figurines. Mailing: 333 N Portage Path Beechwood #11 Akron OH 44303-1218 Home (Summer): 255 The Esplanade N Apt 204 Venice FL 34285-1518 Personal E-mail: atcollier4@comcast.net.

COLLIER, ANNA, photographer; b. LA, Calif., 1970; BFA, Calif. Inst. Arts, Valencia, Calif., 1993; MFA, U. Calif., LA, 2001. Vis. faculty Art Ctr., Pasadena, Calif., 2002—03, Calif. Coll. Arts, San Francisco, 2002—; vis. faculty, New Genres dept. San Francisco Art Inst., Calif., 2003. Solo exhibitions, One on One, Three Day Weekend, LA, Calif., 1995, Inst. Visual Arts, U. Wis., Milw., 1998, MARC FOXX, West Gallery, LA, Calif., 2001, MARC FOXX, 2002, Jack Hanley Gallery, San Francisco, Calif., 2004, group exhibitions, L.A.C.E., video screening of LA video artists, 1993, Summer Group Show, Three Weekend, LA, Calif., 1994, Thank!; Three Day Weekend, 1994, Dave's Not Here; Three Day Weekend, 1995, Eros Travel Com., Studio Neuwirth, Vienna, Austria, 1996, Art Dogs, George's, LA, Calif., 2000, Summer Group Show, Goldman Tevis, 2000, I Want More, Temple Bar Gallery, Dublin, Ireland, 2001, New Wight Art Gallery, UCLA, 2001, MARC FOXX, LA, Calif., 2001, 2003, Group Show, MARC FOXX, 2002, A Show That Will Show That a Show Is Not Only a Show, The Project, 2002, Bay Area Now III, Yerba Buena Ctr. for the Arts, San Francisco, Calif., 2002, Portraiture, Karyn Lovegrove Gallery, LA, Calif., 2003, Makeshift World, Stephen Wirtz Gallery, San Francisco, Calif., 2003, 17 Reasons, Jack Henley Gallery, 2003, Nicole Klagsbrun Gallery, NY, 2004, Whitney Biennial: Day for Night, Whitney Mus. Am. Art, NYC, 2006, mus. collections, San Francisco Mus. Modern Art, Mus. Contemporary Art San Diego, La Jolla, Calif., LA County Mus. Art; curatorial projects Black Rainbow, Lucky Tackle Gallery, Oakland, Calif., 2003, Version, New Langton Arts, San Francisco, Calif., 2004. Address: c/o MARC FOXX Gallery 6150 Wihshire Blvd Los Angeles CA 90048 also: c/o Jack Hanley Gallery 395 Valencia St San Francisco CA 94103*

COLLIER, BEVERLY JOANNE, retired elementary school educator; b. Grand Haven, Mich., Oct. 28, 1936; d. Joseph Frank and Anne (Mary) Snyder; divorced; children: Ann, Cindy. Student, U. Mich., 1955-57; BA, Western Mich. U., 1965. Cert. elem. tchr., Mich. 1st grade tchr. Fruitport (Mich.) Community Schs., 1965-93; retired, 1993. Contbr. articles to local newspapers. Active Grand Haven (Mich.) Presbyn. Ch., 1955—. Mem. ASCD, NEA, Muskegon Edn. Assn., Mich. Edn. Assn. (past regional rep.), West Mich. Edn. Assn. (life), Mich. Assn. Ret. Sch. Personnel (Muskegon County chpt.). Avocations: reading, writing, biking, theater, hiking. Home: 1235 Washington Ave Grand Haven MI 49417-1627 Office: Fruitport Cmty Sch 305 Pontaluna Rd Fruitport MI 49415-9652

COLLIER, CHARISSE AUDRA, family service representative, greeting card designer; b. Phila., Mar. 10, 1973; d. Eleanor Jean and Calvin Charles Cooper; m. Jeffrey Jerome Collier, June 22, 2002. BS in Edn., Temple U., Phila., 2000. Kindergarten tchr. Sch. Dist. Phila., 2000—02, family svc. rep. Pre-Kindergarten/HS, 2005—. Last Dollar scholar, Phila. Edn. Fund, 1991—99. Mem.: Del. Valley Assn. Edn. Young Children (assoc.), Zeta Phi Beta (assoc.; local chpt. pres. 1998—99). R-Consevative. Achievements include design of one of a kind handmade greeting cards. Office: Sch Dist Phila Pre-Kindergarten/HS 13th & Spring Garden St Philadelphia PA 19123 Personal E-mail: colliercreations@aol.com.

COLLIER, HELEN VANDIVORT, psychologist; b. Nagpur, India; d. William Boardley and Stephena Ruth (Hecker) C.; children: Keith Vandivort (dec.), Daniel Vandivort, Heidi Vandivort Zalobowski. BA, Ohio Wesleyan U., 1950; MEd, U. Toledo, 1968, EdD, 1974; postgrad., San Diego Gestalt Tng. Ctr. Lic. psychologist, Ohio, marriage and family therapist, Nev. Tchr. elem. schs., Itasca, Ill.; ednl. cons. Toledo Bd. Edn., 1960-67; elem. counselor Toledo Pub. Schs., 1968; counseling psychologist, asst. prof. U. Toledo, 1968-74; pvt. practice psychotherapy and counseling cons. Bloomington, Ind., 1974—. Asst. dir. adult counseling project Sch. Continuing Studies Ind. U., Bloomington, 1975-76; research assoc. Ctr. for Human of Human Mobility, Ind. U., 1974-75, cons., adj. faculty, 1976-80; ptnr. Nat. Ct. Services, Inc., Reno; adj. faculty Nat. Jud. Coll., Reno; dir. HVC Assocs. Psychotherapy and Orgnl. Cons. Author: Freeing Ourselves: Removing Internal Barriers to Equality, 1979, Counseling Women: A Guide for Therapists, 1982; co-editor: Meeting the Educational and Occupational Planning Needs of Adults, 1975; contbr. articles to jours. Women's Ednl. Equity Act Office of Edn. grantee, 1977—. Mem. Am. Psychol. Assn., Am. Assn. Marriage and Family Therapists. Address: 370 Wheeler Ave Reno NV 89502-1614 Office Phone: 775-786-3097. Office Fax: 775-786-1442.

COLLIER-EVANS, DEMETRA FRANCES, veterans benefits counselor; b. Nashville, Dec. 18, 1937; d. Oscar Collier and Earlee Elizabeth (Williams) Collier-Sheffield; m. George Perry Evans, Dec. 21, 1966; 1 child, Richard Edward. AA in Social Sci., Solano C.C., Suisun City, Calif., 1974; BA in Social Sci., Chapman Coll., Orange, Calif., 1981. Cert. tchr., Calif. Specialist placement, case responsible person employment devel. dept. City of San Diego, 1975-82; vocat. tchr. San Diego Community Coll., 1982-83; specialist placement N.J. Job Service, Camden, 1984-86, mgr. job bank, 1985; specialist placement Abilities Ctr., Westville, N.J., 1987-88; veteran's benifits counselor VA, Phila. 1988-2000, ret., 2000; mem. bd. dirs. Welfare Rights; cons. Bumble Bee Canning Co., San Diego, 1982; developer women's seminar Women's Opportunity Week, City of San Diego, 1982, network seminar Fed. Women's Week, City of Phila., 1986. Bd. dirs. Welfare Rights Orgn., San Diego, 1982; mem. Internat. YWCA. Served with USAF, 1956-59. Recipient Excellence cert. San Diego Employer Adv. Bd., 1981, Leadership cert. Nat. U., San Diego, 1981. Mem. AAUW, NAACP (life, rec. sec. San Diego 1982), Black Advs. State Svc. (charter, corr. sec. San Diego Chpt. 1981-82), Nat. Assn. Female Execs., Am. Fedn. Govt. Employees (officer of yr. award 1999), Bonton Club (svc. award 1998), Chapman Coll. Alumni Assn., Alpha Gamma Sigma. Democrat. Avocation: calligraphy. Office: PO Box 5015 Cherry Hill NJ 08034-0391

COLLINE, MARGUERITE RICHNAVSKY, maternal, women's health and pediatrics nurse; b. Bayonne, NJ, Nov. 30, 1953; d. John P. and Margaret M. (Conaghan) Richnavsky; m. Richard L. Colline, Oct. 8, 1977; children: Jennifer, Nicole, Danielle, James Michael. Diploma in practical nurse, Union County Tech. Inst., Scotch Plains, N.J., 1973; BSN, Seton Hall U., 1978. RN NJ, Md. Practical nurse oncology unit John E. Runnell's Hosp., Berkley Heights, N.J.; staff nurse infant unit Johns Hopkins Hosp., Balt.; staff nurse neonatal unit Overlook Hosp., Summit, N.J.; parish nurse Somerville, NJ. Mem. Sigma Theta Tau.

COLLINS, ALMA JONES, language educator, writer; d. Walter Melville Jones and Anne Teresa Harrington; m. Daniel Francis Collins, Apr. 9, 1994. BA, Conn. Coll., 1943; MA, Trinity Coll., 1952, U. Conn., 1962. Tchr., counselor West Hartford (Conn.) Bd. Edn., 1947-72; pres. Arts Universal Rsch. Assocs., 1978—. Interviewed Salvador Dali (CD located in archives Wadsworth Atheneum Mus. Art), 1978, 79; cons. for corp. product devel.; rep. for artists. Author: Danielle at the Wadsworth, 2004; contbr. articles to profl. jours. Mem. Phi Beta Kappa, Delta Kappa Gamma Internat. Avocation: writing poetry and fiction. Home and Office: 275 Steele Rd A318 West Hartford CT 06117-2763

COLLINS, AMY LYNN, music educator; b. Lufkin, Tex., Feb. 23, 1980; d. Roger B. and Brenda K. Smith; m. James Collins, July 18, 2006. MusB, Henderson State U., Arkadelphia, Ark., 2004; student, John Brown U., Siloam Springs, Ark., 2005—. Tchr. Second Bapt. Child Devel. Ctr., Hot Springs, 1998, 2000, 2003, Gravette Sch. Dist., Ark., 2004—. Piano tchr., 2004—. Tchr. Lake Valley Cmty. Ch., Hot Springs, 1996—2003. Mem.: NEA, Ark. Edn. Assn. Avocations: running, flute, piano, dulcimer, songwriting. Office: Gravette Sch Dist 601 El Paso St Gravette AR 72736

COLLINS, ANGELO, science educator; b. Chgo., June 15, 1944; d. James Joseph and Mary (Burke) C. BS, Marian Coll., 1966; MS, Mich. State U., 1973; PhD, U. Wis., 1986; DHL (hon.), Edgewood Coll. Tchr. h.s. biology various schs., Wis., 1966—81; rsch. asst. U. Wis., Madison, 1981—86; asst. prof. Kans. State U., Manhattan, 1986—87, Stanford U., Calif., 1988—90, Rutgers U., New Brunswick, NJ, 1990—91; assoc. prof. Fla. State U., Tallahassee, 1991—95, Vanderbilt U., Nashville, 1995—2000; exec. dir. Knowles Sci. Tchg. Found., Moorestown, NJ, 2000—. Dir. Sci. Stds., Washington, 1992; sci. com. Nat. Bd. Profl. Tchg. Stds., Washington, 1991—; chmn. adv. bd. BioQuest, Beloit, Wis., 1988-98; bd. dirs. Jour. for Rsch. in Sci. Tchg., ScienceEd, 1995. Editor Tchr. Edn. Quar., 1991; co-editor Jour. Rsch. in Sci. Tchg., 2005—; reviewer several books; contbr. articles to profl. jours. Henry Rutgers fellow Rutgers U., 1990; recipient Devel. Scholar award Fla. State U., 1993-94. Fellow AAAS; mem. Nat. Assn. Biology Tchrs. (Outstandng Biology Tchr. Wis. 1977), Nat. Assn. Rsch. Sci. Tchg., Assn. Edn. Tchrs. Sci., Am. Ednl. Rsch. Assn., Sch. Sci. and Math., Assn. Tchr. Educators, Sigma Xi, Phi Delta Kappa. Office: Knowles Sci Tchg Found 1000 N Church St Moorestown NJ 08057 Office Phone: 856-608-0001. Business E-Mail: angelo.collins@kstf.org.

COLLINS, ANITA MARGUERITE, research geneticist; b. Allentown, Pa., Nov. 8, 1947; d. Edmund III and Virginia (Hunsicker) C. BSc in Zoology, Pa. State U., 1969; MSc in Genetics, Ohio State U., 1972, PhD in Genetics, 1976. Instr. biology Mercyhurst Coll., Erie, Pa., 1975-76; rsch. geneticist Honey Bee Breeding Lab. Agrl. Rsch. Svc., USDA, Baton Rouge, 1976-88, rsch. leader Honey Bee Rsch. Lab. Weslaco, Tex., 1988-95, rsch. geneticist Bee Rsch. Lab. Beltsville, Md., 1995—. Co-author: Bee Genetics & Breeding, 1986; contbr. articles to profl. jours. Mem.: Soc. for Cryobiology, Internat. Union for Study of Social Insects (congress sec. 2006—), Am. Genetics Assn., Am. Beekeeping Fedn. (rsch. com. 1990, 1992—94), Assn. for Women in Sci. (pres. Baton Rouge chpt. 1982), Entomol. Soc. Am. (chair sect. C 1997), Internat. Embryo Transfer Soc., Sigma Xi. Office: USDA ARS Bee Rsch Bldg 476 BARC-East Beltsville MD 20705 Office Phone: 301-504-8570. Business E-Mail: collinsa@ba.ars.usda.gov.

COLLINS, ANNAZETTE R., state representative; b. Chgo., Apr. 28, 1962; m. Keith Langston; children: Angelique, Taylor. BS in Sociology, Chgo. State U., MS in Criminal Justice, 1983. Social worker Ada S. McKinley Interventions, 1982—83; correctional officer Fed. Bur. Prisons, 1983—86; social worker Cook County Social Svcs., 1986—90; adminstr. Dept. Children Family Svcs., 1990—2000, Chgo. Pub. Schs., 2000; mem. Ill. Ho. of Reps., 2000—. Mem. St. Joseph Sch. Bd., 1992—95; v.p. pres.'s club Cosmopolitan Cmty. Ch., 2001. Democrat. Baptist. Office: 252-W Stratton Office Bldg Springfield IL 62706 Home: 3235 W Warren Blvd Apt 2 Chicago IL 60624-2494 Office Phone: 773-533-0010. Personal E-mail: annazette@sbcglobal.net.

COLLINS, ARLENE, secondary school educator; b. Mandan, ND, Sept. 7, 1940; d. John Marcellus and Cecelia Magdalena (Schaaf) Weber; m. Abdul Rahman Rana (dec.); children: Fazale Rahman, Habeeb Rahman; m. Freddie L. Collins. BS in math., N.D. State U., 1962; postgrad., W.Va. Inst. Tech., 1974; M in Edn. Adminstrn., WVCOGS, 1988. Cert. mid. sch. tchr., W.Va. Tchr. physics, math. Montgomery (W.Va.) H.S., 1970; tchr. math., sci. Spencer (W.Va.) Jr. H.S., 1974-80; sci. tchr. Poca (W.Va.) Mid. Sch., 1980—, team leader, 1983-96. W.Va. textbook adoption com., W.Va. Bd. Edn., 1984-90. Leader Girl Scouts U.S.A., Montgomery, 1966-70, 99—, Boy Scouts Am., Montgomery, 1966; bd. dirs. Violet Twp. Womens League, 2002—; vol. Am. Cancer Soc. Fellow: African Am. Law Enforcement Agts. Assn., Inc.; mem.: NOW (bd. dirs. 1986), Am. Fedn. Tchrs., Laurel Soc., VFW Aux., Am. Legion Aux. (sec. 2002—), Buckeye Sertoma, Soroptimists Internat. Home: 7292 Fox Den Ct Pickerington OH 43147-9019 Office Phone: 614-833-5915. Personal E-mail: ac0907@aol.com.

COLLINS, AUDREY B., judge; b. 1945; BA, Howard U., 1967; MA, Am. U., 1969; JD, UCLA, 1977. Asst. atty. Legal Aid Found. LA, 1977-78; with Office LA County Dist. Atty., 1978-94, dept. dist. atty., 1978-94, asst. dir. burs. ctrl. ops. and spl. ops., 1988-92, asst. dir. atty., 1992-94; judge. US Dist. Ct. (Ctrl. Dist.) Calif., 1994—. Dep. gen. counsel Office Spl. Acad. scholar Howard U.; named Lawyer of Yr., Langston Bar Assn., 1988; honoree Howard U. Alumni Club So. Calif., 1989; recipient Profl. Achievement award UCLA Alumni Assn., 1997, Ernestine Stahlhut award Women Lawyers Assn., 1999, Bernard S. Jefferson Justice of Yr. award John M. and Langston Bar Assn., 2006. Mem. FBA, Nat. Assn. Women Judges, Nat. Bar Assn. (life), Assn. Bus. Trial Lawyers (bd. dirs. 2004—), State Bar Calif. (com. bar examiners, chmn. subcom. on moral character 1992-93, co-chmn. 1993-94), LA County Bar Assn. (exec. com. litig. sect. 1999-2002, task force on criminal justice sys. 2002-03), Assn. LA County Dist. Attys. (pres. 1983), Black Women Lawyers LA County, Women Lawyers LA (life, bd. dirs. 2005-, bd. govs. 2005-06), Calif. Women Lawyers (life), Order of Coif, Phi Beta Kappa. Office: US Dist Ct Edward R Roybal Fed Bldg 255 E Temple St Ste 670 Los Angeles CA 90012-3334

COLLINS, BARBARA LOUISE, retired elementary school educator; b. Pasadena, Nov. 6, 1934; d. Harry Carl and Grace Eleanor (Varnum) Wallerman; m. Wayne G. Collins, July 6, 1961; children: Lisa, Garth. BA in Elem. Edn., Calif. State U., LA, 1956; postgrad., U. Vienna, Austria, 1960; Cert. Art Specialist, Clarke Coll., Dubuque, Iowa, 1980. Tchr. Mt. Diablo Sch., Concord, Calif., 1957—60; prin. asst. Regina Pub. Sch., Sask., Canada, 1961—62; tchr. adult basic edn. Dubuque, Iowa, 1966—67; substitute tchr. K-12 Dubuque Pub. Schs., 1967—, substitute art specialist. Tutor trainer Laubach Literacy, Dubuque, Iowa, 1970—90; tchr. pottery, painting, weaving Dubuque Mus. Art, 1985—98; artist-in-residence Cedar Falls (Iowa) Schs., 2000—01. Clay sculpture, pottery, water color paintings, color pencil drawings, exhibitions include Clarke Coll. Gallery, 1985, Dubuque Mus. Art Old Jail Gallery, 1987. Bd. dirs. Dubuque Mus. Art, 1994—97, chair Friends of DUMA, 1995—97. Recipient Best of Show, Grant Wood Art Fest, 1994. United Ch. Of Christ. Avocations: sewing, travel, camping, cooking. Home: 11092 Mound View Rd Dubuque IA 52003

COLLINS, CARDISS, retired congresswoman; b. St. Louis, Sept. 24, 1931; m. George W. Collins (dec.); 1 child, Kevin. Student, Northwestern U.; LLD (hon.), John Marshall Law Sch., 1969, Winston-Salem State U., 1980, Spelman Coll., 1981, BarberScotia Coll., 1986; DHL (hon.), Rosary Coll., 1996; DrPsychology (hon.), Forest Inst. Profl. Psychology, 1993. Barber Scotia Coll.; mem. 93d-104th Congresses from 7th Ill. Dist., 1973-97; ret., 1997. Ranking minority mem. govt. reform & oversight com.; former chair. govt. activity and transp. subcom.; former chair commerce, consumer protection and competition subcom.; former majority whip-at-large; former asst. regional whip; former chair Congl. Black Caucus, sec.; dir. emeritus, former chair Congl. Black Caucus Found.; former chair Mems. Congress for Peace through Law; chairwoman Nielsen Media Rsch. Taskforce TV Measurement. Recipient award Roosevelt U., Loyola U., Scroll of Merit Nat. Med. Assn.; named to Hall of Fame Women's Sports Found. Mem. NAACP, Nat. Coun. Negro Women (past v.p.), Chgo. Urban League, Black Women's Agenda, The Chgo. Network, The Links, Dem. Nat. Com., Alpha Kappa Alpha. Democrat. Baptist. Home: 1110 Roundhouse Ln Alexandria VA 22314-5934

COLLINS, CARLITA RAULERSON, mathematician, educator; d. Daisy Beatrice Green and Frank Raulerson. M in Ednl. Leadership, U. North Fla., Jacksonville, 2006. Cert. 6-12 math. tchr. Fla., 1995. Tchr. math. Duval County Sch. Dist., Jacksonville, Fla., 1995—; chair dept. math. William M. Raines H.S., Jacksonville, Fla., 2000—. Coord. of Fla. Comprehensive Assessment Test fun day William M. Raines H.S., Jacksonville, Fla., 2006—06. Recipient Tchr. of Yr. award, Willaim M. Raines H.S. Faculty, 2002-2003. Mem.: Nat. Coun. of Tchrs. of Math. (assoc.), Nat. Educators Assn. (assoc.), Fla. Coun. of Tchrs. of Math. (assoc.). Home: 11869 Ashbrook Cir N Jacksonville FL 32225 Office: Duval County Sch Dist 3663 Raines Ave Jacksonville FL 32209 Office Phone: 904-924-3049. Personal E-mail: collinsc@educationcentral.org.

COLLINS, CYNTHIA JANE, marriage and family therapist, priestess; b. Florence, Ala., Oct. 21, 1950; d. William Lee and Johnie Glenn (Lutts) Collins; m. Christopher Martin Waldeck, Oct. 2, 1996 (dec. Mar. 1998); m. Harry Blaise Spirito, July 31, 1999; children: Stephanie Kim Collins Newburger Bush, Samuel Collins Newburger, Allan Lee Collins Sylvester. BA in Fine Arts and Philosophy (mark of distinction), Franklin Coll., 1985; MDiv cum laude, Christian Theol. Sem., Indpls., 1989; MS in counseling, U. Evansville, 1991. Lic. marriage and family therapist Ind.; ordained high priestess Cir. of Silver Cauldron. Domina Re:Creations, 1968—; career counselor, 1974-78; counselor, tchr., 1978-86; pastor, counselor South Ind. Conf. hdqs. United Meth. Ch., Indpls., 1986-91; marriage and family therapist Collins Counseling Svcs., 1991—. Bd. dirs. Maine Pagan Clergy, 2001—, chair ordination and licensure com., 2001—. Author: Building a Magical Relationship: The Five Points of Love, 2002—; author, workshop leader: Women in the History of the Church, 1987, Vacation Pagan Sch. First, Second and Third, 1998—; one-woman shows include Ceres St., Portsmouth, N.H., 2001—, 100-piece exhbn., Abrams Gallery Exhbn., 1981; prodr., dir. (radio program) CTS Today, 1986—87; mental health columnist: Our Maine, 2000—. Bd. dirs. Hist. Cannelton, Ind., 1990, 93, Leadership Perry County, 1993, 94; advisor Perry County Devel. Corp., 1994; elder, founding mem., Domina Cir. of the Silver Cauldron, 1994—. Recipient Svc. award Mental Health Assn., 1995. Mem. Am. Assn. for Marriage and Family Therapy (clin. mem.), Mental Health Assn. Spencer County (pres. 1992-94), Perry County Meth. Clergy Assn. (v.p. 1989-91), Kiwanis Internat. (pres. 1992-93, 93-94), Mensa (Officially Overworked Vol. 1998, 99), Phi Kappa Phi. Wiccan. Office: Re Creations 86 High St Saco ME 04072 E-mail: thea@loa.com.

COLLINS, DELORIS WILLIAMS, secondary school educator; b. Jackson, Miss., Oct. 24, 1959; d. Eddie (Stepfather) and Mary Louise Lewis; m. Bobby Collins, July 18, 1981; children: Garrian V., Bryan L. AA, Hinds Jr. Coll., Jackson, Miss., 1987; BBA in Office Adminstrn., Jackson State U., 2000. Circulation clk. Eudora Welty Libr., Jackson, Miss., 1989—91; tech. specialist, libr. circulation clk. H.T. Sampson Libr. Jackson State U., 1991—93; libr. media tech. specialist Canton Pub. Schs. Dist., 1993—96; with U.S. Postal Svc., Jackson, 1999—2000; limited svcs. instr., substitute tchr. Jackson Pub. Schs. Dist., Jackson, 2000—. Cert. facilitator Family Connections, Jackson, 1999; seminar and workshop condr. Author: They Are Throwing Rocks, 1997, Chasing After the Wind, 1998, Anointed Hyms-Poems, 1999, Treasured Recipes, 1999, Marriage in Yesterday and Today Society: There is Hope, Its All in the Lord, 2000, The Talking Partridge, 2003; author: (musical works of published poetry on CD) Inspirations, 1997—2003; actor: (cookbook) DIPS, 2005. Nominee Poet of the Yr., 2003, 2004, 2005—06; named Internat. Educator of Yr., 2004—05; named to Wall of Tolerance, Civil Rights Meml. Ctr., 2003; recipient Editors Choice award, 2003, Achievement Edn. award, Inter-Biog. Ctr., Cambridge, Eng., 2006, Internat. Educator Yr., 2005. Mem.: Internat. Soc. of Poets (hon.). Achievements include patents for The Life's Gadgets Learning Tool; The Prayer Doll Learning Tool. Avocations: reading, cooking. Home: 403 Stillwood Dr Jackson MS 39206

COLLINS, DIANA JOSEPHINE, psychologist; b. Potsdam, N.Y., Apr. 27, 1944; d. Philip Joseph and Janet Dorothy (Lynke) C Grad. with high honors, SUNY; PsyD, Mass. Sch. Profl. Psychology, 1981. Psychologist N.H. Hosp., Concord, 1974-79, asst. dir. forensic unit, 1979-80; founder, dir. Victim/Witness Svc. Country of Hillsborough, Manchester, N.H., 1980-84; pvt. practice Bedford, N.H. Adj. assoc. prof. U. N.H., 1974; adj. assoc. prof. Antioch Coll. of New Eng. Mem. APA, Assn. Applied Psycholphysiology and Biofeedback, Biofeedback Soc. Am. (cert.), N.H. Psychol. Assn. (bd. dirs.), Mass. Psychol. Assn., Ea. Psychol. Assn., Internat. Assn. Psychotherapists and Counselors, Am. Assn. Female Execs. Roman Catholic. Home: 17 Pine Ln Warner NH 03278-4630 Office: 40 S River Rd Unit 63 Bedford NH 03110-6724 Office Phone: 603-626-1446.

COLLINS, EILEEN MARIE, astronaut; b. Elmira, NY, Nov. 19, 1956; d. James Edward and Rose Marie (O'Hara) C.; m. James Patrick Youngs, Aug. 1, 1987; 2 children. AS in Math., Sci., Corning C.C., 1976; BA in Math., Econs., Syracuse U., 1978; grad., USAF Undergrad. Pilot Tng., Vance AFB, Okla., 1979, USAF Test Pilot Sch., Edwards AFB, Calif., 1990; MS in Ops. Rsch., Stanford U., 1986; MA in Space Systems Mgmt., Webster U., 1989; student, Air Force Inst. Techology, 1986; grad., Air Force Test Pilot Sch., Edwards AFB, Calif., 1990. Commd. 2d lt. USAF, 1978, advanced through grades to col., 1993, T-38 instr. pilot 71st flight tng. wing Vance AFB, 1979-82, C-141 aircraft comdr. and instructor pilot, 86th mil. airlift squadron Travis AFB, Calif., 1983-85, ret., 2005; asst. prof. math., T-41 instr. pilot USAF Acad., Colorado Springs, Colo., 1986-89; astronaut Johnson Space Ctr. NASA, Houston, 1991—2006. Served on astronaut support team responsible for Orbiter prelaunch check-out, final launch configuration, crew ingress/egress, landing/recovery; spacecraft communicator, CAPCOM, also served as the astronaut office spacecraft systems branch chief, chief information officer, shuttle branch chief, astronaut safety branch chief; pilot, space shuttle Discovery (STS-63), 1995 (first women pilot of space shuttle), space shuttle Atlantis (STS-84), 1997; comdr. space shuttle, Columbia (STS-93), 1999 (first women shuttle comdr.); crew comdr. space shuttle, (STS-114) Discovery; during this Return To Flight mission, the crew tested and evaluated new procedures for flight safety, shuttle inspections and repair techniques, 2005. Col. USAF. Decorated Air Force Commendation medal with one oak leaf cluster, Air Force Meritorious svc. medal with one oak leaf cluster, Armed Forces Expeditionary medal for svc. in Grenada (Operation Urgent Fury, 1983), Def. Superior Svc. medal, Def. Meritorious Svc. medal, Disting. Flying Cross, French Legion Honor, Disting. Flying Cross, NASA Outstanding Leadership medal, NASA Space Flight medals; recipient Harmon Trophy, 1995, Free Spirit award, 2006. Mem.: Am. Inst. Aeronautics and Astronautics, US Space Found., Order of Daedalians, Air Force Assn., The Ninety-Nines, Women Military Avaitors. Avocations: running, golf, hiking, camping, reading, photography, astronomy.*

COLLINS, ELIZABETH BROOKE, theater educator; b. Albany, Ga. d. David Benjamin and Kay Annelle (Brooks) Collins. AA in Speech and Drama, Gainesville Coll., Ga., 2001; BA in Theatre and English, Brenau U., Gainesville, Ga., 2003. Stage mgr. Va. Stage Co., Norfolk, Va., 2003—04; edn. and prodn. asst. Ga. Shakespeare, Atlanta, 2004; stage mgr. Ctr. Puppetry Arts, 2004—05; summer camp coord. Imagine It! Children's Mus., 2005; summer camp tchr. Art Sta. and Ga. Shakespeare, 2005; stage mgr. Actor's Express, 2005; asst. theatre for youth Alliance Theatre, 2005—06; edn. assoc. and co. mgr. Ga. Shakespeare, 2006—. Freelance tchr. Art Sta., Atlanta, 2005—, Ga. Shakespeare, 2005—, Alliance Theatre, 2005—. Mem.: Am. Alliance Theatre and Edn., Art Search/TCB. Avocations: travel, art history, drawing, painting, reading.

COLLINS, GAIL, editor; BA in Journalism, Marquette U., 1967; MA in Govt., U. Mass., 1971. Founder Conn. State News Bur., 1972—77; freelance writer, 1977—79; sr. editor Conn. Mag.; columnist Conn. Bus. Jour., 1977—79; host pub. affairs program Conn. Pub. TV, 1977—79; instr. journalism So. Conn. State Coll., 1977—79; fin. reporter UPI, N.Y.C., 1982—85; columnist N.Y. Daily News, N.Y.C., 1985—91, N.Y. Newsday, N.Y.C., 1991—95; mem. editl. bd. The N.Y. Times, N.Y.C., 1995—, host This Week Close-Up cable news program, 1997—, columnist op-ed page, 2000—01, editl. page editor, 2001—. Author (with Dan Collins): The Millennium Book, 1991; author: Scorpion Tongues, 1998, America's Women: Four Hundred Years of Dolls, Drudges, Helpmates and Heroines, 2003. Recipient Meyer Berger award, Columbia U., 1987, Matrix award, Women in Comm, 1989, award for commentary, AP, 1994; Bagehot fellow, Columbia U., 1981—82. Office: Editl Page The NY Times 229 W 43d St New York NY 10036 Office Fax: 212-556-3815. Business E-Mail: editorial@nytimes.com.

COLLINS, GWENDOLYN BETH, health facility administrator; b. Akron, Ohio; d. Emmert Samuel and Lillice Elizabeth (Matthews) Shaffer; 1 child, Holly Marie. BA, Case Western Res. U. Exec. dir. Canton Area Regional Health Edn. Network, 1981-88; project dir. Region VII Cancer Registry, Canton, Ohio, 1984-88; program dir. Diabetes Mgmt. Ctr., St. Petersburg, Fla., 1988-89, 92-94, Pasadena Sr. Health Ctr., St. Petersburg, 1995-96; health mgmt. and mktg. cons. Largo, Fla., 1986-88, 95—; practice adminstr. Santiago Morales, MD, P.A., Largo, Fla., 2000—02, Diagnostic and Consultative Cardiology, Brandon, Fla., 2003—04, John F. Spallino M.D. PA, Tampa, Fla., 2005, Stein Med. Inst. Inc., Tampa, Fla., 2006—. Mem. continuing med. edn. com. Aultman Hosp., 1983-88; planner and evaluator Directions for Mental Health, Inc., Clearwater, Fla., 1990-92. Mem. adv. com. Camp Y-Noah, 1985-86. HHS grantee, Canton, 1986-88. Mem. Cancer Control Consortium Ohio (mem. cancer incidence mgmt. com. 1986-87). Republican. Avocations: reading, music, walking. Home: 9508 Cavendish Dr Tampa FL 33626 Personal E-mail: wendyc28@verizon.net.

COLLINS, IRMA HELEN, music educator, consultant; b. Horatio, Ark., May 15, 1930; d. Roy DeWitt Hopkins and Irma Virginia Morgan; m. Walter Ray Collins, Aug. 27, 1960 (div. Feb. 15, 1976). BA, Ouachita Coll., 1952; BS in Music, Southwestern Sem., 1954; MusM, George Peabody Coll., 1958; D in Musical Arts, Temple U., 1979. Instr. Mars Hill (N.C.) Coll., 1954—57; assoc. prof. W.Va. Wesleyan Coll., Buckhannon, 1958—65; tchr., adminstr. Bd. Edn., Pitts., 1965—68; chair dept. music Ea. Coll., St. Davids, Pa., 1968—72; prof. music Murray (Ky.) State U., 1976—93; adj. prof. music Shenandoah U. Conservatory, Winchester, W.Va., 1998—. Arts cons.; founder Jour. Music Tchr. Edn.; rschr., writer stds. of learning in music Commonwealth Va., 2001; tchr./curriculum com. Shenandoah U. Coll. of Lifelong Learning. Author: (songs) I Call to Thee, 1988, In the Eyes of a Child, 1990; reviewer (jours.) including Southeastern Music Edn. Jour.; contbr. articles to profl. jours. Violinist Ark. State Symphony, Carnegie-Mellon Symphony, Nashville Symphony, Paducah Symphony; soloist Temple Sinai Synagogue, Pitts. Mem.: Ky. Music Educators Assn. (Tchr. of Yr. award), Soc. Music Tchr. Edn. (nat. chairperson), Sigma Alpha Iota (Outstanding Mem. award).

COLLINS, JACKIE (JACQUELINE JILL COLLINS), writer; b. London, Oct. 4, 1937; m. Wallace Austin 1955 (div.); 1 child; m. Oscar Lerman, 1966 (dec. 1992); 2 children. Author: The World Is Full of Married Men, 1968, The Stud, 1969, Sunday Simmons and Charlie Brick, 1971 (pub. as The Hollywood Zoo, 1975), Lovehead, 1974 (pub. as The Love Killers, 1977), The World Is Full of Divorced Women, 1975, Lovers and Gamblers, 1977, The Bitch, 1979, Chances, 1981, Hollywood Wives, 1983, Sinners, 1984, Lucky, 1985, Hollywood Husbands, 1986, Rock Star, 1987, Lady Boss, 1989, American Star, 1993, Hollywood Kids, 1994, Vendetta: Lucky's Revenge, 1997, Thrill, 1998, L.A. Connections, 1998, Dangerous Kiss, 1999, Lethal Seduction, 2000, Hollywood Wives: The Next Generation, 2001, Deadly Embrace, 2002, Hollywood Divorces, 2003, Loves & Players, 2006. Office: c/o Simon & Schuster 1230 Ave of Amer New York NY 10020*

COLLINS, JACQUELINE F., nurse, case manager; d. John Francis and Velmah Grace Conroy; m. Richard F. Collins Jr., Sept. 11, 1971; children: Kathleen Fisher, Kelly Maskiell, Kristin Heanssler, Kevin. Diploma in nursing, St. Mary's Sch. Nursing, Lewiston, Maine, 1971; BSN, St. Joseph's Coll., 1997. RN, cert. Internat. Bd. Lactation Examiners, inpatient obstetric nursing, NAACOG, case mgr., Commn. for Case Mgmt. Cert. RN, staff nurse med./surg. unit Brighton Med. Ctr., Portland, Maine, 1986, RN, staff nurse ob. unit, 1986—95, RN, asst. mgr. ob., 1995; RN, staff nurse NICU/Family Ctr. Maine Med. Ctr., Portland, 1995—98, RN, lactation cons., 1999—2002; RN, case mgr. Anthem, South Portland, Maine, 1998—2004, Martin's Point Health Care, Portland, 2004—. Chair Portland walk com. March of Dimes, 2002. Mem.: Case Mgmt. Soc. Am., Assn. Woman's Health Ob. and Neonatal Nurses, Sigma Theta Tau. Democrat. Roman Catholic. Avocations: reading, walking, cross country skiing, kayaking.

COLLINS, JACQUELINE WIGHT, secondary school educator; b. New Rochelle, N.Y., July 17, 1930; d. Alvin D. and Cora A. (Gunthorpe) Wight; m. LeRoy M. Collins, July 26, 1952; children: LeRoy Wight, Laurie Ann. MusB., Syracuse U., 1952; MS in Edn., Hoftra U., 1971. Cert. guidance counselor. Case worker Westchester County Dept. Social Svcs., White Plains, N.Y., 1952-54; tchr. Meml. Jr. High Sch., 1954-59, 68-70; edn. coord. Summer Sch. E.O.C. Corrdinated Program, Inwood, N.Y., 1967-68; guidance counselor Roosevelt Pub. Schs., Roosevelt, N.Y., 1970—. Piano tchr., Nassau County, 1954-85. Treas., Am. Field Svc., N.Y.; pres. PTA, Inwood, 1967-68; v.p. Five Towns Child Care Ctr., Inwood, 1987-88, bd. dirs., 1986-90. Recipient Jenkins award N.Y. PTA. Mem. L.I. Counselors Assn., N.Y. Pers. Assn., L.I. Black Educators and Counselors Assn., Suburban League, Jack and Jill Am. Assocs., N.Y. Holidays (sec.), Alpha Kappa Alpha. Episcopalian.

COLLINS, JACQUELINE Y, state senator; b. McComb, Miss., Dec. 10; Grad. journalism, Northwestern Univ.; MA, Harvard's John F. Kennedy Sch. of Gov.; MA Human Svc. Admin., Spertus Coll.; MA Theol. Studies, Harvard Divinity Sch., 2003. State Senator 11 Senate, Dist. 16Ill., 2003—; min. of Comm. St. Sabina Cath. Ch., Chgo.; journalist in print, radio and TV; press sec. Congressman Gus Savage. Mem. Appropriations I, Environ. and Energy, Revenue (VC), Revenue Subcommittee on Spl. Issues. Recipient Emmy Award - nominated news editor, CBS-TV/ Chgo.; Legislative fellow with US Senator Hillary Rodham Clinton. Democrat. Catholic. Office: Capitol Bldg M-118 Springfield IL 62706 also: 1155 W 79th St Chicago IL 60620

COLLINS, JANET L., psychiatrist; M in Clin. Psychology, San Diego State U.; PhD in Ednl. Psychology, Stanford U. Acting dir. Nat. Ctr. for HIV, Sexually Transmitted Diseases and Tuberculosis Prevention Centers for Disease Control and Prevention, acting dir. Adolescent and Sch. Health Divsn., dep. dir. Nat. Ctr. Chronic Disease Prevention and Health Promotion, dir. Nat. Ctr. Chronic Disease Prevention and Health Promotion. Office: Nat Ctr Chronic Disease Prevention & Health Promotion Centers for Disease Control 2900 Woodcok Bldv Rm 3008 Atlanta GA 30341 Office Phone: 770-488-5401.*

COLLINS, JEAN KATHERINE, language educator; b. Norfolk, Va., June 14, 1928; d. Elwood Brantley and Katherine Belle (Lambertson) C. BA in Liberal Arts, James Madison U., Harrisonburg, Va., 1945-49; MA in English, U. Richmond, 1950-51; edn. credits, U. Va., Eastern Shore of Va., 1950, 60; art edn. credits, Millersville State Tchrs. Coll, summer 1970. Continuity writer Radio Station WLEE, Richmond, Va., 1949; English, critic tchr. Farmville H.S., Longwood Coll., Va., 1951-53; English tchr., art tchr. Hermitage H.S., Richmond, Va., 1953-55; prin., art tchr. Cape Charles (Va.) H.S., 1957-59; head English dept., tchr. Northampton H.S., Eastville, Va., 1960-63; art tchr. Pvt. Studio, Cape Charles, Va., 1964-90. Pres. Lambda chpt. Delta Kappa Gamma Soc., Eastern Shore of Va., 1966-68; recording sec. Iota State Delta Kappa Gamma Soc., Headqtrs., Richmond, Va., 1967-69; adv. bd. Eastern Shore Pub. Libr., Accomac, Va., 1981-89; bd. dirs. Eastern Shore of Va. Hist. Soc., Onancock, Va., 1957-60. Author: (poetry) Madison Quarterly, 1948, 49; author, illustrator: An Eastern Shore Sampler, 1975; author: History of Trinity United Methodist Church, 1993. Named Woman of Yr. Young WOmen's Club of Cape Charles, Va., 1958. Mem. Eastern Shore of Va. Hist. Soc., Cape Charles Hist. Soc., Trinity United Meth. Ch., Delta Kappa Gamma Soc. Republican. Methodist. Avocations: painting, needlecrafts, history, theater, dance, writing.

COLLINS, JENNIFER L., intercultural studies educator; b. Decatur, Ind. m. J. D. Collins. BS in Computer Sci./Sys., Taylor U., Upland, Ind., 1989; MA in Religion, Trinity Internat. U., Deerfield, Ill., 2000. Dir. internat. svc. learning, adj. instr. Taylor U., Upland, Ind., 1994—2003, asst. prof. intercultural studies, 2003—. Mem. exec. com. Nat. Com. for Stds. of Excellence in Short-Term Mission, Mpls., 2005—. Contbg. author: (non-fiction) Overcoming the World Missions Crisis. Chair, mem. missions team 1st Ch. of God, ECI, Muncie, Ind., 2001—. Named Outstanding Student in Systems Analysis, Taylor U., 1989. Mem.: Assn. for Christians in Student Devel. Office: Taylor U 236 W Reade Ave Upland IN 46989-1001 Office Phone: 765-998-5362.

COLLINS, JESSICA ANN, military officer; b. Tulsa, Okla., May 31, 1981; d. Kenneth Matthew Collins, Jr. and Mai Hoa Collins. BS in Sociology, U. Tulsa, 2005, cert. in womens studies, 2005. Vol. Veterans Assistance Hosp., Tampa, Fla., 2005, VFW, Tulsa, 2001—03. Cpl. USMC, 1999—. Decorated

Selected Marine Corps Res. medal USMC, Nat. Def. medal, Global War on Terrorism Svc. medal, Marine Corps Good Conduct medal, Armed Forces Res. medal with M Device, Global War on Terrorism Expeditionary medal, Sea Svc. Deployment ribbon, Navy and Marine Corps Commendation medal U.S. Sec. of Navy; Simon Estes Merit scholar, Simon Estes Ednl. Found., Inc., 1999—2003. Mem.: NOW, Women Marine Assn. Okla. Chpt., Women in Mil. Svc., Nat. Coalition Against Domestic Violence. Office: US Marine Forces Central Command 7115 S Boundary Blvd MacDill AFB FL 33621 Office Fax: 813-827-7011. Business E-Mail: collinsja@marcent.usmc.mil.

COLLINS, JOAN HENRIETTA, actress; b. London, May 23, 1933; came to U.S., 1938; d. Joseph William and Elsa (Bessant) C.; m. Maxwell Reed (div.); m. Anthony Newley (div.); children: Tara, Sacha; m. Ronald S. Kass, Mar., 1972 (div.); 1 child, Katy; m. Peter Holm (div.); m. Percy Gibson, 2002. Student, Francis Holland Sch., London, Royal Acad. of Dramatic Art. Actor: (films) Cosh Boy, 1952, Our Girl Friday, 1953, I Believe in You, 1952, The Good Die Young, 1954, Land of the Pharoahs, 1955, The Virgin Queen, 1955, Girl in the Red Velvet Swing, 1955, The Opposite Sex, 1956, Sea Wife, 1957, Island in the Sun, 1957, Rally Round the Flag Boys!, 1958, The Bravados, 1958, Seven Thieves, 1960, Esther and the King, 1960, Road to Hong Kong, 1962, Warning Shot, 1967, Subterfuge, 1969, The Executioner, 1970, Up in the Cellar, 1970, Revenge, 1971, Quest for Love, 1971, Tales From the Crypt, 1972, Tales That Witness Madness, 1973, Drive Hard, Drive Fast, 1973, Dark Places, 1973, I Don't Want to be Born, 1975, The Bawdy Adventures of Tom Jones, 1976, Empire of the Ants, 1977, The Stud, 1978, The Big Sleep, 1978, The Bitch, 1979, Sunburn, 1979, Game for Vultures, 1979, Homework, 1982, Nutcracker, 1982, Decadence, 1994, In the Bleak Mid-Winter, 1995, The Clandestine Marriage, 1998, The Flintstones-Viva Rock Vegas, 1999, Joseph and His Technicolor Dreamcoat, 1999, Ozzie, 2001, Ellis in Glamourland, 2004, and several others; (TV films) Drive Hard, Drive Fast, 1973, The Man Who Came to Dinner, Paper Dolls, 1982, The Wild Women of Chastity Gulch, 1982, The Cartier Affair, 1983, Making of a Male Model, 1983, Her Life as a Man, 1984, Hart to Hart: Two Harts in Three Quarters Time, 1995, and several others; (TV miniseries) The Moneychangers, 1976, Sins, 1986, Monte Carlo, 1986, Tonight at 8:30, 1991, Dynasty: The Reunion, 1992, Dynasty Reunion:Catfights & Caviar, 2006; (TV series) Dynasty, 1981—89, Faerie Tale Theater, 1982, Pacific Palisades, 1997, Footballers Wives, 2005, Hotel Babylon, 2005; (TV films) Mama's Back, 1993, Annie: A Royal Adventure, 1995, Hart to Hart, 1995; actor, actor: (TV films) Sweet Deception, 1998, These Old Broads, 2000, (video) Secrets of Fitness and Beauty, 1994, (theater) Jassey, Claudia, The Skin of Our Teeth, The Praying Mantis, The Last of Mrs. Cheyney, The 7th Veil, A Doll's House, Private Lives, 1990, Love Letters, 2000, Over the Moon, 2001, Full Circle, 2004, An Evening With Joan Collins, 2006, Legends, 2006; guest appearances Mission Impossible, 1969, Baretta, 1976, Police Women, 1976, Starsky & Hutch, 1977, Fantasy Island, 1980, The Love Boat, 1983, The Nanny, 1996, Roseanne, 1993, Will & Grace, 2000, Guiding Light, 2002, Who Wants to Be a Millionaire, 2005, The British Soap Awards, 2005, TV Land Confidential, 2005, Loose Women, 2005, The L Word, 2005, Breakfast, 2005, and several others; author: Past Imperfect, 1978, Second Act, 1996, Katy, A Fight for Life, Joan Collins Beauty Book, 1980, Prime Time, 1988, Love and Desire and Hate, 1991, My Secrets, 1994, Too Damn Famous, 1995, My Friends Secrets, 1999, Star Quality, 2002, Joan's Way, 2002, Misfortune's Daughters, 2005. Decorated Order of Brit. Empire; recipient Emmy nomination, Golden Globe award, Ace award, People's Choice award; named to Order Brit. Empire. Avocations: travel, 18th century art. Address: 16 Bulbecks Walk South Woodham Ferrers Essex CM3 52N England Office Phone: 011 44 1245 328367. E-mail: pkeylock@aol.com.

COLLINS, JODI M., utilities executive; BBA, U. Redlands; MBA, Pepperdine U. Joined So. Calif. Edison Co., Rosemead, Calif., 2000, dir. info. tech. application services, now v.p. info. tech., 2003—. Named one of 100 Premier IT Leaders, Computerworld, 2005. Office: So Calif Edison Co 2244 Walnut Grove Ave Rosemead CA 91770

COLLINS, JOE LENA, retired secondary school educator; b. Mt. Pleasant, Tenn., Nov. 18, 1922; d. Morton Daniel and Rosetta Francis C. BS in English, Tenn. Tech., Cookeville, 1949; MA in English, George Peabody, Nashville, 1968, EdS in English, 1975. Cert. tchr. Sec. to Dr. G.C. English and Dr. C.D. Walton, Mt. Pleasant, Tenn., 1942-46; tchr. Maury Co. Schs., Mt. Pleasant, Tenn., 1949-51, Tenn. Tech., Cookeville, Tenn., 1951; acct. Cookeville Prodn. Credit, Tenn., 1951-52; tchr. Metro Nashville Schs., 1952-88. Lectr. Ret. Learning Vanderbilt U., 2000—. Com. worker Dem. Party, 1980—2003. Mem. AAUW (pres.), Tenn. Writers Alliance, Tenn. Hist. Soc., Women in the Arts, United Meth. Women (Woman of Purpose award), Belle Meade Book Club (leader), Metro Ret. Tchrs. Assn. Avocations: reading, writing, painting, sports. Home: 6212 Henry Ford Dr Nashville TN 37209-1738

COLLINS, JOYCE A.P., minister, librarian, educator, realtor; b. Memphis, June 12, 1948; d. Joe Harry (Stepfather) and Lelia Mae (Strickand Powell) Armstrong; m. Warren Eugene Collins, Sept. 4, 1971 (div. 1994); adopted children: Evangeline, Warren Gabriel. BA cum laude, LeMoyne-Owen U., Memphis, 1970; MLS, Western Mich. U., Kalamazoo, 1971. Cert. tchr. Tenn., 1970, lifetime tchr. cert. La., cert. realtor La. Circulation libr. Tenn. State U., Nashville, 1971—72; catalog libr. La. State U., Baton Rouge, 1972; dir. info. and rsch. ARIC, Nashville, 1973—74; asst. prof., head libr. media svcs. Fisk U., Nashville, 1974—75; libr., lectr. Pub. Schs. Davidson Co., Nashville, 1975—77; libr., head circulation dept. Southern U., Baton Rouge, 1977—78, social sci. libr., 1978—80; realtor Baton Rouge, 1980—; dir. JACPO Ministries, Nashville, 1997—. Faculty sen. La. State U., Baton Rouge, 1970—80; reader svcs. coord. Fisk U., Nashville, 1975. Mem.: AAUW, Nat. Assn. U. Women, La. Libr. Assn. Baptist. Home: PO Box 1601 Madison TN 37116-1601

COLLINS, JUDY MARJORIE, singer, songwriter; b. Seattle, May 1, 1939; d. Charles T. and Marjorie (Byrd) Collins; m. Peter A. Taylor, Apr. 1958 (div.); 1 child, Clark Taylor (dec.). Pvt. study piano, 1953-56. Debut as profl. folk singer, Boulder, Colo., 1959; has since appeared in numerous clubs, U.S. and around world; performer concerts including Newport Folk Festival, maj. concert halls and summer theatres, throughout U.S. and Europe; also appeared radio and TV, including HBO TV spl. Judy Collins: From the Heart, 1989; recording artist, Elektra; profl. acting debut as Solveig in N.Y. Shakespeare Festival prodn. of Peer Gynt, 1969; producer, dir. documentary movie Antonia: A Portrait of the Woman, 1974; composer songs including Albatross, 1967, Since You've Asked, 1967, My Father, 1968, Secret Gardens, 1972, Born to the Breed, 1975; albums include Bread & Roses, Colors of the Day, So Early in the Spring/The First Fifteen Years, 1977, Hard Times for Lovers, 1979, Running for My Life, 1980, Trust Your Heart, 1987, Sanity and Grace, 1989, Recollections, Fires of Eden, 1990, Judy Sings Dylan: Just Like a Woman, 1993; author: (autobiography) Trust Your Heart, 1987, Sanity and Grace, A Journey of Suicide, Survival and Strength, 2003. Recipient Grammy award, 1968, 6 Gold LP's., Silver medal Atlanta Film Festival, Blue Ribbon award Am. Film Festival, NYC, Christopher award. Office: care Charles Rothschild Prodns 330 E 48th St New York NY 10017-1766 also: Mesa/Blueman Records 209 E Alameda Ave Ste 101 Burbank CA 91502-2673

COLLINS, KATHERINE LOUISE, elementary school educator; b. Terre Haute, Ind., May 9, 1960; d. William S. and Bonnie M. (Jones) Mattox; m. Tom K. Collins, June 25, 1982; children: Casey Dawn, Kyle Kevin. BS in Elem. Edn., Ind. State U., 1982, MS in Elem. Edn., 1987. Elem. tchr. Met. Sch. Dist. of Shakamak, Jasonville, Ind., 1984—. Contbr. articles to profl. jours. Coach girls high sch. basketball. Mem. NEA, Ind. Tchrs. Asns., Internat. Reading Assn., Shakamak Classroom Tchrs. Assn. (treas.), Kappa Delta Pi. Home: RR 3 Box 1337 Linton IN 47441-9760 Office: RR 2 Box 42 Jasonville IN 47438-9511

COLLINS, KATHLEEN, academic administrator, art educator; b. Chgo., BA in psychology, minor in fine arts, Stanford U.; MFA in photography. Chmn. applied photography dept. Sch. Photographic Arts & Sci., Rochester Inst. Tech., coord. summer workshops; dean Sch. Art & Design, NY State Coll. Ceramics, Alfred U., prof.; pres. Kans. City Art Inst., 1996—. Represented in permanent collections, Art Inst. Chgo., Cleve. Art Mus., Centro Cultural/Arte Contemporaneo, Mex. City, Mex., Chrysler Mus., Norfolk Va. Office: Office of President Kansas City Art Inst 4415 Warwick Blvd Kansas City MO 64111

COLLINS, KATHLEEN, mathematics educator; d. Phillip McGregor and Janice Mcafee; m. Tim Majoras, July 13, 2001; children: Jennifer Majoras, Ian Majoras. BS Math. in Math., U. Tenn., Chattanooga, 1990. Lic. tchr. Tenn., 1990. Tchr. Hamilton County Sch., Chattanooga, 1990—. Recipient Tchr. of Yr., WTVC, 2006. Mem.: Nea Tea (assoc.). Office: Hamilton County Sch Ridge Trail Rd Soddy Daisy TN 07379 Office Phone: 423-843-4733. Office Fax: 423-843-4719.

COLLINS, KATHLEEN ANNE, artistic director; b. Elmira, N.Y., Dec. 20, 1951; d. James G. and Joyce (Balmer) C.; m. Andrew Stephon Elston, May 28, 1977; children: Megan, Kate. BA, SUNY, Albany, 1974; MA in Theatre, U. Wash., 1976, MFA in Theatre, 1979. Dir. edn. Seattle Children's Theatre, 1975-78; instr. drama Lakeside Sch., Seattle, 1978-79; artistic dir. Honolulu Theatre for Youth, 1979-83, Fulton Opera House, Lancaster, Pa., 1983-98; prof. Cornish Coll. of Arts, Seattle, 1999—. Guest lectr. U. Hawaii, Honolulu, 1981, U. Wash., Seattle, 2002—04; guest dir. Seattle Children's Theatre, 2002—03; adj. faculty Lesley U., 2000—; guest dir. Six Minutes, Seattle Rep. Woman's Playwriting Festival, Seattle, 2004. Contbg. author: Drama With Children, 1979. Bd. dirs. PTO, Lancaster, 1990-98; pres. Winifred Ward Found. Mem. Am. Assn. Theatre Educators, Assn. and Soc. for Theatre and Children. Democrat. Personal E-mail: kalcollins@comcast.net.

COLLINS, KATHLEEN ELIZABETH, pharmaceutical company official; b. Rock Island, Ill., Jan. 14, 1951; d. A. Phillip and Henrietta (Zeis) C.; m. David Mark Hasenmiller, June 23, 1973 (div. June 1975). Fgn. student, U. Grenoble, 1970; student, Barat Coll., 1968-70, U. Wis., 1970-71; BA in French and English, St. Ambrose Coll., Davenport, Iowa, 1972; postgrad. secondary edn., Augustana Coll., Rock Island, 1975, U. Iowa, 1979, 84; M Counseling, Western Ill. U., 1996. With quality assurance dept. U.S. Army, Savanna, Ill., 1975-76; sales rep. Burroughs Wellcome Co., Research Triangle Park, N.C., 1976-81; vol. nutritionist Peace Corps, Niger, 1981-82; sales rep. Phil Collins Co., Rock Island, 1982-85; med. rep. Lederle Labs., Overland Park, Kans., 1985-88, Summit Pharms. Co. divsn. Ciba-Geigy, NJ, 1988-93, Circle of Excellence; pharm. purchasing specialist John Deere Health Care, Inc., Moline, 1994—96; market devel. assoc. Merck & Co., Inc., 1996—98; Shamanic counselor, 1998—; pharm. sales rep. PDI, Inc., 2001—04; counselor Robert young Ctr., 2004—06. Vol. Big. Bros./Big Sisters, Moline, 1984-85, Pathway Hospice, Luth. Hosp., Moline, 1984-86, 88; vol. domestic violence/sexual assault advocacy Family Resources, Davenport, Iowa; vol. for parent support Network of the Child Abuse Counsel; disaster relief counselor ARC, 1998—. Mem. Quad Cities Pharm. Assn. (treas. 1978, 86, v.p. 1979, sec. 1987, sec./treas. 1988), Jr. League Quad Cities. Roman Catholic. Avocations: swimming, holistic medicine. Home and Office: 3649 Cedarview Ct Bettendorf IA 52722-2877 Office Phone: 563-332-4361. E-mail: ostrichkc@hotmail.com.

COLLINS, LAURA JANE, music educator, singer; b. Mauston, Wis., Mar. 25, 1957; d. Horace Rexford and Mary Jean Collins; m. Thomas Henry Buchholz, Dec. 30, 1977 (div. Dec. 19, 1982); 1 child, Erik. Student, Viterbo Coll., LaCrosse, Wis., 1977; BA, Cameron U., Lawton, Okla., 1979. Cert. music educator K-12 Okla., 1979, Yamaha Music Sch. Tchr. Yamaha Internat. Corp., 1980. Yamaha music sch. tchr. Keynote Music Co., Tulsa, Okla., 1980—82; vocal, gen. music educator Tulsa (Okla.) Pub. Schs., 1981—. Tchr. Tulsa Opera Childrens Workshop, 1986—87; chapel accompanist All Souls Unitarian Ch., 1993—96, choir accompanist, 1995—96; chapel organist Hillcrest Hosp., Tulsa, 1998—; jazz ensemble vocalist R.F. Singers, 2003—04. Vol. Tulsa Boy Singers; co-mgr. office Anderson for Pres., Tulsa, 1980; vol. Jones for U.S. Senate, 1980; vol. Orza for Gov., Tulsa, 2002; liason Dem.Tulsa Pub. Sch. Tchrs.; mem. Children's Advocacy Team of All Souls Unitarian Ch., Tulsa, 1993. Mem.: NEA (del. 2002—05), AAUW, Okla. Choral Dir. Assn., Am. Choral Dir. Assn. (vol. boy singers 2001—03), Music Edn. Nat. Assn., Okla. Music Edn. Assn., Music Tchr. Nat. Assn. (accredited voice and piano 1982), Okla. Edn. Assn. (del. 2003—05), Tulsa Classroom Tchrs. Assn. (bd. dir. 2003—05). Democrat. Unitarian. Avocations: gardening, reading, walking, composing, politics. Home: 3903 S Rockford Ave Tulsa OK 74105 Office: Hoover Elementary Sch 2327 S Darlington Tulsa OK 74114 Office Phone: 918-746-9120. Business E-Mail: collila@tulsaschools.org.

COLLINS, LINDA L., reading specialist, consultant; b. Avenal, Calif., June 13, 1949; d. Albert and Pauline Coffman; m. Daniel Leo Collins, Dec. 8, 1973; children: Daniel Jr., Shawn. BA, Calif. State U., Fresno, 1972; reading credential, U. Calif., Davis, 2000. Tchr. music Reef Sunset Sch. Dist., Avenal, 1974—80, Coalinga (Calif.) Unified Sch. Dist., 1981—82; title I tchr. Big Valley Sch. Dist., Bieber, Calif., 1983—88; reading specialist Ready Springs Sch. Dist., Penn Valley, Calif., 1988—. Reading cons. Houghton Mifflin, 2002—. Bd. dirs. Big Bros. and Sisters, Grass Valley. Named Tchr. of Yr., Big Valley Sch. Dist., 1987, Ready Springs Sch. Dist., 2000; recipient Tchr. Makes a Difference award, Nevada County, 1998. Mem.: Internat. Reading Assn. Avocations: travel, water sports. Home: 17741 Foxtail Dr Penn Valley CA 95946-1201 Office: Ready Springs Sch Dist 10862 Spenceville Penn Valley CA 95946

COLLINS, LUCINDA VARN, occupational therapist; d. Gerhard DeLoach and Gwendolyn Brunson Varn; m. James Terry Collins (div. Mar. 1992); children: Ariel Sarada, Ian Gabriel. Attended, Limestone Coll., Gaffney, S.C., 1973—74; AA, DeKalb Cmty. Coll., Atlanta, 1976; BS, Sch. Applied Health Med. Sch. Ga, Augusta, 1979. Registered occpl. therapist Ga. State Bd. Occpl. Therapy, S.C. State Bd. Occpl. Therapy, cert. Nat. Occpl. Therapy Bd., health and Fitness Phoenix Rising, yoga therapist Phoenix Rising, Pilates instr. Phoenix Rising, 2005, yoga instr. Phoenix Rising, 2005, minister Mother Earth Ch., Culver City, Calif., 1980. Staff occupl. therapist SC Home Health Svcs., Allendale, Barnwell and Bamberg counties, SC, 1980—90, Home Health Profls., Roxboro, NC, 1995—99; rehab. mgr. White Oak Manor, Greensboro, 2000—01; contract occupl. therapist Thematx Rehab., Greensboro, 1994—96, Sunbance Health Care, Mebane, 2000—02, Legacy Healthcare, Greensboro, 2000—02; staff occupl. therapist Peoplefirst Rehab. Kindred Healthcare, Inc., Graham, 2002—. Participant Stewart Wilde's Warrior's Wisdom Course, Taos, N.Mex., 1989, Landmark Edn. Corp. Curriculum Living, Durham, NC, 1992—97, Intro. to Forum Program, 1996—97; yoga and Pilates instr. Mebane Yoga Ctr., 2004—05. Sponsor Christmas Cheer Club, Burlington, NC, 1991—2005, Doctors Without Borders, 2003—05, Amnesty Internat, 2003—05; mem. Women's Resource Ctr., Burlington, 1996—; host parent Youth for Understanding, 1996—99; vol. chaperone HS ednl. trips River Mill Acad., Graham; precinct chair Alamance County Dem. Party, Mebane, 2006. Recipient Appreciation awards, River Mill Acad. Booster Club, 1998—2004. Mem.: N.C. Occupl. Therapy Assn., Alamance County Dem. Women's Assn. Unitarian Universalist. Avocations: dancing, movies, skiing, music festival camping, reading. Home: 413 S Fifth St Mebane NC 27302-2707 Office: Peoplefirst Rehab Kindred Healthcare Inc 779 Woody Dr Graham NC 27253

COLLINS, LYNDA B., biology educator; b. Jackson, Miss., Aug. 5, 1966; d. Robert C. and Mary Helen King Brown; m. Kerry W. Collins, Aug. 1, 1998; children: Caleb, Joshua. BS, Miss. Coll., Clinton, 1988, MSc, 1993. Life scis. tchr. Jackson Pub. Schs., Miss., 1989—97; biology instr., lab. coord. Miss. Coll., Clinton, 1997—2002; life scis. tchr. Hinds County Schs., Terry HS, Miss., 2004—. Mem. Jr. Aux. of Clinton Miss., 1999—. Mem.: NSTA. Office: Terry HS 235 W Beasley St Terry MS 39170

COLLINS, MARIBETH WILSON, retired foundation administrator; b. Portland, Oreg., Oct. 27, 1918; d. Clarence True and Maude (Akin) Wilson; m. Truman Wesley Collins, Mar. 12, 1943; children: Timothy Wilson and Terry Stanton (twins), Cherida Smith, Truman Wesley Jr. BA, U. Oreg., 1940. Pres. Collins Found., Portland, 1964—2006; ret. Trustee Collins Pine Co., Collins Found. Life trustee Willamette U., Salem, Oreg., also mem. campus religious life. Mem. Univ. Club, Gamma Phi Beta. Republican. Methodist. Home: 2275 SW Mayfield Ave Portland OR 97225-4400 Office: Collins Found 1618 SW 1st Ave Ste 505 Portland OR 97201-5708 Personal E-mail: maribeth@teleport.com.

COLLINS, MARTHA, English language educator, writer; b. Omaha, Nov. 25, 1940; d. William E. and Katheryn (Essick) C.; m. Theodore M. Space, Apr. 1991. AB, Stanford U., 1962; MA, U. Iowa, 1965, PhD, 1971. Asst. prof. NE Mo. U., Kirksville, 1965-66; from instr. to prof. English U. Mass., Boston, 1966—2002, co-dir. creative writing, 1979—2000; Pauline Delaney prof., co-dir. creative writing Oberlin Coll., Ohio, 1997—. Author (poetry): The Catastrophe of Rainbows, 1985, The Arrangement of Space, 1991, A History of Small Life on a Windy Planet, 1993, Some Things Words Can Do, 1998, Blue Front, 2006; translator: The Women Carry River Water, 1997 (winner, American Literary Translators Assn. award, 1998), Green Rice, 2005. Fellow Bunting Inst., 1982-83, Ingram Merrill Found., 1988, NEA, 1990; grantee Witter Bynner/Santa Fe Art Inst., 2001, Lannon Found. Residency, 2003; recipient Pushcart prize, 1985, 96, 98, Di Castagnola award, 1990. Mem. Poetry Soc. Am., Assoc. Writing Programs. Democrat. Office: Oberlin Coll Rice Hall Oberlin OH 44074

COLLINS, MARY, writer, educator; b. Hartford, Ct., June 24, 1961; BS cum laude, Gettysburg Coll., 1983; MA, U. Va., 1986. Editor Nat. Geographic Soc., Washington, 1999—2002; prof. grad writing program, non-fiction adv. Johns Hopkins U., 1996—; editor, writer Smithsonian Instn., Washington, 2002—04. Author: The Essential Daughter: Changing Expectations for Girls at Home, 2002, Airborne: A Photo Biography of Wilbur and Orville Wright, 2003. Home: 513 Robinson Ct Alexandria VA 22302

COLLINS, MARY ALICE, psychiatric social worker, educator; b. Everett, Wash., Apr. 20, 1937; d. Harry Edward and Mary (Yates) Caton; BA in Sociology, Seattle Pacific Coll., 1959; MSW, U. Mich., 1966; PhD, Mich. State U., 1974; m. Gerald C. Brocker, Mar. 24, 1980. Diplomate Am. Bd. Social Workers. Dir. teenage, adult and counseling depts. YWCA, Flint, Mich., 1959-64, 66-68; social worker Catholic Social Services, Flint, 1969-71, Ingham Med. Mental Health Center, Lansing, Mich., 1971-73; clin. social worker Genesee Psychiat. Center, Flint, 1974-82, Psychol. Evaluation and Treatment Ctr., East Lansing, Mich., 1982-84; pvt. practice, East Lansing, 1984—; instr. social work Lansing C.C.; lectr. Mich. State U., 1974, 87-93, part-time adj. asst. prof., 1993-2005. ret.; vis. prof. Hurley Med. Center, 1979-84; v.p. Brief Psychotherapy Coalition, 1994; cons. Ingham County Dept. Social Services, 1971-73. Advisor human relations Youth League, Flint Council Chs., 1964-65; sec. Genesee County Young Democrats, 1960-61, pres. Round Lake Improvement Assn., 1984-87. Mem. NASW, Acad. Cert. Social Workers, Phi Kappa Phi, Alpha Kappa Sigma. Contbr. articles to profl. jours. Home: 5945 Round Lake Rd Laingsburg MI 48848-9454

COLLINS, MARY ANN, lawyer; b. Aurora, Colo., May 12, 1953; d. Harold Ernest and Gertrude Elizabeth (Shannon) C.; m. Ronald Jay Sklar, Jan. 20, 1984; 1 child, Jacob Michael. BA, Western Ill. U., 1974; MA in Polit. Sci., U. Ill., 1976; JD, Loyola U., 1980. Bar: Ill. 1980, Calif. 1984. Assoc. Chapman and Cutler, Chgo., 1980-83, Orrick, Herrington & Sutcliffe, San Francisco, 1983-88, ptnr., 1988—. Chair transp. fin. group. Orrick, Herrington & Sutcliffe, San Francisco, co-chair health care, higher edn., and 501(c) revenue transactions group. Contbr. articles to profl. jours. Mem. ABA, Calif. Bar Assn., San Francisco Mcpl. Forum. Office: Orrick Herrington & Sutcliffe 405 Howard St San Francisco CA 94105 Office Phone: 415-773-5998. E-mail: marycollins@orrick.com.

COLLINS, MARY SHAFFER, community nursing educator; b. Sayre, Pa., Nov. 13, 1945; d. Robert L. and Dorothy Mae (McCormick) Shaffer; m. Christopher M. Collins, June 25, 1966; children: Robert M. Collins, Charles A. Collins. BS, Keuka Coll., 1966; MS, Syracuse U., 1975, PhD, 1981. RN, N.Y. Pub. health nurse City-County Health Dept., Colorado Springs, Colo., 1966-69; instr. Broome C.C., Binghamton, N.Y., 1972-74; lectr. Binghamton (N.Y.) U., 1976-81, asst. prof., 1981-86, dean Decker Sch. Nursing, 1988—2002, Decker chair in cmty. health nursing, 2002—. Mem. N.Y. State Bd. for Nursing, 1995—. Contbr. articles to profl. jours. Bd. dirs. Fairview Good Shepard Home, Binghamton, 1986—; mem. accreditation rev. com. Commn. on Collegiate Nursing Edn., 1998—. Mem. ANA, Am. Assn. Colls. Nursing (edn. and credentialing 1986—), N.Y. State Coun. Deans (pres. 1992-94), Sigma Theta Tau (Zeta Iota chpt. pres., v.p. 1980-87). Home: 2529 E Lake Rd Skaneateles NY 13152 Office: Binghamton Univ Decker Sch Nursing PO Box 6000 Binghamton NY 13902-6000

COLLINS, MELANIE JEAN, elementary school educator; d. William Daniel Jr. and Betty Jean Hunt; m. Michael Richard Garrison (div.); m. Paul Vernon Collins Jr., Dec. 17, 1983. BS, U. Tenn., 1979; MEd, Covenant Coll., 1997. Cert. legal sec. Legal sec., paralegal Office of Joe Binkley Jr., Nashville, 1986—91; kindergarten tchr. Mt. Juliet (Tenn.) Christian Acad., 1992—95; prin. Lord's Chapel Christian Acad., Nashville, 1996—99; 5th grade tchr. Woodbine Christian Acad., Nashville, 1999—2000; 1st grade tchr. Lighthouse Christian Sch., Nashville, 2000—02, Metro Nashville Pub. Schs., 2002—04, reading specialist, 2004—. Contbr. poetry to lit. publs. Pres. Tenn. Assn. Legal Secs., Nashville, 1987—89, Davidson County Legal Secs., Nashville, 1988—89; sec. Murfreesboro (Tenn.) Soroptomist Club, 1990—91. Named Legal Sec. of Yr., Davidson County Legal Secs., 1990. Mem.: NEA, Cedars Club of Nashville (sec. 2005—06), Mid. Tenn. Reading Assn. (pres.-elect 2006—), Internat. Reading Assn., Met. Nashville Edn. Assn. (bd. dirs. 2005—06). Avocations: reading, travel. Home: 429 Clearwater Dr Nashville TN 37217 Office: Bordeaux Enhanced Option Elem Sch 1910 S Hamilton Rd Nashville TN 37218 Office Phone: 615-291-6355 ext. 109. E-mail: Cmelpaul@aol.com.

COLLINS, MICHELLE L., venture capitalist; b. 1960; BS in Econ., Yale Univ., 1982; MBA, Harvard Univ., 1986. With corp. fin. dept. William Blair & Co., 1986—91, ptnr., 1991—98; co-founder, mng. dir. Svoboda Collins LLC, Chgo., 1998—. Bd. dir. Coldwater Creek, Inc., CDW Corp., 1996—, Molex, Lisle, Ill., 2003—. Bd. dir. Chgo. Sinfonietta, Erikson Inst.; bd. trustees Field Mus. Named one of 100 Most Influential Women, Crain's Chicago Business, 2004. Mem.: Harvard Bus. Sch. Club, Chgo., Comml. Club Chgo. Office: Svoboda Collins LLC Ste 1500 One N Franklin St Chicago IL 60606 Office Phone: 312-267-8750. Office Fax: 312-267-6025. Business E-Mail: mlc@svoco.com.

COLLINS, N. DANA, art gallery owner, consultant, retired art educator; d. Harold Emile and Nathalie Margaret Collins; m. C. Stephen Rhoades, May 20, 2000 (dec. 2004); children: Jenny Rose, Caitlin Dane(dec.). Student, Yale U., 1964, Sch. Art Inst. Chgo.; BFA, Washington U., 1965; MFA, Pratt Inst., 1967; postgrad., U. Tenn., Columbia Coll., U. Ill., North Adams Coll., Gov.'s State U., Ea. Ill. U., Ill. State U. Prof. fine arts Ill. Valley C.C., Oglesby, 1981—2004, ret., 2004; prin., owner Collins & Co. Studio, Princeton, Ill., 2003—. Tchr. L.I. U., Bklyn., 1967—68, Bay Path Coll., Longmeack, Mass., 1973—74; prof. humanities Ill. Consortium Internat. Edn., London, 1987, Coll. St. Francis, Joliet, Ill., 1991, 94; prof. art Berkshire C.C., Pittsfield, Mass., 1970—80; presenter, tchr., cons. in field. Author: Teaching Studio Art to Diverse Students, 1998; co-editor: The Second Berkshire Anthology, 1975; one-woman shows include The Bklyn. Ctr., 1967, Becket Art Ctr., Mass., 1971, Berkshire Athenaeum, 1979, The Art Gallery, Boston, 1980, McAuley Gallery, Iowa, 1988, The Row Ho. Gallery, Ill., 1993, Prairie Arts Ctr., Princeton, 2006, exhibited in group shows at Pratt Inst., 1968, 1969, 1970, SUNY, New Paltz, 1970, Pratt Manhattan Ctr., 1970, The Bklyn. Mus., 1970, Berkshire Mus., 1975, 1976, 1980, Berkshire C.C., Pittsfield, 1975, Paddlewicker Gallery, Lenox, Mass., 1976, Williams Coll., Williamstown, Mass., 1979, Art Gallery Boston, 1981, Rockford Coll., 1989, Thomas Gallery, Ill., 1991, 1992, Tri-State Gallery, Platteville, Wis., 2003, Art Space, Muscatine, Iowa, 2005—06. Dir. mural projects St. Margaret's Hosp., Spring Valley, Ill.; hot line crisis counselor Battered Woman's Task Force, Pittsfield, 1978—80; bd. dirs. Against Domestic Violence, Streator, Ill., 1983—87, Prairie Arts Ctr., Princeton, Ill.; adv. bd. Ill. Valley Fine Arts Trust, LaSalle, 1992—97. Scholar, Norfolk Sch. Painting, 1964. Mem.: NOW (v.p. 1983—89), Bur. County Big Sister Program, Ill. Fedn. Tchrs. Democrat. Avocations: music, poetry. Home: 19186 Norwood Dr Princeton IL 61356 Office: Collins & Co Studio Gallery 537 S Main St Princeton IL 61356 Office Phone: 815-872-7054.

COLLINS, NANCY LEE, mathematician, educator; b. St. Louis, May 17, 1925; d. Charles Alonzo and Leno Rosie (Squires) Roberts; m. Major Charles Brown Sr., Dec. 23, 1946 (dec. Feb. 1984); children: Major Charles Brown Jr., Victor Ivy Brown; m. James Pickett Collins, Nov. 29, 1986. BA, Harris Stowe State Coll., 1947; MEd, St. Louis U., 1955; MA in Counseling, Washington U., St. Louis, 1968. Cert. elem. and secondary counselor, Mo. Elem. tchr. St. Louis Bd. Edn., 1947-87, adult basic edn. tchr., 1967-72, secondary counselor, 1967-87; supr. computer math. lab. Meramec C.C., St. Louis, 1989—90. Counselor seven up program Villa Duschesne, Ladue, Mo., summer, 1970; tutor continuing edn. program. Univ. City, Mo., 1972-74. Author: Potpourri and Remembrances, 2003; co-editor: Profiles and Silhouettes: The Contribution of Black Women in Missouri, 1979; contbr. poetry to publ. Nat. Libr. of Poetry, 1997; artist compact disc For God and Country, 2004. Spl. advocate vol. Juvenile Ct., St. Louis, 1989-95; mem. exec. bd. Women's Missionary Soc., St. James A.M.E. Ch.; vol peer counselor Older Adult Svcs. Info. Sys. Parsons Blewett scholar St. Louis Bd. Edn., 1977; NSF fellow, 1963; recipient Top Teens Thrust award Top Ladies of Distinction, Inc., St. Louis, 1993, Black History in Mo. Appreciation award AAUW, 1994, Cert. Appreciation Ct. Appointed Spl. Advocates, 1994, Editor's Choice award Outstanding Achievement in Poetry, 2001, Internat. Libr. Poetry, 2003; named Best Poet of Yr.,2002-05; honoree St. James Ch., 1997. Mem. Mo. Conf. Womens Missionary Soc. (membership, recruitment chair 1995), Mo. Conf. Lay Orgn. (local pres. 1993-95, now 3d v.p.), Internat. Soc. Poets (life), Order Eastern Star (worthy matron), Delta Sigma Theta (choir mem. 1986-95, 50 Yr. Mem. award 1995, Cert. Appreciation award 1993), Am. Assn. U. Women, Nat. Assn. U. Women, Mo. State Tchrs. Assn., Retired Sch. Employees of St. Louis. Democrat. African Methodist Episcopalian. Avocations: mathematics, reading, piano, aerobics, Scrabble. Home: 955 Jeanerette Dr University City MO 63130-2719

COLLINS, NANCY WHISNANT, foundation administrator; b. Dec. 20, 1933; d. Ward William and Marjorie Adele (Blackburn) Whisnant; m. James Quincy Collins, Jr., Apr. 25, 1959 (div. 1974); children: James Quincy III, Charles Lowell, William Robey; m. Richard F. Chapman, May 29, 1982. Student, Queens Coll., Charlotte, 1951—53; AB in Journalism, U. N.C., Greensboro, 1955, MS in Pers. Adminstrn., 1967; postgrad., Cornell U., Ithaca, N.Y., 1955—56. Pers. asst. R.H. Macy & Co., Inc., N.Y.C., 1955; jr. exec. placement dir. Scofield Placement Agy., San Francisco, 1956—57; freelance journalist London, Paris, and Frankfurt, Germany, 1957—59; program dir. Girl Scouts U.S.A., Hampton, Va., 1959—61; dir. tour Tokyo, Hong Kong, Singapore, 1965—66; asst. dir. Sloan Exec. Program Stanford (Calif.) U., 1968—78; asst. dir. Hoover Instn., 1979—81; asst. to pres. Palo Alto (Calif.) Med. Found., 1981—2000; asst. to chmn. Novo Ventures, Menlo Park, Calif., 2000—; acting exec. dir. Marconi Soc., 2006. Bd. dir. Am. Healthway Sys.; fund raising cons. Stanford U. Equestrian Ctr., 1994—2004; mgr. Marconi Soc. Ann. Mtg., 2006. Author: Professional Women and Their Mentors, 1988, Women Leading: Making Tough Choices on the Fast Track, 1988, Love at Second Sight, 2003, Playing the MidLife Dating Game, 2003; editor: Have a Great Day: Today and Every Day of Your Life; contbr. articles short stories, and poems to mags. and newspapers. Fundraiser Cornell U., N.Y.C., 1975—81; fundraising consultant Stanford Univ., Equestrian Cender, 1994—2004; mem. coun. Trinity Episcopal Ch., Menlo Park, Calif., 1975—80; mem. leadership team Menlo Park Presbyn. Ch.; bd. dirs. Santa Clara County coun. Girl Scouts U.S.; mem. exec. coun. Stanford area coun. Boy Scouts Am., 1980—81; mem. San Mateo County Charter Rev. Com.; mem. pers. bd. City of Menlo Park, 1979—; mem. women's program bd. Coro Found.; trustee Pacific Grad. Sch. Psychology; sec.-treas. Chapman Rsch. Fund. Fellow, Cornell U.; grantee, Richardson Found., 1967. Mem.: AAUW, Catalyst, Peninsula Profl. Women's Network, Am. Mgmt. Assn., Menlo Circus Club, Overseas Press Club, Commonwealth Club, Mayflower Soc. Club, Kappa Delta. Home: 1850 Oak Ave Menlo Park CA 94025-5842 E-mail: collinsnw@aol.com.

COLLINS, PATRICIA ANN, pastor, pastoral counselor; d. Verner and Mittie Bell Patton; m. Raymond Collins, Sept. 13, 1971; children: Raymond Jr., Annetra Deonette, Sonja Raynette Anthony, Kimberly Dianne, Teon Lavance. A. in Nursing, Lawson State Coll., 1975; BA in Christian Edn., Birmingham-Eastsonian Bible Coll., 1988; MDiv, Samford U-Beeson Div., 1994. Registered nurse, Ala., 1975; pastoral counselor Carraway/United Meth. Counseling Ctr., Ala., 1997, bereavement coord. Am. Acad. Bereavement, N.Y., 2003. Registered nurse Cooper Green Hosp., Birmingham, 1975—77; nursing supr. Lloyd Nolan Hosp., Fairfield, Ala., 1977—83; trauma registered surg. nurse Carraway Meth. Hosp., Birmingham, 1983—92; nurse chaplain Carraway Med. Ctr., Bessemer, Ala., 1992—93, chaplain hospice, 1994—; asst. dir. pastoral svcs. UAB Med. West, Bessemer, 2004—; sr. pastor Faith Missionary Bapt. Ch., Birmingham, 2004—. Bereavement coord. UAB Med. West Hosp., 1995—; pastoral counselor U. Ala. Bessemer Hosp., 1997—, dir. cancer support group touch, 1998—. Mem. Nat. Bapt. Conv., Nashville, 1980—2005, Peace Bapt. Assn., Birmingham, 2005. Mem.: Ala. Nurses Assn. (assoc.), Mary Mahoney Nurses Assn. (assoc.; chaplain 1993—2004, Leadership), Racial - Ethnic Multicultural Assn. of Chaplains (assoc.), Assn. Clin. Pastoral Edn. (assoc.). Baptist. Achievements include first African American woman to become senior pastor of a Black Baptist Church in the state of Alabama. Avocations: singing, reading, music, painting, travel. Home: 1301 Ave H Birmingham AL 35218 Office: UAB Medical West 995 9th Ave Hwy 11 South Bessemer AL 35021 Office Phone: 205-481-7531. Home Fax: 205-780-9128; Office Fax: 205-481-7498. Personal E-mail: pac4567@aol.com. Business E-Mail: pcollins@uabmw.org.

COLLINS, ROSE ANN, minister; b. Pitts., July 5, 1935; d. Joseph and Rochelle (McCrary) Covington; m. Frank Collins, June 30, 1960 (div. 1978); children: Gar Andre, Guy Tracy. BA, Ctrl. Bible Coll., Springfield, Mo., 1987; MDiv, Assemblies of God Theol. Sem., Springfield, Mo., 1989. Ordained to min. 1990. Assoc. min. Deliverance Temple World Outreach Ministries, Springfield, Mo., 1988-90, evangelist Springfield and Pitts., 1991-93; chaplain Western Ctr., Canonsburg, Pa., 1993-96; min. New Jerusalem Holiness Ch., Pitts., 2002—. Trustee Northside Ch. of God in Christ, Pitts., 1982-87, bd. dir., 1983-87. Vol., Ctr. for Victims Violent Crime; vol. mentor Lydia's Pl., Pitts., Pa., 2003—. Mem. Soc. Chaplains (Western chpt.), Pa. Coun. Chs., Ret. Enlisted Assn. (hon., Steel City chpt. 72 chaplain 1994-96). Avocations: reading, walking. Home: 6290 Auburn St Apt 622 Pittsburgh PA 15206-3136 E-mail: rocolli4@aol.com.

COLLINS, ROSEMARIE MARROCCO, psychotherapist; b. Cumberland, Md., Jan. 1, 1939; d. Armand O. and Ethelyn R. (Ross) Marrocco; children: Stephen, Michael, Brian, Laura Diploma, Bon Secours Sch. Nursing, 1960; BS magna cum laude, Neumann Coll., 1976; MSN, U. Pa., 1977, MA Gerontology, 1982, PhD, 1985; postgrad. structural family therapy, Child Guidance Clinic Phila.; postgrad. family therapy, Ea. Pa. Psychiat. Inst. RN, Pa., N.J., Md. Instr. nursing Villanova U., Pa., 1977—79; pvt. practice psychotherapy Wallingford and Glen Mills, Pa., 1977—2002; therapist, dir. Pastoral Counseling Svc., Marianist Ctr., Chester, Pa., 1978—; rsch. asst. Ea. Pa. Psychiat. Inst., Phila., 1980. Asst. prof. Widener U., 1982-85; adj. assoc. prof. LaSalle U., 1986; presenter in field Contbr. articles to profl. publs Recipient Marek Gold medal for Gen. Excellence in Nursing; NIMH grantee, 1976, 77, 79, 80 Mem. ANA, AANC, Pa. Nurses Assn., Family Inst. Phila., AAUP (treas. Villanova chpt. 1979), Am. Orthopsychiat. Assn., Greater Phila. Soc. Clin. Hypnosis, Gerontol. Soc. Am., Bon Secours Alumni Assn., Neumann Coll. Alumni Assn., U. Pa. Alumni Assn. (nominating com. 1983-84), Politically Responsible Nurses, Am. Assn. Nurse Entrepreneurs Home: 69 Stoney Bank Rd Glen Mills PA 19342-1711

COLLINS, RUTH ANN, principal; d. Carl Alvin Pettis, Jr. and Lois Marie Pettis; m. Timothy Paul Collins; children: Thomas Paul, Megan M., Deanna M., Brandon J. BSc, Minn. State U., 1985, MSc cum laude, 1994; postgrad., U. St. Thomas, 1997, postgrad., 1998, postgrad., 2000, U. Loyola, 2000, U. Minn., 2001—04, postgrad., 2005—. Lic. adminstrv. leadership Minn., tchr. Minn., spl. edn. Minn. Tchr. grade 5, 1985—87; tchr. spl. edn., 1987—2005; specialist autism resource Waterville Elysian Morristown Pub. Schs., 1996—2000; intern spl. edn. Roosevelt Sch., Faribault, 2003—04, coord., 2005—; dir. Faribault Spl. Edn. Office, 2005—. Mem. resource and referral com. Gov.'s Coun.; presenter in field. Co-editor: FOCUS - Parent Newsletter, 1996—2000, Faribault Edn. Assn. Newsletter, 2000—02; contbr. A Taste of McKinley, A Quilter's Christmas Cookbook. Mem.: Tchrs. Retirement Assn., Twin Cities Autism Soc., Minn. Assn. Sch. Adminstrs., Nat. Elem. Sch. Prins. Assn., Edn. Minn. (state com., chmn. membership com., co-editor, editor newspaper, bldg. rep., v.p. local chpt., co-chmn. com.), Cath. Dau. of Am., Minn. Deer Hunters Assn., Rotary. Avocation: quilting. Office: Faribault Pub Schs 925 Parshall St Faribault MN 55021

COLLINS, SARAH JANE, secondary school educator; b. Paterson, N.J., Aug. 28, 1965; d. Charles Lewis and Phyllis Mae (Garner) D. Student, Ocean County Coll., Toms River, N.J., 1988—89, Georgian Ct. Coll., 1989—92; postgrad., Georgian Ct. U., 2003—; BS in Biology, Richard Stockton Coll. N.J., 1995. Teller First Nat. Bank of Toms River, 1985-87; legal and exec. sec. Shackleton, Hazeltine & Bishop, Ship Bottom, N.J., 1987-91; tchr. Blessed Sacrament Regional Sch., 1997-99; biology tchr. So. Regional High Sch., 1999—. Avocations: swimming, aerobics, softball. Home: 264 Forge Rd West Creek NJ 08092 Office: So Regional High Sch 600 N Main St Manahawkin NJ 08050-3093

COLLINS, SHERRI SMITH, music educator; b. Winston-Salem, N.C., Apr. 5, 1954; d. Roland Wilson and Foye Cook Smith; m. Paul Steven Collins, Dec. 29, 1979; children: Daniel Joseph, Carrie Elizabeth. BS in Instrumental Music, Western Carolina U., 1976; M in Music Edn., U. N.C.G., 1990. Legal sec. Smith Atty. At Law, Pilot Mountain, NC, 1973; salesperson Southwestern Book Co., Nashville, 1974—76; band dir. East Surry H.S., Pilot Mountain, 1976—88; music specialist Surry County Schs., Dobson, NC, 1990—. Sec. Pilot Mountain Auditorium Restoration, 2000—; pianist, organist First Presbyn. Ch., Pilot Mountain, 1976—, mem. pulpit com., 1977, elder on session, 1993—96. Grantee, Altrusa of Mountain Arry. N.C., 1997—98. Mem.: N.C. Music Educators, N.C. Assn. Educators. Republican. Presbyterian. Avocations: clogging, tennis.

COLLINS, SHERRIE LYNNE, secondary school educator; b. Harlan, Ky., June 18, 1968; d. Shirley Jean and Ronald Lynne Robbins; m. Joel Lee Collins, Dec. 26, 1994; children: Eric Lee, Katherine Emily, Erin Elizabeth. BS in English Edn., U. Tenn., Knoxville, 1990; M in Curriculum and Instrn., Lincoln Meml. U., Harrogate, Tenn., 1992. Cert. tchr. Tenn., 1990, sch. media specialist U. Tenn., 2004. Tchr. Union County Pub. Sch. Sys., Maynardville, Tenn., 1991—. Mem.: Delta Kappa Gamma (chpt. pres. 2005—, Louise Oakley scholar Xi chpt. 2003). Methodist. Avocations: travel, cooking, gardening, reading. Home: 112 Clinch View Dr Corryton TN 37721 Office: Union County High Sch 150 Main St Maynardville TN 37807 Office Phone: 865-992-5232. Home Fax: 865-992-5724; Office Fax: 865-992-5724.

COLLINS, SUSAN BAER, theater director, actor, educator; b. Detroit, May 21, 1951; d. Lesem James and Katheryn Groom Baer; m. Carl Steven Beck, Aug. 14, 1977 (div. 1996); 1 child, Benjamin Wyman Beck; m. Dennis William Collins, Nov. 28, 1998. Student, U. Nebr., Lincoln, 1969—73. Assoc. artistic dir. Omaha Cmty. Playhouse, 1987—. Voice talent dir. DIC Prodns., LA, 2006—. Author (with composer Jonathan D. Cole): (musical for children) Conestoga Stories, 1989, Alice: A Curious Adventure, 1991, Take the Sky, 1993. Recipient various awards for play/musical direction, Theatre Arts Guild, 1988—. Democrat. Avocations: theater, films, travel, swimming, knitting, acting. Office: Omaha Cmty Playhouse 6915 Cass St Omaha NE 68132 Office Phone: 402-553-4890 ext 158. Office Fax: 402-553-6288. E-mail: scollins@omahaplayhouse.com.

COLLINS, SUSAN MARGARET, senator; b. Caribou, Maine, Dec. 7, 1952; BA in Govt. magna cum laude, St. Lawrence U., 1975. Prin. advisor bus. affairs to Senator William S. Cohen US Senate, 1975—78; commr. Maine Dept. Profl. and Fin. Regulation, 1987—92; dir. New England ops. U.S. Small Bus. Adminstrn., 1992—93; exec. dir. Ctr. Family Bus., Husson Coll., Bangor, Maine, 1993—96; US Senator from Maine, 1997—. Staff dir. Senate Subcom. on Oversight Govt. Mgmt., 1981-87; chair Cabinet Coun. on Health Care Policy, State of Maine; mem. U.S. Senate com. health, edn., labor and pensions, 1997—, subcom. on children and families, 1997—, subcom. on pub. health and safety, 1997—, com. on govtl. affairs, 1997—; chmn. permanent subcom. on investigations, 1997—; mem. spl. com. on aging; spl. inspector gen. to handle Hurricane Katrina Relief, 2005- Author (with Catherine Whitney): (Books) Nine and Counting: The Women of the Senate, 2000. Rep. candidate for Gov., State of Maine, 1994. Recipient Outstanding Alumni award St. Lawrence U., 1992, Nat. Public Policy Leadership award Am. Diabetes Assn., Tchr. Leader award Reading Recovery Coun. N. Am., 2004, Public Svc. award Emergency Nurses Assn., 2004, Outstanding Legis. award Triangle Coalition Sci. and Technology Edn., 2005, Port Person of Yr. Am. Assn. Port Authorities, 2006, Congressional Leadership award Nat. Urban League, 2006. Mem. Bangor Rotary Club, Phi Beta Kappa. Republican. Roman Catholic. Office: US Senate 461 Dirksen Sen Office Bldg Washington DC 20510 also: Margaret Chase Smith Fed Bldg 202 Harlow St Rm 204 PO Box 655 Bangor ME 04402-4919 Office Phone: 202-224-2523, 207-945-0417. Office Fax: 202-224-2693, 207-990-4604.*

COLLINS, SUSAN V., secondary school educator; b. Seoul, Republic of Korea, Jan. 22, 1963; d. Joseph D. McCartt and Su Yon Kim Russell; m. Charles W. Collins, June 13, 1987; children: Kalen M., Drew W. BA in Edn., Clinch Valley Coll., Wise, Va., 1989. Cert. coll. profl. tchr. Va. Tchr. St. Paul HS, Wise County Schs., Va., 1990—2006, J.J.H. Kelley HS, Wise County Schs., Va., 1989—90. Grantee, Annenberg Rural Initiative, 1993—98. Mem.: NEA, Va. Edn. Assn. (assoc.). Achievements include development of WDSN school television station. Office: Wise County Schs 1217 Lake street Wise VA 24293 Office Phone: 276-328-8017. Personal E-mail: coolins@charter.net.

COLLINS-BROWN, E. DORLEE (E. DORLEE WOODYARD), registrar; b. Crown City, Ohio, July 10, 1954; d. Walter Woodyard and Ruth Evelyn Simmons; m. Jeffrey Lynn Brown, Feb. 14, 2004; children from previous marriage: Brian Scott Brown, Angela Nycole Collins, Tiara Dorlee Elizabeth Collins. AA, We. Wyo. Coll., 1986; BS in Women's Studies, U. Utah, 1991, BS in Psychology, 1994. Cert. hypnotherapist, child protection svcs./youth and family, adult protection; cert. bus. counselor. Rsch. asst. U. Utah, Salt Lake City, 1988-91; sales mgr. Life and Safety, Sandy, Utah, 1992-94; edn. specialist ITT Tech. Inst., 1994-95; br. mgr. SOS Staff Svcs., Inc., Jackson Hole, Wyo. br., Salt Lake City, 1995-96; social worker Wyo. Dept. Family Svcs., Rock Springs, 1991—99; bus. counselor Small Bus. Devel. Ctr., U. Wyo., Rock Springs, 2000—01; social sci. rschr. U. Mich., Ann Arbor, 2002—; employment trainer Affiliated Computer Svcs., 2004—; outreach parent liaison Parent Edn. Network, 2004. Mem. Nat. Inst. Survey Rsch. U. Mich., Ann Arbor, 2002. Named Miss Regal USA, Amarillo, Tex., 1981, Ms. Wyo. USA, 1997. Mem. AAUW, LWV, Psi Chi. Mem. Lds Ch. Avocations: reading, skiing. E-mail: radardorlee@aol.com.

COLLINSON, VIVIENNE RUTH, education educator, researcher, consultant; b. Kitchener, Ont., Can., July 30, 1949; d. Earl Stanley and Mary Magdalena (Sauder) Feick; m. Charles L. Collinson, May 21, 1983. BA, Wilfrid Laurier U., Waterloo, Ont., 1974; EdM, U. Windsor, Ont., 1989; PhD, OH State U., Columbus, 1993. Cert. adminstr. Tchr. Waterloo County Bd. Edn., 1969-84, Windsor Bd. Edn., 1984-89; vis. asst. prof. U. Windsor, 1989-90, U. Md., College Park, 1993-94, asst. prof. edn., 1994-98; assoc. prof. Mich. State U., 1999—2005. Author: Teachers As Learners, 1994, Reaching Students, 1996, Organizational Learning, 2007. Charter mem. Eleanor Roosevelt Found., 1989—; benefactor Stratford (Ont.) Shakespearean Festival Found. Recipient Ont. Silver medal for piano U. We. Ont. Conservatory of Music, 1965, McGraw-Hill awrd, 1969; Ont. scholar, 1968; Wilfrid Laurier U. grad. scholar. Mem. AAUW, Am. Ednl. Rsch. Assn., Fedn. Women Tchrs. Assn. Ont. (provincial resource leader 1988-94), Nat. Soc. for Study of Edn., Delta Kappa Gamma (Doctoral Dissertation award 1994), Phi Kappa Phi. Avocations: music, theater, travel. Fax: 313-824-2949. E-mail: vrcollinson@yahoo.com.

COLLISCHAN, JUDY KAY, art gallery and museum director, critic, artist; b. Red Wing, Minn., Oct. 19, 1940; d. Michael J. and Olive Amanda (Sundberg) Collischan; 1 son, Brien Grey Collischan Van Wagner. BA, Hamline U., 1962; postgrad. Nat. U. Mex., summer 1963; MFA, Ohio U., 1964; PhD, U. Iowa, 1972. Asst. prof. art history U. No. Iowa, Cedar Falls, 1970-71, U. Nebr.-Omaha, 1971-75; assoc. prof. SUNY-Plattsburgh, 1975-82; dir. Hillwood Art Gallery, LI U., C.W. Post Campus Greenvale, N.Y., 1982—94; assoc. dir. Neuberger Mus. Art, SUNY, Purchase, N.Y., 1995-2000; pvt. practice cons., 2001—; art critic Arts, Art Express, NYC, 1982-; field rep. N.Y. State Council on Arts, NYC, 1983, mem. visual arts panel, 1986—; cons. Gen. Motors art collections, NYC 1983. Author: Women Shaping Art, 1984, Lines of Vision: Drawings by Contemporary Women, 1989, Welded Sculpture of The 20th Century, 2000; contbr. articles to profl. jours. Fellow Kress Found., 1970; recipient award SUNY, 1981. Mem. Am. Assn. Mus. Office Phone: 212-505-9657. Personal E-mail: jcollischan@nyc.rr.com.

COLLISTER, NICOLE S., counselor; b. Williamsport, Pa., Feb. 8, 1978; d. Mark A. Woolever and Raenell A. Mull; m. Mark L. Collister, Nov. 21, 2003; children: Amber L. Hicks, Isaac W. Way. BS in Applied Human Scis., Pa. Coll. Tech., 2003. Residential worker Cmty. Svcs. Group, Williamsport, 1998—2003; vocat. rehag. counselor Suncare Industries Inc., Northumberland, Pa., 2003—, comm. mentor, 2005—. Mem.: ACA, Nat. Assn. Dually Diagnosed, Bloomsburg U. Alumni Assn., Pa. Coll. Alumni Assn. Democrat. Baptist. Avocations: antiques, reading, writing. Home: 10 Catherine Dr Williamsport PA 17701 Office: Suncare Industries Inc 128 Water St Northumberland PA 17857

COLMAN, JENNY MEYER, psychiatrist; b. Livingston, NJ, Apr. 23, 1968; d. Robert Osborne and Margaret Saur Meyer; m. William Woodruff Colman, June 20, 1998; children: Thomas Emory, Sean Robert. BA, Harvard Coll., Cambridge, 1990; MD, Columbia Coll., NYC, 1997. Diplomate Am. Bd. Psychiatry and Neurology. Resident in psychiatry Columbia Presbyn./NY Hosp., NYC, 1997—2000, U. Calif., San Francisco, 2000—01; attending psychiatrist St. Mary's Med. Ctr., San Francisco, 2001—03, med. dir. adolescent inpatient unit, 2002—03; pvt. practice San Francisco, 2001—03, Poughkeepsie, NY, 2003—04, Fishkill, NY, 2004—. Mem.: Am. Acad. Child and Adolescent Psychiatry, Am. Psychiatric Assn. Avocations: hiking, skiing, running. Office: 1081 Main St Ste G Fishkill NY 12524

COLMAN, WENDY See ERSKINE, KALI

COLMENARES, LETICIA, chemistry professor; d. Eduardo Uro and Abundia Chiong; m. Serafin Colmenares Jr.; children: Serafin III, David Roy. BS in Chemistry, Mindanao State U., Marawi, Philippines, 1975; MS in Chemistry, U. Philippines, Quezon City, 1982; PhD in Chemistry, U. Hawaii, Honolulu, 1991. Instr. Mindanao State U., 1975—77; asst. prof. Mindanao State U.-Iligan Inst. Tech., Iligan City, Philippines, 1980—87; jr. rschr. U. of Hawaii, 1991—99; asst. prof. U. Hawaii-Windward C.C., Kaneohe, 1999—. Mem. info. tech. task force Filipino Cmty. Ctr., Waipahu, Hawaii, 2005—. Contbr. articles to profl. jours. Named one of 10 Outstanding Hawaii Filipino Women of Yr., Filipino Women Civics Club, 2003; recipient Excellence in Tchg. award, U. Hawaii Bd. Regents, 2003, Progress award in sci. and tech., United Filipino Coun. of Hawaii, 2003; fellow East-West Ctr., 1987—91; grantee NOAA, 2002—05, Biomed. Rsch. and Infrastructure Network, 2003—04, IDeA Networks of Biomed. Rsch. Excellence, 2005, Ifuku Family Found., 2006—. Mem.: Am. Chem. Soc. (treas. 2001—02), Congress of Visayan Orgns. (Lapulapu award in sci. 2004), Filipino Assn. Univ. Women (pres. 2003—03). Roman Catholic. Avocations: gardening, line dancing.

COLOMB, MARJORIE MONROE, investor, volunteer; b. New Orleans, Sept. 9, 1929; d. Joseph Percy and Mary Velma Monroe; m. Charles McConvill Hardie, June 6, 1953 (div. Nov. 1972); m. John Joseph Colomb, Jr., Sept. 28, 1983 (dec.). BA Art History, La. State U., New Orleans, 1973; BS Bus., U. New Orleans, 1982. Adv. coun. fanfare/columbia U. SE La., Hammond; adv. bd. dirs. New Orleans Mus.; bd. dirs. Easter Seals La., New Orleans; trustee J.Edgar Monroe Found., New Orleans. Fellow: New Orleans Mus. Art; mem.: Raintree Svcs. (hon. bd. dirs.). Republican. Roman Catholic. Home: 4840 Highway 22 Apt 628 Mandeville LA 70471-2685

COLOMBO, ROSE MARIE, freelance/self-employed newswriter, television personality; d. James Santo Colombo and Maria Vigil; children: Robert, Rochelle, Theresa, Holly. Grad., Elegance Acad. Profl. Makeup, 1984; postgrad., Dermatol. Inst. Advanced Skin Care, Torrance, Calif., 1986. Founder, pres., CEO Women Fight Back for Legal Justice, Inc., Calif., 1989—. Freelance writer, 1980—; pres., CEO Jovone Skin Care, 1984—; TV host, prodr., writer Issues of the Day, Calif., 1989—; columnist Sunset Pub., Costa Mesa, Calif., 1995—2003. Author: How to Protect Yourself From Your Own Attorney, 2005. V.p., editor No. Long Beach Fedn. Rep. Women's Club, Calif., 1970—74; mem. Com. to Oppose Recall of Judge Nancy Stock, Orange County, Calif., 1997; past mem. Pres. Reagan's Task Force. Named Crusader for Equal Rights, 2003; recipient Journalism of Arts award, City News Svc., 1996, Jeanne Angel award, So. Calif. Motion Picture Coun., 2005, Eng. Poet award, Internat. Soc. Poets, 2006, Bronze Poet award, 2006; Poet fellow, Noble House, London, 2006. Mem.: L.A. Press Club. Avocations: poetry, music. Office Phone: 714-223-9895. Personal E-mail: jovoneskincare@aol.com.

COLOMER, VERONICA, medical educator, researcher; b. Mexico City, Mex., Nov. 9, 1957; married. BS, U. Mexico City, Mex., 1983; PhD, NYU, 1990. Postdoctoral fellow in lab. dept. cell biology NYU Med. Ctr., 1990-94; instr. lab. dept. cell biology Cornell Med. Coll., 1995; instr. in lab. dept. psychiatry Johns Hopkins U. Sch. Medicine, 1996—. Guest investigator in lab. dept. cellular physiology and immunology Rockefeller U., 1982-84. Contbr. articles to profl. jours. Recipient Minority Scientist Devel. award Am. Heart Assn., 1996, Career award MSDA Am. Heart Assn., 1996—; Undergrad. Student fellowship Consejo Nacional de Ciencia y Tecnologia, 1981-82, Grad. Student fellowship, 1984-87, Ella Fitzgerald fellow Am. Heart Assn., 1991, Postdoctoral Participating Lab. award fellowship Am. Heart Assn., 1991-94. Mem. Am. Soc. Cell Biology, Royal Soc. Tropical Medicine and Hygiene, N.Y. Acad. Scis., Mex. Soc. Biochemistry, Mex. Soc. Immunology. Office: Johns Hopkins U Sch Medicine Dept Psychology 720 Rutland Ave # 618 Baltimore MD 21205-2109

COLÓN, EUGENIA VALINDA, development executive; b. N.Y.C., N.Y., Nov. 24, 1955; d. Israel H.D. and Inez Genevieve (Cavallaro) C. BA in Medieval English Lit., SUNY, Purchase, 1978; MPA, George Washington U., 1996. Cert. fund raising exec. Spl. asst. to asst. chancellor NYU, N.Y.C., 1985-87; ESL tchr. CES Sch., N.Y.C., 1984-88; spl. asst. to v.p. acad. affairs George Washington U., Washington, 1989-93, spl. asst. to dean Sch. Bus. and Pub. Mgmt., 1993-94; devel. cons. in pvt. practice, Vienna, Va., 1990-97; nat. dir. corp. devel. United Negro Coll. Fund, Farifax, Va., 1997-2001; v.p. devel. AFP Found. Philanthropy, 2001—02; pres., CEO Colon & Assocs., LLC, Devel. Cons., 2002—. Freelance writer, ind. cons., 1978—. Author: (collected poems) Volume I: Collected Poems, 1989; author short story and play. Vol.

cons. Literacy Vols. of Am., Washington. Mem. Assn. Fundraising Profls. Democrat. Avocations: creative writing, reading, dance, painting, music. Office: Colon & Assocs LLC 2914 Cashel Ln Vienna VA 22181 Office Phone: 703-319-0619.

COLÓN, NIVIA ENID, counseling administrator; d. Pablo Colón and Emma Santiago; m. Víctor Luis Oquendo. MEd, Pontificia Universidad Católica, Ponce, 1992. Cert. elem. sch. tchr. Dept. Edn., 1977, sch. counselor Dept. Edn., 1992, profl. counselor Junta Examinadora de Consejeros Profesionales de PR, 2005, vocat. evaluator Univ. Interamericana de PR, 2005. Elem. sch. tchr. Dept. Edn., Ponce, PR, 1977—92, sch. counselor, 1992—2001, Fajardo, PR, 2001—. Recipient Tchr. of Yr., Escuela Pastillo de Canas, 1987. Master: Departamento de Trabajado Social y Consejería Escolar (assoc.; v.p. 2005—06), Asociación de Maestros de PR (assoc.; mem. 1977—2006), Asociation Puertorriqueña de Consejería Profesional (assoc.; pres. elect 2004—05), Asociation Puertorriqueña de Consejería Profesional (assoc.; pres. 2005—06); mem.: FAPOAL (assoc.), Asociación de Profesionales de Orientación y Consejería Escolar (assoc.), ACA (assoc.; pres. PR br. 2005—06). Determination Party. Catholic. Avocations: travel, reading. Office: Josefina Ferrero Sch Monte Brisas Esq Ave El Conquistador Fajardo PR 00738 Office Phone: 787-863-6770. Office Fax: 787-863-3917. E-mail: niviacolon@yahoo.com.

COLÓN, PHYLLIS JANET, retired city manager; b. Taylor, Tex., Sept. 1, 1938; d. Jack and Lydia Windmeyer; m. Henry J. Colón, Feb. 12, 1977; children: Walter N. Barnes III, Bradley H. Barnes, Mark A. Barnes. AA in Pub. Adminstrn., Del Mar Coll.; postgrad. in Acctg., Durham Jr. Coll.; BAAS in Pub. Adminstrn., Tex. A&M U., 1987; postgrad., Art Inst. Dayton. Registered profl. appraiser, Tex., assessor, Tex.; cert. tax adminstr., Tex.; lic. real estate borker, Tex. Mgr. info. Med. Arts Lab., Dayton, Ohio, 1970-73; appraiser Nueces County Appraisal Dist., Corpus Christi, 1973-82; tax assessor, collector Flour Bluff Ind. Sch. Dist., Corpus Christi, 1982, dir. spl. svcs., 1992-93; tax assessor, collector City of Laredo, Tex., 1993—. Mem. Profl. Stds. Com. Bd. Tax Profl. Examiners, 1991, vice chmn., 1992, chmn. 1994—. Mem. advance planning bd. Corpus Christi Libr.; chmn. ad hoc planning com. Del Mar Coll., 1989—; US rep. Brindas Meijer celebration Tex. A&M Internat. U.; com. mem. Katy Ind. Sch. Dist., Tex. Recipient achievement award State of Tex., Hero award City of Corpus Christi. Mem. NAFE, AAUW (bd. dirs. Corpus Christi br.), Tex. Assn. Assessing Officers, Tex. Sch. Assessors Assn., Inst. Cert. Tax Adminstrs., Am. Soc. Notaries, Corpus Christi C. of C., Art Mus. South Tex., Kiwanis (treas. Corpus Christi 1989-90, pres. 1990—; 2d v.p. Laredo United Way, 1995-2003, master gardner. Laredo chpt. 2004). Republican. Lutheran. Avocations: art, photography, reading, gardening. Office: City of Laredo PO Box 329 1110 Houston St Laredo TX 78040-8019 Home: 2615 Falcon Knoll Ln Katy TX 77494-2419

COLONA, FRANCES ANN, elementary school educator; b. Bryn Mawr, Pa., Dec. 3, 1949; d. Frank and Rose (Biondi) C. BA, Alvernia Coll., 1971; MEd, Millersville U., 1976. 6th grade tchr. Twin Valley Elem. Ctr., Elverson, Pa., 1971-88, Morgantown Elem. Ctr., Pa., 1988-91; 7th grade lang. arts tchr. Twin Valley Mid. Sch., Elverson, 1991—2005. Cooperating tchr. for student tchr. Twin Valley Elem. Ctr., Elverson, 1975, 90, 94; sci. task force Twin Valley Sch. Dist., Elverson, 1987, lang. arts task force, 1988—; team leader TV Middle Sch., Elverson, 1991, 92, 93, 94; mentor Morgantown Elem. Sch., Elverson, 1990. Office: Twin Valley Middle School RR 3 Box 53 Elverson PA 19520-9306

COLONY, PAMELA CAMERON, medical researcher, educator; b. Boston, Apr. 18, 1947; d. Donald Gifford Colony and Priscilla (Adams) Pratley; m. E. Paul Cokely Jr., Apr. 26, 1986 (div. 2000); children: Daniel Patrick Cokely, John Travis Cokely; m. Richard M. Sparling, June 1, 2003. BA, Wellesley Coll., Mass., 1969; PhD, Boston U., Mass., 1976. Rsch. asst. sch. medicine Boston U., 1969-71, U. Hosp., 1971-73, Peter Bent Brigham Hosp., Boston, 1973-75; instr. dept. anatomy Harvard Med. Sch., 1975-77; assoc. staff in medicine Peter Bent Brigham Hosp., Boston, 1976-79; sr. fellow, instr. Harvard Med. Sch., Boston, 1979-81; asst. prof. anatomy and medicine Pa. State Coll. Medicine, Hershey, Pa., 1981-88; assoc. prof. rsch., pre-health advisor Franklin and Marshall Coll., Lancaster, 1988-91; adj. assoc. prof. of surgery Pa. State Coll. Medicine, Hershey, 1988-91, sr. rsch. assoc. dept. surgery, 1991-95; asst. prof. SUNY, Cobleskill, 1995-97, assoc. prof., 1997-99, program dir. histotech., 1995—, prof. biology, 1999—, co-dir. Women in Sci., 1996—. Bd. dirs. N.Y. State Histotechnol. Soc.; ind. assessor Nat. Health and Med. Rsch. Coun., Australia, 1985—98; ad-hoc reviewer NIH and Nat. Cancer Inst., Bethesda, Md., 1986; lectr. and adj. instr. Harrisburg Area Cmty. Coll., 1991—95. Contbr. articles to profl. jours. Fellow Nat. Found. Ileitis and Colitis, 1979-81; grantee Fed. Republic Germany, 1978, Cancer Rsch. Ctr., 1982-83, NIH, 1982-91. Mem.: Nat. Soc. for Histotech., N.Y. Histotechnol. Soc. (bd. dirs. 2001—05), Am. Soc. Clin. Pathology. Avocations: breeding Am. quarter horses, showing Am. quarter horses, endurance and competitive trail riding. Office: SUNY Cobleskill Dept Natural Scis Main St Cobleskill NY 12043 E-mail: colonyp@cobleskill.edu.

COLPITTS, GAIL ELIZABETH, artist, educator; b. Chgo., Nov. 26, 1954; d. Robert Moore and Mary Lee (Means) C. BA, Greenville Coll., 1976; MA, No. Ill. U., 1984, MFA, 1990. Grad. tchg. asst. No. Ill. U., DeKalb, 1982—83, tchg. intern, 1990, instr. Office Campus Recreation, 1989—90; artist-tchr. MFA program Vt. Coll., Montpelier, 1993; instr. Harold Washington Coll., Chgo., 1993, Columbia Coll., Chgo., 1995; artist, lectr. Judson Coll., Elgin, Ill., 1995, asst. prof. art, 1996—2000, assoc. prof. art and design, 2000—, chair dept. art and design, 2001—; artist-in-residence Studio Midwest (with Knox Coll.), Galesburg, Ill., 2005. Surbeck summer scholar Judson Coll., 2005. One-woman shows include No. Ill. U., DeKalb, 1990, Bethel Coll., Arden Hills, Minn., 1995, Greenville (Ill.) Coll., 1993, Wheaton (Ill.) Coll., 1996, Trinity Christian Coll., Palos Heights, 1998, Cliff Dwellers, Chgo., 1999, Northwestern Coll., St. Paul, Minn., 2000, Judson Coll., Elgin, Ill., 2003; assoc. editor: Shoal Dance, 1995-96, contbr. revs. and news; contbr. poetry to mags.; included in Best of New Ceramic Arts, 1997, Making Visible the Invisible, 2003, Civa Silver, 2005. Dir. Christians in the Visual Arts, 2003. Fellow Grad. Sch. fellow, No. Ill. U., 1987—88. Mem. Christians in Visual Arts, Chgo. Artists Coalition, Ill. Higher Edn. Art Assn. (bd. dirs., Founds. in Art, Theory and Edn. Wesleyan. Avocations: genealogy, reading, travel. Office: Judson College Dept Art and Design 1151 N State St Elgin IL 60123-1404 Office Phone: 847-628-1032. E-mail: gcolpitts@judsoncollege.edu.

COLSON, DAVID A., lawyer; BA, Calif. State Coll., Haywood, 1966; JD, U. Calif., Berkeley, Boalt Hall, 1975. Bar: Calif., DC. Served in Legal Advisor's Office US Dept. of State, Washington, 1975—90, dep. asst. sec. for oceans, Bur Oceans & Internat. Environ. & Sci. Affairs, 1990—96; of counsel LeBoeuf, Lamb, Greene & MacRae LLP, Washington, 1996—, chmn. Internat. Boundary Disputes Dept. Author: Transboundary Fishery Stocks in the Exclusive Economic Zone, 1984—85, How Persistent Must the Persistent Objector Be?, 1986. Office: LeBoeuf Lamb Greene & MacRae LLP 1875 Connecticut Ave NW Ste 1200 Washington DC 20009-5715 Office Phone: 202-986-8024. Office Fax: 202-986-8102. Business E-Mail: dacolson@llgm.com.

COLSON, JUDY C., music educator; b. Leavenworth, Kans., Nov. 4, 1951; d. Robert A. and Doris D. Lange; m. Ed L. Colson, Aug. 7, 1982; children: Amanda L. Zinn, Ed R. MusB in Edn., Baker U., Baldwin City, Kans., 1974, MLA, 1988. Cert. tchr. Kans. State Dept. of Edn., 1974, Mo. Dept. of Edn., 1974. Band dir., Olathe, Kans., 1980—. Founding com. mem. John Philip Sousa Kans. Jr. Honors Band, Lawrence, Kans., 2002. Recipient elem. tchr. of yr., N.E. Kans. Music Educators Assn., 2003—04. Mem.: Women Band Dirs. Internat., Kans. Music Educators (assoc.; dist. one sec. 1982—84), Kans. Bandmasters Assn. (assoc.), Internat. Assn. Jazz Educators (assoc.), Music Educators Nat. Conf. (assoc.). Home: 13283 S Kimberly Circle Olathe KS 66061 Office: Olathe Northwest High Sch 21300 College Blvd Olathe KS 66061 Business E-Mail: jcolsononw@olatheschools.com.

COLSON, ROSEMARY, music educator; b. Madison, Ind., July 15, 1937; d. Howard Paul and Mary Wilder Colson. Student, Georgetown Coll., 1955—56; MusB, George Peabody Coll., 1960; MusM, Yale U., 1965. Tchr. piano Wilmington Music Sch., Del., 1965—66, Settlement Music Sch., Phila., 1966—77, Chestnut Hill Acad., Phila., 1969—78; piano tchr. Acad. Cmty. Music, Ft. Washington, Pa., 1993—; tchr. pvt. piano Phila., 1967—; organist, choir master Grace Epiphany Episcopal Ch., Phila., 1987—2000. Contbr. articles to profl. jours. Treas. West Ctrl. Germantown Neighbors, Phila., 1981—83; bd. dirs. YWCA Germantown, Phila., 1990—94, Women's Sacred Music Project, 2003—05. Mem.: Am. Guild Organists, Delta Omicron (advisor to U. Pa. chpt. 1963—64). Democrat. Presbyterian. Avocations: gardening, reading, travel. Home: 6021 McCallum St Philadelphia PA 19144 Personal E-mail: rsmrclsn@aol.com.

COLTON, BONNIE MYERS, folklorist, writer; b. Oswegatchie, N.Y., Dec. 7, 1931; m. Donald M. Colton, Jan. 4, 1952; children: Cherie Binns, Tricia Kennison, Jean Balch, Roger, Ben, Lin Sawyer, Neil. Record keeper, tax acct. Homewood Farm, Boonville, NY, 1958-89; cons./oral history interviewer Tug Hill Commn., Watertown, 1988-91; ind. oral history interviewer, 1991—. Freelance writer, columnist, 1981—2003; newsletter editor various orgns., 1972—; pres. THRIFT, 2006. Author: (essays) Walking a Roundabout Path, 2004, I Tell You All This Because., 2005. Pres. Tug Hill Resources Investment for Tomorrow, 2006—. Mem. Lewis County Hist. Assn. (life, videotape and hist. programs), N.Y. Forest Owners Assn. (Heiburg Award for svc. to forestry 1992), Adirondack Mus., Acad. Am. Poets. Avocations: museums, woodland conservation. Home and Office: 5595 Trinity Ave Lowville NY 13367-1416 E-mail: authorplus@yahoo.com.

COLTON, ELIZABETH WISHART, government agency administrator; b. Rockville Centre, N.Y., June 25, 1929; d. Ronald Sinclair Wishart and Elizabeth Lathrop Phillips. BA cum laude, We. Coll. for Women, 1951; postgrad., Am. U., 1951—52, Bowie State Coll., 1989—90. Jr. mgmt. asst. U.S. C.S.C., Washington, 1954, test developer, 1954—55, civil svc. insp., 1955—58, stds. developer and writer of qualification and classification stds., 1958—59, developer and implementer nationwide evauation plans of maj. fed. depts., 1958—62; developed and implemented bureauwide pers. mgmt. improvement programs Bur. of Reclamation Dept. of Interior, Washington, 1962—65, asst. dir. of pers. for nat. pk. svc., 1965—70, staff specialist dir. equal opportunity Office of Equal Employment Opportunity Programs, 1970; dep. dir. of pers. for pers. mgmt. evaluation and asst. to dep. dir. for classification and pay Dept. of Treasury, Washington, 1970—78; dir. divsn. pers. sys. imrprovement Office Asst. Sec. Health and Human Svcs., Washington, 1978—85. Real estate broker, Annapolis, Md., 1985—2003; antique dealer, Annapolis, 1985—2003. Job counselor displaced homemakers YWCA, Annapolis, 1985—92, active, 1985—92; ct. -apptd. spl. advocate for a foster child; developer and leader inner-city boys cooking class N.Y. Ave. Presbyn. Ch., Washington, 1960—69. Mem.: We. Coll. Alumnae Assn. Miami U. (trustee 2004—06), Victoria Walk Unit Owners Assn. (sec. treas. 2003—). Presbyterian. Avocations: ancient history, gardening, travel, genealogy. Home: Greens of Cross Court 1200 S Washington St Apt 304 Easton MD 21601 E-mail: bcolton@goeaston.net.

COLTON SKOLNICK, JUDITH A., artist; b. Washington, Jan. 31, 1947; d. Bernard and Helen (Glick) Colton; 2 children. Student, Corcoran Sch. Art, 1964, student, 1993—94; BA in Art and Art History with honors, U. Md., 1972; postgrad., Montgomery Coll., 1990—91. Tchr. faux painting workshop The Artful Framer, 1991, Craft Country, Olney, Md., 1991; artist guest lectr. Radford U., spring 1996; supr. painting Paint Out Aids Ea. Market, Washington, 1992; asst. to art cons. Capitol Arts, Washington, 1992-96; tech. illustrator Vitro Corp., 1981-86; artist assoc. Mary Anne Reilly, 1995; founder Unity in Diversity Women's Exhibn. Group; interviewer, active Va. Juvenile Detention Ctr., 1993; spkr., presenter in field. One-woman shows include Beltone Hearing Aid, Washington, 1963, New Trends, Springfield, Va., 1971, Artful Framer, Olney, Md., 1991, Kurz, Koch, Doland and Dembling, Washington, 1992, Heartland Cafe, 1992, "R" St. Gallery Jackson Sch., 1993, Franklin Ct. Gallery, 1994, Parish Gallery, 1995, Flossie Martin Gallery Radford U., Blacksburg, Va., 1996, Sunrise Gallery, Kilmarnock, Va., 1997, Nat. Press Club Bldg., Washington, 1997—98, Art Mine Agora Gallery, N.Y.C., 1998—2005, Very Spl. Arts Online Gallery, Washington, 1998—2001, Articulate Gallery, 1999, numerous group shows including most recently, exhibited in group shows at Castel S. Pietro Terme, Italy, 1999—, Feminist Expo, Balt., 2000, Art Expo N.Y., 2000, King St. Stephen Mus., Hungary, 2000, Jemison-Carnegie Heritage Hall Mus., Ala., 2001, Attleboro Mus., Mass., 2001, Maison Francois de Bologne, Italy, Sung Kyun Kwan U., Seoul, Korea, Amsterdam Whitney Gallery, NYC, 2002—03, Nat. Assn. Women Artists, 2002—03, Poughkeepsie Art Mus., N.Y., 2004, Kostia, Palkane, Finland, 2005, Centro Culturale, Campamation, Italy, 2005; (command murals, faux painting); contbr. to profl. mags. and pubs. Mem. Nat. Assn. Women Artists Inc., Nat. Mus. Women in Arts, Corcoran Sch. Art Alumni Assn. (presenter). Republican. Jewish. Avocations: poetry, reading, walking, boating. Home: 2301 E St NW A1115 Washington DC 20037

COLUCCI, JACQUELINE STRUPP, insurance agent, sculptor, management consultant; b. Montevideo, Uruguay, July 24, 1963; d. Gunther and Silvia (Klemens) Strupp; m. John Michael Colucci, Sept. 6, 1997; children: Matias Camprubi-Soms, Mercedes Camprubi-Soms. BA cum laude, NYU, 1986. AFLAC rep. Customer svc. mgr. Games Mag./Mail Order, N.Y.C., 1984-86; treas., property mgr., asst. to CEO Hudson Properties, Lyndhurst, NJ, 1986-90; sales assoc. Bloomingdale's, Palm Beach Gardens, Fla., 1990-91, staff tng. supr. and pers. asst., 1991-92; legal asst., bookkeeper Gov.'s Bank and Bruce W. Keihner, Palm Beach, Fla., 1993; assoc. Ideas & Things, 1994-97; freelance bus. mgr., 1993—; personal and bus. coach, 1993-97; bus. mgr. MCR/Michael Colucci Race Engring., Inc., Jupiter, Fla., 1997—; spl. projects coord. AFLAC, 2003—. Office: MCR/Michael Colucci Race Engineering Inc 1092 Jupiter Park Ln Ste 270 Jupiter FL 33458-6024 E-mail: jackiecolucci@bellsouth.net.

COLVIN, CAROLYN W., state agency administrator; BS in Bus. Adminstrn., Morgan State U., MBA; postgrad., Harvard U. Sec. Md. Dept. Human Resources; dep. commr. for policy and external affairs Social Security Adminstrn., Balt., 1994-96, dep. commr. for programs and policy, 1996-98, dep. commr. for ops., 1998—2001; dir. DC Dept. of Human Svcs., Washington, 2001—. Grad. Greater Balt. Leadership Program. Mem. Nat. Coalition 100 Black Women, Nat. Forum Black Pub. Adminstrs. (Md. chpt.), Nat. Acad. Social Ins., Women Execs. in State Govt. Office: DC Dept Human Svcs John A Wilson Bldg 1350 Pennsylvania Ave, NW Washington DC 20004

COLVIN, SHAWN, recording artist, songwriter; b. Vermillion, SD, Jan. 10, 1956; m. Mario Erwin, 1997; 1 child, Caledonia Jean-Marie Erwin. Past mem., founder Shawn Colvin Band, Carbondale, Ill.; past mem. Dixie Diesels, Austin, Tex. Albums include Live Tape, 1988, Steady On, 1989 (Grammy award, Best Contemporary Folk Album, 1991), Fat City, 1992, Cover Girl, 1994, Round of Blues, 1995, Live '88, 1995, Few Small Repairs, 1996, (2 Grammy awards: Record of the Year, Song of Year for Sonny Came Home, 1998), Holiday Songs and Lullabies, 1998, 2005, Whole New You, 2001, These Four Walls, 2006, (single) I Don't Know Why, 1992, (extended play single) Every Little Thing, 1994; background vocals, arranger I Know, 1987; background vocals Solitude Standing, 1987, Ghosts Upon the Road, 1989, Ben & Jerry's Newport Folk, 1989, Festival, 1989, State of the Heart, 1989, Long Road, 1990, Days of Open Hand, 1990, Stages, 1991, Come on Come on, 1992, Life is Messy, 1992, Stones in the Road, 1994, House on Fire, 1995, Strangers World, 1995, Down in There, 1996, Last Tango, 1996; vocals, guitar Samp, 1988, Bob Dylan's 30th Anniversary, 1993, Concert, 1993, Columbia Records Radio Hour (vol. 1), 1994, Best of Columbia Records Radio Hour, 1996; vocals Standing Eight, 1989, Time Was, 1995; harmony vocals Land of the Bottom Line, 1992, Road to Ensenada, 1996; vocals, prodr., Tin Cup, 1996; prodr. Tide, 1994; vocals, background vocals Shooting Straight in the Dark, 1990, others; appearances include (off-broadway) Pump Boys and Dinettes, Diamond Studs, Lie of the Mind, (film) It Could Happen to You, Grace of My Heart, (TV) TNN's presentation of The Players, 1999, An All Star Tribute to Joni Mitchell, 2000.

COLVIN, TINA POWELL, elementary school educator; b. Greenville, Ala., Dec. 8, 1962; d. Albert Wendell and Fay Phelps Powell; m. Mark Douglas Colvin, Feb. 5, 1983; children: Nicholas Dean, Mitchell Douglas. AA, LB Wallace Coll., Ala., 1983; BEd, Auburn U., Ala., 1985; MEd, Auburn U., 1991. Cert. early childhood, elem. edn. Ala. Tchr. Greenville Acad., 1986—91, Lowndes County Bd of Edn., Hayneville, Ala., 1991—94, Hooper Acad., Hope Hull, Ala., 1995—98, Huntsville (Ala.) City Schs., 2002—04, Elmore County Bd. of Edn., Wetumpka, Ala., 1998—2002, 2004—. Family support mem. 1-131 Aviation Battalion, Hope Hull, 2005—. Named Tchr. of Yr., Ft. Deposit Elem., 1993; Academic scholarship, LB Wallace Coll., 1983. Mem.: NEA, Ala. Edn. Assn. Bapt. Avocations: reading, cooking, writing. Office Phone: 334-285-2115. Personal E-mail: tkaycolvin@bellsouth.net.

COLWELL, HEATHER THORSTAD, secondary school educator; b. Wichita Falls, Tex., Feb. 23, 1977; d. James and Alice Thorstad; m. Scott Colwell, Oct. 23, 2004. BA, Greensboro Coll., 1999. Tchr. Prince William County Schs., Woodbridge, Va., 1999—, 10th grade gifted coord., 2003—; EIP tchr. George Mason U., Fairfax, Va., 2002—.

COLWELL, RITA ROSSI, microbiologist, former federal agency administrator, medical educator; b. Nov. 23, 1934; BS in Bacteriology with distinction, Purdue U., 1956, MS in Genetics, 1958; PhD, U. Wash., 1961; DSc, Heriot-Watt U., Edinburgh, Scotland, 1987; DSc (hon.), Hood Coll., 1991; DSc, Purdue U., 1993; DSc (hon.), U. Surrey, Eng., 1995, U. Bergen, Norway, 1999, Coastal Carolina U., 1999, U. Md. Balt. County, 1999, St. Mary's Coll., 1999, Mich. State U., 2000, Washington Coll., 2000, U. Conn., 2000, Williams Coll., 2000, SUNY, Albany, 2000, U. Ancona, Italy, 2001, George Washington U., 2001, Mount Holyoke, 2001, Washington U., St. Louis, 2001, Calif. Poly. Inst., San Luis Obispo, 2001, Renssalaer Poly. Inst., 2001, U. Newcastle, U.K., 2001, Mercy Coll., 2002, U. Queensland, Australia, 2002; DSc, U. Glasgow, 2002, Weizmann Inst. Sci., Israel, 2002, Tuskegee Inst., 2003, U. Ill., 2003, Dartmouth Coll., 2003; LLD, U. Nebr., 2003, Notre Dame Coll., 1994; DHL (hon.), U. Ala., 2001. Rsch. asst. genetics lab. Purdue U., West Lafayette, Ind., 1956—57; rsch. asst. U. Wash., Seattle, 1957—58, predoctoral assoc., 1959—60, asst. rsch. prof., 1961—64; asst. prof. biology Georgetown U., Washington, 1964—66, assoc. prof. biology, 1966—72; prof. microbiology U. Md., 1972—98, v.p. for acad. affairs, 1983—87; dir. Ctr. Marine Biotech., 1987—91; founder, pres. Biotech. Inst. U. Md., 1991—98; dir. NSF, Arlington, Va., 1998—2004; chmn. Canon US Life Scis., Inc., 2004—; Disting. Univ. prof. U. Md., College Park, 2004—, Johns Hopkins Bloomberg Sch. Pub. Health, 2004—. Hon. prof. U. Queensland, Brisbane, Australia, 1988; mem. ocean scis. bd. NAS, 1977—80; hon. prof. Quindao U., China, 1995; cons. Washington area comms. media, congressman, legislators, 1978—; external examiner various univs. abroad, 1964—; vice chmn. polar rsch. bd. NAS, 1990—94; mem. Nat. Sci. Bd., 1984—90; mem. sci. adv. bd. Oak Ridge Nat. Labs., 1988—90, 1993—96; adv. com. FDA, 1991—92, food adv. com., 1993—96, sci. bd., 1996—; Koch lectr., Berlin, 2000. Author (manual numerical taxonomy): Collecting the Data, 1970; author: (with M. Zambruski) Rodina-Methods in Aquatic Microbiology, 1972; author: (with L.H. Stevenson) Estuarine Microbial Ecology, 1973; author: (with R.Y. Morita) Effect of the Ocean Environment on Microbial Ecology, 1973; author: (with A. Sinsky and N. Pariser) Marine Biotechnology, 1983; author: Vibrios in the Environment, 1985, Nucleic Acid Sequence Data, 1988; author: (with others) Marine Biotechnology, 1995; Microbial Diversity, 1996; author: Viable But Nonculturable Microorganisms in the Environment, 2000, others; mem. editl. bd.: Microbial Ecology, 1972—91, Applied and Environ. Microbiology, 1969—81, Oil and Petrochemical Pollution, 1980—91, Jour. Washington Acad. Scis., 1981—87, Johns Hopkins U. Oceanographic Series, 1981—84, Revue de la Fondation Oceanographique Ricard, 1981—, Estuaries, 1983—89, Zentralblatt fur Bacteriologie, 1985—, Jour. Aquatic Living Resources, 1987—, Sys. Applied Microbiology, 1985—2000, World Jour. Microbiology and Biotech., 1988—95, Environ. Microbiology, 2001—; contbr. articles to profl. jours.; (Koch lecture) Anatomy Lesson, Amsterdam, 2002. Named Prof. Extraordinairo, U. Catolica Valparaiso, Chile, 1976, Scholar of Yr., Phi Kappa Phi, 1992; recipient Gold medal, Internat. Biotech. Inst., 1990, Purkinje Gold medal for achievment in sci., Czechoslavakian Acad. Sci., 1991, Civic award, Gov. Md., 1990, Woman of the Yr. award, Women Legis. of Md., 1996, Cert. of Recognition, NASA, 1984, Alice Evans award, Am. Soc. Microbiol., 1988, Andrew White medal, Loyola Coll., 1994, medal of distinction, Barnard Coll./Columbia U., 1996, Gold medal, Charles U., Prague, 2000, Gold medals, UCLA, 2000, Alumna Summa Laude Dignata award, U. Wash., 2000, Achievement award, AAUW, 2001, Carey award, Am. Assn. Adv. Sci., 2001, Thomas award, Explorer's Club Lowell, 2000. Fellow: AAAS (chmn. sect. biol. scis. 1993—94, pres. 1995, chmn. bd. 1996, Carey award 2001), Marine Tech. Soc. (exec. com. 1982—88), Washington Acad. Scis. (bd. mgrs. 1976—79, pres. 1996—98), Am. Acad. Microbiology (chmn. bd. govs. 1989—99), Grad. Women. Sci., Can. Coll. Microbiologists; mem.: NAS, Royal Swedish Acad. Sci., Soc. Gen. Microbiology, Internat. Coun. Sci. Unions, Am. Soc. Limnology and Oceanography, World Fedn. Culture Collections, Classification Rsch. Group Eng. (charter), Am. Soc. Microbiology (hon.; various sci. coms. 1961—, pres. 1985, chmn. program com. REGEM-1 1988, Fisher award 1985), U.K. Soc. Applied Microbiology (hon.), Bangladesh Soc. Microbiology (hon.; fgn.), French Soc. Microbiology (hon.), Israeli Soc. Microbiology (hon.), Australian Soc. Microbiology (hon.), Soc. Indsl Microbiology (bd. govs. 1976—79, Charles Thom award 1998), U.S. Fedn. Culture Collections (governing bd. 1978—88), Internat. Coun. Sci. Unions (exec. bd. 1993—96, gen. com.), Am. Inst. Biol. Scis. (bd. govs. 1976—82), Internat. Union Microbiol. Soc. (v.p. 1986—90, pres. 1990—94), World Fedn. Culture Collections, Royal Soc. Can., Explorers Club (Lowell Thomas award 2000), Omicron Delta Kappa, Phi Beta Kappa, Sigma Delta Epsilon, Sigma Xi (nat. pres. 1991, Ann. Achievement award 1981, Rsch. award 1984), Delta Gamma (Delta Gamma Rose award 1989). Achievements include research in marine biotechnology; marine and estuarine microbial ecology; survival of pathogens in aquatic environments; ecology of Vibrio cholerae and related organisms; microbial systematics; marine microbiology; antibiotic resistance; environmental aspects of Vibrio cholerae in transmission of cholera; global climate and cholera transmission.

COMAR, MARY ALICE, retired art educator, farmer; b. Adrian, Mich., Mar. 2, 1945; d. Rae Jack and Pauline Isabelle Comar; children: Jack Michael Findley, J. Brent Findley. MA in Humanities, Ctrl. Mich. U., 1993; BS, Siena Heights U., 1967. Teaching Cert. State of Mich., 1967. K-12 art tchr. Benton County Cmty. Schools, Oxford, Ind., 1967—68; sr. high art instr. Lafayette Diocese, Lafayette, Ind., 1968—71; instr. speech comm. Alpena C.C., Oscoda, Mich., 1979; instr. secondary art and English Alpena Pub. Schools, Mich., 1974—2005; ret., 2005. Set dir./play dir. sch. musicals Lafayette Diocese, Lafayette, Ind., 1969—70; practicing artist, photographer, videographer, Ossineke, Mich.; yearbook advisor/drama club advisor/play dir. Alpena H.S., 1985—99; secondary curriculum revision com. mem.; designed course Film as Lit. Alpena Pub. Schools; mem. sch. improvement team Alpena H.S. Exhibited in group shows at Greater Lafayette Art Festival, 1968 (Grand prize), Indpls. 500 Festival of Arts, 1968 (2d Most Meritorious Work amateur divsn.), Detroit Inst. of Arts Rental Gallery; author: numerous poems. Mem., sec. and vice chairperson Alpena Twp. Planning and Zoning Commn., 1980—88; vol. prop artist Alpena Civic Theatre and Thunder Bay Theatre, 1972—84; program com. Very Spl. Arts Festival Mich. Coun. for Very Spl. Arts, Alpena, 1980—80; vol. docent Jesse Besser Mus., Alpena, 1978; 4-H youth leader Mich. State County Ext. 4H Program, Alpena, 1978; vol. demonstrator artist Mich. Art Train Mich. Coun. for Arts, Alpena, 1978; vol. art work contbr. Jesse Besser Mus. Art Auction Fund Raiser, Alpena, 1980; adv. for those too young, old, sick, or unborn toward clean air and a healthy environment Citizen and registered voter of Mich. and the USA, Alpena, Mich., 1972—2003; bd. mem., sec., spkrs. bur., com. co-chairperson toxic and hazardous waste study com., chairperson ERA study com. Alpena County LWV, 1977—80; religious edn. tchr. St. John the Bapt. Cath. Parish, Alpena,

1999; lectr. and eucharistic min. St. Bernards Cath. Ch., Alpena, 1983—85; initiated a ch. youth group St. Bernard's Parish, Alpena, 1983—85. Recipient Classrooms of Tomorrow Tchr., Mich. Gov. Blanchard, 1990. Mem.: So. Poverty Law Ctr. (charter mem., leadership coun.), Siena Heights U. Alumni Assn., Nat. Mus. of Women in Arts (corr.). Democrat. Roman Catholic. Avocations: horse training, swimming, dance, golf.

COMBIE, VALERIE AUDREY, communications educator; b. Antigua, W.I., Mar. 24, 1949; d. Leonard George (Oliver) Knowles and Winifred Grace (Olive) Francis; m. Christopher Combie, Aug. 6, 1983; 1 child, Christopher Colby. BEd in Secondary Edn., W.I. Coll., Jamaica, 1972; MA in Cmty. Counseling, Andrews U., Mich., 1992; MA in English, Andrews U., 1978; PhD in English and Comm., Pacific Western U., Calif., 1987. Chair dept. English Good Hope Sch., St. Croix, V.I., 1985—90, guidance counselor, 1993—2004; asst. prof. humanities U. V.I., 1992—98, chair humanities divsn., 2001—04, dir. writing ctr., 2005—, assoc. prof. humanities, 1998—, dir. V.I. writing project, 2004—, chair English proficiency exam, 1997—. Cons. V.I. Housing Authority, St. Croix, 1996—2004; coord. reading is fundamental U.V.I. and V.I. Pub. Schs., 2002—. Author: The Best of Crucian Corner, 1997, Free From the Chains of Prison, 2003; editor: Colloquium on Crime, 2005. Pres. St. Croix Orchid Soc., 1998—2000; sec. Caribbean Prison Ministry Assn., St. Croix, 1998—2000. Named Outstanding Educator, U. Chgo., 1996. Mem.: Am. Counseling Assn. of V.I. (sec. 2002—04), Speech Comm. Assn. P.R., Nat. Coun. Tchrs. English. Avocations: reading, writing, growing orchids, quilting, landscaping. Office: Univ Virgin Islands RR 1 10000 Kingshill St Croix VI 00820

COMBS, DIANE LOUISE, elementary school educator, music educator; b. Amittyville, N.Y., Feb. 8, 1952; d. Earl Foster and Eloise Mae Jones; m. Gary Stephen Combs, June 30, 1979; children: Steven Richard, Jason. BS, Jacksonville U., 1974, MA in Tchg., 1977. Phys. edn. tchr. Clay County Schs., Green Cove Springs, Fla., 1974—79, music tchr., 1983—2006; phys. edn./music tchr. Seminole County Schs., Sanford, Fla., 1979—83; accredited music tchr. St. John's Country Day, 2006—. Dir. music, organist Ortega Presbyn., Jacksonville, 1968—69; organist, dir. Lakewood Presbyn., Jacksonville, 1970—78; dir. music, organist Trinity Luth., Jacksonville, 1978—79; organist Riverside Pk. United Meth., Jacksonville, 1978; dir. music, organist Ch. of the Messiah, Winter Garden, Fla., 1979—83, Orange Pk. (Fla.) Presbyn., 1983—97; organist, asst. dir. Orange Pk. United Meth. Ch., 1997—. Chair Clay County Elem. Music Festival, Orange Park, 1994—2006; scholarship chairperson Concert on the Green, Orange Park, 2002—; design team mem. Southeastern Conf. of Meth. Musicians, Nashville, 2003—06; chair Sch. Adv. Com., Middleburg, Fla., 2003—06. Mem.: Meth. Conferece The Fellowship (assoc.; design team mem. 2003—), Fla. Music Educator's Assn. (assoc.), Am. Guild English Handbell Ringers (chair-elect). Methodist. Avocations: swimming, reading, guitar, piano, organ. Home: 2559 Brockview Pointe Orange Park FL 32073 Office: St Johns Country Day Coll Preparatory Sch 3100 Doctors Inlet Dr Orange Park FL 32073 Personal E-mail: bellringertoo@aol.com.

COMBS, HOLLY MARIE, actress; b. San Diego, Dec. 3, 1973; m. Bryan Travis Smith, Feb. 28, 1993 (div. 1997); m. David W. Donoho, Feb. 14, 2004; children: Finley Arthur, Riley. Actor: (films) Walls of Glass, 1985, Sweet Hearts Dance, 1988, New York Stories, 1989, Born on the Fourth of July, 1989, Simple Men, 1992, Dr. Giggles, 1992, Chain of Desire, 1993, A Reason to Believe, 1995; (TV films) A Perfect Stranger, 1994, Sins of Silence, 1996, Love's Deadly Triangle: The Texas Cadet Murder, 1997, Daughters, 1997, See Jane Date, 2003; (TV series) Picket Fences, 1992—96 (best young actress in a new TV series Young Artist award, 1993), Charmed, 1998—2006; prodr.:, 2000—06. Office: c/o SFM 1122 S Robertson Blvd #15 Los Angeles CA 90035*

COMBS, JUDY DIANE, elementary school educator, civic association administrator; b. Adams County, Iowa, Aug. 6, 1939; d. Carlton Matthew and Faye Maxine Stewart; m. Donald Dean Combs, June 24, 1956; children: Jeffery Dean, Victor Lee. BS in Elem. Edn. summa cum laude, N.W. Mo. State U., 1965, MS in Elem. Adminstrn., 1970; MS in Elem. Tchg., U. Mo., 1969. Cert. tchr. Iowa. Elem. tchr. North Nodaway Sch., Hopkins, Mo., 1965—66, South Page Cmty. Sch., College Springs, Iowa, 1966—73; instr. dept. elem. edn. N.W. Mo. State U., Maryville, 1973—75; mid. sch. tchr. Fox Valley Cmty. Sch., Milton, Iowa, 1975—77; gifted edn. coord., tchr. Davis County Cmty. Sch., Bloomfield, Iowa, 1977—98; student tchg. supr. Iowa State U., 2001—. Mem. gifted edn. and history day adv. com. So. Prairie Edn. Agy., Ottumwa, Iowa, 1983—98. Sec. Bloomfield Hist. Preservation Commn., 1994—; dir. program Bloomfield Main St., 1998—2002, pres. bd. dirs., 2003—05; bd. dirs. Humanities Iowa, 2005—. Named Iowa History Day Tchr. of Yr., State Hist. Soc. Iowa, 1998; recipient Gov.'s Vol. award in econ. devel., State of Iowa, 2001. Mem.: NEA (life), Iowa Reading Assn. (local v.p., pres., state com. chmn. 1966—98, Iowa Reading Tchr. of Yr. 1985), Nat. Reading Assn., Nat. Trust for Hist. Preservation, Delta Kappa Gamma (local v.p., pres.). Republican. Methodist. Avocations: environmental restoration, gardening, antiques, reading, quilting. Office Phone: 641-664-2309.

COMBS, LINDA MORRISON, federal official; b. Lenoir, N.C., June 29, 1946; d. Robert Hugh and Vera Ludema (Bryant) Morrison; m. David Michael Combs, June 20, 1970. AA, Gardner Webb Coll., 1966, PhD (hon.), 1985; BS, Appalachian State U., 1968, MA, 1978; EdD, Va. Poly. Inst. and State U., 1985. Tchr., adminstr. Winston-Salem (N.C.)/Forsyth County Schs., 1968-79, sch. bd. mem., 1980-82; exec. sec., dep. U.S. Dept. Edn., Washington, 1982-84, dep. under-sec. mgmt., 1984-86; pub. edn. advisor State of N.C., Raleigh, 1986-87; owner Combs Group Cons., Winston-Salem, 1987; acting asst. dir. for mgmt. U.S. Dept. Vet. Affairs, Washington, 1987-89; asst. sec. mgmt. U.S. Dept. Treasury, Washington, 1989—91; CFO EPA, Washington, 2002—04; asst. sec., budget & fin. mgmt., CFO U.S. Dept. Transport., Washington, 2004—05; contr., Office Fed. Fin. Mgmt. Office Mgmt. & Budget, Washington, 2005—. Pres., founder Combs Music Internat., Winston-Salem, NC, 1991—2001. Gov.'s advocate Com. for Children and Youth, Winston-Salem, 1974-75; treas. Michael Britt for N.C. Senate, Forsyth County, 1976; v.p. Forsyth County Young Reps. Club, 1980-81. Recipient Honor and Outstanding Svc. award Combined Fed. Campaign, Washington, 1983, Alumnus of Yr. award Gardner Webb Coll., Boiling Springs, N.C., 1987, Disting. Alumnus of Yr. Appalachian State U., Boone, N.C., 1986. Mem. Forysth County Rep. Womens Club, Pres.'s Coun. on Mgmt. Improvement (vice chair, Outstanding Leadership award 1989), Phi Delta Kappa, Delta Kappa Gamma. Republican. Baptist. Avocations: running, cooking, tennis. Office: Office Mgmt & Budget 1650 Pennsylvania Ave NW Rm 263 Washington DC 20503

COMBS, ROBERTA, political organization administrator; m. Andy Combs (dec.); children: Karen, Michele. Bus. homebuilder, developer, 1976—90; polit. cons., 1990—99; exec. v.p. Christian Coalition of Am., 1999—2001, chmn., pres., 2001—. Office: Christian Coalition of America PO Box 37030 Washington DC 20013 Office Phone: 202-479-6900. Business E-Mail: roberta.combs@cc.org.

COMBS, SUSAN, state agency administrator; married; 3 children. Grad., Vassar Coll.; JD, U. Tex. Formerly asst. dist. atty., Dallas; mem. Tex. Legislature, 1993-96; owner, operator ranch in West Tex.; commr. of agr. State of Tex., 1999—. Named Outstanding Legis. Crimefighter, Greater Dallas Crime Commn., 1993. Mem. Tex. Wildlife Assn. (bd. dirs., Tex. and Southwestern Cattle Raisers Assn. (bd. dirs.). Office: Tex Dept Agr PO Box 12847 Austin TX 78711-2847 Business E-Mail: commissioner@agr.state.tx.us.

COMEAU, CAROL SMITH, school system administrator; b. Berkeley, Calif., Sept. 4, 1941; d. Floyd Franklin and Bessie Caroline (Campbell) Smith; m. Dennis Rene Comeau, Dec. 27, 1962; children: Christopher, Michael, Karen. BS in Edn., U. Oreg., 1963; M in Pub. Sch. Adminstrn., U. Alaska, 1985. Third grade tchr., Springfield, Oreg., 1963-64; elem. sch. tchr. Ocean View Elem. Sch., Anchorage, 1975-84, 2d-6th grade tchr.; 6th grade tchr. Spring Hill Elem. Sch., Anchorage, 1985-86; adminstrv. intern Tudor Elem. Sch., Anchorage, 1986-87; prin. Orion Elem. Sch., Anchorage, 1987-89; prin. Spring Hill Elem. Sch., 1989-90; exec. dir. elem. edn. Anchorage Sch. Dist., 1990-93; asst. supt. instrn., 1993-2000; supt., 2000—; mem. exec. com. Coun. Great City Schools, 2003—; community activist ednl. issues. Chair Anchorage United Way, 2004--; bd. dirs. KAKM pub. TV, 1990-92, Alaska Ctr. Performing Arts. Named Tchr. of Yr., Anchorage Sch. Dist. PTA Coun., 1976, Top 25 Most Powerful Alaskans, 2002, Alaska Supt. of Yr., 2003; recipient ATHENA award, Anchorage C. of C., 2004; Mem. NEA (Alaska Renowned Educator, 2003, Nat. Assn. Elem. Sch. Prins., Alaska Assn. Elem. Sch. Prins., Anchorage Edn. Assn. (Tchr. of Yr. 1986), Phi Delta Kappa, Kappa Delta Pi. Democrat. Home: 13632 Jarvi Dr Anchorage AK 99515-3934 Office: Anchorage Sch Dist Adminstrn Bldg 4600 Debarr Rd Anchorage AK 99519-6614 Office Phone: 907-742-4312. Business E-Mail: comeau_carol@asdk12.org.

COMEAU, HEATHER MARIE, dance instructor, administrator; b. Ft. Lauderale, Fla., Jan. 18, 1967; d. Marion Eugene Cochran and Judith Menard Lamport; m. Peter David Comeau, Apr. 8, 1993; children: Matthew David, Sarah Anne Galiatsatos, Jubilee Dawn. Cert. instr. Dance Educators Am. Owner, dir. A Class Apart, Inc., Deltona, Fla., 1999—, ACA Gymnastics, Lake Helen, Fla., 2005—. Office: 3090 Sixma Rd Deltona FL 32738-0903

COMEAU, TRACY LYNNE, small business owner, tax specialist; b. Westfield, Mass., Feb. 15, 1964; d. Bernard Leo Comeau and Sandra Kay Thomas; m. Lee Robert Fobes, Jan. 9, 2001; children: Vitaly Robert Fobes, Nikolai Robert Fobes, Cassandra Ann Fobes. Cert. enrolled agt., IRS, 2000. Contr. Delton Sci. Inc, Huntington Beach, Calif., 1986—92; tax preparer H & R Block, Libby, Mont., 1993—99, owner franchise, 1999—. Instr. H & R Block, 2001—. State coord. Ind. Ukrainian Adoption Family Network, Libby, Mont., 2002—05. Mem.: Mensa. Home: 275 Dawson Street Libby MT 59923 Office: H & R Block 609 East 9th Street Libby MT 59923 Office Phone: 406-293-7434.

COMEAUX, KATHARINE JEANNE, realtor; b. Richland, Wash., Jan. 18, 1949; d. Warren William and Ruth Irma (Remington) Gonder; m. Jack Goldwasser, May 25, 1992; children: Aaron Warren Jacob. AA, West Valley Coll., 1970; student, San Jose State U., 1970-71. Cert. realtor. Realtor Value Realty, Cupertino, Calif., 1975-79, Valley of Calif., Cupertino, 1979-81, Coldwell Banker, Cupertino, 1981-82, Fox & Carskadon, Saratoga, Calif., 1984-90. With Los Gatos-Saratoga Bd. Realtors Polit. Action, 1984-89; v.p. Hospice of Valley Svc. League, Saratoga, 1984-89; Big Sister Big Bros./Big Sisters, San Jose, Calif., 1976-90; bd. dirs. Mountain Energy Inc., Energia Natural, Honduras, Boys and Girls Club, 1996-98, United Way of Josephine Co., 1995-98. Avocations: reading, drawing, writing, needlepoint, photography. Home: 4330 Fish Hatchery Rd Grants Pass OR 97527-9547

COMELLA, CYNTHIA LOUISE, psychologist, neurologist, sociologist, educator; b. Cleve., May 4, 1954; d. Charles Michael and Janet (Jeffries) C. BA in Biochemistry, Smith Coll., 1976; MD, U. Cinn., 1980. Diplomate Am. Bd. Neurology and Psychiatry, Am. Bd. Sleep Medicine. Instr. dept. internal medicine Rush-Presbyn.-St. Luke's Med. Ctr., Chgo., 1980—, instr. dept. neurol. scis., 1983-89, asst. prof. movement disorders sect., 1989-94, asst. prof. dept. psychology and social scis., 1993—, assoc. prof. dept. psychology and social scis., 1995—, assoc. prof. dept. neurol. scis., 1995—2005; prof. neurological sci. Rush U. Med. Ctr., 2005—. Sect. editor Clin. Neuropharmacology Jour., 1997-99, Movement Disorders Jour., 1998-99. Fellow Am. Acad. Neurology; mem. Am. Neurol. Assn. Office: Rush Presbyn St Luke's Med Ctr 1725 W Harrison St Ste 1106 Chicago IL 60612-3828 Office Phone: 312-563-2900.

COMER, BRENDA WARMEE, elementary school educator, real estate company officer; b. Lakewood, Ohio, May 14, 1938; d. Walter Byron and Annabelle (Broderick) Warmee; m. Gerald Edmund Comer, June 30, 1962; children: Brian, James, David, Kristen. BS, Kent State U., 1961; postgrad., Bowling Green State U., 1981, 82, 83-84; reading cert., Baldwin Wallace Coll., 1987. Elem. tchr. Lorain (Ohio) Bd. Edn., 1961-63, tchr. aux. svcs. remedial reading and math., 1979-87, tchr. Chpt. I reading program, 1987—2004; pvt. practice tutor Lorain, 2004—. V.p. Warmee, Inc., real estate. Vice pres. Lakeland Woman's Club, Loraine, 1972, scholarship chmn., 1973-76. Grantee, NEA, 2004—05. Mem. NEA, Ohio Edn. Assn., Loraine Edn. Assn., Internat. Reading Assn., Daniel T. Gardner Reading Coun., AAUW (v.p. Lorain 1981-82, scholarship chmn. 1986-90). Home: 1075 Archwood Ave Lorain OH 44052-1248

COMERFORD, CRISTETA, chef; b. Philippines; naturalized, US; m. John Comerford; 1 child. B in Food Tech., U. Philippines; studied classic French cooking, Vienna. Chef La Ciel Restaurant, Vienna, Westin Restaurant, Washington, ANA Restaurant, Washington; asst. to exec. chef The White House, Washington, 1995—2005, exec. chef, 2005—. Achievements include being first woman appointed head chef of The White House. Office: The White House 1600 Pennsylvania Ave Washington DC 20500

COMERFORD, JANE DEIRDRE, lawyer; b. Stamford, Conn., Sept. 12, 1957; d. John Joseph and Antoinette Andrea Comerford; m. Jonathan Reed Sporn, Sept. 25, 1999; children: Eric, Scott. BA in Math. and Econs. summa cum laude, Boston Coll., Chestnut Hill, 1979; JD, U. Conn., Hartford, 1982; MPH, U. Conn., Storrs, 1997; cert. vet. asst., Middlesex CC, Conn., 2005. Bar: Conn. 1982. Asst. atty. gen. Atty. Gen.'s Office, Hartford, Conn., 1983—. Lectr. in law U. Conn. Sch. Law, Hartford, 1998—, moot ct. competition judge, 1986—88; adj. prof. U. Conn. Grad. Sch., Storrs, 2004—; exam grader Conn. Bar, 1989—96; bd. dirs. Conn. Bar Jour., 1985—89. Exec. editor: U. Conn. Law Rev. Coach West Hartford Youth Soccer Assn., 1997—98, bd. dirs., treas., 2000—04; mem. bd. selectmen Rocky Hill, Conn., 1987; bd. dirs., treas. West Hartford Little League, 2004—; vol. Elizabeth Park Rose Garden, 2003—; treas. State Sen. Cynthia Matthews Re-election Campaign, 1988—89; mem. Dem. Town Com., Rocky Hill, 1984—86. Mem.: Omicron Delta Epsilon, Phi Beta Kappa. Office: U Conn Health Ctr 263 Farmington Ave Farmington CT 06030-0002

COMERFORD, SHALEIGH MARIE, dancer, educator, choreographer; d. Barry William Wright and Margaret Sue Turner Wright; m. Edward Anthony Comerford, Oct. 9, 1999. BA in Studio Art cum laude, Hollins U., Roanoke, 1998; cert. of completion, Am. Dance Festival, N.Y.C., 2001; MA in Liberal Studies in Visual and Peforming Arts, Hollins U., Roanoke, 2004. Performer, outreach educator Young Audiences of Va., Roanoke, 2002—04; instr. dance, choreographer Roanoke Ballet Theatre, 2002—04, co-founder Ariel Ballet, 2003; instr. dance/visual art Art Mus. We. Va., Roanoke, 2004; instr. dance Durham Arts Coun., NC, 2004—05, Ninth St. Dance, Durham, 2004—06; prodn. mgr. Gina Gibney Dance, N.Y.C., 2005—; studio mgr. Studio 5-2, NYC, 2002—. Guest artist Va. Sch. of the Arts, Lynchburg, Va., 2004, Auldern Acad., Pittsboro, NC, 2004; choreographer in residence Mill Mountain Theater, Roanoke, 2005; founder ShaLeigh Dance Works; choreographer and performer U. N.C., Chapel Hill, 2005—06, Duke U., Durham, 2005—06; choreographer and lectr. The Rice Diet, Durham, 2005. Dir.: (documentaries) Woven Identities; co-founder: RealWomen Mag. Dance instr. Triangle Rsch. Options of Substance Abusers, Durham, 2005. Joe Turner scholar, Hollins Coll., 1996, 1997, Nancy Campbell Williamson scholar, 1996, Margaret Jones Irvin scholar, Found. Roanoke Valley, 1997, Betty and Martin Halsell scholar, Hollins Coll., 1996, 1997, Nancy Campbell Williamson scholar, 1997, Freya scholar, Mems. of Freya, 1997, Janet McDonald Travel and Rsch. grantee, Hollins U., 2002, Mimi Babe Harris Arts scholar, dept. art Hollins U., 2003, Janet McDonald Travel and Rsch. grantee, Hollins U., 2003, Co-Operative scholar, dept. dance Hollins U. and Am. Dance Festival, 2003. Mem.: Womens e-News, N.C. Dance Alliance. Avocations: photography, painting, writing, outreach programs, music.

COMFORT, HEATHER E., education educator; b. Charlottesville, Va., Dec. 29, 1971; d. Ronald Comfort, Peter (Stepfather) and Margaret Scherman. BA in English & Art History, James Madison U.; MFA in Creative Writing/Poetry, Arizona State U. Asst. prof., writing & rhetoric James Madison U., Harrisonburg, Va., 2004—. Mem.: MLA. Home: 2376 Breckenridge Ct Harrisonburg VA 22801-8787 Business E-Mail: comforhe@jmu.edu.

COMFREY, KATHLEEN MARIE, lawyer; b. Boston, July 9, 1951; d. George A. and Mary E. (Burke) C.; m. Peter Joseph McCabe, Aug. 23, 1975; children: Peter Joseph, Michael George. BA, Duquesne U., 1973; JD, U. Notre Dame, 1976. Bar: N.Y. 1977, U.S. Dist. Ct. (so. and ea. dists.) N.Y. 1977, U.S. Ct. Appeals (2nd cir.) 1988, U.S. Supreme Ct. 1991, U.S. Dist. Ct. (we. dist.) N.Y. 1994. Assoc. Shearman & Sterling, N.Y.C., 1976-84, ptnr., 1985—; atty. litig. divsn. NYC Law Dept., 2004—. Mem. ABA, Assn. Bar City of N.Y., Women's Bar Assn. State of N.Y. Office: NYC Law Dept 100 Church St New York NY 10007-2601

COMINI, ALESSANDRA, art historian, educator; b. Winona, Minn., Nov. 24, 1934; d. Raiberto and Megan (Laird) C. BA, Barnard Coll., 1956; MA, U. Calif., Berkeley, 1964; PhD with distinction, Columbia U., 1969. Tchg. asst. U. Calif., Berkeley, 1964, vis. instr., 1967; preceptor Columbia U., 1965-66, 67-68, instr., 1968-69, asst. prof., 1969-74; vis. asst. prof. So. Methodist U., summers 1970, 72, assoc. prof. art history, 1974-75, prof., 1975—, univ. disting. prof., 1983—. Alfred Hodder resident humanist Princeton U., 1972-73; disting. vis. lectr. Oxford U., 1996; vis. asst. prof. Yale U., 1973; vis. humanist various univs.; lectr. in English, German and Italian; keynote spkr. Gewandhaus Symposia, Leipzig, Germany, 1983, 85, 87, 89, Mahler Internat Congress, Amsterdam, 1988, 95, Hamburg, 1989, Oxford, 1996, Montpellier, 1996, Internat. Mahler Fest, Boulder, Colo., 1998; featured spkr. Purchase, N.Y., 1989, Leningrad, 1990, Stockholm, 1991, Berlin, 1993, Bethoven Extravaganza, Milw., 1994, Schiele Symposium, Indpls., 1994, Helsinki, 1996, Schubertiads at Curtis Inst., Phila., Reed Coll., Oreg. and So. Meth. U., 1997, Santa Fe Opera, 1997-02, 06, Dallas Symphony Orch., 1998-2006, Brahmsfest of So. Meth. U., 2005, Mozart Internat. Symposium U. Dublin, Ireland, 1999, San Diego Mus., 1999-2005, Giacometti Symposium, Nasher Sculpture Ctr., Dallas, 2005, 06, Neu Galerie, 2005, 06, Mozartfest of So. Meth. U., 2006; panelist NEH Mus. and Pub. Programs, 1978—; vis. scholar Kalamazoo Coll., 1999. Author: Schiele in Prison, 1973, Egon Schiele's Portraits, 1974 (Nat. Book award nominee 1975, reissued 1990, Charles Rufus Morey Book award 1975), Gustav Klimt, 1975, reissued 1986, 90, 93, 01, also German, French and Dutch edit., Egon Schiele, 1976, reissued 1986, 94, 01, also German, French and Dutch edits., The Fantastic Art of Vienna, 1978, The Changing Image of Beethoven, 1987, Egon Schiele: Nudes, 1995, In Passionate Pursuit: A Memoir, 2004; contbg. author: World Impressionism, 1990, Käthe Kollwitz, 1992, Egon Schiele, 1994, Violetta and her Sisters, 1994, Salome, 1996, By a Finnish Fireside: An Evening with Akseli Gallen-Kallela and Gustav Mahler, 1997, The Visual Wagner, 1997, Irony and Gustav Mahler, 2000, Toys in Friend's Attic, 2001, Beethoven and His World, 2000, Pilgrimage to Schiele, 2005; contbr. numerous articles to Stagebill, Arts Mag., English Nat. Opera, Chgo. Lyric Opera; also author various catalogue and book introductions, also book revs. for N.Y. Times, Women's Art Jour. Awarded Grand Decoration of Honor for svcs. to Republic of Austria, 1990; recipient Charles Rufus Morey Book award Coll. Art Assn. Am., 1976, Laural award AAUW, 1979; named Outstanding Prof., 1977, 79, 83, 85, 86, 87, 88, 90, 98, 99, 2000, 01, 02, 03, 04, Laurence Perrine prize Phi Beta Kappa Gamma of Tex., 2003; AAUW travel fellow, 1966-87; NEH grantee, 1975; named Meadows Disting. Tchg. Prof., 1986-87, Tchr./Scholar of Yr., United Meth. Ch., 1996; Comini Lectr. Series in Art History named in his honor So. Meth. U., 2005. Mem. ASCAP, Nat. Mus. for Women in the Arts (nat. bd. 1997—), Coll. Art Assn. Am. (bd. dirs. 1980-84), Women's Caucus for Art (bd. dirs. 1974-78, Life Achievement award 1995, Tex. Women's Hall of Fame 2002), Tex. Inst. Letters. Democrat. Home: 2900 McFarlin Blvd Dallas TX 75205-1920 Office: So Meth U Divsn Art History Dallas TX 75275 Business E-Mail: acomini@smu.edu.

COMISKEY, ANGELA PICARIELLO, accountant; b. Alexandria, Va., Oct. 4, 1971; d. Ralph C. Picariello and Martha Eileen Garretson-Worley; m. John J. Comiskey, Sept. 9, 2000. Student, George Mason U., Fairfax, Va., 1989-91; B Acctg., George Washington U., Washington, 1993. CPA, Va.; registered investment advisor, securities lic., life and health ins. lic. Fin. mgr. Linnhoff March, Houston, 1989-93; acct. Rosenblum, et. al., Rockville, Md., 1993-95; fin. cons. Merrill Lynch, Vienna, Va., 1995-96; acct. Regardie, Brooks, et. al., Bethesda, Md., 1996—. Treas. R.P. Tools, Inc., Falmouth, Va. Mem. AICPA, Va. Soc. CPAs (com. mem. 1995—), Beta Gamm Signa. Repubican. Roman Catholic. Avocations: painting, home renovating, crafts, dogs and cats. Office: Regardie Brooks & Lewis 7101 Wisconsin Ave Ste 1012 Bethesda MD 20814-4876 Home: 12839 Old Bridge Ln Woodbridge VA 22192-5044 E-mail: arp@rblcpa.com.

COMISKY, HOPE A., lawyer; b. Phila., Apr. 23, 1953; married; three children. BA with distinction, Cornell U., 1974; JD, U. Pa., 1977. Bar: Pa. 1977, U.S. Dist. Ct. (ea. dist.) Pa. 1978, D.C. 1979, U.S. Ct. Appeals (3d cir.) 1979, (6th cir.) 1996, (7th cir.) 2005, U.S. Supreme Ct. 1987, U.S. Dist. Ct. (mid. dist.) Pa. 1991, N.Y. 1993. Law clerk ea dist. U.S. Dist. Ct., Pa., 1977-78; assoc. Dilworth, Paxson, Kalish & Kauffman, Phila., 1978-84, ptnr., 1985-91, Anderson Kill & Olick, P.C., Phila., 1992-98, mng. ptnr. Phila. office, 1995-98; ptnr. labor and employment law group Pepper Hamilton LLP, Phila., 1998—, co-chair ERISA and employment litigation practice group, 2005—. Spkr. in field. Contbr. articles to profl. jours. Bd. dirs. Phila. Sch., 1989-2003, pres. 2001-03, hon. bd. dirs., 2004—; bd. dirs. Fedn. Day Care Svcs., 1991-97, mem. exec. com., chmn. pers. practices com., 1985-91; bd. dirs. Ctr. for Literacy, 1996-, v.p., 2004-06, pres. 2006-, chmn. pers. com. 2000-; bd. dirs. Women's Law Project, 1998-2004, Fedn. Early Learning Svcs., 2003-. Mem. Am. Arbitration Assn. (comml. and employment arbitrator), the Coll. of Labor and Employment Attys. (elected mem.), Mortar Board, Phi Beta Kappa. Office: Pepper Hamilton LLP 3000 Two Logan Sq 18th & Arch Sts Philadelphia PA 19103-2799

COMMENT, ANNA MAE, retired principal; b. St. Thomas, V.I., Jan. 26, 1947; d. Warren Elson and Eugenia Eudora Brown; m. Denis X. Comment, May 16, 1970; children: Angela Jeanne McRae, Xavier Warren. BA in English, St. Mary-of-the-Woods Coll., Terre Haute, Ind., 1969. Cert. French/English transls. Nestle Co., Vevey, Switzerland, 1972. Coord. Farley Manning Pub. Rels. Firm, N.Y.C., 1969—70; typist, transl. Nestle Co. S.A., Vevey, Switzerland, 1971—72; adminstrv. asst. Petro Cons. S.A., Geneva, 1973—74; tchr. English grade 12 Eudora Kean H.S., St. Thomas, V.I., 1982—84; exec. asst. Dept. Econ. Devel., St. Thomas, V.I., 1984—89; prin. Sts. Peter and Paul Cath. Sch., St. Thomas, V.I., 1989—94; ret. Commr. 1st Bd. Civil Rights Commn., V.I., 1985; coord. for V.I. 1st V.I. Smithsonian Exhibit on Washington Mall, 1989; con. World of Difference/Anti-Defamation League, Palm Beach, Fla. Columnist: newspaper column; contbr. poetry to anthologies. Active Journey to Justice St. Jude Cath. Ch. Named Woman of Yr., Bus. and Profl. Women of U.S. V.I., 1994. Mem.: LWV (Vol. award 2003). Avocations: reading, writing, travel, music appreciation. Home: 4551 NW 26 Pl Boca Raton FL 33434

COMMERFORD, PATRICIA BERGMAN, elementary school educator; d. John Carl and Mary Rebecca Bergman; divorced; 1 child, Jennifer Christina Davis Kastner. B of Music Edn., Henderson State U., Arkadelphia, Ark., 1975. Pvt. practice, Springdale, Ark., 1985—96, Huntsville, Ark., 1996—; music tchr. Huntsville Sch. Dist., 2003—. Mem.: Music Educators Nat. Conf., NW Ark. Music Tchrs. Assn., Am. Orff-Schuelwerk Assn., Am. Choral Dirs., Springdale Music Club (clinic chair). Republican. Roman Catholic. Avocations: canoeing, camping, hiking, gardening. Home: 1106 Madison 2305 Huntsville AR 72740 Office: Huntsville Intermediate Sch PO Box H 437 Park Ave Huntsville AR 72740

COMMIRE, ANNE, playwright, writer, editor; b. Wyandotte, Mich., Aug. 11, 1939; BS, Eastern Mich. U., 1961; postgrad., Wayne State U., NYU. Author: (plays) Shay, 1973, Transatlantic Bridge, 1977, Put Them All Together, 1978, Sunday's Red, 1982, Melody Sisters, 1983, Starting Monday, 1988; author: (with Mariette Hartley) (book) Breaking the Silence, 1990; editor: Something About the Author, 1970—90, Yesterday's Authors of Books for Children, 1977—78, Historic World Leaders, 1994, Women in World History: A Biographical Encyclopedia, 1999—2002 (Dartmouth medal, 2002), Dictionary of Women Worldwide, 2006. Recipient Eugene O'Neill Theatre award, 1973, 1978, 1983, 1988; grantee, Creative Artists Program, 1975; playwriting grant, Rockefeller Found., 1979. Mem.: PEN, Writers Guild Am., Dramatists Guild, Authors Guild. Home: 11 Stanton St Waterford CT 06385-1400

COMPO, SUSAN ANN, writer, educator; b. N.Y.C., Sept. 19, 1955; d. Leroy Gordon and Yvonne Louise Compo. BA, Calif. State U., Long Beach, 1973—77; MFA, U. So. Calif., L.A., 1986—88. Faculty U. So. Calif., 1999—; vis. artist Cal. Arts, 2002. Author: Life After Death, 1990, Malingering, 1994, Pretty Things, 2001. Office: U So Calif Taper Hall 355 Los Angeles CA 90089 Business E-Mail: compo@usc.edu.

COMPO-PRATT, PAULA ANITA, secondary school educator; b. Camden, NJ, Dec. 22, 1950; d. Peter Compo and Vera Bush; m. Thomas Calvin Pratt, May 10, 1992; 1 child, Lauren Ashley Pratt. BA in English, Rutgers U., 1973; cert. in design, Branch Acad. Floral Design, 1984. Lang. arts tchr., writing specialist, tchr. academically talented program Camden (NJ) Bd. Edn., 1973—. Floral designer, 1983—91; head designer Grove Floral Shop, Deptford, NJ, 1990—91; artist, 1998—; dep. dir. gen. Internat. Biog. Ctr. Ams., 2005. Contbr. poetms, short stories to lit. publs.;, author curriculum materials. Named Outstanding Leader in Elem. and Secondary Edn., Washington, 1976, Woman of Yr., Am. Biog. Inst., 2005; recipient Creativity and Speed award, Br. Acad. Floral Design, 1984, award for cognetics, Nat. Talent Network of E.R.I.C., NJ, 1992—93, Tchr. Recognition award, MIT, 1996, Gov. N.J., 1999, Lifetime Achievement award, Am. Biog. Inst., 2005, Honor medal, 2005, World Freedom medal, 2005, Editors Choice award, Internat. Libr. Poetry, 2005, Lifetime Achievement award, Internat. Biog. Inst., 2005, Universal Achievement Accomplishement award, Am. Biog. Inst., 2005. Russian Orthodox. Avocations: floral design, painting, travel, skiing, horseback riding. Home: 504 Almonesson Rd Westville NJ 08093

COMPSTON, MARION F., small business owner; b. San Francisco, June 5, 1928; d. Stephen James Gilbert and Lorene Alice Schenkel; m. James Compston, Nov. 13, 1948; children: Linda, Kathryn, Mary, Garey, Nancy, Sharon. Attended, San Jose State, 1946-48. Cert. tchr. Diocese of Reno Dept. Relious Edn. Kindergarten tchr. Nev. Dept. Edn., Carson City, 1969-73; owner, bookkeeper Wellington (Nev.) Sta. Resort, 1969—. Dir. religious edn. St. John's Cath. Ch., Wellington, 1972—; mem. (life) Nev. PTA, pres., 1972; active, sec.-treas. parish coun., 1990—; active, treas. Smith Valley Cmty. Hall Bd., Wellington, 1973-98; active, v.p. Lyon County Br. Libr. Bd., Wellington, 1990-98; active, treas. Lyon Co. Park and Recreation Bd., 1988-90; leader 4-H, 1960-85. Mem. Beta Sigma Phi Internat. Republican. Avocations: gardening, stamp collecting/philately, antiques. Home: PO Box 36 Wellington NV 89444-0036 Office: Wellington Station Resort 2855 State Route 208 Wellington NV 89444-9701

COMPTON, ANN WOODRUFF, news correspondent; b. Chgo., Jan. 19, 1947; d. Charles Edward and Barbara (Ortlund) C.; m. William Stevenson Hughes, Nov. 25, 1978; children: William Compton, Edward Opie, Ann Woodruff, Michael Stevenson. BA, Hollins Coll., Va., 1969. Reporter, anchorwoman WDBJ-TV (CBS), Roanoke, Va., 1969-70, polit. reporter, state capitol bur. chief Richmond, Va., 1971-73; fellow Washington Journalism Center, 1970, trustee, 1978-93; corr. ABC News, N.Y.C., 1973-74, White House corr. Washington, 1974-79, 81-84, 89—, 2005—, congl. corr., 1979-81, 84-86, chief Ho. of Reps. corr., 1987-88. Trustee Hollins Coll., 1987-93; bd. dirs. Freedom Forum Ctr. for Media Studies, N.Y., 1984-2000. Named Mother of Yr., Nat. Mother's Day Com., 1987, inducted into Radio Hall of Fame, 2005. Mem. White House Corrs. Assn. (dir. 1977-79), Radio-TV Corrs. Bd. (chmn. 1987). Office: ABC News Washington Bur 1717 DeSales St NW Washington DC 20036-4407*

COMPTON, DIANE GROAT, professional counselor, researcher; b. Long Branch, N.J., July 25, 1958; d. Richard Boyd and Alicia Elizabeth (Winsch) Groat; m. Robert Dale Compton, Aug. 21, 1977; 1 child, Robert Dale Jr. AA with spl. honors, Gulf Coast CC, Miss., 1992; BS summa cum laude, U. So. Miss., Hattiesburg, 1994, MS in Counseling Psychology, 1997. Cert. Nat. Bd. Cert. Counselors, 1998, lic. profl. counselor Miss. State Bd. Lic. Profl. Counselors, 1999. Lic. profl. counselor Meml. Behavioral Health, Gulfport, 1998—2003, Renaissance Counseling Ctr., Gulfport, 2003—04; lic. profl. counselor in pvt./solo practice Changes, Biloxi, Miss., 2004—06, Synergy Behavioral Health Gulf Coast, Biloxi, 2006—. Intrusive thought and social-cognitive devel. following hurricane Katrina rsch. asst. USM Prof., Dr. Manuel Sprung, Long Beach, Miss., 2006—. Author: (poster presentation) Measuring Religiosity: Differences in Liberals and Conservatives, (paper presentation) Physical Child Abuse and Religion: A Look at the Effect of Religious Values on the Perception of Corporal Punishment and Abuse. Vol. Harrison County Family Ct. Youth Shelter, Gulfport, 1991—96; various local ch. positions Christ United Meth. Ch., Long Beach, Miss., 1989—; bd. mem. Harrison County Habitat for Humanity, Gulfport, 1991—94. Named to Hall of Fame, Gulf Coast C.C., 1991—92, Nat. Deans List, 1992, Pres.'s List, U. So. Miss., 1992—94; recipient Honors Program scholarship, Gulf Coast C.C., 1992, Morton scholarship, Bd. Higher Edn. and Ministry of the United Meth. Ch., 1992—93, Jr. Coll. Achievement award, U. So. Miss., 1992—94, Nat. Deans List, 1993, Fielding Grad. U. Psychology Faculty Honors award, Fielding Grad. U., 2006. Mem.: APA (assoc.), U. SO. Miss. Alumni Assn. United Methodist. Avocations: hiking, backpacking, travel. Office Phone: 601-914-4895. E-mail: Comptond1@cableone.net.

COMPTON, DORIS MARTHA, lay worker; b. Eudora, Kans., July 9, 1927; d. Roscoe John and Mabel Ann Robinson; 1 child, Christine Lee Compton-Smith. BA, Ft. Hays State U., Hays, Kans., 1949; MA, U. Ark., Fayetteville, 1951; Cert. Lay Pastor, Sterling Coll., Kans., 2000. Commissioned Lay Pastor Presbytery of No. Kans./Kans., 2000; life credential tchr. Dept. of Edn./Kans., 1951. Tchr. of English, speech, journalism, drama, and Latin Kans. Pub. Schs., Winfield, Ashland, Marysville, Washington, 1951—71; English instr. Am. U. Cairo, 1972—74; founder and dir. Colegio Internacional Miguel Otero Silva, Ciudad Guayana, Venezuela, 1975—80; speech and linguistics U. P.R./Interamerican U., Rio Piedras, PR, 1982—84; temp. English instr. Kans. State U., Manhattan, 1987—89; chmn. English dept. Ramses Coll. for Girls, Cairo, 1989—93; stated supply pastor Little Blue River Parish, Narka, Kans., 1993—97; commd. lay pastor Faith United Ch. Presbyn., Clifton, Kans., 2000—. English instr. for an immersion sch. for ESL Fordham U., San Juan, PR, 1982; completed evaluation for Commonwealth HS, Rio Pedro, P.R. Mid. States Assn., Phila., 1981—82, mem. evaluation team for St. Dunstan's Sch., St. Croix, U.S. Virgin Islands, 1982. Author: (book of poetry) Whisper In The Pines (awards for individual poems); contbr. poems to lit. jours. ($1000 by Am. Poetry Assn., San Francisco, 1985, $200 by Internat. Soc. Poets, Washington, D.C., 1996, First Pl. by Kans. Author's Club, 2000); singer: (solo vocal concerts) Egypt, Venezuela, Am.; performer: (47 dramatic prodns.) Egypt, Venezuela, P.R., Am. Spkr. Presbyn. Ch., 81 cities in Kans., Nebr., Iowa, Mo., Ill.; author of VBS curriculum Presbyn. Ch., Clifton, Kans., 2001—03; display of art and antiquities for schools pub. schs., 5 cities in Kans., 1996—2003. Recipient numerous scholarships for internat. peacemaking, Presbyn. Ch., 1994—. Mem.: Synod of Mid Am. (assoc.; commr. of higher edn. 2001—03), Presbytery of No. Kans. (assoc.), Clifton (Kans.) C. of C. (assoc.). Presbyterian. Avocations: music, collecting art and antiquities, poetry, travel, caring for two grandchildren. Home: 207 East Bartlett Clifton KS 66937 Office: Faith United Ch Presbyterian PO Box 156 Clifton KS 66937 Office Phone: 785-455-3482.

COMPTON, MARY BEATRICE BROWN (MRS. RALPH THEODORE COMPTON), public relations executive, writer; b. Washington, May 25, 1923; d. Robert James and Abia Eliza (Stone) Brown; m. Ralph Theodore Compton, Mar. 18, 1961. Grad., Thayer Acad. Chandler Sch., 1940, Leland Powers Sch. Radio, TV and Theatre, Boston, 1942. Radio program dir. Converse Co., Malden, Mass., 1942—45; head radio continuity dept. Sta. WAAB, Yankee Network, Worcester, Mass., 1945—46; asst. dir. radio Leland Powers Sch. Radio, TV and Theatre, Boston, 1946—49, dir., 1949—51; program asst. Sta. KNBH, Hollywood, Calif., 1951—52; v.p. Acorn Film Co., Boston, 1953—54; dir. women's comm., editor Program Notes, radio interviewer NAM, N.Y.C., NY, 1954—61. Celebrities pub. rels. Nat. Citizens for Nixon, 1968, Kennedy Ctr. Pub. Info., 1985—89, Washinton Nat. Cathedral Visitor's Svcs., 1989—2001. Mem.: Magna Carta Dames, Soc. Old Plymouth Colony Descs., Conl. Country Club (Bethesda, Md.). Home: 15300 Wallbrook Ct Apt 3F Silver Spring MD 20906-1455

COMPTON, MILDRED LEE, retired elementary school educator; d. Virgil Mackey Carpenter and Mary Elizabeth Glasgow; m. Sam Ray Compton, Aug. 13, 1940 (dec. Oct. 13, 1988); 1 child, Sam Ray Jr. BS, East Ctrl. Tchrs. Coll., Ada, Okla., 1941. Elem. tchr. Pontotoc (Okla.) County Schsc., 1942—44; tchr. Calvin (Okla.) Sch. Dist., 1944, Allen (Okla.) Sch. Dist., 1944—48, Wewoka (Okla.) Sch. Dist., 1948, Tulsa (Okla.) Sch. Dist., 1953—55, substitute tchr., 1970—79; tchr. Abilene (Tex.) Sch. Dist., 1961—66, Oklahoma City Sch. Dist., 1966—70. Treas. Fine Arts in Rockbridge, Lexington, Va., 1994—2002, fin. advisor, 2002—05, dir. Goshen outreach, 2002—05; telephone chmn. Tulsa, Okla. Mem.: Okla. Ret. Educators Assn. (life; chmn. tel. com.), Delta Kappa Gamma (v.p. 1950—52, 50 yr. honors). Avocations: building houses, gardening, fishing, dogs. Home: 175 Lutherie Ln Natural Bridge Station VA 24579

COMPTON, NORMA HAYNES, retired dean, artist; b. Washington, Nov. 16, 1924; d. Thomas N. and Lillian (Laffin) Haynes; m. William Randall Compton, Mar. 27, 1946; children: William Randall, Anne Elizabeth. AB, George Washington U., 1950; MS, U. Md., 1957, PhD, 1962; D of Letters, Purdue U., 1996. Rschr. Julius Garfinckel & Co., Washington, 1955; tchr. Montgomery Blair High Sch., Silver Spring, Md., 1955-57; instr. U. Md., 1957-60, teaching and rsch. fellow Inst. Child Study, 1960-61, assoc. prof., 1962-63; psychology extern St. Elizabeths Hosp., Washington, 1962-63; assoc. prof. Utah State U., 1963-64, prof., 1964-68, head dept. clothing and textiles, 1963-68, dir. Inst. for Rsch. on Man and His Personal Environment, 1967-68; dean Sch. Home Econs. Auburn (Ala.) U., 1968-73; dean Sch. Consumer and Family Scis. Purdue U., 1973-87, prof. family studies, 1987-90; faculty The Edn. Ctr., Longboat Key, Fla., 1991-2000, mem. ednl. adv. bd., 1995-98. Cons. Burgess Pub. Co., Mpls., 1975-81, Nat. Advt. Rev. Bd., N.Y.C., 1978-82; bd. dirs. Armour & Co., Phoenix, 1976-82, Home Hosp., Lafayette, Ind., 1983-89; adv. com. Women's Resource Ctr. of Sarasota, Fla., 1992-96; chair Adv. Commn. Status Women, Sarasota, 1993-96; mem. advocates coun. Family Law Network Sarasota, 1994-2000; exec. bd. Sarasota-Manatee Phi Beta Kappa Assn., 1996-99. Author: (with Olive Hall) Foundations of Home Economics Research, 1972, (with John Touliatos) Approaches to Child Study, 1983, Research Methods in Human Ecology/Home Economics, 1988; contbr. articles to profl. jours. Trustee Plymouth Harbor Inc., Sarasota, 2003—; pres. Plymouth Harbor Residents Assn., Sarasota, 2005—. Recipient Woman of Impact Lifetime Achievement award, 1997. Mem.: PEO, APA, Nat. League Am. Pen Women (v.p. Sarasota br. 2000—04), Am. Assn. Family and Consumer Sci., Bird Key Yacht Club, Sigma Xi, Phi Beta Kappa, Psi Chi, Omicron Nu, Phi Kappa Phi. Congregational United Ch. Christ. E-mail: normahc@aol.com.

COMPTON, VALENCIA, pharmacist; b. Beaumont, Tex., May 12, 1975; d. Lionel Compton and Sophia Wright. BS in Chemistry, Southwestern U., Georgetown, Tex., 1997; PharmD, U. Tex., Austin, 2002. Pharmacist Walgreens, Beaumont, 2000—. Mem.: Delta Sigma Theta Sorority, Inc. Office: Walgreens 3605 College St Beaumont TX 77701 Office Phone: 409-832-7374. Office Fax: 409-832-7863.

COMSTOCK, AMY L., social services administrator; BA, Bard Coll.; JD, U. Mich. Atty., U.S. Dept. Edn., 1988—93; asst. gen. counsel for ethics Dept. of Education, 1993—98; assoc. counsel to the Pres. White House, 1998—2000; dir. U.S. Office of Govt. Ethics, 2000—03; CEO, Parkinson's Action Network, Washington, 2003—. Office: Parkinsons Action Network Ste 1120 1025 Vermont Ave NW Washington DC 20005 Office Phone: 202-638-4101. Business E-Mail: acomstock@parkinsonsaction.org.

COMSTOCK, BETH (ELIZABETH J. COMSTOCK), marketing executive; b. Aug. 30, 1960; married; 2 children. BS in Biology, Coll. of William and Mary, 1982. Program dir. Nat. Cable TV Assn., Washington, Arlington Cmty. TV, Va.; publicist, media mgr. NBC, Washington, 1986, corp. comm. mgr. NYC; publicity dir. media rels. Turner Broadcasting, NYC, 1990-92; dir. entertainment publicity CBS/Broadcast Group, NYC, 1992-93; v.p. news media rels. NBC, NYC, 1993-96, sr. v.p. corp. comm. and media rels., 1996—98; v.p., corp. communications GE Co., NYC, 1998—2003, corp v.p. mktg., chief mktg. officer, 2003—05, pres., NBC Universal digital media, mkt. devel., 2005—. Dir. Genworth Financial, 2004—. Named Mktg. Executive of the Year, BtoB mag., 2003, PR Professional of the Year, PR Week mag., 2004; named one of Magnificent Seven Gurus of Innovation, BusinessWeek, 2005; recipient Clarion award Women in Comm., 1995, Matrix award for Corp. Comm., NY Women in Comm. Inc., 2006. Mem.: Assn. of Nat. Advertisers, Inc. (bd. dir.). Office: NBC Universal 30 Rockefeller Plz Ste 4225 New York NY 10112-4225*

COMSTOCK, DIANE ELAINE, science educator, consultant; b. Baton Rouge, La., Sept. 10, 1947; d. Thomas E. and Marie H. Zammit; m. Richard Lee Comstock, Dec. 13, 1975; 1 child, Anne Marie. BS in Elem. Edn., La. State U., Baton Rouge, 1969; MA in Reading Curriculum and Instrn., U. Colo., Colorado Springs, 1999; MA in Tchg. Integrated Natural Scis., Colo. Coll., Colorado Springs, 2002. Lic. tchr.'s provisional La., 1969, Tex., 1981, Colo. Dept. Edn., 1993. Lunar sample libr. NASA, Clear Lake City, Tex., 1969—71; mid. sch. tchr. LaPorte Ind. Sch. Dist., Tex., 1971—74; tchr. Humble Ind. Sch. Dist., Kingwood, Tex., 1987—92, Cheyenne Mountain Sch. Dist. 12, Colorado Springs, 1993—2002; sci. resource tchr. STEP-uP NSF Grant, Colorado Springs, 2002—. Ednl. cons. EZTeach.net, Colorado Springs, 2004—. Author: (profl. devel.) Pathway to Inquiry, Process Skills, Literacy in Science, Science First, Connections to Kits. Sec. treas. Nat. Charity League, Colorado Springs, 1994—97. Named Tchr. of Yr., Cheyenne Mountain Sch. Dist. 12, 1998; recipient UnSung Hero- Top 100 Educators in Am., ReliaStar, 1998, Excellence in Edn., City of Colo. Springs, 1999; grantee Sci. in Edn., Hewlett Packard, 1995, Sci. and Edn., El Pomar, 1996. Mem.: Colo. Assn. Sci. Tchrs., NSTA. Lutheran. Avocations: travel, reading. Office: Cheyenne Mountain Sch Dist 1118 W Cheyenne Rd Colorado Springs CO 80906 Office Phone: 719-475-6100. Business E-Mail: comstock@cmsd.k12.co.us.

COMSTOCK-JONES, JANIS LOU, business owner, consultant; b. Royal Oak, Mich., Nov. 17, 1956; d. Robert Ulysses and Mary Sue Comstock; m. David Todd Jones, July 29, 1983. BS, Rio Grande Coll., 1978; postgrad., Ohio U., Athens, 1978-79, Columbus Tech. Inst., 1986-87, Bennington Coll., Vt., 1977. IBM cert. specialist CAIX. Fiscal officer County Govt., Columbus, Ohio, 1979-85; instr. Columbus Tech. Inst., 1986-87; data processing coord. Am. Red Cross, Columbus, 1987-92, asst. dir., 1992-93; dir. ARC, 1993-95; pres. Gallifrey Enterprises, 1995—. Nat. instr. ARC, Washington, 1990-95. Author: MIS Manual, 1992. Fundraising chair United Way/Assn. Retarded Citizens, Columbus, 1990-91; dir. Nat. Standardbred-Pleasure Horse Orgn., 1989-2003; pres. Ctrl. Ohio Driving Assn., Mt. Vernon, 1992—. Mem. Ohio Standardbred Breeders and Owners Assn., Ohio Harness Horsemen's Assn., U.S. Trotting Assn., Am. Dairy Goat Assn., Ohio Dairy Goat Assn., Nat. Saanan Breeders Assn., Alpines Internat. Avocations: travel, antiques. Mailing: PO Box 65 Centerburg OH 43011 E-mail: web@gallifrey.org.

COMTOIS, TIFFANY LYNN, academic advisor; b. Walnut Creek, Calif., July 7, 1979; d. David Spencer and Kathy Gordon Comtois. AA in Psychology, Los Medanos Coll., Pittsburg, Calif., 0200; BA in Psychology, Calif. State U., Hayward, 2002; MEd in Counseling, UCLA, 2004. Human resources asst. Contra Costa Child Care Coun., Concord, Calif., 2001—03; acad. advisor Calif. State U., Hayward, 2002—03; orientation advisor Stanford (Calif.) U., 2004; acad. advisor U. So. Calif., LA, 2004—. Home: 1484 S Beverly Dr Apt 202 Los Angeles CA 90035

COMUNE, KATHRYN ANN, counselor; b. Newark, Nov. 2, 1951; d. James Charles Camparo and Helen Mildred DeCostanza; children: Tracey Ann, Russell William. BA in Edn., Kean U., 1973; M in Counseling and Edn., William Paterson U., 1996. Lic. profl. counselor NJ, cert. counselor. Elem. sch. tchr. Nutley (N.J.) Bd. Edn., 1973—96, h.s. guidance counselor, 1996—, intervention and referral svc. team, 2001—. Vol. spkr. Internat. Union Against Tuberculosis and Lung Disease, Vancouver, Canada, 2005. Mem.: NEA, ACA, Essex County Sch. Counselors Assn., Edn. Assn. Nutley, N.J. Edn. Assn., Am. Coll. Counselors Assn., N.J. Mental Health Counseling Assn., N.J. Counselors Assn., Am. Sch. Counselors Assn. Home: 24 Ben Franklin Dr Franklin NJ 07416 Office: Nutley High Sch 300 Franklin Ave Nutley NJ 07110 Office Phone: 973-661-8843. Personal E-mail: kcomunelpc@aol.com.

CONANT, DORIS KAPLAN, sculptor, civic worker, real estate developer; b. Phila., Apr. 28, 1925; d. Benjamin A. and Rae (Shander) Kaplan; B.A., U. Pa., 1945; postgrad. U. Havana, 1945, Art Inst. Chgo., 1962; m. Howard R. Conant, Dec. 14, 1947; children— Alison, Howard, Meredith Ann. One man shows Glenview Pub. Library, Northbrook Library,; exhibited in group shows Art Inst. Chgo. Sales and Rental Gallery, Design Unlimited, New Horizons in Sculpture, Old Orchard Art Fair, Lake Forest Coll. Exhbn. Sec. to consul Argentine Consulate, Phila., 1945-47; sec., dir. Interstate Steel Co., Des Plaines, Ill., 1948-1990; organizer proposed 1st Women's Bank Chgo.; dir. Upper Ave. Nat. Bank, Chgo., 1976-81; founder, v.p. Urban Innovations Ltd.First pres. ERA Ill.; mem. Chgo. Network.; bd. dirs. Chgo. Found. for Women, 1986-1989; pres. Conant Family Found., 1995—, treas., 1995—; dir. WBEZ Chgo. Pub. Radio Sta. Recipient Glenview Brotherhood award, 1965; named one of outstanding women P.U.S.H., 1975. Clubs: Carlton, East Bank. Home: 736 Greenacres Ln Glenview IL 60025-3204 also: 180 E Pearson St Chicago IL 60611-2130 Office: 445 North Wells St Chicago IL 60610-4501

CONANT, KIM UNTIEDT, retired elementary school educator; b. Del Norte, Colo., July 26, 1944; d. Warren Malvern and Annine (Gredig) Untiedt; m. Spicer Van Allen Conant, July 9, 1966 (div. Mar. 1983); children: Spicer V., Reid F., Lee G. BA in Am. Studies, Scripps Coll., 1966; MA in Secondary Reading, San Diego State U., 1996. Cert. elem. tchr., Calif. Tchr. asst. Greenwich (Conn.) Country Day Sch., 1966-67; tchr. Katherine Delmar Burke Sch., San Francisco, 1969-70, Cupertino (Calif.) Schs., 1968-69, Kachina Country Day Sch., Phoenix, 1980-83, Paterson (N.J.) Schs., 1985, Black Mountain Mid. Sch., San Diego, 1985-89, Bernardo Heights Mid. Sch., San Diego, 1989—2004, ELD coord., 2000—04; ret., 2004. Tchr. trainer Poway (Calif.) Unified Schs., 1996—2004. Fulbright Exch. tchr. Exeter, Eng., 1998-99. Avocations: swimming, reading, gardening. Home: 14735 Poway Mesa Dr Poway CA 92064-2961

CONANT, MARGARET CANEY, art educator; b. Waterbury, Conn., May 13, 1949; d. Wilbur Hinds and Josephine (Buckingham) Caney; m. Stephen Wright Conant, May 24, 1980; children: Sarah Alden, Margaret Newlin. BA, U. Vt., 1971. Cert. tchr., Vt. Tchr. art John J. Flynn Elem. Sch., Burlington, Vt., 1971-75; spl. edn. aide Early Essential Edn. Ctr., Burlington, Vt., 1976; tchr. art Burlington H.S., 1976—. Alumnae liaison Emma Willard Sch., Troy, N.Y. 1967—; mem. adv. bd. Champlain Valley Sr. Art Show Com., Burlington, 1982—; adj. faculty U. Vt., 2001-. Exhibited in groups at Met. Gallery, Burlington, Vt., 1989, Colburn Gallery, U. Vt., 1991, Fletcher Free Libr., Burlington, Vt., 1991, 2005, Firehouse Gallery, Burlington City Arts, 2005. Tchr. adv. bd. Shelburne Mus., Vt., 1988-1995, ednl. task force, 1990-91; organizer Earth Week Burlington High Sch., 1990. Recipient Outstanding Tchr. award Burlington Sch. Commr., 1982, Tchr. Yr. Burlington H.S., 2001. Mem. Nat. Arts Edn. Assn., Vt. Edn. Assn., Burlington Edn. Assn., Vt. Alliance for Arts Edn. (Arts Educator award 1997), Book Arts Guild Avocations: bookmaking, painting, boating, writing. Home: 69 Mansfield Ave Burlington VT 05401-3323 Office: Burlington High Sch 52 Institute Rd Burlington VT 05401-2721

CONAWAY, CYNTHIA ELIZABETH, parochial school educator, department chairman; d. Erwin and Josephine Antoni; m. Donald Conaway, June 7, 1975; children: Douglas, Donald Jr., Timothy. BS in Biology, Chestnut Hill Coll., Phila., 1975; MEd, Gwynedd Mercy Coll., Gwynedd Valley, Pa., 2004. Tchr. biology, zoology and physics, chair sci. dept. Gwynedd Mercy Acad. HS, Gwynedd Valley, 1975—; chair sci. dept. Gwynedd Mercy Acad., 1986—. Coord. Mid. States evaluation process Gwynedd Mercy Acad., 1999—2005, Kairos retreat coord., 2002—, coach field hockey and softball, 1975—78, coord. ednl. field trips, 1987—98; v.p. Home and Sch. Assn. of Holy Martyrs Grade Sch., Oreland, Pa., 1989—94. Eucharistic min., retreat coord., leader Gwynedd Mercy Acad., 1980—2006. Named Outstanding Tchr. of Yr., Montgomery County Commrs.; recipient Outstanding Sci. Tchrs. award, Phila. U., cert. of appreciation, Soc. Plastics Engrs. Mem.: Nat. Cath. Educators Assn. (assoc.), Montgomery County Sci. Tchrs. Assn. (assoc.). Office: Gwynedd Mercy Acad 1345 Sumneytown Pike Gwynedd Valley PA 19437 Office Phone: 215-646-8815 ext 336.

CONAWAY, JANE ELLEN, elementary school educator; b. Fostoria, Ohio, July 9, 1941; d. Robert and Virginia C. BA in Elem. Edn., Mary Manse Coll., Toledo, Ohio, 1966—67; MEd in Elem. Edn., U. Ariz., 1969; postgrad. in reading, U. Toledo, 1975—77; postgrad., U. Wis., 1987—. Cert. reading specialist in diagnostic and remedial reading Wis. Tchr. Sandusky pub. schs., Ohio, 1969—70; coord. 1st grade small group instrn. program St. Mary's Grade Sch., Sandusky, 1970—71; tchr. Title I remedial reading Eastwood Local schs., Pemberville, Ohio, 1971—87; dist. dir. Right to Read program; reading specialist Middleton-Cross Plains (Wis.) Area Sch. Dist., 1987—. Mem.: NEA, Wis. State Reading Assn., Madison Area Reading Coun., Middleton Edn. Assn., Wis. Edn. Assn., Delta Kappa Gamma. Home: 1302 Wexford Dr Waunakee WI 53597-1842 Office: Middleton Cross Plains Sch Dist Sauk Trail Sch 2205 Branch St Middleton WI 53562-2840 Office Phone: 608-829-9190.

CONAWAY, MARGARET GRIMES (PEGGY CONAWAY), library administrator; b. Minot, N.D., June 6, 1944; d. John Francis and Veronica Ann (McCarthy) Grimes; m. Steven L. Conaway, July 15, 1967 (div. July 1991); 1 child, Anne Marie. BS in Edn., Minot State Coll., 1966; MA in English, San Jose State U., 1978, MLS, 1988. Cert. secondary tchr., Calif.; cert. c.c. tchr., Calif. Instr. Boise (Idaho) Ind. H.S., 1966-67, Santa Maria (Calif.) Joint Union H.S. Dist., 1967-72; libr. asst. San Jose (Calif.) Pub. Libr., 1984-86, libr., 1986-89, sr. libr., 1989-97, divsn. mgr., 1997—2000; libr. dir. Los Gatos (Calif.) Pub. Libr., 2000—. Oper. design project mgr. San Jose Pub. Libr./San Jose State U. Joint Libr., 1998—2000; vice chmn. adminstrv. coun. Silicon Valley Libr. Sys., 2001—02, chmn. adminstrv. coun., 2002—03. Contbr. articles to encys., to profl. jours.; author: Images of America: Los Gatos, 2004; co-author: Images of Rail: Railroads of Los Gatos, 2006. Recipient Helen Putnam award for excellence League of Calif. Cities, 1997. Mem. ALA, Calif. Libr. Assn., Pub. Libr. Assn., Libr. Adminstrn. and Mgmt. Assn. Avocations: writing, antiques, history, travel. Office Phone: 408-354-6895. Business E-Mail: pconaway@losgatosca.gov.

CONDIE, CAROL JOY, anthropologist, science administrator; b. Provo, Utah, Dec. 28, 1931; d. LeRoy and Thelma (Graff) Condie; children: Carla Ann, Erik Roy, Paula Jane. BA in Anthropology, U. Utah, 1953; MEd in Elem. Edn., Cornell U., 1954; PhD in Anthropology, U. N.Mex., 1973. Edn. coord. Maxwell Mus. Anthropology, U. N.Mex., Albuquerque, 1973, interpretation dir., 1974-77; asst. prof. anthropology U. N.Mex., 1975-77; cons. anthropologist, 1977-78; pres. Quivira Rsch. Ctr., Albuquerque, 1978—.

Cons. anthropologist U.S. Congl. Office Tech. Assessment, chair Archeol. Resources Planning Adv. Com., Albuquerque, 1985-86; leader field seminars Crow Canyon Archeol. Ctr., 1986-97; appointee Albuquerque dist. adv. coun., bur. land mgmt. U.S. Dept. Interior, 1989; study leader Smithsonian Instn. Tours, 1991; mem. Albuquerque Heritage Conservation Adv. Com., 1992. Author: The Nighthawk Site: A Pithouse Site on Sandia Pueblo Land, Bernalillo County, New Mexico, 1982, Five Sites on the Pecos River Road, 1985, Data Recovery at Eight Archaeological Sites on the Rio Nutritas, 1992, Data Recovery at Eight Archaeological Sites on Cabresto Road Near Questa, 1992, Archaeological Survey in the Rough and Ready Hills/Picacho Mountain Area, Dona Ana County, New Mexico, 1993, Archaeological Survey on the Canadian River, Quay County, New Mexico, 1994, Archaeological Testing at LA 103387, Nizhoni Extension, Gallup, McKinley County, New Mexico, 1995, Two Archaeological Sites on San Felipe Pueblo Land, New Mexico, 1996, Four Archaeological Sites at La Cienega, Santa Fe County, New Mexico, 1996, A Brief History of Berino, Berino Siding, and Early Mesilla Valley Agriculture, Dona Ana County, New Mexico, 1997; author: (with M. Kent Stout) Historical and Architectural Study of the Old Peralta Elementary School, Valencia County, New Mexico, 1997, Archaeological Survey of 720 Acres on Ball Ranch, Sandoval County, New Mexico, 1998; author: (with H.H. Franklin and P.J. McKenna) Results of Testing at Three Sites on Tesuque Pueblo Land, Santa Fe County, New Mexico, 1999, Cultural Resources Investigations at the Old Roswell Airport for the Proposed Cielo Grande Recreation Area, Chaves County, New Mexico, 2000, Archaeological Survey in Las Lomas de la Bolsa, Santa Fe County, New Mexico, 2001, A Plethora of Walls.the Vigil Properties, Old Town Albuquerque, 2002; author: (with P.W. Bauer, R.P. Lozinsky and L.G. Price) Albuquerque: A Guide to Its Geology and Culture, 2003; author: (with Carol Raish) Indigenous and Traditional Use of Fire in Southwestern Grassland, Woodland, and Forest Ecosystems, 2003; author: (with Susan Dewitt) Doves Along the Ditchbank: La Orilla de la Acequia Historic District, 2003; author: Main Street Project, Aztec, New Mexico, 2004, Testing and Data Recovery at Seven Sites Cabezon Subdivision Sandoval Co., 2005, Archaeological Survey of 355 Acres.on the San Clemente Grant, Valencia County, N.Mex., 2006; co-editor: Anthropology in the Desert West, 1986. Mem. Downtown Core Area Schs. Com., Albuquerque, 1982. Ford Found. fellow, 1953-54; recipient Am. Planning Assn. award, 1985-86, Gov.'s award, 1986. Fellow: Am. Anthrop. Assn.; mem.: Albuquerque Archaeol. Soc. (pres. 1992), N.Mex. Archaeol. Coun. (pres. 1982—83, Hist. Preservation award 1988), Archaeol. Soc. N.Mex. (trustee 2001—), Soc. Am. Archaeology (chmn. Native Am. rels. com. 1983—85), Hist. Albuquerque Inc., The Archaeol. Conservancy (bd. dirs. 2003—), N.Mex. Heritage Preservation Alliance, Maxwell Mus. Assn. (bd. dirs. 1980—83), Las Arañas Spinners and Weavers Guild (pres. 1972). Democrat. Avocations: spinning, weaving, gardening. Home and Office: Quivira Research Ctr 1809 Notre Dame Dr NE Albuquerque NM 87106-1011 Office Phone: 505-255-9264. E-mail: cjc1540@qwest.net.

CONDIT, LINDA FAULKNER, retired economist; b. Denver, May 30, 1947; d. Claude Winston and Nancy Isobel (McCallum) Faulkner; m. John Michael Condit, Dec. 20, 1970; 1 child, David Devin. BA, U. Ark., 1969; MA, U. Wis., 1970; postgrad., U. Minn., 1974-77. Rsch. asst. U. Wis., Madison, 1969—70; economist St. Louis Fed. Res. Bank, 1971—73; ops. analyst No. States Power co., Mpls., 1973-76; energy economist, 1976—78; from ecoomist to v.p. Pennzoil Co., Houston, 1978—95, v.p., 1995—98; v.p., corp. sec. Pennzoil-Quaker State Co., Houston, 1998—2002. Econ. cons. Jr. Achievement, 1983. Recipient Alumni award, U. Ark., 1969. Mem. Internat. Assn. Energy Economists (pres., v.p., treas.), Nat. Assn. Bus. Economists, Internat. Bus. Coun. (v.p.), Am. Econ. Assn., N.Am. Soc. Corp. Planners, Am. Soc. Corp. Secs. (membership chmn.), Hits Theatre (bd. dirs.), Corp. Alliance To Eliminate Ptnr. Violence (bd. dirs.), Leadership Am., Harvard Discussion Group Indsl. Economists, Forst Club, River Oaks Women's Breakfast Club (v.p., pres.), Mortar Bd., Phi Beta Kappa, Kappa Alpha Theta. Home: 11822 Village Park Cir Houston TX 77024-4418

CONDITT, MARGARET KAREN, research scientist; b. Mobile, Ala., Aug. 7, 1953; m. David Joseph Bruno, Feb. 13, 1988; 2 stepchildren: Josh, Holly. BS in Chemistry, U. Ala., Tuscaloosa, 1975; PhD in Chemistry, U. Colo., 1984. Field hydrologist U.S. Geol. Survey, Tuscaloosa, 1975; sci. aide II Geol. Survey Ala., Tuscaloosa, 1975-77; tchg. asst. U. Ala., Tuscaloosa, 1977-79; rsch. asst. U. Colo., Boulder, 1979-84; sr. scientist Procter & Gamble, Cin., 1984—. Reviewer sci. edn. grant proposals NSF, Washington, 1988; mem. water sci. and tech. bd. com. Nat. Acad. Scis., Washington, 1989-91. Author: (chpt.) Advanced Techniques in Synthetic Fuels Analysis, 1983; contbr. articles to profl. jours. Intern Colo. Gov.'s Sci. and Tech. Adv. Coun., 1981—83; appointee Liberty Twp. Bd. Zoning Appeal, 1994—97; elected trustee Liberty Twp., 1998—2001. Recipient fellowship Mining and Mineral Resources and Rsch. Inst., 1980, Rsch. fellowship U. Colo. Grad. Sch., 1981, Browns-Rickett grant AAUW, 1982. Mem. Am. Chem. Soc. Roman Catholic. Avocations: collecting antiques, boy scouts. Home: 6959 Rock Springs Dr Liberty Township OH 45011-9376

CONDON, ANN BLUNT, psychotherapist; b. Brockton, Mass., Sept. 25, 1938; d. Hugh Francis and Ann Collins Blunt; m. John Weston Condon, Jan. 2, 1965 (div. Feb. 1966); 1 child, Pamela Condon Porter. BA, Newton Coll. Sacred Heart, 1960; MSW, Boston U., 1981. LCSW Mass.; cert. profl. coach. Pvt. practice psychotherapy, Centerville, Mass., 1982—; pvt. career coach, 1998—; pvt. writing coach, 2000—; profl. coach, owner The Joy of Success. Seminar leader Landmark Edn., Quincy, Mass., 1986—92; workshop leader Greening Prodns., Centerville, 1988—. V.p. Svc. Employees Internat. Union, Boston, 1965—69; town meeting mem. Town of Barnstable, 1973—75; trustee Cape Cod C.C., 1975—82, Ball Team Platinum, Hashpee, Mass., 2006—. Mem.: NASW (ACSW, diplomate), Cape Cod Chamber Am. Bus. Women Assn., Altrusa Club Cape Cod (founding mem., 1st pres.). Democrat. Roman Catholic. Avocations: gardening, writing, cooking, baseball. Office: PO Box 58 7 Woodvale Ln Centerville MA 02632 Office Phone: 508-775-2059. E-mail: thejoyofsuccess@comcast.net.

CONDON, VANETA MABLEY, medical/surgical nurse; b. Calgary, Alberta, Can., Apr. 1, 1939; d. Orlo William and Florence Isabel (Thompson) Mabley; m. Stanley Charles Condon, May 19, 1963; children: Lori, Brian, David. BSN, Loma Linda U., 1960, MSN, 1964; Phd., Claremont Grad. Sch., Calif., 1996. Charge nurse surg. unit Loma Linda (Calif.) U. Hosp., 1960-61; clin. nurse Loma Linda (Calif.) U. Med. Ctr., 1981-82, facilitator LAP Program, 1982-84, coord. LAP Program, 1984—, instr. med./surg. nursing, 1983—, skills lab. coord., dir. Learning Resource Ctr., 1990—; charge nurse surg. unit White Meml. Hosp., L.A., 1961-63; instr. in med./surg. nursing Pacific Union Coll., Glendale, Calif., 1963-65; curriculum cons. Mountain View Coll., Malaybalay, Philippines, 1965-72. Cons./learning assistance Pacific Union Coll., 1983-92, Santa Monica (Calif.) Coll., 1988-90; asst. prof. med.-surg. nursing Loma Linda U., 1986—; lectr. in field; mem. Nursing Info. Coun., 1990—. Contbr. articles to profl. jours. Elder Redlands (Calif.) Seventh-Day Adventist Ch., 1988-92; dir. Sucess in Nursing, Indiviudalized Pathway Program, 1999-2004, Pipeline to Registered Nursing, Increasing Diversity, 2004-. Grantee Area Health Edn. Coun., 1981-86, HSRA Nursing Workforce Diversity, 1999-2006. Mem. Loma Linda U. Sch. Nursing Alumni Assn. (bd. dirs. 1986-90), Assn. Seventh-Day Adventist Nurses, Nat. League Nurses. Avocations: camping, writing, reading victorian prose. Home: 11524 Ray Ct Loma Linda CA 92354-3630 Office: Loma Linda U 127 West Hall Campus St Loma Linda CA 92350

CONDOS, BARBARA SEALE, real estate broker, developer, investor; b. Kenedy, Tex., Feb. 24, 1925; d. John Edgar and Bess Rochelle (Ainsworth) Seale; m. George James Condos, Dec. 24, 1955 (dec.); 1 child, James Alexander. MusB magna cum laude, U. Incarnate Word, San Antonio, 1946. Lic. real estate broker, Tex. Ptnr., CEO Mountain Top-V.I. Devel. Properties, V.I., 1977-85; pres. Investment Realty Co., L.C., San Antonio, 1978—. Choreographer, dancer San Antonio Symphony's Youth Concerts and Opera Festival; actress San Antonio Little Theatre-Patio-Players 1948—. Trustee San Antonio Little Theatre, 1953-76; mem. coun. McNay Mus., 1986—, chmn. coun., 1987—, chair coun., 1988—, trustee, 1989-97, trustee emerita, 1997—; bd. dirs. San Antonio Performing Arts Assn., 1978—; mng. trustee Russell Hill Rogers Fund for Arts. Mem. Internat. Real Estate Fedn., Internat. Real Estate Inst., Nat. Assn. Realtors, Tex. Assn. Realtors, San Antonio Bd. Realtors, Tex. Watercolor Soc. (signature mem.), The Argyle Club. Avocation: painting. Home: 217 Geneseo Rd San Antonio TX 78209-5913 Office: Investment Realty Co 1635 NE Loop 410 San Antonio TX 78209-1625 Business E-Mail: bsc@investmentrealty.com.

CONDRAN, CYNTHIA MARIE, gospel musician; b. Avon Park, Fla., Apr. 29, 1953; d. Kenneth Dale and Ruth Mae (Garber) Grubb; m. Lee Light Condran, July 3, 1971. Student, Lebanon Valley Coll., 1970—72. Piano tchr., Sebring, Fla., 1968-70, Annville, Pa., 1971—; gospel musician, writer, arranger Condran Music Co., Annville, Pa., 1972—, also recording engr. Sang by spl. invitation at Elipse of The White House, 1982; composer The Only Thing Holding You Back, 1977, Just A Few More Rivers, 1975, The Patchwork Quilt, 1978, Freedom, 1976, The Little Things, 1980, We're America, Heavens Fiesta, He's the Lord of Everyday, 1989, I've Never Known Such Love, 1990, I Just Want To Talk To You, 1990, Sweep Our Sins, 1990, Eternal Friends, 1991, The Precious Jewels At Christmas Time, 1992, Lost On My Way Back Home, 1993, I Believe in the Power of Love, 1993, To Speak Your Name, 1994, Forever, 1994, We Praise You Lord, 1994, R.D. #11, Heaven, 1996, Surprise, 1997, Patience, 1998, His Healing Blood, 1999, Back Door Blessings, 2000; writer comml. jingles. Recipient Contemporary Country Artists of Yr. award Internat. Country Gospel Music Assn., 1995, Internat. Star Music award, 1997, Contemporary Country Duo of Yr. award, 1999, Entertainer of Yr. Silver Heart award, 1999, Female Vocalist of Yr. northeast region, 1999, Golden Heart award for the Nat. Female Vocalist of Yr., 1999; named Female Vocalist of the Yr., Country Gospel Music Assn., 1999, Reciter of the Yr., Country Gospel Music Assn., 2000, 2002. Mem. Gospel Music Assn., Broadcast Music Inc., Christian Bus. and Prof. Women (music chmn.), So. Gospel Music Guild. Republican. Avocations: skiing, golf, swimming, tennis, racquetball. Home: 935 N Route 934 Annville PA 17003-9803 Office Phone: 717-867-4137. Personal E-mail: leecindyco@aol.com.

CONDRILL, JO ELLARESA, freelance/self-employed small business owner, writer, consultant; b. Hull, Tex., Oct. 25, 1935; d. Freddie (dec.) and Ida (Donatto) Founteno; m. Edwin Leon Ellis, Jan. 9, 1955 (div. 1979); children: Michael Edwin, James Alcia, Resa Ann, Thomas Matthew; m. Donald Richard Condrill, Sept. 21, 1980 (div. 1985). BSBA, Our Lady of the Lake U., 1982; MS in Pub. Adminstrn., Ctrl. Mich. U., 1987; grad., U.S. Army War Coll., 1993. Editorial asst. Airman Mag., San Antonio, 1978; mgmt. analyst San Antonio Air Logistics Ctr., San Antonio, 1979-82; inventory mgr. ground fuels Detachment 29, Alexandria, Va., 1982-83; logistics plans officer Mil. Dist. Washington, 1983-85, chief logistics plans ops. and mgmt., 1985-88; chief integration br. Office of the Dep. Chief of Staff for Logistics, 1990-95; deputy chief logistics plans and ops. div. Hdqs. U.S. Army, The Pentagon, 1995-97; owner Seminars by Jo, Alexandria, Va., 1984-86, GoalMinds, Beverly Hills, Calif., 1997—. Author: Leadership: From Vision to Victory in Six Powerful Steps, 1996, 101 Ways to Improve Your Communication Skills Instantly, 1998, A Millennium Primer: Take Charge of Your Life, 1999, From Book Signing to Best Seller: An Insider's Guide to a Successful Low-Cost Booksigning Tour, 2001 (Best Writer's Ref. Guide, Bay Area Ind. Pubs. Assn. 2001-2002), Take Charge of Your Life: Dare to Pursue Your Dreams, 2003. Civilian v.p. student coun. Army War Coll., Carlisle, Pa. Recipient decoration for Exceptional Civilian Svc., U.S. Army, 1997; Best Speaker award Def. Logistics Agy. Mem. NAFE, Nat. Spkrs. Assn., Rotary Internat., Toastmasters Internat. (dist. 27 gov. 1991-92, internat. dir. 1994-96, top ranking dist. gov. in internat. orgn. 1991-92, Internat. Pres. Disting. Dist. award 1991-92). Roman Catholic. Avocations: travel, dance, reading. Office: Goal Minds Inc 6300 Rue Marielyne #308 San Antonio TX 78238 Office Phone: 310-993-7553. Business E-Mail: condrill@goalminds.com.

CONDRON, BARBARA O'GUINN, philosopher, educator, academic administrator, writer; b. New Orleans, May 1, 1953; d. Bill Gene O'Guinn and Marie Gladys (Newbill) Jackson; m. Daniel Ralph Condron, Feb. 29, 1992; 1 child, Hezekiah Daniel. BJ, U. Mo., 1973; MA, Coll. Metaphysics, Springfield, Mo., 1977, DD, D in Metaphysics, 1979. Cert. counselor; ordained min. Interfaith Ch. Metaphysics. Field rep. Sch. Metaphysics, New Orleans, 1978-80; dir. Interfaith Ch. Metaphysics, 1884-89; pres. Nat. Hdqs., Sch. Metaphysics, Windyville, Mo., 1980-84, prof., 1989—, chmn. bd. dirs., 1991-98, mem. coun. elders, bd. govs. internat. edn., 1998—; CEO SOM Pub., Windyville, 1989-98. Creator Sch. Metaphysics Assocs., 1992; initiator Universal Hour Peace, 1995; initiator, internat. coord. Nat. Dream Hotline, 1988—; radio and TV guest, 1977—; creator Maker's Dozen-Visionary Schs. Recognition, 1999, Taraka Yoga Psi Counseling Program; initiator Spiritual Focus Sessions, 1997—; internat. coord. Peace Dome dedication and One Voice Initiative, 2003, Soc. for Intuitive Rsch., 2003—; presenter in field; lectr. in field. Author: What Will I Do Tomorrow?, Probing Depression, 1977, Search for a Satisfying Relationship, 1980, Strangers in My Dreams, 1987, Total Recall: An Introduction to Past Life & Health Readings, 1991, Kundalini Rising, 1992, Dreamers Dictionary, 1994, The Work of the Soul: Past Life Recall & Spiritual Enlightenment, 1996, Uncommon Knowledge, 1996, Firsst Opinion: 21st Century Wholistic Health Care, 1997, Spiritual Renaissance Elevating Your Conciousness for the Common Good, 1999, The Bible Interpreted in Dream Symbols, 2000, Remembering Atlantis: The History of the World Vol. 1, 2002, How to Raise an Indigo Child, 2002, Peacemaking: 9 Lessons for Changing Yourself, Your Relationships and Your World, 2003, The Wisdom of Solomon, 2004, The Invitation: A Play and Film in Four Acts, Satyagraaha: A Play Based on the Life of Mohandas K. Gandhi, Every Dream is About the Dreamer, 2004, Master Living: 10 Essential Life Skills for Health, Prosperity, Success and Peace of Mind, 2005; author series When All Else Fails, editor-in-chief Thresholds Jour., 1990—2001, editor Wholistic Health and Healing Guide, 1992—2000, dir. film Making Peace, 2003, prodr., dir. films The Silver Cord, 2004, The Invitation-8 Nobel Peace Laureates Meet in the Peace Dome, 2006, dir. documentary Vision Quest, 2005, numerous poems. Mem. Internat. Platform Assn., Am. Bus. Women's Assn., Interfaith Ministries, Kundalini Rsch. Network, Planetary Soc., Heritage Found., Mo. Writers Guild, Sigma Delta Chi. Office: Sch Metaphysics World Hdqs Windyville MO 65783 Office Phone: 417-345-8411. Business E-Mail: bcondron@som.org, bgc@dreamschool.org.

CONE, CAROL LYNN, public relations executive; b. NYC, June 7, 1950; d. William Addison Cone and Harriet (Gurney) Brown. BA, Brandeis U., 1972; MS, Boston U., 1978. Account exec. Newsome and Co., Boston, 1977-80; pres., CEO Cone Comm. Inc., Boston, 1980—. Mem. Gov.'s Entrepreneurial Adv. Council, Boston, 1982, Dukakis for Pres. campaign nat. fin. com., Boston, 1987. Named Outstanding Female Entrepreneur La Salle Jr. Coll., Newton, Mass., 1986, YWCA Achievement Entrepreneur, Boston, 1986, Entrepreneur of Yr. Arthur Young/Venture Mag., 1988; recipient Golden Quill award Internat. Assn. Bus. Communicators, 1987. Mem. Counselor's Acad. of Pub. Relations Soc. Am., Pub. Relations Soc. Am. (Silver anvil 1987), Am. Mktg. Assn. Avocations: skiing, windsurfing, walking. Office: Cone Communications 855 Boylston St Boston MA 02116

CONE, FRANCES MCFADDEN, data processing consultant; b. Columbia, S.C., Oct. 20, 1938; d. Joseph Means and Francis (Graham) McFadden: m. Charles Cone Jr., May 1962 (div. Sept. 1964); 1 child, Deborah Ann Cone Craytor. BS, U. S.C., 1960, MEd, 1973, M Math., 1977. Systems svc. rep. IBM, 1960-62; programmer/analyst Ga. Power Co., Atlanta, 1964-68, S.C. Fin. and Data Processing, Columbia, 1968-69; instr., head dept. Midlands Tech. Coll., Columbia, 1969-75; tng. coord. S.C. Nat. Bank, Columbia, 1975-79; systems analyst S.C. Dept. Health and Environ. Control, Columbia, 1979-80; project analyst So. Co. Svcs., Atlanta, 1980-89; cons. George Martin Assocs., Atlanta, 1989-93; sr. sys. developer Emory U., Atlanta, 1993-97; sys. analyst Southland Life Ins. Co., Atlanta, 1997-99; team leader ING-Life of Ga., Atlanta, 1999—2002; ret., 2002. Adj. prof. Golden Gate U., Sumter, SC, 1976—80. Vol. Ga. Wildlife Found., 1989—2002, Save the Manatee Club, 1989—2002, Names Project, 1995—97, Ellijay Wildlife Rehab. Sanctuary, 2000—02, Shepherd Spinal Ctr., 2000—01, Alpha Delta Pi 150-Yr. Conv., 2001; mem./vol. Winyah chpt. Sierra Club, 2003—; vol. Humane Soc. of U.S., 2005—, S.C. United Turtle Enthusiasts, 2005—, Waccamaw River Keeper, 2005—; chair Silver Polishing Daughters of the King Cathedral of St. Philip, 1994—2000; mem./vol. Holy Cross Faith Meml. Epsicopal Ch. Women, 2004—. Mem. Nat. Mgmt. Assn. (sec., treas., awards comn. 1981-89), Episcopal Ch. Women (treas. 2006—). Episcopalian. Avocations: reading, embroidery. E-mail: fcone@mindspring.com.

CONE, MARLA, environmentalist, writer; BA in Journalism, Polit. Sci., Univ. Wis., Whitewater, 1979. Reporter Fla. Today, Orange County Register, Calif.; environ. reporter LA Times, Long Beach, Calif., 1990—. Author: Silent Snow: The Slow Poisoning of the Arctic, 2005; contbr. more than 1,000 newspaper and magazine articles on environ. issues. Recipient Meeman award in environ. journalism, Scripps Howard, 1983, 1994, Oakes award for disting. environ. journalism (hon. mention), 1995, 1996, Am. Lung. Assn. Media award, 1997; grantee Environ. Journalism Teaching Fellowship, Univ. Calif. Berkeley, 1999, Pew Found. Fellowship in Marine Conservation, 1999. Mem.: Soc. Environ. Journalists (bd.dir. 1992—99). Office: Environmental Writer LA Times 5271 E Broadway Long Beach CA 90803 Office Fax: 213-237-7000. Business E-Mail: marla.cone@latimes.com.

CONE, VIRGINIA WILLIAMS, retired historian; b. Noble, Ill. d. George Washington and Ella (Maddox) Williams; m. Elmer Newton Searls, Nov. 27, 1933 (div. 1948); children: Leslie, Janice; m. Leon Winston Cone, Mar. 25, 1948; children: Henrietta Maria, Winston George. BA in History summa cum laude, U. Ill., 1943, MA, 1946; student, Blackburn Coll., 1930-32. Educator U. Ill., Champaign, 1943-48, Purdue U., LaFayette, Ind., 1948-62, U. Ghana, Accra, 1958-59, U. Dar es Salaam, Tanzania, 1962-64, Kenya Inst. Adminstrn., Nairobi, 1964-66; assoc. prof. African history So. Conn. State U., New Haven, 1967-82, adj. prof. of women in U.S. history, 1982—. Author: Africa: A World in Progress, 1961, Kenya Women Look Ahead, 1965. Mem. AAUW (del. to Forum '85), Pnenex Soc. (pres.), Phi Beta Kappa. Republican. Congregationalist. Avocation: leading african tours. Home: 9 Cedar Rd Woodbridge CT 06525-1642

CONELLI, MARIA ANN, art educator, dean, architect; b. Bklyn., Nov. 1, 1957; d. Carmine S. and Mary Conelli; m. Kim J. Hartswick, May 11, 1990. BA in Art History, Bklyn. Coll., 1980; MA, NYU, 1983; MPhil, Columbia U., PhD in Archtl. History, 1992. Educator Met. Mus. Art, NYC, 1981—84; instr. Parsons Sch. Design, NYC, 1983—2001; chair Parsons/Smithsonian Inst., NYC, Washington, 1992—2001; dean Fashion Inst. Tech., NYC, 2001—05; dir. Am. Folk Art Mus., NYC, 2005—. Co-editor: Newsletter Decorative Art Soc., 1995—2005; contbr. articles to profl. jours., books. Trustee Skyscraper Mus., N.Y.C., 1999—2005; mem. mus. com. Coll. Art Assocs., N.Y.C., 2003—. Pub. Works Challenge grantee, Nat. Endowment for the Arts, Washington, 2002—03, J. Paul Getty Postdoctoral fellow, 1997. Fellow: Am. Acad. in Rome (fellow 1987—88); mem.: Coll. Art Assn. Roman Catholic. Office: Am Folk Art Mus 45 W 53d St New York NY 10019-5401 Office Phone: 212-265-1040 ext. 114. Office Fax: 212-265-2350. Business E-Mail: mconelli@folkartmuseum.org.

CONEY, STEPHNÉ RENIÁ, communications educator; b. Camden, N.J., Oct. 29, 1963; d. Douglas Tyrone and Bette Louise Coney; 1 child, Sescily Reneé. BA, Johnson C. Smith U., Charlotte, N.C., 1986; MA, Tex. So. U., Houston, 1988; postgrad., U. Santa Barbara. Prof. edn. Hargest Coll., Houston, 1988-90; tax examiner IRS, Phila., 1990-96; founder, exec. dir. Nat. Stop the Violence Alliance, Inc., Camden, 1991—. Founder, exec. dir. Camden County Internat. Nat. Festival, 1994—, Actors, Artists and Athletes Against Violence, 1995—, Facing Attitudes Concerning Ednl. Spirits, 1996, Peace Troopers: A Youth Partnership with Law Enforcement, 1998. Recipient Stop the Violence award Assembly of N.J./Camden City Coun., 1995. Mem. Delta Sigma Theta. Democrat. African Methodist Episcopal. Avocations: directing, acting, singing, reading, writing. Office: Nat Stop the Violence PO Box 1293 Camden NJ 08105-0293

CONGALTON, SUSAN TICHENOR, lawyer; b. Mt. Vernon, N.Y., July 12, 1946; d. Arthur George and M. Marjorie Tichenor; m. Christopher William Congalton, May 29, 1971. BA summa cum laude, Loretto Heights Coll., 1968; JD, Georgetown U., 1971. Bar: N.Y. 1972, Ill. 1986, Colo. 1990. Assoc. Reavis & McGrath (now Fulbright & Jaworski), N.Y.C., 1971-78, ptnr., 1978-85; v.p., gen. counsel, sec. Carson Pirie Scott & Co., Chgo., 1985-87, sr. v.p. fin. and law, 1987-89; mng. dir. Lupine LLC (formerly known as Lupine Ptnrs.), Chgo., 1989—; chmn., CEO Calif. Amforge Corp., 2002—. Bd. dirs. Harris Fin. Corp., Harris Bankcorp, Inc.; chmn. Cmty. Reinvestment Act Com., 1990-97, chmn. audit com., 1997—; chmn. bd., CEO, Calif. Amforge Corp., 2002—. Mem. editorial staff Georgetown U. Law Jour., 1969-70, editor, 1970-71. Mem. bd. overseers Ill. Inst. Tech., Chgo., Chgo. Kent Coll. Law, 1985-89; mem. bus. adv. coun. Bus. Sch., U. Ill., Chgo., 1987-90; mem. planning com. Ann. Corp. Counsel Inst., 1986-89; bd. dirs. Ill. Inst. Continuing Legal Edn., 1992-95; mem. Chgo. Workforce Bd., 1995-98; chmn. Strategic Planning Task force, 1995-96, chmn. Performance Rev. Com., 1996-98. Mem. ABA, Nat. Assn. Corp. Dirs. (bd. dirs. Chgo. chpt. 2001—), Econ. Club Chgo., Chgo. Club (bd. dirs. 1996—2004, treas. 1999-02, sec. 2002—04). Office: Lupine LLC 1520 Kensington Rd Ste 112 Oak Brook IL 60523-2140

CONGDON, AMANDA, actress, web video blogger, writer; b. NYC, 1981; Grad. magna cum laude, Northwestern U., Evanston, Ill.; additional edn., King's Coll., London, Eng., U. New South Wales, Sydney, Australia. With Saatchi & Saatchi Advertising Agy.; co-scripter, co-prodr, Jet Set Show, 2006; co-prodr., anchor, daily online news show Rocketboom.com, 2004—06, part owner, 2004—. Comp, mem. Playground Improv Troupe, NY Comedy Club. Maintains (blog website) amandacongdon.com, amandaunboomed.blogspot-.com, co-star CSI, Las Vegas, spl. guest Attack of the Show!, season regular The Restaurant, Season 2, guest appearance The Chris Rock Show, Hey Ya, My Coolest Years, co-host Jean Carlo Cooking Show, Northstar Music video, lead performer (theatre) Independence, Manhattan Theatre Source, Waafrica, Red Room Theatre, Manhattan. Avocations: writing, videoblogging, sketching, improv, bungee-jumping, hula hooping, horseback riding, swimming, volleyball, skiing, rollerskating, kayaking, soccer. Address: Endeaver Agy 9601 Wilshire Blvd Beverly Hills CA 90210 E-mail: unboomed@gmail.com.*

CONGDON, SARAH-BRAEME BIRD, medical equipment company executive; b. East Orange, NJ, Aug. 10, 1952; d. Alfred Bird Jr. and Barbara-Anne (Jones) Stewart; m. James Boote Congdon, Feb. 21, 1976; children: Arthur Edward, James Westbrook. AA, Katharine Gibbs Sch., Montclair, N.J., 1973; BBA, U. Pa., 1989. Bus. adminstr. U. Pa., Phila., 1976-82, U. City Sci. Ctr., Phila., 1982—96; CEO Med. Diagnostic Rsch. Found., Phila., 1996—. Co-founder Optical Devices, Inc., 1998—. E-mail: sbcongdon@aol.com.

CONGER, CYNTHIA LYNNE, financial planner; b. Omaha, Dec. 8, 1948; d. Bob Bruce Ashton and Cleo (Artz) Ashton Taplin; m. Terry H. Conger, Dec. 21, 1969 (div. June 1989); children: Cynthia T., Scott A. BA Acctg., U. Ark., Little Rock, 1980, MBA Fin. and Econ., 1983. CPA, Ark.; cert. fin. planner. V.p., fin. planner Ark. Fin. Group, Inc., Little Rock, 1984—94, pres., 1995—2005, Cynthia L. Conger, CPA, PA, Little Rock, 1989—. Mem. found. bd. U. Ark., 2002—. Mem.: LWV (adv. bd. 1997—), Registry Fin. Planning Practitioners, Internat. Assn. Fin. Planning (Ark. chpt., v.p. 1986—87, pres. 1987—89, nat. bd. dirs. 1994—98). Methodist. Avocations: reading, travel, cooking. Office: Cynthia Conger CPA PA 2300 Andover Ct #560 Little Rock AR 72227 Office Phone: 501-374-1174. Business E-Mail: cindy@cindyconger.com.

CONGER, LUCINDA, retired librarian; b. Ft. Bragg, NC, June 11, 1941; d. Meredith Moore and Ann Oliver (Mumford) Dickinson; m. Bruce C. Conger, June 25, 1966. BA, Radcliffe Coll., 1963; MLS, Rutgers U., 1964; student,

Wesley Sem., Washington, 1990. Reference libr. U. Calif., Davis, 1964-65; cataloger Libr. of Congress, Washington, 1965, reference libr., 1966; compact storage libr. Princeton (N.J.) U., 1966-70; dir. reclassification Albion (Mich.) Coll., 1970-71, serials libr., 1971-73; reference libr. Yale U., New Haven, 1973-75, U.S. Dept. State, Washington, 1976—2000; chief Reader Svcs. Br., 1994—2000; ret., 2000. Author: Online Command Chart, 1977, 81; columnist Database Mag., 1980-90; contbr. articles to profl. jours. Vol., Washington Cathedral, 1976—, Smithsonian, 2001—. Recipient Govt. Computer News award, 1992, Sec. Career Achievement award, 2000. Mem.: DAR, Archaeological Inst. Am., Harvard Club Washington, Nat. Soc. Colonial Dames. Democrat. Episcopalian. Avocations: classical greek, archaeology, genealogy, travel. Home: 4906 Jamestown Rd Bethesda MD 20816-2709 Personal E-mail: congerld@msn.com.

CONIGILARO, PHYLLIS ANN, retired elementary school educator; b. Ilion, N.Y., Nov. 27, 1932; d. Gus Carl and Jennie Margaret (Marine) Denapole; m. Paul Anthony Conigilaro, July 16, 1983. BS cum laude, SUNY, Cortland, 1955; MA in Edn., Psychology, Cornell U., 1961. Cert. tchr., N.Y. Elem. classroom tchr. Mohawk (N.Y.) Central Sch., 1955-88. Contbr. articles to profl. jours. Bd. dirs. United Fund of Ilion, Herkimer, Mohawk and Frankfort, 1984-86, pres., 1986; pres. bd. edn. St. Mary's Parochial Sch., 1978; mem. Herkimer County Hist. Soc., 1988—, trustee, 1994-97; bd. dirs. local Federal Emergency Mgmt. Agy., 1987-96. Recipient Outstanding Elem. Tchrs. of Am. award, Outstanding Elem. Tchrs. of Am. Wash. D.C., 1974. Mem. N.Y. State United Tchrs., Mohawk Tchrs. Assn. (past pres.), AAUW (pres. Herkimer chpt. 1981-82), N.Y. State Ret. Tchrs. Assn. (past legis. chmn. Herkimer County chpt.), Rep. Women's Club, Kappa Delta Pi. Republican. Roman Catholic. Avocations: golf, travel, reading, music. Home: 137 7th Ave Frankfort NY 13340-3612 E-mail: pconigil@twcny.rr.com.

CONIGLIO, JUDITH, music educator; b. N.Y., Feb. 27, 1943; d. Sidney and Anita Halpern; m. Joseph Coniglio, Oct. 6, 1989; children: Geoffrey Ian Cox, Tracey Brady, Cindy Federici. BS in Music Edn., SUNY, Potsdam, 1964; MS in Edn. Tech., LI U., Piermont, N.Y., 1990. Cert. tchr. State Edn. Dept. N.Y., 1974, State Edn. Dept. Conn., 2002. Music tchr. Syosset Pub. Schs., NY, 1964—66, East Ramapo Sch. Dist., Spring Valley, NY, 1966—70; adj. prof. Rockland C.C., Suffern, NY, 1970—74; music tchr. Pearl River Sch. Dist., NY, 1971—2001, Cmty. Sch., Prospect, Conn., 2001—. Musician: (performance) Saratoga Performing Arts Festival (Performance Cert., 1977); author: (article in music jour.) For The Boys (Outstanding Musical - female performer, 2000); prodr.: (musical theatre prodn.) The Sound of Music. Sec. RCMEA, Spring Valley, 1996—98. Recipient Music Educator of Yr., New Haven Symphony Orch., 2004. Mem.: Music Educators Nat. Conf. (life). Office Phone: 203-758-6674.

CONKLIN, PEGGY BROWN, history professor; d. Bill L. and Dixie L. Brown; 1 child, Melissa Kathryn. MA, Morehead (Ky.) State U., 1981. Adj. instr. Morehead State U., 1982—89; student affairs coord.-residence life U. South Fla., Tampa, 1989—2000; asst. prof. history SE Ky. Cmty./Tech. Coll., Whitesburg, 2002—. Cons. Nat. History Day Project-State of Ky., Frankfort, 2003—. Social studies coach for academic team Christ Ctrl. Acad., Pikeville, Ky., 2005; judge for regional history day competition Ky. Hist. Soc., Frankfort, 2003; presenter, vol. Wilderness Rd. Girl Scouts, Pikeville, 2003. Recipient Excellence award, NISOD Inst., 2005, 2006, New Horizons Faculty award of excellence, Ky. Cmty. and Tech. Coll. Sys., 2006. Mem.: Orgn. Am. Historians, Pi Gamma Mu, Phi Alpha Theta (pres. 1978—79). Avocations: traveling to historical places, cooking, reading, dance.

CONKLIN, SUSAN JOAN, psychotherapist, educator, television personality, realtor; b. Bklyn., Feb. 7, 1950; d. Joseph Thomas Hallek and Stella Joan Kuceluk; m. John Lariviere Conklin, July 25, 1961; children: Genevieve Therese, Michelle Therese. BA, CCNY, 1972; MSW, Hunter Coll., N.Y.C., 1975. LCSW; lic. NJ Real Estate 2003, bd. cert. diplomate. Shop counselor Assn. for Help of Retarded Citizens, N.Y.C., 1971-75; dir. social svcs., acting exec. dir. North Berkshire Assn. for Retarded Citizens, North Adams, Mass., 1975-77; project dir. Title XX tng. grant State of Mass., North Adams, 1978-79; pvt. practice Williamstown, Mass., 1979—; jr. realtor assoc. Century 21 Alliance. Adj. asst. prof. Mass. Coll. Liberal Art, 1977—2000, Berkshire CC, Pittsfield, Mass., 1985—86, Pittsfield, 1995—; docent Clark Art Inst., 1995—; Therapeutic Touch practitioner, 1978—; talk show host Pub. Access TV, 1998—2003; bd. dirs. Willinet TV Channel 17, 1999—2003; vol. Salvation Army. WTC Disaster Relief Family Assistance Ctr., 2001, 9/11 United Svcs. Group, 2002; adj. faculty Springfield Coll. Sch. Social Work, 2002. Pres. Williamstown PTO, 1989—91; bd. dirs., edn. com., spl. events coord. Hospice No. Berkshire, Inc., 1989—94; fundraising coord. Mainland Regional Edn. Found., Lindwood, NJ, 2004—05; sec. bd. trustees Pumpkin Hollow Farm. Named Berkshire County Social Worker of Yr., 1999, Mass. Social Worker of Yr., 2002; recipient Cmty. Svc. award, Salvation Army, North Berkshire, Mass., 2004. Mem.: LWV, NASW (bd. dirs. 1981—83, regional coun. mem. 1980—83, 1993—2003), Nurse Healers-Profl. Assn. (trustee 1981—83, rec. sec., editor-in-chief Coop. Connection newsletter 1983—88). Democrat. Episcopalian. Office: Susan Conklin LICSW BCD 85 Hawthorne Rd Williamstown MA 01267-2700 Office Phone: 413-884-4129. Personal E-mail: susanconklin@hotmail.com. Business E-Mail: conklin.susan@gmail.com.

CONLAY, LYDIA, anesthesiologist, educator, health science association administrator; b. Natchitoches, La., June 30, 1952; d. Floyd R. and Lou Althea (Roberts) Conlay. BS, Northwestern State U., Natchitoches, 1972; MD, La. State U., Shreveport, 1976; PhD in Neurochemistry, MIT, 1983; MBA with high honors, Boston U., 1995. Intern Johns Hopkins Hosp., Balt., 1976-77; residnet in anesthesia Mass. Gen. Hosp., Boston, 1977-79; asst. prof. anesthesia Harvard Med. Sch., Boston, 1984-89, assoc. prof. anesthesia, 1989-97; lectr. brain and cognitive scis. MIT, Cambridge, Mass., 1986-88; dir. ambulatory recovery svcs. Mass. Gen. Hosp.-Harvard Med. Sch., Boston, 1996-97; prof., chair dept. anesthesiology Temple U. Sch. Medicine, Phila., 1997—. Mem. practice plan bd. Temple U. Practice, Phila., 1977—. Assoc. editor Survey in Anesthesiology, 1996—; contbr. articles to Sci., Nature, Jour. AMA, Prcs. Nat. Acad. Scis., others. Chair Ether Monument Restoration Group, Boston Pub. Garden. Grantee NIH, Glaxo-Welcome Pharms., Marion-Merrell Dow. Mem. Soc. for Ambulatory Anesthesia (bd. dirs. 1996—, treas. 2000—, pres.-elect 2001—), Assn. Univ. Anesthesiologists (mem. coun. 1999—, treas. 2000), Coll. Phys. Phila., Union Club of Boston, Alpha Omega Alpha. Office: Temple U Sch Medicine Dept Anesthesia 3401 N Broad St Philadelphia PA 19140-5103

CONLEY, ELLEN ALEXANDER, writer, educator; b. Carbondale, Pa., Nov. 5, 1938; d. Howard and Sylvia (Eisner) Alexander; m. Stephen Conley; children: Dalton, Alexandra. BS, Pa. State U., 1960; Degree in Clin. Lab. Sci., Jefferson Med. Sch., 1961; MS, Wagner Coll., 1972. Gen. technologist Hosp. for Spl. Surgery, N.Y.C., 1962-64; with Hosp. Albert Schweitzer, Haiti, 1964-65; microbiology technologist N.Y. Infirmary, N.Y.C., 1965-68; instr. microbiology, parasitology, immunology Beth Israel Hosp., N.Y.C., 1967-68; supr. Boro Med. Ctr., N.Y.C., 1968-70; bacteriologist L.I. (N.Y.) Coll. Hosp., 1970-72; lectr., coord. Hostos Cmty. Coll., CUNY, N.Y.C., 1972-74; internship instr. S.I. Cmty. Coll., N.Y., 1974-75; credit evaluator, lectr., tutor Empire Coll., N.Y.C., 1975-78; dir. hosp. internships N.Y. Lab. Sch., 1976-77; asst. prof. Pratt Inst., Bklyn., 1976—; prof. Borough Manhattan Coll., CUNY, N.Y.C., 1984—. Judge Pa. Coun. Arts Awards to Fiction, 1993, Md. Coun. Arts Awards to Fiction, 1995. Author: Soho Madonna, 1980, Soon To Be Immortal, 1982, Bread and Stones, 1986, The Chosen Shore: Stories of New Immigrants, 2004; co-author: (film) The Marble Living Room, 1991; author short stories and poems; contbr. articles to mags. Recipient Creative Artist award N.Y.; Creative Artist in Pub. Svc. grantee N.Y. Coun. on the Arts, 1978, Mellon grantee, 1989, 93. Home: 55 Bethune St # 318C New York NY 10014-2010

CONLEY, OLGA L., retail executive; CPA. Audit staff Coopers & Lybrand; corp. contr. Project Software and Devel. Inc.; with J. Jill Group, Quincy, Mass., 1991—, various sr. fin. positions, 1991—96, treas., 1993—, CFO, 1997—2003, v.p. fin., 1996—98, sr. v.p. fin., 1998—2001, pres. corp. svc., 2001—03, exec. v.p., CFO, 2003—, chief adminstrv. officer, 2005—. Office: J Jill Group 4 Batterymarch Park Quincy MA 02169

CONLEY, RUTH IRENE, poet; b. Seattle, Jan. 26, 1920; d. Irving Birch Anderson and Gertrude Evelyn Unsworth Edwins; m. Samuel Glenn Conley, June 12, 1946 (div. Nov. 1963); children: Joan Evelyn, Mary Jacquelyn, James Harper. BA in Gen. Studies, U. Wash., 1964, BA in English, 1965, MA in English, 1966, MA in Comparative Lit., 1970; studied with Theodore Roethke. Editor publs. office U. Wash., Seattle, 1965—66, acctg. asst., 1973—86. Author numerous poems; author: (poet) (chapbooks) Time of Apple Harvest, Icicle River, and Short Poems from the Japanese. With U.S. Army, 1944—46. Democrat. Avocation: gardening.

CONLIN, KATHRYN MARIE, social studies educator; b. Greensburg, Pa., Mar. 26, 1949; d. Leo Joseph and Mary Ann Bell; m. James Joseph Conlin, June 8, 1974; children: Tad, Joe. BA, U. Pitts., 1971. Tchr. social studies Greater Latrobe Sr. HS, Pa., 1971—2006. Bldg. rep. Greater Latrobe Edn. Assn., Pa., 1999—2002; advisor Greater Latrobe Sr. H.S. Young Republicans, 2004—06. Recipient Tchr. Excellence awards. Avocations: gardening, interior decorating, acting, reading. Home: 621 Westshire Dr Greensburg PA 15601 Personal E-mail: kconlin2@verizon.net.

CONLIN, LINDA MYSLIWY, bank executive, former federal agency administrator; b. Springfield, Mass. m. Joseph F. Conlin Jr. Pres. Park-Main Travel Agy.; protocol visits officer US Dept. State; from corp. liaison officer for US/USSR intiatives to assoc. dir. Office of Pvt. Sector Coms. U.S. Info. Agy.; asst. sec. commerce for mktg. U.S. Travel and Tourism Adminstrn., 1989—93; dir. Office Travel and Tourism NJ Dept. Commerce, 1994—98; exec. dir. Office Travel and Tourism NJ Commerce & Econ. Growth Commn., 1998—99; dep. to program chmn. 2000 Rep. Nat. Conv.; sr. campaign coord. Bush/Cheney 2000-Southeastern Pa. Region; asst. sec. trade devel. US Dept. Commerce, Washington, 2001—04; v.p. Export-Import Bank of the US, 2006—. Bd. dirs. Export-Import Bank of the US, 2004—. Republican. Office: Export Import Bank of the US 811 Vermont Ave NW Washington DC 20571*

CONLIN, ROXANNE BARTON, lawyer; b. Huron, SD, June 30, 1944; d. Marion William and Alyce Muraine (Madden) Barton; m. James Clyde Conlin, Mar. 21, 1964; children: Jacalyn Rae, James Barton, Deborah Ann, Douglas Benton BA, Drake U., 1964, JD, 1966, MPA, 1979; LLD (hon.), U. Dubuque, 1975. Bar: Iowa 1966. Assoc. Davis, Huebner, Johnson & Burt, Des Moines, 1966-67; dep. indsl. commr. State of Iowa, 1967-68, asst. atty. gen., 1969-76; U.S. atty. So. Dist. Iowa, 1977-81; ptnr. Conlin, P.C., Des Moines, 1983—. Adj. prof. law U. Iowa, 1977-79; chmn. Iowa Women's Polit. Caucus, 1973-75, del. nat. steering com., 1973-77; cons. U.S. Commn. on Internat. Women's Year, 1976-77; gen. counsel NOW Legal Def. and Edn. Fund, 1985-88, pres., 1986-88; lectr. in field. Co-editor: ATLAs Litigating Tort Cases, 6 vols., 2003; contbr. articles to profl. jours. Nat. committeewoman Iowa Young Dems.; pres. Polk County Young Dems., 1965-66; del. Iowa Presdl. Conv., 1972; Dem. candidate for gov. of Iowa, 1982; bd. dirs. Riverhills Day Care Ctr., YWCA; chmn. Drake U. Law Sch. Endowment Trust, 1985-86; bd. counselors Drake U., 1982-86; pres. founder Civil Justice Found., 1986-88; pres. Roscoe Pound Found., 1994-97; chair Iowa Dem. Party, 1998-99; chair Edwards For Pres. Iowa, 2004. Named scholarship in her honor, Kansas City Women Lawyers; named one of Top Ten Litigators, Nat. Law Jour, 1989, 100 Most Influential Attys., 1991, 50 Most Powerful Women Attys., Nat. Law Jour., 1998, 10 Most Influential Women Attys., 2002; recipient award, Iowa ACLU, 1974, Alumnus of Yr. award, Drake U. Law Sch., 1989, Ann. award, Young Women's Resource Ctr., 1989, Verne Lawyer Outstanding Mem. award, Iowa Trial Lawyers Assn., 1994, Rosalie Wahl award, Minn. Women Lawyers, 1998, Marie Lambert award, 2000, Mary Louise Smith award, YWCA, 2001, Lifetime Achievement award, Des Moines Human Rights Commn., 2003, Ruth Bader Ginsberg award, 2004, Iowa Juneteenth award, State of Iowa, 2005, Feminist Activist award, Bus. Record and Drake U., 2006; scholar Reader's Digest scholar, 1963—64, Fishcher Found., 1965—66. Mem.: ATLA (chmn. consumer and victims coalition com. 1985—87, chmn. edn. dept 1987—88, parliamentarian 1988—89, sec. 1989—90, v.p. 1990—91, pres.-elect 1991—92, pres. 1992—93, Lifetime Achievement award 2003, Champion of Justice award 2006, Leonard Ring Champion of Justice award 2006), ABA, NOW, Nat. Ctr. State Ct. Lawyers Com. (com. mem. 2003—), Nat. Inst. Trial Advocacy (bd. trustees 2003—06), Trial Lawyers Care (bd. dirs.), Inner Circle of Advocates, Higher Edn. Commn. Iowa (co-chmn. 1988—90), Iowa Acad. Trial Lawyers, Internat. Acad. Trial Lawyers, Assn. Trial Lawyers Iowa (bd. dirs.), Iowa Bar Assn., Chi Omega, Alpha Lambda Delta, Phi Beta Kappa. Office: Griffin Bldg 319 7th St Ste 600 Des Moines IA 50309-3826 Office Phone: 515-283-1111. Business E-Mail: rconlin@roxanneconlinlaw.com.

CONLON, PEGGY EILEEN, publisher; b. Santa Monica, Calif., Mar. 2, 1951; d. Daniel Francis and Mary Eileen (Garrity) C.; m. Robert J. Reale, May 21, 1993. AA, Victor Valley Jr. Coll., Apple Valley, Calif.; BA, Calif. State U., Fullerton; MA, U. So. Calif.-Annenberg, L.A. Account exec. Dozier Eastman, Santa Ana, Calif., 1973-75; advt. and pub. rels. mgr. ITT Marine Divsn., Costa Mesa, Calif., 1975-80, EECO, Santa Ana, 1980-82; group pub. CMP Publs., Manhasset, N.Y., 1982-92; pub. Broadcasting & Cable, N.Y.C., 1992—; pres. The Advt. Coun., 1999—. Lt. USNR, 1974-81. Mem. Internat. Radio and TV Soc. (bd. dirs. 1993-96), exec. coun. The Quills. Office: Advertising Council Fl 11 261 Madison Ave New York NY 10016 also: Broadcasting And Cable 360 Park Ave S New York NY 10010-1710

CONLON, SUZANNE B., federal judge; b. 1939; AB, Mundelein Coll., 1963; JD, Loyola U., Chgo., 1968; postgrad., U. London, 1971. Law clk. to judge U.S. Dist. Ct. (no. dist.) Ill., 1968-71; assoc. Pattishall, McAuliffe & Hostetter, 1972-73, Schiff Hardin & Waite, 1973-75; asst. U.S. atty. U.S. Dist. Ct. (no. dist.) Ill., 1976-77, 82-86, U.S. Dist. Ct. (cen. dist.) Calif., 1978-82; exec. dir. U.S. Sentencing Commn., 1986-88; spl. counsel to assoc. atty. gen., 1988; judge U.S. Dist. Ct. (no. dist.) Ill., 1988—. Asst. prof. law De Paul U., Chgo., 1972-73, lectr., 1973-75; adj. prof. Northwestern U. Sch. Law, 1991-95; vice chmn. Chgo. Bar Assn. Internat. Inst., 1993—; vis. com. U. Chgo. Harris Grad. Sch. Pub. Policy, 1997—; bd. mem. DePaul U. Coll. Law, Internat. Human Rights Law Inst. Bd. mem. Ill. St. Andrew Soc. Mem. ABA, FBA, Am. Judicature Soc., Internat. Bar Assn. Judges Forum, Lawyers Club Chgo. (pres. 1996-97). Office: US Dist Ct No Dist Everett McKinley Dirksen Bldg 219 S Dearborn St Ste 2356 Chicago IL 60604-1878

CONLON KHAN, LORI ELLEN, music educator; b. Great Falls, Mont., Dec. 30, 1958; d. Clifford Gayle Conlon and Patty Ann Breipohl Conlon; m. Ather Ayaz Khan, June 26, 1986; children: Sidrah Khan, Sharif Khan, Khadija Khan. BA in Music Edn., Rocky Mountain Coll., 1982. Cert. tchg. Idaho. Music specialist Boise Sch. Dist., 1983—. Music specialist Northview Montessori, Boise, 1989—. Mem. Idaho Peace Coalition. Mem.: Boise Edn. Assn., Am. Orff Schulwerk Assn., Music Educators Nat. Conf., Idaho Orff Assn. (pres.), Delta Kappa Gamma. Democrat. Avocations: music, dance, scrapbooks, gardening, needlecrafts.

CONNALLY, SANDRA JANE OPPY, retired art educator, freelance/self-employed artist; b. Crawfordsville, Ind., Feb. 10, 1941; d. Thomas Jay and Helen Louise (Lane) Oppy; m. Thomas Maurice Connally, Nov. 9, 1962 (dec. May 2004); children: Leslie Erin Connally Hosier Dakins, Tyler Maurice. BS, Ball State U., 1963, MA, 1981. Freelance writer, Muncie, Ind., 1971-76; art/freelance, 1964-81; substitute tchr. Muncie (Ind.) Cmty. Schs., 1980—81, art tchr., 1981—2003; ret., 2003. Lectr. Ind. U. Art Mus., Ind., docent; substitute tchr. Monroe County Cmty. Sch. Corp. Two women shows include Emens Auditorium, Ball State U., 1983; exhibited in group shows at Ball State U., 1964, Alford House/Anderson (Ind.) Fine Arts Ctr., 1979-81, Historic 8th St. Exhbn., 1981, Patrons Watercolor Gala, Oklahoma City, 1983, Whitewater Valley Annual Drawing, Painting and Printmaking Competition, Richmond, Ind., 1983; represented in pvt. collections; contbr. short stories to profl. publs. Grantee Container Corp. Am., 1981, Ball State U. Mus. Art/Margaret Ball Meml. Fund, 1992, Robert B. Bell, 1993-95; recipient Achievement award Ind. Dept. Edn., 1992-94, Nat. Gallery Videodisc Competition, 1993; named disting. UniverCitizen Ball State U., 1992, Tchr. Intergalactic Art First Place Ind. State winner, 1998. Mem. Nat. Art Edn. Assn. (del. nat. convention 1998, 2000-03). Republican. Methodist. Avocations: computers, painting, handmade paper and glass fusing, travel. Home: 1932 Bay Pointe Dr E Bloomington IN 47401-8136

CONNELL, BONNIE BLEIER, mathematics educator; b. Rochester, N.Y., Dec. 1, 1950; d. William James and Betty Costain Bleier; m. Francis X. Connell, May 13, 1972; children: Daniel F., Deana B., Courtney A. BS, SUNY, Brockprt, N.Y., 1972, MS, 1984. Cert. Tchr. N.Y. Tchr. East Trondequoit Sch. Dist., Rochester, NY, 1972—77, Greece Ctrl. Sch. Dist., Rochester, NY, 1977—78, Wehster Ctrl. Sch. Dist., Webster, NY, 1980—81, Monroe C.C., Rochester, NY, 1981—. Adj. coord. Monroe C.C., Rochester, 1999—, mid. states study team, 2004—05, faculty exec. com., 2004—05, chair faculty senate planning com., co-chair colls. strategic planning com. Election inspector Greece Ctrl. Sch., Rochester, NY, 1990—2002. Mem.: N.Y. State Math. Assn. of Two Yr. Coll., Math. Assn. of Am. Avocations: crocheting, walking, tropical fish, reading, gardening.

CONNELL, MARY ELLEN, diplomat; b. Laconia, N.H., Jan. 20, 1943; d. Howard Benjamin and Jessie Louise Smith Naylor; m. O. J. Connell III, Nov. 4, 1969 (div. Aug. 1988); 1 child, Piers Andrew. BA, Smith Coll., Northampton, Mass., 1964; MPhil, U. Kans., 1969; MS, Nat. War Coll., 1992. Info. ctr. dir. U.S. Fgn. Svc., Nairobi, Kenya, 1978-80, pub. affairs officer Bujumbura, Burundi, 1980-82; officer African affairs USIA, Washington, 1982-85, exec. asst. to assoc. dir. for policy, 1985-86; counselor pub. affairs U.S. Fgn. Svc., Copenhagen, 1986-90; vis. scholar St. Deiniol's Wales, 1991; exec. sec. USIA, Washington, 1992-95; pub. affairs advisor U.S. Mission to NATO, Brussels, 1995-97; spl. asst. to asst. sec. defense for pub. affairs Washington, 1997-99; mem. policy planning staff Dept. of State, Washington, 1999—; sr. policy analyst Ctr. for Naval Analyses, 2001—. Mem. Internat. Inst. Strategic Studies, Am. Fgn. Svc. Assn., Atlantic Coun., Army and Navy Club. Episcopalian. Office: CNA 4825 Mark Ctr Dr Alexandria VA 22311-1850 Office Phone: 703-824-2281. E-mail: connellme@aol.com.

CONNELL, SHIRLEY HUDGINS, public relations professional; b. Washington, Oct. 5, 1946; d. Orville Thomas and Mary (Beran) H.; m. David Day Connell, Dec. 13, 1980 (div. 1985). BA, U. R.I., 1968, MA, 1970. Lic. property, casualty broker, N.Y. Clk., editor MGM Studios, Culver City, Calif., 1970-72; scriptor, talent Monarch Records, Studio City, 1972-73; communications specialist U. So. Calif., L.A., 1973-81; dir. pub. rels. Six Flags Movieland, Buena Park, Calif., 1981-82, Donald J. Fager & Assocs., N.Y.C., 1982-93, dir. policy holder/pub. rels., 1993-99, asst. v.p., 1999—. Cons. Children's TV Workshop, N.Y.C., 1978; ind. beauty cons. Mary Kay Cosmetics, 1991—; instr. Princeton Rev., 1990-91. Editor: Coastal Ocean Space Utilization III, 1995; contbr. articles to profl. jours.; contbg. editor Greater N.Y. Doctor's Shopper mag., 1987—. Pres. bd. trustees Oaks at North Brunswick Condominium Assn., 1987-2000; founding mem. Mcpl. Svcs. Com., North Brunswick; mgr. Animal Rescue Force, 1988—; chair environ. com. Twp. of North Brunswick, 1990-2001, vice chair, 2001—06; snuggler pediat. and neonatal units St. Peter's Hosp.; Blue Belt Tiger Schulmann's Karate, 1997; founding mem., trustee, bd. dirs. Lawrence Brook Watershed Partnership, 1998—. Mem. NAFE, Marine Tech. Soc. (vice chmn. 1980-81), Mensa (pub. rels. adv. com. 1989—, pub. rels. coord. Ctrl. N.J. chpt. 1992—, bd. dirs. 1992—), Oceanic Soc. (bd. dirs. 1979-81), Stony Brook Millstone Watershed Assn. (water qualification monitor 1994—), Ctrl. N.J. Mensa (trustee, chair pub. rels. 1990—). Avocations: photography, reading, swimming, wood finishing, writing. Office Phone: 212-576-9843. E-mail: sconnell@mlmic.com.

CONNELL-ALLEN, ELIZABETH ANN, elementary school educator; b. Portsmouth, Va., Sept. 21, 1949; d. Robert Joseph and Juanita Georgia (Harrill) C.; m. Larry Allen. BS in Edn., Old Dominion U., Norfolk, Va., 1971; MA in Reading Edn., U. No. Colo., Greeley, 1975; PhD in Edn., Lit. and Curriculum, U. Colo., Boulder, 1991. Cert. elem. edn. K-6, reading edn. K-12, K-12 adminstrn. Tchr. 6th grade Norfolk Pub. Schs., 1971-74; tchr. Littleton (Colo.) Pub. Schs., 1975—2004, Peoria Unified Sch. Dist., Ariz., 2004—. Tchg. assoc. U. Colo., Boulder, 1988-90; instr. U. Colo., Denver, 1994; lit. com. When Author Meets Author, Colo. Coun. of Internat. Reading Assn., Denver; judge children's writing contest Friends of the Libr., Littleton, 1992-96. Author: A Community of Learners Selecting and Developing Writing Topics, 1991, Eternal Portraits, 2003. Recipient Outstanding Tchr. award Assn. for Childhood Edn. Internat., Denver, 1992; multicultural grantee Summit CHART: Pub. Edn. Coalition, Denver, 1994. Mem. ASCD, NEA, Internat. Reading Assn., Colo. Edn. Assn., Littleton Edn. Assn., Phi Delta Kappa. Avocations: reading, singing, playing piano. Office: Peoria Unified Schs Marshall Ranch Glendale AZ 85308

CONNELLY, DEIRDRE P., pharmaceutical executive; b. San Juan, Puerto Rico; BA, Lycoming Coll., 1983; grad. Advanced Mgmt. Program, Harvard Univ., 2000. Sales rep. Eli Lilly & Co., 1983—84, mktg. assoc. San Juan, PR, 1984—89, sales supervisor Phila., 1989—90, product mgr. diabetes San Juan, PR, 1990—91, nat. sales mgr., 1991—92, mktg. & sales dir., 1992—93, mktg. & sales dir. Caribbean, 1993—95, gen mgr. Eli Lilly Puerto Rico SA, 1995—97, regional sales dir., exec. dir. global mktg. Evista Indpls., 1997—2001, leader women's health bus. Lilly USA, 2001—03, exec. dir. human resources Lilly USA, 2003, v.p. human resources, 2004, sr. v.p. human resources, 2004—05, pres. Lilly USA, 2005—. Named one of 50 Most Powerful Women in Bus., Fortune mag., 2006. Office: Eli Lilly & Co Lilly Corp Ctr Indianapolis IN 46285*

CONNELLY, DIANE, elementary school educator; b. Logan, Utah, Sept. 27, 1952; d. Melvin Abraham and Grace Huppi; m. Alvin Lee Connelly, July 14, 1990. BS, Utah State U., 1973, MEd, 1988. Elem. tchr. Uinta County Sch. Dist., Evanston, Wyo., 1975—. Presenter in field. Tchr. Cmty. Edn., 1977-78; student body vol. dir. Student Svcs., Logan, Utah, 1972-73; pres. Uinta County Reading Coun., 1988, 98; bd. dirs. Girl's Youth Volleyball, Evanston; rep. youth com. Evanston Parks and Recreation. Named Vol. of Yr. Utah State Student Svcs., 1973, Elem. Tchr. Qtr. Tchrs. Assn. Mem. NEA, Wyo. Edn. Assn., Evanston Edn. Assn., Internat. Reading Assn., Delta Kappa Gamma. Avocations: reading, pets, working with youth. Office: Uinta Meadows Elem Sch PO Box 6002 Evanston WY 82931-6002

CONNELLY, JENNIFER, actress; b. Catskill Mountains, NY, Dec. 12, 1970; d. Gerard and Eileen Connelly; m. Paul Bettany, Jan. 1, 2003; children: Stellan Bettany, Kai Dugan. Actress: appeared in Italian, Canadian, British, Argentinian, and U.S. films: Once Upon a Time in America, 1984, Phenomena, 1985, The Valley, 1985, Labyrinth, 1986, Seven Minutes in Heaven, 1986, Some Girls, 1988, Etoile, 1988, The Hot Spot, 1990, Career Opportunities, 1991, The Rocketeer, 1991, Higher Learning, 1994, Far Harbor, 1996, Mulholland Falls, 1996, Of Love and Shadows, 1996, Dark City, 1997, Inventing the Abbots, 1997, Waking the Dead, 2000, Requiem for a Dream, 2000, Pollock, 2000, A Beautiful Mind, 2001 (Best Supporting Actress Acad. award 2001, Golden Globe, 2001, Am. Film Inst. award, Brit. Acad. award, Golden Satellite award, KCFCC award, OFCS award, SEFCA award and BFCA award 2001-2002, nominee Best Actress SAG award 2001, Featured Actor of Yr. Female Movies AFI Film award 2002), The Hulk, 2003, House of Sand and Fog, 2003, Dark Water, 2005; TV movies: The Heart of Justice, 1993; TV series: The $treet, 2000. Office: Internat Creative Mgmt 8942 Wilshire Blvd Beverly Hills CA 90211-1934

CONNELLY, KORI ANN, lawyer; b. Phila., Oct. 25, 1975; BA summa cum laude, LaSalle U., 1997; JD, Temple U., 2000. Bar: Pa. 2000, NJ 2000, US Dist. Ct., NJ 2000, US Dist. Ct. (ea. dist.) Pa. 2001, US Ct. Appeals (3rd cir.) 2002, US Dist. Ct., Middle Dist. Pa. 2003. Assoc. Swartz Campbell LLC. Contbr. articles to profl. jours. Mem. Phila. bd. dirs. Habitat for Humanity.

Mem.: Soc. for Human Resources Mgmt., Phila. Bar Assn., Pa. Bar Assn. Office: Swartz Campbell LLC 1601 Market St, 34th Fl Philadelphia PA 19103 Office Phone: 215-299-4260. Office Fax: 215-299-4301. E-mail: kconnelly@swartzcampbell.com.*

CONNELLY, SHARON RUDOLPH, lawyer; b. Kingwood, W.Va. d. John E. and Lorene E. Rudolph; 1 child, John. BS, W.Va. State U., 1966; MBA, Ind. U., 1968; JD, Cath. Univ., 1976; LLM in Taxation, Georgetown U., 1995. Bar: Va. 1977. Mgr. IRS, Washington, 1969-76; asst. contr. Mfrs. Hanover, N.Y.C., 1976-77; compliance chief D.C. Dept. Labor, Washington, 1977-79; dir. compliance U.S. Dept. Commerce, Washington, 1979-82; asst. insp. gen. NASA, Washington, 1982-84; dir. insp. office Nuc. Regulatory Commn., Washington, 1984-89, spl. asst. internal controls, 1989-98. Financier, 1998—. Contbr. articles to profl. jours.

CONNER, BEVERLY T., counseling administrator, educator; m. Charles E. Conner, Aug. 10, 1996; 1 child, Morgan Zachary Taylor. BS, U. Ark., Pine Bluff; MS, Tex. So. U., Houston. Cert. sch. counselor/tchr. Payroll officer Tex. So. U., Houston; counselor high sch. Galena Park Ind. Sch. Dist., Houston; adj. prof. Coll. of Mainland, Tex. City. Recipient Dazzling Diamond, Galena Park Ind. Sch. Dist. Grant Found., 2004—06. Mem.: Alpha Kappa Alpha. Home: 17207 Grey Mist Dr Friendswood TX 77546 Office: Northshore HS 13501 Hollypark Dr Houston TX 77015

CONNER, JUDITH G., elementary school educator; b. Islip, NY, June 2, 1966; d. Roberts M. and Anne D. Germeroth; m. Philip J. Conner, July 4, 1992; children: Robert J., Ethan G. BS in special edn., elem. edn., Geneseo State Coll., 1988; MS in reading, Buffalo State Coll., 1993. Special edn. tchr. Niagara Falls BOE, Niagara Falls, NY, 1988—92; grad. asst. Buffalo State Coll. Reading Lab. Clinic, Buffalo, 1994—97; elem. tchr. Niagara Falls BOE, Niagara Falls, NY, 1992—. Presenter various profl. conf. Mem.: Internat. Reading Assn., Niagara Frontier Reading Assn., NY Reading Assn., Alpha Upsilon Alpha, Delta Kappa Gamma. Home: 264 Darwin Dr Amherst NY 14226

CONNERLY, DIANNA JEAN, business official; b. Urbana, Ill., June 7, 1947; d. Ellsworth Wayne and Imogene (Sundermeyer) C. Student, Ill. Comml. Coll., 1967. Bookkeeper Jerry Earl Pontiac, 1968-72; office mgr. Jack Nicklaus Pontiac, 1972-76, Simon Motors Inc., Palm Springs, Calif., 1977-83, bus. mgr., 1983—. Vol. counselor How Found., 1992. Mem. Am. Bus. Women's Assn. (dir. pub. rels. Trendsetter chpt. 1983-85). Office: 78-611 Hwy 111 La Quinta CA 92253

CONNIFF, ALEXANDRA ACOSTA, secondary school educator; b. Eufaula, Ala., June 2, 1970; d. Yamandu Pereyia and Syliva Viroga Acosta; children: Robert Nicholas-Acosta, Stephen Daniel-Acosta. BS, Auburn U., 1993, ME, 1997. Tchr. Eufaula City Bd. Edn., Morris, Ala., 1997—2003, Eufaula City Bd. Edn., 2003—. Roads scholar, Divsn. Learning Disabilities, 2004. Mem.: NEA, Coun. Exceptional Children, Delta Kappa Gamma. Democrat. Methodist. Avocations: travel, reading, cooking. Home: 403 N Randolph Ave Eufaula AL 36027 Office: Eufaula High Sch 530 Lake Dr Eufaula AL 36027 Office Phone: 334-687-1110 x132. Personal E-mail: conniffaa@yahoo.com.

CONNIFF, TAMARA, editor; b. Hollywood, Calif. d. Ray and Vera Conniff. Writer Music Connection mag., Seconds mag., LA Times, Boston Globe; sr. editor Amusement Bus.; music editor Hollywood Reporter; exec. editor Billboard mag., 2004—, assoc. publisher. Named one of 40 Under 40, Crain's NY Bus., 2006. Office: Billboard Mag 6th Floor 770 Broadway New York NY 10003 Office Phone: 646-654-4626. Office Fax: 646-654-4681. E-mail: tconniff@billboard.com.*

CONNOLLY, CARLA MARIE, librarian; b. Chgo., Mar. 27, 1952; d. Thomas Patrick and Alma Eleanor Connolly. BA, Monmouth Coll., Ill., 1974; MS in Edn., Chgo. State U., 1980. Children's libr. Midlothian Pub. Libr., Ill., 1977—78; faculty asst. Chgo. State U., 1978—80; libr. South Suburban Coll., South Holland, Ill., 1981—. Mem.: ALA, Ill. Libr. Assn. Avocations: reading, travel. Office: South Suburban College Library 15800 S State St South Holland IL 60473

CONNOLLY, JANET ELIZABETH, retired sociologist, retired criminal justice educator; b. New Rochelle, N.Y., June 28, 1929; d. Michael A. and Vincentia (Bonitatibus) Dandry; m. Edward C. Connolly, June 7, 1952; children: Michael, Matthew, Christopher, Benedict, Andrew. BA, Chestnut Hill Coll., Phila., 1951; MA, Temple U., Phila., 1970, PhD, 1975; degree (hon.), Rilski Neofit U., Blagoevgrad, Bulgaria, 1992. Intelligence clk. CIA, Washington, 1951-52; tchr. Prince George's County Bd. Edn., Hyattsville, Md., 1952-53; rsch. assoc. Pa. Prison Soc., Phila., 1974-76; field dir. rsch. Georgetown U. Law Sch., Washington, 1976-77; rsch. dir. Phila. Commn. for Effective Criminal Justice, 1977-78; mem. faculty dept. criminal justice Temple U., Phila., 1980-91; mem. faculty dept. sociology Am. U. in Bulgaria, Blagoevgrad, 1991-96; guest lectr. Sch. Law Kiril E Metodi Univerzitet, Skopje, Macedonia, 1993. Cons. Bucks County Correctional Facility, Doylestown, Pa., 1987-91; evaluator Phila. Prison System, 1973. Campaign chairperson, Doylestown, Pa., 1980, 82, 84, 86, 90; pres. Bucks County Assn. for Corrections and Rehab., Doylestown, 1988-91; trustee Bucks County Community Coll., Newtown, Pa., 1989-91; bd. dirs. ARC, Bucks County chpt., Doylestown, 1980-82; mem. New Hope (Pa.) Civil Svc. Commn., 1986-91; bd. dirs. Planned Parenthood, 1986-88. U.S. Justice Dept. dissertation grantee, Washington, 1972. Mem. ACLU, LWV, Law and Soc. Assn., Am. Correctional Assn., Balkan Ednl. and Sci. Assn. (mem. sci. senate). Democrat. Avocations: gardening, embroidery, painting. Home: 762 Fairview Ave Apt C Annapolis MD 21403-2962 E-mail: janet.r.connolly@comcast.net.

CONNOLLY, MELISSA KANE, public relations executive; b. Wilmington, Del., Aug. 8, 1967; BA, Hofstra U., 1989. Bus. mgr. Fairchild Pub., N.Y.C., 1990—93; VISTA vol. Project Challenge, Long Beach, NY, 1993—94; dir. circulation and mktg. Richner Pub., Lawrence, NY, 1994—97; dir. mktg. Farrell Fritz P.C., Uniondale, NY, 1997—2001; dir. comm. Senator Kemp Hannon, Albany, NY, 2001—03; v.p. u. rels. Hofstra U., Hempstead, NY, 2003—. Mem. govt. affairs team. Commn. Indep. Coll. and U., Albany, NY, 2003—; adv. bd. Inst. Devel. and Advancement of Edn. in Sci., Hempstead, 2004—. Adv. bd. PULSE, NY, 2003—; pres. legis. affairs Long Island Women's Agenda, Plainview, NY, 2004—. Named one of Top 50 Women on L.I., L.I. Bus. News, 2006, 40 Under 40, 2000—01. Mem.: Internat. Assn. Bus. Comm. (pres. L.I. chpt. 2000—01, com. chmn., Achievement in Comm. award 1998, 1999, Pres. Achievement award 2001, Achievement in Comm. award 2006), Pub. Rels. Soc. Am. Office: Hofstra Univ 202 A Hofstra Hall Hempstead NY 11549

CONNOLLY, MICHELLE MARIE, athletic trainer; b. Buffalo, Sept. 25, 1979; d. Joseph Frank and Suzanne Marie Connolly; m. Sean Thomas McNamee, Oct. 9, 2004. BS, U. Fla., Gainesville, 2001; MA, U. South Fla., Tampa, 2004. Bd. cert. athletic trainer Nat. Athletic Trainers' Assn., 2002, cert. strength and conditioning specialist Nat. Strength and Conditioning Assn. Cert. Commn., 2005. Student athletic trainer U. Fla., Gainesville, 1999—2001; intern athletic trainer Calif. State U., Chico, 2001; grad. asst. athletic trainer U. South Fla., Tampa, 2002—04; athletic trainer CORA Rehab. Svcs., Kissimmee, 2004—05, Fla. Orthop. Inst., Tampa, 2005—. Vol. Spl. Olympics, Tampa, Fla., 1995—97. Scholar, Fla. Bright Futures, 1997—2001, US Army, 1997. Mem.: Nat. Athletic Trainers' Assn. (assoc.). Roman Catholic. Avocations: golf, rollerblading, soccer, kickball, reading.

CONNOLLY, SARAH THIEMANN, lawyer; b. St. Louis, Mo., 1972; AB magna cum laude, Georgetown U., 1994; JD, NYU, 1997. Bar: Mass. 1997. Ptnr. Nixon Peabody LLP, Boston. Bd. dirs. Family Svc. Greater Boston, Inc., East Boston Social Centers, Inc.; mem. planned giving com. United Way of Mass. Bay. Mem.: Boston Bar Assn. (mem. new developments com., trusts sect. and estates sect.), Phi Beta Kappa. Office: Nixon Peabody LLP 100 Summer St Boston MA 02110 Office Phone: 617-345-1000. Office Fax: 617-345-1300.*

CONNOLLY, VIOLETTE M., small business owner; b. N.Y.C., Nov. 25, 1918; d. Gysbert Martens and Marie Therese dePont; m. Joseph Vincent Connolly Jr., Feb. 27, 1957 (dec.). BA, Hunter Coll., 1940; MS, Columbia U., 1941. Accredited Pub. Rels. Soc. Am. Analyst The Payne Fund, N.Y.C., 1941-53; ptnr. Elser & Assocs., N.Y.C., 1954-56, The J.V. Connolly Co., N.Y.C., 1957-64; cons. on pub. rels., radio and TV Assn. of the Jr. Leagues of Am., N.Y.C., 1964-72; asst. dir. N.Y. Assn. for Brain Injured Children, N.Y.C., 1973-74; circulation mgr. Plants and Gardens Bklyn. Botanic Garden, N.Y.C., 1974-82; adminstr. Nat. Broadcasting Co., N.Y.C., 1983-86; owner, mgr. The White House, Block Island, R.I., 1986—; clk. Town of New Shoreham, Block Island, 1986—. Bd. mem., publicist The Village Art Ctr., N.Y.C., 1944-54; pres. Washington Sq. Bus. and Profl. Women's Club, N.Y.C., 1953-55; founder, chair House and Garden Tours Com., Block Island Hist. Soc., 1971-96; pres. Block Island Gardeners, 1986-97. Capt. First Assembly Dist., Rep. Club, N.Y.C., 1945-57; mem. Bishop's com. St. Ann's Ch., 1995—. Republican. Avocations: antiques, travel.

CONNOR, DANIELLE BROUCQSAULT, secondary school educator; b. Goleta, Calif., Jan. 24, 1969; d. Gerard Charles and Louise Broucqsault; m. Michael John Connor, Dec. 16, 1966. B, U. San Francisco, 1992; student, Sorbonne U., Paris, 1994; tchg. credential, Calif. State U., Fullerton, 2001. ESL asst. French Govt., Reims, 1992—94; ESL instr. U. Bari, Puglia, 1994—97, Cal Poly, Pomona, Calif., 1994—2000; tchr. Kennedy H.S., La Palma, Calif., 2000—01, Valenica H.S., Placentia, Calif., 2002—. Avocations: travel, running, reading, gardening. Home: 2900 Birch Pl Fullerton CA 92835 Office Phone: 714-996-4970. Office Fax: 714-996-3159.

CONNOR, ULLA M., linguistics educator; m. John M. Connor; 1 child, Timo. BA in English Philology, U. Helsinki, 1970, MA in English Philology magna cum laude, 1974; MA in English Lit., U. Fla., 1971; MA in Comparative Lit., U. Wis., 1973, PhD in Edn., English Linguistics, 1978. Asst. prof. Georgetown U., Washington, 1980—83, Ind. U.-Purdue U. Indpls., 1984—87, assoc. prof., 1987—93, prof., 1993—, founder, dir. ESL program, 1985—94, 1997—98, dir. Ind. Ctr. Intercultural Comm., 1997—, Barbara E. and Karl R. Zimmer chair in intercultural communication, 2003—. Asst. dean grad. sch. Purdue U., West Lafayette, Ind., 1988—90; donner guest prof. Abo Akademi U., Finland, 1994, 2000; vis. prof. Temple U. Japan, 1995; vis. rschr. U. Jyvaskyla, Finland, 1995; guest prof. Lund U., Sweden, 1998; academic advisor dept. of fgn. langs. Poly. U. Hong Kong, China, 1999—2001. Author: Contrastive Rhetoric: Cross-cultural Aspects of Second Language Writing, 1996; co-author (with others): Successful Grant Proposals. A Guide for Researchers in the European Union; co-editor (with R.B. Kaplan): Writing Across Languages: Analysis of L2 Text, 1987; co-editor: (with A.M. Johns) Coherence in Writing: Research and Pedagogical Perspectives, 1990; co-editor: (with D. Becker) Reflections on Multiliterate Lives, 2001; co-editor: (with T.A. Upton) Applied Corpus Linguistics: A Multidimensional Perspective, 2004, Discourse in the Professions: Perspectives from Corpus Linguistics; guest editor: Multilingua: Jour. Cross-Cultural and Interlanguage Communication, 2004, Jour. English Academic Purposes Spl. Issue, guest editor with T. Seiler: jour. New Directions for Philanthropic Fundraising. Understanding and Improving Lang. Fundraising. Recipient Glenn Irwin Experience Excellence Recognition award, Ind. U. -Purdue U. Indpls., 1992; Internat. Peace scholarship, U. Fla., 1970-1971, grant, Exxon Edn. Found., 1985-1987, Finland's Acad. Scis. and Tech. (TEKES), 1995, Philanthropy grant, Ind. U., 1999. Mem.: Finnish Soc. Scis. and Letters (elected fgn. mem. 2000), Tchrs. English to Spkrs. of Other Langs., Nat. Coun. Tchrs. English, Am. Assn. Applied Linguistics. Office: Indiana Ctr Intercultural Comm 620 Union Dr Rm 411 Indianapolis IN 46202 Office Phone: 317-278-2441. Office Fax: 317-274-5616. Business E-Mail: uconnor@iupui.edu.

CONNOR-DOMINGUEZ, BILLIE MARIE, science information professional; b. Brighton, Mo., Oct. 4, 1934; d. Clifford Delmar and Naomi Marie (Calhoun) Batten; m. John Michael Connor, Dec. 18, 1968 (dec. 1978); m. Ramon Rosa Dominguez, Sept. 10, 1999. BS, S.W. Mo. State U., Springfield, 1955; MLS, Rutgers U., N.J., 1959. Tchr. Auburn (Ill.) H.S., 1955-58; ext. libr. S.W. Regional Libr., Bolivar, Mo., 1959—62; info. specialist, bus. and tech. svc. Wichita (Kans.) Pub. Libr., 1962-68; subject specialist, SCAN L.A. Pub. Libr., 1969-70, sr. librarian, bus./econ., 1970-77, subject dep. mgr. bus./econs., 1977-79, subject dept mgr. sci./tech./patents, 1979-96, mgr. bus./econs., sci./tech./patents, water and power libr., 1996—. Co-compiler Ottemiller's Index to Plays in Collections, 5th edit., 1971, 6th edit., 1976, 7th edit., 1988; editor Communicator, 1971-74, 95—; contbr. articles to profl. jours. Bd. dirs. Cmty. Career Devel., Inc., L.A., 1995-02. Recipient Supporter of Support Staff award, Libr. Mosaics and Coun. Libr./Media Technicians, 2002. Mem. AAAS, Spl. Librs. Assn. (bd. dirs. 1992-95, Billie Connor award for Outstanding Contbns. So. Calif. chpt. 1994, Rose Vormelker award 2002), Patent and Trademark Depository Libr. Assn. (pres. 1988). Achievements include redevelopment of major science and technology collection following devastating fire. Home: 1707 Micheltorena St Apt 312 Los Angeles CA 90026-1142 Office: Sci/Tech/Patents LA Pub Libr 630 W 5th St Los Angeles CA 90071-2002 Office Phone: 213-228-7201. Business E-Mail: bconnor@lapl.org.

CONNORS, CORNELIA KATHLEEN, marketing services company executive; b. Omaha, Nov. 25, 1958; d. Edward Krueger and Winifred Loretta (Baumer) C. BA, U. Santa Clara, 1981. Dir. project Stan Goldberg Computer Workshops, N.Y.C., 1983; cons. Scholastic Software, N.Y.C., 1983-85; owner, founder Connors Communications, N.Y.C., 1985—. Feature story on Connors Communications, Home Office Computing mag., Mar. 1991; contbr. articles to mags. Mem. Software Pub. Assn., Am. Women's Econ. Devel., Nebr. Soc. of N.Y. (bd. dirs. 1987—). Avocations: teaching aerobics, travel, writing. Office: Connors Comm 7 West 22nd St Fl 7 New York NY 10010

CONNORS, MARY EILEEN, psychologist; b. Springfield, Mass., Sept. 15, 1953; d. John Joseph and Mary Ellen (Teahan) Connors; m. Roger F. Thomson, Nov. 10, 1984. BA, New Coll., Sarasota, Fla., 1975; MA, DePaul U., Chgo., 1980; PhD, DePaul U., 1983. Diplomate in clin. psychology Am. Bd. Profl. Psychology; lic. clin. psychologist. Psychol. intern Michael Reese Hosp., Chgo., 1980-81; staff psychologist DePaul U. Counseling Ctr., Chgo., 1981-83; rsch. assoc. Northwestern U., Chgo., 1984-86, faculty, 1984-91; core faculty mem. Ill. Sch. Profl. Psychology, Chgo., 1989—; pvt. practice psychology Chgo., 1983—; cons. Michael Reese Hosp., 1984-91. Author: Sumpton-Focused Dunamic Psychotherapy, 2005; co-author: Etiology and Treatment of Bulimia Nervosa: a Biopsychosocial Perspective, 1987; contbr. articles to profl. jours. Schmitt fellow, DePaul U., 1979, Phalin fellow, 1980. Mem. Am. Psychol. Assn., Ill. Psychol. Assn., Chgo. Assn. for Psychoanalytic Psychology. Avocations: reading, gardening, cooking. Home: 1925 N Howe St Chicago IL 60614-5127 Office: 55 E Washington St Ste 2007 Chicago IL 60602-2224

CONNORS, MARY JEAN, communications executive; V.p. human resources Phila. Newspapers, Inc., 1989—95; asst. to sr. v.p. news and ops. Knight Ridder, Inc., San Jose, Calif., 1988—89, sr. v.p. human resources, 1996—2003, sr. v.p., 2003—. Chmn. bd. Bd. Calif. Strategic Human Resources Partnership. Office: Knight Ridder Inc 50 W San Fernando St Ste 1500 San Jose CA 95113-2429 Office Phone: 408-938-7700. Office Fax: 408-938-7766.

CONOLLY, KATHARINE FARNAM, editor; b. Rochester, N.Y., Dec. 2, 1969; d. Henry W. III and Bonnie Lou (Ewell) Farnam; m. Christopher Jason Conolly, Oct. 10, 1998. BA in Psychology and English Lit. summa cum laude, St. John Fisher Coll., Rochester, 1998. Cert. in publishing/editing U. Calif. Berkeley. Exec. asst. Chase Manhattan Bank, Rochester, 1992-98; editor New World Libr., Novato, Calif., 1999—. Presenter N.Y. State English conf. Recipient Sholastic Gold Key award in photography. Mem. Sigma Tau Delta (pres. Coll. chpt. 1997-98), Psi Chi, Delta Epsilon Sigma, Alpha Xi Delta. Avocations: hiking, outdoor activities, reading, writing, photography. Office: New World Library 14 Pamaron Way Novato CA 94949-6215 Fax: 415-884-2199. E-mail: katie@nwlib.com.

CONOLLY-WILSON, CHRISTINA, psychologist; m. Gregory Wilson. BS in Biology and Psychology, Loyola Coll., 2000; MA in Sch. Psychology, James Madison U., 2001, PsychD in Sch. and Clin. Psychology, 2005. Cert. sch. psychologist, lic. specialist in sch. psychology. Intern psychology Houston (Tex.) Ind. Sch. Dist., 2004—05; psychologist Waukegan (Ill.) Pub. Schs., 2005—. Team leader dist. crisis intervention Waukegan (Ill.) Pub. Schs., 2005—. Named Outstanding Grad. Student, James Madison U., 2003; recipient Outstanding Grad. Rsch. award, 2002. Mem.: APA (rep. 2003—04), NAACP, Nat. Coun. Educating Black Children, Nat. Assn. Sch. Psychologists, Assn. Black Psychologists (pres. chpt. 2003—05), Delta Sigma Theta. Bapt. Office: Waukegan Public Schs 1201 N Sheridan Rd Waukegan IL 60085 Business E-Mail: cconolly@waukeganschools.org.

CONOLY, KIMBERLY LANE, dance studio owner; b. Dallas, Tex., Sept. 10, 1976; d. Emmett Eugene Conoly and Laura Nan Terrill. BBA, Tex. A&M U., Coll. Sta., 1999. Tech. rep. Info. Plus Corp, Irving, Tex., 1999—2000; demonstration specialist Digital Convergene, Dallas, 2000—01; network engr., contract mgr. Sprint, Irving, 2001—03; pres. K.C's Danceand Cheer Ctr., Inc., Saetise, Tex., 2003—. Mem.: Dallas Dance Coun. Avocations: exercise, running, bicycling. Home: 9006 Longmont Dallas TX 75238 Office: KCs Dance and Cheer Ctr Inc 6300 Industrial Dr #1 Sachse TX 75048

CONOVER, MONA LEE, retired adult education educator; b. Lincoln, Nebr., Nov. 9, 1929; d. William Cyril and Susan Ferne (Floyd) C.; m. Elmer Kenneth Johnson, June 14, 1953 (div. 1975); children: Michael David, Susan Amy, Sharon Ann, Jennifer Lynne. AB, Nebr. Wesleyan U., 1952; student, Ariz. State U., 1973-75; MA in Edn., No. Ariz. U., 1985. Cert. tchr., Colo., Ariz. Tchr. Jefferson County R-1 Sch., Wheat Ridge, Colo., 1952-56, Glendale (Ariz.) Elem. Sch. 40, 1972-92; dir. Glendale Adult Edn., 1987-92; ret., 1992. Author: ABC's of Naturalization, 1989. Mem. FOGG, Garden of Gods volunterr Information Ctr.,, NIA (Nat. Assn for Interpretation), NEA Ret. Life, Heard Mus., Cheyenne Mountain Zoo, Order of Ea. Star. Republican. Methodist. Avocations: music, travel, photography, history.

CONOVER, NANCY ANDERSON, retired secondary school counselor, small business owner; b. Manhattan, Kans., July 8, 1943; d. Howard Julius and Wilma June (Katz) Anderson; m. Gary Hites Conover, Aug. 10, 1968; children: Chad Anderson, Cary Hites. BS in Edn., Kans. State U., Manhattan, 1965; MEd, Wichita State U., Kans., 1991. Cert. sch. counselor, tchr., Kans.; lic. profl. counselor, Kans. Tchr. Flint Sch. Dist., Mich., 1965-66, Unified Sch. Dist. 259, Wichita, Kans., 1967-68, Overland Park Sch. Dist., Kans., 1968-70; bus. mgr., sec.-treas. Gary Conover, D.D.S., Wichita, 1985-94; sch. counselor Unified Sch. Dist. 259, Wichita, 1991-94; secondary sch. counselor Unified Sch. Dist. 385, Andover, Kans., 1994—2002; ret., 2002; owner Creative Classics Home Accents, 2004. Sec. Gilded Lilies Investment Club, Luth. Women's Missionary League, 2003—, pres., 2006—; bd. dirs. Friends Wichita Art Mus. Mem. ACA, Kans. Sch. Counselors Assn., Kans. Assn. Counselors, Mental Health Counselors Assn., Kans. Dental Aux. (sec. 1970-74), Wichita Dist. Dental Aux. (pres. 1970-75), Luth. Women's Missionary League (pres. 2006-), Lr. League Wichita (adminstrv. v.p. 1978-82), Gilded Lilies Investment Club (sec. 2005-06), Gamma Phi Beta, Phi Kappa Phi Republican. Lutheran. Avocations: golf, reading. E-mail: gcoo810000@cox.net.

CONOVER, PAMELA C., cruise line executive; married. Cashier Wells Fargo Bank, London, with NYC, 1979—81; asst. treas. US Line, 1981—85; various positions to mng. dir. N. Am. ship financing divsn. Citicorp, 1985—94; pres. Epirotiki Cruises, Carnival Corp., 1994; v.p. strategic planning Carnival Corp., 1994—98; COO Cunard Line Ltd., Carnival Corp., 1998—, pres., 2001—. Achievements include only female pres. major cruise line; Cunard Line Ltd. launched Queen Mary II in 2004, largest transatlantic cruise ship to date.

CONOVER-CARSON, ANNE, writer; d. George Richards and A. Louise (Pinkerton) Conover; m. Thomas N. Ambrose, June 22, 1959 (div. Oct. 1967); 1 child, Natalie Anne Ambrose; m. Thomas B. Carson, Nov. 14, 1970 (dec. June 2002). BA, Stanford U., 1959, MA, 1966. Editor Curtis Pub. Co., Phila., 1959—61, Johns Hopkins Press, Balt., 1966—68; editor, writer Libr. Congress, Washington, 1968—76, U.S. Info. Agy., 1976—90; editor-in-chief Anne Carson Assocs., 1990—. Author: Caresse Crosby: From Black Sun to Roccasinibalda, 1990, Ezra Pound and the Crosby Continental Editions, 1993; author: (with Julia Montgomery Walsh) Risks and Rewards: A Memoir, 1998; author: Olga Rudge and Ezra Pound: What Thou Lovest Well, 2001, Olga Rudge: Pound's Muse and the Circe of the Cantos in Ezra Pound: Nature and Myth, 2003. Nominee Best Scholarly Biography of Yr., Yale Press, 2001. Mem.: MLA, Author's Guild, Am. Acad. Poets, Nat. Coalition Ind. Scholars, Knickerbocker Club (N.Y.C.), Met. Club (Washington). Democrat. Episcopalian. Avocations: chamber and early music, Chinese brush painting, travel.

CONQUEST, CLAIRE M., secondary school counselor; d. Archie Jones and Cabelle Harris-Smith; m. John E. Conquest, Apr. 8, 1972; 1 child, Alicia 1 stepchild, Troy. BA, So. U., 1966; MA, Queens Coll., NY, 1974; degree in Adminstrn., Coll. New Rochelle, 1990. Cert. in counseling edn. N.Y. Tchr. home econs. Dawnwood Jr. H.S., Centereach, NY, 1967—69; counselor Bellport (N.Y.) H.S., 1969—71, Ea. H.S., Balt., 1971—73, Longwood H.S., Middle Island, NY, 1974—2001, ret., 2001. Spkr. in field. Co-editor: The African American Church, 1996. Commr. Brookhaven Black History Commn., Medford, 1997—; chmn. scholarship com. Faith Bapt. Ch., Coram, NY, 2000—; adv. bd. Brookhaven Town Office Women's Svcs., Medford, NY, 1999—. Recipient Outstanding Educator award, Bus. and Profl. Women, 1998, Educator of Yr. award, Brookhaven Town NAACP, 1999, Outstanding Educator award, Brookhaven Town Office Women's Svcs., 2000. Mem.: We. Suffolk Counselors Assn., Ea. L.I. Black Educators Assn. (treas. 1990—, chmn. scholarship com. 1990—), L.I. Urban League High Achievers (mem. com. 1999—), Delta Sigma Theta (pres. 2000—02, chmn. scholarship com. 2002—). Democrat. Baptist. Avocations: travel, theater, Scrabble, mahjong.

CONRAD, JANILYN MCNEES, special education educator; b. Elmhurst, Ill, Apr. 18, 1956; d. Hobart Eugene and Margaret Evelyn (Musselman) McNees; m. William August Conrad, Feb. 28, 1979; children: Krista, Jenna. BS in Elementary Edn., Ind. U., 1978; MS in Adminstrn., Calif. State U., Long Beach, 1988. Tchr. Bur. of Indian Affairs, St. Michaels, Ariz., 1978, Long Beach Unified Sch. Dist., 1979—, resource specialist, 1982—99, mentor tchr., 1988-89, inclusion specialist, 1999—2003, spl. edn. team leader, 2003—. Mem. Amigos de Bolsa Chica, Huntington Beach, Calif., 1985. State of Calif. CTIIP grantee, 1985. Mem. Coun. Exceptional Children, mem. Calif. Assn. of Resource Specialists, 1991-pres., Inclusion Specialist., 1999-pres. Avocations: reading, jogging, sailing. Home: 20762 Farnsworth Ln Huntington Beach CA 92646-5550 Office Phone: 562-422-6868 X255. Personal E-mail: jconrad@socal.rr.com.

CONRAD, MARIAN SUE (SUSAN CONRAD), retired special education educator; b. Columbus, Ohio, May 3, 1946; d. Harold Marion Griffith and Susie Belle (House) Goheen; m. Richard Lee Conrad, Jan. 23 1971. BS, Ohio State U., 1967. Tchr. spl. edn. West High Sch., Columbus, Ohio, 1967-70; spl. edn. work study coord. North High Sch., Columbus, 1974-79, Whetstone High Sch., Columbus, 1979-80, Briggs High Sch., Columbus, 1980-97, West High Sch., Columbus, 1970-97; ret., 1997. Bd. dirs. Jr. Div., The Columbus Symphony Club, 1972-79; vice chmn. Zoofari, Columbus, 1978-97; bd. dirs., life mem. Wazoo, Columbus, 1974-87; bd. dirs., chair coms. Jr. League, Columbus, 1982-99; vice chmn. devel. com. Dublin (Ohio) Counseling Ctr., 1987-97; trustee Columbus Zoo, 1991—. Recipient Mayors Award for Vol.

Svc., Columbus, 1988. Mem. Am. Bus. Women's Assn. (v.p. 1979-80, bd. dirs., Woman of Yr. 1980), Coun. Exceptional Children (pres. 1988-89, Educator of Yr. 1989), Ohio Assn. Suprs. and Work Study Coords., Dublin Women in Bus. and Professions, Country Club at Muirfield, Dublin Women's Club, Iota Lambda Sigma. Republican. Methodist. Avocations: golf, gardening, travel, cooking. Home: 8039 Crossgate Ct S Dublin OH 43017-8432

CONRAD, MARY TRENCH, elementary school educator; b. St. Louis, Sept. 25, 1940; d. Joseph Michael and Rosemary O'Reilly Flynn; m. Robert Daniel Conrad, June 13, 1964; children: Elizabeth Colleen Mortimer, Sean Robert. BA in Elem. Edn., Webster U., Webster Groves, Mo., 1962. Tchr. Bayless Sch. Dist., St. Louis, 1962—63, Diocese San Francisco, 1963—67, Ritenaur Sch. Dist., St. Louis, 1968—71, Archdiocese St. Louis, 1971—86, 1990—, Diocese Trenton, Mo., 1986—88. Vice prin. Ascension Sch., Chesterfield, Mo., 1983; dir. religion St. Blaise, Maryland Heights, Mo., 1986—88; chmn. sch. self study St. Angela Merici, Florissant, Mo., 1997—98. Nominee Tchr. of Yr. award, Disney, 2000. Mem.: Assn. Cath. Elem. Tchrs., Nat. Cath. Tchr. Assn., U.S. Golf Assn., Ladies Ancient Order Hibernians (pres. St. Louis chpt. 1995—96, v.p. St. Louis chpt. 1992—95, chmn. freedom for Ireland St. Louis chpt. 1991—99, chmn. state missions Mo. chpt. 1999—2001). Avocations: golf, travel, reading. Office: St Angela Merici 3860 North Hwy 67 Florissant MO 63034

CONRAD, SHERRY K. LYNCH, counselor; b. Nov. 20, 1957; d. Robert Emmett and Norma Lea Lynch; married Nov 20, 2004. BA, Randolph-Macon Woman's Coll., 1979; MS, Emporia State U., Kans., 1980; PhD, Kans. State U., 1987. Vocat. rehab. counselor Rehab. Svcs., Topeka, 1980—81, cmty. program cons., 1981—86; counseling intern Winthrop Coll., Rock Hill, SC, 1986—87; counselor Ripon Coll., Wis., 1987—90, Va. Poly. Inst. and State U., 1991—. Exec. com. Sexual Assault Counseling Program, Topeka, 1983-86, recruitment coord., 1983-86, counselor, 1981-86, Nat. Singles Conf. Planning Com., Green Lake, Wis., 1987-90; area admissions rep. Randolph-Macon Woman's Coll., Lynchburg, Va., 1981-87; mem. Student Outreach Schs. coun. Northbrooke Hosp., 1988-90; mem. Student Affairs Devel. Com., 1991-94, chair, 1992-94, mem. Sexual Assault Victim Edn. and Support Com., 1991-95, Wellness Com., 1993-2000, Leadership Resource Team, 1994-96; sec. Ripon Chem. Abuse and Awareness Program, 1987-90; bd. dirs. New River Family Shelter, sec., 1993-98; pro bono counselor Mental Health Assn. of New River Valley, 2002—; clin. mental health counselor certification exam com. Nat. Bd. Cert. Counselors, 1996—. Bd. dirs. Haymarket Sq. Homeowners Assn., 1992-2004, treas., 1993-2004; chair ch. and soc. com. Blacksburg United Meth. Ch., 1992-94, mem. coun. ministries, 1992-94; asst. class agt. Class of 1979, Randolph-Macon Woman's Coll., 2000-04, mem. reunion com., 2005—. Recipient Kans. 4-H Key award Ext. Svc. of Kans. State U., 1974; named Internat. 4-H Youth Exch. Amb. to France, 1977. Mem. ACA, Nat. Rehab. Counseling Assn. (bd. dirs. 1982-88, chair br. devel. subcoun. 1982-87, chair policy and program coun. 1987-88), Gt. Plains Rehab. Counseling Assn. (newsletter editor 1982-85, bd. dirs. 1983-87, pres. 1984-85, sec. 1986-87), Gt. Plains Rehab. Assn. (bd. dirs. 1983-85, awards chairperson 1984-85), Kans. Rehab. Counseling Assn. (bd. dirs. 1983-86, pres. 1984-85), Kans. Rehab. Assn. (bd. dirs. 1982-85, advt. chair 1983-85), Topeka Rehab. Assn. (bd. dirs. 1982-85, sec. 1982-83, pres. 1983-84), Am. Coll. Pers. Assn. (chair commn. VII counseling and psychol. svcs. 1996-98, directorate body 1989-93, 95-99, 2004—, membership commn. 1990-93, planning com. 1997-99, sec. 2000-02, exec. coun. 2000-02, archivist 2004—, continuing edn. com. 2004—, Outreach and Advocacy Core Coun., sec. 1999-2000), Wis. Coll. Pers. Assn. (bd. dirs. 1988-90), Assn. for Specialists in Group Work, Va. Coll. Pers. Assn. Methodist. Avocation: tennis. Home: 6317 Old Ferry Rd Hiwassee VA 24347 Office: Va Tech Counseling Ctr 240 McComas Hall Blacksburg VA 24061 Office Phone: 540-231-6557. Business E-Mail: sklynch@vt.edu.

CONRAD-ENGLAND, ROBERTA LEE, pathologist; b. Meriden, Conn., Aug. 25, 1950; d. Hans and Emma Ann (Bort) Conrad; m. Gary Thomas England, June 6, 1976; children: Eric Bryan, Christopher Ryan. BS in Microbiology, U. Ky., 1972, MD, 1976. Diplomate Nat. Bd. Med. Examiners, Bd. Am. Pathologists. Resident anatomic and clin. pathology Emory U. Affiliated Hosps., Atlanta, 1976-80; pathologist Western Bapt. Hosp., Paducah, Ky., 1980—2005. Cons. Marshall County Hosp., Benton, Ky., 1985-2005, chair infection control com., 1985-2005 Mem., com. chairperson PTA, Poducah, Ky., 1993-94; mother's asst. Boy Scouts Am., Poducah, 1991-94. Fellow Coll. Am. Pathologists, Am. Soc. Clin. Pathologists; mem. Ky. Med. Assn., Ky. Soc. Pathologists, Ky. Women Mentors in Sci., Alpha Omega Alpha, Phi Beta Kappa. Avocations: swimming, snorkeling, interior decorating.

CONRADER, CONSTANCE RUTH, artist, writer; b. Vandalia, Mo., Apr. 13, 1919; d. Gilbert Fordyce and Elizabeth Florence (Cleghorn) Stone; m. Jay Merten Conrader, Nov. 29, 1941 (dec. 1996). Student, Carroll Coll., 1938-40, North Park Coll., 1940-41. Cert. pub. libr. Artist, author, Oconomowoc, Wis., 1940—. Libr. Oconomowoc Pub. Libr., 1947-82, vol. 1982—; illustrator Turtox classroom charts Gen. Biol. Supply House, Chgo., 1940-60; manuscript critique Baha'i Pub. Trust, Wilmette, Ill., 1970-89, editor, 1988. Author, illustrator: Blue Wampum, 1958; co-editor: Tokens From the Writings of Baha'u'llah, 1973; illustrator: Northwoods Wildlife Region, 1983; co-author, illustrator articles to profl. jours.; co-editor regional Baha'i Newsletter, 1997-2006 Chair UN Day, Oconomowoc, 1976-86. Avocations: gardening, music, reading, cooking. Home: 738 E Washington St Oconomowoc WI 53066-3110

CONRADT, JODY, basketball coach; b. Goldthwaite, Tex., May 13, 1941; BS in Phys. Edn., Baylor U., 1963, MS in Phys. Edn., 1969. Women's basketball, volleyball and track head coach Sam Houston State U., Huntsville, Tex., 1969—73; women's basketball, volleyball and softball head coach U. Tex., Arlington, 1973—76, head women's basketball coach Austin, 1976—, women's athletic dir., 1992—2001. Mem. Coaches vs. Cancer/Am. Cancer Soc.; hon. chair Susan B. Komen Race for the Cure fundraising walk/run, Austin, 2003; vol. annual walk Austin's SafePlace. Named one of Top 50 Women's Sports Execs. in the nation, Street & Smith's Sports Bus. Jour., 1998; named to Internat. Women's Sports Hall of Fame, N.Y.C., 1995, Naismith Meml. Basketball Hall of Fame, 1998, Women's Basketball Hall of Fame, 1999, Internat. Scholar-Athlete Hall of Fame, 2003, Tex. Women's Hall of Fame, 1986, Tex. Sports Hall of Fame, 1998, U. Tex. Women's Athletics Hall of Honor, 2000; recipient John and Nellie Wooden Nat. Coach of the Yr. award, 1996—97, Nat. Coach of the Yr. award, ESPN.com, 2002—03, Harvey Penick award for Excellence in the Game of Life, Caritas, Austin, 2003, Carol Eckman award, Women's Basketball Coach's Assn., 1987, Nat. Award for outstanding commitment to women's athletics, Nat. Assn. for Girls and Women in Sports, 1991, award for contbn. to sports, NCAA, 1992. Office: Univ of Texas Athletics Office PO Box 7399 Austin TX 78713

CONROW, ANN E., music educator; b. Franklin, Ind., Apr. 12, 1951; d. Ross Arden and Margaret Evelyn Becker; m. David Bruce Conrow, Sept. 2, 1972; children: Karen D. Linville, Sarah J. Vivo. BA in Music Edn., Butler U., 1993; MA, U. Indpls., 2000. Choral dir. Clark Pleasant Schs., Whiteland, Ind., 1995—99, Ctr. Grove Schs., Greenwood, Ind., 2000, Mooresville Cons. Schs., Ind., 2001, Clark Pleasant Sch. Corp., Whiteland, 2002—. Bright Ideas grant, Vectren/Peyton Manning Peyback Found., 2003. Mem.: Am. Choral Dirs. Assn., Music Educators Nat. Conf. Office: Whitehead Cmty HS 300 Main St Whiteland IN 46184 Office Phone: 317-535-7562.

CONROY, FRANCES, actress; b. Monroe, Ga., Nov. 13, 1953; m. Jan Munroe, 1992. Student, The Neighborhood Playhouse Sch. of the Theatre, New York, Dickinson Coll., Carlisle, Penn.; degree in Drama, Juilliard Sch., New York. Actor: (films) Manhattan, 1979, Othello, 1979, Falling in Love, 1984, Amazing Grace and Chuck, 1987, In the Hands of the Enemy, 1987, Rocket Gibraltor, 1988, Another Woman, 1988, Dirty Rotten Scoundrels, 1988, Hostile Witness, 1988, Crimes and Misdemeanors, 1989, Billy Bathgate, 1991, Scent of a Woman, 1992, Sleepless in Seattle, 1993, The Adventures of Huck Finn, 1993, Angela, 1995, The Neon Bible, 1995, Developing, 1995, The Crucible, 1996, Maid in Manhattan, 2002, Die, Mommie, Die, 2003, Catwoman, 2004, The Aviator, 2004, Broken Flowers, 2005, Shopgirl, 2005, Ira and Abby, 2006, The Wicker Man, 2006; (plays, stage debut) Measure for Measure, 1978; (Broadway plays) The Lady from Dubuque, 1980, The Secret Rapture, 1990 (Drama Desk Award, 1990), The Ride Down Mt. Morgan, 2000 (Tony Award nom., Outer Critics Circle Award, 2000); (TV series) Six Feet Under, 2001—05 (Emmy Award nom., 2002, Golden Globe award for best actress in a dramatic series, 2004, Screen Actors Guild Award for best actress in a drama series, 2004); (TV films) Carl Sandburg: Echoes and Silences, 1982, The Royal Romance of Charles and Diana, 1982, Kennedy, 1983, LBJ: The Early Years, 1987, Terrorist on Trial: The United States vs. Salim Ajami, 1988, Our Town, 1989, One More Mountain, 1994, Journey, 1995, Innocent Victims, 1996, Thicker Than Blood, 1998, Murder in a Small Town, 1999; (TV miniseries) Queen, 1993.*

CONROY, MARY ELIZABETH, history professor; b. Hammond, Ind., Sept. 2, 1937; d. Edward Michael and Branche Gisela (Schellenbauer) Schaeffer; m. Thomas Francis Conroy, June 19, 1965; children: Alexandra Blanche, Margaret Eleanor. BA, St. Mary's Coll., South Bend, Ind., 1959; MA, Ind. U., Bloomington, 1962, PhD, 1964. Asst. prof. Kans. State U., Manhattan, 1964—65, U. Ill., Chgo., 1965—68, U. Colo., Denver, 1975—78, assoc. prof., 1978—85, prof. Russian and Soviet hist., 1985—2005, prof. emerita, 2005. Author: P.A. Stolypin: Practical Politics in late Tsarist Russia, 1977, In Health and In Sickness: Pharmacy Pharmacists and the Pharmaceutical Industry in late Imperial Russia, 1994 (George Urdang award, 1997), The Soviet Pharmaceutical Business During Its First Two Decades 1917-1937, 2005; editor: Emerging Democracy in Late Imperial Russia, 1998. Grantee, Ford Found., 1960—64, Internat. Rsch. and Exchange, 1990. Mem.: Slovak Soc. Colo. (pres. 2006), Assn. Study of Health Democracy in Former Soviet Union, Am. Inst. Hist. Pharmacy, Am. Hist. Assn., Am. Assn. Advancement Slavic Studies. Republican. Roman Catholic. Avocations: art, music, architecture, travel. Home: 3825 Colorado Blvd Cherry Hills Village CO 80113-4202 Fax: 303-761-6273. Personal E-mail: maryesconroy@earthlink.net.

CONROY, SARAH BOOTH, columnist, writer, educator; b. Valdosta, Ga., Feb. 16, 1927; d. Weston Anthony and Ruth (Proctor) Booth; m. Richard Timothy Conroy, Dec. 31, 1949; children: Camille Booth, Sarah Claire. BS, U. Tenn., 1950. Continuity writer Sta. WNOX, 1945-48; commentator, writer Sta. WATO, 1948-49; reporter, architecture columnist Knoxville News Sentinel, 1949-56; assoc. editor The Diplomat mag., 1956-58; columnist Washington Post, 1957-58, design editor, columnist, editor in chief Living in Style, 1970-82, feature writer, columnist, 1982-94, Chronicles columnist, 1986—; reporter, art critic Washington Daily News, 1968-70; regular contbr. N.Y. Times, 1968-70. Mem. adv. bd. Horizon mag., 1978-85 Author: Refinements of Love A Novel about Clover and Henry Adams, 1993. Recipient Raven award Mystery Writers Am., 1990, U. Tenn. Disting. Alumni award, 1995, Mortar Bd. award, 1997. Mem.: AIA (hon. first recipient Glenn Brown award 2000). Home: 122 Sherman Ave Takoma Park MD 20912-5744

CONROY, TAMARA BOKS, artist, special education educator, retired nurse; b. Most, Bohemia, Czechoslovakia; came to U.S., 1947; d. Alois and Tatiana (Shapilova) Boks; m. John P. Conroy, Aug. 19, 1950 (dec. Oct. 1973); 1 child, Michael Thomas (dec.). Student, U. Graz, Austria, 1945-47; RN, New Rochelle (N.Y.) Med. Ctr., 1950; student, Coll. of William & Mary, 1958, 59, Cath. U. Am., 1960; BS in Nursing Edn., Columbia U., 1963, MA in Spl. Edn., 1965. RN, N.Y.; cert. spl. edn. tchr., N.Y. Nurse accident rm. New Rochelle Hosp./Med. Ctr., 1950-51; pub. health nurse Va. Dept. of Health, Richmond, 1958-59; tchr. spl. edn. Southern Westchester Bd. Coop. Edn. Svcs., Portchester, NY, 1965-83; freelance artist and painter N.Y.C. and Pelham, NY, 1969—. Asst. to chmn. math. dept. Columbia U., N.Y.C., 1975-76. Author math. program Learning Numbers-Step by Step, 1977. Pres., founder Classical Music Lovers' Exch., Pelham, N.Y., 1980-98. Mem. Am. Fedn. Tchrs., N.Y. State United Tchrs., BOCES Tchrs. Assn. (profl.), Women's Mus. Group, Mamaroneck Artists Guild, Silvermine Artists Guild, Westchester Musicians Guild (assoc.), Kappa Delta Pi. Avocations: flying, reading, music, fashion designing, painting and drawing.

CONRY, MAURA, pharmacist, social worker; b. New Orleans, July 15, 1940; d. Melvin Raymond Elliott and Mary Byrne O'Connell; 1 child, Michael Sean. BS, MSW, PharmD, Loyola U., 1964; MSW, U. Kans., 1998. Registered pharmicist Kans., 1982, Mo., 1973, La., 1964; LCSW Kans., 1998, Mo. Clin. pharmacist Dept. of VA, Leavenworth, Kans., 1987—97, eeoc counselor Kansas City, Mo., 1989—91, women veterans coord. Leavenworth, Kans., 1993—96; dir., owner Pharmacy and Social Work, Shawnee Mission, Kans., 1998—; psychiat. clin. coord. Shawnee Mission Med. Ctr., 2001—. Presenter World AIDS Conf., Geneva, 1998—98; bd. dirs. Kans. City Friends of Jung, Kansas City, 2000—; educator U. Kans., Lawrence, 2001—; cons., rschr. Brigham & Womens Hosp., Harvard Med. Sch., Boston, 2003—, co-dir. rsch. grant, 2004—. Author: (monograph) Recognizing Elder Abuse; contbr. chapters to books, articles to profl. jours. Recipient Innovative Practice award, Kans. Pharmacist Assn., 1996, Nat. Leadership in Edn. award, Am. Soc. Cons. Pharmacists, 2002; fellow, McLean Hosp., Harvard Med. Sch., Am. Soc. Cons. Pharmacists, 2000; grantee, Cmty. Pharmacist Assn., 2003. Mem.: NASW, Kans. Assn. Social Workers, Am. Soc. Cons. Pharmacists (cons. advisors rsch. and edn. 2003—06). Unitarian. Achievements include research in pharmacy amd social work; development of safe and accurate medication management using pharmacists and social workers; polypharmacy managmenet using pharmacists and social workers. Avocation: painting. Office: Pharmacy & Social Work 7923 Halsey St Shawnee Mission KS 66215-2718 Office Phone: 913-599-4469.

CONSAGRA, SOPHIE CHANDLER, academic administrator; b. Radnor, Pa., Apr. 28, 1927; d. Alfred D. and Carol (Ramsay) Chandler; children: Maria, Pierluigi, Francesca, George. BA, Smith Coll., 1949; MA, Cambridge U., Eng., 1952. Exec. dir. Del. Arts Council, 1972-78; dir. visual arts and architecture N.Y. State Council Arts, 1978-80; dir. Am. Acad. in Rome, 1980-84, pres., 1984-88, pres. emerita, vice chmn./spl. projects, 1988-90. Cons. Nat. Endowment Arts. Recipient Smith Coll. award, 1986, Centennial medal Am. Acad. in Rome, 1995. Address: 955 Lexington Ave New York NY 10021-5128

CONSIDINE, JILL M., securities trader; b. Aug. 14, 1944; m. Martin Rettinger; 1 child, Danielle. BS in Biology, St. John's U., 1965, LLD (hon.), 1986; postgrad. in biochemistry, Bryn Mawr Coll., 1965-67; MS, Grad. Sch. Bus., Columbia U., 1980. V.p. Chase Manhattan Bank, N.Y.C., 1971-81, Bankers Trust, N.Y.C., 1981-83; pres., CEO The First Women's Bank, N.Y.C., 1984-85; supt. banks N.Y. State Banking Dept., N.Y.C., 1985-91; mng. dir., chief admin. officer American Express Bank Ltd., 1991—93; pres. New York Clearing House Assn., N.Y.C., 1993-99; chmn., CEO The Depository Trust Co., N.Y.C., 1999—. Bd. dirs. Fed. Res. Bank N.Y., 2002—, Atlantic Mut. Ins. Comps., Ambac Fin. Corp., The Interpublic Group of Cos. Mem. Coun. Fgn. Rels., Japan Soc., Group of 30 Steering Com., N.Y.C. Partnership, Securities Industry Found. Econ. Devel.; dir., cons. Sept. 11 Fund, Alliance Downtown N.Y. Named equities achiever of the yr., Equities Mag., 2000; named one of 100 Most Influential Women in Bus., Crain's NY mag., 1999; recipient Star award, NY Women's Agenda, 1995, Six Sigma CEO of the Yr. award, 2006. Mem.: Coun. Fgn. Rels. Office: The Depository Trust Co 55 Water St New York NY 10041-0001*

CONSILIO, BARBARA ANN, legal association administrator, management consultant; b. Cleve., June 22, 1938; d. Joseph B. and Anna E. (Ford) C. BS, Kent State U., 1962; MA, U. Detroit, 1973. Cert. social worker Mich. Tchr. Chagrin Falls (Ohio) High Sch., 1962-64; probation officer Macomb County Juvenile Ct., Mt. Clemens, Mich., 1965-68, casework supr., 1968-74, dir. children's svcs., 1974-79; mgr. foster care and instns. Oakland County Juvenile Ct., Pontiac, Mich., 1979-83; ct. adminstr. Oakland County Probate Ct., Pontiac, 1983-93, ret., 1993. Bd. dirs. Children's Charter Cts. of Mich., Lansing, Statewide Adv. Bd. on Sexual Abuse, Lansing, Havenwyck Hosp., Auburn Hills, Orchards Children's Svcs., Southfield, Oakland County Coun. Children at Risk, Pontiac; mem. Nat. Women's Polit. Caucus, N.Y.C.; bd. dirs. Care House, Pontiac. Mem. Nat. Coun. Juvenile and Family Ct. Adminstrs. Group, Mich. Probate and Juvenile Register's Assn., Mich. Juvenile Ct. Adminstrs. Assn., Nat. Assn. Ct. Mgrs., Supreme Ct. Task Force on Racial and Ethnic Bias, Office of Children and Youth Svcs. (state foster care system rev. com.), Nat. Coun. Juvenile and Family Ct. Judges (Outstanding Ct. Adminstr. award, 1993). Avocations: music, sports, sports cars. Home: 2961 Middleton Pl Hendersonville NC 28791

CONSOLO, FAITH HOPE, real estate broker; b. Ohio; BFA, NYU; MFA, Parsons Sch. Design; AA in Real Estate Studies, NYU. Owner internat. promotional modeling agy.; owner interior design studio; small stores real estate broker; joined Garret-Aug Assocs. Store Leasing Inc., N.Y.C., 1985, sr. mng. dir., vice chmn., 1999—; founder, vice chmn. Garrick-Aug Worldwide. Apptd. cons. The 42nd St. Redevel. Corp., N.Y.C., Penn Sta. Redevel., N.Y.C., The Downtown Alliance, N.Y.C.; lectr. Assn. Women on Econ. Devel., Nat. Assn. Women Bus. Owners, The Women's Econ. Roundtable, Inst. Internat. Rsch., Nat. Assn. Appraisers & Planners, Women Inc.; bd. dirs. The Real Estate Bd. N.Y., Internat. Coun. Shopping Ctrs., Nat. Broker's Network; advisor Mayor's Coun. on the Aging Related Issues; instr. NYU Parsons Sch. Design, The Wharton Bus. Sch.; lectr. in field. Author: (internet newsletter) The Faith Report; contbr. N.Y. Post, The N.Y. Times, Crain's N.Y. Bus., Real Estate Weekly, N.Y. Real Estate Jour., Real Estate N.Y., others. Named Woman of Yr., Associated Builders and Owners of Greater N.Y., 1999, Woman of Outstanding Achievement, Assn. Real Estate Women, 2003, Woman of Valor, Capuchin Food Pantries of St. John the Bapt. Friary, 2003; named one of N.Y. Most Influential Women in Bus., Crain's N.Y. Bus., 1996, 1999. Mem.: Young Men's/Women's Real Estate Assn., Assn. Real Estate Women (past pres., creator The Founder's award). Office: Garrick-Aug 360 Lexington Ave 4th Fl New York NY 10017

CONSTANT, ANITA AURELIA, publisher; b. Youngstown, Ohio, Jan. 5, 1945; d. Sandu Nicholas and Erie Marie (Tecau) C. BA, Ind. U., 1967; postgrad., Northwestern U., Evanston, Ill., 1991. Sales rep. Economy Fin. Inc., St. Louis, 1967-69; recruiter Case Western U. Hosp., Cleve., 1969-70; sales rep. Internat. Playtex Inc., Chgo., 1970-71, John Wiley & Sons, Inc., Chgo., 1971-77; sr. product mgr. CBS Pub. Inc., The Dryden Press, Chog., 1977-80; exec. editor Dearborn Fin. Pub., Inc., Chgo., 1980-81, v.p., 1981-89, sr. v.p., prin., 1989-97; cons. to pub. industry, 1997-98; prin. Ea. European investment venture EUROTEC, 1997-99; sr. v.p., editor-in-chief Southwestern Coll. Pub. divsn. ITP Inc., 1988-94; sr. v.p. new bus. devel. South-Western/Thomson Learning, 2000—; v.p. devel. and contract mgmt. Riverside Pub. Divsn. Houghton Mifflin, 1995—. Bd. dirs. Romanian Heritage Ctr., Detroit, 1988—, Orthodox Brotherhood of Am., Detroit, 1985—. Mem.: Nat. Assn. Women Bus. Owners, Chgo. Book Clinic (bd. dirs. 1987—88, v.p. 1988—90, pres. 1990—91, past pres. 1991—92, Mary Alexander award 1995), Internat. Assn. Fin. Planners, Real Estate Educators Assn., Chgo. Women in Pub. Eastern Orthodox. Avocations: property development and renovation, hiking, bicycling. Office: 425 Springlake Dr Itasca IL 60143

CONSTANTINE, JESSICA LEE, elementary school educator; b. White Plains, NY, Sept. 19, 1980; d. Kenneth Eugene and Lucille Mary Folden; m. Peter Joseph Constantine, Apr. 15, 2005. MS, Columbia U., 2004. Cert. tchr. NY. 6th grade sci. tchr. Pelham (NY) Mid. Sch., 2003—.

CONSTANTINE, KATHERINE A., lawyer; b. 1955; BS magna cum laude in Fgn. Svc., Georgetown Univ., 1977, JD, 1980. Bar: Minn. 1980. Assoc., gen. litig. Nichols, Kruger, Starks and Carruthers, 1980—83; assoc. Fabyanske Svoboda & Westra PA, 1983—85, Dorsey & Whitney LLP, Mpls., 1986—88, ptnr., banking comml. dept., 1989—, and co-chair, bus. restructuring and bankruptcy. Assoc. editor Georgetown's The Tax Lawyer, 1979—80. Named a Leading Atty. in bankruptcy law, Minn. Bus. Guidebook to Law and Leading Attorneys, 1994—96, Guide to Leading Am. Attorneys, 1998, Minn. Super Lawyer, 2000—03. Mem.: ABA, Am. Bankruptcy Inst., Minn. Women Lawyers, Hennepin Co. Bar Assn., Minn. State Bar Assn., Phi Beta Kappa. Office: Dorsey & Whitney LLP Ste 1500 50 S Sixth St Minneapolis MN 55402-1498 Office Phone: 612-340-8792. Office Fax: 612-340-2868. Business E-Mail: constantine.katherine@dorsey.com.

CONSTANTINE, MARGARET L(OUISE) (PEGGY CONSTANTINE), newspaper reporter, freelance writer; b. Racine, Wis. d. Charles Ezra and Margaret (Moore) C. BA, Duke U., 1952; MSJ, Northwestern U., 1954. Biography editor World Book Ency., Chgo., 1957-60; reporter, book columnist, copy editor Chgo. Sun-Times, 1960-87. Contbr. book revs. to N.Y. Times, 1990—. Rockefeller Found. fellow for tng. music critics, 1967. Episcopalian. Avocation: golf. Home: 1225 S Main St Racine WI 53403-1928

CONSTANTINI, JOANN M., small business owner, systems administrator, consultant; b. Danbury, Conn., July 30, 1948; d. William J. and Mathilda J. (Ressler) C. BA, Coll. White Plains, N.Y., 1970; postgrad., Ctrl. Conn. State Coll., 1977-78, U. Hartford, 1985-88, U. Jacksonville, 1991; MS, Nova Southeastern U., 1996. Cert. records mgr., 1987; lic. realtor, N.C. Psychiat. social worker N.Y. State Dept. Mental Hygiene, Wassaic, 1970-73; with N.E. Utilities, Hartford, Conn., 1973-88, methods analyst, 1979-82, records and procedures mgmt. adminstr., 1982-88; document contr., mgr. Ralph M. Parsons Co., Fairfield, Ohio, 1990-91, St. Johns River Power Park, Jacksonville, 1991—2001; dir. Jacksonville Elec. Authority, 2001—03; owner Contantini & Assocs., 1988—, Family Threads, 1997—; v.p. new mktg. Utility Devel. Corp., 2006—. Mem. faculty Ctrl. Piedmont C.C., 1989-90, Fla. C.C., Jacksonville, 1993-95. Bd. dirs. Meriden YWCA, Conn., 1978-79; vol. Queen City Friends, Charlotte, 1988-89, Cath. Charities AIDS Ministries, Jacksonville, 1996-99; mem. Greater Charlotte Bd. Realtors, 1989-91, First Coast Chorus, 1998-2002; mem. adv. coun. Greater Hartford C.C., 1986, Clermont Coll., Cin., 1990-91, Jacksonville C.C., 1991-94; mem. com. St. Augustine Diocesan Task Force Alternative Ministries, 1997—2003. Mem.: NACDLGM (nat. v.p. 1999—2001, bd. dirs. 1999—2004, mem. Human Rights Campaign 1999—, bd. dirs. Riverwoods HOA 2000—02, nat. pres. 2002—03), AAUW, Jacksonville Small Bus. Network, Am. Platform Assn., Inst. Cert. Records Mgrs., Nat. Trust for Hist. Preservation, Coll. White Plains Alumnae Assn., Electric Coun. New Eng. (chair records mgmt. com. 1985—87), Assn. Configuration Data Mgmt., Women Bus. Owners, Assn. Image and Info. Mgmt. (dir. 1984—86), Assn. Record Mgmt. and Adminstrs. (sec. 1984—85, bd. dirs. 1984—86, chair industry action com. for pub. utilities 1986—89, internat. chair industry action program 1989—93, profl. issues com. 1997—99), N.E. Utilities Women's Forum Club (treas. 1983—88), Beta Sigma Phi. Democrat. Roman Catholic. Avocations: antiques, online auctions, travel, investing. Home: 11538 Jonathan Rd Jacksonville FL 32225-1314 Personal E-mail: constantiniaassocs@yahoo.com, joann.constantini@gmail.com.

CONSTANTINO-BANA, ROSE EVA, nursing educator, researcher, lawyer; b. Labangan Zamboanga delSur, Philippines, Dec. 25, 1940; arrived in U.S., 1964, naturalized, 1982; d. Norberto C. and Rosalia (Torres) Bana; m. Abraham Antonio Constantino, Jr., Dec. 13, 1964; children: Charles Edward, Kenneth Richard, Abraham Anthony III. BS in Nursing, Philippine Union Coll., Manila, 1962; MNursing, U. Pitts., 1971, PhD, 1979; JD, Duquesne U., 1984. Lic. clin. specialist in psychiatric-mental health nursing, RN. Instr. Philippine Union Co., 1963-65, Spring Grove State Hosp., Balt., 1965-67, Montefiore Sch. Nursing, Pitts., 1967-70, U. Pitts., 1971-74, asst. prof., 1974-83, assoc. prof., 1983—, chmn. Senate Athletic Com., 1985-86, 89-90, sec. univ. senate, 1991-92, v.p., 1993-95. Project dir. grant divsn. nursing HHS, Washington, 1983-85; bd. dir. Am. Jour. Nursing; prin. investigator NIH NINR, 1991-94; bd. dir. Internat. Coun. Women's Health Issues, 1986—; CEO PALAW, 1997. Author (with others): Principles and Practice of Psychiatric Nursing, 1982; contbr. chapters to books, articles to profl. jours. Mem. Presdl. Task Force, Washington, 1980, Rep. Senatorial Com., Washington, 1980. Fellow: Am. Coll. Forensic Examiners, Am. Acad. Nursing; mem.: ANA, ABA, ATLA, Am. Nurses Found. (v.p. 2004—), Sexual Assault Nurse Examiners, Am. Assn. Legal Nurse Cons., Allegheny County Bar

Assn., So. Poverty Law, Pa. League Nursing, Nat. League Nursing, Pa. State Nurses Assn. (sec. 1994—98, chairperson area 6), Women in the Profession, Pa. Bar Assn., Allegheny County Bar Assn. (bd. cert. forensic examiner), Nat. Coun. Jewish Women (Pitts. sect.), U. Duquesne Law Alumni Assn., U. Pitts. Sch. Nursing Alumni Assn., Phi Alpha Delta, Sigma Theta Tau. Mem. Seventh Day Adventist Ch. Avocations: cooking, piano. Home: 6 Carmel Ct Pittsburgh PA 15221-3618 Office: U Pitts Sch Nursing 4500 Victoria St Rm 415 Pittsburgh PA 15261-0001 Office Phone: 412-624-2063. E-mail: rco100@pitt.edu.

CONSTANTINOPLE, ALEXANDRA, communications executive; d. Nicholas and Donna Constantinople; m. Jordan Hoffner, Oct. 2, 1999; 1 child, Nicholas. BA in English lit., Dennison U. Sr. publicist Larry King Live, CNN, Wash., DC, 1991—93; sr. publicist news info. Today Show and Meet the Press, NBC, NYC, 1993; dir. corp. media rels. NBC, NYC, 1997—98, v.p. news comm., 1998—2002; gen. mgr. corp. and mktg. comm. Gen. Electric, 2002—. Mem.: NY Women in Comm.

CONTE, JEANNE L., writer, photographer; d. Ray Albert and Jeanne Steele Larner; m. Jos Francis Conte, June 7, 1947; children: Joseph, Richard, Susan, Kathryn, John Christopher. Studied, Lindenwood Coll., Mo., 1946, U. Ala., Tuscaloosa, 1949, Ohio Dominican U., Columbus, 1966. Photographer; cloissone enamalist; sculptor. Author: German Village, 1994, Advent Anticipations, 1999, The Wonder of Christmas, 2001, Lenten Reflections, 2001; photographer, writer: articles in books, mags. and calendars. Avocations: travel, gardening.

CONTE, JULIE VILLA, nurse, administrator; b. Manila, July 4, 1951; came to U.S., 1970; d. Gregorio Cortes and Lourdes (Villa) Dirige. BSN, Calif. State U., L.A., 1974; MBA, U. Phoeniz, San Diego, 1993. RN, Calif. Staff nurse Santa Monica (Calif.) Hosp., 1976-78; pub. health nurse Kaiser Found. Hosp., Panorama City, Calif., 1978-85; nursing supr. Nat. Med. Homecare, L.A., 1985-86; dir. home health Holy Cross Hosp., Mission Hills, 1986-88; dir. profl. svcs. Care Home Health, San Diego, 1988; dir. nursing Health Prime Home Health Svcs. of San Diego, Inc., 1988-92; dir. home health svcs. Alvarado Home Health Agy., San Diego, 1993-94; expert consulting Home Health and Bus. Cons., San Diego, 1994—; dir. patient care svcs. Unlimited Care, Inc., 1995-96; CEO, pres., adminstr. We Care Home Health Svc., Inc., 1996—. Cons. in field. Mem. Bapt. Nursing Fellowship (pres. Calif. chpt. 1997-2004, nat. pres., pres.-elect 1999-2003), Alpha Delta Chi Republican. Avocations: travel, foreign language, collecting, piano, organ. Office Phone: 619-229-3800. Personal E-mail: juliecare1@aol.com.

CONTENTO COVEY, NICKI ANN, counselor; b. Cortland, N.Y., Feb. 14, 1975; d. James Contento and Carol Ann Richards-Hall; m. Scott Lynn Covey, Sept. 22, 2002. BSc in Psychology, No. Ill. U., 1998; student in Mental Health Counseling, Shippensburg U., Pa., 2004—. Grad. asst. Drug and Alcohol Program Shippensburg (Pa.) U., 2004—; intern Adams-Hanover Counseling Svcs., Gettysburg, Pa., 2006—. Author: (poem) A Celebration of Poets, 1998. Treas. exec. bd. Pa. Mental Health Counseling Assn. Mem.: Nat. Mental Health Assn., Am. Mental Health Counseling Assn., Am. Counseling Assn. Home: 62 Ball Park Drive Gardners PA 17324 Personal E-mail: nac75@aol.com.

CONTI, JOAN NOEL, social worker; b. Rome, N.Y., May 21, 1958; d. Joseph J. and Jean (Norelli) c.; m. Stewart B. Whitney III.; 1 child, Stewart Bowman Whitney Jr. BA in Sociology, Niagara U., 1980; MSW, SUNY, Buffalo, 1987. Cert. sch. social worker, N.Y.; cert. social worker N.Y. Human svc. data base adminstr. Cen. Referral Svc., Inc., Buffalo, 1985-87; editl. asst., rschr. Niagara Rsch. Inst., Niagara Falls, N.Y., 1980-85; sch. social worker, employee assistance program coord. Cheektowaga (N.Y.) Cen. Sch. Dist., 1988—; pvt. practice E. Amherst Counseling Ctr., 1995—. Mem. Nat. Assn. Social Workers, N.Y. State Sch. Social Workers Assn., N.Y. State Coun. Family Rels. Office Phone: 716-686-3631. E-mail: jconti@cheektuwayacentral.org.

CONTI, JOY FLOWERS, judge; b. Kane, Pa., Dec. 7, 1948; d. Bernard A. Flowers and Elizabeth (Tingley) Rodgers; m. Anthony T. Conti, Jan. 16, 1971; children: Andrew, Michael, Gregory. BA, Duquesne U., 1970, JD summa cum laude, 1973. Bar: Pa. 1973, U.S. Dist. Ct. (we. dist.) Pa. 1973, U.S. Ct. Appeals (3d cir.) 1976, U.S. Supreme Ct. 1993. Law clk. Supreme Ct. Pa., Monessen, 1973-74; assoc. Kirkpatrick & Lockhart, Pitts., 1974-76, 82-83, ptnr., 1983-96; shareholder Buchanan, Ingersoll, P.C., Pitts., 1996—2002; dist. judge U.S. Dist. Ct.(we. dist.) Pa., Pitts., 2002—. Prof. law Duquesne U., Pitts., 1976-82; hearing examiner Pa. Dept. State, Bur. Profl. Occupation and Affairs, 1978-82; chairperson search com. for judge U.S. Bankruptcy Ct. (we. dist.) Pa., 1987, 95; active Pa. Futures Commn. on Justice in 21st Century, 1995-97. Contbr. articles to profl. jours. Mem. disciplinary hearing com. Supreme Ct. Pa., 1982-88; v.p. Com. for Justice Edn., Pitts., 1983-84; mem. Leadership Pitts., 1987-88. Named one of Ten Outstanding Young Women in Am., 1981. Fellow Am. Bar Found. (Pa. state chair 1991-97); mem. ABA (ho. of dels. 1980-86, 91-97), Am. Law Inst., Am. Coll. Bankruptcy, Pa. Bar Assn. (gov. 1993-95, ho. of dels. 1978—, corp. banking and bus. law sect. coun. 1983-89, treas. 1991-93, v.p. 1993-95, chair-elect 1995-97, chmn. 1997-99, chmn. commn. comml. law 1990-93, co-chair 1995-2002, chair civil rights and responsibilities com. 1986-89, Achievement award 1982, 87, 99, Anne X. Alpern award 1995), Nat. Conf. Bar Pres. (exec. coun. 1993-96), Am. Inns Ct. (Pitts. chpt., counselor 2004—), Nat. Assn. Women Judges, Fed. Judges Assn., Allegheny County Bar Assn. (adminstrv. v.p. 1984-86, 90, chairperson corp. banking and bus. law sect. 1987-89, treas. 1988-90, gov. 1991, pres.-elect 1992, pres. 1993), Internat. Women's Insolvency and Restructuring Confedn. (chair Tri-State Network 1996), Pa. Bar Inst. (dir. 1991-97), Duquesne Club. Roman Catholic. Office: US Dist Judge 5250 US Courthouse and Post Office 700 Grant St Pittsburgh PA 15219 Office Phone: 412-208-7330.

CONTILLO, DEBBIE B., performing arts educator; d. Frank J. and Ethel Contillo; m. Gregory A. Wohar, Oct. 19, 2002; 1 child, Brittany Rene Frankel. BA, Queensboro CC, Queens, 1980. Cert. tchr. NJ. Dance studio owner Just Dance, Princeton, NJ, 1999—; group fitness instr. Princeton Fitness and Wellness, 2004—06. Recipient Ultimate Choreographer award, Beyond the Stars Dance Competition, 2006. Mem.: SAG. Office: Just Dance 4437 Rt 27 Princeton NJ 08540 Office Phone: 609-924-5446. Personal E-mail: dk1695@aol.com.

CONTRADY, ERIN SHAW, music educator; d. William M. and Beverly V. Shaw; m. Ronald James Contrady, Oct. 11, 1987; children: Jason, Peter, Matthew, Andrew, Paul. BA in English and Journalism, SUNY, New Paltz, 1988, BA in Piano and Vocal Performance, 1998; MS in Music Edn., Coll. St. Rose, Albany, NY, 2004. Cert. music tchr. NY. Music tchr., choral dir. St. Mary of the Snow Sch., Saugerties, NY, 1997—99, Kingston Cath. Schs., NY, 1997—99, Kingston City Schs., 1999—. Organizer 9/11 tribute Where Words Fail, Music Speaks, 2001; Cub Scout den leader Boy Scouts Am., Kingston, 1995—98. Mem.: Music Educators Nat. Conf., NY State Sch. Music Assn. Roman Catholic. Avocations: trail biking, singing, knitting, reading, jazz. Office: Frank L Meagher Elem Sch 61 Wynkoop Pl Kingston NY 12401

CONTRERAS, DAWN RACHELLE, performing arts educator; b. Newberg, Oreg., Nov. 8, 1968; d. Donald Earl and Vicki Charlene Allen; m. David Anthony Contreras, Aug. 8, 1992; 1 child, Darren Anthony. BA in Edn., Western Oreg. State Coll., Monmouth, 1990. Tchr. Bend-LaPine Sch. Dist., LaPine, Oreg., 1991—95; dance studio owner All That Jazz Dance Studio, 1993—2004. Recipient Best Choreography award, Access Broadway, 1998. Mem.: PTA (v.p. 2005—06).

CONTRERAS, DEE (DOROTHEA CONTRERAS), municipal official, educator; b. Kansas City, Mo., Nov. 13, 1945; d. Robert MacGregor Hubsch and Dorothea Ann (Bauer) Wilson; m. Michael Raul Contreras, May 1969 (div. Nov. 1979); 1 child, Jason Michael Raul. BA in Anthropology, UCLA, 1967; JD with honors, Thomas Jefferson Sch. Law, 1979. Bar: Calif. 1979. Sr. social worker San Diego County, 1968-80; sr. field rep. Svc. Employees Internat. Union Local 535, San Diego, 1980-88; bus. rep. Stationary Engrs. Local 39, Sacramento, 1988-90; sr. employee rels. rep. City of Sacramento, 1990-95, dir. labor rels., 1995—. Mem. exec. bd. San Diego Imperial County Labor Coun., 1985-88; tchr. labor history U. Calif. Davis Ext., Sacramento, 1989—. Recipient Bread and Roses award Coalition of Labor Union Women, San Diego, 1981, Outstanding Tchr. award U. Calif. Davis Extension, 1993. Mem. Indsl. Rels. Assn. No. Calif. (exec. bd. 1988-94, pres. exec. bd. 1994-96). Democrat. Avocations: reading, writing, scrapbooks, art. Office: City of Sacramento Rm 4133 915 I St Sacramento CA 95814 Business E-Mail: deecon45@aol.com.

CONTRERAS-SWEET, MARIA, bank executive; b. Guadaljara, Mex., Dec. 24, 1955; came to U.S., 1960; d. Rafael Quintero and Maria Guadalupe (Torres) Contreras; m. Raphael Raymond Sweet, Feb. 7, 1981; children—Rafael, Francesca, Antonio. A.S. in Sec. Legal, Mt. San Antonio Coll., 1975; B.S. in Polit. Sci., Calif. State U.-Los Angeles, 1977. Field rep. Calif. State Speaker State Legis., Los Angeles, 1974-75; adminstrv. asst. to Senator Joseph Montoya, Calif. State Senate, Los Angeles, 1975-79; dist. mgr. U.S. Census Bur., US Dept. Commerce, Los Angeles, 1979-80; former dir. pub. affairs 7-Up Bottling Co., Westinghouse Beverage Group, Los Angeles, former sec., Dept. Bus., Transport. & Housing Agy, State of Calif., mng. ptnr, co-founder, FORTIUS Holdings, LLC, chmn., Promerica Bank, 2006-; Bd. Mex.-Am. Opportunity Found., Los Angeles, 1982—, Rossi Youth Found., Los Angeles, 1978—; fund com. mem. E. Los Angeles Little Sisters, 1983; adv. council Hispanic Women's Council, Los Angeles, 1982—; active Industry Environ. Council, Sacramento, Recipient Mother of Yr. award La Clinica Famillar del Barrio, Los Angeles, 1983; Humanitarian award Rossi Youth Found., 1983; Woman of Yr. award Mex.-Am. Opportunity Found., 1983. Mem. Internat. Assn. Bus. Communicators, Calif./Nev. Soft Drink Assn., RecyCal (fin. chair.). Democrat. Roman Catholic. Office: FORTIUS Holdings LLC 13191 Crossroads Pkwy N Ste 565 City Of Industry CA 91746*

CONVERSE, SANDRA, city finance director, financial planner; b. Galion, Ohio, July 23, 1949; d. Mervin E. Harper and Phyllis R. Bowden (dec.); m. Robert W. Marsh, June 19, 2001; children: Kimberly Spencer, Kelly Converse. Payroll clk. Neighborhood Youth Corps., Mansfield, Ohio, 1977-78; asst. fin. dir. Mansfield City, 1978-93, fin. dir., 1993—. Charter commn. mem. City of Mansfield, 1988. Mem. NAFE, La. Edn. Assn., Govt. Fin. Officers Assn. U.S. and Can., Mcpl. Treas. Assn. U.S. and Can., Nat. Assn. Tax Preparers, Ohio Govt. Fin. Officers Assn., Mcpl. Fin. Officers Assn. Ohio (at-large bd. mem.). Democrat. Pentecostal. Avocations: reading, learning, sewing, painting. Office: City of Mansfield 30 N Diamond St Mansfield OH 44902-1738 Home: 155 W Prospect St Mansfield OH 44907-1305 Office Phone: 419-755-9775. E-mail: sconverse@CI.mansfield.oh.us.

CONVERTINO, CHARLENE D., language educator; b. Scranton, Pa., Aug. 04; d. Henry Jackewicz and Alberta; m. Joseph Convertino, Nov. 24. BA, Sacred Heart U., 1977; MS, So. Conn., 1981; 6th Yr. in Adminstrn. and Leadership, U. Bridgeport, 2000. Tchr. Hall Brooke, Westport, Conn., 1977—78; tchr. dept. chmn. Milford Pub. Schools, Conn., 1978—. Adv. Spanish Nat. Honor Soc. and Spanish Club, Milford; adult edn. tchr. Milford Summer Sch. Named Tchr. of Yr., Foran HS, 2002; recipient Spanish award, 1978; Multi grant, State of Conn., Commn for the Arts, 2000—, Milford Mini grants, 2001—06. Mem.: ASCD, Am. Coun. Tchrs. Spanish and Portugese, Am. Coun. Tchrs. of Fgn. Lang., Conn. Coun. Lang. Tchrs. (Pegasus award 1998, 2000), Phj Kappa Phi. Avocations: travel, cooking, reading. Office: Joseph A Foran 80 Foran Rd Milford CT 06460 Business E-Mail: cconvertino@milforded.org.

CONWAY, ANNE MARIE, psychologist, social worker; d. John Joseph and Judith Anne Conway. BA in Psychology and Sociology, Merrimack Coll., North Andover, Mass., 1990; MA in Psychology, Cath. U., Washington, 1992; MSW, U. Mich., Ann Arbor, 1998, MS in Devel. Psychology, 2001, PhD in Devel. Psychology and Social Work, 2005. Mental health counselor Human Svc. Options, Quincy, 1988—90; preschool tchr. Wesley Childcare Ctr., Boston, 1988—90; rsch. asst. psychology Cath. U., Washington, 1990—92; psychologist NIMH, Bethesda, Md., 1992—97; child psychiat. specialist Children's Nat. Med. Ctr., Washington, 1994—97; grad. rsch. asst. U. Mich., Ann Arbor, 1997—2002; clin. social worker Devel. Centers, Detroit, 1998—99; rsch. and tng. coord. Children's Ctrs. U. Mich., Ann Arbor, 2002—03; grad. student instr. U. Mich., 2004; postdoctoral rsch. fellow Pa. State U., University Park, 2004—. Dept. faculty assoc. U. Mich., 1999—2000; exec. com. mem. Children's Ctr. U. Mich., 2002—03; ad hoc reviewer Social Devel., Arlington, Va., 2005—06, Emotion, N.Y.C., 2006—; reviewer childhood: emotional processes and personality Soc. for Rsch. Child Devel., Ann Arbor, 2006—. Contbr. articles to profl. jours. Vol. HOME, Orland, Maine, 1987—88; union mem. Am. Fedn. Tchrs., Washington, 1997—2004, Grad. Student Orgn., Ann Arbor, 1997—2004. Recipient Rackham Travel awards, Grad. Sch. U. Mich., 1999—2000, Internat. Inst. Travel award, U. Mich., 2000, Pub. Svc. award, Grad. Sch. U. Mich., 2002, Nat. Rsch. Svc. award, NIMH, 2004—06, Nat. Inst. Child Health & Human Devel., 2006—; fellow, U. Mich., 1999—2000, Grad. Sch. U. Mich., 2005; grantee, Positive Psychology Orgn., 2002, Psychology Dept. U. Mich., 2003, Grad. Sch. U. Mich., 2003; scholar, Merrimack Coll., 1988; Margaret Towsely scholar, Ctr. Edn. Women U. Mich., 2000. Mem.: APA, World Assn. Infant Mental Health, Soc. Social Work and Rsch., Internat. Soc. Infant Studies, Soc. Rsch. Child Devel., Assn. Psychol. Sci., NY Acad. Scis. Office: Pa State U 820 N University Dr University Park PA 16802 Office Phone: 814-863-5664. E-mail: amc21@psu.edu.

CONWAY, CONNIE ANNE See HELLYER, CONSTANCE

CONWAY, EVELYN ATKINSON, accountant, financial analyst; b. Goose Creek, Tex., Aug. 14, 1922; d. George Henry and Sadie Ray (Bouldin) Atkinson; m. Lucian Gideon Conway, Nov. 2, 1945; children: Lucian Gideon Conway Jr., Karen Elizabeth Conway, Rebecca Annette Conway, Terri Ruth Conway, Jerry Andrew Conway, Priscilla Janice Conway. BS in Acctg., La. Tech. U., 1943; postgrad., New Orleans Bapt. Theol. Sem., 1949—51. Sr. acct. McGuire & Mazur CPAs, Houston, 1943—45; math. tchr. Enterprise Sch., Summit, Miss., 1953—54; sr. ptnr. Conley & Conway, Coushatta, La., 1955—56; office mgr. Annuity Bd. Rep. SBC, Alexandria, La., 1959—83; regional mgr., pers. fin. analyst Primerica Life & PFS Investments, Inc., Alexandria, La., 1984—. Auditor The Bapt. Message, Alexandria, 1962—64. Emergency evacuation officer Civil Def., Coushatta, 1955—57; treas. Dist. 8 La. Bapt. Missions, Coushatta, 1955—56. Named Hometown All Am., Alexandria Daily Town Talk, 1995. Republican. Baptist. Avocations: sewing, music. Home: 118 Pearce Rd Pineville LA 71360

CONWAY, JAIME J., science educator; d. Edwin O. and Connie J. Eades; m. Garrett M. Conway, June 20, 1998; children: Trevor Vincent, Jered Aiden. BS, Ea. Ill. U., Charleston, 1998. Lic. Ill., 1998. Paraprofl. Belleville (Ill.) Pub. Sch., 1999—2000, 7th grade sci. tchr., 2000—. Jr. high sunday sch. tchr. Signal Hill Luth. Ch., Belleville, 2004—06. Office Phone: 618-233-5377.

CONWAY, LYNN, computer scientist, electrical engineer, educator; b. Mt. Vernon, N.Y., Jan. 2, 1938; BS, Columbia U., 1962, MSEE, 1963; D (hon.), Trinity Coll., 1997. Rsch. staff IBM Corp., Yorktown Heights, NY, 1964-68; sr. staff engr. Memorex Corp., Santa Clara, Calif., 1969-73; rsch. staff Xerox Corp., Palo Alto, Calif., 1973-78, rsch. fellow, mgr. VLSI systems area, 1978-82, rsch. fellow, mgr. knowledge systems area, 1982-83; asst. dir. for strategic computing Def. Advanced Research Projects Agy., Arlington, Va., 1983-85; prof. elec. engrng. and computer sci., assoc. dean U. Mich. Coll. Engrng., Ann Arbor, Mich., 1985—98, prof. emerita elec. engrng. and computer sci., 1999—. Vis. assoc. prof. elec. engrng. and computer sci. MIT, Cambridge, Mass., 1978-79; sci. adv. bd. USAF, 1987-90. Co-author: textbook Introduction to VLSI Systems, 1980; contbr. articles to profl. jours.; patentee in field. Mem. coun. Govt.-Univ.-Industry Rsch. Roundtable, 1993-98; mem. corp. Charles Stark Draper Lab., 1993—; mem. bd. visitors USAF Acad., 1996-2000, presdl. appt.; mem. Air Force Sci. and Tech. Bd., Nat. Acads., 2000—. Recipient Ann. Achievement award Electronics mag., 1981, Harold Pender award U. Pa., 1984, Wetherill Medal Franklin Inst., 1985, Sec. of Def. Meritorious Civilian Svc. award, 1985; named to Electronic Design Hall of Fame, 2002. Fellow IEEE; mem. NAE, AAAS (named Engr. of Yr. 2005), Soc. Women Engrs. (Ann. Achievement award 1990), Assn. Computing Machinery. Avocations: canoeing, natural landscaping, travel. Office: U Mich 3640 CSE Bldg Ann Arbor MI 48109 Business E-Mail: conway@umich.edu.

CONWAY, MARY MARGARET, social studies educator; b. Omaha, Feb. 15, 1955; d. Ccharles Emmanuel and Cecelia Anne (Kraft) Vanderbur; m. Timothy Patrick Conway, Nov. 23, 1983; children: Michaela Anne, Timothy John. BA, Creighton U., Omaha, 1977. Tchr. English Papillion-LaVista High Sch., Nebr., 1977—80, Bartlett Wheeler Ctr. High Sch., 1980—81, Tri-Ctr. High Sch., Ncola, Iowa, 1981—96; tchr. English, social studies Crete Jr./Sr. High Sch., Nebr., 1996—. Coach track, 1978—2005; coach volleyball, 1989—2002; presenter in field. Mem. PEO, 1973—2006; pres. Prins. Adv. Coun., Ncola, 1990—96. Named Coach Yr., ICA, Des Moines, 1992, Tchr. Yr., DAR, Lincoln, Nebr., 2002. Mem.: NEA, Nebr. Coaches Assn., Alpha Sigma Nu. Avocations: reading, travel. Home: 395 County Rd 2100 Crete NE 68333 Office: Crete High Sch 1500 E 15th St Crete NE 68333

CONWAY, TERESA J., secondary school educator; b. Cin., Oct. 14, 1953; d. Clarence Joseph Conway and Grace Katherine Romohr. MEd, U. Cin., 1983; MA, Xavier U., 1988. Cert. tchr. Ohio. Adminstrv. asst. C.E. Healy Co., Cin., 1974—76; tchr. Indiana Hill Schs., Cin., 1979—80; English tchr. West Clermont Sch./Amelia HS, Batavia, Ohio, 1980—. Mem.: SW Ohio Edn. Assn. (mem. exec. com. 2000—05), West Clermont Edn. Assn. (pres. 1984—2000, chmn. grievance com. 2000—), Delta Kappa Gamma. Democrat. Methodist. Avocations: gardening, boating, motorcycling.

CONWAY-LANGGUTH, REBECCA JOAN, dance instructor, dance school owner; b. Altoona, Pa., Dec. 4, 1979; d. Paul Robert and Joan Anita Conway; m. Matthew Patrick Langguth, Aug. 6, 2005. BA in Dance, Slippery Rock U., Pa., 2002. Owner Blair Dance Acad., Altoona, Pa., 2002—; artistic dir. Blair Dance Co., Altoona, Pa., 2002—. Office Phone: 814-943-7174. Business E-Mail: becky@blairdanceacademy.com.

CONWAY-WELCH, COLLEEN, dean, nurse midwife; b. Monticello, Iowa, Apr. 26, 1944; d. John Andrew and Lorraine (Digman) Conway; m. Ted Houston Welch, Mar. 31, 1985. BSN, Georgetown U., 1965; CNM, Catholic Maternity Inst., 1969; MSN, Catholic U., Washington, 1969; PhD, NYU, 1973. Staff nurse Georgetown U. Hosp., Washington, 1965; staff nurse labor & delivery Queens Med. Ctr., Honolulu, 1966; nurse cons. U. So. Calif. Med. Ctr., L.A., 1967; staff assoc. Nat. League Nursing, N.Y.C., 1969-70; asst. prof. Downstate Med. Ctr., Bklyn., 1970-74, Georgetown U., 1974-76, assoc. dean, 1975-76; assoc. prof. George Mason U., Fairfax, Va., 1976-78, Calif. State U., Long Beach, 1978-80; prof. nursing U. Colo., Denver, 1980-84; dean Vanderbilt Sch. Nursing, Nashville, 1984—. Mem. Presdl. Commn. on HIV Epidemic, Washington, 1988, adv. coun. NIH Nat. Ctr. Nursing Rsch., Washington, 1989-93, bd. trustees Healthcare Leadership Coun., Washington, 1990-; chair nursing leadership coun. Inst. Healthcare Improvement, 1992; bd. dirs. Diversicare, Franklin, Tenn., Nat. League Nursing Community Health Accreditation, N.Y.C., Commonwealth Fund Nurse Exch. Fellowship Program, N.Y.C. Contbr. articles to profl. jours. Bd. govs. United Way, Middle, Tenn., 1989; active Mayor's Task Force for Substance Abuse, 1990, JFK Adv. Com. on Arts, Washington, 1991, Jr. League, 1973. Recipient Dempsey Humanitarism award St. Clare's Hosp. AIDS Ctr., 1989; commencement speaker, Columbia Sch. Nursing, 1991. Fellow Am. Acad. Nursing; mem. Soc. Advancement Women's Health Rsch. (bd. dirs. 1991—), Rotary Club, Cosmos Club, Sigma Theta Tau (bd. dirs. 1968—). Avocations: skiing, scuba diving, hiking, reading. Home: 109 Lynnwood Ter Nashville TN 37205-2911 Office: Vanderbilt U Sch Nursing 111 Godchaux 461 21st Ave S Nashville TN 37240-1104*

CONWELL, ESTHER MARLY, physicist, researcher; b. N.Y.C., May 23, 1922; d. Charles and Ida (Korn) C.; m. Abraham A. Rothberg, Sept. 30, 1945; 1 son, Lewis J. BA, Bklyn. Coll., 1942, DSc, 1992; MS, U. Rochester, N.Y., 1945; PhD, U. Chgo., 1948. Lectr. Bklyn. Coll., 1946-51; mem. tech. staff Bell Tel. Labs., 1951-52; physicist GTE Labs., Bayside, NY, 1952-61, mgr. physics dept., 1961-72; vis. prof. U. Paris, 1962-63; Abby Rockefeller Mauze prof. MIT, Cambridge, 1972; prin. scientist Xerox Corp., Webster, NY, 1972-80, rsch. fellow, 1981-98. Adj. prof. U. Rochester, 1990—2001, prof., 2001—; cons., mem. adv. com. engrng. NSF, 1978—81. Author: High Field Transport in Semiconductors, 1967, also rsch. papers; mem. editl. bd. Jour. Applied Physics, Proc. of IEEE, patentee in field. Fellow IEEE (Edison medal 1997), Am. Phys. Soc. (sec.-treas. divsn. condensed matter physics 1977-82); mem. AAAS, NAS, NAE, Soc. Women Engrs. (Achievement award 1960, Susan B. Anthony Lifetime Achievement award 2006). Office: U Rochester Dept Chemistry and Physics Rochester NY 14627 Business E-Mail: conwell@chem.rochester.edu.

CONWELL, RUTH INGRID, assistant principal, educator; b. Hanover, N.H., May 27, 1954; d. Carl Einar and Kathryn Elizabeth Carlson; m. Scott Davidson Conwell, July 20; children: Tyson Greenwood, Tara Greenwood, Meghan, Jason. BS, Ann Hurst Coll., Conn., 1976; MEd, Plymouth State Coll., N.H., 1998, CAGS, 2003. Cert. suprintendant, prin., math. 7-12 N.H. Tchr. Cardigan N.H. Sch., Canaan, 1988—99; math. tchr., dept. chair Hillsboro Deering HS, NH, 1999—2005; asst. prin. Oxbow HS, Bradford, Vt., 2005—06. Home: 24 Reagan Rd Canaan NH 03741-7293

CONWILL, LINDA JILL, enterostomal therapist; b. Wauwautosa, Wis., June 12, 1949; d. Daniel Frederick and Georgia (Sanders) Bishop; m. Michael G. Conwill, Mar. 26, 1983. Diploma in nursing, St. Luke's Hosp. Sch. Nursing, Racine, Wis., 1970; student, Abbott Northwestern Sch. Enter, Mpls., 1981; BSN, Corpus Christi State U., 1987, MSN, 1992. RN Cert. wound/ostomy nurse. Charge nurse St. Catherine's Hosp., Kenosha, Wis., 1970-82; asst. dir. nurses Home Health, Inc., Kenosha, 1982-83; enterostomal therapist Spohn Hosp., Corpus Christi, Tex., 1983—. Mem. Wound, Ostomy and Continence Nurses Soc., Sigma Theta Tau. Home: 601 Monette Dr Corpus Christi TX 78412-3024 Office: Christus Spohn Hosp-Shoreline 600 Elizabeth St Corpus Christi TX 78404-2235 E-mail: lconwill@infionline.net, jill.conwill@christushealth.org.

CONYERS, JEAN LOUISE, chamber of commerce executive; b. Memphis, Nov. 10, 1932; d. Marshall Daniel and Jeffie (Ledbetter) Farris; m. James E. Conyers, June 4, 1956 (div.); children: Judith, James Jr., Jennifer. BA, LeMoyne Coll., 1956; MBA, Atlanta U., 1967. Exec. sec. Dept. Zoology, Wash. State U., Pullman, 1958-62, Sch. Bus., Atlanta U., 1965-68; dep. dir., planner Community Action Agy, Terre Haute, Ind., 1968-78, exec. dir., 1978-79; sr. assoc. exec. United Way of Genesee/Lapeer, Flint, Mich., 1980-82; pres., chief exec. officer Conyers & Assocs., Flint, 1982-86, Met. C. of C., Flint, 1986—, Ultimate Learning Systems, Inc., Flint, 1990—. Program coord. Greater Flint OIC, 1983-85. Bd. dirs. Urban Coalition, Flint, 1988—, Dort-Oak-Pk. Neighborhood Ho., Flint, 1982—. Recipient Cmty. Svc. award Negro Bus. and Profl. Women, Terre Haute, 1977, Supportive Svcs. award Top Ladies of Distinction, Flint, 1989, Black Caucus Found. of Mich.'s Cmty. Svc. award, 1994, Nat. Negro Bus. and Profl. Women's Club Sojourner Truth award, 1994; named Woman of Distinction for contbns. to minority bus. U. Mich., Flint, Mott Coll., Mayor of Flint, Mich. legis., Mich. Dept. of Labor, 1992; enshrined Zeta Phi Beta Hall of Fame, Flint, 1988. Mem. Kiwanis, Zonta Club of Flint II, Alpha Kappa Alpha (Outstanding Grad. Soror of Great Lakes Region 1992). Avocations: reading, travel. Office: 400 N Saginaw St Ste 101A Flint MI 48502-2045 E-mail: metro@tir.com.

COOEY, KATHLEEN MARIE, mathematics educator; b. Garfield Heights, Ohio, Jan. 31, 1975; d. Bruce and Judith Cooey. BS, Boston U., 1997. Cert. tchr. secondary math. Ohio, 2000. Tchr. math. Robinson Secondary, Fairfax, Va., 1997—2000, West Geauga H.S., Chesterland, Ohio, 2000—. Recipient Tchr. of Month, West Geauga Local Schs., 2004. Independent. Avocations: baseball, travel. Office: West Geauga HS 13403 Chillicothe Rd Chesterland OH 44026

COOGAN, MELINDA ANN STRANK, biology professor, chemistry professor; b. Davenport, Iowa, Mar. 29, 1955; d. Gale Benjamin and Margie Delene (Admire) Strank; children: James Benjamin, Jessica Ann. AA, Stephens Coll., Columbia, Mo., 1975; BS, E. Carolina U., Greenville, N.C., 1978; MS, Western Ill. U., 2004. Biology and phys. sci. educator York (Pa.) Catholic H.S., 1989-90; sci. advisor Bettendorf (Iowa) Children's Mus., 1993; gifted, chemistry and physics educator St. Katherine' Coll. Prep. Sch., Bettendorf, 1994; biology educator Lewisville (Tex.) H.S., 1996-99, chemistry educator, 1996-99; ALS rsch. asst. U. Tex. Southwestern Med. Ctr., Dallas, 1998; chemistry, biology and human anatomy educator Milford HS, Ill., 2000—04; rsch. asst., PhD candidate U. No. Tex., Dept. Environ. Scis., Tex., 2004—. Violinist Augustana Symphony Orch., Rock Island, Ill., 1993-94; pres. bd. dirs. Flower Mound (Tex.) Cmty. Orch., 1994-95; founder, instr. Northlakes Violin Acad., Flower Mound, 1994-99; violinist Waterforde Women's String Ensemble, Lewisville, 1995-98, Clinton Symphony, 1999-2001, Country Theater, Cissna Park, Ill., 2002-2004; bd. dirs. Family Mus. Art and Sci., Bettendorf, 2000-01. student mentor, Earthwatch Prog., We. Ill. U. 2003. Student mentor Earthwatch, 2003. Mem. Roanoke Art Mus. (docent 1983-86), Jr. Bd. of Quad City Symphony (chair promotion 1987-88), Jr. Svc. League Moline (Ill.) (chair Riverfest 1987-88), Jr. League of York (Pa.) (chair thrift shop spl. sales 1989-92), Jr. League of Quad Cities (nom./placement 1993-94), Jr. League of Dallas (sustaining 1995-96), Gamma Beta Phi, Chi Beta Phi, Phi Kappa Phi. Democrat. Roman Catholic. Home: 2100 Preston Pl Denton TX 76209 E-mail: mcoogan@verizon.net.

COOK, ALLYSON LEA, secondary school educator; b. Torrance, Calif., Nov. 27, 1963; d. Brian King and Karen Janelle Sobetzer; m. Douglas Ian Cook; children: Sarah Janelle, Benjamin Ulysses-King. BA, San Diego State U., 1986; MEd, Chapman U., 2006. Cert. profl. clear single subject tchr. Calif. Educator LA Unified Schs., 1989—95; educator, Title 1 coord. West Valley HS, Hemet, Calif., 1995—. Asst. leader Girl Scouts Am., Hemet, 2003—05. Office: West Valley HS 3401 Mustang Way Hemet CA 92545 Office Phone: 951-765-1600. Office Fax: 951-765-1607. Personal E-mail: allycookie@hotmail.com. E-mail: acook@hemetusd.k12.ca.us.

COOK, ANDA SUNA, civil rights advocate; b. Riga, Latvia, Mar. 15, 1935; came to U.S., 1952. d. Janis Suna and Erna Alexandra (Kletnieks) Sirmais; m. William E. Cook, May 27, 1961; children: Lisa Inara Cook, Inta Marie Mitterbach, John William. Student, Augustana Coll., Sioux Falls, S.D., 1954-55, Cleve. State U., 1970-85; MS, Case Western Res. U., 1989. Lic. real estate agt. With Cuyahoga Plan of Ohio, Inc., Cleve., 1976-91, dir. resource devel., 1988-91; exec. dir. Living in Cleve. Ctr., 1992—2000; v.p. regional div. U.S. Orgn. Internat. Trade, Inc., Cleve., 1989—. Pres. ASC Cons.-Orgn. Devel., Cleve., 1988; presenter World Latvian Sci. Congress, Riga, 1991. Writer 60 Years of League of Women Voters, 1980; writer, prodr. Vol. Affirmative Mktg. Agreement in Action, 1989, music rev., Laiks. Bd. dirs. Dept. Human Svcs., Cuyahoga County, 1984-93; trustee Friends of Cleve. Met. Housing Authority, 1986-92, Citizens League, Cleve., 1989-95, Housing Advocates, 1996—; pres. Louisa May Alcott Elem. Sch. PTA, Cleve., 1974-76, LWV, Cleve., 1975-77, Tyrian, Inc., 2006—; mem. adv. bd. Cleve. Pub. Radio, 1999-2005; foreman Grand Jury, Cuyahoga County, 2998. Recipient Dedicated Svc. award The Cuyahoga Plan of Ohio, Cleve., 1985, Cleve. Leadership award United Way, 1976, Fair Housing award Cleve. Area Bd. Realtors, 1993, E.R. Gerson Leadership in Social Justice award Greater Cleve. Cmty. Shares, 2000. Mem. Am. Soc. Tng. and Devel. Democrat. Lutheran. Avocations: reading, writing, gardening, promoter and appreciator of arts, travel. Home: 9801 Lake Ave Cleveland OH 44102-1230 Office: US Orgn Internat Trade Inc 9801 Lake Ave 4d Cleveland OH 44102 Office Phone: 216-651-0486. E-mail: AndanBill@aol.com.

COOK, ANN JENNALIE, literature educator, cultural organization administrator; b. Wewoka, Okla., Oct. 19, 1934; d. Arthur Holly and Bertha Mable (Stafford) C.; children: Lee Ann Merrick, Amy Ceil Leonard; m. Gerald George Calhoun, Apr. 1994. BA, U. Okla., 1956, MA, 1959; PhD, Vanderbilt U., 1972. Instr. English U. Okla., 1956-57; tchr. English NC, 1958—61, Conn., 1958—61; instr. So. Conn. State Coll., 1962-64; asst. prof. U. SC, 1972—74; adj. asst. prof. Vanderbilt U., Nashville, 1977-82, assoc. prof., 1982-89, prof., 1990-98, prof. emerita, 1999—. Exec. sec. Shakespeare Assn. Am., 1975-87; chmn. Internat. Shakespeare Assn., 1988-96, v.p. 1996—. Author: Privileged Playgoers of Shakespeare's London, 1981, Making a Match: Courtship in Shakespeare and His Society, 1991; assoc. editor Shakespeare Studies, 1973-80; contbr. articles to profl. jours. Trustee Folger Shakespeare Libr., 1985—90, Shakespeare Birthplace Trust (life), Friends of the Shakespeare Birthplace Trust, Nashville Symphony, 2000—06, Univ. Sch. Nashvillle, 2000—04, Nashville Opera Guild, 2000—03, Nashville Shakespeare Festival, 2002—, Shakespeare League of Nashville; pres. English-Speaking Union, 2003—, nat. bd. dirs., 2004—. Recipient Letseizer award, 1956, Nat. Leadership award Delta Delta Delta, 1956; Danforth fellow, 1968-72, Folger summer fellow, 1973, Donelson fellow, 1974-75, fellow Rockefeller Found., 1984, Guggenheim Found., 1984-85; grantee Folger seminar NEH, 1992-93. Mem. MLA, AAUP, Shakespeare Assn. Am., Shakespeare Inst., German Shakespeare Soc., Renaissance Soc. Am. (bd. dirs.), Vanderbilt Libr. Heard Soc. (pres. 2004-06), Phi Beta Kappa. Episcopalian. Office: Vanderbilt U Dept English Nashville TN 37235 Home: 6666 Brookmont Terr Apt 207 Nashville TN 37205 Office Phone: 615-322-2541. Personal E-mail: gercalhoun@aol.com.

COOK, BETH MARIE, volunteer, poet; b. Electra, Tex., Jan. 4, 1933; d. Charles Bolivar Allen and Ida Marie (Nelson) Burton; m. William H. Cook, May 30, 1955 (div. Nov. 1981); children: David M., Dianne M. Gleason. Student, Rockmont Coll., 1951-54; BA, Antioch U. West, 1981. County coord. office econ. opportunity Upper Arkansas Coun., Salida, Colo., 1974-76; dir. area agy. on aging Upper Arkansas Coun./Dept. Social Svcs., State of Colo., 1976-80; specialist community devel. Mountain Plains Congress Sr. Orgns., Denver, 1980-82; sr. adminstrv. asst. Digital Rsch. Inc., Monterey, Calif., 1983-85, asst. to pres., 1985-87, retail rep., 1987-88; co-owner, ptnr. Scotia Gallery, Monterey, 1983-86; COO MiniSoft, Inc., Phoenix, 1988-89; property mgr. Parklane Arms Apts., 1989-92; exec. asst. Ft. Collins (Colo.) Housing Authority, 1989-92, occupancy specialist, 1992-95; vol. Peace Corps, Kingdom of Tonga, 1995-97, U.S. Dept. Commerce Census Bur., 1998-2000, 2002—. Hostess Sr. Sound-Off show, Sta. KVRH-AM/FM, Salida, 1978-80; cons. Devel. Assocs. Inc., Denver, 1982. Author: (poem) Jessie, 1989-90. Coord. crisis intervention line Chaffee County Comty. Crisis Ctr., Salida, 1976-80; committeewoman Chaffee County Dem. Ctrl. Com., Salida, 1979-80; speaker, program com. Colo. Gov.'s Conf on Aging, Denver, 1980; docent Lincoln Ctr.; vol. food distbn. SHARE; youth Bible tchr., deacon Westminster Presbyn. Ch.; mem. bd. dirs. Fort Collins Housing Corp., Neighbor to Neighbor. Recipient Human Devel. Svc. award HHS, 1980, Golden Poet award, 1989; named Woman of Yr. Chaffee County Bus. and Profl. Women's Club, 1978. Mem. Am. Assn. Ret. Persons, Nat. Mus. Women in Arts. Presbyterian. Avocations: art, study of ancient mexican civilizations, travel.

COOK, BLANCHE WIESEN, historian, educator, journalist; b. NYC, Apr. 20, 1941; d. David Theodore and Sadonia (Ecker) Wiesen. BA, Hunter Coll., 1962; MA, Johns Hopkins U., 1964, PhD, 1970; DHL (hon.), Russell Sage Coll., 1998. Instr. Hampton Inst., Va., 1963; instr. Stern Coll. for Women, Yeshiva U., N.Y.C., 1964-67; prof. history John Jay Coll., Grad. Faculty CUNY, 1968—, disting. prof., 1995—. Prodr., broadcaster program stas. WBAI and WKPFK Radio Pacifica, N.Y.C. and L.A., 1978—; prodr.-host Jewish Women in Am., CUNY-TV, 2004-05; vis. prof. UCLA, 1982-83; syndicated journalist; bd. dirs. Women's Fgn. Policy Adv. Coun., v.p., co-chair Fund for Open Info. and Accountability; mem. freedom to write com. PEN; elected univ.-wide union officer PSC-CUNY, 2000. Author: Crystal Eastman on Women and Revolution, 1978, Declassified Eisenhower, 1981 (N.Y. Times Notable Book), Biography of Eleanor Roosevelt, vol. 1, 1992 (L.A. Times Book award, N.Y. Times Notable Book, Lambda Lit. prize for biography), vol. 2, 1999, ER I, ER II (Best Books), Christian Sci. Monitor, 1999 (Notable Book award 1999); sr. editor: The Garland Library of War and Peace, 360 vols., 1970-80, Bella Abzug in Jewish Women's Encyclopedia, 1997; contbr. articles to various publs. Appointed to com. on documents for fgn. rels. U.S. Dept. State, 1986-90. Named Scholar of the Yr. NY Coun. Humanities, 1996, Alumna of Yr. Hunter Coll. Hall of Fame, 1999; recipient Breakthrough award Women, Men and Media, 1992, Feminist of Yr. award Feminist Majority Found., 1992, Lambda Lit. Pioneer award, 2005; faculty fellow CUNY, 1978, 84, 91. Mem. Orgn. Am. Historians (co-chair freedom of info. com.), Am. Hist. Assn. (v.p. for rsch. 1991-94), Coordinating Com., Women in Hist. Profession (pres. N.Y.C. chpt. 1969-71), Berkshire Women Historians, Soc. Historians Am. Fgn. Rels., Conf. on Peace Rsch. in History (bd. dirs., v.p.), Peace History Soc. Women's Internat. League for Peace and Freedom, Pi Sigma Alpha, Phi Alpha Theta. Office: CUNY John Jay Coll Dept History 445 W 59th St New York NY 10019-1104 Office Phone: 212-237-8827.

COOK, C. COLLEEN, librarian, dean; BA, MLS, U. Tex.; MA, Tex. A&M U., PhD Higher Edn. Adminstrn. Serials cataloger Tex. A&M Univ. Librs., assoc. dean adminstrn. tech. svcs., 1993, exec. assoc. dean, 1996—2003, interim dean, 2003—04, dean, 2004—. Co-prin. investagator LibQUAL+ project; lectr. in field. Mem. editl. adv. bd. Performance measurement and metrics; contbr. articles to profl. jours. Recipient Disting. Librarianship Award, Tex. A&M U. Assn. of Former Students, 1992. Mem.: ALA, Am. Ednl. Rsch. Assn., Tex. Libr. Assn. Office: Tex A&M U Librs College Station TX 77843-5000 Office Phone: 979-845-5741.*

COOK, CAMILLE WRIGHT, retired law educator; b. Tuscaloosa, Ala. d. Reuben Hall and Camille Tunstall (Searcy) Wright; children: Sydney, Reuben, Cade, Camille. AB, U. Ala., 1945, JD, 1948. Bar: Ala. 1948. Asst. prof. law, Law Sch. Auburn (Ala.) U., 1968; mem. faculty Sch. Law U. Ala., 1968-93, assoc. dean, dir. continuing legal edn., prof. law, Law Sch., 1975-93, asst. acad. v.p., 1984-85; prof. emeritus, 1993—. Bd. dirs. U. Ala. Law Sch. Found., Am/South. Mem. Smithsonian Coun., Washington, 1972-78, Ala. Air Pollution Commn., 1971-81; vestry Christ Episcopal Ch. Recipient outstanding commitment to tchg. award U. Ala., 1990, disting. alumni award, 1996, Algernon Sydney Sullivan award, 1999. Fellow Am. Bar Found., Ala. Bar Assn. (award merit 1973); mem. ABA (Rawles Spl. Merit award 1983), Farrah Law Soc. (trustee 1972—, disting. alumnae award 1992), Am. law Inst. (coun., Rawles Spl. Merit award 1983). Episcopalian. Home: 32 Ridgeland Tuscaloosa AL 35406-1607 Personal E-mail: camillewcook1@comcast.net.

COOK, CHARLENE LAMAR, elementary school educator, music educator; b. Rockwood, Tenn., June 1, 1958; d. Harold Lamar Potts and Elizabeth Ann Copenhaver-Potts; m. Howard Wayne Cook, June 24, 1989; 1 child, Monica Elizabeth. MusB, Mid. Tenn. State U., 1980; MEd in Ednl. Leadership, Trevecca Nazarene U., 2001. Asst. dir. band Dade County Schs., Trenton, Ga., 1980—82, Cleve. (Tenn.) Jr./Sr. H.S., 1982—89, Cheatham County H.S., Ashland City, Tenn., 1991—92; music specialist elem. sch. Clarksville (Tenn.) Montgomery County Schs., 1992—99, Hamilton County Schs., Chattanooga, 1999—. Troop leader Girl Scouts USA, Chattanooga, 2002—. Mem.: NEA, Music Educator's Nat. Conf., American Orff-Schulwerk Assn., Tenn. Music Edn. Assn. (mem. coun. 2001—), East Tenn. Elem. Music Edn. Assn. (pres. 2001—). Meth. Avocations: quilting, handbells. Office: McBrien Elem Sch 1501 Tombros Ave Chattanooga TN 37412

COOK, CHARLOTTE C., psychologist; b. Lowndesville, SC, June 20, 1943; d. William Curtis and Marion Juanita Cook. BA, Wesleyan Coll., 1964; MS, Univ. Ga.-Athens, 1965; PhD, Calif. Sch. Profl. Psychology, 1971. Asst. prof. Kennesau Coll., Marietta, Ga., 1969—70, 1971; vis. prof. Stanislau State Coll., Turlock, 1971—72; chief psychologist Napa County Mental Health Clin., Napa, Calif., 1972—73; cons. psychologist Bibb County Mental Health Clin., Macon, Ga., 1974—78; pvt. practice self employed, Macon, Ga., 1978—. Active supporter Rep. Party. Mem.: APA, Am. Assn. of Christian Counselors, Ga. Psychol. Assn., Order of Eastern Star (worthy matron). Home: 5389 Riverside Dr Rt32 Macon GA 31210

COOK, DEBORAH L., federal judge, former state supreme court justice; b. Pittsburgh, Feb. 8, 1952; BA in English, U. Akron, 1974, JD, 1978, LLD (hon.), 1996. Ptnr. Roderick & Linton, Akron, 1976-91; judge 9th dist. Ohio Ct. Appeals, 1991-94; justice Ohio Supreme Ct., 1995—2003; judge U.S. Court of Appeals, 6th cir., Cincinnati, Ohio, 2003—. Bd. trustees Summit County United Way, Vol. Ctr., Stan Hywet Hall and Gardens, Akron Sch. Law, Coll. Scholars, Inc.; bd. dirs. Women's Network; vol. Mobile Meals, Safe Landing Shelter. Named Woman of Yr., Women's Network, 1991. Fellow Am. Bar Found.; mem. Omicron Delta Kappa, Delta Gamma (pres., Nat. Shield award). Office: 532 Potter Stewart US Courthouse 100 E Fifth St Cincinnati OH 45202-3988*

COOK, DORIS ADELE, artist; b. Ligonier, Pa., Apr. 16, 1930; d. William Issac and Adele Henrietta (Siebert) Routch; m. David Glen Eckholm, Feb. 14, 1956 (div. 1969); 1 child, Melissa Marie Schoenberg; m. George E. Cook, Apr. 13, 1973 (dec. 1992). AB, U. Houston. Sec. to dean of men Clarion (Pa.) State Tchr. Coll., 1948-49; sec. dean of edn. U. Houston, 1951-57; sec., v.p. Napko Corp., Houston, 1959-62; adminstrv. sec. Ben Taub Hosp., Houston, 1968-73; victim/witness coord Cherokee County Dist. Atty., Rusk, Tex., 1992—99; cmty. edn. coord. Hospice of Ea. Tex., 2000—. Bd. child advocacy ctr. Crisis Ctr., Cherokee, Jacksonville, 1996—; lay rep., libr. Rusk Libr., 1994—; east Tex. handweaver guild, Nacogdocher, Tex., 1985-92; coord. Anderson County Hospice of East Tex., 2002—. Sgt. USAF, 1949—51. Mem. Tyler Art League, Nat. Women's Mus., Cherokee County Art League (pres., sec., treas.). Home: RR 1 Box 221 Rusk TX 75785-9742 Office: Cherokee County 502 N Main St Rusk TX 75785-1337

COOK, DORIS MARIE, retired accountant, educator; b. Fayetteville, Ark., June 11, 1924; d. Ira and Mettie Jewel (Dorman) Cook. BSBA, U. Ark., Fayetteville, 1946, MS, 1949; PhD, U. Tex., Austin, 1968. CPA Okla., Ark. Jr. acct. Haskins & Sells, Tulsa, 1946-47; instr. acctg. U. Ark., Fayetteville, 1947-52, asst. prof., 1952-62, assoc. prof., 1962-69, prof., 1969-88, Univ. prof. and Nolan E. Williams lectr. in acctg., 1988-97, emeritus disting. prof., 1997—. Mem. Ark. State Bd. Pub. Accountancy, 1987-92, treas., 1989-91, vice chmn. 1991-92; mem. Nat. Assn. State Bds. of Accountancy, 1987-92; appointed Nolan E. Williams lectureship in acctg., 1988-97; Doris M. Cook chair in acctg. U. Ark., Fayetteville, 2000. Mem. rev. bd. Ark. Bus. Rev., Jour. Managerial Issues; contbr. articles to profl. jours. Recipient Bus. Faculty of Month award Alpha Kappa Psi, 1997, Outstanding Faculty award Ark. Tchg. Acad., 1997, Charles and Nadine Baum Outstanding Tchr. award, 1997, Outstanding Leadership and Svc. award for Women's History Month, 1999, AAUW, others. Mem. AICPA, Ark. Bus. Assn. (editor newsletter 1982-85), Am. Acctg. Assn. (chmn. nat. membership 1982-83, Arthur Carter scholarship com. 1984-85, membership Ark. 1985-87), Am. Women's Soc. CPAs., Ark. Soc. CPA's (life, v.p. 1975-76, pres. N.W. Ark. chpt. 1980-81, sec. Student Loan Found. 1981-84, treas. 1984-92, pres. 1992-97, chmn. pub. rels. 1984-88, 93-95, Outstanding Acctg. Educator award 1991, Outstanding Com. Svc. award 1995, Student Loan Found. Bd. award 2001, 21 Yrs. Outstanding Svc. award 2001), Acad. Acctg. Historians (life, trustee 1985-87, rev. bd. of Working Papers Series 1984-92, sec. 1992-95, pres.-elect 1995, pres. 1996), Ark. Fedn. Bus. and Profl. Women's Clubs (treas. 1979-80), Fayetteville Bus. and Profl. Women's Clubs (pres. 1973-74, 75-76, Woman of Yr. award 1977) Mortar Bd., Beta Gamma Sigma, Beta Alpha Psi (editor nat. newsletter 1973-77, nat. pres. 1977-78, Outstanding Alumni in Edn. Iota chpt. 1999, Outstanding Svc. award Iota chpt. 1997), Phi Gamma Nu, Alpha Lambda Delta, Delta Kappa Gamma (sec. 1976-78, pres. 1978-80, treas. 1989-2000), Phi Kappa Phi. Home: 1655 Amy Ave Glendale Heights IL 60139

COOK, FAYE HAMLETT, secondary school educator; b. Goodlettsville, Tenn., Jan. 9, 1944; d. Arthur Thomas and Flara Mae Hamlett; m. Howell Lewis Cook, June 14, 1980; children: Richard Todd Whitaker, Aaron Brandon. BS, David Lipscomb U., Nashville, 1966; MS, Athens State U., Ala., 1970. Cert. tchr. Ala., 1966. English tchr. Woodville H.S., Woodville, Ala., 1967—. Mayor Town of Woodville, Ala., 2000—06. Mem.: NEA (assoc.), Ala. Edn. Assn. Office: Woodville High School 290 Co Rd 63 Woodville AL 35776 Office Phone: 256-776-2874.

COOK, FRANCES D., management consultant; b. Charleston, W.Va., Sept. 7, 1945; d. Nash and Vivian Cook. BA, Mary Washington Coll. of U. Va., 1967; MPA, Harvard U., 1978; LLD, Shenandoah U., 1998. Certificats d'Etudes, Université d'Aix-Marseille (France), 1966. Commd. fgn. svc. officer Dept. State, 1967; spl. asst. to R.S. Shriver amb. to France, Paris, 1968-69; mem. U.S. Del. Paris Peace Talks on Viet-Nam, 1970-71; cultural affairs officer, consul Am. Consul Gen., Sydney, Australia, 1971-73; cultural affairs officer, first sec. Am. Embassy, Dakar, Senegal, 1973-75; personnel officer for Africa USIA, Washington, 1975-77; dir. office public affairs African Bur. Dept. State, Washington, 1978-80, amb. to Republic of Burundi at Bujumbura, 1980—83, consul gen. Alexandria, Egypt, 1983-86, dep. asst. sec. of state for refugees Washington, 1986-87, dir. Office of West African Affairs, 1987-89, amb. to Cameroon Yaoundé, 1989-93, U.S. coord. for Sudan, 1993; dep. asst. sec. of state for political-military affairs Dept. of State, Washington, 1993-95, amb. to Oman Muscat, 1996-99; founder The Ballard Group, LLC, 2002. Bd. dirs. ATK, Pegasus Energy Ltd., Corp. Coun. in Africa; chmn. bd. dirs. Gulf Environment, 2005—. Recipient various honor awards Dept. State and Def. Mem. Am. Fgn. Svc. Assn., Coun. of Fgn. Rels., Harvard Club of N.Y.C., Washington Inst. Fgn. Affairs, Phi Beta Kappa (alumni). Home: PO Box 40882 Washington DC 20016-0882 Business E-Mail: francesdcook@ballardgroupllc.com.

COOK, IVA DEAN, education educator; b. Palmero, W.Va., Jan. 13, 1927; d. Hobert and Elwa (Hill) Lovejoy; m. George William Cook, July 16, 1943; children: Brenda Sue Burford, Pamela Ann Marks. BA, Marshall U., 1963, MEd, 1967. Cert. in elem. and spl. edn., W.Va. Instr. Marshall U., Huntington, W.Va., 1966-67; spl. edn. tchr. Fairfield Spl. H.S., Huntington, 1963-65, 67-70; demonstration tchr. W.Va. Grad. Coll., Institute, 1969, asst. prof. spl. edn., 1970-79, assoc. prof., 1979-86, prof., mental retardation progrm coord., 1986-91, prof. spl. edn., 1970-91, prof. spl. edn. emerita, 1991—. Coord., adj. fculty orientation W.Va. Grad. Coll., 1992-94; mem. mental retardation task force W.Va. Dept. Edn., Charleston, 1984-88; cons. W.Va. Dept. Edn., 1970-91, U. Mo., Columbia, 1987-88. Author: Occupational Notebook Program, 1971; co-author: (5 books and 5 cassette tapes) Learning Through Reading, 1987; contbr. articles to profl. jours. Mem. adv. bd. W.Va. Senator Robert Holiday, 1987-88. Recipient awards for teaching and service. Mem. W.Va. State Coun. on Vocat. Edn., Coun. for Exceptional Children (past pres. div. on career devel.). Democrat. Presbyterian. Avocations: cooking, walking, writing, entertaining, volunteering.

COOK, JENIK ESTERM (JENIK ESTERM COOK SIMONIAN), artist, educator; b. Rezaieh, Iran, July 7, 1940; came to U.S., 1964; d. Sameual Amijon and Nanajan (Amreh Sarkissian) Simonian; m. Carrol Ross Cook, Sept. 28, 1961; children: Fiona Gitana Cook Anderson, Herold H. Studied with Hossein Delrish, Iran, 1968-70; studied with Barbara Lae, Scotland, 1970-78; studied with Chalita Robinson, 1981-87, studied with Jake Lee, 1987-90, studied with Dr. Alex Vilumsons, 1988-94. Tchr. art. Resident artist Orlando Gallery, L.A.; art tchr. U. Judaism, Bel Air. One-woman shows include Pacific Design Ctr., L.A., 1996, Orlando Gallery, 1997, 98, Bakery Digital Post Prodn. Ctr., L.A., West Wood Fed. Bldg., L.A., 1999, Hilton Hotel, L.A., 1999; exhibited in groups shows at Orlando Gallery, 1998, L.A. Conv. Ctr., 1998. Rheinfelden (Germany) Town Hall, 1998, Gallery Merkel, Grenzack, Germany, 1998, L.A. Art Expo, 1998, MGM Conf. Ctr., 1999, Long Beach Conv. Ctr., 1999, Art 21, Las Vegas MGM Conv. Ctr., 1999, Art Expo, N.Y., 2000; set designer, scenic artist North Hollywood Ch. of Religious Sci., 1999. Office: Everywomans Village 5650 Sepulveda Blvd Van Nuys CA 91411-2981 Home: 5643 Norwich Ave Van Nuys CA 91411-3233

COOK, JO ANN LIKINS, psychologist; b. Bowling Green, Ky., Mar. 18, 1946; d. John Thomas and Aurora Quinones Likins; m. Lonnie M. Cook, Nov. 24, 1984. BM, We. Ky. U., 1968, MA, 1972; postgrad., U. Ala., 1975; EdD, Vanderbilt U., 1983. Tchr. Bowling Green (Ky.) Schs., 1971—72, Bessemer (Ala.) Schs., 1972—73; counselor, testing coord. Midfield (Ala.) Schs., 1973—75; fgn. student adv. Ky. State U., Frankfort, Ky., 1975—78; co-dir. Diagnostic Ctr. We. Ky. U., Bowling Green, 1980—83; specialist child devel. pediats. Med. Sch. U. Fla., Gainesville, Fla., 1983—86; pvt. practice psychologist Winter Pk., Fla., 1985—. Mem. interdisciplinary team Ctrl. Fla. Craniofacial Team, Orlando, Fla.; adv. bd. Nana's Mental Health Svc., Phoenix, 2001; devel. sch. psychologist. Co-author: Play and the Growth of Competency, 1993, Play Therapy for Selective Mutism, 1997. Mem.: Assn. Play Therapy, Fla. Assn. Sch. Psychology, Nat. Assn. Sch. Psychology, Ky. Cols., APA, Hon. Order Cols., Delta Omicron, Kappa Delta, Kappa Delta Pi. Avocations: music, reading, travel. Office: 1316 Palmetto Ave Winter Park FL 32789

COOK, JOAN, Canadian senator; b. English Harbor West, Newfoundland, Can., Oct. 6, 1934; children: Diane, Jean. V.p. Automobile Dealership; mgr. CJON Radio-TV; with Robert Simpson Ea. Ltd., Halifax; senator The Senate of Can., Ottawa, 1998—. Liberal. Office: 253 East Block The Senate of Canada Ottawa ON Canada K1A 0A4

COOK, JOANN CATHERINE, computer professor; children: Jeffrey, James, Joseph, Jodie Gray, Janet. AS in Data Processing, Jefferson Jr. Coll., Hillsboro, Ill., AA in Bus. Adminstrn.; BS in Info. Mgmt., Maryville U., St. Louis; MBA, North Ctrl. Coll., Naperville, Ill. Regional computer analyst Prime Computer, St. Louis, 1983—87; regional tech. support mgr. Prime Computer/Computervision, Oakbrook, Ill., 1987—94; assoc. prof. Coll. DuPage, Glen Ellyn, Ill., 1995—. Computer cons., Naperville, 1994—99. Office: Coll DuPage 425 Falwell Blvd Glen Ellyn IL 60137 Office Phone: 630-942-2674. Business E-Mail: cookjo@cod.edu.

COOK, JONI LEANN, science educator; d. Clem Howard and Dorothy Jean Cook. BSE, Ctrl. Mo. State U., Warrensburg, 1988. Tchr. St. Mary's Sch., Montrose, Mo., 1987—89; libr. Montrose R-14 Sch. Dist., Mo., 1991—94, Davis R-12 Sch. Dist., Clinton, Mo., 1994—97, Leesville R-9 Sch. Dist., Mo., 1994—96; libr., social scis. tchr. Calhoun R-8 Sch. Dist., Mo., 1996—2003, social scis. tchr., 2004—. Bd. mem. Calhoun Libr. Bd., Mo., 1996—; com. chair Calhoun R-8 Sch. Dist., Mo., 1999—2002, com., 2004—05. Mem.: Montrose Hist. Soc. Home: 103 Michael Dr Clinton MO 64738 Office: Calhoun R-8 Sch Dist 409 S College Calhoun MO 65323

COOK, JURENA RENEÉ, pastor; b. Phila., June 1, 1952; d. Henry John Capaldi (Stepfather) and Frienzella Louise Chestang; m. Alvin Seymour Cook, Sept. 11, 1981; children: Joseph Henry Anderson children: Samuel Vernon Anderson, Solomon David Anderson. Degree in pastoral ministries, Ch. of Messiah Yeshiva, Cherry Hill, N.J., 1989. Praise and worship leader Ch. of Messiah, Cherry Hill, 1984—89, Victory Ch., North Charleston, SC. Head dir. Songs of the Bride Messiah's Ch., Summerville, SC, 1990—2005. Composer: (harp and bowl psalm) Into the WhirlWind (Most Creative Spontaneous Song award, 2004). Nat. prophetic ministry Mantle Ch. Ministries, Charleston, 1995—2005. Named Most Anointed Praise and Worship Leader, Mantle Ch. Ministries, 2004. Republican. Avocations: travel to all nations, philanthropist missions support, raising up of leaders, church planting, support for Israel. Home and Office: 104 Newington Rd Summerville SC 29485 Office Phone: 843-693-0034. Home Fax: 843-873-1098. Personal E-mail: messiahschurch7@hotmail.com.

COOK, KATE SIEVERT, lawyer; b. K.I. Sawyer AFB, Mich., May 10, 1977; m. Matthew Evan Cook, May 15, 1999; children: Madeleine Eleanor, Caroline Laura. BA magna cum laude, U. of South, 1998; JD magna cum laude, Mercer U., 2002. Bar: Ga. 2002. Law clk. to presiding judge Hon. Clay D. Land U.S. Dist. Ct. Ga., Columbus, 2002—04; assoc. Butler Wooten, Columbus, Ga., 2004—. Team leader Relay for Life, Am. Cancer Soc., Columbus, 2003; bd. dirs. Concharty coun. Girl Scouts USA, Columbus, 2005. Woodruff scholar, Mercer U. Sch. of Law, 1998—2002, Biehl grantee for internat. rsch., U. of South, 1997. Mem.: Ga. Trial Lawyers Assn. (assoc.), Columbus Trial Lawyers Assn. (assoc.; sec. 2005—06), Ga. Assn. Women Lawyer (assoc.; v.p. 2005—06). Methodist. Avocation: travel. Office: Butler Wooten 105 13th St Columbus GA 31901 Office Phone: 706-322-1990. Personal E-mail: cookmkjd@yahoo.com. Business E-Mail: kate@butlerwooten.com.

COOK, KELLI BROOKE, elementary school educator; b. Tifton, Ga., Oct. 4, 1973; d. Randy and Marta Walker; m. Mark Cook, Apr. 17, 1993; children: Marlli Brooke, Elexis Hunter. BS in Health and Phys. Edn., Valdosta State U., Ga., 1995. Cert. tchr. Ga., Tex., 1995. Phys. edn. tchr., coach Cedar Valley Mid. Sch., Austin, Tex., 2000—. Ch. youth leader, Austin, 1998. Home: 3111 Aquila Ct Round Rock TX 78681 Office: Cedar Valley Middle School 8139 Racine Trail Austin TX Office Phone: 512-428-2364. Home Fax: 512-428-2420; Office Fax: 512-428-2420. Personal E-mail: kellibrooke1@yahoo.com.

COOK, KIMBERLY SUE, music educator; b. Huntington, W.Va., Dec. 16, 1964; d. George Walter and Phyllis Gay Chapman; m. David Shane Cook, Dec. 21, 1991; 1 child, Caleb C. BA in Music Edn., Marshall U., Huntington, W.Va., 1987; MA in Music Edn., Marshall U., 1999. Music/chorus/band tchr. Harts H.S., W.Va., 1987—94, Hamlin Jr./Sr. H.S., W.Va., 1994—2006; band/dance/music appreciation tchr. Lincoln County H.S., Hamlin, 2006—. Sunday sch. tchr. Lincoln Bapt. Ch., Branchland, W.Va., 1995—. Mem.: W.Va. Music Educators Nat. Conf. Democrat. Baptist. Avocations: reading, cooking.

COOK, LIA, art educator; b. Ventura, Calif., Nov. 25, 1942; d. James and Esther Miriam (Holman) Polese. BA, U. Calif., Berkeley, 1965, MA, 1973. Prof. art Calif. Coll. Arts and Crafts, Oakland, Calif., 1976—. Lectr. art various univs. and orgns., U.S. One-woman shows include B.Z. Wagman Gallery, St. Louis, 1985, The Allrich Gallery, San Francisco, 1984, 82, 81, 78, No. Ill. U. Gallery 200, De Kalb, 1984, Galerie Nationale de la Tapisserie et d'Art Textile, Beauvais, France, 1983, San Jose (Calif.) Mus. Art, 1980, R. Levy Gallery, Austin, Tex., 1986, Allrich Gallery, San Francisco, 1987, Foster/White Gallery, Seattle, 1988; exhibited in group shows at Tulsa, Okla., 1988, Am. Craft Mus., 1987, Milw. Art Mus., 1986, Three Rivers Art Festival, Pitts., 1986, Albuquerque Mus. Art, History and Sci., 1985, Susan Cummins Gallery, Mill Valley, Calif., 1985, Evanston (Ill.) Art Ctr., 1984, First Street Forum, St. Louis, 1984, The Hand and the Spirit Crafts Gallery, Scottsdale, Ariz., 1984, Ill. State U., Normal-Bloomington, 1984, Kohler Arts Ctr., Sheboygan, Wis., 1984, Meadows Mus., So. Meth. U., Dallas, 1984, Schick Art Gallery, Saratoga Springs, N.Y., Southwest Tex. State U., San Marcos, 1984, Stanislaus State Coll., Turlock, Calif., 1984, Swan Galleries, Phila., 1984, The Allrich Gallery, San Francisco, 1983, Traver Sutton Gallery, Seattle, 1983, Hillwood Art Gallery, Long Island (N.Y.) U., 1983, Brunnier Gallery and Mus. Iowa State U., 1982, Mus. of Art, R.I. Sch. Design, 1982, Cooper-Hewitt Mus., N.Y.C., 1982, 1982, Nelson Gallery of Art, Akins Mus. Fine Arts, Kansas City, Mo., 1982, Oakland Mus., Spencer Mus. Art, Lawrence, Kans, IBM, Rochester, Minn., Met. Mus., N.Y.C. numerous others; represented in permanent collections Mus. Modern Art, N.Y.C., Galerie Nat. de la Tapisserie et d'Art Textile, Am. Craft Mus., N.Y.C., Univ. Tex. Art Mus., Austin, Rensselaer Poly. Inst., AT&T Co., N.Y.C., Art in Architecture Program U.S. GSA, Richmond, Calif., numerous others; contbr. articles, chpts. and revs. to books, catalogues, profl. jours. Fellow NEA, 1974, 77, 86; Jacquard grantee NEA, 1981. Home: 2127 Bonar St Berkeley CA 94702-1805 Office: Calif Coll Arts and Crafts Dept Crafts 5212 Broadway Oakland CA 94618-1426

COOK, LINDA Z., utilities executive; b. Kansas City, June 1958; m. Steve Cook; 3 children. Grad. degree in Petroleum Engring., U. Kans. Various tech. and managerial positions Shell Oil Co. (Houston and Calif.), 1980—98; dir., strategy & bus. develop. Shell Exploration & Prodn. Global Exec. Com., The Hague, Netherlands; CEO Shell Gas & Power, 2000—03, 2004—; pres., CEO, bd. dir. Shell Can. Ltd., 2003—04; mng. dir. Royal Dutch Petroleum Co., 2004—; group exec. dir., gas and power Royal Dutch/Shell Group, 2004—. Bd. dir. Boeing Co., 2003—. Named one of 100 Most Powerful Women in World, Forbes Mag., 2005—06, 50 Women to Watch, Wall Street Journal, 2005, 50 Most Powerful Women in Global Bus., Fortune Mag., 2005. Mem.: Soc. Petroleum Engrs. Office: Shell International BV FSK Division PO Box 162 2501 AN The Hague Netherlands*

COOK, LISA MARIE, mathematics professor, mathematics learning center coordinator; b. Manhasset, N.Y., Apr. 7, 1980; BS in Applied Math. with Computer Sci., L.I. U.-C.W. Post Campus, 2002, MS in Applied Math., 2004. Academic asst. L.I U.-C.W. Post Campus, Brookville, N.Y., 2001—02, grad. asst., 2002—04, student coord. tutoring program, 2002—04; instr. Suffolk County CC, Selden, N.Y., 2004—, coord. math. learning ctr., 2004—. Mem. mediated math. com. Suffolk County CC, 2004—, mem. precalculus com., 2004—. Mem.: Am. Math. Soc., N.Y. State Math. Assn. Two-Year Colls., Kappu Mu Epsilon (sec. 2002, N.Y. Lambda chpt., Nat. Honor Soc., treas. 2004). Roman Catholic. Achievements include guest presenter of honors thesis, Hot Hands in Basketball: Myth or Math?, at the Annual Kappa Mu Epsilon Banquet, 2002. Avocations: cooking, sports. Home: 2678 Martin Ave Bellmore NY 11710 Office: Suffolk County Community Coll 533 College Rd Selden NY 11784 Office Phone: 631-451-4717. Office Fax: 631-451-4887. Business E-Mail: cookl@sunysuffolk.edu.

COOK, SISTER MARY MERCEDES, school system administrator, director; b. Hagerstown, Md., Dec. 18, 1939; d. Garland and Anita Rideoutt (Willis) C. Student, Fordham U.; BA, Ea. Conn. State U., 1974, MS, 1983; grad., Norwich Dicocesan Prins. Acad., Conn., 1991; postgrad., U. Dayton, 1999. Joined Sistes of Charity of Our Lady of Mother of the Ch., Roman Cath. Ch.; cert. tchr., Conn. Tchr., prin. St. Joseph Sch., Baltic, Conn., 1959-61; tchr. Sacred Heart Sch., Byram, Conn., 1961-63, Bloomfield, Conn., 1963-66, Taftville, Conn., 1966-67, Acad. of Holy Family, Baltic, 1967-84; vice-prin., tchr., chair dept. English, guide counselor Acad. of the Holy Family, Baltic, Conn., 1990—2000; tchr., vice prin. Assumption Sch., Manchester, 1984—; dir. Sacred Heart Ednl. Ctr., Baltic, 2003—. Mem.: Nat. Cath. Ednl. Assn., Math. Assn. Am., Nat. Coun. Tchrs. English. Republican. Avocations: reading, writing, painting, cooking, interior decorating.

COOK, MARY PHELPS, chemistry professor; b. Memphis, Tenn., Sept. 21, 1960; d. James Burnette Phelps and Mary Margaret Botteron Jorgensen; m. Stephen D. Cook, Aug. 7, 1982; children: Daniel, Amy, Paul. BS, Christian Brothers Coll., 1982; PhD, Memphis State U., 1990. Grad. asst. U. Memphis, 1983-90; adj. prof. S.W. Tenn. C.C., Memphis, 1990-93, asst. prof., 1993-98, assoc. prof., 1998—. Mem. adv. bd. dept. chemistry Christian Bros. Coll., Memphis, 1996-97. Author: in-house lab. manual; contbr. article to profl. jour. Com. chmn. troop 255 Boy Scouts Am., Bartlett, Tenn., 1997-2000, asst. den leader, 1999—, mem., 2000-02, treas., 2002—; mem. staff N.E. dist. Cub Scout roundtable, 1998-99, dir. day camp, 1999-2001; mem. Girl Scouts USA, Bartlett, 1995—. Van Fleet fellow Van Fleet Found., 1987-89. Mem. Am. Chem. Soc., Assn. Career and Tech. Edn. Office: SW Tenn CC 5983 Macon Cv Memphis TN 38134-7642 Business E-Mail: mcook@southwest.tn.edu.

COOK, MELANIE K., lawyer; b. Salt Lake City, June 3, 1953; BS, UCLA, 1974, JD, 1978. Bar: Calif. Ptnr. Bloom Hergott Cook Diemer & Klein, Beverly Hills, Calif., 1987—2002, Bloom Hergott Diemer & Cook, Beverly Hills, Calif., 1992—2002, Ziffren, Brittenham, Branca, Fischer, Gilbert-Lurie, Stiffelman & Cook, LLP, L.A., 2004—. Office: 1801 Century Park W Los Angeles CA 90067-6406 Office Phone: 310-552-6535.*

COOK, MELISSA ANN, elementary school educator; children: Christopher, Megan. BS, Maryville U., Chesterfield, Mo., 1999; MAT, U. St. Mary, Kans., 2006. Tchr. Hoech mid. sch. Ritenour Sch. Dist., St. Ann, Mo., 1999—. Office: Ritenour Sch Dist 3312 Ashby Rd Saint Ann MO 63074

COOK, MYRTLE, special education educator, elementary school educator; b. New Orleans, June 15, 1936; d. John Henry and Angeline (Gray) C.; m. Marshall Butler, Dec. 22, 1979 (dec. July 1981). Student, So. U., 1954-55; BA, Southeastern La. U., 1960, MEd, 1971, postgrad., 1975. Cert. elem. tchr., tchr. mentally retarded, student tchr. supr., prin., La., reading specialist. Elem. tchr. Tangipahoa Parish Sch. System, Hammond, La., 1960-61, Ponchatoula, La., 1961-62, 65-67, Kentwood, La., 1963-65, tchr. Headstart Ponchatoula, 1965-65, prin. Headstart, 1965, tchr. spl. edn., 1967-72, Hammond, 1972—, mem. spl. edn. adv. coun. Amite, La., 1987—; 1st and 3d grade tchr. Greenville Park Elem. Sch.; elem. tchr. 1st, 4th and 6th grades O.W. Dillon Elem. Sch., Crystal St. Sch., D.C. Reeves Elem. Sch., Ponchatoula, La., spl. edn. tchr.; 6th grade tchr. Perion Jr. HS, Ponchatoula; 7th and 8th grade tchr. spl. edn. Hammond Jr. HS. Participant and presenter workshops in field. Vol., coach La. Spl. Olympics; active Girl Scouts U.S.A., United Way Tangipahoa Parish, La. Heart Fund; music dir., pianist, piano tchr. children's choir cmty. Greenfield Bapt. Ch., Hammond, La., 1961—, sec. sr. women's aux., 1961—; music dir., organist choirs Little Bethel Bapt. Ch., Amite, 1961—; organist, chmn. music La. Home and Fgn. Mission Bapt. Sr. Women's Aux., 1961—; tchr. Parish Tangipahon; also others. Named Tangipahoa Parish Tchr. of Yr., La. Edn. Assn., 1974, Educator of Yr. award, Amite, 1975; Spl. Edn. Tchr. of Yr, Tangipahoa Parish Sch. System, 1987; T.H. Harris scholar So. U., 1954-55. Mem. Tangipahoa Parish Edn. Assn., Tangipahoa Fedn. Tchrs. Democrat. Achievements include being one of the frist African American students at Southeastern Louisiana University. Avocations: reading, piano, singing, aerobics, music. Home: 105 Kansas St Hammond LA 70403-3943

COOK, NENA, lawyer; b. Salt Lake City, Jan. 25, 1966; BA, Gonzaga U., 1988; JD, Willamette U., 1991. Bar: Oreg. 1991, U.S. Dist. Ct. Oreg. 1992, U.S. Dist. Ct. Ea. and We. Dist. Wash. 2000. Ptnr. Sussman Shank LLP, Portland, Oreg. Chair employment law group Sussman Shank LLP; spkr. in field. Prodn. editor: Willamette Law Rev., 1990—91; contbr. articles to profl. jours. Named one of Forty under 40 Outstanding Leadership in Bus. and Civic Affairs, Portland Bus. Jour., 2002. Mem.: ABA, Soc. Human Resource Mgmt., Portland Human Resource Mgmt. Assn., Fed. Bar Assn., Oreg. Women Lawyers, Oreg. State Bar Assn. (mem. fed. practice procedure com. 1997—99, chmn. 1998—99, ninth cir. jud. conf. rep. 2000—03, mem. bd. govs. 2002—, pres.-elect 2004, mem. jud. screening com.), Wash. State Bar Assn. Office: Sussman Shank LLP 1000 SW Broadway Ste 1400 Portland OR 97205 Office Phone: 503-227-1111. Office Fax: 503-248-0130. E-mail: nena@sussmanshank.com.

COOK, REBECCA MCDOWELL, former state official; m. John Larkin Cook; children: Hunter, and Morgan. BA in Polit. sci., U. Mo., 1972, JD, 1975; D (hon.), Mo. We. State Coll., 1997. Former clk., assoc., ptnr. Limbaugh, Limbaugh, and Russell Law Firm, Cape Girardeau, Mo.; v.p. Oliver, Oliver, Waltz, and Cook Law Firm, 1979-92; del. to Mo. State Dem. Conv., 1980; mem. Mo. State Bd. Elem. and Sec. Edn., 1990-94; sec. of state State of Mo., 1994—2001. Mem. Future of South Commn., Dem. Nat. Com., 1995—. Recipient Order of Barristers Award., 1992, Woman of Achievement Award., Cape Girardeau Zonta Club, 1994, James C. Kirkpatrick Excellence in Governance Award; Henry Toll fellow. Mem. S.E. Mo. State U. Found., S.E. Mo. Hosp. Found., Nat. Assn. Secretaries of State (dir., exec. com.), Coun. Econ. Edn., Mo. K-16 Coalition, Lift Mo., Inc. Democrat. Presbyterian.

COOK, RENAY, elementary school educator; b. Cleve., Oct. 19; d. Luke Owens Sr. and Marjorie Redmond; m. Stanley Rephael Cook, Aug. 13, 1994. BA, U. Akron, 1979; MEd, Ashland U., 2002. Mem.: NEA, East. Cleve. Edn. Assn., Ohio Edn. Assn., Delta Sigma Theta. Avocations: reading, walking, theater, travel. E-mail: naydolldst@msn.com.

COOK, RUTH ELLEN, athletic trainer; b. Creighton, Nebr., June 26, 1960; d. Ronald Laverne and Carol Marie Cook. BS, U. Nebr., Lincoln, 1983, MA, 1995. Lic. athletic trainer Ill., cert. Nat. Athletic Trainers Assn. Tchr., athletic trainer Bel Air HS, El Paso, Tex., 1984—93; grad. asst. athletic trainer U. Nebr., 1993—95; asst. athletic trainer U. Ill., Champaign, 1995—2002; athletic trainer Decatur Meml. Hosp., Decatur, Ill., 2002—05; student health coord., head athletic trainer Lincoln Christian Coll., Ill., 2005—. Sunday school tchr. Our Savior Luth. Ch., El Paso, Tex., 1990—91, dir. childhood edn., 9293. Office: Lincoln Christian Coll 100 Campus View Dr Lincoln IL 62656-2167

COOK, SARAH SHEETS, women's health nurse; b. Paterson, NJ, Apr. 27, 1940; d. Jack H. and Maxine E. (Merrill) Sheets; m. Floyd Harrison Cook III; 1 child, Keith. BSN magna cum laude, U. Mich., 1962; MEd, Columbia U., 1969. Cert. perinatal clin. nurse; RN, N.Y., Conn. Instr. in nursing Columbia U., 1964-68, asst. prof. nursing, 1969-72, cons. human grown devel., 1973-79; exec. dir., co founder, chief programmer Stamford Family Life Workshops Parenting Edn. Group, Inc., 1975-85; dir. The Women's Ctr., Stamford, Conn., 1978-79; clin. instr. maternal child health Columbia U. Sch. Nursing, 1979-83, program dir. and developer, 1984-85, asst. prof. clin. nursing, 1985-86; clin. nurse specialist Dr. Richard S. Banfield, Jr., 1980-85, Dr. Corrine E. de Cholnoky, 1985—; asst. dean adminstrv. affairs, asst. prof. clin. nursing, Sch. Nursing Columbia U., NYC, 1987-88, assoc. dean for academic and clin. affairs, asst. prof. clin. nursing, Sch. Nursing, 1988-91, assoc. dean for academic and clin. affairs, assoc. prof. clin. nursing, Sch. Nursing, 1991-94, sr. assoc. dean, assoc. prof. clin. nursing, Sch. Nursing, 1994, vice dean nursing, Dorothy M. Rogers prof. clinical nursing. Faculty coun. Faculty of Medicine, Health Scis. Campus Columbia U., 1991—, facilities task force, 1989-92, parking com. health scis. divsn., 1987—, classroom mgmt. com., 1985-86; dean's exec. com., Columbia U. Sch. Nursing, 1989—, Theresa Marcos Jansson Meml. lectr. planning com., 1989—, cons. program dirs. com., 1988—, centennial adv. planning com., 1986-92, acad. nurse adv. devel. com., 1986—, curriculum com., 1986—, 66-72, dean's adv. com., 1985—, and many others; internat. nursing cons., Sweden, Denmark, England, Australia, Armenia, Thailand, 1986—; lectr. in field. Peer reviewer Jour. Profl. Nursing, 1988—; contbr. numerous articles to profl. jours. Cons. growth and devel. and parent support Stamford Day Care Ctrs., Inc., 1980-81; bd. dirs. The Stamford Counseling Ctr., 1980-86; child care advisor LaLeche League, 1972—; cons. Early Childhood Developmental Ctr. YMCA, 1979-86. Grantee U.S. Dept. HEW, 1978, U.S. Dept. Labor, 1976-78, Stamford Found., 1975, NIH, 1967-68; recipient O'Neil Prize for Acad. Execellence. Fellow Nat. Academies of Practice; mem. ANA, AAUP, NAACOG, Am. Pub. Health Assn. (maternal child health sect., breastfeeding com. 1993—), Nat. Assn. Nurse Practitioners in Women's Health, N.Am. Menopause Soc., Assn. of Reproductive Health Profls., Internat. Coun. on Women's Health Issues, Jacobs Inst. for Women's Health, Internat. Lacatation Cons. Assn. (nomenclature com. 1991-93), N.Y. Acad. Scis., Conn. Nurses Assn. (dist. II legis. network), Sigma Theta Tau, Phi Kappa Phi, Mortar Bd. Office: Columbia U Sch Nursing 617 W 168th St Rm 139 New York NY 10032-3702*

COOK, SHARON LEE DELANCEY, retired elementary school educator, musician; b. Manchester, Iowa, May 15, 1939; d. Donald Wesley Delancey and Alta Grace Haynes; children: Eric LeRoy, Melanie Mae Mead, Keith Delancey. At, Iowa State Tchr's Coll., Cedar Falls, 1956—58; BA, Upper Iowa U., Fayette, 1971. Cert. tchr. Iowa. Tchr. pre-kindergarten Valleybrook Sch., Falls Church, Va., 1958—59; typist-receptionist Libr. of Congress, Washington, 1959—60, 1966—68; tchr. grade 1 Maquoketa Valley Schs, Hopkinton, Iowa, 1968—69; tchr. grades 2.3 and 5 West Del. Schs., Manchester, 1969—97. Accompanist West Del. Pub. Schs., Manchester, Iowa, 1969—2000; repertoire asst. Pvt. Music Tchr's Assn., Cedar Rapids, 1999—; ch. organist and pianist, Manchester, Iowa, 1969—. Chairperson McGee Brick Sch. Found., Manchester, Iowa, 1999—; prayer chairperson Christian Women's Club, 2005—. Mem.: Fed. Women's Club (v.p. 2005—). Achievements include restoration of historic one-room brick school. Avocations: poetry, writing. Office: McGee Brick Sch Found 608 E Union St Manchester IA 52057

COOK, SHARON WARREN, social worker, educator; d. Shirley Whitaker and Johnnie Warren; 1 child, Talia Senai. M in Social Work, U. N.C., Chapel Hill, 1992—95. Asst. prof. social work Winston-Salem State U., NC, 1995—, asst. chair, dept. social sciences, 2003—. Bd. mem. Mental Health Assn. Forsyth County, Winston-Salem, 2000—, Youth Opportunities Homes, Inc., Winston-Salem, 2001—; cons./trainer Novant Healthcare Sys., Winston-Salem, 2005—. Author: (book chapter) Mary Church Terrell. Bd. mem. Mental Health Assn. Forsyth County, Winston-Salem, 2001—06. Recipient Faculty Tchg. awards, Wisnton-Salem State U., 2004, 2003, 2001, 1999, Nat. Recipient, Founding Mem. of Rosa PArks Wall of Tolerance, So. Poverty Law Ctr., 2004. Avocations: boating, pool, golf. Office: Winston-Salem State Univ 601 Martin Luther King Dr Winston Salem NC 27110 Office Phone: 336-750-2625. Home Fax: 336-778-1044; Office Fax: 336-750-2647. Personal E-mail: swarrencook@yahoo.com. Business E-Mail: cooksw@wssu.edu.

COOK, SUSAN FARWELL, director; b. Boston, Apr. 28, 1953; d. Benjamin and Beverly (Brooks) Conant; m. James Samuel Cook Jr., Aug. 17, 1985; children: Emily Farwell, David McKendree. AB, Colby Coll., 1975; MBA, Thomas Coll., 2002. Bank teller Boston 5 Cent Savs. Bank, 1975-76; asst. technician plan cost John Hancock Mut. Life Ins. Co., Boston, 1976-77, technician plan cost, 1977-78, sr. technician plan cost, 1978-79, asst. mgr. group pension plan cost, 1979-81; assoc. dir. alumni rels. Colby Coll., Waterville, Maine, 1981-86, dir. alumni rels., 1986-97, assoc. dir. planned giving, 1997—2005, asst. dir. campaign, 2005, dir. planned giving, 2005—. Co-dir. adv. bd. women's studies Colby Coll., 1987-89, adv. women's group, 1987-89; bd. dirs. Maine Planned Giving Coun., 2001-04, treas., 2002-04. Bd. dirs., newsletter sec. Literacy Vols. Am., Waterville, 1986—89, 1991—92, v.p., 1995—97, pres., 1997—99; treas. Pitcher Pond Improvement Assn., 1988—95, Gagnon/100 Campaign, 1996, 1998; coach Waterville Area Youth Hockey Assn., 1997—2001; bd. dirs. Youth Hockey Assn., 2001—05; treas. Gagnon for Senate, 2000, 2002; trustee Universalist-Unitarian Ch., Waterville, 2001—, v.p., 2003—05, pres., 2005—; bd. dirs. Congress Lake Assns., Yarmouth, Maine, 1988—92, Waterville Youth Soccer Assn., 2001—, pres., 2002—05; bd. dirs. Kennebec Montessori Sch., 1999—2001, Soccer Maine, 2004—, sec., 2005—. Mem. AAUW (sec. Waterville br. 1989-91, pres. 1991-93, co-pres. 1993-95, treas. 2003-06), Coun. Advancement and Support of Edn., CASE Dist. I (exec. bd. dirs. 1994-97, sec. 1996-97, nominating com. 1997-99). Avocations: skiing, sewing, golf. Home: 6 Pray Ave Waterville ME 04901-5339 Office: Colby Coll 4372 Mayflower Hl Waterville ME 04901-8843

COOK, SUSAN J., human resources specialist, manufacturing executive; BA, U. Colo.; MBA, Loyola U., 1977. Various positions in human resources including personnel mgr. IBM Corp.; v.p human resources Tandem Computers, Inc., Eaton Corp., Cleve., 1995—. Bd. dirs. Human Resources Policy Assn., CCL Industries, Inc. Office: Eaton Corp Eaton Ctr 1111 Superior Ave Cleveland OH 44114-2584 Office Phone: 216-523-5000. Office Fax: 216-523-4787.

COOK, TRACI, sports association executive; BA in History, English and Polit. Sci., U. Miss., 1987. With Nat. Dem. Inst., Malawi, Central African Republic; staff mem. Sr. Christopher Dodd (Conn.), 1992; mktg., bus. devel. exec. Physicians' Online; v.p. mktg. comm. Shepardson, Stern and Kaminsky; sr. dir. strategic and corp. rels. Women's Nat. Basketball Assn., N.Y.C., 2001—. Office: Women's Nat Basketball Assn Olympic Tower 645 Fifth Ave New York NY 10022

COOK, VIOLETTA BURKE, university administrator; b. Monroe, Mich., Dec. 13, 1941; d. Vangel and Jordonna (Tomova) Dimeff; m. Dock D. Burke Jr., Nov. 30, 1963 (div. Apr. 1976); children: Jennifer, Jonathan; m. Earl Ferguson Cook, Aug. 9, 1981 (dec. Oct. 1983). Student, U. Mich., 1959-62; BA, Tex. A&M U., 1970, MA in Polit. Sci., 1974. Legis. asst. U.S. Senate, Washington, 1962-64; instr., reseach assoc. geoscience Tex. A&M U., Coll. Sta., 1970-82; instr. Blinn Coll., Coll. Sta., 1982—98; dir. sponsored student programs Tex. A&M U., Coll. Sta., 1982—. Precinct chair Dem. Party, Brazos County, Tex., 1978—; vice-chmn. Planning and Zoning Commn., Coll. Sta., 1976-79; chmn. Zoning Bd. Adjustments, Coll. Sta., 1980-84. Groundwater Shell fellow, 1978. Mem. Southwest Social Sci. Assn., Assn. Univ. Dirs. Internat. Agrl. Programs (bd. dirs. 1985-87). Democrat. Avocation: internat. travel. Office: Sponsored Student Programs Tex A&m U College Station TX 77843-1226

COOK, WANDA REEDY, music educator; d. Cloyce Welborn and Mildred Irene Reedy; children: Kimberly Kristen Grammer, Christopher Ryan. BFA, U. Okla., Norman, 1970; M, U. Ctrl. Okla., Edmond, 1978. Prof. music appreciation OCCC, Oklahoma City, 1976—78; tchr. vocal music, gen. music Cashion Sch. Dist., Okla., 1981; tchr. vocal music Lake Pk. Elem. Sch., Bethany, 1986—; prof. music Am. Bible Coll., Oklahoma City, 1999—2001. Tchr. vocal music Midwest City-Del City Sch. Sys., Okla., 1970—76; dir. Putnamcity Honor Chorus, Oklahoma City, 2001—03; pianist Enterprise Bapt. Ch., Norman, 2000—; tchr. piano pvt. studio, Oklahoma, 1966—. Named Tchr. Yr., Lake Pk. Elem. Faculty, 1995; recipient Outstanding Choir award, DC Festivals, 2002. Mem.: Parent Tchr. Assn., Assn. Classroom Tchrs., Nat. Educators Assn., Okla. Educators Assn. (assoc.), ACACIA's Moms Club (pres. 1998—2002, Cofounder), Chi Omega (hon.; pres. mom's club 1997—98), Beta Sigma Phi (life; pres., v.p. 1995—2003, Woman of the Yr. 2003). Baptist. Avocations: travel, tennis, bridge, piano. Home: 8809 N Kensington Rd Oklahoma City OK 73132 Office: Putnam City Schs 3821 NW 30th Bethany OK 73132

COOKE, CHANTELLE ANNE, writer; b. Denver, Apr. 9, 1971; d. Frederick Blaize and Claire Gail (Jones) C. Student, Collin County C.C., Plano, Tex., 1989-93. Author: (poetry chapbook) Songs From Stars, 1995, (poetry chapbook) Wild Irises on God's Mountainside, 1999, (poetry cassette tape) Visions, 1997; contbg. editor tech. articles for computer industry, 1994-96; freelance writer articles and poems. Recipient Star of Loyalty, Paralyzed Vets. Am., 1996. Mem. Internat. Soc. Poets, Acad. Am. Poets, Poetry Connection, Magic Cir. Democrat. Roman Catholic. Avocations: mosaic art, home interior decorating, pistol target shooting, needlepoint.

COOKE, HONORE GUILBEAU, artist, educator; b. Baton Rouge, Feb. 11, 1907; d. Braxton Honoré Guilbeau and Mary Bangs Magruder; m. Edmund Vance Cooke Jr., Oct. 1930 (dec. Oct. 1978); children: Jennifer Gail, Jeremy Vance. Student, So. Meth. U.; grad., Sch. Art Inst. Chgo., 1926-29. Instr. Art Sch. Akron (Ohio) Art Inst.; artist, tchr. Nat. Mus. Women in the Arts, Washington. Works exhibited at The Cleve. Mus. Art, Phila. Mus. Art, Whitney Mus. Am. Art, N.Y., Cleve. Artist's Show in Miami Beach, Fla., Syracuse (N.Y.) Nat. Ceramic Exhbn., Massillon (Ohio) Mus., Instituto de Rels. Cultural, Mexico City, 1969, Sylvia Ullman Am. Crafts Gallery, Cleve., N.E. Ohio Mus. Art, Cleve., Akron Art Mus., 1995, N.Y. Art Assn. Nat., Cooperstown, 1995, 96, Fla. Pastel Assn., 1995, 96, Coopers Town Art Assn., 2001; author, illustrator: Mrs. Magpie's Invention, 1971; illustrator: The Adventures of Hajji Baba of Ispahan, 1947, A Connecticut Yankee in King Arthur's Court, 1948, Shaving Shagpat, 1955, I Know a Farm, 1960, The Birthday Tree, 1961, Who Goes There in My Garden?, 1963, Hundreds and Hundreds of Strawberries, 1969, Treemendous Gifts (Buck Cooke), 2000. Avocation: gardening. Home (Winter): 3605 E Shore Rd Miramar FL 33023-4953

COOKE, MARCIA GAIL, federal judge, lawyer; b. Sumter, S.C., Oct. 16, 1954; d. Heyward and Ella (Randolph) C. BS in Fgn. Services, Georgetown U., 1975; JD, Wayne State U., 1977. Bar: Mich. 1978, U.S. Dist. Ct. (ea. dist.) Mich. 1978, U.S. Ct. Appeals (6th cir.) 1983, Fla. 2001. Staff atty. Wayne

County Legal Services, Detroit, 1978-79; asst. defender Detroit Defender's Office, 1979-80; asst. atty. U.S. Atty.'s Office, Detroit, 1980-83; assoc. Miro, Miro & Weiner, Bloomfield Hills, Mich., 1983-84; magistrate judge U.S. Dist. Ct. (ea. dist.), Detroit, 1984—92; dir. professional devel. & training U.S. Atty.'s Office (so. dist) Fla., 1992, 1994—99, exec. asst. U.S. atty., 1992—94, acting adminstr. atty., 1996—97; chief insp. gen., Exec. Office of the Gov. State of Fla., 1999—2002; asst. county atty. Miami-Dade County, 2002—04; judge U.S. Dist. Ct. (so. dist) Fla., 2004—. Mem. ABA, Fed. Bar Assn. (bd. dirs. 1986), Nat. Bar Assn., Wolverine Bar Assn., Order of Barristers, NCCJ (Pathfinder award 1986), Women's Econ. Club. Roman Catholic. Avocations: film, lit., tennis. Office: US Dist Ct 301 N Miami Ave Miami FL 33128 Office Phone: 305-523-5150.

COOKE, SARA MULLIN GRAFF, daycare provider, kindergarten educator, medical assistant; b. Phila., Dec. 29, 1935; d. Charles Henry and Elizabeth (Mullin) Brandt Graff; m. Peter Fischer Cooke, June 29, 1963 (div. July 1994); children: Anna Cooke Smith, Peter Fischer Jr., Elizabeth Cooke Haskins, Sara Cooke Lowe; m. Laina Cooke Driscoll, Dec. 18, 1999. AA, Bennett Coll., 1955; BE in Child Edn., Westchester State Tchrs. Coll., 1956. Asst. to tchr. 1st grade The Woodlyn Sch., 1956-58; tchr. Sara Bircher's Kindergarten, Germantown, Pa., 1958-62, Chestnut Hill Acad., Pa., 1962-63, Tarleton Sch., Devon, Pa., 1963-64; with F.C.I. Mktg. Co-ordinators Inc., NYC, New Canaan, Conn., 1980-86; fundraiser Children's Hosp., Phila., 1989-92, pres. women's com., 1987-88; coord., master of ednl. ceremonies Phila. Soc. for Preservation Landmarks, 1991-93; coord. Elderhostel Program Landmarks Soc., 1992-93. Pvt. day caretaker Spl. Care, Inc., 1988—; pvt. daycare and doctor's asst., 1994—. Kindergarten tchr. Sunday Sch., 2004-06; bd. aux. Children's Hosp. Phila., 1970-76, women's bd., 1977—, pres., 1987-88; commonwealth bd. Med. Coll. Pa., 1984-99, Gimbel award com., 1994; alt. del. Rep. Nat. Conv., 1992; co-chmn. benefit St. Martin in the Fields, London, 1997, usher, 2003-06, tchr. Chestnut Hill Sunday Sch., 2005-; vol. with parents of very sick children Connelly Family Resource Ctr./Children's Hosp. of Phila., 1999—, chmn., 2003; vol. Rep. Nat. Conv., 2000; press vol. Polit. Fest in Laura Bush Libr., 2000. Nominee Pa. Soc., 2004; recipient Silver Cup award, Children's Hosp. Phila., 2002. Mem. Pa. Assn. Hosp. Auxs. (health rep.) Nat. Soc. Colonial Dames (garden com. 1988—), Alumnae Assn. Madeira Sch. (class sec., 1997-2003, class agt., Vol. Svc. award 1997), Pa. Soc. (life), Phila. Cricket Club, Jr. League Garden Club (co-chmn. Daisy Day Children's Hosp. 2001), Colonial Dames Pa., Pa. Soc. Reps. Republican. Episcopalian. Home and Office: Penns Wood G-26 20 Haws Ln Flourtown PA 19031

COOKE, WALTA PIPPEN, automobile dealership owner; b. Shreveport, La., Oct. 18, 1940; d. Billy Burt and Eula (Heaton) Pippen; m. John William Cooke II, Dec. 20, 1958; children: Cheryl Cooke Williams, John William III. BA, Baylor U., Waco, Tex., 1963. Co-owner, sec.-treas. Pippen Motor Co., Carthage, Tex., 1972-80, owner, sec.-treas., 1980—. Bd. dirs. Sabine River Authority of Tex., 1993-99, pres. bd., 1996-97; past dir. Toledo Bend Joint Project; chmn. lower basin project com. Sabine River Authority Tex., 1999, mem. by-laws com., chmn. 50th ann. com., 1999. Pianist for sanctuary choir Ctrl. Bapt. Ch., Carthage, 1986—; chmn. 50th anniversary celebration com. Sabine River Authority of Tex., 1999; mem. Panola Co. Heritage Found., 2000—, patron mem., mem. ednl. found. steering com., 2002—; mem. task force Groundwater Conservation, East Tex. Area.; mem. Panola County Groundwater Dist. Bd.; mem. Panola County Appraisal Dist.; founding dir. Carthage Ind. Sch. Dist. Edn. Found.; mem. Panola County Rep. Adv. Com., 2004—, Panola County Groundwater Mgmt. Study Com.; bd. mem. Panola County Appraisal Dist. Mem. Carthage Book Club (rec. sec. 1995-97), The Carthage Club (dir., 2006—). Avocations: reading, gardening, travel, music. Home: 200 Timberlane Dr Carthage TX 75633-2231 Office: Pippen Motor Co 1300 W Panola St Carthage TX 75633-2346 Office Phone: 903-693-6691.

COOK-ELKINS, SHANA FREE, elementary school educator; b. Clarksville, Tenn., Nov. 15, 1978; d. Roger Dale and Cindy Ann Cook; m. Shannon Warren Elkins. BA in Elem. Edn., Murray State U., Ky., 2000, MA in Reading and Writing, 2006. Cert. tchr. Tenn. Dept. Edn., 2001. Tchr. Dover (Tenn.) Elem. Sch., 2001—. Team leader Am. Cancer Soc. Relay for Life, Dover, 2004—05; tchr. Sunday sch. Ch. Christ, Bumpus Mills, Tenn., 1997—2006. Scholar, Ret. Tchrs. Stewart County, 1997. Mem.: Tchr. Assn. Home: 434 Lakeland Drive Dover TN 37058 Office Phone: 931-232-5442. Personal E-mail: shanaelkins@stewart.k12.tn.us.

COOKS, PAMALA ANIECE, insurance agent; b. Harvey, Ill., Dec. 31, 1973; d. Anthony T. Washington and Deloris Townsend; m. Paul Anthony Cooks, Dec. 8, 2002; 1 child, Olivia Janai Washington. BA, Govenors State U., 2001. Lic. prodr. Ill., 2000. Sales assoc. Aetna Inc., Chgo., 1996—. Evangelism ministry St. Mark Missionary Bapt. Ch., Harvey, 2002—03. Mem.: Nat. Campaign for Tolerance (assoc. Wall of Tolerance award 2002, 2003). Office Phone: 847-619-5590, 708-880-0436. Office Fax: 847-619-4936. Personal E-mail: pamalawashington@msn.com.

COOKSON, LINDA MARIE, retired elementary education educator; b. Emporia, Kans., Feb. 15, 1944; d. Fred Rolum and Mary Lavern (Bennett) C. BS, Emporia State U., 1966, MS, 1970. Cert. tchr., Kans. Tchr. 2d grade Howard Wilson Sch., Leavenworth, Kans., 1966-67; tchr. 5th and intermediate Unified Sch. Dist. 253, Emporia, 1967-74; youth advisor Lyon County Youth Ctr., Emporia, summer 1975; lectr. in edn. Emporia State U., 1975-80; art tchr. K-8 Unified Sch. Dist. 251, Admire and Americus, Kans., 1980-81, title I, art K-8 Americus, 1981-82, tchr. 6th grade, 1982-84, art tchr. K-8, 1984-94, comms. tchr. mid. sch., 1994-99. Field editor Country Discoveries. Mem. PTO, 1980—; pres., life mem. PTA, 1966-80. Mem. NEA, Kans. Nat. Edn. Assn. (Sunflower Uniserv region 1 adminstrv. bd. 1995-99), Americus Site Based Coun. (sec. 1994-96). Republican. Methodist. Avocations: travel, photography, antiques. Home: 645 Wilson St Emporia KS 66801-2452

COOL, MARY L., education specialist; b. Buffalo, Dec. 7, 1954; d. Paul G. and Dorothy R. (O'Brien) Wailand; m. Ronald J. Cool, June 23, 1979; children: Logan Elizabeth, Colin Jeffery. BS in Elem. Edn. cum laude, SUNY, Fredonia, 1976; MS in Ednl. Leadership, Nova Southeastern U., 1996, EdD in Ednl. Leadership, 2006. Cert. tchr., N.Y., Fla. Tchr. grade 1, Buffalo, 1976—77; tchr. grade 5 Orange County, Orlando, Fla., 1979—85; tchr. grade 1, head tchr. ESEA Title I Manatee County, Myakka City, Fla., 1977—79; tchr. grade 5, media specialist Volusia County, Osteen, Fla., 1985—89; resource techr. intermediate S.W. Volusia County, 1989—91; dist. elem. resource tchr., elem. tchr. specialist Volusia County Schs., 1991—97, specialist staff devel., 1997—98, coord. elem. and sch. improvement, 1998—2002; sch. improvement coord. initiative implementation Charter Sch. Dist., 2002—, coord. elem. edn., 2003—06, prin., 2006—. Grade level chair, sci. chair, reading chair, facilitative leader, coop. learning trainer, tchr. coach, tech. edn. coach, tchr. asst. coord., student success team coord., tchr. induction coord. Volusia County Schs.; ednl. cons. Scholastic, Inc., Sports Illus. for Kids, Kids Discover, Marvel Comics, Time for Kids, UNICEF, Miami Mus. Arts and Scis. Mem. ASCD, AAUW, Nat. Coalition for Sex Equity in Edn., Nat. Staff Devel. Coun., Fla. Coun. Elem. Edn., Kappa Delta Pi. Home: 1566 Gregory Dr Deltona FL 32738-6159 Office: PO Box 2410 Daytona Beach FL 32115-2410 Office Phone: 386-255-6475. Business E-Mail: mcool@volusia.k12.fl.us.

COOLBAUGH, CARRIE WEAVER, librarian; b. Pocatello, Idaho, Dec. 26, 1945; d. Elmer Dever and Pearl (Cutting) Weaver; 1 child, Marc Harry Pachon; m. J.D. Coolbaugh, June 15, 1992. BA, Calif. State U., L.A., 1972; MS, U. So. Calif., 1974; DPA, U. La Verne, 1993. Reference librarian L.A. County Pub. Library, 1974; adminstrv. asst. Lansing (Mich.) Parks and Recreation, 1975-76; cons. Applied Mgmt. Systems, Silver Spring, Md., 1977; reference librarian Fairfax (Va.) County Pub. Library, 1978, children's librarian, 1979-81, regional children's librarian, 1981-83, br. mgr., 1983-88; coord. Downey (Calif.) City Library, 1987-88; asst. city librarian Commerce (Calif.) Pub. Library, 1988-97, city libr. dir., 1997—. Adj. faculty mem. U. LaVerne, Calif., 1992—. Mem. ALA, Calif. Libr. Assn., Libr. Adminstrn. and Mgmt. Assn., Pub. Libr. Assn., Met. Coop. Libr. System (chmn. adult svcs. com. 1988-89, Reforma, Spl. Libr. Assn.). Home: 404 Damien Ave La Verne CA 91750-4104 Office: Commerce Pub Library 5655 Jillson St Los Angeles CA 90040-1493

COOLEY, FANNIE RICHARDSON, counselor, educator; b. Tunnel Springs, Ala., July 4, 1924; d. Willie C. Richardson and Emma Jean (McCorvey) Stallworth. BS, Tuskegee Inst., Ala., 1947, MS, 1951; PhD, U. Wis., 1969. Cert. counselor. Asst. inst. Tuskegee Inst., 1947-48, prof. counseling, 1969-2000, prof. emeritus, 2000—. Instr. Alcorn A&M Coll., Lorman, Miss., 1948-51; asst. prof. Ala. A&M Coll., Normal, 1951-62, assoc. prof., 1964-65; grad. fellow Purdue U., West Lafayette, Ind., 1962-64; house fellow U. Wis., Madison, 1965-69; cons. VA Med. Ctr. Tuskegee, 1969—. Mem. AAUW, AAUP, ASCD (bd. dirs., Disting. Svc. award 1985), Ala. Assn. Counseling and Devel. (pres. 1976-77, Svc. award 1978-79), Ala. Assn. for Counselor Edn. (pres. 1985-86), Aassn. Specialists in Group Work (pres. 1989-90, Career award 1998), Internat. Platford Assn., Chi Sigma Iota. Episcopalian. Home: 802-C Avenue A Tuskegee Institute AL 36088-2402 Office: Tuskegee Inst Coll Liberal Arts and Edn Bioethics Ctr Tuskegee Institute AL 36088

COOLEY, HILARY ELIZABETH, county official; b. Leesburg, Va., May 8, 1953; d. Thomas McIntyre and Helen Strong (Stringham) C. BA in Econs., U. Pitts., 1976; postgrad. in bus. adminstrn., Hood Coll., Frederick, Md., 1985-90. Mgr. Montgomery Ward, Frederick, 1976-80, merchandiser, 1980-82; asst. bus. mgr. Arundel Comm., Leesburg, 1982-84; bus. mgr. Loudoun Country Day Sch., Leesburg, 1984-85, bd. trustees, 1989-93, sec. bd. trustees, 1989-90, v.p., 1990-92; contr. Foxcroft Sch., Middleburg, Va., 1984-86, 91-92; corr. Loudoun Times Mirror, Leesburg, 1985-87; estate mgr. Delta Farm Inc., Middleburg, Va., 1988-98; cmty. ctr. mgr. County of Loudoun, 1998—. Area chmn. Keep Loudoun Beautiful, Middleburg, 1983-90, pres., bd. dirs. 1993-96; pres. Waterford (Va.) Citizens' Assn., 1985-86, Waterford Players, 1986-88; bd. dirs. Waterford Found., Inc., 1992-95, pres. 1995-98; bd. dirs. Loudoun Hist. Soc., Leesburg, 1987, Mt. Zion Ch. Preservation Assn., 1996-99; treas. Amendment 1 Inc., 1997-99, pres., 1999-2005; bd. dirs. Loudoun County Arbor Day Commn. 2003-05; mem. Friends of Happy Retreat, 2006-. Mem. Penn Hall Alumnae Ann. (pres. 1987-92). Democrat. Episcopalian. Avocations: photography, music, drama, tennis. Home and Office: 197 Maple Ridge Ln Harpers Ferry WV 25425 Office Phone: 703-771-5282.

COOLIDGE, MARTHA, film director; b. New Haven, Aug. 17, 1946; m. Michael Backes (div.). MFA, RISD, 1968; student, Columbia U.; MA, NYU, 1971. Dir.: (films) David: Off and On, 1972, Old-Fashioned Woman, 1974, More Than a School, 1974, (also prodr.) Not a Pretty Picture, 1975, Employment Discrimination: The Troubleshooters, 1976, Bimbo, 1978, Valley Girl, 1983, City Girl, 1984, Joy of Sex, 1984, Real Genius, 1985, Plain Clothes, 1988, Rambling Rose, 1991, Lost in Yonkers, 1992, Angie, 1994, Three Wishes, 1995, Out to Sea, 1997, Introducing Dorothy Dandridge, 1999, If These Walls Could Talk II, 2000, The Prince & Me, 2004, Material Girls, 2006; (TV films) Trenchcoat in Paradise, 1989, Bare Essentials, 1991, Crazy in Love, 1992, Flaming Rising, 2001, The Ponder Heart, 2001, The Twelve Days of Christmas Eve, 2004; (documentaries) David; On and Off, 1972 (Am. Film Festival award), More Than A School, 1973 (Am. Film Festival award), Old Fashioned Woman, 1974 (Am. Film Festival award), Not A Pretty Picture, 1975 (Am. Film Festival award); (TV series) Winners, 1978, The Twilight Zone, 1985, Sledge Hammer, 1986, Sex and the City, 1998, Leap Years, 2001, Related, 2005—; exec. prodr.: (TV films) Rip Girls, 2000. Recipient Best Dir. and Picture Rambling Rose, Independent Spriit Awards, nomination for If These Walls Could Talk II, Emmy awards. Mem.: Dir. Guild of Am. (pres. 2002—03).*

COOLS, ANNE C., Canadian senator; b. Barbados, Aug. 12, 1943; BA, McGill U., 1981; LLD (hon.), Can. Christian Coll., 2004. Social worker; senator Senate of Canada, Ottawa, 1984—. Named Spiritual Mother of Year, Internat. Jewish Women's Orgn., 1997, Person of Year, REAL Women of Can., 1999, Greatest Canadian, CBC-TV, 2004, Top Twenty Canadian Women, 2004, 10 Top Women, Toronto Sun Newspaper, 2004; named to These 50 Made a Difference, 2006; recipient Outstanding Achievement award politics, Pride Mag., 1997, Toronto Bob Marley Day award, 2001, Women of Excellence Leadership award, Nat. Ctr. Strategic Nonprofit Planning and Cmty. Leadership, 2004. Conservative. Avocations: reading, classical music, piano, gardening, dogs. Office: 178-F Centre Block The Senate of Canada Ottawa ON Canada K1A 0A4 Office Phone: 613-992-2808. Business E-Mail: coolsa@sen.parl.ca.

COOMBS, JOANNE DININNY, kindergarten educator; b. Corning, N.Y., May 25, 1947; d. John Hubert and Carrie Jean (Pierson) Dininny; m. Allan Kent Coombs, Feb. 8, 1969; children: Laura, Aaron, Matthew, Graham. AS, Corning C.C., 1972; BS, Elmira Coll., 1987, MS, 1990. Cert. tchr., N.Y. Teaching asst. Addison (N.Y.) Cen. Sch., 1983-85, kindergarten tchr., 1987—; tchr. Bonny Helen Nursery Sch., Corning, 1985-87. Pres. bd. trustees Addison Pub. Libr., 1986-87; supt. Addison Meth. Sunday Sch., 1972-85. So. N.Y. Tchrs. Ctr. grantee, 1988. Mem. N.Y. State Pre-First Grade Coun., Nat. Assn. for Edn. of Young Children. Republican. Avocations: cooking, reading, swimming, needlepoint, hiking. Office: Tuscarora Elem Sch 7 Cleveland Dr Addison NY 14801-1397

COOMER, DONNA R., communications executive; b. Wise, Va., June 21, 1957; d. Martin B. and Anna L. (Noe) C. BA in English and Advt. summa cum laude, Tex. Tech U., 1983. Local sales mgr. KTVT-TV, Gaylord Broadcasting, Dallas/Ft. Worth; account exec. KXAS-TV, Ft. Worth; nat. sales mgr. KTVT Gaylord Broadcasting, Dallas, Ft. Worth; gen. mgr. MMT Sales Cox Comms., Dallas/Ft. Worth. Mem. NAFE, Am. Women in Radio & TV, Phi Beta Kappa. Address: 8022 Fair Oaks Ave Dallas TX 75231-4719

COON, ELIZABETH M., artist; b. Hartselle, Feb. 27, 1932; d. Hubert R. Mitchell and Ola B. Tanner; m. Arthur George Howell, Jr. (dec.); children: Lisa Beth, Amy Ann, Arthur George III; m. Clarence Lee Coon, Dec. 27, 1990; 5 stepchildren. BA, Birmingham So. Coll., Ala., 1955. Art dir. Hubert Mitchell Industries, Hartselle, 1949—55; tchr. Eva HS, 1957—58, Morgan County HS, Hartselle, 1965—67; owner, CEO United Stage Equipment, Hartselle, 1985—2000; owner Mitch Howell Studio, Hartselle, 1960—. Founding mem. Decatur Arts Guild & Coun., 1953—54; originator, HS art dept., Hartselle, 1965; bd. mem. Fine Arts Ctr., Hartselle, 1997—. Watercolor portrait, Gov. Guy Hunt of Ala., 1987, V.P. George H.W. Bush, 1987, books, Southern Scrumptious, 1997, 2002. Charter mem. Birmingham Mus., 1967; county chmn. Rep. Party, Morgan County, 1976; bd. trustees Hartselle First United Meth. Ch., 2003—; bd. mem., archivist Hist. Soc., 1998—. Republican. Methodist. Avocations: travel, reading. Home: 805 Barkley St SW Hartselle AL 35640 Office Phone: 256-773-5745. Personal E-mail: leecoon@yahoo.com.

COONEY, JOAN GANZ, broadcast executive, director; b. Phoenix, Nov. 30, 1929; d. Sylvan C. and Pauline (Reardan) Ganz; m. Timothy J. Cooney, 1964 (div. 1975); m. Peter G. Peterson, 1980. BA, U. Ariz., 1951; degrees (hon.), Boston Coll., 1970, Hofstra U., Oberlin Coll., Ohio Wesleyan U., 1971, Princeton U., 1973, Russell Sage Coll., 1974, Harvard U., 1975, Allegheny Coll., 1976, Georgetown U., 1978, U. Notre Dame, 1982, Smith Coll., 1986, Brown U., 1987, Columbia U., 1991, NYU, 1991. Reporter Ariz. Republic, Phoenix, 1953—54; publicist NBC, 1954—55, U.S. Steel Hour, 1955—62; prodr. Sta. WNET, Channel 13, pub. affairs documentaries N.Y.C., 1962—67; TV cons. Carnegie Corp. N.Y., N.Y.C., 1967—68; exec. dir. Children's TV Workshop (producers Sesame Street, Electric Company, others) (name changed to Sesame Workshop 2000), N.Y.C., 1968—70, pres., trustee, CEO, 1970—88, chmn., CEO, 1988—90, chmn. exec. com., 1990—. Bd. dirs. Johnson & Johnson; bd. dirs. Met. Life Ins. Co. Mem. Pres.'s Commn. on Marijuana and Drug Abuse, 1971—73, Nat. News Coun., 1973—81, Pres.'s Commn. for Agenda for 80's, 1980—81, Adv. Com. for Trade Negotiations, 1978—80, Carnegie Found. Nat. Panel on High Sch., 1980—82, Gov.'s Commn. on Internat. Yr. of the Child, 1979; Mus. TV and Radio; bd. dirs. Edison Schs.; trustee N.Y. Presbyn. Med. Ctr. Named to Hall of Fame, Acad. TV Arts and Scis., 1990; recipient numerous awards for Sesame Street and other TV programs including Nat. Sch. Pub. Rels. Assn. Gold Key, 1971, Disting. Svc. medal, Columbia Tchrs. Coll., 1971, Soc. Family Man award, 1971, Nat. Inst. Social Scis. Gold medal, 1971, Frederick Douglass award, N.Y. Urban League, 1972, Silver Satellite award, Am. Women in Radio and TV, Woman of Yr. in Edn. award, Ladies Home Jour., 1975, NAEB Disting. Svc. award, NEA Friends of Edn. award, Kiwanis Decency award, 5th Women's Achiever award, Girl Scouts U.S.A., Stephen S. Wise award, 1981, Harris Found. award, 1982, Ednl. Achievement award, AAUW, 1984, Disting. Svc. to Children award, Nat. Assn. Elem. Sch. Prins., 1985, DeWitt Carter Reddick award, Coll. Comm., U. Tex.-Austin, 1986, Emmy Lifetime Achievement award, Acad. TV Arts and Scis., 1989, Presdl. medal of Freedom, 1995, Nat. Humanities Medal, 2003. Mem.: NATAS, Am. Women in Radio and TV, Internat. Radio and TV Soc., Nat. Inst. Social Scis. Office: Sesame Workshop 1 Lincoln Plz New York NY 10023-7129

COONEY, MARY ANN, public health service officer, community health nurse; B nursing, Saint Anselm Coll.; MS, Univ. N.H. Supr. sch. health Manchester Public Health Dept., NH; adminstr. chronic disease prevention N.H. Dept. Health & Human Svc., Concord, dir. div. public health svc., 2003—. Mem.: Am. Nurses Assn., N.H. Nurses Assn. (Nurse of the Yr. 1995), N.H. Public Health Assn. (past pres.). Office: Dept Health & Human Svc 6 Hazen Dr Concord NH 03301-6527*

COONEY, PATRICIA RUTH, civic worker; b. Englewood, N.J. d. Charles Aloysius and Ruth Jeannette (Foster) McEwen; m. J. Gordon Cooney, June 8, 1957; 1 child, J. Gordon, Jr. Student, Fordham U., 1950-51; DHL honoris causa, Phila. Theol. Sem. St. Charles Boromeo, 1991. Blood bank chmn. Strafford Village Civic Assn., 1968-69, sec., 1970-71; vice chmn. Spl. Gifts Com. Cath. Charities Appeal of Archdiocese of Phila., 1980—, chmn., 1985. Mem. Coun. of Mgrs. Archdiocese of Phila., 1982-88, sec., exec. com., 1983-88; bd. dirs. Cath. Charities of Archdiocese of Phila., sec., exec. com., 1988-90, v.p., exec. com., 1991—; bd. dirs. Village of Divine Providence, Phila., sec., 1983-85, v.p. exec. com., 1990—; bd. dirs. St. Edmond's Home for Crippled Children, Phila., v.p. exec. com., 1990—; bd. dirs. Don Guanella Village of Archdiocese of Phila., v.p. exec. com., 1990—; v.p. exec. com. St. Francis Homes for Boys, 2000—, St. Joseph House for Boys, 2000--, St. Vincent Svcs. for Women and Children, 2000—, St. Joseph Cath. Home for Children, 2000—, St. Gabriel's Sys., 2000—, St. Vincent's Home, Tacony, 2003—; mem. Archdiocesan Adv. Com. on Renewal, 1991-2000; Women's Com. Wills Eye Hosp., 1973—, mem.-at-large, 1st v.p.; mem. Women's Aux. St. Francis Country House, Darby, Pa., 1976—, treas., 1978-82; exec. com. United Way of Southeastern Pa., 1984-90, sec., 1986-88; bd. dirs. Chapel of Four Chaplains, 1984-89, Phila. Criminal Justice Task Force, 1989-90. Decorated Cross Pro Ecclesia et Pontifice, 1982, Lady Order St. Gregory the Gt., 1998. Republican. Avocations: reading, tennis, sailing. Home: 320 Gatcombe Ln Bryn Mawr PA 19010-3628

COONEY, SONDRA MILEY, literature and language educator; b. Mt. Vernon, Ohio, May 31, 1936; d. Wilbert H. and Orpha K. Miley; m. James F. Cooney, June 16, 1968; children: Margaret Cecilia, Charles Michael. BA, Manchester Coll., Ind., 1958; MA, U. Mich., Ann Arbor, 1959; PhD, Ohio State U., Columbus, 1970. Instr. U. Wis., Madison, 1967—68; asst. prof. English Kent State U., Ohio, 1970—79, assoc. prof. English, 1979—2005. Author: Oxford Dictionary of National Biography, 2005, Dictionary of Literary Biography, 1991, 3d edit., 1995. John Hill Burton fellow, Scottish Centre of Book, 1998. Mem.: Nat. Conf. Tchrs. English, AAUW (fellow 1966—67), Rsch. Soc. for Victorian Periodicals, AAUP, Soc. History of Authorship, Reading, and Pub. Episcopalian. Avocations: gardening, sewing. Home: 384 Burr Oak Dr Kent OH 44240 Office: Kent State Univ/Stark Campus 6000 Frank Ave NW North Canton OH 44720 Personal E-mail: scooney@kent.edu.

COONROD, DELBERTA HOLLAWAY (DEBBIE COONROD), retired elementary school educator, consultant; b. Eldon, Mo., Oct. 21, 1937; d. Delbert Leland and Zealoth (Stevens) Hollaway; m. Charles Ralph Coonrod, Aug. 26, 1961; children: Charles Leland, Marcia Renee. BS in Edn., U. Kans., 1961; MS in Edn., Ind. U., 1972, EdD in Edn., 1977; postgrad., U. Tex., Tex. Women's U. Cert. elem. tchr., Kans. Classroom tchr. Hood Sch. & Heizer Elem., Barton County, Kans., 1957-60, Emporia (Kans.) Pub. Schs., 1961-62, Lincoln (Nebr.) Pub. Schs., 1964-66, South Bend (Ind.) Sch. Corp., 1967-72; assoc. instr., vis. asst. prof. Ind. U., Bloomington, 1972-79; asst. prof. Ind. State U., Terre Haute, 1975-76; pres. Debcon, Inc., Bloomington, 1979-81; pvt. practice cons. Bloomington, 1981-85; classroom tchr. Ft. Worth Ind. Sch. Dist., 1985—2001; assoc. prof., dir. tchr. edn. Culver-Stockton Coll., Canton, Mo., 2001—02; ret., 2002. Cons. Ft. Hays State U., Kans., 1990, Edison C.C., Piqua, Ohio, 1994; instr. Tarrant County (Tex.) Jr. Coll., 1992-94; adj. asst. prof. Tex. Woman's U., Denton, 1987-2000; adj. prof. Tex. Christian U., Ft. Worth, 1991-92; adminstrv. project dir. Monroe County Sch. Corp., Bloomington, 1983-85; instr. Weatherford (Tex.) Coll., 1996-97; kindergarten cons. Penn-Harris-Madison Sch. Corp., Mishawaka, Ind., 1970-71; head adminstr. Hoosier Cts. Nursery Sch., Ind. U., 1978-79; nat. approved trainer Head Start, 1982-85; chair emeritus Who's Who in Am. Edn. adv. bd.; mem. FWISD Dist. adv. com., 1996-98. Reporter Shelby County Herald, Shelbyville, Mo., 2003—; contbr. articles to profl. jours. Bd. dirs. 4C's of Monroe County, 1979—85; mem. Greater Ft. Worth Lit. Coun., 1990—99; mem. Hist. Commn. City of Bedford, Tex., 1993—97; chmn. early literacy com. Tex. State Reading Assn., 1993—96; com. co-chair Campaign for Children, 1st Tex. coun. Camp Fire, 1992—94; educator Ft. Worth Sister Cities, 1991—2001; Harashin Educator scholar Nagaoka, Japan, 1992; bd. dirs. Ft. Worth Assn. Edn. Young Children, 1986—87; chmn. spkrs. bur. Ind. Gov.'s Com. for Internat. Yr. of the Child, 1979—80; mem. Shelby County Outreach and Ext. Coun. U. Mo., 2003—; host parent Am. Field Svc., 2003—; others. Recipient Excellence in English Edn. award Tex. Joint Coun. Tchrs. English, 1990, Ethel M. Leach award Tex. Woman's U., 1990, Outstanding Tchr. award Fort Worth Bus. Cmty./Adopt-A-Sch. Adv. Com., 1991; named Woman of Yr., Monroe County (Ind.) Girls Club, 1985, Yellow Rose of Tex., 1989, Dillard Tchr. of Week, 1992-93; named to Hon. Order Ky. Cols., 1987; Joe E. Mitchell Disting. Educator honoree Tex. Wesleyan U., 1991; honored Tex. Edn. Agy. Early Childhood Promising Practices (inclusion model), 1993-94, NYL Care Health Plans Chair for Tchg. Excellence in Early Childhood Edn., 1997-98, Extension Leaders Honor Roll, U. Mo.-Columbia, 2004. Mem. Ind. Assn. Edn. Young Children (bd. dirs. 1974-80, pres. 1979-80), Pi Lambda Theta (nat. v.p. 1985-89, pres. 1982-84, pres. Great Lakes Region II 1993-97, internat. 1st v.p. 2003, Greater Ft. Worth area chpt. Internat. Recognition award region VII Outstanding Pi Lambda Thetan 1992, pub. adv. bd. 1995-97, Edn. Endowment bd. 1996-2002), PEO (M chpt.), Delta Theta Tau, Delta Kappa Gamma; Am. Field Svc. Host parent, 2003-04. Republican. Baptist. Avocations: poetry, piano, photography, public speaking, journalism. Home: 1362 J Spur Bethel MO 63434-2312 Personal E-mail: coonrod@marktwain.net.

COONS, BARBARA LYNN, public relations executive, librarian; b. Peoria, Ill., June 1, 1948; d. Harold Leroy and Norma (Brauer) C. BA, Stephens Coll., Columbia, Mo., 1970; MA, U. N.C., 1972; MLS, Cath. U., 1982. Rsch. asst. Am. Revolution Bicentennial Office Libr. of Congress, Washington, 1974-76, editl. asst., office of the Asst. Librarian, 1976-78; ednl. liaison specialist Libr. of Congress, Washington, 1978-82; dir. rsch. svc. Gray and Co., Washington, 1982-85, v.p., 1985-86; from v.p., dir. rsch. svcs. to sr. mng. dir. Hill and Knowlton Pub. Affairs Worldwide, Washington, 1986—96; U.S. dir. rsch. svcs. Hill and Knowlton USA, 1996—2004; sr. v.p., dir. media analysis and competitive intelligence Strategy One, Washington, 2004—. Pres. Library of Congress Profl. Assn., 1982. Mem. Spl. Libraries Assn., Stephens Coll. Alumnae Club of Greater Washington (pres. 1987). Lutheran. Home: 709 Arch Hall Ln Alexandria VA 22314-6208 Office Phone: 202-326-1733. E-mail: barbara.coons@strategyone.net.

COONS, HELEN L., clinical psychologist; b. Harrisburg, Pa., Feb. 11, 1958; d. Albert and Louise (Lyons) C. BA with distinction, U. Wis., 1980, MS, 1985; PhD, Temple U., Phila., 1990. Lic. psychologist, Pa. Asst. prof. dept. mental health sci. Hahnemann U., Phila., 1990-94, clin. asst. prof. psychiatry, 1994—; dir. evaluation The Health Fedn. Phila., 1994—2000; pres. Women's Mental Health Assn., 2000—. Bd. dirs. YWCA, Madison, Wis., 1982-84. Mem. APA (chair com. on women and health, div. health psychology 1989-92, 98-99), Pa. Psychol. Assn. Office: Women's Mental Health Assn 255 S 17th St Ste 2701 Philadelphia PA 19103

COONS-LONG, BRITTNEY LEIGH, defender; b. Winfield, Ala., Feb. 17, 1972; d. Fred and Patricia Coons; m. Darren Long, June 2, 2001; 1 child, Abbigayle Long. BS, Judson Coll., Marion, Ala., 1993; JD, U. Ala., Tuscaloosa, 1996. Bar: Ala. 1996, Ga. 2001. Atty. Smith, Hannah & Parker, Valdosta, Ga., 2001—05; asst. dist. atty. Dist. Attorney's Office, Tuscaloosa, 1996—2000; asst. pub. defender Cir. Pub. Defender Office, Valdosta, 2005—. Mem.: Ga. Bar Assn., Ala. Bar Assn., Nat. Assn. Criminal Def. Lawyer's, Ga. Assn. Criminal Def. Lawyer's, Valdosta Assn. Criminal Def. Lawyers, Valdosta Bar Assn. Office: Cir Pub Defender PO Box 1586 Valdosta GA 31603 Office Phone: 229-671-2812. Personal E-mail: bcoons-long@lowndescounty.com.

COONTZ, STEPHANIE JEAN, history professor, writer; b. Seattle, Aug. 31, 1944; d. Sidney Coontz and Patricia (McIntosh) Waddington; 1 child, Kristopher. BA with honors, U. Calif., Berkeley, 1966; MA, U. Wash., Seattle, 1970. Mem. faculty Evergreen State Coll., Olympia, Wash., 1975—. Dir. rsch. and pub. edn. Coun. Contemporary Families, 1993—. Author: The Way We Never Were: American Families and the Nostalgia Trap, 1992, The Social Origins of Private Life: A History of American Families, 1988, The Way We Really Are: Coming to Terms With America's Changing Families, 1997, Marriage, A History: From Obedience to Intimacy, or How Love Conquered Marriage, 2005; (with others) Women's Work, Men's Property: On the Origins of Gender and Class, 1986, History and Family Theory, vol. II, 1989; contbr. numerous articles to profl. jours. Woodrow Wilson Found. fellow, 1968-69; recipient Washington Gov's. Writer's award, 1989, Dale Richmond award Am. Acad. Pediatrics, 1995, Visionary Leadership award Coun. Contemporary Families, 2004. Mem. Am. Studies Assn., Am. Hist. Assn., Orgn. Am. Historians. Office: Evergreen State Coll 2700 Evergreen Pwy NW Olympia WA 98505-0001 Address: c/o Viking Publicity 375 Hudson St New York NY 10014 Office Phone: 360-867-6703. Business E-Mail: coontz@evergreen.edu.

COOPER, APRIL HELEN, family practice nurse practitioner; b. Evergreen Park, Ill., Dec. 24, 1951; d. Frank and Anne (Mirocha) Stevens; m. Michael Dennis, June 20, 1970; children: Christine Michelle, Brian Michael, Jeannette Michelle. AAS, Ohio U., 1981, BSN, 1996; MS, Wright State U., 2000. RN Ohio; cert. family nurse practitioner, ANCC. Supr. home health care Med. Pers. Pool, Cambridge, Ohio, 1989-91; primary nurse pediat. home care Primary Care Nursing Svcs., Dublin, Ohio, 1989-91; case mgr. Buckeye Home Health Svc., Zanesville, Ohio, 1990-91; with home health svcs. Genesis Home Care, Zanesville, 1981-98; family practice nurse practitioner Bucyrus Cmty. Hosp., 2001—. Mem. ANA, Golden Key. Phi Kappa Phi, Sigma Theta Tau, Gamma Pi Delta. Republican. Methodist. Avocations: reading professional journals, travel. Home: 3172 Oak Dr Bucyrus OH 44820-9654

COOPER, CARLOTTA ARLENE, writer, animal breeder; b. Jasper, Tenn., Feb. 21, 1962; d. Carl Otis and Betty Charlsie MacNabb Cooper; life ptnr. Desterie Shane Grimes; 1 child, Orion Hunter Grimes. B. U. South, Sewanee, 1984. Programming dir. Miller Plz., Chattanooga, 1987—89, exec. dir., 1989—91; writer Blue Cross and Blue Shield Tenn., Chattanooga, 1993—95; writer, columnist Dog News and other nat. mag., N.Y.C., 1996—; writer TriCities.com, Media Gen., Bristol, Va., 2004—06. Showdog owner, breeder, handler Hever English Setters, Kingsport, Tenn., 1987—; adj. prof. Va. Intermont Coll., Bristol, 2004—. Author: (making your home safe from puppies) Puppy-Proofing Your Home; contbr. articles to profl. jours. Recipient Guerryaward, U. South, 1984; fellow, U. Va., 1985—87; scholar, U. South, 1983; Wilkins scholar, 1991—94. Mem.: English Setter Assn. Am. (Previous awards for my dogs include awards as best bred by exhibitor, best puppy 1997, 1998, 1999), Ctrl. Carolina English Setter Club, Phi Beta Kappa. D-Liberal. Episcopalian. Avocations: dogs, horses, history, literature, photography. Office: Virginia Intermont Coll 1013 Moore St Bristol VA 24201 E-mail: carlottacooper@vic.edu.

COOPER, CHARLEEN FRANCES, special and elementary education educator; b. Jamaica, N.Y., Oct. 23, 1948; d. Charles and Dolly (Oakes) Fells; m. Chris M. Cooper, June 23, 1969 (div.); children: Chris A., Scott F. BS in Spl. Edn. cum laude, Coll. of St. Joseph, Rutland, Vt., 1985; postgrad., The Provider; MA in Edn., Castleton State Coll., 1994. Cert. spl. and elem. edn. tchr., Vt.; cert. learning specialist/consulting tchr. spl. edn. Spl. edn. and resource rm. tchr. Rutland City Pub. Sch., 1985-88; tchr. spl. edn., multi-handicapped Rutland Cen. Supervisory Union, 1988-91; spl. edn. and resource rm. tchr. Addison-Rutland Supervisory Union, 1991-92; mktg. instr. Stafford Tech. Ctr., Rutland City Pub. Schs., 1992-93; vocat. rehab. employment facilitator State of Vt., 1995-96; chpt. 1 title 1 head instr. Bennington Sch., Inc., 1996-97; title 1 head instr. Catamount Elem., Bennington, Vt., 1997—2002, resource rm. tchr., 1998; tchr. resource rm. Poultney Elem. Sch., Poultney, Vt., 2002—. Coord. program, instr. Integration of Proctor High Sch. Students with Spl. Needs, 1989-91. Coll. of St. Joseph scholar. Avocations: gardening, motorcycling, flying. Home: PO Box 40 North Clarendon VT 05759-0040 Office: Pooultney Elem Sch Circle Poultney VT Personal E-mail: coopsmom@vermontel.net.

COOPER, CONSTANCE CARTER, academic administrator, education consultant, researcher; b. Detroit, Dec. 2, 1935; d. Emmett Cornelius and Earline Maxine (Boone) Carter; divorced; 1 child, Chauncey Lance. BA, U. Mich., 1953; MA, Wayne State U., 1963, EdD, 1971. Secondary sch. tchr. Detroit Pub. Schs., 1958-66, adminstr., 1968-77; adj. prof. Wayne State U., Detroit, 1966-68; adminstr. West Harvey (Ill.) Schs., 1977-78; prof. edn. Northern Ill. U., DeKalb, 1978-79, Seattle U., 1979-82; dean Coppin State Coll., Balt., 1982-86; dean, assoc. provost U. Akron, Ohio, 1986-89; provost, v.p. U. D.C., Washington, 1989—. Cons. Seattle Pub. Schs., 1981-82, Ky. State Dept. Edn., Louisville, 1984-86, Ednl. Testing Svcs., Princeton, N.J., 1984-86 Author: (textbook) Public Education, 1981; contbr. articles to profl. jours. Chair Human Rights Commn., Detroit, 1976-77; chair, exec. bd. mem. Nat. Alliance Black Sch. Educators, Washington, 1985-87; bd. dirs. U. Mich. Alumni Assn., 1987—, YMCA, Akron, 1987-89. Regents-Alumni scholar U. Mich., 1953, Regents scholar Wayne State U., 1961, Fulbright-Hayes scholar, 1987. Mem. Nat. Assn. Women's Deans (adminstrn. counselor), Am. Assn. Higher Edn., Assn. Acad. Affairs Officers, Orgn. Instl. Affiliates (exec. bd.), Delta Sigma Theta (pres. 1950-53), Eta Phi Beta (pres. 1985-86). Democrat. Episcopalian. Avocations: theater, skiing, sports, reading. Office: U DC 4200 Connecticut Ave NW Washington DC 20008-1176

COOPER, CORINNE, communications consultant, lawyer; b. Albuquerque, July 12, 1952; d. David D. and Martha Lucille (Rosenblum) C. BA magna cum laude, U. Ariz., 1975, JD summa cum laude, 1978. Bar: Ariz. 1978, U.S. Dist. Ct. Ariz. 1978, Mo. 1985. Assoc. Streich, Lang, Weeks & Cardon, Phoenix, 1978—82; asst. prof. U. Mo., Kansas City, 1982—86, assoc. prof., 1986—94, prof., 1994—2000, prof. emerita, 2000—; pres. Profl. Presence, Comm. Cons., Tucson, 2001—. Vis. prof. U. Wis., Madison, 1985, 91, U. Pa., Phila., 1988, U. Ariz., 1993, U. Colo., 1994. Author: (with Bruce Meyerson) A Drafter's Guide to Alternative Dispute Resolution, 1991, How to Build a Law Firm Brand, 2005; editor: The Portable UCC, 1993, 3d edit., 2001, 4th edit., 2004, Getting Graphic I and II, 1993, 94, The New Article 9, 1999, 2d edit., 2000; editor in chief Bus. Law Today, 1995-97; mem. editl. bd. ABA Jour., 1999-05; author, editor: Attorney Liability in Bankruptcy, 2006; contbr. articles to profl. jours., chpts. to books. Legal counsel Mo. for Hart campaign, 1984; dir. issues Goddard for Gov. campaign, 1990. Mem. ABA (mem. coun. bus. sect. 1992-96, uniform comml. code com., chmn. bus. sect. membership com. 1992-94, editl. bd. Bus. Law Today, 1991-97, sect. of bus. law pubs. 1998-02, standing com. on strategic comm. 2001-2003, coun. gen. practice sect. 2003-2005, mem. coun. gen. practice divsn. 2004-), Am. Law Inst., Am. Assn. Law Schs. (comml. law 1982-00), Ariz. Bar Assn., Mo. Bar Assn. (comml. law com.), Order of Coif, Phi Beta Kappa, Phi Kappa Phi. Democrat. Jewish. Office: Profl Presence 4558 N 1st Ave Tucson AZ 85718 Office Phone: 520-795-0522. Business E-Mail: c2@professionalpresence.com.

COOPER, DEBORAH KAY, forensic psychologist; b. Durango, Colo., Sept. 30, 1955; d. Cecil Eugene and Margaret Elaine Cooper. BS, San Jose State U., 1990; PhD, U. Ga. Lic. clin. psychologist Va. Postdoctoral fellow in forensic psychology U. Mass. Med. Ctr., Worcester, 1996; forensic psychologist Forensic Health Svcs., Bridgewater, Mass., 1996—98, Dept. Mental Health, Mental Retardation and Substance Abuse Svcs., Petersburg, Va., 2001—; psychologist Dept. Juvenile Justice, Beaumont, Va., 1998—2001. Author: Behavioral Sciences and the Law, 1997; co-author: Behavioral Sciences and the Law, 5-year update, 1997. Recipient Spl. Recognition award, Dept. Mental Health, Mental Retardation and Substance Abuse Svcs., 2005. Mem.: APA, Am. Psychology-Law Soc. Home: PO Box 765 Glen Allen VA 23060 Office: DMHMRSAS PO Box 1797 Richmond VA 23803

COOPER, DORIS JEAN, market research executive; b. NYC, Dec. 17, 1934; d. James N. and Georgina N. (Cassidy) Breslin; m. S. James Cooper, June 17, 1956; 1 son, David Austin. Student, Sch. of Commerce, NYU, 1953-55, Hunter Coll., N.Y.C., 1956-57. Asst. coding supr. Crossley S-D Surveys, N.Y.C., 1955-57; asst. field supr. Trendex, Inc., N.Y.C., 1957-59; coding dir. J. Walter Thompson Co., N.Y.C., 1960-63, Audits & Surveys, N.Y.C., 1964-65; pvt. practice cons. N.Y.C., 1965-73; pres. Cooper Svcs., Hastings-on-Hudson, NY, 1973—; pres., CEO computer tabulation and lang. manipulation Doris J. Cooper Assocs., Hastings-on-Hudson, 1989—. Cons. market rsch. Dir. citizen corps. Hastings on Hudson. Mem. Am. Mktg. Assn. (N.Y. chpt.), nat. Bus. Women Owners Assn., Am. Assn. Pub. Opinion Researchers (N.Y. chpt.), Acad. Health Svcs. Mktg., Hastings C. of C. Republican. Episcopalian. Personal E-mail: doris.cooper@verizon.net.

COOPER, ELVA JUNE, artist; b. Wilmore, Ky., Mar. 18, 1933; d. Scott Combs and Rhoda Mae (Hundley) Bishop; m. Lowell Howard Cooper, Nov. 29, 1952; children: Lowell Scott, Linda Janet, Candace Lea, Connie Lynn, June Roxanne. Student, Georgetown Coll., 1952-53, Southwestern Jr. Coll., 1961, U. West Fla., 1994, Pensacola Jr. Coll., 1998. Owner June Bug Art and Gifts, Pensacola, Fla., 1973—2003, The Studio, Pensacola, Fla., 1986—. Cons. editor Church Recreation, 1993-95; contbr. articles to mags. Drama writer, dir. Myrtle Grove Bapt. Ch., Pensacola, Fla., 1977-96, artist in residence, 1973-96, discipleship tng. dir., 1973-79, 88-97; sec. Lillian (Ala.) First Bapt. Ch., 1984-95; writer Bapt. Sunday Sch. Bd., Nashville, Tenn., 1987-98; state recreation counselor Fla. Bapt. Conv., Jacksonville, 1994—; discipleship tng. dir. Pensacola Bay Bapt. Assn., 1994-96. Three time winner of Peggy award Popular Ceramics Mag., 1970; numerous other awards in art shows; inducted into Internat. Soc. Poetry as Disting. Mem. Mem. Quayside Art Gallery (asst. publicity 1984, pub. rels. dir. 2005—, bd. dirs. 2005—), Art Study Club. Baptist. Avocations: porcelain doll making, sewing, flower arranging, stained glass artist.

COOPER, GINNIE, library director; b. Worthington, Minn., 1945; d. Lawrence D. and Ione C.; m. Richard Bauman, Dec. 1995; 1 child, Daniel Jay. Student, Coll. St. Thomas, U. Wis., Parkside; BA, S.D. State U.; MA in Libr. Sci., U. Minn. Tchr. Flandreau Indian Sch., SD, 1967-68, St. Paul Pub. Schs., 1968-69; br. libr. Wash. County Libr., Lake Elmo, Minn., 1970-71, asst. dir., 1971-75; assoc. adminstr., libr. U. Minn. Med. Sch., Mpls., 1975-77; dir. Kenosha Pub. Libr., Wis., 1977-81; county libr. Alameda County Libr., Calif., 1981-90; dir. librs. Multnomah County Libr., Portland, Oreg., 1990—2003; exec. dir. Brooklyn Pub. Libr., NY, 2003—06, DC Pub. Libr., 2006—. Chair County Mgr. Assn.; county adminstr. Mayor's Exec. Roundtable. Mem. ALA (mem. LAMA, PLA and RASD coms., elected to coun. 1987, 91, mem. legislation com. 1986-90, mem. orgn. com. 1990—), Calif. Libr. Assn. (pres. CIL, 1985, elected to coun. 1986, pres. Calif. County Librs. 1986), Oreg. Libr. Assn., Pub. Libr. Assn. (pres. 1997-98). Office: DC Pub Libr 901 G St NW Washington DC 20001*

COOPER, GLORIA, editor, press critic; b. Oak Park, Ill., Jan. 8, 1931; c. Sam and Madelyn (Brandt) Glaser; m. Wallace J. Cooper, June 3, 1950; children— Alison, Julie BA summa cum laude, Briarcliff Coll., 1970; MA, Columbia U., 1974. From asst. editor to mng. editor to dep. exec. editor Columbia Journalism Rev., N.Y.C., 1974—. Editor: Squad Helps Dog Bite Victim, 1980, Red Tape Holds Up New Bridge, 1987; contbr. articles, revs., editorials to Columbia Journalism Rev., 1974— Mem. Soc. Prof. Journalists, Princeton Club (N.Y.C.). Home: 91 Long Hill Rd E Briarcliff Manor NY 10510-2611 Office: Columbia U Columbia Journalism Rev 207 Journalism Bldg New York NY 10027 Office Phone: 212-854-1887. Business E-Mail: gc15@columbia.edu.

COOPER, ILENE LINDA, magazine editor, author; b. Chgo., Mar. 10, 1948; d. Morris and Lillian (Friedman) C.; m. Robert Seid, May 28, 1972 (div. 1995). BJ, U. Mo., 1969; MLS, Rosary Coll., 1973. Head of children's svcs. Winnetka (Ill.) Libr. Dist., 1974-80; editor children's books Booklist Mag., ALA, Chgo., 1981—. Author: Susan B. Anthony, 1983, Choosing Sides, 1990 (Internat. Reading Assn.-Children's Book Coun. choice 1990), Mean Streak, 1991, Jewish Holidays All Year Round, 2002, Sam I Am, 2004, (series) Frances in the Fourth Grade, 1991, The Dead Sea Scrolls, 1997, numerous others. Mem. Soc. Midland Authors, Soc. Children's Book Writers, Children's Reading Roundtable. Jewish. Office: Booklist Mag 50 E Huron St Chicago IL 60611-5295

COOPER, IVA JEAN, special education educator; b. Newark, Mar. 6, 1950; d. William Brady McClintock and Aleata Margaret Locke-McClintock; m. Jeffrey Lamont Cooper, Oct. 18, 1986; children: Brianna, Jasmine. BS Comms., Howard U., 1973; MA Comms., Mich. State U., 1976. Intern Crippled Children's Soc., Hollywood, Calif., 1979—80; speech & lang. therapist pediats. Sierra Permanente Med. Grp., Fontana, Calif., 1980—81; supr. speech & lang. pathology Head Start Devel. Coun., Stockton, Calif., 1981; spl. edn. educator Manteca Unified Sch. Dist., Calif., 1981—. Mem.: Internat. Soc. Poets, AAUW, Am. Speech Hearing & Lang. Assn. Home: 1928 W Bristol Ave Stockton CA 95204

COOPER, JAMIE LEE, writer; d. Ralph Francis Cooper and Esther Allene Kellner, Lee Frederick Kellner (Stepfather). Grad., Fairfax Hall, Waynesboro, Va., 1947. Radio comml. writer Sta. WKBV, Richmond, Ind., 1947—49; profl. writer, novelist, short stories, essays, libretti various pubs., N.Y.C., Paris, 1955—; creative writing tchr. Ind. U., Bloomington, 1964—88, Ball State U., Muncie, Ind., 1964—88, Evansville (Ind.) U., 1964—88. Liaison, mentoring, judging novel scholarships, nat. competitions Ind. U., Ball State U., Evansville U., judging competitions for several out of state univs., Ind., 1963—88. Author: The Horn in the Forest, 1963 (Most Disting. Fiction of Midwest, 1964), Shadow of a Star, 1965 (Most Disting. Fiction of Midwest, 1966), Rapaho, 1967 (Most Disting. Fiction of Midwest, 1968), The Castaways, 1970 (Most Disting. Fiction of Midwest, 1971), The Great Dandelion, 1972 (Most Disting. Fiction of Midwest, 1973), Grasshopper Summer, 1974 (Most Disting. Fiction of Midwest, 1975); librettist: chorale Song of Mankind, 1970 (Friends of Am. Writers award, 1971), We, the Dreamers, 1975 (Friends of Am. Writers award, 1976), Bad That Woman, 1976 (Friends of Am. Writers award, 1977). Grantee, NEA, 1976. Mem.: PEN, Nat. Writers' Union, Authors Guild. Avocations: playing the sitar, cooking, gardening. Home: 111 S 34th St Richmond IN 47374 Personal E-mail: jleighcooper@aol.com.

COOPER, JANELLE LUNETTE, neurologist, educator; b. Ann Arbor, Mich., Dec. 11, 1955; d. Robert Marion and Madelyn (Leonard) C.; children: Lena Christine, Nicholas Dominic. BA in Chemistry, Reed Coll., 1978; MD, Vanderbilt U., 1986. Diplomate Nat. Bd. Med. Examiners; diplomate in neurology Am. Bd. Psychiatry and Neurology; registered med. technologist Am. Soc. Clin. Pathologists. Med. technologist Swedish Hosp. Med. Ctr., Seattle, 1978-80, U. Wash. Clin. Chemistry, Seattle, 1980-82, Vanderbilt U. Hosp., Nashville, 1983-84; intern medicine Vanderbilt U. Med. Ctr., Nashville, 1986-87, resident neurology, 1987-90; instr. neurology Med. Coll. Pa., Phila., 1990-91, asst. prof., clerkship dir., 1991—, mem. curriculum com., 1990-91, vis. asst. prof., 1991-95; neurologist Greater Ann Arbor Neurology Assocs., 1991-93; dir. neurol. svcs., med. dir. Indsl. Rehab. Program St. Francis Hosp., Escanaba, Mich., 1993-98; founder, dir. No. Neuroscis., Escanaba, 1993-98; pres. HolderLady, Ltd., 1996—; chmn. dept. medicine St. Francis Hosp., Escanaba, Mich., 1998-99; dir. Affinity Health Sys., Oshkosh, Wis., 1998—; med. dir. Memory Clinic of the Upper Peninsula, Escanaba, Mich., 1998—. Neurologist Affinity Med. Group, Oshkosh, Wis., 1998—; physician MCP Neurology Assocs., Phila., 1990-91; emergency rm. physician Tenn. Christian Med. Ctr., 1989-90. Contbr. articles to Annals of Ophthalmology, Ophthalmic Surgery. Vol. Rape and Sexual Abuse Ctr., Nashville, 1988-90; mem. adminstrv. bd. Edgehill United Meth. Ch., Nashville, 1989-90; mem. editorial bd. Nashville Women's Alliance, 1989-90; bd. dirs. Upper Peninsula Physicians Network, 1995-98; mem. adv. bd. Perspective Adult Daycare Ctr., 1996-99; founding dir. Memory Clinic of Upper Peninsula, 1998-00; profl. adv. com. NE Wis. Alzheimer's Assn., 1999—. Recipient Svc. award for outstanding contbns. Rape and Sexual Abuse Ctr., 1990; epilepsy minifellow Bowman Gray U., 1995. Mem. AMA (physician's Recognition award 1989—), AAAS, Am. Med. Women's Assn., Am. Acad. Neurology, Am. Psychol. Soc., Wis. State Med. Soc., N.Y. Acad. Scis., Upper Peninsula Neuro Assn. (v.p. 1998-99, trustee 1998-99), Upper Peninsula Physician Network (bd. dirs. 1995-98), Aircraft Owners and Pilots Assn., Women in Aviation Internat. (charter), Air Force Assn. (life patron). Methodist. Achievements include first synthesis of Difluoromethanedisulfonic Acid; research on neurobehavioral disorders; on neuroendocrinology of sexual development, identity and orientation; on the history of women in medicine on effects of dietary lipids on the etiology of Alzheimer's disease; clinical investigation trials for new medications for dementias and epilepsy. Office: Affinity Med Group Dept Neurology 2725 Jackson St Oshkosh WI 54901-1513 Home: 2819 Hughes St Oshkosh WI 54902-7158 E-mail: jcooper@affinityhealth.org.

COOPER, JEAN SARALEE, judge; b. Huntington, N.Y., Mar. 7, 1946; d. Ralph and Henrietta (Halbreich) Cooper; stepchildren: Mitzi Concklin Prochnow, John Todd Concklin. BA, Sophie Newcomb Coll. of Tulane U., 1968; JD, Emory U., 1970. Bar: La. 1970, Ga. 1970, U.S. Dist. Ct. (ea. dist.) La. 1970, U.S. Ct. Appeals (5th cir.) 1972, U.S. Ct. Appeals (2d cir.) 1976, U.S. Ct. Appeals (4th cir.) 1977, U.S. Ct. Appeals (fed. cir.), U.S. Supreme Ct. 1974. Trial atty. Office of Solicitor, U.S. Dept. Labor, Washington, 1970-73, spl. projects asst., 1973, sr. trial atty., 1973-77; adminstrv. judge Bd. Contract Appeals, HUD, Washington, 1977—2003, acting chmn. and chief judge, 1980-81, vice chmn., 1983—2003; bd. mem. Coalition for Free Trade, 2003—. Cons.; lectr. Contbr. articles to profl. jours. Recipient Moot Ct. award, Tulane Law Sch., 1968. Fellow: Am. Bar Found. (vice chair debarment and suspension com. pub. contracts sect. 1992—97, sr. vice chair alcohol beverage com., adjudication com., adminstrv. law sect.); mem.: ABA (sec. jud. conf. 1979—, sec. jud. divsn. Nat. Conf. Adminstrv. Law Judges 1979—, standing com. on jud. selection, tenure and compensation. 1992—95, chair 1999—2000, standing com. on fed. jud. improvements 2000—01, adminstrn. law sect), Nat. Conf. Bd. Contract Appeals Mems., Prettyman-Leventhal Am. Inn of Ct. (past pres., master of bench), Am. Law Inst. (life), Am. Inns of Ct. Found. (trustee 1992—98, leadership com. 1998—), La. Bar Assn. Republican. Home: 2800 Flagmaker Dr Falls Church VA 22042-2200 Personal E-mail: jeansaralee@cs.com.

COOPER, JEANNE A., retired pathologist; b. Pitts. d. Lardin Monroe Cooper and Antoinette S. Swartz; m. James Thomas Ault, May 14, 1953 (dec. Feb. 1979); 1 child, Toni Lynn Ault. BS, Waynesburg Coll., Pa., 1946; MD, Hahnemann Med. Coll. (now Drexel U.), Phila., 1947. Gen. practitioner, Punxsutawney, Pa., 1949—52; resident VA and Presbyn. Hosp., Pitts., 1952—56; mem. med. staff VA Rsch. Hosp., Chgo., 1956—58; vis. prof. Teheran U. Med. Sch., Iran, 1958—59; dep. med. examiner L.A. County, Calif., 1959—61; pathologist, vice chmn. and chmn. Mercy Hosp., Pitts., 1961—91; ret., 1992. Instr. pathology Northwestern U. Med. Sch., Chgo., 1956—58; instr. Duquesne U., Pitts., 1966—74; clin. asst. prof. U. Pitts. Med. Sch., 1962—74, clin. assoc. prof., 1974—80, clin. prof., 1980—93; med. cons. Centro de Obras Sociales, Chimbote, Peru, 1991—2003; sec. Jefferson County Med. Soc., 1949—52; mem. exec. coun. Penna Assn. Pathologists, 1975—81, 1985—87, sec., 1979—81, v.p., 1981—83, pres., 1983—85. Mem. bd. Blue Shield Med. Bd., 1986—92, Family Hospice, South Hills, Pa., 1986—91, Pitts. Mercy Found., 1997—2005, Found. for History of Women in Medicine, Phila., 1998—2001. Recipient Staff Leadership award, Mercy Hosp., 1986, Tchg. award, Pitts. Med. Sch. Dept. Pathology, 1988, Manifesting the Kingdom award, Diocese of Pitts., 1999. Fellow: Am. Soc. Clin. Pathology (Penna del. 1986—89), Coll. Am. Pathologists (mem. ho. of dels. 1980—93, mem. at large governing bd. 1986—90, sgt.-at-arms governing bd. 1990—92); mem.: U.S. and Can. Acad. Pathology, Pa. Assn. Pathology, Pitts. Pathology Soc. (sec.-treas. 1970—75, pres. 1975—76), AMA, Pa. Med. Soc., Allegheny County Med. Soc.

COOPER, JENNIFER ROYANN, psychiatrist; b. Valdosta, Ga., Jan. 18, 1973; d. Michael Thomas and Margaret Ann Cooper. BA magna cum laude, DePauw U., Greencastle, Ind., 1995; MD, Johns Hopkins U., Balt., 1999. Lic. physician NY, diplomate Am. Bd. Psychiatry and Neurology, Am. Bd. Addiction Psychiatry. Resident in psychiatry NY Presbyn. Hosp./Weill Cornell Med. Ctr./Payne Whitney Clinic, NYC, 1999—2003; fellow in addiction psychiatry Weill Med. Coll. of Cornell U., NYC, 2003—04; staff psychiatrist Bridge Back to Life, NYC, 2004—05; pvt. practice psychiatry NYC, 2004—; med. dir. drug treatment Exponents, NYC, 2004—. Clin. instr. psychiatry Weill Med. Coll. of Cornell U., 2006—. Named Career Directions Resident of the Yr., Pfizer Inc., 2002; recipient Alumni award for resident tchg., Payne Whitney Clinic, 2003. Mem.: AMA (Physician Recognition award 2002—03), Am. Acad. Addiction Psychiatry, Am. Soc. Addiction Medicine, Am. Psychiat. Assn. Avocations: skiing, scuba diving. Office: 239 E 73d St Ste 1W-A New York NY 10021

COOPER, JO MARIE, principal; b. L.A., Oct. 13, 1947; d. Joseph M. Langham and Christina (Burton) Lister; m. Leonard Cooper Jr., May 13, 1967; children: Leonard Joseph, Jo-Lynne Louise, Layton Bishop. Grad., Chgo. State Coll., 1967; MA, Governor State U., University Park, Ill., 1975; MA in Ednl. Adminstrn., Gov. State U., University Park, Ill., 1997. Postal worker, mail handler Chgo. Post Office, 1966-67; tchr. Chgo. Bd. Edn., 1968-75, resource tchr., 1975-93, instrnl. adminstrv. asst., 1993—, dean of girls; interim prin. Oglesby Elem. Sch., 1998, prin., 1998—2004; ret. Advisor Homewood (Ill.) Full Gospel Ch., 1992-94, Homewood Christian Acad., 1994—. Pres. South Ctrl. Women's Aglow, Chgo., 1983-85; chair women's ministries Homewood Full Gospel Ch., 1990-94; South Chicago area leader Marriage Ministries Internat., University Park, 1994—; advisor Human Rels. Commn., University Park, 1987-89. Mem. ASCD. Pentecostal. Avocations: reading, walking, hooklatching, bowling. Office: Oglesby Elem Sch 7646 S Green St Chicago IL 60620-2854

COOPER, JOSEPHINE SMITH, trade association and public affairs executive; b. Raleigh, N.C., Aug. 2, 1945; d. Joseph W. and Marie (Peele) S. BA in Bus. and Econs., Meredith Coll., Raleigh, 1967; MS in Mgmt., Duke U., 1977. Program analyst Office of Air & Quality Planning and Stds. EPA, Rsch., Triangle Park, NC, 1968-78; environ. protection specialist Office of Rsch. and Devel., Washington, 1978-80; mem. profl. staff majority leader Howard H. Baker, Jr., U.S. Senate Com. on Environ. and Pub. Works, Washington, 1980-83; asst. adminstr. for external affairs EPA, Washington, 1983-85; asst. v.p. for environ. and health program Am. Paper Inst., Washington, 1985-86; sr. v.p. for policy Synthetic Organic Chem. Mfrs. Assn., Washington, 1986-88; sr. v.p., dir. environ. policy Hill & Knowlton, Inc., Washington, 1988-91; founder, dir. Capitoline Internat. Group, Ltd., Washington, 1991-92; v.p. environ. and regulatory affairs Am. Forest & Paper Assn., 1992-99; pres., CEO Alliance of Automobile Mfrs., Washington,

1999—2004; group v.p. for govt. and industry affairs Toyota Motor N.Am., 2004—. Treas. RTP Fed. Credit Union, 1969—72, pres., CEO, 1975; pres. Women's Coun. on Energy and Environment, 1986—88, Nat. Coun. on Clean Indoor Air, 1988—96; mem. nat. adv. environ. health scis. coun. NIH, 1990—94; mem. adv. com. EPA Clean Air Act, 1994—2005; liaison mem. trade and environ. policy adv. com. USTR, 1994—2002; chmn. bd. Nat. Urban Air Toxic Rsch. Ctr., 2003—; bd. dirs. Washington First Bank. Bd. visitors Duke U. Nicholas Sch. Environment, 1994—2002, Duke U. Fuqua Sch. Bus., 2004—; bd. dirs. Washington Performing Arts Soc., 2005—. Congl. fellow, 1979-80. Mem.: NAM (coun. bd. dirs. 2000—04), Orgn. of Internat. Auto Assn. (pres.), Orgn. d'Internationale Constructeurs d'Automobiles (chmn. 2003—04), Am. Soc. Assn. Execs. (bd. dirs. 2000—03), U.S. C. of C. (Com. of 100 2000—04), Women in Govt. Rels., Federally Employed Women (pres. 1972—77, treas.). Mem. Christian Ch. (Disciples Of Christ). Office Phone: 202-463-6830. Business E-Mail: jo_cooper@tma.toyota.com.

COOPER, JOY FRANCES, mayor; b. Trenton, N.J., May 14, 1960; d. Peter Emil and Patricia Ventura; m. Harry A. Cooper, Oct. 13, 1985; children: Jamie Melissa, Alana Stephanie, Matt Charles. AA in Bus. Adminstrn., Braward County Cmty. Coll., Laighome, Pa. Auditing asst. State of N.J.; mgr. Bucks County Orthop. Group, Fairless Hills, Pa., Rita's Italian Ices, Hollywood and Avatura, Fla.; commissioner City of Hallandale Beach, vice mayor, mayor. Bd. mem. Fla. League of Cities; v.p. Broward League of Cities; pres. cmty. redevelopment agy. City of Hallandale Beach; weekly columnist South Fla. Sun Times, Hallandale. Democrat. Jewish. Office: Mayor City of Hallandale Beach 400 S Fed Hwy Hallandale Beach FL 33009-6433 Home: 301 Holiday Dr Hallandale Beach FL 33009 Office Phone: 954-457-1300.

COOPER, JOYCE BEATRICE, medical/surgical nurse; b. Marston, Mo., Sept. 29, 1941; d. Lester Hendrex and Fannie Beatrice (McCool) McGruder; m. Joe Taylor Cooper, Oct. 4, 1957; children: Terry Joe, Tracy James, Timothy John. Creative writing degree, Chgo. Writers Inst., 1973; diploma, Kokomo Sch. Practical Nursing, 1977; ADN, Marian Coll., 1987; BSBA, Ind. Wesleyan U., 1996. Cert. ob-gyn. nurse, trauma nurse, cardiac and respiratory nurse, life support care nurse. Nurse Vis. Nurse Assn. North Ctrl. Ind., Elwood; dir. nursing Tipton Nursing Ctr., Ind., 1991—97, Windsor Estates, Kokomo, Ind., 1997—98; intake coord. SCCI-Kokomo-Long-Term Acute Care Hosp., 1998—2002, nurse exec., 2002—. Coord. MDS Madison Pl. Long Term Care, 2005—, dir. mktg., 2004—; cons. Summit Ctr., 2005—. Mem. NAACOG, ANA, Vis. Nurse Assn., Soc. Nursing Profls. Home: Box 205 309 McClellan Windfall IN 46076

COOPER, JUDITH KASE, retired theater educator, playwright; b. Wilmington, Del., Dec. 13, 1932; d. Charles Robert and Elizabeth Edna (Baker) Kase; stepchildren: James, Elizabeth, John, Katherine, Ann, Patty, Doreen, Jeff. BA, U. Del., 1955; MA, Case Western Res. U., 1956. Tchr., dir. children's theatre Agnes Scott Coll., 1956, U. Tenn., 1957, U. Md., Germany, 1958-60, Denver Civic Theatre, Denver U., Kent Sch., 1960-61; dir. children's theatre U. N.H., Durham, 1962-69; dir. theatre resources for youth Somersworth, NH, 1966-69; assoc. prof. theatre U. South Fla., Tampa, 1969-74, assoc. prof. edn., 1975-83, prof., 1984—99, artistic dir. ednl. theatre, 1976—99, ret., 1999. Project dir. Hillsborough County Artists-in-Schs. Evaluation and Inservice Project, 1980—82; dir. Internat. Ctr. for Studies in Theatre Edn.; mem. Nat. Theatre Conf., Coll. Fellows Am. Theatre. Author: The Creative Drama Book: Three Approaches, other books; editor: Creative Drama in a Developmental Context; Children's Theatre, Creative Drama and Learning, Drama as a Meaning Maker, Introduction to Drama Teacher Resource Guide, Interconnecting Pathways to Human Experience, Teaching the Arts Across the Disciplines; contbr. articles to profl. jours.; pub. (plays) Snow White and The Seven Dwarfs, 1960, The Emperor's New Clothes, 1966, Southern Fried Cracker Tales, 1995. Bd. dirs. Fla. Alliance for Arts Edn., sec., 1976-77, vice-chmn., 1979-82, chmn., 1982-84; chmn. Wingspread Conf. on Theatre Edn., 1977; drama adjudicator Nat. Arts Festival, Ministry of Edn., Bahamas, 1975, 76, 79, 80; regional chmn. Alliance for Arts Edn., chmn. nat. adv. coun., mem. edn. adv. com., 1986—; trustee Children's Theatre Found.; bd. dirs. Coll. Fellows Am. Theatre of J.F. Kennedy Ctr. for Performing Arts, 1991-93, Fla. Assoc. Theatre Ed., exec. dir. 1995-99, Coll. Bus., 1993—; cons. S.E. Ctr. for Edn. in Theatre, 1995, Fla. Dept. Edn., 1994-96; cons. theatre edn. and prodn.; steering com. Arts for a Complete Edn., 1991-92; mem. curriculum writing com. Fla. Dept. Edn., 1994-96; active St. Marks Episcopal Parish, Tampa. Recipient Disting. Book of Yr. award, 1989, Arts Recognition award, Arts Coun. Hillsborough County, 1995. Mem. Children's Theatre Assn. Am. (pres.-elect 1975-77, pres. 1977-79, chmn. symposia 1981-85, spl. recognition citation 1984), Am. Theatre Assn. (chief divsn. pres.'s coordinating coun. 1977-78, commn. on theatre edn. 1982—, elected), Am. Alliance for Theatre and Edn. (dir. and project dir. theatre literacy collaborative study Internat. Ctr. for Studies in Theatre Edn., Presdl. award 1992), Speech Comm. Assn. (membership dir. 1961), Southeastern Theatre Confs. (Sara Spencer award 1980), Fla. Theatre Confs. (Disting. Career award), Nat. Theatre Conf., Internat. Assn. Theatres for Children and Youth, Internat. Amateur Theatre Assn. (N.Am. bd. dirs.), Fla. Assn. for Theater Edn. (Theatre Edn. of Yr. award 1986, exec. dir. 1994-99), Arts Coun. Hillsborough County (Arts Recognition award), Children's Theatre Found. Am. (trustee 1977-), Tampa Mus., Cosmopolitan Club of Tampa, Coterie Club. Republican. Episcopalian.

COOPER, KAREN RENÉ, health facility administrator, nursing administrator; b. Pleasanton, Calif., Oct. 15, 1957; d. Homer L. and Rosa B. (Upton) C.; m. Tommy Joe McCarty, Nov. 1, 1981. BSN, U. Ala., Birmingham, 1980. Cert. in profl. healthcare quality; healthcare cert. Bd. Nat. Commn. Certifying Agencies; cert. in profl. utilization rev.; cert. Interqual Nat. Registry; cert. chemotherapy, rehab. nurse, tissue therapy. Internship in SICU/MICU Cedars of Lebanon Hosp., Miami, Fla., 1980; mem. head injury/CVA and chronic pain team Spain Rehab. Ctr. U. Ala. Hosps., Birmingham, 1980-82, rheumatology charge nurse Spain Rehab. Ctr., 1982-88, staff nurse, 1988-90, coord. utilization rev./quality assurance med. care rev., 1990-91, coord. quality improvement med. care rev., 1991-93, sr. nurse coord. med. care rev., 1993, interim dir. med. care rev., 1993-94, sr. coord. dept. quality resources, 1994-2000; quality improvement coord. Dept. Joint Commn./ Regulatory Affairs, 2000—04, Dept. of Quality Resources, 2004—05, U. Health Sys., Dept. Quality, 2005—. Mem. Com. for Quality Improvement U. Ala. Birmingham Hosps., mem. Discharge Planning Com., Emergency Svcs. Quality Improvement, 1991-93, Key 100 Com., Med./Dental Staff Task Force, Mobile Med. ICU Quality Com. APACHE Study, 1990-92, Neurology Quality Com., 1990-92, Nursing Stds. Com., 1982-85, Nursing Task Force Com., 1984-88, Resuscitation Com., 1990-94, 98--, Skin Care/Tissue Therapy Com., 1986-89, Surg. Quality Improvement Com., 1991-93; mem. Arthritis Newsletter Com. U. Ala. Birmingham Multi-Purpose Arthritis Ctr., 1983-89; active Value Improvement Project of Birmingham Hosp. Network; participant, presenter numerous confs. and workshops in field. Contbr. articles to Arthritis Today and Arthritis Newsletter of U. Ala. Birmingham Multi-Purpose Arthritis Ctr., 1983-90. Pres. Coalnugget Ala. Mining Mus., 1987-89, chair literacy daycamp, 1990-92; participant Ala. State Fair Family Craft Divsn., 1975-94; co-chair AHPA Nat. Nursing Coun., 1986-88; vol. Children's Hosp., Dixie Wheelchair Assn. Regional Wheelchair Games, Goodwill Industries Doll Sale, Caring and Sharing Drive; troop leader Cahaba Coun. Girl Scouts Am., 1982—, POGO advisor, 1985-93, advisor outdoor interest group, 1995-98, mem. program operating unit, 1984-93, coun. trainer, 1984—, cons. svc. area events/programs, 1984-92, bd. dir., 1992-94, svc. area mgr. Upper 78 West, 1995-98, assn. chair, 1991-92, 2002-04, camp nurse, 1992—, mem. nominating com., 1993-95, facilities com., 1992-94, chair long-range property planning com., 1993, del. to nat. coun., 1993-99, life mem., 1993, mem. World of People Interest Group, 1997-98; mem. Ala. Assn. Healthcare Quality, Am. Juvenile Arthritis Orgn., 1982-88, Arthritis Found., 1982-90, liaison ACT Club support group, 1984-86; mem. UHC: Quality and Risk Mgmt. Com., 1993-2001, United Way/Benevolent Fund com. U. Ala. Birmingham Hosps., 1990, 2000-01; chair Honor the Children NA Festival, 2001—, Williamsburg Farm Fall NA Festival, 2003—, Blackwater Creek AI Fest., 2003—; coord. Hawks in Wind Family Clothing and Food Pantry, 1998—; bd. dirs. Am. Indian Scouting Assn., 2005—; bd. dirs. Walk of Faith Ministry, bd. sec., 2003—. Recipient Thanks award Girl Scouts Am. Cahaba Coun., 1989, Thanks II badge, 2005, Grey Wolf award Am. Indian Scouting Assn., 2004; fellow Girl Scouts U.S.A., 1976. Mem. NAFE, Nat. Assn. Healthcare Quality, U. Ala. Birmingham Alumni Assn. Avocations: painting, poetry, crafts. Home: 30 Scurlock Rd Dora AL 35062-4221 Office: Univ Health Sys/Quality Resources U Ala Birmingham Hosp Birmingham AL 35294-6558

COOPER, KATHLEEN BELL, dean, former federal agency administrator; b. Dallas, Feb. 3, 1945; d. Patrick Joseph and Ferne Elizabeth (McDougle) Bell; m. Ronald James Cooper, Feb. 6, 1965; children: Michael, Christopher. BA in Math. with honors, U. Tex., Arlington, 1970, MA in Econs, 1971; PhD in Econs, U. Colo., 1980. Research asst. econs. dept. U. Tex., Arlington, 1970-71; corp. economist United Banks of Colo., Denver, 1971-79, chief economist, 1980-81; v.p., sr. fin. economist Security Pacific Nat. Bank, Los Angeles, 1981-83, 1st v.p., sr. economist, 1983-85, sr. v.p., economist, 1985-86, sr. v.p., chief economist, 1986-87, exec. v.p., chief economist, 1988-90; chief economist Exxon Corp., Irving, Tex., 1990-99, chief economist, mgr. econs. & energy divsn. corp. planning, 1999-2001; under sec. for econ. affairs & statistics adminstrn. US Dept. Commerce, Washington, 2001—05; dean Coll. Bus. Adminstrn. U. N. Tex., Denton, 2005—. Bd. dirs. The Williams Companies, Inc., 2006—. Trustee Scripps Coll., 1987-2001, Com. for Econ. Devel.1993-2001; mem. Coun. on Fgn. Rels., Internat. Women's Forum. Mem. Nat. Assn. Bus. Economists (past pres. Denver and L.A. chpts.; bd. dirs. 1975-78, pres. 1985-86), Nat. Bur. Econ. Rsch. (bd. dirs. 1987-2001, 05-, exec. com. 1999-2001, 06-), Am. Bankers Assn. (econ. adv. com. 1979-81, 86-90, chmn. 1989-90), U.S. Assn. Energy Econs. (pres. 1996), Am. Econ. Assn., Conf. Bus. Economists (tech. cons. to bus. coun. 1993-94).

COOPER, KATHLEEN K., music educator; m. Jerry Lee Cooper, May 22, 1977; 1 child, Erin Kathleen. B of Music Edn., Southwestern Okla. State U., Weatherford, 1979. Cert. music tchr. Okla., 1979. Elem. music tchr. Checotah Pub. Schs., Okla., 1980—. Ch. choir dir. First United Meth. Ch., Checotah, 1981—82. Mem.: Okla. Music Educators Assn. Liberal. Methodist. Achievements include serving as music tchr. to American Idol Carrie Underwood. Avocations: travel, shopping, reading. Office: Checotah Inermediate School 1401 SW 2nd Checotah OK 74426 Office Phone: 918-473-2384.

COOPER, LOUISA SINCLAIR, artist; b. Honolulu, July 24, 1931; d. William Taylor and Mary Lydia (Barrette) S.; m. George Dunton Witter, July 4, 1952 (div. May 1966); children: Martha S., George D. Jr., Elizabeth, James; m. Clifford Dennis Cooper, June 19, 1976. Student, U. Calif., Berkeley, 1949-51; BA in Studio Art, U. Calif., Irvine, 1976; postgrad., Laguna Beach Sch. Art, Ecole Migros, Geneva. One-woman shows include Pauahi Tower Gallery, Honolulu, 1989, 91, Contemporary Mus., Honolulu, 1992, Queen Emma Gallery, Honolulu, 1993; exhibited in group shows at Am. Artists Profl. League, 1986, 88, Salamagundi Artists Non-Members Show, N.Y., 1991, Women Artists of West, L.A., 1991, Nat. Art League 61st Ann. Exhbn., N.Y., 1991, Oil Painters Am., Chgo., 1993. Mem. Am. Artists Profl. League, Oil Painters Am., Nat. Mus. Women in Arts, Honolulu Acad. Arts, Rockport Art Assn., Catherine Lorizladd Wolff Art League N.Y., Plein Air Painters of Hawaii, Calif. Art Club. Avocations: travel, pottery, swimming, architecture, interior decorating. Home: 1036 Mokulua Dr Kailua HI 96734-3243 E-mail: runtpig@aol.com.

COOPER, LYNNE MARIE, veterinarian, educator; d. John Terry and Deanna Marie Homer; m. Anthony Wayne Cooper, Feb. 18, 2002; children: Anna Marie, Katherine Cecilia. BS, Okla. State U., 1991, DVM, 1995, MS, 2000. Lic. veterinarian Okla., Pa. Veterinarian All Pets Veterinarian Hosp., Stillwater, Okla., 1996—97; tchg. asst. Okla. State U., Stillwater, 1998—2000; asst. prof. Wilson Coll., Chambersburg, Pa., 2001—. Mem.: AVMA, N.Am. Vet. Technician Educators Assn., Am. Assn. Lab. Animal Scis., Am. Holistic Vet. Med. Assn., Am. Soc. Microbiologists, Okla. Vet. Med. Assn., N.Am. Vet. Technician Assn. (assoc.). Avocations: reading, tennis, cross stitch, bicycling. Business E-Mail: lcooper@wilson.edu.

COOPER, MARGARET J., cultural organization administrator; Pres. Nat. Assn. Colored Women's Clubs, Inc., 2002—. Named one of 100 Most Influential Black Americans, Ebony Mag., 2004, 2006. Office: Nat Assn Colored Womens Clubs 1601 R St, NW Washington DC 20009 Office Phone: 202-667-4080. Office Fax: 202-667-2574. E-mail: mcooper@nacwcya.org.*

COOPER, MARGARET LESLIE, lawyer; b. Geneva, N.Y., Apr. 13, 1950; d. Jack Frederick and Barbara Ann (Hitchings) C. BA in Math., Rollins Coll., 1972; JD, Mercer U., 1976. Bar: Fla. 1976, U.S. Dist. Ct. (so. dist.) Fla. 1977, U.S. Dist. Ct. (mid. dist.) Fla. 2001, U.S. Ct. Appeals (5th cir.) 1977, U.S. Ct. Appeals (11th cir.) 1981, U.S. Supreme Ct. 03, bd. cert. civil trial advocacy: Nat. Bd. Trial Advocacy 2002; bd. cert. civil litigation and bus. litigation Fla. Bar Assn. Assoc. Jones, Foster, Johnston & Stubbs, PA, West Palm Beach, Fla., 1976-81, ptnr., 1981—. Assoc. prof. Palm Beach Jr. Coll., West Palm Beach, 1985-86. Pres. Young People's Pres.'s Coun., Norton Gallery Art, West Palm Beach, 1982—84; bd. trustees Norton Sculpture Gardens; chmn. campaign Lou Frey for Gov., Palm Beach County, 1986; bd. dirs. Planned Parenthood of Palm Beach. Named to Sports Hall Fame, Rollins Coll., 1986, Winter Park H.S. Sports Hall of Fame, 1998. Fellow: Am. Bar Found. (Best Lawyers in Am. 2003); mem.: Fla. Bar (chmn. grievance com. 15th Jud. Cir., mem. client security fund com.), Fla. Tennis Assn. (treas. 1992—98, pres.-elect. 1999), U.S. Tennis Assn. (vice chair grievance com., capt. Maria Bueno Cup Team, fin. com., adult sn. competitive com.), Women's Internat. Tennis Assn. (disciplinary rev. bd. 1985), Palm Beach Jr. League, Exec. Women Palm Beach, Palm Beach County Bar Assn., The Beach Club. Republican. Avocations: tennis, skiing. Home: 2121 S Flagler Dr West Palm Beach FL 33401-8005 Office: Jones Foster Johnston & Stubbs PA PO Box 3475 West Palm Beach FL 33402-3475

COOPER, MARIANNE (ABONYI COOPER), librarian, educator; b. Budapest, Hungary, Apr. 14, 1938; came to U.S., 1957, naturalized, 1962; d. Laszlo and Elisabeth (Lengyel) Abonyi; m. Herbert W. Cooper, June 11, 1961; children— Deborah S., Evelyn Ann. B.A., Syracuse U., 1960; M.L.S., Columbia U., 1961, D.L.S., 1980. Chemistry librarian Columbia U., N.Y.C., 1961-66; sr. info. scientist Am. Inst. Physics, N.Y.C., 1967-70; instr. Grad. Sch. Library and Info. Studies, Queens Coll., Flushing, N.Y., 1975-80, asst. prof., 1980—; invited participant Inst. for Library Sci. Faculty, ARL and Council on Library Resources, 1986. Author: (with E. Terry) Secondary Services in Physics, 1969; (with C.W. Thayer) Primary Journal Literature of Physics, 1969; (with H.M. Watterson) Institutional Producers of Physics Literature, 1969; also articles and papers in info. sci. field. Editor: Secondary Information Services: Development and Future, 1982. Chmn. edn. com., mem. bd. dirs. West Birchwood Civic Assn., Jericho, N.Y., 1970-80. Mem. ALA, Am. Soc. for Info. Sci. (chpt. program chmn. 1981, chpt. rep. to nat. orgn. 1983-85, mem. and nominating com. 1983-84, chmn. edn. com. 1985—), Assn. for Library and Info. Sci. Edn., Library Assn. CUNY, Spl. Libraries Assn., Phi Beta Kappa. Recipient George Virgil Fuller award Columbia U., 1972; Faculty-in-Residence award Queens Coll., 1982; grantee Council on Library Resources, 1986-87. Office: Queens College of NY Rm 254 Grad Sc of Library Flushing NY 11367 Home: 725 Avalon Court Dr Melville NY 11747-4281

COOPER, MARY CAMPBELL, information services executive; b. Meadville, Pa., Aug. 14, 1940; d. Paul F. and Margaret (Webb) Campbell; m. James Nicoll Cooper, June 8, 1963; children: Alix, Jenny. BA, Mt. Holyoke Coll., 1961; MLS, Simmons Coll., 1963; MEd, Harvard U., 1965. Cert. museum adminstrn. With Harvard U. Libr., Cambridge, Mass., 1961-63, Carleton U. Libr., Ottawa, Can., 1965-85; archive cons. U.S., Can., 1985-86; info. mgr. Haley & Aldrich Inc., Cambridge, 1986-88, Tsoi/Kobus & Assocs., Cambridge, 1988-90; pres., founder Cooper Info., Cambridge, 1990—. Bd. dirs. Mass. Com. for Preservation of Archtl. Records, Boston. Author: Records in Architectural Offices, 1992, Records and Information Management: Meeting the Challenge, 1994, Records and Information Management: Order Out of Chaos, 1996. Bd. dirs. Berkshire Hist. Soc., Pitts., Mass. Travel grantee Nat. Hist. Pub. Records Commn., 1991. Mem. Spl. Librs. Assn., Am. Mus. Assn., Assn. Ind. Info. Profls., Assn. Moving Image Archivists, Assn. Records Mgrs. and Adminstrs. (nat. com. 1991—). Avocations: travel, tennis, swimming. Home and Office: 5 Ellery Pl Cambridge MA 02138-4200

COOPER, MARY ELLEN, writer; b. Augusta, Ga. BA in Psychology, Augusta Coll., 1983, BA in Music, 1984; MA in Counseling, Liberty U., 1990; PhD in Human Svcs., Walden U., 1992; MBA in Leadership Devel., Brenau Online U., 2003. Lic. prof. counselor Ga., 1996. Author: (novels) The Greeter. Mem.: ACA (assoc.). Avocations: writing, walking, reading, travel.

COOPER, MARY LITTLE, judge; b. Fond du Lac, Wis., Aug. 13, 1946; AB in Polit. Sci. cum laude, Bryn Mawr Coll., 1968; JD, Villanova U., 1972; LLD (hon.), Georgian Ct. Coll., 1987. Bar. N.J. 1972. Assoc. McCarter & English, Newark, 1972-80, ptnr., 1980-84; commr. N.J. Dept. Banking, Trenton, 1984-90; assoc. gen. counsel Prudential Property & Casualty Ins. Co., Holmdel, NJ, 1991-92; judge U.S. Dist. Ct. N.J., 1992—. Chmn. bd. Pinelands Devel. Credt Bank. Bd. trustees Exec. Commn. Ethical Standards, Trenton, 1984-90, Corp. Bus. Assistance, Trenton, 1984-91, NJ Housing & Mortgage Fin. Agy., Trenton, 1984-90, NJ Cemetery Bd. Assn., 1984-90, NJ Hist. Soc., 1976-79., YMCA of Greater Newark, 1973-76; civil practice com. Supreme Ct. NJ, 1982-84, dist. ethics com., 1982-84 Fellow Am. Bar Found.; mem. John C. Lifland Am. Inn of Ct Office: US Courthouse 402 E State St Ste 5000 Trenton NJ 08608-1507 Office Phone: 609-989-2105.

COOPER, MELONEE V., music educator; b. DeQuincy, La. d. Bevil Jesse and Capitola Jacobs Van Winkle; m. Timothy Williams Cooper, Sept. 12, 1981; children: Katherine Grace, Timothy Luke. MusB, McNeese State U., Lake Charles, La., 1991, M in Music Edn., 2002. Cert. Kodaly edn. McNeese State U., 1994. Tchr. Calcasieu Parish Sch. Bd., Lake Charles, La., 1991—. Mailing: 435 Peach St Dequincy LA 70633-3915

COOPER, NANCY E., computer software company executive; b. 1954; With IBM, 1976—98, dir. fin. mgmt. sys., pricing and fin. planning, 1982—92, CFO global industries divsn., asst. corp. controller, controller, treas.; ptnr. Gen. Atlantic Ptnrs., 1998; CFO Pitney Bowes Credit Corp., 1998—2000, Reciprocal, Inc., 2000—01; sr. v.p., CFO IMS Health Inc., 2001—06; exec. v.p., CFO CA, 2006—. Office: CA One CA Plz Islandia NY 11749*

COOPER, NANNIE COLES, education educator, consultant; b. Washington, Oct. 25, 1930; d. Harry Willie and Lucy Jackson Coles; m. Clement Theodore Cooper; children: Patricia, Karen, Stephanie, Bridgette, Stacy. BS, D.C. Tchrs. Coll., 1964; M in Art of Tchg., Trinity Coll., Washington, 1973. Cert. nat. tchrs. exam. Elem. sch. tchr. D.C. Pub. Schs., 1964—77; reading and SAT preparation specialist Cromwell Acad., Washington, 1978—82; adj. prof. U. D.C., 1984—87; magnet sch. substitute tchr. Montgomery County (Md.) Pub. Schs., 1988—96; adj. prof. reading Am. English Lang. Program Montgomery Coll., Takoma Park, Md., 1986—2002; cons. prescriptive and diagnostic testing Washington, 2002—. Curriculum developer D.C. Pub. Schs., 1980—84, instr. SAT rev., 1984—86; instr. SAT preparation U. D.C., 1984—87; tutor writing and reading skills Montgomery Coll. Takoma Park campus, 2005—. Vol. Ward 4 Dem. race, Washington, 1996, Dem. Women, Washington, 1998—99; mem. choir Trinity Episcopal Ch., 1984—88. Named Outstanding Parent, Parent Tchrs. of Parochial Schs., Washington, 1985—87, Reading is Fundamental honoree, 1986. Mem.: Alpha Wives of D.C., Alpha Kappa Alpha. Avocations: reading, travel, writing. Home: 1220 East West Hwy Apt 821 Silver Spring MD 20910 Personal E-mail: ncooper760@aol.com.

COOPER, NICOLE ROBYN, writer; b. Concord, Mass., July 8, 1975; d. James William and Vicki Cooper. BA, Princeton U., NJ, 1997. Editl. asst. Simon & Schuster, Stamford, Conn., 1997—98, copywriter, 1998; med. writer Q.E.D. Comm., Hawthorne, NY, 1998—2000, editl. mgr. and sr. med. writer, 2000—01; mgr. sci. comm. DesignWrite, Princeton, NJ, 2001—03; pres. Cooper Johnson Comm., LLC, Princeton, NJ, 2003—. Editor: Pathway to Control: Pairing Mechanisms With Treatment in Type 2 Diabetes, 2000, Health, Hormones, and Happiness: Creating Wellness for Midlife and Beyond, 2001, Healing Horizons in Acid Reflux Disease, 2001. Cmty. svc. chair Cloister Inn, Princeton, 1996—97. Named Academic All Am., U.S. Swimming, 1993; named to U.S. Nat. Open Water Swimming Team, 1991—92; scholar, Nat. Merit Scholarship Corp., 1992—97, Thomas J. Watson scholar, IBM Corp., 1992—97. Mem.: Am. Med. Writers Assn., Sigma Phi. Democrat. Avocations: swimming, writing, reading, music.

COOPER, PAULA, art dealer; b. Mass., Mar. 14, 1938; Student, Pierce Coll., Athens, Greece, Sorbonne, Paris, Goucher Coll., Inst. Fine Arts, NYU; DFA (hon.), R.I. Sch. Design, 1995. Asst. World House Galleries, N.Y.C., 1959-61; pvt. dealer, 1962-63; with Paula Johnson Gallery, N.Y.C., 1964-65; dir. Park Place Gallery, N.Y.C., 1965-67, Paula Cooper Gallery, N.Y.C., 1968—. Chmn. bd. dirs. Kitchen Ctr., N.Y.C., 1985-95. Named honoree, N.Y. Studio Sch., 2001; recipient Art Table award for disting. svc. to the visual arts, 2001. Mem.: Art Dealers Assn. Am. (bd. dirs. 1982—86, 1988—90, 1997—2000, v.p. bd. dirs. 1997—2000), Art Students League. Office: Paula Cooper Gallery 534 W 21st St New York NY 10011-2812 Office Phone: 212-255-1105. Office Fax: 212-255-5156.

COOPER, REBECCA, art dealer; b. Phila., July 11, 1947; d. Frank N. Cooper and Bernice Silverstein; m. Michael J. Waldman, June 27, 1982. BA, MA, NYU; postgrad. Cert. appraiser. Owner Gallery Rebecca Cooper, Washington; pres. Rebecca Cooper Fine Art Tours, N.Y.C., 1980—90; owner The Gallery in Sag Harbor, NY. Hon. chairperson N.Y. Women Bus. Owners Art Roundtable, 1981; lectr. Resources Coun., 1983, N.Y. Mayor's com. on interior design and furnishings, 1983; sec. bd. assocs. Am. Craft Mus., lectr. Collectors Circle; nat. patron Am. Fed. Art., Ind. Curators Inc. Patron, Mus. Modern Art; benefactor New Mus. Dirs. Forum; exhbn. mem. dirs. coun. Whitney Mus.; founder The Gallery in Sag Harbor, N.Y.; art tours, cons. Mem. Am. Appraisers Assn. (assoc.), Dame de la Chaine des Rotisseurs, Pvt. Art Dealers Assn., The Guild Hall of East Hampton, The Parish Art Mus. South Hampton, The Gallery in Sag Harbor, Women's 008 Investment Club, Nat. Arts Club, Lotos Club, Guggenheim Mus. (internat. cir.). Office Phone: 631-725-7707. Personal E-mail: rebeccacooperart@aol.com.

COOPER, SARAH JEAN, nursing educator; b. Wallace, Idaho, Oct. 3, 1940; d. Kenneth Albert and Jean Saxsonia (Horton) Merryweather; m. George Harlan Cooper, Aug. 5, 1961; children: John, Matthew, Thomas. Diploma, Sacred Heart Sch. Nursing, 1961; BSN, Pacific Luth. U., 1974; MN, U. Wash., Seattle, 1979. Assoc. dir. nursing St. Alphonsus Hosp., Boise, Idaho; asst. dir. nursing and staffing St. Luke's Regional Med. Ctr., Boise, mgr. patient care support svcs.; nursing dept. Walla Walla Cmty. Coll., Wash. Instr. nursing Walla Walla C.C. Kellogg Found. fellow; Pew grantee. Mem. Sigma Theta Tau. Office: Nursing Dept Walla Walla Cmty Coll 500 Tausick Way Walla Walla WA 99362 E-mail: sargeo@bmi.net.

COOPER, SHARON CROFT, aerospace engineer; BSME, U. Md., 1987, postgrad., 1987—89. With Goddard Space Flight Ctr. NASA, Greenbelt, Md., 1983—87, aerospace engr. Goddard Space Flight Ctr., 1987—. Avocation: Avocations: gardening, jazz and ballroom dancing, horseback riding, flying. Office: NASA Goddard Space Flight Ctr Mail Stop 442 0 Bldg 29 Rm 111 Greenbelt MD 20771

COOPER, SIGNE SKOTT, retired nursing educator; b. Clinton County, Iowa, Jan. 29, 1921; d. Hans Edward and Clara Belle (Steen) Skott. BS, U. Wis., 1948; MEd, U. Minn., 1955. Head nurse U. Wis. Hosp., Madison, 1946—48; instr. U. Wis. Sch. Nursing, Madison, 1948—51, asst. prof., 1952—57, assoc. prof., 1957—62, prof., assoc. dean, 1962—83, prof.

emeritus, 1983. Prof. U. Wis. Extension, 1955-83. Contbg. author: American Nursing: A Biographical Dictionary, Vol. 1, 1988, Vol. 2, 1992, Vol. 3, 2000; contbr. articles to profl. jours. 1st Lt. U.S. Army Nurse Corps, 1943-46. Recipient NLN Linda Richards award, ANA Honorary Recognition award, Adult Edn. Assn. Pioneer award; named to Nursing Hall of Fame, 2000. Fellow Am. Acad. Nursing (named Living Legend 2003); mem. Am. Assn. for History Nursing (Pres.'s award 2003), Wis. Nurses Assn. (pres.).

COOPER, VALERIE GAIL, minister; b. Houston, May 30, 1962; d. Rev. M.C. and Mildred Chappel Cooper. BS in Pre-Medicine, Paul Quinn Coll., 1985; MDiv in Theology and Ministry, Interdenominational Theol. Ctr. Sem., 1998; D in Theology, Immauel Sch. Bible, 2000, DMin, 2005. Elder Full Gospel Bapt. Ch., 2001. Pastor Vistors Chapel African Meth. Episc. Ch., El Paso, Tex., 1998—2000; asst. pastor Morning Star Full Gospel Bapt. Ch., Houston, 2001—05; CEO, founder Faithful Anointed Victories Always with God Ministries, Houston, 2005—. Mem.: Sigma Gamma Rho. Home: 3805 Brill St Houston TX 77026 Personal E-mail: drvalcoop@yahoo.com. E-mail: favawithgod@yahoo.com.

COOPER, VELMA J., elementary school educator; b. Craig, Nebr., Dec. 16, 1920; d. Orrin Smith and Jennie Hampton; m. Phillip H. Cooper, June 29, 1941 (dec. Jan. 2003); children: Phillip L., Carol J., Michael A., Wayne O. BS in Edn., Dana Coll., 1968. Tchr. pub. schs. Nebr. and Iowa, 1939—42, 1961—83. Author, compiler, rschr., spkr., tchr. in genealogy and local history, Burt County, Nebr., 1977—2005. Author: Prairie View Years, 1981; co-editor: Lyons Heritage, 1884-1984, 1983; editor, compiler: Tekamah, Nebraska, Cemetery, 1984, Craig Cemetery, 1993, Hillcrest Cemetery, Decatur, Nebraska, 1990. Bd. mem., planner Burt County Mus., Tekamah, Nebr., 1976—2003. Mem.: Northeastern Nebr. Geneal. Soc. (pres., charter), Nat. Geneal. Soc., Nebr. State Geneal. Soc. (charter, area rep.), Burt County Mus., Inc. (pres. 1995—2001). Methodist. Home: 921 K St Tekamah NE 68061-1415

COOPER-CHEN, ANNE, journalism educator, researcher; b. Pitts., July 19, 1944; d. George Henry and Dorothy Louise (Pursley) Messerly; m. Charles Chin-tse, July 12, 1986; stepchildren: Diana, Derek. AB, Vassar Coll., 1966; MA, U. Mich., 1969; MS, Va. Commonwealth U., 1979; PhD, U. N.C., 1984. Feature writer Daily News, V.I., 1963; writer, editor Asahi Evening News, Tokyo, 1966-68; editor, book pub. John Weatherhill, Inc., Tokyo, 1969-70; writer, columnist Sunday News, York, Pa., 1971-72; writer, editor Commonwealth mag., Richmond, Va., 1974-76; asst. prof. journalism So. Meth. U., Dallas, 1982-83, Mary Baldwin Coll., Staunton, Va., 1983-85; prof. Ohio U., Athens, 1985—. Author: Games in the Global Village, 1994, Mass Communication in Japan, 1997, Global Entertainment Media, 2005; co-author: Idols, Victims, Pioneers, 1976, contbg. author (chpt.) Global Journalism, Covering Africa, International Public Relations, Comics & Ideology; contbr. articles to profl. jours. Fulbright Sr. Rsch. scholar, Japan, 1992-93. Mem. Assn. for Edn. in Journalims and Mass Communications (various offices, disting. svc. award 2005), Intenat. Assn. Media & Comm. Rsch., Kappa Tau Alpha. Office: Ohio U Scripps Sch Journalism 102 Sing Tao Ctr Athens OH 45701 Office Phone: 740-593-2598. E-mail: acooper_chen@hotmail.com.

COOPER-RUSPOLI, ANNIE NATAF, psychiatrist, director; d. Victor and Arlette Nataf; m. Stephane Frank Ruspoli, June 9, 1997; 1 child, Jonathan Cooper. MD, U. Paris, 1975. Resident psychiatry Emory U. Sch. Medicine, Atlanta, 1975—78, fellow child psychiatry, 1978—79; med. dir. child and adolescent unit Ga. Regional Hosp. Atlanta, 1980—91; psychiatrist Piedmont Psychiat. Clinic, Atlanta, 1996—. Mem. Conseil Nat. de l'Ordre des Medecins, Paris, 1991—. Trustee Atlanta Internat. Sch., 1985—97, bd. dirs., 1997—2005; trustee Alliance Francaise d'Atlanta, 1992—95, Ga Casa, Atlanta, 1992—2001. Mem.: Atlanta Med. Assn., Ga. Med. Assn., Ga. Psychiat. Assn., Am. Psychiat. Assn. Independent. Office: Piedmont Psychiatric Clinic 1938 Peachtree Rd Ste 505 Atlanta GA 30309 Office Phone: 404-355-2914. Office Fax: 404-355-2917. Personal E-mail: acooperrus@aol.com.

COOTS, LAURIE, advertising executive; 1 child, Christopher. Student, Colorado State U. Joined Chiat/Day as exec. on Apple Computer bus., 1984; named new bus. coord., 1986; dir. new bus. and adminstrn., 1989; COO LA office, 1993—97; (Chiat/Day merges with TBWA, 1995); chief mktg. officer N. Am. TBWA/Chiat/Day, LA, 1997—2001, chief mktg. officer worldwide, 2001—. Office: TBWA Chiat/Day LA 5353 Grosvenor Blvd Los Angeles CA 90066

COPE, JEANNETTE NAYLOR, executive search consultant; b. Corpus Christi, Tex., Feb. 9, 1956; d. Glen R. and Jeannine (Withington) N.; m. John R. Cope, May 22, 1993. BA in Psychology and Sociology, Trinity U., 1978. Asst. fin. dir. Jim Baker for Atty. Gen. Campaign, Houston, 1978; fin. dir. Rep. Party of Tex., Austin, 1979-81; regional Eagle rep. Rep. Nat. Com., Washington, 1981-83; devel. officer Nat. Endowment for the Arts, Washington, 1983-87; sr. project mgr. Internat. Skye Assocs., Washington, 1988; spl. asst. to Pres. of U.S. The White House, 1989-90, dep. asst. to Pres. of U.S., dep. dir. of presdl. pers., 1990-93; pres. J. Naylor Cope Co., Washington, 1994—. NEA liaison Pres.' Com. on Arts and Humanites, Washington, 1985-87; dir. Internat. Skye Advisor, Washington, 1988; bd. dirs. Bush/Quayle Alumni Assn., TransTech. Corp.; mem. Officer Pers. Mgmt.'s Task Force on Exec. and Mgmt. Devel., Washington, 1990; bd. dirs. Washington First Bank. Mem. Pres.'s Com. Arts and Humanities, 2001—; chmn. alumni admissions coun. Trinity U., Washington, 1986—87; mem. Bush Cheney Transition Team, 2001; vestrywoman St. John's Episcopal Ch., Washington, 1990—94, co-chmn. outreach com., 1991—94, chmn. search com. for 14th rector, jr. warden, 1994—97, sr. warden, 1998—2001; bd. dirs. The Compass Rose Soc. Anglican Communion, 1999—2005, exec. com., 2000—04; trustee Protestant Episcopal Cathedral Found., 2004—; bd. dirs. Coop. Urban Ministry Ctr., Washington, 1987—89, Pennsylvania Ave. Devel. Corp., 1993—96, Decatur House, Washington, 1998—, exec. com., 2000—, vice-chmn., bd. dirs., 2001—03, chmn. bd. dirs., 2004—; bd. visitors Kanuga Confs., 2001—. Scholar, Tex. Coun. of Ch. Related Colls., 1974. Mem. Am. Soc. Assn. Execs. (exec. recruiter), Tex. State Soc. (chmn. membership com. 1981), Nat. Trust for Hist. Preservation (bd. dirs. 2005—), Smithsonian Instn., Am. Film Inst., Mcpl. Art Soc. (N.Y.C.), 1925 F Street Club (chmn. mems. com.), Pres.'s Club, Columbia Country Club (Chevy Chase, Md.), Tex. Breakfast Club, Blue Key (sec. 1976-78), City Tavern Club, Chi Beta Epsilon (v.p. San Antonio coun. 1976). Republican. Episcopalian. Office: J Naylor Cope Co PO Box 40069 Washington DC 20016-0069 Business E-Mail: jnc@jnaylorcopecompany.com.

COPE, KATHLEEN ADELAIDE, critical care nurse, parish nurse, educator; b. Bethlehem, Pa., Sept. 12, 1926; d. Harry Raymond and Mabel Eva (Newhard) Stine; m. Robert Clayton Cope, Aug. 9, 1951; children: Debra Kathleen Howard, Terry Faye Cicero. BA in Psychology summa cum laude, Bellevue (Nebr.) Coll., 1972; diploma, St. Luke's Hosp., Bethlehem, 1951; student, Whitworth Coll., Spokane, 1989, Wash. State U., 1989. RN, Pa., Wash.; cert. nutrition support nurse; cert. critical care nurse, quality improvement, health promotion specialist. Pvt. duty nurse Exeter (N.H.) Hosp., 1957-60; nurse Red Cross Blood Mobile, Portsmouth area, N.H., 1961-65; staff nurse Clarkson Hosp., Omaha, 1966, asst. head nurse, 1966-67, head nurse, 1967-68, supr., organizer coronary care ctr., 1968-70; staff nurse ICU/critical care Sacred Heart Med. ctr., Spokane, 1973—; founder, dir. nutritional risk/identification network Health Improvement Partnership, Spokane, Wash., 1997—. Mem. adv. coun. edn. com. Nutrition Screening Initiative, Washington, 1992—, Nutrition Inst. La., New Orleans, 1993—; apptd. del. by U.S. Senate to White House Conf. on Aging, 1995; developer Body Mass Index awareness cmty. action project through Leadership Spokane Class, 1999; presenter Spokane's body mass index project U.S. Surgeon Gen.'s Inaugural Session on Obesity, 2001. Author: (manual) Malnutrition in the Elderly: A National Crisis, (resolution) Ensuring the Future of the Medicare Program presented to White House and Congress; contbr. articles to profl. jours. Apptd. Silver Senator by U.S. Senate for Wash. in Nat. Silver Haired Congress, 1997. Recipient Cmty. Leadership Recognition award, YWCA, Spokane, 1993, commendation for developing a model for nation from former U.S. Surgeon Gen. C. Everett Koop, 1999, Spl. Recognition award for contrbn. to malnutrition awareness, U.S. Adminstrn. on Aging, 2000. Mem. ANA, Wash. State Nursing Assn., Nat. Coun. on Aging, Am. Soc. for Critical Care Nursing (founding), Am. Soc. for Parenteral and Enteral Nutrition, U.S. apptd. Silver Senator for Wash. State in Nat. Silver Haired Congress, Sigma Theta Tau. Avocations: reading, walking, hiking, bicycling, cooking, crafts. Home: 8315 N Lucia Ct Spokane WA 99208-9654 Office Phone: 509-466-4514. Home Fax: 509-468-1026. Personal E-mail: kcope@mindspring.com.

COPE, MELBA DARLENE, volunteer, photographer; b. Des Moines, Iowa, Feb. 16, 1944; d. Murray J. and Mary Lorena Van Hemert; m. Harvey J. Helgeland, 1964 (dissolved 1971); 1 child, Ingrid; m. Thom K. Cope, Nov. 8, 1980. Student, Nebr. Wesleyan U., Lincoln, 1975—76; BA in Women's Studies, U. Nebr., 1996. Bus. mgr. Williamson Olds/Honda, Lincoln, 1982—88; Granny Smith Washington Apple Commn., Wenatchee, Wash., 1999—2000; photographer Images by Melba, Tucson, 2002—. Photographer Habitat for Humanity Bldg. Project, Lincoln, Nebr., 1998. Contbr. chapters to books. Bd. dirs., sec., v.p. Rape Spouse Abuse Crisis Ctr., 1993—2002; active Older Women's League, 1998—2002, Bd. Friends Commn., 2000—01; mentor Women in Trades program YWCA, Lincoln, 1999; big sister Heartland Big Bros./Big Sisters Orgn., 2001—02; com. mem. Girls and Women in Sports and Fitness, 2001—02; co-chair Am. Cancer Soc. Annual Climb to Conquer Cancer, Tucson, 2005; bd. dirs. YWCA, 2001; bd. dirs., v.p. Women's Studies Adv. Coun., Tucson, 2004—06; commr., mem. exec. bd., v.p. Lincoln Lancaster Women's Commn., 1997—2001; bd. dirs. Coll. Arts and Scis. Alumni Assn. U. Nebr., 1997—2000; com. mem. Women in Transition, 1999; comms. com. Sunflower Cmty. Assn., Tucson, 2002—04. Recipient Elizabeth Kurtz Vol. award, Rape Spouse Abuse Crisis Ctr., Lincoln, Nebr., 2000, Outstanding Vol. award, United Way, Lincoln, 2000, Alice Paul award, Lincoln/Lancaster Women's Commn., Lincoln, 2001. Mem.: Sigma Alpha Iota (Sword of Honor award 1994), Phi Beta Kappa. Avocations: photography, hiking, reading, music, travel.

COPE, RHIAN BRIANNA, toxicologist, educator; b. Brisbane, Australia, Oct. 1, 1965; B in Vet. Sci., U. Queensland, 1989; BSc with 1st class honors, Murdoch U., 1991; PhD, U. Sydney, 1996. Clinician dept. companion animal medicine and surgery U. Queensland, 1990; rsch. asst. Sch. Vet. Sci. Murdoch U., 1991—92; lectr. lab. animal medicine and animal genetics TAFE, Perth, Australia, 1991—92; clinician emergency medicine Ku-Ring-Gai Vet. Hosp., Sydney, 1997—98; postdoctoral rsch. asst. Australian Photobiology Testing Facility, 1997; hon. postdoctoral rsch. fellow dept. animal sci. U. Sydney, 1997; postdoctoral rsch. fellow Commonwealth Sci. and Indsl. Rsch. Orgn., 1998; postdoctoral rsch. assoc. dept. vet. bioscis. U. Ill., Urbana, 1999, asst. prof. morphology dept. vet. bioscis., 1999—2002; asst. prof. toxicology dept. biomed. scis. Oreg. State U., Corvallis, 2002—. Contbr. articles to profl. jours., chpt. to book. Del. People to People Amb. Program, Internat. Union Toxicology, China, 2003. Recipient award for outstanding presentation, Am. Coll. Vet. Microbiologists, 2002; grantee, U. Ill., 2000—01, USDA, 2000—01, Ill. Dept. Agr., 2001, Am. Cancer Soc., 2001—02, Oreg. State U., 2003. Fellow: Am. Acad. Toxicology, Am. Acad. Vet. and Comparitive Toxicology; mem.: Am. Soc. Photobiology, Soc. Toxicology. Office: Oreg State U Coll Vet Medicine Corvallis OR 97331 Office Phone: 541-737-6946. Business E-Mail: rhian.cope@oregonstate.edu.

COPELAN, ANN HANSON, artist, psychologist; d. Jewell Joe and Emily Blanche (Peacock) Hanson; m. Thomas J. Phillips, Jr. (div.); children: Trae Phillips, Dean Phillips, Phoelicia Canup, Cindy McNally, Clay Phillips, David Phillips. Student, U. Ga., Athens, 1966—68; BS in Psychology, Ga. Coll. and State U., Milledgeville, 1981, MS in Psychology, 1986. Asst. to Curator U. Ga. Mus. Art, Athens, Ga., 1967—69; asst. dir., behavior specialist Putnam Jasper Support Svcs., Eatonton, Ga., 1984—; owner Ann H. Copelan Gallery, Greensboro, Ga., 1987—. Cons. Coliseum Psychiat. Hosp., Macon, Ga., 1986—88. One-woman shows include People's Bank, Eatonton, Ga., 1989, Little Acorn, Atlanta, 1989, Cathreen's Gallery, 1990—93, Ga. Coll. and State U. Blackbridge Hall Mus., Milledgeville, 1990, Left Bank Art Gallery, St. Simons Island, Ga., 1991, Sutton Galleries, New Orleans, 1992, 1996, Richard Guritz Antiques, Highlands, NC, 1993—94, Lawrence Charles Gallery, Tampa, Fla., 1993, Magnolia Gallery, Lake Oconee, Ga., 1999—2000, exhibited in group shows at People's Bank, Eatonton, 1987, Festival of the Arts, Moultrie, Ga., 1988, Buckhead Gallery, Atlanta, 1988, Winter Arts Festival, Macon, Ga., 1989, LA Art Expo., 1989, Ansley Inn, Atlanta, 1989, Left Bank Art Gallery, St. Simons, 1989—90, 1992, 1994—95, 1999, Cloister, Sea Island, Ga., 1989—96, 1998—2000, Art Expo., NY, 1990, Leon Loard Art Gallery, Montgomery, Ala., 1992, 1996, 1998, Little Acorn, Atlanta, 1992, 1994—97, 1999—2002, Magnolia Gallery, Lake Oconee, 2001, Harbor Club, 2003, represented in numerous pub. and pvt. collections. Founding bd. trustees John Milledge Acad., Milledgeville, Ga., 1972; bd. dirs. Eatonton-Putnam County Hist. Soc., Eatonton, Ga., 1986—88, Peoples Bank Found., Eatonton, 1988—. Named Outstanding Young Alumni, Ga. Coll. and State U., 1992. Mem.: Nat. Mus. Women in the Arts, Greene County Arts Alliance, Ga. Citizens for the Arts, Gamma Beta Phi. Republican. Baptist. Avocations: writing, reading, walking, painting, interior decorating. Home: Lake Oconee 1134 Harbor Ridge Dr Greensboro GA 30642

COPELAND, ANITA BOB, director, retired elementary school educator, senior consultant; b. Memphis, July 23; d. Bobbie and Margo Jewell; m. Bob Copeland, July 15, 1961; children: Cara Wynn, Robert Ryan. BS, Tex. Wesleyan U., Ft. Worth, 1964, MS. Classroom tchr. Arlington Ind. Sch. Dist., Tex.; ret., 2000. Twirling dir. Tex. Stars and Starlettes, Arlington, 1961—2005; tchr., judge Nat. Baton Twirling Assn., 1961—2005; asst. exec. sec. region 5 U. Interscholastic League, 2000—; sr. cons. Creative Memories, 2003—05; dir. Ignite Stream Energy, 2004—. Mem.: Ret. Tchrs. Assn. (historian dist. 11), Ret. Sch. Employees Arlington (historian), Arlington Women Rotary (pres. 1977—78, 1984—85, past pres.), Encore Club (officer 2000—, historian, publicity 2006—), Arlington Women's Club (officer 1979—). Home: 1811 Mossy Oak Arlington TX 76012 Personal E-mail: anita_copeland@yahoo.com.

COPELAND, BONNIE S., former school system administrator; b. Lima, Ohio, Nov. 27, 1949; BS, Miami U., 1971, MEd, 1972; PhD, St. Louis U., 1978. Supr. reading Lindburgh, Mo. Pub. Schools, 1972—78; exec. asst. supt. Anne Arundel Co. Pub. Schools, 1979—82; asst. state supt., dir. assessment ctr. program Md. State Dept. Edn.; assoc. supt. instr. Balt. Co. Pub. Schools; dept. state supt., acting supt. Md. State Dept. Edn., 1990—94; supt. Balt. Pub. Schools, 1994—2006. Exec. v.p. Greater Balt. Com., 1994—99; pres. Fund for Edn. Excellence, 1999—. Named to Wapakoneta High Sch. Hall of Fame, 2002. Mem.: Balt. Ctr. Performing Arts (chmn. edn. com. 2001—). Office Phone: 410-396-8700.*

COPELAND, DEBORAH GAYLE, education educator; d. William McLeod and Willa Faye Copeland; 1 child, William McLeod. BA, Geneva Coll., Beaver Falls, Pa., 1978; MA, Calif. State U.- Fresno, 1992, U. Kans., Lawrence, 1983, PhD, 1998. Profl. social studies sec. Calif., 1988. Tchr. Am. Acad., Larnaca, Cyprus, 1979—84, Fresno Christian H.S., 1984—88, Sanger H.S., Calif., 1988—93; asst. prin. Ctrl. H.S., Fresno, 1993—95; instr. U Kans., Lawrence, 1995—98; prof. Baylor U., Waco, Tex., 1998—99, Calif. State U., Fresno, 1999—2003; chair, edn. dept. Geneva Coll., Beaver Falls, Pa., 2003—. Author: various ednl. rsch. and opinion. Mem. bd. edn. and publ. Ref. Presbyn. Ch., Pitts., 1990—94; bd. trustees Geneva Coll., 1990—95. Recipient Dissertation Rsch. scholarship, U Kans., 1996—98. Mem.: AACTE, History Edn., ASCD. Democrat. Reformed Presbyterian. Avocations: travel, outdoor sports, bungee jumping. Office: Geneva Col 3200 College Ave Beaver Falls PA 15010 Office Phone: 724-847-6538. Office Fax: 724-847-6855. Business E-Mail: dgcopela@geneva.edu.

COPELAND, ELIZABETH JANE, special education educator; b. St. Petersburg, Fla., Aug. 25, 1946; d. Wesley Jenkins and Jane Iris Alonso; m. McNair Oscar Copeland, Sept. 5, 1969; children: Patricia Dawne Brzostowicz, Christina Marie. BA, Scarritt Coll., 1966—68, MA, 1968—70; Ednl. Specialist, Valdosta State U., 1997—99. T-6, Tchg. Cert. in four fields Ga. Profl. Standards, State of Ga., 1999. Tchr., 5th grade Waycross Bd. Edn., Ga., 1971—72; dir., christian edn. Trinity United Meth. Ch., Waycross, 1972—73; dir. Waycross Day Care Ctr., 1974—77; tchr. Brantley County Bd. Edn., Hoboken, Ga., 1977—78; sales rep. Met. Ins. Co., Waycross, 1978—86; spl. agt. Prudential Ins. Co., Waycross, 1987—88; tchr., ged program Concerted Svcs, Inc., Waycross, 1989—90; tchr., 5th grade Charlton County Bd. Edn., Folkston, 1990—91; tchr., spl. edn. Ware County Bd. Edn., Waycross, 1992—. Mem. Pilot Club Internat., Waycross, 1986—; troop leader, area dir. Girl Scouts Am., Waycross, 1976—86; founder Satilla Habitat for Humanity, Waycross, 1991—. Recipient Past Presidents award, Pilot Club of Waycross, 1992, Jesse Harris Achievement award, 1994, Jim Harley award, Kiwanis Club of Waycross, 1996. Mem.: Okefenokee Pilot Club (pres. 2004—05). Avocations: travel, cross stitch, piano, hiking, sewing. Home: 1700 Marshall Dr Waycross GA 31501 Office: Ware County HS 700 Victory D Waycross GA 31503 Office Phone: 912-287-2371. E-mail: ecopeland@ware.k12.ga.us.

COPELAND, JACQUELINE TURNER, music educator; b. Birmingham, Ala., Mar. 22, 1939; d. Charles Smith and Julia (Northrop) Turner; m. William Edward Copeland, Apr. 20, 1962; children: Denise Arlene, Dawn Alane. B in Music Edn., Birmingham-So. Coll., 1960; M in Music Edn., Wichita State U., 1977. Cert. music tchr. grades K-12, Ala., Ga., Kans., La., Va. Music tchr. Jefferson County Bd. Edn., Birmingham, 1960-62, 63-64, DeKalb County Bd. Edn., Decatur, Ga., 1965-68; choral music tchr. Fairfax (Va.) County Bd. Edn., 1968-69, Derby (Kans.) Unified Sch. Dist. #260, 1977-80, Maize (Kans.) Unified Sch. Dist. #266, 1980-84; music tchr. Montgomery (Ala.) County Pub. Schs., 1984-85; instr. voice and piano Acad. Performing Arts, Montgomery, 1985-95, Studio of Jacqueline T. Copeland, Montgomery, 1995—. Accompanist County-Wide Music Festivals, Birmingham, 1960-65; sect. leader Dekalb Cmty. Chorus, Decatur, Ga., 1965-68; sect. leader, exec. bd. New Orleans Concert Choir, 1970-74; asst. dir., dir. chorale Wichita Choral Soc., 1974-84; dir. opening ceremony Bicentennial Fair, Wichita, 1976; mem. Montgomery (Ala.) Civic Chorale, 1984-87; musical dir. for theatre depts. Performing Arts Jr. High, Performing Arts H.S., Faulkner U., 1986—. Author: Music Teacher Handbook, 1967; editor, contbg. author: Teacher Advisement Handbook, 1980. Secret svc. wife White House Wives, Washington, 1968-70; leader, trainer, area chmn. Camp Fire Girls, New Orleans, 1970-74; leader, membership com., exec. bd. Camp Fire Girls, Wichita, 1974-82; elected ofcl. Citizens Participation Orgn., Wichita, 1984; area chmn. Am. Heart Assn., Montgomery, 1988-94; vol. DA Election, Montgomery, 1994. Recipient Groovey Tchr. award WQXI Radio, Atlanta, 1967, Gov.'s commendation Revolutionary Bicentennial Com., Wichita, 1976; named Outstanding Young Women of Am., New Orleans, 1971. Mem. NOW, AAUW, Music Tchrs. Nat. Assn., Ala. Music Tchrs. Assn., Montgomery Music Tchrs. Forum, Alpha Chi Omega (Montgomery chpt. treas. 1995-99, pres. 1999—), Alpha Chi Omega Alumnae (del. to 4 nat. convs., pres., v.p.). Democrat. Baptist. Avocation: searching for collectibles for country decor. Home: 6121 Bell Road Mnr Montgomery AL 36117-4362

COPELAND, LOIS JACQUELINE, physician; b. Malden, Mass., Sept. 16, 1943; d. Arnold Alan and Ann Copeland; m. Richard A. Sperling, June 7, 1970; children: Mark Edward, Larissa Lynn, Lauren Anne, Lorraine Elizabeth. BA magna cum laude with distinction, Cornell U., 1964, MD, 1968. Intern N.Y. Hosp., N.Y.C., 1968-69, resident, 1969-70, Bellevue Hosp., NYU Med. Ctr., 1970-72; tchg. asst. internal medicine NYU Med. Ctr., 1971—; attending physician Pascack Valley Hosp., Westwood, N.J., 1974—. Mem. courtesy staff Valley Hosp., Ridgewood, N.J., 1980—. Mem. secondary schs. com. Cornell U., 1978—; bd. dirs. Found. for Free Enterprise, 1994—; steering com. physicians coun. Heritage Found., 1993—; pres. Coun. Cornell Women, 1993-95 Mem. Assn. Am. Physicians and Surgeons (bd. dirs. 1991-99, pres. 1994), Assn. Liberty Choice and Self-Autonomy (pres. 1998—), Phi Beta Kappa, Phi Kappa Phi, Alpha Lambda Delta. Achievements include being originator and physician-plaintiff of landmark constitutional lawsuit Stewart v. Sullivan, which reaffirmed the right of senior citizens to contract privately with physicians, and Amicus in United Seniors v. Shalala for the right to pay privately for medical services. Home: 25 Sparrowbush Rd Upper Saddle River NJ 07458-1400 Office: 47 Central Ave Hillsdale NJ 07642-2118 Office Phone: 201-664-1212. Personal E-mail: loisjcope@aol.com.

COPELAND, MICHELLE, plastic surgeon; b. NYC, July 15, 1948; DMD magna cum laude, Harvard Dental Sch., 1977; MD, Harvard Med. Sch., 1980. Cert. Am. Bd. Plastic & Reconstructive Surgery. Oral maxillofacial surgery residency Mass. General Hospital, Boston, 1977—79; fellowship NY Hosp. Cornell Med. Ctr., NYC, 1980—82, Mt. Sinai Hospital, NYC, 1982—83, SUNY Downstate Med. Ctr., NYC, 1983—85; staff mem., div. plastic surgery Mount Sinai Med. Ctr.; former chief, div. plastic surgery City Hosp. Ctr., Elmhurst, NY; pvt. practice plastic surgery NYC; assist. prof. surgery Mount Sinai Sch. of Medicine, NYC; attending surgeon Mount Sinai Med. Ctr. & Manhattan Eye, Ear and Throat Hospital, NYC. Mem. med. advisory bd. Soc. for Advancement of Women's Health Rsch. Co-author: Change Your Looks, Change Your Life, 2002, 2d edit., 2003; commentator NBC Today Show, ABC Good Morning America; contbr. articles to newspapers & magazines; author: numerous articles for scientific publications. Fellow: Am. Coll. Surgeons; mem.: Lipoplasty Soc., Am. Soc. for Laser Medicine and Surgery, Am. Med. Women's Assn., Am. Coll. of Maxillofacial Surgeons, Am. Soc. of Plastic & Reconstructive Surgeons, Am. Soc. for Aesthetic Plastic Surgery. Achievements include development of line of skin care products. Office: Cosmetic Plastic & Reconstructive Surgery 1001 Fifth Ave New York NY 10028 E-mail: mcopland@drcopeland.com.

COPELAND, PATRICIA RUTH, elementary school educator; b. Columbus, Ohio, Apr. 14, 1948; d. George Ralph Jones and Dorothy Mae Ailiff; m. John Richard Copeland, July 10, 1993; m. Jerry Thomas Crouch (div.). BS in Sacred Lit., Circleville Bible Coll., Ohio, 1970; BA in Elem. Edn., Cedarville U., Ohio, 1976; MA in Early Childhood Edn., Tenn. Technol. U., Cookeville, 1984. Cert. career level III tchr. State of Tenn. Dept. of Edn. First grade tchr. Fentress County Schs., Jamestown, Tenn., 1977—. Ednl. workshop trainer Fentress County Schs., Jamestown, 1979—, substitute tchr. trainer, 1984—, chairperson first grade sys., 1984—99, parenting classes for sch. readiness trainer, 1986, tech. staff devel. trainer, 1993—. Mem. child abuse rev. team Dept. Human Svcs., Jamestown, 1986—2000. Recipient Nutrition Edn. grant, Tenn. Dept. Health, 1990; grantee Parenting Edn. grant, 1986, Goals 2000 Tech. grant, 2000. Mem.: NEA (assembly del. to Reps. Assembly 1984, 1988), Fentress County Edn. Assn. (sec. 1979—80, pres.-elect 1982—83, pres. 1983—84, contract chief negotiator 1984—88, 1994—), Tenn. Edn. Assn. (del. to Rep. Assembly 1978, 1979, 1983, 1984), Delta Kappa Gamma (chpt. pres. 1993—96), Kappa Delta Pi, Pi Lambda Theta. Methodist. Avocation: community choir. Home: 2803 Rugby Pike Jamestown TN 38556 Office: Allardt Elem Sch 220 Portland Ave Allardt TN 38504 Office Phone: 931-879-9515. Office Fax: 931-879-2702. Personal E-mail: copelandjp@twlakes.net.

COPELAND, SUZANNE JOHNSON, real estate company executive; b. Chgo., Aug. 01; d. John Berger and Eleanor (Dreger) Johnson; m. John Robert Copeland, Aug. 1, 1971 (div. June 1976). Assoc. French Lang. and Literature, Richland Coll., Dallas, 1974; BFA, Ill. Wesleyan U., Bloomington, 1965. Commercial artist Barney Donley Studio, Inc., Chgo., 1966-69; art dir. Levines Dept. Store, Dallas, 1970-74; creative dir. Titche-Goettinger, Inc., Dallas, 1974-78; catering mgr. Dunfey Hotel, Dallas, 1978-82; regional dir. corp. sales Rayburn Country Resort, Austin, Tex., 1982-84; real estate sales assoc. Henry S. Miller, Dallas, 1984-86; v.p. Exclusive Properties Internat., Inc., Dallas, 1986—. Cons. North Tex. Commn., Dallas, 1988. Acquisitions editor: Unser, An American Family Portrait, 1988. Mem. The Rep. Forum, Dallas, 1983-94; vol. Stars for Children, Dallas, 1988, Soc. for Prevention of Cruelty to Animals, Dallas, 1973-92, Preservation of Animal World Soc., 1986-92, Sedona Acad., 1996—, Sedona Humane Soc., 1996—, Sedona Women, 2001—; charter mem. P.M. League Dallas Mus. Art.; mem. Keep Sedona Beautiful, 1999—, Sedona Art Ctr., 2001—. Mem. Nat. Assn.

Realtors, Tex. Assn. Realtors, Greater Dallas Assn. Realtors (com. chmn., Summit award 1984, 85), North Tex. Arabian Horse Club (bd. dirs. 1975-76, Pres.'s award 1978), Dallas Zool. Soc., Humane Soc. Dallas County (v.p. 1973-74), Humane Soc. U.S./Gulf States Humane Edn. Assn. (bd. dirs. 1990-91), Am. Montessori Soc., VASA Order of Am. (bd. dirs. Nordic Red Rocks Lodge 2004-), Delta Phi Delta, Phi Theta Kappa. Lutheran. Avocations: Arabian and thoroughbred horses, scuba diving. Office: Exclusive Properties PO Box 1973 Sedona AZ 86339 Office Phone: 928-203-9999. Personal E-mail: azmtnlion@aol.com.

COPELAND, TATIANA BRANDT, accountant; b. Dresden, Germany; came to U.S., 1959, naturalized, 1967; d. Cyril Alexander and Maria (von Satin) Brandt; m. Gerret van Sweringen Copeland, May 12, 1979. BS summa cum laude, UCLA, 1964; MBA, U. Calif., Berkeley, 1966. Sr. tax cons. Price Waterhouse & Co., L.A., 1966-72; asst. tax mgr. Whittaker Corp., L.A., 1972-75; mgr. internat. dept. E.I. Du Pont de Nemours, Wilmington, Del., 1975-80; pres. Tebec Assocs., Ltd., Wilmington, 1980—. Co-owner, CFO, Bouchaine Vineyards, Inc., Napa, Calif.; owner The Wine & Spirit Co., Greenville, Del.; co-owner, v.p. Rokeby Realty Co., Wilmington; pres. Napa Valley Holdings, Inc., Tebec Realty Internat. Co. Bd. dirs. Del. Symphony, Grand Opera House, Washington; mem. President's Adv. Com. for Trade Negotiations, 1982-87. Mem. AICPA, Am. Woman's Soc. CPA's, Am. Soc. Women Accts., Internat. Fiscal Assn., Del. Soc. CPA's, Phi Beta Kappa. Home: 175 Brecks Ln Wilmington DE 19807-3008 Office: PO Box 3662 Wilmington DE 19807-0662

COPENHAVER, MARION LAMSON, retired state legislator; b. Andover, Vt., Sept. 26, 1925; d. Joseph Fenwick and Christine (Forbes) Lamson; m. John H. Copenhaver, June 30, 1946; children: John III, Margaret, Christine, Eric, Lisa. Student, U. Vt., 1945-46. Mem. N.H. Ho. of Reps., Concord, ranking Dem. health and human svcs. com., 1973-2000, mem. adminstrv. rules com., 1982-2000, mem. health and human svcs. oversight, 1990-2000; ret., 2000. Chair Grafton County Dems., 1986-91; assoc. supr. Grafton County Soil Conservation Dist., 1980-2002, supr., 2002—; supr. Hanover (N.H.) Dem. Town Com., 1992; mem.-at-large Dem. State Com., Concord, 1992; bd. dirs. Dartmouth Hitchcock Found., Hanover, 1991—; bd. incorporators Dartmouth Hitchcock Med. Ctr., Lebanon, N.H., 1984—; bd. dirs. Grafton County Sr. Citizens Coun., Inc., 1995-96, 2001, vice chair, Outreach House, an Assisted Living Facility, 2001—, Hanover, Friends of Norris Cotton Cancer Ctr., Women's Policy Inst. N.H. Named N.H. Legislator of Yr. N.H. Nurses Assn., 1989; recipient Meritorious award N.H. Women's Lobby, 1996, James A. Hamilton award N.H. Hosp. Assn., 1997. Mem. NOW, Bus. and Profl. Women's Club (Outstanding Mem. award 1990). Democrat. Unitarian Universalist. Avocations: golf, skiing. Home: 80 Lyme Rd 158 Hanover NH 03755

COPLEY, CYNTHIA SUE LOVE, insurance adjuster; b. Defiance, Ohio, Oct. 26, 1957; d. Thomas Lee and Pauline Ann (Brandt) Love, Jr.; m. James Earl Copley, Jr., Oct. 19, 1985. B in Criminal Justice, Ohio U., Athens, 1981, A in Law Enforcement, 1979, A in Fire and Safety Tech., 1982. Cert. profl. ins. woman. With Spangler Candy Co., Bryan, Ohio, 1976-77; guard Juvenile Detention Ctr., Chillicothe, Ohio, 1978; security officer J.C. Penney Corp., Inc., Chillicothe, Ohio, 1979, Rink's Bargain City, Chillicothe, Ohio, 1979; with Rubbermaid Sales Corp., Chillicothe, Ohio, 1980; asst. dept. sec. and computer lab asst. Ohio U., Chillicothe, 1977-81; supr. collections and investigation Bur. of Support, Ross County, Chillicothe, 1981-82; asst. mgr. Tecumseh Claims Svc., Chillicothe, 1982—; owner Copley Adjusting, Chillicothe, 1982—. Part-time employee Ross County Bd. Elections, 1998-2003. Poll worker Rep. Party, Chillicothe, 1983-98; mem. Rep. Women Ross County, sec., 2000-2004. Mem. So. Ohio Claims Assn., Ohio Assn. Ind. Ins. Adjusters (sec.-treas. 1994, v.p. 1995, pres. 1996), Ohio Assn. Mut. Ins. Cos., Nat. Soc. Profl. Ins. Investigators. Lutheran. Avocations: golf, cooking, weekend trips. Home and Office: Tecumseh Claims Svc PO Box 15 Chillicothe OH 45601-0015

COPLEY, EDITH ANN, music educator; b. Davenport, Iowa, Oct. 24, 1952; d. Robert H. and Lottie J. Copley. BA in Music Edn., Luther Coll., 1974; MM in Conducting, U. Cin., 1987, DMA in Conducting, 1990. Music educator 6-12 Norwalk (Iowa) Pub. Schs., 1974-77; h.s. choral dir. Waterloo (Iowa) Pub. Schs., 1978-82; fine arts coord. Am. Internat. Sch., Vienna, 1982-86; asst. dir. of choral studies No. Ariz. U., Flaggstaff, 1990-93, dir. of choral studies, 1993—. Music dir. Am. Choral Soc., Vienna, 1983-86, Master Chorale of Flagstaff, 1993—; resident conductor Flagstaff Symphony, 1999-2000; guest clinician/conductor all-state choirs. Mem. Ariz. Choral Dirs. Assn. (pres. 1999-2001, Music Educators Nat. Conf., Chorus Am., Coll. Music Soc., Am. Choral Dirs. Assn. (western divsn. pres. 2005-). Avocations: golf, hiking, skiing, travel. Home: 791 N Canyon Terrace Dr Flagstaff AZ 86001-4804 Office: No Ariz U PO Box 6040 Flagstaff AZ 86011-0001

COPPENBARGER, CECELIA MARIE, special education educator; b. Kansas City, Mo., Nov. 3, 1961; d. Theodore Francis Bowman, Jr., Betty Marie Bowman; m. Charles Loren Coppenbarger, Jr.; children: Charles Loren Coppenbarger, III, Craig James, Cliff Robert, Joshua Richard, Elena Marie. A Liberal Arts, Longview C.C., 1983; BA Secondary Edn., U. Mo., 1998, BA Eng., 1998; postgrad., Ctrl. Mo. State U. Cert. cross categorical spl. edn. tchr. K-12, secondary Eng.tchr. 9-12. Tchr. cross-categorical spl. edn. Raytown C-2 Sch. Dist., Mo., 1998—2004, Fort Osage R1 Sch. Dist., 2004—. Sponsor Raytown chpt. Mo. State Tchrs. Assn.-Future Tchrs. Am., 2000—04. Active James Lewis Elem. PTA, 2002—; mem. Plaza Heights Bapt. Ch. Choir, Blue Springs, 1998—; tchr. Plaza Heights Bapt. Ch. Sunday Sch., Blue Springs, 1999—; mem. Lucy Franklin Elem. Sch. PTA, Blue Springs, 1998—2001, Blue Springs H.S. Parent Tchr. Student Assn., 1998—2001, 2003—, Brittany Hills Mid. Sch. Parent Tchr. Student Assn., 1998—2003; educator Raytown South H.S. Parent Tchr. Student Assn., Raytown, 1998—2004. Recipient Outstanding Scholastic Achievement and Excellence award, Golden Key Nat. Honor Soc., 1997, Outstanding Omer award, Odyssey of Mind Program, 1997; scholar, U. Mo., Kansas City, 1997—98. Mem.: Mo. State Tchrs. Assn., Raytown Cmty. Tchrs. Assn., Coun. Exceptional Children (nomination chmn. Mo. divsn. learning disabilities 2005—), Pi Lambda Theta. Home: 2114 NE 3rd St Blue Springs MO 64014 Office: Osage Trail Mid Sch 2101 N Twyman Rd Independence MO 64056 Office Phone: 816-650-7151. Personal E-mail: ccoppen@sbcglobal.net. Business E-Mail: ccoppenbargerc@fortosage.net. E-mail: Coppen@Discoverynet.com.

COPPENS, LAURA KATHRYN, special education educator; b. Hoddesdon, England, Jan. 12, 1948; d. Tomas Adriaan and Sylvia Helen Coppens; m. G. Lawrence McQueen (div. 1985); children: Isaac David, Sean Little Hawk. BA in Edn., John F. Kennedy Coll., Wahoo, Nebr., 1970; MEd in Spl. Edn., William Paterson U., 1976. Spl. edn. tchr. Bellmar (N.J.) Schs., 1970—71, N.J. Commn. for Blind, Teaneck, 1972—76; dir. Randolph County Learning Ctr., Roanoke, Ala., 1976—80; spl. edn. tchr. Lineville (Ala.) H.S., 1980—89, BOCES Alternative Program, Apalachin, NY, 1989—93, Owego (N.Y.) Apalachin Middle Sch., 1993—98, Owego Free Acad., 1998—. Dir. Youth Group, Owego, 2000—; co-coord. Inst. of Arts in Edn., Owego, 1996—; mentor tchr. Owego Apalachin Ctrl. Schs., 1999—. Pres. Randolph County Assn. for Retarded Citizens, Roanoke, 1980—83; lay reader St. Paul's Episc. Ch., Owego, 1998—. Recipient Outstanding Tchr. award, So. Tier Inst. of Arts, Binghamton, N.Y., 1998. Mem.: Broome Tioga Autism Soc. Am., Owego Apalachin Tchrs. Assn. (sec. 1998—), Coun. for Exceptional Children. Episcopalian. Achievements include creation of school for the handicapped in Roanoke; creation of first high school program for the multihandicapped in Lineville. Avocations: tenor recorder, reading, singing in church choir. Home: 412 Forest Hill Rd Apalachin NY 13732 Office: Owego Apalachin Ctrl Schs Talcott St Owego NY 13827 E-mail: lcoppens@oagw.stier.org.

COPPERSMITH, SUSAN NAN, physicist; b. Johnstown, Pa., Mar. 18, 1957; d. Wallace Louis and Bernice Barbara (Evans) C.; m. Robert Daniel Blank, Dec. 20, 1981. BS in Physics, MIT, 1978; postgrad., Cambridge U., 1979; MS in Physics, Cornell U., 1981, PhD in Physics, 1983. Rsch. assoc. Brookhaven Nat. Labs., 1983-85; postdoctoral mem. tech. staff AT&T Bell Labs., Murray Hill, N.J., 1985-86, mem. tech. staff, 1987-90, disting. mem. tech. staff, 1990-95; prof. physics U. Chgo., 1995—2001; prof., chair dept. physics U. Wis., Madison, 2001—. Vis. lectr. Princeton U., 1986-87; vis. professorship for women NSF, 1986-87; gen. mem. Aspen Ctr. for Physics, 1991—2006; chancellor's disting. lectr. U. Calif., Irvine, 1991. Trustee Aspen Ctr. for Physics, 1993-96. Winston Churchill scholar, 1978-79, Bell Labs. GRPW fellow, 1979-83. Fellow AAAS, Am. Phys. Soc., Am. Acad. Arts and Scis. Office: Univ Wis Dept Physics 1150 University Ave Madison WI 53706 Office Phone: 608-262-8358. E-mail: snc@physics.wisc.edu.

COPPERSMITH FREDMAN, MARIAN UNGAR, magazine publisher; b. Wilkes-Barre, Pa., June 11, 1933; d. Max H. and Tillie (Landau) Ungar; m. Sy Barash, Jan. 31, 1954 (dec. Feb. 1975); children: Carol Lynn, Nan Ruth; m. W. Louis Coppersmith, Apr. 29, 1978 (dec. Jan. 1989); m. Samuel G. Fredman, Feb. 24, 1990. BA in Journalism with honors, Pa. State U., 1953; postgrad., 1953-55. Tech. writer Kling Studios, Chgo., 1951; editl. dir. Daily Collegian, State College, Pa., 1953; grad. asst., instr. dept. speech Pa. State U., State College, 1953-55, 61; instr. mktg., 1974-75, 78; writer, salesman Friedman & Barash, State College, 1956-59; ptnr. Barash Advtsg., 1959-60, Morgan Signs, Inc., 1960-75; pub. State College Town-Gown, Where & When, 1959—; pres. The Barash Group, 1975—2000, chmn., 2000—. Bd. dir. Milton S. Hershey Med. Sch.; cons. mktg. and pub. rels. to various fin. instns.; guest lectr. speech, journalism, mktg. Pa. State U., 1965—; v.p Palmer Mus Adv. Bd., 1998-99, pres., 1999-2001 Contbr. articles to profl. jours. Chmn. Art Alliance Fund Campaign, 1971; mem.pub. rels. com. Ctrl. Pa. Heart Assn., 1973; chmn. Cancer Crusade, State College, 1973-74; mem. Pa. Commn. for Women, 1980-87; bd. govs. Pa. Free Enerprise Week, 1981-85; chmn. bd. govs. Ctr. County Cmty. Found., 1987-89; pres. Nittany Coun. Rep. Women, 1960-61; bd. dirs. United Fund, 1965-70, asst. chmn., 1969; alumni trustee Pa. State U., 1976-97, vice-chmn., 1988-91, chmn., 1991-93; bd. dirs. Pennsylvanians for Effective Govt., 1978, United Way Pa., 1977-82, treas., 1978; bd. dirs. Capital Blue Cross, 1978-84, Women's Campaign Fund., 1982-85, Pa. Ben Franklin Partnership, 1983-87, Mercy Hosp., Johnstown, Pa., 1983-89, Ctrl. Pa. Festival of the Arts, 1995—2000, Allegheny Highlands Regional Theatre, Pa. Ctr. Stage, Pa. Humanities Coun., Pa. Women's Campaign Fund., Renaissance Scholarship Fund Pa. State U., 1976—; bd. advs. Palmer Mus. Art, 1994—; mem. leadership coun. Ctr. Performing Arts SUNY, Purchase, 1994—96; mem. adv. coun. subcom. small bus. and commerce com. Pa. Ho. of Reps., 1983-86; mem. B'nai B'rith; chair Women's Resource Ctr, Hemlock Girl Scout Council; bd. adv., Palmer Museum Art, 1994-; trustee emerita, Penn State U.; capital campaign coord. Alpha Com. Ambulance, 2001-04 Alumni fellow Pa. State U., 1997; recipient Kiwanis award, 1976, Small buisnessperson of Yr., 1981, Svc. to Soc. award Coll. Liberal Arts Pa. State U., 1984; named Disting. Pennsylvanian, Pa. Gov., 1981, Phila. C. of C. (Disting. Dau. Pa. 1990), One of Pa.'s Best 50 Women in Bus., Pa. Commn. Women, 1996, Crl. Pa. Entrepreneur of Yr., Ctrl. Pa. Bus. Jour., 1996, Disting. Alumna, Pa. State U., 1998; Paul Harris fellow, Rotary, 2004. AAUW, LWV, Mem. Eight-sheet Outdoor Adv. Assn., Nat. Cable TV Assn. (pub. rels. com. 1972-73), Outdoor Adv. Assn., Outdoor Adv. Inc., Pa. Cable TV Assn. (pub. rels. counsel 1967-75), Pa. Outdoor Adv. Assn., Eight-sheet Outdoor Adv. Assn., Specialties Adv. Assn., Inc., Women in Comms., Friends of Palmer Mus. Art, Pa. State U., Friends of Schlow Libr., Clearwater Conservancy, Mt. Nittany Conservancy, Delta Sigma Rho, Omicron Delta Kappa, Nittany Lion Club. Office: Morgan Signs Inc 403 S Allen St Ste 77 State College PA 16801-5252 Office Phone: 814-238-5051. E-mail: mimi@barashgroup.com.

COPPOCK, DORIS ELLEN, retired physical education educator, retired music educator; b. Chgo., May 18, 1927; d. Xury Landon and Martha Ellen (Evans) Coppock. AB, McPherson Coll., 1948; MA, U. Iowa, 1954, PhD, 1964. H.S. tchr. English, phys. edn., music, Hamilton, Kans., 1948—49; social worker Montgomery County Welfare Dept., Independence, Kans., 1949—50; from instr. to prof. McPherson (Kans.) Coll., 1950—92; ret., 1992. Tchr. Colo. State U., Gunnison, 1992; pres. Kans. Assn. Intercollegiate Athletics for Women, 1967—68, Ctrl. Assn. Phys. Edn. for Coll. Women, 1975—77. Active Meals on Wheels, McPherson, 1996—2000; ct. apptd. spl. advocate A Voice for Children, Inc., 2004—; ch. choir dir. Luth. Ch., McPherson, 1956—63, Presbyn. Ch., McPherson, 1964—77, Meth. Ch., McPherson, 1978—89; min. music Ch. of the Brethren, McPherson, 1993—2002. Named Coach of Yr. (Tennis), McPherson Coll., 1976, 1977, Woman of Yr., Soroptimist Internat. (McPherson, Kans. chpt.), 1977; named to Hall of Fame, Nat. Assn. Intercollegiate Athletics, 1993, Athletic Hall of Fame, McPherson Coll., 1999; recipient Honor award, Kans. Assn. for Health, Phys. Edn. and Recreation, 1980, Alumni Citation of Merit, McPherson Coll., 1993, Project Acclaim award, Nat. Assn. Girls and Women's Sports, 1996, Pathfinder award, 2004; grantee, NEH, 1987. Mem.: AAHPERD (life). Avocations: golf, music, reading, travel. Home: 1015 Darlow Dr Mcpherson KS 67460 E-mail: decop@sbcglobal.net.

COPPOLA, SARAH JANE, special education educator; b. Alton, Ill., Apr. 20, 1957; d. Howard Earl and Dorothy Elizabeth (Eads) Cox; children: Daniel Joseph III, Shawn Marie. BS, Trenton State Coll., 1979; M in Counseling Edn., Kean Coll. N.J., 1995. Cert. guidance counselor, substance abuse counselor N.J., early childhood cert., CIE coop. coord. cert., WECEP cert. Substitute tchr. Dunellen (N.J.) Bd. Edn., 1979-87, Greenbrook (N.J.) Bd. Edn., 1979-87, Middlesex (N.J.) Bd. Edn., 1979-87, Bound Brook (N.J.) Bd. Edn., 1983-84; tchr. handicapped Piscataway (N.J.) Bd. Edn., 1987—, prin. adv. bd., 1990-91, editl. yearbook advisor, 1998—. Youth group advisor Trinity Reformed Ch., North Plainfield, NJ, 1983—91, deacon, 1985—87, 2001—04, elder, 1997—2005, head Christian edn., 1997—, v.p. consistory, 2000, 2005. Recipient Internat. Educator of Yr. award, 2003, Servant of Hope award, 2005, Recognition award, Synod of Mid-Atlantics Reformed Ch. Am., 2006. Mem.: NEA, Piscataway Edn. Assn., N.J. Edn. Assn., Kean Coll. Alumni Assn. (vol. Fish Hospitality program). Avocations: reading, needlecrafts, church choir. Home: 200 Barclay Ct Piscataway NJ 08854 Office: Piscataway Bd Edn 100 Behmer Rd Piscataway NJ 08854-4161 Office Phone: 732-981-0700 7130. E-mail: sarahjcoppola@yahoo.com.

COPPOLA, SOFIA CARMINA, film director, scriptwriter, actress; b. N.Y.C., May 1971; d. Francis Ford and Eleanor Coppola; m. Spike Jonze, 1999 (div.). Intern with Karl Lagerfield Chanel; designer Milk Fed. Actor: (films) The Godfather, 1972, The Godfather: Part II, 1974, The Outsiders, 1983, Rumble Fish, 1983, The Cotton Club, 1984, Frankenweenie, 1984, Peggy Sue Got Married, 1986, Anna, 1987, The Godfather: Part III, 1990, Inside Monkey Zetterland, 1992, Star Wars: Episode I-The Phantom Menace, 1999, CQ, 2001; dir., prodr., screenwriter (films) Lick the Star, 1998, Lost in Translation, 2003 (Golden Athena, Athens Intl. Film Festival, 2003, Boston Soc. of Film Critics award for best dir., 2003, Nat. Bd. of Review award for special achievement, 2003, NY Film Critics Circle award for best dir., 2003, Toronto Film Critics Assoc. award for best screenplay, 2003, Golden Globe for best screenplay, 2004, Academy award for best screenplay, 2004), Marie Antoinette, 2006, dir., screenwriter The Virgin Suicides, 1999, host (TV series) Hi-Octane, 1994, segment writer N.Y. Stories, 1989, costume designer, 1989, series creator Platinum, 2003, writer, 2003; exec. prodr.: (TV series) Platinum, 2003; costume designer (plays) The Spirit of '76, 1990.

COPPOLA, TALIA ROSE See SHIRE, TALIA ROSE

COPPS, SHEILA, former Canadian government official; b. Hamilton, Ont., Can., Nov. 27, 1952; d. Victor Kennedy and Geraldine (Guthro) C.; m. Austin Thorne; 1 child, Danelle. BA in French, English with hons., U. Western Ont., London; postgrad., U. Rouen, France, McMaster U., Hamilton. Reporter Ottawa Citizen, 1974-76, Hamilton Spectator, 1977; asst. to Ont. Liberal leader Stuart Smith, Hamilton, 1977-81; mem. Legis. Assembly Ont., Toronto, 1981-84, House of Commons, Ottawa, 1984-97; apptd. dep. leader Liberal Party Can., Ottawa, Ont., 1990—; dep. prime min. Govt. of Can., Ottawa, 1993-97, min. environ., 1993-96, min. of Can. heritage, 1996—2003. Author: Nobody's Baby, 1986. Mem. Liberal Party. Office: House of Commons Rm 509-S Ottawa ON Canada K1A 0A6

COPT, PHYLLIS JEAN, secondary school educator; b. Emporia, Kans., Jan. 25, 1950; d. Arthur and Nettie Marie Weidner; m. Louis Joseph Copt, Oct. 23, 1971; 1 child, Nathaniel Louis. MSE, U. Kans., Lawrence, 1993. MCSE tchr. Kans., 1976. Tchr. Lawrence Pub. Schs., Kans., 1984—. SEGUE sponsor Women's Study Club, Lawrence, 1989—2006; hirstsuka, japan sister city organizer City of Lawrence, Kans., 1990—93. Fund raiser NOW, Lawrence, 2004—06. Mem.: NEA (assoc.), Nat. Coun. Tchrs. English (assoc.), Kans. Land Trust (assoc.). Democrat. Avocations: travel, gardening, reading, writing. Office Phone: 785-832-6050.

CORA, CAT, chef; b. Jackson, Miss. 1 child. BS in Exercise Physiology, Biology; grad., Culinary Inst. Am., Hyde Park, NY. Apprentice to George Blanc, France, Roger Verge, France; sous chef Old Chatham Shepherding Co., NYC; chef de cuisine Bistro Don Giovanni, Napa Valley; exec. chef Postino, East Bay. Co-host, Kitchen Accomplished Food Network, LA, 2004, co-host, Melting Pot, mem., Iron Chef Am., 2005—; ptnr. 3 Street Media. Co-author (with Ann Kreuger Spivak): (cookbooks) Cat Cora's Kitchen, 2004; columnist Cooking from the Hip, Contra Costa (Calif.) Times. Founding mem. Chefs for Humanity, 2004—. Mem.: SAG. Achievements include being named first female Iron Chef. Mailing: Food Network Ste 220 5757 Wilshire Blvd Los Angeles CA 90036*

CORASH, MICHÈLE B., lawyer; b. May 6, 1945; BA, Mt. Holyoke Coll., 1967; JD cum laude, NYU, 1970. Legal advisor to chmn. FTC, 1970-72; dep. gen. counsel U.S. Dept. Energy, 1979; gen. counsel EPA, 1979-81; ptnr. Morrison & Foerster, San Francisco and L.A. Bd. editors Toxics Law Reporter; bd. advisors Jour. Environ. Law and Corporate Practice, Ecology Law Quarterly; mem. nat. editl. adv. bd. Prop 65 Clearingho. Bd. dirs. Calif. Counsel on Environ. and Econ. Balance, 1991—; mem. blue ribbon commn. Calif. Environ. Protection Agy. Unified Environ. Statute; mem. V.P. Bush Regulatory Task Force, 1981, mem. adv. council Environ. Curriculum Stanford Law Sch., bd. adv. Hastings West-Northwest Jour. Environmental Law & Practice. Named one of Best Lawyers in Am., Environ. Law, Corp. Counsel, Am. Lawyer, 2003, Top 50 Women Litigators in Calif., Daily Journal Extra, 2003, 100 Most Influential Lawyers in Calif., Daily Journal, 2002, 2005, Top 30 Women Litigators in Calif., 2002—05. Mem. ABA (mem. standing com. on environ. 1988-91, chair com. environ. crimes 1990), Inter-Pacific Bar Assn. (chair environ. law com.). Office: Morrison & Foerster 425 Market St San Francisco CA 94105-2482 Business E-Mail: mcorash@mofo.com.

CORATHERS, LORNA JOAN, artist; b. New Denver, B.C., Can., Aug. 12, 1931; d. Harold Thatcher Onstine and Elizabeth Jean (Nelson) Philmallee; m. John Franklin Corathers, July 26, 1957 (wid. Oct. 1990). Student, Denver Art Students League, 1987-88. Sec. USAF, various locations; artist, owner Lorna Studio, Aurora, Colo., 1986—. Tchr. pvt. art lessons, art/parks and recreation, Aurora, 1987—. Exhibited in Hist. Mus. New Denver. Donated paintings to Channel 6 TV auction, Denver, Al-Anon Svc. Ctr., Denver Auction for Abused Children, Hawk Creek Wildlife Ctr., Inc., N.Y. Recipient numerous local art awards. Mem. Denver Art Students League, Aurora Artist Guild (pres. 1985-86), Art Soc. Ea. Wash., Mont. Watercolor Soc. (signature), Wildlife Artist Assn., Coeur d'Alene Art Assn. Roman Catholic. Home: 610 S Clinton St Apt 10d Denver CO 80247-1536

CORAZZO, MICHELE, artist, educator; b. Chgo., Ill., July 13, 1951; d. Alexander and Gretchen (Schoeninger); m. Gus Sisto (div.); children: Aaron, Alexander. BA, Ind. U., 1973; MFA, U. Chgo., 1977. Adj. art instr. Roosevelt U., Chgo., 1981—; adj asst. art prof. Valparaiso U., Ind., 1988—; art instr. Chesterton Montessori Sch., Ind., 1996—. Adv. fed. arch. project Gov. Svc. Adminstrn., Hammond, Ind., 1997—99; curator Take A Peek, ARC Gallery, Chgo. Ceramics, Strictly Functional Pottery Nat., 2004, Represented in permanent collections Nat. Field Mus., Chgo., one-woman shows include Brauer Mus. Art, Valparaiso U., 1995, 2006, Represented in permanent collections Hilliard Conservatory, Ind. Continental Bank, Chgo. Vol. Ind. Dunes State Park, Porter, Ind., Hageman Libr., Porter. Avocations: cooking, hiking, reading, guitar, gardening. Home: 551 Graham Dr Chesterton IN 46304 Office: Valparaiso U VUCA Valparaiso IN 46383 Office Phone: 219-465-7929.

CORBET, KATHLEEN A., financial information company executive; b. Feb. 22, 1960; m. Randy Corbet; children: Dylan, Ian. BS in mktg. and computer sci., Boston Coll., 1982; MBA in fin., NYU, 1989. Chmn. Alliance Capital, Australia, New Zealand, chief investment ops. and global trading, 1997—99; CEO Alliance Capital Ltd., London, 1998—2000; CEO fixed income divsn. Alliance Capital Mgmt., 2000—04; pres. Standard & Poor's, 2004—. Mem. bd. trustees Boston Coll. Mem.: Coun. Fgn. Rels. Office: Standard & Poor's 55 Water St New York NY 10041*

CORBETT, ALICE CATHERINE, investor; d. Marshal Richard and Coralyn Estelle Reckard; BS, U. Oreg., 1943. Tchr. Portland (Oreg.) Dept. Edn., 1944—47; mem. Oreg. Senate, Salem, 1950—58; commr. Multnomah County, Portland, 1964—68; investor Portland, 1964—. Mem.: Multnomah Club. Home: 2947 SW Plum Ct Portland OR 97219

CORBETT, HELEN A., chemist, chemical engineer; b. Berkeley Springs, W.Va., Jan. 28, 1972; d. Harry Ralph and Florence Louise Barker; m. James Jay Corbett, Nov. 6, 1996. BS, Towson U., 1995. Lab. tech. State Hwy. Adminstrn., Hancock, Md., 1990-96; R&D chemist Garden State Tanning, Inc., Williamsport, Md., 1996-99; plant process engr. Rust-Oleum Corp., Hagerstown, Md., 1999—. Mem. Am. Chem. Soc., Fedn. Socs. for Coatings Tech. Episcopalian. Avocations: reading, walking. Home: 1051 Lindsay Ln Hagerstown MD 21742-4612 Office: Rust-Oleum Corp PO Box 1008 Hagerstown MD 21741-1008

CORBETT, LENORA MEADE, mathematician, community college educator; b. Reidsville, NC, Aug. 1, 1950; children: Kenneth Russell Johnson, Ralph Nathaniel Brown. AAS in Electromechanics, Tech. Coll. of Alamance, 1985, AAS in Electronics, 1986; BS in Indsl. Tech., Electronics, N.C. A&T State U., 1996; candidate, World Acad. Letters, 2004. Cloth insp. Burlington (N.C.) Industries, 1971-74; electrician's helper Williams Electric, Greensboro, NC, 1978, Nobility Mobile Homes, Reidsville, NC, 1979; instr. math. and physics Alamance C.C., Graham, NC, 1985—2002, chmn. learning resources, 1993. Author: numerous poems. Sr. choir Jones Cross Rd. Ch., Reidsville, 1988-94, pastor's aide mem., 1988-90, jr. Sunday sch. tchr., 1989-91, asst. choir sec., 1988-94; bd. dirs. Nu Generation Enrichment Program, Nu Generation Enrichment Ctr., Teach Tolerance Nat. Campaign Tolerance, 2002-03 Nominee Poet of Yr., 2002, Internat. Poet of Merit, 2002, Noble Laureats, 2004, World Champion Amateur Poet; named Famous Poet, 1996, Poet of Yr., 2000, Best Love Poems from Sparrowgrass, 2001, Famous Poet, 2002, Poet of Yr., 2004, Outstanding Achievement in Poetry, 2004; named to Best Poets of 2000, 2000, Best Poems and Poets, 2001, Internat. Poetry Hall of Fame, 2003, Women's Internat. Hall of Fame; recipient Merit award, 1990, Golden Poet award, 1991, Merit award, 1992, Editor's Choice award, 1997, Recognition award, Famous Poets Soc., 1998, Famous Poet, 2000, Noble prize outstanding achievement and contbn. to soc., 2001. Mem. AAUP, AAUW, Alamance C.C. Alumni Assn., Golden Key, N.C. A&T State U. Alumni Assn. Baptist. Avocations: cooking, reading, poetry, drawing, singing.

CORBETT, REBECCA, editor; With Jour. Inquirer, Manchester, Conn., Morning Sentinel, Maine; asst. mng. editor, projects Baltimore Sun; enterprise editor NY Times Washington bur., Washington, 2004—. Office: NY Times 7th Fl 1627 I St NW Washington DC 20006 Office Phone: 202-862-0300. Office Fax: 202-862-0340. E-mail: rcorbett@nytimes.com.*

CORBETT, SUSAN, mathematics educator; b. Houston; d. Mary Alice and Franklin Fite; m. Steven Corbett; children: Robert, Rachael. BA in Math. and Stats., Miami U., Oxford, Ohio, 1978; BS in Meteorology, N.C. State U., Raleigh, 1979; MS Math. in Math., U. Nev., Las Vegas, 1991. Math lectr. U.

Nev., 1991—94, U. Md., Yokota Air Base, Japan, 1994—96; math tchr. Rancho HS, North Las Vegas, 1997—. Capt. USAF, 1979—81. Named to Hall of Fame, Clark County Sch. Dist., 2004; recipient Advanced Placement Award for Math and Sci., Siemens Found., 2005. Mem.: Nat. Coun. Tchrs. Math. Office: Rancho High Sch 1900 Searles Ave Las Vegas NV 89101 Office Phone: 702-799-7000. E-mail: corbetts@interact.ccsd.net.

CORBI, LANA, communications executive; Sr. v.p. network distbn. Fox Broadcasting Co., 1994—95, exec. v.p. network distbn., 1996—97, pres. network distbn., 1997—99; pres., COO Blackstar, L.L.C., 1995—96; COO Odyssey Holdings, 1999—2000; exec. v.p., COO Crown Media Holdings, 2000—01; CEO Hallmark Channel, Coral Gables, Fla., 2001—.

CORBIERE, MARY LOUISE SAMBATARO, music educator, musician; b. Lawrence, Mass., Dec. 12, 1942; d. Louis John Sambataro and Geneva Mary Cascone; m. Paul Arthur Corbiere, Nov. 9, 1963 (div. July 7, 1995); children: Paul, Arthur, Geneva, Jacqueline. MusB, U. of Miami, Coral Gables, FL, 1960—65, MA iin Music Edn., 1982—85. Cert. tchr. Fla., 1965. Music tchr. Pine Ridge Elem. Sch., Fort Lauderdale, Fla., 1965—70, Sungate Acad., Hollywood, Fla., 1973—76, Cooper City (Fla.) Elem. Sch., 1976—90; music tchr. and magnet coord. Bethune Performing Arts Magnet, Hollywood, 1990—98; music tchr. Fox Trail Elem. Sch., Davie, 1998—2001, Pembroke Pines Charter H.S., 2001—. Dir. of music St. Bernadette Cath. Ch., Davie, 1977—89; parish dir. of music St. Mark Cath. Ch., S.W. Ranches, Fla., 1990—. Recipient Tchr. of Yr., Cooper City Elem. Sch., 1982, Bethune Elem. Performing Arts Magnet, 1985, Fox Trail Elem. Sch., 2000, Master Tchr. award, State of Fla., 1985. Mem.: Music Educators Nat. Conf., Fla. Music Educators Assn., Broward County Elem. Music Tchrs. Assn., St. Mark Women's Club. Roman Catholic. Avocations: children and grandchildren, entertaining, visiting, baking, sports. Office: Pembroke Pines Charter HS 17189 Sheridan Street Pembroke Pines FL 33331 E-mail: mcorbiere@pinescharter.com.

CORBIN, LYNN ANN, music educator, conductor; d. Robert Lyle and Edith Peters Corbin; m. Lester Rolland Seiple, Aug. 28, 1997. PhD, Ohio State U., Columbus, 1982. Asst. prof. Ill. State U., Normal, 1982—83; vis. asst. prof. Butler U., Indianapolis, Ind., 1983—84; from asst. to assoc. prof. Ohio State U., Marion, 1984—94; music cons. State of Ohio, 1994—96; prof. Valdosta State U., Ga., 1996—. Music dir. Valdosta Choral Guild, 1998—, Madison First United Meth. Ch., Fla., 2004—. Contbr. articles to profl. jours. Mem.: Ga. Music Educators Assn. (chmn. coll. divsn. 2003—05). Avocations: scuba diving, horseback riding. Office: Valdosta State U Dept Music 1500 N Patterson St Valdosta GA 31698 Office Phone: 229-333-5804. Office Fax: 229-333-5578. Business E-Mail: lcorbin@valdosta.edu.

CORBIN, ROSEMARY MACGOWAN, former mayor; b. Santa Cruz, Calif., Apr. 3, 1940; d. Frederick Patrick and Lorena Maude (Parr) MacGowan; m. Douglas Tenny Corbin, Apr. 6, 1968; children: Jeffrey, Diana. BA, San Francisco State U., 1961; MLS, U. Calif., Berkeley, 1966. Libr. Stanford (Calif.) U., 1966-68, Richmond (Calif.) Pub. Libr., 1968-69, Kaiser Found. Health Plan, Oakland, Calif., 1976-81, San Francisco Pub. Libr., 1981-82, U. Calif., Berkeley, 1982-83; mem. coun. City of Richmond, 1985-93, vice mayor, 1986-87, mayor, 1993—2001. Mem. Solid Waste Mgmt. Authority, 1985-2001, Contra Costa Hazardous Materials Commn., Martinez, Calif., 1987-2001, San Francisco Bay Conservation and Devel. Commn., 1987-2001; mem. League of Calif. Cities Environ. Affairs Com., 1994-2001; mem. energy and environ. com. U.S. Conf. Mayors and Nat. League of Cities, 1993-2001. Contbr. articles to profl. publs. Pres. Ujima Family Svcs.; chair Richmond Historic Preservation Com.; mem. Rosie the Riveter Trust Bd., San Francisco Bay Trail Bd.; bd. mem. Libr. Found., Inst. for Local Govt. Mem. LWV, NOW, Nat. Women's Polit. Caucus, Calif. Libr. Assn., Sierra Club. Democrat. Avocations: reading, hiking, golf, gardening, quilting. Home: 114 Crest Ave Richmond CA 94801-4031

CORBIN, VERONICA L., secondary school educator, information scientist, consultant; d. Joyce P. Corbin. BS in Chemistry, Va. Union U., 1999; MS in Computer Networking, Strayer U., 2003. Lab. specialist Dept. Gen. Svcs., Richmond, 1999—2001; educator Richmond (Va.) Pub. Schs., 2001—05, Henrico County Pub. Schs., Richmond, Va., 2005—; prin., owner Platinum Networking Svs., Richmond, Va. Computer cons. Platinum Networking Svcs., Richmond, 2001—, Nehemiah Cmty. Ctr., Richmond, 2004—05. Office Phone: 804-651-5523.

CORBITT, ANN MARIE, municipal official; b. Jersey City, N.J., Nov. 28, 1966; d. Andrew M. and Maria Gisondi; m. Frederick William Corbitt, Sept. 18, 1988; children: Frederick Francis, Benjamin Brandon, Kristofer Kevin. Cert. Tax Collector, Rutgers U., 1988. Cert. fire fighter, EMT. Work study program in tax office Twp. of Parsippany, N.J., 1983-84, acct. clk. tax office, 1984-87, sr. acct. clk., 1987-88, dep. tax collector, 1988-94; tax collector Twp. Morris, N.J., 1994-99, City of East Orange, N.J., 1999—. Vol. Denville Fire Dept., 1992—. Mem. Essex County Tax Collectors Assn., Tax Collectors and Treasurers N.J. Republican. Roman Catholic. Office: 44 City Hall Plz East Orange NJ 07017-4104

CORBITT, EUMILLER MATTIE, special education educator; b. Detroit, Jan. 07; d. Harrison and Arnetha (Tatum) Jones; m. Luther Corbitt (div. Dec. 1976); children: Tonya, Stephen. BS, Wayne State U., 1969, MEd, 1976, EdS, 1995. Cert. elem. and secondary sch. tchr., cert. tchr. spl. edn. emotionally and mentally impaired, grades K-12, elem. secondary sch. and central office administration. Tchr. mentally impaired Detroit Pub. Schs., 1969-72, tchr. emotionally impaired, 1972-75, spl. edn. tchr. cons., 1975—, Title I tchr. math. and sci., summers 1993-96; mediator Spl. Edn. Mediation Svcs., Lansing, Mich., 1986-96, Spl. Edn. Mediation Svcs. State Project PL 94-142, Lansing, Mich., 1985—; spl. edn. hearing officer Mich. Dept. Edn., Lansing, 1985—. Developer at-risk program for emotionally impaired, socially maladjusted and ADHD students 12-17 yrs. Wolverine Human Svcs., Detroit, Mich. 1998—; mem. U.S. del. educators and attys. to South Africa for evaluation of schs. and govtl. agys. under leadership of Nelson Mandella Citizen Amb. program People to People, Spokane, Wash., 1996; mem. citizens alliance to uphold spl. edn. study adv. com. Emotionally Impaired Children in Mich./Lansing, 1986; mem. North Ctrl. Assn. accreditation com. Grand Rapids (Mich.) Pub. Schs., 1981; presenter profl. devel. conf. Detroit Fedn. Tchrs. and Det. Pub. Sch. Adminstrs., 1996. Chair Met. Detroit chpt. March of Dimes, 1987; chair Women Who Dare to Care com. United Negro Coll. Fund, Detroit, 1987-89; gen. coord. Mus. African Am. History, Detroit, 1987; tutor, usher, chairperson Hartford Meml. Bapt. Ch., Detroit, 1979—. Recipient Mayor's award of merit for Cmty. Svc., City of Detroit, 1987, plaque and cert. March of Dimes, 1987; recognized as outstanding educator Detroit Tchr., Detroit Fedn. Tchrs., 1987, 94. Mem. Coun. for Exceptional Children (presenter nat. conv. 1983, cert. 1983), Soc. Profls. in Dispute Resolution, Wayne State U. Alumni Assn., Delta Sigma Theta (chairperson 1965—), Phi Delta Kappa (chairperson). Avocations: golf, poetry, racquetball, painting, reading. Office: Martin Luther King Jr Sr HS 3200 E Lafayette Detroit MI 48207 Home: 1249 Navarre Pl Detroit MI 48207 Office Phone: 313-396-5241. Personal E-mail: eumillercorbitt@aol.com.

CORCORAN, BARBARA, real estate company executive; b. Edgewater, N.J. m. Dale Barlow, 1979 (div.); m. Bill Higgins, 1988; 1 child, Thomas. BA in English and Theology, St. Thomas Aquinas Coll.; D (hon.), Marymount Coll. Founder Corcoran Group, NYC, 1973, founder, chmn., 1980—2005, Barbara Corcoran Prodn., NYC, 2005—. Author: If You Don't Have Big Breasts, Put Ribbons in Your Pigtails, 2003, Use What You've Got: And Other Business Lessons I Learned From Mom, 2003, (newsletter) Corcoran Report, 1981—. Former chair NY chpt. Young Pres. Orgn.; former bd. govs. Real Estate Bd. NY. Recipient Harry B. Helmsley Disting. New Yorker award, 2006. Office: 1318 Madison Ave 4 New York NY 10128 also: 210 11th Ave 11th Fl New York NY 10001 Office Phone: 212-937-1000.

CORCORAN, DEBORAH B., geographer, educator; b. Chgo., Mar. 16, 1955; d. Robert and Lucille Borchers; m. William Corcoran, Aug. 9, 1980; children: Kevin, Anne. BS, Mich. State U., East Lansing, 1977; MA, Mich. State U., 1980. Rsch. asst. Mich. Dept. Pub. Health, Lansing, 1979—80; data analyst MOAF Inc. Ptrofl. Stds. Rev. Orgn., Springfield, Mo., 1981—83; data mgr. S.W. Mo. Health Care Found., Springfield, 1983—84; lectr. Mo. State U., Springfield, 1995—. Freelance translator. Pres. Parkview H.S. PTA, Springfield, 2001—03, Rountree Elem. Sch., Springfield, 1993—94; chair edn. dept. Nat. Ave. Christian Ch., Springfield, 1994—95; mem. Rountree Neighborhood Assn., Springfield, 2004—06; pres. Parkview H.S. Site Coun., 2003—04, Christian Women's Fellowship, Springfield, 1989—95. Recipient Tchg. award, Coll. Natural and Applied Scis., 2003, 2006. Mem.: Assn. Am. Geographers, Nat. Coun. Geog. Edn. Office: Missouri State University 901 S National Ave Springfield MO 65897

CORCORAN, MARY ELIZABETH, educational psychology professor emeritus; b. Providence, Aug. 15, 1921; d. Charles M. and Katherine (Weeden) C. BA cum laude, Hunter Coll., 1947; MA, Stanford U., 1948; PhD, U. Minn., 1957. Instr. psychology U. Vermont, Burlington, 1948-50; assoc., editor Edn. Testing Service, Princeton, N.J., 1950-53; asst., then assoc. prof. U. Minn., Mpls., 1957-67, prof. edn. psychology and higher edn., 1967-86, prof. emeritus, 1987—. Research dir. internat. study univ. admissions Internat. Assn. Univs., Paris, 1961-63; vis. prof. Ont. Inst. Studies in Edn., Toronto, 1968-69, Ind. U., Bloomington, 1975-76; cons. various colls., higher edn. systems and research projects. Contbr. articles to profl. jours. Mem. adv. bd. retirees and sr. groups U. Minn. Recipient Disting. Alumni award, 2006. Mem. Assn. Instl. Research (bd. dirs., Disting. Mem. 1981), Assn. Studies in Higher Edn. (bd. dirs., chmn., Merit award 1980), Am. Psychol. Assn. Episcopalian. Avocations: family history study, nature study. Home: 400 Groveland Ave Apt 209 Minneapolis MN 55403-3206 Office: U Minn 178 Pillsbury Dr SE Minneapolis MN 55455-0296

CORCORAN, NANCY LEE, retired elementary school educator; d. Henry Lee and Lillie Eva Jurica; m. James William Corcoran, Dec. 23, 1967; children: Christopher Paul, Kelly Stephen, Jamie Leigh. BS in Elem. Edn., Tex. A&I U., Kingsville, 1966; MEd, U. of Houston, 1975. Cert. life provisional tchg. Tex. Tchr. Victoria Ind. Sch. Dist., Tex., 1965—66, N.E. Ind. Sch. Dist., San Antonio, 1966—67, Pasadena Ind. Sch. Dist., Tex., 1967—73, Ft. Bend Ind. Sch. Dist., Sugar Land, Tex., 1975—76, Austin Ind. Sch. Dist., Tex., 1977—86, Hays Consol. Ind. Sch. Dist., Kyle, Tex., 1986—2003; ret., 2003. Dept. chmn., lead tchr. Dahlstrom Mid. Sch., Buda, Tex., 1995—2003, Univ. Interscholastic League coach and coord., 1986—2003; mentor, dist. mentor advisor Hays Consol. Ind. Sch. Dist., Kyle, 1995—2003. Co-author: (curriculum guides) Writing. Leader, bd. mem., chmn. Boy Scouts of Am., Austin, 1978—89; leader, chmn. Girl Scouts of Am., Austin, 1986—92; mem., chmn. Bowie H.S. Football Booster Club, Austin, 1989—91; mem., pres. cheerleader booster club Hays H.S., Buda, 1994—98, mem., co-chmn. Project Graduation, 1997—98; com. mem. Homeless Advocacy Com., Austin, 1998—2006; mem., pres. ladies club St. Catherine Cath. Club, Austin, 2000—; lay eucharistic min. St. Catherine Cath. Ch., Austin, 2001—. Named Tchr. of the Yr., Austin Ind. Sch. Dist.-Porter Jr. High, 1980, Hays Consol. Ind. Sch. Dist.-Dahlstrom Mid. Sch., 2000. Mem.: Ret. Tchrs. of Tex. (assoc.), Hays Edn. Assn. (assoc.; sch. rep. 1986—2003), Tex. State Tchrs. Assn. (life). Roman Catholic. Home: 3606 Saddlestring Trail Austin TX 78739 Office Phone: 512-268-2141. Personal E-mail: ncorc@yahoo.com.

CORDELL, JOANN MEREDITH, music educator; b. Memphis, Tenn., Jan. 16, 1952; d. Lena Clark Hurd; m. Ronald Eugene Cordell, Sept. 24, 1976; children: David Chadwick, Andrea Kristin. BS, U. Memphis, 1975; BA in Vocal Performance, U. Charleston, 1998. Cert. Orff Music Level 1 U. Memphis, 1998, Kodaly Level 1 Colorada Coll., 1997, Kindermusik Kindermusik Internat., 1996, tchr.spl. edn. Nat. Tchr. Assn. Spl. edn. tchr. Memphis City Sch. Sys., Memphis, 1975—81; children's music dir. St. Matthew's Episcopal Ch., Charleston, W.Va., 1993—96, St. Anthony Cath. Sch., Charleston, W.Va., 1997—2001, Christ Ch. United Meth., Charleston, W.Va., 1997—2000; Kindermusik instr. Bapt. Temple Ch., Charleston, W.Va., 1999—; founder/artistic dir. WomanSong Chorale, Charleston, W.Va., 1997—; assoc. dir. Appalachian Children's Chorus, Charleston, W.Va., 2000—; music instr. leap program Kanawha County Schs., Charleston, W.Va., 2000—02; coord. of soothing sounds music program for pregnant women and high risk teens Charleston Area Med. Ctr., Charleston, W.Va., 2001—. Creator Cantus Early Childhood Music Edn. Program Appalachian Children's Chorus, Charleston, W.Va., 2000—; music clinician arts camp Charleston Stage Co., Charleston, W.Va., 1999—; music clinician for Camp William U. of Charleston, Charleston, W.Va., 2003—; founder of childsong music edn. program, 2004—. Dir.(artistic director): (choral performance) Kennedy Ctr. Performing Arts (womanSong Chorale chosen by jury to represent W.Va. at the nation's capitol for WV day, 2001). Campaign mgr. Com. to elect Nancy Kessel, Charleston, W.Va., 1993—97; state legis. chairperson W.Va. State Med. Alliance, W.Va., 1993—95; dir. of program to fundraise for W.Va. chpt. Susan G. Komen Assn. WomanSong, Charleston, W.Va., 2002; dir. of choral program to raise funds for Ronald McDonald Ho. of So. W.Va. WomanSong and Ronald McDonald Charities of So. W.Va., Charleston, W.Va., 2003; creator of children's early childhood music program Christ Ch. United Meth., Charleston, W.Va., 1990—2000; v.p. Jr. League of Charleston, Charleston, W.Va., 1990—91; mem. Cantori Montani Choral Ensemble, Charleston, W.Va., 1993—98. Grantee, W.Va. Humanities Found. and W.Va. Fund for the Arts, 2003. Mem.: Am. Guild Organists (bd. dirs. 2002—03), Music Educators Nat. Coun., Am. Orgn. Kodaly Educators, Am. Choral Dirs. Assn. (stds. and repertoir chmn. for women's choirs, W.Va. divsn. 2003—), W.Va. Orff Schulwerk Assn. (assoc.; none). Democrat. United Meth. Achievements include development of a pilot music education for kindergarten, 1st and 2d graders. Avocations: creating English gardens, reading, playing piano/autoharp, cooking, scuba diving.

CORDES, KATHLEEN ANN, retired physical education educator, director; d. Rita Ann and Edrick John Cordes. BS, Ind. U., Bloomington, 1972; MA, Ball State U., Muncie, 1973. Grad. asst., coach Ball State U., 1972—73; prof., coach Hanover Coll., Ind., 1973—75, U. Notre Dame, Ind., 1976—77; athletic dir. St. Mary's Coll., Notre Dame, 1977—79; prof. Whittier Coll., Calif., 1979—90; prof. emeritus, honors coord. Miramar Coll., San Diego, 1990—98. Interim exec. dir. Am. Alliance for Health, Phys. Edn., Recreation, and Dance, Reston, Va.; vis. prof. U. Zulia, Maracaibo, Venezuela, 1990—91, U. Andes, Merida, Venezuela, 1995. Author: (book) America's National Historic Trails, America's National Scenic Trails, America's Millennium Trails: Pathways to the 21st Century, 2002, official project of the White House Millennium Council, 2001, (textbook) Applications in Recreation, 3rd edit., 2002 (Chinese Transl., 2001), Parks, Recreation, and Leisure Service Management, 2003, Outdoor Recreation, 2d edit.; editor: (book) National Girls' and Women's Sports Tennis Guide, 1986. V.p. YMCA, Whittier, 1988—90. Recipient Merit Svc. award, Am. Assn. Leisure and Recreation, 1997, Outstanding Achievement award, 2001, Dist. Svc. to Recreation award, CAHPERD, 1998, Past Pres. award of merit, 2005. Fellow: Am. Leisure Acad.; mem.: Calif. Assn. Health, Phys. Edn., Recreation, and Dance. Independent. Roman Catholic. Achievements include first to first woman to coach a varsity sport at the University of Notre Dame. Avocations: tennis, hiking, swimming, golf, gardening. Home: 3848 Flowerwood Ln Fallbrook CA 92028

CORDES, MARY KENRICK, psychologist, retired; b. Flint, Mich., Aug. 6, 1933; d. Charles Fay and Margaret Lydia (Mitchell) Kenrick; m. John Cordes, July 30, 1955 (dec. 1970); children: James Charles, Mari Kenrick Cordes. BA, Denison U., 1955; MA, Oakland U., 1969. Ltd. lic. psychologist, Mich. Rsch. asst. Lafayette Clinic, Detroit, 1968; sch. psychologist Roseville (Mich.) Community Schs., 1968-93; assoc. Rochester (Mich.) Psychol. Clinic, 1970-82. Mem. State Licensure Bd. of Psychology, Lansing, Mich., 1978-81, Spl. Edn. Adv. Com., Lansing, 1984-88. Vol. counselor Crossroads-St. Paul's Cathedral, Detroit, 1982-90; singer Rochester Community Chorus, 1986—. Mem. APA (assoc.), Nat. Assn. Sch. Psychologists, Mich. Assn. Sch. Psychologists (regional bd dirs. 1973-77, Outstanding State Sch. Psychologist 1979), Macomb County Psychol. Assocs. (pres. 1972-73), Oakland County Dem. Party, Alternate State Dem. (exec. bd., 2004—, precinct del. 2003—). Avocation: travel. Home: 2452 Blockton Rd Rochester MI 48306-3902 Personal E-mail: mimicor@aol.com.

CÓRDOVA, FRANCE ANNE-DOMINIC, academic administrator, astrophysicist; b. Paris, Aug. 5, 1947; came to U.S., 1953; d. Frederick Ben Jr. and Joan Francis (McGuinness) C.; m. Christian John Foster, Jan. 4, 1985; children: Anne-Catherine Cordova Foster, Stephen Cordova Foster. BA in English with distinction, Stanford U., 1969; PhD in Physics, Calif. Inst. Tech., 1979. Staff scientist earth and space sci. div. Los Alamos Nat. Lab., 1979-89, dep. group leader space astronomy and astrophysics group, 1989; prof., head dept. astronomy and astrophysics Pa. State U., University Park, 1989-93; chief scientist NASA, Washington, 1993-96; vice chancellor for rsch. U. Calif., Santa Barbara, 1996—2002, chancellor Riverside, 2002—. Mem. Nat. Com. on Medal of Sci., 1991-94; mem. adv. com. for astron. scis. NSF, 1990-93, external adv. com. Particle Astrophysics Ctr., 1989-93; bd. dirs. Assn. Univs. for Rsch. in Astronomy, 1989-93; mem. Space Telescope Inst. Coun., 1990-93; mem. com. space astronomy and astrophysics Space Sci. Bd., 1987-90, internat. users com. Roentgen X-ray Obs., 1985-90, extreme ultraviolet explorer guest observer working group NASA, 1988-92, com. Space Sci. and Applications Group, NASA, 1991-93; mem. Hubble Telescope Adv. Camera Team, 1993; chair Hubble Fellow Selection Com., 1992. Guest editor Mademoiselle mag., 1969; editor: Multiwavelength Astrophysics, 1988, The Spectroscopic Survey Telescope, 1990; contbr. over 150 articles, abstracts and revs. to Astrophysics Jour., Nature, Astrophysics and Space Scis., Advanced Space Rsch., Astron. Astrophysics, Mon. Nat. Royal Astron. Soc., chpts. to books. Named One of Am.'s 100 Brightest Scientists under 40, Sci. Digest, 1986; numerous grants NASA, 1979—, recipient group achievement award, NASA, 1991, Distinguished Svc. medal, NASA, Kilby Laureate, 2000. Mem. Internat. Astron. Union (U.S. nat. com. 1990-93), Am. Astron. Soc. (v.p. 1993-96, chair high energy astrophysics divsn. 1990, vice chair 1989), Sigma Xi. Achievements include analysis of ultra-soft x-ray emission from active galactic nuclei; observations and modeling of the winds from accretion disks; studies of the interstellar medium using ultraviolet spectroscopy of nearby hot binary stars; observations and modeling of extended x-ray emitting regions in close binary systems; understanding the accretion geometry of magnetic binaries with accreting white dwarfs; coordinating radio and x-ray observations of x-ray binaries in an effort to find a unified model for correlated behavior; search for evidence of galactic magnetic monopoles by identifying a class of ultrasoft x-ray emitters; studying the multispectial emission from neutron stars; making observations of x-ray emitting pulsars and their associated supernova remnants in the radio and infrared; conceiving space instruments and data systems for imaging detectors (U.S. principal investigator for optical/UV Telescope launched 1999 on ESA's X-Ray Multi-Mirror mission); making multifrequency observations of high-energy sources. Office: U Calif Riverside Office of Chancellor 900 University Ave Riverside CA 92521*

CORDOVA, MARIA ASUNCION, dentist; b. Punta Arenas, Magallanes, Chile, May 14, 1941; came to U.S., 1972; d. Miguel Cordova and Maria Asuncion Requena; m. Carlos F. Salinas, July 27, 1963; children: Carlos M., Claudio A., Lola. DDS, U. Chile, Santiago, 1965; DMD, Med. U. S.C., 1986. From instr. to assoc. prof. physiology U. Chile, Valparaiso, 1965—72; postdoctoral fellow Johns Hopkins U., Balt., 1972-75; from instr. to asst. prof. dept. physiology Med. U. S.C., Charleston, 1975—86; pvt. practice Charleston, 1986—. Vis. scientist N.Y. Med. Coll., 1975. Contbr. articles to profl. jours. Pres. Circulo Hispanic Charleston; country specialist Amnesty Internat. U.S.A., Spoleto, Charleston, mem. outreach com.; past mem. Hispanic coun. Charleston C. of C.; past bd. dir. Trident Urban League; former bd. dir. YWCA; bd. dir. Robert Ivey Ballet, S.C. Humanities Coun., 1996—2002. Mem. Acad. Gen. Dentists, Charleston Women's Network (pres. 1989-90). Roman Catholic. Office: 159 Wentworth St Charleston SC 29401-1731 Office Phone: 843-577-2898.

CORDRAY-VAN DE CASTLE, KAREN, elementary school educator; b. Key West, Fla., Dec. 20, 1953; d. Richard Palmer and Jzere Marlene Cordray; m. Lance Whitney Van de Castle, Aug. 6, 1983. AS, Northern Va. CC, Annandale, Va., 1973; BS in Ele. Edn., George Mason U., Fairfax, Va., 1975, EdM in New Profl. Studies, 2000. Cert. Va. Tchr. 5th grade Lightfoot Elem. Sch., Unionville, Va., 1977—80, Orange Elem. Sch., 1981; tchr. 6th grade Lightfoot Elem. Sch., Unionville, 1981—2003, Locust Grove Elem. Sch., 2003—. Mem. health com. Lightfoot Elem. Sch., Unionville, Va., 1981—84, mem. curriculum and instrn. com., 1998—2003; mem. countywide sch. climate com. Orange County, Va., 2001—03; Md. testing program proctor, 2002—; new yr. tchr. mentor Locust Grove Elem. Sch., 2003—04, sci. club sponsor, 2003—04, mem. staff devel. com., 2003—04, mem. curriculum and instrn. com., 2003—, tchr. mentor, 2005—06, sci. dept. leader grades 6-8, 2005—06; presenter to profl. meetings and confs. Featured: film, 1985; contbr. articles to profl. jours. Mem. Humane Soc. of Madison Va., 1998—2002. Co-recipient Dedication to Learning and Cmty. award, George Mason U., 2000; named one of Nat. Sci. Tchrs. of Yr., Va., 1982; recipient recognition, Ho. Dels. Va. Gen. Assembly, 1998, Tchr. of Yr., Locust Grove Optimist Club, 2005; fellow, George Mason U., 2000; grantee, Orange County, Va., 1984—86. Avocations: environmental edn., conservation activities with students. Home: 583 Courtney Hollow Lane Madison VA 22727 Office: Locust Grove Mid Sch 31208 Constitution Hwy Locust Grove VA 22508-2631 Office Phone: 540-661-4444. Personal E-mail: kcordraylvdec@ns.gemlink.com.

CORDY, JANE, Canadian senator; b. Sydney, Nova Scotia, Can., July 2, 1950; Tchg. cert., Nova Scotia Tchrs. Coll.; BEd, Mount Saint Vincent U. Tchr. Sydney Sch. Bd., Halifax County Sch. Bd., New Glasgow Sch. Bd., Halifax Regional Sch. Bd.; senator The Senate of Can., Ottawa, 2000—. Vice-chair Halifax-Dartmouth Port Devel. Commn.; chair bd. referees Halifax Region of Human Resources Devel. Can.; bd. dirs. Phoenix House; mem. judging com. Dartmouth Book Awards, 1993—95, 1999—2000; mem. strategic planning com. Colby Village Elem. Sch.; vol. religious edn. program St. Clement's Ch., Dartmouth. Liberal. Office: 314 Victoria Bldg The Senate of Canada Ottawa ON Canada K1A 0A4

CORELL, MARCELLA ANNE, community worker, retired educator; b. Denver, Mar. 2, 1919; d. Berton Wilson and Marcella Jacobs; m. Allen Lawrence Corell, Sept. 25, 1950 (dec. June 1996); children: Michele Anne, Lawrence Robert. AA, Colo. Woman's Coll., 1939; BA, Denver U., 1948. Tchr. Kiowa Sch. Dist., Colo., 1939-40, Jefferson Co. Sch. Dist., Arvada, Colo., 1941-49, Dept. Edn. Hawaii, Spreckelsville, 1949-50, substitute tchr. Kihei, Wailuku, Kahului, 1962-72. Mem. adv. bd. Maui Cmty. Mental Health Ctr., Wailuku, 1968-72; coord. Crisis Phoneline, 1971-81; founder Mental Health Assn. Maui, 1972, pres., 1972-75, bd. dirs., 1975-81, chmn. membership com. 1978-99, edn. com. 1985—, hon. mem. bd. 1991. Recipient 1st Lady's Outstanding Vols. award Vols. in Paradise, Hawaii, 1974, 76, 84, vol. award Maui United Way, 1975, Golden Rule award J.C. Penney, Honolulu, 1994, 98, Jefferson award Honolulu Advertiser, 1987. Avocation: organic gardening. Home: 357 Auhana Rd Kihei HI 96753-8519

CORELLO, SARA A., lawyer; b. NYC, Aug. 27, 1964; BA cum laude, Amherst Coll, 1986; JD, Columbia Univ., 1992. Bar: NY 1993, US Dist Ct (so., ea. dists.) NY 1993, US Ct. Appeals (2nd cir.) 1997, US Ct. Appeals (9th cir.) 2004. Law clerk to Hon. Eugene H. Nickerson US Dist. Ct (ea. dist.), NY, 1992—93; ptnr. Spivak, Lipton, Watanabe, Spivak & Moss LLP, NYC. Legal counsel Actor's Equity Assn. Mem. Columbia Law Rev., 1990—91; editor: Columbia Law Rev., 1991—92; contbr. articles to profl. journals. Mem.: ABA, NY State Bar Assn., Assn. of Bar of City of NY. Office: Spivak Lipton Watanabe LLP 21st Fl 1700 Broadway New York NY 10019 Office Phone: 212-765-2100. Office Fax: 212-541-5429.

CORETTE, DEBORAH WEST, elementary school educator; d. John and Thelma West; m. William Pauly Corette, Nov. 20, 1965; children: William, Krista, Kara, Candace. BA, U. Mont., Missoula, 1965; MS, Pepperdine U.,

Culver City, Calif., 1990. Tchr. Ridgecrest Intermediate Sch., Rolling Hills Estates, Calif., 1967—68, Rolling Hills Country Day Sch., 1981—. Pres. Rolling Hills Womens Club, 1972; assistance league Cmty. Svc., San Pedro, Calif., 1981. Mem.: ASCD, Internat. Reading Assn., Calif. Assn. Tchrs. English, Nat. Coun. Tchrs. English, Kappa Kappa Gamma. Avocations: piano, flute, horseback riding, golf. Office: Rolling Hills Country Day Sch 26444 Crenshaw Blvd Rolling Hills Estates CA 90274

COREY, CANDY ABRAMSON, oncologist; m. Seth Corey. BS, U. Minn., Mpls., 1977, MD, 1982. Cert. oncology, hematology, internal medicine. Oncologist Health Ptnrs., Mpls. Med. dir. oncology Lakeview Hosp., Stillwater, Minn. Mem.: Am. Soc. Clin. Oncology. Office: Health Partners 2220 Riverside Ave S Minneapolis MN 55454 Personal E-mail: cacorey55@aol.com.

COREY, KAY JANIS, small business owner, apparel designer, nurse; b. Detroit, Aug. 22, 1942; d. Alexander Michael Corey and Lillian Emiline (Stanley) Kilborn; divorced; children: Tonya Kay, William James, Jason Ronald. Student, C.S. Mott Community Coll., 1960-62, Mich. State U., 1962-64; AA, AS in Nursing, St. Petersburg Jr. Coll., 1978; student, U. South Fla., 1985-86. RN; cert. perioperative nurse; cert. varitypist. Mgr. display Lerner Shops, Flint, Mich., 1960-62; layout artist Abdulla Advt., Flint, 1966-67; varitypist, artist City Hall Print Shop, Flint, 1967-70; nurse Suncoast Hosp., Largo, Fla., 1976-78; nurse, coord. plastic surgery svc., perioperative staff nurse Largo Med. Ctr. Hosp., 1978-81, 84-90; assoc. dir. nursing Roberts Home Health Svc., Pinellas Park, Fla., 1982-84; co-owner Sand Castle Resort, White Bay, Jost Van Dyke, Brit. Virgin Island, 1990-95; perioperative nurse HCA Gulf Coast Surgery Ctr., 1995-99; perioperative nurse, surg. nurse Blake Med. Ctr. Hosp., 2000—. Designer, artist K.J. Originals clothing line, 1990-95, The Magic Needle clothing line, 1998; insvc. edn. instr., dir. video edn., team leader oncology dept. Largo Med. Ctr. Hosp., 1980-81; designer, mfr. Haelan Jewelers--Fine Custom Jewelry, 1999. Editor, illustrator: (book) Some Questions and Answers About Chemotherapy, 1981, Thoughts for Today, 1981; illustrator (cookbooks) Spices and Spoons, 1982, Yom Tov Essen n' Fressen, 1983; various brochures and catalogues; art work in permanent collection of C.S. Mott Jr. Coll., Flint, 1962; artist, designer of casual and hand painted clothing for children and adults. Historian Am. Businesswomen's Assn., Flint, 1968-73 (scholarship 1976); outreach chmn. Temple B'nai Israel, Clearwater, Fla., 1981-85; regional outreach coord. Union of Am. Hebrew Congregations, N.Y.C., 1983-85. Mem. Assn. of Oper. Rm. Nurses, Phi Theta Kappa. Republican. Jewish. Avocations: sailing, scuba diving, tennis, original teddy bear making, golf. Address: 4080 Kingsfield Dr Parrish FL 34219 Personal E-mail: bubbekay@msn.com.

COREY, MARA J., language educator; d. Vija Rumpe Kelly; m. Matthew E. Corey, Sept. 3, 1994. MEd, U. Minn., Twin Cities, 2000. Tchr. English Prior Lake H.S., Minn., 1999—2000, St. Louis Pk. H.S., St. Louis Park, Minn., 2000—01, Irondale H.S., New Brighton, Minn., 2001—. Grantee, 621 Found., 2004. Dfl. Avocations: travel, reading, training dogs. Office: Irondale HS 2425 Long Lake Rd New Brighton MN 55112 Office Phone: 654-786-5200 4308. Business E-Mail: mara.corey@moundsviewschools.org.

CORINBLIT, NITA GREEN, artist, educator; b. Detroit, Mar. 3, 1924; d. Leo and Gussie Green; m. Jack Corinblit, Mar. 9, 1944; children: Meryl Daniels, Barbara Graff, Nancy Montgomery. BFA, Art Inst. Chgo., 1949; MA, Calif. State U., 1971. Cert. art tchr., Calif. Art, history of art and English tchr. jr. and sr. H.S., L.A., 1963-85; arts and humanities cons. L.A. Unified Sch. Dist., 1982-86; methods tchg. crafts instr. Calif. State U., Northridge, 1969-71; humanities instr. Lee Coll. U. Judaism, L.A., 1989-91. Participant NEH project, Greensboro, NC, 1982; adjudicator Emerging Young Artists competition Calif. Alliance for Arts Edn., 2002—. Exhibited in group shows at Libr. of Congress, Washington, others. Witness U.S. House Ways and Means com., Am. Assn. Mus., Washington, 1980; docent L.A. Mus. Contemporary Art, 1987-92; mem. exec. bd. Fine Arts Coun., Platt Gallery, U. Judaism, L.A., 1990—; mem. Women's Polit. Com., L.A., 1992—, Taube Found. Jewish Life and Culture, 2006. Grantee Calif. Coun. for the Humanities, NEH, 1986, 99, Calif. Arts Coun., 1983-84, U.S. Arts for the Aging, 1980-81. Mem. Calif. Humanities Assn. (pres. 1986-87, newsletter editor 1988-2002, treas. 1978-85, Perlee award 1991), LA Printmaking Soc., Acad. TV Arts and Scis. Found. (edn. adv. bd. 1995-99). Avocation: photography. Home: 5854 Hillview Park Ave Valley Glen CA 91401-4022

CORKERY, ANTOINETTE ELIZABETH, literature and language educator; d. William John and Elizabeth Althea Jugon; m. Dennis Francis Corkery, Aug. 18, 1973; children: Michael William, Dennis Andrew. BA, Middlebury Coll., Vt., 1965; MAT in English, Brown U., Providence, 1966; M A in English, Middlebury Coll., 1972. Cert. secondary tchr. lang. arts Mass., 1969. Secondary English tchr. Johnsburg Ctrl. Sch., North Creek, NY, 1966—69, Danvers H.S., Mass., 1969—, AP English tchr., 1979—. Grad. sch. tchr. NE Consortium/Salem State, Mass., 1996—. Campaign vol. Dem. Party, Gloucester, Mass., 1984—2006; mem. and vol. St. Vincent de Paul Soc., Gloucester, Mass., 1994—2006. Recipient Cert. of Merit, DEEP, 2006; grantee, Nat. Found. for the Humanities, 1966; scholar Regents scholar, N.Y. State, 1961. Mem.: Mass. Tchrs. Assn. Democrat-Npl. Roman Catholic. Avocations: gardening, cooking/baking, hiking. Home: 7 Gee Ave Gloucester MA 01930 Office: Danvers HS 60 Cabot Rd Danvers MA 01923 Office Phone: 978-777-8925.

CORKRAN, VIRGINIA B., retired real estate agent; b. NYC, Feb. 13, 1924; d. Stuart H. and Bessie (Moses) Bowman; m. Sewell H. Corkran, Jr., June 15, 1946; children: Sewell H. III, Leslie C. Price. BA, Conn. Coll., 1945. Tchr. Low-Heywood Sch., Stamford, Conn., 1946—47; editor North Shore Calendar, Winnetka, Ill., 1955—59; real estate assoc. Lodge McKee Realty Inc., Naples, Fla., 1963—2001; ret., 2001. Mem. Naples City Coun., 1974-78; pres. Old Naples Assn., 1995-97; past bd. dirs. Big Cypress Nature Ctr., Naples, The Conservancy, Inc., Collier County LWV, Naples Garden Club, Collier Co. Audubon; hon. bd. dirs. S.W. Heritage, Inc., Naples, 2002 Recipient Guy Bradley award Collier County Audubon, ONA award Old Naples Assn., 1998.

CORLESS, DOROTHY ALICE, nursing educator; b. Reno, Nev., May 28, 1943; d. John Ludwig and Vera Leach (Wilson) Adams; children: James Lawrence Jr., Dorothy Adele Carroll. RN, St. Luke's Sch. Nursing, 1964. Clinician, cons., educator, grant author, adminstr. Fresno County Mental Health Dept., 1991—94; instr. police sci. State Ctr. Tng. Facility, 1991-94; pvt. practice, mental health cons., educator, 1970—; sr. assoc. guidance distbn. disaster svcs. ARC, 2003—04; mental health nurse Calif. Dept. Corrections and Rehabilitation, 2006—. Res. officer ARC, Disaster Mental Health Svcs., 1993-2003. Maj. USAFR, 1972-94. Mem. USAF Acad. Assn. Grads. (assoc. life), Forensic Mental Health Assn. Calif., Calif. Peace Officers Assn., Critical Incident Stress Found. Office: 1849 E Everglade Fresno CA 93720 Office Phone: 559-325-9599. E-mail: dorothydmh@aol.com.

CORLEY, CATHY F., elementary school educator; b. Victoria, Tex., July 15, 1955; d. William Earnest and Lillian Frances Fenner; m. Rick L. Corley, Mar. 23, 1974; children: Cari Michelle, Ashley Frances, Gregory Brent. BA, U. Houston, 1994. Teller 1st Nat. Bank Alvin, Tex.; asst. v.p. Bank One, Houston, 1979—91; tchr. Friendswood Ind. Sch. Dist., 1994—. Grantee, Friendswood Edn. Found., 1991—. Mem.: Tex. Sci. Tchrs. Assn., Nat. Sci. Tchrs. Assn. Avocation: gardening. Home: 906 Knights Ct Friendswood TX 77546

CORLEY, ROSE ANN MCAFEE, government official; b. Lawton, Okla., Aug. 21, 1952; d. Claude James and Mary Margaret (Holman) McAfee; m. Gary Michael Griffin, Feb. 14, 1973 (div. Oct. 1984); m. Terry Joe Corley, July 31, 1988 (div. Oct. 2002); stepson Troy Justin Corley. BS, Cameron U., Lawton, Okla., 1970; diploma, Army Command and Staff Coll., Ft. Leavenworth, Kans., 1989; MCJA, Oklahoma City U., 1990; cert., Army Mgmt. Staff Coll., Ft. Belvoir, Va., 1991. Cert. in distbn. mgt., Fed. Exec. Inst. Supply clk. Dept. of Army, Ft. Sill, Okla., 1972-80, supply mgmt. asst., 1980-82, supply systems analyst Ft. Lee, Va., 1982, supply tech. Ft. Sill, Okla., 1982-83, supr. inventory mgmt. specialist, 1983-86, manprint program mgr., 1986-91; weapon system advisor Def. Logistics Agy., San Antonio, 1991-96, customer svc. rep. Robins AFB, Ga., 1996-98; dir. supply mgmt. NIH, Rockville, Md., 1998—2002, dir. divsn. logistics svcs., 2002—05; deputy assoc. commr., publications and logistics Social Security Adminstrn., 2005—. Equal employment counselor USA Field Artillery Sch., Ft. Sill, Okla., 1976-82; mentor Fed. Women's Program, Kelly AFB, Tex., 1991-96. Active Md. Citizen Foster Care Rev. Bd., 1999-2001. Decorated Order of St. Barbara U.S. Army Arty. Sch., Ft. Sill; recipient cert. Appreciation, U.S. Sec. of Def., 1984, Directorate of Engrng. and Housing, Ft. Sill, 1986; Excellence in Govt. Sr. fellow, Council for Excellence in Govt., 2001—. Mem. Fed. Women's Program, Soc. Logistics Engrs., Fed. Mgrs. Assn., Kelly Mgmt. Assn., World Affairs Coun. of San Antonio, Internat. City Mgmt. Assn., Tex. Corvette Assn. Avocations: auto racing, reading, golf, crafts. Office: Social Security Adminstrn 1540 Annex 6401 Security Blvd Baltimore MD 21235 also: SSA 1540 Annex 6401 Security Blvd Baltimore MD 21235 Office Phone: 410-965-9297, 410-965-9297. Business E-Mail: rose.ann.corley@ssa.gov. E-mail: ra.corley@verizon.net.

CORLISS, DEANE KENWORTHY, lawyer; b. Phila., Oct. 18, 1945; d. Joseph Edmund and Edith Mae Kenworthy; m. David Alexander Corliss, June 22, 1968; 1 child, Jonathan David. BSN cum laude, Duke U., NC, 1967; MS in nursing, Ohio State U., 1970; JD summa cum laude, Cumberland Sch. Law, Birmingham, 1989. Bar: Ala. 1989, DC 1992, admitted to US Dist. Ct. for Northern Divsn. Ala.:. Staff nurse PeterBent Brigham Hosp., Boston, 1967—68; instr. sch. nursing Northeastern U., Boston, 1968—69, U. Ala., Birmingham, 1970—73, health edn. coord., ob/gyn, 1978—80, asst. prof. medicine dept. ob/gyn, 1983—86; nursing dir., pub. health area III Ala. Dept. of Pub. Health, Birmingham, 1980—83; assoc. Bradley Arant Rose & White LLP, Birmingham, 1989—95, ptnr., chair of health law practice group, 1996—. Adv. com. Samford U. Inst. for Healthcare Ethics and Law, Birmingham, 1999—2000. Bd. dirs. Unitarian Universalist Svc. Com., Boston, 1978—81; regional perinatal adv. com. Region III, 1980—88, Region VIII, 1988—96; adv. com. Jefferson County Healthy Start Infant Mortality Advisory Com., 1994—95; bd. dirs. VSA Arts of Ala., Inc., Birmingham, 2003—; mem. steering com., adv. bd. UAB Palliative Care Ctr., Birmingham, Ala., 2005—. Named one of Best Lawyers in Am., 2001—. Mem.: Birmingham Bar Assn. (bd. dirs. women lawyers sect. 1999—, sec. treas. women lawyers sect. 2000—03, corr. sec. 2005), ABA Health Law Sect., Am. Health Lawyers Assn., ABA. Avocations: scuba diving, jewelry making. Office: Bradley Arant Rose & White LLP 1819 5th Ave N Birmingham AL 35203 Office Phone: 205-521-8633. Office Fax: 205-488-6633. Business E-Mail: dcorliss@bradleyarant.com.

CORMIER, LORETTA A., anthropologist; b. NYC, Apr. 6, 1962; d. Annette Chappell Garrison; m. James P. Cormier, Aug. 22, 1989. PhD, Tulane U., New Orleans, 2000. Asst. prof. U. Ala., 2000—04, assoc. prof., 2004—. Tribal anthropologist MOWA Band of Choctaw Indians, McIntosh, Ala., 2001—. Author: Kinship with Monkeys: The Ethnoprimatology of the Guaja Foragers, 2003. Recipient Roy A. Rappaport Student Paper prize, Am. Anthrop. Soc., 1999; Fulbright fellow, Inst. for Internat. Edn., 1996—97. Mem.: Soc. for Anthropology of Lowland S.Am. (sec.-treas. 2005—). Office: U Ala at Birmingham 338 Ullman Bldg Birmingham AL 35294-3350 Office Phone: 205-934-3508. E-mail: lcormier@uab.edu.

CORMIER, LORRAINE R., secondary school educator; b. Fall River, Mass., Oct. 15, 1950; d. William J. and Therese M. (Francoeur) Paul; children: Jeffrey A., Jacqueline M. AA in English/History magna cum laude, Bristol C.C., Fall River; BA in English cum laude, R.I. Coll. Lab. tech. Union Hosp., Fall River, 1968-72, Damon Med., Fall River, 1972-75; dir. St. Catherine of Siena Ch., Little Compton, R.I., 1978-97; tchr., head tchr. grades 7-8 St. James St. John Sch., New Bedford, Mass., 1991—. Phelobotomist, cons. Little Compton Vis. Nurses, 1975-79. Girl Scout leader Girl Scouts U.S., Little Comptn, 1982-87, den mother Boy Scouts Am., Little Compton, 1978-84; candidate for sch. com. Dem. Party, Little Compton, 1978; mem. Tax Payers Assn., Little Compton, R.I. Recipient Tchg. in Excellence award, New Bedford, 2003. Mem. Nat. Cath. Tchrs. Assn., Nat. Coun. Tchrs. of English, New Eng. Coun. Tchrs. of English. Roman Catholic. Avocations: reading, ceramics, exercise, skiing, interantional travel. Office: St James St John Sch 180 Orchard St New Bedford MA 02740-3471

CORMIER, PATRICIA PICARD, academic executive; AS, Univ. Bridgeport, 1958; BS, Boston Univ., 1964; MEd, Univ. Va., 1969, EdD, 1975. Pvt. practive, 1958-64; instr. Northeastern Univ., Boston, 1964-68; instr. social dentistry Tufts Univ., Boston, 1964-68; instr. pediatrics Univ. Va., Charlottesville, 1968-72, rsch. assoc., 1969-72; asst. dean. dental auxiliary Univ. Pa., Phila., 1975-79, assoc. dean acad. affairs, assoc. prof. dental care, 1979-82; spl. asst. to pres. Wilson Coll., Chambersburg, Pa., 1982-83, acting dean, 1983-84, v.p., dean of coll., 1984-88; v.p. devel. and alumnae rels. Medical Coll. Pa., Phila., 1989-93; v.p. acad. affairs, prof. ednl. leadership Winthrop Univ., Rock Hill, S.C., 1993-96; pres., prof. edn. Longwood Coll., Historic Farmville, Va., 1996—. Regional v.p. devel. Allegheny Health, Edn. and Rsch. Found., 1991-93; exec. dir. Am. Diabetes Assn., Phila., 1988-89. Named Outstanding Young Women of Am., 1969. Fellow Coll. Physicians of Phila., Am. Coun. on Edn.; mem. Sigma Phi Alpha, Phi Delta Kappa. Home: 1403 Johnston Dr Farmville VA 23901-2807 Office: Longwood Coll 201 High St Farmville VA 23909-1800

CORN, MELISSA ANN, secondary school educator; b. South Bend, Ind., Sept. 10, 1975; d. Michael Lee and Leslie Jane Corn. MS, NC State U., Raleigh, 1999; BA, U. NC, Chapel Hill, 1997. Cert. tchr. NC, Ga. Tchr. R.L. Osborne HS, Marietta, Ga., 2002—05, Apex HS, Raleigh, 2005—. Home: 7005 Bellard Ct Raleigh NC 27617 Office: Apex High Sch 1501 Laura Duncan Rd Apex NC 27502 Office Phone: 919-387-2208. Personal E-mail: cornm5@yahoo.com.

CORN, WANDA MARIE, fine arts educator; b. New Haven, Nov. 13, 1940; d. Keith M. and Lydia M. (Fox) Jones; m. Joseph J. Corn, July 27, 1963. BA, NYU, 1963, MA, 1965, PhD, 1974. Instr. art history Washington Sq. Coll., NYU, 1965-66; lectr. U. Calif.-Berkeley, 1970, vis. asst. prof., 1976; lectr. Mills Coll., Oakland, Calif., 1970, vis. asst. prof., 1971, asst. prof., 1972-77, assoc. prof., 1977-80; assoc. prof. Stanford U., Calif., 1980-89, prof., 1989—, chair dept. art, 1989-91; acting dir. Stanford Mus., 1989-91; dir. Stanford Humanities Ctr., 1992-95; Clark prof. Williams Coll., 2004; vis. curator Fine Arts Mus., San Francisco, 1972, 73, 76; vis. curator Mpls. Inst. Arts, 1983-84, Grant Wood travelling exhbn. to Whitney Mus. Am. Art, N.Y.C., Art Inst. Chgo., Mpls. Inst. Arts, Fine Arts Mus. San Francisco. Author: The Color of Mood, American Tonalism, 1880-1910, 1972; The Art of Andrew Wyeth, 1973; Grant Wood: The Regionalist Vision, 1983, The Great American Thing: Modern Art and National Identity 1915-35, 2000, The Great American Thing exhbn. Figge Art Mus., Davenport, Iowa, 2005, Tacoma Art Mus., 2006; contbr. articles to profl. jours. Commr. Smithsonian Am. Art Mus., 1988—95; bd. dirs. Terra Found. Am. Art, 1999—, Wyeth Found. for Am. Art, 2002—. Ford Found. fellow, 1966-70, Radcliffe Inst., 2003-04; recipient Graves award 1974-75; Smithsonian fellow, 1978-79; Woodrow Wilson fellow, 1979-80; Stanford Humanities Ctr. fellow, 1982-83, Regents fellow Smithsonian Instn., 1987; Am. Coun. Learned Socs. grantee, 1982, 86; rsch. assoc. Smithsonian Instn., 1983—; Phi Beta Kappa scholar, 1984-85. Mem. Coll. Art Assn. (bd. dirs. 1970-73, 1980-84, program chmn. ann. meeting, 1981, mem. numerous coms.), Women's Caucus for Art, Am. Studies Assn. (nat. coun. 1986-89), Assn. Historians of Am. Art. Office: Stanford U Dept Art and Art History Stanford CA 94305-2018 Office Phone: 650-723-6282. Business E-Mail: wcorn@stanford.edu.

CORNELIUS, LAURA ELIZABETH, music educator; b. Tulsa, Nov. 6, 1968; d. Donald Rex and Marcile Lavonne Stroup; m. Kevin Ray Cornelius, June 5, 1993; children: Jessica Anne, Caleb Ray. MusB in Edn., So. Nazarene U., Bethany, Okla., 1987—91. Music tchr. Sand Springs Pub. Schs., Okla., 1991—95; choral dir., music tchr. Maries Co. R-II Schs., Belle, Mo., 1995—2000; choral dir. Arkadelphia Pub. Schs., Ark., 2000—. Mem., rep. Clark Co. Arts & Humanities Coun., Arkadelphia, Ark., 2001—04. Religious edn. tchr., bd. mem. First Ch. of the Nazarene, Arkadelphia, Ark., 2000—. Named Resource Tchr. of Yr., Ctrl. Elem. Sch., 2000; grantee, Ross Found., 2001. Mem.: Ark. Choral Dirs. Assn., Ark. Music Educators Assn., Music Educators Nat. Conf. Republican. Avocations: piano, graphic design. Office: Arkadelphia Pub Schs 401 High School Rd Arkadelphia AR 71923

CORNELIUS, MARIA G., financial advisor; b. Washington, Apr. 19, 1961; d. James C. and Rose Marie; m. Frederick J. Cornelius, Apr. 13, 1991; children: Patrick Joseph, Michael James. BS, Mt. St. Mary Coll., 1983. CFP, Coll. Fin. Planning, 1989. Adminstrv. asst. AFC Adv. Svcs., Silver Spring, Md., 1984-89, fin. planner, 1990-91, Nat. Bank Washington, Rockville, Md., 1989-90, Montgomery Advisors, Rockville, Md., 1990-91, Profl. Fin. Planning, Gaithersburg, Md., 1991-93; exec. v.p. Burt Assocs., Inc., Rockville, Md., 1992—; pres. MGC Fin. Advisors, Rockville, Md., 1993—2003. Mem. Inst. CFP, Fin. Planning Assn. (Md. chap.), Bethesda C. of C. (com. svcs. mem. 1998). Avocations: walking, bicycling, spending time with family, basketball. Office: Burt Assocs Inc 6010 Executive Blvd Rockville MD 20852-3809

CORNELIUS, TIA MARIE, physical education educator; m. Ian Luke Cornelius, Dec. 15, 2001; 1 child, Lucas Ian. BS, Brigham Young U., Provo, Utah, 2004. Cert. tchr. Idaho and Utah. Phys. edn. tchr., soccer coach, softball coach Rigby H.S., Idaho, 2004—; dep. sheriff res. Jefferson County Sheriff, Rigby. Youth leader LDS Ch., Ammon, Idaho, 2004—. Mem.: Idaho Tchr. Assn. (assoc.).

CORNELL, ANNIE AIKO, nurse, administrator, retired military officer; b. L.A., Sept. 23, 1954; d. George and Fumiko (Iwai) Okubo; m. Max A. Cornell, Dec. 10, 1990. BSN, U. Md., 1976. RN, Calif. Enlisted U.S. Army, 1972, advanced through grades to maj., clin. staff nurse surg. ICU Presidio of San Francisco, clin. head nurse ICU Seoul, Korea, clin. head nurse gen. medicine ward Ft. Ord, Calif., chief nursing adminstrn., ret., 1992; nursing supr. Home Health Plus; dir. patient svcs. Hollister Vis. Nurses Assn., Calif.; asst. dir. patient svcs. Monterey Vis. Nurses Assn., Calif.; case mgr. supr. Cmty. Hosp. Home Health Svcs., Monterey, asst. mgr. Recipient Walter Reed Army Inst. nursing scholarship. Mem. Sigma Theta Tau. Home: 11725 Fir Dr Reno NV 89506

CORNELL, CAROLE ANNE WALCUTT ARNOLD, nurse; b. Paris, Ky., Apr. 29, 1957; d. Hardin Owsley and Cecele Christine (Smith) Walcutt; m. Richard Wood Arnold, Feb. 22, 1976 (dec. Apr. 1993); children: Richard Wood Jr. (dec.), John Walcutt; m. Duane F. Cornell; stepchildren: Robert F., Joseph E. ADN, Midway Coll., 1975; BSN summa cum laude, St. Joseph's Coll., 1992. RN; cert. family genealogist. Nurse Bapt. Hosp. East, Louisville. Mem. Harrison County Fine Arts Coun., 1980-92 Ky. Heritage Woman's Mus., Inc., Harrison Hosp. Aux., pres.,1979-80. Recipient Woman of Achievement award YMCA, 1982; named to hon. order Ky. Cols., 1986-87; fellow U. Ky. Mem. ANA, DAR (1st vice regent Lexington chpt., state program chmn. 1987-89, state corr. sec. 1989-92, state jr. mem. chmn. 1992-95, nat. vice chmn. scholarships 1992—, Good Citizenship award 1975, Outstanding Young Woman, 1st alt. nat. conv. 1980, Ky. State Page 1987-89, Nat. Congl. Page 1987-89, Nat. Personal Page to Pres. Gen. 1990, state mem. chmn. 1995—, state chaplain 1998-2001, nat. chmn. guest hospitality, chmn. debutante presentation, 2000, chpt. regent 2005—, 1st vice regent John Marshall chpt., Ky., 2005-, Ky. state chmn. nat. spkr's staff, 2005-), Ky. Nurses Assn., Ky. Hist. Soc., Blue Grass Trust, The Hereditary Register of the U.S., Daus. of 1812 (rec. sec. River Raisin chpt. 1989—, 1st v.p. 1988-90, 2d v.p. 1990-92, rec. sec.), Sovereign Soc., Harrison County Women's Club (fine arts chmn. 1978-80, 1st v.p. 1981-83), Colonial Dames 17th Century (hon. pres., 1st v.p. Sarah Morgan Boone chpts., nat. outstanding young woman of yr. 1990-91, nat. chmn. jr. membership, state officer Ky., state corr. sec. 1990-92, historian, state libr., state nat. def. chair, chmn. membership com. 1988—, state first v.p., state pres. 2001—, nat. chaplain gen.), Manikin Huquenot Soc. (past state rec. sec.), Family of Bruce Soc. Am., Owsley Family Soc. Am. (recipient merit award 1987), Sovereign Colonial Soc., Ams. Royal Descent, Daus. Colonial Wars, Order St. Andrew of Jerusalem, Magna Charta Dames (soc. herald), Colonial Order of Crown in Am., Soc. Washington's Army Valley Forge, Jr. League Louisville, Colonial Dames Am. (registrar chpt. 7), Colonial Dames 17th Century (chaplain gen. 2003-05), Order Ams. Amorial Ancestry (rec. sec. 2003-05, pres. gen. 2005—), Sons and Daus. Pilgrims (state gov. Ky. 2005—), The Jamestowne Soc. (state dep. gov. Ky.), Order of Three Crusades, Descendants Knights Most Noble Order Garter, Dau. British Empire, Dames of Colonial Cavaliers, Nat. Soc. Daus. Am. Colonists, Descendants of Early Quakers, Nat. Soc. Colonial Physicians and Chirugions, Hugenot Soc. in Va. Manikin Hugenots, Nat. Soc. So. Dames Am., United Daus. Confederacy, Sons and Daus. Colonial and Antebellum Bench and Bar, Guild of Colonial Artisans and Tradesmen, Sons and Daus. Colonial and Antebellum Planters, Order of Ams. of Armorial Ancestry (2d v.p. gen. 2005-), English Speaking Union, Pendennis Club Louisville, Cornell Club N.Y., Jr. League Louisville (sustaining), Midway Coll. Alumni Assn. (named Miss Midway Coll. 1975, Disting. Alumnae award 1989), Order of the Crown of Charlemagne, Woman's Club Louisville, Presdl. Families Am., Thoroughbred Club Am., Cornell Club, Phi Theta Kappa. Personal E-mail: 10503kc@earthlink.net.

CORNELL, DEBORAH A., artist, educator; b. Natick, Mass., Mar. 31, 1947; d. Richard Johnston and Dorothy Darling; m. Richard E. Cornell, June 25, 1967. BFA, RI Sch. of Design, 1969; MFA, Vermont Coll., 1996. Founder, dir. Experimental Etching Studio, Boston, 1972—2002; vis. artist Radcliffe Coll., Harvard U., Cambridge, Mass., 1987—90; dir. visual arts Boston U. Tanglewood Inst., Lenox, Mass., 1995—97; asst. prof. Boston U. Coll. of Fine Arts, 1997—2005, assoc. prof., 2005—. Vis. artist Royal Acad., London, 1999, Russian Art Acad., St. Petersburg, Russia, 2002, U. Tex., Arlington, Tex., 2000. Author (contr.): (hist. catalogue) Working Proof: Experimental Etching Studio, 1992; Tracer, 2003—05, Represented in permanent collections Boston Mus. Fine Arts, Australian Print Collection, U. West England, Bank of Am., IBM, Boston Pub. Libr. Recipient Purchase prize, Purdue U., 2004; fellow, Bunting Inst., 1987—88. Mem.: Boston Printmakers (exec. bd. 1999—2006), Southern Graphics Coun. (bd. mem. 2002—04), Am. Print Alliance (bd. mem. 1999—). Office: Boston U Coll of Fine Arts Visual Arts 855 Commonwealth Ave Boston MA 02215 Office Phone: 617-353-3373 3. E-mail: dcornell@bu.edu.

CORNING, JOY COLE, retired state official; b. Bridgewater, Iowa, Sept. 7, 1932; d. Perry Aaron and Ethel Marie (Sullivan) Cole; m. Burton Eugene Corning, June 19, 1955; children: Carol, Claudia, Ann. BA, U. No. Iowa, 1954; degree (hon.), Allen Coll. Nursing. Cert. elem. tchr., Iowa. Tchr. elem. sch. Greenfield (Iowa) Sch. Dist., 1951-53, Waterloo (Iowa) Cmty. Sch. Dist., 1954-55; mem. Iowa Senate, Des Moines, 1984-90, asst. Rep. leader, 1989-90; lt. gov. State of Iowa, Des Moines, 1991-99. Past chmn. Nat. Conf. Lt. Govs. Bd. dirs. Inst. for Character Devel.; mem. policy bd. Performing Arts Ctr., U. No. Iowa, also trustee UNI Found.; bd. dirs. Nat. Conf. Cmty. and Justice, Des Moines Symphony, Planned Parenthood of Greater Iowa. Named Citizen of Yr., Cedar Falls C. of C., 1984; recipient ITAG Disting. Svc. to Iowa's Gifted and Talented Students award, 1991, Pub. Svc. award Iowa Home Econs. Assn., 1994, Friend of Math. award Iowa Coun. Tchrs. of Math., 1995, Iowa State Edn. Assn. Human Rights award, 1996, Govs. Affirmative Action award, Spl. Recognition award Nat. Foster Parent Assoc., Des Moines Human Rights Commn. award, Pub. Svc. award Coalition for Family and Children's Svcs in Iowa, Friends of Iowa Civil Rights, Inc. award, Martin Luther King Jr. Lifetime Svc. award, 1999, Svc. award Des Moines Area Religious Coun., 2002, NCCJ Brotherhood-Sisterhood award, 2003, Senator Barry Goldwater award Planned Parenthood Fedn. Am., 2003; recognized for Extraordinary Advocacy for Children of Iowa chpt. Nat. Com. for Child Abuse, award for leadership Early Care and Edn. Congress, Alumni Achievement award U. No. Iowa; named among YWCA Women of Achievement, 2000, Woman of Influence, Bus. Record, 2003; Nat. Conf. for Cmty.

and Justice honoree, 2003; named to Iowa Women's Hall Fame, 2004. Mem. AAUW, LWV, PEO, Nat. Assn. for Gifted Children (mem. adv. bd. 1991-99), Rotary Club, Delta Kappa Gamma, Alpha Delta Kappa. Republican. Mem. United Ch. Of Christ. Home: 4323 Grand Ave No 324 Des Moines IA 50312-2443 Personal E-mail: corningj@aol.com.

CORNISH, BONITA CLARK, retired secondary school educator; b. Live Oak, Calif., Feb. 18, 1911; d. Cyrus Benito Clark and Anna Margretha Carstenbrook; m. Edwin Robert Cornish, July 23, 1935 (dec. Mar. 31, 1970); children: William Robert, Susan Margretha. AB, U. Calif., Berkeley, 1932, MA, 1933; postgrad., Fresno State U., 1944—2001, Coll. Pacific, 1956; EdD, Calif. Coast U., 2001. Life tchg. cert. Calif. Phys. edn., music and math. tchr., dean of girls Dunsmuir (Calif.) Internat. Union, 1934—38; pvt. music tchr. Yosemite Valley, Calif., 1943; asst. to prin. Fresno (Calif.) County Sys., 1944; spl. edn. tchr. Fresno City Sys., 1946—72; tchr. Bullard HS, Fresno, 1972, Roosevelt HS, Fresno, 1973—76; ret., 1976. Dramatics Calif. Ret. Tchrs. Assn., Fresno, 1976—2001; lectr. gerontology classes Fresno State U., 1990—2001; tchr. Elderhostel-Wonder Valley, Fresno, 1990—95. PTA pres. Coll. Elem., 1940—60; city coun. Assembly Woman, Calif., 1980—93; assembly women Calif. Sr. Legis., 1980—86; bd. mem. YWCA, Fresno, 1985—90. Mem.: AARP, Fresno County Dem. Women's Club (pres. 1990), Order of Ea. Star (life; conductress 1937), Alpha Delta Kappa (Ca Xi cptr. charter pres. 1945). Avocations: camping, gardening, reading, folk art, cooking. Home: Apt 320E 9525 N Ft Washington Rd Fresno CA 93720-0681

CORNISH, ELIZABETH TURVEREY, retired investment advisor; b. Ionia, NY, Dec. 31, 1919; d. Clifford Dwight and Mildred Althea (Spicer) T.; m. Louis Joseph Cornish, June 21, 1941 (div. June 1955); 1 child, Carol Cornish Reeves. BS, Cornell U., 1941. Lic. stockbroker N.Y. Stock Exch., Prin. Reg. Options Prin., Commodity prin., Insur. prin. Teletype operator, sec. to mgr. Carl M. Loeb Rhoades & Co., Ithaca, N.Y., 1955-65, reg. rep., 1962-75; br. mgr. Loeb, Rhoades & Co., Ithaca, 1975-82; registered rep. Shearson Loeb Rhoades, Shearson Am. Express, Ithaca, 1982-86, Hutton, Shearson, Ithaca, 1986-88, First Albany Corp., Ithaca, 1988-91; registered rep., br. office mgr. A.G. Edwards & Sons, Inc., Ithaca, 1991-97, investment broker, 1998—2004; ret., 2004. Charter mem. Nuveen Adv. Coun., 1984, 85, 86; instr. stock market and various br. office jobs for coll. interns; bd. dirs. McGraw House, 1996-2004. Mem. Planning Com. Downtown Mall, Ithaca, N.Y., 1972-75; chmn. campaign United Way Tompkins County, Ithaca, 1983, dir., 1983-89; bd. dirs. Ithaca Neighborhood Housing, Leadership Tompkins, 1986-88; pres. Friends of Ithaca Coll., 1985-86; mem. adv. coun. Ithaca Coll., 1986—; comdr. Ithaca Squadron of U.S. Power Squadron, 2003-04. Mem. Downtown Bus. Women (pres. l971-72), Tompkins County C. of C. (bd. dirs. l974-77, 83-86, v.p. l980-8l, pres.-elect l989, pres. l990, ambs. coun. 1997—), Ithaca Yacht Club (bd. dirs. l988-90). Republican. Episcopalian. Avocations: boating, reading, letter writing, tai chi.

CORNISH, JEANNETTE CARTER, lawyer; b. Steelton, Pa., Sept. 17, 1946; d. Ellis Pollard and Anna Elizabeth (Stannard) C.; m. Harry L. Cornish; children: Lee Jason, Geoffrey Charles. BA, Howard U., 1968, JD, 1971. Bar: N.J. 1976, U.S. Dist. Ct. N.J. 1976. Atty. Newark-Essex Law Reform, 1971-72; technician EEOC, Newark, 1972-73; atty., asst. sec. Inmont Corp., N.Y.C., 1974-82, sr. atty., asst. sec. Clifton, N.J., 1982-85; sr. atty. BASF Corp., Mt. Olive, N.J., 1986-99. Speaker on diversity in bus. Past mem., bd. dirs. YWCA, Paterson, N.J.; trustee Barnert Hosp., Paterson; bd. dirs. Lenni-Lenape coun. Girl Scouts Am. Mem. ABA (commn. on opportunities for minorities in the profession, minority in-house counsel group, diversity vice chair gen. practice sect. corp. counsel com.), Nat. Bar Assn., Assn. Black Women Lawyers, Am. Corp. Counsel Assn., Internat. Trademark Assn. (past mem. editorial bd. The Trademark Reporter, exec. commn. com., meetings com., program quality and evaluation subcom.). Business E-Mail: jeannettecornish@1stcounsel.com.

CORNISH, NANCY LEE, music educator; b. Providence, R.I., Sept. 21, 1946; d. Arthur Jeremiah, Jr. and Doris Helen Latham; m. James Elden Cornish; children: Stephen James, Christopher Samuel. BME, U. Kans., 1969, MME, 1975. Music tchr. Leavenworth (Kans.) West Jr. High, 1970—71, Chanute (Kans.) HS, 1972—74, Allen County CC, Iola, Kans., 1980—86, Neosho County CC, Chanute, Kans., 1991—2000; grad. tchg. asst. U. Kans., Lawrence, Kans., 2001—03; music instr. Laramie County CC, Cheyenne, Wyo., 2003—. Dir. St. Cecilia Choir, Chanute, Kans., 1975—90; music dir. First United Meth. Ch., Chanute, Kans., 1990—2000; dir. St. Mary's Cathedral Choir, Cheyenne, Wyo., 2004—. Pres. Neosho Valley Arts Council, Chanute, Kans., 1974—76; sec. Hist. Govs. Mansion Found., Cheyenne, Wyo., 2003—05. Mem.: Am. Choral Dirs. Assn., Music Educators Nat. Conf., Wyo. Music Educators Assn. (v.p. higher edn. 2004—06). Mem. Cmty. Of Christ Ch. Avocations: sailing, skiing. Home: 408 W 1st Ave Cheyenne WY 82001 Office: Laramie County CC 1400 E College Dr Cheyenne WY 82007

CORNO, DONNA A., retired public relations executive, consultant; b. St. Louis, Feb. 9, 1942; d. Charles F. and Cecelia J. Zorumski; children from previous marriage: Vincent, Suzanne, Lisa. B in Polit. Sci., U. Mo., St. Louis; AA Summa Cum Laude, St. Louis C.C.; accredited in pub. relations, PRSA, 2003. Cert. pub. rels. 2003. Cmty. rels. dir. Ferguson-Florissant Sch. Dist., Florissant, Mo.; reporter various St. Louis Jour. newspapers; cons. in pub. rels., crisis mgmt., strategic comm., 2003—. Bd. dirs. North County, Inc., Florissant Valley C. of C. Recipient numerous awards in writing field. Mem.: Mo. Sch. Pub. Rels. Assn. (pres., v.p. 1983—2001, numerous state and nat. awards), Nat. Sch. Pub. Rels. Assn. (numerous awards). Avocation: tennis, biking, skiing. Home: 223 Kehrs Mill Trail Ballwin MO 63011

CORNO, LYN, psychology educator; b. Williams, Ariz., May 25, 1950; d. Edward Eugene and Verla (Hornbacher) C.; m. William Fairfax Herbert, Aug. 4, 1984; children: William Fairfax Herbert Jr., Leigh Carter Herbert. BA, Ariz. State U., 1972; MA, Stanford U., 1977, PhD, 1978. Rsch. assoc. SWRL Edn. Rsch. and Devel., Los Alamitos, Calif., 1972-74, Ctr. for Edn. Rsch. at Stanford, Calif., 1974-77; asst. prof. edn. Stanford U., 1977-82; prof. edn., psychology Columbia U., N.Y.C., 1982—. Editor: Am. Ednl. Rsch. Jour., 1992—95, Ednl. Psychologist, 2000—05, Tchrs. Col Record, 2001—. Fellow APA, AAAS, Am. Psychol. Soc. Democrat. Episcopalian. Avocations: running, dance, tennis. Personal E-mail: lycorno@pipeline.com.

CORNWELL, NANCY DUNN, secondary school educator; b. Franklin, Va., May 19, 1950; d. Robert James Dunn, Jr. and Catherine Edwards Dunn; m. Ronald Boothe Cornwell, Nov. 18, 1972; children: Matthew(dec.), Christopher, Ashley. BS, Longwood Coll., 1972; cert. in Tech., U. Va., Charlottesville, 2000, cert. in Gifted and Talented, 2005. Cert. collegiate profl. Va., 1972. HS art tchr. Sussex County Pub. Schs., Sussex, Va., 1972—77; K-12 art tchr. Southampton Acad., Courtland, Va., 1977—88; tchr. art adolescent edn. dept. Ctrl. State Hosp., Petersburg, Va., 1988—98; tchr. art and social studies Merrimac Juvenile Detention Ctr., Williamsburg, Va., 1998—; tchr. Gov.'s Sch. for Gifted and Talented (Sci. and Tech.), Windsor (Va.) HS, 2003—04, 2005. Mem. character edn. com. Williamsburg/James City County Schs., Williamsburg, Va., 2002—03; presenter Va. Character Edn. Program, Richmond, Va., 2000—03; Stop Violence in Classroom com. Va. Dept. Edn., Richmond, Va., 1998—2003. Sunday Sch. tchr. Millfield Bapt. Ch., Ivor, Va. Mem.: Va. Art Edn. Assn. Personal E-mail: mcnasmom@aol.com.

CORNWELL, PATRICIA DANIELS, writer; b. Miami, Florida, June 9, 1956; d. Sam and Marilyn Daniels; m. Charles Cornwell, 1980 (div. 1989). BA in English, Davidson Coll., 1979. Police reporter Charlotte Observer, NC, 1979-81; tech writer to computer analyst Office Chief Med. Examiner, Richmond, Va., 1984—90. Author: A Time for Remembering: The Story of Ruth Bell Graham, 1983 (Medallion award), Life's Little Fable, 1999, Food to Die For, 2001, Portrait of a Killer: Jack the Ripper, Case Closed, 2002, (novels) Postmortem, 1990 (only novel ever to simultaneously win Edgar, Creasey, Anthony and Macavity awards), Body of Evidence, 1991, All That Remains, 1992, Cruel and Unusual, 1993, The Body Farm, 1994, From Potter's Field, 1995, Cause of Death, 1996, Hornet's Nest, 1997, Unnatural Exposure, 1997, Point of Origin, 1998, Southern Cross, 1998, Scarpetta's Winter Table, 1998, Black Notice, 1999, The Last Precinct, 2000, Isle of Dogs, 2001, Blow Fly, 2003, Trace, 2004, From Potter's Field, 2005, At Risk, 2006 (No. 1 Publishers Weekly Hardcover Bestseller List, 2006). Vol. police officer. Address: ICM 40 W 57th St Fl 16 New York NY 10019-4001 Office: Cornwell Enterprises 2260 High Bush Cir Glen Allen VA 23060-2258*

CORNWELL, SUSAN, music educator; b. St. Louis, Mo. m. Ronald Cornwell. B of Music Edn., Kans. U., Lawrence, 1988; M in Reading, Washburn U., Topeka, 2005. Tchr. Unified Sch. Dist. 345, Topeka, 1988—. Named Tchr. of Yr., Indian Creek Elem. Sch., 2003; scholar, Kans. U., 1983—88, Washburn U., 2003—04. Mem.: Kans. Reading Assn. Business E-Mail: scornwell@usd345.com.

CORPENING, DEBORAH WEEMS, dance educator; b. Johnson City, Tenn., Dec. 25, 1955; d. Worley Emerson and Shirley Ann (Wright) Weems; m. Richard Randall Corpening, Aug. 28, 1976; children: Lindsey Paige, Brandon Michael. BS in Elem. Edn., East Tenn.State U., Johnson City, 1978. Dance instr. The Dance Co., Johnson City, Tenn., 1971—2006; owner Ctr. Stage, Johnson City, 1979—85; tchr. Johnson City Pub. Sch., 1980—83; bus. mgr. The Dance Co., Johnson City, 1992—2006. Pres. bd. Dance Odyssey, Johnson City, 1992—95; choreographer Cmty. Theater, 1992—2006. Pres., sec. Jr. League, 1990—94; corresponding sec. Jr.Monday Club, 1989—90; mem. bd. Coalition for Kids, 2004—06. Recipient David Kent Miller Outstanding Tchr. Republican. Christian. Avocations: golf, dance. Home: 1913 Villa Ct Johnson City TN 37615 Office: The Dance Co Johnson City TN 37604

CORPORA, KATHLEEN M., middle school educator, technology integration specialist; b. Allentown, Pa., Apr. 6, 1959; d. Thomas Robert and Mary Ann (Polaha) Burns; m. James Corpora, June 30, 1985. BS, West Chester U., Pa., 1981; Instructional Tech. Specialist, DeSales U., Center Valley, Pa., 2004. Cert. athletic trainer Nat. Athletic Trainers Assn., 1983. Tchr. Bethlehem Area Sch. Dist., Pa., 1981—; asst. girls' basketball coach Notre Dame HS, Easton, Pa., 2004—. New tchr. induction program mentor Bethlehem Area Sch. Dist., 2003—. Lector, vol. Holy Trinity Cath. Ch., Whitehall, Pa., 2003—, St. John the Bapt. Ch., Whitehall, 1990—2003. Mem.: NEA, Rails to Trails Conservancy, Nat. Athletic Trainers Assn., Appalachian Trail Conservancy. Democrat. Roman Catholic. Avocations: hiking, travel, computers. Office: East Hills Middle School 2005 Chester Rd Bethlehem PA 18017

CORPREW, HELEN BARBARA, mental health services professional; b. N.Y.C., Sept. 20, 1928; d. Charles August Shipley and Florence Lillian Musgrave-Shipley; m. Gerald Wilson Corprew, June 3, 1953 (div. May 1974); 1 child, Gerald Wilson Jr. BSW, Temple U., Phila., 1971; MSW, Temple U., 1980. LCSW. Tng. supr. Bell Telephone of N.Y., N.Y.C., 1947—70; dir. girls' day care Wissahickon Boys/Girls Social Programs Cmty. Club, Phila., 1970—73; dir. juvenile justice spl. svcs. programs Phila. Family Ct., 1973—; SCOH program supr. Sleighton Sch., Lima, Pa., 1991—; clin. therapist Harmony Mental Health, Phila., 1989—. Cons. home assignment Sleighton Sch., Phila., 1995—. Mem. cmty. recourse devel. com. Summit Presbyn. Ch., Phila., 1990—93, bd. deacons, 1972—78, bd. mem. elders session, 1979—87; cmty. coord. resources Wissahickon Boys and Girls Club, Phila., 1972—75. Recipient Disting. Outstanding Svc. award, Ct. Judges, Phila., 1986. Mem.: NASW, Acad. of Clin. Social Workers. Presbyterian. Avocations: travel, camping, dance, reading, swimming. Mailing: 6701 Wissahickon Ave Philadelphia PA 19119

CORRADINI, DEEDEE, real estate company executive, former mayor; Student, Drew U., 1961—63; BS, U. Utah, 1965, MS, 1967. Adminstrv. asst. for pub. info. Utah State Office Rehab. Svcs., 1967-69; cons. Utah State Dept. Cmty. Affairs, 1971-72; media dir., press sec. Wayne Owens for Congress Campaign, 1972; press sec. Rep. Wayne Owens, 1973-74; spl. asst. to N.Y. Congl. Rep. Richard Ottinger, 1975; asst. to pres., dir. cmty. rels. Snowbird Corp., 1975-77; exec. v.p. Bonneville Assocs., Inc., Salt Lake City, 1977-80, pres., 1980-89, chmn., CEO, 1989-91; mayor Salt Lake City, 1992—2000; prin. Corradini & Co., Salt Lake City, 2000—; sr. v.p. Prudential Utah Real Estate, 2004—. Pres. U.S. Conf. of Mayors, 1998—, mem. unfunded fed. mandates task force, mem. crime and violence task force; chair Mayor's Gang Task Force; mem. intergovtl. policy adv. com. U.S. Trade Rep., 1993-94, 99—; mem. transp. and comm. com. Nat. League of Cities, 1993-94. Bd. trustees Intermountain Health Care, 1980-92; bd. dirs., exec. com. Utah Symphony, 1983-92, vice chmn., 1985-88, chmn., 1988-92; dir. Utah chpt. Nat. Conf. Christians and Jews, Inc., 1988; bd. dirs. Salt Lake Olympic Bid Com., 1989—; chmn. image com. Utah Partnership for Edn. and Econ. Devel., 1989-92; co-chair United Way Success by 6 Program; pres. Shelter of the Homeless Com.; active Sundance Inst. Utah Com., 1990-92; disting. bd. fellow So. Utah U., 1991; v.p. Internat. Women's Forum, co-chair program com.; trustee Am. Comm. Sch., Beirut; vice-chair 2012 Bid Selection Com., U.S. Olympic Com.; active numerous other civic orgns. and coms. Fellow Disting. sr. fellow in Urban Studies, Richard Riley Inst. Govt., Politics and Pub. Adminstrn., Furman U., 2000—. Mem. Salt Lake Area C. of C. (bd. govs. 1979-81, chmn. City/County/Govt. com. 1976-86). Democrat.

CORRALES, CARMEN AMALIA, lawyer; b. Santiago, Cuba, July 24, 1964; BA, U. Pa., 1986; JD, Harvard U., 1989. Bar: NJ 1990, NY 1991. Assoc. Clearly Gottlieb Steen & Hamilton LLP, NYC, 1990—98, ptnr. sovereign govt, internat. inst., Latin Am. practices, 1998—. Office: Cleary Gottlieb Steen & Hamilton LLP 1 Liberty Plz New York NY 10006 Office Phone: 212-225-2982. Office Fax: 212-225-3999. E-mail: ccorrales@cgsh.com.

CORRAO, ANGELA M., psychologist; b. Mora, N.Mex., May 26, 1941; d. Robert and Marie (Romero) Romero; m. Anthony A. Corrao, Nov. 25, 1964; children: Karen Thomas, Michael, Stephanie Comstock, Maria. BA in Psychology, Conn. Coll., 1984, MA in Clin. Psychology, 1987, U. Hartford, 1992, D in Psychology, 1994. Lic. psychologist Dept. Health Conn. Vis. prof. psychology N.Mex. Highlands U., Las Vegas, 1994—95; staff clin. psychologist, clin. med. liaison Cmty. Health Ctr., Middletown, Conn., 1995—98; clin. psychologist Old Lyme (Conn.) Psychotherapy Ctr., 1998—99; staff clin. psychologist Spring Street Psychiat. Group, Middletown, Conn., 1998—, Child Guidance Clinic Southeastern Conn., New London, Conn., 1999—. Invited faculty advisor ethics and rsch. com. Las Vegas Med. Ctr., 1994—95; presenter in field. Vol. Conn. Hospice, Branford, 1987—91; active Lyme-Old Lyme Lions, 1995—2004. Mem.: APA, Conn. Psychol. Assn. Avocations: writing, piano, bicycling, sewing, cooking. Home: 74 Ayers Point Rd Old Saybrook CT 06475 Office: Box 1018 7 Spring St Middletown CT 06457 Office Phone: 860-344-9558.

CORRELL, SALLY RUTH, elementary school educator; b. Lincoln, Ill., Dec. 10, 1952; d. Hubert Lloyd and Eileen Cross Kohl; m. Ronald Correll, Apr. 8, 1978. BA, Millikin U., Decatur, Ill., 1975. Cert. gifted tng. U. Ill., Springfield, 1988. Sci. tchr. Ball-Chatham Dist. #5, Ill., 1975—; dept. coord. Glenwood Mid. Sch., Chatham, 1994—. Active Our Savior's Luth. Ch. Mem.: NEA (assoc.), Ball-Chatham Edn. Assn. (assoc.; bldg. rep. 1985—90), Ill. Edn. Assn. (assoc.). Avocations: piano, organ. Office: Glenwood Middle School 595 Chatham Rd Chatham IL 62629 Office Phone: 217-483-2481. Business E-Mail: scorrell@chathamschools.org.

CORREU, SANDRA KAY, special education educator; b. Crowley, La., Aug. 24, 1938; d. Edward Dorsey and Elizabeth Mays (Wiggins) Peckham; m. Donald Audrey Correu, Sept. 5, 1959; children: Lisa G., Donald Andrew. BS in Edn., Mo. Western State Coll., 1976; postgrad., N.W. Mo. State Coll., 1980-86. Cert. in learning disabilities, behavior disordered, educable mentally handicapped, trainable mentally handicapped. Tchr. Autistic children Helen Davis State Sch., St. Joseph, Mo., 1976-78; tchr. behavior disordered St. Joseph (Mo.) Sch. Dist., 1978—. Pres., v.p., mem. Assn. for Retarded Citizens, St. Joseph, 1976-86; bd. mem. United Cerebral Palsy, St. Joseph, 1980-86; devel. dir. summer program for MRDD youth in cooperation with Mo. Western State Coll.; presenter in field. Elder Presbyn. Ch. Mem. Nat. Dem., Coun. for Exceptional Citizens, Assn. for Retarded Citizens, Mo. State Tchrs. Assn., Greenpeace, Gorilla Found., Humane Soc. U.S., Habitat for Humanity. Avocations: reading, sewing, crafts. Home: 500 NE 44th St Kansas City MO 64116 Office: St Joseph Sch Dist 10th and Edmond Saint Joseph MO 64507

CORRIGAN, CAROL A., state supreme court justice; b. Stockton, Calif., Aug. 16, 1948; d. Arthur Jospeph and Genevieve Catherine (Green) C. BA, Holy Names Coll., 1970; postgrad., St. Louis U., 1970-72; JD, U. Calif., San Francisco, 1975. BAr: Calif. 1975, U.S. Dist. Ct. Calif. 1975. Dep. dist. atty. Office Dist. Atty. Alameda County, Oakland, Calif., 1975—85; adj. prof. law U. Calif. Hastings Coll. Law, San Francisco, 1981-87, 89, U. Calif., Berkeley, 1984-87, U. San Francisco, 1987—89; sr. dep. dist. atty. Office Dist. Atty. Alameda County, Oakland, 1985-87; mcpl. ct. judge Oakland, Piedmont and Emeryville Jud. Dist., Oakland, 1987-91; judge Alameda County Superior Ct, 1991-94; assoc. justice Calif. Ct. Appeals, 1994—2006, Calif. Supreme Ct., San Francisco, 2006—. Adj. prof. sociology and polit. sci. Holy Names Coll., Oakland, 1976-80; vis. prof. law U. Puget Sound Sch. Law, Tacoma, 1981; spl. cons. Pres.'s Task Force on Victims of Crime, Washington, 1982, White House Conf. on Drug Free Am., 1988; mem. Pres.'s Commn. on Organized Crime, Washington, 1983-86; mem. faculty, cons. Nat. Inst. Trial Advocacy, South Bend, Ind., 1982—, Alaska Dept. Law, Fairbanks, 1983, Hawaii Dist. Atty. and Pub. Def.'s Office, Honolulu, 1981-83, Nat. Coll. Dist. Attys., Houston, 1984-87; trustee Holy Names Coll., 1987—. Author: Report Task Force on Victims of Crime, 1982, book chpts.; contbr. articles to profl. jours.; editor Point of View, 1981-84. Bd. dirs. Goodwill Industries of East Bay, Oakland, 1984-87, St. Vincent's Day Home, Oakland, 1984—; mem. adv. bd. St. Mary's Community Ctr. for Elderly, Oakland, 1985-87; trustee Holy Names Univ., Oakland, 1988—, chair, 1990-95. Mem. ABA, Calif. State Bar Assn., Alameda County Bar Assn., Asia Found. (advisor 1987), Calif. Dist. Attys. Assn. (bd. dirs.). Roman Catholic. Office: Calif Supreme Ct 350 McAllister St San Francisco CA 94102

CORRIGAN, DARA A., lawyer, former federal agency administrator; b. Queens, N.Y., Nov. 5, 1965; m. Naftali Bendavid; 1 child, Geffen. BA in History, Baylor U., 1986; JD, U. Va., 1990. Bar: Penn., DC. Trial lawyer civil fraud sect. US Dept. Justice, 1991—95, asst. U.S. atty. DC, 1995—99; dep. chief counsel Heath Care Financing Adminstrn., 1999—2003; dir. program integrity Centers for Medicare & Medicaid Svcs., Washington, 2003; acting prin. dep. insp. gen. U.S. Dept. Health and Human Svcs., Washington, 2003, acting insp. gen., 2003—04; ptnr. Arnold & Porter LLP, Washington, 2004—, co-head Pharm. & Med. Device practice group. Named Star of the Bar, Women's Barr Assn. DC, 2003; recipient Atty. Gen's award for Disting. Svc., 1997, 1999. Office: Arnold & Porter LLP Thurman Arnold Bldg 555 12th St NW Washington DC 20004 E-mail: Dara_Corrigan@aporter.com.

CORRIGAN, FAITH, journalist, educator, historian; b. Cleve., Oct. 16, 1926; d. William John and Marjorie (Wilson) C.; m. Sigvald Matias Refsnes, Sept. 18, 1957 (dec. Feb. 1994); children: Marjorie Refsnes, Sunniva Collins, Stephen Refsnes. BA, Ohio State U., 1948; MAT, Kent State U., 1987. Cert. tchr. English, reading, Ohio. Staff writer women's news N.Y. Times, N.Y.C., 1953-57; investigative reporter Cleve. Plain Dealer, 1962-66; dir. pub. info. Cuyahoga County Bd. Commrs., Cleve., 1966-69; dir. news, publs. Huron Rd. Hosp., East Cleveland, Ohio, 1970-73; lectr. II U. Akron, Ohio, 1990-91; adj. prof. Kent State U., North Canton, Ohio, 1996-97, Ashtabula br. Kent State U., Geauga/Twinsburg, Ohio, 1999—2005, Willoughby Hills br. Bryant and Stratton Coll., 2005—06; English instr. Bryant and Statton Coll., Willinglgy Hills, Ohio, 2005—. Lectr. Fordham U., N.Y.C., 1956; expert witness U.S. Senate Medicare Hearings, Cleve., 1965; mgr. Cuyahoga County Welfare Levy Campaign, Cleve., 1966; owner Willoughby Antiques Pub Author: First Generation, 2002, Bread Glass and History, 2003; contbr. articles to newspapers. TESOL, Lit. Vols. Am.; mem. bd. mgrs. Eleanor B. Rainey Meml. Inst., Cleve., 1966-78; officer, trustee Lake County Cmty. Svcs. Coun., 1984-90; mem. adv. bd. Lake Geauga Legal Aid Soc., Painesville, Lake County, 1984-87; chair Initiative Petition Campaign on Environ. Waste Plant Issue, Willoughby, Ohio, 1991; officer, founder Ohio State U. chpt. Am. Newspaper Guild, 1947-48; del. rep. assembly N.Y. Newspaper Guild, 1954-57; poll judge Lake County Bd. Elections, 1984-2006; field rep. U.S. Census Bur., 1989—; recruiter, crew leader U.S. Census 2000. Recipient award of achievement Press Club of Cleve., 1964, Pulitzer nominee Cleve. Plain Dealer, 1964, 1st in state Ohio Newspaper Women's Assn., 1964, 1st in state Pub. Contest of Am. Heart Assn., 1972, 1st pl. publs. award Internat. Assn. Bus. Communicators, 1971-72. Mem. VFW (Ladies Aux.), Willoughby Hist. Soc. (trustee, v.p. 1997-2002, Heritage chmn. 2003-), Ohio Bicentennial Hist. Markers Rsch., Early Am. Pattern Glass Soc. Democrat. Irish Catholic. Avocations: expert on American china, glass, american labor history. Home: 37550 Euclid Ave Willoughby OH 44094-5622

CORRIGAN, HELEN GONZÁLEZ, retired cytologist; b. San Diego, Tex., Sept. 30, 1922; d. Rodrigo Simon and Eva Ruby (Corrigan) Gonzalez. BS, Our Lady of Lake, San Antonio, 1943. Registered cytologist Internat. Acad. Cytology. Tchr. San Diego HS, 1943-45; microbiologist Nix Hosp. Profl. Lab., San Antonio, 1952-59; med. technologist Tucson Med. Ctr., 1959-60; cytologist in charge Jackson-Todd Cancer Detection Ctr., San Antonio, 1961-64; cytologist in charge cytology sect. Pathology Lab. 4th and 5th U.S. Army Ref. Area Lab., Ft. Sam Houston, Tex., 1964-78; instr. trouble shooters, quality control analyst cytology sect. Brooks Med. Ctr., Fort Sam Houston, 1978-81; owner Corrigan Enterprises, San Diego, 1981-91; ret., 1997. Cytologist Waco Med. Lab. Svc., Waco, Tex., 1988—89, Nat. Health Lab., San Antonio, 1989—90, Internat. Cancer Screening Lab., San Antonio, 1990—91; head cytologist Dr. R. Garza & Assocs., Weslaco, Tex., 1992—. Adv. bd. mem. EEO, Ft. Sam Houston, 1972—74. Mem.: NAFE, Am. Soc. Clin. Pathologists (assoc. registered cytologist, registered med. technologist), Greater San Antonio Women's C. of C. Republican. Roman Catholic. Avocations: fishing, hunting, tennis, skiing, dance. Home: 147 Perry Ct San Antonio TX 78209-6211

CORRIGAN, JANET M., health science association administrator; MBA, U. Rochester, M in Cmty. Health; M in Indsl. Engring., U. Mich., PhD in Health Svcs. Orgn. and Policy. V.p. planning and devel. Nat. Com. for Quality Assurance, 1991-95; prin. rschr. Ctr. for Studying Health Sys. Change Robert Wood Johnson Found., 1995—98; exec. dir. consumer protection and quality in health care industry Pres.'s Advisory Commn., 1998; dir. Health Care Svcs. Bd. Inst. Medicine of Nat. Academies, 1998—. Office: Inst Medicine Nat Acad Scis Health Care Svcs 500 5th St, NW, Rm 760 Washington DC 20418-0007 Fax: 202-334-1463. E-mail: jcorriga@nas.edu.

CORRIGAN, MAURA DENISE, state supreme court justice; b. Cleve., June 14, 1948; d. Peter James and Mae Ardell (McCrone) Corrigan; m. Joseph Dante Grano, July 11, 1976 (dec.). BA with hon., Marygrove Coll., 1969; JD with hon., U. Detroit, 1973; LLD (hon.), No. Mich. U., 1999, Mich. State U., 2003; JD (hon.), Mercy Law Sch., 2002, Ea. Mich. U., 2004, Schoolcraft Coll., 2005. Bar: Mich. 1974. Jud. clk. Mich. Ct. Appeals, Detroit, 1973—74; asst. prosecutor Wayne County, Detroit, 1974—79, asst. U.S. atty., 1979—89, chief appellate divsn., 1979—86, chief asst. U.S. Atty., 1986—89; ptnr. Plunkett & Cooney PC, Detroit, 1989—92; judge Mich. Ct. Appeals, 1992—98, chief judge, 1997—98; justice Mich. Supreme Ct., Detroit, 1999—, chief justice, 2001—04; mem. Family Support Coun. MIch. Vice chmn. Mich. Com. to formulate Rules of Criminal Procedure, Mich. Supreme Ct., 1982-89; mem. Mich. Law Revision Commn., 1991-98; mem. com. on standard jury instrns., State Bar Mich., 1978-82; lectr. Mich. Jud. Inst., Sixth cir. Jud. Workshop, Inst. CLE, ABA-Cin. Bar Litigation Sects., Dept. Justice Advocacy Inst.; v.p. Conf. Chief Justices, 2003-04; bd. dirs. Vista Maria. Co-author: book on civil procedure; contbr. chpt. to book, articles articles to legal revs. Vice chmn. Project Transition, Detroit, 1976-92; mem. citizens Adv. Coun. Lafayette Clinic, Detroit, 1979-87; bd. dirs. Detroit Wayne County Criminal Advocacy Program, 1983-86; pres., bd. dirs. Rep. Women's Bus. and Profl. Forum, 1991; mem. Pew Commn. on Children in Foster Care,

2003-05. Named disting. Alumna, Marygrove Coll., 2003, U. Detroit Mercy Law Sch., 2004, Detroit News Michiganian of Yr., 2005, Vista Maria Child Advocate of Yr., 2005, Angel in Adoption, Congl. Coalition on Adoption, 2005, Jurist of Yr., Police Officers Assn. Mich., 2006, Outstanding Judge, Spectrum Human Svcs., 2006; recipient award of merit, Detroit Commn. on Human Rels., 1974, Dir.'s award, Dept. Justice, 1985, Outstanding Practitioner of Criminal Law award, Fed. Bar Assn., 1989, award, Mich. Women's Commn., 1998, Grano award, 2001, Disting. Svc. award, HHS, 2002, disting. Alumna, St. Joseph Acad., 2004. Mem. Mich. Bar Assn., Detroit Bar Assn., Fed. Bar Assn. (pres. Detroit chpt. 1990-91), Inc. Soc. Irish Am. Lawyers (pres. 1991-92, Achievement award 2001), Federalist Soc. Office: Mich Supreme Ct 8-500 3034 W Grand Blvd Detroit MI 48202 Office Phone: 313-972-3232.

CORRIGAN, MAUREEN, book critic, English educator; b. Long Island City, N.Y., July 30, 1955; d. John Joseph and Johanna Alice (Dobosz) C.; m. Richard Jay Yeselson, July 21, 1990, 1 child. BA in English, Fordham U., 1977; MA in English, U. Pa., 1978, PhD in English, 1987. Prof. English Haverford Coll., Phila., 1981-84, Bryn Mawr Coll., Phila., 1981-87; book critic The Village Voice, N.Y.C., 1981-93; book reviewer, commentator Nat. Pub. Radio, Phila., 1989—; prof. English Georgetown U., Washington, 1990—; book critic The N.Y. Observer, N.Y.C., 1994-96; mystery critic, columnist The Washington Post, 1993—; book critic Newsday, N.Y.C., 1995—, The Nation, N.Y.C., 1996—. Author: Leave Me Alone, I'm Reading: Finding and Losing Myself in Books, 2005. NEH grantee Yale U., 1993. Mem. Nat. Writers Union, Nat. Women's Book Assn., Nat. Book Critics Cir., assoc. bd. mem., Mystery Writers, 1998. Mailing: Stuart Krichevsky Lit Agy Ste 914 381 Park Ave South New York NY 10016

CORRIGAN, MEG M., psychiatrist; d. Timothy Edward and Margaret Mary Corrigan. BA, Vanderbilt U., Nashville, 1999, MD, 2003. Resident physician Barnes Jewish Hosp., Washington U., St. Louis, 2003—. Home: 18 Kingshighway Blvd Apt 8E Saint Louis MO 63108-1318

CORRIGAN, PAULA ANN, military officer, internist; b. Cheyenne, Wyo., Feb. 17, 1961; d. Patrick Joseph and Eleanor Marie (Kasun) C. BS, U. Notre Dame, 1983; MD, U. N.Mex., 1987; M in Pub. Health in Tropical Medicine, Tulane Sch. Pub. Health, 1999. Diplomate Am. Bd. Internal Medicine, Am. Soc. Tropical Medicine and Hygiene, Am. Bd. Preventive Medicine, in Aerospace and Preventive Medicine. Advanced through ranks to col. USAF, 2005, chief internal medicine clinic Holloman AFB, N.Mex., 1990-93, flight surgeon Hosp. 48 RQS, 1993-94, flight comdr. 18 AMDS/SGPF Kadena AB, Japan, 1996-98; res., Aerospace Med. Brooks AFB, 1999—2001, aeromedical cons. svc., 2006—; exch. assignment RAAF Aviation Medicine Policy, Canberra, Australia, 2001—04; ADS comdr. Tyndall AFB, Fla., 2004—. Fellow: Aerospace Med. Assn. (assoc.), Am. Heart Assn. (assoc.; mem. coun. 1992—93); mem.: ACP, Australasian Soc. Aerospace Medicine, Soc. USAF Flight Surgeons, N.Mex. Med. Soc., Am. Soc. Tropical Medicine and Hygiene. Roman Catholic. Avocation: scuba diving. Home: 1334 Arrow Spring San Antonio TX 78258 Personal E-mail: pacorrigan@hotmail.com.

CORRIHER, SHIRLEY, food writer; b. Atlanta, Feb. 23, 1935; d. A.J. and Clide (Mann) Ogletree; m. Theodore Hecht, 1958 (div. 1970); children: Terron Jan, Sherron Ann, Theodore Jr. BA in Chemistry cum laude, Vanderbilt U., 1956. Cert. culinaryn profl. Rsch. biochemist Vanderbilt Med. Sch., Nashville, 1956-58; co-founder, tchr. Brandon Hall, 1959, food svc. mgr., 1959-69; a founder First Montessori, 1963; traveling tchr., writer and cons., 1975—. Cons. DK's Desserts, Fine Cooking, Cook's Illus., others. Regular columnist, contbg. editor Fine Cooking, 1994—; author: CookWise, 1998; contbr. articles to Food and Wine, Ladies Home Jour., Fine Cooking, Martha Stewart Living, The Phoenix, Jour. Biol. Chemistry, others. Trustee Cooking Advancement, Rsch. and Edn. Found., 1984, chair, 1985. Recipient Best Reference Book of Yr. award, James Beard Awards, 1998, Best Tchr. of Yr. award, Bon Apetit's Food and Entertaining Awards, 2001. Mem. Internat. Assn. Cooking Profls. (bd. dirs. 1982, 83-84), Les Dames d'Escoffier, Inst. Food Technologists, Am. Inst. Wine and Food, Am. Assn. Cereal Chemists Home: 3152 Andrews Dr NW Atlanta GA 30305-2013

CORRIN, LISA G., museum director; BA in Art History, with honors, Mary Washington Coll.; grad. studies, SUNY, Stony Brook, Johns Hopkins U. Co-founder & chief curator The Contemporary Mus. of Balt., 1989—97; chief curator The Serpentine Gallery, London, 1997—2001; dep. dir. art & Jon and Mary Shirley curator of modern and contemporary art Seattle Art Museum, 2001—05; dir. Williams Coll. Mus. Art, Williamstown, Mass., 2005—. Curator (exhibitions) Mining the Museum: An Installation by Fred Wilson, 1992 (Named Exhbn. of Yr., Am. Assn. Museums, 1992, Wittenborn Prize for book on exhbn., North Am. Assn. Art Librarians). Rockefeller Fellow for Multicultural Scholarship in Visual Arts, Coll. Art Assn., 1993. Office: Williams Coll Mus Art Ste 2 15 Lawrence Hall Dr Williamstown MA 01267

CORRIVEAU, HEATHER M., II, social studies educator; d. Robert L. and Kim E. Patterson; m. Troy T. Corriveau, July 5, 1997; 2 children. BA in Liberal Arts & Am. Studies magna cum laude, Franklin Pierce Coll., Rindge, NH, 2001—04. Cert. basic acct., NH Tech. Inst., Condord, 1999; counseling for children & adolescents So. NH U., Manchester, 2005. Children & adolescent counseling internship Prospect Mountain HS, Alton, NH, 2005, social studies tchr., 2005—. Jv girls volleyball coach Prospect Mountain HS, 2005. Grantee ROTC scholarship, US Army, 1993. Office: Prospect Mountain HS 242 Suncook Valley Rd Alton NH 03809

CORROTHERS, HELEN GLADYS, criminal justice official; b. Montrose, Ark., Mar. 19, 1937; d. Thomas and Christene (Farley) Curl; m. Edward Corrothers, Dec. 17, 1968 (div. Sept. 1983); 1 child, Michael Edward. AA in Liberal Arts magna cum laude, Ark. Bapt. Coll., 1955; BS in Bus. Adminstrn. Mgmt., Roosevelt U., 1965; grad. officer leadership sch., WAC Sch., 1965; grad. Inst. Criminal Justice, Exec. Ctr. Continuing Edn., U. Chgo., 1973; postgrad., Calif. Coast U., 1981—. Enlisted U.S. Army, 1956, advanced through grades to capt., 1969, chief mil. pers. Ft. Meyer, Va., 1965-67; dir. for housing Giessen Support Ctr., Germany, 1967-69; resigned, 1969; social interviewer Ark. Dept. Corrections, Grady, 1970-71, supt. women's unit Pine Bluff, 1971-83; commr. U.S. Parole Commn., Burlingame, Calif., 1983-85, U.S. Sentencing Commn., Washington, 1985-91; fellow U.S. Dept. Justice, Washington, 1992-95; criminal justice cons., 1996—. Instr. women and crime U. Md., College Park, 1994; instr. corrections U. Ark.-Pine Bluff, 1976-79; mem. bd. visitation Jefferson County Juvenile Ct., Pine Bluff, 1978-81; bd. dirs. Vols. in Cts., 1979-83, Vols. Am., 1985-94; mem. Am./Can. study team Mex. penal system Am. Correctional Assn., Islas Marias, Mex., 1981; mem. Ark. Commn. Crimes and Law Enforcement, 1975-78; mem. U.S. Atty. Gen.'s Correctional Policy Study Team, 1987. Mem. Ark. Commn. on Status of Women, 1976-78; bd. dirs. Com. Against Spouse Abuse, 1982-83; mem. nat. adv. bd. dept. criminal justice Xavier U., Cin., 1993-97; bd. dirs. Bapt. Mission Found. of Md./Del., Columbia, Md., 1993-98. Recipient Ark. Woman of Achievement award Ark. Press Women's Assn., 1980, Human Rels. award Ark. Edn. Assn., 1980, Outstanding Woman of Achievement award Sta. KATV-TV, Little Rock, 1981, Correctional Svc. award Vols. Am., 1984, William H. Hastie award Nat. Assn. Blacks in Criminal Justice, 1986, Outstanding Victim Advocacy award Nat. Victim Ctr., 1991, Appreciation cert. Dept. Justice Office for Victims of Crime, 1994; recipient testimonial for svc. to fed. judiciary Adminstrv. Office of Cts., 1991. Mem.: NAFE, Am. Soc. Criminology, Nat. Coun. on Crime and Delinquency, Ark. Law Enforcement Assn., N.Am. Assn. Wardens and Supts., Am. Correctional Assn. (treas. 1980—86, v.p. 1986—88, pres. 1990—92, mem. Del. Assembly 1993—, chmn. rsch. coun. 1997—2000, chmn. Correctional awards com. 2001—05, chmn. retirees com. 2005—, mem. pres.'s field adv. task force 2005—, E.R. Cass Correctional Achievement award 1993), Ark. Sheriff's Assn. (hon.), Delta Sigma Theta (local sec. 1976—79, local parliamentarian 1983). Baptist. Avocations: reading, music. Office: Am Correctional Assn 4380 Forbes Blvd Lanham Seabrook MD 20706-4863

CORRY, ALINE LAHUSEN, art educator; d. Alfred Gustave Lahusen and Marianna Posey; m. Henry Cecil Corry, Apr. 23, 2004; children: Christa, Amy 1 stepchild, Elaine. BA, U. La., Lafayette, 1973, MEd, 1980. Tchr. secondary sch. art St. Landry Parish, Opelousas, La., 1975—85; tchr. elem. sch. art Houston Ind. Sch. Dist., 1986—88; tchr. mid. sch. art Galena Park Ind. Sch. Dist., 1988—89, 1997—98; tchr. elem. art Katy Elem. Sch. Dist., 1989—93; tchr. art Ft. Bend Ind. Sch. Dist., Sugarland, 1993—97; tchr. elem. sch. art Clear Creek Ind. Sch. Dist., League City, 1999—. Cons. Transdesigns, Atlanta, 1983—85; instr. Art Alliance Ctr., Nassau Bay, Tex., 2004—. Sponsor Youth Art Coun. Am., La., 1976—81, Gifted Talented Conv., Baton Rouge, 1981; vol. Houston Art Educators Assn., 1987. Mem.: Houston Art Educators Assn., Phi Delta Kappa. Avocations: painting, drawing, sailing. Office Phone: 281-284-6300.

CORRY, DALILA BOUDJELLAL, internist, educator; b. El-Arrouch, Algeria, July 7, 1943; came to U.S., 1981; MD, U. Algiers, 1974. Diplomate in internal medicine and nephrology Am. Bd. Internal Medicine. Intern Hosp. Mustapha Algiers, 1972-73; resident Hosp. Tenon, Paris, 1975-79; fellow in nephrology UCLA, 1981-83; chief renal divsn. Olive View-UCLA Med. Ctr., Sylmar, Calif., 1983—; from asst. prof. to prof. clin. medicine UCLA, 1993, prof. clin. medicine, 2001—. Fellow Am. Heart Assn. Office: Olive View-UCLA Med Ctr Dept Medicine 2B182 14445 Olive View Dr Sylmar CA 91342-1437 Office Phone: 818-364-3205. Business E-Mail: dbcorry@ucla.edu.

CORS, JEANNE MARIE, lawyer; b. Bowling Green, Ohio, Jan. 7, 1968; BA in French, Marquette U., 1989, BA in German, 1989, BA in Polit. Sci., 1989; MA in Polit. Sci., U. Mich.; JD, Georgetown U. Law Ctr., 1999. Bar: Ohio 1999. Legis. asst. Senator Herb Kohl; assoc. Taft, Stettinius & Hollister LLP, Cin., mem., Women's Resource Grp. Named one of Ohio's Rising Stars, Super Lawyers, 2005, 2006; named to Leading Lawyers list, Cincy Bus. Mag., 2006. Mem.: Ohio State Bar Assn. (mem., Bd. Governors, Antitrust Sect.). Office: Taft Stettinius & Hollister LLP 425 Walnut St Ste 1800 Cincinnati OH 45202-3957 Office Phone: 513-381-2838. Office Fax: 513-381-0205.*

CORSELLO, LILY JOANN, minister, counselor, educator; b. Newark, Mar. 30, 1953; d. Joseph DiFalco and Antonietta (Gandolfo) Corsello. BA, Fla. State U., 1974; MEd, Fla. Atlantic U., 1977; MA, Southwestern Bapt. Theol. Sem., 1987; D in Ministry, Luther Rice Sem., 2003. Lic. profl. counselor Tex., mental health counselor Fla.; ordained min. Maranetta Ch., Pompano Beach, Fla., 1969. Lang. arts tchr. Broward County Pub. Schs., Fla., 1974-80, guidance counselor Fla., 1980-85; min. of single adults Park Pl. Bapt Ch., Houston, 1985-87; founder, exec. dir. SinglePlus, Inc., Flower Mound, Tex., 1989-96; guidance counselor Palm Beach and Broward County Pub. Schs., 1996-99; pastor Maranatha Ch., Pompano Beach, Fla., 2000—01; lic. counselor mental health In Spirit and In Truth Counseling Svs., Pompano Beach, 1999—. Writer, lectr. singles ministry and Christian Single mag. So. Bapt. Conv., Nashville, 1979—89. Mem.: Am. Assn. Christian Counselors, Women's Club Flower Mound (pres. 1989—90), Pilot Club Ft. Lauderdale (chaplain 1982—83), Phi Delta Kappa, Lambda Iota Tau. Democrat. Home and Office: PO Box 811 Pompano Beach FL 33061-0811 Office Phone: 954-784-7046.

CORSO, SUSAN FALK, minister; b. Mineola, N.Y., Oct. 12, 1957; d. Morris Stephen and Linda (Jackson) Falk; m. Antony Corso, Jan. 23, 1987 (div. Mar. 1991); 1 child, Isaac Stephen (dec.); m. Sheriden Thomas, Oct. 31, 2005 BA, Smith Coll., Northampton, Mass., 1979; DDiv, Coll. Divine Metaphysics, Pasadena, Calif., 1992. Ordained to ministry, 1991. Mgr. profl. theater; min. Celebration Unity, Richland, Wash., 1992—93; min., ch. cons. River of Life Met. Cmty. Ch., Richland, 1992—93; cons. U.S. Dept. Energy, Richland, 1993—95; min., spkr. Vaud, various locations, 1993—. Author: The Peace Diet, 1996 Mem. Smith Coll. Alumni Assn Office: 101 School St Somerville MA 02143

CORTES, CAROL SOLIS, school system administrator; b. N.Y.C., N.Y., Aug. 16, 1944; d. Jesus and Dora Solis; m. Fernando Miranda, June 25, 1964 (div. Apr. 1978); children: Christopher, Christina Guerra; m. Jose Cortes (div. Nov. 1, 1983). BEd with hon., U. Miami, 1970; MSc, Fla. Internat. U., 1974. Cert. in Social Sci. & Adminstrn. Supr. From tchr. to dep. supt. Miami-Dade County Pub. Sch., Miami, Fla., 1970—96, dep. supt., 1996—. Exec. bd. Gender Equity Network. Exec. bd. Women's C. of C., Miami, Fla., 2000—01. Recipient Hispanic Educator award, Nova U., 1999, Cervantes Outstanding Educator award, 1999, Educator of Yr. award, 1999. Mem.: Phi Delta Kappa. Avocations: travel, dominoes. Home: 2105 SW 123rd Court Miami FL 33175 Office: Miami Dade Pub Schs 1450 NE 2nd Ave Miami FL 33132-1308

CORTESE, JULIA F., retired elementary school educator; b. Reading, Pa., Mar. 2, 1922; d. Frederick Hagman and Elizabeth Hartman Dechant; m. Sam Saunders Fitzsimmons, June 16, 1946 (dec. Aug. 1959); children: Samuel, Elizabeth Barclay, Carol Sargent, Sarah; m. Joseph Robert Cortese, June 20, 1964. BA, Lake Erie Coll., 1943; MEd, Western Res. U., 1961. Cert. tchr. comprehensive sci., Ohio. Rsch. chemist Hercules Powder Co., Wilminton, Del., 1943-44; rsch. biochemist Rockefeller Inst. for Med. Rsch., N.Y.C., 1944-46; rsch. asst. Maclean Hosp. Harvard Med. Sch., Boston, 1946-49; sci. tchr. Monticello Jr. High, Cleveland Heights, Ohio, 1959-64; sci. tchr., dept. chair Hathaway Brown Sch., Shaker Heights, Ohio, 1966-83; sci. tchr. U. Sch., Shaker Heights, 1985-96; ret. Bd. mem., trustee Ind. Schs. Assn. Ctrl. States, Downers Grove, Ill., 1976-79, Nat. Assn. Ind. Schs., Washington, 1980-83; bd. mem. Andrews Sch. for Girls, Willoughby, Ohio, 1984—, chmn., 1995—. Bd. dirs. Global Issues Resource Ctr., Cleve., 1988—; docent Cleve. Mus. Natural History, 1996—, Great Lakes Sci. Ctr., Cleve., 1996—. Recipient Disting. Tchg. award Ind. Schs. Assn. Ctrl. States, Downers Grove, 1974. Mem. ACLU, Nat. Assn. Biology Tchrs., Nat. Sci. Tchrs. Assn., Sierra Club, Common Cause. Democrat. Episcopalian. Avocations: reading, sewing, family activities. Home: 3911 Lander Rd # 2 Chagrin Falls OH 44022-1328

CORTINA, BETTY, magazine editor; B in journalism, U. Fla., 1992. City hall reporter Miami Herald; LA staff corr. People Weekly, 1995—96; assoc. editor People En Espanol, 1996—99; sr. writer Entertainment Weekly, 1999; founding news editor O, the Oprah mag., 1999—2001; editl. dir. Latina mag., 2001—. Adv. coun. Journalism Dept., U. Fla. Office: Latina Mag 1500 Broadway Ste 700 New York NY 10036 E-mail: betty@latina.com.

CORTNER, HANNA JOAN, retired research scientist, political scientist; b. Tacoma, May 9, 1945; d. Val and E. Irene Otteson; m. Richard Carroll Cortner, Nov. 14, 1970. BA in Polit. Sci. magna cum laude with distinction, U. Wash., 1967; MA in Govt., U. Ariz., 1969, PhD in Govt., 1973. Grad. tchg. and rsch. asst. dept. govt. U. Ariz., Tucson, 1967-70, rsch. assoc. Inst. Govt. Rsch., 1974-76, rsch. assoc. forest-watershed and landscape resources divsns. Sch. Renewable Natural Resources, 1975-82, adj. assoc. prof. Sch. Renewable Natural Resources, 1983-89; exec. asst. Pima County Bd. Suprs., 1985-86; adj. assoc. prof. renewable natural resources, assoc. rsch. scientist Water Resources Rsch. Ctr. U. Ariz., Tucson, 1988-89, prof., rsch. scientist Water Resources Rsch. Ctr., 1989-90, prof., rsch. scientist, dir. Water Resources Rsch. Ctr., 1990-96, prof., rsch. scientist Sch. Renewable Resources, 1997-2000; rsch. prof., assoc. dir. Ecol. Restoration Inst. No. Ariz. U., Flagstaff, 2001—04; ret. Program analyst USDA Forest Svc., Washington, 1979-80; vis. scholar Inst. Water Resources, Corps of Engrs., Ft. Belvoir, Va., 1986-87; com. arid lands AAAS, 1986-89; com. natural disasters NAS/NRC, 1988-91, com. on planning and remediation of irrigation-induced water quality impacts, 1994-95; rev. com. nat. forest planning Conservation Found., Washington, 1987-90; chair adv. com. renewable resources planning techs. for pub. lands Office of Tech. Assessment U.S. Congress, 1989-91; policy coun. Pinchot Inst. Conservation Studies, 1991-93, bd. dirs. 2005-; co-chair working party on evaluation of forest policies Internat. Union Forestry Rsch. Orgns., 1990-95, chair working party on forest instns. and forestry adminstrn., 1996; vice-chair Man and the Biosphere Program, Temperate Directorate, US Dept. State, 1991-96; cmtys. com. steering com., Am. Forest Congress, 1996-2004, rsch. com., 1996-97; sci. adv. com. Consortium for Environ. Risk Evaluation, 1996-97; cons. Greeley and Hansen, Cons. Engrs., US Army Corps Engrs., Ft. Belvoir, US Forest Svc., Washington, Portland, Oreg., Ogden, Utah. Assoc. editor Society and Natural Resources, 1992-94; book reviewer We. Polit. Sci. Quar., Am. Polit. Quar., Perspectives, Natural Resources Jour., Climatic Change, Society and Natural Resources, Jour. of Forestry, Environment; mem. editl. bd. Jour. Forest Planning, 1995—, Forest Policy and Econs., 1999-2002; co-author: The Politics of Ecosystem Management, 1999, George W. Bush's Healthy Forests, 2005; co-editor: The State and Nature, 2002; contbr. articles to profl. jours. Bd. dirs. Planned Parenthood So. Ariz., 1992-94, planning com., 1992, bd. devel. and evaluation com., 1994; bd. dirs. N.W. Homeowners Assn., 1982-83, v.p., 1983-84, pres., 1984; vice chmn., chmn. Pima County Bd. Adjustment Dist. 3, 1984; active Tucson Tomorrow, 1984-88; water quality subcom. Pima Assn. Govts., 1983-84, environ. planning adv. com., 1989-90, chmn., 1984, mem. Avra Valley task force, 1988-90; bd. dirs. So. Ariz. Water Resources Assn., 1984-86, 87-95, sec., 1987-89, mem. com. alignment and terminal storage, 1990-94, CAP com., 1988-92, chair, 1989-90, basinwide mgmt. com., 1983-86, chair, 1992-93; active Ariz. Interagy. Task Force on Fire and the Urban/Wildland Interface, 1990-92; wastewater mgmt. adv. com. Pima County, 1988-92, subcom. on effluent reuse Joint CWAC-WWAC, 1989-91, citizens water adv. com. Water Resources Plan Update Subcom., 1990-91; bd. dirs. Ctrl. Ariz. Water Conservation Dist., 1985-90, fin. com., 1987-88, spl. studies com., 1987-88, nominating com., 1987; mem. Colo. River Salinity Control, 1989-90; chair adv. com. Tucson Long Range Master Water Plan, 1988-89; water adv. com. City of Tucson, 1984. Travel grantee NSF/Soc. Am. Foresters; Rsch. grantee US Geol. Survey, US Army Corps of Engrs., USDA Forest Svc., Soil Conservation Svc., Utah State U., Four Corners Regional Commn., Office of Water Rsch. & Tech.; Sci. & Engring. fellow AAAS, 1986-87; recipient Copper Letter Appreciation cert. City of Tucson, 1985, 89, SAWARA award, 1989. Mem. Am. Water Resources Assn. (nat. award com. 1987-90, statues and bylaws com. 1989-90, tech. co-chair ann. meeting 1993), Am. Forests Assn. (forest policy ctr. adv. coun. 1991-95), Soc. Am. Foresters (task force on sustaining long-term forest health and productivity 1991-92, com. on forest policy 1994-96, sci. and tech. bd. 2001-04), Am. Polit. Sci. Assn., Western Polit. Sci. Assn. (com. on constrn. and bylaws 1976-80, chair 1977-79, exec. coun. 1980-83, com. on profl. devel. 1984-85, com. on status of women 1984-85), Nat. Fire Protection Assn. (tech. com. on forest and rural fire protection 1990-94), Phi Beta Kappa. Democrat. Achievements include research in political and socioeconomic aspects of natural resources policy, administration, and planning, water resources management, ecosystem management, wildland fire policy and management. Home: 6064 E Mountain Oaks Flagstaff AZ 86004-7222 Personal E-mail: hannacortner@aol.com.

CORTO, DIANA MARIA, coloratura soprano; b. N.Y. d. Samuel and Margaret C.; 1 child, Christian Miles Stomsvik. BA, CUNY, 1977, MA, 1984; studied drama, Am. Place Theatre; studied voice with Maria Kurenko, Bolshoi Theatre, Moscow, studied ballet with Maria Nevelska. Founder, dir. Am. Opera Musical Theatre Co., Inc., 1995—. Prof. drama for musical theatre Pace U., N.Y.C.; mem. voice faculty Calif. State U., L.A., also stage dir. opera program; founder, dir. Am. Opera/Mus. Theatre Co. Starred as Maria in West Side Story in numerous opera houses in Spain, Germany, Switzerland, Austria, 1984; appeared on Broadway in Her First Roman, Status Quo Vadis, Thirteen Daughters, West Side Story Revival, Stop the World, I Want To Get Off; concert tours in U.S., S.Am., Moscow, 1989-91; lead singer City of Angels Opera, Met. Studio; lyric-coloraturist in operas in U.S. and Europe; road tours include King and I, Man of La Mancha, Kismet; prodr. (N.Y. debut performance) The Jewel Box by Mozart/Griffiths; co-prodr. The Jewel Box with N.J. State Opera, Dmitiri Shostakovich concert with Fedn. of Russia, La Bohéme, and others; prodr., dir. Am. premiere of La Molinara by Paisiello at Town Hall, La Boheme; prodr.: Iolanta by Tchaikowski at Town Hall, Embassy of Russian Fedn., La Boheme, Rigoletto, Nat. Performing Arts Ctr. Taiwan; prodr., dir. Stars of the Bolshoi Opera at Carnegie Hall, 2006. E-mail: corto@mindspring.com.

CORVINI, MARGUERITE, social worker; b. Smithtown, NY, Nov. 4, 1979; d. Robert Henry and Joann DeFalco Corvini. BA, Wake Forest U., Winston-Salem, NC, 2001; MSW, NYU, 2004. LMSW NY. Social worker Pederson-Krag, St. James, NY, 2003—04; child psychotherapist Ctr. for Life Mgmt., Salem, NH, 2005—06. Presdl. scholar, Wake Forest U.

CORVINO, BETH BYSTER, lawyer; b. Dec. 8, 1956; m. John Corvino. BA, Ind. U.; JD with honors, DePaul U. Assoc. Katten Muchin Zavis Rosenman, 1982—83; various positions Am. Hosp. Supply Corp., Staley Continental Inc., 1983—89; asst. gen. counsel Whitman Corp., 1989—92; with Gen. Instrument Corp., 1992—98; v.p., gen. counsel, corp. sec. Chas. Levy LLC, 1998—2004; exec. v.p., gen. counsel, corp. sec. Laidlaw Internat. Inc., 2004—. Office: Laidlaw Internat Inc 55 Shuman Blvd Ste 400 Naperville IL 60563 Office Fax: 630-848-3167. Business E-Mail: bcorvino@laidlaw.com.

CORWIN, JOYCE ELIZABETH STEDMAN, construction company executive; b. Chgo. d. Cresswell Edward and Elizabeth Josephine (Kimbell) Stedman; m. William Corwin, May 1, 1965; children: Robert Edmund Newman, Jillanne Elizabeth McInnis. Pres. Am. Properties, Inc., Miami, Fla., 1966-72; v.p. Stedman Constrn. Co., Miami, 1971—. Owner Joy-Win Horses, Gray lady ARC, 1969-70. Guidance worker Youth Hall, 1969-70; sponsor Para Med. Group of Coral Park H.S., 1969-70; hostess, Rep. presdl. campaign, 1968; aide Rep. Nat. Conv., 1972. Mem. Dade County Med. Aux. (chmn. directory com. 1970), Marion County Med. Aux., Fla. Psychiat. Soc. Aux., Fla. Morgan Horse Assn., Fla. Thoroughbred Breeders Assn., Coral Gables Jr. Women's Club (chmn. casework com.), Royal Dames of Ocala. Home: Windrift Farm 8500 NW 120th St Reddick FL 32686-4513

CORWIN, VERA-ANNE VERSFELT, small business owner, consultant; b. Glen Ridge, N.J., Nov. 12, 1932; d. Porter LaRoy and Vera Anna (Price) Versfelt; m. John M. Corwin, Apr. 9, 1955; children: Gail Elizabeth Corwin Bayne, Gregory John, Lynn B. Corwin Byers. BS, Upsala Coll., East Orange, N.J., 1954; MEd, Wayne State U., Detroit, Mich., 1972, PhD, 1977. Instr. Wayne (N.J.) Sch. Dist., 1954-55; engr., spec., analyst Chrysler Corp., Highland Park, Mich., 1955-56, 78-85; instr. Royal Oak (Mich.) Sch. Dist., 1968-78; sr. systems engr. Electronic Data Systems, Troy, Mich., 1985-87; owner, pres. Unique Solutions, Inc., Royal Oak, 1987—. Adj. prof. U. Mich., Dearborn, 1989, Wayne State U., 1989; expert cons. Teltech, Inc., Mpls., 1990—. Author: (tng. manuals) Statistical Process Control Philosophies and Tools, 1988, Design of Experiments Philosophies and Tools, 1989. Pres. Arlington Pk. Homeowners Assn., Royal Oak, 1984—85, rd. commr., 1984—90; sec. bd. dirs. Cmty. Concert Assn. Troy, 1996—99, 2d v.p. bd. dirs., 2002—05, 1st v.p. bd. dirs., 2005—; vol. Oakland County Mobile Meals, 1996—; trustee First Presbyn. Ch. Royal Oak, 1990—93, 2004—, sec., 1993, Presbies sec., 1994, choir, 1958—72, 1997—, ch. children's computer lab. cons., instr., 1997—, Christian edn. com., 2000—, adult computers instr., 2001—. N.J. scholar, 1950—51. Fellow: Am. Soc. Quality (standing rev. bd. 1996—); mem.: Am. Statis. Assn., Soc. Mfg. Engrs. (trainer 1987—91), Soc. Automotive Engrs. (sr.; trainer 1991—), Automotive Industry Action Group (chmn. design expts. subgroup 1988—94). Avocations: skiing, piano, travel. Office Phone: 248-435-5307. E-mail: corwinvj@aol.com.

CORY, CYNTHIA STRONG, mathematics professor; b. Rochester, Ind., Nov. 11, 1954; d. Clair Eugene and Betty Jane Strong; m. Timothy James Cory, Aug. 6, 1983; children: Bettina Jane, Kevin Scott, Nicholas David, Christopher Steven. BS, Purdue U., 1973—77; MBS, Morehead U., 2000—03. Teacher Certification Ind. U. Purdue U. at Indpls., Indpls., IN, 1989. Math. instr. Hazard Cmty. and Tech. Coll., Hazard, 2000—, challenger learning ctr. of Ky., 1999—2000; math. tchr. Perry County Schools, Hazard, Ky., 1996—99; fin. officer US Army Reserves, 1983—89, US Army, 1977—83. Dir., soapbox derby Kiwanis Club of Hazard, 2001—05; parish planners Mother of Good Counsel Cath. Ch., Hazard, 2003—05. Capt. U.S. Army, 1977—83, Korea, Fort Harrison, Fort Knox. Decorated Parachutist

Badge US Army, Army Commendation medal; recipient, 1982, Coach of the Yr., Ky. Track and Cross Country Coaches Assn., 2003, 2004, Unsung Hero award for Volunteerism, US Army, Ft. Ord, Calif., 1992, 1993. Mem.: Math. Assn. of Am., Nat. Coun. of Teachers of Math., Kiwanis Club of Hazard, Phi Kappa Phi, Delta Mu Delta. Home: PO Box 472 Dwarf KY 41739 Office: Hazard Cmty and Techl Coll 1 Community College Drive Hazard KY 41701 Office Phone: 606-436-5721. Personal E-mail: ccory1234@msn.com. Business E-Mail: cynthia.cory@kctcs.edu.

CORZINE, JENNIFER JEAN, music educator; b. Evanston, Ill., Apr. 2, 1946; d. Raymond Alfred and Majorie Palmer; children: Christopher, Lindsay, Erin. MusB with hon., Wis. State U., 1968; MA, U. Hawaii, 1970; MS, Fla. State U., 1991, MSW, 1994. Cert. tchr. NY, Fla. Vocal music tchr. Tomorrow River Sch., Amherst, Wis., 1968—69, Greece Ctrl. Sch. Dist., Rochester, NY, 1970—71; instrumental music tchr. Pittsford Ctrl. Sch., NY, 1971—72; gen. music tchr. Evansville-Vanderburgh Sch. Corp., Ind., 1972—73; instrumental music tchr. Maclay Sch., Tallahassee, 1973—. Vol. choir mem. various ch., 1970—85; vol. family counselor Family Living Ctr., Tallahassee, 1986; vol. Am. Heart Assn., 1999—2005; vol. supr. social work interns Maclay Sch., 2002—06. Mem.: Fla. Bandmasters Assn., Fla. Music Educators Assn., Music Educators Nat. Conf. Achievements include established instrumental music program at Maclay School. Avocations: travel, reading, gardening. Office: Maclay Sch 3737 N Meridian Rd Tallahassee FL 32312 Office Phone: 850-893-2138. Business E-Mail: jcorzine@maclay.org.

COSEY PULLEY, BERNICE, volunteer; b. Blaine, Miss., Sept. 23, 1927; d. Sampson M. and Slenner (McGee) Cosey; m. Arthur L. Pulley, Sr., June 13, 1955; children: Arthur L.(dec.), Nicholas S. BA, Ohio State U., Columbus, 1950; DD, Yale U., New Haven, Conn., 1955. Spkr. in field. Author: Homes Are the Strangest Things, 1968, Thinking About the YWCA 1894-1994, 1994, 2027, 2004. Active ACLU, N.Y., 1970—2004, Dem. Party, Westchester County, NY, 1955—; bd. dirs. YWCA-USA World Svc. Coun., N.Y., 1964—76, 1986—, Am. Bapt. Assembly, Grero Lake, Wis., 1996—2000. Named Yale Black Seminarian, 2000; recipient Contribution award, Fedn. Women's Clubs, 1986, Appreciation cert., Yale Dvinity Sch., 1986, Recognition award, YWCA, 1991. Mem.: NAACP (life; adv. youth coun. 1950—2000, Outstanding Svc. award 1992, honoree 2006), Ch. Women United, Assn. Former Internat. Civil Servants (life), Yale U. Alumni Assn. (life), Assn. Advancement Colored People (life), Nat. Coun. Colored Women's Club, Inc. (life). Democrat. Bapt. Home: 381 Fifth Ave New Rochelle NY 10801 Office: Arthur L Pulley Jr Meml Ctr PO Box 247 Greenfield Park NY 12435-6247

COSGROVE, ANNMARIE, special education educator; b. Freeport, N.Y., Jan. 7, 1962; d. Cosmo and Rose Marie (Tarantino) L. BS, L.I. U., Greenvale, 1984, MS, 1986. Cert. elem. tchr., spl. edn., N.Y. Presch. tchr. spl. edn. Nassau Ctr. for Devel. Disabled, Woodbury, N.Y.; tchr. pre-kindergarten Manhasset (N.Y.) Unified Free Sch. Dist.; learning disabilities specialist DRS-PC, Merrick, N.Y.; ptnr. Melted Ice Prodns., North Merrick, N.Y.; elem. edn. tchr. North Merrick Unified Free Sch. Dist., 1990—. Cooperating tchr. student teaching program Hofstra U. Hon. life mem. PTA, NY. Mem. N.Y. State United Tchrs. Assn. E-mail: anname40@optonline.net.

COSMAN, FRANCENE JEN, former government official; b. Windsor, Ont., Can., Jan. 14, 1941; d. John Douglas and Dorothy Mae (Machel) McCarthy; m. David Killam Cosman, July 25, 1964 (div.); children: Lara Machel, Andrea Leigh; m. Aza Avramovitch, June 27, 1998 (dec.). Diploma in Nursing, St. John Gen. Hosp., N.B., 1962; postgrad. diploma, Margaret Hague Hosp., Jersey City, 1963. RN Can., cert. healing touch practitioner. Various nursing positions, 1963-68; county councillor County of Halifax, N.S., 1976-79; mayor Town of Bedford, N.S., 1979-82; pres. Adv. Coun. on Status of Women, N.S., 1982-86; exec. dir. N.S. Liberal Party, 1989-93; mem. Legis. Assembly, House of Assembly of N.S., Halifax, 1993-99, dep. spkr., min. comty. svcs., 1995-99; ret. Chair Sr. Citizens Secretariat, 1997-99; min. responsible administrn. Adv. Coun. Status Women Act, 1997-99; min. Cmty. Svcs., 1997-99; min. responsible Disabled Persons Commn. Act, 1997-99; mem. Healing Touch Ministry, 2000—. Contbr. numerous reports, brief, documents to provincial and fed. levels of govt.; opinion col. writer Chronicle Herald Newspaper, 1987-88. Liberal. Mem. United Ch. Avocations: artist, poetry, swimming, healing touch practitioner. E-mail: fjc@eastlink.ca.

COSS, SHARON ELIZABETH, counselor; b. Bellingham, Wash., Aug. 25, 1950; d. Frank LeRoy and Margaret Elizabeth (Pierre) Coss; children: Terry David Fast Horse, Anne Celeste Fast Horse, Jonathon Michael Lane. BA, Western Wash. U., 1986, M.Psychology, 1991. Customer svc. rep. Std. Ins. Co., Portland, 1972-76; sec./bookkeeper Lummi Tribal Ent., Bellingham, 1976-78; rsch. asst. Portland State U., 1985; teaching asst. Western Wash. U., Bellingham, 1986-87, rsch. asst., 1988, counselor-in-tng., 1987-88, counselor; counselor-in-tng. Seattle Indian Health Bd., 1987—88; retention/transfer specialist NW Indian Coll., Bellingham, 1989—92; counselor Whetcom CC, 1998—2001; domestic violence advocate Lummi Victims of Crime, 2001—. Author poetry anthology in Fern Shadows, 1990. Mem., officer Indian Child Welfare Adv. Com., Bellingham, 1985-88, Indian Edn. Parent Com., Bellingham, 1983-88; vol. Coalition for Child Advocacy, Bellingham, 1985-87, Whatcom Youth Diversion Program, Bellingham, 1980; bd. dirs. Bellingham YWCA, 2003-, bd. pres., 2006. Dept. Edn. Am. Indian fellow, 1986, 88. Mem. NAFE. Avocations: writing, reading, jogging. Office: # 507 177 Telegraph Rd Bellingham WA 98226-8079

COSSON, MARY GWENDOLYN, music educator; b. Eufaula, Ala., Feb. 15, 1962; d. Wayne Clevester and Sara Dean Cosson. MusB in Edn., Samford U., 1985; MusM in Ch. Music, Southwestern Bapt. Theol. Sem., 1988. Min. music Omega (Ga.) Bapt. Ch., 1989; tchr. music Omega (Ga.) Elem., 1990—92, Tiftthea Acad., Tifton, Ga., 1990—95, Turner County Schs., Ashburn, Ga., 1995—96, Berrien County Schs., Nashville, Ga., 1996—. Min. music Unity Bapt. Ch., Sylvester, Ga., 1994—99; dir. music Alapaha (Ga.) Cmty. choir, 2000—; dir. children's choir First Bapt. Ch., Tifton, Ga., 1990—, mem. adult emsemble, 1990—. Singer: Samford U. Acapella Choir, 1982—83, Acapella Alumni Choir, 1996, 1998. Orch. flutist First Bapt. Ch., Tifton, Ga., 1998. Scholar Camerata T.D. scholar, Camerata Chorus, 1980. Mem.: Nat. Fedn. Music Clubs, NEA-Ga. Assn. Educators, Tifton Choral Soc., Tifton Music Club (pres. 1994). Republican. Baptist. Avocations: piano, flute, violin, reading, exercise. Home: 104 Maple St PO Box 742 Omega GA 31775 Office: Berrien Elementary 305 N Anne st Nashville GA 31639

COSTA, JUDITH ANN, secondary school educator; b. N.Y.C., Nov. 8, 1928; d. Michael and Ida (Gold) Petrella; m. Ernest F. Costa, Dec. 26, 1953; children: Deirdre Costa Major, Christopher. AB, Hunter Coll., 1950, AM, 1952; Cert. in Guidance, C.W. Post Coll., 1974. Tchr. Flushing (N.Y.) High Sch., 1964-78; guidance counselor Middle Coll. High at LaGuardia Coll., L.I.C., 1978-80, B.N. Cardozo High Sch., Bayside, N.Y., 1980-87. Freelance writer. Mem. Community Sch. Bd. 26, Bayside, 1983-89; founder Prospect Ave. Block Assn., Douglaston, 1975—; trustee Rogers Meml. Libr., Southampton, N.Y., 2006. Mem. AAUW, (pres. Queens br. 1991-93, Excellence and Equity in Edn. award 1986, Choices grantee 1987), Ams. of Italian Heritage (chmn. cultural com.), Costa Assocs. (dir. 1999—). Democrat. Roman Catholic. Home: PO Box 1478 Southampton NY 11969-1478 Office Fax: 631-728-0549.

COSTA, MARY, soprano; b. Knoxville, Tenn. Student, LA Conservatory of Music; PhD (hon.), Hardin-Simmons U., 1973. Film voice of Aurora Disney's Sleeping Beauty, 1959; appeared TV commls., 1955—57; debut LA Opera, 1958; appeared Glyndebourne Opera House, 1958; v.p. Calif. Inst. Arts; in La Boheme, San Francisco Opera, 1959; recorded "La Boheme" for RCA Victor from the stage of Rome Opera Ho., 1961; soloist John F. Kennedy Meml. Svc. at Sports Arena, LA, 1963; as Violetta in La Traviata Met. Opera, NYC, 1964; appeared Royal Opera House Covent Garden, Teatro Nacional de San Carlos, Grand Theatre de Geneve, Vancouver, Lisbon, Kiev, Leningrad, Tbilisi, Boston, Cin., Hartford, Newark, Phila., San Antonio, Seattle; toured US with Bernstein's Candide; appeared English prodn. Candide; tour Soviet Union, 1970; Bolshoi debut in La Traviatta, 1970; revival Bernstein's Candide at John F. Kennedy Ctr. for Performing Arts, 1971; starring role motion picture The Great Waltz, 1972; v.p. Hawaiian Fragrances, Honolulu, 1972; appeared internat. recitals, orchs.; command performance at the White House, 1974; Met. Opera hist. tour of Japan as Musetta in La Boheme, 1975. Named Woman of Yr., LA, 1959, Tenn. Woman of Distinction, Am. Lung Assn., 2000; recipient DAR Honor medal, 1974, Tenn. Hall of Fame award, 1987, Women of Achievement award, Northwood Inst., Palm Beach, Fla., 1991, So. Birmingham Coll., 1993, Tenn. Achievement award, Gov. of Tenn., 1998, Disney Legends award, 1999, Disting. Verdi performances of 20th Century, Met. Opera Guild, 2001; Mary Costa Scholarship established at U. Tenn., 1979. Achievements include apptd. by Pres. to serve on Nat. Coun. on the Arts, 2003; featured artist at Hollywood Bowl tribute to "Walt Disney: 75 Years of Music", 2004.*

COSTANTINI, MARY ANN C., writer, editor, adult education educator; b. Steubenville, Ohio, June 13, 1955; d. Thomas and Anna M. (Slabdorf) Colsh; m. William J. Costantini; children: Thomas Kyle, Susan Michelle. BS in Elem. Spl. Edn., U. Steubenville, 1977; MS in Sch. Counseling, U. Dayton, Steubenville, 1986; MS in Multihandicapped Edn., Ohio U., St. Clairsville, 1991. Cert. K-8 spl. edn., elem. tchr., Ohio. Substitute tchr. St. John's Elem. Sch., Wellsburgh, W.Va., 1977-78; mid. sch. tchr. All Saints Consol. Elem. Sch., Steubenville, 1979-80; elem. tchr., tchr. spl. edn. Steubenville City Sch. System, 1978-79; pvt. tutor, counselor, 1976-79; elem. tchr., tchr. spl. edn. Edison Local Sch. Dist., Hammondsville, Ohio, 1985-90; freelance writer and editor Steubenville, Ohio, 1995—; former supr. aquatic safety and instrn. Millsop Cmty. Ctr., Weirton, W.Va. Freelance writer. Coach Spl. Olympics, 1977, 79; instr. ARC; mem. Girl Scouts USA. With USMC, 1981-82, ret. Mem. APA, Epilepsy Found. Am., Nat. Writers Assn, Internat. Soc. Poetry, Am. Acad. Poetry, Women Marines Assn., DAV.

COSTANZO, NANCI JOY, art educator; b. New Britain, Conn., June 2, 1947; d. Edward Francis and Vivian Evelyn (Allen) Sarisley; m. Joseph Paul Costanzo, Apr. 10, 1974; 1 child, Ashley Allen Bailey. BA, Cen. Conn. State U., New Britain, 1973; MAE, R.I. Sch. Design, 1979; cert. advanced grad. study in Expressive Art Therapy, European Grad. Sch., Leuk, Switzerland, 1999. Assoc. prof. art Elms Coll., Chicopee, Mass., 1985—, also chair dept. visual arts. Exhibited at Western New Eng. Coll., 1977, Springfield Art League Show, 1978, Zone Gallery, 1981, Westfield State Coll., 1985, Valley Women Arts Show, 1980, 83, 85-89, New Britain Mus. Am. Art, 1987-90, Borgia Gallery Elms Coll., 1989-92, Hampden Gallery at U. Mass., 1990, Sino-Am. Women's Conf., Beijing, People's Republic of China, 1990, Monson Arts Coun., 1995, Elms Coll., 1997, European Grad. Sch., Switzerland, 1998-99, Dane Gallery, 2001-02, NY Am. Mus. Illustrators, 2002, Yorktown Mus., NY, 2002, others; one woman shows include Thronja Art Gallery, 1979-80, Elms Coll., 1992, 2002, Dane Gallery, 2001-02, 03-04, 04-05, RI Sch. Design Alumni Show, 2004, Monson Art Juried Exhbn. (hon. mention), 2005; represented in pvt. collections in Mass., RI, Wash., NY, Italy, corp. collections in RI and Conn.; creator Cmty. Art Exhibit for 9-11; contbr. articles to profl. jours.; lectr. Greece, Mex. and China. Recipient Outstanding Arts Educator in Mass. award Mass. Alliance for Arts Edn., 1985, New Britain Mus. Am. Art, 1987, 88; Nat. Endowment for Humanities grantee, 1987, 88; Faculty Devel. grantee, Beijing, 1989, 90. Mem. Nat. Art Edn. Assn., Valley Women Artists, Mass. Art Edn. Assn. (mem. coun. 1984-86, v.p. 1986-88), Nat. Mus. of Women in the Arts, Coll. Art Assn., Nat. Women's Studies Assn., Internat. Soc. for Edn. through Art, Women's Caucus for Art. Avocations: painting, reading, gardening, skiing, sailing. Office: Elms Coll 291 Springfield St Chicopee MA 01013-2837

COSTELLA, LORRAINE ADELE, state agency administrator; b. N.Y.C., Apr. 25, 1936; children: Margaret F., Robert B., Richard L. BS, Bowling Green State U., 1958; MEd, U. Md., 1973, PhD, 1981. Tchr. Prince George's County Pub. Schs., 1968—70, pupil pers. worker, 1970—77, prin., 1977—85; supr. spl. edn. Howard County Pub. Schs., 1985—87; asst. supt. Frederick County Pub. Schs., 1987—92; state asst. instrn. Md. State Dept. Edn., 1992—94; supt. Kent County Pub. Schs., 1994—. Bd. dirs. Upper Shore Bus. and Mfg. Coun. 1st v.p. Kent County United Way, 1997—; bd. dirs. Kent County Cancer Soc., 1994—. Named Educator of Yr., Kent County C. of C., 2000, one of Md.'s Top 100 Women, 1999; recipient Minority Achievement award, Md. State Dept. Edn., 2000, Gov.'s citation, Svc. to Challenge Schs., 1994. Mem.: Md. Assessment Consortium (bd. dirs. 1994—), Md. Assn. Supervision and Curriculum Devel. (pres. 1995), Ea. Shore Supt.'s Assn. (pres. 1997—98), Pub. Sch. Supt.'s Assn. (sec. 1998—99, pres. 2000), Md. State Parent Tchr. Assn. (life) (hon.), Chestertown Rotary Club. Office: 215 Washington Ave Chestertown MD 21620

COSTELLO, CHRISTINE ANN, fine arts director, church organist; b. Webster, Mass., Sept. 13, 1966; d. Robert Ashmore Cozzens and Joyce Alice Redlitz-Cozzens; m. James J. Costello, Dec. 10, 1988; 1 child, Jonathan Ashmore. BA in Music, Mount Holyoke Coll., 1988; MA in Music, U. Conn., 2000. Lic. tchr. Mass. Dept. Edn., cert. dir. fine arts Fitchburg State Coll., 2002. Dir. vocal music Southbridge Pub. Schs., Mass., 1993—99; middle sch. music specialist Auburn Pub. Schs., Mass., 1999—2001; dir. fine arts Tantasqua Regional/Union 61 Schools, Fiskdale, Mass., 2001—. Mem. Music Educators Nat. Conf., 1993—. Mem.: Assn. Supervison and Curriculum Devel., Nat. Art Educators Assn. Luth. Avocation: gourmet cooking. Home: 77 Vinton Rd Holland MA 01521 Office: Tantasqua Regional Schools 320 Brookfield Rd Fiskdale MA 01518 Office Phone: 508-347-7381 x28. Business E-Mail: costelloc@tantasqua.org.

COSTELLO, JOAN, psychologist; b. Lawrence, Mass., Jan. 16, 1937; d. William Agustine and Helen Mary (Dolfe) C.; B.S., Boston Coll., 1959; M.S., Ill. Inst. Tech., 1963, Ph.D., 1967; 1 dau., Cathleen. Clin. psychologist Cath. Charities Chgo., 1960-70; research scientist Ill. Inst. Juvenile Research, 1964-70; asst. prof. Yale U., 1970-77; dean, Erikson Inst., Chgo., 1977-79; assoc. prof. Sch. Social Service Adminstrn., U. Chgo., 1979-85, faculty assoc. ctr. for children Chapin Hall Forum U. Chgo., 1985-2001; adj. assoc. prof. U. Ill. Coll. Medicine, Dept. Psychiatry; pvt. practice clin. psychology, 1985-2001; cons. U.S. Dept. Health and Human Services. Mem. AAAS, Am. Psychol. Assn., Soc. Research Child Devel., Am. Orthopsychiat. Assn. Office: Ste 305 601 Skokie Blvd Northbrook IL 60062-2819 Office Phone: 847-291-0151. E-mail: joan.costello@sbcglobal.net.

COSTELLO, KATHARINE PACELLA, lawyer; b. Washington; BA, Princeton U., 1993; JD magna cum laude, Boston Coll., 1996. Bar: Mass. 1996, US Dist. Ct. (Dist. Mass.) 1997. Ptnr. Pepe & Hazard, Boston. Mem.: Women's Bar Assn., Boston Bar Assn., Mass. Bar Assn., ABA. Office: Pepe & Hazard LLP Floor 16 225 Franklin St Boston MA 02114-2804 Office Phone: 617-748-5522. Office Fax: 617-748-5555. E-mail: kcostello@pepehazard.com.*

COSTELLO, SHERI ANN, primary school educator; b. Grand Rapids, Mich., Nov. 14, 1967; d. Gary Allen and Ellen Hedderman Robbins; m. James Cloyd Costello, June 29, 1991. AA, Grand Rapids Jr. Coll., Mich., 1987; BA, Mich. State U.; BS in Edn., Athens State U., Ala., 1999; MEd, Ala. A&M U., 2002. Social worker Dept. Human Resources, Camden, Ark., 1992—94; counselor/supr. Three Springs, Courtland, Ala., 1995—2000; tchr. kindergarten Decatur City Schs., Ala., 2002—. Mem.: Internat. Reading Assn. Lutheran. Home: 1070 W Sternberg Rd Norton Shores MI 49441 Office: Decatur City Schs Somerville Rd Elem Sch 910 Somerville Rd Decatur AL 35601

COSTELLO, STACY ANN, elementary school educator; b. Camp Zama, Japan, Oct. 26, 1972; d. Ronald Earl and Ellen Louise Boliski; m. Merle B. Costello, Aug. 2, 1997; children: Ethan Paul, Michael Merle. BS in Biology, MA in Curriculum and Instrn., Va. Tech, Blacksburg. Lic. tchr. Va., 2005. Tchr. Chesterfield County Pub. Schs., Richmond, Va., 1995—96, 1997—99, Reynoldsburg Pub. Schs., Ohio, 1996—97, VBCPS, Virgina Beach, 1999—. Curriculum writer NASA, Houston, 2005—. Coord. children's liturgy of the word St. Stephen Martyr Cath. Ch., Chesapeake, Va., 2005—06. Grantee, VBCPS, 2003. Mem.: NSTA. Catholic. Avocation: dance. Office: Ocean Lakes HS 885 Schumann Dr Virginia Beach VA 23454 Office Phone: 757-721-4110. Office Fax: 757-721-4309. Business E-Mail: stcostel@vbschools.com.

COSTIGAN, CONSTANCE FRANCES, artist, educator; b. Hoboken, N.J., July 3, 1935; d. Charles Francis and Joan Aletta (Visser) C.; m. John Francis Christian, June 6, 1959 (div. 1972); m. Michael Krausz, May 14, 1976. BS, Simmons Coll. and Boston Mus. Sch. Fine Arts, 1957; MA, Am. U., 1965; postgrad., U. Calif.-Berkeley, 1971, U. Va.-Fairfax, 1968-69, U. D.C., 1972-73. Cert. tchr. Va. Designer Smithsonian Instn., Washington, 1957-59, mus. svcs. staff mem., 1962-68, drawing and design instr., 1971-76; art and crafts instr. Arlington County (Va.) Pub. Schs., 1970-75; prof. fine arts George Washington U., Washington, 1976—2002, prof. fine arts emeritus, 2003—; curator Arlington Art Ctr., Va., 1980; disting. vis. prof. Am. U. in Cairo, 1980-81; vis. prof. in drawing Haystack Mt. Sch. Crafts, Deer Isle, Maine, 1990. Jurist and judge art show D.C. area, 1975, 76, 90, 82, area show Del. Ctr. for Contemporary Arts, 1985; judge art show Sussex County Arts Coun. Mems. Show, 1991; mem. adv. bd. So. Del. Ctr. for the Arts and Humanities, 2003—; panelist Del. Divsn. of the Arts, 2004— Author: Leonardo, 1982, Elements of Art: Line, 1980; one-woman shows Hodson Gallery, Hood Coll. Frederick, Md., 2005, Visual Arts Gallery, Habitat Ctr. for the Arts, Dehli India, 2003, Lavinia Ctr., Milton, Del., 2003, Soho 20 Gallery, N.Y.C., 1997, Hampshire Coll. Gallery Hampshire Coll., Amherst, Mass., 1996, Dimock Gallery, George Washington U., 1987, Franz Bader Gallery, Washington, 1985, 90, No. Va. C.C., Alexandria, 1983, Barbara Fiedler Gallery, Washington, 1979, 82, Phillips Collection, Washington, 1977, Gulbenkian Gallery, U. Kent, Canterbury, Eng., 1975, Talbot Rice Arts Ctr., Edinburgh, Scotland, 1974, Design Ctr. Gallery, Cleve., 1974, Annenburg Arts Ctr., Phila., 1973; represented pub. collections Hirschhorn Mus. and Sculpture Garden, Washington, Phillips Collection, Washington, U. Iowa Mus., Iowa City, Dimock Gallery, George Washington U., Del. Mus. Art, others; included in numerous pvt. collections USA and abroad Sec. steering com. Del. chpt. Nat. Mus. for Women in the Arts, Newark, 1997—01. Named to Nat. Mus. for Women in Arts to represent Del., 1998; recipient Jurors award, Del. Ctr. Contemporary Art, Wilmington, 2006; fellow, Macdowell Colony, 1977, Ossabaw Island project, 1980; grantee, Lester Hereward Cooke Found., 1978—79, GSAS Facilitating Fund, 1990. Fellow Royal Soc. Arts. Home: 210 NE Market St Lewes DE 19958-1574 Office: 210 NE Market St Lewes DE 19958-1574 Business E-Mail: cfc@gwu.edu.

COSTON, BRENDA MARIA BONE, language arts educator; b. Pensacola, Fla., Sept. 25; d. Marvin Ralph and Irmgard Maria (Minna) Bone; m. Glen Howard Coston, Dec. 21, 1994. AA in Tchr. Edn., Pensacola Jr. Coll., Fla., 1981; BA in English and Comm. Arts, U. West Fla., 1983, MA in English, 1984; MS in Counseling and Human Devel., Troy State U., Pensacola, 1994. Cert. K-12 counseling, tchr. 6-12 English, tchr. 5-9 social sci. Tchr. 8th grade English Warrington Middle Sch., Pensacola, Fla., 1992—93; adj. instr. English Pensacola Jr. Coll., 1995—. Recipient Tchg. Excellence (Golden Apple) award, Pensacola Jr. Coll., 1999—2000, Award of Support for Student Support Svcs., 2002. Mem.: Phi Theta Kappa. Avocations: reading, writing, poetry, feeding wild animals. Home: 3022 N 14th Ave Milton FL 32583-5885

COTE, CHARLOTTE JUNE, social sciences educator, consultant; d. Grace and Jack Georg. BA in Polit. Sci., Simon Frasier U., Burnaby, BC, Can., 1992; MA, U. Calif., Berkeley, 1996, PhD, 2001. Counsellor Nuuchahnulth Tribal Coun., Port Alberni, British Columbia, Canada, 1991—94; prof. Am. Indian studies U. Wash., Seattle, 2001—06. Cons., Seattle, 1999—; longhouse project coord. U. Wash., 2005—. Scholar, U.S.-Canada Fulbright Program, 1996. Mem.: Native Arts Coun. (assoc.; membership chair 2006—06). Achievements include first woman from Nuu-cha-nulth Native Nation to receive doctoral degree. Avocations: reading, travel. Office: Univ Wash Box 354305 Seattle WA 98195 Office Phone: 206-221-6549.

COTÉ, DEBRA NAN, surgical nurse; b. White Plains, N.Y., Apr. 16, 1960; d. Morton and Sheila (Pshedesky) Schwam; children: Matthew Jonathan, Eric Martin. AAS, Rockland Community Coll., Suffern, N.Y., 1981. Staff nurse neurol./nuerosurg. flr. Columbia Presbyn. Med. Ctr., N.Y.C., 1981-84, staff nurse neurol. ICU, 1984-87, rsch. nurse clinician neurosurg. dept., 1987—; mgr. pharmacology unit Health and Scis. Rsch. Inc., Englewood, N.J.; clin. rsch. assoc. Regeneron Pharms., Tarrytown, N.Y., 1991-94, med. safety officer, 1994-96; dir. clin. coordination Mt. Sinai, N.Y.C., 1996-97; cons. Regions Ltd., 1997—99, Noven Pharm., 1999—2001; sr. cons. Ivax Rsch., Miami, Fla., 2001—03; project mgr. oncology PPD Devel., Wilmington, NC, 2003—. Instr. Am. Cancer Soc., N.Y.C., 1989-90; cons. in field. EMT, Spring Hill Ambulance Corps, Spring Valley, N.Y., 1978-81. Mem. Am. Assn. Neurosci. Nurses, Oncology Nurses Assn., Am. Clin. Pharmacology. Home: 3104 Joe Wheeler Dr Wilmington NC 28409

COTE, DENISE LOUISE, federal judge; b. St. Cloud, Minn., Oct. 13, 1946; d. Donald Edward and Dorothy (Garberson) C.; m. Howard F. Maltby, Dec. 24, 1987. BA, St. Mary's Coll., 1968; MA, Columbia U., 1969, JD, 1975. Bar: N.Y. 1976, U.S. Dist. Ct. (so. and ea. dist.) N.Y. 1976, U.S. Ct. Appeals (2d cir.) 1984. Law clk. to Hon. Jack B. Weinstein U.S. Dist. Ct. (ea. dist.) N.Y., 1975-76; assoc. Curtis Mallet-Prevost, N.Y.C., 1976-77; asst. U.S. Attys. Office (so. dist.), N.Y.C., 1977-85; dep. chief criminal divsn. so. dist. U.S. Attys. Office, N.Y.C., 1983-85, chief criminal divsn. so. dist., 1991-94; atty. Kaye Scholer Fierman Hays & Handler, N.Y.C., 1985-88, ptnr., 1988-91; judge U.S. Dist. Ct. (so. dist.) N.Y., 1994—. Mem. Assn. of Bar of City of N.Y. Office: US District Court 500 Pearl St Room 1040 New York NY 10007-1316

COTÉ, KATHRYN MARIE, psychotherapist, stress management educator; b. Oceanside, Calif., May 31, 1953; d. Richard Alfred Kauth and Carole Maxine Brue Potter; m. Dennis Malcolm Coté, Dec. 23, 1983; children: Claire Marie, Simone Gloria, Jesse Patrick. BA, St. Norbert Coll., DePere, Wis., 1975; MSSW, U. Wis., 1977. Lic. clin. social worker, Calif.; cert. clin. social worker, N.H. Psychiat. social worker Napa (Calif.) State Hosp., 1977-79, team leader, 1979-80; supr. adolescent clin. svcs. Solano County Mental Health, Vallejo, Calif., 1980-83; sect. head of residential svcs. for children and adolescents London Borough of Camden, 1983-84; mental health program mgr. Solano County Mental Health, Fairfield, Calif., 1985-87; clin. social worker, county liaison West Ctrl. Cmty. Svc. Ctr., Montevideo, Minn., 1987-90; pvt. practice as psychotherapist and stress mgmt. educator Berlin, NH, 1990—2001; outpatient therapist N.E. Kingdom Human Svcs., St. Johnsbury, Vt., 2000—02; pvt. practice St. Johnsbury, Vt., 2002—. Profl. cons. North Bay Suicide Prevention and Stressline, Napa, 1985-87. Bd. dirs. Coos County Family Health, Berlin, 1990—. Recipient Cert. of Appreciation, Solano County Mental Health Adv. Bd., 1987. Democrat. Roman Catholic. Avocations: hiking, travel, bicycling, cooking, reading. Office Phone: 802-748-1700. Personal E-mail: cote5@kingcon.com.

COTE ROBBINS, RHEA JEANNINE, writer, educator; b. Waterville, Maine, May 26, 1953; d. G. Raymond and Rita Lucille (St. Germain) Cote; m. David Maurice Robbins, July 3, 1971; children: Bridget, Benjamin, Jesse. AA in Liberal Arts, U. Maine, Presque Isle, 1982; BS in Edn. with honors, U. Maine, Orono, 1985, MA in Liberal Studies, 1997; LHD (hon.), U. Maine, Farmington, 2004. Cert. tchr., Maine. Comm. coord. Franco-Am. Ctr., Orono, 1986-96; founder, exec. dir. Franco-Am. Women's Inst., Brewer, Maine, 1996—; adj. asst. prof. U. Maine, Orono, 1999—. Co-editor, designer: I Am Franco-American and Proud of It, 1995; editor Initiative, 1996; co-author: Old Women's Wisdom, 1996; author: Wednesday's Child, 1997, 2d edit., 1999 (Maine Writers Chapbook award 1997). Mem. sys. diversity com. U. Maine, 1998—; mem. grants rev. com. Susan G. Komen Race for the Cure, 1999—; mem. adv. bd. edn. and cultural Franco-Am. Heritage Ctr., Lewiston. Recipient Terry Plunkett Maine Writers Collection, U. Maine, Augusta, 1998, Maine Women Writers Collection, Abplanalp Libr., 1999, Yale Collection Am. Lit. award Yale U., 1999. Mem.: Franco-Am. Studies Com., Maine

Franco-Am. Studies Alliance, Maine Women's Studies Consortium. Avocations: web page authoring, boating, walking, quilting. Home and Office: 641 S Main St Brewer ME 04412-2516 E-mail: RJCR@aol.com.

COTHERMAN, AUDREY MATHEWS, educational association administrator, management consultant; b. St. Paul, May 20, 1930; d. Anthony Joseph and Nina Grace (Harmon) Mathews; m. Richard Louis Cotherman, Dec. 30, 1950 (div. 1973); children: Steven, Michael, Bruce, Gen Elizabeth. BA, Hamline U., 1952; MA, U. Wyo., 1973, EdD, 1977. Comm. coord. Natrona Sch. Dist., Casper, Wyo., 1968—69; hostess TV program KTWO-TV, Casper, 1970—71; exec. dir. United Way, Casper, 1971—73, Wyo. Coun. Humanities, Laramie, 1973—79; dep. state supt. pub. instrn. Wyo. Dept. Edn., Cheyenne, 1979—90; devel. officer Coll. Edn. U. Wyo., Laramie, 1990—91; pres. Connections: Mgmt. and Policy Cons., Casper, 1991—96; spl. asst. U.S. Dept. Edn. Region VIII, 1996—99; asst. dir. U. Wis. Comprehensive Ctr., 1999—2000, dir., 2001—06, North Ctrl. Comprehensive Ctr., 2006—. Exec. sec. Wyo. Bd. Edn., 1979-90; dir. comty. programs HSS, Cheyenne, 1986-90; cons. Wyo. Atty. Gen., Cheyenne, 1990; dealer Profiles, Internat. Dem. precinct chair, Laramie, 1986—90. State exec. policy fellow U.S. Dept. Edn., 1985. Mem. LWV (past pres. local chpts., Wyo. chpt.), Am. Assn. Pub. Adminstrs. (pres. 1987-88), Wyo. Assn. Pub. Adminstrs. (Pub. Adminstr. of Yr. 1982), Phi Delta Kappa. Presbyterian. Avocations: writing, reading, antiques, politics. Home: 704 E 11th Casper WY 82601

COTHRAN, ANNE JENNETTE, academic administrator; b. Buffalo, Nov. 28, 1952; d. Raymond John and Thelma Lorraine C. BA in English, Gordon Coll., 1975; MBA in Specialization Mktg., U. Chgo., 1989; MEd, Loyola U., Chgo., 2000, EdD, 2004. Mgr. 1776 House, Salem, Mass., 1974-75; dept. mgr. Goldblatt's Dept. Store, Chgo., 1975-77; sales rep. Sta. WWMM, Arlington Heights, Ill., 1977-79, Sta. WYEN, Des Plaines, Ill., 1979-81; coop. mgr. Southtown Economist Newspapers, Chgo., 1981-83, div. sales mgr., 1983-88; retail advt. mgr. Lansing (Mich.) State Jour., 1988-90; advt. & mktg. dir. Herald-Bulletin Newspapers, Anderson, Ind., 1990-92; mgr. Dealer Network Advt. Sys. Newspaper Assn. of Am., Chgo., 1993-94; pub. dir. Standard Rate and Data Svc., Chgo., 1994—95; exec. dir. Sylvan Learning Systems, Contract Svcs. Divsn., Balt., 1996-98; tchr. Chgo. Pub. Schs., 1998-2000; dean J. Sterling Morton H.S. Dist. 201, 2000—02; sys. dir. Sch. Dist. 201, 2002—. Bd. dirs. Cabrini Green Legal Aid Clinic, Chgo., 1981-83. Mem.: ASCD, Internat. Tech. Edn. Assn., Internat. Reading Assn., Nat. Mid. Sch. Assn., Am. Ednl. Rsch. Assn., U. Chgo. Women's Bus. Group (bd. dirs. chpt. devel., chair 1987), Ikebana Internat., Rotary (v.p. Anderson suburban chpt. 1992—93). Avocations: theater, ikebana, gardening.

COTHREN, EVANGELINE (MRS. J.C.), retail store owner; b. Light, Ark., May 16, 1925; d. Vance and Laura May (Newberry) Cupp; m. J.C. Cothren; 1 child, Jackson David. BS, Ark. State U., 1944; MA in Bus. Edn., Peabody Coll., 1952. Bookkeeper Vance Cupp & Sons, Light, 1935—, Union Auto Sales, Memphis, 1945-46; tchr. bus. edn. Greene County Tech. High Sch., Paragould, Ark., 1947-74; propr. Evangeline's Footwear, Paragould, 1974—. Sec. Chaffin-Cothren Auto Sales, Paragould, 1983—; co-chair Greene County Courthouse Preservation Soc. Inc., 1991-; chmn. Greene County Scholarship Fund, 1988-, Beaark Endowment Found. Greene County, 2001-; bd. mem. Ark. Cmty Found., 1996-2002. Mem. Paragould Centennial Celebration, 1986, Greene County Sesquicentennial, Paragould, 1986, Ark. Sesquicentennial, Little Rock, 1986; v.p. Northeast Ark. Devel. Council, Jonesboro, 1987— Named Ark. Tchr. Yr., Ark. Edn. Com., 1971, Disting. Educator, Peabody Coll.; 1971. Mem. Paragould C. of C. (pres. 1986—), Delta Kappa Gamma (scholarship com. 1985—, various nat. offices held 1948—). Baptist. Office Phone: 870-236-8137. Personal E-mail: efgc@grnco.net.

COTMANS, SHARON JENKINS, computer scientist, educator; MBA, Old Dominion U., Norfolk, Va., 1983; MA in Computer Edn., Hampton U., Va., 1993; EdS, George Washington U., Hampton, 2006. Sec. NASA, Hampton, 1973—79; computer programmer IBM, White Plains, NY, 1979—81, City of Newport News, Va., 1981—83; computer analyst New Hampton Inc., Hampton, 1983—84; prof. of info. tech. Thomas Nelson C.C., Hampton, 1984—. Office Phone: 757-825-2750. E-mail: cotmans@tncc.edu.

COTRONE, JANICE LYNNE, nursing consultant; b. Arlington, Va., Sept. 11, 1956; d. James Franklin and Ferne Smith Cooper; m. Mitchell John Cotrone, July 6, 1996; children: Philip Joseph, Joshua John, Francia Marie. BSN, Ind. Wesleyan U., 1978, MS in Cmty. Health Nursing, 1995. RN Va. Charge nurse Shenandoah County Meml. Hosp., Woodstock, Va., 1978—79; asst. head nurse Arlington Hosp., 1979—81; staff nurse, cardiac ICU Fairfax (Va.) Hosp., 1981—84; dir. mission clinic Petit Goave, Haiti Wesleyan World Missions, Indpls., 1981, missionary nurse to Haiti, 1984—94, 1997—2001; nurse case mgr. Samaritan Bethany Home Health Agy., Rochester, Minn., 1995—96; RN cons. Hope Wesleyan Ch., Naples, Fla., 2002—. Dir. mission clinic in Haiti Wesleyan World Missions, Indpls., 1981, adminstr. La Gonave (Haiti) Wesleyan Hosp., 1984—94, prof. nursing La Gonave (Haiti) Wesleyan Hosp., 1985—88, med. dir. Wesleyan Ch. Haiti, 1986—88, DON Wesleyan Hosp. La Gonave, 1984—94, dir. surgery Wesleyan Hosp. La Gonave, 1984—94, mission sta. mgr. Wesleyan Mission Haiti, 1991—94, mission/hosp. bookkeeper and acct. Wesleyan Mission Haiti, 1985—2001; spkr. seminars, confs., retreats, and convs. Author: (book) Nutritional Assessment of American School-Age Children; contbr. articles to mags.; featured on radio and TV interviews regarding work in Haiti. Transl., cons. local health dept., physician's and dentist's offices, local nursing homes, Naples, 2002—05; vol. liaison Am. and Haitian comty., 2002—05; poll worker, poll inspector, Creole transl. for 2004 presdl. election, 2004; English tchr. to Haitian nurses Wesleyan Mission to Haiti, Petit Goave and La Gonave, 1981—2001, vol. meal server to 9 Haitian sch. children La Gonave, 1984—94, funded sch. for 15 Haitian children, 1984—2004; field dir. child-sponsorship program World Hope Internat., Haiti, 1997—2001. Recipient Continuing Edn. scholarship, Ind. Wesleyan U., 1994. Mem.: Wesleyan Women (work dir. 2004—05), Wesleyan Med. Fellowship (Continuing Edn. scholarship 1994), Sigma Theta Tau. Republican. Avocations: knitting, travel, composing music and writing lyrics, piano, tutoring school students. Home: 1740 45th St SW Naples FL 34116 Office: Hope Wesleyan Ch 4445 17th Ct SW Naples FL 34116 Office Phone: 239-455-1825.

COTSONAS, ELENA CATHERINE, music educator; b. Oak Park, Ill., Nov. 14, 1955; d. Nicholas John Cotsonas, Jr. and Dorothy Frances Johnson Cotsonas; m. Steve Herbert Fouts, July 15, 1989; m. Walter Donald Otey, July 23, 1975 (div. June 22, 1987); 1 child, Gregory Carson Otey. BS in Music Edn., U. Ill., Champaign-Urbana, 1975. Nat. Bd. Certification 2002. Tchr. grades 1-6 music East Peoria Elem. Sch. Dist. #86, Ill., 1975—77; tchr. grades k-5 music Knoxville City Schs., Tenn., 1979—82, Buncombe County Schs., Asheville, NC, 1989—. Recipient Fulbright Meml. Fund Scholarship, 2003. Office: Avery's Creek Elementary Sch 15 Park South Blvd Arden NC 28704 Office Phone: 828-654-1810. E-mail: elena.cotsonas@bcsemail.org.

COTTEN, ANNIE LAURA, psychologist, educator; b. Oxford, NC, Nov. 18, 1923; d. Leonard F. and Laura Estelle (Spencer) Cotten; children: Hollis W., Rebecca Ann, Laura Cotten. Diploma, Hardbarger Bus. Coll., 1944; AB, Duke U., 1945; MEd, U. Hartford, Conn., 1965; PhD, The Union Inst., 1979. Diplomate Am. Bd. Sexology, lic. Am. Assn. Marriage & Family Therapists, 1987. Asst. to pres. So. Meth. U., 1953; rsch. asst. Duke U., 1947-49; exec. sec. Ohio Wesleyan U., 1955-56, Conn. Coun. Chs., 1958-60; adj. prof. U. Hartford, 1976-78, 1976-78; clin. pastoral counselor Hartford Hosp., 1962-65; asst., then assoc. dir. social svcs. Hartford Conf. Chs., 1965-67; tchg. fellow U. NC, 1970-71; assoc. prof. Ctrl. Conn. State U., New Britain, 1967-93, adj. prof., 1994—2002. Adj. prof. St. Joseph Coll., 1986-96; clin. intern Montefiore Med. Ctr., 1995; dir. elderhostel programs Ctrl. Conn. State U., 1989-93, organizer ctr. adult learners, 1991-93; cons. Somers Correctional Ctr., Conn., 1980-81, instr./rschr., 1980-81; cons. Conn. Life Ins. Mktg. Rsch., 1981-1982; amb. to China, spring, 1986; presenter 3d Internat. Interdisciplinary Cong. on Women, 1987; vis. prof., scholar Duke U., 1989; adj. prof. health and human svcs. Ctrl. Ch. St. U., 1995-2002; vis. prof. Conn. Coll., New London, 1990; mem. clin. faculty, Am. Bd. Sexology, 1994; land developer NC Triangle, 1995—. Author: Comparisons of Gender Differences in Sexuality 1970s/1990s; cons. editor: Jour. Feminist Family Therapy, 2000—, reviewer: Contemporary Sexuality, 2003, Sexual and Relationship Jour., 2005. Fellow: Am. Acad. Clin. Sexologists (clin. faculty 1994—, founder), Nat. Coun. Family Rels.; mem.: APA (chair divsn. 1987—91), AAUW, Soc. Sci. Study of Sexuality (presenter ann. meeting 2003), Conn. Assn. Marital and Family Therapists (clin.) (bd. dirs. 2000—02), Sex Info. and Edn. Coun. of Conn. (bd. dirs. 1994—2002, Human Sexuality Leader of Yr. 1997), Conn. Psychol. Assn., Am. Assn. Sex Educators Counselors and Therapists (supr. sex therapy 2005—, sex therapy cert. com. 2005, Disting. Svc. award 1998), Hartford Women's Network. E-mail: anniecotten@nc.rr.com.

COTTER, EMILY REXANN, social worker, marriage and family therapist; b. Ft. Sill, Okla., Aug. 31, 1974; d. Richard and Mary Frances Enevoldsen; m. Robert Edward Cotter, Sept. 2, 2000; 1 child, Matthew Dylan. BA in Psychology, Rockhurst Coll., 1997; MS in Counseling Psychology, Calif. Bapt. U., 2000. Therapist CBU Counseling Ctr., Riverside, Calif., 1999—2000; social worker Angelica Foster Family Agy., Perris, Calif., 2000; sr. social worker Inland Empire Residential Ctr., Redlands, Calif., 2000—01; social worker Internat. Foster Family Agy., Moreno Valley, Calif., 2001, Walden Family Svcs., Riverside, Calif., 2001—03, ABC Foster Family Agency, San Bernardino, Calif., 2004. Mem.: Am. Psychol. Assn., Calif. Assn. Marriage and Family Therapists. Avocations: son, movies, reading.

COTTER, KA, real estate company executive; Founding mem. The Staubach Co., Addison, Tex., 1979, exec. v.p., S.W. regional mgr., 1987—92, vice chmn., mem. exec. com. and bd. dirs. Office: The Staubach Co Ste 400 15601 Dallas Pkwy Addison TX 75001

COTTER, PATRICIA O'BRIEN, state supreme court justice; b. South Bend, Ind., 1950; m. Michael W. Cotter, 1979; 2 children. BS in Polit. Sci. and History with honors, We. Mich. U, 1972; JD, Notre Dame, 1977. Pvt. practice, South Bend, 1977—83, Great Falls, Mont., 1984; ptnr. Cotter & Cotter, Great Falls, 1985—2000; justice Mont. Supreme Ct., 2001—. Chair lawyer representatives Ninth Circuit Judicial Conf., 1996—98, exec. com., 1998; mem. commn. on judicial conduct Mont. Supreme Ct. Mem.: Mont. Trial Lawyers Assn. (chair amicus com. 1993—99, Public Service award 1992, 1998). Office: Rm 323 PO Box 203003 Helena MT 59620*

COTTER, ROBERTA L., elementary school educator; b. Streator, Ill., Mar. 14, 1954; d. Irvin J. and Lillian M. Morgensen; m. Thomas J. Cotter, Aug. 19, 1978; children: Jessica, Meegan. BS in Edn., Ill. State U., 1976; postgrad., U. Oreg., Portland (Oreg.) State U. Tchr. 4th grade Newtown Elem. Sch., Oakwood, Ill., 1976-80; elem. tchr. Elmira (Oreg.) Elem. Sch., 1980—. Co-chairperson Western Lane Youth Svcs. Team, Lane County, Oreg., 1996—; mem. Crisis Response Team for Children, Elmira, Lane County, 1991—. Asst. coach soccer Territorial Sports, Veneta, Oreg., 1996; co-leader Girls Sci./Math. Club, Veneta, 1996—. Home: 88098 Huston Rd Veneta OR 97487-9525

COTTINGHAM, JENNIFER JANE, city official; b. Salt Lake City, July 10, 1961; d. Miles Dixon and Ruth Eugenia (Skeen) Cottingham; m. Richard Frame Cavenaugh, July 23, 1983 (div. Apr. 1989); 1 child, John Douglas. BS in Civil Engring., So. Meth. U., 1984; MBA, U. Dallas, 2001. Lic. profl. engr., Tex. Estimator Avery Mays Constrn., Dallas, 1981-83, project engr., 1984; owner, gen. contr. Dallas, 1985-89; asst. project mgr. Austin Comml., Dallas, 1989; ct. appointed receiver 14th Dist. Ct., State of Tex., Dallas, 1990-91; mgr. project Dallas Water Utilities, 1990—91, project mgr., program mgr. capital improvements, 1991—2004; adv. bd., vice chmn. environ. and civil engring. program Southern Meth. Univ., 2004—. Dir. CBC Investors, L.P., Dallas. Goodwill ambassador City of Dallas Water Utilities, 1990-92, 95-96, fin. strength com., 1991. Mem. CBC Investments (founding pres.), DAR (pres. jr. group 1989-92), Cotillion Book Club (founding mem.). Republican. Episcopalian. Avocations: creative writing, reading, travel. Office: City of Dallas Water Utilities 2121 Main St Ste 300 Dallas TX 75201-4336

COTTINGHAM, MARTHA MAXFIELD, journalist, volunteer; b. Dallas, Sept. 1, 1952; d. Jack G.S. and Louise Maxfield; m. Lon Worth Cottingham, Apr. 7, 1979; children: Lara Elizabeth, Sara Worth. BFA, So. Meth. U., 1974. Adminstrv. asst. sci. com. U.S. Ho. Reps., Washington, 1975-76; flight attendant Am. Airlines, N.Y.C., 1976-79; contbg. writer Observer-Sun Newspapers, Kingwood, Tex., 1996-97, staff reporter, 1997-98; editor Humble Observer and Sun, 1998-99, sr. writer, 1999-2000; freelance writer, 2000—. Mem. cmty. adv. bd. Childhood Decides at North Harris Coll. Participant class II, Leadership North Houston, 1996-97. Recipient Best Original News Story, Tex. Cmty. Newspaper Assn., 1998, Cmty. Svc. award Tex. Cmty. Newspaper Assn., 1999, award of merit Med. Journalism Awards, Harris County Med. Soc., 2000, 3d Pl. award for Print Journalist of Yr., Houston Press Club, 2000. Mem. Leadership North Houston Alumni Assn. (v.p. 1997-98, sec.-treas. 1998-99, 99-2000), Assn. Jr. Leagues (state pub. affairs com., sec. 1994-95, resolutions com. 1998-2000), Jr. League North Harris County, chair pub. affairs com. 1993-94, treas. 1994-95, fin. v.p. 1995-96, sustaining adv. to fin. com. 1996-97), So. Meth. U. Alumni Assn. (life), Zeta Tau Alpha Alumnae Chpt. (treas. 1991-92, 92-93, historian/reporter 1993-94, 94-95, 95-96, 96-97, 99, corr. sec. 1994-95, 95-96, nominating com. chair 1994-95, pres. 1997-98, 98-99, Alumnae Cert. of Merit 1994).

COTTLE, DEBORAH ELLEN, elementary school educator; b. Argentia, Nfld., Canada, Nov. 15, 1953; US, 1954; d. Robert Allen and Eleanor Ruth Cheever; m. David F. Cottle, June 20, 1981; 1 child, Aaron David. BS, Purdue U., West Lafayette, Ind., 1974; MS, Purdue U., 1975. Cert. Reading Specialist. Tchr. Kanakee Valley Sch. Corp., Wheatfield, Ind., 1976—78, mid. sch. guidance counselor, 1978—86; program developer Westerville City Schools, Ohio, 1993—94, autism cons., 1994—96; reading specialist The Columbus Acad., Gahanna, Ohio, 1996—. Presenter in field. Mem.: Internat. Dyslexia Assn. Avocations: reading, writing, travel, gardening, hiking. Office: Columbus Acad 4300 Cherry Bottom Rd Columbus OH 43230

COTTLE, KAREN OLSON, lawyer; b. Aug. 14, 1949; m. Robert Cottle. BA, Pomona Coll., Claremont, Calif., 1971; JD, U. Calif., Berkeley, 1976. Bar: Calif., Utah. Law clk. to Judge Spencer Williams U.S. Dist. Ct. (no. dist.) Calif., San Francisco, 1976-78; assoc., ptnr. Farella, Braun & Martel, San Francisco, 1978-86; corp. counsel Raychem Corp., Menlo Park, Calif., 1986-96, gen. counsel, 1996—99; v.p., gen. counsel Vitria Technology Inc., 2000—02; sr. v.p., gen. counsel, corp. sec. Adobe Systems Inc., San Jose, 2002—. Office: Adobe Systems Inc 345 Park Ave San Jose CA 95110-2704

COTTON, SALLY JEAN, retired music educator; b. East St. Louis, Ill., July 5, 1955; d. Clifford Leroy and Shirlee Ruth Corbier; children: Daniel Joseph, Julie Ann. BS Edn., Grand Canyon U., 1992; MEd, No. Ariz. U., Flagstaff, 1999, postgrad. studies Yamaha Sch. of Music, 2000—. Conductor piano ensemble ASMTA, MTNA, Phoenix, 1982—2000; music tchr. piano, voice, guitar self-employed, Glendale, Ariz., 1982—; music tchr. Glendale Elem. Sch., Ariz., 1992—2001. Co-author: (pamphlet) Ascending and Descending Melodic Intervals in Song, 1985. Singer Cactus Country Singers Sweet Adelines; pres. Phoenix chpt. Nat. Jr. Fedn. Music Clubs, 1989—2000. Grantee Technology in Music, 1993. Mem.: NEA (rep 1987—), Music Educators Nat. Conf. (co-conductor 1992—2000), Music Tchrs. Nat. Assn. (spkr. 1997), Ariz. State Music Tchrs. Assn. (sec. 1987—88). Democrat. Nazarene. Home: 5747 W Missouri Ave #37 Glendale AZ 85301 Office Phone: 602-290-5299.

COTTRELL, JANET ANN, controller; b. Berea, Ohio, Dec. 2, 1943; d. Carmen and Hazel (French) Volpe; m. Melvin M. Cottrell, Mar. 2, 1963; children: Lori A., Gregory C. Student, Los Angeles State Coll., 1961-63. Lic. ins. agt., Calif. Loan processing Eastern Lenders, Covina, 1962-64; asst. bookkeeper Golden Rule Discount Stores, Rosemead, Calif., 1964-66; acctg. supr. Walter Carpet Mills, Industry, Calif., 1967-69; co-owner Motorcycle Specialties Co., Industry, 1969-78, Covina (Calif.) Kawasaki, 1978-84; v.p., contr. M.C. Specialties Inc., Covina, 1984—, Aviation Communications Inc., Covina, 1992—. Active various coms. relating to promotion, safety and advancement of the recreational vehicle and auto industry, So. Calif., 1981—. Mem. com. Miss Covina Pageant, 1986—, presdl. task force, nat., 1982—, Rep. nat. com., 1986—. Mem. Covina C. of C., Calif. Motorcycle Dealers Assn., Nat. Auto Dealers Assn., Internat. Jet Ski Boating Assn. Republican. Avocations: travel, gourmet cooking. Office: Aviation Comm Inc 1025 W San Bernardino Rd Covina CA 91722-4106

COTTRELL, JEANNETTE ELIZABETH, retired librarian; b. Buffalo, Dec. 10, 1923; d. Benjamin Birch and Mary Jeannette (Ashdown) Milnes; m. William Barber Cottrell, Jan. 21, 1944 (dec.); children: Karen Jean, Susan Marie, William Milnes, Scott Barber, Stephen Ashdown. BA in Sociology, U. Tenn., 1970, MS, 1976; student, Alfred U., 1940-43. Cert. tchr. libr., Tenn. Nursery sch. tchr. Concord Meth. Ch., Knoxville, Tenn., 1964-65; libr. City Sch. Sys., Knoxville, Tenn., 1971-84, ret., 1984. Author: (with husband) An American Family in the 20th Century, 1987; recorder textbooks for the blind, 1983—. Libr. Concord United Meth. Ch., Knoxville, 1975—, reading chair Suzanna Wesley Circle. Mem. DAR, Phi Kappa Phi, Beta Phi Mu. Republican. Methodist. Avocations: singing, bridge, cooking, travel, reading. Home: 308 Camelot Ct Knoxville TN 37922-2076

COTTRELL, LINDA BILLOPS, retired elementary school educator; b. Milan, Tenn., Jan. 2, 1945; d. H. Leon and Dean Billops; m. Dan Fesmire Cottrell, Aug. 16, 1964; children: Chris, Craig, Cindy. BS, Lipscomb U., Nashville, 1964—67; MEd, Tenn. State U., Nashville, 1981—83. Tchr. Chester Co. Jr. High, Henderson, Tenn., 1974—75, Freed-Hardeman U., Henderson, Tenn., 1976—78, David Lipscomb Mid. Sch., Nashville, 1980—2006; ret., 2006. Tchr. So. Hills Ch. of Christ, Franklin, Tenn., 1992—. Mem.: Tenn. Sci. Tchrs. Assn., Nat. Sci. Tchrs. Assn. Avocations: reading, travel.

COTTRELL, MARY-PATRICIA TROSS, bank executive; b. Seattle, Apr. 24, 1934; d. Alfred Carl and Alice-Grace (O'Neal) Tross; m. Richard Smith Cottrell, May 17, 1969 (dec. 1995). BBA, U. Wash., 1955. Sys. svc. rep. IBM, Seattle, Endicott, NY, 1955-58, customer edn. instr. Endicott, 1958—65; cons. data processing Stamford, Conn., 1965-66; asst. treas. Union Trust Co., Stamford, 1967-68, asst. v.p., 1969-76, v.p., 1976-78, v.p., head corp. svcs., 1978-83; v.p. corp. fin. svcs. Citytrust, Bridgeport, Conn., 1983-90, sr. v.p. cash mgmt. svcs., 1990-91; v.p. cash mgmt. Chase Manhattan Bank Conn., N.A., 1991-92, Centerbank, New Haven, 1992-95; v.p. corp. svcs. Lafayette Am. Bank, Bridgeport, 1995-97; sr. v.p. corp. svcs. Union Savs. Bank, Danbury, Conn., 1997—. Bd. dirs. Family and Children's Agy., 1982—; trustee Norwalk Seaport Assn., 1997—2001; bd. dirs. Danbury Vis. Nurse Assn., 2003—; pres. Danbury Vis. Nurses Assn., 2006—; bd. dirs. New Eng. Network, Inc., Bank Mktg. Assn., 1988—91, Bridgeport Housing Svcs., 1985—91, Danbury Cemetery Assn., 2002—04, Gaylord Hosp., 1986—92, 1998—2004, vice chmn., 1991, chmn., 2003—04, chmn. develop. com., 1992—2004; chmn. Family and Children Agy., 1986—87; bd.dirs. Stamford Rehab Ctr., 1996—2004, chmn., 2003—04. Mem.: New Eng. Automated Clearing House Assn. (bd. dirs. 1995—97), Fairfield County Bankers Assn. (dir., pres. 1984—85), Electronic Funds Transfer Assn. (chmn. bd. dirs. 1983—84, vice chmn., bd. dirs.), Phi Beta Kappa, Beta Gamma Sigma. Republican. Roman Catholic. Office Phone: 203-830-6927. Business E-Mail: mcottrell@unionsavings.com.

COTTRELL-ADKINS, LEONE, opera company director; Artistic dir., founder Kitsap Peninsula Opera, Bremerton, Wash., 1992—. Office: Kitsap Peninsula Opera PO Box 1071 Bremerton WA 98337-0223 Office Phone: 360-377-8119.

COTTRILLE, PATRICIA ANNE, retired pediatrician; b. Jackson, Mich., June 25, 1927; d. William Harvey and Audra Powell Cottrille; m. J. Leonard Azneer, Dec. 5, 1974. DO, Coll. Osteo Medicine & Surgery, 1951; MSc in Pediats., Phila. Coll. Osteo. Medicine, 1960. Gen. practice, Erie, Pa., 1952-57; pediatric resident, 1957-60; pvt. practice pediats. Grand Rapids, Mich., 1960-74; pediat. cons. Grand Rapids Osteo. Hosp., 1960-74, chmn. dept. pediats., 1961-74, vice chief of staff, 1972; prof. pediats. Coll. Osteo. Medicine and Surgery, Des Moines, 1974-93, chmn. dept. pediats., 1974-84, assoc. dean student affairs, 1979-93, asst. dean clin. affairs, 1983-93, interim dean acad. affairs, 1985-86, med. dir. Tower Med. Clinic, 1987-93; ret., 1994. Commr. Accreditation of Birth Ctrs., 1993—2001. Contbr. numerous articles to profl. jours. Mem. Nat. Adv. Coun. on Health Professions Edn., Washington, 1982-87, Des Moines Child Abuse and Neglect Coun., 1982-86, Des Moines Select Com. on Drug Abuse, 1990-91. Recipient Alumni of Yr. award Coll. Osteo. Medicine and Surgery, 1983, Extraordinary Leadership and Svc. in Higher Edn. award Carnegie Found., 1986, Alumni Achievement award in medicine Hillsdale Coll., 1996. Fellow Am. Coll. Osteo. Pediatricians (pres. 1971-72); mem. Am. Osteo. Assn., Fla. Osteo. Med. Assn., Nat. Acad. Practice in Osteo. Medicine (chmn. 1984-90). Avocations: fishing, bird watching, reading. Home: 962 Marco Dr NE Saint Petersburg FL 33702-2727

COUCH, KATRINA DENISE, elementary school educator; b. Grand Rapids, Mich., Oct. 26, 1972; d. Kathy L. (Couch) Matthews-Walker and James Lee Couch; 1 child, Trevian Javon. BS, Oakwood Coll., Ala., 1995; MS (hon.), Walden U., 2005. Profl. Ednl. Cert. Mich., 2005. Wyo. pub. schs. diversity com. Diversity Coun. for the Wyo. Pub. Schs., Wyoming, Mich., 1996—2005; climate com. leader Taft Elem., 2004—. Singles ministry leader Bethel Seventh-day Adventist Ch., 2002—03, women's ministries leader Grand Rapids, Mich., 2003—05; music ministries dir. Bethel SDA, 2006. Recipient Least Restrictive Environment award, Wyoming Pub. Sch., 2000. Office: Taft Elem 2700 Taft SW Wyoming MI 49519 Office Phone: 616-249-7627 4542. Business E-Mail: couchk@wyoming.k12.mi.us.

COUCH, MIRIAM KNOWLES, retired special education educator; b. Phila., Dec. 31; d. Matthew and Rosa Knowles; m. James W. Couch (div.); children: Jamir R., Sasha D. BS in Elem. Edn., Cheyney U., 1962, BS in Spl. Edn., 1962; M in Reading, Hofstra U., 1968, ESL cert., 1979. Cert. tchr., N.Y. Tchr. blind retarded, Camden, N.J., 1963; tchr. 1st grade; tchr. mentally retarded, Englishand Spanish manpower program Mineola, N.Y., 1965; ESL tchr. Trenton, 1965; resource tchr. Brentwood Schs., NY, learning disability specialist NY, 1985-94; tchr. retarded Brentwood; tchr. ESL adults; drama tchr. South Mid. Sch., 1988-95; advisor S.A.D.D. Club, 1990; advisor mid. sch. girls SUNY, Stony Brook; ret., 2000. Columnist Amsterdam Newspaper, 1975-77. Pres., nat. nominating com. LI Links, Inc., 1987-91, Nassau and Suffolk, NY, 1987-89; chair youth svcs. com. Am. Diabetes Assn., Melville, NY, 1988, chair bd. dirs. -elect LI chpt., 1987-95, chair bd. dirs., 1994-97, chair minority initiative com., LI Leadership Coun.; bd. dirs. Head Start, Patchogue-Suffolk County; mem. adv. bd. Suffolk County Literacy; vol. Urban Leauge LI, United Way Youth Devel. Bd., Children and Family Mental Health Svcs., Inter-Faith Anti-Bias Task Force, Suffolk County, Erase Racism Com., Intergenerational Com. Stragedies, SAJES -CPR, numerous others; mem. Freeport Arts Coun., LI Women's Agenda, Coalition 100 Black Women, Suffolk County, Am. Assn. U. Women, Islip Br. Mem. Alpha Kappa Alpha (pres. Suffolk County chpt. 1989). Republican. Episcopalian. Home: 18 Greenview Cir West Sayville NY 11796-1603 Office: South Middle School 785 Candlewood Rd Brentwood NY 11717-6600

COUDERT, DALE HOKIN, real estate executive, marketing consultant; b. Chgo., Nov. 29, 1941; d. Sidney and Ruth (Brower) Manowitz; m. Frederic R. Coudert (div.); children Dana, Alexandra. BA, Northwestern U., 1964. V.p. Cross & Brown, N.Y.C., 1975-86; dir., sec. First Women's Bank, N.Y.C., 1980-87; head bus. devel., office of pres. 1st N.Y. Bank for Bus., 1988-91; mktg. dir. Lafer Mgmt., N.Y.C., 1993-94; pres., CEO Coudert Assocs. Ltd., N.Y.C., 1991—; broker Brown Harris Stevens Palm Beach Real Estate, Pal, 1999—; founder, pres. Coudert Inst., 2001—. Dir. Hosp. Tak Co., L.I., NY, 1979—98; creator, chmn., CEO Coudert Inst. at Villa Dei Fiori, Palm Beach, Fla., 2001—. Pub., editor: (book) Business and Pleasure, 1986-87. Bd. dirs.

Women's Rep. Club, N.Y.C., 1994, N.Y. Drama League, N.Y.C., 1975—; mem. nat. bd. dirs. Aspen Art Mus., Kennedy Ctr., 1996-98; trustee, treas. Zoo of the Palm Beaches at Dreker Park, 1996-98, bd. dirs., 1996—; regent St. John the Divine, N.Y.C., 1988. Fellow Aspen Inst. (life); mem. Internat. Womens Forum, Met. Opera Club, Women's Forum Fla. Avocations: piano, voice, dance, golf, tennis. also: Brown Harris Stevens Palm Beach Real Estate Ste 329 340 Royal Poinciana Plz Palm Beach FL 33480-4048 Home: 163 Seminole Ave Palm Beach FL 33480-3732 E-mail: dal1129@aol.com.

COUGHENOUR, CARRIE LEE, music educator; b. Randolph, Vt., Apr. 26, 1981; d. Ronald Lee and Reeta Jeanne Coughenour; m. Gordon Rinker Kohl, July 15, 2006; 1 child, Geoffrey Lee Kohl. BA in Music Edn., Castleton State Coll., 2004. Music tchr. Reading (Vt.) Elem. Sch., 2004—, Orange North Supervisory Union, 2005—. Trumpet player Vt. Philharm. Orch. Choir mem. Pittsfield (Vt.) Federated Ch., 1986—2006, Sumday sch. supt., 2002—. Mem.: Nat. Assn. Music Educators. Home: 96 Music Mountain Rd Pittsfield VT 05762 Office: Orange Center Sch 357 US Rte 302 East Barre VT 05649 Office Phone: 802-476-3278. Personal E-mail: smurfmusicmtn@msn.com. Business E-Mail: ckohl.wvs@ensu.org.

COUGHLIN, ANNE M., law educator; b. NJ, 1956; BA, Tufts U., 1978; MA, Columbia U., 1979; JD, NYU, 1984. Bar: NY 1987. Law clk. to Hon. Jon O. Newman US Ct. Appeals 2nd Cir., Hartford, Conn., 1984—85; law clk. to Hon. Lewis F. Powell, Jr. US Supreme Ct., Washington, 1985—86; assoc. Cravath, Swaine & Moore, NYC, 1986—88, Miller, Cassidy, Larroca & Lewin, Washington, 1988—91; asst. prof. Vanderbilt U. Law Sch., 1991—94, assoc. prof., 1994—96; prof. U. Va. Sch. Law, 1996—, now O.M. Vicars prof. law, Barron F. Black rsch. prof. Vis. assoc. prof. U. Va. Sch. Law, 1995—96. Office: U Va Sch Law 580 Massie Rd Charlottesville VA 22903-1789 Office Phone: 434-924-3520. E-mail: amc6z@virginia.edu.

COUGHLIN, JEANNINE MARIE, music educator; b. Midland, Mich., May 30, 1969; d. Jeremiah Thomas and Marciann Coughlin. BA in Music Edn., Saginaw Valley State U., 1992, postgrad., 1996, postgrad., 2003. Instrumental music tchr. Saginaw (Mich.) Pub. Schs., 1993—. Tennis coach Saginaw H.S., 1998—2000, softball coach, 2001—; dir. Herter Band Camp, 1995—, Mich. H.S. All Star Band, 2001—; cons., presenter Reading and Writing in the Arts, Bay City, Mich., 2001, Success of Baldridge in the Classroom, Saginaw, Bay City, 2001—03. Co-author: (anthology) Reflections: Threads-Words that Bind Us, 2001. Leader Arenac County 4-H Club, Standish, Mich., 1999—. Named Saginaw Valley Tchr. of the Yr., Mich. H.S. Athletic Assn., 2000; recipient Excellence in Edn. award, Mich. Edn. Assn., 1996. Democrat. Roman Catholic. Avocations: reading, writing, sports, music. Home: 2640 Midland Rd Saginaw MI 48603 Office: Saginaw High Sch 3100 Webber St Saginaw MI 48601

COUGHLIN, NATALIE, Olympic athlete; b. Vallejo, Calif., Aug. 23, 1982; d. Jim and Zennie Coughlin. Student, U. Calif., Berkeley. Swimmer U.S. Olympic Team, Athens Olympic games, 2004. Co-author (with Michael Silver): Golden Girl: How Natalie Coughlin Fought Back, Challenged Conventional Wisdom, and Became America's Swimming Champion, 2006. Named Nat. High School Swimmer of the Yr., 1998, NCAA Swimmer of the Yr., 2001, 2002, 2003; recipient Female Swimmer of the Yr., Swimming World Mag., 2002. Achievements include world record-holder in 100m back (first woman under one minute - 59.58); world record-holder in the 100m and 200m back (short course); first U.S. woman to break 54 seconds in 100m free (long course) - 53.99; gold medal, 100m back, 800m free relay, World Championships, 2001; Am. record-holder in over 10 events, including the 50m, 100m and 200m back (long course); won 9 NCAA Titles, University of California-Berkeley, 2001-03; gold medal, 100m backstroke, 4x200m free relay, Silver medal, 4x100m free relay, 4x100m MR, Bronze medal, 100m free, Athens Olympic games, 2004. Office: c/o USA Swimming One Olympic Plaza Colorado Springs CO 80909

COUILLARD, ELIZABETH L., secondary school educator, department chairman; m. Patrick Couillard, 1986; children: Ashley, Jason. BS in English and Econ., U. Wis., River Falls, 1993, MA in Tchg., 1995. Educator Wis. English instr. Wabeno HS, Wis., 1998—, English dept. chair, 2005—. Alternative edn. instr. Tech. Alternatives Plus program Nicolet Coll. Distance Edn. Network, Rhinelander, Wis., 2004—. Author: (book of poetry) Labyrinth, 1995. Achievements include teaching and learning among the Potawatomi. Avocations: writing, photography, travel, music. Personal E-mail: ecouillard@wabeno.k12.wi.us.

COULSON, ELIZABETH ANNE, physical therapist, educator, state representative; b. Hastings, Nebr., Sept. 8, 1954; d. Alexander and Marilyn (Marvel) Shafernich; m. William Coulson, Feb. 14, 1986. Student, Wellesley Coll., 1972-73; BS in Edn., U. Kans., 1976; cert. in phys. therapy, Northwestern U., Chgo., 1977; MBA, Keller Grad. Sch. Mgmt., 1985; postgrad., U. Ill., 1991. Lic. phys. therapist, Ill. Assoc. prof. dept. phys. therapy Chgo. Med. Sch., North Chicago, Ill., chmn. dept. phys. therapy, 1993-96. Contbr. articles to profl. jours. Trustee Northfield Twp., Ill., 1993-97; Ill. state rep. 17th dist., 1997—. Mem. APHA, Am. Phys. Therapy Assn. (Ill. del. 1986-93, chief del. 1991-93), Ill. Phys. Therapy Assn. (chmn. jud. com. 1989-91). Home: 1701 Sequoia Trl Glenview IL 60025-2022

COULSON, ZOE ELIZABETH, retired consumer marketing executive; b. Sullivan, Ind., Sept. 22, 1932; d. Marion Allan and Mary Anne (Thompson) C. BS, Purdue U., 1954; AMP, Harvard Bus. Sch., 1983. Asst. dir. home econs. Am. Meat Inst., Chgo., 1954-57; acct. exec. J. Walter Thompson Co., Chgo., 1957-60; creative consumer dir. Leo Burnett Co., Chgo., 1960-64; mag. editor-in-chief Donnelley-Dun & Bradstreet, N.Y.C., 1964-68; food editor Good Housekeeping, N.Y.C., 1968-75; sr. editor, dir. G H Inst., 1975-81; corp. v.p. Campbell Soup Co., Camden, N.J., 1981-91. Bd. dirs. RubberMaid Inc.; mktg. cons. Internat. Exec. Svc. Corp., Russia, 1998-99. Author: Good Housekeeping Cookbook, 1972, Good Housekeeping Illustrated Cookbook, 1980. Trustee Cooper Hosp./Univ. Med. Ctr., 1982-91; elder Old Pine Presbyn. Ch., 1992-96. Named Disting. Alumni Purdue U., 1971. Mem. Women's Econ. Bus. Alliance (bd. govs. 1987-91), Food and Drug Law Inst. (food bd. dirs. 1979-81), Soc. Hill Towers Owners Assn. (mem. coun. 1996-99), Harvard Bus. Sch. Club (Phila. v.p. budget 1994-95, chmn. program com. 2003-04, bd. dirs. 2001—), Purdue Club Phila. (pres. 1999-), Friends Old Pine (bd. dirs. 1995-, chmn. awareness com. 2005—), Kappa Alpha Theta (pres. house corp. Beta Eta chpt. 1991-2000). Republican. Avocation: Meso-Am. archaeology. Home: 220 Locust St Apt 18B Philadelphia PA 19106-3931 Home Fax: 215-922-4233. Personal E-mail: zcoulson@aol.com.

COULSON-GRIGSBY, CAROLYN, theater educator; d. Eric Oliver and Joan Melonie Coulson; m. Bryon Grigsby, Oct. 13, 1996; children: Eliza, Henry. BA in Theatre Arts, Santa Clara U., Calif., 1987; MA in Medieval Studies, U. Conn., 1994, PhD in Medieval Studies, 2006. Asst. prof. theatre and humanities Centenary Coll., Hackettstown, NJ, 2001—. Dir.: (numerous prodns.) Centenary Stage Co.; contbr. articles to profl. jours. Mem. pastor-parish com. Waterloo United Meth. Ch., Stanhope, NJ, 2001—06. Mem.: MLA, Medieval Acad. Am., Medieval and Renaissance Drama Soc. Office: Centenary College 400 Jefferson St Hackettstown NJ 07840 Office Phone: 908-852-1400 2309. Business E-Mail: coulsongrigsbyc@centenarycollege.edu.

COULTER, ANN, writer, political columnist, lawyer; b. New Caanan, Conn., Dec. 8, 1961; d. John V. and Nell Martin Coulter. BA cum laude, Cornell U., 1985; JD, U. Mich. Law Sch., 1988. Law clk. to Hon. Pasco Bowman II US Ct. Appeals (8th cir.), Kansas City, 1989; atty. US Dept. Justice Honors Program for outstanding law sch. grads.; corp. lawyer, pvt. practice NYC; handled crime and immigration issues for Senator Spencer Abraham Senate Judiciary Com., Mich., 1994—96; polit. commentator MSNBC, 1996; litigator Ctr. Individual Rights, Wash., DC; legal affairs corr. Human Events. Writer syndicated column, Universal Press Syndicate; guest appearances Politically Incorrect, Larry King Live, Hannity and Colmes, The O'Reilly Factor, Am. Morning with Paula Zahn, Crossfire, "This Week", ABC, Good Morning Am., The Leeza Show. Author: High Crimes and Misdemeanors: The Case Against Bill Clinton, 1998, Slander: Liberal Lies About the American Right, 2002, Treason: Liberal Treachery From the Cold War to the War on Terrorism, 2003, How to Talk to a Liberal (If You Must), 2004, Godless: The Church of Liberalism, 2006; editor: The Mich. Law Review. Named one of Time Mag. 100 Most Influential People, 2005. Office: Human Events One Mass Ave NW Washington DC 20001*

COULTER, BEVERLY NORTON, singer, pianist, opera director; b. Dallas, Feb. 27, 1953; d. George Melville Norton and Dorothy May Morrison; m. Fred P. Coulter, Apr. 24, 1981. BFA, Fla. Atlantic U., 1975; MusM, U. Miami, 1977, D of Mus. Arts, 1985. Grad. asst. U. Miami, Coral Gables, Fla., 1976—80; founder, artistic dir. Riuniti Opera, Inc., Miami, 1999—; prof. music. Miami-Dade C.C., 1981—2002, prodr. cmty. outreach program, 1992—; Stanley Sutnick endowed tchg. chair Miami-Dde C.C., 1994—97; prof. music, dir. opera and musical theatre Barry U., Miami Shores, Fla., 2002—. Adjudicator Silver Knight award Miami Herald, 2000, 01. Prodr., dir. numerous operas, musical and shows. Musician Ctrl. Presbyn. Ch., Miami, 1992—2001, Christ the King Luth. Ch., Miami, 2002—, Temple Judea, Miami, 2002—. Mem.: Miami Music Tchrs. Assn. (rec. sec. 2000—01), Music Tchrs. Nat. Assn., Nat. Assn. Tchrs. of Singing. Democrat. Avocations: running, caring for homeless animals, collecting ethnic sculptures, collecting historical manuscripts. Home: 7345 SW 108 Ter Miami FL 33156 Office: Barry U 11300 NE 2d Ave Miami FL 33161-6695

COULTER, CAROL ANN, retired secondary school educator; b. Peru, Ill., July 9, 1946; d. Walter Harold and Pearl Grace C. AA, LPO Junior Coll., LaSalle, Ill., 1966; BS in English, Ill. State U., 1968, MS in English, 1977. Instr. Dixon (Ill.) H.S., 1968-69, Dwight (Ill.) H.S., 1969—2004; instr./coord. Joliet (Ill.) Jr. Coll., 1985—2004. Poet. Bd. dirs. Cmty. Found. for Acad. Advance., Dwight, 1994—. Recipient Tchr. of the Yr. award Ill. Bd. Edn., Springfield, 1985. Mem. Ill. Edn. Assn., Nat. Edn. Assn., Dwight Edn. Assn., Delta Kappa Gamma. Avocations: theater, travel, reading, films. Home: 404 S Saint Louis St Dwight IL 60420-1524 E-mail: cjc404@sbcglobal.net.

COULTER, CAROLYN KAY, information technology executive; b. Aurora, Ill., Apr. 1, 1962; d. John Russell and Sandra Kay (Thomas) Coulter; life ptnr. Constance Dudgeon. BA in History, Pittsburg State U., Kans., 1992; MLS, Emporia State U., Kans., 1995. Chief tech. officer Boston Pub. Libr., 2000—05; info. tech. officer Pikes Peak Libr. Dist., Colorado Springs, Colo., 2005—. Kans. State scholar, Kans. Legislature, 1980, Thomas Jefferson scholar in history, Pittsburg State U., 1991. Mem.: ALA (mem. website adv. com. 2004—), Pub. Libr. Assn., Phi Alpha Theta, Phi Kappa Phi. Home: 88 Stockwell St Castle Rock CO 80104 Office: Pikes Peak Libr Dist 5550 N Union Blvd Colorado Springs CO 80918 Office Phone: 719-531-6333 1100. Business E-Mail: ccoulter@ppld.org.

COULTER, CATHERINE, writer; b. Tex. married. BA, U. Tex.; MA, Boston Coll. With human resources, N.Y.C., San Francisco. Author: The Countess, 1978, rewritten, 1999, The Rebel Bride, 1979, 94, Lord Harry's Folly, 1980, rewritten as Lord Harry, 1995, Lord Deverill's Heir, 1980, rewritten as The Heir, 1996, The Generous Earl, 1981, rewritten as The Duke, 1995, An Honorable offer, 1981, rewritten as The Offer, 1999, Devil's Embrace, 1982, An Intimate Deception, 1983, rewritten as The Deception, 1998, Sweet Surrender, 1984, Devil's Daughter, 1985, Chandra, 1984, Fire Song, 1985, Aftershocks, 1985, Midnight Star, 1986, The Aristocrat, 1986, Wild Star, 1986, Midsummer Magic, 1987, Afterglow, 1987, Jade Star, 1987, Moonspun Magic, 1988, Calypso Magic, 1988, Night Shadow, 1989, Night Fire, 1989, An Intimate Deception, 1989, False Pretenses, 1989, Night Storm, 1990, Impulse, 1990, Earth Song, 1990, Secret Song, 1991, Season of the Sun, 1991, The Hellion Bride, 1992, The Heiress Bride, 1992, The Sherbrooke Bride, 1992, Beyond Eden, 1993, Lord of Hawkfell Island, 1993, The Wyndham Legacy, 1994, Lord of Raven's Peak, 1994, The Nightingale Legacy, 1995, Lord of Falcon Ridge, 1995, The Cove, 1996, Rosehaven, 1996, The Valentine Legacy, 1996, The Maze, 1997, The Wild Baron, 1997, The Target, 1998, Mad Jack, 1999, The Courtship, 2000, Riptide, 2000, Evening Star, 2000, The Scottish Bride, 2001, Warrior's Song, 2001, Pendragon, 2002, Eleventh Hour, 2003, The Penwyth Curse, 2003, The Sherbrooke Twins, 2004, Lyon's Gate, 2005, Point Blank, 2005. Recipient Romantic Times award for best historical romance author, 1989. Mem. Mystery Writers Am., Romance Writers Am., Novelists' Ink. Address: PO Box 17 Mill Valley CA 94942-0017 Business E-Mail: readmoi@aol.com.

COULTER, CYNTHIA JEAN, artist, educator; b. Lincoln, Nebr., Jan. 16, 1951; d. George Wallace and Arlene Jean (Winzenburg) C. Student, U. Tex., 1971; BFA in Sculpture, U. Colo., 1975; postgrad., U. Iowa, 1976-77; MFA in Sculpture, U. Okla., 1980. Instr. Arts Annex, Oklahoma City, 1977-78, Firehouse Art Ctr., Norman, Okla., 1979-80, U. Chgo. Lab. Sch., 1984—85, Francis Parker Sch., Chgo., 1986-87, Express-Ways Children's Mus. Art, Chgo., 1987, Wai Sch., Hong Kong, 1987, Field Mus. Natural History, Chgo., 1987-88, Oklahoma City Pub. Schs., 1988-90, Fine Arts Inst. of Edmond, Okla., 1990-91, U. Okla. Mus. Art, 1991, Okla. Sch. Sci. and Math., Oklahoma City, 1992, St. Michael's Presch., Amagansett, L.I., 1994—, Country Sch., Amagansett, 1994—, Guild Hall, East Hampton, N.Y., 1994—. Instr. SPARK Program for Inner City Children, Oklahoma City, 1989; instr., artist-in-residence State Arts Coun., Oklahoma City, 1989-92, City Arts Coun., Oklahoma City, 1977, 89-92, State Arts Coun. Colo., Denver, 1990-95, BOCES Program, Suffolk County, N.Y., 1994-2003; art dir. Hampton Day Sch. Summer Camp, Bridgehampton, N.Y., 1993; set designer Okla. Children's Theater, 1992; instr. adult art edn. City Coll., Chgo., 1982-84; vis. artist Sch. of Art Inst. Chgo., 1980; instr. art fundamentals program U. Okla., 1979-80; NYFA grantee Children's Art Workshop, Libr., Livingston, N.Y., 1999. One-woman shows include Ctrl. Innovative Gallery, Oklahoma City, 1979, Alternative Space, Norman, Okla., 1979, U. Nev. Sheppard Fine Arts Gallery, Reno, 1981, Lenore Gray Gallery, Providence, 1981, Sch. of Art Inst. Chgo. Sculpture Gallery, 1981, ABC No Rio, N.Y.C., 1984, Gas Sta./Performance Space, N.Y.C., 1987, 1997 Gallery with Alvin Gallery, Hong Kong, 1988, Kirkpatrick Ctr., Mus., Oklahoma City, 1989, Helio Gallery, N.Y.C., 1989, Okla. State U. Gardiner Art Gallery, Stillwater, 1990, Oklahoma City Art Mus., 1991, City Arts Ctr., Oklahoma City, 1992, Brickhouse Gallery, Tulsa, 1992, Conscience Point Yacht Club, Southampton, N.Y., 1993, Ashawagh Hall, East Hampton, N.Y., 1994, TSL Warehouse, Hudson, N.Y., 1996, Leslie Urbach Gallery, 1998, Albright Coll., 1999, Upstate Art, Phoenicia, N.Y., 2001, Saratoga (N.Y.) Arts Ctr., 2004, others; exhibited in group shows at M.A. Doran Gallery, Tulsa, 1991, Individual Artists of Okla. Gallery, Oklahoma City, 1992 (award), U. Ctrl. Okla. Mus. Art, Edmond, 1989-93, Brickhouse Gallery, Tulsa, 1992, Ea. N.Mex. U., Portales, 1992 (award 1992), Spazi Fine Art, Housatonic, Mass., 1992-95, Ashawagh Hall, 1994-95, Gallery North, Setauket, N.Y., 1994 (award), Danette Koke Fine Art/Ramscale Art Assocs., N.Y.C., 1995, Kendall Art & Design, Hudson, N.Y., 1998, Albany (N.Y.) Ctr. Galleries, 1998, N.Y. State Mus., Albany, 1998, Rentschler/Law Gallery, Hudson, N.Y., 1998-1999, Schenectady Mus., 1998, Kendall Art & Design, Hudson, 1999, Upstate Art, 1999, SUNY Albany Art Mus., 2000, Firehouse Gallery, Bainbridge, Ga., 2000, Upstate Art, 2000, Carrie Haddad Gallery, Hudson, 2000-2001, Albany Inst. History and Art, 2002, Arts Ctr. Capital Region, Troy, N.Y., 2002, Upstate Art, Phoenicia, NY, 2003, Columbia Country Coun. Arts, Hudson, NY, 2003, BCB Art, Hudson, N.Y., 2003, Arts Ctr. Gallery, Saratoga County Arts Coun., Saratoga Springs, N.Y., 2004, others; represented in permanent collections at Oklahoma City Art Mus., U. Okla. Mus. Art, also pvt. collections; represented in catalog Exhibition by Artists of the Mohawk/Hudson Region, 2002. Bd. dirs. Renaissance Arts Found., Oklahoma City, 1977. Grantee Inst. for Art and Urban Resources P.S. 1, N.Y.C., 1980-81, Ill. Arts Coun., Chgo., 1983-84, Artists Space Exhbn., N.Y.C., 1987, Columbia Coll., Chgo., 1988, Okla. Visual Arts Coalition, 1990, Pollack-Krasner Found., Inc., 1991, Eben Demarest Trust, 1995, N.Y. Found. for the Arts, N.Y.C., 1998, 2003, N.Y. Found. Arts, 2003, Resident Studio Artist award Pvt. Sch. 1, 1980-81.

COULTER, FERN GOSHEN, retired secondary school educator; b. Zanesville, Ohio, Jan. 29, 1916; d. Charles Mauderson and Janey W. (Miller) Goshen; m. George E., Sr. Coulter, July 10, 1944 (dec.); children: George (Skip) E. Jr., Christine E. Waltz, Margaret A. Nelson. BA, Greenville Coll., Ill., 1938; MA, U. Mich., Ann Arbor, 1943; postgrad., Kent State U., Ohio. Cert. tchr. English, Latin, biology. Tchr. Orrville (Ohio) Pub. Schs., 1938—44, El Paso (Tex.) Pub. Schs., 1944—45, El Paso Tech. HS, 1947—48, Canton S. HS, North Industry, Ohio, 1940—41, Plain Canton Jr. HS, North Canton, 1947—48; tchr., guidance counselor Marlington HS, Alliance, Ohio, 1961—71; guidance counselor Lousville Jr. HS, Louisville, Ohio, 1971—74; ret., 1974. Contbr. articles to mags. Rep. Nat. Hist. Preservation, Zoar, Ohio, 1975—84; bd. dirs. Salvation Army, Louisville, 1971—74; vol. counselor, youth leader Orrville Meth. Ch., 1938—44; tchr. Bible study group, 1998—. Recipient mounted emblem, Salvation Army, 2005. Republican. Avocations: antiques, reading. Home: 3010 OConner Ct Helena AL 35080

COULTER, KATHLEEN MARIE, psychotherapist, consultant; b. Norristown, Pa., July 19, 1970; d. David George and Maryann Gullick; m. Michael Patrick Coulter, Sept. 13, 1997; children: Shawn Cullin, Aiden Kheil. BS in Psychology, U. Mary Washington, 1992; MSc, Hahnemann U., 1996. Lic. Profl. Counselor Pa., 2003, cert. Masters' Level Psychologist PA, 2003, Elementary School Counselor Pa., 2005. Tng. coord., specialist United Human Svcs., North Wales, Pa., 1995—97; behavior specialist, mobile therapist Northwestern Human Svcs., Lansdale, 1997—2000; neurodevelopmentalist Nat. Assn. Child Devel., West Chester, 2000—01; individual, group psychotherapist, clin. supr. Creative Health Svcs., Pottstown, 2001—04; individual, group psychotherapist Psychology & Counseling Assocs., P.C., Pottstown, 2004—. Parent and cmty. trainer, cons. Goddard Sch., Sanatoga, 2003; spkr. in field, Pa., 2003—. Youth group leader Mary Mother of Redeemer Cath. Ch., North Wales, 1996—97. Mem.: ACA. Avocations: volunteerism, coaching, reading. Office: Psychology Counseling Assocs PC 2091 E High St Pottstown PA 19464 Office Phone: 484-686-4855.

COUPEY, SUSAN MCGUIRE, pediatrician, educator; b. Montreal, Que., Can., June 29, 1942; came to U.S., 1978; d. Clarence Herbert and Paulette (Lefevre) McGuire; m. Pierre M.L. Coupey, July 1964 (div. 1981); children: Marc M.R., Ariane S.; m. James R. English III, Nov. 23, 1988. BA, Queen's U., Kingston, Ont., Can., 1962; postgrad., McGill U., Montreal, 1962-63; MD, U. B.C., Vancouver, Can., 1975. Diplomate Am. Bd. Pediatrics, subboard in adolescent medicine. Devel. chemist Merck, Sharp & Dohme, Ltd., Montreal, 1963-64; rotating intern Montreal Gen. Hosp., 1975-76; resident in pediatrics Montreal Children's Hosp., 1976-78; fellow in adolescent medicine Montefiore Med. Ctr., Bronx, NY, 1978-79, attending pediatrician, 1980—; rsch. asst. Cancer Rsch. Ctr., U. B.C., 1967-72; instr., asst. prof. pediatrics Albert Einstein Coll. Medicine, Bronx, 1979-85, assoc. prof., 1985-93, prof., 1993—, assoc. dir. div. adolescent medicine, 1984—2001, course dir. introduction to clin. medicine, 1989—, mem. faculty senate, 1983-84, 88-90, co-chair divsn. edn., 2000—, chief adolescent medicine, 2002—. Attending pediatrician North Ctrl. Bronx Hosp., 1979-97; cons. in adolescent medicine Flushing (N.Y.) Hosp. and Med. Ctr., 1982-96; Maricopa-Pima vis. prof. U. Ariz., 1989; vis. prof. Children's Hosp. Ea. Ont., U. Ottawa and Ea. Can. chpt. Soc. for Adolescent Medicine, 1990; vis. prof. Philippine Children's Med. Ctr., U. Philippines Coll. of Medicine, 1997; chmn. health svcs. adv. com. Children's Aid Soc., 1985—, bd. trustees, 1993—; mem. adv. bd. Office Substance Abuse Ministry, Archdiocese of N.Y., 1983-85; spkr. Hosp. Italiano, Buenos Aires, Argentina, 1999, Israeli Soc. Adolescent Medicine, Jeruseleum, Israel, 2000, Greek Soc. Adolescent Med., Athens, Greece, 2000. Editor: Primary Care of Adolescent Girls, 2000; assoc. editor Adolescent Medicine Clinics, 1990—; assoc. editor Jour. Devel. & Behavioral Pediatrics, 1992-96, editl. bd., 1996-00; assoc. editor Jour. Pediat. & Adolescent Gynecology, 1992-98, editl. bd. 1998—; editl. bd. Jour. of Youth and Adolescence, 1998-04; contbr. articles to med. jours., also chpts. to books and monographs Fellow Am. Acad. Pediatrics (exec. com. sect. on adolescent health 1993-96, Adele Dellenbaugh Hofman award for excellence in adolescent health, 2005); mem. Soc. for Adolescent Medicine (nominations com. 1984-85, chmn. jour. adv. com. 1987-97, program com. 1991-93, awards com. 1992-95, bd. dirs. 1997-2000), Am. Pediat. Soc. (abstract review com. 1999—2001), Soc. for Behavioral Pediatrics, N.Am. Soc. Pediat. and Adolescent Gynecology (bd. dirs. 1993-96, sec. 1996-2001, chair publs. com. 1996-2001, pres.-elect 2001-2002, pres. 2002-03), Sex Info. and Edn. Coun. U.S., Am. Acad. Physicians and Patients, Albert Einstein Coll. Medicine Alumni Assn. (v.p. pediatrics 1983-84, pres. 1984-85), Alpha Omega Alpha (Kappa chpt. councilor, Harry F. Gordon award for outstanding clin. tchg. at Albert Einstein Coll. Medicine, 2002). Office: Albert Einstein Coll Medicine Montefiore Med Ctr 111 E 210th St Bronx NY 10467-2401 Office Phone: 718-920-6781. Business E-Mail: scoupey@montefiore.org.

COURIC, KATIE (KATHERINE ANNE COURIC), newscaster, journalist; b. Arlington, Va., Jan. 7, 1957; d. John and Elinor; m. John Paul (Jay) Monahan III, 1989 (dec. Jan. 24, 1998); children: Elinor Tully Monahan, Caroline Couric Monahan. BA in Am. Studies, U. Va., 1979. Desk asst. ABC News, Wash., 1979; prodr. news show CNN, Atlanta, 1980; reporter, WTVJ NBC, Miami, 1984—86, reporter, WRC-TV Washington, 1987—89, Pentagon reporter, 1989; nat. corr. NBC News Today (The Today Show), Washington, 1990—91, co-anchor, 1991—2006; anchor, mng. editor CBS Evening News, 2006—. Contbg. anchor Dateline NBC, 1994—2006; co-host Macy's Thanksgiving Day Parade, 1991—, Summer Olympics, Barcelona, 1992; contbr. 60 Minutes, 2006—. Anchor: (documentaries) Everybody's Business: America's Children, 1995; author: The Brand New Kid, 2000, The Blue Ribbon Day, 2004; actor: (films) Austin Powers in Goldmember, 2002, Shark Tale (voice only), 2004; guest appearances Murphy Brown, 1992, Cheers, 1993, Will & Grace, 2002, and several others. Co-founder Nat. Colorectal Cancer Rsch. Alliance (NCCRA), 1999. Named News Person Yr., TV Guide, 2001; named one of 25 Most Intriguing People, People mag., 2001, 100 Most Powerful Women, Forbes mag., 2005—06, 100 Most Influential People, Time Mag., 2006; recipient six Emmys, Associated Press award, Nat. Headliner award, Sigma Delta Chi award, Nat. Soc. Profl. Journalists, Matrix award, Gracie Allen award, Peabody award, 2001, Julius B. Richmond award, Harvard Sch. Pub. Health, 2003. Achievements include being the first woman sole anchor of a major US network evening newscast in 2006 (CBS Evening News). Office: CBS Evening News 524 W 57th St New York NY 10019*

COURSON, MARNA B.P., public relations executive; b. Waynesboro, Pa., Feb. 22, 1951; d. Eugene Perry and Charlotte Mae (Sherman) Roschli; m. Sydney E. Courson, May 24, 1982 (dec. 1999); 1 child, Sydney Alexandra. BA, Franklin and Marshall Coll., 1973; postgrad., U. Kans., Kansas City. Reporter Beach Haven Times/The Beacon, Manahawkin, N.J., 1973-74, Dailey Observer Newspaper, Toms River, N.J., 1974-76; comm. mgr. Frick India Ltd., New Delhi, 1976-77; reporter, dictationist UPI, Washington, 1978-80, reporter Richmond, Va.; reporter, editor AP, Balt., 1980-84; comm. coord. St. Luke's Hosp. Found., Kansas City, Mo., 1986-88; exec. v.p. pub. rels. Spaw and Assocs., Inc., Overland Park, Kans., 1988-89; exec. v.p. CCI Pub. Rels. & Mktg. Comm., Inc., Shawnee Mission, Kans., 1990-92, pres. Kansas City, Mo., 1992—. Former bd. dirs. Wonderscope Children's Mus.; active Kansas City Downtown Coun.; bd. mem. Notre Dame de Sion; bd. dirs. Platte County Citizens Coalition, mem. exec. com.; mem. econ. devel. coun. Plate County; former bd. dirs., former exec. com. Mid Am. Youth Aviation Assn. Recipient Prism award for Fund Raising, numerous awards and honors for reporting, 1973—80, pub. rels. awards, 1988—2006. Mem.: Platte County Econ. Devel. Coun., Nat. Assn. Women Bus. Owners, Pub. Rels. Soc. Am. (Pres.'s award with GKC), Internat. Assn. Bus. Communicators, World Futurists Soc., Greater Kansas City C. of C., Northland Sertoma Club, Northland Regional C. of C. Office: CCI Pub Rels and Mkgt Comms 601 Walnut St Ste 200 Kansas City MO 64106 Office Phone: 816-471-2900. Business E-Mail: marna@cci-pr.com.

COURT, KATHRYN DIANA, editor; b. London, Dec. 23, 1948; came to U.S., 1976; d. Ian Howard and Elizabeth Irene (Freeman) Onslow; m. David Court, Mar. 25, 1972; m. Jonathan Coleman, July 8, 1978 (div.); m. Michael

Stephensen, Mar. 26, 1993. BA in English with honors, U. Leicester, 1970. Editor William Heinemann Ltd., London, 1971-76, Penguin Books, N.Y.C., 1977-79, editl. dir., 1979-83; editor-in-chief Viking Penguin Inc., 1984-87, v.p., sr. exec. editor, 1987-92; pub., editor-in-chief Penguin Books, N.Y.C., 1992—, pres., 2000—. Office: Penguin USA 375 Hudson St New York NY 10014-3658 E-mail: kcourt@penguinputnam.com.

COURTENAYE, CATHERINE, artist; b. Madrid, Sept. 18, 1957; d. Richard Hubert and Norma Jean C. Student, U. Bath, Eng., 1977; BA in English magna cum laude, Colby Coll., 1979; postgrad., Mass. Coll. Art, 1980; MA in Painting and Drawing, U. Iowa, 1983, MFA in Painting and Drawing, 1984. Grad. teaching asst. in painting U. Iowa, 1982-84; guest artist Dominican Coll., San Rafael, Calif., 1985; artist in residence Va. Ctr. Creative Arts, Sweet Briar, 1985; instr. Emeryville (Calif.) Youth Art Program, 1985-86; guest artist Calif. Coll. Arts and Crafts, Oakland, 1988, 89, 90, panelist, 1999; artist in residence Ucross Found., Clearmont, Wyo., 1991; instr. So. Oreg. U., Ashland, 1993, guest artist, 1999. One-woman shows include Iannetti-Lanzone Gallery, San Francisco, 1988, Kouros Gallery, NYC, 1989, Bank of Am. World Hdqrs., San Francisco, 1990, Gallery Paule Anglim, San Francisco, 1992,Andrew Shire Gallery, L.A., 1994, Grover/Thurston Gallery, Seattle, 1997, LIMN, San Francisco, 1999, Shaker Mus., S. Union, Ky., 2000, Hunsaker/Schlesinger Fine Arts, Santa Monica, Calif., 2000, Oakland Mus. Latham Sq., Calif., 2002, Stremmel Gallery, Reno, Nev., 2004, Bentley Projects, Phoenix, 2005; exhibited in group shows at U. Iowa Mus. Art, Iowa City, 1984, Art: The Other Industry, Emeryville, 1987, 90, ProArts Ann., Oakland, 1987-88, Oakland Mus. Collectors' Gallery, 1987, Richmond (Calif.) Art Ctr., 1987, 95, San Francisco Arts Commn. Gallery, 1988, Internat. LA Art Fair, 1989, Galleria San Benigno, Genoa, Italy, 1989, Gallery Paule Anglim, 1990, Elizabeth Leach Gallery, Portland, Oreg., 1991, Asher/Faure Gallery, L.A., 1991, Vladimir (Russia)/Emeryville Cultural Exch., 1992, Schneider Mus. Art, So. Oreg. U., 1993, San Francisco Mus. Modern Art Rental Gallery, 1996, Sherry Frumkin Gallery, Santa Monica, Calif., 1996, Jewish Mus., San Francisco, 1997, Patricia Sweetow Gallery, San Francisco, 1998, Jan Baum Gallery, LA, 1998, Jeffrey Coploff Gallery, NYC, 1999, Art Mus. Missoula, Mont., 2000. Bedford Gallery, Dean Lesher Regional Ctr. for the Arts, Walnut Creek, Calif, 2000, LIMN Gallery, San Francisco, 2001, Yellowstone Art Mus., Billings, Mont., 2002, Kala Art Inst., Berkeley, Calif., 2002, San Francisco State U. Fine ARts Gallery, 2006; represented in pub. and pvt. collections including Bank of Am., Folger & Levin, Matsushita Investment & Devel. Co., Osaka, Japan, Pillsbury, Madison & Sutro. Individual Artist grantee NEA, 1989; Ford Found. fellow, 1982-84. Mem. Emeryville Artists Cooperative (bd. dirs. 1994-99), Phi Beta Kappa. Home: Apt 43 1420 45th St Emeryville CA 94608-2928

COURTNEY-WILDS, NOREEN, air transportation executive; b. 1971; married; 2 children. Grp. sales rep. Aer Lingus, 1993; interline sales mgr. Virgin Atlantic Airways; mgr. Bus. Devel., JetBlue, 2000—03; dir. sales JetBlue Airways Corp., Salt Lake City, 2003—. Contbr. author (Bus. Travel Coalition's BTC TravelBlog). Named one of the travel industry's "Rising Stars", Travel Agent magazine, 2002. Mem.: Airline Competition Panel. Office: JetBlue Airways Corp PO Box 17435 Salt Lake City UT 84117 Office Fax: 801-365-2440.*

COURY, KRISTEN, theater director, theater producer; b. Rochester, N.Y., Dec. 28, 1968; d. Gerard Thomas and Gail Hilliard Coury; m. Laurent Chevalier, June 17, 2001. Bachelor's, U. N.Y., Albany, 1992. Cert. arts adminstrn. N.Y., 1996. Dir., N.Y.C., 1998—2000; dir./dramaturg Waiting for the Glaciers to Melt the Musical, N.Y.C., 2001—03; founder and producing artistic dir. Gulfshore Playhouse, Naples, Fla., 2004—. Exec. prodr., N.Y.C., 2004—. Writer (screenplay) Noble Rot. Mem. Bonita Springs C. of C. Recipient Gt. Dane award - President's Undergraduate Leadership award, U. N.Y. at Albany, 1992, Gold award for Best Comedy, Worldfest Houston, 2001, Dir.'s Club award: Best Feature, Fresno REEL Pride, 2002, Disting. Alumnus award, WCDB 90.9FM/U. N.Y. at Albany, 2003.

COUTANT, MARY MCELWEE, retired editor; b. Charleston, Ill., Oct. 14, 1919; d. William Willard Merritt and Mary Emma Turman; m. Laurence Allen McElwee (dec.); m. Albert Syze Coutant. Cert., Utterback's Bus. Coll., 1943. Catalog editor Ea. Ill. U., Charleston, 1967—86. Mem. Coles County Farm Bureau, Coles County Tax Payers Assn. Named to Wall of Tolerance, Nat. Campaign for Tolerance, 2002, Legion of Honor., NRA. Mem.: AARP, Ill. Sheriff's Assn., Coles County Taxpayers Assn., Kaskaskia Archeol. Soc., Ea. Ill. U. Found., Ea. Ill. U. Annuitants Assn., Coles County Hist. Assn. (v.p. 1992—98), Nat. Assn. Ednl. Office Personnel (life), Ill. Assn. Ednl. Office Personnel (life), Nat. Arbor Day Found., Smithsonian Instn., Nat. Audubon Soc., Ea. Ill. U. Alumni Assn., Defenders of Wildlife, Coles County Arts Coun., M.J. Hummel Club, Epsilon Sigma Alpha. Republican. Methodist. Home: 9228 N County Rd #1840 Charleston IL 61920

COUTTS, LINDA DALE, elementary school educator, consultant; b. St. Louis, Sept. 7, 1947; d. John Leonard Dale and Mayrose (Koenig) Fischer; m. John Herbert Coutts, Dec. 15, 1979; children: Christina Lynn, Michael John. AS, Florissant Valley Jr. Coll., 1968; BS in Edn., U. Mo., 1970; MA in Tchg., Webster U., 1975. Tchr. St. Lawrence the Martyr, Bridgeton, Mo., 1970-78; elem. and mid. sch. math. coord. Columbia (Mo.) Pub. Schs., 1978—. Cons. Ctr. for Edn. Assessment, Columbia, 1985-92, Project Construct Nat. Ctr.; presenter Columbia Pub. Schs., 1987—; cons. in field. Editor: MCTM-Drive-In Conference Book, 1989. Co-lay coord. Newman Ctr. Christian Edn. Program, Columbia, 1988-93. Exxon Ednl. Found. grantee, N.J., 1989-, Leroy Sachs award, 2000, Outstanding Educator in Specialized Area, 2005. Mem. ASCD, Nat. Coun. Tchrs. Math. (ctrl. region rep., regional svcs. com. 1998-2000), Nat. Coun. Suprs. Math.(ctrl. region dir., 2000-04), Mo. Coun. Tchrs. Math. (v.p. elem. 1985-86, treas. 1987-92, 98—, pres.-elect 1993, pres. 1994), Delta Kappa Gamma (Beta chpt. 1st v.p. 1986-88, fin. chair 1988-89), Phi Delta Kappa. Roman Catholic. Office Phone: 573-214-3920. Business E-Mail: lcoutts@columbia.k12.mo.us.

COUTURE, SISTER DIANE RHEA, sister, artist, educator; b. Hartford, Conn., Jan. 8, 1952; d. Rheal Paul Couture and Mary O'Shea. BA, Flagler Coll., 1979; student, U. North Fla., 1979—80; student in Pastoral Studies, Baptist Hosp., 1981—82; student in Spiritual Direction, San Pedro Ctr., 1989—92; student in Painted Glass, Klopfenstein Studios, 1995—98; student in Glass Painting, Millard Studio, 2002—03. Sister St. Joseph of St. Augustine, Fla., 1973. With Pine Hills Bike & Mower Shop, Orlando, Fla., 1968—72, Senco of Fla., Orlando, Fla., 1972—73; psych. counselor Flagler Hosp., St. Augustine, Fla., 1975—76; pastoral asst. St. Catherine Laboure Manor, Jacksonville, Fla., 1979—83; counselor Oncology Unit Mercy Hosp., Miami, Fla., 1983—87; youth minister St. Agnes Cath. Ch., Key Biscayne, Fla., 1987—89; dir. social svcs. Fla. Manor Nursing Home, Orlando, 1989—94; dir. Sisters of St. Joseph Archl. Stained Glass Studio, Orlando, 1992—99, Sisters of St. Joseph Stained Glass Studio, Orlando, 2000—. Adj. art prof. Flagler Coll., St. Augustine, Fla., 2000—05; spkr. in field. Prin. works include Meml. Window for 9/11 Victims, N.Y., Meml. Window, St. Francis of Assisi Nat. Shrine, Meml. Window for bay, St. Louis, recovery team for stained glass destroyed by Hurrican Katrina, New Orleans. Recipient Nat. Leadership award, Pres. U.S., 2003. Mem.: Stained Glass Assn. Am. Roman Catholic. Avocations: fishing, hiking. Office: SSJ Stained Glass 2745 Industry Ctr Rd 6 Saint Augustine FL 32084 Office Phone: 904-823-1918. Business E-Mail: LiteArt@aol.com.

COUZENS, LINDA LEE ANDERSON, oncology nurse; b. Alpena, Mich., May 10, 1957; d. Roy James and Celia Jeanette (Swartzinski) Anderson; m. Frank Couzens, Jr., Nov. 1, 1997. ADN, Lake Superior State U., Sault Ste. Marie, Mich., 1977; BSN, Wayne State U., 1980; MS, U. Mich., 1988. Staff nurse Alpena Gen. Hosp., 1977-79, U. Mich. Med. Ctr., Ann Arbor, 1980-81, Catherine McAuley Health Ctr., Ann Arbor, 1981-89; case mgr. Harper Hosp., Detroit Med. Ctr., Detroit, 1989-91; clin. nurse specialist McLaren Regional Med. Ctr., Flint, Mich., 1991-93; nurse practitioner Harper Hosp., Detroit Med. Ctr., Detroit, 1993-96, Oakwood Hosp. and Med. Ctr., Dearborn, Mich., 1996-98. Co-editor chpt. Oncology Nursing, 3d edit., 1997. Mem. St. Paul Altar Soc. (sec. 2001-02, pres. 2002-05). Roman Catholic. Avocations: walking, quilting, reading, movies, home decoration. Home: 14 Windemere Ct Grosse Pointe Farms MI 48236 Personal E-mail: Lroyceland@aol.com.

COVALT, EDNA IRENE, retired medical/surgical nurse; b. May 3, 1935; married; 5 children. Grad., Sch. Nursing, Blackwell, Okla., 1957; AS in Nursing, Grayson State U., 1971; BSN, Wichita State U., 1979. Charge nurse Blackwell Gen. Hosp., 1957—71, Madill (Okla.) Hosp., 1957—71; dir. nursing Christ Villa Nursing Home, 1974—79, Seneca Manor, 1979—83; contract nurse Nebr., Kans., Tex., Okla., 1983—98; ret. Nurse med. pers. pool, 1974—79. Sec. First Christian Ch., Lamont, Okla., 1998-99. Home: PO Box 213 302 S Walnut Lamont OK 74643 E-mail: Landpub@yahoo.com.

COVARRUBIAS, SHERRIE, nurse anesthetist; b. Bessemer, Ala., Aug. 28, 1956; d. John Thomas and Willo Dean (Walker) Kniphfer; m. Armando Covarrubias, Nov. 6, 1986 (div.); children: Melissa Ann, Robert Layne. ADN, Mobile Coll., 1980; BSN, U. Ala., Birmingham, 1990; MS in Nursing Anesthesia, Baylor Coll., Houston, 1992. RN, Tex., Ala.; cert. RN anesthetist. Critical care nurse U. Ala., Birmingham, 1990-92; nurse anesthetist Carraway Meth. Med. Ctr., Birmingham, 1992—. Mem.: AANA. Home: 6020 Longmire Tr Conroe TX 77304 Personal E-mail: sherriecovarrubias@yahoo.com.

COVASSIN, TRACEY, athletic training educator; b. Mississauga, Ont., Canada, Mar. 25, 1972; d. Gino and Joyce Covassin. PhD, Temple U., Phila., 2003. Asst. prof. Shippensburg U., Pa., 2003—05; asst. prof., program dir. undergraduate athletic tng. Mich. State U., East Lansing, 2005—. Contbr. articles to profl. jours. Mem.: Am. Psychology Assn., Assn. for Advancement Applied Sport Psychology, Am. Coll. Sports Medicine, Nat. Athletic Trainers' Assn. (cert., grantee 2002). Office Phone: 517-353-2010.

COVENSKY, EDITH, language educator, poet; b. Bucharest, Romania, Apr. 14, 1945; arrived in U.S., 1965, naturalized; d. Moshe Friedrich Michaeli and Gizy Heinish Michaeli Bizaoui; m. Harvey Covensky, June 26, 1969; children: Jeffrey, Laurice. BA, MA, Wayne State U., 1971, PhD qualifications, 1980. Tchr. Congregation Shaarey-Zedek, Southfield, Mich., 1968—75; instr. Hebrew Wayne State U., Detroit, 1987, lectr. Hebrew, 1998—. Author: Other Words, 1985, Syncopations, 1987, Night Poems, 1992, An Anatomy of Love, 1992, Partial Autobiography, 1993, Origins, 1994, Synesis, 1995, Jerusalem Poems, 1996, Poetics, 1997, After Auschwitz, 1998, Metamorphosis and Other Poems, 1999, Steps, 2000, Electrifying Love, 2000, Collage, 2002, Zohar, 2002, Anatomy of Love: Selected Poems, 1992-2002, 2005; contbr. poetry to numerous publs. Scholarship chair Hillel Found. of Met. Detroit, 2000—, bd. dirs., 1991—. Sgt. comm. corps Israeli Army, 1963—65. Finalist, Nat. Libr. Poetry, 1995; recipient Editor's Choice award, 1995, Internat. Poet of Merit award, 1996. Mem.: Internat. Soc. Poets (disting., nominee Poet of Yr. 1996). Avocations: reading, running, music, tennis. Home: 3816 Columbia Bloomfield Hills MI 48302 Office: Wayne State U 455 Manoogian Hall Detroit MI 48202 Office Phone: 313-577-6267. Home Fax: 248-865-9242. E-mail: edithpoet@aol.com.

COVERT, ADDEY ELIZABETH, art educator; b. Casper, Wyo., Oct. 4, 1977; d. Tom and Kaley Ann Covert; m. Steven D. Lloyd. A, Casper, Wyo., 1999; BS in Edn. and Art, Black Hills State U., Spearfish, S.D., 2001. Summer coord. Arc of Natrona County, Casper, 2000—03; art tchr. Natrona County Sch. Dist., Casper, 2002—. Mem. Cmty. Emergency Response Team, Casper, 2005—. Green Party. Roman Catholic. Avocations: painting, gardening, cooking. Address: Grant Elem Sch 1536 S Oakcrest Ave Casper WY 82601 Office Phone: 307-577-4538. Business E-Mail: addey-covert@ncsd.k12.wy.us.

COVERT, SARAH JANE (SALLY), elementary school educator; b. Waterloo, N.Y., June 6, 1960; d. Robert C. and Barbara (Dorwald) Gerlach; m. Christopher Covert, Mar. 30, 1985; children: Carah Irene, Zachary George, Alexander Duke. BS in Edn., SUNY, Geneseo, 1982; MA, Elmira (N.Y.) Coll., 1988. 4th grade tchr. Romulus (N.Y.) Cen. Sch. Mem. Lake Counties Coun. Reading Assn., Kappa Delta Pi. Home: PO Box 263 Willard NY 14588-0263

COVEY, NORMA SCOTT, travel service executive; b. Cambridge, Mass., Feb. 16, 1924; d. Irving Osgood and Leah (Crowell) Scott; m. Myles Edward Covey, July 8, 1950; children: Chrisann and Cynthia (twins). BE, Boston U., 1947. Tchr. East Hartford (Conn.) Schs., 1947-57; mgr., owner, pres. Myles Travel, Glastonbury, Conn., 1975—. Bd. dirs. C&W Mfg., Glastonbury; computer instr. Conlin-Hallissey Travel Sch., Glastonbury, 1984-86. Columnist for 3 local newspapers. Vol. Foster Parents Plan Outreach Group, 1984—. Mem. Am. Soc. Travel Agts., Internat. Airlines Travel Agts. Assn., Cruise Lines Internat. Assn., Pacific Area Travel Assn., Bus. and Profl. Women, Nat. Assn. Female Execs. Clubs: Boston U. Alumni. Republican. Congregationalist. Avocations: travel, photography, interior decorating, physical fitness.

COVILLE, ANDREA, public relations executive; BA in English Lit. and Journalism, U. N.H. With Franson & Assocs.; joined Infocom, 1984, Brodeur Worldwide, Boston, 1987, mng. ptnr., gen. mgr., pres., C.E.O., founding ptnr. Began career in New England Newspapers and magazines. Mem. Brodeur Worldwide Global Bd. Avocations: family activities, outdoor activities. Office: Brodeur Worldwide 855 Boylston St Boston MA 02116-2622

COVINGTON, ANN K., lawyer, former state supreme court justice; b. Fairmont, W.Va., Mar. 5, 1942; d. James R. and Elizabeth Ann (Hornor) Kettering; m. James E. Waddell, Aug. 17, 1963 (div. Aug. 1976); children: Mary Elizabeth Waddell, Paul Kettering Waddell; m. Joe E. Covington, May 14, 1977. BA, Duke U., 1963; JD, U. Mo., 1977. Bar: Mo. 1977, U.S. Dist. Ct. (we. dist.) Mo. 1977. Asst. atty. gen. State of Mo., Jefferson City, 1977-79; ptnr. Covington & Maier, Columbia, Mo., 1979-81, Butcher, Cline, Mallory & Covington, Columbia, Mo., 1981-87; justice Mo. Ct. Appeals (we. dist.), Kansas City, 1987-89, Mo. Supreme Ct., 1989—2001, chief justice, 1993-95; ptnr. Bryan Cave, St. Louis, 2001—. Bd. dirs. Mid Mo. Legal Services Corp., Columbia, 1983-87; chmn. Juvenile Justice Adv. Bd., Columbia, 1984-87. Bd. dirs. Ellis Fischel State Cancer Hosp., Columbia, 1982-83, Nat. Ctr. for State Cts., 1998—; chmn. Columbia Indsl. Revenue Bond Authority, 1984-87; trustee United Meth. Ch., Columbia, 1983-86, Am. Law Inst., 1998—. Recipient Citation of Merit, U. Mo. Law Sch., 1993, Faculty-Alumni award U. Mo., 1993; Coun. of State Govt. Toll fellow, 1988. Fellow Am. Bar Found.; mem. ABA (jud. adminstrv. divsn., mem. adv. com. on Evidence Rules, U.S. Cts.), Mo. Bar Assn., Boone County Bar Assn. (sec. 1981-82), Am. Law Inst., Acad. Mo. Squires, Order of Coif (hon.), Mortar Bd. (hon.), Phi Alpha Delta, Kappa Kappa Gamma. Office: Bryan Cave One Metropolitan Sq 211 N Broadway Ste 3600 Saint Louis MO 63102-2750

COVINGTON, EILEEN QUEEN, secondary school educator; b. Washington, May 25, 1946; d. Louis Edward and Evelyn (Travers) Q.; m. Norman Francis Covington; children: Norman, Marina, Deanna, Trena. BS, D.C. Tchrs. Coll., 1971; postgrad., George Washington U., 1978-81. Tchr., coach Evan Jr. High Sch., D.C. Pub. Schs., Washington, 1971, Woodrow Wilson H.S., Washington, 1971-95, chmn. phys. edn. dept., 1971-75, 77-81, 1984-87, athletic dir., 1988-95, Anacostia Sr. H.S., Washington, 1995—, chmn. dept. health and phys. edn., tchr. health/phys. edn., 1995—, swim coach, 1996, softball coach, 1996—, student activities dir., 1995. Cons. Coaches Assn., Washington, 1973-76; athletic dir. Woodrow Wilson H.S., 1988-95; pres. DCAA Athletic Dir. Assn., 1997—; sports chmn. in field. Named Coach of Yr., Ea. Bd. Ofcls., 1977, Nat. Coaches Assn. 2d Region, 1982, 86, Nat. Fedn. State H.S. Assns., 2000, Winningest Coach Washington Coaches Assn., 1982, Coach of Yr. U.S., 1986, Coach of Yr. Washington Post, 1987, Athletic Dir. of Yr., 1989, Volleyball All-Interhigh Coach, 1989; recipient Billie Jean King award Women Sports and Am. Fedn. Coaches, 1980-81, Disting. Women award D.C. Polit. Women Com., 1996, D.C. Women's Bd. Affiliated Chs., 1996; inducted into Nat. High Sch. Athletic Coaches Assn. Hall of Fame, 2000. Mem. NAFE, Nat. High Sch. Athletic Coaches Assn. (bd. dirs., named to Hall of Fame 2000, regional dir. region II), D.C. Coaches Assn. (3rd v.p., v.p. volleyball 1981-83, softball coach 1990, Athletic Dir. of Yr. 1992, pres. 1993-96, chmn. crew coun. 1994, Regional Softball Coach of the Yr. 1993, Coach of the Yr. in Volleyball and Softball 1993, Softball Coach of Yr. 1994, 95, Coach/Athletic Dir. of Yr. 1988), NIAAA and D.C. Coaches Assn. (named Athletic Dir. of Yr. 1998, mem. dir.), Assn. Health, Phys. Edn. Athletics, D.C. High Sch. Coaches Club, Women's Sports Found., DCIAA (pres. athletic dir. 1997—). Home: 7601 Ingrid Pl Landover MD 20785-4624 Office: Anacostia Sr HS 16 & R Sts SE Washington DC 20020 Office Phone: 202-698-2173. Personal E-mail: ecovin@hotmail.com.

COVINGTON, GERMAINE WARD, municipal agency administrator; BS in Social Work, Ind. State U., 1966; MA in Urban Studies, Occidental Coll., 1972; postgrad., Harvard U., 1998. Budget analyst City of Seattle, Office Mgmt. and Budget, 1978-87; cmty. affairs mgr. City of Seattle, Engring. Dept., 1987-90, property and ct. svcs. mgr., 1990-91, dir. exec. mgmt., 1993-94, acting dir. drainage and wastewater utility, 1993-94; dep. chief staff City of Seattle, Mayor's Office, 1991-93; dir. office for civil rights City of Seattle, 1994—. Office: Seattle Office for Civil Rights 700 3rd Ave Ste 250 Seattle WA 98104-1827 Office Phone: 206-684-4500. E-mail: germaine.covington@seattle.gov.

COVINGTON, PATRICIA ANN, university administrator; b. Mt. Vernon, Ill., June 21, 1946; d. Charles J. and Lois Ellen (Combs) C.; m. Burl Vance Beene, Aug. 10, 1968 (div. 1981). BA, U. N.Mex., 1968; MS in Ed., So. Ill. U., 1974, PhD, 1981. Prof. art, asst. dir. Sch. Art So. Ill. U., Carbondale, 1974-88, asst. dir. in admissions and records, 1988-95, assoc. dir. in admissions and records, 1995—2003; cons. records/registration & academic affairs, 2003—04; land developer Fla., 2004—. Mem. Am. Coun. on Edn., Nat. Com. for Army, Registry Transcript, AARTS SMART (Sailor, Marines Registry Transcript); mem. tech. com. Ill. Articulation Initiative, Ill. Bd. Higher Edn.; vis. curator Mitchell Mus., Mt. Vernon, 1977-83, judge dept. conservation; mem. panel Ill. Arts Coun., Chgo., 1982; faculty advisor European Bus. Seminar, London, 1983; edn. cons. Ill. Dept. Aging, Springfield, 1978-81, Apple Computer, Cupertino, Calif., 1982-83; mem. adminstrv. profl. coun. Soc. Ill. U., 1989-93; presenter in field. Exhibited papercastings in nat. and internat. shows in Chgo., Fla., Calif., Tenn., N.Y. and others, 1974—; author: Diary of a Workshop, 1979, History of the School of Art at Southern Illinois University at Carbondale, 1981, Guidelines of Transcripts & Records, 2003; co-author: AACRAO Transcript and Record Guide, 2003; reviewer Mayfield Pub., Random House, William C. Brown, Holt, Reinhart & Winston. Bd. dirs. Humanities Couns. John A. Logan Coll., Carterville, Ill., 1982-88; mem. Ill. Higher Edn. Art Assn., chmn. bd. dirs., 1978-88; mem. Post-Doctoral Acad., 1981-95; sec. adminstrv. profl. coun., 1989-90; del. Girl Scouts USA, 1992-93, 97-2004, bd. dirs., mgmt. com., bldg. com., devel. com., nominating com., Shagbark Coun., treas., 2003, fin. com., 2003—, chair assessment com., 2003-04. Grantee Kresge Found., 1978, Nat. Endowment for the Arts, 1977, 81, Ill. Bd. Higher Edn. HECA grantee, 1994, 95; named Outstanding Young Woman of Yr. for Ill., 1981, Woman of Distinction Girl Scouts U.S.A., Thanks Badge, 2004, Pride of Shagbark, 2003. Fellow Ill. Ozarks Craft Guild (bd. dirs. 1976-83); mem. Am. Assn. Coll. Registrars and Admissions Officers (task force on transcript guidelines 2001-03), Ill. Assn. Coll. Registrars and Admissions Officers (chair so. dist., exec. com. 1992-93, nominating com. 1993-94), Spinx (hon.), Rhen Soc., Chancellor's Coun., Phi Kappa Phi. Presbyterian. Home: 3415 Ceitus Pkwy Cape Coral FL 33991 Business E-Mail: mmouse@siu.edu.

COVINGTON, STEPHANIE STEWART, psychotherapist, writer, educator; b. Whittier, Calif., Nov. 5, 1942; d. William and Bette (Robertson) Stewart; children: Richard, Kim. BA cum laude, U. So. Calif., 1963; MSW, Columbia U., 1970; PhD, Union Inst., 1982. Diplomate Am. Bd. Sexology, Am. Bd. Med. Psychotherapists. Pvt. practice Inst. for Relational Devel., La Jolla, Calif., 1981—; co-dir. Ctr. for Gender and Justice, La Jolla, Calif., 1981—. Instr. U. Calif., San Diego, 1981—, Calif. Sch. Profl. Psychology, San Diego, 1982-88, San Diego State U., 1982-84, Southwestern Sch. Behavioral Health Studies, 1982-84, Profl. Sch. Humanistic Psychology, San Diego, 1983-84, U.S. Internat. U., San Diego, 1983-84, UCLA, 1983-84, U. So. Calif., L.A., 1983-84, U. Utah, Salt Lake City, 1983-84; co-dir. Inst. Relational Devel.; cons. L.A. County Sch. Dist., N.C. Dept. Mental Health, Nat. Ctrs. Substance Abuse Treatment and Prevention, Nat. Inst. Corrections, others; designer women's treatment, cons. Betty Ford Ctr.; presenter and lectr. in field; addiction cons. criminal justice sys. Author: Leaving the Enchanted Forest: The Path from Relationship Addiction to Intimacy, 1988, Awakening Your Sexuality: A Guide for Recovering Women, 2000, A Woman's Way Through the Twelve Steps, 1994, Helping Women Recover: A Program for Treating Addiction (with spl. edit. for criminal justice sys.), 1999, A Womans Way Through the Twelve Steps Workbook, 2000, Beyond Trauma: A Healing Journey for Women, 2003, Voices: A Program of Self-Discovery and Empowerment for Girls, 2004; contbr. articles to profl. jours. Mem. NASW (diplomate), Am. Assn. Sex Educators, Counselors and Therapists, Am. Pub. Health Assn., Am. Assn. Marriage and Family Therapy, Assn. Women in Psychology, Calif. Women's Commn. on Alcoholism (Achievement award), Am. Soc. Criminology, Western Soc. Criminology, Internat. Coun. on Alcoholism and Addictions (past chair women's com.). Avocations: reading, theater, raising orchids. Office: 7946 Ivanhoe Ave Ste 201B La Jolla CA 92037-4517 Office Phone: 858-454-8528. Personal E-mail: sc@stephaniecovington.com.

COWAN, AMY MICHELLE, elementary school educator; b. Huntington, W.Va., Dec. 27, 1975; d. Glenn Thomas and Sandra Lynn Hall; m. David Eddie Cowan, Aug. 10, 2002; 1 child, Dylan Thomas. BA in Humanities, Bluefield State Coll., 2001, BA in Social Studies, 2002. Mem. direct care staff Autism Services Ctr., Huntington, 1996—98; clin. supr. ResCare, Princeton, W.Va., 1999—2003; tchr. exceptional children Person County Schs., Roxboro, NC, 2003—. Mem.: Pi Gamma Mu (hon.). Democrat. Home: 358 Water Front Lane Timberlake NC 27583 Office: Northern Middle Sch 1935 Carver Drive Roxboro NC 27573 Office Phone: 336-599-6344. Personal E-mail: acowan29@yahoo.com. Business E-Mail: cowana@person.k12.nc.us.

COWAN, JOYCE A., lawyer; BA in Polit. Sci. cum laude, U. Wash., 1983; JD with honors, George Washington U., 1986. Ptnr. Epstein Becker & Green, Washington, Sonnenschein Nath & Rosenthal LLP, Washington, 2004—. Mem.: ABA (mem. health law sect.), Am. Health Lawyers Assn. Office: Sonnenschein Nath & Rosenthal LLP Ste 600, E Tower 1301 K St NW Washington DC 20005 Office Phone: 202-408-3239. Office Fax: 202-408-6399. Business E-Mail: jcowan@sonnenschein.com.

COWAN, MARIE JEANETTE, dean, nurse, medical educator; b. Albuquerque, July 20, 1938; d. Adrian Joseph and Leila Bernice (Finley) Johnson; m. Samuel Joseph Cowan, Aug. 14, 1961; children: Samuel Joseph, Kathryn Anne, Michelle Dionne. Diploma, Mary's Help Coll., 1961; BS, U. Wash., 1964, MS, 1972, PhD, 1979. Charge nurse Herrick Meml. Hosp., Berkeley, Calif., 1961-62; staff nurse ICU Univ. Hosp., Seattle, 1966-68; asst. prof. Seattle U., 1972-75; from asst. prof. to prof. nursing U. Wash., Seattle, 1979-97, assoc. dean rsch., 1985-96; dean UCLA Sch. Nursing, 1997—. Rsch. grant reviewer Am. Heart Assn. Wash., Seattle, 1977-82, divsn. rsch. grants reviewer nursing study sect., 1987-90; chair CVN AHA, 1989-91. Mem. editl. bd. Ann. Rev. Nursing Rsch., Rsch. in Nursing and Health, Nursing Rsch.; contbr. articles to profl. jours. Grantee, NIH, 1977, 1981, 1984, 1985, 1991, 1996, 2000. Fellow: Am. Acad. Nursing; mem.: ANA, AACN, Wash. State Nurses Assn., Calif. State Nurses Assn. Roman Catholic. Office: UCLA Sch Nursing PO Box 951702 Los Angeles CA 90095-1702

COWAN, RHONDA RENEE, nurse, social worker; d. Joe Walker Lassiter and Opal Orene Jordan; m. Robert Allen Cowan, Jr, Jan. 29, 1999; children: Kevin Lloyd Cottrell, Meredith Renee Cottrell. AS in Nursing, Jefferson Davis Coll., Brewton, Ala., 1979, AA, 1987; BA in Social Work, U. W.Fla., Pensacola, 1998; postgrad. in Pub. and Cmty. Health Nursing, U. S.Ala., Mobile, 2005—. RN Fla., gen. nursing practice cert., ANCC, 1995. Staff RN State Fla. Dept. Corrections, Milton, 1999—2001, W.Fla. Hosp., Pensacola,

2002—04; admissions nurse Covenant Hospice, Pensacola, 2003—04; case mgr./discharge planner Santa Rosa Med. Ctr., Milton, Fla., 2004—05. Mem.: ANA, Fla. Nurses Assn. Avocations: walking, tennis, reading, crafts/cross stitch & quilting.

COWARD, PATRICIA ANN, language educator; b. Oswego, N.Y., Nov. 2, 1954; d. Charles John and Ann Elizabeth (Daly) C.; m. Sanford J. MacMillen, Dec. 26, 1980; children: Emma Rose, Kathrine Daly, Therese Burns. BA, SUNY, Fredonia, 1976, MA, 1978; PhD, Bowling Green State U., 1990. Instr. SUNY, Oswego, 1979-81, Wayne State Coll., Nebr., 1981-84; grad. fellow Bowling Green State U., Ohio, 1984-88; lectr. Bowling Green State U., 1988-90; assoc. prof. Frostburg State U., Md., 1990—96, prof., 1996—2005; dir. faculty devel. and ctr. for tchg. excellence Canisius Coll., Buffalo, 2005—. Bd. dirs. Family Crisis Resource Ctr., Cumberland, Md., 1991-2005. Mem. MLA (field bibliographer 1987-2000), Coll. Conf. on Composition and Comm., NCTE. Office: Frostburg State U Frostburg MD 21532 Home: 218 N Forest Rd Williamsville NY 14221

COWEN, JEAN, employee benefits consultant; b. Winthrop, Mass., Jan. 9, 1965; d. George Milton and Barbara Jean Cowen; m. Michael David Violet, Oct. 15, 1994; children: William Michael Violet, Caitlin Elizabeth Violet, Caitlin Elizabeth Violet. BS in Psychology, U. Mass., 1988, BA in Econs., 1988; MBA, Clark U., 1994. Cert. profl. ins. woman; cert. ins. svc. rep. Multiple employeer trust coord. Home Life, Wellesley Hills, Mass., 1988-91; agt. svc. rep. Consol. Group, Framingham, Mass., 1991-92; sr. account exec. Roblin Ins. Agy., Needham, Mass., 1992-94; account mgr. William Gallager Assocs., Boston, 1994-95; prodr. Van Gilder Ins. Corp., Colorado Springs, Colo., 1996-99; sr. account exec. McLean (Va.) Ins. Agy., 2001—. Mem. citizens goals Leadership Pikes Peak, 1988; active Jr. League, Colorado Springs; mem. nominating and fin. com. Wagon Wheel coun. Girl Scouts U.S., 1988—; vol. Women's Resource Ctr., Colorado Springs, 1996-98; sponsor Air Force Cadet Sponsor Program, 1995-97. Mem. Nat. Assn. Health Underwriters (pres.'s coun. 1988), Ins. Women Colorado Springs (pres. 1997-99, dir. 1996-97, Ins. Profl. of Yr. award 1995—), So. Colo. Assn. Health Underwriters, Colo. U. Exec. Club, Clark U. Alumni Assn., U. Mass. Alumni Assn., Soc. Cert. Ins. Svc. Reps., So. Colo. Ins. Profls., Soc. Cert. Resume Writers. Avocations: scuba, Tae Kwon Do, running, downhill skiing.

COWGER, KARIN R., literature and language educator; b. Waterloo, Iowa, Jan. 25, 1968; d. Richard Paul and Hildegard Mehlich; m. James P. Cowger, June 13, 1998. B, U. Iowa, Iowa City, 1990, M, 1991. Tchr. English Richland Sch. Dist. #1, Columbia, SC, 1991—95, Chariton Cmty. Schs., Iowa, 1995—99, Ankeny Cmty. Schs., 1999—. Yearbook advisor Ankeny Cmty. Schs., Iowa, 1999—2005. Mem.: NEA. Avocations: reading, writing, photography. Office: Ankeny HS 1302 N Ankeny Blvd Ankeny IA 50023-4010

COWGER, SHARI ANN, music educator; d. Richard Paul and Janet Leatrice Negley; m. Jerry W. Cowger, Sept. 18, 1999; children: Savannah Paige Boggess, Kylie Glen Boggess, Noah Paul Boggess. BS in Edn., N.W. Mo. State U., Maryville, 1980; MEd, U. of Idaho, Moscow/Boise, 2006. Classified sales mgr. The Daily Tribune, Ames, Iowa, 1986—90; advt. sales KMVT TV, Twin Falls, Idaho, 1990—98; elem. music tchr. Twin Falls Sch. Dist., 1998—. Pvt. music instr. Magic Valley Sch. of Performing Arts, Twin Falls, 2002—. Sunday sch. tchr. Twin Falls Ref. Ch., Twin Falls, 2000—02, pianist, 2005. Mem.: Nation Orff Orgn. R-Consevative. Office: Oregon Trail Elementary School 660 Park Ave Twin Falls ID 83301 Office Phone: 208-733-8480. Home Fax: None. E-mail: cowgersh@tfsd.k12.id.us.

COWGILL, URSULA MOSER, biologist, educator, environmental consultant; b. Bern, Switzerland, Nov. 9, 1927; came to U.S., 1943, naturalized, 1945; d. John W. and Mara (Siegrist) Moser. AB, Hunter Coll., 1948; MS, Kans. State U., 1952; PhD, Iowa State U., 1956. Staff MIT, Lincoln Lab., Lexington, Mass., 1957-58; field work Doherty Found., Guatemala, 1958-60; research assoc. dept. biology Yale U., New Haven, 1960-68; prof. biology and anthropology U. Pitts., 1968-81; environ. scientist Dow Chem. Co., Midland, Mich., 1981-84, assoc. environ. cons., 1984-91; environ. cons., 1991—. Environ. measurements adv. com. Sci. Adv. Bd. EPA, 1976-80; Internat. Joint Commn., 1984-89. Contbr. articles to profl. jours. Trustee Carnegie Mus., Pitts., 1971-75. Grantee NSF 1960-78, Wenner Gren Found., 1965-66, Penrose fund Am. Philos. Soc., 1978; Sigma Xi grant-in-aid, 1965-66 Mem. AAAS, Am. Soc. Limnology and Oceanography, Internat. Soc. Theoretical and Applied Limnology. Achievements include research in ecology, biology and minerology. Home and Office: PO Box 1329 Carbondale CO 81623-1329 E-mail: ucowgill@sopris.net, ucowgill@direcway.com.

COWIN, JUDITH ARNOLD, state supreme court judge; b. Boston, Apr. 29, 1942; m. William I. Cowin, 1965; 3 children. BA, Wellesley Coll., 1963; LLD, Harvard U., 1970. Asst. legal counsel Mass. Dept. Mental Health, 1971—72; legal counsel for chief justice Mass. Dist. Ct., 1972—79; asst. dist. atty. Norfolk County, 1979—91; judge Mass. Superior Ct., 1991—99; justice Mass. Supreme Jud. Ct., Boston, 1999—. Clinical field supervisor Harvard Law Sch., 1980. Office: Mass Supreme Judicial Ct One Pemberton Sq #2 Boston MA 02108

COWLES, ELIZABETH HALL, program consultant; b. Wichita Falls, Tex., Aug. 27, 1936; d. Eugene DeWitt and Lorena (Perry) Hall; m. James Edgar Cowles, Dec. 26, 1957 (div. Jan. 1989); children: Gary Randall, Jan Alison Cowles Sendker, Richard Scott. BS in Edn., North Tex. State U., Denton, 1958; MAIS, U. Tex., Dallas, 1994. Elem. tchr. Long Beach (Calif.) Ind. Sch. Dist., 1958—59; tchr. 6th grade Austin (Tex.) Ind. Sch. Dist., 1960—62; statewide project dir. Rainbow Days, Inc., Dallas, 1989—90; LIFESPAN exec. dir. Dallas County Hosp. Dist., Dallas, 1990—94; Dallas Healthy Start exec. dir. Fed. Initiative Dallas County Hosp. Dist., Dallas, 1994—98; nat. cons. cmty. collaboration, program devel., resource devel., 1999—. State pres. Tex. Coalition for Juvenile Justice, Dallas, 1983-84; mem. adv. com. Tex. Juvenile Probation Commn., Austin, 1987-88. Author: Early Influences on Development of English Language, 1994; initiated Listener Project, 1981. Pres. bd. dirs. Lone Star coun. Camp Fire, Dallas, 1986-87; mem. nat. steering com. Camp Fire, Inc., Kansas City, Kans., 1989; bd. dirs. United Way of Met. Dallas, 1988-89; pres. bd. dirs. Women's Coun. Dallas County, 1988-89; mem. pub. affairs com. Mental Health Assn.; mem. cmty. leaders forum Ctr. for Non-Profit Mgmt., 1996-97; mem. cmty. action com. Dallas Coun. on Alcohol and Drug Abuse, 1996-97; chair adminstrv. bd. Lovers Lane United Meth. Ch., 1997; dir. Juvenile Justice. Recipient Cmty. Advocacy award Dallas County Juvenile Dept., 1985, Gulick award for cmty. svc. Camp Fire, Inc., 1989, Women Helping Women award Women's Ctr. of Dallas County, 1995, Susan B. Anthony award United Meth. Ch., 1997, Award for Ednl. Excellence in Programming Planned Parenthood of Dallas, 1998. Mem. LWV (bd. dirs. 1982-85), Nat. Assn. Healthy Start (founding mem. bd. dirs. 1998). Avocations: travel, reading, swimming, tennis, family.

COWLES, LOIS ANNE FORT, social worker, educator, poet; b. Providence, Dec. 26, 1933; d. Charles M. and Rebecca Parker (Latham) Fort. AB in Philosophy, Ind. U., 1955, MA in Sociology, 1964; MSW, Ind. U., Indpls., 1966; PhD, U. Wis., 1990. Social worker Meth. Hosp., Indpls., 1963-67, Community Svc. Coun., Indpls., 1967-69, Indpls. Pub. Schs., 1969-74, Middleton (Wis.) Pub. Schs., 1974-75; rsch. asst. Wis. HHS, Madison, 1976-77, 80-81; rsch. assoc. U. Wis., 1981-83, tchg. asst., 1983; ind. rschr., 1983-89; asst. prof. social work Ind. State U., Terre Haute, 1989-93; assoc. prof. social work Idaho State U., Pocatello, 1993—2003, prof. emerita, 2003—; social worker St. Thomas Free Clinic, Franklin, Ind., 2003—; instr. Sch. Social Wk., Ind. U., 2003—04. Author: (textbook) Social Work in the Health Field: A Care Perspective, 2000, 2d edit., 2003; contbr. articles to profl. jours., poetry to anthologies. Mem. NASW, ACSW, Am. Pub. Health Assn., Coun. on Social Work Edn., Soc. Social Work Leadership in Health Care, Phi Kappa Phi. Personal E-mail: cowllois@isu.edu.

COWLES, MILLY, education educator; b. Ramer, Ala., May 29, 1932; d. Russell Fail and Sara (Mills) C. BS, Troy State U., 1952; MA in Edn., U. Ala., 1958, PhD (grad. fellow), 1962. Tchr. pub. schs., Montgomery, Ala., 1952-59; grad. tchg. fell Coll. Ed. U. Ala., 1959-62; asst., then assoc. prof. Grad. Sch. Edn. Rutgers U., 1962-66; assoc. prof. U. Ga., 1966-67; prof., dir. early childhood devel. and edn. Sch. Edn. U. S.C., Columbia, 1967-73; assoc. dean, prof. Sch. Edn. U. Ala., Birmingham, 1973-80, dean, prof., 1980-87, disting. prof. edn., 1987—; assoc. prof. edn. Coll. Edn. U. Ga., 1996-97. Dir. Williamsburg County Schs. Career Opportunity Program, 1970-73; cons. So. Edn. Found., Atlanta, Ga. Inst. Higher Edn. U. Ga., also numerous sch. systems throughout Northeast and South. Editor, contbg. author: Perspectives in the Education of Disadvantaged Children, 1967; co-author: Taming the Young Savage, Developmental Discipline; author: Quality Early Childhood Education in the South, 1991, Activities in Early Childhood Education, 1992, The Civilized Child: A Practical Guide to Discipline, 1998; mem. editorial bd. Dimensions, 1987—, The Profl. Educator, 1986—. Bd. dirs. S.C. Assn. on Children Under Six, 1969-73. Recipient Outstanding Pub. Educator award Capstone Coll. Edn. Soc. U. Ala., 1977, Outstanding Alumna award Troy State U., 1984, Early Childhood Edn. Leadership award S.C. State Coll., 1992. Mem. AAAS, AAUP, ASCD (mem. coun. on early childhood edn. 1969—, dir. 1978-82), NCATE (bd. examiners 1990), Am. Ednl. Rsch. Assn., Soc. for Rsch. Child Devel., Nat. Coun. Tchrs. English, Internat. Reading Assn., So. Assn. for Children Under Six (bd. dirs. 1985-87, chmn. editorial bd. 1989-91, Outstanding Mem. award 1992), Nat. Assn. Edn. Young Children (tchr. edn. panel 1991-94, editorial panel 1994—), Ala. Assn. Young Children (pres. 1984-85), Ala. Assn. for Colls. Tchr.Edn. (pres.1986-88), Ala. Assn. Supervision and Curriculum Devel. (pres. 1985-86), N.Y. Acad. Scis., Kappa Delta Pi (chpt. treas. 1964-66), Delta Kappa Gamma. Achievements include rsch. and publs. on psycholinguistic behaviors of rural children.

COWLISHAW, MARY LOU, government educator; b. Rockford, Ill., Feb. 20, 1932; d. Donald George and Mildred Corinne (Hayes) Miller; m. Wayne Arnold Cowlishaw, July 24, 1954; children: Beth Cowlishaw McDaniel, John, Paula Cowlishaw Rader. BS in Journalism, U. Ill., 1954; DHL, North Ctrl. Coll., 1999; DHL (hon.), Benedictine U., 2000. Mem. editorial staff Naperville (Ill.) Sun newspaper, 1977-83; mem. Ill. Ho. of Reps., Springfield, 1983—2003, chmn. elem. and secondary edn. com., 1995—97, vice-chmn. pub. utilities com., 1995—2003, mem. joint Ho.-Senate edn. reform oversight com., 1985—97; assoc. Ctr. for Govtl. Studies No. Ill. U., 2003—; adj. prof. North Ctrl. Coll., Naperville, Ill., 2003—. Mem. Ill. Task Force on Sch. Fin., 1990-96; vice chmn. Ho. Rep. Campaign Com., 1990—; co-chair Ho. Rep. Policy Com., 1991-2003; chmn. edn. com. Nat. Conf. State Legislatures, 1993-97; mem. Joint Com. Adminstrv. Rules, 1992-2003; commr. Edn. Commn. of the States, 1995-2002; chair, Ill. Women's Agenda Task Force, 1994—; mem. Nat. Edn. Goals Panel, 1996—, bd. govs. Lincoln Series for Excellence in Pub. Svc., 1996—. Author: This Band's Been Here Quite a Spell, 1983; columnist Ill. Press Assn., 2003—. Mem. Naperville Dist. 203 Bd. Edn., 1972-83; co-chmn. Ill. Citizens Coun. on Sch. Problems, Springfield, 1985-2003. Recipient 1st pl. award Ill. Press Assn., 1981, commendation Naperville Jaycees, 1986, Golden Apple award Ill. Assn. Sch. Bds., 1988, 90, 92, 94, Outstanding Women Leaders of DuPage County award West Suburban YWCA, 1990, Activator award Ill. Farm Bur., 1996, 98, Bd. of Dirs. award Little Friends, Inc., 1998, Honor award Ill. Math. and Sci. Acad., 2002, Pub. Svc. award West Suburban Higher Edn. Consortium, 2002; named Best Legislator, Ill. Citizens for Better Care, 1985, Woman of Yr., Naperville AAUW, 1987, Best Legislator, Ill. Assn. Fire Chiefs, 1994, Outstanding Edn. Adv. Indian Prairie Sch. Dist. 204, 1994, Legislator of Yr., Ill. Assn. Pk. Dists., 1995; commr. Edn. Commn. of the States, 1994-2002; Mary Lou Cowlishaw Elem. Sch. named in her honor, 1997, Legislator of Yr., Ill. Assn. Mus., 1998. Mem. Am. Legis. Exch. Coun., Conf. Women Legislators, Nat. Fedn. Rep. Women, DAR, Naperville Rep. Women's Club (pres. 1994—). Methodist. Avocation: the violin. Home: 924 Merrimac Cir Naperville IL 60540-7107 Office: North Central Coll 30 N Brainard St Naperville IL 60540-4690

COWSER, MARY ELLEN, literature and language professor; d. Edmund Michael Duffley and Ruth Duffley Sanderock; m. Robert Gene Cowser, Mar. 27, 1967; children: Mary Catherine Holtz, Robert Duffley, Ruth Anne McCluskey, James Corley. BS, Marquette U., Milw., Wis., 1958; MA, U. Conn., Storrs, 1966. Med. technologist Charity Hosp., Cleve., 1958—60; instr. of English, Univ. Tenn., Martin, 1990—2006. Writing ctr. attendant U. Tenn., Martin, 1988—90. Reviewer: She Said What?, by Molloy Ivins (Reagan award for rsch., 2003). Pres. We Care Ministries, Martin, Tenn., 1988—89. Mem.: Philharm. Music Guild (pres. 2004—06). Independent. Avocations: swimming, travel. Office: Univ Tenn University St Martin TN 38238 Office Phone: 731-881-7296.

COX, ALMA TENNEY, retired language educator, retired science educator; b. Sand Run, W.Va., Apr. 6, 1919; d. Albert Law and Viola Columbia (Gooden) Tenney; m. James Carl Cox Jr., Sept. 8, 1945; children: James Carl III, Joseph Merrils II, Alma Lee, Elizabeth Susan, Albert John. BA, W.Va. Wesleyan Coll., 1946; MEd, West Tex. State U., 1975. Elem. sch. tchr. Floyd (Va.) County Schs., 1940-42, Nicholas County Schs., Summersville, W.Va., 1942-43; high sch. English tchr. Harrison County Schs., Lewisburg, W.Va., 1943-45; English tchr. am. Embassy, Baghdad, 1956-58; high sch. English and Sci. tchr. Tulsa Sch. System, 1965-68, Plainview (Tex.) Ind. Sch. System, 1969-86, ret., 1986. Author: Birds in Plainview, 1998. Pres. Plainview Federated Women's Club, 1988-90, Hale County Retired Tchrs., 1990-91, Hale County Hist. Com., 1985-91, United Meth. Women; sec. Disable Am. Vet. Aux., 1990. Named Woman of Yr. Plainview Federated Women's Club, 1991, Hale County Retired Tchrs., 1990-91, Disable Am. Vet. Aux., 1991, Hale County Hist. Com., 1991; recipient Woman of Distinction AAUW, 1997, disting. youth educator award, Coprock Dist. Federated Womens Club & Texas State Federated womens club, 1997, Delta Kappa Gamma Soc. Internat. Pres. Achievement award, 2000. Mem. Delta Kappa Gamma (pres. Gamma Iota chpt. 1990-92, pres. Epsilon Alpha chpt. 1998-2001). Republican. Avocations: painting, reading, travel, tatting, crochetting, flower gardening. Home: 5105 Stacey Ave Fort Worth TX 76132-1628

COX, ANA MARIE, writer, former political blogger; b. 1972; m. Chris Lehmann. Grad., U. Chgo., 1994. Editor Mother Jones, The Chronicle of Higher Edn., The American Prospect; with Feedmag.com, inside.com; sr. editor In These Times; former exec. dir. Suck.com; founding editor, polit. blog Wonkette.com, 2003—06, wonkette emerita, 2006; Washington editor Time.com, 2006—. Author: Dog Days, 2006; contbg. writer Time Mag., 2006—, maintains personal website anamariecox.com, guest appearances Scarborough Country, 2006, Fox News Channel, 2006, MSNBC, 2006. Office: Time Time & Life Bldg Rockefeller Ctr 1271 Avenue of the Americas New York NY 10020-1393 Office Phone: 212-522-1212. E-mail: dogdaysgirl@gmail.com.*

COX, ANNA LEE, retired administrative assistant; b. Knoxville, Tenn., Feb. 18, 1931; d. Carter Calloway and Fairy Belle (Byers) Bayless; m. William Smith Cox, Sept. 4, 1952; 1 child, Catherine Anne Cox Faust. Grad. high sch., Knoxville. Sec. Am. Mut. Liability Ins. Co., Knoxville, 1948-53; flight procedures clk. FAA, Atlanta, 1963-66; legal sec., paralegal U.S. Atty.'s Office for Dist. S.C., Greenville, 1972-79; sec. criminal investigation div. IRS, Knoxville, 1981-84; sec., adminstrv. asst. CIA, Knoxville, 1984-88; adminstrv. asst. U.S. Dept. Def., Knoxville, 1988-91, ret., 1991. Tutor Greenville Literacy Assn., 1977-79; founder, dir. NATO Womens Chorus, Izmir, Turkey, 1969-71; choir dir., pres. United Meth. Women, Stephenson Meml. United Meth. Ch., Greenville, 1972-79; bd. dirs. Fountainhead Conservatory Music, Knoxville, 1983-85, 92-95, sec. of bd. dirs., 1994-95; singer Knoxville Choral Soc., 1955-56, Atlanta Symphony Chorus, 1971, Greenville Civic Chorale, 1973-79; vol. Farragut Folklife Mus., Concord United Meth. Ch. Republican. Avocations: music, drama. Home: 619 Farragut Commons Dr Knoxville TN 37934-1673 Personal E-mail: annaleecox@aol.com.

COX, BARBARA JOANNE, psychologist, consultant; b. Norristown, Pa., Jan. 11, 1967; d. Gary John and Donna Diane Hagstrom; m. David Andrew Cox, July 8, 1995; 1 child, Delilah Anicia. BA in Biology, U. Calif., LaJolla, 1990; MA in Psychology, Calif. Sch. Profl. Psychology, San Diego, 1996, PhD in Psychology, 1999. Lic. psychologist Calif., 2002. Environ. protection specialist Navy Pub. Works, San Diego, 1991—94; grad. rsch. asst. Calif. Sch. Profl. Psychology, 1994—99; psychol. asst., cons. CDM, Inc., San Diego, 1999—2002; psychologist Psychiat. Ctr. San Diego, 2002—04; psychologist/coach pvt. practice, 2005—. Developer continuing edn. courses The Zur Inst., Sonoma, Calif., 2005—. Author: (CD) Guided Imagery and Relaxation Techniques for Parents, 2005. Mem.: San Diego Profl. Coaches Alliance, Bus. Networking Internat., San Diego Psychol. Assn. (mem. profl. affairs com. 2004—05). Avocation: travel. Office: Huntington Ctr 8950 Villa LaJolla Dr Ste 1241 La Jolla CA 92037 Business E-Mail: drbarbara@mind-body-tools-for-life.com.

COX, BEULAH ELIZABETH, violinist, music educator; b. Newport News, Va., Mar. 15, 1955; d. Willis Franklin and Rosemary Christian Coates Cox. BA, Coll. of William and Mary, 1973—77. Violinist Colonial Williamsburg Found., Williamsburg, Va., 1975—78, Hudson Valley Philharm., Poughkeepsie, NY, 1984—95, The Greenwich Symphony, Conn., 1984—; violinist/founder The Ambrosia Trio, NYC, 1990—; violin soloist Allegro Chamber Ensemble, New York, NY, 1991, Virtuoso Strings, NYC, 1992, Doansburg Chamber Ensemble, Brewster, NY, 1993; violinist Nat. Chorale, NYC, 1994—; violin soloist Buglisi/Foreman Dance Co., NYC, 1996; violinist, founder Hudson String Quartet, N.Y.C., 2006—. Violinist Joseph Fuchs Chamber Music Inst., Alfred, NY, 1976—83, Grand Teton Music Festival, Teton Village, Wyo., 1984, Am. Inst. of Musical Studies, Graz, Austria, 1985, Banff Chamber Music, Banff, Canada, 1995; adj. prof. of violin Fordham U., Bronx, NY, 2000—; string tchr. Ethical Culture Sch., NYC, 1997—; violin and piano tchr. Riverdale YM-YWHA - Rhoda Grundman Sch. of Music, Bronx, 1999—; violin tchr. Bronx Arts Ensemble Sch., Bronx, 2000—05; founder The Hudson String Quartet, 2006—. Musician: (recording) Peter and the Wolf, 1999, Baroque Sonatas and Trios, 1975, Berlioz Te Deum - Voices of Ascension, 1996, Meet The Ambrosia Trio!, 1997, The Ambrosia Trio Close Up, 2000. Mem.: Am. Fedn. of Musicians, Chamber Music Am.

COX, CAROL YVONNE, counselor; b. Pavo, Ga., Apr. 29, 1951; d. Joseph Elza and Carolyn Virginia (Sandifer) C.; 1 child, Kayla Cynthia. BA, Emory U., 1973; MEd, Ga. State U., 1979; PhD, U. Ga., 1991. Lic. profl. counselor, Ga., Tex. Dir. counseling Grady Rape Crisis Ctr., Atlanta, 1979-80; social worker Ga. Highlands Ctr., Dalton, 1980-85; program coord. N.E. Ga. Health Dist., Athens, 1985-92; dir. family therapy Burke Ctr., Lufkin, Tex., 1992-95; exec. dir. Covenant Counseling Ctr., Moultrie, Ga., 1995—99; pvt. practice Moultrie, 2000—. Adj. faculty Stephen F. Austin U., Nacogdoches, Tex., 1994-95; cons. N.W. Ga. Headstart, Dalton, 1980-85, Ga. Sheriff's Youth Estates, Dalton, 1983-85, Ga. Network to End Sexual Assault, Athens, 1986-92; cons., mem. adv. bd. Ga. Coun. on Child Abuse, Athens, 1986-92. Author: Safety Kid: A Child Abuse Prevention Curriculum, 1987. Office: 600 1st St SE Moultrie GA 31768-5508 Office Phone: 229-985-8452. Business E-Mail: docvon@planttel.net.

COX, CAROLYN, healthcare educator; b. Pitts., Jan. 16, 1960; d. Joseph and Margaret Cox. BS, U. Pa., Slippery Rock, 1982; MEd, U. Pa., Shippensburg, 1984; PhD, Pa. State U., University Park, 1994. Cert. health edn. specialist Nat. Commn. Health Edn. Credentialing, 1995. Health & phsyical edn. tchr. Big Spring Sch. Dist., Newville, Pa., 1988—92; paraprofessional tchr. Capitol Area Intermediate Unit, Carlisle, Pa., 1992—94; adj. instr. health edn. Pa State U., University Park, Harrisburg, 1993—94; assoc. prof. health & exercise scis. Truman State U., Kirksville, Mo., 2000—. Reviewer of abstracts and symposia Rsch. Consortium, Reston, Va.; tchg. techniques reviewer Am. Sch. Health Assn., Kent, Ohio; editl. assoc. Eta Sigma Gamma Health Educator Jour., Muncie, Ind. Author: (textbook) ACSM's Worksite Health Promotion Manual: A Guide to Building and Sustaining Healthy Worksites; prodr.: (CD) Health Commns. Commr. Nat. Commn. For Health Edn. Credentialing, Allentown, Whitehall, Pa., 2004—; exec. bd. mem. Adair County Family YMCA, Kirksville, Mo., 1996—. Recipient Robert Taylor Profl. Svc. Honor award, MO Assn. for Health Phys. Edn. Recreation & Dance, 2005, Health Educator of Yr. award, Mo. Alliance, 2005; fellow, Assn. Worksite Health Promotion, 1997. Mem.: Eta Sigma Gamma (life Disting. Svc. award 2001). Avocations: walking, swimming. Home: 1709 East Laharpe St Kirksville MO 63501 Office: Truman State U 329 Pershing Bldg Kirksville MO 63501 Home Fax: 660-785-7492; Office Fax: 660-785-7492. Business E-Mail: ccox@truman.edu.

COX, CARRIE, pharmaceutical executive; b. 1957; m. Ken Cox; 2 children. BS, Mass. Coll. Pharmacy and Health Sci., 1981. With Sandoz Pharm., 1982—92; v.p. women's healthcare Wyeth-Ayerst; sr. v.p. & head global bus. mgmt. Pharmacia & Upjohn, 1997, exec. v.p., 1999; exec. v.p., pres. global perscription Pharmacia, 2002; pres. global pharm. Shering-Plough, 2003—, also exec. v.p., 2003—. Mem. bd. dir., audit com. Texas Instruments, 2004—. Named Healthcare Businesswoman of Yr., Healthcare Businesswomen's Assn., 2001; named one of 50 Most Powerful Women in Bus., Fortune mag., 2005, 2006, 10 Most Powerful Women in NJ Bus., Star-Ledger, 2006. Office: Shering-Plough Corp Headquarters 2000 Galloping Hill Rd Kenilworth NJ 07033-0530 Office Phone: 908-298-4000.*

COX, CATHLEEN RUTH, zoologist, educator; b. Vallejo, Calif., Oct. 20, 1948; d. Charles W. and Betty B. (Born) Cox; m. William S. Bain, Dec. 14, 1985. BA, U. Calif., San Diego, 1970; PhD, Stanford U., 1976. Postdoctoral fellow Am. Mus. Natural History, N.Y.C., 1976—78; rsch. assoc. Barnard Coll., N.Y.C., 1978—79; rsch. zoologist UCLA, 1979—82, lectr., 1985—. Asst. prof. Calif. State U., Northridge, Calif., 1980—84; dir. rsch. LA (Calif.) Zoo, 1981—. Contbr. articles to profl. jours. Recipient W.C. Allee award, Animal Behavior Soc., 1976; grantee, NSF, 1978. Mem.: Am. Primatol. Soc., Animal Behavior Soc., Am. Ornithol. Union, Am. Assn. Zool. Pks. and Aquaria. Office: 5333 Zoo Dr Los Angeles CA 90027-1451 Office Phone: 323-644-4204. Business E-Mail: ccox@zoo.lacity.org.

COX, CATHY, state official; b. Bainbridge, Ga., July 18, 1958; d. Walter Cox; m. Mark Dehler. A.Agr., Abraham Baldwin Agrl. Coll., 1978; BJ summa cum laude, U. Ga., 1980; JD magna cum laude, Mercer U., 1986. Newspaper reporter The Gainesville Times, Gainesville, 1980-82, Post-Searchlight, Bainbridge, 1982-83; atty. Hansell & Post, Atlanta, 1986-88, Lambert, Floyd & Conger, Bainbridge, Ga., 1988-95; mem. Dist. 160 Ga. Gen. Assembly, 1993-96; asst. sec. of state State of Ga., Atlanta, 1996-98, sec. of state, 1999—. Editor Mercer U. Law Rev. Named Conservation Legislator of Yr., Ga. Wildlife Fedn., 1994, Woman of Courage award, Woman's Policy Group, 1995, Woman of Yr., Ga. Commn. on Women, 2000, named one of 11 Pub. Officials of Yr., Governing Mag., 2002. Democrat. Methodist. Office: Office Sec of State 214 State Capitol SW Atlanta GA 30334-1600 Office Phone: 404-656-2881. Office Fax: 404-656-0513. E-mail: sosweb@sos.state.ga.us.*

COX, CHRISTINE K., secondary school educator; b. Decatur, Ill., Jan. 5, 1950; d. Max G and Lois Marie Roberts; m. Victor B. Cox, May 12, 1979; children: Jay D. Reed, Nathan Cody, Andrew Christopher. BA, U. Ill., 1976, MEd, 1982. Tchr. Urbana (Ill.) H.S., 1977—. Recipient Outstanding Cooperating Tchr. award, U. Ill., 1992, Tchg. Recognition award, NAACP, 2003. Mem.: NEA, Urbana Edn. Assn., Ill. Edn. Assn., Nat. Coun. Teachers of English. D-Liberal. Avocations: travel, water aerobics. Office Phone: 217-384-3524. Personal E-mail: c-cox@insightbb.com.

COX, CYNTHIA A., art education specialist; b. Cleve., Mar. 29, 1957; d. Jerry L. and Lynn (Hargrove) C. BFA, Kent State U., 1979; MSEd with all honors, Lake Erie Coll., 1996. Cert. visual arts K-12, edn. specialist, Ohio. Art edn. specialist East Cleveland Schs., 1980-86, Kenston Schs., Chagrin Falls, Ohio, 1987—. Instr. profl. devel. grad. program Lake Erie Coll., Painesville, Ohio, 1996, in-svc. spkr. Kenston Schs., Chagrin Falls, Ohio,

1993, East Cleveland Schs., 1981; spkr. U.S. Joint Conf. on Edn., Beijing, 1992; vis. tchr. J.F.K. Schule, Berlin; Am. spkr. 1994 Commemorative Ceremony for Tearing Down Berlin Wall, 1994; apptd. del. leader People to People, Japan, 1999. Author, designer: Building Bridges: An International Approach to the Fine Arts, 1996; author: A Social, Cultural and Political Comparison Study of Children's Art Work from China, Germany, Bosnia and the United States, 1996. Elder Lake Shore Christian Ch., 1986-93. Mem. Ohio Art Edn. Assn., Ohio Edn. Assn., Internat. Assn. Edn. Through Art, Dwight D. Eisenhower Citizen Ambassador Program, Am. Acad. Disting. Students, Internat. Assn. of Asian Studies (presenter conf. 2000). Office: Kenston Schs 9421 Bainbridge Rd Chagrin Falls OH 44023-2703

COX, DARLENE BETH, secondary school educator; b. Cin., Oct. 28, 1952; d. Kenneth and Ruth Janet Cox. BS, U. N.Mex., Albuquerque, 1996. Cert. level two tchr. N.Mex. Dept. Edn., 1999, lab. animal tech. Am. Assn. for Lab. Animal Sci., 1982, radiation protection tech. U. N.Mex., 1982. Lab. animal tech. U. N.Mex., Albuquerque, 1977—91; h.s. sci. tchr. Moriarty Mcpl. Schs., N.Mex., 1996—. Chmn. regional exam. bd. #19 Am. Assn. for Lab. Animal Sci., Albuquerque, 1991—92. Primary contbr.: Training Manual Series, American Association for Laboratory Animal Science. Dream Fund grantee, Ctr. for Tchg. Excellence, Ea. N.Mex. U., 1999, 2000. Mem.: NSTA, World Class Tchrs. Network, N.Mex. Sci. Tchrs. Assn., SW Dairy Goat Assn., Am. Goat Soc., Am. Dairy Goat Assn. (life), SW Nigerian Dwarf Dairy Goat Club (bd. mem. 2003—05), Golden Key Nat. Honor Soc., Phi Beta Kappa. Independent. Avocation: showing and breeding of Nigerian dwarf dairy goats. Home: 27 Nizhoni Ln Tijeras NM 87059 Office: Moriarty HS 2000 Center St Moriarty NM 87031 Office Phone: 505-832-4254. Personal E-mail: caprinz@aol.com.

COX, DAWN EVERLINA, protective services official; d. Donald Lewis and Everlina Cox. AS in Criminal Justice Magna Cum Laude, Johnson Wales U., 1997, BS in Criminal Justice Magna Cum Laude, 1999, MA in Tchg., 2001. Lic.: N.Y. State Licensed Security Officer, cert.: RI Pistol Revolver Cert.; Am. Red Cross. Govt. intern Office Pub. Defender, Providence, 1997—98; intern Mayer Buddy Cianci Providence Police Dept., 1997; tchg. asst., special needs tutor Johnson Wales U., 1995—99; edn. outreach specialist Cmty. Care Svcs. Inc., Attleboro, Mass., 2000—01; court adv. Riker's Island Prison Women's Prison Assn., N.Y.C., 2001; clinician heroin addiction Cmty. Substance Abuse Clinic, Fall River, Mass., 2001; corrections officer R.I. Dept. Corrections, 2004—. Organizer, writer NAACP, Bklyn.; elder R.I. Indian Coun. Recipient Most Studious award, Johnson Wales U., 1997, Tutor award, 1997. Mem.: Amnesty Internat. (charter mem.), Silver Key Honor Soc., Zeta Phi Beta, Delta Theta Phi. Democrat. Roman Catholic. Avocation: travel. Home: 438 Kosciusko St Brooklyn NY 11221 Office: Home Office 60 Radcliffe Ave Providence RI 02908 Personal E-mail: dawn_everlinacox@hotmail.com.

COX, JOY DEAN, small business owner; b. Oklahoma City, Sept. 13, 1940; d. Wordy John Neely and Ethel (Russell) Neely Biggs; m. Sidney Lee Johnson, Sept. 10, 1958 (div. 1963); m. Ronald Gene Cox, Sept. 22, 1964; children: Beverly Kay, Jeffrey Wilson; 1 stepchild, Ronald D. Student pub. schs., Oklahoma City. Long-distance operator S.W. Bell Tel. Co., Oklahoma City, 1958-59, L.A., 1959-60; clk. John Pilling Shoes, Oklahoma City, 1960-62; cashier Dial Fin. Co., Houston, 1966; file clk., typist N.Am. Ins. Co., Oklahoma City, 1966-67, bookkeeper, co-owner farm and ranch ops. Dewey County, Okla., 1968—78, Panola, Okla., 1977-2001; bookkeeper, co-owner farm and ranch ops., co-op R&J Farms-Ranch, Dewey County, 1991—. Co-owner, operator Apco Svc. Sta. and Bulk Fuel Plant, Taloga, Okla., 1972-76, D&R Svc. & Supply Co., Panola, 1979-89, Eufaula, Okla., 1989-95, Taloga, 1993—; co-owner, operator Panola Store, 1980-85; dealer, co-owner Cox Chevrolet, Wilburton, Okla., 1985. Contbr. articles to newspapers and jours. Pres. Taloga Ext. Homemakers, 1971-73, sec.-treas. 1973-75; entertainer Dewey County Rest Homes, 1969-78, Latimer County Rest Homes, Wilburton, 1978-88, County of McIntosh, Eufaula, 1990-93; leader, contbr. funds to drug abuse program Latimer County 4-H, Wilburton, 1979-89; fund raiser ARC, Am. Heart Assn., Girl Scouts U.S., Panola PTA, Drug Abuse Program, Panola 4-H, Latimer County, 1979-89, Salvation Army Donations, Pittsburg County, 1977-91, Am. Cancer Soc., Taloga, 1968-78, Panola, 1978-88, McIntosh Co., Eufaula, 1988-92, Nat. Help Hospitalized Vets., 1978-90; contbr. funds to drug abuse program Wilburton, Quinton and Okla. Police Dept., McIntosh County 4H; bd. dirs. Latimer County Pick-A-Star, 1985, Clown for Eufaula and Stigler Christmas Parade, Okla., 1989-93; clown, singer McIntosh Rest Homes, 1989-93; participant Paradeentry Desert Storm Support Day, 1991; singer Eufaula Arts and Crafts Festival, 1991-93, entertainer, 1991-92; clown, singer 4th July Parade and Arts Festival, Eufaula, 1992-93; fundraiser Dewey County Hist. Jail House Mus., 1993-2000, pres., 2000; singer Pittsburg County Ann. Masons Widows Banquet, 1993. Recipient Leadership award Latimer County 4-H, 1983, Citizen of Yr. award Com. to Keep and Bear Arms, 1986. Mem. Lake Eufaula Assn. (bd. dirs. 1990-91, entertainer ann. fund raiser 1989, Friendly Lake Eufaula Area Supporters (entertainer ann. fleas Christmas parties and talent show 1991-92), Lake Eufaula Area Flying Coun. (pub. rels. rep.), Taloga Kiwanis Club (v.p. 1999-2000, pres. 2000-01). Republican. Avocations: bicycling, sewing, swimming, walking, reading.

COX, JULIA DIAMOND, lawyer; b. Winfield, Ill., Mar. 1, 1971; d. Darrough Blain and Linda Mann Diamond; m. John Francis Cox, Jan. 7, 1995. BS, U. Ill., 1992; JD, U. Chgo., 1995. Bar: Ill. 1995, Ohio 1996, Fla. 1996. Assoc. McDermott, Will & Emery, Chgo., 1995-99, of counsel, 1999-2000; ptnr. McDermott, Will & Emery LLP, Chgo., 2001—. Mem. Phi Beta Kappa. Office: McDermott Will & Emery LLP Ste 3100 227 W Monroe St Chicago IL 60606-5096 Office Phone: 312-984-7628. Office Fax: 312-984-7700. Business E-Mail: jcox@mwe.com.*

COX, KATHLEEN, broadcast executive, lawyer; BS, U. Va.; JD, U. Chgo., 1979; M of Pub. Policy, Georgetown U., 1996. Atty., Washington, LA; intellectual property counsel Bell Atlantic Corp., Washington; assoc. gen. counsel Corp. Pub. Broadcasting, 1997, gen. counsel, 1998, sr. v.p., gen. counsel and corp. sec., 1999—2002, exec. v.p. and COO, 2002—04, pres. & CEO, 2004—05.

COX, KATHY, school system administrator; m. John Hamilton Cox Jr.; children: John, Alex. BA, Emory U., Atlanta, MA in Polit. sci. Tchr. social studies McIntosh H.S., Fayette County Bd. Edn., Atlanta, 1987—2002; rep. Ga. Ho. of Reps., Atlanta, 1998—2002; supt. of edn. State of Ga., Atlanta, 2002—. Supporter Boy Scouts Am. Cub Scout Pack 201, Boy Scout Troop 275. Mem.: Kiwanis, Phi Beta Kappa. Meth. Office: Ga Dept Edn 2054 Twin Towers E Atlanta GA 30334

COX, LYNNE CRAIGE, music educator, composer; b. N.Y., May 19, 1944; d. Richard Ervin (Stepfather) and Evelyn Avante Smith, Edwin M. Craige; m. Jerry D. Cox, Jr, June 20, 1964; children: Trevor B., Sean Dixon. MusB, East Carolina U., Greenville, N.C., 1966. Cert. tchr. pub. sch. music East Carolina U., 1992. Pvt. piano tchr., Belhaven, NC, 1966—91; tchr. music Beaufort County Schs., Washington, NC, 1991—. Presenter S.C. Early Childhood Assn., Myrtle Beach, 2004, various music orgns. & tchr.'s groups, SC, NC; owner/pub. Sea Zoo music products. Composer: (music for children) 'Sea Zoo' Collection of Piano solos (Best Composition for Elem. Music N.C. Fedn. Music Tchrs., 1984); contbr.: ednl. projects in virtual reality Introduction of Virtual Reality Through Music, Cruising Down the Nile; author: (article) www.kidsmusicweb.com; music CD, Piano Classics, American Eagle; composer: Myklas Music Press and Alfred Music Publishing. Ch. musician various chs., Belhaven & Bath, NC. Finalist Sarah Belk Gambrell award for Excellence in Pub. Sch. Music, N.C. Arts in Edn. Found., 1998; named to Hall of Fame, Nat. Guild Piano Tchrs.; recipient Disting. Music Alumni award, Sch. Music, East Carolina U., Greenville, 2004; grantee various music grants, local bus.; scholar, N.C. Ctr. Advancement of Tchg., 1996, 1998, N.C. Ctr. Advancement for Tchg., 2000, 2002. Mem.: Music Educators Nat. Conf. (assoc.), Nat. Fedn. Music Clubs (life). Methodist. Office Phone: 252-946-1611.

COX, M. CAROLYN, lawyer; b. June 10, 1949; BA, Agnes Scott Coll., 1971; JD, Yale Univ., 1974. Bar: Ala. 1975, DC 1976. Law clk. Judge Frank M. Johnson, US Dist. Ct., Middle Dist. Ala., 1974—75; ptnr., Corp. dept., chmn. Ethics com. Wilmer Cutler Pickering Hale & Dorr, Washington. Dir. Yale Barristers Union. Office: Wilmer Cutler Pickering Hale & Dorr 1801 Pennsylvania Ave NW Washington DC 20006 Mailing: Wilmer Cutler Pickering Hale & Dorr 2445 M St NW Washington DC 20037 Office Phone: 202-663-6645. Office Fax: 202-663-6363. Business E-Mail: carolyn.cox@wilmerhale.com.

COX, MARGARET STEWART, photographer; b. Indpls., Jan. 9, 1948; d. Douglass Falconer and Margaret Geraldine (Gates) Stewart; m. Herbert Leo Cox Jr., Dec. 21, 1977 (dec. Nov. 1985); 1 child, Matthew Michael. Student, Butler U., 1965-67, Rollins Coll., 1990—93. Real estate agt. Don Asher & Assocs., Orlando, Fla., 1972-80; real estate agt., appraiser Mary P. Logvin Real Estate, Orlando, 1987-90; freelance photographer Orlando, 1990—. Exhibited photographs in group shows at Marie Selby Bot. Gardens, 1993, 94, 98 (Merit awards), 1999 Exhibit, Orlando Artists Biennial Exhbn., 1992 (Merit award), Mt. Dora Ctr. for the Arts, 1994 (Merit award), others. Bd. dirs. Adult Literacy League, Inc., Orlando, 1987-95, pres., 1994; active Fla. Literacy Coalition, 1988-96; vice chair Orange City Devel. Adv. Bd., Orlando, 1991-95; active United Way Spkrs. Bur., 1994, 95; judge Chertok Nature Photo Contest, 1993, chairperson, 1995, 96, 98; mem. Lake County Dem. Exec. Com., 1997-2001. Recipient Spl. Mission Recognition award United Meth. Women, 1985. Mem. High Country Art and Craft Guild, Nat. Audubon Soc., Fla. Audubon Soc. (bd. dirs. 1998-99), Audobon Fla. (bd. dirs. 2003-), Orange Audubon Soc. (bd. dirs. 1993-96, 97—, 98-99, rec. sec. 1996, bd. pres. 1998—2002, conservation chmn. 2002-). Democrat. Avocations: reading, travel, wildlife art, birdwatching, gardening. Office: 9410 Oak Island Ln Clermont FL 34711-7304 Office Phone: 352-429-1042.

COX, MARY ANTHONY, musician, educator; b. Birmingham, Ala. Studies with Rosina Lhevinne and Jeaneane Dowls; student, Conservatoire National Supérieur de Musique, Paris; studies with Annette Dieudonné, studies chamber music with Pierre Pasquier, piano with Jean Battalla, Alice Gaultier-Leon, Robert and Gaby Casadesus; MusB, Juilliard Sch., 1965; MS, Julliard Sch., 1967; studies with Nadia Boulanger. Performer, faculty mem. Congregation of Arts, Dartmouth Coll., Hanover, N.H., 1963, 65; educator in musical ear training Juilliard Sch., N.Y.C., 1964—. Music dir. Craftsbury Chamber Players; vis. prof. U. Montreal, Que., Can., 1968-69; mem. faculty music theory, Curtis Inst. Music, 1969-74. Office: The Juilliard Sch Lincoln Ctr New York NY 10023

COX, NANCY JANE, microbiologist; b. Emmetsburg, Iowa, July 21, 1948; d. Emmett Stanley and Verna Lucille (Olson) Cox; B.S. with honors, Iowa State U., 1970; Ph.D., Cambridge, (Eng.) U., 1975; m. M. Evan Lindsay, Apr. 11, 1981; 1 child, Julia Claire Lindsay. Postdoctoral fellow Muscular Dystrophy Assn., Balt. and Atlanta, 1975-77; staff fellow Centers for Disease Control, Atlanta, 1978-80, research chemist, 1980—, now dir. Influenza Divsn. Recipient Marshall Scholarship for study abroad, 1970; postdoctoral fellow Muscular Dystrophy Assn. Am., 1975. Nmed one of 100 Most Influential People, Time Mag., 2006. Mem. AAAS, Am. Soc. Virology, Am. Soc. Microbiology, Sigma Xi. Methodist. Contbr. articles to profl. jours. and books. Office: Div Viral Diseases 7-111 Centers for Disease Control 1 600 Clifton Rd Atlanta GA 30316-2228*

COX, PAULYN MAE, retired elementary school educator; b. Oberlin, Ohio, Apr. 19, 1930; d. Lafayette Clinton and Magdalene Elizabeth Cox. AAS, SUNY, 1953; BA, Ithaca Coll., 1958. Cert. tchr. N.Y. Elem. tchr. Bd. Edn., Elyria, Ohio, 1964-65, reading tchr. Grafton, Ohio, 1966-67, St. Colombas Sch., Schenectady, NY, 1967-68; elem. tchr. Bd. Edn., Fonda, NY, 1968-94; ret., 1994. Active YWCA, Schenectady, Deaf Ctr., Schenectady; mentor Brown Sch., Schenectady, 1996—; sponsor Pearl S. Buck Found., World Vision and Children Inc.; coord. coun. Inter-faith Comty., Schenectady, NY. Named Top Fund Raiser, Crop Walk for Hunger, Schenectady County; recipient Sister Rachel award, Schenectady Inner city Ministries, 1998. Mem.: AAUW, N.Y. State United Tchrs., Am. Fedn. Tchrs., Upper Montgomery County Ret. Tchrs., Amnesty Internat. Avocations: reading, music, walking, mentoring, gardening. Home: PO Box 404 1561 Main St Rotterdam Junction NY 12150-9759

COX, ROSSALENE MULLINS, art educator; d. Roscoe Mullins and Evealeene Mullins Sluss; m. Gary Wayne Cox, June 28, 1975; children: Alison Tegan Cox Maynard, Lauren Alyssa Cox Runyon. Degree, Pikeville Coll., Ky., 1975, Morehead State U., 1979, degree, 1990. 5th grade tchr. Pigeon Roost Elem. Sch., Pilgrim, Ky., 1975—76; tchr. h.s. art Sheldon Clark H.S., Inez, Ky., 1976—. Mem. Martin County Libr. Bd., Inez, 1980—88. Mem.: Ky. Edn. Assn., Ky. Edn. Assn. Republican. Baptist. Avocations: reading, quilting, painting, crafts, tennis. Home: HC 63 Box 660 Inez KY 41224

COX, RUTH MILLER, music educator; b. Balt., Sept. 25, 1923; d. Lawrence Lefever and Florence Fortiner Miller; children: Jennifer, Heather(dec.). BS in Music Edn., West Chester U., Pa., 1945; MS in Edn., Temple U., Phila., 1948. Permanent tchg. cert. Pa., cert. supr. Pa. Tchr. elem. music Upper Darby (Pa.) Sch. Dist., Haverford Township Sch. Dist., Havertown, Pa.; tchr. secondary music Lansdowne (Pa.)-Aldan Sch. Dist. (now William Penn Sch. Dist.). Supr. music William Penn Sch. Dist., Lansdowne, dept. chair; condr. Cultural Alliance Choir, Lansdowne, 1979—90, Havertown Choristers, 1989—; pres. Main Line Symphony, Wayne, Pa., 1983—2000. Recipient Thanks Badge award, Girl Scouts Am., 1973, Disting. Alumna, West Chester U., 1997. Mem.: Am. Choral Dirs. Assn., Pa. State Edn. Assn., Pa. Music Edn. Assn. (pres. S.E. region 1972—76). Presbyterian. Home: 253 Merrybrook Dr Havertown PA 19083-1320

COX, TERI POLACK, public relations executive; b. Pitts., May 21, 1952; d. Meyer and Faye Helen (Tischler) Polack; m. William R. Cox, Jan. 1, 1982. BA, U. Pitts., 1974; MBA in Mktg., NYU, 1989. Info. dir. United Mental Health; prodr., host weekly PA radio program; pub. rels. dir. Atlanta Merchandise Mart; mktg. rsch., pub. rels. cons. Pfizer Inc., NYU Stern Sch. Bus.; acct. supr. Burson-Marsteller; mng. ptnr. Cox Comms. Ptnrs., Lawrenceville, N.J., 1992-98, sr. mng. ptnr., 1998—. Chair Bd. Devel. Workgroup; mem. Advocacy Leadership Team, Prevention and Detection Workgroup; legis. amb. Am. Cancer Soc. Named Pharma Voice 100 Most Inspiring and Influential Individuals Life Scis. Industry, 2005. Mem.: Nat. Am. Cancer Soc. (Capitol Dome award, NJ Gov.'s Task Force on Cancer Prevention, St. George Medal award), Women Execs. in Pub. Rels., Health-care Businesswomen's Assn. (past pres., adv. bd.), Pub. Rels. Soc. Am. Office: Cox Comm Ptnrs 2 Roseberry Ct Lawrenceville NJ 08648-1058 Office Phone: 609-896-3250. Personal E-mail: coxcomptnr@aol.com.

COX ARQUETTE, COURTENEY, actress; b. Birmingham, Ala., June 15, 1964; d. Richard L. Lewis and Courteney Bass-Copland; m. David Arquette, June 12, 1999; 1 child, CoCo. Attended, Mt. Vernon Coll. Spokesperson Kinerase skin care products, 2005—; co-founder Coquette Prodns. Appearances include (music video) Bruce Springsteen's Dancing in the Dark, 1984, The Rembrandts I'll Be There For You, 1995; (TV series) As The World Turns, 1984, Murder, She Wrote, 1984, Misfits of Science, 1985-86, Family Ties, 1987-88, Dream On, 1990, Seinfeld, 1990, The Larry Sanders Show, 1992, The Trouble with Larry, 1993, Friends, 1994-2004; (TV pilots) Sylvan in Paradise, 1986; (TV films) If It's Tuesday, It Still Must Be Belgium, 1987, A Rockport Christmas, 1988, Roxanne: The Prize Pulitzer, 1989, Judith Krantz's Till We Meet Again, 1989, Curiosity Kills, 1990, Morton and Hays, 1991, Topper, 1992, Sketch Artist II: Hands That See, 1995; (films) Down Twisted, 1986, Masters of the Universe, 1987, Cocoon: The Return, 1988, Mr. Destiny, 1990, Blue Desert, 1990, Shaking the Tree, 1992, The Opposite Sex (and How to Live with Them), 1993, Ace Ventura, Pet Detective, 1994, Scream, 1996, Commandments, 1996, Scream 2, 1997, The Runner, 1999, Scream 3, 2000, 3000 Miles to Graceland, 2001, The Shrink Is In, 2001 (also exec. prodr.), Get Well Soon, 2001, Alien Love Triangle, 2002, November, 2004, The Longest Yard, 2005, Alpha Dog, 2006, (voice) Barnyard: The Original Party Animals, 2006, Zoom, 2006; exec. prodr. TV Series Mix It Up, 2003; actor, exec. prodr. Dirt, 2006. Office: Brillstein Grey Entertainment 9150 Wilshire Blvd Beverly Hills CA 90212*

COX-HAYLEY, DEON MELAYNE, geriatrics services professional; b. Trenton, NJ, 1960; MD, U. Health Scis., Coll. Osteopathic Medicine, 1986. Cert. internal medicine 1990, geriatric medicine 1992, internal medicine 2000, geriatric medicine 2002. Intern Riverside Hosp., Wichita, Kans., 1986—87; resident U. Kans. Sch. Medicine, Wichita, 1987—90; fellowship U. Chgo. Hosps., Chgo., 1990—92; assoc. prof., medicine U. Chgo. Pritzker Sch. Med., Dept. Medicine, Divsn. Biological Scis.; med. dir. Windermere Sr. Health Ctr., Chgo. Office: 5841 S Md Ave MC 6098 Chicago IL 60637 Address: Windermere Sr Health Ctr and Dental Assoc 5549 S Cornell Ave Chicago IL 60615

COYE, JUDY, science educator; d. Robert and Alice Wilkinson; m. Jim Coye, Aug. 3, 1985; children: Jenny, Ryan. Master's, Cortland U., N.Y., 1987. Cert. tchr. sci. N.Y., 1987. Tchr. sci. Auburn H.S., NY, 1987—. Office: Auburn HS Lake Ave Ext Auburn NY 13021 Office Phone: 315-255-8300.

COYLE, ALLISON BROOKE, director; d. John and Susan Howard; m. Michael Coyle, June 29, 2002. MusB in Music Edn., U. Ariz., Tucson, Ariz., 1999; MusM in Wind Band Conducting, U. Ariz., Tucson, Ariz, 2004. Music tchr. Sierra Mid. Sch., Tucson, 1999—2002; grad. tchg. asst. U. Ariz. Bands, Tucson, 2002—04; dir. of bands Sunnyside HS, Tucson, 2004—06, Rio Rico HS, 2006—. Clinician So. Ariz. Honor Band, Tucson, 2002—02. Mem.: Music Educators Nat. Conf., Tau Beta Sigma (hon.), Kappa Kappa Psi (hon.). Avocations: photography, kickboxing. Office: Rio Rico HS 1374 W Frontage Rd Rio Rico AZ 85648

COYLE, DIANE BONANOMI, special education educator; b. Philadelphia, Pa., Apr. 26, 1950; d. Fernand Joseph Bonanomi and Alice Mabel Pooler; m. James Edward Coyle Jr., Oct. 10, 1981; children: Kathryn Janine, Susan Elizabeth, Caryn Marie. BS in Elem. Edn., Gwynedd Mercy Coll., Pa., 1972; MEd, Lehigh U., Bethlehem, Pa. Cert. elem. edn. tchr. Pa., tchr. socially and emotionally disturbed Pa., spl. edn. tchr. Pa. 2nd grade tchr. St. Stanislaus Sch., Lansdale, Pa., 1969—72, resource rm. tchr., 1972—76; learning disabilities cons. READS, Montgomery County, Pa., 1976—78; spl. edn. tchr. New Hope-Solebury Jr./Sr. HS, New Hope, Pa., 1978—83; acting spl. edn. supr. New Hope - Solebury Sch. Dist., New Hope, 1983—88; 4th grade and spl. edn. tchr. New Hope - Solebury Elem. Sch., New Hope, 1990—. Math and reading tutor, Bucks County, Pa., 1982—; multisensory lang. tchr. Wilson Reading Sys., Bucks County, 2000—; tchr. Confraternity of Christian Doctrine Queen of Universe Parish, St. John the Evangelist Parish, Levittown/Yardley, Pa., 1990—95. Leader Girl Scouts USA, Bucks County, 1986—96; asst. children's summer theater Ocean Grove Youth Assn., NJ; costume dir. Drama Works, Yardley, 1997—2000; mem., co-chmn. costume com.Youth Club, Morrisville Presbyn. Ch., Pa., 2000—06, chmn. youth bd., 2004—06; jr. Christian Youth Orgn. bd. St. John the Evangelist Parish, Morrisville, 1993—97, chmn. social concerns com., 2005—06, mem. peace and justice com., 2000—05. Recipient Apple award, New Hope Solebury Upper Elem. Sch., 2005. Mem.: New Hope-Solebury Edn. Assn. (pres. 2000—02), Coun. Exceptional Children (assoc.). Democrat. Roman Catholic. Avocations: reading, swimming, gardening, travel, sewing. Home: 300 Hollow Branch Ln Yardley PA 19067 Office: New Hope Solebury Sch Dist 180 W Bridge St New Hope PA 18938 Office Phone: 215-862-8026. Business E-Mail: dcoyle@nhsd.org.

COYLE, DIANE R., artist, educator; b. Seattle, Jan. 25, 1933; d. Raymond E. and Dorothy H. (Larson) Manning; m. Jack G. Coyle, Feb. 7, 1953; children: Michael Gordon, Patrick Colin, William Scott, Linda Diane. Comml. art tech., Sinclair C.C., 1980. Instr. mixed media Riverbend Art Ctr., Dayton, Ohio, 1983-87; instr. watercolor Sinclair C.C., Dayton, Ohio, 1984—, Kettering Adult Sch., Ohio, 1986-93, Centerville Adult Sch., Ohio, 1988-92. Chmn. Dayton Fine Art Expo, 1986, 89, 95, Art in the Park, Dayton, 1984; pres. Tri Art Club, Dayton, 1986-88; juror of awards Ohio Arts and Crafts Guild, 1997; tchr. summer workshops, 1992—, watercolor on cruise-line, 2004. One-woman shows include Children's Med. Ctr. and Miami Valley Hosp., 1990-95, Gallery Ten, 1993, Benham's Grove, Centerville, 1994, 95, Thum'prints Gallery, Sea Pines Ctr., Hilton Head Island, S.C., 1994, 98, Miami Valley Gallery, 1996, Lumpkins Gallery, Centerville, 1996, Preble County Art Ctr., Eaton, Ohio, 1996, numerous others; exhibited in group shows at Ohio State U., Columbus, 1991, Middletown Fine Arts Ctr., 1992, Jade Gallery, Centerville, Ohio, 1997—, numerous others; represented in permanent collections Kettering Meml. Hosp., Miami Valley Hosp., Children's Med. Ctr., WHIO Radio/TV, Four Seasons Country Club, Sunrise Fed. Savs. and Loan, Pridgen Jewelers, Mattec Corp., Hospice of Dayton, Dayton Soc. Painters & Sculptors. Mem. Ohio Watercolor Soc. (assoc.), Western Ohio Watercolor Soc., Dayton Soc. Painters and Sculptors (pres. 1986-88). Republican. Roman Catholic. Studio: Coyle Studio 1610 Ambridge Rd Centerville OH 45459-5104

COYLE, DOROTHY, government agency administrator; Grad., Marquette U., Milw., Northwestern U. Kellogg Sch. Mgmt., 2001. Dir. Chgo. Office of Tourism, 1999—. Bd. dirs. Visit Ill. Named one of Top 40 Under 40, Crain's Chgo. Bus., 2006. Office: Chgo Office of Tourism Chgo Cultural Ctr 78 E Washington St 4th Fl Chicago IL 60602-4801 E-mail: dcoyle@cityofchicago.org.*

COYLE, DOROTHY SHERIN BEHEN, medical/surgical nurse; b. Jackson Heights, N.Y., Oct. 14, 1939; d. George William and Helen I. (Thompson) Sherin; m. David E. Behen, Nov. 25, 1967; m. John E. Coyle, May 3, 1997. RN, Sisters of Charity Hosp., Buffalo, 1960; BSN, SUNY, Buffalo, 1975, MS in Nursing Adminstrn., 1992. Surgery coord. Sisters of Charity Hosp., Buffalo, 1979-83, staff nurse operating rm., 1960-79; head nurse oper. rm. Dept. Vets. Affairs Med. Ctr., Buffalo, 1983-96; staff nurse oper. rm. VA Western N.Y. Healthcare System, 1997—2001; ret., 2001. Mem. Assn. Oper. Rm. Nurses, Assn. Oper. Rm. Nurses of Western N.Y. (past treas., bd. dirs.).

COYLE, LINDA MARIE, elementary school educator; d. Francis Thomas and Mary Anita Flynn; m. Michael Coyle, May 24, 1986. AAS, Scottsdale C.C., Scottsdale, Ariz., 1992; BS, Ea. Mich. U., Ypsilanti, Mich., 1978; MA, Ariz. State U., Tempe, Ariz., 1989. Sci. tchr. Paradise Valley Unified Sch. Dist., Phoenix, Ariz., 1980—, sci. program area coord., 1997—2004. Cmty. mem. representing sci. edn. Paradise Valley Learning Connections, Phoenix, Ariz., 2002—04. Recipient Greenway Mid. Sch. Tchr. of the Yr., Ctrl. Ariz. Mid. Level Tchg. Assn., 1999, Sch. Bus. Partnership, Grand Canyon Nat. Pk.-Revegetation, 1995-1999; grantee Environ. Edn. Rsch. Grant, Ariz. Adv. Coun. on Environ. Edn., 2001, Project Resource Grant for Environ. Edn., Salt River Project, 1995-1997. Mem.: NEA, NSTA, Paradise Valley Edn. Assn., Ariz. Sci. Coord. Assn., Ariz. Sci. Tchrs. Assn. Independent. Achievements include Ariz. Sci. Tchr. of the Yr; Crescordia Award for Environl. Edn.- Valley Forward Assn. Avocations: horseback riding, hiking, reading, travel. Office: Mountain Trail Mid Sch 2323 E Mountain Gate Pass Rd Phoenix AZ 85024 Office Phone: 480-538-7100.

COYLE, MARIE BRIDGET, retired microbiologist, retired lab administrator; b. Chgo., May 13, 1935; d. John and Bridget Veronica (Fitzpatrick) Coyle; m. Zheng Chen, Oct. 30, 1995 (div. Aug. 2000). BA, Mundelein Coll. (now part of Loyola U.), Chgo., 1957; MS, St. Louis U., 1963; PhD, Kans. State U., Manhattan, 1965. Diplomate Am. Bd. Med. Microbiology. Sci. instr. Sch. Nursing Columbus Hosp., Chgo., 1957-59; research assoc. U. Chgo., 1967-70; instr. U. Ill., Chgo., 1970-71; asst. prof. microbiology U. Wash., Seattle, 1973-80, assoc. prof., 1980-94, prof., 1994-2000; ret., 2000. Assoc. dir. Univ. Hosp., Seattle, 1973—76; dir. microbiology labs Harborview Med. Ctr. U. Wash., Seattle, 1976—, co-dir. postdoctoral tng. clinic microbiology,

1978—96, dir. postdoctoral tng. clinic microbiology, 1996—2000. Contbr. articles to profl. jours. Recipient Pasteur award, Ill. Soc. Microbiology, 1997, Profl. Recognition awards, Am. Bd. Med. Microbiology, Am. Bd. Med. Lab. Immunology, 2000. Fellow: Am. Acad. Microbiology; mem.: Am. Soc. Microbiology (chmn. clin. microbiology divsn. 1984—85, mem. coun. policy com. 1996—99, bd. govs. 2000—, bioMerieux Vitek Sonnenwirth Meml. award 1994), Acad. Clin. Lab. Physicians and Scientists (sec.-treas. 1980—83, mem. exec. com. 1985—90), Kappa Gamma Pi. Avocation: hiking. Business E-Mail: mbcoyle@u.washington.edu.

COYNE, ANN, social work educator; b. Medford, Mass., June 26, 1936; d. Edward James Jr. and Catherine Mary (Stokes) Gaffey; m. Dermot Patrick Coyne, June 15, 1957; children: Patrick J., Brian D., Thomas M., James E., Catherine A., Gerard W. BA, Cornell U., 1958; MSW, U. Nebr., 1975, PhD, 1980. Dir. community services Lancaster Office Mental Retardation, Lincoln, Nebr., 1971-75; assoc. prof. social work U. Nebr., Omaha, 1975-88, prof. social work, 1988—; dep. dir. State Dept. Social Services, Lincoln, 1981-82. Pres. Coyne & Assocs., Lincoln, 1978—; project dir. Child Welfare Tng. Inst., Lincoln, 1982-87; bd. dirs. Adoption Links Worldwide. Contbr. articles to profl. jours. Bd. dirs. Child Guidance Ctr., Lincoln, 1975-81, Crime and Community, Lincoln, 1983-85, Nebraskans for Peace, Lincoln, 1985, Nebraskans for Nicaraguan Children, 1987-95, Voices for Children in Nebr., 1987-92, Assn. Pediatricians United Health Children Nicaragua, 1995, v.p.; chmn. Gov.'s Planning Coun. on Devel. Disabilities, 1986-90. Mem. Nat. Assn. Social Workers, Child Welfare League of Am. (cert.), Sigma Xi. Democrat. Roman Catholic. Avocation: photography. Home: 1130 N 79th St Lincoln NE 68505-2007 Office: U Nebr Sch Social Work Annex 40 Omaha NE 68182-0293 Business E-Mail: acoyne@mail.unomaha.edu.

COYNE, JUDITH, editor; With Glamour mag., 1986—98, sr. editor articles dept., 1989—92, exec. editor, 1992—98; editor-in-chief New Woman, 1998—2000; v.p., editor-in-chief Women.com networks, 2000—01; exec. dir. Good Housekeeping, 2001—. Office: Good Housekeeping 959 Eighth Ave New York NY 10019

COZAD, RACHAEL BLACKBURN, museum director; Exec. dir. Iris and B. Gerald Cantor Found., L.A., 1994—2001; dir. Kemper Mus. Contemporary Art, Kansas City, Mo., 2001—. Office: Kemper Mus Contemporary Art 4420 Warwick Blvd Kansas City MO 64111-1821 Office Phone: 816-753-5784. Business E-Mail: rbcozad@kemperart.org.

COZART, HELEN RAY, church administrator, educator; b. Yonkers, N.Y., Dec. 31, 1928; d. Winston Anthony and Helen Mary (Sims) Mack; m. William Edward Cozart, Sr., June 21, 1947; children: Susanne, William Jr., Winston. Student, Trinity Coll. Bible, 1988—93. Supt. Sunday Sch. Smith Thompson's African Meth. Episcopal Zion Ch., Spring Valley, NY, 1991—98; dir. children and youth St. paul's Am. Meth. Zion Ch., 1999—. Dir. Westchester (N.Y.) children N.Y. Conf. African Meth. Episc. Zion Ch., 2001—, dir. L.I. (N.Y.) children N.Y. Conf., 1993—2000, mem. N.Y. conf.; supr. buds promise St. Paul's Am. Meth. Zion Ch., 1988—99, coord. first acobytles, 1989, dir. christian edn., 1989—99, coord. first vacation bible sch., 1989—, dir. Findley Youth Choir, 1991—, dir. adults, 2006. Reporter: Star of Zion, 1998—; editor: The Pulse Newsletter, 2000; author: The Black Church The Beginning, 2005. Committee person Clarkstown Dem. Com., New City, NY, 1988—92. Named Mother of Yr., St. Paul's Am. Meth. Zion Ch., 1997; recipient Humanitarian award, Town Ramapo, 1987, Mother's Day honoree, Smith Thompson Am. Meth. Zion Ch., 2001, Lifetime Achievement Trailblazer award, NAACP, 2004, honoree, New Beginnings Dignity Svcs., 2004, Spl. Recognition award, Christian Edn. A.M.E. Zion NY Conf., 2005. Democrat. Meth. Episc. Avocation: writing. Home: 13 Dickinson Ave Nyack NY 10960

COZZA, HELEN ROCK, art educator, artist; b. Auburn, N.Y., Jan. 16, 1956; d. Ralph and Patricia Ann Gannetti. BS, Buffalo State Coll., 1978, cert in graphic design, 1988; postgrad., Cleve. State U., 1998-99; grad. student, U. New Mex., 2003—. Asst. dir. People Art Gallery, Buffalo, 1982-84; art tchr. Brecksvill-Broadview H.S., Ohio, 1999—2002. Exhibited in group shows at Butler Inst. Art, 1989, U. Wis., 1999, 37th Annual Juried Internat. Exhbn., El Paso, Tex., 2004. Personal E-mail: cozzatron@qwest.net.

COZZENS, MIMI, actress, director; b. Bklyn. d. Milton L. Cozzens and Dorothy Pitt. Student, Emerson Coll., 1952—54; BA in Drama Speech, Hofstra Coll., 1956. Tchr., dir. Va. Ave. Project, L.A., 1991—92; with Interact Theatre Co., 2005—. Actor: (TV series) Malcolm in the Middle, Cold Case, The Practice, Will & Grace, Providence, 3d Rock From The Sun, Seinfeld, Chgo. Hope, Seventh Heaven, The Drew Carey Show, Diagnosis Murder, Star Trek; (TV films) The Pandora Project, Perfect Prey, Tell Me No Secrets, Liz: The Elizabeth Taylor Story, Livewire, Daddy, Night Of The Cyclone, Spring Break; (Broadway plays) I Ought To Be In Pictures, Children Of A Lesser God, Same Time Next Year; (plays) The Dining Room, Mornings At Seven, Prisoner Of Second Ave, Fallen Angels, Tribute, regional prodns., Her Majesty the King, 2006, I Coulda Been a Kennedy, 2006. Rep. Valley Theatre League, North Hollywood, Calif., 1992—94. Mem.: Women In Film (co-chmn. dirs. workshop 1990—96), Acad. TV Arts and Scis. Achievements include John Powers model since age 2 1/2; former champion water skier, 14 trophies in the 1950's. Avocations: water-skiing, scuba diving, sculpting.

CRABB, BARBARA BRANDRIFF, federal judge; b. Green Bay, Wis., Mar. 17, 1939; d. Charles Edward and Mary (Forrest) Brandriff; m. Theodore E. Crabb, Jr., Aug. 29, 1959; children: Julia Forrest, Philip Elliott. AB, U. Wis., 1960, JD, 1962. Bar: Wis. 1963. Assoc. Roberts, Boardman, Suhr and Curry, Madison, Wis., 1962-64; legal rschr. Sch. Law, U. Wis., 1968-70, Am. Bar Assn., Madison, 1970-71; US magistrate US Dist Ct (we. dist.) Wis., Madison, 1971-79; judge U.S. Dist. Ct. (we. dist.) Wis., Madison, 1979—, chief judge, 1980-96, 2002—. Mem. Gov. Wis. Task Force Prison Reform, 1971-73 Membership chmn., v.p. Milw. LWV, 1966-68; mem. Milw. Jr. League, 1967-68. Mem. ABA, Nat. Assn. Women Judges, State Bar Wis., Dane County Bar Assn., U. Wis. Law Alumni Assn. Office: US Dist Ct PO Box 591 120 N Henry St Madison WI 53701-0591

CRABB, VIRGINIA GEANY RUTH, librarian; b. Whittier, Calif., Dec. 30, 1951; d. Lawrence Guerro and Nellie Aguilar Gutierrez; m. Rod D. Crabb, Sept. 8, 1973; 1 child, Adam Matthew. AA in Fgn. Lang., Calif. State U., Fullerton, 1973. Children's librarian-sr. libr. asst. Orange County Libr., La Palma, Calif., 1975—76, Brea, Calif., 1976—81, sr. libr. asst. Mission Viejo, Calif., 1981—83, Orange County Libr.-University Park, Irvine, Calif., 1982—83, Orange County Libr., San Juan Capistrano, Calif., 1983—96; libr. - part time in absence of regular libr. Laguna Beach Sch. of Arts, Laguna Beach, Calif., 1988—88; sr. libr. asst. Orange County Libr., Garden Grove, Calif., 1996—98, Orange County Library-Costa Mesa, Costa Mesa, 1998—2001; children's librarian Orangewood Children's Home Libr., Orange, Calif., 2001—. Art asst. vol. Irvine Fine Arts, Irvine, Calif., 1985—85. Recipient Perspectives Study Program Cert., U. S. Ctr. for World Mission, 2003. Avocation: art travel.

CRABTREE, BEVERLY JUNE, retired dean; b. Lincoln, Nebr., June 22, 1937; d. Wayne Uniack and Frances Margaret (Wibbels) Deles Dernier; m. Robert Jewell Crabtree, June 1, 1958; children: Gregory, Karen. BS in Edn., U. Mo., 1959, MEd, 1962; PhD, Iowa State U., 1965. Tchr. home econs. area pub. schs., Pierce City and Sarcoxie, Mo., 1959-61; mem. faculty home econs. Mich. State U., East Lansing, 1964-67; assoc. prof. U. Mo., Columbia, 1967-72, coord. home econs. edn., 1967-73, prof., 1972-73, assoc. dean home econs., dir. home econs. extension programs, 1973-75; dean Coll. Home Econs. Okla. State U., Stillwater, 1975-87; dean Coll. Family and Consumer Scis. Iowa State U., Ames, 1987-97, ret., 1997. Mem. faculty Family Impact Seminar Inst. Ednl. Leadership, George Washington U., 1976-82, Cath. U. Am., 1982-87; mem. nat. panel cons. for Vocat. Ednl. Pers. Devel., 1969-70; mem. nat. com. on future of coop. extension USDA and Nat. Assn. State Univs. and Land Grant Colls., 1982; mem. joint coun. on food and agrl. scis., 1987-91. Contbr. articles in field to profl. jours. Gen. Foods fellow, 1963-64; recipient Centennial Alumni award Coll. Home Econs. Iowa State U., 1971, Alumni Citation of Merit, Coll. Home Econs. U. Mo., 1976, Profl. Achievement award Iow State U., 1983. Mem. Am. Home Econs. Assn. (pres. 1977-78, chmn. adv. coun. Ctr. for Family 1982-83, mem. coun. profl. devel. 1980-83, a leader to commemorate 75th anniversary 1984, pres. found. 1987-88, chair Coun. for Certification 1991-92, chair Coun. for Accreditation 1997-98, Disting. Svc. award 1993), Okla. Home Econs. Assn. (Profl. Achievement award 1983), Nat. Assn. State Univs. and Land Grant Colls. (mem. commn. home econs. 1981-84), Assn. Tchr. Educators, Home Econs. Edn. Assn., Nat. Coun. of Adminstrs. of Home Econs., Am. Ednl. Rsch. Assn., Am. Assn. Higher Edn., Nat. Assn. Tchr. Educators for Home Econs. (pres. 1969), Nat. Coun. on Family Relations, Mortar Bd., Golden Key, Omicron Nu, Phi Upsilon Omicron, Phi Delta Kappa, Omicron Delta Kappa, Pi Lambda Theta, Phi Kappa Phi, Gamma Sigma Delta. Methodist. Home: 3113 Rosewood Cir Ames IA 50014-4589

CRABTREE, DAVIDA FOY, minister; b. Waterbury, Conn., June 7, 1944; d. Alfred and Davida (Blakeslee) Foy; m. David T. Hindinger Jr., Aug. 28, 1982; stepchildren: Elizabeth Anne, David Todd. BS, Marietta Coll., 1967; MDiv, Andover Newton Theol. Sch., 1972; D of Ministry, Hartford Sem., 1989. Ordained to ministry United Ch. of Christ, 1972. Founder, exec. dir. Prudence Crandall Ctr. for Women, New Britain, Conn., 1973-76; min., dir. Greater Hartford (Conn.) Campus Ministry, 1976-80; sr. min. Colchester (Conn.) Federated Ch., 1980-91; bd. dirs. Conn. Conf. United Ch. of Christ, Hartford, 1982-90; conf. min. So. Calif. Conf., United Ch. of Christ, Pasadena, 1991-96, Conn. Conf., United Ch. of Christ, Hartford, 1996—. Rsch. assoc. Harvard Div. Sch., Cambridge, Mass., 1975—76. Author: The Empowering Church, 1989 (named one of Top Ten Books of Yr. 1990); editorial advisor Alban Inst., 1990-98. Bd. dirs. Hartford region YWCA, 1979-82, Christian Conf. of Conn., 1997—; trustee Cragin Meml. Libr., Colchester, 1980-91, Hartford Sem., 1983-91, Sch. of Theology at Claremont, 1993-96, Andover Newton Theol. Sch., 1997—; founder Youth Svcs. Bur., Colchester, 1984-89; pres. Creative Devel. for Colchester Inc., 1989-91; coun. Religious Leaders of L.A., 1991-96; v.p. Hope in Youth Campaign, 1992-96; dir. UCC Ins. bd., 1993-2000, 06—; bd. dirs. Amistad America, 1998—; trustee UCC Cornerstone Fund, 2000-04; chair Coun. of Conf. Mins., United Ch. of Christ, 2004-06. Named one of Outstanding Conn. Women, UN Assn., 1987; recipient Antoinette Brown award, Gen. Synod, United Ch. of Christ, 1977, Conf. Preacher award, Conn. Conf. United Ch. of Christ, 1982, Woman in Leadership award, Hartford region YWCA, 1987, Pres.'s award, Conn. Coalition Against Domestic Violence, 1997, Somos Uno award, United Neighborhood Orgn., 1995, award, Vet. Feminists Am., 2005. Mem. Nat. Coun. Chs. (bd. dirs. 1969-81), Christians for Justice Action (exec. com. 1981-91). Mem. United Ch. Of Christ. E-mail: dfc@ctucc.org.

CRABTREE, VALLERI JAYNE, real estate company executive, educator, lawyer; b. Columbus, Ohio, Feb. 22, 1957; d. Ralph Dale and Ida Mae (Call) C. BS in Bus. Adminstn., Ohio State U., 1979; JD, Capital U., 1983. Bar: Ohio 1983; lic. real estate broker, Ohio, Fla.; CLU; FLMI; accredited buyers rep. Various mgmt. positions Nationwide Life Ins. Co., Columbus, 1980-87, dir. group annuity underwriting, adminstr., 1987-91; pvt. practice Columbus, 1991—95, 1999—; real estate salesperson Metro II Realty, Henderson Realty, Columbus, 1991-94; pres., broker Onyx Real Estate Svcs., Inc., Columbus, 1994—2003, Condos to Castles Realty, Inc., 2003—; atty., owner Crabtree & Assocs., Attys. at Law, Columbus, 1995-99; owner Crabtree Jocularities, 2002—, Quixtar IBO, 2003—. Adj. faculty Columbus State C.C., 1995-2002; instr. Inst. Fla. Real Estate Careers, Inc., 2003—, dir. of instr. and course devel., 2005—; mem. equal opportunity com. Columbus Bd. Realtors, 1996-98, 2000-2002. Chair various coms. Welsh Hills Sch. Parent Orgn., 2000—02; asst. brownie leader Girl Scouts USA, 2002—03; pres. Royal Ballet Parents Orgn., 2002—05, Dems. of Celebration, 2004—; vice chair Osceola County Dem. Exec. Com., 2005—; trustee Unity Ch. Christianity, Columbus, 1991—94, 1999—2000, usher, 1990—2000, chair devel. com., 1996—99; vol. bus. mgr. Light in the Woods Ch., 2000—03; bd. dirs. Royal Celebration Ballet, Inc., 2003—. Mem. AAUW, ACLU. Democrat. Avocation: toy collecting. Office: Inst Fla Real Estate Careers Inc 5029 Edgewater Dr Orlando FL 32810 Office Phone: 321-246-0361.

CRACAUER, CYNTHIA PHIFER, architectural firm executive; BA magna cum laude, Princeton U., NJ, MArch. From arch. to prin. Swanke, Hayden, Connell Archs., N.Y., 1989—99, prin., 1999—, mng. prin. N.Y. Office, 2000—. Mem. exec. com. Swanke, Hayden, Connell Archs., prin.-in-charge spl. projects; adj. asst. prof. Sch. Architecture N.J. Inst. Tech.; vis. critic Princeton (N.J.) U., U. Va. Mem. Nat. Trust Hist. Preservation; active Ptnrs. Sacred Places. Office: SHCA 295 Lafayette St New York NY 10012

CRADDOCK, CATHERINE TODD, accountant; b. Dallas, June 28, 1948; d. Milton Whaley and Margaret Mary Todd; m. John Parker Craddock, May 21, 1970; children: Cliff, Ashley, J. Forrest. BA, Austin Coll., Sherman, Tex., 1970. CPA, Tex. Med. technologist M.D. Anderson Hosp., Houston, 1972-74; acct. Price Waterhouse, Sydney, Australia, 1981, Greenstein Logan & Co., Houston, 1982-86; pvt. practice acctg., Houston, 1986—. Elder, mem. session St. Thomas Presbyn. Ch., Houston, 1990—; mem. steering com. Robert E. Lee H.S., Houston, 1994-98, treas. PTO, 1994-97, pres., 1997-98, mem. adv. com. for Houston Ind. Sch. Dist., 1997-98. Mem. Tex. Soc. CPA's, Houston Estate and Fin. Forum. Avocations: reading, cooking. Office: PO Box 5829 Leander TX 78645-0028

CRADDOCK, MARY SPENCER JACK, volunteer; b. Greensboro, Ala., Dec. 12, 1912; d. Theodore Henley Jack and Alice Searcy Ashley; m. George Barksdale Craddock, Feb. 1, 1941 (dec. Dec. 11, 1985); children: George B. Jr., Theodore J., Alice (Craddock) Massey. BA, Emory U., 1933. Pres. Lynchburg Jr. League, Va., 1944—45; founder, bd. dirs. Seven Hills Sch., Lynchburg, 1959—70; Va. regent Gunston Hall Plantation, Commonwealth Va., 1980—92; pres. Family Svc., Lynchburg. Founder, bd. dirs. Lynchburg Mus. Sys., 1975—79; 30 yr. chmn. Lunchburg Friends Stratford Plantation; bd. dirs. Meals on Wheels, Lynchburg, 1993—96, Lynchburg Bicentennial Commn., 1973—76, Greater Lynchburg Cmty. Trust, 1991—99. Mem.: Nat. Soc. Col. Dames of Am. (Roll of Honor 1992—93), Garden Club Va., Boonsboro Country Club, Phi Beta Kappa. Episcopalian. Avocations: travel, bridge, reading, historic preservation. Home: 3249 Landon St Lynchburg VA 24503

CRADLER, JUDITH A., science educator; d. Robert E. and Ruth H. Keller; m. Burton C. Cradler, Dec. 22, 1973; children: Christopher, Tyler. BA, SUNY, Geneseo, 1968; MEd, U. Buffalo, N.Y., 1973; postgrad., U. Mass., Amherst. Cert. tchr. biology, social studies N.Y., tchr. sci. Mass. Sci. tchr. Lew-Port Ctrl. Sch., Youngstown, NY, 1968—70; sci. tchr. grade 7 Starpoint Ctrl. Sch., Lockport, NY, 1970—74; sci. tchr. grades 7 and 9 Worcester Pub. Schs., Mass., 1994—. Design team mem. New Eng. Small Sch. Network, Worcester, 2001; rep. U.S. People to People, Beijing, 2005. Contbr. articles to profl. jours. Mem. Northbor Jr. Woman's Club, 1998—; chmn bd. Boy Scout Am., Southboro, Mass., 1992—96. Named Tchr. of the Yr., Worcester Pub.Schs., 2000. Mem.: ASCD, NEA, Edn. Assn. Worcester, Mass. Edn. Assn., Nat. Assn. of Rsch. in Sci., Nat. Sci. Tchrs. Assn. Avocations: gardening, reading, American revolution history. Home: 78 Indian Meadow Dr Northborough MA 01532

CRADY, PAULA GANNON, secondary school educator; b. Peoria, Ill., Oct. 1, 1946; d. Walter Franklin and Alma Edgcomb Gannon; children: Marc J., Sarah C. Rood. BS, Bradley U., Peoria, 1969; MS in Sch. Adminstrn., Olivet U., Bourbonais, Ill., 2005. English tchr. Peoria Pub. Schs. 150, 1970—71; history/English tchr. Scott Ctr. Sch., Bloomington, Ill., 1999—2001; English tchr. Kankakee Sch. Dist. III, Ill., 2001—. Program dir. Newcomers, Charleston, Ill., 1976; v.p. Welcome Wagon, Carbondale, Ill., 1977. Office: Kankakee Sch Dist III Salt Program 710 N Chicago Kankakee IL 60901

CRAFT, CHERYL MAE, neurobiologist, anatomist, researcher; b. Lynch, Ky., Apr. 15, 1947; d. Cecil Berton and Lillian Lovelle C.; m. Laney K. Cormney, Oct. 14, 1967 (div. Sept. 1980); children: Tyler Craft Cormney, Ryan Berton Cormney (dec.); m. Richard N. Lolley (dec.). BS in Biology, Chemistry and Math., Valdosta State Coll., 1969; cert. in Tchg. Biology and Math., Ea. Ky. U., 1971; PhD in Human Anatomy and Neurosci., U. Tex., San Antonio, 1984. Undergrad. rsch. asst. Ea. Ky. U., Richmond, 1965-67; tchg. asst. dept. cell-structural biology U. Tex. Health Sci. Ctr., San Antonio, 1979-84; postdoctoral fellowship lab. devel. neurobiology NICHD and LMDB/NEI, Bethesda, Md., 1984-86; instr. dept. psychiatry U. Tex. Southwestern Med. Ctr., Dallas, 1986-87, asst. prof., 1987-91; dir. lab. Molecular Neurogenetics Schizophrenia Rsch. Ctr., VA Med. Ctr., Dallas, 1988-94; dir. Lab. Molecular Neurogenetics Mental Health Clinic Rsch. Ctr., U. Tex. Southwestern Med. Ctr., 1990-94; assoc. prof. U. Tex. Southwestern Med. Ctr., 1991-94; Mary D. Allen chair Doheny Eye Inst. U. So. Calif. Keck Sch. Medicine, L.A., Calif., 1994—, founding chmn. dept. cell and neurobiology, 1994—2004. Ad hoc reviewer NEI/NIH, Bethesda, 1993—; reviewer Molecular Biology, NSPB Fight for Sight Grants, 1991-94; STAR-sci. adv. bd. U. So. Calif./Bravo Magnet H.S., L.A., 1995—. Contbr. author: Melatonin: Biosynthesis, Physiological Effects, 1993; exec. editor Exptl. Eye Rsch. jour., 1993—; editor Molecular Vision. Recipient Merit award for rsch. VA Med. Ctr., 1992, 93, 94, nomination for Women in Sci. and Engring. award Dallas VA, 1992, 93; NEI fellow, 1986, NICHD/NIH fellow, 1986. Mem. AAAS, AAUW, Assn. for Rsch. in Vision and Ophthalmology (chair program planning com. 1991-94), Am. Soc. for Neurochemistry (Jordi Folch Pi Outstanding Young Investigator 1992), Sigma Xi (sec./treas. 1986-93, pres. 1993-94). Avocations: reading, travel. Office: U So Calif Keck Sch Medicine 1355 San Pablo St Rm 405 DVRC Los Angeles CA 90033 Office Phone: 323-442-6694. Personal E-mail: eyesightresearch@hotmail.com. Business E-Mail: ccraft@usc.edu.

CRAFT, LIZ, artist; b. LA, 1970; BA, Otis Parsons, 1994; MFA, UCLA, 1997. One-woman shows include, Richard Telles Fine Art, LA, 1998, Centrum fur Gegenwartskunst Oberosterreich, Linz, Austria, 2001, Galerie Nathalie Obadia, Paris, 2001, Public Art Fund, NY, 2002, A Real Mother For Ya, Sadie Coles HQ, London, 2002, Marianne Boesky Gallery, 2003, exhibited in group shows at Happy Trails, Coll. Creative Studies, U. Santa Barbara, 1999, Hot Spots, Weatherspoon Gallery, U. NC, 1999, Good Luck for You, Transmission Gallery, Edinburgh, 2000, Calif. Dreamin', Gallery Art, Carlsen Ctr., Johnson County Cmty. Coll., Kans. City, 2000, Young & Dumb, ACME, LA, 2001, Play it as it Lays, The London Inst. Gallery, 2002, Wheeling - Krad Kult Tour! Motorcycles in Art, Frankfurt am Main, Germany, 2002, 3-D, Friedrich Petzel Gallery, 2003, The Thought That Counts, Sister, LA, 2003, It's All An Illusion, Migros Museum fur Gegenwartskunst, Zurich, 2004, Whitney Biennial, Whitney Mus. Am. Art, 2004, Seeing Other People, 2004. Mailing: c/o Marianne Boesky Gallery 535 West 22st St New York NY 10011

CRAFT, MARY FAYE, public relations executive, consultant, television producer, poet; b. Glennville, Ga., Jan. 20, 1936; d. James Levy Durrence and Mary Frances (Merritt) Thompson; widow; children: James P. Craft, Joseph A. Craft. DD, Calvary Grace Bible Inst., Rillton, Pa., 1975; cert. of journalism arts, CNS Internat., Willow Springs, Mo., 1991; D of Phil. in Film and Video, LaSalle U., Mandeville, La., 1995. Cert. tchr., Protocol Sch. of Washington, D.C., 1993. Dist. mgr. Family Record Plan, Honolulu, 1963-64; acct. exec. Heirloom Inc., Honolulu, 1964-65; pres. Durracraft Advt. and Photography, Cocoa Beach, Orlando, Fla., 1965-71; CEO Western American Corp., Orlando, 1971-73; pres. MF Craft & Assoc. Travel, Orlando, 1972-73, Mary Faye Craft & Assocs., Washington, 1977—; prodr., host FCAC Ch. 10, Fairfax, Va., 1990—; editor MFDC Rev., Springfield, Va., 1992—; CEO Facets, Inc., Savannah, Ga., 2004—. Owner, mgr. Gallery Unique, Alexandria, Va., 1974-75. Author: Poems of Perception, 1984, Gifts of Poetry, 1986, Poems by Mary Faye Craft, 1988, Poems A to Z, 1997, MFDC Rev. Millennium edit., 1999, Christmas Poems and Songs, 2000, The Legend of Tattnall Count and other Poems, 2001, MFDC Rev. edit., 2002, True to the Red White and Blue, 20 Facets of Life, 2003, Life is a Poem, 2005; composer, performer music album Facets of Music, 1989 (Mid Atlantic Contest winner 1990). Bd. dirs. Jacksonville Sister's City Assn., 1996—; active Nursing Home Ministries, 1985—, Homeless Ministries, 1989—. Recipient Paul E. Garber award, Grover Loening award, Gill Robb Wilson award Civil Air Patrol, Maxwell AFB, Ala., 1982, 83, Golden Poets award, World of Poetry, Las Vegas, 1987, Tattnal County Bicentennial Poet Laureate award, 2001. Mem. AAUW, Nat. Press Club, Nat. Space Club, C. of C., Garden Club, Mil. Officers Assn., Air Force Assn., Marine Corps Assn., Rotary (Paul Harris fellow), Phi Theta Kappa. Republican. Roman Catholic. Avocations: photography, television production. Home: PO Box 220 Glennville GA 30427 Office Phone: 202-737-2249. Personal E-mail: mfctv@aol.com.

CRAFT DAVIS, AUDREY ELLEN, writer, educator; b. Vanceburg, Ky., June 9, 1926; d. James Elmer and Lula Alice (Vance) Gilkison; m. Vernon Titus Craft, Nov. 5, 1943 (dec. Aug. 1979); children: James Vernon Craft, Alice Ann Craft Schuler; m. Louis Amzie Davis, Oct. 22, 1986. PhD, Ohio U., 1964; Dr. of Metaphysics, Coll. Divine Metaphysics, 1968; DD, Ohio U., 1971; postgrad., St. Petersburg Jr. Coll., 1975; DD (hon.), Assoc. Minister, Coll. Metephysical Studies, 1998. Owner beauty salon Audrey Craft Enterprises, Tampa Bay, Fla., 1970-83, owner cosmetic co. Portsmouth, Ohio, 1958-70; owner, distbr. Nightingale Motivation, Tampa Bay, 1960—; tchr., counselor Bus. Coll. U., Tampa Bay, 1965—; ins. staff Investors Heritage & Wabash, Portsmouth, 1967-70; ins. broker Jackson Nat. & Wabash, Tampa Bay, 1971-91; pres. The Gardens 107, Inc., Tampa Bay, 1987—. Travel writer, counselor Cruises/Travel & Etc., Fla., 1981—. Author: (poetry) Pathways, 1990, Metaphysical Techniques That Really Work, 1994, (Spanish translation), 2nd edit., 2002, Metaphysical Encounters, 1992, How to Stay Secure in a Chaotic World, 1993, Metaphysics Encounters of a Fourth Kind, 1995, How to Safeguard Your World and Avoid Becoming a Target, 1996, Angel Trails, 2003, Hidden Truths and Unusual Events of the Bible, 2002, Making Love with God, 2006, Metaphysical Encounters of a 4th Kind, An Exciting Science, 2006, Magnificent Journey Into Prosperity Consciousness; contbr. articles to profl. jours. Bd. dirs. The Gardens Domicurculums, Cmty. Coun., 1987—; bd. dirs. State Bd. Cosmetology, Columbus, Ohio, 1962-63, Bus. and Profl. Women, Portsmouth, 1967-69, Sci. Rsch., Portsmouth, 1965-69, Tampa Bay, 1972-74. Recipient Key to Miami, Office of Mayor Claude Kirk, 1969, Million Dollar trophy Lt. Gov. John Brown Ohio; commd. Ky. Col. by Gov. Edward T. Breathitt, 1968, Gov. Wendell Ford, 1969. Mem. AARP, S.E. Writers Assn., Christian Writers Guild, Writers Digest Book Club, Nat. Assn. Retired Fed. Employees (assoc.), Am. Heart Assn. (chmn. Seminole area 1994). Democrat. Avocations: writing, lectures, counseling, travel, meditation. Home and Office: 102 Saint Petersburg Dr W Oldsmar FL 34677-3620

CRAFTON-MASTERSON, ADRIENNE, real estate company executive; b. Providence, Mar. 6, 1926; d. John Harold and Adrienne (Fitzgerald) Crafton; m. Francis T. Masterson, May 31, 1947 (div. Jan. 1977); children: Mary Victoria Masterson Bush, Kathleen Joan, John Andrew, Barbara Lynn Harrison Student, No. Va. C.C., 1971-74; A in Biblical Studies, Christ to World Bible Inst., Jacksonville, Fla., 1992; A in Pastoral Leadership, Calvary Bible Inst., Jacksonville, Fla., 1993. Mem. staff Senator T.F. Green of R.I., Washington, 1944-47, 54-60, with U.S. Senate Com. on Campaign Expenditures, 1944-45; asst. chief clk. Ho. Govt. Ops. Com., 1948-49; clk. Ho. Campaign Expenditures Com., 1950; asst. appointment sec. Office of Pres., 1951-53; with Hubbard Realty, Alexandria, Va., 1962-67; owner, mgr. Adrienne C. Masterson Real Estate, Alexandria, 1968-82; pres. Adrienne Investment Real Estate (AIRE) Ltd., Alexandria, 1982-91; devel. staff writer Calvary Internat., Jacksonville, Fla., 1992-93; Adrienne Crafton-Masterson Real Estate, Winchester, Va., 1993-94, owner, prin., broker Haymarket, Va., 1994—. Pres. AIRE-Merkli developers, 1988-92; founder AIHRE USA, Inc., 1993—. Mem. adv. panel Fairfax County (Va.) Coun. on Arts, 1987-88; founder, pres. Mt. Vernon/Lee Cultural Ctr. Found., Inc. 1984-92; mem. Haymarket (Va.) Hist. Commn., 1994-95, 97-2001, chmn., 1999-2001. Fellow Internat. Biog. Ctr. (dep. dir. gen.); mem. Internat. Orgn. Real Estate Appraisers (sr.), Nat. Assn. Realtors, No. Va. Assn. Realtors (chmn. comml.

and indsl. com. 1982-83, cmty. revitalization com. 1983-84, pres. land comml. indsl. mems. 1985, v.p. land comml. and indsl. mems. 1989), Fairfax Affordable Housing Inc. (sec. 1990-91), Haymarket-Gainesville (Va.) Busl. and Profl. Assn. (bd. dirs. 1996-99, sec. 1998-99), Alexandria C. of C., Mt. Vernon/Lee C. of C., Friends of Kennedy Ctr. (founder), Optimist Club Gainesville-Haymarket (charter, bd. dirs. 1997-99). Mailing: 353 Plymouth St Safety Harbor FL 34695 Office Phone: 703-754-1166. Personal E-mail: aihrecraft@earthlink.net.

CRAGER, GINNY LEE, gifted and talented educator; b. Parker Valley, Idaho, Oct. 29, 1941; d. John Loren Wingler and Isabel Sylvia Parker-Wingler; m. J.L. Crager, Apr. 21, 1963; children: Raven Jennifer Barkley, Brenny Gail, Latika Black Horse Hope. BA, U. So. Miss., Hattiesburg, 1975, MS, 1982, D of Adminstrn., 1984. Log comptr. Martin Bros. Container Corp, Oakland, Oreg., 1960—64, Ga. Pacific Corp, Coos Bay, 1964—68; instr. gifted elem. Buckatunna Elem. Sch., Miss., 1988—96; instr. gifted art history Wayne County H.S., Waynesboro, 1996—. Design cons. Neshtas Creations, Waynesboro, 1999—, Raven Clothiers, Inc., 1994—; v.p. C & C Agy. Inc., 2002—. Singer: (Operas) Madam Butterfly (Lead Singer, 1960). Chair Am. Cancer Soc., Waynesboro, 1998—2006, luminaria chair relay life, 1998—2006. Recipient Tchr. of Yr., Oak Grove, 1976—77, Outstanding Tchr., Buckatunna Parent Org, 1994, Golden Apple award, WDAM TV/ Alfa Ins., 1994, Allen R. Barton award, Miss. Power, 1995; fellow, 1996; grantee, Hewlett Packard, 2002. Mem.: Miss. Profl. Educators (hon.; legis. del. 1987—2006). Independent. Baptist. Achievements include design of Native American Clothing Designer. Avocations: landscape painting, jewelry designing, leather work, horseback riding, swimming. Home: POBox 833 Waynesboro MS 39367 Office: Wayne County High School 1325 Azalea Drive Waynesboro MS 39367 Office Phone: 601-735-2405. Home Fax: 601-671-8944; Office Fax: 601-671-8944. Personal E-mail: ladyelvis1941@hotmail.com.

CRAGLE, DONNA LYNNE, medical researcher, director; b. Ft Knox, Ky., Oct. 14, 1953; BA in Biol. Scis., Ind. U., 1974; MS in Human Genetics, Med. Coll. Va., 1978; PhD in Environ. Epidemiology, U. N.C., 1984. Med. lab. technologist Blood Bank, N.C. Meml. Hosp., Chapel Hill, 1977-81; tchr. asst. dept. epidemiology U. N.C., Chapel Hill, 1979-80; epidemiologist Ctr. Epidemiol. Rsch., Oak Ridge Assoc. Univs., 1981082, epidmiology rsch. sect. leader, 1983-85, epidemiology rsch. sect. leader, dep. dir., 1986-91, epidemiology rsch. leader, dir., 1991—; dir. basic and applied rsch. Oak Ridge Assocs. Univs., 1998—. Tchr. gen. genetics Pellissippi State Tech. C.C., 1993-96; cons. in field. Contbr. articles to profl. jours. Office: Oak Ridge Assoc Univs Oak Ridge Inst Sci and Edn PO Box 117 Oak Ridge TN 37831-0117

CRAGNOLIN, KAREN ZAMBELLA, real estate developer, lawyer; b. Boston, May 19, 1949; d. John T. Zambella and Corrine M. (Feeney) Zenga; m. Robert Louis Cragnolin, Sept. 8, 1974; 1 child, Nikki Josephine. BA, Georgian Ct. Coll., 1971; JD, New Eng. Sch. Law, 1974. Bar: N.Y. 1974, D.C. 1981. Sr. tax editor Prentice-Hall, Englewood Cliffs, N.J., 1974-76; dir. pub. affairs Am.-Arab Affairs Coun., Washington, 1981-83; founder, dir. Am. Bus. Coun., Dubai, United Arab Emirates, 1983-86; dir. River Link, Inc., Asheville, N.C., 1987—. Bd. trustees Clean Water Mgmt. Trust Fund, 1996-, chair acquisitions com.; bd. trustees WNC Tommorrow, Complemtary Health Care, Inc. Pres. Young Dems., Georgian Court, N.J., 1970-71; chair Greenway Commn., Asheville, N.C., 1990—; pres., bd. dirs. Leadership Asheville, 1993—, Asheville Area C. of C., 1992-96; bd. dirs. Hand Made Am., Asheville, 1994—, Handi-Skills, Asheville, 1986-90, chmn., 1986-88; bd. dirs. French Bd. River Garden Club Found., 2005—. Recipient Downtown Hero award Asheville Downtown Assn., 1991, Cir. Excellence Leadership Asheville, 1995, Friend of River award Land Regional Coun., 1995, Athena award Asheville C. of C., 1999. Mem. D.C. Bar Assn., N.Y. Bar Assn. Avocations: gardening, cooking, paddling. Home: 7 Cedarcliff Rd Asheville NC 28803-2905 Office: RiverLink Inc PO Box 15488 Asheville NC 28813-0488 Office Phone: 828-252-8474 110. Business E-Mail: Karen@riverlink.org.

CRAHALLA, JACQUELINE R., state representative; b. Phila., Oct. 8, 1940; m. Benjamin R. Crahalla; children: Benny, Richie(dec.). BA in English, Gwynedd-Mercy Coll. Supr. Lower Providence Twp.; twp. liaison Lower Providence Sewer Authority; Pa. state rep., 2002—06. Mgr. corp. contbn. AstraZeneca; human health divsn. Merck & Co., Inc. Feature writer, weekly corr. (newpaper) Today's Post. Republican. Lutheran. Office: 161B East Wing Harrisburg PA 17120-2020

CRAHAN, ELIZABETH SCHMIDT, librarian; b. Cleve., Oct. 6, 1913; d. Edward and Margaret (Adams) Schmidt; m. Kenneth Acker, 1938 (div. 1968); children: Margaret Miller, John Acker, Steven Acker, Charles Acker; m. Marcus E. Crahan, Dec. 16, 1968. Student, Wellesley Coll., 1931—32; BArch, U. So. Calif., 1937, MLS, 1960. Reference libr. Los Angeles County Med. Assn., L.A., 1960—61, head reference libr., 1961—67, asst. libr., 1967—78, dir. libr. svcs., 1978—90. Mem.: Fletcher Soc., Am. Assn. History Medicine, George Dock Soc. History of Medicine, Med. Libr. Group So. Calif. and Ariz., Med. Libr. Assn., Friends of the UCLA Libr. (pres. 1977—79, sec. 1978—97), Zamorano Club. E-mail: escrahan@mcn.com.

CRAIG, CAROL MILLS, marriage, family and child counselor; b. Berkeley, Calif. BA in Psychology (hon.), U. Calif., Santa Cruz, 1974; MA in Counseling Psychology, John F. Kennedy U., 1980; doctoral student, Calif. Sch. Profl. Psychology, Berkeley, 1980-87, Columbia Pacific U., San Rafael, Calif., 1987—. Psychology intern Fed. Correction Inst., Pleasanton, Calif., 1979-81, Letterman Army Med. Ctr., San Francisco, 1980-82, VA Mental Hygiene Clinic, Oakland, Calif., 1981-82; instr. Martinez Adult Sch., 1983, Piedmont Adult Edn., Oakland, 1986; biofeedback and stress mgmt. cons. Oakland, 1986—; child counselor Buddies-A Nonprofit, Counseling Svc. for Persons in the Arts, Lafayette, Calif., 1993—; founder Chesley Sch., 1994, Healing with Music for People and All Animals, 1996, Music Therapy for animals, 1998—. Rsch. asst. Irvington Pubs., N.Y.C., 1979, Little, Brown and Co., Boston, 1983; music therapist for people and animals, 1998—. Mem. Calif. Scholarship Fedn. (life). Avocations: music-guitar, violin, folk and opera singing, song writing, art. Office Phone: 707-279-1743. Personal E-mail: carches@sbcglobal.net.

CRAIG, CYNTHIA MAE, mathematics professor; b. Brownsville, Tex., Jan. 22, 1951; d. Richard Virgil and Mae Margaret (Phillips) Cole; m. Daniel Baxter Craig, Jan. 15, 1971; children: Tammy Michelle Craig Black, Heather Elizabeth Craig Rios. BA, Augusta (Ga.) Coll., 1985, MEd, 1989, specialist in edn., 1993. Cert. devel. specialist; cert. tchr., Ga. Tchr. 5th-6th grade tchr. Blessed Sacrament Sch., El Paso, Tex., 1981-82; tchr. 4-8th grade honors math. St. Mary on the hill Cath. Sch., Augusta, Ga., 1985-87; tchr. Aquinas H.S., Augusta, 1987-88; asst. prof. of math. in learning support Augusta State U., 1989—, assoc. chair dept. learning support, 1998—2002, acting chair dept. learning supoort, 2002—04; dir., chair learning support Augusta State U. Coll., 2004—. Presenter at profl. confs. in field. Contbr. articles to profl. jours. Mem. ASCD, Ga. Assn. of Devel. Educators, Nat. Assn. for Devel. Edn., Phi Delta Kappa (newsletter editor 1990-93, v.p. membership 1993-94, newsletter editor 1989-92, 94-96, 97-98, found. rep. 1996-97, newsletter editor 1997-98, rsch. rep. 1998—). Avocations: reading, educational research, travel. Office: Augusta State U Learning Support 2500 Walton Way Augusta GA 30904-4562 Office Phone: 706-737-1685. Business E-Mail: ccraig@aug.edu.

CRAIG, JESSICA ANN, secondary school educator; d. Jeff and Mary Craig. BS, Ea. Ill. U., Charleston, 2003. Cert. secondary edn. Ill. Tchr. Rich Ctrl. HS, Olympia Fields, Ill., 2004—; all-star cheerleading coach Tumbling and Cheerleading Acad., Orland Park, Ill., 2005—. Mem.: NEA, Ill. Edn. Assn. Office: Rich Ctrl HS 3600 W 203d St Olympia Fields IL 60461 Office Phone: 708-679-5600. Personal E-mail: ja_craig17@yahoo.com. E-mail: jcraig1@rich227.org.

CRAIG, JOAN CARMEN, secondary school educator, performing arts educator; b. Sacramento, Calif., July 13, 1932; d. Frank Hurtado and Enid Pearl (Hogan) Alcalde; m. Elmer Lee Craig, Aug. 14, 1955 (dec. Jan. 1981); children: Shelley, Wendy, Cathleen, Scott; m. Donald E. Peterson, 1997. BA, San Jose State U., 1954, gen. secondary cert., 1955; postgrad. studies, various univs., 1956—. Cert. tchr. (life), Calif. Drama tchr. Willow Glen High Sch. San Jose (Calif.) Unified Sch. Dist., 1955-58, Kennedy Jr. High Sch. Cupertino (Calif.) Sch. Dist., 1968-93. Cons. Cupertino Unified Sch. Dist., 1990—; coord. program activiy Growth Leadership Ctr., Mountain View, Calif., 1993; presenter Computer Use in Edn., 1990-93. Author, coord.: Drama Curriculum, 1971-93, Musical Comedy Curriculum, 1985-93, (Golden Bell, Calif. 1992). Dir. Nat. Multiple Sclerosis Soc., Santa Clara County, 1983-86. Recipient Spl. Svc. award Nat. Multiple Sclerosis Soc., Santa Clara, Calif., 1986, Hon. Membership award Nat. Jr. Honor Soc., 1990, Hon. Svc. award Calif. Congress Parents, Tchrs. and Students, Inc., 1992; named Tchr. of Year, Kennedy Jr. High, Cupertino Union Sch. Dist., 1993. Mem. AAUW, NEA, Calif. Tchrs. Assn., Cupertino Edn. Assn. (rep. 1982). Avocations: theater, hiking, biking, writing, swimming. Home: 3381 Brower Ave Mountain View CA 94040-4512

CRAIG, JUDITH MARIE, history educator; b. Sterling, Ill., Feb. 3, 1958; d. Herbert Joseph and Helen A. (Elmendofr) Adams; m. David W. Craig, July 24, 1982; 1 child, Kelley Marie. BA, Western Ill. U., Macomb, 1980; MS in Edn., No. Ill. U., DeKalb, 1992. Tchr. Minooka Cmty. High Sch., Ill., 1980—. Mem.: World History Assn., Nat. Coun. Social Studies. Office: Minooka Cmty High Sch 301 Wabena Ave Minooka IL 60447

CRAIG, LINDA (TERI) CAROL, science educator; b. Susanville, Calif., Nov. 3, 1947; d. Wayne and Hazel Marie Craig. AA, Fresno City Coll., Calif., 1969; BA, Fresno U., Calif., 1972; MSc, Jacksonville U., Ala., 1979. Resource tchr. Clay County Bd. Edn., Ashland, Ala., 1977—, dir. alternative sch. Lineville, Ala. Chmn. Spl. Olympics, Ashland, 1982—90; pres. Clay County Animal Welfare, Ala., chmn. bd. dirs. 2d lt. U.S. Army, 1977—83. Mem.: Ala. Edn. Assn., Women's Army Corp. Vets. Assn. Avocations: hiking, animals.

CRAIG, MARY LAURI, accountant; b. Helena, Mont., Jan. 19, 1936; d. Henry and Hilma (Newman) Lauri; m. William Craig (div. 1982); children: Nona Marie, Lauri Sue. BS cum laude, Rocky Mtn. Coll., 1973. CPA. Acct. various firms, Billings, Mont.; sole practice CPA Billings, 1973-78; dir. Mont. Dept. Revenue, Helena, 1979-81; sole practice CPA Helena, 1982—. Commr.'s adv. group IRS, Washington, 1994-96; exec. com. Multi-State Tax Commn., Denver. Co-author: Adventure Bound in Montana. Mem. Am. Soc. Women Accts. (pres. chpt. 100 1976), Mont. Soc. CPAs. Avocations: fly fishing, gold mining, woodworking, watercolors, music. Home and Office: 408 Washington Dr Helena MT 59601-3911

CRAIG, PAMELA J., management consulting firm executive; married; 2 children. B in Econs., Smith Coll., 1979; MBA, NYU. CPA. With Accenture Ltd., NYC, 1982—, ptnr., 1991—, positions in media & entertainment practice Comm. & High Tech oper. group., group. dir. bus. ops. & services, sr. v.p. fin., 2004—06, CFO, 2006—. Bd. dirs. Comprehensive Devel. Inc., NYC, Avanade Inc. Named one of Top 100 Women in Corp. Am. Mem.: C200. Office: Accenture Ltd 1345 Ave of the Americas 6th Fl New York NY 10105*

CRAIG, PATRICIA, voice educator, opera singer; b. Kew Gardens, NY, July 21, 1943; d. William A. and Dorothy H. Duncklee; m. Donald E. Craig, July 23, 1966 (div. 1976); m. Richard Cassilly BS Music Edn., Ithaca Coll., 1965; postgrad., Manhattan Sch. Mus. Prin. artist N.Y.C. Opera, 1971—81, Met. Opera, 1978—91. Tchr. voice New Eng. Conservatory Music; condr. master classes various locations; advisor Longwood Opera; chair bd. overseers Opera Boston; bd. dirs. Am. Inst. Musical Studies, Graz, Austria; adv. bd. Bay Area Summer Opera Theater Inst. Operatic debut as Marenka in The Bartered Bride, Met. Opera, 1978; appeared in Madama Butterfly, Carmen, La Boheme, I Pagliacci, The Rise and Fall of the City of Mahagonny, Les Dialogues des Carmelites, Pique Dame, Turandot, Peter Grimes, La Rondine, Zaza, Un Ballo in Maschera; appeared in maj. opera houses around the world Home: 33 Pond Ave #920 Brookline MA 02445 Office: New England Conservatory 290 Huntington Ave Boston MA 02115-5018 E-mail: casamagda@aol.com.

CRAIG, SUSAN LYONS, library director; b. Barksdale Air Force Base, La., Feb. 23, 1948; BA, Trinity Coll., Washington, 1971; MSLS, Fla. State U., 1976; MBA, Rosary Coll., 1989. Pub. svcs. libr. St. Mary's Coll., Moraga, Calif., 1976-79; head pub. svcs. Hood Coll., Frederick, Md., 1979-85, Dominican U. (formerly Rosary Coll.), River Forest, Ill., 1985-87; dir. libr. Aurora (Ill.) U., 1987-97; dir. libr. and acad. info. svcs. Trinity Coll. Libr. (now Trinity U.), Washington, 1997—. Adj. assoc. prof Rosary Coll. Grad. Sch. Libr. and Info. Sci., 1990-97. Mem. ALA, Assn. Coll. and Rsch. Librs. (nat. adv. com., rep. Ill. chpt. 1991-95), Pvt. Acad. Librs. of Ill. (pres. 1994-96), Ill. Libr. Assn. (del. pre-White House Conf., Chgo., 1989-90), Beta Phi Mu, Phi Eta Sigma (hon.). Office: Winter Park Campus Valencia Cmty Coll 850 W Morse Blvd Winter Park FL 32789 Business E-Mail: scraig8@valenciacc.edu. E-mail: Susancraig23@yahoo.com.

CRAIG, SUSAN VIRGINIA, librarian; b. Newton, Kans., Nov. 10, 1948; d. Theodore James and Dorothy Mae (Davis) C. BA, U. Kans., 1970; MLibrarianship, Emporia (Kans.) State U., 1971. Indexer for art index H.W. Wilson Co., N.Y.C., 1971-74; art history and classics libr. U. Calif., Berkeley, 1975-81; head Fine Arts Librs., U. Kans., Lawrence, 1981—. Mem. Am. adv. bd. Art Bibliographies:Modern, Oxford, Eng., 1982—. Named Chancellor's Disting. Libr., U. Kans., 1992. Mem. ALA, Art Librs. Soc. N.Am. (pres. 1986-87), Art Librs. Soc. Ctrl. Plains (chmn. 1983-84), LWV, Sisters in Crime. Home: 1717 Indiana St Lawrence KS 66044-4049 Office: U Kans Art And Architecture Libr Lawrence KS 66045-0001

CRAIG, VIKI PETTIJOHN, language educator; b. Ft. Worth, Nov. 1, 1947; d. James Newton Jr. and Annie Marie (Spivey) Spencer; m. Carl H. Pettijohn, Feb. 14, 1969 (div. Dec. 1987); m. Richard L. Craig, Apr. 19, 1997 (dec. 2002). BA in English, Tex. Wesleyan U., 1969; MAT in English, Jacksonville U., 1972; PhD in 20th Century Brit. and Am. Lit., Fla. State U., 1994. Tchr. O.D. Wyatt High Sch., Ft. Worth, 1969-70; tchr. English, Spanish Virginia Beach (Va.) Jr. High Sch., 1972-77, Englewood High Sch., Jacksonville, Fla., 1977-84; teaching asst. Fla. State U., Tallahassee, 1985-89, instr. English, 1989-90; instr. English and Spanish Southwestern Okla. State U., Weatherford, 1990-94, from asst. prof. to assoc. prof., 1994—2005, prof., 2005—. Dir. freshman English, 1995-96; presenter in field. Contbr. papers to pubs. Trustee Okla. Found. for Humanities, 1997—; mem. exec. bd. Okla. Humanities Coun., 1998—, vice chair, sec.; pub. outreach task force Nebr. Consortium Regl. Humanities Ctr. Okla. Found. Humanities grantee, 1991, Okla. Regents grantee, 1992, 93, 98, NEH grantee, 2000; Chautauqua scholar, 1997, scholar Liberty Fund Colloquium, 2003; listed in Nat. Chautauqua Tour Roster. Mem. AAUW, MLA, South Ctrl. Modern Lang. Assn., Pop Culture Assn., Western Lit. Assn. Independent. Presbyterian. Avocations: acting, vocal music, cooking, writing, cats. Office: Southwestern Okla State U Lang Arts Dept Weatherford OK 73096 Home: 1316 Linwood St Weatherford OK 73096-2416 Office Phone: 580-774-3094.

CRAIK, MARY BERNICE, artist, art gallery owner; b. Louisville, Ky. d. Huse and Grace Wilhite; m. James Craik Jr. (dec.); children: Earl Richard Wilhelm, Jr., Stephen, Juliet. AA, Armstrong Jr. Coll., Savannah, Ga., 1953; BA in Tchg., U. Tex., El Paso, 1960, MA, 1963; PhD, U. Iowa, Iowa City, 1968. Lic. tchr. Tex., 1960. Tchr. Bowie H.S., El Paso, Tex., 1960—62; instr., rschr. U. Tex., El Paso, Tex., 1962—64; instr. U. N.Mex., Silver City, N.Mex., 1965; prof. St. Cloud (Minn.) State U., 1968—83; freelance artist Louisville, 1997—; prin., owner Mary Craik Gallery, Louisville, 2004—. Numerous one-woman shows including most recently, one-woman shows include Makeready Gallery, Montclair, N.J., 2004, Ekstrom Libr., U. Louisville, 2004, Meidinger Tower Lobby Show, Louisvill, 2004, Baer's Gallery, Louisville, Ky., 2005, Portland Mus., 2005, Numerous group exhibitions including most recently, exhibitions include Ky. Mus. Art and Craft, Louisville, 2000—06, Louisville (Ky.) Pub. Libr., 2006, Thrust Theater, Louisville, Ky., 2006. Named to Hall Fame, Shawnee H.S., 1997; recipient Outstanding Svc. to Univ. Women award, Inter Faculty Orgn., 1984, Sex Equity Policy award, Women Educators Nat. Orgn., 1984, Achievement award, Women's Equality Group, 1985, Ednl. Equity award, 1995, Salute to Seven Sisters Star award, The Plaiades Theater Co., 2005, Women Leaders in Edn. Tower award, Presentation Acad., 2000, numerous art awards, 2001—06, Lucy Friebert award, Project Women, U. Louisville; grantee, Ky. Found. Mem.: Louisville (Ky.) Arts Coun., Alliance Am. Quilts, Am. Quilters Soc., Louisville (Ky.) Artisans Guild, Louisville (Ky.) Visual Arts Assn., Louisville (Ky.) Area Fiber and Textile Artists, Artcentric, Nat. Mus. Women in Arts.

CRAIN, GAYLA CAMPBELL, lawyer; b. Cleburne, Tex., June 13, 1950; d. R. C. and Marilyn Ruth (McFadyen) Campbell; m. Howard Leo Crain, May 27, 1978; 1 child, Robert Leo. BA, Baylor U., 1972, JD, 1974. Bar: Tex. 1974, U.S. Dist. Ct. (no., ea., we., and so. dists.) Tex., U.S. Ct. Appeals (5th cir.) 1988, U.S. Ct. Appeals (10th cir.) 1994, U.S. Supreme Ct. 1999, U.S. Supreme Ct. 1999. Asst. counsel Trailways, Inc., Dallas, 1975-79; counsel Schering Plough, Inc., Kenilworth, NJ, 1979—81; assoc. Epstein Becker Green Wickliff & Hall, P.C., Ft. Worth, 1985-86, ptnr. Dallas, 1986—. Contbg. author: State by State Guide to Human Resources Law, 1990, 91; editl. adv. bd. Employee Rels. Law Jour., Tex. Employment Law, 1998. Trustee Dallas Bapt. U., 1989-97, 98—. Office: Epstein Becker Green Wickliff & Hall 500 N Akard St #2700 Dallas TX 75201-3306

CRAIN, MARY ANN, elementary school educator; b. Dallas, Sept. 5, 1951; d. Robert Lee and Mary Ann (T.) Crain. MusB in Edn., Fla. State U., 1973; MusM, Ohio State U., 1974; EdS, U. Ga., 1998. Cert. tchr. T-6, music, early childhood edn., mid. grades, ednl. leadership Ga. First clarinet Vienna Kursalon Orch., Vienna, 1975—77; band dir. Sch. Bd. of Broward County, Ft. Lauderdale, Fla., 1977—78; teller Fla. Coast Bank, Coral Springs, Fla., 1978—79; strings tchr., grades 6-7 DeKalb County Bd. of Edn., Decatur, Ga., 1979—82, band tchr., grades 6-7, 1982—86, classroom tchr., grades 4-7, 1986—96, math. specialist, grades 2-5, 1996—2000, early intervention math. and reading specialist, grades 2-5, 2000—02; math. specialist, grades K-5 Bethesda Elem. Sch., Lawrenceville, Ga., 2002—. Mem.: Phi Delta Kappa (chpt. v.p. for membership). Office: Bethesda Elem Sch 525 Bethesda Sch Rd NW Lawrenceville GA 30044 Personal E-mail: corkgrease@msn.com.

CRAMBLIT, MIGGIE E., lawyer; BA, Cornell Coll.; JD, Hamline U.; attended, Kellogg Grad. Sch. Exec. Mgmt. Prog., Northwestern U. Law clerk for Justice James C. Otis Minn. Supreme Ct.; v.p., gen. counsel CenterPoint Energy Minneagasco; COO Family Fin. Strategies; counsel, corp. sec. Greater Minnesota Synergy; v.p., gen. counsel, corp. sec. DPL, Inc., 2003—, corp. sec., 2004. Adj. prof. William Mitchell Coll. Law, St. Paul. Trustee Dayton Philharm. Orch., Miami Valley Childhood Devel. Ctr.; former trustee William Mitchell Coll. Law, The House of Hope Presbyn. Ch., St. Paul and Greater Mpls. C. of C. Office: DPL Inc 1065 Woodman Dr Dayton OH 45432 Office Phone: 937-259-7214. Business E-Mail: miggie.cramblit@dplinc.com.

CRAMER, LISA M., elementary school educator; b. Wynne, Ark., July 21, 1966; d. Donald Lee Martin and Arbie Della Moye; m. James Gregory Cramer, Aug. 20, 1988; children: Emily LeeAnne, Hannah Catherine. B in Elem. Edn., U. Ctrl. Ark., Conway, 1992. Tchr. first grade Ark. Bapt. Christian Sch., Little Rock, 1992—94; tchr. gifted and talented lang. arts, social studies Rock Hill Sch. Dist. 3, SC, 2000—. Mem.: York County Ballet (life; v.p. 2005—06). Southern Baptist. Avocations: reading, cooking, scrapbooks. Home: 1325 Beckton Court Rock Hill SC 29732 Office: Rawlinson Road Middle School 2631 West Main Street Rock Hill SC 29732 Office Phone: 803-981-1500.

CRAMER, PHEBE, psychologist; b. San Francisco, Dec. 30, 1935; children: Mara, Julia. BA, U. Calif., Berkeley, 1957; PhD, NYU, 1962. Clin. psychologist Malmonides Hosp., Bklyn., 1962-63; asst. prof. Psychology Barnard Coll., N.Y.C., 1963-65; vis. asst. prof. Psychology U. Calif., Berkeley, 1965-70; assoc. prof. Psychology Williams Coll., Williamstown, Mass., 1970-73, prof. Psychology, 1973—. Pvt. practice in clin. psychology, Williamstown, 1970—; chief psychologist Berkshire Mental Health Ctr., Pittsfield, Mass., 1978-86. Author: Word Association, 1968, Understanding Intellectual Development, 1972, The Development of Defense Mechanisms, 1991, Story-telling, Narrative, and the Thematic Apperception Test, 1996, Protecting the Self, 2006; mem. editl. bd. Jour. of Personality, 1987-96, assoc. editor, 1991-96; mem. editl. bd. Jour. of Personality Assessment, 1989—, European Jour. Personality, 2000—, Jour. Rsch. Personality, 2003—. Judge U.S. Figure Skating Assn., 1989—. Mem.: APA, Soc. Personality and Social Psychology, Soc. for Personality Assessment. Office: Williams Coll Dept Psychology Bronfman Sci Ctr Williamstown MA 01267 Home: 20 Forest Rd Williamstown MA 01267-2029 Office Phone: 413-597-2463. Business E-Mail: phebe.cramer@williams.edu.

CRANDALL, ELIZABETH WALBERT, retired home economics professor; b. Columbus, Kans., Jan. 18, 1914; d. Stanley Giltner and Edna Maude (Daniel) Walbert; m. Robert Dalton Crandall, Aug. 3, 1946 (dec. Sept. 1999). BS, Kans. State Coll., 1935, MS, 1939; EdD, Boston U., 1962. Tchr. Cedar Point (Kans.) H.S., 1935-36, Ellsworth (Kans.) H.S., 1936-38; instr., asst. prof. home econs. Mich. State Coll., East Lansing, 1939-46; instr., asst. prof., assoc. prof. home econs. R.I. State Coll., Kingston, 1946-62; prof. home econs., dept. chair U. R.I., Kingston, 1962-73, acting dean, Coll. Home Econs., 1973-76, dean, Coll. Home Econs., 1976-77, prof. emerita, 1977—. Vice chair R.I. Consumer Adv. Com., Office Price Stabilization, Providence, 1952-53; mem. adv. com. R.I. Office Vocat. Rehab., Providence, 1962-64, Cmty. Homemaker Svcs. R.I., Inc., Providence, 1965-79; mem. various coms., U. R.I., 1961-77. Co-author (coll. textbooks): Home Management in Theory and Practice, 1946, Management for Modern Families, 1st edit., 1954, 2d edit., 1963, 3d edit., 1973, 4th edit., 1980. Mem. So. Poverty Law Ctr., Montgomery, Ala., 1974—, Equal Rights for Maine Coalition, Augusta, 1984; citizen lobbyist, Maine Women's Lobby and Women's Devel. Inst., Hallowell, 1989—; legis. chair Maine Home Econs. Assn., rep. Women's Legis. Agenda Coalition, Augusta, 1984-93, rep. Maine Choice Coalition, Augusta, 1990-93; mem. campaign com. for Hon. Sophia Pfeiffer's election to Maine Ho. of Reps., 1990; adv. com. Bath-Brunswick Child Care Svcs., Inc., 1994-95; various other civic activities. Recipient Presdl. award for courage, svc. and integrity, Maine Lesbian/Gay Polit. Alliance, Augusta, 1987; recipient Maine Women's Hall of Fame award Maine Fedn. Bus. & Profl. Women's Clubs and U. Maine, 1996. Mem. AAUW (hon. life mem.; pres. R.I. divsn. 1977-79, rep. New England Energy Task Force 1978-79, 79-81, mem. exec. bd. 1982-90, 92-95, chair legis. program 1984-86, chair women's issues com. 1986-88, chair legal advocacy fund 1992-95; Elizabeth "Liz" W. Crandall Rsch. & Projects Endowment, AAUW of Maine, 1996), LWV (exec. bd. Brunswick, Maine league 1981-93, pres. 1983-85), NOW, Family Planning Assn. Maine, Phi Kappa Phi, Phi Upsilon Omicron, Omicron Nu (nat. editor 1953-55, nat. pres. 1957-59). Democrat. Episcopalian. Avocations: philanthropy, feminism, physical fitness, social action, wildflowers. Home: 34 Belmont St Brunswick ME 04011-3051

CRANDELL, SUSAN, magazine editor; b. Troy, N.Y., July 31, 1951; d. Irwin Norton and Grace (Thompson) C.; m. Stephan Wilkinson, June 24, 1978; 1 child, Brook Crandell. BA in History cum laude, Middlebury Coll., 1973. Mng. editor Flying Mag., N.Y.C., 1973-79; editor-in-chief Direct Mag., N.Y.C., 1982-84; editor publ. devel. Comp-U-Card Internat., Stamford, Conn., 1985-86; editor custom media group Am. Express Publs., N.Y.C., 1986-90; exec. editor Travel & Leisure, N.Y.C., 1990-93; cons. editor Smart Money, N.Y.C., 1995, In Style, N.Y.C., 1993-95; exec. editor Ladies' Home Jour., N.Y.C., 1995-2000, MORE mag., N.Y.C., 1998—2000, editor, 2000—02, editor-in-chief, 2002—04. Office: More 125 Park Ave New York NY 10017-5529

CRANE, BARBARA BACHMANN, photographer, educator; b. Chgo., Mar. 19, 1928; d. Burton Stanley and Della (Kreeger) Bachmann; children: Elizabeth, Jennifer, Bruce. Student, Mills Coll., 1945-48; BA in Art History, NYU, 1950; MS in Photography, Inst. Design, Ill. Inst. Tech., 1966. Prof. photography Sch. Art Inst. Chgo., 1967-93, prof. emeritus, 1993—; vis. prof. Phila. Coll. Art (now Univ. of the Arts), 1977, Sch. Mus. Fine Arts, Boston, 1979, Cornell U., Ithaca, NY, 1983; represented by Stephen Daiter Gallery, Chgo., Flatfile Photography Gallery, Chgo., Francoise Paviot Gallery, Paris. Vis. prof. Bezalel Acad. Art and Design, Jerusalem, 1987. Author: (retrospective monograph) Barbara Crane: 1948-80, (exhibn. catalog) Barbara Crane: The Evolution of a Vision, 1983, Barbara Crane: Chicago Loop, 2002, Barbara Crane Urban Anomalies: Chicago, 2002, Barbara Crane Still Lifes: Natures Mortes, 2004, Barbara Crane: Grids, 2005. Grantee, Polaroid Corp., 1979—95, Ill. Arts Coun., 1985, 2001; Photography fellow, NEA, 1975, 1988, Guggenheim Meml. fellow in photography, 1979—80. Mem.: Soc. Photog. Edn. (Nat. Honored Educator award 1993). Studio: 1017 W Jackson Blvd 1A Chicago IL 60607-2918

CRANE, CHARLOTTE, law educator; b. Hanover, N.H., Aug. 30, 1951; d. Henry D. and Emily (Townsend) C.; m. Eric R. Fox, July 5, 1975; children: Hillary, Teresa. AB, Harvard U., 1973; JD, U. Mich., 1976. Bar: N.H. 1976, Ill. 1978. Law clk. to presiding judge U.S. Ct. Appeals (6th cir.), Detroit, 1976-77; law clk. to presiding justice U.S. Supreme Ct., Washington, 1977-78; assoc. Hopkins & Sutter, Chgo., 1978-82; asst. prof. Northwestern U., Chgo., 1982-86, assoc. prof., 1986-90, prof., 1990—. Contbr. articles to profl. jours. Mem. U.S. Women's Nat. Crew Team, 1976. Mem. ABA, Chgo. Tax Forum. Office: Northwestern U Sch Law 357 E Chicago Ave Chicago IL 60611-3059 Office Phone: 312-503-4528. E-mail: ccrane@law.northwestern.edu.

CRANE, DEBRA K., lawyer; b. 1957; BBA, U. Cinn.; JD, No. Kentucky U. Bar: 1996. Asst. treas. Ohio Casualty Corp., Fairfield, Ohio, 1996—99, v.p., 1999—2002, gen. counsel, 2000—, sr. v.p., sec., 2002—. Mem.: Assn. Corp. Counsel S.W. Ohio Chpt. Office: Ohio Casualty Corp 9450 Seward Rd Fairfield OH 45014-5456 Office Phone: 513-603-2400. Office Fax: 513-603-3179. E-mail: debra.crane@ocas.com.

CRANE, FRANCES HAWKINS, artist, educator; b. July 8, 1928; d. Henry Cleo and Laura Elizabeth (Jenkins) Hawkins; m. Gene Calvin Crane, May 10, 1946; children: Cindie Crane Reynolds, Cheryl Crane Garcia. Student, Del Mar Coll., 1948; studied with, Frederick Taubes, N.Y.C. Exhibitions include Highland Mall Gallery, Austin, Tex., Prichard Gallery, Houston, Salado Gallery, Tex., Bellas Artes Gallery, Kerrville, Tex., Jerry Smith Gallery, Alice, Tex., Corpus Christi Mus., Tex., M. and N. Originals, Corpus Christi, Represented in permanent collections Corpus Christi Mus., Lyndon Baines Johnson Libr. Recipient, top awards local, state, nat., internat. shows. Mem.: Internat. Soc. Artists, Hill Country Arts Found., Intenat. Platform Assn., Nat. League Am. Pen Women, South Tex. Traditional Art Assn. Home: 2802 Cimarron Blvd #210 Corpus Christi TX 78414

CRANE, KATHLEEN DICKINSON, elementary school educator, writer; b. Mt. Pleasant, Utah, Mar. 22, 1957; d. Eldon and Theresa (Hansen) Dickinson; m. Scott L. Crane, Sept. 30, 1977; children: Lyndsey, Shawn. AA, Brigham Young U., Provo, Utah, 1977; BA, Idaho State U., Pocatello, 1991. Tchr. Blackfoot Sch. Dist., Idaho, 1993—. Author: Preparing to Read, 2002, Phonics, Book 1, 2004, Phonics, Book 2, 2004, Phonics, Book 3, 2004. Mem. Friends of Libr., PTA. Mem.: NAEYC, Delta Kappa Gamma Lambda (pres. 2004—). Mem. Lds Ch.

CRANE, LAURA JANE, retired chemist; b. Middletown, Ohio, Nov. 2, 1941; d. David R. and Frances T. (Watkins) Scott; m. Robert K. Crane, Apr. 13, 1972. BS, Carnegie Inst. Tech., 1963; MS, Harvard U., 1964; PhD, Rutgers U., 1972. Postdoctoral fellow Roche Inst. Molecular Biology, 1972-74, rsch. assoc., 1974-75; analytical chemist Eastman Kodak Co., Rochester, NY, 1962; asst. scientist Warner-Lambert Co., Morris Plains, NJ, 1965, 67-68; English tchr. Am. Sch., Manila, 1966; assoc. scientist W.R. Grace & Co., Clarksville, Md., 1969; sr. scientist diagnostic enzymology Warner-Lambert Co., 1975, group leader coagulation rsch., 1976-79; mgr. lab. products rsch. J.T. Baker Inc., Phillipsburg, NJ, 1979, asst. dir. R&D, 1980-85, dir. R&D, 1986-92; sr. dir. new product innovation Schering-Plough Health Products, Inc., Memphis, 1992-93, sr. dir. adv. products rsch. and new product innovation, 1993—2003, rsch. fellow, 2003—04, ret., 2004. Mem. faculty Seton Hall U., 1979; participant profl. symposia; mem. R&D coun. N.J., state sci. adv. coun. Rutgers U.; pres. Am. Clerical Soc. Memphis Section, 2005-, Delta Dressage Assn., 2005-; cons. in field. Contbr., editor sci. articles and books. Judge U.S. Dressage Fedn. US Dressage Federation Bronze Medalist, 2003, Armco Corp. scholar, 1959-63; Women's Dormitory Coun. scholar; William Connelly scholar: nat. Merit scholar; NSF fellow; DuPont fellow; NDEA fellow, 1969-72, others. Mem. AAAS, Am. Chem. Soc. (pres. Memphis chpt. 2005), U.S. Dressage Fedn., Delta Dressage Assn. (pres. 2005—, jduge 2005—), Arabian Horse Registry Assn., Al Khamsa Arabian Horse Breeders Assn. (pres.). Home: 7155 Highway 194 Williston TN 38076-3511 Office: Schering-Plough Health Products Inc 3030 Jackson Ave Memphis TN 38112-2020 Personal E-mail: ljcrane@bellsouth.net.

CRANE, REA BABCOCK, retired nurse; b. Oakland, Calif., June 2, 1942; d. William Joy and Adeline Hazel (Gunnufson) Babcock; m. Charles Truman Crane, Apr. 2, 1966 (div. 1977); children: Audra Joy, Elise Deborah. Diploma, Calif. Hosp. Sch. Nursing, Los Angeles, 1963. RN, Calif.; cert. disability mgmt. specialist; cert. case mgr. Emergency room nurse Kaiser Found., San Francisco, 1963-64, Santa Monica Hosp., Calif., 1964-65; med.-surg. floor nurse West L.A. VA Hosp., 1964-65; rehab. nurse Internat. Rehab. Assocs., L.A., 1970-76, Fremont Compensation Ins. Co., L.A., 1976-79, rehab. supr., 1979-84, asst. dir. rehab., 1984-86, dir. rehab., 1986-91; rehab. mgr. T.I.G. Ins. (formerly TransAmerica), Woodland Hills, Calif., 1991-95; med. dir. Calif. Worker's Compensation Inst., San Francisco, 1995—2005; ret., 2005. Mem. Cert. Ins. Rehab. Specialist Commn., chair, 2001-02. Mem. Rehab. Nurses Soc. (pres. 1978-82, T. Gucker award 1992), Nat. Assn. Rehab. Profls. in Pvt. Sector (founding pres. Calif. chpt. 1984-86, regional rep., chmn. constn. by-laws 1986-2005, Bd. Mem. of Yr. 1985, Lifetime Contbn. to Pvt. Sector Rehab. award 1989), Rehab. Pres.' Coun. (founder), Calif. Workers Compensation Inst. (chair rehab. com. 1995), Ins. Rehab. Study Group (sec. 1995). Democrat. Episcopalian. Avocations: reading, theater, arts, cooking, travel. Personal E-mail: reacrane@verizon.net.

CRANFILL, VIRGINIA MAY, retired nursing administrator; b. Winfield, Kans., Jan. 28, 1931; d. Archie Lewis and Eva Dell (Martin) Fisher; m. B. Charles Smith, Aug. 3, 1949 (div. Nov. 1978); children: Charles David Smith, Terry Lee Smith (dec.), Bruce Wayne Smith, Nancy Ann Smith Barnhurst; m. Bert D. Cranfill, Oct. 1, 1981. Grad. with honors, Hinsdale (Ill.) Hosp. Sch. Practical Nursing, 1964; student, South Fla. C.C., Avon Park, 1971—73; AS with honors, Polk C.C., Winter Haven, Fla., 1975; student, Fla. So. Coll., Lakeland, 1983—84. Diplomate coord. Am. Bd. Quality Assurance Utilization Rev. Physicians, Inc., cert. case mgr. Am. Bd. Quality Assurance Utilization Rev. Physicians, Inc.; RN Fla., Ga., Tenn., Calif., LPN III, Tenn., Fla., cert. profl. healthcare quality, Nat. Assn. Health Care Quality; vegetarian cooking, vegetarian food instr. Emergency rm. nurse Hinsdale (Ill.) Hosp., 1964—65; office receptionist, dental asst. Dr. J.C. Trivett, DDS, Madison, Tenn., 1965—66; charge nurse Little Creek Sanitarium and Hosp., Concord, Tenn., 1966—68; nurse and surg. tech. Walker Meml. Hosp., Avon Park, Fla., 1968—73, circulating surg. nurse, 1975—76, charge nurse and head nurse, 1979—86, house supr., 1982—86; office nurse Dr. S.A. King, Gen. Practice, 1973—75; asst. DON Hillcrest Nursing Home, Avon Park, 1975; charge nurse med./surg. unit Smyrna (Ga.) Hosp., 1976; insvc. dir. and asst. DON Jellico (Tenn.) Cmty. Hosp., 1976—77; charge nurse maximum security infirmary Avon Park Correctional Instn., 1978—79; charge nurse med./surg./orthop. unit Med. Ctr. Hosp., Punta Gorda, 1979; circulating surg. nurse St. Helena Hosp., Deer Park, Calif., 1981-82; DON Lake Wales (Fla.) Convalescent Ctr., 1987-88; nursing quality assurance coord. Fla. Hosp. Heartland Divsn., 1988—92, med. staff quality assurance, 1988—92, asst. dir. and coord. case mgmt., 1992—93, physician liaison, 1993—95, part-time internal auditor, 1996—97; ret., 1997; part-time nurse Ctr. Wound Care Fla. Hosp. Heartland Divsn., 2004—05. Past mem. adv. bd. Home Health Agy., Sebring, Fla.; asst. to physicians regarding rules and guidelines of Fed. Govt. Health Care Fin. Adminstrn., 1990-1996; participant profl. seminars and workshops. Author: Our Heavenly Messenger, 2001. Cmty. instr. ARC; past vol. EMT and nurse Jellice Ambulance Svc., vol. Fla. Hosp. Heartland Divsn.; spiritual mentor Walker Meml. Jr. Acad.; deaconess, hostess, active in evangelism outreach Walker Seventh-Day Adventist Ch., parish nurse, 2000, coord. health clinic and lectr. Philippines mission, 2004. Recipient Outstanding Achievement in Nursing, Lakeland (Fla.) Hosp., 1984. Mem.: Am. Bd. Quality Assurance Utilization Rev. Physicians, Inc, Fla. Utilization Rev. Assn., Fla. Assn. Health Care Quality, Assn. Seventh-Day Adventist Nurses (bd. dir., pres.-elect), Nat. Assn. Health Care Quality, Case Mgmt. Soc. Republican. Avocations: church activies, reading, crafts, sewing, music. Home: 1417 W Avon Blvd Avon Park FL 33825-9511 E-mail: vcran@tnni.net.

CRANFORD, JUDITH, medical association administrator; Head, healthcare, advocacy practice Ruder Finn Pub. Rels., London; asst. exec. dir., devel., mktg., comm. Nat. Osteoporosis Found., Washington, 2001—02, acting exec. dir., 2002, exec. dir., 2002—. Mem.: Inst. of Pub. Rels., UK, Assn. for Healthcare Philanthropy, Am. Soc. Assn. Execs. Office: Nat Osteoporosis Found 1232 22nd St nW Washington DC 20037-1292 Office Phone: 202-223-2226. Business E-Mail: judith@nof.org.*

CRANNA, CHRISTINA M., social services specialist; b. Poughkeepsie, N.Y., May 27, 1975; d. Charles Francis and Mary M. Lauria. BS in Psychology, St. Thomas Aquinas Coll., 1997; MSW, Adelphi U., 2001. Mental health worker Rockland County Dept. Mental Health, Pomona, NY, 1997—98; svc. coord. Ulster-Green ARC, Kingston, NY, 1998—; social worker Aster Home for Children, 2000—. Mem.: NASW. Roman Catholic. Avocations: crafts, crocheting, swimming, travel, history. Home: 2 Woods Rd Tivoli NY 12583-5429

CRANSTON, MARY BAILEY, lawyer; b. Palo Alto, Calif., Dec. 29, 1947; d. James Alfred and Bettye (Luhnow) Bailey; m. Harold David Cranston, Aug. 15, 1970; children: Susan Anne, John David. AB in polit. sci., Stanford U., 1969, JD, 1975; MA in psychology, UCLA, 1970. Bar: Calif. 1975. Assoc. atty. Pillsbury, Madison & Sutro, San Francisco, 1975-82, ptnr., 1983—2001, firm chair, 1999—2001; (Pillsbury, Madison & Sutro merged with Winthrop, Stimson, Putnam & Roberts, 2001); ptnr. Pillsbury Winthrop LLP, San Francisco, 2001—, firm chair, 2001—04; (Pillsbury Winthrop LLP merged with Shaw Pittman LLP, 2005); firm chair Pillsbury Winthrop Shaw Pittman LLP, San Francisco, 2005—. Faculty The Rutter Group, 1984—, Calif. Continuing Edn. of the Bar, 1985—, Nat. Inst. Trial Advocacy, San Francisco, 1986—; bd. dirs. GrafTech Internat. Ltd., 1999—, Bay Area Coun., 1999—; editl. bd. Nat. Law Jour., 2004—. Contbr. articles to profl. journals. Trustee San Francisco Ballet, 1996, Stanford U., 2000—; mem. The Yosemite Fund; mem. nat. centennial com. Girl Scouts USA, 2001; bd. dirs. Legal Services for Children, San Francisco, 1983—87, San Francisco C. of C., 1999—2001; bd. dirs. hist. soc. US Dist. Ct. No. Dist. Calif., 2001—; bd. mem. Episcopal Charities, 2003—; exec. com. bd. visitors Stanford Law Sch., 1977—80, 1996—, chair bd. visitors, 2001; chair bd. advisors we. region Catalyst, 2004—; bd. governors Commonwealth Club of Calif. Named one of The 100 Most Influential Lawyers in Calif., LA Daily Jour., 1999—2002, The 50 Most Influential Bus. Women in the Bay Area, San Francisco Bus. Times, 1999—2003, The 100 Most Influential Lawyers in Am., Nat. Law Jour., 2000, The 2 Best Law Firm Leaders in the US, Of Counsel, 2002; recipient Stanford Associates Award for disting. svc., Stanford U., 1999, Disting. Jurisprudence Award, Anti-Defamation League, 2000, Award of Merit, Bar Assn. San Francisco, 2002, Athena Award, 2004. Fellow: Am. Coll. Trial Lawyers; mem.: Assn. Bus. Trial Lawyers (bd. dirs. 1993—97), Calif. State Bar (mem. com. on women 1986—89, chair sect. of antitrust and trade regulation 1998—99), ABA (mem. commn. on women 1993—2000, coun. mem. antitrust sect. 1994—97, officer antitrust sect. 1997—2000), Am. Law Inst., Stanford Alumni Assn. (bd. dirs. 1986—93, 2001—, pres. 1990), Cap & Gown (Stanford) (treas. 1974—75). Avocations: reading, sports. Office: Pillsbury Winthrop Shaw Pittman 50 Fremont St Ste 1474 San Francisco CA 94105 Office Phone: 415-983-1621. Office Fax: 415-983-1200. Business E-Mail: mary.cranston@pillsburylaw.com.

CRAVEN, BETTY, educational association administrator; b. Petersburg, Va., July 10, 1955; d. Richard Wilson and Helen Rose (Ellington) Cheely; m. Thomas Leake Millner, June 5, 1976 (div. Feb. 1987); m. Erle Bulla Craven, IV, Apr. 29, 1989; children: Hannah Elizabeth, Erle Bulla V. Student, Randolph-Macon Coll., Ashland, Va., 1973-74, 74-75. Pres., dir. exercise leader Fitness Motivations, Greensboro, N.C., 1986-89; cultural arts, reflections chmn. Cash Elem. Sch., Kernersville, N.C., 1999—, PTA pres., 1998-99; mem. Zone 2 adv. bd. Winston-Salem/Forsyth County PTA Coun., N.C., 1998-00; vice dir. Dist. 16 N.C. State PTA, Raleigh, 1999-00, reflections chair, 1998—. Pres., dir. Eclectic Creations, Kernersville, 1985—. Recipient Outstanding Vol. award Cash Elem. PTA, 1997-98, 98-99, 99-00. Democrat. Presbyterian. Avocations: gardening, reading novels, drawing, music, piano. Mailing: 4921 Lombardy Ln Winston Salem NC 27103-5213

CRAVEN, DEBORAH, performing arts educator; b. Birmingham, Ala., Mar. 17, 1950; d. Jesse Auborn Adams and Jimmie Louise Myers; m. T. Judson Revelle; 1 child, Myer Brookins Craven. BS in Edn., Samford U., 1970; MA, PhD, Trinity U. Tchr. Birmingham Pub. Schs., 1970-73; newspaper columnist The Daily Herald, Houston, 1974-76; accompanist Suzuki Acad., Mt. Prospect, Ill., 1977-79; tchr., dir., CEO Craven Acad., Lake Forest, 1991—. Dir. CATSS Internat. Mus. Touring Co., Grayslake, Ill., 1996—. Author: Miss Debbie Series, 1996, Miss Debbie Coloring Books, 1996, Adagio Pedagogy, 1998, Andante Pedagogy, 1997, Allegro Pedagogy, 1998. Active People to People Amb. Program. Mem. Music Educators Nat. Conf., Internat. Soc. for Musical Edn., Nat. Assn. for Music Edn., Nat. Guild Piano Tchrs., Am. Coll. Musicians, Music Tchrs. Nat. Assn., Ill. State Music Tchrs. Assn., North Suburban Music Tchrs. Assn., Downtown Assn., Grayslake C. of C., Kiwanis, Exch. Club. Office: The Craven Acad Performing Arts 408 Center St Grayslake IL 60030-1626

CRAVEN, PAMELA F., lawyer; b. Bloomfield, NJ, 1953; m. Bill Craven; 2 children. BA in English, U. Pa., 1974, JD, 1977; LLM in taxation, NYU, 1981. Bar: 1977. Assoc. McCarter & English, 1977—79, Coudert Brothers, 1979—82; asst. gen. counsel, asst. sec. NCR Corp., 1982—92; atty. AT&T, 1992—96; v.p. law Lucent Technologies Inc., Murray Hill, NJ, 1996—2000, sec., 1999—2000, v.p., gen. counsel, sec. Enterprise Networks Group, 2000; v.p., gen. counsel, sec. Avaya Inc., Basking Ridge, NJ, 2000—02, sr. v.p., gen. counsel, sec., 2002—. Bd. overseers U. Pa. Law Sch., 2004—; bd. managers U. Pa. Law Alumni Assn.; chair cmty. adv. bd. NJ Network. Recipient Alumni Award of Merit, U. Pa. Law Alumni Soc. Office: Avaya Inc 211 Mount Airy Rd Basking Ridge NJ 07920

CRAVEN, STELLA MARIS, principal; d. John Evangelist and Erline Viola (Meyer) Craven. BS in Secondary Edn., Seton Hall U., 1967; MAT in Adminstrn. and Supervision, The Citadel, 1973. Cert. elem., secondary, biology, math tchr., elem. adminstrn. and supervision SC. Tchr. Sacred Heart Sch., Charleston, 1953—57, 1960—61, St. Angela Acad., Aiken, SC, 1957—58, Cathedral Sch., Charleston, 1958—60, Immaculate Conception Sch., Charleston, 1967—68, Bishop Engle Grad. HS, Charleston, 1969—70; tchr., prin. Our Lady of Mt. Virgin, Middlesex, NJ, 1964—67, 1968—69, St. Andrew's Sch., Myrtle Beach, SC, 1969—70; prin. Christ Our King-Stella Maris Sch., Mt. Pleasant, SC, 1980—2006. Mem., sec., vicar Sisters of Charity of Our Lady of Mercy, Charleston, 1970—80, 1996—2000. Mem.: ASCD, Nat. Cath. Ednl. Assn., Nat. Assn. Elem. Sch. Prins. Roman Catholic. Avocations: music, reading, cooking. Office: Christ Our King-Stella Maris Sch 1183 Russell Dr Mount Pleasant SC 29464

CRAVEY, PAMELA J., librarian; b. Washington, Mar. 6, 1945; d. Jack M. and Marjorie M.W. Bristow; m. G. Randall Cravey; 1 child, Christopher B. BA, Baldwin Wallace Coll., Berea, Ohio, 1967; MS, Fla. State U., Tallahassee, 1968; PhD, Ga. State U., Atlanta, 1989. Libr., instr. Fla. State U., Tallahassee, 1968-69, U. Ga., Athens, 1969-72; asst. then assoc. libr. U. Ctrl. Fla., Orlando, 1973-75; asst. then assoc. prof., libr. Ga. State U., Atlanta, 1975-2000; pvt. practice $D, Decatur, 2000—. Author: Protecting Library Staff, Users, Collections, and Facilities, 2001; contbr. articles to profl. jours. and books. Libr. Svc. Enhancement Program grantee Coun. Libr. Resources; personal grantee Coun. Libr. Resources. Mem. ALA, Assn. Coll. Rsch. Librs. Home: 2413 Harrington Dr Decatur GA 30033-4903 Office: 2107 N Decatur Rd #308 Decatur GA 30033-5305 Office Phone: 404-636-6338. E-mail: pcraveyi2s@comcast.net.

CRAWFORD, ANDREA KIRVENE, business educator; b. Detroit, Mich., Apr. 21, 1945; d. Kirven and Verna Louise Crawford; 1 child, Jonathan Andreaoff. BA in Edn., Social Studies, Lang. Arts, Mich. Stae U., East Lansing, 1975; MA in Edn., Urban Tchg., Media Sci., Mich. State U., East Lansing, 1979; EdS in Math., Wayne State U., 1987, EdS in Gen. Adminstrn. and supervision, 1990. Combined adjuster/intermediate fire and allied lines Allstate Ins. Co., Mich. Claims Dept.; waste info. series for edn. Mich. Dept. of Natural Resources, Waste Mgmt. Divsn., comprehensive sch. health edn., mid. sch. grades 6, 7, 8 Mich. Model Steering Com., tchr. State of Mich. Dept. of Edn. Info. operator Mich. Bell Tel. Co., Detroit, 1964—67; drapery buyer's asst. JL Hudson Co., Detroit, 1967—69; mgr. savs. dept. 1st Independence Nat. Bank, Detroit, 1969—73; oper. computer sys. Kelly Svcs., East Lansing, Mich., 1973—76; cross-combined adjuster Allstate Ins. Co., Lansing, Mich., 1976—79; instr. Detroit Pub. Schs., 1979—2003; area mgr. BioPerformance/Premium Performance Fuel Additive, Detroit, 2006—. Extern in ednl. adminstrn. Mich. State U., Troy, 1982. Recipient Silver Bell Pin, Gold Bell Pin, Excellent Svc. Pin, Mich. Bell Tel. Co., 1964—67, Womans Arts and Econs. Guild award, 1st Independence Nat. Bank, 1971. Mem.: Nat. Coun. for Social Studies (corr.), Mich. Alt. Edn. Assn. (corr.), Met. Detroit Sci. Tchrs. Assn. (corr.), Detroit Area Coun. Tchrs. of Math. (corr.), Am. Fedn. Tchrs. (life), Detroit Fedn. Tchrs. (life). Avocations: flower arranging, travel, walking, boating. Home: 14411 Harbor Island Detroit MI 48215 Office: BioPerformance-Premium Fuel Additive 14411 Harbor Island Detroit MI 48215 Office Phone: 313-821-8950. Office Fax: 313-821-8950. Personal E-mail: ak14411@sbcglobal.net.

CRAWFORD, ANNETTE LAMBSON, elementary school educator; b. Balt., Nov. 30, 1951; d. Calvin George and Norma Barnum Lambson; m. David C. Miller, Apr. 9, 1994; 1 child, Kimya Dawn. BA, U. Md., 1973; MS, Johns Hopkins U., Baltimore, Maryland, 1999—2001. Cert. advanced profl. educator Md. Math. tchr. Balt. County Pub. Schools, Balt., 1973—74, Balt. City Pub. Schs., 1974—81, 1983—85, 1988—90, math. sci. tchr., 1990—; math. tchr. Pensacola (Fla.) Jr. Coll., 1981—83, Cath. HS Balt., 1985—88. Lyricist Christian Music Anthology, 2004. Choir mem. Forest Pk. Cmty. Ch., Balt., 1963—2006, leader girls youth group, 1985—88, v.p. Women in the Ch., 1988—90, chmn. pastoral search com., 2002—04. Fellow: Marylan Writing Project (assoc.; tchr. cons.); mem.: NSTA (assoc.), Nat. Coun. Tchrs. Math. (assoc.). Presbyterian. Avocations: music, poetry. Home: 2218 Clove Terr Baltimore MD 21209-4631 Office: Rosemont Elem Sch 2777 Presstman St Baltimore MD 21216 Office Phone: 410-396-0574. Personal E-mail: annettecm@comcast.net.

CRAWFORD, BRENDA R., music educator; d. Arthur and Marilyn Hummel; m. Clifford P. Crawford, June 18, 1994. B Music Edn., Greenville Coll., Ill., 1975; postgrad., U. Minn., Mpls., 1986—87. Cert. Orff Schulwerk level I Minn., tchr. Oreg. Band and vocal tchr. Rhame Sch. Dist., ND, 1975—76; vocal music tchr. Belfield Sch. Dist., ND, 1976—77; elem. gen. music tchr. Dickinson Sch. Dist., ND, 1978—86, 1987—89; elem. tchr. music methods, tchg. asst. U. Minn., 1986—87; elem. music tchr. Klamath Falls City Schs., Oreg., 1989—. Pvt. piano and voice tchr., 1975—. Office: Fairview Elem Sch 1017 Donald St Klamath Falls OR 97601-6572

CRAWFORD, CAROL ANNE, marketing professional; b. San Francisco, Jan. 17, 1945; d. Kenneth H. and Marcella (Schloesser) Crawford. BA, San Jose State U., Calif., 1967; MBA in Mktg., Golden Gate U., 1985. Food publicist J. Walter Thompson, San Francisco, 1967—70; asst. mktg. and sales promotion dir. Eastridge Shopping Ctr., San Jose, 1970—72; consumer info. specialist Carl Byoir & Assocs., San Francisco, 1972—78; account supr. Ketchum Pub. Rels., San Francisco, 1978—80; v.p. dir. pub. rels. Grey Advt., San Francisco, 1980—82; dir. corp. comms. S&O Cons., San Francisco, 1982—84; mgr. mktg. and pub. rels. GTE Sprint, 1984—86; dir. pub. rels. U.S. Sprint, 1986; prin. Crawford Comms., San Francisco, 1986—. Instr. pub. rels. Golden Gate U., 1987—94; instr. pub. rels. U. Extension U. Calif., Berkeley, 1994—97; cons. in field; lectr. in field. Adv. bd. Hospice by the Bay; bd. mgrs. YMCA, Embarcadero, Calif., 1980—82. Mem.: San Francisco Publicity Club, San Francisco PR Roundtable, Home Economists in Bus. (past chpt. chmn., past chmn. nat. pub. rels.), San Francisco (Calif.) Profl. Food Soc. (recording sec. 1992—94, com. svcs. chmn. 1995), Pub. Rels. Soc. Am. (past chpt. pres. San Francisco chpt.), Commonwealth Club. Office: Crawford Comms 423 Lansdale Ave San Francisco CA 94127-1616

CRAWFORD, CAROL TALLMAN, law educator; b. Mt. Holly, NJ, Feb. 25, 1943; m. Ronald Crawford; children: Timothy, Jeffrey, Richard. BA, Mt. Holyoke Coll., 1965; JD magna cum laude, Washington Coll. Law, Am. U., 1978. Bar: Va. 1978, DC 1979. Legis. asst. to Senator Bob Packwood, Washington, 1969-75; assoc. firm Collier, Shannon, Rill & Scott, Washington, 1979-81; exec. asst. to chmn. FTC, Washington, 1981-83, dir. bur. consumer protection, 1983-85; assoc. dir. Office of Mgmt. & Budget, Washington, 1985-89; asst. atty. gen. legis. affairs U.S. Dept. Justice, Washington, 1989-90; commr. U.S. Internat. Trade Commn., 1991-2000; disting. vis. prof. law George Mason U., Arlington, Va., 2000-01. Bd. dirs. European Inst., Ind. Women's Forum, Smithfield Foods, Inc. Trustee Barry Goldwater Chair of Am. Instns., Ariz. State U., Phoenix, 1983—; chair internat. trade and investment subcom. Federalist Soc., 1998—99, chair internat. and nat. security sect., 1999—2003; adv. com. NAFTA Labor Agreement, 2002—; bd. trustees Torray Fund, 2006—. Republican.

CRAWFORD, CHARLOTTE JOANNE, psychologist, psychoanalyst, psychological anthropologist; b. Santiago, Chile, June 10, 1942; came to U.S., 1953; d. Randall LaVern and Florence Ahleen (Bamber) C.; m. José Maria Garcia-Diez, Dec. 28, 1969 (div. Sept. 1986); children: S. Amaya Garcia, Tamara S. Garcia. BA in Sociology, U. Wash., 1965; MA in Anthropology, Columbia U., 1969; Lic. Psychology, U. Barcelona, Spain, 1974, PhD in Psychology, 1982. From asst. prof. to assoc. prof. U. Basque Country, Bilbao, Spain, 1970-90; vis. scholar Harvard U., Cambridge, 1990-91; rsch. assoc. U. Calif., Berkeley, 1991-92; clinician Children's Health Coun., Palo Alto, Calif., 1992-95, San Jose (Calif.) Unified Sch. Dist., 1995-96; pvt. practice Berkeley. Adj. faculty Wright Inst., Berkeley, 1991-93, Pacific Grad. Sch. Psychology, Palo Alto, 1991-93, Saybrook Inst., San Francisco, 1992—; pvt. practice clinician, Bilbao, 1975-90, Oakland, Calif., 1997. Author, editor: Identidad: Norma y Diversidad, 1988; author: La Psicoterapia de Inspiración Psicoanalítica, 1989, Estudio Integral de la Personalidad, 1990. Study fellow for internat. devel. Ford Found., 1966-68, grad. fellow Govt. of Spain, 1975-77; Barandiaran grantee Soc. for Basque Studies, 1981-83, rsch. grantee U. Basque Country, 1987-88, 90-91, 91-92, grantee Govt. of Spain, 1988-90, 90-91. Mem. APA, Calif. Psychol. Assn., Inst. Psychoanalytic Studies, Alameda County Psychol. Assn. (pres. 2001, chair colleague assistance com., rep. 2002-05, bd. dirs.), Internat. Psychoanalytical Studies Orgn. (pres. 1983-85), Soc. Psychol. Anthropology, Am. Anthropol. Assn., Rotary Club (Berkeley chpt.), Crawford Assn. (chair). Democrat. Avocations: sailing, swimming, reading, classical music. Home: 7 Commodore Dr Apt 357 Emeryville CA 94608-1670 Office: 3036 Regent St Berkeley CA 94705 Office Phone: 510-658-3396. Personal E-mail: jcrawfordphd@sbcglobal.net.

CRAWFORD, CINDY (CYNTHIA ANN CRAWFORD), model, actress; b. Dekalb, Ill., Feb. 20, 1966; d. Dan Crawford and Jennifer Moluf; m. Richard Gere, Dec. 12, 1991 (div. 1995); m. Rande Gerber, May 29, 1998; children: Presley Walker, Kaya Jordan. Student, Northwestern U. Model for Victor Skrebneski, 1984-86; signed with Elite Modeling Agy., 1986; spokesperson Revlon, 1989—. JH Collectibles, Pepsi Cola, Kay Jewelers, Blockbuster Video, others; host MTV's House of Style, 1989-95. Released Cindy Crawford Fragrance, 2003. First featured on cover Vogue, 1986; has appeared on covers of W, People, Harper's Bazaar, ELLE, Allure, many others; Actor: (films) Fair Game, 1995, 54, 1998, The Simian Line, 2000; (exercise videos): Cindy Crawford's Shape Your Body Workout, 1992, The Next Challenge Workout, 1993. Host: (TV specials) Sex With Cindy Crawford, 1998. Supporter breast cancer rsch.; active Leukemia Soc. of Am.

CRAWFORD, DENISE F., lawyer; BS, Calif. Polytechnic Univ., 1999; JD, Univ. San Diego, 2002. Bar: Calif. 2002. Assoc., criminal defense Law Offices of Jennifer L. Keller, Irvine, Calif. Named a Rising Star, So. Calif. Super Lawyers, 2006. Office: Law Offices of Jennifer L. Keller Ste 560 18500 Von Karman Ave Irvine CA 92612-1043 Office Phone: 949-476-8700. Office Fax: 949-476-0900.*

CRAWFORD, HELENE HOPE, elementary school principal; b. N.Y.C. d. Jerome I. and Ethel Emily Lipson; m. Jon Kent, May 6, 1973 (div. Feb. 1984); m. John Larry Crawford, July 11, 1987. BA, Hunter Coll.; MS in Edn., CUNY, 1971; MS in Spl. Edn., Coll. of New Rochelle, 1978. Cert. sch. adminstr., supr., N.Y.; cert. intermediate supr., Conn. Tchr. I.S. 162, Bronx, N.Y., 1971-73, I.S. 183, Bronx, 1973-86; spl. edn. supr. Cmty. Sch. Dist. 7, 1986-95; asst. prin. P.S. 31X, Bronx, 1995-97; prin. P.S. 5X, Bronx, 1997—. Mem. ASCD, Nat. Trust for Historic Preservation, Orton Dyslexia Soc., Phi Delta Kappa. Avocations: reading, walking, movies, cooking.

CRAWFORD, JENNY LYNN SLUDER, medical/surgical nurse, educator; b. Asheville, NC, Oct. 14, 1952; d. Fletcher Sumpter and M. Orva (Yost) Sluder; m. Thomas Rodney Crawford, Jan. 21, 1984; children: Orva Marie, Sara Lynn. AA, Stephens Coll., 1972; BSN, Baylor U., 1974; MSN, U. NC, Charlotte, 1998. RN, Ola.; cert. med.-surg. nurse ANA. Staff nurse Comanche County Hosp., Lawton, Okla., 1974, VA Hosp., Asheville, 1975-77, VA Med. Ctr., Durham, NC, 1977-84, Presbyn. Hosp., Charlotte, NC, 1984-95; health occupations instr. Garinger HS, Charlotte, 1995—2002; health occupations inst. Independence HS, Charlotte, 2002—. Nursing instr. Presbyn. Hosp., Charlotte, 1989-95; instr. basic life support and CPR Am. Heart Assn., others. Mem.: ANA, Sigma Theta Tau. Avocations: camping, swimming, crosstitch, needlepoint, reading. Home: 8941 Dartmoor Pl Charlotte NC 28227-8983 Office Phone: 980-343-6900.

CRAWFORD, JUANITA GATEWOOD, nursing technician; b. Wadesboro, NC, Jan. 17, 1937; d. Huey and Ola Tillman Gatewood; m. James Crawford, July 2, 1961; 1 child, Gerald B. AA, Carver Coll., 1961; A, Ctrl. Piedmont, 1975. Nursing tech. Carolina Med., Charlotte, NC, 1967—97. Sec. Seversville Neighborhood Assn., Charlotte, NC, 1994—2006; chmn. Seversville Arch., Charlotte, NC, 2003—06; v.p. Healthy Families, Charlotte, NC, 2004—05. Adult I Sunday sch. clerk Shiloh Bapt. Ch., Charlotte, NC, 1985—2006, church missionary, 2000—06, Sunday sch. clerk, 2003—06. Home: 405 State St Charlotte NC 28208

CRAWFORD, LINDA SIBERY, lawyer, educator; b. Ann Arbor, Mich., Apr. 27, 1947; d. Donald Eugene and Verla Lillian (Schenck) Sibery; m. Leland Allardice Crawford, Apr. 4, 1970; children: Christina, Lillian, Leland. Student, Keele U., 1969; BA, U. Mich., Ann Arbor, 1969; postgrad., SUNY, Potsdam, 1971; JD, U. Maine, 1977. Bar: Maine 1977, U.S. Dist. Ct. Maine 1982, U.S. Ct. Appeals (1st cir.) 1983. Tchr. Pub. Sch., Tupper Lake, N.Y., 1970-71; asst. dist. atty. State of Maine, Farmington, 1977-79, asst. atty. gen. Augusta, Maine, 1979-95; prin. Linda Crawford and Assoc., 1985—, Litigation Consulting Firm, N.Y.C., 1986—. Legal adv. U. Maine, Farmington, 1975; legal counsel Fire Marshall's Office, Maine, 1980-83, Warden Svc., Maine, 1981-83, Dept. Mental Health, 1983-90, litigation divsn. 1990-95; tchg. team trial advocacy Law Sch., Harvard U., 1987—; lectr. Sch. Medicine Harvard U., 1991, 2004—; counsel to Bd. of Registration in Medicine, 1994-95; chmn. editl. bd. Mental and Physical Disability Law Reporter, 1993-95; arbitrator Am. Arbitration Assn., 1995—; facilitator Nat. Constrn. Task Force, St. Louis, 1995. Contbg. editor: Med. Malpractice Law and Strategy, 1997—, Managed Care Law Strategist, 1999—2002. Bd. dirs. Diocesan Human Rels. Coun., Maine, 1977-78, Arthritis Found., Maine, 1983-88; atty. expert commn. experts UN War Crime Investigation in the former Yugoslavia, 1994. Named one of Outstanding Young Women of Yr., Jaycees, 1981. Mem. ABA (com. on disability 1992-95), Nat. Assn. State Mental Health Attys. (treas. 1984-86, vice chmn. 1987-89, chmn. 1989-91), Nat. Health Lawyers Assn. Home and Office: 150 Orleans St PH 1 East Boston MA 02128 also: 45 Rockefeller Plz Fl 20 New York NY 10111-2099 Office Phone: 800-208-6117. Business E-Mail: crawford@lcandassociates.com.

CRAWFORD, MALLORY, counselor; b. Sweetwater, Tex., Jan. 4, 1942; d. Leslie Charles and Marjorie Eloise (Crawford) Edie; children: Alma Willow Whitten, Amedeo Michael Cacciutto. BA, Barnard Coll., N.Y.C., 1964; MA, Beacon Coll., Leesburg, Fla., 1981. Co-dir. Crisis Ctr. Touch, alcohol counselor Tri-County Alcohol Coun., Middletown, Conn., 1973-76; dir. social svcs. Town of Portland, Conn., 1977-78; counselor, group leader YWCA, Hartford, Conn., 1978-80; pvt. practice psychotherapy Hartford, Conn., 1980-95; counselor Parent and Child Guidance Ctr., Pitts., 1996-97; pvt. practice Pitts., 1998—; founder, pres. Earth Mother Enterprises. Speaker at profl. confs.; ambassador to China Citizen Ambassador Program. Mem. Out Town/Our Planet; adv. bd. Hartford area Birthright, La Leche League; past pres. Hartford Gay and Lesbian Health Collective. Grantee Conn. Humanities Coun. Mem. ASGPP, Gestalt Therapists Assn., Capitol Region Conf. Chs. (chair sexual minorities com.), Hartford Women's Ctr., Mensa, Barnard Alumnae Coun. Office Phone: 412-381-4877. Personal E-mail: mallory2@peoplepc.com.

CRAWFORD, MANETTE SUE, parochial school educator; d. Norman Robert and Virginia Anita Crawford. BS in Elem. Edn., Concordia Tchrs. Coll., Seward, Nebr., 1981; profl. edn. cert., U. Mich., 1999; MA in Edn. Tech., Ctrl. Mich. U., 2003. Tchr. Immanuel Luth. Sch., Mercedes, Tex., 1981—83, Trinity Luth. Sch., Warren, Mich., 1983—84, Mt. Hope Luth. Sch., Allen Park, Mich., 1984—86, St. John the Bapt. Cath. Sch., Dearborn Heights, Mich., 1987—95, Taylor (Mich.) Cath. Sch., 1995—. Tech. coord. Taylor Cath. Sch., Taylor, Mich., 1995—, adminstrv. asst., 1997—2002, yearbook advisor, 1997—. Mem.: Internat. Tech. Edn. Assn., Internat. Soc. Tech. in Edn., Mich. Assn. Computer Users in Learning (dir. spl. interest group for profl. devel. 2005—06). Home: 714 Kings Hwy Lincoln Park MI 48146 Office: Taylor Cath Sch 8070 Roosevelt Taylor MI 48180 Office Phone: 313-291-6650.

CRAWFORD, MARIA LUISA BUSE, geology educator; b. Beverly, Mass., July 18, 1939; d. William Theodore Buse and Barbara (Kidder) Aldana; m. William A. Crawford, Aug. 29, 1963. BA, Bryn Mawr Coll., 1960; postgrad., U. Oslo, 1960-61; PhD, U. Calif., 1965. Asst. prof. Bryn Mawr (Pa.) Coll., 1965-73, assoc. prof., 1973-79, prof., 1979-92, prof. environ. studies and sci., 1992—2006, William R. Kenan Jr. prof., 1985-92, chmn. dept. geology, 1976—88, 1998—2005; mem. U.S. Nat. Com. Geology, 1994-97. Chmn. women geoscientists com. Am. Geol. Inst., 1976-77; mem. U.S. Nat. Com. Geochemistry, 1980-82; organizing com. 28th Internat. Geol. Cong., 1987-89. MacArthur fellow, 1993-98; grantee NASA, 1973-76, NSF, 1967—. Fellow Geol. Soc. Am. (councillor 1982-85), Mineral Soc. Am. (councillor 1989-92);mem. Mineral Assn. Can. (councilor 1985-87), Am. Geophys. Union, Norwegian Geol. Soc., Phila. Geol. Soc., Assn. Women in Sci. Office: Bryn Mawr Coll Dept Geology Bryn Mawr PA 19010 Office Phone: 610-526-5111. Business E-Mail: mcrawfor@brynmawr.edu.

CRAWFORD, MARY LOUISE PERRI, career officer; b. Grand Haven, Mich., Nov. 26, 1949; d. Louis and Helen Marie (Buckley) Perri; m. Keith Eugene Crawford, Feb. 23, 1974 (dec. Oct. 1986); children: Matthew Perri, Michael Kirk. AA, Muskegon County C.C., 1969; BA, U. Mich., 1971. Commd. ensign U.S. Navy, 1972, advanced through grades to capt., 1993; pub. affairs officer Naval Air Sta., Key West, Fla., 1974-77, adminstrv., personnel officer Naval Air Res. Detachment, Patuxent River, Md., 1977-78, adminstrn. br. head Strike Aircraft Test Directorate, Naval Air Test Ctr., Patuxent River, 1978-80, ops. watch officer Command Ctr., Comdr.-in-Chief Naval Forces Europe Staff, London, 1980-84, officer-in-charge Personnel Support Activity Detachment, Patuxent River, 1984-86; engring. officer Chief Test and Evaluation Div., Strategic C3 Systems Directorate, Ctr. for Command, Control, and Communications, Def. Communications Agy., Washington, 1986-89; mgr. ultra high frequency Joint Satellite Communications Ctr., Joints Chiefs Staff, Pentagon, Washington, 1989-91; comdr. N.Y. Mil. Entrance Processing Sta., 1991-94; dir. personal, family & cmy support divsn. Bur. Navy Pers., Washington, 1994-95; head surveillance & navigations programs Office of Chief Naval Ops., Washington, 1996—. Mem. AAUW, Armed Forces Comm. & Electronics Assn., Women's Overseas Svc. League, U. Mich. Alumni Assn. Roman Catholic. Avocations: painting, ballet. Office: Office of CNO-N633 2000 Navy Pentagon Washington DC 20350-2000 Home: 4316 Chancery Park Dr Fairfax VA 22030-8103

CRAWFORD, MURIEL LAURA, lawyer, educator, writer; d. Mason Leland and Pauline Marie (DesIlets) Henderson; m. Barrett Matson Crawford, May 10, 1959; children: Laura Joanne, Janet Muriel, Barbara Elizabeth. BA with honors, U. Ill., 1973; JD with honors, Ill. Inst. Tech., 1977; cert. employee benefit splst., U. Pa., 1989. Bar: Ill. 1977, Calif. 1991, U.S. Dist. Ct. (no. dist.) Ill. 1977, U.S. Dist. Ct. (no. dist.) Calif. 1991, U.S. Ct. Appeals (7th cir.) 1977, U.S. Ct. Appeals (9th cir.) 1991; CLU; chartered fin. cons. Atty. Washington Nat. Ins. Co., Evanston, Ill., 1977-80; sr. atty., 1980-81; asst. counsel, 1982-83; asst. gen. counsel, 1984-87; assoc. gen. counsel, sec., 1987-89; cons. employee benefit splst., 1989-91; assoc. Hancock, Rothert & Bushoft, San Francisco, 1991-92. Author: (with Beadles) Law and the Life Insurance Contract, 1989, (sole author) 7th edit., 1994, Life and Health Insurance Law, 8th edit., 1998; co-author: Legal Aspects of AIDS, 1990; contbr. articles to profl. jours. Recipient Am. Jurisprudence award Lawyer's Coop. Pub. Co., 1975, 2nd prize Internat. LeTourneau Student Med.-Legal Article Contest, 1976, LOMA FLMI Ins. Edn. award, 1999. Fellow Life Mgmt. Inst.; mem. Ill. Inst. Tech./Chgo.-Kent Alumni Assn. (bd. dirs. 1983-89, Bar and Gavel Soc. award 1977). Democrat.

CRAWFORD, SARAH CARTER (SALLY CARTER CRAWFORD), broadcast executive; b. Glen Ridge, NJ, Oct. 3, 1938; d. Raymond Hitchings and Katherine Latta (Gribbel) Carter; m. Joseph Paul Crawford III, Sept. 10, 1960 (div. 1966). BA, Smith Coll., Northampton, Mass., 1960. Media dir. Kampmann & Bright, Phila., 1961-64; sr. media buyer Foote, Cone & Belding, N.Y.C., 1964-69; assoc. media dir. Grey Advt., L.A., 1969-75; account exec., research dir. Sta. KHJ-TV, L.A., 1975-76; mgr. local sales Sta. KCOP-TV, L.A., 1977-82; gen. sales mgr. Sta. KTVF-TV, Fairbanks, Alaska, 1982-96; nat. sales mgr. KTVF, KTVA, Fairbanks, 1996-97; gen. sales mgr. Sta. KYES-FM, Anchorage, 1997-2000; sta. and gen. sales mgr. mgr. Sta. KATN, Fairbanks, 2000—03; owner Crawford Commns. of Ala., 2004—; acct. rep. GCI, Fairbanks, 2003—. Adv. com. Golden Valley Electric Corp., Fairbanks, 1984-86; mem. coun. UAF Tanana County Campus, 1989-96, 2000-01. Chmn. Fairbanks Health and Social Svc. Commn., 1986—93; vice chmn. Fairbanks North Star Borough Health and Social Svc. Commn., 1993—96; pres. Fairbanks Meml. Hosp. Aux., 1988—90, creator trust fund, 1990—94, chmn. fin. com., 1990—94; active Fairbanks Health Ctr. Coalition, Tesoro Citizens Adv. Coun., Alaska, 1999, Fairbanks Chamber Membership Com., 2000—04; search com. UAF Tanana Valley Campus Dir.; pub. rels. chair Kids Vote Anchorage; chmn. mktg. com. Gov.'s Coun. on Youth Substance Abuse Prevention, 1999—2003; bd. dirs. Breast Cancer Detection Ctr., 2002—06; mem. U. Alaska Fairbanks Intercollegiate Athletic Coun., 2002—; promotions com. Fairbanks Downtown Assn., 2000—05; mktg. vol. FCVB, 2003—; mktg. coord. World Eskimo Indian Olympics, 2003; founder scholarship found. FBK Meml. Hosp. Aux., 1990; mem. Fairbanks City Bed Tax Com., 2003—; mktg. legis. liaison Arctic Alliance For People, 2002—; bd. dirs. Interior Regional Health Corp., 1992—97. Recipient Vol. of Yr. award, Fairbanks Downtown Assn., 2002, Flag and Citation, U.S. Senator Stevens, Cmty. Svc. award, Arctic Alliance for People, 2003, 1st Lady Vol. of Yr., 2006. Mem.: Alaska Broadcasters Assn. (bd. dirs. 1995—, founder scholarship found. 2001, pres. 2001—02, lobbyer, Broadcaster of the Yr. 2001, First Lady's Vol. of Yr. award Gov. 2006). Avocations: weightlifting, stock and real estate investments, running, motorcycling. Home: 107 Maple Dr Fairbanks AK 99709-2956 Office Phone: 907-452-1395.

CRAWFORD, SHEILA JANE, librarian, reading specialist; b. Beckley, W.Va., Mar. 1, 1943; d. Roger and Ruth (Ashworth) Crawford; m. Lloyd E. Johnston, June 4, 1966 (dec.); 1 child, Jacqueline; m. Troy Thomason, June 28, 2000. BA, Tenn. Tech. U., 1963; MA in Christian Edn., Seabury Western Theol. Sem., 1965; MS in Curriculum and Instrn., U. Tenn., Martin, 1989; EdD in Instrn. and Curriculum Leadership, U. Memphis, 1994; postgrad., San Jose State U., U. Calif., Berkeley, U. Utah, Tex. Woman's U. Cert. tchr. Tenn. Dir. Christian edn. St. Luke's Episcopal Ch., Rochester, Minn., 1965-66; elem. tchr. Santa Catalina Sch. Girls, 1967-69, Rowland-Hall St. Mark's Sch., Salt Lake City, 1968-69, Union City (Tenn.) Christian Sch., 1984-87; libr. Dept. Edn. U. Tenn. at Martin, 1987-89; rsch. asst. U. Memphis, 1989-92, adj. prof., 1996; prof., edn. dept. chair Lane Coll., Jackson, Tenn., 1992-94; reading tchr., drama club sponsor Ashland (Miss.) Mid. Sch., 1994-95; workshop presenter Jackson, Tenn., 1989-96; ednl. cons. Delta Faucet of Tenn. divsn. Masco Corp., Jackson, 1995—; homebound tchr. Jackson-Madison County Schs., 1996-97; instr., libr. LaGrange-Moscow (Tenn.) Sch., 1997-99; libr. Lauderdale Sch., Memphis. Mem. campus All Stars, Honda, Jackson, Tenn., 1992—93; cons. in field. Contbr. articles to profl. jours. Mem. story telling conf. Internat. Assn. Sch. Librs., Dublin, 1999, 2004. Mem. AAUW, DAR, Nat. Libr. Assn., Ch. and Synagogue Libr. Assn., Order Eastern Star (worthy matron 1980-81), Sch. Libr. Assn., Internat. Reading Assn., Sigma Tau Delta, Kappa Delta Pi Anglican. Achievements include research in the effect of chess on predicting and summarizing skills; Presentation of For You Stories from Primary Children in Memphis to Children in Ireland in the International Association of School Librarians Storytelling Convention in Dublin. Office Phone: 901-365-4863. Personal E-mail: crawfords444@cs.com.

CRAWFORD, SUSAN, library director, educator, editor, writer; b. Vancouver, BC, Can. d. James Y. and S. Young; m. James Weldon Crawford, July 5, 1955; 1 son, Robert James. BA, U. B.C., 1948; MA, U. Toronto, 1950, U. Chgo., 1954, PhD, 1970. With bur. libr. and indexing svc. ADA, 1954-56; with office exec. v.p. AMA, Chgo., 1956-60, dir. divsn. libr. and archival svcs., 1960-81; assoc. prof. Sch. Libr. Sci., Columbia U., N.Y.C., 1972-75; prof., dir. Sch. Medicine Libr. and Biomed. Comm. Ctr. Washington U., 1981-92; adj. prof. U. Ill., Chgo., 1994—. Internat. steering com. Royal Coll. Physicians and Surgeons. Mem. internat. steering com. Universal Guide Sci. Publs.; mem. editl. bd. Med. Socioecon. Rsch. Sources, Index to Sci. Revs., Jour. Am. Soc. Info. Sci., Med. Libr. Assn. News, Health and Info. Librs., Budapest, Health Librs. Rev., London, Health Info. and Librs. Jour., Oxford, Eng., 2003—; assoc. editor Jour. Am. Soc. Info Sci., 1979-82; editor Med. Info. Sys., 1988-90; editor-in-chief Jour. Med. Libr. Assn., 1982-88, 91-92; contbr. aticles to profl. jours. Bd. regents Nat. Libr. Medicine, NIH, 1971-75; mem. bd. overseers for univ. librs. Tufts U., 1988-89 Janet Doe hon. lectr., 1983; recipient Disting. Alumni award U. Toronto, 1987, Grad. medal U. Toronto, 1989. Fellow AAAS (chmn. coms.), Med. Libr. Assn. (life, Eliot award 1976, chmn. com. on surveys and stats. 1966-75, publs. panel 1977-80, chmn. consulting editors panel 1981-88, 91-92, spl. award to editor of bull. 1988, Noyes award 1992, Pres.'s award 1992, Centennial award), Med. Libr. Assn. (100 Most Notable 1998); mem. ALA, Soc. Social Studies Sci., Am. Soc. Info. Sci. and Tech. (chmn. med. info. sys. 1987-88, outstanding splty. group award 1988, 89, bd. and program chair Chgo. chpt. 1993-95), Am. Med. Informatics Assn., Acad. Health Info. Profls. (disting. mem.), European Assn. Health and Info. Librs. (U.S. rep. 1989-94), Sigma Xi (chmn. coms.). Achievements include research in scientific and biomed. comm., statis. surveys, info. sys. Home: 2418 Lincoln St Evanston IL 60201-2151 Office Phone: 847-869-3108. Personal E-mail: sjcrawf@aol.com.

CRAWFORD, SUSAN JEAN, federal judge; b. Pitts., Apr. 22, 1947; d. William Elmer Jr. and Joan Ruth (Bielau) C.; m. Roger W. Higgins; 1 child, Kelley S. BA, Bucknell U., 1969; JD, New Eng. Sch. Law, 1977. Bar: Md. 1977, D.C. 1980, U.S. Ct. Appeals for Armed Forces 1985, U.S. Ct. Appeals (4th cir.) 2003, U.S. Supreme Ct. 1993. Tchr. history, coach Radnor (Pa.) H.S., 1969-74; assoc. Burnett & Eiswert, Oakland, Md., 1977-79; ptnr. Burnett, Eiswert and Crawford, Oakland, 1979-81; prin. dep. gen. counsel U.S. Dept. Army, Washington, 1981-83, gen. counsel, 1983-89; insp. gen. U.S. Dept. Def., Arlington, Va., 1989-91; judge U.S. Ct. Appeals for the Armed Forces, Washington, 1991-99, 2004—, chief judge, 1999—2004. Asst. states atty. Garrett County, Md., 1978-79; instr. Garrett County C.C., 1979-81. Del. Md. Forestry Adv. Commn., Garrett County, 1978-81, Md. Commn. for Women, Garrett County, 1980-83; chair Rep. State Cen. Com., Garrett County, 1978-81, Bucknell U., 1988—, chair bd. trustees, 2003—; trustee New Eng. Sch. Law, 1989—. Mem. FBA, Md. Bar Assn., D.C. Bar Assn., Edward Bennett Williams Am. Inn of Ct. Presbyterian. Office: US Ct Appeals Armed Forces 450 E St NW Washington DC 20442-0001

CRAWFORD, SUSAN LEE, health educator; b. Newark, Ohio, Aug. 10, 1951; d. Robert D. Field and Shirley J. Gregg; m. Duane E. Crawford, Oct. 24, 1970; children: Carrie, Susan. BS, Coll. St. Francis, Joliet, Ill., 1980; MEd, U. Phoenix, 1992; PhD, Walden U., 2000. RN, Ariz.; cert. health education specialist. Staff nurse Mesa (Ariz.) Gen. Hosp., 1980-85; occupl. health nurse Medtronics, Tempe, Ariz., 1986-87; staff nurse Scottsdale (Ariz.) Healthcare, 1988-89; health edn. specialist Motorola, Inc., Mesa, 1989-99. Adj. faculty Maricopa County C.C., Mesa, 1989-99; mem. pub. health month task force Ariz. Dept. Health Svcs., Phoenix, 1994-99. Columnist Pub. Health Month, 1994-99. Recipient Cmty. Svc. award United Blood Svcs., 1994, Corp. Wellness award Ariz. Gov.'s Coun. Health, Phys. Fitness and Sports, 1996, Pub. Health Partnership award Ariz. Dept. Health Svcs., 1998. Mem. Nat. Wellness Assn., Assn. Workplace Health Promotion. Home: 3234 S Allred Dr Tempe AZ 85282-4118 Office: Motorola 2100 E Elliot Rd Tempe AZ 85284-1806

CRAWFORD, VICKY CHARLENE, perinatal clinical nurse specialist, nursing administrator; b. Waynesville, NC, Aug. 20, 1959; d. Jerry Harrell and Geneva Pauline (Parker) C. BSN, Med. U. of S.C., 1981; MS in Maternal/Infant Nursing, Clemson U., 1991. Cert. in inpatient obstet. nursing. Staff nurse II ob Greenville (S.C.) Gen. Hosp., 1981-83; staff nurse labor and delivery Lexington County Hosp., West Columbia, S.C., 1983-84; staff RN III high risk ob-gyn Greenville Meml. Hosp., 1984-85, ob-gyn. clinician, 1985-91, ob-gyn. clin. nurse specialist, 1991-94; perinatal clin. nurse specialist Ctr. for Women's Medicine-Maternal Fetal Medicine Divsn., Greenville, 1994-2000; clin. nurse specialist, clin. mgr. high risk pregnancy unit Gwinnett Women's Pavilion, Lawrenceville, Ga., 2000—. Counselor, program coord. Resolve Through Sharing Bereavement Svcs.; developer Mother-Baby Care Cross-Tng. Program, 1989. Contbr. articles to profl. jours. Mem. Assn. Women's Health, Obstetrics and Neonatal Nursing (conv. speaker), Sigma Theta Tau. Office Phone: 678-442-3075. E-mail: vcrawford@ghsnet.org.

CRAWFORD-LARSON, KRIS, minister; b. Port Lavaca, Tex., July 17, 1957; d. Fred Morris Thedford and Wanda Qualls; m. Stanley A. Larson, May 5, 2001; children: John Patrick Crawford, Carly Crawford, Tara Shea Crawford. BS in Home Econs., Tex. Tech. U., 1980; MDiv, Austin Presbytery Theol. Seminary, 1994. Ordained min. Mission Presbytery P.C., 1995. Assoc. pastor Grace Presbyn. Ch., Victoria, Tex., 1995—2001; pastor First Presbyn. Ch. P.C., Morrilton, Ark., 2001—. Leader Mission Trip to Kenya, 2001; mem. com. on ministry P.C. Presbytery Ark., 2002—03. Chair founding bd. dirs. Conway County Christian Clinic, Morrilton, Ark., 2003. Mem.: Rotary Internat. Avocations: scrapbooks, reading, walking. Office: First Presbyn Ch 105 W Church St Morrilton AR 72110 Office Phone: 501-354-2187.

CRAWFORD-MASON, CLARE WOOTTEN, television producer, journalist; b. Durham, N.C., July 22, 1936; d. Charles Thomas and Clare (Erly) Wootten; m. Robert Watts Mason; children: Victor Lawrence Crawford Jr., Charlene Elizabeth Crawford; stepchildren: John Mason, Robert Mason 3d. BA, U. Md., 1958. Reporter, columnist Washington Daily News, 1961-72; columnist Washington Star News, 1972-74; Washington bur. chief People mag., 1974-82; reporter, sr. prodr. NBC-TV, 1969-80; pres. CC-M Prodns. Inc., Washington, 1981—, managementwisdom.com. Prodr. 1st network documentary on spouse abuse NBC-TV, 1975 (blue ribbon San Francisco Film Festival), 1st network documentary on child sexual abuse NBC, TV, 1977, People of the Year (CBS), 1982, If Japan Can, Why Can't We, 1980 (Dupont award Columbia U. Sch. Journalism), It's Up to the Women, 1984, The Issues Hit Home, 1986, Windows on Women, 1986, How To Fix Up a Little Old American Town, 1987, Work Worth Doing, 1987 (Golden Eagle award Coun. on Internat. Non-theatrical Events), The Deming Library: Vols. I-27, Implementing Deming, vols. 1-4; co-author: Thinking About Quality, Progress, Wisdom and the Deming Revolution, 1995; prodr., dir. documentary series Quality of Else, 1991, W. Edwards Deming: The Prophet of Quality, 1994; co-author: Quality or Else: The Revolution in World Business, 1991, The Nun and the Bureacrat: How They Found an Unlikely Cure for America's Sick Hospitals, 2006; prodr., dir. How Everyone Wins: Joy, Meaning and Profit in the Workplace, 1997, The Enneagram Nine Paths to a Productive and Fulfilling Life, 1999, Good News: How Hospitals Heal Themselves, 2006. Recipient Bill Pryor Meml. award, 1st prize Washington Newspaper Guild, 1966; Disting. Pub. Affairs Reporting award Am. Polit. Sci. Assn., 1967; Nat. Assn. Broadcasters award, 1971, 2 Emmy awards Nat. Acad. TV Arts and Scis., 1972, award for broadcast investigative reporting AAUW, 1972, award for investigative reporting Chesapeake Press Assn., 1971, Douglas Southall Freeman award for pub. service Va. Assn. Press Broadcasters, 1972; Washington Newspaper Guild award, 1974, Blue Ribbon Am. Film Festival, 1977, 1st place award Nat. Edn. Film Festival, 1985, documentary award Am. Women in Radio and TV, 1986, Golden Eagle award, 1986, 87, Award of Excellence Soc. Tech. Communication, 1988. Mem. AFTRA, SAG. Democrat. Roman Catholic. Office: 7755 16th St NW Washington DC 20012-1460 Office Phone: 202-882-7430.

CRAYBAS, JILL, professional tennis player; b. Providence, July 4, 1974; d. Norbert and Camille. Degree in telecom., U. Fla., 1996. Profl. tennis player, 1996—. Recipient Ranked #8 in U.S. 18s, 1992, NCAA Champion, 1996, Ranked #97, WTA, Ranked #14 Among U.S. Players, Highest Season Ending Singles Rank #57, 2002, 1WTA Tour Singles Title, Japan, 2002, 1 WTA Tour Doubles Title, Madrid, 2003, 2 ITF Women's Circuit Tour Titles, 8th Place Wimbledon, 2005. Office: WTA Tour Corporate Headquarters One Progress Plz Ste 1500 Saint Petersburg FL 33701

CREA, VIVIEN S., career military officer; BA, U. Tex.; MS, Mass. Inst. Tech.; MA, Ctrl. Mich. U. Advanced through grades to vice admiral USCG, 2006, chief office of programs, Coast Guard Hdqs., commdg. officer Air Station Clearwater, exec. asst. to commandant, commdg. officer Air Station Detroit, ops. officer Air Station Borinquen PR, coast guard aide to Pres. Reagan, comdr. First Coast Guard Dist., chief info. officer, comdr. Coast Guard Atlantic Area, comdr. U.S. Maritime Def. Zone, 2004—06, vice comdt., 2006—. Decorated Legion of Merit, Def. Superior Svc. Medal, Coast Guard Commendation Medal; Sloan Fellow. Office: USCG US Dept Homeland Security 2100 2d St SW Washington DC 20593*

CREAMER, DEBORAH, library director, educator; MDiv, Vanderbilt Div. Sch., Nashville, 1993; PhD, U. of Denver, 2004. Coord. libr. svcs. Iliff Sch. of Theology, Denver, 1997—2005, asst. prof. of theol. studies, 2005—, interim dir. of libr. and info. svcs., 2005—. Co-chair religion and disability studies group Am. Acad. of Religion, Atlanta, 2003—; cons. editor Jour. of Religion, Disability, and Health. Contbr. articles to profl. jours. Mem.: Am.

Theol. Libr. Assn., Assn. of Physically Challenged Pastors, Colo. Assn. of Librs., Soc. for Disability Studies, Am. Acad. of Religion. Office: Iliff Sch of Theology 2233 S University Blvd Denver CO 80210 Office Phone: 303-765-3178. Business E-Mail: dcreamer@iliff.edu.

CREAMER, KATHY JAYNE, writer; b. Logansport, Ind., Dec. 10, 1959; d. James Hensley and Evelyn Lois (Good) Logan; m. Randall Wayne Creamer, Oct. 15, 1983; children: Jennifer Lois, Krysta Elizabeth. Lic., Beer Sch. Real Estate, 1987. Lic. real estate agt. Ind. Agt. Era Real Estate Co., Warsaw, Ind., 1987—88; referral agt. various real estate cos., Warsaw, 1988—89; freelance writer, 1992—. Author: (children's book) Case of the Missing Books, 1993, (novels) Shadows Dark, 1995. Vol. Am. Party, Ind., 1978; treas. sr. class Lakeland Christian Acad., Winona Lake, Ind., 1977—78. Republican. Baptist. Avocations: photography, quilting, reading, crafts, book collecting. Home: PO Box 184 Atwood IN 46502 E-mail: kjlc78@yahoo.com.

CREASIA, JOAN CATHERINE, dean, nursing educator; b. Burlington, Vt., Aug. 14, 1941; d. Ramon J. and Marjorie E. (Rising) LaBelle; m. Donald A. Creasia, June 29, 1963; children: Karen, Tracey. BSN, U. Vt., 1964; MSN, U. Tenn., 1978; PhD, U. Md., 1987. Staff nurse psychiat. unit Mass. Mental Health Ctr., Boston, 1964-65; instr. D'Youville Sch. Nursing, Cambridge, Mass., 1965-66; staff nurse Boston Lying-In Hosp., 1966-67; staff nurse med. surg. units Norwood (Mass.) Hosp., 1967-70; staff nurse, nursing supr. Oak Ridge (Tenn.) Hosp., 1971-74; staff nurse, supr. Frederick (Md.) Meml. Hosp., 1977-78, 86-92; instr. in nursing U. Tenn., Knoxville, 1974-77; rsch. asst. U. Md., Balt., 1980-83; instr., coord., asst. prof. med. surg. nursing Frederick (Md.) C.C., 1978-80, 81-83; asst. prof., coord. RN-BSN program U. Md. Sch. Nursing, Balt., 1983-90, assoc. prof., chair RN-BSN/MS programs, 1990-94, dir. statewide programs, 1991-94; assoc. dean for acad. programs and interim dean Med. U. of S.C. Coll. Nursing, Charleston, 1994-95; dean, Coll. Nursing, U. Tenn., Knoxville, 1995—. Cons. in field. Author: Conceptual Foundations of Professional Nursing Practice, 1991, 96 (Book of Yr. award Am. Jour. Nursing 1992), Conceptual Foundations: The Bridge to Professional Nursing Practice, 2001, 2d edit., 2006; contbr. articles to profl. jours. and books. Bd. dirs. Tenn. Ctr. for Nursing. Recipient Outstanding Achievement in Indirect Nursing Rsch. award, 1987, Nat. Rsch. Svc. award, 1982, 83, Profl. Nurse Traineeship award, 1981, Outstanding Leadership award Md. Nurses Assn., 1990, Excellence in Nursing Leadership award Tenn. Orgn. Nurse Execs., 2006. Mem.: ANA, Am. Assn. Colls. Nursing (bd. dirs.), Nat. League Nursing, Phi Kappa Phi, Sigma Theta Tau. Home: 605 Scotswood Cir Knoxville TN 37919-7457 Office Phone: 865-974-7583. Personal E-mail: joan.creasia@comcast.net. Business E-Mail: jcreasia@utk.edu.

CREBO, MARY ELIZABETH, state agency official, assessor; b. Chgo., Oct. 30, 1939; d. George Henry Browne and Nellace Marie Kamman; m. Frank S. Crebo, Jan. 11, 1958; children: Tracey E., Jeanne M., Frank Andrew, Daniel J. Student, Sauk Valley Cmty. Coll. State appraiser State of Ill., 1993-99; assessing officer State Ill., Dept. of Revenue, 1983-99; adminstr., assessor Coloma Twp., Ill.; owner Mary Crebo, Appraisals, 1986-99. Mem. Rock Falls (Ill.) Sch. Bd., 1972-74. Mem. Whiteside County Assessors Assn. (sec. 1998-99, acting pres. 1985-86, v.p. 1984-85). Avocations: painting, writing, camping, travel, photography. Home: 1307 Riverdale Rd Rock Falls IL 61071-2433 Office: 1200 Prophetstown Rd Rock Falls IL 61071-1064

CRECELIUS, BRIDGET MICHELLE, counselor; b. Hot Springs, Ark., Jan. 2, 1976; d. Lee Cleveland McNeely and Diana Lynn Bowen; m. Norman Hogan Crecelius, II, Aug. 11, 2001; 1 child, Elijah (Eli) Tucker. Diploma in edn. psychology and counseling, Ark. State U., 2001. Lic. counselor MSHS, Jonesboro, Ark., 2000—02, Child & Youth Pediatric Day Clinic, Jonesboro, 2002—. Mem.: Ark. Counseling Assn., Assn. Play Therapy, Am. Counseling Assn. Avocations: scrapbooks, travel, reading. Home: 4705 Gregory Dr Jonesboro AR 72401 Office: Child and Youth Pediatric Day Clinic 806 Glendale Jonesboro AR 72401

CREDLE, GINA C., mathematics educator; BS in Math., East Carolina U., Greenville, NC, 1987. Nat. bd. cert. tchr. NC, 1999. Math tchr. Hyde County Schs., Swan Quarter, NC, 1987—. Office: Mattamuskeet HS 20392 US 264 Swanquarter NC 27885 Office Phone: 252-926-0221.

CREECH, REBECCA J., science educator; b. Naperville, Ill., Mar. 26, 1974; d. Thomas H. and Margaret A. Potratz; m. Brett A. Creech, June 11, 2005. BS, Purdue U., West Lafayette, Ind., 1996, MS, 2001. Sci./math tchr. LaSalle-Peru Twp. H.S., Ill., 1996—98; bioscope tchr.-in-residence Purdue U., West Lafayette, 1998—99, sci. advisor, 1999—2000; sci. tchr. Harrison H.S., West Lafayette, 2000—. Chair sci. dept. Tippecanoe Sch. Corp., Lafayette, Ind., 2004—; coach varsity softball Harrison H.S., 2002—04. Grantee, Pub. Schs. Found., 2001, 2003, 2006. Mem.: Hoosier Assn. Sci. Tchrs., Inc., NSTA, Golden Key Honor Soc., Phi Beta Kappa. Office: Harrison HS 5701 N 50 W West Lafayette IN 47906

CREECH, SHARON, children's author; b. South Euclid, Ohio; d. Arvel and Ann Creech; m. Lyle Rigg; children: Rob, Karin. BA, Hiram Coll.; MA, George Mason U. Editl. asst., indexer Congl. Quarterly, Washington; rschr. Libr. Congress. Author: Recital, Nickel Malley, Walk Two Moons, 1994 (School Library Journal Best Book of 1994, ALA Notable Children's Book Award, 1995, John Newbery medal 1995), Absolutely Normal Chaos, 1995, Pleasing The Ghost, 1996, Chasing Redbird, 1997, Bloomability, 1999, The Wanderer, 2000 (Newbery honor), Fishing in the Air, 2000, A Fine, Fine School, 2001, Love That Dog, 2001, Ruby Holler, 2002, Heartbeat, 2004. Office: care HarperCollins Children's Bks c/o Author Mail 1350 Ave of the Americas New York NY 10019

CREED, BARBARA ELLEN, music educator; d. Richard Thomas Carpentier and Dorothy Mary Henry; m. Robert Thomas Creed, Aug. 17, 1974; children: Robert Edward, Charles Thomas, Catherine Therese. MusB in Music Edn. with highest honor, De Paul U., Chgo., 1976. Music tchr. Ascension Cath. Sch., Oak Park, Ill., 1994—. Cantor Ascension Cath. Ch., Oak Park, 1986—. Recipient Heart of the Sch., Ascension Cath. Sch., 2004, Devel. Impact award, 2006, Exemplary Website award, Ill. Computer Educators, 2005, Recognized Web Showcase Winner, 2004. Mem.: Nat. Assn. of Pastoral Musicians, Music Educators (assoc.), Music Educators Nat. Conf. (assoc.). Roman Catholic. Avocations: reading, music, travel. Office: Ascension School 601 Van Buren Oak Park IL 60304 Office Phone: 708-386-7282. E-mail: bcreed@ascension-school.com.

CREEDON, GERALDINE, state legislator; b. Springfield, Mass., Sept. 26, 1945; m. Robert Stanton Creedon Jr.; children: Jennifer, Robert S. BA, Emmanuel Coll., 1967. Vice chair edn. Mass. Ho. of Reps., Boston, mem. house ways and means com., mem. election laws, mem. Dist. 11, 1995—. Mem. Brockton (Mass.) City Coun., 1992-95, pres., 1995; bd. dirs. Charity Guild, 1990-97; mem. Dem. City Com. Roman Catholic. Office: Mass State Legis Rm 473G State House Boston MA 02133 Office Phone: 617-722-2070.

CREEL, SUE CLOER, retired secondary school educator; b. Columbus, Miss., July 4, 1943; d. Cornelius Ducler Cloer and Sara Verna (Shackelford) Cloer Mackie; children: Ricky (dec.), Ronny. BA, Harding U., 1982, MEd, 1986; grad., Jackson State U., 1996. Nat. bd. cert. Adolescent and Young Adult English Lang. Arts, 2000. Tchr. 8th grade English Alfh Jr. H.S., Searcy, Ark., 1982-87; part-time editor, writer for neurosurgery Miss. Med. Ctr., Jackson, 1987-89; adminstrv. asst. to dean of nursing U. Miss. Med. Ctr., Jackson, 1988-89; tchr. advanced placement English and creative writing Jackson Pub. Schs., 1990—2006; ret., 2006; adj. instr. world lit. and Brit. lit. Holmes C.C. Adj. prof. Holmes C.C., 1999-2000; adj. instr. English Hinds C.C., Raymond, Miss., 1987-89; cons. Nat. Writing Project, 1985, Univ. Ctrl. Ark., Conway, Ark., Nat. Writing Project; session chair Writing-Across-the-Curriculum K-12, Charleston, S.C., 1997; tchr. long distance learning interactive video ETV, 1998-99, 2000-2001; presenter Nat. Coun. Tchrs. English, 2001; instr. U.S. Army, 2006. Contbg. poet: Moments in the Garden, 1998, Miss. Musings, Miss. Poetry Soc., 1997, The Drifting Sands, 1999. With USN, 1962—63. Grantee Entergy, Jackson, 1994-96; fellowship Jackson (Miss.) State U., 1996; recipient 3 Editor's Choice awards, Beyond Call of Duty award JPSD, 1999; named tchr. excellence Calloway H.S., 2000; finalist Sharp Wave award U.S. Army, 1962. Mem. Nat. Coun. Tchrs. of English, Miss. Poetry Soc. (v.p. ctrl. br. 2002-), The Poetry Guild (poetry included Best Poems of the 90s, 1998), Phi Kappa Phi, Beta Sigma Phi (v.p. XI chpt. 2002—, pres. 2003, Valentine Ball Queen 2003, mem. Internat. Queen's Ct. 2003), Alpha Chi, Kappa Delta Pi, Sigma Tau Delta, Phi Alpha Theta. Mem. Ch. Of Christ. Avocations: reading, writing, theater, gardening, competitions. Home: 625 Choctaw Rd Jackson MS 39206-5325

CREEM, CYNTHIA STONE, state legislator, lawyer; BSBA, JD, Boston U. Mem. Mass. Senate, Boston, 1998—, chair revenue com., vice chair pub. health com., mem. econ. devel. com., bonding capital expenditures com., telecomm. com. Mem. Newton Bd. Aldermen, Gov.'s Coun. Fellow Women's Bar Assn.; mem. Mass. Bar Assn. Democrat. Office: Mass State Senate State House Rm 416B Boston MA 02133 E-mail: cynthia.creem@state.ma.us.

CREENAN, KATHERINE HERAS, lawyer; b. Elizabeth, N.J., Oct. 7, 1945; d. Victor Joseph and Katherine Regina (Lederer) Petervary; m. Edward James Creenan; 1 child, David Heras. BA, Kean Univ., 1968; JD, Rutgers U., 1984. Bar: N.J. 1984, Maine 1996, N.Y. 2005, U.S. Dist. Ct. N.J. 1984, U.S. Ct. Appeals (3d cir.) N.Y., 2005. Various tchg. positions including, Union and Stanhope, NJ, 1968-81; law clk. to presiding judge Superior Ct. of N.J. Appellate Div., Newark, 1984-85; assoc. Lowenstein, Sandler, Kohl, Fisher & Boylan, Roseland, NJ, 1985-88, Kirsten, Simon, Friedman, Allen, Cherin & Linken, Newark, 1988-89, Whitman & Ranson, Newark, 1989-93; sr. atty. Whitman Breed Abbott & Morgan LLP, Newark, 1993-99; assoc. Skadden, Arps, Slate, Meagher & Flom LLP, Newark, 1999—2004, sr. staff assoc. NYC, 2004—. Mem. ABA, N.J. State Bar Assn. Office: Skadden Arps Slate Meagher & Flom LLP Four Times Sq New York NY 10036-6522 Office Phone: 212-735-2832. Business E-Mail: kcreenan@skadden.com.

CREGAN, NORA C., lawyer; b. Phila. BA magna cum laude, Middlebury Coll., 1984; JD with honors, U. Chgo., 1991. Bar: Calif. 1991, U.S. Dist. Ct., Ctrl. & No. Dist. Calif. 1992, U.S. Ct. Appeals, ninth cir. 1992, Wash. 1995, U.S. Dist. Ct., We. Dist. Wash. 1995. With Morgan Stanley, N.Y.C.; law clk. to Hon. Eugene A. Wright U.S. Ct. Appeals, ninth cir., Seattle; ptnr. Bingham McCutchen LLP, San Francisco, co-chairperson pro bono com. Mem.: San Francisco Lawyers Com., Nat. Lawyers Com. Civil Rights Under Law (bd. dirs.). Office: Bingham & McCutchen LLP 3 Enbarcader Ctr San Francisco CA 94111 Office Phone: 415-393-2060. Office Fax: 415-393-2286. Business E-Mail: nora.cregan@bingham.com.

CREIGHTON, JOANNE VANISH, academic administrator; b. Marinette, Wis., Feb. 21, 1942; d. William J. and Bernice Vanish; m. Thomas F. Creighton, Nov. 9, 1968; 1 child, William. BA with honors, U. Wis., 1964; MA, Harvard U., 1965; PhD, U. Mich., 1969. From instr. to prof. English Wayne State U., Detroit, 1968—85; assoc. dean liberal arts, 1983—85; dean arts and scis., prof. English U. N.C., Greensboro, 1985—90; v.p. acad. affairs, provost, prof. English Wesleyan U., Middletown, Conn., 1990—94, interim pres., 1994—95; pres., prof. English Mt. Holyoke Coll., South Hadley, Mass., 1995—. Author: William Faulkner's Craft of Revision, 1977, Joyce Carol Oates, 1979, Margaret Dabble, 1985, Joyce Carol Oates: Novels of the Middle Years, 1992. Grantee, Am. Coun. Learned Socs. Mem.: Phi Kappa Phi, Phi Beta Kappa. Home: 45 College St South Hadley MA 01075-1403 Office: Mount Holyoke Coll Office of Pres 50 College St South Hadley MA 01075-1423 Office Phone: 413-538-2500. Office Fax: 413-538-2391.*

CREIGHTON, PEGGY MILAM, media specialist, writer; b. Richmond, Va., Sept. 8, 1953; d. Robert Charles and Nola Maxine (Brisentine) Squier; married; children: Ryan Wesley Milam, Sara Kristen Milam. BS in Elem./Spl. Edn., Ga. State U., 1975, postgrad., 1999; MEd in Early Childhood, Mercer U., 1992; EdS in Media/Inst. Tech., State U. West Ga., 2002. Cert. libr. media specialist Nat. Bd. Cert., 2003. Tchr. 6th grade lang. arts Newton County Bd. Edn., Covington, Ga., 1975—76, Gwinnett County Bd. Edn., Lawrenceville, Ga., 1976—80; elem. tchr. Mt. Vernon Presbyn. Sch., Atlanta, 1986—99; from dir. media svcs. to coll. dean Interactive Coll. Tech., Chamblee, Ga., 1999—2001; libr. media specialist Cobb County Bd. Edn., Marietta, Ga., 2001—. Mem. Media Leadership Team, Marietta, 2001—05; tchr. support specialist, 2005—; presenter in field. Author: Infoquest: A New Twist on Information Literacy, 2002, National Board Certification in Library Media: A Candidates Journal, 2005; contbr. articles to profl. jours. New tchr. mentor Mighty Mentors, 2000—01; relay for life fundraiser Am. Cancer Soc., Atlanta, 2000—; amb. People to People: Spl. Needs Delegation to China, 2006. Named Most Outstanding Specialist in Media, State U. West Ga., 2003; recipient Extra Mile award, Interactive Coll. Tech., 2000. Mem.: ASCD, ALA, Ga. Assn. Sch. Libr. Media Specialists, Cobb County Assn. Libr. Media Specialists (pres.-elect 2004—05, pres. 2005—06), Internat. Soc. for Tech. in Edn. (sec. 2004—, pres.-elect 2006—), Pi Lambda Theta. Avocations: reading, writing, sewing, quilting. Office: Compton Elem Sch 3450 New Macland Rd Powder Springs GA 30127 Office Phone: 770-222-3700 227. Personal E-mail: peggymilam@hotmail.com.

CREMONA, RACHEL KAREN, political science professor; b. Kent, England, Dec. 28, 1968; d. Paul Raphael and Gwendoline Anita Cremona; m. James Robert Spathelf, Dec. 29, 2004; 1 child, Gabriel James Spathelf. BA, U. Kent, Canterbury, Eng., 2000; MA in Am. Politics, U. Essex, Eng., 2001; MA in Political Sci., Binghamton U., NY, 2003; PhD, Binghamton U., 2006. Asst. prof. Flagler Coll., St Augustine, Fla., 2004—. Named to Deans Honor Roll, U. Calif. Berkeley, 1999; recipient Best Degree Performance award, Am. Studies Dept., Kent U., 2000; Travel grant, Am. Polit. Sci. Assn., 2004. Mem.: Brit. Politics Group, Western Polit. Sci. Assn., So. Polit. Sci. Assn., MidWest Polit. Sci. Assn., Am. Polit. Sci. Assn. Office: Flagler Coll 75 King St St Augustine FL 32085 Office Phone: 904-819-6272. Business E-Mail: rcremona@flagler.edu.

CRENSHAW, KIMBERLE WILLIAMS, law educator; b. 1959; BA, Cornell U., 1981; JD, Harvard U., 1984; LLM, Wis. U., 1985. Law clk. to Hon. Shirley S. Abrahamson Wis. Supreme Ct., 1985-86; asst. prof. UCLA, 1986-89, acting prof., 1989, prof. law, Columbia U., NYC. Co-founder African-American Policy Forum, 1996. Co-author: Words that Wound: Critical Race Theory, Assaultive Speech and the First Amendment, 1993, Critical Race Theory, 1995; contbr. articles to law jours. Office: UCLA Sch Law 405 Hilgard Ave Los Angeles CA 90095-9000 also: 435 W 116th St New York NY 10027 E-mail: crenshaw@law.columbia.edu, crenshaw@law.ucla.edu.

CRENSHAW, MARJORIE JUANETA, retired music educator; d. Perry and Etta Hollins; m. Willie Newton Crenshaw, Nov. 8, 1959 (dec.); children: Lisa Jeannette, Perry Newton. BA in Music Edn., Wiley Coll., Marshall, 1948; MA in Music Edn., U. N.Tex., Denton, 1963. Cert. tchr. NY, Tex. Music & English tchr. Atlanta I.S.D. Pruitt HS, Tex., 1948—50; elem. music tchr. Ft. Worth I.S.D., 1950—85. Pianist St. Andrew's United Meth. Ch.; bd. dirs. Imagination Celebration; mem. measures & benefits com. A.F.M., Las Vegas, Nev., 1991; mem. panel on jazz Ft. Worth Libr., 2002. Recipient Outstanding Contributions in Entertainment/Commitment to Black Texans, Legis. Black Caucus Tex., 1989, Outstanding Contributions in Jazz Edn. award, Black Jazz Music Caucus, 1993, T.W. Micheaux Outstanding Svc. award, St. Andrew's United Meth. Ch., 2001, Traditional Jazz Coord. Dir. Jazz award, Ft. Worth, 2001, Marion Brooks award; Humanities grant, Ford Found., U. N.Tex. Mem.: IAJE, MENC, TMEA, Duke Ellington Soc., Ft. Worth Elem. Music Tchrs. Assn., Ft. Worth Jazz Soc. (charter mem., pres., program chmn.), Delta Sigma Theta. Democrat. United Methodist.

CRENSHAW, PATRICIA SHRYACK, sales executive, consultant; b. Kansas City, Mo., Oct. 7, 1941; d. George Randolf and Velma Irene (Carroll) Shryack; m. Paul Burton, Mar. 24, 1961 (div. 1971); m. Peter Frederick Schmidt, Jan. 21, 1989. Student, William Jewell Coll., 1959—60, S.W. Mo. State U., 1960—61; BEd, U. Mo., 1967; postgrad., Cen. Mo. State U., 1971—73. Cert. tchr. secondary edn. and history, Mo. Tchr. Lillis H.S., Kansas City, 1967—69, Park Hill H.S., Kansas City, 1969-73; terr. mgr. Hollister, Inc., Kansas City, 1973-75, field trainer, 1974-75, sales edn. mgr. Chgo., 1975; dist. sales mgr. Detroit Mich., 1976-81; regional sales mgr. Chgo., 1981-84; dir. contract sales Chgo. Serta, Inc., 1984-86, nat. dir. contract sales divsn., 1987-89, v.p. nat. contract sales, 1989-90; area v.p. B G Industries, Northridge, Calif., 1990-91, v.p. sales, 1992-95, v.p. internat. sales, 1995-97, v.p. clin. svcs., 1998—2002; ret., 2002. Mem. women's com. Young Reps., Kansas City, 1962. Mem. NOW, U.S. Golf Assn., Lake Barrington Shores (Ill.) Golf Club. Republican. Avocations: golf, skiing, scuba diving, racquetball, reading, gardening. Home (Winter): PO Box 511182 Key Colony Beach FL 33051 Personal E-mail: Crenshawpt@cs.com.

CRENSHAW, REBECCA SUE, physician; b. Ponca City, Okla., Jan. 9, 1956; d. Lee Arthur and Lovina Sue Crenshaw. BA in Biology and Psychology, Rice U., 1979; MD, U. Tex., Galveston, 1985. Diplomate Am. Bd. Neurology. Organist Grace Episcopal Ch., Galveston, Tex., 1973-74; exam. asst. Samuel Simkin, ND, MPH, Houston, 1977-79; emergency rm. clk. N.W. Med. Ctr., Houston, 1979-80; rsch. asst. U. Tex. Health Sci. Ctr., Houston, 1980-81; resident in internal medicine U. Kans. Affiliated Schs., Wichita, 1985-87; resident in neurology, chief resident U. Kans. Med. Sch., Wichita, 1987-90; neurologist Shannon Clinic, San Angelo, Tex., 1990—2002; occupl. therapy dir. Shannon Hosp., San Angelo, Tex., 1992-94; neurologist West Tex. Med. Assocs., San Angelo, 2002—04, CMA, San Angelo, 2004—. Contbr. articles to profl. jours. Mem. AMA, Am. Nuerol. Assn. Avocations: piano, golf, water sports, skiing, archery. Office: CMA 2141 Hamilton Way #106 San Angelo TX 76904

CREPPEL, CLAIRE BINET, hotel owner; b. New Orleans, Nov. 30, 1936; d. Albert Leo and Leocadie (Dominique) Binet; m. Jacques Jules Creppel, Feb. 2, 1957; children: Ingrid, Foster, Collette and Gregg (twins), Lisa, Morgan. BA in English, U. Southwestern La., 1971; MEd in Guidance/Counseling Psychology, Loyola U., New Orleans, 1975; postgrad. adminstrn., mgmt., supervision, Tulane U., New Orleans, 1978. Instr. English and Spanish Booker T. Washington Sr. High Sch., 1972-74, instr. English and reading, 1974-76, guidance counselor, 1976-77; intervention counselor Sophie B. Wright Middle Sch., 1977-79; owner, gen. mgr. Columns Hotel, New Orleans, 1980—; owner Woodland Plantation, 1997—. New Orleans regional dir. La. Coun. on Child Abuse, 1985—87; v.p. bd. Barataria Terrebne Estuary Found. (Save the Wetlands), 2000—02; mem. adv. bd. Le Petite Thetre du Vieux Carre, 2000—; mem. citizens adv. bd. Jo Ellen Smith Hosp.; mem. task force Ct. Appointed Spl. Advocate; bd. dirs. So. Repertory Theatre of New Orleans, Odyssey House, Bravo, Arts Coun., Overture to the Cultural Season, pres., 1997—98. Named one of Top Exec. Women New Orleans, 1990, one of Top Women New Orleans Bus. Owners, 1997. Mem. Am. Pers. and Guidance Assn., AAUW, La. Pers. and Guidance Assn., Orleans Sch. Counselors Assn., St. Charles Ave. Bus. Assn., Street Car Inns, Fgn. Rels. Assn. New Orleans, Am. Heart Assn. (pres. elect, New Orleans chpt.), New Orleans Opera Assn. (bd. govs. 2006), Kappa Delta Pi, Sigma Delta Pi. Republican. Roman Catholic. Avocations: skiing, real estate market, scuba diving, water-skiing, travel. Home: 7927 St Charles Ave New Orleans LA 70118-2724 Office: Columns Hotel 3811 Saint Charles Ave New Orleans LA 70115-4681 E-mail: clairecreppel@aol.com.

CRESCENZ, VALERIE J., music educator; b. Bethlehem, Pa., Mar. 8, 1956; d. George Henry and Florence Showers; m. Joseph Martin Crescenz, July 26, 1980; children: Monica Lynn, Melanie Jane. BS in Music Edn., West Chester State Coll., Pa., 1978, MusM in Piano Performance, 1980. Music instr. West Chester State Coll., 1979—80, Delaware County C.C., Media, Pa., 1990—95; composer Hinshaw Music, Inc., Chapel Hill, NC, 1994—; music tchr., dir. Downingtown (Pa.) Sch. Dist., 1995—. Composer (choral music): various titles, including 3 written with composer James Green of Durham, N.C.; composer: (commd. works) Durham Sch. Arts, 2002. Mem.: Music Educators Nat. Conf., ASCAP, NEA, Pa. State Edn. Assn., Pa. Music Educators Assn. (commn. 2001, 2002). Home: 10 Juniata Dr Coatesville PA 19320 Office: West Bradford Elem Sch 1475 Broad Run Rd Downingtown PA 19335

CRESPIN, LESLIE ANN, artist; b. Cleve., Sept. 30, 1947; d. Edwin Creaver and Eunice Jane (Pierce) Ulrich; m. Raimondo J. Vinella; children: Greg, Chris, Tony. Student, Cleve. Art Inst., U. Capetown (S. Africa), Hiram (Ohio) U. Instr. Taos (N.Mex.) Sch. Fine Art. Works in permanent collections at Johnson Humrick House Mus., Ohio, Harwood Found., Mus. Taos Art, Midland Savs. and Loan, Denver, Monsanto Internat., N.Y.C., St. Louis, Carlsbad Fine Art Mus., Tubac Ctr. for the Arts, Rolm Corp., Dallas, Wichita Art Assn., Kans. Exhibits include Cleve. Mus. Art, Jewish Community Ctr., Cleve., Hiram U., U. Capetown, N.Mex. State U., Peyton Wright Gallery, Santa Fe, Roanoke (Va.) Fine Arts Mus., The New Gallery, Taos, 1981-84, Amarillo Art Ctr., 1983, Carlsbad Fine Arts Mus., 1984, Beachwood Mus., Ohio, 1985, Tubac Ctr. for Arts, Ariz., 1985, Erie (Pa.) Art Mus., 1986, Albuquerque Mus., 1991—, Harwood Found. Mus. Taos Art, 1987, Fenix Gallery, N.Mex., 1990-91, 92, 93, Sharon Blaustein, N.J. and N.Y., 1990—, Lumina Gallery, 1994—, Van Vechten Lineberry Taos Art Mus., 2000; represented in permanent collections Harwood Found., Maytag, Wichita Art Assn., Kans., Monsanto Internat., Carlsbad Fine Art Mus., Tubac Ctr. for the Arts, Am. Express-Mus. Collection I.B.M., Dallas, Rolm Corp., Johnson Humrick House Mus., N. Pajarola Museumstrasse, Switzerland, Carson County Square House Mus. Recipient numerous purchase awards; Masterfield award, North Coast Collage Soc., 1985, Grumbacher award, Beachwood Mus., Ohio, 1986, Master Field award, KennedyCtr. Gallery, 1987, Taos Spring Arts 1st pl. award, 1999. Mem. Soc. Layerists in Multi Media, Taos Art Assn. Avocations: western history, wildlife study, travel. Home and Office: 414 Camino De La Placita Apt 9 Taos NM 87571-6193

CRESPO DE SANABIA, MARÍA MILAGROS, retired education educator; b. Mayaguez, Puerto Rico, June 5, 1948; d. Osvaldo J. Crespo Salas and Joaquina Reyes Rivera; m. Aníbal Sanabia, June 24, 1972; children: Aníbal Iván Sanabia Crespo, Aníbal Osvaldo Sanabia Crespo. MA in Edn., U. Phoenix, PR, 1996. Sci. tchr. Dept. Edn., Río Piedras, 1978—2001; asst. project dir. Ednl. Linkages Demonstration Project, Bronx, 1999—2001; coord. PR Statewide Systemic Initiative, San Juan, 1994—2000; ednl. cons. Evans Newton Inc., Scottsdale, Ariz., 2004—06; prof. (part time) Universidad del Este, Carolina, 2006—. Coord. profl. devel. program Evans Newton Inc., 2005—06. Recipient Tchr. of Yr., Dept. of Edn. - Converse, Sci. Tchr. of P. R., Dept. of Edn., 1992. Mem.: NSTA (assoc.), ASCD (assoc.). Achievements include design of profl. devel. programs; acad. for new tchrs. of sci. and math. Avocations: travel, craftman, reading, exercise. Home: Colinas de Fair View 202 St 4E-#26 Trujillo Alto PR 00976 Personal E-mail: maria_s@prw.net.

CRESWELL, DOROTHY ANNE, computer consultant; b. Burlington, Iowa, Feb. 6, 1943; d. Robert Emerson and Agnes Imogene (Gardner) Mefford; m. John Lewis Creswell, Aug. 28, 1965. AA, Burlington CC, 1963; BA in Math., U. Iowa, 1965; MS in Math., We. Ill. U., 1970; postgrad., Iowa State U., 1974. Computer programmer Mason & Hanger, Silas Mason Co., Inc., Burlington, 1965—74; sys. programmer Contractor's Hotline, Ft. Dodge, Iowa, 1974; dir. data processing Iowa Ctrl. CC, Ft. Dodge, 1975—80; mgr. sys. programming Norand Corp., Cedar Rapids, Iowa, 1980—82; mgr. spl. svcs. Pioneer Hi-Bred Internat., Inc., Cedar Rapids, 1982—87; owner, pres. D.C. Cons., Inc., Ankeny, Iowa, 1987—2003. Computers-in-edn. del. to China People to People Internat., Kansas City, Mo., 1987. Contbr. articles, papers to profl. publs. Mem.: Ind. Computer Cons. Assn. (editl. bd. 1989—96, chpt. pres.-at-large 1993—95), DEC Users Group (v.p. Ea. Iowa chpt. 1981—82), Hawkeye Pers. Computer Users, Assn. Computing Machinery, Adminstrv. Mgmt. Soc. (sec. 1985—86, v.p. 1986—90, Merit award 1987), Data Processing Mgmt. Assn. (bd. dirs. 1986—87, v.p. 1988, 1991—93, pres. 1993—94). Democrat. Methodist. Avocations: jogging, travel.

CREWE, NANCY MOE, retired psychologist; b. Mpls., Aug. 27, 1939; d. Arnold O. and Ruby V. Moe; m. James C. Crewe (div.); 1 child, Laurel; m. John Pond. BA, U. Minn., 1961, MA, 1964, PhD, 1967. Lic. psychologist, Mich. Staff psychologist Am. Rehab. Found., Mpls., 1966-69, Robbinsdale (Minn.) Sch. Dist., 1969-71; asst. prof. psychology U. Minn., Mpls., 1971-78, assoc. prof. psychology, 1978-87; postdoctoral fellow New England Rehab. Hosp., Boston, 1985-86; prof. Mich. State U., East Lansing, 1987—2006, ret., 2006. Co-author: Employment After Spinal Cord Injury, 1978, Psychology of Disability, 2004; co-editor: Independent Living for Disabled People, 1983. Bd. dirs. Accessible Space, Mpls., 1980-82, Met. Ctr. for Ind. Living, Mpls., 1983-85; bd. dirs., chairperson Comprehensive Svcs. for Disabled Citizens, Mpls., 1980-87, Capital Area Ctr. for Ind. Living, 2000-05. Recipient Disting. Faculty award, Mich. State U., 1997. Fellow: APA (pres. divsn. 22 1987—88, Disting. Contbns. to Rehab. Psychology award 1993, Roger Barker Disting. Career award 2001); mem.: ACA, Nat. Coun. Rehab. Edn. (Disting. Career in Rehab. Edn. award 2004), Nat. Rehab. Assn., Am. Rehab. Counseling Assn., Am. Assn. Spinal Cord Injury Psychologists and Social Workers (bd. dirs. 1995—98, Disting. Svc. award 1990), Am. Congress Rehab. Medicine (Licht award 1981, Disting. Mem. award 1990), Phi Beta Kappa. Office: Mich State Univ 459 Erickson Hall East Lansing MI 48824-1034 Business E-Mail: ncrewe@msu.edu.

CREWSON, WENDY JANE, actress; b. Hamilton, Ontario, Canada, May 9, 1956; d. Robert Binnie and June Doreen (Thomas) C.; m. Michael George Murphy, Mar. 7, 1988; children: Margaret Mary, Branton. BA, Queen's U., 1977; postgrad., Weber-Douglas Acad. Drama, London, England, 1979. Actor: (films) Skullduggery, 1983, The Sight, 1985, Mark of Cain, 1985, The Doctor, 1991, I'll Never Get to Heaven, 1992, Folks!, 1992, The Good Son, 1993, Corrina, Corrina, 1994, The Santa Clause, 1994, To Gillian on Her 37th Birthday, 1996, Air Force One, 1997, Gang Related, 1997, Sleeping Doges Lie, 1998, At the End of the Day: The Sue Rodriguez Story, 1998, Escape Velocity, 1998, The Eighteenth Angel, 1998, Where's Marlowe?, 1998, Better Than Chocolate, 1999, Question of Privilege, 1999, Bicentennial Man, 1999, Mercy, 2000, What Lies Beneath, 2000, The 6th Day, 2000, Suddenly Naked, 2001, Between Stangers, 2002, Perfect Pie, 2002, The Santa Clause 2, 2002, The Clearing, 2004, Niagara Motel, 2005, Eight Below, 2006, The Covenant, 2006, Away from Her, 2006, Who Loves the Sun, 2006, The Santa Clause 3: The Escape Clause, 2006, (TV films) War Brides, 1980, Mazes and Monsters, 1982, Heartsounds, 1984, The Guardian, 1984, Murder: By Reason of Insanity, 1985, My Father, My Rival, 1985, Murder in Space, 1985, Whodunit, 1986, Perry Mason: The Case of the Shooting Star, 1986, Covert Action, 1987, A Hobo's Christmas, 1987, Getting Married in Buffalo Jump, 1990, Lives of Girls & Women, 1994, Spenser: The Judas Goat, 1994, Spenser: A Savage Place, 1995, Ebbie, 1995, Summer's End, 1999, Love and Murder, 2000, Deadly Appearances, 2000, The Wandering Soul Murders, 2001 A Colder Kind of Death, 2001, The Many Trials of One Jane Doe, 2002, Verdict in Blood, 2002, An Unexpected Love, 2003, Jack, 2004, Hunt for Justice, 2005, The Man Who Lost Himself, 2005; (TV series) Keep the Home Fires Burning, 1981-85 (Best Actor award 1985), Night Heat, 1985, Hard Copy, 1987, Studio 5-B, 1989, The Beast, 2001, Crimes of Passion, 2006, TV guest appearances include Adderly, 1986, Street Legal, 1990, Due South, 1997, Black Harbour, 1997, 24, 2003. Recipient Lorne Greene award Queen's U., 1977.*

CRIBBS, MAUREEN ANN, artist, educator; b. Marinette, Wis., Feb. 17, 1927; d. Roy Cecil Hubbard and Lillian Worner (Hubbard) Yeoman; m. James Milton Cribbs, Apr. 22, 1950; children: Cynthia, Valerie. BA, DePauw U., Greencastle, Ind., 1949; student, Sch. of Art Inst., Chgo., 1971-72, 79-81; MA, Govs. State U., 1973. Cert. secondary sch. tchr., Ill. Tchr. art Sch. Dist. 163, Park Forest, Ill., 1960-78; instr. humanities Sch. Dist. 227, Park Forest, Ill., 1978-79; artist, painter, printmaker Park Forest, 1979—; instr. painting Village Artists, Flossmoor, Ill., 1980-87. Lectr. Chgo. State U., 1980—81; chair study group Homewood-Flossmoor cmty. assocs. of woman's bd. Art Inst. Chgo., 1989—95, sec., 1995—96; adj. prof. Govs. State U., University Park, 1995; artist-in-residence Ox Bow Sch. of Art, 1993; docent presenter Art Insights, Art Inst. of Chgo., 1995—; docent Nathan Manilow Sculpture Park, Govs. State U., 1996—2004; instr. art, art history Robert Morris Coll., Orland Park, Ill., 1996—2001; woodcut printing and presenter Sr. Celebrations, Art Inst. Chgo., 1998—2006; participant printmaking Santa Reparata Graphic Art Ctr., Florence, Italy, 1999; faculty Tall Grass Arts Assn. Sch., Park Forest, Ill., 2000—. Exhibitions include Union St. Gallery, Chicago Heights, 2001, Recent Work South Suburban C.C., Thornton, Ill., 2001, Farnsworth House Gallery, Plano, Ill., 2001—03, Art de Chgo. Gallery, Highland Park, Ill., 2001, Union St. Gallery, Chicago Heights, 2002, Creative Experience Gallery, Frankfort, Ill., 2002—05, Ox Bow Benefits, 2002—06, A Portrait of Music, Ill. Philharm. Orch., 2003, 2005—06, Ill. Theatre Ctr., 2003, Sanctuary Gallery, Clifton, Ill., 2005, 2006, Steeple Gallery, St. John, Ind., 2005, 2006, one-woman shows include S. Suburban Coll., 2001, Moraine Valley CC, 2001, Tall Grass Arts Assn. Gallery, Park Forest, 2002, Prairie State Coll., 2002, No. Ind. Arts Assn., 2002, U. Wyo., 2002, Denver Internat. Airport, 2002, Lessedra Gallery, Sofia, Bulgaria, 2003—05, U. Kans., 2004, Palace of Culture, Sofia, Prairie State Coll., 2006, U. Ohio, 2006, Represented in permanent collections Amity Found., Woodbridge, Conn. Bd. dir. Ill. Philharm. Orch., Park Forest, 1981-83, Grace Migrant Day Care, Park Forest, 1981-85, LWV, Park Forest chpt., 2003-05, 06—; adminstrv. chair Grace United Protestant Ch., Park Forest, 1984-94, v.p. Women's Christian Assn., 1999-2003, pres. 2004-06; lay mem. No. Ill. Ann. Conf. of United Meth. Ch., 1996—, mem. commn. on christian unity and interreligious concerns, 1996-2004. Monetary grantee to produce 15 works Freedom Hall, 1982, Ill. Arts Coun. and Park Forest Cmty. Arts Coun.; Artist-in-Residence Cmty. Arts Coun. Park Forest, 1983, Sch. of Art Inst. of Chgo. at Ox Bow, 1993; recipient Russia Peace ribbon, 1987—. Mem. LWV, Mid-Am. Print Coun., Am. Print Alliance, Chgo. Artists Coalition, Chgo. Methodist. Avocations: reiki master, studying herbs & wildflowers, reading, travel, swimming. Home: 74 Blackhawk Dr Park Forest IL 60466-2146 Studio: 266 Somonauk St Park Forest IL 60466-2241 Office Phone: 708-748-5883.

CRICHTON, FLORA CAMERON, volunteer, foundation administrator; b. Waco, Tex. d. William Waldo and Helen Emelyn (Miller) Cameron; m. John H. Crichton, 1989; children: Ike Simpson Kampmann III(dec.), Megan Cameron Kampmann. Dir., mem. exec. com. Certain-Teed Corp., 1971—78; exec. com. San Antonio World's Fair, 1968. Mem. Pres.'s Mission to Latin Am., 1969; U.S. del. Inter-Am. Commn. Women, 1969—72; mem. nat. adv. coun. Georgia O'Keefe Mus.; mem. citizens stamp adv. commn. U.S. Postal Svc., 1969—71; cons. Bur. Inter-Am. Affairs, Dept. State, 1972—75; pres. Flora Cameron Found.; trustee Trinity U., San Antonio, 1965—2005, chmn., 1976—78; trustee Sweet Briar Coll., 1969—78; mem. Pres.'s Commn. German-Am. Tricentennial, 1983—84; bd. govs. East-West Ctr., Honolulu, 1989—92; vice chmn. exec. com. Tex. Rep. Party, 1958—60; del. Rep. Nat. Conv., 1960, 1964, alt. del., 1968, sec. platform com., 1960; former mem. Rep. Nat. Fin. Com., 1965—, pres., chmn., 1976—78; vice chmn. nat. fin. com. George Bush for Pres., 1987—88; mem. Tex. Rep. Nat. Com., 1960—65; former mem. bd. dirs. San Antonio Art Inst., Sch. Am. Rsch., Santa Fe; former mem. nat. coun. Met. Opera. Mem.: San Antonio Jr. League, Colonial Dames Am. Home: 315 Westover Rd San Antonio TX 78209-5653 Office: 5701 Broadway St San Antonio TX 78209-5722

CRIDER, MELINDA GRAY, artist; b. Hattiesburg, Miss., Aug. 6, 1951; d. Howard R. and Sylvia O'Kain Gray; m. Claude J. Crider, Feb. 7, 1976; children: Shae Marcus Adams, Lindsay Jeanne-Catherine. Student, Atlanta Coll. Art, 1975-77, 83, 84, Callanwolde Fine Arts Ctr., Atlanta, 1978-81. Dir. Claybasket Coop., Alpharetta, Ga., 1981-83; owner, dir. Studio III, Roswell, Ga., 1985-87, Heaven Blue Rose Gallery, Roswell, 1989-91; owner, Crider Studio, Alpharetta, 1982—. Exhibited in group shows at Arts Festival Atlanta, 1986, Roswell (Ga.) Arts Alliance, 1987, Highland Gallery, Atlanta, 1987-93, Novus Gallery, 1989-93, Roswell Visual Arts Ctr., 1991, Reinhardt Coll. Gallery, Canton, Ga., 1991-92, Quinlan Arts Ctr., Gainesville, Ga., 1991, Ga. Inst. Tech. Gallery, Atlanta, 1991-92, Emory Gallery, 1989—, Heaven Blue Rose Gallery, 1991—, Perrin Ctr. for Arts, 1992—, Art South Gallery, 1993—, Albany Mus., 1994, Taylor Kinzel Gallery, Roswell, Ga., 2005; represented in permanent pub. collections. Fine arts juror Congregation Etz Chaim Arts Festival; visual arts orgns. selection panel Fulton County Arts Coun. Recipient Sculpture award Roswell Arts Festival, 1983, Merit award Creative Art Guild, Dalton, Ga., 1983, Dick Blick Painting award Rheinhart Coll., 2002. Mem. Roswell Arts Alliance (v.p. 1994). Avocations: swimming, horseback riding. Home: 850 Liberty Grove Rd Alpharetta GA 30004-2451 Personal E-mail: mgcart@mindspring.com.

CRIER, CATHERINE, newscaster; b. Dallas; BA in Polit. Sci., Univ. Tex.; JD, So. Meth. Univ., Dallas. Asst. dist. atty., felony chief prosecutor Dallas Co. Dist. Atty. Off., 1978—81; civil litig. atty. Dallas, 1982—84; former judge 162nd Dist. Ct. Tex., 1984-89; anchor Cable News Network, 1989-92; corr. ABC 20/20, 1993-95; news corr. ABC News, 1995—96; anchor Crier Report Fox News, 1996—99; exec. show host and editor legal news spls. Courtroom TV Network LLC, 1999—, host Catherine Crier Live, 2001—. Author: The Case Against Lawyers, 2002 (NY Times bestseller), Contempt-How the Right is Wronging American Justice, 2005 (Number One NY Times bestseller, 2005); co-author (with Cole Thompson): A Deadly Game: The Untold Story of the Scott Peterson Investigation, 2005 (Number One NY Times bestseller). Named one of the Dynamic Dozen, TV Guide Mag., 1990, Twenty Young Lawyers Who Make a Difference, ABA Barrister Mag., 1990; recipient Outstanding Young Tex. Ex award, Univ. Tex., Austin, 1990, Les Femmes du Monde award, Dallas Coun. on World Affairs, 1996, Emmy award, 1996, duPont-Columbia award, 2001, two Gracie Allen awards, Found. Am. Women in Radio and TV. Avocations: golf, scuba diving, raising, training Arabian horses. Office: Courtroom TV Network LLC Frnt 2 600 3rd Ave New York NY 10016 Business E-Mail: info@criercommunications.com.

CRILE, SUSAN, artist; b. Cleve., Aug. 12, 1942; d. George Jr. and Jane (Halle) C.; m. Joseph S. Murphy, May 18, 1984. Student, NYU; BA, Bennington Coll., 1965. Mem. faculty Fordham U., NYC, 1972-76, Princeton U., NJ, 1974-76, Sarah Lawrence Coll., Bronxville, NY, 1976-79, Sch. Visual Arts, NYC, 1976-82, Barnard Coll., NYC, 1983-86, Hunter Coll., NYC, 1983—. Travelling rep. to Hungary and Portugal with exhbn. Am. Paintings in the Eighties, Internat. Comm. Agy., Washington, 1981; resident-in-painting Am. Acad. in Rome, 1990. One-woman shows include Kornblee Gallery, NYC, 1971-73, Fischbach Gallery, NYC, 1974-75, 77, Brooke Alexander Gallery, NYC, 1975, Phillips Collection, Washington, 1975, New Gallery, Cleve., 1977, Ctr. Gallery Bucknell U., Lewisburg, Pa., 1978, Droll Kolbert Gallery, NYC, 1978, 80, Ivory Kimpton Gallery, San Francisco, 1981, 84, 88, Van Straten Gallery, Chgo., 1983, Lincoln Ctr. Gallery, NYC, 1983, Cleve. Ctr. for Contemporary Art, 1984, Nina Freundenheim Gallery, Buffalo, NY, 1980, 84, Graham Modern, NYC, 1985, 87-88, 90, Adams Middleton Gallery, Dallas, 1986, Gloria Luria, Bay Harbor Island, Fla., 1987-88, 90, St. Louis Art Mus., 1994, Blaffer Gallery- U. Houston, 1994, Univ. Art Mus. U. So. Calif., Long Beach, 1994, Fed. Reserve Bd., Washington, 1995, Herbert Johnson Mus. Cornell U., Ithaca, NY, 1995, Middlebury Coll. Mus. Art, Vt., 1995, James Graham & Sons, NYC, 1995, 98, 2001, Nat. Coun. for Culture, Art and Letters, Kuwait City, Kuwait, 1996, U. Ariz. Mus. Art., Tucson, 2003, James Graham and Sons, NYC, 2004, Bertha and Karl Leubsdorf Gallery, Hunter Coll., 2006; exhibited in group shows at Whitney Mus. Art, NYC, 1972, 82, Indpls. Mus. Art, 1972, 74, Kent State U., 1972, Art Inst. Chgo., 1972, Corcoran Gallery Art, Washington, 1973, Va. Mus. Fine Arts, 1975, USLA., 1979, Grey Art Gallery, NYC, 1979, 83, Janie C. Lee Gallery, Houston, 1979, Meml. Art Gallery, U. Rochester, 1980, Bklyn. Mus., 1980-81, 83, Carnegie Inst., Pitts., 1981, Inst. Contemporary Art, 1981, Am. Acad. Arts and Letters, 1983, 94, 99, Weatherspoon Gallery, Greensboro, NC, 1984, Columbus Mus. Arts and Sci., Ga., 1985, Queens Mus., 1986, Portland Mus. Art, Maine, 1986, Mus. Fine Arts, Boston, 1986, Cleve. Mus. Art, 1987, Mt. Holyoke Coll. Art Mus., South Hadley, Mass., 1987, Hudson River Mus., 1988, Bowdoin Coll. Mus. Art, Brunswick, Maine, 1992, Denver Art Mus., 1993-94, Am. Acad. Arts & Letters, NYC, 1994, Fla. Internat. U., Miami, 1995, James Graham & Sons, NYC, 1997, 99, 2003, Times Sq. Gallery, NYC, 2000, Art in Gen., NYC, 2000, U. Ariz. Mus. Art, Tempe, 2001, Smith and Eds, Palo Alto, Calif., U. Colorado Springs, Colo., 2002, Lehman Coll. Art Gallery, NYC, 2004, MOCA, Cleve., 2005, Detroit Mus. Art, 2005; poster commn.: Live from Lincoln Ctr., NYC, 1980, Mostly Mozart, 1985, IBM Gallery Aci. & Art, NYC, 1989, Nat. Gallery Art, Washington, 1989, Detroit Inst. Art, 1991, Nat. Mus. Women in the Arts, Washington, 1991, William Proctor Art Gallery, Bard Coll., Annandale-on-Hudson, NY, 1992, Bowdoin Coll. Mus. Art, Brunswick, Maine, 1992, Andre Emmerich Gallery, NYC, 1992, Denver Art Mus., 1993, Cleve. Ctr. for Contemporary Art, 1993; represented in permanent collections Albright-Knox Art Gallery, Buffalo, Bklyn. Mus., Mus. Art Carnegie Inst., Pitts., Guggenheim Mus., NYC, Hirshhorn Mus., Washington, Met. Mus. Art, NYC, Phillips Collection, Washington, Cleve. Mus. Art, Libr. Congress, Washington, Denver Mus. Art, Middlebury Coll. Mus. Art, Ariz. State U. Art Mus., Tempe, Bowdoin Coll. Mus. Art, Brunswick, Fed. Res. Bd., Washington, Portland Mus., Weatherspoon Art Gallery, Greensboro. Trustee Bennington Coll., 1979-81; active Yaddo Corp., 1986—, bd. dirs., 1991—. Resident grantee Yaddo, 1970-71, 74-75, 78, MacDowell Colony, 1972, grantee Ingram Merrill Found., 1972; fellow Nat. Endowment for Arts, 1982, 89-90. Home: 168 W 86th St New York NY 10024-4033 E-mail: scrile@rcn.com.

CRILL, ALICE EILEEN, music educator; b. Hubbard, Ohio, Apr. 15, 1914; d. John Wilson Fairbanks and Ola Gardner Fairbanks; m. Chester C. Crill, Aug. 12, 1937 (dec.); children: Charles, Carole Anne, Virginia Lea. BA, Greenville Coll., 1936; MusM, U. Okla., 1941; attended, Eastman Sch. of Music, 1938. Tchr. Auburn (Ill.) Pub. Sch., 1936—37, Bethany (Okla.) Nazarene Coll., 1938—47; pvt. piano tchr. Pasadena, Calif., 1949—73, San Diego, 1975—. Organist Bresee Ch. Nazarene, Pasadena, Calif., 1948—67, St. James Meth. Ch., Pasadena, 1967—73, La Jolla First Bapt., San Diego, 1974—77, Ocean Beach First Bapt. Ch., San Diego, 1977—93. Donor student music scholarships Pt. Loma Nazarene U., San Diego, 1993, donor student music scholarship, 1996, Greenville Coll., Greenville, Ill., 2003, So. Nazarene U., Bethany, Okla., 1997, Roberts' Wesleyan Coll., Rochester, NY, 2003. Republican. Achievements include co-organizer of Ch. Cmty. orangization called Point Loma United Seniors or PLUS in San Diego. Avocation: growing cymbidium orchids. Home: 1130 Catalina Blvd San Diego CA 92107

CRIMLISK, JANE THERESE, probation officer; b. Boston, Dec. 2, 1945; d. Herbert Leo and Grace Beatrice (McGilvray) C. AS, Aquinas Coll., Newton, Mass., 1968; BA in Sociology cum laude, Boston Coll., 1974; MS in Bus. Edn., Suffolk U., Boston, 1978; MEd in Rehab. Counseling, U. Mass., 1991, Cert. of Advanced Grad. Study, 1995. Tchr. religious edn., 1965-88, 93—; legal sec. Hale, Sanderson, Byrnes & Morton, Boston, 1968-69; sec. Boston Coll. Law Sch., Chestnut Hill, 1969-74, Life Resources, Inc., Boston, 1974-75; tchr. Archbishop Williams High Sch., Braintree, Mass., 1975-78; exec. sec. Cramer Electronics, Newton, Mass., 1978-79; jud. sec. Com. of Mass. Ct. Systems, Boston, 1979-95; probation officer Probate and Family Ct., Boston, 1995—; tchr. adult edn. Aquinas Coll., Milton, 1989—. Vol. counselor Pregnancy Help, Brighton, Mass., 1992, Arthur Clark for U.S. Congress campaign, Newton, 1980, Marian Walsh for State Senate campaign, 1992, 94, Mass. Citizens for Life. Mem. Boston Coll. Alumni Assn. (bd. dirs. 1982-84), Boston Coll. Evening Coll. Alumni Assn. (bd. dirs., past pres.), Aquinas Coll. Alumni Assn. Democrat. Roman Catholic. Avocations: swimming, ice skating, crewel, cross stitch, music. Home: 416 Belgrade Ave Apt 25 West Roxbury MA 02132-1540 Office: Probate and Family Ct Dept 24 New Chardon St Boston MA 02114-4703

CRIMMEL, CYNTHIA EILEEN, rail transportation executive; b. Ft. Wayne, Ind., Apr. 4, 1964; d. John Edward and Sharon Thomas Crimmel. BSBA, U. Phoenix, 2003; MBA, Pa. State U., University Park, 2005. Preload supr. United Parcel Svc., St. Augustine, Fla., 1992—98; svc. coord. Svc. Mgmt./CSX Tech., Jacksonville, 1998—99; mgr. customer ops. CSX Transp., 1999—2002, mgr. coal ops., 2002—03, mgr. customer svc., 2003—05, dir. curfew planning, 2005—. Facilitator City of Jacksonville Racial Rels. Study Circles, Fla., 2006—06; task force mem. Jacksonville's Blueprint Prosperity, 2005—06; mem. CSX Diversity Coun., 2004—06. Liberal. Presbyterian. Avocations: exercise, reading, travel. Office: CSX Transportation 3027 Warrington Street Jacksonville FL 32254

CRIMMINS-SNYDER, CAROLINE JEAN, secondary school educator, paralegal; d. Thomas Allen Crimmins and Dorothy Louise Voss; m. Ronald Snyder, Oct. 15, 1994; children: Clare Rose Snyder, Karla Marie Snyder, Cortney Leigh Snyder. BS, Ill. State U., Normal, 1986; M of Tchg., Nat. Louis U., Chgo., 2002. Cert.: Roosevelt U., Chgo. (paralegal) 1986. Paralegal Jenner & Block, LLP, Chgo., 1992—2002, McGuire Woods, LLP, 2002—03; tchr. Hillcrest H.S., Country Club Hills, 2003—. Office: Hillcrest High School 17401 S Crawford Ave Country Club Hills IL 60478 Office Phone: 708-799-7000. E-mail: csnyder@bhsd228.com.

CRINCOLI, TRACY ANNE, athletic trainer; b. Roselle, NJ, Mar. 8, 1979; d. Thomas and Cynthia Crincoli. Degree in Sports Medicine and Athletic Training with honors, Lenoir-Rhyne Coll., Hickory, NC, 2001. Cert. athletic trainer Nat. Athletic Trainers Assn., 2001. Asst. athletic trainer Lenoir-Rhyne Coll., 2001—05; athletic trainer Frye Regional Med. Ctr., Hickory, 2005—; head athletic trainer West Lincoln HS, Lincoln, 2005—. Com. mem. Frye Regional Med. Ctr., Lake Hickory Triathlon, NC, 2005—. Mem.: NATA (licentiate). Roman Catholic. Avocations: golf, dance, sports, twirling. Personal E-mail: tracy.crincoli@tenethealth.com.

CRINKLAW, KATHERINE MARY, artist; b. Newman, Calif., Feb. 11, 1959; d. John Joseph and Dorothy Ann (Oliviera) Menezes; m. Jerry Frank Palermo, Sept. 21, 1981 (dec. 1984); children: Jason; m. Michael John Crinklaw, Feb. 22, 1986; children: Mark, Morgan. Grad. h.s., Gustine, Calif. Self-employed artist, Calif., 1977—. Vol. art instr. Bonita Elem. Sch., Crows Landing, Calif., 1990-93. Group shows include Haggin Mus., 2000, 02; paintings publ. on cover of 3 Internat. Fairs and Expos Mag., 1998, 2000, 02; Contbr. poems to publs. of Nat. Libr. Poetry, 1995, 96, 97. Recipient Mayor's award Turlock (Calif.) Art League, 1993; 1st Pl. Watercolor Turlock City Art Commn., 1998, 2d Pl. Watercolor, 2000, Mayor's award, 2003, 04, 3d Pl. Watercolor, 2004, 1st Pl. Watercolor, 2005, Merit award State Fair, 2003, best of Show Merrit County Spring Fair, 2003. Mem. Ctrl. Calif. Art League (mem. coun. 1991-93, honorable mention award 1992, 93), Internat. Soc. Poets. Republican. Roman Catholic. Avocations: golf, gardening, guitar, reading. Office Phone: 209-862-3523. E-mail: kateartbuiz@hotmail.com.

CRINO, MARJANNE HELEN, anesthesiologist; b. Rochester, N.Y., Aug. 18, 1933; d. Michael Jay and Helen Barbara (Kennedy) C.; m. Michael Anthony La Iuppa, Nov. 12, 1960 (dec. Feb. 1996); children: James Michael, Barbara Helen, John Christopher. BS, Coll. St. Teresa, 1955; MD, Med. Coll. Wis., 1959; MA in Theology, St. Bernard's Inst., 1991. Diplomate Nat. Bd. Med. Examiners. House staff Genesee Hosp., Rochester, 1959—61; perinatal mortality rsch., resident in anesthesiology Jackson Meml Hosp.-U. Miami, 1962—65; attending staff in anesthesiology Genesee Hosp., Rochester, 1969—2000, mem. exec. com., med. staff sec., 1980, Rochester, 1982, acting chmn. dept. anesthesiology, 1989, 1991, chmn. pain control com., 1989—95; clin. instr. anesthesiology U. Rochester Sch. Medicine, 1983—99; ret., 1999. Cons. anesthesiology Rochester Psychiat. Ctr., 1975-85; instr. anesthesiology U. Miami Sch. medicine, 1966, 67; attending staff anesthesiology Jackson Meml. Hosp., Miami, 1966, 67. Mem. adv. bd. Isaiah House Hospice, 1994-2000, com. Pittsford (N.Y.) Rep. Party, 1970's-80's; vol. chaplain Genesee Hosp. Mem. N.Y. State Soc. Anesthesiologists (bd. dirs., vice spkr. 1983-86, del. 1971-82, 87-2002), Am. Soc. Anesthesiologists (del. 1979-86, 97), AMA, N.Y. State Med. Soc., Med. Soc. County of Monroe, Rochester Acad. Medicine, Cath. Physicians Guild Rochester (bd.dirs., pres. 1988-89), Margaret Roper Guild (pres. 1975-76), Cath. Women's Club (Diocese of Rochester). Roman Catholic. Avocations: reading, gardening, music.

CRIPE, ELIZABETH ANN (BETTY CRIPE), investment company executive; b. Seneca, Kans., Dec. 25, 1940; d. August Joseph and Getrude Marie (Stueve) Glissman; m. Luor L. Cripe, Jan. 28, 2003; children: Scott D. Duermeier, Kevin J. Duermeier. Sec.-treas. Capital City, Inc., Topeka, 1958—66; office mgr. women's div. Manpower, Inc., Topeka, 1966—68; agt. Old Am. Life Ins. Co., 1968—69; rep. B.C. Christopher & Co. Securities, 1969—74; v.p. securities, investment adv. WZW Fin. Services Inc. (formerly Weinrich-Zitzmann-Whitehead, Inc.), Topeka, 1974—86; investment advisor VSR Fin. Svcs., Inc., 1985—87; prin., founder BBI Investments (affiliate VSR Fin. Services), 1987—96; investment advisor Archer-Alexander Securities, 1997—2000, Woodbury Fin. Svcs., 2001—04, specialist, 2000—; regional investment adviser Nat. Planning Corp., 2004—. Bd. dirs. Topeka Youth Project; v.p. Topeka C. of C., 1972—73, pres. women's divsn., 1972—73, bd. dirs., mem. econ. devel. com., 1987—; chmn. fundraising, 1998—99; mem. fin. com. Most Pure Heart of Mary Cath. Ch. Mem.: Sales and Mktg. Execs. (bd. dirs. Topeka chpt.), Am. Bus. Womens Assn. (hospitality chmn. career chpt.), Topeka Cosmopolitan Club (gov. Mo.-Kans. fedn. 1999—2000, Cosmopolitan Internat. Gov. of Yr. 2000). Home: 617 W 4th St Holton KS 66436-1402 Office: 3735 SW Wanamaker Rd Ste A Topeka KS 66610 Office Phone: 785-364-5319.

CRISCI, PAT DEVITA, retired psychology educator; b. N.Y.C., Oct. 29, 1931; d. Victor Anthony and Christine Marie (Capobianco) De V.; m. S. George Crisci, Jan. 10, 1954; children: Debra Leah, George Sabato, Wayne Lawrence, Lorraine I. BA, CUNY, 1952; MA, John Carroll U., 1968; PhD, Kent State U, 1974. Lic. psychologist, Ohio; cert. sch. supt., counselor, sch. psychologist, Ohio. Psychology intern Cleveland Heights-University Heights (Ohio) City Sch. System, 1968-69, sch. psychologist, counselor, 1969-70, supr. intern sch. psychologists, 1970-71, supr. spl. edn., 1971-72, dir. edn., 1972-74; supt. schs. Tallmadge (Ohio) City Sch. System, 1974-78; asst. supr. pub. instrn. Dept. Edn. State Ohio, Columbus, 1978-79; assoc. prof. then prof. ednl. psychology and leadership Kent (Ohio) State U., 1979-93, dir. Ctr. for Sch. Pers. Rels., 1981-93, dir. KEDS Desegregation Assistance Ctr., 1986-88; prof. emeritus, 1993—. Cons. numerous orgns. including Greater Cleve. Rouondtable, The Cleve. Found., Shaker Heights Bd. Edn., Lakewood Bd. Edn., Cleve. Bd. Edn., Youngstown City Sch. Dist., others. Contbr. numerous articles to profl. jours. Mem. Am. Ednl. Rsch. Assn., Am. Assn. Sch. Adminstrs. (chmn. governance subcom. platform and resolutions com. 1987-88, mem. Blue Ribbon task force on evaluation 1988, exec. com. Women's Caucus), Am. Edn. Finance Assn., Am. Psychol. Assn., Nat. Assn. Mediation in Edn., Assn. Negotiators and Contract Adminstrs. (adv. bd.), Nat. Coun. Profs. of Edn. Adminstrn., Nat. Assn. Sch. Psychologists, Ohio Assn. Gifted Children, Ohio Assn. Children with Learning Disabilities, Phi Delta Kappa.

CRISLER, DONNA, music educator; b. Columbia, SC, June 1, 1952; d. Robert Minor and Lottie Faye Whitten; m. Tommy Crisler, Aug. 1, 1996; children: David Allen Jennings children: Douglas Allen Jennings, Jr. MusB in Edn., U. Miss., University, 1973. Tchr. Norris Elem. Sch., Memphis, 1975—76, Lester Elem. Sch., Jackson, Miss., 1976—78, Yamaha Music Sch., Jackson, 1978—87, Jim Hill HS, Jackson, 1987—93; choral music tchr. Siwell Mid. Sch., Jackson, 1992—95, Madison Mid. Sch., Miss., 1995—. Treas. Dist. VI Choral Dirs., Jackson, 1993—; children's choir dir. Broadmoor Bapt. Ch., 1993—95. Recipient Top Twelve Metro Area Tchr. award, Jackson C. of C., 2003, Music Educator of Yr. award, Miss. Music Educators Assn., 2006. Mem.: Delta Kappa Gamma (assoc.; music chmn. 1994—95), Am. Choral Dirs. Assn. (assoc.), Miss. Music Educators' Assn. (assoc.), Music Educator's Nat. Assn (assoc.), Sigma Alpha Iota (assoc.). Conservative. Avocations: travel, reading. Home: 126 Greenridge Dr Madison MS 39110 Office: Madison Mid Sch 1365 Mannsdale Rd Madison MS 39110 Home Fax: 601-853-2254; Office Fax: 601-853-2254. Business E-Mail: dcrisler@madison.k12.ms.us.

CRISMAN, MARY FRANCES BORDEN, librarian; b. Tacoma, Nov. 23, 1919; d. Lindon A. and Mary Cecelia (Donnelly) Borden; m. Fredric Lee Crisman, Apr. 12, 1975 (dec. Dec. 1975). BA in History, U. Wash., 1943, BA in Librarianship, 1944. Asst. br. libr. in charge work with children Mottet br.

Tacoma Pub. Libr., 1944-45, br. libr., 1945-49, br. libr. Moore br., 1950-55, asst. dir., 1955-70, dir., 1970-74, dir. emeritus, 1975—; mgr. corp. libr. Frank Russell Co., 1985-96, ret., 1997. Chmn. Wash. Cmty. Libr. Coun., 1970-72. Hostess program Your Libr. and You, Sta. KTPS-TV, 1969-71. Mem. Highland Homeowners League, Tacoma, 1980-04, incorporating dir. 1980, sec., registered agt., 1980-82; mem. Denham West Condominium Assn., Sun City, Ariz., 1995—, chair by laws com., 1999, sec., 2002-05. Mem. ALA (chmn. mem. com. Wash. 1957-60, mem. nat. libr. week com. 1965, chmn. libr. adminstrn. divsn. nominating com. 1971, mem. ins. for librs. com. 1970-74, vice chmn. libr. adminstrn. divsn. personnel adminstrn. sect. 1972-73, chmn. 1973-74, mem. com. policy implementation 1973-74, mem. libr. orgn. and mgmt. sect. budgeting acctg. and costs com. 1974-75), Am. Libr. Trustee Assn. (legis. com. 1975-78, conf. program com. 1978-80, action devel. com. 1978-80), Pacific N.W. (trustee divsn. nominating com 1976-77), Wash. Libr. Assn. (exec. bd. 1957-59, state exec., dir. Nat. Libr. Week 1965, treas., exec. bd. 1969-71, 71-73), Urban Librs. Coun. (editl. sec. Newsletter 1972-73, exec. com. 1974-75), Ladies Aux. to United Transp. Union (past pres. Tacoma), Friends Tacoma Pub. Libr. (registered agt. 1975-83, sec. 1975-78, pres. 1978-80, bd. dirs. 1980-83), Smithsonian Assocs., Nat. Railway Hist. Soc., U. Wash. Alumni Assn., U. Wash. Sch. Librarianship Alumni Assn. Clubs: Quota Internat. (sec. 1957-58, 1st v.p. 1960-61, pres. 1961-62, treas. 1975-76, pres. 1979-80) (Tacoma). Home: 9054 N 109th Ave Sun City AZ 85351-4676

CRISMOND, LINDA FRY, public relations executive; b. Burbank, Calif., Mar. 1, 1943; d. Billy Chapin and Lois (Harding) Fry; m. Donald Burleigh Crismond, 1965 (dec.). BS, U. Calif.-Santa Barbara, 1964; M.L.S., U. Calif.-Berkeley, 1965. Cert. county libr., Calif., assn. exec. Reference libr., EDP coordinator San Francisco Pub. Library, 1965—72; head acquisition San Francisco Pub. Libr., 1972-74; asst. univ. libr. U. So. Calif., L.A., 1974-80; chief dep. county libr. L.A. County Pub. Libr., L.A., 1980-81, county libr. Downey, 1981-89; exec. dir ALA, Chgo., 1989-92; v.p. public rels. Profl. Media Svc. Corp., Chgo., 1992-98; v.p. pub. rels. Follett Media Distbn., Crystal Lake, Ill., 1999—2003; nat. media cons. BWI, Lexington, Ky., 2003—. Western rep. quality control council Ohio Coll. Libr. Ctr., Columbus, 1977-80; mem. Am. Nat. Standards Inst., N.Y.C., 1978-80; bd. councillors U. So. Calif. Sch. Libr. and Info. Mgmt., 1980-83; adv. bd. mem. UCLA Libr. Sch., 1981-89; chmn. bd. dirs. L.A. County Pub. Libr. Found., 1982-85; mem. OCLC Users Coun., 1988-89; mem. exec. com. L.A. County Mgmt. Coun., 1986-88, pres., 1988; cons. libr. Trinity Coll., 1995-99; prin. The Charleston Group, Inc., 1996—. Author: Directory of San Francisco Bay Area, 1968, Against All Odds, 1994; editor; Urban Librs. Coun. Exch., 1994-2005, The Charleston Report, 1996-99 Bd. dirs. So. Meth. U. Libr., 1992-98. Named Staff Mem. of Year San Francisco Pub. Libr., 1968 Mem. ALA, Calif. Libr. Assn. (council 1980-82), Calif. County Libr. Assn. (pres. 1984), L.A. County Mgmt. Assn. (pres. 1988). Home: 303 Mariner Dr Tarpon Springs FL 34689-5840

CRISP, SALLY CHANDLER, writing educator; b. Knoxville, Tenn., Oct. 9, 1946; d. David W. and Lucille Kelly Chandler; m. Huey D. Crisp, Sept. 14, 1974; children: Mitchell, Molly. BA, U. Ark., Little Rock, 1968, EdD, 1996; MA, U. Ark., Fayetteville, 1970. Instr. Richland Coll., Dallas, 1972—79; dir. writing ctr. U. Ark., Little Rock, 1981—98, instr., 1998—, dir. Little Rock writing project, 2004—. Editor, co-author: Steps We Took, 1990, Carry This Message, 2002; co-author: Widowed, 2000. Grantee, Nat. Writing Project, 2005—. Mem.: Coun. Writing Program Adminstrators, Nat. Coun. Tchrs. English. Office: U Ark Little Rock Dept Rhetoric and Writing 2801 S University Ave Little Rock AR 72204

CRISSEY, REBECCA LYNN, special education educator; b. Denver, Mar. 9, 1977; d. James Edward and Timber Smith Crissey. EdB, Auburn U., 1999; EdM, Vanderbilt U., 2000. Cert. early childhood spl. edn. State of Va., class B early childhood spl. edn. State of Ala. With E. Ala. Friends of Life, Auburn, 1997—99; ednl. asst. Blakemore Children's Ctr., Nashville, 1999; pvt. therapist, tutor Nashville, 1999—2000; spl. edn. tchr. Stafford County Pub. Schs., Fredericksburg, Va., 2000—02; presch. autism tchr. Fairfax County Pub. Schs., Va., 2002—04, applied behavior analysis resource tchr., 2004—. Early interventionist, therapist Chesapeake Ctr., Inc., Springfield, Va., 2002—; spl. edn. dance instr. Dance Abilities, Inc., Fairfax, 2004—. Spl. needs vol. Fairfax County Park Authority, 2002—03. Early Intervention grant, Vanderbilt U., 1999—2000. Mem.: Coun. for Children with Behavioral Disorders, Coun. Exceptional Children (mem. divsn. early childhood), Gamma Sigma Alpha, Alpha Chi Omega, Golden Key, Mortar Board, Phi Eta Sigma, Lambda Sigma, Omicron Delta Kappa, Phi Kappa Phi. Republican. Lutheran. Avocations: dance, swimming. Home: 4462 Oakdale Crescent Ct #1232 Fairfax VA 22030 Office: Belle Willard AdminstrvCtr Fairfax VA 22030 Office Phone: 703-246-7767. E-mail: rlcrissey@hotmail.com.

CRIST, CHRISTINE MYERS, consulting executive; b. Harrisburg, Pa., Feb. 5, 1924; d. John Eyster and Eunice Horton (Ingham) Myers; m. Robert Grant Crist, June 25, 1949; children: Catherine Ingham Crist Marcson, Jessica Rogers Crist, Robert Jeffrey Myers Crist. BA, Dickinson Coll., 1946. Reporter The Patriot, Harrisburg, Pa., 1946-49; editor West Shore Times, Lemoyne, Pa., 1964-65; adminstr. arts in edn. Pa. Dept. Edn., Harrisburg, 1974-77, dir. leadership in arts edn., 1977-79; press sec. gov.'s office Pa. Commn. for Women, Harrisburg, 1980-83, dir. Gov.'s Commn. for Women, 1983-87; exec. dir. com. for women Evang. Luth. Ch. in Am., Chgo., 1987-90; ptnr. Crist and Crist, Cons., Camp Hill, Pa., 1990—. Mem. State Employees Retirement Bd., 1986-88; state coord. We the People Edn. Program. Editor: Song As A Measure of Man, 1975 (excellent pub. 1975). Mem. Camp Hill (Pa.) Sch. Bd., 1967-73, Capital Area Intermediate Bd., Lemoyne, Pa., 1970-73; pres. Camp Hill (Pa.) Civic Club, 1970-72, women's orgn. Trinity Lutheran Ch., 1999; chair Ch. in Society, Lower Susquehanna Synod, Evang. Lutheran Ch. in Am.; mem. coun. Trinity Congregation, 1991-94; mem. Harrisburg Choral Soc., Dickinson Alumni Coun., 1992—; bd. dirs. Women's Polit. Network Pa., Camp Hill Cmty. Found., 1996—; mem. candidacy bd. Luth. Ch., 1992—; Pa. bd. Common Cause, 1997—; mem. Envision Capital Region Task Force, 2000-02; mem. Nat. Assn. Comms. for Women, 1987. Recipient Women in Comms. Freedom of Info. award, 1982, Great Commicators award, 1985, Pa. Women's History award, Pa. Com. for Women, 2003, Women Inventing Future award, Cumberland County, 2003. Mem. Monday Club, Cumberland County Fedn. Women's Clubs (pres. 1996—), Coll. Club Harrisburg (pres. 2004—). Lutheran. Home and Office: Crist and Crist 1915 Walnut St Camp Hill PA 17011-3854 Personal E-mail: camcrist@paonline.com.

CRIST, GERTRUDE H., civic worker; b. Barnard, S.D. d. Jacob H. and Lillian Belle (Freeman) Hartman; m. Howard Grafton Crist, Jr., Nov. 2, 1940; children: Howard Grafton III, Douglas Freeman. Student, S.D. State Coll., 1936-38. Owner, ptnr. Farm and Home Svc. Chmn. Westmoreland County chpt. ARC, 1946, sec., 1943-45, chmn. vol. spl. svcs., 1944-45; dist. chmn. Cancer drive Howard County; mem. Howard County Bd. Edn., 1953-70, pres., 1963-65; bd. dirs. Howard County Tb Assn.; adv. coun. Catonsville C.C., 1962-70; chmn. Emergency Civil Def. Hosp. Howard County, 1961-62; sec. Cmty. Action Coun. Howard County, 1965, dir., 1966; bd. dirs. Girl Scout Coun. Ctrl. Md., 1967-68; mem. Md. Coun. Higher Edn., 1968-76, State Bd. for C.Cs., 1968-80; trustee Howard C.C., 1968-70, v.p., bd. dirs. Howard County chpt. ARC, 1973-77, v.p., 1976-77; mem. Md. Bd. for Higher Edn., 1977-86, Howard County Commn. on Arts, 1975-77; v.p. Farm and Home Svc., Inc., 1968-78. Mem. LWV (county sec. 1957-59, dir. 1960-62, pres. 1959), Nat. Sch. Bds. Assn. (dir. 1968-71), Nat. Congress Parents and Tchrs. (hon. life mem.), Md. Congress Parents and Tchrs. (life), Md. Assn. Bds. Edn. (pres. 1966, 67), W. Friendship PTA (sec. 1949-51), Delta Kappa Gamma (hon. Alpha Beta State and Lambda chpts.), Cattail River Garden Club. Episcopalian (vestryman, chmn. parish day sch. bd. 1970-73). Home: Fairhaven C-87 7200 Third Ave Sykesville MD 21784

CRIST, JUDITH, film and drama critic; b. NYC, May 22, 1922; d. Solomon and Helen (Schoenberg) Klein; m. William B. Crist, July 3, 1947 (dec. Apr. 1993); 1 son, Steven Gordon. AB, Hunter Coll., 1941; tchg. fellow, State Coll. Wash., 1942-43; MSc in Journalism, Columbia, 1945; DHL (hon.), SUNY, New Paltz, 1994. Civilian instr. 3081st Army AFB Unit, 1943-44; reporter N.Y. Herald Tribune, 1945-60, editor arts, 1960-63, assoc. theater critic, 1957-63, film critic, 1963-66; film, theater critic NBC-TV Today Show, 1963-73; film critic World Jour. Tribune, 1966-67; critic-at-large Ladies Home Jour., 1966-67; contbg. editor and film critic TV Guide, 1966-88; founding film critic N.Y. mag., 1968-75; film critic The Washingtonian, 1970-72, Palm Springs Life, 1971-75; contbg. editor, film critic Saturday Rev., 1975-77, 80-84, N.Y. Post, 1977-78, MD/Mrs., 1977—, 50 Plus, 1978-83, L'Officiel/USA, 1979-80; arts critic Sta. WWOR-TV, 1981-87; critical columnist for Coming Attractions, 1985-93; cons. editor Hollywood Mag., 1985-93; contbg. editor Columbia Mag., 1993-95. Instr. journalism Hunter Coll., 1947, Sarah Lawrence Coll., 1958-59; assoc. journalism Columbia Grad. Sch. Journalism, 1958-62, lectr. journalism, 1962-64, adj. prof., 1964—; host Judith Crist Film Weekends at Tareytown House, NY, 1971— Author: The Private Eye, The Cowboy and the Very Naked Girl, 1968, Judith Crist's TV Guide to the Movies, 1974, Take 22: Moviemakers on Moviemaking, 1984, rev. edit., 1991; contbr. articles to popular mags. Trustee Anne O'Hare McCormick Scholarship Fund. Named to 50th Anniversary Honors List, Columbia Grad. Sch. Journalism, 1963, Hunter Alumni Hall of Fame, Hunter Coll., 1973; recipient Page One award, NY Newspaper Guild, 1955, George Polk award, 1950, Newswomen's Club of NY award, 1955, 1959, 1963, 1965, 1967, Edn. Writers Assn. award, 1952, Alumni award, Columbia Grad. Sch. Journalism, 1961, 50th Anniversary Award, 1965, Centennial Pres.'s medal, Hunter Coll., 1970, Hall of Fame award for outstanding profl. achievement, 2003, Grad. Sch. Journalism's Faculty and Alumni award, Columbia U., 1998, Univ. Alumni Fedn. medal for conspicuous svc., 2003. Mem.: Soc. of the Silurians, Columbia Journalism Alumni Exec. Com. (pres. 1967—70), Sigma Tau Delta. Office: 180 Riverside Dr New York NY 10024-1048

CRISWELL, ELEANOR CAMP, psychologist; b. Norfolk, Va., May 12, 1938; d. Norman Harold Camp and Eleanor (Talman) David; m. Thomas L. Hanna (dec. 1990). BA, U. Ky., 1961, MA, 1962; EdD, U. Fla., 1969. Asst. prof. edn. Calif. State Coll., Hayward, 1969; prof. psychology, former chair Calif. State U., Sonoma, 1969—. Faculty adviser Humanistic Psychology Inst., San Francisco, 1970-77; dir. Novato Inst. Somatic Rsch. and Tng.; editor Somatics jour.; cons. Venturi, Inc., Autogenic Sys., Inc.; clin. dir. Biotherapeutics, Kentfield Med. Hosp., 1985-90; founder Humanistic Psychology Inst. (now Saybrook Grad. Sch.), 1970. Author: How Yoga Works, 1987, Biofeedback and Somatics, 1995; co-editor: Biofeedback and Family Practice Medicine, 1983; patentee optokinetic perceptual learning device. Mem. APA (past pres. divsn. 32), Biofeedback Soc. Calif. (past pres.), Assn. for Humanistic Psychology (past pres.), Somatic Soc. (pres.), Equine Hanna Somatics (founder), Internat. Assn. Yoga Therapists (sec./treas.). Office: Novato Inst 1516 Grant Ave #212 Novato CA 94945 Office Phone: 415-897-0336. Business E-Mail: ecriswel@ix.netcom.com.

CRISWELL, KIMBERLY ANN, executive coach, communications consultant, performance artist; b. L.A., Dec. 6, 1957; d. Robert Burton and Carolyn Joyce (Semko) C. BA with honors, U. Calif., Santa Cruz, 1980; postgrad., Stanford U., 1993-94, Coaches Tng. Inst., 2000. Cert. profl. co-active coach. Instr. English Lang. Svcs., Oakland, Calif., 1980-81; freelance writer Verbum mag., San Diego, 1986, Gambit mag., New Orleans, 1981; instr. Tulane U., New Orleans, 1981; instr., editor Haitian-English Lang. Program, New Orleans, 1981-82; instr. Delgado Coll., New Orleans, 1982-83; instr., program coord. Vietnamese Youth Ctr., San Francisco, 1984; dancer Khadra Internat. Folk Ballet, San Francisco, 1984-89; dir. mktg. comm. Centram Sys. West, Inc., Berkeley, Calif., 1984-87; comm. coord. Safeway Stores, Inc., Oakland, 1985; dir. corp. comm. TOPS divsn. Sun Microsystems, Inc., 1987-88; pres. Criswell Comm., 1988—. Dir. corp. comm. CyberGold, Inc., Berkeley, 1996-97; co-founder, v.p. Conferenza, Inc., 1998-99. Vol. coord. Friends of Haitians, 1981, editor, writer newsletter, 1981; dancer Komenka Ethnic Dance Ensemble, New Orleans, 1983; mem. Contemp. Art Ctr.'s Krewe of Clones, New Orleans, 1983, Americans for Nonsmokers Rights, Berkeley, 1985. Mem. Mem. Sci. Meets the Arts Soc. (founding). Democrat. Avocations: visual arts, travel, creative writing.

CRITCHFIELD, TAMMY K., elementary school educator; b. Chickasha, Okla., Nov. 12, 1965; d. Larry J. Cook and Linda K. Ferrell; m. Ernie Critchfield, May 17, 1997; children: Kami Nicole Loveless (Critchfield), Tara Le'Chelle, Caitlin Breann. BS, U.S.A.O, Chickasha, 1998. Tchr. Union City Pub. Schs., Okla., 1999—2005, Friend Pub. Schs., Chickasha, 2005—. Recipient Masonic Tchr. of the Yr., 2001, 2002, 2005. Home: PO Box 162 Amber OK 73004 Office: Friend Public Schools 1307 County Rd 1350 Chickasha OK Office Phone: 405-224-3822.

CRITELLI, NANCY BARBARA, music educator, cellist; b. Billings, Mont., Dec. 4, 1927; d. Frank S. and Inez Estell (MacDonald) C. MusB, Mont. State U., 1950, MusM, 1963; D of Mus. Arts, U. Mich., 1976. Orch. dir., tchr. Flathead County H.S., Kalispell, Mont., 1950-52; string instr. El Paso (Tex.) Pub. Schs., 1952-55; instrumental instr. Lansing (Mich.) Pub. Schs., 1957-62; instr. theory, cello, bass Wis. State U., Eau Claire, 1965-66; asst. prof. orch., chamber music theory, appreciation Rocky Mountain Coll., Billings, 1967-69; asst. prof. Western Ill. U. Lydian Quartet, Macomb, 1972-73; asst. prof. cello, bass, chamber music, theory Appalachian State U., Boone, N.C., 1974-80; instr., adj. prof. Ea. Mont. Coll., Billings, 1987; adj. prof. Rocky Mountain Coll., Billings, 1988—. Clinician N.W. Music Edn. Conv., Boise; workshop leader 7th Ann. Coulee region Festival of Arts, LaCrosse, Wis., 1966; organizer Solo and Small Ensemble Festival, Boone, N.C., 1977-78; adjudicator Orch. Contest Festival, Winston-Salem, N.C., 1978, Mont. Music Tchrs. Dist. Festival, Billings, 1982, NE Wyo. Music Festival, Sheridan, 1997, 98; dir., founder Flathead County Symphony, Kalispell, 1951-52, Lansing Jr. Symphony, 1959, Red Lodge (Mont.) Music Festival, 1964-73; cellist Mont. Suzuki Inst., 1980-90, mem. faculty, 1985-95. Performer (cellist) U. Mont. Orch., Western Ill. Symphony, Appalachian State U. Symphony, Billings Symphony, others; composer: (for cello and piano) Variations on Three Blind Mice Mem. Nat. Music Tchrs. Assn. (cert.), Music Educators Nat. Assn., Am. String Tchrs. Assn., Yellowstone Chamber Music Players, Suzuki Assn., Billings Music Tchrs. Assn. (commd. composing tchg. pieces) Avocations: birding, outings with sierra club, instrument repair, gardening.

CRITTENDEN, DANIELLE ANN, writer, journalist; b. Toronto, Ont., Can., Apr. 20, 1963; d. Maxwell John Crittenden and Yvonne Ann (Wilson) Worthington; m. David Jeffrey Frum, June 26, 1988; children: Miranda Ann, Nathaniel Saul. Reporter Toronto Sun, 1983-86; founding editor Women's Quar., Arlington, Va., 1994-99; columnist The Nat. Post, NYC, 1999; contbr. Nat. Pub. Radio; contbr. blogger The Huffington Post, 2005—. Author: What Our Mothers Didn't Tell Us: Why Happiness Eludes the Modern Woman, 1999, Amanda Bright@home, 2003. Jewish. Office: c/o William Morris Agency 1325 Avenue of the Americas New York NY 10019 E-mail: danielle@daniellecrittenden.com.*

CRITTENDEN, ETTA MARIE, elementary school educator; b. Tulsa, Okla., Dec. 17, 1953; d. Johney Franklin and Etta Belle Crittenden. BA, Free Will Bapt. Bible Coll., 1976, BS, 1980; MEd in Reading, Tenn. State U., 1993. Cert. elem. edn. grades 1-8, reading grades K-8. Tchr. Guin Kindergarten Kampus, Ala., 1976—77; sec. Gibbon, Gladd, Clark, Bornes & Taylor, Tulsa, 1977—78; tchr. Woodbine Christian Acad., Nashville, 1979—84, Pk. Ave. Christian Sch., Nashville, 1984—86; receptionist 22nd & State Med. Clinic, Nashville, 1986—87; tchr. Metro-Davidson County Pub. Schs., Nashville, 1987—2001; reading coord., cons. Tenn. Dept. Edn., Nashville, 2001—. Math manipulative tng. for tchrs. Metro-Nashville Pub. Schs., 1997—99; tchr. edn. adv. bd. Free Will Bapt. Bible Coll., Nashville, 1999—; dir., facilitator Tenn. Reading Panel, Nashville, 2004—. Pres. Monticello Manor Homeowners Assn., 2000—04; mem. greeters svcs. com. First Bapt. Nashville, 1994—. Mem.: Internat. Reading Assn., Delta Kappa Gamma. Baptist. Avocations: reading, cross stitch, paper cutting. Home: 163 Harbor Village Dr Madison TN 37115 Office: State Tenn Dept Edn 710 James Robertson Pkwy Nashville TN 37243

CRITTENDEN, MARTHA A., rehabilitation services professional; b. Georgiana, Ala., Nov. 2, 1957; d. Walter Ray and Martha Pugh C. AA, Lomax - Hannon Jr. Coll., Greenville, Ala., 1978; BS, Troy State U., 1987, MS, 1993. Cert. counselor Am. Counseling Assn./Ala. Alochol and Drug Abuse Assn.; cert. instr. HIV & AIDS, ARC; cert. criminal justice addiction profl., Ala.; foster care parent cert. Shelby County, 2005. Patient care asst. Jackson Hosp., Montgomery, Ala., 1978-89, psychiat. tech., 1989-90; drug program specialist Bullock County Correctional, Union Spring, Ala., 1990-95; drug treatment counselor Montgomery Cmty. Based Facility, Mt. Meigs, Ala., 1995-99, Ala. Dept. Corrections, Birmingham, 1999-2000; disability specialist Ala. Dept. Edn. Birmingham Disability Determination Svcs., 2000—. Vol. Neighbors Who Care, 1999; tchr. Bethel Full Gospel Ch., Montgomery, 1986—, Faith Chapel Christian Ctr. Ch., 1986—. Recipient Supr. of Yr. award Ala. Dept. Corrections, 1994. Mem. Ala. Alcohol and Drug Abuse Assn., Ala. Dept. Corrections (supr. 1990-95, Supr. of Yr. 1994), Addiction and Offender Counselors, Gamma Beta Phi. Avocations: reading, church, walking or jogging, school. Office: Birmingham Disability Determination Svcs PO Box 830300 Birmingham AL 35283 also: Faith Chapel Christian Ctr 800 Quebec St Birmingham AL 35224-1571 Home: 140 Shady Acres Rd Alabaster AL 35007-4631 E-mail: goeque12@yahoo.com.

CRITTENDON, DONNA ELIZABETH, customer service administrator; b. San Diego, Aug. 3, 1954; d. Clayton Thomas and Bessie Mae Foster; m. Paul Gregory Crittendon, Mar. 14, 1955; children: Orin, Michelle. AA, Sacramento City Coll., 1975; BS in Bus. Adminstrn., U. Phoenix, Sacramento, 1999. Tchr. asst. Sutter County Schs., Yuba City, Calif., 1976, media clk. Comprehensive Employment Training Act program, 1977—79; svc. rep. Pacific Gas and Electric, Marysville, Calif., 1979—, safety coord., 1998—, Cordaptix trainer, 2002. United Way chairperson Pacific Gas and Electric Co., Marysville, 1998—; voter registration vol. Sutter County, Yuba City, Calif., 2000; corp. sec., treas., bookkeeper, media person Christ Temple Cmty. Ch., 1976—; vol. Women's Ministry at Convelesant Home, 1999—. Mem.: Calif. Dist. Coun. (sec./treas. 2001—, dist. #5 2001—03). Apostolic. Avocations: creating media, sewing, bookkeeping, gardening, cooking.

CRIVELLI-KOVACH, ANDREA, public health and nutrition consultant, educator; b. Drexel Hill, Pa., Sept. 27, 1947; d. Albert Francis and Philomena Maria Crivelli; m. Gerald Charles Scullin, Apr. 24, 1971 (div. 1980); m. Edward Raphael Kovach, Aug. 6, 1982. BA in Biology, Immaculata Coll., 1969, MA in Nutrition Edn., 1988; PhD in Cmty. Health, Temple U., 1995. Cert. health edn. specialist. Info. specialist E.I. DuPont de Nemours & Co., Wilmington, 1969-83, contract info. specialist, 1987-91; nutrition cons. Health Choices Unltd., Media, Pa., 1988—; asst. prof., cmty. health coord. Phila. Coll. Osteopathic Medicine, 1994-96; rsch. evaluation cons. Crivelli Assocs., Media, Pa., 1996—; asst. prof., dir. cmty. health programs Arcadia U., Glenside, Pa., 1996—. Adj. prof. women's studies U. Pa., Phila., 1996-2002. Contbr. articles to profl. jours. including Jour. of Human Lactation, Birth, Jour. Korean Acad. Nursing, Jour. Osteo. Medicine. Chair Media Bd. of Health, 1997—; dep. health officer Media Borough, 1994—97; mem. nutrition adv. bd. Nursing Mothers Network, Springfield, Pa.; mem. profl. adv. bd. Breastfeeding Ctr. Mont. County, Women's Health and Environ. Network. Mem. Am. Dietetic Assn., Am. Pub. Health Assn., Soc. of Pub. Health Educators, Soc. of Nutrition Edn. (Del. Valley chpt.), Kappa Omicron Nu. Democrat. Achievements include development of a measurement instrument to evaluate hospital breastfeeding policies based on the UNICEF/WHO baby-friendly hospital initiative; research in cross-cultural international breastfeeding; the role of community lay health advocates in empowering low income pregnant women. Avocations: biking, swimming, boating, gardening, hiking, cross country skiing. Office: Arcadia U 450 S Easton Rd Glenside PA 19038-3215

CRNKOVICH, RUTH ANNE, art appraiser, museum director; b. Dayton, Ohio, Aug. 31, 1967; d. Donald Paul and Odette Maria Burks; children: Maxwell Thomas, Trevor Paul. AA in Art, South Suburban Coll., 1989; BA in Art, Governors State U., 1992, MA in Art History, 1997. Cert. Appraisers Assn. Am., NYC, 2004, Appraisers Assn. Am., NYC, 2002. Curator Brauer Mus. Art, Valparaiso U., Ind., 1998—99; dir. exhbns. No. Ind. Arts Assn., Munster, 2000—04; founder and pres. CRN Fine Art Svcs., Chgo., 2002—; exec. dir. Nat. Vietnam Veterans Art Mus., Chgo., 2004—, Tall Grass Arts Assn., Park Forest, Ill., 2006. Cons. No. Ind. Arts Assn., Munster, 2004—, Shimmery Gallery, Munster, 2004—; fundraising chair Bridge Mag., Chgo., 2004—. Dir., curator (exhibitions) That 70s Show: The Age of Pluralism in Chicago, Karamu: Remnants of Ritual, Imagined Vistas: Paintings By Paul Sierra, Children of War, Valor: The Warsaw Uprising, Emergence: Women Artists in the New Millennium, Relections in Silver, Sideshow of the Absurd, Celebration in Glass, Emergence: Women Artists in the New Millennium, Beyond Icons: Contemporary Art in Armenia, prodr., curator Semper fidelis: How I Met My Father. Vol. FRIENDS of Braur Mus. Art, Valparaiso, Ind., 2002—04; mem. Columbia Coll. Photography Mus. Auxillary Bd., Chgo., 2004—05. Scholar, Governors State U., 1995-1997. Mem.: AAM (assoc.), Appraisers Assn. Am. (assoc.), Aumni Assn. Governors State U. (assoc.), Soc. Contemporary Art (assoc.), Am. Craft (assoc.), Arts Club of Washington DC (assoc.). Home: 10033 Gettler St Dyer IN 46311 Office Phone: 219-313-9960. Personal E-mail: info@crnart.com.

CROCE, ARLENE, critic; b. Providence, May 5, 1934; d. Michael Daniel and Louise Natalie (Pensa) C. Student, Women's Coll., U. N.C., 1951-53; BA, Barnard Coll., 1955. Founder, editor Ballet Rev., 1965-78; dance critic New Yorker mag., 1973-98. Dance panelist Nat. Endowment for Arts, 1977-80. Author: The Fred Astaire & Ginger Rogers Book, 1972, Afterimages, 1977, Going to the Dance, 1982, Sight Lines, 1987, Writing in the Dark, Dancing in the New Yorker, 2000. Recipient AAAL award 1979, award of Honor for Arts and Culture Mayor N.Y.C., 1979, Janeway prize Barnard Coll., 1955; Hodder fellow Princeton U., 1971; Guggenheim fellow, 1972, 86, NEH fellow 1992, Nat. Arts Journalism Program sr. fellow, 1999. Office: New Yorker Mag 4 Times Sq New York NY 10036-6561 Office Phone: 212-286-2860.

CROCKER, JANE LOPES, library director; b. Mass., Sept. 19, 1946; d. Joseph Barros and Mary (Faria) Lopes; m. Lowell Steven Crocker, Feb. 14, 1976; children: Susan J., Jennifer L., Jacqueline M. BA in English, Bridgewater State Coll., 1968; MS in Libr. Sci., Simmons Coll., 1971. Cert. libr., Mass.; cert. secondary edn. tchr., Mass. Libr. New Bedford (Mass.) Pub. Libr., 1968-71; pub. svcs. libr. Simmons Coll. Libr., Boston, 1971-73; head libr. Boston City Hosp., 1973-76; libr. dir. Gloucester County Coll., Deptford, NJ, 1976—. Pres. Libr. Network Rev. Bd., 1994-95, vice-chmn., 1996-97; assoc. prof. Gloucester County Coll., 1995—. Editor Bay State Libr., 1974-76; contbg. author: Reference and Information Service, 1978, N.J. Libraries, 1984, 89-90, 94, Vocat. and Tech. Resources for C.C. Librs., Laun, Mary Ann Assn. of Coll. and Rsch. Librs., ALA. Vice chair Gloucester County Coll. Acad. Assembly, 1996-98, co-chair Tech. Roundtable, 2000—; sec. Internat. Union of Electronic, Elec., CWA Local #442, 1996—; pres. GCCEA, dir.'s group, 2002-. Recipient Ray Murray award, NJ Assn. Libr. Assts, 1991, Disting. Svc. award, Coll. and Univ., 2004, cert. of commendation, Gloucester County Bd. Freeholders, 2004. Mem. ALA (chpt. rels. coun. 1995—, chpt. councilor 1997—), NJ Libr. Assn. (pres.-elect 1991-92, pres. 1992-93, vice-chair pub. policy com. 1996-97, exec. bd. 1997—, newsletter editor 2003—, pres. Dirs.' assn. 2002—, Pres. award 2004), NJ Edn. Assn. Dirs. Assn. (pres. 2002—), VALE (exec. com. 2002-05), South Jersey Regional Libr. Coop. (pres. 1988-90, exec. bd. 1985—, Resolution of Appreciation award 1990, Pres.'s award 1993). Roman Catholic. Office: Gloucester County Coll 1400 Tanyard Rd Sewell NJ 08080-4222 Office Phone: 856-415-2250. Business E-Mail: jcrocker@gccnj.edu.

CROCKER, JEAN HAZELTON, elementary school educator, consultant, environmental services administrator; b. Hyannis, Mass., Nov. 7, 1930; d. James Barnard and Helene Snow (Cahoon) Hazelton; m. Merle McDonald Crocker, Sept. 13, 1952; children: Carolyn, James Lauchlan. BS, U. Mass., 1952; MS in Med. Sci., SUNY, New Paltz, 1978; postgrad., Fitchburg State Coll., Mass., 1981, Troy State U., Montgomery, Ala., 1970. Cert. tchr., N.Y., Mass. Kindergarten - 6th grade tchr. Dept. Def., Heilbronn, Germany, 1953-54; tchr. 6th grade Fred Lynn Mid. Sch., Woodbridge, Va., 1965-68, curriculum resource dir., 1968-69; tchr. 6th grade Dept. Def. Edn. Overseas, Heidelberg, Germany, 1960-61, tchr., supr., asst. prin. Frankfurt, Germany, 1974-75, tchr. 4th grade Boeblingen, Germany, 1972-73; tchr. 7th and 8th grades, reading specialist N.Y. Mil. Acad., Cornwall-on-Hudson, NY, 1977-78; tchr. Mt. Watchusett C.C., Watchusett, Mass., 1979-80, Lowell Jr. Coll., Ft. Devens, Mass., 1980-81; tchr. ESL Manter Hall Sch., Osterville, Mass., 1981-83, Barnstable Cmty. Sch., Hyannis, 1982; tchr. Cape Cod C.C., West Barnastable, Mass., 1984-90. Author: (poetry) Songs of Psychosis, Camp Edwards: Seasons, Environs, Issues, Seaside Garden of Verses, A Cape Cod Pilgrim Sings, In Memoriam, A Cape Cod Pilgrim Grieves; writer articles, curricula, poetry. Co-founder and chair Save The Reservation and Our Nat. Guard, 1998-2002; mem. Otis Civilian Adv. Coun.; mem. citizen adv. bd. Internat. Ctr. for Clubhouse Devel.; adv. mem. Cape Cod Dept. Mental Health. Recipient Pres. award, Nat. Guard AMA, 2001, George Washington Honor medal, Freedoms Found. at Valley Forge, 2002, Appreciation citation, Mass. Army Nat. guard, 2002. Mem.: AAUW, Nat, Alliance for the Mentally Ill, Patriots Advocating Camp Edwards Restoration and Survival, Friends of Mass. Mil. Reservation, Order of Ea. Star (Rainbow chpt. #123), Kappa Kappa Gamma (Cape Cod Alumnae chpt.). Methodist. Avocations: walking, biking, flower arranging, crafting. Home: 40 Tracy Rd Cotuit MA 02635-3417 Personal E-mail: jeancrocker@hotmail.com. Business E-Mail: jhccotuit@comcast.com.

CROCKER, SAONE BARON, lawyer; b. Bulawayo, Zimbabwe, Jan. 11, 1943; came to U.S., 1963; d. Benjamin and Rachel (Joffe) Baron; m. Chester Arthur Crocker, Dec. 18, 1965; children: Bathsheba Nell, Karena Wynne, Rebecca Masten. BA, U. Cape Town, 1961, BA with honors, 1962; MA, Johns Hopkins U., 1966; JD cum laude, Georgetown U., 1983. Bar: DC 1983, U.S. Ct. Appeals (DC cir.) 1985, U.S. Dist. Ct. DC 1990, U.S. Supreme Ct. 1990, U.S. Ct. Appeals (7th cir.) 1991, U.S. Ct. Appeals (4th cir.) 1998. Adminstr. Guinea program African Am. Inst., Washington, 1965-66, author Africa Report, 1966; writer fgn. affairs divsn. Am. U., 1967—68; freelance writer, 1968—80; atty. firm Wilmer, Cutler & Pickering, 1983—84; clk. to judge U.S. Ct. Appeals for DC Circuit, 1984—85; atty. firm O'Melveny & Myers, 1985—90, Beveridge & Diamond, 1990—92, Wright & Talisman, P.C., 1992—2001; pvt. practice, 2001—. Contbg. author: Zambia Handbook, 1967. AAUW fellow, 1963-65; Fulbright fellow, 1963; Johns Hopkins U. fellow, 1964-65; recipient Lawyers Coop. Pub. Co. awards, 1980. Mem. ABA, AAUW (state pres. 1992-94), Fulbright Assn. Office Phone: 202-256-3366. Personal E-mail: saonec@aol.com.

CROCKER, SUZANNE, painter; m. Peter Crocker; children: Travis, Hayden. BA in History of Art cum laude, U. Pa., 1987; student, Montserrat Coll. Art, 1997—2000; studied with, Wolf Kahn and Cynthia Packard. One-woman shows include Hamilton Pub. Libr., Mass., 2000, Conomo Cafe, Essex, Mass., 2001, Copley Soc., Boston, 2004—06, Woodstock Folk Art, Vt., 2005—06, exhibited in group shows at Wenham Mus., Mass., 2000, Northshore Art Assn., 2001—04, Lyme Art Assn., Conn., 2002, 2004, Boltax Gallery, N.Y., 2002—05, Mingo Gallery, Mass., 2002, Nat. Arts Club Galleries, N.Y., 2002, River Gallery, Mass., 2002—03, Newburyport Art Assn., 2002—05, Michael Price Gallery, 2003, Powers Gallery, 2004—06, Woodstock Folk Art, Vt., 2005—, This Old House Designer Showhouse (PBS TV), Mass., 2005, Green Mountain Cultural Ctr., Vt., 2005, Rocky Neck Art Gallery, Mass., 2005, Trinity Ch., 2005, Bennett St. Gallery, Atlanta, 2006, Gardner Colby Gallery, Martha's Vineyard, 2006, Left Bank Gallery, Wellfleet, Mass., 2006. Named Copley Artist, 2005; fellow, Vt. Studio Ctr., 2002, 2005. Mem.: North Shore Arts Assn., Newburyport Art Assn., Artists' Fellowship, Inc., Copley Soc. Art, Audubon Artists (assoc.), Allied Artists Am. (assoc.). Independent.

CROCKETT, DODEE FROST, brokerage house executive; b. Oklahoma City, Oct. 19, 1956; d. Carl S. Frost and Mikki (Matheny) Marcus; m. Billy Crockett. M in Theol. Studies, So. Meth. U., 2003. Chartered advisor in philantropy 2005, cert. divorce fin. analyst 2006. 1st v.p., wealth mgmt. advisor Merrill Lynch Pvt. Client, Dallas, 1980—. Bd. dirs. Ronald McDonald House of Dallas, 1992—, Dallas Social Venture Ptnrs., 2003—, chair of bd., 2005; trustee Dallas Opera, 1991—; exec. bd. Perkins Sch. Theology, So. Meth. U., Dallas, 2003-; found. adv. bd. Dallas Found.; pres. Cir. Shared Housing Ctr., Dallas. Mem. Nat. Assn. Securities Dealers (gen. securities prin., mcpl. securities rulemaking bd. prin., registered options prin., bd. arbitrators), NYSE (com. mem.), Merrill Lynch Dirs. Cir., Park Cities Exch. Club (charter). Office: Merrill Lynch Pierce Fenner and Smith 2000 Premier Pl 5910 N Central Expy Ste 2000 Dallas TX 75206-5152

CROCKETT, JOAN M., human resources executive; B in Polit. Sci., John Carroll Univ., 1972. Underwriter, various positions in human resources Allstate Ins. Co., 1973—94, sr. v.p. human resources, 1994—. Bd. dirs. INROADS; adv. bd. Univ. Ill. Chgo. Internat. Student Exchange Program; ptnr., bd. dirs. Ctr. for Human Resource Mgmt. Univ. Ill., gov. coun. Good Shepherd Hosp., Barrington, Ill. Named Human Resource Exec. of Yr., Human Resource Exec. mag., 1997. Mem.: Nat. Acad. Human Resources. Office: Allstate Corp 2775 Sanders Rd Northbrook IL 60062-6127 Office Phone: 847-402-5000. Office Fax: 847-326-7519.

CROFT, CANDACE ANN, psychology professor, academic administrator, small business owner; b. Lancaster, Wis., Jan. 14, 1957; d. Wilford Stanley and Myrna Viola Croft. BA, St. Olaf Coll., 1979; MS, U. Ariz., 1980; PhD, Pa. State U., 1984. Psychotherapist Forrester Clinic, Chgo., 1984-86; dir. rsch. on child and adolescent health Am. Acad. Ped., Elk Grove Village, Ill., 1986-92; dir. rsch. and sci. affairs Am. Acad. Orthop. Surgeons, Rosemont, Ill., 1992-94; sr. program assoc. Aon Found., Chgo., 1994-95; dir. Strong Spirit Wellness Ctr., Chgo., 1995-96; adj. prof. DePaul U., Chgo., 1993-96; assoc. prof. psychology, chmn. dept. psychology Clarke Coll., Dubuque, Iowa, 1996—2003, chair instl. rev. bd., 2000—03; dean Health & Human Svc. Occupations, SW Tech. Coll., Fennimore, Wis., 2003—; pres. Tabankhu, LLC, 2005—. Textbook reviewer McGraw-Hill, 1998-2003; media contact Nat. Coun. Family Rels., St. Paul, 1998—, Clarke Coll.-Fox-40, Dubuque, Iowa, KWWL Channel 7, Dubuque, Iowa; adv. Clarke Coll.; owner Heart Light Shining; cert. aromatherapist, appreciative inquiry facilitator. Author: Annalia's Simply Splendid, 2003, Growing Good Hearts: The Rooting Years, 2005, The Tao of the Magician, 2005; contbr. articles to sci. and profl. jour.; exec. prodr. film Heart of the Matter, 1991 (bronze award Houston Internat. Film Festival 1991); contbr. column to on-line pub., Living With Heart, 2002—. Mem. liturg. ministry St. Mary's Ch., Platteville, Wis., 1999—2001. Mem. Nat. Coun. Family Rels. (cert. family life educator, sect. religion and the family, sect. on family and health), Assn. Humanistic Psychology, Inst. Noetic Scis., Assn. for Transpersonal Psychology, Phi Kappa Phi, Omicron Nu. Avocations: writing, music, aerobics, swimming, photography. Home: 119 North Monroe Lancaster WI 53813 Office: SW Tech Coll 1800 Bronson Blvd Fennimore WI 53809 Personal E-mail: cacroft@chorus.net.

CROFT, KATHRYN DELAINE, social worker, consultant; b. Eastover, S.C., Jan. 13, 1944; d. Randolph and Ethel (Williams) Lloyd; m. Daniel Marranzini, June 26, 1987. BS, Wilberforce U., 1965; MS, Columbia U., 1982, New Sch. for Social Rsch., 1988. Cert. social worker, N.Y. Exec. dir. Family Dynamics, Inc., N.Y.C., 1987—92; asst. provost Columbia U., N.Y.C., 1992—94; commr. N.Y.C. Child Welfare Adminstrn., N.Y.C., 1994—96; dir. ops. Just One Break, Inc., N.Y.C., 1997—2000, exec. dir., 2000—02; chief program officer ARC Greater N.Y.C., 2002—04; adminstrv. dir. supported housing and real property Women-in-Need, Inc., 2004—. Cons. various nonprofit orgns., N.Y.C., 1996—. Bd. dirs. Artsgenesis, N.Y.C., 1993—, chmn., 1996-99; bd. dirs. Ackerman Inst., N.Y.C., 1997-2000. Recipient scholarships New Sch. for Social Rsch., 1985-88, Columbia U., 1978-82. Mem. NAFE, Assn. Black Women in Higher Edn. Avocations: travel, reading, photography.

CROMBIE, PAMELA GASPARIN, restaurant and commercial property owner; b. Springfield, Ill., Jan. 22, 1949; d. Stephen Lewis and Rita Imogene (Donaldson) Gasparin; div.; 1 child, Kimberly;div.; 1 child, Katherine. AA, Springfield Coll., Ill., 1969; BS, So. Ill. U., 1973; postgrad., U. Ill., 1976-79. Cert. appraiser, New Eng. Ins. investigator Equifax, Chgo., 1973-79; pres. Internat. Antiques, Chgo., 1980—; v.p. Moncrieff Enterprises, Chgo., 1989—; ptnr., owner Mid-Atlantic Properties, Chgo., 1991—. Appraisals cons. Internat. Art and Antiques Ctr., Chgo., 1991—; antiques expert guest Oprah Winfrey Show, 1994; resturant owner The Duke of Perth; comml. property owner, Chgo. Co-chair, commr. Chgo. Spl. Svcs. Area # 8, 1989-92. Mem. ACLU, Citizens Utility Bd., NOW, Greenpeace, Lakeview C. of C. Avocations: rollerblading, antiques, architecture, skiing.

CROMWELL, ADELAIDE M., sociology educator; b. Washington, Nov. 27, 1919; d. John Wesley Jr. and Yetta Elizabeth (Mavritte) Cromwell; 1 child, Anthony C. Hill. AB, Smith Coll., 1940; MA, U. Pa., 1941; cert. in Social Work, Bryn Mawr Coll., 1943; PhD, Radcliffe Coll., 1952; LHD (hon.), U. Southwestern Mass., 1972, George Washington U., 1989, Boston U., 1995. Mem. faculty Hunter Coll., 1942—44, Smith Coll., 1945—46, Boston U., 1951—85, prof. sociology, 1971—85, dir. Afro-Am. studies, 1969—88, prof. emerita sociology, 1985—; mem. faculty Harvard U. Ext., 1965—66. Mem. adv. com. vol. fgn. aid AID, 1964-80; mem. NEH, 1968-70; adv. com. corrections Commonwealth Mass., 1955-68; mem. commn. instns. higher edn., 1973-74; adv. com. to dir. IRS, 1970-71, to dir. census, 1972-75. Bd. dirs. Wheelock Coll., 1971-74, Nat. Ctr. Afro-Am. Artists, 1971-80, African Am. Scholars Coun., 1971—, Nat. Fellowship Fund, 1974-75, Mass. Hist. Commn., 1993; bd. dirs. Sci. and Tech. for Internat. Devel., 1984-86; mem. exec. com. Am. Soc. African Culture, 1967. Mem. AAAS, African Studies Assn. (bd. dir. 1966-68), Am. Acad. of Arts and Scis., Am. Sociol. Assn., Coun. on Fgn. Affairs (bd. fgn. scholarships 1980-84), Mass. Hist. Soc., Phi Beta Kappa. Home: 51 Addington Rd Brookline MA 02445-4519

CROMWELL, FLORENCE STEVENS, occupational therapist; b. Lewistown, Pa., May 14, 1922; d. William Andrew and Florence (Stevens) Cromwell. BS in Edn., Miami U., Oxford, Ohio, 1943; BS in Occupl. Therapy, Washington U., St. Louis, 1949; MA, U. So. Calif., 1952; cert. in health facility adminstrn., UCLA, 1978. Mem. staff, then supervising therapist Los Angeles County Gen. Hosp., 1949—53; occupl. therapist Goodwill Industries, L.A., 1954—55; staff therapist Vis. Nurse Assn., Phila., 1955—56; rsch. therapist United Cerebral Palsy Assn., L.A., 1956—60; dir. occupl. therapy Orthopaedic Hosp., L.A., 1961—67; coord. occupl. therapy Rsch. and Tng. Ctr. U. So. Calif. Med. Sch., L.A., 1967—70; assoc. prof. U. So. Calif., L.A., 1970—76, acting chmn. dept. occupl. therapy, 1973—76, mem. adv. bd. project SEARCH, Sch. Medicine, 1969—72; founding editor Occupl. Therapy in Health Care jour., 1984—88, editor emerita, 1988—. Assoc. dir. L.A. Job Corps Ctr., 1977—78; cons. in edn. and program devel., 1976—95; freelance editor, 1986—. Author: Manual for Basic Skills Assessment, 1960; contbr. articles to profl. jours. Mem. scholarship com. L.A. March of Dimes, 1963—70; mentor U. Tex.-Galveston Class 1990 Occupl. Therapy; bd. dirs. Am. Occupl. Therapy Found., 1965—69, v.p., 1966—69; bd. dirs. Nat. Health Coun., 1975—78. Served to lt. (j.g.) WAVES USNR, 1943—46. Recipient Disting. Alumni award, Washington U., 1978, Disting. Lectr., Calif. Occupl. Therapy Found., 1986. Fellow: Am. Occupl. Therapy Assn. (pres. 1967—73, Pres.'s WLWest commendation AOTA-AOTF 1999); mem.: Assn. Schs. Allied Health Professions (dir. 1973—74), Coalition Ind. Health Professions (chmn. 1973—74), So. Calif. Occupl. Therapy Assn. (pres. 1950—51, 1975—76), Inst. Medicine NAS (emerita 2002), Cwen, Kappa Kappa Gamma, Kappa Delta Pi, Mortar Bd. Personal E-mail: fscromwell@aol.com.

CRONE, ANNA LISA, Russian literature educator; b. Bklyn., June 9, 1946; d. James Clarence Jr. and Ethel Margaret (Donnelly) C.; m. Vladimir Donchik, July 12, 1982; 1 child, Liliana Donchik. BA in Russian Lit., Goucher Coll., 1967; MA in Russian Lang. and Lit., Harvard U., 1969, PhD in Russian Lang. and Lit., 1975; LHD (hon.), Goucher Coll., 1988, DHC (hon.), 1998. From instr. to asst. prof. Russian and Russian lit. Goucher Coll. Johns Hopkins U., Balt., 1971—74; tchr., translator Associated Jewish Charities, Balt., 1974—75; rschr. Radcliffe Inst., Harvard U., Cambridge, Mass., 1975—76; from asst. prof. to prof. Slavic langs. and lits. U. Chgo., 1977—. Hon. vis. fellow Slavonic Inst. U. London, 1998—; internat. lectr. on Russian topics. Author: (scholarly study) Rozanov and the End of Literature, 1978; author: The Daring of Derzhavin, 2001, My Petersburg/Myself, 2004; editor, contbr.: New Studies in Russian Language and Literature, 1986; mem. editl. bd. Russian Lang. Jour., Ency. of Russian Literature, Ency. of the Essay; contbr. articles to profl. jours. Mem. Univ. Senate U. Chgo., 1992-95. Nat. Def. Fgn. Lang. fellow, 1967-71, Woodrow Wilson fellow, 1967: recipient Quantrell Tchr. of Yr. award, U. Chgo., 1985, Best Grad. Tchr.award, 2000, Barbara Heldt prize for scholarship and mentoring in Slavic studies, 2004, Main Nat. Lifetime Achiev. award for woman in the Slavic field. Mem. Am. Assn. Tchrs. of Slavic and East European Langs. (Best Grad. Prof. award 2000), Am. Assn. Advancement of Slavic Studies, Stochastic Soc. (pres. 1991-92, 96-97), Phi Beta Kappa. Democrat. Avocations: music, travel, intellectual history, history of culture, amateur acting. Office: U Chgo Slavic Dept 1130 E 59th St Chicago IL 60637-1539 Personal E-mail: liscron@yahoo.com. Business E-Mail: acrone@midway.uchicago.edu.

CRONE, PATRICIA ANN, gifted and talented educator; d. Edward Vincent and Marian Luszczynski; m. Michael Crone, Aug. 13, 1983; children: Matthew David, Tricia Ann. MA in English and Elem. Ed, Bowling Green State U., Ohio, 1981; BA in Elem. Edn. magna cum laude, Mary Manse Coll., Toledo, 1974. Cert. elem. edn. Ohio, 1974, N.J., 1974. Tchr. grade one Immaculate Conception Sch., Port Clinton, Ohio, 1974—77; tchr. grade two Holy Angels Sch., Sandusky, Ohio, 1977—78; tchr. grade one St. Aloysius Sch., Bowling Green, 1978—85; gifted edn. specialist Thomas Jefferson Sch., Turnersville, NJ, 1985—. Parish coun. St. Mary's Ch., Malaga, NJ, 1993—98. Grantee, Washington Twp. Edn. Found., 2003—04, 2004—05, 2005—06. Mem.: NJ Assn. Gifted Children, NJ Edn. Assn. Roman Catholic. Avocations: reading, gardening, travel, flower arranging. Office: Thomas Jefferson Elementary 95 Altair Dr Turnersville NJ 08012 Office Phone: 856-589-8248.

CRONHOLM, LOIS S., academic administrator; b. St. Louis, Aug. 15, 1930; d. Fred and Emma (Tobias) Kisslinger; m. James Cronholm, Sept. 15, 1965 (div. 1974); children: Judith Frances, Peter Foster, Mark Steven Feldman; m. Stuart E. Neff, Apr. 11, 1975. BA, U. Louisville, 1962, PhD, 1966. Asst. prof. biology dept. U. Louisville, 1973-76, assoc. prof., 1976-80, dean arts and scis., 1979-85, prof. 1980—, 1980-85; dean arts and scis., prof. Temple U., Phila., 1985-92; sr. v.p. acad. affairs, prof. Baruch Coll., CUNY, 1992-98, interim pres., 1998-99; CEO Ctr. for Jewish History, N.Y.C., 1999—2001; sr. v.p., chief operating officer CCNY, 2001—. Bd. dirs. J. History Ideas, 1987—93. Contbr. articles to profl. jours. Chmn. Human Relations Commn., Louisville, 1976-79; group capt. Dems., Valley Station, Ky., 1975-78; sec. Grass Roots Dem. Club, Valley Station, 1975; chmn. Southwestern Jefferson County Econ. Devel. Com., Valley Station, 1983-84; pres. Hampden-Booth Theater Libr., 1997-99. Recipient Pre-Doctoral fellowship NIH, 1963-66, Post-Doctoral fellowship NIH, 1967-70. Mem. Nat. Assn. Land Grant and Urban Univs. (chmn. com. arts and scis. 1987-89, bd. dirs. divsn. urban affairs 1988-90, sec. bd. dirs. internat. divsn. 1991-92), Coun. Colls. Arts and Scis. (bd. dirs. 1987-90, pres.-elect 1989-90, pres. 1990-91, chair commn. on faculty recruitment ethics 1991-93), Players Club N.Y.C. (sec. bd. 1994). Democrat. Jewish. Avocations: gardening, cooking. Office Phone: 212-650-7309. Business E-Mail: lcronholm@ccny.cuny.edu.

CRONIN, BONNIE KATHRYN LAMB, museum director; b. Mpls., Mar. 11, 1941; d. Edwin Rector and Maude Kathryn (MacPherson) Lamb; m. Barry Jay Cronin, Jan. 23, 1963 (div. Feb. 1972); 1 son, Philip Scott. BA, U. Mo., 1963, BS, 1964; MS, Ill. State U., 1970. Copywriter Neds & Wardlow Advt., Columbia, Mo., 1962-64; tchr. Columbia Sch. Sys., 1964-68, Normal (Ill.) Sch. Sys., 1968-69; asst. gen. mgr. Sta. WGLT, Normal, 1969-70; dir. devel. Radio Sta. WBUR, Boston, 1970-71, program dir., 1971-75, gen. mgr., 1975-78; dir. pub. rels. Joy of Movement Ctr., 1978-80; dep. scheduler Anderson for Pres., 1980; scheduler Spaulding for Gov., 1980-81; dir. scheduling John Kerry Campaign, 1982; dir. of scheduling Mass. Lt. Gov.'s Office, dir. ops., 1983-84; dep. campaign mgr. Kerry for Senate Com., 1984; dir. ops. Senator John Kerry, Washington, 1985-86, dir. constituency outreach Boston, 1986-92, exec. asst., 1992-95; chief staff to Senator John Kerry Boston, 1995-97; dir. devel. and pub. affairs Working Capital, 1997-2001; dir. found. rels. USS Constn. Mus., 2001—. Chair Mass. Micro Enterprise Coalition, 2000-01. Commr. Melrose Human Rights Commn., Mass., 2004—; active Melrose Econ. Devel. Coun., 2002—04. Mem.: Mass. Broadcasters Assn. (dir. 1973—78, chair scholarship com., pub. svc. com., adminstrv. oversight com.), Polymnia Choral Soc. (pres. 2002—04), Nat. Pub. Radio (dir. 1974—77, chairperson devel. com.). Office: Box 1812 Boston MA 02129 Office Phone: 617-426-1812. E-mail: bonniemelrose@aol.com.

CRONIN, DOREEN, writer, former lawyer; b. Queens, N.Y. m. Andrew Cronin. Grad., Pa. State U., St. John's U. Former comml. and civil litigation atty., NY; children's book author, 2000—. Author: Click, Clack, Moo: Cows That Type, 2000 (Caldecott Honor, 2000, Red Clover award, N.Y. Times best-seller, Cuffie award, Simington Black Honor, BookSense Honor, The Bill Martin Jr. award Kans. Reading Assn., 2003, The Charlotte award NYSRA, 2002, The Md. Sunflower award, 2002, The Smart award, 2002), Giggle, Giggle, Quack, 2000, Diary of a Worm, 2003, Duck for President, 2004 (Book Sense Book of Yr. for children's illustrated book, 2005). Office: Simon & Schuster Childrens Pub 1230 Ave of the Americas New York NY 10020*

CRONIN, KATHLEEN M., lawyer; b. Montclair, NJ, 1963; BA cum laude, Boston Coll., 1985; JD cum laude, Northwestern U., 1989. Bar: Ill. 1989. Chief counsel corp. fin. Sara Lee Corp., 1995—97; corp. atty. Skadden, Arps, Slate, Meagher & Flom, 1989—95, 1997—2002; corp. sec., acting gen. counsel Chgo. Mercantile Exchange, 2002—03, mng. dir., gen. counsel, corp. sec., 2003—. Office: Chgo Mercantile Exchange Inc 20 S Wacker Dr Chicago IL 60606 Office Phone: 312-930-1000. Office Fax: 312-930-3323.

CRONIN, PATRICIA ROMERO, computer company executive; m. Kevin Cronin; children: Briana, Meaghan, Alyse. BSc, U. Santa Clara; MBA, Golden Gate U. Dir. worldwide mktg., database products IBM, 1994, dir. mktg. strategy and bus. devel., 1996, gen. mgr. global ins. solutions, 1997, v.p. Olympic tech. integration, 1999; current v.p. transformation initiative IBM Global Svc. Mem. Pan Am. Roundtable; with Nat. Charity League; co-chair LaFamilia; bd. mem. Jr. Achievement. Named Elite Hispanic Woman, Hispanic mag., 2002; named one of 100 Top Latinas, 2003, 50 Most Important Hispanics in Tech. & Bus., Hispanic Engr. & Info. Tech. mag., 2005; recipient Exec. Excellence award, 1st female recipient, HENAAC, 2001. Avocation: playing and coaching soccer. Office: IBM Corp 4000 Executive Pkwy Ste 300 San Ramon CA 94583*

CRONSON, MARY SHARP, foundation administrator; Prod., works & process Guggenheim Mus., NYC; pres. Evelyn Sharp Found. Bd. trustee Solomon R. Guggenheim Mus., NYC; secy. NYC Opera.

CROOK, ANNA MARIE, legislator; b. Crossroads, N.Mex., Dec. 6, 1934; d. Joe H. and Esther Jane (McClure) Barnes; m. Jerry W. Crook; m. Keigm, Kevin. BA, Ea. N.Mex. U., 1959. With Midwest Rsch., Kansas City, Mo., 1956; legal dept. Skelly Oil Co., Kansas City, 1957-58; property mgr., bus. mgr. Jerry Crook, 1958—. Fashion cons. Doncaster, 1983-99. Republican. Baptist. Avocation: golf. Home: 1041 Fairway Ter Clovis NM 88101-2806

CROOK, LORRAINE PARKER, secondary school educator; d. Woodrow and Wanda Parker; m. S. Lee Crook, Aug. 25, 1967; children: Nate B., Brad E., Eric L., Scott P., Marci. BA, Idaho State U., Pocatello, 1969. Cert. tchr. K-8 Idaho. Tchr. 6th grade Sch. Dist. #25, Pocatello, 1985—2004, tchr. 7th grade lit., 2004—. Regional dir. Alliance of Idaho Geographers, 1995—2001. Pres. Pocatello Music Club, 1983—85; choir coord. Idaho Internat. Choral Festival, Pocatello, 1999—2000, program dir., 2000—02. Mem. Lds Ch. Office: Franklin Mid Sch 2271 E Terry Pocatello ID 83201 Office Fax: 208-233-1024. Business E-Mail: crooklo@k25.k12.id.us.

CROOK, WENDY P., management consultant, educator; b. Trenton, N.J., May 28, 1952; B. Psychology, Trenton State Coll., 1979; MSW, Rutgers U., 1986, PhD, 1996. Rsch. asst. Princeton (N.J.) U., 1977-79; shelter mgr. Womanspace, Inc., Trenton, 1980-82; asst. exec. dir. Mercer unit N.J. Assn. Retarded Citizens, Inc., Trenton, 1982-87; acting exec. dir. United Cerebral Palsy Assns. of N.J., Inc., Trenton, 1988; exec. dir. United Cerebral Palsy of Mercer County, Inc., Hamilton, N.J., 1987-93; mgmt. cons. DWC Enterprises, 1993—. Adj. prof. Columbia U., N.Y.C., 1993-96, Temple U., Phila., 1993-96, Rutgers U., 1993-96, Monmouth Coll., 1993-96, Ocean County Coll., 1993-96; field cons. Sch. Social Work, Rutgers U., 1993-96, rsch. asst., 1993-96; asst. prof. Fla. State U., Tallahassee, 1996—. Author: (manual) Accessary and ECHO Housing, 1994. Team leader Stand Down for Homeless Vets., 1994; chmn. Mercer County Disabilities Coalition, 1991-93; peer mentor UCPA Regional Adminstrs. Coun., chmn. N.E. region, 1988-93; mem. contracting task force N.J. Dept. Human Svcs., 1992-93; mem. steering com., vice chmn. Mercer County Human Svcs. Coalition, 1986-89; mem. N.J. Ctrl. Region Human Rights Com., 1986-88; mem. United Way Spkrs. Bur., mem. allocations com., Princeton area, Ocean County, Delaware Valley, 1985-93; mem. Mayor Holland's Task Force on Emergency Housing, Trenton, 1981; steering com. Mercer County Food Coalition, 1980-81; pres. bd. dirs., chmn. pers. com. Womanspace, Inc., 1983-84; bd. pres. Tallahassee Coalition for the Homeless, 1998-99. Mem. NASW (conf. chmn., co-chair Ctr. for Social Policy Campaign), N.J. Assn. Cmty. Providers (bd. trustees 1983-93, past v.p.). Avocations: sailing, scuba diving, travel. Home: 277 Stormant Dr Tallahassee FL 32303-4218 Office: Fla State U UCC 2511 Tallahassee FL 32306-2570

CROOKE, ROSANNE M., pharmacologist; b. Pittsfield, Mass., Oct. 30, 1955; d. Myron Michael and Marian Geneva (Russell) Muzyka; m. Stanley T. Crooke, Sept. 5, 1986. BA, Williams Coll., 1978; PhD, U. Pa., 1986. Rsch. asst. endocrine sec. dept. medicine U. Pa., Phila., 1978-81; fellow Wistar Inst. Anatomy and Biology, Phila., 1986-89; prog. leader cardiovasc. disease, dir. antisense drug discovery ISIS Pharms., Carlsbad, Calif., 1989—. Contbr. articles to profl. jours. Mem.: AAAS, Am. Heart Assn. Avocations: hiking, gourmet cooking, bicycling. Home: 3211 Piragua St Carlsbad CA 92009-7840 Office: ISIS Pharms 1896 Rutherford Ave Carlsbad CA 92008 Business E-Mail: rcrooke@isisph.com.

CROOKER, BARBARA ANN, writer, educator; b. Cold Spring, NY, Nov. 21, 1945; d. Emil Vincent and Isabelle Charlotte Poti; m. Michael James Gilmartin, 1967 (div. 1973); 1 child, Stacey Erin Gilmartin Krastek; m. Richard McMaster Crooker, 1975; children: Rebecca Cameron Crooker Ceartas, David MacKenzie. BA, Rutgers U., 1967; MSEd, Elmira Coll., 1975. Adj. instr. English Elmira (NY) Coll., 1975, Corning (NY) CC, 1974—76, Tompkins Cortland CC, Dryden, NY, 1975—76, County Coll. Morris, Randolph, NJ, 1978—79; instr. cmty. svcs. Leigh County CC, Schnecksville, Pa., 1980, 1993; adj. asst. prof. Northampton (Pa.) Area CC, 1980—82; instr. women's ctr. Cedar Crest Coll., Allentown, Pa., 1982—85, adj. prof., 1999—. Contbr. (poetry) lit. mags., anthologies, textbooks, online mags.; author: Writing Home, 1983, Starting From Zero, 1987, Looking for the Comet Halley, 1987, Obbligato, 1992, The Lost Children, 1989, In the Late Summer Garden, 1998, The White Poems, 2001, Ordinary Life, 2002, Paris, 2002, Greatest Hits, 1980—2003, Impressionism, 2004, Radiance, 2005. Finalist, The Paterson Poetry prize, 2006; nominee Pushcart prize, 1978, 1989, 1998, 1999, 2001, 2002, 2003, 2005; named winner, Passages North and NEA Emerging Writers Competition, 1987, Karamu poetry contest, 1997, Byline Chapbook Competition, 2001, winner Thomas Merton Poetry of the Sacred award, 2003, winner Public Poetry Project, 2004, winner Chapbook Competition, Grayson Books, 2004, winner, Labyrinth Soc., 2005, Rosebud Ekphrastic Poetry Contest, 2006, winner April is the Cruelest Month award; recipient Phillips award, Stone Country, 1988, Y2K writing prize, New Millenium Writings, 2000, Grand prize, Dancing Poetry Contest, 2000, First Book award, Word Press, 2005; fellow lit., Pa. Coun. Arts, 1985, 1989, 1993, Va. Ctr. for Creative Arts, 1990, 1992, 1994, 1995, 1995, 1997, 1998, 2000, 2001, 2003, 2004, 2006. Mem.: Am. Acad. Poets. Avocations: gardening, camping, cross country skiing. Home: 7928 Woodsbluff Run Fogelsville PA 18051 Personal E-mail: bcrooker@ix.netcom.com.

CROONQUIST, CHERYL, music educator, realtor; d. Ellard and Joan Larson; m. James Croonquist, Apr. 20, 1974. BS, St. Cloud State U., Minn., 1974; MS magna cum laude, Tri-College U., Moorhead, Minn., 1980. Cert. tchr. ND, lic. real estate salesperson ND. Dir. instrumental music Bishop Ryan HS, Minot, ND, 1980—87; residential real estate agt. Prudential Preferred Properties, Inc., Minot, ND, 1987—; dir. music edn. Carpio (ND) Pub. Sch., Glenburn (ND) Pub. Sch., 1989—. Chair vocat. edn. com. Glenburn Pub. Sch., 2004—. Recipient Spirit of Am. Award, Nat. Independance Day Com., 1984. Mem.: NEA, Glenburn Edn. Assn. (collaborative bargaining com. 2005—), Nat. Assn. Realtors, ND Assn. Realtors, ND Am. Choral Director's Assn., ND Edn. Assn., Music Educators' Nat. Conf., Phi Beta Mu, Phi Delta Kappa. Office: Glenburn Pub Sch 102 Raymond St Glenburn ND 58740 Office Phone: 701-362-7426. Office Fax: 701-362-7349. E-mail: croonqui@minot.com.

CROPPER, SUSAN PEGGY, veterinarian; b. N.Y.C., Feb. 11, 1941; d. Eli and Ruth (Rader) Abrahams; divorced; 1 child, Tracy Lynn. BS, Kans. State U., 1962, DVM, 1964. Assoc. veterinarian Asbury Park (N.J.) Animal Hosp., 1964-65; instr. in Vet. Sci. Kans. State U., Manhattan, 1965-66; owner, veterinarian Markle (Ind.) Vet. Clinic, 1966-71, Meisels Animal Hosp. Clinic, Elmwood Park, N.J., 1971-73, Ridgewood (N.J.) Animal Hosp., 1973-75, Cropper House Call Practice, Wyckoff, N.J., 1975—. Editor Nat. Assn. Women Vets., 1966-68; mem. Audibon Soc. Mus. Natural History. Co-author: Loving and Losing a Pet; editor WJMA Jour., 1973; photographer: Best Diving Spots in Western Hemisphere, 1987. Leader Brownie troop Girl Scouts U.S., Glen Rock, N.J., 1976-77, Wyckoff, 1977-83; chairperson No. Jersey Tridents, Ridgefield, N.J., 1985-86. Mem. AVMA, Soc. Aquatic Vet. Medicine (treas.), No. N.J. Vet. Med. Assn. (pres. 1972-73), Met. Vet. Med. Assn., N.Y. Zool. Soc., Van Saun Zool. Soc., N.J. Acad., Ski and Scuba Club of Westwood, North Jersey Tridents Club (Ridgefield, chair 1985-86, Millennial Cert. for philanthropic recognition). Avocations: scuba diving, underwater photography, travel, racquetball, markmanship practice. Office: 310 Newtown Rd Wyckoff NJ 07481-2608 Office Phone: 201-444-6254. Personal E-mail: dvm2go@optonline.net.

CRORY, ELIZABETH LUPIEN, retired state legislator; b. Gardner, Mass., Sept. 12, 1932; d. James Quaiel and Mary (Reilly) Lupien; m. Frederick E. Crory, Aug. 21, 1954; children: Thomas, David, Ellen, Ann, Edward, Stephen. AB, U. Mass., 1954; MALS, Dartmouth Coll., 1975. Tchr. Amherst (Mass.) Schs., 1954, Lyme (N.H.) Schs., 1972-76; mem. N.H. Ho. of Reps., 1977-87, 92-96, mem. commerce/consumer affairs com., 1977-87, 93-96, mem. spl. com. on med. malpractice, 1984; exec. dir. Children's Ctr. of Upper Valley, 1986-90. Bd. dirs. Mascoma Savs. Bank. Mem. character and fitness com. N.H. Supreme Ct., 1998-2005; chair N.H. Health Svcs. Planning and Rev. Bd., 1999-2005; bd. dirs. Kendal at Hanover, 2001—. Roman Catholic. Home: 40 Rip Rd Hanover NH 03755-1614

CRORY, MARY, town official; b. Concord, Mass., Sept. 27, 1932; d. Lennart William and Mary Susan (Sullivan) Fougstedt; m. Arthur Donald Crory, Jan. 31, 1953; children: Michael, Patricia, Joanne, Paul, Mary Susan, Mark; m. John W. Leahy, Dec. 22, 2004. Tax collector Town of Littleton, Mass., 1963-99, town clk. Mass., 1976—2003. Sec., St. Anne Sodality, 1960-76. Democrat. Roman Catholic. Avocations: golf, needlepoint. Home: P O Box 216 Littleton MA 01460-0216

CROSBY, DEBORAH BERRY, artist; b. Gulfport, Miss., Oct. 9, 1930; d. Thomas Davis and Deborah Bennett (Hewes) Berry; m. Charles E. McHale Jr., Nov. 23, 1950 (div. 1952); 1 child Deborah Bennett McHale; m. Hueston T. Fortner, Jr., Mar. 17, 1957 (div. 1963); 1 child, Hueston G. Fortner; m. Richard Louis Crosby, Dec. 27, 1981. BA, Sophie Newcomb Coll., 1951; MA, Ind. State U., 1968; postgrad., Utah State U., 1969, Tulane U., 1979; BA (hon.), U. New Orleans, 1984. Educator Wesleyan Coll., Rocky Mt., NC, 1969-70; prof. Spanish, Bay de Noc Coll., Escanaba, Mich., 1970-72; instr. yoga, Spanish, U. So. Miss.-Gulf Park Campus, Long Beach, 1972-78, Miss. Gulf Coast Jr. Coll. Dist., Keesler AFB Ctr., 1972-78; instr. reading, English, Miss. Gulf Coast Jr. Coll. Dist.-Jefferson Davis Campus, Keesler AFB Ctr., 1972-78; freelance artist Metairie, La., 1988—. Vis. artist at various galleries. One-woman shows include Dixie Art Co., Jefferson, La., 1990, World Trade Ctr., New Orleans, 1993—, Reginelli's Eating Gallery, 1994, Marceline Bonorden Fine Arts Gallery, 1998, 1999, Agora Gallery, Soho, N.Y.C., 2000, Movie Pitchers, 2000—01, Ambassador Hotel, New Orleans, 2002—04, Leahy Gardens, Covington, La., 2005, exhibited in group shows at Artists Showroom Gallery, 1993—95, Rivertown Art Gallery, Kenner, La., Slidell Cultural Ctr., La. State Archives, Baton Rouge, La., Martin Hall, U. of Mobile, Ala., George E. Ohr Arts and Cultural Ctr., Biloxi, Miss., Stamford (Conn.) Mus., Havre de Grace (Mich.) Mus., West Wind Gallery, Casper, Wyo., Jefferson SQ, Klamath Falls, Oreg., Destrehan (La.) Plantation, Lexington (Ky.) Mus., Falls River Mills, Calif., Our Lady of the Rosary Gallery, NOLA Pitot Historic Ho., New Orleans, Marceline Bonorden Fine Arts Gallery, Agora Gallery, Soho, NYC, The Purple Mullet Gallery, Ala., Serenity Gallery, The Artisan Mkt., Riverview Gallery, Zigler Art Mus., Jennings La., Amsterdam Whitney Internat. Fine Arts Gallery, Inc., NYC, 2002—06, Regional Art Ctr., Hammond, La., 2004, New Orleans Mus. Art, New Orleans Art Assn. Fine Arts Festival (1st place), St. Charles Art Assn. (1st place), Metairie Art Guild, 1996 (1st place), Oil Met. Art Guild (1st place), Grumbacher (1st, 2d and 3d place, 2002), Rivertown Gallery, Kenner, La., 2005, La. Archives, Baton Rouge, 2006—, Riverstone Gallery, New Orleans, Represented in permanent collections World Trade Ctr., prin. works include Juvenile Diabetes Assn., 2001, Exhibited in group shows at WTC, New Orleans, 1995—2001; designer, executor (cover chess book) The Art of Bisguier, 2003; coloring book for Children's Life on a Louisiana Plantation, 2006. Chmn. auction Heart Ambs., 1995; mem. Ladies Leukemia League, 1994-, program chmn., 1996; mem. Goodwill Industries VS, 1995-2002, BRAVO Ballet, 1995—; spring fiesta hostess Napoleon's Home, Spring Fiesta Assn., 2002, 05; bd. dirs. Profl. Women's Adv. ABI, Inc., 2003, East Jefferson Hosp. Aux., 2005—; active Contemporary Arts Ctr. NOLA, 2003, 05, New Orleans Arts Coun., 2003—; bd. dirs. East Jefferson Gen. Hosp. Aux., 2005—. Named Sweetheart, Local Br. Am. Heart Assn. Heart Ambs., 2001, Hawk as lyricist of Archbishop Nannah's Fight Song, New Orleans; recipient Lyricist award, U. New Orleans, 1984, Spl. Painting award, Winsor-Newton, 1994, Great Lady award, New Orleans Met. area by East Jefferson Hosp. Aux., 2000, Spl. award for lyricist for, Archbishop Hannan Sch. Song, New Orleans, 2006. Mem. Nat. League Am. Pen Women (chaplain 1996—, v.p. 1998-2000), New Orleans Art Assn. (v.p. 1995-98), Le Petit Art Guild (program chair 1995-97, Le Grand chair, 1995-2003, officer 1995-97), St. Charles Art Assn. (pres. 1994-95, Artist of Yr. award 1991-92), Nat. Mus. Women in the Arts, Newcomers Club, East Jefferson Gen. Hosp. Aux. (bd. dirs. 2005-). Avocations: yoga, community activist, languages, travel, songwriting. Home: 5600 Kawanee Ave Metairie LA 70003-1414 Office Phone: 504-455-1275.

CROSBY, JACQUELINE GARTON, newspaper editor, journalist; b. Jacksonville, Fla., May 13, 1961; d. James Ellis and Marianne (Garton) Crosby. ABJ, U. Ga., 1983; MBA, U. Cen. Fla., 1987. Staff writer Macon Telegraph & News, Ga., 1983-84; copy editor Orlando Sentinel, Fla., 1984-85; dir. spl. projects Ivanhoe Communications, Inc., Orlando, Fla., 1987-89; producer spl. projects Sta. KSTP-TV, Mpls., 1989-94; asst. news editor Star Tribune Online, Mpls., 1994—2003, reporter, 2003—. Recipient award for best sports story Ga. Press Assn., 1982; award for best series of yr. AP, 1985, Pulitzer prize, 1985 Mem. Quill Avocations: competing in triathlons, playing electric bass, tutoring, reading. Home: 5348 Drew Ave S Minneapolis MN 55410-2006 Office: Star Tribune 425 Portland Ave Minneapolis MN 55488-0001

CROSBY, JANE WATTS, science educator; b. Fort Myers, Fla., Sept. 10, 1945; m. Michael Crosby, Dec. 12, 1947; children: John Marshall, Kate. BS, Mars Hill Coll., 1967; MEd, U. N.C., Charlotte, 2003. Cert. environ. educator NC Dept of Environment and Natural Resources, 2004. Sci. tchr. South Iredell H.S., Troutman, NC, 1994—2000, Statesville H.S., Statesville, NC, 2000—. Named Environmentalist of the Yr., Keep Am. Beautiful and County. Mem.: Alpha Delta Kappa, Kappa Delta Pi. Office: Statesville High School 474 N Center St Statesville NC 28677 Office Phone: 704-873-3491. E-mail: jwcrosby@iss.k12.nc.us.

CROSBY, KATHRYN GRANDSTAFF (GRANT CROSBY), actress; b. Houston, Nov. 25, 1933; d. Delbert Emery and Olive Catherine (Stokely) Grandstaff; m. Harry L. (Bing) Crosby, Jr., Oct. 24, 1957 (dec. Oct. 1977); children: Harry Lillis III, Mary Frances, Nathaniel Patrick. BFA, U. Tex., 1955; RN, Queens of Angles Sch. Nursing, Los Angeles, 1964; attended, UCLA; teaching credential, Immaculate Heart Coll., L.A., 1965. Actress: in plays including Sunday in New York, 1963, Pygmalion, Sabrina Fair, 1964, Peter Pan, 1965, Arms and the Man, 1965, Mary, Mary, 1966, The Guardsman, 1967, The Prime of Miss Jean Brodie, 1969, Same Time Next Year, 1977-78; films include Rear Window, Unchained, Reprisal, Operation Mad Ball, 1958, others; hostess daily TV talk show, Sta. KPIX, San Francisco; TV appearances Bing Crosby Christmas Specials, Suspense Theater, Ben Casey; Author: Bing and Other Things, 1967, My Life With Bing, 1983; also column Texas Gal in Hollywood, 1952-54. Mem. advisory com. arts State Dept.; Co-chmn. bd. trustees Immaculate Heart Coll.; trustee Eisenhower Med. Center. Named Distinguised Alumae U. Tex., 1969, Rodeo Queen Houston Fatstock Show, 1950 Mem. Am. Conservatory Theatre. Roman Catholic.

CROSBY, LETITIA JORDAN, science educator; b. St. Croix, V.I., Mar. 21, 1975; d. Leonard and Angela Bernadette Jordan; m. Dalton Glenn Crosby, July 17, 1998; children: Dalton Glenn II, Jordan Xavier. BS in Biology and Chemistry, Xavier U., New Orleans, 1997, MEd in Secondary Edn., 1999; EDs in Ednl. Supervision and Adminstrn., Lincoln Meml. U., Harrogate, Tenn., 2003. Tchr. biology Duval County Pub. Schs., Jacksonville, Fla., 1998—2000, Gwinnett County Pub. Schs., Norcross, Ga., 2000—05, Coweta County Pub. Schs., Newnan, Ga., 2005—. Recipient Outstanding Recognition of Tchrs. award, Burger King Corp., 2000. Mem.: NEA, ASCD, Nat. Sci. Tchrs. Assn. Avocations: singing in choir, reading, cooking, baking. Home: 116 Paxton Pl Newnan GA 30263 Office: East Coweta H S 400 McCollum Sharpsburg Rd Sharpsburg GA 30277 Office Phone: 770-254-2850. E-mail: letitia.crosby@cowetaschools.org.

CROSBY, MARENA LIENHARD, retired academic administrator; b. Shreveport, La., Mar. 2, 1948; d. John Joseph and Clara Curtis (Lawton) L.; m. H.W. Patrick Obrien, Sept. 23, 1977; m. John L. Crosby, Nov. 23, 1997. MEd, U. New Orleans; JD, Loyola U., New Orleans. Bar: La. 1971; lic. profl. counselor, La.; diplomate Am. Coll. Profl. Mental Health Practitioners. Instr. Delgado C.C., New Orleans, 1973-80, counselor, 1980-86, coord. testing, 1986-88, dir. admissions, 1988-90, dir. counseling and mktg., 1990-93, dir. degree audit program, 1993-97, asst. to v.p. student affairs, 1997-98, ret., 1998. Mem. DAR, FBA, ACA, Internat. Assn. for New Sci., Assn. for Rsch. and Enlightenment, Am. Psychotherapy Assn., Inst. Noetic Scis., Theosophical Soc. Am., Family Mediation Coun., La. Bar Assn., La. Notary Assn., La. Assn. Spiritual and Religious Values in Counseling, New Orleans Bar Assn., New Orleans Womens Opera Guild, New Orleans Mus. Art, Colonial Dames, Magna Charta Dames. Republican. Avocations: reading, piano. Home: 811 Rue Royal Metairie LA 70005 Personal E-mail: cmloc18@aol.com.

CROSER, MARY DOREEN, educational association executive; b. N.Y.C., June 22, 1944; d. Charles William and Rita Mary (Lalor) C. BS, SUCNY, Buffalo, 1969; MS, Va. Commonwealth U., 1975. Cert. spl. edn., vocat. rehab. counseling tchr. Spl. educator Hampton (Va.) City Schs., 1971-73, dean of students, 1973-75; dir. devel. disabilities svcs. Cmty. Svc. Bd., Portsmouth, Va., 1975-79; assoc. dir. Welfare Rsch. Inc., N.Y.C., 1979-83; asst. dir. Md. Dept. Health and Mental Hygiene, Balt., 1983-88; exec. dir. Am. Assn. on Mental Retardation, Washington, 1988—. Free-lance cons. on disabilities; lectr. on nat. disabilities issues; active Gov.'s Coun. on Devel. Disabilities, 1993—. Contbr. articles to profl. jours. Mem. Gov.'s Com. on Employment of the Handicapped, 1987-88, Pres.'s Com. on Employment of People with Disabilities, 1989-93, adv. com. Pres.'s Com. on Mental Retardation, 1990-91. Fellow Am. Assn. on Mental Retardation (pres. Md. chpt. 1988); mem. Internat. Assn. for Sci. Study of Intellectual Disabilities, Am. Soc. Assn. Execs. Avocations: sailing, photography, music, art, travel. Office: Am Assn on Mental Retardation 444 N Capitol St NW Ste 846 Washington DC 20001-1512 Business E-Mail: dcroser@aamr.org.

CROSKELL, MADELON BYRD, music educator, classical vocalist; b. Ardmore, Okla., Nov. 16, 1937; d. Lyndall Rae Byrd and Avis Madeline Bradshaw; m. Henry Croskell, July 24, 1955; children: Maralyn Lee and Mark Henry Student, U. N.Mex., 1955, S.E. U. Okla., 1956—58; MusB cum laude, U. Mo., St. Louis, 1979. Nat. cert. tchr. music - piano and theory. V.p. Ind. Piano Tchrs. Guild, Indpls., 1964—69, Okla. Music Tchrs. Assn., Bartlesville, 1969—72, St. Louis Area Music Tchrs. Assn., 1974—89; tchr. music, dir. choir Parkway Ctrl. Jr. H.S., St. Louis, 1979—80. Performed 32 oratories with Indpls. Symphonic Choir, St. Louis Symphony; contbr. articles to Mo. Music Tchrs. Notes, 1980-89 Vol. sr. tour guide Mo. Bot. Garden, St. Louis, 1978-89 Mem. Nat. Fedn. Music Clubs (jr. counselor), Music Tchrs. Nat. Assn., Tex. Music Tchrs. Assn., Dallas Music Tchrs. Assn. (bd. dirs., founder Playathon 2004), Richardson Music Tchrs. Assn. (bd. dirs., pres. 1989-2006, founder Playathon 1995-2006), St. Louis Area Music Tchrs. Assn. (founder Music Masters 1984-2006), Sigma Alpha Iota (Sword of Honor award St. Louis chpt., pres. alumnae chpt. 1974-89) Republican. Presbyterian. Avocations: gardening, horseback riding, swimming, reading. Home and Office: 6817 Cliffbrook Dr Dallas TX 75254 Office Phone: 972-233-9990. Personal E-mail: madelonbc88k@earthlink.net.

CROSMER, JANIE LYNN, insurance company executive; b. Sioux City, Iowa, Nov. 8, 1969; d. William J. and Penny Lou Crosmer; m. Scott Thomas Clifford, Feb. 14, 1971. BS, Iowa State U., Ames, 1993; MS, Tex. Woman's U., Denton, 2000, MBA, 2006, post grad., 2002—. Cert. cmty. health edn. specialist The Nat. Commn. Health Edn. Credentialing, Inc., 1997, gen. lines agent Tex. Dept. Ins., 2000. Managed care technician Medicap Pharmacies, Inc., West Des Moines, Iowa, 1993—94; mktg. coord., fitness dir. Sports-Ridge Athletic Club, Richardson, Tex., 1994—95; response Coord., profl. rels. and customer svc. rep. PCA Health Plans Tex., Dallas, 1995—97; sr. client svc. specialist UnitedHealth Group, Plano, Tex., 1997—99; account exec. Waldman Bros., Dallas, 1999—2001; dental strategic account exec. UnitedHealth Group, Plano, Tex., 2001; strategic account exec. Optum, 2006—. Tchg. asst. Tex. Woman's U., Denton, Tex., 2002—. Pres. bd. dirs. Grand Park Estates Homeowners Assn. Named Outstanding Sr. in Cmty. Health Edn., Iowa State U., 1993; recipient Top Dental Sales Achievement award, UnitedHealthcare Dental, 2004, UnitedHealthcare Pinnacle award, 2001; scholar, Iowa State U., 1992. Mem.: Am. Alliance for Health, Phys. Edn., Recreation and Dance, DFW Cyclone Club, Iowa State Alumni Assn. (ambassador). Methodist. Avocations: swimming, exercise, piano, reading. Home: 2021 Cartwright Ct Flower Mound TX 75028 Office: Optum PO Box 9472 Minneapolis MN 55440-9472 Office Phone: 972-874-2062. Home Fax: 972-355-0487. Personal E-mail: jlcrosmer@verizon.net. Business E-Mail: janie_l_crosmer@uhc.com.

CROSON, CHARLOTTE JOANNE, retired language educator; b. Cleve., Mar. 15, 1938; d. Stanley John and Marie Croson. BE cum laude, Kent State U., 1960, MA in English cum laude, 1976. English tchr. New Carlisle Sch. Dist., Ohio, 1960—62, Hayward Unified Sch. Dist., Calif., 1962—68, Monrovia Unified Sch. Dist., Calif., 1968, Glendale Unified Sch. Dist., Calif., 1968—97; ret., 1997. English dept. chair Wilson Jr. HS, Glendale Sch. Dist., 1972—92; mem. curriculum study com. Glendale Unified Sch. Dist., 1972—92. Recipient Outstanding Svc. award, So. Council Tchrs. English, 1974, Increasing Membership award, Calif. Retired Tchrs. Assn., 2003. Mem.: Calif. Retired Tchrs. Assn. (officer 1998—), Inst. Survival Through Design (officer 1980—), Lambda Iota Tau, Gamma Phi Beta (chair, pres. 1959—60). Avocations: travel, reading, piano, hiking. Home: 2440-A Neutra Pl Los Angeles CA 90039

CROSS, CHARLOTTE LORD, retired social worker, artist; b. Andalusia, Ala., Dec. 1, 1941; d. Roy Olice and Laura Emily (Smith) Lord; m. Jack Allen Cross, May 5, 1960; children: Jack Allen III, James Duane, Jeffrey Miles. BA in English, Auburn U., Montgomery, Ala., 1979, MS in Psychology, 1980, MS in Secondary Edn./English, 1993. Social worker dept. human resources State of Ala., Andalusia, 1980—2002; ret., 2002. Tchr. English conservation Nat. Cancer Inst. Rsch. Scientists, Tokyo, 1965—66; adj. instr. psychology Lurieen B. Wallace State Jr. Coll., 1988—98, Troy State U., Ft. Rucker, 1991; owner Capriccio's Coffee Bar; portrait artist. Recipient Commr.'s Merit award, Dept. Human Resources, 1989. Baptist. Home: PO Box 1364 Andalusia AL 36420-1364

CROSS, DOROTHY ABIGAIL, retired librarian; b. Bangor, Mich., Sept. 9, 1924; d. John Laird and Alice Estelle (Wilcox) C. BA, Wayne State U., 1956; MA in Libr. Sci., U. Mich., 1957. Jr. libr. Detroit Pub. Libr., 1957-59; adminstrv. libr. U.S. Army, Braconne, France, 1959-61, Poitiers, France, 1961-63, area libr. supr., 1963, asst. commd. libr. Kaiserslautern, Germany, 1963-67, acquisitions libr. Aschaffenburg, Germany, 1967, Munich, 1967-69, sr. staff libr. specialist, 1969-72, commd. libr. Stuttgart, Germany, 1972-75, dep. staff libr. Heidelberg, Germany, 1975-77; chief libr. 18th Airborne Corps and Ft. Bragg, N.C., 1977-79; chief ADP sect. Pentagon Libr., Washington, 1979-80, chief readers svcs. br., 1980-83, dir., 1983-91. Mem. ALA, U. Mich. Alumni Assn., Delta Omicron. United Methodist. Home: 6511 Delia Dr Alexandria VA 22310-2609 E-mail: dacross@starpower.net.

CROSS, E. ASHLEY, special education educator; b. Benton, Ill., Aug. 24, 1979; d. Jack Dean and Kerrie Anne Stewart; m. Ryan Lee Cross, Oct. 9, 2004. AA, Rend Lake Coll., Ina, IL, 1999; BS, Murray State U., Ky., 2001; MEd, Olivet Nazarene U., Bourbonnais, Ill., 2005. Cert. Elem. and Spl. Edn. Ill., 2002. Tchr. behavior disorders Franklin Jefferson Spl. Edn. Coop., Benton, 2001—02; tchr. kindergarten Vienna Grade Sch., Ill., 2002—04; resource tchr. mid. sch. Grant Park Mid. Sch., Ill., 2004—. R-Consevative. Baptist.

CROSS, EUNICE D., elementary school educator; b. Foley, Minn, May 28, 1932; d. William Joseph and Elizabeth Agnes Latterell; m. Alan Viking Cross; children: Carol, Michael, Mari, Elizabeth, Jon, Catherine. BS, St. Cloud State U., 1956, MS, 1964. Rural sch. tchr. Dist. Common Sch. 51, North Benton, Minn., 1958-59; tchr. 4th grade Ind. Dist. 51, Foley, 1960-64, tchr. 1st grade, 1964-66, tchr. 6th grade, 1966-85, Chpt. I tchr., 1985-96, chairperson Chpt. 1 dept., 1986—98. Sec. Benton unit Am. Cancer Soc., 1985—89, pres., 1989—2006, daffodil chair, 1986—2006; active Foley Pub. Sch. Bd., 1999—2006, treas., 2001—04, v.p., 2005, chair, 2006; active Foley Connection Team, 1987—99, Foley Found., 2003—04. Recipient Leadership in Edn. Excellence award Ctrl. Minn. Edn. Rsch., 1996. Mem.: Minn. Sch. Bd. Assn. (del. to assembly 2003—06, bd. dirs. 2004—05), Ret. Tchr. Assn. Ctrl. Minn. (v.p. 1998—2003, bd. dirs. 2004—05), Foley Edn. Assn. (pres. 1970—85, Tchr. of Yr. 1971). Democrat. Roman Catholic. Home: 50 6th Ave Foley MN 56329 E-mail: alanv@cloudnet.com.

CROSS, GOLDIE K., telecommunications engineer; b. Grosse Pointe, Mich., Aug. 4, 1955; d. William Issac Fowler and Garnet Christine Potter; m. Jamie John Cross, June 30, 1983 (div. May 1991). AAS in Electronics Engring. Tech., Macomb C.C., Warren, Mich., 1985; BAS in Electronics Engring. Tech., Sienna Heights Coll., 1992. Sec. Alexander & Alexander, Detroit, 1973-74; stage technician Detroit Pub. Schs., 1974-78, audio-visual technician, 1978-82, tchr. electronics and telecomm., 1982-87; telecomm. specialist Mich. Bell-Ameritech, Dearborn, 1987-96; network engr. I and II Bakersfield (Calif.) Cellular, 1996—2000; network engr. III Bell South Mobility, Birmingham, Ala., 1998—2000; prin. mem. tech. staff Cingular Wireless, Atlanta, 2000—05, network sales support mgr. Hawaii Honolulu, 2000—. Chair tech. ops. com. Mich. Emergency Patrol-REACT, Detroit, 1979-84; past mem. Mich. Woman's Missionary Union, state rec. sec., 1995-97, Calif. Woman's Missionary Union, Calif. Girls in Action Cons., 1997-98. Recipient letter of commendation FBI, Bakersfield, 1998. Mem. Ala. Woman's Missionary Union (missions edn. vol.). Republican. Baptist. Avocations: scuba diving, bowling, travel, flying, photography. Office Phone: 818-627-8686. E-mail: goldie.cross@cingular.com.

CROSS, JOAN RUSSIN, medical technologist; b. Wilkes-Barre, Pa., July 11, 1935; d. Harry S. Russin and Helen R. Ralick; m. George A. Cross, Feb. 3, 1957; children: Gregory G., Jennifer G. Med. tech., Wilkes Coll., Wilkes-Barre, Pa., 1955, Jefferson Med. Coll. Sch., Phila., Pa., 1956. Cert. Med. Technologist ASCP, 1956. Med. technologist Mercy Hosp., Wilkes-Barre, Pa., 1956—57, Allentown Hosp., Allentown, Pa., 1960—62, Mercy Hosp., Wilkes-Barre, Pa., 1962—63; med. technologist, hemotology dept. head St. Francis Hospital, New Castle, Pa., 1967—2002. Pres. Jr. Women's Club, 1967—68; chmn. Lawrence County March of Dimes, Lawrence, 1968. Mem.: Fedn. Jr. (pres. 1976—77, Named Jr. Women of the Yr. 1968), La. Co. Garden Club (pres. 1996—98), New Castle Coll. Club. Avocations: music, bridge, needlecrafts, gardening.

CROSS, KATHRYN PATRICIA, education educator; b. Normal, Ill., Mar. 17, 1926; d. Clarence L. and Katherine (Dague) C. BS, Ill. State U., Normal, 1948; MA, U. Ill., Urbana, 1951, PhD, 1958; LLD (hon.), Ill. State U., 1970; DS (hon.), Northeastern U., Boston, 1975; HHD (hon.), Grand Valley State Colls., Mich., 1975; D in Pedagogy (hon.), Our Lady of Lake U., Tex., 1977; LHD (hon.), Hood Coll., Md., 1979; DS (hon.), Loyola U., Chgo., 1980; LHD (hon.), Marymount Manhattan Coll., NY, 1982, Coll. St. Mary, 1985, De Paul U., Chgo., 1986, Thomas Jefferson U., Pa., 1987; LittD (hon.), SUNY, 1988; DHL (hon.), Open U., The Netherlands, 1989; LHD (hon.), Rider Coll., NJ, 1992, U. Mass., Lowell, 1995, Coll. Lifelong Learning, NH, 1999. Math. tchr. Harvard (Ill.) Community High Sch., 1948-49; rsch. asst. dept. psychology U. Ill., Urbana, 1949-53, asst. dean of women, 1953-59; dean of women then dean of students Cornell U., Ithaca, N.Y., 1959-63; dir. coll. and univ. programs Ednl. Testing Svc., Princeton, N.J., 1963-66; rsch. educator Ctr. R&D in Higher Edn. U. Calif., Berkeley, 1966-77; rsch. scientist, sr. rsch. psychologist, dir. univ. programs Ednl. Testing Svc., Berkeley, 1966-80; prof. edn., chair dept. adminstrn., planning & social policy Harvard U., Cambridge, Mass., 1980-88; Elizabeth and Edward Conner prof. edn. U. Calif., Berkeley, 1988-94, David Pierpont Gardner prof. higher edn., 1994-96. Mem. sec. adv. com. on automated personal data sys. Dept. HEW, 1972-73; del. to Soviet Union, Seminar on Problems in Higher Edn., 1975; vis. prof. U. Nebr., 1975-76; vis. scholar Miami-Dade CC, 1987; trustee Berkeley Pub. Libr., 1998-2002; spkr., cons. in field; bd. dirs. Elderhostel, 1999-; nat. adv. bd. Ctr. for First-Year Experience, 2000-. Author: Beyond the Open Door: New Students to Higher Education, 1971 (Sch. and Soc. Outstanding Books in Edn. award, 1971); author: (with S. B. Gould) Explorations in Non-Traditional Study, 1972; author: (with J. R. Valley and Assocs.) Planning Non-Traditional Programs: An Analysis of the Issues for Postsecondary Education, 1974; author: Accent on Learning, 1976 (Am. Coun. Edn. Borden medal, 1976), Adults as Learners, 1981; author: (with Thomas A. Angelo) Classroom Assessment Techniques, 1993; author: (with Mimi Harris Steadman) Classroom Research, 1996; author: (with Elizabeth Barkley and Claire Major) Collaborative Learning Techniques: A Handbook for College Faculty, 2005; contbr. articles, monographs to profl. publs., chapters to books; mem. editl. bd. several ednl. jours., cons. editor (ednl. mag.) Change, 1980—. Active Nat. Acad. Edn., 1975—, Coun. for Advancement of Exptl. Learning, 1982-85; trustee Bradford Coll., Mass., 1986-88, Antioch Coll., Yellow

Springs, Ohio, 1976-78; mem. nat. adv. bd. Nat. Ctr. of Study of Adult Learning, Empire State Coll.; mem. nat. adv. bd. Okla. Bd. Regents; mem. higher edn. rsch. program Pew Charitable Trusts; mem. vis. com. Harvard Grad. Sch. Edn., 1998—; bd. dirs. Elderhostel, 1999—; trustee Berkeley Pub. Libr., 1999—, Carnegie Found., 1999—. Named to Hall of Fame, Internat. Adult and Continuing Edn., 1997; recipient Leadership award, Assn. Continuing Higher Edn., 2000, Lifetime Contbns. to Learning Assistance and Devel. Edn. award, Am. Coun. Devel. Edn., 2000, Morris Keeton award, Coun. For Adult Exptl. Learning, 2005, Tchrs. Coll. medal, Columbia U., 2006. Fellow League for Innovation in CC (nat. adv. bd. Learning Coll. Project 2000-); mem. Am. Assn. Higher Edn. (bd. dirs. 1987—, pres. 1975, chair 1989-90), Am. Assn. Comty. and Jr. Colls. (vice chair commn. of future comty. colls.), Carnegie Found. Advancement of Tchg. (adv. com. on classification of colls. and univs., trustee 1998-), Nat. Ctr. for Devel. Edn. (adv. bd.), New Eng. Assn. Schs. and Colls. (commn. on instns. higher edn. 1982-86), Am. Coun. Edn. (commn. on higher edn. and adult learner 1986-88). Business E-Mail: patcross@berkeley.edu.

CROSS, MARCIA, actress; b. Marlborough, Mass., Mar. 25, 1962; d. Mark and Janet Cross; m. Mahoney Tom Cross, June 24, 2006. Grad., Julliard Sch., NYC; M in Psycology, Antioch U., LA, Calif. Actress (TV series) The Edge of Night, 1984, One Life to Live, 1986—87, Another World, 1986, Knots Landing, 1991—92, Melrose Place, 1992—93, 1994—97, Everwood, 2003—04, Desperate Housewives, 2004— (Screen Actors Guild Award for outstanding performance by an ensemble in a comedy series, 2005, 2006), (TV films) Brass, 1985, The Last Days of Frank and Jesse James, 1986, Pros & Cons, 1986, Almost Grown, 1988, Storm and Sorrow, 1990, M.A.N.T.I.S, 1994, All She Ever Wanted, 1996, Target Earth, 1998, Eastwick, 2002, (TV miniseries) George Washington II: The Forging of a Nation, 1986, (films) Bad Influence, 1990, Ripple, 1995, Female Perversions, 1996, Always Say Goodbye, 1996, Dancing in September, 2000, Living in Fear, 2001, Bank, 2002, The Wind Effect, 2003; performer: (plays) La Ronde, Twelfth Night, Gentleman of Verona; guest appearances Tales From the Darkside, 1986, Cheers, 1989, 1990, Booker, 1989, "Who's the Boss?", 1989, Doctor Doctor, 1989, Quantum Leap, 1990, Jake and the Fatman, 1991, Murder, She Wrote, 1992, Herman's Head, 1992, Raven, 1993, Ned and Stacey, Burke's Law, 1995, Seinfeld, 1997, The Outer Limits, 1999, Boy Meets World, 1999, Touched by an Angel, 1999, Profiler, 2000, Spin City, 2000, Ally McBeal, 2000, Strong Medicine, 2001, CSI: Crime Scene Investigation, 2001, The King of Queens, 2002, 2003, Life & Style, 2004, "Corazón, Corazón", 2005. Address: Desperate Housewives Touchstone Television 100 Universal City Plaza Bldg 2128 Ste G Universal City CA 91608

CROSS, MEREDITH B., lawyer; b. Oct. 14, 1957; BA cum laude, Duke Univ., 1979; JD, Vanderbilt Univ., 1982. Bar: Ga. 1983, DC 1998. Law clk. Judge Albert J. Henderson, US Ct. Appeals (11th cir.); atty. fellow Div. Corp. Fin., SEC, Washington, 1990—92, chief counsel, 1992—94, assoc. dir., Internat. Corp. Fin. & Small Bus. sect., 1994, dep. dir., 1994—98; ptnr. Wilmer Cutler Pickering Hale & Dorr, Washington, 1998—, co-chmn. Corp. dept. Frequent speaker at securities law conferences. Mem.: Order of the Coif. Office: Wilmer Cutler Pickering Hale & Dorr 1899 Pennsylvania Ave NW Washington DC 20006 Mailing: WIlmer Cutler Pickering Hale & Dorr 2445 M St NW Washington DC 20037 Office Phone: 202-663-6644. Office Fax: 202-663-6363. Business E-Mail: meredith.cross@wilmerhale.com.

CROSS, NADINE DEBRA-ANN, pharmacist; b. Santa Cruz, Jamaica, W.I., Mar. 7, 1965; d. Nigel Bartley and Gertrude Thelwell; m. Ellsworth Alton Cross, Feb. 15, 1991; children: Renae Simone, Jovan Barrington. Diploma in pharmacy, Coll. Arts, Sci. and Tech., Mona, Jamaica, 1988; diploma in comp. program, Morse Sch. Bus., Conn., 1990; BSc in Pharmacy summa cum laude, U. Conn., 1995. Registered pharmacist, Conn. Staff pharmacist Mt. Sinai Hosp., Hartford, Conn., 1995-97; pharmacist NeighborCare Pharmacy, Windsor, Conn., 1997-99; pharmacy mgr. JP Rogers Pharmacy, Hartford, 1999—. Career counselor Weaver H.S., Hartford, 1997. Mem. Am. Pharm. Assn., Conn. Pharmacist Assn., Rho Chi. Seventh-Day Adventist. Avocations: photography, reading. Home: 392 Mile Hill Rd Tolland CT 06084-3605 Office: J P Rogers Pharmacy 100 Wells St Ste 1E Hartford CT 06103-2920

CROSS, RUTH CHAIKEN, retired educational administrator; b. Irvington, N.J., Mar. 22, 1941; d. Edward and Miriam (Rothman) Chaiken; m. Arnold Gross, July 4, 1960; children: Ira, Allen. BA in Edn., Newark State Coll., N.J., 1962; collateral in Judaic studies, Kean Coll. of N.J., 1987. Cert. religious tchr., cert. prin. Tchr. Temple Sinai, Summit, NJ, 1966-76, Temple Emanu-El, Westfield, NJ, 1972-77, Temple Beth-El, Cranford, NJ, 1975-78; dir. high sch. program Temple Beth Ahm, Springfield, NJ, 1975-85; dir. edn. Congregation Beth Israel, 1985—2006; ret., 2006. Co-author: Ulpan for the Afternoon Hebrew School, 1991. Mem. N.J. Region Commn. on Jewish Edn., United Synagogue of Am. publs. com., Jewish Fedn. of Ctrl. N.J. edn. com.; founding mem. Project Manna; co-chair Soviet Jewry Action Com. Ctrl. N.J. Fedn.; mem. cmty. svcs. com. Nat. Conf. on Soviet Jewry; chair Profl. Educators Com. Jewish Fedn. Ctrl. N.J. Recipient Chai award Jewish Edn. Assn., 1985, Cmty. Svcs. award Jewish Federation Ctrl. N.J., 1999, Vol. of Yr., 2006, Nathan H. Winter Profl. Excellence award N.J. Region United Synagogue, 2005. Mem. Coalition for Advancement Jewish Edn. (charter), Coun. for Jewish Edn., Jewish Educator's Assembly, Assn. Jewish Spl. Educators, Women's League for Conservative Judaism.

CROSS, WILDA SUE, secondary school educator; b. Waurika, Okla., Oct. 25, 1952; d. Clyde Franklin and Mary Wilda (Fulton) C. BA, Southea. State Coll., Durant, Okla., 1974; MS, Emporia State U., 1986. Tchr. English and fgn. lang. Unified Sch. Dist. 322, Onaga, Kans., 1975-80; tchr. English, fgn. langs. and forensics Consol. Unified Sch. Dist. 101, Erie, Kans., 1980—. Mem. NEA, Nat. Coun. Tchrs. of English, Kans. Speech Comm. Assn.

CROSSER, CARMEN LYNN, marriage and family therapist, social worker, consultant; b. Iowa Falls, Iowa, Jan. 17, 1970; d. Gary Laverne Sr. and Karen Dorothy (Ulrich) C. AA, Ellsworth C.C., 1990; BS, Iowa State U., 1993; MSW, U. Iowa, 1995; PhD, U. Chgo., 2006. Lic. clin. social worker, marriage and family thrapist, Ill.; ACSW. Grad. teaching asst. U. Iowa, Iowa City, 1994-95; mental health therapy intern Mid-Eastern Cmty. Mental Health Ctr., Iowa City, 1994-95; clin. social worker Sinnissippi Ctrs., Inc., Dixon, Ill., 1995-97; family therapist Ctr. for Counseling, DeKalb, Ill., 1997—2005; pvt. practice DeKalb, 2005—, St. Charles, Ill., 2005—. Cons. sexual abuse svcs. Sinnissippi Ctrs. Inc., 1997—98; rsch. asst. U. Chgo., 1998—2000, tchg. asst., 1999—2001; revs. asst. Jour. of Marital and Family Therapy, 1999—2000; adj. prof. Dominican U., River Forest, Ill., 2002—, Am. Family Therapy Acad., 2003—. Mem. Dekalb Area Women's Ctr., 1997—2000; mem. instnl. rev. bd. No. Ill. U., DeKalb, 1997—2000. All-Am. scholar, 1995. Mem. ACA, NASW, NOW, Am. Soc. Prevention Cruelty Animals (voting mem.), Am. Assn. Marriage and Family Therapy (clin. mem.), Am. Coll. Counselors, Internat. Assn. Marriage and Family Counselors, Ill. Soc. Clin. Social Work, Assn. Play Therapy, Nat. Fedn. Socs. for Clin. Social Work, Golden Key, Phi Kappa Phi, Phi Alpha. Office: 400 E Hillcrest Dr Ste 100A Dekalb IL 60115 Office Phone: 630-845-1529. Business E-Mail: c-crosser@uchicago.edu.

CROSSLAND, MARY HELEN, language educator; d. James and Estella Campbell; 1 child, Dawn Felice. BS, Prairie View A&M Coll., Tex., 1965; MEd, Prairie View A&M U., Tex., 1977. Tchr. Dallas Sch. Dist., 1969—71, tchr. English as 2d lang., 1971—2005, bilingual tchr., 2005—. Chair instructural leadership Donald Sch., Dallas, 1997—2002, chair grade level, 1980—2003, acad. coach, 2001—06. Sec. Missin Bd. BBC, Dallas, 1980—2006. Recipient Golden Oak award, Oak Cliff C. of C., 1987. Democrat. Evangelical. Avocations: reading, gardening, numismatics, movies, walking. Home: 3733 Olney Ct Dallas TX 75241 Office: L O Donald Sch 1218 Phiney Ave Dallas TX 75211

CROSSLEY, DOLLY MADENA JOHNSTON, retired elementary school educator; b. Tex., Jan. 21, 1934; d. Glenn Harrison and Abbie Elizabeth (Snipes) Johnston; 1 child, Elizabeth Lorraine Draper. BS, U. North Tex., Denton, 1955, MEd, 1969; postgrad., U. North Tex., 1970—87. English, phys. educator Ft. Worth Ind. Sch. Dist.; tchr. 5th grade Highland Park Ind. Sch. Dist., Dallas; ret. Substitute tchr. Highland Park Ind. Sch. Dist., Dallas; presenter in field. Author: numerous poems. Active First United Meth. Ch., Ft. Worth. Named Tchr. of Yr., U. Park Elem., Dallas, 1984, Highland Park Ind. Sch. Dist., Dallas, 1985, U. North Tex., Denton, 1990; grantee, Freedom's Found., Dallas, 1982. Mem.: Delta Kappa Gamma (Chpt. Achievement award 1989). Republican. Methodist. Avocations: writing, reading, classical music.

CROSSLEY, HELEN MARTHA, public opinion analyst, research consultant; b. Phila., Sept. 8, 1921; d. Archibald Maddock and Dorothy (Fox) C BA Govt. cum laude, Harvard U., 1942; MA Social Sci. and Pub. Opinion, U. Denver, 1948; postgrad., Heidelberg U., Germany, Am. U., Washington, George Washington U., Yonsei U., Korea. Jr. info. analyst Office War Info., Washington, 1942—43; rsch. specialist, bus. analyst War Food Adminstrn., Washington, 1943—45; data analyst, field supr. Crossley Inc., N.Y.C., 1945—47; from grad. rsch. asst. to sr. analyst Opinion Rsch. Ctr. U. Denver, 1947—49; from study dir. to chief attitude rsch. br. Dept. Def., Heidelberg, Germany, 1950—53; sec., treas., v.p., pres., project dir. ArchCross Assocs., Inc., Princeton, NJ, 1954—85; survey specialist U.S. Info. Agy., Washington, 1955—60, rsch. specialist, 1979—92, ret., 1992; tng. evaluation officer Internat. Coop. Adminstrn., Seoul, 1960—63; ind. cons. Princeton, 1964—78. Trustee Gallup Internat. Inst., Princeton, 1995-99; co-organizer Korean Soc. for Social Sci. Rsch., 1961-62; technical dir. Nat. Coun. Pub. Polls, 1969-71; rsch. cons., 1993— Author: Highlights of Population Shifts, 1944, Evaluation Survey of Korea/U.S. Participant Training Program, 1955-60, 1963; co-author: (with Don Cahalan and Ira Cisin) American Drinking Practices, 1970; contbr. articles to profl. jours Sec., treas., pres. Penzance Players, Woods Hole, Mass., 1939-45 Recipient Ann Radcliffe scholarship Radcliffe Coll., 1938, Cert. Appreciation Korean Ministry Pub. Info., 1962, Merit Cert. Nat. Safety Coun., 1965, Career Achievement award, U.S. Info. Agy., 1992 Mem. AAUW, AARP, NOW, Am. Assn. Pub. Opinion Rsch. (pres. Washington chpt. 1956, 77-78, councillor-at-large 1970-72, sec., treas. 1973-75, conf. com. 1994-95, endowment com. 2003-06), World Assn. Pub. Opinion Rsch. (sec., treas. v.p., conf. chmn., pres. 1960-62, historian 1993-2003), Princeton PC Users Group, U.S. Info. Agy. Alumni Assn., Harvard Club Princeton, Harvard Club Wash., Women's Coll. Club (scholarship prize 1938), Woods Hole Yacht Club, Nassau Club Avocations: travel, photography, music, sailing, history. Home and Office: 21 Battle Rd Princeton NJ 08540-4901 Office Phone: 609-924-0848.

CROSSLEY, NANCY RUTH, retired federal agency administrator; b. San Jose, Feb. 2, 1944; d. Edward and Ruth Flesher Crossley. Grad., San Francisco Bus. Sch., 1964. Adminstr. U.S. Geol. Survey, Menlo Park, Calif., 1965—88, internat. program specialist Reston, Va., 1988—89, Menlo Park, Calif., 1989—97, ret., 1997. Sec. Nat. Heart Inst., Taipei, Taiwan, 1962—63. Vol. Lee Meml. Health Sys., Cape Coral, Fla., 2001—02. Avocations: travel, swimming, games, puzzles.

CROSSWHITE, JEANETTE ELVIRA, art educator; b. Halifax County, Va., Nov. 2, 1941; d. Miles Emory Elder and Elise Elizabeth Guthrie; m. Dean Harlow Crosswhite, Dec. 27, 1968. B in Music Edn., Longwood Coll., Farmville, Va., 1964; B in Ch. Music, So. Bapt. Theol. Sem., Louisville, 1966, M in Ch. Music, 1967; PhD in Music Edn., U. N.C., Greensboro, 1996. Assoc. prof. music Milligan Coll., Milligan College, Tenn., 1967—93, chair music dept., 1983—91; music cons. Tenn. Dept. Edn., Nashville, 1994—99, dir. arts edn., 2000—. Dean Tenn. Arts Acad., Nashville, 2000—; liaison to Tenn. Art Edn. Assn., 2000—, Tenn. Music Edn. Assn.; facilitator Arts Suprs. of Tenn., 2000—; bd. dirs. Tenn. Performing Arts Ctr., Nashville; evaluator Tenn. Bd. Examiners, 1999—; columnist Tenn. Musician, 1994—. Vol. Reach to Recovery, Am. Cancer Soc., Nashville, 1998—. Mem.: Tenn. Music Edn. Assn., Tenn. Art Edn. Assn. (Adminstr. of Yr. award 2005), Nat. Ednl. Theatre Assn., Nat. Art Edn. Assn., Music Educators Nat. Conf. (local chair for nat. conf. 2002), Tenn. Assn. of Dance (Dance Adv. of Yr. 2005), Sigma Alpha Iota. Avocations: walking, crocheting, knitting, cooking. Office: Tenn Dept Edn Andrew Johnson Tower 5th fl 710 James Robertson Pkwy Nashville TN 37243 Office Phone: 615-532-6278. Business E-Mail: jeanette.crosswhite@state.tn.us.

CROST, KATHARINE I., lawyer; b. Bryn Mawr, Pa., 1952; BM cum laude, Mich. State U., 1974; JD, U. Va., 1978. Bar: N.Y. 1979, U.S. Dist. Ct., So. Dist. N.Y, U.S. Dist. Ct., Ea. Dist. N.Y. Ptnr. Orrick, Herrington & Sutcliffe LLP, N.Y.C., chairperson structured fin. group. Mem.: Am. Secularization Forum. Office: Orrick Herrington & Sutcliffe LLP 666 Fifth Ave New York NY 10103 Office Fax: 212-506-5151, 212-506-5070. Business E-Mail: kcrost@orrick.com.

CROSTHWAITE, DIANE LOUISE, secondary school educator; d. Russell Elmer and Alberta Marie Shepherd; m. Kevin Rae Crosthwaite; children: Candy Lynn Brown, Mark Henry, George Russell, Natalie Marie Watkins, Peter Shepherd. BSc in Microbiology, Ohio State U., Columbus, 1975; MEd, U. Dayton, Ohio, 1998. Cert. profl. educator Ohio Dept. Edn. Technician dept. microbiology Ohio State U., Columbus, 1975—77; med. technologist Meml. Hosp. Union County, Marysville, Ohio, 1980—83; tchr. North Union HS, Richwood, Ohio, 1992—. Elder, deacon, Sunday sch. tchr. First Presbyn. Ch., Marysville, 1977—2006. Grantee, Ohio Sch.-To-Work, 1997. Mem.: Nat. Assn. Sci. Tchrs., Nat. Assn. Biology Tchrs. Presbyterian. Avocations: reading, travel, trivia, theater. Office Phone: 740-943-3012.

CROTEAU, PATRICIA A., nursing case manager; b. Barre, Vt., June 14, 1949; d. Augustus Guido Storti and Geraldine Lucy Sayers; m. David Armand Croteau, May 16, 1969; children: Karen, David. Diploma in nursing, Henry Heywood Sch. Nursing, Gardner, Mass., 1970. RN; cert. case mgmt. Staff nurse/charge nurse hosps., N.H., Mass., Md., Vt., 1970-88; case mgr. utilization rev. Lincoln Nat. Ins. Co., Pleasanton, Calif., 1989-92; case mgr. United Health Care, Long Beach, Calif., 1992—. Avocations: swimming, reading, alternative medicine. Home: 503 Springbrook N Irvine CA 92614-7561 Office: United Healthcare 180 E Ocean Blvd Ste 500 Long Beach CA 90802-4708

CROTTA, ANNETTE GUNTER, retired educator; b. Brunswick, Ga., Sept. 24, 1930; d. William Van and Cora Mae (Young) Gunter; m. William Jackson Saunders, Dec. 11, 1948 (dec. Dec. 1977); m. Joseph Louis Crotta, June 2, 1989; children: Amanda Lou Aycock, Michael William. BS, Ga. State U., 1971, M in Bus. Edn., 1978, EdS, 1991. Billing clerk Hoffman-LaRoche Inc., Decatur, Ga., 1965-66; statis. asst. TB program Ctr. Disease Control, Atlanta, 1966-68; educator Blayton Bus. Coll., Atlanta, 1971-72, Fulton County Bd. Edn., Roswell, Ga., 1972-94; ret., 1994. Cons. Crotta Cons. Svcs., Roswell, 1980—; tech. coord. Roswell H.S., 1990-94. Recipient Outstanding Svc. award Ga. Vocat. Assn., 1979, 81; named Educator of Yr. 5th Congressional Dist., 1977, 81. Mem. DAR, Nat. Bus. Edn. Assn., Am. Soc. Curriculum Devel., Ga. Bus. Edn. Assn., Delta Pi Epsilon, Mu Rho Sigma. Republican. Episcopalian. Avocations: travel, golf, opera. Home: 721 Fairway Dr Jasper GA 30143-7257

CROTTO, DENICE, elementary school educator; b. Bell, Calif., Sept. 15, 1946; d. James Maurice Johnson and Eunice Elaine Brown; m. James Nicholas Crotto, Dec. 21, 1963; children: James Bradley Crotto, Denein Elaine Cusack. BS Elem. Edn. cum laude, S. Oregon U., 1986; MA in Counseling and Guidance, Pacific Lutheran U., 1994. Tchr. Franklin Pierce Sch. Dist., Tacoma, 1987-2000. Mem. AAUW, Humane Soc., Audubon, Kappa Delta Pi, Phi Kappa Phi. Democrat. Roman Catholic. Home: 9218 Milton Ave Gig Harbor WA 98332-1085 Office: Franklin Pierce Sch Dist 315 129th St S Tacoma WA 98444-5099

CROTTY, LADONNA DEANE, librarian; b. Williamson, W.Va., July 22, 1939; d. Kenneth B. and M. Virginia (Parcell) Crockett; m. Robert E. Crotty, Nov. 25, 1959; 4 children. BA, Marshall U., 1960. English instr. Northwest HS, McDermott, Ohio, 1976—79; media specialist, libr. Valley Mid. Sch., Lucasville, Ohio, 1979—. Mem.: NEA, Valley Tchrs. Assn., Ohio Edn. Assn. Home: 228 Pleasant Dr Lucasville OH 45648-9008 Office: Valley Mid Sch 393 Indian Dr Lucasville OH 45648

CROTTY, TERI, education educator; b. South Bend, Ind., June 10, 1950; d. Grayson Michael and Alice Elizabeth (Schneider) C. BS in Elem. Edn., Ind. U., 1972, MS Counseling and Guidance, 1981, PhD in Ednl. Psychology, 1992. Lic. elem. and cert. middle sch. tchr. Tchr. Edwardsburg and Cass Dist., Mich., 1972-75; cost analyst Bendix Corp., South Bend, Ind., 1975-81; career counselor Ind. U., South Bend, 1981-83, asst. dir. bus. outplacement svc. Bloomington, 1983-86, assoc. dir., 1987, assoc. instr. South Bend, 1988-90; asst. prof. U. Wis., River Falls, 1990-95, asst. dean, assoc. prof., 1995—, prof., coord. internat. program, 2004—. Vis. prof. Ind. U., Bloomington, 1990, 91; presenter in field. Grantee 3M, 1991, U. Wis., 1991. Mem. ASCD, APA, Am. Ednl. Rsch. Assn. (divsn. K), Am. Assn. of Colls. for Tchr. Edn. Democrat. Avocations: swimming, bicycling, skiing. Office: U Wis River Falls Wyman Edn Bldg River Falls WI 54022

CROUCHET, KATHLEEN HUNT, elementary school educator, reading educator; b. Dec. 30, 1946; d. Abram Davis Sr. and May (Botsay) Hunt; m. Courtland Adam Crouchet, Sr., Feb. 5, 1966; children: Chantelle C. McInerney, Courtland Adam. BS in Elem. Edn., Our Lady of Holy Cross, New Orleans, 1983; MEd in Curriculum and Instrn., U. New Orleans, 1990, PhD in Curriculum and Instrn., 1998. Cert. reading specialist, supr. student tchg., parish and city sch. supervision of instrn. tchr. assessment, elem. and secondary prin., La. Tchr. Archdiocesan Schs., Arabi, La., 1965-84, Orleans Parish Schs., New Orleans, 1984-94, St. Bernard Parish Schs., Chalmette, La., 1994-97; reading instr. Nunez C.C., Chalmette, 1996—. Lectr., cons. Our Lady of Holy Cross Coll., New Orleans; adj. asst. prof. U. New Orleans; participant Model Career Option program State of La., New Orleans, 1991-92; tchr. assessor State of La., St. Bernard, 1994—; curriculum writer St. Bernard Parish Schs., 1997; cooperating tchr. U. New Orleans, 1989-90, 94; insvc. lectr. Co-author: Teacher Professionalism and Leadership in Louisiana, 1992. Moderator, 4-H Cleanest Parish Competition, St. Bernard, 1995. Mem. ASCD, Internat. Reading Assn., Nat. Coun. Tchrs. English, La. Middle Sch. Assn., Phi Delta Kappa, Kappa Delta Pi (historian, sec.). Avocations: reading, travel, gardening. Office: Nunez CC 3700 La Fontaine St Chalmette LA 70043-1249 Home: 14244 Riverlake Dr Covington LA 70435-5786

CROUGHAN, MARY, medical educator; BS in Cmty. Health, U. Calif., Davis, 1982; PhD in Epidemiology, Johns Hopkins U. Sch. Hygiene and Pub. Health, 1987. Asst. rsch. epidemiologist dept. family and cmty. medicine U. Calif., San Francisco, 1987—88, hon. postdoctoral fellow Pew health policy prog. at Inst. Health Policy Studies, 1987—89, asst. adj. prof. depts. family and cmty. medicine and epidemiology and biostatistics, 1989—96, assoc. prof., 1996—, prof., 2002—04, prof. dept. ob-gyn. and reproductive scis. and epidemiology and biostatistics, 2004—. Vice chair dept. family and cmty. medicine U. Calif., San Francisco, 1999—2004. Contbr. articles to profl. jours. Recipient RESOLVE No. Calif. Vol. of Yr. award, 1998. Office: Comprehensive Cancer Ctr U Calif San Francisco Box 1793 San Francisco CA 94143-1793 E-mail: mary.croughan@ucsfmedctr.org.*

CROUSE, CAROL K. MAVROMATIS, elementary school educator; d. George and Helen Mavromatis; m. David Crouse (dec. Dec. 1998). BS in Edn., Temple U., 1972, MEd in Curriculum and Instrn., 1981. Elem. tchr. grades 1, 3, 4, 5, Upper Darby (Pa.) Sch. Dist., 1974—, mem. Sci. Curriculum Writing Commn., 1974—99. Mem. excellence edn. team Hillcrest Elem. Sch., Pa., 1987; cert. NASA Lunar Rock and Meteorite Edn. Program, 1993—; tchr. adv. bd. Phila. Zoo, 1995—; mem. writing and evaluation team Schuykill Valley Nature Ctr., 1993—94; mem. Highland Park Elem. Sch. Learn and Serve Cmty. Svc. Ctr., Kids Care Club, 2000—02, Safety Patrol Advisor, 2002—. Recipient Howard W. McComb award, Temple U. Phi Delta Kappa, 1981. Mem.: NSTA, ASCD, Upper Darby Recreation Tennis Players (First Serve Tennis Racket stringer 1981—, tournament co-dir. 1983—92, supr. summer camp 2004—). Home: 122 Crestview Rd Upper Darby PA 19082

CROUT, ELIZABETH ROOP, retired elementary school educator; b. Linwood, Md., Aug. 25, 1925; d. John Daniel and Edith Elizabeth (Pfoutz) Roop; m. Alan Lee Crout, Mar. 31, 1951; children: J. Daniel, Peter A., John W., Ruth Ann. BS in Gen. Edn., Manchester Coll., North Manchester, Ind., 1948; postgrad., Miami U., Oxford, Ohio, 1963-87. Med. technologist State of Md., Sykesville, 1945-46, Ch. of Brethren, Castañer, P.R., 1946-47, Middletown Hosp., Ohio, 1949-53, Hughes Hosp., Hamilton, Ohio, 1956-63; tchr. Middletown Bd. Edn., 1964-87; ret., 1987. Prayer warrior Oasis Ch., 1980—; Aglow treas., 1998—; tutor, Trenton, Ohio, 1987—. Mem. AAUW. Mem. Full Gospel Ch. Avocation: sewing. Home: 5389 Wayne Madison Rd Trenton OH 45067-9548

CROW, LYNNE CAMPBELL SMITH, insurance company representative; b. Buffalo, Oct. 13, 1942; d. Stephen Smith and Jean Campbell (Ruggles) Hall; m. William David Crow II, Apr. 16, 1966 (div. Dec. 1989); children: William David III, Alexander Fairbairn, Margaret Campbell. BA, Sweet Briar Coll., Va., 1964; postgrad., Am. Coll., 1986. CLU; ChFC; registered rep. Claims rep. Liberty Mut. Ins. Co., Bklyn. and N.Y.C., 1964-66; with McGraw-Hill Corp., N.Y.C., 1966-67; claims rep. Liberty Mut. Ins. Co., East Orange, N.J., 1967-68; sales assoc. Realty World/Allsopp Realtors, Millburn, N.J., 1981-82; field rep. Guardian Life Ins. Co., 1982—; registered rep. Park Ave. Securities. Bd. dirs. Jr. League Oranges and Short Hills, Millburn, 1979-80, 95-96, Millburn LWV, 1979-80, Cheshire Homes, 2004-05; campaign chair, bus. chair, bd. dirs. United Way Millburn/Short Hills, 1981-88, 90-96, sec., 1990-91; adult planning chair Cora Hartshorn Arboretum, 2000-03, bd. dirs., trustee, 2000-04, sec., 2003-04; bd. dirs. Cheshire Homes, 2005—. Named Life Underwriter of Yr., 1996. Mem. AAUW, Nat. Assn. Ins. and Fin. Advisors (Nat. Quality award 1988, 91, 95, Nat. Health Achievement award 1988, 90), Nat. Assn. Health Underwriters, Am. Soc. Fin. Svc. Profls. (bd. dirs. 1994-99), N.J. Assn. Ins. and Fin. Advisors (dir. region II 1993-95, health chair 1995—, sec. 1998-99, 2d v.p. 1999-2000, 1st v.p. 2000-01, pres. 2001-02), Newark Assn. Life Underwriters (bd. dirs. 1986-94, sec. 1987-88, treas. 1988-89, 3d v.p. 1989-90, 2d v.p. 1990, pres.-elect 1991-92, pres. 1992-93, health chair 1995-98, Life Underwriter of Yr. 1986), Nat. Assn. of Ins. and Fin. Advisors (governance com. 2003-04, com. on assns. 2004—), Women in Fin. Svcs., Leader's Recognition Soc., Million Dollar Round Table (life, capt. focus session on non-core products and investments 1999-2000, chair spl. events 2000-01, asst. dir. program gen. arrangements 2006), Million Dollar Round Table Found. (trustee 2002-05, platinum knight, trusteeship com. 2003-04), Assn. Health Ins. Advisors, Nat. Assn. Security Dealers, Chatham (Mass.) Beach and Tennis Club. Republican. Episcopalian. Avocations: travel, sailing, reading, hiking, photography. Home: 22 Winding Way Short Hills NJ 07078-2530 Office: Cert Fin Svcs LLC 52 Forest Ave Paramus NJ 07652 Office Phone: 201-843-7700 x358. Personal E-mail: lscrow22ww@aol.com. E-mail: lcrow@glic.com.

CROW, MARTHA ELLEN, lawyer; b. Bryan, Tex., Dec. 7, 1944; d. Elvin Earl and Walteen (Daly) Burnett; m. Michael Paine Crow, Apr. 20, 1968; children: Jennifer Johanna, Emily Jeanne, Bryan Jacob. BA, Baker U., 1966; JD magna cum laude, Washburn U., 1992. Bar: Kans. 1993. Tchr., jr. high Shawnee Mission Schs., Johnson County, Kans., 1966-68; legal intern Speaker's Office Kans. Legislature, Topeka, 1991; law clk. Freilich, Leitner, Shortlidge and Carlisle, Kansas City, Mo., 1992-93; planning cons. Kans. Dept. Health and Environment, Topeka, 1993-95; ptnr. Crow, Clothier & Assocs., Leavenworth, Kans., 1995—. Comments editor: Washburn Law Jour., Vol. 31, 1991-92. Mem. Kans. Ho. of Reps., 41st dist., 1996—, agenda chair Ho. Dems., 2001—; mem. Kans. Continuing Legal Edn. Commn., 1993—99, chmn., 1997—99; bd. dirs., founding mem. Leadership Leavenworth, 1988-90; chmn., vice chmn. Leavenworth City Planning Commn.,

1978-90, 94-96; v.p. to pres. Leavenworth Bd. Edn., 1983-96; chmn. Leavenworth Bd. Zoning Appeals, 1979-89, 94-96; pres. Downtown Leavenworth Revitalization, Inc., 1988-90, Leadership Kans. Class of 1986; bd. dirs. YWCA, 1974-82, pres., 1977-79; bd. dirs. Leavenworth C. of C., women's divsn., 1980-86, Baker U. Alumni Assn., 1978-80, Mother to Mother Ministry, 1996—, Richard Allen Cultural Ctr., 2000-, Northeast Kans. Mental Health and Guidance Ctr., 1997—2003; co-chmn. residential divsn. United Way Drive, 1977, 78, numerous others. Recipient Michaud, Cordry, Michaud, Hutton scholarship, Wichita, Kans., 1991, scholarship Washburn Law Sch., 1991. Mem. ABA, Kans. Bar Assn., Kans. Trial Lawyers Assn., Washburn Sch. of Law (women's legal forum), Phi Kappa Phi, Phi Delta Phi, Phi Gamma Mu, Delta Delta Delta, PEO. Democrat. Methodist. Home: 1200 S Broadway St Leavenworth KS 66048-3118 Office: Crow Clothier & Assocs PO Box 707 302 Shawnee St Leavenworth KS 66048-2063 Office Phone: 913-682-0166.

CROW, SHERYL, singer, songwriter, musician; b. Kennett, Mo., Feb. 11, 1962; Degree in classical piano, U. Mo., 1984; Ph.D (hon.), S.E. Mo. St. U. Backup singer Bad tour Michael Jackson, 1987; backup singer The End of the Innocence tour Don Henley, 1989; also backup singer George Harrison, Joe Cocker, Stevie Wonder, Rod Stewart. Singer: (albums) Tuesday Night Music Club, 1993, Sheryl Crow, 1996, The Globe Sessions, 1998, Sheryl Crow and Friends: Live in Central Park, 1999, C'mon, C'mon, 2002 (Grammy award best female rock vocal performance, 2003), Live at Budokan, 2003, The Very Best of Sheryl Crow, 2003, Wildflower, 2005, (songs) Leaving Las Vegas, 1994, All I Wanna Do, 1994 (Grammy awards for Record of Year and Female Pop Vocal, 1995), Strong Enough, 1994, Can't Cry Anymore, 1995, Everyday Is a Winding Road, 1996, If It Makes You Happy, 1996, My Favorite Mistake, 1998, Anything But Down, 1999, Soak up the Sun, 2002, The First Cut Is the Deepest, 2003; singer: (with Kid Rock) Picture, 2001; participant Lilith Fair, 1998, 1999. Recipient Grammy award for Best New Artist, 1995, Favorite Female Artist award Pop or Rock, Am. Music Awards, 2004, Favorite Artist award Adult Contemporary Music, 2004.

CROWDER, BARBARA LYNN, judge; b. Mattoon, Ill., Feb. 3, 1956; d. Robert Dale and Martha Elizabeth (Harrison) C.; m. Lawrence Owen Taliana, Apr. 17, 1982; children: Paul Joseph, Robert Lawrence, Benjamin Owen. BA, U. Ill., Urbana, 1978; JD, U. Ill., 1981. Bar: Ill. 1981. Assoc. Louis E. Olivero, Peru, Ill., 1981—82; asst. state's atty. Madison County, Edwardsville, Ill., 1982—84; ptnr. Robbins & Crowder, Edwardsville, 1985—87, Robbins, Crowder & Bader, Edwardsville, Ill., 1987—88, Crowder, Taliana, Rubin, and Buckley, Edwardsville, 1988—98; assoc. judge 3d Jud. Cir. Madison County, Edwardsville, 1999—. Spkr. Ill. Inst. CLE seminars Family Law Update, 1993—; co-chair 3d. Jud. Cir. Family Violence Coord. Coun., 1999—, chair ct. com., 1999—; presiding judge Family divsn. 3d Jud. Cir., Edwardsville, 2000, 2003—04, 2005—06; spkr. edn. Conf. Adminstrn. Office Ill. Ct., 2002—06; mem. spl. com. child custody issues Supreme Ct., Ill., 2002—; spkr. in field. Co-author chpts. in ISBA Family Law Handbook, 1995, Maintenance Chapter Ill. Family Law Ill. Inst. CLE, 1998, supplement, 2001; contbr. articles to profl. jours Chmn. City of Edwardsville Zoning Bd. Appeals, 1986-87; committee woman Edwardsville Dem., Precinct 15, 1986-98; mem. City of Edwardsville Planning Commn., 1985-87; bd. dirs. Madison-Bond County Workforce Devel. Bd., 1995-96, 96-97 Named Best Oral Advocate, Moot Ct. Bd., 1979, Outstanding Young Career Woman, Dist. XIV, Ill. Bus. and Profl. Women, 1986; recipient Alice Paul award Alton-Edwardsville NOW, 1987, Woman Achievement YWCA, 1996; recipient Athena award Edwardsville/Glen Carbon C. of C., 1991, V-Day Warrior Phoenix Crisis Ctr. and U.S. Women of Steel, 2006, Ptnrs. in Peace award 3d Cir. Family Violence Coordinating Coun., 2006. Mem. Ill. Bar Assn. (family law coun. sect. 1990-99, chair 1997-98, co-editor Family Law newsletter 1993, vice chair 1996-97, Bench and Bar sect. coun. 2002—, sec. 2004-2005, vice chair, 2005-2006, chair Bench and Bar section coun., 2006-), Ill. Judges' Assn. (bd. dirs.), Nat. Assn. Women Judges, Ill. Fedn. Bus. and Profl. Women (parliamentarian dist. XIV 1991-92, Outstanding Working Woman Ill. 1988-89), Women Lawyers Assn. Met. East (pres. 1986), Edwardsville Bus. and Profl Women's Club (pres. 1988-89, 95-96, treas. 1989-90, Woman of Achievement award 1985, Jr. Svc. award 1987), U. Ill. Alumni Assn. (v.p. met.-east club 1994-95, bd. dirs. 1995-97, alumni bd. vis., 2005-) Democrat. Office: Madison County Cthse 155 N Main St Edwardsville IL 62025-1955 Office Phone: 618-296-4411. Business E-Mail: blcrowder@co.madison.il.us.

CROWDER, BONNIE WALTON, small business owner, composer; b. Lafayette, Tenn., Apr. 14, 1916; d. Edward Samuel Bailey and Nannie Elizabeth (Goad) Walton; m. Reggie Ray Crowder, Nov. 19, 1936; 1 child, Rita Faye Grad., Nashville Beauty Coll. Owner, operator Bonnie's Beauty Salon, Tampa, Fla. Composer: A Man of Faith, 1988, This Miracle, 1988; (with Willard E. Walton) God Bless Our President, 1988, Awake, Arise America, 1989, Touching My Jesus, 1990, (with W.E. Walton) Muscle Jerky Boogie, 1992 Active ch. choir, Tampa; mem. Bus. and Profl. Women's Chorus, 1960-70's, U. South Fla. Cmty. Chorus, 1973-81 Mem. Beta Sigma Phi Home and Office: 266 Oak Knob Rd Lafayette TN 37083-4137

CROWDER, ELIZABETH See WADDINGTON, BETTE

CROWDER, HEATHER ELIZABETH, mental health services professional, consultant; d. Henry A. and Beth M. Crowder. BA, Newberry Coll., SC, 1999; MS, Capella U., 2003. Customer svc. rep. ULTA Cosmetics and Salon, Fayetteville, Ga., 1998—99, beauty advisor, 1999, store supr., 1999—2000; program asst. A Friend's Ho., Inc., McDonough, Ga., 2000—01; mental health profl. Greenwood (S.C.) Mental Health Clinic S.C. Dept. Mental Health, 2001—03, clin. counselor Greenwood (S.C.) Mental Health Clinic, 2001—03, mental health profl. Pickens (S.C.) Mental Health Clinic, 2004—. Quality assurance com. Pickens (S.C.) Mental Health Clinic S.C. Dept. Mental Health, 2004—, cons. Pickens (S.C.) Mental Health Clinic, 2004—; adj. faculty Piedmont Tech. Coll., Greenwood, SC, 2004. Mem.: APA (assoc.), Alpha Xi Delta (life; scrapbook chair, new mem. educator, marshall, panhellenic del., named Alumni of Yr. 1999). Office: Pickens Mental Health Center 314 W Main St Pickens SC 29671 Office Phone: 864-878-6830. Personal E-mail: hec1687@yahoo.com.

CROWDER, MARJORIE BRIGGS, lawyer; b. Shreveport, La., Mar. 26, 1946; d. Rowland Edmund and Marjorie Ernestine (Biles) Crowder; m. Ronald J. Briggs, July 11, 1970 (div. Nov. 2000); children: Sarah Briggs, Andrew Briggs. BA, Carson-Newman Coll., 1968; MA, Ohio State U., 1969, JD, 1975. Bar: Ohio 1975, U.S. Ct. Appeals (6th cir.) 1983, U.S. Ct. Claims 1992, U.S. Supreme Ct. 2001. Asst. dean of women Albion Coll., Mich., 1969-70; dir. residence hall Ohio State U., Columbus, 1970-71, acad. counselor, 1971-72; assoc. Porter, Wright, Morris, Arthur, Columbus, 1975—83, ptnr., 1983-2000; AmeriCorps atty. Southeastern Ohio Legal Svs., Portsmouth, Ohio, 2000—02, staff atty., 2002—03; domestic violence team leader Legal Aid Soc. Columbus, 2003—04. Legal aide Cmty. Law Office, Columbus, 1973—74. Co-author: (book) Going to Trial, A Step-By-Step Guide to Trial Practice and Procedure, 1989. Trustee, pres. Epilepsy Assn. Ctrl. Ohio, Columbus, 1977—84; bd. dirs. Scioto County Domestic Violence Task Force, 2001—04, v.p., 2001—; bd. dirs. Action Ohio Coalition Battered Women, 2002—, Columbus Speech & Hearing, 1977—82. Fellow: Columbus Bar Found. (trustee 1993—95); mem.: Scioto County Bar Assn., Columbus Bar Assn. (com. chmn. 1979—83, docket control task force 1989—91, editor 1981—83), ABA (mem. gavel awards com. 1989—96, gen. practice sect. 1983—, chair litig. com. 1987—89, mem. exec. coun. 1989—93, dir. bus. com. group 1990—91, chair program com. 1991—93, torts and ins. practice sect. 1993—, vice chair health ins. law com. 1993—96), Ohio Bar Assn. (mem. joint task force gender fairness 1991—93), Scioto County Bar Assn. Office: 209 E Pacemont Rd Columbus OH 43202 E-mail: mcrowder@columbuslegalaid.org.

CROWDER, REBECCA BYRUM, music educator, elementary school educator; b. Suffolk, Va., Apr. 27, 1951; d. Joseph Etheridge and Jane Carroll Byrum; m. Melvin Linnwood Crowder, July 19, 1977. BS in Music Edn., Radford U., 1973, MS in Music Edn., 1976. Cert. music tchr. grades K-12, tchr. grades 4-7. Profl. musician, 1973—; music tchr. East Salem Elem., Salem, Va., 1973—78; music dir. Colonial Ave. Bapt., Roanoke, Va., 1973—79; music tchr. Andrew Lewis Jr. High, Salem, 1979—83, Salem High and Glenvar High, Salem, 1983—84, Glenvar High, Salem, 1984—90, Oak Grove Elem., Roanoke, 1990—. Music tchr. Hollins U., Roanoke, 2000; pianist, accompanist Colonial Ave. Bapt., Roanoke, 1963—79, Shady Grove Bapt., Thaxton, 1979—92, First Bapt., Roanoke, 1992—97, Salem Ch. of Christ, 1997—. Mem.: Music Educators Nat. Conf., Va. Congress Parents and Tchrs., Phi Kappa Phi. Avocations: ballroom dancing, reading, playing piano, crossword puzzles, singing. Home: 1606 Mountain Hgts Dr Salem VA 24153

CROWDER-PAGANO, LINDA LOUISE, special education educator; b. Queens, NY, Apr. 9, 1956; d. Roy Miller Crowder and Edith Elizabeth Sisson Crowder; m. Theodore Joseph Pagano, Apr. 26, 1996; children: David Theodore, Christopher Alexander, Jeffrey Joseph. BA in Edn., Dowling Coll., 1978; MSc in Spl. Edn., Adelphi U., 1981, MSW, 1993. Cert. sch. social worker NJ; elem. tchr. NY, tchr. handicapped NJ, tchr. psychology NJ, hypnotherapist Nat. Assn. Cert. Hypnotherapists. Tchr. spl. edn. Saxton Jr. H.S., NY; tchr. Patchogue-Medford Sch. Dist.; tchr. resourse and self contained Ocean Ave. Elem. Sch., Middleton, NJ, 1988—. Freelance tutor, NY, NJ. Recipient Tchr. of Yr. award, Gov., 1992. Mem.: Psi Chi. Avocations: antiques, tennis, music, writing. Home: 14 Boxwood Dr Colts Neck NJ 07722 Office Phone: 732-787-0092.

CROWE, JENNIFER, newspaper reporter; b. L.A., Apr. 17, 1973; d. Timothy James and Beverly Jean Crowe. BA in Print Journalism and Polit. Sci., U. Nev., Reno, 1995. Intern Reno Gazette-Jour., Gannett Newspapers, 1993-95, feature writer, 1995-96, police reporter, 1996-98, edn. reporter, 1998—2000, legis. reporter, 2000—01, asst. opinion editor, 2001—02; congl. fellow Am. Polit. Sci. Assn., 2002—03; with Office of Sen. Maria Cantwell, Washington, 2003—. Reporting fellow Knight Ctr. for Journalists, College Park, Md., 1998. Vol., Salvation Army, Reno, 1997; Career Day spkr. Washoe County Schs., Nev., 1997—; coord. Make Time for Kids Vols., 1999—. Recipient Best Spot News Story award Nev. Press Assn., 1998, Best of Gannett 2d pl. award Gannett Newspapers Inc., 1996, Well Done news series award, 1996, Well Done news enterprise Gannett, 1999. Mem.: Soroptimists Internat. Avocations: downhill skiing, snowboarding, hiking, fishing. Office: Reno Gazette-Jour 955 Kuenzli St Reno NV 89502-1160

CROWE, VIRGINIA MARY, retired librarian; b. Meadville, Pa., Mar. 8, 1933; d. Harold Augustus and Daisy Lee (Ervin) Shartle; m. Robert William Crowe, Mar. 22, 1951; children: Thomas Robert, David William, Steven Michael. BS in Edn., Edinboro U. of Pa., 1965; MLS, U. Pitts., 1967, PhD, 1973. Elem. sch. librarian Saegertown (Pa.) Area Schs., 1965, Gen. McLane Sch. System, Edinboro, 1965-67, sec. sch. librarian, 1967-68; asst. prof. libr. sci. Edinboro Univ. of Pa., 1968-72, dept. chair of libr. sci. and assoc. prof., 1972-82; asst. dir. outreach svcs. U. Libr. Svcs., Va. Commonwealth U., Richmond, 1982-83, assoc. dir. for pub. svcs., 1983-87; dean libr. and media svcs Shippensburg U. of Pa., 1987-95; ret., 1995. Adj. faculty Cath. U. Am., Washington, 1984-87; cons. Weston Woods Studios, Conn., 1980-85. Contbr. articles to profl. jours. Pres. Venango (Pa.) Borough Coun., 1973-79; dir. Cambridge Springs Joint Sch. Bd., 1958-69; trustee Venango Pub. Libr., 1975-80. U.S. Office of Edn. grantee, 1975, 77, 79. Mem. ALA, Pa. Libr. Assn., State System of Higher Edn. Librs. Coun. (chair 1989-91). Home: 1041 Capri Isles Blvd Apt 225 Venice FL 34292-1585

CROWELL, ROSEMARY ELAINE, social services administrator; b. Monroe, N.C., Sept. 14, 1942; d. Frederick Perry and Berthenia (Alexander) C. AA, Clinton Jr. Coll., 1961. Mem. staff Betty Bacharach Home Afflicted Children, Atlantic City, 1964-66, Murdoch Ctr., Butner, N.C., 1964-66; cottage parent N.C. Dept. Human Resources, Butner, 1966-68, cottage parent, then cottage mgr. C.A. Dillon Sch. div. youth svcs., 1968-82, asst. unit adminstr., 1982—98. Del. to Dem. Nat. Conv., Atlanta, 1988; Dem. precinct chmn., Butner, 1989; active Dem. presdl. candidate campaigns, 1988; mem. Dem. Leadership Coun., 1990; mem. Granville County Dem. Steering Com. for N.C. Gov., 1996; mem. Granville County Steering Com. for Sen. John Edwards, 1998; com. mem. Granville County 2015 Task Force Comprehensive Land Devel. Plan, 2002. Mem. Nat. Abortion Rights Action League, Elks. Episcopalian. Avocations: reading, travel, politics. Home: PO Box 334 Butner NC 27509-2144

CROWELL, SHERRY DIEGEL, psychologist; BA, Tex. Tech U., 1983, MA, 1985, PhD, 1992. Lic. psychologist, Tex. Sr. dir. Psychol. Clinic, Lubbock, Tex., 1987-89; psychometrist Med.-Surg. Neurology Clinic, Lubbock, 1987-89; assoc. clin. psychologist Big Spring (Tex.) State Hosp., 1987-89; psychology intern Austin (Tex.) State Hosp., 1989-90; pvt. practice psychotherapy Abilene, Tex., 1990-93; clin. psychologist Abilene Regional Mental Health Mental Retardation Ctr., 1991-93; pvt. practice psychology Abilene; cons. and chief psychologist Young County Family Resource & Advocacy Ctr., Child Advocacy of Tex., 1995—. Adj. prof. psychology McMurry U., 1994—98; chmn. symposium Tex. Assn. on Mental Retardation, 1992; presenter in field. Contbr. rsch. articles to profl. pubs. Mem. adv. bd. Big Country AIDS Support Group, Abilene, 1992—; mem. Lubbock AIDS Health Care Planning Group, Lubbock, 1987-89; founding mem., trustee West Tex. AIDS Found., Lubbock, 1986-89, mentoring program, 1995—; patron Abilene Cmty. Theatre. Mem. APA, Tex. Psychol. Assn. (chair symposium 1987, 88, 92-93, Alexander award for Rsch. Excellence in Psychobiologic Field 1992). Avocations: reading, music, painting. Office: 3301 N 3d St Ste 113 Abilene TX 79603-7033

CROWELL, TANGIE MICHELLE, elementary school educator; b. Tuskegee, Ala., June 19, 1974; d. Thomas Groce and Eva Mae Williams; m. Platon Renard Crowell, Aug. 19, 2000; children: Lauryn Marie, Dequadri Q. Jefferson. BS in English Edn., Ala. State U., Montgomery, Ala., 1997; MS in English Edn., Troy State U., Phenix City, Ala., 1998; student in Orgnl. Leadership, Nova Southeastern U., Miami, Fla., 1997—. Tchr. english Goodwyn Jr. H.S. Montgomery Co. Pub. Schs., Ala., 2001—03; tchr. lang. arts Booker T. Wash. Mid. Sch. Mobile County Pub. Schs., Ala., 2004—. Tutor Ala. League Montgomery Ala. State U., Ala., 1996—97; mem. tchr. leader network Ala. State Dept. Edn.; tutor in field. Dir. women's ministry Faith Baptiat Ch., Mobile, Ala., 2004—06, instr., choreographer praise dance ministry. Named Tchr. of Yr., 2002, Most Influential, 2000. Mem.: Ala. Edn. Assn. Office: Mobile Co Public Sch Washington Middl 1961 Andrews Road Mobile AL 36617 Office Phone: 215-221-2361. Personal E-mail: tangie@nova.edu. Business E-Mail: tcrowell@mcpss.com.

CROWLEY, CYNTHIA WARNER JOHNSON, secondary school educator; b. Summit, N.J., June 28, 1930; d. Theodore Eames and Frances Lysett (Wetmore) J.; m. Robert J. Crowley, Sept. 6, 1952 (dec.); children: David Cochrane II, Cynthia Wetmore BA, U. Pa., 1952; MA, Fairleigh-Dickinson U., 1980. Cert. English tchr., NJ. Tchr. econs. and reading St. Mary's Sch., Peekskill, NY, 1952—53; tchr. humanities Henry Hudson Regional Sch., Highlands, NJ, 1969—92, coord. gifted program, 1983—92. Pres. Associated Ednl. Svcs.; with N.J. Curriculum Revision Project; adv. bd. mem. N.J. Coun. U.S. Congl. Awards Program; ednl. cons.; cons., lectr. creative writing workshops; mem. secondary sch. admissions com. U. Pa Prodr. TV Tutor Series for Home and Schs. Former mem. Atlantic Highlands Bd. Edn., also past pres.; mem. adv. bd. Women's Athletic bd. U. Pa., 1992—, chair, 1999—; former mem. exec. com. Monmouth County Sch. Bds. Assn. Basketball. Team Room named in her honor U. Pa., Palestra, 1997; named to Hall of Fame, U. Pa., 1998; recipient U. Pa. Alumni award, 1997, Alumni Merit award U. Pa., 2004 Mem. ASCD, Nat. Coun. Tchrs. English, NATAS (N.Y. chpt.), Gifted Educators (exec. com. 1986—), Alumni Pres.'s Coun. Ind. Secondary Schs. (life, past pres.), Phi Delta Kappa, Kappa Alpha Theta Home and Office: 245 Shore Rd Westerly RI 02891-3707 Office Fax: 401-322-8379.

CROWLEY, CYNTHIA WETMORE, real estate broker; d. Robert James and Cynthia Johnson Crowley. BA, Princeton U., Princeton, N.J., 1982. Dir. of relocation Olshan Realty Inc., N.Y., 1984—. Founding dir. Manhattan Assn. of Realtors, N.Y., NY, 1999—, pres., 2004—. Com. mem. N.Y. Women's Found., NY, 2002—; del. N.Y. Assn. of Realtors, Albany, NY, 2003—. Achievements include 4 Time National Tae Kwon Do Champion. Avocations: athletics, travel, reading. Office: Olshan Realty Inc 641 Lexington Ave 22nd Flr New York NY 10022 Office Phone: 212-751-3300. E-mail: cwc@olshan.com.

CROWLEY, JUANITA A., lawyer; b. Jan. 11, 1953; BA, Trinity Coll., 1974; JD, Georgetown Univ., 1977. Bar: DC 1977. Law clk. Judge Herbert F. Murray, US Dist. Ct. (Md. dist.), 1977—78; ptnr., co-chmn. Litigation dept. Wilmer Cutler Pickering Hale & Dorr, Washington. Prof. Nat. Inst. Trial Advocacy, Boulder, Colo. Editor (exec.): Georgetown Law Jour. Mem.: ABA, Phi Beta Kappa. Office: Wilmer Cutler Pickering Hale & Dorr 2445 M St NW Washington DC 20037 Office Phone: 202-663-6207. Office Fax: 202-663-6363. Business E-Mail: juanita.crowley@wilmerhale.com.

CROWLEY, MONICA, political commentator; BA in Polit. Sci., Colgate U., 1990; Ph.D in Internat. Rels., Columbia U., 2000. Fgn. policy asst. to Pres. Richard Nixon, 1990—94; fgn. affairs analyst, polit. analyst Fox News Channel, NYC, 1996—2004; host The Monica Crowley Show WABC Radio, NYC, 2002—; co-host Connected: Coast to Coast MSNBC, 2004—. Term mem. Coun. Fgn. Rels.; host The Monica Crowley Show, Westwood One Radio, 2002—. Author: Nixon off the Record: His Candid Commentary on People and Politics, 1996, Nixon in Winter, 1998. Office: c/o MSNBC TV One MSNBC Plz Secaucus NJ 07094

CROWLEY, ROSA QUINONEZ, literature and language educator; b. Quininde, Ecuador, July 1, 1966; d. Victor Edilfonso Quininez and Maria Reneira Quinonez; m. Frederic C. Crowley, Apr. 25, 2001. Degree in edn., U. Guayaquil, Ecuador, 1992; BA in Spanish, RI Coll., Providence, 2002. Tchr. Spanish Aida Lara Sch., Guayaquil, 1992—98, St. Mary Acad., Riverside, RI, 2002—03, Ctrl. Falls High Sch., 2004, Woonsocket High Sch., 2003—. Elected mem. Cumberland Sch. Com., RI, 2004—. Mem.: ASCD, RI Fgn. Lang. Assn. (bd. dirs. 2003—), Am. Coun. Tchg. Fgn. Langs., Am. Assn. Tchrs. Spanish and Portuguese. Avocations: travel, writing, reading, gardening, soccer. Home: 15 Liberty St Cumberland RI 02864 Office: Woonsocket High Sch 777 Cass Ave Woonsocket RI 02895

CROWN, MICHELE FLEURETTE, lawyer; b. NYC, Nov. 16, 1943; d. Louis and Sophia C.; m. Norman R. Williams, Dec. 2, 1972; children: Zachary Crown Williams, Oliver Crown Williams. BA, Queens Coll., CUNY, 1965; JD, Brooklyn Law Sch., 1967. Bar: N.Y. 1968, D.C. 1969. Trial atty. FTC, Washington, 1967-72, 1975-79; gen. counsel Am. Meat Inst., Washington, 1979-82; of counsel Perito, Duerk & Pinco, Washington, 1982-84, Olsson, Frank & Weeda, Washington, 1984—, Venable LLP, Washington, 2001—. Author reports to Congress; contbr. articles to profl. jours. Mem. ABA, FDLI (mem. academic oversight com.), Pi Sigma Alpha. Office: Venable LLP 575 7th St NW Washington DC 20004 Office Phone: 202-344-4778. Office Fax: 202-344-8300. Business E-Mail: mfcrown@venable.com.

CROWN, NANCY ELIZABETH, lawyer; b. Bronx, NY, Mar. 27, 1955; d. Paul and Joanne Barbara (Newman) C.; children: Rebecca, Adam. BA, Barnard Coll., 1977, MA, 1978; MEd, Columbia U., 1983; JD cum laude, Nova Law Sch., 1992. Cert. tchr.; Bar: Fla. 1992. Tchr. Sachem Sch. Dist., Holbrook, N.Y., 1978-82; v.p. mail order dept. Haber-Klein, Inc., Hicksville, N.Y., 1984-88; mgr. mdse., dir. ops. Sure Card Inc., Pompano Beach, Fla., 1988-89; legal intern Office U.S. Trustee/Dept. Justice, 1992; assoc. John T. Kinsey, P.A., Boca Raton, Fla., 1993-95; pvt. practice Nancy E. Crown, P.A., Boca Raton, Fla., 1995—; owner Crystal Title, Inc., 1999—. Recipient West Pub. award for acad. achievement, 1992. Mem. NOW, Fla. Bar Assn., South Palm Beach County Bar Assn., Bus. Partnership Coun., Fla. Assn. Women Lawyers Democrat. Jewish. Avocations: theater, walking, reading, jazz. Office Phone: 561-447-8750. E-mail: necrownpa@aol.com.

CROWN, ROBERTA, artist, educator; b. N.Y.C., Sept. 9, 1946; d. Louis and Sophia (Siegal) C. BA, Queens Coll., MA, 1970. Art tchr. N.Y. Bd. Edn., N.Y.C., 1969—. One-woman shows include Harbor Sq., Washington, 1970, Andalusia Arts, Inc. Gallery, N.Y.C., 1974, Women's Studio Workshop Gallery, Rosendale, N.Y., 1988, Queens Coll. Art Ctr., Flushing, N.Y., 1989, Dag Jammaraskjold Tower, N.Y.C., 1997, Uniproperty Gallery, N.Y.C., 1998; group shows include Air Naval Res. Show (1st prize oils, 3d prize watercolors), 1969, East Meadow Outdoor Show, N.Y.C., 1970, Aorta, East Hampton, N.Y., 1971, United Art Group, N.Y.C., 1976, WIA Gallery, N.Y.C., 1978-80, Bklyn. Coll. (2d prize oils), 1978, One Hundred Artists Show, N.Y.C., 1979, Picture Show Gallery, N.Y.C., 1979, Contemporary Arts Ctr., 1980, Fed. S.I. Artists, Lever House, N.Y.C., 1980, Fine Arts Gallery Ocean County Coll., 1980, Panassus Gallery, Woodstock, N.Y., 1980, Gallery 14, Copenhagen, 1980, Newhouse Gallery, 1981, Queens Mus., 1981, 84, Off the Wall Show, 1982, Cork Gallery, 1983-84, 86-87, Nugent Gallery, Marymount Manhattan Coll., 1983, 84, Garcia Gallery, Bronx, N.Y., 1983, City Gallery, N.Y.C., 1984, Franklin Furnace, N.Y.C., 1984, Lehigh U., Bethlehem, Pa., 1984, Chgo. Gallery, U. Ill., 1984, Tokyo Met. Mus., 1984, Arsenal Gallery, 1984, 86, Art and Design HS, N.Y.C., 1985, Janco-Dada Mus., Ein-Hod, Israel, 1985, Passaic CC, Patterson, N.J., 1986, Todd Capp Gallery, N.Y.C., 1986, Castillo Gallery, N.Y.C., 1987, WRIC Ctr., 1987, Appalachian State U., Boone, N.C., 1988, Transco Energy Gallery, Houston, 1988, Rice Gallery, 1991, Sotherby's, 1991, Nat. Mus. Women in Arts, 1991, NAWA Traveling Show, 1992, Tesori Gallery, 1993, Queens Coll., 2005, Broome Street Gall, 2005. Mem. Women in the Arts Found., Inc. (exec. coord. 1980—), Women Caucus in Art, NY State Assn. Tchrs. Art. Studio: 365 Canal St New York NY 10013

CROWNING, LISA L., secondary school educator, horticulturist, consultant; b. Point Pleasant, NJ, Aug. 6, 1963; d. John Robert and Margaret Lee Kelley; m. Jeffrey Crowning, Apr. 19, 1986; children: K. Maxwell, Sam Jeffrey, Nick Thomas, Quinn Margaret. BS, U. Del., Newark, 1985. Cert. tchr. NJ, 1985. Aide III Conn. Agrl. Expt. Sta., New Haven, 1985—87; chief horticulturalist Thompson & Morgan Seed Co., Jackson, NJ, 1990—95; hort. cons. Rutgers Coop. Ext. NJ, Toms River, 1995—; educator Manasquan H.S., NJ, 1999—. Cons. in field, NJ, 1990—; lectr. in field. Facilitator Environ. groups. Avocations: landscaping, gardening. Home: 1408 Northstream Pkwy Point Pleasant NJ 08742 Office: Manasquan Board of Education 167 Broad St Manasquan NJ 07526 Office Phone: 732-528-8820.

CROYLE, BARBARA ANN, health facility administrative executive; b. Knoxville, Tenn., Oct. 22, 1949; d. Charles Evans and Myrtle Elizabeth (Kellam) C. BA cum laude in Sociology, Coll. William and Mary, 1971; cert. corp. tax and securities law, Inst. Paralegal Tng., 1971; JD, U. Colo., 1975; cert. program mgmt. devel., Colo. Women's Coll., 1980; MBA, U. Denver, 1983. Bar: Colo. 1976. Paralegal Holland & Hart, Denver, 1972-73; law clk. Colo. Ct. Appeals, Denver, summer 1976; assoc. firm Shaw Spangler & Roth, Denver, 1976-77; mgr. acquisitions/lands Petro-Lewis Corp., Denver, 1977-85; mgr. strategic planning Westinghouse, Transp. Divsn., Denver, 1985-87; mng. dir. Benefit Resource Mgmt. Group subs. Blue Cross We. Pa., 1987-92; COO, v.p. D.T. Watson Rehab. Hosp., 1992-93; v.p. ambulatory care svcs., compliance officer Franciscan Med. Ctr., Dayton campus, Ohio, 1994-2000; exec. dir. Swedish Am. Ctr. for Complementary Medicine, Rockford, Ill., 2000—02; v.p., legal advisor Peninsula United Meth. Homes, Inc., Hockessin, Del., 2003—. Tchr. oil and gas law Colo. Paralegal Inst., 1978, 79; arbitrator Am. Arbitration Assn.; mediator Dayton Mediation Ctr. Mem. ABA, Del. Bar Assn., Inst. Noetic Scis., Am. Coll. Healthcare Execs. Home: 150 Mercer Mill Rd Landenberg PA 19350 Office: Peninsula United Meth Home 726 Loveville Rd Hockessin DE 19807 Office Phone: 302-235-6823. Personal E-mail: bcroyle@earthlink.net.

CROZIER, PRUDENCE SLITOR, economist; b. Boston, Oct. 27, 1940; d. Richard Eaton and Louise (Bean) S.; m. William Marshall, June 20, 1964; children: Matthew Eaton, Abigail Parsons, Patience Wells. BA with honors, Wellesley Coll., 1962; MA in Econs., Yale U., 1963; PhD in Econs., Harvard

U., 1971. Rsch. asst. Fed. Res. Bank, Boston, 1963-64; tchg. fellow, tutor Harvard U., Cambridge, Mass., 1966-69; instr. Wellesley Coll., Mass., 1969-70; sr. economist Data Resources Inc., Lexington, Mass., 1973-74; bd. dirs. Omega Fund, 1984-87, Mass. Ednl. Facilities Authority, 1985-93, Boston Pub. Libr. Found., 1994—, vice chmn., 1996—. Vis. com. Harvard Sch. Pub. Health, 1993—2000, Coll. des Conseillers French Libr. and Cultural Ctr., Boston, 1995—, trustee, 1996—2002. Contbr. articles to profl. jours. Trustee Newton Wellesley Hosp., Mass., 1978—90; overseer Ctr. Rsch. of Women, Wellesley, 1982—83, Mus. Fine Arts, Boston, 1999—; trustee Wellesley Coll., 1980—98, Nantucket Hist. Assn., 1997—2002, Nantucket Atheneum, 2001.

CRUDDEN, ADELE LOUISE, social work research educator; b. New Orleans, Sept. 25, 1957; d. Edwin Francis and Eunice Louise (Courtault) C.; m. Curtis Edward Alford; children: Abigail Louise Alford. BS, Miss. State U., Starkville, 1979; MEd, Miss. State U., 1980, PhD, 1997; MSW, La. State U., 1989. Lic. social worker, profl. counselor; cert. rehab. counselor, ins. rehab. specialist. Vocat. therapist Developmental Ctr., Decatur, Ala., 1981-82; supr. New Orleans Assn. Retarded Citizens, 1982-84; rehab. specialist Sullivan Rehab., New Orleans, 1984-90; social worker Nat. Med. Care, New Orleans, 1990-91; adminstr., dir. Vocat. Rehab. for Blind, Jackson, Miss., 1991-94; rsch. sci. Miss. State U., Starkville, 1994—, dir. social work program. Counselor Children's Hosp., New Orleans, 1988, social work cons., 1989; social work cons. La. State U. Human Devel. Ctr., 1989. Active NOW, PTA, Coalition for Citizens with Disabilities, Miss., Parents for Pub. Schs., Starkville. Grantee Miss. Dept. Human Svcs., 1995-96, Nat. Inst. for Disability on Rehab. Rsch. Mem. NASW, Assn. Edn. and Rehab. Blind and Visually Impaired. Office: Miss State U SASW PO Box C Mississippi State MS 39762-6189 Office Phone: 662-325-2173, 662-325-8859. Business E-Mail: crudden@ra.msstate.edu.

CRUDUP, PAMELA TRACY PARHAM, science educator, writer; 1 child, Courtney Allison. Cert. cardiovasc. technologist, Shelby State Coll., 1996; BS in Biology, Crichton Coll., Memphis, Tenn., 2001, BS in Secondary Edn., 2001; MS in Pub. Health, Walden U., 2005. Cardiovasc. technologist, catheter lab. mgr. Meth. Hosp., Somierville, Tenn., 1995—96, radiology physician liaison Memphis, 1996—2004. Instr. anatomy/physiology, Memphis, 2001—06. Author: The Hat Box, 2003, The Mist of Mineral Springs, 2004, The Slipper Club, 2006. Mem.: APHA, NEA, Endometriosis Assn. (West Tenn. support group leader), Authors for Charity, Nat. Trust for Hist. Preservation, Arlington Womens Club, Kiwanis Club Arlington. Republican. Baptist. Avocations: travel, antiques, tennis, writing. E-mail: InstructorCrudup@aol.com.

CRUIT, WENDY, mechanical engineer; d. Steve Richards; m. Brian Cruit; 1 child. BSME, U. Ala., 1992. With NASA Marshall Space Flight Ctr., Huntsville, Ala., 1992—95, mem. Fastrac team, 1995—. Vol. Shriners Hosps. Crippled and Burned Children. Avocation: restoring antique furniture and clocks. Office: NASA Marshall Space Flight Ctr Huntsville AL 35812 Business E-Mail: wendy.d.cruit@msfc.nasa.gov.

CRUM, GLENDA M., elementary school educator; b. Butte, Mont., May 13, 1966; d. Keith M. and Glenda J. Crum; m. Scott Smith, Aug. 8, 1992 (div. Jan. 3, 1994); 1 child, Kaitlyn M. BS, Western Mont. Coll., Dillon, 1989. Cert. tchr. Mont., 1989, Idaho, 1996, Nev., 2003. Tchr. Butte Ctrl. Sch., Mont., 1991—93, Misson Mountain Sch., Condon, 1994—95, Vallivue Sch. Dist., Caldwell, Idaho, 1996—2001, Nampa Sch. Dist., Nampa, Idaho, 2001—02, Meridian Sch. Dist., 2002—03, Virgin Valley Schs., Mesquite, Nev., 2003—04, Glenns Ferry Schools, Idaho, 2004—. Mem.: NEA. Home: PO Box 1244 Glenns Ferry ID 83623 E-mail: gmcrum@hotmail.com.

CRUMBLEY, ESTHER HELEN KENDRICK, retired real estate agent, retired secondary school educator, councilman; b. Okeechobee, Fla., Oct. 3, 1928; d. James A. and Corrine (Burney) Kendrick; m. Chandler Jackson, Oct. 24, 1949 (dec.); children: Pamela E., Chandler A., William J. BS in Math. Edn., Ga. So. Coll., 1966; M in Math., Jacksonville (Fla.) U., 1979. Cert. secondary edn. tchr., Ga. Secondary edn. tchr. Camden County Bd. Edn., St. Mary's, Ga., 1958-92, ret.; realtor Watson Realty, St. Mary's, 1985-98, ret., 1998. Dept. chairperson Camden H.S., St. Mary's, 1966-72. Reporter: for hometown newspaper. Councilwoman City of St. Mary's, 1979-86, mayor pro tem, 1981-86. Mem. Camden Ga. Assn. Educators (pres. 1976, sec.-treas. 1977-78, star tchr. 1972), PAGE (biog. com. rep. 1984-92, 1992 retired, named outstanding 8th dist. bldg. rep.), Camden Gen. Mcpl. Assn. (pres., sec.-treas. 1979-88), fin. and budget coms.), Math. Assn., Internat. Platform Assn. Internat. Dictionary Ctr., ABI. Republican. Baptist. Avocations: reading, art. Home: RR 3 Box 810 Folkston GA 31537-9729

CRUMMIE, ANN VAUGHN, mental health services professional; d. Edward McDonald Vaughn and Ruth Leila Vaugh-Martin; m. Robert Gwinn Crummie, Nov. 21, 1990; children: Robin, Ruby, Rebecca, Robert, Ryan, Rhett, Reid, Virginia; m. Nolan Paul Clark (div.); children: Jennifer, Scotty, Glenn, Carolyn. BS in Biology and Chemistry, Methodist Coll., Fayetteville, N.C.; MA in Edn., NC State U., MS in Psychology; PhD in Psychology, Union Univ. APA, NCMFT, AAMFT, LPC, NAADAC, CCAS, SAP. Profl. dancer, N.Y.C.; operator, instr. Ann Clark Schs. of Dance, Fayetteville, Elizabethtown, Clinton, NC; psychology instr. Meth. Coll. Ft. Bragg Edn. Ctr. Pembroke (N.C.) Univ.; mental health profl. Raintree Clinic, Rutherfordton, NC. Recipient Ronald Reagan award, 2004, 2005. Home: 236 Charlotte Rd Rutherfordton NC 28139-2914 Office Phone: 828-287-8861. E-mail: dravc@bellsouth.net.

CRUMP, ANN, artist; b. Cleve., June 13, 1939; d. Philip Chandler Hintz and Bessie Ann Leckie; m. Walter Gray Crump III, Dec. 28, 1968; children: Sarah Crump Collins, Walter Gray IV. BA, Skidmore Coll., 1961. Sys. engr. IBM, Detroit, Chgo., San Jose, San Francisco, 1961-68. Pvt. collections include St. Francis Yacht Club, San Francisco, Pier 39 San Francisco. Mem. Nat. Watercolor Soc. (signature mem.), Calif. Watercolor Assn. (signature mem.). Home: 11 Tamalpais Ave Belvedere CA 94920-2457

CRUMP, CLAUDIA, geographer, educator; BS in Elem. Edn., Western Ky. U., 1952; MS in Elem. Edn., Ind. U., 1957, EdD in Elem. Edn., 1969. Co-author: Teaching for Social Values in Social Studies, 1974, Indiana Map Studies, 1983, Indiana Yesterday and Today, 1985, Teaching History in the Elementary School, 1988, People in Time and Place: Indiana Hoosier Heritage, 1992. Recipient First Educator of Yr. award, Nat. Coun. Internat. Visitors, 2005. Home: 309 Whippoorwill Hts New Albany IN 47150-4255 Office: Ind U Southeast Sch Edn New Albany IN 47150 E-mail: ccrump700@cs.com.

CRUTCHFIELD, SUSAN RAMSEY, neurophysiologist; b. Pasadena, Calif., Oct. 7, 1941; d. Henry Colwell Ramsey and Rowena Ruth (Lockett) Banning; m. Ralph L. Crutchfield, Sept. 26, 1964 (div. Sept. 1973); children: Pamela Montague, Ashley Noland. AA, Pine Manor Coll., 1961; student, Sorbonne U., Paris, 1961-62; BA, George Washington U., 1964; MA, U. Calif., San Diego, 1978; PhD, Aston U., Birmingham, Eng., 1986. Rsch. assoc. U. Calif. Med. Ctr., San Diego, 1978-80, rschr., 1986-89, clin. instr. dept. pediats. divsn. neonatology, 1989-94, asst. clin. prof. depts. ophthalmology and pediat., 1994-98, clin. prof. dept. pediat., 1998—; rschr. Birmingham U., England, 1980-86. Owner Daisy's Bookstore and the Ute Theater, LLC. Mem. AAAS, NY Acad. Scis., European Neurosci. Soc., Internat. Soc. Clin. Electrophysiology Vision, Assn. Rsch. Vision and Ophthalmology, Brit. Soc. Neurophysiology, La Jolla Beach and Tennis Club, Univ. Club (San Diego). Avocations: camping, horseback riding, hiking, photography, gardening. Office: Univ Calif San Diego Pediat Divsn San Diego CA 92103-0831 Home: PO Box 190 Embudo NM 87531 Office Phone: 303-818-5180. Personal E-mail: daisyute@earthlink.net.

CRUTE, BEVERLY JEAN, minister; b. Kansas City, Mo. d. Robert Scott and Rossie Nell (Locke) C. BA, Baker U., Baldwin City, Kans., 1961; MA, U. Mo.-Kansas City, 1969; PhD, Boston Coll., 1981; MDiv, Princeton Theol. Sem., 1984. Ordained to ministry Presbyn. Ch. (USA), 1985; cert. chaplain Assn. Profl. Chaplains. Summer intern Berkeley Presbyn. Ch., Mo., 1981-83; sem. asst. Faith Presbyn. Ch., Medford, N.J., 1981-82, First Presbyn. Ch., Morrisville, Pa., 1982-83, asst. pastor Willmar, Minn., 1984-85, assoc. pastor, 1986-92; dir. pastoral care Rice Meml. Hosp., Willmar, 1992—. Vis. lectr. Washington U., St. Louis, 1980; lectr. Boston Coll., Chestnut Hill, Mass., 1974-79; instr. North Shore Cmty. Coll., Beverly, Mass., 1972-79; dean women Baker U., Baldwin City, Kans., 1967-71, instr. sociology, 1967-71; tchr. Shawnee Mission H.S. Dist., Kans., 1961-67; chair Presbytery Social Justice Com., Willmar, 1985-90, 94—, chair, 1994-96; mem. Synod Work Group in Social Justice, 1989-94, moderator, 1991-92; co-chair ethics com. Rice Meml. Hosp., 1993—; pastor United Presbyn. Ch., Kerkhoven, Mich., 1997—, First Presbyn. Ch., Maynard, Minn., 1997—. Author: (instr.'s guide) Introduction to Sociology, 1979; contbr. numerous book revs. in Theology Today, 1982-85. Mem. City of Willmar Heartland Express Bd., 1990-92, Kandiyohi County Probation Coun. Adv. Bd., 1991-94, Willmar Cmty. Edn. Adv. Bd., 1996—, Kandiyohi County Children's Trust Fund Coun., 1990-94, Willmar Ministerial Assn., 1985—, pres., 1989-90, bd. dirs. 1996—. Recipient Disting. Svc. award, Kiwanis, 1990, Spiritual Aims award, Minn.-Dakotas Dist., 1989-90. Mem. AAUW (bd. dirs. 1992—, pres. elect 2005—), Am. Sociol. Assn., Kiwanis (bd. dirs. 1991-94, v.p. 2005-06), Zeta Tau Alpha. Office: Rice Meml Hosp 301 Becker Ave SW Willmar MN 56201-3395 Home: 111 15th Ave Nw Willmar MN 56201-2193

CRUTHIRD, BRANDY K., gym owner and fitness instructor; BS in Communications and Pub. Rels., James Madison Univ., Harrisonburg. VA. Former mktg. rep. Reebok Internat., Inc.; founder, owner, pres. Body by Brandy Fitness, Boston, 1996—. Contbr. articles to profl. online jours. Fitness demonstrator YWCA Breast Cancer Awareness Day, Af. Am. Women on Tour Convention; co-organizer Everybody Walk Your Body Fitness and Health Fair, Boston, 1997—. Named Rookie Yr., NCAA Women's Basketball; named one of 40 Under 40, Boston Bus. Jour., 2005; recipient Girl Scout's Leading Women award, 2001, Rebecca Lee award, Harvard Univ., 2002. Home: Body by Brandy 2181 Washington St Roxbury MA 02119*

CRUVER, SUZANNE LEE, communications executive, writer; b. Indpls., Mar. 24, 1942; d. William Edward and Margaret Rosetta (McArtor) Ozzard; m. Donald Richard Cruver, June 9, 1963 (div. Feb. 1989); children: Donald Scott, Kimberly Sue, Brian Richard. BA in English, Rutgers U., 1964; postgrad., Rice U., 1990—. Asst. dir. pub. rels. dept Upsala Coll., East Orange, N.J., 1964-65; asst. planner, pub. editor N.J. Divsn. State & Regional Planning, Trenton, 1967-68; realtor Vonnie Cobb Realtors, Houston, 1979-81; owner Sugar Land Comm., 1980-94; exec. v.p., mktg. mgr. Photoflight Aviation Corp., Sugar Land, Tex., 1982; exec. v.p., artist mgr. H. McMillan Orgn., Inc., Sugar Land, 1983-85; account exec. Mel Anderson Comm., Inc., Houston, 1986; exec. dir. Ft. Bend Arts Coun., Sugar Land, 1986-87; dir. resource devel., vol. svcs., pub. info. Richmond (Tex.) State Sch., Tex. Dept. Mental Health/Mental Retardation, 1987-93; dir. corp. and found. giving Meml. Found., Meml. Healthcare Sys., Houston, 1993-94; owner SLC Comms., Houston & Englewood, Fla., 1994-2000; mktg. coord., pub. info. officer Gulf Coast Workforce Bd. Houston-Galveston Area Coun., 2000—. Mem. adv. bd. Ft. Bend Regional Coun. on Alcoholism and Drug Abuse, Rosenburg, Tex., 1989—. Writer, editor: PATCH Handbook: A Parent to Parent Guide to Texas Children's Hospital, 1983, Ft. Bend mag., 1985-86; book editor, contbg. writer: Fort Bend County, Texas - A Pictorial History, 1996. Pres. Ft. Bend Arts Coun., Ft. Bend County, Tex., 1987-89; founding dir. PATCH, Tex. Children's Hosp., Houston, 1982; mem. adv. bd. Challenger Ctr. of Ft. Bend; committeeman Houston Livestock Show & Rodeo, 1996—; co-coord. 25th Anniversary of lunar landing celebration and internat. space expo, Houston, 1994; bd. dirs. United Way South Sarasota County. Mem. NAFE, Nat. Soc. Fundraising Execs., Women in Comm., Ft. Bend Profl. Women, Pub. Rels. Soc. Am., Houston (Tex.) Advt. Fedn., Houston World Trade Assn., Ft. Bend C. of C., Rosenberg/Rich C. of C., Leadership Tex. Alumni Assn., Exch. Club of Sugar Land, Ft. Bend Exch. Club (charter bd. mem.). Republican. Presbyterian. Avocations: travel, scuba diving, golf, dance, photography. Business E-Mail: sue.cruver@theworksource.org.

CRUZ, CASSANDRA, elementary school educator; b. Ga. m. Paul Cruz; children: Kierra, Kianna. M in Acctg., Ga. So. U. 6th grade math tchr. Long County Bd. Edn., Ludowici, Ga., 2004—. Vis. scholar HOPE scholar, 1997—2002. Mem.: PA Ga. Educators. Office Phone: 912-545-2069.

CRUZ, PENELOPE, actress; b. Madrid, Apr. 28, 1974; d. Eduardo and Encarna Cruz. Studied classical ballet, Nat. Conservatory, Madrid. Actor: (films) El Laberinto griego, 1991, Belle époque, 1992, Jamón, jamón, 1992, La Ribelle, 1993, La Celestina, 1996, Más que amor, frenesí, 1996, Et Hjørne af paradis, 1997, Carne trémula, 1997, Abre los ojos, 1997, Don Juan, 1998, The Man with Rain in His Shoes, 1998, Talk of Angels, 1998, La Niña de tus ojos, 1998, The Hi-Lo Country, 1998, Todo sobre mi madre, 1999, Volavèrunt, 1999, Woman on Top, 2000, All the Pretty Horses, 2000, Blow, 2001, Captain Corelli's Mandolin, 2001, Sin noticias de Dios, 2001, Vanilla Sky, 2001, Waking Up in Reno, 2002, Masked and Anonymous, 2003, Fanfan la tulipe, 2003, Gothika, 2003, Noel, 2004, Head in the Clouds, 2004, Sahara, 2005, Chromophobia, 2005, Bandidas, 2006, Volver, 2006 (Hollywood Actress of the Yr. award, Hollywood Awards, 2006); (TV films) Framed, 1992. Founder Sabera Found. Named a Knight in Order of Arts and Letters, France, 2006. Office: Creative Artists Agy 9830 Wilshire Blvd Beverly Hills CA 90212*

CRUZ, ROSALINA SEDILLO, marriage and family therapist; b. Dumaguete City, The Philippines, Apr. 1, 1933; came to U.S., 1957; d. Dionisio Sedillo and Simplicia Raagas; m. Anatolio Benedicto Cruz Jr., Apr. 28, 1955; children: Raquel Regina, Anatolio Benedicto III, Anthony Bradley, Roselle Regina. BS in Edn., U. of the Philippines, Manila, 1955; MEd in Guidance Counseling, Trinity U., San Antonio, 1972; Specialist Degree Marriage/Family Therap, St. Mary's U., San Antonio, 1980. Cert. marriage and family therapist, Tex. Tchr. Roosevelt H.S., Manila, 1955-57, Holy Spirit Cath. Sch., San Antonio, 1968-70; counselor Holy Spirit Sch., San Antonio, 1972-75, part-time counselor, 1990—; pvt. practice marriage and family therapy San Antonio, 1980—. Adv. bd. Child Abuse Prevention Svcs., San Antonio, 1994—; chmn. family adv. bd. St. Mary's U., San Antonio, 1985-86. Named Vol. of Yr., Child Abuse Prevention Svcs., 1991. Mem. Am. Assn. Marriage and Family Therapy (clin.), Tex. Counseling Assn. (mem. lobbying-licensure com. 1980, ethics com. 1985—), San Antonio Marriage and Family Therapy (pres. 1985-86), South Tex. Assn. Marriage and Family Therapy, Lic. Profl. Counselors of Tex. (ethics com. 1995—). Roman Catholic. Avocations: tennis, reading, jogging, swimming, cooking. Home: 1118 Mount Eden Dr San Antonio TX 78213-2226 Office: 4402 Vance Jackson Rd San Antonio TX 78230-5336

CRUZ, TEOFILA PEREZ, nursing administrator; AS, U. Guam, 1970; BSN, St. Louis U., 1973; MS in Nursing Adminstrn., U. Hawaii, 1989. Founder 1st hemodialysis unit Guam Med. Hosp., Agana, Guam, 1974, hosp. nurse supr. II critical care units, 1978-85; with various hemodialysis units, 1974-77; emergency rm. dept. nurse III then headnurse Med. Ctr. Marianas, Guam, 1977; instr. Sch. Nursing U. Guam, 1978; nurse examiner adminstr. Dept. Pub. Health and Social Svcs., Guam, 1985-88, health profl. lic. adminstr., 1988-97, 98—; clin. svc. adminstr. Guam Meml. Hosp. Authority, 1997-98. —dminstr. Guam Bd. Nurse Examiners, Guam Bd. Med. Examiners, Guam Bd. Examiners for Pharmacy, Guam Bd. Examiners for Dentistry, Guam Bd. Examiners Optometry, Guam Bd. Allied Health Examiners, Commn. on Healing Arts of Guam, Bd. Cosmetology; mem. exam. com. computer adaptive test Nat. Coun. State Bds. Nursing, 1991-92, com. alt., 1993-98, mem. exam. com., 1998—; past mem. com. and chmn. Emergency Med. Svcs. Commn. Mem. Young Men's League of Guam Women's Aux., ROTC Parents Com., Sigma Theta Tau. Office: Guam Bd Medical Examiners PO Box 2816 Hagatna GU 96932

CRUZ, WILHELMINA MANGAHAS, critical care physician, educator; b. Bulacan, Philippines, July 20, 1942; d. Rectorino Bernardo and Mercedes Correa (Mangahas) C.; m. Antonio I. Lee, May 28, 1977; children: Richard Anthony, Alexander Victor. AA, U. Santo Tomas, The Philippines, 1960, MD, 1965. Diplomate in internal medicine and critical care medicine Am. Bd. Internal Medicine; diplomate Am. Bd. Nephrology. Intern Meml. Hosp., Albany, NY, 1967-68; resident in internal medicine Coney Island Hosp., Bklyn., 1968-71; fellow in nephrology VA Hosp., Bronx, 1971-72, SUNY Downstate Med. Ctr., Bklyn., 1972-73; staff physician King's County Hosp. Ctr., Bklyn., 1973-76; coord. in medicine Kingsbrook Jewish Med. Ctr., Bklyn., 1976—. Assoc. med. dir. ICU Drs. Cmty. Hosp., Lanham, Md., 1977-99; med. dir. Critical Care Svcs., 1999—; clin. asst. prof. SUNY Downstate Med. Ctr., 1977—. Mem. ACP, Med. and Chirurg. Soc. Md., Prince George's Med. Soc., Soc. Critical Care Medicine, Philippine Med. Assn. Washington. Roman Catholic. Office: 7700 Old Branch Ave Ste D205 Clinton MD 20735-1611 Office Phone: 301-868-3858.

CRUZ, ZOE, diversified financial services company executive; b. Feb. 2, 1955; m. Ernesto Cruz. BA in Literature, Harvard U., 1977, MBA, 1982. With Morgan Stanley, 1982—, v.p., 1986—88, prin., fixed income, 1988—90, mng. dir., fixed income, 1990—93, co-chief, fgn. exch., 1993—2000, head of worldwide fixed income, fgn. exch. and commodities, 2000—05, acting pres., 2005—06, co-pres., 2005, 2006—, bd. dirs., 2005—. Named one of Most Powerful Women, Forbes mag., 2005—06, Top 50 Women To Watch, Wall St. Jour., 2005, 50 Most Powerful Women in Bus., Fortune mag., 2006. Office: Morgan Stanley 1585 Broadway New York NY 10036*

CRUZ-CONNERTON, MAYRA, elementary school educator; d. Louis Cruz and Maria Christina Quiñones-Cruz; m. Christopher Charles Connerton, Aug. 29, 1998; children: Isabella Maria Connerton(dec.), Julian Christopher Connerton, Gabriel Ryan Connerton. BA in English Lit., Georgian Ct. Coll., 1993, postgrad., 1994—. Tchr. Atlantic City (N.J.) Bd. Edn., 1997—. Adj. prof. Atlantic Cape C.C., NJ, 2006. Author: When Children Go to Heaven, 2004. Named Gov.'s Tchr. of Yr., State of N.J., 1998—99. Democrat. Roman Catholic. Avocations: reading, writing.

CRUZE, JENNIFER LEA, secondary school educator; b. Hurst, Tex., Oct. 2, 1970; d. David Roy and Betsy Carolyn Esslinger; m. Dennis Wayne Cruze, Apr. 27, 1997; children: Nathaniel, Miranda; m. Gerald Irwin Appel (div.); 1 child, Maxwell. BA in Biology, Tex. Christian U., Ft. Worth, Tex., 1993; MS in Chemistry and Physics, U. Tex., Arlington, Tex., 2005. Tchr. chemistry LD Bell H.S. Hurst-Euless-Bedford (Tex.) Ind. Sch. Dist., 1999—. Coord. drug edn. L.D. Bell H.S., Hurst, 2002—06, organizer Key Club, 1999—2006; writer curriculum Hurst Euless Bedford (Tex.) Ind. Sch. Dist., 2005—06; presenter in field; lectr. U. Tex., Arlington, 2006—. Named Tchr. of Yr., L.D. Bell H.S., 2003, Runner Up, Dist. Secondary Tchr. of Yr., Hurst-Euless-Bedford Sch. Dist., 2002—03; grantee, Meadows Found., 2003—06. Mem.: NEA, Nat. Sci. Tchrs. Assn., Kiwanis. Avocations: painting, reading, sudoku, home improvement projects. Home: 1100 Roundhouse Dr Saginaw TX 76131 Office: LD Bell High Sch 1601 Brown Trail Hurst TX 76054 Office Phone: 817-282-2551 x7364. Business E-Mail: cruzej@hebisd.edu.

CRUZ-MANRIQUE, DIANA ELIZABETH, elementary school educator; d. Gloria Edith Cuevas; m. Abel Ernesto Manrique, Feb. 20, 2005; 1 child, Jaiden Elizabeth Manrique. BA in Elem Edn., Northeastern Ill. U., 1995; MA in Reading, Chgo. State U., 2000; MA in Ednl. Leadership, U. Nev., 2006. Reading program coord. Chgo. Pub. Schs., 2001—03; 4th gr. lead tchr. Clark County Sch. Dist., Las Vegas, 2003—05, English lang. learner facilitator, 2005—. Office: Clark County Sch Dist 4850 Kell Ln Las Vegas NV 89115 Office Phone: 702-799-8820. Personal E-mail: cruzdi32@hotmail.com. Business E-Mail: cruzdi32@yahoo.com.

CRUZ-MYERS, THERESA, finance company executive; V.p. Nationwide Finl. Retirement Plans, Columbus, Ohio. Co-chmn. corp. adv. coun. Nat. Conf. Black Mayors; contbr. Nat. Assn. Govt. Defined Contbn. Adminstrs. Named to Elite Women, Hispanic Bus. Mag., 2005. Office: Nationwide Fin One Nationwide Plz Columbus OH 43215 Office Phone: 614-435-1564. Office Fax: 303-987-5370. Business E-Mail: myerst9@nationwide.com.

CRUZ-ROMO, GILDA, soprano; b. Guadalajara, Jalisco, Mexico; came to U.S., 1967; d. Feliciano and Maria del Rosario (Diaz) C.; m. Robert B. Romo, June 10, 1967. Grad., Coll. Nueva Galicia, Guadalajara, 1958; student, Nat. Conservatory of Music of Mexico, Mexico City, 1962-64. Tchr. voice U. Tex., Austin, 1990—. Assoc. prof., coach, voice tchr. U. Tex., Austin, 1990—. With Nat. and Internat. Opera, Mexico City, 1962-67, toured, Australia, N.Z., S.Am., with, Dallas Civic Opera, 1966-68, N.Y.C. Opera, 1969-72, Lyric Opera Chgo., 1975, Met. Opera debut as Madama Butterfly, 1970, leading soprano, 1970—, appeared in U.S. and abroad including Covent Garden, La Scala, Vienna State Opera, Rome Opera, Paris Opera, Florence Opera, Torino Opera, Verona Opera, Portugal, Buenos Aires, others, concert appearances in U.S., Can., Mexico; U.S. rep. World-Wide Madama Butterfly Competition, Tokyo, 1970; La Scala rep. in: Aida, USSR, 1974; appeared on radio, TV; filmed and recorded: Aida, with Orange Festival, France, 1976; roles include Aida, Madama Butterfly, Suor Angelica, Tosca, Odabella in Attila; Manon Lescaut, Leonora in Il Trovatore; Norma; Maddelena in Andrea Chenier; Desdemona in Otello; Donna Anna in Don Giovanni; Santuzza in Cavalleria Rusticana; (title role) La Gioconda; Adriana Lecouvreur; Luisa Miller; Elisabetta in Don Carlo; Margherite in Faust; Venus in Tannhauser; Giorgetta in Il Tabarro; also roles in Macbeth, Turnadot, Norma, Medea. Named Winner Met. Opera Nat. Auditions, 1970, Best Singer, 1976—77, honoree, Opera Guild of San Antonio, 2003; recipient Critics award, Union Mexicana de Cronistas de Teatro y Musica, 1973, Minerva al Arte award, Mexico, 1991, Silver Bird award, Govt. of Jalisco, Mexico, 1998, season Cronistas de Santiago de Chile, 1976, Baccarat 2001 award, The Licia Albanese-Puccini Found., 2001, Lifetime Achievement award, Nat. Opera Assn., 2003, Pedro Sarquis Merrewe Found., 2004, Gold medal fine arts, Bellas Artec, Mex., 2006. Personal E-mail: bobgilda2@sbcglobal.net.

CRUZ-WEAVER, BONNIE E., elementary school educator; b. Fremont, Ohio, Jan. 1, 1977; d. Erasmo Cruz Jr. and Elphida Jaramillo; m. Brian E. Weaver, Dec. 14, 2005. AA, Terra C.C., Fremont, 1998; BS in Edn., Bowling Green State U., Ohio, 2001, MEd, 2004. Server Ponderosa Steakhouse, Fremont, Ohio, 1993—95, Ryns Steakhouse, 1995—2001; site dir. Tex. Migrant Coun., 1999—2001; tchr. 4th grade Stamm Elem. Sch., 2001—04; specialist English as 2d lang. Cooghan Elem. Sch., 2004—. Mem.: Vaces Unides Sandusky. Office: Fremont City Schs 1115 Chestnut St Fremont OH 43420

CRYAR, RHONDA LYNN, elementary school educator; b. Demopolis, Ala., Jan. 10, 1967; d. Ronald Alvin and Nancy Stewart Melton; m. Steven Glenn Cryar, Feb. 5, 2000; children: Steven Ray, Terry O'Neal Melton. BS in Elem. Edn., Judson Coll., Marion, Ala., 1989; M in Elem. Edn., U. Montevallo, Ala., 1992. Cert. elem. edn. Ala., 1989. 4th grade tchr. Hale County Pub. Schs., Greensboro, Ala., 1989—93; 3rd grade tchr. Mobile County Pub. Schs., Ala., 2000—04; lang. arts tchr. Baldwin County Pub. Schs., Bay Minette, Ala., 2004—. Partner's in edn. liason Mobile County Pub. Schs., 2000—04; ARI reading/writing connection presenter South Ala. Rsch. and Inservice Ctr., Mobile, 2003—04; master tchr. Ala. Reading Acad. Ala. State Dept. Edn., Montgomery, 2003—04; writing curriculum task force mem. Mobile Pub. Schs., 2003—04. Named Ella Grant Elem. Tchr. of Yr., Mobile County Commn., 2002, Ella Grant Tchr. of Yr., 2004, Tchr. of Quarter, Baldwin EMC, 2005. Mem.: NEA, Ala. Edn. Assn. Office Phone: 251-937-9243.

CUARTAS, BEATRIZ H., humanities educator; b. Bucaramanga, Santander, Colombia, June 9, 1977; arrived in US, 1992, naturalized, 1999; d. Sergio Leon Cuartas and Clotilde Jaimes-Duran; life ptnr. Hans-Filip Jorgen Fex; 1 child, Ulysses Del Mar Chaslus. BA in Internat. Affairs & Polit. Sci., U. Maine, Orono, 1999; DEA in Comparative Polit. Sci., Polit. Sci. Inst., France, 2002. Cert. notary pub. Tex. Sec. State, Dallas, 2004. ESOL instr. Colombo-

Am. Alliance, Bucaramanga, Colombia, 1993—94; rsch. intern OAS, Washington, 1999; exec. asst. Inter-Am. Devel. Bank, 2002—03; French, Spanish instr. Pk. U., El Paso, Tex., 2003—04; analyst US Govt. Accountability Office, Dallas, 2004—05; govt. instr. El Paso CC, 2005—. Writer Norton Pub. Co., NYC, 2005—; faculty coord., sen. El Paso CC, 2005—. Vol. dep. registrar Tex. Sec. State, El Paso, 2005; moderator El Paso CC Candidate Awareness Debate; vol. Get Out the Vote. Recipient Vol. of Yr. award, Socorro Head Start, 2003, Cmty. Svc. Achievement award; scholar, Pi Sigma Alpha Honors Soc. Mem.: El Paso CC Faculty Senate, Upper Rio Grande Econs. Assn. Independent. Roman Catholic. Avocations: swimming, sports, reading, writing, travel. Office: El Paso CC PO Box 20500 El Paso TX 79998-0500 Home Fax: 915-831-5122; Office Fax: 915-831-5122. Business E-Mail: bchaslus@epcc.edu.

CUBA, MATTIE DENEICE, elementary school educator; b. Tyler, Tex., Oct. 1, 1958; d. Will Oscar and Frances Marie Arps; m. Larry Darnell Arps, Feb. 14, 1986. BA, Prairie View A&M U., Tex., 1981. Cert. tchr. Tex., 1981. Theatre arts tchr. 6-8 grades Foster Mid. Sch., Longview, Tex., 1990—2006; theatre arts tchr. Longview ISD, Tex., 1990—. Mem.: Tex. Classroom Tchrs. Assn. (life), Delta Sigma Theta (parliamentarian 1991—2006). Home: 1313 Fairmont Longview TX 75601-4320 Office: Foster Middle School 410 S Green St Longview TX 75602 Office Phone: 903-753-1692. Home Fax: 903-753-0559. E-mail: mcuba@lisd.org.

CUBBERLEY, GAYLE SUSAN, band director; b. Trenton, N.J., Aug. 18, 1952; d. Carlton Burton Cubberley and Mary Elizabeth Tantum. BMus in Edn., U. Miami, 1974, MusM in Edn., 1975. Cert. tchr. Fla. Music tchr. Homestead (Fla.) Jr. H.S., Homestead, 1976—78, Campbell Jr. H.S., Florida City, 1978—79; band dir. Nautilus Jr. H.S., Miami Beach, Fla., 1979—80, West Miami Mid. Sch., Miami, 1980—2003, Lamar Louise Curry Mid. Sch., 2003—. Solo 1st chair clarinetist Greater Miami Symphonic Band, 1976—; clarinetist Klezmer Band, 2002—. Mem.: Dade County Music Educators Assn., Fla. Bandmasters Assn., Music Educators Nat. Conf. Avocations: tennis, sailing, scuba diving, skiing. Home: 11281 SW 88th St K-216 Miami FL 33176-1158 Office: Lamar Louise Curry Mid Sch 15750 SW 47th St Miami FL 33185

CUBIN, BARBARA LYNN, congresswoman; b. Salinas, Calif., Nov. 30, 1946; d. Russell G. and Barbara Lee (Howard) Sage; m. Frederick William Cubin, Aug. 1; children: William Russell, Frederick William III. BS in Chemistry, Creighton U., 1969. Chemist Wyo. Machinery Co., Casper, Wyo., 1973-75; social worker State of Wyo.; office mgr. Casper, Wyo.; mem. Wyo. Ho. Reps., 1987-92, Wyo. Senate, 1993-94; pres. Spectrum Promotions and Mgmt., Casper, 1993-94; mem. US Congress from Wyo., Washington, 1995—; mem. resources com., energy and commerce com. Mem. steering com. Exptl. Program to Stimulate Competitive Rsch. (EPSCOR); mem. Coun. of State Govts.; active Gov.'s Com. on Preventive Medicine, 1992; vice chmn. Cleer Bd. Energy Coun., Irving, Tex., 1993—; chmn. Wyo. Senate Rep. Conf., Casper, 1993—; mem. Wyo. Rep. Party Exec. Com., 1993; pres. Southridge Elem. Sch. PTO, Casper, Wyo. Toll fellow Coun. State Govts., 1990, Wyo. Legislator of Yr. award for energy and environ. issues Edison Electric Inst., 1994. Mem. Am. Legis. Exch. Coun., Rep. Women. Republican. Avocations: bridge, golf, singing, reading, hunting. Office: US House of Reps 1114 Longworth House Office Bldg Washington DC 20515-5001 also: Dist Office 100 East B St Ste 4003 Casper WY 82601*

CUDAK, GAIL LINDA, lawyer; b. Bellville, Ill., July 13, 1952; d. Robert Joseph and Margaret Lucille Cudak; m. Thomas Edward Young, Sept. 15, 1979. BA, Kenyon Coll., 1974; JD, Case Western Res. U., 1977, MBA, 1991. Bar: Ohio 1977, U.S. Dist. Ct. (no. dist.) Ohio 1977, U.S. Ct. Appeals (6th cir.) 1977, U.S. Ct. Appeals (fed. cir.) 1989. Assoc. Fuerst, Leidner, Dougherty & Kasdan, Cleve., 1977-79; staff atty. The B.F. Goodrich Co., Akron, Ohio, 1979-84, sr. corp. counsel Independence, Ohio, 1985-89, divsn. counsel Brecksville, Ohio, 1990-98, group counsel, 1998-99; counsel ops. Eaton Corp., Cleve., 1999—. Trustee Great Lakes Theater Festival, 1992—, mem. exec. com. Mem.: ABA, Assn. Corp. Counsel (trustee N.E. Ohio chpt. 2006—), Cleve. Internat. Lawyers Group, Cleve. Bar Assn. (past chair corp. sect.), Ohio State Bar Assn. Home: 12520 Edgewater Dr Apt 1405 Lakewood OH 44107-1639 Office: Eaton Corp 1111 Superior Ave E Cleveland OH 44114-2507

CUDDIHY, JUNE TUCK, pediatrics nurse; b. Buffalo, June 15, 1936; d. John R. Sr. and Monica A. (Donahue) Tuck; m. Robert V. Cuddihy, Aug. 24, 1957; children: Robert V., Timothy, Kathleen. BSN, D'Youville Coll., Buffalo, 1957; MA, Seton Hall U., 1972, MSN, 1979. Cert. primary care nurse practitioner. Pub. health nurse Monroe County, Rochester, N.Y.; health coord. Early Childhood Learning Ctrs. N.J., Morristown; asst. prof. Seton Hall U., South Orange, N.J., 1977-81, William Paterson Coll., Wayne, N.J., 1981-94; clin. assoc. Coll. Nursing Ohio State U., 1994-97; cons. Berkeley BioMedical Group, Inc., 1991—; mem. faculty Western Mich. U., Kalamazoo, 1997—. Contbr. articles to profl. jours. Named Outstanding Grad. Student, Seton Hall U., 1979. Mem. ANA (vice chmn. bd. examiners for cmty. health nursing practice, chmn. sch. nurse practice subcom.), N.J. State Nurses Assn., Nat. Child Abuse Assn., Nat. Burn Victim Found., Pub. Health Assn., Sigma Theta Tau. Office: Ohio State U Coll Nursing Dept Cmty Parent Child Psyc 1585 Neil Ave Columbus OH 43210-1216 Home: 399 Meyersville Rd Gillette NJ 07933-1209

CUDNEY, AMELIA HARRISON, medical/surgical nurse, obstetrics/gynecological nurse; b. Eatonton, Ga., Apr. 5, 1961; d. Patrick Wesley and Mary Lee (Covert) Harrison; m. Phillip M. Sperin (div. Dec. 1987); children: Phillip Wesley, Lauren Heicha; m. Lester Cudney, Aug. 6, 2005. LPN, Pickens Vocat. Tech. Sch., 1980; BSN, Med. Coll. Ga., 1984. RN, Ga. Med.-surg. nurse Cobb Gen. Hosp., Austell, Ga., 1983-85; nurse case mgr. N.W. Home Health, Jasper, Ga., 1991-93; nurse Northside Hosp.-Cherokee at R.T. Jones Campus, Canton, Ga., 1987—. Active mem. Jasper First Bapt. Ch. Office: Northside Hosp-Cherokee 201 Hospital Rd Canton GA 30114-2408 Office Phone: 770-720-5300.

CUEBAS IRIZARRY, ANA E., director; b. Mayaguez, P.R., Apr. 29, 1944; d. Francisco Cuebas and Isidora Irizarry. BA in Econ., Coll. Agr. & Mechanics Arts, Mayaguez, 1965; MLA, Pratt Inst., 1967; MPA, U. P.R., Rio Piedras, 1972; postgrad., U. P.R., San Germán, 2001—. Head reference collection Gen. Libr. U. P.R., Mayaguez, 1972—75, dir. pub. svcs., 1975—78, dir. documentation ctr. and cultural promotion, 1978—79, head purotorrican collector, 1978—80, head serials dept., 1980—86, project dir. title III Auguadilla, 1986—88, dir. continuing edn. and profl. studies, 1988—. Part-time prof. U. P.R., Mayaguez, 1972—82, mem. libr. personal com., Aguadilla, 1988—, coord. students deanship, 1990—, pres. continuing edn. dirs. com., Rio Piedras, PR, 1994—97; mem. consultive bd. Coun. Superior Edn., Rio Piedras, 1995; trustee Consorcio del Noroeste. Author: (book) Diccionario de siglas en uso en PR, 1979, En busca de una bibliografía para Mayagüez, 1982; contbr. articles to profl. jours. Mem. Cultural: Eugenio María de Hostos, Mayaguez, 1985—94. Recipient Spl. recognition, Altrusa Internat. Mayaguez, 1996—98, plaque of Recognition, Sindrome Down Assn., 2002, 2004, Altrusa Internat. Ing. 14th Dist., 1992—94, cert. of Recognition, Coun. Superior Edn. P.R., 2002; grantee, 2002, P.R. Humanities Endowment, 1998, Consejo de Desarrollo Ocupacional y Recursos Humanos, 1998, Works Rights Adminstrn., 2000, Dept. Edn., Rincón Sch. Dist., 2002, Dept. Edn., P.R., 2002, San Sebastián Sch. Dist., P.R., 2002. Mem.: PR ASCD, ASCD, Puertorrican Assn. Continuing Edn., Asociación Puertorriqueña Educación Continua, Phi Delta Kappa. Avocations: cooking, reading, Three Kings collector. Home: 626 Yaurel ST Mayaguez PR 00682-6233 Office: U PR Bell St Aguadilla PR 00604-0160 Personal E-mail: a_cuebas@hotmail.com.

CUENCA, CARMEN, piano teacher; b. Oct. 25, 1960; M of Music, U. Miami, 1996. Piano tchr. Fla. State Music Tchrs. Apprentice Judging, Miami, 1983—. Mem. Am. Coll. Musicians/Guild Piano Tchrs. (adjudicator), Nat. Music Tchrs. Assn., Fla. State Music Tchrs., Miami Music Tchrs. Assn. (v.p. 1999—, pres. elect 2005—, chair).

CUETO, ROCHELLE E., elementary school educator; b. Chgo., Nov. 19, 1949; d. Morris and Marsha L. (Rotman) Federman; m. Fernando J. Cueto, Sept. 13, 1979 (div. Aug. 1987); children: Steven, Jennifer; children: Eric Raymond, Laura Raymond. BA Spl. Edn., Northeastern Ill. U., 1974, MA Spl. Edn., 1980. Cert. tchr. Ill., spl. edn., lang. arts cert./endorsement, mid. sch. endorsement, sci. endorsement, cert. family life coord., Golden Tchr. coach. Tchr. elem. Jordan Cmty. Sch. Chgo. Pub. Schs., 1975—. Judge Chgo. Bd. Elections, 1977. Mem.: NSTA, Ill. Sci. Tchrs. Assn. Jewish. Avocations: needlepoint, reading, gardening. Home: 7233A N Campbell Ave Chicago IL 60645 Office: Jordan Cmty Sch 7414 N Wolcott Ave Chicago IL 60626 Office Phone: 773-534-2220.

CUFF, VIRGINIA EVELYN, architectural firm executive, consultant; d. Raymond and Dorothy Edwina Williams; m. Elliott Cuff, Dec. 9, 1989. MPA, Baruch Coll., NY, 1998. Founding exec. dir. Family & Life Ctr. Mt. Ararat, Bklyn., 1994—2004; exec. asst. to exec. commr. NYC Human Resources Adminstrn., 1996—97; cons., pres. Virgelli-Snu, Inc., Mason, Ohio, 2006—; archtl. adminstr. DHArchitects, Inc., Fairfield, 2006—. Bd. mem. Scholarship Found. Mt. Ararat, Bklyn., 1995—2004; vp bus. devel. Greater Cin. C. of C., Cin., 2004—05; mem. bd. Help, USA, Bklyn., 2003—04; treas. Northridge Village Assn., Mason, 2006; adv. bd. mem. universal pre-kindergarten fed. initiative Dept. Edn., Dist. 23, 1998—2002. Recipient DAR Good Citizenship award, DAR, Va. Chpt., 1982, Disting. Leadership award, 2001, Ezra award Excellence, Mt. Ararat, 1999, Vigorous Spririt award, Elon Cosmetics, 2005; fellow, Nat. Urban and Rural Fellows, Inc., 1996—98. Mem.: Golden Key Nat. Honor Soc. Baptist. Achievements include development of Music & Arts Academy Serving inner-city children; Assisted in developing an economic development corporation for African American families in the inner-city; Summer Cultural Camp for inner-city children; School-Age program for inner-city children; School with an emphasis on Early Childhood Education for inner-city children. Avocations: tennis, golf, travel, reading, writing. Office: Virgelli-Snu Inc PO Box 132 Mason OH 45040 Office Phone: 513-258-8137. E-mail: consulting@virgelli-snu.com.

CULBERTSON, DEBORAH JEAN, educational consultant; b. Corpus Christi, Tex., May 9, 1957; d. Michael R. and Ottilia Elise Manning; m. Paul Michael Culbertson, Dec. 27, 1980; 1 child, Cassandra Michelle. BA in Edn., Va. Wesleyan Coll., Norfolk, 1991; MEd, Prairie View A&M U., Tex., 2002. Cert. prin. Tex. Dir. edn. Sylvan Learning Ctr., Houston, 1991—93; tchr. Banff Pvt. Sch., Houston, 1993—95, Cypress Fairbanks Ind. Sch. Dist., Houston, 1995—98, asst. to curriculum coord., 1998—2004; reading/dyslexia cons. Edn. Svc. Ctr., Corpus Christi, 2005—. Tutor Culbertson Tutoring, Houston, 1995—98. Vol. ARC, 1982—84. Named Spotlight Tchr., Cypress Fairbanks Ind. Sch. Dist., 1995—96. Mem.: ASCD, Internat. Dyslexia Soc., Nat. Coun. Tchrs. English, Internat. Reading Assn. Avocations: reading, genealogy, gardening, painting. Home: 3006 Moore Ave Portland TX 78374 Office Phone: 361-851-8559. E-mail: dculbertson@esc2.net.

CULBERTSON, JANE YOUNG, statistician; b. Phila., Pa., Sept. 9, 1917; d. Samuel Lemon Young and Jennie Goddard Harper; m. Harry Edward Culbertson (dec.); children: Karen Ruth Corbin, Harry Edward III. BS in Edn., Temple U., Phila., 1938. Statistician Farm Jour., Phila., 1937; sec. to supt. DuPont, Phila. Soloist Local churches in NJ and Pa.; pres., treas. Free Pub. Libr., 1990—92. Recipient Citizen of Yr., Sentinel Ledger, Ocean City, NJ, 1998, Libr. Citation, Ocean City C. of C., 2000. Mem.: MENSA, Ocean City Hist. Mus. Republican. Presbyn. Avocations: bridge, crossword puzzles, Scrabble. Home: 416 W Surf Rd Ocean City NJ 08226

CULBERTSON, JANET LYNN, artist; b. Greensburg, Pa., Mar. 15, 1932; d. Joseph F. and Helen C. (Moore) Culbertson; m. Douglas I. Kaften, Sept. 30, 1964. BFA, Carnegie Inst. Tech., 1953; MA, NYU, 1963. Instr. art Pace Coll., N.Y.C., 1964-68, Pratt Art Inst., Bklyn., 1973; assoc. prof. Southampton Coll., 1976; drawing instr. Parrish Art Mus., 1979. Exhibited one-woman shows 20th Century West Gallery, N.Y.C., 1967, Molly Barnes Gallery, L.A., 1970, Midtown Gallery, Atlanta, 1971, Lerner-Misrachi Gallery, N.Y.C., 1971, Lerner-Heller Gallery, N.Y.C., 1973, 75, 77, Tower Gallery, Southampton, N.Y., 1976, Benson Gallery, Bridgehampton, N.Y., 1978, 81, 89, Interart Gallery, N.Y.C., 1979, Harriman Coll., N.Y., 1980, Nardin Gallery, N.Y.C., 1981, Aronson Gallery, Atlanta, 1982, Harrisburg State Mus. Pa., 1988, Women Artists Series Rutgers U., N.J., 1988, Carnegie Mellon U., Pitts., 1991, Acme Art Co., Columbus, Ohio, 1992, Islip (N.Y.) Mus., 1992, Suffolk Coll., Riverhead, N.Y., 1996, Stone Quarry Art Park, Cazenovia, N.Y., 1996, Wave Hill, Bronx, N.Y., 1997, Atelier A/E Gallery, N.Y.C., 1997, U. Alaska, Anchorage, 1997, Nat. Acad. Scis., Washington, 1998, Hoyt Mus., New Castle, Pa., 1998, U. Nebr., Omahá, 2002, Huntington Arts Coun. Gallery, N.Y., 2002-03, Cambridge Multicultural Arts Ctr., 2003, Nat. Mus. of Women in the Arts, Washington, 2004, Nassau County Mus., Hewlett-Woodmere Gallery, 2004, Ill. Ctrl. Coll., Ohio, 2005, Seton Hill U., Greensburg, Pa., 2006, deCordora Gallery, Greenfort, N.Y., 2006, Hunterdon Mus., Clinton, N.Y., 2006; two-women shows Women's Art Ctr., San Francisco, 1975; four-women show Heckscher Mus., Huntington, N.Y., 1980; numerous group exhbns.from 1953 to present including most recently Parrish Art Mus., Southampton, N.Y., 2000, N.J. Ctr. Visual Arts, Summit, 2000, Toxic Landscapes, Puffin Found. traveling exhib., Morning, Noon and Night, The Long Island Mus. of Stony Brook, N.Y., Earth 2002, U. Miami Coral Gables, Denise Bibro Fine Art, N.Y.C., 2002, Soho Photo, N.Y.C., 2002, Savannah Coll. Art and Design, Ga., 2002, Long Beach Found. for Arts, NJ, 2002, Antioch Coll., Ohio, 2004, Telfair Mus., Savannah, Ga., Silverpoints, 2006, Hunterdon Mus., Clinton, N.J., 2006, others; contbr. collage to Attica Book, 1972; contbr. articles to profl. jours., prodr. and contbr. Heresies #13 mag. Creative Artists Pub. Svc. grantee, 1979. Recipient Shirk Meml. award for oil painting Nat. Assn. Women Artists, Inc., 1993, first place award Notorious L.I. exhibit Hillwood Art Mus., Brookville, N.Y., 1994, Purchase award Hoyt Art Inst., 1995, Purchase award Nassau County Mus. Art, 1997, Print Ctr. Excellence award, Phila., 2001; fellow Ossabaw Found., 1981, Dorland, 1983, Ucross Found., 1989, 99, Blue Mt. Found., 1991, 94, 96, 2000, 02, VCCA Ctr. Found., Ragdale Found., 1984, 2001; David and Julia White Colony, Costa Rica, 2003, 05, Ludwig Vogelstein grantee, 2004, Puffin grantee, 2004. Home: PO Box 455 Shelter Island Heights NY 11965 E-mail: jan@janetculbertson.net.

CULBRETH, LUCRETIA JOY, science educator; d. Dewey N. and Ruth A. (Hughes) Walls, Josephine M. (Bennett) Walls (Stepmother); m. Larry McCoy Culbreth; children: Lauren Nicole (Culbreth) Duty, Lance McCoy. BS in Mid. Grades Edn., North Ga. Coll. and State U., Dahlonega, 1965; MS in Mid. Grades Edn., Columbus Coll. and State U., Ga., 1984; EdS in Curriculum, Instrn., Mgmt., Adminstrn., NOVA Southeastern U., Ft. Lauderdale, Fla., 2003. Cert. elem. tchr. with ednl. specialist degree Ga., 2003. Tchr. sci. Ft. Benning Dependent Sch. Sys., Ga., 1982—85, Coweta County Sch. Sys., Newnan, Ga., 1985—. Chair dept. sci. Madras Mid. Sch., Newnan, Ga., 2001—04, 7th grade tean leader, 2002—03. Recipient Tchr. of Month award, Madras Mid. Sch. Faculty, 2005. Avocations: collector, crochet. Office: Madras Mid Sch 240 Edgeworth Rd Newnan GA 30263 Office Phone: 770-254-2744. E-mail: lucretia.culbreth@cowetaschools.org.

CULLEENEY, MAUREEN ANN, information technology executive, educator; d. Robert P. and Marlene A. Culleeney. PhD, Loyola U. Chgo., 1996; MBA, DePaul U., 1983; EdM, U. Ill., Urbana-Champaign, 1992; BSW, U. Ill., 1976. Registered Social Worker State of Ill., 1982. Med. social worker St. Joseph Hosp., Elgin, Ill., 1977—81; co-founder and prin. Bus. Computer Edn., Inc., Chgo., 1981—84; regional mgr., tng. & product support ICC, Schaumburg, 1984—86; corp. trainer Ashton-Tate, Chgo., 1986—87; computer coord. Village of Schaumburg, Schaumburg, Ill., 1987—89; assoc. prof. and chair bus. comm., chairperson ednl. policy com. Lewis U., Romeoville, Ill., 1989—. Author: WordStar Simplified: Mastering the Essentials on the IBM PC, WordStar Simplified: Mastering the Essentials; contbg. author: Lotus 123: A Business Guide to Productivity; author: Utiliser WordStar. Mem.: Assn. for Bus. Comm., Delta Epsilon Sigma, Delta Sigma Pi.

CULLEN, VALERIE ADELIA, secondary school educator; b. Northampton, Mass., May 28, 1948; d. Stanley Walter and Wanda Mary (Rup) Helstowski; m. Lawrence Joseph Cullen, June 26, 1982; 1 child, Shanna Valerie. BA, Westfield (Mass.) State Coll., 1970; MALS, SUNY, Stony Brook, 1975. Cert. secondary math. tchr., N.Y., Mass. Tchr. math. Brentwood (N.Y.) Pub. Schs., 1970-71, Center Moriches (N.Y.) Jr.-Sr. High Sch., 1971-88, BOCES I, Alternative High Sch. and Adolescent Pregnancy Program, Riverhead, N.Y., 1988-90, Ctr. Moriches (N.Y.) Jr.-Sr. High Sch., 1990—2002. Mem. Nat. Com. to Preserve Social Security and Medicare. Mem.: N.Y. State Ret. Tchrs., N.Y. Math. Tchrs. Assn., N.Y. State United Tchrs., Nat. Coun. Tchrs. Math., Smithsonian Assocs. Home: 4 Keswick Dr East Islip NY 11730-2808

CULLEY, DEBORAH ANITA, science educator; d. Robert H. and Effie A. Dolan; children: Chad, Eric, Joanna, Janelle. BA in Biology, Gettysburg Coll., 1973. Cert. instrnl. II tchng. Pa. Tchr., biology Norristown (Pa.) HS, 1974—77, Conestoga HS, Berwyn, Pa., 1978—80; tchr., life sci. Santa Fe Christian Schs., Solana Beach, Calif., 1989—, sci. dept. chair, 2000—05. Women's gymnastic coach Norristown HS, 1974—77; jr. varsity coach, field hockey Conestoga HS, 1978—80. Mem.: NSTA. Office: Santa Fe Christian Schs 838 Academy Dr Solana Beach CA 92075 Office Phone: 858-755-8900.

CULLINA, JOANNE FRANCES, medical/surgical nurse; b. Evergreen Park, Ill., Apr. 23, 1960; d. William J. Jr. and Alice (Rowland) C. BSN, St. Mary's Coll., Notre Dame, Ind., 1982. RN, Ill. Commd. 2 lt. USAF, 1982, advanced through grades to maj., 1986; coord. adult systic fibrosis clin. Northwestern U., Oak Lawn, Ill. Capt. USAFR, 1991. Mem. Officers Assn., Air Force Assn., Assn. Mil. Surgeons U.S., Respiratory Nursing Soc. Home: 11021 S Ridgeway Ave Chicago IL 60655-4026 Office: St 14-002 675 N St Clare Chicago IL 60611

CULLINAN, BERNICE ELLINGER, education educator; b. Hamilton, Ohio, Oct. 12, 1926; d. Lee Alexander and Hazel (Berry) Dees; m. George W. Ellinger, June 5, 1948 (div. 1966); children: Susan Jane Ellinger, James Webb Ellinger; m. Paul Anthony Cullinan, June 9, 1967 (div. 1994); m. Kenneth Seeman Giniger, Apr. 13, 2002. BS, Ohio State U., 1948, MA, 1951, PhD, 1964. Cert. elem. educator Ohio, N.Y. Tchr. Maple Pk. Elem. Sch., Middletown, Ohio, 1944-46, Trotwood (Ohio) Elem. Sch., 1946-47, Columbus (Ohio) Pub. Schs., 1948-50, Upper Arlington (Ohio) Pub. Schs., 1950-52; instr. Ohio State U., Columbus, 1959-64, asst. prof., 1964-67, Ohio State U./Charlotte Huck prof. children's lit., 1997; assoc. prof. NYU, N.Y.C., 1967-72, prof. reading, 1972-97, prof. emeritus, 1998—; editor-in-chief Wordsong Books, Honesdale, Pa., 1990—. Chair selection com. Ezra Jack Keats New Writer award, 1984—2000; exec. sec. English Stds. Project, 1993—94. Author (with Lee Galda): Literature and the Child, 1989, 6th edit., 2006; author: Children's Literature in the Classroom: Weaving Charlotte's Web, 1989, 2d edit., 1994, Read to Me: Raising Kids Who Love to Read, 1992, 3d edit., 2006, Let's Read About: Finding Books They'll Love to Read, 1993; author: (with Brod Bagert) Helping Your Child Learn to Read, 1993; author: (with Dorothy Strickland and Lee Galda) Language Arts: Learning and Tchg., 2003; author: (with L. Galda and D. Strickland) Language, Literacy and the Child, 1993; author: 3d edit., 2002; author: (with Marilyn Scala and Virginia Schroder) Three Voices: Invitation to Poetry Across the Curriculum, 1995; author: 75 Authors and Illustrators Everyone Should Know, 1994; author: (with David Harrison) Poetry Lessons That Dazzle and Delight, 1999; editor: Children's Literature in the Reading Program, 1987, Invitation to Read: More Children's Literature in the Reading Program, 1992, Black Dialects and Reading, 1974, Fact and Fiction: Literature Across the Curriculum, 1993, Children's Voices, 1993, Pen in Hand, 1993, A Jar of Tiny Stars, 1996; editor: (with Diane Person) The Continuum Encyclopedia of Children's Literature, 2003; editor: (with Bonnie L. Kunzel and Deborah A. Wooten) The Continuum Encyclopedia of Young Adult Literature, 2005; author (with M. Jerry Weiss): Books I Read When I Was Young, 1980; author: (with Carolyn Carmichael) Literature and Young Children, 1977; author: Children's Literature in the Classroom: Extending Charlotte's Web, 1993; mem. editl. bd. Nat. Coun. Tchrs. English, Champaign, Ill., 1973—76, New Adv., 1987—99, Ranger Rick Mag., 1992—; contbr. articles to profl. jours. Adv. bd. Reading Rainbow, 1979—, Sta. WGBH-TV, 1989—; mem. selection com. Caldecott award ALA, Chgo., 1982—83; trustee Highlights Children Found., 1993—. Named Outstanding Educator in Lang. Arts, Nat. Coun. Tchrs. English, 2003; named to Ohio State U. Coll. Edn. Hall of Fame, 1995; recipient Ind. U. Citation for outstanding contbn. to literacy, 1995. Mem.: Reading Hall of Fame (pres. 1998—99, inducted 1989), Internat. Reading Found. (trustee 1984—91, Jeremiah Ludington award 1992), Internat. Reading Assn. (bd. dirs. 1979—84, pres. 1984—85, chair Tchrs. Choices 1988—91, chair spl. svc. award selection com. 2005—, Arbuthnot award for outstanding tchr. children's lit. 1989), Ch. Club N.Y., Century Assn., Alpha Chi Omega. Avocations: tennis, reading for pleasure, poetry. Home: 1045 Park Ave Apt 6A New York NY 10028 Office: 3 Tudor Ln Sands Point NY 11050-1104 Office Phone: 212-369-7899. Personal E-mail: bernicecullinan@verizon.net.

CULLINAN, MARY PATRICIA, academic administrator, literature and language professor; BA, U. Pa., 1972; MA, U. Wis., 1973, PhD in English Lit., 1978. Writing cons. MBA Program U. Calif., Berkeley, 1980—81; lectr. Dept. Mktg. Calif. State U., Hayward, 1981—87, assoc. prof., dir. Composition Program, 1987—91, prof. Dept. English, 1992, interim dean Sch. Arts, Letters and Social Scis., 1992—93, dir. Office of Faculty Devel. and Faculty Ctr. for Excellence in Tchg., 1994—96, dean Coll. Arts, Letters and Scis. Stanislaus, 1996—2003; provost, v.p. Academic Affairs, prof. English Stephen F. Austin State U., 2003—06; pres. So. Oreg. U., Ashland, 2006—. Author: Susan Ferrier, Business Communication: Principles and Processes, Business English for Industry and the Professions; co-editor: American Women Writers: Diverse Voices in Prose Since 1845. Office: So Oreg U Office of Pres 1250 Siskiyou Blvd Ashland OR 97520-5032 E-mail: cullinanm@sou.edu.*

CULLINGFORD, HATICE SADAN, chemical engineer; b. Konya, Turkey, June 10, 1945; d. Ahmet and Emine Harmanci. Student, Mid. East Tech. U., 1962-66; BS in Chem. Engring. with high honors, N.C. State U., 1969, Engring. Honors Cert., 1969, PhD, 1974. Statis. clk. Rsch. Triangle Inst., 1966; reactor engr. AEC, Washington, 1973-75; spl. asst. ERDA, Washington, 1975; mech. engr. U.S. Dept. Energy, Washington, 1975-78; staff mem. Los Alamos (N.Mex.) Nat. Lab., 1978-82; sci. cons. Houston, 1982-84; environ. control and life support systems test bed mgr. Johnson Space Ctr., NASA, Houston, 1984-85, sr. project engr. advanced tech. dept., 1985-86, sr. staff engr. divsn. solar system exploration, 1986-88, asst. divsn. advanced devel., 1988-90; sr. sys. engr. Exploration Programs Office NASA, Houston, 1990-92. Founder Peace U., 1993; internal adv. com. Ctr. for Nonlinear Studies Los Alamos Nat. Lab., 1981; organizer tech. confs., sessions at soc. meetings; lectr. in field; docent Mus. Fine Arts, Houston. Contbr. articles to profl. jours.; inventor and patentee in field. Mem. curriculum rev. com. U. N.Mex., Los Alamos, 1980. Recipient Woman's badge Tau Beta Pi, 1968, ERDA Spl. Achievement award, 1976, Inventor award Los Alamos Nat. Lab., 1982, Group Achievement award NASA Johnson Space Ctr., 1987, Outstanding Performance award NASA Johnson Space Ctr., 1987, 89, Superior Performance award NASA Johnson Space Ctr., 1987, 89, Cert. of Recognition for Inventions, NASA, 1988, 89, 90, 92, 93. Mem. AIAA (organizer, 1st chmn. human support com. Houston chpt. 1988-93), AIChE (organizer, 1st chmn. No. N.Mex. club 1980-81, organizer and chmn. low-pressure processes and tech. 1981-89), Am. Nuc. Soc. (sec.-treas. fusion energy divsn. 1982-84, vice chmn. South Tex. sect. 1984-86, local sects. com. 1986-88, meeting session chair, organizer topical meetings), Am. Chem. Soc., Soc. for Risk Analysis (organizer, sec. Lone Star chpt. 1986-88, chmn. soc. publicity 1990-93), No. N.Mex. Chem. Engrs. Club, Sierra Club, Houston Orienteering Club, Phi Kappa Phi, Pi Mu Epsilon.

CULLITON, BARBARA J., publishing executive; b. Buffalo, May 2, 1943; Grad., Vassar Coll. Founder, dep. editor and head editl. ops. N.Am. Nature Publs. Nature Medicine, Structural Biology, Nature Genetics., 1991—99; founder, sci. comm. and exec. editor GeneWire.com Celera Genomics, 1999—2001; v.p. for pub. The Inst. for Genomic Rsch., Rockville, Md., 2001—; editor-in-chief Genome News Network, Rockville, 2001—. Times Mirror vis. prof. and dir. Writing About Sci. The Writing Seminars, Johns Hopkins U., Balt., 1990—98; advisor Am. Bd. Internal Medicine; adv. com. Knight Journalism Fellows, MIT, Cambridge; journalism advisor Fulbright Scholars program; advisor Sound Print, the radio series; panelist Sci. Jour., a Pub. Broadcasting prodn. Editor (founding editor-in-chief): Nature Genomics, Nature Structural Biology, Nature Medicine. Bd. overseers Darmouth Med. Sch. Co-recipient George Polk award for journalism. Mem.: Coun. for Advancement of Sci. Writing (pres. 1985—89, bd. dirs.), Nat. Assn. Sci. Writers (pres. 1981—82), Inst. of Medicine of NAS (mem. governing coun.), Italian Soc. for Molecular Medicine (hon.), Sigma Xi (hon.). Episcopalian.

CULP, DORIE, marketing executive; married; 1 child. BA in History, Princeton U. Sales and mgmt. positions IBM; with First Fidelity Bank; v.p., gen. mgr. Manchester Partners Internat.; v.p. human resources Safeguard Scientifics (parent comp. of Aligne, Inc.); prin. Aligne, Inc.; v.p. human resources, Away From Home Divsn. Campbell Soup; v.p. sales & mktg. The Leader's Edge, Bala Cynwyd, Pa. Office: The Leaders Edge Two Bala Plz Ste 300 Bala Cynwyd PA 19004 Office Phone: 610-660-6684. Office Fax: 610-617-1051.

CULP, FAYE BERRY, state legislator; b. Kilmichael, Miss., Dec. 6, 1939; d. Otis Milton and Drapa (Clark) Berry; m. James H. Culp, Dec. 28, 1966; children: James Jr., David. BS in Bus. Edn., Miss. U. for Women, 1961; postgrad., Ga. State U., 1965-66; M, U. South Fla., Tampa, 1993. Tchr. Atlanta Pub. Schs., 1961-66; ednl. svcs. rep. IBM, San Francisco, 1966, Poughkeepsie, NY, 1967-68; real estate salesperson Yates Realty, Tampa, 1975-79; mem. sch. bd. Hillsborough County, Tampa, 1988-92; mem. Fla. Ho. of Reps., Tallahassee and Tampa, 1994—, majority whip, 1996-98. Mem. State Task Force Tech. Fla. Sch. Bds. Assn.; chmn. legis. subcom. on spl. legislation, chmn. bylaws com. Fla. Sch. Bds. Assn.; mem. State Instrnl. Coun. Textbook Selection; vice chmn. gen. edn. com. Fla. Ho. Reps., children's svcs. com.; mem. appropriations com. Fla. Ho. Reps., tourism com.; chmn. juvenile justice com. Fla. Ho. Reps, 2004—; chair Joint Ho. and Senate Com. Legis. Info. Tech. Resources Procedural Coun. Fla. Ho. Reps.; leader Nat. Delegation Women Legislators to Bahrain, Nat. Delegation to Taiwan Nat. Found. Women Legislators. Asst. dir. Theatre Atlanta prodns.; dir., prodr. musicals First United Meth. Ch., Tampa. Mem. Govs. Task Force for Prevention Teen-Age Suicides; del. Fla. Fedn. Rep. Women's Conv.; 1st pres. Child Abuse Coun. Aux.; pres. Hillsborough Women's Rep. Club, Tampa Realistic Artists, Inc., United Meth. Women, 1st United Meth. Ch., Tampa, Plant High Sch. Parent Student Tchrs. Assn.; v.p. various PTAs; area v.p. Hillsborough County Coun.; juvenile protection chmn. Hillsborough PTA County Coun.; Fla. del. Nat. White Ho. Conf. on Aging, Washington, 2006; youth coord., bd. trustees First United Meth. Ch.; bd. mem. Nat. Coun. Christians and Jews, Coun. Downtown Chs.; treas. West State Archaeol. Soc.; chmn. internat. affairs Tampa Civic Assn.; leader, den mother Cub Scouts; chmn. Just Friends Mentoring Program; bd. mem., officer Friends of Pub. Edn.; chmn. Masterpiece Morning. Named Woman of Distinction Girl Scouts Am., Tampa, Pacesetter in Ky. So. Women in Pub. Svc., 1997, Disting. Alumni of Yr. U. South Fla. Coll. Fine Arts, Tampa, 1997, Legislator of Yr. Internat. Coun. Shopping Ctrs., Orlando, Fla., 1997, 2003, One of Top 40 Legislators, Fla. C. of C., 1997, Legislator of Yr. Fla. Sch. Bds. Assn., 1997, Alliance Homeowners Assn., 2003, Elected Official of Yr, Tampa Rep. Women, 2004, Pacesetter So. Women in Pub. Svc. San Antonio, 2005, Pacesetter So. Women in Pub. Svc. Nashville, 2006; recipient over 150 awards in photography, 40 awards in painting, 3 awards in poetry, others. Mem. LWV (mem. justice coun., 2004-06, Polit. Courage award, 2006), Nat. Order Women Legislators (stakeholder, regional dir. nat. conf., nat. pres. 2005—), Nat. Found. Women Legislators (chmn. bd. 2005), PEO (chpt. historian), Miss. U. Women Alumni Assn. (pres. Suncoast chpt.), Hillsborough County Pres. Roundtable, Greater Tampa C. of C. (mem. edn. coun.), South Tampa C. of C., Greater Town n' Country C. of C., Lamplighters, Red Cross Angels, Friends of the Arts, Fla. Orch. Guild, Port Tampa Civic Assn., Alpha Republican. Methodist. Avocations: photography, painting, travel. Personal E-mail: faye.culp@myfloridahouse.gov.

CULP, KRISTINE ANN, dean, theology studies educator; B in Gen. Studies with distinction, U. Iowa, 1978; MDiv, Princeton Theol. Sem., 1982; PhD in Religion, U. Chgo., 1989. Vis. instr. theology St. Paul Sch. Theology, Kansas City, Mo., 1985-86, instr. theology, 1986-89, asst. prof. theology, 1990-91; dean Disciples Div. House U. Chgo., 1991—, sr. lectr. theology Div. Sch., 1991—. Contbr. articles to profl. jours. Office: U Chgo Disciples Divinity House 1156 E 57th St Chicago IL 60637-1536 also: The Divinity Sch-U Chgo Swift Hall S-406 1025 E 58th St Chicago IL 60637-1509

CULP, MILDRED LOUISE, corporate financial executive; b. Ft. Monroe, Va., Jan. 13, 1949; d. William W. and Winifred (Stilwell) C. BA in English, Knox Coll., 1971; AM in Religion and Lit., U. Chgo., 1974, PhD Com. on History of Culture, 1976. Faculty, adminstr. Coll. 1976—81; dir. Exec. Résumés, Seattle, 1981—; pres. Exec. Directions Internat., Inc., Seattle, 1985—2000, Clive, Iowa, 2000—03, Crete, Ill., 2003—. Mem. MBA mgmt. skills adv. com. U. Wash. Sch. Bus. Adminstrn., 1993; spkr. in field; contract rschr. U.S. Army Recruiting Command, 1997. Author: Be WorkWise: Retooling Your Work for the 21st Century, 1994; columnist Seattle Daily Jour. Commerce, 1982-88; writer Singer Media Corp., 1991-98, Worldwide Media, 1999-2002, Globalvision, Inc., 2002-06, WorkWise syndicated column, 1994—, Universal Press Syndicate, 1997-01, WorkWise Interactive syndicated column, 2004-, WorkWise Advice column, 2004-; WorkWise Internet audio program, 2000—; featured on TV and radio; contbr. articles to profl. jours.; presenter WorkWise Report, Sta. KIRO, 1991-96. Admissions counselor U. Chgo., 1981—, vol. Jeff Metcalf Fellow Program, 2006—; mem. Nat. Alliance Mentally Ill, 1984-91; life mem. Alliance Mentally Ill Hamilton County, 1984—; founding mem. People Against Telephone Terrorism and Harassment, 1990; co-sponsor WorkWise award, 1999-2000. Recipient Alumni Achievement award Knox Coll., 1990, 9 other awards; named Hon. Army Recruiter. Mem.: U. Chgo. Puget Sound Alumni Club (bd. dir. 1982—86), Knox Coll. Alumni Network. Personal E-mail: culp@workwise.net.

CULPEPPER, MABEL CLAIRE, artist; b. St. Louis, June 20, 1936; d. John Raymond and Mabel Lorene (Hardy) Bondurant; m. James William Culpepper, Dec. 24, 1957; children: Julie Ann, James Jeffrey, John William. AA, Columbia Coll., Mo., 1956; BS in Edn., U. Mo., Columbia, 1958, MEd, 1965. Represented by Artel Gallery, Emmitsburg, Md., 1987-88, Nob Hill Artisans, Albuquerque, 1993-94, Amapola Gallery, Albuquerque, 1995—, Nob Hill Gallery, 2006—. Art tchr. Twinbrook Bapt. Ch., Rockville, Md., 1972-75. One-woman shows include Artel Gallery, 1987, exhibited in group shows at Rockville (Md.) Art League, 1987, N.Mex. Watercolor Soc., 1989—2005, Nat. Watercolor Soc. Nat. Exhbn., Brea, Calif. Host parent, officer Am. Field Svc., Damascus, Md., 1978-80; program chmn. Albuquerque Newcomers, 1989-91; docent Albuquerque Mus., 1990-94; co-chair care com. Hope Evang. Free Ch., 2000-2005, deacon; vol. worker N.Mex. Autism Soc. Recipient First Prize Rockville Art League, 1987. Mem.: Soc. Layerists in Multi-Media, Frederick County Art Assn. (pres. 1988), N.Mex. Watercolor Soc. (pres. 1992—93, hosp. chair We. Fedn. Show 2002, 1st prize 1990, Best of Show 1993, 1st prize 1998, Best of Show 1999, Peter Walker award 2001, Collectors Guide award 2002, Village Framers award 2003, Connoisseur award 2004, Daniel Smith award 2005, Western Fedn. Show award 2006), Nat. Watercolor Soc. (signature mem.), Nat. League Am. Penwomen (pres. Yucca br. 1998—2000, art awards chmn. 2000—05, editor newsletter 2001, sec. 2004—), Nat. Mus. Women in the Arts, Mortar Board, Delta Gamma. Avocations: hiking, singing in church choir, crafts, bible study, travel. Home: 3208 Casa Bonita Dr NE Albuquerque NM 87111-5610

CULPEPPER, MARY KAY, publishing executive; With Weight Watchers; exec. dir. Coastal Living, 2000—01; exec. editor Cooking Light Mag., editor-in-chief, 2001—, v.p., 2002—. Office: Cooking Light Magazine 2100 Lakeshore Dr Birmingham AL 35209 Office Phone: 205-445-6600. Office Fax: 205-445-6600.*

CULTON, SARAH ALEXANDER, psychologist, educator; b. Burwell, Nebr., Nov. 12, 1927; d. James Claude and Frances Ann (Evans) Alexander;m. Verlen Ross Culton, June 19, 1949; children: James Verlen, Sarah Ann. BA in Edn., Ea. Wash. U., 1953, MA in Edn., 1956; EdD in Psychology, U. Idaho, 1966. Tchr. pub. schs., Kennewick, Northport, Wash., Potlatch, Idaho, 1946-56; prof. Lewis-Clark U. of Idaho, Lewiston, 1956-59, North Idaho Jr. Coll., Coeur d'Alene, 1961-66; sch. psychologist Sch. Dist. 81, Spokane, Wash., 1966-67; prof. psychology Spokane Falls Community Coll., 1967-88; author Colville, Wash., 1988—; sch. psychologist Adna (Wash.) Spl. Edn. Coop., 1994; mid. sch. counselor Soda Springs (Idaho) Sch. Dist., 1994-98; sch. psychologist Canyon-Owyhee Spl. Svc. Agy., Caldwell, Idaho, 1998—. Sch. psychologist, sch. counselor vol. Northport Schs., 1989-92; presenter convs. in field. Author: Psychology of Stress and Nutrition, 1992, Documentary of the Scotch-Irish Alexander Family History, 2002, 3d edit., 2005; contbg. editor: Gen Weekly, 2004—05. Doctoral fellow Wash. State U., 1959, U. Idaho, 1964; recipient Faculty Achievement award Burlington No. Found., 1988. Fellow Am. Inst. Stress; mem. NEA, APA, Internat. Coun. Psychologists, Internat. Stress Mgmt. Assn. (newsletter editor), Nat. Stroke Assn., Western Psychol. Assn., Am. Counseling Assn. (writer invitation 1992), Nat. Assn. Sch. Psychologists, Internat. Soc. Family History Writers and Editors, Alpha Delta Kappa. Baptist. Achievements include design of Alexander family history website www.houseofalexander.com. Avocations: travel, painting, photography, genealogy, writing. Mailing: 717 Prouty Corner Loop Rd Colville WA 99114-9208 Office Phone: 509-684-2070. Personal E-mail: versar@theofficenet.com.

CULVER, CATHERINE MARIE, secondary school educator; d. David Larry Culver, Sr. and Mary Ann Culver. BS in Edn., Calif. U. of Pa., California, 2001; postgrad., Morgan State U., Balt., 2006—. Cert. tchr. Pa., 2001, Md., 2002, athletic trainer Nat. Athletic Trainers' Assn. Bd. of Certification, 2002. Records clk. Howrey, Simon, Arnold, & White LLP, Washington, D.C. / Largo, Md., 2001—02; 9th, 10th, and 12th grade English tchr. Charles County Pub. Schs., La Plata / Waldorf, Md., 2002—05, athletic trainer, 2002—05; 8th grade English tchr. Anne Arundel County Pub. Schs., Annapolis / Millersville, Md., 2005—, athletic trainer, 2005—. Mem.: Edn. Assn. Charles County (gen. counsel 2003—04, bldg. rep. 2002—05, co-chair new educators voice com. 2003—05), Tchrs. Assn. of Anne Arundel County, Mid-Atlantic Athletic Trainers Assn., Md. Athletic Trainers Assn., Nat. Athletic Trainers Assn. (home course study reviewer bd. cert. 2004—), Nat. Coun. Tchrs. English, Md. State Tchrs. Assn. (new mem. task force 2003—05). D-Liberal. Roman Catholic. Avocations: creative writing, swimming, hiking, reading. Office: Old Mill Middle School South - AACPS 620 Patriot Ln Millersville MD 21401 Office Phone: 410-969-7000.

CULVER, JENNIFER LYNN, secondary school educator; b. Pontiac, Ill., Sept. 7, 1970; d. John Murray Lehman and Lynn Elizabeth Payette, Lois Jane Lehman (Stepmother) and Jay Payette (Stepfather); m. Richard Bruce Culver; children: John Raven McCarthy, Catharine Elizabeth Falka 1 stepchild, Richard Heinrich. BA, Tex. Woman's U., Denton, 1996; postgrad., U. North Tex., Denton, 2004—. Cert. tchr. Tex. English tchr., gifted and talented and creative writing tchr. Hebron HS, Carrollton, Tex., 2002—. Curriculum advisor Tex. Edn. Agy., Austin, 2005—; nat. writing project mentor U. North Tex., 2005—; dist. writing/literacy project mentor Lewisville Ind. Sch. Dist., Flower Mound, Tex., 2002—; presenter in field. Vol. Habitat for Humanity, Plano, Tex., 2004—06. Grantee, NEH, 2004. Mem.: Mortar Bd., Sigma Tau Delta (v.p. 1994—96). Home: 5520 Rutledge The Colony TX 75056 Office Phone: 972-862-1600. Personal E-mail: ferrrr@msn.com. Business E-Mail: culverjl@lisd.net.

CULVER, MONA CAPRICIA, retired elementary school educator; m. Donald L. Culver (dec.); 1 stepchild; 3 children from previous marriage. BA, Pomona Coll., Calif., 1959; postgrad., Claremont Grad. U., 1960. Elem. tchr. Pomona Unifed Sch. Dist., 1959—60; elem, mid. sch. tchr. San Miguel Joint Union, Calif., 1970—98; ret., 1998. Coop. tchr. for many student tchrs. Reader toddler storytime Paso Robles Libr., Calif., 1998—; bd. mem. Project Theatre Found., 1998—. Named Tchr. Yr., San Miguel Joint Union Sch. Dist., 1986, Woman of Distinction, AAUW, Paso Robles, 2004; recipient Franny award, Pioneer Players Cmty. Theatre Group, 2000. Mem.: Calif. Ret. Tchrs. Assn. (v.p. 2004—), PEO Chpt. HL (recording sec., pres.), Delta Kappa Gamma (Alpha Mu chpt.).

CULVERWELL, ROSEMARY JEAN, principal, retired elementary school educator; b. Chgo., Jan. 15, 1934; d. August John and Marie Josephine (Westermeyer) Flashing; m. Paul Jerome Culverwell, Apr. 26, 1958; children: Joanne, Mary Frances, Janet, Nancy, Amy. BEd, Chgo. State U., 1955, MEd in Libr. Sci., 1958; postgrad., DePaul U., 1973. Cert. supr., tchr. Tchr. Otis Sch., Chgo., 1955-59; tchr., libr. Yates Sch., Chgo., 1960-61, Nash Sch., Chgo., 1962-63, Boys Chgo. Parental, 1969-72, Edgebrook and Reilly Schs., Chgo., 1965-67; counselor, libr. Reilly Sch., Chgo., 1968, tchr., libr., asst. prin., 1973, prin., 1974—97. Reviewer Ill. State Bd. Edn. Quality Review Team. Pres. Infant Jesus Guild, Park Ridge, Ill., 1969-70; troop leader Girl Scouts U.S., Park Ridge, 1967-69; sec. Home Sch. Assn., Park Ridge, 1969, v.p. spl. projects, 1970; mem. Ill. Svc. Ctr. Six Governing Bd., 1994; vol. Ctr. of Concern, Park Ridge, Ill., 1997; quality reviewer Ill. State Bd. Edn., 1998; mem. Ill. Quality Edn. Rev. Team, 1998; v.p. Renaissance Art Club, 1999-05. Recipient Outstanding Prin. award Citizens Schs. Com., Chgo., 1987, For Character award, 1984-85, Whitman award for Excellence in Edn. Mgmt., 1990, Local Sch. Coun. award Ill. Bell Ameritech, 1991, Ill. Disting. Educator award Milken Family Found. Nat. Educators, 1991, Ill. Edn./Bus. Partnership award, 1994, 96. Mem. AAUW, LWV (chmn. speakers bur. 1969), Delta Kappa Gamma, Phi Delta Kappa. Avocations: acrylic painting, reading, swimming, making doll houses and furniture. Home: 1929 S Ashland Ave Park Ridge IL 60068-5460 Personal E-mail: rmaryculverwell@aol.com.

CUMMINGS, ANDREA J., lawyer; b. 1967; BA in Polit. sci., BS in Journalism, Boston U., 1990; JD, U. Va., 1995. Bar: Tex. 1995, Calif. 1999, Ill. 2000. With Locke Purnell Rain Harell, Tex., 1995—97, Weil, Gotshall Manges LLP, 1997—98, Nomura Asset Capital Corp., 1998—99, Gray Cary Uare Freidenrich, 1999—2000, Sidley Austin LLP (formerly Sidley Austin Brown & Wood LLP), Chgo., 2000—, ptnr., 2003—. Office: Sidley Austin LLP 1 S Dearborn Chicago IL 60603 Office Phone: 312-853-2107. Office Fax: 312-853-7036. Business E-Mail: acummings@sidley.com.*

CUMMINGS, CATHERINE T., elementary school educator; b. Phila., Apr. 4, 1963; d. Edward W. and Agnes M. Cummings. BS in Edn., West Chester U., Pa., 1983—86; MA in Edn., LaSalle U., Phila., 1990—92. Cert. Tchr. K-8 & K-12 Spl. Edn. Va. Dept. Edn., 1986, Pa. Dept. Edn., 1986, N.J. Dept. Edn., 1986. Tchr. St. Timothy Sch., Phila., 1986—95, St. Charles Borromeo Sch., Cinnaminson, NJ, 1996, Corp. Landing Mid. Sch., Virginia Beach, 1997—. Adult advisor Cath. Youth Orgn., Phila., 1986—97; adult educator/advisor Ch. Youth group, Virginia Beach, 1997—2001. Mem.: NEA, VBEA. Roman Catholic. Avocation: travel. Office: Corporate Landing Mid Sch 1597 Corporate Landing Pkwy Virginia Beach VA 23454 Office Phone: 757-437-6199.

CUMMINGS, EDITH JEAN, small business owner; b. La Salle, Colo., June 11, 1931; d. John Wesley Benson and Beaulah (Fay) Ellis; m. Robert Lee Meserault Sr., Nov. 10, 1951 (div.); children: Judy Kay Jensen, Robert Lee Jr.; m. Bob Cummings, 1999 (dec. 2002). Grad., Southwestern Coll., 1950; degree in bus., DeLake Hosp., Oreg., 1954; cert., Universal Beauty Acad., Concord, Calif., 1970. Lic. cosmetologist. Nurse in tng. DeLake Hosp., 1952-54; nurse Rossmore Hosp., Walnut Creek, Calif., 1960-70; with Joseph Magin Salon, Walnut Creek, 1970-78, Bullocks Salon, Walnut Creek, 1978-82, San Jose, 1982-84; prin., owner Edie's Natural Tips and Toes Salon, Morgan Hill, Calif., 1984—99; with Affinity Hair Design, Lakewood, Colo., 2005—. Recipient certs. of profl. creativity, 1985, 91. Republican. Avocations: painting, flower arrangemnts, travel.

CUMMINGS, ELLEN FINAN, special education educator; d. Jerome Ferdinand and Anne Cawley Finan; m. James Patrick Cummings, Sept. 26, 1980; 1 child, Kevin. MS in Spl. Edn., Marywood, Scranton, 2006. Exec. dir./pres. Jr. Achievement NE PA, Inc., Scranton, 1988—97; grantwriting & cmty. resource Career and Tech. Ctr. Lackawanna County, Scranton, 1997—2000; tng. and tech. asst. Northeastern Ednl. Intermediate Unit, Archbald, 2000—. Mem. Skills in Scranton, Scranton, 1990, LIFE, Greater Scranton C. of C., Scranton, 1989; perkins adv. coun. Career and Tech. Ctr., Scranton, 1997. Office: Northeastern Ednll Intermediate Un 1200 Line St Archbald PA 18403 Office Phone: 570-876-9200. Business E-Mail: cumminge@neiu.org.

CUMMINGS, ERIKA HELGA, financial consultant; b. Offenbach, Germany; came to U.S., 1978; d. Erwin and Edith (Trunski) Maier; 1 child, Marisa Anne. BSBA, Calif. State U., Bakersfield; MBA in Internat. Mgmt., Am. Grad. Sch. Internat. Mgmt., Glendale, Ariz., 1983. Inflight supr. TWA, Paris; internat. ops. mgr. Cooper LaserSonics, Santa Clara, Calif., 1983-85; bus. cons. Suncoast Bus. Industries, Sarasota, Fla., 1985-89; cert. fin. planner Am. Express Fin. Advisors, Sarasota, 1989-94; Peace Corps. vol. City Adminstrn. of Vladimir, Russia, 1994-96; internat. cons. Solutions Internat., Sarasota, Fla., 1996—. Mem. Toastmasters, Beta Gamma Sigma. Avocations: travel, tennis, reading, langs. E-mail: ericum@aol.com.

CUMMINGS, JOAN, history educator; b. St. Elizabeth, Jamaica, July 28, 1949; arrived in U.S., 1954; d. Adrian Braganza and Winnifred Icylin (Reid) Cummings; children: Safiya, Sajid. AS, Bronx CC, NY, 1981; BA, CCNY, 1985. Stock clk. N.Y. Stock Exchange, N.Y., 1969—70; reservations sales agent United Airlines, N.Y., 1970—71; restauranteur Cummings & Co., Ltd., Kingston, Jamaica, 1971—78; tchr. N.Y. Bd. Edn., 1985—88; artist, designer Kingston, 1988—91; tchr. Dade County Pub. Schs., Miami, Fla., 1992—2002; tchr. history L.A. (Calif.) Unified Sch. Dist., 2002—; prin., owner Samples, Hollywood, Calif. Tutor L.A. (Calif.) Unified Sch. Dist., 2003—05; instr. Dade County Pub. Schs., Miami, 1994—95. Author: Caribbean Cameos, 2005. Vol. plant a tree program City N.Y., 1985. Mem.: United Tchrs. L.A. Avocations: horseback riding, driving, clayworks restoration, interior decorating. Office: Samples PO Box 3786 Hollywood CA 90078 Home: 703 Washington Ave 1 Santa Monica CA 90403

CUMMINGS, JOAN E., health facility administrator, educator; BA, Trinity Coll., 1964; MD, Loyola U., 1968. Diplomate Am. Bd. Internal Medicine, Geriatric Medicine. Med. intern St. Vincent Hosp., Worcester, Mass., 1968-69; med. resident Hines VA Hosp., Hines, Ill., 1969-71, sr. resident in nephrology, 1971-72, ambulatory care svc. chief gen. med. sect., 1971-84, med. dir., hosp. based home care, 1972-87, chief, intermediate care svc., 1984-87, assoc. chief of staff, extended care and geriatrics, 1987-90, med. dir., extended care center, 1987-90, dir., 1990—; asst. prof. clin. medicine U. Ill., 1976-82, Loyola U., 1983-91, assoc. prof. clin. medicine, 1991—; network dir. Dept. Vet. Affairs, Hines, Ill., 1995—2005. Mem. ad hoc com. on primary care U. Ill., 1980-82, coll. edn. policy com. U. Ill., 1980-82, State Ill. Emergency Med. Svc. Coun., 1981-83, Comprehensive Health Ins. Plan Bd. State Ill., 1990—, Med. Licensing Bd. State Ill., 1992—, exec. com. Chgo. Fed. Exec. Bd. State Ill., 1992—; program dir. Loyola/Hines Geriatric Fellowship Program, 1987-90; mem. bd. trustees Rosalind Franklin U. Medicine and Sci., 2005-; mem. bd. dirs. Ismie Mutual Ins. Co., 2003-. Contbr. to profl. mags. and jour. Recipient Disting. Svc. award Abraham Lincoln Sch. Med. Univ. Ill., 1979, 81, Leadership award VA, 1980, Certificate of Appreciation award VA, 1980, Laureate award Am. Coll. Physicians, 1990. Fellow ACP; mem. AMA (Ill. delegation 1985—, vice speaker ho. of dels. 1987-89), Chgo. Med. Soc. (pres. Hines-Loyola br. 1982-83), Ill. State Med. Soc. (trustee 1984—, chmn. com. on Ill. med., 1988—, spkr. ho. of dels. 1989-91, exec. com., 1989-91, policy com., 1989—), Chgo. Geriatric Soc., Am. Geriatric Soc. Office: 772 St Charles Rd Glen Ellyn IL 60137 Personal E-mail: joanecum@msn.com.

CUMMINGS, JOSEPHINE ANNA, writer, consultant, advertising executive; b. Gainesville, Fla., July 12, 1949; d. Robert Jay and Marcella Dee (Mount) Cummings. ABJ./Design cum laude, U. Ga., Athens, 1971; MA, NYU, 1999. Copywriter William Cook, Jacksonville, Fla., 1971-73; creative dir. Leo Burnett, Chgo., 1973-76; sr. v.p., group creative dir. D. D. B. Needham, Chgo., 1976-84; sr. v.p., creative dir. Saatchi-Saatchi, N.Y.C., 1984; sr. v.p., sr. creative dir. Ted Bates, N.Y.C., 1984; exec. v.p., chief creative officer Tracy-Locke, Dallas, 1985-87; exec. v.p., exec. creative dir. Bozell, Chgo, 1989; exec. v.p., creative dir. Y&R, N.Y.C., 1990-92; pres. The Joey Co., N.Y.C., 1992—. Author: (play) Azaleas, 1988, (short story collection) Crimes of Passion, 1988, (childrens' book) The Hospital is a Funny Place, 1988, (short film) Night Magic, 1989. Named as creator One of Hundred Best TV Commls. Advt. Age, 1978-79, one of Advt. 100 Best Advt. Age, 1986, one of People to Watch Fortune mag., 1986, Ad Age one of Best and Brightest, N.Y. Mem. Amelia Earhard, Ninety Niners Club, N.Y. Women in Film. Avocations: reading, writing, golf. Office: The Joey Company Ste 632 45 Main St Brooklyn NY 11201 Business E-Mail: joey@thejoeycompany.com.

CUMMINGS, KAREN SUE, retired corrections classification administrator; b. Ft. Wayne, Ind., July 15, 1939; d. Floyd Henry and Mary Emma (Wolfe) Kneller; m. Oswald Wade Cummings, Feb. 16, 1962; children: Ruth Marie Cummings Everett, John Phillip. BA, Bethal Coll., 1976; MA, Webster U., 1989; grad., Corrections Mgmt. Sch., La., 1991. Sub. tchr. various sch., Mishawaka, Ind., La., 1978-82; classification dir. Work Tng. Facility North La. Dept. Corrections, Pineville, La., 1978-82; eligibility worker Office of Family Security, Alexandria, La., 1982-84; classification officer Work Tng. Facility North La. Dept. Corrections, Pineville, 1984-92, classification dir. Work Tng. Facility North, 1992—, ret., 2002—. Big sister Big Bros./Big Sisters, Mishawaka, 1974-76, Pineville, 1990-91. With USAF, 1957-65. Mem. Am. Correctional Assn., So. States Corrections Assn. Republican. Baptist. Avocation: travel. Office: 1519 Dupree Rd Pineville LA 71360-8718

CUMMINGS, KELLI DAWN, psychology professor; d. Gary Thomas and Diane Marie Cummings. BA with honors, Oreg. State U., 1999; MS, U. Oreg., 2003, PhD, 2004. Grad. tchg. fellow U. Oreg., Eugene, 2000—04; predoctoral rsch. assoc. NW Media Inc., Eugene, 2001—04; asst. prof. U. Mont., Missoula, 2004—, rsch. asst. prof., 2005—. Mem. Comprehensive Sys. Profl. Rev., Missoula, 2004—, AOA Team, Missoula, 2004—; cert. trainer Dynamic Measurement Group, Eugene, 2005—. Contbr. chpt. to book; mem. editl. bd.: Jour. Psychoednl. Assessment, 2004—. Mem.: APA, Nat. Assn. Sch. Psychologists. Office: U Mont Corbin Hall-Bioethics Missoula MT 59812

CUMMINGS, MARY VOIGT, counselor; b. Eagle Grove, Iowa, Sept. 23, 1937; d. Wilson Burns and Evelyn Louise (Allen) Voigt; m. William Grosvenor Cummings, Jr.; children: William Grosvenor III, Grace Ann, Mary Joan, Margaret Louise, Nancy Elizabeth. BS, Northwestern U., 1959; MA, U. South Fla., 1977. Counselor Pinellas Park H.S., Largo, Fla., 1977-84; guidance coord. Clearwater (Fla.) H.S., 1984—2000. Bd. dirs. Samaritan Counseling, Clearwater, 1984, Fla. Bot. Gardens, 2003-05; bd. dirs., trustee MPM Health Systems, Clearwater, 1991-97; pres. Jr. League, Clearwater, 1975; altar guild, 2002-05, Christcare leader, 2003-; active in PTAs, sch. adv. bds., etc. Named Outstanding Young Woman, Jr. Woman's Club, Clearwater,

1975, Beautiful Activist, Burdines, Clearwater, 1977, Master Tchr., State of Fla., 1986. Mem. Am. Counselors Assn., Fla. Counselors Assn., Suncoast Counselors Assn., Pinellas County Counselors, Phi Kappa Phi, Carlouel Yacht Club (oversight com.). Episcopalian.

CUMMINGS, MAXINE GIBSON, elementary school educator; b. Tupelo, Miss., Oct. 7, 1940; d. T. Ruben and Maggie (Ruff) Gibson; m. Willie B. Cummings, Aug. 15, 1964; 1 child, Stanley. BS, Barber-Scotia Coll., Concord, N.C., 1962; MA, Northeastern Ill. U., Chgo., 1974. Cert. tchr., N.C., Ill. Tchr. Walter Reed Elem. Sch., Chgo., 1963-75, reading tchr., 1975-82, social studies tchr., 1982-85; reading resource tchr. Arna Bontemps Sch., Chgo., 1985-91, ESEA lab. tchr., 1991—; Title I reading/math tchr. St. Sabina Acad., Chgo. Mentor tchr. Tchrs. for Chgo. Program, Arna W. Bontemps Sch. Site, 1996—; counselor Westside YWCA, Chgo., 1963-68; chmn. reading com. Bontemps Sch., 1986-92, chmn. activity com., 1992-93; mentor tchr. Bontemps Tchrs. for Chgo. Program; mem. staff devel. team Reading Tchrs. Acad. for Profl. Growth, Chgo. Bd. Edn.; Title I tchr., presenter in field. Contbr. articles to profl. jours. Vol. Edna White Century Garden; sec. S.W. Morgan Park Civic Assn., Chgo., 1990-92; block rep. Neighborhood Watch Program, Chgo., 1989-90; trustee, elder Morgan Park Presbyn. Ch., peace and justice com., mem. choir, tchr. vacation bible sch., coord. lunches, 2005—; Great Books Discussion leader Walker Br. Libr., 1999; race rels. com. Beverly/Morgan Park Neighborhood-Task Force; coord. garden site Metra Train Sta., hist. rschr. family reunions. Recipient Regional Cmty. Gardening award, Morgan Park Neighborhood, Chgo., 1998, Mayor Daley's Landscpae Improvement Program award, 1999, 2d place award, City Scape Gardening Corner, Chgo., 1999; grantee, Chgo.-Incentive, 1987, NEH, 1984, Northeastern Ill. U., 1980. Mem. Minority Students of Chgo. Area (recruiter), Barber-Scotia Alumni Club (sec. 1989-92), Pi Lambda Theta. Avocations: biking, walking, reading, travel, gardening. Home: 11116 S Longwood Dr Chicago IL 60643-4043 Office: St Sabina Acad 7801 S Throop St Chicago IL 60620- Office Phone: 773-535-3596. Business E-Mail: mcummings@cps.k12.il.us.

CUMMINGS, MELVA ANDREWS, music educator; b. N.Y.C., Oct. 7, 1943; d. Arnold and Margaret Meyer Andrews; children: Catherine Margaret Poling, Victoria Paige Bailey. BA, Cedar Crest Coll., Allentown, Pa., 1965; MusM, Boston U., Mass., 1967. Cert. vocal music tchr. N.J., 2 certs. Mozcertcum, Salzburg, Australia, 1965. Tchr. music Sparta Bd. Edn., NJ, 1968—, tchr. vocal music, 1968—72, 1974—79, 1981—. Pres. Sparta Edn. Assn., NJ, 1994—. Recipient Tchr. of Yr. award, Sparta Bd. Edn., 1989. Mem.: MENC, NEA, Sparta County Edn. Assn., N.J. Edn. Assn. Avocations: golf, Broadway shows, travel, family. Home: 25 Hickory Tr Sparta NJ 07871 Office: Mohawk Ave Sch 18 Mohawk Ave Sparta NJ 07871 Office Phone: 973-886-6486. E-mail: mcummings6762@earthlink.net.

CUMMINGS, PEGGY ANN, counseling administrator; b. Plainfield, N.J., May 18, 1957; d. Peter James Cummings and Marjorie Ann Pope. BA Spl. Edn., Rowan U., Glassboro, N.J., 1979; MA Student Pers. Svcs., Rowan U., 1986; AS Restaurant Mgmt., Restaurant Sch. Phila., 1989; EdS Marriage and Family Therapy, Coll. N.J., Ewing, 2006. Lic. profl. counselor N.J., cert. tchr. handicapped N.J., nat. counselor, nat. dietary mgr., food mgr./operator Pa., student pers. svcs. N.J. Tchr. spl. edn. Montgomery Twp. Sch. Dist., Skillman, NJ, 1995—99, sch. counselor, 1999—. Dir. Camp Jotoni Somerset County Assn. for Retarded Citizens, Manville, NJ, 1979—82; tchr. spl. edn. Haddon Heights Sch. Dist., NJ, 1979—88; dir. food svc. Nutrition Mgmt. Svcs. Co., Kimberton, Pa., 1990—94, mgr. dist., 1994—95. Sch. rep. Rocky Hill/Montgomery Twp. Mcpl. Alliance, Belle Mead, 2002—03; donor membership Sharing Network Organ and Tissue Donation Svcs., Springfield, NJ, 2001—; vol. Challenger Little League Montgomery Twp. Edn. Assn., Belle Mead, 2001—05, co-pres. Challenger Little League, 2002—05. Mem.: PTA, NEA, Am. Assn. Marriage and Family Therapists, N.J. Edn. Assn., N.J. Sch. Counselor Assn. (Somerset County Counselor of Yr. 2002—03), Am. Sch. Counselor Assn., Kappa Delta Pi, Gamma Tau Sigma, Mortar Bd., Chi Sigma Iota. Achievements include development of Elementary School Peer Mediation Student Leader and Peer Partners Programs. Avocations: golf, swimming, hiking, gardening, bicycling. Home: 423 Jackson Ave Manville NJ 08835 Office: Montgomery Township School District 1014 Rte 601 Skillman NJ 08558 Business E-Mail: pcummings@mtsd.k12.nj.us.

CUMMINGS, RAMONA, music educator; b. Waynoka, Okla., Jan. 2, 1957; d. Merton Kenneth Roberts and Roberta Lou Newton; m. John Franklin Cummings; 1 child, Connor. BME, Southwestern Okla. State U., 1978, MEd, 1979. Cert. elem. and secondary adminstr. Vocal music tchr. Dumas Elem. Schs., Tex., 1980—81, Dumas Jr. High Sch., 1981—82, Alva Pub. Schs., Okla., 1982—. Mem. Okla. Secondary Schs. Activities Assn., 1987—2003. Entertainment dir. Nescatunga, Alva, 1990, scholarship chair, 1999—. Named Tchr. of Yr., Alva Pub. Schs., 1998, Dir. of Distinction, Western Okla. Choral Assn., 1990. Mem.: Okla. Choral Dir.'s Assn. (treas.), Okla. Music Adjudicator Assn., Am Choral Dir. Assn., Okla. Music Educators Assn., Delta Kappa Gamma. Baptist. Avocations: walking, bicycling, singing, piano, gardening. Office: Alva HS Choir 501 -14th Alva OK 73717 Personal E-mail: rcummings73717@yahoo.com.

CUMMINGS, RAYANN BURNHAM, minister; b. Paris, Maine, Mar. 26, 1938; d. George Raymond and Alice Marian (Welch) Burnham; m. Ronald J. Haines (div.); children: Stuart T. Haines, Melony Lynn Haines. BS, Gorham State Coll., 1960; MA, U. Conn., 1972; postgrad., Sacred Heart U., Bridgeport, Conn., 1977—80; MDiv, Andover Newton Theol. Sch., 1984; postgrad., Hartford Seminary, 1991—94. Tchr. social studies Lyman Moore Jr. H.S., Portland, Maine, 1960—61; tchr. English/social studies Nathan Hale - Ray Jr./Sr. H.S., East Haddam, Conn., 1968—81; tchr. distance edn. Bibl. studies SUNY, Empire Coll., Utica, NY, 1989—92; min., tchr. Deansboro/Paris (N.Y.) United Ch. of Christ, 1984—89, First Federated Ch., United Ch. of Christ and Unitarian/Universalist, Beverly, Mass., 1989—98, Mayflower Congregational United Ch. of Christ, Sioux City, Iowa, 1998—2003; ret. Host exch. students Rotary Internat., 1972—73, 1978—79, 1980—81; contbg. mem. Interprofessional Inst., Sioux City, 1999—2004; mem., chair Spiritual Leadership Coalition Siouxland, Sioux City, 2000—03; tutor ESL Sioux City Sch. Sys., 2000—03; mem., sec. bd. dirs. Calico Kids Preschool, Sioux City, 2000—03; bd. dirs., program chair Mary Treglia Cmty. House, Sioux City, 2001—03; founder, facilitator Ecumenical Discussion Group, Sioux City, 2002—03; tutor Literacy Vols. Am., Ft. Myers, Fla., 2004—; active Rep. Town Com., East Hampton, Conn., 1978—80; founder, mem. Interfaith Coun., Beverly, Mass., 1995—98; bd. dirs. Coun. of Chs., Utica, NY, 1985—89; trainer Connecticut Trails coun. Girl Scouts Am., New Haven, 1974—79. Recipient award, Beverly (Mass.) Citizen Newspaper, 1996. Mem.: PEO, Friendship Force, Girl Scouts Am. (life). Mem. United Ch. Of Christ. Avocations: singing, theater, writing, sailing, entertaining. Home: 6803 Bogey Dr Fort Myers FL 33919

CUMMINGS, TONI MARIE, language educator; b. Rogers City, Mich., Apr. 16, 1947; d. Arthur Dale and Margaret Maxine Freel; m. William John Cummings (div.); children: Michelle Lee Zambon, Emily Alice. BA, Mich. State U., East Lansing, 1969. Spanish/English tchr. Maple Valley HS, Vermontville, Mich., 1969—71; English tchr. Camp Zama Am. HS, Japan, 1971—72; clk., computer specialist Colenso & Co. CPAs, Iron Mountain, Mich., 1985—89; libr. Dickinson County Libr., Iron Mountain, 1989—91; Spanish/English tchr. Goodman-Armstrong Creek HS, Wis., 1991—. Advisor Nat. Honor Soc., Goodman, Wis., 1992—2005; mem. scholarship selection com. Goodman-Armstrong Creek HS, 2000—, mentor, 2005—. Treas. Dickinson County Geneal. Soc., Iron Mountain, 1979—83, Friends of the Libr., Iron Mountain, 1980; elder, ch. session 1st Presbyn. Ch., Kingsford, Mich., 1982—; sec. non-Roman coun. Cursillo Movement, Garden, Mich., 1990. Finalist Herb Kohl Fellowship, Madison, Wis., 2005. Mem.: NEA, Wis. Edn. Assn., Wis. Assn. Fgn. Lang. Tchrs. Avocations: travel, reading, cross stitch, puzzles, genealogy. Office: Goodman-Armstrong Creek HS 1 Falconcrest Goodman WI 54125

CUMMINGS ROCKWELL, PATRICIA GUILBAULT, psychiatric nurse; b. Ludlow, Mass., June 22, 1939; d. Lee Allen and Mavis Isabella (White) Guilbault; m. Philip W. Cummings, Oct. 23, 1960 (dec. Jan. 1978); children: Sharon Ellen Timmons, Geoffrey Scott Cummings, Susan Mavis Lornitzo, Lee Millett Cummings, Mary Rockwell Thon; m. William Leonard Rockwell Jr., Aug. 18, 1990. ADN, Vt. Coll., 1982; BSN, Norwich U., 1987. RN, Vt. Staff nurse Ctrl. Vt. Hosp. Nursing Home, Berlin, 1982-84, 87—; staff psychiat. nurse Va. Hosp. Ground East, White River Junction, Vt., 1987-94; owner Globe Travel, Bradford, Vt., 1988-94; rschr. Norwich U., Northfield, Vt., 1988—. Nurse-entrepeneur Globe Travel, 1988—. Tchr. adult edn. ARC, Bradford, Vt., 1988, 89; bd. dirs. Fedn. of Vt. Lakes and Ponds, Inc.; v.p. Vale Hospice Internat.; dir. Fedn. Vt. Lakes and Ponds Inc. Mem. ANA (nat. and Vt. chpts.), AAUW, New Eng. Hist. Geneal. Soc. Avocations: writing, travel, medical genealogy, genetics and geneology. Home: 307 Godfrey Rd East Thetford VT 05043-9517 Office Phone: 802-785-4812. Personal E-mail: patsy@together.net.

CUMMINS, KATHLEEN K., retired elementary school educator; b. Fountain County, Ind., June 20, 1919; d. Homer Elston Krout and Edith Zerilda Allen; m. Robert E. Cummins, Oct. 4, 1940 (dec. Mar. 1984); 1 child, Robert E. Jr. BS in Edn., Ind. State U., 1952. Elem. tchr. East Allen Cmty. Schs., New Haven and Ft. Wayne, Ind., 1940—76; ret., 1976. Deaconess Trinity English Luth. Ch., Ft. Wayne, 1982—. Recipient Ret. Tchr. of Yr. award, Instant Copy, Ft. Wayne, 1993. Mem.: AAUW (grantee 1984), Allen County Ret. Educators Assn. (pres. 1986—88), Ft. Wayne Hist. Mus. (past pres. Barr St. Irregulars), Ft. Wayne Women's Club (bd. dirs. 1988—, chmn. fine arts dept.), Fortnightly Club (pres. 1994—96), Delta Kappa Gamma (chpt. pres. 1964—66). Democrat. Lutheran. Avocations: painting, reading, bridge, knitting, gardening. Home: 3808 Oak Park Dr Fort Wayne IN 46815

CUMMINS, NANCYELLEN HECKEROTH, electronics engineer; b. Long Beach, Calif., May 22, 1948; d. George and Ruth May (Anderson) Heckeroth; m. Weldon Jay Cummins, Sept. 15, 1987; children: Tracy Lynn, John Scott, Darren Elliott. Student, USMC, Memphis, 1966-67. From tech. publ. engr. to engring. instr. Missile and Space divsn. Lockheed Corp., Sunnyvale, Calif., 1973-77; test engr. Gen. Dynamics, Pomona, Calif., 1980-83; quality assurance test engr. Interstate Electronics Co., Anaheim, Calif., 1983-84; quality engr., certification engr. Rockwell Internat., Anaheim, 1985-86; sr. quality assurance programmer Point 4 Data, Tustin, Calif., 1986-87; software quality assurance specialist Lawrence Livermore Nat. Lab., Yucca Mountain Project, Livermore, Calif., 1987-89, software quality mgr., 1989-90; from sr. constrn. insp. to sr. quality assurance engr. EG&G Rocky Flats, Inc., Golden, Colo., 1990-91, engr. IV software quality assurance, 1991-92, instr., developer environ. law and compliance, 1992-93; software, computer cons. CRI, Dabois, Wyo., 1993-97; contractor Dept. of Energy, Golden, Colo., 1997-98; test mgr. Keane Inc., Lakewood, Colo., 1998, project officer, 1998—. Customer engr. IBM Gen. Sys., Orange, Calif., 1979; electronics engr. Exhibits divsn. LDS Ch., Salt Lake City, 1978; electronics repair specialist Weber State Coll., 1977-78. Author: Package Area Test Set, 6 vols., 1975, Software Quality Assurance Plan, 1989. Vol., instr. San Fernando (Calif.) Search and Rescue Team, 1967-70; instr. emergency preparedness and survival, Claremont, Calif., 1982-84, Modesto, Calif., 1989; mem. Lawrence Livermore nat. Lab. Employees Emergency Vols., 1987-90, EG&G Rocky Flats Bldg. Emergency Support Team, 1990-93, Dubois Search and Rescue, 1995-97. Mem. NAFE, NRA, Nat. Muzzle Loading Rifle Assn., Am. Soc. Quality, Job's Daus. (majority mem.), Ea. Starr. Republican. Avocations: history, weapons, camping, native American crafts. Office Phone: 406-882-4513. E-mail: whltierna@fortinedsl.net, fallingleafcircle@fortinedsl.net.

CUMMINS, PATRICIA ANN, lawyer, educator; b. Portland, Maine, Sept. 29, 1945; d. Arther M. and Eunice G. (Swan) Peterson Griggs; m. Gerald D. Cummins, July 4, 1964 (div. 1971); children: Mark David, Christine Dianne, Scott David; m. Michael Hoxsey, Dec. 1988 (div. Sept. 1992); m. Harris R. Angell, June 3, 1995. AA, San Diego City, 1967; BA magna cum laude, Nat. U., 1977, MBA, 1977; D in Bus. Adminstn., U.S. Internat. U., 1980; JD with internat. legal cert., Western State U., San Diego, 1996. Bar: Calif. 1997. Real estate broker Carlton Oaks Realty and Investment, Santee, Calif., 1967-86, Century 21 Teamwork, Santee, Calif., 1987-90; atty. San Diego and V.I., 1997—2005. Tax acct. Larson CPA, San Diego, 1966-86, asset mgr. Mesa Mortgage, San Diego, 1970-80; bus. prof. U.S. Internat. U., San Diego, 1980-82; instr. Grossmont Coll., El Cajon, Calif., 1982; prof. U. V.I., 2000-2002. Author: (with others) Inside Secrets IRS, 1981, Tax Dictionary, 1981; producer broadway mus., San Diego, 1980. Active Boy Scouts Am., Pop Warner youth softball league, Santee, 1972-80; dir. Calif. Performing Arts, San Diego, 1980-2000, Pistarckle Theatre, 2002-2005; reader 1st Ch. Christ Scientist, Lakeside, Calif., Christian Sci. Soc. St. Thomas and St. John, 2005; mem. Christian Sci. Com. on Publ., 2003-2005. Mem. ABA, Nat. Lawyers Guild, Nat. Assn. Realtors, Supreme Ct. of U.S. Bar Assn., Calif. Assn. Realtors, State Bar Calif., San Diego County Bar Assn., William B. Enright Am. Inn of Ct., Planned Parenthood, Santee C. of C., Lawyers Club San Diego, Flying Club, Los Ancianos Club, Delta Theta Phi. Republican. Avocations: performing arts, humanity rights advocacy. Home: PO Box 900164 San Diego CA 92190-0164 E-mail: patriciaacummins@aol.com.

CUMMINS, WILMA JEANNE, actress, comedienne; b. Guthrie, Okla., Sept. 25, 1927; d. Chauncey Dewitt and Etta (Marshall) Anderson; m. Joseph Sylvester Cummins, May 24, 1952; children: Jeanetta Kay Arnold, Bunny Gail Cline, Mary Jo Stoops, Susan Dee. BA, Phillip's U., 1948; MA, U. Tulsa, Okla., 1980. Cert. tchr., lic. real estate broker. Ops. base payload control United Air Lines, Denver, 1948-50; lab. tech. Barnes Hosp., St. Louis, 1950, Coffeyville, Kans., 1951—53; elem. tchr. Kansas City, Mo., 1951-53; actress Gaslight Dinner Theatre, Tulsa, 1984, Discoveryland's Okla., Prattville, 1985; tchr. Tulsa Pub. Schs., 1970-78; part time tchr. Tulsa Jr. Coll., 1987-89; freelancer in TV and radio SAG, AFTRA, Dallas, Tulsa, 1991—. Real estate broker, Tulsa, 1981—93. Performer: (radio) Grasso's Barn Dance Festival, 1950, Mayfest, 2003, (plays) Whales of August, 2005; actor: (films) The Ripper, 1985, UHF, 1988, Christmas Child, 2003; (TV series) Rosie O'Donnell Show, 1997, America's Funniest People, 1991, Howie Mandel Show, 1999, Tonight Show with Jay Leno, 2001, 30 Seconds to Fame, 2002, Lawrence Welk Champagne Theatre, 1997, Spotlight Theatre, 1983—, (commercial) Tex. Transp. Inst., 2002. Vol. Gilcrease Mus., Tulsa, 1995—2002; pres. Internat. Club, Tulsa, 1996, Pan-Am. Round Table, Tulsa, 1990—92, Altrusa Club, Tulsa, 1985, Christian Women's Fellowship, 1983, Conversing Couples, 1986—, Pro-Am., 2001—02. Recipient 1st pl. monologue, Internat. Platform Assn., 1989, 2d pl., 1991, 1st pl., Srs. Take Ctr. Stage, Welk Resort, 2000. Republican. Methodist. Avocations: theater, commercials. Office Phone: 918-628-1359. Personal E-mail: wilmajeannecummins@sbcglobal.net.

CUNDIFF, LOU WILLIE, artist, sculptor, writer; b. Nashville, Mar. 20, 1926; d. John Melvin and Bertha Agnes (Johnson) Gibson; m. James Howard Cundiff, Sept. 16, 1944; children: Billie June, James Howard, Jr., Michael Douglas. Diploma, Howard H.S., Nashville. Typist clk. City of Nashville Ct., 1944; sales asst. mgr. Spartan Dept. Store, Nashville, 1966-70; credit clk. Woolco Credit Office, 1970-72; sec. H.D. Lee, Nashville, 1972-75; exec. sec. Red Kap Industries, Nashville, 1972-75; vol. Art judge AT&T Pioneers of Am., Nashville, 1990, Cheatham County H.S., Ashland City, Tenn., 1993, 94, 95. Maury County, Columbia, Tenn., 1994; Tenn. Art League Sch. Auctions, Tenn. Art League Gallery, Nashville, 1990-96. Author, illustrator: Miss Cundiff Speaking, 1975; editor, illustrator: Tennessee Art League Cookbook, 1995-96; compiler, illustrator: Word and Image Guild Manual, 1995-96; writer, compiler, illustrator: Steps of Time Chapbook, 1995. Speaker, artist 55 Health Fair Symposiums, Two Rivers Bapt. Ch., 1991; sec., scrapbook host Christian Women Club, Internat. Soc. Poets, Nashville; TV interview CT 39 TV, Murfreesboro, Tenn., 1993, WAGG Channel 3, Franklin, Tenn., 1987-90. Recipient 1st Oil 1982, 85, 92, Tenn. State Fair, Nashville, CASE Parthenon Ctrl. South Art Exhbn., Nashville, 1991, Solo 1992 Show Cheekwood Art Ctr., Pineapple Rm., Nashville, 1992, Ornament 1991 Trees nat, Mus. Women in Arts, Washington, 1991. Tenn. Art League Gallery, Tenn. Art League Gallery, Word and Image Guild, Friends of Tenn. Art League Gallery, Hendersonville Artists Guild. Mem. Two Rivers Baptist Ch. Avocations: bowling, reading, creative writing, sculpting, computers. Home: 909 Drummond Dr Nashville TN 37211-2730

CUNDIFF, VICTORIA ANNE, lawyer; d. Jerome W. and Anne C. BA summa cum laude, U. Denver, 1977; JD, Yale U., 1980. Bar: N.Y. 1981, U.S. Dist. Ct. (so. and ea. dists.) N.Y. 1981, U.S. Ct. Appeals (2nd cir.) 1984, U.S. Ct. Appeals (3rd cir.) 1988, U.S. Supreme Ct. 1991, U.S. Ct. Appeals (11th cir.). Assoc. Breed Abbott & Morgan, NYC, 1980-82, Milgrim Thomajan & Lee, P.C., NYC, 1982-87, mem., 1987-92; ptnr. Paul, Hastings, Janofsky & Walker, NYC, 1992—. Intellectual property adv. bd. mem. Practicing Law Inst. Author: Maximum Security: How to Prevent Departing Employees From Putting Your Trade Secrets to Work for Your Competitors, 1992, Trade Secrets and the Internet: Preventing the Internet from Being an Instrument of Destruction, Strategic Planning for Strategic Alliances: An Intellectual Property Perspective, How to Hire Your Competitor's Employee: A Trade Secret's Perspective, What you Need to Know About Economic Espionage act, The New York Law of Trade Secrets: A Practical Guide; contbg. editor Intellectual Property Law. Bd. dirs. Yale Law Sch. Fund, 1990-95, Yale Law Sch. Alumni Assn., NYC; Practicing Law Inst. Intellectual Property Adv. Bd. 2000. Fellow: ABA 2003; mem. ABA (mem. com. on intellectual property litigation 1988-93, chairperson subcom. on trade secrets litigation 1990-93, lectr. ABA Nat. Inst. on Corp. Litigation), N.Y. State Bar Assn. (chair intellectual property sect. 2000-02, co-chair com. trade secrets 1992-2006), Assn. of Bar of City of N.Y. (mem. com. on sci. and law, 1991-93, com. trademarks and unfair competition 1987-90, chair PLI program on trade secret protection and litigation 1992-2002), Intellectual Property Owners Assn. (com. trade secrets 2005). Avocations: art history, historic preservation. Office: Paul Hastings Janofsky & Walker LLP Park Avenue Tower 75 E 55th St, 1st Fl New York NY 10022 Office Phone: 212-318-6030. Office Fax: 212-230-7643. Business E-Mail: victoriacundiff@paulhastings.com.

CUNNIFF, SUZANNE, surgical technician; b. Detroit, Dec. 3, 1960; d. Louis Thomas and Joyce Lenore (Barkell) C. AA in Surgical Tech., Marygrove Coll., 1986; BS Med. Tech., Mich. State U., 1984. Cert. surgical technologist. Surg. technologist Botsford Gen. Hosp, Farmington Hills, Mich., 1986-88, St. Joseph Mercy Hosp., Pontiac, Mich., 1988-91; cardiothoracic surg. asst. Cardiothoracic Surgeons, Pontiac, 1991-97, Lynchburg, Va., 1997—. Mem. Assn. Surg. Technologists. Avocations: figure skating, volleyball, bowling, wool spinning.

CUNNINGHAM, ALICE JEANNE, chemistry educator, author, consultant; b. Walnut Ridge, Ark., Sept. 23, 1937; d. Percy Smith and Barbara Beryl (Fry) C. Student, Vanderbilt U., 1955-57; BA in Chemistry, U. Ark., 1959; PhD in Chemistry, Emory U., 1966. Chemist Layne Rsch., Memphis, 1959; instr. Secondary Schs., Gainesville, Atlanta, Ga., 1959-62; postdoctoral rsch. assoc. U. Tex., Austin, 1967-68; asst., assoc. prof. Agnes Scott Coll., Decatur, Ga., 1968-79, chair dept. chemistry, 1978-90; prof. W.R. Kenan Jr., 1979-92; prof. emerita, 1992. Vis. asst. prof. Agnes Scott Coll., Decatur, 1966-67; vis. scholar Emory U., Atlanta, 1984-85; vis. prof., 1985-86. Contbr. articles to profl. jours. Active Hazardous Waste Mgmt. Authority, Ga., 1991-94. Fellow AAAS; mem. Am. Chem. Soc. (com. on profl. tng. mem. 1979-88, chair 1983-88, cons., com. profl. tng. 1989-93), Sigma Xi, Iota Sigma Pi, Sigma Delta Epsilon (Hon. Mem. award 1990). Avocations: walking, reading, fishing.

CUNNINGHAM, ALICE NORIDA, retired physician; b. Princeton, W. Va., Jan. 26, 1931; d. Geroge Elliott and Mamie Virgina (Smith) Cunningham; m. Richard Eugene Spindler, Nov. 29, 1970; children: Eugene Nolan Spindler, Timothy Elliott Spindler. BA, Columbia Union Coll., Takoma Pk., Md., 1953; MD, Loma Linda U., Loma Linda, Calif., 1957. Internship Wash. Adventist Hosp., Takoma Pk., Md., 1957—58; ob-gyn resident Luth. Hosp. Md., Balt., 1958—61; ob-gyn practice pvt., Brunswick, Maine, 1961—98. Hosp. bd. Parkview Adventist Hosp., Brunswick, Maine, 2002—; bd. dirs. Child Devel. Svcs., Brunswick. Mission, Singapore, 1983—85; dir. Seventh Day Adventist Cmty Svc., Branswich, 1998—. Mem.: AAUW. Avocations: knitting, cross stitch, cmty. vol.

CUNNINGHAM, ALICE WELT, law and mathematics educator; b. Washington, Aug. 18, 1949; d. Samuel Louis and Beatrice (Boxer) Welt; m. Daniel Paul Cunningham, Aug. 10, 1975; adopted children: Stephen Paul, Philip James 1 child, Samuel Paul (dec.). BA summa cum laude, Yale U., 1971; JD, Harvard U., 1974; MA in Math. Edn., Columbia U., 2001, postgrad., 2001. Bar: N.Y. 1975, Calif. 1975, U.S. Dist. Ct. (no. dist.) Calif. 1975, U.S. Ct. Appeals (fed. cir.) 1980, U.S. Tax Ct. 1976. Assoc. Shearman & Sterling, N.Y.C., 1974-75, Heller Ehrman, White & McAuliffe, San Francisco, 1975-78, Debevoise & Plimpton, N.Y.C., 1978-83; assoc. prof. N.Y. Law Sch., N.Y.C., 1983-86. Contbr. articles to profl. jours. Mem.: ABA, Assn. Bar City N.Y., N.Y. State Bar Assn., Kappa Delta Pi, Phi Beta Kappa. Personal E-mail: acunnin167@aol.com.

CUNNINGHAM, BETTY JEAN DE BOW, adult education educator; b. Venice, Ill., Apr. 11, 1942; d. John Wells and Anna DeBow; m. Langford Allen Cunningham, July 18, 1967 (div. Dec. 1976); 1 child, Langford Allen Jr. BS in Elem. Edn., So. Ill. U., 1967; M in Secondary Edn. and Adult Edn., U. Mo., St. Louis, 1991. Dir. Madison (Ill.) County Equal Opportunity Ctr., 1966—67; reading tchr. Venice-Lincoln Tech. Ctr., 1968—. Mem. Metro East Literacy Adv. Coun., East St. Louis, Ill., 1989—94. Vol. Des Peres Hosp., St. Louis, 1993—95. Recipient Steward of Records, Bethel A.M.E. Ch., 2003. Mem.: Ill. Adult and Continuing Educators Assn., Inc. (jr. dir. Region V 1996—97, sr. dir. Region V 1997—98). Office: Venice-Lincoln Tech Ctr 300 S Fourth St Venice IL 62090

CUNNINGHAM, DONNA LYNN, library director; d. Donald and Maxine Mills; m. Scott Lee Cunningham, July 4, 1988; 1 child, Angela. BA, U. Ill. (formerly Sangamon State U.), Springfield, 1989. Cert. elem educator Ill. Children's libr. Elkhart (Ill.) Pub. Libr. Dist., 1989—90, libr. dir., 1990—. Avocations: travel, crafts, fishing, swimming. Office: Elkhart Pub Libr Dist 121 Bohan St Elkhart IL 62634 Office Phone: 217-947-2313.

CUNNINGHAM, ELIZABETH ANN, librarian; b. Troy, Mo., Dec. 14, 1953; d. Harley Charles William and Shirley Ann (Thompson) Tretow; children: Amanda Sadie, James William. BA, Lawrence U., 1976. Periodicals libr. Lawrence U., Appleton, Wis., 1976-79; mgr. info., libr. svcs. Hollister Inc., Libertyville, Ill., 1979—. Leader Girl Scouts U.S.A., 1990-92. Recipient Spl. Libr. of Yr. award North Suburban Libr. System, 1991-92. Mem. Spl. Librs. Assn., North Suburban Spl. Librarians, No. Ill. Libr. Consortium (coord. 1987). Office: Hollister Inc 2000 Hollister Dr Libertyville IL 60048-3781

CUNNINGHAM, ISABELLA CLARA MANTOVANI, advertising executive, educator; b. Milan, Apr. 1, 1942; came to U.S., 1967; d. Fortunato and Anna (Sinigaglia) Mantovani; m. William H. Cunningham, Dec. 30, 1970; 1 child, John William. JD, Faculdade de Direito da Universidade Catolica, Sao Paulo, Brazil, 1964; MBA, Escola de Aministracao de Empresa, Sao Paulo, 1966, Mich. State U., 1968, PhD, 1972. Asst prof. Escola de Administracao de Empresas de Sao Paulo, 1969-71; asst. prof. St. Edward's U., Austin, Tex., 1971-72, acting dean, 1972-73; vis. asst. prof. U. Tex., Austin, 1973-74, asst. prof., 1974-76, assoc. prof., 1976-81, prof. advt., 1981-83, chair dept. advt., 1978-85, Ernest A. Sharpe Centennial prof. in communication, 1983—. Cons. in field, spkr., presenter to numerous univs., orgsn., confs.; bd. dirs. Franklin Fed. Bancorp; mem. Sunset Commn. for State of Tex. Author: (with others) A Study of Consumer Behavior in Brazil, 1976, Selling: The Personal Force in Marketing, 1977, rev. edit., 1988, Effective Selling, 1977, Investment Management: A Book of Readings, 1979, Marketing: A Managerial Approach, 1980, 2d edit., 1987, Metodos Efectivos de Venta, 1980, Advertising and Marketing Communication Management, 1993; editorial bd. Jour. Current Issues and Rsch. in Advt., 1979—, Jour. Managerial Issues, 1988—, Jour.

Mktg., 1992—; reviewer major publs.; contbr. articles to profl. jours. Chair Daughters of Charity Health Svcs. of Austin Planning Coun., 1987—; mem. Internat. Business Fellows, 1987, Austin Child Care Commn., 1987, exec. bd. Boy Scouts Am., 1987-92, Tourism Adv. Com. Tex. Dept. Commerce, 1988-90, Austin Diocesan Forum, 1988-92, bd. Communities in Schs.-Austin, 1989-90, campaign exec. com. Allan Shivers Radiation Therapy Ctr., 1991—; assoc. mem. Settlement Club, 1991—; bd. dirs. Austin Mental Health Assn., 1985-86, Tex. State Com. Nat. Mus. of Women in the Arts, 1987-92, Susan G. Komen Found., 1990—, Austin Smiles, 1992—, Nat. Mus. of Natural History (Smithsonian), 1993—; trustee Holy Cross Hosp., 1985-86, St. Edward's U., 1985—, Austin Lyric Opera, 1986-87, adv. bd. Nat. Wildflower Rsch. Ctr., 1986—. Rsch. grantee various orgns. Mem. Am. Acad. Advt., Am. Mktg. Assn., Brazilian Bar Assn., So. Mktg. Assn., Austin Advt. Club (pres. 1978-79), Am. Advt. Fedn., Phi Kappa Phi, Beta Gamma Sigma. Avocations: tennis, skiing, reading. Office: Univ Tex Dept Advirtising Coll Communication 1 University Station A1200 Austin TX 78712 Office Phone: 512-477-1145. E-mail: i.cunningham@mail.utexas.edu.

CUNNINGHAM, JACQUELINE LEMMÉ, psychologist, educator, researcher; b. Biddeford, Maine, Apr. 22, 1941; d. S. James and Alice (Fréchette) Lemmé; m. Seymour Cunningham II, Dec. 16, 1960 (dec. 1987); children: Macklin Todd, Danielle, Alyssa. BA in Psychology cum laude, U. Maine, Orono, 1963; MS in Psychology, U. South Ala., 1983; PhD in Ednl. Psychology, U. Tex., 1994. Tchr. Mobile (Ala.) Pub. Schs., 1976-81; psychology intern Devereux Found., Devon, Pa., 1988-89; fellow in developmental disabilities Children's Hosp. Harvard Med. Sch., Boston, 1990; prof. U. S.D., Vermillion, 1994-95; fellow in pediat. neuropsychology Children's Nat. Med. Ctr., George Washington U. Med. Ctr., Washington, 1995—97; psychologist pvt. practice, Wilmington, Del., 1997—2000, Children's Hosp. of Phila., Phila., 2000—. Cons. in field. Contbr. articles to profl. jours., chapters to books. Mem. Am. Psychol. Assn. (outstanding dissertation of yr. award 1994), Internat. Neuropsychol. Soc., Nat. Acad. Neuropsychology, Soc. History Behavioral Scis., Phila. Neuropsychology Soc. (bd. dirs. 1998-2002), Phi Kappa Phi. Avocations: travel, writing. Office: Children's Hosp of Phila 34th St & Civic Ctr Blvd Philadelphia PA 19104 Business E-Mail: cunningham@email.chop.edu.

CUNNINGHAM, JANIS ANN, lawyer; b. Seattle, May 13, 1952; d. Luvern Victor and Anna Jane (Bierstedt) Rieke; m. D. John Cunningham, June 10, 1972; children: Emily Jane, Laura Christine. BS with honors, U. Wis., Milw., 1973; JD, U. Wash., 1976. Bar: Wash. 1976, U.S. Dist. Ct. (we. dist.) Wash. 1976, U.S. Ct. Appeals (9th cir.) 1976. Law clk. to Hon. Eugene A. Wright U.S. Ct. Appeals (9th cir.), Seattle, 1976-77; assoc. Karr, Tuttle, & Campbell, Seattle, 1977-84; ptnr. Karr, Tuttle, Koch, Campbell, Mawer & Sax, Seattle, 1984-89; ptnr., Personal Planning Area Perkins Coie LLP, Seattle, 1989—. Lectr. community property law U. Wash., Seattle, 1984, mem. estate planning coun. adv. bd., 1984-85. Co-author: Washington Practical Probate, 1982, 5th rev. edit., 1988; editor in chief U. Wash. Law Rev., 1975-76. Mem. estate plnning com. Am. Heart Assn., Seattle, 1978; bd. dirs. Community Services for the Blind, Seattle, 1977-79. Fellow Am. Coll. Trust and Estate Counsel; mem. Wash. State Bar Assn. (Real Property, Probate & Trust Section, exec. com. 1988-95, chmn. 1993-94), Seattle Estate Planning Coun.; King County Bar Assn. (Real Property, Probate & Trust Section, pres 1986-87), Order of Coif. Republican. Lutheran. Avocations: hiking, canoeing. Office: Perkins Coie LLP 1201 3rd Ave 48th Fl Seattle WA 98101-3029 Office Phone: 206-359-8607. Office Fax: 206-359-9607. Business E-Mail: jcunningham@perkinscoie.com.

CUNNINGHAM, JOYCE WENTWORTH, retired secondary school educator; b. Sanford, Maine, Aug. 29, 1930; d. Norman Lowd and Helen Martha (Dunnells) Wentworth; m. Ralph Clifford Cunningham, Feb. 6, 1954; children: Cynthia, Alan. BS in Edn., Gorham (Maine) State Tchrs. Coll., 1951. Cert. elem., secondary, occupl. English, and social studies tchr. Mass. Tchr. social studies City of Wallingford, Conn., 1951-54; tchr. English Town of Westboro, Mass., 1956-57; tchr. Town of Grafton, Mass., 1968-74, Assabet Valley Regional Vocat. Sch. Dist., Marlboro, Mass., 1974-90, lead tchr., 1978-90, adult continuing edn. tchr. bus. comm. Assabet Valley Regional Vocat. High Sch., 1979-82, trainer, 1982-85; ret. Docent Willowbrook Mus. Village, Newfield, Maine, 2005—; dir. Christian edn. Bangor (Maine) Theol. Sem., 1999. Named Disting. Tchr. of the Yr.; recipient Horace Mann award, Commonwealth of Mass., 1986—87, 1987—88, Outstanding Instrnl. Materials for Profl. Devel. award, Am. Vocat. Assn. Mem.: NEA (life), Actor Shapleigh Hist. Soc., York County Ret. Tchrs. Assn., PEO. Mem. United Ch. Of Christ. Avocations: reading, painting, golf, bridge. Home: PO Box 868 Acton ME 04001-0868 Personal E-mail: joycliffc@yahoo.com.

CUNNINGHAM, JUDY MARIE, lawyer; b. Durant, Okla., Sept. 7, 1944; d. Rowe Edwin and Margaret (Arnott) C. BA, U. Tex., 1967, JD, 1971; postgrad., Schiller Coll., Heidelberg, Fed. Republic Germany, 1976. Bar: Tex. 1972. Quizmaster U. Tex. Law Sch., Austin, 1969-71; rschr. Tex. Law Rev., Washington, 1970; staff atty. Tex. Legis. Coun., Austin, 1972-75; adminstrv. law judge, dir. sales tax div., assoc. counsel Comptr. of Pub. Accounts, Austin, 1975-85; owner, editor J.C. Law Publs., Austin, 1986—; pvt. practice Austin, 1986—. Author: (with others) Texas Tax Service, 1985; pub., editor, contbr. (newsletter) Tex. State Tax Update, 1986—; contbr. articles to Revenue Adminstrn.; assoc. editor Tex. Law Rev., 1968-71. State del. Dem. Party, Ft. Worth, 1990, county del., Austin, 1972, 88, 90, 92; vol. numerous Dem. campaigns, Austin, 1972-90. Mem. Industry Practitioners Liaison Group (comptr. pub. accts.), State Bar Tex. (taxation sect.), Austin (Tex.) Bar Assn. (bus. corp. and taxation sect.), Tex. Taxpayers and Rsch. Assn. Avocations: travel, cooking, reading mysteries, photography, swimming. Office: 4905 W Park Dr Austin TX 78731-5535 Office Phone: 512-459-3810. Personal E-mail: judymcunningham@earthlink.net.

CUNNINGHAM, JULIA WOOLFOLK, author; b. Spokane, Oct. 4, 1916; d. John George and Sue (Larabie) C. Grad., St. Anne's Sch., Charlottesville, Va., 1933. Author: (juveniles): The Vision of Francois the Fox, 1960, Dear Rat, 1961, Macaroon, 1962, Candle Tales, 1964, Dorp Dead, 1965 (Children's Spring Book Festival award), Violet, 1966, Onion Journey, 1967, Burnish Me Bright, 1970, Wings of the Morning, 1971, Far in the Day, 1972, The Treasure Is the Rose, 1973, Maybe, A Mole, 1974, Come to the Edge, 1977 (Christoper award 1978), Tuppenny, 1978, A Mouse called Junction, 1980, Flight of the Sparrow, 1980 (Commonwealth Club Calif. award, Honor Book award Boston Globe), The Silent Voice, 1981, Wolf Roland, 1983, Oaf, 1986, (with Betsy Hearne) Dorp Dead, 2002; (poetry) Shadow Heart, 1999, The Stable Rat and Other Christmas Poems, 2001, Cicada, 2001. Mem. Authors Guild. Home: Rancho Santa Barbara 333 Old Mill Rd Space 88 Santa Barbara CA 93110-4429

CUNNINGHAM, JULIE KAYE, music educator; b. Ackerman, Miss., Feb. 7, 1958; d. Ethel Rone Brunt; children: Katie, Emily, Philip. B Music Edn., Miss. U. Women, Columbux, 1980. Piano instr. Naxapater HS, Miss., 1980—82; music tchr. Winson Acad., Louisville, Miss., 1982—88, Chocktaw Ctrl. Sch., Philadelphia, Miss., 1988—89, Fair Elem. Sch., Louisville, 1989—2000, Neshoba Ctrl. HS, Philadelphia, 2000—, chmn. music dept., 2006—. Pianist, accompanist 1st Presbyn. Ch., Louisville, 1981—. Sch. nurse grantee, State of Miss., 1988. Mem.: Miss. Profl. Educators, Miss. Music Educators Assn., Music Educators Nat. Conf. Home: 624 Albert McMIllin Rd Louisville MS 39339

CUNNINGHAM, KAREN LYNN, social worker; b. Chapel Hill, NC, Dec. 12, 1975; d. Timothy Clontz and Wendelin Jones McBride; m. John David Cunningham, Oct. 8, 2005. BA in Internat. Studies, U. N.C., Chapel Hill, 1998; MSW, U. Md., Balt., 2001. Lic. ind. clin. social worker. Case worker Bread for the City/Zacchaeus Free Clinic, Washington, 1998—99; social worker intern Yorkwood Health Ctr., Balt., 1999—2000; rsch. asst. Family Connections U Md., Balt., 2000—01; social work intern Adoptions Together, Silver Spring, Md., 2000—01, contract social worker, 2001—; clin. case mgr. PSI Family Svcs., Lanham, Md., 2001—02; social worker Child and Family Svcs. Agy., Washington, 2002—. Recipient Ruth H. Young Endowment award for excellence in child welfare, U. Md., Balt., 2001. Mem.: Nat. Assn. Social Workers. Democrat. Mem. United Ch. Of Christ. Avocations: reading, singing, crafts. Office: Child and Family Svcs Agy 400 6th St SW Washington DC 20024

CUNNINGHAM, KARLA, political scientist, researcher; b. Rochester, N.Y. d. Carl Cunningham and Margaret Frances Jones Springer, Richard Springer (Stepfather); m. Christopher Brown; 1 child, Hayden Mairead Cunningham Brown. PhD, U. Buffalo, 1997. Analyst U.S. Dept. Def., Md., 1998—99; asst. prof. SUNY, Geneseo, 1999—2006; polit. scientist The RAND Corp., Pitts., 2006—. Author: Encyclopedia of Women's History; contbr. articles to profl. jours. V.p. Upper Monroe Neighborhood Assn., Rochester, NY, 2005—06. Fellow, USIA/NMERTP, 1995. Office: The RAND Corp Ste 600 4570 Fifth Ave Pittsburgh PA 15213 Office Phone: 412-683-2300.

CUNNINGHAM, KATHLEEN ANN, researcher; b. St. Louis, May 1, 1952; d. Russell Martin Hagan and Helen Marie Hogan; children: Merrit Cunningham-Neptune, Clayton. LPN, Waukesha County Tech. Inst., 1976. Dep. property tax assessor New Trier Twp., Winnetka, Ill., 1988—89; trustee Northfield Twp., Glenview, Ill., 1984—90; v.p. Cunningham Fluid Power, Inc., Ocala, Fla., 1993—2003; staffing coord. Donbar Svc. Corp., Tampa, 2001—02; head human resources, purchasing specialist Odyssey Marine Exploration, Tampa, 2003—. Cons. John F. Kennedy Assassination Records Rev. Bd., Washington, 1993—98. Contbr. Killing the Truth, 1993, Killing Kennedy, 1995, Between the Signal and the Noise, 1995, Not In Your Lifetime, 1998, Assassination Science: Experts Speak Out on the Death of JFK, 1998; contbr. articles to profl. jours. Precinct capt. Northfield Twp. Rep. Orgn., Glenview, 1981—83, election judge, 1979—88, area chairperson, 1983—90; chmn. bd. dirs. Northshore Rehab. Fund, Northbrook, Ill., 1987—90; bd. dirs. Citizens for the Truth in the Kennedy Assassination, L.A., 1995—2001; bd. trustees Northfield Twp., Glenview, Ill., 1984—90. Achievements include donation of large collection of documents relating to John F. Kennedy's assassination to the Special Collections department at University of South Florida. Avocations: canoeing, reading, writing, historic research. Home: 18307 Aintree Ct Tampa FL 33647 Office: Odyssey Marine Exploration 5215 W Laurel St Tampa FL 33607 Office Phone: 813-876-1776 2238. E-mail: kathy@shipwreck.net.

CUNNINGHAM, KATHY, artist, educator; b. New Brunswick, NJ, Oct. 12, 1947; d. John Christopher and Josephine Wilkens; m. Robert Edward Cunningham, Jan. 19, 1985; children: Kevin, Darren; m. Stephen Dennis Lane (div.). BS in Art Edn., St. John's U., Jamaica, NY, 1974; MS in Art Edn., C.W. Post, LI U., Greenvale, NY, 1978. Cert. art tchr. K-12 NY, elem. tchr. N-6 NY. Art tchr. K-6 South Huntington Pub. Schs., NY, 1974—75, North Merrick Pub. Schs., NY, 1977—81, 1987—, kindergarten tchr., 1981—86, art tchr., 1986—; art tchr. 5-12 Tapei Am. Sch., Taipei, Taiwan, 1975—76. Developed and taught tchr. workshops Art for Classroom Teachers, North Merrick, 2005, North Merrick, 06. One woman show, West Islip (N.Y.) Pub. Libr., 2002, 2006; contbr. articles to Arts and Activities mag., Sch. Arts mag. Mem.: Am. Press Assn., L.I. Art Tchrs., NY State Art Tchrs. Avocations: running, reading, drawing. Office Phone: 516-379-3732.

CUNNINGHAM, KINA ANN, media specialist, educator; b. Winchester, Ind., June 13, 1954; d. Francis Leon and Anna Mae Addington; m. Les E. Cunningham, Nov. 29, 1974; children: Hannah Beth MacGilrvay, Rhett Lester. AS, Ball State U., 1983, BS, 1992—97, MA, 2004. Librarian V Ind. Libr. and Hist. Bd., 1994, Librarian IV Ind. Libr. and Hist. Bd., 1998. Sch. media specialist, tchr. Monroe Ctrl. Elem. Sch., Parker City, Ind.; head tchr. United Day Care Ctr., Muncie, Ind., 1985—87; children's libr. Winchester Cmty. Libr., Ind., 1987—98, libr. dir., children's libr., 1995—98. Grantee, Target, 2004. Mem.: Assn. for Ind. Media Educators, Internat. Reading Assn., Tri Kappa. Home: PO Box 28 Albany IN 47320-0028 Office: Monroe Ctrl Elem Sch 10421 W State Rd 32 Parker City IN 47368-9791 Office Phone: 765-468-7725. Office Fax: 765-468-8409. Personal E-mail: kinaacelk@aol.com. E-mail: kinac@monroec.k12.in.us.

CUNNINGHAM, MARY ANN MICHAEL, secondary school educator; b. Jackson, Pa., Mar. 5, 1947; d. Chester Benjamin and Wanda Mae (Plew) Michael; m. Donald Lewis Cunningham, Apr. 16, 1976; children: Courtney A., Donald M. AA, Keystone Coll., LaPlume, Pa., 1967; BS, Bloomsburg U., Pa., 1969; MA, U. Scranton, Pa., 1971; post grad, 1971—. Faculty Montrose Area Sch. Dist., Pa., 1969—. Chair and fund raiser Sunshine Club, Montrose, Pa., 1977—2003; Advisor Key Club, 1992—2002; adj. instr. Luzerne C.C., Wilkes-Barre, 1998—; exch. tchr. Northeastern Ill. U. Sponsor Big Brothers Big Sisters Susquehanna County, Montrose, 1990—94. Named Woman of Distinction, Alpha Alpha State; recipient Cmty. Svc. citations (4), Susquehanna County Commrs., 1994—98, Fundraising award, March of Dimes, Svc. award, Garden Club Montrose. Mem.: Montrose Edn. Assn. (dir. activities 1969—), Delta Kappa Gamma (pres. 1990—92), Phi Alpha Theta, Phi Theta Kappa. Republican. Avocations: gardening, reading, nature, travel. Home: RD2 177B New Milford PA 18834 Office: Montrose Area Sch Dist RD3 Montrose PA 18801

CUNNINGHAM, MILAMARI ANTOINELLA, retired anesthesiologist; b. Cody, Wyo., Oct. 4, 1949; d. Milo Leo and Mary Madeline (Haley) Olds; m. Michael Otis Webb, June 4, 1970 (div. Feb. 1971); m. James Kenneth Cunningham, June 14, 1975. BA with honors, U. Mo., 1971, MD, 1975. Diplomate Am. Bd. Anesthesiologists. Intern and resident U. Mo., Columbia, 1975—78; jr. ptnr. Anesthesiologist, Inc., 1979—82, ptnr., 1982—86; owner Cunningham Anesthesia, 1986—2003; dir. anesthesia dept. Ellis Fischel Cancer Ctr., 1991—92; acting chief anesthesia Harry S. Truman Meml. Vets. Hosp., 1994—95; instr. U. Mo. Columbia Anesthesia Dept. Mem. med. staff U. Mo. Hosp. and Clinics, Columbia; vice chair Mo. Health Facilities Rev. Com., 2004—05. Mem. editl. bd.: Mo. Medicine Jour., 2001—. Active Mo. Med. Polit. Action Com., 1991-2000, Friends of Music, Friends of Libr., Boone County Fair, 1978-94, with ham breakfast divsn., 1978-85, with draft horse and mule show, 1986-88; Mo. bd. dirs. A Call to Serve, 1996-2004, program mgr., 2004. Fellowship Am. Coll. Anesthesiologists, 1977; named Lifetime Senator, World Nations Congress, 2003. Mem.: AMA (life Physicians Recognition award 1978, 1985, 1987, 1991, 1995), Vis. Nurses Assn. (bd. dirs. 1982—89, adv. bd. 1989—93), Am. Soc. Anesthesiologists (alt. dir. dist. 17 2003, Mo. dist. dir. 2003—05), Mo. State Med. Assn. (commn. econs. third party payors 1986—89), Boone County Med. Soc., Mo. Soc. Anesthesiologists (membership chair 1982—84, v.p. 1986—87, pres. 1988—89, spkr. ho. dels. 1992—2002, sec.-treas. 1996, bd. dirs. 1996—99, del. various yrs. including 1996—2004), Phi Beta Kappa. Home and Office: 8202 S Bennett Dr Columbia MO 65201-9178 E-mail: mila@tranquility.net.

CUNNINGHAM, PATRICIA ANN CAHOY, band director, musician; d. Arnold Stephan Cahoy and Carolyn Ann Thiry; m. Gregg A. Cunningham, July 30, 1988. MusB Edn., U. No. Iowa, Cedar Falls, Iowa, 1980; MusM, Boston U., Boston, Mass., 1997. Band dir. Allamakee Cmty. Sch., Waukon, Iowa, 1981—81, Ventura Cmty. Sch., Ventura, Iowa, 1981—83, Ctrl. City Cmty. Sch., Central City, Iowa, 1983—85, Merrimack Cmty. Sch., Merrimack, NH, 1986—. Prin. clarinetist N.H. Philharm. Orch., Manchester, NH, 1985—; clarinetist New Eng. Wind Symphony, Manchester, NH, 1985—, New Eng. Symphony Orch., North Conway, NH, 1998—, Granite State Symphony, Concord, NH, 2000—02, Gt. Waters Music Festival Orch., Wolfeboro, NH, 1999—, North End Marching Band, Boston, 2001—. Musician: (featured soloist) North Iowa Wind Ensemble, N.H. Philharmonic Orch. Music merit badge advisor Boy Scouts, Nashua, NH, 1990; sec. N.H. Philharm. Orch., Manchester, NH, 1987—95. Scholar Meritorious Performer, Boston U., 1996. Mem.: NEA (assoc.), Merrimack Teachers' Assn. (assoc.), N.H. Music Educators' Assn., Internat. Clarinet Assn. (assoc.), Nat. Band Assn. (assoc.), Iowa Bandmasters' Assn. (assoc.), Pi Kappa Lambda (assoc.). Achievements include Merrimack High School Band receives top ratings at competitions. Avocations: travel, gardening, tennis. Office: Merrimack H S 38 McElwain St Merrimack NH 03054 Business E-Mail: patricia.cunningham@merrimack.k12.nh.us.

CUNNINGHAM, VALERIE S., historic preservationist, researcher; b. Portsmouth, N.H., May 31, 1941; d. Clarence Woodrow and Augusta Serena Ragland Cunningham; children: Bradley D. Randolph, Kirby A. Randolph. B of Gen. Studies, U. Sys. N.H., 1988. Rschr., writer, lectr. and cons. African Am. Resource Ctr., Portsmouth, 1988—. Mem., former trustee Strawbery Banke Mus., Portsmouth, 1996—2002; mem., past sec. New Eng. chpt. Afro-Am. Hist. & Genealogical Soc., Bedford, Mass., 1998—2000; exec. bd. Seacoast African Am. Cultural Ctr., Portsmouth, 2000—05; founder, pres. Portsmouth Black Heritage Trail, Inc., 1995—2005; co-founder, past pres., exec. bd. Blues Bank Collective, Inc., 1985—2005; co-founder Chichester Connections/N.H. Cir. Friends; mem. commn. status women N.H., 2005—. Co-author: (book) Black Portsmouth: Three Centuries of African-American Heritage, Portsmouth Black Heritage Trail Resource Book; contbr. articles to profl. jours., essays to enycs. Apptd. N.H. Commn. Status of Women, 2005. Named Outstanding Woman N.H., Keene State Coll., 2004; recipient Achievement award, U. N.H. Commn. Status Women, 1991, Cmty. Svc. award, N.H. Coalition MLK Holiday, 1991, Pres.'s award Excellence, U. N.H., 1992, Race Amity award, Seacoast Area Baha'i Cmty., 1994, Spirit Seacoast award, Cmty. Resource Network, 1997, Jefferson award, Am. Inst. Cmty. Svc., 1999, A. J. Gerrier award History, Portsmouth Advocates, 2000, Am. History award, Ranger chpt. DAR, 2001, Robert Frost Contemporary Am. award, Plymouth State U., 2005. Mem.: Schomburg Ctr. Rsch. African-Am. Life and Culture, N.H. Hist. Soc., Nat. Trust Hist. Preservation, Mus. African-Am. History, New Eng. Hist. Assn., Am. Assn. State and Local History, N.H. Preservation Alliance, Assn. Black Women Historians, Afro-Am. Hist. and Geneal. Soc. (New Eng. chpt.), Portsmouth Athenaeum, Nat. Ctr. Black Philanthropy. Unitarian-Universalist. Avocations: travel, jazz, movies. Office: Portsmouth Black Heritage Trail Inc PO Box 5094 Portsmouth NH 03802 Office Phone: 603-862-3520, 603-431-2768. Personal E-mail: nhblackhistory@aol.com. Business E-Mail: pbhtrail@aol.com. E-mail: vc@unh.edu.

CUNNINGHAM, VICTORIA L., secondary school educator; BS, Towson U., 1976, MEd, 1985, MS, 2002. Cert. EMT intermediate Nat. Registry EMTs; tchr. Md. Tchr. Edgewood Mid. Sch., 1976—86, Aberdeen HS, 1986—, chmn. instrnl. leadership bd., 2000—04. EMT intermediate Harford County Fire and EMS Assn., Fallston, Md., 1981—; sci. dept. chair Aberdeen HS, 2003—; with Harford County Leadership Inst., 2005—06. V.p. Fallsont Vol. and Ambulance Co., 1989—90. Mem.: NSTA. Office Phone: 410-273-5500.

CUPKA, NANCY IRVINE, artist, educator; b. Indpls., Oct. 9, 1942; d. Don E. and Marie Irvine; m. W. Roger Cupka, Apr. 8, 1961; children: Gregory, Thomas. Group shows include Am. Artists Profl. League Nat. Exhbn., N.Y.C., 2001, Lafayette Art Assn.,1997, Hoosier Salon, 1970, 89, 92, 93, 97, 98, 2001, 2002, Ind. Heritage Arts Exhbn. Contemporary Ind. Artists, 1991, 92, 93, 94, 97, 98, 99, 2000, 01, Southside Art League, Inc., 1992, 93, 94, 95-97, Ind. Artist's Club, Indpls., 1995, 98, 2000, 01, Brown County Art Gallery, Nashville, 1988-97, Renditions Fine Art Gallery, Indpls., 1998-2002, Honeysuckle Gallery, Nashville, 1998-2002; permanent collections include St. Elizabeth's Hosp., Lafayette, Ind., Ind. State Mus., Indpls., Franklin (Ind.) Coll. Past bd. dirs. Brown County Art Gallery, Nashville, Southside Art League, Indpls.; founder Eastview Women's Support Group for Women with Chronic Pain, Martinvsville, Ind.; assoc. mem. So. Ind. Ctr. for the Arts, Brown County Art Gallery Hist. Assn. Recipient numerous awards. Mem. Am. Artists Profl. League (artist mem.), Allied Artists Am. (assoc.), Southside Art League, Hoosier Salon Patron's Assn., Ind. Heritage Arts (artist mem.), Brown County Art Guild (assoc.), Ind. Artists Club. Avocations: walking trails, photography. Home: 819 N Indiana Ave Auburn IN 46706-1105

CUPO, JANINE, secondary school educator; b. Bklyn., June 5, 1963; d. John Paul and Beatrice Fitzgerald; m. Thomas Robert Cupo; children: Thomas M., Jessica C. BS, SUNY, Oswego, 1985; MS, SUNY, Stony Brook. Tchr. Seaford H.S., NY, 1988—. Office: Seaford High School 1575 Seamans Neck Rd Seaford NY 11783 Office Phone: 516-592-4305. Business E-Mail: janine_cupo@mail.seaford.k12.ny.us.

CUPP, ANETA JOAN, music educator; b. Bonham, Tex., Dec. 30, 1940; d. Emmett Morgan and Hattie Fay (Taylor) Northcutt; m. Charles Daniel Cupp, Mar. 8, 1980; 1 son, Daniel Emmett, B.Mus., North Tex. State U., 1963; M.Ed., U. Houston, 1983. Sec. health workshop North Tex. State U., Denton summer 1963; sec. to recreation music dir. Parks and Recreation Dept. Houston, summers 1964, 65, 66, 68; tchr. elem. itinerant music Houston Ind. Sch. Dist., 1963-96; substitute tchr. H.I.S.D. and Meml. Hall Sch., 1996-2002, Meml. Hall Sch., 2002—. Named Tchr. of Yr., Houston Ind. Sch. Dist., 1976, named to Hall of Honor, 1984; Jim Collins scholar Corsicana Sr. H.S., 1959. Mem. Congress Houston Tchrs. Lutheran. Home: 1237 Althea Dr Houston TX 77018-5230 Office: Memorial Hall Sch 3721 Dacoma Houston TX 77092

CUPP, LUCY PASCHALL, retired elementary school educator, minister; b. Portsmouth, Va., Sept. 18, 1949; d. John Robert Paschall and Frances Wright Pridgen; m. Daniel Lee Cupp, Aug. 17, 1968; children: Jeannie Kay, Paul Daniel. BS in Elem. Edn., Old Dominion U., 1970, MS in Edn. Adminstrn./Supervision, 1980; MA in Counseling, Liberty U., 1987; post-grad., various instns. Cert. elem. tchr., 1-7, elem. prin., elem. supr., elem. counselor, Va; ordained minister, 1999. Tchr. elem. edn. Norfolk (Va.) Pub. Schs., 1970-86, 90-92, tchr. regular elem. edn., 1986-90; SPIRAL educator. Ednl. adminstr. Ingleside Bapt. Ch., Norfolk, Va., 1990-92; assoc. pastor, sch. adminstr. Bayview Baptist Ch., 1999-2001; guidance counselor Ryan Acad., 2004-06. Recipient Sch. Bell award, Norfolk Pub. Schs., Honor Citation, AWANA Clubs Internat., Meritorious Achievement award. Mem. AACD, Am. Assn. Elem. Sch. Guidance Counselors, Am Sch. Counselor Assn., Am. Assn. Christian Counselors. Personal E-mail: funcupp@aol.com.

CURCI, PAULA, counseling administrator, poet, television personality; b. Bklyn., Oct. 11, 1962; d. Michael C. and Angela (Surace) Curci; m. Emilio Squillante III, Dec. 4, 2005; stepchildren: Melissa Squillante, Nick Squillante. BA, Adelphi U., 1984; MS, L.I. U., 1986, PhD, 2006. Cert. sch. counselor, sch. adminstr. N.Y. Sch. counselor L.I. Luth. HS, 1986—88, Sevanhaka HS, 1988—. Talk show host WRHV Radio Hofstra U., Hempstead, NY, 2000—; founder Acoustic Poets Network, 2004—. Author (prodr.): (book and CDs) Letters Never Sent, 1998, Emissary, 2000, Bittersweet, 2005. Chairperson Drug Free Sch. Com., Sevanhaka, 2005—. Named Best Poet, Vault Artist Cmty., 2000, 2004; recipient Guardian Angel award, Hope for the Children Found., 2005. Office: Sevankala HS 500 Tulip Ave Floral Park NY

CURETON, CLAUDETTE HAZEL CHAPMAN, biology professor; b. Greenville, S.C., May 3, 1932; d. John H. and Beatrice (Washington) Chapman; m. Stewart Cleveland Cureton, Dec. 27, 1954; children: Ruthye, Stewart II, S. Charles, Samuel. AB, Spelman Coll., 1951; MA, Fisk U., 1966; DHum (hon.), Morris Coll., Sumter, S.C., 1996. Tchr. North Warren High Sch., Wise, N.C., 1952-60; tchr. Sterling High Sch., Greenville, 1960-66, Wade Hampton High Sch., Greenville, 1967-73; instr. Greenville Tech. Coll., 1973-95, ret., 1995. Bd. dirs. State Heritage Trust, 1978-91; commr. Basic Skills Adv. Program, Columbia, 1990—; mem. adv. bd. Am. Fed. Bank, NCNB Bank, Greenville, 1991—; mem. Higher Edn. S.C. Com. for Selection Prof. of Yr., 1995 Mem. Greenville Urban League, NAACP, S.C. Curriculum Congress; v.p. Woman's Bapt. E.& M. Conv. of S.C.; mem. S.C. Commn. on Higher Edn. Com. for Selection of the 1995 Gov.'s Prof. of the Yr.; mem. Gov.'s Task Force on Juvenile Crime, S.C., Gov.'s Juvenile Justice Task Force, 1997, S.C., Gov.'s Juvenile Justice Youth Coun., S.C., 1996—, Best Chance Network Task Force of Am. Cancer Soc., 1995—, Mental Health Bd.; bd. dirs. Sisters Saving Sisters, Roper Mountain Sci. Ctr., 2003—. Recipient Presdl. award Morris Coll., 1987, 91, Svc. award S.C. Wildlife and Marine Dept., 1986, Outstanding Jack and Jill of Am. citation, 1986, Excellence in Tchg. award Nat. Inst. for Staff and Orgnl. Devel., U. Tex., Austin, 1992-93, Educator of Yr. award Greenville chpt. Am. Cancer Soc., 1994, Outstanding Svc. award Best Chance Network/Am. Cancer Soc., 1994, Citation S.C. House of Reps., 1995, Outstanding Svc. award Ready River Bapt. Assn., 2001; named Unsung Hero of the Cmty. for Outstanding Svc. to Humankind

Greenville Tech. Coll., 1999. Mem. AAAS, AAUW, Nat. Assn. Biology Tchrs., S.C. Curriculum Congress, Nat. Coun. Negro Women, Inc., Delta Sigma Theta (past v.p. Greenville chpt. alumnae). Home: 501 Mary Knob Ct Greenville SC 29607-5242

CURIALE, GINA, secondary school educator, director; d. Raymond and Josephine Curiale; BSc, C.W. Post Coll., Greenvale, N.Y., 1986; MA in Liberal Studies, SUNY, Stony Brook, 1988; profl. diploma, Dowling Coll., Oakdale, N.Y., 1992. Phys. edn. tchr. Longwood Ctrl. Sch. Dist., Middle Island, NY, 1986—91, Kings Park Sch. Dist., 1992—96, Longwood Ctrl. Sch. Dist., Middle Island, 1996—2001, dept. chair, 2001—02, dir. phys. edn. and health, 2002—. Athletic coun. rep. sect. XI N.Y. State H.S. Athletic Assn., Smithtown, NY, 2002—, fin. com. rep. srct. XI, 2004—. Named to C.W. Post Women's Hall of Fame. Mem.: Am. Alliance Health and Phys. Edn., Recreation and Dance, N.Y. State Assn. Health and Phys. Edn. Avocations: golf, boating, fishing, cooking. Office: Longwood Ctrl Sch Dist Athletic Office 100 Longwood Rd Middle Island NY 11953-2056 Office Phone: 631-345-9260.

CURL, MACKENZIE ELIZABETH, secondary school educator; b. Erie, Pa., Sept. 21, 1978; d. Greg and Diane Williams; m. Eric Curl, July 14, 2001. BS in Secondary Edn., Bowling Green State U., Ohio, 2000; EdM, Marygrove Coll., Detroit, 2004. Cert. tchr. Mich., Ohio, Pa., 2000. Tchr. John Glenn H.S., Westland, Mich., 2000—01, Sherman Mid. Sch., Holly, Mich., 2001—. Soccer coach Holly H.S., 2001—; student coun. sponsor Sherman Mid. Sch., Holly, 2001—. Recipient Outstanding Tchr. award, Nat. Honor Roll, 2006. Mem.: MEA. Democrat. Roman Catholic. Avocations: travel, camping, hiking, sports, fitness. Office Phone: 248-328-3400 5453.

CURLE, ROBIN LEA, computer company executive; b. Denver, Feb. 23, 1950; d. Fred Warren and Claudia Jean (Harding) C.; m. Lucien Ray Reed, Feb. 23, 1981 (div. Oct. 1984). BS in Bus. Comm., U. Ky., 1972. Systems analyst 1st Nat. Bank, Lexington, Ky., 1972-73, SW BancShares, Houston, 1973-77; sales rep. Software Internat., Houston, 1977-80; dist. mgr. UCCEL, Dallas, 1980-82; v.p. and gen. mgr. Southeastern region Info. Sci., Inc., Atlanta, 1982-83; v.p. sales and mktg. TesserAct, San Francisco, 1983-86, Foothill Rsch., San Francisco, 1986; pres., founder Curle Cons. Group, San Francisco, 1986-89; mgr. strategic mktg. MCC, Austin, Tex., 1989-90; founder, exec. v.p. Evolutionary Tech., Inc., Austin, 1991-99; pres., CEO Journée Software, Austin, 1999-2000; founder, mng. dir. CEO Partnerships, Austin, 2000—02; pres., CEO Zebra Imaging, 2002—. Bd. dirs. Evolutionary Techs. Internat., Austin Software Coun., Tex. Property and Casualty, Zebra Imaging, Govs. Bus. Coun.; adv. bd. 360 Summit; dir. adv. bd. U. Tex. Engrng. Sch. Mem. bus. adv. com. Rep. Party, Austin. Recipient Ma Ferguson award Exec. Women Internat. 1997, Grad of Yr. award Nat. Bus. Incubator Assn. 1996, Profiles in Power award, 1999, Entrepreneur of Yr. award 360 Summit Adv. Bd.; feature in Forbes Mag., 1996, Entrepreneur Mag., 1997; named top 50 most prestigious people Digital South; profile documentary Entrepreneurial Revolution, 1997, Inc 500 List, 1997, 98. Mem. U. Ky. Alumni Assn., Women in Tech., Women of Austin, Software Exec. Com., Inc. 500 Cos., Austin C. of C. (bd. dir.), Delta Gamma (pres. 1969). Avocations: scuba diving, running, skiing, cooking. Home: 7009 Quill Leaf Cv Austin TX 78750-8306 Office Phone: 512-633-3011. E-mail: rcurle@austin.rr.com.

CURLEE, CAROL WYNETTE, mathematics educator, science educator, small business owner, Internet company executive; b. Terrell, Tex., June 16, 1948; d. Stacy A. and Vera F. Calvin; m. Larry L. Curlee, Aug. 14, 1971; children: David Calvin, Gregory Wade, Marcy Deann Hicks. BS, Tex. Wesleyan U., 1991, M, 1998. Cert. state tchr. Tex. Edn. Agy., 1991. Bookkeeper, payroll Acme Brick, Ft. Worth, 1985—88; bookkeeper Albertsons, Ft. Worth, 1988—99; tchr. Burleson ISD, Tex., 1992—98; mid. sch. math tchr. FWISD, Ft. Worth, 1998—2002, tech. specialist, 2002—03; math and sci. tchr. Plum Creek Elem., Joshua, Tex., 2003—. V.p. United Educators Assn. Ft. Worth, 2000—02. Choreographer (Internat. Assn. Rebekahs Assembly talent show) Thriller (1st Pl., 1992). Dir. Miss Burleson Scholarship Pageant, 1984—91; mem. Bus. and Profl. Women, Burleson, 1988—92, Burleson Rep. Women, 1985—2005. Named State Advisor of Yr., Theta Rho, Rebekah, 1984, 1985, 1991, 1992, 1993; Tchr. scholar, Radio Shack, 2002. Mem.: Nat. Coun. Tchrs. Math., United Educators Assn. (v.p. 2000—02), Rebekah. R-Conservative. Methodist. Avocations: travel, sewing, needlepoint. Home: 7 Fox Hollow Rd Joshua TX 76058 Office: Plum Creek Elem 500 Plum St Joshua TX 76058 Office Phone: 817-475-4940. Personal E-mail: cwcurlee@dot11net.net. E-mail: curleec@joshuaisd.org.

CURNAN, SUSAN P., social policy and management educator, consultant; b. Hyde Park, N.Y., Mar. 7, 1949; d. Charles Agustus and Mildred (Kron) C. BA cum laude, Stony Brook U., 1971; MS, SUNY, New Paltz, 1972; MFS, Yale U., 1978. Cert. tchr. K-12. Rsch. assoc. Yale U., New Haven, 1976-78; dir. New England Non-Profit Corp., Vt., 1978-82, Brandeis U. Ctr. for Youth and Comtys., Waltham, Mass. Co-founder, pres. ER's Kitchen Cabinet, spec. food co., 2001. Co-pub. CYD Jour.; contbr. articles to profl. jours. Trustee Taconic Found., N.Y.C., 1987—93; co-founder, chmn. Inst. for Just Cmtys., 2001. Fellow Berkley Coll. Yale U., 1985, 88; Grad. fellow Yale U., 1976-78; recipient Key to City and Cert. Hon. Citizenship, New Orleans Mayor and City Coun., 1991, Outstanding Young Woman in Am. award, 1982. Home: 174 Boston Post Rd Sudbury MA 01776-3102 Office: Brandeis U 60 Turner St Waltham MA 02453-8923

CURNS, EILEEN BOHAN, counselor, author, speaker; b. Chgo., May 22, 1927; d. Alvin Joseph and Lorraine Bohan; m. John R. Curns, July 1, 1950 (div. 1975); children: James, Barbara. BA in Sociology, DePaul U., Chgo.; MEd in Psychology and Edn., Loyola U., Chgo.; postgrad. in health edn., U. Wis. Cert. Gestalt therapist, Gestalt Inst. Chgo.; Ill. lic. clin. profl. counselor; cert. energy healer Jaffe Inst. for Spiritual Healing, Anguin, Calif. Prin. ACCORD, Vernon Hills, Ill. Cons. in health care cost containment, stress rschr., inner healing; lectr. on the five stress signals leading to disease and how to reverse them. Author: First Aid for Stress charts, 5 workbooks. Recipient Golden Deeds award Exch. Club, 1965, commendation Queen Mary Vets. Hosp., Montreal, 1975. Mem. Am. Bd. Med. Psychotherapists (cert.). Home: 1400 Pauly Apt 307 Gurnee IL 60031

CURNUTTE, MARY E., artist; b. Valera, Tex., Dec. 15, 1920; d. Robert Franklin and Mary Elizabeth (Walker) Line; m. James Richard Curnutte, Oct. 14, 1950 (dec. Feb. 1972); 1 child, Sandra Elizabeth Curnutte; m. Robert Frederick Furman, Apr. 27, 1985 (dec. Apr. 2003). Bookkeeper, sec. drug stores, 1942-49, NCO Club, Goodfellow AFB, San Angelo, Tex., 1949-51; bookkeeper Boyce Hardware and Fuel Oil, Portsmouth, Va., 1953; artist/logs/filing Christian Broadcasting Network, Portsmouth, 1972-73; tchr. art Frederick Mil. Acad., Portsmouth, 1978-82, Alliance Christian Sch., Portsmouth, 1981-85; artist and pvt. tchr. art and music, restorer of art Portsmouth, 1959-89; artist Winter Haven, Fla., 1989—. Recipient Silver Cup award Alliance Christian Sch., 1984. Mem.: DAV Aux., Nat. Assn. Ret. Fed. Employees, Nat. Mus. Women in the Arts (charter), Nat. Ret. Tchrs. Assn. Baptist. Avocations: photography, reading, fishing, music, travel.

CUROE, BERNADINE MARY, counselor; b. Cascade, Iowa, Nov. 20, 1930; d. Harold Richard and Naomi Cecelia (Dahlem) V. BA, Clarke Coll., 1959; MA, Loras Coll., 1969. Tchr. schs. in Iowa, 1950-70; counselor Wahlert HS, Dubuque, Iowa, 1970-79, Loras Coll., Dubuque, 1979—, dir. Ctr. for Counseling and Student Devel., 1986-2002; counselor Archdiocesan Deacons, Waterloo, Iowa, 1978-85; v.p. Sisters of Visitation, Dubuque, 1991—2000, pres. 2000-. Mem. Iowa Dist. Jud. Nominating Commns., 1986-91. Mem. Am. Assn. Counseling and Devel., Am. Coll. Personnel. Assn. Religious Value Issues (dir. 1979-82), Iowa Student Personnel Assn. Democrat. Roman Catholic. Avocations: canoeing, swimming, hiking. Office: Loras Coll 1450 Alta Vista St Dubuque IA 52001-4327 Office Phone: 563-588-7256. Business E-Mail: bernadine.curoe@loras.edu.

CUROL, HELEN RUTH, librarian, English language educator; b. Grayson, La., May 30, 1944; d. Alfred John and Ethel Lea (McDaniel) Broussard; m. Kenneth Arthur Curol, June 25, 1967 (div. 1988); children: Edward, Bryan. BA, McNeese State U., 1966; postgrad., L.I. U., 1969—70; MLS, La. State U., 1987. Tchr., libr. Cameron Parish Schs., Grand Lake, La., 1966—67; media specialist Brentwood Sch. Dist., NY, 1967—69; sch. libr. Patchogue H.S., NY, 1969—70, 1976—95; reference libr., mgr. circulation dept. McNeese State U., Lake Charles, La., 1976—96; test adminstr. Edn. Testing Svc., Princeton, NJ, 1987—95; asst. prof. McNeese U., 1989—95; owner Curol Consulting, Lake Charles, 1995—2002; head adult svcs. Laman Pub. Libr., North Little Rock, Ark., 1996; media libr., tech. rep. LaGrange H.S., Lake Charles, 1997—2004; libr. cons. Calcasieu Parish Sch. Sys., La., 2004—. Rschr. Boise Cascade, DeRidder, La., 1987-88, Vidtron, Dallas, 1990-92, Nat. Archives, Washington, 1989; cons. Cmty. Housing Resource Bd., Lake Charles, 1988-93, Boyce Internat. Engrs., Houston, 1988-89, La. Pub. Broadcasting, Baton Rouge, 1989; devel. cons. Calcasieu Women's Shelter, 1988-92; reference cons. Calcasieu Parish Pub. Libr., 1990-95; presenter at confs. Sr. arbitrator Better Bus. Bur., Lake Charles, 1986-95; local facilitator La. Com. for Fiscal Reform, Lake Charles, 1988; state bd. dirs. PTA, Baton Rouge, 1981-83, LWV La., Baton Rouge, 1983-85; chairperson budget panel com. United Way S.W. La., Lake Charles, 1992-94, bd. dirs., 1995-96; judge La. region IV Social Studies Fair, 1979-89; program spkr. region IV tng. conf. HUD, El Paso, 1992; rep. on Nat. Taxpayer Advocacy Panel, 2002-05, to La.'s Virtual Libr. Commn., 2000—; mem. I-10 Petrochemical Industry's Citizen Adv. Panel, 2003—; apptd. City of Lake Charles Alcohol Rev. Bd., 2003—; bd. dir. SWLA 2005-. Named Citizen of the Day, Sta. KLOU, 1978; grantee La. Endowment for Humanities, 1987, La. Divsn. Arts, 1989, Fair Housing Initiative Program, 1990, HUD, 1992, La. Ctr. Women and Govt. of Nicholls State U., 1993. Mem. ALA (sec. coun. 1988-90, chairperson coun. 1990-91), AAUW (chairperson intellectual freedom com. 1988-89), La. Libr. Assn. (chairperson reference group 1988-90, spkr. Ann. State Convention, 2006), La. Assn. Coll. and Rsch. Librs. (chairperson 1995-96), Ark. Libr. Assn., McNeese U. Alumni Assn., S.W. La. C. of C. (legis. com. 1992), Krewe du Feteurs (Mardi Gras Ct. Duchess 1992), Beta Sigma Phi (pres. Lake Charles chpt. 1983-84, Pres. USA Freedom Corp Silver medal of appreciation, 2000), Beta Phi Mu. Republican. Lutheran. Address: 1005 Cherryhill St Lake Charles LA 70607-4911 Office: Calcasieu Parish School Board's Library Services 2423 6th St Lake Charles LA 70601 Office Phone: 337-437-1211.

CURRAN, BARBARA A., superior court judge; Degree with hon., St. Mary of Woods Coll.; MA with High hon., Syracuse U.; JD, Seton Hall U., 1977. Bar: NJ 1977. Ptnr. Publs. Ltd.; editor Rahway News-Record, Clark Patriot; mem. N.J. Gen. Assembly, Trenton, 1974-80; pres. N.J. Pub. Svc. Commn., Newark, 1980-87; with Chubb & Son Ins. Co., Drexel Burnham Lambert; judge Superior Ct. NJ, Jersey City, 1993—. Contbr. articles to profl. jours. Exec. dir. N.J. Rep. Com.; rep. Am. Coun. Young Polit. Leaders in Romania, Belgium and Eng. Named Woman of Yr., N.J. Fedn. Rep. Women, Most Powererful Woman, N.J. Monthly mag. Office: Superior Ct NJ 595 Newark Ave Rm 806 Jersey City NJ 07306-2394 Office Phone: 201-795-6971.

CURRAN, EMILY K., music educator; b. Duluth, Minn., Mar. 15, 1979; d. Patrick J. and Nicole M. Curran (Stepmother), Peg S. and Bill Klieforth (Stepfather). BME, Valparaiso U., Ind., 2002. Cert. tchr. Wis., 2005. Music tchr. Trinity Cath. Sch., Green Bay, Wis., 2004—, Our Lady of Lourdes Cath. Sch., DePere, Wis., 2005—.

CURRAN, EMILY KATHERINE, museum director; b. Boston, Mar. 27, 1960; d. George Morton and Gloria Rose (Martino) C.; m. John Vincent Callahan, Oct. 8, 1989; 1 dau., Clara Huiru. AB in Fine Arts, Bard Coll., 1982; MS in Mus. Leadership, Bank Street Coll., 1992. Sr. developer The Children's Mus., Boston, 1982-88; dir. edn. The Old South Meeting House, Boston, 1988-92, exec. dir., 1992—. Vis. cmty. artist Great George's Project, Liverpool, Eng., 1983. Author: Science Sensations, 1989, An Architectural History of the Old South Meeting House, 1995. Bd. dirs. Freedom Trail Found., Boston, 1992-97; elected mem. Colonial Soc. Mass., 1996—; mem., exec. com. mem. cmty. adv. bd. WGBH, Boston, 1996-99, vice chair, 1998-99. Mus. edn. fellow Bank Street Coll., 1989-91. Fellow Mass. Hist. Soc.; Mem. Am. Assn. Mus., Am. Assn. State and Local History, New Eng. Mus. Assn., Boston Mus. Educators' Roundtable (chair steering com. 1989-91). Office: Old South Meeting House 310 Washington St Boston MA 02108-4616

CURRAN, LEIGH, actress, playwright; b. Santa Barbara, Calif., Dec. 5, 1943; d. John Van Benschoten and Barbara (Hansl) Griggs; m. Edward Herrmann, Sept. 9, 1978. Grad., Am. Mus. and Dramatic Acad., 1964. Mem. L.A. Women's Shakespeare Co., 1992—. Actress: (Broadway debut) How Now, Dow Jones, Lunt-Fontanne Theatre, 1968, (stage prodns.) The Lunch Girls, 1977 (also author), 'night, Mother, 1985, Stitchers and Starlight Talkers, 1986, Walking The Blonde, 1989 (also author), The 52nd Street Project, 1987-91, (feature films) I Never Promised You a Rose Garden, 1977, Reds, 1981, (TV series) Adam's Rib, 1974, St. Elsewhere, 1985, Another World, 1986, L.A. Law, 1991, West Wing, 2002, Judging Amy, 2002 author: (play) Alterations, Useful Trash, Zone 13 Hair, Michelle Hammer, Girl Detective, Destiny, Destiny, Destiny, Pressed Against Strangers; (teleplays) The Paper Chase, St. Elsewhere; founder, artistic dir. The Virginia Avenue Project, 1991—. Mem. AFTRA, Actors' Equity Assn., Screen Actors Guild, Writers Guild, Dramatists Guild, Women in Film. Office: Va Ave Project 3000 W Olympic Blvd Santa Monica CA 90404 Office Phone: 310-264-4224.

CURRAN, LISA M., environmental scientist, educator; AB with honors in Anthropology, Harvard U., 1984; PhD in Ecology and Evolutionary Biology, Princeton U., 1994. Mercer postdoctoral fellow Harvard U., 1994—96; asst. prof. ecol. sustainability dept. biology U. Mich., 1996—2001; assoc. prof. tropical resources Sch. Forestry and Environ. Studies Yale U., 2001—06, prof., 2006—. Bd. mem. Tropical Forest Found., 1999—; vis. rsch. fellow ecosystems and governance prog. East West Ctr., Honolulu, 2001—02; John Musser dir. Yale U. Tropical Resource Inst., 2001—; external faculty Santa Fe Inst., 2003—; cons. Contbr. articles to profl. jours.; mem. editl. bd.: Environ. Rsch. Letters, 2006—. MacArthur fellow, John D. and Catherine T. MacArthur Found., 2006. Mem.: Soc. Conservation Biology, Internat. Soc. Tropical Foresters, Assn. Tropical Biologists, Am. Geophys. Union, AAAS, Ecol. Soc. Am. (Aldo Leopold Leadership Program fellow 2004—). Office: Sch Forestry & Environ Studies Yale U 370 Prospect St New Haven CT 06511 E-mail: lisa.curran@yale.edu.*

CURRAN, MARY ANN, chemical engineer; b. Cin., Oct. 1, 1957; d. Ernst Carl and Marilyn W. Braun; m. Roger Wayne Curran, July 16, 1982 (div. May 1998); children: Amanda, Margo. BS in Chem. Engrng., U. Cin., 1980; MSc, Lund (Sweden) U., 1996. Chem. engr. U.S. EPA, Cin., 1980—. Editor: Environmental Life Cycle Assessment, 1996. Mem. AIChE (chmn. 1989-90). Office: US EPA 26 W Ml King Dr Cincinnati OH 45268-0001 Home: 804 Andrea Dr Loveland OH 45140-6740 E-mail: curran.maryann@epa.gov.

CURRAN, PATRICIA A., retail executive; Positions from hourly assoc. through regional v.p. & div. mdse. mgr. Wal-Mart Stores Inc., Bentonville, Ark., 1983—2003, sr. v.p. store ops., 2003—05, exec. v.p. store ops., 2005—. Mem. Coca-Cola Retailing Rsch. Council, Ctr. for Retailing Excellence, Sam M. Walton Coll. Bus., Univ. Ark. Mem. Single Parent Scholarship Fund Wash. County. Named one of 50 Most Powerful Women in Bus., Fortune mag., 2006. Mem.: Network of Exec. Women. Office: Wal-Mart Stores Inc 702 SW Eighth St Bentonville AR 72716*

CURRAN-SMITH, ANITA STILES, retired public health medicine educator, dean; b. Northampton, Mass., 1929; BA, U. Conn., 1951; MD, N.Y. Med. Coll., 1955; MPH, Col. U., 1974. Diplomate Am. Bd. Preventive Medicine (bd. dirs.). Intern Mountainside Hosp., Montclair, N.J., 1955-56; house officer Maryview Hosp., Portsmouth, Va., 1960-63; pediat. clinic physician Met. Hosp., N.Y.C., 1963-65; med. dir. Newark Presch. Coun., 1965-70; child health physician N.J. Dept. Health, 1965-73; resident in pub. health N.Y.C. Dept. Health, 1974-75, dir. lead poisoning control program, 1974-78, dep. com., 1976-78; com. health Westchester County (N.Y.) Health Dept., 1978-89; prof. clin., environ. and cmty. medicine U. Medicine and Dentistry N.J. R.W. Johnson Med. Sch., New Brunswick, 1989—, assoc. dean cmty. health, 1992-96. Mem. exec. com. Am. Bd. Med. Specialists, 1995-98; chair residency review com. coun. Accreditation Coun. for Grad. Med. Edn., 1992-94. Fellow Am. Coll. Preventive Medicine, N.Y. Acad. Medcine, N.Y. Acad. Scis.

CURRENCE, GLENNDA KAY, elementary school educator; b. Davenport, Iowa, Feb. 4, 1954; d. Glenn Elston and Ethel Lucille (Watts) C. BME, Augustana Coll., 1976; M in Counseling, We. Ill. U., 1995. Tchr. elem. vocal music Clinton (Iowa) Cmty. Sch. Dist., 1976-77, Davenport (Iowa) Cmty. Sch. Dist., 1977-95, elem. counselor, 1995—. Organist, pianist Faith United Meth.Ch., Davenport, 1968-77. Mem. NEA, ACA, Am. Sch. Counselors Assn., Internat. Assn. for Addictions and Offender Counselors, Iowa Music Educators Assn. Methodist. Avocations: reading, music, piano, exercise. Office: Davenport Cmty Schs Davenport IA 52803-5025 Home: 2653 N Stark St Davenport IA 52804-5012

CURRIE, BARBARA FLYNN, state legislator; b. LaCrosse, Wis., May 3, 1940; d. Frank T. And Elsie R. (Gobel) Flynn; m. David P. Currie, Dec. 29, 1959; children: Stephen Francis, Margaret Rose. AB cum laude, U. Chgo., 1968, AM, 1973. Asst. study dir. Nat. Opinion Rsch. Ctr., Chgo., 1973-77; part time instr. polit. sci. DePaul U., Chgo., 1973-74; mem. Ill. Ho. of Reps., 1979—, chmn. House Dem. Study Group, 1980-83, asst. majority leader, 1993, asst. minority leader, 1995, majority leader, 1997. V.p. Chgo. LWV, 1965-69; mem. Hyde Park-Kenwood Cmty. Conf., Ind. Voters of Ill., Ill. Conf. Women Legislators, Ind. Precinct Orgn., Hyde Park Coop. Soc., Ams. for Dem. Action., Women United for S. Shore. Named Best Legislator, Ind. Voters of Ill., 1980, 1982, 1984, 1986, 1986, 1990, 1992, 1994, 1996, 1998, Ill. Credit Union League, Outstanding Legislator, Ill. Hosp. Assn., 1987, Legislator of Yr., Ill. Nurses Assn., 1984, NASW, 1984, Ill. Women's Substance Abuse Coalition, 1984, Illinoisan of Yr., Ill. News Broadcasters Assn., 2001; recipient Leon Despres award, 1991, Ill. Environ. Coun. award, Lottie Holman O'Neill award, Ill. Women's Polit. Caucus, Susan B. Anthony award, honor award, Nat. Trust Historic Preservation, awards, Welfare Rights Coalition of Orgns., Ill. Pub. Action Coun., Chgo. Heart Assn., BEST BETS award, Nat. Ctr. Policy Alternatives, 1988, Svc. award, Nat. Ctr. for Freedom of Info. Studies, 1989, Beautiful Person award, Chgo. Urban League, 1989, Friend of Labor award, Ill. AFL-CIO, 1990, Ill. Maternal and Child Health Coalition award, 1990, Ill. Hunger Coalition award, 1991, cert. of appreciation, SEIU Local 880, 1989, March of Dimes, 1988, Chgo. Tchrs. Union, Ill. Hosp. Assn., Ptnr. Vision award, Families' and Children's AIDS Network, Woman of Vision award, Women's Bar Assn. Ill., 1997, Nat. Elected Pub. Ofcl. award, NASW, 1997, Outstanding Working Woman of Ill. award, Ill. Fedn. Bus. and Profl. Women, Dist. Pub. Health Legislator award, Am. Pub. Health Assn., 1999, Legis. award, Ill. Primary Health Care Assn., 2002, Ill. Press Assn., 2003, Legis. of Yr. award, Access Living, 2003, others. Mem.: LWV, ACLU (bd. dirs. Ill.). Office: Ill Gen Assembly 300 State House Springfield IL 62706-0001 Office Phone: 773-667-0550.

CURRIE, JANET M., economics professor; b. Kingston, Ont., Can., Mar. 29, 1960; came to U.S., 1983; d. Kenneth Lyell and Edrith Delores Currie; m. William Bentley MacLeod, May 18, 1996; children: Joana Marion, Daniel Bentley. BA, U. Toronto, 1982, MA, 1983; PhD in Econs., Princeton U., 1988. Asst. prof. econs. UCLA, 1988-91, MIT, Cambridge, Mass., 1992, assoc. prof. econs., 1993, UCLA, 1994-95, prof. econs., 1995—, Charles E. Davidson prof. econs., 2005—; prof. econs. Columbia U., NYC, 2005—. Panel mem. NAS, Washington, 1998-99, 2000-01, NSF, Washington, 1998-2001; rsch. assoc. Nat. Bur. Econ. Rsch., 1995—; mem. Brookings Roundtable on Children and Families, 1998—; affiliate Joint Ctr. Poverty Rsch., 1998—; cons. RAND, 1993—. Author: Welfare and the Well Being of Children, 1994; contbr. chpts. to books, articles to profl. jours.; co-editor Jour. Labor Econs., 1994-2000; mem. edit. bd. Quar. Jour. Econs., 1995—; assoc. editor Jour. Health Econs., 2000—02. Alfred P. Sloan Found. fellow, 1993-95, Olin fellow Nat. Bur. Econ. Rsch., 1993, Can. Inst. Advanced Rsch. fellow, 1998-2000. Avocation: gardening. Office: UCLA Dept Econs 405 Hilgard Ave Los Angeles CA 90095-1477 also: Columbia U Econs Dept Internat Affairs Bldg, MC 3323 420 W 118th St New York NY 10027 Office Phone: 212-854-4520. E-mail: jc2663@columbia.edu.

CURRIER, PATTY, physiologist; With bone lab. NASA, Calif.; payload scientist NASA Kennedy Space Ctr., Fla.

CURRY, ANN, correspondent, anchor; b. Agana, Guam, Nov. 19, 1956; d. Robert Paul and Hiroe (Nagase) Curry; m. Brian Wilson Ross, Oct. 21, 1987; children: Anna McKenzie, William Walker. Student, U. Oreg., 1974—78. Reporter Sta. KTVL-TV, Medford, Oreg., 1978—81; reporter, weekend anchor Sta. KGW-TV, Portland, Oreg., 1981—84; reporter Sta. KCBS-TV, L.A., 1984—90; corr., anchor NBC News at Sunrise NBC News, N.Y.C., 1991—96; news anchor Today Show, 1997—. Nominee Emmy award, 1985, 1986, 1987, 1988; recipient Golden Mike award, RTNA, 1986, 1987, 1989, Cert. Excellence award, AP, 1987, 1988, Greater L.A. Press Club, 1987, Superior Reporting award, NAACP, 1989, Emmy award, Acad. TV Arts and Scis., 1987, 1989, Nat. award, AAJA, 2000, AmeriCares Humanitarian Medial award, 2002. Avocation: art history. Office: NBC News 30 Rockefeller Plz # 374E New York NY 10112-0002

CURRY, CATHARINE TERRILL, marketing executive, health facility administrator, sales executive; b. Mobile, Ala., Sept. 27, 1950; d. Edward Chapin Jr. and Danie (Convey) Terrill; m. Wiliam Thomas Curry Jr., June 27, 1988. BS in Social Sci., Eastern Mich. U., 1974; MA in Counseling, La. State U., 1986. Mgr. Terrill Realty Co., Mobile, 1975-84; dir. community rels. ARC, Mobile, 1981-83; mktg. rep. Ochsner Found. Hosp., New Orleans, 1986-87; dir. mktg. HCA Coliseum Med. Ctrs., Macon, Ga., 1987-88; dir. coop. edn. Mercer U., Macon, 1988-90; sr. med. sales specialist Mead Johnson Labs., Bristol-Myers Squibb, Macon, 1990—2002; reg. sales coord. Hearthstone/Carestone Assisted Living, 2002—04; sales dir. Classic Residence by Hyatt, 2004—. Mem. NAFE, Internat. Assn. Female Execs., Ga. Coll. Placement Assn., Am. Coll. Placement Assn., Nat. Disting. Svc. Regtistry (chartered), Nat. Coop. Edn. Assn., Art Patrons League, Am. Hosp. Assn., Soc. for Healthcare Pub. Rels./Mktg. and Healthcare Strategic Planning, Kappa Kappa Gamma Alumnae, Phi Beta Kappa. Republican. Avocations: painting, cooking, scuba diving. Office Phone: 775-223-0022. Personal E-mail: mardanne@sbcglobal.net.

CURRY, DALE BLAIR, retired journalist; b. Memphis, May 30, 1941; d. Hamilton Minter and Doris (Terry) Blair; m. Douglas Hester Curry, Dec. 21, 1963; children: Jennifer, Elizabeth. BA, U. Miss., 1963. Reporter The Commerical-Appeal, Memphis, 1962-63, Atlanta Constn., 1963-65, The States-Item, New Orleans, 1969-72, The Morning Advocate, Baton Rouge, 1974-76, 82-84; food editor The Times-Picayune, New Orleans, 1984—2004; columnist New Orleans Mag.; food and travel freelance writer. Elder St. Charles Ave. Presbyn. Ch., New Orleans, 1984-87, 91-94. Recipient award AP, UPI, New Orleans Press Club; named among Top 50 alumni 50th Anniversary U. Miss. Sch. Journalism, 1998. Mem. Assn. Food Journalists (pres. 1994-96), Theta Sigma Phi (Alumni of Yr. U. Miss. chpt.). E-mail: dalecurry2004@yahoo.com.

CURRY, DENISE, women's college basketball coach; BS, UCLA, 1982, MA in Humanities, 1985. Asst. coach Calif., San Jose Lasers, 1996; head coach Calif. State Fullerton, 1997—2000; asst. coach women's basketball Long Beach State, Calif. Named to Naismith Meml. Basketball Hall of Fame, 1997, Women's Basketball Hall of Fame, 1999; French Profl. Player of the Decade 1980's, Three-time Kodak All-Am.; recipient Olympic gold medal. Office: Long Beach State Women's Basketball 1250 N Bellflower Blvd Long Beach CA 90840

CURRY, ELLEN R., academic administrator, educator; b. New Rochelle, N.Y. d. Joseph Francis and Helen (McGuinness) C.; m. William D. Damato. BS, Good Counsel Coll., 1965; MS, Boston Coll., 1970, Pace U., 1980; PhD, NYU, 1994. Cert. sch. dist. adminstr., N.Y.; cert. sch. adminstr. and supr., N.Y. Chemistry tchr. Acad. Our Lady of Good Counsel, White Plains, N.Y., 1967-68; sci. and math. tchr. John F. Kennedy H.S., Somers, N.Y., 1970-85, sci. chairperson, 1979-85; prin. Acad. Our Lady of Good Counsel, White Plains, 1985-95; asst. v.p. acad. affairs Coll. New Rochelle, 1995-98, exec. asst. to pres., 1998—2001, exec. v.p., 2001—. Cons. EME Software Co., Fla., 1986-97; presenter, cons. HRM Software/Queue Software, Pleasantville, N.Y., 1985-89; presenter N.E. Solar Energy Ctr., Boston, 1979-81; curriculum developer Energy Edn. Project, Albany, N.Y., 1977-81. Creator (software) The Periodic Law. Mem. planning com. N.Am. Ursuline Educators, Louisville, 1998, N.Am. Ursuline Administrators, New Rochelle, 1999; bd. dirs. Mercy Secondary Edn., NY, 1996—, Notre Dame H.S., 2001—. Recipient Spl. Olympics proclamation Westchester County Bd. Legis., 1983, scholarship NYU, 1984. Mem. NSTA, AAUP, AAUW. Roman Catholic. Home: 112 Winchester Dr Yonkers NY 10710-2319 Office: Coll of New Rochelle 29 Castle Pl New Rochelle NY 10805-2338 Office Phone: 914-654-5854. E-mail: ecurry@cnr.edu.

CURRY, ESTELLA ROBERTA, education educator, school psychologist, consultant; d. John Henry and Grace Gannon; m. Carl Alton Curry, Apr. 7, 1950 (dec. Feb. 1986); children: John, Carl, Carla, David. BS cum laude, Ohio U., 1968, postgrad., 1973—2002; MA, Marshall U., 1969, postgrad., 1971—73. Cert. elem. tchr. Ohio, 1961, sch. counselor Ohio, 1969, sch. psychologist Ohio, 1973. Middle sch. tchr. South Point (Ohio) Local Schs., 1961—64, elem. sch. tchr., 1964—68, elem. guidance counselor, 1969—72; grad. asst. Marshall U., Huntington, W.Va., 1968—69; sch. guidance counselor Fairland Local Schs., Proctorville, Ohio, 1972—73; G.E.D. adminstr., coordinator of psychological svcs., sch. psychologist/counselor Lawrence County Ednl. Svc. Ctr., Ironton, Ohio, 1973—. Therapist, clin. supr. Prestera Mental Health Ctr., Huntington, 1991—96; instr. Ohio U., Ironton, 1999—; ednl. cons. Oakridge Treatment Ctr., Ironton, 1999—. Mem.: Sch. Psychology Assn. South Ea. Ohio, Ohio Sch. Psychologist Assn., Coun. for Exceptional Children. Avocations: reading, travel, cooking, art collecting, gardening. Home: 3964 County Rd 15 South Point OH 45680 Office: Lawrence County Ednl Svc Ctr 111 S 4th St Ironton OH 45638 Office Phone: 740-532-4223. Personal E-mail: ecurry3600@aol.com.

CURRY, JANE ANNE, writer, educator, performer; b. Indpls., Mar. 23, 1945; d. James Alton and Norma (Werden) C.; m. David Lee Lund, Mar. 25, 1978. BA in English, Hanover Coll., 1967; MA in Am. Studies, U. Mich., 1970, PhD, 1975. English tchr. Waterford (Conn.) High Sch., 1967-69; asst. prof. English and Am. Studies Lafayette Coll., Easton, Pa., 1974-78; free lance writer, performer Mpls., 1978—; ind. scholar-performer Minn. Chautauqua, 1981-84, 88-92. Author: The River's in My Blood, 1983, Marietta Holley, 1996; editor, performer Samantha Rastles the Woman Question, 1983; writer-performer Just Say Know, Nice Girls Don't Sweat, Miz Wizard's Science Secrets, Sisters of the Quill and Skillet; contbr. essays, articles and book revs. to various publs. Vol. Big Sisters, Big Brothers, Mpls., 1985-87; coach girl's basketball Seward Cmty. Ctr., Mpls. 1988, '89; vol. Dowling Elem. Sch., 2001—. Grantee NEH summer stipend, 1977, Am. Coun. Learned Socs., 1977, Minn. Hist. Soc., St. Paul, 1991, Minn. Ind. Schloar of Yr., 1984. Mem. AAUW, Nat. Women's Studies Assn., Women's Sports Found. Avocations: scuba diving, racquetball, travel, reading. Home and Office: 5048 37th Ave S Minneapolis MN 55417-1525

CURRY, JANE LOUISE, writer; b. East Liverpool, Ohio, Sept. 24, 1932; d. William Jack and Helen Margaret (Willis) C. Student, Pa. State U., University Park, 1950-51; BS, Ind. U. of Pa., 1954; postgrad., UCLA, 1957-59; AM, Stanford U., Calif., 1962, PhD, 1969. Tchr. art East Liverpool schs., 1955, L.A. schs., 1956-59; teaching asst. dept. English Stanford U., 1959-61, 64-65, acting instr., 1967-68, instr., 1983-84, lectr., 1987. Storyteller, 1962—. Author: Down from the Lonely Mountain, 1965, Beneath the Hill, 1967, The Sleepers, 1968, The Change-Child, 1969, The Daybreakers, 1970, Mindy's Mysterious Miniature, 1970, Over the Sea's Edge, 1971, The Ice Ghosts Mystery, 1972, The Lost Farm, 1974, Parsley Sage, Rosemary and Time, 1975, The Watchers, 1975, The Magical Cupboard, 1976, Poor Tom's Ghost, 1977, The Birdstones, 1977, The Bassumtyte Treasure, 1978, Ghost Lane, 1979, The Wolves of Aam, 1981, Shadow Dancers, 1983, The Great Flood Mystery, 1985, The Lotus Cup, 1986, Back in the Beforetime, 1987, Me, Myself and I, 1987, The Big Smith Snatch, 1989, Little Little Sister, 1989, What the Dickens?, 1991, The Great Smith House Hustle, 1993, The Christmas Knight, 1993, Robin Hood and his Merry Men, 1994, Robin Hood in the Greenwood, 1995, Moon Window, 1996, Dark Shade, 1998, Turtle Island, 1999, A Stolen Life, 1999, The Wonderful Sky Boat, 2001, The Egyptian Box, 2002, Hold Up the Sky, 2003, Brave Cloelia, 2004, The Black Canary, 2005. Scholar Fulbright Scholar, U. London, 1961—62; Leverhulme Fellow, 1965—66. Office: Simon & Schuster Children's Publ Divsn 1230 Ave of Ams New York NY 10020

CURRY, JOAN R., medical/surgical nurse, emergency nurse; b. Vandalia, Ill., Dec. 16, 1953; d. Melvin and Ruby I. (Wheatley) Maroon; m. Thomas D. Terry, Apr. 19, 1974 (div. Apr. 1985), m. James Roger Curry, June 10, 2004; children: Jeremy D., Renae I. Student, Kaskaskia Coll., Centralia, Ill., 1983, Greenville (Ill.) Coll., 1983; AAS, Parkland Coll., Champaign, Ill., 1988. Ward sec. Edward A. Utlaut Meml. Hosp., Greenville, 1969-85; nursing asst. Piatt County Nursing Home, Monticello, Ill., 1985-87; staff nurse John and Mary E. Kirby Hosp., Monticello, 1988-91, Carle Found. Hosp., Urbana, Ill., 1992-97, med. intensive care stepdown nurse, 1997—. Home: 519 E Franklin St Paxton IL 60957-1640

CURRY, JULIE A., state official; b. Granite City, Ill., June 7, 1962; 1 child, Evan Curry-Dennison. BA, Eastern Ill. U., 1984, MA, 1985. Ill. state rep. Dist. 101, 1995—2003; deputy chief staff, economic devel. and labor State of Ill., 2003—. Democrat. Office: 207 State Capitol Bldg Springfield IL 62706

CURRY, KATHLEEN BRIDGET, retired librarian; b. Parnell, Iowa, May 19, 1931; d. John Michael and Ellen Theresa (Clear) Curry. BSLS, Marycrest Coll., 1953. Head libr. Moline (Ill.) Sr. HS, 1953-90; ret., 1990. Part-time libr. Moline Pub. Hosp. Sch. Nursing, 1957—66; mem. sch. nursing libr. St. Anthony's Hosp., Rock Island, Ill., 1955; hist. libr. Rock Island Hist. Libr., Moline, 1956—59; libr. Black Hawk Coll., Moline, 1958—59. Guild mem. Quad City Symphony Orch., Davenport, 1972—; bd. dirs. Quad City Arts Coun., Davenport, 1990, Miss Black Hawk Coll., Moline, 1986—; exec. bd. Miss Iowa Pageant, Davenport, 1987—. Recipient Disting. Svc. award, Moline HS PTA, 1983, Marycrest Coll., 1987. Mem.: AAUW, NEA, Iowa Libr. Assn., Moline Edn. Assn., Ill. Sch. Libr. Assn., Ill. Edn. Assn., Zonta Internat., Delta Kappa Gamma. Democrat. Roman Catholic. Avocations: playing the piano, cooking. Home: 3646 71st St Ct Moline IL 61265-1833 E-mail: gmedhus@aol.com.

CURRY, NANCY ELLEN, psychologist, psychoanalyst, educator; b. Brockway, Pa., Jan. 26, 1931; d. George R. and Mary F. (Covert) C. BA, Grove City Coll., 1952; MEd, U. Pitts., 1956, PhD, 1972; grad., Pitts. Psychoanalytic Inst., 1988, grad. child analytic program, 1992. Lic. psychologist, Pa. Tchr. public schs., East Brady and Oakmont, Pa., 1952-55; presch. demonstration tchr. Arsenal Family and Children's Center, U. Pitts., 1955-79, assoc. dir., 1971-79; from instr. in psychiatry to prof. child devel. Sch. Social Work, U. Pitts, 1957-93; prof. emeritus Sch. Social Work, U. Pitts.; also mem. faculty U. Pitts Sch. Medicine, Sch. Edn., Sch. Health Related Professions.; pvt. practice in psychanalysis and psychotherapy; ret., 2000. Supr., cons.; Fulbright exchange tchr. North Oxford Nursery Sch., Oxford, Eng., 1957-58; vis. prof. Oreg. State U., summer, 1964, Ariz. State U., summer, 1969; assoc. dir. early childhood project Edn. Professions Devel. Act, U.S. Office of Edn., 1970-74; cons. in field. Co-producer 12 films on children's play; co-author Beyond Self-esteem, 1990; editor The Feeling Child; author numerous articles on child devel. Adv. bd. Fred Rogers Ctr; bd. mem. Family Commn. Mem. APA, Assn. Child Psychoanalysis Home: 149 Shadow Ridge Dr Pittsburgh PA 15238-2133 Personal E-mail: NCU149@comcast.net.

CURRY, SADYE BEATRYCE, gastroenterologist, educator; b. Reidsville, N.C., Oct. 17, 1941; BS cum laude, Johnson C. Smith U., 1963; MD, Howard U., 1967. Intern Duke U. Med. Ctr., Durham, N.C., 1967-68, fellow in gastroenterology, 1969-72; instr. dept. medicine Duke U., Durham, 1969-72; resident medicine VA Hosp., Washington, 1968-69; asst. prof. medicine divsn. gastroenterology Howard U. Coll. Medicine, Washington, 1972-78, assoc. prof. medicine divsn. gastroenterology, 1978—; asst. chief med. officer Howard U. Med. Svc., D.C. Gen. Hosp., Washington, 1973-74; asst. chief medicine in-charge of undergrad. med. edn. Howard U., Washington, 1974-77. Contbr. articles to profl. jours. Mem. bd. trustees Lake Land 'Or Property Owners Assn., Ladysmith, Va., 1989-90. Recipient Howard U. Coll. Medicine Student Coun. Faculty award for Teaching Excellence, 1975, Kaiser-Permanente Faculty award for excellence in teaching, Howard U. Coll. Medicine, 1978, Howard U. Coll. Med. Student/Am. Med. Women's Assn. woman of yr., 1990; named U.S. Friendship Force amb. to West Berlin, 1980. Mem. AAUW, AMA, Nat. Med. Assn., Am. Soc. Internal Medicine, Medico-Chirurgical Soc. D.C., Med. Soc. D.C., Am. Digestive Diseases Soc., Leonidas Berry Soc. for Digestive Diseases, Nat. Coun. of Negro Women, Alpha Kappa Alpha, Beta Kappa Chi, Alpha Kappa Mu.

CURRY, SHEILA DIANE, secondary school educator, athletic trainer; b. Washington, June 30, 1953; d. Robert William and Janet Louise Miller; m. Robert Frederic Curry, May 19, 1973; children: Lee Patrick, Wayne Robert. BSc, Shepherd Coll., 1976; MSc, Marshall U., 1985. Lic. athletic trainer 1992. Tchr., coach Richwood Jr. H.S., Richwood, W.Va., 1978—83, tchr., athletic trainer, 1983—84; grad. asst. Marshall U., 1984—85; tchr., athletic trainer Allendale Fairfax H.S., 1985—92, Dutch Fork H.S., Irmo, 1982—2001, Dorman H.S., Roebuck, SC, 2001—. Recipient Region Coach of Yr., 1986—87, 1987—88, 1988—89, State Coach of Yr., 1986—87, 1987—88. Mem.: SC Athletic Trainers Assn., Nat. Athletic Trainers Assn. Office: Dorman HS 1020 Cavalier Way Roebuck SC 29376

CURRY, SHERRIE DONELL, real estate agent; b. Huntsville, Ala., Apr. 29, 1969; d. Charles Boyd Anderson and Donell Mae (Koch) Koch; m. Mathew Joseph Curry, Sept. 26, 1987. Grad. H.S., Wichita, Kans. Real estate agt. Coldwell Banker, Wichita, 1999—2004, Allegiant GMAC, Wichita, 2004—. Fellow: Ea. Star; mem.: Wichita Area Assn. Realtors. Avocations: fishing, quilting, art, crafts. Home: 943 W 61st St Wichita KS 67217 Office: Allegiant GMAC Realty 4601 E Douglas Wichita KS 67208

CURRY, VIRGINIA FRANCES, retired language educator; b. Kansas City, Kans., Feb. 20, 1922; d. Garfield Allen and Pauline Charlton Curry. AB, U. Kans., Lawrence, 1943, MA, 1944; PhD, Ind. U., Bloomington, 1947. Tchr. Langston U. Coll., Okla., 1949—50, Spelman Coll., Atlanta, 1950—52, Tex. So. U., Houston, 1953—57, Fla. A&M U., Tallahassee, 1958—60; tchr., dept. head Fayetteville State U., NC, 1961—92; ret., 1992. Scholar, Ford Found., Kansas City, 1939. Mem.: NAACP, Phi Sigma Iota, Pi Lambda Theta, Phi Beta Kappa. Home: 1846 Broadell Dr Fayetteville NC 28301

CURRY-CARLBURG, JOANNE JEANNE, elementary school educator; b. Cleve., Oct. 11, 1947; d. James Michael and Joan Marie (Bukky) Curry; m. Stan R. Carlburg. BS, Villa Maria Coll., Erie, Pa., 1973; MEd, Edinboro U. Pa., 1975; EdD, SUNY, Buffalo, 1987. Cert. tchr., reading specialist, Pa. Tchr. Erie Diocese, 1966-76; reading specialist N.W. Tri-County Intermediate Unit 5, Edinboro, Pa., 1976—. Cons. Erie Diocese Cath. Schs., 1990—; adj. faculty Gannon U., Erie, 1991—. Author: Pseudoword Phonics Test, 1986. Active Flagship Niagara League, Erie, Erie Zool. Soc.; pres. bd. trustees Villa Maria Acad., 1999-2001. Recipient Friends of Edn. award Gannon U., 1993; finalist Elem. Sch. Tchr. of Yr. 1995, Commonwealth of Pa., Disting. Alumni award Gannon U., 1998. Me. ASCD, AAUW, NEA, Pa. State Edn. Assn., Internat. Reading Assn. (Celebrate March 1998 Literacy award, with Erie Reading Coun.), Erie Reading Coun. (pres.-elect), Keystone Reading Assn., U. Buffalo Alumni Assn., Grad. Sch. Edn. Alumni Assn. U. Buffalo, Gannon U. Alumni Assn. Avocations: outdoor activities, golf, walking, photography, reading. Office: Northwest Tri-County Intermediate Unit 5 252 Waterford St Edinboro PA 16412-2373

CURRY SCOTT, SHIRLEY GOODMAN, retired director; b. Perry, Fla., Nov. 14, 1935; d. Hezekiah and Vivian Inez Goodman; children: Gherry Monte Rolle, Veleta Inez Roberson. BS in Phys. Edn., Health, Fla. A&M U., Tallahassee, 1961, MEd. in Guidance, 1969. Phys. edn. tchr. Taylor County Sch. Bd., Perry, Fla., 1961—74, dean, 1975—82, 1988—90, dir. student svcs., 1983—87, 1991—97; ret., 1997. Bd. dirs. Big Bend Hospice, Perry, 1994—, United Way of Big Bend, Perry, 2004—. Coun. mem. City of Perry, 1992—2000, mayor, 1995, vice mayor, 1996; Sunday sch. supt. Stewart Meml. AME Ch., 1995—2005, Sunday sch. tchr., 2005—06. Named to Wall of Tolerance, So. Poverty Law Ctr., 2005. Mem.: Taylor County Ret. Tchrs. Assn., Taylor County FAMU Alumni Chpt., Vogue XIII, Inc. (life; pres. 1982—2000). Methodist. Achievements include First woman elected to serve as council member, vice mayor, and mayor of the City of Perry, Florida; first African American inducted into the Taylor County Educator's Hall of Fame. Avocations: reading, travel.

CURTIN, CONSTANCE O'HARA, language educator, writer; b. N.Y.C., Mar. 11, 1927; d. V. Winthrop and Belle Callum O'Hara; m. David Yarrow Curtin, July 1, 1950; children: Susan M., David F., Jane C. Jones. AB, Mt. Holyoke Coll., Mass., 1948; MA in Chemistry, Columbia U., 1950, PhD in Chemistry, 1953; MAT in Russian, U. Ill., Urbana, 1966. Author of cyrillic alphabet lesson PLATO (Programmed Logic for Automatic Tchg. Ops.), U. of Ill., Urbana, Ill., 1966—89; author of Russian reading program PLATO U. Ill., 1966—89, author of lab. material Slavic 101-104 PLATO, 1966—82, tchr. of Russian U. H.S., 1966—89; ret. Project dir. Apple Edn. Found., Urbana. Author (cd) Russian Alphabet Program for TRS80, Apple II and IBM PC; author: (cd) Language Review Packets for Apple II and IBM; author: (software designer) (cd for lang. learning) Conversations Around the World: in French, German, Russian, Spanish. Recipient Outstanding Tchr. of Russian, Ill. Fgn. Lang. Assn., 1986, Achievement award, Mt. Holyok Coll. Alumnae Assn., 1989; NEH grant, Apple Edn. Found. Mem.: Am. Assn. of Tchrs. Slavic and East European Langs. (sec., treas., v.p., pres. 1980—85), Phi Beta Kappa. Home: 12114 Lakewood Court Fort Myers FL 33908

CURTIN, JANE THERESE, actress, writer; b. Cambridge, Mass., Sept. 6, 1947; d. John Joseph and Mary Constance (Farrell) C.; m. Patrick F. Lynch, Apr. 31, 1975; 1 child, Tess. AA, Elizabeth Seton Jr. Coll., 1967; student, Northeastern U., 1967-68. Appeared in plays The Proposition, Cambridge and N.Y.C., 1968-72, Last of the Red Hot Lovers touring co., 1973; Broadway debut in Candida, 1981; author, actress Off-Broadway mus. rev. Pretzels, 1974-75; star TV series NBC Saturday Night Live, 1975-79, Kate & Allie, 1984-88, Working It Out, 1990, 3rd Rock from the Sun, 1996-2001 (Golden Satellite for best actress 1996), Crumbs, 2006-; appeared in films including Mr. Mike's Mondo Video, 1979, How to Beat the High Cost of Living, 1980, O.C. and Stiggs, 1987, Coneheads, 1993, Antz, 1998, Geraldine's Fortune, 2004, Brooklyn Lobster, 2005, The Shaggy Dog, 2006; TV films include Divorce Wars-A Love Story, 1982, Suspicion, 1988, Maybe Baby, 1988, Common Ground, 1990, Tad, 1995, Christmas in Washington, 1996, Catch a Falling Star, 2000, Our Town, 2003, The Librarian: Quest for the Spear, 2004; TV guest appearance Recess, 1997. Recipient Emmy nomination, 1977, 87; Emmy awards for outstanding actress in comedy series, 1984, 85 Mem. Screen Actors Guild, Actors Equity, AFTRA. Office: ICM care Boaty Boatwright 40 W 57th St Fl 16 New York NY 10019-4098*

CURTIN, LEIGH, media consultant, writer; b. Denville, N.J., May 18, 1954; d. Howard Steven and Eleanor Catherine Wilding; children: Kevin Steven, Keith Francis. AA in Theater Arts, Ocean County Coll., Toms River, N.J., 1978—80; BA in Journalism, U. Okla., Norman, 1980—82. Dir., pub. rels. WWOR-TV, Secaucus, NJ, 1985—89; mgr., media rels. - nat. brands Pepsi-Cola Co., Somers, NY, 1990—93; ea. european events cons. & exec. speechwriter Pepsi-Cola Internat., Vienna, 1994—97; spl. events cons. AC Nielsen, Brussels, 1997—98; media & mktg. advisor Reader's Digest Books, N.Y.C., 1998—. Freelance bus. writer Avon, Andersen Consulting, NBC Broadcasting Network, Macmillan Publ. Contbr. articles to profl. jours. Mem.: Nat. Writer's Union. Avocations: travel, music, reading, gardening. Office Fax: 732-775-8827.

CURTIN, PHYLLIS, music educator, dean, vocalist; b. Clarksburg, W.Va. d. E. Vernon and Betty R. (Robinson) Smith; m. Eugene Cook, May 6, 1956 (dec.); l child, Claudia Madeleine. BA, Wellesley Coll., 1943. Prof. Yale Sch. Music, New Haven, 1974-83; master Branford Coll. Yale U., New Haven, 1979-83; dean Coll. Fine Arts, prof. music Boston U., 1983-91, prof. music, 1983—, dean emerita, prof. music, 1991—; artist-in-residence Tanglewood Music Ctr., Tanglewood, Lenox, Mass., 1965—. Named Amb. for the Arts; tchr. master classes U.S., Can., Beijing, Moscow. Recital debut Town Hall, NYC, 1950, opera debut, NYC Opera in U.S. premiere of The Trial, 1953, recitals throughout, U.S. and fgn. countries; soprano soloist leading symphony orchestras; performer, tchr., Aspen Mus. Festival, 1953-57, appeared as Cressida in, Walton's Troilus and Cressida in, NY premiere, 1955; title role in Floyd's: Susannah, world premiere, Tallahassee, 1955; title role in: Darius Milhaud's Medea, U.S. premiere, Brandeis U., 1955; world premiere Floyd's opera Wuthering Heights, 1958, Floyd's Passion of Jonathan Wade, 1959, Flower and Hawk, 1971; U.S. Premier Peter Grimes, 1946; leading soprano: Vienna Staatsoper, 1960, 61; debut as Fiordiligi in Cosi Fan Tutte, Met. Opera Co., 1961, La Scala Opera, Milan, 1962; U.S. premiere Benjamin Britten's War Requiem, with Boston Symphony, 1963; world premiere of Darius Milhaud's opera La Mére Coupable, Geneva, 1966; U.S. premiere Dimitri Shostakovitch's Symphony No. 14, with, Phila. Orch., 1971. Recipient Alumnae Achievement award, Wellesley Coll., Nadia Boulanger Achievement award, Longy Sch. Music, Letter of Distinction for Svc. to Am. Music, Am. Music Ctr., Lifetime Achievement award, Nat. Opera Assn., 2005. Home: 9 Seekonk Rd Great Barrington MA 01230-1558 Personal E-mail: curtinphyllis@msn.com.

CURTIS, ANN B., utilities executive; Mgr., adminstr. Gibbs & Hill, Inc.; v.p. mgmt. and fin. svcs. Calpine Corp., 1984—92, sr. v.p., 1992—98, dir., 1996—, exec. v.p., sec., 1998—, vice chmn., 2002—. Office: Calpine 50 W San Fernando St 5th Fl San Jose CA 95113

CURTIS, BARBARA, consumer products company professional; b. Cleve., Nov. 4, 1953; d. Ralph Willis Sr. and Alice Pearl Kitzmiller; m. Marc David King (div.); 1 child, Justin Matthew; m. David Charles Curtis, Sept. 28, 1995. MA in Psychology, Shelbourne U.; postgrad., Andersonville Bapt. Sem. Cert. Langevin tng. mgr./dir., DDI facilitator, achieve global facilitator, Corey facilitator, William Bridges facilitator. Teller/operator C&P Tel. Co., Laurel, Md., 1972-76; transp. clk. Ryder Truck Rental, Houston, 1976-78; lease/rental mgr. Lawrence Marshall Chevrolet-Oldsmobile, Hempstead, Tex., 1978-80; contr./treas. Bluebonnet Sungs, Hempstead, 1980-84; br. mgr. Heights Savs., Hempstead, 1984-89; sr. performance and devel. specialist Cingular Wireless, Houston, 1990—. Trainer, facilitator A.J.R.S., Houston, 1995-98. Editor Ralston Meml. Pres. Ch., Houston, 1999. Mem. ASTD. Avocations: cooking, gardening, horseback riding. Home: 11205 Debra Rd Houston TX 77013-3319

CURTIS, CAROLE ORTALE, executive recruiter, consultant; b. Inglewood, Calif., Aug. 15, 1944; d. Albert Thomas and Ann Irene Ortale; m. John Joseph Curtis, Oct. 19, 1968; children: Mark Gregory, Michelle Ann. BA in English and Edn., Cal State U., Long Beach, 1967, Grad. Cert. in Career Counseling, 1982. Career, image cons. Image Plus, Rancho Palos Verdes, Calif., 1996—. Pers. mgr. Savage Info. Svcs., Torrance, 1989—91; career counselor Ednl. and Tutorial Svcs., Palos Verdes Peninsula, Calif., 1994—96; guidance counselor So. Calif. Regional Ctr., Torrance, 1997—98; career ctr. dir., career counselor Career Planning Ctr., Marina Del Rey, Calif., 2000—02. Author: (poetry) A Time of Strife, 2003, The Tribute, 2004, A New Decade, 2004, Eyes of the Moon, 2006, To Die and Be Forgotten, 2006; photographer Artistic Visions; contbr. poetry to anthologies. Advocate Alzheimers Orgn., Rancho Palos Verdes, 2001—06; legislative chair Soleado Sch., Rancho Palos Verdes, Calif., 1980—81; assoc. Nat. Career Devel. Assn., 1997—2004; membership chair Las Ayudas, Rancho Palos Verdes, 1998—2000; minister St. John Fisher, Rancho Palos Verdes, Calif., 1995—99, co-chair women's group, 2006—; bd. dirs. Casa Verde de L.A., 2006. Nominee Poet of Yr., 2006; named Most Disting. Alumni, El Camino Coll., 1998. Mem.: Internat. Soc. Poets, Calif. Assn. Career Counselors (assoc.), Beta Sigma Phi (v.p., treas. 1987—93). Avocations: writing poetry, photography, travel, dance. Home: 27510 Halescorner Rd Rancho Palos Verdes CA 90275 Business E-Mail: cccounselor@juno.com.

CURTIS, DEANA A., electronics executive, small business owner; b. Rochester, N.Y., July 31, 1953; d. Dean A. and Patricia A. Prevost; m. Michael J Curtis, July 4, 2004. AS in Fashion and Interior Decorating, John Robert Powers, 1972. With advt. divsn. Dem. & Chronicle, Rochester, 1971—73; leasing adminstr., property tax mgmt. Xerox Corp., Webster, NY, 1976—; prin., owner Impressions Dating Svc., Rochester, 1996—98, Shadows of the Past, Rochester, 1996—; prin., co-owner Niagara Elec. Sales, Rochester, 1987—94. Vol. Holy Cross Ch., Rochester, 1980—96. Recipient Recognition award, Astoria, 1993. Republican. Roman Cath. Home: 4625 Kear Rd Canandaigua NY 14424 Office: Xerox Corp 800 Salt Rd Bldg 843 Webster NY 14580 Office Phone: 585-393-1975.

CURTIS, DOLORES ROGERS, writer; b. Columbus, Ohio, Apr. 16, 1929; d. Charles William and Lillian Beatrice Rogers. Student, Ctrl. State U., Xenia, Ohio, 1956—57; B.Elem.Edn., Ohio State U., 1963; attended, John Carroll U., 1980. Bookkeeper Spiegel's, Chgo., Kronfeld's, Manhattan, NY; libr. U.S. Govt. Facility, Columbus; sec. to traveling entertainer, 1949—54; tchr. Columbus Pub. Schs., 1963—68, Cleve. Bd. Edn., 1968—93. Author: Rhyming Pretzels, 2002. Avocations: reading, art, playing piano and organ, writing.

CURTIS, JAMIE LEE, actress; b. LA, Nov. 22, 1958; d. Tony Curtis and Janet Leigh (dec. 2004); m. Christopher Guest, Dec. 18, 1984; children: Annie, Thomas. Student, U. Pacific, Stockton, Calif., 1976. Actress: (films) Halloween, 1978, The Fog, 1980, Prom Night, 1980, Terror Train, 1980, Halloween II, 1981, Road Games, 1981, Trading Places, 1983, Love Letters, 1984 Grandview USA, 1984, The Adventures of Buckaroo Banzai: Across the 8th Dimension, 1984, Perfect, 1985, Welcome Home, 1986, A Man in Love, 1987, Amazing Grace and Chuck, 1987, Dominick and Eugene, 1988, A Fish Called Wanda, 1988, Blue Steel, 1990, Queens Logic, 1991, My Girl, 1991, Forever Young, 1992, My Girl 2, 1994, Mother's Boys, 1994 True Lies, 1994 (Golden Globe award Best Actress - Musical or Comedy), House Arrest, 1996, Ellen's Energy Adventure, 1996, Fierce Creatures, 1997, Homegrown, 1998, Halloween H2O, 1998, Virus, 1999, Drowning Mona, 2000, The Tailor of Panama, 2001, Daddy and Them, 2001, Rudolf the Red-Nosed Reindeer and the Island of Misfit Toys (voice), 2001, Halloween: Resurrection, 2002, Freaky Friday, 2003, Christmas with the Kranks, 2004, The Kid and I, 2005; (TV movies) Colombo: Bye-Bye Sky-High I.Q. Murder Case, 1977, Death of a Centerfold: The Dorothy Stratten Story, 1981, Money on the Side, 1982, As Summers Die, 1986, The Heidi Chronicles, 1995, Nicolas' Gift, 1998; (TV series) Operation Petticoat, 1977-78, She's in the Army Now, 1981, Anything but Love, 1990-93, Pigs Next Door, 2000; (TV appearances) Quincy, 1977, Hardy Boys/Nancy Drew Mysteries, 1977, Charlie's Angels, 1978, The Love Boat, 1978, Buck Rogers in the 25th Century, 1979, The Drew Carey Show, 1996; dir.: Anything But Love, 1990; author (children's books): When I Was Little: A Four-Year-Old's Memoir of Her Youth, 1993, Today I Feel Silly, 1998, Where Do Balloons Go? An Uplifting Mystery, 2000, I'm Gonna Like Me: Letting Off a Little Self-Esteem, 2002, It's Hard to Be Five, 2004, Is There Really a Human Race?, 2006. Office: Creative Artists Agy c/o Rick Kurtzman 9830 Wilshire Blvd Beverly Hills CA 90212-1804*

CURTIS, KATHERINE LANAE, pharmacist; b. Bossier City, La., Apr. 4, 1973; d. Clarence Rayson III and Sara Vernelda White; m. Juvar Nakia Curtis, Jan. 26, 2003; 1 child, Juvar Pierre. Assoc. Electronics, C.C. Air Force, Randolph AFB, Tex., 1997; BS, Wayne State U., 2001, D Pharmacy, 2003. Registered pharmacist Mich. Pharmacy intern Bon Secour Hosp., Grosse Pointe, Mich., 1999—2001, VA Hosp., Detroit, 2000—03, Meijer's Pharmacy, Livonia, Mich., 2001—03; pharmacist Walgreens, Detroit, 2003; staff pharmacist Semper Care Hosp., Kalamazoo, 2003—04, A&P Great Atlantic Tea Co., Detroit, 2004—. Counselor Camp Tomahawk, Enid, Okla., 1996; vol. Vol. Impact, Detroit, 2001—03; med. min. Straight Gate Ch., Detroit, 1999—2001. With USAF, 1994—97. Mem.: Wayne State Alumni Assn., Am. Pharm. Assn. Democrat. Mem. Full Gospel Ch. Avocations: reading, writing, singing. Personal E-mail: katherin_curtis@sbcglobal.net.

CURTIS, KATHRYN FAYE, medical laboratory technician; b. Liberty, Tex., Oct. 29, 1953; d. James Thomas Hays Jr. and Bonnie Lois Griffin; m. Harry Owen Hardison, Sept. 12, 1973 (dec. Dec. 1976); children: Michael Scott, Stephen Owen; m. Van Eldon Curtis, Mar. 31, 1979; 1 child, Brandon Lynn. Cert., Twin Lakes Vocat. Tech. Sch., 1973; EMT cert., High Plains Vocat. Tech. Sch., 1994. Cert. lab. asst. Lab. asst. Laverne (Okla.) Hosp., 1973-76; lab. technician Med. Arts Clinic, Laverne, 1978-94; med. lab. technician Laverne Med. Clinic, 1994-2000, Woodward Hosp. & Health Ctr., Woodward, Okla., 2000—04, Woodward Orthopedics, Woodward, 2004—. Paramed. examiner Is. Exams., Colwich, Kans.; mem. Laverne adv. com. Woodward Hosp. and Health Ctr., 1997-98. Vol. EMT Laverne Emergency Med. Svc., 1995—; asst. coord. Heartland Shares, Laverne, 1998-99; standby vol. Fed. Emergency Mgmt. Agy., Laverne, 1998-99. Mem. Am. Soc. Clin. Pathologists (assoc.). Democrat. Baptist. Avocations: gardening, computing. Office: Woodward Orthopedics 1650 Main St Woodward OK 73801 E-mail: kittykat@ptsi.net.

CURTIS, LINDA KATHRYN, elementary school educator; b. Jacksonville, Ill., Dec. 5, 1944; d. Robert Lukeman Zeller and Wanda Lee Ervin; m. Frederick Antony Curtis, Mar. 29, 1969; children: Karin Lynn, Michael Anthony, Scott Frederick, Jeffrey Adam. BS, So. Ill. U., 1967, MS, 1973. Elem. tchr. Hurst-Bush Sch., Herrin, Ill., 1967—69, Alexander-Franklin, Ill., 1969—72, Jacksonville SD 117, Ill., 1986—2005. Mem. adv. bd. MacMurray Coll., Jacksonville, Ill., 2002—05. Life mem. Passavant Hosp. Aux., Jacksonville, Ill.; Eucharistic min. Our Saviours Cath. Ch., Jacksonville, Ill., religious edn. tchr., 1973—93. Mem.: Ill. Reading Coun., Right to Life, Inc. Roman Catholic. Avocations: arts and crafts, gardening. Home: 210 Leland Lake Jacksonville IL 62650 Office: Sch Dist 117 North Elem 1626 State Hwy 78 Jacksonville IL 62650

CURTIS, LISA A., accountant, administrator; b. Syracuse, N.Y. d. David William and Barbara Ann Barron; m. Douglas Garfield Curtis, June 27, 1998. BS in Mech. Engring., Ga. Inst. Tech., 1992. Engr. in tng. Lockwood Greene Engrs., Atlanta, 1992-96; acctg. mgr. No. Trust Retirement Cons. LLC, Atlanta, 1996—. Named Young Engr. of Yr. Ga. Soc. Profl. Engrs., 1994. Mem. ASME (chair). Avocations: stained glass design, walking. Office: Northern Trust & Retirement Cons LLC Ste 850 400 Perimeter Center Ter NE Atlanta GA 30346-1299

CURTIS, MARY E. (MARY CURTIS HOROWITZ), publishing executive; d. Lloyd E. and Jean Curtis; m. Irving Louis Horowitz, Oct. 30, 1979 AB cum laude, Washington U., St. Louis, 1968. Editl. dir. Transaction Pubs., New Brunswick, NJ, 1968-74, exec. v.p., 1987-97, pres., 1997—, chmn. bd. dirs., 1994-97; editor in chief Praeger Pubs. subs. CBS Ednl. Pub., N.Y.C., 1974-79; v.p., pub. periodicals John Wiley and Sons, N.Y.C., 1979-87; v.p. Scripta Techica subs. John Wiley and Sons, Washington, 1984-87; mem. mgmt. bd. MIT Press, 1998—; vice chair, trustee Horowitz Found. for Social Policy, 1998—. Chair adv. com. Serials Industry Systems, 1985-88; dir. Transaction Pubs. (U.K.) Ltd.; lectr. in field. Contbr. articles to profl. jours. Mem. Soc. Scholarly Pubs. (bd. dirs. 1984-88), Assn. Am. Pubs. (Freedom to Read com.). Jewish. Office Phone: 732-445-2280. Business E-Mail: mcurtis@transactionpub.com.

CURTIS, RACHAEL ELIZABETH, music educator; b. Springfield, Oreg., Nov. 17, 1971; d. Steve and Bettie Frances Woodard; m. Tim Glen Curtis, Jan. 22, 1964; children: Gabriel Ronald, Evelyn Lorelei. MusB, U. Oreg., Eugene, 1994. Cert. music edn. Oreg., 1994. Tchr. music Clear Lake Elem., Keizer, Oreg., 1995—2001, Grant Cmty. Sch., Salem, Oreg., 2004—. Tutor Willamette ESD, Salem, 2005—06. Musician (dancer, singer): (church worship) New Hope Foursquare, Fern Ridge Foursquare. Conservative. Christian. Avocations: travel, reading.

CURTIS, SALLY DIANE, educational consultant; b. Boston, Mass., Nov. 22, 1939; d. Merton Elden and Hazel Parker Curtis; m. John Quayle Brennan, Apr. 5, 2004; 1 child, Jon D. AB, Union Coll., Barbourville, Ky., 1961; MEd, U. Hartford, Hartford, Conn., 1972; Cert. Advanced Grad. Study, U. Mass., Amherst, Mass., 1992. Lic. Child Care Dir. II Mass. Dir. Hill House Assoc., Pitts., 1965—66; lead tchr. Lowell Day Nursery, Lowell, Mass., 1967; exec. dir. United Way Child Care, Springfield, Mass., 1968—72; dept. chair Springfield Tech. CC, Springfield, Mass., 1972—2002. Ednl. cons. Curtis Ednl. Group, Killington, Vt., 2002—. Treas. Chaffee Art Ctr., Rutlaud, Vt., 2006; sec. Killington Arts Guild, 2006; trustee Sherburne Libr., Killington, 2006; sec. Killington Pico Rotary, Killington, Vt., 2006. Mem.: Internat. Reading Assn., Nat. Assn. Edn. Young Children. Avocations: hiking, bicycling, kayaking, travel. Office: Curtis Ednl Group PO Box 156 Killington VT 05751

CURTIS, SUSAN GRACE, lawyer; b. N.Y.C., Apr. 24, 1950; d. Henry G. and Helen Curtis; m. Robert Y. Pelgrift Jr., June 8, 1974; children: Robert III, Henry, Victoria. A.B., Yale Coll., 1971; J.D., Columbia U., 1974. Bar: N.Y. 1975, U.S. Ct. Appeals (2d cir.) 1975. With Lord, Day & Lord, N.Y.C., 1974-79, Shearman & Sterling, N.Y.C., 1979-84, Proskauer, Rose, 1984-87, 93-98; ptnr. Epstein, Becker & Green, N.Y.C., 1987-93; of counsel White & Case, N.Y.C., 1998—; adj. asst. prof. law NYU Sch. Law, 1995-98; mem. faculty Practising Law Inst., 1990—. Contbg. editor: Jour. Pension Planning and Compliance, 1991—; mem. editl. adv. bd. BNA Pension Reporter, 1993—, tax mgmt. adv. bd., 1993—; contbr. articles to profl. jours. Mem. ABA (com. employee benefits), N.Y. State Bar Assn. (com. employee benefits), Assn. Bar City N.Y. (sec. com. employee benefits 1987-90).

CURTIS, SUSAN M., lawyer; b. Nashville, 1956; BA summa cum laude, U. Tenn., Knoxville; JD, Vanderbilt Univ., 1981. Bar: NY 1982. Ptnr., structured fin. Skadden, Arps, Slate, Meagher & Flom, N.Y.C. Mem.: Phi Beta Kappa. Office: Skadden Arps Slate Meagher & Flom 4 Times Sq New York NY 10036 Office Phone: 212-735-2119. Office Fax: 917-777-2119. Business E-Mail: scurtis@skadden.com.

CURTIS, SUSAN VIRGINIA, social worker; b. N.Y.C., Apr. 19, 1943; m. Robert Maxwell Curtis, July 30, 1967; children: Benjamin William, Rebecca Elizabeth. BA in Lit., William Smith Coll., Geneva, N.Y., 1965; M of Social Scis. Adminstrn., Case Western Res. U., 1980; student Anglo-Irish Lit., Trinity Coll., Dublin, Ireland, 1964; grad. in Gestalt Therapy, Gestalt Inst. Cleve., 1983. Lic. social worker, Ohio; cert. social worker; diplomate Am. Bd. Social Work; cert. introductory level FEMA, NIMS, Emergency Mgmt. Inst. Grant asst. Wenner Gren Found., N.Y.C., 1965-66; editorial asst. Edn. and World Affairs, N.Y.C., 1966-67; tchr. Birch Wathen Sch., N.Y.C., 1967-68; adminstrv. asst. Columbia U. Tchrs. Coll., N.Y.C., 1968-69; with VISTA, OEO, Dahlonega, Ga., 1969-70; tchr. Tng. in Lamaze Childbirth, Chesterland, Ohio, 1973-76; social worker Lake County Mental Health Ctr., Mentor, Ohio, 1980-88; pvt. practice Highland Counseling Svcs., Inc., Cleve., 1987—2006; ret., 2006. Bd. mem. Greater Cleve. Audubon Soc. Mem. NASW, Acad. Cert. Social Workers (diplomate), Stepfamily Assn. Am.., Amnesty Internat., World Wildlife Fund. Avocation: walking. Office Phone: 440-461-1255. Business E-Mail: scurtis@highlandcounseling.com.

CURTIS CRANEY, KAREN B., reading specialist; b. Corpus Christi, Tex., June 23, 1962; d. Charles Robert and Jane Bainbridge Curtis. Tchr. Frederick County Pub. Schools, Md., 1984—93, reading specialist, 1994—. Instr. Frederick County Pub. Schools, 1998—2001. Mem.: Internat. Reading Assn., Frederick County Reading Coun. Home: 6147 Fieldcrest Dr Frederick MD 21701 Office: Frederick County Pub Schools 9051 Ridgefield Dr Frederick MD 21701

CURTISS, CAROL PERRY, health facility administrator, consultant, nurse; b. Worcester, Mass., Dec. 9, 1946; d. Joseph Anthony and Marjorie Ruth (Riedle) Perry; m. Jack Daniel Curtiss, Feb. 8, 1970; children: Paul Daniel, Jennifer Perry. Diploma in nursing, Mass. Gen. Hosp. Sch. Nursing, Boston, 1967; BS, Am. Internat. Coll., Springfield, Mass., 1978; MSN, Yale U., 1981. RN Mass. Staff nurse Franklin Med. Ctr., Greenfield, Mass., 1970, Greenfield Ob-Gyn. Assocs., 1972-74, Greenfield Vis. Nurses, 1974-75; instr. Slim Living Program YMCA, Greenfield, 1977-78; instr. nursing Greenfield C.C., 1978; asst. prof. nursing Elms Coll., Chicopee, Mass., 1981-84; oncology program mgr. Franklin Med. Ctr, Greenfield, 1986-93; cancer care cons. Curtiss Cons., Greenfield, 1981—. Mem. faculty Greenfield C.C., 1985—87; vis. lectr., clin. instr. Fitchburg (Mass.) State Coll., 1985—86; vis. lectr. Elms Coll., Chicopee, Mass., 1984—85; mem. adj. faculty SUNY, 1987—90, U. Mass., Amherst, 1989—2005; peer reviewer Agy. for Health Care Policy and Rsch., Cancer Pain Gidelines, HHS, 1993; presenter in field, U.S. and abroad, 1981—; adj. faculty Sch. Nursing U. So. Ind.; adj. clin. instr. Tufts U. Sch. Medicine, 2005—. Co-author: Cancer Doesn't Have to Hurt, 1997; guest editor Oncology Nursing Forum, 1993; contbr. articles to profl. jours. Bd. dirs. Franklin County, Am. Cancer Soc., Greenfield, 1979-95, mem. nurse and social work scholarship com., 1988-96, nursing com. liaison, 1990-98; mem. steering com. Mass. Cancer Pain Initiative, 1988-90, 2002—, liaison, 1990-97, cons. chmn., 2002—; trustee Oncology Nursing Found., 1995-2000. Recipient Am. Alliance of Cancer Pain Initiatives award, Dahl Lectureship: Leadership in Systems Change, Am. Alliance of Cancer Pain Initiatives, 2003. Mem.: Internat. Union Against Cancer, Am. Soc. Pain Mgmt. Nurses, Am. Pain Soc., Internat. Union Against Cancer (U.S. com. 1992—2000), Oncology Nursing Soc. (mem. numerous sub coms. 1987—, mem. numerous subcoms. 1987—, pres.-elect 1991—92, 1991—92, corp. adv. bd. 1991—93, 1991—93, bd. dirs. 1991—, 1991—, nat. pres. 1992—93, Oncology Nursing Press pres. 1992—94, pres. Oncology Nursing Press 1992—94, pres. 1993—94, co-chair conf. on pain 1994, Disting. Svc. award 1999), Am. Soc. Pain Mgmt. Nurses (Master Faculty 2005—), Am. Pain Soc., Sigma Theta Tau. Avocations: bicycling, skiing, tennis, carpentry. Home: 73 James St Greenfield MA 01301-3607 Office Phone: 413-774-5238. E-mail: carol.curtiss@verizon.net.

CURTISS, CATHERINE, lawyer; b. July 29, 1950; BA, U. Mich., 1972, MA cum laude, 1973; JD cum laude, Georgetown U., 1980. Bar: DC 1980, Calif. 1982, admitted to practice: US Dist. Ct. (DC), US Dist. Ct. (No. Dist.) Calif., US Dist. Ct. (Ea. Dist.) Calif., US Ct. Internat. Trade (Fed. Cir.). Ptnr. Hughes, Hubbard & Reed. Office: Hughes Hubbard & Reed 1775 Eye St NW Washington DC 20006-2401 Office Phone: 202-721-4660. Office Fax: 202-721-4646. E-mail: curtiss@hugheshubbard.com.

CURTIS-TWEED, PHYLLIS MARIE, humanities educator; d. Cecil Morris and Alice Marie Curtis; m. Nicholas Genevieve-Tweed, May 30, 1992; 1 child, Lauren Genevieve-Tweed. BA, U. Md., College Park, 1978, MEd, 1985; PhD, Emory U., 1993. Rsch. assoc., instr. psychology dept. psychiatry Harvard Med. Sch., Judge Baker Children's Ctr., Boston, 1995—2001; assoc. prof., dir., freshman yr. program Medgar Evers Coll. CUNY, Bklyn., 2001—05; asst. prof. Medgar Evers Coll. CUNY, 2005—. Contbr. entry, articles to profl. publs. Leader Reach Out and Touch/Macedonia AME Ch., Flushing, NY, 2002. Recipient postdoctoral fellowship in psychology dept. psychiatry, Harvard U., 1993—95, Rsch. award, Childrens Studies at Harvard U., 1998—99, U.S. Achievement Acad. Nat. award, 1994; grantee, NIMH, 1995—2001. Mem.: Assn. for Moral Edn. (exec. bd. mem. 2005—). African Methodist Episcopal Church. Avocations: reading, writing, travel. Office: Medgar Evers Coll 1650 Bedford Ave Brooklyn NY 11225 Office Phone: 718-270-4960. E-mail: ptweed@mec.cuny.edu.

CURZAN, ANNE, linguist, educator; d. Myron and Mary Curzan. BA, Yale U., New Haven, Conn., 1991; PhD, U. Mich., Ann Arbor, Mich., 1998. Asst. prof. English U. Wash., Seattle, 1998—2002, U. Mich., Ann Arbor, Mich., 2002—04, assoc. prof. English, 2004—. Dir. undergraduate studies Dept. English U. Mich., 2004—. Author: Gender Shifts in the History of English, 2003; co-author: First Day to Final Grade: A Graduate Student's Guide to Teaching, 2000, How English Works: A Linguistic Introduction, 2006. Recipient Henry Russel award, U. Mich., 2006. Mem.: MLA, Dictionary Soc. N.Am., Internat. Computer Archives Modern and Medieval English (bd. dirs. 2004—), Nat. Coun. Tchrs. English, Linguistic Soc. Am. Avocations: triathalons, marathons. Office: University of Michigan Dept of English 3187 Angell Hall Ann Arbor MI 48109-1003 Office Phone: 734-936-2881.

CURZON, SUSAN CAROL, academic administrator; b. Poole, Eng., Dec. 11, 1947; came to U.S., 1952. d. Kenneth Nigel and Terry Marguerite (Morris) C. AB, U. Calif., Riverside, 1970; MLS, U. Wash., 1972; PhD, U. So. Calif., 1983. Spl. libr. Kennecott Exploration, San Diego, 1972-73; various positions L.A. County Pub. Libr., 1973-89; dir. libr. Glendale (Calif.) Pub. Libr., 1989-92; dean univ. libr. Calif. State U., Northridge, 1992—, 1992—. Cons. Grantsmanship Ctr., L.A., 1981-83; vis. lectr. Grad. Sch. Libr. and Info. Sci. UCLA, 1986-92. Author: Managing Change, Managing the Interview. Libr. of the Year, Libr. Jour., 1993. Mem. ALA, Calif. Libr. Assn. Democrat. Avocation: history. Office: Calif State U Libr Office of the Dean 18111 Nordhoff St Northridge CA 91330-8326 Office Phone: 818-677-2271.

CUSACK, JOAN, actress; b. NYC, Oct. 11, 1962; d. Richard and Nancy C.; m. Richard Burke 1993; 2 children. BA, U. Wis., 1985. Stage appearances include Road, 1988, Brilliant Traces, 1989, Cymbeline, 1989; TV appearances include Saturday Night Live (regular 1985-86 season), The Mother, 1994, What About Joan, 2001-02, A Very Merry Muppet Christmas, 2002; film appearances include Cutting Loose, 1980, My Bodyguard, 1980, Class, 1983, Grandview USA, 1984, Sixteen Candles, 1984, The Allnighter, 1987, Broadcast News, 1987, Stars and Bars (aka An Englishman in New York), 1988, Married to the Mob, 1988, Working Girl, 1988 (Acad. award nominee best supporting actress 1989), Say Anything, 1989, Men Don't Leave, 1989, My Blue Heaven, 1990, The Cabinet of Dr. Ramirez, 1991, Hero, 1992, Toys, 1992 (also musician), Addams Family Values, 1993, Corrina, Corrina, 1994, Nine Months, 1995, Two Much, 1996, Mr. Wrong, 1996, A Smile Like Yours, 1997, In and Out, 1997, Grosse Pointe Blank, 1997, Arlington Road, 1999, Runaway Bride, 1999, (voice) Toy Story 2, 1999, Arlington Road, 1999, Cradle Will Rock, 1999, High Fidelity, 2000, Where the Heart Is, 2000, School of Rock, 2003, Looney Toons-Back in Action, 2003, Raising Helen, 2004, The Last Shot, 2004, Ice Princess, 2005, (voice) Chicken Little, 2005, Friends With Money, 2006. Office: United Talent Agy Inc 9560 Wilshire Blvd Fl 5 Beverly Hills CA 90212*

CUSACK, REGINA M., psychology professor, lawyer; BA, Columbia U., NYC, 1974; JD, St. Mary's U., San Antonio, 1977, PhD, 1999, MBA, 2002. Bar: Tex. 1978, US Dist. Ct. (we. dist.) Tex. 1981, NJ 1985, NY 1985, US Dist. Ct. NJ 1985. Atty. Lawfirm Evans & Marshall, San Antonio, 1977—90; asst. atty. gen. Atty. Gen. for the State NJ, Trenton, 1986; magistrate City of San Antonio, 1990—2000; prof. psychology Our Lady of the Lake U., San Antonio, 1990—. Cons. Bd. Disciplinary Appeals, Austin, Tex., 2001, Tex. Lawyer's Assistance Program, State Bar Tex., Austin, 2001—. Home: PO Box 790966 San Antonio TX 78279 Office: Our Lady of the Lake University 411 SW 24th St San Antonio TX 78207 Office Phone: 210-434-6711 8170. Office Fax: 210-431-3927. Business E-Mail: cusar@lake.ollusa.edu.

CUSHMAN, BEVERLY WHITE, religious studies educator; b. Orlando, Fla., Oct. 22, 1952; d. Arthur Wilson and Roberta Beckett White; m. David Oeth Cushman, Dec. 29, 1973; children: Jeremiah David, Amanda Katherine. BA, Stetson U., DeLand, Florida, 1974; MDiv, Vanderbilt U., Nashville, 1977; MA, Vanderbilt U., 1991, PhD, 1999. Ordination - Presbyn. Ch. Presbytery South La., 1977. Pastor Raceland Presbyn. Ch., La., 1977—81; assoc. pastor Lakeview Presbyn. Ch., New Orleans, 1981—85; interim pastor Eastminster Presbyn. Ch., New Orleans, 1985—86; parish assoc. Tims Meml. Presbyn. Ch., Lutz, Fla., 1988—92; lectr. U. Sask., Saskatoon, 1993—94, St. Thomas More Coll., Saskatoon, 1994—98, Luth. Theol. Sem., Saskatoon, 1998; adj. asst. prof. and registrar Coll. of Emmanuel and St. Chad, Saskatoon, 1998—2002; assoc. prof. religion Calvin Coll., Grand Rapids, Mich., 2002—04; asst. prof. religion and Christian edn. Westminster Coll., New Wilmington, Pa., 2004—. Area supr. Excavation Sepphoris U. South Fla., Sepphoris, Israel, 1988—92; lectr. St. Andrew's Coll., Saskatoon, 1996—97. Author: (journal article) The Politics of the Royal Harem and the Case of Bat-Sheba. Recipient J. D. Owen Prize in Bibl. Studies (Old Testament), Vanderbilt Div. Sch., 1977, Enhancement award, Vanderbilt U., 1992; Henry B. Carre Fellowship, 1986—87. Mem.: Shenango Presbytery, Ea. Gt. Lakes Bibl. Soc. (com. on regional scholars 2006—), Religious Edn. Assn., Soc. Bibl. Lit., Assn. Presbyn. Christian Educators, Am. Schs. Oriental Rsch. Achievements include First woman ordained in the state of Louisiana 1977. Avocations: music, gardening. Office: Westminster College 319 Market Street New Wilmington PA 16172 Office Fax: 724-946-7256. E-mail: cushmabw@westminster.edu.

CUSHMAN, HELEN MERLE BAKER, retired management consultant; b. Perth Amboy, N.J. d. Ivan F. and Lucile (Atkinson) Baker; m. Robert Arnold Cushman, June 2, 1945; children— Lucinda Ann, Robert Rorem. AB in History, Barnard Coll., 1942; postgrad., NYU, 1944. Route analyst intelligence divsn. Air Transport Command, Washington, 1943-44; personnel asst. Gen. Cable Corp., N.Y.C., 1944-45; sr. staff asst. to chmn. bd. Trans World Airlines, N.Y.C., 1945-50; pres. H.M. Baker Assocs., Westfield, N.J., 1958-93; ret., 1993. Past archivist-historian N.J. chpt. Am. Records Mgmt. Assn. Author: ARMA-New Jersey, The Founding Years, 1972, A History of Shreve, Crump and Low, 1974, Butterick and the Story of Sewing, 1975, The Anniversary Manual, 1976, Gears, Machines, Systems, 1978, Mountainside Chapel: Yesterday, Today, Tomorrow, 1981, Serving Westerly Since 1800, 1985, The Mill on the Third River, 1992, From Seed to Harvest, 1993, The Church at the Crossroads, 1999, Walter's World: Memoirs of W.E. Atkinson 1856-1944, 2004; editor, pub. Ministry Press, The Bus. History Letter; contbr. to Am. Archivist. Recipient Lit. award Am. Records Mgmt. Assn., 1972. Mem.: PEO Sisterhood (pres. chpt. AE,.Princeton N.J.), various hist. socs., Newcomen Soc., Barnard Coll. Club North Ctrl. NJ (past pres.). Address: 321 Sharon Way Monroe Township NJ 08831-1561

CUSHMAN, ORIS MILDRED, retired nurse, hospital education director; b. Springfield, Mass., Nov. 22, 1931; d. Wesley Austin and Alice Mildred (Vaile) Stockwell; m. Laurence Arnold Cushman, Apr. 16, 1955; children: Lynn Ann Cushman Wronker, Laurence Arnold III. Diploma in nursing, Hartford Hosp. Sch. Nursing, Conn., 1953; BS, Western Mich. U., 1978, MA, 1980. Staff nurse Wesson Maternal Hosp., Springfield, 1953—54, acting supr., 1954—55; staff nurse Hartford Hosp., 1955—56, head nurse, 1956, staff nurse, 1957—59; staff nurse, charge nurse Reed City Hosp. (Mich.), 1961—67; supr. Meml. Hosp. (Mich.), St. Joseph, 1967—75; clin. supr. maternal/child health Meml. Hosp., St. Joseph, 1975—77, dir. maternal/child health, 1977—80; dir. edn. Pawating Hosp. (Mich.), Niles, 1980—87; ret., 1987. Sec. Women's aux. Reed City Hosp., 1964—65, v.p., 1965—66, pres., 1966—67; program com. Venice (Fla.) Presbyn. Ch., 2000—02, mem. health ministries cabinet, 2002—; mem. adv. bd. on family life edn. St. Joseph Sch. Bd. (Mich.), 1979—80, Krasl Art Ctr., St. Joseph, 1987—94. Republican.

CUSHWA, PATRICIA K., commissioner; b. Aug. 1938; m. Victor Cushwa (dec.); 3 children. BA, MA, Hood Coll. Mem. Md. State Senate, 1990; chair, commr. Md. Parole Commn., 1992—2004; commr. U.S. Parole Commn., 2004—. Adj. faculty mem. Hagerstown C.C.; established Ctr. Against Spousal Abuse, Washington County; former mem. Md. Human Relations Commn., Md. State Sch. Bd. Mem. bd. trustees Hagerstown C.C., 2003—. Democrat. Office: US Dept Justice 950 Pennsylvania Ave, NW Washington DC 20530-0001 Office Phone: 301-492-7014. Business E-Mail: patricia.cushwa@usdoj.gov.

CUSICK, PATRICIA A., information technology executive; b. Scranton, Pa., Nov. 5, 1948; BS in Math., Marywood Coll., Scranton, 1970. Plant mgr., sys. supplies IBM, dir., info. sys. and logistics for comm. product group; dir., computer integrated mfg., mktg. & devel. IBM U.S.; dir., acct. technical programs IBM at Fort Motor Co.; mgr., info. tech. Digital Equipment Corp., Maynard, Mass.; joined Xerox Corp., 1991, v.p., info. mgmt., bus. group ops., v.p. & chief info. officer Webster, NY, 1999—. Named Woman of Yr. in Bus. and Industry, Raritan Valley C. of C., 1984. Office: VP & CIO Xerox Corp M/S 102-12A 800 Phillips Rd Webster NY 14580

CUSICK REIMINK, RUTH ELIZABETH, community health nurse; b. Nunica, Mich., Oct. 26, 1929; d. Jacob A. Venema and Nellie K. Holtrop-Venema; m. Roger Duane Cusick, Sept. 26, 1953 (dec. Apr. 1994); children: Mary Kay, William Roger, Beth Ann; m. Harvey Reimink, June 28, 1997 (dec. Nov. 1997). BS, St. Joseph's Coll., North Windham, Maine, 1989; RN, Hackley Hosp. Sch. Nursing, Muskegon, Mich., 1951. Nurse mgr. Holland (Mich.) City Hosp., 1953—54; nurse North Ottowa Cmty. Hosp., Grand Haven, Mich., 1955—66, St. Mary's Hosp., Grand Rapids, Mich., 1982, Butterworth Hosp., Grand Rapids, Mich., 1982—84, Hackley Hosp., Muskegon, 1966—2002, Hackley Vis. Nurses, Muskegon, 2003—. Mem.: Assn. Women's Health Ob-Gyn. and Neonatal Nursing, Am. Nurses Assn. Office: Hackley Vis Nurses 888 Terrace St Ste 150 Muskegon MI 49440 E-mail: ruthcusick@mgn.com.

CUSSON-CAIL, KATHLEEN, consulting company executive; b. Manchester, N.H., Mar. 17, 1971; m. Alan Cail, Feb. 26, 2000. AS in Archtl. Engring. Tech., N.H. Tech. Inst., 1994; BS in Mgmt., Franklin Pierce Coll., 1995, MBA, 2000. Lic. securities, life, property, casualty. Personal fin. analyst Primerica Fin. Svcs., Nashua, NH, 1996—2003; instructor Introduction to Windows and Word Processing, Adult Comm. Education program Merrimack Sch. District, 2000—02; prin., owner Aggregate Bus. & Comm. Cons., Inc., Manchester, NH, 2002—, Collabresource, Manchester, 2002—, Ideal Instr., Manchester, 2002—. Vol. Vt. Adaptive Ski and Sport, 1996—98, Jerry Lewis Labor Day Telethon, 1998—2003, Riverfest, 1999. Recipient Good Citizenship award DAR, 1985. Avocations: volleyball, horseshoes, motorcycling, winter hiking. Office: Aggregate Business & Communication Cons Inc 1361 Elm Street Ste 208 Manchester NH 03101

CUSTER, MARY JO, university official; b. Cortland, N.Y., Aug. 1, 1955; d. Edward Daniel and Nancy Janet (Burdick) Dwyer; children: Jessica Lynn, Kristi Marie. Student, Nazareth Coll., Rochester, N.Y., 1973-75; BS Liberal Arts Syracuse U., 1978, BS in Psychology, 1978, MS in Higher Edn., 1993. Cert. in sanitation and tng. Nat. Inst. Foodservice Industry. Service supr. dining services Syracuse U. (N.Y.), 1978-79, asst. mgr. dining services, 1979-81, dir. sanitation and tng. dining services, 1981-82, asst. to v.p. instnl. services, 1983-85, asst. to sr. v.p. student svcs., 1985-89, asst. to v.p. student affairs, 1989-1992, dir. student affairs, assoc. to sr. v.p., dean, 1992—; lectr. in field. Contbr. articles to profl. jours. Mem. lector, St. Mary's, 2003—, Firemen's Aux., Cuyler, N.Y., 1980—, pres., 1987-91; sec. Tioughnioga Lake Assn., 1972-80. Recipient award for disting. service Nat. Inst. Foodservice Industry, 1983, Chancellor's Citation Disting. Svc. award, 2001. Mem. Nat. Assn. Coll. and Univ. Food Services (pubs. officer, Meritorious Service award 1983), Nat. Restaurant Assn., Nat. Assn. Student Personnel Adminstrs., Assn. Coll. Personnel Adminstrs., VA. Republican. Roman Catholic. Office: 306 Steele Hl Syracuse NY 13244-0001 Home: 4772 Portzline Rd Truxton NY 13158

CUSTURERI, MARY CATHERINE FOCA, literature educator; b. Jersey City, Dec. 28, 1929; d. Joseph and Rosa (Scala) Foca; m. Domenick Custureri, July 31, 1948; children: Frank, Richard. BS, Fla. Atlantic U., 1969,

MEd, 1972, EdS, 1986, EdD, 1989. English lectr. Embry Riddle Aeronautical U., Daytona Beach, Fla.; lectr., coll. instr., 1999—. Tchr.-trainer learning strategies, speaker at confs. in field and at Internat. Reading Assn., Nat. Coun. of Tchrs. of English. Instructional Strategies: Helping all Students Succeed, 2004; contbr. articles to profl. jours. Grantee Palm Beach County Edn. Found., 1985, Fla. Atlantic U., 1980, Cardinal Newman H.S., Latner Found., Nat. Cath. Edn. Assn., Good Sam Wallmart. Mem. Internat. Reading Assn. (spkr. 1988), Nat. Cath. Edn. Assn., Fla. Reading Assn., Nat. Coun. Tchrs. English (spkr.), Fla. Writers Assn., Assn. for Supervision and Curriculum Devel. (spkr. various confs.), Fla. Devel. Assn. (spkr. 2003), Delta Kappa Gamma (North Palm Beach chpt., spkr.). Roman Catholic.

CUSWORTH, CHRISTYL J., conservator, artist; b. Neptune, NJ, Mar. 14, 1963; d. Christopher and Dorothy Cusworth. BA, Coll. N.J., 1986; student, Am. Coll. Greece, Athens, 1984; sculpture student, U. New Orleans, 1994. Registered profl. assoc. Am. Inst. for Conservation of Hist. and Artistic Works. Artist, bronze caster Antietam, Trenton, NJ, 1987—91; paintings conservator, artist Christyl Cusworth Paintings Conservator, Lambertville, NJ, 1995—. Bronze caste, art installer Artist Julian Schnabel, NYC, 1989—90; apprentice, artist Salah Hudson Conservation Studio, New Orleans, 1991—95; art installer Artist/Photojournalist Melina Mara, Washington, 2003. Oil painting, Star night over Lambertville (Bob and Joyce Byers award, 2004). Office: Christyl Cusworth Paintings Conservator 28 N Union St Lambertville NJ 08530 Personal E-mail: cus@pil.net.

CUTCHER, KRESTA KING, photojournalist, educator; b. Mountain View, Calif., Nov. 28, 1972; d. John McCormick Cutcher and Christine Edwards (Stepmother); life ptnr. Graham Wentworth Venning. BA in Psychology, U. Ariz., Tucson, 1997. Cert. tchr. K-12 Ariz., 1997. Photographer; educator. Photographer Gisimba Meml. Ctr., Kigali, Rwanda, 2005. Photographer: (documentaries) Orphans of Rwanda; Orphans of Uganda. Grantee, Kodak SNAP Found., 2005; Kate Farness scholar, U. Ariz., 1997. Mem.: Christian Photojournalists. Episcopalian. Avocation: yoga.

CUTHBERT, EMILIE ANN (EMILIE WINTHROP), interior designer; b. Denver, Apr. 13, 1932; d. Theodore Kostitch and Florence Engelbach; m. Robert Whiting Caulfield, Mar. 4, 1955 (dec. May 1961); 1 child, Emilie Florence; m. William Kendal Cuthbert, June 7, 1968 (dec. Apr. 1994). Student, Pomona Coll., 1949—50; grad., Parson's Sch. Design, 1953; student, U. Calif., San Diego. Designer Guy Brink, Inc., Pasadena, Calif., 1954—55; sr. designer Gerald Jerome, Inc., La Jolla, 1960—65; owner, designer Emilie Winthrop, 1965—; entertainment editor San Diego Writers Monthly, 1998—2003; writer The News Chronicle Mag., Encinitas, 1994—95; writer, arts editor Calif. Women Mag., 1995—97; exec. editor San Diego Decor & Style, Solana Beach, 1998; editor Mt. LaJolla News, 1975—84. Bd. govs. Mt. La Jolla, 1973—75. Avocations: travel, gardening, genealogy, gemology. Home: 3207 La Costa Ave Carlsbad CA 92009 E-mail: follee@sbcglobal.net.

CUTLER, AMY, artist; b. Poughkeepsie, NY, 1974; Attended, Staatliche Hochschule für Bildende Künste, Germany, 1994—95, Cooper Union Sch. Art, NY, 1997, Skowhegan Sch. Painting & Sculpture, 1999. Exhibitions include, Miller Block Gallery, Boston, 2000, Dialogues: Amy Cutler/David Rathman, Walker Art Ctr., Mpls., 2002, Inst. Contemporary Art, Phila., 2002, Once Upon A Time, Kohler Art Center, Sheboygan, Wis., 2003, Kemper Museum of Contemporary Art, Kansas City, Mo., 2004, exhibited in group shows at Small Works, 80 Washington Square East Galleries, NY, 1998, Art for Parks, Bklyn. Mus., 1999, Summer Voices, Miller Block Gallery, Boston, 1999, Rural Crossing, 195 Bedford Avenue, NY, 1999, Artists in the Marketplace, Bronx Mus., 2000, Terrors and Wonders: Monsters in Contemporary Art, De Cordova Museum & Sculpture Park, Lincoln, Mass., 2001, Stranger Than You, New Langton Arts, San Francisco, 2001, Works on Paper, The Weatherspoon Art Museum, Greensboro, NC, 2002, Rendered, Sara Meltzer Gallery, NY, 2003, Open House: Working in Bklyn., Bklyn. Mus. Art, 2004, Whitney Biennial, Whitney Mus. Am. Art, 2004, The Drawn Page, Aldrich Mus. Contemporary Art, Ridgefield, Conn., 2004, About Painting, Tang Mus., Saratoga Springs, NY, 2004. Roma Hort Mann Found. Grant, 1999. Office: c/o Whitney Museum American Art 945 Madison Ave New York NY 10021

CUTLER, CAROLE MARIE, music educator; b. Seattle, July 28, 1954; d. Virgil Earl and Jessie Margaret Cutler. BA in Music, U. Calif., Santa Barbara, 1976. Cert. tchr., Calif. Founder, dir., owner Jr. Music Acad., Ventura, Calif., 1976—. Author music instrn. manuals, 1976, 88, 91. Mem. Music Tchrs. Assn. Calif., Assn. Female Execs. Democrat. Avocations: music, flying. Home: 697 Via Cielito Ventura CA 93003-1236 Business E-Mail: redredtiger@aol.com.

CUTLER, RONNIE, artist; b. NYC; d. Leo and Sarah (Saks) C.; m. Mar. 1, 1951 (dec. May 1990). Student, Columbia U., 1955—56, Bklyn. Mus. Art, 1958, Art Students League, NYC, 1959—60. One-woman shows include SW Minn. State U. Art Mus., 2005, exhibited in group shows at Whitney Mus. Am. Art, 1954, Delgado Mus. Art, New Orleans, 1955, Berkshire Mus. Art, Pittsfield, Mass., 1955, 1956, Bklyn. Mus., 1956, 1958, Springfield (Mass.) Mus. Art, 1957, Riverside Mus. Art, NYC, 1957, Nat. Acad. Art, 1958, Am. Watercolor Soc. 132d Ann. Internat., 1999, 2000, 133d Ann. Internat., 2000, Monique Goldstorm Gallery, NYC, 2002, Internat. Works on Paper, Watercolor, 2003, William Whipple Mus. and Gallery SW State U. Minn., 2005, permanent collection, S.W. Minn. State U. Art Mus. Recipient Sherwood prize in oil, Silvermine Guild Artists, 1955, 1st prize, Riverside Mus. Art, 1957, alumni purchase award, Art Students League, 1960, 1st ptize in oil, So. Berkshire Assn., 1979, 1st prize in oil, 1980, Painters and Sculptors Soc., 1955, Frederix/Tara prize, Audubon Artists 58th Ann., First prize Oil Works on Canvas, Pen and Brush, NYC, 2003. Mem. Am. Watercolor Soc. Internat., Salmagundi Club (Thomas E. Picard award, artist exhbn. NYC 2006). Home: 175 W 12th St Apt 11J New York NY 10011-8206 Office Phone: 212-242-7934.

CUTNAW, MARY-FRANCES, retired communications educator, writer, editor; b. Dickinson, N.D., June 15, 1931; d. Delbert A. and Edith (Calhoun-Pritchard) C. BS, U. Wis., 1953, MS, 1957, postgrad., 1967—68. Life tchg. license in speech, English and French, Wis. Vol. tchr. Vocat. Sch. for World War II Displaced Persons, Stevens Point, Wis., 1951-52; speech tchr. Pulaski H.S., Milw., 1953-55; tchg. asst. dept. speech U. Wis., Madison, 1956-57, spl. asst. Sch. Edn., summer 1957; instr. speech U. Wis.-Stout, Menomonie, 1957-58, dean of women, 1958-59, asst. prof. speech, 1959-64, assoc. prof. speech, 1964-74, prof. emeritus, 1974—. Comm. and pers. cons., St. Paul, 1974—; writer, editor, pub. New Legal Press, 1995—. Author: How to Settle a Living Trust, 1996, 4th edit., 2003. Organizer, past advisor Young Dems., Menomonie, 1959—; founder Edith and Kent Cutnaw Scholarship, U. Wis., Stevens Point, 1960—; bd. dirs. Blaisdell Place, Mpls., 1980-85. Hon. scholar U. Wis., Madison, 1959-60, 67-68. Mem. ACLU, NOW, Internat. Platform Assn., Nat. Women's History Mus., Wis. Acad. Arts and Scis., Wis. Women's Network, Progressive Roundtable (Mpls.), Calhoun Beach Club (Mpls.), Amnesty Internat., World Jewish Congress (charter), U. Club St. Paul, Greenpeace, Dunn County Humane Soc., Sierra Club, Soc. for Prevention of Cruelty to Animals, Humane Soc. U.S., Gamma Phi Beta, Phi Beta, Sigma Tau Delta, Pi Lambda Theta. Roman Catholic. Office: New Legal Press PO Box 282 Menomonie WI 54751-0282 Business E-Mail: cutnawm@uwstout.edu.

CUTTER MODLIN, BEVERLY WRIGHT, management consultant; b. N.Y.C., Dec. 31, 1947; d. Thomas Wright and Ruth Louise (Litchfield) Northrop; children: Ernest III, Katherine Virginia. Student, Goucher Coll., 1965-68; BS in Family Services, U. N.H., 1978. Devel. asst. Duke U., Durham, N.C., 1969-71, coordinator of spl. programs, 1978-80; cons., corp. dir. and officer Ross, Johnston & Kersting, Inc., Durham, 1980-84; dir. devel. Nat. Child Welfare Leadership Ctr., Chapel Hill, N.C., 1984-85; asst. dean for devel. sch. law U. N.C., Chapel Hill, 1985-89, vice chancellor for univ. rels. Asheville, 1989—2003; prin. Beverly Cutter Modlin Consulting, 2003—. Mem. Council for Advancement and Support of Edn., Nat. Soc. Fund Raising Execs. E-mail: modlinconsult@aol.com.

CUTTING, PATRICIA GRACE, publishing executive, educator; d. Winfred James and Alma Marie Morrison; m. Dale Emerson Cutting (dec.); children: Paula, Elizabeth, David. BS, U. Utah, Salt Lake City, 1966; MA in Philosophy, U. N.Mex., Albuquerque, 1971, PhD in Philosophy, 1976. Lectr. U. N.Mex., Albuquerque, 1975; adj. prof. U. Albuquerque, 1975—78; prof. philosophy, head dept. Northland Coll., Ashland, Wis., 1978—79; adj. assoc. prof. Coll. of Santa Fe, 1979; mgr. DalPat Pub. Co., Salt Lake City, 2002—. Pres. Philosophy Colloquium, U. N.Mex., 1972—73. Author: A Saga: Choosing Yourself an Ontology, 2002, Tacking with the Wind, 2003. Advocacy contbr. Amnesty Internat., N.Y.C., 2002; mem. Citizens for Global Solutions, Washington, 2002; contbr. Sierra Club, Salt Lake City, 2005—. Recipient scholarship, U. N.Mex., 1972, Fulbright Found., 1973—74, 1st place award, Scottish Internat. Poetry Competition, 1994. Mem.: UN Assn., Acad. Am. Poets, Am. Philos. Assn., Phi Sigma Tau (v.p., sec. 1970—76). Presbyterian. Avocations: skiing, poetry readings and writing, public speaking. Office: DalPat Pub Co 4500 W 3650 S Salt Lake City UT 84120 Personal E-mail: patcutting30@aol.com.

CUTTNER, JANET, hematologist, educator; b. N.Y.C. d. William Robert and Ida Edith C. BA, NYU, 1953; MD, Med. Coll. of Pa., 1957. Diplomate Am. Bd. Internal Medicine, Am. Bd. Hematology. Intern, resident King's County Hosp., Bklyn., 1957-61; hematology fellow Mt. Sinai Med. Ctr., N.Y.C., 1961-63, rsch. assoc. hematology, 1963-65, asst. prof. medicine, 1965-72, assoc. prof. medicine, 1972-86, prof. medicine, 1986—. Recipient Jacobi Medallion, Alumni Mt. Sinai Med. Ctr., 1999. Fellow N.Y. Acad. Scis.; mem. Am. Soc. Hematology, Am. Soc. Clin. Oncology, Am. Assn. for Cancer Rsch. Office: 1735 York Ave Ste P2 New York NY 10128 Office Phone: 212-860-9055.

CUTUJIAN, PAULETTE SUE, school psychologist; b. Cleve., Aug. 6, 1961; d. Boghos Hagop and Barbara Jean (Kuzak) C. BA, Baldwin-Wallace Coll., Berea, Ohio, 1983; MEd, John Carroll U., 1995, Postmaster's Sch. Psychology Cert., 1996. Cert. sch. psychologist, Ohio; nationally cert. sch. psychologist. Counselor, sr. counselor Glenbeigh Hosp., Cleve., 1983-86, patient care coord., dir., 1986-88; profl. svc. rep. Laurelwood Hosp., Willoughby, Ohio, 1988-92; intern sch. psychologist Brunswick (Ohio) City Schs., 1995-96, intervention cons., spl. edn. coord., 1997—98; sch. psychologist PSI Inc., Twinsburg, Ohio, 1996-97, West Geauga Local Schs., 2004—. Mem. Nat. Assn. Sch. Psychologists, Cleve. Assn. Sch. Psychologists. Home: 6885 Carriage Hill Dr Apt 67 Brecksville OH 44141-1251 Office: 13738 Caves Rd Novelty OH 44072 Office Phone: 440-729-5990 4342. E-mail: cutup@westgeauga.k12.oh.us.

CYFORD, JANET IRENE, Spiritualist medium, meditation consultant; b. Walthamstow, London, Eng., June 21, 1939; d. Leonard George and Irene Olive Chapman; m. Albert Howard Cyford, Feb. 14, 1987; m. Michael Ernest Morton, Sept. 23, 1961 (div. Feb. 9, 1977); children: Angela Morton, David Morton. Diploma in bus. adminstrn. (hon.), Ramsgate Coll., 1976. Window display artist various stores, London, 1959—61; self employed restuarant owner Broadstairs, Kent, England, 1965—77; office mgr. Baverstock Pollock Accts., Great Dunmow, England, 1977—80; legal cashier Wade & Davis Solicitors, Barristers, Great Dunmow, England, 1980—; spiritualist medium, lectr., tchr. self employed, Balt., 1987—2006; meditation cons. Dept. of Pub. Safety & Correction Detention Ctr. SAP, ACT, Balt., 2000—02; pvt. practice medium Balt., 2002—06. Asst. sec. Inst. of Spiritualist Mediums, London, 1965—85; bd. mem. Stepping up & Helping Out Recovering Drug Addicts, Balt., 2001—02; meditation cons. Families in Recovery Maintenance, Balt., 2000—02. Author: The Ring of Chairs A Medium's Story, 2000; featured in book: Witness to the Unsolved by Edward Olshaker. Recipient Cert. of Appreciation, SAP/ACT Dept of Pub. Safety & Correctional Svcs., 2001. Mem.: Co-Freemasonry (master mason 1982—2002). Office Phone: 410-235-9116. Personal E-mail: JCMedsp@aol.com.

CYGANOWSKI, MELANIE L., bankruptcy judge; b. Chgo., June 8, 1952; d. Daniel F. and Sophia A. C.; married, 1989. AB in anthropology, Grinnell Coll., 1974; postgrad. in urban devel., Cornell U., 1975; JD magna cum laude, SUNY, Buffalo, 1981. Bar: N.Y. 1982, U.S. Supreme Ct., U.S. Ct. Appeals (2d cir.), U.S. Dist. Ct. (so., ea. and we. dists.) N.Y. Coord. program planning, planner, cons. dept. community devel. and human resources City of Buffalo, N.Y., 1974-78; dir. individual referral program Broadway-Filmore Area Coun., Inc., Buffalo, 1978-79; summer assoc. Hodgson, Russ, Andrews, Wood & Goodyear, Buffalo, 1980; law clk. to Hon. Charles L. Brieant U.S. Dist. Ct. (so. dist.) N.Y., 1981-82; litigation assoc. Sullivan & Cromwell, N.Y.C., 1982-89; sr. atty. Milbank, Tweed, Hadley & McCloy, 1989-93; judge U.S. Bankruptcy Ct. (ea. dist.) N.Y., Ctrl. Islip, 1993—. Adj. prof. law bankruptcy program St. John's U. Sch. Law. Contbr. articles to legal jours. Fellow Am. Bar Found, ABA; mem., Nat. Conf. Bankruptcy Judges, N.Y. State Bar Assn. Roman Catholic. Avocations: bicycling, gardening, fishing. Office: US Bankruptcy Ct The Long Island Fed Ct 290 Federal Plz Central Islip NY 11722 Office Phone: 631-712-5682. Business E-Mail: melanie_cyganowski@nyeb.uscourts.gov.

CYPRUS, RHONDA RENEÉ, marriage and family therapist, social worker; b. San Diego, Sept. 24, 1959; d. Gerald Price and Norma Helan (Miller) Wynns; m. Clarence Earl Hann (div.); children: Tarrah Reneé Mundy, Chadnay Earl Hand. BA in Christian Edn., Jackson Coll., Miss., 1978; BSW, Ball State U., Muncie, Ind., 1996; MA in Marriage and Family Counseling, Ind. Wesleyan U., Marion, 2002. Ministerial coord. United Pentecostal Ch., St. Louis, 1978—93; social svc. dir. Yorktown Health Care Ctr., Ind., 1996—2000; marriage and family therapist Directions for Mental Health, Clearwater, Fla., 2002—. Sign lang. instr. VA, Marion, 1979—80. Fundraiser United Way, Muncie, 1990—91. Mem.: Nat. Assn. Christian Social Workers, Am. Counseling Assn. Republican. Apostolic. Avocation: reading.

CYR, LISA WATSON, lawyer; BA summa cum laude, U. Minn., Duluth, 1995; JD magna cum laude, William Mitchell Coll. Law, 1998. Bar: Minn. 1998. Atty. McCullough, Smith, Williams & Cyr, P.A., St. Paul. Guest lectr. Family Law Inst. Named a Rising Star, Minn. Super Lawyers mag., 2006. Mem.: Ramsey County Bar Assn. (mem. family law sect., co-chair family law sect. 2001—02), Minn. State Bar Assn. (mem. family law sect.), Phi Kappa Phi. Office: McCullough Smith Williams & Cyr PA 905 Parkway Dr Saint Paul MN 55117 Office Phone: 651-772-3446. E-mail: lwatsoncyr@mcculloughlawyers.com.*

CZACH, GABRIELA BOZENA, personal care industry executive; b. Nidzica, Poland, Aug. 1, 1953; arrived in U.S., 1983; d. Jenryk and Janina Krystkiewicz; m. Witold Edmund Czach, Dec. 1, 1951; 1 child, Jaroslaw. Midwife Gen. Swierczewski Hosp., Gdansk, 1975—78; mgmt. specialist Techino Svc. Co., 1978—83; med. asst. Phila. Med. Coll., 1983—86; manicurist Jean Marlyn Salon, Kenkintown, 1986—87; esthetician Pierre and Carlo Spa, Phila., 1990—97; esthetician cons. Metropolis Spa, Princeton, NJ, 1998—2002; owner Amber Spa, Pennington, 2003—. Cosmetic cons. Pierre and Carlo Spa, Phila., 1991—98, asst. mgr., 1993—96. Ind. cons. Women Cmty., Pennington, 2002; leader Girl Scouts Poland, Nidzica, 1966—72; asst. troop leader Girls Scouts U.S.A., Bucks County, Pa., 1996—99. Mem.: Polish Am. Mothers Assn. (sec. 1989—99), Polish Am. Orgn. (sec. 1986—95), Internat. Spa Assn. Republican. Roman Catholic. Avocations: skiing, travel, bicycling, gardening, tennis. Home: 1139 Buttonwood Ave Bensalem PA 19020 Office: Amber Spa 16 S Main St Pennington NJ 08534

CZARNIAK, JULIA A., lawyer; b. Moscow, 1968; BA, Moscow State U., 1990; MA, Yale U., 1993; JD, Georgetown U., 1997. Bar: NY 1998. Legal intern (spring) Export-Import Bank US, 1997; legal intern Hogan & Hartson LLP, Moscow, 1996; summer assoc. Skadden, Arps, Slate, Meagher & Flom LLP, assoc. NYC, ptnr., 2005—. Office: Skadden Arps Slate Meagher & Flom LLP Four Times Square New York NY 10036 Office Phone: 212-735-4194. Office Fax: 917-777-4194. E-mail: jczarnia@skadden.com.

CZESAK, LINDA SUSAN, secondary school educator, education educator; b. Waukegan, Ill., Oct. 2, 1954; d. Ralph and MaryJane Hersick; children: Thomas, Susan, Felicia Maclean, David Maclean. AAS, McHenry CC, Crystal Lake, Ill., 1985; BS, Northern Ill. U., Dekalb, Ill., 1987; MA, Northeastern Ill. U., Chgo., 1995. Classroom tchr. Arch. Chgo., Chgo., 1987—95, City Chgo. Bd. Edn., 1995—. Coll. instr. Triton Coll., River Grove, Ill., 2001—04, Northwestern Bus. Coll., Chgo., 2001—. Mem. St. Cornelius Ch., Chgo., 1999—. Roman Cath. Avocation: swimming.

CZIN, FELICIA TEDESCHI, Italian language and literature educator, small business owner; b. Vallata, Avellino, Italy, Jan. 20, 1950; came to U.S., 1958; d. Pasquale Aurelio and Maria (Branca) Tedeschi; m. Peter Czin, Oct. 19, 1972; children: Jonathan, Michael. BA, Rutgers U., 1972; MA, NYU, 1978, ABD, 1981, postgrad. Prodr. RAI Corp. Italian TV, N.Y.C., 1973-84; tchg. asst. dept. Italian NYU, 1977-79, adj. instr. dept. English, 1979-81; asst. prof. Vassar Coll., Poughkeepsie, N.Y., 1981-84; co-owner Czin Opticians, Teaneck, N.J., 1984—. Coord. Symposium on Italian Poetry, N.Y.C., 1978; adj. prof. SUNY at the Fashion Inst. Tech., N.Y.C., 2000—. Editor Out of London Press, N.Y.C., 1977-82, dir. pub. rels., 1977-82; editor jour. Yale Italian Studies, 1979-82; translator for jours. Avocations: hiking, swimming, knitting, cooking, sewing. Home and Office: 489 Cedar Ln Teaneck NJ 07666-1710

CZNARTY, DONNA MAE, secondary school educator; b. Bridgeport, Conn., Aug. 17, 1950; d. Richard W. and Dorothy Mae (Kosturko) Oefinger; m. Wiliam C. Cole, Jr., July 11, 1970; 1 child, Michael William Cole; m. Thomas Robert Cznarty, Apr. 29, 1983. BS in Edn., So. Conn. State U., 1973, MS in Edn., 1977. English and reading tchr. Shelton Bd. Edn., Conn., 1973-82; English tchr. Millbrook Bd. Edn., N.Y., 1985-86; sec., bd. dirs. Hopewell Precision, Inc., Hopewell Junction, N.Y., 1986—, CEO, 1999—, 1999. Bd. dirs. Dutchess Arts Coun. Mem. NAFE. Republican. Avocations: interior decorating, antiques, doll collecting. Home: Field Haven Stanfordville NY 12581 Office: Hopewell Precision Inc Ryan Rd Hopewell Junction NY 12533

DABBS RILEY, JEANNE KERNODLE, retired public relations executive; b. Corsicana, Tex., 1922; d. Robert and Anne (Forrest) McCluer; m. John David Kernodle, June 27, 1942 (div. 1968); 1 child, Elizabeth Kernodle Cabell; m. Jack Autrey Dabbs, Feb. 14, 1981 (dec. 1992); m. James J. Riley, Jr., June 28, 1997 (dec. 1999). BS in Sociology, Tex. Woman's U., 1970. Supr., writer pub. rels. St. Paul's Hosp., Dallas, 1974-76; dir., v.p. mktg. svcs. Fidelity Union Life Ins. Co., Dallas, 1976-81, ret., 1981. Pres. aux. Seton Med. Ctr., Austin, 1985—86; mem. Dallas Civic Chorus, Austin Choral Union. Recipient Editl. medal Freedoms Found. Valley Forge, 1973, Eddy award Internat. Assn. Bus. Communicators, 1974, 76, 79, Matrix award Women in Comm., Inc., 1975, Best of Show award Life Ins. Advts. Assn., 1980, Sr. Vol. award Retirees Coordinating Bd., 1989. Mem. Tex. Women's U. Alumnae Assn. (pres. Capital Area chpt. 1987-89), Tuesday Book Club Austin (pres. 1986), Austin Poetry Soc. Methodist. Avocations: book reviewer, singing. Home: 7200 E Quincy Ave # 226 Denver CO 80237

DABINETT, DIANA FRANCES, artist; d. Leslie Frank and Ivy Annie May; m. Patrick Dabinett, Aug. 1969; children: Emily Thomas. BA in fine arts, U. Cape Town, 1963. H.S. art tchr., Zimbabwe, 1965-66; H.S. English tchr. Eng., 1967-69; asst. curator London (Ont.) Art Gallery, 1969-73. Visual arts advisor, adv. panel Fed.-Prov. Cultural Agreement, Nfld., Canada, 1992—2000; Can. artists rep., Nfld. and Labrador, 1980—97; artist in residence, Hopedale, Labrador, 1988—99, Gros Morne Park, Nfld., 2001. One-woman shows include St. John's, 1989-92, 06, Lunenberg, N.S., 1992, Christina Parker Fine Art St. John's, 1994, 98, 00, 02, 04, 05, 06, Can. Embassy Tokyo, 2001, Can. Embassy Washington, 2003, Argyle Fine Art Gallery, Halifax, 2003, Prince Edward Island, Can., 2004, Devel. House, St. John's, 2006; two-person exhbn. Pathways, 1997-99; exhibited in group shows at Discovery Travelling Maritimes, 1997; commd. works at Birthing Ctr. and Cancer Ctr., Cmty. Hosp. of the Monterey Peninsula, St. Lawrence Hosp. and Labrador Health Ctr., Newfoundland, N.S. Health and Welfare Dept. Halifax, Labrador Straits; illustrator: Iceburgs-Castles in the Sea, 2000; collection HRH Queen Elizabeth II. Mem.: Canadian Soc. Water Colour Painters. Avocations: reading, snow shoeing, hiking. Address: Box 1005 Torbay NL Canada A1K 1K9 Business E-Mail: dianadabinett@nl.rogers.com.

DABLE, CAROL M., primary school educator; b. New Ulm, Minn., Jan. 14, 1943; d. Edwin A. and Emma Clara Helen (Laeslin) Nolte; m. Paul D. Dable, July 22, 1967; children: Ami McClure, Kala McClellan, Marci Gorman, Jon. BS, Dr. Martin Luther Coll., Minn., 1965. 1st and 2d grade tchr. Trinity Luth. Sch., Waukesha, Wis., 1965—71; elem. and HS substitute tchr. Lake Mills, Wis., 1971—74; pre-K, grades 3-5 and kindergarten tchr. Christ Luth., West Salem, Wis., 1975—. Bd. mem. Hist. Soc., West Salem, Wis.; dir. handbell choir Christ Luth. Avocations: reading, crocheting, canvas craft-stitching. Personal E-mail: cdable@christstjohns.org.

DABNEY, MICHELLE SHEILA, administrative assistant; b. Newark, Oct. 19, 1959; d. Charlie Louis and Agatha Cecelia Talley; m. James Charles Dabney, Oct. 3, 1981; children: Jameel Charles, Nadiyah Aliyah. Student, Del. State Coll., 1977-79, Union County Coll., 1979-83; certificate, Taylor Bus. Inst, Bridgewater, N.J., 1985; BS in Sociology, Kean Coll., 1997; postgrad., Rutgers U. Sec., adminstrv. asst. Newark Beth Israel Med. Ctr., 1978-85; sec. AT&T Info. Svcs., Piscataway, N.J., 1985-87; legal sec. Timins & Lesniak, Esq., Elizabeth, N.J., 1987; assoc. mgr. AT&T Communications, Bedminster, N.J., 1987—, AT&T, Bedminster, N.J., 1992—. Mem. NAACP, Plainfield Teen Parenting Program. Mem. IDE Alliance of Black Telecommunications Employees (co-chair profl. devel.), Plainfield Tsunami Track Club (dir.). Democrat. Avocations: cooking, jogging, knitting. Office: AT&T Comm Rt 22/206 N Bedminster NJ 07921 Home: 1021 E 7th St # 1 Plainfield NJ 07062-1901

D'ABO, OLIVIA, actress; b. London, Jan. 22, 1967; d. Mike D'Abo and Maggie London; m. Patrick Leonard; 1 child, Oliver. Actress (films) Conan the Destroyer, 1984, Bolero, 1984, Flying, 1986, Bullies, 1986, The Mission-.Kill, 1987, Into the Fire, 1988, Beyond the Stars, 1989, Another Chance, 1989, The Spirit of '76, 1990, Point of No Return, 1993, Bank Robber, 1993, Wayne's World 2, 1993, The Last Good Time, 1994, Greedy, 1994, Clean Slate, 1994, The Big Green, 1995, Kicking and Screaming, 1995, Live Nude Girls, 1995, Hacks, 1997, The Velocity of Gary, 1998, Soccer Dog: The Movie, 1999, A Texas Funeral, 1999, Seven Girlfriends, 1999, Jonni Nitro, 2000, It Had to Be You, 2000, The Enemy, 2001, (TV films) Really Weird Tales, 1987, Crash Course, 1988, Midnight's Child, 1992, For Love and Glory, 1993, Dad's Week Off, 1997, Batman Beyond: The Movie, 1999, The Triangle, 2001, (TV series) The Wonder Years, 1988—92, (TV films) Star Trek: The Next Generation, 1992, Party of Five, 1994, (TV series) Mortal Kombat: The Animated Series, 1995, The Single Guy, 1995, 3rd Rock from the Sun, 2000, Spin City, 2001, The Legend of Tarzan, 2001, Invader Zim, 2001—02, The Twilight Zone, 2002, Justice League, 2002—05, actress (voice) (films) The Raccoon War, 1994, Titanic Explorer, 1997, Tarzan & Jane, 2002, The Animatrix, 2003, Matriculated, 2003, Medal of Honor: European Assault, 2005, appearanced in (TV series) Alias, Law & Order: Criminal Intent, 2002, actress (Broadway plays) The Odd Couple, 2005. Office: ICM 8942 Wilshire Blvd Beverly Hills CA 90211-1934*

D'ABRUZZO, STEPHANIE, actress; Grad., Northwestern U. Actor: (off-broadway plays) Avenue Q, 2003 (Drama Desk nominee, 2003); (TV series) Sesame Street, 1993—, The Wubbulous World of Dr. Seuss, 1996—98, Oobi, 2003—04, (voice actor) Sheep in the Big City, 2000—01, The Book of Pooh, 2000—01, Proof of Life on Earth, 2005,: (films) The Adventures of Elmo in

Grouchland, 1999, Sesame Street 4D, 2003; (Broadway plays) Carnival, 2002, Chess, 2003—, Avenue Q, 2003 (Tony nominee, 2004, Theatre World award, 2004, Outer Critics Circle Special Ensemble award); (plays) I Love You Because, 2006.

DABUL, BARBARA LOHMAN, speech pathologist; b. Evergreen Park, Ill., Oct. 5, 1942; d. Wilfred Goetzinger Lohman and Barbara (Murray) Seagreaves; 1 child, Amy. Student, Occidental Coll., 1960-61; BA, U. So. Calif., 1965, MA, 1967, PhD, 1970. Lic. speech pathologist, Calif. Asst. prof. speech pathology Calif. State U., Northridge, 1969-70; speech pathologist VA Outpatient Clinic, L.A., 1970-76; assoc. prof. La Verne (Calif.) Coll., 1977-78; asst. dir. Am. Speech Lang. Hearing Assn. Clinic and Hosp. Programs, Rockville, Md., 1978-79; assoc. prof. Calif. State U., L.A., 1979-80; chief speech svcs. Sepulveda (Calif.) VA Hosp., 1980-83; speech pathologist L.A. County U. So. Calif. Med. Ctr., 1983-85; dir. speech svcs. San Gabriel Valley (Calif.) Med. Ctr., 1985-89; speech pathologist Jerry L. Pettis Meml. VA Hosp., Loma Linda, Calif., 1989—. Mem. bilingual adv. com. Fremont Sch., 1979-80, Dir.'s Council So. Calif. Mem. AAUW (v.p. program com. 1980), Am. Speech Lang. Hearing Assn. (cert., quality assurance com.), Calif. Speech Lang. Hearing Assn. (sec. 1982-84, commr. rsch., pubs. and documents 1986-87), Calif. Assn. Bilingual Lang. Speech Specialists (treas. 1986-90), Mensa. Democrat. Congregationalist. Home: 96 Via San Carlos Paso Robles CA 93446

DACBERT-FRIESE, SHARYN VARHELY, social worker, evangelist; b. Utica, N.Y., Dec. 10, 1947; d. Henry Alexander Varhely and Elouise Fulmore; m. Thomas Jewett Mitchell III, Oct. 20, 1968 (div. Dec. 1982); children: Sharyn Mitchell, James Bailey Mitchell, Jaclyn Ashley Mitchell; m. Guenther Roland Friese, Dec. 16, 1998. BA, U. Ala., 1968; MSW, Our Lady of the Lake U., San Antonio, Tex., 1991. Lic. master social worker Advanced Clin. Practitioner, 1991, cert. clin. supr. 1998, LCSW 2003. Entrepreneur, Laredo, Tex., 1972—85; founder, owner Jacob's Well, Laredo, 1980—87; corp. v.p. Dacbert Music Co., San Antonio, 1992—94; psychotherapist individual and family Fuller & Assocs., San Antonio, 1991—94; pvt. practice San Antonio, 1994—; sr. pastor, founder, pres., chmn. Sheepgate Fellowship, San Antonio, 1997—; dir., founder, pres., chmn. Christian Family Counseling Ctr., San Antonio, 1997—. Radio personality, counselor Sta. KSLR-AM, San Antonio, 1997—2001; individual and family psychotherapist Adult Parent Child, San Antonio, 1991—92. Contbr. articles to profl. jours. Mem.: NASW, Nat. Assn. Bus. and Profl. Women, Am. Assn. Christian Counselors, Play Therapy Assn., Tuesday Musical Club. Avocations: painting, camping, drawing, cooking, quilting. Office: Christian Family Counseling Ctr 233 Carolina St San Antonio TX 78210 Office Phone: 210-533-9250. Personal E-mail: sdacbert1@aol.com.

DACEK, JOANNE CAROLE, psychologist; b. Oceanside, N.Y., July 26, 1963; d. Gerald S. and Teresa E. (Iusi) Martinis; m. Stephen T. Dacek, Jan. 17, 1988; children: Stephen Thomas, Mark Brendan, Megan Michelle, Phoebe Lauren, Benjamin Ryan. BA, Adelphi U., 1984; MS, Syracuse U., 1987; MA, Sem. of Immaculate Conception, 1995. Cert. sch. psychologist. Psychologist Greece (N.Y.) Ctrl. Schs., 1987-90, Bellmore (N.Y.) Union Free Sch. Dist., 1990-95; chair C.S.E., Bellmore Unified Sch. Dist., 1995—98; psychologist Bellmore Pub Schs., 2006—. Office: Bellmore Union Free School District 580 Winthrop Ave Bellmore NY 11710-4237

DACEY, KATHLEEN RYAN, lawyer, former federal judge; b. Boston; m. William A. Dacey (dec. Aug. 1986); 1 child, Mary Dacey White AB with honors, Emmanuel Coll., 1941; MS in L.S., Simmons Coll., 1942; JD, Northeastern U., 1945; postgrad., Boston U. Law Sch., 1945-46; LLD (hon.), Suffolk Law Sch., 1990, Emmanuel Coll., 1992. Bar: Mass. 1945, U.S. Supreme Ct. 1957. Law clk. to justices Mass. Supreme Jud. Ct., 1945-47; Practiced in Boston, 1947-75; asst. dist. atty. Suffolk County, Mass., 1971-72, Mass., 1971-72; auditor, master Commonwealth of Mass., Boston, 1972-75, Suffolk and Norfolk Counties, Mass., 1972-75; asst. atty. gen., chief civil bur. Mass. Dept. Atty. Gen., Boston, 1975-77; U.S. adminstrv. law judge Commonwealth of Mass., Boston, 1977-99; of counsel Cushing & Dolan P.C., Mass., 1999—; asst. dist. atty. Suffolk County, Mass., 1971-72. Mem. panel def. counsel for indigent persons U.S. Dist. Ct. Dist. Mass.; lectr., speaker in field Contbr. articles to profl. jours. Bd. dirs. Mission United Neighborhood Improvement Team, Boston; mem. Boston Sch. Com., 1945-46, chmn., 1946-47 Recipient Silver Shingle award Boston U. Sch. Law, 1980; named Alumnae Woman of Yr., Northeastern U. Law Sch. Assn., 1976 Mem. ABA (ho. of dels. 1982—, exec. com. conf. of adminstrv. law judges jud. adminstrn. divsn. 1987—), Internat. Bar Assn., Mass. Bar Assn., Boston Bar Assn., Norfolk Bar Lawyers Assn., Nat. Assn. Women Lawyers (pres.), Mass. Assn. Women Lawyers, Internat. Fedn. Women Lawyers, Boston U. Law Sch. Alumni Assn. (corr. sec. 1974-76), Boston U. Nat. Alumni Coun. Office Phone: 617-361-6070.

DACONS, GWENDOLYN BROWN, educator; b. Whiteville, NC, Aug. 6, 1951; d. Elmore and Catherine Martin Brown; m. Pierre Wyatt Dacons, June 28, 1980; children: Donovan Pierre, Dion Jerard. M, Gardner-Webb U., Boiling Springs, NC, 1982. Tchr. Iredell-Statesville Schs., NC, 1975—, Mitchell C.C., 2003—04. Mem.: NC Assn. Educators, NC Tchrs. Math. Home: 126 Timberbrook Lane Statesville NC 28625 Office: Statesville High School 474 North Center Street Statesville NC 28677 Office Phone: 704-873-3491. Personal E-mail: gbdacons@iss.k12.nc.us.

DACOSTA, CAROLINE LEE, small business owner; b. Slippery Rock, Pa., Dec. 13, 1941; d. John Edward and Eleanor Rose Allen; children: Yvonne Rene Shawgo, Tamara Kay Hufnagel, Andrea Lee Douds. Student Elem. Edn., Slippery Rock State Tchrs. Coll., 1960. Cert. Fingerprint Analyzation, Criminal Divsn. FBI, Wash., D.C., 1961. Asst. to pathologist and lab technician Grove City Hosp., Pa., 1962—64; book keeper Rice Clin. Lab, Santa Ana, Calif., 1964—65; exec. asst. to prin. Slippery Rock Area Sch. Dist., 1966—74; account exec. WMGW/WZPR AM/FM Radio, Meadville, Pa., 1975—76; account exec., office mgr. Butler Eagle Newspaper, Pa., 1975—81; account exec. UNSCO Linens, Youngstown, Ohio, 1981—83; owner, mgr. DaCosta Properties, Mercer, Pa., 1985—, Casa DaCosta Bed & Breakfast, Mercer, 2004—. Pub. spkr., presenter, specialist Mercer County Vocat., Tech. Sch., 1987—91. Author: (cookbook) My Kitchen Also Has a Stove. Make up artist Theater in Park, Grove City, 1975—76; asst. chairperson Heart Assn. Fund, Grove City, 1976—77; pub. spkr., adv. for elderly to obtain affordable prescription drugs Citizens for Consumer Justice, Phila., 2001—05. Mem.: Mercer County C. of C., Mercer County Conv. and Visitors Bur., Pa. Soc. Bed and Breakfast (co-founder, asst. dir.), Zelienople Lions Club (assoc.). Presbyterian. Achievements include One of the first women to be initiated as a full fledged Lion in Pennsylvania. Avocations: painting, hist. preservation and restoration of homes, travel, reading. Home: 116 West Market St Mercer PA 16137 Office: DaCosta Properties Casa DaCosta B & B 116 West Market St Mercer PA 16137 Office Phone: 724-662-5681. Home Fax: 724-662-1617; Office Fax: 724-662-1617. Personal E-mail: casadacosta@zoominternet.net.

D'ADDARIO, JODY ANN, science educator; b. Bridgeport, Conn., Jan. 4, 1973; d. Gerald Bennett and Linda Ann Wright; m. Robert Joseph D'Addario, June 22, 1999; children: Max Anthony, Cameron Lynn. BS, U. Conn., Storrs, 1991—95, MS, 1995—96. Cert. Tchr. Conn. Dept. Edn., 2005. Tchr. Madison Mid. Sch., Trumbull, 1996—, sci. team leader, 2005—. Student govt. advisor Madison Mid. Sch., 1998—. Den mother Boy Scouts Am., Trumbull, 2005—. Mem.: Conn. Edn. Assn. (life). Methodist. Avocations: horseback riding, volleyball. Office: Madison Mid Sch 4630 Madison Ave Trumbull CT 06611 Office Phone: 203-452-4499. Office Fax: 203-452-4490. Business E-Mail: daddarij@trumbullps.org.

DADLEY, ARLENE JEANNE, retired sleep technologist; b. Cleve., Sept. 13, 1941; d. Bernard and Bernice Anne (Selleck) Davis; m. Charles Dadley, Sept. 15, 1967 (div. Oct. 1977); children: Anitra, Charles. BA in Bus., Ursuline Coll., 1980; postgrad., Case Western Res. U., 1983-85, Stanford U., 1988. Registered polysomnographic technologist. Jr. fund acct. Am. U., Washington, 1967-70; htn and cancer rsch. asst. Case Western Res. U., Cleve., 1976-87, gastroent. rsch. assoc., 1984, sleep rsch. assoc., 1985-87; sr. clin. sleep technologist Metrohealth Med. Ctr., Cleve., 1987—2006, sleep diagnostics tchr., trainer, 1987—2006; ret., 2006. Judge regional and state sci. fairs. Exhibited in group shows at Cleve. Mus. Art, Butler Inst. Art, Corcoran Gallery Art, Washington, Internat. Traveling Am. Artists Exhibit (Jury 1st award); contbr. articles to profl. jours. Recipient Presdl. Lit. Achievement citation, League Am. Pen Women, 1974, citation, ARC, 1991; scholar, Case Western Res. U., 1976—80, Yale U., 1982, Respironics, Inc., 1988; Pell grantee, 1976—80, Ohio Instl. grantee, 1976—80. Mem.: Am. Acad. Sleep Medicine, Midwest Polysomnographic Technologists, Assn. Polysomnographic Technologists, Sleep Rsch. Soc., Am. Acad. Sleep Medicine. Avocations: painting, gardening. Home: PO Box 894 Columbia Station OH 44028-0894

DADURIAN, MEDINA DIANA, pediatric dentist, educator; b. Landstuhl, Germany, Apr. 12, 1964; arrived in US, 1964; d. John Gulbenc Jr. and Alice Nartouhi (Vosgeritchian) D.; m. Gregory Sarkis Kinoian, July 3, 1993 (div.); children: Melissa Marie, Natalie Anoush. BS, Allegheny Coll., Meadville, Pa., 1986; DMD, U. Medicine and Dentistry N.J., Newark, 1991. Resident in hosp. gen. practice dentistry Hackensack (N.J.) Med. Ctr., 1991-92; tng. in pediatric dentistry Columbia U. Sch. Dental and Oral Surgery, N.Y.C., 1994-96; assoc. dentist pvt. practices, 1992-93, Assocs. for Dental Care, Hackensack, 1993-95; assoc. dental specialist Denville (N.J.) Dental Assocs., 1997—99; owner, pediatric dentist in pvt. practice, Rochelle Park, N.J., 1996—, Fair Lawn, N.J., 1999—; pvt. practice Fair Lawn, N.J., 1999—. Assoc. clin. prof. Hackensack U. Med. Ctr., 1993—; dental adminstr. Hackensack Bd. Edn., 1993—95; dental cons. Hovnanian Sch., New Milford, NJ, 2000; pediatric dental cons. Howard Karaghensian Med. Benevolent Social Orgn. Children's Dental Clinics of Am., 2000—, Howard Karaghusian Commemorative Found., 2001—. Author in field. Dental dir. Bergen County Head Start, Englewood, N.J., 1993-95. Cerebral Palsy fellow United Cerebral Palsy Found., 1995-96; Gulbenkian Found. grantee, 1983-86. Fellow Acad. Gen. Dentistry; mem. ADA, Am. Acad. Pediatric Dentistry, Am. Armenian Dental Soc. Mem. Armenian Apostolic Ch. Avocations: reading, cooking, horseback riding, martial arts, needlecrafts. Home: 377 Elliot Pl Paramus NJ 07652-4647 Office: 18-00 Fair Lawn Ave Fair Lawn NJ 07410-2330 also: 315 Rochelle Ave Rochelle Park NJ 07662-3916 Office Phone: 201-791-4113. Business E-Mail: mdadurian@juno.com.

DAFFRON, MARYELLEN, retired librarian; b. Richmond, Va., Nov. 12, 1946; d. William Charles and Ellen (Ahern) D. BA, Coll. Mt. St. Joseph on Ohio, Cin., 1968; MLS, Drexel U., 1970. Libr. Richmond Pub. Libr., 1969-73, FMC, Washington, 1973—93; with U.S. Immigration and Naturalization Svc. Office of Gen. Counsel, Washington, 1993—2003; law libr. Office of Prin. Legal Advisor, U.S. Immigration and Customs Enforcement, Washington, 2003—05, ret., 2005. Vol. No. Va. Hotline, Arlington, 1974-79. City of Richmond fellow, 1968. Mem. Law Libr. Soc. Washington, Beta Phi Mu. Roman Catholic.

DAFFRON, MITZI LYNNAE, quality improvement specialist; b. New Orleans, Sept. 27, 1965; d. Jerry Lee and Betty Jean (Dougherty) Need; m. Stanley William Daffron, Oct. 15, 1988; children: Lauren Alexandra, Joseph Duncan. BSN magna cum laude, U. Indpls., 1988. RN, Ind. Surg. nurse Meth. Hosp., Indpls., 1988-89; nurse telemetry unit Good Samaritan Hosp., Vincennes, Ind., 1989-91; home health care nurse, case mgr. Daviess County Hosp. Home Health, Washington, Ind., 1990-92; quality assurance nurse Meml. Hosp. Home Health Care, Jasper, Ind., 1992; nurse tng. and edn. health care quality improvement specialist Health Care Excel, Inc., Terre Haute, Ind., 1993—. Recipient Am. Legion scholarship, 1986. Mem. Sigma Theta Tau Internat. Avocations: reading, tennis, bowling, word games. Home: 11278 N State Road 63 Farmersburg IN 47850-8225 Office: Health Care Excel Inc 2901 Ohio Blvd Terre Haute IN 47803-2239

DAFTARY, MONIKA NEIL, pharmacist, educator; BS in Pharmacy, Howard U., Washington, 1994; PharmD, Howard U., 1998. Registered pharmacist DC. Staff pharmacist CVS Pharmacy, Washington, 1994—98; asst. prof. Howard U., 1999—2004, assoc. prof., 2004—; treatment adherence specialist HUH Cares, Howard U. Hosp., Washington, 2003—05; treatment adherence specialist, clin. pharmacist Ctr. for Infectious Diseases Mgmt. and Rsch., Washington, 2005—06. Preceptor pharmacy residency program Howard U. Hosp., 1999—2006; cons. Adherence Techs., Sterling, Va., 2000—02; dir. cmty. residency program Howard U., 2000—02; preceptor non-traditional PharmD program Shenendoah U., Winchester, Va., 2003. Named Disting. Young Pharmacist of Yr., DC Soc. Pharmacists, 1998; grantee, Ryan White Title I/II Grants Program, Washington, 2003—05, IACP, PI, 2000—02, AHRQ Minority Rsch. Infrastructure Program, 2002—05. Mem.: Am. Soc. Health-Systems Pharmacists, Am. Pharmacists Assn. Achievements include research in HIV Diagnosis and Treatment Using Medical Expenditure Panel Survey Data, 1996 — 1999. Avocations: travel, scrapbooking, cooking, party planning. Office: Howard U 2300 4th St NW Washington DC 20059 Office Phone: 202-806-4206. Office Fax: 202-806-4478. E-mail: mdaftary@msn.com.

DAGAVARIAN, DEBRA A., college administrator, consultant; b. N.Y.C., Oct. 26, 1952; d. Harry O. Dagavarian and Norma Siran (Cazanjian) Hansen; m. James B. Bonar, Dec. 26, 1988. BA, SUNY, New Paltz, 1973; MA, SUNY, Albany, 1975; EdD, Rutgers U., 1986. Transfer admissions counselor Mercy Coll., Dobbs Ferry, NY, 1976—79, asst. dir. spl. sessions, 1979—81, dir. evening programs, 1981—86, dir. acad. advising, 1986—87; asst. dean for assessment Empire State Coll., Hartsdale, NY, 1987—88; dir. testing assessment Thomas Edison State Coll., Trenton, NJ, 1988—96, dep. vice provost, 1996—2002; asst. provost Richard Stockton Coll. NJ, Pomona, 2002—. Adj. prof. Empire State Coll., Mercy Coll., 1979-95; cons. various instns. and corps., 1987—. Author: Saying It Ain't So: American Values as Revealed in Children's Baseball Stories, 1987; author, editor: A Century of Children's Baseball Stories, 1990, (jour.) Jour. of the Nat. Inst. on Assessment of Experiential Learning, 1989-2002; contbr. articles to profl. jours., periodicals, books. Mem. Soc. Am. Baseball Rsch., Coun. Adult and Experiential Learning, Assn. Continuing Higher Edn. Democrat. Avocations: baseball, singing, jewelry making. Office: Richard Stockton Coll of NJ PO Box 195 Jim Leeds Rd Pomona NJ 08240 Business E-Mail: dagavarian@stockton.edu.

DAGGETT, KATHLEEN, special education educator; b. Hannibal, Mo., Mar. 22, 1947; d. Harry Richard and Anna Mary (Morriss) Snyder; m. Boyd Reed Ludwick, Oct. 11, 1981 (dec. Mar. 1990); m. David C. Daggett, June 23, 2000; m. Bill Pruett, 1963; children: Deanna Marie Maddox, Mark William Pruett, Deidre Michelle Powell. BA, Avila Coll., 1978; M in Edn., U. Kans., 1990. Cert. special edn./learning disabilities K-12. Tchr. Belton Sch. Dist., Mo., learning disability resource tchr. Mo. Former bldg. coord. Belton H.S., Mo. Office: Belton Sch Dist 107 Pirate Pkwy Belton MO 64072 Office Phone: 816-348-2736. Business E-Mail: kdaggett@bsd.124.net.

DAGLIS, LISA GENINE, deputy attorney general; b. Northridge, Calif., Feb. 28, 1969; d. Abraham and Rosalynd Rohrberger; m. John P. Daglis, Apr. 21, 1988; 1 child, Brett John. AA pre law, Atlantic C.C., Mays Landing, N.J., 1985; BA Govt. and Politics, Widener U., Chester, Pa., 1997; JD, Widener U. Law Sch., Wilmington, Del., 2003. Bar: N.J. 2003. Staff South Jersey Legal Svcs., Atlantic City, 2004; law clk. Superior Ct. N.J., Mays Landing, 2004—; dep. atty. gen. State of NJ, 2006—. Legal aid vol. South Jersey Legal Svcs., 2004; campaign vol. Rep. Club, Atlantic County, Hamilton Twp., NJ. Recipient Zelda K. Hermann award, Widener Sch. of Law, 2003. Mem.: ABA, U. S.Holocaust Meml. Mus. Soc., So. Poverty Law Ctr., Phi Kappa Phi. Avocations: sailing, interior decorating, painting. Office Phone: 609-633-2038.

DAGNA, JEANNE MARIE, special education educator; b. Flushing, N.Y., July 28, 1959; d. Renato Lawrence and Norma Jeanne (Leuchtman) D. BS in Elem. and Spl. Edn., L.I. U., 1982, MS in Spl. Edn., 1984. Cert. spl. edn. tchr., N.Y., Pa. Adminstrv. asst. N.Y. State Dept. Edn., Greenvale, 1983-85; spl. edn. tchr. Baldwin (N.Y.) Sch. Dist., 1985-87, Advances of Wiley House, Reading, Pa., 1989-90; master tchr. Centennial Sch./Lehigh U., Bethlehem, Pa., 1990-92; student assistance liaison Alcohol & Adddictions Dept. of Delaware County, Media, Pa., 1992-93; spl. edn. tchr. children and adolescent units Horsham Psychiat. Clinic, Ambler, Pa., 1993-95; spl. edn. tchr. learning and emotional support Lower Merion H.S., Ardmore, Pa., 1994-2000, spl. edn. liaison in pupil svcs., 2000—. Sec. Main Line Youth Alliance, Wayne, Pa., 1996-99. Contbr. articles to profl. jours. Mem. Crohn's and Colitis Assn., United Ostomy Assn., Coun. for Exceptional Children, Pa. Coun. for Exceptional Children (conf. presenter 1998, 99, Gay, Lesbian, Straight Educators Network. Avocations: reading, flute/oboe, drawing, bicycling. Office: Lower Merion HS 245 E Montgomery Ave Ardmore PA 19003-3339 E-mail: dognaj@lmsd.org.

DAGUE, TERESA, elementary school educator, music educator; b. Bluffton, Ind., Dec. 18, 1972; d. Jeffrey and Mary Ogan; m. Robert Dague, Dec. 4, 1993; 1 child, Janelle Marie. BEd, Ind. U., Fort Wayne, Ind., 1997. Lic. tchr. Ga., 2005, Ind., 2005. Tchr. music Bluffton-Harrison (Ind.) Mid. Sch., 2001—03; dir. music Banks County Mid. Sch., Homer, Ga., 2004—. Dir. choir St. Joseph's Cath., Bluffton, 1996—98. Mem. praise team Meth. Ch., Bluffton, 2002—03. Recipient John Phillip Sousa award, Norwell H.S., 1991, Concerto award, Ft. Wayne Cmty. Orch., 1997. Mem.: NEA (assoc.), Bluffton-Harrison (Ind.) Tchr. Assn. (assoc.; v.p. 2001—02), Sigma Alpha Iota (life). Republican. Meth. Home: 145 Atlanta Ave Commerce GA 30529 Office: Bansk County School System 712 Thompson Street Homer GA 30547 Office Phone: 706-677-2277. Personal E-mail: trjd6129@peoplepc.com. Business E-Mail: tdague@banks.k12.ga.us.

D'AGUSTO, KAREN ROSE, lawyer; b. Phila., Jan. 4, 1952; d. Les and Anne Heilenman; m. Stephen Joseph Bernasconi, Aug. 21, 1976; children: Lesley Anne D. Bernasconi, Stephanie Kalena D. Bernasconi. BA in History cum laude, Immaculata Coll., 1974; JD, U. San Diego, 1977; postgrad., U. So. Calif., 1983—. Bar: Conn. 1977, Hawaii 1978, S.C. 1986. Tng. coord. Protection and Advocacy, Honolulu, 1978, adv. coord., 1979, staff atty., 1980-81, assoc dir., 1982, project dir., 1983—; regional coord. S.C. Protection and Adv. Sys., 1986-88; dep. dir. Hawaii Protection and Advocacy, 1989-91; pvt. practice law Mililani, Hawaii, 1980—. Instr. Hawaii Pacific Coll., Honolulu, 1982-84; adj. prof. Immaculata Coll., 1998-2003; legal cons., 1999—; asst. prof. dept. history, polit. sci. and internat. rels. Immaculate U., 2003—. Author: Legal Rights of Persons with Disabilities, 1980; author, editor curriculum Vol. I Guardians Ad. Litem, 1983, Nursing and Law Module, 2000, revised 2004; editor Jour. Comparative Legis. Analysis of Protection and Advocacy System, 1991. Pres. Ctrl. Oahu Mental Health Ctr., Pearl City, Hawaii, 1981-82; officer Kings Grant Assn., Summerville, S.C., 1988; rep. St. Andrews Priory Parent-Tchr. Fellowship Bd., 1990-91; mem. John B. Dey PTA, mem. bd. dirs., chair legis. com.; leader Girl Scouts Am., svc. unit mgr., trainer, cons. Cape Henry Svc. unit, Colonial Coast coun.; mem. PTA legis. com.; vol. Great Neck Mid. Sch.; co-chair Tower Hill Camp Fair, 1998-2002; chair Family Appeal Brandywine Valley Girl Scout Svc. Unit, 1996-2004; mem. events com. Bayard Taylor Libr., 2000-04; chmn. thinking day event Girl Scouts, Brandywine; chair libr. commn. Immaculata U.; bd. dirs. YWCA of Chester Co., 2005. Recipient Exceptional Achievement award, 1989-90, Disting. Contbn. to Civil Rights of Persons with Disabilities award, 1991, Outstanding Svc. to Hawaiis Disabled Citizens award, 1982, Outstanding Vol. of Yr. award Colonial Coast coun. Girl Scouts U.S., 1995, Vol. of Yr. award Great Neck Middle Sch., 1996; named Outstanding Adv., 1985, Outstanding Vol. of Yr. award Brandywine Svc. Unit, Freedom Valley Girl Scouts, 2002, Appreciation pin, 2006. Mem. ABA, Hawaii State Bar Assn., S.C. Bar Assn., Conn. Bar Assn., Hawaii Lawyers Care, Am. Assn. Counsel for Children Counsel, Wimbledon on the Bay Homeowners Assn. (v.p. 1992-93, chair by-laws com. 1993-94). Office Phone: 610-647-4400 ext. 3458. Personal E-mail: kdagusto@aol.com. Business E-Mail: kdagusto@immaculata.edu.

DAHEIM, MARY RENE RICHARDSON, writer; b. Seattle, Nov. 7, 1937; d. Hugh Emery and Monica Mary (Dawson) Richardson; m. David Charles Daheim, Dec. 18, 1965; children: Barbara, Katherine, Magdalen. BA in Communications, U. Wash., 1960. Mng. editor Anacortes (Wash.) Am. Bull., 1960; mgr. Pacific NW Bell Tel. Co., Seattle, 1960-66; reporter, columnist Port Angeles (Wash.) Evening News, 1966-69; pub. rels. cons. Pacific N.W. Bell, U.S. West, Seattle, 1969-86; writer Seattle, 1983—. Author: Love's Pirate, 1983, Destiny's Pawn, 1984, Pride's Captive, 1986, Passion's Triumph, 1988, King's Ransom, 1990, Improbable Eden, 1991, Just Desserts, 1991, Fowl Prey, 1991, Holy Terrors, 1992, Gypsy Baron, 1992, Alpine Advocate, 1992, Dune to Death, 1993, Alpine Betrayal, 1993, Bantam of the Opera, 1993, The Alpine Christmas, 1993, A Fit of Tempera, 1994, The Alpine Decoy, 1994, Major Vices, 1995, The Alpine Escape, 1995, Murder, My Suite, 1995, The Alpine Fury, 1995, Auntie Mayhem, 1996, The Alpine Gamble, 1996, Nutty as a Fruitcake, 1996, The Alpine Hero, 1997, September Mourn, 1997, The Alpine Icon, 1997, The Alpine Journey, 1998, Wed and Buried, 1998, Snow Place to Die, 1998, The Alpine Kindred, 1999, Legs Benedict, 1999, The Alpine Legacy, 1999, Creeps Suzette, 2000, Suture Self, 2001, Silver Scream, 2002,Alpine Obituary, 2002, This Old Souse, 2004, The Alpine Pursuit, 2004, Hocus Croakus, 2004, The Alpine Quilt, 2005, Dead Man Docking, 2005, The Alpine Recluse, 2006. Mem. Romance Writers Am., Mystery Writers Am., Authors Guild. Roman Catholic. Avocations: gardening, reading, history, travel, opera. Mailing: c/o Maureen Moran Agency Park West Station PO Box 20191 New York NY 10025*

DAHL, ARLENE, actress, writer, designer, cosmetics executive; b. Mpls., Aug. 11, 1928; d. Rudolph and Idelle (Swan) D.; m. Marc A. Rosen; children: Lorenzo Lamas, Carole Christine Holmes, Stephen Andreas Schaum. Student, U. Minn., 1943-44, Mpls. Inst. Art, 1945, Minn. Coll. Music, 1944, Minn. Bus. Coll., 1944. Pres. Arlene Dahl Enterprises, 1952-67; v.p. Kenyon & Eckhart, 1967-72; pres. Woman's World divsn. Kenyon & Eckhart Advt. Agy., 1967-72; nat. beauty and health advisor Sears Roebuck Co., 1970-75; internat. dir. Sales and Mktg. Execs. Internat., 1972-75; fashion dir. O.M.A., 1975-78; pres. Dahlia Parfums, Inc., 1975-80, Dahlia Prodns., Inc., 1978-81, Dahlmark Prodns., 1981—; pres., CEO Scandia Cosmetics, Ltd., 1978-80; pres., chmn. Lasting Beauty Ltd., 1986—. Author: Always Ask a Man, 1965, 12 Beautyscope books, 1968, rev. edit., 1978, Arlene Dahl's Secrets of Hair Care, 1969, Arlene Dahl's Secrets of Skin Care, 1972, Beyond Beauty, 1980, Arlene Dahl's Lovescopes, 1983, Arlene Dahl's Weekly Astro Forecast, yearly from 1991-2005, The Enquirer, 1991-2005, Celebrity Living mag. Weekly Forecast, 2005-, Arlene Dahl's Hollywood Horoscope internat. mag. weekly column, 1990-2005; actress: (Broadway plays) including Mr. Strauss Goes to Boston, Questionable Ladies, Cyrano de Bergerac, Applause (Tony award musical), (films) including (debut) My Wild Irish Rose, The Bride Goes Wild, Reign of Terror, A Southern Yankee, Ambush, The Outriders, Three Little Words, Watch the Birdie, Scene of the Crime, Inside Straight, No Questions Asked, Desert Legion, Slightly Scarlet, Sangaree, Caribbean Gold, Jamaica Run, Diamond Queen, Here Come the Girls, Bengal Brigade, Kisses for My President, Woman's World, Journey to the Center of the Earth, Wicked as They Come, She Played with Fire, Les Poneyettes, Du Blé Enliases, The Land Raiders, The Way to Kathmandu, Fortune Is a Woman, The Big Bank Roll, Who Killed Maxwell Thorn?, Midnight Warrior, 1991, (TV shows) Lux Video Theatre, 1952-53, guest starring appearances on The Love Boat, Fantasy Island, Love American Style, One Life to Live, 1981-84, Night of 100 Stars, 1983, Happy Birthday Hollywood, 1987, All My Children, 1995, Renegade, 1995, 96, 97, Air America, 1999; hostess (TV series): Pepsi-Cola Theatre, 1954, Opening Night, 1958, Arlene Dahl's Beauty Spot, 1966, Arlene Dahl's Starscope, 1979-80, Arlene Dahl's Lovescope, 1980-82; played throughout U.S. in One Touch of Venus, The Camel Bell, Blithe Spirit, Liliom, The King and I, Roman Candle, I Married an Angel, Bell, Book and Candle, Applause, Marriage Go Round, Pal Joey, A Little Night Music, Forty Carats, Life with Father, Murder Among Friends, Dear Liar; nightclub acts

Flamingo Hotel, Las Vegas, Latin Quarter, N.Y.C., musical stage appearances: Carnegie Hall, 1997, London Paladium, 1992, 1998, Salute to MGM Musicals; internat. syndicated beauty columnist Chgo. Tribune/ N.Y. News Syndicate, 1950-70, Arlene Dahl's Lucky Stars Column, Globe Communications, 1988-90, Arlene Dahl's Starscope Weekly Column, 1991, 92, 93, 94, 95, 96, 97, 98, 99, 00, 01, 02, 03, 04, 05, Horoscope Yearly Forecast 1991-02; designer sleepwear for A.N. Saab & Co., 1952-57, In Vogue with Arlene Dahl (Vogue Patterns), 1980-85, Arlene Dahl Pvt. Collection Jewelry, 1989-94, Arlene Dahl's Jewels of Fortune Home Shopping Network, 1996. Hon. life mem. Father Flannagan's Boys Town; internat. amb. Pearl Buck Found.; founder, pres. Broadway Walk of Stars Found., Inc., 1999—; bd. dirs. Hollywood Mus. Recipient 10 Box Office Laurel awards, Hollywood Walk of Fame Star, 1961, Coup de Chapeau Deaville Film Festival award, 1982, 92; named Best Coiffed, Heads of Fame awards, 1967-72, 80; named Woman of the Yr., Advt. Club of N.Y.C., 1969, Mother of the Yr., 1982, Lifetime Achievement award WorldFest, 1994, Leadership in the Arts, 1997; named to Scandinavian Hall of Fame, 1997. Fellow: Vesterheim Norwegian/Am. Found. (life); mem.: UNIFEM, NATAS (trustee), Film Soc., Edward Grieg Soc., Authors Guild, Acad. Motion Picture Arts and Scis. (vice chair N.Y. spl. events), Acad. TV Arts and Scis. (bd. govs., v.p.), Smithsonian Assocs., Nat. Trust for Hist. Preservation, Commanderie de Bordeaux (N.Y.), Commanderie de Bontemps du Medoc et Graves, France. Office: Dahlmark Prodns PO Box 116 Sparkill NY 10976-0116

DAHL, LAUREL JEAN, human services administrator; b. Chgo. d. James Edward and Gladys Uarda (Boquist) Findlay; m. Philip Nels Dahl, Aug. 29, 1970; children: Eric Nels, John Philip. BA, Trinity Coll., 1970; MS in Human Svcs., Nat. Louis U., 1992. Cert. sr. alcohol and other drug preventionist. Tchr. Grove Sch., Lake Forest, Ill., 1971, Little Bear Child Care Ctr., Waukegan, Ill., 1975-77; sec. to dir. Strang Funeral Home, Antioch, Ill., 1981-87; comptroller, office mgr. Village of Antioch, 1987-92; prevention specialist Lake County Dept. of Health: Mental Health Div., 1992; community coord. Fighting Back Project of Lake County, Round Lake, Ill., 1992-94; dir. prevention svcs. Nicasa, Lake, 1994—. Adj. faculty Nat. Louis U., 1994—; adv. bd. U. Ill. Extension, 1999; dir. Lake County Gang Prevention Alliance, 2000—03; mem. Character Matters in Lake County Found., 1999—, treas., 2001—03, pres., 2003—. Mem. editl. adv. bd. Family Times. Mem. Antioch Cmty. H.S. Bd. Edn., 1987—95, pres., 1991—95, sec., 1989—91; mem. Antioch Cmty. H.S. Drug Task Force, MADD; past pres. PTO; vice chair Human Svc. Coun., 1994—96, chmn., 1996—98, 1999—2003; mem. peer rev. com. Ill. Alcohol and Other Drug Abuse Profl. Cert. Assn., 1996—; mem. women's bd. No. Ill. Coun. on Alcoholism and Substance Abuse, 1996—2003, v.p. for programs, 1997—2003; mem. Cmty. Partnership Bd., 2003—. Recipient commendation for Gt. Lakes Naval Tng. Ctr. for Drug Edn. for Youth, 1994-95, Disting. Svc. award Ill. chpt. Nat. Sch. Pub. Rels. Assn., Enrique Camarena "One Person Can" award, 1995, State Prevention Leadership award Ill. Alcoholism and Drug Dependence Assn., 1996, Individuals in the Forefront for Lake County award, 1998; Paul Harris fellow. Mem.: Ill. Assn. for Prevention, Ill. Student Assistance Profls., Alliance Against Intoxicated Motorists, Round Lake Exch. Club (charter mem. 1999). Home: PO Box 613 Antioch IL 60002-0613

DAHL, LINDA M., writer; b. Omaha, Oct. 27, 1949; d. Robert A. and Marilyn (DeCamp) Dahl; m. A. J. Vogl, July 19, 1986; children: Timothy Vogl, Katrina Vogl. BA with honors, U. Wis., 1972; MA, Hunter Coll., 1985. Author: Stormy Weather, 1984, Morning Glory: a Biography of Mary Lou Williams, 2000, Come Back, Carmen Miranda, a Collection of Short Stories, 2002, Haunted Heart, a biography of Susannah McCorkle, 2006. Com. chair St. Luke's Ch., Somers, NY, 1992—. Mem.: St. Luke's Book Club. Episcopalian. Avocations: gardening, swimming, jazz. Home: 281 Allview Ave Brewster NY 10509-3405 E-mail: dahljazz@comcast.net.

DAHL, MARILYN GAIL, psychotherapist; b. Louisville, Dec. 6, 1946; d. James Blair and Dorothy Emma (McDermott) Swartzwelder; m. Charles Dalton Weaver, Dec. 30, 1967 (div. Apr. 1969); m. Donald Allan Dahl, Sept. 18, 1985 (div. Oct. 2005). BSN, U. Ky., 1968; MEd in Clin. Counseling, The Citadel, 1987. Lic. profl. counselor, Ill. Instr. med.-surg. nursing Sch. Nursing Ky. Bapt. Hosp., Louisville, 1973-79; child psychiat. nurse Norton's Children's Hosp., Louisville, 1980-81; asst. prof., psychiat. nurse Sch. Nursing, U. Louisville, 1981-82; primary therapist/child psychiat. nurse Children's Treatment Svc., Louisville, 1982-83; instr. psychiat. nursing Sch. Nursing Bellarmine Coll., Louisville, 1983-84; adult and geriat. therapist Seven Counties Svcs., Louisville, 1984; psychiat. nurse So. Pines Hosp., Charleston, SC, 1985-86; rev. specialist S.C. Peer Rev. Orgn., Charleston, 1986-87; psychotherapist Ctr. for Change, Charleston, 1987-88; pvt. practice North Charleston, 1988-94; hospice nurse Condell Home Health Agy., Libertyville, Ill., 1994-95; home health nurse Manpower Temporary Agy., Waukegan, Ill., 1996-97; staff nurse Hospice of Highland Park (Ill.) Hosp., 1996-99; pvt. practice psychotherapy Goshen, Ky., 1999—; home health nurse Manpower Temp. Agy., Waukegan, 1996-97. Hospice nurse Hospice of Charleston, Inc., 1991-92; pub. health nurse Trident Home Health Svcs., 1992; mental health profl. Charleston/Dorchester Mental Health Ctr., 1993. Vol. Hospice of Louisville, Inc., 1978-85, ARC State and Nat. Response Team, 1996—, Hospice and Palliative Care Louisville, Inc., 1999—; mem. steering com. Highlands Adult Day Ctr., Louisville, 1984-85; bd. dirs. Ashley River Fire Dept., Charleston, 1986-90, chair, 1989-90, mem. ladies aux., 1985-94; mem. test rose panel Jackson & Perkins, 1989-91. Named to Honorable Order Ky. Cols., Commonwealth of Ky., 1977. Mem. ACA, Am. Assn. for Mental Health Counselors. Avocations: cross stitching, raising roses, wildflower gardening, singing, making stained glass projects.

DAHLEN, TRACY, music educator; d. Barbara and Richard Youngberg; m. John Dahlen, May 21, 1994; 1 child, Benny. BS in Music Edn., N.D. State U., Fargo, 1991; M in Music Edn., U. St. Thomas, St. Paul, 2004. Tchr. music Ind. Sch. Dist. 535, Rochester, Minn., 1995—. Co-chair, dist. diversity com. Ind. Sch. Dist. 535, Rochester, Minn., 2001—05, lead grant writer, 2001—, Harriet Bishop staff devel. com., 2002—. Musician: (Swing Street jazz band) performances; composer (elementary choir): (songs) Wouldn't It Be Grand. Edn. ministry team Homestead United Meth. Ch., Rochester, Minn., 2006—06. Mem.: NEA, Rochester Edn. Assn., Music Educators Nat. Conf. Office: Harriet Bishop Elem Sch 406 36th Ave NW Rochester MN 55901 Office Phone: 507-281-6063. E-mail: trdahlen@rochester.k12.mn.us.

DAHLGREN, DOROTHY, museum director; b. Coeur d'Alene, Idaho; BS in Museology and History, U. Idaho, 1982; M in Orgnl. Leadership, Gonzaga U., 1998. Dir. Mus. North Idaho, Coeur d'Alene, 1982—. Mem. Kootenai County Hist. Preservation Commn. Author: (with Simone Carbonneau Kincaid) In All the West No Place Like This: A Pictorial History of the Coeur d'Alene Region, 1996. Mem. no. region com. Idaho Heritage Trust. Office: Mus N Idaho PO Box 812 Coeur D' Alene ID 83816 Office Phone: 208-664-3448. E-mail: dd@museumni.org.

DAHLIN, ANGELA DENISE, language educator; d. Meridith Ann and Jan Olof Dahlin. MA, Oreg. State U., Corvallis, 2002. Tchr. English Nyssa H.S., Oreg., 2003—. Leader single mothers group Resilient Empowered Single Moms Trusting God, Ontario, Oreg., 2004—05. Mem.: NEA.

DAHLINGER, MARTHA LOUISE, elementary school educator; b. Tampa, Fla., Mar. 28, 1936; d. Carl Bowman and Etta Louise Burkhalter; m. Russell Allen Dahlinger, 1958 (div. 1968); children: Jeffrey, Deborah, Daniel, Maria. BA in Edn., Mich. State U., 1965; MA in Edn., Western Mich. U., 1988. Classroom tchr. Vicksburg (Mich.) Pub. Schs., 1958—60, Kalamazoo (Mich.) Pub. Schs., 1969—94, Numazu (Japan) Bd. Edn., 1994—95, Kalamazoo (Mich.) Pub. Schs., 1995—98. Co-chair program and events Kalamazoo County Juvenile Home, 1963—65; troop leader Girl Scouts Am., 1965; tchr. rep. ARC, 1971—91; host family exchange students Western Mich. U., 1971—80; chair pub. affairs Kalamazoo Edn. Assn., 1972; appt. by state rep. to Friend of Ct. rev. com. Mich. Women's Commn., 1979—80; pub. affairs com. Planned Parenthood, 1977—79, state del., 1978—85; bd. dirs. Western Mich. U. Partners in Dance, 2001—05, v.p., 2003, pres., 2004, co-chair programs and events, 2003—05; vol. Portage Pub. Libr., 2002—06, 2002—05; mem. exec. com. Dem. Party Kalamazoo County, 1972—86, county and state convs. del., 1972—86, mem. state platform com., 1978, candidate county commn., 1987, mem. state ctrl. com., 1979—84, campaign mgr. 6th congl. dist., 1986; bd. dirs. South Ctrl. Mich. ACLU, 1983—93, pres., 1988—90, bd. dirs. Mich. affiliate, 1986—93, mem. exec. bd., 1987—93, nat. del., 1989—91, chair Mich. delegation, 1989; bd. dirs. Planned Parenthood/Reproductive Health South Ctrl. Mich., Inc., 1972—85; mem. polit. action com. Mich. Edn. Assn., 1975—89, mem. governing bd., 1976—78, chair 3d congl. com., 1976, 1978, 46th dist. house com. chair, 1976, 1978. Named Outstanding Vol., Planned Parenthood South Ctrl. Mich., 2005; recipient award, Kalamazoo Pub. Schs. Hispanic Program, 1983, award for participation in Classrooms of Tomorrow Computer Program, Gov.of Mich., 1990. Mem.: Western Mich. Univ. Ptnrs. in Dance (bd. dirs. 2001—05, v.p. 2003, program and events co-chair 2003—05, pres. 2004), Kalamazoo/Numazu Sister City Com. (life; host family com. chair 2003, exch. tchr. com. chair 2003, 2004). Democrat. Unitarian Universalist. Avocations: reading, music, dance, water related activities, gardening. Home: 2612 Chopin Kalamazoo MI 49024-6634

DAHLMANN, MARY ELSA, secondary school educator; b. Pitts., Sept. 3, 1954; d. Raymond Anthony and Hilda Teresa (McGuire) Hahn; m. Thomas Lynn Dahlmann, Sept. 4, 1976; 1 child, Charles Thomas. BS in Biology, California U. of Pa., California, Pa., 1975; BS in Med. Tech., California U. of Pa., 1976; M.H.A., Wilkes U., Wilkes Barre, Pa., 2000; Secondary Edn. Cert., Susquehanna U., Selinsgrove, Pa., 2003. Tchr. C.W. Rice Mid. Sch., Northumberland, Pa., Shikellamy HS, Sunbury, Pa. Adj. faculty Thomas Jefferson U. Merit badge counselor Boy Scouts Am., Selinsgrove, 1996—, troop com. sec., 1999—2004, dist. roundtable commr. Williamsport, Pa., 2001—04, dist. tng. chair, 2004—. Recipient Dist. Award of Merit, Boy Scouts Am., 2004. Mem.: Assn. for Profls. in Infection Control (N.E. Pa. chpt. bd. dirs., pres.). Avocation: gardening.

DAHL REEVES, GRETCHEN, occupational therapist, educator; b. Highland Park, Mich., July 20, 1949; d. Henry Raymond and Dorothy Ann (Canavan) Dahl; m. Jerry Charles Reeves, Dec. 30, 1970; children: Branden Levi, Garrett Whitney. BS magna cum laude, Mich. State U., 1970, MA, 1973; M of Occupl. Therapy, Western Mich. U., 1974; PhD, U. Mich., 1994. Cert. occupl. therapist. Staff therapist State of Mich., Howell, 1974-75, Clinton County Intermediate, St. Johns, Mich., 1975-78, City of Pontiac (Mich.) Schs., 1978-80; owner, oeprator Devel. Therapy Svc., Oxford, Mich., 1980—; asst. prof Med. Coll. Ohio, Toledo, 1996—. Vis. asst. prof. Oakland U., Rochester, Mich., 1993-96. Contbr. chpt. to books, articles to profl. jours.; presenter/spkr. in field. Bd. dirs. North Star Acad., Southfield, Mich., 1995-96. Recipient Dean's award for tchg. excellence Med. Coll. Ohio, 1997, Jane Walter award for acad. excellence Oakland U., 1998. Fellow Am. Occupl. Therapy Assn.; mem. Nat. Rehab. Assn., Soc. for Rsch. in Child Devel. Office: Med Coll Ohio Dept Occupl Therapy 3015 Arlington Ave Toledo OH 43614-2570 E-mail: greeves@mco.edu.

DAHLSTROM, BECKY JOANNE, journalist; b. Olympia, Wash., Sept. 24, 1957; d. Timothy Craddick and Shirleen (Stout) Roan; m. Kenneth W. Dahlstrom, Mar. 17, 1978 (div. Aug. 1984); children: Levi, Olivia; m. Robert Salley, Sr., Feb. 21, 1986 (div. Sept. 1994); 1 child, Robert, Jr. Student, Am. Coll., 1985-86. Writer Hospital, 1988-89; admitting clerk County Ventura (Calif.) Healthcare Agy., 1989—. Writer, editor West Fork (Ark.) Elem. Sch., 1970-73. Author: (poem) My Authority, 1980 (Hon. mention 1980). Mem. Future Bus. Leaders Am. Republican. Baptist. Avocations: drawing, writing, horseback riding, ceramics.

DAHLSTROM, PATRICIA MARGARET, real estate appraiser; b. L.A., Calif., Apr. 29, 1951; d. Colin Rose, Jr. and Patricia Rose; m. David Keith Dahlstrom, July 15, 1989; m. Peter Klaus Reese, Dec. 3, 1972 (div. Dec. 31, 1983); 1 child, Steven Eric Reese. BA in Urban Econ. Geography, Calif. State U., Northridge, 1976, MA in Urban Econ. Geography, 1984; BSN, UCLA, Westwood, Calif., 1995, MSN, 1997. Cert. profl. logistician, Soc. of Logistics Engrs., 1987; RN Calif., 1995, lic. Nurse Practitioner, Bd. of Registered Nursing, Calif., 1997, cert. Pediatric Nurse Practitioner, Nat. Certification Bd. of Pediatric Nurse Practitioners, 1997. Instr. Moorpark (Calif.) Coll., 1977—78; rsch. analyst Natelson Co., Westwood, Calif., 1976—78; logistics engr. Litton, Data Systems Divsn., Van Nuys, Calif., 1980—84; program mgr. Micom, Simi Valley, Calif., 1984—86; logistics engr. Allied Signal, Ocean Systems, Sylmar, Calif., 1986—87; logistics engr./project lead Litton, Data Systems Divsn., Van Nuys/Agoura Hills, Calif., 1987—91; PNP Children's Hosp., Los Angeles, Calif., 1997—98, Lavin and VanDopp, MDs, Tarzana/Van Nuys, Calif., 1998—99, Kaiser Permanent, Panorama City, Calif., 2000—01; part-time faculty instr. Calif. State U., Dept. Health Scis., Northridge, 1998—2002; appraiser Graphic Appraisal Svcs., Sherman Oaks, Calif., 2003—; tchg. asst. UCLA Sch. Nursing, Westwood, Calif., 1995—97. Workshop leader Profls. Plus Networking Group, Lancaster, Calif., 1991—92; cons. AMEX, Compton, Calif., 1986—86. On-screen nurse practitioner & co-author: (instructional video) Physical Assessment: Head to Toe Examination in 45 Minutes. Fundraiser Am. Stroke Assn., L.A., Calif., 2003; pres. Calif. Coalition of Nurse Practitioners, Region 16, San Fernando Valley, 1999—2000; sec. Calif. Coalition of Nurse Practitioners, Region 13, L.A., 1998—99; ch. coun. Ch. of the Foothills, Sylmar, Calif., 2002—. Fellow: Nat. Assn. of Pediatric Nurse Practitioners; mem.: Soc. for Adolescent Medicine, Am. Acad. of Pediat., Calif. Coalition of Nurse Practitioners, Golden Key, Sigma Theta Tau. Democrat. Lutheran. Avocations: travel, walking marathons, reading, gardening, music, theater, movies.

DAHMUS, TERESA A., lawyer; BA magna cum laude in Internat. Studies and French, Tex. A&M U., Coll. Sta., 1997; student, Université Stendhal, Grenoble, France, 1997; M of Pub. Affairs, U. Tex. Lyndon B. Johnson Sch. Pub. Affairs, 2003; JD, U. Tex. Sch. Law, 2003. Bar: Tex. 2003. Atty. Eggleston & Briscoe, Houston, 2003—04, Popp & Ikard, L.L.P., Austin, Tex., 2004—05, Ikard, Wynne & Ratliff, L.L.P., Austin, Tex. Contbr. articles to profl. jours. Named a Rising Star, Tex. Super Lawyers mag., 2006. Mem.: Austin Young Lawyers Assn., Austin Bar Assn. Office: Ikard Wynne & Ratliff LLP 515 Congress Ave Ste 1320 Austin TX 78701 E-mail: teresa@iwrlaw.com.*

DAHSE, LINDA JEWELL, social studies educator; b. Jersey City, Feb. 28, 1949; d. Richard Walter and Eleanor Gertrude Jewell; m. Kenneth William Dahse, Feb. 23, 1974; 1 child, Shannon Beth. BA in History, Fairleigh Dickinson U., Teaneck, NJ, 1971; MA in Social Sci., William Paterson U., Wayne, NJ, 1990, postgrad., 1992. Secondary tchr. social studies Rutherford Pub. Schs., NJ, 1981—86, 1991—. Adj. prof. history Bergen CC, Paramus, NJ, 2003—. Mem.: Rutherford Edn. Assn. (rep. 2005—), NJ Edn. Assn., Humane Soc., NJ Coun. Social Studies, Nat. Coun. Social Studies. Avocations: reading, travel, politics, horseback riding, kayaking. Home: 50 Catherine Ct Ringwood NJ 07456 Office: Rutherford HS 56 Elliott Pl Rutherford NJ 07070

DAI, WEILI, information technology executive; b. China; m. Sehat Sutardja; 2 children. BS in Computer Sci., U. Calif., Berkeley. Positions in software devel. and project mgmt. Canon Rsch. Ctr. Am., Inc.; co-founder Marvell Tech. Grp. Ltd., 1995, v.p., corp. sec., bd. dirs., 1995, exec. v.p. and gen. mgr. comm. and consumer bus. grp., 1999—, COO, 2006—. Named one of 400 Richest Ams., Forbes mag., 2006. Office: Marvell Semiconductor Inc 5488 Marvell Ln Santa Clara CA 95054*

DAIE, JALEH, investment company executive; Exec. ptnr. Aurora Equity; head sci. & tech. The David and Lucile Packard Found.; prof., dept. chair Rutgers U., New Brunswick, NJ, dir. plant biology grad. program, dept. chmn., founder, dir. Interdisciplinary Ctr.; sr. sci. advisor U. Wis. System, Madison; prof. U. Wis. Sci. liaison to pres.'s nat. sci. and tech. coun.; spl. asst. office of chief scientist NOAA, U.S. Dept. Commerce, Commn. Biotech. and Global Food Security, Ctr. Internat. Strat. Studies; dir. Leadership Found.; treas., exec. com. U.S. Space Found.; treas. Legacy Found.; trustee World Affairs Coun. No. Calif.; spkr. in field; mem. White House Fellow selection panel; mem. adv. bd. Nokia/Innavent, Investigen, Teksia, U. Calif., Davis, Common Wealth Club, Lightfull Foods. Inducted into Hall of Fame Women in Tech. Internat.; named to 25 Smartest, Madison mag., Internat. Women Forum; featured Leaders of Sci., The Scientist; Henry Rutgers Rsch. fellow, Tchg. Acad. fellow U. Wis.; recipient lifetime achievement award Teksia. Fellow: AAAS; mem.: Coun. of Sci. Soc. Presidents (chmn.), Assn. Women in Sci. (pres.), Band of Angels, Phi Kappa Phi, Sigma Xi (bd. dirs.).

DAIGLE, BARBARA DIANNE, elementary school educator; b. East Liverpool, Ohio, Feb. 2, 1960; d. Jack Earl and Barbara Ann Talbott; m. Kenneth Alan Daigle, July 24, 1982; children: Kellie Elise, Emily Kate. BA in Polit. Sci., Youngstown State U., 1982; MEd, Marygrove Coll., 1999. Cert. tchr. in elem. edn. (K-8) Ohio, 1988, reading validation (K-12) 1987. Reading, math. tchr. E.J. Blott Elem. Sch., Youngstown, Ohio, 1988—90; elem. tchr. Roosevelt Elem. Sch., McDonald, Ohio, 1992—, mem. textbook selection com.; mem. sch. improvement com. Bldg. rep. teaming to impact student achievement Trumbull County, 2005; mem. textbook com. Roosevelt Elem. Sch., McDonald, Ohio, 2003—04, mem. sch. improvement com., 2004—05. Co-author (editor): (plays) The Rainforest, 2000; contbr. columns in newspapers. Participant Hands Across Am., Salem, Ohio, Relay for Life, Youngstown, 2005, com. mem., 2005; missions com. mem. United Meth. Ch., Girard, Ohio, 2004, 2005. Mem.: NEA, Trumbull Area Reading Coun., OH Edn. Assn., McDonald Edn. Assn., Nat. Sci. Tchrs. Assn. Democrat. Methodist. Avocations: reading, exercise, photography, travel, theater. Office: Roosevelt Elem Sch 410 W 7th St Mc Donald OH 44437 Personal E-mail: iluvrus43@yahoo.com.

DAIGLE, SARA ELIZABETH, elementary school educator; b. Bryn Mawr, Pa., July 17; d. Jess Joseph and Mary Elizabeth (McMahon) Diefenderfer; m. Richard Allan Daigle, Apr. 10, 1987. BS, West Chester (Pa.) U., 1977, M in Elem. Edn., 1989. Cert. elem. tchr., Pa. Grade 4 tchr. Coatesville (Pa.) Area Sch. Dist., 1978-84, adult educator, 1979-81, second/third split position, 1984-85, grade 2 tchr., 1985—, grade 2 and 3 chairperson, 1989—, math coord., 1990—. Tchr. expectation student achievement pers. Carl Benner Sch., 1990—; cooperating tcht. West Chester U., 1988—; tutor Coatesville Area Sch. Dist., 1980—, homebound instr., 1987, 92, 2001, 2002; writing second grade math curriculum Math Steering Com., 1989—; mem. Lang. Arts, Social Studies and Crisis Com., 2001- Recipient Gift of Time Tribute parent award, 1991-1995, 2003 Fellow ASCD, NEA, Pa. State Edn. Assn., Coatesville Are Tchrs. Assn. Roman Catholic. Avocations: reading, hiking, continuing education. Home: 129 S Christiana Ave Gap PA 17527 Office: Friendship Elem Sch 296 Reeseville Rd Coatesville PA 19320

DAILEADER, CELIA ROSE, literature educator; b. Huntington, N.Y., Mar. 1, 1968; d. William James Caputi and Dorothy Louise Otto; m. Gary Lynn Taylor, Oct. 24, 2004. PhD, Brandeis U., Waltham, Mass., 1996. Asst. prof. English U. Ala., Tuscaloosa, 1995—99, assoc. prof. English, 1999—2005; prof. English Fla. State U., Tallahassee, 2006—. Author: Racism, Misogyny, and the Othello Myth: Inter-racial Couples from Shakespeare to Spike Lee, Eroticism on the Renaissance Stage: Transcendence, Desire, and the Limits of the Visible; contbg. author: Shakespeare and Race, Shakespeare and Sexuality; editor: (plays) The Tamer Tamed. Mem.: Group for Early Modern Cultural Studies, Shakespeare Assn. Am., Internat. Shakespeare Assn. Avocations: Italian language and culture, swimming, drawing, beach-combing. Office Phone: 850-645-6478.

DAILEY, COLEEN HALL, magistrate; b. East Liverpool, Ohio, Aug. 10, 1955; d. David Lawrence and Deloris Mae (Rosensteel) Hall; m. Donald W. Dailey Jr., Aug. 16, 1980 (div. May 2001); children: Erin Elizabeth, Daniel Lester. Student, Wittenberg U., 1973-75; BA, Youngstown State U., 1977; JD, U. Cin., 1980. Bar: Ohio 1981, U.S. Dist. Ct. (no. dist.) Ohio 1981. Sr. libr. assoc. Marx Law Libr., Cin., 1979-80; law clk. Kapp Law Office, East Liverpool, 1979, 1980-81, assoc., 1981-85; pvt. practice East Liverpool, 1985-95; magistrate Columbiana County, Ohio, 1995—. Spl. counsel Atty. Gen. Ohio, 1985-92. Pres. Columbiana County Young Dems., 1985-87; bd. dirs. Big Bros./Big Sisters Columbiana County, Inc., Lisbon, Ohio, 1984-87, Planned Parenthood Mahoning Valley, Inc., 1993-97; trustee Ohio Women Inc., 1991-95; mem. Columbiana County Progress Coun., Inc. Mem.: ABA, Ohio Women's Bar Assn. (trustee 1997—99), Columbiana County Bar Assn., Ohio Assn. Magistrates (chmn. domestic rels. sect. 1998—2000, 2002—06), Ohio Bar Assn. (Ohio Supreme Ct. Joint Task Force on Gender Fairness, family law specialization bd.). Democrat. Lutheran. Office: Columbiana County Common Pleas Court 105 S Market St Lisbon OH 44432-1255 Office Phone: 330-424-7777 ext 1102. Business E-Mail: cdailey@ccclerk.org.

DAILEY, DIANNE K., lawyer; b. Great Falls, Mont., Oct. 10, 1950; d. Gilmore and Patricia Marie (Linnane) Halverson. BS, Portland State U., 1977; JD, Lewis & Clark Coll., 1982. Assoc. Bullivant, Houser, Bailey PC, Portland, Oreg., 1982-88, ptnr., 1988—, pres., 2002—06. Contbr. articles to profl. jours. Fellow: Am. Bar Found.; mem.: ABA (chair task force on involvement of women 1990—93, governing coun. 1992—99, liaison to commn. on women 1993—97, vice chair tort and ins. practice sect. 1995—96, chair-elect tort and ins. practice sect. 1996—97, standing com. environ. law 1996—99, chair tort and ins. practice sect. 1997—98, chair sect. officers conf. 1998—2001, governing coun. 2003, del. 2003, ins. coverage litigation com., chair task force CERCLA reauthorization, law practice mgmt. sect., comm. com.), Fedn. Ins. and Corp. Counsel, Def. Rsch. Inst., Multnomah Bar Assn. (bd. dirs. 1994—95), Oreg. State Bar, Wash. Bar Assn. Office: Bullivant Houser Bailey PC 300 Pioneer Tower 888 SW 5th Ave Ste 300 Portland OR 97204-2089 Office Phone: 503-499-4430. Business E-Mail: dianne.dailey@bullivant.com.

DAILEY, JANET, writer; b. Storm Lake, Iowa, May 21, 1944; d. Boyd and Louise Haradon; m. William Dailey; 2 stepchildren. Student pub. schs., Independence, Iowa. Sec., Nebr., Iowa, 1963-74. Author: No Quarter Asked, 1976, After the Storm, 1976, Boss Man From Ogallala, 1976, Savage Land, 1976, Land of Enchantment, 1976, Fire and Ice, 1976, The Homeplace, 1976, Dangerous Masquerade, 1977, Night of the Cotillion, 1977, Valley of the Vapors, 1977, Fiesta San Antonio, 1977, Show Me, 1977, Bluegrass King, 1977, A Lyon's Share, 1977, The Widow and the Wastrel, 1977, Giant of Mesabi, 1978, The Ivory Cane, 1978, The Indy Man, 1978, Darling Jenny, 1978, Reilly's Woman, 1978, To Tell the Truth, 1978, Sonora Sundown, 1978, Big Sky Country, 1978, Something Extra, 1978, Master Fiddler, 1978, Beware of the Stranger, 1978, The Matchmakers, 1978, For Bitter or Worse, 1979, Green Mountain Man, 1979, Six White Horses, 1979, Summer Mahogany, 1979, Touch the Wind, 1979, Strange Bedfellow, 1979, Low Country Liars, 1979, Sweet Promise, 1979, For Mike's Sake, 1979, Sentimental Journey, 1979, A Land Called Deseret, 1979, The Bride of the Delta Queen, 1979, Tidewater Lover, 1979, Lord of the High Lonesome, 1980, Kona Winds, 1980, The Boston Man, 1980, The Rogue, 1980, Bed of Grass, 1980, The Thawing of Mara, 1980, The Mating Season, 1980, Southern Nights, 1980, Ride the Thunder, 1980, Enemy in Camp, 1980, Difficult Decision, 1980, Heart of Stone, 1980, One of the Boys, 1980, Wild and Wonderful, 1981, A Tradition of Pride, 1981, The Traveling Kind, 1981, The Hostage Bride, 1981, Dakota Dreamin', 1981, For the Love of God, 1981, Night Way, 1981, This Calder Sky, 1981, Lancaster Men, 1981, Terms of Surrender, 1982, With a Little Luck, 1982, Wildcatter's Woman, 1982, Northern Magic, 1982, That Carolina Summer, 1982, This Calder Range, 1982, Foxfire Light, 1982, The Second Time, 1982, Mistletoe and Holly, 1982, Stands a Calder Man, 1983, Separate Cabins, 1983, Western Man, 1983, Calder Born, Calder Bred, 1983, Best Way to Lose, 1983, Leftover Love, 1984, Silver Wings, Santiago Blue, 1984, The Pride of Hannah Wade, 1985, The Glory Game, 1985, The Great Alone, 1986, Heiress, 1987, Rivals, 1989, Masquerade, 1990, Aspen Gold, 1991, Tangled Vines, 1992, Riding High, 1994, The Proud and The Free, 1994, Touch the Wind, 1994, Summer Mahogany, 1995, Legacies, 1996, Homecoming, 1997, Illusions: A Novel, 1997, The Prodigal Daughter, 1998, This Calder Sky, 1999, Calder Pride,

1999, A Capital Holiday, 2001, Green Calder Grass, 2002, Calder Promise, 2004, Lone Calder Star, 2005. Recipient Golden Heart award Romance Writers Am., 1981, Romantic Times Contemporary award, 1983.

DAILEY, LYNNE, secondary school educator; Physical education teacher. Recipient Secondary Sch. Physical Educ. Teacher of the Yr. awd., Nat. Assn. for Sport and Physical Education, 1993. Office: 3760 W Bilby Rd Tucson AZ 85746-3517

DAILEY, MARILYN, elementary school educator; b. Lucedale, Miss., Apr. 30, 1957; d. Jesse Lee and Vera Mae Chambers; m. William Harry Dailey, July 27, 1985. BS, William Carey Coll., Hattiesburg, Miss., 1982; MS, Ala. State U., 1995, EdS, 2001. Tchr. spl. edn. New Augusta (Miss.) H.S., 1982-83, Richton (Miss.) H.S., 1983-85; tchr. 1st grade Frisco City (Ala.) Elem. Schs., 1985-86; tchr. 4th grade Southside Elem. Sch., Evergreen, Ala., 1987-89, Thurgood Marshall Elem. Sch., Evergreen, 1989—. Named Tchr. of Yr., Conecuh County Bd. Edn., 1997-98. Mem. Internat. Reading Assn., Ala. Edn. Assn., Assn. Supervision and Curriculum, Nat. Assn. Elem. Sch. Prins., Nat. Coun. Tchrs. English, Sigma Gamma Rho, Kappa Delta Pi, Phi Delta Kappa. Avocations: singing, art. Home: PO Box 917 Evergreen AL 36401-0917

DAILY, ANNA WILKINS, science educator; b. Louisburg, N.C., Feb. 15, 1943; d. Ernest and Susie Anna (Collins) Wilkins; m. Albert James Daily, Jr., May 21, 1965 (dec.); children: Albert J. III, Dwayne G., Letecia A. BS Biology, St. Augustine's Coll., 1965; EdM Urban Edn., Rutgers U., 1972; MA in Couseling Edn., Kean U., Union, NJ, 2003. Tchr. Tri-County Headstart, Louisburg, N.C., 1966; lab. technician Perth Amboy (N.J.) Gen. Hosp., 1966-70, Med. Lab., Metuchen, N.J., 1970-71; tchr. Plainfield (N.J.) Bd. Edn., 1971-72, Perth Amboy Bd. Edn., 1972—2005; urban tchr. intern AT&T, Murray Hill, N.J., 1989; ret., 2006. Adviser Health Occupation Students of Am., Perth Amboy, 1976-83, Health Career Awarness Club, 1990-93; mentor/adviser Celebration of Tchg., Perth Amboy, 1986—; mentor tchr. Perth Amboy Afro-Am. Club, 1994—97; adj. instr. Jersey City State Coll., 1989-91; adj. tchr. prep program, NJ City U., 1989-1991. Women's Day chmn. 2d Bapt. Ch., Perth Amboy, 1984-86, pres. edn. com., 1973-90, sec. usher bd., 1968-90; pres. First Bapt. Ch. Pastor's Aid Ministry, 1994—; trustee Perth Amboy Pub. Libr., 1994—, sec., 2004—; mem. exec. bd., com. chair Perth Amboy area NAACP, 1976—, 3d v.p. NJ State NAACP; vol. Domestic Violence Response Team, 1995—; mem. parents group Rutgers Upward Bound. Recipient N.J. Disting. H.S. Tchr. award Princeton U., 1983, Perth Amboy Tchr. of Yr., 1982, Middlesex Tchr. of Yr., 1982, N.J. Gov.'s Tchr. award, 1995 Mem. NAACP (3d v.p. N.J. state chpt. 2005), Nat. Sci. Tchrs. Assn. (Nat. Exemplary H.S. Sci. Tchr. award 1984), N.J. Edn. Assn. (local pres. 1994—2000), N.J. Biology Tchrs. Assn. Home: 439 Bruck Ave Perth Amboy NJ 08861-2120

DAILY, DIANA SMITH, music educator; b. Livermore, Calif., July 25, 1968; d. Charles Arthur Smith; m. David Douglas Daily, Aug. 6, 2002. MusB, U. of the Pacific, Stockton, Calif., 1990. Cert. tchr. Calif., 1990. Tchr. music Tracy Unified Sch. Dist., Calif., 1996—2006. Children's tchr. Calvary Cmty. Ch., Manteca, Calif., 2002—06. Mem.: Music Eductors Nat. Conf. Republican. Home: 16109 Bizzibe St Lathrop CA 95330

DAILY, FREDA SMITH, superintendent; b. Calberty County, Ala., Jan. 30, 1940; d. Cletus V. and FloElla Elliot Smith; m. Marvin Andrew Daily, June 29, 1957; children: Rebecca Susan, Mark Andrew. BSc, U North Ala., 1972; MA, U. North Ala., 1976; D of Edn., U. Ala., 1992. Cert. Education Specialist U. North Ala., 1978. Tchr. Colbert County Sch., Tuscumbia, 1972—93, dir. programs, 1993—2000, supt. Tuscumbia, Ala., 2000—03. Author: (book) A Heritage to Treasure, 2004, The Riverton Rose Trial, 1971. Democrat. Meth. Avocations: genealogy, writing. Home: 2775 Moody Lane Cherokee AL 35616

DAILY, GRETCHEN CARA, ecologist, environmental services administrator; b. Washington, Oct. 19, 1964; d. Charles Dennis and Suzanne Rachel (Schubert) D. BS, Stanford U., 1986, MS, 1987, PhD, 1992. Ctr. for Conservation Biology/Nature Conservancy fellow Stanford (Calif.) U., 1988-92; Winslow/Heinz postdoctoral fellow U. Calif., Berkeley, 1992—; assoc. prof. biology Stanford (Calif.) U., dir., Tropical Rsch. Program, Ctr. for Conservation. Sci. advisor IPAT Prodns. (film), Stanford, 1995. Author (with PR Ehrlich & AH Ehrlich) The Stork and the Plow: The Equity Solution to the Human Dilemma, 1995, Nature's Services: Societal Dependence on Natural Ecosystems, 1997, (with Katherine Ellison) The New Economy of Nature: The Quest to Make Conservatoin Profitable, 2002; Contbr. over 150 articles to profl. jours. Recipient Frances Lou Kallman award Stanford U., 1992, 21st Century Scientist award, 2000; Named Pew scholar in conservation and environ., Pew Found., 1994, Fellow, Aldo Leopard Leadership Program, 1999, Smith Sr. Scholar, The Nature Conservancy, 2003. Mem. Rocky Mtn. Biol. Lab; Fellow, Am. Acad. Arts & Sciences, NAS. Office: Stanford U Ctr Conservation Biology 385 Serra Mall Stanford CA 94305 Office Phone: 650-723-9452. Office Fax: 650-725-1992. E-mail: gdaily@stanford.edu.

DAILY, JEAN A., marketing executive; b. Bloomington, Ill., Nov. 20, 1949; d. William H. and Niola N. (Thompson) D.; m. Ronald R. Willis, June 14, 1968 (div. 1972); m. Rodger D. Melick, Aug. 15, 1981. BS, Ill. State U., 1975. Sr. acctg. clk. Country Cos., Bloomington, 1976-78; owner, mgr. Danvers (Ill.) Motor Co., 1979-85; office mgr., ops. mgr. Goods Carpet, Bloomington, 1986-87; dir. mktg. Westminster Village Inc., Bloomington, 1987—. Chair Com. to Elect Judge Prall, Bloomington, 1996; publ. chair Danvers Days, 1982—85; bd. dirs., publ. rels. & devel. advisor Twin Cities Ballet, Bloomington, 1994—96; bd. dirs. ARC, 1991—94; pres. Chestnut Health Sys. Aux., 1995—98, 1999, treas., 1997—2001; vol. Arthritis Telethon, St. Jude Golf Tournament, 1997—2004; publicity chair Gardenwalk 97; mem. adv. bd. Arthritis Found., 1997—2001; apptd. cabinet bd. Ill. Life Svcs. Network Assisted Living, 1997—2003, sec., 1997—99, 2006—, pres. housing cabinet, 2003, 2004—, corp. bd., 2004—, sec., 2006. Mem. Women in Comms., Nat. Soc. Fund Raising Execs. (co-editor chpt. newsletter 1989-91). Avocations: reading, crafts, golf, photography, square dance. Office: Westminster Village 2025 E Lincoln St Bloomington IL 61701-5995 Office Phone: 309-663-6474. Business E-Mail: jdaily@westminstervillage.inc.com.

DAJANI, VIRGINIA, art association administrator; Exec. dir. Am. Acad. Arts and Letters, N.Y.C., 1990—. Office: Am Acad Arts and Letters 633 W 155th St New York NY 10032-7501 Office Phone: 212-368-5900. E-mail: academy@artsandletters.org.

DAKE, MARCIA ALLENE, retired nursing educator, dean; b. Bemus Point, N.Y., May 22, 1923; d. Earl B. and Bernice DeLeo (Haskin) D. Diploma, Crouse Irving Hosp., 1944; BS, Syracuse U., 1951; MA, Columbia U., 1955, EdD, 1958. RN. Tchr., sch. nurse various locations, 1946—48; chmn. health dept. SUNY, Oneonta, 1952—56; dean coll. nursing U. Ky., Lexington, 1958—72; dir. dept. nursing edn. ANA, Kansas City, 1972—74; project dir. program devel. nursing ARC, Washington, 1975—79; dir. nursing edn. James Madison U. Coll. Nursing, 1979—81; prof. dean Coll. Nursing, 1981—88; ret., 1988. Editor, resident photographer: Greenspring Village Photo Directories, 2000—; programmer, host Closed Circuit TV Studio, 2000. Mem. Ky. Bd. Nursing Edn. Nurse Registration, 1969-72, pres., 1970-72; pres. Va. Coun. Deans of Baccalaureate Nursing Programs, 1981-84; nurse officer Civil Def. Otsego County, N.Y., 1953-56; mem. Def. Adv. Com. on Women in Svcs., 1963-65; mem. Ky. Comprehensive Health Planning Coun., 1968-71; pres. Ky. League for Nursing, 1961-65; bd. dir. Cmty. Ch. Coll., Sun City Ctr., Fla., 1989-92, Sun City Ctr. Guardianship Found., 1990-98; trustee United Cmty. Ch., Sun City Ctr., 1993-96, chmn. pers. com., 1994-96, fin. com., 1994-95, vice chmn. bd. trustees, 1995-96, stewardship com., 1996-98, mem. pastoral rels. com., 1996-98, mem. long range planning com., 1996-97, chmn. pastoral rels. com., 1998—; sec. Caloosa Women's Golf Assn., Sun City Ctr., 1991-92; treas. Greater Sun City Ctr. Disaster Coun., 1992-94; mem., vice chmn. resident adv. com. Greenspring Village, Springfield, Va., 1999-2000, corr. sec. resident adv. com., 2001; prodr., host Channel 6 T.V Greenspring Village, 2001; prodr., pub. resident/staff photo directories, 2000-. 1st lt. U.S. Army Nurse Corps., 1945—46. Fellow Nat. League Nursing; mem. ANA, Va. Nurses Assn. (pres. dist. 9 1983-85), Va. Soc. Profl. Nurses (treas. 1983-88), Va. Assn. Colls. Nursing (sec. 1980-82, pres. 1982-85), Alliance Nursing Orgns. (chmn. Va. 1985-88), LWV, Delta Kappa Gamma, Kappa Delta Pi, Pu Lambda Theta. Address: 222 7442 Spring Village Dr Springfield VA 22150-4444

DAKELMAN, RHONDA ELYSE, physical education educator; b. New Brunswick, NJ, July 14, 1958; d. Jay H. and Thelma N. Dakelman. BS, Pa. State U., University Park, 1980. Cert. secondary edn. NJ, 1976. Personal trainer Gold's Gym, Monmouth Junction, NJ, 1994—2004; phys. edn. tchr. Perth Amboy Bd. Edn., NJ, 1996—. Track and field coach Perth Amboy Pub. Schs., 1996—. Mem. Hadassah, Highland Park, NJ, 1998—2006. Mem.: AAPHERD (assoc.). Achievements include Champion Body Builder from 1993-2000. Home: 3072 Cypress Ct Monmouth Junction NJ 08852 Office: Perth Amboy Board of Education 178 Barracks St Perth Amboy NJ 08861 Office Phone: 732-376-6030. Business E-Mail: rhondakelman@paps.net.

DAKIN, CHRISTINE WHITNEY, dancer, educator; b. New Haven, Aug. 25, 1949; d. James Irving, Jr. and Jean Evelyn (Coulter) Crump; m. Robert Ford Dakin, June 21, 1969 (div. Sept. 1982); m. Stephen J. Mauer, Aug. 1, 1985. Student, U. Mich., 1967-71; D of Arts (hon.), Shenandoah U., 1996. Performer, teacher Ann Arbor Dance Theater, Mich., 1965-71; tchr. Ann Arbor Pub. Schs., 1967-70, Lincoln Ctr. Inst., N.Y.C., 1978, Guanajuato U., Mex., 1982; vis. artist USIA Vladivastock, Vladivastock, Russia, 1992; ArtsLink grantee, vis. artist Vladivastock, 1996; tchr., faculty advisor, choreographer Ballet Nacional de Mex., 1993—, U. Colima, Mexico, 2000—; vis. artist USIA Ballet Contemporaneo, Buenos Aires, 1993; prin. dancer Martha Graham Dance Co., N.Y.C., 1976—. Dancer, rehearsal dir. Pearl Lang. Dance Co., 1972-76, Kazuko Hirabayashi Dance Co., 1974-76; faculty Martha Graham Sch., 1972—, Juilliard Sch., 1992—, Alvin Alley Am. Dance Ctr., 1989-93. Appeared in: It's Hard to Be a Jew, 1972, The Dybuk, 1975; appeared (with Martha Graham Dance Co.) Covent Garden, London, 1976, Met. Opera, 1980, Bklyn. Acad. Music, 1994, Sta. WNET Dance in Am. Series, 1979; Young Artist in Performance at The White House, Sta. WNET, 1982, (with Rudolph Nureyev) Paris Opera, Berlin Opera, 1984, N.Y. State Theater, 1985; NHK Film, Japan, 1990, Paris Opera Film, 1991, (documentary film) Les Printemps du Sacre, 1993; assoc. founder Buglisi/Foreman Dance, 1994, (with Buglisi/Foreman Dance) Runes of the Heart, Kennedy Ctr., 1997; assoc. artistic dir. Martha Graham Dance Co., 1997, artistic dir., 2001. Am. Dance Festival scholar, 1969, Garcia-Robles Sr. scholar Fulbright Found., 1999; recipient award Dance Mag., 1994, U. Mich. Alumni award, 2000, Bessie award, 2004; grantee Rockefeller U.S.-Mex. Fund for Culture, 1997-98, 2001. Mem. Am. Guild Mus. Artists (life, bd. govs.) Office: Martha Graham Dance 344 East 59th Street New York NY 10022 Business E-Mail: cdakin@marthagrahamdance.org.

DAKOFSKY, LADONNA JUNG, medical counseling physician, radiation oncologist; b. N.Y.C., Oct. 30, 1960; d. George S. and Kay (Han) Chung. BA magna cum laude, Columbia U., N.Y.C., 1982; MD, NYU, 1987. Bd. cert. radiation oncologist. Rsch. asst. dept. neurology UCLA, 1980-81, Harvard U., Boston, 1982; tchr. chemistry St. Ann's Sch., Brooklyn Heights, N.Y., 1982-83; resident in internal medicine Lenox Hill Hosp., N.Y.C., 1987-88; resident in radiation oncology Hosp. of U. Pa., Phila., 1988-91; instr. in radiation oncology New Eng. Med. Ctr., Boston, 1991-92; attending physician Norwalk (Conn.) Hosp., 1992—. Clin. asst. prof. radiation oncology Yale U., 1994—; prin. investigator RTOG cancer rsch. Norwalk Hosp., exec. com. hosp. staff, IPA chair of quality improvement subcom.; physician adminstr. Norwalk Radiology Cons.; acad. advisor, intern mentor devel., med. counseling U. Conn., 2004. Mem. jr. com. Boys Club N.Y.; sponsor Mus. City of N.Y.; mem. com. Vocat. Found., N.Y.C.; mem. Jr. League of Stamford-Norwalk. Marine Biol. Lab. scholar, 1981. Mem. AMA, Assn. Therapeutic Radiology and Oncology, Fairfield County Med. Assn. (Melville Magida award 1998, Best Younger Physician in Fairfield County 1998), New Eng. Cancer Soc., Met. Breast Cancer Group. Presbyterian. Avocations: writing, sailing, voice. Office: Expert Med Counseling 7 Sweetheart Ln Sandy Hook CT 06482-1481 Office Phone: 203-270-6913, 203-270-6913.

DALE, ADRIANNE MARIE, information technology executive, consultant; d. Almore Marcus and Marie Antoinette (Dale) Dale. BS, Howard U., Washington, 1961. Cert. med. technologist Am. Soc. for Clin. Pathology, 1967. Med. technologist Providence Hosp., Washington, 1967—71; med. tech. instr. D.C. Gen. Hosp., 1971—72; assoc. prof., med. tech. Prince Georges C.C., Largo, Md., 1972—87; cons. D.C. Commn. Women, Washington, 1987—87; adminstrv. asst. Episcopal Ch. Women Diocese of Washington, 1989—90; program officer Episcopal Diocese of Washington, 1990—99; founder and CEO Mouse Calls, LLC, 2000—. Editor: (anthology) People of the Promise; author: (biography) Earl Neil: Black Civil Rights Reformer. Vol. D.C. Crisis Hotline, Washington, 1995, Arena Stage, 2003—; diocesan/parish cons. Episcopal Diocese Washington, 1985—99; lay leader Trinity Epic. Ch., Washington, 1987—2003; mem. All Souls Unitarian Choir, 2003—; sec. Episcopal Sr. Ministries, 1993—99; mem. ByteBack Cmty. Computer Ctr., 2005, Oracle Set Found., 1999—. Recipient Vol. of the Yr. cert., ByteBack Cmty. Computer Ctr., 2005. Episcopalian. Avocations: yoga, crossword puzzles, reading, jazz piano, travel. Office: Mouse Calls LLC Washington DC 20017-2621 Office Phone: 202-529-8934. Personal E-mail: info@mousecalls-llc.com.

DALE, BRENDA STEPHENS, gifted and talented educator; b. Hickory, N.C., Sept. 24, 1942; d. John Doyle and Bertha (Barger) Stephens; m. James Darrell Dale, June 13, 1964; children: Ginger Leigh Rizoti, Jami Lynne Price. BS in English, Appalachian State U., 1964, MA in Reading Edn., 1977; cert. edn. academically gifted, Lenoir Rhyne, Hickory, N.C., 1982. H.S. tchr. Moore County Schs., Carthage, N.C., 1964, Asheboro (N.C.) City Schs., 1964-65; 8th grade tchr. Davidson County Schs., Thomasville, N.C., 1967-68; reading specialist Randolph County Schs., Trinity, N.C., 1970-72, Wilkes N.C. Schs., Wilkesboro, 1972-82, tchr. acad. gifted, 1982—. Tchr. Davidson County C.C., Lexington, N.C., 1965-68, Wilkes C.C., Wilkesboro, 1982-87, 97—; adult literacy tutor, 1997-99. Edn. chair, bd. dirs. Am. Cancer Soc., North Wilkesboro, N.C., 1985-90; mem. Wilkes Regional Med. Ctr. Aux., 1992—; adminstrv. coun. Wilkesboro Meth. Ch., 1997-1999; vol. Samaritan's Purse, 1997-99, 2005—. Tchr. scholar fellow N.C. Ctr. for Advancement of Tchg., Western Carolina U., 1990; recipient C.B. Eller Tchg. award C.B. Eller Found., 1991; finalist Gifted Tchr. of Yr. N.C., 2003 Mem. AAUW (charter, fundraiser 1977-78, bd. dirs., chmn. edn. found. 1992-96), NEA, N.C. Assn. Educators (state del. 2002, intellectual profl. devel. com. 2003-05), Internat. Reading Assn. (sec. 1985-86), Mary Hemphill Svc. Group, So. Appalachian Leadership on Cancer, Lynnwoode Recreation Club, United Meth. Women (dist. membership chair Western N.C. conf. 1996-97, nominating com. 1997-98), Alpha Delta Kappa. Methodist. Avocations: writing, reading, piano. Home: 187 Laurel Mountain Rd North Wilkesboro NC 28659-8122 Office: Wilkes County Schs Main St Wilkesboro NC 28697 Office Phone: 336-667-1121. Business E-Mail: Mustang35@earthlink.net.

DALE, CANDACE L., lawyer; m. Craig Dale. BSW magna cum laude, U. Minn., 1983; JD (hon.), William Mitchell Coll. Law, 1986. Cert.: Nat. Bd. Trial Advocacy (civil trial specialist). Assoc. Burke & Hawkins, Mpls., 1986—87, Schwebel, Goetz & Sieben, P.A., Mpls., 1987—. Named a Top 100 Super Lawyer, MN Law and Politics- Peers, 2000—05; named one of Top 40 Personal Injury Super Lawyers, 2006. Mem.: Minn. Trial Lawyers Assn. Office: Schwebel Goetz & Sieben PA 5120 IDS Center 80 So 8th Street Minneapolis MN 55402 Office Phone: 612-344-0406, 612-333-8361. Office Fax: 612-333-6311. Business E-Mail: cdale@schwebel.com.

DALE, DEBORAH, foundation executive; b. 1967; Chief devel. officer Primavera Found., Tucson. Involved with Voices for Edn., Ariz. Women's Conf., Southern Ariz. Ctr. Against Sexual Assault; Taste of Nation founding com. mem. Share Our Strength; com. mem. Mayor's Costume Ball for Arts; former bd. mem. Cmty. Shares; former bd. chair Mus. Contemporary Art; co-chair Tucson Suffragettes Virgin Voter Ball. Named one of 40 Under 40, Tucson Bus. Edge, 2006. Mem.: Assn. Fundraising Professionals (govt. rels. chair). Office: Primavera Foundation 702 S 6th Ave Tucson AZ 85701 Office Phone: 520-623-5111. Office Fax: 520-623-6434.*

DALE, JUDY RIES, religious organization administrator, consultant; b. Memphis, Dec. 13, 1944; d. James Lorigan and Julia Marie (Schwinn) Ries; m. Eddie Melvin Ashmore, July 12, 1969 (div. Dec. 1983). BA, Rhodes Coll., 1966; M in Religious Edn., So. Bapt. Theol. Sem., 1969, grad. specialist in religious edn., 1969. Cert. tchr. educable mentally handicapped, secondary English, adminstrn. and supervision spl. edn. EMH tchr., curriculum writer, tchr. trainer Jefferson County Bd. Edn., Louisville, 1969-88, ednl. cons., 1988-90; dist. coord. Gt. Lakes dist. Universal Fellowship Met. Cmty. Chs., 1990—2002, spl. asst. comm. and lay resources, 2006—. Lectr. U. Louisville, 1976—77, 1987—90, Jefferson CC, Louisville, 1987—93; mem. program adv. com. Internat. Conf. Spl. Edn., Beijing, 1987—88; mem. faculty Samaritan Inst. Religious Studies, 1992—98. Editor, writer: A Manual of Instructional Strategies, 1985, Handbook for Begining Teachers, 1989. Bd. sec. Com. Ten, Inc., Louisville, 1987—91; v.p. GLUE, 1988—92, pres., 1992—94; mem. steering com. Ky. Fairness Alliance, 2005—, treas., 2005—; mem. membership com. Cmty. Health Trust, 1991—94; chair acad. affairs com. Samaritan Inst. Religious Studies, 1996—97, trustee, 1992—98; mem. programs and budget divsn. Universal Fellowship Met. Cmty. Chs., 1990—97, mem. gen. coun., 1990—2002, active women's secretariat steering com., 1991—95, mem. core team, 1993—2000, chair, 1997—2000, fin. team, 2000—, bd. adminstrn., 2003—05, chmn. risk mgmt. team, 2003—05, sec., 2004—05, chair, 2005. Named Outstanding Elem. Tchr. Am., 1975; recipient Hon. Order of Ky. Cols., 1976, MCC Disting. Lay Leadership award, 1999. Mem.: ACLU, NOW, AAUW, Ky. Coun. Exceptional Children (bd. dirs. 1978—90, Mem. of the Yr. 1987), Coun. Exceptional Children (keynote spkr., mem. exec. com. 1984—88, internat. pres. 1986—87, bd. govs. 1981—88), Women's Alliance, Parents, Family and Friends Lesbians and Gays, Nat. Gay & Lesbian Task Force, Nat. Ctr. Lesbian Rights, Internat. Platform Assn., Gay and Lesbian Assn. Anti-Defamation, Lambda Legal Def. and Edn. Fund, Phi Kappa Phi. Democrat. Avocations: reading, handwork. Home and Office: 1300 Ambridge Dr Louisville KY 40207-2410 Office Phone: 502-897-3821. Personal E-mail: judydale13@aol.com.

DALE, SHANA L., federal agency administrator; b. 1964; BS, U. Tulsa; JD, Calif. Western Sch. Law. Bar: Calif. 1991, DC 1991. Asst. vice-chancellor fed. rels. U. Tex.; Rep. counsel sci., space com. US House Com. Sci., Space, Tech., 1991—95, staff dir. subcommittee Space, Aeronautics, 1995—2000; chief of staff, gen. counsel Office of Sci., Tech. Exec. Office Pres., 2005, dep. dir. Homeland & Nat. Security; dep. adminstr. NASA, 2005—. Spkr. in field. Mem.: Women in Aerospace (Outstanding Alumnus award 2000). Achievements include becoming highest ranking female official in histroy of NASA, 2005. Office: NASA HQ Suite 1M32 Washington DC 20546-0001*

DALE, SHARON KAY, real estate broker; b. San Franciso, July 14, 1940; d. Terrill Odin and Alice Ernestine (Anthony) Glenn; divorced; 1 child, Kimberly Kay. AS, Fresno City Coll., Calif., 1982; student, Calif. State U., Fresno, 1983—. Lic. real estate broker, Calif. Sales assoc. Red Carpet Realtors, Fresno, 1974-77; broker, owner U.S. Cities Realtors, dba, Pierson & Planamento, Inc., Fresno, 1977-80; broker assoc. Easterbrook Constrn., Fresno, 1980-81, 1983-84; exec. sec. Valley Med. Ctr., Fresno, 1981—96; broker Assoc. Adanalian & Jackson Real Estate, Fresno, 1981—83, 1984—85. Dir. div. II U.S. Cities Realtors, Inc. No. Calif, Nev., 1978-80. Vol. St. Agnes Service Guild, Fresno, 1974—, Mental Health Assn., Fresno, 1982-83, Ednl. T.V. Channel 18, Fresno,1983, Valley Med. Ctr. Aux., Fresno, 1985-96, Holiday Guild Children's Hosp. Ctrl. Calif., 2000—. Mem. Fresno County, City C. of C. (Ambassadors Club), Calif. Assn. Realtors, Fresno Bd. Realtors, Multiple Listing Svc., Nat. Bd. Realtors, Fresno State Alumni Assn., Sierra Sport & Racquet Club (Fresno, Calif.) (charter mem.). Republican. Avocations: golf, tennis, photography, travel. Office: Adanalian & Jackson Real Estate 1515 W Shaw Ave Fresno CA 93711-3503 Home: 2823 W Kensington Ln Fresno CA 93711-1157

DALE, SONIA IVETTE, principal; d. Pedro Jesus and Carmen Ilia Rosado; m. Jimmy Earl Dale, June 14, 1969; children: Ivette Michele Beach, Nicole Monique Carsten, Cory Shane. BS in Chemistry, Cameron U., Lawton, Okla., 1972; MEd, U. Montevallo, Ala., 1993; cert. in adminstrn., Jacksonville U., Fla., 2005. Chemistry tchr. Cherokee HS, Canton, Ga., 1974—75; chemistry tchr., dept. chair John Carroll Cath. HS, Birmingham, Ala., 1975—77, 1990—99; pres., mgr. Snelling & Snelling, Birmingham, 1980—89; chemistry tchr. Pell City (Ala.) HS, 1999—2005; prin. W.M. Kennedy Elem., Pell City, 2005—. Adj. prof. Birmingham So. Coll., 1995—2000; adult tutor, cert. reading and ESL tutor Literacy Coun., Pell City, 2001—; presenter in field. Founder, bd. dirs., chmn., sec. Safe Ho. of Shelby County, Pelham, Ala., 1989—99; v.p. St. Clair Literacy Coun., Pell City, 2000—; bd. dirs. Literacy Coun. Ctrl. Ala., Birmingham, 2000—. Nominee Pell City Citizen of Yr., 2003, 2005; named Tchr. of Yr., Birmingham So. Coll., 1999; recipient Svc. to Mankind award, Cahaba Valley Sertoma Club, 1996. Mem.: NEA, Pell City Edn. Assn., Ala. Edn. Assn., Nat. Sci. Tchrs. Assn., Delta Kappa Gamma (sec.). Roman Catholic. Avocations: water sports, reading, sewing, hiking, camping. Office: W M Kennedy Elem 250 Otis Perry Dr Pell City AL 35128 Office Phone: 205-538-7876. Office Fax: 205-538-1659. E-mail: wmksdale2000@yahoo.com.

D'ALENE, ALIXANDRIA FRANCES, human resources professional; b. Buffalo, Oct. 21, 1951; d. Fern (Hill D'A. BA, Canisius Coll., Buffalo, 1973, MS, 1975, MBA, 1980. Tchr. Buffalo pub. schs., 1973-76; pers. cons. Sanford Rose Assocs., Williamsville, NY, 1976-78; mgr. benefits adminstrn. Svc. Sys. Corp., Clarence, NY, 1978-80; mgr. employee rels. Del. Monte Corp., Walnut Creek, Calif., 1980-82; human resource mgmt. cons. H.R.S., Inc., Winston-Salem, NC, 1982-87; corp. pers. specialist Advance Stroes Co., Inc., Roanoke, Va., 1987-90; pers. dir. Alfred (N.Y.) U., 1990-94; dir. human resources Framtone Connectors USA, Inc., Norwalk, Conn., 1994—; mgr. Lord Corp., Shelton, Conn., 1994-96; dir. human resources Energy Scis., Inc., Wilmington, Mass., 1999—. Mem. Assn. Pers. Adminstrs., Indsl. Pers. Soc., Coll. and U. Pers. Assn., Phi Alpha Theta. Episcopalian. Home: 250 Lynnfield St # A Peabody MA 01960-4921 Office: 42 Industrial Way Wilmington MA 01887-4605 Office Phone: 978-694-9000. E-mail: tighee@comcast.net.

D'ALESSIO, JACQUELINE ANN, English educator; b. Morristown, N.J., Jan. 26, 1943; d. Clifford Corbet and Helen Ann (Chrenko) Compton; m. Harold F. D'Alessio, Oct. 28, 1967. BA in English, Coll. New Rochelle, 1964; MA in English, Seton Hall U., 1969. Tchr. Bridgewater-Raritan Regional Sch. Dist., NJ, 1964—. Advisor dramatics Bridgewater-Raritan Mid. Sch., 1983—. Chmn. pub. rels. Mt. St. Mary Devel. Office, 1985-2000; stewardship com. St. Ann's Ch., 2005—. Recipient Gov. Tchr. Recognition, N.J. Dept. Edn., Trenton, 1989, Disting. Svc. award Bridgewater-Raritan Regional Sch. Dist., 2001; named Outstanding Elem. Tchr. in U.S., 1971. Mem. AAUW (N.J. pres. 1990-94, program v.p. 1988-90, rep. Women's Agenda 1989-94, dir. pub. policy 1997-99, treas. 1999-2003, dir. mid-Atlantic region 2001-05, pres. Raritan Valley 2005—). Roman Catholic. Avocations: travel, golf, biking, gardening. Home: 30 Putnam St Somerville NJ 08876-2737 Personal E-mail: jqline@att.net.

D'ALESSIO, VALAIDA CORRINE, artist, consultant; b. Dwight, Ill., Jan. 7, 1938; d. Roy Selmer and Agnes Irene (Seversen) Christiansen; m. Terald Ramon Stevens, July 5, 1958 (div. Dec. 1974); children: Christian Stevens, Curt Stevens, Kirsten Stevens, Karlin Stevens; m. Paul D'Alessio, July 16, 1976 (dec. Apr. 2000). Student, Joliet (Ill.) Jr. Coll., 1957, Aurora (Ill.) Coll., 1964, Am. Acad. Art, Chgo., 1969. Experienced-based master ednl. resources Joliet Twp. High Schs. Adult art educator Joliet Jr. Coll., 1980-88; art workshop leader various art leagues, Chgo. area, 1980-96, State of Ill. Gallery, Lockport, 1994. Art cons. Lockport St. Gallery, Plainfield, Ill., 1994—96, Prairie View Gallery, Lockport, 1999—2000. Contbr. (paintings and mixed media collages) Watercolor and Collage Workshop, 1988, (books) Layering: An Art of Time and Space, 1992, Creative Collage Techniques,

1994, Best of Watercolor 2, 1997, Best of Watercolor 2 Painting Texture, 1997, Bridging Time and Space, Essays on Layered Art, 1998, Art and Healing (Barbara Ganin), 1999, The Art of Layering Making Connections, 2004. Vol. Crisis Line Will County, 1990—96. Mem.: North Coast Collage Soc., Soc. Exptl. Artists, Soc. Layerists Multi-Media. E-mail: valaida@aol.com.

DALEY, ANN SCARLETT, curator; b. Havre, Mont., Jan. 26, 1935; d. Frederick William and Clara Scarlett; m. James Burger Daley, Feb. 22, 1958 (div. 1981); children: James Bruce, Kathryn Scarlett, John Edward, Matthew Frederick; m. John Charles Emerson, June 6, 1987. AA, Colo. Womans Coll., 1955; BA, U. Wyo., 1958; MA, Denver U., 1981. Curator Am. art Denver Art Mus., 1977-81; curator Foxley & Co., Denver, 1980-81, Captiva Corp., Denver, 1985—. Advisor Holme, Roberts & Owen, Denver, 1989—; assoc. curator Denver Art Mus., 1993—; curator Nat. Western Stock Show Art Exhibit, 1994—97; cons. in field. Contbr. articles to profl. jours. Mem. Mayor's Art Culture & Film Com., Denver, 1995-2003; bd. dirs. Met. State Coll. Ctr. Visual Arts, Denver, 1991-96. Mem.: Assn. Profl. Art Advisors, Phi Beta Kappa. Avocations: bicycling, skiing. Office: 1700 Lincoln St Ste 4750 Denver CO 80203-4511 E-mail: ann@captiva-resources.com.

DALEY, BARBARA SABIN, clinical psychologist; b. Washington, Sept. 19, 1949; d. Hilbert Speich and Katherine (Keet) Sabin; m. Paul Patrick Daley, May 24, 1980; 1 child, Patrick Sabin. BS, Duke U., 1972; MSN, Yale U., 1975; PsyD, Mass. Sch. Profl. Psychology, 1992. Lic. psychologist, health svc. provider, Mass. Staff nurse Durham (N.C.) County Mental Health Ctr., 1972-73; coord. after-care svcs. Emerson Hosp., Concord, Mass., 1975-77; clin. specialist in mental health Harvard Cmty. Health Plan, Cambridge, Mass., 1977-88; dir. pediatric behavioral medicine Cambridge Hosp., 1994—; pvt. pracitce child assessment and treatment. Clin. fellow in psychiatry Harvard U. Med. Sch., Cambridge, 1990-93, clin. instr., 1993—. Mem. APA, Internat. Soc. Behavioral Medicine, Mass. Psychol. Assn., Assn. Advancement Behavioral Therapies. Home: 9 Crofton Rd Waban MA 02468-1931 Office: Cambridge Hosp Cambridge St Cambridge MA 02139

DALEY, DEBORAH ANN, assistant principal; d. William Andrew Dabilis and Margaret Mary Gibbons; m. Gerald Nugent Daley, Jan. 8, 1972; children: Elisha Gerolyn, Theresa Marie Beausoleil, Melissa Ann Hibbard. BA in Psychology, Clark U., 1994, MA in Edn., 1997; MEd in Sch. Leadership and Adminstrn., Worcester State Coll., Mass., 2002. Creative writing specialist Worcester Arts Magnet Sch., 1997—2001, curriculum specialist, 2001—03, No Child Left Behind implementation tchr., 2003—04; asst. prin. City View Elem. Sch., Worcester, 2004—. Co-tournament dir. Mass. ASA Girls Softball, Chelmsford, Mass., 1985—2005; mem. Friends of Chelmsford Libr., 1995—; fundraiser Dance Guild-Ballet, Chelmsford, 1987—90. Recipient cert. of achievement, Greater Boston Undergrad. Psychol. Rsch. Conf., 1993, Literacy award, Alliance For Edn., 1997, 1998, 1999, 2000; grantee, Mass. Dept. Edn., 1997—2003, 2003, Nat. Gardening Assn., 2003, St. Gobain Corp., Worcester, 2005. Mem.: ASCD, NSBA, NCTM, ACEI, MESPA, NCTE, Internat. Reading Assn., Phi Delta Kappa. Home: 10 Leedburg St North Chelmsford MA 01863 Office: City View Sch 80 Prospect St Worcester MA 01605 Office Phone: 508-799-3670. Personal E-mail: debdaley@comcast.net. E-mail: daleyd@worc.k12.ma.us.

DALEY, LINDA, lawyer; b. Newark, N.J., Jan. 19, 1954; d. Charles and Margaret Mongiovi; m. Rodger Cleveland Daley, Oct. 7, 1978. Student, Upsala Coll., 1971—74; BS, Regis Coll., 1975; JD, U. of Denver, 1982. Bar: Colo. 1982. Loan svc. clk. World Savs. & Loan Assn., Denver, 1975—76; rschr. Eleanor Roosevelt Inst. for Cancer Rsch., Denver, 1976—79; legal asst. Robert T. Hinds, Jr. & Associates, P.C., Littleton, Colo., 1979—82, assoc., 1982—86; law clerk to Hon. Donald P. Smith Colo. Ct. Appeals, 1987—89; assoc. staff atty. Colo. Ct. of Appeals, Denver, 1989—95, dep. chief staff atty., 1995—. Contbr. articles to profl. jours. Mem.: Colo. Bar Assn. (Amicus com.), YMCA, Denver Law Jour., Phi Beta Kappa. Avocations: walking, pets, knitting, crocheting. Business E-Mail: linda.daley@judicial.state.co.us.

DALEY, PAMELA, diversified services, technology and manufacturing company executive; b. Springfield, Mass., Oct. 1, 1952; d. Edward Murray and Elizabeth Bloom Daley; m. Randall Lee Phelps, Aug. 26, 1995. AB summa cum laude in Romance Langs. and Lit., Princeton U., 1974; JD magna cum laude, U. Pa., 1979. Bar: Pa. 1979, N.Y. 1991. Lectr. partnership taxation law U. Pa., Phila., 1982-89; assoc. tax sect. Morgan, Lewis & Bockius, Phila., 1979-86, ptnr., 1986-89; tax counsel GE, Fairfield, Conn., 1989-91, v.p., sr. counsel for transactions, 1991—2004, sr. v.p. bus. devel., 2004—. Bd. outside advisor Va. Tax Review assn., 1982-92. Editor-in-chief U. Pa. Law Review; contbr. articles to profl. jours. Trustee MacDuffie Sch., Springfield, 1986-92; bd. govs. Pa. Economy League, 1986-89; mem. bd. overseers Law Sch. U. Pa., 1999—; bd. dirs. G.E. Found., 1999—, Genworth Fin., Inc.; bd. dirs. World Wildlife Fund, 1999—. Teaching fellow Salzburg Seminar on Am. Law and Legal Instns., 1986; named to Acad. Women Achievers YWCA, 1992. Mem. Order of Coif, Phi Beta Kappa. Office: GE 3135 Easton Tpke # E3 Fairfield CT 06828*

DALEY, RUTH MARGARET, advertising agency administrator; b. Buffalo, Apr. 12, 1950; d. Russell Short and Emma Pleasant (Wear) Garrick; m. Jeffrey George Vanghel (dec. 1988); m. Patrick L. Daley. Student, Villa Maria Coll., Buffalo. Sec. McKesson & Robbins Drug Co., Cheektowaga, NY, 1972-78; sales rep. Nasco Inc., Springfield, Tenn., 1978-80; telemktg. sales rep. L.M. Berry & Co., Amherst, NY, 1980-81, mgr. telemktg. sales unit, 1981-83, mgr. telemktg. sales dept., 1984-90; mgmt. cons. Ameritech, Troy, Mich., 1990-92; mgr. tng. White Directory Pub. (The Talking Phone Book), Buffalo, 1992—2002, telephone sales mgr., 2002—. Grad. asst. Dale Carnegie Inst., Buffalo, 1985. Avocations: dance, reading, travel. Home: 66 Parktrail Ln Buffalo NY 14227-2545 Office: The Talking Phone Book 1945 Sheridan Dr Buffalo NY 14223-1203 Office Phone: 716-875-9100 x80142. Business E-Mail: rdaley@talkingphonebook.com.

DALEY, SANDRA, retired artist, filmmaker, photographer; b. Fargo, ND, Feb. 28, 1940; d. Cecil Raymond and Margaret (Anderson) D. AB cum laude, Oberlin Coll., Ohio, 1961; MFA with high distinction, Calif. Coll. Arts and Crafts, Oakland, 1965. Co-editor (Geoffrey C. Ward): Contemporary Photographer Magazine, 1960; show (with Andy Warhol and Roy Lichtenstein), Dwan Gallery, LA, 1964, show (with Nicholas Quennell), 1965, Experiments in Art and Tech., Osaka Pavilion, World's Fair, 1970; prodr., dir.: (film (with Sally Potter) London Mysteries, 1964; (film (with Robert Mapplethorpe and Patti Smith) Robert Having His Nipple Pierced, 1970; (film (Patti Smith, Sam Shepard and Vali) Patti Having Her Knee Tattooed, 1971; prodr., dir. (live mixed media performance (with Alan Lanier and Patti Smith) Cine Probe, The Mus. of Modern Art, N.Y.C., 1971. Avocations: writing, drawing.

DALEY, SUSAN JEAN, lawyer; b. New Britain, Conn., May 27, 1959; d. George Joseph and Norma (Woods) Daley. BA, U. Conn., 1978; JD, Harvard U., 1981. Bar: Ill. 1981. Assoc. Altheimer & Gray, Chgo., 1981-86, ptnr., 1986—2003, Perkins Coie LLP, Chgo., 2003—. Mem.: ABA (real property, probate and trust law sect. 1983—, employee benefits com. taxation sect. 1984—, chmn. welfare plans com. real property, probate and trust law sect. 1989—95, chmn. employee benefits, securities law com. taxation sect. 2001—), Chgo. Coun. Fgn. Rels., Chgo. Bar Assn. (chmn. employee benefits divsn. fed. taxation com. 1985—86, chmn. employee benefits com. 1990—91, chmn. fed. taxation com. 1992—93), Ill. Bar Assn. (chmn. employee benefits divsn. fed. taxation sect. 1984—86, chmn. employee benefits sect. 1995—96), Nat. Assn. Stock Plan Profls. (pres. Chgo. chpt. 1995—). Avocation: marathons. Home: 1636 N Wells St Apt 415 Chicago IL 60614-6009 Office: 131 S Dearborn St STE 1700 Chicago IL 60603-5559 Office Phone: 312-324-8645. Business E-Mail: SDaley@perkinscoie.com.

DALGLISH, LUCY ANN, lawyer, organization executive; b. Mpls., Mar. 24, 1959; d. James Mark and Joanne Elizabeth (Speikers) D. BA, U. N.D., 1980; MSL, Yale U., 1988; JD, Vanderbilt U., 1995. Bar: Minn. 1995, D.C. 2001. Reporter Grand Forks (N.D.) Herald, 1978-80, St. Paul Dispatch, 1979, 80-81, St. Paul Pioneer Press., 1981-89; night city editor St. Paul Pioneer Press, 1989-90, nat./fgn. editor, 1991-93; rsch. asst. Freedom Forum, Nashville, 1993-95; assoc. Dorsey & Whitney, Mpls., 1995-2000; exec. dir. Reporters Com. for Freedom of Press, Arlington, Va., 2000—. Instr. Hamline U., St. Paul, 1989, 90. Nat. chair Project Watchdog, Greencastle, Ind., 1990-92. Inducted into Nat. Freedom of Info. Act Hall of Fame, Washington, 1996; Yale Law Sch. fellow, 1987-88. Mem. Soc. Profl. Journalists (bd. dirs. 1987-91, nat. chairwoman, freedom of info. com. 1991-95; recipient Wells Meml. Key 1995), First Amendment Congress (nat. bd. mem. 1991-97), Minn. AP Assn. (v.p. 1991-93), Sigma Delta Chi Found. (bd. dirs. 1990-91), Minn. Bar Assn. (bar/media com. 1992-93, 95-97, bar-media chairwoman 1997-2000). Roman Catholic. Avocations: downhill and water skiing, golf, reading, antiques, gardening. Office: Reporters Com for Freedom of Press 1101 Wilson Blvd Ste 1100 Arlington VA 22209 Office Phone: 703-807-2100.

DALIA, VESTA MAYO, artist; b. Atlanta, Aug. 14, 1932; d. Frank and Winnifred (Layton) Mayo; m. William Barber Macke, May 30, 1952 (div. 1971); children: William Barber Jr., Michael Mayo, Vesta Melissa, Mary Sue Macke Mullen; m. Joseph William Dalia, Aug. 31, 1973 (dec. 1990); stepchildren: Joseph W. Jr., Jeffrey Meade, Denise Marie Dalia Cooper, Nancy Dalia Cook. Student, U. Ga. Tchr. art Cen. Piedmont Coll., Charlotte, N.C. Exhibited art in shows in Charlotte and Atlanta. Bd. dirs., officer Caribbean Condo; poll worker Fla. elections. Mem. Nat. Tole and Decorative Painters (past pres. Dogwood chpt., recipient Golden Palet award 1990), Missle Tole Decorative Painters, Team Network S.E. Painters, Weinman Mineral Mus., West Fulton Owls Club, Frog Club, Zoo Atlanta, Friendship Force, Native Atlantans Club, The Etowah Found. NATAS (Atlanta chpt.), NRA, Ga. Ensemble Theatre. Republican. Episcopalian. Home: 2814 S Peninsula Dr Daytona Beach FL 32118 E-mail: vdalia@cfl.rr.com.

DALIS, IRENE, mezzo soprano, performing arts association administrator; b. San Jose, Calif., Oct. 8, 1925; d. Peter Nicholas and Mamie Rose (Boitano) D.; m. George Loinaz, July 16, 1957; 1 child, Alida Mercedes. AB, San Jose State Coll., 1946; MA in Teaching, Columbia U., 1947; MMus (hon.), San Jose State U., 1957; studied voice with, Edyth Walker, N.Y.C., 1947-50, Paul Althouse, 1950-51, Dr. Otto Mueller, Milan, Italy, 1952-72; MusD (hon.), Santa Clara U., 1987; DFA (hon.), Calif. State U., 1999. Prin. artist Berlin Opera, 1955-65, Met. Opera, N.Y.C., 1957-77, San Francisco Opera, 1958-73, Hamburg (Fed. Republic Germany) Staatsoper, 1966-71; prof. music San Jose State U., Calif., 1977—2004; founder, gen. dir. Opera San Jose, 1984—. Dir. Met. Opera Nat. Auditions, San Jose dist., 1980-88. Operatic debut as dramatic mezzo-soprano Oldenburgisches Staatstheater, 1953, Berlin Staedtische Opera, 1955; debut Met. Opera, N.Y.C., 1957, 1st Am.-born singer, Kundry Bayreuth Festival, 1961, opened, Bayreuth Festival, Parsifal, 1963; commemorative Wagner 150th Birth Anniversary; opened 1963 Met. Opera Season in Aida; premiered: Dello Joio's Blood Moon, 1961, Henderson's Medea, 1972; rec. artist Parsifal, 1964 (Grand Prix du Disque award); contbg. editor Opera Quar., 1983. Recipient Fulbright award for study in Italy, 1951, Woman of Achievement award Commn. on Status of Women, 1983, Pres.'s award Nat. Italian Am. Found., 1985, award of merit People of San Francisco, 1985, San Jose Renaissance award for sustained and outstanding artistic contbn., 1987, Medal of Achievement Acad. Vocal Arts, 1988; named Honored Citizen City of San Jose, 1986; inducted into Calif. Pub. Edn. Hall of Fame, 1985, others. Mem. Beethoven Soc. (mem. adv. bd. 1985—), San Jose Arts Round Table, San Jose Opera Guild, Am. Soc. Univ. Women, Arts Edn. Week Consortium, Phi Kappa Phi, Mu Phi Epsilon. Office: Opera San Jose 2149 Paragon Dr San Jose CA 95131 Office Phone: 408-437-4450. Business E-Mail: dalis@operasj.org.

DALLAS, DONNA ANN, music educator; b. Bellevue, Pa., May 17, 1969; d. Donald Daniel and Janet Elaine Sporny; m. Joseph Anthony Dallas, July 1, 1994; 1 child, Jaina Jo. BS in Music Edn., Clarion U. Pa., 1991; MusM, Youngstown State U., Ohio, 1993. Instrumental dir. Adams County/Ohio Valley Sch. Dist., Manchester, Ohio, 1993—96, Horace O'Bryant Mid. Sch., Key West, Fla., 1996—. Music tchr. leader Monroe County Schs., Key West, 2000—03; mentor tchr. Horace O'Bryant Mid. Sch., 2005—06. Musician: Paradise Big Band, 1997—, Keys Chorale, 1997—, Keys Pops Orch., 2000—. Recipient Tchr. Recognition, Key West C. of C., 1996, Tchr. of Yr. award, Horace O'Bryant Mid. Sch., 2000. Mem.: Fla. Bandmasters Assn., Fla. Music Educators Assn. (Enrollment award 1998). Avocations: reading, crocheting, cooking.

DALLAS, SANDRA, writer; b. Washington, June 11, 1939; d. Forrest Everett and Harriett (Mavity) Dallas; m. Robert Thomas Atchison, Apr. 20, 1963; children: Dana Dallas, Povy Kendal Dallas. BA, U. Denver, 1960. Asst. editor U. Denver Mag., 1965-66; editl. asst. Bus. Week, Denver, 1961-63, 67-69, bur. chief, 1969-85, 90-91, sr. corr., 1985-90; freelance editor, 1990—2001. Book reviewer Denver Post, 1961—, regional book columnist, 1980—. Author: Gaslights and Gingerbread, 1965, rev. edit., 1984, Gold and Gothic, 1967, No More Than 5 in a Bed, 1967, Vail, 1969, Cherry Creek Gothic, 1971, Yesterday's Denver, 1974, Sacred Paint, 1980, Colorado Ghost Towns and Mining Camps, 1985, Colorado Homes, 1986, Buster Midnight's Cafe, 1990, reissued, 1998, The Persian Pickle Club, 1995, The Diary of Mattie Spenser, 1997, Alice's Tulips, 2000, The Chili Queen, 2002, The Quilt that Walked to Golden, 2004, New Mercies, 2005; editor: The Colorado Book, 1993; contbr. articles to popular mags. Bd. dirs. Vis. Nurse Assn., Denver, 1983—85, Hist. Denver, Inc., 1979—82, 1984—87, Rocky Mountain Quilt Mus., 2001—04, Historic Georgetown, Inc., 2002—05. Recipient Wrangler award Nat. Cowboy Hall of Fame, 1980, Lifetime Achievement award Denver Posse of Westerners, 1996, disting. svc. award U. Colo., 1997; named Colo. Exceptional Chronicler of Western History by Women's Library Assn. and Denver Pub. Library Friends Found., 1986; finalist Spur award We. Writers of Am., 1998, recipient, 2003, Benjamin Franklin award Ind. Book Pub. Assn., 2005 Mem. Women's Forum Colo., Denver Woman's Press Club, Western Writers Am. (Spur award 2003), Women Writing the West. Democrat. Presbyterian. Home and Office: 750 Marion St Denver CO 80218-3434

DALLOLIO, JANELLE K., language educator, literature and language educator; b. Twin Falls, Idaho, July 14, 1956; d. Luther Emmet and Lois Elaine Morton; m. Shane Dallolio, Nov. 21, 1982 (div. July 1992); children: Darren, Heidi. AA, Coll. of Southern Idaho, Twin Falls, 1989; BA, Idaho State U., 1992; MEd, U. Idaho, 2000. Cert. reading endorsement K-12 Idaho State U., 1992. Tchr. Minico Pub. HS, Rupert, Idaho, 1995—, Southern Idaho CC, Twin Falls, Idaho, 2003—. Supr. com. Minico HS, Rupert, Idaho, 1995—. Mem.: Idaho Edn. Assn., NEA. Avocations: fishing, dance, travel.

DALLY, LYNN, choreographer, performing company executive, educator; d. Jimmy Rawlins. Student, Honi Coles, Eddie Brown, Jimmy Rawlins. Cofounder Jazz Tap Ensemble, LA, 1979, artistic dir., 1986—; now adj. prof., Dept. World Arts & Cultures UCLA. Choreographer (film) Tribute, (ballet) Black Iris, (play) Speak Low; appearances include (film) Tapdancin'. Fellow, Nat. Endowment Arts; artist fellow, Calif. Arts Coun., 1991, Irvine Fellowship in Dance, 2000, Guggenheim Fellowship in Choreography, 2001, City of LA Fellowship, 2002. Office: Jazz Tap Ensemble 1416 Westwood Blvd Ste 207 Los Angeles CA 90024 Office Phone: 310-475-4412. Office Fax: 310-475-4037. E-mail: lynndally@aol.com.

DALMAS-BROWN, CARMELLA JEAN, special education educator; b. Dec. 31, 1959; d. Bruno L. and Mary S. (Pashinski) Dalmas; m. Charles T. Brown; 1 child, Kathlina. AS in Edn., Luzerne County C.C., 1979; BS in Spl. and Elem. Edn., Coll. of Misericordia, 1981; MS in Elem. Edn., Wilkes Coll., 1989. Cert. mentally/physically handicapped tchr., Pa. Substitute tchr. Luzerne Intermediate Unit 18, Kingston, Pa., 1983-84, Pope John Paul II Sch., Nanticoke, Pa., 1983-84, Genesis Sch./First Hosp. Wyo. Valley, Wilkes-Barr, Pa., 1983-84, tchr., 1984-88, head tchr., 1988-94; dir. edn. Genesis Sch., 1995—2000; tchr. spl. edn. Greater Nanticoke Area Sch. Dist., 2000—. Presenter in field; spl. edn. advisor Best Buddies chpt., cheerleader advisor Greater Nanticoke HS. Tchr. Diocese of Scranton, St. Mary's Parish, Nanticoke; former leader brownie troop Girl Scouts USA, now junior leader. Mem. Coun. of Exceptional Children. Democrat. Roman Catholic. Avocations: reading, sports, arts and crafts, photography. Home: 124 W Broad St Nanticoke PA 18634-2205 Office: Greater Nanticoke Area Sch Dist Nanticoke PA 18634-

DALOIA, RACHEL ROSEMARY, music educator; b. New Hyde Park, NY, Nov. 2, 1976; d. Gregory Francis and Rose Mary Spano; m. Michael Nicholas Daloia, Oct. 18, 2003; 1 child, Gianna Lahela. B Voice Performance, B Music Edn., U. Del., 1999; M Music Edn., Five Towns Coll., 2004. Cert. K-12 music tchr. NY. 5th-6th grade choir dir. Island Trees Mid. Sch., Levittown, NY, 1999—2000; jr. high choir dir. North Country Rd. Mid. Sch., Miller Place, NY, 2000—00; jr./sr. high choir dir. Sewanhaka HS, Floral Park, NY, 2000—. Varsity and jr. high gymnastics coach Roslyn (NY) HS/Mid. Sch., Roslyn, NY, 2002—03. Mem.: Nassau Music Educator's Assn., Music Educator's Nat. Conf. Republican. Roman Catholic. Avocations: gymnastics, camping, crafts, musical theater. Home: 1602 Broadway New Hyde Park NY 11040 Office: Sewanhaka HS 500 Tulip Ave Floral Park NY 11001 Office Phone: 516-488-9627. Personal E-mail: musicdaloia@yahoo.com.

DALPHOND-GUIRAL, MADELEINE, member of Canadian parliament; b. Monteal, Quebec, Can., June 6, 1938; BS in Nursing. Mem. parliament from Laval Centre Parliament of Canada, Ottawa, 1993.

DALPINO, IDA JANE, retired secondary school educator; b. Newhall, Calif., Oct. 20, 1936; d. Bernhardt Arthur and Wahneta May (Blyler) Melby; m. Gilbert Augustus, June 14, 1963 (div. 1976); 1 child, Nicolette Jane. BA, Calif. State U., Chico, 1960; postgrad., Sacramento State, 1961—65, Sonoma State, 1970—71; MA, U. San Francisco, 1978. Cert. cmty. counselor, learning handicapped, c.c. instr., exceptional children, pupil pers. specialist, secondary tchr., resource specialist. Tchr. Chico High Sch., 1959-60; counselor Mira Loma High Sch., Sacramento, 1960-66; tchr. ESL Phoenix Ind. High Sch., 1968-69; resource specialist Yuba City (Calif.) High Sch., 1971-2000; ret., 2000. English tchr. Rough Rock Demonstration Sch., summers, 1975, 76. Office sec. Job's Daus., North Bend, Oreg., 1953—; active Environ. Def. Fund, Centerville Hist. Assn., Chico, 1991—. Mem. NEA, Calif. Tchrs. Assn., Chico State Alumni Assn., Sierra Club, Nature Conservancy, Audubon, Greenpeace, Sigma Kappa Alumni. Democrat. Mem. Science of the Mind Church. Avocations: reading, ecology, genealogy. Home: 6 Navajo Ln Corte Madera CA 94925 Personal E-mail: idajane@comcast.net.

DALRYMPLE, MARILYN ANITA, small business owner, photographer; b. Vancouver, B.C., Can., Apr. 2, 1945; d. Herbert Walter and Eudora Ethelyn (Walters) Hortin; m. Randall William Duffey (div. Jan. 1971); m. Ronald Vern Dalrymple, Sept. 27, 1972; children: Valerie Ann, Leslie Thomas, Kelly Walter Duffey. AA, Antelope Valley Coll., 1987. Cert. fine art photography, Calif. Pvt. practice writer, photographer, Lancaster, Calif., 1987-89; owner Images by Marilyn, Lancaster, 1989—, Red Rose Fine Photography, Lancaster, 1998—. Author: My Lives as an Editor, 1993, To Catch a Butterfly, 1993, Have You Tried Everything, 1996, Bartholomew's Buttons, 1997; work included in Photo Forum (intrnet), The Art of Seeing (virtual photo mag.). Dir., pres. Antelope Valley Com. Aging, Lancaster, 1994—; v.p. Antelope Valley Calif. Rep. League; mem. Calif. Coalition Juvenile Justice, Lancaster citizens and govt., Lancaster City Planning Commn.; founder Respect for Parents Day-Aug. 1st. Recipient Excellence award, Photographer Forum's Mag., 1993, L.A. County New Photography Silver award, 1994, 1995, Merit award, World Poetry, 1997, Profl. Photographers of Am., 2001. Mem. Photographic Soc. Am., Profl. Photographers Am. (Merit award), Profl. Photographers Calif., Photo Mktg. Assn., Assn. Photo Educators, Royal Photographic Soc. (licentiateship distinction, associateship distinction 2005). Home: PO Box 1563 Lancaster CA 93539-1563 Office: Images by Marilyn/Red Rose Fine Photography PO Box 1563 Lancaster CA 93539-1563 E-mail: mailyn@rglobal.net.

DAL SANTO, DIANE, retired judge, writer, arbitrator, mediator; b. East Chicago, Ind., Sept. 20, 1949; d. John Quentin and Helen (Koval) D.; m. Fred O'Cheskey, June 29, 1985. BA, U. N.Mex., 1971; cert., Inst. Internat. and Comparative Law, Guadalajara, Mex., 1978; JD, U. San Diego, 1980. Bar: N.Mex. 1980, U.S. Dist. Ct. N.Mex. 1980. Ct. planner Met. Criminal Justice Coordinating Coun., Albuquerque, 1973-75; planning coord. Dist. Atty.'s Office, Albuquerque, 1975-76, exec. asst. to dist. atty., 1976-77, asst. dir. atty. for violent crimes, 1980-82; chief dep. city atty. City of Albuquerque, 1983; assoc. firm T.B. Keleher & Assocs., 1983-84; judge Met. Ct., 1985-89, chief judge, 1988-89; judge Dist. Ct., 1989-2000. Mem. faculty Nat. Jud. Coll., 1990-95, 97-, trustee, 1995-96; adj. faculty Internat. Law Enforcement Acad., Roswell, N.Mex., 2002-. Columnist Albuquerque Jour., 1996-98. Bd. dirs. Nat. Coun. Alcoholism, 1984, S.W. Ballet Co., Albuquerque, 1982-83, Pennies for Homeless, 2000—, Youth Devel., Inc., 2004—; mem. Mayor's Task Force on Alcoholism and Crime, 1987-88, N.Mex. Coun. Crime and Delinquency, 1987-97, bd. dirs., 1992-94, Task Force Domestic Violence, 1987-94; pres. bench, bar, media com., 1987, pres. 1992, rules of evidence com. Supreme Ct., 1993-96, chair com. access to pub. records Supreme Ct., 1988; steering com. N.Mex. Buddy Awards, 1995—; mem. Metro. Criminal Justice Coordinating Coun., 1998-2000. U. San Diego scholar, 1978-79; recipient Women on the Move award YWCA, 1989, Disting. Woman award U. N.Mex. Alumni Assn., 1994, Outstanding Alumnus Dept. Sociology U. N.Mex., 1995; named Woman of Yr. award Duke City Bus. and Profl. Women, 1985. Mem. ABA (Nat. Conf. State Trial Judges Jud. Excellence award 1996), LWV, AAUW, Am. Judicature Soc., N.Mex. Women's Found., N.Mex. State Bar Assn. (silver gavel award 1997), N.Mex. Women's Bar Assn. (bd. dirs. 1991-92, Power and Caring award 2000), Albuquerque Bar Assn., Nat. Assn. Women Judges (bd. dist. dirs. 1999-00), Greater Albuquerque C. of C. (steering com. 1989), N.Mex. Magistrate Judges Assn. (v.p. 1985-89), Dist. Judges Assn. (pres. 1994-95). Personal E-mail: dianedalsanto@aol.com.

DALTCHEV, ANA RANGUEL, sculptor; b. Sofia, Bulgaria, Jan. 25, 1926; came to U.S., 1979; d. Ranguel and Struma Popov; m. Lubomir Daltchev, Jan. 23, 1949; 1 child, Lubomir. MA, Higher Inst. Visual Arts, Sofia, Bulgaria, 1952. Registered sculptor, Europe, 1953-79; free-lance sculptor U.S.A., 1979—. Exhibited in U.S., Germany, Bulgaria, France, Yugoslavia, India, Greece, Rumania; prin. works include Motherhood, Fount, Weaver, Joy, Sophia, Youth, California Women, Torso, Spouse, Awakening, Dance; participation with sculptures in XIV World Biennial of Sculpture, Middleheim, Antwerpen, Pagani Biennial of European Sculpture Milan, European Biennial of Small Sculpture, Budapest, Hungary. Selected Biennale Internazionale dell' Arte Conteporanea, Italy. Mem. San Francisco Mus. Modern Arts, Women in Arts. Achievements include: half a century dedicated to research and creation of new feminine forms in sculpture. Office: PO Box 70054 Sunnyvale CA 94086-0054

DALTON, CHERYL RENEE, entrepreneur; b. Jersey City, May 16, 1960; d. Ronald McGowan and Marie Funchess; m. Allen Brett Dalton, Sept. 3, 1995; children: Sha-nia Nell Smith, Ebony Elisa Casley 1 stepchild, Ebony Johnsen. Student, Barnwell Vocat. Sch., 1992. Cert. nursing asst., S.C. Pvt. nurse Atty. George Crawford, Orangeburg, SC, 1992—95; nursing asst. Dehec Home Health, 1992—95; asst. dir. CMC Group Home, 2004—. Founder, dir. Edisto Fork Family Info. Referral, Orangeburg, 2003—. Author: A Path From Destruction (Then & Now), 2001; writer poetry for gospel songs:. Mem.: NAACP, Order Ea. Star. Methodist. Achievements include patents pending for adhesive weave. Avocation: softball. Home and Office: 356 Cimmaron St Orangeburg SC 29115 Office Phone: 803-533-5599. E-mail: crdalton_29115@hotmail.com, orangeburgrenee@aol.com.

DALTON, CLAUDETTE ELLIS HARLOE, anesthesiologist, educator, dean; b. Roanoke, Va., Jan. 18, 1947; d. John Pinckney and Dorothy Anne (Ellis) Harloe; m. Henry Tucker Dalton, May 17, 1973 (div. 1979); 1 child, Gordon Tucker; m. H. Christopher Alexander, III, Apr. 29, 2000. BA, Sweet Briar Coll., 1969; MD, U. Va., 1974. Resident anesthesiology U. N.C., Chapel Hill, 1974—77; med. edn. Lenoir County Meml Hosp./East Carolina U.,

Kinston, 1978—80; med. edn. intensive care Presbyn Hosp., Charlotte, NC, 1981—82; practice anesthesiology Charlotte Eye, Ear, Nose and Throat Hosp., 1982—85, Medivision Charlotte and Orthop. Hosp. Charlotte, 1985—89; asst. prof. U. Va. Health Scis. Ctr., Charlottesville, Va., 1992—2006; dir. Office Cmty. Based Med. Edn., Charlottesville, 1994—2006; asst. dean cmty. based med. edn. U. Va., Charlottesville, 1996—2006, med. dir. Pre-Anesthesia Clinic, 1996—2006, asst. prof. anesthesiology and med. edn., 1996—2006; med. dir. perioperative svcs. Rockingham Meml. Hosp., 2006—; founder med. team for the remote area med. clinic in Wise Cmty. Svc./Outreach, 1999—. Adv. bd. Nat. Bd. Med. Examiners, 2004; exec. com. Accreditation Coun. Continuing Med. Edn., 2004; mem. Va. Bd. Medicine, 2005—; spkr. in field. Author: emergency med. svc. tng. program, 1981, patient edn. materials for illiterate patients, 1979—. Bd. dirs. Charlottesville Family Svcs., Family Svcs. Albemarle County, 1992—93, Coun. Aging, Am. Cancer Soc.; exec. dir. Cmty. Involvement Coun. Lenoir County, Kinston, 1979; county coord. Internat. Yr. of Child, Kinston, 1979; bd. dirs. U. Va. Women's Ctr., Lenoir County CC; mem. sch. medicine com. women U. Va. Med. Sch. Recipient Gov.'s award, State of N.C., 1980, Outstanding Tchg. award, U. Va. Sch. Medicine, 1993, Sharon L. Hostler U. Va. Outstanding Woman in Medicine award, 2002, Svc. to Disadvantaged Populations award, AMA-Hosp. Rsch. and Edn. Trust, 2005, Cert. of Merit award, NC Dept. Human Resources, 2005. Mem.: AMA (Coun. on Med. Edn.), Va. Soc. Anesthesiology, Albemarle County Med. Soc., Med. Soc. Va. (bd. dirs. Va. Health Quality Coun. 1995—97, chair ad hoc com. on telemedicine 1996—99, 2d v.p. 1998—99, chair scope of practice com. 1999—2002, dist. dir. 1999—2005, editor med. news Va. Med. Quar., legis. com., health access com., strategic planning and implementation com., women's com., med. affairs com., bd. medicine adv. com., Cmty. Svc award 2003), Alpha Omega Alpha, U. Va. Med. Alumni Assn. (assoc. bd. dirs. 1989—92, chair women in medicine leadership conf. 1998—99). Avocations: natural history, environment, dance, writing, gardening. Office: U Va Med Sch PO Box 800325 Charlottesville VA 22908-0325

DALTON, JEANNE M., musician, music educator; d. Carl B. and Ethel Bauer Houseman. BS in Music Edn., Duquesne U., Pitts., 1965; MEd, George Mason U., Fairfax, Va., 2002. Music tchr. Hollidaysburg Area Sch. Dist., Hollidaysburg, Pa., 1965—67, Hopewell Valley Regional Sch. Dist., Pennington, NJ, 1967—68, Loudoun County Pub. Schs., Ashburn, Va., 1978—. Violinist Fairfax Symphony Orch., Fairfax, Va., 1989—. Mem.: NEA, Music Educators Nat. Conf.

DALTON, LINDA CATHERINE, university administrator; b. Seattle, May 5, 1945; d. Chester Carlton and Dorothy Catherine (Salladay) Little; m. Thomas Barron Fitzpatrick, June 10, 1967 (div. 1983); children: Pandora Catherine, Benjamin Lawrence; m. Thomas Carlyle Dalton, Aug. 16, 1984. AB magna cum laude, Radcliffe Coll., 1967; M.Urban Planning, U. Wash., 1974, PhD in Urban Planning, 1978. Archtl./historic preservation staff Boston Redevel. Authority, 1967-68; long-range campus planner MIT, Cambridge, Mass., 1969-71; environ. impact analyst Kelly Pittelko Fritz & Forssen Cons., Seattle, 1974-76; lectr. Seattle U., 1976-78, asst. prof., 1978-82, assoc. prof., 1982-83, Calif. Poly. State U., San Luis Obispo, 1983-87, prof. city and regional planning, 1987—, dept. head city and regional planning, 1989-95, interim assoc. v.p. acad. resources, 1995-97, vice provost for instnl. planning, 1997—2001, exec. vice provost, chief planning officer, 2002—. Contbr. articles to profl. jours.; mem. editl. bds. profl. jours. Mem. Citizen Transp. Adv. Com., San Luis Obispo, 1990-94; mem. vis. com. Coll. Arch. and Urban Planning, U. Wash., Seattle, 1982-83; mem., vice chair, chair Seattle City Planning Commn., 1979-83; mem. Planning Accreditation Bd., 1992-97, chair, 1993-97; co-chair, City San Luis Obispo, Housing Element Task Force, 2003. Am. Coun. on Edn. fellow, 1994-95; Nat. Merit scholar, 1963-67. Mem. Am. Inst. Cert. Planners (cert.), Am. Planning Assn., Assn. Collegiate Sch. of Planning (exec. com. 1990-97), Calif. Planning Found. (v.p. 1995-98, pres. 1999-2001), Calif. Planning Rroundtable (pres, 2006), Soc. Coll. and Univ. Planning. Avocation: wildflowers. Office: California Poly State Univ San Luis Obispo CA 93407

DALTON, MARY M., communications educator, documentary filmmaker; b. Winston-Salem, NC, Jan. 20, 1962; BA, Wake Forest U., Winston-Salem, 1982; MA, U. NC, Greensboro, 1986; PhD, U. NC, 1995. Assoc. prof. comm. Wake Forest U., 1986—. Dir.: (documentary film) Martha in Lattimore (Best Documentary, Reel to Real Film Festival, 2005, Ofcl. Selection Silverdocs Documentary Festival, 2006), Sam McMillan: The Dot Man (Best Ind. Documentary, Carolina Film and Video Festival, 2003); author: The Hollywood Curriculum: Teachers in the Movies, 2004. Mem. Piedmont Triad Film Commn., NC, 2003—. Mem.: Univ. Film and Video Assn. (editl. bd. of the Jour. of Film and Video 2005—). Office: Wake Forest U PO Box 7347 Winston Salem NC 27109 Office Phone: 336-758-6120.

DALTON, PHYLLIS IRENE, library consultant; b. Marietta, KS, Sept. 25, 1909; d. Benjamin Reuben and Pearl (Travelute) Bull; m. Jack Mason Dalton, Feb. 13, 1950. BS, U. Nebr., 1931, MA, 1941, U. Denver, 1942. Tchr. City Schs., Marysville, Kans., 1931-40; reference libr. Lincoln (Nebr.) Pub. Libr., 1941-48; libr., asst. state libr. Calif. State Libr., Sacramento, 1948-72; pvt. libr. cons. Scottsdale, Ariz., 1972—. Libr. U. Nebr., Lincoln, 1941-48. Author: Library Services to the Deaf and Hearing Impaired Individuals, 1985, 91 (Pres.' Com. Employment of Handicapped award 1985), also poems; contbr. chpt., articles, reports in books and publs. in field. Mem. exec. bd. So. Nev. Hist. Soc., Las Vegas, 1983-84; mem. So. Nev. Com. on Employment of Handicapped, 1980-89, chairperson, 1988-89; mem. adv. com. Nat. Orgn. on Disability, 1982-94; mem., sec. resident coun. Forum Pueblo Norte Retirement Village, 1990-91, pres. resident coun., 1991-94; bd. dirs. Friends of So. Nev. Libraries; trustee Univ. Libr. Soc., U. Nev.-Las Vegas; mem. Allied Arts Coun., Pres.' Com. on Employment of People with Disabilities, emeritus, 1989—, Ariz. Gov.'s Com. on Employment of People with Disabilities, 1990—, Scottsdale Mayor's Com. on Employment of People with Disabilities, 1990—, chmn., 1996—; mem. Scottsdale Publ Libr. Ams. With Disabilities Com., 1994—; coord. writers' group Pueblo Norte, 2002—. Recipient Libraria Sodalitas, U. So. Calif., 1972, Alumni Achievement award U. Denver, 1977, U. Nebr., Lincoln, 1983, Outstanding Sr. Citizen Vol. award City of Scottsdale, 1997, citation for svc. to people with disabilities Mayor of Scottsdale, 1999; named Mover and Shaker Scottsdale Mag., 1994. Mem. LWV, ALA (councilor 1963-64, Exceptional Svc. award 1981, award com. O.C.L.C. Humphreys Forest Press award 1994), AAUW, Assn. State Librs. (pres. 1964-65), Calif. Libr. Assn. (pres. 1969), Nev. Libr. Assn. (hon.), Internat. Fedn. Libr. Assns. and Instns. (chair working group on libr. svc. to prisons, standing com. Sect. Librs. Serving Disadvantaged Persons 1981-95), Nat. League Am. Pen Women (Las Vegas chpt. 1988-94, com. on qualifications for Letters membership 1994—, parlimentarian Scottsdale chpt. 1989-94, v.p. 1992-94, 96-98, v.p. state chpt. 1996-98, sec. 1998-2001), Am. Correctional Assn. (libr. svcs. instns. com. 1994—), Internat. Soc. Poets (disting.), Pilot Internat. (at-large). Home: 7100 E Mescal St # 215 Scottsdale AZ 85254-6126

DA'LUZ VIEIRA-JONES, LORRAINE CHRISTINE C., acupuncturist, researcher; b. London, Apr. 30, 1955; arrived in U.S., 1999; d. Archibald Carlyle and Christine Heather Da Luz Vieira; m. Schuyler M. Jones, Dec. 23, 1998; children: Jesse Christopher, Cassandra Laurie. Licentiate in Acupuncture, C.T.C.M., Leamington Spa, Eng., 1983, B in Acupuncture, 1986, M in Acupuncture, 1989; M in Anthropology, Oxford U., Eng., 1994; MPh in Med. Anthropology, Oxford U., 1995, DPhil, 1999; DOM (hon.), Chelsea U., Eng., 2004; diploma in Acupuncture (hon.), 2002. Lectr. Coll. Traditional Chinese Medicine, England, 1985-96; cons. Drug and Alcohol Rehab. Centre, London, 1994-97; pvt. practice acupuncturist Oxford, 1982—99, Wichita, Kans., 2000—. Cons. to various clinics, Canada, United States, Europe, 1983—, England, 1987—; lectr. hosps., England, 1984—, Acad. 5 Element Acupuncture, Miami, Fla., 2002—; lectr., cons. 10 hosps., China, 1993; adj. prof. WSU, Kans. Bd. dirs. O.A.C.M., Oxford, England, 1981, W.I.S.E., Netherlands, Denmark, 1979—82. Grantee, Oxford U., 1997. Fellow: Am. Assn. Integrative Medicine, Am. Integrative Medicine Assn.; mem.: Traditional Acupuncture Soc., Brit. Acupuncture Coun., Am. Assn. Oriental Medicine. Avocations: travel, reading, cooking, tapestry, music. Mailing: 1570 N Ridgewood Dr Wichita KS 67208 Office Phone: 316-841-4745. Personal E-mail: drlorijones@cs.com.

D'ALVIA, MARLENE, medical social worker, clinical social worker; b. Peekskill, N.Y., Aug. 10, 1941; d. Edward and Ethel (Robinson) Beisser; m. Raymond D'Alvia (div. Feb. 1975); children: Carl, Jennafer, Thea. BS in Edn., Oneonta (N.Y.) State U., 1963; MSW, Fordham U., Tarrytown, N.Y., 1986. Cert. social worker. Sr. caseworker Dept. Social Svcs., White Plains, N.Y., 1983-92; supr. child profl. svcs. Dept. Social Svcs. Westchester County, Yonkers, N.Y., 1992-95; coord. ptnrs. in parenting No. Westchester Guidance Clinic/ Mental Health Assn. Westchester County, Mt. Kisco, N.Y., 1995-99; med. social worker Hospice of Rockland, Pomona, N.Y., 1999—. Foster parent traine Dept. Social Svcs., White Plains, 1989-92. Mem. NASW. Avocations: sculpture, walking, dance. Home: PO Box 255 Cornwall On Hudson NY 12520

DALY, ANN MICHELLE, broadcast executive; BA in Economics, U. Calif., LA. Pres. N.Am. Buena Vista Home Video; head feature animation DreamWorks SKG, 1997—2004; COO DreamWorks Animations SKG, 2004—. Mailing: Dreamworks Animations Inc 1000 Flower St Glendale CA 91201*

DALY, CHERYL, communications executive, broadcast executive; b. Providence, Apr. 20, 1947; d. Francis Patrick and Mary Ann (Wallis) D.; m. Arthur James Generas, July 18, 1970; 1 child, Caroline. BA, Rutgers U., 1969; postgrad., New Sch. for Social Rsch., 1975-78. Account exec. Phil Dean Assocs., N.Y.C., 1969—72; dir. pub. rels. Kirkland Coll., Clinton, 1972—75; mgr. press svcs. CBS Radio, N.Y.C., 1976—80; assoc. dir. internal comm. CBS, Inc., 1980—81, dir. corp. info., 1981—83; v.p. pub. rels. Group W Satellite Comm., 1984—95, sr. v.p. pub. rels., 1995—97, CBS Cable, 1997—2000; sr. v.p. comm. TNN, MTV Networks, 2000—01; v.p. media relations MSNBC, 2002; pub. rels. cons. N.Y.C., 2002—05; dir. comms. NATAS, 2005—. Examiner Westinghouse Quality Awards, Pitts., 1990. Recipient Best Co. Comm. award Cable TV Bus., 1986, Mktg. award Westinghouse Broadcasting Co., 1991. Mem. Cable TV Pub. Affairs Assn. (bd. dirs. 1985-87), Media Mommies (co-founder 1987). Democrat. Roman Catholic. Home: 1 W 67th St New York NY 10023-6200 Office: NATAS 111 W 57th St Ste 600 New York NY 10019 Office Phone: 212-484-9446. E-mail: dcheryl311@aol.com, cdaly@emmyonline.tv.

DALY, ELLEN M., pediatrics nurse, educator; b. Boston, Nov. 20, 1941; d. George W. and Anna M. McInnis; m. Gordon P. Daly, Nov. 20, 1959; children: Gordon P. Jr., Glenn W., Geraldine L. Ciardelli. MS, U. Lowell, Mass., 1989. RN Mass., 1978, N.H., 1978. Asst. prof. Rivier Coll., Nashua, NH, 1993—2001, Regis Coll., Weston, Mass., 2002—. Contbr. articles to profl. jours. Vol. Big Bros./Big Sisters, Nashua, NH, 1998—2002. Mem.: ENRS. Home: PO Box 682 Glen NH 03838 Office: Regis College 235 Wellesley Street Weston MA 02493 Office Phone: 781-768-7099. Personal E-mail: maidski@verizon.net.

DALY, GAIL M., law librarian, educator; b. Detroit; BA in Edn., U. Mich., 1968, MA in Libr. Sci., 1969; JD, U. Minn., 1989. Former assoc. dir. U. Minn. Law Sch. Libr.; assoc. dean for libr. and tech., assoc. prof. law So. Meth. U. Dedman Sch. Law, Dallas. Former mng. editor Minn. Law Rev.; vis. assoc. law Rsch. Librs. Group Stanford U., Mountain View, Calif.; mem. Nat. Mus. and Libr. Svcs. Bd., Washington, 2004—. Mem.: ABA, Am. Assn. Law Librs., Assn. Am. Law Schs. Office: So Meth Univ Underwood Law Libr 6550 Hillcrest Ave Dallas TX 75275

DALY, KATHLEEN ANN, elementary school educator; b. Ft. Belvoir, Va., July 10, 1956; d. Hugh Francis and Helen Margaret (Breen) Daly; m. David Whitton, Mar. 8, 1985; children: Patrick Brendan, Sean David. AB in Elem. Edn., U. Ky., 1978; MS in Elem. Edn., No. Ky. U., 1990. Reading tchr. Covington Cath. H.S., Park Hills, Ky., 1979-80; tchr. math and reading St. Mary's Sch., Alexandria, Ky., 1980-81; tchr. grades 7-8 St. Leo's Sch., Versailles, Ky., 1981-82, Menwith Hill Sch., Harrogate, Eng., 1982—. Recipient Presdl. Award for Excellence in Sci. and Math. Teaching, NSF, 1993. Mem. Nat. Coun. Tchrs. Math., Coun. of Presdl. Awardees in Math. Office: Menwith Hill Sch APO AE 09468

DALY, KAY R., public relations professional; b. Santa Monica, Calif., Oct. 31, 1966; d. Walter Francis and Joy Ray Ryon; m. Jack Williams Daly, Dec. 14, 1996; children: Patrick Bryan, Jack Reagan. BA in Comms., U. Calif., San Diego, 1989; postgrad., George Washington U. Prodn. intern TV show Dukes of Hazzard, fall 1982, Hill Street Blues, spring 1984; lab. asst. George C. Page Mus., summer 1983; salesperson Saks Fifth Ave., Beverly Hills, summer 1985; intern Phillips-Ramsey Advt. & Pub. Rels., fall 1987; press intern U.S. Sen. Pete Wilson Washington, summer 1988; press intern Senate campaign Californians for Pete Wilson, fall 1988; press asst. to campaign mgr. Sen. Pete Wilson's Campaign for Gov., 1989; state projects asst. U.S. Sen. Phil Gramm, 1989-91; dir. polit. analysis Booz-Allen & Hamilton, Inc., 1991-92; chief of staff Office of Tex Lezar, 1992-94; press sec., dep. campaign mgr. Tex Lezar for Lt. Gov., 1994; press sec., projects dir. U.S. Rep. Fred Heineman, 1995-96; rsch. cons. U.S. Rep. Robin Hayes' Campaign for Gov., 1996; comms. cons. N.C. Rep. Party, 1996, dir. comm., 1996-97; v.p., Wash. ops & publ. rels. dir. Signature Agy., 1997—2003; pres. Daly & Assocs., Inc. Various positions Mitsui Mfrs. Bank, summer 1984, 86, 87; rsch. dir. radio/TV talk show The Tom Joyner Show, N.C., mng. editor newsletter The Amen Corner, 1996; dir. Am. for Ashcroft Comm., 2001; spokesperson Coalitian for a Fair Judiciary. Asst. editor: (book) Making Government Work, 1992; newsletter editor: N.C. Fed. Rep. Women; host radio talk show The Daly Report, website; frequent columnist, radio/TV guest. Mem. exec. com. Wake County GOP, 4th Congl. Dist. GOP; bd. dirs. state coord. Ronald Reagan Legacy Project. Recipient speech and debate awards Nat. Forensics League, commendation letter U. So. Calif. Reading Ctr. for Tapes for the Blind, Top Honors in Crisis Comm., Infogroup, 2000, Ronald Reagan award Am. Conservative Union, 2003. Fellow (sr.) Ctr. for Individual Freedom; mem. Internat. Rep. Inst. (trainer issue advocacy/campaign comms. seminar in Ukraine), Internat. Assn. Bus. Communicators, Rep. Comms. Assn., Ind. Women's Forum, Coalition Fair Judiciary (pres.), Mil. Order of World Wars (hereditary mem.), Delta Delta Delta. Republican. Avocations: gourmet cooking, politics, travel. Home: 6035 Woodlake Ln Alexandria VA 22315 Office: 5810 Kingstowne Ctr Dr Ste 120 PMB 166 Alexandria VA 22315 Personal E-mail: krdaly@aol.com.

DALY, MARKATE, philosophical researcher, counselor; d. Jerome Aloysius Daly and Helen Boemer Wall; children: Kristin Ann Bugge, Laura Jean Schroeter, Jill Wynn. BS, Marquette U., 1958; MS, U. Wis., 1982, PhD in Philosophy, 1984. Pres. Ctr. Pub. Philosophy, Berkeley, Calif., 1994—; philosophy tchg., asst. prof. Mills Coll., Santa Clara U., U. Calif., Calif., 1984—93. Counselor Philisophical Counseling Svc., Berkeley, 1994—. Editor: (anthology) Communitarianism: A New Public Ethics; author, 1994. Grass roots organizing MoveOn.org, Berkeley, Calif., 2004—. Mem.: Am. Philos. Assn. (licentiate). Unitarian Universalist. Achievements include research in naturalized social metaphysics and ethics. Office: Philos Counseling 2714 Telegraph Ave Berkeley CA 94705 Office Phone: 510-703-8748. Personal E-mail: markatedaly@comcast.net. Business E-Mail: philosophycounsel@comcast.net.

DALY, MARY BERYL, health facility administrator; d. Kenneth and Stella Jeannette Kimmerlin; m. James L. Borders, Oct. 4, 1997; children: Joseph, Justine, Roisin Gael. BA in Biology, Coll. New Rochelle, N.Y., 1965; MPH in Epidemiology, U. N.C., Chapel Hill, 1971, PhD in Epidemiology, 1973, MD, 1978. Diplomate Am. Bd. Internal Medicine, 1981, Am. Bd. Med. Oncology, 1983. Tchr. St. Josephs H.S., Nkubu, Kenya, 1965—68; intern internal medicine U. Tex. Health Sci. Ctr., San Antonio, 1978—81, fellow med. oncology, 1981—83; chmn. Dept. Hematology, Oncology Hall Med. Ctr. USAF, San Antonio, 1983—89; sr. v.p. population sci. divsn. Fox Chase Cancer Ctr., Phila., 1989—2005, sr. v.p. Divs. Population Sci., 2006—. Col. USAF, 1983—89. Recipient Best in Show award, Printing Coun. N.J., 2005. Fellow: ACP; mem.: Am. Soc. Clin. Oncology, Am. Soc. Preventive Oncology (pres. 2001—02). Avocations: lithography, kayaking, bicycling. Office: Fox Chase Cancer Ctr 333 Coltman Ave Philadelphia PA 19111 Office Phone: 215-728-2791.

DALY, MARY C., dean, law educator; BA, Thomas More Coll., 1969; JD cum laude, Fordham U. Sch. Law, 1972; LLM in Comparative Law, NYU Sch. Law, 1975—78. Assoc. Rogers & Wells, 1973—75; asst. U.S. Atty. Civil Div., 1975—80; chief of civil div. U.S. Atty. Office, So. Dist. N.Y., 1981—83; prof. Fordham Law Sch., 1983—2004, co-dir. Louis Stein Ctr. for Law and Ethics, dir. Grad. Prog., James H. Quinn Prof. Legal Ethics; dean, John V. Brennan Chair Law and Ethics St. John's U. Sch. Law, 2004—. Grantee Zichkla Fellow, Université de Paris, Faculté de Droit, 1973. Mem.: ABA (reporter Commn. Multidisciplinary Practice 1998—2000, mem. Out-of-the Box Com.), Fed. Bar Coun. (trustee 1997—2004), Assn. Bar N.Y.C. (chair Com. Profl. and Judicial Ethics 1996—99, mem. Delegation to Chile, Rwanda and Brazil 2002—03). Office: St Johns U Sch Law 8000 Utopia Parkway Jamaica NY 11439 E-mail: dalym@stjohns.edu.

DALY, MIRIAM SHAMER, retired family physician; b. Balt., Jan. 26, 1925; d. Maurice Emory and Bertha (Tapman) Shamer; m. Harold L. Daly, Jr., June 28, 1948 (dec. July 2, 1989); children: John, Martha, Thomas, David. AB, Goucher Coll., 1946; MD, U. Md., 1950. Diplomate Am. Bd. Family Practice. Intern Luth. Hosp. of Md., Balt., 1950-51, resident, 1951-52; clinic physician Balt. City Health Dept., Md. State Health Dept., 1952-55; practicing physician Balt., 1952-55; physician pvt. practice Albion, Mich., 1955-93; ret., 1993. Leader, camp counsellor Girl Scouts, South Ctrl. Mich., 1955—, pres. Irish Hills Coun., 1993-97, coord. Albion ARC blood drives, 1994—, mem. Sweet Adelines, 2003-05; bd. dir., 1990-97, Albion Ambulance Svc., 1989-95, ARC Calhoun County chpt., 1993—, Great Lakes Region Blood Svcs., ARC, 1994-95; mem. bd. Albion-Homer United Way, 1999-2005, pres., 2001, 2002. Recipient Girl Scouts Thanks Badge, Irish Hills Girls Scouts Coun., 1977, 1993, Cmty. Recognition award, Albion Coll., 1996, Athena award, Greater Albion C. of C., 2000. Mem. AMA, AAUW, NAACP (exec. bd. 2005—, bd. mem. Albion br.), Mich. State Med. Soc. (Frederick and Besse Moulton Plessner Meml. award 1996), Calhoun County Med. Soc., Am. Acad. Family Practice, Mich. Acad. Family Practice, S.W. Mich. Perinatal Assn., Rotary. Avocations: piano, photography, gardening. Personal E-mail: msdaly@hotmail.com.

DALY, TYNE, actress; b. Madison, Wis., Feb. 21, 1946; d. James Daly and Hope Newell; m. Georg Stanford Brown (div.); children: Alyxandra, Kathryne, Alisabeth. Student, Brandeis U., Am. Music and Dramatic Acad. Performed at Am. Shakespeare Festival, Stratford, Conn.; appeared on Broadway in Gypsy, 1990, 91 revivals, The Seagull, 1992, Rabbit Hole, 2006; films include Angel Unchained, 1970, The Enforcer, 1976, The Entertainer, 1976, Speed Trap, 1977, Telefon, 1977, Zoot Suit, 1982, The Aviator, 1985, Movers and Shakers, 1985; made TV debut in series The Virginian; guest appearances in various TV series including Veronica's Closet, 1996, appearances in TV series include Cagney & Lacey, 1982-88 (Emmy awards 1983, 84, 85, 88), Christy, 1994, (Emmy award 1996), Judging Amy, 1999-, (Emmy award best sup. actress, 2003); TV films include In Search of America, 1971, A Howling in the Woods, 1971, Heat of Anger, 1972, The Man Who Could Talk to Kids, 1973, Larry, 1974, Intimate Strangers, 1977, Better Late Than Never, 1979, The Women's Room, 1980, A Matter of Life and Death, 1981, The Great Gilly Hopkins, 1981, Your Place or Mine, 1983, Kids Like These, 1987, Stuck With Each Other, 1989, The Last to Go, 1990, Face of a Stranger, 1991, On the Town, 1993, Scattered Dreams, 1994, Colombo: Bird in the Hand, 1994, Bye Bye Birdie, 1994, Columbo: Undercover, 1994, The Forget-Me-Not Murders, 1994, Cagney and Lacey: The Return, 1994, Cagney and Lacey: Together Again, 1995, A Perfect Mother, 1996, Autumn Heart, The Simian Line, Shades of Gray, Three Secrets, Tricks, 1997, The Perfect Mother, 1997, Vig, 1998, Execution of Justice, 1999, The Wedding Dress, 2001; appearance one-woman show Mystery School. Recipient Tony award for Mama Rose role in Gypsy, 1990; nominated 2nd Antoinette Perry (Tony) award role in Rabbit Hole, 2006. Address: 272 S Lasky Dr Unit 402 Beverly Hills CA 90212-3671

DALY-GAWENDA, DEBRA, health facility administrator, nursing educator; b. Chgo., Aug. 30, 1956; m. Tom Gawenda; children: Christopher, Haley, Zachary. Diploma, Michael Reese Hosp. Sch. Nsg., 1978; AA in Liberal Arts, Richard J. Daley Coll., 1982; BSN, Rush U., 1983; MS, U. Ill., Chgo., 1984. RN, Ill. Staff nurse emergency room Rush Med. Ctr., Chgo., Mercy Hosp. and Med. Ctr., Chgo.; asst. prof. Rush U., Chgo.; dir. employee & corp. health svcs. Rush-Presbyn.-St. Luke's Med. Ctr., Chgo. Lectr. in field. Author 2 books; contbr. articles to profl. publs. Mem. NAFE, Nat. Wellness Inst., Am. Assn. Occupl. Health Nurses, Internat. Platform Assn., Ill. Hosp. Assn. Occupl. Health Nurses (pres.), Ill. Coun. Nurse Mgrs., Worksite Wellness Coun. Ill. (bd. dirs.), Sigma Theta Tau (mem. nominating com.). Home: 11580 Circle DR Burr Ridge IL 60527-8012

DAM, CHRISTINA MALO, secondary school educator; b. Leyden Twp., Ill., May 20, 1976; d. Ted O. and Pat A. Malo; m. Steve Gerrit Dam; 1 child, Gerrit Tyler. BS, Western Ill., Macomb, 1999; M in Tchg. in Leadership, St. Xavier, Chgo., 2006. Cert. tchr. Ill. 6th grade sci. tchr., Prairie Grove, Ill., 2000—01; h.s. sci. tchr. Johnsburg HS, McHenry, Ill., 2001—. Cross country and track coach Johnsburg Dist. 12, McHenry, 2001—05. Children's ministries Crystal Lake (Ill.) Evang. Free Ch., 2005—06. Office: Johnsburg HS 2002 W Ringwood Rd Mchenry IL 60050 Office Phone: 815-385-9233 ext 201. Business E-Mail: cdam@kidsroe.org.

DAME, CATHERINE ELAINE, acupuncturist; b. Holyoke, Mass., Oct. 1, 1951; d. Josaphat Charles and Lillian Geneva (Archer) Boulanger; m. William Henry Dame, Jan. 9, 1970 (div. May 1999); 1 child, Cristinna Lian. Acupuncture Diplomate, N.E. Sch. Acupuncture, Watertown, Mass., 1992; student, Ind. U., 1988-93; MEd, Cambridge Coll., 1994. Lic. acupuncturist, Mass.; nat. bd. cert. in acupuncture. Dept. mgr. Zayre Dept. Store, Chicopee, Mass., 1969; retail sales clk. Woodward & Lothrop Store, Alexandria, Va., 1971-72; dept. mgr. Steiger Dept. Store, Enfield, Conn., 1972-73; retail sales clk. Point Dept. Store, Ft. Walton Beach, Fla., 1973-74; assembly, repair mfg. Texas Instruments, Ft. Walton Beach, 1974-75; tller Third Nat. Bank, Springfield, Mass., 1975-81, customer svc. rep., 1981-82; teller Bank of N.E./Fleet Bank, Springfield, 1990-93; owner, mgr. Acupuncture Svcs., Chicopee, 1994—. Cons. Cambridge Coll., Springfield, Mass., 1994-95; bus. office liaison Cambridge Coll., 1995-98; Traditional Chinese Med. tour, China, 2001. Mem. People to People Internat. Mem.: Acupuncture Soc. Mass., Nat. Commn. Cert. of Acupuncturists Directory, Am. Assn. Oriental Medicine, Assn. Profl. Genealogists, New Eng. Hist. Geneal. Soc., Chicopee C. of C., Kings Bridge Equine Rescue, Inc., Granby Regional Horse Coun. Office: Acupuncture Svcs Chicopee 665 Prospect St Chicopee MA 01020-3064 Office Phone: 413-536-4534.

DAMIANO, CATHY, elementary school educator; BS in Elem. Edn., Shippensburg U., Pa., 1987. Tchr. St. Rose of Lima Sch., Altoona, Pa., 1987—. Office: St Rose of Lima Sch 5519 6th Ave Altoona PA 16602 Office Phone: 814-942-7835.

DAMICO, DEBRA LYNN, academic administrator, language educator; b. Passaic, N.J., Apr. 15, 1956; d. Nicholas Biagio and Eleanore Lorraine (Hugle) D. BA, Montclair State U., 1978, MA, 1989. Cert. tchr., N.J, reading specialist. Tchr. adult basic edn., gen. edn devel. and ESL Montclair State U., 1974—2001, coord. EXCEL program, 1993—2001; tchr. St. Francis Sch., Hackensack, NJ, 1978—79, Saddle Brook (NJ) HS, 1979-80, St. Dominic Acad., Jersey City, 1980-84; internat. student advisor Manhattan Coll., Bronx, NY, 1984—, ESL instr., 1986—, instr. French, 1988—, dir. internat. student svcs., coord. academic programming residence life, 2006—. Instr. Writing

Inst. Adult Edn. Resource Ctr., Jersey City State Coll., 1987—; Outstanding Internat. Student advisor, 1989—. Mem. Dist. Wide Curriculum Council, Lodi, N.J., 1977-78; ch. cantor and musician. Named Outstanding Young Woman Am., 1986; grantee, Assn. Internat. Educators, 1985—86. Mem. Nat. Assn. Tchrs. of English as a Fgn. Lang., N.Y. Tchrs. of ESL, Assn. of Internat. Educators, Metro-Internat., Am. Assn. Tchrs. French, NAFSA:Assn. of Internat. Educators, Kappa Delta Pi, Pi Delta Phi. Democrat. Roman Catholic. Avocations: singing, playing and teaching guitar, cantor and musician at church. Office: Manhattan Coll 4513 Manhattan College Pkwy Bronx NY 10471-4998 Fax: 718-862-8016. Business E-Mail: debra.damico@manhattan.edu.

D'AMICO, SANDRA HATHAWAY, art educator; b. Torrington, Wyo., Dec. 3, 1954; d. Stanley Knapp and Roberta Harley Hathaway; m. John Chris D'Amico, May 24, 1980; children: Andrew, Christine. BFA, U. Denver, 1977; M of Humanities, U. Colo., Denver, 1998. Tchr. art Aurora (Colo.) Pub. Schs., 1977—81; artist-in-residence Wilder Elementary Sch., Littleton, 1988—90; art tchr. on spl. assignment Littleton Pub. Schs., 1989—90; tchr. art Creekside Elem. Sch., Aurora, 1990—92, Laredo Mid. Sch., 1992—98, Smoky Hill H.S., 1998—. Visual arts coord. Smoky Hill H.S., Aurora, Colo., 2000—. Mem.: ArtSource Colo. (adv. coun., chair staff devel. 2003—), Colo. Art Edn. Assn. (Outstanding H.S. Art Educator 2003). Office: Smoky Hill HS 16100 E Smoky Hill Rd Aurora CO 80015

DAMON, SHERRI MARCIA, music educator; b. Wilson, NC, Nov. 23, 1964; d. Alvin Earl and Shirley Woodard Damon. MusB, Cleve. Inst. Music, 1986; MusM, U. NC, Greensboro, 1994, D in Musical Arts, 1999. Lic. K-12 Music NC Dept. Pub. Instrn. Vis. asst. prof. music Valley City (ND) State U., 1999—2000; dir. bands Chewning Mid. Sch., Durham, NC, 2000—05; asst. prof. music, instrumental music dir. Mt. Olive (NC) Coll., 2005—. Prin. trombone Salisbury (NC) Symphony Orch., 1992—99; adj. brass instr. Livingstone Coll., Salisbury, NC, 1997—99; member, arranger Brass-on-the-Slide Trombone Ensemble, Chapel Hill, NC, 2000—05; performer, clinician NC Trombone Festival, Greensboro, NC, 2002—05; guest conductor, clinician Sampson County All-County Band, NC, 2006—. Featured arranger (Ea. Trombone Workshop); composer: (brass quintet) The Watchman, The Journey: A Celebration of Epiphany; musician (guest performer): Thoughts of Love for Trombone and Band; musician: Wayne Cmty. Coll. Band, 2006. Mem. First Assembly God, Goldsboro, NC, 2005. With USN, 1986—91, Cinclantflt Band. Mem.: Music Educators Nat. Conf., Kappa Delta Pi. Office: Mt Olive Coll 634 Henderson St Mount Olive NC 28365 Office Phone: 919-653-0854 ext. 4079. Business E-Mail: sdamon@moc.edu.

DAMON, SHIRLEY STOCKTON, art gallery owner; b. San Francisco, Apr. 29, 1931; d. Andrew Benton and Melva Laverta (Harbin) Stockton; m. Terry Allen Damon, Oct. 20, 1956 (div. 1980); children: Benton Allen (dec.), Diana Clare, Denise Yvonne, Andrew Allen. BA, U. Calif., Santa Barbara, 1953; MA, Stanford U., 1956, postgrad., 1958. Tchr. Santa Barbara City Sch., 1953-54; demonstration tchr. U. Calif., Santa Barbara, 1954; dir. CIT program, asst. camp dir. Montecito Camp for Girls, Calif., 1955-57; tchr. Santa Clara County Sch., 1957; instr. Stanford U., 1958; tchr. Escambia County Sch., Pensacola, Fla., 1959; pres. Damon Galleries, Ltd., Vienna, Va., 1973—. Chair archtl. rev. bd. Town of Vienna, 1994—, mem., 1991—; mem. Police Chiefs Adv. Bd., Vienna, 1993-96; pres. Vienna Commons Assn., 1990-96; adult leader Girl Scouts USA Mem.: Vienna's Windover Historic Dist. Bd., Am. Soc. Philat. Exhibitors, Internat. Soc. Japanese Philately, Ryukyu Philat. Soc. (charter), Profl. Picture Framers Assn. (assoc. regional dir. 1984—90, pres. 1990—93), judge framing competitions 1990—, chmn. cert. com. 1993—98, nat. instr. in tng. courses, awards recognition com. 2001—, award for svc. 1994), Am. Philat. Soc. (life). Republican. Episcopalian. Office Phone: 703-938-7000.

D'AMOUR, MICHELLE ALINE, principal; b. Malone, N.Y., Oct. 12, 1948; d. Carmen Lawrence D'Amour and Pierrette Jeanette Quenneville; m. Steven Craig Podd, Oct. 7, 1980; 1 child, Lindsay D'Amour Podd. BA, Nazareth Coll., Rochester, N.Y., 1970; postgrad., Sarah Lawrence Coll., Terryville, N.Y., 1977, U. Tucson, 1976; Grad. Diploma, McGill U., Montreal, 1972; MS, L.I. U., Brookville, N.Y., 1980. Cert. tchr. K-23, French, Spanish, art. Instr. French North Country C.C., Malone, NY, 1970—73; tchr. Spanish and French No. Adirondack Ctrl. Sch. Dist., Ellenburg, NY, 1970—71, Malone Ctrl. Sch. Dist., 1970—73; tchr. French, Spanish, art Three Village Sch. Dist., Setauket, NY, 1973—79; chairperson fgn. lang. Gelinas Jr. H.S., Setauket, 1979—82; adminstrv. asst. W.C. Mepham H.S., Bellmore, NY, 1982—84; asst. prin. West Islip H.S., NY, 1984—92, Beach St. Mid. Sch., 1992—95; prin. Oquenock Elem. Sch., 1995—. Contbr. articles to profl. jours. Recipient Acad. Excellence award in ednl. leadership and adminstrn., C.W. Post Ctr., L.I. U., 1980. Mem.: ASCD, Nassau Suffolk Coun. of Adminstrv. Women in Edn. (v.p. 1980—83), West Islip Assn. Sch. Adminstrs. (sec. 1987—92, v.p. 1992—94, pres. 1994—96, negotiation team 1994—), Sch. Adminstrs. Assn. N.Y. State, Nat. Assn. Elem. Sch. Prins., Internat. Reading Assn., PTA (hon.), Phi Delta Kappa. Avocations: reading, painting, travel. Home: 293 Northern Blvd Saint James NY 11780 Office: Oquenock Elementary School 425 Spruce Ave West Islip NY 11795

DAMPIER, CARYN, self-defense instructor; b. San Angelo, Tex., June 9, 1956; d. Clyde Hampton and Betty Jean Harville; m. David Anthony Dampier, Feb. 4, 1983; children: David, Michael, Nicholas. BA, U. Tex., El Paso, 1978. Teen psychiat. counselor St. Joseph Hosp., El Paso, 1978-82; vol., counselor Ft. Stewart (Ga.) Drug Abuse Program, 1984-87; vol. Ft. Stewart Children's Camp, 1984-87; adminstrv. asst. Naval Rsch. Lab., Monterey, Calif., 1988-2000; claims asst. William Beaumont Army Med. Ctr., El Paso, Tex., 1988-2000; transp. specialist The Mil. Traffic Command, Washington, 1988-2000; rape/aggression/def. instr. Fairfax (Va.) County Police, 1999-2000, Miss. State U., 2000—, com. specialist Social Sci. Rsch. Ctr., 2000—02; program dir. First United Meth. Ch., 2002—. Chief instr., regional dir. Naval Postgrad. Sch. Tae Kwondo Assn., 1997—, master instr., 1999—. Vol. First United Meth. Ch. TV Ministry, Missions Team. Recipient Presdl. Sports award Pres. Coun. on Phys. Fitness, 1998, 2000, 01, 02. Mem. Am. Legion Aux., Civitan. Republican. Methodist. Home: 801 Cathys Pond Starkville MS 39759-7008 Office Phone: 662-323-5722. Business E-Mail: caryn@first-umc.org.

DAMROSCH, LORI FISLER, law educator; b. Santa Monica, Calif., Nov. 4, 1953; d. Peter D. and Jean (Bauer) Fisler; m. David Damrosch, May 18, 1974; children: Diana Helen, Eva Katherine, Peter Leopold. BA summa cum laude, Yale U., 1973, JD, 1976. Bar: Conn. 1976, DC 1980, NY 1982, US Supreme Ct. 1982. Law clk. US Dist. Ct., New Haven, 1976-77; atty. US Dept. State, Washington, 1977-80; assoc. Sullivan & Cromwell, NYC, 1981-84; assoc. prof. law Columbia U. Sch. Law, NYC, 1984-89, prof. law, 1989—, Henry L. Moses prof. law and internat. organ., 1999—. Mem. adv. com. internat. law U.S. Dept. State, Washington, 1986—. Editor: The International Court of Justice at a Crossroads, 1987 (recipient Am. Soc. Internat. Law cert. of merit 1988); bd. editors Am. Jour. Internat. Law, 1990—; co-author: United States Law of Sovereign Immunity, 1983, Law and Force in the New International Order, 1991, Collective Restraint: Intervention in Internal Conflicts, 1993. Mem. Human Rights Watch, N.Y.C., 1987-. Recipient Superior Honor award Dept. State, Washington, 1980. Mem. ABA, Am. Soc. Internat. Law (exec. coun. 1985-88, Francis Deak Prize 1981), Assn. of Bar of City of N.Y. (sec. internat. law com. 1981-84), Phi Beta Kappa. Home: 138 St Johns Pl Brooklyn NY 11217-3402 Office: Columbia Law Sch Jerome L Greene Hall 435 W 116th St New York NY 10027-7297 E-mail: damrosch@law.columbia.edu.

DAMROSCH, SHIRLEY PATCHEL, social psychologist, educator; b. Wilkes-Barre, Pa. d. Charles and Sophie (Ruch) Petchel; m. William Ludlow Damrosch, June 4, 1970; 1 child, Guy Donahoo. BA, Ohio State U.; PhD, U. Minn., 1975. Assoc. prof. social psychology and rsch. cons. Ctr. for Methodological Rsch., Sch. Nursing, U. Md., Balt., 1977—. Contbr. articles to profl. jours., chpts. to books. Mem. AIDS Prevention Edn. Adv. Com. of the Howard County Pub. Sch. System, Columbia, Md., 1990-94. Mem. APA, Phi Beta Kappa. Office Phone: 410-706-7556, 410-730-6917.

DAMS, JEANNE M., writer; b. Ind., 1941; married. Graduate, Purdue U., U. Notre Dame, Ind. Author: (novels) (Dorothy Martin Series) Body in the Transept, 1995 (Agatha award for best novel, Macavity award nominee), Trouble in the Town Hall, 1996, Holy Terror in the Hebrides, 1997, Malice in Miniature, 1998, The Victim in Victoria Station, 1999, Killing Cassidy, 2000, To Perish in Penzance, 2001, Sins Out of School, 2003, Winter of Discontent, 2004, (Hilda Johansson Series) Death in Lacquer Red, 1999, Red White and Blue Murder, 2000, Green Grow the Victims, 2001, Silence is Golden, 2002, Crimson Snow, 2005. Mem.: Sisters in Crime, Mystery Writers of Am., Midwest Chpt. (past pres.). Mailing: c/o Kimberley Cameron Reece Halsey North # 704 98 Main St Belvedere Tiburon CA 94920 Home: South Bend IN Business E-Mail: jdams@jeannedams.com.

DAMSGAARD, PATRICIA RAE, artist, educator; b. Chgo., Ill., Dec. 29, 1931; d. Harold John Carlson and Rachel Marie Berti; m. Conrad Damsgaard; children: Susan Rae, Kristine Anita, Elizabeth Lynn. BA, Ill. Coll., Jacksonville, 1953, DHL (hon.), 2004. Cert. tchr. Mo. Legal sec. Gilbert & Polance, Chgo., 1954—56; alumni sec. Ill. Coll., Jacksonville, 1956—57; legal sec. Irwin, Deneke & Penner, Chgo., 1957—59; tchr. art Parkway Continuing Edn., St. Louis, 1979—81; tchr. art, program coord. St. Louis Artist Guild, 1986—89; tchr. art Spring Branch Continuing Edn., Houston, 1992—2000, Houston, 2000—04. Paintings, Casa Tavanoti-Watercolor USA, 2000. Trustee Ill. Coll., Jacksonville, 1996—2004; tutor Literacy Advance, Houston, 1992—94; moderator Ivy Chapel, St. Louis, 1984—86. Mem.: St. Louis Art Assn. (show chmn. 1976—77), St. Louis Watercolor Soc., Soc. Watercolor Artists, Houston Watercolor Soc. (mem. nominating com. 1999—2000, 2004—05), St. Louis Artist Guild (life). Democrat. United Church Of Christ.

DANA, JANE T., lawyer; BA with honors, U. NC, Chapel Hill, 1975; JD, Columbia U. Sch. Law, 1978. Law clerk to Hon. Leonard P. Moore US Ct. Appeals, 2nd Cir.; atty. US Dept. State; practiced law McGuire, Woods, Battle & Booth, Wilmer, Culter and Pickering; dep. gen. counsel US Dept. Commerce, Washington, 2003—, acting gen. counsel, 2004—. Scholar Harlen Fiske Stone. Mem.: Phi Beta Kappa. Office: Dept Commerce Herbert C Hoover Bldg Rm 5870 1401 Constitution Ave NW Washington DC 20230 Office Phone: 202-482-4772. Office Fax: 202-482-0042.

DANA, MARIE IMMACULÉE, education educator, department chairman; b. Albany, N.Y., Oct. 28, 1931; d. Peter Theodore and Frances Veronica (Karger) D. BA, Rosemont Coll., Phila., 1953; MA, McGill U., Montreal, Que., Can., 1962; PhD, U. Pa., 1968; postgrad., U. Paris, 1972. Cert. secondary tchr., Pa. Tchr. St. Agnes Sch., Pitts., 1953-54, Our Lady of Mercy Acad., Pitts., 1955-60, St. Peter High Sch., MeKeesport, Pa., 1960-63; prof. Carlow Coll., Pitts., 1967—, chm. div. edn., 1975-92, chmn. modern lang. divsn., 1970-90, v.p. for academic affairs, academic dean, 1993—. Presenter in field. Fulbright fellow, 1963, fellow Am. Coun. on Edn., 1974; travel grantee U. Pa., 1966. Mem. Assn. Tchr. Educators (resolution com. 1991-93), Pa. Assn. Colls. and Tchr. Educators (bd. dirs. 1990-93), Mercy Higher Edn. Colloquium (exec. com. 1988-94). Democrat. Roman Catholic. Office: Carlow Univ 3333 5th Ave Pittsburgh PA 15213-3109 Office Phone: 412-578-8865. E-mail: danami@carlow.edu.

DANAHER, MALLORY MILLETT (MALLORY JONES), actress, photographer, film and theater producer; b. St. Paul, 1939; d. James Albert and Helen Rose (Feely) Millett; m. Thomas C. Danaher, Mar. 1985; 1 child from previous marriage, Kristen Vigard. BA, U. Minn. CFO Sheets & Co., N.Y.C., Happy Camper Inc., N.Y.C., Everwarm, Inc., Mallory Inc. Actress: original cos. of Annie, The Best Little Whorehouse in Texas; stage roles: Dodsworth, Berkshire Theatre Festival; House of Blue Leaves; Hedda Gabler; Kennedy's Children; Edward Albee's Everything in the Garden (dir. Shelley Winters); Lincoln Ctr. Libr. Theatre; Stella; Cocteau's one-character play The Human Voice at Deutsches-Haus, NYU; Full Moon and High Tide; (off-Broadway prodn.) Loose Connections, Judith Anderson Theatre; actor: (TV series) Love of Life, Another World, Hunter, Thirtysomething, Superior Court, Divorce Court, The Judge, Eischied: Only the Pretty Girls Die (NBC Movie of the Week); (films) Tootsie, Hell Hath No Fury with Barbara Eden, Alone in the Dark; exhibitions include Third Eye Gallery, NYC, Modernage Discovery Gallery, Gallery of St. Clement's; author: Fatherless Child, numerous poems; co-prodr.: (films) Three Lives; exec. prodr., lead actress: Deleting Spam; prodr.: (Broadway plays) Epic Proportions. Active Creative Coalition, NY Theatre; bd. dirs. David Horowitz Freedom Ctr. Mem.: Women in Theatre, Legatus, The Actors Studio (chmn. auditions 2002—06), The Friars Club.

DANAO-SALKIN, JULIE, actress; b. Philippines; Student, Fla. Internat. U. Actress (Off-Broadway plays) The Karaoke Show, (nat. tours plays) Miss Saigon, 1992, (Broadway plays) Rent, 1997, Saturday Night Fever, 1999—2000, Lennon, 2005, (films) 101 Ways, Three Penny America, Reading Lessons, playwright (plays) Thank You, Something More, featured performer Concert of Excellence, Second Generation Productions, Lincoln Ctr., 2003, 2004.

DANCE, GLORIA FENDERSON, dance studio executive, ballet administrator; b. Portsmouth, Va., Mar. 10, 1932; d. Charles Bourrell and Ottillia Lavinia (Korn) Fenderson; m. Walter Forrest Dance III, June 4, 1951; children: Walter Forrest IV, Jon Marlon, Gloria Cherie. Student pub. schs., Petersburg. Cert. promotional dir., modeling/finishing and charm sch., cosmotologist. Assoc. tchr. Boyer/Traylor Dance Acad., Richmond, Va., 1952-60; founder, owner, dir. Gloria F. Dance Sch. Dancing, Petersburg, 1960—; artistic dir. Petersburg Ballet, Inc., 1984—. Block leader Ind. Voters, Walnut Hill, 1955—; chairwoman Jr. Woman's Club, Petersburg; Va. chairwoman Petersburg Dance Festival, White House Performance, Aug. 1984; chairwoman 1985 July 4 Festival, Petersburg. Recipient hon. award Optimist Club, Colonial Heights, Va., 1950-63, Va. Hon. award Va. Nat. Dance Week, 1984, Petersburg Pub. Service award Alumni Gloria F. Dance Sch., 1980, award Best Actress-Actress/Dancer, Liot, South Pacific, Mosque, Richmond, 1950; named Miss Virginia in Miss Am. Pageant, Atlantic City, Sept., 1950; prin. judge Miss America Preliminaries, Va., Md., N.C., Tenn., 1950's-80's; Dance Library Dedication (Gloria F. Dance Collection), Petersburg Pub. Library. Mem. Dance Educators of Am. (life), Profl. Dance Tchrs., Miss America Sorority (life). Clubs: Petersburg Country Club; Ft. Lee Country Club (Va.); Battlefield Park and Racquet, Duck Woods Country Club (Nags Head N.C.). Presbyterian. Avocations: boating, swimming, skiing, dance. Home: 1806 Brandon Ave Petersburg VA 23805-1612 also: 413 E Albatross St Nags Head NC 27959 Office: Petersburg Ballet Inc 44 Goodrich Ave Petersburg VA 23805-2120 Office Phone: 804-733-9998. E-mail: gloriadance@50470.com.

DANCE-KAYE, PAMELA, equestrian educator, consultant; b. Darien, Conn., May 13, 1949; d. Chauncey Berkeley and Rhoda Wuensch Dance; m. Gary D. Kaye, Jan. 22, 2005; 1 child, Gregory P. Colbath. Riding Instr.-Advanced Am. Riding Instrs. Assn., 1988, Intermediate Instr. Brit. Horse Soc., 1969, Advanced Instr. Physical & Cognitive Disabilities North Am. Riding for the Handicapped Assn., 2002, Special Olympics Equestrian Coach U. S. Spl. Olympics Com., 2001. Owner Tin Roof Farms, Inc., 1984—; co-founder, coach intercollegiate equestrian team Mont. State U., Bozeman, 1999—2001; equestrian dir. Gallatin River Ranch, Manhattan, Mont., 1999—2002; dir. of therapeutic svcs. Good Shepherd Therapeutic Ctr., Warm Springs, Ga., 2002—04; equestrian dir. Wills Pk. Equestrian Ctr., Alpharetta, Ga., 1996—98; coach, intercollegiate equestrian team U. of Ga., Athens, Ga., 1989—91; owner Equilink, Inc., Helena, Mont., 1983—; equestrian dir. Eagle Mt. Therapeutic Ctr., Helena, Mont., 2005—; v.p. Big Sky Horse and Hound, Three Forks, Mont., 2006—. Piroplasmosis control contractor Internat. Olympic Games, Atlanta, 1996—96; adv. bd. mem. Emory U. Cmty. Health Clinics, 1997—98. Columnist The Horseman's Corner. Equestrian coach U. S. Spl. Olympics, Atlanta, 2001—05; bd. mem. St. Francis Inst., Helena, Mont., 2006—; judge & clinician Am. Competition Opportunity for Riders With Disabilities, 1997—98; vol. Pan Am. Games - Combined Tng. Event, Chatsworth, Ga., 1992—92; judge, coach, clinician US Pony Clubs, 1976—83; judge, coach 4-H Clubs of Ga., 1989—91; cons., guest spkr. Mont. Farm Bur. Fedn., Bozeman, Mont., 2000—05. Recipient Nat. Instr. of The Yr., Am. Riding Instrs. Assn., 2000, Test Ctr. Adminstr. Yr., 2004, State Rep. Yr., 2004. Mem.: N.Am. Riding for the Handicapped Assn. (licentiate; site visitor 2001—06), Am. Riding Instrs. Assn. (licentiate; regional rep. 1999—2006). Achievements include patents for Equipparel Equestrian Visual Training Aid. Avocation: snow skiing. Office: 6700 Birdseye Rd Helena MT 59602 Office Phone: 406-443-3735. E-mail: pamsubaru@yahoo.com.

DANCYGER, RUTH, art historian; b. Cleve., Nov. 11, 1918; d. Henry and Nellie (Friedman) Steuer; married, Dec. 21, 1939; widowed, July 1968; children: Polly Sherard, Emily Edelstein. Student, Goucher Coll., 1936-38; BA, Case Western Res. U., 1942; MA, John Carroll U., 1966. Art historian John Carroll U., Cleve., 1987-93, Cleve. Artists Found., 1986—, also bd. dirs.; art historian Cleve. Artists Now, 1993-95; archivist, historian Temple Tifereth Israel, Cleve., 1998—. Lectr. Midwest Art History Found., 1995-96; catalogue rsch. asst. Cleve. Mus. Art and Ohio Univ. Press, 1996. Author (book) The Temple Tifaruth Israel 1850-2000, 1999, Kubinyi and Hall: Cleveland Partners in Art, 1988, Edris Eckhardt, Cleveland Sculptor, 1990, Samuel Bookatz, Cleveland Artist in the Nation's Capital, 1993, Phyllis Seltzer Cleveland Printmaker, 1996. Bd. dirs. Temple Mus., 1984—; mem. mayor's com. Adopt-A-Sculpture, 1993; women's coun. Cleve. Mus. Art, 1994-2004, Cleve. Ctr. for Contemporary Art, 1985—, docent coun. of Mus. of Contemporary Art Ctr., 1989-2000; mem. Cleve. Artists' Found., 1987—, recording sec., 1990-93. Ohio Bell Telephone Co. grantee, 1987. Mem. Cleve. Soc. for Contemporary Art (program and travel planner 1989-96), Print Club of Cleve. (recording sec., 2000-04), Dirs. Cir. Cleve. Mus. Art. Home: 2632 S Green Rd Cleveland OH 44122-1536

DANDEKAR, SWATI, state representative; b. Mar. 1951; arrived in US, 1973; m. Arvind Dandekar; children: Ajai, Govind. BS in Chem. & Biology, Nagpur U., India, 1971; postgrad. diploma in Dietetics, Bombay U., 1972. Mem. Iowa Ho. Reps., DesMoines, 2003—, mem. appropriations com., mem. econ. growth com., mem. edn. com. Active Linn-Mar Cmty. Sch. Dist. Bd. Edn., 1996—, Vision Iowa Bd., 2000—; bd. dir. Iowa Assn. Sch. Bds., 2000—; bd. dirs. Liars Holographic Radio Theatre, 2001—. Recipient JC Penney Edu. Golden Rule award, 2000. Mem.: Jr. League Cedar Rapids (pres. sustainers, chair diversity com.). Office: State Capitol East 12th and Grand Des Moines IA 50319 Office Phone: 515-281-3221. E-mail: swati.dandekar@legis.state.ia.us.

DANDENEAU, BILLIE JO, retired data processing executive; b. Port Arthur, Tex., May 31, 1938; d. Joseph Richard and Ida Ann (Daigle) Barrows; m. Richard Joseph Dandeneau, July 23, 1987; m. Milton S. King (div.); children: Kelly Lynn Muschong, Kevin Wayne King. AA, Lamar U., Beaumont, Tex., 1958; BBA, Ea. Ky. U., Richmond, 1976, MBA, 1978. Sec. English dept. Southea. La. U., Hammond, 1965, Miss. State U., Starkville, 1968; part-time instr. bus. adminstrn. Ea. Ky. U., Richmond, 1978; computer programmer/analyst Square D Co., Lexington, Ky., 1978—81, First Security Bank & Trust Co., Lexington, 1981—85, IBM, Lexington, 1985—91, data base adminstr. Clear Lake, Tex., 1991—93; ret., 1993. Named Outstanding Chemistry Student, Am. Chem. Soc., 1956. Mem.: Gardening Angels Garden Club (treas.), Mensa. Avocations: genealogy, photography, gardening, travel, music.

DANDONOLI, PATRICIA A., not-for-profit fundraiser; b. 1954; V.p. devel. & exec. dir. planning Am. Mus. Nat. Hist., NYC; dir. strategic initiatives Sundance Inst., Beverly Hills, Calif.; dir. resource devel. Office of Her Majesty Queen of Jordan Rania al-Abdullah, NYC; pres., CEO WaterAid Am., NYC, 2006—. Office: WaterAid Am 1221 Avenue of the Americas New York NY 10020 Office Phone: 646-344-7201.*

DANDOY, MAXIMA ANTONIO, retired education educator; b. Santa Maria, Ilocos, Sur., Philippines; came to U.S., 1949, naturalized, 1951; d. Manuel and Isidra (Mendoza) Antonio. Tchg. cert., Philippine Normal Coll., 1938; AB, Nat. Tchrs. Coll., Manila, 1947; MA, Arellano U., Manila, 1949; Ed.D. (John M. Switzer scholar, Newhouse Found. scholar), Stanford U., 1951, postgrad. (Calif. Fedn. Bus. and Profl. Women's Club scholar), 1952. Tchr. elem. sch., Philippines, 1927-37; lab. sch. tchr. Philippine Normal Coll., Manila, 1938-49; instr. Arellano U., Manila, 1947-49; lab. sch. prin. U. of East, Manila, 1953-54, assoc. prof., 1952-55; prof. edn. Calif. State U., Fresno, 1956-82, prof. edn. emeritus, 1982—. Curriculum writer, gen. office supr. Manila Dept. Edn., 1944-45; Mem. com. for the selection social studies textbooks for state adoption Calif., 1970-71; vis. prof. UCLA, 1956; Floro Crisologo Meml. lectr. U. No. Philippines, 1977 Author: Teaching Competencies, A Workbook and Log, 1985. Mem. Friends of the Stanford (Calif.) U. Sch. Edn., 1993, Sch. of Edn. and Human Devel. Alumni and Friends, Calif. State U., Fresno, 1992-93; mem. Calif. Gov.'s Conf. on Traffic Safety, 1962, Calif. Gov.'s Conf. Delinquency Prevention, 1963. Named Disting. Woman of Year, Fresno Bus. and Profl. Women's Club, 1957, Woman of Achievement, 1973, Outstanding Filipino, 1982, 98; recipient Higher Edn. and Internat. Understanding award Philippine Normal Coll. Alumni Assn., 1986, One Moment in Time award Calif. Fedn. Bus. and Profl. Women, 1997-98. Mem. AAUW (liaison Calif. State U. Fresno 1970-71, bridge gen. coord. 1995--), Nat. Coun. Social Studies (chmn. sec. internat. understanding, nat. conv. 1966), Calif. Fedn. Bus. and Profl. Women's Clubs (state chmn. scholarships 1961-63, treas. Fresno), Calif. Tchrs. Assn., Orgn. Filipino-Am. Educators Fresno (pres. 1977-95, Outstanding Svc.), Filipino-Am. Women's Club (adv. 1969-74), Internat. Platform Assn., Phi Delta Kappa, Pi Lambda Theta, Kappa Delta Pi (counselor 1972-79, nat. com. attendance and credentials 1975, nat. com. regional confs. 1966). Home: 1419 W Bullard Ave Fresno CA 93711-2324

D'ANDREA, KATHLEEN CLAIRE, speech therapist; b. Montclair, N.J., Aug. 22, 1950; d. Raymond and Claire (Delezenski) Klimaski; m. William R. McLellan, July 9, 1976 (div. Aug. 1988); 1 child, Sean W.; m. Salvatore D'Andrea, July 11, 1999. BA, William Paterson Coll., Wayne, N.J., 1972; MA, Montclair State U., Upper Montlcair, N.J., 1981. Cert. clin. competency Am. Speech and Hearing Assn.; cert. speech/lang. specialist, N.J.; lic. speech pathologist, N.J. Speech, lang. specialist Paterson Pub. Schs., NJ, 1972—2006; speech pathologist Vis. Health Svcs., Totowa, NJ, 1988—; pvt. practice speech pathology Nutley, NJ, 1989—; treas. N. Jersey Speech Pathology Assocs., Wayne, NJ, 1991-97; speech clin. supr. William Paterson U., 2002—. Pres. Am. Inst. Self Improvement, Nutley-Brielle, N.J., 1988-90, participant in grant project State of N.J. Mem. Am. Speech-Lang.-Hearing Assn. (ACE award 1991-94), N.J. Speech-Lang.-Hearing Assn., Toastmasters Internat. (past. pres. Clifton chpt. 1986-88). Avocations: bicycle riding, swimming, walking, tennis. Home and Office: 4 Adams Rd Wayne NJ 07470-2527 E-mail: kmc822@aol.com.

DANDRIDGE, LENOR, paralegal; d. LeRoy and Lucille Dandridge; 1 child, LaMont Warren. Student, Malcolm X Coll., 1976—79, Roosevelt U., 1979—83, Harold Washington Coll., 2002—. Owner Dandridge Tutoring and Mentoring, Chgo., 1998—. Author: (children's coloring book) Color N History, 1992, poetry. Cons., vol. Home-Along-With Home, Chgo., 1987—; tutor, mentor YMCA, Chgo., 1998, Hull House, Chgo., 2002; vol., asst. Play and Learn Daycare, Burham, Ill., 1999—; respite worker Ada S. McKinley, Chgo., 2002; vol. Lincoln Park Zoo, Chgo., 2003. Avocations: writing, bowling, modern jazz dancing, exercising. Home: PO Box A3203 Chicago IL 60690-3203

DANES, CLAIRE, actress; b. NYC, Apr. 12, 1979; d. Chris and Carla Danes. Attended, Lee Strasberg Theater Inst., Yale U., 1998—2002. TV role as Angela Chase in series My So-Called Life, ABC, 1994-95 (nominee Emmy award for Best Lead in Drama Series 1995, Golden Globe award for Best Actress in a Drama 1995); appeared in HBO spl. More Than Friends: The Coming Out of Heidi Leiter, 1994; guest appearances on TV series Law and

Order, 1990; film appearances include: Dreams of Love, 1992, 30, 1993, Little Women, 1994, Dead Man's Jack, 1994, How to Make an American Quilt, 1995, Home for the Holidays, 1995, The Pesky Suitor, 1995, I Love You, I love You Not 1996, To Gillian on Her 37th Birthday, 1996, as Juliet in William Shakespeare's Romeo and Juliet, 1996, Mononoke-hime (voice only), 1997, U-Turn, 1997, The Rainmaker, 1997, Les Misérables, 1998, Polish Wedding, 1998, The Mod Squad, 1998, Brokedown Palace, 1999, Hercules (voice only), 1998, Igby Goes Down, 2002, The Hours, 2002, It's All About Love, 2003, Terminator 3: Rise of the Machines, 2003, The Rage in Placid Lake, 2003, Stage Beauty, 2004, Shopgirl, 2005, The Family Stone, 2005; NYC Theatre appearences include Christina Olson: American Model, 2005. Named one of 50 most beautiful people in the world, People mag., 1997.*

DANFORD, ARDATH ANNE, retired librarian; b. Lima, Ohio, Feb. 11, 1930; d. Howard Gorby and Grace Rose (Klug) D. BA, Fla. State U., 1951, MA, 1952. Head tech. services Lima Pub. Library, 1956-60; librarian Way Pub. Library, Perrysburg, Ohio, 1960-70; asst. dir. Toledo-Lucas County Pub. Library, 1971-77, dir., 1977-85, ret., 1985. Author: The Perrysburg Story, 1966, Perrysburg Revisited, 1992. Bd. dirs. Toledo Cmty. Found., Sunset House, Way Libr. Found., Sisters of Mercy No. Health Found.; mem. adv. bd. St. Charles Hosp. Recipient Toledo Headliner award Women in Communication, 1978, Boss of Yr. award PerRoMa chpt. Am. Bus. Women's Assn., 1978 Mem. Ohio Libr. Assn. (Libr. of Yr. 1985, Hall of Fame 1993), Toledo Club, Perrysburg Garden Club, Zonta (pres. Toledo club 1975-76). Methodist. Home: 4780 Tranquility Ln Zanesville OH 43701-7664

DANFORTH-MORNINGSTAR, ELIZABETH, obstetrician, gynecologist; b. Sioux Falls, S.D., July 3, 1951; d. George Jonathan and Mina (Schumacher) Danforth; m. John Wesley Morningstar III, May 29, 1976; children: John Wesley Morningstar IV, George Danforth, Charles Alexander. BA, Grinnell (Iowa) Coll., 1972; MD, Med. Coll. Va., Richmond, 1976. Intern Strong Meml. Hosp.-U. Rochester, 1976-77, resident ob/gyn, 1977-80; MD Genesee Hosp., Rochester, N.Y.; clin. assoc. prof. U. Rochester Sch. Medicine. Pres. Women Gynecology and Childbirth Assocs., 1989—; adv. bd. Rochester Individual Practice Assocs. Adv., mem. Monroe County Bd. for Infant Mortality, Rochester, N.Y. Mem. Monroe County Med. Soc., Am. Coll. Obstetricians/Gynecologists. Address: 378 Beach Ave Rochester NY 14612-2010

D'ANGELO, RENÉE YOUNG, special education educator; d. William and Iva Mae Young; m. Thomas C. D'Angelo, Aug. 15, 1981. BS, Ea. Nazarene Coll., 1981; MS, Nova U., 1991. Cert. profl. educator's cert. Fla., elem. edn. Fla., emotionally handicapped Fla., specific learning disabilities Fla., English to spkrs. of other langs. Fla. Tchr. specific learning disabilities Palm Beach County Schs., Belle Glade, Fla., 1986—88, tchr. emotionally handicapped, 1988—92, Loxahatchee, Fla., 1992—95, pre-kindergarten tchr. of autistic, 1995—. Recipient Seldon Waldo Meml. award, Fla. Jr. C. of C., 1998. Mem.: Royal Palm Beach Jaycees (sec. 1995—97, pres. 1997—98, mgmt. v.p. 1998—99), Palm Beach County Chpt. 200, Coun. for Exceptional Children (sec. Palm Beach County chpt. 2001—02, pres. Palm Beach County chpt. 2003—04). Avocations: reading, travel, cooking, walking.

D'ANGELO MELBY, DONNA MARIE, lawyer; BA, U. Calif., 1972; JD, Calif. Western Sch. Law, 1978. Bar: Calif. 1979. Ptnr. Sonnenschein, Nath & Rosenthal LLP, L.A. Apptd. Jud. Sect. Adv. Panel; spkr. in field. Contbr. articles to profl. jours. Bd. dirs. Wellness Cmty. Foothills. Named one of Top 30 Women Litigators, L.A. and San Francisco Daily Jour., 2002, 2003, 2004, 100 Most Influential Attys. in Calif., L.A. Daily Jour., San Francisco Recorder, 2004, Top 5% So. Calif. Super Lawyers, Los Angeles Mag. & Law and Politics, 2004, 2005. Fellow: Internat. Soc. Barristers, Am. Coll. Trial Lawyers; mem.: ABA (mem. litigation sect., labor sect., employment sect), Fedn. Def. and Corp. Counsel, Internat. Assn. Def. Counsel, Def. Rsch. Inst., State Bar Calif. (trustee legal svcs. trust fund commn. 1985—86, 1997), L.A. Bar Assn. (mem. labor and employment law sect.), Fed. Bar Assn., Women Lawyers Assn. L.A., Calif. Women Lawyers, Am. Bd. Trial Advocates (exec. com. L.A. chpt. 1995—, mem. pres.'s coun. 1997, co-chair civil justice and nat. office com. 2001, nat. bd. dirs., nat. pres. 2005, pres. L.A. chpt. 2004). Office: Sonnenschein Nath & Rosenthal LLP 601 S Figueroa St Ste 1500 Los Angeles CA 90017 Office Phone: 213-892-5027. Business E-Mail: dmelby@sonnenschein.com.

DANIEL, ANN CUMMINS, psychotherapist, consultant; b. Indpls., Dec. 14, 1940; d. William Richard and Thelma Elizabeth (Macy) Cummins; m. Eric Hansen Helt, Aug. 17, 1963 (div. Oct. 1985); 1 child, Bethany Ann Helt Winston; m. Terry White Daniel, Oct. 8, 1989; 1 stepchild, Jason Wallace Daniel BS Home Econs. Edn., Purdue U., 1962; MSW, Ind. U., Indpls., 1989. Lic. clin. social worker, marriage and family therapist. Mental health clinician Cmty. Hosp. Indpls., 1985—89, psychiat. social worker, 1989—96, dir. relationship tng. for staff, 1998—, coord. marital and family wellness program, 1998—2001. Pvt. practice psychotherapy, Indpls., 1987—; mem. adj. faculty Ind. U. Sch. Social Work, 1991-96; numerous presentations on marital and family topics to local, regional and national workshops, 1987—Contbr. articles to profl. jours Participant women's movement, 1969—, anti-war movement, 1969-73, Ann Arbor (Mich.) Ecology Ctr., 1969-71, Natural Organic Farmers Assn., 1974-80, Vt. Alliance, 1974-75, Breakthrough Found., 1980-84 Mem. NASW (clin.), Acad. Cert. Social Workers (clin.), Am. Assn. Marriage and Family Therapists (clin.), Mental Health Assn. Marion County, Kappa Delta Pi, Alpha Delta Mu Avocations: hiking, bicycling, skiing. Home: 21215 Little Chicago Rd Noblesville IN 46062-8519 Office: Cmty Health Network 1500 N Ritter Ave Indianapolis IN 46219

DANIEL, BETH, professional golfer; b. Charleston, S.C., Oct. 14, 1956; d. Robert and Lucia D. Grad., Furman U., 1978. Profl. golfer Ladies Profl. Golf Assn. tour, 1979—. Mem. U.S.A. World Cup Team, 1978, U.S.A. Solheim Cup Team, 1990, 92, 94, 96, 2000, 02, 03, LPGA Executive Com., 2002—03. Winner U.S. Amateur Title, 1975, 77; winner 33 LPGA events including World Series Women's Golf, 1980, 81, Columbia Savs. Classic, 1980, 82, LPGA Championship, 1990, Big Apple Classic, 1994; Named Rolex Rookie of Yr., 1979, Rolex Player of Yr., 1980, 90, 94, A.P. Female Athlete of Yr., 1990; recipient Vare Trophy, 1989, 90, 94, The Heather Farr Player Award, 2003. Achievements include being the leading money winner in LPGA, 1980, 81, 90; inducted into LPGA Tour Hall of Fame, 1999, inducted World Golf Hall of Fame, 2000; named in the top 50 LPGA Players All-time, 2000.

DANIEL, CATHY BROOKS, educational consultant; b. Nashville, Sept. 1, 1946; d. Conway William and Alliene Marie (Gilliam) B.; m. James Newton Daniel Jr., Dec. 29, 1967 (div. July 1988); children: Laura Marie, James Newton III. Student, Memphis State U., 1964—66; BS, George Peabody Coll., 1968, MA, 1971. Cert. elem. tchr., special edn. tchr., learning disabilities and behavior disorders. Tchr. Fairview (Tenn.) Elem. Sch., 1968-69; special edn. tchr. Ross Elem. Sch., Nashville, 1969-70, Rosebank Elem. Sch., Nashville, 1970-71, Graymar Elem. Sch., Nashville, 1971-73, Norman Binkley Elem. Sch., Nashville, 1973-74; cons. ednl. and family counseling, ednl. testing Franklin, Tenn., 1975—. Methodist. Avocation: tennis. Home and Office: 2203 Springdale Dr Franklin TN 37064-4962 Office Phone: 615-794-0705.

DANIEL, DEANNA ALANE, music educator; b. Lamar, Colo., Aug. 10, 1954; d. Marvin Clair and Ruth Elizabeth Hamilton; m. David Lawerence Daniel, Oct. 27, 1984; children: Kathryn Elizabeth, Douglas Hamilton, Jonathan David. B in Music Edn., Okla. Bapt. U., 1977; MusB, Okla. Bapt. U., Shawnee, 1976; MusM, Southwestern Bapt., Ft. Worth, Tex., 1981. Music asst. Casa View Bapt. Ch., Dallas, 1981—90; music tchr. Holly Pub. Sch., Colo., 1994—99, Lake George Charter Sch., Colo., 1999—2006; ch. pianist Lake George Bible Ch., 2001—06, ch. sec., 2003—06, worship coord. Pvt. piano tchr., 1981—; handbell dir., Lake George. Recipient Marie Patterson Piano award, Okla. Bapt. U., 1975. Home: 623 Fossil Creek Rd Florissant CO 80816 Office: Lake George Charter Sch P O Box 420 Lake George CO 80827

DANIEL, ELINOR PERKINS (PERKY DANIEL), clergywoman; b. Louisville, Dec. 9, 1952; d. James Gordon and Lenora (Lisle) Perkins; m. James Wallace Daniel III, Sept. 21, 1974; one child. BA in Music, Agnes Scott Coll., 1974; MDiv, Columbia Sem., 1986; PhD of English, Ga. State U., 1994. Ordained to ministry Presbyn. Ch., 1986. Founding team, assoc. music dir. Young Singers of Callanwolde, Atlanta, 1975—82; dir., developer youth, children, handbell choirs Peachtree Presbyn. Ch., Atlanta, 1976—78; dir., developer youth, handbell choirs Decatur Presbyn. Ch., Ga., 1978—84; sr. pastor Morningside Presbyn. Ch., Atlanta, 1984—92; interim pastor Decatur Presbyn. Ch., 1994—96; mem., project coord. Romans 2000 Bib. On-Line Collaborative Commentary Project, www.romans2000.org, 1998—2003; founding pastor Genesis Cmty. Congregation, Decatur, 2001—. Pres. alumni assn. Columbia Sem., 1993, 1st alumna baccalaureate preacher, 90; baccalaureate preacher Agnes Scott Coll., 1990; preacher, England, Scotland, Switzerland, United States. Co-creator, author mus.: Petros/Life of Peter, 1980; co-creator, composer mus.: Innkeeper, 1982, The Room, 1983; contbr. articles and book revs. to profl. jours. Mem. Leadership Ga., 1990; trustee Westminster Homes, 1991—93; founding co-chair (with Imam Plemon el-Amin) Interfaith Coalition of Metro Atlanta, 1992—94; mem. fundraising com. Glenn Sch. for Young Children, 1994—99; mem. adv. bd. Atlanta Young Singers, 1996—2002, Pastoral Leadership Search Effort, 2001—03; mem. tech. com. Greater Atlanta Presbytery, 2002—04. Office: Genesis Cmty Congregation Decatur GA 30030 E-mail: genesiscommunity@mindspring.com.

DANIEL, ELNORA D., academic administrator; d. Stephen and Cecelia Bell; m. Herman Daniel, Mar. 25, 1961; 1 child, Michael. BS, N.C. Agrl. and Tech. U., Greensboro, 1964; MEd, Columbia U., N.Y.C., 1968; EdD, Columbia U., 1978. RN N.C., 1964. V.p. for acad. affairs Hampton U., Va., 1991—93, v.p. for health, 1994—95, exec. v.p. and provost, 1995—98; pres. Chgo. State U., 1998—. Bd. dirs. LaRabida Children's Hosp., Am. Assn. State Colls. and Univs. (AASCU), Am. Coun. Edn. (ACE), Commn. Adult Edn., Nat. Assn. Equal Opportunity Higher Edn. (NAFEO), Beverly Bank & Trust Co., Little Co. Mary Hosp., Seaway Nat. Bank; nat. adv. bd. Millennium Leadership Initiative Am. Assn. State Colls. and Univs. (AASCU). Contbr. articles to profl. jours., chpts. to books. Mem. LWV Chgo., 1999, Ill. Commn. 50th Anniversary Brown vs. Bd. Edn.; mem. advisory bd. Cmty Violence Prevention Program Ctrl State. U.; prin. mem. Chgo. United; mem. Econ. Club Chgo., Women's Network Chgo., Chgo. Consortium Higher Edn., Comml. Club Chgo., Univ. Club Chgo.; mem. women's bd. Field Mus. Ret. col. Nurses Corp. U.S. Army, 1991. Named to Hall of Fame, Today's Chgo. Woman, 2002; recipient Dir.'s Oustanding Achievement award, Ill., 2002. Fellow: Am. Acad. Nursing; mem.: Jr. Achievement Chgo. Independent. Office: Chicago State Univ 9501 S King Dr ADM/313 Chicago IL 60628 Office Phone: 773-995-2400. Business E-Mail: ed-daniel2@csu.edu.

DANIEL, KAREN, engineering and design company executive; BS in Acctg., N.W. Mo. State, 1980; MS in Acctg., U. Mo., Kansas City, 1981. CPA. With KPMG Peat Marwick, 1981—92, Black & Veatch, Overland Park, Kans., 1992—, now CFO. Mem. bd. commrs. Kansas City Pks. and Recreation, 1999—2003; bd. dirs. Cmty. Found., Women's Employment Network, Black Econ. Union; mem. bd. regents N.W. Mo. State U., 2003—. Recipient Nat. Profl. Achievement award, Nat. Women of Color, 2002. Office: Black & Veatch 11401 Lamar Overland Park KS 66211

DANIEL, MARGARET HAGEN, music and voice educator; b. Eau Claire, Wis., Sept. 9, 1949; d. Harold Odin and Genevieve (Kjendalen) Hagen; m. Douglas Vaughn Daniel, Aug. 9, 1975; children: Nathan Elliot, Adam Stuart, Jason Christopher (dec.). MusB in Voice, Wis. State U., Eau Claire, 1971; postgrad., Boston U., 1971; MusM in Voice, U. Wis., 1973; pvt. studies in piano and voice. Pvt. instr. piano, 1965-71; instr. music, voice U. Southwestern La., Lafayette, 1973-80, asst. prof. music, voice, class piano and music fundamentals, 1980-93, assoc. prof. music, voice, diction, pedagogy, 1993—; mem. faculty, coord. vocal studies U. La., 1995—. Asst. to dir. Sch. Music, U. Southwestern La., 1991-95; guest faculty summer music symposium Kansas State U., 1994; adjudicator mus. competitions and auditions, 1974—; presenter vocal clinics Grace Presbyn. Ch., Lafayette, 1983, 85, Chorale Acadienne, Lafayette, 1985, 86, First Bapt. Ch., Lafayette, 1989, Cantors of St. Joseph Ch., Milton, La., 1991; guest artist Luther Northwestern Theo. Sem., St. Paul, 1991, McNeese State U., Lake Charles, La., 1993, Troy (Ala.) State U., 1993, Nicholls State U., Thibodaux, La., 1994-95, New Orleans, 1995, Houston, 1996, Monroe, La., 1996, Shreveport, La., 1997; lectr./recital performer So. Chpt. Coll. Mus. Soc., 1993, 95, 96, La. Music Tchrs. Assn., 1993, 95, 2003, 05, La. Music Educators Assn., 1994, 95; presenter in field. Performer operas, including Roméo et Juliette, 1973, Rigoletto, 1974, La Traviata, 1978, others, also leading roles in musicals; oratorios include Handel's Messiah, 1980, Haydn's The Creation, 1982, Brahms' Ein Deutsches Requiem, 1989, Mendelssohn's Elijah, 1992, others; contbr. articles to profl. publs. Dir. music summer bible sch. Grace Presbyn. Ch., 1986-90, dir. children's choir, 1987-88; mem. cultural arts com. Plantation Elem. PTO, 1991-93; team coord. Cajun Sports Assn., 1991-93, Lafayette Youth Soccer Assn., 1991-93; active L.J. Alleman Mid. Sch. PTO, 1992; guest soloist numerous chs., 1966—; organist Grace Presbyn. Ch., 1997-04. Recipient Cert. of Appreciation, Coun. Devel. of French in La., 1975, Plantation Elem. Sch., 1989, 90, 91, 92; music scholar U. Wis., Eau Claire, 1967-71. Mem. AAUP, Nat. Assn. Tchrs. of Singing (v.p. South La. chpt. 1988-90, pres. 1990-92), Music Educators Nat. Conf., La. Music Tchrs. Assn., Music Tchrs. Nat. Assn. (nat. cert.), Coll. Music Soc., Sigma Alpha Iota (life, pres. 1978-80, 87-88, editor 1983-85, faculty advisor 1980—, Sword of Honor 1982), Pi Kappa Lambda (pres. 1990-92), Phi Kappa Phi. Avocations: travel, camping, reading, sewing. Office: Univ Louisiana Lafayette PO Box 41207U Lafayette LA 70504-0001 Office Phone: 318-482-5202. Business E-Mail: mdaniel@louisiana.edu.

DANIEL, MARILYN S., lawyer; b. Tulsa, Okla., July 30, 1940; d. Basil M. and Kathryne (Shannon) Stewart; m. John A. Daniel, June 15, 1962; 1 child, John S. BA, Rhodes Coll., 1962; JD, U. Ky. Coll. of Law, 1976. Bar: Ky. Sec. math. tchr., Ky, NJ, 1962—71; legal clerk U.S. Dist. Judge, Lexington, Ky., 1977; asst. U.S. atty. U.S. Dept. Justice, Lexington, 1978—81; gen. counsel Mason & Hanger Corp., Lexington, 1982—, v.p. adminstrn., 1992—96, sr. v.p., 1996—99. Dir. The Mason Co., Lexington, 1990—99, Ky. Bar Assn. for Women, 1991—93; vol. dir. Maxwell St. Legal Clinic, 1999—. Mem. Fayette County Bd. Edn., 1985—88; trustee Transylvania Presbytery, 1985—98; elder Maxwell St. Presbyn. Ch., 1993—. Recipient Women of Achievement award YWCA, 1993. Mem. ABA, KBA (CLE chair ann. conv. 1992), Fayette County Bar Assn. (Henry T. Duncan award 1994. Avocations: gardening, cooking, hiking, quilting, handwork.

DANIEL, SUSAN QUALLS, secondary school educator; b. Gary, Ind., Apr. 11, 1958; d. Raymond Dee Qualls; 1 child, Jordan Taylor. BA, Nat. U., San Diego, 1986, MA, lifetime CC credential, Nat. U., San Diego, 1988. Tchr. Oceanside Unified Sch. Dist., Calif., 1990—, night sch. adult edn. tchr., 1997—2001; ESL instr. Mira Costa C.C., Oceanside, 1986—90. Gifted and talented class tchr. Murrieta Sch. Dist., Calif., 1988—90. Author: (anti-graffiti video) California Youth Against Graffiti Video (Outstanding Educator Appreciation award City of Oceanside, 1995). Recipient Marvin T. Levin scholarship. Mem.: Oceanside Tchrs. Assn. (corr.; site rep. 2000—02), Calif. Tchrs. Assn. (life). Avocations: writing, reading, oil painting. Home: 31130 El Torito Ct Temecula CA 92592 Office: Ocean Shores Continuation High School 3131 Oceanside Blvd Oceanside CA 92056 Office Phone: 760-439-3142. Office Fax: 760-439-5588. Personal E-mail: susieqintemecula@aol.com.

DANIEL, WINIFRED YVONNE, elementary school educator; d. William Clair Goatley and Imogene Gregory Shelby; 1 child, Jacquelyn Marie. BS in Elem. Edn., Ctrl. State U., 1960. Profl. cert. elem. edn. Ohio. Tchr. grade 1 Cleve. Pub. Schs., 1960—72; tchr. grades 1 and 4 Maple Heights Pub. Schs., Ohio, 1972—77; tchr. grades 4-8 Warren City Schs., Ohio, 1977—2000. Substitute tchr. Warren City Schs., 2000—. Jennings scholar, Martha Holden Jennings Found., 1966—67. Mem.: Delta Sigma Theta. Baptist. Avocations: reading, baking, quilting.

DANIEL-DREYFUS, SUSAN B. RUSSE, information technology executive; b. St. Louis, May 30, 1940; d. Frederick William and Suzanne (Mackay) Russe; m. Don B. Faerber, Nov. 27, 1962 (div. Nov. 1968); 1 child, Suzanne Mackay; m. Marc Andre Daniel-Dreyfus, Aug. 9, 1969; 1 child, Cable Dunster. Student, Smith Coll., 1958-60, Corcoran Sch. Fine Arts, 1960-61, Washington U., St. Louis, 1961-62; MEd, Cambridge Coll., 1991. Mng. ptnr. Comm., Inc., 1980-82; asst. dir. Harvard Bus. Sch. Fund, Cambridge, 1982-86; pres. SCR Assocs. Corp., Cambridge, 1986—. Mem. bd. advisors Odysseum, Inc.; bd. dirs. Future Mgmt. Systems. Mem. St. Louis-St. Louis County White House Conf. on Edn., 1966-68; mem. Mo. 1st Gov.'s Conf. on Edn., 1966, 2d Conf., 1968; bd. dirs. Tunbridge Sch., 1973-78, St. Louis Smith Coll.; hon. bd. dirs. New Music Circle; mem. woman's bd. dirs. Washington U., New Music Circle, 1963-67; mem. woman's bd. Mo. Hist. Soc.; bd. dirs. Non-Partisan Ct. Plan for Mo., Young Audiences Inc., 1967-69; bd. dirs. Childrens Art Bazaar, 1968-70; founder St. Louis Opera Theater; chmn. Art. Mus. Bond Issue election St. Louis, 1966; jr. bd. dirs. St. Louis Symphony, 1966-68, Opportunities Indsl. Center, Boston; legis. chmn. bd. dirs. Boston LWV, 1969-72; mem. coun., bd. dirs. Jr. League Boston, 1970-72, 74-76, v.p. Bd. of Family Counseling Services-Region West, Boston, 1979—; pres. Family Counseling Bd., Brookline, Mass.; trustee Chestnut Hill Sch., Boston, Brookline Friendly Soc.; mem. steering com. ann. fund Boston Children's Hosp. Med. Center, 1980-84; v.p. Nat. Friends Bd., Joslin Diabetes Found., 1980-83; mem. corp. bd. Joslin Diabetes Ctr.; v.p. bd. dirs. Boston Ctr. Internat. Visitors, 1979-82; Boston bd. dirs. Mass. Soc. Prevention of Cruelty to Children, 1980-84; exec. v.p. Ctr. for Middle East Bus., 1978-82; pres. bd. Brookline Community Fund, 1984—; overseer Old Sturbridge Village, 1987—. Mem. Colonial Dames, Soc. Art Historians. Clubs: Women's City (dir., Boston); Vincent (dir.). Home: PO Box 638 Altona 3018 Australia

DANIELEWSKI, DONNA KRYSTYNA, secondary school educator; b. Poland, Jan. 4, 1942; came to U.S., 1947; d. Walter and Alice Wojec; m. George L. Danielewski, June 7, 1969; children: Eva, Christopher, Paul. BA, Beaver Coll., 1963; MA, Temple U., 1966. Cert. tchr., Pa. Classroom tchr. Upper Dublin Sch. Dist., Dresher, Pa., 1963-77; classroom tchr., scholars bowl coach Pennsbury H.S., Fairless Hills, Pa., 1989—. Instr. Holy Family U., Phila., 1993. Cub scout den leader Boy Scouts Am. Mem. AAUW, Polish Heritage Soc. Phila. (pres. 1996), Nat. Coun. for the Social Studies, Delta Kappa Gamma. Avocations: reading, travel, walking.

DANIELIDES, JOANNIE C., public relations executive; m. Nicholas Danielides; children: Philippe, Alexander. BA in art history, Finch Coll.; MA in art history, Queens Coll. With Met. Mus. Art, NYC, lectr.; with Ruder Finn, Burson-Marsteller, Ogilvy & Mather, Spencer & Rubinow; press sec. for Donna Hanover, others; founder, pres. Danielides Comm., 1986—. Bd. sec. Am. Farm Sch., 2005—. Recipient Media award, Am. Acad. Nursing, 1998. Mem.: NY Women in Comm. (pres. 2003—04, found. pres. 2004—05). Office: Danielides Comm 9 E 53rd St New York NY 10022-4220 Office Phone: 212-319-7566. Business E-Mail: joannie@danielides.net.

DANIELS, ALBERTINA DIANA, secondary school educator; b. Jacksonville, Fla., Aug. 30, 1948; d. David and Petronita Josephine Daniels. BS, Edward Waters Coll., Jacksonville, 1971; MA in Tchg., Marygrove Coll., Detroit, 2003. Cert. notary pub. N.J., N.J. Dept. Banking and Ins. Prodr. Bus. edn. tchr. Camden City Sch. Dist., NJ, 1976—, resource tchr., 1991—96, GED examiner, 1998—2001, GED chief examiner, 2001—, career counselor, 1999—. Coord. food basket drive Cmty. Sharing and Caring, Camden, 1994—, sch. book asst., 1995—, summer food program asst., 1998—. Mem.: Camden Edn. Assn. (exec. bd. 2004—, chair sunshine com. 2005—), Women's Internat. Bowling Congress, Club Docetts, Order of Ea. Star (grand organizer 1988—, assoc. matron). Baptist. Avocations: bowling, sewing, reading, travel, computer programs. Office: Cmty Sharing and Caring Corp 2656 Baird Blvd Camden NJ 08105 Office Phone: 856-962-7170. Personal E-mail: tindaniels@aol.com.

DANIELS, ARLENE KAPLAN, sociology educator; b. N.Y.C., Dec. 10, 1930; d. Jacob and Elizabeth (Rathstein) Kaplan; m. Richard Rene Daniels, June 9, 1956. BA with honors in English, U. Calif., Berkeley, 1952; MA in Sociology, 1954, PhD in Sociology, 1960. Instr. dept. speech U. Calif., Berkeley, 1959-61; rsch. assoc. Mental Rsch. Inst., Palo Alto, Calif., 1961-66; assoc. prof. sociology San Francisco State Coll., 1966-70; chief Center for Study Women in Soc., Inst. Sci. Analysis, San Francisco, 1970-80; mem. faculty Northwestern U., Evanston, Ill., 1975-95, prof. dept. sociology, 1975-95, dir. Women's Studies, 1992-94, prof. emerita. Vis. prof. dept. sociology U. Calif., Berkeley, 1997—; cons. NIMH, 1971-73, NEH, 1975-80, Nat. Inst. Edn., 1978-82 Editor: (with Rachel Kahn-Hut) Academics on the Line, 1970; co-editor: (with Gaye Tuchman and James Benét) Hearth and Home: Images of Women in the Mass Media, 1978, (with James Benét) Education: Straightjacket or Opportunity?, 1979, (with Rachel Kahn-Hut and Richard Colvard) Women and Work, 1982, (with Alice Cook and Val Lorwin) Women and Trade Unions in Eleven Industrialized Countries, (with Teresa Odendahl and Elizabeth Boris) Working in Foundations, 1985, Invisible Careers, 1988, (with Alice Cook and Val Lorwin) The Most Difficult Revolution: Women in the Trade Union Movement, 1992; editor: Jour. Social Problems, 1974-78; assoc. editor: Contemporary Sociology, 1980-82, Symbolic Interaction, 1979-84, Am. Sociol. Rev., 1987-90. Trustee Bus. and Profl. Women's Rsch. Found. Bd., 1980-85, Women's Equity Action League Legal and Ednl. Def. Fund, 1979-81; mem. Chgo. Rsch. Assoc. Bd., 1981-87. Recipient Social Sci. Rsch. Council Faculty Rsch. award, 1970-71; Ford Found. Faculty fellow, 1975-76; grantee Nat. Inst. Edn., 1978-79, 1979-80, NSF, 1974-75, NIMH, 1973-74 Mem. Inst. Medicine NAS, Sociologists Women in Soc. (pres. 1975-76), Am. Sociology Assn. (coun. 1979-81, chmn. occupations and orgns. 1987, chmn. pubs. com. 1985-87, sec. 1992-95, Jessie Bernard award 1995), Soc. Study Social Problems (v.p. 1981-82, pres. 1987 Lee Founders award 1988), Soc. Study Symbolic Inter-Action. E-mail: akdaniels@aol.com.

DANIELS, ASTAR, artist; b. Fostoria, Ohio, Nov. 27, 1920; d. Alfred Henry and Edna Mae (Roush) Shultz; m. Bert Franklin Daniels, May 17, 1942 (div. Sept. 1976); children: Larry Bert, Cheri, N. Dana Rahbar-Daniels. Grad. (hon.), Art Instrn., Inc., Mpls., 1952; student, Toledo Mus. Sch. Design, 1950—52; studied with Emerson C. Burkhart, 1952—54; student, Thomas Moore Coll., 1971—73; diploma summa cum laude, U. Cin., 1977; student, Ohio U., 1984—85. Tchr. art pvt. adult and youth art classes, Forest and Cin., Ohio, 1950-57; portrait demonstrator numerous galleries, colls., museums, TV nationwide, 1951-79; dir. art, tchr. Defiance (Ohio) Coll., 1956-57; tchr. art and drama Meth. Ch. Camp, Sabina, Ohio, 1960-64; lectr. on liturgical art Hyde Park Cmty. Ch., Cin., 1960-79; tchr. art and drama Fairview Arts Ctr., Cin., 1977-78; tchr. art Losantiville Summer Sch. Disadvantaged Youth, 1996. Judge, mem. jury art shows, 1956—70; gallery guide Contemporary Art Ctr., Cin., 1972—73; costume designer Girl Scouts Symphony Music Hall, Cin., 1960, Cin., 62, Cin., 66; dir. art Ohio State Fair, Columbus, 1955—57; nat. art dir. Sr. Girl Scout Round-up, Button Bay, Vt., 1962; founder, chairperson Fine Arts Com. Ecclesia, Cin., 1960—79. Exhibitions include Schaff Gallery, Cin., 1996, Represented in permanent collections Richard Nixon, Dr. A. B. Graham, James Arness; author, illustrator: Aiming in His Direction, 1971; illustrator Woman Spirit Bonding, 1983. Art therapist Christ Hosp. Psychiat. Ward, Cin., 1959—61; citizen diplomat Soc. Positive Future, 1986; youth liturgical dance dir. Hyde Park Cmty. Ch., Cin., 1959—66. Recipient Scouters award for tng. leadership, Boy Scouts Am., Forest, 1957, Cert. of Achievement, Charlotte R. Schmidlapp Found., Cin., 1977, Exptl. Inst. Human Devel. award, Hyde Park Cmty. Ch., 1976. Mem.: Nat. Mus. Women in Arts, Soc. Universal Human (founding mem. 1996). Achievements include third oldest participant to fly zero-gravity. Avocations: travel, exploring Incan and Mayan sites, reading, metaphysical phenomena. Home and Office: 101 Solway Ct Cary NC 27511

DANIELS, BENITA JEAN, special education educator; b. Demopolis, Ala., Jan. 15; d. Eugene and Bertha (Lomax) D. BS in Bus. Edn., Ala. A&M U., 1979; MS in Spl. Edn., Livingston U., 1985, ednl. specialist, 1991. Tchr. of multi-handicapped Eutaw (Ala.) Schs., 1980-86, tchr. of educable mentally retarded, 1986-89, tchr. of learning disabled, 1989—; spl. svcs. dept. chmn. Carver Middle Sch., 2005—. Special svcs. dept. chairperson Carver Mid. Sch., 2005—06. Coach Spl. Olympics, Eutaw, 1989—; advisor Parental Involvement, Eutaw, 1980—; sponsor Eutaw Cheerleaders, 1991—; active Eutaw PTA, 1991—. Named one of Outstanding Young Women of Am., 1987. Mem. NEA, Ala. Edn. Assn., Martin L. King Svc. Orgn. (asst. sec., cert. 1975), Zeta Phi Beta (pres. 1979-91, plaque), Phi Chi Theta (pres., plaque 1976), Phi Beta Lambda (cert. 1976). Baptist. Avocations: sewing, piano, travel, working with children, creative arts and crafts. Home: 719 E Decatur St Demopolis AL 36732-2505 Office: Carver Middle Sch PO Box 527 Greensboro Rd Eutaw AL 35462 also: Eutaw High Sch 623 Mesopotamia St Eutaw AL 35462-1013 Office Phone: 372 4816.

DANIELS, CARA J., lawyer; b. Newburgh, NY, Aug. 11, 1973; BA, Boston Coll., 1995, JD, 2000. Bar: Mass. 2000, NY 2000. Assoc. Rackemann, Sawyer & Brewster PC, Boston. Mem.: NY State Bar Assn., Mass. Bar Assn. Office: Rackemann Sawyer & Brewster PC One Financial Center Boston MA 02111 Office Phone: 617-951-1194. Office Fax: 617-542-7437. E-mail: cdaniels@rackemann.com.*

DANIELS, CARLA LEE, information technology specialist; b. Beaufort, S.C., Aug. 23, 1957; d. Pervis C. and Alyse Haynes Lee; m. Osborne L. Daniels, Apr. 14; children: Matthew, Michelle. BA, U. S.C., Columbia, 1978, MLS, 1981; EdD, U. Sarasota, Fla., 2001. Cert. libr. media Nat. Bd. Profl. Tchg. Stds. Tchr. English Richland County Sch. Dist. 1, Columbia, 1981—84, info. tech. specialist, 1984—. Named Tech. Laureate, Smithsonian Inst. internat. ceremony, 1999; recipient 2-Yr. grant, Apple Computer Co., 1997, Living the Legacy award, Nat. Coun. Negro Women, 2004. Mem.: NEA, S.C. Coun. on Accreditation and Sch. Improvement, So. Assn. Colls. and Schs. (commr. 2006), S.C. Assn. Sch. Librs., Girls' Leadership Club (sponsor, founder 2006), Pi Lambda Theta, Alpha Kappa Alpha. United Methodist. Avocations: reading, travel, sailing, horseback riding, snorkeling. Office: Eau Claire H S 4800 Monticello Rd Hopkins SC 29061

DANIELS, CAROLINE, publishing executive; b. San Francisco, Dec. 11, 1948; d. William L. and Gladys Daniels; m. Jack Wernick, Nov. 30, 1985 (div.); children: Martin Wernick, Katherine Wernick. Student, U. Dijon, France, 1965; BA in Psychology, U. Colo., 1970; postgrad., Harvard U., 1983-85. Export agt. Air Oceanic Shippers, San Francisco, 1972-73; library supr. Aircraft Tech. Pubs., San Francisco, 1973-75, ops. mgr., 1975-80, v.p., 1980-82, exec. v.p. Brisbane, Calif., 1982-84, pres., CEO, chmn. bd. dirs., 1984—. Pres. adv. bd. Embry Riddle Aero. U.; bd. dirs. Acad. Art U., San Francisco; past bd. dirs. Jr. Achievement of Bay Area. Mem.: Gen. Aviation Mfg. Assn. (bd. dirs., former exec. com., former chmn. pub. affairs com., chmn. safety affairs com.), San Francisco Opera Guild (bd. dirs.). Office: Aircraft Tech Pubs 101 S Hill Dr Brisbane CA 94005-1251 Office Phone: 415-330-9500.

DANIELS, CASSANDRA DIANE, secondary school educator, choreographer; b. Columbus, Ohio, July 24, 1968; d. Clyde William and Ethel Ghene Nelson; m. Clarence Waymonn Daniels. Jr., Nov. 29, 2003; children: April Marie Nelson, Aaron Joseph Nelson, Alexis Nicole Ballentine, Clarence Waymonn Daniels III, Chance Gabriel, Armani Marie. A in Applied Tech. Studies, Columbus State CC, Ohio, 1994; BS in Human Ecology, Ohio State U., Columbus, 1999, MS in Edn., 2002. Cert. pharmacy technician Columbus, 1986, min. dance Set Free Ministries, 2006. Tchr./educator Columbus City Sch., 2000—; choreographer Mt. Hermon Missionary Bapt. Ch., Columbus, 2004—. Tutor, educator Columbus City Sch., 2002—; summer sch. instr. Columbus City Schs., 2003—, curriculum writer, 2005—. Cheer coach Little League Mifflin Youth Assn., Columbus, 2001—04; cheer coach Mifflin H.S., Columbus, 2004—06, Columbus Africentric Early Coll., 2006—, softball coach, 2006—, Columbus City Sch., 2004—06. Home: 3179 Crossing Hill Way Columbus OH 43219 Office: Africentric Early College - CPS 300 E Livingston Ave Columbus OH 43219 Office Phone: 614-365-8675. Personal E-mail: cassandradaniels@hotmail.com. Business E-Mail: cdaniels3977@columbus.k12.oh.us.

DANIELS, CHERYL LYNN, pediatrics nurse; b. Paterson, NJ, June 15, 1951; d. Nathan and Frances Avonna (Bradshaw) D. RN, Martland Hosp. Sch. Nursing, Newark, 1971; AAS in Health and Community Svc., NYU, 1984, BA in Journalism, 1987. Evening charge nurse Martland Hosp. Unit, Newark, 1971-73; staff nurse Heal Econs. Advancement League, Paterson, N.J., 1972-74; neonatal intensive care nurse St. Joseph's Hosp. & Med. Ctr., Paterson, N.J., 1973-77, charge nurse neonatal intensive care, 1977—79, pediat. neonatal ICU, 1979-89, intensive care nurse, pediatric HIV outpatient nurse, 1989-90; rsch. outpatient HIV/SJH case mgmt. nurse Aids Clin. Trial Group, 1990-2001; case mgr. outpatient pediat. HIV Clinic, 1989—; pediat. sedation nurse for CT scan procedures, 2001—02. Mentor Career Beginning Program, Paterson, 1988-90. Recipient Gobetz award, NYU, 1984. Mem. ARC, AACN (cert. pediat. nursing), Alpha Sigma Lambda. Baptist. Avocations: clarinet, swimming, reading, writing, painting. Office: Saint Joseph Hosp 703 Main St Paterson NJ 07503-2691 Business E-Mail: danielscheryl@msn.com, danielsc@sjhmc.org.

DANIELS, CINDY LOU, aerospace transportation executive; b. Moline, Ill., Sept. 24, 1959; d. Ronald McCrae and Mary Lou (McLaughlin) Guthrie; m. Charles Burton Daniels, June 19, 1982. Student, Augustana Coll., Rock Island, Ill., 1977-78; BS cum laude, No. Mich. U., 1981; MS in Info. Sys., George Washington U., 1999, M Engring Mgmt., 2000. Field engr. Ford Aerospace, Houston, 1982-83; engr. flight ops. McDonnell Douglas Corp., Houston, 1983-85; electronics engr. Johnson Space Ctr. NASA, Houston, 1985-89, project mgr. multiple program control ctr., 1989-90, project mgr. Houston, 1989-91, mission control ctr. upgrade project mgr., 1990-91, mgr. program control office, 1991-93; mgr. ground facilities Space Sta. Program Office NASA, Houston, 1993-94; engring. and ops. mgmt., space sta. program NASA Hdqrs., Washington, 1994-96; spl. assessments and acquisition mgr. NASA Langley Rsch. Ctr., Hampton, Va., 1996—. Dynamics contr. NASA Johnson Space Ctr., 1982-83; payload data engr. NASA, 1983-84, earth radiation budget satellite joint ops. integration plan mgr., 1984; mem. payload assist module team NASA-McDonnell Douglas Corp., 1984-85. Home: 200 Barrington Ln Yorktown VA 23693 Office: NASA Langley Rsch Ctr 12 W Taylor Ave Hampton VA 23663-2206

DANIELS, DAVETTA MILLS, principal; b. Austin, Tex., July 31, 1952; d. Carole Athene and David Crockett Hill; m. Ray McCoy Daniels, Feb. 17, 2001; 1 child, Joelle Devee Mills. EdD, Nova Southeastern U., 2003. Cert. tchr. Tex. Edn. Agy., 1978. Social work Houston Area Urban League, Houston, Tex., 1975—76; tchr. Houston Ind. Sch. Dist., Houston, Tex. Prin. Houston Ind. Sch. Dist., Houston, 1995—2003, Hartsfield Elem., Houston, Texas, Tex.; founder/dir. Nat. Counseling and Referral Svcs., Houston; presenter Oxford (Eng.) U., 1999. Greeter/welcome Wheeler Ave. Bapt. Ch., Houston, 2002—03; bd. mem. Women's Ctr., Houston, 2000—02; dir. Pass It On Mentorship/Guidance Program for Male Students, Houston. Fellow: Tenn. State U. (life; sec. 1999—2002); mem.: NAACP, Tex. Assn. Secondary Sch. Prins. (Outstanding Prin. of Yr. 1999—2000), Phi Delta Kappa, Delta Sigma Theta, Alpha Kappa Alpha. Home: 12714 Water Oak Drive Missouri City TX 77489 Office: Hartsfield Elem Sch 5001 Perry St Houston TX 77021 Personal E-mail: ddaniel1@houstonisd.org.

DANIELS, DELORIA, elementary school educator; b. Baconton, Ga., Feb. 13, 1943; d. Charles E and Mary Liza Daniels. BSc, LSc, Ft. Valley State U., 1965; M in edn., U. Ga., 1973. Kindergarten tchr. Elbert County Bd. Edn., 1965—67, libr., 1967—68, tchr., 1968—83, 1983—2005. Pres. Albany Reading Area Council; exec. bd. Mitchell County NAACP, 1983—; youth dir. Camilla Bapt. Assn., Mitchell County, 1997—, Camilla Progress of Christian Edn., Albany, 2000—; presenter in field. Named Tchr. of Yr., Mitchell County Primary, Reading Tchr.l of Yr., Ga. Reading Coun., 1995. Mem.: Ga. Reading Assn., Ga. Internat. Reading Assn., Ga. Assn. Edn. (chmn. 1983—2005). Democrat. Bapt. Avocations: reading, aerobics, antiques, dance. Office: Mitchell County Primary Sch 50 Griffin Rd Camilla GA 31730

DANIELS, DIANA M., lawyer, publishing executive; b. Dillon, Mont. BA, Cornell U., 1971; JD, Harvard U., 1974; M of City Planning, MIT, 1974; diploma, U. Edinburgh, 1976. Bar: N.Y. 1975, U.S. Dist. Ct. (ea. and so. dists.) N.Y. 1975, U.S. Ct. Appeals (2d cir.) 1975, D.C. 1978, U.S. Supreme Ct. 1988. Assoc. Cravath, Swaine & Moore, N.Y.C., 1975—78; asst. counsel Washington Post newspaper, 1978—79; gen. counsel Washington Post Co., 1988—89, v.p., gen. counsel, 1989—91, v.p., gen. counsel, sec., 1991—; v.p., counsel Newsweek, N.Y.C., 1979—85, v.p., gen. counsel, 1985—88. Mem. legal adv. com. NYSE, 2003—. Trustee Cornell U., 1995—, ABA Mus. Law, 1997-04, Appleseed Found., 1998-2004, Ctr. Study of Presidency, 1997-01, Am. Law Inst., 2003—; mem. legal adv. com. NYSE, 2003— Office: Washington Post Co 1150 15th St NW Washington DC 20071-0002

DANIELS, ELIZABETH ADAMS, English language educator; b. Westport, Conn., May 8, 1920; d. Thomas Davies and Minnie Mae (Sherwood) Adams; m. John L. Daniels, Mar. 21, 1942; children: John L., Eleanor B. (dec.), Sherwood A., Ann S. AB, Vassar Coll., 1941; A.M., U. Mich., 1942; PhD, N.Y. U., 1954. From instr. to prof. English Vassar Coll., Poughkeepsie, NY, 1948-85, dean freshmen, 1955-58, dean studies, 1965-73, chmn. dept. English, 1974-76, 81-84, acting dean faculty, 1976-78, chmn. self-study, 1978-80, Vassar historian, 1985—. Author: Jessie White Mario, Risorgimento Revolutionary, 1972, Main to Mudd, Bridges to the World, 1994, Main to Mudd, and More, 1996; co-author: (with Clyde Griffen) Full Steam Ahead in Poughkeepsie, The Story of Coeducation at Vassar 1966-74, 2000, (with Maryann Bruno) Vassar College 1861-2000, 2000, (with Ron Patkus, Kari Strickland and Marian Thomas) Administrative History of Vassar College, 2004; contbr. articles to publs. Bd. dirs. Alzheimer's Assn. Mid-Hudson Valley, World Affairs Coun. Hudson Valley. Recipient Grad. award Alumnae Assn. N.Y. U., 1954, Spirit of Vassar Alumnae award, 2006; Vassar fellow, 1941; Nat. Endowment Humanities summer stipend, 1981. Mem. MLA, AAUP, Poughkeepsie Tennis Club, Phi Beta Kappa. Democrat. Home: 56 Muirfield Ct Poughkeepsie NY 12603 Office: Vassar Coll PO Box 74 Poughkeepsie NY 12602-0074

DANIELS, FAITH, former newscaster; b. Pitts., 1957; d. Steven and Mary Skowronski; m. Dean Daniels, 1981; children: Andrew, Alyx Rae, Aidan Rose. Grad., Bethany Coll. Co-anchor CBS Early Morning News, 1985—87, CBS Morning News, 1987—90; host A Closer Look with Faith Daniels NBC, 1991-93; news anchor Today Show NBC, 1990-92; correspondent Dateline NBC, 1993—95. Actor: (films) Man of the Year, 2006. Mem. Nat. Coun. Adoption; pres. bd. trustees Dystrophic Epidermolysis Bullosa Rsch. Assn. Am. Roman Catholic. Office: c/o DebRA of Am Inc 5 W 36th St Ste 404 New York NY 10018*

DANIELS, JUDITH WALL, education educator, retired principal; d. Frederick George and Helen Clarice Wall; 1 child, Frederick John Jr. BA, Douglass Coll., New Brunswick, NJ, 1966; MAT, U. NJ, Trenton, 1969; EdD, Rutgers U., New Brunswick, 1989. Tchr. Berkeley Twp. Schs., Bayville, NJ, 1966—67, Birck Twp. Schs., 1967—70, Jersey City Pub. Schs., 1970—75; cons. Toms River Regional Sch. Dist., 1976—86, prin., 1993—96; asst. prof. edn. Georgian Ct. U., Lakewood, 1996—. Mem.: Delta Kappa Gamma, Kappa Delta Pi. Avocations: Arabian horses, scuba diving. Office: Georgian Ct U Sch Edn 900 Lakewood Ave Lakewood NJ 08701

DANIELS, KAREN S., mathematics educator; b. Britt, Iowa, July 4, 1968; d. George C. and Marie E. Tlach; m. John J. Daniels, July 10, 1995; children: Lucas J., Landon J. BS in Edn., Mankato State U., Minn., 1990. Tchr. Webster City (Iowa) Cmty. Sch. Office: Webster City Cmty Sch 1001 Lynx Webster City IA 50595 Office Phone: 515-832-9210.

DANIELS, LYDIA M., health care administrator; b. Louisville, Dec. 21, 1932; d. Effort and Gladys T. (Turner) Williams; children by previous marriage: Danny Winston, Jeffrey Bruce, Anthony Wayne. Cert., Samuel Merritt Hosp. Sch. Med. Record Adminstrs., 1959; student, Ctrl. State Coll., Wilberforce, Ohio, 1950—52, Calif. State U., Hayward, 1967, student, 1969—72; BA, Golden Gate U., 1992, MS, 1993; postgrad., Argosy U., 2005. Sec. chemistry dept. Ctrl. State Coll., Wilberforce, 1950-52; co-dir. Indian Workcamp Pala (Calif.) Indian Reservation, 1956-58; clk.-typist Camarillo (Calif.) State Hosp., 1956-58; student med. record adminstr. Samuel Merritt Hosp., Oakland, Calif., 1958-59, asst. med. record adminstr., 1962-63, asst. chief med. record adminstr., 1965, chief med. record adminstr., 1965-72; med. record adminstr. Albany (Calif.) Hosp., 1964-65; asst. med. record adminstr. Children's Hosp., San Francisco, 1960; co-dir. interns in cmty. svc. Am. Friends Svc. Com., San Francisco, 1960-61; med. record adminstrs. Pacific Hosp., Oakland, 1963-64; med. record cons. Tahoe Forest Hosp., Truckee, Calif., 1969-73; chief med. record adminstr. Highland Gen. Hosp., Oakland, 1972-74; dir. med. record svcs. U. Calif. San Francisco Hosps. and Clinics, 1975-82; mgr. patient appointments, reception/registration Kaiser-Permanente Med. Ctr., 1982-88, dir. ambulatory adminstrv. svcs., 1988-94, asst. dir. human resources, 1994-96; dir. human resources Brookside Hosp., San Pablo, Calif., 1996-97; cons. human resources Daniels Consultation Svcs., San Pablo, 1996-98; dir. human resources Alameda County Med. Ctr., San Leandro, Calif., 1998—2002. Adj. prof. human resources mgmt., labor mgmt. rels. Golden Gate U., 1978—; adj. prof. human resources mgmt. Dominican U. Calif., San Rafael, 2002—; pres. Daniels Consultation Svcs., Albany, 1988—, mgmt. tng. human resources cons., 1997—. Author: Health Record Documentation: A Look at Cost, 1981; Inservice Training as a Tool in Managing the Changing Environment in the Medical Record Department, 1983; The Budget as a Management Tool, 1983; issues editor: Topics in Health Record Management, Parts I and II, 1983. Leader Girl Scouts Am. Oakland area coun., 1960-62; Sunday Sch. tchr. Soc. of Friends, Berkeley, Calif., 1961-63, mem. edn. com., 1965-68; mem. policy and adv. bd. Far West Lab Demonstration Sch., Oakland, 1973-75; bd. dirs. The Californians, Oakland, 1993-97, Patrons of the Arts and Humanities, Oakland, 1994-97, YWCA, Berkeley, 1995-2001, Operation Dignity, Inc., 2002-2004. Recipient Mgmt. Fellowship award U. Calif., San Francisco, 1979-80. Mem. Am. Med. Record Assn., Calif. Med. Record Assn. (editl. bd. 1976-77, pres. 1974-75), East Bay Med. Record Assn. (chmn. edn. com. 1971-72, pres. 1969-70), Assn. Systems Mgmt., Am. Mgmt. Assn., San Francisco Med. Records Assn. (pres.-elect 1982-83, pres. 1983-84), Am. Assn. Tng. and Devel. (Golden Gate chpt., v.p. prof. devel. 1994-96). Home: 545 Pierce St Apt 1105 Albany CA 94706-1048 Office Phone: 510-525-0848. E-mail: ldancon@aol.com.

DANIELS, MARY P., academic administrator, technologist; b. P.G. County, Md., Feb. 16, 1961; d. William Clarence Proctor and Eva Rostta Bricsoe; children: Zanisha, Bobby Jr., Nathaniel, Jeremiah. BBA, BRE, Mgmt. Wash. Sat. Coll., Wasgington, D.C., 1993; MRE, DD, Breakthrough Bible Coll., Suithand, Md., 2003; DHL, Breakthrough Bible Coll., Md., 2005. Commn. technologist WMATA, Washington, 1981—2000; v.p. fin./bus. Breakthrough Bible Coll., Suitland, Md., 2000—; commn. technologist Met. Area Transit Authority, Washington, 2000—. Bd. dirs., CEO Wells of Water Ministries, Inc., Washington, 1989—; bd. dirs. Britt Quinn Enterprise, Md., 2003—; exec. bd. dirs. Breakthrough Bible Coll., 2000. Author: Establishing Your Church, Church Law, 2004. Democrat. Avocations: walking, travel, cooking, reading. Office Phone: 202-546-8228. E-mail: drmarypdaniels@aol.com.

DANIELS, SUSANNE, broadcast executive; m. Greg Daniels. Grad., Harvard U. Asst. mgr. devel. Broadway Video Entertainment, mgr. devel.; dir. variety, reality and specials ABC TV Network; dir. comedy devel. The Fox Broadcasting Co.; pres. entertainment, lifetime svcs. entertainment The WB Network, Burbank, Calif., 2005; pres. entertainment Lifetime Entertainment Services, 2005—. Spkr. in field; developer (for Lorne Michaels) Saturday Night Live, Kids in the Hall, Am. Detective, America's Funniest People, Living Single, Martin, Buffy the Vampire Slayer, Dawson's Creek, Felicity, Roswell, Angel, Gilmore Girls, 7th Heaven; responsible for overseeing (ABCs spls.) Academy Awards, Muhammad Ali's 50th Birthday Spl., Am. Comedy Awards. Bd. dirs. The Nat. Campaign to Prevent Teenage Pregnancy. Named in the Power Issue Entertainment Weekly, 1997, one of most powerful women in entertainment, The Hollywood Reporter, 1998, 1999, 2000; named one of, 2005; recipient Gemini award, Am. Women in Radio & Television, 2001. Mem.: Acad. TV Arts and Sci.*

DANIELS, TINA LYNN, special education educator; b. Waynesville, N.C., May 5, 1958; d. James Truett and Betty Jean (Kilpatrick) Parham; m. Jon Mark Daniels, Feb. 16, 1980; children: Valerie Diane, Tiffany Ann. BA, Bethany Coll., 1984; MA, Wichita State U., 1989; MA in Adminstrn., Kans. State U., 1994. Behavior disorder tchr. United Sch. Dist. 305, Salina, Kans., 1986—97; adminstr. Schilling Elem., 1997—99; tchr. Coronado Elem., Salina, 2000—. Baptist. Office: Coronado Elem 518 Neal Salina KS 67401 Office Phone: 785-309-4100.

DANIELS-ROGERS, LATAUSHA, social sciences educator, entrepreneur; d. David D. and Lenora Daniels; m. Marcus Diego Rogers, Nov. 3, 2001 (div. Oct. 14, 2003); 1 child, Marcus Diego Rogers Jr. BS in Secondary Social Sci. Edn., Judson Coll., Marion, Ala., 2001; postgrad., Lesley U., Cambridge, Mass., 2005—. Cert. tchr. Ala., highly qualified tchr. Ala. Dept. of Edn. and No Child Left Behind. Social studies tchr. permanent supply Birmingham City Schs., 2002—03, social studies tchr., 2004—, Holy Family Cath. HS, Birmingham, 2003—04. Cheer coach Ala. HS Athletic Assn., Birmingham, 2003—; tchr. cons. and presenter Nat. Urban Alliance, Birmingham, 2005—; tchr. rep. Whatley Cmty. Forum, Birmingham, 2004—05; tchg. Am history grant tech. asst., 2006; founder Rebirth Soc. Women, 2006. Grantee Generation Text: Promoting Change, Cmty. and Voting Literacy, Columbia U. Tchrs. Coll., 2005. Mem.: AAUW, NEA, Birmingham Edn. Assn., Nat. Coun. Social Studies. Avocations: poetry, dance, Christian education, civic literacy. Office: Birmingham Bd of Edn Whatley K-8 Sch 549 43rd St Birmingham AL 35222 Office Phone: 205-231-3800. Personal E-mail: latausharogers@bellsouth.net.

DANIEWICZ, SUSAN CARNEY, education educator, social worker; b. Chgo., Apr. 20, 1943; d. Thomas Francis and Alice Boehler Carney; m. John L. Daniewicz, Nov. 18, 1967; children: Amy, Katie. BA, Marquette U., Milw., 1965; MSW, U. Hawaii, 1971; PhD, Iowa State U., 1987. ACSW Acad. Cert. Social Workers, 1990, LMSW Tex., 1991. Social worker Tama Co. Dept. Social Svcs., Tama, Iowa, 1972—73; asst. dir. Ctrl. Iowa Family Planning, Marshalltown, Iowa, 1973—82; asst. prof. U. Northern Iowa, Cedar Falls, Iowa, 1986—87, Mount Mercy Coll., Cedar Rapids, Iowa, 1987—90; field dir., asst. prof. U. Ctrl. Tex., Killeen, Tex., 1990—99, Tarleton State U., Killeen, Tex., 1999—2000; chair, assoc. prof. U. Mary Hardin-Baylor, Belton, Tex., 2000—. Dir. social work program UMHB, Belton, Tex., 2000—, chair instn. effectiveness com., 2003—05; site visitor Coun. on S.W. Edn., 2004—. Chair faculty senate U. Ctrl. Tex., Killeen, 1992—93; program chair NASW/Tex., 1996—2003; vol. Caritas, Austin, 2004—. Mem.: Tex. Assn. Deans and Dirs. of Social Workers (sec. 2000—), Nat. Assn. Social Workers (Lifetime Achievement 2006), Acad. Cert. Social Workers. Democrat. Roman Catholic. Avocations: hiking, gardening, quilting. Office: Univ Mary Hardin-Baylor 900 College St Belton TX 76515 Business E-Mail: sdaniewicz@umhb.edu.

DANILOW, DEBORAH MARIE, realtor, vocalist, composer, musician, rancher; b. Mineral Wells, Tex., Dec. 9, 1947; d. Stanton Byron and Irval Leona (Vanhoosier) D.; m. William Paul Cook Jr., June 1965 (div. Oct. 1967); m. Chance Gentry, Oct. 1971 (div. May 1974); m. Ellis Elmer Aldridge, Dec. 3, 1977 (div. Nov. 1984); children: Chandra Desiree, Anthony Ellis; m. Carl Graham Quisenberry, Feb. 7, 1992 (div. May 1997). Student, Brantley Draughon Bus. Coll., Ft. Worth, 1965-66, Tex. Christian U., 1965-67, U. Ariz., 1967-69. Lic. residential, farm and ranch real estate Tex. Real Estate Commn., comml. real estate Tex. Real Estate Commn. Asst. to pres. Hollywood Video Ctr., L.A., 1969-72; producer Western Inst. TV, L.A., 1972-77; owner Chanelde Ranch, Weatherford, Tex., 1977-84; band musician Bonnie Raitt, Jerry Williams, Malibu, Calif., 1984, Mick Fleetwood, Malibu, 1984; lead musician Jazz Talk, Ft. Worth, 1985-96; owner Brazos Valley Ranch Inc., 1987—97, AAA Bail Bonds, Seymour, 1990-96; mgr., team leader Keller Williams Realty, Arlington, Tex., 2002—03, Mansfield, Tex., 2002—03, realtor assoc. Ft. Worth, 2003—. Composer numerous pub. songs, 1969—; lead musician Debbie Danilow and Soul Full o' Jazz, 1996—; debut solo CD Primordial Heart, 1999. Active Sheriffs Assn. Tex., Seymour, 1991-97, North Tex. Taxpayers League, Wichita Falls, Tex., 1991-96, Tex. State Notary Bd., Austin, 1990-99. Mem. NRA, Nat. Assn. Realtors, Tex. Realtors Assn., Greater Ft. Worth Bd. Realtors, Greater Lewisville Bd. Realtors, Arlington Bd. Realtors, Tex. Limousin Assn., Tex. Southwestern Cattle Raisers Assn., Tex. Cattlewomen's Assn., Am. Quarter Horse Assn. (life), Nat. Found. Quarter Horse Assn., Dallas-Ft. Worth Profl. Musicians Assn., Ft. Worth Jazz Soc. (sec. 1987-89), N.Am. Limousin Found. (life), Australian Shepherd Club Am., Marchigiana Cattle Assn. (life), Greater Ft. Worth Assn. Realtors. Avocations: music, investments, writing, performing, real estate. Home and Office: Debbie Danilow Inc 524 Pineview Ln Fort Worth TX 76140 Office Phone: 817-919-8284. Personal E-mail: debbie@debbiedanilow.com.

DANIN, MARY ANN, artist, designer, educator; b. L.A., Apr. 21, 1928; d. Dan and Edith (Shorr) D.; m. Marvin Rand, 1988; children from previous marriage: Sharon, David. AB, UCLA, 1951, MA, 1965; MFA, Claremont Grad. Sch., 1973. Free-lance textile designer, 1947-52; high sch. tchr. L.A. Pub. Schs., 1951-55; instr. interior design and crafts L.A. Pierce Coll., 1954-55, 63-69; prof. art, design, computer drafting Calif. State U., Northridge, 1969—, chmn. 3-D dept., 1985-87, head interior design program, 1987—. Freelance design cons., Venice, Calif., 1968—; colorist, designer: Colorways, 1980—, Am. Haiku Scrolls, Venice, 1980-85; Author: Catalog Tapestry and Other Forms in Fiber, 1974; One-woman exhbn. City Gallery, Sacramento, 1985; exhbns. Art Park-Los Angeles, 1976, Toys by Artists, Security Pacific Plaza, 1977-78, Fiber Artists, Ten from Calif. State U. Northridge, 1978, City Gallery, 1985. Active program devel. interdisciplinary, univ. level fin. planning, color rsch.; mem. Venice Community Planning Coun., 1975-77. Mem. AAUP, Am. Craft Coun., Handweavers Guild Am., Siggraph, Nat. Computer Graphics Assn., Am. Soc. Interior Designers, So. Calif. Hand Weavers Guild, Women in Design, Caucus for Art, Town Hall Inter Soc. Color Council, Venice C. of C. Democrat. Jewish. Home: 1310 Abbot Kinney Blvd Venice CA 90291-3758 Office: Calif State U Art 3D Media Northridge CA 91330-0001

DANIS, JULIE MARIE, writer, advertising executive; b. Dayton, Ohio, Aug. 19, 1955; d. Charles Wheaton and Elizabeth Jane (Sliter) D. BS, Northwestern U., 1977; AM, U. Chgo., 1979, MBA, 1984. Juvenile justice planner Ill. Law Enforcement Commn., Chgo., 1979-80; prin. budget analyst City of Chgo., 1980-82; account mgmt. intern Foote, Cone & Belding, Chgo., 1983; product mgr. Frito-Lay, Inc., Dallas, 1984-87; advt. account exec. Leo Burnett Co., Chgo., 1987-88; ptnr., mgmt. cons. The Everest Group, Chgo., 1988-94; writer, columnist, humorist, pub. spkr. Chicago Tribune, 1994—; sr. v.p., dir. Mind & Mood Foote, Cone & Belding Advt., Chgo., 1994—. Commentator PRI Marketplace radio. Cons. United Way of Chgo.; ex-officio Discovery Bd. Goodman Theatre; trustee Chgo. Trustee Group Goodman Theatre, active in Leadership Am., Metro Help Svcs., Am. Cancer Soc., Social Venture Ptnrs., Mercy Home for Boys and Girls, 1990-94. Mem. U. Chgo. Women's Bus. Group, Pi Beta Phi. Roman Catholic. Avocations: theater, dance, long distance running, tennis, travel. Home: 2047 N Howe St Chicago IL 60614 Office: Foote Cone & Belding 101 E Erie St Fl 14 Chicago IL 60611-2850

DANITZ, MARILYNN PATRICIA, choreographer, video specialist; b. Buffalo; BS in Chemistry, Le Moyne Coll.; MS in Chem. Engring., Columbia U. Artistic dir. High Frequency Wavelengths/Danitz Dances, 1976—. Assoc. prof. Tainan Cheng Chuan Coll., Taiwan, 1984; profl. dancer Ballet Mcpl. Strasbourg, France, Ballet Mcpl. Geneva, Switzerland; choreography comms. performances include The 11th Internat. Ballet Comp. Varna, Bulgaria, 1983, Tbilisi Ballet co., USSR, Nat. Ballet of Colombia, Nat. Inst. Arts,

Taiwan, Nanatsudera Theatre, Nagoya, Japan, Shanghai Ballet and Shanghai Jiao Tung U., People's Republic of China, Nat. Cheng Kung Dance Group, Taiwan, Jacob's Pillow Dance Festival, Mass., 6th Internat. Dance Theatre Festival, Poland, 5th Anniversary Celebration Kannon Ctr., St. Petersburg, Russia, 15th Internat. Festival of Modern Choreography, Belarus, Opening Ceremony World Congress UNESCO, Larnace, Cyprus, 2005, others; master choreography workshops include Ctrl. Ballet, Beijing, Chinese Cultural U., Taipei, Taiwan, Okuda Studio, Nagoya, Ballet Philippines, Manila, NSW Coll. Dance, Sydney, The Ballet Sch., Bogota, Colombia, Lublin, Lodz, Poznan and Bytom, Poland, Vitebsk, Belarus, UNESCO 19th World Congress on Dance Rsch., Cyprus, others; video prodn. Real Art Ways Nat. Residency, funded by NEA, 1990; video art collaboration with Allen Ginsberg. Presentations include Internat. Conf. on Dance and Tech., 1993, Naropa Inst. 20th Anniversary Celebration, 1994; video work presented at Lincoln Ctr., N.Y.C., 1995, Hanyang U., Seoul, Korea, 1997, others; video work in permanent collection Lincoln Ctr. Dance Collection; TV prodns. of works include Nat. Broadcasting, Venezuela, Colombia, Bulgaria, Poland, Russia, Belarus, Cyprus, Pub. Broadcasting, Albany, N.Y.C., Mpls.; works performed by Nat. Ballet with the Nat. Philharm. Orch. of Colombia Gala Performance, 1984; co. tours include China, Japan, Taiwan, Europe, Hawaii, Philippines, Can, Europe, S.Am., Russia and Belarus, Cyprus; co-editor Branching Out, Oral Histories of the Founders of Six National Dance Orgns.; juror competitions. Recipient Outstanding Dance-Theater Work of 1986 award Dance Brew-ATV Cable Manhattan, award for disting. choreography Nat. Assn. Regional Ballet, 1982; Bessie Schoenberg Lab. for Experienced Choreographers Dance Theater Workshop; NIH fellow; Gold Medal scholar Conservatoire Geneve, N.Y. State Regents scholar, Le Moyne Coll. Chemistry scholar, others. Mem. UNESCO Internat. Dance Coun., Dance Theater Workshop, Am. Dance Guild (pres., editor Am. Dance, bd. dirs., nat. conf. planning com.), Soc. Dance History Scholars, Dance Films Assn., Congress on Rsch. in Dance Address: 560 Riverside Dr Apt 16E New York NY 10027-3208 also: PO Box 216 Sand Lake NY 12153-0216 also: 3200 Holly Rd Apt 2 Virginia Beach VA 23451-2926 Office Phone: 212-222-7204, 757-422-1240. E-mail: HFW2000@aol.com.

DANKE, VIRGINIA, educational administrator, travel consultant; b. Spokane, Wash., Mar. 9, 1925; d. William Ernest and Daisy May (Norton) Danke. BS, Wash. State U., 1947; MEd, Whitworth Coll., 1950; postgrad., LaSalle U., 1973. Cert. tchr. Counselor Clarkston (Wash.) Sch. Dist., 1947—48; head phys. edn. dept. Lewis & Clark H.S., Spokane Sch. Dist., 1948—77; travel cons. Viking Travel, Spokane, 1982—, Empire Tours, Spokane, 1982—. Co-author (editor): Marching Together, 1955. Treas. Fedn. Western Outdoor Clubs, 1980—92; com. mem. Future Spokane, 1981—, bd. dirs., Pacific Crest Trail Conf., Santa Ana, Calif., 1984; mem. Friends Centennial Trial, 1992—, bd. dirs., 1994—96; mem. Am. Red Cross Disaster Unit; vol. Meals on Wheels, 2004—. Named to Wash. State Officials Hall of Fame, 2003, Inland Empire Softball Hall of Fame, 2004; recipient Scroll of Honor-Hall of Fame, Spokane C. of C., 1983, Greater Spokane Sports Assn., 1973, Wash. Interscholastic Activites Assn., 1990, State Officiating, 1992, Red Cross award, 2006, spl. award, ARC, 2006. Mem.: Spokane Ret. Tchrs. Assn. (pres. 1981—82), Wash. State Ofcls. Assn. (Meritorious Svc. award 2002, named to Hall of Fame 2003), Wash. State Ret. Tchrs. Assn. (bd. dirs. 1987—), Nat. Ret. Tchrs. Assn., Wash. Edn. Assn., Spokane Edn. Assn. (com. chmn. 1960—70), Soroptimist (pres. 1970), Hangman Golf Club (Spokane pres. 1997), Hobnailers Club (pres. 1966—67, 1986—87). Home: 1103 E 14th Ave Spokane WA 99202-2541

DANKO, CASSANDRA DAWN, educational consultant, researcher; b. Pitts., Feb. 13, 1968; d. John A. and Frances J. Danko; m. Stephen D. Scott, Oct. 4, 2003; 1 child, Zetta C. BS, U. Pitts., 1989; MEd, Duquesne U., Pitts., 1994; PhD, U. NC, Chapel Hill, 2004. Sr. project assoc. Early Learning Inst., Pitts., 1993—95; cons. behavior specialist PErsonal Touch Home Health Svcs., 1995; cons. state-wide health U. Colo., Denver, 1995—2000; rsch. asst. U. NC, Chapel Hill, 2000—02, project coord., 2003—04. Mem.: Autism Soc. NC, Autism Soc. Am.

DANKO-MCGHEE, KATHERINA ELAINE, art educator, consultant; b. Derry, Pa., May 1, 1952; d. George Danko and Margaret Scholastica Mlinarchek; m. Jimmy Scott McGhee, July 31, 1977; children: Windsor Castille McGhee, Caribbea Laise McGhee. BS, W.Va. Wesleyan, Buckhannon, 1974; MS, Ind. State U., Terre Haute, 1979; PhD, Ohio State U., 1988. Art tchr. Upshur County Sch. Dist., Buckhannon, W.Va., 1974—82; art edn. coord. U. Ctrl. Fla., Orlando, 1989—95; art edn. dir. Tenn. Technol. U., Cookeville, 1995—2000; early childhood art edn. coord. U. of Toledo, 2000—. Early childhood cons. Toledo Mus. Art, 2000—; art cons. to Reggio Emilia study group NW Ohio Spl. Edn. Regional Resource Ctr., Bowling Green, Ohio, 2003—; early childhood art edn. cons. Harcourt Ednl. Pub. Co., Orlando, Fla., 2003—. Author: The Aesthetic Preferences of Young Children, 2000; contbr. articles to profl. jours. Grantee, NEA, 1999—2000; Artist in Residence project grantee, Tenn. Arts Commn., 1997—2000. Mem.: Toledo Assn. Edn. of Young Children (historian 2003—), Assn. Edn. of Children Internat. (assoc.), Nat. Assn. Edn. of Young Children (assoc.), Ohio Art Edn. Assn. (assoc.), Nat. Art Edn. Assn. (assoc.; southeast dir. higher edn. 1997—2001). Avocations: travel, jewelry making, painting, gardening. Office: U Toledo Art Dept 620 Grove Place Toledo OH 43620 Business E-Mail: kdankom@pop3.utoledo.edu.

DANLEY, LINDA SHARON, elementary school educator; b. Glendale, W.Va., July 15, 1951; d. Harold and Mildred Henrietta Cunningham; m. William F. Danley, July 22, 1975. AB in Edn., Fairmont State Coll., W.Va., 1974; MEd, Marygrove Coll., Detroit, 1998. Reading tchr. Calcutta Elem. Sch., Ohio, 1974—75; kindergarten tchr. West Point Elem. Sch., 1975—85; 1st grade tchr. Calcutta Elem. Sch., 1985—2001; 5th grade tchr. Beaver Local Mid. Sch., Lisbon, Ohio, 2002—. Mem. sch. improvement team Calcutta Elem. Sch., 1990—2001, mem. crisis intervention team, 1996—2001; ednl. adv. YMCA, Calcutta, 1999—. Recipient Tchr. of Yr. award, Walmart, Calcutta, Ohio, 2006. Mem.: NEA, Ohio Ednl. Assn., Beaver Local Ednl. Assn. Avocations: reading, boating. Home: 49068 S Park Cir E East Liverpool OH 43920 Office: Beaver Local Mid Sch State Rte 7 Lisbon OH 44432

DANN, EMILY, mathematics educator; b. Albany, Ga., July 26, 1932; d. Jesse Lyman and Evelyn (Calhoun) Dann; m. Christian A. Hansen, June 7, 1977; children: Leslie Montgomery Przybyzewski, Ann Christiansen, Robin Hansen, Randall Hansen, Rhonda Hansen McAleaivey, Rheta Hansen. BA, Huntingdon Coll., 1954; MS in Math., U. Houston, 1964; EdD, Rutgers U., 1976. Instr. Lee Coll., Baytown, Tex., 1965-67; prof. Middlesex County Coll., Edison, N.J., 1967-81; dir. human resources Hanlin Group (formerly LCP Chem. & Plastics Co.), Edison, N.J., 1981-84, systems analyst, 1986-89; v.p. Assoc. Svcs., Edison, N.J., 1989-91; sr. math. edn. assoc. Rutgers U. Sch. Edn., New Brunswick, N.J., 1991-95, 99—, sr. math. edn. specialist, 1995-99; asst. prof. edn. CCNY, N.Y.C., 1995-99; sr. math. edn. specialist Rutgers U. Grad. Sch. Edn., 1999—. Vis. assoc. prof. math. Drew U., 1984-86; cons. Title I math. program Bedminster (N.J.) Pub. Sch., 1976-77; mem. co-adj. faculty Grad. Sch. Edn., Rutgers U., 1976-81, Kean Coll., 1980-81. Contbr. articles to profl. jours. Mem. ASTD, Acad. Mgmt., Orgn. Devel. Network, Am. Math. Assn., Jean Piaget Soc. Home: 1 Scenic Dr Highlands NJ 07732-1329 Personal E-mail: edann75@comcast.net.

DANNER, BLYTHE, actress; b. Phila., Feb. 3, 1943; d. Harry Earl and Katharine D.; m. Bruce W. Paltrow, Dec. 14, 1969 (dec. Oct. 3, 2002); children: Gwyneth Kate, Jake, Laura. BA in Drama, Bard Coll., 1965, D.F.A. (hon.), 1981; L.H.D. (hon.), Hobart-Smith Coll., 1981. Appeared as Laura in Glass Menagerie, 1965; repertory at Theatre Co. Boston, The Knack, and 7 new Am. Plays, 1965-66; appeared as Helena in repertory Midsummer Night's Dream, Trinity Sq. Playhouse, R.I.; appeared as Irena in repertory Three Sisters, Trinity Sq. Playhouse, R.I., 1967; with Lincoln Ctr. Repertory Co. in Summertree, 1968, Cyrano de Bergerac, 1968, Elise in the Miser, 1969 (Theatre World award); appeared on Broadway as Jill Tanner in Butterflies Are Free (Tony award 1971); also appeared in Major Barbara, 1971, Twelfth Night, 1972, The Seagull, 1974, Ring Around The Moon, 1975, Betrayal, 1980 (Tony award nominee), Blithe Spirit, 1987, A Streetcar Named Desire, 1988, Sylvia, 1995, Moonlight, 1995, Suddenly Last Summer, 2006; actor (films) 1776, 1972, To Kill a Clown, 1972, Lovin' Molly, 1974, Hearts of the West, 1975, The Seagull, 1975, Futureworld, 1976, The Great Santini, 1980, Too Far to Go, 1982, Man, Woman, And Child, 1983, Brighton Beach Memoirs, 1986, Another Woman, 1988, Mr. and Mrs. Bridge, 1990, Alice, 1990, The Prince of Tides, 1991, Husbands and Wives, 1992, To Wong Foo, Thanks for Everything, Julie Newmar, 1995, The Myth of Fingerprints, 1997, The X Files, 1998, The Farmhouse, 1998, Forces of Nature, 1999, The Love Letter, Meet the Parents, 2000, The Invisible Circus, 2001, 3 Days of Rain, 2002, The Quality of Life, 2003, Sylvia, 2003, Meet the Fockers, 2004, (voice) Howl's Moving Castle, 2004, The Last Kiss, 2006; (TV movies) To Confuse the Angel, 1970, Dr Cook's Garden, 1971, George M!, 1972, The Scarecrow, 1972, F. Scott Fitzgerald and "The Last of the Belles", 1974, Sidekicks, 1974, Eccentricities of a Nightingale, 1976, The Court-Martial of George Armstrong Custer, 1977, A Love Affair: Eleanor and Lou Gehrig, 1978, Are You in the House Alone?, 1978, Roots: The Next Generations, 1979, Too Far to Go, 1979, You Can't Take It With You, 1979, Inside the Third Reich, 1982, In Defense of Kids, 1983, Helen Keller-The Miracle Continues, 1984, Guilty Conscience, 1985, A Streetcar Named Desire, 1988, Tattinger's, 1988, Judgment, 1990, Never Forget, 1991, Cruel Doubt, 1992, Getting Up and Going Home, 1992, Homage, 1995, Saint Maybe, 1998, We Were the Mulvaneys, 2002, Back When We Were Grownups, 2004; (TV series) Adam's Rib, 1973, Healthcare Crisis, 2000, Presidio Med, 2002-03, Huff, 2004- (Emmy award for outstanding supporting actor in a miniseries or a movie, 2005, Emmy award for outstanding supporting actress in a drama series, 2006). Recipient Theatre World award, 1969; Best Actress award Vevey Film Festival, Switzerland, 1982*

DANNER, JULIE A., literature and language educator; b. Tulsa, Dec. 10, 1958; children: Kathryn Elizabeth Bass, Anna Kristine Shelton, Kelsey Lynn Shelton. BA, U. Ctrl. Okla., Edmond, 1981. Cert. Lang. Tchr. State Okla., 1981. Retail buyer and mgr. The Sutlery, Inc., Oklahoma City, 1976—91; tchr. English Edmond Pub. Schs., 1991—. Retail cons. Mem.: NEA, Edmond Assn. Classroom Tchrs., Okla. Edn. Assn. Avocations: swimming, fishing, reading. Office: Edmond Public Schools 215 W Danforth Edmond OK 73003 E-mail: julie.danner@edmondschools.net.

DANNER, PATSY ANN, former congresswoman; b. Louisville, Ky., Jan. 13, 1934; d. Henry J. and Catherine M. (Shaheen) Berrer; children: Stephen, Stephanie, Shane, Shavonne.; m. C.M. Meyer, Dec. 30, 1982. Student, Hannibal-LaGrange Coll., 1952; BA in Polit. Sci. cum laude, N.E. Mo. State U., 1972. Dist. asst. to Congressman Jerry Litton, Kansas City, Mo., 1973-76; fed. co-chmn. Ozarks Regional Commn., Washington, 1977-81; mem. Mo. State Senate, 1983-1992, 103rd-106th Congress from 6th Mo. dist., 1993-2001. Mem. internat. rels. com., transp. and infrastructure com. Mem.: LWV (bd. mem., health chairwoman Columbia-Boone County, Mo.). Democrat. Roman Catholic.

DANNIN, ELLEN JEAN, lawyer; b. Flint, Mich., Aug. 3, 1951; d. Arthur Edwin and Jean Rogers (Smith) Dannin; m. Francis Robert Shor, May 17, 1981; 1 child, Emma Simone Shor. BA with high honors and high distinction, U. Mich., 1975, JD with honors, 1978. Bar: Mich. 1978. Teaching fellow, Women's Studies Dept. U. Mich., 1977—78; law clk. to Hon. Cornelia G. Kennedy US Dist. Ct. (Ea. Dist.) Mich., Detroit, 1978—79, US Ct. Appeals (6th cir.), 1979—80; atty., seventh region NLRB, Detroit, 1980—91; prof. law Calif. Western Sch. Law, San Diego, 1991—2002, Wayne State U. Law Sch., Detroit, 2002—. Vis. prof., Dept. Commerce Massey U., Palmerston, New Zealand, 1990; scholar in residence, Ctr. Indsl. Relations Victoria U., Wellington, New Zealand, 1992, scholar in residence, Law Dept., 94, Wellington, 97; scholar in residence Otago U., Dunedin, New Zealand, 1996, Waikato U., Hamilton, New Zealand, 1996; vis. prof. U. Mass., Amherst, 1999—2002; vis. prof. law U. Mich., 2002. Contbr. articles prof. jour. Office: Wayne State Univ Law Sch 471 Palmer St Detroit MI 48202 Office Phone: 313-577-3941. Office Fax: 313-577-9016. E-mail: e.dannin@wayne.edu.

DANTAS, STELLA MARIE, obstetrician, gynecologist; d. Paul and Leonora Dantas; m. Adam Coutu, June 7, 1997; 1 child, Kieran. BA, U. Calif., Berkeley, 1993; MD, Oreg. Health Scis. U., Portland, 1997; postgrad., U. Hawaii, Honolulu, 1997—2001. Ob-gyn. Northwest Permanents, Portland, 2001—. Mem.: Portland Soc. Ob-gyn. Office: Northwest Permanente 4855 SW Western Ave Beaverton OR 97007 E-mail: maddogcoutu@yahoo.com.

D'ANTONIO, CYNTHIA MARIA, sales and marketing executive; b. Chgo., Sept. 12, 1956; d. Michael Patrick and Joan Marie (Funk) D'A. BS in Natural Resource Devel., Mich. State U., 1979. Chemist Aqualab, Streamwood, Ill., 1980-83; R&D specialist Seaquist Closures, Crystal Lake, Ill., 1983-87; internat. sales & mktg. exec. Seaquist-Valois Australia, Sydney, 1987-93; internat. v.p. sales and mktg. cosmetics Pfeiffer Inc., Princeton, N.J., 1993—. Spkr. in field. Contbr. articles and photos to profl. jours. Mem. NAFE, Plastic Inst. Australia. Republican. Roman Catholic. Avocations: foreign current events, photography, golf, bike tours.

D'ANTUONO, ELEANOR, ballet director, educator, coach; b. Cambridge, Mass., Oct. 13, 1939; d. Lou and Marie (D'Antuono) Jacobs; m. John b. Vrabel, Oct. 25, 1986. AA, Columbia U. Dancer, mem. co., soloist Ballet Russe de Monte Carlo, N.Y.C., 1954-60, Joffrey Ballet, N.Y.C., 1960; prima ballerina Am. Ballet Theatre, N.Y.C., 1961-81; artistic dir. Festival Dance Theatre, N.Y.C., 1981-83; artistic assoc. dir. N.J. Ballet, 1986—; resident artistic advisor Nutmeg Ballet, 1990—; faculty Joffrey Ballet Sch., 1990—; artistic dir., coach N.Y. Internat. Ballet Competition, 1996—; dir. Joffrey Workshop, San Antonio, 1997—. Artistic dir. N.Y. Internat. Ballet Competition, 1996—. First Am. ballerina to appear as guest artist with Chinese cos., Kirov Ballet, Leningrad; leading roles include Coppelia, Giselle, Raymonda, The Sleeping Beauty, Swan Lake, Les Sylphides, Tales of Hoffman, La Fill Mal Gardee, also many original roles created by leading choreographers; appeared with Internat. Ballet Festival, Havana. Bd. dirs. Harkness Ballet Found., 1981-84; panelist N.Y. Coun. Arts, 1987-89; advisor Conn. Coun. Arts, 1997; nominated UN Internat. Femme Mythique, 1000 Legendary Women divsn. UNICEF, 1997. Roman Catholic. Office: NY Internat Ballet Competition 250 W 57 St Ste 1023 New York NY 10107

DANTZIC, CYNTHIA MARIS, artist, educator; b. NYC, Jan. 4, 1933; d. Howard Arthur and Sylvia Hazel (Wiener) Gross; m. Jerry Dantzic, June 15, 1958; 1 son, Grayson Ross. Student, Brooklyn Mus. Art Sch., Bklyn., 1947—50, Bard Coll., 1950—52; BFA, Yale U., 1955; MFA, Pratt Inst., 1963. Tchr. art Baldwin Sch., Bryn Mawr, Pa., 1955-58; head art dept. Bentley Sch., N.Y.C., 1958-62; coord. art prog., instr. North Shore Cmty. Arts Ctr., Roslyn, NY, 1962-64; instr. art CUNY-Bronx, N.Y.C., 1963-64; faculty L.I. U., Bklyn., 1964—, prof., 1975—, chair art dept., 1980-86. Adj. assoc. prof. art Cooper Union, 1992—99, adj. prof. art, 1999—2002; lectr., presenter in field. One-woman shows include Resnick Gallery, L.I. U., Bklyn., 1983, 89, 95, 2000, East Hampton Gallery, N.Y.C., 1965-66, St. John's U. Gallery, 1995, Crosby Studio Gallery, N.Y.C., 2005; exhibited in group shows at Blue Mountain Gallery, N.Y.C., 1984-85, 94-98, 2001, 2002, 2004-06, Hillwood Gallery, Greenvale, N.Y., 1985, Spring St. Gallery, N.Y.C., 2005-06; commd. artist edit. of photo collages Bklyn. Arts and Culture Assn., 1983; represented in permanent collections Bklyn. Mus., N.Y., Rose Art Mus., Mass., Bard Coll., N.Y., Adirondack Mus., N.Y.; author, illustrator: Stop Dropping BreAdcrumBs on my YaCht, 1974, Sounds of Silents, 1976, Design Dimensions: An Introduction to the Visual Surface, 1990, Drawing Dimensions: A Comprehensive Introduction, 1999, Antique Pocket Mirrors: Pictorial & Advertising Minatures, 2002, 100 New York Painters, 2006; contbr. articles to profl. jours. Trustee Park Slope Civic Coun., 1991—. Mellon grantee, 1984, L.I. Univ. faculty rsch. grantee, 1985—; recipient Newton Teaching Excellence award, 1988, Trustees award single work, 1990, Trustees lifetime award for Scholarly Achievement in art and art edn. L.I. Univ., 1999. Mem. AAUP, Internat. Soc. Copier Artists, L.I. U. Faculty Fedn. (exec. com. 1975—), Coll. Art Assn., Soc. Scribes (bd. govs. 2003—). Avocations: piano, travel, collecting americana and tribal and folk art. Home: 910 President St Brooklyn NY 11215-1604 Office: LI U Art Dept University Pla Brooklyn NY 11201 Office Phone: 718-488-3350. Business E-Mail: cdantzic@liu.edu.

DANTZLER, DERYL DAUGHERTY, lawyer, educator, dean; b. Macon, Ga., Jan. 26, 1944; d. Marshall Harrison and Gertrude Earle (Baker) Daugherty; m. L. Keitt Dantzler, June, 1968 (div. 1975); 1 child, Kennon Otis. BA, Mercer U., Macon, Ga., 1964, JD, 1970. Bar: Ga. 1970, U.S. Dist. Ct. (mid. dist.) Ga. 1970, U.S. Ct. Appeals (5th and 11th cirs.) 1970, U.S. Supreme Ct. 1973. Assoc. Mincey, Kenmore & Bennett, Macon, 1970-73; ptnr. Bennett, Mobley & Dantzler, Macon, 1973-78; pvt. practice Macon, 1978-79; asst. prof. Law Sch., Mercer U., Macon, 1979-84, prof., 1984—, dir. trial practice, 1985—; dean Nat. Criminal Def. Coll., Inc., Macon, 1985—. Mem. Nat. Assn. Criminal Def. Lawyers (Presdl. Commendation 1985, 89, Lifetime Achievement award 1996), Assn. Continuing Legal Edn. Adminstrs., Ga. Bar Assn. Office: Mercer U Law Sch Macon GA 31207-0001 Office Phone: 912-746-4151. E-mail: dean@ncdc.net.

DANTZSCHER, JAMIE, gymnast; b. Canoga Park, Calif., May 2, 1982; d. John and Joyce Dantzcher. Student, UCLA, 2001—. Mem. U.S. Nat. Team, 1994—2001, U.S. Gymnastic Team, Sydney Olympics, 2000. Mem. Charter Oaks Gliders. Named NCAA Champion, All-around, Vault and Floor Competitions, 2002, NCAA Co-Champion, Uneven Bars, 2003; recipient 1st pl. vault, Coca-Cola Nat. Championships, 1995, 1st pl. all-around, City of Popes (France) Competition, 1996, 1st pl. (tied) vault, Am. Classic, 1998, 1st pl. uneven bars, John Hancock U.S. Gymnastics Championships, 1999. Address: c/o UCLA Athletic Dept JD Morgan Ctr PO Box 24044 Los Angeles CA 90024

DANZIGER, GERTRUDE SEELIG, retired metal fabricating executive; b. Chgo., Oct. 24, 1919; d. Isidor and Clara (Fuchs) Seelig; widowed; children: Robert, James. With Homak Mfg. Co., Inc., Chgo., 1966-79, pres., 1979—2005; ret., 2005. Patentee in field.

DANZIGER, LUCY, editor; married; 2 children. Grad., Harvard U. Reporter Star-Ledger, Newark, 1982—86; mag. assoc. editor, 1986—88; founding mng. editor 7 Days, 1988—90; exec. editor Manhattan, Inc., NYC, 1990—92; freelance writer, 1992—95; freelance editor Allure; editor style and news dept. NY Times, NYC, 1994—95; founding editor Women's Sports & Fitness, 1997—2001; editor-in-chief SELF mag., NYC, 2001—. Office: Salf Mag 4 Times Sq New York NY 10036

DANZIS, ROSE MARIE, emeritus college president; b. Adrian, Pa. d. Paul A. and Josephine (Bugala) Manger; m. James Gordon Channing, Jan. 24, 1954 (dec. 1973); children: Rose Marie Buhrman, Lorraine Genieczko; m. Sidney Danzis, June 1, 1986. Diploma, Jersey City Hosp. Sch. Nursing, 1949; BS, N.Y. U., 1954; MA, Columbia U., 1961, M.Ed., 1971, Ed.D., 1973. Staff nurse, asst. supr. Pub. Health Nursing Svc., Jersey City, 1949-55; dir. health and recreation, clin. coordinator, asso. dir. nursing edn. Charles E. Gregory Sch. Nursing, Perth Amboy (N.J.) Gen. Hosp., 1958-66; chmn. dept. nurse edn., dir. health techs., dean div. health techs. Middlesex County Coll., Edison, NJ, 1966-78, pres., 1978-86; ret. Mem. Middlesex County Comprehensive Health Planning Coun., 1973-75, N.Y. Com. Regents External Degree in Nursing, 1972-80, Council on Continuing Edn. for Allied Health Pers., N.J.; Regional Med. Program, 1968-71; chmn. N.J. Health Professions Edn. Adv. Council, N.J. Dept. Higher Edn., 1979-82, chmn. nursing subcom., 1975-78; mem. health careers com. J.F. Kennedy Hosp., 1972-75; chmn. Middlesex County Coll. Assembly, 1975-77; mem. Pres.'s Adv. Com. Sch. Allied Health, Coll. Medicine and Dentistry of N.J., 1976-79; commr. Middle States Assn. of Colls. and Schs.; chmn. Commn. High Edn., 1984-85; mem. liaison com. Am. Assn. Cmty. and Jr. Colls. and Nat. League for Nursing, 1978-82; chmn. acad. affairs com. N.J. Coun. of C.C., pres., 1978-82; trustee Nat. Bank of N.J., 1979-81; exec. com. Acad. Pres.'s, Am. Assn. Community and Jr. Colls.; also exec. com. Internat./Intercultural Consortium. Contbr. articles to profl. jours. Recipient Torch of Liberty award Anti-Defamation League, 1981, Disting. Service award U. Medicine and Dentistry of N.J. Sch. Health Related Professions, 1983; named to Hall of Fame, Perth Amboy High Sch., 1985 Mem. Council of County Coll. Presidents, Am. Nurses Assn., Nat. League for Nursing, Am. Soc. Allied Health Professions, Am. Coun. on Edn., Am. Assn. Cmty. and Jr. Colls. (bd. dirs. 1984-86), Coll. Consortium for Internat. Studies., Jersey City Sch. Nursing Alumni Assn., N.Y. U. Alumni Assn., Tchrs. Coll., Columbia Alumni Assn., Kappa Delta Pi. Home: 5055 Collins Ave Apt 8C Miami Beach FL 33140

DAOUD, JULIE PERRY, literature and language professor; b. Cin., May 30, 1970; d. James and Renee Perry; m. Alexander Jamal Daoud. BA, Miami U., Oxford, Ohio, 1992; MA, U. Cin., 1994, PhD, 1999. Assoc. prof. Thomas More Coll., Crestview, Ky., 1999—. Grantee Seminar on Islam, Jordan, ACOR/U.S. State Dept., 2004—05. Mem.: Jr. League Cin. Avocations: cooking, travel, running, tennis, art. Office: English Dept Thomas More Coll 333 Thomas More Pkwy Crestview Hills KY 41017 Office Fax: 859-344-5385. Business E-Mail: julie.daoud@thomasmore.edu.

DARABAN, VICKIE LEIGH PLOTT, secondary school educator; b. Salt Lake City, Jan. 15, 1957; d. Leon Taylor and Betty May (Mower) Plott; m. Paul Alex Daraban, Dec. 21, 2005; children: Natalie Ann Mac Donald, Melissa Rae Bona. BS, So. Utah State Coll., Cedar City, 1979. Tchr. Granite Sch. Dist., Salt Lake City, 1979—. Named Tchr. of Yr., Granite Sch. Dist., 1993, Excel Outstanding Educator, 1993, Sci. Tchr. of Yr., Nat. Sci. Tchrs. Assn., 2004. Mem.: Nat. Sci. Tchr. Assn. (Sci. Tchr. of Yr. 2004). Home: 10104 S Dunsinane Dr South Jordan UT 84095 Office: Matheson Jr High Sch 3650 S Montclair Dr Magna UT 84044 Office Phone: 801-646-5290. E-mail: vickie.bona@granite.k12.ut.us.

DARAGAN, PATRICIA ANN, librarian; b. Ft. Worth, Mar. 3, 1953; BA with honors, Syracuse U., 1975, MLS, 1976. Libr. clk. Danbury (Conn.) Pub. Libr., 1969-74; grad. asst., libr. intern Canal Mus., Syracuse, N.Y., 1975-76, libr., registrar, 1976-78; fed. women's program mgr. USCG Acad. Libr., New London, Conn., 1979-80, cataloger, 1978-80, head tech. svcs., 1980-89, acting dir., 1989-90, libr. dir., 1990—. Adj. faculty Mohegan C.C., Norwich, Conn., 1989—, mem. libr. tech. program regional adv. bd., 1989—; vice-chair Coun. Conn. Acad. Libr. Dirs., 1998-99. Bd. dirs. YWCA, Groton, Conn., 1981-83. Recipient Excellence in Equity award AAUW, 1992. Mem. ALA, Spl. Librs. Assn., Am. Soc. for Engring. Edn., Southeastern Conn. Libr. Assn. (bd. dirs. 1982-83), New Eng. Morgan Horse Assn. (membership chairperson 1983-90), Assn. Coll. Rsch. Librs. (com. bibliog. instrn. sect., planning com. 1994-96). Office: USCG Acad Libr 35 Mohegan Ave New London CT 06320-8105

D'ARBANVILLE, PATTI, actress; b. NYC, May 25, 1951; m. Roger Mirmont, 1976 (div. 1977); m. Steve Curry, 1980 (div. 1981); m. Terry Quinn, June 15, 1993 (div. 2000); children: Emmelyn, Alexandra, Liam, Jesse. Appeared in films Flesh, 1968, Bilitis, 1976, Big Wednesday, 1978, Time After Time, 1979, The Fifth Floor, 1980, Modern Problems, 1981, THe Boys Next Door, 1985, Call Me, 1988, Fresh Horses, 1988, Crossing the Mob, 1988, Wired, 1989, Snow Kill, 1990, The Fan, 1996, Father's Day, 1997, I Know What You Did Last Summer, 1997, Archibald the Rainbow Painter, 1998, Bad to the Bone, 1997, Celebrity, 1998, Personal Velocity: Three Portraits, 2002, A Tale of Two Pizzas, 2003, World Trade Center, 2006, (TV series) Another World, 1992-93, New York Undercover, 1994-97, The Guiding Light, 1998-2000, (TV episodes) Eddie Capra Mysteries, 1978, Barnaby Jones, 1980, Charlies Angels, 1980, Darkroom, 1982, Murder, She Wrote, 1984, Miami Vice, 1985, Crime Story, 1986, Midnight Caller, 1988, The Hitchhiker, 1989, Wiseguy, 1989, Law & Order, 1992, South Beach, 1993, L.A. Law, 1994, Nip/Tuck, 2003, The Sopranos, 2004, Third Watch, 2004-05, Rescue Me, 2006.*

DARBY, JOANNE TYNDALE (JAYE DARBY), arts and humanities educator; b. Tucson, Sept. 22, 1948; d. Robert Porter Smith and Joanne Inloes Snow-Smith; stepchildren: Margaret Loutrel, David Michael. BA, U. Ariz., 1972; MEd, UCLA, 1986, PhD, 1996. Cert. secondary tchr., gifted and talented tchr., Calif. Tchr. English, chmn. dept. Las Virgenes Unified Sch. Dist., Calabasas, Calif., 1979-82; tchr. English and gifted and talented edn. Las Virgenes Unified Sch.Dist., Calabasas, Calif., 1983-84; sch. improvement coord./lang. arts/social studies/drama tchr Las Virgenes Unified Sch. Dist., Calabasas, Calif., 1991-92; tchr. English and gifted and talented edn. Beverly Hills (Calif.) Unified Sch. Dist., 1982-83, 84-89, English and drama tchr., 1994; tchr., cons. Calif. Lit. Project, San Diego, 1985-87; cons., free lance editor L.A., 1977—; dir. Shakespeare edn. and festivals project Folger Libr., Washington, 1990-91; field work supr. tchr. edn. program Ctr. X, Grad. Sch. Edn. and Info. Studies, UCLA, 1992-96, Ctr. X postdoctoral scholar, tchr. edn. program, 1996-97; asst. rschr. Am. Indian Studies Ctr., UCLA, 1997—2000; asst. prof. Coll. Edn. San Diego State U., 2000—; founding co-dir. Project HOOP Am. Indian Studies, UCLA, 1997—. Cons. arts and edn., L.A., 1991—. Co-editor (with Hanay Geiogamah) Stories of Our Way: An Anthology of American Indian Plays, 1999, American Indian Theater in Performance: A Reader, 2000, (with Stephanie Fitzgerald) Keepers of the Morning Star: An Anthology of Native Women's Theater, 2003; contbr. articles to profl. publs. Mem.: MLA, Assn. for Theatre in Higher Edn., Nat. Coun. Tchrs. English, Am. Ednl. Rsch. Assn., Phi Beta Kappa, Alpha Lambda Delta, Phi Beta Phi. Home: 11811 Venice Blvd Apt 118 Los Angeles CA 90066 Business E-Mail: jdarby@mail.sdsu.edu.

DARBY, NANCY, secondary school educator; d. Almas Joiner and Mattie Lambirth; m. George Darby, Dec. 1, 1969; children: Katherine Merrick, Jeremy. BA in English Edn., Wash. State U., Pullman, 1992, M in English, 2000. Cert. profl. tchr. Wash., 1992. Instr. English Columbia Basin Coll., Pasco, Wash., 1994—2000; contract learning dir. River's Edge H.S., Richland, 1995—. Chair entrance com. River's Edge H.S., 1998—2006, tech. coord., 1999—. Author: (poetry) 'The First Time'. Leader 4-H, Kennewick, Wash., 1986—89; pres. Riverview H.S. Booster Club, 1986—88; elected rep. state assembly Wash. Edn. Assn., Richland, 1999—2006. Grantee, Pacific NW Nat. Lab., Battelle, U.S. Dept. Energy, 2004—; Eva Peterson English fellow, Wash. State U., English Dept., 1992, 1998—2000, Paul Douglas Tchg. scholar, Wash. State Higher Edn. Bd., 1989—92, Bundy English scholar, Wash. State U. English Dept., 1991—92. Mem.: Richland Edn. Assn. (recorder 2004—), NW Inland Writing Project, Wash. Assn. Learning Alternatives, Nat. Sci. Tchrs. Assn., Gamma Pi Delta, Phi Beta Kappa. Baptist. Avocations: birdwatching, bicycling, reading, writing, travel. Office: River's Edge High School 975 Gillespie Richland WA 99352

DARBY, SHANNON SMITH, social studies educator; b. Lumberton, N.C., Apr. 17, 1975; d. Rebecca and James Smith; m. Drury James Darby, Mar. 27, 1999. BA in Elem. Edn., Converse Coll., Spartanburg, S.C., 1997, M in Elem. Edn., 2003; cert., Conerse Coll., Spartanburg, S.C., 2005. Social studies tchr. RP Dawkins Mid. Sch., Moore, SC, 1997—2006. Mem. Assn. Jr. Leagues Internat., Spartanburg, 1997—2006; leader YoungLife, Spartanburg, 1995—98; Sunday sch. leader Westminster Presbyn. Ch., Spartanburg, 1996—99; nominating chair Assn. Jr. Leagues Internat., Spartanburg, 1997—2006. Named Tchr. of Yr., RP Dawkins Mid. Sch., 2003—04. Mem.: S.C. Mid. Sch. Assn. (assoc.). R-Consevative. Avocations: running, travel. Home: 38 Woodwind Dr Spartanburg SC 29302 Office: RP Dawkins Mid Sch 1300 E Blackstock Rd Moore SC 29369 Office Phone: 864-576-8088. Personal E-mail: darbyss@spartanburg6.k12.sc.us. E-mail: darbyss@spart6.org.

D'ARCY, PAULA, writer; b. Fall River, Mass., Nov. 6, 1947; d. Raymond Vincent and Barbara (Waite) Pettine; m. Roy Thomas D'Arcy, Jan. 6, 1973 (dec. Aug. 1975); children: Sarah (dec.), Beth; m. Charles Granville Verge, Nov. 7, 1987. BA, Stonehill Coll., 1969; M in Counseling, U. N.H., 1970. Lic. allied mental health counselor. Counselor Mattatuck C.C., Waterbury, Conn., 1970-73; pvt. practice psychotherapy Newton, Mass., 1988—. Pub. author, 1979—, speaker, 1980—; cons. dept. ministry & guidance Peale Ctr. for Christian Living, Pawling, N.Y., 1981—. Author: Song for Sarah, 1979, Where the Wind Begins, 1984, When Your Friend is Grieving, 1990, Gift of the Red Bird, 1996, A New Set of Eyes, 2002, Seeking with All My Heart, 2003, Sacred Threshold, 2004. Mem. ch. Christian edn. com. Union Ch., Newton, 1993—, ch. search com., 1991-93. Mem. ACA, Internat. Graphoanalysis Soc. Avocations: reading, travel, biking, tennis, music.

DARDEN, BARBARA S., library director; b. Cleve., Apr. 6, 1947; d. Curley and Cora (Chambliss) Brown; m. Joseph S. Darden; children: Michelle, Crystal. BS, Ohio State U., 1967; MS in Edn. Media, Kent State U., 1971, MLS, 1971; PhD, Rutgers U., 2002. Adminstrv. supr. Cleve. Pub. Schs., 1968-70; libr. Cuyahoga C.C., 1972-75, coord., 1975-77, interim dir., 1977-78, asst. dean, 1978-80, dir., 1980-84; dir. libr. Kean Coll., Union, N.J., 1984—. Cons. Dembsy Assocs., Boston, 1967-81; editl. cons. Max Pub. Co., N.Y.C., 1967-81; cons. reader U.S. Office Edn., Washington, 1979-80; editl. cons. Jossey-Bass Pub. Co., 1979. Cons. editor Probe, 1976, Sch. Media Ctr., 1968, Booklist, 1969; contbr. articles to profl. jours. Bd. dirs. N.J. Adv. Bd. on Status of Women, 1988, Africana Studies, 1988; mem. N.J. State Libr. Adv. Bd.; bd. dirs. N.J. Ednl. Activities Task Force Libr. Com. Recipient Phillips award Kent State U., 1970. Mem. ALA (chmn. pay equity com. 1996, chair LAMA-COLA 1999), Higher Edn. Reps., N.J. Acad. Libr. Network (chmn. 1987, bd. dirs. 1995—), Coun. N.J. Librs. (prs. 1987—), N.J. Libr. Assn., Oral History Soc., N.J. Hist. Soc., Libr. Adminstrn. Mgmt. Assn. (chair 1997-99, bd. dirs. 1999), Coun. N.J. Coll. and Univ. Libr. Dirs. (pres. 1999—), Jr. League (Cleve. vice chmn. 1981, 83), Concerned Parents Club (pres. 1984), Women's City Club (adv. bd. 1997—). Avocations: music, reading. Office: Kean Univ Libr Morris Ave Union NJ 07083 E-mail: bsimpson@kean.edu.

DARDEN, LAURETTA, elementary school educator; b. Kinston, N.C., Dec. 1, 1956; d. Robert Lee and Sallie Lorraine Brown; m. Gregory Maurice Darden, July 2, 1988; 1 child, Loreal Sallie Lorraine. BA, Fayetteville State U., N.C., 1978. Elementary Education NJ, 1979, Nursery NJ. Elem. tchr. Paterson Bd. of Edn., Paterson, NJ, 1979—. Recipient Governor's Tchr. Recognition, Paterson Bd. of Edn., 2001, Mayor's Award (outstanding civic contbn.), Mayor Barnes Paterson, N.J., 2001, Golden Apple Award, The NJ. Herald News, 2002. Mem.: NJ. Edn. Assn. (assoc.), Paterson Edn. Assn. (assoc.), Alpha Kappa Alpha Sorority Inc. (life). Avocations: reading, sewing, drawing, travel. Personal E-mail: hunnybrown2@yahoo.com.

DAREN, SYLVIA, poet; b. NYC, Apr. 2, 1920; d. Louis Millman and Rose Beresnoger; m. Joseph Daren, Dec. 24, 1939; children: Edythe Hepner, Marsha. Student, grad. H.S., 1937. Lectr. Singles Group, N.Y.C.; poet laureat Temple Emeth; bd. mem. & by-law co-chair Temple Emeth Sisterhood; Instalation Chmn. Gold Coast Cancer Rsch. of Palm Greens, Women's Club of Palm Green; fund raising chair Delray B'nai B'rith; Poet and Mistress of Ceremonies Palm Greens Entertainers; actor, poet, story teller Yiddish Club of Palm Greens. Author (childrens poetry): Moses, The Hebrew Giant; author: (poetry book) How I Earned My Bachelor of Life Degree --You Can COunt Your Credits Too !!!; author: (plays and poetry) various including Temple Emeth of Delray Beach (Poet Laureat); co-dir.: Oakland Sr. Citizens -Oakland Jewish Ctr., 1962—80; editor (newspaper): Palms West O.R.T.; actor(co-author): (plays) My Unfair Lady. Leader Girl Scouts of Am., Queens, NY, 1953—54; vol. Creedmore Hosp., Queens; v.p. and trustee, adv. girls, fund raising, cmty. svc., jewish edn., Aid to Israel for Queens, vol. B'nai B'rith, Bayside, NY, 1953—2003, various Fla., 1953—2003; founder Marsha Daren Fund Long Island Jewish Med. Ctr., Long Island, 1975—89. Recipient Honorary Mem. of Am. Legion, Am. Legion, 1933, Honoree- This is Your Life, Oakland B'nai B'rith, 1959, Honoree, Org. of people Undaunted by Stroke, 1976, United Jewish Appeal & Federation of Jewish Philanthropies, 1976, Jewish Nat. Fund Temple Emeth, 0955—2003, Mem. award, B'nai B'rith Dist. 5, Woman of Achievement award, Women's League of Conservative Judaism, 2005. Mem.: Bowling League, B'nai B'rith. Jewish. Avocations: poetry, acting, bowling, golf, volunteering.

DARGAN, CATHERINE JANINE, lawyer; b. Feb. 15, 1970; AB with honors, Stanford U., 1991; JD cum laude, Harvard U., 1994. Bar: Calif. 1994, DC 1995. Law clk. for Judge Matthew J. Perry US Dist. Ct., SC; with Covington & Burling, DC, 1995—, ptnr., Corp. & Securities Practice Group, co-chmn. recruitment com. Office: Covington & Burling 1201 Pennsylvania Ave NW Washington DC 20004-2401 Office Phone: 202-662-5567. Office Fax: 202-662-6291. Business E-Mail: cdargan@cov.com.

DARGAN, PAMELA ANN, systems engineer, consultant; b. Norfolk, Va. d. Thomas J. and Stana E. (Verich) Piazza; m. W. Scott Dargan, Dec., 1990. BS in Math., Va. Poly. and State U., 1979; MS in Computer Sci., George Mason U., 1993. Programmer Control Data Corp., Rockville, Md., 1979—80; tech. staff BDM Corp., McLean, Va., 1980—81, TRW Fed. Sys. Group, McLean, 1981—87; dep. program mgr. Mystech, Inc., Alexandria, Va., 1987—89; lead engr. MITRE Corp., McLean, 1989—98, prin., 2001—02, Litton Tasc, Inc., Chantilly, Va., 1998—2001; sr. cons. Scitor Corp., Chantilly, 2002—03; prin. sys. engr. SAIC, Reston, Va., 2003—. Program chair East Coast Artificial Intelligence Work Sta. Users Group, 1984-85; author on open sys. for internat. confs. and publs. Author: Open Systems and Standards for Software Product Development, 2005; contbr. chpts. to books, articles to profl. jours. Mem. IEEE, Assn. Computing Machinery, Internat. Coun. on Sys. Engring. E-mail: pdargan@erols.com, pamela.a.dargan@saic.com.

DARISH, BERNICE STEIMAN, realtor; b. Everett, Mass., July 25, 1928; d. Samuel and Lena (Taple) Steiman; m. Joseph Darish, Oct. 27, 1951 (dec. Apr. 1989); children: Lee Raymond, Jay Lawrence, Neil Phillip, Susan Beth. Student, Boston Dispensary, 1948-49, Boston Evening Clinic, 1949-50, Northeastern U. Med. technologist Dr. Albert S. Lappin, Hyde Park, Mass., 1951-53, Dr. H. Archer Berman, Chelsea, Mass., 1953-56; auditor USMC Exch., Boston Naval Shipyard, 1961-70; office mgr. Torf Funeral Svc., Chelsea, 1982-90; realtor DeLuca Real Estate, Medford, Mass., 1990—. Leader workshops. Pres. Greater Boston Coun., 1993-96, mem. nat. bd. dirs. 1993—; mem., chair Malden (Mass.) Sch. Com., 1979. Mem. Internat. Tng. in Comm. (coun. 3 of Colonial Region sec., coun. v.p., coun. 3 pres. 1995-96, northeast region sec., pres. elect, pres., 2003-04), Malden Cultural Coun. (chair 1990-93), Mass. Cultural Coun. (vice chair). Democrat. Avocations: travel, creative cooking, knitting and crocheting, reading, crossword puzzles. Home: 63 Maple St Malden MA 02148-3828

DARKOVICH, SHARON MARIE, nursing administrator; b. Ft. Wayne, Ind., Dec. 10, 1949; d. Gerald Antone LaCanne and Ida Eileen (Bowman) LaCanne Cutler; m. Robert Eliot Ness, July 17, 1971 (dec. Aug. 1976); m. Paul Darkovich, Jan. 23, 1981 (div. May 1994); 1 child, Amy Elizabeth. BSN, Case Western Res. U., 1973, BA in Psychology, 1978; cert. in advanced bioethics, Cleve. State U., 1990, MA in Philosophy and Bioethics, 1994. RN, Ohio. Staff nurse Univ. Hosps., Cleve., 1973, asst. head nurse, 1973-76; quality improvement coord. St. Luke's Med. Ctr., Cleve., 1976-83, 84-97, dir. nursing, 1983-84, quality improvement dir., 1997-98; dir. quality svcs. Lake Hosp. Sys., Inc., Painesville, Ohio, 1998-2000, corp. quality and compliance officer, 2000—. Cons. to long-term care facilities, 1986-92, pressure ulcer dressing devel. B.F. Goodrich Co., 1988-92; cons. to ambulatory facility for Joint Commn. for Accreditation of Health Care Orgns., Oakbrook, Ill., 1994, cons. to cmty. hosp. med. staff, bylaws, 1996; lectr. U. Akron, 1992-93, Northeast Ohio U. Coll. Medicine, 1993-95; bd.dir. Bioethics Network Ohio. Mem. ANA, Am. Soc. for Healthcare Bioethics, Am. Soc. for Quality, Greater Cleve. Nurses Assn. (mem. dist. coun. on practice, 1982-84), Sigma Theta Tau. Avocations: reading, needlecrafts, sewing, camping. E-mail: sharon.darkovich@lhs.net.

DARLING, ALBERTA HELEN, state legislator, art gallery director, marketing professional; b. Hammond, Ind., Apr. 28, 1944; d. Albert William and Helen Anne (Vaicunas) Statkus; m. William Anthony Darling, Aug. 12, 1967; children— Elizabeth Suzanne, William Anthony. BS, U. Wis., 1967. English tchr. Nathan Hale High Sch., West Allis, Wis., 1967—69, Castle Rock High Sch., Castle Rock, Colo., 1969—71; mem. Wis. State Assembly, 0990—1992, Wis. Senate from 8th dist., Madison, 1992—. Cons. orgn. devel., Milw., 1982—; dir. mktg. and communications Milw. Art Mus., 1981-88; exec. dir. mktg. architectural firm, 1988-90; State Rep. Wis., 1990—, mem. urban edn. com., children and human svcs. com., tourism com., homelessness com., teenage pregnancy com., vice chmn. gov.'s housing policy commn., assembly coms. Pres. Community Action Seminar for Women, 1979-80; a founder Goals for Greater Milw. 2000, 1980-84; co-chair Action 2000, 1984-86; co-chmn. Icebreaker Am. Winterfestival; chmn. Community Action Seminar for Women, 1988; bd. dirs., exec. com. United Way, Milw., 1982-1992, chair project 1985, 1984-85, chmn. policy com. 1988; founder Today's Girls/Tomorrow's Women, Milw., pres. Jr. League Milw., 1980-82, Planned Parenthood Milw., 1982-84, Future Milw., 1983-85; vice chmn. State of Wis. Strategic Planning Council, 1988—, chmn. small bus./entrpreneur com.; mem. Greater Milw. Com.'s Mktg. Task Force, 1987-88; chmn. United Way Policy Com., 1987-88; participant Bus. Ptnrs. White House Conf., 1987; mem. summerfest adv. com. on Winter Festivals, 1989; founder Women's Fund of Milw. Found; active Juvenile Justice Leadership Com. Recipient Vol. Action award Milw. Civic Alliance, 1984, Community Service award United Way, 1984, Leader of Future award Milw. Mag., 1988, Nat. Assn. Community Leadership Orgn. award, 1986, Today's Girls/Tomorrow's Women Leadership award, 1987, Future Milw. Community Leadership award, 1988, Friend of Edn. Leadership award Head Start, 1994, William Steiger Humanitarian award, 1994. Mem. Greater Milw. Com., TEMPO Profl. Women, Am. Mktg. Assn. (Marketer of Yr. 1984), Pub. Relations Soc. Am., Ctr. for Pub. Representation (state bd. 1988), ARC (bd. dirs., exec. fin. coms. 1987—), Women's Fund (steering com. 1988), Internat. Assn. Bus. Communicators, Greater Milw. Com. Republican. Avocations: travel, art history, contemporary american literature, golf, tennis. Home: 1325 W Dean Rd Milwaukee WI 53217-2537 Office: State Capitol PO Box 7882 Madison WI 53707-7882 Office Phone: 608-266-5830. Business E-Mail: sen.darling@legis.state.wi.us.

DARLING, HELEN, health services consultant; b. Fla., Mar. 1, 1942; d. Henry B. and Ann B. D.; m. John M. Nail Jr., Aug. 31, 1961 (div. Aug. 1970); children: John M. III, Ann Darling Nail Turner; m. Bradford H. Gray, Jan. 15, 1983. BA, Memphis State U., 1965, MA, 1970. Rsch. assoc. R.I. Health Svcs. Rsch., Providence, 1970-75; spl. asst. Dept. health, Edn. & Welfare, Washington, 1975-78; study dir. Inst. Medicine, Nat. Acad. Scis., Washington, 1979-82; v.p. Govt. Rsch. Corp., Washington, 1982-86; sr. policy advisor U.S. Senate, Washington, 1986-88; sr. cons. William M. Mercer, Stanford, Conn., 1988-92; mgr. health care benefits Xerox Corp., Stanford, Conn., 1992-98; sr. cons. Watson Wyatt Worldwide, Stanford, Conn., 1998—2002; pres. Washington Bus. Group on Health, Washington, 2002—. Bd. trustees Gaylord Rehab. Hosp., Conn., 1993-97, 99—; pres. citizenz bd. Providence Hosp., Washington, 1985-88; pres ARPHA Ctr., Washington, 1980-95. Episcopalian. Office: Washington Bus Group in Health 50 F St NW Washington DC 20001

DARLING, RANDI A., science educator; d. Walter and Janet Engle; m. Jerry Darling; children: Alexander, Trevor. BS, Cornell U., Ithaca, N.Y., 1987; MS, U. Calif.-San Diego, La Jolla, 1989; PhD, Dartmouth Coll., Hanover, N.H., 1995. Assoc. prof. Westfield (Mass.) State Coll., 1995—. Contbr. articles to sci. publs. Named a Disting. Scientist, Outstanding Scientists of 21st Century. Mem.: Nat. Assn. Biology Tchrs., Soc. for Coll. Sci. Tchrs., Assn. Coll. and Univ. Biology Educators, Nat. Sci. Tchrs. Assn., Sigma Xi. Office: Westfield State Coll 577 Western Ave Westfield MA 01086

DARLINGTON, HILDA WALKER, real estate company officer; b. Anderson, SC, May 3, 1923; d. Dewey Columbus White and Julia Elizabeth Davis; m. Thomas M. Darlington; m. Roy Jones Walker, June 28, 1945 (div. July 1962); children: Stephen D. Walker, Karon Elaine Meehan. Diploma in History. Adminstrv. acct. So. Railway, Atlanta and Washington, 1960—76, Human Resources/State of Va., Arlington, 1978—85; real estate cons. Arlington, Va., 1986—98; real estate entrepreneur, 2000—. Adv. for adminstrv. manual Human Resources, Richmond, Va., 1988—93. Vol. adminstrv. asst. Kennedy Ctr., Washington, 1986—96; civic assn. sec. Lyon Village, Arlington, Va., 1985—97; proprietor homeless shelter Courtlands, Arlington, Va., 1995—99. Mem.: Women's Investment Club, Profl. Business Women's Club. Republican. Avocation: aerobics, gardening, reading.

DARLOW, JULIA DONOVAN, lawyer; b. Detroit, Sept. 18, 1941; d. Frank William Donovan and Helen Adele Turner; m. George Anthony Gratton Darlow (div.); 1 child, Gillian; m. John Corbett O'Meara. AB, Vassar Coll., 1963; postgrad., Columbia U. Law Sch., 1964-65; JD cum laude, Wayne State U., 1971. Bar: Mich. 1971, U.S. Dist. Ct. (ea. dist.) Mich. 1971. Assoc. Dickinson, Wright, McKean, Cudlip & Moon, Detroit, 1971-78; ptnr. Dickinson, Wright, Moon, Van Dusen & Freeman and predecessor, Detroit, 1978—2001; sr. v.p. Detroit Med. Ctr., 2001—01; cons. mem. Dickinson, Wright PLLC, Detroit, 2002—04; counsel Varnum, Riddering, Schmidt & Howlett, LLP, 2005—. Chair corp. governance com. Internat Corp., 2004-05; adj. prof. Wayne State U. Law Sch., 1974-75, 96; commr. State Bar Mich., 1977-87, mem. exec. com., 1979-83, 84-87, sec. 1980-81, v.p., 1984-85, pres.-elect 1985-86, pres. 1986-87, coun. corp. fin. and bus. law sect. 1980-86, coun. computer law sect. 1985-88; mem. State Officers Compensation Commn., 1994-96; chair Mich. Supreme Ct. Task Force on Gender Issues in the Cts., 1987-89 Bd. dirs. Hutzel Hosp., 1984—2003, chair, 2002—03; bd. dirs. Mich. Opera Theatre, 1985—, mem. exec. com., 1992—; bd. dirs. Mich. Women's Found., 1986—91, Detroit Med. Ctr., 1990—2003, Marygrove Coll., 1996—, sec., 2003—; trustee Internat. Inst. Met. Detroit, 1986—92; trustee Mich. Met. coun. Girl Scouts USA, 1988—91; trustee Detroit coun. Boy Scouts Am., 1988—98; mem. exec. com. Mich. Coun. Humnanities, 1988—92; mem. Blue Cross-Blue Shield Prospective Reimbursement Com., Detroit, 1979—81; v.p., mem. exec. com. United Found., 1988—95; mem. Mich. Gov.'s Bilateral Trade Team for Germany, 1992—98. Fellow Am. Bar Found. (Mich. State chair 1990-96); mem. Detroit Bar Assn. Found. (treas. 1984-85, trustee 1982-85), Mich. Bar Found. (trustee 1987-94), Am. Judicature Soc. (bd. dirs. 1985-88), Internat. Women's Forum (global affairs com. 1994-03), Women Lawyers Assn. (pres. 1977-78), Mich. Women's Campaign Fund (charter). Democrat. Office: Ste 400 200 E Liberty St Ann Arbor MI 48104 Address: Varnum Riddering Schmidt & Howlett LLP 39500 High Pointe Blvd Ste 150 Novi MI 48375 Office Phone: 313-690-3054. Business E-Mail: jdarlow@varnumlaw.com.

DARNELL, DORIS HASTINGS, performance artist; b. Chgo., Sept. 14, 1916; d. Willard Seth and Faith Emily (Olmstead) Hastings; m. Howard Clayton Darnell, Aug. 27, 1938; children: Elizabeth Loyd, John Hastings, Eric Allen. BA in Latin, Bryn Mawr Coll., 1939. Head resident, asst. to dir. Pendle Hill Grad. Sch. Religious and Social Concerns, Wallingford, Pa., 1939-40; libr. Res. Rm. and sci. Bryn Mawr (Pa.) Coll., 1950-52; acting head libr. Westtown (Pa.) Friends Sch., 1952-53; head libr. Westtown Sch., 1954-55; libr. Res. Rm. Haverford (Pa.) Coll., 1953-54; exec. dir., editor Westtown Alumni Assn., 1955-64; from coord. recruitment to assoc. exec. sec. pers. Am. Friends Svc. Com., Phila., 1964-78; creator, owner A Century of Elegance in Costume and Story, State College, Pa., 1980—. Gov. com. Pendle Hill, Westtown Sch., Friends Select Sch., Pa., 1948—78; mem. Rufus Jones Assocs., Haverford Coll.; founding trustee Allen Hilles Fund, 1982—91, trustee emerita, 1991—; lectr., exhibitor 19th and 20th century fashions, 1980—. Mem.: Women's Nat. History Mus., Women in the Arts, Internat., Palmer Art Mus., Costume Soc. Am. Mem. Soc. Of Friends Quaker. Home and Office: #C 36 500 Marylyn Ave State College PA 16801 E-mail: eleganztoo@juno.com.

DARNELL, MICHELLE R., philosophy educator; d. Rebecca Deasey; m. Jamey A. Darnell. BA, U. San Diego, 1998; MA, Purdue U., West Lafayette, Ind., 2001, PhD, 2004. Asst. prof. philosophy Meth. Coll., Fayetteville, NC, 2004—05, Fayetteville State U., 2005—. Recipient Grad. Student Outstanding Paper award, Am. Philos. Assn., 2003, Outstanding Creative Work award, Fayetteville State U., 2006; Travel grantee, Purdue U. Grad. Student Assn., 2003, Rsch. grantee, Purdue U., 2003—04. Mem.: North Am. Sartre Soc., Am. Philos. Assn. Office: Fayetteville State U 1200 Murchison Road Fayetteville NC 28301 Office Phone: 910-672-1573. Business E-Mail: mdarnell@uncfsu.edu.

DARNELL, SUSAN LAURA BROWNE, retired air force officer; b. Milw., Mar. 11, 1955; d. William George Jr. and Jean Marie (Gable) Browne; m. Kevin Scott Charles Darnell, Oct. 4, 1984; children: Emily Elizabeth Browne, Katherine Maureen Browne. BSN, U. Md., 1982; MS in Sys. Mgmt., U. So. Calif., Okinawa, Japan, 1988; postgrad., Roger Williams U., 2001—. Cert. RN, Aeronautical Rating of Sr. Navigator. Commd. 2d lt. USAF, 1982, advanced through grades to maj., 1995; Army spl. 7th Army Soldiers Chorus, Heidelberg, 1975-78; AWACS navigator 964 AWAC Squadron, Tinker AFB, Okal., 1983-85; instr. navigator 961 AWAC Squadron, Kadena, Japan, 1985-90; flight comdr. 451 Flying Training Squadron, Mather AFB, Calif., 1990-92; chief current ops. 12 Ops. Support Squadron, Randolph AFB, Tex., 1992-94; asst. ops. officer 12 Ops. Support Squadron, Randolph AFB, Tex., 1994-95; asst. chief Comdr.'s Action Group 12 FTW, Randolph AFB, Tex., 1995; chief of counter-drug plans 24 ASG, Howard AB, Panama, 1996-97; dep. dir. for plans and policy Joint Inter-Agy. Task Force South, Howard AB, Panama, 1997—99. Leader Girl Scouts U.S., 1997—; v.p., pres. Newport Officer Spouses, 1999—2001. Recipient Appreciation award Girl Scouts of U.S., San Antonio, 1996. Mem. Air Forces Assn. (life), Women Mil. Aviators, Inc., Women Mil. Svc. for Am.Meml. Avocation: public speaking.

DARNLEY, KATHERINE E., elementary school educator; b. Junction City, Kans., Nov. 17, 1978; d. Kenneth R. and Michele I. Darnley. BA, Canisius Coll., Buffalo, NY, 2000; MA in Edn., East Carolina U., Greenville, NC, 2006. Mid. sch. tchr. Randolph County Schools, Ramseur, NC, 2001—. Democrat.

D'ARPA, JOSEPHINE, music educator; b. Tampa, Fla., Oct. 26, 1936; d. Jerome F. and Susie G. D'Arpa. Student, U. Tampa, 1956-58; MusB, William Carey Coll., 1960; M of Ch. Music, Southwestern Theol. Sem., 1964. Min. of music 1st Bapt. Ch., Forrest City, N.C., 1964-65; assoc. prof. music William Carey Coll., Hattiesburg, Miss., 1965—, Winters endowed chair music, 1991-93. Mem., soloist Bapt. Hour Choir, So. Bapt. Conv. Radio and TV Commn., Ft. Worth; jr. choral dir. Grace Luth. Ch., Ft. Worth; min. music Bay Springs (Miss.) Bapt. Ch., 1971-75; dir. choral activities 1st Presbyn. Ch., Hattiesburg, 1975-79; interim min. music Bellevue Bapt. Ch., Hattiesburg, 1980; interim children's choral dir., soloist Broadstreet Meth. Ch., Hattiesburg, 1983; min. of music Court St. United Meth. Ch., 1997—; condr. vocal workshops; adjudicator choral festivals Ga. Bapt. Conv., 1965, 85, Miss. Bapt. Conv., 1965—, Jones Jr. Coll., Ellisville, Miss., others. Opera performances include Noye's Fludde (The Chester Miracle Play), Amahl and the Night Visitors, La Boheme; recital soloist Southwestern Bapt. Theol. Sem. and 1st Bapt. Ch. of Tampa, 1963, Harrisburg Bapt. Ch., Tupelo, Miss., Ridgecrest (N.C.) Bapt. Assembly, others. Mem. Music Tchrs. Nat. Assn. (guest collegiate artist so. divsn. 1960), Nat. Assn. Tchrs. of Singing, Miss. Music Tchrs. Assn., Ch. Music Conf. of So. Bapt. Conv., Ch. Music Conf. of Miss. Bapt. Conv., Condrs. Conf. of U. of So. Miss., Omicron Sigma chpt. Delta Omicron (chpt. advisor 1974—). Avocations: swimming, reading, singing. Home: 620 S 28th Ave Hattiesburg MS 39402-2518

DARR, CAROL C., lawyer; b. Apr. 24, 1951; d. Patt M. and Justine D.; m. Albert Louis May III Dec. 19, 1992. BA, U. Memphis, 1973, JD, 1976; M.Litt, Christ's Coll., Cambridge U., 1978. Bar: Tenn. 1977, DC 1981. Atty. Fed. Election Commn., 1976-77; asst. counsel U.S. Senate Com. on Rules & Adminstrn., 1977-79; dep. gen counsel Carter/Mondale Presidential Com., 1979-81; in house counsel Dem. Nat. Com., 1981-82; assoc. Skadden, Arps, Slate, Meagher & Flom, 1983-85; chief counsel Dukakis/Bentsen Com., Inc., 1987-91; gen. counsel Dem. Nat. Com., 1991-92; with Clinton/Gore Transition Com., 1992-93; actg. gen. counsel, dep. gen. counsel U.S. Dept. Commerce, 1993-94; assoc. Adminstrn. Nat. Telecom. and Info. Agy., Office Internat. Affairs, 1994-96; v.p. govt. affairs Info. Tech. Industry Coun., Washington, 1996-98; sr. v.p. bus. and pub. affairs Interactive Digital Software Assn., 1998-2001; dir. careers and external programs Grad. Sch. Polit. Mgmt. George Washington U., 2001—, sr. rsch. staff scientist. Author:

Political Parties, Presidential Campaigns, and National Party Conventions, 1992; Contributions and Expenditures by National, State, and Local Party Conventions, 1990; Active Corporate Participation, 1993; Candidates and Parties 1982, Registration and Reporting, 1981. Recipient U. Memphis Outstanding Young Alumnus award 1982. Mem. ABA, Fed. Bar Assn. (chair. com. on political campaigns and election laws 1983-85. Mailing: Columbian Sch Arts and Sci George Washington Univ Washington DC 20052 Office Phone: 202-994-5141. E-mail: dar@gwu.edu.

DARR, CLARISSA MCCUDDEN, psychiatric clinical nurse specialist; b. Orange, N.J., Nov. 27, 1950; d. Francis E. McCudden and Clarissa C. Brady; children: Brendan T., Gillian C. BSN, Ball State U., Muncie, Ind., 1972; MSN, Cath. U., Washington, 1977. RN, CNS, cert. psych-mental health nurse, group therapist, AAGP. Sr. nurse Montimone Hosp., Bronx, NY, 1972—75; staff nurse St. Elizabeth's Hosp., Washington, 1975—76; staff nurse CCU Providence Hosp., Washington, 1975—77; nursing coord. Georgetown U. Hosp., Washington, 1977—81; nursing coord. psychiat. in-patient unit Georgetown Hosp., Washington, 1981—89; program coord. Psych Day Hosp., Washington, 1989—94; pvt. practice nurse/therapist Chevy Chase, Md., 1994—. Clin. instr. dept. psychiatry Georgetown U., 1981—94. Mem. D.C. Nursh Push, 1979—84; tchr. CCD St. Raphael's Ch., Rockville, Md., 1994—2000. Scholar, Fed. Govt., 1975—77. Mem.: Am. Assn. Group Psychotherapists, Am. Psychiat. Nursing Assn., Md. State Nursing Assn. Roman Catholic. Avocations: gardening, sewing, music, children's sports. Office: 5530 Wisconsin Ave #660 Chevy Chase MD 20815 Office Phone: 301-986-1481. Personal E-mail: clarissadarr@verizon.net.

DARROW, EMILY M., public relations executive, writer; b. Kingston, N.Y., Sept. 21, 1964; d. H. Van Wyck and Marianne Darrow; m. Brendon Paul McCrane, Oct. 5, 2002. Student, Vassar Coll., 1983—84; BA, Hunter Coll., 1989; postgrad., Inst. of FIne Arts, NYU, 1992. Mus. mgr., edn. mgr. Hist. Hudson Valley-Montgomery Pl., Annandale-on-Hudson, NY, 1995; dir. pub. rels. and promotions Mohonk Mountain Ho., New Paltz, NY, 1997—98; pub. rels. assoc. Bard Coll., Annandale-on-Hudson, 1998—; asst. to exec. dir. Inst. Advanced Theology Bard Coll., Annandale-on-Hudson, 2001—. Rschr. Salander O'Reilly Gallery-Stuart Davis Catalogue Raisonne Project, N.Y.C., 1989—90; writer, rschr. Art Commn. City of N.Y., 1989—90; internship in pub. rels. Opera Garnier de Paris-Paris Opera Ballet, Paris, 1990—91, N.Y.C. Ballet, 1982—84; cons., writer Vikarmasila Found., N.Y.C., 1999—; mem. Woodstock Arts Bd., 2004—. Mem. Woodstock (N.Y.) Arts Bd., 2004—. Recipient Zabar grad. scholarship, Hunter Coll., 1989; fellow Leon Levy and Shelby White, Inst. of Fine Arts/NYU, 1990. Mem.: Coll. Art Assn. and Pub. Rels. Soc. Am., Jr. League Kingston (rec. sec. 1991—96, pub. rels. dir. 1991—96). Home: 250 Morton Rd Rhinebeck NY 12572 Office: Bard Coll Annandale Hotel Annandale On Hudson NY 12504 Personal E-mail: EMDarrow87@alum.vassar.edu.

DARROW, GRETCHEN, costume designer; b. Ithaca, N.Y., Apr. 5, 1970; d. Frank William and Catherine (Twomey) D. MusB, U. Hartford, 1992; MFA, U. Conn., 1995. Asst. mgr. box office Hangar Theatre, Ithaca, 1992, mgr. box office, 1993-94, asst. shop mgr., 1995, mgr. costume shop, costume designer, 1996-99; sales assoc. JoAnn Fabrics, Ithaca, 1995; foreman costume shop Syracuse (N.Y.) Stage Co., 1996-99, mgr. costume shop, 1999—. Office: Syracuse Stage Co 820 E Genesee St Syracuse NY 13210-1508

DARROW, JANE, artist; b. Hollywood, Calif., Apr. 9, 1936; d. Reginald Ivan and Dorothy Gertrude Bauder; m. Henry Frank Smith, Oct. 1954 (div. June 1967); children: Michael Henry, Linda Lee, Nancy Ann; m. Lee Hunter Darrow, Nov. 21, 1981 (dec. 7/2005). Student, U. So. Calif., 1953-55, U. Oreg., 1960-61. Art tchr. and exhibiter Los Abrigados, Sedona, Ariz., 2002—. Art instr. Sedona Art Ctr., Ariz., 1995; tchr. art Los Abrigados, 2002—; represented by Raku Gallery, Jerome. One-woman shows include Miramar, San Juan, P.R., El Dorado Gallery, San Juan, Excelsior Hotel, San Juan, Conservation Soc., P.R., Galeria Isabella, Vieques, P.R., 1992-94, Inst. Culture, San Juan, 1995, Ch. of the Red Rocks, Sedona, 1996, Creekside Gallery, Sedona, 1997; exhibited in group shows at P.R. and Fla. Watercolo Assn. Shows, 1989, 90, Phila. Watercolor, 1992, Catherine Lorillard Wolfe Art Club, 1992-95, Rocky Mountain Nat., 1992, 97, San Diego Watercolor, 1993, Ariz. Aqueous, 1993, 94, 97, La. Watercolor, 1994, Salmagundi Non-members, 1994, Ariz. Watercolor Assn., 1994-97, N.W. Watercolor, 1994-98, No. Ariz. Watercolor Assn., 1995, 97, Allied Artists, N.Y., 1995, 96, Phippen Mus., Prescott, Ariz., 1999; commd. artist Mariott Hotel, San Juan, 1994, Piñon Pointe Hyatt Hotel, Sedona; represented in permanent collections Condado Plaza Hotel, San Juan, Law Offices Guzman Esquilin and Assocs., San Juan, Crow's Nest Hotel, Vieques, Danmar Corp., San Juan. Mem. N.W. Watercolor Soc. (Miva/Walter Welt award 1997, No. Ariz. Watercolor Soc. (v.p. 1995-97, pres. 1997—, award of excellence 1996, best in show award 1997-99), Ariz. Watercolor Assn. (award of excellence 1995), Catherine Lorillard Wolfe Art Club. Home: 45 Ridge Rd Sedona AZ 86336-4035

DARROW, JILL E(LLEN), lawyer; b. NYC, Jan. 6, 1954; d. Milton and Elaine (Sklarin) D.; m. Michael V.P. Marks, May 14, 1987. AB in English, Barnard Coll., 1975; JD, U. Pa., 1978; LLM in Tax Law, NYU, 1983. Bar: Pa. 1978, NY 1979, US Tax Ct. 1982. Assoc. Shearman & Sterling, NYC, 1978-79, Rosenman & Colin, NYC, 1979-86, ptnr., 1987—2002, Katten Muchin Rosenman LLP, NYC, 2002—. Mem. ABA, NY State Bar Assn., Pa. Bar Assn., Phi Beta Kappa. Home: 300 Central Park W New York NY 10024 Office: Katten Muchin Rosenman LLP 575 Madison Ave Fl 12 New York NY 10022-2511 Office Phone: 212-940-7113. Business E-mail: jill.darrow@kattenlaw.com.

DARSCH, NANCY, former professional basketball coach; b. Plymouth, Mass., 1951; BS, Springfield (Mass.) Coll., 1973. Coach Longmeadow (Mass.) H.S.; asst. coach U. Tenn., 1978-85; coach Ohio State U., 1985-97; head coach N.Y. Liberty, WNBA, 1997-98, Washington Mystics, WNBA, 1998—2000; asst. coach Minn. Lynx, 2003—. Coach U.S.A. Olympic trials, 1980, 88, U.S.A. Pan Am. Games trials, 1979, 83; head coach U.S.A. Jr. Nat. basketball team, 1990; asst. coach U.S. Olympic team, 1984, 96.

DARST, MARY LOU, elementary school educator; b. Houston, Aug. 12, 1943; d. Carl Kennedy and Sara Catharine (Emmott) Hughes; m. William Maury Darst, Apr. 20, 1963 (dec. May 1990); children: Robert Maury, Catharine Fontaine Darst Knight. Student, Stephen F. Austin State Coll., 1961—63, Galveston Coll., 1970-72, 76-77, U. Tex. Med. Br., 1983—84; BA, U. Houston, Clear Lake, 1989, BA, 1993, MS, 2001; Gifted and Talented Cert., U. St. Thomas, 1999—2002; Adv. Placement Cert., Rice U., 2003. Cert. tchr. elem. edn., secondary English, ESL. Sec. William Temple Found., Galveston, 1979-80; new accounts Tex. First Bank, Galveston, 1981-84; med. sec. U. Tex. Med. Br., Galveston, 1984-87; tchr. Galveston Ind. Sch. Dist., 1990—2002, Galveston Coll., 1995-96; ESL tchr. Clear Lake H.S., 2002—04; tchr. 3d grade St. Thomas the Apostle Episc. Sch., 2004—05; ESL instr. Alvin CC, 2004—05, Coll. of the Mainland, 2005—. Mem. Jr. League of Galveston, 1966-69; bd. dirs. YWCA, Galveston, 1972-73. Recipient Title VII grantee, U. Houston at Clear Lake, Houston, 1991—93. Mem.: Galveston Art League, Tex. Neurofibromatosis Found. (sec. 1987—89, pres. 1989—91), Assn. Tex. Profl. Educators, Mus. Fine Arts Houston, Scenic Galveston, Sierra Club, Delta Kappa Gamma, Alpha Chi Omega. Democrat. Episcopalian. Avocations: travel, music, swimming, walking, writing. Home: 1431 San Sebastian Ln Houston TX 77058-3451 Personal E-mail: mldarst@juno.com.

DARVAROVA, ELMIRA, musician, concertmaster; b. Bulgaria; came to U.S., 1986; MusB, State Conservatory, Sofia, Bulgaria, 1977, MusM, 1979; certificate, Guildhall Sch. Music, London, 1982; artist's diploma, Ind. U., 1987. Concertmaster Plovdiv (Bulgaria) Philharm. Orch., 1979-86, Owensboro (Ky.) Symphony Orch., 1986-88, Evansville (Ind.) Philharm., 1987-88; artistic dir., concertmaster Evansville Chamber Orch., 1987-88; assoc. instr. violin Ind. U. Sch. Music, Bloomington, 1986-88; acting concertmaster Rochester (N.Y.) Philharm., 1988. Vis. lectr. Ind. U. Sch. Mus., 1988; guest concertmaster Columbus Symphony Orch., Columbus, Ohio, 1988; concertmaster Met. Opera Orch., NYC, 1989-2002, Chgo. Grant Park Symphony, 1990-2003; founding mem. New World Trio, 1991; performer at various recitals and concerts throughout the world. Recipient 1st medal internat. competition, Barcelona, Spain, 1979, hon. diploma, prize Tchaikovsky competition, Moscow, 1982, silver medal Viotti internat. competition, Vercelli, Italy, 1984, 3d prize internat. competition, Sion, Switzerland, 1985. Achievements include first woman concertmaster in Metropolitan Opera history. Avocations: reading, languages.

DASILVA, DINA PATRICIA, science educator; b. Freeport, Bahamas, Apr. 18, 1976; d. Arthur and Donna DaSilva. BSc in Zoology, U. Fla., Gainesville, 1998, MSc in Edn., 2000. Tchr. biology Stonewall Jackson H.S., Manassas, Va., 2000—; tchr. biology EIP summer acad. George Masion U., Manassas, 2004—. Coord. sci. fair Stonewall Jackson H.S., 2005—. Office Phone: 703-365-2900.

DASILVA, LYNN JUDITH, special education educator; d. John and Sonia Luz DaSilva; children: Christian Daniel, Samantha Lillian. M in profl. studies, Adelphi U., Garden City, 1985. Cert. advanced studies Coll. St. Rose, N.Y., 2005, administrative supr. Coll. St. Rose, N.Y., 2005, dist. adminstr. Coll. St. Rose, N.Y., 2005, physical edn. tchr. K-12 1985. Pre-school hearing and speech impairments tchr. North Shore Hosp. Affiliate, Westbury, NY, 1984; physical edn. tchr. grades 1-8 Rockville Ctr. Union Free Sch. Dist., NY, 1985—; in-state head coach Nassau County Spl. Olympics, NY, 2000—02, area coord. NY, 2000—02. Roundtable spkr. N.Y. Health Dept., NY, 2005. Author: (book) Theatre of the Mind, 2005. Recipient Jenkins award, Spl. Edn. PTA, 1997, Jennie E. Hewitt PTA, 2002, Master Educator award, RVC Dist. Tchrs., 2003, Cert. of Achievement, N.Y. Health Dept., 2003, 2004, 2005, 2006. Mem.: Assn. for Athletics, Physical Edn., Recreation and Dance, N.Y. Assn. for Health, Physical Edn., Recreation and Dance. Avocations: writing, painting, bicycling, hiking, running. Home: 437 Little East Neck Rd S Babylon NY 11702 Personal E-mail: ldasilva21@optonline.net.

DASSEL-STUKE, DONNA JANE, psychologist, educator; b. Evansville, Ind., Feb. 29, 1956; d. Forrest James Dassel and Doris Eileen (Edmonson) Vowels; m. Michael Charles Stuke, July 7, 1985; 1 child, James Conrad. Student, Harlaxton Coll., England, 1976; BS cum laude, U. Evansville, 1977, MS, 1981; postgrad., Kans. State U., Fort Hays State U., Emporia State U., Peru State Coll., Pitts. State U. Cert. sch. psychologist (nat.), 1988, endorsement early childhood 1992. Work adjustment supr. So. Ind. Rehab. Ctr., Boonville, 1978, work adjustment specialist, 1978—79; grad. asst. U. Evansville, 1979; vocat. evaluator Rehab. Ctr., Evansville, 1979—81; intern Evansville Vanderburgh Sch. Corp. & Rehab. Ctr., 1981; sch. psychologist Twin Lakes Co-op., Clay Center, Kans., 1981—83, Marshall-Nemaha Co. Edn. Svc. Co-op., Seneca, 1983—99; substitute tchr. Holton, 1999—2005, Sabetha, 1999—2005, Wetmore, Kans., 1999—2005, Hiawatha, Kans., 1999—2005, Fall City, Nebr., 1999—2005; prof. Highland C.C., Kans., 2000—. Mem.: Kans. Assn. Sch. Psychologists, Nat. Assn. Sch. Psychologists, Delta Kappa Gamma, Alpha Lambda Delta. Democrat. Presbyterian. Avocations: piano, swimming, fishing, baseball, basketball. Home: 311 S Mathews St Bern KS 66408-0151

DASSINGER, KRISTINE R., literature and language professor; M in English, U. Alaska, Fairbanks, 2000. Asst. prof. English and journalism Genesee C.C., Batavia, NY, 2000—. Office: Genesee Community College One College Rd Batavia NY 14020 Office Phone: 585-343-0055.

DASTRUP-HAMILL, FAYE MYERS, city official; b. Sanford, Colo., Dec. 15; d. Earl Dixon and Kady Florence (Cornum) Faucett; m. Sherly K. Myers (dec.); children: Carla Pearce, Susan Kitley (dec.), Mary Jane James, Elizabeth Ireland; m. Merrill E. Dastrup, Sept. 22, 1972 (dec. July 1987); m. Wayne A. Hamill, Mar. 23, 1991. Student, L.D.S. Bus. Coll., 1934-35; grad., Dale Carnegie Inst., 1953; degree in mcpl. works adminstrn., Mt. San Antonio Coll., 1960; student, Syracuse U. Inst., 1968; degree in tech. reporting, Chaffey Coll., 1970. Legal sec. W. W. Platt, City Atty., Alamosa, Colo., 1935-40; sec. pub. works dept. City of Ontario, Calif., 1957-60, dep. city clk., dep. city treas. Calif., 1960-64, city clk. Calif., 1964-73, city coun. mem., mayor and mayor pro tem Calif., 1974-92; mem. part 150 implementation com. Ontario Airport, Calif., 1993—, chmn. noise adv. com., dept. trans. State of Calif., 1994—. Sec. pers. dept. L.A. Housing Authority, 1948; mem. legis. subcom. So. Calif. Assn. Govts., chmn. hist. preservation and cultural arts com.; mem. revenue and taxation com. League of Calif. Cities, vice-chmn., chmn. Clks. Inst., gen. resolutions com., com. on environ. quality Inland Empire divsn.; chmn. San Bernardino County Planning Com., Criminal Justice; prese. So. Calif. City Clks. Assn., chmn. legis. com.; mem. exec. com. Valley Assn. of Cities; city coun. rep. Ontario Libr. Bd. Trustees. Escort sch. classes through City Hall; judge sci. fairs and sch. and comty. events; life mem. Friends of Ontario Libr.; mem., donor Friends of Mus. of History and Art, Ontario; pres., treas., trustee Ontario (Calif.) City Libr., 1993—; choir dir., life mem. Ch. of Jesus. Recipient plaque with gold gavel So. Calif. City Clks. Assn., 1972, Women Helping Women award Soroptomist Internat. of Ontario, 1981, 1990 Woman of Yr. award State Legislature, State of Calif., 1990, Woman of Achievement award 90s Women's Conf., 1990, 1994 YWCA Woman of Achievement award West End YWCA, 1994, Elizabeth S. Genee Lifetime Achievement award, West End YWCA, 1994, Bryce Denton award Mus. of History and Art, 1996, Outstanding Effort with Calif. Water plaque San Bernardino County Waterworks Dist. #8, 1986, Outstanding Svc. plaque Ontario Air N.G., 1990, Leadership plaque San Bernardino County Sheriff's Dept., 1993, Founding, Support and Encouragement of Crime Stoppers Spl. Recognition plaque Ontario Police Dept., 1993, Outstanding Comty. Svc. plaque U.S. Congressman Jay Kim, 1994, Plaque and Spl. Cert. congratulating receipt of Elizabeth Genee Lifetime Achievement award, 1994, Pub. Svc. Award trophy Adrian Meewis, 1972, plaque for dedicated and meritorious svc. to Ontario, as mayor City Coun. and City Clk., 1986, Lifetime Achievement plaque San Bernardino County Supr. Larry Walker, 1994, Svc. plaque South Coast Air Quality Mgmt. Dist., 1987, decorated plaque Salvation Army, 1992, others. Mem. Calif. Assn. Libr. Trustees and Commrs., Comty. Concert Assn. Pomona Valley (donor), Ontario C. of C. (life, Svc. Award plaque 1992), Musicians Club of Pomona Valley. Mem. Ch. of Jesus Christ of LDS. Avocation: vocal soloist. Home: 761 W Hawthorne St Ontario CA 91762-1510

DATCU, IOANA, artist; b. Bucharest, Romania, Apr. 22, 1944; d. Marin and Niculina Datcu; m. Vasile Porcisanu, Aug. 5, 1967 (div. 1983); 1 child, Isabelle Ioana. BA, Pedagogical Inst., Bucharest, 1967; BFA summa cum laude, U. Minn., 1987, MFA, 1991. Tchr. biology high sch., Argova, Preasna, Romania, 1967—74; photography asst. U. Minn., St. Paul, 1985—86; photographer civil rights dept. City Hall, St. Paul, 1986—87; darkroom supervisor Film in the Cities, St. Paul, 1987—88; gallery asst., curator Paul Whitney Gallery, St. Paul, 1987—91; art instr. Minn. Mus. Am. Art, St. Paul, 1993—94; instr. drawing & painting U. Minn., Mpls., 1996—97. One-woman shows include Flanders Contemporary Art, Mpls., 1994, Winona (Minn.) State U, 1995, Mont. State U., Billings, 1996, Ea. Wash. U., Cheney, 1996, Indpls. Art Ctr., 1996, Kansas City (Mo.) Artists Coalition, 1997, Grants Pass (Oreg.) Mus. Art, 1997, Trinity Presbyn. Ch., Denton, Tex., 1998, South Bend (Ind.) Mus. Art, 1998, U. Dayton, Ohio, 2000, Concordia U., Seward, Nebr., 2004, exhibited in group shows at North Park Coll., Chgo., 1991, Hist. Trinity, Detroit, 1993, 1995—96, Barrett House Galleries, Poughkeepsie, N.Y., 1994, 1996, Katherine E. Nash Gallery, Mpls., 1992, 1995—96, Minot (ND) State U., 1995, Coll. St. Catherine, St. Paul, 1995, St. John's U., NY, 1995, Focal Point Gallery, NYC, 1996, SoHo Photo Gallery, 1997, Greater Lafayette Mus. Art, 1997, Truman State U., Mo., 1998, McNeese State U., La., 1998, Attelboro (Mass.) Mus. Art, 1998—99, New World Art Ctr., NYC, 1999, Ctrl. Mo. State U., 1999, Am. Bible Soc. Gallery, NYC, 2000, Internat. Print Triennial, Cracow, Poland, 2000, 2006, Krakow Nürnberg, Messezentrum Mus., Germany, 2000, Jewish Cmty. Ctr. Greater New Haven, Woodbridge, Conn., 2001, Open Studio Press, 1995, Images of the Spirit Traveling Exhibit, 1995—97, CIVA CODEX III traveling exhibit, 1997—2001, Korean Cultural Ctr., LA, 2001, Grand Forks Art Gallery, Can., 2004, represented in, CD-Rom collections of Art Comms. Internat., 1995, Artmax Internat., 1995, Ency. Internat. Women Artists, Alliance Women Artists, 1997, New Art Internat., Book Art Press, 1997, Christianity and the Arts Jour., Internat. Print Triennial, 1999, Bridge to the Future, Nurnberg, 2000, The Missing Mary (by Charlene Spretnak), 2004, Faith and Vision: Twenty Five Years of Christians in the Visual Arts, 2005. Grantee Pollock-Krasner Found., 1992, Minn. State Arts Bd., 1994; Jerome Found. Residency fellow, 1994; McKnight Photography fellow, 1992, fellow Arts Midwest NEA, 1994-95, Clowes Fund regional residency fellow, Indpls., 1997; Vt. Studio Ctr. Residency award, Johnson, Vt., 1997. Mem. Christians in the Visual Arts, Nat. Assn. Women Artists, Inc. Mem. Eastern Orthodox Ch. Avocations: classical music, movies, yoga, literature. Home: 507 W 5th St Vermont IL 61484 Office Phone: 309-784-6208. Personal E-mail: ioanadatcu@yahoo.com.

DATE, ELAINE SATOMI, physiatrist, educator; b. San Jose, Calif., Feb. 19, 1957; BS, Stanford U., 1978; MD, Med. Coll. Pa., 1982. Diplomate of Nat. Bd. Med. Examiners. Diplomate Am. Bd. Phys. Medicine and Rehab. Dir. phys. medicine and rehab. Stanford (Calif.) U. Sch. Medicine, 1985—, rehab. medicine sect. chief, 1988-90, head phys. medicine and rehab. div., 1990—, assoc. prof. dept. functional rehab., 1995—; rehab. medicine chief Palo Alto (Calif.) VA Med. Ctr., 1988—. Fellow Am. Acad. Phys. Medicine and Rehab., Am. Assn. Electromyography and Electrodiagnosis. Avocations: reading, jogging.

DAUB, PEGGY ELLEN, library administrator; b. Bluffton, Ohio, Oct. 15, 1949; d. Perry J. and Olive L. (Hoover) D.; m. Jeffrey H. Cooper, Dec. 13, 1975; 1 child, William P. Cooper-Daub. MusB summa cum laude, Miami U., 1972; MA, Cornell U., 1975; MSLS, U. Ill., 1980; PhD, Cornell U., 1985. Acting asst. music libr. Yale U., 1980-81, head of music tech. svcs., rare books libr. Music Libr., 1981-82; head Music Libr. U. Mich., Ann Arbor, 1982-89, head Spl. Collections & Arts Librs., 1989-99, head Spl. Collections Libr., 2000—. Presenter Rare Books and Manuscript Sect. Pre-Conf., New Orleans, 1993, Bloomington, 1995 and others. Contbr. articles to profl. jours. Co-clk. Ann Arbor Friends Meeting, 1997-2001. Travel grantee Ctr. for Internat. Studies, Cornell U., 1977. Mem. ALA (Assn. Coll. and Rsch. Librs. rare books and manuscripts sect., mem. task force on interlibr. loan 1991-93, mem. preconf. program planning com. 1992-94), Music Libr. Assn. (bd. dirs. 1985-87, mem. resource sharing and collection devel. com. 1982-91), Rsch. Librs. Group (chairperson music program com. 1985-87, mem. steering com. 1982-87), Am. Musicol. Soc. (mem. coun. 1988-91, mem. coun. com. on minorities/diversity 1988-91), Phi Beta Kappa. Mem. Soc. Of Friends. Office: U of Mich Spl Collections Libr 711 Graduate Libr Ann Arbor MI 48109-1205 Office Phone: 734-764-9377. E-mail: pdaub@umich.edu.

DAUBE, LORRIE O., sales executive; b. Toledo, Ohio, Feb. 3, 1951; d. Stanley and Marian Oberlin; m. Jeffrey Daube, Aug. 31, 1975; children: Ryan Oberlin, Danielle Elyse. BS in Comm., U. Ill., 1973. Media sales WDAI-ABC-FM, Chgo., 1973—74; media sales rep. Jack Masla, Chgo., 1974—75; media sales WMET Metromedia, Chgo., 1976—79, WIND-Westinghouse, Chgo., 1980—82; copywriter Burgess, Heynssen and Oberlin, Deerfield, Ill., 1983—85; sales cons. Coldwell Banker, Deerfield, 1990—. Girls tennis coach asst. Deerfield (Ill.) H.S., 2000—. Charity fundraiser Med. Rsch. Inst., 1985—90, Jewish United Fund, Chgo., 1995—; active guest svcs. 2002 Winter Olympics, Deer Valley, Utah, 2002; asst. coach girls jr. varsity and varsity tennis Deerfield High Sch., Ill., 2002—. Named Multi million dollars producer, Coldwell Banker. Mem.: North Shore Women's Tennis League (pres. 1986—88). Republican. Avocations: skiing, tennis, golf, platform tennis, swimming. Home: 8 Dunsinane Ln Bannockburn IL 60015 Office Phone: 847-945-7100. E-mail: motherlod@aol.com.

DAUGHERTY, DEBRA L., science educator; b. El Centro, Calif., Jan. 2, 1961; d. Gerald T. Chastain and Laura A. Jewell, James W. Stepp (Stepfather); m. Dwight D. Daugherty, Apr. 1, 1980; 1 child, Brianna C. BA, Harding U., Searcy, Ark., 2006. Cert. mid. level math and sci. Ark. Dept. of Edn., 2003, mid. level English and soc. studies Ark. Dept. of Edn., 2003. 7th grade CMP math tchr. Cabot (Ark.) Jr. H.S. North, 2003—04, math tchr., 2003—05, astronomy club sponsor, 2004, earth sci. tchr., 2005—, quiz bowl sponsor, 2005—. Strive rsch. participant Ark. Strive Program, UALR, Little Rock, 2005—. Astronomy grant, Ark. Space Consortium, 2005—06. Mem.: Nat. Coun. Math. Tchrs. R-Consevative. Baptist. Avocations: reading, cooking, horseback riding, sports, travel. Home: 815 Gravel Hill Rd Romance AR 72136 Office: Cabot Jr High Sch North 38 Spirit Dr Cabot AR 72023 Office Phone: 501-605-8470. Personal E-mail: debra.daugherty@cps.k12.ar.us.

DAUGHERTY, LINDA HAGAMAN, real estate company executive; b. Denver, Jan. 25, 1940; d. Charles B. and Agnes May (Wall) Hagaman; m. Thomas Daniel Daugherty, Nov. 20, 1965; children: Patrick, Christina Marie. BS in Bus., U. Colo., 1961; postgrad., Tulane U., 1963-64, U. St. Thomas, 1990-91. Sr. systems analyst Lockheed Electronics NASA, Houston, 1966-73; sr. systems cons. TRW Systems Internat., Caracas, Venezuela, 1973-74; sy. systems cons. TRW Systems, L.A., 1974-75; mng. ptnr. TDD-LHD Investments, LP, Katy, Tex., 1976—; pres. Nottingham Country Day Sch., Katy, 1977—2006; sr. systems analyst Intercomp, Houston, 1979-80; pres. Daugherty Fin. Svcs., Inc., Katy, 1979—91, Williamsburg Country Day Sch., Katy, 1983—2006. Mem. Epiphany Ch. Social Works Commn., San Antonio World Affair Coun.; pres. Mason Creek Women Reps. Club, Katy, 1980; treas. Nottingham Country Civic Club, Katy, 1979; mem. adv. bd. Nottingham Country Club, 1982—85; co-founder Friends of Archaeology U. St. Thomas, pres., 1991—93; pres., treas. Friends of Boerne Pub. Libr., 1997—99; asst. curator Archaeology Gallery, U. St. Thomas. Mem. Houston Archeology Soc., Tex. Archeology Soc., Archaeology Inst. of Am., Boerne Women's Club. Roman Catholic. Avocations: archaeology, bridge. Office: Motivated Child Learning Ctr PO Box 489 Boerne TX 78006-0489

DAUGHERTY, LYNN BAYLISS, psychologist, consultant; b. Durham, N.C., Aug. 24, 1947; d. Welden Cushman and Vivian Lynn (Burroughs) Bayliss; m. Charles Hines Daugherty, June 11, 1968 (div. 1979); m. Lawrence Gabriel Michelsohn, Sept. 29, 1984; children: Moses James, Aaron Bayliss. Student, Middlebury Coll., 1965—68; BA, U. Tulsa, 1970; PhD, U. Mont., 1977. Lic. psychologist. Psychologist Warm Springs State Hosp., Mont., 1975—80; dir. N.Mex. Forensic Evaluation Team, Roswell, 1980—81; psychologist Cmty. Counseling Ctr., Roswell, 1981—83; pvt. practice psychology Roswell, 1981—. Cons. psychologist Tabosa Tng. and Devel. Ctr., Roswell, 1983—84, bd. dirs., 1984; cons. psychologist Roswell Girls Club, 1984—, Roswell Ind. Sch. Dist., 1984—86, Roswell Job Corps Ctr., 1986—, Roswell Refuge Battered Adults, 1983, bd. dirs., 1984—86. Author: Why Me? Help for Victims of Child Sexual Abuse, 1984; contbr. articles to profl. jours. Chmn. area selection com. Am. Field Svc., Missoula, Mont., 1974—76; pres. adv. bd. Chaves County Widowed Person's Svc., Roswell, 1984—86. Fellow, NSF, 1970—74; Am. Field Svc. scholar, Italy, 1964—65. Mem.: APA, Nat. Audubon Soc., Am. Psychology-Law Soc., Nat. Acad. Neuropsychologists, N.Mex. Psychol. Assn., Sigma Xi. Office: 200 W 1st St Ste 323 Roswell NM 88203-4674 Office Phone: 505-623-1943.

DAUGHERTY, PATRICIA ANN, retired elementary school educator; b. Rockford, Ill., May 19, 1949; d. Bjarne John and Mary Rita (Ryan) Jacobsen; m. Greg A. Kramer, June 23, 1973 (div. Apr. 1988); 1 child, Josie Kramer. BS, No. Ill. U., 1971, MS, 1978. cert. elem. tchr., Ill., spl. edn. tchr., Ill. Tchr. Aurora (Ill.) East Sch. Dist., 1971—2004, ret., 2004; adj. faculty dept. edn. Aurora U., 2004—. Mem. choir Our Lady of Mercy Cath. Ch. Mem. AAUW (2d v.p. membership 2005—, gift honoree 1996), Am. Fedn. Tchrs. (bldg. rep. 1995-2004), Ill. Ret. Tchrs. Assn. Avocations: reading, gardening, skiing, golf. Home: 340 Inverness Dr Aurora IL 60504-6925

DAUGHERTY, RUTH ALICE, religious association consultant; b. Shenandoah, Va., Feb. 21, 1931; d. Lee Earl and Lena Alice (Heishman) Sheaffer; m. Robert Mowery Daugherty, July 11, 1953; children: Carole Ruth Daugherty Haigh, Steven Robert, Beth Anne Daugherty Carr. AA, Shenandoah Jr. Coll., 1950; BA, Lebanon Valley Coll., 1952; HHD (hon.), Albright Coll., 1982, Shenandoah U., 1986. English and history tchr. Bruce H.S., Westernport, Md.,

1952-53, Trotwood (Ohio) H.S., 1953-55; officer United Meth. Women, Pa., 1956-72, nat. pres., 1980-84, dir. women's divsn., 1976—84; mem. gen. coun. on ministries United Meth. Ch., 1972—76, nat. chair ministry study, 1984-92; nat. v.p. United Meth. Comm. Commn., 1984-88; v.p. United Bd. for Christian Higher Edn. in Asia, N.Y.C., 1984-87. M. faculty Drew Theol. Sem., 2001; cons. for gen. commn. Christian unity and interreligious concerns United Meth. Ch., 2001—04. Author: (booklet) United Methodist Women in Mission, 1994, (study guide) John Wesley Study, 1996, The Missionary Spirit: History of the Methodist Protestant Church, 2004. Trustee Lebanon Valley Coll., Annville, Pa., 1971—89; chair pers. com., chair mus. com. Scarritt-Bennett Ctr., Nashville, 1991—96, sec., 1996—99; pres. Lumina Bd., Lancaster, Pa., 1998—; co-chair addressing world and cmty. issues EPA Conf., 2000—04, del. to quad gen. confs., 1972—; sec. NE jurisdiction United Meth. Ch., 2003—; bd. dirs. United Meth. Pub. House, 2003—; chair policy program com., chair directions for the '90s United Bd. for Christian Edn. in Asia, 1990—98, trustee emeritus, 1998—; sec. trustees Ea. Pa. Conf. United Meth Ch., Valley Forge, 1992—98; gen. commn. Christian unity and interreligious concerns United Meth. Ch., 1992—2000, sec., 1996—2000, Otterbein dist. lay leader, 1998—2001, cons., 2000—04, bd. ordained ministry Ea. Pa. chpt., 2004—, mem. nat. adv. com. ch. and cmty. workers, 2004—, mem. 50th anniversary taks force ordination of women, 2002—06; pres. S.W. Dist., United Meth. Women, 2005—. Recipient Disting. Alumni award Shenandoah U., 1996, Alumni award Lebanon Valley Coll., 1979, Woodrow B. Seals Laity award Perkins Sch. Theology, 1997, Anna Howard Shaw award Anna Howard Shaw Ctr., Boston U. Avocations: making yeast breads, making quilts, reading, gardening. Home: 1936 N Eden Rd Lancaster PA 17601-4952 Personal E-mail: rdaugherty@mycyberlink.net.

DAUGHTREY, MARTHA CRAIG, federal judge; b. Covington, Ky., July 21, 1942; d. Spence E. Kerkow and Martha E. (Craig) Piatt; m. Larry G. Daughtrey, Dec. 28, 1962; 1 child, Carran. BA cum laude, Vanderbilt U., 1964, JD, 1968. Bar: Tenn. 1968. Pvt. practice, Nashville, 1968; asst. U.S. atty., 1968—69; asst. dist. atty., 1969—72; asst. prof. law Vanderbilt U., Nashville, 1972—75; judge Tenn. Ct. Appeals, Nashville, 1975—90; assoc. justice Tenn. Supreme Ct., Nashville, 1990—93; circuit judge U.S. Ct. Appeals (6th cir.), Nashville, 1993—. Lectr. law Vanderbilt Law Sch., Nashville, 1975—82, adj. prof., 1988—90; mem. faculty NYU Appellate Judges Seminar, N.Y.C., 1977—90, N.Y.C., 1994—. Contbr. articles to profl. jours. Pres. Women Judges Fund for Justice, 1984—85, 1986—87; active various civic orgns. Named Woman of the Yr., Women Prof. Internat., 1976; recipient Athena award, Nat. Athena Program, 1991. Mem.: ABA (chmn. appellate judges conf. 1985—86, ho. of dels. 1988—91, chmn. jud. divsn. 1989—90, standing com. on continuing edn. of bar 1992—94, commn. on women in the profession 1994—97, bd. editors ABA Jour. 1995—2001, Margaret Brent award 2003), past mem., bd. visitors, Memphis State Sch. of Law, past mem., ed. bd., Judge's Journal, Lawyers Assn. for Women (pres. Nashville 1986—87), Nat. Assn. Women Judges (pres. 1985—86), Am. Judicature Soc. (bd. dirs. 1988—92), Nashville Bar Assn. (bd. dirs. 1988—90), Tenn. Bar Assn. Office: US Ct Appeals 300 Customs House 701 Broadway Nashville TN 37203-3944*

DAUM, CARYN LYNN, lawyer; BA in Polit. Sci., U. Vt.; JD cum laude, Suffolk U. Bar: Mass. 2001, US Dist. Ct. (Dist. Mass.). Assoc. Trial and Appellate Group Robinson & Cole LLP, Boston. Mem.: Boston Bar Assn. (panel counsel Volunteer Lawyers Project 2004—), Mass. Bar Assn., ABA, Women's Bar Assn. (com. mem. New Lawyer's Sect. 2004—). Office: Robinson & Cole LLP One Boston Place Boston MA 02108-4404 Office Phone: 617-557-5904. Office Fax: 617-557-5999. E-mail: cdaum@rc.com.*

DAUPHIN, SUE, writer, producer; b. Balt., Sept. 1, 1928; d. William Goll and Elsie Elizabeth (Lipps) Helfrich; m. Vernon Mayfield Dauphin, Feb. 7, 1959; children: William Mayfield, Katie Dauphin Collins. BA cum laude, U. Houston, 1976, MA, 1979; Cert., Boston Mus. Sch. Fine Arts. Exec. prodr. and writer videos: LAMPS Light: A Support Group Profile, 1993, Safe Handling of Sharps, 1991, Safe Cytotoxics, 1990, Beyond Apothecary: The Pharmacists in Today's Hospital, 1989; writer radio drama broadcast by KUHF, Psyche and the Pskyscraper, 1985; prodr., writer, host Sue Dauphin's Curtain Call weekly radio program, KUHF-FM, Houston, 1975-87, Diversions, weekly radio program KLYX-FM, Houston, 1974-75. Author: Understanding Sjogren's Syndrome, 1993 (Japanese transl. 1994), Parkinson's Disease: The Mystery, the Search, and the Promise, 1992 (Japanese transl. 1995), Sjogren's Syndrome: The Sneaky "Arthritis", 1988 (Japanese transl. 1990), Houston by Stages, A History of Theatre in Houston, 1981; contbr. theatre revs. to Miami Herald, 1987-88, Palm Beach Post, 1992—; contbr. articles to profl. jours.; prodr. play: Transit, 1983. Mem. The Am. Theatre Critics Assn., Internat. Theatre Critics Assn., Internat. Assn. Ind. Pubs., Nat. Sjogren's Syndrome Assn. (pres. 1994, 97, bd. dirs. 1991, 97), Palm Beach Macintosh Users Group, Fla. Motion Picture and TV Assn. (State Crystal Reel award for documentary scriptwriting 1990, 91, 92, for documentary prodn. 1992).

DAUTH, FRANCES KUTCHER, journalist, editor; b. St. Louis, Aug. 20, 1941; d. David Jacob Kutcher and Dorothy Marie (Baugh) Hedges; m. Jerry Donald Dauth, July 5, 1964 (div. Dec. 1980). BA, U. Colo., 1963; cert. mgmt. program, Smith Coll., 1989. Staff writer Alameda (Calif.) Times Star, 1966—67, Contra Costa Times, Walnut Creek, Calif., 1968—69, Oakland (Calif.) Tribune, 1969—77; project editor San Francisco Examiner, 1977—82; asst. city editor Phila. Inquirer, 1982, dep. N.J. editor, 1983, suburban editor, 1984—85, city editor, 1985—89, nat. editor, 1989—91, fgn. editor, 1991—94, assoc. mng. editor, 1994—96; mng. editor Star Ledger, Newark, 1996—2004, editor editl. pages, 2004—. Office: Star Ledger Newark NJ 07102 Office Phone: 973-392-1536. Business E-Mail: fdauth@starledger.com.

DAVAROVA, ELMIRA, musician; Concertmaster Met. Opera Orch., N.Y.C., 1989—. Office: Met Opera Assn Lincoln Ctr New York NY 10023

DAVE', ANNE DUPREE, music educator; b. Camp Springs, Md., June 21, 1960; d. Forist Gleaton and Jaline Gilbertson Dupree; m. Jitendra Narmdashankar Dave', Feb. 2, 1985; children: Jivan Dupree, Noelle Elise. BFA, Coll. of Charleston, SC, 1982; MEd, Columbia Coll., SC, 2005. Cert. educator SC. Music tchr. Sumter (SC) Sch. Dist. 2, 1984—97, Sumter Sch. Dist. 17, 1997—. Pianist Alice Dr. Bapt. Ch., Sumter, 1990—. Named Campus Tchr. of Yr., Alice Dr. Elem. Sch. Faculty, 2005—06. Mem.: SC Music Educators Assn. (treas. elem. divsn. 2000—05), Music Educators Nat. Conf. Baptist. Home: 141 Chappell St Sumter SC 29150 Office: Alice Dr Elem Sch 251 Alice Dr Sumter SC 29150 Office Phone: 803-775-0857.

DAVENPORT, DONNA JEANNE SWANSON, elementary school educator; b. Houston, Jan. 11, 1953; d. Edwin Bernard and Margie Oneala (Gholson) Swanson; m. Ronald Travis Davenport, May 26, 1972; children: Shelley, Jennifer, Rebecca. BS in Edn., U. Houston, 1978; MS in Edn., Stephen F. Austin State U., 1987. Cert. elem. tchr., Tex. Tch. bus. Crosby (Tex.) High Sch., 1974-81; grade tchr Newport Elem. Sch., Crosby, 1989—; 4th grade tchr. Newport Elem., 1985—99; math. coord. K-6 Crosty Ind. Sch. Dist., 1999—. Author story Tex. Coach, 1980. Pres. Crosby Sick-Leave Bank, 1990—. Named Outstanding Young Woman of Am., 1982, Tchr. of Yr., CISD, 1994-95. Mem. PTA (life, 3d v.p. 1979-81), Nat. Sci. Tchrs. Assn., Nat. Coun. Tchrs. Maths. Baptist. Avocations: coaching, softball.

DAVENPORT, LINDSAY, professional tennis player; b. Palos Verdes, Calif., June 8, 1976; d. Wink and Ann Lindsay; m. Jon Leach, 2003. Profl. tennis player, 1993—. Mem. U.S. Women's Olympic Tennis Team, Atlanta, 1996, Sydney, 2000, U.S. Fed Cup Team, 1993—2000, 2002. Named Rookie of the Yr., TENNIS Magazine, 1993, World Team Tennis, 1993, MVP, 1997, Player of the Year, TENNIS Magazine, 1998, Tour Player of the Year, WTA, 1998, 1999. Achievements include winning a gold medal in US Women's singles, Atlanta Olympic Games, 1996; singles champion, US Open, 1998, Wimbledon, 1999, Australian Open, 2000; doubles champion, Roland Garros (with Mary Jo Fernanadez), 1996, U.S. Open (with Jana Novotna), 1997, Wimbledon (with Corina Morariu), 1999; being WTA Tour Champion, 1999; winner of 48 career singles titles, 35 doubles titles, WTA Tour. Office: US Tennis Assn 70 W Red Oak Ln White Plains NY 10604-3602

DAVENPORT, MARGARET ANDREWS, lawyer; b. Nov. 1, 1961; BA magna cum laude, Amherst Coll., 1983; JD, U. Chgo., 1987. Bar: NY 1988. Assoc. Debevoise & Plimpton LLP, NYC, 1987—95, ptnr., 1995—, co-head pvt. equity group. Mem.: ABA, Assn. of Bar City of NY. Office: Debevoise & Plimpton LLP 919 Third Ave New York NY 10022-3904 Office Phone: 212-909-6667. Office Fax: 212-909-6836. E-mail: madavenport@debevoise.com.

DAVENPORT, SANDRA, cultural organization administrator; d. Charles Adams and Katy Ann Davenport; 1 child, Suerain S. BA in Classics, St. John's Coll., Annapolis, Md., 1975; MSW, Ariz. State U., 1986. Lic. master social worker Ariz. Bd. Behavioral Health Examiners. Dir. Home Based Montessori Pre-Sch., Tucson, 1980—82; counselor, program coord. Family Counseling Agy., Tucson, 1986—89; therapist Tri Cmty. Counseling, Oracle, 1989—92; med. social worker Carondelet St. Mary's Hosp., Tucson, 1993—2001; exec. dir. Pima County/Tucson Women's Commn., Tucson, 2003—. Presenter, trainer Ariz. Child Abuse Prevention Conf., Phoenix, 1999; mem. steering com. Ariz. Women's Conf., Tucson, 2003—04; mem. hon. com. Micro Bus. Advancement Ctr. Luncheon, Tucson, 2004—05; founding mem., facilitator Pay Equity Initiative Cmty. Collaboration. Active Mayor's Task Force on Domestic Violence, Tucson, 1995; coord. Cmty. Collaboration on Domestic Violence Intervention in Healthcare, 1998—2001; mem. site visit team Ariz. Perinatal Trust, Phoenix, 2000; bd. mem., com. chair Am. Friends Svc. Com., Tucson, 2002—04. Recipient Mayor's cert. of recognition for role in Elder Shelter Program Devel. Team, award excellence, Mayor George Miller, Tucson, 1998, Cmty. Collaboration award, Carondelet Cmty. Trust, 1999. Mem.: NASW (Ariz. br. steering com., Social Worker of Yr. 2000), Black Women's Task Force, Ariz. Women's Polit. Caucus. Achievements include developed and implemented area protocol for domestic violence screening in hospitals. Avocations: painting, hiking, dance. Home: 3242 N El Tovar Tucson AZ 85705 Office: Pima County/Tucson Womens Commn 240 N Court Ave Tucson AZ 85701

DAVES, SANDRA LYNN, poet, lyricist; b. Sacramento, Mar. 14, 1950; d. Willard Glen and Rachel Lucille Humbert; m. Tommy Wilburn Daves, Nov. 16, 1971 (dec. 2006); children: Todd Eric, Brice Aaron. Student, Internat. Libr. Poetry, 2003. Sec. McClellan AFB, Sacramento, 1969, Fish and Game Dept., Sacramento, 1970—71; poet, 1994—. Lyricist: songs Songs of Praise, Star of Bethlehem, America At War!, Gospel Millennium Celebration, Home For Christmas, Your Very Special Place, Kingdom of Angels (Four Star award for song Pray Without Ceasing, 2004), Celebrating Christmas with Jesus, The Joy and Splendor of Christmas, America, Producer's Showcase, Land That I Love, Hurricane, Songs of Love and Romance, 2006, Christmas By Candle Light, 2006; contbr. poetry to lit. pubs. Recipient Poet of Merit, Fla., 2005. Mem.: ASCAP, Internat. Libr. Poetry, Am. Soc. Poets (founding laureate mem., founding laureate), Internat. Soc. Poets (Editor's Choice award Poet of Merit, Md. chpt. 2000—05, Poet of Merit Hollywood chpt. 2002, Poet of Merit Fla. chpt. 2003, Poet of Yr. Fla. chpt. 2003, Poet Laureate 2003, Poet of Merit DC chpt. 2003, Poet of Merit Fla. chpt. 2004, 2005, named Poet of Merit Las Vegas chpt. 2006, Poet of Merit Washington chpt.), Am. Biog. Inst. (life), Internat. Biog. Assn. (life). Avocations: reading, writing, walking, crossword puzzles. Home: 6825 Susanna Ct Citrus Heights CA 95621

DAVEY, ELEANOR ELLEN, science educator; b. Colorado Springs, Colo., Aug. 28, 1910; d. Stanley James and Elizabeth (Bays) Britton; m. Herbert Merritt, Aug. 9, 1932; children: Ted H. Davey, Ronald B. Davey, Betty Nell Davey Ferraro AB, U. No. Colo., 1934; MS, Ariz. State U., 1967. Cert. tchr., Wyo., Ariz. Credit advisor Montgomery Ward, Denver, 1936-38; swimming instr. Colo. State U., Ft. Collins, 1938; English tchr., swimming tchr. East H.S., Cheyenne, Wyo., 1939-40; dir. phys. edn. Xavier H.S., Phoenix, 1955—63, biology tchr., sci. dept. chair, 1963-76; sci. awards dir. Ariz. State U., Tempe, 1974-88; biology prof. U. Ariz., Tucson, 1980; Ariz. dir. presdl. awards program NSF, Arlington, Va., 1983—2000. Author: (with others) Air Pollution: Man and the Environment, 1971, Mothers of Achievement in American History 1776-1976, 1976; co-author: Strength Through Leadership, 1963. Foster care bd. dirs. Ariz. Dept. Econ. Security, Phoenix, 1978-84. Named Outstanding Secondary Educator of Am., 1974; named to Hall of Fame, Palmer Alumni Assn, 1987; recipient Am. Soc. Microbiology award, 1973—75, Cert. of Recognition, Sigma Xi, 1986, Disting. Svc. award, Ariz. Alliance for Math., Sci. & Tech. Edn., 2000. Fellow Ariz. Nev. Acad. Sci. (Ariz. Outstanding Sci. Tchr. Yr. 1965, dir. Ctrl. Ariz. chpt. 1971-82, chair outstanding sci. tchr. com. 1982-86, chair scholarship com. 1990-95, exec. bd. dirs. 1980-90, Outstanding Svc. award 1997); mem. NSTA (mem. at large, exec. bd. dirs. 1974-76, chair awards com. 1976-77, chair S.W. area conv. 1976, internat. com. h.s. com. nominations 1976, Ariz. contact 1972-99, 2003—, Disting. Svc. to Sci. Edn. award 1975), Nat. Assn. Biology Tchrs. (Ariz. state rep. 1975-80, coord. Region VII 1980-86, 89-91, exec. bd. dirs. 1984-86, chair nominating com. 1987-89, Outstanding Biology Tchr. Ariz. 1973), Ariz. Sci. Tchrs. Assn. (membership sec. 1973-88, pres. 1973-74, exec. bd. dirs. 1973-98, chair nomination/election com. 1990-97, hon. life mem., contact 1973-98, 2003—, Cmty. Svc. award 35+ Yrs., 2000). Avocations: volunteer education programs, reading, swimming, watching basketball and football games. Home and Office: 242 E McLellan Blvd Phoenix AZ 85012-1141

DAVID, MARTHA LENA HUFFAKER, retired music educator, retired sales executive; b. Susie, Ky., Feb. 7, 1925; d. Andrew Michael and Nora Marie (Cook) Huffaker; m. William Edward David, June 24, 1952 (div. Jan. 1986); children: Edward Garry, William Andrew, Carolyn Ann, Robert Cook. AB in Music magna cum laude, Georgetown (Ky.) Coll., 1947; postgrad., Vanderbilt U., 1957-58; Spanish cert., Lang. Sch., Costa Rica, 1959; MEd, U. Ga., 1972. Elem. tchr. Wayne County Bd. Edn., Spann, Ky., 1944-45; music tchr. Mason County, Mayslick, Ky., 1947-49, Hikes Grade Sch., Buechel, Ky., 1949-53; English and Spanish tchr. Jefferson (Ga.) High Sch., 1961-63; music and English tchr. Athens (Ga.) Acad., 1967-71; music tchr. Barrow County Bd. Edn., Winder, Ga., 1971-88; real estate agt. South Best Realty, Athens, 1986-90; ret., 1988. Data collector Regional Ednl. Svcs. Agy., Athens and Winder, 19176-78; tchr. music Union Theol. Sem., Buenos Aires, 1957-60. Author: (poems) Parcels of Love, Book I, 1984, Book II, 1999, Poems and Reflections; composer (music plays) The B.B.'s, The Missing Tune, A Dream Come True, The Stars Who Creep Out of Orbit, 1976-86. Active cultural affairs orgns., Athens, 1962—, Athens Area Porcelain Artists, YWCO; entertainer nursing homes and civic orgns., Athens, 1962; chmn. cancer drives, heart fund drive United Way, March of Dimes, Athens, 1962—; historian, elder, pianist Christian Ch. Winner regional piano competition Ky. Philharm. Orch., 1946; nominated Tchrs. Hall of Fame, Barrow County, 1981. Mem. Ret. Tchrs. Assn., Writer's Group, Ga. Music Tchrs., Nat. Music Tchrs. Assn., Athens Music Tchrs. Assn. (pres. recital chmn.), Ga. World Orgn. China Painters, Athens Area Porcelain Artists, Women's Mus. Arts (assoc.), Women's Mus. Art (Washington), Touchdown Club, Band Boosters, Alpha Delta Kappa (Fidelis Nu chpt., historian), Delta Omicron (life, scholar 1944). Democrat. Mem. Christian Ch. Avocations: porcelain art, oil and acrylic painting, swimming, square dancing, round dancing. Home: 105 Nassau Ln Athens GA 30607-1456

DAVID, SUSAN HOLCOMBE, child and family therapist; b. Plainfield, N.J., Aug. 29, 1949; d. Paul Thorne Holcombe and Marilyn Jean Lennon; children: Mark Christian, Jason Esser, Michael John, Karen Marie. BA in Edn., Clemson U., S.C., 1971; MA in Cmty. counseling, U. Phoenix, 2002. Lic. profl. counselor, nat. bd. cert. counselor. Tchr. Cath. Elem. Sch., Tampa, Fla., 1971; cons., internet healthcare Unicity Network, Mesa, Ariz., 1992—; therapist Jewish Family & Childrens Svc., Phoenix, 2002—; therapist, educator E. Valley Family Resource Ctr., Mesa, Ariz., 2002—; therapist Child Crisis Ctr., Mesa, Ariz., 2003—04. Co-chmn., co-founder Morton Plant Hosp. Cruisin' the 60s Ann. Fund-raiser; co-founder Kimberly Home, Kimberly-Brian David Birthing Ctr., Jr. League Clearwater Dunedin, 1986—90. Mem.: Chi Sigma Iota (treas. 2002), Chi Omega. Roman Catholic. Avocations: art, sewing, scrapbooks, theater. Office: Jewish Family & Childrens Svc 1930 S Alma Sch Rd Ste A-104 Mesa AZ 85210 Personal E-mail: powerperson@cox.net.

DAVID, VALENTINA S., physics professor; d. Samuel and Mercy Yohan; m. Sunil Kumar David, June 4, 1971. BS in Edn., U. Indore, India, 1970; BSc in Biology, U. Poona, Pune, India, 1972; MSc in Botany, U. Poona, 1974, PhD in Physics, 1983. Cert. tchr. U. Indore, 1970. Instr. biology Vidya Bhavan Jr. Coll., Pune, Maharastra, India, 1981—91; biology lab. mgr. Bethune-Cookman Coll., Daytona Beach, Fla., 1992—93, instr., 1994—96, asst. prof., 1996—2003, assoc. prof., 2003—. Lead tchr. VISION, Daytona Beach, 1999—2002; lead tchr. MASTT project Bethune-Cookman Coll., Daytona Beach, 2003—04, project mgr. MASTT project, 2004—, project dir. UNCF-FAPT project, 2002—; lectr. in fiel; condr. workshops in field. Author: online course in phys. sci.; contbr. articles to profl. jours. Recipient Faculty Honors award, Bethune-Cookman Coll., 1999, Provost's award for Outstanding Svc., 1999, award Divsn. Sci. and Math., 2003, Pres.'s award for Faculty Mem. of the Yr., 2003, Best Paper award, CIBER/TLC Conf., Las Vegas, 2004, ABR/TLC Conf., Orlando, 2005, cert. of achievement for completing GLOBE Land Cover, Hydrology, and Soil Protocol, NASA Stennis Space Ctr., 2005; fellow, So. Edn. Found., 2003—04; grantee, NASA, 2004—05. Mem.: Assn. for Advancement of Computing in Edn. (corr.). Office: Bethune-Cookman Coll 621 Dr Mary McLeod Bethune Blvd Daytona Beach FL 32114 Office Phone: 386-481-2667.

DAVIDOFF, JOANNE MALATESTA, multi-media specialist; d. John Ruben and Erma Carpinelli Malatesta; children: Cynthia Louise Bernstiel, Michael John. BA, Chestnut Hill Coll., Phila, 1954; MEd., Temple U., 1959. Cert. tchr. visually and multihandicapped Cath. U. Am., Washington, D.C., 1952, tchr. Commonwealth Pa., 1963. Dir. Upsal Day Sch. for Blind Children, Phila., 1955—69; coord. Nat. Exhibits for Blind Artists, Phila., 1981—82; coord. first GED for disabled persons Phila. Free Libr., 1981—83; classroom tchr. K-12 Overbrook Sch. for Blind, Phila., 1985—2000; educator for ind. living skills Del. County Assn. for Blind, Chester, Pa., 1996—2004; braille specialist, lang. arts Overbrook Sch. for the Blind, Phila., 2000—. Bd. mem. Associated Svcs. for the Blind, Phila., 1982—, pres., 1984—87, Overbrook Sch. for Blind Alumni, Phila., 1985—90, Liberty Bell Chpt. Pa. Assn. for Blind, Phila., 1990—; bd. mem. Nat. Exhibits for Blind Artists, Phila., 1990—, Montgomery County Assn. for Blind, North Wales, Pa., 1995—2004, Pa. Council of the Blind, Harrisburg, 1997—2001. Coord. Cath. Christian Doctrine Classes, Seven Dolors, Wyndmoor, Pa. Named Most Beautiful Blonde Girl in Am., NY Assn. Mem.: Cath. League of Persons with Disabilities (pres. 2001—04), Phila. Reg. Chpt. Pa. Council of Blind, Nevilaires (pres. 2000—), Oreland Lions Club. Roman Catholic. Avocations: music, reading, tandem cycling. Home: 7808 Pine Rd Wyndmoor PA 19038 Office: Overbrook Sch for the Blind 6333 Malvern Ave Philadelphia PA 19151

DAVIDOV, LUDMILA G., psychiatrist; arrived in U.S., 1993; d. Grigoriy Solomonovitch Davidov and Alexandra Yakovlevna Davidova; m. Alex P. Levy, July 4, 1974; children: Elena Levy, Alla Levy. MD, Med. SCh., Tajikistan, 1975. Cert. Bd. Cert. Psychiatry NY, 2003. Fellowship Citi Hosp., Tajikistan, 1975—77; internist City Hosp., Tajikistan, 1975—84, chief of dept., 1984—93; interperter 113 Hillside Divsn., Great Neck, NY, 1996—97, mental health worker, 1997—98; residency Nassau Univ. Med. Ctr., NY, 1998—2002; MD Comprehensive Counseling Ctr., Rego Pk., NY, 2003—; staff psychiatrist HIP Mental Health Clin., NY, 2002—; pvt. practice Rego Pk., 2006—. Contbr. articles to profl. jour. Recipient Best Physician of Year, Tajikistan, 1979. Mem.: Am. Psychiatric Assn. Avocations: piano, travel, reading, music. Office: 64-33 99th St Rego Park NY 11374 Office Phone: 718-459-1225.

DAVIDOW, JENNY JEAN, counselor, writer; b. Santa Monica, Calif., Mar. 25, 1953; d. Ray M. Davidow and Caroline D. (Kos) Lackmann. BA, UCLA, 1974; MA, Internat. Coll., Santa Monica, 1981; D Clin. Hypnotherapy, Am. Inst. Hypnotherapy, Honolulu, Hawaii, 1994. Cert. clin. hypnotherapist. Pvt. practice, L.A., 1981-92, Santa Cruz, Calif., 1992—. Seminar leader, L.A., 1981-92, Santa Cruz, 1992—; bd. dir. Tidal Wave Press, Santa Cruz; featured guest various TV and radio shows, L.A., 1983-88; spkr. Whole Life Expo, L.A., 1983-87; mem. Am. Bd. Hypnotherapy, 1989—. Author: Dream Therapy Workbook, 1983, Embracing Your Subconscious, 1996, Corners of the Soul, 1998; contbg. author: anthology Dreamscaping, 1999; Love Games, 2000, The Spirit of Writing, 2001; contbr. articles to various pubs.; creator, presenter (audiotape collection) Comfortable and Capable, 1994. Mem.: Resource Ctr. for Nonviolence, World Wilflife Fund (ptnr. in conservation 1995, Mono Lake com., Treepeople), Focusing Inst., Found. for Shamanic Studies, Assn. for Humanistic Psychology, Sierra Club (life). Democrat. Avocations: photography, gardening. E-mail: twave@cruzio.com.

DAVIDS, JODY R., information technology executive; BBA, MBA, San Jose State U. Computer programmer Apple Computer, Inc., Cupertino, Calif., 1982, various positions, including Asia Pacific divsn., dir. supply chain reengring.; dir. tech. svcs. Nike, Inc., Beaverton, Oreg., 1997—2000; sr v.p. IT pharm. distbn. bus. unit Cardinal Health, Inc., Dublin, Ohio, 2000—03, exec. v.p., chief info. officer, 2003—. Office: Cardinal Health Inc 7000 Cardinal Pl Dublin OH 43017 Office Phone: 614-757-5000.

DAVIDSON, ANN D., lawyer, aerospace transportation executive; b. Upper Montclair, NJ, 1952; BA, Ohio U.; JD, U. Dayton, 1979; attended, Georgetown U. Sch. of Foreign Service. Bar: 1979. Assoc. Coolidge, Wall, Womsley & Lombard, Dayton, Ohio, 1979—80; atty. US Navy, 1980—83; various positions including assoc. gen. counsel Honeywell, 1983—90; dep. gen. counsel Alliant Techsystems, 1990—93; v.p., gen. counsel, corp. sec. Power Control Technologies, Inc., Kalamazoo, 1993—98; assoc. gen. counsel, asst. sec. Parker Hannifin Corp., Cleveland, 1998—2001; v.p., gen. counsel Alliant Techsystems, 2001—03, v.p., gen. counsel, corp. sec., 2003—04, sr. v.p., gen. counsel, corp. sec., 2004—. Office: Alliant Techsystems Inc 5050 Lincoln Dr Edina MN 55436

DAVIDSON, ANNE STOWELL, lawyer; b. Rye, N.Y., Feb. 24, 1949; d. Robert Harold and Anne (Breeding) D. BA magna cum laude, Smith Coll., 1971; JD cum laude, George Washington U., 1974. Bar: D.C. 1975, U.S. Dist. Ct. D.C. 1975, U.S. Ct. Appeals (D.C. cir.) 1975, U.S. Supreme Ct. 1980. Asst. chief counsel drugs and enforcement FDA, Rockville, Md., 1974—78; counsel Abbott Labs., North Chicago, Ill., 1978—79, U.S. Pharm. Ops. Schering-Plough Corp., Kenilworth, NJ, 1979—83; sr. counsel Sandoz Pharms. Corp., Inc., East Hanover, NJ, 1983—86, v.p., assoc. gen. counsel, 1987—96; assoc. gen. counsel Novartis Pharms. Corp., East Hanover, NJ, 1997—2000; legal cons. Alamo Pharm., LLC, Parsippany, NJ, 2004—. Contbr. articles to profl. jours. Trustee N.J. Pops Orch.; patron St. Hubert's Giralda Animal Shelter, N.J. Recipient Dawes prize Smith Coll., 1971. Mem. ABA, Pharm. Mfrs. Assn., Food and Drug Law Inst., Healthcare Businesswomen's Assn., Non-prescription Drug Mfrs. Assn. (govt. affairs com.), Smith Coll. Club (pres. 1981-82). Republican. Presbyterian. E-mail: missy224@optonline.net.

DAVIDSON, BONNIE JEAN, gymnastics educator, sports management consultant; b. Rockford, Ill., Nov. 19, 1941; d. Edward V. and Pauline Mae (Dubbs) Welliver; m. Glenn Duane Davidson, June 4, 1960 (dec. Oct. 1993); children: Lori Davidson Aamodt, Wendy Davidson Seerup; m. James A. Johnson, Sept. 15, 2001. Student, Rockford Coll., Ill., 1965, Rock Valley Coll., Rockford, Ill., 1969—77. Founder, owner, dir. Gymnastic Acad. Rockford, 1977-95; pres., dir., owner Springbrook, Ltd., swim and tennis club, Rockford, 1986-95. Rep. trampoline and tumbling com. AAU, 1989-99; coach nat. and world champion athetes; mgr., judge, head del. U.S.A. gynmastics teams, 1980—2004; speaker, lectr., clinician in field.; mem. organizing coms. world championships, also others, 1982-99. Contbr. World

Book Ency. Bd. dirs. U.S. Olympic Com., 1995-2005, U.S.A. Gymnastics, 1991-2005; instr. ARC. Named one of Most Interesting People, Rockford mag., 1987; named to USA Gymnastics Hall of Fame, 2003; recipient YWCA Janet Lynn Sports award, 1996. Mem. Internat. Fedn. Trampoline and Tumbling (internat. judge, mem. tech. com. 1986-99—, del. to congress 1976-86, hon. lifetime mem. 1998), Internat. Fedn. Sport Acrobats (internat. judge), U.S.A. Trampoline and Tumbling Assn. (hon. life; nat. tumbling chairperson 1980-88, advisor 1988-99—, Coach of Yr. award 1980, Outsanding Contbn. to the Sport award 1987, 96, Master of Sport award 1989), U.S. Sports Acrobatics Fedn. (hon. life; v.p. 1984-95), Nat. Judges Assn. (exec. dir.). Republican. Avocations: skiing, boating, bicycling, birdwatching, flying. E-mail: johnsonbj11@insightbb.com.

DAVIDSON, CYNTHIA ANN, elementary school educator; b. Neosho, Mo., Nov. 21, 1953; d. Richard Thomas and Cora Nadine (Mitchell) Morrison; m. Charles Richard Davidson, Aug. 3, 1985; children: Tony, Daniel. AA, Crowder Coll., Neosho, Mo., 1973; BS in Edn., Mo. So. State Coll., 1975; MS in Edn., S.W. Mo. State U., 1977. Tchr. 1st grade Exeter (Mo.) R 6, 1975-76; tchr. 3rd grade East Newto R 6, Stella, Mo., 1976—. Mem. prin.'s adv. com. Triway Elem. Sch., Stella, 1986—. Mem. East Newton CTA (mem. exec. com., bldg. rep.), Internat. Reading Assn., Mo. State Tchrs. Assn. Mem. Ch. of Christ. Avocations: yardwork, 4 h club, horses. Home: 18755 Nettle Dr Neosho MO 64850-8796 Office: Triway Elem Sch Third Grade Stella MO 64867

DAVIDSON, DIANE (MARIE DAVIDSON), publisher; b. L.A., Mar. 6, 1924; d. Charles Casper and Stella Ruth (Bateman) Winnia; divorced, 1953; children: David William, Ronald Mark. AB, U. Calif., Berkeley, 1943; MA, Calif. State U., Sacramento, 1959. cert. secondary tchr., 1944. Tchr. Campbell (Calif.) High Sch., 1944-45; actress Pasadena (Calif.) Playhouse, 1945, U.S.O. Camp Shows, N.Y.C., 1946-47; tchr. El Camino H.S., Sacramento, 1954-85. Illustrator, pub. and editor Swan Books, Fair Oaks, Calif., 1979—99. Author: Feversham, 1069, "18 easy-to-read Shakespeare plays without changing the words; editor: History of Trinity Episcopal Church, Folsom, California, 1856-1994, 1996; contbr. articles to Shakespeare mag. Mem. NEA, PEN, Authors Guild, Calif. Writers Club, Calif. Tchrs. Assn., Phi Beta Kappa, Pi Lambda Theta. Democrat. Episcopalian. Avocations: gardening, writing. Home: 11390 Coloma Rd Gold River CA 95670 Personal E-mail: swanbks@aol.com.

DAVIDSON, DONETTA LEA, federal official, former state official; b. Liberal, Kans., Aug. 14, 1943; d. Edwin Donald Owens and Loretta May (Conrad). County clk. and recorder Bent County, Las Animas, Colo., 1978-86; dir. of elections State of Colo., Denver, 1986-94; county clerk & recorder Arapahoe County, Littleton, Colo., 1995—99; sec. state State of Colo., Denver, 1999—2005; commr. US Election Assistance Commn., 2005—. Accreditation bd. Nat. Assn. State Election Directors Voting Sys./Ind. Test Authority, 1998—; bd. dirs. Election Ctr., 1998—. Henry Toll Fellowship of Coun. of State Govts., 1993. Mem.: Nat. Assn. Secretaries of State (treas. 2003—04, pres. elect 2004—05, pres. 2005), Postal Svc. Task Force (chairperson, joint elections officials liaison cmty. 1997—), Fed. Election Commn. Adv. Panel (mem. 1995—), Internat. Assn. Clks., Recorders, Election Officials, and Treasurers (mem. 1995—), Nat. Assn. State Election Dir. (pres. 1994), Colo. State Assn. of County Clk. and Recorders (pres. 1983—84). Republican. Office: US Election Assistance Commn 1225 NY Ave NE Ste 1100 Washington DC 20005 Office Phone: 303-894-2200. Business E-Mail: sos.admin1@sos.state.co.us.

DAVIDSON, HEATHER JEAN, gifted and talented educator; b. Pa., May 28, 1970; d. Nancy DePuy; m. Dana Davidson, June 19, 1993; children: Hunter Dylan, Cayde Anthony. BS in Edn., Westminster Coll., New Wilmington, Pa., 1992; MEd in Reading, Slipper Rock U., Pa., 1994, prin. cert., 2003. Title I kindergarten tchr. Grove City (Pa.) Sch. Dist., 1994—96, title I reading and math grades 3-6, 1996—2004, gifted support tchr. grades 1-8, 2004—. Academic games coach Grove City Sch. Dist., 2004—. Home: PO Box 341 104 Parkview Dr Clark PA 16113 Office: Grove City School District Hillview Int 482 East Main St Grove City PA 16127 Office Phone: 724-458-7570.

DAVIDSON, JANET G., telecommunications industry executive; b. Short Hills, N.J. B in Physics, Lehigh U.; M in Elec. Engring., Ga. Tech., 1979; M in Computer Sci. Joined Bell Labs., 1978; various positions Bell Labs. & Lucent Techs.; v.p. access product mgmt. Lucent Techs., Murray Hill, NJ, 1996—98, v.p. access, switching and access solutions, 1998, v.p. N.Am. emerging markets, 1999, pres. Access Networks divsn. InterNetworking Sys., 2000, group pres. InterNetworking Sys., 2000, group pres. Network Ops. Software, 2000, group pres. InterNetworking Sys. and Switching Solutions, 2001, pres. Integrated Network Solutions, 2001—. Named one of Top 50 Most Powerful Women in Bus., Fortune 500, 2001; named to Acad. Women Achievers, YWCA, N.Y.C., 1999; recipient Women Enabling Sci. and Tech. award, Working Woman Found., 2001. Office: Lucent Techs 600 Mountain Ave Murray Hill NJ 07974

DAVIDSON, JEANNIE, costume designer; b. San Francisco, Mar. 21, 1938; d. Willis H. and Dorothy J. (Starks) Rich; children from previous marriage: David L. Schultz (dec. Jan. 1996), Mark P. Schultz, Seana Davidson, Michael Davidson; m. Bryan N. St. Germain, June 14, 1980. BA, Stanford (Calif.) U., 1961, postgrad., 1965-68. Resident costume designer Oreg. Shakespearean Festival, Ashland, 1969-91; owner, designer Ravenna Fabric Studio, Inc., Medford, Oreg., 1994—. Mfr. custom ch. vestments and hand-dyed wearable art. Designer over 150 prodns. including all 37 of Shakespeare's plays. Recipient numerous awards for excellence in costume design. Mem. U.S. Inst. for Theatre Tech., Phi Beta Kappa. Avocations: fabric design, painting, writing, quilting. E-mail: jsaintg@earthlink.net.

DAVIDSON, JO ANN, political organization executive, retired state legislator; children: Julie, Jenifer. Mem. Ohio Ho. of Reps., Columbus, 1981—2001, minority leader, speaker, 1995—2001; interim dir. Ohio Dept. Jobs and Family Services, 2001; owner JAD & Assoc. Government Cons. Firm, 2001; campaign chmn. Ohio Valley Bush-Cheney '04, 2004; co-chmn. Rep. Nat. Com., Washington, 2005—. Chmn. Ohio Ho. Rep. Campaign Com., 1986-2000. Mem. Reynoldsburg (Ohio) City Coun., 1968-77; former vice chmn. Ohio Turnpike Commn.; trustee Franklin U., U. Findlay, Ohio, Ohio State U. Named Legislator of Yr., Nat. Rep. Legislators Assn., 1991; named to Ohio Women's Hall of Fame, 1991. Republican. Office: Rep Nat Com 310 First St SE Washington DC 20003

DAVIDSON, JOAN ELIZABETH GATHER, psychologist; b. Long Branch, NJ, Jan. 26, 1934; d. Ralph Paul and Hilde (Bresser) Gather; m. Harry Gene Davidson, Sept. 14, 1957; children: Guy, Marc, Kelly. BA, Shorter Coll., 1956; BA cum laude, U. South Fla., 1982; MS, Fla. Inst. Tech., 1986, PsyD, 1987. Lic. psychologist, Fla., RN, Ga. Clin. instr. Ga. Bapt. Sch. Nursing, Atlanta, 1956-59; dir. nurses Aidmore Hosp., Atlanta, 1959-60; dir. insvc. edn., asst. dir. nurses Bayfront Med. Ctr., St. Petersburg, Fla., 1960; instr. St. Petersburg Jr. Coll., 1971-76; pvt. practice St. Petersburg-Clearwater, 1987—2001. Mem. Am. Psychol. Assn., Fla. Psychol. Assn., Nat. Register Health Svc. Providers in Psychology, Assn. for Advancement Psychology, Am. Assn. Christian Counselors, Psi Chi, Phi Kappa Phi. Republican. Baptist. Home: 2507 SW Sandlewood Ave Gresham OR 97080-9458

DAVIDSON, JOANN W., retired elementary school educator; b. Newark, Apr. 12, 1931; d. Donald Franklin and Helen Wallace; m. Robert Louis Davidson, Nov. 29, 1952; children: John, Betsy, Sam. BA, Smith Coll., 1952; MSEd, Western Conn. State Coll., Danbury, 1968; postgrad., Bank St. Coll., Fairfield U., Conn. State Insts., 1969-88. Cert. tchr. Conn. Tchr. Westport (Conn.) Bd. Edn., 1968-92; ret., 1992. Founder, co-chair Parents as Tchrs., Westport, 1992—; mem., mentor Ret. Tchr. Corps, Westport, 1992—2004; cons. peer coaching Westport Tchr. Ctr., 1992—93, sci. resource tchr., 1998—2003; presenter sci. workshop, Moscow. Author, illustrator: Our Town Has a River, 1996; Exhibited in group shows, 2000—, one-woman shows include Watercolors, 2005. Mem. Conservation Commn., Westport, 1994—2003, Westport Tree Bd., 2002—03; elected Westport Rep. Town Meeting, 2003—. Recipient Unsung Hero award, ARC, 1998. Mem.: LWV (v.p. 1997—99, town bds. observer 1995—99), NEA, Westport Hist. Soc., Westport Arts Ctr., Rowayton Arts Ctr., Y's Women (mem. program com. 1992—99). Republican. Congregationalist. Avocations: gardening, painting, tennis, reading, birdwatching. Home: 15 Whitney St Westport CT 06880-3736 Personal E-mail: JoAnnDvdsn@sbcglobal.net.

DAVIDSON, JOY ELAINE, retired mezzo soprano; b. Ft. Collins, Colo., Aug. 18, 1940; d. Clarence Wayne and Jessie Ellen (Bogue) Ferguson; m. Robert Scott Davidson, Aug. 9, 1959; children: Lisa Beth, Robert Scott II, Jeremy Fergus, Bonnie Kathleen, Jordan Christian. BA, Occidental Coll., Los Angeles, 1959; postgrad., Fla. State U., 1961-64. Dir. vocal/opera dept. New World Sch. Arts Coll./Conservatory Divsn., Miami, Fla., 1992—2002; ret., 2001. Robert A. Carrie Mastronardi endowed prof., 1995—. Debut 1965 with Miami Opera; has performed with Met. Opera, opera cos. throughout U.S. and Can., La Scala, Vienna State Opera, Bayerische State Opera, Lyons (France) Opera, Welsh Opera, Florence (Italy) Opera, Torino (Italy) Opera. (recipient Gold medal Internat. Competition Young Opera Singers, Sofia, Bulgaria 1969), Rio de Janeiro; performed with numerous orchs. including N.Y. Philharm., Los Angeles Philharm., Boston Orch., Pitts. Orch., Columbus (Ohio) Orch.; rec. artist. Named Outstanding Miami Artist at Orange Bowl; recipient Mastronardi endowed chair, 1995, NISOD award for tchg. excellence, 1996, Roberta Rymer Balfe award Fla. Grand Opera. Mem. PEO, United Meth. Women, Sigma Alpha Iota, Zeta Tau Zeta. Methodist. Avocations: swimming, camping, bicycling, church activities. Home: 413 Walnut St #5032 Green Cove Springs FL 32043 Office Phone: 305-510-5131. E-mail: davidsons123@hotmail.com.

DAVIDSON, JUDI, public relations executive; b. Bklyn., June 06; d. Samuel Lewis and Esther (Friedman) Swiller; m. Gordon Davidson, Sept. 21, 1958; children: Adam, Rachel Davidson-Janger. BA, Vassar Coll., 1957. Writer Charm Mag., N.Y.C., 1957-59; press agt. various theatrical prodns., N.Y.C., 1959-64; prin. Judi Davidson Publicity, L.A., 1972-84; ptnr. Davidson & Choy Publicity, L.A., 1984—. Bd. dirs. Bet Tzedek Ho. Justice, L.A., 1989—99, Blue Ribbon, L.A., 1990—2006, L.A. Music Ctr., 1995—99. Mem.: Pub. Rels. Soc. Am. (bd. dirs. 1997—98), Entertainment Publicists Profl. Soc. (bd. dirs. 1996—99), Assn. Theatrical Press Agts. and Mgrs. (bd. dirs. 1996—97). Democrat. Jewish. Avocations: cooking, gardening, reading. Office: Davidson and Choy Publicity 4311 Wilshire Blvd Los Angeles CA 90010-3708 Office Phone: 323-954-7510. Business E-Mail: j.davidson@dcpublicity.com.

DAVIDSON, KAREN SUE, computer software designer; b. Chgo., July 24, 1950; d. Woodrow Wilson and Velma Louise (Dickinson) D. BS in Comm., U. Ill., 1972; MBA, De Paul U., 1977. Microsoft cert. profl. News prodr. Sta. WIND, Westinghouse Broadcasting Co., Chgo., 1973-75; mktg. rep. divsn. data processing IBM, Chgo., 1977-80, process industry specialist, 1980, industry applications specialist White Plains, N.Y., 1981-83; sr. sales rep. Wang Labs., Chgo., 1983-84; ptnr. KDA-K Davidson & Assocs., Centralia, Ill., 1984-88; pres. KDA Software Inc., Centralia, 1988—. Instr. Belleville (Ill.) Area Coll., 1992, mem. office and tech. adv. bd., 1998—, chair, 1999—; vis. lectr. So. Ill. U., Carbondale, 1994; mem. rev. bd. State of Ill. Pvt. Enterprise. Author/designer software programs; contbr. articles to profl. pubs. State of Ill. Small Bus. Adv. Bd., Internat. Trade/Export Rep., 1990-93; WordPerfect cert. resource instr. WordPerfect Corp., 1991—; apptd. to State of Ill. Small Bus. 100, 1996. Named Outstanding Working Woman of Ill. Fedn. Bus. & Profl. Women's Clubs, 1990. Mem. Soc. Profl. Journalists, Ind. Computer Cons. Assn. (pres. St. Louis chpt. 1998-99), Ill. Software Assn., Chgo. High Tech. Assn. Assn. St. Louis Info. Sys. Trainers (v.p. 1988), Centralia Cultural Soc., Inventors' Assn. St. Louis, Greater Centralia C. of C. (bd. dirs. 1990-93, good will amb. 1990), Rotary, Zeta Tau Alpha. Presbyterian. Office: KDA Software Inc PO Box 1163 315 E 3rd St Centralia IL 62801-3919

DAVIDSON, LISA RAE, physician; BS, Creighton U., 1988; MD, U. S.D., 1993. Intern U. S.D., Sioux Falls, 1993-94; resident in neurology U. Wis. Hosp. & Clinics, Madison, 1994-97; chief neurology Ireland Army Hosp., Ft. Knox, Ky., 1997—. Mem. AMA, Am. Acad. Neurology.

DAVIDSON, MARILYN COPELAND, writer, music educator, musician; b. New Castle, Ind., Sept. 2, 1934; d. Clyde Harrison and Hazel Uva Copeland; m. Douglass Albert Davidson, Dec. 28, 1961; children: Jennifer Juntwait, Diana Valencia. BS, Ball State U., 1955; diploma in piano, Juilliard Sch., 1956. Music tchr. Dallas Public Schs., 1956—57, Shortridge H.S., Indpls., 1957—62, Port Washington (NY) Pub. Schs., 1962—66, Troy State U., Troy, Ala., 1966—70, South Lyon (Mich.) Middle Sch., 1970—72, Fairleigh Dickinson U., Teaneck, NJ, 1979—83, Bergenfield (NJ) Pub. Schs., 1972—84, Our Redeemer Luth. Ch., Dumont, NJ, 1973—78, Evangelical Luth. Ch., Hasbrouck Heights, NJ, 1980—82, Pequannock (NJ) Pub. Schs., 1986—90, 1992—95; coord. author MacMillan/McGraw Hill, Inc., NYC, 1984—. Presenter Internat. Reading Assn., NJ, 1995, N.J. Music Supervisors Assn., 1985, Bruno Walter Hall, Lincoln Ctr., NYC, 1994, Carnegie Hall, NYC, 2000, Technology Symposium, Fla. State U., Tallahassee, 2000, Suffolk County Music Educators, 2001, workshops, throughout U.S.; presenter in field. Author: (textbook series) Music and You, 1988, 1991, Spotlight on Music, 2005; author: (with Bob McGrath) Music for Fun, 2000; author: (textbook series) Share the Music, 1992, 1995; composer: (orchestrations) Tops in Pops, 1995, An Acoustic Jam, 1996, Folk Songs From A World Apart, 2004; contbr. articles to profl. newsletters, teacher's guides and other publs.; author (with Bob McGrath): (profl. training video) Music and the Curriculum; author: Using Music to Help Children Learn, 2004, It's Elementary, 2005. Coun. mem., soloist and accompanist for recitals Bergenfield Coun. for the Arts, 1974—80; accompanist Carley Singers Chamber Choir, Indpls., 1957—61; educational cons. New Jersey Symphony, 1987—92; education com. mem., clinician, tnr. N.J. Symphony Master Tchr. Project; lectr. N.Y. Philharm. Children's Series, 1995; lectr., performer Bergenfield Pub. Libr., 1996; piano soloist Hawthorne Chamber Symphony, 1996, 1997, 1998, North Jersey Symphony, Tenafly, 1996, 2001, Rockland NY Symphony, 2003. Named Outstanding Alumnus, Ball State U. Sch. Music, 1993; recipient Young Artists award, Muncie Symphony, 1953, Gov.'s Tchr.'s Recognition award, NJ, 1995. Mem.: NEA, N.J. Edn. Assn., Music Educators Nat. Conf. (music selection com. 1993, nat. assembly, writer for teacher's guides), N.J. Music Educators Assn. (writer "It's Elementary" 1988—96), Northern N.J. Orff Schulwerk Assn. (co-founder, treas., sec., pres., mem-at-large), Am. Orff-Schulwerk Assn. (hon.; life mem., regional rep., chairperson higher edn., nat. v.p., nat. pres., higher edn. post-level III adv. com., AOSA celebrity advocacy panel selection com.), Orgn. Am. Kodaly Educators, Delta Kappa Gamma, Pi Kappa Lambda, Sigma Alpha Iota. Home and Office: 31 Martin St Bergenfield NJ 07621 Office Phone: 201-385-8521.

DAVIDSON, MARTHA W., elementary school educator; b. Phila., Feb. 20, 1952; d. William Belsterling and Frances H. Welte; m. Gary E. Davidson, Oct. 27, 1979; children: Amanda, Alan. BA, Mary Washington Coll., Fredericksburg, Va., 1974; MA, Fla. State U., Talahassee, 1975. Cert. educator U. Tex. Arlington, 1994. Adminstrv. mgr. Champion Internat., Franklin Park, Ill., 1977—81; adminstrv. and acctg. mgr. Fortier USA, Inc., Denver, 1981—83; tchr. grade 6 Arlington Ind. Sch. Dist., Tex., 1993—. Intermediate math liaison Arlington Ind. Sch. Dist., Tex., 1996—, team leader, 1996—, gifted and talented liaison, 2003—, coach Lone Star Challenge, 2006. Named lifetime mem., Ellis Elem. Sch. PTA, 2004. Office: Ellis Elem Sch 2601 Shadow Ridge Dr Arlington TX 76006 Office Phone: 682-867-7900.

DAVIDSON, MARY ANN, information technology executive; BSME, U. Va.; MBA, U. Pa., Wharton Sch. Commd. officer U.S. Navy Civil Engineer Corps; various positions in product devel. and security Oracle Corp., 1988—2001, chief security officer, 2001—. Ed. review bd. Secure Business Quarterly; testified before Congress on info. security four times. Recipient Navy Achievement Medal, U.S. Navy Civil Engr. Corps. Mem.: Info. Tech. Info. Security Analysis Ctr. (bd. dirs.). Avocations: outdoors, surfing, skiing. Office: Oracle Corp 500 Oracle Pkwy Redwood City CA 94065

DAVIDSON, NANCY BRACHMAN, artist, educator; b. Chgo., Nov. 3, 1943; d. Philip and Jane (Blanch) Brachman; m. Donald Davidson, July 15, 1961 (div. 1977); 1 child, Lance A.; m. Greg Drasler, June 15, 1985. BEd, Northeastern Ill. U., 1965; BA, U. Ill., Chgo., 1972; MFA, Sch. Art Inst., Chgo., 1975. Vis. asst. prof. U. Ill., Champaign, 1977-79, Williams Coll., Williamstown, Mass., 1980-84; vis. artist, assoc. prof. SUNY, Purchase, 1984—. One-woman shows include Berkshire Mus., Pittsfield, Mass., 1982, Marianne Deson Gallery, Chgo., 1978, 1981, 1983, 1988, Richard Anderson Gallery, N.Y.C., 1991, 1993, 1995, Shoshana Wayne Gallery, Santa Monica, Calif., 1997, Nova Sin Gallery, Prague, Czech Republic, 1998, Neuberger Mus., Purchase, N.Y., 1998, Dorsky Gallery, N.Y.C., Inst. Contemporary Art, U. Pa., Phila., 1999, Vedanta Gallery, Chgo., 2000, The Contemporary Arts Ctr., Cin., 2001, Robert Miller Gallery, N.Y.C., 2001, Regina Gouger Miller Gallery, Carnegie Mellon U., Pitts., 2002, exhibited in group shows at Albright-Knox Gallery, Buffalo, 1980, Mus. Contemporary Art Chgo., 1984, Art Inst. Chgo., 1974, 1978, 1979, Bad Girls West-UCLA, 1994, Corcoran Biennial, 2002. Fellow NEA, 1978, Mass. Coun. Arts, 1981, Ford Found., 1978; Mass. Coun. Arts grantee, 1984, Anonymous Was a Woman grantee, 1997, Pollock-Krasner grantee, 2001, Creative Capital Artist grantee, 2005. Home: 137 Duane St Apt 4W New York NY 10013-3892

DAVIDSON, SARA, writer; b. L.A., Feb. 5, 1943; d. Marvin Harold Davidson and Alice Sarah Wass; m. Jonathan Schwartz, 1968 (div. 1975); m. Glen Strauss, June 28, 1981 (div. 1990); children: Andrew, Rachel. AB, U. Calif., Berkeley, 1964; MS with honors, Columbia U., 1965. Creator Jack and Mike-ABC, L.A., 1986-87; prodr. Heartbeat-ABC, L.A., 1988-89; co-exec. prodr. Dr. Quinn, Medicine Woman-CBS, Hollywood, Calif., 1992-95; writer, exec. prodr. My Ptnr., 1995, I.D., 1997, Bloodhound Red, 1998, The River Goddess, 1999. Author: Loose Change, 1977, Real Property, 1980, Friends of the Opposite Sex, 1984, Rock Hudson: His Story, 1986, Cowboy: A Love Story, 1999; contbg. editor: O The Oprah Winfrey Mag.; contbr. articles and essays. Mem. Phi Beta Kappa. Avocations: reading, skiing, hiking, horseback riding, wilderness trips. Home: 2135 Knollwood Dr Boulder CO 80302

DAVIDSON, SARAH J., educational consultant, healthcare educator; b. North Little Rock, Ark., Nov. 26, 1947; d. Earnest Jefferson and Alice Sanders D.; 1 child, DeAngelo Kinard. BA in Sociology, Howard U., 1970; MA in Edn., Catholic U., 1971. Elem. sch. tchr. DC Pub. Schs., 1971-72; rsch. assoc. Pres. Nat. Adv. Coun. on Edn., Washington, 1972-74; sr. info. specialist Howard U. Children's Ctr., Washington, 1974-75; head start edn. dir. Wash., DC Parent Child Ctr., Washington, 1975-77; dir. office of field svcs. Child Devel. Assn. Consortium, Washington, 1977-78; child devel. assoc. Enterprise for New Directions, Washington, 1978-79; state coord. children's health DC Dept. of Health Medicaid, Washington, 1979—2000; pres. Nat. Inst. of Family Svcs., 2000—. Child devel. assn. rep. Coun. for Early Childhood Recognition, Wash., 1976—; proposal reader Dept. Edn., 1979; review panelist Dept. Edn., 1986. Assoc. editor: (nat. newsletter) Parent Preschool Press, 1981. Bd. sec. Nat. Fed. Black Women Bus. Owners, 1992—; pub. rels. coord. Coun. of 100 Black Repubs., 1986-91; pres., founder Assn. for the Presevation of N. Little Rock, Ark. African Am. History, 2000; bd.mem. Howard Univ. Alumni Assn., 2002-05. Named Outstanding Arkansan Living in DC Arkansas Dem. Gazette, Little Rock, 1993; participant Nat. Security Seminar, U.S. Army War Coll., Carlisle, Pa., 1994. Mem. Nat. Black Child Devel. Inst., Delta Sigma Theta. Republican. Baptist. Avocations: writing, reading, tennis, travel. Personal E-mail: nifamserv@aol.com. Business E-Mail: sdavidson.doh@dcgov.org.

DAVIDSON, SHEILA KEARNEY, lawyer, insurance company executive; b. Paterson, NJ, Dec. 16, 1961; d. John James and Rita Barbara (Burke) Kearney; m. Anthony H. Davidson, Oct. 5, 1996; children: Andrew John, Patrick Kearney. BA cum laude, Fairfield U., 1983; JD, George Washington U., 1986. Bar: N.Y. 1987, U.S. Dist. Ct. (so. dist.) N.Y. 1987, D.C. 1989. Assoc. Shearson Lehman Bros., Inc., NYC, 1986-87; staff atty. Nat. Assn. Securities Dealers, NYC, 1987-89, regional atty., 1989-90, sr. regional atty., 1990-91; regional counsel NY Life Ins. Co., NYC, 1991-93, assoc. counsel, 1993-94, asst. gen. counsel, 1994-95, v.p., assoc. gen. counsel, 1995-97, sr. v.p. in charge of corp. compliance dept., 1998-00, sr. v.p., gen. counsel, 2000—05, exec. v.p. law and corp. adminstrn., 2005—. Trustee Fairfield U., 2003—, Madison Sq. Park Conservancy, 2004—. Mem.: D.C. Bar Assn., Phi Delta Phi. Republican. Roman Catholic. Office: NY Life Ins Co 51 Madison Ave New York NY 10010-1603

DAVIDSON, SUSAN BETTINA, editor, writer; b. Wolverhampton, Eng., June 6, 1942; came to U.S., 1957; d. Basil Thomas and Hedi (Liebermann) Goldfarb; m. Daniel Ira Davidson, Mar. 13, 1966; 1 child, Jill. Student, Nat. U. Mex., Mexico City, 1962; BA in Langs., Ohio State U., 1963; postgrad., New Sch. for Social Rsch., 1963, Columbia U., 1963—65, Alliance Française, Paris, 1968, George Washington U., 1995—97. Editl. asst. Harcourt, Brace & Co., N.Y.C., 1963-64; asst. to prodr. ABC-News, N.Y.C., 1964-65; prodn. asst. UPI, N.Y.C., 1965-66; news prodr. Ind. TV News, Washington, 1966-69; freelance prodr. London Weekend TV, Washington, 1969-75; arts editor Washingtonian mag., Washington, 1977—. Contbg. editor Women's Work, 1972—75; Washington editor Changing Homes, 1985—87; nominator Helen Hayes Awards, Washington, 1983—99, Ortho 21st Century Women Awards; judge Washington Craft Show, 1996; reader Fund for New Am. Plays, Washington, 1997, Washington, 98, Washington, 99, Washington, 2000, Washington, 01; reviewer, rschr., editor books and plays. Contbr. articles to newspapers and various publs. Panelist Prince George's County Arts Awards, Washington, 1992, Mayor's Arts Awards, Washington, 1993, Mayor's Arts Edn. Awards, Washington, 1996, USIA Selection Bd., Washington, 1997; vol. Women's Health Initiative. Mem.: Travel Journalists Guild. Democrat. Jewish. Avocations: theater, reading, music, dance, travel. Home: 2900 Brandywine St NW Washington DC 20008-2138 Office: Washingtonian Mag 1828 L St NW Ste 200 Washington DC 20036-5169 Office Phone: 202-296-3600. Personal E-mail: s.davidson@starpower.net. Business E-Mail: sdavidson@washingtonian.com.

DAVIDSON, TARA BETH, secondary school educator; b. Pitts., Dec. 4, 1980; d. John L. and Paula Beth Davidson. BS, Davidson Coll., 2002; MA, City Coll., NYC, 2004; student in Urban Edn. Policy, Rutgers U. Cert. secondary social studies tchr. N.Y. State, 2005. Tchr. N.Y.C. Pub. Schs., 2002—. Fellow, Gotham Ctr., N.Y., 2004—05. Mem.: Nat. Coun. for Social Studies. Personal E-mail: tdavids2@pegasus.rutgers.edu.

DAVIES, ALMA (ALMA ROSITA), theater producer, composer, playwright, lyricist, sculptor; b. Bloemfontein, South Africa; d. Walter David Davies and Elizabeth (Van der Kar); m. Lee Kaye, Dec. 9, 1956 (dec. Jan. 1967); children: Walter Ian Kaye, Elena-Beth Kaye; m. Edwin William Williams, June 22, 1985 (dec. Mar. 1997). Grad. BMI musical theater workshop, Comml. Theatre Inst., N.Y.C. Tchr., choreographer Spanish dance, ballet Sch. Dance Arts, Carnegie Hall, N.Y.C. Toured as solo dancer, actress with Manhattan Opera Co. in Desert Song, with Ana Maria Spanish Dance co.; soloist Dances of Spain, Am. Mus. Natural History, N.Y.C., featured soloist Jose Greco Dance Co., Washington; soloist, choreographer Jacobs Pillow Dance Festival, Mass.; soloist Radio City Music Hall, Am. Youth Ballet, N.Y.C.; guest artist, soloist, choreographer Syracuse (N.Y.) Philharm. Orch.; soloist, dancer, actress Voice of Firestone NBC-TV, N.Y.C.; guest artist Simmons Cruise Concert-S.S. Olympia, Caribbean Seas; exhbns. for sculpted 3-D pictures include Schumacher Fabrics, N.Y.C., Warner Bros., Hollywood others; puppeteer Rose Rivero Charity Showcase, N.Y.C.; jewelry designer, manufacturer, marketer Saks Fifth Ave., Lord & Taylor, Bloomingdales, Bergdorf Goodman; author, composer, dir., prodr. musicals: Princessa, Moon Holiday, Little Lord, Dorinmore, Lord Fauntleroy, (TV film) Clash of Wills; author: I Blow Myself Away, Memoirs of a Remarkable Diva; composer music video, United In Spirit, We'll Never Forget, America's Homeland

Security Anthem (featured on U.S. Dept. Def. website, 2005). Recipient First prize for costume design Beaux Arts Ball, N.Y., Internat. Beaux Arts Ball, N.Y.; featured in Fashion mag. Mem. ASCAP, Dramatists Guild, The Drama League, Internat. Platform Assn. Avocations: sculpture, scenic design, costume design. Office Phone: 702-254-3775.

DAVIES, COLLEEN T., lawyer; b. Sacramento, Oct. 22, 1958; married; children: Katie, Patrick. BA with honors in English lit., U. Calif., Davis, 1980; JD, Santa Clara U., 1983. Bar: Calif. 1983. With Crosby, Heafey, Roach & May (combined with Reed Smith LLP, 2003), 1983—2003; ptnr., mem. exec. com. Reed Smith LLP, Oakland, Calif., 2003—. Comments editor Santa Clara Law Rev., 1982—83; mem. Product Liability Adv. Coun. Mem.: ABA, Def. Rsch. Inst. (pharm. & med. device sect.), Alameda County Bar Assn., Calif. State Bar, Phi Beta Kappa. Office: Reed Smith LLP 1999 Harrison St Ste 2400 Oakland CA 94612 Office Phone: 510-763-2000. Office Fax: 510-273-8832. Business E-Mail: cdavies@reedsmith.com.

DAVIES, FONDA WOODELL, minister of music, music teacher; b. Atchison, Kans., Oct. 6, 1952; d. Victor Allen and Jean R. Woodell; m. William O. Davies, June 21, 1975; children: Denny R., Bradley W. BMusic magna cum laude, U. Miami, 1973; MS in Music Edn. magna cum laude, Fla. Internat. U., Miami, 1980. Tchr. North Miami Beach Sr. H.S., Miami, 1973-75; dir. music, organist St. Andrews Presbyn. Ch., Hollywood, Fla., 1976-81, Ch. of the Palms, Sarasota, Fla., 1983-88, St. Armands Key Luth. Ch., Sarasota, 1989-94; min. of music Pine Shores Presbyn. Ch., Sarasota, 1996—2002; owner, mgr. Svc. Master of N.W. Sarasota, Svc. Master of the Meadows, 1989—. Accompanist Sarasota Choral Soc., 1994-2004. Composer choral anthems and solos, 1990—. Vol., chair fundraising Sarasota H.S. Band, 1994—. Republican.

DAVIES, GRACE LUCILLE, real estate educator; b. Providence, Apr. 6, 1926; d. Leonard Cerulle and Eleanor De Prete; m. David John Davies, Feb. 8, 1948; children: Mary Ellen, David L., Pamela, Amy. AA, Long Beach City Coll., 1946; BA, U. Calif., Berkeley, 1948; MA, Calif. State U., Long Beach, 1965. Gen. elem. credential Calif., life elem. credential Calif., elem. sch. adminstr. credential Calif., life elem. sch. adminstr. Calif. Elem. educator ABC Unified Sch. Dist., Artesia, Calif., 1956—85, MGM coord., 1960—70, bilingual coord., 1960—70, asst. prin., 1970—80; real estate, bus., investment D. Davies & Assoc., Long Beach, Calif., 1985—. Clk. Long Beach (Calif.) Election Bd., 1990—; mem., vol. Long Beach City Campaign, 1998. Mem.: Calif. Ret. Tchrs. Assn. (legis. chair 1985—, pres. 2000—), Apt. Mgmt. Assn., Delta Kappa Gamma (v.p., pres., Golden Rose award 1996), Pi Lambda Theta (treas., v.p., pres., Outstanding Contbn. Edn. award 1996). Avocations: travel, reading, theater, camping, music. Home: 6215 Parima St Long Beach CA 90803

DAVIES, LAURA, professional golfer; b. Coventry, Eng., Oct. 5, 1963; Profl. golfer LPGA, 1987—. Mem. European Solheim Cup Team, 1990, 92, 94, 96, 98. 15 career victories, including Circle K LPGA Tucson Open, 1988, Jamie Farr Toledo Classic, 1988, Lady Keystone Open, 1989, Inamori Classic, 1991, McDonald's Championship, 1993, Standard Register Ping, 1994, 95, 96, 97, Sara Lee Classic, 1994, Chick-fil-a Charity Championship, 1995, Star Bank LPGA Classic, 1996, LPGA Tour Championship, 1996, L.A. Womeen's Championship, 2000, The Philips Invitational, 2000; recipient Rolex Player of Yr. award, 1996; named Mem. Brit. Empire, Queen Elizabeth II, 1988. Office: care LPGA 100 International Golf Dr Daytona Beach FL 32124-1082

DAVIES-MCNAIR, JANE, retired educational consultant; b. Topeka, May 21, 1922; m. K. Robert Davies, Aug. 27, 1949; m. John D. McNair June 4, 1989. BE, Nat. Louis U. (formerly Nat. Coll. Edn.), Evanston, Ill., 1944, ME, 1958; postgrad., Columbia U., Ill. State U., Nat. Coll. Edn. Tchr. various schs., Oak Park, Ill., Hillside, N.J., Elmont, N.Y., 1944-58, Sch. Dist., Dwight, Ill., 1959-67, Streater, Ill., 1968; asst. county supt. Livingston County, Pontiac, Ill., 1969-72; project cons., supr., trainer early prevention of sch. failure K-W Curriculum Svc. Office, Peotone, Ill., 1972-77; freelance cons., speaker early childhood edn. Ill., 1977-80; ret., 1980. Author: Resource Guide for Developing Pre-Academic, Learning Skills and Other guides for the Early Prevention of School Failure, The Gifted and the Biligual and Migrant Programs. Mem.: DAR, ASCD, AAUW, Childhood Edn. Internat., Internat. Platform Assn., Ill. Edn. Assn. (life and ret. life com.), Ill. Ret. Tchrs. Assn. (dir. region II), Assn. Childhood Edn. (early childhood), Nat. Assn. Edn. Young Children, State Evaluation Team, U.S. Holocause Meml. Mus. Circle of Life (charter supporting mem.), Nat. Mus. Am. Indian (charter), Smithsonian Mus. Am. India, Nat. Soc. Sons and Daus. of Pilgrims, Am. Assn. Ret. Persons, Gen. Fedn. Women's Club, Delta Kappa Gamma, Order Eastern Star.

DAVILA, ELISA, language educator, literature educator; b. Libano, Tolima, Colombia, May 29, 1944; arrived in U.S., 1974; d. Rafael Antonio Davila and Amalia Parra; m. Bruce Roger Smith, Oct. 17, 1973 (div. 1981). BA, U. Pedagogica Nat., Bogota, Colombia, 1966; MA, U. Pacific, 1972; PhD, U. Calif., Santa Barbara, 1983. Asst. prof. U. Valle, Cali, Colombia, 1968-73; rschr. Inst. Colombiano de Pedagogia, Bogota, Colombia, 1973-73; assoc. U. Calif., Santa Barbara, 1974-78, 78-80; instr. W. Tex. State U., Canyon, Tex., 1978-80, Def. Lang. Inst., Calif., 1981-82; prof. SUNY, New Paltz, 1999—, chair fgn. langs., 1990—94, 1996—2004, dir. Latin Am. studies, 1991—. Vis. lectr. U. Calif., Santa Cruz, 1982—; reader, evaluator N.J. Dept. Higher Edn., Princeton, 1987—89; reader Ednl. Testing Svc., Princeton, 1987—89; acad. dir. Spanish Immersion Inst. Bd. Edn. and Office Mental Health, N.Y.C., Albany, 1987—90; project dir. title VI grant undergraduate internat. and fgn. lang. program U.S. Dept. Edn., 2000—. Recipient Disting. Tchr. award, Alumni Assn., 1996; scholar Heloise Brainer, 1964, Latin-Am. Scholarship Program, Am. Univs. Mem.: MLA, Latin-Am. Studies Assn., Am. Assn. Tchrs. Spanish and Portuguese. Avocations: creative writing, poetry. Home: PO Box 423 Hurley NY 12443-0423 Fax: 845-257-3512. Office Phone: 845-257-3489. Business E-Mail: davilae@newpaltz.edu.

DAVILA - MADERA, MARIA L., mathematics educator; b. Arroyo, P.R., July 25, 1967; d. Jose M. Davila - Lopez and Candy Madera de Davila; m. Jose E. Soler, Dec. 27, 1992; children: Jose G. Soler - Davila, Manuel A. Soler - Davila. BA in Environ. Design, U. P.R., San Juan, 1992; postgrad., U. Ctrl. Fla., Orlando, 2005—. Cert. educator Fla. Dept. Edn., 2004. Interior/archtl. designer various firms, San Juan, 1992—2000; math. educator Orange County Pub. Sch., Orlando, Fla., 2001—. Math tutor GSCS Youth Ministry, Orando, 2004—05. Cathechist St. Isaac Cath. Ch., Orlando, 2004—06. Named Math Tchr. of Yr., Colonial H.S., 2005—06, Support Pers. of Yr., 2005—06; recipient Disting. Scholar award, Valencia C.C., 2001. Mem.: Orange County Coun. Tchrs. Math. Office: Colonial High School 6100 Oleander Dr Orlando FL 32807 Office Phone: 407-482-6300. Business E-Mail: davilam2@ocps.net.

DAVILIS, KATRINA LYN, music educator; b. Hammond, Ind., Mar. 20, 1976; d. Carol and Spirio Davilis. BS in Instrumental Music Edn., Ball State U., Muncie, Ind., 1999; M in Instrumental Music Edn., Morehead State U., Ky., 2004—05. Registered Teacher Va., 2005. Dir. bands Roosevelt M.S., Monticello, Ind., 1999—2004; asst. band dir. Twin Lakes H.S., Monticello, Ind., 1999—2004. Host Morehead State H.S. and Mid. Sch. Honor Band, Morehead, Ky., 2004—05, Ind. Bandmasters Assn., Monticello, Ind., 2003, Solo and Ensemble Contest, Monticello, 2001—04, Marching Band Invitational, Monticello, 2001—03, Mid. Sch. Orgnl. Contest, Monticello, 2000—04; adjudicator Ind. State Sch. Music Assn., Indpls., 2002—04. Music scholarship, Women Band Dir. Internat., 2005. Mem.: Va. Music Educations Assn. (assoc.), Music Educators Nat. Conf. (assoc.), Nat. Band Assn. (assoc.), Pi Kappa Lambda (life). Democrat-Npl. Avocations: hiking, poetry, musical instruments, reading. Office: Thoreau MS 2505 Cedar Lane Vienna VA 22181 Office Phone: 703-846-8046.

DAVION, ETHEL JOHNSON, school system superintendent, curriculum specialist; b. Raleigh, N.C., July 21, 1948; d. John Arthur and Ethel Mae (Morgan) Johnson; 1 child, Laura Christal. BA, Livingstone Coll., Salisbury, N.C., 1971; MA, Glassboro State U., N.J., 1983. Cert. tchr., prin., supr., N.J. Sr. English tchr. Camden Bd. Edn., N.J., 1977-81; tchr. of English Westfield Bd. Edn., N.J., 1982-85, Union County Regional Dist. 1, Berkeley Heights, N.J., 1981-82, Hillside Bd. Edn., N.J., 1985-87; supr. English, lang. arts Irvington Bd. Edn., N.J., 1987-92; vice prin. Frank H. Morrell H.S., Irvington, N.J., 1992-95, prin., 1996—2000, asst. supt. acad. affairs, 2000—. Writer, researcher Collegiate Rsch. Systems, Camden, 1976-77; participant profl. devel. programs Harvard U., 1989, Notre Dame U., 1990; participate Oxford Univ. Roundtable, Oxford, Eng., 2002. Author: A Tutorial Approach to Teaching English, 1983, Teachers' Resource Manual, 1987; contbr. articles to jours. Bd. dirs., sec. Emmanuel Tabernacle, Linden, N.J., 1988; com. chair Narrowing the Achievement Gap for Kean Univ.'s Diversity, 2000—. Recipient Resolution Town Coun. Irvington, 1992. Fellow N.J. Edn. Assn., Nat. Coun. Tchrs. English; mem. ASCD, NAFE, Am. Assn. Sch. Adminstrs., Linden Scholarship Guild (sec. 1985—), Prin. and Suprs. Assn., Irvington Adminstrs. Assn. (treas.), Internat. Platform Assn., Good Samaritans Club, Obsidian Civic Club (Westfield, historian 1985—), Diversity 2000 Coun. (sec. 1997—). Democrat. Baptist. Office Phone: 973-399-6800 ext. 2100. Business E-Mail: ejdavion@irvington.k12.nj.us.

DAVIS, ADA ROMAINE, nursing educator; b. Cumberland, Md., June 7, 1929; d. Louis Berge and Ethel Lucy (Johnson) Romaine; m. John Francis Davis, Aug. 1, 1953; children: Kevin Murray, Karen Evans-Romaine, William Romaine. Diploma in nursing, Kings County Hosp., Bklyn., 1949; BSN, U. Md., Balt., 1973, MS, 1974; PhD, U. Md., 1979, postdoctoral student, 1985—89. Cert. editor in life scis. Asst. prof. grad. program U. Md., Balt., 1974-79; chmn. dept. nursing Coll. of Notre Dame, Balt., 1979-82; assoc. dean grad. program Georgetown U. Sch. Nursing, Washington, 1982-87; nurse cons. Health Resources and Svcs. Adminstrn., Rockville, Md., 1987-93, HHS, USPHS, Bur. Health Profls., Rockville, 1987-93; assoc. prof. and dir. undergrad. program Johns Hopkins U. Sch. of Nursing, Balt., 1993-98, prof. emeritus, 1998—. Reviewer Choice, ALA; evaluator methodology and findings for rsch. studies; hist./med. biographer; prof., editor Johns Hopkins U. Sch. Nursing, 2003—. Author: John Gibbon and His Heart-Lung Machine, 1992, Advanced Practice Nurses: Education, Roles and Trends, 1997; editor: Ency. of Home Care for the Elderly, 1995; contbr. articles to nursing jours.; assoc. editor Hopkins InteliHealth, Johns Hopkins Family Health Guide, 1999, Johns Hopkins Insider, 1998; sr. editor: Am. Nurses Certification Ctr., 2000-01. Recipient excellent performance award HRSA; rsch. grantee U. Md. Grad. Sch. Mem. AAAS, ANA (cert. adult nurse practitioner), Soc. for Neoplatonic Studies, Nat. Orgn. Nurse Practitioner Faculties, Am. Acad. Nurse Practitioners, APHA, Gerontol. Soc. Am., Nat. Trust for Hist. Preservation, Am. Geriat. Soc., Md. History of Medicine Soc., Soc. for the Social History of Medicine (Oxford U.), N.Y. Acad. Scis., Coun. Sci. Editors, Sigma Theta Tau. E-mail: adarom@earthlink.net.

DAVIS, ADDIE L., mathematics educator; d. Joe Smith and Margieree Crosby; m. Clarence L. Davis, June 27, 1970; children: Raymond DeJoe Smith, Maurice Lamar. BSBA, Roosvelt U., Chgo., 1975; MA, Chgo. State U., 1979; ABD, Capella U., 2003. Assoc. prof. Olive-Harvey Coll., Chgo., 1983—. Sr. faculty advisor Phi Theta Kappa Olive-Harvey Coll., 2002—. Women's dept. chair Little Mountain Hope, Chgo., 2005—. Recipient Woman of Yr., Assn. Women in Cmty. Colleges-Local, 2003—04, Dist. Prof., Olive-Harvey Coll., 2003—04, Dist. Adv. Paragon award, Phi Theta Kappa, 2005. Mem.: Am. Assn. Math. (assoc.). Democrat-Npl. Avocations: reading, travel, swimming, singing. Office: Olive-Harvey Coll 10001 S Woodlawn Ave Chicago IL 60628 Office Phone: 773-291-6428. Office Fax: 773-291-6304. Business E-Mail: addavis@ccc.edu.

DAVIS, AIMEE SLAUGHTER, social studies educator; b. Atlanta, May 15, 1947; d. Ellinor Whiteford and Paul Slaughter; m. Manson Luther Davis III, June 14, 1969; children: Cameron Wesley, Julie Davis Charles, Andrew Scott. BA, W.Ga. Coll., Carrollton, 1969; MEd, Ga. State U., Atlanta, 1975. Lic. Ga., 2005. Tchr. Ronald E. McNair Sr. H.S., Atlanta, 1985—, dept. chairperson social studies, career acad. coord. Named Tchr. of Yr., McNair H.S. Faculty and Staff, 1996. Mem.: GCSS, NCSS. Achievements include implemented careers academies within our high school creating small learning communities. Home: 4250 Inns Brook Dr Snellville GA 30039 Office: Ronald E McNair Sr High Sch 1804 Bouldercrest Rd SE Atlanta GA 30039 Office Phone: 678-874-4902. Office Fax: 678-874-4910. Personal E-mail: aimeesdavis@comcast.net. E-mail: aimee_s_davis@fc.dekalb.k12.ga.us.

DAVIS, ALICE MARLECE See DAVIS, MARLECE

DAVIS, AMANDA, newscaster; m. Steve Grierson, 1996; 1 child, Melora. Degree, Clark Coll. Anchor, host WRET-TV, Charlotte, NC; Washington (D.C.) corr. Satellite News Channel; anchor, reporter Sta. WSB-TV, Atlanta; anchor Sta. WAGA-TV, Atlanta. Recipient Cmty. Svc. award, Clark Coll., Emmy award, 1999, Gabby award, Ga. Assn. Broadcasters, EdwardR. Murrow Award, 1998, 2000. Mem.: Atlanta (Ga.) Assn. Black Journalists (Kenan's Kids Found. Media award, named Best Anchor 2000, named Pioneer Black Journalist of Yr. 2002). Office: WAGA TV 1551 Briarcliff Rd NE Atlanta GA 30306

DAVIS, AMANDA NICOLE, elementary school educator; b. Peoria, Ill., Oct. 10, 1981; d. Tom R. and Jan E. Davis. Degree in elem./mid. edn., St. Norbert Coll., 2002. Spl. edn. tchr. Green Bay (Wis.) Pub. Sch. Dist., 2003; 5th grade tchr. Antioch (Ill.) C.C. Sch. Dist., 2003—04, Unified Sch. Dist. of De Pere, Wis., 2004—. Soccer coach De Pere HS, 2004—06. Home: 932 Hilly Haven Ct Green Bay WI 54311 Office: Unified Sch Dist of De Pere 650 S Michigan St De Pere WI 54115 Office Phone: 920-337-1036. Personal E-mail: adavis@depere.k12.wi.us.

DAVIS, ANGELA YVONNE, political activist, educator, writer; b. Birmingham, Ala., Jan. 26, 1944; D.B. Frank and Sally E. Davis. Studied under Theodor Adorno, Frankfurt Sch., 1960-62; student, U. Paris, 1963-64; BA magna cum laude, Brandeis U., 1965; MA, U. Calif., San Diego, 1968. Mem. faculty San Francisco State U.; tchr. U. Calif., San Diego, 1968; asst. prof. philosophy UCLA, 1969; prof. history of consciousness dept. U. Calif., Santa Cruz, 1991—, presdl. chair in African American and feminist studies, 1995-97. Adv. bd. Prison Activist Resource Ctr., spkr. in field. Removed from teaching position in philosophy dept., UCLA, 1969. On FBI's 10 Most Wanted List, 1970. Captured, tried and acquitted, 1972. Gov. Ronald Reagan vowed she would never teach in Univ. Calif. sys. Candidate for US v.p., Communist Party ticket, 1980. Author: If They Come in the Morning: Voices of Resistance, 1971, Angela Davis: An Autobiography, Women, Race, and Class, 1981, Women, Culture, and Politics, 1989, Violence Against Women and the Ongoing Challenge to Racism, 1992, Resisting State Violence: Radicalism, Gender, and Race in US Culture, 1996, The Angela Y. Davis Reader, 1998, The House That Race Built, 1998, Blues Legacies and Black Feminism: Gertrude "Ma" Rainey, Bessie Smith, and Billie Holiday, 1998, Are Prisons Obsolete?, 2003. Mem. Black Panthers. Mem. Communist Party. Office: History of Consciousness Dept UC Santa Cruz 1156 High St Santa Cruz CA 95064 Office Phone: 831-459-0111.

DAVIS, ANN CALDWELL, history educator; b. Alliance, Ohio, June 3, 1925; d. Arthur Trescott and Jane Caldwell D. BA, Western Reserve U., 1947; MA, Columbia U., 1955; PhD, Columbia Pacific U., 1987. Cert. tchr., Ill., Ohio. Pres. The Clio Found. Inc., Gulfport, Fla., 1955—; tchr. Supr. Child Enterprise, Evanston, Ill., 1956-60; human rels. coun. U. Chgo., 1957-58, asst., 1961; tchr., dept. chair Evanston Pub. Schs., 1961-85; project English Northwestern U., Evanston, 1963-64. Cons. Dist. #65 Sch., Evanston, 1985-90. Presenter, author: (speech) Do-it-Yourself Help For The Top 10%, 1964, The Non-Graded School, 1976, Social Studies Reading & Reference Skills, 1979; author: (video) U.S. & Ill. Constn., 1986. Vol. Meals ON Wheels, Treasure Island, Fla., 1990-94, Pinellas County Schs., Fla., 1991, steering com. St. Petersburg, Fla., 1995, health care chair Older Women's League, St. Petersburg, 1995. Mem. Am. Assn. of U. Women, Orgn. of Am. Historians, Ill. & Nat. Edn. Assn. Office: The Clio Found Inc PO Box 5110 Gulfport FL 33737-5110 Office Phone: 727-367-6771. E-mail: cliofdn@aol.com.

DAVIS, ANNA JANE RIPLEY, elementary school educator; b. Uhrichsville, Ohio, Sept. 7, 1931; d. Emmet Frank and Lillie Hazel (Kinsey) Ripley; m. H. Joe Davis, Mar. 16, 1951; children: Alan Joe, Kendal Jay. A, Asbury Coll., 1953; BS with honors, Kent State U., 1962, MEd with honors, 1978, postgrad., 1980—96; student, Richmond Coll., London U., St. Andrews U., Dundee U., Cambridge U., U. Paris, U. Rome, U. Amsterdam, Ohio U. Cert. elem. tchr., Ohio. Tchr. Kenston Schs., Chagrin Falls, Ohio, 1953-55, 58-62, Firestone Rubber Plantation, Harbel, Liberia, West Africa, 1962-64, Newbury (Ohio) Schs., 1964-65, Orange Schs., Pepper Pike, Ohio, 1965-99. Chaperone, counselor Am. Inst. for Fgn. Study, British Isles and Europe, summers 1968-81. Author children's books. Active Kenston PTA, Chagrin Falls and Pepper Pike PTA, Am. Field Svc., Chagrin Falls, Geauga County Personal Growth Com. for workshops; bd. dirs. Friends Geauga County Pub. Libr.; bookmobile project vol. traveling libr. Geauga County Pub. Libr. for Amish Schs., traveling libr., 1994—; elem. sch. tutor, 1998—; vol. ARC, 1955—, Food Pantry and Clothing for Needy, Kiwanis, bookmobile projects Geauga County Pub. Lib. Friends; mem. edn. com., libr., home care, Care Bears com., Prayer Chain, Sunday sch. com., Sunday Sch., membership com., libr. com. Pepper Pike Garfield Meml. United Meth. Ch. Mem. NEA (life), ASCD, Ohio Edn. Assn., N.E. Ohio Tchrs. Assn., Orange Tchrs. Assn. Avocations: travel, bicycling, hiking, reading, writing.

DAVIS, AQUILLA, diversified financial services company executive; d. Mallie Harmon Woodberry and Rosa Lee Davis; children: Meshelliah Davis Hayward, Genonyus Damorris, Jawanda Lecress. BSc, Benedict Coll., 1973—77; MA, Webster U., 2001—05. Data entry operator Champus BC/BS, Florence, SC, 1989—92; asst. mgr. J.L. Income Tax & Gen. Acctg. Svc, Georgetown, SC, 1993—2005. County office clk. Farmers Home Adminstrn., Kingstree, SC, 1979—86; owner Davis Tax & Poetry Svc, Johnsonville, SC, 2002—05. Author: (poem writer) Inspire Poems of Love, Joy and Peace (Editors award, 2003). Asst. vp dir. Young People Dept., Johnsonville, SC, 1997—2005. Scholar, Minority Access, Inc, 2005. Ame. Avocations: reading, singing, travel. Home: 718 Poston Rd Johnsonville SC 29555 Office Phone: 843-386-3973. Personal E-mail: aquilladavis2003@yahoo.com.

DAVIS, BARBARA ANN LANE, retired elementary school educator, retired realtor; b. Hamilton, Ohio, Jan. 20, 1932; d. Charles Lyn Lane and Myrtle Emily Corwin; m. Edwin Lee Davis, Sept. 16, 1950; children: Jeffrey Lee, Cynthia Lynn. BE, Miami U., Oxford, Ohio, 1967. Kindergarten tchr., Waynesville, Ohio, 1952—54; elem. tchr. McKinley-Ridgewood Schs., Springfield, Ohio, 1970—73; pub. rels. dir. Am. Cancer Soc., Springfield, 1974—75; rental mgr. Forest Oak Towers, Gaithersburg, 1981—82; pre-sch. tchr. YMCA, Gaithersburg, Md., 1982—83; realtor Long & Foster, Gaithersburg, 1982—90; ret., 1990. Charter mem. Nat. Alliance for Mentally Ill, 1980—; mem. Jr. Svc. League, Springfield, 1960—69, Ohio Vet. Aux., Springfield, 1955—80; Sunday sch. tchr., deaconess Highlands UCC, Springfield, 1976—78; bd. dirs. Ohio Schizophrenic Soc., 1975—78, Gatepost Halfway Ho., Springfield, 1976—79; mem. Haxley Inst. Biosocial Rsch., 1974—78. Mem.: Warren County Hist. Soc., Lebanon Conservancy Orgn., Kiwanis. Avocations: walking, choir, bridge, dance. Home: 1110 E Main St # 801 Lebanon OH 45036

DAVIS, BARBARA JUDY, counselor, mental health educator; b. Lewisburg, W.Va., Apr. 27, 1955; d. Harris Wilson and Dorthea Pearl (Baker) Judy; m. Robin John Otis, May 10, 1980 (div. Nov. 1987); 1 child, Tamara; m. Ancel Barbour Davis Jr., Mar. 4, 1989; 1 child, Shannon. BA, U. Va., 1980, MEd, 1993. Lic. profl. counselor; cert. counselor. Benefits specialist Charlottesville (Va.) Dept. of Social Svc., 1988-91, social worker, 1991—96, Cumberland County (N.C.) Mental Health, 1996-97; coord. Thomas S program Edgecombe-Nash (N.C.) Mental Health Ctr., 1997-99; dir. mental health edn. Area L Area Health Edn. Ctr., Rocky Mount, N.C., 1999—. Adj. asst. prof. dept. psychiatry Sch. Medicine U. N.C., Chapel Hill, 2002—; bd. dirs. Tar River Mental Health Assn. Mem. adv. bd. Region X Cmty. Svc. Mental Retardation Divsn., Charlottesville, 1989-96; founding mem. planning com. Disability Awareness Day, Charlottesville, 1992-95, chair fund raising, 1993; mem. Thomas S. Provider/Area Program Work Group, 1998-99; elder First Christian Ch., Rocky Mount.; mem. exec. bd. S.W.I.M. Network, Inc., affiliate Christian Women's Job Corp., 2000—. Recipient Outstanding Vol. Svc. award, Office Gov., N.C., 2004. Mem.: ACA, Mental Health Assn. (mem. ea. region client's rights com. 2005—), Counselors for Social Justice, Nat. Bd. Cert. Counselors, Chi Sigma Iota. Avocations: alpine skiing, hiking, church choir. Office: Area L Area Health Edn Ctr 1631 S Wesleyan Blvd Rocky Mount NC 27803-5627 E-mail: Barbara.Davis@ncmail.net.

DAVIS, BARBARA SNELL, education educator; b. Painesville, Ohio, Feb. 21, 1929; d. Roy Addison and Mabelle Irene (Denning) Snell; children: Beth Ann Davis Schnorf, James Lee, Polly Denning Davis Spaeth. BS, Kent State U., 1951; MA, Lake Erie Coll., 1981; postgrad., Cleve. State U., 1982-83. Cert. reading specialist, elem. prin., Ohio. Dir. publicity Lake Erie Coll., Painesville, 1954-59; tchr. Mentor (Ohio) Exempted Village Sch. Dist., 1972-86, prin., 1986-97; prof., supr. Lake Erie Coll., 1997—. Author: Who Says You Can't Change the World?, 2005; contbr. articles to profl. jours. Former trustee Mentor United Meth. Ch. Mem. Delta Kappa Gamma (pres. 1982-84), Phi Delta Kappa (pres. 1992-93), Theta Sigma Phi (charter). Home: 7293 Beechwood Dr Mentor OH 44060-6305 Office: 326 College Hall Lake Erie Coll Painesville OH 44077 Office Phone: 440-375-7159.

DAVIS, BERTA, psychologist; b. Bklyn., June 1, 1942; d. Harry Davis and Helen (Schwartz) Snyder; m. Benjamin W. Nitzberg; 1 child, Hersh Davis-Nitzberg. BA, Bklyn. Coll., 1963; MS, CCNY, Bklyn., 1965; PhD, NYU, 1976. Lic. psychologist, Calif.; cert. sex therapist. Lectr. Lehman Coll., CUNY, 1970-75; co-dir. Inst. for Internal Living, Tokyo, 1980-82; pvt. practice psychology Encino, Calif., 1982—; clin. assoc. U. So. Calif., L.A., 1990—. Weekly columnist Japan Times, 1981-84. Mem. L.A. County Psychol. Assn. (newsletter editor, bd. dirs., past pres.); fellow Am. Bd. Sexology (Diplomate). Office: 16055 Ventura Blvd Ste 1128 Encino CA 91436-2612

DAVIS, BETH, elementary school educator; b. Collins, Miss., Sept. 24, 1940; d. Richard Alexandria McDonald and Vaudril Lindell Taylor; m. James Stancel Davis, Oct. 28, 1960; children: James Stancel II, Tracy Lynd Davis-Blomgrist. AS, Brevard C.C., Cocoa, Fla., 1972; BS in Elem. Edn., Rollins Coll., 1975; M in Adminstrn., Nova U., 1978. Tchr. Golfview Elem., Rockledge, Fla., 1975-93, 97—, Saturn Elem., Cocoa, Fla., 1993-96, Riverview Elem., Titusville, Fla., 1996-97. Tchr. TK-1 workshops Brevard County Sch., Rockledge; spkr. Fla. Reading Assn., Orlando, 1985, U. Ctrl. Fla., 1994. City coun. candidate City of Rockledge. Mem. Elks (Cocoa, Lady Elk of Yr. lodge 1532, 1st Woman Exalted Ruler 1999), Delta Kappa Gamma, Phi Delta Kappa. Republican. Presbyterian. Avocations: decorating, flower garden, college football, fishing, golf.

DAVIS, BETSY RAE, nurse; b. Newport, R.I., Sept. 18, 1939; d. J. Raymund and Anna Maria Fritz; m. Gary Thayne Davis (div.); children: Gary Thayne Jr., Alisa Diane Lindsey. BS in nursing, Salve Regina U., R.I., 1963. RN R.I., N.Y., Ill., Calif., Mich., Colo., Guam. Staff nurse U.S. Naval Hosp., Newport, RI, 1963—64; pub. health nurse Providence Dist. Naval Nursing Assn., 1965—66, Govt. of Guam, Aguana, 1976—77; sch. nurse Family Svcs. Ctr., Honolulu, 1978—81; RN III Porter Hosp., Denver, 1982—88, Children's Hosp., Denver, 1988—2001; sr. RN Apria Healthcare, Littleton, Colo., 2001—. Founder, dir. child care ctr. U.S. Naval Hosp., Agana, Guam, 1974—77; Vietnemese pediat. RN Operation Neno Life, Agana, Guam, 1975;

v.p., sec. treas. Lexington Village Homeowners Assn., Littleton, Colo., 1997—99. Republican. Roman Catholic. Avocations: camping, skiing, crafts, reading, music. Home: 9626 Fox Dew Dr Littleton CO 80125 Personal E-mail: takzb@msn.com.

DAVIS, BETTYE JEAN, school system administrator, state legislator; b. Homer, La., May 17, 1938; d. Dan and Rosylind (Daniel) Ivory; m. Troy J. Davis, Jan. 21, 1959; children: Anthony Benard, Sonja Davis Wade. Cert. nursing, St. Anthony's, 1961; BSW, Grambling State U., 1971; postgrad., U. Alaska, 1972. Psychiat. nurse Alaska Psychiat. Inst., 1967-70; asst. dir. San Bernardino (Calif.) YWCA, 1971-72; child care specialist DFYS Anchorage, 1975-80, soc. worker, 1980-82, foster care coordinator, 1982-87; dir. Alaska Black Leadership Edn. Program, 1979-82; exec. dir. Anchorage Sch. Bd., 1982-89; mem. Alaska Legislature, 1990—2000, Alaska Senate, 2000—. Chair Children's Caucus Alaska Legis., 1992—. Pres. Anchorage Sch. Bd., 1986-87; bd. dirs. Blacks in Govt., 1980-82, March of Dimes, 1983-85, Anchorage chpt. YWCA, 1989-90, Winning with Stronger Edn. Com., 1991, Alaska 2000, Anchorage Ctr. for Families, 1992—, active Anchorage chpt. NAACP, bd. dirs., 1978-82; mem. State Bd. Edn., 1997-2000. Toll fellow Henry Toll Fellowship Program, 1992; named Woman of Yr., Alaska Colored Women's Club, 1981, Child Care Worker of Yr., Alaska Foster Parent Assn., 1983, Social Worker of Yr., Nat. Foster Parents Assn., 1983, Outstanding Bd. Mem. Assn. Alaska Sch. Bds., 1990,; recipient Outstanding Achievement in Edn. award Alaska Colored Women's Club, 1985, Outstanding Women in Edn. award Zeta Phi Beta, 1985, Boardsmanship award Assn. Alaska Sch. Bds., 1989, Woman of Achievement award YWCA, 1991, Outstanding Leadership award Calif. Assembly, 1992. Mem. LWV, Nat. Sch. Bd. Assn., Nat. Caucus of Black Sch. Bd. Mems. (bd. dirs. 1986-87), Alaska Black Caucus (chair 1984—), Alaska Women's Polit. Caucus, Alaska Black Leadership Conf. (pres. 1976-80), Alaska Women Lobby (treas.), Nat. Caucus of Black State Legis. (chair region 12, 1994—), Women Legislators Lobby, Women's Action for New Directions, North to Future Bus. and Prof. Women (pres. 1978-79, 83), Delta Sigma Theta (Alaska chpt. pres. 1978-80). Clubs: North to Future Bus. and Profl. Women (past pres.). Democrat. Baptist. Avocations: cooking, Scrabble, stamp collecting/philately, coin collecting/numismatics, reading. Home: 2240 Foxhall Dr Anchorage AK 99504-3350 E-mail: bdavis@ak.net.

DAVIS, BEVERLY WATTS, federal agency administrator; b. Cincinnati; BS in economics, polit. sci., and social sciences, Trinity U., San Antonio; postgrad. in mgmt. and human resources, Webster U., Jeffersonville, Ind. Statewide coord. Texans' War on Drugs, 1988; cons., then dir. cmty. health Travis County Tex. Health Dept.; exec. dir. San Antonio Fighting Back Anti-Drug Cmty. Coalition; sr. v.p. United Way of San Antonio and Bexar County; dir. Ctr. for Substance Abuse Prevention, Substance Abuse and Mental Health Svcs. Adminstrn., Rockville, Md., 2003—. Mem. Minority- and Women-Owned Bus. Commn. Named Vol. of the Yr., U.S. Atty. Gen., 1997, Advocate of the Yr., Palmer Drug Abuse Program, Yellow Rose of Tex., Gov. of Tex., Outstanding Minority Bus. Owner, Greater Austin C. of C., 1985; named to San Antonio Women's Hall of Fame, 1998; recipient Dir.'s Award for Cmty. Leadership, FBI, Commendation Award, US Dept. Justice, Comdr.'s Award for Outstanding Leadership, Dept. Def., Vol. Award, Gov. Tex., Award for Neighborhood Action, Tex. Atty. Gen.'s Office, Outstanding Citizen Advocate Award, Nat. Crime Prevention Coun. Office: Substance Abuse and Mental Health Svc Adminstrn Rm 4-1057 1 Choke Cherry Rd Rockville MD 20857 Office Phone: 240-276-2420.*

DAVIS, BONNIE CHRISTELL, judge; b. Petersburg, Va., July 13, 1949; d. Robert Madison and Margaret Elizabeth (Collier) Davis. BA, Longwood Coll., 1971; JD, U. Richmond, 1980. Bar: Va. 1980, U.S. Dist. Ct. (ea. dist.) Va. 1980, U.S. Ct. Appeals (4th cir.) 1982. Tchr. Chesterfield County Schs., Chesterfield, Va., 1971-77; pvt. practice Chesterfield, 1980-83; asst. commonwealth atty. Chesterfield County, 1983-93; judge Juvenile and Domestic Rels. Ct. for 12th Jud. Dist. Va., 1993—. Adviser Youth Svcs. Commn., Chesterfield, 1983-93; cons. Task Force on Child Abuse, 1983-93, Met. Richmond Multi-Discipline Team on Spouse Abuse, 1983-93, Va. Dept. of Children for handbook "Step by Step Through the Juvenile Justice System in Virginia, 1988; mem. nat. adv. com. for prodn. on missing and runaway children Theatre IV; mem. adv. group to set stds. and tng. for Guardians Ad Litem, Supreme Ct. Va., 1994; chmn. jud. adminstrn. com. Jud. Conf. Va. for Dist. Cts., 1995-97, 2001-03; mem. state adv. com. for CASA and children's Justice Act, 1998-2002. Co-author: Juvenile Law and Practice in Virginia, 1994. Mem. Chesterfield County Pub. Schs. Task Force on Core Values, 1999. Mem.: Chesterfield-Colonial Heights Bar Assn., Met. Richmond Women's Bar Assn., Va. Trial Lawyers Assn., Va. Bar Assn., Va. State Bar (bd. govs. family law sect. 1997—2001, bd. govs. sr. lawyers conf. 2005—, bd. govs. gen. practice sect. 2005—), State-Fed. Jud. Coun. Va. Home: 415 Lyons Ave Colonial Heights VA 23834-3154 Office: Chesterfield Juvenile and Domestic Rels Dist Ct 7000 Lucy Corr Blvd Chesterfield VA 23832-6717 Office Phone: 804-751-4115.

DAVIS, CAROL LYN, museum administrator; b. West Palm Beach, Fla., Oct. 22, 1953; d. Robert Lee and Barbara Jean (Collett) D. BFA in Studio Arts, Tex. Christian U., Ft. Worth, 1975; MA in Am. Studies, Tex. Christian U., 1977. R&D product line designer Am. Handicrafts/Merribee Needlearts, Ft. Worth, 1977-81; ceramics/china sales cons. Dillard's, Ft. Worth, 1981-82; dept. mgr. Stripling-Cox, Ft. Worth, 1982-83; freelance ceramic and string art designer, 1982-83; rschr. with phase III, IV, V hist. sites inventory Tarrant County (Tex.) for Hist Preservation Coun., 1983-86, Page, Anderson & Turnbull, Inc., San Francisco, 1983-86; rschr. Tarrant County Greater Ft. Worth Housing Starts Tex. Update, Inc., 1987-94; rschr. M/PF Rsch., Inc., Dallas, 1989-94; sales adminstrv. asst. Trail Ridge, Bellaire Park, Summer Creek, Hulen Bend subdiv., Ft. Worth, 1994-2001, Summer Creek Ranch subdiv. Perry Homes, A Joint Venture, Ft. Worth, 2001—05; mus. mgr. White Settlement Hist. Mus., Tex., 2006—. Author pamphlets in field. Mem. mgmt. adv. panel Chem. Week, 1981; alternative precinct election judge Dem. Party, 1994—; mem. Tarrant County Dem. Party; mem. Arts Coun. Ft. Worth and Tarrant County; mem. Family History Soc. Newfoundland and Labrador, Inc.; mem. Tarrant County Hist. Soc. Mem.: Royal Over-Seas League (London). Democrat. Episcopalian. Home: 7800 Garza Ave Fort Worth TX 76116-7717 Office Phone: 817-246-9719. E-mail: hanontc@lycos.com.

DAVIS, CAROLYN JEAN, music educator; b. Thomasville, NC, Mar. 14, 1957; d. George and Helen Davis. MusB in Edn., Appalachian State U., 1979. Choral dir. Grayson County HS, Independence, Va., 1979—. Choir dir. Hillcrest Bapt. Ch., Galax, Va., 1991—. Mem.: Delta Kappa Gamma (pres. 1994—96). Avocations: music, crafts, reading, travel. Office: Grayson County HS 110 Blue Devil Ln Independence VA 24348 Office Phone: 276-773-2131.

DAVIS, CARYLON LEE, mortgage company executive, real estate broker; d. Palmus Dupree and Alice Enolia Strickland Dupree; m. Willie Davis, June 2, 1973. AA, L.A. City Coll., 1966; student, L.A. State Coll., 1967—69. Clk.-typist Gold's Furniture and Appliances, L.A., 1960—63, Dept. Def., L.A., 1963—69, sec., 1969—72, adminstrv. asst., 1972—78, exec. sec., 1983—85; office mgr. Dept. Air Force, L.A., 1978—83; bus. owner, pres. Kari's Profl. Svcs., Carson, Calif., 1989—98; real estate agt. Frank Jones Realty, Carson, 1989—98; real estate broker Kari's Enterprises, Carson, 1998—; mortgage broker A Plus Fin., Carson, 1998—. Avocation: piano. Office: A Plus Fin 20715 S Avalon Blvd #300 Carson CA 90746 Office Phone: 310-538-5254. E-mail: carylon@sbcglobal.net.

DAVIS, CLARICE MCDONALD, lawyer; b. New Orleans, Jan. 20, 1941; d. James A. and Helen J. (Ross) McDonald. BA cum laude, U. Tex., 1962, MA, 1964; JD magna cum laude, So. Meth. U., 1968. Bar: Tex. 1969, U.S. Dist. Ct. (no. dist.) Tex. 1970, U.S. Ct. Appeals (5th cir.) 1971, U.S. Supreme Ct. 1973. Law clk. to presiding justice U.S. Ct. Appeals (5th cir.), Dallas, 1969-71; ptnr. Akin, Gump, Strauss, Hauer & Feld LLP, Dallas, 1971—, gen. counsel. Comments editor Southwestern Law Jour., 1967-68; instr. Southern Methodist Univ. Sch. of Law, 1968-69. Bd. visitors So. Meth. U., Dallas, 1979-82, v.p. Law Sch. Alumni Adv. Coun., 1992, pres. 1993-94, mem. bd. govs., 1995-98. Avocations: photography, swimming, running, golf. Office: Akin Gump Strauss Hauer & Feld LLP 1700 Pacific Ave Ste 4100 Dallas TX 75201-4675 Office Phone: 214-969-2711. Office Fax: 214-969-4343. Business E-Mail: cdavis@akingump.com.

DAVIS, CONNIE WATERS, public relations executive, marketing professional; b. Gainesville, Ga., July 3, 1948; d. Starling Randolph and Evelyn Jeanette (Bonds) Waters; m. John W. Davis Jr., Sept. 24, 1971; 1 child, John Christopher. AA, Gainesville Jr. Coll., 1968; BA in Human Resources Mgmt., Brenau U., 1988; postgrad., Student Evaluation Inst. of Washington, 1988, U. Ga., 1972-73, 85—. Project evaluator Model Cities Program, Gainesville, 1970-74; pers. dir. Lanier Pk. Hosp., Gainesville, 1977-79; asst. dir. Ga. Mountains Ctr., Gainesville, 1979-83; owner, CEO Models by Davis and Davis, Gainesville, 1979—; dir. pub. rels. and sales Ramada Hotel, Gainesville, 1985—; dir. corp. devel. Chestatee Regional Hosp. Dir. Fashion Works, Gainesville; pres. Davis Consulting; owner & pres. Tastefully & Properly Growing Up, 1998—; cons. pub. rels. and mktg., dir. of pub. rels. UP Corp. Devel. Specialty Clinics Ga. Prodr., writer, implementor Gracefully and Properly Growing Up; contbr. articles to mags. and newsletters; writer nat. poulty industry publ., 1990, 95. Publicity chmn. Cancer Soc., 1982, 83, 85; mem. Theatre Wings and Arts Coun.; bd. dirs., mem. mktg. com. Gainesville Jr. Coll., 1985—, trustee, 1995—; bd. dirs. ARC, 1978-79; co-chmn. Flag Com. for Olympics; bd. dirs. Greater-Hall C. of C., 2003—. Recipient Peach award Lions Club, 1979, Vol. award ARC, 1978, various modeling awards So. Models Assn., 1983, 2 Silver Shovel award 1993, 94, state vol. award, 1995; named Best Dressed Woman, Fashion Tour Group, 1984. Mem. Am. Heart Assn. (pres. 1995-96), Am. Lung Assn. (state bd. dirs., Vol. of Yr.), Greater Hall C. of C. (bd. dirs.), Gainesville C. of C., Gainesville Coll. Exec. Coun., Tourism and Conv. Bur. (chmn. 1983-84), N.E. Ga. Advt. Club, Pers. Adminstrs. Group, Ga. Hospitality and Travel Assn., Phoenix Soc., Greater Hall C. of C. (bd. dirs. 2003-), Rotary (cotillion dir. 1998—), Fashion Club (bd. dirs.). Avocations: exercising, skiing, boating, jogging, writing, music, arts. Home: 1214 Chestatee Rd Gainesville GA 30501-2816

DAVIS, D. LAVELDA, dean, academic administrator; d. Howard and Alice Mae Davis; 1 child, Shawnelle Tatianna White. BA in Polit. Sci., Syracuse U., NY, 1980; MDiv, All Faiths Sem. Internat., NYC, 2003; PhD in Divinity, Commonwealth Open U., NY, 2004, Dr of the Univ. (hon.), 2006. Lic. interfaith min. New Light Temple, NY, 2002, cert. theol. youth leader NY Theol. Sem., 1996, ordained deaconess Bapt. Ch., 1996. Human resouce generalist GreenPoint Bank, Lake Success, NY, 1998—2001, mem. staff NYC, 2001—05; assoc. dean All Faiths Sem. Internat., NYC, 2004—05, dean, 2005—; engring. adminstr. Hofstra U., Hempstead, NY, 2006—; sr. pastor New Light Temple, 2005—. Owner, CEO Davida Enterprises, Bklyn., 2003—; founder Counseling for Clerics, Bklyn., 2005—; spiritual advisor All Faiths Sem., NYC, 2002—03; founding mem. Tribeca Spiritual Ctr., NYC, 2001—03, celebration chmn., 2001—03, chmn. bd. trustees, 2001—03. Contbr. audio book New Light Temple Internat. Contbr. United Spinal Assn., Milford, NH, 1997—2006. Mem.: Assn. Interfaith Ministers, Nat. Notary Assn., So. Poverty Law Ctr. (assoc.; named to Wall of Tolerance 2005—06), Thirteen NY, Build the Dream (assoc.; founding sponsor 2006), Wildlife Conservation (assoc.), Schomberg Soc. (assoc.). Dfl. Avocations: sports, travel, reading, crafts, crocheting. Home: P O Box 470888 Brooklyn NY 11247-0888 Office: All Faiths Sem Internat 7 West 96th St Ste 19B New York NY 10025 Office Phone: 212-866-3795. Personal E-mail: revdavida@verizon.net.

DAVIS, DAISY SIDNEY, history professor; b. Matagorda County, Tex., Nov. 7, 1944; d. Alex C. and Alice M. (Edison) Sidney; m. John Dee Davis, Apr. 17, 1968; children: Anaca Michelle, Lowell Kent. BS, Bishop Coll., 1966; MS, East Tex. State U., Commerce, 1971; MEd, Prairie View A&M U., Tex., 1980; postgrad., U. Tex., Tex. A&M U. Cert. profl. lifetime secondary tchr., Tex.; mid-mgmt. adminstr. Tchr. Dallas Pub. Schs., 1966—2004, history dept chairperson, 1998—2004, substitute tchr., 2004—. Instr. Am. History El Centro Coll., 1991-98; scorer SAT and Tex. Assessment of Knowledge Skills; adv. Am. history telecourse Dallas Cournty C.C. dist. Coord. Get Out the Vote campaign, Dallas, 1972, 80, 84, 88, 92, 94, 96, 98, 2000, 02, 04; sec., bd. trustees St. John Bapt. Ch., 1995-98; pres. The Amazons. Recipient Outstanding Tchr. award Dallas pub. schs., 1980, Jack Lowe award for ednl. excellence, 1982; Free Enterprise scholar So. Meth. U., 1987; Constl. fellow U. Dallas, 1988; named to Hall of Fame, Holmes Acad., 1979. Mem. NEA, Tex. State Tchrs. Assn., Classroom Tchrs. Dallas (faculty rep. 1971-77, 95—), Dallas County History Tchrs., Afro-Am. Daus. Republic of Tex. (founder), Top Ladies of Distinction, Zeta Phi Beta. Clubs: Jack & Jill Assocs., (Dallas) (rec. sec., v.p., chair Beautillion Ball, pres., Disting. Mother award, Nat. Committment award 1997). Democrat. Baptist. Home: 1302 Mill Stream Dr Dallas TX 75232-4604

DAVIS, DARNA BETTS, elementary school educator; b. Glendale, Ariz., Feb. 14, 1979; d. Darnell and Edna Rallos Betts; m. George Earl Davis, Nov. 12, 1999; 1 child, Alexander Keoki. BA in Elem. Edn., Ariz. State U., Phoenix, 1997—2001. 5th grade tchr. Moon Mountain Elem. Sch., Phoenix, 2001—05, Sunnyslope Elem. Sch., Phoenix, 2005—; reading intervention tchr., 2006—. Sec. Ariz. State U. Coll. of Tchr. Edn. and Leadership Alumni Bd., 2005—06. Grantee Leadership scholarship, Ariz. State U., 1997—2001, Pepsi Cola, 1999—2001; scholar medallion of Merit, Ariz. State U. Alumni Assn., 1997—2001. Mem.: NEA, ASCD, Internat. Reading Assn., Ariz. State U. Alumni Assn. (life), Golden Key Nat. Honor Soc. Democrat. Office: Sunnyslope Elem Sch 801 W Peoria Ave Phoenix AZ 85029 Office Phone: 602-347-4300. Personal E-mail: supersmileymom@gmail.com. Business E-Mail: ddavis@ss.wesd.k12.az.us.

DAVIS, DEBORAH ANN ST. CYR, elementary school educator; b. Oklahoma City, Dec. 30, 1956; d. Lester Adrian and Maxine Gladys (Smith) St. Cyr; m. Kenneth N. Davis, May 25, 1980; children: Dustin, Adrienne. B Art Edn., U. Ctrl. Okla., 1978, MEd, 1980. Cert. tchr., Ark. Art tchr. Mustang (Okla.) Pub. Schs., 1978-81, art and 2d grade tchr., 1985-90; 2d, 3d and 6th grade tchr. Eureka Springs (Ark.) Pub. Schs., 1990—; owner bed and breakfast Old Orchard Inn, Eureka Springs, 19936; elem. prin. Springdale Schs., Ark., 2004—. Commr. Hist. Dist. Commn., Eureka Springs, 1993—. Recipient 2d Pl.-Open award Internat. Paper Co. Found./Nat. Coun. Econ. Edn., 1993. Mem. Eureka Springs Edn. Assn. (membership chair 1994-95, pres. 1993), Preservation Soc. (v.p. 1994-95, award 1994). Mem. Lds Ch. Avocations: painting, weaving, historic preservation. Home: 403 JTL Pkwy E Springdale AR 72762-8405

DAVIS, DEBRA ANN, secondary school educator; b. Houston, Nov. 2, 1967; d. James Lawrence Camden and Marilyn Lee De Moss; m. Mark Alexander Davis, Mar. 9, 2002. BS in Animal/Equine Sci., Colo. State U., Ft. Collins, 1993; postgrad., Colo. State U., 1994—96. Cert. secondary edn. tchr. Rsch. asst. Colo. State U. Vet. Tchg. Hosp., Ft. Collins, 1993—96; agr. tchr. Columbia Brazoria Ind. Sch. Dist., Brazoria, Tex., 1997—99; biology tchr. Humble Ind. Sch. Dist., Tex., 1999—2003; physics and chemistry tchr. Cypress Fairbanks Ind. Sch. Dist., Houston, 2003—05, physics tchr., 2005—. Recipient Tchr. Appreciation award, FFA, 1998. Mem.: Houston Livestock Show and Rodeo, Assn. of Tex. Profl. Educators, Nat. Sci. Tchrs. Assn. Republican. Methodist. Avocations: travel, Collies, music, photography. Home: 7006 Autumn Flowers Dr Katy TX 77449 Office: Cypress Ridge High School 7900 N Eldridge Pkwy Houston TX 77041

DAVIS, DEBRA GREER, educational association administrator; b. Crocker, Mo., Mar. 4, 1956; d. Clifford Eugene and Emogene Telitha (Bullock) Greer; m. Rodney Neal Davis, July 1, 1978; children: Neal Stephen, Kimberly Reneé, Paul Andrew. B of Music Edn., S.E. Mo. State U., 1978. Cert. vocal music educator, K-12; cert. tchr., Mo., Iowa. Pvt. piano instr., Cape Girardeau, Mo., 1980-96; ch. pianist First Bapt. Ch., Cape Girardeau, Mo., 1987-90; music educator Cape Girardeau (Mo.) Pub. Sch., 1987-91, St. Augustine Sch., Kelso, Mo., 1991-93, Altenburg (Mo.) Pub. Sch., 1991-96; nursing libr. St. Francis Med. Ctr., Cape Girardeau, 1992-96; music educator Spickard (Mo.) R-2 Sch., 1996-97, Harrison R-IV Sch., Gilman City, Mo., 1997, Scott County R-IV Schs., Benton, Mo., 2003—04; adminstr. The Christian Acad., Sikeston, Mo., 2004—. Instr. Music Preparatory Program, S.E. Mo. State U., Cape Girardeau, 1990-92; dist. music try-out judge S.E. Mo. Dist. Music Educators, Cape Girardeau, 1992; sr. grant coord. disease prevention com. St. Francis Med. Ctr., Cape Girardeau, 1995-96, mem. healing environment, 1994-96. Accompanist: (cassette tape) Open Your Hear's Door-Charlene Peyton, 1994; editor: (booklet) Ann. Nursing Report-St. Francis Med. Ctr., 1995. Accompanist L.J. Schultz Mid. Sch. Choir, Cape Girardeau, 1992-93, Cape Girardeau H.S. Chamber Choir, 1993, Charles Clippard Elem. Sch. Choir, Cape Girardeau, 1996, Mo. Bapt. Conv., Cape Girardeau, 1994. Mem. Mo. Educators Assn., Music Educators Nat. Conf. Avocations: counted cross stitch, music.

DAVIS, DIANN HOLMES, elementary school educator; b. NYC, July 5, 1949; d. Henry F. and Pearl B. Holmes; m. Milton Davis, July 24, 1973; children: Milton, Keith, Madelyn. AA, N.Y. Tech. Coll., 1971; BS cum laude, Medgar Evers Coll., Bklyn., 1981; MA, Columbia U., N.Y.C., 1994. Lic. reading and early childhood. Sci. tchr. JHS 166, IS 302 Future Day Care, Bklyn.; tchr. N.Y. Bd. Edn., Bklyn. Dance tchr. Faith Hope and Charity Day Care Ctrs.; parent rep. Start Smart; mem. Bklyn. (N.Y.) Reading Coun. Common Brs.; tchr. Nat. Bapt. Congress. Mem. Hall of Sci., Bklyn. Children's Museum, Assn. for Study of Curriculum Devel. Avocations: bicycle riding, ice skating, roller skating, dance, sewing.

DAVIS, DIANNE, music educator; b. Cleve. d. Lee Frederick and Mary Kate McQueen; 1 child from previous marriage, Travis. BS in Music Edn., Ky. State U., 1966. Cert. Ohio Bd. Edn. Vocal music tchr., Gary, Ind., 1966—68; vocal instr. Cleve. Music Sch. Settlement, 1977—82; dir. Sanaa Music Sch., Cleve., 1982—, Music Inc., Cleve., 1991—; vocal music tchr. East Cleveland City Schs., 1997—. Bd. dirs. The Cleve. Fine Arts Soc., 1995. Mem.: Ohio Edn. Assn., Music Educators Nat. Conf., Alpha Kappa Alpha. Baptist. Avocations: cooking, designing, home remodeling, gardening, entertaining. Home: 24412 Emery Rd Cleveland OH 44128 Office: East Cleveland City Schs 15320 Euclid Ave East Cleveland OH 44112 Personal E-mail: diannedavis@msn.com.

DAVIS, DORINNE SUE, audiologist; b. East Orange, N.J., Mar. 29, 1949; d. William Henry and Evelyn Doris (Thorp) Taylor; children: Larissa Louise, Peter Alexander. BA, Montclair State Coll., 1971, MA, 1973. Cert. tchr. of hearing impaired, speech correctionist, tchr. speech and drama, supr. nursery sch. endorsement, N.J. Ednl. audiologist Kinnelon (N.J.) Bd. Edn., 1972-94, kindergarten tchr., 1994-97; ednl. audiologist Inst. for Career Advancement, Inc., 1980-82, Dover Gen. Hosp., 1984-86; pres. Hear You Are, Inc., 1987-98, Davis Ctr. Hearing Speech and Learning, Inc., Budd Lake, NJ, 1998—2002; with Davis Ctrs., Inc., 2002—05, The Davis Ctr., 2005—. Adj. prof. Kean Coll., Union, NJ, 1993—95, Ctr. Mich. U., 2005—06. Mem. NEA, Internat. Orgn. Educators Hearing Impaired, Am. Speech and Hearing Assn. (cert. clin. competence in audiology), Am. Acad. Audiology, N.J. Speech and Hearing Assn., N.J. Edn. Assn., Ednl. Audiology Assn. (past pres.). Methodist. Home: 51 King Rd Landing NJ 07850-1308 Office: The Davis Ctr 200 Valley Rd Ste 205 Mount Arlington NJ 07856 Office Phone: 973-398-2710. Business E-Mail: ddavis@thedaviscenter.com.

DAVIS, DORIS JOHNSON, retired music educator; b. Yazoo City, Miss., Nov. 26, 1947; d. Floyd Lee and Bessie Louvenia Johnson B of Music Edn., Jackson State U., 1970; B of Music Therapy, Loyola U., 1973; M of Music Edn., William Carey Coll., 1975; postgrad. in Computer Tech. and Adult Edn., U. So. Miss. Cert. tchr. spl. subjects, Miss.; registered music therapist. Music tchr. Ft. Wayne (Ind.) Cmty. Schs., 1970-71; clin. intern, music therapy Cen. La. State Hosp., 1973; music therapist Ellisville (Miss.) State Sch., 1974-75; music tchr. Forrest County Sch. Sys., Hattiesburg, Miss., 1976-81; music instr. Prentiss (Miss.) Jr. Coll., 1975-76, 81-82; clk. typist Hattiesburg Pub. Libr., 1983-87; ch. musician Zion Chapel AME Ch., Hattiesburg, 1982-95, True Light Bapt. Ch., Hattiesburg, 1995-2000; music tchr. Hattiesburg Pub. Sch. Dist., 1987—2002; ret., 2002. Tchr. from home, Hattiesburg, 1998—. Vol. youth dept. Star Light Band, True Light Bapt. Ch., Hattiesburg, 1999—; mem. NAACP, Hattiesburg. Named to Outstanding Young Women of Am., 1979, 82; recipient scholarship So. Ill. U., 1965. Mem. Am. Fedn. Tchrs., Music Educators Nat. Conf. Democrat. Avocations: genealogy, computers, reading, walking. Home: 703 Myrtle St Hattiesburg MS 39401-4850 Personal E-mail: djdavis@megagate.com.

DAVIS, DORIS ROSENBAUM (DEE DAVIS), artist, writer; b. N.Y.C., Nov. 7, 1919; d. Lewis Newman and Bella (Wretnikow) Rosenbaum; m. Lewis F. Davis, Aug. 13, 1940 (div. Dec. 1989); children: Laurie, Peter. BA, Sarah Lawrence Coll., 1941. Crafts instr. Cooper Hewitt Mus., N.Y.C., 1977-87, Pratt Inst., N.Y.C., 1988-92, Am. Craft Mus., N.Y.C., 1996—2004, Adventures in Crafts, N.Y.C., 1971—2006. Represented in permanent collections Cooper-Hewitt Mus., Am. Craft Mus., Mus. City of N.Y., Gracie Mansion, Sarah Lawrence Coll.; author: Découpage, 1995, Decoupage, A Practical Guide, 2000; co-author: Step by Step Découpage, 1976, The Découpage Gallery, 2001, The Victorian Scrap Gallery, 2003; contbr. articles on découpage, faux finishes, gilding to craft mags.; appeared in (TV series) Our Home, 1997—98, HGTV, 2001. Democrat. Jewish. Avocations: traveling abroad, visiting museums, galleries, reading, classical music. Office Phone: 212-410-9793. Personal E-mail: deecoupage@aol.com.

DAVIS, DOROTHY SALISBURY, writer; b. Chgo., Apr. 26, 1916; d. Alfred Joseph and Margaret Jane (Greer) Salisbury; m. Harry Davis, Apr. 25, 1946 (dec.). AB, Barat Coll., Lake Forest, Ill., 1938. Mystery and hist. novelist, short story writer. Author: A Gentle Murderer, 1951, A Town of Masks, 1952, Men of No Property, 1956, Death of an Old Sinner, 1957, A Gentleman Called, 1958, The Evening of the Good Samaritan, 1961, Black Sheep, White Lamb, 1963, The Pale Betrayer, 1965, Enemy and Brother, 1967, God Speed The Night, 1968, Where the Dark Streets Go, 1969, Shock Wave, 1972, The Little Brothers, 1973, A Death in the Life, 1976, Scarlet Night, 1980, A Lullaby of Murder, 1984, Tales for a Stormy Night, 1985, The Habit of Fear, 1987, In the Still of the Night, 2000. Recipient Life Achievement award Bouchereon, 1989. Mem. Authors Guild, Mystery Writers of Am. (former pres., recipient Grand Master award 1985), Adams Roundtable. Home: PO Box 595 Palisades NY 10964-0595

DAVIS, ELBA LUCILA, veterans affairs nurse; b. San Juan, P.R., Feb. 25, 1945; d. Eladio Millan and Fidencia Walker; m. Joseph Edward Davis; children: Pauly Lucille, Joelyne Lucille. BS Mgmt., Columbian Union Coll., 1995; Cosmetology degree, Hollywood Acad., College Park, Md., 1988; Principles of Real Estates degree, Prince Georges C.C., Largo, Md., 2001. RN P.R., 1971. Student aide Columbus Hosp., N.Y.C., 1963—64; med. asst. Dr. Durruthy's Office, Bronx, NY, 1964; officinist P.R. Lottery, Rio Piedras, 1965—67; nurse Saint Martin's Hosp., Rio Piedras, PR, 1971, Carolina (P.R.) Mcpl. Hosp., 1971—76, Walter Reed Army Med. Ctr., Silver Spring, Md., 1976—80; cosmetologist Hair Cuttery, Wheaton, Md., 1993—93; nurse VA Med. Ctr., Washington, 1980—. Unit preceptor VA Med. Ctr., Washington, 1985—, chairperson edn. IV Team, 2001—, rep. safety com., 1995—96, rep. product com., 1995—96, rep. standard of care com., 1992—94, rep. quality assurance com., 1981—83, rep. scheduling com. IV Team, 2001—. Actor: (video prodn.) Annual Infection Control Review Video, 1997, (Video) VA Med. Ctr. BCMA Sys./Japanese Prodn., 2001; (films) The Replacements, 1999. Active Wild Life Defendant, Washington, 2001; RN Anthrax Hotline Channel 9 News on Anthrax, Washington, 2001. Mem.: Fed. Women's Program, Washington DC Nurses Assn. Mem. Seventh Day Adventist. Avocations: reading, bicycling, exercise, crafts, singing.

DAVIS, ELENA DENISE, accountant; b. Rome, NY, June 24, 1953; d. Robert Frederick and Arlene Ruth (Fravor) Vrooman; m. Joseph E. Davis, Dec. 24, 1975 (div. Nov. 1988); children: JoAnna Lynn, Robert George, Crystal Leigh. AS, Jefferson C.C., Watertown, N.Y., 1975; BSBA, Orlando Coll., 1995, BS in Acctg., 1995; MBA in Acctg., Fla. Met. U., 2001. Staff acct., asst. mgr. Vrooman's Tire & Rd. Svc. Inc., Adams, N.Y., 1975-89; claim assoc. Hartford Ins., Maitland, Fla., 1989-97; acct. Raybob Plumbing Co. Inc., Orlando, 1997-98, Ctrl. Sweeping Svc., Inc., Winter Garden, Fla., 1998-99; staff acct., office mgr. Engelmeier Roofing & Sheet Metal Co., Inc., Lockhart, Fla., 1999—2003; acct. Mr. Foamy of Cen. Fla., LLC, Orlando, 2004—; owner Vrooman's, 2000—. Active Boy Scouts Am., Girl Scouts Am., PTA; Sunday sch. tchr. Methodist Ch., 1984-89; coord. Meth. Ch. Nursery. Mem.: NAFE, Nat. Notary Assn. (signing agent). Home: PO Box 721 Ocoee FL 34761-0721

DAVIS, ELISABETH BACHMAN, librarian, library administration educator; b. Effingham, Ill., Mar. 13, 1932; d. Raymond Lawrence and Serena Mildred (Houston) Bachman; m. James Henry Davis, June 27, 1954; children: Stephen James, Kristin Elisabeth, Leah Elisabeth. BS in Bacteriology, U. Ill., 1954, MS in LS, 1970. Bacteriologist Mich. Dept. Health, Lansing, 1956-59; asst. biology libr. U. Ill., Urbana, 1969-70, biology libr., 1971-96; prof. libr. adminstrn., 1987-96; prof. emeritus, 1996—. Author: Using the Biological Literature, 1995, Guide to Information Sources in the Botanical Sciences, 1995; also numerous articles. Mem. World Heritage Mus. Guild, Urbana, 1990—. Mem. AAAS, Spl. Librs. Assn. (chmn. biol. scis. div. 1983), Med. Libr. Assn. (cert.), Coun. on Bot. and Hort. Librs., Phi Beta Kappa, Alpha Lambda Delta, Phi Kappa Phi, Beta Phi Mu. Avocations: reading, swimming. Office: U Ill Biology Libr 101 Burrill Hall 407 S Goodwin Ave Urbana IL 61801-3704

DAVIS, ELIZABETH EILEEN, education educator; b. West Point, NY, Nov. 3, 1967; d. Buster Keaton and Rita Ann Davis. AA in Info. Sys., Anne Arundel Cmty. Coll., 1990; BS in Info. Systems, U. Balt., 1992, BS in Bus. Mgmt., 1992; advanced tchg. cert., Coll. Notre Dame, 1996, MEd, 2000. Computer operator Nat. Security Agy., Ft. Meade, Md., 1985—86; mktg. rep. Spl. Programs Inc., Glen Burnie, Md., 1990—96; elem. sch. tchr. Balt. City Sch. Sys., 1996—, spl. edn. tchr., 2003—04. Coord. Balt. symphony orch. Balt. Pub. Sch., 1996—98. Sunday sch. tchr. Glen Burnie Evangelical Presbyn., 1987. Mem.: ASCD.

DAVIS, EMMY MAE, school system administrator; b. Painsville, Ohio, July 29, 1976; d. William Harris Chapek and Kathlynn Jo Davis; children: Abby Kathlynn, Jesse Elias. Bachelor's degree, Ohio Dominican Coll., Columbus, Ohio, 1997; Master's degree, U. Findlay, Ohio, 2005. Tchr. grades 5-8 St. John's Luth. Sch., Marysville, Ohio, 1998—2000; tchr. grades 7-12 Elgin Local Schs., Marion, Ohio, 2000—01; tchr. 12th grade Tri-Rivers Career Ctr., Marion, 2002—05; curriculum dir. Benjamin Logan Local Schs., Belfontaine, Ohio, 2005—. Pub. spkr Tri-Rivers Career Ctr., Marion, 2002—05. Prayer chmn. Marysville Aglow, Marysville, 1999—2004. Recipient Gene Glick Action Rsch. grant, Ohio ASCD, 2005. Mem.: ASCD. Avocations: writing, reading, painting, public speaking, travel.

DAVIS, EVANGELYN S., elementary school educator; d. Thomas Hosea and Janie Melrose Singleton; m. Ronald B. Davis, Mar. 15, 1985; children: Keith A. Jackson, Tasha L. BS, Bethune-Cookman Coll., Daytona Beach, 1970—74. Lic. tchr. Fla., 1974. Tchr. Enterprise Elem. Sch., Fla., 1974—75; tchr./reading coach Holly Hill Elem. Sch., Fla., 1995—. Christian edn. dir. Allen Chapel A.M.E. Ch., Daytona Beach, 2005—06. Recipient Tchr. of Month, Holly Hill Elem. Sch., 2004—05. Mem.: Alpha Kappa Alpha Sorority, Inc. (life; epistelous 1995—96). Democrat-Npl. African Methodist Episcopal. Home: 2 Indianbow Ln Ormond Beach FL 32174 Office: Holly Hill Elem Sch 1500 Center Ave Holly Hill FL 32117

DAVIS, FLOREA JEAN, social worker; b. Crossett, Ark., Jan. 10, 1953; d. Richard Davis and Geneva (Bedford) Williams. BA in Psychology and Social Work cum laude, Park Coll., Parksville, Mo., 1975; MSW, Kans. U., 1982. Cert. secondary tchr. social studies; lic. social worker, Kans.; lic. specialist clin. social work. Asst. dir. Northeast Coordination and Devel. Ctr., Kansas City, Kans., 1975; asst. dir., clin. supr. DRAG Alcohol Ctr., Kansas City, 1975-83; substance abuse counselor Johnson County Substance Abuse Ctr., Shawnee, Kans., 1983-85; clin. social worker Family & Children Services, Inc., Kansas City, 1975-88; area svc. mgr. Agy. Heart of Am. Family Svcs., Kansas City, 1988-90; sr. practitioner Crittenton, Kansas City, Mo., 1990—; dir. Wyandotte Christian Counseling Ctr., Kansas City, Kans., 1995—; employee asst. counselor St. Luke Health Sys., 2002—; social work instr. U. Kans. Social Welfare Dept., 2006. Instr. U. Kans., Lawrence, 1976: substance abuse specialist, cons. Kansas City area, 1985—; part-time instr. Avila Coll., Kansas City, Mo., 1987—; sr. practitioner Kansas City Outpatient Clinic, Crittenton, Kans., 1990—; behavioral health cons. KCMC Child Devel. Ctr., 1999-2000; counselor Saint Luke EAP Office, Kansas City, 2002—; ednl. cons., presenter Donnelly Coll., 2002—; lectr. in field. Co-author: Human Services and Social Change: An African-American Church Perspective, 1992. Vol. United Way Spkrs. Bur., 1986—. Named to Wall of Tolerance, Nat. Campaign for Tolerance, 2004. Mem. NASW (clin. diplomat), Acad. Cert. Social Workers, Next Step Counseling & Consulting Assn. (pres., founder). Avocations: reading, singing, tennis, travel. Home: 1216 N 77th St Kansas City KS 66112-2408 Office: Crittenton S Kans City 10920 Elm Ave Kansas City MO 64134-4108 Personal E-mail: Flo_rejoice@sbcglobal.net.

DAVIS, FLORENCE ANN, lawyer; b. Pitts., Feb. 22, 1955; d. Richard Davis and Charlotte (Saul) McGhee; m. Kevin J. O'Brien, May 28, 1978; children: Rebecca Davis, Sarah Davis. AB, Wellesley U., 1976; JD, NYU, 1979. Bar: N.Y. 1980, U.S. Dist. Ct. (ea. and so. dists.) N.Y., N.Y. Ct. Appeals (2d cir.), U.S. Tax Ct., U.S. Supreme Ct. Assoc. atty. Sullivan & Cromwell, N.Y.C., 1979-86; litigation counsel Morgan Stanley & Co., N.Y.C., 1986-88, v.p., 1988-90, dir. compliance, 1989-90, prin., 1990-95; v.p., gen. counsel Am. Internat. Group, N.Y.C., 1995—. Pres. Starr Found. Root-Tilden scholar NYU Law Sch., 1976-79. Mem. Securities Industry Assn. (v.p. edn. Compliance and Legal div. 1992, exec. com. Compliance and Legal div. 1990-92). Office: American International Group Inc 70 Pine St New York NY 10270-0094*

DAVIS, GEENA (VIRGINIA DAVIS), actress; b. Wareham, Mass., Jan. 21, 1957; m. Richard Emmolo, March 25, 1982 (div. Feb. 26, 1983); m. Jeff Goldblum, Nov. 1, 1987 (div. Oct. 17, 1990); m. Renny Harlin, Sept. 18, 1993 (div. June 21, 1998); m. Reza Jarrahy, Sept. 1, 2001; children Alizeh Keshvar Davis Jarrahy, Kian William, Kaiis Steven. BFA, Boston U., 1979; attended, New England Coll., Henniker, N.H. Founder Genial Pictures; mem. My. Washington (N.H.) Repertory Theatre Co. Actor: (films) Tootsie, 1982, Fletch, 1985, Transylvania 6-5000, 1985, The Fly, 1986, Beetlejuice, 1988, The Accidental Tourist, 1988 (Academy award Best Supporting Actress, 1989), Earth Girls Are Easy, 1989, Quick Change, 1990, Thelma and Louise, 1991 (Acad. award nominee Best Actress 1991, British Acad Film and TV Arts award Best Actress in leading role 1991, Golden Globe award nominee Best Actress 1991), A League of Their Own, 1992, Hero, 1992, Princess Scargo and the Birthday Pumpkin (voice), 1993, Angie, 1994, Speechless, 1994 (also prodr.), Cutthroat Island, 1995, The Long Kiss Goodnight, 1996, Stuart Little, 1999, Stuart Little 2, 2002; TV series: Buffalo Bill, 1983-84 (also wrote), Sara, 1985, The Geena Davis Show, 2000 (also co-exec. prodr.), Commander-in-Chief, 2005-06(Best Performance by an Actress in a TV Series-Drama, Hollywood Fgn. Press Assn (Golden Globe award), 2006; appeared in TV film Secret Weapons, 1985; exec. prodr. Mistrial, 1996; TV appearances include Knight Rider, 1983, Fantasy Island, 1984, Family Ties 1984, Remington Steele, 1985, Will & Grace, 2004. Recipient Matrix award for arts & entertainment, NY Women in Comm. Inc., 2006. Avocation: archery. Office: Creative Artists Agy 9830 Wilshire Blvd Beverly Hills CA 90212*

DAVIS, GLORIA WHITTIE, educational association administrator; d. Jim Daniel Whittie and Sadie Whittie Smith; m. Clarence Earl Davis, June 10, 1995; 1 child, Eric Wayne Whittie. BA in Criminal Justice, Lamar U., 1991; MA in Counseling, Prairie View A&M U., 1998, MA in Vocat. Edn., 2005. Dir. Tobacco Prevention Program, Beaumont, 2000; program coord. Family Literacy Program, Beaumont, 2001—. Employment supr. Tex. Work Force, Beaumont, 1973—99. Singer, writer, actor (performance) Gospel Music Work Shop of America (Excellence award, 2005). Registrar Tex. Mass Choir, Beaumont, 1993; bd. mem. Even Start, Beaumont, 2000, com. mem. Austin, Tex., 2004; instr. Texas Honors Leadership Program; choir pres. City Wide Musical; vol. Cmty. Outreach Program; deaconess Word of God Christian Ch., Beaumont, 1999. Recipient Beaumont Leadership award, 1984, Tex. Honors Leadership award, Tex., 2001-2004, Black Gospel Music award, Beaumont, 2004, Leadership Coun. Wall of Tolerance, So. Poverty Law Ctr., 2004. Mem.: Am. Counselling Assn., Nat. Ctr. Family Literacy, Internat. Assn. Pers. Employment Sys., Ea. Star. Home: 13350 Moss Hill Dr Beaumont TX 77713 Office: Lamar U PO Box 10034 Beaumont TX 77710 Home Fax: 409-753-2261; Office Fax: 409-880-1880. Personal E-mail: gdavis@aol.com. E-mail: gdavis7646@aol.com.

DAVIS, GWENDOLYN LOUISE, military officer, literature educator; b. Toledo, Dec. 8, 1951; d. Robert Louis and Marietta Beatrice (Sautter) Davis; m. Barry Dennis Fayne, Jan. 6, 1979 (div. Feb. 2001); children: Ashleigh Elizabeth, Zachary Alexandur-John. BFA, So. Meth. U., 1972; MEd, U. North Tex., 1978; MA, U. Denver, 1987. Cert. tchr., Tex., Ala.; cert. secondary tchg. Am. Montessori Soc. Substitute tchr., Toledo and Dallas, 1972-73; film dir. Channel 39 Christian Broadcasting Network, Dallas, 1973-75; engr., air oper. Channel 40 Trinity Broadcasting Network, Tustin, Calif., 1978; commd. 2d lt. USAF, 1978, advanced through grades to maj., 1989, ret., 1995; mgr. western area Hdqrs. USAFR Officers Tng. Corp., Norton AFB, Calif., 1979-81; chief tng. systems support Hdqrs. Air Force Manpower Pers. Pentagon, Washington, 1981-84; pers. policies officer J1, Orgn. of Joint Chiefs of Staff Pentagon, Washington, 1984-85; asst. prof. English, dir. forensics USAF Acad., Colorado Springs, Colo., 1987-92; adj. faculty mem. dept. English Auburn U., Montgomery, Ala., 1994-95; adj. faculty mem. dept. arts and scis. Troy State U., Montgomery, 1994-96; dir. Bullock County HS Learning Ctr., Union Springs, Ala., 1995-96; tech. and acad. tchr. Ctr. for Advanced Tech. Booker T. Washington Magnet H.S., Montgomery, 1996; tchr. speech and English Mountain Brook H.S., Birmingham, Ala., 1997-98; tchr. humanities Joseph Bruno Montessori Acad., Birmingham, 1998-2000; upperschool dir. Sacred Heart Ch. Sch., 2000—01, ednl. cons., 2001—; founder, dir. Shiloh Village Montessori H.S., 2002—04; tchr. Spring Valley Sch., 2004—. Assoc. editor Airpower Jour., Maxwell AFB, Ala., 1992-94, mil. doctrine analyst, 1994-95; chmn. mil. affairs Jr. Officer's Coun., Norton AFB, 1981; invited spkr. in field; chmn. program devel. com. for nat. orgn. Cross Exam. Debate Assn., 1990-91. Contbr. articles to profl. jours. Tchr., mem. choir, soloist various chs., 1973; chair publicity com. Birthright, Inc., Woodbridge, Va., 1983. Named Command Jr. Officer of Yr., Hdqrs. USAFR Officers Tng. Corps, 1979. Mem. Nat. Parliamentary Debate Assn. (co-founder, editor Parliamentary Debate jour. 1992-95), Am. Montessori Soc., Phi Upsilon Omicron. Avocations: reading, antiques, sight-seeing. Home: 2526 Acton Park Ln Birmingham AL 35243 Personal E-mail: gwendavis1@aol.com.

DAVIS, HELEN GORDON, retired state senator; b. NYC, 1926; m. Gene Davis; children: Stephanie, Karen, Gordon. BA, Bklyn. Coll.; postgrad., U. South Fla., 1967—70. Tchr. High Sch. Commerce, N.Y.C., Hillsborough High Sch., Tampa, Fla.; grad. asst. U. South Fla., 1968; mem. Fla. Ho. of Reps. (1st woman to be elected in 1974 from Hills Co., 1st woman to chair the legis. del.), 1974-88; state senator Fla., 1988-92; mem. Fla. Supreme Ct. Commn. on Gender Bias in the Cts., 1988-90, Fla. Supreme Ct. Commn. on Mediation and Arbitration, 1987—. Chmn. senate appropriations subcom. human svcs., mem. rules com., internat. trade and econ. devel. com., health and rehab. svcs. com. Jud. chmn. Local Govt. Study Commn. Hillsborough County (Fla.), 1964; mem. Tampa Commn. on Juvenile Delinquency, 1966-69, Mayor's Citizens Adv. Com., 1966-69, Quality Edn. Commn., 1966-68, Gov.'s Citizen Com. for Ct. Reform, 1972, Hillsborough County Planning commn., 1973-74; mem. Gov.'s Commn. on Jud. Reform, 1976; mem. employment com. Commn. Cmty. Rels., 1966-69; by-laws chmn. Arts Coun. Tampa, 1971-74; 1st v.p. Tampa Symphony Guild, 1974; bd. dirs. U. South Fla. Found., 1968-74, Stop Rape, 1973-74; past pres. PTA; active adv. commn. Nat. Child Care Action Campaign, Nat. Ctr. for Crime and Delinquency; chair Hillsborough Dem. Exec. Com., also pres.; active Fla. Com. on the Status of Women, 2001. Recipient U. South Fla. Young Dems. Humanitarian award, 1974, Diana award NOW, 1975, Woman of Achievement in Arts award Tampa, 1975, Tampa Human Rels. award, 1976, Hannah G. Solomon Citizen of Yr., 1980, St. Petersburg Times/Fla. Civil Liberties award, 1980, Friend of Edn. award, 1981, Fla. Alliance for Responsible Parenting award, 1981, Humanitarian award Judeo-Christian Clinic, 1984, Fla. Network of Runaway Youth award, 1985, Ctr. for Women Leader-adv. Friend award, 1985, Nat. Assn. Juvenile Ct. Judges Appreciation award, 1987, AAUW Leadership award, 1987, Hillsborough County Halfway House appreciation award, 1988, Martin Luther King award City of Tampa, 1988, Appreciation award Nat. Fedn. Dem. Women, 1989, Dept. Legal Affairs appreciation, 1990, Superwoman award Mus. Sci. and Industry, 1990, Nat. Childcare Merit award NASP, 1992, Am. Judicature award Am. Judicature Assn., 1993, Woman of Courage award City of Tampa, 2000, Liberty Bell award, Hillsborough Bar Assn., 2005; named Fla. Motion Picture and TV Outstanding Legislator, 1990; named to Fla. Women's Hall Fame, 1999. Mem. LWV (pres. Hillsborough County 1966-69, lobbyist, Fla. adminstrn. of justice chmn. 1969-74, First Leadership Achievement award 2004), Am. Arbitration Assn., Hills County Bar Assn. (Liberty Bell award 2005), Hills County Expy. Authority, Fla. Supreme Ct. Commn. Arbitration Democrat. Home: 45 Adalia Ave Tampa FL 33606-3301 Home Fax: 813-253-0393.

DAVIS, JACI CARROLL, elementary school educator, musician; b. Batavia, NY, July 8, 1962; d. John Aaron and Nina Maxine (Tucker) Davis; m. Anthony David Gardner (div.). Student, Oberlin Conservatory, Ohio, 1980—81; MusB, U. Mich., Ann Arbor, 1981—84; MusM, U. Minn., Mpls., 1997. Cert. tchr. Mich., Wash., Idaho, Minn., Wis. Ins. agt. Fidelity Union Life Ins. Co., Pullman, Wash., 1985—86; regional sales mgr. Internat. Comm. Mgmt., Redmond, Wash., 1986—88; adminstrv. asst. Indsl. Supply Co., Plymouth, Minn., 1988—91; pvt. practice St. Louis Park, Minn., 1991—2001; music tchr. Milw. Pub. Sch. Dist., 2001—02, Palmyra (Wis.)-Eagle Area Sch. Dist., 2001—. Adj. piano faculty Bethel Coll., St. Paul, 1995—98. Musician: (CD) On Moonlit Waters, 1999. Union steward Teamsters-Indsl. Supply Co., Plymouth, 1989—91; accompanist, dir. United Meth. Ch., Minn., 2002—. Named Salesman of Qtr., Fidelity Union Life Ins., 1987. Mem.: Music Educators Nat. Conf., Am. Choral Dirs. Assn., Alpha Omicron Pi. Avocations: cooking, exercise, travel, wine tasting. Home: 107 Forest Ave Edgerton WI 53534 Office: Palmyra-Eagle Area Sch Dist 123 Burr Oak St Palmyra WI 53156

DAVIS, JANE G., lawyer; b. Norwich, NY, May 3, 1949; BA in French, Elmira Coll., NY, 1971; MA in French, U. Pitts., 1973; JD, Duquesne U., 1978. Bar: Pa. 1978, US Dist. Ct. We. Dist. Pa. 1978. Assoc. gen. counsel Limbach Co., Pitts., 1978—81; atty. Joy Technologies Inc., Pitts., 1981—88, v.p., gen. counsel, sec., 1988-95, York Internat. Corp., York, Pa., 1995—. Mem. ABA, Pa. Bar Assn. Office: York Internat Corp 631 S Richland Ave York PA 17403

DAVIS, JANET MARIE GORDEN, secondary school educator; b. Springfield, Mo., Jan. 6, 1938; d. Ura Arlond and Evelyn Ruby (Nickols) Gorden; m. Benjamin George Davis, June 21, 1980; children: Leslie Anne, John Nathan. BS, Mo. State U., 1960, MA, 1969; PhD, U. Md., 1992. Tchr. Springfield Schs., 1960-64; instr. USAFE-U. Md., Germany, 1965-67, S.W. Mo. U., Springfield, 1969-70; tchr., dept. chair Baltimore County, 1977—. Cons. in internat. edn. World Relief Corp., Wheaton, Ill., 1984; asst. prof. Balt. Internat. Coll., 1993-95. Author: For the Love of Literature: A Survey of Fiction, 1989, For the Love of Literature: Reading and Writing Nonfiction, 1989. Fulbright fellow, Eng., 1980-81. Mem. Dickens Fellowship, Fulbright Assn., Phi Kappa Phi. Baptist. Avocations: piano, poetry. Home: 6580 Madrigal Ter Columbia MD 21045-4628

DAVIS, JANET R. BEACH, science educator; b. Davenport, Iowa, Jan. 25, 1960; d. James R. and Fern Louise Munday Beach; m. Dennis Kay Davis, Jan. 31, 1978; 1 child, Matthew Glenn. AA, Heartland C.C., Bloomington, Ill., 1995; BA, U. Ill., Springfield, 2004. Sr. sci. lab. tech. Heartland C.C., Bloomington, 1994-99, supr. sci. lab., 1999—. Founder, pres. environ club Heartland C.C., Bloomington, 1993—99; advisor First STEP Environ. Club, 2000—; facilitator Ill. Dept. Natural Resources, 1998—, citizen scientist forest watch, 1999. Author: Earth Science Lab, 1999. Vol. worker Audubon Soc., Bloomington, 1996—; adv. bd. Ecology Action Ctr., Normal, Ill., 1997—, bd. dirs., 2002— Recipient Paul Simon award Ill. C.C. Trustee Assn., 1996; mem. USA Today Ill. Acad. Team, 1995, 96. Mem.: Am. Assn. Women in C.C. (pres.-elect 2001, pres. 2002—04), Bloomington Normal Women Writers Group (founder), Ill. Power Customers United to Save Our Trees (founding mem.), First Step Environ. Club (founder, pres. 1993—), Phi Theta Kappa (founder). Avocations: needlecrafts, reading, mahjong. Office: Heartland CC ICB 1006 1500 W Raab Rd Normal IL 61761 E-mail: janet.beach-davis@heartland.edu.

DAVIS, JANICE, school system administrator; BS, U. NC, Chapel Hill, MA in Tchg., PhD in Curriculum and Instruction. Asst. supt. Granville County, NC, supt. NC, 1994—2000; asst. supt. for curriculum and instruction Durham, NC, 2000—03; dep. state supt. NC Dept. Pub. Instrn., 2003—, interim supt., 2005. Office: NC Dept Pub Instrn 301 N Wilmington St Raleigh NC 27601 Office Phone: 918-807-3441. E-mail: jdavis@dpi.state.nc.us.

DAVIS, JEAN E., bank executive; b. Durham, N.C., Dec. 9, 1955; BS in Polit. Sci. and Indsl. Rels., U. N.C.; MBA, Duke U. Joined Wachovia Corp., Charlotte, NC, 1985, regional v.p. Piedmont Triad Region, 1996—98, merger coord. Va. ops., 1998, exec. v.p., dir. human resources, 1998—99, sr. exec. v.p., dir. human resources, 1999—2000, sr. exec. v.p., chief tech. and ops. officer, 2000—01, sr. exec. v.p., divsn. head info. tech., e-commerce and ops., 2001—. Mem. Fin. Svcs. Roundtable; bd. trustees U. N.C., Greensboro, bd. visitors, Chapel Hill. YMCA of Greater Charlotte. Named one of 25 Women to Watch, US Banker Mag., 2003. Office: Wachovia Corp 301 South College St Charlotte NC 28288-0570

DAVIS, JESSICA G., geneticist; b. Bklyn., Apr. 3, 1934; d. Nathan S. and Sylvia (Teplitz) Grosof; m. Andrew R. Davis, June 17, 1956; children: Jennifer Davis Hall, David. BA, Wellesley Coll., 1955; MD, Columbia U., 1959. Diplomate Am. Bd. Med. Genetics. Intern pediatrics St. Luke's Hosp.-Columbia U.; fellow Albert Einstein Coll. Medicine Yeshiva U., N.Y.C., 1961-68, instr. Albert Einstein Coll. Medicine, 1962, asst. prof. Albert Einstein Coll. Medicine, 1968-74; assoc. prof. clin. pediatric Well Coll. Medicine Cornell U., N.Y.C., 1974—. Cons. March of Dimes, N.Y.C., 1974—, Hastings Inst., Garrison, N.Y., 1979—; mem. sickle cell adv. com. NIH. Contbr. articles to profl. jours. Recipient Antoine Marfan award Nat. Marfan Found., 2005, numerous grants. Fellow: Am. Coll. Med. Genetics (founding fellow, CME officer); mem.: N.Y. Acad. Medicine, Coun. Regional Genetics Network (pres. 1991—94), Am. Soc. Human Genetics. Office: Weill Med Coll Cornell U NY-Presbyn Hosp 525 E 68th St Rm Box 128 New York NY 10021-4870 Office Phone: 212-746-1496. Business E-Mail: jgdavis@med.cornell.edu.

DAVIS, JEWEL BETH, literature and language professor, writer, actress; b. Boston, May 1, 1951; d. Bernard and Frances Lowe Davis. BA in Theatre, U. N.H., Durham; MA in Theatre Movement, Wesleyan U., Middletown, Conn.; MFA in Writing, Vermont Coll., Montpelier; grad., New England Artists' Tng. Program Handicapped, Boston, 1988. Creator and dir. Alpha Hispanic Youth Theatre, Manchester, NH; SAT and GRE tutor Princeton Rev., Exeter; SAT tutor A1 Tutoring, Melrose, Mass.; artistic dir. Classics Repertory Co., Dover, NH; prof. Maine C.C., South Portland, Middlesex C.C., Lowell, Mass., N.H. Cmty. Tech. Coll., Stratham. Actress Maine Photographic Film Inst., Seacoast Rep. Theatre, Looking Glass Theatre, Chamber Theatre Prodns. Home: 91 Rollins Rd Rollinsford NH 03869 Office Phone: 978-239-4500. Personal E-mail: bugjewel@verizon.net.

DAVIS, JO ANN S., congresswoman; b. Rowan County, NC, June 29, 1950; m. Charles E. Davis II; children: Charlie, Chris. Student, Hampton Roads Bus. Coll., Va. Owner Davis Mgmt. Co., 1988, Jo Ann Davis Realty, 1990; mem. Va. State Gen. Assembly, 1997—2001, mem. gen. laws com., mem. health welfare & insts., mem. sci. & tech. com., mem. claims com., mem. Chesapeake and its tributaries com.; mem. US Congress from 1st Va. dist., 2001—, mem. armed svcs. com., mem. internat. rels. com., mem. permanent select com. on intelligence, chair terrorism, human intelligence, analysis and counter-intelligence subcommittee, mem. def. rev. threat panel. Republican. Mem. Assembly Of God Ch. Office: US Ho Reps 1123 Longworth Ho Office Bldg Washington DC 20515-4601 Office Phone: 202-225-4261.*

DAVIS, JOAN CARROLL, retired museum director; b. Sept. 20, 1931; d. Homer Leslie and Ruby Isabelle (Stone) G.; m. Frederic E. Davis, Aug. 22, 1953; children: Timothy, Terri, Tami, Traci, Todd, Tricia. Student, Bob Jones U., 1949-52. Supr. Day Care Ctr. Bob Jones U., Greenville, SC, 1953-63; docent Univ. Art Gallery, Greenville, 1964-73, dir., 1974—; ret., 1999. Republican. Baptist. Office: 217 Stadium View Dr Greenville SC 29609 Personal E-mail: fedjed@juno.com.

DAVIS, JOAN ELAN, artist; b. Queens, N.Y., June 6, 1963; d. Gerald and Selma Pearl Kushel; m. James Clarke Davis, Nov. 26, 1989; children: Matthew, Alexander. BS in Journalism, Ohio U., Athens, 1985. Painter, fine artist Linda Zweig Fine Art (Art Smart), San Francisco, 1998—2001, Sightings Gallery, San Francisco, 1997—2001, Lionheart Gallery, Louisville, 1999—, Ebert Gallery, The Project Rm., San Francisco, 1999—, North Beach Galllery, San Francisco, 2002—. Co-chair, art from the heart com. Schs. of the Sacred Heart, San Francisco, 2000—01; docent San Francisco Mus. Modern Art, 1999—; pub. spkr., lectr. on art appreciation, nationwide; fall lectr. series chair San Francisco Art Inst. One-woman shows include San Francisco Sch. Art Gallery, 1999—, San Bernardino County Mus., Redlands, Calif., 2000—01, Period Gallery, Omaha, 2000, Walter Anderson Mus. Art, Ocean Springs, Miss., 2000, Bolinas (Calif.) Mus., 2000, Southeastern C.C., Whiteville, N.C., 2000, Coos Art Mus., Coos Bay, Oreg., 2000, Chatahoochee Valley Art Mus., LaGrange, Ga., 2000, Nathan B. Rosen Mus. and Gallery, Boca Raton, Fla., 2000, eklektikos gallery of art, Washington, 2000, Springfield (Mo.) Mus. Art, 2001, Lionheart Gallery, Louisville, 2001, North Beach Gallery, San Francisco, 2002, San Francisco Mus. Modern Art Auction, 2002, San Francisco Art Inst. Auction, 2002, many others, —, Represented in permanent collections Chevron Energy Solutions, San Francisco, Joseph Piedot Advt., San Francisco, Represented in permanent collections numerous pvt. owners, Artfully Yours, Inc., San Francisco, Am. Embassy, Budapest, Hungary. With U.S. in Embassies art program, Budapest, 2002—; docent Columbus (Ohio) Mus. Art, 1994—96, Houstong Mus. Fine Art, 1996—97, San Francisco Mus. Fine Art, 1998—; Edgewood vol. children's orgn., San Francisco, 2000—01; pres. Joan Davis Art.com. Republican. Jewish. Avocations: exercise, reading, writing, skiing. Home: 66 Sea View TER San Francisco CA 94121-1024

DAVIS, JOANNE FATSE, lawyer; m. Thomas J. Davis, Jr. BS, Boston U., 1977; JD, U. Bridgeport, 1982. Bar: Conn. 1982, N.Y. 1983. Motions law clk. U.S. Ct. Appeals (2d cir.), N.Y.C., 1982-83; assoc. Debevoise & Plimpton, N.Y.C., 1983-89; sr. corp. counsel Uniroyal Chem. Co., Middlebury, Conn., 1989-99; asst. gen. counsel, fin. and adminstrn. Crompton Corp., 1999—. Mem. Am. Corp. Counsel Assn., Conn. Bar Assn., The Corporate Bar, Assn. Bar City of N.Y., Soc. Farsarotul. Eastern Orthodox.

DAVIS, JOY LEE, language educator; b. NYC, Apr. 3, 1931; d. William Henry and Genevieve (Rhein) Belknap; m. Peter John King, Aug. 26, 1955 (div. Feb. 1985); children: William Belknap King, Russell Stuart King; m. John Bradford Davis, Jr., July 5, 1986. AB, Wellesley Coll., Mass., 1952, AM, 1953; PhD, Rutgers U., 1968; postgrad., Oxford U., Eng., 1978. Tchr. English Dana Hall Sch. for Girls, Wellesley, Mass., 1953-54; instr. English U. Mo., Columbia, 1954-55, Boston U., 1955-56; tchr. English Brookline H.S., Mass., Spartanburg H.S., S.C., 1956-60; prof. English Ohio Wesleyan U., Delaware, 1966-71, Hamline U., St. Paul, 1972-74, U. Minn., Mpls., 1974-77, Coll. St. Thomas, St. Paul, 1977-88; lectr., dir. Joy Davis Seminars, St. Paul, 1988—.

Prof. MA in Liberal Studies Program Hamline U., 1993—; lectr. compleat scholar program Univ. Minn., 2003. Author: Everything But: An Education Memoir, 1999, The Hero in Literature: Prometheus to Prufrock, 2003, Money Talks: Jane Austen and the Almighty Pound, 2005; pub. poetry in New World Writing and Crisp Pine Anthology; lit. criticism in Midwest Quar., 1993, Jour. Grad. Liberal Studies, 1996. Wellesley Coll. scholar, 1952. Mem. AAUW (bd. dirs., v.p. ways and means, 2003—, Svc. awrd St. Paul br. 1983), Midwest MLA, Mpls. Inst. Fine Arts, Minn. Club (bd. dirs. 1982-88), Schubert Club (bd. dirs., chmn. mus. com.), Wellesley Coll. Club (regional campaign com.), Jane Austen Soc. N.Am., Delta Kappa Gamma. Republican. Presbyterian. Avocations: reading, travel, creative cuisine. Home and Office: 4312 Pond View Dr Saint Paul MN 55110-4155 Personal E-mail: kinnijohnbdavis@aol.com.

DAVIS, JUDITH LEE, medical/surgical nurse; b. Terre Haute, Ind., Mar. 12, 1940; d. Fred William and Jean (Champer) Schwartz; m. Ben F. Davis, May 29, 1960; children: Debroah Jean, Susan Louise Davis Dawson. Diploma, St. Anthony Hosp. Sch. Nursing, 1961; B of Edn., U. Toledo, 1982. RN. Office nurse, instr. Sch. Nursing, Corpus Christi, Tex., 1961—64; office nurse, hosp. mgr. Terre Haute, Ind., 1964—67; office nurse Decatur, Ill., 1969—71; insvc. dir., dir. nursing Monroe Care Ctr., Mich., 1974—75; nurse St. Lukes Hosp., Toledo, 1974—76; sch. nurse Toledo Pub. Schs., 1976—95; parish nurse Luth. Ch. of Lakes, Addison, Mich., 1995—2004, Lamb of God, Haines City, Fla., 2004—. Mem. Trinity Luth. Sch. Bd., 1975—81, chair, 1980—81. Mem.: Northwest Ohio Assn. Sch. Nurses (pres. 1985—87, rep. 1992—), Sch. Nurses Toledo Pub. Schs. (dept. chair 1991—), Swiss Golf & Tennis Club (chair sunshine com.). Avocations: shuffle board, swimming. Home: 334 N Putter Cir Winter Haven FL 33881 Personal E-mail: benjudydavis@aol.com.

DAVIS, JUDY, actress; b. Perth, Australia, Apr. 23, 1955; m. Colin Friels, 1984; children: Jack, Charlotte. Student, Nat. Inst. Dramatic Art, Sydney, Australia. Appearances include: (films) Clean Straw for Nothing, 1976, High Rolling, 1977, My Brilliant Career, 1979 (Best Actress Sammy award Australian Film and TV Awards 1979, Best Actress award Brit. Acad. Film and TV Arts 1981, Best Newcomer Brit. Acad. Film and TV Arts 1981), Hoodwink, 1981 (Best Supporting Actress Sammy award Australian Film and TV Awards 1981), Winter of Our Dreams, 1981 (Best Actress Sammy award Australia Film and TV Awards 1981), Heatwave, 1982, The Final Option, 1983, A Passage to India, 1984 (Acad. award nominee for best actress 1984), Kangaroo, 1986, High Tide, 1987, Georgia, 1988, Alice, 1990, Impromptu, 1991, Barton Fink, 1991, Naked Lunch, 1991 (Best Supporting Actress award N.Y. Critics Cir. 1991), Where Angels Fear to Tread, 1991, Husbands and Wives, 1992 (Acad. award nominee for best supporting actress 1992), The Ref, 1994, The New Age, 1994, Children of the Revolution, 1996, Absolute Power, 1996, Blood and Wine, 1996, Deconstructing Harry, 1996, Celebrity, 1997, The Echo of Thunder, 1998, Gaudi Afternoon, 2000, The Man Who Sued God, 2001, Swimming Upstream, 2003, Marie-Antoinette, 2006, The Break-Up, 2006; (TV movies) Water Under the Bridge, 1980 A Woman Called Golda, 1982 (Emmy award nominee 1982), The Merry Wives of Windsor, 1982, Rocket to the Moon, 1986, One Against the Wind, 1991, Serving in Silence: The Margarethe Cammermeyer Story, 1995 (Emmy award), Echo of Thunder (Emmy nomination), 1997, Dash & Lily, 1997 (Emmy nomination), A Cooler Climate, 1998, Life With Judy Garland: Me and My Shadows, 2000 (Golden Globe award, Am. Screen Actors award, Golden Satellite award, Broadcast Critics Choice award, Am. Film Inst. award, Emmy award), The Reagans, 2003, Coast to Coast, 2004, A Little Thing Called Murder, 2006. Office: care Shanahan Mgmt PO Box1509 Darlinghurst NSW 1300 Australia*

DAVIS, JULIA A., lawyer, retail executive; BA in Economics, John Carroll U., 1982; JD with honors, Ohio State U. Sch. of Law, 1985. Assoc. then prtnr. Vorys, Sater, Seymour and Pease, Columbus, Ohio, 1987—2003; exec. v.p., gen. counsel Retail Ventures (Value City Dept. Stores), Columbus, Ohio, 2003—. Nat. bd. mem. ACLU, nat. bd. mem. exec. com., 1999—, nat. affirmative action officer, 2000—. Mem.: Columbus Bar Assn. (ethics com.). Office: Retail Ventures Inc 3241 Westerville Rd Columbus OH 43224

DAVIS, JULIA MCBROOM, college dean, speech pathology and audiology educator; b. Alexandria, La., Sept. 29, 1930; d. Guy Clarence and Addie (McElroy) McBroom; m. Cecil Ponder Davis, Aug. 25, 1951 (div. 1981); children: Mark Holden, Paul Houston, Anne Hamilton; m. David G. Reynolds, Aug. 26, 1987. BA, Northwestern State U., Natchitoches, La., 1951; MS, U. So. Miss., 1965, PhD, 1966. Asst. prof. U. So. Miss., Hattiesburg, 1966-69, assoc., 1969-71; assoc. prof. Southwestern State U., Hammond, 1971; faculty U. Iowa, Iowa City, 1971-87, prof., chmn. dept. speech pathology and audiology, 1980-85, assoc. dean Coll. Liberal Arts, 1985-87, dir. Speech and Hearing Ctr., 1979-80; dean Coll. Social and Behavioral Scis. U. South Fla., Tampa, 1987-90, assoc. provost, 1990-91; dean Coll. Liberal Arts, U. Minn., Mpls., 1991-96, prof., 1991-97. Author (with Edward J. Hardick)): Rehabilitative Audiology for Children and Adults, 1981; editor: Our Forgotten Children, 3d edit., 2001; assoc. editor: Jour. Speech Hearing Research, 1975—77, Jour. Speech Hearing Disorders, 1982—83. Pres., bd. of trustees Minn. Foun. for Better Hearing & Speech; bd. trustees Mpls. Found., Ballet Arts of Minn., Johnson County Crisis Ctr., Am. Speech-Lang.-Hearing Assn. Found.; bd. dirs. Crisis Intervention Ctr. Fellow Am. Speech-Lang.-Hearing Assn. (cert. in clin. competence in audiology, chmn. program com. 1980-81, found. trustee 2001-), Iowa Speech and Hearing Assn. (v.p.-liaison 1972-73, honors 1985); mem. Acad. Rehabilitative Audiology (pres. 1979-80), Iowa Conf. for Hearing Impaired (pres. 1975-76), Sigma Xi. Democrat. Methodist.

DAVIS, KAREN, insurance company executive, educator; b. Blackwell, Okla., Nov. 14, 1942; d. Walter Dwight and Thelma Louise (Kohler) Padgett; 1 child, Kelly Denise Collins. BA, Rice U., 1965, PhD, 1969. Asst. prof. econs. Rice U., 1969—70; econ. policy fellow Social Security Adminstrn. Brookings Instn., Washington, 1970—71, rsch. assoc., 1971—74, sr. fellow, 1974—77; dep. asst. sec. for planning and evaluation, health HEW, Washington, 1977—80; adminstr. health resources adminstrn. USPHS, Washington, 1980—81; prof. Johns Hopkins U., Balt., 1981—92, chmn., 1983—92; exec. v.p. Commonwealth Fund, N.Y.C., 1992—94, pres., 1995—. Mem. Physican Payment Rev. Commn., 1986-94; dir. Commonwealth Fund Commn. on Elderly People Living Alone, 1985-91; vis. lectr. Harvard U., 1974-75; nat. adv. com. Agy. for Health Care Rsch. and Quality, 1999-2003; bd. dirs. Geisinger Health Sys. Author: National Health Insurance: Benefits, Costs and Consequences, 1975, Health and the War on Poverty, 1978, Medicare Policy: New Directions for Health and Long-Term Care, 1986, Health Care Cost Containment, 1990. Mem.: Inst. Medicine, Phi Beta Kappa. Democrat. Methodist. Home: 1365 York Ave 27K New York NY 10021 Office: The Commonwealth Fund The Harkness House 1 E 75th St New York NY 10021-2692 Office Phone: 212-606-3825. Business E-Mail: kd@cmwf.org.

DAVIS, KAREN ANN (KAREN ANN FALCONER), special education educator; b. Rockford, Ill., Sept. 24, 1948; d. Duane Fay and Vivian Marie (Milani) Falconer. BS in Edn., Ill. State U., 1971; MBA in Mgmt., Kennedy-Western U., 1994; MA in Tchg., Rockford Coll., 1996. Cert. Ill. assessing ofcl. Spl. edn. tchr. Winnebago Co-op, Rockton, Ill., 1971-76; assessor Winnebago Twp., Ill., 1977-85; program coord. Ill. Growth Enterprises, Rockford, Ill., 1977-87; substitute tchr. Rockford Pub. Schs., 1987-89, 92—; estate planner Bradford and Assocs., Rockford, 1988-89, A. Bergners, Rockford, 1989-91; spl. edn. tchr. Eisenhower Middle Sch., Rockford, 1992—. Pub. ofcl. Assessor-Winnebago Twp., 1977-85. Mem. Twp. Assessor's Assn. (treas. 1985), Nat. Audubon Soc. Roman Catholic. Avocations: photography, birdwatching, gardening, travel, antiques.

DAVIS, KAREN SUE, hospital nursing supervisor; b. Owensboro, Ky., June 5, 1950; d. Robert J. and Mona F. (Urlaub) D. Diploma, Deaconess Sch. Nursing, 1971. RN, Ky.; cert. in pediatric nursing; cert. PALS. Charge nurse pediatrics Daviess County Hosp., 1971-89; clin. supr. pediatrics 11-7 shift Owensboro Med. Health Sys., 1989—2005, charge nurse, 2005—. Republican. Lutheran. Avocations: needlecrafts, reading, travel, cooking, decorating. Home: 686 N Fairview Ct Rockport IN 47635

DAVIS, KATHERINE LYON, former lieutenant governor; b. Boston, June 24, 1956; d. Richard Harold and Joy (Hallum) Winer; m. John Marshall Davis, Feb. 22, 1992; 1 child, Madeline Felton. BS, MIT, 1978; MBA, Harvard U., 1982. Engr. Cambridge (Mass.) Collaborative, 1978-80; mfg. mgr. Cummins Engine Co., Columbus, Ind., 1982-87, bus. dir., 1987-89; dep. commr. Ind. Dept. Transp., Indpls., 1989-95; budget dir. State of Ind., Indpls., 1995-97; exec. sec. Ind. Family and Social Svcs. Commn., Indpls., 1997-99; city contr. City of Indpls., 1999—2003; lt. gov. State of Ind., Indpls., 2003—05; CEO Global Access Point, South Bend, Ind., 2005—. Mem. Transp. Rsch. Bd., 1990-93. Recipient commendation Dept. Transp., Fed. Hwy. Adminstrn., 1991. Democrat. Avocations: running, swimming, bicycling, hiking, photography. Office: Global Access Point 4001 Technology Dr South Bend IN 46628 Office Phone: 574-472-0750.*

DAVIS, KATHERINE SARAH, physical therapy educator; b. Landstuhl, Germany, Oct. 14, 1960; (parents Am. citizens); d. Quentin Duane and Jean Elizabeth (Marshall) D. BS in Health and Phys. Edn., West Chester U., 1982; MA in Phys. Edn., U. No. Colo., 1983; BS in Phys. Therapy, U. Md., Balt., 1991, DSc in Physical Therapy, 2006. Lic. phys. therapist, Colo., Md. Tchr. phys. edn. Baltimore County Pub. Schs., Essex, Md., 1983-85, St. Joseph Sch., Perry Hall, Md., 1985-89; phys. therapist Meml. Hosp., Colorado Springs, Colo., 1991-93; asst. prof. phys. therapy, acad. coord. clin. edn. U. Md., Balt., 1993—2006. Mem. AAUW, Am. Phys. Therapy Assn., Am. Assn. Therapeutic Humor, Kappa Delta Pi. Avocations: golf, hiking, bicycling.

DAVIS, KATHRYN WASSERMAN, foundation executive, educator, writer; b. Phila., Feb. 25, 1907; d. Joseph and Edith (Stix) Wasserman; m. Shelby Cullom Davis, Jan. 4, 1932; children: Shelby M. Cullom, Diana Davis Spencer, Priscella Alden (dec.). BA, Wellesley Coll., 1928; MA, Columbia U., 1931; D of Polit. Sci., U. Geneva, 1934; law degree (hon.), Columbia U., 1997. Researcher Coun. on Fgn. Rels., N.Y.C., 1934-36, State of Pa., Phila., 1936-37; writer and lectr. on fgn. affairs N.Y., 1937—; ptnr. Shelby Cullom Davis & Co., N.Y.C., 1985—; pres. The Shelby Cullom Davis Found., N.Y.C., 1985—. Lectr. on fgn. affairs. Author: Soviets at Geneva, 1934. Trustee Wellesley Coll., 1983—2003; v.p. Women's Nat. Rep. Club, 1976—, chmn. internat. affairs com.; bd. govs. Harvard U., mem. vis. com. Russian studies, 1986—; past pres. LWV. Recipient life achievement award Women's Nat. Rep. Club, 1990, gold medal for disting. svc. to humanity Nat. Inst. Social Scis., 1990, Claire Booth Luce medal Heritage Found., 1991, Plymouth Com. award Mayflower Soc., 1992, Life Accomplishment award Internat. House, 1995. Mem. Cosmopolitan Club (N.Y.C., com. fgn. visitors), Sleepy Hollow Club (Scarborough N.Y.), N.Y. Harbor Club, Seal Harbor Club (Maine), Jupiter Island Club (Hobe Sound, Fla.), The Everglades Club, Inc. (Palm Beach, Fla.), Knickerbocker Club, Univ. Club. Avocations: skiing, tennis, swimming, travel. Office: Shelby Cullom Davis & Co LP 609 5th Ave New York NY 10017-1021 Home: 2 Riverview Rd Hobe Sound FL 33455-2324 Office Phone: 800-232-0303. E-mail: k.w.d33455@aol.com.

DAVIS, KATHY E., information analyst; b. Kansas City, Kans., Sept. 14; d. James Thomas and Mary Katherine Davis. AA in Computer Sci./Data Processing, Kansas City Kans. C.C., 1980; BS in Computer Sci./Data Processing, Avila Coll., 1982. Supr. ops. Western Auto, Kansas City, Mo., 1979-85; info. analyst Electronic Data Sys., Kansas City, Kans., 1985—. Democrat. Mem. Assembly of God Ch. Avocations: singing, bible teaching, embroidery, cooking, aerobics. Office: Electronic Data Sys 3201 Fairfax Trfy Kansas City KS 66115-1307

DAVIS, KEIGH LEIGH, aerospace engineer; b. Mitchell, SD, Oct. 6, 1954; d. Clarence Ralph and Katherine Lee Schilling; m. Glenn Nickerson Davis, Nov. 24, 1992; children: Tasha Clare Marie, Anastasia Lynn Marie. BS in Aerospace Engring. & Mechanics, U. Minn., 1976; MS in Aerospace Engring., U. Dayton, 1983. Stability and control project engr. Flight Stability and Control Br., USAF, Wright Patterson AFB, Ohio, 1976-85, E-3/Joint Stars Program Office, Wright Patterson AFB, 1985-86; lead stability, control & flying qualities project engr. Advanced Tactical Fighter Program, Wright Patterson AFB, 1986-88, Advanced Tactical Fighter Sys. Program Office, Wright Patterson AFB, 1988-90; stability and control project engr. Joint Tactical Autonomous Weapon Sys. Program Office, Wright Patterson AFB, 1990-91; lead br. engr. Flight Stability and Control Br., Wright Patterson AFB, 1991-94; stability and control tech. specialist Flight Mechanics Br., Wright Patterson AFB, 1993—2001. Chmn. MIL-STD-1797 pilot-in-the-loop oscillation update team ASC/ENFT, Wright Patterson AFB, 1992-95, responsible engr. for flying qualities of piloted aircraft mil. std., 1992-97, mil. handbook, 1997-2003; co-chmn. USAF flying qualities devel. process team, 1995-97. Mem. AIAA (sr.), Soc. Women Engrs. (life), Order of Ea. Star (pres.).

DAVIS, KRISTIN, actress; b. Boulder, Feb. 23, 1965; d. Keith and Dorothy Davis. BFA, Rutgers U Mason Gross Sch of the Arts, 1987. Spokesperson Maybelline cosmetics. Actor: (TV series) General Hospital, 1991, "Melrose Place", 1995—96, Sex and the City, 1998—2004 (Women in Film Lucy Award, 1998, Award for Outstanding Ensemble in a Comedy Series, 2001); (TV films) N.Y.P.D. Mounted, 1991, Alien Nation: Body and Soul, 1995, The Ultimate Lie, 1996, Deadly Vision, A., 1997, Atomic Train, 1999, Take Me Home: The John Denver Story, 2000, Sex and the Matrix, 2000, Someone to Love, 2001, Three Days, 2001; (films) "Doom Asylum", 1987, Nine Months, 1995, Sour Grapes, 1998, Traveling Companion, 1998, Blacktop, 2000, The Adventures of Sharkboy and Lavagirl 3-D, 2005, The Shaggy Dog, 2006.*

DAVIS, LANITA IRENE, secondary school educator; d. George Michael and Beulah Elizabeth Soffa; m. James Edward Davis, May 6, 2000; children: Brittany Sue, Adam James. BS in Secondary Math., U. Colo., Denver, 1993, MA in Curriculum and Instrn., 1997. Cert. tchr. Colo. Mid. sch. math. tchr. Douglas County Sch. Dist., Highlands Ranch, Colo., 1996—, sports coach, 1998—2005. Eucharistic min. St Francis Cath. Ch., Castle Rock, Colo., 2000—06. Mem.: Nat. Coun. Tchrs. Math. Office Phone: 303-387-3300.

DAVIS, LAURA ARLENE, retired foundation administrator; b. Battle Creek, Mich., Apr. 14, 1935; d. Paul Bennett and Daisy E. (Coston) Borgard; m. John R. Davis, Aug. 7, 1955; children: Scott Judson, Cynthia Ann Davis Welker. BS, Ctrl. Mich. U., 1986. Sec. Mich. Loan Co., Battle Creek, 1952-56; legal sec. Ryan, Sullivan & Hamilton, Battle Creek, 1957-64; exec. sec. W.K. Kellogg Found., Battle Creek, 1965-76, adminstrn./program asst., 1976, fellowship dir., 1977, asst. v.p. adminstrn., asst. corp. sec., 1978-84, v.p. corp. affairs, corp. sec., 1984-95, spl. asst. to pres., CEO, 1996-97. Cons. Mich. State U., 1998—2000. Pres. bd. dirs. Charitable Union, Battle Creek, 1983-85; mem. allocations panel United Way of Battle Creek, 1983, v.p. cmty. rels., 1990-91, 1st v.p., 1994, pres. of bd., 1995-97; bd. dirs. Battle Creek Gas Co., 1988—2004, Riding for the Handicapped Cheff Ctr., 1991-96, sec., 1992; trustee Binder Park Zoo; mem. adv. coun. Argubright Bus. Coll., 1989-90; mem. Visionquest 5000, 1989; mem. selection com. Cmty. Leadership Acad.; bd. dirs. Coun. Mich. Founds., 1994-97; mem. membership com. Recipient Athena award C. of C., Cmty. Svc. award J.C. Penney. Mem. Adminstrv. Mgmt. Soc. (pres. chpt. 1982-83), Am. Mgmt. Assn., Nat. Touring Network (bd. mem. 1997-99, sec. 1998-99), Battle Creek C. of C. Home: 101 Brighton Park Battle Creek MI 49015-9615

DAVIS, LAUREN ALEXIS, science educator; b. Morgantown, W.Va., July 6, 1971; d. Lynette and Rick Davis. BS, Longwood U., Farmville, Va., 1993; MEd, Marymount U., Arlington, Va., 1998. Emergency med. technician Office Emergency Med. Svc., Commonwealth of Va., 2004; lic. State Bd. Edn., Commonwealth of Va., 2001. Tchr. 8th grade phys. sci. Carl Sandburg Mid. Sch., Alexandria, Va., 1998—99; tchr. 7th grade life sci. Joyce Kilmer Mid. Sch., Vienna, Va., 1999—, sci. dept. chair, 2000—. Mem.: NSTA. Home: 12001 Market St #31 Reston VA 20190 Office: Joyce Kilmer Mid Sch 8100 Wolftrap Rd Vienna VA 22182 Office Phone: 703-846-8909.

DAVIS, LINDA LENNON MCCONNELL, critical care nurse; b. Kingstree, SC, Mar. 1, 1943; d. Murdoch and Vandetta (Vandergrift) Lennon; m. Robert John McConnell, Apr. 20, 1963 (div. 1971); children: Susan McConnell Kennedy, Amber Virginia Smith; m. S.E. Felkel, 1974 (div. 1984); m. Hal Davis, 1998. Grad. with honors, Mercy Sch. Nursing, 1968; student, U. NC, 1972; BS in History with honors, Charleston So. U., 1990. Cert. BLS; RN SC, NC, Fla. Head nurse neurosurgery intensive care Med. U. Hosp., Charleston, SC, 1968—70; head nurse respiratory intensive care Duke U. Med. Ctr., 1971—73. Author: Charleston's Historical Churches and Chapels of Ease, 1998; co-author: Angel Oak Story, 1981. Hist. guide City of Charleston, 1983; active Gibbes Mus. Art Women's Coun., 1978—; vol. Hospice, Jacksonville, Fla., 2001; women's council Gibbes Mus. Art; women's coun. membership chair Unitarian Ch., Charleston, SC, 1979, religious edn. tchr., 1980. Recipient Svc. award, Gibbes Mus. Art Women's Coun., 1997. Mem.: AAUW. Home and Office: The Grand Reserve #926 13810 Sutton Park Dr N Jacksonville FL 32224 Office Phone: 904-821-9479. E-mail: revolution1779@aol.com.

DAVIS, LISA, elementary school educator; d. J. W. and B. J. Davis; 1 child, Caitlin. BS, U. Fla., Gainesville, 1982. Cert. Tchr. Fla., 1982. Tchr. Seminole County Pub. Schs., Sanford, Fla., 1983—. Named Tchr. of Yr., Seminole County Pub. Schs., 2002. Mem.: Fla. APHERD (life). Democrat-Npl. Roman Catholic. Office: RT Milwee Middle School 1341 S Ronald Reagan Boulevard Longwood FL 32750 Office Fax: 407-320-3899. E-mail: lisa_davis@scps.k12.fl.us.

DAVIS, LISA E., lawyer; b. Flushing, NY, Feb. 6, 1960; BA, Harvard U., 1981; JD, NYU Sch. Law, 1985. Bar: NY 1986. Law clk. to Honorable Constance Baker Motley, US Dist. Ct., So. Dist. NY, 1985—86; assoc. Kramer Levin Naftalis & Frankel LLP; ptnr., entertainment, publ., media Frankfurt Kurnit Klein & Selz, PC, NYC. Contbr. articles to law jour. Named one of Top 50 Black Power Brokers in Entertainment, Black Enterprise Mag., 2002, Am. Top Black Lawyers, 2003; recipient Jacob K. Javits Achievement award, Bedford Stuyvesant Restoration Corp., 2003. Mem.: Black Entertainment and Sports Lawyers Assn., Nat. Bar Assn. (Intellectual Property Sect.), Assn. Bar City of NY. Office: Frankfurt Kurnit Klein & Selz PC 488 Madison Ave New York NY 10022 E-mail: ldavis@fkks.com.

DAVIS, LISA RENE, special education educator, consultant; b. Tracy, Calif., Aug. 23, 1970; d. Buddy Ray and Shirley Mae Davis. BA in Psychology, U. Calif., San Diego, 1994; MS in Edn. and Psychology, Calif. State U., Hayward, 1997. Cons., contractor, Calif., 1994—; spl. edn. tutor, 1994—. Cmty. health analyst First Steps Collaborative, Tracy, 1994-95; student health educator U. Calif., San Diego. Author reports; contbr. essays, poetry, screenplays and book revs. to various publs. Chair Libr. Adv. Bd., Tracy, 1999—2001; mem. Deuel Vocat. Inst. Literacy Program, Tracy, 1995—96; advisor San Joaquin Family Preservation and Family Support Program Survey, Stockton, Calif., 1994; mem. Hosp. Found. Com., Tracy, 1994. Recipient Recognition awards Sierra Health Found., 1995, City of Manteca, 1995, U. Calif., San Diego, 1992, Excellence award Give Every Child a Chance, 1998. Mem.: APA, Toastmasters Internat. (v.p. edn. 1999—2001). Avocations: arts and crafts, sailing, tennis, golf.

DAVIS, LOIS ANN, computer specialist, educator; b. Thermopolis, Wyo., Nov. 29, 1945; d. Hester Oliver and Ruth Louise (Baker) Davis; m. Harold W. Wright, Dec. 22, 1969 (div. 1988); children: Geraldine Ann, Harold W. III. BS in Bus. Edn. cum laude, U. Wyo., 1968, MS in Bus. Edn., 1988. Cert. office automation profl., Wyo. Instr. Lander (Wyo.) Valley High Sch., 1968-70, Cath. Sch., Chandler, Ariz., 1970-71; part-time instr. Casper (Wyo.) Coll., 1981-83, instr. bus. div., 1983-94, network support specialist, acad. computing, 1994-95, acting dir. acad. computing, 1995-96, dir. acad. computing, 1996—2005, dean edn. resources, 2005—. Textbook reviewer Prentice-Hall, Englewood, N.J., 1989-91; co-dir. Casper Regional Tech. Ctr., 1999-2000; mem. computer sys. adv. bd. Casper Coll., 1995-2002; chair Casper Coll. Adminstrv. Alliance, 1996-97. Author: Electronic Communications, 2d edit., 1996. Bd. dirs. Murie Audubon Choir Nat. Audubon, 1995—97. Mem. Office Systems Rsch. Assn. (conf. co-chair 1999), Wyo. Bus. Edn. Assn. (sr. rep. 1991-92), Beta Gamma Sigma (life), Phi Kappa Phi (life). Avocations: cross country skiing, hiking, gardening, reading. Home: 1514 Jim Bridger Ave Casper WY 82604-3186 Office: Casper Coll Academic Affairs 125 College Dr Casper WY 82601-4612 Office Phone: 307-268-2703. Business E-Mail: ldavis@caspercollege.edu.

DAVIS, LORI, not-for-profit developer; children: Jacob, Josh, Caitlin, Michael, Eric, Travis. Grad. in acctg., Fresno State C.C., Fresno, Calif. Acctg. position with a cons. co.; acctg. position with a bank; engring. asst. for an ind. oil prodr.; asst. dir. Tread Lightly!, Ogden, Utah, exec. dir. Office: Tread Lightly 298 24th St Ste 325 Ogden UT 84401-1482

DAVIS, LORRAINE JENSEN, writer, editor; b. Omaha, Apr. 2, 1924; d. Theron R. and L. Mildred (Henkel) Jensen; m. Richard Morris Davis, Apr. 4, 1959 (dec.); 1 child, Laura Jensen. BA, U. Denver, 1946. Copywriter Glamour mag., N.Y.C., 1946-54, prodn. editor, 1954-61, Vogue Children mag., N.Y.C., 1963-66. Writer, assoc. features editor, Vogue mag., N.Y.C., 1966-77; mng. editor, writer women's news column, 1977-88; editorial dir. Condé Nast Books, 1988-91; editor: Vogue Living and Food Guide, 1975; editorial cons.: Vogue Beauty and Health Guide, 1979-82; editor: Cooking with Colette (by Colette Rossant), 1975, Fairchild Dictionary of Fashion (by Charlotte Calasibetta), 1975, English translation Paul Bocuse's French Cooking, 1977. Recipient Disting. Citizen award Alpha Gamma Delta, 1981 Mem. NOW, Phi Beta Kappa. Democrat. Episcopalian. Home: 200 Leeder Hill Dr Apt 538 Hamden CT 06517-2729

DAVIS, LYDIA, writer, educator; Assoc. prof. lit. Bard Coll., 1986—2001; prof. Eng., writer in residence SUNY, Albany, 2001—. Author: (book) Break it Down, 1986, The End of the Story, 1995, Almost No Memory, 1997, Samuel Johnson Is Indignant, 2001. Fellow N.Y. State writers Inst., U. of Albany, MacArthur Found., 2003. Office: U Albany Humanities 350 1400 Washington A Albany NY 12222

DAVIS, LYNN ETHERIDGE, political scientist, educator; b. Miami, Fla., Sept. 6, 1943; d. Earl DeWitt and Louise (Featherston) Etheridge. BA, Duke U., 1965; MA, Columbia U., 1967, PhD, 1971; DHL (hon.), Va. Theol. Sem., 2000. Lectr. Miles Coll., Birmingham, Ala., 1966-67; asst. prof. polit. sci. Barnard Coll., Columbia U., N.Y.C., 1970-74; rsch. assoc. Internat. Inst. for Strategic Studies, London, 1973; program analysis staff Nat. Security Council, 1974; asst. prof., lectr. dept. polit. sci. Columbia U., 1974-76; prof., staff mem. Senate Select Com. on Intelligence, 1975-76; dep. asst. sec. of def. for policy plans and nat. security affairs Office of the Under Sec. for Policy, Dept. Def., Washington, 1977-79, asst. dep. under sec. for policy planning, 1979-81; rsch. Internat. Inst. Strategic Studies, London, 1981-82; prof. national security affairs National War Coll., Washington, 1982-85; dir. studies Internat. Inst. Strategic Studies, London, 1985-87; hon. sr. rsch. fellow, dept. war studies Kings Coll., London, 1988-90; rsch. fellow John Hopkins Fgn. Policy Inst, Paul H. Nitze Sch. Advanced Internat. Studies, 1988-91; v.p. army rsch. divsn., dir. Arroyo Ctr. RAND, Santa Monica, Calif, 1991-93, sr. fellow Washington, 1997—2001, sr. polit. scientist, 2001—; under sec. for arms control and internat. security affairs Dept. State, Washington, 1993-97. Author: The Cold War Begins, Soviet American Conflict Over Eastern Europe, 1974. Woodrow Wilson fellow, 1965-66, 69-70, 81-82; Columbia U. fellow, 1965-66, 68-69; recipient David D. Lloyd prize Harry S. Truman Library, 1976 Mem.: Coun. on Fgn. Rels., Phi Beta Kappa. Home: 827 S Lee St Alexandria VA 22314-4333 Office: RAND 1200 S Hayes St Arlington VA 22202-5050 Office Phone: 703-413-1100 x5399. E-mail: Lynn_Davis@rand.org.

DAVIS, MAMIE (DENISE DAVIS), writer; b. Florence, SC, July 28, 1943; divorced; 1 child, Jacqueline J. Maslin. Cert. IBM data entry, N.Y.C., 1981. From clk grade 2 to prin. admin. assoc. NYC Civil Svc., 1962—86; freelance writer, composer N.Y.C. and, SC, 1986—. Tchg. coord., cons. NYC-DSS/HRA, 1980—86; stock actor Pilgrim Dramatic Playhouse. Author: (plays) So Many Drops of Rain (showcased at NATAS), Sam Blood's Secret, Sibling of Evil, Agency Procedures: Lust and Corruption, 2002, (novel and screenplay) Jessie's Folly, 2000, over 30 short stories; actor: numerous feature films, (Off-Broadway plays) Medea, Damn That Miss Anne, The Nurse, Civil Rights Worker. Mem.: ASCAP. Avocations: fashion design, dressmaking, book cover design. Personal E-mail: bernetha8000@yahoo.com.

DAVIS, MARCIE L., public health and human services consultant; b. Jackson, Miss. d. William Franklin and Gillie Neel Davis; m. Franz Joseph Freibert, May 8, 1987. BS, U. So. Miss., 1987, MLS, 1989. Dept. head Fla. State U., Tallahassee, 1989—92; bureau chief Fla. Atty. Gens. Office, Tallahassee, 1992—96; exec. dir. Crisis Response of Santa Fe, 1996—98; dir. student wellness Santa Fe Pub. Schs., 1998—99; dir. victims svcs. N.Mex. Atty. Gens. Office, 1999—2002; project dir. N.Mex. Coalition Sexual Assault, Albuquerque, 2002—; pres. Davis Innovations, Inc., Santa Fe, 2002—. Pres. Working Like Dogs LLC, Santa Fe, 2001—. Bd. chmn. Am. Red Cross, Santa Fe, 2001—04, mem. nat. diversity coun., 2002—04. Named Santa Fe Bus. Woman of Yr., Capital City Bus. and Profl. Women, 1997; recipient, 1997, Southwest Star award, ARC, 2001, Up & Comers award, U. Mex., Anderson Sch. Mgmt., 2001, Governor's Outstanding Woman award, N.Mex. Women's Commn., 2002; N.Mex. Friends grant, N.Mex. Friends, 2003. Mem.: Habitat for Humanity Women's Build, N.Mex. Crime Victim Reparation Commn. (violence against women team mem. 2000—), Internat. Women's Forum. Avocation: travel. Office: Davis Innovations Inc 59 Wildflower Way Santa Fe NM 87506 Business E-Mail: mdavis@davisinnovates.com.

DAVIS, MARGARET BRYAN, paleoecology researcher, educator; b. Boston, Oct. 23, 1931; AB, Radcliffe Coll., 1953; PhD in Biology, Harvard U., 1957; DSc (hon.), U. Minn., 2002. NSF fellow dept. biology Harvard U., Cambridge, Mass., 1957-58; dept. geosci. Calif. Inst. Tech., Pasadena, 1959-60; rsch. fellow dept. zoology Yale U., New Haven, 1960-61, prof. biology, 1973-76; rsch. asoc. dept. botany U. Mich., Ann Arbor, 1961-64, assoc. rsch. biologist Gt. Lakes Rsch. divsn., 1964-70, rsch. biologist, assoc. prof. dept. zoology, 1966-70, rsch. biologist, prof. zoology, 1970-73; head dept. ecology and behavioral biology U. Minn., Mpls., 1976-81, prof. dept. ecology, evolution and behavior, 1976-82, Regents prof. ecology, 1983—2000. Vis. prof. Quaternary Rsch. Ctr., U. Wash., 1973; vis. investigator environ. studies program U. Calif., Santa Barbara, 1981-82; adv. panel ecology NSF, 1976-79; sci. adv. com. biology, behavior and social scis., 1989-91; adv. panel geol. record of global change, NRC, 1991-92, planetary biology com., 1981-82, global change com; 1987-90, mem. screening com. in plant scis., internat. exch. of persons com., 1972-75, sci. and tech. edn. com., 1984-86, vis. rsch. scientist scholarly exch. com. NAS/NRC, People's Republic China, mem. grand challenges in environ. sci. com., 1999-2000; U.S. nat. com. internat. Union Quaternary Rsch., 1966-74; bd. trustees Inst. for Ecosys. Studies, 2000—. Mem. editl. bd. Quaternary Rsch., 1969-82, Trends in Ecology and Evolution, 1986-92, Ecosystems, 2000-03. Bd. dir. Ricon Inst., 2005—. Recipient Sci. Achievement award Sci. Mus. Minn., 1988, alumnae Recognition award Radcliffe Coll., 1988, Nevada medal, 1993, Merit award Bot. Soc. Am., 1998, award for Contbn. Grad. Edn., U. Minn., 1999. Fellow: AAAS, Geol. Soc. Am., Am. Acad Arts and Scis.; mem.: NAS, Am. Quaternary Assn. (councillor 1969—70, 1972—76, pres. 1978—80, Dist. Career award 2001), Brit. Ecol. Soc. (hon.), Am. Soc. Naturalists (hon.), Ecol. Soc. Am. (pres. 1987—88, Eminent Ecologist award 1993), Nature Conservancy (bd. dirs. Minn. chpt. 1979—85), Internat. Assn. Gt. Lakes Rsch. (bd. dirs. 1970—73), Sigma Xi, Phi Beta Kappa. Office: U Minn Dept Ecology Evolution & Behavior 100 Ecology Bldg 1987 Upper Buford Cir Saint Paul MN 55108-1051 Business E-Mail: mbdavis@ecology.umn.edu.

DAVIS, MARICA NANCI ELLA RIGGIN, retired artist; b. Phila., Apr. 13, 1934; d. Dale Thomas and Anna (Kudla) Purtle; m. Donald Allen Riggin, Sept. 11, 1954 (dec. Nov. 10, 1970); children: Ralph Allen Riggin, Ronald Dale Riggin, David Wayne Riggin; m. Leonard Nettleton Davis, July 3, 1976; 3 stepchildren. Student, Montgomery Coll., Rockville, Md., 1975—78, student, 1983, student, 1988, student, 1993. Electro-mech. drafter Philco, Phila., 1952—55, Vitro Labs. Automated Industries, Aspen Hill, Md., 1971—73; designer, printer Sears Roebuck, Bethesda, Md., 1970; drafer, illustrator Watkins-Johnson Co. divsn. CEI, Gaithersburg, Md., 1973—86, IDEAS/SAIC, Columbia, Md., 1987—98. Instr. adult edn. craft class Montgomery County, Md.; jury Damascus County Fair Art Show. Juried and award winning shows, Sugar & Frichtle, Kensington, Md., Town Ctr., Ten Oaks, Md., Gurmukh Galleries, Md., Gaithersburg Coun. Arts, Woodlawn Mansion, Md., Kentland Mansion, McCrillus Gardens, Audubon Soc., Unitarian Universalitic Ch., Pyramid Atlantic, Sandy Spring Mus., Visual Sys. Art Ctr., Strathmore Hall, Rockville Arts Pl., Delapaine Visual Arts Ctr., Md., Café Monet, Kensington, Kent Island Federation Art, Md., Sumner Mus., Washington, Saxon Swan Gallery, Del., Dietricks Gallery, Sta. Gallery, Dover (Del.) Art League, one-woman shows include Open Studio Gallery, 2000, 2001, 2002, 2004, Kent Island Fedn. Art, Md., 2003, 2004. Pres. Episcopal Ch. Women, Beathany Beach, Del., 2003. Mem.: Ga. Miniature Art Soc., Miniature Art Soc. Fla. Inc., Cider Painters Am., Printmakers Plus, Olney Art Assn. (pres. 1995, 1996), S. Ea. Del. Artists Studio Tour, Miniature Painters Sculptors and Gravers Soc. (receiver 1989—98), Nat. League Am. Pen Women (membership chair Holly chpt.), Md. Printmakers (assoc.; folio chair 1996), Phi Theta Kappa. Home: 306 Steamboat Ln Dagsboro DE 19939-9226 Personal E-mail: ezdavis306@aol.com.

DAVIS, MARILYN JEAN, medical educator; b. St. Louis, Mo., Sept. 8, 1935; d. Charles Paul and Josephine Lorraine Davis, Julia Mary Davis (Stepmother). BSBA, St. Louis U., 1973, MBA, 1975; MA, Calif. Inst. of Integral Studies, San Francisco, 1999. Cert. Rosen Method practitioner Rosen Method: Berkeley Ctr. Budget dir., medicare coord. SSM St. Mary's Hosp. Med. Ctr., Madison, Wis., 1975—83; fin. cons. SSM Health Care Sys., St. Louis, 1983—85; treas. Franciscan Sisters of Mary, St. Louis, 1985—95. Mem. governing bd. SSM Health Care Sys., St. Louis, 1995—; assoc. woman'Space, St. Louis, 2001—. Author: (textbook) The Rosen Method: Coming Alive and Staying Alive in the 21st Century. Home: 1 Provincial Ct Kirkwood MO 63122-1501 Office: Spiritual Connection 1009A Taman Ct Kirkwood MO 63122-6807 Office Phone: 314-768-1759.

DAVIS, MARLECE (ALICE MARLECE DAVIS), secondary school educator, director; d. Rex S. and E. Lucille Treadwell; children: Lindsey, Cody. BA in Elem. Edn. and English, Houston Bapt. U., Tex., 1970; MEd, Stephen F. Austin U., Nacogdoches, Tex., 1981, degree in Mid-Mgmt., 1981. Cert. tchr. Tex., 1970. Tchr. elem., mid. schs. Humble Ind. Sch. Dist., Tex., 1974—81, administrator, 1981—2004; tchr. mid. sch. Holy Trinity Episc. Sch., Houston, 2004—, dir. devel., 2005—. Adj. prof. Kingwood Coll., Tex., 2000—; sponsor sch. newspaper Holy Trinity Sch., 2003—06; student sponsor svc. learning Rosemont Assisted Living, Atascocita, Tex., 2002—06, Jesse Jones State Pk., Houston, 2005—06. Author: Creative Writing for Teachers, 1985. Bd. dirs. Kingwood Christian Ch., 1991—93, dir. edn., 2001—03, dir. small group, 2003—05. Named Tchr. of Yr., Humble (Tex.) Walmart, 2006; grantee, Houston Endowment, 2005—06, Astro-CocaCola-Minute Maid, 2006. Mem.: PTA (life). Democrat. Home: 1303 St Andrews Kingwood TX 77339 Office: Holy Trinity Episc Sch 11810 Lockwood Houston TX 77044

DAVIS, MARTHA FRANCES, lawyer; b. Wichita, Kans., Apr. 4, 1957; d. Robert Louis and Marian (Larson) D. AB in Anthropology, Harvard U., 1979; BA, Trinity Coll., Oxford, Eng., 1981, MA in Jurisprudence, 1987; JD, U. Chgo., 1983. Bar: Ill. 1983, N.Y. 1985, U.S. Supreme Ct. 1988. Law clk. to judge U.S. Dist. Ct. (no. dist.) Ind., Hammond, 1983-85; assoc. Cleary, Gottlieb, Steen & Hamilton, N.Y.C., 1986-90; staff atty. NOW Legal Def. and Edn. Fund, 1990—. Bd. dirs. Ctr. for Immigrants Rights; Kate Stoneman vis. prof. Albany Law Sch., 2000; adj. prof. NYU Sch. Law. Author: Brutal Need: Lawyers and the Welfare Rights Movement, 1960-73. Bunting Inst. fellow, Radcliffe Coll., 1988-89; Wasserstein fellow, Harvard Law Sch., 1998. Mem. N.Y.C. Bar Assn. (chair adminstrv. law com.). Mem. Soc. Of Friends. Avocations: music, writing. Office: NOW Legal Def & Edn Fund 99 Hudson St Rm 12R New York NY 10013-2815

DAVIS, MARY BRONAUGH, music educator; b. Kansas City, Kans., June 28, 1937; d. John Esme and Martha Lucinda (Wilson) Bronaugh; m. William D. Davis, Jr., Jan. 1, 1983. AB, William Jewell Coll., Liberty, Mo., 1959; MA, Conservatory Music, U. Mo., Kansas City, 1974. Cert. tchr. piano, service playing Am. Guild Organists, 2006. Piano tchr. Leshosky Music Store, Gladstone, Mo., 1959-61; organist Pres. Hotel, Kansas City, 1965-67; piano tchr. Maple Woods C.C., Kansas City, 1972-81; ind. piano/organ tchr. Gladstone, Mo., 1962—; min. music, organist Barry Christian Ch., Kansas City, 1960—. Trustee Mo. 4-H Found., 2004—. Mem.: Federated Music Tchrs. Greater Kansas City (pres. 1969—70, 1984—85), Kansas City Music Tchrs. Assn. (pres. 1988—90), Mo. Music Tchrs. Assn. (pres. 1995—96, Outstanding Svc. award 2004), Mo. Fedn. Music Clubs (handbell chair 1999—, Ch. Musician of Yr. 1998, 1999), Am. Guild Organists (svc. playing cert. 2006), Music Tchrs. Nat. Assn. (bd. dels. 1995—96). Home: 1400 NE 76th Ter Kansas City MO 64118-1907

DAVIS, MARY BYRD, conservationist, researcher; b. Cardiff, Wales; came to U.S., 1947; d. John Dymond and Joanna Inger (Falconer) Byrd; m. Robert Minard Davis; children: Carol, John. BA, Agnes Scott Coll., 1958; MA, U. Wis., 1968, PhD, 1972; MLS, Simmons Coll., 1974. Acquisitions libr. No. Mich. U., Marquette, 1974—75; asst. libr. Georgetown (Ky.) Coll., 1975—78; libr. U. Ky., Lexington, 1978—83; freelance writer and editor Georgetown, 1983-90, 93—; staff writer, office mgr. Earth First Jour., Canton, NY, 1990; co-founder and pub. Wild Earth, Canton, NY, 1991—92, assoc. editor Richmond, Vt., 1993—98; dir. Yggdrasil Inst., Georgetown, Ky., 1994—. Author: The Military Civilian Nuclear Link, 1988, Guide de L'Industrie Nucleaire Francaise, 1988, The Green Guide to France, 1990, Going Off the Beaten Path: An Untraditional Travel Guide to the U.S., 1991, Old Growth in the East: A Survey, 1993, rev. edit., 2003, La France nucléaire: matières et sites, 1997, 2002, The U.S. Enrichment Establishment 1999, 1999; co-author: Les Déchets nucléaires militaires Français, 1994, Weapons of Mass Destruction, 2005; editor: Eastern Old-Growth Forests: Prospects for Rediscovery and Recovery, 1996, Eastern Old-Growth Notes, 1997-2000. Bd. dirs. Centre de Documentation et de Recherche sur la Paix et les Conflits, Lyon, France, 1989—, Wildlands Ctr. for Preventing Roads, Missoula, Mont., 1996-99. Mem. Nat. Writers Union, Sierra Club (editor energy report 1986-87, exec. com. Cumberland chpt. 1982-84), Phi Beta Kappa. E-mail: yggdrasili@yahoo.com.

DAVIS, MARY ELLEN K., library director; MLS, U. Ill.; MA, Ctrl. Mich. U. Sr. assoc. exec. dir. Assn. Coll. and Rsch. Librs., 1993—2001, exec. dir., 2001—, dir. comm. and systems, publs. program officer; ref. libr., bibliographer Ctrl. Mich. U. Recipient Girl Scouts Outstanding Vol. award. Mem.: ALA, Libr. Sch. Alumni Assn. (bd. dirs.), Am. Soc. Assn. Execs., Soc. Scholarly Publishing, Phi Kappa Phi, Beta Phi Mu. Office: 50 East Huron St Chicago IL 60611 Office Phone: 800-545-2433. E-mail: acrl@ala.org.

DAVIS, MARY HELEN, psychiatrist, educator; b. Kingsville, Tex., Dec. 2, 1949; d. Garnett Stant and Emogene (Campbell) D. BA, U. Tex., 1970; MD, U. Tex., Galveston, 1975; grad. in adult and child psychoanalysis, Inst. for Psychoanalysis, Chgo., 1982-92. Cert. Nat. Bd. Med. Examiners, Am. Bd. Psychiatry and Neurology, Child and Adolescent Psychiatry. Intern, then resident in psychiatry SUNY, Buffalo, 1975-78; fellow in child psychiatry U. Cin., 1978-80; asst. prof. Med. Coll. Wis., Milw., 1980-89, clin. assoc. prof., 1989-93; med. dir. adolescent treatment unit Milw. Psychiat. Hosp., 1981-86, Schroeder Child Ctr., 1986-89; pvt. practice, 1989-93; med. dir. Devereux-Victoria (Tex.) Psych. Residential Treatment Ctr., 1993-94; pvt. practice Lancaster, Pa., 1995—. Cons. Milw. Mental Health Cons., 1980-93, Children's Svc. Soc., Milw., 1982-93, Cath. charities, Harrisburg, Pa., 1996—, Sch. Dist. Lancaster, 1998—. Bd. dirs. Next Generation Theatre, Milw., 1988-90, Next Act Theatre, Milw., 1990-92, Lancaster Guidance Ctr., 2002-06. Mem. Am. Med. Women's Assn., Assn. for Child Psychoanalysis, Am. Psychoanalytic Assn., Am. Acad. Child and Adolescent Psychiatry. Baptist. Avocations: science fiction, music, computers, crochet. Office Phone: 717-392-7062. E-mail: mdsquare@juno.com.

DAVIS, MARY KATHRYN, marketing professional; b. Clearwater, Fla., Jan. 10, 1966; d. John Minor, Lee Marie Zuberer; m. James R. Davis (div.); children: Rachel Frances, Joshua Edward Leo; m. Michael C. Sultzbach, Sept. 8, 2001. BA in Mass Comm., U. Denver, 1987. Reporter Del. Bus. Rev., Wilmington, 1988—90; mktg. coord. Del. Dept. Transp., Dover, 1990—93; mktg. mgr. MBNA Am. Bank, Wilmington, 1993—99; mktg. and pub. rels. dir. The Grand Opera House, Wilmington, 1999—. Contbr. articles to profl. jours. Bd. dirs. Wilmington Drama League, Chapel St. Players. Avocations: writing, community theatre. Office: The Grand Opera House 818 N Market St Wilmington DE 19801

DAVIS, MARY MARTHA (MARTY DAVIS), small business owner, consultant; b. Canton, Ohio, May 6, 1939; d. John Newton Reed and Mary Maria Schrengost; m. Richard Paul Davis, Dec. 23, 1961; children: John Newton, Scott Reed. BA, Grove City Coll., Pa., 1961; post grad., Pa. State U., State Coll., 1961—. Cert. YMCA PE Springfield, Mass., 1985, grad. Sheffield Sch. Design, N.Y.C., 1995. Tchr. Spanish Penn Hills H.S., Pitts., 1962; tchr. English Corning & Elmira Sch. Dists., NY, 1963, 1964; mgr. and buyer Smith's Dept. Store, 1973—76; assoc. exec. dir., instr. and program mgr. YMCA, 1980—93; owner Marty R. Davis Interior Design, Corning, Chautauqua and Hilton Head, NY, 1995—. Cons. and workshop presenter Coop Ext. Ctr., Ithaca, NY, 1972—75, Hosp. Aux. N.Y. State, 1975—89; pres., dir. and advisor Women's Ctr., Corning, 1980—89. Campaign dir Easter Seals, St. Lawrence County, NY, 1974; dir. and legis. liaison 7 Lakes Coun. Girl Scouts U.S.A., 1982—96; spkr. hosp. assn. and aux. convs., 1981—89; pres. Kiwanis, Corning, 1994; trustee, elder 1st Presbyn. Ch., Corning, NY, 1980—99; trustee Corning Philharmonic Soc., Corning and Elmira, NY, 1984—94; bd. trustees Hosp. Assn. N.Y. State, Albany, 1981—83, chair Com. on Hosp. Aux., 1981—83; trustee Presbyn. Ho. Assn., chair auqua bldg. and grounds com., 2000—; trustee Hist. Assn., Canton, NY, 1973—79, Corning, NY, 1985—90. Master: Am. Contract Bridge League (life; cert. dir.); mem.: Investment Club (sec. Hilton Head chpt. 2000), Palmetto Rowing Club (treas. 2003—, instr.), Northshore at Chautauqua (trustee 2004—). Republican. Avocations: golf, reading, bridge, rowing. Home: 5 Yard Arm Palmetto Dunes Hilton Head Island SC 29928-5247 Address: Chautauqua Institution 20 Elm Lane c1 Chautauqua NY 14722 E-mail: martyrdid@yahoo.com.

DAVIS, MEGAN J., consulting firm executive; b. 1967; Pres. The Davis Consulting Grp., Inc. Mem. Ariz. Humanities Coun., Women at the Top Bd.; adv. coun., Women's Studies U. Ariz. Chairwoman Jewish Fedn. Southern Ariz., Planned Parenthood Southern Ariz. Bd. Named one of 40 Under 40, Tucson Bus. Edge, 2006. Office: The Davis Consulting Group Inc S 6th Ave Tucson AZ 85701 Office Phone: 520-615-1842.*

DAVIS, MELODIE MILLER, writer, editor; b. Sarasota, Fla., Dec. 2, 1951; d. Vernon U. and Bertha Mae (Stauffer) Miller; m. Stuart Perry Davis, May 29, 1976; children: Michelle Dawn, Tanya Ruth, Doreen Estella. Student, U. Barcelona, 1973-74; BA, Eastern Mennonite Coll., 1975. Sec., rschr., writer Mennonite Broadcasts, Inc., Harrisonburg, Va., 1975-77; prodr. Mennonite Media, Harrisonburg, Va., 1977-79, exec. prodr., 1979-81, print prodr., 1981-97, columnist (syndicated by Globe Syndicate 1997—), 1987—; editor Shalom Found., Grottoes, Va., 1995—. Author: Becoming a Better Friend, 1988, Working, Mothering, and Other Minor Dilemmas, 1983, Departure, 1991, Why Didn't I Just Raise Radishes?, 1994 (Angel award 1995); compiler (perpetual calendar) 366 Ways to Peace, 1999; editor: Reinvating Aging, 2003. Big Sister Big Bros./Big Sisters, Harrisonburg, 1977-80. Recipient Woman of Distinction award, Girl Scouts USA, 1995, Gracie Allen award, Am. Women in Radio & TV, 2004, Disting. Svc. Alumni award, Eastern Mennonite U., 2005. Mem. Va. Press Women (treas. 1993-95), Nat. Fedn. Press Women (Va. Communicator of Achievement award 1993), Internat. Women's Media Found., Coun. on Ch. and Media. Presbyterian. Avocations: travel, gardening, flowers, hiking. Office: Mennonite Media 1251 Virginia Ave Harrisonburg VA 22802-2434

DAVIS, MERRILL, public relations executive; Various positions including creation of training programs for new policy initiatives within the electric-utility industry, Tex.; formerly with Gov. Office, Tex.; joined Public Strategies, Inc., Austin, 1994—, now mng. dir. Contbr., rsch. project Nat. Sci. Found. Office: Public Strategies Inc Ste 1200 98 San Jacinto Blvd Austin TX 78701

DAVIS, MICHELE A., mortgage company executive, former federal agency administrator; b. Louisville, Ky. BS in Fgn. Svc., Georgetown U., Washington, 1988; M in Econs., Am. U. Economist Citizens for Sound Economy; economist minority leader staff Joint Econ. Com. Washington; chief spokesperson majority leader's office; adv. house Rep. leadership; comms. dir. house majority leader Dick Armey, 1997—2001; asst. sec. for pub. affairs US Dept. Treasury, Washington, 2001—02; sr. v.p. regulatory policy Fannie Mae, Washington, 2003—. Republican. Office: Fannie Mae 3900 Wisconsin Ave NW Washington DC 20016*

DAVIS, MICHELLE MARIE, elementary school educator; b. Cleve., Jan. 7, 1956; d. Frank Charles and Rita Theresa (Zdrojewski) Koran; m. Gary Wayne Davis, Sept. 24, 1976; children: Benjamin, Zachary. BA, Ball State U., 1978, MA in Edn., 1989; postgrad., U. S.C., 2003—. Substitute tchr. Baugo Cmty. Schs., Elkhart, Ind., 1982-83, Middlebury (Ind.) Schs., 1982-84, Goshen (Ind.) Cmty. Schs., 1982-84, Elkhart (Ind.) Cmty. Schs., 1984-87; elem. tchr. Ft. Wayne Diocese, Elkhart at St. Thomas, 1987-91, Williamsburg County Schs., Kingstree, SC, 1991—2003, Richland One Sch. Dist., 2003—. Lead tchr. homework ctr. Kingstree Elem. Sch., 1992—93; chair S.C. grammar and composition textbook rev. com., 1996; presenter, lectr. in field. Adminstr. food bank St. Ann's Ch., Kingstree, 1992—94, mem. pastoral coun., 1992—2002, sec., 1992—94, pres., 1995—96, vol. outreach ctr., 1992—. Grantee, SC Dept. Edn., 1994. Mem.: ASCD, SC Coun. Tchrs. Social Studies, SC Coun. Tchrs. English, Nat. Coun. Tchrs. English, SC Reading Assn., Internat. Reading Assn., SC Coun. Tchrs. Math. (grant), St. Ann's Women's Club. Office: John P Thomas Elem Sch 6001 Weston Ave Columbia SC 29203 Home: PO Box 306 Gaston SC 29053-0306 E-mail: mdavis1756@yahoo.com, midavis@richlandone.org.

DAVIS, MINNIE LOUISE, writer; b. Chattanooga, Tenn., Sept. 5, 1935; d. Moses McKelton and Lillie Mae (Glover) Smith; m. Robert Lee Martin, 1952 (div. 1964); children: Bobby Lee, Loretta, Enrico, Alexander, Jacqueline; m. Will Davis Jr., Feb. 18, 1979. BS, Va. State U., 1979. Lic. cosmetologist, Ohio, Va. Background artist various films. Author: (books) Brittini in ABC Land, 1994, (poem) Green & Gold, 1997, A Mother's Prayer, 1998, (screenplay) A Mother's Prayer, 2002. Mem., tchr. Meml. Chapel, Ft. Lee, 1980—; vol. Am. Red Cross. Mem. Ladies Auxilliary VFW, Disabled Am. Vets., NCO Wives Club (v.p. 1997-98), Sigma Gamma Rho. Home: 20124 Gandy Ave Ettrick VA 23803-1666

DAVIS, MINNIE P., minister; d. George Andrew Prince and Dorothy Prince Blakely, Rosevelt Blakely (Stepfather); m. Fred Davis, July 3, 1971; children: Gregory David Prince, Tammy LaVette, Dontrece, Denita La'Chele, Nicolette Robertson. Attended, Reading Area CC, 1977—79, Pace Bus. Inst., 1980—81, Urskin Theol. Seminary, 1989—90. Pastor Sandy Grove AME Ch., Warrenton, Ga., 1988—91, Mt. Taber AME Ch., Keysville, Ga., 1991—95, Liberty Hill AME Ch., Thomson, Ga., 1995—98, St. James AME Ch., Tennile, Ga., 1998—2000, Wesley Chapel AME Ch., Milledgeville, Ga., 2000—01, Ward Chapel AME Ch., Augusta, Ga., 2001—02, Spring Bethel AME Ch., Louisville, Ga., 2004—. Chaplain U. Hosp., Augusta, 1989—92, mem. bd. ethics, 1990—92; adv. bd. mem. Ga. Health Decisions, Atlanta, 1995—99; tchr. African Meth. Bd. Examiners, Augusta, 1997—; bd. trustees AME Ch., Augusta, 2001—; spkr. Predatory Lending Practices US Senate. Founder Citizens Addressing Pub. Svcs. Trustee AME Ch., Atlanta, 1997. Recipient Unsung Heroine, Top Ladies of Distinction, 1995, Citizen of Yr., Kappa Chpt. TAU Gamma Delta Sorority, 1995, Cmty. Svc. award, Augusta Lincoln League, 1995. Mem.: Women in Ministries AME Ch. (assoc.). Home: 3534 Prince Rd Augusta GA 30906 Office Phone: 706-589-1316.

DAVIS, NANCY COSTELLO, retired elementary school educator, retired vice principal, adult education coordinator; b. Manchester, Conn., May 16, 1939; d. Lawrence Fredrick Costello and Agnes Imalda (Dailey) Schmidt; m. Paul Hawley Davis, Aug. 23, 1958; children: Mark A., Susan A., Linda J., Dianne M., Maryellen L. BS, Cen. Conn. State U., 1978, MS, 1986, 6th yr. diploma adminstrn.-supervision, 1990. Computist UTC div. Pratt & Whitney, East Hartford, Conn., 1958-59; program dir. YWCA, East Hartford, 1966-68; dean mid. age religious edn. St. Mary's Ch., East Hartford, 1972-77; tchr. Bennet Jr. High Sch., Manchester, Conn., 1978—91, chmn. data processing, 1983—91, also dir. computer edn.; vice prin. Bennet Middle Sch., 1991—2000; ret., 2002; regional program coord. Vernon Regional Adult Basic Edn. Program, Conn., 2000—. Insvc. instr. Manchester Bd. Edn., 1981, 83—; adj. instr. Cen. Conn. State U., 1987, program coord., Vernon Adult Edn., 2000-. Treas. Lullaby Club of Hartford, Conn., 1966, 2d v.p., 1967, pres., 1968. Democrat. Roman Catholic. Avocations: sewing, gardening, golf, dance. Office: Vernon Adult Edn 70 Loveland Hill Rd Vernon Rockville CT 06066

DAVIS, NATALIE ZEMON, retired history professor; b. Detroit, Nov. 8, 1928; d. Julian Leon and Helen (Lamport) Zemon; m. H. Chandler Davis, Aug. 16, 1948; children: Aaron Bancroft, Hannah Penrose, Simone Weil. BA summa cum laude, Smith Coll., 1949, DHL (hon.), 1977; MA, Radcliffe Coll., 1950; PhD, U. Mich., 1959; D (hon.), U. Lyon II-France, 1983; DHL (hon.), Northwestern U., 1983, U. Rochester, 1986, U. Chgo., 1992, George Washington U., 1987, Reed Coll., 1988, Muhlenberg Coll., 1989, New Sch. for Social Rsch., 1989, Colby Coll., 1990, U. Pa., 1992, U. Chgo., 1992, U. Pa., 1992; LLD (hon.), Tufts U., 1987, Williams Coll., 1987, Goucher Coll., 1989, Muhlenberg Coll., 1989, New Sch. for Social Rsch., 1989, Columbia U., 1990, U. Toronto, 1991. Lectr. to asst. prof. Brown U., 1959-63; asst. prof. to assoc. prof. U. Toronto, 1963-71, Northrop Frye vis. prof. literary theory, 1996—97, adj. prof. history, anthropology, 1997—, prof. medieval studies, 1997—; prof. history U. Calif.-Berkeley, 1971-77, Princeton U., 1978—81, Henry Charles Lea prof. history, 1981—96, Henry Charles Lea prof. history emeritus, 1996—, dir. Shelby Cullom Davis Ctr. for Hist. Studies, 1990—94; Henry Luce vis. prof. humanities Yale U., 1987. Author: Society and Culture in Early Modern France, 1975 (Berkeshire Conf. spl. award 1976), The Return of Martin Guerre, 1983, Fiction in the Archives: Pardon Tales and Their Tellers in Sixteenth-Century France, 1987, Women on the Margins: three Seventeenth-Century Lives, 1995, Slaves on Screen: Film and Historical Vision, 2000, The Gift in Sixteenth-Century France, 2000; co-editor: A History of Women, vol. 3: Renaissance and Enlightenment Paradoxes, 1993; editl. bd. Comparative Studies in Society and History, History and Memory, Yale Journal of Law and Humanities, Literature and History, Historical Reflections; historical cons. (opera) The House of Martine Guerre, 1993, 96, 97. Bd. trustees Ctrl. European U., Budapest, 2000—05. Recipient teaching citation U. Calif.-Berkeley, 1974, Outstanding Achievement award U. Mich., 1975, Disting. Achievement medal, Radcliffe Grad. Soc., 1983, Howard T. Berhman award for Disting. Achievement in Humanities, Princeton U., 1983, New Eng. Hist. Assn. Media award, 1985; decorated Chevalier Ordre des Palmes Academiques France, 1976 Fellow Am. Acad. Arts and Scis.; cooresp. fellow Royal Hist. Soc.; sr. fellow Ctr. Comparative Lit.; cooresponding fellow British Acad.; mem. Internat. Congress Hist. Scis. (bureau mem. 1990-95, first v.p. 1995-2000), John Simon Guggenheim Meml. Found. (selection com. 1988-2003), Can. Inst. Advanced Rsch. (rsch. council 2001-), Renaissance Soc. Am., Soc. French Hist. Studies (pres. 1976-77), Am. Hist.

Assn. (council 1972-75, pres. modern history sect. 1980, pres. 1987, Eugene Asher Disting. Tchg. award, 1994), Soc. Reformation Research, Am. Antiquarian Soc. (selected mem. 1987), Phi Beta Kappa Soc. (Sidney Hook Meml. award, 2000). Democrat. Jewish.

DAVIS, NICOLE D., executive secretary, entrepreneur; d. Mace Green and Anna L. Davis; children: Anthony R, David T, Thomas J. AAS in Secretarial Arts, Gibbs Coll., 1992; BTh, MDiv, Christian Life Sch. Theology, 1999; student, Sacred Heart U., 2004—. Min. Shabach Christian Ctr., 2000. Sec. Shabach Ministries, Norwalk, Conn., 1992—; exec. sec. Fairfield County Coun., Boy Scouts Am., Norwalk, 1992—94; adminstrv. sec. Norwalk Pub. Schs., 1994—2000, exec. sec., 2000—. Owner secretarial svcs. AnRay Tobiah, Norwalk, 1998—. Vol. Shabach Christian Ctr., Norwalk, 1992—2000. Scholar, Katharine Gibbs Sch.-Gibbs Coll., 1990. Avocations: dance, reading, writing. Personal E-mail: nicoledd72@yahoo.com.

DAVIS, NIGHTA J., photographer, artist; d. Betty J. Stephens Spratling and Elmer R. Spratling; m. Reuben G. Davis, Sept. 12, 1992; 1 child, Vanessa Alana Flanders-Freuen. AA, GTC, Ga., 1985. Pres./chairwoman Ltd. Signature Edit., Hiawassee, Ga., 1999—. Prin. works include ltd. signature edit. photographic art. Mem. apptd. by the gov. Children and Youth Coordinating Coun. of Ga., Statewide, Ga., 2004—. Mem.: Blue Ridge Art Assn., Ga. Mountain Cultural Alliance, Ga. Assembly Cmty. Arts, Ga. Born Artists Group (founder), North Ga. Arts Guild, Soc. of Children's Book Writers and Illustrators (assoc.), Mountain Arts Assn. (assoc.). Achievements include Her work hangs in the Atlanta Capitol Building in Atlanta, Ga., the Congressional and US Senate Building in Washington, D.C.as well as many prestigous institutions and homes throughout the world; Some of her finest works hang in the homes and offices of U.S. Senators, Governors and State Senators. Avocations: travel, collecting various items of interest, classical music, writing, hiking. Office: Ltd Signature Edit 794 Ramey Mountain Rd Hiawassee GA 30546 Office Phone: 706-896-9021. Personal E-mail: nider77777@alltel.net.

DAVIS, PAM N., literature and language professor; d. J.B. and Cleta Mae Weeks; m. Chris T. Davis, May 27, 1989; 1 child, Emily Brooke. BS, U. Ala., Tuscaloosa, 1982, MA, 1984. Instr. English, Shelton State C.C., Tuscaloosa, Ala., 1984—. Sprk., presenter in field. Vol. Red Cross, Tuscaloosa, Ala.; cons., vol. Hillcrest PTO, Tuscaloosa, Ala. Recipient Achievement award, Shelton State C.C. Mem.: Ala. Assn. Devel. Edn., 2 Yr. English Coll. Assn., Nat. Coun. Tchrs. of English, Kappa Delta Epsilon. Avocations: crossword puzzles, reading, spending time with family. Home: 10750 Winding Way Tuscaloosa AL 35405 Office: Shelton State CC 9500 Old Greensboro Rd Tuscaloosa AL 35405 Office Phone: 205-391-2267. Business E-Mail: pdavis@sheltonstate.edu.

DAVIS, PAMELA BOWES, pediatric pulmonologist; b. Jamaica, NY, July 20, 1949; d. Elmer George and Florence (Welsch) Bowes; m. Glenn C. Davis, June 28, 1970 (div. Mar. 1987); children: Jason, Galen. AB, Smith Coll., 1968; PhD, Duke U., 1973, MD, 1974. Cert. Am. Bd. Internal Medicine, 1977, in Pulmonary Diseases 1980, Am. Bd. Pediat., 1996, in Pediatric Pulmonology 2000. Internal medicine intern Duke Hosp., 1973-74, resident in internal medicine, 1974-75; sr. investigator NIAMD/NIH, Bethesda, Md., 1977-79; asst. prof. U. Tenn. Coll. Medicine, Memphis, 1979-81, Case Western Res. U. Sch. Medicine, Cleve., 1981-85, assoc. prof., 1985-89, prof., 2002, Arline H. and Curtis F. Garvin Rsch. prof., 2005—, chief pediatric pulmonary divsn., 1985—, vice chmn. rsch. dept., 1994—96, vice dean rsch., 2005—, interim dean, v.p. med. affairs. Pres. Am. Fedn. for Clin. Rsch., Thorofare, NJ, 1989—90; trustee Rsch. Am, Arlington, Va., 1989—90; mem. adv. coun. Nat. Inst. Diabetes, Digestive and Kidney Diseases, 1992—96; mem. bd. sci. counselors NHLBI, 2001—06, chmn., 2004—06; founding scientist Copernicus Therapeutics, Inc., Cleve. Contbr. articles to profl. jours. Chmn. med. adv. coun. Cystic Fibrosis Found., Bethesda, 1988-90. With USPHS, 1975—79. Named to, Clevel. Med. Hall of Fame, 2001; recipient Samuel Rosenthal award in acad. pediat., 1996, Maurice Saltzman award, Mt. Sinai Health Care Found., 1998, Smith Coll. medal, 2001, Rainmaker of Yr., Edn. Rsch. Northeast Ohio Live Mag., 2002. Fellow ACP; mem. Am. Pediatric Soc., Am. Acad. Pediatrics, Am. Physiol. Soc., Am. Thoracic Soc., Am. Soc. Gene Therapy, Biophys. Soc., Soc. for Pediatric Rsch., Assn. Am. Physicians, Phi Beta Kappa, Sigma Xi, Alpha Omega Alpha. Achievements include 7 patents in field. Office: Rainbow Babies/Child Hosp 2101 Adelbert Rd Cleveland OH 44106-2624 Business E-Mail: pbd@case.edu.

DAVIS, PAMELA F., orthopedist, surgeon; b. Tulsa, Okla., Sept. 9, 1959; d. Charles Jerry and Jan Suzanne Fillebrown; m. Taylor S. Davis, Dec. 28, 1985; children: Sarah, Suzanne. BS in Phys. Therapy, U. Tex. Med. Br., Galveston, 1981; MD, Baylor Coll. Medicine, Houston, Tex., 1987. Diplomate Am. Bd. Orthop. Surgeons, 1995. Intern Baylor Coll. Medicine Hosps., Houston, 1987—88, resident, 1988—92, fellow, 1992—93; ptnr. Orthop. and Rheumatology Assocs., Moline, Ill., 1982—2004; pvt. practice Davenport, Iowa, 2005—. Fellow: Am. Acad. Orthop. Surgeons; mem.: AMA, Am. Orthop. Foot and Ankle Soc. Episc. Avocations: skiing, volleyball, fitness. Office: Foot & Ankle Specialists 4622 Progress Dr Ste C Davenport IA 52807

DAVIS, PAMELA MARIE, administrative analyst; b. New Orleans, Jan. 22, 1961; d. David James Davis Sr. and Anita Hurst Davis. B in Pub. Adminstrn., Loyola U., 1983. Adminstrv. analyst divsn. housing and neighborhood devel. City of New Orleans, 1988—2002, prin. analyst divsn. housing and neighborhood devel., 2003—; civil svc. trainer Civil Svc. Dept., New Orleans, 1991—. Mem. City Civil Svc. Commn., New Orleans, 1999—. Contbr. (employee newsletters) The Link/Our Beat, 1999—. Lector St. Peter Claver Ch., New Orleans, 1971—, lector tng. coord., 1991—, chairperson worship commn., 1988—92; assoc. mem., pres. St. Vincent de Paul Conf., New Orleans, 1994—99; del. Nat. Black Cath. Congress, 1992; mem. parish coun. St. Peter Claver Ch., New Orleans, 1985—97; bd. dirs. Outstanding Young Ams., 1996—98. Named one of Outstanding Young Women of Am., 1983, 1988; recipient Order of St. Louis medallion, Archdiocese of New Orleans, 1988, Hibernia Merit award, Bur. Govtl. Rsch., 1997. Mem.: Legion of Mary (assoc.). Democrat. Roman Catholic. Avocations: reading, playing table tennis, travel. Office: Divsn Housing and Neighborhood Devel 1340 Poydras St 10th Fl New Orleans LA 70112

DAVIS, PATRICIA HEWSON, elementary school educator; d. Robert Emmet and Julia Waters Hewson; m. James F. Davis, Esq., Aug. 7; children: Michael B., Victoria Ashley. BA in Psychology, Edn., Spl. Edn., Marymount Manhattan Coll., N.Y.C., 1970; MEd in Spl. Edn., U. Del., Newark, 1976. Tchr. spl. needs N.Y.C. PUb. Schs., 1970—71, Upper Merion Sch. Dist., Pa., 1971—72, Rex Clay Sch. Dist., Wilmington, Del., 1972—83; tchr. pre-sch. St. David's Day Sch., Wilmington, Del., 1983—86; tchr. math. Wilmington Friends Sch., Del., 1986—2002; head lower sch. St. Anne's Episcopal Sch., Middletown, Del., 2002—. Home: 138 Marcella Rd Wilmington DE 19803-3451

DAVIS, PATRICIA MARGARET ALICE, psychology and religion educator; b. LA, Mar. 2, 1955; d. Robert Joseph and Sallianne Nissen Davis; m. Daniel Sperling, June 28, 1981; 1 child, Rhiannon Elizabeth Davis Sperling. BA, U.C. San Diego, 1978; MBA, U.C. Berkeley, 1982; MA in theol. studies, San Francisco Theol. Seminay, 2004. Rsch. analyst Calif. Pub. Utilities Commn., San Francisco, 1978—80, So. Pacific RR, San Francisco, 1982—83, asst. mgr., 1984; supr., planning and analysis Am. Pres. Lines, Oakland, Calif., 1985—86, mgr., planning and control, 1987—88; instr., psychology and religion Grad. Theol. Union Summer Session, Berkeley, Calif., 2005—. Instr. summer session Pacific Sch. Religion, 2006. Co-author: (book) Future Drive: Electric Vehicles and Sustainable Transportation; contbr. chapters to books. Mem.: Soc. for the Sci. Study of Religion, Am. Acad. of Religion, APA, Internat. Assn. for the Study of Dreams, Met. Club (mem. com. 2003—05). Office: San Francisco Shakespeare Festival PO Box 460937 San Francisco CA 94146-0937

DAVIS, PAULA MAY, music educator; b. Huntington, W.Va., Feb. 17, 1957; d. Paul Adair and Frances Edwards Warren; m. Donald Allen Davis, June 17, 1996; 1 child, Christina Marie Lewis. B.A. in music edn., Marshall U., 1984—88, M.S. in adult and tech. edn., 1998—99. Choral dir. Vinson H.S., Huntington, W.Va., 1988—89; elem. music tchr. Prichard Elem. Sch., Prichard, W.Va., 1988—89; choral dir. Buffalo H.S., Kenova, W.Va., 1989—91; gen. music Buffalo Mid. Sch., Kenova, W.Va., 1991—2000; choral dir. Spring Valley H.S., Huntington, W.Va., 2000—02. Choral dir. Lavalette United Meth. Ch., W.Va., 1997—2000, Steele Meml. United Meth. Ch., Barboursville, W.Va., 1991—97, music ministry dir., 2003—; spkr. in field; substitute tchr. Wayne County Schs. Scholarship com. mem. Huntington Area Postal Credit Union, W.Va., 1999—2003; corr. sec. WV Alpha Delta Kappa, 2000—02; altruistic chmn. Alpha Delta Kappa, Huntington, W.Va., 1998—2000. Mem.: Huntington Centennial Toastmasters Club, KYOVA Quilt Soc., WV Alpha Delta Kappa (historian 2002—04, pres.-elect 2004—, state pres. 2006—). Avocations: reading, quilting, singing. Office: Wayne County School System PO Box 79 Wayne WV 25570 Personal E-mail: singingquilter96@yahoo.com.

DAVIS, PAULETTE JEAN TURNER, secondary school educator, editor, consultant; b. Racine, Wis., Apr. 9, 1946; d. Thomas Elmer and Lorraine Lucille (McClure) Turner; m. Wesley Kent Davis, June 1, 1968; children: Rebecca Lynn, Rachel Marie, Shannon Ruth. BS cum laude, U. Wis., Whitewater, 1968. Cert. secondary edn. English and math. tchr., Wis. Tchr. Ft. Atkinson Schs., Wis., 1968-69, Janesville Sch. Dist., Wis., 1969—74, Wis., 2000—06, Beloit Pub. Schs., Wis., 1984, Blackhawk Tech. Inst., Janesville, 1984, U. Wis.-Rock Ctr., Janesville, 1985. Editor joint project for Janesville Found., Janesville Pub. Sch. Dist. and Janesville Pub. Libr., 1983-85; del. White House Conf. on Domestic and Fgn. Affairs, 1980; tchr. U. Wis Rock Ctr., 1996, 97 (summers). Prodr.: (local cable show) Community Corner, 1998—. Com. mem. Wis. Dem. Com., 1983-85; dir. edn. St. Mark's Luth. Ch., Janesville, 1984-86; co-chmn. numerous local and state campaigns, 1983—; vice chmn. 1st Congl. Dist. Dem. Com. Wis, 1989—; mem. Nat. Women's Polit. Caucus; bd. dirs. Janesville br. Ch. Women United, 1980—, pres., 1990-91. Named to Hall of Fame, Washington Park HS, 2000. Mem. AAUW (pres. 1998-2000), NEA, Wis. Edn. Assn., Janesville Edn. Assn., Rock Valley United Tchrs. Assn. (bd. dirs. 1973-74), AAUW (women's chmn. Janesville br. 1980-82, bd. dirs. 1980-89, pres.-elect 1997-98). Avocations: reading, writing, yoga, history, politics. Home: 4210 Castlemoor Drive Janesville WI 53546 Personal E-mail: wpsdavis@charter.net.

DAVIS, PEGGY COOPER, law educator; b. Hamilton, Ohio, Feb. 19, 1943; d. George Clinton and Margarett (Gillespie) Cooper; m. Gordon Jamison Davis, Aug. 24, 1968; 1 child, Elizabeth Cooper. BA, Western Coll. for Women, 1963; student, Barnard Coll., 1963-64; JD, Harvard U., 1968; student, NY Soc. for Freudian Psychologists, 1972-73. Bar: NY, 1969, US Supreme Ct., 1976. Staff atty. Williamsburg Legal Services, NYC, 1968-69; Reginald Heber Smith Fellow Cmty. Action for Legal Services, 1969-70; assoc. Poletti, Freidin, Prashken, Feldman & Gurtner, 1970-72; law clk. to Hon. Robert L. Carter, US Dist. Ct. So. Dist. NY, 1972-73; asst. counsel capital punishment project NAACP Legal Def. Fund, 1973-77; dep. criminal justice coord. City of NY, 1979-80; judge Family Ct. State of NY, 1980-83; assoc. prof. law Rutgers U., Newark, 1977-78, NYU Sch. Law, 1983-86, prof. 1987-, now John S.R. Shad prof. lawyering & ethics, also dir. lawyering program. Author: Neglected Stories: The Constitution and Family Values, 1997. Bd. dirs. Russell Sage Found., 1989-99, chair, 1996-99. Office: NYU Sch Law Vanderbilt Hall Rm 302D 40 Washington Sq S New York NY 10012-1099 Office Phone: 212-998-6465. E-mail: davisp@juris.law.nyu.edu.

DAVIS, PENNI THARP, science educator; b. Jackson, Miss., July 24, 1966; d. Jack Earl and Gladys Nell (Davis) Tharp; m. Christopher Calvin Davis, July 6, 1991; children: Peyton Frances, Jacob Christopher. BS in Elem. Edn., Miss. Coll., 1989. Cert. mid. sch. sci. educator Miss. Elem. tchr. Jackson Pub. Sch. Dist., 1989—93; mid. sch. sci. tchr. Madison County (Miss.) Sch. Dist., 1993—. Co-chmn. scholarship fund Jr. Auxiliary Madison-Ridgeland, Miss., 1998, chmn. britekids project, 1999, co-chmn. book rocks for kids, 2001; chmn. summer reading camp Jr. League Jackson, 2002, chmn. habitat for humanity, 2004, co-chmn. aas for heats, 2006. Sci. grant, Jr. Auxilary Madison-Ridgeland. Mem.: Madison County Rep. Women, Am. Revolution, Symphony League Jackson. Republican. Roman Cath. Avocations: exercise, volunteering, children's sports. Home: 377 Kings Bridge Rd Morton MS 39117 Office: Olde Town Med Sch 210 Sunnybrook Rd Ridgeland MS 39157 Personal E-mail: ppjdavis@bellsouth.net.

DAVIS, PHYLLIS J., education educator; b. Grundy, Va., Dec. 22, 1944; d. Anderson and Mildred Dora Dales; m. Henry Larry Davis, July 11, 1965; 1 child, Karen Suzanne. AA, J. Sargeant Reynolds CC, Richmond, Va., 1987, AS in Bus. Adminstrn., 1987, AS in Edn., 1987; BA in English/Secondary Edn., U. Richmond, Va., 1987—90; MA in Lit., Va. Commonwealth U., Richmond, 1990—91. Indices clk., stenographer FBI, Washington, 1963—65; sec. Page Comm. Engrs., Inc., Washington, 1965—68; math. tchr. Johns Hopkins U., Richmond, Va., 1986—89; resident asst. Gov.'s Sch., Richmond, 1989; English tchr. Hermitage HS, Richmond, 1989, Richmond Montessori Sch., 1993; English instr. J. Sargeant Reynolds CC, 1991—. Mem. human resources com. J. Sargeant Reynolds CC, 1991—; guest lectr. Va. Commonwealth U., 1991; forensic judge Galwin HS, Richmond, 2001; poetry judge J. Sargeant Reynolds CC, 2006, mem. English forum, 06; presenter in field. Editor: (book) To Catch a Butterfly, 2000, Mountain Clay, 2002. Dir. Project Clothing for S.W. Va., Richmond, 2004—05. Recipient Outstanding Svc. award, J. Sargeant Reynolds CC, 1993; grantee English grant, 1991; Va. scholar, 1987. Mem.: Phi Beta Kappa (scholarship judge 2001—), Delta Kappa Gamma (mem. telephone com. 2004—). Avocations: art, antiques, poetry, genealogy. Office: J Sargeant Reynolds CC PO Box 85622 Richmond VA 23285

DAVIS, ROBIN, publishing executive; b. 1969; With Deloitte & Touche, St. Louis, 1991—95; v.p., CFO, Pulitzer Newspapers, Inc., St. Louis, 1998—2005; controller, newspaper divsn. E.W. Scripps, Cin., 2005—. Office: The E W Scripps Co 28th Fl 312 Walnut St Cincinnati OH 45202 Office Phone: 513-977-3000. Office Fax: 513-977-3810.

DAVIS, ROBIN JEAN, state supreme court chief justice; b. Boone County, W.Va., Apr. 6, 1956; m. Scott Segal; 1 child, Oliver. BS, W.Va. Wesleyan Coll., 1978; MA in Indsl. Rels., W.Va. U., 1982, JD, 1982. With Segal & Davis L.C., 1982-96; justice W.Va. Supreme Ct. of Appeals, 1996—, chief justice, 1998, 2002, 2006. Mem. W.Va. U. Law Inst., W.Va. Bd. of Law Examiners, 1991-96. Contbr. articles to W.Va. Law Rev.; co-author Litigation Handbook on West Virginia Rules of Civil Procedure. Recipient Dist. West Virginian award, 2000. Mem. ABA, Assn. of Trial Lawyers of Am., Kanawha County Bar Assn., Am. Acad. Matrimonial Lawyers. Office: Supreme Ct of Appeals Bldg 1 Rm E 301 State Capitol Charleston WV 25305 Office Phone: 304-558-4811. Business E-Mail: robindavis@courtswv.org.*

DAVIS, RUBY DEE See DEE, RUBY

DAVIS, RUTH CAROL, pharmacist, educator; b. Wilkes-Barre, Pa., Oct. 27, 1943; d. Morris David Davis and Helen Jane Gillis. BS, Phila. Coll. Pharmacy and Sci., 1967; PharmD, Ohio State U., 1970; AA in Elec. Engring., ITT Tech. Inst., 1999. Cert. pharmacist, Pa., Md. Mgr. pharmacist Fairview Pharmacy, Etters, Pa.; mgr., pharmacist Neighborcare Pharmacy, Balt.; dir. ambulatory svcs. Rombro Health Svcs., Balt.; tchr., pharmacist Boothwyn Pharmacy, Phila.; pharm. cons. Nat. Rx Svcs. of Pa.; Eagle Managed Care, 1996; pharmacist Pharmastat Inc., 1996—; pharmacy supr. Johns Hopkins Hospice Pharmacy, 2000—; asst. prof. pharmacy Anne Arundel C.C., 2001—. Adj. prof. Essex C.C., 1999, Balt. City C.C., 2000; pharmacy instr. Sch. Sisters of Notre Dame, 2003. Republican. Baptist. Avocations: music, reading. Home and Office: 75 Lion Dr Hanover PA 17331-3849 E-mail: ladypharm@hotmail.com.

DAVIS, RUTH MARGARET (MRS. BENJAMIN FRANKLIN LOHR), information technology executive; b. Sharpsville, Pa., Oct. 19, 1928; d. W. George and Mary Anna (Ackermann) D.; m. Benjamin F. Lohr, Apr. 29, 1961. BA, Am. U., 1950; MA, U. Md., 1952, PhD, 1955; PhD (hon.), CMU, 1978, U. Md., 2000. Statistician FAO, UN, Washington, 1946-49; mathematician Nat. Bur. Standards, 1950-51; head ops. rsch. div. David Taylor Model Basin, 1955-61; staff asst. Office Dir. Def. Rsch. and Engring. Dept. Def., 1961-67; asso. dir. rsch. and devel. Nat. Libr. Medicine, 1967-68; dir. Lister Hill Nat. Center for Biomed. Communications, 1968-70; dir. Inst. for Computer Scis. and Tech. Nat. Bur. Standards, 1970-77; dep. undersec. def. for rsch. and engring., 1977-79; asst. sec. resource applications U.S. Dept. Energy, 1979-81; chmn., pres., CEO Pymatuning Group Inc. FMR, 1981-2000. Chmn. Aerospace Corp., 1994—2001; lectr. U. Md., 1955—57, Am. U., 1957—58; vis. prof. computer sci. U. Pa., 1969—72; adj. prof. U. Pitts.; mem. Md. Gov.'s Sci. Adv. Coun., 1971—77; chmn. nat. adv. coun. Elec. Power Rsch. Inst., 1975—76. Contbr. articles to profl. jours. Recipient Rockefeller Tech. Mgmt. award, 1973, Fed. Woman of the Yr. award, 1973, Systems Profl. of Yr. award, 1979, Disting. Svc. medal, U.S. Dept. Def., 1979, U.S. Dept. Energy, 1981, Gold medal, 1981, Ada A. Lovelace award, 1984, Disting. Alumnus award, U. Md., 1993, Disting. Alumna award, 1995, Alumna of Yr. in Math. and Sci. award, 2003; inducted into Computer News Hall of Fame, 1988. Fellow AIAA, Soc. for Info. Display; mem. AAAS, Am. Math. Soc., Math. Assn. Am., Nat. Acad. Engring. (counselor), Nat. Acad. Pub. Adminstrn., Nat. Acad. Arts and Scis., Washington Philos. Soc., Sigma Pi Sigma, Tau Beta Pi. Office: Pymatuning Group Inc 1500 N Beauregard St Ste 101 Alexandria VA 22311-1878 Office Phone: 703-671-3500. Personal E-mail: rmdavis5@aol.com.

DAVIS, SARAH C., elementary school educator; b. Copperhill, Tenn., May 5, 1971; d. Bradley L. and Dorothy J. Davis. B, Brenau U., Gainesville, Ga., 1994; M, Piedmont Coll., Demorest, Ga., 1998; specialist, Lincoln Meml. U., Harrogate, Tenn., 1999. Cert. early childhood edn. Ga. Profl. Stds. Commn., 1994, ednl. leadership PreK-12 Ga. Profl. Stds. Commn., 1999, tchr. support specialist Ga. Profl. Stds. Commn., 2005. Educator East Fannin Elem., Morganton, Ga., 1994—. Mem. East Fannin Sch. Coun., Morganton, 2003—05, Sch. Improvement Team, Morganton, 2005—06. Mem.: Profl. Assn. Ga. Educators. Baptist. Avocations: poetry, reading, travel, gardening. Office: East Fannin Elem One Elementary Cir Morganton GA 30560 Office Phone: 706-374-6418. E-mail: sdavis@fannin.k12.ga.us.

DAVIS, SARAH IRWIN, retired language educator; b. Louisburg, NC, Nov. 17, 1923; d. M. Stuart and May Amanda (Holmes) Davis; m. Charles B. Goodrich, Nov. 18, 1948 (div. 1953). AB, U. N.C., 1944, AM, 1945; PhD, NYU, 1953. Tchg. asst. English dept. NYU, 1948-51; tchr. English Elizabeth Irwin H.S., N.Y.C., 1951-53; editor coll. texts Henry Holt, N.Y.C., 1953-55; editor coll. texts, encylopedias McGraw-Hill, N.Y.C., Rome, 1955—60; asst. prof. English Louisburg (N.C.) Coll., 1960-63, Randolph-Macon Woman's Coll., Lynchburg, Va., 1963-70, assoc. prof. English, 1970-75, chairperson Am. studies, 1971-87, prof. English and Am. studies, 1975-87, ret., 1987. Contbr. articles to profl. jours. Mem. MLA, Am. Studies Assn., N.C.-Va. Coll. English Assn. (various coms.), Franklin County Hist. Soc. (pres. 1989-94). Address: Carol Woods 139 750 Weaver Dairy Rd Chapel Hill NC 27514

DAVIS, SHIRLEY ROSS See SULLIVAN, SHIRLEY ROSS

DAVIS, STACY NICOLE, religious studies educator; b. Waukegan, Ill., Oct. 6, 1973; d. John Michael and Melissa Ann Davis. BA, U. Tulsa, 1996; M. in Theol. Studies, Phillips Theol. Sem., 1998; PhD, U. Notre Dame, 2003. Instr. theology U. Notre Dame, 2002; asst. prof. religious studies St. Mary's Coll., Notre Dame, Ind., 2003—. Mem. African Am. bibl. hermeneutics steering com. Soc. Bibl. Lit., 2004—. Contbr. articles to profl. jours. Mem. Amnesty Internat., 1992; advisor Sex Offense Svcs., South Bend, Ind., 2004. Grantee Ctr. for Academic Innovation faculty tchg. grant, St. Mary's Coll., 2005. Mem.: Soc. Bibl. Lit., Phi Beta Kappa. Avocations: reading, listening to music, traveling. Office: Saint Mary's Coll Box 38 161 Madeleva Hall Notre Dame IN 46556 Office Phone: 574-284-4700. Business E-Mail: dsn1973@aol.com.

DAVIS, SUE ELLEN H., elementary and secondary music educator; b. Girard, Ohio, May 26, 1952; d. Edgar J. and Jane A. (O'Brien) Harris; 1 child, Heidi Elizabeth. BM, Youngstown (Ohio) State U., 1975, MS in Edn./Sch. Counseling, 1985. Cert. counselor, music tchr. K-12, sch. counselor. Tchr. vocal music, kindergarten-12th grade Girard City Schs. Grant coord. Tng. Ohio Parents for Success, Girard City Schs. Active in ch. and community orgns.; co-founder Cmty. Band, 2002. Mem. NEA, Ohio Edn. Assn., Girard Edn. Assn., Nat. Assn. Tchrs. Singing (high sch. div. competition judge), Music Educators Nat. Conf., ASCD, Ohio Sch. Counselor Assn., Ohio Career Devel. Assn., Ohio Assn. Counseling and Devel., Eastern Ohio Counselor's Assn., Ohio Assn. Counselor Educators and Suprs., Ohio Coll. Pers. Assn., Ohio Mental Health Counselors Assn., Ohio Assn. for Specialists in Group Work, Phi Delta Kappa, Delta Kappa Gamma, Sigma Alpha Iota.

DAVIS, SUSAN A., congresswoman; b. Cambridge, Mass., Apr. 13, 1944; m. Steve, 1970; children: Jeffrey, Benjamin. BA in Sociology, U. Calif., Berkeley, 1965; MA in Social Work, U. N.C. Social worker; exec. dir. Aaron Price Fellowship Program, 1990-93; served Calif. State Assembly, 1994-2000; mem. U.S. Congress from 53rd Calif. dist., 2000—, Ho. Com. on Veteran Affairs. Mem. Congressional com. House Armed Svcs., Edn. and Workforce; chaired Women's Caucus for Senate and Assembly, Consumer Protection, Govt. Efficiency, Econ. Devel. com.; created and co-chaired Select com. on Adolescence. Mem. San Diego City Sch. Bd., 1983-1992, pres. and v.p.; pres. League of Women Voters San Diego., Democrat. Office: US Ho Reps 1224 Longworth House Office Bldb Washington DC 20515-0553

DAVIS, SUSAN F., human resources specialist; BS, MS, Beloit Coll.; MBA, U. Mich. From strategic planner to corp. mgr. tng. and devel. Hoover Universal Corp., 1983-85; various positions including v.p. orgnl. devel. automotive group Johnson Controls, Inc., Milw., 1983—94, corp. officer, v.p. human resources, 1994—. Bd. dirs. Quanex Corp., Butler Mfg. Co. Mem.: HR Policy Assn. (vice chair). Office: Johnson Controls Inc 5757 N Green Bay Ave Milwaukee WI 53209-4408 Office Phone: 414-228-1200. Office Fax: 414-524-2077.

DAVIS, SUSAN LYNN, music educator, musician; b. Arcadia, Calif., May 4, 1963; d. David Russell Aronovici and Merlyn Sue Smith, Herb Moreno (Stepfather) and Kathryne DeLorme (Stepmother); m. John Edward Davis, June 10, 1990; children: Evan William, Andrew Russell. AA, Cabrillo Coll., 1983; MusB, San Francisco State U., 1986, MusM, 1990; Tchg. Certification in Music, U. Ariz., 1995. Cert. tchr. support specialist Ga. Profl. Standards Commn., 2004, music in edn. Yamaha Nat. Tchg. Inst., Mich., 1999, Orff-Schulwerk: Levels 1 & 2 U. Ariz., 1994. Music specialist Rome City Schs., Rome, Ga., 1995—; flute and saxophone instr. ABC Music Store, San Bruno, Calif.; flute instr. Rome Music Acad., 1996—2000; kindermusik instr. Berry Coll., Mt. Berry, Ga., 1996—99; flute instr. Shorter Coll. Prep. Dept., Rome, 1996—99, Tanque Verde Sch. Dist., Tucson, 1992—95; music technician Red Rock Elem. Sch., Red Rock, Ariz., 1991—94. Flutist Specifically Winds Woodwind Quintet, San Francisco, 1985—91, City Winds Woodwind Trio, San Francisco, 1985—91; prin. flutist Palo Alto Chamber Orch., 1987—91, San Francisco City Coll. Summer Opera Orch., 1987—91; flutist Twentieth-Century Forum, San Francisco, 1988—91; saxophonist San Francisco City Coll. Cmty. Jazz Band, 1988—90; prin. flutist Redwood Symphony, Redwood City, 1989—91; flutist and saxophonist So. Ariz. Light Opera Co., Tucson, 1994—95; prin. flutist Chamber Players of the South, Rome, 1996—; flutist Dogwood Chamber Ensemble, Rome, 1998—; prin. flutist Catalina Chamber Orch., Tucson, 1991—95; flutist Davis/Harding Flute and Guitar Duo, Tucson, 1991—95; prin. flutist Master's Sinfonia Orch., Belmont, Calif., 1991; flutist Davis/Huckabee Flute and Guitar Duo, Rome, 1996—99; saxophonist Clocktower Jazz Ensemble, Rome, 1996—; prin. flutist Rome Symphony Orch., Rome, 1999—. Musician: (flutist) Nat.

Flute Assn. Conv. Profl.l Flute Choir, (flute soloist) Miss Calif. State Pageant Contestant (First Pl. Talent award, 1982), (saxophonist) Aptos HS Jazz Band (European Jazz Festival Concert Tour, 1981), (flutist) Santa Cruz County Symphony Talent Bank (First Pl. Flute and Chamber Ensemble Winner, 1983). Flutist/chorus dir. Floyd Med. Ctr. Arts Program, Rome, 2003—; vol. (music & charities) Westminster Presbyn. Ch., Rome, 1997—2005; bd. dir. Rome/Floyd (Ga.) Humane Soc., 2000—; sch. improvement com. West Ctrl. Elem. Sch., Rome, 1997—2005; profl. devel. steering com. mem. Berry Coll./West Ctrl. Elem., Rome, 2002—05; tchr. mentor Berry Coll. Sch. of Edn., Ga., 2002—05. Recipient Tchr. of Year, West Ctrl. Elem., 2004—05. Mem.: Nat. Flute Assn. (assoc.), Ga. Music Educator's Assn. (assoc.), Music Educator's Nat. Conf. (assoc.), PA of Ga. Educators (assoc.). Democrat. Presbyterian. Avocations: travel, tennis, reading, movies, animals. Home: 121 E Clinton Dr Rome GA 30165 Office: West Central Elem Sch 409 Lavender Dr Rome GA 30165 Office Fax: 706-234-5854. Business E-Mail: susdavis@rcs.rome.ga.us.

DAVIS, SUZANNE SPIEGEL, retired information specialist; b. St. Louis, Sept. 27, 1935; d. Albert Louis Jr. and Dorothy Lydia (Grafeman) Spiegel; m. Glenn Guy Davis Jr., Sept. 23, 1961 (div. Mar. 1986); 1 child, Wendy Sue. BA, U. Okla., 1957; MLS, U. Ill., 1958. Reference asst. Atlanta Pub. Libr., 1958-59, head adult dept. Ida Williams br., 1959-61, head Fulton County dept., 1961-62; pub. svcs. and documents libr. Queens Coll. Libr., Charlotte, 1969-83; info. specialist Pub. Libr. Charlotte and Mecklenburg, NC, 1983—96. Pres. Charlotte Panhellenic Congress, 1965-66, Charlotte Nature Mus. Guild, 1969-70; rec. chmn. ARC, Mecklenburg County Unit, Charlotte, 1968-69, tng. chmn., 1969-70. Mem. Southeastern Libr. Assn., N.C. Libr. Assn., Charity League, Guild of Nature Mus. and Discovery Place, Beta Phi Mu, Phi Alpha Theta, Alpha Phi. (Michaelanean award 1984). Republican. Presbyterian.

DAVIS, TAYLOR, sculptor; Diploma in Fine Arts, Sch. Mus. Fine Arts; BS in Edn., Tufts U.; MFA, Milton Avery Grad. Sch. Arts, Bard Coll. Asst. prof. Mass. Coll. Art, 1999—; faculty mem. Milton Avery Sch. Arts Bard Coll., 2003—. Exhibitions include Whitney Biennial, Whitney Mus. Am. Art, 2004, Triple Candie, NY, Inst. Contemporary Art, Boston, Green Street Gallery, Boston, Chgo. Arts Coun. Recipient Artist Prize, Inst. Contemporary Art, 2001, Assn. Internat. Art Critics Award, 2002; grantee St. Botolph Found. Grant, 2003; Mass. Cultural Coun. Grant, 1999.

DAVIS, TERESANN WELLER, social worker; b. Sharon, Pa., Mar. 9, 1946; d. Frank and Teresa (Phelan) Weller; m. Ronald E. Davis, Nov. 24, 1972 (div. 1979); 1 child, Jeanne Marie Reighard. BA, Youngstown State U., 1969; MSSA, Case Western Res. U., 1978. Lic. ind. social worker, profl. clin. counselor, Ohio. Therapist Child and Adult Mental Health Ctr., 1969-72; social worker, supr. adult svcs. Valley Counseling, Warren, Ohio, 1973—. Bd. dirs. Someplace Safe, Warren, Rape Crisis Team, Warren; mem. adv. bd. Warren Health Dept.; mem. Child Abuse and Neglect Team, Warren; mem. Pleasant Valley Ecumenical Ch. Mem. NASW. Avocations: reading, youth baseball.

DAVIS, TERRI MYRL, theater educator; d. Gerald Charles and Patsy Ann Hawkins; m. Randall Keith Davis, May 7, 1994. BFA in Theatre Arts, S.W. Tex. State U., San Marcos, 1984. Cert. lifetime secondary theatre arts tchg. Tex., 1995. Theatre and dance tchr. Austin Ind. Sch. Dist., Tex., 1996—; fine arts dept. chair Dobie Mid. Sch., Austin, 2000—; elective team leader, 2000—, campus adv. coun., 2004—. Sunday sch. tchr. Bastrop Christian Outreach Ctr., Tex., 1998—2006, play dir., choreographer, 2000—06. Office Phone: 512-841-2887.

DAVIS, VICKIE B., pre-school educator, director; b. Maryville, Tenn., Dec. 4, 1959; d. Lenword Clay and B. Sue Bolinger; children: Kelsey, Bo. AA in Child Devel., Roane State C.C., 2001. Dir., gymnastics coach The Sch. Perpetual Motion, Maryville, Tenn., 1980—96, dir., 2000—, lead tchr., 2000—; lead tchr. Early Childhood Edn. Ctr. Fort Craig Sch., Maryville, 1997—2000. Mentor Roane State C.C., Oak Ridge, Tenn., 2001—. Named Dir. of Yr., Success By 6, 2004. Mem.: Nat. Assn. Edn. Young Children. Baptist. Avocations: gymnastics, travel, outdoors. Home: 542 Hopewell Rd Maryville TN 37801 Office: The School Perpetual Motion 1452 E Brown Sch Rd Maryville TN 37801

DAVIS, VIRGINIA, trade show producer; b. Waycross, Ga., Nov. 14, 1933; d. Arthur Lewis and Mina (Hyers) Davis; m. Edward Anthony Carfano, July 3, 1954 (div. June 1976). Adminstrv. asst. Mills Music Ltd., N.Y.C., 1960-67; v.p. Edward Carr Prodns., Ltd., N.Y.C., 1990-96; owner Virginia Davis Trade Shows, Convs., Meetings, N.Y.C. and Phoenix, 1973—; asst. at trade shows and press confs. William Campeau Pub. Rels., 1983—. Democrat. Avocations: reading, dance, yoga, animals. Home: 10216 W Campana Dr Sun City AZ 85351-1159 Office Phone: 623-846-2685.

DAVIS, WANDA ROSE, lawyer; b. Lampasas, Tex., Oct. 4, 1937; d. Ellis DeWitt and Julia Doris (Rose) Cockrell; m. Richard Andrew Fulcher, May 9, 1959 (div. 1969); 1 child, Greg Ellis; m. Edwin Leon Davis, Jan. 14, 1973 (div. 1985). BBA, U. Tex., 1959, JD, 1971. Bar: Tex. 1971, Colo. 1981, U.S. Dist. Ct. (no. dist.) Tex. 1972, U.S. Dist. Ct. Colo. 1981, U.S. Ct. Appeals (10th cir. 1981), U.S. Supreme Ct. 1976. Atty. Atlantic Richfield Co., Dallas, 1971; assoc. firm Crocker & Murphy, Dallas, 1971-72; prin. Wanda Davis, Atty. at Law, Dallas, 1972-73; ptnr. firm Davis & Davis Inc., Dallas, 1973-75; atty. adviser HUD, Dallas, 1974-75, Air Force Acctg. and Fin. Ctr., Danver, 1976-92; co-chmn. regional Profl. Devel. Inst. Am. Soc. Mil. Comptrollers, Colorado Springs, Colo., 1982; chmn. Lowry AFB Noontime Edn. Program, Exercise Program, Denver, 1977-83; mem. speakers bur. Colo. Women's Bar, 1995—, Lowry AFB, 1981-83. Mem. fed. ct. liaison com. U.S. Dist. Ct. Colo., 1983; mem. Leaders of the Fed. Bar Assn. People to People Del. to China, USSR and Finland, 1986. Contbr. numerous articles to profl. jours. Bd. dirs. Pres.'s Coun. Met. Denver, 1981-83; mem. Lowry AFB Alcohol Abuse Exec. Com., 1981-84. Recipient Spl. Achievement award USAF, 1978; Upward Mobility award Fed. Profl. and Adminstrv. Women Denver, 1979, Internat. Humanitarian award CARE, 1994. Mem. Fed. Bar Assn. (pres. Colo. 1982-83, mem. nat. coun. 1984—, Earl W. Kintner Disting. Svc. award 1983, 1st v.p. 10th cir. 1986-97, Internat. Hummanitarian award CARE, 1994), Zach Found. for Burned Children (award 1995), Colo. Trial Lawyers Assn., Bus. and Profl. Women's Club (dist. IV East dir. 1983-84, Colo. pres. 1988-89), Am. Soc. Mil. Comptrollers (pres. 1984-85), Denver south Met. Bus. and Profl. Women's Club (pres. 1982-83), Denver Silver Spruce Am. Bus. Women's Assn. (pres. 1981-82; Woman of Yr. award 1982), Colo. Jud. Inst., Colo. Concerned Lawyers, Profl. Mgrs. Assn., Fed. Women's Program (v.p. Denver 1980), Colo. Woman News Community adv. bd. 1988—), Dallas Bar Assn., Tex. Bar Assn., Denver Bar Assn., Altrusa, Zonta, Denver Nancy Langhorn Federally Employed Women (pres. 1979-80). Christian.

DAVIS DECKARD, DIANE A., art educator; b. Denver, Colo., Aug. 18, 1949; d. William Alexander and Dorothy Alice Adam; m. Donald Lowell Deckard, Jan. 26, 1980; 1 child, William Lee Davis. BA in fine arts, Ind. U., 1973, MS in edn., 1985. Cert. tchg. Ind. U., 1979. Art tchr. Monroe County Cmty. Sch., Bloomington, Ind., 1980—81, Spencer Owen Cmty. Sch., Spencer, Ind., 1981—83, Martinsville Sch., Martinsville, Ind., 1983—84, Monroe County Cmty. Sch., Bloomington, Ind., 1984—. Coord. Monroe County Art Tchrs., Bloomington, Ind., 1990—91, 1994—95, 1998—99, 2003—04, exhibit coord., 1995—. Facilitator Bloomington Hosp. Student Mural, Bloomington, Ind., 1998, Bloomington Hosp. Student Landscape Paintings, 1999—2004, Bloomington Hosp. Student art works for 100th Anniversary, 2004—05, Jiffy Treet Student Mural Project, 2005; artists in residence Monroe County Cmty. Sch. Found., 1987—90. Named Monroe County Educator of Yr., 2005. Mem.: Ind. State Tchrs. Assn., Monroe County Edn. Assn., Nat. Art Edn. Assn., Pi Lambda Theta, Phi Delta Kappa Internat. Presbyn. Avocations: painting, photography, reading, hiking, embroidery. Office: Bloomington HS N 3901 N Kinser Pike Bloomington IN 47404 Business E-Mail: ddavis@mccsc.edu.

DAVIS-FERNANDES, TINA DENISE, secondary school educator, coach; b. LA, Dec. 10, 1967; d. Lenious Samuel Davis and Martha Lee Callegari-Davis; m. Sean Anthony Fernandes, June 29, 1991; children: Anthony Fernandes, Denise Fernandes. MEd, Argosy U., Orange, 2005. Coach girls head track & field Compton Unified Sch. Dist., Calif., 1991—95; tchr. spl. ecdn. ECKO-Multi-Center, 1992—95; tchr. Lynwood Unified Sch. Dist., 1995—; coach track & field U. So. Calif., LA, 1999—. Recipient West Regional Asst. Coach Yr. Sprints/Hurdles, NCAA, 2005. Mem.: Women's Track & Field, AAHPERD (none), USA Track & Field (none). Achievements include Coached over 20 All-American Titles for USC; Assisted USC Track & Field Team to the First National Title in 2001. Office: USC / Lynwood Unified School District 3501 Watt Way Los Angeles CA 90089 Office Phone: 213-821-2170. Home Fax: 213-740-7289; Office Fax: 213-740-7289. Personal E-mail: davisfer@usc.edu.

DAVIS-JEROME, EILEEN GEORGE, educational consultant, principal; b. NYC, Nov. 10, 1946; d. Rennie and Flora May (Compton) George; m. Bruce Davis, Aug. 8, 1970 (div. 1978); m. Frantz Jerome, Sept. 7, 1982; 1 child, Thais Davis BFA, Pratt Inst., Bklyn., 1968; MA, CUNY, 1971, PD, 1990; EdD, Nova Southeastern U., Ft. Lauderdale, Fla., 1998. Lic. ednl. adminstr., prin., instrn. specialist, N.Y. Tchr. fine arts Herbert Lehman H.S., Bronx, NY, 1971—75; tchr. English, fine arts Jr. H.S. 131, Bronx, 1975—76; tchr. English Jr. H.S. 22, Bronx, 1976—79; admissions counselor Fashion Inst. Tech., SUNY, 1983—85; tchr. fine arts Andrew Jackson H.S., Cambria Heights, NY, 1979—83, coord. art dept., 1986—92; project dir. Andrew Jackson Magnet H.S., Cambria Heights, 1993—, prin. Humanities and Arts, 1994—2003, project dir. Humanities and Arts, 1994—; coord. Queensborough Coll. Project Prize, Bayside, NY, 1991—92; ednl. adminstr. Queens H.S. Office, N.Y.C. Pub. H.S., Corona, NY, 1993—94. Coord. internat. studies Friends Jackson H.S., Cambria Heights, 1986-93, equal opportunity coord., 1989-92; exam asst. N.Y.C. Bd. Edn., Bd. Examiners, Bklyn., 1983-87; curriculum/career cons. Fashion Inst., SUNY, Detroit, Washington, Phila., 1983-86 Curriculum writer N.Y. State Project Implement Career Edn., 1975, N.Y. State Futuring, 1984; proposal writer Magnet Sch. Funding, 1993; author: Resource Book, 1989 Mem., spkr. Cambria Heights Civic Assn., 1983; mem. N.Y. Urban League, N.Y.C.; vol. Mayor's Vol. Action/Alpha Sr. Cr., Cambria Heights, 1984; vol. Black Spectrum Theatre Co., 1983-86; mem. coord. coun. h.s. divsn. N.Y.C. Bd. Edn., 1997—; v.p. for edn. Madam C.J. Walker Found., 2001— Named Educator of Yr., NAACP/ACT-S0, N.Y.C., 1992; recipient Recognition award, Black Spectrum Theatre Co., 1983, Spkrs. award, N.Y.C. Bd. Edn. Open Doors, 1983—84, Black Exec. Exch. Program Nat. Urban League, N.Y.C., 1984, Developer Grant award, Impact II Grant, N.Y.C., 1989, Laurelton Club Prol. award, 1996, Disting. Educator award, L.I. br. Nat. Assn. U. Women, 2001, Life Membership award, NAACP, N.Y.C., 2001, Excellence in Edn. award, Omega Psi Phi, 2002, Disting. Educator award, Newsday, 2003, Outstanding Citizen citation, N.Y.C. Coun., 2003, Performace award, N.Y.C. Dept. Edn., N.Y.C. Coun. Suprs. and Adminstrs, 2002—03. Mem. ASCD, UN Assn., N.Y. State Art Tchrs. Assn., N.Y.C. Art Tchrs. Assn. (v.p., sec. 1983-85, cert. 1983-86), Cultural Heritage Alliance (assoc., Recognition award 1986), Greater Queens Chpt. The Links, Inc., Delta Sigma Theta (chair arts and letters 1991-97, Golden Life award 1991), Phi Delta Kappa (Disting. cert. 1994) Democrat. Episcopalian. Avocations: painting, travel, dance, writing, theater. Office: Magnet HS Humanities and the Arts 20701 116th Ave Jamaica NY 11411-1038

DAVIS-KEITH, MADELYN MICHELLE, elementary school educator; b. Birmingham, Ala., Dec. 28, 1971; d. Troy and Stevie Davis; m. Michael Guy Keith, Sept. 5, 2004; 1 child, Saydee Morgan. BS in Biology, U. Ala., Birmingham, 1995, BS in Edn., 1997; JD, Birmingham Sch. Law, 2005. Bar: Ala.; cert. tchr. Ala. Swim tchr. Wald Pk., Vestavia Hills, Ala., 1993—; tchr. Sumiton Sch., Ala., 1999—. Office Phone: 205-648-5032.

DAVIS-LEWIS, BETTYE, nursing educator; b. Egypt, Tex., Sept. 19, 1939; d. Henry Sr. and Eliza (Baylock) Davis; divorced; children: Kim Michelle, Roderick Trevor. BS, Prarie View A&M U., 1959; BA in Psychology, U. Houston, 1972; MEd, Tex. Southern U., 1974, EdD, 1982. Dir. edn. Houston Internat. Hosp., 1987—; dir. nurses Mental Health & Mental Retardation Auth. Harris County, Houston, 1982-87, Riverside Gen. Hosp., Houston; CEO, owner Diversified Health Care Systems, Inc., Houston, 1985—; asst. clin. prof. psychiat. nursing U. Tex., 1987-88; asst. prof. allied health sci. Tex. So. U., Houton, 1989—. Adj. prof. Coll. Nursing, Prairie View A&M U., 1986—; lectr. in field; leadership extern. Mem. Harris County Coun. Orgns., 1987—; mem. polit. action com. Coalition 100 Black Women, 1988—; founder, mem. Hattie White Aux. br. NAACP, 1988; mem. grievance com. State Bar Tex., 1988—; chmn. S.W. Regional Nat. Black Leadership Initiative on Cancer, 1988—; grad. Leadership Tex.; bd. dirs. Theatre Under the Stars. Recipient Disting. Rsch. award Internat. Soc. Hypertension, Disting. Crystal award, Impact award Wheeler Ave. Bapt. Ch.; fellow Internat. Leadership Forum, Am. Leadership Forum; named one of Most Influential Black Americans, Ebony mag., 2005, 06. Fellow Internat. Soc. Hypertension in Blacks; mem. ANA, Nat. Black Nurses Assn. (past mem. bd. dirs., pres.), Sigma Theta Tau, Chi Eta Phi. Office: Diversified Health Care Sys Inc #2 4811 Jackson Houston TX 77004 also: Nat Black Nurses Assn 8630 Fenton St, Ste 330 Silver Spring MD 20910-3803*

DAVISON, DAWN SHERRY, correctional administrator, educator; b. Chgo., Nov. 3, 1956; d. Henry and Teresa (Lombardo) Foreman; m. Wayne Thomas Davison, Apr. 21, 1979; children: Laurenne Teresa, Celise Arielle. BS, Loyola Marymount U., 1978; MS, Calif. State U., Fullerton, 1982. Personnel officer Calif. Instn. Women, Frontera, 1986-93; correctional bus. mgr. Calipatria (Calif.) State Prison, 1994-97; assoc. warden, correctional administrator Calif. State Prison L.A. County, Lancaster, 1997—, equal employment opportunity program coord. Mem. NAFE, Chicano Correctional Workers Am., Assn. Black Correctional Workers. Democrat. Avocations: theater, jazz music, reading, sketching. Office: Calif State Prison L A County 44750 60th St W Lancaster CA 93536-7619

DAVISON, KIM M., elementary school educator; b. Buffalo, Dec. 20, 1955; d. George Turpie and Ida Lorraine (Ramsey) D. BS, Daemen Coll., Buffalo, 1978; MA, Mich. State U., 1986. Cert. tchr. Tchr. Calasanctius Sch., Buffalo, 1979-81, coord. enrichment program, 1980-81; tchr., grade level coord. The Am. Sch. Guatemala, 1981-85; tchr. Kalamazoo (Mich.) Pub. Schs., 1986—. Founding mem. Learning to Give. Producer, editor video What I Want to Be When I Grow Up, 1988. Singer St. Augustine's Cathedral, Kalamazoo, 1986—, Kalamazoo Community Chorale, 1988—. Recipient Excellence in Edn. award Kalamazoo County Excellence in Edn. Found., 1989, 92, Presdl. award, 1991; Kalamazoo Pub. Edn. Found. mini-grantee, 1988, 90, 91, Mich. Dept. Edn. mini grantee, 1991. Roman Catholic. Avocations: travel, recycling, video production, photography, singing. Office: Kalamazoo Pub Schs 1220 Howard St Kalamazoo MI 49008-1871 Business E-Mail: davisonkim@kalamazoo.k12.mi.us.

DAVISON, LESLI ANNE, elementary school educator; b. Carmichael, Calif., July 31, 1966; d. Barry Gene and Linda Higgins Flanary; m. Paul Alan Davison, June 16, 1990; children: Austin, Grant. BS in Elem. Edn., Miami U., Oxford, Ohio, 1988; MEd, Wright State U., Fairborn, Ohio, 1995. 4th grade tchr. Kings Local Sch. Dist., Kings Mills, Ohio, 1989—99, Olentangy Local Sch. Dist., Lewis Center, Ohio, 2000—. Vol. Cozy Cat Cottage/Human Soc. for Cats, Powell, Ohio, 2005—. Named Walmart Tchr. of the Yr., 2003, Oak Creek Tchr. of the Yr., Olentangy Local Sch. Dist., 2002—03, Coach of the Yr., Kings Local Sch. Dist., 1990—91. Republican. Avocations: camping, soccer. Home: 2643 Silverleaf Dr Powell OH 43065 Office: Olentangy Local School District 814 Shanahan Dr Lewis Center OH 43035

DAVIS-TOWNSEND, HELEN IRENE, retired art educator; b. North Adams, Mich., July 25, 1910; d. Bert and Jennie Louisa (Martin) Smith; m. Donald Hicks Davis, Mar. 21, 1931 (dec. Nov. 1944); children: Donald H. Jr., Bernard S., Bruce M., William J.; m. Loal Wendell Townsend, Dec. 27, 1971. BA, Mich. State U., 1952, MA, 1959. Permanent tchg. cert., Mich. Typist, sec. Buermann-Marshall Co., Lansing, Mich., 1928-30; pvt. sec. Frank L. Young, Jr., LLD, Lansing, 1930-31; typist Buermann-Marshall Co., Lansing, 1932-36, Olds Motor Co., Lansing, 1936-37; art tchr. Okemos (Mich.) Pub. Schs., 1952-72. Art club dir. Okemos H.S., 1952-72, tchr. adult edn. classes, 1962-70; supervising tchr. tchr. edn. program Mich. State U., East Lansing, 1960-72; region 8 rep., liaison officer Mich. Art Edn. Assn. State Bd., East Lansing, 1962-70; vis. artist John Wesley Coll., Owosso, Mich., 1979. Author, composer: (children's mus.) That Star Is Shaking Up Our Town, 1974, (song and music) Life Is a Road, 1974; artist numerous paintings. Sec.-typist Mich. Rep. Party, Lansing, 1932; children and youth choir dir. Wesleyan Meth. Ch., Lansing, 1939-72, choir mem., 1929-72; choir mem. Stockbridge (Mich.) United Meth. Ch., 1972-80. Recipient Bonderenco award, 1987; Hinman scholar Mich. State U., 1950, Alumni scholar, 1951-52. Mem. NEA (life), Mich. Edn. Assn. (life), Nat. Mus. of Women in Arts (charter), Art Ctr. Manatee, Lansing Art Gallery (charter). Methodist. Avocations: painting, playing piano and organ, bowling, theater, travel.

DAVIS-WEXLER, GINIA, singer, director; b. Phila., Mar. 10, 1918; d. Meyer and Hilda (Emery) D.; m. Morris M. Wexler, Oct. 1968 Student drama, Carnegie Inst. Tech., 1939—41; vocal pupil, Frances Lewando, Doris Monteux, 1939—50; coached with, Povla Frijsh, Pierre Monteux, Queena Mario, Pablo Casals, Madeleine Grey. Voice tchr. Mich. State U., East Lansing, 1962; dir. Hancock County Chamber Music Soc. (now Hancock County Friends of Arts), East Sullivan, Maine, 1962—; dir. free programs for children Farmstead Barn, Sullivan, Maine, 1970—. Performed as Polly Peachum in The Beggar's Opera, 1941, Bar Harbor (Maine) Stock Co., Chautauqua, N.Y. Bucks County Playhouse; leading roles New Moon, Toledo Light Opera Co., 1945; appeared on Broadway in Susan and God, 1942, Call Me Mister, 1946; made operatic debut as Gretel in Hansel and Gretel with Pitts. Opera Soc., 1943; ann. recital N.Y.C., 1948-65; toured U.S.A., 1947-67, Europe, 1949, 50; appeared at Holland Festival, 1950; in 1st U.S. performances of Flaminio of Pergolesi, 1953; performances at Royal Opera of Brussels, 1955, broadcasts, U.S., Europe; appeared with symphony orch., U.S., Europe, Mid.-East, 1955-67; made six months world tour, Africa, Asia, 1966, guitar concerts, 1965; dir. performing arts for children series, Hancock Grand County Auditorium, 1976-89, h.s. touring program, 1980-89, recs. songs Music Libr. Records, Inc., folk music divsn., Libr. Congress; mem. Surry, Maine Opera Co., 1984-90; dir. Sullivan Bicentennial Chorus, 1989; lead role in play All Thru the Night, 1989; appearances Am. Folksong Festival; adviser folk music, Nat Arts Found.; authority on folksongs; collector, transcriber, interpreter: (with Jean Thomas) folklore Ky. mountains (the Traipsin' Woman), 1950-55, also other locations; entertainer Armed Forces, U.S., Europe. (Recipient grand prize Internat. contest interpretation French song 1958) Chmn. Sullivan Conservation Commn., 1973-83; interim pres. Pierre Monteux Sch., Hancock, Maine, 2005-06. Developer unique recital program Portraits in Song, 1947. Home: The Farmstead 2816 US Hwy 1 Sullivan ME 04664-3522 Personal E-mail: gdwexler@msn.com.

DAVIS-YANCEY, GWENDOLYN, lawyer; b. Jackson, Mich., Apr. 6, 1955; d. Wendell Norman Sr. and Jean Davis; children: Natosha, Michael, Nicole, Jennifer, Cyril; m. Kenneth Donald Yancey, Dec. 9, 1995. BS, Wayne State U., 1990; JD, U. Detroit Mercy, 1994. Bar: Mich., U.S. Dist. Ct. (ea. dist.) Mich.; cert. tchr., Mich. Legal sec. Dykema, Gossett, Detroit; chemistry tchr. Detroit Bd. Edn., 1990-92; atty. Misdemeanor Def.'s Office, Detroit, 1994-95, Legal Aid and Def.'s Office, Detroit, 1995-96, Davis-Yancey Law Office P.L.L.C., Southfield, Mich., 1996—; ptnr., owner Men's Legal Svc., 1999—. Mem. ABA, State Bar of Mich. (family law sect., real estate sect., bus. law sect., litig. sect.), Wayne County Family Law Bar. Office: Davis-Yancey Law Office PLLC # 703A W 15565 Northland Dr Southfield MI 48075

DAVLANTES, ANNA, newscaster; b. Chgo. Degree, Northwestern U.; postgrad., Oxford U., Eng. Formerly with WTTW, Chgo., WXIN-TV, Indpls., WPTA-TV, Ft. Wayne, Ind.; former primary anchor KRIV-TV, Houston; co-anchor weekend evening newscasts WMAQ-TV, Chgo., 2000—. Mem. Coun. of 100 Women Northwestern U. Nominee Nat. Emmy award; recipient Chgo. Emmy award, Headliner award. Office: WMAQ-TV NBC Tower 454 N Columbus Dr Chicago IL 60611-5555 Business E-Mail: anna.davlantes@nbc.com.

DAVLIN, MARY CLEMENTE, literature and language professor, sister; b. Chgo., Mar. 6, 1929; d. John Joseph Davlin and Margaret Mary Ryan. BA, Rosary Coll., River Forest, Ill., 1950; MA, U. Wis., Madison, 1951; PhD, U. Calif., Berkeley, 1964. Tchr. Aquinas H.S, Chgo., 1952—53, DuSable H.S., 1953—54; instr. to prof. Edgewood Coll., Madison, Wis., 1956—59, 1963—70; prof. Rosary Coll. (now Dominican U.), River Forest, Ill., 1970—2005, prof. emerita, 2005—. Tchr.-scholar Ill. Humanities Coun., Starved Rock, 2000. Author: A Game of Heuene, 1989, Place of God in Piers Plowman and Medieval Art, 2001. Violinist Oak Park-River Forest Symphony, Ill., 1971—; spkr. River Forest Pub. Libr., 1994—2006. Recipient Excellence in Tchg. award, Dominican U., 1973, 1997, Diversity award, 2003; fellow, Newberry Libr., Chgo. and Brit. Acad., London, 1981, NEH, 1991. Mem.: Langland Soc., Modern Lang. Assn., Medieval Acad. Home: Dominican U 7900 Division St River Forest IL 60305-1066

DAWDY, SHANNON LEE, archaeologist, historical anthropologist; BA in Anthropology, Reed Coll., Portland, Oreg., 1988; MA in Anthropology, Coll. William and Mary, Williamsburg, Va., 1994; MA in History, U. Mich., Ann Arbor, 2000, PhD in Anthropology and History, 2003. Docent coun. adminstr. Fine Arts Mus. San Francisco, 1989—92; archaeologist Colonial Williamsburg Found./Coll. William and Mary, Va., 1992—93; consulting ethnohistorian Meherrin Indian Tribe, Winton, NC, 1994—95; project mgr. Earth Science, Inc., New Orleans, 1994—95; rsch. assoc., dir. greater New Orleans archaeology program U. New Orleans, 1995—98, vis. scholar, Coll. Urban and Pub. Affairs, 2004—; grad. student instructor, dept. anthropology and history U. Mich., Ann Arbor, 1999—2001; adj. instructor, dept. history Triton Coll., River Grove, 2003; lectr., dept. social sciences Harold Washington Coll., Chgo., 2003; asst. prof. anthropology and social sciences in the coll. U. Chgo., 2004—. Fieldwork experience in Oreg., So. New England, Va., NC, Cuba, New Orleans, La., 1987—; reading group coord., doctoral program in anthropology and history, 1998—99; dept. rep. Grad. Employee Orgn., 1999—2000; grant writer for team project Social Sci. Rsch. Coun., Cuba Program, 2001—02; spkr. in field. Contbr. articles to prof. jours., chapters to books; manuscript reviewer Jour. of Social History, Louisiana History, bd. dir., newletter editor La. Archaeological Conservancy, 1996—98, guest editor Historical Archaeology, Vol. 34, 1999—2000. Rackham Regents Fellowship, 1998—2001, Inst. for Humanities Fellow, 2001—02, Am. Soc. for Eighteenth Century Studies Fellow, Newberry Libr., 2002. Mem.: La. Archaeological Soc., Soc. for Am. Archaeology (session organizer, chair, Cuban Archaeology for conf. 2002), French Colonial Hist. Soc., La. History Assn., Soc. for Hist. Archaeology (session organizer, chair, Creolization for conf. 1998), Am. Anthropology Assn. Office: Dept Anthropology Haskell 202 U Chgo 1126 E 59th St Chicago IL 60637 Office Phone: 773-834-0829. Business E-Mail: sdawdy@uchicago.edu.*

DAWICKI, DOLORETTA DIANE, analytical chemist, research biochemist, educator; b. Fall River, Mass., Sept. 13, 1956; d. Walter and Stella Ann (Olszewski) D. BS, S.E. Mass. U., 1978; PhD, Brown U., 1986. Rsch. assoc. Meml. Hosp. R.I., Pawtucket, 1986-92; asst. prof. Brown U., Providence, 1986-96; rsch. assoc. VA Med. Ctr., Providence, 1992-96; quality control tech. svcs. assoc. dir. Genzyme Corp., Framingham, Mass., 1996—. Contbr. articles to profl. jours. Mem. AAAS, Am. Soc. for Biochemistry and Molecular Biology, Parenteral Drug Assn. Achievements include research on in vivo antiplatelet mechanism of action of the clinical agent dipyridamole, endothelial cell injury, effects of nucleotides on leukocyte-endothelial cell interaction; assay development, optimization, and validation to monitor drug identity, safety, and efficacy; product testing and quality control release of commercial therapeutic finished drug products. Home: 3 Odyssey Ln Franklin MA 02038-2460 Office: Genzyme Corp PO Box 9322 Framingham MA 01701-9322 Office Phone: 508-424-4241. E-mail: dale.dawicki@genzyme.com.

DAWKINS, AMY, artist; b. Moberly, Mo., May 11, 1969; d. Frederick Eugene and Carol June D.; 1 child, James Eugene Dorman. BFA, Md. Inst. Coll. Art, 1991. Delivery truck driver UPS, Columbia, Mo., 1995-99; artist Dogkins Studio, Sturgeon, Mo., 1999—. Author: poems. Juror State of Mo., Columbia, 1999; student youth amb. People to People (Eisenhower) Program, Moberly, 1987. Scholar, grantee Md. Inst. Coll. Art, 1987-91; scholar Little Divie Art Assn., 1987; named Honor Top of Class Moberly Rotary Club, 1991. Mem. Columbia Art League, Women in Arts Mus., Humane Soc. Columbia, Nat. ARbor Day Found. Avocations: painting, drawing, writing, photography, running. Home and Office: Dogkins Studio 19101 N Route V Sturgeon MO 65284-9470

DAWKINS, BARBARA ELAINE, retired secondary school educator; b. Willimantic, Conn., Feb. 21, 1938; d. Stanley Potter and Gladys Mae (Buskard) Lamberton; m. James Elbert Dawkins, Aug. 7, 1965. BA in Math., U. Del., 1960; postgrad. studies, Brown U., 1963-64. Math. tchr. Bloomfield (N.J.) Pub. Schs., 1960-63, Dept. of Defense, Crailsheim, Germany, 1964-66, Nurenberg, Germany, 1966-67, Freehold (N.J.) High Sch., 1967-68, Lakes High Sch., Tacoma, 1973-74, Empire Sch., Duncan, Okla., 1977—95. Recipient scholarship Brown U. Nat. Sci. Found. Acad., 1963-64. Mem. NEA, AAUW (treas. Lawton chpt. 1984-85, 88-90), Okla. Edn. Assn., Empire Edn. Assn. (Tchr. of Yr. 1982), Nat. Coun. Tchrs. Math., Okla. Coun. Tchrs. Math., Delta Kappa Gamma (treas., 1998—). Republican. Presbyterian. Avocations: needlecrafts, knitting, golf, reading, bowling. Home: 2329 NE Village Dr Lawton OK 73507-2346 Office: Empire Sch RR 1 Box 155 Duncan OK 73533-9713

DAWKINS, TERESA GILLILAND, elementary school educator; b. Oneonta, Ala., June 4, 1955; d. Russel Ervin and Gertrude Lera Gilliland; m. Robert Anthony Dawkins, Sept. 13, 1981; children: Alan Keith, Rachel Diane. BS, Auburn U., Ala., 1979, MS, 1981; MEd, Jacksonville State U., Ala., 1989. Lab technician Auburn U., 1981—85; tchr. Ft. Payne City Schs., Ala., 1989—. Author: (rsch.) Comp. Immunology Microbiol. Infectious Diseases, 1982. Tchr. Sunday sch. Union Grove Bapt. Ch., Crossville, Ala., 1999—2006. Achievements include research in Published in Comp. Immun. Microbiol. Infect. Dis. Vol. 5 No 4 pp. 457-468, 1982. Office Phone: 256-845-0535.

DAWSON, ARLETA M., history educator; b. Downey, Calif., Oct. 18, 1955; d. Stanley Donal and Mary Jane Glassgow; m. Jess Paul Dawson, June 23, 1977; children: Jess Patrick, Brian Paul. BA, George Mason U., Fairfax, Va., 1996; MS, Troy State U., Dathan, Ala., 1999. Tchr. social studies Green Run H.S., Virginia Beach, Va., 1999—. With U.S. Army, 1977—78. Home: 3825 Bent Branch Dr Virginia Beach VA 23452 Office: Green Run HS 1700 Dahlia Dr Virginia Beach VA 23453 Office Phone: 757-431-4040. Business E-Mail: arleta.dawson@vbschools.com.

DAWSON, BESSE MALINDA BARKER, secondary school educator, department chairman; b. South Charleston, W.Va., June 20, 1948; d. Carroll Teass and Hester Mitchell Barker; m. Robert Maitland Dawson, Oct. 26, 1986; 1 child, Malinda Virginia Fields. BA in Geneal. Sci. and Art, Marshall U., 1970; MS in Biology, Marshall U., 76. Tchr. Washington Jr. HS, Winfield, W.Va., 1969—70, Montgomery (W.Va.) Sr. and Jr. HS, 1970—71, Alleghany County HS, Covington, Va., 1971—73, Dunbar (W.Va.) Jr. HS, 1974—79, Andrew Jackson Jr. HS, Cross Lanes, W.Va., 1981—84, Johnson HS, Savannah, Ga., 1984—85, Pearland (Tex.) Ind. Sch. Dist., 1985—, head dept., 1993—. Mentor, advisor Tchrs. Experiencing Antarctica and The Arctic, 1998—2002; presenter in field. Pres. Landing Coun. Co-owners, El Lago, Tex., 2002—05; adv. trustee Galveston Bay Found., Webster, Tex., 1999—2000, mem., officer edn. com., 1993—2002; vol. Tex. Marine Mammal Stranding Network, Galveston, 1993—2006. Named Dist. Secondary Tchr. Of The Yr., Pearland Ind. Sch. Dist., 1995; recipient Radioshack Nat. Tchr. award, Radioshack/Tandy Corp., 2000; grantee, NSF, 1997—98, 2000. Mem.: NEA. Avocations: camping, guitar, travel, birdwatching, sailing. Office: Pearland Ninth Grade Ctrr 4717 Bailey Rd Pearland TX 77581 Home: 1 Hermann Museum Cir # 4030 Houston TX 77004 Office Phone: 281-727-1600. Personal E-mail: dawfun@houston.rr.com.

DAWSON, CAROL GENE, former commissioner, writer, consultant; b. Indpls., Sept. 8, 1937; d. Ernest Eugene (dec.) and Hilda Lou (Carroll) D.; m. Robert Edmund Bauman, Nov. 19, 1960 (div. 1982); children: Edward Carroll, Eugenie Marie, Victoria Ann, James Shields; m. Franklin Dean Smith, Aug. 2, 1986. BA, Dunbarton Coll., Washington, 1959, Cath. U., 1960; MA in Internat. Transactions, George Mason U., 1994. Staff asst. Senator Kenneth B. Keating, Washington, 1959; exec. asst. Americans for Constl. Action, Washington, 1959; exec. sec. Youth for Nixon Lodge, Washington, 1959-60; legis. asst. Rep. Donald C. Bruce, Washington, 1961-63; dep. dir., pub. info. Goldwater for Pres. Campaign and Rep. Nat. Com., Washington, 1963-64; editor, assoc. editor The New Guard Mag., Washington, 1965-66; dir. info. Am. Conservative Union, Washington, 1966-67; publs. and news analyst White House, Washington, from 1969; staff reporter Easton (Md.) Star-Democrat, 1971-72; freelance writer Easton, 1972-77; real estate salesperson Latham Realtors, Easton, 1977-80; sr. staff asst. presdl. transition U.S. Office of Personnel Mgmt., Washington, 1980-81; dep. press sec. U.S. Dept. Energy, Washington, 1981-82, dep. spl. asst. to sec., 1982-84; commr. U.S. Consumer Product Safety Commn., Washington, 1984-93. Editor Cath. Currents newsletter, Washington, 1969-70. Bd. visitors Inst. Polit. Journalism Georgetown U., 1985—89; mem. Nat. Policy Forum, Coun. of Free Individuals in a Free Soc., Coun. on Internat. Trade, 1994—97; bd. dirs. Consumer Alert, 1995—; mem. Commonwealth of Va. Bd. Phys. Therapy, 2000—04; bd. dirs. Nat. Conservative Campaign Fund, Washington, 1999—; chmn. Lancaster County (Va.) Rep. Com., 1996—2002, 99th Legis. Dist. Rep. Com., 2000—; mem. Va. Rep. State Ctrl. Com., 2001—; bd. dirs. Va. Horse Coun., 2004—. Recipient Award of Merit Young Americans for Freedom, 1970. Mem. The Charter 100, Reagan Appointees Alumni, The Fairfax Hunt Club (bd. govs. 1989-91). Roman Catholic.

DAWSON, CARON, medical and legal consultant; b. London, Sept. 21, 1956; d. Douglas and Patsy Dawson. Diploma, NW Surrey Dist. Sch. Nursing, Chertsey, England, 1978; BA in Polit. Sci. (hon.), Old Dominion U., Norfolk, Va., 1987; JD, U. Miami, 1990, LLM in Internat. Law, 1991. Bar: Fla. 1991; RN Fla., 1978, Ill., 2001. Med.-legal cons. pvt. practice, Chgo., 1991—. Recipient Outstanding Polit. Sci. award, Old Dominion U., 1986—87. Mem.: ATLA, Phi Kappa Phi. Personal E-mail: carondawson@cdrnjd.com.

DAWSON, CINDY MARIE, lawyer; b. Oklahoma City, May 3, 1960; d. Alva Glenn and Ethel Estelle Horner; m. Ronnie L. Dawson, July 14, 1977; children: Kristina Lee Ann, Kathryn DeeAnn, Shaunna Renee. AA, Rose State Coll., Midwest City, Okla., 1993; BBA, U. Ctrl. Okla., 1994, postgrad., 1997—; JD, Oklahoma City U., 1997. Bar: Okla. 1997. Leasing agt. Brentwood Apts., Shawnee, Okla., 1988; bus. advisor Triple H Constrn., Eufaula, Okla., 1989-96; pvt. practice atty. Edmond, Okla., 1997-2000; asst. dist. atty. Shawnee, Okla., 2000—01; pvt. practice atty. Eufaula, 2001—. Mem.: Okla. Criminal Def. Lawyers Assn., Okla. Bar Assn. (family law section, criminal law section, mgmt. and tech. section), Eufaula Alumni Assn., Phi Delta Phi. Avocations: reading, cooking, sports, travel. Office: 112 Selmon Rd Eufaula OK 74432 Office Phone: 918-689-3600. E-mail: dawsonpc@hotmail.com.

DAWSON, DAWN LOUISE, elementary school educator, church administrator; d. William Allen Dawson and Joyce Lynn Berg. BS in Edn., Mont. State U., 1996; MEd, U. Gt. Falls, 2005. Cert. elem. prin. Mont. Adminstrv. asst. Belt (Mont.) Cmty. Ch., 1996—; Saturday sch. tchr. Gt. Falls Pub. Sch., 1997—; supervising tchr. Benton Lake Sch., Floweree, Mont., 1998—. Home: 3408 13th Ave S Great Falls MT 59405 Office: Benton Lake Sch 17557 Bootlegger Trl Floweree MT 59440 Office Phone: 406-452-9023.

DAWSON, GERALDINE, medical educator, social worker; b. Huntington, Pa., Oct. 2, 1945; d. Donn and Evelyn Koontz; m. Nathan Maniam. BA, Pa. State U., 1967; MSW, Smith Coll., 1969; MD, Albert Einstein Coll. Medicine, 1988. Fellow Harvard Med. Sch.-Mass. Gen. Hosp., Boston, 1980—82, All India Inst. Med. Sci., New Delhi, 1987—88; med. resident Lenox Hill Hosp., N.Y.C., 1988—89; cons. Dept. of Def., Washington, 1990—92; assoc. prof. Marywood U., Scranton, Pa., 1993—. Contbr. articles to profl. jours. Mem. adv. coun. Regional Health Edn. Ctr. N.E. Pa., Scranton, 2001—; mem. Pa. Health Edn. Interdisciplinary Task Force, Hershey, 2002—. Named N.E. Woman, Scranton Times, 2000, Excellence in Their Field, Johnstown Tribune Democrat, 2000. Mem.: Pa. Nat. Alliance Mentally Ill, Pa. Nat. Assn. Social Workers (chairperson profl. stds. com. 1997—2003), Am. Psychotherapy Assn. (diplomate). Office Phone: 570-348-6282 ext 2390. Business E-Mail: dawson@marywood.edu.

DAWSON, JESSICA, art critic; Writer Washington City Paper; art critic, galleries column Washington Post; art critic Washington Post.com, 2001—. Freelance art critic. Office: Washington Post 1150 15th St NW Washington DC 20071

DAWSON, JOAN MARIE, elementary school educator; b. Niles, Kans., July 2, 1937; d. Clifford C. and Lura M. (Allison) Geske; m. Glen E. Dawson, Jan. 1, 1956; children: Justin G., Geffrey B. BS, Marymount Coll., 1972; MS, Kans. State U., 1979. Cert. elem. edn. tchr. Tchr. Unified Sch. Dist. 473, Chapman, Kans., 1972—. Grantee Southwestern Bell, 1990-91, 92-93, Wolfcreek Generating Sta., 1992-93; recipient Presdl. award NSF, 1993-94. Mem. NSTA, Kans. Sci. Tchrs. Assn., Eisenhower Reading Coun., Chapman Edn. Assn. (pres., sec. 1972-95, Master Tchr. 1988). Lutheran. Avocations: walking, gardening, reading. Home: 609 NW 10th St Abilene KS 67410-2380 Office: Chapman Elem Sch 622 N Marshall Chapman KS 67431

DAWSON, M. SUSAN, nursing educator, mental health services professional; b. St. Louis, June 9, 1950; d. Lester A. and Natalie J. (Federer) Liebmann; m. W.M. Mark Dawson, Jan. 1, 1993; children: Jessica M. Patton, Jillian L. Countryman. ADN, St. Louis C.C., 1974; BSN, Webster U., 1988, MA in Edn., 1990; MSN, So. Ill. U., 1993; EdD, U. Mo., 1997. RN;bd. cert. psychiat. advanced practice nurse. Nurse, various locations, 1974—; nursing instr. Luth. Sch. Nursing, St. Louis, 1990-93, Lewis and Clark C.C., Godfrey, Ill., 1993-95; prof. nursing St. Louis C.C., 1992—; prof. Goal Program Greenville Coll., Ill., 1997—; assoc. faculty Jewish Coll. Nursing/Washington U., St. Louis, 1998—. Mem. Nat. League of Nurses, Sigma Theta Tau. Office: St Louis CC at Meramec 11333 Big Bend Rd Saint Louis MO 63122-5720

DAWSON, MARTHA BROMLEY, retired software developer; b. Whitewater, Wis., Feb. 25, 1940; d. Fred G. and Ruth O. (Hackett) Bromley; m. James R. Dawson, June 10, 1959; children: Heather Joy Dawson Cudworth, Jamie Ruth Dawson Strebing. Student, U. Wis.-Stout, Menomonie, 1957-59, Ind. U., 1977-78. Cert. computer profl. Inst. for Cert. Computing Profls. Sys. analyst, programmer Johnson Controls, Milw., 1963-69; software developer various orgns., Bloomington, Ind., 1969—2000; sys. analyst, programmer Westinghouse Electric, Bloomington, 1973-75; adminstrv. asst. Bloomington (Ind.) Twp., 1979-2000; mem. com. new ch. devel. South Ind. conf. United Meth. Ch., 1998—, bd. ch. location and bldg. Bloomington dist., 2001—. Bd. dirs. Youth For Christ, Bloomington, 1989-93. Methodist. Avocation: genealogy. E-mail: mdawson@bluemarble.net.

DAWSON, MARY E., lawyer; b. Halifax, N.S., Can., June 23, 1942; d. Thomas Paul and Florence Margaret (Thurston) McMillan; m. Peter Dawson, Aug. 30, 1969; children: David, Emily. BA in Philosophy with honors, McGill U., 1963, BCL, 1966; DESD, U. Ottawa, 1968; LLB, Dalhousie U., 1970. Tax rschr. Revenue Can., Ottawa, 1967-68, legal counsel, 1968-69; tchg. fellow Dalhousie U., 1969-70; legis. drafter Dept. of Justice, Ottawa, 1970-79, assoc. chief legis. counsel, 1980-86, asst. dep. minister pub. law, 1986-88, assoc. dep. minister, 1988—2005. Mem. adv. bd. Ctr. Rsch. and Edn. Women and Work, Sch. Bus., Carleton U. Recipient Lyon William Jacobs Q. C. award, 1965, Queen's Counsel award, 1978; scholar, McGill U., 1960. Mem.: Ont. Bar, Que. Bar, N.S. Bar, Internat. Bar Assn. (chmn. govt. law com. 1998—2002, mem. coun. 2002—04, mem. constitution com. 2005—). Avocations: nordic skiing, swimming, theater, reading, skating.

DAWSON, MARY RUTH, curator, educator; b. Highland Park, Mich., Feb. 27, 1931; d. John Elson and Olga Josephine (Down) D. BS, Mich. State Coll., 1952; postgrad., U. Edinburgh, 1952-53; PhD, U. Kans., 1957; D of Humanities (hon.), Chatham Coll., 1983; DSc (hon.), Mich. State U., 2005. Instr. zoology Smith Coll., 1958-61; asst. program dir. NSF, Washington, 1961-62; mem. staff Carnegie Mus., Pitts., 1962—, curator, 1971—, chmn. earth sci. div., 1973-97, acting dir., 1982-83, curator emeritus, 2003. Adj. prof. earth scis. U. Pitts., 1971—. Named Disting. Dau. Pa., 1987; recipient Arnold Guyot award, Nat. Geog. Soc., 1981, Woman in Sci. award, Chatham Coll., 1983, Disting. Alumni award, Mich. State U., 2003, Romer-Simpson medal, Soc. Vertebrate Paleontology; fellow, AAUW, 1958—59; Fulbright scholar, 1952—53, rsch. grantee, NSF, 1961—62, 1965—. Fellow Geol. Soc. Am., Arctic Inst. N.Am., Paleontol. Soc.; mem. Soc. Vertebrate Paleontology (hon.; v.p. 1972-73, pres. 1973-74), Paläontologische Gesellschaft, Bernese Mountain Dog Club Am., Am. Soc. Mammalogists, Phi Beta Kappa. Achievements include research and publication on Tertiary Lagomorpha, 1957—, early Tertiary Holarctic rodents, 1960—, Arctic paleontology, 1975—. Office: Carnegie Mus 4400 Forbes Ave Pittsburgh PA 15213-4080 Business E-Mail: dawsonm@carnegiemnh.org.

DAWSON, PATRICIA LUCILLE, surgeon; b. Kingston, Jamaica, W.I., Sept. 30, 1949; arrived in U.S., 1950; d. Percival Gordon and Edna Claire (Overton) D.; children: Alexandria Zoe Hiserman, Wesley Gordon Hiserman BA in Sociology, Allegheny Coll., 1971; MD, N.J. Med. Sch., Newark, 1977; MA in Human and Orgn. Devel., The Fielding Inst., 1996, PhD in Human and Orgnl. Sys., 1998. Membership dir. N.J. ACLU, Newark, 1972; resident in surgery U. Medicine and Dentistry N.J. N.J. Med Sch., 1977-79; resident in surgery Virginia Mason Med. Ctr., Seattle, 1979-82; pvt. practice specializing in surgery Arlington, Wash., 1982-83; dir. med. staff diversity Group Health Coop., Seattle, 1993-98, staff surgeon, 1983-98; pvt. practice Seattle, 1998—2003; breast surgeon Swedish Cancer Inst., 2004—. Author: Forged by the Knife—The Experience of Surgical Residency from the Perspective of a Woman of Color, 1999 Fellow ACS, Seattle Surg. Soc.; mem. Physicians for Social Responsibility, Assn. Women Surgeons, Wash. Black Profls. in Health Care, NOW. Avocations: fiction, walking, cooking. Office: Providence Comp Breast Ctr Jefferson Twr 1600 E Jefferson St Ste 300 Seattle WA 98122-5645 Office Phone: 206-320-4880.

DAWSON, ROSARIO, actress, singer; b. NYC, May 9, 1979; Actor: (films) Kids, 1995, Girls Night Out, 1995, He Got Game, 1998, Side Streets, 1998, Light It Up, 1999, Down to You, 2000, Josie and the Pussycats, 2001, Sidewalks of New York, 2001, Trigger Happy, 2001, Chelsea Walls, 2001, King of the Jungle, 2001, Love in the Time of Money, 2002, Ash Wednesday, 2002, The First $20 Million Is Always the Hardest, 2002, Men in Black II, 2002, The Adventures of Pluto Nash, 2002, 25th Hour, 2002, This Girl's Life, 2003, Shattered Glass, 2003, The Rundown, 2003, Alexander, 2004, This Revolution, 2005, Sin City, 2005, Little Black Dress, 2005, Rent, 2005, A Guide to Recognizing Your Saints, 2006, Clerks II, 2006. Mailing: 1635 N Cahuenga Blvd Los Angeles CA 90028

DAWSON, ROSE DOROTHY, elementary school educator; b. Waukesha, Wis., Feb. 16, 1931; d. Frank Peter and Rose M. (Cisler) Zaic; m. Keith W. Dawson, June 13, 1953 (dec. May 1987); children: Kenneth, Richard, Michael, Gail, Allen. BS, U. Wis., Whitewater, 1970; postgrad., U. Wis., Parkside, 1983-85. Cert. elem. tchr., Wis. Tchr. Magee Sch., Genesee Depot, Wis., 1951-53, Union Grove (Wis.) Grade Sch., 1953-54, 65-86, Union Grove Middle Sch., 1986-91, Union Grove (Wis.) Grade Sch., 1991-94, ret., 1994. Mem. NEA, Wis. Edn. Assn., Union Grove Area Edn. Assn., Am. Rose Soc. Lutheran. Avocations: gardening, crocheting, knitting, stamp collecting/philately, hummel collection. Home: 18906 58th Rd Union Grove WI 53182-9611 Office: 1745 Milldrum St Union Grove WI 53182

DAWSON, STEPHANIE ELAINE, city manager; b. Norwalk, Conn., Nov. 12, 1956; BA, Cornell U., 1979; MPA, Marist Coll., 1994. Cert. Project Mgmt. Inst., Inst. for Cert. Computing. Ops. analyst Irving Trust Co., N.Y.C., 1981-82, ops. mgr., 1982-85; sys. analyst Dept. Gen. Svcs., N.Y.C., 1986-88, sr. project mgr., 1988-91, dir., 1991-95; project mgr., cons. Port Authority N.Y. and N.J., N.Y.C., 1995-98, mgr. capital programs, 1998—. Dir. projects, chpt. liaison Project Mgmt. Inst.-Info. Sys. Spl. Interest Group, Panel leader emerging tech. Am. Soc. Pub. Adminstrn., 1993; mem. Emerging Tech. Adv. Group Assn. for Info. and Image Mgmt., 1995-99; del. to South Africa, People to People Mission, 1997. Maj. Army Nat. Guard, 1979—. Recipient Women in Law and Govt. recognition Nat. Assn. Negro Bus. and Profl. Women's Clubs, N.Y., 1999. Mem. Alpha Kappa Alpha. Office: One Madison Ave New York NY 10010 Fax: 212-435-4537. E-mail: srpdawson@aol.com, sd@panynj.gov.

DAWSON, SUZANNE STOCKUS, lawyer; b. Chgo., Dec. 29, 1941; d. John Charles and Josephine (Zolpe) Stockus; m. Daniel P. Dawson Sr., Sept. 1, 1962; children: Daniel P. Jr., John Charles, Michael Sean. BA, Marquette U., 1963; JD cum laude, Loyola U., Chgo., 1965. Bar: Ill. 1965, U.S. dist. Ct. (no. dist.) Ill. 1965. Assoc. Kirkland & Ellis, Chgo., 1965-71, ptnr., 1971-82, Arnstein & Lehr, Chgo., 1982-89, Foley & Lardner, Chgo., 1989-94; spl. counsel publicly held corps., 1995-97; corp. counsel Baxter Healthcare Corp., Deerfield, Ill., 1997-98, sr. counsel, 1998—2004, asst. gen. counsel, chief transactions counsel, 2004—06. Mem. various coms. United Way Chgo.; corp. adv. bd. Sec. State of Ill., 1973; past mem. bd. advisors Loyola of Chgo. Law Sch.; trustee Lawrence Hall Youth Svcs., Chgo., 1983-98, pres., 1991-93, chair 1993-96; mem. adv. bd. Cath. Charities Chgo., 1985—, bd. dirs., 2002—, chair north suburban regional adv. bd., 2002—; mem. exec. com., bd. governance Notre Dame High Sch., Niles, Ill., 1990-97. Recipient Founder's Day award Loyola U., 1980, St. Thomas More award Loyola of Chgo. Law Sch., 1983. Mem. ABA, Am. Arbitration Assn. (appointed mem. nat. panel of comml. arbitrators 1996—), Ill. Bar Assn. Roman Catholic. Avocations: piano, choir singing, gardening, skiing, gourmet cooking. Office Phone: 847-948-3636. Personal E-mail: suzannedawson@auditrecovery.net.

DAWSON, VALINA L., science educator; BS in Environ. Toxicology, U. Calif., Davis, 1983; PhD in Pharmacology, U. Utah, 1989. Fellow dept. neurology Hosp. of U. Pa., Phila., 1989—90; fellow Addiction Rsch. Ctr. Nat. Inst. Drug Abuse, Balt., 1990—93; dir. neurobiology of disease program dept. neurology Johns Hopkins U. Sch. Medicine, Balt.; assoc. prof. neurology, neurosci., and physiology Johns Hopkins Hosp., 1994—2001, prof., vice chmn. neurology, prof. neurosci. and physiology, 2001—. Contbr. articles to profl. jours. Named Internat. Soc. for Neurochemistry Young Investigator, 1999, Staglin Music Festival Investigator, 1998; recipient Mary Lou McIlhany scholarship, 1999, Am. Heart Assn. Grant-in-Aid award, 1996, award, Muscular Dystrophy Assn., 1995, Alzheimer's Assn. Scholar award, 1994, Am. Heart Assn. Grant-in-Aid award, 1994, AmFar Scholar award, 1994, ADAMHA Intramural Rsch. Tng. award, 1992, Nat. Inst. Drug Abuse Staff Fellow award, 1992, Winter Conf. on Brain Rsch. fellowship, 1991, NIH PRAT fellowship, 1990. Achievements include research in molecular mechanisms of neurodegeneration and regeneration; experimental models of stroke; gene discovery of novel cell survival pathways; cell based therapies for the treatment of neurologic disorders. Office: Inst for Cell Engring Dept Neurology 733 N Broadway St Ste 711 Baltimore MD 21205 E-mail: vdawson@jhmi.edu.

DAWSON, VIRGINIA SUE, retired editor; b. Concordia, Kans., June 6, 1940; d. John Edward and Wilma Aileen (Thompson) Morgan; m. Neil S. Dawson, Nov. 28, 1964; children: Shelley Diane Dawson Sedwick, Lori Ann Dawson Hughes, Christy Lynn. BS in Home Econs. and Journalism, Kans. State U., 1962. Asst. publs. editor Ohio State U. Coop. Ext. Svc., Columbus, 1962-64; home editor Ohio Farmer mag., Columbus, 1964-78; food editor Columbus Dispatch, 1978—2000, ret. Recipient Commn. award Ohio Poultry Assn., 1980. Mem. Assn. Food Journalists. Avocations: biking, reading, cooking, hiking. Personal E-mail: ndawson1@cox.net.

DAY, ANN ELIZABETH, artist, educator; b. Valetta, Malta, June 1, 1927; came to U.S., 1940; d. John Dwight and Joyce Elizabeth (Marett) Harvey; m. George Frederick Day, Oct. 23, 1948 (div. Oct. 1979); children: Georgianna Day Ludcke, John F., David S.; m. Donald Monturean Mintz, Dec. 30, 1980. BA, Mt. Holyoke Coll., South Hadley, Mass., 1948. Asst. to dir. advanced studies Nat. Ctr. Atmospheric Rsch., Boulder, Colo., 1962-67; edn. dir. Waterloo Recreation and Arts Ctr., Iowa, 1967-76; curator edn. svcs. Utah Mus. Fine Arts, Salt Lake City, 1976-80; lectr. art history YMHA of No. N.J., Wayne, 1982—, RSVP, Paramus, NJ, 1994—, Art History Tours of France, Tour de France, Ltd., 1994—, Classic Residence, Teaneck, N.J., 1995—, Belleville Libr., N.J., 1995—, Montclair Adult Sch., N.J., 2001—, Teaneck Sr. Ctr., N.J., 2003—; freelance artist Ringwood, N.J., 1982—; represented by Jacklyn Kling Gallery, Montclair, NJ, 2005—. Vice chair, panelist Fed. State Ptnrship., NEA, Washington, 1972-77; mem. exec. com. Nat. Assn. Community Arts Agys., Washington, 1975-77. Author of poems; represented in permanent collections Utah Mus. of Fine Arts, also U.S. and abroad. Recipient Silver medal Utah Watercolor Soc., Salt Lake City, 1976, Lake Mohawk Club award Sussex County Art Assn., Sparta, N.J., 1992, 93, Best in Show award Sussex County Art Assn., 1997, Artists Mag. award (NWS juried exhbn.), 1996, Am. Artists Profl. League award for representational art, 2004. Mem. Nat. Watercolor Soc., N.J. Watercolor Soc. (Heimrod award for NJWSC exhibit 1991), Phi Beta Kappa. Democrat. Avocations: walking, swimming, collecting tribal art. Home and Office: 29 Whig St Trumansburg NY 14886

DAY, ANNE WHITE, retired nurse; b. Cin., July 9, 1926; d. Pinkney McGill and Anna Pearl (Glendenning) White; m. Raymond Eric Parker, Mar. 6, 1948 (div. 1969); children: Douglas McGill, Stephanie Morse. Diploma, Christ Hosp. Sch. Nursing, Cin., 1947. RN, Ohio; cert. chem. dependency nurse Consol. Assn. Nurses in Substance Abuse. Staff nurse to asst. head nurse Holmes divsn. U. Cin., 1948-84; nursing supr. Villa Hope Extended Care Facility, Cin., 1970-72; staff nurse Hillenbrand Nursing Home, Cin., 1980-82, Emerson A. North Hosp., Cin., 1982-94. Vol. Group Against Smoke Pollution, Cin., 1989—; donor Zoo, Cin., 1989—, Voters for Choice, Ohio, 1989—, Ams. for Non-Smokers Rights, Calif., 1989—, Action on Smoking or Health, 1989—, Stop Teenage Addiction to Tobacco. Mem. DAR (life). Episcopalian. Avocations: swimming, reading, knitting, crocheting, pattern dancing.

DAY, COLIEN, retired secondary school educator; b. Roxboro, N.C., Nov. 3, 1927; d. Luther Davis and Cornelia Lou (Allen) Long; m. Russell Van Buren Day (dec. 1981). AB in English, Trevecca U., Nashville, 1951; MEd, U. N.C., 1955; Sectl. Cert., Elon Coll., 1944-45. With Burlington Ind., Burlington, NC, 1945-48; tchr. Bartlett-Yancey High Sch., Yanceyville, NC, 1951-53, Sumner High Sch., Greensboro, NC, 1953-59; tchr. English Asheboro (N.C.) City Schs., 1959-61; librarian Randolph County Schs., Asheboro, 1961-64; tchr. English Marysville (Calif.) Joint Unified Sch. Dist., 1964—91. Tutor in English to Asian immigrants, 1988—. Mem. AAUW, Nat. Geographic Soc., Nat. Edn. Assn., Smithsonian Instn. Democrat. Home and Office: 1739 Glen St Marysville CA 95901-4018

DAY, DIANE ELAINE, science educator, researcher; b. Portsmouth, Va., Jan. 14, 1961; d. Charles Henry and Melba Joyce Day; m. Christopher D. Balch (div.). BA, Wesleyan Coll., 1996; PhD, Ga. State U., 2003. Adj. instr. Spelman Coll., Atlanta, 2004; lectr. Ga. State U., Atlanta, 2004—. Co-author: Progress in Psychobiology and Physiological Psychology, 2003. Vol. Brain Awareness Week, Atlanta, 1998—2006, Brain's Rule, Atlanta, 2004—06, Save the Leatherneck Sea Turtle, St. Croix, 2005, Etowan Indian Mounds, Cartsville, Ga., 2006. Recipient Travel award, NIMH Soc. Behavioral

Neuroendocrinology, 2001; Neurobiology and Behavior scholar, Ga. State U., 2003. Mem.: Soc. Behavioral NeuroEndocrinology, Soc. Study Ingetive Behavior (New Investigator award 2003), Soc. Neuroscience. Avocation: jewelry making. Office: Ga State U Dept Biology PO Box 4018 Atlanta GA 30302-4010

DAY, FRANCES ANN, writer, educator; b. Grant, Nebr., June 30, 1942; d. Jay and Rachel Ellen Day. BA magna cum laude, Kearney (Nebr.) State Coll., 1964; MA, U. Colo., 1969, EdS, 1979. Cert. lang. and culture tchr., Colo. Tchr. Kearney Pub. Schs., 1961-64, Cherry Creek Schs., Englewood, Colo., 1965-93; lectr. Sonoma State U., Rohnert Park, Calif., 1999—. Grant dir. Village East Schs., Englewood, 1984-90; chair Village East Multicultural Edn. Com., Aurora, Colo., 1989-91. Author: Multicultural Voices, 1994, 2d edit., 1999, Latina and Latino Voices, 1998, Lesbian and Gay Voices, 2000; author column and revs. Sec., East Arapahoe County Coun. on Human Rels., 1971-73; mem. adv. bd. U. San Francisco Ctr. for Multicultural Lit., U.S. Bd. on Books for Young People. Recipient Colo. Tchr. of Yr. Honorable Mention award Colo. Dept. Edn., 1974, Women's History award of excellence Colo. Com. for Women's History, 1988, Denali Press award Am. Libr. Assn., 1998. Mem. Nat. Assn. for Multicultural Edn., Calif. Assn. for Bilingual Edn. Avocations: reading, walking. Office: Heinemann Pubs 361 Hanover St Portsmouth NH 03801-3959

DAY, JANET S., academic administrator; Sr. v.p. Robert Morris Coll., Ill.; pres. Art Inst. Ill., 1998—. Office: Art Institute Atlanta 6600 Peachtree Dunwoody Rd 100 Embassy Row Atlanta GA 30328

DAY, JOYCE CEREJO, school psychologist; b. Hartford, Conn., Oct. 21, 1975; d. Armindo Goncalves and Maria Lourdes Cerejo; m. Michael D. Day, July 2, 2004. BA, St. Joseph Coll., 1997; MS, Northeastern U., 2000, cert. advance grad. study, 2001. Cert. early intervention specialist Mass. Dept. Pub. Health. Crisis intervention worker Intercommunity Mental Health Group, East Hartford, Conn., 1996—97; emergency rm. admitting registrar St. Francis Hosp., Hartford, Conn., 1997—98; early intervention intern Dimock Early Intervention Program, Brighton, Mass., 1998—99; grad. rsch. asst. Northeastern U.-Bouve Grad. Sch., Boston, 1998—2000; site testing coord. Am. Guidance Svc., Circle Pines, Minn., 1999—2000; sch. psychologist C.B. Jennings Elem. and New London (Conn.) H.S., 2000—01; neuropsychology assessment asst. Conn. Pediat. Neuropsychology Assocs., West Hartford, 2002; sch. psychologist Edna C. Stevens Elem. Sch., Cromwell, Conn., 2001—04, Wintergreen Interdist. K-8 Magnet Sch., 2004—. Reviewer Practicing Leadership: Principles and Applications, 2d ed., 2000; psychology mentor Northeastern Sch., 1999—2000; guest lectr. and spkr. in field; conf. presenter. Contbr. articles to profl. jours. Social svcs. cons. Cromwell (Conn.) Coop. Nursery Sch., 2002—; student vol. New Solutions for the Millennium: Violence Prevention for Children and Youth, 1999, Student Affiliates in Sch. Psychology: Grad. Student Mini Conf., 1999. Avocation: yoga.

DAY, KATHRYN ANN, history educator; b. Montpelier, Ohio, July 3, 1955; d. Karlen E. and Jessie D. Day. MA in History, Sam Houston State U., Huntsville, Tex., 2001. Tchr. secondary history Navasota H.S., Tex., 1981—. Spkr. on local history, Navasota, Tex., 2001—. Contbr. articles on history to newspapers. Hon. mem. Daus. of the Republic of Tex., Navasota, Tex., 2005—06; dir. Navasota History Fair, Tex., 2005—06. Recipient Tchr. of Yr. award, Navasota H.S., 1994, 2001, 2003, VFW Tchr. of Yr. award, Grimes County VFW, 2004, DAR Outstanding Tchr. award, Robert Raines DAR, Navasota, Tex., 2006, Outstanding Regional History Fair Coord., Brazos Valley Regional History Fair, 2006; Joan Verilli Outstanding Grad. Student scholarship, Sam Houston State U., 2001. Mem.: Tex. Social Studies Assn., DAR. Achievements include research on Frank Hamer-used in upcoming movie. Avocations: travel, research. Home: 1405 Stacey St Navasota TX 77868 Office: Navasota HS #1 Rattler Dr Navasota TX 77868 Office Phone: 936-825-4250. Office Fax: 936-825-8539. Personal E-mail: kaday@tca.net. E-mail: dayk@navasotaisd.org.

DAY, LUCILLE LANG, museum administrator, educator, writer; b. Oakland, Calif., Dec. 5, 1947; d. Richard Allen and Evelyn Marietta (Hazard) Lang; m. Frank Lawrence Day, Nov. 6, 1965 (div. 1970); 1 child, Liana Sherrine; m. Theodore Herman Fleischman, June 23, 1974 (div. 1985); 1 child, Tamarind Channah Fleischman; m. Richard Michael Levine, Aug. 25, 2002. AB, U. Calif., Berkeley, 1971, MA, 1973, PhD, 1979; MA, San Francisco State U., 1999, MFA, 2004. Tchg. asst. U. Calif., Berkeley, 1971-72, 75-76, rsch. asst., 1975, 77-78; tchr. sci. Magic Mountain Sch., Berkeley, 1977; specialist math. and sci. Novato (Calif.) Unified Sch. Dist., 1979-81; instr. sci. Project Bridge Laney Coll., Oakland, 1984-86; sci. writer and mgr. precoll. edn. programs Lawrence Berkeley Nat. Lab., 1986-90, life scis. staff coord., 1990-92, mgr. Hall of Health, Children's Hosp. & Rsch. Ctr. at Oakland, 1992—2004, dir. Hall of Health, 2004—. Lectr. St. Mary's Coll. Calif., Moraga, 1997—2000. Author: numerous poems, articles and book reviews; author: (with Joan Skolnick and Carol Langbort) How to Encourage Girls in Math and Science: Strategies for Parents and Educators, 1982; author: Self-Portrait with Hand Microscope, 1982, Fire in the Garden, 1997, Wild One, 2000, Lucille Lang Day, Greatest Hits, 1975-2000, 2001, Infinities, 2002, Chain Letter, 2005, The Book of Answers, 2006. Recipient Joseph Henry Jackson award in lit., San Francisco Found., 1982; Grad. fellow, NSF, 1972—75. Mem.: Soc. Pub. Health Edn. (No. Calif. chpt.), Math./Sci. Network, Nat. Assn. Sci. Writers, No. Calif. Sci. Writers Assn., Phi Beta Kappa, Iota Sigma Pi. Home: 1057 Walker Ave Oakland CA 94610-1511 Office: Hall of Health 2230 Shattuck Ave Berkeley CA 94704-1416 Office Phone: 510-549-1564. Business E-Mail: lucyday@hallofhealth.org.

DAY, MARGARET ANN, research librarian, information specialist; b. Butler, Pa., Nov. 15, 1941; d. Edwin James and Helen Louella (Christy) Longwell; m. Donald Emery Day, Dec. 15, 1961; children: Catherine Anne (dec.), Donna Lau, Donald Edwin. BS in Edn. magna cum laude, Clarion U. Pa., 1972, MS in Libr. Sci., 1986. Cert. tchr., profl. libr., Pa.; lic. real estate salesperson, Pa. Substitute tchr. Karns City (Pa.) Area Schs., 1976, 79-85; grad. asst. Clarion U. Pa., 1985-86; libr., info. specialist Interactive Media Corp., Butler, 1987—94. Real estate sales assoc. Ed Shields, Realtor, Butler, 1994. Pres. Bruin (Pa.) Borough Coun., 1984. DAR, Breth and Wahr scholar, 1959. Mem. Beta Phi Mu. Avocations: reading, gardening, sewing, cooking and nutrition, continuing education. Home: PO Box 85 Bruin PA 16022-0085 Office: Interactive Media Corp 292 Three Degree Rd Butler PA 16002-3860

DAY, MARLENE E., elementary school educator; b. Biddeford, Maine, July 16, 1955; d. Vincent Louis and Marguerita Marcella Noella Angelosante; widowed; children: Shauna, Chaz; m. Charles E. Day Jr., Oct. 1, 2003. BS, U. Maine, 1977; MS in Reading, U. So. Maine, 1982. Tchr. Old Orchard Beach (Maine) Elem. Sch., 1977—80, Lorange Mid. Sch., Old Orchard Beach, 1980—. Mem. Commn. for Children with Spl. Needs., Augusta, Maine, 1983—84, Gov.'s Commn. Excellence in Edn., Augusta, 1983—85; religious edn. tchr., lectr. St. Margaret Cath. Ch., Old Orchard Beach. Named Maine State Tchr. of Yr., 1983; recipient Project Seed award, 1994. Mem.: Maine Tchrs. Assn., Phi Delta Kappa (past sec.). Roman Catholic. Avocations: reading, gardening, travel. Home: 1 Smith Ave Old Orchard Beach ME 04064 Office: Old Orchard Beach Sch Dept Loranger Mid Sch 148 Saco Ave Old Orchard Beach ME 04064 Business E-Mail: mday@oobschools.org.

DAY, MARY ANN, medical/surgical nurse; b. Covington, Tenn., Apr. 9, 1944; m. George Day, Jan. 17, 1980; children: Maurice, Michele, Shawn, Corey. AAS, Joliet (Ill.) Jr. Coll., 1989; BSN, Lewis U., 1995; student, U. St. Francis, 1998—. RN, Ill.; cert. emergency nurse pediat. course. Staff nurse Michael Reese Hosp., Chgo., 1989-91, MacNeal Hosp., Berwyn, Ill., 1991-99, Westlake Hosp., Melrose Park, Ill., 1999—; adj. faculty/LPN program Triton Coll., River Grove, Ill., 1996—, instr. RN continuing edn. course, 1998—; asst. patient care mgr. St. Joseph Hosp., Joliet, Ill., 1999—; IV therapist Ctrl. Dupage Hosp., Winfield, Ill., 1999—; nursing supr. St. Anthony's Hosp., Chgo., 2001—. Mem. diversity task force com., Westlake Hosp., 1999; instr. in nursing assistance Waubonsee Coll., 2002; weekend supr. VNA Home Health; adj. faculty nurse asst. program, Moraine Valley CC, 2005. Nominee Black Profl. Female scholarship, Minority Student of Yr., 1989. Avocations: classical music, classical pianist. Home: 6 Puffin Cir Bolingbrook IL 60440-1236

DAY, MARY CAROL, human factors psychologist; b. Gainesville, Fla. d. Noah Jefferson and Rosemary (Morgan) Halbrook; m. Paul Benjamin Newland, Mar. 14, 1984. BA in Libr. Sci., Fla. State U., 1967, MA in Psychology, 1968; EdD in Human Devel., Harvard U., 1975. Assoc. in rsch. Yale U., New Haven, 1968-69; rsch. assoc. Grad. Ctr. CUNY, N.Y.C., 1969-70; various positions in rsch. and policy planning Harvard U., Cambridge, Mass., 1970-75; postdoctoral fellow U. Pitts., 1974-75; asst. prof. psychology U. Houston, 1975-80; mem. tech. staff AT&T Bell Labs., Holmdel, N.J., 1980-84, tech. supr., 1987—; dist. mgr. AT&T Corp. Hdqrs., N.Y.C., 1984-87; pres. M.C. Day Cons., 1998—2004; dir., user interface sys. Angel Med. Sys., 2004—. Editor: The Preschool in Action, 1977; contbr. numerous articles to profl. jours. Mem. AAMI (human factors engring. standards com. 2004—), Am. Psychol. Assn., Human Factors and Ergonomics So. (sec.-treas. 1991, 97), Southern Poverty Law Ctr., Planned Parenthood. Office: Angel Med Sys Tinton Falls NJ 07724

DAY, MARY LOUISE, volunteer; b. LaGrange, Ill., May 22, 1917; d. Kenneth Farwell Burgess and Louise Frances Todd; m. J. Edward Day, July 2, 1941; children: Geraldine Day Zurn, Mary Louise Day Himmelfarb, James E. Jr. (dec.). AB, Vassar Coll., 1939. Bd. dirs. YWCA, Washington, 1962-80, chmn. internat. fair, 1966, 82; active YWCA World Svc. Coun.; mem. adv. bd. The Hospitality Info. Svc., Washington, 1964—, chmn., 1969-71; chmn. women's bd. Am. Heart Assn., Washington, 1981-83; mem. Smithsonian Women's Com., Washington, 1982—; co-chmn. Smithsonia Craft Show, 1987. Democrat. Home: 5901 MacArthur Blvd NW Apt 400 Washington DC 20016-2547

DAY, SARAH JANE, actor; b. Madison, Wis., Oct. 30, 1958; d. Roland Bernard and Mary Jane (Purcell) Day. BA, U. Wis., 1980. Mem. Core Co. Am. Players Theatre, Spring Green, Wis., 1986—; actor Milw. Repertory Theater, Milw. Chamber Theater, First Stage Milw., Next Act Theatre, Milw., Madison Repertory Theatre, Madison. Guest artist Univ. Theatre, Madison. Bd. mem. Spring Green Literary Festival, Wis., Friends of the Spring Green Library; founding bd. mem. Spring Green Area Arts Coalition. Democrat. Home: E3516 US Hwy 14 & 60 Spring Green WI 53588

DAY, SUSAN BRENT, assistant principal, educator; b. New Orleans, Aug. 26, 1952; d. Will Francis and Mabel Mae Brent; m. Ora Coe Day, III, May 18, 1974; children: Courtney, Ryan, Lindsay. BA, Southeastern La. U., Hammond, 1974, MA, 1976. Cert. tchr. La. Edn. specialist La. Assn. Bus. and Industry, Baton Rouge, 1976—80; libr., tchr., asst. prin. Trafton Acad., Hammond, La., 1990—. Office: Trafton Acad PO Box 2845 Hammond LA 70404-2845

DAY, SUSAN MARIE, music educator, composer; b. Kingston, NY, June 12, 1949; d. Joseph and Esther Besdesky Hartman; children: Andrew, Casey. BSc in Music Edn., Ithaca Coll., 1971; MA in Music Edn., Columbia U., 1972. String tchr. Cherry Creek Schs., Englewood, Colo., 1972—80, Douglas County Schs., 1988—. Violinist Arapahoe Philharm., Englewood, Colo., 1984—; guest condr. youth symphonies, Colo., 1994—; contest adjudicator in field, Colo., 1994—. Composer: SMHD Music, 1994—, ASCAP, 2005, Reverie, 2004, over 25 other compositions in field; author: Teaching Orchestra on a Year Round Calendar, 1996. Recipient Winner String Orch. Composition Contest, Tex. Orch. Dirs. Assn., 2006. Mem.: Nat. Sch. Orch. Assn., Am. String Tchrs. Assn. (mem. string industry coun., named Outstanding String Tchr. 2000), Music Educators Nat. Conf., Colo. Music Educators' Assn. Avocations: hiking, bicycling, Scrabble, reading, movies. Home: 8091 S Albion St Littleton CO 80122 Office Phone: 303-387-2845. Personal E-mail: sday@ecentral.com.

DAY, TWILA M., food service executive; b. Champaign, Ill. m. Bill Day; 5 children. B in Bus. Mgmt., Our Lady of the Lake, San Antonio, Tex., 1989. Various position in the banking and oil industry, 1983—92; sr. programmer analyst, information tech. dept. Sysco Corp., Houston, 1992—93, team leader, Sysco Uniform Systems, 1993—95, project mgr., 1995—96, sr. mgr., application develop., 1996—97, sr. dir., operating comp. support team, 1997—99, sr. dir., application develop., 1999—2000, asst. v.p., tech. and applications, 2000—05, v.p., information tech., 2005, v.p., CIO, 2005—. Office: Sysco Corp 1390 Enclave Pkwy Houston TX 77077-2099*

DAY, TYANNA YONKERS, religious studies educator, minister; b. Hagerstown, Md., Feb. 9, 1959; d. Gerald Edward Yonkers and Lillian Belle Ruth Yonkers Pickens; m. Gregory Allen Day, July 14, 1979; 1 child, Joshua Caleb. AA in Liberal Arts, Hagerstown Jr. Coll., Md., 1979; BA in Spl. Edn., Hood Coll., Frederick, Md., 1981; MDiv, Southea. Bapt. Theol. Sem., Wake Forest, NC, 1990; DMin, Bapt. Theol. Sem. at Richmond, Va., 1999; postgrad., Cath. U. Am., Washington. Ordained to Gospel Ministry Calypso Bapt. Ch., NC, lic. to preach Paramount Bapt. Ch. Spl. edn. tchr. Berkeley County Bd. of Edn., Martinsburg, W.Va., 1981—82, Washington County Bd. of Edn., Hagerstown, Md., 1982—87; after-sch. coord. Wake Forest Bapt. Ch., 1987—90; edn. assessment specialist Duplin County Bd. of Edn., Kenansville, NC, 1990—95; pastor Garner's Chapel Bapt. Ch., Mt. Olive, NC, 1992—97; assoc. prof. religion Mt. Olive Coll., 1995—; pastor Holly Grove Presbyn. Ch., Clinton, NC, 2001—. Coun. mem. NC Bapt. State Conv. Coun. on Christian Life and Pub. Affairs, 1998—2001; mem. com. Coop. Bapt. Fellowship, 1998—2004, chairperson 2000 gen. assembly program com., NC, 1999—2000, moderator-elect, moderator, past moderator, 2000—03. Bd. mem., leader Bus. and Profl. Women's Orgn. So. Wayne Dist., NC Bapt. Women in Ministry, 1996—98; bd. mem., sec. NC chpt. Alliance of Baptists, 1991—95. Named NC State Young Careerist, Bus. and Profl. Women's Clubs, 1994; recipient award, So. Bapt. Religious Edn. Assn., 1990, Thomas R. Morris award for excellence in tchg., Mt. Olive Coll., 2001; Risden P. Reece scholar, Southea. Bapt. Theol. Sem., 1989. Mem.: Religious Edn. Assn., N.Am. Bapt. Profs. of Religion, Am. Acad. Religion, Bapt. Women in Ministry (convenor, co-convenor 1996—98, Anne Thomas Neil award 1999). Democrat. Avocations: reading, environmental issues, nature. Office: Mt Olive Coll 634 Henderson St Mount Olive NC 28365 Office Phone: 919-658-2502. E-mail: tday@moc.edu.

DAY, VALERIE MARIAN, mechanical engineer; b. Annapolis, Md., July 21, 1962; d. Ernest O. and Virginia G. (Gleason) Crocker; m. Mark A. Young, May 18, 1991 (div. Apr. 1997); m. Christopher J. Day, Sept. 22, 2001. BS in Engring., Bioengring., U. Vt., 1984; MS in Biomed. Engring., Duke U., 1986; MBA, San Diego State U., 2002. Rehab. engr. Tufts U./New Eng. Med. Ctr., Boston, 1983; rsch. engr. Harvard Med. Sch., Southborough, Mass., 1987—88; project engr. surg. devices ETHICON Inc., Somerville, NJ, 1988—90; sr. mech. project engr. Abbott Labs., San Diego, 1990—92, supr. disposables mfg., 1992—94, mgr. mech. engring., R&D, 1994—2001, sr. program mgr., 2001—03; v.p. product devel. Gen-Probe, Inc., San Diego, 2003—. Contbr. articles to profl. jours. Avocations: triathalons, ocean swimming, marathons, bicycling, skiing. Home: 7644 Hillside Dr La Jolla CA 92037 Office: Gen-Probe Inc 10210 Genetic Ctr Dr San Diego CA 92121 E-mail: valerieday@gen-probe.com.

DAYA MATA, SRI (FAYE WRIGHT), clergywoman; b. Salt Lake City, Jan. 31, 1914; d. Clarence Aaron and Rachel (Terry) Wright. Grad. high sch., 1931. Ordained to ministry Self-Realization Fellowship, 1935. Min. Self-Realization Fellowship, L.A., 1935—, bd. dirs., 1941—, sec., 1944—45, treas., 1945—71, lectr., 1952—; pres. brs. U.S., Can., Mex., S.Am., Europe, Africa, Asia, Australia and New Zealand Self-Realization Fellowship/Yogoda Satsanga Soc. of India, 1955—. Gemeinschaft der Selbst-Verwirklichung, 1974—, Self Realization Inst. of Va., Inc., 1981—. Author: Only Love, 1976, Finding the Joy Within You, 1990, Enter The Quiet Heart, 1998, Intuition: Soul-Guidance for Life's Decisions, 2003; (videos) Security in a World of Change, 1989, Him I Shall Follow, 1997, Living in the Love of God, 2002, A Scripture of Love, 2005; contbr. articles to mags. Pres. Yogoda Satsanga Homeopathic Mahavidyalaya, Yogoda Satsanga Mahavidyalaya, Yogoda Satsanga Vidyalaya, Yogoda Satsanga Kanya Vidyalaya, Yogoda Satsanga Sangeet Kala Bharati, Yogoda Satsanga Shilpa Kala Bharati, Yogoda Satsanga Balkrishnalaya, Yogoda Satsanga Sevashram Hosp., Worldwide Prayer Circle, others. Home and Office: Self-Realization Fellowship 3880 San Rafael Ave Los Angeles CA 90065-3298

DAYHARSH, VIRGINIA FIENGO, secondary school educator; b. New Haven, Dec. 2, 1942; d. Edward Arthur and Rose (Giaquinto) Fiengo; m. George R. Dayharsh, Dec. 31, 1966 (div. Nov. 1983); children: Regina Lynn Santanello, Jennifer Allison Mullen. BA, Coll. of New Rochelle, N.Y., 1964; MA, So. Conn. State U., 1974, cert. advanced study, 1985. Cert. social studies tchr., Conn. Tchr. Troup Jr. High Sch., New Haven, 1964-65, East Haven (Conn.) Jr. High Sch., 1965-69; tchr., dept. chairperson Lauralton Hall, Milford, Conn., 1979-81; tchr. Nathan Hale Ray High Sch., East Haddam, Conn., 1981-85, Naugatuck (Conn.) High Sch., 1985—2002. Mem. Rep. Town Com., East Haven, 1968-72, Library Bd., East Haven, 1968-81, Bd. of Edn., East Haven, 1986-87. Mem.: Retired Conn. Edn. Assn., Retired Nat. Edn. Assn., New Eng. Assn. History Tchrs., New Eng. Assn. Schs. and Colls., Conn. Coun. Social Studies, New Haven County Ret. Tchrs. Assn., Assn. Ret. Tchrs. Conn., East Haven Hist. Soc., Coun. Cath. Women. Home: 1360 N High St East Haven CT 06512-1156

DAYHOFF, DIANE, retail executive; B in Polit. Sci., Northwestern U., MBA. CFO Birraporitti's Restaurant; staff v.p. fin. Continental Airlines; v.p. investor rels. Home Depot, 2003—. Office: Home Depot 2455 Paces Ferry Rd Atlanta GA 30339 E-mail: diane_dayhoff@homedepot.com.*

DAYMON, JOY JONES, school psychology specialist; b. Prescott, Ark. d. Coy A. and Alma E. (Honea) Jones; m. Jack C. Daymon, May 3, 1947; children: Jim, Michael, David, Deborah. BA, Long Beach State Coll.; MS in Ednl. Psychology, U. So. Calif., 1974; student, UCLA. Cert. elem. tchr., sch. psychologist specialist, Ark.; lic. profl. counselor, Ark. Tchr. Redondo Beach (Calif.) Sch. Dist.; ednl. examiner El Dorado (Ark.) Schs. Adj. instr. So. Ark. U., Magnolia; presenter workshop on assessment of severe and multi-handicapped various state and nat. convs. Author: Rabbit Pancakes, 1995, Princess Diana the Lamb to the Slaughter, 2002. Mem. NASP (state del., 1984-86), APA, Ark. Psychol. Assn. (treas. 1978-80), Ark. Sch. Psychologists Assn. (state del.), Ark. Counseling Assn., Nat. Bd. Cert. Counselors, Ark. Assessment in Counseling (pres., 1980-81), Delta Kappa Gamma (pres. 1986-87), Phi Delta Kappa. Home: 2202 N Wyatt Dr El Dorado AR 71730-9262 Office: 108 Randolph El Dorado AR 71730

DAY-SALVATORE, DEBRA LYNN, medical geneticist; b. Hoboken, N.J., Oct. 23, 1953; m. Francis P. Salvatore, Sr., Dec. 24, 1988. BA in Biology, Harvard U., 1975; MS in Pharmacology, NYU, 1979, PhD in Pharmacology, 1982; MD, Case Western Res. U., 1986. Diplomate Am. Bd. Med. Genetics, Am. Bd. Pediats. Grad. fellow dept. pharmacology NYU Med. Ctr., 1978-79; sr. rsch. asst. dept. medicine Case Western Res. U., Cleve., 1979-82, rsch. assoc. dept. molecular biology and microbiology, 1982-84; pediatric and adolescent medicine resident Cleve. Clinic Found., 1986-89; med. genetics fellow Robert Wood Johnson Med. Sch., New Brunswick, NJ, 1990-91, asst. prof. pediatrics, 1990—, coord. perinatal genetics dept. ob-gyn., 1991-92, dir. divsn. reproductive and perinatal genetics dept. ob-gyn., 1992—, asst. prof. ob-gyn. and reproductive scis. and pediatrics, 1992—, acting chief divsn. clin. genetics, dept. ob-gyn. and reproductive scis., 1993—; physician Robert Wood Johnson Univ. Hosp., New Brunswick, 1990—, St. Peter's Med. Ctr., 1992—, chief divsn. clin. genetics, 1996—. Mem. genetic adv. bd. N.J. State Dept. Health's Parental and Child Adv. Com.; mem. med. adv. bd. Cryo-Cell Internat. Genetics editor Jour. of Perinatology, 1993—; contbr. articles, abstracts to profl. jours. Cons. N.J. Interagency Adoption Coun. Mem. AAAS, AMA, Am. Acad. Pediatrics (mem. N.J. chpt.), Am. Soc. Cell Biology, Am. Soc. Human Genetics, Human Genetics Assn. N.J. (mem. legis. com.), N.Y. Acad. Sci. Office: Saint Peter's Univ Hosp 254 Easton Ave # 4410 New Brunswick NJ 08901-1766 E-mail: Day-Salva@comcast.net.

DAYSON, DIANE HARRIS, parks director, cultural organization administrator; b. N.Y.C., Feb. 14, 1953; d. Robert Gene and Dessie Lee (Osborne) Harris; m. Kevin Maurice Dayson, Sept. 15, 1978; children: Dayna Renee, Kyle Ryan. BA in Early Secondary Edn. and Am. History, SUNY, Cortland, 1975; MS, NYU, 2000; Sr. Exec. Svc. grad., U.S. Dept. Interior, 2000. With Nat. Pk. Svc. U.S. Dept. Interior, 1975—, law enforcement ranger, 1977-79, concessions specialist, 1979-81, site mgr. Nat. Pk. Svc. N.Y.C., 1984-87, supt. Nat. Pk. Svc. Oyster Bay, N.Y., 1987-90, Morristown, N.J., 1990-93, Hyde Park, N.Y., 1993-95; supt. Statue of Liberty Ellis Island, N.Y.C., 1996—. Adj. prof. NYU Wagner Sch. of Pub. Adminstrn.; ambassador to Amsterdam, 1998; ambassador on geneology to Paris, France, 2000, Bremehaven, Germany, 2000, San Marino, Italy, 1997. Active United Way, Dutchess County; exch. steward, Manchester, Eng., 1994; bd. dirs. Christian Ministry in Nat. Parks, 1997—. Mem. NAFE, Oyster Bay C. of C. Republican. Roman Catholic. Avocations: travel, knitting, reading. Office: Statue of Liberty Ellis Island Liberty Is New York NY 10004-1467

DAYTON, JEAN, principal; b. Belleville, Ill., Jan. 6, 1957; d. Charles John and Marjorie Jane Hempen Mueth; m. Michael Louis Dayton, Oct. 26, 1996. BS in Spl. Edn. & Elem. Edn., So. Ill. U., 1980, MS in Spl. Edn., 1993; PhD in Edn., St. Louis U., 1998. Tchr. spl. edn. Cmty. Consol. Sch. Dist. 110, Fairview Heights, Ill., 1980-92, behavior devel. coord., 1992-93; spl. edn. advisor So. Ill. U., Edwardsville, 1993-98; supr. spl. edn. program Cmty. Unit Sch. Dist. #10, Collinsville, Ill., 1998-2000; prin. Caseyville (Ill.) Elem. Sch., 2000—, Hollywood Heights Elem. Sch., 2003—. Leader Tchr. Support Team, St. Clair County, Ill., 1989-91; mem. Transition Planning Com., St. Clair County, 1992-93. Tchr. in space applicant NASA, Cape Canaveral, Fla., 1985. Mem. Coun. Exceptional Children. Office: Caseyville Elem Sch 433 S 2d St Caseyville IL 62232

DAYTON, KATHLEEN G., nurse; b. San Bernardino, Calif., June 22, 1963; d. Ronald Jack and Carol Bernice (Walton) Kelly; m. Darren R. Dayton, Jan. 4, 1999; children: Amanda May, Andrea René. Diploma, United Health Careers, San Bernardino, Calif., 1984. Hemodialysis nurse San Bernardino Valley Dialysis, San Bernardino, 1984-94; staff nurse Blood Bank San Bernardino/Riverside Counties, San Bernardino, 1994-96; rsch. nurse Ariz. Rsch. and Edn., Phoenix, 1996—2003; hospice case mgr. Hospice Inspiris, Phoenix, 2003—. Mem. ACRP, Am. Nephrology Nurses Assn., Nat. Kidney Found., Ariz. Hospice Palliative Care, Hospice and Palliative Nurses Assn. Office Phone: 602-712-1000. Business E-Mail: kathy.clayton@hospiceinspiris.net.

DAYTON, LEAH JANE, secondary school educator; b. Fort Worth, Tex., Apr. 27, 1953; d. Robert Hartwell and Vernon Elizabeth Mitchell; m. John Leon Dayton, Aug. 21, 1971; children: Amy E. Gausin, Jonathan L. Cert. tchr. psychology and English. Med. transcriptionist Robert H. Mitchell, MD, Plainview, Tex., 1970—84, Carl P. Weidenbach, MD, Plainview, Tex., 1984—91; English tchr. Plainview (Tex.) Ind. Sch. Dist., 1995—. Mem. dist. writing com. Plainview (Tex.) Ind. Sch. Dist., 1995—, mem. ednl. improvement coun., 1997—2000, mem. textbook adoption com., 2000—01; adv. bd. dirs. Houston Sch., Plainview, Tex.; mem. TAKS II com. Tex. Edn. Agy., Austin, 2000—01. Life mem. PTA, Plainview, Tex., 1978—. Recipient Outstanding Educator award, Plainview Daily Herald, 1998, Tchr. of Yr. award, Walmart Distbn., Plainview, Tex., 1998—99. Mem.: AAUW (sec. 1995—2001), Tex. Classroom Tchrs. Assn. (campus rep.), Tex. Assn. Alternative Schs., Psi Chi (life). Republican. Episcopalian. Avocations: reading, camping, water activities. Home: 513 W 8th Plainview TX 79072 Office: Houston Sch 2417 Yonkers Plainview TX 79072 Office Phone: 806-296-4184. Business E-Mail: ldayton@plainview.k12.tx.us. E-mail: ldayton@cox.net.

DAYTON, REGINA LAUDI, secondary school educator; b. Cleve., Apr. 27, 1952; d. Peter Rocco and Gretchen Margaret (Schoen) Laudi; m. Timothy John Dayton, July 28, 1978. BA in Am. Studies and Social Studies in Edn., Heidelberg Coll., 1974; MA in Am. Studies, Bowling Green State U., 1975. Cert. tchr., Ohio. Tchr. social studies Nordonia City Schs., Northfield, Ohio, 1975-77, Strongsville (Ohio) City Schs., 1977—2002. Served to lt. comdr. USNR, 1980—96. Recipient Points of Light award, 2002, Proclamation for vol. work, City of Strongsvilleand State of Ohio. Mem. Naval Res. Assn., U.S. Naval Inst. Republican. Roman Catholic. Avocations: reading, summer sports, travel, volunteer work.

DE ABREU, SUE, elementary school educator; b. Honolulu, Dec. 29, 1947; d. Lawrence and Mary (Jones-Howard) de Abreu-Morris; 1 child, Steven. AA, Gulf Coast Coll., Panama, 1967; BA, Fla. State U., 1971; BS, Harvard U., 1968; MS, Ga. So. Coll., 1984; MA, U. West Fla., 1985. Cert. art edn. tchr. K-12th, elem. tchr., sci. specialist 5th-6th grades, Fla. Reading specialist Craig Elem. Sch., Vail, Colo., 1980; tchr. sci. 7th-8th grade Ludowic County Schs., Jesup, Ga., 1981-84; tchr. sci. 5th-6th grade Gulf County Pub. Schs., Port St. Joe, Fla., 1985-98. State judge Fla. State Sci. and Engring. U. Fla, instr.; spl. news cons. Time Mag., 2001. Inventor Learning Through Creative Designs series, 2000. Chmn. Gulf County-N.W. Fla. chpt. Nat. Dem. Senatorial Com., 2001; pres. DeAbreu Plantation Nurseries; landscape designer, pres. Abreu Landscaping Design Svcs. Recipient Outstanding Fla. Artist award, Fedn. Fla. Women's Clubs Am., 2000-01. Mem. NEA, ASCD, Nat. Art Edn. Assn., Nat. Middle Sch. Assn., Nat. Wildlife Fedn. (Gulf County dir.), Wewahitchka Fedn. Women's Club (v.p. 1994-96). Home: 211 Abreu Rd Wewahitchka FL 32465-7719

DEACH, JANA AUNE, lawyer; b. Fergus Falls, Minn. BA magna cum laude, U. ND, 1993; JD with distinction, U. ND, Grand Forks, 1999. Bar: Minn. 1999, US Dist. Ct. (dist. Minn.) 1999. Assoc. Moss & Barnett, P.A., Mpls. Contbr. articles to profl. publs.; symposium editor: U. ND Law Rev. Named a Rising Star, Minn. Super Lawyers mag., 2006. Mem.: ABA, Minn. State Bar Assn., Hennepin County Bar Assn., Phi Alpha Theta. Office: Moss & Barnett PA 4800 Wells Fargo Ctr 90 S 7th St Minneapolis MN 55402 Office Phone: 612-877-5305. E-mail: deachj@moss-barnett.com.*

DEAL, JILL B., lawyer; b. Stockton, Calif., Sept. 3, 1942; d. Ronald Emerson and Otilia (MacDonald) Brady; m. Timothy E. Deal, Sept. 5, 1964; children: Christopher, Bartholomew. BA, U. Calif., Berkeley, 1964; JD, Cath. U., 1979. Bar: D.C. 1979. Rsch. asst. FTC, Washington, 1974-78, policy analyst, 1978-79; atty. Arnold & Porter, Washington, 1979-81; Am. legal advisor Gen. Electric Co., p.l.c., London, 1981-85; atty. Rogers & Wells, Paris, 1985-88, of counsel Washington, 1988—96; principal, regulatory group Fish & Richardson, 1996—2000; ptnr., FDA, bioscience and pharmaceuticals Venable LLP, Washington, 2000—. Speaker FDLI Conference on Generic Biologics, 2003, CBI Annual Forum on Generic Drugs, 2003, Biopharmaceutical Comparability Conference, 2004. Contbr. articles to profl. jours.; co-author Biotechnology: Patents, Licensing and FDA Practice, 2001, Liability for Generic Drug Products: Issues to Consider, 2003. Mem. ABA (secs. on antitrust, bus. and internat. law), Club L (Paris). Office: Venable LLP 575 7th St NW Washington DC 20004 Office Phone: 202-344-4713. Office Fax: 202-344-8300. Business E-Mail: jdeal@venable.com.

DEAL, KATE, language educator; b. Susanville, Calif., July 17, 1979; d. Rocky and Gail Deal. BA, Stanford U., Calif., 2000; MA, Stanford U., 2000. Cert. Surface Warfare Officer USN, 2002. Tchr. English, coach St. Francis H.S., Mountain View, Calif., 2004—. Lt. USS McCampbell USN, 2000—04. Fellow, Amy Biehl Found., 1998. Mem.: Phi Beta Kappa.

DEAL, MARCI SMITH, social studies educator, consultant; b. Fort Worth, Tex., July 22, 1961; d. Hulin Hoot Henry and Patricia Ann Smith; m. John David Deal, July 8, 2000; 1 child, Jackson Reed. BS in Econs., U. Tex. Arlington, 1984; MEd, U. North Tex., Denton, 1987. Cert. Tchr. 1-12 Tex., 1984. Tchr. Hurst-Euless-Bedford ISD, Bedford, Tex., 1984—94; coord. K-12 social studies Hurst-Euless-Bedford Ind. Sch. Dist., Bedford, 1994—. Tchr. cons. Nat. Geog. Soc., Washington, 1990—. Author: Geography Textbook, 2003. Mem.: Nat. Coun. Social Studies, Assn. Tex. Profl. Educators (Outstanding Adminstr. Region XI 1995), Geography Educators of Metroplex (pres. 2004—06), HEB Ednl. Found. Cornerstone Club, Nat. Coun. Geog. Edn. (Disting. Tchg. Achievement Award 2001), Tex. Alliance Geog. Edn. (Disting. Svc. Award 2000), Tex. Social Studies Supervisors Assn. (pres. 2001—02), Mid-Cities Coun. Social Studies (pres. 1996—97), Nat. Social Studies Supervisors Assn., Tex. Coun. Social Studies (v.p. 1995—96). Avocation: travel. Home: 1132 Woodvale Dr Bedford TX 76021 Office: Hurst-Euless-Bedford Ind Sch Dist 1849 Central Drive Bedford TX 76022 Office Phone: 817-399-2068. Office Fax: 817-354-3311. E-mail: marcideal@hebisd.edu.

DEAL, REBECCA L., art educator; d. Gary M. and Ruth E. Sibley; children: Rachel Marlene, Jonathan David. BS in Art Edn., Edinboro U. of Pa., 1993. Cert. instructional II tchr. H.s. art tchr. Rochester Area Schs., Pa., 1997—2005, elem. art tchr., 2005—. Mem.: PSEA, Nat. Art Edn. Assn.

DEALBUQUERQUE, JOAN MARIE, conductor, music educator; b. Grosse Pointe, Mich., Feb. 1, 1967; d. Angela May and Anthony Joseph deAlbuquerque. MusB in Edn., Mich. State U., East Lansing, 1993, MusM in Wind Conducting, 1999; DMA, U. North Tex., Denton, 2005. Tchg. fellow U. North Tex., Denton, 2000—03; assoc. dir. of bands Calif. State U., Long Beach, 2003—. Music dir, choir dir., vocal soloist Unity Ch. of Rochester, Mich., 1994; asst. condr. Mich. State U. Concert Band, East Lansing, 1997—99; H.S. band adjudicator No. N.Mex. Dist., 2000; condr. U. North Tex. Concert Band, Denton, 2000—03, H.S. Honor Band, Alamosa, Colo., 2000—00; cantor/vocal soloist Immaculate Conception Cath. Ch., Denton, Tex., 2001—03; rec. prodr. John Wacker, solo trumpet, Denton, Tex., 2002—02; mgr. Conductors Collegium, Denton, Tex., 2002—03; condr. Octet by Stravinsky/Grad. Chamber Group, Denton, Tex., 2003—03. Author: (book) 4 articles in Teaching Music Through Performance in Band. Scholar, Macomb C.C., 1990-1991, Toulouse Grad. Dept., 2000; Tchg. fellowship, U. North Tex., 2000-2003. Mem.: Music Educators Nat. Conf., So. Calif. Sch. Band and Orchestra Assn., Calif. Band Dirs. Assn., Coll. Band Dirs. Nat. Assn., Golden Key Nat. Honor Soc., Pi Kappa Lambda, Phi Kappa Phi. Roman Catholic. Home: 35444 Stillmeadow Ln Clinton Township MI 48035 Office: Calif State Univ 1250 Bellflower Blvd Long Beach CA 90840-7101 Office Phone: 562-985-4533. Personal E-mail: jdealbuq@csulb.edu.

DEALEY, AMANDA MAYHEW, former foundation administrator; b. Dallas, July 17, 1950; d. Charles Milton and Audrey (Overton) Mayhew; m. Joe M. Dealey Jr., Nov. 4, 1972 (div. 1978); 1 child, Christopher Charles; m. Lawrence W. Speck, Oct. 3, 1992 (div. 2005). BA in Art History, U. Tex., 1972; M in pub. affairs, U. Tex. at Austin, 2003. Bd. dirs. Mid Am. Arts Alliance, Kansas City, Mo., 1987-90, James Dick Found., 1978—, Planned Parenthood Fedn. Am., 2005—, Planned Parenthood Action Fund, 2006—; mem. adv. coun. Sch. Nursing U. Tex., Austin, 1987—1994; sec.-treas. Tex. Assn. for Symphony Orchs., Austin, 1988-89, vice-chmn. Tex. Arts Alliance, 1986-89. Mem. Mental Health Assn. Tex. (v.p. 1995—98), Tex. Lyceum Assn. (pres. 1995, chair 1996). Home: 1210 W 13th St A Austin TX 78703-4106

DEALEY, LYNN TOWNSEND, artist; b. Smithfield, NC, July 16, 1954; d. John Sims and Rebecca Barnes Townsend; m. Russell Edward Dealey, May 4, 1985. AS in Advt. Design, Art Inst. Ft. Lauderdale, 1977; BS in Health Edn., U. N.C. Greensboro, 1976. Mem. adv. bd. Artreach, Dallas, 1991—92; spkr. in field. Illustrator: A Coon Creek Chronicle, 1992; featured, Texans and Their Pets, 2006, cover, Philanthropy in Tex., 2002, featured, Texas Women: Trailblazers, Shining Stars and Cowgirls, 2003, Enchanted Galleries, 2004—, mural, Dallas Zoo, 1998; co-author: Splenda: Is It Safe?, 2005. Recipient award, United Way, U. Tex., Austin, 1997—2002. Mem.: Dallas Country Club, Dallas Social Dir. Avocations: science, biology, cartooning, travel, cooking. Office: PO Box 191406 Dallas TX 75219

DEAMANT, CATHERINE D., internist; b. 1960; MD, Rush Med. Coll., 1987. Resident Michael Reese Hosp.; founder Connections' Health Svc., Chgo., 1990—; internist, dir., palliative care program Cook Co. Bur. Health Svcs., Chgo., 2001—. Named one of Chgo.'s 100 Most Influential Women, Crain's Chicago Business, 2004. Office: Cook County Bur Health Svcs 1835 W Harrison St Chicago IL 60612*

DEAMER, PEGGY, architecture educator; BA, Oberlin Coll.; BArch, Columbia U.; PhD in Arch. History, Theory and Criticism, Princeton U. With Pasanella & Klein Arch., N.Y.C.; instr. archtl. design and theory Cooper Union-Columbia U., Princeton U.; prin. Dreamer & Phillips Archs., N.Y.C., 1987—; assoc. dean, assoc. prof. Yale Sch. Arch., New Haven. Co-author: Re-Reading Perspecta: The First Fifty Years of the Yale Architectural Journal, 2004. Mailing: Dreamer & Phillips 149 Franklin St New York NY 10013 Office: Yale Sch Arch PO Box 208242 New Haven CT 06520-8242 also: Yale Sch Arch 180 York St New Haven CT 06520-8242

DEAN, BARBARA W., elementary school educator; b. Pitts., Pa., Aug. 23, 1938; d. Lawrence Kennedy and Dorothy Burrall Whitfield; m. George W. Dean, June 26, 1983; children: Elizabeth Anderson, Andrea Young; m. James D. Lynn (div.); children: David L. Lynn, Pamela L. Seavers, Jonathan M. Lynn. BA, U. Redlands, 1960. Cert. learning handicapped credential Calif. State U., 1987, life elem. tchg. Calif. Second grade tchr. Alexander Hamilton Sch., Morristown, NJ, 1960—62; preschool tchr. Marian Anderson Child Care, Sacramento, 1973—78; tchr. Harkness Elem. Sch., Sacramento, 1978—86; resource specialist Chgo. Pk. Sch. Dist., 1986—2003. Leader, Calif. lit. project CSUS, Sacramento, 1983—86; fellow U. Calif., Davis, 1986—2000; tutor Self-Emplyed, Chgo. Pk., Calif., 2000—05. Vol. Hospitality Ho., Grass Valley, Calif., 2006; mem. Habitat for Humanity, 2001—06; bd. mem. Chernobyl Children's Project, Nevada City, 1986—88, Pacific Network for Mission Edn., 2000—06; mem., actor Foothill Theatre Co., Nevada City, Calif., 1980—86, Cmty. Asian Theatre, NevadaCity, 2003—06; facilitator Stephens Ministry Program, 2002—06. Named one of Tchrs. who Make a Difference, Nevada County Bd. Edn., 2000; scholarship, State of Calif., 1956—60. Democrat. United Meth. Avocations: art, music, theater, raising sheep. Home: 17671 Donner Oaks Rd Grass Valley CA 95945

DEAN, CAROLE LEE, film company executive; b. Dallas, Mar. 23, 1939; d. Roy Webster and Dorothy Lee Dean; children: Richard Dean, Carole Joyce. Student, UCLA. Pres. Studio Film and Tape, LA, 1969-2000, NYC, 1970-2000, Chgo., 1994—2000, From the Heart Prodn., LA, 1992—. Spkr. in field. Prodr., host Health Styles, 1994-97; author: Heal Thyself, 1999, The Art of Funding Your Film: Alternative Financing Concepts, 2003, The Art of Manifesting: Create Your Future, 2005. Established Roy W. Dean film, video and writing grants, 1992. Mem. Nat. Arts Club. Republican. Avocations: skiing, equesterian. Personal E-mail: caroleedean@att.net.

DEAN, DIANE (H.) SWEET, artist, retired credit manager; b. Glendale, Calif., May 7, 1953; m. Bill J. Dean, Aug. 27, 1994; children: Aaron J., Brian W. Wallace. AA in Graphics, Pierce Coll., 1971; studied with The Samsel's, Calif., 1963—69; studied with Vel Miller, Reseda, Calif., 1969—73; studied with Hal Reed, Van Nuys, Calif., 1971—74; studied with Lisette De Winne, L.A., 1973—. Credit mgr. Syncor Internat., Woodland Hills, Calif., 1984—2000. Exhibited in group shows at Santa Clarita Art Guild (1st Place award, 1978, Best of Show award, 1979, 1st Place award, 2000, 2001), 1979, Art Classic XII, Santa Clarita, 2001 (1st in Theme award, 1st in Colored Graphics award, 2d in Peoples' Choice award), Santa Paula Art Exhibit, 2002 (1st People's Choice award, 1st jury of peers award, 2002), Southwest Art Mag., 2002. Recipient Artist of Yr., San Gabriel Fine Art Assn., 2001, Don Roche Meml. award, 2002. Mem.: River Valley Art Assn. (1st pl. award 2003), Pastel Soc. Am. (signature), Havasu Art Assn. (1st Pl. award 2003, People's Choice award 2003). E-mail: ddsweet7@frontiernet.net.

DEAN, DOROTHY G., psychologist, social sciences educator, researcher; b. Oyster Bay, N.Y., Jan. 28, 1919; d. William Miles and Georgiana Goodrich Dean; widowed; children: Ellen, Arthur, Robert. BA, St. Lawrence U., 1940; MA in Religion, Yale U., 1973; EdD, Boston U., 1985. Personnel testing R.H. Macy & Co., N.Y.C., 1940—41; advt. rsch. Newell-Emmett Co., N.Y.C., 1941—44; coll. admissions Albertus Magnus Coll., New Haven, 1964—65; ref. asst. Yale U. Libr., New Haven, 1966—70; chaplain trainee Boston City Hosp., 1971—72; clinician trainee Conn. Mental Health Ctr., New Haven, 1972—73; therapist intern Cambridge (Mass.) Family & Children's Svc., 1975—76; pvt. practice Brookline, Mass., 1975—86. Family counselor First and Second Ch., Boston, 1975—85; rsch. fellow, Bainton assoc. Yale Divinity Sch., New Haven, 1984; presenter in field. Contbr. articles to profl. jours. and mags.; author: Transforming Violence: Teaching Democracy and Civility. Del. Nat. Impact, Washington; mem. Robert Shaw Collegiate Chorale, 1942—44; mem. great decisions com. Learning in Ret., 2002—05; mem. Nat. Women's Hist. Mus. Mem.: AAUW (pres. 1956—57, pub. chair 1955—56), LWV (v.p. 1950—52, co-founder Rutland chpt.), Rutland Players (v.p. 1950—52), Pi Lambda Theta. Mem. United Church Of Christ. Avocations: singing, acting, music, theater, bridge. Home: 52 Firethorn Ln Northampton MA 01060

DEAN, KATHERINE S., physical education educator, consultant; children: Zach, Josh, Kate. BA, Ind. State U., Terre Haute, 1981; MA, Ind. State U., 1985. Lic. tchr. Ind., Ariz. Phys. edn. and athletic dir. Diocese of Phoenix, 2001—04; phys. edn. and wellness tchr. Carmel Clay Schs., Ind., 2005—. Wellness cons., 1987—. Theology tchr., choir dir. Diocese of Phoenix, 1997—2004. Named Wayne Twp. Tchr. of Yr.; recipient Extra Mile award; grantee Am. Heart Assn., 1986, 2001, 2002, Ind. Dept. Edn., 1987. Mem.: AAHPERD (assoc.), Am. Coll. Sports Medicine Fitness Alliance (assoc.), Ind. AAHPERD (assoc.; bd. mem. 1987—, Outstanding Young Profl. 1992), Alpha Chi Omega (life; social dir., rush advisor 1980—82). Avocations: health and fitness, piano, coaching. Office Phone: 480-783-3000. Personal E-mail: ksdean@cox.net.

DEAN, KRYSTEN, manufacturing engineer; Assembly plant vehicle engr. DaimlerChrysler Corp., Newark, Del. Recipient Women of Color Tech. award, 2005. Office: DaimlerChrysler AG Newark Assembly Plant 550 S College Ave Newark DE 19713 Office Phone: 302-453-5221.*

DEAN, LISA, foundation executive; b. New Castle, Pa., Aug. 8, 1968; d. Wayne Ernest and Theresa May Dean. BA, St. John's U., 1992; postgrad., Columbia U., 1992-94. V.p. for tech. policy Free Congress Found., Washington, 1994—. Editor The Privacy Papers, 1997—; host nat. syndicated TV show Endangered Liberties, 1997-99; bd. dirs. Am.'s Voice TV Network, Free Congress PAC, Com. for an Effective State Govt. Republican. Eastern Orthodox. Avocations: travel, orgnizational and charitable work. Office: Free Congress Found 717 2d St NE Washington DC 20002

DEAN, MARGARET JUSTICE, literature and language professor; b. Logansport, Ind., Apr. 19, 1950; d. Robert Scott and Catherine Leirer Justice; m. Claude de Seze Dean, Apr. 14, 1973; children: Celeste de Seze Dean, Jesse de Seze Dean. AB, Radcliffe Coll., Cambridge, Mass., 1972; MA, U. Colo., Boulder, 1985; PhD, U. Ky., Lexington, 1998. Cert. secondary English tchr. Mass., Colo. Tchr. secondary English, Salem Pub. Schs., Mass., 1973—76, Jefferson County Pub. Schs., Colo., 1985; dir. writing ctr. Ea. Ky. U., Richmond, 1986—98, assoc. prof., 1999—2006, prof., 2006—. Office: Ea Ky Univ Dept English Theatre 467 Case Annex 521 Lancaster Ave Richmond KY 40475-3102

DEAN, NANCY, literature educator, retired playwright; d. Archie Leigh Dean and Ella Cecile Lang; life ptnr. Beatrice Eva Eastman, Sept. 2, 1963. BA with honors, Vassar Coll., 1952; MA in Tchg., Radcliffe Coll., 1953; PhD, NYU, 1963. Tchr. The Madeira Sch., Greenway, Va., 1953—55, Wakefield H.s., Arlington, Va., 1955—56; instr. Robert Coll., Istanbul, Turkey, 1956—59; from instr. to full prof. Hunter Coll., CUNY, NYC, 1963—90; ret. Author: (plays) Ophelia's Laughter, 1988, Blood and Water, 1988, Burning Bridges, 1991, Upstairs? In the Afternoon?, 1995, That Ilk, 2000, Criseyde, 2003, Libretto, Criseyde, 2005; author: (as Elizabeth Lang) (novels) Anna's Country, 1981; author: (screenplay) Ophelia's Rainbow, 2005; co-editor: (short stories) In the Looking Glass, 1977, (plays) Intimate Acts, 1997; translator: Molière's Misanthrope, 1991. Founder The Astraea Found., NYC, 1977—85; co-founder with Beatrice Eva Eastman Open Meadows Found., NYC, 1986. Recipient Significant Achievement As Playwright & Supporter of Other Lesbian Playwrights, Sisters On Stage, 1995; Ford fellow, Vassar Coll., 1953, Louise Hart Van Loon fellow, 1959—60, Woodrow Wilson fellow, NYU, 1962—63, Penfield scholar, 1961, Jay F. Krakauer Meml. grantee, NYU Grad. Sch. Alumni, 1962—63. Mem.: AAUW, Pen and Brush (chair playwrights 2002—04), Washington Sq. Playwrights, Times Sq. Playwrights, Dramatists Guild (assoc.). Democrat. Buddhist. Office: Grimalkyn Ltd 620 King Ave Bronx NY 10464 Personal E-mail: enndean@mindspring.com.

DEAN, NAT, artist, designer, educator; b. Redwood City, Calif., Jan. 13, 1956; d. Richard William and Marianne Ridley (Smith) D.; m. Paul Singdahlsen, May 24, 1987. Student, Calif. Inst. of Arts, 1972-76, Cooper Union Coll., 1975; BFA, San Francisco Art Inst., 1977. Freelance artist, educator, Fla./Calif, 1978-95; annual workshop leader, lectr. Calif. Inst. of Arts, Valencia, 1985—; dir. career planning Calif. Inst. Arts, Valencia, 1986-89; dir. of career ctr. Ringling Sch. of Art and Design, Sarasota, Fla., 1989-92; conf. co-organizer Arts Placment Profls. Groups, 1989, 91, 92, 93; pres., owner Ruta Zinc Fine Arts Agy., San Francisco, NY and L.A., 1980-89; freelance artist, educator N.Mex./Calif., 1995—; owner Ruta Zinc Handmade, San Francisco, 1999—, N.Mex., 1999—, NY, 1999—. Guest lectr. Iowa State U., Ames, 1992; adj. faculty Md. Inst., Balt.; lectr. L.A. Internat. Art Fair, 1988-94; dir., organizer annual Dialogue Among Peers, Santa Fe, 1995-2005, numerous others; spkr. in field. One-person shows and group exhbns. include Valencia C.C., Orlando, Fla., 1995, Durango (Colo.) Art Ctr., 1995, Manatee C.C., Bradenton, Fla., 1994, Ormond Beach (Fla.) Meml. Art Mus., 1994, Oreg. Sch. of Arts & Crafts, Portland, 1993, The Edn. Ctr. Gallery, Longboat Key, Fla., 1993, NutraLife, Buena Park, Calif., 1993, Sarasota County (Fla.) Arts Coun., 1993, ARTarget, Sarasota, Fla., 1993, Selby Gallery, Sarasota, Fla., 1992, Ctr. Gallery, Miami-Dade C.C., 1991, NCCA Gallery/New Ctr. for Creative Awareness, Sarasota, 1990, Scottsdale (Ariz.) Ctr. for Arts, 1992, 95, Boca Raton (Fla.) Mus. Art, 1991, Coll. Creative Studies, U. Calif., Santa Barbara, 1990, San Francisco Mus. Modern Art Rental Gallery, 1986, 89, Galerie Anton Meir, Geneva, 1988, Orange County Ctr. Contemporary Art, Santa Ana, Calif., 1990, The Fukuoka Mcpl. Mus., Japan, 1987, Berlin Transit, 2001, San Francisco Ctr. for the Book, 2002, North 4th Art Ctr., Santa Fe, 2005, 06, Santa Fe Ann. Design Conf., 2006, Govs. Office on Disabilities, N.Mex., 2004, 05, 06, Capital Rotunda Gallery, 2006, The Roundhouse, Santa Fe, 2006, Gallery for the State of N.Mex., Santa Fe, 2006, Kitchen Angels Invitational, Santa Fe, 2006 others; co-author: The Visual Artist's Business and Legal Guide, 1995; contbr. Artmaker Mag., 2002. Chmn. visual artists task force Sarasota County Arts Coun., 1991-92; AIDS subcom. Planned Approach to Community Health, Sarasota, 1991-92; visual aids com., Visual Aids: Day Without Art, 1989—; program adv. Regional Occupational Program, Contra Costa Bd. Edn., 1986, numerous others; mem. Mayor's Com. Disabilities, Santa Fe, 2000—. Recipient Residency award The Bemis Project, Omaha, 1986, Profl. Devel. grant Ringling Sch. of Art and Design, Sarasota, 1990, Merit award Calif. Inst. of Arts, Valencia, 1976, others. Mem. Coll. Art Assn. (speaker 1992, 93), Nat. Artists Equity (speaker 1992), Women's Caucus for Art (speaker 1993), Nat. Soc. Exptl. Learning (speaker 1988, 89, 92, 93), Nat. Art Edn. Assn. (speaker 1992), Nat. Assn. Artists Orgns., Coll. Placement Coun., others. Home and Studio: 110 Sierra Azul Santa Fe NM 87507-0188 Office Phone: 505-474-6257. Business E-Mail: natdean@hubwest.com.

DEAN, PATRICEA LOUISE, lawyer, law educator, small business owner; b. Kansas City, Mo., Sept. 25, 1928; d. Merville Francis Davies and Marie Margaret (Dorsch Davies) Damron; m. Richard Wallace Dean, Mar. 14, 1948 (dec. July 20, 1987); children: Phyllis Carol(dec.), Katherine Ann, Carol Anne. AA, Met. Jr. Coll., Kansas City, 1947; BA, Pepperdine U., 1968, JD, 1971. Bar: Calif. 73, U.S. Supreme Ct. 87, U.S. Tax Ct. 92. Pvt. practice, Anaheim and Sacramento, Calif., 1973—2001; instr. various colls. and law schs., Calif., 1975—2001; continuing edn. instr. N.W. Coll., Powell, Wyo., 2001—04; founder, pres. Office@Home, Inc., 1998—. Legis. coord. Western Manufactured Housing Inst., 1977—83; atty., lobbyist, presenter seminars Golden State Manufactured Home Owners League, 1984—89; dir., pres. telecomms., software and internet businesses, 1990—. Author: Guide to Manufactured Housing, 1980; contbr. articles to profl. publs. Pres. Friends of Cody Libr., 2002—04; precinct worker Dem. Party, Mo. and Calif., 1949—53; campaign mgr. Dist. Atty. race, Iron County, Utah, 1962—63; precinct committeewoman Rep. Party, Park County, Wyo., 2002—03. Achievements include helped draft federal and state laws on building, siting, zoning and taxation of manufactured homes. Office: Office@Home Inc PO Box 836 Powell WY 82435

DEAN, SHERRY LYNN, language educator, speech professional; b. New Albany, Ind., July 1, 1960; d. Oscar L. and Betty L. (Jason) Brown; m. A. L. Dean Jr. BA in French, Speech Comm., Secondary Edn., Asbury Coll., 1983; MA in French, U. Tex. Arlington, 1990; Cert. pratique de francais commercial, Chambre de Commerce de d'Industries, Paris, 1990; MA in Interdisciplinary Studies, U. Tex., 1999; PhD in Higher Edn. Adminstrn., U. Tex. Austin, 2003. Mem. adj. French faculty Mountain View Coll., Dallas, 1986—91, mem. French faculty, 1991—, prof. French and speech comm., 1993—. Sponsor French Club, Mountain View Coll., 1989—, chair honors program, 1996—98, sponsor Senegal Studies Club, 1997—98, 1999—2000, coord. Study Abroad Programs, 1998—, mem. study abroad coords., 1998—, chair cultures course com., 1999—, mem. core curriculum cultures course com., 1999—, coord. intercultural spkr. series, 1995, coord. Europe 1992 Conf., 1991—92, mem. numerous other coms.; mem. North Tex. C.C. Consortium for Internat. Edn., 1997—; presenter in field. Compiler AATF Travel Guide, 1996, reviewer Little-known Museums In and Around Paris; author: (book) Discover French-speaking Louisiana: A Brief Guide to Creating An Acadiana Adventure Tour. Dir. DCCC Senegal, West Africa Profl. Devel. Seminar, 2005. Named Outstanding Young Woman of Yr., 1986, Chevalier, Knight of the Acad. Palm, French Govt., 2003; recipient internship, French Cultural Svcs., Washington, 1981; grantee, Dallas County C.C. Dist., 1995—2000; Fulbright/Hays, U.S. Dept. Edn. Mem.: Am. Assn. Tchrs. of French (v.p. North Tex. chpt. 1994—96, com. chair Task Force for Promotion of French in U.S. 1995—97, pres. North Tex. chpt. 1996—98, mem. Commn. for Promotion of French 1999—2000, mem. Nat. French Week Commn. 1998—, co-chair Nat. C.C. Commn. 2000, Coll. Tchr. of Yr. award 1999, Dorothy S. Ludwig Excellence inTchg. award 2000), Tex. Fgn. Lang. Assn. (Coll. Tchr. of Yr. award 1998), l'Alliance Francaise (hon.). Home: 1329 Primrose Ln Desoto TX 75115 Office: Eastfield Coll 3737 Motley Dr Mesquite TX 75150 E-mail: sherrydean@dcccd.edu.

DEANDRADE, KRISTY A., elementary school educator; d. Alan and Joyce Kirkland; m. Richard Floyd; children: Katee, Elizabeth; m. William DeAndrade (dec.). B of Edn., U. Md., College Park, 1998; postgrad., U. Md., Balt., 2004—. Advanced Profl. Cert. Md., cert. group cycling instr. Tchr. Ctr. Marine Biotech., Balt., 1998; tchr. 6th grade sci. and math. Meade Mid. H.S., Ft. Meade, 1998—; counselor, tchr. Md. Sci. Ctr., Balt., 2000—. Faculty coun. chair, regional rep. Meade Mid. Sch., Ft. Meade, 1999—2005, team leader, 2004—, mem. materials of instrn. selection bd. Anne Arundel County Pub. Schs., Annapolis, Md., 1999—2003. Youth fitness instr., 2003—; liaison, staff mem. Young Marines, Laurel, Md., 1997—2001; liaison svc. learning Meade Mid. Sch., Ft. Meade, 2004—. Cpl. USMC, 1992—94. Nominee Disney Tchr. of Yr., 2001, 2002, 2005; recipient U.S. Achievement Acad. scholarship, 1996, 1997, Chancellor's award, U. of NC, Wilmington, 1996. Mem.: Am. Fitness and Aerobics Assn. (cert. group fitness instr.), Phi Theta Kappa, Lambda Delta. Avocations: fitness, bicycling, bowling, music, reading.

DEANE, DEBBE, psychologist, journalist, editor, consultant; b. Coatesville, Pa., July 30, 1950; d. George Edward and Dorothea Alice (Martin) Mays; widowed; children: Theo, Vonisha, Lorise, Voniece. AA in Psychology, Mesa Coll., 1989; BA Psychology, San Diego State U., 1993; MA in Psychology, Nat. U., 1995; D of Psychology, Calif. Sch. Profl. Psychology, 2005. Announcer Sta. KBPI, Denver, 1969-70, Sta. WKXI, Jackson, Miss., 1970-72; news anchor Sta. WNGE-TV, Nashville, 1973-76; news dir. Sta. KLDR, Denver, 1976-78; host, reporter Sta. KMGH-TV, Denver, 1978-81; news anchor, editor Sta. KHOW, Denver, 1978-79; news & pub. affairs dir. Sta. KLZ, Denver, 1979-80, Sta. KCBQ, San Diego, 1980-82; news anchor Sta. KOGO, San Diego, 1983-84; news anchor, reporter Sta. KCST-TV, San Diego, 1984-87; dir. comm. Omni Corp., San Diego, 1987—; news anchor Sta. KFI, L.A., 1990-91; sr. psychiat. therapist Behavioral Health Group, San Diego, 1993—. Media liaison United Negro Coll. Fund, San Diego, 1990-92; dir. comm. United Chs. of Christ, San Diego, 1989-92; cons. San Diego Assn. Black Journalists, 1985-92, San Diego Coalition Black Journalists, 1985-92; cons. in field. Campaign fin. analyst San Diego County Registrar of Voters, San Diego, 1990; cons. San Diego County Office Disaster Preparedness, 1990-91, Nu Way Youth Ctr. & Neighborhood House, Inc., San Diego, 1991-92; counselor Project STARRT, San Diego, 1991-92; cons. United Way Home Start, Inc. Family Self-Sufficiency Program, 1996—; cons. and program coord. San Diego Healthy Start, Inc., 1997—, Samuel L. Gompers Secondary Inst. Math., Sci. & computer Tech., 1997—; coord. Clin. program rsch. treatment, TeleCare, Inc., 1999-. Recipient San Diego Black Achievement award Urban League, 1989, Best News Show & Spot News award San Diego Press Club, 1985, Golden Mike award So. Calif. Broadcast Assn., L.A., 1986; named one of Top 25 Businesswomen Essence Mag., 1978, Outstanding Humanitarian Worldvision, 1993, Outstanding Humanities Alumna Mesa Coll., 1993, Woman of the Year, Outstanding Humanitarian, Habitat for Humanity, Outstanding Humanitarian, Feed-the-Children, Outstanding Humanitarian, Teach Tolerance Project. Mem. AFTRA, APA, Am. Women in Radio & TV, Women in Comm., Black Students Sci. Orgn. (sec. 1989-91), Africana Psychol. Soc. (media coord. 1990-92), San Diego Assn. Black Psychologists (media coord. 2003-06), Psi Chi. Democrat. Achievements: first African-Am. in U.S. lic. to teach radio & TV broadcast prodn. Home: 3545 Valley Rd No 1 Bonita CA 91902-4164 Personal E-mail: debbedeane@msn.com.

DEANE, SALLY JAN, health facility administrator, consultant; b. Downey, Calif., Sept. 24, 1948; d. Virgil Eldred and Pearl Jan (Kettell) D. BA, Whittier Coll., 1970; MEd, Boston U., 1971, MPH, 1988. Mgr. community health Peter Bent Brigham Hosp., Boston, 1974-76; coord. WIC program Martha Eliot Health Ctr., 1976-78; dir. S.W. Boston WIC program Shattuck Hosp. Corp., 1978-80; exec. dir. Fenway Community Health Ctr., 1980-84; exec. asst. commr. Boston Dept. Health & Hosps., 1984-86; assoc. dir. spl. projects Health Policy Inst. Boston U., 1986-87; dir. ambulatory reimbursement Mass. Medicaid, 1987-88; assoc. Cambridge (Mass.) Mgmt. Group, 1989; ptnr. Integrated Health Strategies Inc., Cambridge, Mass., 1990-96; adj. asst. clin. prof. Pub. Health Boston U., 1994—; v.p. Chadwick Martin Bailey, Boston, 1996-98; mng. ptnr. Strategic Healthcare Innovations LLC, Boston, 1999—; instr. Boston U., 1999—. Cons. Mass. Dept. Pub. Health, Boston, 1978-80, Citicorp Corp. Hdqrs., N.Y.C., 1986; lectr. Grad. Sch. Mgmt., Boston U., 1999—; bd. visitors Boston U. Sch. Pub. Health, 1999—; innkeeper Charles St. Inn, 1999—. Mem. Mayor's Task Force on AIDS, Boston, 1983—86; v.p. Trustees Charitable Donations, Boston, 1984—88; chair bd. dirs. Boston Women's Health Book Collective, 2000—05; chmn. bd. dirs. N.E. Eye Inst., 2001—06. Presbyterian. Personal E-mail: sallydeane@yahoo.com.

DEANGELIS, CATHERINE D., pediatrics educator; b. Scranton, Pa., Jan. 2, 1940; m. James C. Harris. BA, Wilkes Coll., 1965; MD, U. Pitts., 1969; MPH, Harvard U., 1973. Diplomate Nat. Bd. Med. Examiners, Am. Bd. Pediat.; RN Pa., N.Y. Intern in pediat. Children's Hosp., Pitts., 1969—70; resident in pediat. Johns Hopkins Hosp., Balt., 1970—72, teaching fellow pediat. dept. internat. health Sch. Pub. Health, 1972; pediatrician Roxbury Comprehensive Health Clinic, Boston, 1972—73; asst. prof. pediat. Coll. Physicians and Surgeons, asst. prof. health svc. adminstrn. Sch. Pub. Health Columbia U., 1973—75; mem. staff divsn. pediatric ambulatory care, dir. med. edn. Child Care Project Columbia Presbyn. Med. Ctr., 1973—75; asst. prof. pediat. Sch. Medicine U. Wis., 1975—77, assoc. prof. pediat. Sch. Medicine, 1977—78; dir. ambulatory pediatric svcs. U. Wis. Hosps., 1975—78; assoc. prof. pediat. Johns Hopkins Sch. Medicine, 1978—85; dir. pediatric primary care and adolescent medicine Johns Hopkins Hosp., 1978—84, co-dir. adolescent pregnancy program, 1979—82; with dept. health svcs. adminstrn. and dept. internat. health Johns Hopkins Sch. Hygiene and Pub. Health, 1980—90; dir. residency tng. dept. pediat. Johns Hopkins Hosp., 1983—90, dir. divsn. gen. pediat. and adolescent medicine, 1984—90; deputy chmn. dept. pediat. Johns Hopkins Sch. Medicine, 1983—90, prof. pediat., 1986—90, assoc. dean acad. affairs, 1990—93, sr. assoc. dean acad. affairs and faculty, 1993—94, vice dean acad. affairs and faculty, 1994; editor Jour. AMA, 2000—. Mem. Gov.'s Task Force to Evaluate Health Care in Wis. State Prisons, 1975—78; chmn. ambulatory care com. U. Wis. Hosp., 1976—78; mem. med. sch. admissions com. U. Wis. Sch. Medicine, 1976—78, chmn., 1977—78; mem. exec. coun. dept. pediat. and Children's Ctr. Johns Hopkins U. Sch. Medicine, 1982—90, chmn. fin. com. dept. pediat., 1984—85, chmn. assoc. prof.'s promotion com., 1985—88, chmn. com. developing Women's Health Ctr. at Johns Hopkins Med. Instns., 1993; mem. Md. Gov.'s Task Force on Women's Health, 1993—, chair, 1994; mem. search com. U. Wis., 1976, Johns Hopkins Sch. Medicine, 1984, 88, 92, 93; mem. nat. rev. com. for accreditation of nurse practitioners Am. Nurses' Assn., 1975—79, co-chmn., 1977; mem. peer rev. com. nurse practitioner programs divsn. nursing Health Resources Agy., Dept. HEW, 1979—81. Author: Basic Pediatrics for the Primary Care, 1984; editor: An Introduction to Clinical Research, 1990; editor: (with others) Principles and Practice of Pediatrics, 1990, 1994; assoc. editor Pediatric Annals, 1990, editor Archives of Pediatrics and Adolescent Medicine, 1993—. Cons. Robert Wood Johnson Found., 1973—; mem. adv. group on improving outcomes for children Pew Charitable Trusts, 1991—92; mem. adv. panel medicine Pew Health Profn.'s Commn.; mem. nat. adv. com. Robert Wood Johnson Clin. Scholars Program, 1992—; mem. steering com. Rural Health Planning, Wis. Recipient George Armstrong award, Ambulatory Pediatric Assn., scholarship, Acad. Adminstrn. and Health Policy, Assn. Health Ctrs., 1993; fellow NIH, 1973. Fellow: APHA, Am. Acad. Pediat. (govt. affairs com. 1984—88, chpt. III youth com. N.Y. chpt. 1974—75, chmn. adolescent com. Md. chpt. 1981—84); mem.: Inst. Medicine Coun., Soc. Adolescent Medicine, Am. Bd. Pediat. (examiner 1986—, long-range planning com. 1990—91, chmn. long-range planning com. 1992—, bd. dirs. 1990—, fin. com. 1991—, sec., treas. 1993—95, chair-elect 1995—96, chair 1996, search com. 1990), Am. Pediatric Soc. (sec., treas. 1989—), Alpha Omega Alpha. Address: JAMA 515 N State St Chicago IL 60610-4325 Office: Johns Hopkins Sch Medicine 720 Rutland Ave Ste 106 Baltimore MD 21205-2109*

DE ANGELIS, JUDY, anchorwoman; b. Passaic, N.J., Oct. 1, 1949; d. Fredrick and Patricia (Zollo) De An.; m. Barry Sheffield, Aug. 28, 1977; children: Alexader, Katelin, Corrine. Student, Hartt Sch. Music, Hartford, Conn., 1968-69; BA in Speech and Drama, U Hartford, 1971; MA in Edn., Montclair State U., 1973. Lic. 3d class operator FCC. Anchor Sta. WALK-AM-FM, Patchogue, NY, 1978-79, Sta. WGBB-FM, Freeport, NY, 1979-80, Sta. WKJY-FM, Hempstead, NY, 1980, Sta. WHLI, Hempstead, 1980, Sta. WCBS-FM, N.Y.C., 1980-81; reporter, anchor Sta. WNBC, N.Y.C., 1981-88; morning anchor Sta. WINS, N.Y.C., 1988—; morning drive anchor WNEW-FM, N.Y.C., 2004—; co-owner Sheffield Studios, Mahwah, NJ. Freelance anchor The Source, 1982-88; freelance anchor NBC Radio Network, 1982-888, host talk-net, 1989-90; news anchor HBO Entertainment, 1988; indsl. voice-over Odyssey Prodns., N.Y.C., 1981-88; comml. voice-over DWJ, Ridgewood, N.J., 1994—, Gourvitz Comm., N.Y.C., 1995—; cons. Media Placement Svcs., Glen Rock, N.J., 1994—. Author: (documentary) Child Abuse: The Darker Side of Growing Up, 1982 (Olive awrd N.Y.C. Coun. of Chs., 1983; appeared on Broadway in Rockabye Hamlet, 1976. Lectr. on broadcasting all ednl. levels, 1985—; dir. religious edn. Christ Episcopal Ch., Ridgewood, 1995—; troop leader Girl Scouts U.S.A., 1994—. Recipient award for pub. svc. N.Y. Deadline Club, 1982, spl. citation Office N.Y.C. Comptr., 1983; name Best Radio Newscaster, N.Y. AIR, 2000, 01. Mem. AFTRA, Actors Equity, Ramapo-Bergen Animal Refuge. Democrat. Avocations: carpentry, gardening, crossword puzzles, sailing, swimming. Office: 1010 WINS Radio 888 7th Ave New York NY 10106-0001

DE ANGELIS, ROSEMARY ELEANOR, actress; b. Bklyn., Apr. 26, 1933; d. Francis and Antoinette (Donofrio) De A.; m. Kenneth Richard Bridges, Sept. 12, 1965 (div. 1983); 1 child, Laurel Ann. BA, Empire State Coll., 1998. Tchr. HB Studio, N.Y.C., 2004—, Uta Hagen Herbert Berghof Studio. Tchr. Practice of Acting HB Studios, N.Y.C. Appeared in plays Spinning into Butter, Over The River and Through the Woods, Queen and the Rebels, High Time, Six Characters in Search of an Author, Mrs. Klein (Barrymore award 1993), The Paradise Kid, In the Summer House, The Transfiguration of Benno Blimpie (Drama Desk award-Best Actress), N.Y. Sharespeare Fest. (with Joseph Papp dir.), numerous others; appeared in movies Frequency, Hit and Runway, Two Family House, The Wanderers, Enormous Changes at the Last Minute, Nothing Lasts Forever, Out of Darkness, Household Saints, Mamma Mia, Angie, Two Bits, The Juror; appeared in TV shows 100 Centre St., Guiding Light, As The World Turns, Monkey, Monkey, The Death of Ivan Ilyich, P.B.S. Theatre in Am., Baker's Dozen, The Equalizer, Law and Order; co-writer (screenplay) Burning Intentions, 1992-99; dir.: Shadow Boxers, 1998; author: The Nightingales; author numerous poems. Recipient residency award, Edna St. Vincent Millay writer's colony, N.Y.C. Mem. AFTRA, SAG, Actors Equity Assn. Avocations: painting, photography. Personal E-mail: redtoes100@aol.com.

DEANGELO, JUDITH, artist; b. Conn., July 17, 1944; d. Carl Carlson and Mildred Baker; m. Lawrence DeAngelo, Sept. 29, 1990; children: Robin Dawson, Kirsta Migliaro. Oil/alkyd paintings on exhbn. at Hargis Unique Art Gallery, Corona, Calif.; other exhbns. include Spectrum Fine Art, Westhampton Beach, N.Y., 1996, Mus. of Modern Art, Miami, Redding Mus. of Art, Calif., Art for AIDS, Milw., 1995; work displayed in pvt. collections of Sally Marr, Kitty Bruce, John Cestare, Ed Zwirn, Hugo DeVillar. Recipient award of Excellence, Manhattan Arts Internat. Competition, 1998. Office Phone: 800-326-3935.

DEAN-PRATT, BRIDGET, secondary school educator; b. Hornell, NY, Sept. 7, 1953; d. James Martin Dean and Mary Jane McDonald; m. Robert Eller Pratt, Oct. 8, 1995. Student, Gwynedd-Mercy Coll., Pa., 1971—73; BA in English, Temple U., Phila., 1975; MA, St. Johns Grad. Inst., Annapolis, Md., 1991. Tchr. St. Francis H.S., SD, 1976—79, Mission H.S., 1979—80; stockbroker Walford Demaret, Denver, 1981—83; ins. sales JC Penny, Boulder, 1983—84; tchr., counselor Alexander Danson, Lafayette, 1985—90; tchr. Browne Acad., Alexandria, Va., 1990—91, George Mason H.S., Falls Church, 1991—. Rep. Profl. Educators Nat. Com., Falls Church, 1994—. Grantee, NEH, Palo Alto, Calif., 1988, NEH, Tempe, Ariz., 2000, NEH, Cortez, Colo., 2002. Mem.: Va. Edn. Assn. (rep. 1996—2006), Nat. Mus. Am. Indian, Nat. Coun. Tchrs. English. Avocations: skiing, hiking, running, writing. Home: 10003 Blackman Ct Fairfax VA 22030 Office: George Mason H S 7124 Leesburg Pike Falls Church VA 22046

DEANS, PATRICIA HERRMANN, investment banker; b. Monmouth Beach, N.J., Oct. 28, 1956; d. Joseph Charles and Caroline (Hauck) Herrmann; m. Jamie Robertson Deans, Feb. 29, 1981 (div. Mar. 1992). BA, U. Mass., Boston, 1980; M Internat Fin, Rutgers U., 1984. Account mgr., media & telecomm. Bank Montreal, N.Y.C., 1984-86; v.p. Media corp. fin. Chase Securities, Inc., N.Y.C., 1986—, mng. dir., sr. ptnr. in global syndicated fin., 1996—; head telecomm. media and tech. Syndicated Leveraget Fin., J./P. Morgan, 2002—. Mem. Lawrence Beach Club, Norfolk Country Club, Phi Beta Kappa. Roman Catholic. Avocations: skiing, running, travel, violin. Office: Chase Securities Inc 5th Fl 270 Park Ave Fl 5 New York NY 10017-2014 Address: 771 W End Ave Apt 4D New York NY 10025-5537 also: 26 Windom Rd Norfolk CT 06058-1126 Office Phone: 212-270-4872.

DEANY, DONNA JEAN, radiology technologist; b. Fairbury, Ill., Aug. 14, 1959; d. Paul Leroy and Jean Avis (Donley) D. Cert., Bloomington-Normal Sch. Radiog, 1979. Registered radiologic technologist. Staff technologist Mennonite Hosp., Bloomington, Ill., 1979-80, asst. chief technologist, 1981-85; radiology mgr. BroMenn Healthcare, Normal, Ill., 1985—. Clin. instr. Bloomington-Normal Sch. Radiography, 1980-85. Mem. Am. Registry Radiologic Technoloigsts, Ill. State Soc. Radiologic Technologists (sec. 1985-87, v.p. 1989-91, pres. 1992-94, treas. 1994-95). Avocations: skiing, reading, gardening. Office: BroMenn Healthcare Virginia at Franklin Normal IL 61761

DEAN-ZUBRITSKY, CYNTHIA MARIAN, psychologist, researcher; b. Urbana, Ill., Oct. 27, 1950; d. William Bonaparte and Lois (Doran) Dean; m. John Jay Zubritsky, Sept. 15, 1979; 1 child, Grant Doran. BA, Ind. U., 1972; M in Psychology, Pa. State U., 1978; PhD, Temple U., 1989. Counselor New Castle (Pa.) Youth Devel. Ctr., 1972-76; dir. Ill. Family Edn. Ctr., Danville, 1976-77; researcher Pa. State U., University Park, 1977-78, 89—; film cons. Ill. Devel. Disabilities Council, Springfield, 1978; psychologist Atkins House, York, Pa., 1978-82; quality assurance specialist Pa. Office Mental Retardation, Harrisburg, 1982-84; dir. tng. and staff devel. Pa. Office Mental Health, Harrisburg, 1984-89; pvt. practice psychology Harrisburg, 1989—. Bd. dirs. children and youth svcs. Vermilion County Mental Health Program, Danville, 1975-77; psychologist Loysville (Pa.) Youth Devel. Ctr., 1981-82; tchr. Danville Community Coll., 1975; cons. U. Ill., Urbana, 1976, Danville Sch. System, 1975-76; asst. prof. dept. psychiatry U. Pa., 1989—; rsch. alliance for mentally ill Pa., 1989-92. Vol. ARC, 1967-87, YWCA, 1970-89; mem. Pa. Task Force on Mental Health: Women, Harrisburg, 1986-87. Fed. rsch. grantee NIMH, CSAD, AOA; Human Resource Devel. grantee NIMH, 1985-88, Office of Substance Abuse Prevention grantee, 1992-97, Pew Charitable Trust grantee, 1997—, SAMHSA grantee, 1997—. Mem. Internat. Psychogeriatric Assn., Nat. Assn. State Mental Health Program Dirs., Gerontol. Soc. Am., Am. Soc. Aging, Am. Horticulture Soc., Phi Delta Kappa, Phi Mu. Republican. Presbyterian. Avocations: horticulture, interior design. Office: U Pa Dept Psychiatry Philadelphia PA 19104 Business E-Mail: cdz@mail.med.upenn.edu.

DEARBORN, MAUREEN MARKT, speech and language clinician; b. Brockton, Mass., Jan. 19, 1948; d. Francis Joseph and Marjorie Agnes (White) M.; m. James Clement Bovin, Nov. 6, 1970 (div. June 1973); m. David C. Dearborn, Jan. 14, 1989. BA in Speech Pathology and Audiology, U. Mass., 1970; MA in Ednl. Psychology, Am. Internat. Coll., Springfield, Mass. Speech and lang. clinician Holyoke (Mass.) Pub. Schs., 1970—. Chmn. Holyoke Cancer Crusade, 1985; voter registration chmn. Holyoke Dem. Com., 1987; chmn. deaconesses 2d Congl. Ch. Holyoke. Mem.: DAR (historian Eunice Day 1984—), Mass. Tchrs. Assn., Mass. Speech, Hearing and Lang. Assn., Am. Speech, Hearing and Lang. Assn. (continuing edn. adv. bd. 1988—91, congl. action contact 1988—90), Holyoke Tchrs. Assn., Hampden County Tchrs. Assn. (pres. 1981, 1987, sec. 1982, v.p. 1984—86, treas. 1988—), Dorchester Hist. Soc., Wrenthan Hist. Soc., Assn. for Gravestone Studies, Friends of the Libr. Coun. (treas. 1992—2000), Mass. Geneal. Soc., New Eng. Hist. and Geneal. Soc. Avocations: bicycling, antiques, genealogy, aerobics. Home: 257 W Franklin St Holyoke MA 01040-2210 Office: Holyoke Pub Schs 57 Suffolk St Holyoke MA 01040-5015 Office Phone: 413-534-2067. E-mail: dearborn@massed.net.

DEAS, ALBERTA D., educator, educational administrator; b. Charleston, S.C., Mar. 15, 1934; d. Michael and Carrie Lee (Waring) D.; m. Joe Major Williford, Dec. 19, 1957 (div. Oct. 1964); children— Joel Major, Jon Michael. B.S., S.C. State Coll., 1956; M.Ed., U. Mass., 1975, Ed.D., 1978. Gen. mgr. Sta. WMOZ, Mobile, Ala., 1959-62; chmn. bus. edn. dept. Carver Tech., Mobile, 1962-68; project dir. Westfield State Coll., Mass., 1975-77; asst. prof. S.C. State Coll., Orangeburg, 1977-82; gen. mgr. Sta. WLGI-FM, Hemingway, S.C., 1982-84; sch. adminstr. Louis Gregary Inst., Hemingway, 1980-85; owner, dir. Tiny Tot Presch., Mobile, 1961-65; adminstr. Ind. State U., Terre Haute, 1968-69; owner Garden of Eden, Orangeburg, S.C.; program analyst Office of Econ. Opportunities, Charleston, 1969-71; adminstr. Baha'i Regional Office, Goose Creek, S.C., 1971-74; del UN Internat. Women's Conf., Nairobi, Kenya. Author: (filmstrip) Parenting: Early Childhood, 1980; (manual) Exchange Student/Australia, 1976. Mem. Children Defense Fund, Washington, 1985. Mem. Nat. Council of Women, Nat. Spiritual Assembly of Baha'is of U.S., Phi Delta Kappa (Coll. Tchr. Yr. 1979). Avocations: health and fitness; dancing; travel; reading. Home: PO Box 2152 Orangeburg SC 29116-2152 Office: Garden of Eden 389 Russell St Orangeburg SC 29115

DEASON, ELLEN MURIEL See WELLS, KITTY

DEASY, IRENE M., retired protective services official; d. Earnest August Markley and Clara Matilda Larson; m. Howard Gale Ledgerwood (dec.); m. William H. Deasy (dec.). Grad., Sarachon-Hooley Secretarial Sch., Kansas City, Mo., 1942; RN, BSN, Hunter Coll., 1973. Stenographer clk. US Naval Air Sta., Olathe, Kans., 1942—43, stenographer, disc jockey Jacksonville, Fla., 1943—45; stenographer, sec. US Dept. Immigration, NYC, 1945—49; policewoman NYC Police Dept., 1949—73. Co-author: In That Very Day, 1995, The Civil War, 1996, The Holy Spirit, Your Divine Companion, 1996, Money Is Power, 1997. Vol. Marantha Internat., Sacramento; mem. Internat. Effort for Am. Armed Forces; v.p., treas. Consolidated Mgmt. Corp.; nominee v.p. U.S.A. Ind. Prty, 2004. Scholar, Bellevue Hosp., Hunter Coll.; Four scholarships NYC policewoman. Mem.: AAUW. Avocations: reading, political activities. Home: 2025 Jerry Murphy Rd Apt 101 Pueblo CO 81001

DEATER, ELOISE ELAINE, mental health services professional; b. Corpus Christi, Tex., Mar. 25, 1943; d. Fred Thomas and Martha Leona (Soloma) Paine; m. Glen D. Scott (dec.); children: Larry L. Scott, Sherry L. Scott. Student, Fresno City Coll., Calif., U. Alaska, Juneau and Anchorage, Anchorage C.C., Harlingen Tech. Coll., Tex. Cert. in Tex. Patient and Family Edn. Program Mental Health. Acct. State of Alaska, Juneau, 1974—79; mgr. of restaurants, apt. bldgs., mobile home parks Alaska and Tex., 1979—96; acct. of farm Harlingen, 1996—99; chair Silver Star, Rosenberg, Tex., 2000—02, Survivors of Mental Adversity, Rosenberg, Tex., 1998—. Office Phone: 281-239-1331.

DEATON, FAE ADAMS, social worker, consultant, artist, graphics designer; b. Phila., Feb. 19, 1932; d. Charles Sizemore and Dorothea Lucia (Adams) Deaton; children: Dorothea Fae Stein Krause Scott, Caroline Louise Stein Collins, Erich Charles Stein. MusB in Music Edn., Salem Coll., NC, 1953; postgrad., Ohio U., Oxford, 1962, Oxford U., Eng., 1963, U. Alaska, 1969, Wright State U., 1973; MSEd in Guidance & Counselling, Old Dominion U., 1975; MSW, Norfolk State U., 1980; postgrad., Santa Clara U., 1980; BS in Graphic Design summa cum laude, Elizabeth City State U., 2005, BA in Art summa cum laude, 2006. Diplomate Am. Bd. Social Workers; cert. Am. Bd. Clin. Social Workers; cert. Del Giacco art therapist. Tchr. music, Mifflin, Ohio, 1953—54; HS supr. USN Dependents Sch., Argentia, Nfld., Canada, 1956—57; tchr. USAF Dependents Sch., Croughton, England, 1960—63, Upper Heyford, England, 1963—64; substitute tchr. Pontiac Jr. HS, Ill., 1965—66; mag. editor Scott AFB, Ill., 1966—67; substitute tchr. Elmendorf AFB, Alaska, 1967—69; mem. staff Hist. and Fine Arts Mus., Anchorage, 1968—70; publicity chmn., publicity staff Alaska Council on Arts, 1969—70; counselor Youth Svcs. Bur., Dayton, Ohio, 1973; engring. rsch. aide Wright Patterson AFB Biophysics Lab., Dayton, 1973; writer Dayton Daily News, 1973; field rsch. aide Am. Inst. Rsch., Palo Alto, Calif., 1974—75; counselor, patient advocate Norfolk (Va.) Free Clinic, 1975—76; adminstrv. asst. econs. dept. Old Dominion U., Norfolk, 1975—76; tchr., counselor Blessed Sacrament Sch., Norfolk, 1976—77; mental health team, young adolescent unit, milieu therapist Portsmouth (Va.) Psychiat. Ctr., 1977—79, mem. children's unit, 1979—80; child, adult, family and marital therapist sexual trauma treatment Ctr. Psychiatrists/Portsmouth Psychiat. Ctr., 1980—82; psychology faculty Tidewater C.C., Virginia Beach, Va., 1987—88; therapist, social worker children's svcs. sexual trauma treatment unit Cmty. Mental Health Ctr. and Psychiat. Inst. Dept. Psychiatry, Eastern Va. Med. Sch., Norfolk, 1983—88; dir., psychotherapist Hampton Roads Psychotherapy Assocs. and Childhood Trauma Treatment Ctr., Norfolk, 1988—95; lt. gov.'s taskforce on sexual victimization prevention Va., 1992—95; lead clin. social worker Edenton unit Albemarle Mental Health Ctr., 1995—99; pvt. practice Elizabeth City, NC, 1999—2004; mem. Edenton DSS Cmty. Resource Coms., 1999—2001. Substitute tchr. Pontiac Middle School, Ill., 1965, O'Fallon Middle School, Ill., 1965, Elmendorf AFB Schs., 1967—69, Norfolk Sch., 1973—74; proofreader editing Office Printing Pubs. Old Dominion U., 1974; cons. Families United, Norfolk, Va., 2001—02; intern Mus. of Albemarle, 2003; adj. faculty social work dept. Elizabeth City State U., 2003, asst. editor yearbook, 2004—05; lectr. in field; spkr., educator Women Heart, 2006—. Exhibitions include Va. Beach Mother Daughter Art Exhibit, 1957, Va. Beach Boardwalk Art Show, 1957, Norfolk, Va., 1957, Anchorage, Alaska, 1967—70, Elmendorf AFB, Alaska, 1976—70, Christ Episc. Ch., 2004, ECSU, 2004—05; contbr. articles to profl. jours. Pres. Tidewater Profl. Assn. on Child Abuse, 1981—82; active Tidewater Rape Info. Svcs., Norfolk, 1978—88, Norfolk Com. for Prevention of Child Abuse, 1983—95, VBDSS Sexual Abuse Treatment Team, 1979—82; adminstr., author, bd. dirs. Sexual Abuse Helpline of Tidewater, 1979—95; adhoc com. Nat. Coalition on Sexual Abuse, 1980—81; pres. Tidewater Alliance on Sexual Abuse, 1984—87; mem. admissions, release bd. Norfolk Lakehouse Girls Detention Home, 1978—79; program chmn. Conf. Internat. Yr. of the Child, Norfolk, 1979; sec. Middle Atlantic Coalition on Sexual Victimization of Children, 1981—82; multi discipline team Virginia Beach Dept. Social Services, 1983—86; chmn. task force spl. children Children's Art Center, Norfolk, 1979—81; co-chmn. Gov.'s Child Abuse sub-com.; chmn. Families United Va., Inc., 1980—95; founder, sponsor, coord. Virginia Beach chpt. Parents United, chmn. quality assurance com., regional chair mid.-Atlantic chpts., 1987—92, chmn. 20th Anniversary Norfolk, 1991; state dir. Parents United Inc., Va., 1979—92; historian Alaska Artists Guild, 1969—70; mem. Elmendorf AFB Sch. Bd., 1967—68; state dir. parents Famlies United, Tidewater, 1992—95; mem. Messiah concert Evelyn Johnson Cmty. Singers, 2000—06; vol. Hampton Rds. Naval Mus., 2001—, USS Wis., 2001—, Elizabeth City State U. Commuters Club, 2002—06, Hope Cmty.Prescription Project, Elizabeth City, NC, 2003—04, Friends of the Libr., 2003—, v.p., 2005—; vol. Albemarle Hosp., 2005—, Pasquotauk Arts Coun., 2004—; clarinetist Pensacola H.S. Marching Band, 1946—47, Newport Symphony Orch., 1948—49; choir Trinity Luth. Ch., Norfolk, 1970; sr. choir Mount Lebanon AME Zion Ch., 2000—06; campus and worship commn. Christ Episcopal Ch., 2003—05; Sunday Sch. pianist Warrenton Presbyn. Ch., Fla., 1946—47; chorus Salem Coll., 1949—53; active Salem Chapel Quartet, 1952—53; Base Chapel choir RAF, Croughton, 1961—64, jr. choir dir. Base Chapel choir, 1962—64; bd. dirs. Va. chpt. Nat. Com. on Prevention of Child Abuse, 1981—82; bd. dirs. Tidewater Alliance on Sexual Abuse, 1981—88, Tidewater Assembly on Family Life, 1981—82, Parents Anonymous of Va., 1984—86, Norfolk Little Theater, 1977—78, Parents United Internat., San Jose, Calif., 1987—92; bd. mem. Arts Zone, Elizabeth City, NC, 2004—. Recipient Spl. recognition award Peninsular Task Force on Sexual Abuse Child Abuse for work contbr. to the wellbeing of children and family, Gov.'s award for work in child/sexual abuse, Norfolk, Va. Mem. NASW, Am. Profl. Soc. on Abuse of Children (life), Calif. Profl. Soc. on Abuse of Children (life), So. Christian Leadership Conf. Avocations: knitting, needlepoint, photo restoration, painting.

DEATON, VALERIE L., financial researcher, consultant; b. Des Moines, Sept. 19, 1960; d. C. Ray and Patricia Ruth Deaton; m. Stephen R. West, Dec. 22, 1996. BFA magna cum laude, Drake U., 1984. Asst. fin. officer Iowa State Senate, Des Moines, 1984; field dir. Edgar U.S. Senate Campaign, Media, Pa., 1985; mgr. Vanguard Group, Valley Forge, Pa., 1985-86; sr. rsch. assoc. Opinion Rsch. Corp., Princeton, N.J., 1986-89; sr. rsch. mgr. Prin. Fin. Group, Des Moines, 1989-96; prin. Deaton Rsch., Lambertville, N.J., 1996-99; bus. devel. and fin. rsch. cons. Matthew Greenwald and Assocs., Washington/Lambertville, 1999—. Lectr., cons. in field; mktg. advisor U.S. AID, CNFA, Nakhodka, Russia, 1994-96. Bd. dirs. Project Mgmt. inst., Des Moines, 1992-94; rsch. advisor Des Moines C. of C., 1990-93, VA, Des Moines, 1994; mem. comms. com. Planned Parenthood, Des Moines,

1992-95. Mem. Am. Mkgt. Assn., Assn. Profl. Ins. Women, Soc. Ins. Rsch. (v.p. ann. conf. 1998-99), Rock Creek Woods Homeowner Assn. (sec. bd. dirs. 1999—, trustee), Omicron Delta Kappa, Alpha Lmabda Delta, Phi Eta Sigma. Democrat. Avocation: horticulture. Office: Mathew Greenwald & Assocs 4201 Connecticut Ave NW Washington DC 20008-1158 Home: 8013 Ardleigh St Philadelphia PA 19118-3424 E-mail: valeriedeaton@yahoo.com.

DEATS, SUZANNE, writer, editor, artist; b. Abilene, Tex., Nov. 14, 1937; d. Otto and Susan Reynolds Deats; m. Ben Bedford, Aug. 27, 1960 (dec. Jan. 19, 1978); children: Aaron Bedford, John Bedford. BA in Fine Arts, U. N.Mex., 1981. Juror Santa Fe Art Festival, Main St. Show, Ft. Worth, Mus. S.W., Midland, Tex. Author: Evelyne Boren, 1998, Michael Dunbar, 2006; co-author: Santa Fe Design w. Elmo Baca, 1990, Abstract Art w. Stuart Ashman, 2004, Western Traditions w. Michael Duty, 2005, New Mex. Landscape w. Suzan Campbell, 2006; editor: Fresco Fine Art Publ.; exhibitions include Hill's Gallery, Santa Fe, Art du Monde, Japan; exhbn. (catalog) Kevin Red Star, Yellowstone Art Mus., Billings, Mont.; contbr. articles to periodicals. Mem.: Mensa. Avocations: fiction, design, cooking, travel. E-mail: suzdeats@aol.com.

DEATS-O'REILLY, DIANA DAY, educator, journalist; b. Orland, Calif., Jan. 27, 1940; d. Henry William Jr. and Agnes Elizabeth (Walker) Day; m. Thomas Stewart Deats Jr., May 19, 1960 (dec. Feb. 1987); children: Kimberlee Ellen, Lanai Elizabeth, Stewart Allen; m. Edward Joseph O'Reilly, June 30, 1988. BA, Calif. State U., Chico, 1963, MEd, 1969; MA, U. Santa Clara, 1985. Cert. elem. tchr., Calif., Iowa, N.D., Minn. Tchr. Chico Unified Schs, 1963-69, Iowa City Schs., 1969-72, St. Michael's Sch., Grand Forks, N.D., 1974, Sacred Heart HS, East Grand Forks, 1974-78; with div. student affairs U. N.D., Grand Forks, 1978-81; tchr. Grand Forks Pub. Schs., 1978-81, 83—. Editor: The Way West, 1973, With an Everlasting Love, 1984, Bruised Reed, 1986, The Rennie's of Scotland to America, 1987, Six Bishops of Fargo, 1988, The First County Legislator, 1989; author AIP and Nutrition, Porphyria: The Unknown Disease, Acute Porphyria Case Histories. Vol. St. Anne's, 1989—, United Hospice, Grand Forks, 1986—; lay missioner to Chimbote, Peru, 1984; mem. exec. bd. Greater Grand Forks Symphony, 1988—, United Hosp. Aux., Grand Forks, 1985—; CEO Porphyria Ednl. Svcs. Named First Pl. Editor,Fargo, N.D. Cursillo Newsletter, 1982, Excellence Rating Editor, ACPA, 1982, Grand Forks Woman of Yr., Beta Sigma Phi Internat., 1986, Humanitarian award for human rights Grand Forks, 2004; named Woman of Dist. award N.D. AAUW, 2004. Mem. AAUW (past br. pres. 1978), Press Women Internat., Nat. Cursillo Movement, Kappa Phi Alumnae (Young Woman of Yr. 1974). Democrat. Roman Catholic. Avocations: playing organ, writing, genealogy.

DEAVER, BARBARA JEAN, manufacturing executive; b. Pitts., July 26, 1951; d. William Ervin and Dorothy Marie (Wolf) Cain; m. William Lee Gockley, Mar. 29, 1975 (div. Aug. 1989); children: Ervin Cain, Marianne Bellot, William Cain, Malinda Cain; m. John W. Deaver, Dec. 27, 2002 BA in Bus. Mgmt. and Mktg. Mgmt., Alvernia Coll., 1993; MBA, Univ. Wis., 1997. Cert. in purchasing mgmt.; cert. prodn. and inventory mgmt. Asst. materials mgr. Redman Mobile Homes, Ephrata, Pa., 1972-75; mgr. inventory control Gym-Kin, Inc., Reading, Pa., 1975-77; supr. prodn./inventory control Wyomissing Converting, Reading, 1979-82; mgr. prodn./inventory control Dorma Door Controls, Inc., Reamstown, Pa., 1982-85, project mgr., 1985-86; materials mgr. Powder Coatings Group-Morton Internat., Reading, 1986-94; dir. purchasing Dexter Corp., Waukegan, Ill., 1994-99; v.p. global strategic sourcing Spectrum Brands, St. Louis, 1999-2001; dir. global supply chain mgmt. The Falcon Cos., St. Louis, 2001—03; dir. supply chain mgmt. Elkay Mfg., Chgo., 2003—05; dir. material mgmt. Fluid Mgmt., Wheeling, 2005—. Dir. programs Congress for Progress Inc., 1984-88, vice chmn., 1988-89, 99-2000, chmn., 1989-90, 2000-2001; dir. programs PRMS User Group Internat. Conf., 1991, 92; instr. Berks Campus, Pa. State U., Reading, 1985-86. Dir. Reinholds (Pa.) PTA, 1978-81; bd. dirs. Cocalico Sch. Bd., Denver, Pa., 1985-89. Mem.: Nat. Assn. Female Execs., Assn. Mfg. Excellence, Inst. for Supply Mgmt., Am. Prodn. and Inventory Control Soc. (cert. prodn. and inventory mgmt., treas. Schuylkill Valley chpt. 1981—82, pres. 1982—84, dir. membership region IX 1985—86, asst. v.p. 1987, v.p. 1988—89, Internat. Vol. Svc. award 1986). Republican. Presbyterian. Home: 29W725 Waynewood Dr West Chicago IL 60185 Personal E-mail: barbaradeaver@aol.com.

DEBAKEY, LOIS, science administrator, educator; b. Lake Charles, La. d. S. M. and Raheeja (Zorba) DeBakey. BA in Math., Tulane U., MA in Lit. and Linguistics, 1959, PhD in Lit. and Linguistics, 1963. Asst. prof. English Tulane U., 1963—64; asst. prof. sci. communication Tulane U. Med. Sch., 1963-65, assoc. prof. sci. communication, 1965-67, prof. sci. comm., 1967-68, lectr., 1968-80, adj. prof., 1981-92; prof. sci. comm. Baylor Coll. Medicine, Houston, 1968—. Mem. biomed. libr. rev. com. Nat. Libr. Medicine, Bethesda, Md., 1973-77, bd. regents, 1981-86, cons., 1986—, co-chmn. permanent paper task force, 1987—, lit. selection tech. rev. com., 1988-93, chmn., 1992-93, outreach planning panel, 1988-89; dir. courses in med. comm. ACS and other orgns.; trustee DeBakey Med. Found., 1995—; mem. exec. coun. Commn. on Colls. So. Assn. Colls. and Schs., 1975-80; mem. nat. adv. coun. U. So. Calif. Ctr. Continuing Med. Edn., 1981; mem. steering com. Plain English Forum, 1984; mem. founding bd. dirs. Friends Nat. Libr. Medicine, 1985—, chmn. med. media award of excellence com., 1992—; mem. adv. com. Soc. for Preservation English Lang. Lit., 1986; mem. nat. adv. bd. John Muir Med. Film Festival, 1990-92; mem. The Internat. Health and Med. Film Festival, Acad. of Judges, 1992-93; mem. adv. bd. U. Tex. at Austin Sch. Nursing Found., 1993—; cons. legal writing com. ABA, 1983—, Ency. Brit. Biomed. and Health Database, 1999—; former cons. Nat. Assn. Std. Med. Vocabulary; pioneered instrn. in sci. comm. in med. sch. Sr. author: The Scientific Journal: Editorial Policies and Practices, 1976; co-author: Medicine: Preserving the Passion, 1987; Medicine: Preserving the Passion in the 21st Century, 2004; mem editl. bd.: Tulane Studies in English, 1966-68, Cardiovasc. Rsch. Ctr. Bull., 1971-83, Health Comms. and Informatics, 1975-80, Forum on Medicine, 1977-80, Grants Mag., 1978-81, Internat. Jour. Cardiology, 1981-86, Excerpta Medica's Core Jours. in Cardiology, 1981—, Health Comm. and Biopsychosocial Health, 1981-82, Internat. Angiology, 1985—, Jour. AMA, 1988-2002. CV Network, 2003—; mem. usage panel Am. Heritage Dictionary, 1980—; cons. Webster's Med. Desk Dictionary, 1986; editl. advisor Ency. Brit.; contbr. articles on biomed. comm. and sci. writing, literacy, also other subjects to profl. jours., books, encys., and pub. press. Active Found. for Advanced Edn. in Sci., 1977—. Recipient Disting. Svc. award, Am. Med. Writers Assn., 1970, Bausch & Lomb Sci. award, 1st John P. McGovern award, Med. Libr. Assn., 1983, Outstanding Alumna award, Newcomb Coll., 1994. Fellow Am. Coll. Med. Informatics, Royal Soc. for Encouragement of Arts, Mfrs., and Commerce; mem. Internat. Soc. Gen. Semantics, Med. Libr. Assn. (hon.), Coun. Biology Editors (dir. 1973-77, chmn. com. on editl. policy 1971-75), Coun. Basic Edn. (spl. com. writing 1977-79), Assn. Tchrs. Tech. Writing, Dictionary Soc. N.Am., Nat. Assn. Sci. Writers, Soc. for Health and Human Values, Com. of Thousand for Better Health Regulations, Golden Key, Phi Beta Kappa.

DEBAKEY, SELMA, communications educator, writer, editor; b. Lake Charles, La. BA, postgrad., Newcomb Coll., Tulane U., New Orleans. Dir. dept. med. communication Ochsner Clinic and Alton Ochsner Med. Found., New Orleans, 1942-68; prof. sci. communication Baylor Coll. Medicine, Houston, 1968—; editor Cardiovascular Research Ctr. Bull., 1970-84. Mem. panel judges Internat. Health and Med. Film Festival, 1992. Author: (with A. Segaloff and K. Meyer) Current Concepts in Breast Cancer, 1967; past editor Ochsner Clinic Reports, Selected Writings from the Ochsner Clinic; contbr. numerous articles to sci. jours., chpts. to books. Named to Tex. Hall of Fame. Mem. AAAS, Soc. Tech. Communication, Assn. Tchrs. Tech. Writing, Am. Med. Writers Assn. (past bd. dirs.; publ., nominating, fellowship, constn., bylaws, awards, and edn. coms.), Council Biol. Editors (past mem. trn. in sci. writing com.), Soc. Health and Human Values, Modern Med. Monograph Awards Com., Nat. Assn. Standard Med. Vocabulary (former cons.).

DE BARBIERI, MARY ANN, not-for-profit management consultant; b. Winston-Salem, NC, May 1, 1945; d. Robert Carroll and Annie Louise (Neal) Hutcherson; m. Alfredo Emanuele De B.; children: Maria Luisa, Riccardo Roberto. BA in Theatre Arts, Mary Washington Coll., 1967; student, Herbert Berghof Studio, 1967—69. With J. Walter Thompson, N.Y.C., 1967-68; asst. to prodr. Norman Twain Prodns., N.Y.C., 1968-69, Contemporary Theatre Co., N.Y.C., 1971-74; co. mgr. Folger Theatre Group, Washington, 1974-77, bus. mgr., 1977-80; mng. dir. Shakespeare Theatre at the Folger, Washington, 1980-90; performing arts cons. Alexandria, Va., 1990-92; dir. The Found. Ctr., Washington, 1992-94; pres. De Barbieri and Assocs., 1994—. Adj. prof. arts mgmt. grad. program Am. U., 1994-99; treas. League of Washington Theatres, 1983-86; chair selection com. The Washington Post/Washington Coun. Agys. Award for Excellence in Nonprofit Mgmt., 1997, 98, 99, mem. selection com. 1996-99, The Washington Post Grants in the Arts, 1997—; curriculum design cons., core faculty Choral Mgmt. Inst. of Chorus Am., 2002—; presenter in field. Bd. dirs. Washington Area Lawyers for Arts, 1984-94; bd. dirs. Cultural Alliance Greater Washington, 1986-96, v.p., 1990-96; bd. dirs. Nat. Soc. Fundraising Execs., 1993-96, v.p. edn., 1995, treas., 1996; bd. dirs. Ctr. for Nonprofit Advancement, 2000—, pres., 2004-05; chair Performing Arts Coun., Alexandria, Va., 1981-84; founder, first chair Alexandria Commn. for Arts, 1984-88, theater commr., 1984-94; contbr. to study of downtown stages for new theater in Washington, 1985; mem. panel Va. Commn. for the Arts, 1990-96, 2005—. Recipient Outstanding Svc. to Theatre Cmty. award League of Washington Theatres, 1990. Office: 525 Beauregard Dr SE Leesburg VA 20175 Office Phone: 703-777-3585. Business E-Mail: debarasso@aol.com.

DEBARDELEBEN, MARTHA GRAVES, counselor; b. Atlanta, Dec. 26, 1925; d. Charles Wilbur and Edith Helen (Klooz) Graves; m. John Thomas DeBardeleben Jr., 1946 (div. 1989); children: John Thomas III, Charles Graves, Eve Lamar Roebu ck. BA, Vanderbilt U., 1947; MA, Rider U., 1986. Pvt. practice Christian Counseling, Princeton, N.J. Author: Fear's Answer, 1980, Belief Systems Inventory, 1989, Just Leora A Case History in Incest and Multiple Personality, 2005. Home: 219 Mercer St Princeton NJ 08540-6818 E-mail: introit2@aol.com.

DEBARLING, ANA MARIA, language educator; b. Del Rio, Tex., Apr. 30, 1938; d. Octauiano and Guadalupe Dominguez; m. Peter Wesley Barling, June 4, 1968 (div. Oct. 1988); children: Laura Blanche, Wesley Peter. BA, San Jose State U., 1968, M in Hispanic Lit., 1970; DEd, U. Pacific, 2001. Cert. sch. administrn. Calif. Secondary tchr. Fremount Union H.S. Dist., Sunnyvale, Calif., 1968—94, dir. gifted edn., 1980—83; lang. prof. West Valley Coll., Saratoga, Calif., 1994—. Cons. Edn. Testing Svcs., San Antonio, 1992—; bilingual proficiency testing City of Morgan Hill and Campbell, Calif., 1995—. Editor: (booklet) Gifted & Talented Education, 1991. Mem. Latina Leadership, San Jose, 1988—, Immigration Edn. Task Force, Santa Clara, Calif., 1999—. Mem.: Am. Tchrs. Fgn. Lang., Faculty Assn. C.C. Democrat. Roman Catholic. Home: 373 Redwood Ave Santa Clara CA 95051 Office: West Valley Coll 14000 Fruitvale Ave Saratoga CA 95070 E-mail: and_maria_de_baring@wuv.edu.

DEBARTOLO-YORK, DENISE, sports team executive; m. John C. York II; 4 children. Grad., Notre Dame U. Team pres. Pitts. Penguins; exec. v.p. personnel and corp. mktg./comm. The Edward J. Bartolo Corp., vice chmn., 1994; chmn. The Edward J. DeBartolo Corp., 1994—. Supporter DeBartolo Family Found. Mem. fin. adv. bd. Ursuline Sisters; mem. MADD; recognized for contbn. to St. Charles Elem. Sch., Boardman, Ohio. Named to Italian American Sports Hall of Fame, 2003. Office: care San Francisco 49ers 4949 Centennial Blvd Santa Clara CA 95054-1229

DEBAUN, LINDA LOUISE, performing arts educator; b. L.A., Nov. 11, 1946; d. James Irving and Katherine Adeliade deBaun; life ptnr. Heidi Annette Wilson, June 15, 1996. AA, Mt. San Antonio Jr. Coll., 1966; BA in Writing, Pitzer Coll., 1968; MLitt of English, Clairemont U., 1972; M of Theatre, Calif. State U., 1998. Tchr. Azusa (Calif.) H.S., 1972—73, Vol. State Coll., Gallatin, Tenn., 1973—75; tchr., dir. drama Yucaipa (Calif.) H.S., 1980—. Recipient Tchr. of Yr., San Bernadino County, Calif., 2000. Mem.: Internat. Thespian Soc. (state bd. dirs.). Avocations: writing, music. Home: 11666 Pendelton Rd Yucaipa CA 92399 Office: Yucaipa High Sch 33000 Ycuaipa Blvd Yucaipa CA 92399

DEBEERS, SUE, photographer; b. Tarrytown, NY, Aug. 9, 1973; BFA, Parson Sch. Design, NY, 1995; MFA, Columbia U., 1998. Artist-in-residence Wexner Ctr., Ohio, 1999. One-woman shows include Heidi 2, Deitch Projects, NY, 2000, Photographs / project room: Ghost Stories Mag., Sandroni Rey, LA, 2001, Photographs, Kunstlerhaus Bethanian, Berlin, 2002, Hans & Grete, Kunst Werke, Berlin, 2003, The Dark Hearts, Sandroni Rey at Statements, Basel, Miami, 2004, exhibited in group shows at Imaginary Beings, Exit Art, NY, 1995, Terra Bomba, 1996, 26 Positions, Miriam & Ira D. Wallach Gallery, NY, 1997, Scope 3, Artist's Space, NY, 1998, The Searchers, 1999, Death Race, Threadwaxing Space, NY, 2000, Fresh: The Altoids Curiously Strong Collection, New Mus. Contemporary Art, 2001, Desiring Machines, Dorsky Curatorial Projects, NY, 2002, Internat. Monster League, Derek Eller Gallery, NY, 2003, Working in Bklyn., Bklyn. Mus., 2004, Whitney Biennial, Whitney Mus. Am. Art, 2004, SCREAM, Anton Kern Gallery, NY, 2004. Recipient Franklin Furnace Fund for Performance Art, 1998—99, Joan Sovern Award Excellence in Sculpture, 1999, Philip Morris Emerging Artist Prize, Am. Acad. Berlin, 2001. Mailing: c/o Whitney Museum American Art 945 Madison Ave New York NY 10021 E-mail: sue@sevenseven.com.

DEBELLO, JOAN ELIZABETH, mathematics professor; d. Robert N and Marie J DeBello. BS, St. John's U., 1993—97; MA, St.John's U., 1997—99. Asst. prof. of math. and comp. sci. St. John's U., Jamaica, NY, 1999—. Chmn. Theta Phi Alpha Sorority, 2000—05. Recipient Outstanding Prof. of the Yr., Sigma Phi Epsilon Frat., 2000, Pi Mu Epsilon, St. John's U., 1996-present; Scholarship, Columbia U. Teacher's Coll., 2000—01, Women In Sci./Clare Boothe Luce, St. John's U., 1993—97. Roman Catholic. Avocations: baseball, swimming, travel, music, poetry. Office: St John's Univ 8000 Utopia Pkwy Jamaica NY 11439 Office Phone: 718-990-2032. E-mail: debelloj@stjohns.edu.

DEBENEDET, RACHEL, actress; Actor: (Broadway plays) Nine, 2003, Dirty Rotten Scoundrels, 2005—06, (off-broadway plays) The King and I, 1995, Love and War, Adrift in Macao, 2005—06 (Barrymore award Outstanding Leading Actress in a Musical, 2006). Office: Phila Theatre Co 1714 Delancey St Philadelphia PA 19103*

DEBERRY, DONNA, retail executive; b. 1955; Attended, Calif. State U. Worked with NFL, U.S. Olympic Com., The Oprah Winfrey Show; exec. v.p. global diversity and corp. affairs Wyndham Internat. Inc.; CEO, founder DRP Internat.; v.p. diversity Nike, Inc., 2006—. Bd. dirs. Nat. Hispanic Corp. Coun., U.S. Hispanic C. of C., Nat. Coalition of Black Meeting Planners, Nat. Assn. Black Hotel Owners, Operators and Developers; mem. adv. coun. eWomen Network Found. Office: Nike Inc 1 Bowerman Dr Beaverton OR 97005-6453*

DEBERTRAND, LYNETTE MICHELE, clinical nurse specialist, educator; b. Wheeling, W.Va., Feb. 2, 1966; d. Sam and Linda Zavacky; m. Jon Daniel DeBertrand, May 13, 2000; 1 child, Jacob Spencer DeBertand. ADN, Belmont Tech. Coll., St. Clairsville, Ohio, 1986; BSN, Ohio U., Athens, 1989; MSN, W.Va. U., Morgantown, 1990. RN Ohio, cert. authority, Ohio, doula, 2000, cert. inpatient obstetrics, Nat. Cert. Corp, clin. nurse specialist. Staff nurse obstetrics Belmont Cmty. Hosp., Bellaire, Ohio, 1987—98; clin. nurse specialist East Ohio Regional Hosp., Martins Ferry, Ohio, 1998—; part-time obstet. faculty W.Va. No. CC, Wheeling, 1991—. Pres. Dogwood Twig/Hosp. Ladies Aux. (EORH), 2003—. Fellow: Am. Coll. Childbirth Educators of Lamaze; mem.: Assn. Women's Health, Obstetric and Neonatal Nurses, Doulas N.Am., Internat. Childbirth Edn. Assn. Presbyterian. Home: 67568 Elizabeth St Saint Clairsville OH 43950 Office Phone: 740-633-4543.

DEBOLT, NANETTE C., medical/surgical nurse; b. Wheeling, W.Va., Feb. 20, 1955; d. William Edward and Goldie Ann (Brandtner) DeB. Diploma, Ohio Valley Gen. Hosp., Wheeling, 1976; BSN, Wheeling Jesuit Coll., W.Va., 1996. Cert. med.-surg. nurse. Staff nurse Mercy Hosp., Santa Ana, Calif., Long Beach (Calif.) Meml. Hosp., East Ohio Regional Hosp., Martins Ferry, vascular lab. nurse, ultrasound sonographer. Home: 4437 Highland Ave Shadyside OH 43947-1228 E-mail: nandeb55@wmconnect.com.

DE BONO, LUELLA ELIZABETH, music educator; b. Argyle, Iowa, May 15, 1920; d. Albert Fred and Bessie Mae (Langwith) Haffner; m. Charles De Bono, July 26, 1947; 1 child, Douglas. MMus, Sherwood Conservatory Music, Chgo., 1945; M in Counseling and Guidance, U. St. Thomas, St. Paul, 1966; postgrad., U. Minn. Lic. music instr. of keyboard, voice and instrumental. Dir. music Am. Girl's Coll., Assiut, Egypt, 1945-48; music tchr. Argyle Pub. Sch., 1949-54; instr. music MacPhail Coll. Music, Mpls., 1956-66; counselor various pub. schs., Minn., 1966-82; pvt. music instr. Eden Prairie, Minn., 1982—. Profl. accompanist and pianist; adjudicator state music contests, Mpls., 1958—. Nat. honor soc. advisor St. Paul Pk. H.S., 1966-68; Am. field svc. adviser St. Paul Pk. H.S.; counselor Am. Youth Hostel Camp, Europe, 1946. Presbyterian. Avocations: animals, showing horses, volunteering. Home and Office: 17325 Pioneer Trail Eden Prairie MN 55347-3403 Office Phone: 952-937-1947.

DE BOTH, TANYA, statistician; BA in Psychology, U. Wis., 1996; student, Frostburg State U., Md., 1996—97; MSc in Exptl. Psychology, U. Wis., 2000. Outcomes specialist Family Svcs., Green Bay, Wis., 2000—01; data rsch. analyst Agnesian Health Care, Fond du Lac, Wis., 2001—. Contbr. articles to profl. jours. Mem.: AAUW, NOW, APA, ACLU, Nafe, Planned Parenthood Fedn. Am., Exec. Women's Golf Assn., Phi Kappa Phi. Avocations: walking, volleyball, golf, camping, bicycling.

DEBOW, BRIDGETTE M., elementary school educator; b. Jonesboro, Ark., Feb. 28, 1970; d. Isaac M. and Rhynea Debow. BS Early Childhood/Elem. Edn., Ark. State U., Jonesboro, 1994. Cert. Tchr. K-6 Ark., 1995. Tchr. Ark. better chance Miss. County EOC Head Start, Blytheville, 1995—99; tchr. kindergarten Sheffield Elem. Sch., Memphis, 1999; tchr. 1st grade West Elem. Sch., Osceola, Ark., 1999—2006, Tyronza Elem. Sch., Ark., 2006—. Mem. Jr. Aux., Osceola, 2005—06. Named Who's Who Among Am. Tchrs., Who's Who LLC, 2005, 2006, Cmty. Tchr. of Yr., Wal-Mart, 2006; named to Pres.'s List, Ark. State U., 1994. Mem.: Internat. Reading Assn. (assoc.), Ark. Reading Assn. (assoc.). Office: Tyronza Elem Sch 412 S Main St Tyronza AR 72386 Office Phone: 870-487-2259. Personal E-mail: bridgette.debow@yahoo.com.

DE BRETTEVILLE, SHEILA LEVRANT, artist, art educator; b. Bklyn., Nov. 4, 1940; Student, Barnard Coll.; BA in Art History, Columbia U., 1962; MFA in Graphic Design, Yale U., 1964. Dir. Dept. Graphic Design Calif. Inst. Arts, 1970—74; co-founder, editor, designer Chrysalis Mag., 1977; design dir. LA (Calif.) Times; chmn. Dept. Comm., Design and Illustration Otis Art Inst. Parsons Sch. Design, LA, 1981; dir. studies in graphic design Yale Univ., New Haven, 1990—; now prof., and director grad. studies Yale Univ. School of Art, New Haven. Co-founder, pres. Woman's Bldg., 1973—; judge Endowment Arts-Civil Svc. Commn., 1975; lectr. in field. Exhibited in group shows at Am. Inst. Graphics Art, 1972, 5e Biennale des Arts Graphiques, Brno, Czech., 1972, Whitney Mus., 1974, Represented in permanent collections N.Y. Mus. Modern Art, N.Y.C., Cmty. Gallery, LA, Calif., Spl. Collections Victoria and Albert Mus., N.Y. Pub. Libr., commns., Archtl. League, N.Y., 1965, Yale Art Gallery, 1966, publicity, Olivetti, Milan, Italy, 1968, poster design, Calif. Inst. Arts, Valencia, 1970, spl. issue design, Art Soc. Wis., 1970; typographer: Yale U. Press, 1969—74; pub. works, L.A., 1970, New Haven, Conn., 1993, 2005, Boston, 1995, 2006, Cranston, R.I., 1996, N.Y.C., 1995, Flushing, N.Y., 1997. Recipient Grand Excellence award, Soc. Pub. Designers, 1971, AIGA medal, 2004. Mem.: Am. Inst. Graphic Arts (nat. bd. dirs. 1989—, Comm. Graphics awards 1972). Office: Sch of Art-Graphic Design Yale U 1156 Chapel St New Haven CT 06511-4804 Business E-Mail: sheila.debretteville@yale.edu.

DE BRIGARD, EMILIE, anthropologist, consultant; b. NYC, Dec. 11, 1943; d. A. Lincoln and Ruth Emilie (Jaeger) Rahman; m. Raul de Brigard, June 11, 1966; 1 child, George. BA, Harvard Coll., 1963; MA, U. Calif., 1972. Guest curator dept. of film Mus. of Modern Art, N.Y.C., 1972-73; asst. to dir. human studies film archives Smithsonian Instn., Washington, 1975-77; prin. programmer Margaret Mead Film Festival Am. Mus. Natural History, N.Y.C., 1977-78; faculty Harvard Summer Sch., Cambridge, Mass., 1980-86; pres. Internat. Film Seminars, Inc., N.Y.C., 1981-83; vis. lectr. dept. anthropology Yale U., New Haven, 1989-91; pres. Soc. for Visual Anthropology, Washington, 1995-97, FilmResearch, Higganum, Conn., 1970—. Author: The History of Ethnographic Film, 1971, Anthropological Cinema, 1973, Cine Antropológico, 1978; producer (film) Margaret Mead: A Portrait by a Friend, 1978. Trustee Wadsworth Atheneum, Hartford, Conn., 2000—; pres. Friends of the Ixchel Mus., Guatemala, 2005—; adv. bd. Arden Inst., Shakespeare and Co. Fellow Am. Anthrop. Assn., Royal Anthrop. Inst.; mem. Soc. Woman Geographers, Harvard Alumni Assn. (dir. 2002-06, Hiram S. Hunn award 2002), Harvard Club of So. Conn. (v.p. 1995—). Avocation: costume and textiles. Home: 285 Riverside Dr Apt 7D New York NY 10025-5227 Office: FilmResearch 8 Christian Hill Rd Higganum CT 06441-4030 E-mail: debrigard@att.net.

DEBRINCAT, SUSAN JEANNE, nutritionist; b. Detroit, Oct. 7, 1943; d. Lloyd Brode and Florence Claire Greenleaf; m. Raymond Frank DeBrincat, June 19, 1965; children: David Lloyd, Mark Joseph. BS magna cum laude, Mich. State U., 1965. Cert. med. technologist, Am. Soc. Clin. Pathologists. Med. technologist Harper Hosp., Detroit, 1965-66, South Macomb Hosp., Warren, Mich., 1966; art tchr. YWCA, Berkley, Mich., 1969-80; master coord. Shaklee Corp., 1977—, sr. master coord., facilitator Pacific Inst., 1987—, lifetime master, 1990—, nutritional counselor, fashion, color, image and makeup counselor, mgmt. and leadership trainer, motivational spkr. Interior designer. Painter oil, acrylic, watercolors. Mem. Rep. Nat. Com. Pres.'s Club, Found. Club, Phi Kappa Phi, Delta Zeta. Roman Catholic. Avocations: painting, art and antiques, reading, travel, boating. Office Phone: 770-538-9982. E-mail: healthychoices@charter.net.

DEBRUIN, RUTH PEARL, primary school educator; b. Sibley, Iowa, Oct. 13, 1951; d. Arnold and Henrietta (Jansma) Bosma; m. Harold Dean DeBruin, July 9, 1974; children: Rex, Joel, Rachel, Heather. BA in Edn., Dordt Coll., Sioux Center, Iowa, 1973. 6th-8th grade sci. tchr. Pella Christian Schs., Iowa, 1973—75; 4th grade tchr. Oskaloosa Christian Sch., Iowa, 1975—76, kindergarten tchr., 1990—, 5th-8th grade music tchr., 1999—. Leader, dir. 4H, Mohaska County, Iowa, 1993—2000; choir dir. 1st Christian Reformed Ch., Oskaloosa, 1985—2000, organist, 2004—. Republican. Avocations: singing, photography, sewing, gardening, antiques. Office: Oskaloosa Christian Sch 726 N E St Oskaloosa IA 52577

DEBRUIN SAMPLE, ANNE, human resources specialist; Formerly with Whirlpool Corp., Benton Harbor, Mich.; numerous human resources positions including mgr. human resources Pepsi-Cola N.Am. PepsiAmericas, Inc., Mpls., 1988—2001, sr. v.p. human resources, 2001—. Office: PepsiAmericas 4000 Dain Rauscher Plz 60 S Sixth St Minneapolis MN 55402 Office Phone: 612-661-4000. Office Fax: 612-661-3737.

DE BRUN, SHAUNA DOYLE, industrialist, investment banker; b. Boston, June 3, 1956; d. John Justin and Marie Therese (Carey) Doyle; m. Seamus Christopher de Brun, July 24, 1982; children: Brendan Joseph, Kieran Christopher. Student, U. Salzburg, 1974-75; BA, Mt. Holyoke Coll., 1978; postgrad., Harvard U., 1981-82; M in Internat. Fin., Columbia U., 1984. Cert. fin. analyst, 1987. Assoc. Salomon Bros., N.Y.C., 1978; rsch. assoc. Kennedy Sch. Govt., Cambridge, Mass., 1979-80; faculty assoc. Harvard Bus. Sch., 1980-81; fgn. expert Beijing Normal U., Peoples Republic China, 1981-82; assoc. dir. N.Y. Capital Resources, N.Y.C., 1984-85; ptnr. Eppler & Co.,

Denver, 1985-87, pres. Teaneck, NJ, 1987-88; v.p. fin. Patten Corp., Stamford, Vt., 1988-91; pres. Serfimex USA, Inc., 1991-92; pres., CEO Pliana Holdings, Mexico City, 1992—. Columbia U. Internat. fellow, 1982; Sarah Williston scholar Mt. Holyoke Coll., 1975. Mem. AACCLA (v.p., treas.), Am. C. of C./Mex. (past pres., dir.), Navy League U.S., Phi Beta Kappa, Harvard Club. Avocations: piano, horseback riding. Office: Pliana Holdings SA de CV 275 Palmas 5th Fl 11000 Mexico City Mexico

DEBS, BARBARA KNOWLES, former college president, consultant; b. Eastham, Mass., Dec. 24, 1931; d. Stanley F. and Arline (Eugley) Knowles; m. Richard A. Debs, July 19, 1958; children: Elizabeth, Nicholas. BA, Vassar Coll., 1953; PhD, Harvard U., 1967; LLD, N.Y. Law Sch., 1979; LHD, Manhattanville Coll., 1985. Freelance translator editor Ency. of World Art divsn. McGraw-Hill Pub., N.Y.C., 1959-62; from asst. prof. to prof. Manhattanville Coll., Purchase, N.Y., 1968-86, pres., 1975-85; trustee N.Y. Hist. Soc., 1985-87, pres., CEO, 1988-92; cons. non-profit orgns. pvt. practice, 1992—. Contbr. articles on Renaissance and contemporary art to profl. publs. Mem. N.Y. Coun. Humanities, 1978-85; mem. Westchester County Bd. Ethics, 1979-84; trustee N.Y. Law Sch., 1979-89; trustee Geraldine R. Dodge Found., 1985—; bd. dirs. Internat. Found. for Art Rsch., 1985-92; trustee Com. Econ. Devel., 1985-94, Bklyn. Mus. Art, 1996—; mem. Coun. Fgn. Rels., 1983—; mem. exec. bd. Bard Ctr. for Decorative Arts, 1995—; bd. govs. Fgn. Policy Assn., 1996-2002; hon. trustee Manhattanville Coll., 1996—, Midori Found., 1998—. AAUW Nat. fellow and Ann Radcliffe fellow, 1958-59; Am. Council Learned Socs. grantee, 1973; Fulbright fellow, Pisa, Italy, 1953, U. Rome, 1954. Mem. Am. Coun. on Edn. (chmn. commn. acad. affairs 1977-79), Young Audiences (nat. dir. 1977-80), Renaissance Soc. Am., Coll. Art Assn., Phi Beta Kappa. Clubs: Cosmopolitan, Century Assn.

DEBUONO, BARBARA ANN, physician, state official; b. N.Y.C., Apr. 13, 1955; d. Richard Francis and Catherine (Brutto) DeB.; m. David Lavington Farren, June 1, 1980; children: Adam, Douglas. BS, U. Rochester, 1976, MD, 1980; MPH, Harvard U., 1984. Diplomate Am. Bd. Internal Medicine, Nat. Bd. Med. Examiners. Intern in internal medicine New Eng. Deaconess Hosp., Boston, 1980-81, jr. med. resident, 1981-82, sr. med. resident, 1982-83; clin. fellow Brown U., Providence, 1984-86, clin. instr. dept. medicine, 1987-90, clin. asst. prof. medicine, 1990; med. epidemiologist R.I. Dept. Health, Providence, 1986, state epidemiologist, med. dir. Office Disease Control, 1986-91; dir. dept. health State of R.I., 1991—95; commr. NY State Dept. Health, Albany, 1995—98; CEO N.Y. Presbyn. Healthcare Network, 1998—2000; exec. v.p. N.Y. Presbyn. Healthcare System, 1998—2000; sr. med. dir. pub. health Pfizer Inc., 2001—; clin. prof. medicine Columbia U. Coll. Physicians and Surgeons. Lectr. in field; adv. com. to dir. Ctrs. for Disease Control; bd. mem. Ctr. Health Policy Devel.; nat. adv. com. Healthy Steps. Contbr. articles to profl. jours. Robert Wood Johnson Found. Ednl. scholar U. Rochester Sch. Med., 1976-80; recipient James L. Tulis Disting. Study Lectureship award New Eng. Deaconess Hosp., 1992; named Women of Yr. by Bus. and Profl. Women's Club Providence, 1989, Person of Yr. by The Women's Youth League R.I., 1990, Woman of Yr. by R.I. Fedn. Bus. and Profl. Women's Clubs, 1991. Fellow Am. Coll. Internat. Physicians, Am. Coll. Physicians; mem. AMA, APHA, Am. Soc. Microbiology, Infectious Disease Soc. Am., Providence Med. Assn., R.I. Med. Soc., R.I. Med. Women's Assn. (R.I. Women Physician of Yr. 1988), R.I. Environ. Health Assn., Hosp. Assn. R.I., Women Execs. in Govt. Avocations: swimming, tennis, gardening.

DEBUSK, LORRAINE, elementary school educator; b. Bklyn., Oct. 1, 1941; d. John and Muriel Holley; m. Jeffrey Crawford (div.); children: Sean Crawford, Kimberly Crawford; m. Jack DeBusk, Feb. 5, 1987. AA, Clark County CC, 1984; BA, U. Nev., Las Vegas, 1989; degree in Tchg., Nat. U., Las Vegas, 1991; MS, Nova U., Las Vegas, 1994, postgrad. Cert. sch. adminstr. Nev. Pvt. practice, NYC; med. technician, nurse Sunrise Hosp., Las Vegas; GATE specialist Clark County Sch. Dist., Las Vegas, tchr., 1991—. Tchr. English to adults CCSD, Las Vegas, 2002. Mem.: Humane Soc. US, Planetary Soc., Greenpeace. Avocations: raising parrots, gardening. Office: Clark County Sch Dist Doris Reed Elem Sch Las Vegas NV 89108 Office Phone: 702-799-4777.

DE CANDIDO KAMIN, ROSANN THERESE, secondary school educator; b. Englewood, N.J., July 18, 1958; d. Joseph John and Angela (Perrini) De Candido; m. John Russell Kamin, Aug. 24, 1980 (div. Oct. 1994); 1 child, Stefanie Therese. BA with honors, Rutgers U., 1980, MA, 1985, EdD, 2004. English/Spanish tchr. New Milford (N.J.) Bd. Edn., 1980-81; Spanish tchr. Teaneck (N.J.) Bd. Edn., 1981-82; English/Spanish tchr. Maywood (N.J.) Bd. Edn., 1982-83; English tchr. Edison (N.J.) Twp. Bd. Edn., 1983-84; Spanish/ESL tchr. Metuchen (N.J.) Bd. Edn., 1984—; interdisciplinary project coord. Metuchen (N.J.) H.S., 1986—; instr. Rutgers, The Grad. Sch. of Edn., 2005. Part-time lectr. Rutgers U., 2005—06. Brownie and Cadette leader, Older Girl program coord. Girl Scouts USA, Edison, 1993-96. Grantee Geraldine R. Dodge Found., Morristown, N.J., 1995, Playwrights Theatre, N.J., Madison, 1995; recipient best practice in the arts award N.J., 1995-96, Star award Metuchen Cmty., 1998, Appreciation award, Girl Scouts of Del., 2003; named Outstanding Vol. Girl Scouts U.S., 2001-02. Mem. ASCD, Acad. Am. Poets, Am. Ednl. Rsch. Assn., The John Dewey Soc., Fgn. Lang. Educators N.J., N.J. Edn. Assn., Phi Beta Kappa, Phi Sigma Iota, Phi Delta Kappa, Kappa Delta Pi Avocations: travel, dance. Home: 2503 Cricket Cir Edison NJ 08820-4206

DECARLO, MARY KATHLEEN, elementary school educator; b. Johnstown, Pa., Feb. 7, 1952; d. James Francis Gallagher and Mary Margaret Lorditch-Gallagher; m. Keary Leon DeCarlo, Nov. 22, 1950; 1 child, Anthony James. MEd, Baker State U., Overland Park, Kans. Tchr. Archdiocese of Kans. City in KS, Overland Park, 1992—2000; prin. Our Lady of the Presentation, Lee's Summit, Mo., 2000—02; tchr. Frederick County Pub. Schs., Md., 2002—. Recipient Tchr. of Yr., Cure' of Ars Sch., 1997—98. Mem.: VFW (Ladies Aux.). Democrat. Roman Catholic. Home: 99 Plank Rd York Springs PA 17372 Office: Monocacy Mid Sch Opossumtown Pike Frederick MD Personal E-mail: kdecarlo2001@yahoo.com. Business E-Mail: kathe.decarlo@fcps.org.

DECARO, SHANA, lawyer; BA, George Washington U., Washington, DC, 1976; JD, Cardoza Law Sch., N.Y.C., 1980. Bar: N.Y. 1981. Prin. law sec. Supreme Ct. Kings County NY, Bklyn., 1982—84; ptnr. DeCaro & Kaplen LLP, NYC, 1984—. Exec. bd. Traumatic Brain Injury Litigation Group, 2004—; assoc. Trial Lawyers of Am., 2004—; mem. N.Y. State Med. Malpractice Mediation Panel, Supreme Ct., N.Y. State. Mem.: ATLA, N.Y. State Trial Lawyers Assn. Office: 20 Vesey St New York NY 10007

DECASTRO, CRISTINA L., secondary school educator; b. Westerly, RI, Jan. 23, 1973; d. David G. and Nelia L. deCastro. BS in Edn., U. Conn., Storrs, 1995; EdM, U. Hartford, West Hartford, Conn., 2001; M in Math., Quinnipiac U., Hamden, Conn., 2005. Cert. elem. edn. grades K-6 tchr. Conn., 2001, math. tchr. grades 4-8 Conn., 2004. Program dir. St. Paul's Luth. Day Sch., Savannah, Ga., 1997—98; after-sch. program coord. St. Andrew's Sch., Savannah, Ga., 1998—99; math. tchr. summer sch. Rockville H.S., Vernon, Conn., 1999—2002; substitute tchr. Salem Sch., Conn., 2000—02; grade 4 tchr. West Broad St. Sch., Stonington, Conn., 2001—02; grade 6 math./lang. arts tchr. Dr. Robert H. Brown Mid. Sch., Madison, Conn., 2002—03; grade 8 math. tchr. East Lyme Mid. Sch., Niantic, Conn., 2004—. Mem.: NEA, Nat. Coun. Tchrs. Math., Conn. Edn. Assn., Kappa Delta Pi (Pi Phi chpt.). Office Phone: 860-739-4491 3462.

DECATUR, RAYLENE, former museum director; BA, U. Va.; MA, George Washington U. Various positions Md. Sci. Ctr., Balt., Acad. Natural Scis., Phila., Renwick Gallery; pres., CEO Denver Mus. Nature and Sci. (formerly Denver Mus. Natural History), 1995—2004.

DECHERT, WENDY DAWN, speech educator, literature and language educator, writer; b. Machias, Maine, Oct. 20, 1972; d. Lawrence James and Judith Evelyn Loney; m. Stephan Frederich Dechert, Apr. 8, 2000; 1 child, Olivia Rose. BS in Communication Arts Edn. and English Edn., Taylor U., Upland, Ind., 1996; M in Ednl. Leadership, U. Ga., Athens, 2004. Lic. tchr. Ind. English and theater tchr. Plainfield (Ind.) H.S., 1996—99, Franklin County H.S., Carnesville, Ga., 1999—2000; theater tchr. Oconee County H.S., Watkinsville, Ga., 2000—02; speech, theater, and English tchr. Danville (Ind.) Cmty. H.S., 2005—. Contbg. author Authentic Voices: Women of Insight Talk about Real-Life Challenges, 2005. Vol. Trinity Luth. Ch., Athens, Ga., 2002—04. Named Top 15 Hon. Educator, Danville Cmty. Sch. Corp., 2006. Mem.: Ednl. Theater Assn. (assoc.; tchr.), Alpha Psi Omega (assoc.). Conservative. Avocations: acting, singing, writing, reading, dance. Home: 603 Waterford Way Danville IN 46122 Office: Danville Cmty HS 100 Warrior Way Danville IN 46122 Office Phone: 317-745-6411 229. Office Fax: 317-745-3908. Personal E-mail: wdechert@comcast.net. E-mail: wdechert@danville.k12.in.us.

DECHOCHRANTRAUT, LEILA L., education educator; Grad. cum laude, Virgie Meml. Hosp., Ky. Lic. psychology tchr., sociology tchr., sociology history tchr., polit. sci. tchr. Instr. Ams. Naval Base, Ceiba, PR. Organize Horizon Sci. Acad., Ohio; presiding judge Cuyagoha County Bd. Election, Cleve.; vol. Eucharist Minister. Mem.: NAMP, Am. Counseling Assn., Writers Guild of N.Y., Women League of Voters. Home: 27843 Detriot Rd #211 Westlake OH 44145

DECIL, STELLA WALTERS (DEL DECIL), artist; b. Indpls., Apr. 26, 1921; d. William Calvin and Hazel Jean (Konkle) Smith; m. John W. Walters, June 19, 1940 (div. Sept. 1945); m. Casimir R. Decil, Feb. 6, 1965. Grad., Indpls. Acad. Comml. Art, 1939, John Heron Art Inst., Indpls., 1941. Staff artist William H. Block Co., Indpls., 1945-50, art dir., 1952-62, Frank R. Jelleff Co., Washington, 1950-51, Diamonds Dept. Stores, Phoenix, 1962-67; freelance artist, 1967-70. Painting instr. various art groups in Ariz.-N.Mex, 1970—, Phoenix Art Mus., 1975—77; mem. visual arts bd. Prescott Fine Arts Assn., 1990—2000; curator Mature Eye Bi-Ann. Prescott (Ariz.) Fine Arts Assn., 1996—2000; instr. Mountain Artists Guild, Prescott, 1995—97. One-woman shows include Cave Creek, Carefree, Scottsdale, Ariz., N.Mex., exhibited in group shows, Phoenix, Scottsdale, Las Cruces, N.Mex, Hoosier Salon, Folger Gallery, Indpls., Mammen II Gallery, Scottsdale, Thompson Gallery, Garelick Gallery, Hopkins Fine Art, Scottsdale, Ariz., Helen Vohl Gallery, Wickenburg, Ariz., Phippen Mus., Prescott, Ariz., Represented in permanent collections Continental Bank, Humana Hosp., Pueblo Grande Mus., VA Med. Ctr., Prescott, Mayo Ctr. Women's Health, Scottsdale, Proctor Bank Vt., Bank Rio Grande, Las Cruces, Detroit Inst. of Arts, Mich., Trevor Brown H.S., Phoenix, pvt. collections in 20 states. Past pres. Scottsdale Art League, 1973. Named Ad Woman of Yr., Indpls. Ad Club, 1958; recipient Maxine Cherrington Meml. award, Hoosier Salon, 1973. Mem.: No. Ariz. Watercolor Assn., Ariz. Artists Guild, Ariz. Watercolor Assn. (Royal Scorpion Status, past pres.). Home: 9460 E Towago Dr Prescott Valley AZ 86314-7140

DECKER, CAROL ARNE, magazine publishing executive; b. Rochelle, Ill., Apr. 3, 1946; d. Irvin Norman Arne and Edna (Olsen) Stein; m. Charles Levitt Decker, Feb. 17, 1979; children: Katharine Elizabeth. BA, So. Ill. U., 1969. Advt. sales rep. Travel Agent mag., N.Y.C., 1971-74, Business Week mag., N.Y.C., 1974-80, Reader's Digest Publs., N.Y.C., 1980-82; assoc. pub. The Atlantic Monthly, N.Y.C., 1982-84; pub. Personal Investor, N.Y.C., 1984-86, Lear's Mag., 1992-93; pub. cons. C.A. Decker & Assocs., N.Y.C., 1986-94; founder, CEO Western Interiors and Design Mag., LLC, Jackson, Wyo., 1999—. Office: PO Box 14610 Jackson WY 83002

DECKER, CATHERINE HELEN, language educator; b. Lower Merion, Pa., June 1, 1965; d. Leonard Edward and Harriet Anne D.; m. Roland Curt Burgess, May 25, 1991. BA, LaSalle U., 1987; MA, U. Rochester, 1989, PhD, 1994. Instr. English U. Rochester, N.Y., 1989-92; lectr. English SUNY, Geneseo, 1990-91; instr. English Auburn (Ala.) U., 1993, San Bernardino (Calif.) Valley Coll., 1995, 97; prof. lang. arts Chaffey Coll., Rancho Cucamonga, Calif., 1995—; instr. English Calif. State U., San Bernardino, 1995-97; rschr. psychology U. Calif., Riverside, 1992—. Rschr. ESTC, Riverside, Calif., 1993. Editl. asst.: Electric Dreams, 1994—95, webmistress: The Regency Fashion Page, The Regency Page; author (with others): Women, Revolution and the Novel of the 1790's, 1999; contbr. book rev. Wordworth Cir., 1995. Competitive scholar La Salle U., 1983-87; Sproull fellow U. Rochester, 1987-89, fellow, 1989-90, NEH summer seminar fellow, 1995. Mem. Aphra Behn Soc. (comm. chair 1994-95, editor newsletter 1995), Cat Lovers of Am., Freedom Valley Girl Scout Alumnae. Democrat. Unitarian Universalist. Avocations: fashion research, bargello, Cornhusker football fan. Office: Chaffey College English Department 5885 Haven Avenue Rancho Cucamonga CA 91737 Office Phone: 909-941-2412. Business E-Mail: cathy.decker@chaffey.edu.

DECKER, JOSEPHINE I., health clinic official; b. Barling, Ark., May 24, 1933; d. Ralph and Ada A. (Claborn) Snider; m. William Arlen Decker, Feb. 4, 1952; 1 child, Peter A. BS in Health Mgmt., Kennedy Western U., 1986, MS in Bus. Adminstrn., 1987. With Southwestern Bell Tel. Co., Ft. Smith, Ark., 1951-52, Sparks Med. Found. (formerly Holt Krock Clinic), Ft. Smith, 1952—, bus. adminstr., 1970—, reg. dir., 1999—2004; ret., 2004. Bd. dirs. Sparks Credit Union, Bost Found., Crisis Ctr. for Women, Sparks Women's Ctr., Leadership Ft. Smith; mem. adv. coun. Northside H.S., Southside H.S., Ft. Smith, Ft. Smith Girls Shelter, Ft. Smith Credit Bur. Mem. Credit Women Internat., Soc. Cert. Consumer Credit Execs. Office Phone: 479-650-2735.

DECKER, SUE (SUSAN L. DECKER), Internet company executive; married; 3 children. BS, Tufts U.; MBA, Harvard U. Cert. Charterd Fin. Analyst. With Donaldson, Lufking & Jenrette (DLJ), 1986—2000, publ. and advtsg. rsch. anlayst, dir. global head rsch., 1998—2000; sr. v.p. fin. & adminstrn. Yahoo! Inc., Sunnyvale, Calif., 2000—02, CFO, 2000—, sr. v.p. fin. and adminstrn., 2002—. Apptd. to acctg. standards adv. coun. Fin. Acctg. Fedn., 2000—04; bd. dirs. Pixar Animation Studios, 2004—. Office: Yahoo! 701 1st Av Sunnyvale CA 04089*

DECKER-BARNHILL, JENNIFER GRACE, performing company executive, educator; b. Oklahoma City, May 26, 1969; d. John Leslie Hull and Linda Carol (Lay) Ford; m. Timothy James Decker (div.); m. Arthur Wayne Barnhill, May 4, 1963. BA in Creative Writing and English, U. Houston, 2003; MLA, U. St. Thomas, Houston, 2006. Artistic/mng. dir., founder Mildred's Umbrella Theater Co., Houston, 2001—, also bd. dirs. Prof. Houston C.C., 2005—, North Harris Coll., Houston, 2006—; bd. mem. dos Chicas Theater Commune, Houston. Office: Mildreds Umbrella Theater Co PO Box 66686 Houston TX 77266

DECKERT, MYRNA JEAN, nonprofit association administrator; b. McPherson, Kans., Nov. 4, 1936; d. Francis J. and Grace (Killion) George; m. Ray A. Deckert, Sept. 29, 1957; children: Rachelle, Kimberly, Charles, Michael. AA, Coll. of Sequoias, 1956; BBA, U. Beverly Hills, 1983, MBA, 1984. Youth dir. Asbury Meth. Ch., El Paso, Tex., 1960-63; teen program dir. YWCA, El Paso, 1963-69, assoc. exec. dir., 1969-70, CEO, 1970—2002; chair strategic planning com. Tex. Dept. Pub. and Regulatory Svcs., 1994-97; owner, prin. MJD and Assocs., 2002—03; COO Pasodel Norte Group, 2004—; commr. UNESCO, 2004—; prin. UJD & Assocs. Cons. to nonprofits; exec. cons. Bus. Leadership Coun., 2002—. Pres. Exec. Forum, 1991—92; commr. Housing Authority City of El Paso, 1989—92; former chair bd. trustees Columbia Med. Ctr. East, 1992—97; deans adv. com. Tex. Tech. Med. Ctr.; past trustee Dues/High Tower Found.; chair Leadership El Paso, 1994—95; past mem. Tex. Challenge Adv. Com., 1998; chair Change Initiative Com., 1998—2000; adv. dir. M.D. Anderson Hosp., Houston; co-chair El Paso Ind. Sch. Dist. Bd. Com., 2000; mem. City of El Paso Bond Com., 1999—2000; mem. nat. coordinating bd. YWCA of the USA, 2002—04, chair global campaign; commr. UNESCO, 2004; bd. mem. Kids Excel, El Paso, 2005—; bd. dirs. Chase Bank of Tex., El Paso, Blue Cross/Blue Shield Tex., 1999—. Recipient Hannah Soloman Cmty. Svc. award Nat. Coun. Jewish Women, Sertoma Club award Svc. to Mankind, 1974, Cmty. Svc. award League United L.Am. Citizens, 1980, Humanitarian award, 1994, Vol. Svc. award Vol. Bur., 1984, Merit award Adalante Mujer, 1986, Social Svc. award KVIA/Sunturians, 1986, Excellence award Nat. Assn. YWCA Execs., 1990, Racial Justice award YWCA of the U.S.A., 1991, Disting. Svc. award Rotary of El Paso, 1997, Citizen of Yr. award Greater El Paso Assn. Realtors, 1998; named Woman of Yr., AAUW, 1975, Dir. of Yr., United Way El Paso County, 1985, Philanthropy Exec. of Yr., 2003, First Lady of El Paso, Beta Sigma Phi, 1991, One of 10 Most Influential Women, El Paso Times, 1995, Citizen of Yr., Mil. Order of World Wars, 1996; inducted into El Paso Women's Hall of Fame, 1990, El Paso Hist. Soc. Hall of Honor, 1995, Hall of Fame/Coll. of Sequoias, 1995, Hall of Honor, 1996, Jr. Achievement Bus. Hall of Honor, 1998, Bravo award LWV, 1999, Myrna J. Deckert Living Legacy award, 2003; named Citizen of Yr., El Paso Bd. Realtors, 1999; Conquistador award, City of El Paso, 2002; named El Pasoan of Yr., 2003, Philanthropy Exec. of Yr., 2003, Lifetime Achievement award YWCA El Pasodel Norte Region, 2003. Methodist. Home: 4276 Canterbury Dr El Paso TX 79902-1352 Personal E-mail: mjdeckert42202@sbcglobal.net. Business E-Mail: mdeckert@pasodelnortegroup.org.

DECOLLIBUS, PAULA (DILUGLIO), psychologist; d. Domenic R. and Dorothea A. DiLuglio; m. Stephen M. DeCollibus, 1985; 1 child, Marisa J. BA, Brown U., Providence, RI, 1975; MA, U. NC, Chapel Hill, 1977. Sch. psychologist Moore County Schools, NC, 1981—84; psychologist Dept. for Children, Youth and Families, Providence, 1984—85; sch. psychologist Freetown Lakeville Pub. Schools, Mass., 1985—86, Warwick Pub. Schools, RI, 1986—, O'Neal Day Sch., Southern Pines, NC. Mem.: RI Sch. Psychologists' Assn., Nat. Assn. Sch. Psychologists. Home: 111 Harrison St North Kingstown RI 02852 Office: Warwick Pub Sch 34 Warwick Lake Ave Warwick RI 02889

DECOPPET, LAURA LOUISE, writer, editor; b. N.Y.C., June 21, 1946; d. André and Eileen (Johnston) de C; m. Kenneth Archer LaBarre; 1 child, Susanna Jane. BA, Barnard Coll., N.Y.C., 1968. Asst. Avant Guard Art Gallery, N.Y.C., 1972-76; writer, editor Interview Mag., 2003—. Author, editor: The Art Dealers, 1984, 2d edit., 2002. Mem. Ch. Of Eng. Avocations: backgammon, biking, art collecting, mahjonga, bridge. Home: 50 E 10th St New York NY 10003-6221 Office: Interview Mag 500 Broadway New York NY 10012-4416 Office Phone: 212-475-3267.

DECOTIS, RUTH JANICE, career planning administrator, educator; b. Lebanon, N.H., July 3, 1949; d. David Gilman Fowler and Olive Leonie Greenwood; m. Terry L. DeCotis, Sept. 2, 1967; children: Gregory, Curtis, Erin. AS magna cum laude in Sec. Sci., Plymouth State Coll., 1989, BS magna cum laude in Adminstrn. Mgmt. & Comm., 1995, MEd magna cum laude in Counselor Edn. & Human Rels., 1998. Sec. Equity Pub., Orford, NH, 1969—79; sec. social sci. dept. Plymouth State Coll., Plymouth, NH, 1980—86, from program asst. to academic & career adv. ctr., 1986—. Travel agt. Plymouth Travel, Plymouth, 1991—. Co-author: Great Jobs for Math Majors, 1998. Mem.: Assn. for Psychol. Type, Nat. Academic Adv. Assn., Nat. Soc. Experiential Edn., Am. Counseling Assn. Avocations: travel, antiques, restoration of old homes. Office: Plymouth State Coll Academic & Career Adv Ctr 17 High St MSC 44 Plymouth NH 03264 E-mail: rdecotis@mail.plymouth.edu.

DE COURTEN-MYERS, GABRIELLE MARGUERITE, neuropathologist; b. Fribourg, Switzerland, Aug. 8, 1947; came to U.S., 1979; d. Maurice Edmond and Margrit (Wettstein) De Courten; m. Ronald Elwood Myers, Apr. 18, 1981; 1 child, Maximilian. BSBA, Akademikergemeinschaft, Zurich, Switzerland, 1967; MD, U. Zurich, 1974. Resident in psychiatry Hopital Psycho-Geriatrique, Gimel, Switzerland, 1974-75; resident in pediatrics U. Hosp. Zurich, 1977; resident in neuropathology U. Hosp. of Lausanne, Switzerland, 1976-78; rsch. assoc. NIH, Bethesda, Md., 1979-80; fellow in neuropathology Coll. of Medicine U. Cin., 1980-83, asst. prof. neuropathology Coll. of Medicine, 1983-88, assoc. prof. neuropathology Coll. of Medicine, 1988-89, tenured assoc. prof. Coll. of Medicine, 1989—. Cons. Vets. Affairs Med. Ctr., Cin., 1983—, Children's Hosp. Med. Ctr., Cin., 1984—, Good Samaritan Hosp., Cin., 1990—. Grantee VA, 1985—, NIH, 1986-90, 93—, Am. Heart Assn., 1991-94, Am. Diabetes Assn., 1995. Mem. AAAS, Am. Assn. Neuropathologists, Am. Acad. Neurology, AAUP, Soc. Acad. Emergency Medicine, Soc. Exptl. Neuropathology. Office: U Cin Coll of Medicine Dept Pathology PO Box 670529 231 Bethesda Ave Cincinnati OH 45267-0529 Office Phone: 513-558-0148.

DECROSTA, SUSAN ELYSE, graphic designer; b. Cambridge, Mass., Aug. 28, 1956; d. Joseph Mario and Gertrude Ermelinda (Galligani) DeC. BFA, Mass. Coll. Art, 1980. certified art tchr., supr. Graphic artist Nixdorf Computer Corp., Burlington, Mass., 1981—86; artist, illustrator Rivers, Trainor, Doyle, Providence, 1987; lead artist, illustrator Raytheon Co., Andover, Mass., 1986—94; graphic designer Raytheon Svc. Co., Burlington, Mass., 1994—2004; art dir. Raytheon Tech. Svc., Burlington, 2004—. Freelance graphic artist, 1980—; guest spkr. to design and illustration students Northeastern U., 1992. Publ. Graphic Design U.S.A. Mag., 2000 (Am. Graphic Design award, 2000, 2003, 2005). Vol. AIDS Action Com., Boston; bd. dirs. Jeannette Neill Dance Scholarship Program, Boston, 1999-2006. Recipient Excellence award Soc. Tech. Comm. and Art Direction, 1986, In-House Am. Graphic Design awards Graphic Design USA Mag., 2005, 06, others. Mem.: Women's Initiative Network, Art Alumni Assn. Avocations: dance, painting. Office: Raytheon 235 Presidential Way Woburn MA 01801 Office Phone: 339-645-6980. Personal E-mail: sdecrosta1@verizon.net.

DECROW, KAREN, lawyer, educator, writer; b. Chgo., Dec. 18, 1937; d. Samuel Meyer and Juliette (Abt) Lipschultz; m. Alexander Allen Kolben, 1960 (div. 1965); m. Roger DeCrow, 1965 (div. 1972, dec. 1989). BS, Northwestern U., 1959; JD, Syracuse U., 1972; DHL (hon.), SUNY, Oswego, 1994. Bar: NY, US Dist. Ct. (no. dist.) NY. Resorts editor Golf Digest mag., Evanston, Ill., 1959-60; editor Am. Soc. Planning Ofcls., Chgo., 1960-61; writer Ctr. for Study Liberal Edn. for Adults., Chgo., 1961-64; editor Holt, Rinehart, Winston, Inc., N.Y.C., 1965; textbook editor L.W. Singer, Syracuse, NY, 1965-66; writer Ea. Regional Inst. for Edn., Syracuse, 1967-69, Pub. Broadcasting System, 1977; tchr. women and law, 1972-74; nat. bd. mem. NOW, 1968-77, nat. pres., 1974-77, also nat. politics task force chair; cons. affirmative action; pvt. practice, Jamesville, NY, 1974—. Lectr. topics including law, gender, internat. feminism to corps., polit. groups, colls. and univs., US, Can., Mex., Finland, China, Greece, former USSR; nat. coord. Women's Strike for Equality, 1970; moot ct. judge, 1974--; NY State del. Internat. Women's Yr., 1977; originator Schs. for Candidates; participant DeCrow-Schlafly ERA Debates, from 1975; founder (with Robert Seidenberg, MD) World Woman Watch, 1988; gender issues advisor Nat. Congress for Men; mem. Task Force on Gender Bias. Author: (with Roger DeCrow) University Adult Education: A Selected Bibliography, 1967, American Council on Education, 1967, The Young Woman's Guide to Liberation, 1971, Sexist Justice, 1974, First Women's State of the Union Message, 1977, (with Robert Seidenberg) Women Who Marry Houses: Panic and Protest in Agoraphobia, 1983, Turkish edit., 1988, 2d Turkish edit., 1989, United States of America vs. Sex: How the Meese Commission Lied About Pornography, 1988, (with Jack Kammer) Good Will Toward Men: Women Talk Candidly About the Balance of Power Between the Sexes, 1994; editor: The Pregnant Teenager (Howard Osofsky), 1968, Corporate Wives, Corporate Casualties (Robert Seidenberg, MD), 1973; contbr. articles to USA Today, NY Times, NY Times Bus. Sect., LA Times, Chgo. Tribune, Nat. Law Jour., Women Boston Globe, Vogue, Mademoiselle, Ingenue, Newsday, Chgo. Sun Times, Penthouse, Washington Post, LA Times Mag., Policy Review, Miami Herald, Internat. Herald Tribune, Social Problems, Houston Chronicle, Pitts. Press, Nat. NOW Times, Syracuse U. Mag., San Francisco Chronicle, Civil Rights Quar., Women Lawyers Jour., other newspapers, mags.; regular columnist: Syracuse New Times, 1985—; columnist NY Times Spl. Features; recording: Opening Up Marriage, 1980. Hon. trustee Elizabeth Cady Stanton Found.; active Hon. Com. to Save Alice Paul's Birthplace; Liberal party candidate for Mayor of Syracuse, 1969. Recipient Profl. Recognition award for best newspaper column Syracuse Press Club, 1990, 94, 95, 96, 2000, Best Column award, 1994-95, 99, 2001, 02, Best Column award NY Press Assn., 1991-92, 95, award Barnard Coll., Vet. Feminists of Am. and the Barnard Ctr. for Rsch. on Women, Woman of Achievement/Distinction award Gov. George E. Pataki, 1998; Svc. to Soc. award Northwestern U. Alumni Assn., 2002, Achievement award The Post-Standard, Syracuse, 2003. Mem. NOW (pres., 1974-77, bd. mem., 1968-74, v.p.), ACLU (Ralph E. Kharas Disting. Svc. in Civil Liberties award 1985), NY Women's Bar Assn. (ctrl. NY chpt. pres. 1989-90, jud. screening com., Joan L. Ellenbogen Founder's award 2003, Doris Hoffman medal 2005), Women's Bar Assn. State NY (founder, Ctrl. NY chapt., 1977, judicial screening com., ctrl. NY chapt. pres., 1989-90, nom. com., 1996, 2001, Doris Hoffman medal 2005), NY Bar Assn., Onondaga County Bar Assn. (profl. ethics com., fed. Courts com., grievance com., co-chair membership com. 2006, governance com. 2006, nominating com. 2006, bd. dirs. 2005—), Elizabeth Cady Stanton Found. (trustee), Feminists for Free Expression (adv. com.), Abortion Rights Mobilization (bd. dir.), Nat. Coalition Against Censorship, Working Women's Inst. (bd. advisors), Syracuse Friends Chamber Music, Atlantic States Legal Found., Yale Polit. Union (hon. life), Nat. Congress Men (gender issues advisor), Mariposa Edn. and Rsch. Found., Nat. Coun. Children's Rights (adv. panel), Wilderness Soc., Northwestern U. Alumni Assn., Women's Inst. Freedom Press, Art Inst. Chgo., Nat. Women's Polit. Caucus, Theta Sigma Phi. Address: 7599 Brown Gulf Rd Jamesville NY 13078-9636 Office Phone: 315-682-2563.

DECTER, MIDGE, writer; b. St. Paul, July 25, 1927; d. Harry and Rose (Calmenson) Rosenthal; m. Norman Podhoretz, Oct. 21, 1956; children: Rachel, Naomi, Ruth, John. Student, U. Minn., 1945-46, Jewish Theol. Sem. Am., 1946-48. Asst. editor Midstream mag., 1956-58; mng. editor Commentary, 1961-62; editor Hudson Inst., 1965-66, CBS Legacy Books, 1966-68; exec. editor Harper's mag., 1969-71; book review editor Saturday Rev./World mag., 1972-74; sr. editor Basic Books, Inc., 1974-80; exec. dir. Com. for Free World, 1980-90; sr. fellow Inst. on Religion and Pub. Life, 1991—95. Author: The Liberated Woman and Other Americans, 1971, Liberal Parents, Radical Children, 1975, The New Chastity and Other Arguments Against Women's Liberation, 1997, An Old Wife's Tale: My Seven Decades in Love and War, 2001, Losing the First Battle, Winning the War, 2002, Rumsfeld: A Personal Portrait, 2003; mem. editl. bd.: First Things. Bd. dirs. Heritage Found., Ctr. for Security Policy, Phila. Soc.; founding mem. Coalition for Dem. Majority; former dir. Nicaraguan Freedom Fund. Recipient Nat. Humanities medal, 2003. Home: 120 E 81st St New York NY 10028-1428

DEDE, BONNIE AILEEN, librarian, educator; b. Racine, Wis., Mar. 21, 1942; d. Edward Charles and Gracebelle Roeber; children: Suzan A., Ercan M. BA, U. Mich., 1963, MA, 1966, AM in Libr. Sci., 1968; cert., U. Ill., 1970. From mem. staff to head monograph cataloging prodn. U. Mich. Libr., Ann Arbor, 1967—99, head monograph cataloging prodn., 1999—. Mem. part-time faculty libr. and info. sci. program Wayne State U., Detroit, 1993—2000; vis. lectr. Grad. Sch. Libr. and Info. Sci. U. Ill., Urbana-Champaign, 2003—04; cons. Gale Rsch., Detroit, 1993; reviewer Am. Reference Books Ann., 1992—2000; cons. grant projects OCLC, 1991—92, 1994—96; adj. lectr. Law Libr. U. Mich., 2003—04. Mem. editl. bd. MC, Jour. Acad. Media Librarianship, 1992—2002. Grantee Title II-B, U.S. Office Edn., 1970, faculty-libr. coop. rsch. grantee Coun. on Libr. Resources, 1986-88, access grantee NEH, 1990-93. Mem. ALA, Alpha Lambda Delta, Beta Phi Mu (pres. Mu chpt. 1991-96). Office: U Mich 100 Hatcher Libr North Ann Arbor MI 48109-1205

DÉDÉ, BRENDA SANDERS, academic administrator; b. Henderson, Tex., Sept. 12, 1948; d. Leroy and Reneva (Hunt) Sanders; divorced; 1 child, Angelique. BA, Tex. So. U., 1975, MEd, 1985, EdD, 1991. Sec. Tex. So. U., Houston, 1969-87, adminstrv. asst., 1987-88, asst. dir., 1988-91, assoc. dir., 1991-95; dir. faculty rsch. devel. Clarion (Pa.) U., 1995-96, dir. faculty rsch. devel. and interim coord. grad. studies, 1996—2000, asst. v.p. academic affairs, 2000—. Proposal reviewer U.S. Dept. Edn., 1999—; pres. Pa. Black Conf. Higher Edn., 2006-; profl. devel. com. Nat. Coun. U. Rsch. Adminstrs., 2001-02. Vol. Voting Precinct, Houston, 1980-85; alternate del. State Dem. Conv., Houston, 1988; sec. Community Devel. Program, Houston, 1978; v.p. PTO, Concord Elem. Sch., Houston, 1980; bd. dirs. Stop Abuse for Everyone, Clarion, 1998-2004, 06—, Big Brothers/Sisters, 2004, United Way, 2003—; candidate Mayor Clarion Borough, 2005. Recipient Outstanding Svc. award Bethlehem Missionary Bapt. Ch., Houston, 1990, Vol. of the Yr., United Way, 2003, Mary Davis Balt. award, Pa. Black Conf. on Higher Edn., 2002, Woman of the Yr., Clarion U., 2002, Outstanding Equity award, 2002; grantee Women's Bur. Dept. Labor, 1990-91. Mem. NAACP, Am. Assn. Higher Edn. (Black Caucus conf. attendance award 1991), South Tex. Missionary Bapt. Dist. Assn., Pa. System of Higher Edn. Faculty Profl. Devel. Coun., Kiwanis Club of Clarion, Eta Phi Beta (fin. sec.), Alpha Kappa Alpha. Democrat. Baptist. Avocations: sewing, reading, sports. Office: Clarion U Pa 840 Wood St Clarion PA 16214-1240

DEDIEGO, PAULA DAWN, education educator; b. Mass., July 22, 1971; d. Alan Genovese and Anne Roy; m. Robert deDeigo, Jr., June 26, 1990; children: Lori, Justin. AS in Liberal Arts and Sci., Mt. Wachusett C.C., Gardner, Mass., 1991; BA in Natural Sci., Worcester State Coll., Mass., 1993; M in Biology, Fitchburg State Coll., Mass., 1998. Liaison sci. dept. Montachussett Regional Vocat. Tech. Sch., Fitchburg, 1997—; mem. adj. faculty Mt. Wachusett C.C., Gardner, 2001—; mem. faculty Connecting Link, Calif., 2004—. Mentor coord. Montachusett Vocat. Tech. Sch., Fitchburg, 2001; key leader Building a Presence for Sci., 2002. Author: (online course) Best Practices in Teaching, 2001. Mem.: AIA Aero., Mass. Sci. Edn. Leadership, NSTA. Christian. Avocations: piano, guitar, singing, flying. Office: Montachusett Regional Vocat Tech Sch 1050 Westminster St Fitchburg MA 04126 Business E-Mail: dediego@monty.tech.net.

DEDMON, ANGELA MARIE MAXINE, psychologist; b. Oklahoma City, May 25, 1971; d. Hubert Carlton and Patricia Ann Bryan; m. Brian Todd Dedmon, June 15, 1991; children: Caeli Ann Louise, Joshua Todd. BA in Psychology and Sociology magna cum laude, Okla. State U., 1993; MA in Clin. Psychology, Tex. Tech. U., 1997, PhD in Clin. Psychology, 1999. Lic. psychologist Okla. Rsch. asst. Tex. Tech. U., Lubbock, 1995—96; clinic co-dir. Tex. Tech. Psychology Clinic, Lubbock, 1995—97; psychologist in tng. Lubbock County Youth Ctr., 1996—97, Lubbock Ind. Sch. Dist., 1997—98; intern psychology Children's Mercy Hosp., Kansas City, Mo., 1998—99, fellow psychology, 1999—2000; pvt. practice clin. child psychologist Edmond, Okla., 2001—. Clin. child psychologist psychol. evaluations Pauline Meyer Shelter, Oklahoma City, 2001—; spkr. Okla. Foster Care Assn., Oklahoma City, 2002. Contbr. articles to profl. jours. Vol. disaster recovery ARC, Oklahoma City; vol. disaster hotline local TV sta., Oklahoma City, 2001. Mem.: APA, Okla. Psychol. Assn. Avocations: swimming, reading, church activities. Office: 2500 S Broadway #200 Edmond OK 73013 Office Phone: 405-514-1476.

DEDRICK, REBECCA ANN, elementary school educator; b. Sedalia, Mo., Dec. 15, 1961; d. Robert and Mary Bennett; m. Rene' Bennett, Nov. 29, 1985; children: Russell, Richard, Christopher, Chelsey. MEd, Ctrl. Mo. State U., 1992. Cert. tchr. Mo. Dept. Secondary and Elem. Edn., 1992. Tchr. Sedalia Sch. Dist. #200, Mo., 1989—2006. Com. mem. Sacred Heart Cath. Ch., Sedalia, Mo., 2002—06. Mem.: Mo. State Tchrs. Assn. Roman Catholic. Office: Sedalia Mid Sch 2205 S Ingram Sedalia MO 65301

DEE, PAULINE M., artist; b. Concord, N.H., Jan. 9, 1933; d. Arthur Joseph and Anna Marie (Marquis) Champagne; m. Edmond Francis Dee, July 2, 1955; children: James Francis, Diane Mary. Bus. Cert., Burdett Coll., Lynn, Mass. Membership chmn. Danvers (Mass.) Art Assn., 1986-92, v.p., 1990-92; founder Pauline Dee Studio for Oil Painting, 1989; v.p. Lynnfield (Mass.) Art Guild, 1991-93, pres., 1994-96; v.p. Saltbox Gallery, Topsfield, Mass., 1995-2000, pres., 2000—. Demonstrator in field; founder Pauline Dee Studio, 1989; instituted Lynnfield Art Guild Scholarship Fund, 1993. Exhibited in solo shows at Woman's Club of Boston, 1980, Naval Officers Club, Pearl Harbor, Hawaii, 1994; represented in numerous pvt. collections. Cons. Peabody (Mass.) Internat. Festival, 1995; bd. dirs. North Shore Art Assn., Gloucester, Mass., 1996. Recipient achievement awards, 1985-95; Peabody Arts Lottery grantee, 1996. Roman Catholic. Avocations: art, photography. Home: 16 Samoset Rd Peabody MA 01960-3504

DEE, RONDA, poet, photographer, small business owner, journalist; b. Bronx, NY, May 6, 1943; d. Maurice Dee and Rachel Hoffer. AA, Manhattan CC, NYC, 1974; BS, NYU, 1976. Cert. Isadora Duncan Dance Workshop, 1995, Trager massage Dallas. Sec. Book of Knowledge, N.Y.C., 1962; pvt. tutor City Coll., 1963; tchr. head start Lennox Hill Neighborhood Assoc., N.Y.C., 1970; tchr. k-3 NW Harlee Elem. Sch., Dallas, 1977; sec. City of Dallas, 1977; tchr., summer reading prog. Texas Dept. Human Resources, Dallas, 1978; pvt. practice, 1980—83; adminstrv. asst. Contact Dallas Telephone Crisis Counseling, 1980; journalist Brookhaven Sch. News The Courier, Dallas, 1987; pvt. practice, 2004—; distbr., dealer Eco-Quest Internat. Co. Living Air Ozone Machines; journalist, photographer Decoy newspaper, Richland Coll., 2004—05, comedy writer, 2004—05, newspaper comedy writer, 2004—05; journalist Richland Chronicle, Dallas, 2003—; journalist, staff writer The Courier, Brookhaven Coll., 1987; news reporter Richland Coll. Web Radio, 2006. Pupeteer children's ward Mt. Sinai Hosp., 1968; adminstrv. asst. Contact Dallas, 1990; featured reader Barnes & Noble Booksellers, 2000—02; distbr. Cell Tech. Health Foods, 1991—95; radio reporter Richland Coll., 2005. Exhibitions include Brookhaven Coll., Dallas, 1988, Ward Nass Gallery, 1995, Mem. D'Art, Dallas, 1997, Wells Fargo Bldg. Plano, Tex., Richland Coll., 2002—03, 500 X Gallery, Dallas, 2003—04, Richland Coll., 2004—05, exhibited in group shows at Oak Lawn Pub. Libr., Dallas, 2006 (2d pl. digital prints); photographer Photograph: Walls of New York City, 2002, Touch of Tomorrow, 2004, Labour of Love, 2005; author, photographer: Parallex, 2002—05; contbg. writer Rough Diner, 1970; contbr. articles to profl. jours. and newspapers;, author numerous poems; actor: Hands Across the Sea; (documentaries) Homelessness, 1985; extra (films) Veritas, Prince of Truth, 2004. Intake sec. Big Brother adn Big Sisters, Dallas, 1981; mem. Concerned Citizens Pesticide Control, Dallas, 2003—; social svc. worker Holy Trinity Ch., 1983—85. Recipient Founders Day award, NYU, 1976, Juried Art Contest winner for charcoal design collage, Brookhaven Coll., 1986, League Innovation award, Richland Coll., 2002—04, 2006. Mem.: Tex. Visual Arts Assn., Internat. Soc. Photographers, Internat. Soc. Poets, Sierra Club, Phi Theta Kappa. Avocations: camping, theater, films, exercise, drums. Home: PO Box 823478 Dallas TX 75382-3478 Office Phone: 972-221-7511. Personal E-mail: rondadee2001@yahoo.com.

DEE, RUBY (RUBY DEE DAVIS), actress, writer, film director; b. Cleve., Oct. 27, 1924; d. Marshall Edward and Emma (Benson) Wallace; m. Ossie Davis, Dec. 9, 1948; children: Nora, Guy, Hasna. BA, Hunter Coll., 1945; ArtsD (hon.), Fairfield U.; BA (hon. doctorate), Iona Coll., Va. State U.; apprentice, Am. Negro Theatre, 1941-44; LHD (hon.), SUNY, Old Westbury, 1990; DFA, Spelman Coll., 1991. Ind. actress, writer, dir., v.p. Emmslyn II Prodns., 1945—. Author: (poetry) Glowchild, 1972, (musical) Take It from the Top, (collected poetry, humor, short stories) My One Good Nerve; adaptor: (African folk tales) Two Ways to Count to Ten, The Tower to Heaven, (play) Books With Legs, 1993; contbr. column N.Y. Amsterdam News; co-writer (film) Uptight; dir., adaptor (stage prodn.) Zora is my Name!, 1983; stage appearances include Jeb, 1946, Raisin in the Sun, 1959, Purlie Victorious, 1961, The Imaginary Invalid, 1971, Wedding Band, 1972 (Drama Desk award 1972), Boesman and Lena, 1970 (Obie award 1971), Anna Lucasta, Taming of the Shrew, Checkmates, 1988, The Glass Menagerie, 1989, Flyin West, 1994, Two Hah-Hahs and a Homeboy, 1995; actress: (films) Gone are the Days, The Jackie Robinson Story, 1950, Take a Giant Step, St. Louis Blues, A Raisin in the Sun, Purlie Victorious, To Be Young, Gifted and Black, Buck and the Preacher, Countdown at Kusini, Cat People, 1982, Do the Right Thing, 1989 (NAACP Image award as best actress 1989), Jungle Fever, 1991, Cop & 1/2, 1993, Whitewash, 1994, Just Cause, 1995, Simple Wish, A, 1997, Baby Geniuses, 1999, Little Bill, 2001, Feast of All Saints, 2001, Unchained Memories, 2002, Baby of the Family, 2002; narrator: Time to Dance: The Life and Work of Norma Canner, A, 1998, Unfinished Journey, 1999; numerous TV appearances including It's Good to be Alive, 1974, Today Is Ours, 1974, The Defenders, Police Woman, Peyton Place, (TV films) To Be Young, Gifted and Black, All God's Children, The Nurses, Roots: The Next Generation, I Know Why the Caged Bird Sings, Wedding Band, It's Good to Be Alive, Decoration Day (Emmy award for Supporting Actress in a Miniseries or Special 1991), The Atlanta Child Murders, (TV spl. with Ossie Davis) Martin Luther King: The Dream and the Drum, The Winds of Change, Windmill of the Gods, TV miniseries Stephen King's The Stand, 1994, Tuesday Morning Ride, 1995, Mr. & Mrs. Loving, 1996, Captive Heart: The James Mink Story, 1996, Porgy and Bess: An American Voice, 1998, Passing Glory, 1999, Having Our Say: The Delany Sisters' First 100 Years, 1999, Finding Buck McHenry, 2000, A Storm in Summer, 2000, Taking Back Our Town, 2001; co-producer: (TV spl.) Today is Ours, The Ernest Green Story, 1993, (radio show) Ossie Davis and Ruby Dee Story Hour, 1974-78, (TV series) With Ossie and Ruby, 1981, (home videotape) Hands Upon The Heart, 1991, Middle Ages, 1992, Hands Upon The Heart II, 1993; rec. artist poems and stories; host (with Ossie Davis) African Heritage Movie Network. Recipient Martin Luther King Jr. award Operation PUSH, 1972, Drama Desk award, 1974, (with Ossie Davis) Frederick Douglass award N.Y. Urban League, 1970, (with Ossie Davis) NAACP Image award Hall of Fame, Master Innovator For Film award Sony, 1991, Nat. Medal of Arts, 1990; Kennedy Ctr. Honors (with Ossie Davis), 2004. Mem. NAACP, CORE, Student Non-Violent Coordinating Com., SCLC. Address: The Artists Agy 10000 Santa Monica Blvd Los Angeles CA 90067-7007

DEEB, MARY-JANE, editor, educator; b. Alexandria, Egypt, Aug. 27, 1946; arrived in U.S., 1973; d. Alix and Stephanie (Klanscek) Anhoury; m. Marius K. Deeb, Sept. 27, 1969; 1 child, Hadi K. BA in Sociology, Am. U., Cairo, 1967, MA in Sociology, 1972; PhD in Internat. Rels., Johns Hopkins U., 1987. Rsch. assoc. Ford Found., Beirut, 1972-73; cons. UN Econ. Commn. for Western Asia, Beirut, 1980, UNICEF, Beirut, 1980-81; project dir. U.S. AID, Beirut, 1982-83; asst. professorial lectr. George Washington U., Washington, 1988-89, 93, 97, Georgetown U., Washington, 1991, 94; asst. prof. Am. U., Washington, 1989-94, adj. assoc. prof., 1994—; editor Mid. East Jour., Washington, 1995-98; Arab world area specialist Libr. of Congress, Washington, 1998—2004, head Near East sect., 2004—05, chief African and Mid. Ea. divsn., 2005—. External reviewer for grant proposals U.S. Inst. Peace, Washington, 1991, 92, 97, Woodrow Wilson Ctr. for Scholars, 2003, NEH, 2005; testified on subcom. on Africa fgn. rels. com. U.S. Ho. of Reps., 1991, 92, 98; testified before the select com. on intelligence, U.S. Senate, 1996; testified on fgn. rels. com. U.S. Senate, 1997, UN Monitor of Algerian legislative elections, 1997; dir. Algeria program Corp. Coun. on Africa; leader Libr. of Congress Mission to Iraq, 2003; team mem. Libr. Congress Mission to Iran, 2004. Co-author (with Marius K. Deeb): Libya Since the Revolution, 1982; author: Libya's Foreign Policy, 1991; co-editor: Hasib Sabbagh from Palestinian Refugee to Citizen of the World, 1996, Cocktails and Murder on the Potomac, 2001, (novel) Murder on the Riviera, 2004, A Christmas Mystery in Provence, 2004; rev. editor Internat. Jour. Mid.-East Studies, 1989-94; contbr. articles, revs. to profl. jours. and encys., and chpts. to books; interviewed on numerous TV programs, including CBS Evening News, ABC News, NBC Nightly News, CNN Headline News, Fox Morning News, PBS, and in news publs., including N.Y. Times, Washington Post, Time mag., L.A. Times, The Christian Sci. Monitor, U.S.A. Today, Boston Globe, Tokyo Shimbum, Yomouri, others. Mem. UN Assn., Am. Polit. Sci. Assn., Internat. Studies Assn., Mid. East Studies Assn. N.Am., Women's Caucus for Polit. Sci., Am.-Tunisian Assn. (exec. bd. 1989—), Hannibal Club (founding mem. 1999), World Affairs Coun., Women in Fgn. Policy, Mystery Writers Am., Sisters in Crime, Cosmos Club. Roman Catholic. Office: Libr Congress African and Middle Ea Divsn Jefferson Bldg 101 Independence Ave SE Washington DC 20540-0002 Office Phone: 202-707-1221. Business E-Mail: mdee@loc.gov.

DEEDS, VIRGINIA WILLIAMS, volunteer; b. Newark, Ohio, June 28, 1934; d. Theodore Nelson and Nell Elizabeth (Hoover) Williams; m. Charles Lemoin Deeds, Aug. 7, 1955; children: Melinda, Jennifer Giesen, C. Jason, Stephanie Sanda. RN, White Cross Sch. Nursing, 1955. RN, Ohio. RN obstet. dept. Berea (Ohio) Cmty. Hosp., 1955-56; RN emergency dept. White Cross Hosp., Columbus, Ohio, 1956; RN med. & obstetrics Union Hosp., Dover, Ohio, 1961-62; vol. RN United Health Found. Sr. Ctr., Dover, Ohio, 1961—, Office Roy Geduldig, Dover, Ohio, 1967-68. Co-founder, co-dir. Tuscarawas County Teen Pregnancy Prevention Taskforce, 1985-92. Co-editor The Chart newsletter, 1991-98. Bd. dirs. United Health Found., New Philadelphia, YMCA, Dover, Union Hosp. Aux., Chestnut Soc. Kent State U., 1996—, Juvenile Ct. Citizens Review Bd., 1989—; mem. bd. Chestnut Soc. Kent State U., Tuscarawas Campus, 1996-98; mem. Alcohol-Drug Addiction Mental Health Svcs. Bd., 1996—. Recipient Zeisberger award Tusc. County Hist. Soc., 1994. Avocations: golf, reading, needlecrafts.

DEEL, FRANCES QUINN, retired librarian; b. Pottsville, Pa., Mar. 9, 1939; d. Charles Joseph and Carrie Miriam (Ketner) Q.; m. Ronald Eugene Deel, Feb. 5, 1983. BS, Millersville State Coll., 1960; M.L.S., Rutgers U., 1964; M.P.A., U. West Fla., 1981. Post librarian U.S. Army Armor (Desert Tng. Ctr.), Ft. Irwin, Calif., 1964-66; staff librarian Mil. Dist. of Washington, 1966-67; supervisory librarian 1st Logistical Command, APO San Francisco, 1967-68; tech. process specialist Naval Edn. and Tng. Supervisory Command, Washington, 1968-77, Pensacola, Fla., 1968-77; chief tech. library USAF Armament Lab., Eglin AFB, Fla., 1977-81; dir. command libraries Air Force Systems Command (Andrews AFB), Washington, 1981-92; mem. exec. adv. council Fed. Library and Info. Network, Washington, 1983-86; libr. Air Force Dist. of Washington (Bolling AFB), Washington, 1992-94; dir. Navy Dept. Libr., Washington, 1994; ret., 1994. Mem. ALA (dir.-at-large armed forces libraries sect. Chgo. 1983-86), Spl. Libraries Assn., D.C. Library Assn. Roman Catholic. Home: 99 Country Club Dr W Destin FL 32541-4433

DEELEJALDE, ANA LEVY, psychotherapist; b. Rosario, Argentina, Dec. 16, 1936; d. Leon and Rosa Pessah Levy; m. Fernando DeElejalde; children: Hernan, Andrea, Kadina, Paula. B, Washburn U., 1969; MSW, Kans. U., 1973. Clin. social worker Topeka State Hosp., South Fla. State Hosp., Hollywood; psychoanalytic psychotherapist Pvt. Practice, Ft. Lauderdale. Dir. social svcs. South Fla State Hosp. for Children, 1973—79. Author: Halfway House, 1978.

DEEN, PAULA H., television personality, restaurant owner, chef; b. Albany, Ga., Jan. 19, 1947; m. Michael Groover, Mar. 2004; 2 stepchildren;children from previous marriage: Bobby, Jamie. Owner catering bus. The Bag Lady; owner The Lady and Sons restaurant, Savannah, Ga., 1990—. Host (TV series) Paula's Home Cooking, Food Network, 2002—; author: (cookbooks) The Lady and Sons Too, The Lady and Sons Just Desserts, 2002, The Lady and Sons Savannah Country Cookbook, 2005; co-author (with Martha Nesbit): Paula Deen & Friends: Living It Up, Southern Style, 2005; author: (mag.) Cooking with Paula Deen, 2006—; actor: (films) Elizabethtown, 2005. Provided sponsorships and donations of money, cookbooks and other services to cmty. groups and causes. Named Most Memorable Meal Yr. at The Lady and Sons restaurant, USA Today, 1999, Small Bus. Person Yr. in Ga., US Small Bus. Adminstrn., 2003; recipient Ga. Women Entrepreneurs (GWEN) award, Ga. Small Bus. Devel. Ctr., 2003. Office: Food Network Studios 604 W 52nd St New York NY 10019 also: Lady & Sons Restaurant 102 W Congress St Savannah GA 31401*

DEER CLOUD, SUSAN ANN, writer; b. Livingston Manor, N.Y., Oct. 20, 1950; d. Joseph R. and Dorothea Mae Hauptfleisch. BA in Creative Writing and Gen. Lit., Binghamton U., 1980, MA in English Lit. and Creative Writing, 1982; postgrad., Amherst Coll. Instr. creative writing Binghamton (N.Y.) U. Author: The Broken Hoop, 1988, In the Moon When the Deer Lose Their Horns, 1993; editor: (anthology) Confluence; contbr. numerous jours. Recipient Individual Artist's grant Chenango County Council for the Arts, 2005; 1st prize Allen Ginsberg Poetry Awards, 1989, 98, Readers' Choice award Prairie Schooner, 2003; Poetry fellow N.Y. State Found. Arts, 1993. Mem. Wordcraft Cir. Native Am. Authors. Avocations: photography, hiking, poetry readings. Home: 45 Schoolhouse Rd Amherst MA 01002 E-mail: sdeercloud@wildblue.net, sdeerclo@cas.umass.edu.

DEERING, ANNE-LISE, artist, retired real estate salesperson; b. Oslo, June 20, 1935; d. Reidar Ingolf Dahlsrud and Dagny Elfrida (Grönneberg) Nilsen; m. Reginald Atwell Deering, Oct. 20, 1956 (div. July 1992); children: Eric, Mark, Linda, Norman. BA in Art, Pa. State U., 1977, postgrad., 1990—91. Rsch. asst. Yale U., New Haven, 1955-57; ceramic artist/potter State College, Pa., 1977-98. Real estate agt. Coldwell Banker Univ. Realty, State College, 1992-93, Century 21 Corman Assocs., State College, 1993-99; artist mem. Art Alliance Ctrl. Pa., 1977-2000. Editor Ctrl. Pa. Guild of Craftsmen newsletter, 1994; exhibited in group shows at Am. Medallic Sculpture Assn., Newark Mus., 1990, Mountain Tip Gallery, Cresson, Pa., 1998, Pen and Brush Gallery, N.Y.C., 1998, 99, 2000, 01, Queensborough C.C., 2000, FIDEM, Weimar, Germany, 2000, FIDEM, Paris, 2002, Fed. Interat. Medaille, Seixal, Portugal, 2004, ANA, Colorado Springs, 2001, Penn State U., 2002, Wroclav, Poland, 2002, Am. Medallic Sculpture Assn., mems. exhibit, Nat. Ornamental Metal Mus., Memphis, 2003, Ford Gallery, Eastern Mich. U., 2003, Art/Net Terminal Gallery, Seattle, Nordic Heritage Mus., Seattle, 2004, Forest Lawn Mus., Glendale, Calif., 2005. Mem. visual arts adv. com. Ctrl. Pa. Festival of Arts, 1989-93, co-chair, 1991-93, jury and rules co-chmn. for sidewalk sales com., 1993-97, chair AMSA mems. juried exhibit, Nordic Heritage Mus., Seattle, 2004; mem. exhbn. com.; show judge Forest Lawn Mus. Mem.: Wash. Potters Assn. (bd. dirs. 2000—), Art Alliance Ctrl. Pa. (chair mems. juried exhibit 1978, bd. dirs. 1978—79, participant Gallery Shop 1989—99, steering com. 1994—97), Am. Medallic Sculpture Assn. (newsletter editor 2000—, co-chmn. Hands Across the Sea Am./Polish Medals Exhibit 2001—02, sec. 2002—), Am. Mus. Women in Arts (charter), Ctrl. Pa. Guild Craftsmen (pres. 1986—87, 1993—94), Pa. Guild Craftsmen (bd. dirs. 1980—83, v.p. 1985, bd. dirs. 1985—98, v.p. 1991, 1992, coord., chair ann. Christmas sale). Avocations: photography, music, sailing, gardening, wine making. Home: 24229 92nd Ave W Edmonds WA 98020-6503 Personal E-mail: supermedal@verizon.net.

DEES, SANDRA KAY MARTIN, psychologist, research scientist; b. Omaha, Apr. 18, 1944; d. Leslie B. and Ruth Lillian (May) Martin; m. Doyce B. Dees. BA magna cum laude, Tex. Christian U., 1965, MA, 1972, PhD, 1989. Cert. Montessori Soc., 1977. Adminstrv. asst., rsch. coord. Hosp. Improvement Project, Wichita Falls (Tex.) State Hosp., 1968-69; caseworker adoptions Edna Gladney Home, Ft. Worth, 1970-71; psychologist Mexia (Tex.) State Sch., 1971-72; sch. psychologist Ft. Worth Ind. Sch. Dist., 1971-78, program evaluator, 1978-86; pvt. counselor, 1986-88; rsch. scientist Tex. Christian U., Ft. Worth, 1989—2005, mem. adj. faculty, 1991-92, mem. grad. faculty, 1994—2005. Bd. dirs Because We Care, Ft. Worth, 1988-97, Hill Sch., 1994—. Contbr. articles to profl. jours. Dallas TCU Women's Club creative writing scholar, 1962-64, Virginia Alpha scholar, 1963; NASA rsch. asst., 1965-67; USPHS trainee, 1967-68. Mem. APA, Am. Ednl. Rsch. Assn., Mental Health Assn., Mortar Board, Mensa, Sigma Xi, Alpha Chi, Phi Alpha Theta, Psi Chi, Phi Delta Kappa. Home: 29 Bounty Rd W Fort Worth TX 76132-1003 Office: Tex Christian U Dept Psychology Fort Worth TX 76129-0001 E-mail: s.dees@tcu.edu.

DEESE, E(THEL) HELEN, retired literature and language professor; b. San Diego, Sept. 15, 1925; d. Clyde Thomas and Ethel (Findlay) Smith; m. Rupert Julian Deese, Mar. 4, 1951; children: Rupert Thomas, Mary Ann, Franklin William, Richard Samuel. BA, U. Calif., Riverside, 1968, MA, 1970, PhD, 1977. Lectr. U. Calif., Riverside, 1977—79, 1992—2005, Calif. State Poly. U., Pomona, 1979-81; assoc. prof. English Mt. St. Mary's Coll., Los Angeles, 1983-89; Fulbright lectr. Hungary, 1989-90, Macao, 1990-91. Critic So. Calif. drama, Shakespeare Bull., NYC, 1985—; author: Robert Lowell: A Reference Guide, 1982; editor: Robert Lowell: New Essays on the Poetry, 1986, Critical Essays on Wallace Stevens, 1988, Critical Essays on William Carlos William, 1995; contbr. Ency. Am. Poets and Poetry, 2005; contbr. articles to profl. jours. Mem. MLA, Internat. Fedn. Theatre Rsch., Assn. Lit. Scholars and Critics, Shakespeare Assn. Democrat. Unitarian Universalist. Home and Office: 601 E Baseline Rd Claremont CA 91711-2237 Office Phone: 909-626-6135. Personal E-mail: hsdeese@msn.com.

DEESE, PAMELA MCCARTHY, lawyer; b. Abington, Pa., July 4, 1958; d. John Joseph McC. and Penny Ann (Wells) Knight; m. Charles Michael Deese, May 10, 1986; children: Spencer Michael, Charles Jameson, Kendall Ann. BS, The Am. U., 1980, JD, 1983. Bar: Pa. 1984, DC 1990, US Ct. Appeals (8th cir.) 1989 (4th cir.) 1992, US Supreme Ct. 1995, US Ct. Appeals (DC cir.) 1996. Asst. dir. GSP U.S. Trade Rep., Washington, 1978-83; assoc. atty. Ablondi & Foster, Washington, 1983-86, Robins, Zelle, Larson & Kaplan, Washington, 1986-89; ptnr. Robins, Kaplan, Miller & Ciresi, Washington, 1990—99; ptnr., trademark licensing and advertising Dorsey & Whitney, LLP, 1999—2005; mem. intellectual property practice Arent Fox PLLC, Washington, 2005—. Vol. Offender Aid and Rep., Fairfax, Va., 1983-86; pres. Am. U. Alumni Assn., Washington, 1988-97; elder Lewinsville Presbyn. Ch., McLean, Va., 1989-92; trustee Am. U., 2002—; mem. Circles Bd. Kennedy Ctr., 2001—. Mem. ABA (vice chair sci. and tech. tech. stds. com. 2005—), Am. Intellectual Property Lawyers Assn., Licensing Industry Merchandising Assn. Democrat. Presbyterian. Avocations: skiing, reading, cooking, flower arranging, travel. Office: Arent Fox PLLC 1050 Connecticut Ave NW Washington DC 20036-5339 Office Phone: 202-828-3431. Office Fax: 202-857-6395. Business E-Mail: deese.pamela@arentfox.com.

DEETS, MICHELLE LOUISE, secondary school educator; b. St. Louis, Oct. 27, 1961; m. John M. Deets, Feb. 20, 1989; 1 child, Alexandria L. BA, Greenville Coll., Ill., 1983; MA, So. Ill. U., Edwardsville, Ill., 1992. Tchr. english Morton (Ill.) H.S., 1983—84; tchr. spanish Highland (Ill.) H.S., 1984—. Coach dance team Highland (Ill.) H.S., 1993—. Mem.: NEA, Ill. Edn. Assn., Highland (Ill.) Edn. Assn. (pres. 1989—2006), Ill. Drill Team Assn. (sec. 2000—06). Home: 9 Burdick Creek Collinsville IL 62234 Office: Highland High School 12760 Troxler Highland IL 62249 Office Phone: 618-654-7131. Personal E-mail: mdeets@highland.madison.k12.il.us.

DEEVES, MARY ELLEN, medical/surgical nurse, nursing administrator; b. New Rochelle, N.Y., June 19, 1953; d. John Edward and Eleanor (Henderson) D. BSN summa cum laude, Tex. Christian U., 1975; MS, Tex. Woman's U., 1980. RN, Tex., Va., Fla; cert. nursing adminstrn., advanced, ANA. Head nurse St. Luke's Episcopal Hosp., Houston, nursing supr., asst. dir. nursing; dir. med./surg. nursing AMI Pk. Pla. Hosp., Houston; asst. dir. med./surg. MCV Hosp., Richmond, Va., dir. med-surg. nursing; dir. critical care/telemetry nursing Manatee Meml. Hosp., Bradenton, Fla.; dir. progressive care nursing Blake Med. Ctr., Brandenton, Fla. Mem. AACN, Am. Orgn. Nurse Execs., Fla. Orgn. Nurse Execs., Sigma Theta Tau. Office Phone: 941-798-6316.

DEFAZIO, LYNETTE STEVENS, dancer, educator, choreographer, violinist, actress; d. Honore and Mabel J. (Estavan) Stevens; children: J.H. Panganiban, Joanna Pang. Student, U. Calif., Berkeley, 1950—55, San Francisco State Coll., 1950—51; studied classical dance tchg. techniques and vocabulary with Gisella Caccialanza and Harold and Lew Christensen, San Francisco Ballet, 1952-56; D in Chiropractic, Life-West Chiropractic Coll., San Lorenzo, Calif., 1983; cert. techniques of tchg., U. Calif., 1985; BA in Humanities, New Coll. Calif., 1986. Lic. chiropracter, Mich.; diplomate Nat. Sci. Bd.; eminence in dance edn., Calif. C.C. dance specialist, std. svcs., childrens ctrs. credentials Calif. Dept. Edn., 1986. Contract child dancer Monogram Movie Studio, Hollywood, Calif., 1938-40; dance instr. San Francisco Ballet, 1953-65; performer San Francisco Opera Ring, 1960-67; performer, choreographer Oakland (Calif.) Civic Light Opera, 1963-70; dir. Ballet Arts Studio, Oakland, 1960; tchg. specialist Oakland Unified Sch. Dist., 1965-80; fgn. exch. dance dir. Academie de Danses-Salle Pleyel, Paris, 1966; instr. Peralta C.C. Dist., Oakland, 1971—, chmn. dance dept., 1985—. Cons., instr. ext. courses UCLA, Dirs. and Suprs. Assn., Pitts. Unified Sch. Dist., 1971-73, Tulare (Calif.) Sch. Dist., 1971-73; rschr. Ednl. Testing Svcs., HEW, Berkeley, 1974; resident choreographer San Francisco Childrens Opera, 1970—. Oakland Civic Theater; ballet mistress Dimensions Dance Theater, Oakland, 1977-80; cons. Gianchetta Sch. Dance, San Francisco, Robicheau Boston Ballet, TV series Patchwork Family, CBS, NYC; choreographer Ravel's Valses Nobles et Sentimentales, 1976. Author: Basic Music Outlines for Dance Classes, 1960, 1965, rev. edit., 1968, Teaching Techniques and Choreography for Advanced Dancers, 1965, Goals and Objectives in Improving Physical Capabilities, 1970, A Teacher's Guide for Ballet Techniques, 1970, Principle Procedures in Basic Curriculum, 1974, Objectives and Standards of Performance for Physical Development, 1975, Techniques of the Ballet School, 1970, rev. edit., 1974, The Opera Ballets: A Choreographic Manual Vols. I-V, 1986; assoc. music arranger: Le Ballet du Cirque, 1964, assoc. composer, lyricist: The Ballet of Mother Goose, 1968; choreographer Valses Nobles Et Sentimentales (Ravel), Transitions (Kashevaroff), 1991, The New Wizard of Oz, 1991, San Francisco Children's Opera (Gingold), Canon in D for Strings and Continuo (Pachelbel), 1979, Oakland Cmty. Orch. excerpts from Swan Lake, Faust, Sleeping Beauty, 1998, Rodeo, Alameda Coll. Cultural Affairs Program, 2000, The Gershwin Dances, 2004, solo dancer Three Stravinsky Etudes, Alameda Coll. Cultural Affairs Program, 1999, appeared in Flower Drum Song, 1993, Gigi, 1994, Fiddler on the Roof, 1996, The Music Man, 1996, Sayonara, 1997, Bye Bye Birdie, 2000, Barnum, the Circus Musical, 2001; musician (violinist): Oakland Cmty. Concert Orch., 1995—; condr.: Gil Gleason, coord.: Oakland Cmty. Orch., 2001—. Bd. dirs. Prodrs. Assocs., Inc., Oakland, 1999—; coord. Oakland (Calif.) Cmty. Orch., 2002—. Recipient Foremost Women of 20th Century, 1985, Merit award San Francisco Children's Opera, 1985, 90. Mem. Calif. State Tchrs. Assn., Bay Area Chiropractic Rsch. Soc., Profl. Dance Tchrs. Assn. Home and Office: 4923 Harbord Dr Oakland CA 94618-2506 Office Phone: 510-547-5477. Personal E-mail: LynetteDeFazio@comcast.net.

DEFEIS, ELIZABETH FRANCES, law educator, lawyer; b. NYC; d. Francis Paul and Lena (Amendola) D. BA, St. John's U., 1956, JD, 1958, JSD (hon.), 1984; LLM, NYU, 1971; postgrad., U. Milan, Italy, 1963-64, Inst. Internat. Human Rights, 1991. Bar: N.Y. 1959, U.S. Dist. Ct. (fed. dist.) 1960, U.S. Dist. Ct. (so. dist.) N.Y. 1961, U.S. Supreme Ct. 1965, U.S. Dist. Ct. (ea. dist.) N.Y. 1978, N.J. 1983. Asst. U. S. atty. So. Dist. N.Y., Dept. Justice, 1961-62; atty. RCA Corp., 1962-63; assoc. Carter, Ledyard & Milburn, N.Y.C., 1963-69; atty. Bedford Stuyvesant Legal Svcs. Corp., 1969-70; prof. law Seton Hall U., Newark, 1971—, dean Sch. Law, 1983-88. Vis. prof. St. Louis U. Sch. Law, 1988, St. John's U. Sch. Law, 1990, 2001, U. Milan, Italy, 1996; Fulbright-Hays lectr., Iran, India, 1977-79; lectr. Orgn. Security and Cooperation in Europe, Russia, Turkmenistan, Tajikistan, Azerbaijan; vis. scholar Ctr. Study of Human Rights, Columbia U., 1989; project dir. TV series Women and Law, 1974-80; narrator TV series Alternatives to Violence, 1981; mem. com. women and cts. N.J. Supreme Ct., 1982-95; trustee Legal Svcs. N.J., 1983-88; mem. 3rd Cir. Task Force on Equality in the Cts., 1995-98; tech. cons. on Constitution of Armenia, 1992-95; project dir. T.V. series Pub. Internat. Law.; legal expert Armenia election OSCE, 1998; disting. chair fulbright program U. Naples, 2002. Chair Albert Einstein Inst., Boston, 1995—2001. Fulbright-Hays scholar Milan, Italy, 1963-64, Fulbright-Hays, Orgn. for Security and Cooperation in Europe scholar, Armenia, Russia, Italy, 1996; Ford Found. fellow, 1970-71. Mem. ABA, Columbian Lawyers Assn., Assn. of Bar of City of N.Y. (chair, spl. com. United Nations, coun. internat. affairs), N.J. Bar Assn., Nat. Italian Am. Found. Office: Seton Hall U Law Sch One Newark Ctr Newark NJ 07102 Business E-Mail: defeisel@shu.edu.

DEFELICE, FRANCES RADOSTA, restaurateur; b. New Orleans, Feb. 7, 1924; d. Pascal Joseph Sr. and Frances (Sansone) Radosta; m. John Parker Airey, Oct. 7, 1945 (widowed); m. Stephen Joseph DeFelice, Mar. 19, 1950. Student, Loyola U., New Orleans, 1942. Owner Pascal's Manale Restaurant, New Orleans, 1942—. Vice chmn. Regional Experimental Opera, 1960; bd. dirs. Loyola U. Dept. Music, New Orleans, New Orleans Opera Assn. Republican. Roman Catholic. Office: Pascals Manale Restaurant 1838 Napoleon Ave New Orleans LA 70115-5540

DEFELICE, LAURA A., lawyer; BA, Tufts Univ., 1981; JD, Columbia Univ., 1984. Bar: NY 1985. Ptnr., co-head structured fin. practice group Latham & Watkins LLP, NYC. Contbr. articles to profl. jours. Named one of 15 Dealmakers of the Year, Am. Lawyer, 2001. Mem.: ABA, NY State Bar Assn. Office: Latham & Watkins Ste 1000 885 Third Ave New York NY 10022-4834 Office Phone: 212-906-1780. Office Fax: 212-751-4864. Business E-Mail: laura.defelice@lw.com.

DEFILIPPIS, GLADYS LLANES, language educator; b. Bklyn., Dec. 20, 1954; d. Angel Luis and Herminia Llanes DeFilippis; 1 child, David John. BS, Queens Coll., Flushing, N.Y., 1980; MA, C. W. Post, N.Y., 1983; SAS, C. W. Post, SDE, 1998. Spanish tchr. St. Dominic HS, Oyster Bay, NY, 1990—96, Hewlett (N.Y.) Woodmere Mid. Sch., 1994—96, Baldwin (N.Y.) HS, 1996—, ESL, fgn. lang. chair, 2005—. Office: Baldwin Sr HS 841 Ethel Kloberg Dr Baldwin NY 11510

DEFLEUR, LOIS B., academic administrator; b. Aurora, Ill., June 25, 1936; d. Ralph Edward and Isabel Anna (Cornils) Begitske; m. Melvin L. DeFleur (div.) AB, Blackburn Coll., 1958; MA, Ind. U., 1961; PhD in Sociology, U. Ill., 1965; HHD (hon.), U. Alaska, 1999. Asst. prof. sociology Transylvania Coll., Lexington, Ky., 1963-67; assoc. prof. Wash. State U., Pullman, 1967-74, prof., 1975-86, dean Coll. Liberal Arts, 1981-86; provost U. Mo., Columbia, 1986-90; pres. Binghamton U., SUNY, 1990—. Disting. vis. prof. USAF Acad., 1976-77; vis. prof. U. Chgo., 1980-81; bd. dirs. Energy East Corp., HealthNow, N.Y. Author: Delinquency in Argentina, 1965; (with others) Sociology: Human Society, 3d edit. 1981, 4th edit., 1984, The Integration of Women into All Male Air Force Units, 1982, The Edward R. Murrow Heritage: A Challenge for the Future, 1986; contbr. articles to profl. jours. Mem. Wash. State Bd. on Correctional Svcs. and Edn., 1974-77, State of N.Y. Edn. Dept. Curriculum and Assessment Coun., 1991-94, Trilateral Task for N.Am. Ednl. Collaboration, USIA, 1993-95. Recipient Disting. Alumni award Blackburn Coll., 1991, Chief Exec. Leadership awrd Coun. for Advancement and Support of Edn., 1999, Civic Leadership award Greater Binghamton C. of C., 2003, Woman of Distinction award Girl Scout Coun., 2002; grantee NIMH, 1969-79, NSF, 1972-75, Air Force Office, 1978-81. Mem. NCAA (pres. commn. 1996, exec. com. 1997-98), Am. Sociol. Assn. (publs. com. 1979-82, nominations com. 1984-86, coun. mem. 1987-90, com. on exec. office and budget), Pacific Sociol. Assn. (pres. 1980-82), Coun. Colls. of Arts and Scis. (bd. dirs. 1982-84, pres. 1985-87), Aircraft Owners and Pilots Assn., Internat. Comanche Soc., Nat. Assn. State U. and Land-grant Colls. (exec. com. 1990-93, chair coun. of pres. 1994-95, chmn. bd. dirs. 1996-97), Am. Coun. Edn. (bd. dirs. 1994-2000, v.p. chair-elect 1997-98, chair bd. dirs. 1998-99), Consortium Social Sci. Assns. (bd. dirs. 1993-96). Office: Binghamton U Office of Pres PO Box 6000 Binghamton NY 13902-6000 E-mail: ldefleur@binghamton.edu.

DEFORD, RUTH I., music educator; b. Lawrence, Kans., Dec. 8, 1946; d. Donald D. DeFord and Leora M. Adams DeFord; m. Mahesh K. Kotecha, Aug. 20, 1977; children: Vicram Cyrus, Vijay Roy. MusB, BA, Oberlin Coll. Conservatory Music, Ohio, 1968; PhD, Harvard U., 1975. Asst. prof. SUNY, Geneseo, NY, 1975—77; prof. Hunter Coll. and Grad. Ctr. CUNY, N.Y.C., 1977—. Contbr. chapters to books, articles to profl. jours. Office: Music Dept Hunter Coll 695 Park Ave New York NY 10021 Office Phone: 212-772-5537. Business E-Mail: rdeford@hunter.cuny.edu.

DEFOTIS, CONSTANCE, choral conductor; b. Chgo., June 22, 1951; d. George Constantine and Aphrodite (Javaras) DeF. BA summa cum laude, U. Ill., 1973, MusM, 1974; DMA, U. Cin., 1988. Dir. choral activities Lake Forest (Ill.) Coll., 1975-77; music dir. Mt. Washington Presbyn. Ch., Cin., 1978-82; chorus/soloist Deutsche Oper Berlin, Germany, 1983-85; domkapellmeisters asst. Chor der St. Hedwigs-Kathedrale, Berlin, 1984-86; dir. Knabenchor der St. Hedwigs-Kathedrale, Berlin, 1984-86; dir. choral activities Vassar Coll., Poughkeepsie, N.Y., 1986-87, Wellesley (Mass.) Coll., 1988—; Fulbright scholar Germany, 1992-93. Alto Rockefeller Chapel Choir, Chgo, 1974-76, Chgo. Symphony Chorus, 1975-77; mezzo soprano Cin. Opera, 1978-82, Cantata Singers, Boston, 1988—; guest conductor Griffin Ensemble, Boston, 1988-91, Cantata Singers, Harvard, Mass., 1992; guest condr. MENC MA Cen. Dist. Chorus, Worcester, Mass., 1990; adjudicator MA ACDA State Choir Contest, Holden, Mass., 1991. Mem. AAUP, Am. Choral Dirs. Assn. (ea. div. repertoire and stds. chair-women's choral music 1993—), Am. Choral Found., Coll. Music Soc., Internat. Fedn. choral Music, Am. Guild Musical Artists, Mass. Arts Coun. (panelist 1993). Avocations: german literature, psychology. Office: WV Univ Dept Music PO Box 6111 Morgantown WV 26506-6111

DE FOX, MARTA SAHAGUN JIMENEZ, First Lady of Mexico; b. Zamora, Mexico, Apr. 10, 1953; d. Alberto Sahagun; m. Manuel Bribiescal, 1971 (div. 2000); 3 children; m. Vicente Fox (president of Mexico), July 2, 2001; 4 stepchildren. Tchr. English La Salle U., Celaya, Konrad Adenauer Found.; mem. Nat. Action Party, Mexico, 1988—, nat. and state party coun. mem., sec. women's polit. promotion Guanajuato, coord. citizen's environ. protection com., candidate for mcpl. pres. city of Celaya; spokesperson Gov. of Guanajuato Vicente Fox, Mexico, 1995—99; pres. sec. Pres. Vicente Fox, Mexico, 2000—01; head social work found. Vamos Mex., 2001—; first lady of Mex., 2001—. Office: Presidencia de la Republica Residencia Oficial de los Pinos Puerta 1 Col San Miguel Chapultepec 11850 Delegacion Miguel Hidalgo Mexico

DEFRANCIS, SUZY, federal agency administrator; Grad., U. Colo. Speechwriter for Nixon Adminstrn., US Senator Robert P. Griffin, US Sec. Interior Rogers C.B. Morton; dep. dir. comm. and Congl. affairs Rep. Nat. Com.; sr. v.p., dir. pub. affairs Peter Novelli; dep. asst. to pres. for comm. Pres. George W. Bush., 2002—05; asst. sec. pub. affairs HHS, 2005—. Office: US Dept Health and Human Services Rm 647-D 200 Independence Ave SW Washington DC 20201 Office Phone: 202-690-7850. Office Fax: 202-690-5673. E-mail: Suzy.DeFrancis@hhs.gov.

DEFRANTZ, ANITA, sports association executive, lawyer; b. Phila., Oct. 4, 1952; d. Robert and Anita DeFrantz. BA in Political Philosophy, Conn. Coll., 1974; JD, U. Penn., 1977; PhD (hon.), U. RI, Pepperdine U., Mills Coll., Mount Holyoke Coll. Atty. Juvenile Law Center of Phila., 1977—79; admin. Princeton U., 1979—81; counsel Corp. for Enterprise Develop., 1980—81; v.p. L.A. Olympic Organizing Comm., 1981—85; pres. Amateur Athletic Found., 1987—. Mem. U.S. Women's Rowing Team, 1975—80; captain U.S. Olympic Women's Rowing Team, Montreal, 1976, mem., Moscow, 80. Recipient Olympic Bronze medal in rowing, 1976, Olympic Bronze medal of the Olympic Order, 1980, Olympic Torch award, U.S. Olympic Comm., 1988, Black Women of Achievement award, NAACP Legal Defense and Ednl. Fund, Martin Luther King Jr. Brotherhood award, L.A. YMCA, 1990, Award of Excellence, Sports Lawyers Assoc., 1992, Turner Broadcasting Trumpet award, 1993, Billie Jean King Contribution award, 1996. Mem.: Internat. Rowing Fed. (v.p. 1993), U.S. Rowing Assoc. (Jack Kelly award 1991), Vesper Rowing Club, S. Calif. Olympian Soc. (former pres.), Kids in Sports (pres.), Internat. Olympic Comm., 1986- (exec. bd. 1992—2001, v.p. 1997—2001). Office: Amateur Athletic Found 2141 W Adams Blvd Los Angeles CA 90018

DEGANN, SONA IRENE, obstetrician, gynecologist, educator; b. Homs, Syria, 1952; d. Papken Stephan and Helen Irene (Wadsworth) Mugrditchian; m. A. David Degann, May 11, 1983; children: Alexander, Seta. BSc, Am. U. Beirut, Lebanon, 1975; MS, U. Mich., 1976; MD, Johns Hopkins U., 1983. Diplomate Am. Bd. Ob-Gyn. Resident in ob-gyn. N.Y. Hosp., N.Y.C., 1983-87, staff. Clin. instr. Cornell U. Sch. Medicine, N.Y.C., attending Ob-Gyn New York Presbyn. Hosp., N.Y.C. Fellow Am. Coll. Ob-Gyn.; mem. AMA, Med. Soc. State N.Y., N.Y. County Med. Soc.

DEGAYNOR, ELIZABETH ANNE, secondary school educator; d. G. Scott and Maxine DeGaynor. BA in English, U. Mich., Ann Arbor, 1993; MA in English, U. Va., Charlottesville, 1996. Chair dept. English The Covenant Sch., Charlottesville, 1996—. Fellow, Nat. Endowment for the Humanities, 2000. Office: The Covenant School 175 Hickory St Charlottesville VA 22902 Office Phone: 434-220-7329.

DEGENER, CAROL M., lawyer; d. John Michael and Marie-Laure Degener. BA magna cum laude, Barnard Coll., Columbia U.; MA, Columbia U., N.Y.C.; JD, Harvard U., Cambridge, Mass. Bar: Mass. 1988, N.Y. 1990. Assoc. corp. fin. Goldman Sachs & Co., N.Y.C., 1987—89; assoc. corp. dept. Donovan Leisure Newton & Irvine, N.Y.C., 1989—95; counsel corp. fin. dept. Seward & Kissel LLP, N.Y.C., 1996—. Office: Seward & Kissel LLP 1 Battery Park Plz Fl 20 New York NY 10004-1405 Business E-Mail: degener@sewkis.com.

DEGENERES, ELLEN, actress, comedienne, talk show host; b. Metairie, LA, Jan. 26, 1958; d. Elliott and Betty DeGeneres. Began career as emcee local comedy club, New Orleans; performer various comedy clubs. Comedian (TV spls.) Young Comedians Reunion, HBO, Women of the Night, 1986, Command Performances: One Night Stand, 1989; author: My Point.And I Do Have One, 1995, The Funny Thing Is., 2003; actor: (films) Coneheads, 1993, Mr. Wrong, 1996, Goodbye Lover, 1998, (voice) Dr. Doolittle, 1998, EDtv, 1999, The Love Letter, 1999, Reaching Normal, 1999, (voice of Dory) Finding Nemo, 2003 (Annie award for Outstanding Voice Acting in Animated Feature Prodn., 2004); writer, dir., actor (films) My Short Film, 2004; actor: (TV films) On the Edge, 2001; (TV series) Open House, 1989, Laurie Hill, 1992; actor, exec. prodr. (TV films) If These Walls Could Talk 2, 2000, (TV series) The Ellen Show, 2001—02, actor, prodr., writer Ellen (originally named These Friends of Mine from 1993-94), 1993—98 (Emmy award for Outstanding Writing for Comedy Series, 1997, Peabody award, 1997), host, exec. prodr. The Ellen DeGeneres Show, 2003— (Best Talk Show, Daytime Emmy award, Nat. Acad. TV Arts and Sciences, 2005, Best Talk Show Host, Daytime Emmy award, Nat. Acad. TV Arts and Sciences, 2005, People's Choice awards, favorite daytime talk show host, 2006, Outstanding Talk Show, Daytime Emmy award, Nat. Acad. TV Arts and Sciences, 2006, Outstanding Talk Show Host, Daytime Emmy awards, Nat. Acad. TV Arts and Sciences, 2006), star, exec. prodr. (TV spls.) Ellen DeGeneres: The Beginning, 2000 (Am. Comedy award for Funniest Female Peformer in TV spl., 2001), Ellen DeGeneres: Here and Now, 2003, co-host 46th Annual Primetime Emmy Awards, 1994 (Am. Comedy award for Funniest Female Peformer in TV spl., 1995), host 53rd Annual Primetime Emmy Awards, 2001, 54th Annual Primetime Emmy Awards, 2002, 57th Annual Primetime Emmy Awards, 2005, 38th Annual Grammy Awards, 1996, 39th Annual Grammy Awards, 1997, VH1 Fashion Awards, 1998, VH1 Divas Las Vegas, 2002, appeared as herself (documentaries) Wisecracks, 1991. Named one of 100 Most Influential People, Time Mag., 2006; recipient Funniest Person Am. for videotaped club performances in New Orleans, Showtime, 1982, Am. Comedy award for Funniest Female Stand-Up Comic, 1991, Golden Apple award as Female Discovery Yr., Hollywood Women's Press Club, 1994, Lucy award, 2000, Enduring Spirit award, Amnesty Internat., 2000, Funny Female Star, People's Choice Award, 2006, Best Television Series or Special (Variety), The Producers Guild of Am., 2006. Office: c/o Creative Artists Agy 9830 Wilshire Blvd Beverly Hills CA 90212*

DE GENNARO, EIDA MENDOZA, interpreter, real estate agent; b. Havana, Cuba, Sept. 21, 1944; arrived in US, 1961; d. Carlos and Aída Mendoza; m. Antimo G. De Gennaro, July 22, 1967; children: Aída Marie, Carl. BA, U. Nebr., 1967, MA, 1976. Fgn. lang. tchr., 1967—83; internat. lang. cons., 1983—; interpreter US Dept. State, Washington, 1983—; real estate agt. Dreamscape Realty, Inc., Aldie, Va., 1999—. Fundraising com. St. Jude Children's Hosp., Memphis, 1992—. Recipient award, US Dept. State, 2002. Mem.: Nat. Assn. Realtors, No. Va. Assn. Realtors. Republican. Roman Catholic. Avocations: reading, swimming. Home and Office: 6312 John Charles Landing Centreville VA 20121 Office Phone: 703-629-3851.

DEGEORGE, GAIL, retired special education educator; b. Englewood, N.J., Nov. 27, 1950; d. Frank Anthony and Bertha (Zwienzska) DeG.; m. Georges Melhim Mouchantaf, May 7, 1981 (div. Jan. 1985); 1 child, Channing Camille DeGeorge. BA, Ariz. State U., Tempe, 1977, MEd, 1986, EdD, 1998. Cert. elem. edn., spl. edn. tchr., prin., Ariz. Spl. edn. tchr. Ariz. Boys' Ranch (Ariz.)-Helamen House, 1977-80, Ariz. State Hosp., Phoenix, 1980-82, Mesa (Ariz.) Pub. Schs., 1982-84; tng. supr. Am. West Airlines, Tempe, 1984-86; spl. edn. tchr. Phoenix Union High Sch., 1986—2001, ret., 2001. Mem. NEA, Ariz. Ednl. Assn., Profl. Women in Edn., Wine Taster's Guild. Republican. Roman Catholic. Avocations: skiing, reading, cooking, decorating. Home: 814 Clarence Stout Ln Mountain City TN 37683

DE GETTE, DIANA LOUISE, congresswoman, lawyer; b. Tachikawa, Japan, July 29, 1957; came to U.S., 1957; d. Richard Louis and Patricia Anne (Rose) De G.; m. Lino Sigismondo Lipinsky de Orlov, Sept. 15, 1984; children: Raphaela Anne, Francesca Louise. BA magna cum laude, The Colo. Coll., 1979; JD, NYU, 1982. Bar: Colo. 1982, U.S. Dist. Ct. Colo. 1982, U.S. Ct. Appeals (10th cir.) 1984, U.S. Supreme Ct. 1989. Dep. state pub. defender Colo. State Pub. Defender, Denver, 1982-84; assoc. Coghill & Goodspeed, P.C., Denver, 1984-86; sole practice Denver, 1986-93; of counsel McDermott & Hansen, Denver, 1993-96; mem. Colo. Ho. of Reps., 1992-96, asst. minority leader, 1995-96; mem. U.S. Congress from 1st Colo. dist., 1997—; mem. commerce com. Editor: (mag.) Trial Talk, 1989-92. Mem. Mayor's Mgmt. Rev. Com., Denver, 1983-84; resolutions chair Denver Dem. Party, 1986; bd. dirs. Root-Tilden Program, NYU Sch. Law, N.Y.C., 1986-92; bd. trustees, alumni trustee Colo. Coll., Colorado Springs, 1988-94. Recipient Root-Tilden scholar NYU Sch. Law, NYC, 1979, Vanderbilt medal, 1982. Mem. Colo. Bar Assn. (bd. govs. 1989-91), Colo. Trial Lawyers Assn. (bd. dirs., exec. com. 1986-92), Colo. Women's Bar Assn., Denver Bar Assn., Phi Beta Kappa, Pi Gamma Mu. Democrat. Avocations: reading, backpacking, gardening.

DEGIOVANNI-DONNELLY, ROSALIE FRANCES, biologist, educator; b. Bklyn., Nov. 22, 1926; d. Frank and Rose (Quartuccio) DeGiovanni; m. Edward Francis Donnelly, Sept. 23, 1961; children: Edward F. Jr., Francis M. BA, Bklyn. Coll., 1947, MA, 1953; PhD, Columbia U., 1961. Adj. prof. microbiology, genetics George Washington U., Washington, 1968—; rsch. biologist FDA, Washington, 1968-88. Contbr. articles to profl. jours. Recipient Merit award FDA, 1970. Mem. AAAS, AAUW, Italian Cultural Soc., Environ. Mutagen Soc., NY Acad. Scis., Am. Soc. Microbiology, McLean Indoor Club, Sigma Xi, Sigma Delta Epsilon. Democrat. Roman Catholic. Avocations: theater, swimming, tennis, travel, photography. Home: 1712 Strine Dr Mc Lean VA 22101-4744 Personal E-mail: edndol@earthlink.net.

DEGNAN, KERI-JENE, science educator; b. Bethpage, N.Y., Apr. 24, 1970; d. Joseph C. and Sheryl D. Scholpp; m. James Broderick Degnan, June 29, 1996; children: James Jr., Emma. B in Environ. Sci., SUNY, Plattsburgh, 1991; M in Hydrogeology, SUNY, Stony Brook, 1993. Cert. tchr. earth sci. N.Y., 1993. Chemist NYtest Environ. Labs., Port Washington, 1991—94; tchr. sci. Woodmere Mid. Sch., NY, 1994—96, Seaford H.S., NY, 1996—. Tchr. at sea, 2001; with NASA, Stennis, Miss., 2000; Maury project Am. Meterol. Soc./USN, Annapolis, Md. Mem.: Sci. Tchrs. Assn. N.Y. State. Avocations: hiking, bicycling, travel. Home: 1319 Lakeside Dr Wantagh NY 11793 Office: Seaford HS 1575 Seaman's Neck Rd Seaford NY 11783 Office Phone: 516-592-4300.

DE GRAMONT, CAROL CARMEL, writer; b. Cin., Dec. 15, 1934; d. A. Gerson and Cyrilla Elaine Carmel; m. Georges Louis de Gramont, Nov. 3, 1961; children: Alexandre, Nina. BA, Sarah Lawrence Coll., 1956; postgrad., U. Cin., 1958. Copywriter Reader's Digest, N.Y.C., 1958—61. Contbr. stories to literary mags. Mem.: Englewood Writers Club. Avocations: theater, films, reading literature, physical fitness. Home: 200 Winston Dr # 509 Cliffside Park NJ 07010

DEGUTIS, LINDA CHRISTINE, adult education educator, epidemiologist, researcher; b. Chgo., Dec. 16, 1953; d. William Joseph and Genevieve (Karons) D.; m. Robert F. Miller, Aug. 16, 1975 (div. Mar. 1983); m. Bruce Fenton Carmichael, Mar. 26, 1988. BS, DePaul U., 1975; MSN, Yale Sch. of Nursing, 1982; DrPH, Yale Sch. of Medicine, 1994. Cert. RN Conn., Ill. Staff nurse Rush-Presbyn. St. Luke's Med. Ctr., Chgo., 1975-78, Yale-New Haven

Hosp., Conn., 1978-81; trauma program coord. Yale Sch. Medicine, New Haven, 1982-91, 92-95; lectr. in surgery Yale Sch. of Medicine, New Haven, 1984-95, asst. prof. sect. of emergency medicine, 1995—2003, assoc. prof. emergency medicine, pub. health, 2003—; trauma coord. Bridgeport (Conn.) Hosp., 1991-92; Robert Wood Johnson Health Policy fellow Office of Senator Paul Wellstone, Washington, 1996-97. Adv. mem. Conn. State com. on trauma; exec. com. mem. Conn. Adv. for Highway Safety, Hartford, Conn., 1995—. Contbr. articles to profl. jours. Founding mem. MADD-New Haven Chpt., 1983; vol. Conn. Spl. Olympic Games, New Haven, 1990-94, Internat. Spl. Olympic Games, New Haven, 1995; pres. Lake Point Condominium Assn. Bd., 1991. Mem. ACS, AAAS, Am. Pub. Health Assn. (exec. bd., chmn. injury control and emergency health svcs. sect.), Am. Trauma Soc., Nat. Assn. for Pub. Health Policy, Soc. Acad. Emergency Medicine. Office: Yale Sch Medicine 464 Congress Ave New Haven CT 06519-1361

DEHART, DEBORAH LEE, private school educator, composer; b. Woodbury, N.J., Nov. 26, 1953; d. John Walter and Doris Ray DeH. Cert. music tchr. K-12 Del., 1977. Theory tchr. dept. chair Wilmington (Del.) Music Sch., 1976—84; mgr. Minikin Opera Co., Wilmington, Del., 1976—80; music tchr. St. Edmond's Acad., Wilmington, 1977—, dept. chair, 2001—; founder, pres., gen. mgr. Shoestring Prodns., Ltd., Wilmington, 1977—; pvt. tchr., 1977—. Author, composer: music theater for youth, 35 titles, 1981—; composer: (commd. works for) Longwood Gardens, Hellenic Soc., Del. Assn. Early Childhood. Mem.: Del. Music Educators Assn., Music Educators Nat. Conf. Avocations: costuming, gardening, travel, history, reading. Office: 705 Brandywine Blvd Wilmington DE 19809

DEHART, KAREN TRAUTMANN, artist, educator; b. Pitts., Nov. 11, 1953; d. Elmer Martin and Jane Anne (Hesse) T.; m. Shannon Dean DeHart, May 23, 1976; children: Allison Anne, Rebekah Ellen, Rachel Elisabeth. AA, Miami U., 1975; BFA summa cum laude, Wright State U., 1991. Art instr. Troy-Hayner Cultural Ctr., Troy, Ohio, 1991-94; artist Troy, Ohio, 1990—; art tchr., 1991—; drawing tchr. Troy Christian Schs., Troy, Ohio, 1991-92; teaching asst. Wright State Univ., Dayton, Ohio, 1993. Exhibition comm. Troy-Hayner Cultural Ctr., 1991—; chmn. Through Our Eyes Exhibit, 1993-95; adj. instr. Wright State U., 1996. One-woman shows include Preble County Fine Arts Ctr., Eaton, Ohio, 1994, The Crandall Gallery Mount Union Coll., Alliance, Ohio, 1995, MacMurray Coll. Art Gallery, Jacksonville, Ill., 2002; exhibited in group shows at Bowery Gallery, N.Y., 1992, Butler Inst., 1994-98, Trumbull Art Gallery, 1994, Mus. Contemporary Art Wright State U., 1991, 97, Dayton Visual Arts Ctr., 1992, 97, Butler Inst. Am. Art, 1993-95, 97-98, Pearl Conard Gallery, 1993-94, Rosewood Art Ctr. Gallery, Kettering, Ohio, 1993, Olin Fine Arts Ctr. Gallery, Washington and Jeffrson Coll., Washington, Pa., 1994, 97, Books & Co., Kettering, 1994, Fine Arts Inst. San Bernardino County Mus., Redlands, Calif., 1994, Evansville (Ind.) Mus. Arts and Sci., 1994, Wichita (Kans.) Ctr. Arts, 1994, Stables Art Gallery, Taos, N. Mex., 1995, Gallery Alexy, Phila., 1996, Hoyt Inst. Fine Arts, New Castle, Pa., 1997, Troy (Ohio)-Hayner Cultural Ctr., 1997, Valdosta State U. Gallery, Valdosta, Ga., 2002; featured in Nexus Mag., 1990, Art Duck, 1989-91, Dayton Daily News, 1992, 98, Alliance Review, 1995. Com. mem. Troy C. of C., 1993; ad hoc mem. Troy-Hayner Cultural Ctr., 1992, chamn. photography exhibit, 1993-95, chmn. sister-city art exchange Troy-Takahashi City, Japan, 1995-96, mem. exhib. com., 1991-96; curriculum com. Troy Christian Schs., 1992-94. Recipient Grumbacher Gold medallion 16th ann. Hoyt Nat., 1997, 26th Nat. Painting Show, 1994, Winsor Newton award Fine Arts Inst., 1994, Evansville Mus. Contemporaries Purchase award, 1994, Jurors Choice award Butler Inst. Am. Art, 1994, Margaret Kaulback award, 1997, Best of Show award Rosewood Art Ctr., 1992, Award of Excellence Edison State C.C., 1989; Spl. Talent scholar Wright State U., 1989-91. Mem. Dayton Visual Arts Ctr., Phi Kappa Phi, Chi Omega. Home and Office: 1498 Cheshire Rd Troy OH 45373-2602

DE HAVILLAND, OLIVIA MARY, actress; b. Tokyo, July 1, 1916; naturalized, 1941; d. Walter Augustus and Lilian Augusta (Ruse) de H. (parents British subjects); m. Marcus Goodrich, Aug. 26, 1946 (div.); 1 child, Benjamin Briggs Goodrich (dec.); m. Pierre Galante, Apr. 2, 1955 (div.); 1 child, Gisele. Student schs. and convent in, Calif.; DHL (hon.), Am. U., Paris, 1994. Made stage debut as Hermia in: Midsummer Night's Dream (Max Reinhardt prodn.), Hollywood Bowl, 1934; 1st motion picture in same role, 1935; actress: (films) including Captain Blood, Anthony Adverse, Robin Hood, Gone With the Wind (nominated for Acad. award 1939), Strawberry Blonde, Hold Back The Dawn (nominated for Acad. award 1941), Princess O'Rourke, To Each His Own (Acad. award for best actress 1946), Dark Mirror, The Snakepit (nominated for Acad. award 1948, N.Y. Critics Award 1948, Laurel Award for best performance 1948-53), The Heiress (Acad. award for best actress 1949, N.Y. critics award), My Cousin Rachel 1952, Not As A Stranger, 1954, Ambassador's Daughter, 1955 (Belgian Critics Prix Femina), Proud Rebel, 1957, Light in the Piazza, 1961, Lady in a Cage, 1963 (British films and filming award), Hush, Hush Sweet Charlotte, 1964, Airport '77, 1976, The Swarm, 1978, The Fifth Musketeer, 1979; TV appearances include Noon Wine, 1966, The Screaming Woman, 1972, Roots: The Next Generations, 1979, Murder is Easy, 1981, Charles and Diana: A Royal Romance, 1982, North and South, II, 1986, Anastasia: The Mystery of Anna, 1986 (Golden Globe award, Emmy nomination), The Woman He Loved, 1988; theatre includes (on Broadway) Romeo and Juliet, 1951, Candida, 1952, A Gift of Time, 1962, (summer stock) What Every Woman Knows, Westport, Conn., Easthampton, Long Island, 1946, Candida, same plus 9 other summer theatres, 1951; (legitimate) Transcontinental Tour Candida 1951-52, (245 Performances); lecture tours, U.S., 1971-80; toured Army and Navy hosps. in U.S., Alaska, Aleutians, South Pacific, 1943-44, Europe, 1957-61; pres. jury Cannes Film Festival, 1965; participant: narration of France's Bicentennial gift to U.S. Son et Lumiere, 1976, Bicentennial Service, Am. Cathedral in Paris, 1976; author: Every Frenchman Has One, 1962. Trustee Am. Coll. in Paris, 1970-71, Am. Libr. in Paris, 1974-81. Recipient Women's Nat. Press Club award for outstanding accomplishment in theater presented by Pres. Truman, 1950; Am. Legion Humanitarian award, 1967 Mem. Screen Actors Guild, Acad. of Motion Picture Arts and Scis. Democrat. Address: BP 156 75764 Paris Cedex 16 France

DEHLE, JUDY JAYE, education educator; d. Francis and Sandra Mabbott; m. Lawrence Dehle; children: Mykah, Karrina, Nikkita. AA, Spokane Falls C.C., 1984; BA in Ednl. Reading and History, Ea. Wash. U., Cheney, 1987. Educator, computer specialist Christ the King Sch., Richland, Wash., 1990—93; educator athletic dir, head coach Spokane Luth. Sch., 1994—96; help desk mgr. Whitworth Coll., Spokane, 1997—99, adj. instr., 1997—, mgr. instrnl. tech. and media, 1999—. Bd. mem. commn. on tech. CCCU, Washington, 2006—. Digital consultant (book) Voices, digital designer Dipped in Chocolate All Over Again, database and layout consultant Primary Source Collections in the Pacific Northwest, digital editor and consultant Lands of True and Certain Bounty. Leader Spokane County 4-H, Spokane, 1993—2006. Named Profl. Tech. Employee of Yr., Whitworth Coll., 1998. Mem.: CCUMC. Office Phone: 509-777-1000. Business E-Mail: jdehle@whitworth.edu.

DEHN, CATHLEEN PATTERSON, health facility administrator; b. Akron, Feb. 25, 1958; d. James Edward and Doris Elizabeth (Boyd) P.; m. James Keith Dehn, June 27, 1981; children: Benjamin Jameson and Alexander Hudson (twins). BSN, U. Akron, 1980; MSN, Case Western Res. U., 1988; MA Applied Psychology, NYU, 1995, postgrad., 1995—. RN, N.Y.; cert. PNP, ANCC. Nurse technician Children's Med. Ctr. Akron, 1979-80, staff nurse, 1980-81; pediatric and advanced clin. nurse, asst. head nurse, clin. nurse specialist Rainbow Babies and Children's Hosp., Cleve., 1981-91, edn. coord., 1991-93; PNP, project coord. divsn. nursing, NYU The Child Health Ctr., Bklyn., 1994-96; PNP dept. pediat. Inst. for Neurology and Neurosurgery Beth Israel Med. Ctr., N.Y.C., 1996-2000; case mgr. dept. pediats. St. Vincent Hosp. and Med. Ctr., N.Y.C., 2001—05, nurse mgr. NICU, pediat. divsn., 2005—. Lectr., clin. instr. Frances Payne Bolton Sch. Nursing, Case Western Res. U., Cleve., 1990-93; mem. adj. faculty divsn. nursing NYU, 1994-96; project coord. Dance Cleve., 1990-91; regional instr. Neonatal Resuscitation Program, Am. Heart Assn., Am. Acad. Pediatrics. Exec. prodr. videos: Getting to Know the Unique Behavioral Capabilities of the Newborn, 1987, One Step at a Time: A Family's Guide to the Neonatal Intensive Care Unit, 1991. Co-founder Sick Kids Need Involved People, Cleve., 1987; team-walk capt. March of Dimes, Cleve., 1989-92 (Edn. grantee 1991); mem. Nat. Mus. Women in Arts. Recipient Samuel E. and Rebecca Elliott award for Cmty. Svc. Case Western Res. U., 1988; named One of Outstanding Young Women of Am., 1988; Fed. Profl. Nurse Trainee scholar, 1986-87. Mem. APA, Am. Ednl. Rsch. Assn., Kappa Delta Pi, Sigma Theta Tau, Pi Lambda Theta. Avocations: health outcomes research, teaching, educational evaluation. Home: 1 University Pl Apt 10L New York NY 10003-4518 Office Phone: 212-604-7875.

DEHOFF, VALERIE S., music educator; d. Robert Ransome and Hazel Story Stone; m. George W. DeHoff, June 29, 1974; children: George W., Robert Stone, David Alan. BA, David Lipscomb Coll., 1974; MEd, Mid. Tenneessee State U., 1981. Lic. profl. tchr. Tenn., 1974. Pvt. piano tchr., Murfreesboro, Tenn., 1974—85; homebound tchr. Rutherford County Schools, Murfreesboro, 1978—79; English tchr. Thurman Francis Jr. H.S., Smyrna, Tenn., 1979—80; music tchr., choral dir. Mid. Tenn. Christian Sch., Murfreesboro, 1984—. Exec. bd. Mid. Tenn. Vocal Assn., Tenn., 2000—. Mem. Minerva Dr. Ch. of Christ, Murfreesboro, 1989—2005. Named Tchr. of Excellence, Tenn. Gov.'s Sch. for the Arts, 1999, 2003. Mem.: DAR, Am. Choral Dir. Assn. (assoc.), Mid. Tenn. Vocal Assn. (assoc.; elem. honors chairperson 2000—05, exec. bd. 2000—), Mid. Tenn. Choral Soc. (assoc.), Womans Club (assoc.). R-Consevative. Avocation: reading. Office Phone: 615-893-0602.

DEHORITY, MIRIAM ARNOLD NEWMAN (MIRIAM NEWMAN), artist; b. Hampton, Ga., Jan. 6, 1928; d. David Johnson and Ethel (Sloan) Arnold; m. William Truslow Newman, Feb. 12, 1954 (dec.); children: David Arnold Newman, William Truslow III Newman; m. Edward Havens DeHority, Jr., Jan. 1, 1984. BA, Agnes Scott Coll., 1949; student, Atlanta Sch. Art, 1953-55, Ga. State U., 1959-60, Chatov Studios, 1961-63. One-woman shows include Water Color Soc. Ala., Mont., 1963 (1st award), Am. Water Color Soc.-Nat. Acad. Galleries, NYC, 1966, Patricia Cloutier Gallery, 2000, 2002, 2 person show, Heath Gallery, Atlanta, 1968, Soc. Fine Arts, Palm Beach, Fla., 1999, Soc. of 4 Arts, Palm Beach., 1999, Patricia Cloutier Gallery, 2002, William Truslow Newman III, exhibited in group shows at Atlanta Art Assocs., 1958—62, High Mus. Art, Atlanta, 1965, 1971, Soc. Contemporary Art, Mobile, Ala., 1969, Mus. Arts and Sci., Macon, Ga., 1972, Heath Gallery, 1972, Swan Coach House Gallery, Atlanta, 1983, 1988, Patricia Cloutier Gallery, Jupiter, Fla., 1992, 1999—2000, 2003, Lighthouse Gallery, Jupiter, 1997, John Collette Gallery, Highland, N.C., 2003, Donna Tribbe Gallery, West Palm Beach, Fla., represented in permanent collections. Founding pres. Members Guild High Mus., Atlanta, 1966; bd. dir. High Mus. Art, Atlanta, 1966-67, Atlanta Arts Alliance, 1966-67, Jr. League of Atlanta, 1958-68. Avocations: gardening, cooking, design, tennis, golf.

DE HOYOS, DEBORA M., lawyer; b. Monticello, N.Y., Aug. 10, 1953; d. Luis and Marion (Kinney) de Hoyos; m. Walter C. Carlson, June 20, 1981; children: Amanda, Greta, Linnea. BA, Wellesley Coll., 1975; JD, Harvard U., 1978. Bar: Ill. 1978, U.S. Dist. Ct. (no. dist.) Ill. 1980. Assoc. Mayer, Brown & Platt, Chgo., 1978—84, ptnr., 1985—, mng. ptnr., 1991—. Bd. dirs. Evanston Northwestern Healthcare; bd. trustees Providence St. Mel. Sch. Contbr. chpt. to Securitization of Financial Assets, 1991. Trustee Chgo. Symphony Orch. Named one of the Ten Most Influential Women Lawyers in Ill., Am. Lawyer Media, 2000, Fifty Outstanding Women Graduates, Harvard Law Sch., 2003. Office: Mayer Brown Rowe Maw Llp 71L S Wacker Dr Chicago IL 60606-4637

DEIBERT, PATRICIA J., biology educator; b. Meadville, Pa., Feb. 24, 1952; d. Harry Eugene and Barbara Wetherbee Eakin; m. Scott Thomas Deibert, Feb. 26, 1977; children: Thomas William, Jonathan Harry. BS in Secondary Edn. Biology, Edinboro U., Pa., 1974; MEd in Psychology, U. So. Calif., Seoul, Korea, 1978; MEd in Ednl. Computing, Cardinal Stritch U., Milw., 2002; postgrad., Silver Lake Coll., Manitowoc, Wis., Marian Coll., Fond du Lac, Wis. Cert. secondary edn. tchr. Wis., SMART master educator, SMART exemplary educator. Pharm. sales rep. Warner/Chilcott Pharm. Co., Morris Plains, NJ, 1979—80, Boehringer Ingelheim Pharm. Co., Ridgefield, Conn., 1980—87; adminstrv. asst. to pastor St. Paul's United Ch. of Christ, Mechanicsburg, Pa., 1987—89; dir. children's ministry First United Luth Ch., Sheboygan, Wis., 1995—96; tchr. H.S. sci. Sheboygan Falls Schs., 1995—. Presenter in field; instr. Summer Tech. Inst. for Educators in Sheboygan County, 2001, 02, 03; pilot WebGrader program, 05. Mem. Football Adv. Panel, 2005; advisor Key Club, 1998—2005; tchr. leader Chemistry in the Cmty., 2006—; WorkBound Educator Advisor to Students, 1999—2000, 2005—06; Stephen min., 1989—. With U.S. Army, 1976—79. Recipient Recognition for tech. innovations, Faculty Assn., 2002, Scholarship award to attend Leopold Workshop, 2004, Scholarship award to attend Biotech. Boot Camp, Sinclair Coll., Dayton, Ohio, 2004, Scholarship award to attend SMART Master Educator Cert. Tng., 2006. Mem.: NSTA, NEA, Wis. Soc. Sci. Tchrs., Nat. Biology Tchrs. Assn., Am. Chem. Soc., Befriender, Beta Beta Beta Biol. Honor Soc. Home: 434 Pine St Sheboygan Falls WI 53085 Office: Sheboygan Falls HS 220 Amherst Ave Sheboygan Falls WI 53085 Office Phone: 920-467-7890. Fax: 920-467-7825. Business E-Mail: pdeibert@sheboyganfalls.k12.wi.us.

DEICHSTETTER, PEGGY ANN, science educator; b. Chgo., Oct. 3, 1948; d. Ervin Anthony and Dorothy Marie (Gneist) Deichstetter; m. Thomas Charles Mott Sr., June 25, 1988; children: Thomas Jr., Christine. AA, Triton C.C., Ill., 1967; BS in Edn., Northern Ill. U., Dekalb, 1969; MEd, Nat. Louis U., Ill., 1975; MSW, Loyola U., Ill., 1982. Cert. tchr. Ill. Biology educator Guerin HS, Rivergrove, Ill., 1970—75, St. Edward HS, Elgin, Ill., 1975—; Einstein fellow Nat. Inst. Health, Bethsada, Md., 2003—04. Cons. Nat. Inst. Health Office Sci. Edn., Bethesda, Md., 2005—06; mentor Ill. State U. Mentor Program, 2005—06. Author various online lesson plans and rsch. papers. Finalist Outstanding Biology Tchr. award, State Ill., 2001—03; recipient Presdl. award, Ill. State Sci. Tchrs., 2005, Elgin Ednl. Leader award, 2006; Einstein Disting. Educator fellow, 2003—04. Mem.: Nat. Academics Adv. Bd., Nat. Sci. Tchrs. Assn., Nat. Assn. Biology Thcrs., Ill. Assn. Biology Tchrs. (v.p. 1971—), Pi Lambda Theta. Roman Cath. Avocations: scuba diving, cake decorating, jewelry making. Home: 4N610 Wescot Ln West Chicago IL 60185 Office: St Edward HS 335 Locust St Elgin IL 60123 Office Phone: 847-741-7536 X 166. Office Fax: 847-741-8658. Personal E-mail: pdeichstetter@yahoo.com.

DEIHL, SUSAN GALYEN, preservationist; b. Columbus, Miss., May 22, 1973; d. James Bruce Galyen, Jr. and Janice Greear Galyen; m. Joshua John Joseph Deihl; children: Cole children: Grayson. BA, U. Va., 1995; M Hist. Preservation, U. Ga., 1998. Intern Hist. Preservation Soc. Durham, 1997; nat. register asst. Paul Hardin Kapp, AIA, Galax, Va., 1997; preservation planner/grants coord. Mass. Hist. Commn., Boston, 1999—2000; asst. to revolving fund dir. Preservation NC, Raleigh, NC, 2000—01. Mem., vol. Preservation N.C., 2001—04; mem. Capital Area Preservation, Raleigh, NC, 2001—04, Va. Hist. Soc., Richmond, Va., 1995—2004, Colonial Williamsburg Found., Williamsburg, Va., 1993—2004, Nat. Trust for Hist. Preservation, Washington, 1990—2004. Mem.: Student Hist. Preservation Soc. (v.p. 1997—98), Nat. Honor Soc. Hist. Preservation. Home: 605 N Bloodworth St Raleigh NC 27604-1227

DEILY, ANN BETH, special education educator, consultant; b. Albany, N.Y., Oct. 16, 1948; d. Ezra Jack and O. Sonya June (Balshan) Sarachan; m. William Edward Deily, Aug. 13, 1972. BA, U. Rochester, 1970; MA, Vanderbilt U., 1971, MS, 1972; PhD, SUNY, Albany, 1977. Speech-lang. therapist Children's Rehab. Ctr., Kingston, NY, 1972-73; pvt. practice Chatham, NY, 1973—; teaching fellow SUNY, Albany, 1974-75; dir. dept./developer Speech Hearing Dept. St. Mary's Hosp., Troy, 1974-77; instr. communication disorders Coll. St. Rose, Albany, 1977-78, asst. prof. communication disorders, 1978-82, assoc. prof., 1982-87, prof., 1987-91; pvt. practice speech-lang. pathology Chatham Ctr., NY, 1989—. Dir. rural edn. grant Coll. St. Rose, Albany, 1983-86; cons. State of N.Y. Dept. Edn., State of Conn. Dept. Edn., Wildwood Sch., Schenectady, N.Y., Bd. Coop. Ednl. Svcs. (Renssalaer-Columbia-Greene, Schenectady-Albany, Saratoga), East Greenbush, Albany, Columbia County Spl. Needs Group, A.B. Deily Cons. Assocs., 1990—, early intervention program Columbia County ARC, Ctr. for the Disabled, Regents Coll., Columbia County Early Intervention and Preschool Svcs. Author: Working with Communication Disorders in Rural Settings, 1987; contbr. 30 articles to profl. jours. Founder Capital Area Network for Rural Speech-Lang. Pathologists, 1985; co-founder Capital Dist. Computer Users Group in Speech-Lang. Pathology, 1989, Columbia-Greene Rape Crisis Ctr. (edn. and tng. com., coord. com. 1981). Mem. ASTD (mem. exec. bd. Hudson-Mohawk chpt., membership chair), Am. Speech-Lang.-Hearing Assn. (nat. site visitor, nat. computer tutor, nat. faculty-teleconf.), Am. Coun. Rural Spl. Edn. (editorial rev. bd.), AG Bell Assn. for Deaf (editorial rev. bd.), Capital Area Speech and Hearing Assn. (disting. svc. award), Computer Users in Speech Hearing (pres.), Coun. Exceptional Children, Ind. Computer Consulting Assn. (cap. region), Helping Hands Preschool (bd. dirs., Hugs award). Home: 128 Merwin Rd Valatie NY 12184-4404

DEILY, LINNET FRAZIER, former ambassador; b. Dallas, June 20, 1945; d. William Harold and Ruth (White) Frazier; m. Myron Bonham Deily, Apr. 18, 1981. BA, U. Tex. Austin, 1967; MA, U. Tex. Dallas, 1976. Banking officer, asst. v.p., v.p. Republic Bank, Dallas, 1975—80, sr. v.p., 1980—81; v.p. First Interstate Bancorp, L.A., 1981—83; sr. v.p., divsn. mgr. First Interstate Bank of Calif., L.A., 1983—84, exec. v.p., 1988; chmn., pres., CEO First Interstate Bank of Tex., 1988—96; pres. Schwab Institutional, 1996—98, Schwab Retail Group, 1998—2001; vice chmn. Charles Schwab Corp., 2000—01; dep. US Trade Rep. Exec. Office of the Pres., Washington, 2001—05. Bd. dirs. First Interstate Inst., L.A., Lucent Tech. Inc., 2005—, Chevron Corp., 2006—. Mem.: Univ. Club L.A. (fin. com.).

DEINES, BETHANY A., fraternal organization administrator; b. Denver, Jan. 17, 1968; d. Arthur E. and Joan B. Deines. BS, Ariz. State U., Tempe, 1990. Supr. Ariz. State U. Telefund, Tempe, 1987—90; asst. branch mgr. Reese Brothers, Inc., Phoenix, Tempe, 1991—92; asst. panmellenic adv., asst. residence hall dir. Ariz. State U., Tempe, 1992—93; exec. dir. Sigma Sigma Sigma, Woodstock, Va., 1993—97; dir. devel. Phi Kappa Tau Found., Oxford, Ohio, 1997—. Publ. v.p. Sigma Sigma Sigma, 2004—; chmn. Assn. Fraternity Advisors Found., Indpls., 2002—; chpt. adv. Gamma Phi Beta, Oxford, 1998—2005. Mem.: Fraternity Exec. Assn., Assn. Fraternity Adv., Assn. Fundraising Profl., Oxford Rotary Club. Avocations: travel, music, home improvements. Home: 438 Marcia Ave Hamilton OH 45013 Office: Phi Kappa Tau Found 5221 Morning Sun Rd Oxford OH 45056 Office Phone: 513-523-4193. Office Fax: 513-524-4812. Business E-Mail: badeines@phidappatau.org.

DE IORIO, LUCILLE THERESA, retired social worker; b. Utica, N.Y., Mar. 7, 1926; d. Patsy and Elizabeth (Graziano) De I. BA, Syracuse U., 1949, MSW, 1969. Cert. social worker, N.Y. Caseworker Oneida County Dept. Social Svcs., Utica, 1952—65, case supr., 1965-90, tng. supr., 1969-70, dir. staff devel., 1970—2005; ret., 2005. Mem. NASW, Acad. Cert. Social Workers, N.Y. State Assn. for Human Svcs., Staff Devel. Assn. N.Y. State. Republican. Roman Catholic. Avocations: writing, doll collecting. Home: 1306 Sherman Dr Utica NY 13501-5313

DEIOTTE, MARGARET WILLIAMS TUKEY, nonprofit consultant, grants writer; b. Lafayette, Ind., Mar. 6, 1952; d. Ronald B. and Elizabeth A. (Williams) Tukey; m. Charles E. Deiotte, Sept. 11, 1971 (dec.); children: Raymond, Karl, Ronald. Student, U. Wash., 1969-72, 77-79. V.p., treas. Logical Systems, Inc., Colorado Springs, 1982-86; v.p. CEDSYS, Inc., Colorado Springs, 1987-92; pres. Penrose Enrichment Program Found., Colorado Springs, Colo., 1988-89; free lance tech. and grant proposal writer, 1990—; dir. Unicity, Boca Raton, Fla., 1994—. Conf. coord. Colo. Assn. Ptnrs. in Edn., 1994; editor Am. Boarding Kennels Assn., 1995-98; owner Outside The Box, 1996—; grant writing trainer, 2001—; project design cons., 2002—; facilitator spl. edn. adv. com. Sch. Dist. 11, 2005; pres., bd. dirs. Colo. Legends and Legacys Youth Corps, 2005—; presenter in field. Mem. adv. bd. gifted and talented Sch. Dist. 11, 1989—, mem. dist. II found. bd., 1997—2004, OS/CR adv. coun. dist. II, 1999—2001; pres. Penrose Elem. PTA, 1989—91; 1st v.p. El Paso Coun. PTA, 1990—91, treas., 1991—92; mem. grants commn. Colo. State PTA, 1990—91; coach Odyssey of the Mind, 1990, 1991—92, 1995—96; mem. dist. accountability com. Sch. Dist. 38, 1993—94; accountability chmn. Lewis-Palmer Mid. Sch.; mem. gifted and talented com. Sch. Dist. # 38; mem. parent bd., internat. baccalaureate Palmer High Sch., Colorado Springs, Colo., 1994—97, treas., 1995—96, pres., 1996—97; bd. dirs. YMCA Youth Leadership Inst., 1990—92, 1992—93, Ind. Cmty. Partnership, 2001—, Start to Achieve Charter Acad., 2005—. Mem.: Assn. Fundraising Profls. Home and Office: 1221 Mount View Ln Colorado Springs CO 80907-4722 Office Phone: 719-592-1831. E-mail: outsidethebox@adelphia.net.

DEISSLER, MARY ALICE, foundation executive; b. Oneonta, NY, Dec. 30, 1957; d. George W. and Carol (Zorda) Baker; m. James N. Deissler, Nov. 24, 1987; children: Benjamin, Eliza. BA, U. Mass., 1978; MBA, Babson Coll., 1982. Fin. analyst Digital Equipment Corporation, Maynard, Mass., 1978-82; devel. dir. Handel & Haydn Soc., Boston, 1984-89, gen. mgr., 1984-89, exec. dir., 1990—. Pres., bd. dirs. Studebaker Movement Theatre Co., Boston, 1986-88. Bd. dirs. Early Music Am., N.Y.C., 1989—, v.p., 1991—, pres., 1994; bd. dirs. Babson Coll., 1990-94, Chorus Am., 1991—, v.p., 1992, pres.-elect, 1996, pres., 1997, pres. bd. dirs., 1997; mem. bd. Arts/Boston, 1994—, pres. bd. dirs., 2003; bd. dirs. Am. Composers Fourm, 2000, chair, 2004—; bd. dirs. Berkshire Choral Soc., 2000—; treas. Handel House of Am. Found. Mem. Am. Symphony Orch. League. Office: Handel & Haydn Soc 300 Massachusetts Ave Boston MA 02115-4544 Business E-Mail: mdeissler@handelandhaydn.org.

DEITERS, SISTER JOAN ADELE, psychoanalyst, nun, chemistry professor; b. Cin., Apr. 28, 1934; d. Alfred Harry and Rose Catherine (Rusche) Deiters. BA, Coll. Mt. St. Joseph, Cin., 1963; PhD, U. Cin., 1967; M in Christian spirituality, Creighton U., Omaha, 1985. Joined Sisters of Charity, Roman Cath. Ch., 1952; cert. psychoanalyst, Westchester Inst. for Tng. in Psychoanalysis and Psychotherapy, 2000. Prof. chemistry Coll. Mt. St. Joseph, Cin., 1969-78; Matthew Vassar Jr. chair Vassar Coll., Poughkeepsie, NY, 1978-96. Contbr. articles to profl. jours. Mem. Am. Chem. Soc., Sisters of Charity, Sigma Xi; Nat. Assn. for Advancement of Psychoanalysis. Home: 10 Drouilhet Ln Apt 2 Poughkeepsie NY 12603 Office: 39 Collegeview Ave Poughkeepsie NY 12603-2415 Office Phone: 845-485-4920.

DEITZ, PAULA, magazine editor; b. Trenton, NJ, Apr. 26, 1938; d. David and Rosalie (Nathanson) Deitz; m. (George) Frederick Morgan, Nov. 30, 1969 (dec. Feb. 2004). BA, Smith Coll., Northampton, Mass., 1959, LHD (hon.), 2006; MA, Columbia U., NYC, 1969. Asst. editor Bollingen series Bollingen Found., N.Y.C., 1962-67; assoc. editor The Hudson Rev., N.Y.C., 1967-75, co-editor, 1975-98, editor, pres., 1998—. Rsch. asst. Pakistan Mission to UN, N.Y.C., 1961; lectr. Columbia U., N.Y.C., 1962. Contbr. articles on art, architecture, landscape design to newspapers and mags. Bd. counselors Smith Coll., 1992-96. Mem. Cosmopolitan Club, Colony Club, Century Assn. Avocation: swimming. Office: The Hudson Rev 684 Park Ave New York NY 10021-5043

DEITZ, SUSAN ROSE, advice columnist, writer; b. Far Rockaway, NY, Mar. 21, 1934; d. Emanuel and Florence Jean (Goodstein) Davis. Student, Smith Coll., Barnard Coll., N.Y.C., Art Students League, Stella Adler Theater Studio. Advice columnist L.A. Times Syndicate, 1975-2000; syndicated columnist Creators Syndicate, 2000—. Faculty New Sch., N.Y.C., 1977-79; radio host, 1979; singles expert Prodigy Svcs., White Plains, N.Y., 1987-93; spkr. satellite conf. NAFE, 1990; lectr. L.A. Times Syndicate Spkrs. Bur.; guest expert iVillage.com. Author: Valency Girl, 1976, Single File, 1989, paperback edit., 1990. Honored Single Parent Resource Ctr., N.Y.C., 2001. Mem. Women in Comm. (Outstanding Member award 1984), Authors Guild, Newspaper Features Assn., Overseas Press Club (elect.), Smith Coll. Club. Business E-Mail: info@creators.com.

DEJACK, JACQUELINE ELVADEANA, artist, educator; b. St. Louis, Oct. 9, 1938; d. John Allen and Margie Louise (Cooksey) Williams; m. James Patrick DeJack (dec. June 1994); children: Jennifer Lynn, John Patrick. Student, St. Louis U, 1966-67, Webster Coll., 1978-79; AA, East Ctrl. U., 1979; student, U. Mo., 1998. Lic. real estate agt., Mich.; cert. broker sales and tchr. broker, Mo. Sales staff Hudsons Dept. Store, Detroit, 1957; with First Fed. Savs., Detroit, 1961-62; cons. to libr. dir. St. Louis U., 1965-66; bank cons., ins. mgr. Willston (Mo.) State Bank, 1967-68; co-founder, broker, cons. Tri County Real Estate, Pacific, Mo., 1971-89; pvt. practice artist and writer Jacqueline's Affordable Graphics, Pacific, Mo., 1993-2001; pvt. practice broker, sales, 2001—. Fine art tchr., cons. Six Flags Over Mid-Am., Eureka, Mo., summer 1982; cons. wedding portraits. Supr. youth corp. St. Louis U., 1964; bd. mem. U. Mo., St. Louis, 1980; mem. Sears (Mich.) Writer's Guild, 1987. Mem. Cadillac Artis Guild, Phi Theta Kappa. Avocations: writing, art, history research, music, swimming. Personal E-mail: zippburrd@yahoo.com.

DEJARNATT, KITTY M., special education educator; b. Ogden, Utah, Mar. 3, 1947; d. Dean Ward Minson and Kitty Colleen Carr; m. Paul DeJarnatt, Nov. 28, 1964; children: Shalae Michelle, Stephenie Ann Dietz, Shawn Paul, Sheri Sue Giles, Stephen Ward, Sheryl Lynn, Shauna Leigh, Shannon Deane, Scott Thomas. BS in spl. edn., Utah State U., Logan, 1986—94, BS in psychology, 1986—94. Special Education (Severe) Teacher Certification Utah State Bd. of Edn., 1994. Spl. edn. tchr. (severe) Davis H.S., Kaysville, Utah, 1994—99, Davis Sch. Dist. STEPS Program, Farmington, Utah, 1999—. Mandt trainer Davis Sch. Dist., Farmington, 1996—2003, autism team mem., 1998—, transition manual com. mem., 2002—04, spl. edn. graduation com., 2002—04, spl. edn. mentor, 2001—03, Utah spl. edn. program improvement planning sys. interview com., Farmington, 2004—05; best buddies advisor Davis H.S., 1996—99, U. of Utah, 2000—01; spl. edn. para-educator Box Elder Sch. Dist., Garland, 1988—94; presenter in field. Mem.: NEA, Utah Edn. Assn., Davis Edn. Assn. (area rep. 2002—04), Coun. for Exceptional Children (sec./treas. 1997—2000). Republican. Mem. Lds Ch. Achievements include instrumental in development of transition program for students with severe disabilities from the ages of 18 to 22 years. Avocations: travel, crocheting, painting. Business E-Mail: kdejarnatt@dsdmail.net.

DEJOIE, CAROLYN BARNES MILANES, educator; b. New Orleans, Apr. 17; d. Edward Franklin and Alice Philomena (Milanes) Barnes; children: Deirdre, Prudhomme III, Duan. MA, Universidad Nacional de Mexico, Mexico City, 1962; MSW, U. Wis., 1970; PhD, Union U., Cin., 1976. Cert. psychotherapist, Wis. Instr. So. U., Baton Rouge, 1962-63; asst. prof. Va. State Coll., Norfolk, 1963-66; asst. to pres. U. Wis. Sys., Madison, 1970-73, prof. adult edn. U. Wis., Madison, 1973—; fgn. lang cons., Mexico City, 1960-62; pvt. practice psychotherapy, 1980—; bd. dir. Human Rels. Counseling Svc., 1980—; owner Sun and Shadows Pub. Co., 1987; exec. dir. Organ. Hispana Americana, 1974-75; spl. con. on crime prevention, Nassau, Bahamas, 1985; dir. Secutar Humanism, Madison, Wis., 1995; appointed mem. Wis. Bd. Bar Examiners, 2004. Author: Students Speak Out: Racial Problems and What Students Can Do About Them, 1988; mem. adv. editl. bd. Jour. of Negro Edn., 1985—, Negro Ednl. Rev., 1988; editor: Readings from a Black Perspective, 1984, Racism-Sexism: The Interlock of Racist and Sexist Problems, 1986, Wisconsin Minority Women's Perspectives on Women's Issues, 1989; author book of poetry, 1980; producer, hostess TV show Innervisions Sta. WYOU, Madison, 1987, 88; contbr. articles to scholarly jours. Mem. adv. bd. Madison Met. Schs. Human Rels. Coun., 1975-85; mem. exec. bd. Madison chpt. ACLU, 1978-80, Coun. Minority Pub. Adminstrs., Madison, 1980-82; bd. dirs. Dane County Mental Health (Wis.), 1980-82; mem. exec. bd. NAACP. Recipient Recognition award Va. State Coll., 1962, Outstanding Woman award Zeta Phi Beta, 1975, Black Women: Achievements Against the Odds award Wis. Humanities Com., 1983, Gov.'s Spl award State of Wis., 1984, Appreciation award Madison Met. Sch. Dist., 1984, Outstanding Contbn. to Soc. award Alpha Kappa Alpha, 1984, Recognition of Svc. award Nat. Assn. Negro Bus. and Profl. Women, 1986, laudatory resoultion Bd. Commrs. Genessee County, Mich., 1986, Appreciation award City of New Orleans, 1987, Unsung Heroine award NAACP, 1988, La. Black Heritage citation Etches of Ebony La. calendar 1990, Dollars and Sense award, 1991, cert. Recognition of Achievement, Emerita State U., Madison, Wis., 1992; Fulbright scholar, 1966-67. Mem. AAUP, AAUW, Nat. Assn. Media Women (Woman of Yr. 1985, Golden Egg Appreciation award 1987, Cert Recognition for Achievement of Emeritus Dir., 1992), Nat. Assn. Social Workers, Assn. Black Psychologists, Assn. Women in Psychology, Nat. Congress Black Faculty, Links. Home: 5322 Fairway Dr Madison WI 53711-1039 Office: 610 Langdon St Madison WI 53703-1104

DEJUNEAS, PATRICIA ANN, lawyer; b. Elizabeth, NJ, Mar. 4, 1969; d. James Vincent and Patricia Mary Dejuneas. BS magna cum laude, Sacred Heart U., 1993; JD with high honors, U. Conn., 1996. Bar: Conn. 1996, Mass. 2001, US Dist. Ct. (Dist. Mass.) 2002, US Dist. Ct. (Dist. Conn.) 2002, US Ct. Appeals (1st Cir.) 2003. Law clk. to Hon. E. Eugene Spear Conn. Appellate Ct., 1996—97; law clk. to Hon. Donna F. Martinez US Dist. Ct. (Conn.), Hartford, 2000—02; assoc. Shipman & Goodwin, Hartford, Conn., Day, Berry & Howard LLP, Boston, Law Offices of Richard M. Egbert, PC, Boston. Mem.: Mass. Criminal Def. Lawyers Assn. Office: Law Offices of Richard M Egbert Ste 1800 99 Summer St Boston MA 02110-1251 Office Phone: 617-737-8222. Office Fax: 617-737-8223.*

DE KANTER, ELLEN ANN, retired English and foreign language educator; b. Spokane, Wash., Mar. 10, 1926; d. George L. and Alison P. (Christy) Tharp; m. Scipio de Kanter, Feb. 2, 1949 (dec.); children: Scipio, Georgette, Robert, Adriana. BA, Mexico City Coll.-U. of Ams., 1947; MEd, U. Houston, 1972, MA in Spanish, 1974, EdD, 1979. Dir. bilingual edn. U. St. Thomas, Houston, 1979—2005; ret., 2005. Editor Tex. Assn. Bilingual Edn. Jour., 2004-05; Contbr. articles to profl. jours. 11 Tchr. Tng. grants undergrad. and grad. students, U. St. Thomas, 1986—2004. Mem. Nat. Assn. Bilingual Edn. (chmn. conf. 1989, program chmn. conf. 1993), Houston Area Assn. Bilingual Edn. (pres. 1987-88), Inst. Hispanic Culture (bd. dirs. 1989-90). Home: 3015 Meadowview Dr Missouri City TX 77459-3308 E-mail: dekanter@stthom.edu.

DEKIEFFER, KITTY, volunteer; b. San Diego, Nov. 12, 1956; d. Robert Paul and Beverly Ann Cannon; m. Robert Coffin deKieffer, May 18, 1985; 1 child, Hunter Coffin. BA in Acctg., Calif. State U., Fullerton, 1979. Fin. mgr. NREL, Golden, Colo., 1981-84; asst. contr. Boulder (Colo.) Daily Camera, 1984-89; acctg. mgr. Career Track, Boulder, 1989-91. Hon. trustee Boulder Philharm. Orch., pres., 1991—96; dir. Humane Soc. Blair Valley, pres., 1995—96; treas. Fran Ravanbush for Senate, Boulder, 1996; dir. YWCA Boulder County, pres., 1996—; trustee Womens FO of Colo., 1996—; dir. FO for Boulder Valley Schs., sec. and devel. chair and endowment chair, 1998—2002; vol. Douglas Elem. Sch., 1994—2000, Platt vol., 2000—03; dir. Women in the Wilderness Inst., 2000—, pres.; project team Boulder County Attention Homes; fundraising chair Boulder Cmty. Hosp. Aux.; capital campaign chair YWCA Boulder County, 2000—04, Peak to Peak chpt., 2003—; trustee Boulder County Mental Health Found., 2003—04; com. mem. Cmty. for Devel.; treas. Trinity Luth. Ch., 1997—99. Recipient Women Who Light Up Cmty. award Boulder C. of C., 1997, Vol. award 2000 Pacesetter of Boulder County, award Channel 9 (NBC) 9 Who Care, 2000. Mem.: Alpha Chi Omega (past officer and current trustee of AXR Found.). Republican. Lutheran. Home: 3002 Melissa Ln Boulder CO 80301-4841

DEKLYEN, MICHELLE, psychologist; b. Great Falls, Mont., May 31, 1945; d. Charles Linse DeKlyen and Harriet Loraine Thomas; m. Jerome Leslie Silbergeld, June 27, 1970; children: David Silbergeld, Emily Silbergeld. BA, Stanford U., 1967; MA, U. Oreg., 1972; PhD, U. Wash., 1992. Lic. psychologist Wash.; N.J. Dir. Student/Parent Coop. Day Care, Seattle, 1977—80; coord., clinic dir. Presch. Families Project, Seattle, 1987—97; clin. instr. psychiatry U. Wash., Seattle, 1992—97; attending clin. psychologist Children's Hosp. and Regional Med. Ctr., Seattle, 1997—2001; clin. and acting asst. prof. psychiatry U. Wash., Seattle, 1998—2001; assoc. dir. rsch. Inst. Infant and Presch. Mental Health, East Orange, NJ, 2003—05. Rschr., vis. faculty Princeton (N.J.) U., 2001—. Contbr. articles to profl. jours. Recipient Dissertation Rsch. award, APA, 1990, Dir.'s prize, Clin. Psychiat. Internship, U. Wash., 1992; grantee Fragile Families Newark, Fund for N.J., 2004—, Schumann Fund N.J., 2005, Healthcare Found. N.J., 2005—. Mem.: APA, World Assn. Infant Mental Health (mem. N.J. bd. 2005—), Soc. Rsch. Child Devel., Internat. Soc. Rsch. Child and Adolescent Psychopathology. Office: Princeton U 288 Wallace Princeton NJ 08544 Office Phone: 609-258-6977.

DE KRETSER, MICHELLE, writer; b. Colombo, Sri Lanka; arrived in Australia, 1972; Studied French, U. Melbourne, Australia; MA, U. Sorbonne, Paris. Former sr. editor Lonely Planet. Founding editor Australian Women's Book Rev., 1989—92. Author: The Rose Grower, 1999, The Hamilton Case, 2004 (Commonwealth Writers Prize for S.E. Asia and South Pacific Region, 2004, Encore Prize, Brit. Soc. Authors, 2004). Office: Little, Brown & Co 1271 Ave of the Americas New York NY 10020

DEKREY, PETRA JEAN HEGSTAD, retired elementary school educator; b. Oakland, Calif., May 27, 1944; d. Lorentz Reginald and Hazel Dorothy (Danielson) Hegstad; m. Curtis Wayne Martel, Apr. 30, 1966 (div. 1989); children: Christopher W. Martel, Peter L. Martel, Loren R. Martel; m. Donald DeKrey, July 13, 2002. BS in Elem. Edn. and German, Concordia Coll., Moorhead, Minn., 1966; MS in Elem. Edn., Bemidji (Minn.) State U., 1989. Cert. German, elem. edn., reading cons., remedial and devel. reading tchr. K-12, Minn. 2d grade tchr. Rice Creek and Hayes Elem. Schs., Fridley, Minn., 1966-72; chpt. 1 reading tchr. Chief Bug-O-Nay-Ge-Shig Sch., Cass Lake, Minn., 1986-92; tchr. English, reading Rochester (Minn.) Pub. Schs., 1992-93; student newspaper advisor Moorhead (Minn.) Jr. HS, 1993—2001, Chpt. I reading tchr. English, reading, 1993—2004; tchr. 8th grade reading Horizon Mid. Sch., Moorhead, Minn., 2004—05; ret., 2005. Mem. lic. com. Dist. 152, 2000—02. Vol. den mother Cub Scouts, Bismarck, N.D., 1976-77; vol. com. to establish kindergarten Bismarck Pub. Schs., 1974-75; vol. com. to help refugees relocate Bismarck, 1976; vol. Bemidji Sch. System, 1985; vol. Northland Regional Hosp., Bemidji, 2006—. Mem.: NEA, Minn. Edn. Assn., Internat. Reading Assn., Minn. Reading Assn. (sec. 1993—2002), Northland Reading Coun. (pres. 1985—86, honor coun. 1986), Kappa Delta Pi. Avocations: skiing, golf, music, art, travel. Home: 1902 Lakeview Dr Bemidji MN 56601

DE LACERDA, MARIA ASSUNÇAÕ ESCOBAR, retired social worker, consultant; b. Cedros, Faial, Portugal, Aug. 15, 1944; came to U.S., 1948; d. Antonio Garcia de Lacerda and Filomena Escobar de Lacerda. BA in Polit. Sci., U. R.I., 1966; MSW, U. Conn., 1972. Social worker R.I. Dept. Social and Rehab. Svcs., 1969-78, supr., 1978-81, R.I. Dept. for Children and Their Families, 1982; supr. div. retardation and devel. disabilities R.I. Dept. Mental Health, Retardation and Hosps., 1982-90; social worker cons. Alternatives Inc., North Kingstown, R.I., 1990-92, Avatar, Inc., Warwick, R.I., 1992-97. Vol. Peace Corps, Paraguay, 1966-69; pres. bd. dirs. East Bay Community Mental Health Ctr., Barrington, R.I., 1982-85; mem. R.I. Coun. for Mental Health Ctr., 1982-85; chair phonathon U. R.I. Ann. Fund, 1988. Recipient Profl. Recognition award Ocean State Assn. Residential Resources, 1990. Mem. U. R.I. Alumni Assn. (sec. 1990-91). Democrat. Roman Catholic. Avocations: reading, gardening, bicycling, travel. E-mail: mdelacerda@aol.com.

DELACOUR, JONELL, music educator; b. St. Joseph, Mo., Jan. 14, 1952; d. John David and Nellie Mae Roberts; m. Michael Gene Delacour, Nov. 8, 1975; 1 child, Jerad William. B in Music Therapy, U. Kans., 1974; MAT, St. Mary Coll., Leavenworth, Kans., 2002. Music therapist Larned (Kans.) State Security Hosp., 1975—83; paraprofl. Larned Sch. Dist., Garfield, 1983—90; vocal music tchr. United Sch. Dist. 447, Cherryvalle (Kans.) Mid./High Sch., 1991—2000; vocal/gen. music tchr. United Sch. Dist. 446, Independence (Kans.) Mid. Sch., 2000—. Accompanist children's choir Ind. Area, 2002—05. Bd. dirs. Independence Area Childrens' Choir, 2001—03. Mem.: Music Educators Nat. Conf., Kans. Choral Dirs. Assn., Kans. Music Educators Assn. (state tri-m chair 1999—2002, S.E. dist. ms choral chair 2001—03, S.E. dist. pres.-elect 2003—05, S.E. dist. pres. 2005—, SE Dist. Middle Sch. Outstanding Tchr. 2000). Office: Independence Middle Sch 300 W Locust Independence KS 67301 Office Phone: 620-332-1836. E-mail: jdelacour@indyschools.com.

DELACRETAZ, CHERYL DIANE, English educator; b. Garden City, Kans., Jan. 8, 1949; d. Lee Roy and Billie Juanita (Howard) Hollingsworth; m. James Larry DeLacretaz, Jan. 22, 1970; children: Nathan, Vanessa, Ryan. BA in Edn., Northeastern State Coll., Tahlequah, Okla., 1971. Lifetime Tex. cert. tchr. Yoga and aerobics instr. Seminole Jr. Coll., Okla., 1979-82; tchr. English, algebra, phys. edn. Seminole Ind. Schs., 1980-85; tchr. English, dept. head Andress H.S. in El Paso Ind. Sch. Dist., Tex., 1985—97; tchr. English dept. head Dripping Springs HS, Tex., 1997—. Dist. staff devel. and insvc. presenter El Paso Ind. Sch. Dist., 1989-97; chairperson English dept. Andress H.S., El Paso, 1990-97, mem. campus improvement com., 1991-97; mem. Tex. state steering com. Coll. Bd., S.W. region, Austin, Tex., 1992-95; cons. Coll. Bd. Advanced Placement Inst., 1998—. Author Advanced Placement English Curriculum, 1992, (dist. staff devel. modules) Writing With Computers II, 1993, Writing With Computers III, 1996, (workshop module) New Teacher Orientation, 1990. Rep. U.S. tchrs. and students in Hiroshima, Japan at 50th anniversary of dropping of A bomb People to People Internat., 1995. Named One of Top Ten H.S. Tchrs. in Tex., U. Tex. Ex-Students Assn., Austin, 1991, Tex. State Humanities Tchr. of Yr., Tex. Humanities Coun., Austin, 1993; recipient Advanced Placement Recognition award S.W. Region Coll. Bd., Austin, 1996, 2005. Mem. Nat. Coun. Tchrs. English, People-to-People Internat. Office: Dripping Springs HS 111 Tiger Lan Dripping Springs TX 78620

DE LA CRUZ, CARLOS, wholesale distribution executive; b. Havana, Cuba; arrived in Miami, 1975; m. Rosa de la Cruz; 5 children. BS, U. Pa., 1962, MBA in fin., 1963; JD, U. Miami Sch. Law, Fla., 1972. Car dealership exec.; chmn. Eagle Brands, Coca-cola Bottlers, PR, Trinidad and Tobago. Co-founder Cuba Study Group; co-chmn. Mesa Redonda. Named one of top 200 art collectors, ARTnews Mag., 2004; recipient Silver Medallion Brotherhood Award, Nat. Conf. of Christians & Jews, Distinguished Svc. Award, Fla. Internat. U., Social Responsibility Award, Urban League, Alexis de Tocqueville Award for outstanding philanthropy, United Way, 1997, Simon Weisenthal Ctr. Nat. Cmty. Svc. Award, 1998. Achievements include becoming first hispanic chmn. United Way (1990) & U. Miami Bd. Trustees (1999). Avocation: collector of contemporary art, especially Latin Am. Mailing: 5 Harbor Pl Key Biscayne FL 33149-1715

DE LA CRUZ, ROSA, art collector; b. Havana, Cuba; m. Carlos de la Cruz; 5 children. Co-founder Moore Space, Fla., 2001. Curator (exhibitions) THAT PLACE, Moore Space, 2002. Named one of top 200 collectors, ARTnews Mag., 2004; recipient Alexis de Tocqueville Award for outstanding philanthropy, United Way, 1997, Simon Weisenthal Ctr. Nat. Cmty. Svc. Award, 1998. Mem.: Mus. Contemporary Art N. Miami, Miami Art Mus. (aquisition com.), Mus. Contemporary Art Chgo. (exhibitor com.). Avocation: collector of contemporary art, especially Latin Am. Mailing: 5 Harbor Pl Key Biscayne FL 33149-1715 E-mail: rdelacr@aol.com.

DELAGARDELLE, LINDA, food executive; b. Waterloo, Mar. 15, 1953; d. Donald Leo D. and Leona Ann Reuter. AA in Biotechnology, Ellsworth C.C., Iowa Falls, Iowa, 1992; BS in Agronomy, Iowa State U., 1994. Owner, operator dairy farm, Jesup, Iowa, 1979-86; barber, stylist Kathy's Barber Shop, Alden, Iowa, 1986-94; rsch. lab asst. USDA, Ames, Iowa, 1992-94; intern Pioneer Hi-Bred Int., Kekaha, Hawaii, 1995; asst. agronomist Hudson (Iowa) Co-op, 1995-96; area supr. Seneca Foods Corp., Glencoe, Minn., 1996—. Carver scholar, 1992, Transfer scholar, 1992; Pell grantee, 1992. Mem. Nat. Rep. Com., 1996—; co-chair Children's Christmas Party, Glencoe, 1996-98; vice-chair Employee Fund Com., Glencoe, 1996-98; mem. United Fund Com., Glencoe, 1996-98. Mem. Glencoe C. of C. (annual banquet com.), Glencoe Country Club. Roman Catholic. Avocations: golf, biking, skiing, organ. Home: 210 Pleasant Ave Glencoe MN 55336

DELAHANTY, LINDA MICHELE, dietician; b. Boston, Feb. 8, 1957; d. John Joseph and Helen Mary (Salami) D.; m. Paul Joseph Gorski, June 14, 1987. BS summa cum laude, U. Mass., 1978; MS summa cum laude, Boston U., 1980. Adminstrv. dietitian Joslin Diabetic Camp, Charlton, Mass., 1978; nutritional research asst. Lemuel Shattuck Hosp., Jamaica Plain, Mass., 1979; nutrition educator Home Med. Service-Univ. Hosps., Boston, 1980, Boston City Hosp., 1980-81; clin. dietitian Mass. Gen. Hosp., Boston, 1981-88, nutrition counselor, 1988—; rschr. Mass. Gen. Hosp. Diabetes Ctr., Boston, 1983—, chief dietitian, dir. nutrition and behavioral rsch., 2003—. Nutrition coord. Diabetes Control and Complications Trial, NIH, 1987—93, co-investigator Diabetes Prevention Program, 1996—2002; co-investigator LOOK AHEAD (Action for Health in Diabetes), 1999—, Today Study - Treatment Options for Type 2 Diabetes in Adolscents and Youths, 2002—; cons. New Eng. Diabetes and Endocrinology Ctr., Brookline, Mass., 1985—86; panelist NIH Consensuc Devel. Conf., Bethesda, Md., 1986, Am. Diabetes Assn. Consensus Statement on Self Monitoring of Blood Glucose, 1993; expert panelist TV series Doctors on Call, 1997; assoc. lectr. Harvard U. Geriatric Edn. Ctr., 1984—89; instr. Med. Sch. Harvard U., Cambridge, 2002—. Mem. editl. bd. Diabetes Spectrum, 1994-96, Diabetes Forecast, 2001-03, Jour. Am. Dietetic Assn., 2002—; contbr. articles to profl. jours. Recipient Charles H. Best Disting. Svc. medal Am. Diabetes Assn., 1994, Rschrs. award Am. Dietetic Assn., 1998, Mary P. Huddleston award, 2002, First Author award Rsch. Dietetic Practice Group, 2003, Diabetes Care and Edn. Pubs. award, 2004, Annie Galbraith award Outstanding Dietitian Mass., 2004; named Young Dietitian of Yr. Am. Dietetic Assn., 1984. Mem. Mass. Area Rehab. Dietitians (co-chair 1983-84), Diabetes Care and Edn. Practice Group (sec. 1985-87), Mass. Gerontol. Nutrition Practice Group (chair 1984-85), Mass. Dietetic Assn. (chair community dietetics div. 1983-84, coun. on practices), Am. Dietetic Assn. (area coord. gerontol. nutrition and dietetic practice group 1988-90, Rsch. Excellence award 2005). Roman Catholic. Avocations: skiing, photography, travel. Home: 18 Saybrook Rd Framingham MA 01701-7835 Office: Mass Gen Hosp Diabetes Ctr 50 Staniford St Ste 340 Boston MA 02114-2620 E-mail: ldelahanty@partners.org.

DELAHANTY, REBECCA ANN, school system administrator; b. South Bend, Ind., Oct. 18, 1941; d. Raymond F. and Ann Marie (Batsleer) Paczesny; m. Edward Delahanty, June 22, 1963; children: David, Debbie. BA, Coll. of St. Catherine, Minn., 1977; MA, Coll. St. Thomas, Minn., 1983; PhD, Ga. State U., 1994. Cert. in adminstrn. and supervision Ga. Initiator, tchr. gifted kindergarten Dist. 284 Sch., Wayzata, Minn., 1977-83; gifted kindergarten coord. St. Barts Sch., Wayzata, 1983-85; prin. Dabbs Loomis Sch., Dunwoody, Ga., 1987-91; asst. to supt. Buford (Ga.) City Schs., 1993-98, supt., 1998-99; prof. Ga. State U., 1999-2000; ednl. cons., 2000—; adv. bd. U. Saint Thomas, Coll. Edu., 2001—. Staff devel. adv. coun. Ga. Contbr. Mem. adv. bd. Coll. Edn. U. St. Thomas, 2001—. Mem.: ASCD, Minn. Coun. Gifted and Talented, Minn. Assn. Gifted Children, Nat. Assn. Gifted Children, Am. Ednl. Rsch. Assn., Omicron Gamma, Phi Delta Kappa. E-mail: beckydelah@aol.com.

DELANEY, ANNA T., director; b. Phila., May 5, 1963; d. John Ennis S. and Mary Agnes Schmidt; m. Daniel Robert Delaney, June 21, 1985; children: Daniel Robert Jr., Erin Rose. BS, St. John's U., Phila., 1985; postgrad., West Chester U., Pa. Dept. asst. Macy's Inc., Mays Landing, NJ, 1987—89; mgr. Nutri/Sys., Inc., Northfield, NJ, 1990—92, Paoli, Pa., 1992—93; office mgr. Leo J. McCormick, D.C., Wayne, Pa., 1993; sr. sec. to vice dean edn. Office Acad. Programs U. Pa. Sch. Medicine, Phila., 1994—95, adminstrv. coord. I, 1995—96, adminstrv. coord. III, 1994—98, assoc. dir. curriculum office, 1998—2000, dir., chief adminstrv. officer, 2000—. Office: U Pa Sch Medicine 3450 Hamilton Walk Philadelphia PA 19104 Office Phone: 215-898-8091.

DELANEY, BARBARA SNOW, retired editor; d. Raymond Charles and Alma Hopson Snow; m. Edmund Thomas Delaney (dec. 2000); stepchildren: Christopher, Nicholson. BA, Conn. Coll., New London, 1944. Editorial asst. Antiques Mag., N.Y.C., 1947—70, mng. editor, 1947—70; ret., 1970. Author: History of Chester Historical Soc- From Meeting House to Mill, 2005; contbr. articles to Antiques Mag. Mem. Conn. River Mus., 1970—; pres. Rockfall Found., 1990—94; ptnr. Chester Gallery, Conn.; mem. bd. of fin. Town of Chester, Conn., 1980—89; mem. River Estuary Planning Agy. Chester Dept. Conservation, 1980—89, Chester Watershed Project, 1994—97, Chester Vision Commn., 1994; bd. mem. Mcpl. Arts Soc., N.Y.C., 1950—59. Recipient Alumnae medal, Conn. Coll., 1998. Mem.: Conn. Trust Hist. Preservation (sec., incorporator 1975, bd. mem. 1975—80), Nat. Trust Hist. Preservation, Conn. Land Trust, Chester Historical Soc. (pres. 1990—96, honoree, tree planting on Chester Meeting House Green 1990). Democrat. Avocations: reading, landscape planning, cooking.

DELANEY, KIM, actress; b. Phila., Nov. 29, 1961; 1 child, Jack. Appeared in (TV series) All My Children, 1981-84, 94, Tour of Duty, 1987, The Fifth Corner, 1992, NYPD Blue, 1995-2001 (Emmy award 1997), Philly, 2001, CSI: Miami, 2002, 10.5: Apocalypse, 2005 (TV movies) First Affair, 1983, Perry Mason: The Case of the Sinister Spirit, 1987, Cracked Up, 1987, Christmas Comes to Willow Creek, 1987, All My Darling Daughters, Please Take My Daughters, 1988, Something Is Out There, 1988, The Broken Cord, 1992, Lady Boss, 1992, Closer and Closer, The Disappearance of Christina, 1993, Tall, Dark, and Deadly, 1995, Tall Dark and Deadly, 1995, All Lies End in Murder, 1997, The Devil's Child, 1997, Love and Treason, 2001, (films) That Was Then.This Is Now, 1985, The Delta Force, 1986, Hunter's Blood, 1987, Campus Man, 1987, The Drifter, 1988, Hangfire, 1991, Body Parts, 1991, The Force, 1994, Inferno, Darkman II: The Return of Durant, 1994, Dark Goddess, 1994, Serial Killer, 1995, Project: Metalbeast, 1995, Closer and Closer, 1995., Mission to Mars, 2000. Avocations: biking, swimming, working out, watching films. Office: care The Gersh Agy attn Bob Gersh 232 N Canon Dr Beverly Hills CA 90210-5302 also: care Melissa Prophet Mgmt 1041 N Formosa Ave Los Angeles CA 90046 also: CSI Miami Prodn Office El Segundo Studios 2265 E El Segundo Blvd El Segundo CA 90245

DELANEY, MARGARET L., academic administrator; BS in Chemistry summa cum laude, Yale U., 1977; PhD, MIT, 1983. Rsch. scientist Scripps Instn. Oceanography, LaJolla, Calif., 1983—84; asst. prof. marine scis. U. Calif., Santa Cruz, 1983—90, assoc. prof. marine scis., 1990—96, prof. ocean scis., 1996—, interim exec. vice chancellor, provost, 2004—. Mem. U.S. Adv. Com. to the Ocean Drilling Program, 1996—, mem. exec. com., 1998—. Editor: Paleoceanography, 1996; mem. editl. rev. bd.: Marine Geology, 1991—. Fellow: Am. Geophysical Union (mem. com. on paleoceanography 1990—94, 1996—); mem.: Soc. for Sedimentary Geology, Oceanography Soc., Geochemical Soc., Assn. for Women Geoscientists (Outstanding Educator award 1993), Sigma Xi. Office: Interim Campus Provost and Exec Vice Chancellor 280 McHenry Libr Univ Calif Santa Cruz CA 95064

DELANEY, MARIA CISSY, elementary school educator; d. Guadalupe and Carlota Garcia; children: Jonathan Michael, Zachary Michael. BS, S.W. Tex. State U., San Marcos, 1986. Tchg. asst. Sarah Ring Elem. Sch., San Antonio, 1976—80, Irving Mid. Sch., San Antonio, 1979—80, Tafolla Mid. Sch., San Antonio, 1980—84; tchr. Connell Mid. Sch., San Antonio, 1986—88; tchr. math and sci. Tafolla Mid. Sch., San Antonio, 1989—. Bd. pres. Our Lady of Perpetual Help Sch., Selmia, Tex., 1996—99. Recipient Edward's Aquifer Outstanding Tchr. award, 2005. Mem.: NEA, Tex. State Tchrs. Assn. Home: 4810 Bohill San Antonio TX 78217 Office: Tafolla Middle School 1303 W Durango San Antonio TX 78207-3935

DELANEY, MARION PATRICIA, retail executive; b. Hartford, Conn., May 20, 1952; d. William Pride Delaney Jr. and Marian Patricia (Utley) Murphy. BA, Union Coll., Schenectady, N.Y., 1973. Adminstrv. asst. N.Y. State Assembly, Albany, 1973-74; account exec. Foote, Cone & Belding, N.Y.C., 1974-78; sr. account exec. Dailey & Assocs., L.A., 1978-81; pub. rels. cons. NOW, Washington, 1981-83; account supr. BBDO/West, L.A., 1983-85; v.p. Grey Advt., L.A., 1985-87, San Francisco, 1987-89; sr. v.p. McCann-Erickson, San Francisco, 1989-95; sr. v.p., dir. advt./mktg. comms. Bank of Am., San Francisco, 1995-99; cons. Brand Strategy, 1999—2000; mng. dir. doodlebug LLC, San Anselmo, Calif., 2001—. Bd. dirs. Marin Art and Garden Ctr. Del. Dem. Nat. Conv., San Francisco, 1984; bd. dirs. JED Found., Hartford, Conn., 1989—, Easter Seals Soc., Bay Area, 1995-97. Mem. NOW (v.p. L.A. chpt. 1980-83, pres. 1984, advisor 1985-87), Marin Assn. Female Execs., Contemporary Ceramics Studio Assn., Am. Splty. Toy Retailers Assn., Craft and Hobby Assn., Toy Industry Assn., Marin Soc. Artists, Marin Needle Arts Guild, San Anselmo C. of C. (bd. dirs.).

DELANEY, MARY ANNE, retired theology studies educator; b. Waltham, Mass., Feb. 15, 1926; d. Thomas Joseph and Mary Teresa (Berry) D. BA, Regis Coll., 1953; MEd, U. Mass., Boston, 1973; MDiv, Andover Newton Theol. Sch., Newton Ctr., Mass., 1978. Tchr. various schs., Mass., 1953-73; pastoral counselor Boston City Hosp., 1974-76; dir. pastoral care Cape Breton Hosp., Sydney River, N.S., Canada, 1978-81, Nova Scotia Hosp., Dartmouth, 1981-86, Misericordia Hosp., Edmonton, Alta., Canada, 1986-91; pastoral counselor Assn. Pastoral Edn., Waltham, Mass., 1992-96, Emmanuel Coll., Boston, 1996—2001; supr. pastoral edn. Leland Retirement Home, Waltham, 1992—2001; ret., 2001. Vice chair bioethics consultative svc. Misericordia Hosp., Edmonton, 1987-91; vis. scholar Andover Newton Theol. Sch., 1991-92. Trustee Pastoral Inst., Halifax, N.S., Can., 1981-86; mem. commn. on ecumenism Archdiocese of Halifax, 1982-86; mem. of the Congregation of Sisters of St. Joseph, Boston, 1945—. Mem. Can. Assn. Pastoral Edn. (cert. com. 1987-91), Assn. for Clin. Pastoral Edn. (cert. supr., accreditation com. 1993-98, cert. com. 1998-2001). Roman Catholic. Avocations: international travel, classical music, art.

DELANEY, PAMELA DELEO, foundation administrator; b. Providence, May 14, 1947; d. Raymond S. and Anna A. Santulli DeLeo; m. Carroll J. Delaney Jr., Sept. 12, 1970; 1 child, Carroll J. III. BA, Newton Coll., Mass., 1969; MA, Rutgers U., 1970; M in Philosophy, Columbia U., 1978. Dept. sec., asst. to police commr. N.Y.C. Police Dept., 1971-80, dir. civilian programs, 1980-83; pres. N.Y.C. Police Found., 1983—. Chmn. N.Y.C. Civilian Complaint Review Bd, 1974-83; mem. N.Y.C. cmty. Bd., 1998-02.

DELANEY, SHARON ELIZABETH, elementary school educator; b. N.Y.C., May 2, 1957; d. Richard Martin and Florence Philomena (Cappiello) D.; m. Manuel Carmelo Delgado, Aug. 9, 1986; 1 child, Francis Aaron Delgado. BS, St. John's U., 1979, Diploma Adminstrn. and Supervision, 1994; MA, Manhattan Coll., 1982. Cert. tchr. nursery and elem., reading N.Y., tchr. N-6, reading tchr. Tchr. elem. Good Shepherd Elem. Sch., N.Y.C., 1979-82, Intermediate Sch. 174, Bronx, 1983-90, dean of students, 1990—, asst. prin., 2005—, Cmty. Sch. 152, 1990—. Den leader Pack 159 Boy Scouts Am., Bronx, 1993—. Mem. ASCD. Roman Catholic. Avocations: needlepoint, reading. Office: Eugene T Maleska Sch 174 456 White Plains Rd Bronx NY 10473-2211

DELANEY-LAWRENCE, AVA PATRICE, secondary school educator; b. Knoxville, Tenn., Apr. 12, 1960; d. William J. and Lena (Guilford) Delaney; 1 child, Brian. BS, U. Tenn., 1982; MA, Clark Atlanta U., 1994. Cert. English tchr. grades 7-12, Ga., Tenn.; Leadership cert., 2000. Substitute tchr. Knoxville City Schs., 1982; English tchr. Chattanooga (Tenn.) City Schs., 1982-85, Atlanta Pub. Schs., Therrell H.S., 1985-99, Booker T. Washington H.S., 1999—; instr. edn. curriculum Clark Atlanta U., 1997—2002. Testing cons. R&R Evaluations, Decatur, Ga., 1985-87; ednl. cons. Harris Learning Sys., Atlanta, 1988-2000. Mem. Nat. Assn. Educators, Nat. Coun. Tchrs. English, Zeta Phi Beta. Home: PO Box 724373 Atlanta GA 31139-1373

DE LANGE, TITIA, research scientist, educator; BA, MS, U. Amsterdam, PhD in biochemistry; MS, Nat. Inst. Med. Rsch.; PhD in biochemistry, Netherlands Cancer Inst.; postdoctoral fellow, U. Calif., San Francisco, 1989; doctorate (hon.), U. Utrecht. Asst. prof. Rockefeller U., NYC, 1990—94, assoc. prof., 1994—97, prof., 1997—99, Leon Hess prof. and head lab. cell biology and genetics, 1999—. Recipient Rita Allen award, 1995, Burroughs Wellcome Fund Toxicology Scholar award, 1997, Cancer Rsch. award, NY Cmty. Trust, 1997, Sr. Scholar award, Ellison Med. Found., 2000, Paul Marks Prize, Meml. Sloan Kettering Cancer Ctr., 2001, AACR Women in Cancer Rsch. Charlotte Friend Meml. Lectureship, 2004, Dir.'s Pioneer Award, NIH, 2005. Mem.: Dutch Royal Acad. Scis., NAS (assoc.). Office: Rockefeller Univ 1230 York Ave New York NY 10021*

DELANOIS, CYNTHIA SUE, elementary school educator; b. Danville, Ill., Apr. 8, 1951; d. Keith and Rosedna (Winkler) Snider; m. Arthur David Delanois, Apr. 9, 1977; 1 child, Jason Orrick. A in Applied Sci., Danville Area CC, 1986; BS in Edn., Ea. Ill. U., 1987, M in Edn. and Guidance Counseling, 1991. Computer lab tchr. Westville Cmty. Schs., Ill., 1989—91, second grade tchr., 1991—95, first grade tchr., 1995—96, kindergarten tchr., 1996—2000, first grade tchr., 2000—03, second grade tchr., 2003—04, guidance counselor, 2004—06. Mem. profl. devel. units com. Westville Cmty. Schs., 2002—04, peer mediation coord., 2002—06. Author: (children's book) Tidbit, 1986. Santa's anonymous Westville Cmty. Schs., 2004—05, advocate for children in need, 2004—05. Recipient Golden Apple award Excellence in Edn., 1998; Ill. Power grant, Ill. Power Co., 1997, 2003. Mem.: Kappa Delta Pi. Avocations: reading, bicycling, swimming, antiques. Home: 1410 English St Westville IL 61883

DELAP, MIRIAM ANNE, music educator; b. Wichita, Kans., Jan. 9, 1944; d. Ewald William and Norine Bertha (Scar) Nath; m. David Frank, Jr. DeLap, Dec. 21, 1968; children: David William, Lora Colleen. BA, MA, Wichita State U., Kans., 1966. Cert. elem. tchr. Kans., 1966. Tchr. Wichita (Kans.) Sch. Dist. McLean Elem., 1966—68; 6th grade tchr. Anchorage (Alaska) Sch. Dist. Nunaka Valley, 1969—71; 5th and 6th grade tchr. Lake Otis Elem., Anchorage, 1971—73, classroom tchr., 1983—. Prin. bassist Anchorage Symphony Orch., 1969—2004; adj. faculty bass tchr. U. Alaska, Anchorage, 1996—; instr. record for Anchorage Sch. Dist., Alaska, 1997—; adj. faculty music edn. Alaska Pacific U., 2004—. Recipient Oustanding Alaska Music Educators, Alaska Music Educators Assn., 2000, Tchr. of Excellence award, Brit. Petroleum Exploration Inc., 2000. Mem.: Alaska Orff Schulwerk (v.p. 1997—99), Am. Orff Schulwerk Assn., Music Educators Nat. Conf. Achievements include Created Miss Mimi's Music Room, thirty minute music program for preschool children, for sch. dist. TV channel in Anchorage. Office: Lake Otis Elem Sch 3331 Lake Otis Pkwy Anchorage AK 99508 E-mail: delap_miriam@asdk12.org.

DELAPA, JUDITH ANNE, business owner; b. Bad Axe, Mich., Feb. 1, 1938; d. John Vincent and Ellen Agatha (Peters) McCormick; m. James Patrick DeLapa, Jan. 10, 1959; children: Joseph Anthony, James P. II, John M., Gina M. BS, Mich. State U., 1959, MA, 1985. Tchr. various schs., Mich., 1959-64; co-founder Saluto Foods Corp., Benton Harbor, Mich., 1963-76; founder Earthtone Interiors, St. Joseph, Mich., 1977-82, High Impact Coaching and Cons. Inc., Grand Rapids, Mich., 1987—. Mktg. rsch. and mgt. cons., writer various clients, nationwide. Author: High-Impact Business Strategies, 1993, The McCormick-DeLapa Family Cookbook, 1997, A Place Called Ireland, 2000, Was That Really Us God?, 2001. Past vice chair exec. bd. Grand Rapids Symphony Orch.; bd. dirs., pres. The Samaritan Found.; bd. dirs. Grand Rapids Art Mus.; trustee Mich. Colls. Found. Judith A. DeLapa Perennial Garden named in her honor Mich. State U. Avocations: reading, travel, theater. Office: High Impact Coaching & Cons Inc 2505 E Paris Ave SE Ste 195 Grand Rapids MI 49546 E-mail: jdelapa@high-impact.com.

DE LA PAZ, LUCIA, social worker, consultant; b. N.Y.C., Dec. 27, 1960; d. William and Leocadia De La Paz. BS in Edn., SUNY, Old Westbury, 1982; MSW, Fordham U., 1988. Cert. in theory and practice of psychotherapy; lic. social worker Bd. Edn., N.Y.C. Caseworker, supr. Adminstrn. for Children's Svcs., Jamaica, N.Y., 1985-90, tng. devel. specialist, 1990-95, child welfare specialist supr., 1995-96; med. social worker Med. Assistance Program, N.Y.C., 1995-97, Montefiore Home Health Agy., Bronx, N.Y., 1995-99; cons. Local 371 Union, N.Y.C.; asst. dir. tng. dept. N.Y.C. Children's Svcs., 2004—. Mem. NASW, Coalition of Labor Union Women, Labor Coun. for Latin Am. Advancement, Old Westbury Alumni Assn. Avocations: travel, swimming, reading. Office: NYC Adminstrn for Children's Svcs 92-31 Union Hall St Jamaica NY 11433 Office Phone: 718-262-3385.

DELAPLAIN, LAURA ZULEME, psychologist; b. Berkeley, Calif., Oct. 2, 1955; d. James Lisle Jr. and Mary Kathryn (Hickman) D.; m. Donald Richard Zook; children: Nathan Walker Delaplain-Zook, Joshua David Delaplain-Zook. BA, U. Wis., 1977; MDiv., Garrett-Evang., 1981; PhD, Boston U., 1989. Lic. psychologist, Mass.; ordained minister United Meth. Ch., 1980. Clin. fellow Danielsen Inst. for Psychotherapy, Boston, 1984-86; pastor United Meth. Ch., Swampscott, Mass., 1984-88, Hingham, Mass., 1988-90; interim pastor United Ch. of Christ in Abington, Mass., 1990-91; clin. psychologist Beechwood Counseling Svcs. Inc., Quincy, Mass., 1988—98; exec. dir. Norma Kent Pastoral Counseling Ctr., Abington, 1986—. Author: Cutting a New Path, 1997. Named Danielsen fellow Boston U., 1984-86, Johnson Teaching fellow Boston U., 1986-87. Diplomate Am. Assn. Pastoral Counselors. Avocations: running, creative writing, flute. Home: 16 Copeland Tannery Dr Norwell MA 02061-2837 Office: Norma Kent Ctr 10 Bedford St Abington MA 02351-2441 Office Phone: 781-871-2051 ext. 201. Business E-Mail: laura.delaplain@verizon.net.

DELAPP, TINA DAVIS, retired nursing educator; b. LA, Dec. 18, 1946; d. John George and Margaret Mary (Clark) Davis; m. John Robert DeLapp, May 31, 1969; children: Julia Ann, Scott Michael. Diploma, Good Samaritan Hosp., Phoenix, 1967; BSN, Ariz. State U., 1969; MS, U. Colo., Denver, 1972; EdD, U. So. Calif., 1986. Health aide instr. Yukon-Kuskokwim Health Corp., Bethel, Alaska, 1970-71; asst. prof. nursing Bacone Coll., Muskogee, Okla., 1972-74; instr. nursing Alaska Meth. U., Anchorage, 1975-76; prof. nursing U. Alaska, Anchorage, 1976—84, assoc. dean nursing, 1984—92, dir. Sch. Nursing, 1996—2004, emeritus prof., 2004—. Mem. Alaska Bd. Nursing, 1989-92. Mem. editl. adv. bd. Jour. Nursing Edn., 2004—; contbr. articles to profl. jours. Treas. Atlanta Nurses Found., 2004—. Named Legend of Nursing, Alaska March of Dimes, 2004. Fellow: We. Acad. Nursing; mem.: Alaska Nurses Found. (treas. 2004—), Am. Assn. Colls. Nursing (mem. nominating com. 2003, task force 2003—04, emeritus 2005), Nat. League for Nursing Accreditation Comn. (program evaluator 1986—, eval. review panel mem. 2000—05), We. Inst. Nursing (chair program com. 1994—95, sec.-treas. 1995—2005, gov.-at-large 2005—, Jo Elinor Elliott Leadership award 2002, Anna Shannon Mentorship award 2006), Sigma Theta Tau (pres. chpt. 1986—88, v.p. 1988—93, counselor 1995—2000). Office Phone: 907-786-4580. Personal E-mail: tdelapp@ak.net.

DE LARIOS, DORA, artist; b. LA, Oct. 13, 1933; d. Elpidio and Concha (Martinez) De L.; 1 child, Sabrina. BFA, U. So. Calif., 1957. Tchr. ceramics UCLA, 1979, U. So. Calif., L.A., 1959; curator 1st internat. ceramic exhbn., L.A., 1988. Ceramic artist, commd. work for site specific areas, including Montage Resort and Spa, Laguna Beach, Calif., 2003; over 40 major works located in Tahiti, Hawaii, Japan, N.J., Fla., pvt. residential projects. Democrat. Avocations: reading, collecting cook books, cooking, drawing edwin the rabbit. Studio: 8560 Venice Blvd Los Angeles CA 90034-2549 Office Phone: 310-839-8305. Personal E-mail: delarios@comcast.net.

DE LA RIVA, MYRIAM ANN, artist; b. Mexico City, Mex., Oct. 8, 1940; arrived in U.S., 1989; d. Adolfo De La Riva and Marianne Kayser; m. Conrado Gallegos, Feb. 26, 1961; children: Conrado Bernardo, Aileen, Eugenio Eduardo. Grad. Fine Arts, IberoAm. U.; student, Kent State U., U. Femenina Mex., Master Carlos Orozco Romero Studio, Master Gilberto Aceves Navarro Studio. V.p. World Coun. Visual Artists, Mexico City, 1994—96; bd. dirs. Mus. Americas; coord. Artists Libr. European Cmty., 2003; coord. Mex. cultural month Latin Am. Art Mus., Miami, 2004; coord., creator World Trade Ctr., Veracruz, 2004. One-woman shows include over 42 internat. shows, 1988—2006, exhibited in group shows at including over 500 internat. shows, 1988—2006, prin. works include mural Today XX first Century. Vol. Tamayo Contemporary Art Mus., Mexico City, 2000—04, Munal Mus., San Carlos, 2000—02; mem. Miami Art Mus., 1991—2004, Nat. Mus. Women in Arts, 1991—2004, Global Culture Ctr., 1991—98. Named Hon. Mention Women in the Arts, Latin Am. Art Mus., Fla., 1994; recipient 1st prize, Sor Juana Found. Mex.-Lebanon Inst. Cultural, 1998, 3d prize, Francisco Goitia prize, 1994, Francisco Goitia prize, Ateneo del Anahuac, 1991, 1992. Mem.: Assn. Artac Aiap-Unesco, Soc. Mex. de Artistas Plasticos, Mex. Fine Artists Salon. Office: Delariva Bosque de Guayacanes #57 11700 Mexico City Mexico Personal E-mail: delarivamyriam@hotmail.com.

DELATEUR, BARBARA JANE, medical educator; b. Hoquiam, Wash., Nov. 17, 1936; Student, Marylhurst (Oreg.) Coll., 1954-56; BS in Philosophy, St. Louis U., 1959; MD, U. Wash., 1963, MSc, 1968. Diplomate Am. Bd. Phys. Medicine and Rehab.; lic. physiatrist, Wash., Md. Rotating intern U. Hosp., U. Wash., 1963-64, resident dept. phys. medicine and rehab., 1964-67; instr. dept. phys. medicine and rehab. U. Wash. Sch. Medicine, 1967-68, asst. prof., 1968-71, assoc. prof., 1971-76, prof. dept. rehab. medicine, 1976-93; prof., dir. dept. phys. medicine and rehab. Johns Hopkins U. Sch. Medicine, Balt., 1993—2003, Lawrence Cardinal Shehan chair phys. medicine and rehab., 1993—2003, joint prof. health policy & mgmt. Sch. Hygiene & Pub. Health, 1994—; acting physiatrist-in-chief Rehab. Medicine Svc. Harborview Med. Ctr., Seattle, 1970-72, physiatrist-in-chief, 1972-93; dir. Muscular Dystrophy Clinic Meml. Hosp., Yakima, Wash., 1979-88; dir. dept. phys. medicine and rehab. Johns Hopkins Hosp., Balt., 1993—2003; med. dir. dept. rehab. medicine Good Samaritan Hosp., Balt., 1993—2003. Vis. prof. dept. rehab. medicine and dept. internal medicine SUNY, Syracuse, 1988; cons. physiatrist Johns Hopkins Geriatrics Ctr., Johns Hopkins Bayview Med. Ctr., Balt., 1994—; vis. lectr. dept. phys. medicine Coll. Medicine, Ohio State U., 1985; Arthur Grant lectr. U. Tex., San Antonio, 1992; Marquette lectr. Jefferson Med. Coll., Phila., 1993; spkr. various univs. and orgns.; pres. Phys.Medicine and Rehab./Edn. and Rsch. Found., 1990-94; mem. governing coun. sect. rehab. hosps. and programs Am. Hosp. Assn., 1993—; mem. adv. bd. Wash. State Divsn. Vocat. Rehab., 1979-84; vis. prof. U. Wash., 2005, Rehab. Inst. Chgo., 2005; spkr. in field. Contbr. articles to profl. jours.; mem. editl. bd. Archives Phys. Medicine and Rehab., 1978-84, Health After 50, Johns Hopkins Hosp., 1994—; reviewer Jour. Am. Geriatrics Soc., 1994—. Recipient Elizabeth and Sidney Licht award for sci. writing, 1990, Excellence in Tchg. award N.J. Med. Sch., 1992, Excellence in Rsch. Writing award Assn. Acad. Physiatrists and Am. Jour. Phys. Medicine and Rehab., 1992, Golden Goniometer award Phys. Medicine and Rehab. Residents, 1995, 2002, 04, 05, Labe Scheinberg award, Meeting of Consortium of MS Ctrs., Portland, Oreg., 1995. Fellow Am. Acad. Phys. Medicine; mem. AMA, Am. Acad. Phys. Medicine and Rehab. (bd. govs. 1983-90, v.p. 1986-887, pres-elect 1987-88, pres. 1988-89, Disting. Clinician award 1998, Frank M. Krusen award 2004), NAS, Am. Burn Assn., Am. Congress Rehab. Medicine, Assn. Acad. Physiatrists (Disting. Academician award 1998), Internt. Assn. for Study of Pain, King County Med. Assn., Northwest Assn. Phys. Medicine and Rehab. (pres. 1974-76), Gerontol. Soc. Am. (clin. medicine sect.), Wash. State Med. Assn. Office: Johns Hopkins Bayview Med Ctr PM&R AA Bldg Rm 1654 4940 Eastern Ave Baltimore MD 21224

DELAURENTIS, LOUISE BUDDE, writer; b. Stafford, Kans., Oct. 5, 1920; d. Louis and Mary (Lichte) Budde; m. Mariano Anthony DeLaurentis, Mar. 26, 1948 (dec. Oct. 1991); 1 child, Delbert Louis. BA, Ottawa (Kans.) U., 1942. Airport traffic contr. FAA, various cities, 1943-55. Author: Etta Chipmunk, 1962, A Peculiarity of Direction, 1975, Traveling to the Goddess, 1994; editor: Gentle Sorcery by Bessie Jeffery, 1972; author numerous poems various periodicals; contbr. articles to profl. jours. Chairperson Tompkins County Liberal Party, Ithaca, N.Y., 1969-72; mem. local women's spirituality groups. Mem. LWV, AAUW, Writers Assn. of Ithaca Area (pres. 1964-65, co-editor anthology 1967, 95). Avocations: swimming, camping, backpacking, making lunar calendars. Home: 983 Cayuga Heights Rd Ithaca NY 14850-1044

DELAURO, ROSA L., congresswoman; b. New Haven, Conn., Mar. 2, 1943; m. Stanley Greenberg; 3 children. Student, London Sch. Econs. & Polit. Sci., 1962-63; BA in History and Polit Sci. cum laude, Marymount Coll., 1964; MA in Internat. Politics, Columbia U., 1966. Tng. assoc. Community Progress Inc., New Haven, 1967-69; instr. in internat. rels. Albertus Magnus Coll., 1967-68; adminstrv. asst. Nat. Urban Fellows, 1969-72, asst. dir., dir., 1972-75; city coord. Carter-Mondale Presdl. Campaign, New Haven, 1976; exec. asst. Mayor Frank Logue, New Haven, 1976-77, campaign mgr., 1977; exec. asst., devel. adminstr. City of New Haven, 1977-79; campaign mgr. Chris Dodd for U.S. Senate, 1979-80, 86; adminstrv. asst. U.S. Senator Christopher J. Dodd, Washington, 1981-87; state dir. Mondale-Ferraro Presdl. Campaign, NJ, 1986; ptnr. DeLauro-Geller, 1987-88; regional dir. Dukakis for Pres. Campaign, NY, NJ, Conn., 1988; exec. dir. EMILY's List, 1989; mem. U.S. Congress from 3rd Conn. dist., 1991—; mem. house appropriations com. and budget com. Del. to Dem. Nat. Conv., 1984; bd. dirs. Pax Ams. Past pres. New Haven Arts Coun. Assoc. fellow Timothy Dwight Coll., Yale U.; recipient Leadership award Am. Com. on Italian Migration. Mem. Nat. Italian-Am. Found., Dem. Women for Progress. Democrat. Roman Cath. Office: US House of Reps 2262 Rayburn Ho Office Bldg Washington DC 20515-0703 also: District Office 59 Elm Street New Haven CT 06510

DE LA VEGA, DIANNE WINIFRED DEMARINIS (MRS. JORGE DE LA VEGA), government official; b. Cleve., Oct. 30, 1930; d. Gerald M. and Dorothy (Philp) DeMarinis; m. Jorge Alejandro de la Vega, July 19, 1952; children: Constance, Francisco Javier, Alexandra. Student, Case Western Res. U., 1948-50, MA, 1969; BA, U. Am., 1952; PhD in Psychology, Internat. Coll., Los Angeles, 1977; MA, Goddard Coll., 1978. Lic. marriage and family counselor. Faculty Western Res. U., Cleve., 1961-62; instr. Instituto Mexicano-Norteamericano de Relaciones Culturales, Mexico, 1967; supr. fgn. press Mexican Olympic Organizing Com., Mexico, 1968; asst. to producer Producciones Ojo, Canal 8 TV, Mexico, 1969; exec. asst. Internat. Exec. Service Corps, Mexico City, 1969-70; asst. to dir. U.S. Internat. U. Mexico, Mexico City, 1970-75; family planning evaluator for Latin Am. AID, 1976; with dept. spl. edn. region IX Nat. Ctr. Child Abuse/Neglect Children's Bur., Office Child Devel., HEW, Calif. State U., 1977—. Author: Heaven Knows, Anything Goes, 2004 (1st prize Santa Barbara Writers' conf., 2004). Chmn. Puppet's Jr. League, Mexico City, 1967, chmn. ways and means, 1968; sec. Tlaxcala-Okla. Partner's of Alliance for Progress, 1967—; ret. pres. acculturating Hispanic and Asian refugee children Los Angeles Unified Sch. Dist.; bd. dir. Hot Line of Mexico City; mem. Los Angeles adv. com. 1984 Olympics; active LEARN Com., 1995—; mem. steering com. Annenberg/Weingart Grant, 1996—. Mem.: Transactional Analysis Assn., Pro Salud Maternal, Flying Samaritans, Calif. Marriage and Family Therapists Assn. (L.A. chpt.), Jr. League, Order of St. John of Jerusalem (dame). Home: 130 Alta Ave Apt D Santa Monica CA 90402-2737

DE LA VIÑA-SIERRA, DIANA MARIA, music educator; b. Holguin, Cuba, Apr. 22, 1956; arrived in U.S., 1962; d. Santos Rafael de la Viña and Ana Julia Viamonte-de la Viña; 1 child, Michael Arles. BA in Music Edn., Kean U., Union, N.J., 1980; cert., Villa Walsh Acad., 2005. Cert. piano tchr. Nat. Guild Piano Tchrs., 2003. Tchr. music Uruguay USA Sch., Elizabeth, NJ, 1983—86; tchr. voice, piano Newark Cmty. Sch. Arts, 1983—94, chmn. music dept., 1993—; head Dept. Music St. Hegwig's Sch., Elizabeth, NJ, 1997—2002; chmn. Spanish dept. Blessed Sacrament Sch., Elizabeth, 2003—04; chmn. Dept. Music and Spanish St. Mary's Sch., Elizabeth, 2004—. Author: (song) Danza Cubana. Head cultural affairs Pro Cuba Orgn., Elizabethtown, 1990—94. Recipient Piano Competition First prize, Cath. Youth Orgn., 1969, Excellence in Tchg. award, Newark (N.J.) Cmty. Sch. Arts, 1993, Don Galaor award, La Tribuna newspaper; scholar, Villa Walsh Acad., 1971. Home: 151 Morristown Rd Elizabeth NJ 07208-1315

DELBANCO, SUZANNE F., human services administrator; MPH, U. Calif., Berkeley; PhD in Pub. Policy, Goldman Sch. Pub. Policy. With Henry J. Kaiser Family Found.; sr. mgr. Pacific Bus. Group on Health; exec. dir. The Leapfrog Group, Washington, 2000—. Office: Leapfrog Group 1801 K St NW Ste 701L Washington DC 20006

DELBOURGO, JOËLLE LILY, publishing executive; b. Alexandria, Egypt, Sept. 10, 1953; arrived in US, 1960; d. Edward Daniel and J. Andrée (Domergue) D.; m. Lewis Foster Patton, May 16, 1976 (div. May 1996); children: Caroline Emily, Andrew David. Student, Vassar Coll., 1970-72; BA, Williams Coll., 1974; MA, Columbia U., 1975. Editorial asst. Bantam Books, N.Y.C., 1975-76, asst. editor, 1976-78, assoc. editor, 1978-80; sr. editor Ballantine Del Rey Fawcett Books div. Random House Inc., N.Y.C., 1980-81; exec. editor Ballantine Del Rey Fawcett Ivy Books div. Random House Inc., N.Y.C., 1981-83, editor-in-chief, 1983-86, v.p., editor-in-chief trade books, 1986-89, editor-in-chief hard cover books and trade paperback, 1990-95; v.p., editl. dir. HarperCollins, N.Y.C., 1996, sr. v.p., assoc. publ., editor-in-chief, 1997-99; CEO, pres. Joëlle Delbourgo Assocs. Inc. Lit. Mgmt., Pub. Cons., 1999—. Columbia faculty fellow, 1974—75. Mem.: Women's Media Group (bd. dirs., treas.), Phi Beta Kappa. Office: 516 Bloomfield Ave Ste 5 Montclair NJ 07042 Office Phone: 973-783-6800. Business E-Mail: info@delbourgo.com.

DELCAMBRE, LOIS MARIE LUNDBERG, academic administrator; BS in Math., U. Southwestern La., 1972, PhD in Computer Sci., 1982; MS in Math. Scis., Clemson U., 1974. Instr. dept. math. scis. and computer sci. Clemson (S.C.) U., 1973-79; from asst. prof. to prof. engring. U. Southwestern La., Lafayette, 1983-92; assoc. prof. computer sci. engring. dept. Oreg. Grad. Inst., 1993—. Affiliate staff scientist Pacific N.W. Nat. Lab., Richland, Wash., 1993—; dir. Data-Intensive Sys. Ctr., 1993—; assoc. chair edn. computer sci. and engring. dept. Oreg. Grad. Inst., 1996—; assoc. dir. rsch. apparel computer integrated mfg. ctr. U. Southwestern La., 1988-92; cons. divsn. info. sys. devel. Clemson U., 1979; panelist, review bd., NSF; presenter in field. Contbr. articles to profl. jours. Grantee Incremental Specialization Tech., Def. Advanced Rsch. Projects Adminstrn., 1996—, NSF, 1995-97, Dept. of Energy, 1993-97, Office Naval Rsch., 1995—, Dept. Commerce, 1992-93, Dept. Def. Logistics Aty., 1992-94, others. Office: Oreg Grad Inst Sci Tech PO Box 91000 Portland OR 97291-1000

DEL COLLO, MARY ANNE DEMETRIS, school administrator; b. Norristown, Pa., May 10, 1949; d. John and Julia (Chale) Demetris; m. William Paul Del Collo, July 1, 1973; children: Margaux, Julia, Nicole. BS, West Chester State U., 1971; MEd, Rosemont Coll. Tech., 1995; EdD, Widener U., 2001. Cert. elem. tchr. and sch. adminstr., Pa. Tchr. Phoenixville (Pa.) Area Sch. Dist., 1971-97, adminstr., 1997—, Methacton Sch. Dist., Norristown, Pa., 1998—. Mem. AAUW, Pa. Assn. Elem. and Secondary Sch. Prins., Hellenic Univ. Club, Nat. Middle Sch. Assn., Kappa Delta Pi (v.p. Chi Gamma chpt. 1998-2000, pres. 2000-02, past pres. 2002-). Avocations: technology, walking, reading, antiquing, travel. Office: Methacton Sch Dist Eagleville Rd Norristown PA 19403

DEL CONTE, L. CATHERINE, special education educator; b. Montour Falls, N.Y., June 8, 1955; d. Leon Clarence and Dorothy Louise May; m. Douglas Kelsey, Aug. 2, 1973; children: Henry Lee Kelsey, Bryon Douglas Kelsey; m. Richard Ralph Del Conte, Apr. 8, 1995. AA in Human Svcs., Genesee C.C., Batavia, N.Y., 1981; BSW, SUNY-Brockport, 1983, MPA in Geriatrics, 1986; M.Spl. Edn., George Mason U., Fairfax, Va., 2000. Case mgr. We Care, Inc., Washington, 1991—92, Brice Warren Corp., Washington, 1992—94, State of Md./Great Oaks MR Ctr., 1994—95, Jewish Social Svcs., Rockville, Md., 1995—97; learning disabilities/ED tchr. Fairfax County Pub. Schs., Annandale, Va., 1998—2004, Robinson HS, Fairfax, Va., 2004—.

Historian Phi Delta Kappa/George Mason U., 1998—2000; ct. apptd. specialist Fairfax County, Fairfax, Va., 1991—93; lead tchr. remediation program Annandale H.S., 1999—2002, mem. attendance adv. com., 2003—04. Avocations: hiking, reading, working out, poetry. Home: 6006 Scarborough Commons Ln Burke VA 22015 Office: Fairfax County Pub Sch 5035 Sideburn Rd Fairfax VA 22032 E-mail: lcdelconte@cox.net.

DEL CUETO, S. E., Spanish and English language educator; b. Havana, Cuba; arrived in U.S., 1962; d. Luis L. Del Cueto and Leonor C. Alvarez; m. Joseph M. Chapuk, July 14, 1990; 1 child, Ana-Maria Chapuk. BA, Manhattan Coll., Bronx, N.Y.; MA, UCLA, U. Pa., Phila. Cert. tchr. N.Y.C., Calif. Prof. Northampton C.C., Bethlehem, Pa., 1997—. Student adviser Northampton C.C., Bethlehem, Kopecek chair in humanities. Recipient Christensen Excellence in Tchg. award. Office: Northampton C C 3835 Green Pond Rd Bethlehem PA 18020

DEL DUCA, RITA, language educator; b. NYC, Apr. 1, 1933; d. Joseph and Ermelinda (Buonaguro) Ferraro; m. Joseph Anthony Del Duca, Oct. 29, 1955; children: Lynn, Susan, Paul, Andrea. BA, CUNY, 1955. Elem. tchr. Yonkers (N.Y.) Pub. Schs., 1955-57; tchr. kindergarten Sacred Heart Sch., Yonkers, 1962-64; tchr. piano, Scarsdale, N.Y., 1973-79; asst. office mgr. Foot Clinic, Hartsdale, N.Y., 1977-85; tchr. ESL, Linguarama Exec. Sch., White Plains, N.Y., 1985-89; ESL tutor, Scarsdale, 1989—. Dist. leader Greenburgh (N.Y.) Rep. Com., 1991-92. Mem.: ASCAP. Avocations: painting, piano teaching, tennis, theatre arts. Home and Office: Unit 79 10 Old Jackson Ave Hastings On Hudson NY 10706

DELEHANTY, MARTHA, human services administrator; B in Psychology, Mount Holyoke Coll.; M in Bus., U. Tex. With GTE, 1991—2000; field dir. Midwest Area GTE Wireless; joined Verizon Wireless, 2000; exec. dir. employee rels. Verizon Wireless LLC, Bedminster, NJ, 2000—04, v.p. human resources, 2004—. Office: Verizon Wireless LLC 180 Washington Valley Rd Bedminster NJ 07921

DELEHANTY, SUZANNE, museum director; b. Worcester, Mass., July 18, 1944; d. George B. and Catherine (Powers) D. BA with honors, Skidmore Coll., 1965; student, U. Pa., 1966-68. Curatorial asst. Inst. Contemporary Art, Phila., 1968-71, dir., 1971-78, Neuberger Mus., Purchase, NY, 1978-88, Contemporary Arts Mus., Houston, 1989—93; ind. curator and cons. NYC, 1994—95; dir. Miami Art Mus., 1995—. Mem. adv. coun. The Art Mus. at Princeton U., 1984—. Author: Agnes Martin, 1973, Cy Twombly and Video Art, 1975, George Segal/Environments, 1976, Fred Sandback/Sculpture, 1991. Mem. visual arts panel Tex. Commn. on Arts, 1990-91. Mem. Assn. Art Mus. Dirs., Urban League of Greater Miami. Office: Miami Art Mus 101 W Flagler St Miami FL 33130-1504 E-mail: sdeleha@miamidade.gov.

DE LEON, LIDIA MARIA, magazine editor; b. Havana, Cuba, Sept. 10, 1957; d. Leon J. and Lydia (Diaz Cruz) de L. BA in Communications cum laude, U. Miami, Coral Gables, Fla., 1979. Staff writer Miami Herald, Fla., 1978-79; editorial asst. Halsey Pub. Co., Miami, 1980-81, assoc. editor, 1981, editor, 1981—, editor Delta Sky mag., 1983-95. Mem. Am. Soc. Mag. Editors, Am. Assn. Travel Editors, Golden Key, Sigma Delta Chi. Roman Catholic. Avocation: tennis. Office: 12550 Biscayne Blvd # 212 Miami FL 33181

DE LEON, SYLVIA A., lawyer; b. Corpus Christi, Tex., Mar. 2, 1950; m. Lynn R. Coleman; 3 children. BA, Briarcliff Coll., 1972; JD, U. Tex., 1976. Bar: Tex. 1976, DC 1977. Ptnr., founding mem. public law and policy practice group and mem. mgmt. com. Akin, Gump, Strauss, Hauer & Feld LLP, Washington. Adj. prof. law Georgetown U. Law Ctr., 1988-90; bd. dirs. (pres. apptd. senate confirmed) Amtrak, Nat. Railroad Passenger Corp., 1994—, vice chmn. 2003-, chair corp. strategy com. Bd. trustees U. Tex. Law Sch. Found. 2002-, U. Tex. Law Assn., 1985-89, 92-96, 2000-03, U. Tex. Devel. Bd., 1996—, bd. dirs. exec. com. Washington Ballet, 2001-; coord. issues transp. Clinton-Gore Presdl. Transition Team, 1992; presdl. appointee Nat. Commn. Ensure Strong Competitive Airline Industry, 1993, White House Conf. on Travel and Tourism. Mem. Bar Assn. DC, State Bar Tex. (chmn. fed. law and regulations com. 1984-87), Nat. Civil Aviation Rev. Commn. Office: Akin Gump Strauss Hauer & Feld Rm 1214 1333 New Hampshire Ave NW Washington DC 20036-1564 Business E-Mail: sdeleon@akingump.com.

DELESKI, KAREN MARGARET, athletic trainer; b. Bklyn., N.Y., Mar. 5, 1975; d. Martin Michael and Maureen Anne McNeill; m. Peter Deleski, Apr. 30, 2005. BS, Fordham U., Bronx, 1997; MS, L.I. U., Bklyn., 1999. Staff athletic trainer Sports Phys. Therapy of N.Y., Bklyn., 1999—2002, East End Phys. Therapy, East Hampton, NY, 2002—04; head athletic trainer William Floyd H.S., Mastic, NY, 2004—. Mem.: BOC, Nat. Athletic Trainers Assn. Roman Catholic. Avocations: photography, gardening, swimming, boating. Home: 25 Pine Neck Ave Sag Harbor NY 11963 E-mail: kmchamptons@yahoo.com.

DELEUZE, MARGARITA, artist; b. Caracas, Miranda, Venezuela, May 11, 1943; arrived in US, 1982, naturalized, 1992; d. Ivor Hauck and Margarita Schnell; m. Felipe Silén, July 3, 1964 (div. Nov. 1982); children: Anabella, Margarita; m. Eric Charles Deleuze, Nov. 12, 1988. AAS, Bennett Coll., Greensboro, N.C., 1962. Recipient Arts awards Venezuelan VAAUW, Caracas, 1971, 72, San Francisco Mus. Contemporary Hispanic Art award, 1998, Premio Nosotros award, ALAS, Miami, 2000, Artistic Achievement award Five Part Nat. Juried Competition, Artscape Naples, Fla.; named Dressage Nat. Champion, Venezuelan Riding Fedn., Caracas, 1972, 73, 74, 75. Mem. World Wildlife Fund, Nat. Audubon Soc., Humane Soc. Broward County, Defenders Wildlife, Cousteau Soc., Nat. Mus. Women in Arts. Avocations: photography, gardening, travel, music, gourmet cooking. Home: 2698 Cypress Ln Weston FL 33332-3423 Studio: MD Fine Arts Studio 2698 Cypress Ln Weston FL 33332-3423 Personal E-mail: mdeleuze@bellsouth.net.

DELGADO, JANE, health policy executive, writer, psychologist; b. Havana, Cuba, June 17, 1953; d. Juan Lorenzo Delgado Borges and Lucila Aurora Navarro Delgado; m. Mark A. Steo, May 15, 1999; 1 child, Elizabeth A. Steo. BA, SUNY, New Paltz, 1973; MA, NYU, 1975; MS, W. Averell Harriman Sch., 1981; PhD in Clin. Psychology, SUNY, Stony Brook, 1981. Children's talent coord. Children's TV Workshop, 1973-75; rsch. asst. SUNY, Stony Brook, 1975-79; social sci. analyst U.S. Dept. HHS, 1979-83, health policy advisor, 1983-85; pres., CEO Nat. Alliance for Hispanic Health, 1985—; pvt. practice in psychology, 1979—. Bd. dirs. Nat. Health Coun., 1986—97, Carter Ctr. Mental Health Taskforce, 1991—2000, Patient Safety Inst., 2001—; trustee The Kresge Found, 1997—, Found. Child Devel., 1989—97. Author: Salud! A Latina's Guide to Total Health, 1997, 2d edit., 2002. Bd. dirs. Lovelace Respiratory Rsch. Inst., 2002—, Health Found. Am., 2003—. W.K. Kellogg Found. Nat. fellow, 1988, NIMH fellow, 1975-79; recipient Surgeon Gen.'s award, 1992, Florence Kelley award, 2002, Health and Sci. Latina Excellence award, 1995, FDA Commr.'s Citation award, 2005, Hispanic Heritage Found. award, 2005; named SUNY Alumna of Yr., 1993 Office: Nat Alliance for Hispanic Health 1501 16th St NW Washington DC 20036-1401 Office Phone: 202-797-4321. Business E-Mail: jdelgado@hispanichealth.org.

DELGADO, MARICA LADONNE, librarian, educator; b. Murray, Ky., Nov. 28, 1959; d. Billie Ray Roberts and Ada Sue Ross Roberts; m. Jon E. Delgado; children: Maurya, Jessamyn, Ian. BS, Murray State U., 1981; ML, Vanderbilt U., 1982. Libr. spl. projects Tenn. Tech. U., Cookeville, 1982, libr. collection develop./spl. projects, 1983—88, exch. libr. head periodicals and gifts, 1986—88; libr. gifts and exch., instr. Miss. State U., Starkville, 1988—92, libr. govt. documents, asst. prof., 1992—97, coord. govt. documents and microforms, assoc. prof., 1997—2005, prof., 2005—. Contbr. articles to profl. jours. Mem.: ALA (poster sessions rev. panel 1992—2002, 2005—06), Govt. Documents Roundtable, MSU Robert Holland Faculty Senate (sec. 1999—2005), Miss. Libr. Assn. (govt. documents round table sec. 1996—97, chair 2004), Southeastern Libr. Assn. (poster sessions coord. 1992—94, 1998—2000). Avocations: boating, travel, camping, hiking. Home: 507 Sycamore St Starkville MS 39759 Office: Miss State U Libr Hardy Rd Mississippi State MS 39762 Office Phone: 662-325-7660. Office Fax: 662-325-3560. Business E-Mail: ldelgado@library.msstate.edu.

DELGADO, MARY LOUISE, elementary school educator, secondary school educator, consultant, Internet company executive; b. Manitowoc, Wis., June 6, 1943; d. Walter Anthony and Jane Mary Jagodensky; 1 child, Daniel David. BA in English, Edn., Silver Lake Coll., 1971; MA, Govs. State U., Park Forest, Ill., 1983. Cert. tchr. Wis., Ill. Tchr. Colegio San Antonio Abad, Humacao, PR, 1973—75, Chgo. Pub. Schs., 1984—88, Milw. Pub. Schs., 1988—; pres., cons. Quality Online Connections, Milw., 2000—. Presenter in field. Pres. Lenox Heights Neighborhood Assn., Milw., 1999—2002. Fellow, Am. Coun. Learned Socs., 1994, 1995; grantee, Coun. Basic Edn. Ind. Study, 1994, NEH, 2000; Eleanor Roosevelt Tchr. scholar, 1999. Mem.: ASCD, AAUW, Wis. Tchrs. English to Students Second Langs. Democrat. Avocations: bicycling, reading, weaving. Office: Quality Online Connections 6333 W Chambers St Milwaukee WI 53210 Personal E-mail: mdelgado1@wi.rr.com.

DELI, ANNE TYNION, retail executive; b. Milw., Apr. 18, 1956; m. Steven F. Deli; 2 children. BA in History and French, Georgetown U., 1978. Acct. exec. Dancer Fitzgerald Sample, N.Y.C., 1978—80; acct. supr. Grey Advt., N.Y.C., 1980—82; v.p. Wells Rich Greene, N.Y.C., 1982—84; sr. v.p. Lawrence Charles Free, N.Y.C., 1984—86; prin. Anspach Grossman Portugal, N.Y.C., 1986—88; sr. v.p. Siegel & Gale, N.Y.C., 1988—93; v.p., global mktg. Harley-Davidson, Inc., Milw., 1993—95; pres., founder North River Strategies, Milw./Chgo., 1995—2000; pres. Harley-Davidson Am. Rd. LLC/Orlando Harley-Davidson/Harley-Davidson Airport Stores, 2000—. Active Com. of 200; founder's coun. The Field Mus., Chgo.; bd. dirs. Milw. Zool. Soc., 1995—97, Chgo. Shakespeare Theatre, 2001—02, Orlando Mus. Art, 2002—05, Orlando and Orange County Conv. and Visitor's Bur. Named Bus. Woman of Yr., Orlando Bus. Jour., 2005. Mem.: Orlando Regional C. of C. (vice chmn. 2003—05). Republican. Avocations: world travel, tennis, theater, art. Office: H-D Am Rd LLC Ste 2144 875 N Michigan Ave Chicago IL 60611 Office Phone: 312-280-6001. Personal E-mail: annetdeli@aol.com.

DELIA, MARGARET M., elementary school educator; b. Phila., Aug. 24, 1964; d. John and Elsie McLaughlin; m. Christopher C. Delia, Sr., Aug. 16, 1986; children: Christopher, Chad, Curt, Cara. BA, Glassboro State Coll., 1986; MA, Rowan Coll. N.J., 1994. Cert. tchr. health/phys. edn., elem. edn., student personnel svcs., supr., N.J., adminstr., dir. student pers. svcs., prin. Tchr. health/phys. edn. Pitman (N.J.) Mid. Sch., 1986-92; elem. tchr. Kindle Sch., Pitman, 1992—; guidance counselor Glassboro (N.J.) High Sch., 1994—, Pitman H.S., 1994—99, Clearview Mid. Sch., Mullica Hill, NJ, 1999—2006; dir. guidance Delsea Regional H.S., Franlinmills, NJ, 2006—. Writing com. mem. Pitman Schs., NJ, 1992—93; career day chairperson Clearview Mid. Sch., Mullica Hill, 2003—. Chairperson Ch. and Soc. FUMC, Glassboro, 1987-89; mem. PTA Glassboro Schs., 1994-96, Pitman Schs., 1994; presenter/coord. Am. Heart Assn., N.J., 1987-94, coord. Jum Rope for Heart, 1987-94; scholarship selection com. SJCWS, N.J., 1989-92; mem. United Meth. Women Sunday Sch. Class, 1992-96, chairpersoon C/S, United Meth. Ch., 1987-89. Named N.J.'s New Tchr. of Yr., Sallie Mae, 1987, Delsea H.S. Sports Hall of Fame, 2003, Gloucester County Counselor of Yr., 2001—02, 2002—03, 2004—05. Mem. NJAHPERD (cons.), S. Jersey Coaches of Women's Sports (sec./treas. 1989-92, SADD advisor 1997-99), Gloucester County Profl. Mid. Sch. Counselor's Assn. (pres. 2001-03, sec. 2004-06). Avocations: skiing, crafts, crocheting, golf. Home: 155 Ewan Rd Mullica Hill NJ 08062-2901 Office: Delsea Regional High Sch Fries Mill Rd Franklinville NJ 08322 E-mail: deliama@clearviewregional.edu.

DE LIMANTOUR, CLARICE BARR, food scientist; b. Allentown, Pa., Dec. 24, 1918; d. Joseph Robert and Laura (Wirthlin) Barr; m. Julio Edwardo Iturbide Limantour, Sept. 13, 1940 (dec. 1972); children: Jose' Ignacio, Julio Edwardo. BS, Rutgers U., 1938, MS, 1940; postgrad., U. Mexico, 1946-49, Rutgers U., 1949-50. Advisor Nat. Sch. Feeding Program, Mexico City, 1947-49; pres. Factory Feeding Corp., Mexico City, 1950-58; advisor Nat. Factory Feeding Program, Mexico City, 1958-60; developer New Food Product-Gen. Foods, White Plains, NY, 1960-61, New Food Product-Gen. Mills, Reynolds, 1961-63, New Food Product-Miles Labs., 1963-64; cons. New Food Products-various cos., 1964-78; pres., researcher Limantour Devel. Corp., Pa., 1966-91, chmn. of bd. Pa., 1988—; developer Cliffdale Farms, Quakertown, Pa., 1988—; pvt. practice cons. Durham, Pa. Inventor in field of freezing of all classes of emulsions. Mem. Bucks County Conservancy Assn., Doylestown, Pa., 1989-91, Fine Arts Club, N.Y.C., 1984-88, Acad. Sci., N.Y.C., Republican Club, Pa., 1982-89, Citizens Against Govt. Waste, Washington, 1988-91. Republican. Episcopalian. Avocations: reading, music, travel, sailing, bird watching. Office Phone: 610-346-7104.

DELING-LEWIS, ELAINE MARIE, special education educator; b. Miami, Apr. 4, 1969; BS, Fla. Internat. U., 1991, MS, 1995. Cert. Fla. Spl. edn. tchr. Dade County schs., 1991—. CEO The Open Door Way Inc., 2000—. Mem. Autistic Soc. Am., Coun. Exceptional Edn., Autism Rsch. Rev. Internat. Home: 9488 Majestic Way Boynton Beach FL 33437 Office Phone: 561-436-6367.

DELISANTI, MARILYN W., medical/surgical and pediatrics nurse; b. Rochester, NY, Jan. 26, 1937; d. Kenneth and Rita Marie (Zonnevylle) Whitty; children: Ernest, Neil, Maria, Deanna. ADN, Tacoma Community Coll., 1976; BS in Health Care Adminstrn. cum laude, St. Leo's Coll., 1988. hospice case mgr., Calif. Office nurse, Tacoma; team leader Madigan Army Hosp., Tacoma; office mgr., nurse Mease Healthcare, Dunedin, Fla.; training specialist Innovated Dialysis System, Inc., Long Beach, Calif.; hospice case mgr. Garden Grove, Calif. Home: 17200 Newhope St Apt 40A Fountain Valley CA 92708-4237

DE LISI, JOANNE, communications consultant, educator; b. Bklyn. d. Louis Anthony and Maria Anna De Lisi. BA, Hunter Coll., N.Y.C., 1972, MA, 1977; postgrad., NYU. Cert. tchr. N.Y. Asst. instr. Hunter Coll., N.Y.C., 1974-75; instr. NYU, N.Y.C., 1974-78; cons. communication N.Y.C., 1976—; instr. Bklyn. Coll., 1978-82, dir. forensics, 1981-82, asst. dir. acad. prep. program, 1980-82; adj. lectr. City U. Sys., N.Y.C., 1983-91. Profl. entertainer, 1953—75; faculty advisor Alpha Tau Omega, Bklyn. Coll., 1980—82. Contbr. articles to profl. jours., poems to anthologies, radio programs, newspapers. Dep. rep. St. Albans Campus NYVA Harbor Health Care Sys.; mem. pres. adv. bd. N.Y. State Senator Serphin Maltese, Queensboro. Recipient Nat. award of excellence, POW/MIA, Am. Legion Aux., 1995, award, USO and Savs. Bonds Jr. Activities Am. Legion Aux., 1998, Vets. Affairs, 2000, Queens Women of Distinction award, 2005, Iona Kubby Nat. award, Am. Legion Aux., 2005. Mem.: Metro N.Y. Database Internet Users Group, Fencers Am., Hunter Alumni Assn., Am. Legion Aux. (pub. rels. officer Queens County 1991—93, v.p., girls state chmn. 1993—94, pub. rels. officer, newsletter editor, sec. Leonard unit 1993—94, Queens County pres. 1994—95, del. chmn. N.Y. state Dept. Conv. 1995, judge Forensics Tournament 1995—2003, pres. unit 104 1996, nat. security chmn., jr. activity chmn., pub. rels. dir. 1996—98, pres. 10th dist. aux. 2004—05, N.Y. state nat. security chmn. 2004—05, N.Y.S. Am. Legion Aux., Iona Kubby Nat. award in nat. security 2005), Kappa Delta Pi. Roman Catholic. Avocations: antiques, travel, jewelry making. Office: Wyckoff Heights Sta PO Box 370029 Brooklyn NY 11237-0029 Office Phone: 718-381-7042. E-mail: joannedelisi@yahoo.com.

DE LISI, NANCY, corporate financial executive; BA in Psych., U. Tex., Austin, MS in Profl. Acctg. Various exec. positions in multinational cos. and Citibank in internat. fin. and bus. devel., 1976—85; asst. treas. to v.p. fin. and treas. Altria Grp., Inc., NYC, 1985—2002, sr. v.p. mergers and acquisitions, 2002—. Bd. dirs. SABMiller, PLC. Office: Altria Group Inc 120 Park Ave New York NY 10017-5592

DELK, CHARLOTTE TURLEY, elementary school educator; b. Ft. Benning Columbus, Ga., Sept. 27, 1964; d. Lester Albert Turley, Jr. and Charleen Whittle Turley; children: Joshua Turley Rusch, Whittle Harrison. BA, Valdosta State Coll., Ga., 1985; cert. T-4/Mid. Grades, Kennesaw State Coll., Ga., 1991. Staff writer Cherokee Tribune, Canton, Ga., 1986—89; tchr. M.A. Teasley Mid. Sch., Canton, 1991—94, Pelham City Mid. Sch., Pelham, Ga., 1994—97, Pearson Elem. Sch., Ga., 2003—. Hist. homes including home of former pres. Jimmy and wife Rosalyn Carter. Baptist. Avocation: reading. Home: 505 North Chester Ave Douglas GA 31533 Office: Atkinson County Bd of Edn Pearson Elem Sch 1001 King St Pearson GA 31642 Office Phone: 912-422-3882. Fax: 912-389-1774. Business E-Mail: cdelk@atkinson.142.ga.us.

DELL, CHARLENE ELIZABETH, music educator; d. Arthur Kenyon Dell and Gertrude May Poelma. MusB, SUNY, Potsdam, 1984; MS, We. Conn. State U., Danbury, 1989; PhD, U. SC, Columbia, 2003. Music educator Gouverneur Ctrl. Schs., NY, 1984—86, Arlington Ctrl. Schs., Poughkeepsie, NY, 1986—99; asst. prof. music edn. U. Okla., Norman, 2002—. Exec. adminstrv. dir. Sooner String Project, Norman, 2002—; asst. dir. for adminstrn. N.Y. State Summer Sch. of Arts, Saratoga Springs, 1983—96. Musician and soloist First Bapt. Ch., Norman, 2002—06. Tech. Grant, U. Okla. Sch. Music, 2004, Internat. Travel Grant, U. Okla., 2004. Mem.: Nat. Sch. Orch. Assn., Nat. Assn. Music Educators (assoc.), Am. String Teachers Assn. (assoc.; state pres. 2005—06). Office Phone: 405-325-0168.

DELL, SUSAN, foundation administrator, apparel designer; m. Micahel Dell; 4 children. BA in Fashion Merchandising & Design, Ariz. State U. Designer Susan Dell Collections, Austin, Tex., NYC; chmn. bd. Phi, NYC. Co-founder, chmn. bd. Michael & Susan Dell Found.; clothing designs featured in Am. Vogue, French Vogue, Harper's Bazaar, W Mag. Bd. mem. Austin Children's Hosp., Cooper Inst., St. Andrew's Episcopal Sch. Office: Cooper Inst 12330 Preston Rd Dallas TX 75203 also: Michael & Susan Dell Found One Dell Way Round Rock TX 78682*

DELLA, TERESA BRISBON, social studies educator; b. Camden, S.C., Jan. 15, 1971; d. Marie Magazine and James Edward Brisbon. BS in Criminal Justice, U. S.C., 1993; MAT in Social Studies, U. S.C., Columbia, 1994—96, MLS, 1999—2001. Social studies tchr. St. Andrews Mid. Sch., Columbia, 2002—; media specialist Orangeburg Consol. Dist. 5, SC, 2002—03; ind. beauty cons. Mary Kay, Columbia, 2006—. Facilitator Richland Sch. Dist. One, Columbia, 2004—. Chairperson scholarship ministry Bible Way Ch. of Atlas Rd, Columbia, 2002—04. Recipient Add a Diamond Ring, Mary Kay, 2006. Mem.: S.C. Edn. Assn., Alpha Kappa Alpha. Democrat. Avocations: reading, travel. Office: Richland Sch Dist One 1231 Bluefield Rd Columbia SC 29210 Office Phone: 803-731-8910.

DELL'ARINGA, YVONNE SILVIA BOZZINI, elementary school educator; b. Stockton, Calif., Feb. 11, 1951; m. Richard Gene Dell'Aringa, June 1, 1974; 2 children. BS, U. of Pacific, 1973, MEd, 1987. Tchr. St. Luke's, Stockton, 1974—81; tchr., reading recovery tchr., mentor tchr. Lodi Unified Sch. Dist., Calif., 1981—. Mem.: AAUW.

DELLAS, MARIE C., retired psychology educator, consultant; b. Buffalo; d. Theodore Andrew and Katherine (Callos) D. BS cum laude, State U. Coll., Buffalo, 1945; MEd, U. Buffalo, 1967; PhD, SUNY, Buffalo, 1970. Asst. editor Urban Edn. Jour., Buffalo, 1966-67; rsch. asst. SUNY, Buffalo, 1967-69; asst. prof. psychology Ea. Mich. U., Ypsilanti, 1969-73, assoc. prof., 1973-79, prof., 1979-93. Mem. adv. bd. Inst. Study Children and Families, 1983-93. Author: Dellas Identity Status Inventory, 1979, 81, Creative Thinking Applied to Problem Solving Manual, 1993; contbr. articles to profl. jours.; mem. bd. editors Midwestern Ednl. Researcher, 1980-87, Urban Edn. Jour., 1977-94. Recipient Josephine N. Keal award Women's Commn., 1980, 85, 86; Grad. Rsch. grantee Ea. Mich. U., 1980-84. Mem. APA, Am. Ednl. Rsch. Assn., Nat. Assn. Gifted Children, Midwestern Ednl. Rsch. Assn., Midwestern Psychol. Assn., Mich. Acad. Gifted, Am. Assn. Univ. Women, Women's Coun. Cleveland Mus. of Art, Pi Lambda Theta. Home and Office: 2201 Acacia Park Dr Apt 312 Lyndhurst OH 44124-3840

DELLASEGA, CHERYL, humanities educator; b. Patuxant River, Md., Dec. 12, 1953; d. James Robert and Lillian Margaret (Diehl) Miller; m. Paul Dellasega, Aug. 1984; children: Matthew, Ellen, Joe. BSN, Millersville U., 1981; MS in Nursing, C.R.N.P., U. Del., 1982; PhD in Health Edn., Temple U., 1988. RN; cert. gerontologic nurse practitioner. Clin. instr. nursing care of the elderly Sch. Nursing Lancaster (Pa.) Gen. Hosp., 1982; instr. dept. nursing Millersville (Pa.) U., 1982-84, Messiah Coll., Grantham, Pa., 1984-85; asst. prof. Sch. Nursing Pa. State U., University Park, Pa., 1986—; staff nurse PRN Medox Nursing Pool, Phila., 1975-76; staff nurse CCU Lancaster (Pa.) Gen. Hosp., 1976, Muhlenburg Hosp., South Plainfield, NJ, 1977; vis. nurse, team coord. Centre Community Home Health Agy., Bellefonte, Pa., 1977-78; charge nurse infirmary St. Joseph's Hosp. and Health Care Ctr., Lancaster, Pa., 1978-80; staff nurse recovery room Lancaster Gen. Hosp., 1980-81; assoc. prof. medicine, dept. of humanities Pa. State Univ. Coll. Medicine, Hershey, Pa. Nurse practitioner, cons. Dr. B. Eggler, Reedsville, Pa., 1989—, Susquehanna Nursing Svcs., Harrisburg, Pa., 1985; nurse practitioner So. Huntingdon County Family Health Ctr., Orbisonia, Pa., 1988, Rehab Hosp. for Spl. Svcs., Bellefonte, Pa., 1987; cons. devel. of geriatric assessment team Carlisle (Pa.) Hosp., 1985, Mifflin County Area Agy. on Aging, Lewistown, Pa. Author: Surviving Ophelia: Mothers Share Their Wisdom in Navigating the Tumultuous Teenage Years, 2001, Girl Wars, 2003, Mean Girls Grown Up: Adult Women Who are Still Queen Bees, Middle Bees and Afraid to Bees, 2005, contbr. articles to profl. jours. GSA Postdoctoral fellow. Mem. ANA, Pa. Nurses Assn., Am. Pub. Health Assn., Nat. League Nursing (researcher coun.), Am. Soc. Aging, Pa. Long Term Care Coun. (system orgn. subcom. 1988), AAUW (legal advocacy fund rep.), Gerontological Soc. Am., Sigma Theta Tau, Phi Delta Kappa. Office: Pa State Univ Coll Med Dept Humanities 500 University Dr Hershey PA 17033

DELLER, RITA WILLENNAR, elementary school educator; b. Hamilton, Ind., Aug. 9, 1938; m. Ronald K. Deller, Sept. 2, 1956; children: Jodi Anne, Jill Lynn. BS in Edn., Ind. U., Ft. Wayne, 1973, MS in Edn., 1977. Cert. tchr., Ind. Tchr. Met. Sch. Dist. of Steuben County, Angola, Ind., 1974—99; student tchr. supr. Tri-State U., Angola, Ind., 2004—. Mem. Delta Kappa Gamma (Alpha Xi chpt.). Avocations: crocheting, sewing, basket making. Home: 840 S 200 E Angola IN 46703-8993

DELLINGER, MARY, medical/surgical nurse; b. Richmond, Va., Mar. 4, 1952; d. David Marion and Anneke-Jan (Fleetwood) Bounds; m. David Dellinger, May 12, 1979; children: Robert, Michael. BSN, U. Va., 1974. Cert. adult nurse practitioner; CNOR; cert. RN first asst. Staff nurse, head nurse U. Va., Charlottesville, 1974-79; staff nurse Fairfax Hosp., Falls Church, Va., asst. nursing coord. cardiac surgery, clinician IV oper. room, 1979—. Mem. AACN, Assn. Oper. Room Nurses, Sigma Theta Tau. Home: 9254 Longstreet Ct Manassas VA 20110-4901 Personal E-mail: marydellinger@msn.com.

DELO, LYNDA JEANNE, secondary school educator; b. Tulsa, Okla., Apr. 11, 1961; d. Larry Dean and Norma Jeanne Lloyd; m. James Andrew Delo, Aug. 29, 1987; children: Jack, Andrew, Martyn, Derek. BA, Ouachita Bapt. U., Arkadelphia, Ark., 1983. Cert. tchr. Ark., La. Missionary New Tribes Mission, Papua New Guinea, 1988—2000; tutor Shreveport, La., 2001—02; sci. tchr. Caddo Pub. Schs., Shreveport, 2002—. Com. mem., merit badge counselor Boy Scouts of Am., Shreveport, 2001—06. Recipient tchr. mini grant, Alliance for Edn., 2003, 2004, 2005. Mem.: NEA, Nat. Sci. Tchrs. Assn. Avocations: camping, reading, scrapbooks. Office: Captain Shreve High 6115 E Kings Hwy Shreveport LA 71105 Office Phone: 318-865-7137. Personal E-mail: ldeloread@bellsouth.net.

DELOFF, DOLA LOUISE, secondary school educator; b. Fredericksburg, Va., Mar. 31, 1962; d. Newton John and Bertha Lou Coughenour; m. Francis Raymond Deloff, Sept. 1, 1984; children: Jeffrey Francis, Daniel Patrick. BS,

Pa. State U., University Park, 1984; MS in Edn., SUNY, Oswego, 1992, MA, 1992. Cert. tchr. NY, 1992. Tchr. Mexico H.S., NY, 1986—. Adj. prof. SUNY, Oswego, 1993—; instr. IIT Tech. Inst., Ind., 2004—. Home: 120 W Mohawk St Oswego NY 13126 Office: Mexico Central School Main St Mexico NY 13126 Office Phone: 315-963-8400. Personal E-mail: ddeloff1@twcny.rr.com. Business E-Mail: ddeloff@mexico.cnyric.org.

DE LONG, KATHARINE, retired secondary school educator; b. Germantown, Pa., Aug. 31, 1927; d. Melvin Clinton and Katherine Frances (Brunner) Barr; m. Alfred Alvin De Long, June 21, 1947; children: Renée, Claudia, Jane. AA, Mesa Jr. Coll., Grand Junction, Colo., 1962; BA, Western State Coll., Gunnison, Colo., 1964; MA, Colo. State U., Ft. Collins, 1972. Camp dir. Girl Scout Day Camp, 1958—60, Kannah Creek Girl Scout Camp, 1960-64; tchr. Mesa County Valley Sch. Dist. #51, Grand Junction, 1964-84, dept. chmn., 1970-79; ret., 1984; tour coord., escort Mesa Travel, 1990—2002. Substitute instr. Mesa State Coll., 1986-90; student council sponsor Mesa County Valley Sch., 1976-80; bd. dirs. Am. Red Cross, mem. disaster team, 1996-2000, state svc. coun. rep., 1998-2000. Bd. dirs. Chipeta Girl Scout Coun., Grand Junction, 1960-66; pct. committeewoman Mesa County Dem. Party; mem., vice-chmn. Profl. Rights and Responsibilities Commn. for Dist. #51 Schs., Grand Junction, 1978-84; trustee Western Colo. Ctr. for the Arts, Grand Junction, 1987-88; mem. Mesa County Hist. Soc.; mem. Mesa County Coun. on Aging, 1994—, chmn., 2002, 03; rep. Area Agy. in Aging, 2002-05. Mem. AAUW (pres. local chpt. 1979-81, chmn. state cultural interest), AARP (Colo. legis. com. area I, transp. task force, dist. dir. dist. 1, del. to nat. conv., dir. state conv. 1991, legis. com. 1988-90, asst. state dir. 1990-91, dist. dir. 1991-94), LWV (Grand Junction Area, sec. bd. dirs. 1995-2000, Pub. Employees Retirement Assn. (legis. adv. com. 1990-91), Colo. Ret. Sch. Employees Assn. (v.p. 1993, 94), Mesa County Coun. on Aging (rep. to area agy. on aging 2000—, pres. 2002, 2003), Wednesday Music Club (treas. 2002-03, pres., 2003-04), Phi Theta Kappa. Congregationalist. Avocations: music, theater, swimming, hiking, travel.

DELONG, LORI LYNN, physical education educator, athletic trainer; b. Monroe, La., Mar. 16, 1973; d. Bryan Leslie and Linda Diane McGaha; m. Robert James DeLong, July 16, 2005. BA, La. Coll., Pineville, 1991—95; MEd, U. La., Monroe, 1995—97; PhD, La. State U., Baton Rouge, 1999—2006. Cert. athletic trainer BOC, 2001. Asst. women's basketball coach La. Coll., Pineville, 1996—2001, asst. prof., 2001—. Athletic trainer La. Coll., 2001—. Vol. athletic trainer Internat. Sports Fedn., Atlanta, 2003—04, Olympics, Athlens, Greece, 2004. Mem.: NCAA (sr. women's adminstr. 2000), SE Athletic Trainers' Assn. (women in athletic tng. com. 2002—06), La. Athletic Trainers' Assn. (edn. com.), Nat. Athletic Trainers' Assn. Home: 115 Country Club Dr Pineville LA 71360 Office: La Coll 1140 College Dr Pineville LA 71359

DELONG-SMITH, STEPHANIE K., secondary school educator; b. Chadds Ford, Pa., Dec. 20, 1969; d. Warren Earl and Carla Jean (Douthat) DeLong; m. Carl E. Smith, July 27, 1996; 1 child, Laura Eden. BA in History and Social Studies Edn., York Coll. of Pa., 1992; MA in History, U. Ky., 1996. Tchr. 7th grade McCurdy Mission Sch., Espanola, N.Mex., 1992-94; dance instr. Lexington, 1993-94; tchr. 7th grade Woodland Hills Christian Sch., Harlan, Ky., 1996-97; tchr. high sch. social studies-AP U.S. history Cawood H.S., Harlan County Bd. Edn., 1997-99. Intern in mus. edn. Hagley Mus., Wilmington, Del., 1991. Lifeguard and Red Cross swim instr. Kendal and Crosslands, Kennett Square, Pa., 1986-96; advisor Y-Club, Cawood High Sch., 1997—. James Madison Meml. fellow Madison Found., 1993; recipient Ashland Golden Apple Teaching award Ashland Oil, 1999. Mem. Nat. Coun. History Edn., Orgn. Am. Historians, Ky. Assn. Tchrs. of History, Pa. Hist. Assn., Ladies Golf Assn. (v.p. 1999—), Beta Sigma Phi (Zeta Beta chpt.), Phi Sigma Pi. Avocations: ballet dancing, reading, golf, cooking international cuisine, singing in church choir. Home: 1345 Ivy Hl Harlan KY 40831-1550 E-mail: Sdelong@Eastky.net.

D'ELOSUA, JENNIFER DAWN, music educator; b. Fort Sill, Okla., Aug. 19, 1977; d. Ralph Frederick and Kathy Taylor D'Elosua. BA in Music Edn., Shenandoah U., Winchester, Va., 1999. Performer Walt Disney World, Orlando, Fla., 1999—2002; music specialist Fairfax County Pub. Schs., Springfield, Va., 2002—. Tchr. rsch. leader Tchr. Rsch., Springfield, 2005—; dir., tchr. pvt. music studio, Springfield, 2002—; presenter in field; performer various sch. fundraising events. Dir., choreographer: (prodn.) King's Voices; composer various songs for sch. programs. Mem.: Sigma Alpha Iota (corr.). Home: 8225 Crestmont Cir Springfield VA 22153 Office: Kings Park Elem Sch 5400 Harrow Way Springfield VA 22151 Office Phone: 703-426-7000. Personal E-mail: jdznygoof@aol.com.

DELOZIER, DORIS M., retired secondary school educator; b. Hartford, Vt., June 11, 1933; d. Arthur James and Lena Anne Moffitt; m. A. John Lacaillade, Aug. 19, 1958 (div. Sept. 6, 1964); m. Dean K. Delozier, July 9, 1969; 1 child, Tracy. BA, Plymouth State Coll., 1957; MEd, Boston U., 1968; advanced grad. studies, Harvard U., 1987. Lic. tchr. N.H., Mass. Tchr. English Laconia (N.H.) Sch. Dist., 1958—68, reading specialist, 1969—96; ESL specialist Harvard U., Cambridge, Mass., 1984—87; reading cons. Coll. Park Elem. Sch., Ocala, Fla., 1999—2001; ret., 2001. Head Right to Read program Supervisory Assn. Union # 30, Laconia, 1970—80; mem. adv. bd. N.H. Edn. Assn., Concord, 1975—85; literacy chmn. Delta Kappa Gamma, Laconia, 1970—80; reading curriculum devel. Laconia Sch. Sys., 1979; literacy sec. AAUW, Laconia, 1967—77; literacy chmn. Zonta Internat., Laconia, 1990—. Co-author: (booklet) Sign Posts in Reading, 1975; author: (study skills book) Fishing for Success, 1992, (guide booklet) Keep It Simple, 2001 (Am. Assn. Ret. Persons award, 2001). Recipient tchg. fellowship, Harvard U., 1984. Republican. Episcopalian. Avocations: golf, bridge, reading, antiques. Home: 11558 SW 72 Cir Ocala FL 34476-9487

DEL PAPA, FRANKIE SUE, former state attorney general; b. 1949; BA, U. Nev.; JD, George Washington U., 1974. Bar: Nev. 1974. Staff asst. U.S. Senator Alan Bible, Washington, 1971—74; assoc. Law Office of Leslie B. Grey, Reno, 1975—78; legis. asst. to U.S. Senator Howard Cannon, Washington, 1978—79; ptnr. Thornton & Del Papa, 1979—84; pvt. practice Reno, 1984—87; sec. of state State of Nev., Carson City, 1987—91, atty. gen., 1991—2002. Active Nev. Women's Fund; bd. dirs. Sierra Arts Found.; adv. com. Trust for Pub. Land. Democrat. E-mail: renofsdp@aol.com.

DELPH, DONNA JEAN (DONNA MAROC), education educator, consultant, academic administrator; b. Hammond, Ind., Mar. 7, 1931; d. Edward Joseph and Beatrice Catherine (Ethier) Maroc; m. Billy Keith Delph, May 30, 1953 (div. 1967); 1 child, James Eric. BS, Ball State U., 1953, MA, 1963, EdD, 1970. Cert. in ednl. adminstrn./supervision, reading specialist, Ind.; cert. elem. sch. tchr., Ind., Calif. Elem. tchr. Long Beach (Calif.) Community Schs., 1953-54; elem. tchr., reading specialist, asst. dir. elem. edn. Hammond Pub. Schs., 1954-70; prof. edn. Purdue U. Calumet, Hammond, 1970-84, 88-90, prof. emeritus, 1990—, head dept. edn., dir. tchr. edn., 1984-88. Cons. pub. schs., Highland, Ind., 1970-88, Gary, Ind., 1983-88, East Chicago, Ind., 1987-88, Hammond, 1970-88; speaker/workshop presenter numerous profl. orgns., Hammond, 1964—; mem. exec. coun. Nat. Coun. Accreditation Tchr. Edn., 1991-97. Author: (with others) Individualized Reading, 1967; contbr. articles, monographs to profl. jours. Bd. dirs. Bethany Child Care and Devel. Ctr., Hammond, 1972-77. Recipient Outstanding Teaching award Purdue U. Calumet, 1981. Mem. Assn. Tchr. Educators, Assn. for Supervision and Curriculum Devel. (rev. coun. 1987-91, bd. dirs. 1974-85), Internat. Reading Assn., Ind. Reading Profs. (pres. 1985-86), Pi Lambda Theta. Office: Purdue Univ Calumet Dept Education Hammond IN 46323 Personal E-mail: delnjohn@otherside.com.

DELPIT, LISA D., education educator, researcher, consultant; b. Baton Rouge, May 23, 1952; d. Thomas Henry Delpit and Edmae Celestine (La Motte) Butler; 1 child, Maya Adiya. BA in Edn. Psychology, Antioch Coll., 1974; EdM, Harvard U., 1980, EdD, 1984. Administrv. asst. to tchr. Durham Child Devel. Ctr., Phila., 1972-77; lectr. Antioch Coll., Phila., 1976-79; cons. Cambridge (Mass.) pub. sch. system, 1980-81; co-dir. tchr. tng. program U. Mass., Boston, 1979-81; program dir. Earthwatch, Inc., Belmont, Mass., 1981-82; cons. North Solomons provincial govt., Arawa, Papua New Guinea, 1982-83, Atari Rsch. Lab., Cambridge, 1983-84; asst. prof. Reading, Language, Literacy, coord. tchr. edn. program U. Alaska, Fairbanks, 1987-88; assoc. prof. Sch. Edn. Mich. State U., Lansing, 1988—; sr. rsch. assoc. Inst. Urban Rsch. Morgan State U., Baltimore, 1988—. Facilitator Phila. Parent-Tchr. Ctrs., 1975-77; mem. Sch. Employees Action Caucus, Phila., 1975-77; supr. La. State Dept. Edn., Baton Rouge, 1977-79; cons. Roxbury Community Coll., Boston, 1980-81; guest faculty Cleve. State U., 1981; dir. Summer Inst. Cross Cultural Studies, 1985; mem. Internat. Edn. Com., Fairbanks, 1984-85; mem. Minority Task Force, Fairbanks North Star Bourough Sch. Dist., 1987-88; vice-chairperson exec. bd. Alaska State Humanities Forum, 1986-88; rsch. support Nat. Black Child Devel. Inst., Baltimore; co-chair, African and African-American Curriculum Com. Baltimore City Pub. Schs. Author: A Classroom Incident, 1975, Language and Culture: An Evaluation of the North Solomons Viles Tok Ples Skuls, 1986; contbr. articles to profl. jours. Frederick Sheldon Traveling fellow Harvard U., 1981-82, Annie Ryder fellow AAUW, 1981-82, Ednl. Found Dissertation fellow AAUW, 1984, Spencer fellow, Nat. Acad. Edn., 1988, MacArthur fellow, 1990; Harvard U. scholar, 1981-82; named Outstanding Community Contbr. Childhood Learning Ctrs., 1979. Mem. Interat. Reading Assn., Am. Ednl. Rsch. Assn., Nat. Coun. Teaching of English, Nat. Bd. for profl. Teaching Standards, (vice-chairman Standards Com., Early Adolescence/English Lang. Arts Standards Com.), Phi Delta Kappa. Office: Morgan State U Inst for Urban Rsch Baltimore MD 21239

DEL SESTO, JANICE MANCINI, opera company executive; Grad., New England Conservatory. Dir. development and comm. New England Foundation for the Arts, 1983—89; dir. development and public relations Computer Museum, 1989—92; gen. dir. Boston Lyric Opera Co., Boston, 1992—. Office: Boston Lyric Opera Co 45 Franklin St Boston MA 02110-1301

DEL TIEMPO, SANDRA KAY, sales executive; b. Willoughby, Ohio, Nov. 21, 1962; d. Charles Soloman and Lacey Marie (Webb) Eggers; m. Robert Joseph Craig, June 28, 1986 (div. Jan. 1993); 1 child, Misty Marie Mangus; m. Robert David Del Tiempo, Feb. 14, 1995; stepchildren: Jaime Brandon, Joseph David Del Tiempo. AAB cum laude, Shawnee State U., 1985; BBA summa cum laude, Ohio U., 1987; postgrad., Pepperdine U., 1998—2000. From ter. mgr. to sales mgr. ARA Cory, San Diego, 1988—90; sales rep. Rsch. Inst. Am., Riverside, Calif., 1990—92, 1996—2000, regional sales mgr. So. Calif., L.A., 1992—95, leader's coun. Culver City, 1996—2000, pres. bd. dirs., 1996—97, asst. mgr., 1997, 1999—2000, corp. acct. mgr., 1997—2000; mem. sales adv. bd. RIA/CLR Group (formerly Rsch. Inst. Am.), Culver City, 1998—2000; sr. v.p. Media Strategy Lawnmower Media, Culver City, 2000; sr. account exec. SAP Am., Irvine, Calif., 2000—03; acct. mgr. CCH, Inc., 2003—04; cons. internet mktg. LexisNexis, New Providence, NJ, 2004—. Cons. Video Ave., Paradise Pizza, Chillicothe, Ohio, 1987-88; sales rep. to corp. acct. mgr. Rsch. Inst. Am. Orange County, L.A., 1990-2000 Active Girl Scouts U.S., Menifee, 1988—92, Jr. All Am. Football. Mem. NAFE, NOW, Phi Kappa Phi, Phi Theta Kappa, Delta Mu Delta. Democrat. Avocations: travel, reading, jazz. Home: 6732 E Ashler Hills Cave Creek AZ 85331-3130 Office: Martindale Hubbell 123 Chanlon Rd New Providence NJ 07974 Office Phone: 480-575-0050. Personal E-mail: sdeltiempo@yahoo.com. Business E-Mail: sandra.deltiempo@martindale.com.

DEL TORO-POLITOWICZ, LILLIAN, medical association administrator, geriatrics services professional, consultant; b. Bronx, N.Y., Feb. 23, 1954; d. Billie Antonio Del Toro and Eva Luz (Guasp) Toro; 1 child, Yvelise Delilah Chandler; m. Walter Politowicz, Nov. 23, 1997; 1 stepchild, Sebastian. BS in Psychology summa cum laude, Mercy Coll., 1981; postgrad., L.I. U., 1982-83, Harvard U., 1973-74, Lehman Coll., 1972, 75, Nova South-Eastern U., 1998—. Lic. adminstr. adult care facilities, Fla. Mental hygiene therapist Rockland Psychiat. Hosp., Orangeburg, NY, 1975-81; office mgr. Frankart Furniture, Inc., Pelham Pkwy., NY, 1979-84; regional office mgr. W.J. Sloane, Inc., Ridgewood, NY, 1984-86; bookkeeper, asst. dir. mgmt. info. sys. Midland Lumber Supply Co., Midland Pk., NY, 1986-89; adminstr. Fla. Golden Years, Spring Hill, 1991-92, Gallo House II, River Lodge, New Port Richey, Fla., 1994-95, Ranch House, Tarpon Springs, Fla., 1993-94; co-owner Elder Care Foster Home, Spring Hill, Fla., 1992—. Grad. admissions counselor L.I. U., Bklyn., 1981-82; elder-care cons. Fla. Golden Years, Spring Hill, 1991-92. Harvard U. scholar, 1973-74; recipient outstanding achievement, health & human svcs.- cmty. svc. award YWCA and St. Petersburg Times, Tampa, 1997; undergraduate pre-medicine scholar Lehman Coll., Bronx, N.Y., 1972, 75, Harvard U., 1973-74. Mem. AAUW, NAFE, Altrusa Internat. (mem. cmty. projects com. 1997), Fla. Assisted Living Adminstrs. Assn., Alpha, Psi Chi. Avocations: world music and dance, opera, ballet, reading, nature. Home and Office: Elder Care Foster Home 6427 Mayhill Ct Spring Hill FL 34606-6028 E-mail: politowicz@yahoo.com.

DELUCA, ANNETTE, professional golfer; b. North Bergen, N.J., May 13, 1968; Golfer LPGA, 1989—; mem. Asian Tour, 1993; mem. Gold Coast Tour, 1994, 95; 3 Gold Coast victories, 1995; qualifier U.S. Women's Open, 1994, 95. Avocations: fishing, water sports, harley davidson motorcycles, movies, working out. Office: c/o LPGA 100 International Golf Dr Daytona Beach FL 32124-1082

DE LUCA, EVA, vocalist, writer, composer, entrepreneur, inventor; d. John Adolph De Luca and Rosa Maria Litrenta; m. Alfred A. Sima, May 11, 1975 (dec. Dec. 1984); m. Russell Frederick Du Laux, Dec. 24, 1985 (dec. Apr. 2006). Student, Peabody Conservatory, Juilliard Sch., 1943—44, Marymount Coll., 1985; D (hon.), Dewey Internat. Consortium, 1999. Pres. Eva De Luca Co., N.Y.C., 1950, Greeting Scrolls, Ltd., N.Y.C., 1960; mem. adv. bd. Humanity Against Hatred, N.Y.C., 1992—96; cons. Creative Consultations, N.Y.C., 1994; CEO, dir., inventor Creative Ideas Unlimited U.S.A., 2001. Singer: (Operas) (profl. operatic debut) Phila. La Scala Opera Co., (European debut) La Boheme, Madama Butterfly; singer: (starred in 1st recording) (albums) (for Columbia Records) La Rondine (Puccini), 1955; author: poetry; design patent Mirror-View Measuring Stick, 1972, personal dental aid. Active Italian Welfare League, N.Y.C., 1978, Met. Opera Guild, N.Y.C., 1979; mem. Women's Nat. Rep. Club, N.Y.C., 1978—85. Recipient Editor's Choice award for Outstanding Achievement in Poetry, Nat. Libr. Poetry, 1997. Mem.: Am. Soc. Composers, Authors and Pubs., Famous Poets Soc., Russian Nobility Assn. Am., Inc. (mem. benefit com.), Soldiers, Sailors, Marines and Airmen's Club (adv. bd.), Sovereign Order Orthodox Knights Hospitalier St. John of Jersusalem (dame comdr.), Nat. Orgn. Italian-Am. Women. Roman Catholic. Achievements include being an inventor in her field; patents for a mirror-view measuring stick; a personal dental aid. Avocations: reading, politics, theater, opera. Home: 3510 Bainbridge Ave Apt 2F Bronx NY 10467-1419 Office Phone: 718-653-4095.

DELUCA, JENNIE M., English educator; b. Scranton, Pa., Dec. 12, 1964; d. Russell Michael and Mary Ann Nowalk; m. Robert Anthony DeLuca, Sept. 23, 1989; 1 child, Nicole Marie. BS in Secondary Edn., Pa. State U., 1988, MEd in Instructional Sys., 1995; EdD in Ednl. Leadership, Immaculate U., 2000. Tchr. lang. arts Penn Wood West Jr. HS, Darby, Pa., 1988—89, Yeaden, 1989—91, Marple Newton Sr. HS, Newton Square, 1993—. Mem.: ASCD, Am. Ednl. Rsch. Assn., Phi Delta Kappa. Avocations: theater, music, art, travel, tennis. Home: 11 Smedley Dr Newtown Square PA 19073 Office: Marple Newtown Sr High Sch 120 Media Line Rd Newtown Square PA 19073 Office Phone: 610-296-7478. E-mail: dr.deluca@comcast.net.

DELUCA, SUSAN RICE, physical education educator; b. Providence, Dec. 12, 1946; d. Stephen Arnold and Marjorie Campbell Rice; m. Richard James DeLuca, Nov. 24, 1973; 1 child, Amy Lynn DeLuca Stafford. BS, Fla. State U., Tallahassee, 1968; MS, U. Mass., Amherst, 1973. Motor therapist Children's Perceptual Achievement, East Providence, RI, 1969—72; phys. edn. tchr. Warwick Elem. Schs., RI, 1969—72; phys. edn. tchr., coach Coventry Jr. HS, RI, 1973—76, Tri County Regional Vocat. and Tech. HS, Franklin, Mass., 1974—2005; ednl. cons., 2005—. Alpine ski instr. Mt. Sunapee Resort, Newbury, NH, 1984—; lectr., presenter in field. Named to 75th Anniversary Hall of Fame, Whitinsville Golf Club; 31 Ladies Club golf championships, 1977—2005, 21 Ladies Club championships, Whitinsville Country Club. Mem.: AAHPERD, Mass. Tchrs. Assn., Mass. Assn. Health, Phys. Edn., Recreation and Dance, Mass. Women's Golf Assn., US Golf Assn., NH Women's Golf Assn., NEA, Phi Delta Pi. Avocations: golf, skiing, travel, gardening. Home: 73 Summit View Rd New London NH 03257

DELUCCIA, PAULA, artist; b. Paterson, N.J., Sept. 9, 1953; d. Ralph Lincoln and Isabel Miriam (Santucci) DeLuccia; m. Larry Poons, Dec. 18, 1981 Student, Ridgewood Sch. Art, N.J., 1971—73, Kansas City Art Inst., Mo., 1973—74. Exhibited in group shows at Nelson Atkins Mus., Kansas City, 1974, Ridgewood Sch. Art, 1978, Soghor Leonard & Assocs., N.Y.C., 1985, Art & Design, Phila., 1985, Jerusalem Gallery, N.Y.C., 1986, Helander Gallery, Palm Beach, Fla., 1990, 91, 92, 93, Wetherholt Gallery, Washington, 1991, Perspectives, Ghent, N.Y., 1991, Schulte Galleries, South Orange, N.J., 1992, Greene County Coun. Arts, Catskill, N.Y., 1992-93, 2000, 2001, 2002, 2004, 2006, Lorraine Kessler Gallery, Poughkeepsie, N.Y., 1992-93, Philharmonic Ctr. Arts, Naples, Fla., 1993, Farah Damji Fine Art, N.Y.C., 1993, Mountaintop Gallery, Windham, N.Y., 1994, 95, 98, Roger Smith Gallery, N.Y.C., 1994, Art/Omi Studios, N.Y., 1994, Planet Thailand, Bklyn., 1995, 97, 98, Tribes Gallery, N.Y.C., 1996, Sideshow, Bklyn., 1998, 2001, 2004, 2006, Claudia Carr Gallery, N.Y.C., 1998, Steinboum Kraus Gallery, N.Y.C., 1999, Phoenix Gallery, 2002, Perrella Gallery, Johnstown, N.Y., 2003, Hudson (N.Y.) Opera House, 2004, McIninch Art Gallery, Manchester, N.H., 2004, AIR Gallery, N.Y.C., 2005, AAWAA Gallery, Bklyn., 2005, 06, Asian Fusion Gallery, N.Y.C., 2005, GCCA Windham Gallery, 2006, Sideshow Gallery, 2006; two-person exhbns. include Farah Damji Fine Art, 1993, LaCappelli, Cambridge, Mass., 1995; one-woman shows include The Bentley Inn, Bay Head, N.J., 1993, Hair Gallery, N.Y.C., 1995, Side Show Gallery, Bklyn., 2001, 02, 03, C.W. White Gallery, Portland, 2003, Phoenix Gallery, 2003, Richard Sena Gallery, Hudson, 2003, Deborah Davis Fine Art, Hudson, 2004, AAWAA Gallery, 2004, Studio 18, N.Y., 2004, 05, Ceres Gallery, 2006, Side Show, 2006, Brik Gallery, 2006, Jean Eseilich Fine Art, 2006; represented in permanent collections of City of Barcelona, Art Omi, Leshanski, O'Sullivan & Maybaum, N.Y.C., Pondside Press, Ghant, N.Y., and numerous private collections; drawing reproduced in Cover Mag., 1982; paintings reproduced in Long Shot, 1993 Recipient Art Triangle Barcelona, Spain, 1987, Inaugural Yr. award Art/Omi, 1992 Home: 831 Broadway New York NY 10003-4706 Personal E-mail: sixthkid9@yahoo.com.

DELUCIA, CHARLOTTE, psychotherapist; b. Patchogue, NY, Apr. 14, 1975; d. Ralph Richard and Nancy Jane Delucia. BA, NYU, NYC, 1997; MA, Naropa U., Boulder, Colo., 2002. Crisis counselor NYC Dept. Edn., Project Liberty Unit, Bklyn., 2002—03, borough coord., 2003—04; sr. counselor Infant & Child Learning Ctr., SUNY, Bklyn., 2004—06; program coord. Project Renewal Tides Ctr., NYC, 2006—. Office Phone: 212-509-0022. Business E-Mail: cdelvcia@projectrenewaltides.org.

DE LUNA-GONZALEZ, ELMA, accountant, academic administrator; b. Edinburg, Tex., June 22, 1950; d. Emilio De Luna and Julia Andaverde; m. Antonio Gonzalez, Oct. 10, 1975; 1 child, Julissa Priscilla Gonzalez. AA, Houston C.C., Tex., 1986; BA, Houston Internat. U., Tex., 1990, U. Houston, 1997; MA, Prairie View A&M U., Tex., 1999. Bookkeeper Aluminum Industries, McAllen, Tex., 1973—75; estimator Clow Corp., Tarrant City, Ala., 1975—79; acct. Freeman Design and Display Co., Houston, 1980—86, Forrest Mfg. Co., Houston, 1988, Hispanic Bus. and Acctg. Svcs., Houston, 1988—2001; asst. to dean Prairie View (Tex.) A&M U., 2001—06, dir. multicultural affairs, 2006—. Musician, vocalist De Luna Band, Dekalb, Ill., 1968—88. Composer: Impossible Love, 1987. Chair, treas. Gonzalez for Tex. Ho. Reps. Campaign, Houston, 1994. Named Women of the Yr., Ala. Women Soc., 1988; recipient Mayors award, City Kendelton, Tex., 2002. Mem.: ACA, AAUW, Tex. Counseling Assn., Nat. Soc. Pub. Accts., League United L.Am. Citizens, No. Ill. U. Women Club, Phi Delta Kappa, Chi Sigma Iota. Avocations: writing, music, reading. Home: 16614 Dounreay Dr Houston TX 77084 Office: Prairie View A&M U PO Box 4207 Prairie View TX 77446 Office Phone: 936-857-4543. Personal E-mail: elma_gonzalez@aol.com. Business E-Mail: gonzalez_e@pvamu.edu.

DE LUNG, JANE SOLBERGER, independent sector executive; b. Anniston, Ala., July 9, 1944; d. Samuel and Margaret Polk (Oldham) S.; m. Harry Leonard De Lung, Apr. 23, 1965 (div. 1972); m. Charles F. Westoff, May 2, 1997. BA in History, Emory U., Atlanta, 1966; MA in Urban Planning, Roosevelt U., Chgo., 1972. Exec. asst. Cook County Legal Assistance, Chgo., 1967—69; asst. dir. family planning Am. Coll. Ob-gyn., Chgo., 1969—71; v.p. Ill. Family Planning Coun., Chgo., 1971—80; asst. commr. Chgo. Dept. Pub. Health, 1981—82; pres. Pub. Solutions, Princeton, NJ, 1982—88, Population Resource Ctr., N.Y.C., 1988—. Bd. dirs. Planned Parenthood Mercer County, Trenton, NJ, 1986-96, Population Resource Ctr., 1989—, Trenton Head Start, 1993-98; adv. bd. dept. sociology Princeton U., 1991— Mem. APHA, AAUW, LWV, Internat. Union Sci. Study of Population, Population Assn. Am., UN Assn. of U.S.A. (nat. adv. com. 1998-). Democrat. Episcopalian. Office: Population Resource Ctr 1 Highland Rd Princeton NJ 08540 Office Phone: 609-492-7004. Business E-Mail: jdelung@prcnj.org.

DEL VILLAR, AURORA, science educator; d. Enrique and Aurora Del Villar; m. Miguel Angel Casillas, Nov. 5, 2005. BSc, Mt. St. Mary's Coll., L.A., 1992; MSc, Wayne State U., Detroit, 1995. Single Subject Profl. Clear Credential -BCLAD Emphasis Calif. State U. Dominguez Hills, 1998. Lab. rsch. asst. Mt. St. Mary's Coll., L.A., 1989—92; grad. rsch. asst. Wayne State U., Detroit, 1992—95; microbiology lab. technician Daniel Freedman Meml. Hosp., Inglewood, Calif., 1996; tchr. sci. Bell H.S., Calif., 1996—. Sci. instrnl. leader Bell H.S., 2003—; fellow tchg. advisor LA Tchg. Fellows, 2004; biotechnology labs adminstr. Pasadena City Coll., Calif., 2004—. Author: (article) Soc. Neurosci. Sch.-cmty. adv. Bell H.S., 2004, facilitator students-profls. partnership, 1998—2006; biotechnology outreach Calif. Biotechnology Office, Pasadena, 2004—06. Mem.: Nat. Sci. Tchrs. Assn. (assoc.). Achievements include research in memory and learning as well as in high blood pressure. Avocations: roller blading, hiking, dance, nature, travel. Office Phone: 323-560-1800.

DEMA-ALA, RELIE L., medical/surgical nurse; b. Dumangas, Iloilo, Philippines, May 30, 1951; d. Ireneo and Ceferina (Lobaton) D. Diploma, St. Paul's Sch. Nursing, Iloilo, 1972; BSN, St. Paul Coll., Manila, 1974. Cert. med.-surg. nurse. Staff nurse in orthopedics Meml. Med. Ctr., Savannah, Ga.; charge nurse surg. unit Hollywood Presbyn. Med. Ctr., L.A.; staff nurse surg. unit Glendale (Calif.) Meml. Hosp. Mem. Calif. Nurses Assn. (bd. dirs.), St. Paul Nurses Assn.

DEMAIO, BARBARA K., principal; b. NY, May 20, 1961; d. Henry and Rose Kulenovsky. BA, Queens Coll., Queens, NY, 1984; MSE, Fordham U., NY, 2002. Tchr. St. Cecila Sch., Bklyn., 1984—89, Most Precious Blood Sch., Long Island City, NY, 1989—2001, vice prin., 2001—04, prin., 2004—. Office: Most rPreciuos Blood Sch 32 52 37 St Long Island City NY 11103

DEMAIO, BARBARA PATRICIA, social worker; b. Bronx, N.Y., Oct. 29, 1940; d. Alphonse Joseph and Elizabeth Elsie (Vogel) DeM.; children: Antonio, Damon. AAS in Human Svcs., Rockland C.C., 1971; BSW summa cum laude, Fairleigh Dickinson U., 1973; MSW, Yeshiva U., 1975, postgrad., 1981. LCSW, qualified clin. social worker, diplomate. Counselor developmentally disabled ARC, Pomona, 1971-73; counselor foster care Abbott House, Tarrytown, N.Y., 1973-74; psychiat. social worker Mental Health Outpatient Clinic, Pomona, 1974-75; dir. med. social work Dept. Hosps. Robert Yeager Health Ctr., Pomona, N.Y., 1975—. Instr. Yeshiva U. Gerontol. Inst., 1981; cons. Skilled Nursing Facility, 1980; rape crisis counselor, 1983; adj. prof. Albany State U.; field instr. Fordham U., Dominican Coll., St. Thomas Aquinas Coll., Fairleigh Dickinson U., Rockland C.C., 1975—. Mem. NASW, Acad. Cert. Social Workers, Westchester-Rockland Health

Care Social Work Assn., Phi Sigma Omicron, Phi Omega Epsilon. Avocations: reading, art, music, home design. Office: Dr Robt L Yeager Health Ctr Dept Hosps Bldg A Pomona NY 10970

DEMAIO, DONNALEE A., bank executive; BA summa cum laude, Muhlenberg Coll. CPA, cert. internal auditor. Ptnr., banking practice Pricewaterhouse Coopers; CFO MetLife Bank, Bridgewater, NJ, 2002—05, pres., 2005—. Bd. mem. Regional Bus. Assistance Corp. Named one of 25 Most Powerful Women in Banking, US Banker mag., 2005. Mem.: Am. Inst. CPAs, NJ Soc. CPAs. Office: Met Life Bank 501 Rt 22 Bridgewater NJ 08807

DEMANKOWSKI, LISA RENEE, architect, educator; b. Chgo., Apr. 11, 1967; d. William Minto Davis and Judith Ann Dobbs; m. Dale Alvin Demankowski, Jan. 19, 1985; children: Brittany Noel, Gabriel Adam, Collin William. AS with high honors, Charles Stewart Mott C.C., Flint, Mich., 1992; BS, U. Mich., 1994, MArch with distinction, 2000. Registered arch., Mich., 2005, cert. Nat. Coun. Archtl. Registration Bd., 2005, endorsement, Fla., 2005. Arch. THA Archs. Engrs., Flint, 1995—2005; pres. NJB Archs., Inc., Flushing, Mich., 2005—. Adj. faculty Lansing (Mich.) C.C., 2005—. Treas. Shiawassee Twp., Bancroft, Mich., 1994—2004. U. Mich. Alumni scholar, U. Mich., Coll. Arch. and Urban Planning, 1999. Mem.: AIA (sec. Flint chpt. 2005—06), Rotary Club, Golden Key Nat. Honor Soc. Democrat. Avocations: landscaping, construction renovation/restoration/adaptive reuse, reading. Office: NJB Architects Inc 105 1/2 Main St Flushing MI 48433 Office Phone: 810-659-7118. Office Fax: 810-659-7224.

DEMANT, MARGARET H., retired interior designer; d. Walter and Erna Putzel Herz. Mgr., buyer, interior designer Walter Herz Interiors, Detroit and Southfield, Mich., 1944—85. Exec. comm. Internat. Furnishings Design Assn., Dallas, 1974—85. Author: Southern Market: A Market for Interior Designers. Mem. adv. bd. home furnishings mktg. program High Point Coll., 1980—85; chairperson subcom. for interior furnishings gen. adv. com. Detroit Pub. Schs., 1982—85; bd. mem. Detroit Inst. Arts, 1986—2006, mem. acquisitions comm., 1994—2006; trustee Mich. Opera Theatre, 2006—; adv. bd. mem. Jewish Adult Day Care Ctr., 2006—; bd. mem. Resettlement Svc., Detroit, 1987—90, Jewish Resettlement Svc., Detroit, 1987—90, Jewish Family Svc., Detroit, 1990—2006, Project Discovery, 2006—. Recipient Life Time Svc. award, Detroit Inst. Arts, 2004; Fellow mem., Internat. Furnishings Design Assn., 1991.

DEMARCO-MILLER, MARIE LISA, lawyer; d. John Michael DeMarco and Maria Desiderio; m. Gregory Nelson Miller, July 4, 1996; 1 child, Christopher Miller. BS in Acctg., Kean U., Union, N.J., 1987; JD, Stetson U., St. Petersburg, Fla., 1990. Bar: Fla. 1990, Md. 1996, U.S. Tax Ct. 1992. Law clk. U.S. Dist. Ct. No. Dist. Fla., Tallahassee, 1990—91; shareholder MacFarlane, Ferguson & McMullen, Clearwater, Fla., 1991—96; asst. U.S. atty. U.S. Dept. Justice, Orlando, Fla., 1996—2000; mng. ptnr. Overchuck, DeMarco, Byron & Overchuck, Winter Park, Fla., 2000—. Moot ct. bd., mock trial bd. Stetson U. Editor: Stetson U. Law Rev.; contbr. articles to profl. jours. Reader Head Start of Fla., Clearwater, 1991—92; patron various local charities. Named Best Advocate, Am. Coll. Trial Lawyers, 1990. Mem.: ATLA, AIEG, Assn. Fla. Trial Lawyers. Office: Overchuck DeMarco Byron & Overchuck 2709 W Fairbanks Ave Winter Park FL 32789

DEMAREST, SYLVIA M., lawyer; b. Lake Charles, La., Aug. 16, 1944; d. Edmand and Emily Demarest; m. James A. Johnston, Jr., Oct. 31, 1975 (div. Dec. 1979). Student, U. S.W. La., 1963-66; JD, U. Tex., 1969. Bar: Tex. 1969, U.S. Supreme Ct. 1973, U.S. Ct. Appeals (5th cir.) 1970, U.S. Ct. Appeals (7th cir.) 1979, U.S. Ct. Appeals (11th cir.) 1980, U.S. Dist. Ct. (no. dist.) Tex. 1970, U.S. Dist. Ct. (ea. dist.) Tex. 1970, U.S. Dist. Ct. (so. dist.) Tex. 1972. Reginald H. Smith Cmty. Lawyer fellow, Corpus Christi and Dallas, 1969-71; house counsel Tex. Inst. Ednl. Devel., San Antonio, 1972-73; staff atty. Dallas Legal Svsc. Found., Inc., 1973, exec. dir., 1973-76; sole practice Dallas, 1977-78; mgr. product litig., dir. Windle Turley, P.C., Dallas, 1978-83; sole practice Dallas, 1983-85; ptnr. Demarest & Smith, Dallas, 1985—. Mem. faculty trial advocacy program So. Meth. U. Law Sch., 1984; lectr. Contbr. articles to profl. jours. Mem. ABA, State Bar Tex., ATLA, Dallas Bar Assn., Dallas Trial Lawyers Assn. (past pres.), Dallas Inn of Ct. (master of the bar 1989—). Democrat. Home: 1812 Atlantic St Dallas TX 75208-3002 Office: 10440 N Central Expy Ste 1100 Dallas TX 75231

DEMARINIS, NANCY A., state legislator, educator; b. Glen Ridge, N.J., Sept. 11, 1930; d. Edmund Theodore and Sara Antoinette (Rosewater) Nesbitt; m. James Robertson, Feb. 14, 1948 (div. 1976); children: Margaret, Elizabeth, Theodore, Carl; m. Anthony R. Demarinis, Mar. 9, 1979. AS, Mohegan C.C., Norwich, Conn., 1973; BS, U. Conn., 1975; MS, So. Conn. State U., 1981. Cert. guidance counselor. Tchr. Groton (Conn.) Pub. Schs., 1975-78, guidance counselor, 1978-95; ret.; pvt. practice psychotherapist Groton, 1981-87; mem. Conn. Ho. Reps., Hartford, 1992—. Vol., bd. dirs., mem. various commns. United Way Women's Ctr., 1975—; town counselor, Groton, 1987-89. Democrat. Address: 898 Shennecossett Rd Groton CT 06340-6047 Office: Conn Ho of Reps Legis Office Bldg Hartford CT 06106 Office Phone: 240 0082.

DE MARNEFFE, BARBARA ROWE, historic preservationist; b. Boston, June 2, 1929; d. H S Payson and Florence Van Arnhem (Cassard) Rowe; m. James Hopkins, Oct. 9, 1954 (div. 1969); m. Francis de Marneffe, 1969; stepchildren: Peter, Daphne, Colette. BA, Vassar Coll., 1952. Tchr. Chapin Sch., NYC, 1952-54; adminstrv. asst. to dean Sch. of Indsl. Mgmt., MIT, Cambridge, 1959-60; asst. pub. rels. dir. Peter Bent Brigham Hosp., Boston, 1960-61, pub. rels. dir., 1961-63; pub. rels. cons. Diabetes Found. and Joslin Clinic, Boston, 1963-64; pub. rels. dir. McLean Hosp., Belmont, Mass., 1964-68; mgr. pub. affairs Cambridge (Mass.) C. of C., 1975-78; pres. de Marneffe Selections, Cambridge, 1978-90. Trustee Edith Wharton Restoration, Inc, 1999; chair Edith Wharton Restoration, Inc., 2002—03, co-chair, 2003—06, chair, 2006—; corporator Brookline (Mass.) Savs. Bank, 1995—2002. Contbr. articles to profl. jours. Trustee coun. Archives Am. Art, Smithsonian Inst., Washington, 1983—99, 1999—2000; officer, bd. dirs. Family Counseling Svcs. Cambridge, 1969—78; trustee Peterborough (NH) Players, 1983—89; docent NC Mus. Art, Raleigh, 1992—93; chair Friends of Pain Ctr. Mass. Gen. Hosp., Boston, 1995—99; mem. adv. coun. Farnsworth Art Mus., Rockland, Maine, 1995—98; chmn. New Eng. Com., 1982—88, trustee, 1988—2000; state comitteewoman Mass. Rep., 1977—80; exec. sec. Cambridge Rep. City Com., 1956—57; pub. rels. dir. Peabody for Congress Campaign, Newton, Mass., 1968; vestry Emmanuel Episcopal Ch., Dublin, NH, 1995—; com. mem. Ellis Mem. Settlement House Antiques Show, 1968—89; bd. dirs. Friends McLean Hosp, Belmont, Mass., 1967—89, Friends Frances Lehman Loeb Art Ctr., Vassar Coll., 2001—05, Nat. Com. Treatment Intractable Pain, Washington, 1980—90. Mem.: Jewelers Am. Inc., Vassar Club (pres. Boston chpt. 1989). Avocations: medicine, business, politics, history, art. Home: 126 Coolidge Hl Cambridge MA 02138-5522

DE MARR, MARY JEAN, English language educator; b. Champaign, Ill., Sept. 20, 1932; d. William Fleming and Laura Alice (Shauman) Bailey. BA, Lawrence Coll., 1954; MA, U. Ill., Urbana, 1957; PhD, U. Ill., 1963; postgrad., U. Tuebingen, Germany, 1954—55, Moscow State U., 1961—62. Asst. prof. English Willamette U., 1964-65; asst. prof. English Ind. State U., 1965-70, assoc. prof., 1970-75, prof., 1975-95, prof. emerita English and women's studies, 1996—. Author: Colleen McCullough: A Critical Companion, 1996, Barbara Kingsolver: A Critical Companion, 1999, Kaye Gibbons: A Critical Companion, 2003; co-author: Adolescent Female Portraits in the American Novel, 1961-81: An Annotated Bibliography, 1983, The Adolescent in the American Novel Since 1960, 1986; Am. editor: Annual Bibliography of English Language and Literature, 1979-90; editor, contbr. In the Beginning: First Novels in Mystery Series, 1995. Recipient Fulbright assistantship, 1954—55, Dove award, Popular Culture Assn., 1996, Midam. award, Soc. for the Study of Midwestern Lit., 2000. Mem.: ACLU, AAUP, MLA, Modern Humanities Rsch. Assn., Phi Kappa Phi, Phi Beta Kappa. Home: 594 Woodbine Terre Haute IN 47803-1760 Personal E-mail: mjd594@msn.com.

DEMARS, BONNIE MACON, librarian; b. Pensacola, Fla., Jan. 13, 1943; AA Pensacola Jr. Coll., 1963; BS, U. West Fla., 1968; M in Libr. Sci., Fla. State U., 1983. Head cataloging dept. W. Fla. Regional Library, 1969—79, asst. head tech. svcs. Pensacola, 1979—92, head reference dept., 1992—. Mem.: ALA, Fla. Libr. Assn. (mem. employee exec. com., named Employee of Month). Office: W Fla Regional Library 200 W Gregory St Pensacola FL 32502 Office Phone: 850-436-5063. Business E-Mail: bdemars@ci.pensacola.fl.us.

DEMARS, JUDITH M., elementary school educator; b. Cleve., Mar. 17, 1947; d. Edward C. and Ann J. (Sedivy) Nau; m. Gordon DeMars, Mar. 10, 1973; 1 child, Darren Jay. BS in Edn., Cleve. State U., 1969; MA in Edn., Baldwin Wallace Coll., Berea, Ohio, 1984; PhD, U. Akron, 1990. Cert. tchr. Nat. Bd. Edn., early childhood generalist Nat. Bd. Edn. Tchr. Garfield Heights City Sch., Ohio; tchr. 2nd and 3rd grades Warrensville Heights City Sch., Ohio; tutor developmental reading, 6th-8th grades Medina, Ohio; tutor Chpt. I reading, 1st and 2nd grade, multiage tchr. Highland Local Schs., Medina. Ohio Reads coord. Sharon Elem.; presenter in field. Rsch. on beginning reading methods. Mem. adv. com. Medina County Tchrs. Acad. Martha Holden Jennings grantee. Mem. Internat. Reading Assn. (Ohio coun.). Home: 6704 Kennard Rd Medina OH 44256-8559

DEMARY, JO LYNNE, school system administrator, elementary school educator; BEd, DEd, Coll. of William and Mary; MS in Spl. Edn., U. Va. Commonwealth. Tchr. Fairfax County Schs., Va., Henrico County Schs., Va., from tchr. to asst. supt. Va.; asst. supt. pub. instruction Commonwealth of Va., 1994—99, acting supt. pub. instruction, 1999—2000, supt. of pub. instruction, 2000—. Office: Va Dept Edn PO Box 2120 Richmond VA 23218

DEMASI, KARIN A., lawyer; b. San Francisco, July 20, 1971; BS, Northwestern Univ., 1993; JD, Univ. Pa., 1996. Bar: Pa. 1996, NY 1997. Law clk., Hon. D. Brock Hornby US Dist. Ct., Dist. of Maine; assoc. Cravath Swaine & Moore LLP, NYC, 1997—2005, ptnr., litig., 2005—. Editor: Univ. Pa. Law Rev. Office: Cravath Swaine & Moore LLP Worldwide Plz 825 Eighth Ave New York NY 10019-7475 Office Phone: 212-474-1059. Office Fax: 212-474-3700. Business E-Mail: kdemasi@cravath.com.

DE MASSA, JESSIE G., media specialist; BJ, Temple U.; MLS, San Jose State U., 1967; postgrad., U. Okla., U. So. Calif. Tchr. Palo Alto (Calif.) Unified Sch. Dist., 1966; libr. Antelope Valley Joint Union HS Dist., Lancaster, Calif., 1966, ABC Unified Sch. Dist., Artesia, Calif., 1968—72; dist. libr. Tehachapi (Calif.) Unified Sch. Dist., 1972—81; media specialist, free lance writer, 1981—; assoc. Chris DeMassa & Assocs., 1988—. Author: (novel) The Haunting and Murder in Aruba, 2002; contbr. articles to profl. jours. Active Statue of Liberty Ellis Island Found., Inc., Nat. Trust Hist. Preservation; founding mem. Nat. Campaign for Tolerance Wall of Tolerance, Montgomery, Ala., 2005; charter supporter US Holocaust Meml. Mus., Washington; supporting mem. US Holocaust Meml. Coun., Washington; founder Pacific Aviation Mus. Pearl Harbor at Ford Islands, Hawaii, 2006. Named Nat. Women's Hall Fame, 1995. Fellow Internat. Biog. Assn.; mem. Calif. Media Libr. Educators Assn., Calif. Assn. Sch. Librs. (exec. coun.), AAUW (bull. editor chpt., assoc. editor state bull., chmn. publicity, 1955-68), Nat. Mus. Women Arts (charter), Hon Fellows John F. Kennedy Libr. (founding mem.), Women's Roundtable Orange County, Nat. Writer's Assn. (so. Calif. chpt.), Calif. Retired Tchrs. Assn. (Harbor Beach divsn. 77), Heritage Found., Claremont Inst., Nat. Women's History Mus. (charter mem.), Libr. Congress (nat. charter mem.), Nat. World War II Meml. Nat. Mall (charter mem.). Home: 9951 Garrett Cir Huntington Beach CA 92646-3604 Office Phone: 714-962-9810. E-mail: jdwriter10@verizon.net.

DE MATTEO, DREA, actress; b. Queens, NY, Jan. 19, 1973; BFA in film prodn., NYU, Tish Sch. Arts. Owner Filth Mart Clothing, NY. Actor: (TV series) The Sopranos, 1999—2004 (Emmy award Outstanding Supporting Actress in a Drama Series, 2004), Joey, 2004—; (films) Meet Prince Charming, 1999, Sleepwalk, 2000, Swordfish, 2001, The Perfect You, 2002, Deuces Wild, 2002, Love Rome, 2002, Prey for Rock & Roll, 2003, Beacon Hill, 2003, Assault on Precinct 13, 2005.

DEMATTEO, GLORIA JEAN, banker; b. Perth Amboy, N.J., May 23, 1943; d. John J. and Helena (Elias) Kancz; m. Ronald D. DeMatteo, Feb. 20, 1965 (div. Nov. 1987); children: Douglas J., Keith G. Student, Berkeley Sch., 1961. CLU. Exec. sec. Rhodia Inc., New Brunswick, N.J., 1961-65; real estate saleswomen Mid-Jersey Realty, East Brunswick, N.J., 1974-79; pntr. Realty World Garden of Homes, East Brunswick, 1979-81; spl. agt. Prudential Ins. Co. Am., Iselin, N.J., 1981-2000; agt. Rahway (N.J.) Savs. and Ins. Agy., Inc., 2000—01; account exec. retirement svcs. divsn. Citistreet Travelers Educators Retirement, Woodbridge, NJ, 2002—04; asst. v.p. and premier client mgr. Bank of Am., Bridgewater, NJ, 2004—05; asst. v.p. PNC Bank, Bridgewater, 2005—. V.p. Belcourt Condo Assn., North Brunswick, N.J., 1987-88. Mem. Nat. Assn. Life Underwriters (nat. sales achievement award, nat. quality award), Soc. Fin. Svc. Profls., Prudential Leaders Club. Avocations: bridge, hiking, dance, theater. Home: 463 Andover Pl East Brunswick NJ 08816-5121 Office: PNC Bank 1500 Prince Rodgers Ave Bridgewater NJ 08807 Office Phone: 908-459-7598.

DEMBECK, MARY GRACE, artist, writer; b. NYC, Oct. 29; m. John Francis Dembeck (dec.); children: Christine Elizabeth, John Francis Jr. Student, St. John's U., N.Y.C., Fordham U., Fairfield U., 1982-83; studies with Charles Reid, Daniel Green, John Mc Clelland, Leonard Everett Fisher, John C. Pellew and Mary Ann Hoberman, Conn., N.Y., 1974-82. Artist, pres. Pinafore, Ltd., Westport, Conn., 1987—. Works exhibited at Nat. Acad. Design, N.Y.C., 1981; author: Moonsnacks and Assorted Nuts, 1994; contbr. articles and poetry to mags., author numerous short stories; creator cartoon character Harriet; mng. editor, staff artist Carousel Mag., 1988-89; lyricist (with Maureen McGovern): (songs) I'm Mad at the Moon, Sweet Dream, Gadzook Tea; lyricist: (children's musical) Bengal Tiger's Ball, 1999. Designer Mass book cover St. Patrick's Cathedral, N.Y.C., 1977-2000; judge children's poetry and short story Trumbull Arts Festival, 1986-89; artist mem. Italian Apostolate Archdiocese N.Y.C. Recipient Nat. Pub. Radio award, 1987. Mem. ASCAP, Nat. League of Pen Women (poetry award 1983, best humorous poem 1984), Brontë Soc. Roman Catholic.

DEMBER, CYNTHIA FOX, retired clinical psychologist; b. N.Y.C., Feb. 15, 1934; d. Joseph and Florence Fox; m. William Norton Dember, Dec. 21, 1958; children: Joanna, Laura, Greg. AB, Vassar Coll., 1954; MS, Yale U., 1955, PhD, 1959. Dir. psychology Children's Psychiat. Ctr., Cin., 1961-80; pvt. practice Cin., 1962—97; ret. Adj. prof. U. Cin., 1961-97. Contbr. articles to profl jour. Mem. APA, Ohio Psychol. Assn., Cin. Acad. Profl. Psychology (pres. 1984), Clin. Soc. Child Clin. Psychologists (pres. 1982-84). Home: 920 Oregon Trl Cincinnati OH 45215-2536 E-mail: drsdember@aol.com.

DEMBROW, DANA LEE, lawyer; b. Washington, Sept. 29, 1953; parents: Daniel William and Catherine Louise (Carder) D. BA, Duke U., 1975; JD, George Washington U., 1980. Bar: D.C., Md., W.Va. Law clk. D.C. Superior Ct., Washington, 1979—80; mem. com. on constl. and adminstrv. law Md. Ho. of Dels., 1986—92; mem. jud. com. Md. State Legis., 1993—2002. Dir. policy and program devel. Dept. Juvenile Svcs., Balt., 2003-04; chair county affairs com., Montgomery Del., 1994-02; can. for congress, Md.'s 4th Congl. Dist., 1992; chair subcom. on civil law and procedure House Judiciary Com., 1994-02, intergovtl. affairs com., so. legis. conf., 1999-00; mem. bd. contract appeals Md. State, 2006-. Office Phone: 410-767-3524. Personal E-mail: danadembrow@aol.com. Business E-Mail: dembrow@msbca.state.md.us.

DEMEDIO, KATHLEEN MARIE, chemistry educator; b. Norristown, Pa., June 20, 1961; d. John Patrick and Caroline Mary (Conners) Agnew; m. John Francis DeMedio, Nov. 5, 1994; children: Jacqueline, John, Joseph Francis, Kathleen Marie. AB in Biology, Immaculata U., Pa., 1983; MS in Edn., St Joseph's U., Phila., 1996. Cert. biology Pa. Dept. Edn., 1994, chemistry Pa. Dept. Edn., 2000. Tchr. US Peace Corps, Mmadinare, Botswana, 1986—88; chemistry tchr. Acad. Notre Dame de Namur, Villanova, Pa., 1990—97; sci. tchr. St. Aloysius Acad., Bryn Mawr, Pa., 1998—99; chemistry tchr. Norristown Area Sch. Dist., Pa., 1999—. Mem.: NSTA. Democrat. Roman Catholic. Avocations: piano, singing. Home: 1806 Sandy Hill Rd Plymouth Meeting PA 19462 Office: Norristown Area High School 1900 Eagle Dr Norristown PA 19401 Office Phone: 610-630-5090. Personal E-mail: kmd620@aol.com. Business E-Mail: kdemedio@nassd.k12.pa.us.

DE MENIL, LOIS PATTISON, historian, philanthropist; b. NYC, May 15, 1938; d. Charles Krone and Julia Anne (Hasson) Pattison; m. Georges Francois Conrad de Menil, Aug. 3, 1968; children: John-Charles, Joy-Alexandra, Benjamin, Victoria. AB, Wellesley Coll., 1960; diploma, Inst. d'Etudes Politiques, Paris, 1962; Lic. in Law, U. Paris, 1962; PhD, Harvard U., 1972. Pres. D. M. Found., N.Y.C., 1986—2001, Ctr. Khmer Studies, Cambodia, 2001—. Bd. dirs. AXA Art Ins. Corp., 1998—; counsellor to Ministry of Culture, Romania, 1997—2001; mem. Coun. Fgn. Rels., 1976—, Inst. for Strategic Studies, London, 1978—, French Inst. Internat. Rels., Paris, 1980—, U.S. Coun. on Germany, N.Y.C., 1978—, Festival d'Automne, Paris, 1997—. Author: Who Speaks for Europe?, 1978; editor, translator: The African Unity Movement, 1965, French Foreign Policy under De Gaulle, 1967. Internat. coun. Mus. Modern Art, NYC, 1975—; vis. com. to art mus. Harvard U., Cambridge, Mass., 1977—; vice-chair bd. dirs. Dia Ctr. for Arts, N.Y.C., 1985—96; vice-chair trustees coun. Nat. Gallery Art, Washington, 1988—96; bd. dirs. World Monuments Fund, N.Y.C., 1990—, Groton Sch., 1991—2004, NASDAQ Found., 2000—04, Coun. Am. Overseas Rsch. Ctrs., 2003—; bd. trustees Tennis Hall of Fame, 2005. Fulbright scholar, France, 1960-62; Ford Found. fellow, 1966-68. Mem. Century Assn., Univ. Club, Harvard Club, Fishers Island Country Club, Phi Beta Kappa. Episcopalian. Avocations: art, skiing, tennis, travel. Office: D M Found 149 E 63rd St New York NY 10021-7405

DEMENTIEVA, ELENA, professional tennis player; b. Moscow, Oct. 15, 1981; d. Viatcheslav and Vera Dementieva. Profl. tennis player WTA Tour, 1998—. Named WTA Tour Most Improved Player, 2000; recipient Female of Yr. Award, Russia, 2001. Achievements include Winner 6 WTA Tour singles titles: Amelia Island, 2003, Bali, 2003, Shanghai, 2003, Hasselt, 2004, Toray Pan Pacific Open, 2006, JPMorgan Chase Open, 2006; Winner 5 WTA Tour doubles titles: (with Husarova) Moscow, 2002, San Diego, 2002, Berlin, 2002, Season-Ending Championships, 2002, (with Krasnoroutskaya) Hertogenbosch, 2003; Member Russian Olympic Team, 2000, 2004. Office: c/o WTA Tour Corp Hdqs One Progress Plz Ste 1500 Saint Petersburg FL 33701*

DEMER, MADELINE See DIEMER, MADELINE ANN

DEMERS, JUDY LEE, retired state legislator, dean; b. Grand Forks, ND, June 27, 1944; d. Robert L. and V. Margaret (Harming) Prosser; m. Donald E. DeMers, Oct. 3, 1964; div. Oct. 1971; 1 child, Robert M.; m. Joseph M. Murphy, Mar. 5, 1977; div. Oct. 1983. BS in nursing, U. N.D., 1966; M in Edn., U. Wash., 1973, post grad., 1973-76. Pub. health nurse Govt., Wash., DC, 1966-68; Combined Nursing Svc., Mpls., 1968-69; instr. pub. health nursing U. N.D., Grand Forks, ND, 1969-71; assoc. dir. Medex program, 1970-72; rsch. assoc. U. Wash., Seattle, 1973-76; dir. family nurse practitioner program, 1977-82; dir. under grad. med. edn., 1982-83; assoc. dir. rural health ND, 1982-85; mem. N.D. Ho. of Reps., 1982-92; assoc. dean, 1983—; mem. N.D. Senate, 1992-2000. Cons. health manpower devel. staff, Honolulu, 1975-81, Assn. Physician asst. programs, Washington, 1979-82; site visitor cons., AMA Com. Allied Health Edn. Accreditation, Chgo.,1979-81. Author: Educating New Health Practitioners, 1976; mem. editl. bd.: P.A. Jour., 1976-78; contbr. articles to profl. jours. Sec., bd. dirs. Valley Health, Grand Forks, N.D., 1982—; mem. exec. com., bd. dirs. Agassiz Health Systems Agy., Grand Forks, 1982-86; mem. N.D. State Daycare Adv. Com., 1983-93, Mayor's Adv. com. on Police Policy, Grand Forks, 1983-85, N.D. State Foster Care Adv. Com., 1985-87, N.D. State Hypertension Adv. Com., 1983-85, Gov.'s Com. on DUI and Traffic Safety, 1985-91, State wide Adv. Com. on AIDS, 1985-90; bd. dirs. Casey Found., Families First Initiative, 1988-97, Comprehensive Health Assn. N.D., 1993-95, United Health Found., 1990-97, Northern Valley Mental Health Assn., 1994-00, bd. dir., Grand Forks Girl's and Women's Hockey Assn., 1999-2002; bd. dirs., sec.-treas., exec. com., program com., fundraising com., vice-chmn. Devel. Homes, 1999—; adv. bd. Mountainbrooke (formerly Friendship Place), 1992-96; adv. com. Ruth Meiers Adolescent Ctr., Grand Forks, 1988-2002, Altru Health Sys. Corp. Bd., 1997-2006; mem. Commn. on Future Structure of VA Health Care, 1990-91; bd. dirs. Red River Valley Cmty. action Program, 1991—; mem. Resource and Referral Bd. Dirs., 1990-2005; caring coun. N.D. Blue Cross and Blue Shield Caring Program for Children, 1995-99; coun. mem. N.D. Health Task Force, 1992-94; healthcare subcom. Northern Gt. Plains Econ. Devel. Commn., 1995-96; adv. com. on telecomms. and healthcare FCC, 1996; mem., chmn. Grand Forks City and County Bd. Health, 2000—. Named Nurse of Yr., 1983; recipient: Pub. Citizen of Yr. Award, N.D. chpt., Nat. Assn. Social Workers, 1986, Golden Grain Award, N.D. Dietetic Assn., 1988, Person of Yr. Award, U. N.D., Law Women Caucus, 1990, Legislator of Yr. award North Valley Labor Coun., 1990, N.D., Martin Luther King Jr. Award, 1990, Legislator of Yr. Award, Mental Health Assn., N.D., 1993, N.D. Libr. Assn. Legislator of Yr., 1999, Friend of Medicine Award N.D. Med. Assn., 1999, Legislator of Year Award, N.D. Pub. Employees Assn., 1999, Friend of Counseling Award, N.D. State Counseling Assn., 2000, Legislative Svc. Award, ARC of N.D., Friend of Higher Edn. Award, AAUP, 1995; named to Nursing Hall of Fame, 2002. Mem. N.D. Nurses Assn., Assn. Am. Med. Colls. (central region rep. student affairs nat. com. 2002-06.) Alpha Lambda Delta, Sigma Theta Tau, Pi Lampda Theta. Home: Unit 92 N 2200 S 29th St Grand Forks ND 58201-5869 Office: UND Sch Medicine PO Box 9037 501 N Columbia Rd Grand Forks ND 58202-9037 Office Phone: 701-777-4221. Personal E-mail: demersjudy@aol.com. Business E-Mail: jdemers@medicine.nodak.edu.

DEMERS-BOURGEOIS, AIMEE E., physical therapist; d. Peter J. and Marji E. Demers; m. John J. Bourgeois, Aug. 28, 2005. BS in sports medicine, Lynchburg Coll., Va., 1999; D in physical therapy, U. Southern Calif., LA, 2002. Lic. PT and AT N.Y., cert. athletic trainer NATA, strength and conditining specialist NSCA. Physical therapist, athletic trainer Health South, Atlanta, 2002, physical therapist, 2002—03; physical therapist, athletic trainer Sports, Orthopedic & Spines, Plateburgh, NY, 2003—05, Champlain Valley Physician's Hosp., Plateburgh, NY, 2005—; athletic trainer Beecmantown Ctrl. Sch., NY, 2003—. Mem.: Strength & Conditioning Assn., Nat. Athletic Trainer's Assn. Office: CWPH Rehab & Wellness 295 New York Rd Plattsburgh NY 12903 Personal E-mail: ademersdptate@netzero.com.

DEMETRAKEAS, REGINA CASSAR, social worker; b. Detroit, Jan. 23, 1969; d. Rene Antoine and Carol Ann Cassar; m. David Demetrakeas, June 4, 1993. BSW, Wayne State U., 1992, MSW, 1993. Cert. social worker ACSW. Therapist intern Cath. Svcs. Macomb, Sterling Heights, Mich., 1992-93; therapist Judson Ctr., Royal Oak, Mich., 1993-96, supr., 1996—, supr. interns, 1996-97. Contractual therapist Eastwood Clinics, Clinton Twp., Mich., 1999. Mem. NASW, Nat. Honor Soc. Avocations: archery, hunting, nature walks, reading.

DEMICK, BARBARA, journalist; Fgn. corr., Middle East bur. chief Phila. Inquirer, Jerusalem, 1998—2002; fgn. corr, bur. chief LA Times, Seoul, Republic of Korea, 2002—. Recipient Joe & Laurie Dine award, Overseas Press Club, 2006. Office: LA Times 202 W 1st St Los Angeles CA 90012 Office Phone: 213-237-5000. E-mail: barbara.demick@latimes.com.*

DEMING, JOAN, clergy; b. Milw., Nov. 7, 1949; d. Jarvis Roy and Mirabel Fay (Hansen) Deming; m. Kirk Michael Cavallo, Dec. 21, 1974 (div. June 1987); children: Kathryn Joan Cavallo, Anna Lee Cavallo; m. Donald F. Schultz, July 7, 1989. BA, Carroll Coll., Waukesha, Wis., 1972; student, U. Nairobi, Kenya, 1970-71; MDiv, Pacific Sch. Religion, Berkeley, Calif., 1976. Ordained deacon United Meth. Ch., 1974, elder, 1977. Pastor First United Meth. Ch., Milton, Wis., 1976-80, Sherman Ave United Meth. Ch., Madison,

Wis., 1981-82; interim campus min. Madison Campus Ministry, 1985-87; pastor of visitation First United Meth. Ch., Madison, 1985-88; pastor Trinity United Meth. Ch., Montello, Wis., 1988-90, First United Meth. Ch., Waukesha, 1990-94, Madison, 1994—2002; fund devel. dir. United Meth. Childrens Svcs. Wis., Inc., 2002—04; resource devel. dir. Middleton Outreach Ministry, Wis., 2005—. Bd. dirs. United Meth. Children's Svcs., Milw., 1993-97, chmn., 1997-2001; chmn. bd. global ministries Wis. Conf. United Meth. Ch., Sun Prairie, Wis., 1984-92, chmn. commn. status and role of women, 1979-84. Mem. AAUW, Assn. Fundraising Profls., YWCA (racial justice vol). Democrat. Avocations: gardening, yardwork, quilting, knitting. Home: 1541 Comanche Gln Madison WI 53704-1012 E-mail: jdeming7@charter.net.

DEMING, JODY WHEELER, oceanography educator; b. Houston, July 2, 1952; d. Samuel Henry Wheeler and Laverne (Lewis) Kraft. BA in Biol. Scis., Smith Coll., 1974; PhD in Microbiology, U. Md., 1981. Rsch. asst. biology Sloan Found. Rsch. Smith Coll., Northampton, Mass., 1973; field biologist Water Quality Div. Md. State Dept. Natural Resources, Annapolis, 1974; rsch. technician Div. Infectious Diseases Tufts/New Eng. Med. Ctr. Hosp., Boston, 1974-75; rsch. assoc. Bioluminescence Lab. NASA/Goddard Space Flight Ctr., Greenbelt, Md., 1975-77; grad. teaching and rsch. asst. microbiology U. Md., College Park, 1977-81; NSF postdoctoral fellow Marine Biology Rsch. Div. Scripps Inst. Oceanography, La Jolla, Calif., 1981-82; NOAA postdoctoral fellow Office of Marine Pollution and Assessment, Rockville, Md., 1982-83; assoc. rsch. scientist Chesapeake Bay Inst. Johns Hopkins U., Shady Side, Md., 1981-86, rsch. scientist Chesapeake Bay Inst., 1986-88, asst. prof. biology, 1983-86; scientist Ctr. Marine Biotech., U. Md., Balt., 1986-88; dir., Marine Bioremediation Program U. Wash., Seattle, 1993—99; assoc. prof. U. Wash. Sch. Oceanography, Seattle, 1988—95, prof., 1995—, U. Wash. Astrobiology Program, 1998—. Mem. nat. com. ALVIN Rev. Com., 1984-87, internat. Arctic projects and steering coms., numerous proposal review panels for NOAA, NSF and others. Contbr. numerous chpts. to books and articles to profl. jours. Recipient award for Sci. Achievement in the Biol. Scis., Wash. Acad. Scis., 1987, Presdl. Young Investigator NSF award, 1989-94. Mem. AAAS, Am. Soc. for Microbiology, Am. Acad. of Microbiology, Am. Soc. of Limnology and Oceanography, Am. Geophys. Union, The Oceanography Soc., Sigma Xi. Achievements include patents for rapid quantitive determination of bacteria and their antibiotic susceptibilities in a variety of fluid samples. Office: U Wash Sch Oceanography Box 357940 Seattle WA 98195-0001 E-mail: jdeming@u.washington.edu.

DEMING, N. KAREN, lawyer; b. Valdosta, Ga., Sept. 7, 1953; BA magna cum laude, Valdosta State Coll., 1975; JD cum laude, U. Ga., 1978. Bar: Ga. 1978, U.S. Ct. Appeals (4th, 5th and 11th cirs.), U.S. Dist. Ct. (no., mid. and so. dists.) Ga. Assoc. Troutman Sanders LLP, Atlanta, 1978—85, ptnr., 1986—, practice group leader, product liability, mem. exec. com. Mem. editorial bd. Ga. Law Rev., 1976-77, rsch. editor, 1977-78. Named a Super Lawyer, Atlanta Mag., 2004, Legal Elite in personal injury, Ga. Trends Mag., 2004. Mem. ABA, Def. Rsch. Inst., State Bar Ga., Ga. Def. Lawyers Assn., Atlanta Bar Assn., Atlanta Coun. Young Lawyers (bd. dirs. 1983-85), Lawyers Club Atlanta, Order of Coif., Phi Kappa Phi. Office: Troutman Sanders LLP 600 Peachtree St NE Ste 5200 Atlanta GA 30308-2216 Office Phone: 404-885-3124. Office Fax: 404-962-6543. Business E-Mail: karen.deming@troutmansanders.com.

DEMITCHELL, TERRI ANN, law educator; b. San Diego, Apr. 10, 1953; d. William Edward and Rose Annette Wheeler; m. Todd Allan DeMitchell, Aug. 14, 1982. AB in English with honors, San Diego State U., 1975; JD, U. San Diego, 1984; MA in Edn., U. Calif., Davis, 1990; MEd, Harvard U., 1997. Bar: Calif. 1985, U.S. Dist. Ct. (so. dist.) Calif. 1985; cert. elem. tchr., Calif. Tchr. Fallbrook (Calif.) Union Elem. Sch. Dist., 1976-86; adminstrv. asst. gen. counsel San Diego Unified Sch. Dist., 1984; assoc. Biddle and Hamilton, Sacramento, 1986-88; instr. U. N.H., 1990-93. Teaching asst. U. Calif., Davis, 1987. Author: The California Teacher and the Law, 1985, The Law in Relation to Teacher, Out of School Behavior, 1990, Censorship and the Public School Library: A Bicoastal View, 1991, Statutes and Standards: Has the Door to Educational Malpractice Been Opened?, 2003, You Will Come Back, 2004 (Mayhaven award Children's Fiction Mayhaven Pub., 2004) Recipient Mayhaven award for children's fiction, Mayhaven Pub. Co., 2004. Mem. Calif. Bar Assn., Am. Bar Assn.

DEMITRY, ELPIS HOPE, music educator; b. Trenton, NJ, Apr. 4, 1947; d. Lillian and James Demitry. MusB, Trenton State Coll., 1970, MA in Music Edn., 1976. Teacher of Music Mercer County/State of NJ., 1970, Supervisor/Principal Certification Mercer County/State of NJ., 1983, Nursery/Kindergarten Certification Mercer County/State of NJ., 1983. Internal coach,facilitator for the accelerated sch. plus program, our whole sch. reform Trenton Bd. of Edn. - Wash. Elem. Sch., NJ, 1999—; vocal/gen. elem. music tchr. Trenton Bd. of Edn., 1970—2003; pvt. piano tchr. Trenton Conservatory of Music and Home Instrn., 1966—2003; coord. of elem. music faculty meetings Trenton Pub. Schs., 1993—, coord. all city elem. music festivals. Coord. of the all city elem. music festivals Trenton Pub. Schs., Trenton, NJ, 1971—86, coord. of elem. music faculty meetings, 1993—98; acting prin. in principals absence Wash. Elem. Sch., Trenton, NJ, 1998—, profl. devel. coord., 1999—, trainor of staff, 1999—. Nat. grand gov. zone i Daughters of Penelope, 1993—95, dist. gov. NJ, 1982—83; organist St. George Greek Orthodox Ch., Trenton, NJ, 1960—2005; treas. - diocesan svc. Ea. Fedn. of Greek Orthodox Choirs and Musicians, NJ, 1993—2005. Recipient Patriarch Athenagoras I Medal for Ch. Musicians, Diocesan Svc. Award- Ea. Fedn. of Greek Orthodox Ch. Choirs and Musicians, 1999. Mem.: NEA, Assn. Supr. and Curriculum Devel. (assoc.), Am. Choral Dirs. Assn. (assoc.), Trenton Edn. Assn. (assoc.), Music Educators Nat. Conf., NJ. Music Educators Assn. (assoc.), Nat. Forum of Ch. Musicians (life). Greek Orthodox. Avocations: swimming, travel, needlecrafts. Home: 95 Beechwood Ave Trenton NJ 08618 Office: Washington Elem Sch 331 Emory Ave Trenton NJ 08611 Office Phone: 609-656-4960 3714. Personal E-mail: ehoped@comcast.net. E-mail: hdemitry@trenton.k12.nj.us.

DEMONBRUEN, TONYA ROCHELLE, science educator; b. Detroit, Dec. 31, 1961; adopted d. Jane Louise and d. Ernest Leo Demonbruen. AS in Natural Sci., Wayne County C.C., Detroit, Mich., 1982; BS in Natural Sci., Madonna U., Livonia, Mich., 1997; MA in Curriculum and Instrn., U. Detroit, Mich., 1999. Cert. tchr. Mich., 1999. Tchr. sci. Wayne Westland Cmty. Schs., Mich., 2001—; assoc. prof. Wayne County C.C., Taylor, Mich., 2002—05. Counselor/tchr. Hartford Meml. Bapt. Ch., Detroit, 1989—95. Mem.: Kappa Delta Pi (life; Kappa Kappa chpt. v.p. 1999—2000). Liberal. Baptist. Avocations: walking, travel, collecting cats (artifacts), theater, ice skating. Office: Wayne Westland Cmty Schs 36105 Marquette Westland MI 48185 Office Phone: 734-419-2300. Home Fax: 734-595-2338; Office Fax: 734-595-2338. Personal E-mail: demonbruent@wwcsd.net.

DEMONTE, CLAUDIA ANN, artist, educator; b. Astoria, N.Y., Aug. 25, 1947; d. Joseph James and Ammeda Ellen (Heiss) DeM.; m. William Edward McGowin, May 28, 1977. BA, Coll. Notre Dame, 1969; MFA, Cath. U., 1971; D (hon.), Coll. Santa Fe, N.Mex., 2006. Instr. Bowie State Coll., Md., 1971—72, Prince Georges C.C., Largo, Md., 1972; prof. dept. art U. Md., Coll. Pk., 1972—2005, prof. emeritus, 2005—. Dir. Art Workshops, New Sch. Social Rsch., N.Y.C., 1980-94; USIA artist in residene (Sofia) Bulgaria, 1982; mem. art bd. Queens Coll., N.Y. Selected exhbns.: Corcoran Gallery Art, 1976, Contemporary Arts Ctr., New Orleans, Cranbrook Acad., 1978, Marianne-Deson Gallery, 1979, Miss. Mus., Fort Worth Mus., Washington Project for Arts, 1980, Marion Locks Gallery, Miami Dade Gallery, Xochipilli, 1981, 86, 95, New Sch. Social Rsch., 1982, Queens Mus., N.Y., Stamford Mus., Conn., Gallery 121, Antwerp, Belgium, 1985, Gracie Mansion Gallery, N.Y., 1987, Brentwood Art Gallery, St. Louis, 1987, Nina Freunenheim Gallery, Buffalo, 1987, 92, 94, Internat. Rev. of Arts Arsenal, Amalfi, Italy, 1987, Esbo Mus., Helsinki, Finland, 1988, Evanston (Ill.) Art Ctr., 1989, Barbara Gillman Gallery, Miami, 1991, 92, 94, Gallery 86, Lodz, Poland, Slow Art, Painting in N.Y. Now, P.S. 1 Mus., N.Y., 1991, Haggerty Mus., Wis., 1993, Nina Freudenheim Gallery, Buffalo, 1994, Leedy Voulkos Gallery, Kansas City, Mo., 1996, Panaroma Gallery, Barcelona, Spain, Silpakorn U., Bangkok, 1997, Retrospective, Choklalfabuken, Malmo, Sweden, 1998, Liesbeth Lip Gallery, Rotterdam, The Netherlands, 1999, Retrospective Rosemont Coll., Pa., 2000, U. New Eng., Tucson Mus., 2001, Mus. of S.W., Midland, Tex., 2002, Internat. Mus. of Women, San Francisco, 2003, Tallinn Kunsit House, Estonia, Gerdubery Cultural Ctr., Iceland, 2004, Contemporary Art Ctr., New Orleans, 2005, U. Md., 2006; pub. collections include Indpls. Mus., Stamford Mus., Miss. Mus., Prudential Life Ins., Hyatt-Regency, Chem. Bank, Best Products, U. Md., Mus. Modern Art, New Orleans Mus., Minn. Mus., Grand Rapids Mus., Mich., UCLA, Corcoran Gallery of Art, Bklyn. Mus., Bass Mus., Tucson Mus., Boca Raton Mus.; author: (with Judy Bachrach) The Height Report, 1983, (pomegranate) Women of the World: A Global Collection of Art, 2000; commd. works include: U. No.Iowa, 2003. Mem. art bd. Queens (N.Y.) Coll. Recipient award Am.-Italian Assn., 1971, Head Balt. Bus., 1972, Creative award Me., 1974, 77, 83, 87; fellow N.Y. Found. Arts, 1989—, N.Y.C. Dept. Cultural Affairs Art in Pub. Places Sculpture Commn., 1991, N.Y.C. Dept. Cultural Affairs Mural Commn., 1993, sculpture commn. N.Y.C. Dept. Cultural Affairs, 1997, N.Mex. State Art Commn., Sculpture Commn., Socorro, 1998, U. No. Iowa Commn., 2003, N.Mex. State Hwy. Rte. 66 Commn., 2006, Ft. Lauderdale Broward County Sculpture Commn., 2006; grantee Gund Found., 1998, Ancohrage Found. Tex., 1999, Cantor Found., 2004. Democrat. Home: 96 Grand St New York NY 10013-2633 Office Phone: 212-966-4496. Business E-Mail: demonte@umd.edu.

DEMONTE, CYNTHIA MARIA, investor relations and management consultant; b. N.Y.C., May 23, 1956; d. Joseph James and Ammeda Ellan (Heiss) DeM.; m. Abraham Figueroa, Mar. 8, 1991. BA, NYU, 1978. Asst. dir. mktg. Tandem Computers, N.Y.C., Cupertino, Calif., 1978-82; v.p. corp. fin. Gruntal & Co., N.Y.C.; pres. DeMonte Assocs. Cons., N.Y.C., 1995—; v.p. Investor Access Corp., 1992-94; v.p. investor rels., corp. comm. Ruder Finn, 1994—; sr. v.p. investor rels. Fin. Rels. Bd., 1995; pres., founder Cynthia DeMonte Assocs Ltd./DeMonte Assocs., 1996—. Mem. Dinkin's Com., 1990—; Dem. nat. com. Women's Leadership Forum. Mem. NAFE, Nat. Investor Rels. Inst., Nat. Assn. Profl. Organizers, Am. Women's Econ. Devel. Corp., Am. Mgmt. Assocs., Ctr. for Entrepreneurial Mgmt., Am. Mgmt. Assn. Avocations: european travel, foreign language. Office: Cynthia M DeMonte & Assoc 161 W 54th St New York NY 10019-5322 Home: 3124 30th St Astoria NY 11106-2802

DE MONTEIRO, NADSA, chef; b. Cambodia; d. Longteine de Monteiro; m. Bob Perry, Dec. 1986. Studied, Cambridge Sch. Culinary Arts. Travel agt., Boston, 1986—92; owner, sous chef The Elephant Walk, Somerville, Mass., 1992—94, owner, exec. chef Boston, 1994—; owner, chef Carambola, Waltham, Mass., 1997—. Author: The Elephant Walk Cookbook. Office: The Elephant Walk 2067 Massachusetts Ave Cambridge MA 02140*

DE MORNAY, REBECCA, actress; b. Santa Rosa, Calif., Aug. 29, 1962; d. Richard and Julie De Mornay; m. Bruce Wagner, 1989 (div. 1990); m. Patrick O'Neal; 2 children. Student, Lee Strasberg Theatre Inst., Los Angeles; also studied with Kristin Linklater. Apprentice with Francis Coppola's Zoetrope Studio, 1981. Actress: (films) Risky Business, 1983, Testament, 1983, The Slugger's Wife, 1985, The Trip to Bountiful, 1985, Runaway Train, 1985, Cannon Movie Tales: Beauty and the Beast, 1987, And God Created Woman, 1988, Feds, 1988, Dealers, 1989, Backdraft, 1991, The Hand That Rocks the Cradle, 1992, Guilty as Sin, 1993, The Three Musketeers, 1993, Thick as Thieves, 1998, The Right Temptation, 2000, Identity, 2003, Raise Your Voice, 2004, Lords of Dogtown, 2005; (TV films) The Murders in the Rue Morgue, 1986, By Dawn's Early Light, 1990, An Inconvenient Woman, 1991, Blind Side, 1993, Getting Out, 1994, The Con, 1998, Night Ride Home, 1999, Range of Motion, 2000; (TV miniseries) The Shining, 1996, A Girl Thing, 2001; (plays) Born Yesterday, 1988, Marat/Sade, 1990; actor, exec. prodr.: (films) Never Talk to Strangers, 1995, The Winner, 1996; actor, co-exec. prodr.: (films) A Table for One, 1999; TV appearances include The Outer Limits, 1995. ER, 1999, Boomtown, 2003, The Practice, 2004.

DEMORO, ROSE ANN, nursing administrator; Former dir. collective bargaining Calif. Nurses Assn., Oakland, Calif., exec. dir., 1993—. Office: Calif Nurses Assn 2000 Franklin St Oakland CA 94612

DEMORUELLE, CHARMAINE, music educator; b. New Orleans, Sept. 30, 1952; d. James Ivon and Nell Marie (Porbes) deMoruelle; m. Oren Francis Benedic, Nov. 10, 1973 (div. July 1976); m. John Joseph Brion, Oct. 29, 1989; children: Yvette Jeanne Brion, Jean-Paul deMoruelle Brion. AS, Delgado Jr. Coll., New Orleans, 1973; BA, U. New Orleans, 1979. Tchr. instrumental music Jefferson Parish Sch. Bd., Metairie, La., 1979—. Clarinetist Jefferson Parish Cmty. Band, Am. Legion Post 175 Band; chief of Kickapoo YMCA Indian Guides, Metairie; bd. mem. at large 1st Unitarian Universalist Ch. of New Orleans, 1987. Scholar Seymore Weiss scholar, Delgado Jr. Coll., 1972—73. Mem.: La. Band Masters Assn., La. Music Educators Assn. Unitarian Universalist. Avocations: camping, soccer, karate. Office: J D Meisler Middle Sch 3700 Cleary Ave Metairie LA 70002 Home: 356 Devon Dr Mandeville LA 70448-3301

DEMOTT, DEBORAH ANN, law educator; b. Collingswood, N.J., July 21, 1948; d. Lyle J. and Frances F. (Cummings) DeM. BA, Swarthmore Coll., 1970; JD, NYU, 1973. Bar: N.Y. 1974. Law clk. U.S. Dist. Ct. (so. dist.) N.Y., 1973; assoc. Simpson, Thacher & Bartlett, N.Y.C., 1974-75; from asst. prof. to assoc. prof. Duke U., Durham, NC, 1975-80, prof. law, 1980—, David F. Cavers prof. law, 2000—. Vis. asst. prof. U. Tex., Austin, 1977-78; Bost rsch. prof. law, 1981; vis. prof. U. Calif. Hastings Coll. Law, 1986, U. Colo., 1989, U. San Diego, 1991; James L. Lewtas vis. prof. law Osgoode Hall Law Sch., Toronto, Ont., Can., 1991; vis. fellow U. Melbourne, 1993, 95, 98; Huber C. Hurst Eminent vis. scholar U. Fla. Coll. Law, 1996; Frances Lewis Scholar-in-Residence Washington and Lee Law Sch., 1998; centennial vis. prof. law dept. London Sch. Econs., 2000-02; vis. prof. internat. faculty U. Sydney Faculty of Law, 2004, McWilliams vis. prof., 2006. Author: Shareholder Derivative Actions, 1987, Fiduciary Obligation Agency and Partnership, 1991; editor: Corporations at the Crossroads: Governance and Reform; contbr. articles to profl. jours.; bd. advisors Jour. Legal Edn., 1983-86. Trustee Law Sch. Admission Coun., 1984-88; mem. N.C. Gen. Statutes Commn., 1990-98; mem. selection com. Coif Book Award, 1988-90. Recipient Pomeroy prize NYU Sch. Law, 1971-73; AAUW fellow, 1972-73; Fulbright Sr. scholar Sydney U. and Monash (Australia) U., 1986. Mem. ABA, Am. Law Inst. (reporter restatement of agy.) AALS (chmn. sect. bus. assocs. 2006). Office: Duke U Law Sch PO Box 90360 Durham NC 27708-0360 Office Phone: 919-613-7082. Business E-Mail: demott@law.duke.edu.

DE MOTT, MARIANNE, artist, educator, space designer, craftsperson; b. New Rochelle, NY, June 5, 1932; d. Monroe Van Wart and Mathilde Ann De Mott. Student, Coll. New Rochelle, 1950-53; student Sch. Modern Dance, Henry St. Playhouse, N.Y.C., 1958-61; BA, Hunter Coll./CUNY, 1969, postgrad., 1969-71. Cert. tchr., N.Y. Westchester county dir. girls and women's activities Cath. Youth Orgn., Yonkers, NY, 1953-54; tchr. phys. edn. and English, Sacred Heart of Mary Acad./Mother Butler Meml. H.S., Bronx, N.Y., 1954-65; tchr. art Harrison (N.Y.) Jr. Sr. H.S., 1970-71; art tchr., designer, craftsperson Studio of Art, Deming, N.Mex., 1973—. Lectr. on art history, gems and minerals; theater set designer. Designer jewelry with macrame and beads, gems and minerals; painter, creator wood sculptures; finder, exhibitor gems and minerals; lapidarist; photographer. Founder, rschr. Apache Hts. Homeowners Assn., Deming, 1979—88; asst. sec. Cooke's Peak Vol. Fire Dept., Deming, 1993—97; co-founder, life mem. Deming Arts Coun., bd. dirs., 1989—, exhbn. com., 1994—99; chmn. Arts in the Park, 1992—94; chmn. performance com., county-wide youth art show, 1989—; chmn. Arts in the Park, 2003. Named Coach of Yr., Cath. Youth Orgn., 1962, Sculpture award Mamaroneck Artists Guild, 1970, Sculpture award Women's Club Westchester County, 1970, 1971, Cert. of Appreciation for Promoting Cmty. Arts and Cultural Activities, Gov. of N.Mex., 1976, Painting award Luna County N.Mex Southwestern N.Mex. State Fair, 1974-76, Photography award Deming Arts Coun. Juried Exhibition, 1987, Cert. of Appreciation, Deming Arts Coun., 1994, 2000. Mem.: Deming Arts Coun., Am. Fedn. Gem and Mineral Socs. (Bull. Editors Hall of Fame 2000—), Deming Gem and Mineral Soc. (sec. 1974—79, bd. dirs. 1985—89, bull. editor 1991—98, libr. 1999—2006), Rocky Mountain Fedn. Gem and Mineral Socs. Republican. Roman Cath. Avocations: visual and performing arts and cultural events, rockhounding, gardening, swimming. Home and Office: 4320 Cherokee Trl NW Deming NM 88030-8307

DEMOU, DORIS BECK, small business owner, civic leader; b. St. John, Kans., Sept. 17, 1931; d. Charles Clarence and Dorothy Sarah (Hahn) Beck; m. Sam George Demou, June 5, 1960; children: Victoria Demou Hanson, Mary Demou Kleve, George Sam. Student, Hutchinson (Kans.) Community Coll., 1949-51. Operator Southwestern Bell, Hutchinson, 1951-52; receptionist, sec. Bendix Aviation, Davenport, Iowa, 1952-61; hostess Welcome Wagon, Burnsville, Minn., 1975-76; owner, mgr. Garden City Ct. Apts., Burnsville, Minn., 1968—; free-lance writer, pub. Burnsville, 1976—. Distbr. Morris Demou and Assocs., Burnsville, 1976—. Author: (poetry) A Part of Myself, 1976, More to Give, 1990; pub. Mrs. Beck's Cookie Cookbook, 1988. Vol. Met. Mt. Sinai Hosp., Mpls., 1975-87; sec. Met. Med. Ctr. Svc. Guild, Mpls., 1976-78. Mem. DAR (historian 1988-89, regent 1998-2000), Minn. State DAR (nominating bd. 1989-91, chpt. treas. 1989-91), Daus. Penelope, St. Mary Philoptochos Soc., Women's Club Mpls. (com. mem.), Mpls. Woman's Club (com. chmn.). Greek Orthodox. Avocations: reading, writing, travel, walking.

DEMOUY, ALYSON M., social studies educator; d. Patricia Demouy. BA in History, U. So. Miss., Hattiesburg, 2000; EdM in Curriculum and Instrn., Tex. A & M U., College Station, 2005. Cert. tchr. Tex. State Bd. Edn. World geography tchr. Westfield 9th Grade Ctr., Houston, 2002—. Student coun. sponsor Westfield 9th Grade Ctr., Houston, 2005—. Mem.: Kappa Delta Pi. Office: Westfield 9th Grade Center 1500 Southridge Houston TX 77090 Office Phone: 832-446-1401. Business E-Mail: alysond@springisd.org.

DEMPSEY, B., artist; b. Ada, Okla., Nov. 24, 1926; d. John Benjamin Foster and Alma Lula Hubbard; m. Loyd Dempsey, Apr. 21, 1949; children: Ronny DeWayne, Johnny DeWight, Loyd Raymond, Novelia Dianne, Kevin Wendell. Diploma, Byng H.S., Ada, 1945. Sec. First Nat. Bank, Ada, 1945, Ada Welfare Dept., 1946; sorter/packer Hazel-Atlas Glass Co., Ada, 1946-48; tailor, seamstress S & Q Clothiers, Ada, 1971-86. Exhibited in group shows at Okla. State Capitol, 1981-93, Festival of Lights, Oklahoma City, 1983-86, Folklife Festival Art Show, Oklahoma City, 1983-86, Oklahoma City Meml. Bldg.; exhbits in 12 area shows annually. Mem. Ada Artists Assn. (publicity chair), Magic Brush Art Guild (publicity chair), Holdenville Soc. Painters. Democrat. Baptist. Avocations: church choir, sewing and painting crafts, creative doll making. Home: 921 Williams St Ada OK 74820-1822

DEMPSEY, CECELIA See BYRNE-DEMPSEY, CECELIA

DEMPSEY, JANE M., nurse epidemiologist; b. Bklyn., Jan. 29, 1939; d. Robert A. and Sally (Enders) Marci; m. John A. Dempsey, Oct. 19, 1963. BS, Russell Sage Coll., 1960; MS, U. Pa., 1985. RN, R.I.; cert. infection control nurse. Staff nurse recovery rm., thoracic surgery VA Hosp., N.Y.C., 1960-62; staff nurse recovery rm. Children's Hosp., Boston, 1962-63; instr. Roger Williams Hosp., Providence, 1963-72; nurse epidemiologist Women and Infants Hosp., Providence, 1974-90; adminstrv. dir. epidemiology R.I. Hosp., Providence, 1990—2004; ret., 2004. Author: (with others) Perinatal Nursing: Care of the High Risk Mother and Infant, 1986; contbr. articles to profl. jours. Mem. Assn. Profls. in Infection Control (New Eng. chpt., co-chair symposium 1980, chair program com. 1986, pres. 1990, treas. 1993-94), Infection Control Profls. So. New Eng. (co-pres. 1998), Sigma Theta Tau.

DEMPSEY, MARGARET THERESA, psychologist; b. Gainesville, Fla., Nov. 30, 1962; d. Walter Bernard and Annette Shirley Dempsey. BA, U. Tex., 1984, MA, 1992, PhD, 1996. Lic. psychologist La. State Bd. Examiners Psychologists, 2000. Asst. prof. Tulane U., New Orleans, 1996—2002; lic. psychologist Mercy Family Ctr., Mandeville, La., 2002—. Adj. prof. Tulane U., New Orleans, 2002—04; cons. lic. psychologist Counseling and Diagnostic Assoc., Inc., Denham Springs, La., 2002—. Contbr. chapters to books, articles to various profl. jours. Eucharistic min. Holy Name of Jesus Cath. Ch., New Orleans, 1998—. Grantee, U.S. Dept. Housing and Urban Devel., 1996, 1997, 1997—98, Found. for Ind. Higher Edn. and Annenberg Found., 1997—98, U.S. Office of Adolescent Pregnancy Prevention, HHS, Office Pub. Health and Sci., 1997—98. Mem.: APA (assoc.). Office: Mercy Family Ctr 1445 W Causeway Approach Mandeville LA 70471 Office Phone: 985-727-7993. Personal E-mail: mdempseyphd@yahoo.com.

DEMPSEY, MARY A., commissioner, lawyer; m. Philip Corboy, Sept. 4, 1992. BA (hon.), St. Mary's Coll., Winona, Minn., 1975; MLS, U. Ill., 1976; JD, De Paul U., 1982. Bar: Ill. 1982. Libr. Hillside Pub. Libr., Ill., 1976-78; assoc. Reuben and Proctor, Chgo., 1982-85; assoc. gen. counsel Michael Reese Hosp. and Med. Ctr., Chgo., 1985-86; pvt. practice Chgo., 1987-89; counsel Sidley and Austin, Chgo., 1990-93; commr. Chgo. Pub. Libr., 1994—. Adj. prof. law DePaul U. Coll. Law and Health Inst., Chgo., 1986-90; spl. counsel Chgo. Bd. Edn., 1987-89; mem. adv. bd. Dominican U. Grad. Sch. Libr. and Info. Sci., River Forest, Ill. Mem. State Street Commn., Chgo.; bd. dir. Big Shoulders Fund (for inner city Cath. sch.), Urban Libr. Coun.; trustee DePaul U., Chgo.; mem. Ill. State Libr. Adv. Coun. State libr. scholar in Ill. Mem. Chgo. Bar Assn., Chgo. Network. Office: Chgo Pub Libr 400 S State St Chicago IL 60605-1203

DEMSEY, KAREN BOOR, music educator; b. Rochester, N.Y., Oct. 3, 1955; d. Jack LeRoy and Patricia (Gatter) Boor; m. David B. Demsey, Aug. 16, 1980; 1 child, Laura. MusB in Performance (Flute), U. Maine, 1977; MusM in Music Edn., Eastman Sch. of Music, Rochester, N.Y., 1989; DMA., Rutgers U., 1997. Freelance flutist Chamber Orch., Phila., 1977-80; adj. faculty U. Maine at Augusta, 1981-91, coord. dept. music, 1991-92; adj. faculty Rutgers U., New Brunswick, NJ, 1994-96, William Paterson Coll., Wayne, NJ, 1992—96, assoc. prof., 1996—. Freelance flutist, flute/piano duo, flute/guitar duo in field. Contbr. articles to profl. jours. Home: 151 Farmingdale Rd Wayne NJ 07470-6550 Office Phone: 973-720-3199. Business E-Mail: demseyk@wpunj.edu.

DEMUELLER, LUCIA, investment consultant; b. Manizales, Caldas, Colombia, Aug. 14, 1937; came to U.S., 1960; d. Ricardo Aristizabal and Soledad Villegas; m. Harold Charles Mueller, Feb. 26, 1966; children: Christine and Anne Marie (twins). Degree in journalism, U. Caldas, 1960; degree in bus. and fin., NYU, 1965; cert. in gerontology, Marymount Manhattan Coll., 1991; grad., Nat. Def. U., Washington, 2000. Editor Young Women's Mag., Bogota, Colombia, 1959-60; asst. export mgr. M & T Chems. Inc., N.Y.C., 1963-66; mgr. banker acceptances Mitsui & Co., N.Y., N.Y.C., 1970-73; acct. exec. Conn. Mut., N.Y.C., 1976-83; assoc. Cowan Agy., Mass. Fin., N.Y.C., 1983-86; investment cons. Chem. Investment Svcs., N.Y.C., 1993-94; internat. bus. cons., 1994—. Contbr. articles to profl. publs. Mgr. disaster assistance ctr. Fed. Emergency Mgmt., N.Y., 1985, 91. Mem. Nat. Def. Exec. Res. (mgr. various disaster sites), L.Am. Progressive Group (pres. 1990—, founder). Home: 19 Quarry Rd Apt 411 Goshen NY 10924-6006

DEMUNBRUN-HARMON, DONNE O'DONNELL, retired family physician; b. St. Paul, Aug. 26, 1926; d. Francis Joseph and Julia (Hoffmann) O'Donnell; m. Truman Weldon DeMunbrun, Mar. 17, 1948 (dec. Aug. 1996); children: Michael J., Steven M., Julie F., Suzanne B.; m. Donald Laurance Harmon, Aug. 26, 1997. BS, U. Ky., 1948, MS, 1949; MD, U. Louisville, 1954. Diplomate Am. Bd. Family Practice. Rotating intern St. Anthony Hosp., Louisville, 1955—56; pvt. practice Louisville, 1956—85; med. dir. St. Mary and Elizabeth Hosp., Louisville, 1971—76, Parkway Med. Ctr., Louisville, 1976—99, Family Health Ctrs., Louisville, 1985—90; ret., 1999. Case reviewer Health Care Rev., Louisville, 1995-96; criteria writer Nat. Health Svc., Louisville, 1995-96; asst. clin. prof. family practice, U Louisville Med. Sch., 1987-90. Pres. Jacques Timothe Boucher Sieur de Montburn Heritage Soc., Nashville, 1996-97. Recipient mayor's citation Cify of Louisville, 1990, proclamation of tribute Jefferson County, Ky., 1990. Mem.: Jefferson County Med. Soc. (life; v.p. 1976—77), Ky. Acad. Family Practice (life), Ky. Med. Assn. (life; del.), Am. Acad. Family Practice (life), Frazier Arms Mus., Filson Club, Execs. Club, Univ. Club, Sigma Pi Sigma, Pi Mu Epsilon, Alpha Lambda Delta. Avocations: gardening, reading, travel. Home: 3004 Beals Branch Dr Louisville KY 40206-2902 Personal E-mail: d2d.harmon@att.net.

DEMUTH, VIVIENNE BLAKE MCCANDLESS, artist, illustrator; b. Nutley, N.J., Mar. 8, 1916; d. George Wilbur and Hazel Metcalfe Blake; m. Henry DeMuth, July 3, 1935 (div. Sept. 1957); children: Simon (dec.), Vivienne, Shelley, David; m. George Warren McCandless, May 12, 1984 (dec. May 1995). Diploma, Am. Sch. Design, 1932, 33. Designer, artist Norcross Pub. Co., N.Y.C. and West Chester, Pa., 1936-40, 50-75; designer, illustrator Fisher Price Toys, East Aurora, N.Y., 1957-80; freelance book illustrator many pub. cos., 1992-94. Mem. newspaper panel cmty. newspapers Cape Cod, Mass.; artist, crafts tchr. presch. Cape Cod Mus. Natural History, Brewster, Mass., 1994—. Illustrator: Little Golden Book A to Z, 1945, Pre-School Science, 1996, many others. Mem. Nature Conservancy, Mass. Audubon Soc., Cape Cod Mus. Natural History (artist environ. posters). Avocations: cooking, travel, reading. Home: 2300 Herringbrook Rd PO Box 983 North Eastham MA 02651-0983 Business E-Mail: vivienne@c4.net.

DEN BESTEN, PAMELA KAY, biomedical researcher, dentist; b. Iowa City, Iowa, Sept. 20, 1954; d. Lawrence and Shirley Ann (Langeland) Den B.; m. Brian John Awbrey, Aug. 22, 1981; children: Matthew, Nathan. BS in Chemistry, St. Olaf Coll., 1976; DDS, U. Iowa, 1980. Pedodontic resident N.C. Meml. Hosp., Chapel Hill, N.C., 1980-82; clin. asst. prof. U. N.C., Chapel Hill, 1982-85; instr. pediatric dentistry Harvard Sch. Dental Medicine, Boston, 1985—; staff assoc. Forsyth Dental Ctr., Boston, 1985-88, asst. mem. staff, 1988—; asst. in pediatric dentistry Children's Hosp., Boston, 1986—. Ad hoc mem. study sect. NIH, Bethesda, Md., 1990. Editorial rev. bd. Jour. Dental Rsch., 1988—; contbr. articles to profl. jours. Deacon Park Ave. Congl. Ch., Arlington, Mass., 1990—. Mem. AAAS, Am. Acad. Pediatric Dentistry, Am. Soc. Dentistry for Children, Internat. Assn. Dental Rsch. Democrat. Mem. United Ch. of Christ. Achievements include advances made in understanding the mechanisms by which fluoride affects tooth enamel development. Office: UCSF Dept Growth & Develop PO Box 640 San Francisco CA 94143-0001

DENEE, LORI S., elementary school educator; BS in Elem. Edn., U. N.Mex, Albuquerque, N.Mex., 1992, MA in Elem. Edn., 1996. Tchr. lang. arts and lit. Albuquerque (N.Mex.) Pub. Schs., 1996—. Mem.: Albuquerque (N.Mex.) Fedn. Tchrs. (fedn. rep. 2000). Office: Eisenhower Middle School 11001 Camero Road NE Albuquerque NM 87111

DENENBERG, KATHARINE W. HORNBERGER (TINKA DENENBERG), artist, educator; b. Ann Arbor, Mich., Nov. 2, 1932; d. Theodore Roosevelt and Marian Louise (Welles) Hornberger; m. Allan Neal Denenberg; children: Peter David, Thomas Andrew. Student, Brown U., 1950-51; BA, U. Minn., 1953; MAT, Harvard U., 1954. Intern tchr. art Concord (Mass.) H.S., 1954-55; tchr. art Bedford and Pound Ridge (N.Y.) Schs., 1955-56, New Lincoln Sch., N.Y.C., 1956-62, Mus. Modern Art, N.Y.C., 1964-71, Children's Art Workshop, Mamaroneck, N.Y., 1971-81, Pelham (N.Y.) Art Ctr., 1981. One-woman shows include Manhattanville Coll., Purchase, N.Y., 1975, Rye (N.Y.) Libr., 1975, 85, West Cornwall (Conn.) Gallery, 1978, 79, West Cornwall Libr., 1979, 84, Condeso Lawler Gallery, N.Y., 1982, 84, Moviehouse Gallery, Millerton, N.Y., 1987, Larchmont Libr., 1988, St. Peter's Ch., N.Y., 1990; exhibited in group shows at Duffy-Gibbs Gallery, N.Y., Nat. Mus. of Taiwan, Bridge Gallery, White Plains, N.Y., Westport-Weston Arts Coun., Greenwich (Conn.) Libr., Manhattanville Coll., New Britain (Conn.) Mus., Sarah Rentzler Gallery, Condeso-Lawler Gallery, Silvermine Gallery, The Castle Gallery, Coll. New Rochelle, N.Y., Weschester Arts Coun., White Plains, N.Y.; represented in permanent collections at Credit Lyonais, Bank of Boston, Chermayeff and Geismar, Great Lakes Corp., Tex. Comml. Bank, Sohio Petroleum, Cleary Gottlieb, Chemical Bank, Mobil. N.Y.State Coun. for the Arts grantee, 1975. Mem. Phi Beta Kappa.

DENEUVE, CATHERINE (CATHERINE DORLEAC), actress; b. Paris, Oct. 22, 1943; d. Maurice Dorleac and Renee Deneuve; m. David Bailey, 1965 (div. 1970); children: Christian Vadim, Chiara Mastroianni. Student, Lycée La Fontaine, Paris. Co-chair UNESCO campaign to protect World's Film Heritage, 1994—. Films include Les Petits Chats, 1956, Les Collegiennes, 1956, Les portes claquent, 1960, Les Parisiennes, 1961, Et Satan conduit le bal, 1962, Vacances portugaises, 1963, Le Vice et la Vertu, 1963, Les Parapluies de Cherbourg, 1964 (Golden Palm of Cannes Festival), La Chasse à l'homme, 1964, Les Plus belles escroqueries du monde, 1964, Un Monsieur de compagnie, 1964, Repulsion, 1965, Coeur à la gorge, 1965, Le Chant de Ronde, 1965, La Vie de Chateau, 1965, Les créatures, 1966, Les Demoiselles de Rochefort, 1966, Benjamin, 1967, Manon 70, 1967, Belle de Jour, 1967 (Golden Lion of Venice Festival), Meyerling, 1967, La Chamade, 1968, The April Fools, 1968, La Sirène du Mississippi, 1968, Tristana, 1969, It Only Happens to Others, 1971, Dirty Money, Hustle, 1975, Lovers Like Us, 1975, Act of Aggression, 1976, March or Die, 1977, La Grande Bourgeoise, 1977, The Last Metro, 1980, A Second Chance, 1981, Reporters, 1982, The Hunger, 1983, Fort Saganne, Scene of the Crime, Agent Trouble, 1987, FM-Frequency Murder, 1988, Drole d'endroit Pour Une Rencontre, 1988, Helmut Newton: Frames from the Edge, 1989, Indochine, 1992 (César award Best Actress, Acad. award nominee for Best Actress), Ma Saison Preferee, 1993, La Partie d'Echecs, 1994, Les Cent et Une Nuits, 1995, Les Voleurs, 1996, Place Vendome, 1997, Gènéalogies d'un Crime, 1997, Pola X, 1998, Le Temps retrouvé, La Princesse de Clèves, 1999, The Last Napoleon, 1999, Est, ouest, 1999, Le Vent de la nuit, 1999, Belle Maman, 1999, Dancer in the Dark, 2000, Je rentre à la maison, 2001, Absolument fabuleux, 2001, The Musketeer, 2001, Le Petit poucet, 2001, 8 femmes, 2002 (Berlin Film Festival Silver Bear for Individual Artistic Contbn.), Au plus près du paradis, 2002, Um Filme Falado, 2003; TV movies include Les Liaisons dangereuses, 2003, Princesse Marie, 2004; prodr. A Strange Place to Meet, 1988. Recipient Berlin Film Festival Golden Bear for Lifetime Achievement, 1998, Venice Film Festival Silver Lion for Best Actress, 1998, Bangkok Internat. Film Festival Golden Kinnaree Career Achievement award, 2006. Office: 76 Rue Bonaparte 75006 Paris France

DENGLER, EARTHA (ERDMUTH), librarian, archivist; b. Hamburg, Germany, Aug. 15, 1922; came to U.S., 1951; d. Peter Nikolai and Martha Katherine (Jacobsen) Molzen; m. Claus Oscar Dengler, May 3, 1941; children: Anne, Claudia, Thomas. BA magna cum laude, U. Mass., Boston, 1975; MLS, Simmons Coll., 1977; HHD (hon.), Merrimack Coll., 1995ä. Libr. Merrimack Valley Textile Mus., North Andover, Mass., 1977-87; founder, dir. Immigrant City Archives, Inc., Lawrence, Mass., 1978-87, exec. dir., 1987-95, also bd. dirs. With Lawrence Heritage State Park Visitors Ctr., bd. dirs., mem. mgmt. adv. bd. dirs. Author: Lawrence, Massachusetts, 1995. Bd. dirs. YWCA, Lawrence, 1959-71, Internat. Inst., Lawrence, 1972-85, Andover (Mass.) Hist. Soc., 1992—, Mass. Advs. for Arts, Scis. and Humanities, Boston, 1992-96, Lawrence into Action, Inc., 1993-96. Recipient Tribute to Women in Industry award Greater Lawrence YWCA, 1990, Woman of Yr. award Eagle Tribune, newspaper, North Andover, 1992, Immigrant City award Internat. Inst., 1992, leadership award Merrimack Valley C. of C., 1995, Ayer award Bay State Hist. Soc., 1995. Avocations: history, literature, arts, nature, travel. Home: 3663 Park Ctr Blvd Apt 709 Minneapolis MN 55416-2590

DENHAM, CAROLYN HUNTER, academic administrator, statistics educator; b. Abilene, Tex., Sept. 21, 1945; d. J. C. and Mary (Balch) Hunter; m. Robert Edwin Denham, June 3, 1966; children: Jeffrey, Laura. BA, U. Tex., 1966; MEd, Boston Coll., 1967, PhD, 1971. Prof. ednl. rsch. Calif. State U., Long Beach, 1971-88, assoc. dean grad. studies and rsch., 1983-88; prof. ednl. rsch. Calif. State Poly. U., Pomona, 1988-92, assoc. v.p. for acad. programs, 1988-92; dir. Nat. Ctr. Social Work and Edn. Collaboration Fordham U., N.Y.C., 1992—. Appointed mem. Calif. Commn. on Tchr. Credentialing, 1976-80; statis. cons. sch. fin. case, 1973-74. Co-editor: Time to Learn, 1980 (Best in Eric award 1980); editor The Generator, 1978—; cons. editor Jour. Pers. in Edn., 1986—; mem. rsch. adv. coun. Handbook on Tchr. Edn.; contbr. articles to profl. jours. Trustee Westridge Sch., Pasadena, Calif., 1985-89, Cushing Acad., Claremont Grad. Sch.; bd. dirs. Lincoln Found. and Inst., Cambridge, Mass., Access Devel. Corp., The Constn. Works, Children's Aid Soc., Inst. Internat. Edn.; advisor ednl. policy for gubernatorial campaigns. Am. Coun. on Edn. fellow, 1988. Mem. Am. Ednl. Rsch. Assn. (sec. Div. G 1982-84), Nat. Coun. on Measurement on Edn., L.A. Women's Found. (charter founder). Democrat. Espicopalian. Avocations: reading, cooking, hiking, aerobic dancing.

DENHAM, JILL H., bank executive; BBA, U. Western Ont.; MBA, Harvard U., 1990. From asst. v.p. to exec. v.p. CIBC Wood Gundy, Toronto, 1983—2001, sr. exec. v.p. retail markets and small bus. banking, 2001—03, vice chair retail markets, 2003—05.

DENHAM, MARY WASHKO, former college official, civic worker; b. Springfield, Ill., May 29, 1957; d. George Joseph and Betty Jean (Downen) Washko; m. William A. Denham III, Oct. 6, 1984. AA, Sprinfield Coll. in Ill., 1977; BA, Blackburn Coll., 1979; MA in Psychology, Sangamon State U., 1981. Sec. Lincoln Fest, Springfield, Ill., 1982-83; mgr. spl. events Perfect Impressions, Springfield, 1983-88; dir. devel. Springfield Coll., 1988-91. Interpreter Dana-Thomas State Hist. Site, Springfield, 1981—. Recipient Vol. of Yr. award Dana-Thomas Found., 1985. Mem. AAUW (treas. 1984-86, pres. 1988-90, endowment gift named in her honor 1986). Democrat. Lutheran. Avocations: reading, architecture, travel, auto racing, cooking. Home: 40 Westwood Ter Springfield IL 62702-4611

DEN HARTOG, GRACE ROBINSON, lawyer; b. Richmond, Va., Jan. 19, 1952; d. Eldred Hiter and Jane Haddon (Pitt) Robinson; m. Wilhelm H. King, June 14, 1997; children: Jonathan Wilhelm, Mary Douglas. BA, U. Richmond, 1974; JD, U. Va., 1980. Bar: Va. 1980, US Dist. Ct. Ea. and We. Districts Va. 1984, US Ct. Appeals 4th Cir. 1983, Tex. 1993. Assoc. Tremblay & Smith, Charlottesville, Va., 1980-83, McGuire, Woods, Battle & Boothe LLP (McGuire Woods LLP as of 2000), Richmond, Va., 1984—90, ptnr., 1990—2003, chmn., product liability litig. mgmt. group, 1994-97, mem. associates com., 1992-97; sr. v.p., gen. counsel Owens & Minor Inc., Glen Allen, Va., 2003—. Mem. allocations com. United Way, Charlottesville, 1980-83; mem. Jefferson Area Cmty. Corrections Resources Bd., 1983-84. Named one of Nation's Top 50 Women Litigators, Nat. Law Jour., 2001. Mem. Va. Bar Assn., Va. State Bar (bd. governors young lawyers com. 1983-87, chmn. cir. representatives com. 1985-87; chmn. membership com. 1983-85). Office: Owens & Minor Inc 4800 Cox Rd Glen Allen VA 23060-6292

DENICE, MARCELLA LOUISE, counselor; b. 1934; BA in English, Our Lady of the Lake U., 1973, MA in Counseling, 1990. English tchr., volleyball/basketball coach Anson Jones Mid. Sch., San Antonio, 1974—80; head basketball coach Alamo Heights H.S., 1978—80; English tchr., cross-country track coach Burbank H.S., San Antonio, 1983—90; guidance counselor Highland Park Elem. Sch., San Antonio, 1990—. Bd. dirs. Nat. Bd. for Profl. Tchg. Stds.; mem. adv. com. for counselors San Antonio Ind. Sch. Dist., mem. dist. leadership team, 2002—. Mem. spkrs. bur. Am. Cancer Soc. Nominee H.E. Butt Grocery Chain Excellence in Tchg. award, 2005; named Outstanding Counselor of Yr., Tex. Counseling Assn., 1991, Tex. Tchr. of Yr., Peer Assistance Leadership Skills, 2002, Counselor of Yr., So. Tex. Counseling Assn., 2004; recipient Remarkable Woman award, Our Lady of the Lake, 1995. Mem.: So. Tax Counseling Assn. (named counselor of yr. 2004). Office: Highland Park Elem 635 Rigsby San Antonio TX 78210 Business E-Mail: marcella@fittingadventures.com.

DENICOLA, MICHELLE, mathematics educator; b. Bklyn., N.Y., Feb. 10, 1981; d. Frank and Natalie DeNicola. BA (hon.), St. John's U., Staten Island, N.Y., 2003; MA, Bklyn. Coll., N.Y. Math. tchr. Bklyn. Diocese, Bklyn., 2003—; math tchr. NYC Dept. Edn., 2005—. Home: 1553 East 2nd St Brooklyn NY 11230 Office: PS 206 Gravesend Neck Rd Brooklyn NY 11230 Office Phone: 718-768-4406. Personal E-mail: missdenicola@aol.com.

DENIGRIS, CAROLE DELL CATO, artist; b. N.Y.C., May 26, 1936; d. Frederick and Elsie Helen (Dell) Cato; m. Daniel Anthony DeNigris, June 30, 1957; children: Daniel Cary, Carole Lynn. Student, Hunter Coll., 1954-57; studied with Richard Lippold, 1954-57, William Baziotes, 1954-57, studied Oriental art with Diana Kan, 1969-75; grad., Silva Mind Control. Buyer, salesperson Ethel Allan, Stamford, Conn., 1976-79; asst. mgr., buyer Jean Hutchinson, Greenwich, Conn., 1977-85; dir. Decker Studio and Art Gallery Ltd., Glenville, Conn., 1985-88; mgr. Odetta-Women's Fine Apparel, Greenwich, 1988-90; freelance fragrance model Guerlain of Paris, Stamford, 1990—2004; exhbn. chair Oriental Brush Artists Guild. One-woman shows include Greenwich Hosp., 1995, Greenwich (Conn.) Beauty Salon and Spa, 2003, 2 person show, Town and Country Club, Hartford, Conn., 2001, exhibited in group shows at Hammond Mus., North Salem, N.Y., Ferguson Libr., Stamford, Hurlbert Gallery, Greenwich, Wilton (Conn.) Libr., Greenwich Art Soc., Conn. Cmty. Bank, Greenwich, Old Bergen Art Guild, 1977—78, Hobe Sound (Fla.) Art Gallery, Pen and Brush Club, N.Y.C., Port Chester (N.Y.) Libr., Greenwich YWCA, Nat. Arts Club, NYC, 2005. Pres. Newcomers of Port Chester, 1969-70. Mem. Oriental Brush Artists Guild (v.p. 1995-96, pres. 1996-98, publicity chmn., advisor to pres., asst. treas. art exhibit com., asst. hostess art exhibit com., chmn. exhibits 2005—) Republican. Avocations: mycology, metaphysics. Home: 12 Nutmeg Dr Greenwich CT 06831-3211

DENIOUS, SHARON MARIE, retired publishing executive; b. Rulo, Nebr., Jan. 27, 1941; d. Thomas Wayne and Alma (Murphy) Fee; m. Jon Parks Denious, June 17, 1963; children: Timothy Scot, Elizabeth Denious Cessna. Grad. high sch. Operator N.W. Pipeline Co., Ignacio, Colo., 1975-90; pub. The Silverton Standard & The Miner, Colo., 1990-99. Avocations: reading, hiking. Personal E-mail: jondenious@comcast.net.

DENISH, DIANE D., lieutenant governor; d. Libby Donley and Jack Daniels; m. Herb Denish; 3 children. Assoc. pub., bus. devel. and advt. sales Starlight Pub. Ltd., Albuquerque Living and N.Mex Monthly, Albuquerque; state chmn. N.Mex Dem. Party, 1999—2001; former owner Target Group; lt. gov. State of N.Mex, Santa Fe, 2003—. Chair Children's Cabinet, Mortgage Fin. Authority, Mil. Base Planning Commn., Ind. Devel. Account Adv. Coun.; active Equal Pay Task Force, Spaceport Commn., Border Authority, Fin. Independence Task Force, Workforce Devel. Bd., Commn. on Volunteerism; trustee N.Mex. Mil. Inst. Found. Bd.; former chair N.Mex. First, N.Mex. Cmty. Found., N.Mex. Tech. Bd. Regents; former mem. N.Mex. Commn. on the Status of Women; former mem. nat. adv. bd. Small Bus. Adminstrn.; pres. N.Mex. State Senate; bd. mem. Daniels Fund. Named 2003 YWCA New Mexican of Vision; named one of Top 100 New Mexicans in honor of her cmty. leadership. Democrat. Office: Office Lt Governor State Capitol Ste 417 Santa Fe NM 87501*

DENISON, CYNTHIA LEE, accountant, tax specialist; b. Hyannis, Mass., Feb. 1, 1956; d. Gordon Avery Denison, Elizabeth Theresa Bourque-Denison; children: Randall Wayne Brown, Shaun Avery Brown, Kelly Joseph Brown. BS in Bus. Adminstrn., Hawaii Pacific U., 1990. Office mgr., tax preparer H&R Block, Fayetteville, NC, 1979—83; asst. acct., acctg. supr. Dept. of Def. Acctg. and Fin., Stuttgart, Germany, 1984—86; revenue agt. IRS, Bailey's Crossroads, Va., 1990—91, taxpayer rep., 1991—97, lead tax specialist, 1997—2000, sr. tax specialist, taxpayer rep., 2000—. Electronic filing No. Va. coord. IRS, Bailey's Crossroads, 1998—. Unoffical scoutmaster and cubmaster, den mother, com. mem., counselor Boy Scouts Am., Honolulu, 1986—90; football, baseball, soccer coach Moral, Recreation & Welfare, Honolulu, 1986—90; baseball coach Youth Sports, Spring Lake, NC, 1981—83. Mem.: AAUW, Statue of Liberty/Ellis Island Soc., Smithsonian Instn., Nat. Preservation Soc., Nat. Geog. Soc., Denison Soc., Nat. Geneal. Soc., New Eng. Hist. and Geneal. Soc. Avocations: genealogy, historic preservation, reading, crafts. Home: 2909 Marsala Ct Woodbridge VA 22192 Personal E-mail: cdenison88@comcast.net.

DENISTON-TROCHTA, GRACE MARIE, educator, artist; d. Leopold and Amalie (Hotarek) Henzl; m. James Trochta; children: Paul Michael and Maria Suzanne Deniston. BA in Elem. Edn., U. Mich., 1962; MA in Art Edn., U. Iowa, 1984; PhD in Curriculum and Instrn & Art Edn., U. Wis., 1995. Cert. tchr art edn., elem. edn., Wis. 6th grade tchr. Colegio Franklin Roosevelt, Peru, 1963-64; art tchr., dept. chair St. Katharine /St. Mark's Sch., Bettendorf, Iowa, 1975-82; art tchr. U. Chgo. Lab. Sch., The Dewey Sch., 1984-87, Graland Country Day Sch., Denver, 1987-88, Sewickley Acad., Pa., 1988-89, Greenfield Pub. Sch. Dist., Wis., 1990-91; adminstr. People's Rep. China vis. scholar exchange program U. Wis., Madison, 1982-84, career counselor, placement cons., tchg. asst., lectr. dept. art, 1989-96; asst. prof. art U. No. Iowa, Cedar Falls, 1996-98, U. Wis., Oshkosh, 1998—2001; editl. cons. Visual Arts Rsch., 2000—. Co-advisor Student Art Educator's Assn., 1996-98. Exhibited in group shows at U. Chgo. Lab. Sch., 1986, Women's Caucus for Art, Meml. Union, U. Wis., Madison, 1992, Milw. War Meml., 1992, Milw. Inst. Art and Design, 1993, Electronic Gallery, Chgo., 1993; contbg. author: Real-World Readings in Art Ed., 2000; contbr. articles to profl. jour. Mem.: Women's Caucus for Art, U.S. Soc. for Edn. Through Art, Seminar for Rsch. Art Edn., Caucus on Social Theory and Art Edn. (comms. coord., exec. bd. 1998—2000), Nat. Art Edn. Assn., Am. Ednl. Rsch. Assn. Home: 5912 Running Deer Trl Mc Farland WI 53558-9053

DENKO, JOANNE D., psychiatrist, writer; b. Kalamazoo, Mar. 29, 1927; d. John S. and Marian Mildred (Boers) Decker; m. Charles Wasil Denko, June 17, 1950; children: Christopher Charles, Nicholas Charles, Timothey Charles. BA summa cum laude, Hope Coll., 1947; MD, Johns Hopkins U., 1951; MS in Psychiatry, U. Mich., 1963. Lic. psychiatrist Md., Ill, Mich., Ohio. Pvt. practice, Columbus, Ohio, 1961—68; staff psychiatrist Fairview Hosp., Cleve., 1968—97, Cleve. Clinic Health Systems, 1997—2003, Luth. Hosp., Cleve., 1998—2002; pvt. practice Rocky River, Ohio, 1968—2003. Cons. Juvenile Diagnostic Ctr., Columbus, 1967—68, VA Hosp., Cleve., 1968—72, Cmty. Mental Health Ctrs., Greater Cleve., 1974—80; clin. instr. Case Western Res. U., Cleve., 1981—83; adj. prof. Geneva Coll., Beaver Falls, Pa., 2001—. Author: Through the Keyhole at Gifted Men and Women, 1977, The Psychiatric Aspects of Hypoparathyroidism, 1962; author: (pen name Victoria Greenleaf) Interlink: And Other Nature/Humankind Poems, 2005; author: (pen name Victoria C.G. Greenleaf) A Handful of Ashes: One Mother's Tragedy, 2001, Fighting the Good Fight: One Family's Struggle against Adolescent Alcoholism, 2002, Into a Mirror and Through a Lens: Forty Poems on the Mother/Child Relationship from Conception to Marriage, 2003; contbr. articles to profl. jours. Mem. AAAS (reviewer children's books), Cleve. Astron. Soc. (bd. dirs. 1984-86, 96-98), Mensa (Cleve. area br. pres. 1986-87), Great Books Discussion Group (Rocky River, chmn. 1985-92, 94—), Kiwanis Internat. Russian Orthodox. Achievements include naming sexual deviance klismaphilia; research in special problems of adults of high intelligence, educating gifted girls, teenage alcoholism, mental illness in pre-literate peoples, psychiatric aspects of lupus, antisocial personality disorder, adolescent alcoholism. Home and Office: 21160 Avalon Dr Cleveland OH 44116-1120 Office Phone: 440-331-1726. E-mail: charlottegreenleaf@yahoo.com.

DENLINGER, ANN T., school system administrator; b. Waynesville, N.C., July 15, 1944; m. Robert Denlinger; 1 child. B in Elem. Edn., Campbell Coll., 1966; M in Ednl. Adminstrn., Campbell U., 1982, D in Ednl. Adminstrn., 1992. Tchr. Harnett County Schs., 1966—68, Wake County Schs. and Raleigh (N.C.) City Schs., 1968—80; prin. A.V. Baucom Elem. Sch., 1980—82, Lynn Rd. Elem. Sch., 1982—85, Fuquay-Varina Mid. Sch., 1985—87; asst. supt. for elem. curriculum and instrn. Wake County Schs., 1990—92; supt. Wilson County Schs., 1992—97, Durham (N.C.) Pub. Schs., 1997—. Named Supt. of Yr., N.C. Assn. Sch. Adminstrs., 2000; recipient Disting. Alumna award, Campbell U., Reading Recovery Tchr. Leader award, Boston Tchr. Leader Inst., 2002. Avocations: following U. N.C. basketball and football, reading, landscaping, gardening. Office: Durham Pub Schs 511 Cleveland St PO Box 30002 Durham NC 27701

DENLINGER, VICKI LEE, secondary school educator, healthcare educator; b. Dayton, Ohio, June 13, 1961; d. David Lee and Barbara Ann (Zimmerman) D.; 1 child, David Micheal. Student, Ohio State U., 1979-82; BS in Edn., Wright State U., 1982-85; postgrad. studies, Miami U., Oxford, Ohio, 1986-87, U.S. Sports Acad., Daphne, Ala., 1996-97, U. Dayton, 2001—. Cert. phys. edn. and health tchr. Ohio, lic. athletic trainer Ohio, nat. cert. athletic trainer. Student athletic trainer Wright State U., Dayton, Ohio, 1983-85; asst. athletic trainer Oakwood (Ohio) City Sch., 1984-86; grad. asst. athletic trainer Miami U., Oxford, Ohio, 1986-87; subst. tchr. Oakwood City Sch., Kettering Moraine City Schs., Ohio, 1987-89; athletic trainer Kettering Moraine City Schs., Kettering, Ohio, 1987-96, tchr., 1989—; owner VLDInnerPrize, Kettering, 1996—. Pub. spkr. Greater Dayton Athletic Trainers, 1987—, InnerPrize, 1996—; advisor Kettering Fairmont Student Athletic Trainers Assn., Kettering Moraine City Schs., 1989—96; facilitator Student Assistance Support Group, Kettering-Moraine City Schs., 1994—2000; instr. Kettering Awareness Tobacco Edn. Program, 1997—2001; advisor Students Against Destructive Decisions, 1997—2005. Mem. PTA Assns. of various Kettering-Moraine Pub. Schs., 1989-00; co-dir. Kettering 24-Hour Relay Challenge, 1999. Named Jaycee of the Month Region E, 1996, Ohio Jaycees, Most Outstanding Write-Up of the First Quarter, 1996, Ohio Jaycees. Mem. NEA, ASCD, Nat. Athletic Trainer's Assn. (cert. athletic trainer), Ohio Athletic Trainers Assn., Greater Dayton Athletic Trainers Assn., Nat. Strength and Conditioning Assn., Internat. Weight Lifting Assn. (cert. weight trainer), Ohio Edn. Assn., Kettering Edn. Assn., Ohio Assn. for Health, Phys. Edn., Recreation and Dance, Am. Coll. Sports Medicine, Nat. Fedn. Interscholastic Coaches Edn. Program/Am. Coaching Effectiveness Program, Sports First Aid Instr. Avocations: fitness, sports, athletics. Home: 3489 Valleywood Dr Kettering OH 45429-4234 Office: Kettering Fairmont HS 3301 Shroyer Rd Kettering OH 45429-2635 Personal E-mail: vldinrprz@aol.com. Business E-Mail: vicki.denlinger@ketteringschools.org.

DENMARK, FLORENCE HARRIET LEVIN, psychology professor; b. Phila., Jan. 28, 1931; d. Morris and Minnerva (Sharkis) L.; m. Stanley J. Denmark, June 7, 1953 (div. Apr. 1973); children: Valerie, Pamela (dec.) and Richard (twins); m. Robert W. Wesner, Sept. 5, 1973; stepchildren: Kathleen, Michael, Wendy. AB, U. Pa., 1952, AM, 1954, PhD, 1958; DHL, Mass. Sch. Profl. Psychology, 1985, Cedar Crest Coll., 1988; D of psychology, Ill. Sch. Profl. Psychology, 1995; DHL, Alleghany Coll., 1998. Lectr. psychology CUNY, Queens, 1959-66, instr. to prof. N.Y.C., 1964-90, doctoral faculty psychology, 1967-87, prof. psychology, 1984-90; Robert Scott Pace Disting. prof. psychology, chair Pace U., N.Y.C., 1988—; adj. prof. CUNY, N.Y.C., 1990—. Editor: Who Discriminates Against Women?, 1974, Psychology: The Leading Edge Into the Unknown, 1980, (with L.L. Adler) Violence and the Prevention of Violence, 1995, (with M.B. Nadien) Females and Autonomy: A Life-span Perspective, 1999, (with V. Rabinowitz and J. Sechzer) Engendering Psychology, 2000, others; co-editor: Women: Dependent or Independent Variable?, 1975; contbr. various chpts. to books and numerous articles to profl. jours. Mellon scholar St. Olaf Coll., 1977; grantee Ctr. Human Rels. U. Pa., U.S. Office Edn., Rsch. Found. State of N.Y., N.Y. Cmty. Trust, Nat. Sci. Found., Ford Found., Nat. Endowment for Humanities, Nat. Inst. Mental Health, Muskowini Fund, Pace U. Fellow APA (com. on accreditation 1998—, pres. divsn. 52 internat. psychology 1999, pres. 1980, mem. various coms.; Centennial award 1992, disting. contbns. to psychology in pub. interest 1993, disting. contbns. to internat. psychology award 1996, 99), Am. Psychol. Soc. (charter); mem. Internat. Coun. Psychologists (pres. 1989-90), Interamerican Soc. Psychology (Interamerican award in Psychology 1997), Internat. Orgn. for Study of Group Tensions (v.p.), N.Y. State Psychol. Assn. (pres. divsn. social psychology 1989-90, acad. divsn. 1990-91; Kurt Lewin award 1978, Wilhelm Wundt award 1988, Carolyn Wood Sherif award 1992, Allen V. Williams Jr. Meml. award 1994, Margaret Floy Washburn award

1996), N.Y. Acad. Scis. (fellow 1966, v.p. 1984-87, Psychology Adv. Com. 1971—), Eastern Psychol. Assn. (pres. 1986, bd. dirs. 1988-91), Coun. Sci. Pres. (sec., exec. bd. mem. 1983-84), Internat. Coun. Psychologists, Assn. Women in Psychology (Outstanding Women in Sci. award 1980, disting. career award 1996), Soc. for Advancement of Social Psychology, Nat. Coun. of Chairs of Grad. Depts. Psychology, Soc. for Psychol. Study of Social Issues (mem. Otto Klineberg Intercultural and Internat. Rels. Award. Com.), Century Club, Chemists Club, Psi Chi (nat. pres. 1978-80). Avocations: opera, ballet, theater, travel, sports. Office: Pace U 41 Park Row Fl 13 New York NY 10038-1508 E-mail: Fdenmark@pace.edu.

DENNANY, KELLY, mechanical engineer, test engineer; b. Kalamazoo, Sept. 26, 1972; d. Robert Dale Jr. and Debra Lee Dennany. BS in Mech. Engring., GMI Engring. and Mgmt. Inst., Flint, MIch., 1995.; MS in indsl. ops., Lawrence Tech. U., 2004. ABS lab. sr. test engr. Continental Teves, Auburn Hills, Mich., 1995—. Mem. Soc. Automotive Engrs. Republican. Baptist. Avocations: rubber stamping, cooking, crafts.

DENNEHY, MARY NORA, psychologist; b. Phila., Sept. 14, 1933; d. John and Winifred (Byrne) D. BS in Social Studies, Marywood Coll., 1970; MEd in Counseling, Am. U., 1973; PhD in Sch. Psychology, Temple U., 1981. Joined Good Shepherd Sisters, Roman Cath. Ch., 1955; lic. psychologist, Pa., cert. sch. psychologist, Pa. Dir. clin. svcs. Claver Sch., Phila., 1957, Lourdesmont Sch., Clarks Summit, Pa., 1957-61, Tekakwitha Hills Sch., Phila., 1965-67; formation dir. Good Shepherd Sisters, Phila., 1961-64, provincial adminstr. Washington, 1970-76; exec. dir. Lourdesmont Sch., Clarks Summit, 1967-70; psychologist Cora Svcs., Inc., Phila., 1978—; coord. adolescent parenting prog. Cora Lifeline, Phila., 1983—; area coord. Teen Star, Phila., 1985—. V.p., pres., bd. dirs. Good Shepherd Svcs., Scranton, Pa., 1970-76, chmn. Good Shepherd Provincial Adminstr., 1970-1976. Co-author I Only Loved (3d edit.), 1994; contbr. articles to profl. jours. Fellow Pa. Psychol. Assn. Roman Catholic. Office: Cora Svcs Inc 733 Susquehanna Rd Philadelphia PA 19111-1320 also: 5356 Chew Philadelphia PA 19138-2898

DENNERY, LINDA, newspaper publishing executive; b. Phila., July 7, 1947; V.p., gen. mgr. Times-Picayune, New Orleans, 1987—97, pres., mem. of advisory bd., 1997—99; pub. Star-Ledger, Newark, 1999—2004; exec. v.p. benefits Advance Newspaper Group, 2004—. Bd. dirs. Kingsley House, Touro Infirmary, Bur. Govtl. Rsch., So. Newspaper Pub. Assn., Internat. Women's Forum. Mem.: bd. of dir. of Kingsley House, Touro Infirmary, Bureau of Governmental Research, Southern Newspaper Pub. Assoc., International Women's Forum. Office: Exec VP Benefits Advance Publications Inc 950 Fingerboard Rd Staten Island NY 10305 Office Phone: 212-286-2860.

DENNICK, LORI ANN (L. ANNE CARRINGTON), publicist; b. Cannonsburg, Pa., Feb. 8, 1962; d. Albert William and Mary Alice (Baldwin) D. AS, Pa. Comml. Bus. Coll., Washington, 1987; BA, U. Md., 1992; MFA, Hunter Coll., N.Y.C., 1999. Editor, art dir. Common Ground, Pitts., 1995-96. Holdenlog guest product reviewer, 2003; freelance writer Pitts. City Paper, Pitts. Post-Gazette, Pitts. Tribune; reporter Women's Interest Mag.; publicist Mark Castrillion, Pamela Louise Lee. Freelance contbr.: Observer Reporter, 1980—97, staff writer: Women's Interest Mag.; contbr. articles to mags. and jours., columns in newspapers. Mem. daffodil days com. Am. Cancer Soc., Pitts., 1999. Named Miss 16 Plus-Model of Yr., Miami, Fla., 1995, Ms. Plus Internet World, 2002, Miss Pa. Galaxy, 2002, Miss Pa Galaxy, 2003, Miss Am. Rose McKeesport City Queen, 2003, Ms. Pa. Tourism Beauty, 2005; recipient Ms. McKeesport Am. States, 2003. Mem.: NY Press Club, Am. Sportscasters Assn., Models United. Democrat. Presbyterian. Avocations: theater arts, travel, painting, jewelry design.

DENNIES, SANDRA LEE, city official; b. Buffalo, Dec. 26, 1951; d. Norman John and Shirley Edith (Dils) D.; m. Robert Francis Gilbane, Sept. 21, 1974 (div. Apr. 1987); children: Brandon Michael, Gianpatrick. AS in Dental Hygiene, U. Bridgeport, Conn., 1972, BS in Dental Hygiene Edn., 1973; MS in Health Scis., So. Conn. State U., New Haven, 1979. Dental hygienist various orgns., New Haven, 1972-73, Leonard B. Zaslow, DDS, Westport, Conn., 1973-81; lectr. U. Bridgeport, 1973-76; planner City of Bridgeport, 1977-79, planning asst., 1979-81; grants dir. City of Stamford, Conn., 1981—. Sec. Com. Emergency Med. Disaster Planning, Bridgeport, 1978-79; dir., dep. dir. Stamford Coliseum Authority, 1982-91; dep. dir. Stamford Film Commn., 1986-88. Editor, chief Hy-Light Jour., 1973-76. Mem. Stamford Youth Planning Adv. Bd., 1981-91, Stamford Youth Svc. Bur., 1991-95, 2006—, United Way Corp., Stamford, 1986-93; pres., sec. Alcohol Drug Abuse Coun., 1987-92; mem. bd. Christian Outreach North Stamford Congl. Ch., 1988-92, 1995-2000, 2006—; mem. pastoral rels. com., 1995—; mem. Coun. Chs. Synagogues Assembly, Stamford, 1989; pres. Stamford Mcpl. Supervisory Employees Union, 1991-99, mem. 1981—; v.p., sec. Stamford Sch. Readiness Found., 1998—; advisor Stamford Sr. Ctr, 2004—. Democrat. Avocations: piano, guitar. Home: 171 Shadow Ridge Rd Stamford CT 06905-1813 Office: City of Stamford 888 Washington Blvd PO Box 10152 Stamford CT 06904-2152

DENNIS, DIANE JOY MILAM, retired architect; b. Jacksonville, Fla., Oct. 8, 1925; d. Robert Richerson Milam, Meriel Lapham Wilson; m. Thomas Gordon Dennis, Nov. 9, 1974 (dec. Apr. 1999). Grad., Bennington Coll., 1947; MArch, Columbia U., 1955; studied landscape arch., Harvard U., 1998. With several archtl. firms, N.Y.C.; with Edward Durell Stone on Kennedy Ctr. Mem.: AIA. Home: 47 E 64th St Apt 10A New York NY 10021

DENNIS, DONNA FRANCES, sculptor, art educator; b. Springfield, Ohio, Oct. 16, 1942; d. Donald Phillips and Helen Frances (Hogue) D. BA in Art, Carleton Coll., 1964; student, Coll. Art Studies Abroad, Paris, 1964-65, Art Students League, N.Y.C., 1965-66. Instr. Skowhegan Sch. Painting and Sculpture, Maine, 1982, Sch. Visual Arts, N.Y.C., 1983-90, SUNY, Purchase, 1984-85, 87, Princeton U., NJ, 1984; assoc. prof. SUNY Purchase Coll., 1990-96; prof. SUNY, 1996—, Doris and Karl Kempner disting. prof., 2001—03. One-woman shows include Holly Solomon Gallery, N.Y.C., 1976, 80, 83, 98, Contemporary Arts Ctr., Cin., 1979, Neuberger Mus. of SUNY-Purchase, 1985, Univ. Gallery, U. Mass., Amherst, 1985, Bklyn. Mus., 1987, Del. Art Mus., Wilmington, 1988, Indpls. Mus. Art, 1991-98, Sculpture Ctr., N.Y.C., 1993, Dayton Art Inst., 2003, Five Myles, Bklyn., 2005; exhibited in group shows Venice Biennale, Italy, 1982, 84, Whitney Mus., N.Y.C., 1979, 81, Tate Gallery, London, 1983, Hirshhorn Mus., Washington, 1979, 84, Biennial of Pub. Art, Neuberger Mus., 1997, Asheville (N.C.) Mus. Art, 1998, Palazzo Ducale, Genoa, Italy, 2004, Ctr. for Arch., N.Y., 2005, Margulies Collection at the Warehouse, Miami; commd. decorative fence P.S. 234, N.Y.C., I.S. 5, Queens, N.Y., Grey Gallery, NYU, 2006; represented in permanent collections at Wonderland Sta., MBTA, Boston, North Plaza, Klapper Hall, Queens Coll., Queens, N.Y., Am. Airlines Terminal, Terminal One, Kennedy Airport, N.Y.C. Recipient Art award for excellence in design N.Y.C. Art Commn., 1987, Art award Am. Acad. and Inst. of Arts and Letters, 1984, Bessie Set Design award, 1992; grantee N.Y. State Creative Artists, 1975, 81, N.Y. Found. for Arts, 1985, 92; fiscal sponsorship, N.Y. Found. for Arts, 2002-; fellow Guggenheim Found., 1979, NEA, 1977, 80, 86, 94, Pollock-Krasner award, 2001, 05; Doris and Karl Kempner Dist. Prof. award Purchase Coll. SUNY, 2001-03. Democrat. Home: 131 Duane St New York NY 10013-3850 E-mail: tunnelsandtowers@att.net.

DENNIS, GIGI (GINETTE E. DENNIS), state official, former state legislator; b. Kansas City, Mo., Nov. 28, 1961; m. Dean Dennis. Student, Adams State Coll., U. So. Colo., Harvard U. With Band of Monte Vista, 1982-87; customer svc. rep. Pub. Svc. Co. Colo., Alamosa, 1987-91, Pueblo, 1991-94; mem. from Dist. 5 Colo. State Senate, Denver, 1995—2001; dir. rural devel USDA, Denver, 2001—05; sec. of state State of Colo., Denver, 2005—. Bd. mem. El Pueblo Boys and Girls Ranch; active Sangre de Cristo Arts Ctr., Rosemount Mus.; sec., past sec. Rio Grande County Reps.; past chair Ho. Dist. 60; mem. Local, State and Nat. Campaign Com., 1984—. Mem. Pueblo Zool. Soc., Bel Nor Rep. Women, Monte Vista C. of C., Pueblo West Rotary, Colo. Cattle Assn. Republican. Roman Catholic. Office: Office Sec of State Ste 200 1700 Broadway Denver CO 80290 Fax: 719-547-9330. Office Phone: 303-894-2200 ext. 6108. Office Fax: 303-869-4860.*

DENNIS, JESSICA MICHELE, psychology professor; b. Anaheim, Calif., Feb. 16, 1976; d. William Brent Rickard and Cheryl Jean Dennis. PhD, U. Calif., Riverside, 2003. Asst. prof. Calif. State U., LA, 2005—. Mng.editor: Jour. Nonverbal Behavior, 2002—. Fellow Grad. Student Ednl. Fellowship, U. of Calif., Riverside, 1998-2003, Post-doctoral rsch. fellowship, Calif. State U., LA, 2003-2005, Calif. State U., 2003—05. Mem.: Soc. Rsch. Adolescence. Office: California State University Los Angeles 5151 State University Dr Los Angeles CA 90032 Office Phone: 323-343-2276.

DENNIS, LINDA SUSAN, not-for-profit developer; b. Chgo., Mar. 26, 1948; d. William Evert and Edwina Louise (Franke) Dennis; m. William Raymond Parker, Feb. 15, 1969 (div. 1999); children: Anthony Wade, Kathleen Louise, Elizabeth Irene, Sarah Miriam. AA magna cum laude, Kenai Peninsula Coll., 1996; BA, Evergreen State Coll., 1999; postgrad., U. Wash., 1999. Founder, dir. Kenai Peninsula Food Bank, Soldotna, Alaska, 1987-98; co-chmn. Kenai Healthy Start, Soldotna, 1991-98; pres., bd. dirs. Green Stor, 1997-98. Bd. dirs. Bishop's Attic, Soldotna, 1993-98, Fed. Emergency Mgmt. Agy., Soldotna, 1992-98; vol. Boy Scouts Am., Soldotna, 1980-93, Girl Scouts Am., Soldotna, 1980-87, Kenai Peninsula Sch. Dist., Soldotna, 1980-90; co-chair Alaska Food Coalition, 1996-98; established 1st St. Soup Kitchen, 1997. Recipient Vol. of the Yr. award State of Alaska, 1986, Points of Light award Points of Light Found., 1992, Gold award United Way, Kenai, 1990-95, Woman of Distinction award Soroptimist, Person of Yr. award Soldotna C. of C., 1996. Mem. Soldotna C. of C. (bd. dirs. 1996-98, sec.-treas. 1998), Phi Theta Kappa (treas.). Methodist. Avocations: reading, travel, education. Home: 155 SE Washington Ave Chehalis WA 98532-3049

DENNIS, LORRAINE BRADT, psychology educator; b. Norway, Mich., May 11, 1921; d. Maurice Lincoln and Mary Louise (Martini) Bradt; m. Lawrence Edward Dennis, Nov. 24, 1943 (div. 1972); children: Patrick, Brian, Deborah, Thomas. BS, RN, U. Minn., 1943; MS, Kans. State U., 1951; PhD, U. Fla., 1976. Instr. Drake U., Des Moines, 1952-54; rsch. asst. Pa. State U., State College, 1957-60; asst. prof. Marymount Coll., Arlington, Va., 1961-64; cons. Child Study Ctr., Caracas, Venezuela, 1965-67; from instr. to prof. Roger Williams U., Bristol, R.I., 1969-97; ret. prof. emerita. Author: Psychology of Human Behavior for Nurses, 1960; co-author: Introduction Human Development and Health Maintenance, 1982. Home: 47 Seneca Rd Portsmouth RI 02871-4210 E-mail: ldennis471@verizon.net.

DENNIS, PATRICIA DIAZ, lawyer; b. Santa Rita, N.Mex., 1946; d. Porfirio Madrid and Mary (Romero) Diaz; m. Michael John Dennis, Aug. 3, 1968; children: Ashley Elizabeth, Geoffrey Diaz, Alicia Sarah Diaz. BA in English, UCLA, 1970; JD, Loyola U. LA Sch. Law, 1973. Bar: Calif. 1973, DC 1984, Tex. 1998. Law clk. Calif. Rural Legal Assn., McFarland, 1971; assoc. Paul, Hastings, Janofsky & Walker, LA, 1973—76; atty. Pacific Lighting Corp., LA, 1976—78; atty., asst. gen. atty. ABC, Hollywood, 1978—83; mem. NLRB, Washington, 1983—86; commr. FCC, 1986—89; ptnr., head comm. Jones, Day, Reavis & Pogue, 1989—91; v.p. govt. affairs US Sprint/United Telecom, 1991—92; asst. sec. State for Human Rights and Humanitarian Affairs Dept. State, Washington, 1992; special coun. comm. Sullivan & Cromwell, 1993—95; sr. v.p.and asst. gen. counsel SBC Comm., San Antonio, 1995—98, sr. v.p. regulatory and pub. affairs, 1998—2002; sr. v.p., gen. counsel and sec. SBC West, 2002—04; sr. v.p. and asst. gen. counsel AT&T (formerly known as SBC), 2004—. Bd. dir. Mass. Mut. Life Ins. Co., UST Inc.; chmn. US del. Internat. Telecomm. Union Region 2 Broadcasting Conf., Rio de Janeiro, 1988; bd. dir. Telemundo Group Inc., 1989-92, Nat. Pub. Radio, 1993-99, PR Legal Def. and Edn. Fund, 1991-92; mem. adv. bd. Ctr. Telecom. and Info. Studies, Columbia U., 1991-05, Latin Am. Inst., Loyola U. (LA Sch. Law), 1973, Bur. Nat. Affairs, Media Law Reporter, 1990-05; mem. Nat. Adv. Com. (Women Judges' Fund for Justice), 1990-93. Exec. editor Loyola Law Rev., 1972—73. Com. mem. Hispanic leadership program Coro Found., LA, 1981-82; U.S. del. UN Commn. on Status of Women, 30th session Econ. and Social Coun., Vienna, Austria, 1984, World Conf. UN Decade Women, Nairobi, Kenya, 1985; bd. dir. Resources Infant Educators, 1981-83, Nat. Network Hispanic Women, LA, 1983-92, Reading is Fundamental, 1991-98; mem. exec. com., nat. adv. bd. Leadership Am., Found. for Women's Resources, 1989-02, bd. mem.; bd. visitors Pepperdine U. Sch. Law, 1988-92; mem. adv. coun. Ctr. Pub. Utilities, N.Mex. State U., 1988-92; trustee Tomás Rivera Policy Inst., 1991-05, Radio and Television News Dirs. Found., 1993-05,; bd. dir. Women's Mus., 1998-03, Bexar County Women's Bar Assn., 1998-02, Tex. State U. Sys. Bd. Regents, 1999-05, Hispanic Scholarship Fund, 1997-00, Mex. Am. Legal Defense and Ednl. Fund, 1999-01; nat. sec. Girl Scouts US, 1999-02, first vice chair, 2002-05, chair, 2005-; trustee NHP Found., 2003-. Named Hispanic Woman Yr., Houston YWCA, 1992, Alumna Yr., UCLA Latino Alumni Assn., 1999, Corp. Exec. Yr., San Antonio Women's C. of C., 1999; named one of 100 Influentials, Hispanic Bus. mag., 1987, 1988, 1990, 1996, 80 Elite, Hispanic Women Directory, 2002, Top 25 Elite Women, Hispanic Mag., 2004, Top 100 Latinas, 2003, 2004; recipient cert. achievement, L.A. YMCA, 1979, Woman Yr. award merit, Mex. Am. Opportunity Found., 1984, Recognition Outstanding Achievements award, Nat. Coun. Hispanic Women, 1986, Woman Achievement award, City Club Cleve., 1986, Friend of Family award, The Family Place, 1987, Woman Yr. award, Hispanic Women's Coun., Inc., 1989, Exec. of Yr. award, Nat. Hispanic Employee Assn., 1999, Belva Lockwood Outstanding Lawyer award, Bexar County Women's Bar Assn., 2000, Pub. Endeavor award, Assn. Women in Comm., 2001, Leadership award, Cuban Am. Nat. Coun., 2002, Hall of Fame award, San Antonio Women, 2002, Corp. Responsibility Svc. award, MALDEF, 2003, Fortune Dir. award, Hispanic Assn. Corp. Responsibility, 2004, Legacy of Leadership award, Spelman Coll., 2006. Mem. Mex.-Am. Bar Assn. (sec. 1980-81, trustee 1979-80, 81-82), LA County Bar Assn. (child abuse subcom. chmn. barristers sect. 1980-81, exec. com. barristers sect. 1980-82), Hispanic Bar Assn. DC, ABA (com. labor arbitration and law of collective bargaining agreements, labor law sect. 1979-82), Women's Forum Wash., Am. Bar Assn. Commn. (on opportunities for minorities in the profession 1991-92, mem. nominations com., 1991-92, co-chmn. common carrier com., 1990-91), Fed. Comm. Bar Assn. Democrat. Roman Catholic. Office Phone: 210-351-3439. Business E-Mail: pdennis.1@att.com.

DENNIS, PATRICIA LYON, adult education educator; b. Rockford, Tenn., June 13, 1933; d. Howard Stanton and Dora Hester (Maynard) Lyon; m. Norman Bryan Dennis Jr., Jan. 12, 1957 (dec. Jan. 1985); children: Sarah Dennis Banks, Rebecca Dennis Hampton. BS, George Peabody Coll., 1955; postgrad., Auburn U., 1972—73; MA, U. Mo., 1977; postgrad., U. Kans., 1982—92, U. Mo., Kansas City, 1994, U. Mo., 1996. Cert. tchr.; cert. libr. media specialist, Kan; elem. classroom tchr., NC, Mich., Mo., Ala. 3d grade tchr. Ray Street Elem. Sch., High Point, NC, 1955-56; kindergarten and 3d grade tchr. Wurtsmith Dependent Sch., Clark AFB, Philippines, 1957-59; spl. reading tchr., 1st grade tchr. McDonald Elem. Sch., K.I. Sawyer AFB, Mich., 1961-63; kindergarten tchr. Gladden Elem. Sch., Richards-Gebaur AFB, Mo., 1964-65; 2d grade tchr., libr. Goose AFB Dependent Sch., Labrador, 1965-67; 2d grade tchr. Edgewood Acad., Wetumpka, Ala., 1969-70; 1st and 4th grade tchr. Trinity Christian Day Sch., Montgomery, Ala., 1970-72; 2d and 3d grade tchr. Fairview Elem. Sch., Olathe, Kans., 1974-77; libr. media specialist Wash. Elem. Sch., Olathe, 1977-99; instr. continuing edn. Johnson County C. C., Overland Pk., Kans., 1999—. Pres. Pre-Sch. Bd., Gunter AFB, 1968-69; children's choir dir. Leawood (Kans.) Bapt. Ch., 1979-84, Sunday sch. dept. dir., 1987-88, ch. libr., 1990-93; bd. dirs. Scholarship Pageant, Kansas City, 1988-96; chaperone, traveling companion Miss Am.-Kans. Scholarship Pageant, Pratt, Kans., 1989-98; commr., book rev. com. Kans. State Reading Cir. Commn., Topeka, 1985-91, 94-96, 97-99; primary subcom. chairperson Kans. State Reading Circle, 1998-99; pastoral care and counseling com. Village Presbyn. Ch., 2004—, libr. com., 2004—, mem. adult choir, 2004—. Mem.: MLA, NEA, Kans. Reading Assn., Kans. Assn. Sch. Librs. (presenter 1990—97), Olathe Culture Group (v.p. 2002—04), Sigma Alpha Iota (treas. 1954), Alpha Delta Kappa (sec. 1999—2002, mem. cmty. scholarship bd. 2002—03, pres. 2002—04, v.p. 2004—). Republican. Baptist. Avocations: harp, piano, voice, dance, physical fitness. Home and Office: 10525 Chesney Ln Olathe KS 66061-2775

DENNISON, ELIZABETH CORNELIA, special education educator; b. The Philippines, Aug. 7, 1953; d. William Herman and Lucy May Olson; m. John Robert Dennison, July 30, 2000; stepchildren: Jim, Sarah; m. Alan Morgan (div.); 1 child, Kathryn Morgan. BS in Spl. Edn., U. Tulsa, 1976; MEd in Edn. of Blind and Visually Impaired, U. No. Colo., Greeley, 1980; postgrad, Utah State U., Logan, 1991. Cert. tchr. blind and visually impaired Utah. Presch., infant tchr. Little Lighthouse, Inc., Tulsa, 1976—79; vision cons. Utah Schs. for Deaf and Blind, Ogden, 1985—; project dir. INSITE and VIISA SKI-HI Inst., Utah State U., Logan, 1981—, co-dir., 2001—. Editor, writer curriculum for blind VIISA Curriculum and Tng. Package, 1995; asst. editor, prin. writer curriculum for deaf and blind INSITE Curriculum and Tng. Package, 1989. Vol. various charitable, polit. and religious orgns. Grantee, U.S. Office Edn., 1981—98, 1995—2003. Mem.: Assn. for Edn. of Blind and Visually Impaired (sec., chair, bd. dirs. for divsn. 8, Berthold Lawrenfeld award 2000, Outstanding Svc. to Blind award 1994). Democrat. Presbyterian. Avocations: reading, cross country skiing, hiking, sewing, music. Office: Utah State University SKI-HI Institute 6500 Old Main Hill Logan UT 84322-6500

DENNISON, LISA, museum director; b. NJ, May 13, 1953; d. Saul and Ellyn Dennison; m. Roderick Waywell, Sept. 9, 1983; children: Brad, Tyler. BA, Wellesley Coll., 1975; MA in Art History, Brown U., 1978. Intern to dir. Solomon R. Guggenheim Mus., NYC, 1973, asst. curator, 1981-89, assoc. curator, 1990-91, collections curator, 1991—94, curator of collections exhbns., 1994-96, chief curator, 1996—, dep. dir., 1996—2005, dir., 2005—. Instr. Sch. Visual Arts, NYC, 1983—84; mem. ArtTable, NYC. Bd. dir. Byrd Hoffman Found., NYC; mem. NY State Coun. on Arts, NYC. Office: Solomon R Guggenheim Mus 1071 5th Ave New York NY 10128-0112 Office Phone: 212-423-3500.

DENNISON, RAMONA POLLAN, special education educator; b. Floydada, Tex., Jan. 19, 1938; d. William C. and Anne M. (Tivis) Pollan; m. Bob Dennison, Oct. 12, 1956; 1 child, Tajquah. BS, MEd, E. Cen. U., 1972, cert. in psychometry, 1974, lic. in profl. counseling, 1975. Lic. psychometrist, profl. counselor. Tchr. Konawa (Okla.) Pub. Sch., 1972—. Mem. NEA, DAR, PEO, Okla. Edn. Assn., Okla. Assn. Children of Learning Disabilities, Konana Edn. Assn., Lic. Profl. Counselor Assn., Nat. Assn. Children Learning Disabilities, E. Cen. Alumni Assn., Tanti Study Club, Oak Hills Country Club, Delta Kappa Gamma, Phi Delta Kappa. Democrat. Baptist. Avocations: tennis, bridge, walking, cooking, gardening. Home: 18326 County Rd 1542 Ada OK 74820-3072

DENNY, JUDITH ANN, retired lawyer; b. Lamar, Mo., Sept. 18, 1946; d. Lee Livingston and Genevieve Adelpha (Falke) D.; m. Thomas M. Lenard, May 29, 1976; children: Julia Lee, Michael William. BA, La. Tech. U., 1968; JD, George Washington U., 1972. Bar: D.C. 1973. Asst. spl. prosecutor Watergate Spl. Prosecution Force, Washington, 1973-75; pros. atty. U.S. Dept. Justice, Washington, 1975-78; dir. div. compliance U.S. Office Edn. HEW, Washington, 1978-80; acting asst. insp. gen. for investigations U.S. Dept. Edn., Washington, 1980; dep. dir. policy and compliance, office of revenue sharing U.S. Dept. Treasury, Washington, 1980-83, counselor to gen. counsel, 1983-89; insp. gen. ACTION, Washington, 1989-94; cons. Fed. Quality Inst., 1994-95. Mem. D.C. Bar Assn. Home: 2816 Arizona Ter NW Washington DC 20016-2642 E-mail: jadenny@aol.com.

DENNY, MARY CRAVER, state legislator, business owner; b. Houston, July 9, 1948; d. Kenneth and Lois (Skiles) Craver; m. Henry William Denny, Jan. 26, 1969 (div. Aug. 1990); 1 child, Bryan William; m. Norman C. Tolpo, May 6, 2005. Student, U. Tex., 1966—70; BS in Elem. Edn. magna cum laude, U. North Tex., 1973. Cert. tchr. Tex. Mem. Tex. Ho. of Reps., Austin, 1993—, chair ho. com. on elections. Mem. numerous other civic orgns.; del. state and nat. Rep. convs., 1972—; chmn. Denton (Tex.) County Rep. Com., 1983—91; bd. dirs. Tex. Fedn. Rep. Women, 1988—2003, Tex. Com. Humanities, 1990, YMCA, Denton, 1985—; life mem. pres.'s coun. U. N. Tex., Denton, 1974—, chmn., 1983; mem. Denton Benefit League, 1976—, Denton Arts Coun., 1986—. Named Outstanding Rep. Vol., Denton County Rep. Com., 1985, Outstanding Alumna in Edn., U. N. Tex. Coll. Edn., 1993; named one of 10 Outstanding Rep. Women, Tex. Fedn. Rep. Women, 1991. Mem.: Nat. Conf. State Legislature, Am. Legis. Exch. Coun., Ariel Club, Delta Zeta. Episcopalian. Avocations: swimming, bridge. Address: 8684 FM 2153 Aubrey TX 76227-3029 Office: PO Box 2910 Austin TX 78768-2910 also: 1001 Cross Timbers Rd Flower Mound TX 75028 Office Phone: 972-724-8477, 800-371-6179, 512-463-0688. Business E-Mail: mary.denny@house.state.tx.us.

DENNY, TERRY ANNE, elementary school educator; Student, Boston Conservatory, 1976—78; MusB, Berklee Coll., 1980. Cert. U. NC, 1991, Campell U., 2001. Tchr. Lacy Elem. Sch., 1998—. Lectr., clinician Wake County Schs. Vol. NC Mus. Natural Sci., Raleigh, 2000—, N.C. Mus. Life and Sci., Durham, 2000—; dir., arranger The Encore Singers of Cary, 1999—.

DENOON, PATRICIA Y'VETTE, science educator, consultant; d. Donald L. DeNoon and Sandra L. Dean; 1 child, Ruel Mason Alexandr. BS in Speech Communication, Pub. Rels., So. Ill. U., Carbondale, 1997; postgrad., U. Ctrl. Fla., Orlando, 2005—. Edn. cert. Fla. Dept. Edn. Animal keeper Walt Disney World, Orlando, Fla., 1998—2001; 7th grade sci. tchr. Piedmont Lakes Mid. Sch., Apopka, Fla., 2001—02, 6th grade sci. tchr., 2002—. Darden grantee, Found. of OCPS, 2004. Mem.: Orange County Classroom Tchrs. Assn. (north learning cmty. rep. 2004—06), US Track and Field. Democrat. Mem. Lds Ch. Office: Orange County Pub Sch Orlando FL Personal E-mail: pydraptors@juno.com.

DENSLEY, COLLEEN T., principal; b. Provo, Utah, Apr. 12, 1950; d. Floyd and Mary Lou (Dixon) Taylor; m. Steven T. Densley, July 23, 1968; children: Steven, Tiffany, Landon, Marianne, Wendy, Logan. BS in Elem. Edn., Brigham Young U., 1986, MEd in Tchg. and Learning, 1998. Cert. in elem. edn., K-12 adminstrn. Utah. Substitute tchr. Provo Sch. Dist., 1972-85, curriculum specialist, 1999-2001; tchr. 6th grade, mainstreaming program Canyon Crest Elem. Sch., Provo, 1985—94; instructional facilitator Campus Crest Elem., 1994—99; prin. Wasatch Elem. Sch., Provo, 2001—. Tchr. asst., math. tutor Brigham Young U., 1968—69; attendee World Gifted and Talented Conf., Salt Lake City, 1987, Tchr. Expectations and Student Achievement, 1988—89, Space Acad. for Educators, Huntsville, Ala., 1992; supr. coop. tchr. for practicum tchrs., 1987—90; co-chmn. accelerated learning and devel. com.; trainee working with handicapped students in mainstream classroom, 1989; mem. elem. sch. lang. arts curriculum devel. com., 90; mem. task force Thinking Strategies Curriculum, 1990—91; extensions specialist gifted and talented, 1990—91; math, 1991—; master tchr. Nat. Tchr. Tng. Inst., 1993. Co-author: (curricula) Provo Sch. Dist.'s Microorganism Sci. Kit, 1988, Arthropod Sci. Kit, 1988, Tchg. for Thinking, 1990—, PAWS Presents the Internet and the World Wide Web, 1997. Named Utah State Tchr. of the Yr., 1992; recipient Honor Young Mother of Yr. award, State of Utah, 1981, Mayor's award of Excellence, Provo, Utah, 2003. Mem.: NEA, Provo Edn. Assn. (Tchr. of the Yr. 1991—92), Internat. Space Edn. Initiative (adv. bd.), Utah Coun. Tchrs. Math., Utah Edn. Assn., Nat. Coun. Tchrs. Math. Republican. Mem. Lds Ch. Office: Wasatch Elem Sch 1080 N 900 E Provo UT 84604 Office Phone: 801-374-4910. Business E-Mail: colleend@provo.edu.

DENSLOW, DEBORAH PIERSON, primary school educator; b. Phila., May 2, 1947; d. Merrill Tracy Jr. and Margaret (Aiman) D.; m. James Tracy Grey III, Nov. 24, 1972 (div. Dec. 1980); 1 child, Sarah Elizabeth. BS, Gwynedd Mercy Coll., 1971; MA, Marygrove Coll., Detroit, 2000; M in Ednl. Adminstrn., Gwynedd Mercy Coll., Gwynedd, Pa., 2005. Tchr. Willingboro (N.J.) Bd. Edn., 1971—. Union rep. Burlington County Edn. Assn., Willingboro, 1981-82, ednl. adv. Nat. Constitution Ctr., Phila., 2002-.; mem. task force for reoganization Morrisville Sch. Dist., 1991-92. Mem. Borough Coun., Morrisville, 1988—94, pres., 1992—94, rep. candidate, 1986; borough chmn. Am. Cancer Soc., 1986—87; sec. bd. dirs. Morrisville Free Libr., 1988—90, bd. dirs., 1988—2001; mem. Morrisville Mcpl. Authority, chmn., 1994—95, 1996—2000, asst. sec., treas., 1995—96, 2001; judge City Gardens Contest The Pa. Horticultural Soc., Phila., 2002; committeewoman 1st ward Morrisville (Pa.) Rep. Com., 1986—98. Mem. NEA, N.J. Edn. Assn., Willingboro Edn. Assn. (union rep. 1981-82, alt. union rep. 1988-89), Parents without Ptnrs. (bd. dirs. Mercer County chpt. 1981-82, sec. 1982-84), Bucks County Boroughs Assn. (bd. dirs. 1989—, v.p. 1990-92, pres. 1992-93), Pa. Mcpl. Authorities Assn. (profl. devel. com. 2000-2001). Presbyterian. Avocations: swimming, sailing. Home: 1 Garrett Lane Willingboro NJ 08046

DENSMORE, SUSAN ELIZABETH, secondary school educator, music educator; b. Lynn, Mass., Feb. 14, 1966; d. Gordon M. and Marjorie E. Densmore. MusB in Music Edn., U. Vt., Burlington, 1988; MS in Edn., U. New Eng., Biddeford, Maine, 2000. Cert. tchr. music Commonwealth Mass., 1995. Tchr. music Somersworth (N.H.) Sch. Dist., 1988—95, Triton Regional H.S., Byfield, Mass., 1995—. Program coord. Dept. Visual and Performing Arts Triton H.S., 2002—. Singer: (albums) Amazing Love. Worship leader Grace Cmty. Ch., Rochester, NH, 1989, mem. preaching team, 1989. Mem.: NEA, Mass. Tchrs. Assn., Nat. Band Assn., The Nat. Assn. Music Edn., Triton Regional Tchrs. Assn. (v.p. 2005—). Independent. Avocations: musical theater, piano, guitar, drums, French horn. Office: Triton Regional High School 112 Elm St Byfield MA 01922 Office Phone: 978-462-8171 ext. 4271. Business E-Mail: sdensmore@triton.info.

DENT, JULIE, executive director; d. Ernest and Elaine (King) Dent; m. Barry Morrow; 1 child, Christopher Dent Morrow. AAS, Borough Manhattan CC, 1988; BS in Edn., Empire State Coll.; MS with honors in Edn., CUNY, 1995. Tchr. Horace E. Greene Day Care Ctr., Bklyn., 1983—88, adminstrv. dir., 1988—97; exec. dir. Audrey Johnson Day Care, Bklyn., 1997—. Domestic violence prevention counselor Women Working for a Better Cmty., 1996—; exec. bd. 1st vice chair Woodhull Hosp., Bklyn., 1999—; exec. vice chair Cmty. Sch. Bd. Dist. # 32, Bklyn., 2002—; dir. universal pre-K program dept. of edn. Long Island U., 1994—. Recipient award for excellence in early childhood edn., Profl. Assn. Day Care Dirs. Inc., 1989, award for outstanding cmty. svc., City Coun. N.Y., 1996, Key Stone award, Fedn. Protestant Welfare Agy. Inc., 2000, Citation of Honor, Charles J. Hynes, Dist. Atty., 2002, award for dedicated svc. to children, State Senator Martin M. Dilan, 2003, Citizenship award, Assemblyman Vito Lopez, Cmty Svc. award, Hon. D. Towns, 2004, Congressional Recognition award, Hon. E. Towns, 2004. Mem.: Nat. Assn. for Female Exec., Nat. Assn. For the Edn. of Young Children, Phi Delta Kappa (mem. Beta Omicron chpt.). Avocations: reading, dance. Office Phone: 718-574-0130. Personal E-mail: julieeduc@aol.com. Business E-Mail: audreyjo272@aol.com.

DENT, LEANNA GAIL, art educator; b. Manhattan, Kans., Oct. 21, 1949; d. William Charles and Maxine Madeline Payne; children: Laura Michelle, Jeffery Aaron. BS in Edn., U. Houston, 1973; postgrad., U. Tex., 1975-76; MS in Edn., Okla. State U., 1988. Cert. elementary and secondary art tchr., Okla., Tex. Tchr. art Popham Elem. Sch., Del Valle, Tex., 1973-77; graphic artist Conoco, Inc., Ponca City, Okla., 1987-88; tchr. art Garfield Elem. Sch., Ponca City, Okla., 1988-91, Reed Elem. Sch., Houston, 1991-92, Copeland Elem. Sch., Houston, 1992-94, Campbell Jr. High Sch., Houston, 1994—. Cons. and specialist in field. Author: Using Synectics to Enhance the Evaluation of Works of Art, 1988; group exhibitions in Ala., Kans., Nebr., Okla., Tex. and Pa. Vol. 1st Luth. Day Sch., Ponca City, 1977-91, Ponca City Inds. Sch. Dist., 1987-91; work com. Cy-Fair Ind. Sch. Dist., Houston, 1991-94. Acad. and Mem. scholar Okla. State U., 1986-88; named Spotlight Tchr. Yr., 1992-93. Mem. Nat. Art Edn. Assn., Tex. Art Edn. Assn. (judges commendation 1993), Assn. Tex. Profl. Educators, Houston Art Edn. Assn. (v.p. 1992-93, pres.-elect 1993-95, pres. 1995-97, past pres. 1997-99), Phi Delta Kappa, Phi Kappa Phi. Republican. Lutheran. Avocations: riding horses, camping, art, museums, black and white movies. Office: Campbell Jr High Sch 11415 Bobcat Rd Houston TX 77064-3097

DENTLER, ANNE LILLIAN, artist; b. Pitts., Oct. 13, 1937; d. Bailey Kent and Anna Wilhelmina; m. Gary Morgan, July 13, 1957 (div. Mar. 1975); children: Gary, Sherree, Mitch; m. David Daniel Dentler, Aug. 14, 1976; stepchildren: David, Jr., Joseph Charles. Degree in journalism, Pa. State U., 1974; postgrad., McNeese U., 1984, 85, 86, postgrad., 1998-2000; degree in art, Pa. State U., 2002. Clk.-typist Westinghouse Electric, Beaver, Pa., 1956, 57, 58; clk. (part time) J.C. Penney, Baden, Pa., 1974-76; rschr. survey analysis Penn State U., University Park, Pa., 1973-74; dep. prothonotary Beaver County Govt., 1974—78; dist. magistrate Pa. State Govt., Baden, 1976—80. Profl. artist, workshop instr., Pa., La.; with arts immersion program Calcasieu Arts & Humanities, Lake Charles, La., 1989; illustrator, conceptual artist Vol. Ctr. Southwest La., 1989-95; artist in residence Calcasieu Parish Schs., Lake Charles, 1990; assoc. mem. Women in the Arts, Washington, 1995; instr. continuing edn. portraiture McNeese U., Lake Charles, 1998—. Illustrator Jean Lafitte, Louisiana Buccaneer, 1990—, Rhythmic Alphabet, First Step Arithmetic, 1994, My Sister, My Friend, 1994, Birds Gotta Fly, 1995, Many Hats, Many Faces, 1996, The Porcupine Connection, 2003, Adolpheaux the Adventurous Dolphin, 2005, Clyde, The Cajun Calf, 2006; authored Portraiture.in Plain Language, 1993. Bd. dir. Associated La. Artists, 1984—, Gateway Found., Lake Charles, 1988, Martin Luther King Coalition, Lake Charles, 1993, Big Brothers Big Sisters, 2005-. Recipient Best of Show award Arts and Humanities Coun., Southwest La., 1986; named Artist of Yr., Gateway Found., 1988. Mem. Assoc. La. Artists (founder 1984, pres. 1984, 85, 86, 2003-, sec. 1990, workshop instr. 1986-99, 2000—), Beaumont Art League, New Orleans Art Assn., New Brighton Art Assn. Democrat. Avocation: travel. Studio: Annie's Artworks 2223 W Sale Rd Lake Charles LA 70605-2323 Office Phone: 337-478-9405.

DENTON, ESTELLE ROSEMARY, retired federal agency administrator; d. Daniel Poncy and Alice Gardiner; m. Benjamin E. Denton, Jr., May 15, 1948 (dec.); children: David Alan, Benjamin E., Kathleen Ann. AA, Bus. Inst. Pa., Sharon, 1943; student, U. Va., 1965. Asst. clk. Selective Svc., Sharon, 1943—46; adminstrv. sec. Navy Dept., Washington, 1946—57, exec. asst., 1946—57, Dept. Def./Chief Human Resources, Richmond, Va., 1958—62; human resources asst. SBA, Richmond, 1963, loan officer asst., 1964, exec. asst. to dir. fin. assistance, 1964—66, exec. asst. to dist. dir., 1966—73; exec. asst. to exec. dir. Va. Redevel. Housing Authority, 1974—76; exec. asst. pres. Nat. Realty Com., Washington, 1976—78; spl. programs officer Va. Dept. Emergency Svcs., Richmond, 1978—87; ret., 1987. Adv. coun. Congressman Eric Cantor, Richmond, 1998—2004. Recipient Pub. Rels. award, SBA, 1968—71, Cert. of Appreciation, Dept. Emergency Svcs. and Fed. Emergency Mgmt. Agy., 1986—87. Mem.: Profl. and Bus. Woman's Club. Republican. Roman Catholic. Home: 675 Pinehurst Trace Dr Pinehurst NC 28374 Personal E-mail: mrsed10@earthlink.net.

DENTON, JILL B., political science educator; b. Easley, S.C., Dec. 8, 1969; d. James Thomas and Nan McJunkin Boggs; m. M. Chris Denton, June 20; children: Lauren, Kayli. BS in Biology, Furman U., S.C., 1992, MA in secondary adminstrn., 1997; D of Edn. Leadership, NOVA Southeastern U., 2006. Inspector Dept. Health and Environmental Control, Greenville, SC, 1992—93; sci. tchr. Mauldin HS, SC, 1993—97, Pickens HS, SC, 1997—. Office: Pickens HS Sci Dept Chairperson 111 Blue Flame Dr Pickens SC 29671-2821

DENTON, JOY GRIGG, retired music educator; b. Marianna, Fla., Dec. 21, 1943; d. Jesse Edward and Inez Martin Grigg; m. William Warren Denton, June 4, 1965; children: Kathryn Jessica Acree, William Drake. Student, Judson Coll., Marion, Ala., 1962—64; BS in Music Edn., U. Ala., 1966; M.Music Edn., U. Montevallo, Ala., 1994; Cert. Edn. Adminstrn., Samford U., Birmingham, Ala., 1996—97. Elem. music tchr. DeKalb County Schs., Decatur, Ga., 1966—67, Dekalb County Schs., Decatur, 1975—76; pvt. piano tchr. Decatur, 1967—75; presch. tchr. Mountain Park Bapt. Ch., Stone Mountain, Ga., 1976—80; pvt. piano tchr. Stone Mountain, 1980—85; elem. music tchr. Gwinnett County Schs., Lawrenceville, Ga., 1985—88, Jefferson County Bd. Edn., Birmingham, 1989—. Guest presenter music methods class U. Montevallo, 1998; guest presenter Jefferson County Bd. Edn., Birmingham; resource/curriculum presenter Birmingham Internat. Festival for Jefferson County Bd. Edn., 2000—. V.p. Leeds Music Study Club, Ala., 1990—; choir and com. mem. Meadow Brook Bapt. Ch., Birmingham, 1989—. Named Second Mile Tchr., Jefferson County Bd. Edn., 1994, Outstanding Grad. Student in Music, U. Montevallo, 1994; grantee Multicultural Fine Arts grantee, Ala. State. Coun. on the Arts, 1994, Jefferson County Bd. of Edn. Found., for Hansel and Gretel musical prodn., Birmingham Internat. Festival, 1996, for sch.-wide Native Am. Festival, 2000. Mem.: Ala. Music Educators Assn., Ala. Orff Assn., Music Educators Nat. Conf., Am. Fedn. Tchrs., Delta Kappa Gamma, Delta Omicron (life). Baptist. Avocations: southern history, antiques. Office: Leeds Elementary Sch 201 Ashville Rd Leeds AL 35094

DENTON, JUDY ANN, art educator; d. John Lewis and Nellie Ann Yates; m. Charles Theodore Denton, May 31, 1975; children: Janel, Jessica. BS magna cum laude in Art Edn., N.E. Mo. State U. (now Truman U.), Kirksville, 1977, MA in Art Edn., 1984. Art educator Marceline (Mo.) Sch. Dist., 1977—86, libr., 1986—89; art educator Marshall (Mo.) Sch. Dist., 1989—. Educator Marshall Philharm. Orch., Mo., 1993—2006; asst. coach cross country Marshall Sch. Dist., 1998—; mem. fine arts project Dep. Elem. and Secondary Edn., Jefferson City, Mo., 1999—2000. Mem.: Marshall (Mo.) Cmty. Tchrs. Assn., Mo. Art Edn. Assn., Nat. Art Edn. Assn. Avocations: reading, gardening, travel, exercise, artwork.

DENTON, PEGGY, occupational therapist, educator; b. Moose Lake, Minn., Apr. 19, 1950; d. Donald Duane and Ruth Elaine (Stewart) D.; m. Frank William Johonnott, Feb. 22, 1986; 1 child, James Ryan. BS in Occupl. Therapy, U. Minn., 1972; MS in Occupl. Therapy, Boston U., 1979; PhD in Urban Edn., U. Wis., Milw., 1997. Registered occupl. therapist, Wis. Staff occupl. therapist Rogers VA Hosp., Bedford, Mass., 1973-78; asst. prof. U. Wis., Madison, 1979-83; staff occupl. therapist Meth.-Meriter Hosp., Madison, 1983-86, supr. occupl. therapy, 1986-87; occupl. therapy adminstrv. cons. Rock County Health Care Ctr., Janesville, Wis., 1988-99; assoc. prof. occupl. therapy Concordia U., Mequon, Wis., 1995-99, prof., 1999—, dir. divsn. occupl. therapy, 1999—. Bus. dir. Images of Madison, 1981-85; mem. accreditation rev. bd. Accreditation Coun. for Occupl. Therapy Edn., Bethesda, Md., 1995—; mem. profl. jour. rev. bd. Am. Jour. Occupl. Therapy, Bethesda, 1998—. Author: Psychiatric Occupational Therapy: A Workbook of Practical Skills, 1987; co-author: Occupational Therapy for Mood Disorders, 1999; contbr. articles to profl. jours., including Devel. Rev., Hosp. and Cmty. Psychiatry. Mem. employment task force Joint One Sch. Bd., Lake Geneva, Wis., 1998-991 mem. United Ch. Christ Bell Choir. Grantee Aid Assn. for Luths., 1999. Fellow Am. Occupl. Therapy Assn.; mem. Soc. for Rsch. in Child Devel., Wis. Occupl. Therapy Assn. (bd. dirs. 1986-92), award of distinction 1987), Lakeland Players Assn. Avocations: quilting, needle arts, gardening, community theater, music. Office: Concordia U 12800 N Lake Shore Dr Mequon WI 53097-2418

DENTON-MCGREW, SHELA IVA, retired trade association administrator; b. Bklyn., Aug. 27, 1934; d. Elias Kalmonowitz and Fonnie Rochelle Gurwitz; m. Leroy Richard Denton (div.); children: Sharon Lee Marsh, David Denton, Marshall Denton; m. William James McGrew, Dec. 7, 1985. Student, Ithaca Coll., NY, Moravian Coll., Bethlehem, Pa., Bklyn. Coll. V.p. Culton Gold, NYC, 1974; sec. NAPT, West Covina, Calif., 1978—88, exec. dir., 1979—89; ret., 1989. Mem.: Am. Soc. Assn. Execs. Address: PO Box 65 Vail AZ 85641-0065

DENVER, EILEEN ANN, retired editor; b. NYC, Nov. 16, 1942; d. Daniel Joseph and Katherine Agnes (Boland) Denver; m. Duncan C. Stephens, July 2, 1988. BA, Coll. New Rochelle, 1964; certificate, Radcliffe Sch. Pub., 1964; MA, Ind. U., 1967. Editorial asst. Mass. Inst. Tech. Tech. Review, Boston, 1965-66; instr. English St. Peter's Coll., Jersey City, 1967-70; assoc. editor, writer Am. Home mag., N.Y.C., 1971-75; asst. editor Consumer Reports, Mt. Vernon, NY, 1975-77, asst. mng. editor, 1977-79, mng. editor, 1979-91, exec. editor, 1991-96, dir. editl. ops., 1997-2000, assoc. editl. dir./exec. editor, 2000—04; ret., 2003—. Chair Friends Glebe House and Gertrude Jekyll Garden, Woodbury, Conn., 2006—; mem. bd. dirs. Denan Project, 2004—.

DENZEL, NORA, information technology executive; BS in Computer Sci., SUNY, Plattsburgh; MS in bus. admin., Santa Clara U., Calif. Various engring., mktg. and exec. roles to worldwide dir. storage software products IBM, 1984—97; sr. v.p. product operations Legato Systems, 1997—2000; gen. mgr., v.p. network storage solutions orgn. Hewlett Packard Co., 2000—03, sr. v.p. and gen. mgr. adaptive enterprise and software global bus. unit, 2003—05. Spkr. about computer technology and women's advancement in technology careers; mem. tech. adv. bd. of startup co. Mem. adv. bd. Santa Clara Univ. Bus. Sch., Women in Technology Internat., several private technology companies, Calif. C. of C.; mentors young executives in high tech careers WOMEN unlimited Program. Named Most Powerful People in Computer Networking, Networking World Mag.; named one of Top 20 Storage Movers and Shakers, Storage, Inc., Top 50 Tech. Women of the Next Millennium, Feminine Fortunes Mag., 50 Most Powerful People in Networking, Network World mag., 2003; recipient Tribute to Women in Industry, YWCA, Santa Clara County. Office: Hewlett Packard Co 1428 Hamilton Ave Palo Alto CA 94301 Office Phone: 650-327-2697. E-mail: nora.denzel@sbcglobal.net.

DENZLER, NANCY J., artist; b. Newport, Ark., Apr. 17, 1936; d. Walter and Eathel (Faulkner) Blanchard; m. Ronald Ray Hopkins, Dec. 10, 1956; m. Arthur Henry Denzler, Dec. 31, 1969; m. Timothy Joseph Riordan, Apr. 10, 1989; children: Ronald Ray Hopkins Jr., Carrie Jayne Tel-Oren. BFA magna cum laude, SUNY, Buffalo, 1976, MFA, 1978. Instr. sculpture, watercolor, acrylic, pastel and drawing, pvt. groups, 1971—. Works exhibited at Albright-Knox Gallery, Buffalo, 1976, 77, 79, Mainstreams, Marietta, Ohio, 1976, Erie (Pa.) Art Ctr., 1976, AAO Gallery and AC Gallery, Buffalo, 1977, 78, 79, Niagara Falls (N.Y.) Art Ctr., 1977, Patterson Art Gallery, Westfield, N.Y., 1979, Barn Workshop Gallery, Danvers, Mass., 1980, Union Gallery, Boston, 1982, Montserrat Gallery, Beverly, Mass., 1983, Copley Soc., 1997, others. Artists fellow Creative Artists Pub. Svc. Program, N.Y.C., 1980. Mem. Boston Visual Artists Union, The Copley Soc. of Boston. Address: 9685 N Linda Vista Pl Tucson AZ 85742-8576

DEOUL, KATHLEEN BOARDSEN, publishing executive; b. New London, Conn., May 5, 1944; d. Harry Kostrope Boardsen and Elizabeth (Conti) Dunham; m. Neal Deoul, June 20, 1982; 1 child, Shannon Rae. Grad. high sch., New London. Br. mgr. Qwip Sys. divsn. Exxon, Balt.; br. ops. mgr. Exxon Office Sys., Pitts., 1977—82; owner, pres. Bus. Quars., Crystal City, Va., 1983—95, Wellness Alternatives, Balt., 1993—, Cassandra Books, LLC, Balt., 2001; one-star presdl. dir. Bio Pro Tech., 2005—. Author: Cancer Cover-up, 2001. With Safe Wireless Initiative; co-chair Found. Alternative and Complementary Therapies. Named Cons. of Yr., Nikken, Inc., 1999, Bio Pro Tech., 2005. Mem.: Pres.'s Club Nikken, Inc. (Distbr. of Yr. 1999), Pres.'s Club Exxon. Avocations: venture capitalist, travel, writing, interior decorating, public speaking. E-mail: kathleendeoul@comcast.net.

DE PALMA-IOZZI, FRANCES M., music educator, conductor; b. Montclair, NJ, Aug. 27, 1947; d. Anthony Francis De Palma and Edith I. DiIorio; m. Louis A. Iozzi, Aug. 28, 1993; m. Eugene W. McBride (div.). BA in Music, William Patterson U., N.J., 1969; MA in Liberal Studies summa cum laude, Kean U., N.J., 1987. Cert. supr. N.J. Dept. Edn. Music educator and choral conductor West Caldwell Pub. Schs., NJ, 1969—2006; choral dir. Newark Acad., Livingston, NJ, 2006—. Adjudicator N.J. State Honors Choirs, 1986—; mem. Clin. Schs. Network Montclair State U., 1989—96; tchg. fellow Lincoln Ctr. Inst. Arts Edn., N.Y.C., 1995—2005; adj. prof. Montclair State U., NJ, 2001, Caldwell Coll., 2003. Pianist charity big band Reeds Rhythm and All That Brass, Caldwell, NJ, 1989—; founding mem. West Caldwell Performing Arts Com., 1994, program chair, 1994—2000, bd. mem., 1994—2000. Nominee Tchr. of Yr., N.J. Edn. Assn., 1993; named Best Master's Thesis in Humanities, Kean U., 1993; recipient Tchr. Edn. in Democracy award, Montclair State U., 1993; fellow, Cornell U. and NEH, 1989. Mem.: N.J. Jazz Soc., Mensa. Avocations: quilting, cooking, winemaking, reading.

DEPAOLI, GERI M. (JOAN DEPAOLI), artist, art historian; b. June 8, 1941; m. Alexander DePaoli, July 4, 1961; children: Alexander Mark, Michael Alexander. BA, U. Md., 1974, MA, 1978; student, U. Calif., Davis, 1965-68. Art history educator, artist, curator slides and photos Nat. Mus., Bangkok, Thailand, 1968-71; art prof. Montgomery Coll., Rockville, Md., 1978-82; cons. oriental slide and photo collection Princeton U., 1983-84; lectr. Princeton Sch. Visual Arts, 1986-90; curator The Mus. Art, Ft. Lauderdale, Fla., 1986; dir. Coun. for Creative Projects, N.Y.C., 1989-91; faculty artworks Princeton Sch. Visual Arts, 1984-91; exec. dir. EducArt Projects Inc., Davis, Calif., 1991—. Cons. in field. Author: Emmy Lou Packard: A Woman and a Century, 1998, Barbara Spring, Populations from the Collective Unconscious, 1998, Donna Billick: Making Art out of Stone, 1999, Clayton Bailey: Happenings in the Circus of Life, 2000, Lisa Reinertson: Art Out of Experience, 2005; editor (exhbn. catalog): Elvis & Marilyn: 2 X Immortal, Rizzoli, 1994; author (ednl. resource guide) Elvis & Marilyn: 2 X Immortal, 1994, (ednl. program) Images of Power, 1994, video prodr. Images of Power: Balinese Paintings made for Gregory Bateson and Margaret Mead, 1994, editor/co-curator (exhbn. catalog) Transcending Abstraction, 1986, reviewer ArtMatters Newspaper, Phila., 1987—90, author-curator The Trans Parent Thread: Asian Philosophy in Recent Am. Art, 1990, contbg. author Art of Calif. Mag.; one-woman shows include E.W. Gallery, Bethesda, Md., 1978, Upstairs Gallery, Kingston, N.J., 1982, Gallery at the Purple Barge, N.Y.C., 1984, The Art Gallery, Kingston, 1985, Back Door Gallery, Princeton, 1986, Campion Gallery of Art, 1987, AT&T Corp. Gallery, Princeton, 1989, Rider Coll. Gallery, Lawrenceville, N.J., 1990; also numerous group shows. Councilor Nat. Abortion Rights Action League, 1989—. Recipient award for excellence in pub., Office of Pres. of U.S., 1969. Fellow Soc. for Arts Religion and Contemporary Culture; mem. Assn. Ind. Historians of Art (v.p. 1988—), Coll. Art Assn., Princeton Rsch. Forum, Nat. Coalition of Ind. Scholars, Sierra Club, Greenpeace. Buddhist. Avocations: skiing, philosophy discussion groups, intellectual history. Office: EducArt Projects Inc PO Box 267 Davis CA 95617-0267

DEPAOLO, ROSEMARY, academic administrator; b. Bklyn., July 17, 1947; d. Nunzio and Edith (Spano) DeP.; m. Dennis B. Smith, 1977 (div. 1983); m. T. Frederick Wharton, 1984. BA, CUNY, Flushing, 1970; MA, Rutgers U., 1974, PhD, 1979. Asst. prof. to prof., dir. Ctr. for Humanities Augusta (Ga.) Coll., 1975-90; asst. dean Coll. Arts and Sci. Ga. So. U., Statesboro, 1990-93; dean Coll. Arts and Scis. Western Carolina U., Cullowhee, N.C., 1993-97; pres. Ga. Coll. and State U., Milledgeville, 1997—2003; chancellor U. N.C.-Wilmington, 2003—. Office: UNC 601 S College Rd Wilmington NC 28403-3297

DEPARLE, NANCY-ANN MIN, former federal agency administrator, lawyer; b. Cleve., Dec. 17, 1956; m. Jason DeParle. BA, U. Tenn., 1978; JD, Harvard U., 1983; BA, MA, Balliol Coll., Oxford U., Eng., 1981. Past pvt. practice in law; commr. human services State of Tenn., 1987-89; assoc. dir. health and pers. White House Office Mgmt. & Budget, Washington; adminstr. Health Care Financing Adminstrn. HHS, Washington, 1997—2000; now sr. advisor JP Morgan Partners LLC; also cons. on health policy and regulatory affairs. Mem. Medicare Payment Adv. Commn.; adj. prof. health care systems Wharton Sch., U. Pa.; bd. dirs. Cerner Corp., 2001—; mem. bd. DaVita, Guidant Corp., Triad Hospitals, Nat. Quality Forum. Bd. trustees The Robert Wood Johnson Found., 2002—. Rhodes scholar, 1979-81. Address: MedPAC Ste 9000 601 New Jersey Ave NW Washington DC 20001

DEPASS-CREQUE, LINDA ANN, educational consultant association executive, former education commissioner; b. N.Y.C. d. Noel and Enid Louise (Schloss) DePass; m. Leonard J. Creque, July 29, 1967; children: Leah Michelle, Michael Gregory. BS, CUNY-Queens, 1963, MS, 1969; PhD, U. Ill., 1986. Tchr. 2d grade Bd. Edn., N.Y.C., 1963, tchr. demonstrations, team tchr., 1964-65, master tchr., 1965-66; elem. tchr. P.S. 69, Jackson Hgts., N.Y., 1963-67; tchr. English Cath. U., Ponce, P.R., 1967; cmty. exch. elem. tchr. grades K-6 Ponce, 1966-67; tchr. 4th grade Dept. Edn., Virgin Islands, 1967—69, tchr. remedial reading, master tchr. Virgin Islands, 1968—69; program coord. Project HeadStart, Virgin Islands, 1969—73, coord. Inst. Developmental Studies Virgin Islands, 1970—71, acting dir. Virgin Islands, 1972—73; prin. Thomas Jefferson Annex Primary Sch., St. Thomas, Virgin Islands, 1973—80, Joseph Sibilly Elem. Sch., St. Thomas, 1980—87; commr. edn. Dept. Edn., St. Thomas, 1987—94; founder, pres. V.I. Inst. for Tchg. and Learning, St. Thomas, 1995—; pres. LCe Cons. Cons. Edn. Devel. Ctr., Mass. Nat. SSI Project, 1992-93, Coll. V.I., 1978; mem. exec. com., bd. overseers Regional Lab. Ednl. Improvement NE and Islands, Andover, Mass., 1988-92; bd. dirs. V.I. Pub. TV; mem. exec. bd. Leadership in Edn. Adminstrv. Devel., V.I., 1989—; op-ed columnist V.I. Daily News; presenter, keynote spkr. confs. in field. Contbr. articles to profl. publs. Trustee U. V.I., 1989—; mem. V.I. Residential Task Force for Human Svcs., 1989-94, V.I. Labor Coun.; bd. dirs. Nat. Urban Alliance for Effective Edn. Tchrs. Coll. Columbia U., N.Y.C., 1993—, Cultural Inst. V.I., 1989-94; mem. cultural endowment bd., V.I., 1989-94; mem. governing bd. East End Health Ctr., 1979-80; mem. Gov.'s Conf. Librs., 1978. Grantee V.I. Coun. on Arts Ceramics for Primary Children, 1974-78, Comprehensive Employment and Tng. Act, 1977, NSF, 1989-93, Carnegie Found., 1988-90; recipient award NASA, award St. Thomas-St. John Counselors Assn., 1988, Ednl. Excellence award Harvard U. Prins. Ctr., Ill. Edn. Svc. Ctr., 1975, Outstanding Leadership award FEMA, 1990, Disting. Svc. award Edn. Commn. of U.S., 1991, Outstanding Svc. award Coun. of Chief State Sch. Officers, 1995. Mem. LWV, St. Thomas Reading Coun., Nat. Assn. Tchrs. Math., Edn. Commn. of States (commr. 1987-93, steering com. 1988-92, internal audit com. 1988, policies priority com. 1991, exec. com. 1992, alt. steering com. 1991-94), Coun. Chief of State Sch. Officers (chair extra jurisdictions com., bd. dirs., task force early childhood edn., ednl. equity com., restructuring edn. com.), Phi Kappa Phi, Kappa Delta Pi, Phi Delta Kappa. Office: 1-1 Tabor Harmony PO Box 301954 St Thomas VI 00803-1954

DEPAUL, CHRISTINA, dean, artist; b. Pitts., 1959; BFA, Carnegie-Mellon U., 1981; MFA, Temple U., 1984. Assoc. prof. art in metals U. Akron, Ohio, 1986—2002, dir. Mary Schiller Myers Sch. Art Ohio, 1995—2002; dean Corcoran Coll. Art and Design, Washington, DC, 2002—. Office: Corcoran Coll Art and Design 500 Seventeenth St, NW Washington DC 20006-4804 Office Phone: 202-639-1801.

DE PAUW, LINDA GRANT, historian, educator, writer; b. NYC, Jan. 19, 1940; d. Phillip and Ruth (Marks) Grant. BA, Swarthmore Coll., 1961; PhD, Johns Hopkins U., 1964. Asst. prof. history George Mason Coll.-U. Va., Fairfax, 1964-65; spl. asst. to archivist U.S. Nat. Archives, Washington, 1965-66; asst. prof. history George Washington U., Washington, 1966-69, assoc. prof., 1969-75, prof. Am. history, 1975-98, prof. emeritus, 1999—. Editor-in-chief, project dir. Documentary History of the First Fed. Congress, 1966-84; author: The Eleventh Pillar: New York State and the Federal Constitution, 1966, Founding Mothers: Women of America in the Revolutionary Era, 1975, Remember the Ladies, 1976, Seafaring Women, 1982; Baptism of Fire, 1993, Battle Cries and Lullabies, 1998, Sea Changes, 2003; editor, pub. Minerva: Quar. Report on Women and the Mil., 1983-2002, Minerva's Bulletin Bd., 1988-98; writer/prodr. Minerva on the Air (armed forces radio), 1987-89; editor H-Minerva, 1995—, Minerva: Women and War, 2006—. Founder, pres. Minerva Ctr., 1983—. Woodrow Wilson fellow, 1961 Mem. Am. Hist. Assn. (Beveridge award 1964). Home: 20 Granada Rd Pasadena MD 21122-2708 Office Phone: 410-437-5379. Business E-Mail: depauw@minervacenter.com.

DEPEW, CAROL ANN, pharmaceutical sales representative; b. Kalamazoo, Mar. 2, 1962; d. Norman Sylvester and Margaret Ann (Mitscher) D. BA, U. Tenn., Knoxville, Tenn., 1986; MEd, U. Va., 1988. Nat. cert. counselor. Transition resource specialist Project PERT, Woodrow Wilson Rehab. Ctr., Fishersville, Va., 1989-1991; social worker Victor C. Newman Sch., Chgo., 1992-93; marriage and family couns. Community Svcs. Bd., Appomattor, VA, 1993-94; sales rep. Eli Lilly Co., 1994-98, Hoffman LaRoche, 1999—. Home: 25 Easton Ave Lynchburg VA 24503-1605 E-mail: cdepewmed@aol.com.

DEPEW, MAE F., director, educational consultant; d. Dewey and Axie M. Burton; 1 child, Jo M. Lewis. BA in Edn., Fla. Bapt. Coll., Lakeland, 1987, MA in Edn., 1989; MEd in Therapist, Nat. Inst. Learning Disabilites, Norfolk, Va., 1990. Dir. spl. edn. Lock Haven Christian Sch., Orlando, Fla., 1983—89, Master's Christian Sch., St. Cloud, Fla., 1989—92, Pine Castle Christian Acad., Orlando, 1992—2006; dir. pre-sch. Estelle Cmty. Ch. Day Care, Sylacauga, Ala., 2006—. Avocation: singing. Office: 375 Bice Rd Sylacauga AL 35151 Office Fax: 407-438-2739. E-mail: maedepew@juno.com.

DE PLANQUE, E. GAIL, physicist; b. Orange, N.J., Jan. 15, 1945; d. Martin William and Edna de Planque. AB, Immaculata Coll., 1967; MS in Physics, N.J. Inst. Tech., 1973; PhD in Environ. Health Scis., NYU, 1983. Physicist U.S. AEC, U.S. Dept. Energy, N.Y.C., 1967-82; dep. dir. environ. measurement lab. U.S. Dept. Energy, N.Y.C., 1982-87, dir. environ. measurement lab., 1987-91; commr. U.S. Nuclear Regulatory Commn., 1991—95; pres. Strategy Matters, Inc., 1998—; dir. Energy Strategists Consultancy, Ltd., 2000—. Adj. prof. NYU, N.Y.C., 1986—; pres. Pacific Nuclear Coun., 1989-91; mem. engring. sci. dept. adv. com., bd. trustees N.J. Inst. Tech., Newark, 1985-91; bd. dirs. TXU Corp. Landauer, Inc.; mem. visiting com. dept. nuclear engring. MIT, Diablo Canyon Ind. Safety Commn.; mem. TU Electric Ops. Rev. Com.; cons. in field. Contbr. articles to profl. jours. Commr. U.S. Nuclear Regulatory Commn., 1991-95; bd. trustees Northeast Utilities, 1995—; bd. dirs. British Nuclear Fuels, Inc., 1996—; Tex. Utilities Elec. Ops. Review Com., 1996—; cons. United Nation's Internat. Atomic Energy Agy., 1996—; mem. external adv. com., Amarillo Nat. Resource Ctr. for Plutonium, 1996—. Named to Hall of Fame, Women in Tech. Internat., 2004. Fellow Am. Nuclear Soc. (bd. dirs. 1977-80, 84-91, v.p. 1987-88, pres. 1988-89), Health Physics Soc., AAAS, Am. Phys. Soc., Assn. for Women in Sci. (v.p. N.Y. met. sect. 1980-82), Internat. Nuclear Energy Acad., (sec. 1996—); mem. NAE. Achievements include research in environmental radiation, radiation protection, solid state dosimetry, thermoluminescence.

DERAKHSHANI, MANA, literature and language professor; b. Tehran, Iran, Jan. 7, 1956; d. Manuchehr and Mahvash Derakhshani; m. Robert Harold Stockman, May 10, 1992; children: Lua Bahiyeh Derakhshani-Stockman, Nabil Robert Derakhshani-Stockman. PhD, U. Utah, Salt Lake City, 1990. French instr. U. Ga., Athens, 1984—86; vis. prof. French Purdue U., Fort Wayne, Ind., 1986—89; French prof. St. Mary's Coll., Notre Dame, Ind., 1989—. Interim dir. Ctr. Women's Intercultural Leadership St. Mary's Coll., Notre Dame, 2000—02. Chair Coalition for Race Unity, South Bend, 1990—2000; sec. Spiritual Assembly of Baha'is South Bend, 1990—2006; mem. United Religious Cmty., 1996—2002, Urban League, 1993—98; pres. United Religious Cmty., 2000—01. Recipient Ind. French Tchr. of Yr. Higher Edn. award, Ind. Assn. Tchrs. French, 1994; Course Devel. grant, Lilly Found., 1991, Rsch. grant, Nat. Endowment for Humanities, 1993. Mem.: Am. Coun. Tchrs. Fgn. Langs. Bahá'í. Avocations: reading, travel, theater, cooking. Office: St Mary's Coll Dept Modern Langs Notre Dame IN 46556

DERBER, DANA M., graphic designer; b. Beaver Dam, Wis., Oct. 23, 1955; d. Paul Oscar and Virginia May (Linck) Derber; m. Kevin André Sullivan, Sept. 4, 1988; children: Collin Pierce Sullivan, Seth Nathan Sullivan. BS in Art, U. Wis., 1977. Graphic designer Storyboard, Inc., Madison, Wis., 1982-85; dir. advt. C. G. Rein Co., St. Paul, 1985-91; pvt. practice West Salem, Wis., 1991—; adminstrv. asst., graphics and web design Wis. Ann. Conf., United Meth. Ch., 2001—04. Vol. art dir. Madcity Music Sheet, Madison, Wis., 1977-81; photo editor, webmaster, designer Hometown News, 2005 Lutheran. Avocations: computers, art, gardening.

DER BOGHOSIAN, PAULA, computer business consultant; b. Watervliet, NY, Nov. 19, 1933; d. Harry and Osgi (Piligian) der B. BS magna cum laude, Syracuse U., 1964, MS, 1967; postgrad., SUNY, Oswego, 1972, SUNY, Albany, 1974. Cert. profl. sec. Asst. prof. Cazenovia (N.Y.) Coll., 1964-73; instr. Bd. of Coop., Syracuse, N.Y., 1973-76, dir. bus. careers, 1976-92; cons. computer bus., prin. Syracuse, 1984—. Zonta scholar, 1964; Jessie Smith Noyes grantee Syracuse U., 1965. Mem. Assn. Info. Systems Profl. (com. chmn.), Bus. Tchrs. Assn. of N.Y. State, Adminstrv. Mgmt. Soc., Eastern Bus. Tchrs. Assn., Assn. for Supervision and Curriculum Devel., Assn. of Am. Jr. Colls., Assn. of Am. U. Profs., Nat. Assn. for Armenian Studies and Rsch. Harvard U., Internat. Tng. Communications (v.p. 1985-86), Delta Pi Epsilon, Beta Gamma Sigma, Phi Kappa Phi, Pi Lambda Theta, Sigma Lambda Delta. Republican. Mem. Armenian Apostolic. Avocations: music, golf, water colors, designer, travel. Home and Office: 4864 Huntwood Path Manlius NY 13104 Office Phone: 315-637-3050.

DERBY, DEBORAH, retail executive; BA in Econs., Harvard U.; MBA, JD, U. Notre Dame. Fin. analyst Goldman Sachs; atty. Miller, Canfield, Paddock and Stone; various human resources positions Whirlpool Corp., 1992—2000; from v.p. human resources Babies "R" Us Divsn. to exec. v.p. human resources Toys "R" Us, Inc., Wayne, NJ, 2000—03, exec. v.p. human resources, 2003—. Bd. dirs. Jobs for America's Graduates, Inc. (JAG). Mem.: ABA, Soc. Human Resource Profls., Mich. Bar Assn. Office: Toys R Us Inc 1 Geoffrey Way Wayne NJ 07470-2030 Office Phone: 973-617-3500.

DERCHIN, DARY BRET INGHAM, writer, radio personality; b. Camden, N.J., Sept. 15, 1941; d. Charles and Dorothy Roberta (Ingham) Lambiase; m. Michael Wayne Derchin, Dec. 29, 1970; children: Taylor-Leigh, Danielle Ashlin Lacey. BA, Montclair State Coll., 1962; postgrad., NYU, 1965, New Sch., 1966. Tchr., Randolph, N.J., 1962-64; rsch. asst. NYU, N.Y.C., 1965-67, Bolivian Peace Corps Project, N.Y.C., 1966; co-head rsch. Derchin Enterprises, N.Y.C., 1970-75. Author: Real Talk, 1992; playwright Blue No More; contbr. articles to the N.Y. Times, Harper's and book the Big Picture, others; talk show host: The Better Sex with Danna Day, Sta. WALE, 1999—, KFNY, WEVD; spkr., guest talk shows. Mem. Drama League, Lincoln Ctr. Film Soc., Am. Film Inst., Friends of Poets and Writers, Univ. Club, Nat. Art Club (lit. com., film com., Joseph Kesselring Playwright award com.). Home: Laurel Cove PO Box 200 Fair Haven NJ 07704-0200

DERDARIAN, CHRISTINE ANNE, lawyer; b. Highland Park, Mich., Aug. 30, 1948; d. Samuel and Mae Margaret (Mikjian) D. BA in Sociology, U. Mich., 1970; JD, Detroit Coll. Law, 1973. Bar: Mich. 1973. Sole practice, Detroit, 1974; asst. atty. gen. Mich. Dept. Atty. Gen., Lansing, 1974-80, sr. specialist, asst. atty. gen. Detroit, 1980-85, asst. in charge labor divsn. Lansing, 1985—2003; dir. Mich. Atty. Gen. Opinion Rev. Bd., Lansing, 1985—2002; pvt. practice Sylvan Lake, Mich., 2003—. Pres. PAX Resolution Svcs., LLC. Bd. dir. Internat. Inst. Met. Detroit, 1980-84, v.p., 1984-86, pres., 1986-88; bd. dir. Detroit Inst. for Children, 1996-98; trustee Alvin Bentley Found., 1997-2003. Mem. Mich. State Bar (dir. young lawyers coun. 1981-83, comm. com. young lawyers coun. 1982-86, bd. dirs. health com. 1986-91, coun. mem. adminstrv. law sect. 1994-96, assoc. mem. state bar com. on character and fitness 1997-99), Internat. Women's Forum, Mich. Women's Forum (dir. 1985—, pres. 1997-2004), Women's Econ. Club Detroit (pres. 1984-85, bd. trustees Project Discovery, 2004-, Human Spectrum Svcs., 2005—. Democrat. Home: 6952 Sandalwood Dr Bloomfield Hills MI 48301-3025 Office: 2055 Orchard Lake Rd Sylvan Lake MI 48320 Office Phone: 248-538-9737.

DERICKSON, SANDY, bank executive; With GE Capital Corp., 1976—99, officer, 1991—99; pres. GE Capital Auto Fin. Svcs., 1991—99; joined Household Internat. (now HSBC Fin. Corp.), 2000, CEO retail svcs., 2000—04, group exec. retail svcs., insurance svcs. and refund lending bus., vice chair, 2004—; group gen. mgr. HSBC Holdings, plc, 2005—; pres., CEO designate HSBC Bank USA, N.A., HSBC Bank USA, Inc., 2006. Dir. Hexcel Corp., 2002—. Office: HSBC Fin Corp 2700 Sanders Rd Prospect Heights IL 60070 Office Phone: 847-564-5000.

DE RIVAS, CARMELA FODERARO, retired psychiatrist, retired health facility administrator; b. Cortale, Italy, Nov. 25, 1920; arrived in U.S., 1935, naturalized, 1942; d. Salvatore and Mary (Vaiti) Foderaro; m. Aureliano Rivas, Oct. 30, 1948; children: Carmen, Norma, Sandra, David. Student, U. Pa., 1940—42; MD, Women's Med. Coll. Pa., 1946. Diplomate Am. Bd. Psychiatry and Neurology. Intern women's health Med. Coll. Pa. Hosp., 1946—47; resident gen. medicine Chestnut Hill Hosp., Phila., 1947—48; gen. practice Tex., 1948—49; mem. staff Norristown State Hosp., Pa., 1949—63, supt., 1963—70, dir. family planning, 1979—87, clin. dir. spl. assignments, 1979—82. Psychiatrist Penn Found. Mental Health, Sellersville, Pa., 1970—72; dir. intake coping svcs. Ctrl. Montgomery Mental Health/ Mental Retardation Ctr., Norristown, 1972—77, med. dir., 1977—82, psychiatrist, 1980—82; cons. surveyor Health Care Fin. Adminstrn., 1987—2001; dir. program evaluation Norristown State Hosp., 1979—82, med. dir., 1982—87; assoc. psychiatry U. Pa., 1963—75. Named to Hall of Fame S. Phila. H.S., 1968; recipient citation Women's Med. Coll. Pa., 1968, Amita achievement award, 1976, achievement award Grad. Club Phila., 1976; named Woman of Yr. Pa. Fedn. Bus. and Profl. Women, 1979. Disting. life fellow Am. Psychiat. Assn., Pa. Psychiat. Soc. (rep. assembly of dist. brs. 1979-88); mem. AMA, Phila. Psychiat. Soc. (councilor), Montgomery County Med. Soc. (bd. dir., past pres.), Pa. Med. Soc. (chmn. adv. com. to aux. 1981-88, ho. of dels., commn. med. edn. 1991-94, com. continuing med. edn. 1994-98) Home: Dunwoody Village-CH 112 3500 W Chester Pike Newtown Square PA 19073-4101

DERJUE, RITA, artist, educator; b. Warwick, R.I., July 12, 1934; d. Gustav Herman Heinrich and Lisette Anna (Gossler) Derjue; m. Carle C. Zimmerman, Jan. 30, 1960; children: Andrew Erik, Heidi Anna. BFA, RISD, 1956; MA, Cornell U., 1962; postgrad., Akademie den Bildenden Kunste, Munich, Germany, 1956-57. Artist self-employed, Denver, 1963—; artist, mentor tchr. Arapahoe C.C., Littleton, Colo., 1964—84; featured tchr. White River Inst., Beaver Creek, Colo., 1994—98. Workshop leader, painter Truro (Mass.) Ctr. for Arts, 1970-97; workshop tchr. Acapulco (Mex.) Arts Workshop, 1988-2004; cons. Littleton Fine Arts Guild, 1965-75; founder L'Asemblage, Englewood, 1976-86; theater stage designer Friends of Libr./Mus., Littleton, 1988. Exhibited in solo shows at Edgar Britton Gallery, Denver, 1980, Ohio State U., Newark, 1989, Art of Denver Gallery, 1985, Gov.'s Mansion, Colo., 1986, 87, Panache Gallery, Denver, 1988-93, Elizabeth Schlosser Gallery, 1994-2000, Western Fedn. Watercolor Socs., 2000-06, A 50-Yr. Retrospective Littleton History Mus., 2005, DieBurg, Burghausen, Germany, 2006; group shows include Colo. Gallery of Arts, 1987—, U. Colo., Colorado Springs, 1988, 2000, Colo. History Mus., Denver, 1990-2005, Littleton Pub. Libr. Mural, 2004; represented in collections at R.I. Hist. Soc., Littleton Hosp., Women's Bank, Denver, Cornell U.; author Rita Derjue: One Artists Passion, 2005; subject of newspaper and mag. articles. Bd. dirs. Littleton Hist. Mus., 1972-82, Town Hall Art Ctr., Littleton, 1986-90, Rocky Mt. Women's Inst., 2001-; mem. Rocky Mt. Nat. Watermedia; mem. adv. bd. Colo. Gallery of the Arts, Littleton, 1986-91, South Suburban Park Dist., Arapahoe County, Colo., 1994. Recipient numerous awards for art; fellow more than 80 groups exhibits and 19awards. Mem. Denver Art Mus., Colo. Watercolor Soc. (pres. bd. dirs. 1986), Rocky Mountain Women's Inst. (bd. dirs. 2001—), Rocky Mt. Watermedia Soc. Avocations: historical renovations, hiking, interior design. Home: 2539 W Ridge Ct Littleton CO 80120-3029 Office Phone: 303-798-5612.

DERK, DENISE B., nurse; b. Shamokin, Pa., Aug. 18, 1959; d. Daniel Emory and Alma Arleen (Boyer) Carl; m. Donald John Hatzel, Apr. 24, 1982 (dec. Sept. 1982); m. David Brian Derk, Dec. 8, 1984; children: Yvonne Marie. Diploma, Geisinger Med. Ctr., 1979; student, Bloomsburg U., 1981-82, U. Md., 1985-86, Graceland Coll., 1996-98. RN Pa., Fla., Mont.; CA. Staff nurse Geisinger Med. Ctr., Danville, Pa., 1979-83; nurse clinician Holmes Regional Med. Ctr., Melbourne, Fla., 1983-85; charge nurse Landstuhl (Germany) Army Regional Med. Ctr., 1985-89; nurse emergency dept. Desert Springs Hosp., Las Vegas, 1989-92; clin. nurse II Mont. Deaconess Med. Ctr., Great Falls, 1992-97; dir. nursing Rocky Mountain Treatment Ctr., Great Falls, 1996—99; dir. devel. Eagle Mount-Great Falls, 1997-98; nurse educator Rocky Mountain Treatment Ctr., 1997-99; quality assurance analyst Shasta Regional Med. Ctr., 2000—02; asst. dir. program integrity Butte Home Health & Hospice, 2002—06; nurse emergency rm. and surgery Dept. Glenn Med. Ctr., Willows, Calif., 2005—. Guest lectr. Mont. Deaconess Med. Ctr., 1993, Geisinger Med. Ctr., 1989, Great Falls Safety & Health Orgn., 1998. Contbr. articles to profl. jours. Bd. dirs. Am. Cancer Soc., Northumberland County, Pa., 1982-83, Nurse of Hope, 1979-82, Great Falls Studio Theatre, 1997-99, cmty. liason Backstage Theatre, 2005—. Avocations: horseback riding, reading, acting. Home: 12295 Paskenta Rd Red Bluff CA 96080-9720

DERK, PATRICIA KEACH, secondary school educator; b. Lancaster, Pa., June 8, 1935; d. Elmer Robert, Sr. and Emma Keach; m. Richard Elmer Osman, Jr., Apr. 17, 1954 (div. Aug. 0, 1993); children: Ruthann Eileen Black, Richard Elmer Osman III; m. Thomas Lamar Derk, Apr. 30, 1994. BS in Edn., Shippensburg State Tchrs. Coll., Pa., 1956. Cert. tchr. Pa. Social studies tchr. Ctrl. Union Sch. Dist., York, Pa., 1956—58, East Pennsboro Sch. Dist., Enola, Pa., 1959—60, Ctrl. Dauphin Sch. Dist., Harrisburg, Pa., 1962—64, English tchr., 1968—93; Am. govt./economics and st. law tchr. Milton Hershey Sch., Hershey, Pa., 2003—. Animal sci. tchr. summer program Milton Hershey Regional Sch. of Excellence, Hershey, Pa., 2001—03. Mem.: NEA, Nat. Coun. for the Social Studies, Pa. State Edn. Assn., Nat. Guild of Hypnotists (cert.), Order of Ea. Star. Republican. Lutheran. Avocations: raising show sheep, spinning, weaving, travel. Home: 720 Knight Dr Harrisburg PA 17111-4902 Office: Milton Hershey Senior Hall 820 Spartan Ln Hershey PA 17033 Personal E-mail: pkderk566@msn.com.

DERKSEN, CHARLOTTE RUTH MEYNINK, librarian; b. Newberg, Oreg., Mar. 15, 1944; BS in Geology, Wheaton Coll., Ill., 1966; MA in Geology, U. Oreg., 1968, MLS, 1973. Faculty and libr. Moeding Coll., Ootse, Botswana, 1968—71, head history dept., 1970-71; tchr. Jackson (Minn.) Pub. High Sch., 1975-77; sci. libr. U. Wis., Oshkosh, 1977-80; libr. and bibliographer Stanford (Calif.) U., 1980—2004. Acting chief scis., 1985-86, head Sci. and Engring. Librs., 1992-97. Contbg. author: Union List of Geologic Field Trip Guidebooks of North America; contbr. articles to profl. jours. Mem. ALA, Western Assn. Map Librs., Geosci. Info. Soc. (v.p. 1997-98, pres. 1998-99; first Mary B. Anasri Disting. Svc. award, 2005), Am. Geol. Inst. (mem. soc. coun. 2000-02), Geol. Soc. Am. (publ. com. 2002-05), Geoscience World (libr. adv. com., chair 2005—). Republican. Mennonite. Office: Stanford U Branner Earth Scis Library Stanford CA 94305 Home: 12522C 26th Ave NE Seattle WA 98125-8803 E-mail: cderksen@stanford.edu.

DERN, LAURA, actress; b. LA, Feb. 10, 1967; d. Bruce Dern and Diane Ladd; m. Ben Harper, Dec. 23, 2005; children: Ellery Walker, Jaya. Student, Lee Strasberg Inst., Royal Acad. Dramatic Art, London. Appeared in films Alice Doesn't Live Here Anymore, 1975, Foxes, 1980, Ladies and Gentlemen, The Fabulous Stains, 1982, Teachers, 1984, Mask, 1985, Smooth Talk, 1985, Blue Velvet, 1986, Haunted Summer, 1988, Fat Man & Little Boy, 1989, Wild At Heart, 1990, Rambling Rose, 1991 (Acad. award nomination for best actress, Golden Globe nomination for best actress in a drama), Jurassic Park, 1993, A Perfect World, 1993, Citizen Ruth, 1996, Bastard Out of Carolina, 1996, October Sky, 1999, Daddy and Them, 2001, Jurassic Park III, 2001, Novocaine, 2001, I Am Sam, 2001, We Don't Live Here Anymore, 2004, Happy Endings, 2005, The Prize Winner of Defiance, Ohio, 2005; TV appearances include: Afterburn, 1992 (Golden Globe award for best actress in TV movie or mini series), Fallen Angels (Murder, Obliquely), 1993 (Emmy nomination, Best Actress - Drama, 1994), Ruby Ridge, 1996, The Baby Dance, 1998, Damaged Care, 2002 (also co-prodr.); exec. prodr.: (TV film) Down Came a Blackbird, 1995; dir.: (TV film) The Gift, 1994; TV guest appearances include Shannon, 1981, Fallen Angels, 1993, Frasier, 1995, Ellen, 1997, The West Wing, 2002, (voice) King of the Hill, 2003; stage appearances include The Palace of Amateurs (N.Y.), 1988, Brooklyn Laundry (L.A.).

DERNER, CAROL A., retired librarian; b. Evansville, Ind., May 12, 1934; d. Jacob Christopher and Catherine Loretta (Grant) Niedhammer; m. George Bendix Derner, May 4, 1957. BA in Am. Lit., Ind. U., 1956, MA in Libr. Sci., 1958. Children's libr. Monroe County Pub. Libr., Bloomington, Ind., 1958-59, Pub. Librs. of Lake County, Merrillville, Ind., 1959-60; sch. libr. Valparaiso (Ind.) Cmty. Schs., 1960-63; head popular libr. Gary (Ind.) Pub. Libr., 1963-64, head extension dept., 1964-67; head libr. Elmwood Park (Ill.) Pub. Libr., 1968-76; asst. dir. Lake County Pub. Libr., Merrillville, 1976-85, dir., 1985-99. Adj. faculty Ind. U. Sch. Libr. and Info. Sci., Bloomington, 1982—94. Contbr. articles to profl. jours. Mem. edn. com. N.W. Ind. Forum, Portage, 1992-99; mem., sec. Ednl. Referral Ctr., Highland, Ind., 1996-99. Named Woman of Yr., Merrillville Bus. and Profl. women, 1990. Mem. ALA (coun. 1983-87), Ind. Libr. Fedn. (Libr. of Yr. 1997), Exec. Coun., Altrusa Club of Ind. Dunes (pres. 1998-99), Sun City Anthem Book Club (pres. 2004). Avocations: reading, travel, antiques. Home: 2558 Shellsburg Ave Henderson NV 89052-6442 E-mail: carderner@earthlink.net.

DE ROSA, NINON DE VERE, television producer; CEO KidsTalk Prodns., Inc.; founder KidsTalk Found., Inc., Beverly Hills, Calif., 1996—, creator, Youth Training Program, 2000—, creator, A Second Chance, ednl. svc. program, 2004—, creator, Future Leaders Program San Diego, 2005—; real estate investor, CEO NDD Properties LLC, LA, Las Vegas, 2004—. Founder KidsTalk Found., Inc., Beverly Hills, Calif., 1996—. Exec. prodr., host: (TV talk show) Voices of Tomorrow, 1996—2005 (20 Telly awards, Grace Allen award). Founder, Hal Roach Awards, comm. dept. Loyola Marymount U., 1987, bd. mem., fine arts coun.; pres., the assocs. House Ear Inst., chair, the assocs., bd. trustees. Recipient Congl. recognition, Hon. Lucille Roybal Allard, Commendation cert., Gov. Gray Davis, Richard R. Riordan, Mayor of LA, cert., Michael D. Antonovich, County of LA, Zev Yarolslavsky, County of LA, Humanitarian of Yr. award, Am. Mothers Calif., Child Abuse Appreciation award, Environ. Commn., City of Carson, Outstanding Pub. Svc. award, Dept. Recreation, City of LA, 2 Pres.'s Vol. Svc. awards, Diane Feinstein, US Senate, Nat. Philanthropy award, Small Bus. LA Connect award, Parent to Parent award, 72 Media awards, 1996—2006. Home: 7534 Mulholland Dr Los Angeles CA 90046 Office: KidsTalk Foundation Inc 8950 W Olympic Blvd Ste 271 Beverly Hills CA 90211 Office Phone: 323-850-1303. Office Fax: 323-375-0284. Business E-Mail: ninon@kidstalk.org.

DE ROSE, SANDRA MICHELE, psychotherapist, educator, administrator; b. Beacon, NY; d. Michael Joseph Borrell and Mabel Adelaide Edic Sloane; m. James Joseph De Rose, June 28, 1964 (div. 1977); children: Stacey Marie, Harrison Marquisa. Diploma in nursing, St. Luke's Hosp., 1964; BA in Child and Cmty. Psychology, Albertus Magnus Coll., 1983; MS in Counseling Psychology with honors, Century U., 1986, PhD in Counseling Psychology with honors, 1987. Gen. duty float nurse St. Luke's Hosp., Newburgh, N.Y., 1964-65; supr. nurses Craig House Hosp., Beacon, NY, 1965—70; pvt. practice New Haven, 1975—; psychotherapist, in-patient unit Conn. Mental Health Ctr., Outpatient Treatment Svc., 1970—71, psychotherapist, outpatient unit, 1971—75, head nurse, outpatient divsn., 1975—80, clin. instrn., outpatient divsn., 1980—86, dir. staff devel., team dir. divsn. New Haven, 1986-94; dir. edn. Conn. Mental Health Ctr., Outpatient Divsn., New Haven, 1994-95; clin. instr., sch. nursing Yale U., New Haven, 1979-84, clin. instr., dept. psychiatry, 1989-96. Clin. dir. Comprehensive Psychiat. Care, Norwich, Colchester and Willimantic, Conn., 1994-96; group practice Comprehensive Psychiat. Care, Norwich, Conn., 1995-2003, Alternative Paths, Yalesville, Conn., 1995-97. Mem. AAUW, ANA (cert.), Conn. Nurses Assn., Conn. Nurse Psychotherapists Assn., Western New Eng., Psychoanalytic Psychologists Soc., New Haven C. of C., Sigma Theta Tau, Delta Mu, Alpha Sigma Lambda. Avocations: music, theater, antiques, interior design/architecture, travel. Office: 100 Crown St Ste 2 New Haven CT 06510 Office Phone: 203-787-5381.

DE ROSSI, PORTIA, actress; b. Melbourne, Victoria, Australia, Jan. 31, 1973; d. Barry and Margaret Rogers; m. Metcalf Mel de Rossi (div.). Grad., Melbourne U. Actor: (films) Sirens, 1994, Scream 2, 1997, The Invisibles, 1999, American Intellectuals, 1999, Stigmata, 1999, Women in Film, 2001, Who is Cletis Tout?, 2001, I Witness, 2003, The Night We Called It a Day, 2003, Dead & Breakfast, 2004, Cursed, 2004; (TV series) Too Something, 1995—96, Nick Freno: Licensed Teacher, 1996—97, Ally McBeal, 1998—2002, Arrested Development, 2003—; (TV films) Perfect Assassins, 1998, Astoria, 1998, The Glow, 2002, America's Prince:The John F. Kennedy Jr. Story, 2003; TV appearances include Veronica's Closet, 1997, (TV series) Mad TV, 1997, The Twilight Zone, 2002, Mister Sterling, 2003.

DERR, DEBRA HULSE, advertising executive, writer; b. Newark, May 21, 1957; d. Edgar William and Mary Carway Hulse; m. David Derr. Student, Fordham U. Lic. employment agy. operator, N.J. V.p. D2 Studios, Inc., Dover, NJ. Writer, activist, spkr. assoc. prodr.: (off-Broadway) The Female Heart, 2005; assoc. prodr. (off-Broadway) Equality Plays Festival, 2006; editor: Tiny Lion, 1996; co-author: Journeys Into Self-Acceptance, 1994. Prodr. Diverse City Theater Co., Inc., 2006—. Mem.: NAFE, Amnesty Internat. Avocations: historical research, genealogy. Office: D2 Studios Inc 142 Elm St Dover NJ 07801 Personal E-mail: tinylion@d2studios.com.

DERR, TERESA MARIE, social worker; b. Jamaica, N.Y., Nov. 26, 1953; d. Emmanuel Henry and Catherine Elizabeth (Junker) D. BA magna cum laude, Georgian Ct. Coll., Lakewood, N.J., 1975; MDiv, Princeton Theol. Sem., 1980; pastoral counselor in tng., The Westchester Inst. Tng. Psychoanalysis and Psychotherapy, 1983; therapist in tng. Dynamics of Psycho., Washington Sch. Psychiatry, 1989-91; MSW, Cath. U. Am., Washington, 1993; postgrad., Yale U., 1993—94, Wash. Sch. Psychiatry, 1995. Tchr. religion Notre Dame HS, Lawrenceville, NJ, 1975-76; tchr. religion, campus minister Stuart Country Day Sch., Princeton, NJ, 1977-78; chaplain AMI Presbyn.-St. Luke's Med. Ctr., Denver, 1978, 84-85, supr., 1984-85; chaplain Bethesda PsycHealth Sys., Denver, 1978-79; alcohol counselor Rescue Mission Trenton, Inc., NJ, 1979-80; chaplain St. Peter's Med. ctr., New Brunswick, N.J., 1980-83, Children's Hosp., Denver, 1983-84; assoc. dir. pastoral care Luth. Med. Ctr., Bklyn., 1985-88; assoc. dir. pastoral care, dir. clin. pastoral edn. Washington Hosp. Ctr., 1988-90; dep. dir. devel. Women in Mil. Svc. for Am., Meml. Found., Washington, 1990-91; therapist in training Eugene Meyer II Treatment Ctr., 1990-91; chaplain, bereavement coord. Children's Nat. Med. Ctr./Hospice Svcs., Washington, 1991-92; social worker intern outpatient psychiatry Children's Nat. Med. Ctr., Washington, 1992-93; social worker Hospice Care D.C., Washington, 1994—96, Christ Child Sch. Counseling Program, Washington, 1996, Hudson Guild, N.Y.C., 1997; social worker, coord. pastoral care, child life St. Mary's Hosp. for Children, Bayside, NY, 1998—2000; social worker Prison Health Svcs./Crossroads Juvenile Ctr., Bklyn., 2002, Horizon Juvenile Ctr., Bronx, NY, 2002; social worker adolescent inpatient Yale New Haven Psychiat. Hosp., 2002—; social worker Yale U. Sch. Medicine/Psychiatry, New Haven, 2002; asst. clin. instr. Yale Child Study Ctr., 2004—. Lay minister St. Francis Ch., Brant Beach, N.J., summer 1977; dir. children's summer prog. St. Michael's Episcopal Ch., Trenton, summer 1979; workshop leader Ctr. for Humanizing Healthcare, Washington, 1988-90; mem. employee and physician devel. com. Ctr. for Humanizing Healthcare. Choral singer various groups incl. Oratorio Soc. of N.Y. Mem. Bread for World; co-leader, organizer support group for people with cancer, Bklyn., 1985-86; rep. Trenton Diocesan Pastoral Coun., 1976. Yale Child Study Ctr. fellow 1993-94. Mem. NASW, Assn. Clin. Pastoral Edn. (assoc. supr., com. mem. 1986-89), Washington Sch. Psychiatry, Sigma Phi Sigma, Phi Delta Phi. Democrat. Avocations: exercise, reading, acting, music, dance. Home: 115 Wilton Rd Westport CT 06880 Office Phone: 203-688-9871. Personal E-mail: territunes@optonline.net. E-mail: teresa.derr@ynhh.org.

DERRICK, DEBORAH BALL, editor, writer; b. Syracuse, N.Y., Aug. 20, 1952; d. Thomas Martin and Joyce Virginia (DeLine) Ball; m. Thomas Charles Derrick, Sept. 29, 1978; children: Kristina, Jonathan. BA, Drake U., 1981; MA, U. Nebr., Omaha, 2003; postgrad., U. Nebr., 2003. Program specialist City of Syracuse, 1975-77; planner Ctrl. Iowa Regional Assn., Des Moines, 1977-82; MIS supr., contract mgmt. coord. Ctrl. Iowa Employment and Tng. Consortium, Des Moines, 1982-84; adminstrv. asst. Francis & Assocs., Des Moines, 1984-85; mktg. coord. Wells Engrs., inc., Omaha, 1985-90; instr. tech. writing U. Nebr., Lincoln, asst. to dean Med. Ctr. Omaha, 1990-92, comms. specialist Lincoln, 1992—2005, grant writer, 1992—, grant coord. Omaha, 2005—. Presenter in field. Editor: Contacts Mag., 1997—2002 (award of excellence Pub. Rels. Soc. Am., 2002); editor: (with others) PCI Bridge Manual, 1997, Plains Song Rev., 2004—; contbr. feature articles and stories to profl. jours. Dir. Friends Loren Eiseley. Recipient Jim Raglin Media award, Am. Cancer Soc., 1995. Mem.: Soc. Tech. Communication (award for Merit 2003), Nat. Assn. Sci. Writers, Assn. Study Lit. and Environment, Nat. Fedn. Press Women (dir., Mag. and Website Design award 1999). Avocations: writing, travel, quilting, reading, outdoor activities. Home: 5411 Western Ave Omaha NE 68132-2158 Office: Eppley Adminstrn Bldg 60th and Dodge Rm 203 Omaha NE 68182-0210 Business E-Mail: dderrick@mail.unomaha.edu.

DERRICK, KATHRYN THILL, secondary school educator; b. Rochester, Mich., Jan. 9, 1976; d. Thomas Robert Thill, Jr. and Nancy Katherine Christian Thill; m. Brian Alan Derrick, June 7, 2003. BS, U. Conn., 1997; MEd, Peabody Coll.Vanderbilt U., 2000; M in Info. Sci., U. Tenn., 2003. Cert. tchr. Tenn. Dept. Edn., 2002. Environ. scientist IT Corp., Norwood, Mass., 1998—99; tchr. St. Cecilia Acad., Nashville, 2000—01, Met. Nashville Pub. Schs., Nashville, 2001—03, Pope John Paul II H.S., Hendersonville, Tenn., 2003—. Writer of credit recovery curriculum Met. Nashville Pub. Schs., 2002—03; supr./mentor Peabody Coll., 2002; sci. standards com. mem. Met. Nashville Pub. Schools, 2003. Supr. and designer of 9-11 meml. Overton H.S. - MNPS, Nashville, 2001; vol. ARC, Storrs, Conn., 1995—97, Nashville Cath. Diocese, 2003—05. Recipient Fulbright Meml. Fund, Japan-U.S. Ednl. Commn., 2004, The Chancellor's List, Nat. Academic Affairs, 2005. Mem.: ALA, Tenn. Environ. Edn. Assn., Tenn. Acad. Scis., Nat. Assn. Biology Tchrs., Tenn. Sci. Tchr. Assn., Nat. Sci. Tchr. Assn., Libr. and Info. Tech. Assn., Kappa Delta Pi, Golden Key, Phi Kappa Phi. Roman Catholic. Avocations: scuba diving, travel, reading, hiking.

DERUBERTIS, PATRICIA UHL, software company executive; b. Bayonne, N.J., July 10, 1950; d. George Joseph and Veronica (Lukaszewich) Uhl; m. John Stryker, 1975; m. Michael DeRubertis, 1986. BS in Bus. Adminstrn., U. Md., 1972. Account rep. GE, San Francisco, 1975-77; tech. rep. Computer Scis. Corp., San Francisco, 1977-78; cons., pres. Uhl Assocs., Tiburon, Calif., 1978-81; cons. mgr. Ross Sys., Palo Alto, Calif., 1981-83; COO, exec. v.p. Distributed Planning Sys., Calabasas, Calif., 1983-92; pres. DeRubertis & Assocs., Thousand Oaks, Calif., 1992-94, DeRubertis Software Sys., Inc., Windermere, Fla., 1995—. Author: Rose Gardening By Color, 1994. Troop leader San Francisco coun. Girl Scouts Am., 1974; participant Woman On Water, Marina Del Rey, Calif., 1983; vol. Martin County Coun. for the Arts, 1995, Habitat for Humanity, 2002, Windermere Preparatory Sch., 2003—; sec./treas. Windermere Tree Bd., 2005—; vol. Gayle Harrell campaign for state legis., 2000. Mem. AAUW, NAFE, Windermere Garden Club, Lake Eustis Sailing Club, Delta Delta Delta. Democrat. Office: 109 Main St Windermere FL 34786 Office Phone: 407-909-0887. E-mail: dssincpd@aol.com.

DERUYTER, MARILYN, real estate broker; b. Canandaigua, N.Y., May 8, 1942; d. Ernest Robert and Alice Zereda Mason Prober; m. Paul C. DeRuyter, Dec. 29, 1961 (div. July 1990); children: Kristin M. Walters, Paul R. Grad., high sch., Shortsville, N.Y., 1960, Real Estate Inst., 1982. Cert. residential specialist; grad. Real Estate Inst. Exec. sec. Red Jacket Tel., Shortsville, 1966-72; paralegal David G. Retchless Esq., Clifton Springs, N.Y., 1972-80; real estate broker M. DeRuyter Real Estate, Shortsville, 1978—. Recipient Sales Master Gold and Zenith awards for Sales Excellence. Mem.: Clifton Springs Rotary, Lions. Avocations: reading, shopping. Home: 74 E Main St Clifton Springs NY 14432 Office Phone: 315-462-2222. E-mail: mderuyte@rochester.rr.com.

DERVIN, BRENDA LOUISE, communications educator; b. Beverly, Mass., Nov. 20, 1938; d. Ermina Diluiso; adopted d. John Jordan and Marjorie (Sullivan) D. BS, Cornell U., 1960; MA, Mich. State U., 1968, PhD, 1972; PhD (hon.), U. Helsinki, 2000. Pub. info. asst. Am. Home Econ. Assn., Washington, 1960-62; pub. info. specialist Ctr. Consumer Affairs, U. Wis., Milw., 1962-65; instr., rsch. and teaching asst. dept. communications Mich. State U., E. Lansing, 1965-70; asst. prof., Sch. Info. Transfer Syracuse (N.Y.) U., 1970-72; asst. to assoc. prof. U. Wash., Seattle, 1972-85; prof. comm. Ohio State U., Columbus, 1985—. Co-author: The Mass Media Behavior of the Urban Poor, 1980; editor: Rethinking Communication, 1989, Communication A Different Kind of Horserace, 2003, Sense-making Methodology Reader, 2003; editor Progress in Communication Sci., 1981-92; contbr. articles to profl. jours. Grantee U.S. Office Edn., 1974-76, Calif. State Libr., 1974-84, Nat. Cancer Inst., 1984, Ameritech, 1992, Inst. Mus. and Libr. Svc., 2003—. Fellow Internat. Communication Assn. (pres. 1986-87); mem. Internat. Assn. Mass Communications Rsch. (governing coun. 1988-97). Home: 4269 Kenridge Dr Columbus OH 43220-4157 Office: Ohio State U 3016 Derby 154 N Oval Mall Columbus OH 43210-1330 Office Phone: 614-292-3192. Business E-Mail: dervin.1@osu.edu.

DE SÁ E SILVA, ELIZABETH ANNE, secondary school educator; b. Edmonds, Wash., Mar. 17, 1931; d. Sven Yngve and Anna Laura Elizabeth (Dahlin) Erlandson; m. Claudio de Sá e Silva, Sept. 12, 1955 (div. July 1977); children: Lydia, Marco, Nelson. BA, U. Oreg., 1953; postgrad., Columbia U., 1954—56, Calif. State U., Fresno, 1990, U. No. Iowa, 1983; MEd, Mont. State U., 1978. Med. sec., 1947—49; sec. Merced Sch. Dist., Calif., 1950—51; sec., asst. Simon and Schuster, Inc., N.Y.C., 1954—56; tchr. Casa Roosevelt-União Cultural, São Paulo, Brazil, 1957—59, Coquille Sch. Dist., Oreg., 1978—96; tchr. music Cartwheels Pre-sch., North Bend, Oreg., 1997—99, 2001. Tchr. piano, 1967—78; instr. Spanish Southwestern Oreg. C.C., Coos Bay, 1991—94; pianist/organist Faith Luth. Ch., North Bend, Oreg., 1995—2002, New Life Luth. Ch., Florence, Oreg., 2002—04; vocal soloist, 1996—; voice tchr., 1997—99. Chmn. publicity Music in Our Schs. Month, Oreg. Dist. VII, 1980-85; sec. Newcomer's Club, Bozeman, Mont., 1971. Quincentennial fellow U. Minn. and Found. José Ortega y Gasset, Madrid, 1991, Sheffield Berkshire Choral Festival, Sheffield, Mass., 2004, 05. Mem. AAUW (sec., scholarship chmn., co-pres., pres., treas., editor newsletter), Nat. Trust Hist. Preservation, Am. Coun. on Tchg. Fgn. Langs., Am. Assn. Tchrs. Spanish and Portuguese, Nat. Coun. Tchrs. English, Music Educators Nat. Conf., Oreg. Music Educators Assn., Oreg. Coun. Tchrs. English, Confedn. Oreg. Fgn. Lang. Tchrs., VoiceCare Network, Am. Guild Organists, Berkshire Choral Festival. Democrat. Avocations: swimming, walking, travel, drama. Home: 14425 SW Arabian Dr Beaverton OR 97008 Office Phone: 503-524-6036.

DESAI, VEENA BALVANTRAI, obstetrician, gynecologist, educator; b. Karvan, Gujarat, India, Oct. 5, 1931; arrived in U.S., 1973; d. Balvantrai P. and Maniben (Vashl) Desai; m. Vinay D. Gandevia, Sept. 19, 1964. MBBS, Seth G.S. Med. Coll., Bombay, 1957, MD, 1961. Jr. resident Bombay U., 1957-59; house officer gyn. Chalmer's Hosp., Edinburgh, Scotland, 1962-63; registrar ob-gyn. Neath Gen. Hosp., England, 1963-64, Scunthorpe Gen. Hosp., England, 1964-66; chief resident ob-gyn. St. John Gen. Hosp., Canada, 1973-74; attending ob-gyn. Portsmouth Hosp., NH, 1975-84; assoc. prof. Boston U., 1985-86; sr. staff ob-gyn. Santa Clara Valley Med. Ctr., Calif., 1986-87; mem. staff ob-gyn. West Anaheim Med. Ctr., Calif., 1988-98, chief dept. ob-gyn., 1992-93, vice chief of gen. med. staff, 1994—95; ob/gyn Bay State Med. Ctr., Springfield, Mass., 1998—; chief ob-gyn. Mercy Med. Ctr., Springfield, 2002—03. Pres. Desai Med. Corp., Anaheim, 1989—; assoc. clin. prof. ob-gyn. U. Calif., Irvine, 1990—98. Chmn.'s advisor NSC; charter mem. Presdl. Task Force; mem. Reps. Inner Cir., 1984—2003. Named Pioneer of Healthcare Reform, Nat. Rep. Congl. Com., 2004, Merit for Life, Confedn. Chivalry, Sydney, 1989; recipient Presdl. medal of Merit, 1982, award, Spl. Congl. Adv. Bd., 1984, Order of Liberty, US Congress, 1995, medal of Freedom, US Senate, 1994, medal, Ronald Wilson Reagan Eternal Flame of Freedom, 1996, Millennium medal of Freedom, Rep. Senate, 1999, Internat. Peace prize, United Cultural Conv., 2003, Congl. Order of Merit, 2004, Dame, Confedn. Chivalry, Sydney, 1989, Outstanding Achievement in Poetry award, Internat. Soc. Poets, 2005. Fellow: ACOG, ACS, Royal Coll. Ob-Gyn. (chmn. Am. rep. com. 1997—2002), Western Mass. Ob-Gyn. Soc. (pres. 2002—), Internat. Coll. Surgeons; mem.: Buena Park Rotary (pres. 1994, chair internat. svc. 1992—93). Avocations: latchhook work, international politics, travel. Home: 35 Sean Louis Cir West Springfield MA 01089-4547 Personal E-mail: veenadesai@comcast.net.

DESAI, VISHAKHA N., museum director, professional society administrator; b. Ahmedabad, Gujarat, India, May 1, 1949; came to U.S., 1966; m. Robert B. Oxnam, 1993. BA, Bombay U., Elphinstone Coll., 1970; MA in History of Art, U. Mich., 1975, PhD in History of Art, 1984. With edn. div. Bklyn. Mus., N.Y.C., 1972-74; head exhibit resource Mus. sect. edn. dept. Fine Arts, Boston, 1977-80; acting dir. edn. dept. Mus. Fine Arts, Boston, 1980-81, coord. acad. program, 1981-88, asst. curator, 1981-90, mus. pres.; dir. Asia Soc. Galleries, N.Y.C., 1990—; v.p. Asia Soc., 1993—. Adj. asst. prof. Boston U., 1982-87; assoc. prof. U. Mass., Boston, 1986-90; adj. prof. Columbia U., 1995-96, 97; bd. dirs. Am. Com. South/S.E. Asia Art; reviewer Bunting Inst., Radcliffe Coll., Boston, 1990—; bd. dirs. Art Table, N.Y.C., 1991-94. Contbr. articles to profl. jours. Pres. Mass. Found. for Humanities, 1989-91. Outstanding Teaching fellow U. Mich., 1977, Am. Inst. of Indian Studies fellow, 1978; grantee, Nat. Endowment for the Arts, NEM, 1979—, Mus. Sabbaticatal grantee Nat. Endowment for the Arts, 1982. Mem. Coll. Art Assn. (bd. dirs. 1995—), Am. Assn. Art Mus. Dirs. (bd. dirs. 1995—. pres. 1998—). Office: Asia Soc and Mus 725 Park Ave New York NY 10021-5025

DESALVO, CATHERINE GASTON, principal; d. Dale S. and Frances (Pawlowski) Gaston; m. Jules John DeSalvo, June 30, 1979; children: Jules Gaston, John Andrew. BA in English, Benedictine Coll., Atchison, Kans., 1972; MA in English, Creighton U., Omaha, 1974; MS in Spl. Edn., U. Nebr., Omaha, 1978. Cert. tchr. Nebr. From ednl. therapist to assoc. dir. ednl. therapy Nebr. Psychiat. Inst., Omaha, 1974—84; behavioral cons. Loess Hills Area Edn. Agy., Council Bluffs, Iowa, 1984—88; student svcs. cons. Wegner Sch., Boys Town, Nebr., 1988—96, prin., 1996—. Instr. Met. CC, Omaha, 2001—. Mem.: ASCD. Avocations: walking, choral singing. Office: Wegner Sch 14124 Norton Dr Boys Town NE 68010-7556

DESAN, CHRISTINE, law educator; b. Washington, Mar. 20, 1959; AB in Religion, Princeton U., 1981; MALD Fletcher Sch. Law & Diplomacy, Tufts U., 1987; JD, Yale U., 1987. Bar: Mass. 1987, DC 1989. Law clk. to Judge Stephen Breyer US Ct. Appeals 11th Cir.; asst. to Solicitor Gen. Charles Fried; asst. prof. law Harvard Law Sch., Cambridge, Mass., 1992—98, prof., 1998—. Office: Harvard Law Sch 1563 Massachusetts Ave Cambridge MA 02138 Office Phone: 617-495-4613, 617-495-5156. Business E-Mail: desan@law.harvard.edu.

DE SANTIAGO, DENA KALENE, investment company executive, writer; b. Council Bluffs, Iowa, Aug. 19, 1970; d. Savino Michael and Linda Lou (Hannum) De Santiago; life ptnr. Vincent William Young, Jan. 14, 1979; children: Todd Michael Roberts, Isabella Kalene De Santiago-Young. Degree in Pub. Rels./Orgnl. Comm. & Devel., Creighton U., Omaha, Nebr., 1991; degree in Liberal Arts (hon.), Bellevue U., Nebr., 2002, M in Leadership (hon.), 2003; PhD, Walden U., Balt., 2004. Lic. ins. Nebr., 1996; cert. CPR/First Aid Nebr., 2003; Child Care Nebr., 1999; Mergers and Acquisitions Columbia U., 1999, Series 7 NASD, 1996, Series 63 NASD, 1996, Series 65 NASD, 1996, Series 31 NASD and CFTC, 1996, Series 3 NASD and CFTC, 1997. Investment exec. Dain Rauscher, Omaha, 1997—98; devel. dir. First Investment Inc., Omaha, 1998—. Ops. mgr. Law Offices of S.J. Albracht, Omaha, 1991—93; rsch. and fin. coord. Dain Bosworth, Inc, Omaha, 1993—94; mktg. dir. Hawkeye Investment Ctr., Council Bluffs, Iowa, 1994—96; agt./exec. DKD Modeling, Omaha, 1995—96; account exec. Dean Witter Reynolds, Omaha, 1996—97; casting asst. Topeka Prodns., Omaha, 1995—96. Actor: (primetime mini series) Gone in the Night; contbr., vol. (cmty. leader) KPTM Fox News; author: (publs. com.) Omaha Press Club; contbr. speech (1st Pl.); contbr.: speech Why My Family is Important, 1981-1982; contbr. citywide childrens' works (Trophy and Cert., 1978), essay contest (7th Pl. out of 35,000 entries, 1982), essay (1st Pl., 2001). Vol./fundraising Muscular Dystrophy Assn., Council Bluffs, Iowa, 1974—80, Nebr. Aids Project, Omaha, 1991—2000, MADD, Omaha, 1994—2000; vol. Girl's Inc., Omaha, 1995—97; NW divsn. comm. chair Mar. of Dimes, Omaha, 2001—02. Democrat. Catholic And Christian. Achievements include research in prison reform; development of National Issues Forum. Avocations: writing, research, mentoring, public speaking. Office: First Investment Inc PO Box 31616 Omaha NE 68131-0616 Office Phone: 402-689-8792. Business E-Mail: ddesantiago@firstinvestmentinc.com.

DESANTIS, SHEROLYN SMITH, foundation executive; b. Ontario, Oreg., Feb. 7, 1949; d. Ronald Duane Smith and Dorothy Lorene Hergert Smith; divorced; children: Louie Duane, Rhonda Marie, Paul Nunzio. BA, Idaho State U., 1971. Chmn., founder, exec. dir. Diagnostek Charitable Found., Albuquerque, 1990-95, Joshua Chariable Found., Albuquerque, 1995—; chmn., founder, ex-dir. Albuquerque Women's Resource Ctr., 1998—. Bd. dirs. Caballero Norte Neighborhood Assn., Albuquerque, 1985-87; mem. fundraising Albuquerque Pregnancy Ctr., 1984-99, bd. dirs., 1996-98, sec. bd. dirs., 1997-98; mem., del. Rep. State Ctrl. Com., Albuquerque, 1998—; mem. Rep. Assembly, Albuquerque, 1998—, Rep. Ward vice-hmn.; mentor Wise Men & Women, Albuquerque, 1998-99; mem. nat. adv. com. on violence against women U.S. Dept. Justice and U.S. Dept. Health and Human Svcs., 2002—; mem. N.Mex. Crime Victims Reparation Commn., 2004; N.Mex. alt. del. to Rep. Nat. Conv., 2000, 2004; N.Mex. state chmn. W Stands for Women, 2004; mem. Gov.'s Met. Judge Nominating Commn., 2002; elected 2d vice chmn. N.Mex. State Rep. Party, 2001-2003. Mem. N.Mex. Soc. Fundraising Execs. Baptist. Avocations: reading, cooking, entertaining, politics, fundraising. Office Phone: 505-350-2305.

DESANTO, GRACE L., elementary school educator; d. Joseph and Lilla Elizabeth Jekot; m. Andrew C. DeSanto, Dec. 23, 1975; 1 child, Kathleen L. Burghardt. BS in Elem. Edn., West Chester U., Pa., 1965. Cert. tchr. elem. edn. N.J., 1965. Tchr. Woodbury Pub. Schs., NJ, 1965—67, Samuel S. Yellin Sch., Stratford, NJ, 1981—. Recipient Dist. Tchr. of Yr., N.J., 1997. Independent. Episcopal. Avocations: knitting, gardening, travel. Home: 7 South Branch Ct Mullica Hill NJ 08062 Office: Samuel S Yellin Sch 111 Warwick Rd Stratford NJ 08084 Office Phone: 856-783-1094 712.

DESCA, EVA See GARNET, EVA

DESCHAINE, BARBARA RALPH, retired real estate broker; b. Syracuse, N.Y., Feb. 16, 1930; d. George John and Dora Belle (Manchester) Ralph; children by previous marriage: Olav Bernt Kollevoll Jr., Kristan George Kollevoll, Eric John Kollevoll; m. Bernard Richard Deschaine May 23, 1981 (dec. 1994). BA, St. Lawrence U., 1952; postgrad., Pa. State U., 1969-72; grad., Pa. Realtors Inst., 1973; student, Realtors Nat. Mktg. Inst., 1974-75. Salesman Brose Realty, Easton, Pa., 1967—71, assoc. broker/mgr., 1972—73, broker, owner, 1974-85; broker, mgr. John W. Monaghan Corp. Realtors, 1985-91; assoc. broker The Prudential/Paul Ford Realtors, Easton, 1991-99. Mem. Pa. Real Estate Polit. Edn. Com. Bd. dirs. Easton Area C. of C., 1973-79, v.p. organizational improvement, 1975-76, v.p. econ. devel., 1976-77, pres., 1977-78; mem. Greater Easton Corp. Strategy Group, 1977-78; mem. Northampton County Revenue Appeals Bd., 1982-98, co-chmn., 1994-98; trustee Easton area YMCA, 1984-91; bd. dirs. State Theatre for the Arts, 1994-2002. Mem.: NAFE, Sales and Mktg. Execs. (bd. dirs. Easton area chpt. 1976—91, Disting. Sales award 1982), Homes for Living Network (state chmn. 1980), Ea. Northampton County Multiple Listing Svc. (bd. dirs. 1987—91, pres. 1986), Easton Area Bd. Realtors (bd. dirs. 1973—87, sec. 1977, v.p. 1980—81, pres. 1972, Realtor of Yr. 1978), Pa. Assn. Realtors, Nat. Assn. Realtors, Phi Beta Kappa. Republican. Presbyterian. Address: 384 Hobson Place Blue Bell PA 19422

DESCHAMP, GLORIA J., retail liquor store owner; b. Boston, Aug. 22, 1949; d. Frank and Golda Gloria Bugley; m. David Arthur Deschamp, Apr. 21, 1990. AA, Dean Jr. Coll., Franklin, Mass., 1969. Phys. edn. instr. Hollis (N.H.) High Sch., 1971; owner El Jebel (Colo.) Liquors, 1979—; pres., CEO Sun Pro-Tech. Inc., 1996—. V.p. Liberty Resource, Inc., Grand Junction, Colo., 1993; co-founder, co-chmn. El Jebel Bus. Assn., 1992. Author: (cookbook) The Roaring Fork, 1993. Bd. dirs. Aspen Mesa Estate Assn., Carbondale, Colo., 1987-89. Mem. Colo. Lic. Beverage Assn., Small Bus. Assn., Smithsonian. Avocations: tennis, golf, skiing, gardening. Office Phone: 970-245-5342. E-mail: gloriadeschamp@msn.com.

DESCHINNY, ISABEL, elementary school educator; b. Pine Springs, Ariz., Sept. 6, 1943; d. James Clah and Mabel Burnside Myers; m. Daniel Deschinny Sr., Aug. 28, 1965 (dec. Dec. 1997); children: Daniel Jr., Ronald Sr., Mark, Janet. BA, No. Ariz. U., 1986; BS in Elem. Edn., Prescott Coll., 1999. Cert. tchr. Ariz. Nava jo weaving tchr. U. N.M., Gallup, 1992—2006; tchr. Window Rock (Ariz.) Elem. Sch., 1999—2004. Mem. Pine Springs Sch. Bd. (Navajo Nation), Pine Sprs. Houck, Ariz., 1986—92. Scholar, Navajo Tribal Edn. Com., Window Rock, 1963—86. Roman Catholic. Avocation: Navajo weaving. Home: PO Box 4677 Window Rock AZ 86515

DESCHNER, JANE WAGGONER, photo artist, arts in healthcare consultant; b. Bellefont, Pa., Feb. 9, 1948; d. George Ruble and Helen Louise (Talbert) Waggoner; m. William Henry Deschner, July 26, 1969 (div. Dec. 1987); children: John William, Elisabeth Anne. BA in Geography, U. Kans., 1969; BA in Art, Mont. State U., Billings, 1987; MFA in Visual Art, Vt. Coll., 2002. Economist Mid-Am. Regional Coun., Kansas City, Mo., 1970-73; ptnr., owner Castle Art Gallery, Billings, Mont., 1982-88; asst. dir. client svcs. Mont. Inst. of Arts Found., Billings, 1988-89; account exec., artist, writer Exclamation Point Advt., Billings, 1989-94; artist Billings, 1981—; project coord., cons. pub. rels./graphic design, arts in healthcare, 1994—; curator Women's Ctrl. Gallery, Billings, 1991—2005, D.A. Davidson & Co. Gallery, Billings, 2003—. Coord. Art in the Libr. program, adj. art faculty Rocky Mountain Coll., Billings, creative coord. Arts in Medicine St. Vincent Healthcare; adj. faculty Rocky Mountain Coll., Billings. Exhibited at Nicolaysen Art Mus., Casper, Wyo., Toucan Gallery, Billings, U. Mont., Missoula, Mont., Art Mus. Missoula, Mont. State U., Billings, Holter Mus. Art, Helena, Mont., Broken Diamond Gallery, Billings, Mont. State U., Bozeman, Deering Galleries, Taos, N.Mex., Contemporary Art Mus., Sacramento, St. Vincent Healthcare, Billings, Mont. Art of Survival, Healing in Life, 2000-. Bd. dirs. Billings Mental Health Assn., 1988-92, v.p., 1989, 90; bd. dirs. Soc. for Arts in Healthcare, Washington, 2003—; gallery dir., bd. dirs. The Women's Ctr., St. Vincent Healthcare, Billings, 1991-2004; mem. Youth Ct. Conf. Com. 13th Jud. Dist. Mont., Billings, 1992—; Poets on the Prairie artist YMCA Writer's Voice; bd. dirs. InterMountain Planned Parenthood, 1998-2001. Recipient 1st pl. award in non-comml. art Billings Advt. and Mktg. Assn., 1992, 93; Sam and Alfreda Maloof scholar Anderson Ranch Arts Ctr., 1998-99; State of Mont. profl. devel. grantee, 1999. Mem. Yellowstone Print Club (bd. dirs., pres. acquisitions chair), Yellowstone Art Ctr. (Auction Artist 1989-2002). Unitarian Universalist. Avocations: travel, cooking, reading. Studio: 1313 Granite Ave Billings MT 59102-0869 Personal E-mail: jwd@bresnam.net.

DE SCHWEINITZ, JEAN HOWARD, biology professor; b. Fontainebleau, France, Oct. 22, 1956; arrived in U.S., 1958; d. Jack Linwood and Eloise Bentley Howard; m. David Dane de Schweinitz, June 16, 1985; children: Daniel, Sarah, Richard. BS, North Ga. Coll., Dahlonega, 1977; MA, Austin Peay State U., Clarksville, Tenn., 1978; PhD, U. North Tex., Denton, 1986. Postdoctoral fellow U. Tex. Southwestern Med. Sch., Dallas, 1986—89; prof. biology Tarrant County Coll., Ft. Worth, 1993—. Mem.: DAR, Soc. Mayflower Descendants (historian 2004—06), Ft. Worth Woman's Club, Tex. Scottish Rite Hosp. (mem. 500 Club), Delta Kappa Gamma, Phi Theta Kappa (hon.; faculty adviser, Horizon awrd 2004), Kappa Delta. Republican. Methodist. Office: Tarrant County Coll South Campus Dept Natural Scis 5301 Campus Dr Fort Worth TX 76119 Business E-Mail: jean.deschweinitz@tccd.edu.

DESCOTEAUX, CAROL J., health facility administrator; b. Nashua, N.H., Apr. 5, 1948; d. Henry Louis and Therese (Arel) D. BA, Notre Dame Coll., 1970; MEd, Boston Coll., 1975; MA, U. Notre Dame, 1984, PhD, 1985. Jr. high sch. instr., dir. religious studies St. Joseph's Sch., North Grosvenordale, Conn., 1970-73; jr. high sch. tchr., dir. religious edn. Notre Dame Sch., North Adams, Mass., 1973-77, 1978—81; chairperson religious studies discipline Notre Dame Coll. Grad. Theol. Union, U. Notre Dame, Ind., 1982-83, 84-85; jr. high sch. instr. Sacred Heart Sch., Groton, Conn., 1977-78; pres. Notre Dame Coll., Manchester, NH, 1985—99; v.p. mission integration St. Joseph Hosp., Nashua, NH, 2000—. Trustee King's Coll., Wilkes-Barre, Pa., 1987-95; pres. Fedn. of Holy Cross Colls., 1985-96; mem. adv. bd. Manchester Christian Life Ctr., 1978-80; treas. N.H. Coll. and Univ. Council, Manchester, 1985-86; trustee N.H. Higher Edn. Assistance Found., 1986—. Mem. Manchester United Way campaign, 1985—; bd. incorporators, mem. ethics com., instl. research com. Cath. Med. Ctr., Manchester, 1986—99; mem. bd. trustees Dartmouth-Hitchcock Med. Ctr., Marguerite's Place, St. Joseph Cmty. Svcs., N.H. Partnership for End-of-Life Care, Stonehill Coll., Rivier Coll. Named Disting. Woman Leader of Yr., So. N.H. region YWCA, 1985, N.H. Disting. Woman Educator, 1994, Manchester Citizen of Yr., 1995, N.H. Boston Coll. Alumna of Yr., 1990, N.H. U. Notre Dame Alumna of Yr., 1992. Mem. Am. Acad. Religion, Coll. Theology Soc. Am., N.H. Women's Forum, Soc. Christian Ethics, Nat. Hospice and Palliative Care Assn., Cath. Hosp. Assn. Am. Democrat. Roman Catholic. Avocations: art, music, theater, fishing, bowling. Office: St Joseph Hosp 172 Kinsley St Nashua NH 03060-3688

DESFORGES, DEBORAH WALN, music educator; b. Phillippi, W.Va., Nov. 27, 1951; d. Raymond Reeder Waln and Ann Luse Manning; m. Christopher Tracy Sylvester, July 14, 2001; 1 child, Christopher Douglas Sylvester. BA, W.Va. Wesleyan Coll., 1973; MusM, U. Fla., Gainesville, 1993. Cert. profl. educator State of Fla. Dept. of Edn. Music tchr. Collier County Pub. Schs., Naples, Fla., 1974—77, Sch. Bd. of Alachua County, Gainesville, Fla., 1977—. Music workshop cons. Sch. Bd. of Alachua County, Gainesville, mem. music curriculum devel. com.; condr. honor choir Polk County Sch. Bd., Lakeland, Fla., 2002—03, Sch. Bd. of Columbia County, Lake City, Fla., 2003—05; dist. chair Arts for a Complete Edn., Gainesville; chair fine arts Glen Springs Elem., Gainesville, mem. placement rev. com., 2002—; dir. Glen Springs Summer Enrichment Program, Gainesville; yearbook editor Glen Springs Elem., Gainesville; co-chair Glen Springs com. So. Assn. of Colls. and Schs. Rev., Gainesville; performing arts summer symposium co-dir. Sch. Bd. of Alachua County, Gainesville; coord. Glen Springs Summer Sci. Acad., Gainesville, 2004—; founder, dir. choir selected to perform with Vienna Boys Choir European Cultural Initiative for Young Generation, 2002. Author: (mus. play) Florida History Live! (grant Sch. Bd. of Alachua County), (computer program) Computerized Composer Information Retrieval System. Team capt. U.S. Tennis Assn. Women's 3.0 Team, Gainesville, 2000—01; founder, artistic dir. Gainesville (Fla.) Youth Chorus, Inc., 1994—; mem. worship com. 1st Presbyn. Ch., Gainesville; choir mem. 1st Presbyn. Ch. Chancel Choir, Gainesville. Named Outstanding Vol. in the Arts, City of Gainesville Cultural Affairs Bd., 2002. Mem.: NEA, Fla. Elem. Music Educators Assn. (bd. dirs., dist. chair), Alachua County Educators Assn., Am. Choral Dirs. Assn., Music Educators Nat. Conf., DB Racquet Club, Alpha Phi Gamma, Alpha Gamma Delta. Avocations: tennis, singing, gardening, photography, travel. Office: 2826 NW 31st Ave Gainesville FL 32605 Office Phone: 352-955-6708. E-mail: desfordw@sbac.edu.

DESFORGES, JANE FAY, retired internist, hematologist, educator; b. Melrose, Mass., Dec. 18, 1921; d. Joseph Henry and Alics Maher (Fay) Desforges; m. Gerard Desforges, Sept. 11, 1948; children: Gerard Joseph, Jane Alice. BA cum laude (Durant scholar), Wellesley Coll., 1942; MD cum laude, Tufts U., 1945; ScD (hon.), Holy Cross Coll., 1990. Diplomate Am. Bd. Internal Medicine, Am. Bd. Hematology. Intern in pathology Mt. Auburn Hosp., Cambridge, Mass., 1945—46; intern in medicine Boston City Hosp., 1946—47, resident in medicine, then chief resident, 1948—50; USPHS rsch. fellow in hematology Salt Lake Gen. Hosp., Salt Lake City, 1946—47; rsch. fellow in hematology hosp. Thorndike Lab., 1950—52; physician-in-charge RH lab., 1952—53; faculty Tufts U. Med. Sch., 1952—72, prof. medicine, 1972—92, disting. prof., 1992—94, prof. emerita, 1994—; asst. dir. Tufts Med. Svc., Boston City Hosp., 1952—67; assoc. dir. Tufts Med. Svc., 1967—68, acting dir., physician in charge, 1968—73, dir., 1968—69; ret., 1999. Sr. physician in hematology New Eng. Med. Ctr. Hosp., Boston, 1973—, rsch. assoc. blood resch. lab, 1973—92; attending physician VA Hosp., Jamaica Plain; cons. in hematology to various area hosps., 1955—72. Assoc. editor New Eng. Jour. Medicine, 1960—93, mem. editl. bd. Blood, 1976—79; contbr. numerous articles to med. jours. Bd. dirs. Med. Found., Inc., 1976—82; bd. trustees Boston Med. Libr., 1977—81; chmn. automation in med. lab. scis. rev. com. Nat. Inst. Gen. Med. Scis., 1974—76; chmn. consensus com. of infectious disease testing for blood transfusions NIH, 1995—96; mem. subcom. on hematology Am. Bd. Internal Medicine, 1976—82, bd. dirs., 1980—88, exec. com., 1984—88; chmn. blood diseases and resources adv. com. Nat. Heart, Lung and Blood Inst., 1978—81. Named to Internat. Women in Medicine Hall of Fame, Am. Med. Women's Assn., 2003; recipient Disting. Alumna award, Wellesley Coll., 1981; grantee NIH, 1955—88. Fellow: AAAS; mem.: Inst. Medicine, Am. Assn. Physicians, N.Y. Acad. Scis., Mass. Med. Soc. (mem. publs. com. 1995—99, Lifetime Achievement award 2001), Internat. Soc. Hematology, Am. Soc. Hematology (exec. com. 1975—78, adv. bd. 1980—82, v.p. 1982—83, pres. 1984—85), Am. Soc. Clin. Pathology, Am. Fedn. Clin. Rsch., ACP (chmn. med. knowledge self assessment program IX 1989—92, Master 1983, Disting. Tchr. award 1987), Alpha Omega Alpha (Outstanding Tchr. award 1994), Phi Beta Kappa. Home: 49 Lake Ave Melrose MA 02176-2701

DESHAW, MICHELE, principal; b. Portland, Dec. 28, 1950; d. Clayton Paul DeShaw and Millie Estelle Congdon; m. Timothy Michael Smeekens, June 21, 1999. BA, Oberlin Coll., Ohio, 1972; MAT, Reed Coll., Portland, 1976. Tchr. Portland Pub. Sch., 1976—79, Parkrose Pub. Schs., 1979—98; mgr. edn. tech. program Alaska Dept. Edn. & Early Devel., Juneau, 1998—2002; prin. Nondalton K-12 Sch., 2002—03, Alternative HS, Dillingham, 2003—06; prin. Evergreen Sch. Dist. Legacy HS and Evergreen Internat Acad., Vancouver, 2006—. Cons. curriculum & rsch., improvement planning facilitator DeShaw DeSigns, Alaska, 1984—, Oreg., 1984—, Wash., 1984—; adj. instr. U. Alaska Southeast, Juneau, 1999—2002, Mt. Hood C.C., Portland, 1985—98; bd. dirs. Rural Alliance Teens, Bristol Bay, Alaska; mem. adv. bd. Bristol Bay Area Health Corp., Dillingham, 2003—06; mem. tech. planning com. Dillingham City Sch. Dist., 2004—06, mem. strategic planning com., 2005—06. Mem. exec. bd. Dillingham City Pub. Libr., 2003—06; delivery driver Meals-on-Wheels, Portland, 1985—98; mem. East Portland cmty. plan adv. com. City of Portland, 1996—98. Named History Tchr. Yr., DAR, 1988; recipient Outstanding Tchr. award, U. Chgo., 1989; fellow, NEA, 1986, 1988, Freedoms Found., 1989, 1991, 1997, Oreg. Humanities Coun., 1992, Woodrow Wilson History Inst., 1993, Nat. Archives, 1994; William Robertson Coe fellow, Stanford U., 1984. Mem.: ASCD, Alaska Soc. Tech. Edn. (bd. dirs. 1998—2002), Internat. Soc. Tech. Edn., Nat. Assn. Secondary Sch. Adminstrs., Confedn. Oreg. Sch. Adminstrs., Phi Delta Kappa. Avocations: bicycling, photography, gardening.

DESHAZO, MARJORIE WHITE, occupational therapist; b. Syracuse, N.Y., Apr. 25, 1941; d. Rexford Everett and Joyce Winifred Ella (Brown) Young White; m. Del DeShazo, Dec. 22, 1966; stepchildren: Chad A., Karen A. Lynch. BS in Occupl. Therapy, U. Puget Sound, Tacoma, 1964. Lic. occupl. therapist, 1996. Occupl. therapist VA Med. Ctr., Roseburg, Oreg., 1965-70, Salisbury, N.C., 1970-78; occupl. therapist, co-chief VA Domiciliary, White City, Oreg., 1978-80; chief occupl. therapist VA Med. Ctr., Lexington, Ky., 1980-87; pvt. cons. occupl. therapy Camdenton, Mo., 1987—. Coord. TV21 Art Collections, Springfield, Mo. Inventor (in field); exhibitions include Lexington Art League, 1986—87, Artery Gallery, 1990—2005, Laurie Fine Arts Show, 1993, Ozark Art and Palette, 1996, Lisa Frick Gallery, 1996—98, Lake Chorale, 2005—, Landing Art Expo, 2005, Osage Beach City Hall Mural, Represented in permanent collections First Nat. Bank, Lake Ozark, Mo., Ozark Ford Bldg., private collections. Active Greater Lake Area Arts Coun., Osage Beach, Mo., 1987—. Kappa Kappa Gamma scholar U. Puget Sound. Mem. Ozark Art and Palette Club (treas. 1998-2000), Creative Artists Guild (coord. art hanging 1998—), Mo. Watercolor Soc., Nat. Oil and Acrylic Soc. Democrat. Methodist. Avocations: sewing, art, gardening, gourmet cooking. Home: 3730 Brookfield Ln Osage Beach MO 65065 E-mail: del01@charter.net.

DESHIELDS, ELIZABETH PEGGY BOWEN, artist, educator, poet; b. Ada, Okla., Nov. 11, 1928; d. Simuel Archie and Etta Berthel (Flowers) Bowen; m. Amos Jack DeShields, Sept. 19, 1947; children: Dennis Jack, Sheila Beth. BA in English, East Ctrl. Okla. U., 1947, BS Edn., 1947, EdM in counseling, 1977. Bus. tchr. Bearden HS, Okla., 1947-48; confidential sec., prodn. supt. Phillips Chem. Co., Borger, Tex., 1949-53; English tchr. Borger HS, 1954-55; co-owner, bookkeeper Rainbow Hills Ranch, Cromwell, Okla., 1955—; asst. prin., tchr. Ctrl. Oak Elem. Sch., Oklahoma City, 1955-68; tchr. Will Roger's Sch., Shawnee, 1968-70, Butner Pub. Schs., Cromwell, 1970-74; co-owner, bookkeeper DeShields' Energy, 1970—, Jack DeShields' Bldg. Stone, 1970—; tchr. Castle Pub. Schs., 1976-79; counselor Okemah Pub. Schs., Okemah, 1979-85. Reporter Ada Times Democrat, 1947; news corr. Daily Oklahoman, Oklahoma City Times, 1947; abstracting asst. Pontotoc Co. Abstract Co., Ada, 1946; legal sec. C.F. Green Law Offices, Ada, 1944-46. Contbr. poems to profl. publs.; artist, illustrator for books. Mem. choir, Sunday sch. tchr. First Bapt. Ch., Cromwell, chmn. trustees, 1991; tchr. Cromwell Art Club. Named Ret. Tchr. of Yr., Okemah Alumni Assn., 2002; recipient scholarship, Nat. Sch. Bus., 1944, East Ctrl. U., 1944, Spl. Recognition Appreciation of Svc. award, Crooked Oak PTA, 1967, Yearbook Dedication, 1966, Svc. award, 1967, Leadership Svc. award, Girl Scouts U.S., 1968, Leadership Am. Secondary Edn., 1972, Yearbook award, 1971—73, Golden Eagle award for outstanding contbn. to journalism, 1973, Silver award, Columbia Scholastic Press Assn., numerous art awards, Okmulgee, Seminole and Hughes Counties, Okla., 1979—2004, Butner Yearbook Dedication, Appreciation Plaque, Cromwell Headstart, 1985, FFA, 1985, Plaque, First Bapt. Ch., 1991, Editor's Choice award, Nat. Libr. Poetry, 1996, Recognition award, Famous Poets Soc., 1999—2003. Mem. Okla. Ret. Tchrs., Okfuskee County Ret. Tchrs., Nat. Mus. Women in Arts (charter). Democrat. Avocations: painting, writing, gardening. Home: RR 2 Box 71 Okemah OK 74859-9623

DESIATO, DONNA JEAN, superintendent; b. Bridgeport, Conn., Nov. 28, 1949; d. William Joseph and Elvira Rosemarie (Cerreta) Gilberti; 1 child, Danielle DeSiato Creveling. BEd, U. Miami, 1971; MS in Edn., SUNY Cortland, 1977; cert. advanced study, SUNY Oswego, 1983; EdD, Syracuse U., 2004. Cert. permanent tchr. cert. N.Y., 1976, sch. dist. adminstr. N.Y., 1983. Tchr. Syracuse (N.Y.) City Sch. Dist., 1974—79, instrl. specialist, 1979—83, vice prin., 1983—84, prin., 1984—94, dir. elem. edn., 1993—2000, asst. supt., 2000—. Mem. reading and lit. partnership N.Y. State Edn. Dept., Albany, 1999—; mem. lit. collaborative Success By Six, Syracuse, NY, 1999—; mem. edn. adv. bd. Syracuse Newspapers, 1990—95. Mem. Corinthian Club, Syracuse, 2000—. Recipient Outstanding Educator award, Supervisors and Adminstrs. Assn. N.Y. State, 1999, Adminstrs. Excellence award, Supervisors and Adminstrs. Assn. Syracuse, 1996, 1997, 1998, Leadership Recognition award, Commn. on Women in Leadership, 1995, Disting. Alumni award, Onadaga C.C., 2003. Mem.: N.Y. State Assn. Women in Adminstrn. (chair chpt.), Delta Kappa Gamma (Alpha Omega chpt.), Phi Delta Kappa. Office: E Syracuse Minoa Cent Sch Dist 407 Fremont Rd East Syracuse NY 13057

DE SIENA-RAPPA, KELLY ANN, principal; b. Staten Island, NY, Feb. 2, 1974; d. Robert and Carolyn De Siena; m. Marlen Rappa. BA, Rutgers U., New Brunswick, NJ, 1996; MAT, Coll. NJ, Ewing, 2000; MA, Kean U., Union, NJ, 2003. Cert. prin., supr. NJ, tchr. seconday English NJ. Gen. mgr., sales assoc. Kotliar's Cards, Edison, NJ, 1992—96; assoc. mgr., multi-media specialist Zany Brainy, Edison, NJ, 1996—97; English tchr. Edison Bd. Edn., 1997—2004; asst. prin. Herbert Hoover Mid. Sch., Edison, 2004—. Mem.: ASCD, Nat. Mid. Sch. Assn., NJ Principals and Supervisors Assn., Nat. Assn. Secondary Sch. Prin., Alpha Chi (life). Office: Herbert Hoover Mid Sch 174 Jackson Ave Edison NJ 08837 Office Phone: 732-452-2940. Office Fax: 732-452-2949. Business E-Mail: kelly.rappa@edison.k12.nj.us.

DESIO, DELORES JEAN, writer, artist, retired elementary school educator; b. Detroit, May 20, 1933; d. Thomas Matthew Lannie and Anne Charlotte Zambon; m. Anthony William Desio, June 27, 1959; children: Douglas Anthony, Darcy Desio Rouse. BS in Fine Arts and Art Edn., Wayne State U., Detroit, 1955. Life credential tchg. Calif. Art educator Clawson City Schs., Mich., 1955—56; elem. tchr. Redondo Beach Schs., Calif., 1956—57; tchr. Inglewood Schs., Calif., 1957—59, Palo Alto (Unified Schs., Palo Alto, 1959—63, Cupertino Schs., Los Altos, 1963—65, St. John's Sch., Encinitas, 1979—85; art tchr. St. Patrick's Sch., Carlsbad, 1986—87; owner, writer, illustrator Primo Publs. Trustee Interfaith Shelter Network Homeless, San Diego, 1992—, Nev. Mus. Art, Reno, 2000—06; ret., 2006. Author: Rescue of the Gem Children, 1999, Up a Tree with Mary McPhee, 2006; Distinctly Duck, 2003, periodicals. Prin. Anthony and Delores J. Desio Found., 1998—. Recipient Christian Unity award, Ecumenical Coun. of San Diego, 1995. Office Phone: 760-806-8070. Business E-Mail: adesio2210@aol.com.

DESJARDINS, BETTY LEE, histologist; b. Greensboro, NC, Oct. 2, 1928; d. Robert Lester and Lizzie Lee Gray; m. Richard Fernand Desjardins, June 18, 1949; children: Cheryl Lee Greene, David, Frances Ann Pulsifer, James Robert. BSc, Winthrop U., Rockhill, S.C., 1948. Rsch. asst. Roscoe B. Jackson Meml. Lab, Bar Harbor, Maine, 1948—49; histologist Cancer Rsch. and Cancer Control Lab., New England Med. Ctr., Boston, 1949—51. Pres. Va. Mountain Housing, Blacksburg, 1986—88; dir. March of Dimes, 1958; pres. LWV, Blacksburg, Va., 1982, Va. Mountain Housing, Inc., Blacksburg, 1986—88; leader Girl Scouts, 1957—60. Home: 8117 Blue Heron Dr E Apt 204 Wilmington NC 28411

DESJARDINS, JUDITH ANNE, psychotherapist; b. Colorado Springs, Colo., Dec. 21, 1943; d. Herbert T. and Sally H. King; m. Sherwyn L. Drucker, Sept. 3, 1993; children from previous marriage: André, Danielle Anne. BA with honors, U. Wyo., Laramie, 1965; MSW, Ariz. State U., Tempe, 1972. Diplomate Acad. Managed Care Providers; LCSW Calif. Bd. Behavioral Sci. Examiners, bd. cert. diplomate in clin. social work Am. Bd. Examiners Clin. Social Work, master social work addiction counselor Nat. Bd. Addiction Examiners. Counselor, instr. Phoenix Opportunities Industrialization Ctr., 1972—73; med. social worker Maricopa County Hosp., Phoenix, 1973—75; psychiat. social worker St. Joseph's Hosp., Phoenix, 1975—76; oncology social worker St. John's Hosp., Santa Monica, Calif., 1976—78; pvt. practice Santa Monica, 1978—; clin. supr. Turning Point Shelter, Santa Monica, 1987—91; clin. supr. outpatient substance abuse svcs. Didi Hirsch, Venice, Calif., 1990—98; dir. Addiction Recovery Ctr., Santa Monica, 1998—2000. Owner custom jewelry design bus.; lectr. Mt. St. Mary's Coll., LA, 1979, Loyola Marymount U., LA, 1993—96; instr. St. Martin Tours Sch., LA, 1982—88; presenter in field. Contbr. articles to profl. jours. and online. Vol. therapist Pacific Counseling Ctr. AIDS/HIV, L.A., 1991—2004; mem. disaster mental health team Am. Red Cross, Santa Monica, 1999—. Fellow: NASW; mem.: AFTRA, Screen Actors Guild. Avocations: rollerblading, Native Am. art, Australian Shepherds. E-mail: despsych@verizon.net.

DESJARLAIS, GEORGIA KATHRINE, retired military officer; b. Chattanooga, Tenn., Oct. 31, 1958; d. Lowell and Lucy Caroline (Brown) Lawson; m. Daniel Eugene Desjarlais, Apr. 22, 1978 (div. May 1985). AA, Hawaii Pacific Coll., 1980, BS, 1982; MPA, Auburn U., Montgomery, 1999; student, Air U., 1999, Air Command and Staff Coll., 1998—99. Enlisted as E-1 USN, 1976, commd. as ensign, 1983, advanced through ranks to lt. comdr., 1995, ret., 2000; supply officer, food svc. officer NSGA Adak, Alaska, 1984—86; disbursing and stores officer USS Dixon (AS 37), San Diego, 1986—88; material officer COMNAVSUPPFORANTARCTICA, Oxnard, Calif., 1988—91; stock control and AOIC USNS Sirius (TAFS 8), Norfolk, Va., 1991—94; load mgr. COMNAVSURFLANT, Norfolk, 1994—96; asst. supply officer USS Emory S. Land (AS 39), Norfolk, 1996—98; logistics supr. Corning Inc., Oneonta, NY, 1999—2002. Ind. rep. Avon, 2003—. Ensign supply corps USN, 1983. Mem.: AAUW (membership chmn. Memphis br. 2002, pres. Memphis chpt. 2002—, treas Tenn. State divsn. 2003—), Aleutian Vet. Assn., Navy Mustang Assn., Mil. Officers Assn. Am. (mentor 1999—, Memphis chpt. 1st v.p. 2004, Memphis chpt. pres. 2005—), The Women's Meml. (charter mem.). Methodist. Avocations: reading, history, wildlife.

DESLAURIERS, SUZANNE DAWSEY, secondary school educator, artist; b. Wilmington, NC, Sept. 13, 1950; d. Cyrus Bassett and Marshlea (Cottingham) Dawsey; m. Cecil Hörger Knight, Dec. 28, 1972 (dec. Nov. 25, 1995); 1 child, Jesse Hörger Knight; m. E. Joseph Deslauriers, Dec. 16, 1996. BA in Fine Arts, Fla. So. Coll., Lakeland, 1972; MA in Art Edn., U. SC, Columbia, 1985. Nat. bd. cert. tchr. Child care program dir. Appalachia State Wesley Found., Boone, NC, 1977—78; supr. aftercare sch. program Hardin Park Elem., Boone, 1977—78; art tchr., asst. soccer coach Holly Hill-Roberts High Sch., Holly Hill, SC, 1979—88; art tchr., social studies tchr. Hiwassee Dam Sch., Murphy, NC, 1988—2006, A+ Schs. coord., 1994—; tchr. humanities Tri County Early Coll., Murphy, NC, 2006—. Presenter, cons. on integrated instrn. Cherokee County Schs., Murphy, 1994—; mentor for nat. bd. tchr. cert. NEA, Western, NC, 2000—; adj. prof. West Carolina U., Cullowhee, NC, 2002; painting and drawing tchr. John C. Campbell Folk Sch., Brasstown, NC, 1995—. Named Creative Tchr. of the Yr., Western N.C., 1996. Mem.: N.C. Art Educator Assn. (Secondary Art Educator of the Yr. 1999—2000). Home: 24 Lady Slipper Ln Brasstown NC 28902-8073 Office: Tri County Early Coll Murphy NC 28906 E-mail: artedasuzy@verizon.net.

DE SMET, LORRAINE MAY, artist; b. Passaic, N.J., May 5, 1928; d. Peter John and Mary (Lovas) Prevelige; m. Louis John de Smet, May 17, 1952; children: Mary Lizabeth, Jean Marie, Carolyn, Allise Marie. Student, Berkeley Sch., 1945, Art Students League, 1979-82. One woman show Pen and Brush Club, 1984 (Solo Show award). Bd. dirs. Art Ctr. of N.J., 1993—. Recipient 1st prize, Livingston Art Assn., NJ, 1987, 1988, Best in Show award, 2004, Am. Artist award, Ridgewood Art Inst., 1998, Caldwell Progress award, 1998, 2003, 2006, LAA merit award, 1998, 1999, 2001, 2002, 2003, 2004, WEAA award, Caldwell Coll., 1999, merit award, 2000, 3d Pl. award, 2004, 1st pl. award, 2005, Best of the Best exhbn., Trenton Mus., 2001, numerous other awards. Mem. U.S. Coast Guard Artists, Am. Artists Profl. League (Ann Waldron N.J. award 1998, N.J. Disting. Merit award 2002), Ringwood Manor Art Assn. (award 2000), Pen and Brush Club of N.Y. (bd. dirs. 1985-92, v.p. 1989-92, dir. brush divsn. 1987-89, mem. dir. 1990-92, co-chair brush sect. 1994-95, 97), Art Ctr. of N.J. (bd. dirs., sec., membership chair, 1st pl. 2005, Merit award, 2006), West Essex Art Assn. (bd. dirs. 1992-98), Art Students League of N.Y. (life), Millburn-Short Hills Art Assn.(award of excellence 2001, 2002, Louise Melrose Gallery award 2002, Merit award 2004, 05). Home: 33 Campbell Rd Fairfield NJ 07004-1735

DESMOND, BEVIN, investment research company executive; B in Psych., St. Mary's Coll. With Morningstar, Inc., 1993—, mgr. internat. ventures, 1998—2000, pres. internat. bus., 2001—. Named one of Top 40 Under 40, Crain's Chgo. Bus., 2006. Office: Morningstar Inc 225 W Wacker Dr Chicago IL 60606*

DESMOND-HELLMANN, SUSAN, medical products manufacturing executive; b. 1958; BS in Pre-Medicine, U. Nev., MD; M in Epidemiology and Biostats., U. Calif. Sch. Pub. Health, Berkeley. Bd. cert. internal medicine and med. oncology. Trainee U. Calif., San Francisco; assoc. dir. clin. cancer rsch., project team leader Taxol Bristol-Myers Squibb Pharm. Rsch. Inst.; clin. scientist Genentech, Inc., South San Francisco, 1995-96, sr. dir. clin. sci., 1996, v.p. med. affairs, 1996, chief med. officer, 1996—97, v.p. devel., 1997, sr. v.p. devel., 1997, exec. v.p. devel. and product ops., 1999, pres., product devel., 2004—. Vis. faculty Uganda Cancer Inst.; asst. prof. hematology-oncology U. Calif. San Francisco, adj. assoc. prof. epidemiology and biostats; adv. com. regulatory reform, HHS, 2002; bd. dirs. Biotechnology Industry Orgn., 2001-, Am. Assn. Cancer Rsch., 2005-. Named Woman of Yr., Healthcare Businesswomen's Assn., 2006; named one of 50 Most Powerful Women in Bus., Fortune mag., 2001, 2003, 2004, 2006, 100 Most Powerful Women in World, Forbes Mag., 2005, Top 50 Women to Watch, Wall St. Jour., 2004, 2005, Leading Women and Minority Scientists, NY Acad. Sciences, 2005. Office: Genentech Inc One DNA Way South San Francisco CA 94080-4990 Office Fax: 650-225-6000.*

DESNOYERS, MEGAN FLOYD, archivist, educator; b. NYC, Oct. 31, 1945; d. Lawrence Clifford and Frances Irene Floyd; m. David George Desnoyers, Sept. 2, 1967; 1 child, Adam O'Neil. AB, Vassar Coll., 1967; MLS, Rutgers U., 1968. Cert. archivist. Libr. John Jay H.S., Wappingers Falls, NY, 1968-69; archivist Franklin D. Roosevelt Libr., Hyde Park, NY, 1969, John F. Kennedy Libr., Boston, 1970—, curator Ernest Hemingway Collection, 1987—96, 2000—01; instr. in archives adminstrn. Nat. Archives Modern Archives Inst., Washington, 1982-2000. Lectr. archives adminstrn. U. Mass., Boston, 1978-80; lectr. on Hemingway, 1992—2000; mem. Archives Adv. Commn., Boston, 1977-2000; archival advisor Girl Scouts U.S., N.Y.C., 1991—. Contbr. chpt. to book, articles to profl. jours. Mem. adv. bd., chmn. com. Voluntary Action Ctr., Mass. Bay United Way, Boston, 1974-80; mem., chair bd. trustees Randall Libr., Stow, Mass., 1976-80; mem. Mass. Hist. Records Adv. Bd., 1979-2000. Nat. Def. fellow, 1967-68. Fellow Soc. Am. Archivists; mem. New Eng. Archivists (sec. 1976-78), Soc. Am. Archivists (workshop instr. 1978-2000), Acad. Cert. Archivists (task force on recert. 1991-92), Beta Phi Mu. Democrat. Roman Catholic. Office: John F Kennedy Libr Columbia Point Boston MA 02125

DESOER, BARBARA J., bank executive; BA in Math., Mt. Holyoke Coll.; MBA, U. Calif., Berkeley. Various positions to mng. strategy devel. and implementation, consumer banking unit Bank Am. Corp., 1977—96, exec. v.p. Calif. retail banking grp., 1996—98, pres. No. Calif. banking, 1998, mktg. exec., 1999—2001, pres. consumer products, 2001—04, global tech., svc. and fulfillment exec., 2004—. Chmn. internat. diversity adv. coun. Bank Am. Corpn.; mem. adv. coun. Haas Sch. Bus. U. Calif., Berkeley; mem. bus. adv. coun. U. NC Belk Coll. Bus. Adminstrn., Charlotte. Bd. dirs. Providence Day Sch., Charlotte, NC Dance Theatre, Presbyn. Hosp. Found., United Way Ctrl. Carolinas. Office: Bank Am Corpn 100 N Tryon St Charlotte NC 28255*

DE SOTO, LISA, lawyer; Gen. counsel Social Security Adminstrn. Office: Social Security Adminstrn Altmeyer Bldg Rm 617 6401 Security Blvd Baltimore MD 21235-0001 Office Phone: 410-965-0600. Office Fax: 410-966-3146. Business E-Mail: lisa.desoto@ssa.gov.

DESPANZA-SPRENGER, LYNETTE CHARLIE, small business owner; b. New Orleans, June 7, 1948; d. Sylvester Issac and Yverdelle Ida Despanza; m. Charles Ricard II, May 1970 (div. May 18, 1978); m. Paul Henri Sprenger, Oct. 28 (div. June 2002); 1 child, Charles Ricard III. BSN, U. Hawaii, 1995; ASN, St. Pete Jr. Coll., 1988; student, Delgado Jr. Coll., 1972. Cert. respiratory therapist La.; RN La. Sedation rm. dir. King Khalid Eye Specialist Hosp., Riyadh, Saudi Arabia, edn. clin. instr. and stress mgmt. instr., 1989—98; ballroom dance and exercise instr. Inst. Royal Family and We. and European Families in Saudi Arabia, Saudi Arabia, 1990—98; clinic adminstr., dir. Columbia Gia Diah Internat., Vietnam; respiratory therapist Bay Front Hosp., St. Petersburg, Fla.; emergency nurse, ICU nurse Maxim Healthcare Agy. and Agy. Personnel, St. Petersburg, Fla., 1999—2000; owner, chef, operator Lagniappe Bistrot, St. Petersburg; co-operator Swiss Creole Connection, 2002—. Art restorer Leppa Rathner Mus., St. Petersburg. Vol. St. Petersburg Jr. Coll. N.O.L.A., Fla. Recipient pastels and oil painting award, Art Soc. of St. Petersburg, U. New Orleans. Roman Catholic. Avocations: jazz, tap, ballroom dancing, painting, fencing. Home: 732 17th Ave N Saint Petersburg FL 33704 E-mail: despanzalynette@hotmail.com.

DESPOT, SHIRLEY ANN, artist; b. Des Moines, Feb. 25, 1932; d. James David and Bertha Luellen (Eaton) Haines; m. John Despot, Nov. 5, 1950; children: Debra, John, Joann, Tom. BAE, John Herron Art Sch., Indpls., 1963; MS, Butler U., 1983; student, Arrowmont Sch. Arts and Crafts, Gatlinburg, Tenn., U. Indpls. Tchr. art Perry Twp. Schs., Indpls., Center Grove Schs., Greenwood, Ind., Indpls. Art League, 1991-91. Exhibited Mid-States, Evansville, Ind., Ind. State Fair, Wabash Valley, Terre Haute, Ind., Ind. Artists Club, Indpls., Tippecanoe Regional, Lafayette, Ind., Whitewater-Valley, Connersville, Ind., 500 Festival, Indpls., Indpls. Mus. Rental Gallery, Hoosier Salon, 1992, Cen. South Regional, Nashville, 1992. Mem. Watercolor Soc. Ind., Ind. Artists Club (pres. 1965), Ind. Artists and Craftsmen, Indpls. Art League, CCA Gallery, Hoosier Salon.

DESPRES, LOUISE FAY, secondary school educator; b. New Haven, Conn., Feb. 29, 1944; d. Frederick Taylor and Ruth Jean (Lowery) Fay; m. Robert Leon Despres, Feb. 16, 1974; 1 child, Frederick Leon. Studied organ with Nadia Boulanger Fontainebleau, Am. Sch. Music, France, 1965; BA, Conn. Coll., 1966; MAT, Brown U., 1968; MA, Middlebury Coll., France, 1973. Cert. secondary sch. tchr. Conn. French tchr. N. Haven HS, Conn., 1967—69, High Plains Sch., Orange, Conn., 1969—70, New Canaan HS, Conn., 1970—, Spanish tchr., 1979—, advanced placement tchr., 1980—, chair world langs., 2001—06, advisor to Internat. Club, 1986—87, ind. study advisor, 1990—2003, mentor tchr., 1991—93, 2005—, chair ind. study, 1996—2001, mem. ind. study com., 1992—94; coop. tchr. U. Conn., 1985—90. Hs tchr. liaison Am. Field Svc., New Canaan, Conn., 1979—81; sch. liaison Sch. Yr. Abroad, New Canaan, 1983—85; summer sch. tchr. Saxe Mid. Sch., 1984, New Canaan HS, 1986; rev. curriculum com. New Canaan Schs., 1989—91, chair rev. curriculum com., 1999—2001; tchr. assessor State of Conn., 1989—91; cons. in field. Vol. devel. tchr., New Haven, 1968; vol. Recs. for the Blind, New Haven, 1969; participant Conn. Inst. Tchg. and Learning, 1988—90. Recipient Advanced Placement Tchr. Recognition award, New Eng. Coll. Bd., 1994, Pegasus Pride award, Conn. Orgn. Langs., 2001; fellow, NEH, 1983; grantee, North Haven Bd. Edn., Conn., 1968, New Canaan Bd. Edn., 1985, Bd. of A Better Chance, New Canaan, Conn., 2001—06; Higher Edn. Act fellow, 1966—67, French govt. fellow, 1972—73. Mem.: Philanthropic Ednl. Organ., Conn. Orgn. Lang. Tchrs., Am. Assn. Tchrs. French (adminstr. Conn. Nat. French Contest 1980—81). Congregationalist. Avocations: music, theater, reading, travel. Home: 3 Peters Ln Westport CT 06880-3937 Office: New Canaan High Sch 11 Farm Rd New Canaan CT 06840-6608 Office Phone: 203-594-4703. Personal E-mail: duds95@sbcglobal.net. Business E-Mail: louise.despres@newcanaan.k12.ct.us.

DESROCHES, DANIELLE, biology professor, researcher; b. Cap-Haitien, Haiti, Dec. 31; m. Archie Arrington. PhD, CUNY, 1981. Prof. William Paterson U., Wayne, NJ, 1981—. Dir. Support Sys. for Minority Students in Scis., Wayne, 1981—2006. Mem.: Minority Assn. Premed. Students (bd. dirs. 2004—). Achievements include research in in utero effects of alcohol in mice; sex and strain related differences in first pass alcohol metabolism; calcium metabolism and bone. Home: 300 Pompton Road Wayne NJ 07470 Office: William Paterson U 300 Pompton Road Wayne NJ 07470 Home Fax: 973-720-2338. Personal E-mail: desrochesd@wpunj.edu.

DESROSIERS, MURIEL C., music educator, retired nursing consultant; b. Woonsocket, R.I., Jan. 15, 1934; d. Rodolphe J. Desrosiers and Rhea M. Archambault; m. Albert A. Desrosiers; 6 stepchildren. BSN, Boston Coll., 1965; MSN, Boston U., 1967, cert. advanced grad. studies, 1975, EdD, 1977. Instr. St. Anselm's Coll. Sch. Nursing, Manchester, NH, 1968—74; cons. drug abuse prevention N.H. State Dept. Edn., Concord, 1974—75, sch. health cons., 1976—89; instr. piano performance, theory and technique. In-svc. educator N.H. Hosps., 1968—75; instr. leadership workshops, 1969—75; grant writer Sch. Nurse Achievement Program. Vol. Home for Little Wanderers; chair Am. Sch. Health Assn., 1984—87; pres. Nat. Assn. Sch. Health Consultants, 1984—87. Recipient Disting. Svc. award, Am. Sch. Health Assn., 1987, Sch. Nurse Achievement award, 1988. Mem.: N.H. Nurses Assn. (pres. 1976—78), Maine Nurses Assn., Maine Music Tchrs. Assn. (chair program 1990—95), Nat. Assn. Music Tchrs. (emeritus). Avocation: writing. Home: 89 Roderick Rd Winslow ME 04901

DESSASO, DEBORAH ANN, freelance/self-employed writer, corporate communications specialist; b. Washington, Feb. 6, 1952; d. Coleman and Virginia Beatrice (Taylor) Dessaso. AS in Bus. Adminstrn., Southeastern U., 1986, BSBA, 1988; MA in English Composition and Rhetoric, U. DC, 1997. Clk.-stenographer FTC, Washington, 1969—70; sec. NEA, Washington, 1970—72, AARP, Washington, 1972—79, assoc. adminstrv. specialist, 1979—80, adminstrv. specialist, 1979—89, legis. comm. specialist, 1989—2000, mgr. issue response, 2000—01; cons., 2000—. Founding mem., sec. Andrus Fed. Credit Union, 1980; adj. prof. English U. DC, 2002—03, dir. Writing Ctr., 2003—. Mem.: Associated Writing Program. Mem. Faith Outreach Cmty. Ch. Home: 3042 Stanton Rd SE Washington DC 20020-7883 Office Phone: 202-274-5938. Personal E-mail: dessaso749@verizon.net.

DESSEREAU, APRIL, art educator; b. Port Chester, NY, Mar. 4, 1952; d. Francis Gregory and Ruth Helen (Sundberg) Dessereau. BA, SUNY, Oswego, 1975; MS in Art Edn., U. Bridgeport, 1978; MA in Humanities, Manhattanville Coll., 1992. Cert. art tchr. N.Y. Adult edn. instr. art Port Chester (N.Y.) Bd. Edn., 1979-83, art/photography tchr., 1982—. Freelance calligrapher, 1978—92. Mem.: NEA, Westchester Coun. of the Arts, Am. Fedn. Tchrs., N.Y. State Art Tchrs. Assn., Nat. Art Edn. Assn. Avocations: photography, quilting, gardening, drawing, painting. Office: Port Chester HS Tamarack Rd Port Chester NY 10573

DESSERT, KATHRYN ISOBEL, elementary school educator; b. Cornwall, Ontario, Canada, Feb. 6, 1959; d. Allan Borden and Patricia Anne Lougheed; m. Steven Edward Dessert, July 30, 1988; children: William Allan, Andre Steven, Meralyse Renee. BS, U. Tenn.-Chattanooga, 1982. Tchr. St. Vincent de Paul Elem., Mount Vernon, Ohio, 1991—96, Twin Oak Elem., Mount Vernon, 1996—. Lang. arts & math. curriculum writer Mt. Vernon City Schs., 2001—05. Pres. CHADD, Mount Vernon, 1993—98. Recipient Disting. Svc. award, Mt. Vernon City Schs. Mem.: Mt. Vernon Edn. Assn. (assoc.; sch. rep. 2003—), Delta Kappa Gamma. Avocations: snow-skiing, camping, reading, water-skiing, bicycling. Home: 133 Lakeview Heights Dr Howard OH 43028 Office: Twin Oak Elem Sch 8888 Martinsburg Rd Mount Vernon OH 43050 Office Phone: 740-393-5970 ext. 6510. Business E-Mail: kdessert@mt-vernon.k12.oh.us.

DESSYLAS, ANN ATSAVES, human resources and office management executive; b. Bklyn., Jan. 28, 1927; d. Charles and Agnes (Cocoros) Atsaves; m. George Dessylas, Dec. 28, 1969. BA, Bklyn. Coll., 1957; MA, NYU, 1961, MBA, 1977. Exec. asst. W.R. Grace & Co., N.Y.C., 1950-70; asst. sec. St. Joe Minerals Corp., N.Y.C., 1970-81, asst. v.p., 1981-85; cons. Cyprus Minerals, Denver, 1985-91; pres. AAD Enterprises, Forest Hills, NY, 1992—2004. Dir. Continental Owners Corp.; sec. Plato Malozemoff Found. Avocations: music, theater, golf, art, tennis. Home and Office: 70-20 108th St Ste 8-p Forest Hills NY 11375-4449

D'ESTE, MARY ERNESTINE, investment group executive; b. Chgo., Apr. 1, 1941; d. Ernest Gregory and Mary (Turcich) D'E. Student, Mundelein Coll., 1958-61. Sec. MMM, Bedford Park, Ill., 1961-69, Michael Reese Med. Ctr., Chgo., 1969-73; adminstrv. asst. Thomas Jefferson U., Phila., 1973-85, divisional adminstr., 1985-86; adminstr. dept. cardiothoracic surgery Hahnemann U., Phila., 1986-94, Med. Coll. Pa.-Hahnemann U. Hosps., Phila., 1994-96; exec. adminstr., bus. mgr. dept. cardiothoracic surgery Allegheny U. Hosps., 1997-98; v.p. CTS Cardiac & Thoracic Surgeons PC, Phila., 1986-98; adminstrv. coord. Scharf Investment Group, Phila., 1998—. V.p. archtl. review com. GTV Homeowners Assn., Marlton, N.J., 1979-85. Mem. King Charles Spaniel Club (bd. dirs. Delaware Valley chpt. 2004—, show chair 2004—). Roman Catholic. Avocations: gardening, cooking, reading, show dogs.

DESTREMPES, SANDRA LEE, elementary school educator; b. Whitinsville, Mass., May 18, 1960; d. Albert O. Destrempes and Margaret Vincent; children: Kathy Stevens, Sandra, Charles, Ann Smith Ganey, Al Jr. BS in Sociology, Social Work and Recreation, Calvin Coll., Grand Rapids, Mich., 1985; MS in Reading, Calvin Coll., 1995. Cert. tchr. Mich. Tchr. Haili Christian Sch., Hilo, Hawaii, 1991—94; reading tchr. Pine Trails Elem. Sch., Allegan, Mich., 1995—96; kindergarten enrichment tchr. Forest Hills Pub. Schs., Grand Rapids, 1996—97; reading tchr. 1st grade Byron Ctr. Christian Sch., Byron Center, Mich., 1997—98; reading tchr. Grand Rapids Pub. Schs., 1998—99; 2d grade tchr. Gallup McKinley Sch. Dist., Gallup, N.Mex., 2000—01; literacy tchr. Lansing Sch. Dist., Mich., 2001—. Sponsor Rehoboth Christian Sch. Scholarship Program, Gallup, 2001—. Mem.: Mich. Reading Assn., Reading Assn., Reading Recovery Orgn. Christian Ref. Ch. Avocations: birds, running, swimming, backgammon, bicycling. Home: 7829 Trestlewood Dr Apt 1A Lansing MI 48917 Office Phone: 517-325-6796. Personal E-mail: leedestr@msn.com.

DESTRO, (HELEN) JANE, artist, medical illustrator; b. Dayton, Ohio, Oct. 11, 1927; d. Earl Hobart and Cynthia Eldora Allen; m. Vincent Paul Destro (dec.); children: Lucy Schmidt, Maryanna, Molly Destro-Borgen. Student, Stephens Coll., Columbia, Mo., 1945—47, U. Ill., Chgo., 1949—50, LeCole de Beaux Arts, Paris, 1948, Slade Sch., London, 1948. Portraitist, Rochester, Minn., 1945—; freelance med. illustrator Chgo., 1949—51; med. illustrator Mayo Clinic, Rochester, 1951—53. Mem.: Women in Arts, Portrait Soc. Am., Am. Watercolor Soc. Home: 1122 10th St SW Rochester MN 55902

DESUTTER, PAULA A., federal agency administrator; BA, U. Nev., Las Vegas, MA in Econs.; MS in Nat. Security Strategy, Nat. War Coll.; MA in Internat. Rels., U. So. Calif. Profl. staff mem. US Senate Select Com. on Intelligence; staff liaison to Senator Jon Kyl US Sentate; fgn. affairs specialist Bur. of Verification, Compliance, and Implementation, US Dept. State, Washington, spl. asst., asst. sec., 2002—. Sr. vis. rsch. fellow Ctr. for Counter-Proliferation Rsch. Recipient Presidentís Strategic Vision Award for Excellence in Rsch. and Writing. Office: US Dept State 2201 C St NW Washington DC 20520

DETERT, MIRIAM ANNE, chemical analyst; b. San Diego, Sept. 16, 1925; d. George Bernard and Margaret Theresa Zita (Lohre) D. BS, Dominican Coll., San Rafael, Calif., 1947. Chem. analyst Shell Devel. Co., Emeryville, Calif., 1947-72, Houston, 1972-86. Photo participant Wax Rsch.: Quest, 1981; exhibited etchings Sight and Insight Art Studio, Mill Valley, Calif., 2002; contbr. poetry to books including The International Library of Poetry - Best Poems of the 90's, Spirit of the Age, The Nightfall of Diamonds, The Long and Winding Road, Through Oceans of Time. Vol. Falkirk Cultural Ctr., San Rafael, 1987-91, M.D. Anderson Tumor Inst., Houston, 1978-86, Rep. Party, San Rafael, 1990, 94; mem. Jewish Comm. Ctr. Recipient Disting. Alumni award Dominican Coll., 1994. Mem. Marin Geneal. Soc. Republican. Roman Catholic. Avocations: etching, painting, genealogy, swimming. E-mail: mdetert@ix.netcom.com.

DETERT-MORIARTY, JUDITH ANNE, graphic designer, educator, volunteer; b. Portage, Wis., July 10, 1952; d. Duane Harlan and Anne Jane (Devine) Detert; m. Patrick Edward Moriarty, July 22, 1978; children: Colin Edward Moriarty, Eleanor Grace Moriarty, Dylan Joseph Moriarty. BA, U. Wis., Madison, 1973, U. Wis., Green Bay, 1991. Cert. in no-fault grievance mediation Minn. Legis. sec., messenger State of Wis. Assembly, Madison, 1972, 74-76; casualty-property divsn. clk. Capitol Indemnity Corp., Madison, 1977-78; word processor consumer protection divsn. Wis. Dept. Agr., Madison, 1978; graphic arts composing specialist Moraine Park Tech. Inst., Fond du Lac, Wis., 1978-79; freelance artist Picas, Pictures and Promotion (formerly Detert Graphics), 1978-90; prodn. asst. West Bend News, 1980-83; devel. asoc. Riveredge Nature Ctr., Inc., Newburg, Wis., 1983-84; exec. dir. Voluntary Action Ctr. Washington County, West Bend, 1984-86; instr. cmty. svcs. Austin (Minn.) CC, 1988; art and promotional publs. dir. Michael G. and Co., Albert Lea, Minn., 1988-89; corp. art dir. Newco, Inc., Janesville, Wis., 1989-91; owner, artist Art Graphica, 1991-00; knitting instr. Hancock's Fabrics, 2004—05, Blackhawk Tech. Coll., 2004—. Cartooning instr., contbg. artist Janesville Sch. Dist., 1989—93, substitute tchr., 1998—2001. Contbr. articles to profl. jours. Newsletter editor, artist Friends of Battered Women, West Bend, 1983—86; rep. Planned Parenthood of Wis. Bd., 1984—85; fundraiser Victims Crisis Ctr., 1987; cmty. contact, v.p. Caths. Free Choice Wis., 1990—92; newsletter editor Roosevelt Elem. Sch. PTA, 1996—2002, sec., 1999—2001; vol. newsletter editor Badger Coun. Girls Scouts, Inc., 1996—98; founder United Arts Alliance, 1996, pres., 1997—98, 2004—06, sec., 1998—2001; editor ArtRock, 2000—; founder, bd. mem., sec. Bower City Preservation Assn., 1999—; chpt. coord. Janesville/Rock Valley Project Linus, 2000—; founder, instr. after-school knitting clubs Roosevelt and Jefferson Elem. Schs. and Boys and Girls Club, Janesville, 2001—04; organizer Lysistrata Project, Janesville, 2003; vol. Austin Pub. Sch. Omnibus Program, 1987—88; newsletter editor Montessori Childrens House-West Bend, Wis., 1983—85; founder, pres. Parents' Assn. Montessori Childrens House-Janesville, Wis., 1994—97, newsletter editor Wis., 1994—97; founder and coord. Janesville area chpt. "Stitch N' Bitch", 2004—; founder NexusKnit, 2005—; artist LWV Washington County, 1984—86; apptd. Austin (Minn.) Human Rights Commn., 1987—88, Janesville Hist. Commn., 1993—95, sec., 1992—95; student vol. McCarthy for Pres., U. Wis., Madison, 1968; coord. student residences McGovern for Pres., 1972; vol. Udall for Pres., 1976; Washington County Campaign coord. Nat. Unity Campaign for John Anderson for Pres., 1980; publicity coord. Wis. Intellectual Freedom Coalition, 1981; pres., founder People of Washington County United for Choice, 1981—83; bd. dirs., v.p. Wis. Pro-Choice Conf., 1981—82; Washington County ward coord. Earl for Gov., 1982, Mondale/Ferraro, 1984; Washington County campaign chmn. Peg Lautenschlager for Wis. State Senate, 1984; sec., newsletter editor Manitowoc County Dems., Wis., 1986; precinct ofcl., affirmative action officer Mower County Dems., Minn., 1986—88; local chair Women's Polit. Caucus, 1997—98; v.p. commn. officer, newsletter editor Rock County Dems., Wis., 1988—; vol. coord. Rock County Dukakis for Pres., 1988; campaign chair Lew Mittness for Wis. State Assembly, 1990; newsletter editor Rock County Voice for Choice, 1990—94; founding exec. bd. dirs., newsletter editor Moral Alternatives, 1990—92; vol. Rock County Clinton for Pres., 1992, 1996; 1st C.D. 4th vice chair Wis. Dems., 1999—2001; mem. campaign coordinating com. Vote Graf, 2000; Rock County coord. Ralph Nader for Pres., 2000; mem. steering com., bd. mem. Rock County Citizens for Peace, 2001—; Rock County campaign coord. John Kerry for Pres., 2004; vol. bd. dir. and chmn. advt. com. Janesville Concert Assn., 1994—97; bd. dir. Montessori Childrens House-West Bend, Wis., 1983—85; newsletter editor, mem. coms., bd. mem. Planned Parenthood of Washington County, 1980—85, pres., 1984—85. Recipient award of Excellence, Bd. Report Graphic Artists, 1994. Mem.: NOW (newsletter editor Dane County 1977—78, coord. reproductive rights task force North Suburban chpt. 1981—84, coord. Wis. state reproductive rights task force 1982—84, Minn. pub. rels. coord. 1987—88, Wis. state 1994—99), Green-Rock Audubon Soc. (bd. dirs., newsletter editor 2003—04), Forward Janesville (mem. steering com. Celebrate Janesville 1992—94). Mem. Soc. Of Friends. Avocations: reading, bicycling, gardening, knitting, world wide correspondence. Office: 23 S Atwood Ave Janesville WI 53545-4003 Personal E-mail: proartist@aol.com.

DETHRAGE, DEBBIE J, educational consultant; d. Bill Gene and Evelyn Mae Cobb; m. Robert C Dethrage, Feb. 14, 1993; m. Francisco Javier Marticorena, June 6, 1983 (div.); m. Ben E Quintana, Feb. 18, 1973 (div.); children: Francisco Javier Marticorena Jr., April L Quintana, Amy L Quintana. AA, Merced C.C., 1985—87; BA in edn., Stanislaus State U. of Calif., 1987—89; M of edn. adminstrn., Tex. A&M U., 1998—2000. Mid-Management Cert. Tex. A&M U., 2000, Supervision in Curriculum Certification Tex. A&M U., 2000, Teaching Certification Chapman U. of Calif., 1990. Bookkeeper Custom Cleaning & Janitorial Svc., Los Banos, Calif., 1983—89; tchr. Los Banos I.S.D., 1989—92, Wylie I.S.D., Wylie, Tex., 1992—99; edn. cons. Region 10 Edn. Svc. Ctr., Tex., 1999—. Adv. bd. mem. Wylie H.S., 2002—03; edn. cons. Region 10 Edn. Svc. Ctr., Richardson, Tex., 1999—. Author: (math curriculum books) Mathematics Curriculum Alignment Project, (technology math curriculum) TEKStar Math Curriculum. Organizer for food drive for the needy Wylie Intermediate Sch., 1996—97; visit ill members Bapt. Ch., Rockwall, Tex., 1992—2005. Recipient Presdl. award for Excellence in Math. and Sci., Tex. Edn. Agy., 2004, Dynamic Classroom Assessment Facilitator, ETA Cuisenaire, 2004, Cert. of Leadership Devel., Tex. Assn. of Supervisors of Math., 2004. Mem.: Tex. Coun. of Math. Teachers (assoc.), Tex. Assn. for Secondary Math. (assoc.), Nat. Coun. of Teachers of Math. (assoc.). R-Liberal. Bapt. Avocations: travel, gardening, hiking. Home: 6205 Creekhaven Court Sachse TX 75048 Office: Region 10 Edn Svc Ctr 400 E Spring Valley Rd Richardson TX 75081 Office Phone: 972-348-1368. Home Fax: 972-348-1369; Office Fax: 972-348-1369. E-mail: debbie.dethrage@region10.org.

DETMAR-PINES, GINA LOUISE, business strategy and policy educator; b. SI, NY, May 3, 1949; d. Joseph and Grace Vivian (Brown) Sargente; m. Michael B. Pines, Sept. 11, 1988; 1 child, Drue Joseph Pines. BS in Edn., Wagner Coll., 1971, MS, 1972; MA in Urban Affairs and Policy Analysis, New Sch. for Social Rsch., 1987; MPhil, CUNY, 1995; PhD in Bus./Orgn. and Policy Studies, CUNY-Baruch Coll., 1997. Cert. adminstr. and supr., sch. dist. adminstr. Tchr. pub. schs., N.Y.C., 1971-82; coord. spl. projects, pub. affairs N.Y.C. Bd. Edn., 1982, spl. asst. to exec. dir. pupil svcs., 1983, asst. to chancellor, 1983-84, exec. dir. tchr. Summer Bus. Industry Program, 1984-93; prof. pub. adminstrn. and mgmt. John Jay Coll. Criminal Justice CUNY, 1992-93; prof. bus. Ctrl. Conn. State U., 2000—04; assoc. prof. bus. strategy and policy U. Hartford, West Hartford, Conn., 2004—. Vis. prof. Rensselaer at Hartford, 1993—98, Fairfield U., 1998—2000; liaison for the Tech. Industry Program N.Y.C. Partnership, 1985—93; mem. editl. adv. bd. Internat. Jour. Bus. Rsch. Mem. com. to re-elect Borough pres. Lamberti, S.I., 1985-86; chairperson Crystal Ball event Greater Hartford Easter Seals Rehab. Ctr., 1994, trustee, 1994—; bd. dirs. Hartford Symphony, com. mem. 50th Anniversary Gala, 1993. Mayor's scholar, City of N.Y., 1984—96. Mem. ASPA, Fgn. Lang. Instrs. Assn., Strategic Mgmt. Soc., Acad. Mgmt., U.S. Seaplane Pilot's Assn., Internat. Orgn. for Lic. Women Pilots, Jr. League of Hartford, Hartford Task Force on Healthy Families, Chinese-Am. Soc., Am. Mgmt. Soc., Ea. Acad. Mgmt., Acad. of Internat. Bus., Cambridge Flying Group Club. Episcopalian. Avocations: flying, scuba diving, skiing. Office: Univ Hartford 200 Bloomfield Ave West Hartford CT 06117 Business E-Mail: gipines@hartford.edu.

DE TORNYAY, RHEBA, nursing educator, retired dean; b. Petaluma, Calif., Apr. 17, 1926; d. Bernard and Ella Fradkin; m. Rudy de Tornyay, June 4, 1954. Student, U. Calif., Berkeley, 1944-46; diploma, Mt. Zion Hosp. Sch. Nursing, 1949; AB, San Francisco State U., 1951, MA, 1954; Ed.D., Stanford U., 1967; Sc.D. (hon.), Ill. Wesleyan U., 1974; LHD (hon.), U. Portland, 1974, Georgetown U., 1994. Mem. faculty San Francisco State U., 1957-67, prof. nursing, 1966-67, chmn. dept., 1959-67; assoc. prof. U. Calif. Sch. Nursing, San Francisco, 1968-71, prof., 1971; dean, prof. Sch. Nursing UCLA, 1971-75; dean emeritus, prof. U. Wash., Seattle, 1986—. Author: Strategies for Teaching nursing, 1971, 3rd edit., 1987, Japanese transl., 1974, Spanish edit., 1986; co-author: (with Heather Young) Choices: Making a Good Move to a Retirement Community, 2001. Trustee emeritus Robert Wood Johnson Found. Mem. ANA, Am. Acad. Nursing (charter fellow, pres. 1973-75), Inst. Medicine (governing coun. 1979-81). Home: 4540 8th Ave NE Apt 1001 Seattle WA 98105-4795 Business E-Mail: rheba@u.washington.edu.

DETTLOFF, DONNA JEAN, retired social worker; b. Detroit, Mar. 25, 1939; d. Donald Jesse and Mirabel (Hitchcock) Faragher; m. Dennis F. Dettloff (div. 1975); children: Denise Christine, Dennis Michael, Donald Joseph, David Allen. Diploma in practical nursing with honors, U. Hawaii, 1969, AA in Mental Health with honors, 1980; BS in Psychology with honors, Chaminade U., 1980. Lic. realtor, Hawaii. Practical nurse Hawaii State Hosp., Kaneohe, 1968-72, Kailua (Hawaii) Counseling Ctr., 1972-90, social worker, 1990-94; mental health counselor Castle Med. Ctr., Kailua, 1983—2002; ret., 2002. Republican. Avocations: stamps, coins, travel, interior design, hawaiiana. Home: PMB 5029 PO Box 2428 Pensacola FL 32513 Personal E-mail: donnadettloff@aol.com.

DETTWILER, PEGGY DIANE, music educator; b. Freeport, Ill., Dec. 16, 1947; d. Frank F. and Isabel (Yarger) Ochsner; m. Jürgen Thym, June 6, 1992. BS, U. Wis., Platteville, 1970; MusM, U. Wis., Madison, 1980, MusBM, 1982; MusM, U. Tex., San Antonio, 1985; DMA, Eastman Sch., 1991. Vocal music tchr. Mt. Horeb (Wis.) H.S., 1970-77; dir. music Christ Presbyn. Ch., Madison, 1979-84; dir. choral activities St. Mary's U., San Antonio, 1985-88, Mansfield (Pa.) U., 1990—. Guest condr. N.Y. State Sch. Music Assn., 1995, Pa. Music Edn. Assn., 1994, 96, 97, 98, 2000, 2002-04. Contbr. articles to profl. jours. Recipient Concert Choir Gold medal, Robert Schumann Internat. Choral Competition, 2002. Mem.: Music Educators Nat. Conf. (performer 1994—, guest clinician 1995, 1997, 2000, performance choral condr. dir. conv. 2003, guest clinician 2004—06), Collegiate Choral Assn. (pres. 1993—95), Am. Choral Dirs. Assn. (performer 1999—, pres. Pa. chpt. 2001—03). Avocations: photography, horseback riding, travel. Home: 452 N Main St Mansfield PA 16933-1326 Office: Mansfield U Butler 105 Mansfield PA 16933 Office Phone: 570-662-4721. E-mail: pdettwil@epix.net.

DETURK, PAMELA ELIZABETH, retired special education educator, elementary school educator; b. Phila., Aug. 26, 1946; d. Clarence Newton and Myrtle (Stauffer) Herb; m. Jay Ralph DeTurk, June 8, 1968; children: Nathan Jacob, Benjamin Levi, Adam Seth. AS, Harcum Jr. Coll.; BS in Elem. Edn., St. Joseph U.; MEd, U. Colo. Cert. elem., spl. edn. tchr., Colo. Dept. Edn. Tchr. Bryn Mawr (Pa.) Pre-Sch., 1966-68, Boyertown (Pa.) Area Sch. Dist., 1968-70; tchr. trainable mentally retarded Mahoning County Sch. for Retarded, Youngstown, Ohio, 1970-76, El Paso Sch. Dist. #11, Colorado Springs, Colo., 1976—2006; ret., 2006. Pres. PHD Learning Systems, Inc., Colorado Springs, 1982—; v.p. JMJ Imports, Inc., Colorado Springs, 1985—; ptnr. Rampart Kennels, Colorado Springs, 1981—. Mem. Coun. for Exceptional Children, Airedale Terrier Club Am. (pres. Greater Denver chpt. 1991-1994, 1999-2002), Colorado Springs Kennel Club (corr. sec. 1978-1980). Lutheran. Avocations: reading, travel. Home: 5977 Templeton Gap Rd Colorado Springs CO 80918-5108 Home (Summer): Condominios Pilar door 219 Apto 496 San Carlos 85506 Mexico Office Phone: 719-328-4041. Personal E-mail: airemetoo@aol.com.

DEUTSCH, ALLEEN DIMITROFF, university administrator; b. Cleve., Dec. 5, 1946; d. Joseph A. and Mildred A. (Dimitroff) D. BA, Bowling Green State U., 1969; MS, Miami U., Oxford, Ohio, 1973, PhD, 1978. Asst. dean Coll. Arts and Scis. Miami U., Oxford, Ohio, 1973-79; asst. to provost Bradley U., Peoria, Ill., 1979-83, dir. divsn. continuing edn. and profl. devel. Coll. Edn., 1983-87, adj. prof., 1983-87; dean divsn. continuing edn. Auburn U., Montgomery, Ala., 1987-92; assoc. dir. Ctr. Profl. Devel. Fla. State U., Tallahassee, 1993-99, interim dir., 1994-95, dir. devel. Coll. Social Scis., 1999-2000; dir. devel. Coll. of Law, Ga. State U., Atlanta, 2000—; devel. dir. U. Memphis Humphreys Law, 2005—. Pres. Planned Parenthood Greater Peoria, 1983-85, bd. dirs., 1981-87; mem. com. United Way, 1980-87; bd. dirs. Peoria YWCA, 1981-84, Planned Parenthood Ala., 1990-92. Mem. ASTD, Am. Assn. Higher Edn. (women's caucus), Am. Assn. Adult and Continuing Edn., Nat. Assn. Women Deans, Adminstrs. and Counselors, Univ. Continuing Edn. Assn. (Region IV chmn. women's divsn., chmn. awards and honors com., bd. dirs., nat. membership chair, chmn. Region III), Nat. Women's Studies Assn., Phi Delta Kappa, Phi Kappa Phi, Alpha Lambda Delta. Office: U Memphis Humphreys Law Sch Memphis TN 38152 Home: 505 Tennessee St #407 Memphis TN 38103 Office Phone: 901-678-2425. E-mail: adeutsch@memphis.edu.

DEUTSCH, JENNIFER LOREN, mathematics professor; b. St. Louis, June 29, 1978; d. Steven Ira and Vicki Lynn Deutsch; m. Andrew Wade Shrensker. BS in Math. with honors, U. Mo., Columbia, 2000, B in Ednl. Studies, Curriculum and Instrn. magna cum laude, 2000; MA in Math., Washington U., St. Louis, 2004. Permanent substitute tchr. Pky. West Sr. H.S., St. Louis, 2000; grad. tchg. asst. U. Mo., St. Louis, 2001, lectr., 2005—; grad. tchg. asst. Washington U., St. Louis, 2001—04. Supplemental instr. St. Louis U., 2003; adj. faculty Fontbonne U., St. Louis, 2004—, Washington U., St. Louis, 2004—; course coord. for calculus II U. Mo., St. Louis, 2006—. Recipient Robert H. McDowell award for excellent tchg. Math. Dept., Washington U., 2002—03, Dean's award for Tchg. Excellence, Grad. Sch. Arts and Sci., Washington U., 2003—04, Meritorious Svc. award, U. Mo., St. Louis, 2006. Mem.: NEA (pres., mem. student adv. com. 1997—99), Nat. Coun. Tchrs. Math., Am. Math. Soc., Golden Key, Rho Lambda, Alpha Phi (rec. sec., rush chair 1997—98). Office: Univ Missouri St Louis 332 CCB 1 University Blvd Saint Louis MO 63121 Office Phone: 314-516-6353. Business E-Mail: deutschj@umsl.edu.

DEUTSCH, JUDITH, clergywoman; b. N.Y.C., Apr. 18, 1929; d. Charles Shepard and Sadie (Freedman) Greene; m. Marshall E. Deutsch, June 27, 1947; children: Pamina Margret, Ethan Amadeus, Freeman Sarastro. BA, Hunter Coll., 1950; MA, New Sch. Social Rsch., 1965, Boston Coll., 1980. Ordained to ministry Unitarian-Universalist Ch., 1981. Dir. Hexiad, Cambridge, Mass., 1979-80; intern First Parish, Framingham, Mass., 1981; assoc. min. Unitarian-Universalist Soc., Hartford, Conn., 1982-85; interim min. First Parish Petersham, Mass., 1985-87, First Parish Sharon, Mass., 1988-90, Unitarian Universalist Ch., Worcester, Mass., 1990-91; min. Unitarian-Universalist Ch., Rockland, Mass., 1987-88, First Parish Medfield, Mass., 1991-2000, min. emerita Mass., 2000—. Bd. dirs. Internat. League Religious Socialism, Stockholm, 1989—2004, alt. dir., 2004—; trustee Coop. Met. Ministries, 1999—; bd. dirs., former chair religion and socialism commn. Dem. Socialists Am., 1989—95; former chmn. Religious Coalition for Abortion Rights, Boston, 1987—90; acting pres. James Luther Adams Found., Newton, Mass., 1989—91, bd. dirs., sec., 1985—; former sr. co-chair Collegium, former chmn. ethics sect., co-chair faith-in-action com. First Parish. Producer, interviewer TV program Religous Issues in The News, 1994-95; author curriculum materials; op-ed columnist Sudbury Town Cover, 2003—; contbr. articles to profl. publs. Lobbyist Coalition for Choice, Boston, 1988—92; mem. Medfield Alcohol and Other Drug Action Com., 1992—97, Coun. on Aging, Sudbury, 2000—, Mass. LWV Health Care Com.; chair Sudbury LWV Health Care Com.; v.p. Mass-Care, 2004—, chair legis. com., 2005—; mem. Sudbury Cmty. Housing Com., 2005—; co-chair Citizens for Kennedy and Johnson, Morris County, NJ, 1960; mem. Sudbury (Mass.) Dem. Town Com., 1985—; del. Mass. Dem. Conv., 1990, 1994, 1996, 2002, 2003, 2005; candidate for state rep. 13th Middlesex dist., Mass., 2000. Hunter Coll. Hall of Fame inductee, 1999. Mem. Unitarian Universalist Ministers Assn., Liberal Religious Education Dirs. Assn., Mass Bay Ministers Assn. Avocations: folk dancing, cooking, reading, piano. Home and Office: 41 Concord Rd Sudbury MA 01776-2328 E-mail: revjd@aol.com.

DEUTSCH, NINA, pianist, vocalist; b. San Antonio, Mar. 15; d. Irvin and Freda (Smukler) Deutsch. BS, Juilliard Sch. Music, 1964; MMA, Yale U., 1973. Concert pianist internat. and U.S. tours, 1965-82; entertainer, solo pianist Holland Am. Cruise Lines, 1987, 89-90; freelance pianist, lectr. music, 1990—; pianist Royal Caribbean Cruise Lines, 2004. Exec. v.p. Internat. Symphony, N.Y.C., 1978—82. Musician (pianist): (albums) Charles Ives, 1976; author: (plays) Portrait of Clara Schumann, 1987, Portrait of Liberace, 1995; contbr. articles to mags. and newspapers. Bd. dirs. Metzner Found. Overseas Relief; Ft. Lee coord. Channel 13, 1974. Recipient award for Am. music, Nat. Fedn. Music Clubs, 1975; grantee, Philips Petroleum Found., 1982; scholar, Oberlin Coll.; Tanglewood fellow, Wulsin Fellowship, 1966. Mem.: Yale Alumni Assn. Bergen County. Achievements include first American pianist to play all American music in communist China, 1982; first woman pianist to entertain for Holland America; first and only woman to record complete solo piano music of Charles Ives. Avocations: swimming, hiking, baking. Home: PO Box 405 Leonia NJ 07605-0405 Office Phone: 201-947-0087. Personal E-mail: ianist100@aol.com.

DEUTSCHMAN, LOUISE TOLLIVER, curator; b. Taylorville, Ill., Sept. 6, 1921; m. Paul Eugene Deutschman, Dec. 20, 1941 (div. 1966); 1 child, Deborah Elliott. BA, MacMurray Coll., 1937; postgrad., Northwestern U., Sorbonne, Paris, 1950—66. Assoc. dir. Waddell Gallery, NYC, 1966—74, Sidney Janis Gallery, NYC, 1975—78; dir. Alex Rosenberg Gallery, NYC, 1978—80; assoc. Sidney Janis Gallery, NYC, 1980—2000; curator PaceWildenstein, NYC, 2000—. Guest curator Nasher Sculpture Ctr., Dallas, 2004—. Personal E-mail: louisetd@earthlink.net.

DEVAN, DEBORAH HUNT, lawyer; b. Allentown, Pa., Jan. 22, 1950; d. Valerio R. and Audrey (Miller) H.; m. Mark S. Devan, May 30, 1981; children: Emily, David, Eric. BA in Econs. magna cum laude, U. Md., 1972, JD cum laude, 1975. Bar: Md. 1975, D.C. 1976, U.S. Dist. Ct. Md. 1976, U.S. Dist. Ct. D.C. 1987, U.S. Ct. Appeals (4th cir.) 1988, U.S. Ct. Appeals (2d cir.) 1991, U.S. Supreme Ct. 1980, Md. Ct. Appeals 1975, D.C. Ct. Appeals 1976. Ptnr. Weinberg and Green, Balt., 1974-94; prin. Neuberger, Quinn, Gielen, Rubin & Gibber, P.A., Balt., 1994—. Bd. dirs. Lutheran Hosp. Md., Inc., 1981-86, Cystic Fibrosis Found., 1983 (Community Svc. Gold award), Lutheran Health Care Corp., 1988-91, U. Md. Law Sch. Fund, 1991, Balt. Devel. Corp., 1999—, U. Md. Sch. Law Alumni Assn., 2000—; trustee Merry-Go-Round Enterprises, Inc. Named one of Top 100 Md. Women, The Daily Record, 2005. Fellow Am. Coll. Bankruptcy; mem. ABA (bus. bankruptcy com., subcommittee bankruptcy litigation, subcommittee claims and priorities), Am. Bankruptcy Inst., Turnaround Mgmt. Assn., Women's Bar Assn., Assn. Comml. Fin. Attys., Md. State Bar Assn., Inc. (subcommittee creditor's rights, bankruptcy and insolvency), Bankruptcy Bar Assn. Md. (corp. sec., bd. dirs., pres. 1996-97), Exec. and Profl. Women's Coun. Md. (1st v.p. 1984), Network 2000, Comml. Real Estate Women, Bar Assn. Balt. City (profl. ethics com. 1980, publicity com. 1981). Office: Neuberger Quinn Gielen Rubin & Gibber 1 South St Fl 27 Baltimore MD 21202-3282 Office Phone: 410-332-8522.

DEVANE, MINDY KLEIN, financial planner; b. Detroit, May 4, 1954; d. Myer and Maxine (Gold) Klein; m. Kenneth Manuel DeVane, Nov. 20, 1993. BS in Journalism, U. Fla., 1976, MBA in Fin., 1981, MS in Fin. Planning, 2003. CFP. Mktg. rep. IBM, Tampa, 1981-85; account exec. Thomson McKinnon, Tampa, 1985-88, Smith Barney, Miami, 1988-89; underwriter Cigna, North Miami, Fla., 1989-92; sr. account exec. Cohig & Assocs., Tampa, 1992-93; v.p. Josephthal Lyon & Ross, Tampa, 1993-96; v.p. investments Raymond James, Tampa, 1996-99; fin. planner Griffith Bowles Fin. Mgmt. First Union Securities, Tampa, 1999—2001; pres. DeVane Fin. Advisors Inc., Tampa, 2001—. Allocations com. mem. United Way, Pinellas County, Fla., 1998, Hillsborough County, Fla., 1999; founder Hyde Park Exec. Women Leader Club, 1999-2002; bd. dirs. Vivo Fla. Orch. Guild, Sword of Hope; mem. ACS Guild. Recipient Outstanding Fin. Advisor award Asset Mgmt. Svcs. RJF, 1996-97. Mem. Fin. Planners Assn. (pres.-elect), Bus. and Profl. Women (editor 1986-88). Avocations: bicycling, swimming, collectibles. Home: 6308 Jacqueline Arbor Dr Temple Terrace FL 33617-3164 Office: PO Box 16626 Tampa FL 33687 Office Phone: 813-988-3453. E-mail: mdevane@vsrfin.com.

DEVANEY, CYNTHIA ANN, retired elementary school educator, real estate instructor; b. Gary, Ind., Feb. 6, 1947; d. Charles Barnard and Irene Mae (Nelson) Burner; m. Harold Verne DeVaney, Nov. 23, 1974 (dec. 1981). BS, Ball State U., 1970, MS, 1972; postgrad., Ind. U. and Purdue U., 1974-76. Cert. real estate broker, Ind. Real estate broker Century 21 McColly Realtors, Highland, Ind., 1979-86, McColly Realtors, Merrillville, 1986—, with Pres.' Coun.; tchr. Merkley Elem. Sch., Highland, Ind., 1969—2002; student tchr. supr. Ind. U., Bloomington, 2002—. Supr. student tchrs. Ind. U. N.W.; real estate tchr. McColly Sch. Real Estate. Active Schubert Theater Guild, Chgo. Mem. N.W. Ind. Bd. Realtors (Million Dollar Club), Nat. Bd. Realtors, Jr. Ind Hist. Soc., Innsbrook Country Club. Democrat. Methodist. Avocations: golf, tennis, travel, gardening, theater. Home: 607 E 78th Pl Merrillville IN 46410-5624 Office: McColly GMAC 2000 W 45th Ave Highland IN 46322-2504 Office Phone: 219-934-6326. E-mail: cindevaney@aol.com.

DEVANY SERIO, CATHERINE, clinical psychologist; b. N.Y.C., July 27, 1964; d. Edward Heath and Mary Langley (Peebles) Devany; m. Vincent Joseph Serio, III, May 2, 1992. BA in Am. Studies magna cum laude, U. Tex., 1987; MS in Clin. Psychology, Va. Commonwealth U., 1990, PhD in Clin. Psychology, 1993. Rsch. assoc. Dept. Mental Health, Mental Retardation and Substance Abuse, Richmond, 1988-90; extern in family therapy Family Therapy Practice Ctr., Washington, 1993-94; postdoctoral fellow dept. phys. medicine and rehab. Med. Coll. Va., Richmond, 1993-94; clin. dir. Community Rehab. Svcs., Richmond, 1994—. Invited lectr. in field. Contbr. articles to profl. jours. Rehab. Psychology fellow Nat. Inst. Disability and Rehab. Rsch., 1990-92; recipient Young Investigator award Nat. Head Injury Found., 1993. Mem. APA (divsn. family psychology). Avocations: hiking, canoeing, rock climbing.

DEVARD, JERRI, marketing professional; BA in Econs., Spelman Coll., 1979; MBA in Mktg., Atlanta U., 1983. Mktg. asst. The Pillsbury Co., Mpls., 1983—92, group mktg. mgr. cake mixes divsn., 1992—93; dir. suites mktg. Minn. Vikings, 1993—94; v.p. mktg. Harrah's Entertainment, New Orleans, 1994—96; v.p. mktg. Color Cosmetics Revlon, 1996; with Citigroup, chief mktg. officer e-Consumer line of bus.; sr. v.p. brand mgmt. and mktg. comm. Verizon Comms., N.Y.C., 2003—. Bd. dirs. Exec. Leadership Coun. Found. Mem.: Nat. Black MBA Assn., Spelman Coll. Alumnae Assn. Office: Verizon Communications Inc 1095 Ave of the Americas New York NY 10036-6797

DEVARIS, JEANNETTE MARY, psychologist; b. Burbank, Calif., Jan. 7, 1947; d. Nicholas Propper Klein and Elizabeth (Von Lichtenberg) Schaeffer; m. Robert Lee Blake, May 20, 1967 (div. 1979); 1 child: Brendon; m. Panayotis Eric DeVaris, Dec. 5, 1988. BA, Adelphi U., 1968; MA, Fairleigh Dickinson U., 1977; PhD, Seton Hall U., 1987. Lic. psychologist, N.J. Caseworker N.Y.C. Welfare Dept., 1968-72; alcohol and drug rehab. counselor U.S. Army, Ft. Monmouth, NJ, 1972-76; psychol. intern N.J. State Intern Program, Trenton, 1977-78; psychologist Greystone Psychiat. Hosp., Greystone Park, NJ, 1979; sr. psychologist R. Hall Cmty. Mental Health Ctr., Bridgewater, NJ, 1979-90; pvt. practice South Orange, NJ, 1988—. Tng. supr. Grad. Sch. Applied and Profl. Psychology; adj. prof. Seton Hall U.; sponsor and participant in Cable TV program; mem. South Orange Critical Support Team Vol. Group of Psychologists; founder One Braine Integration. Contbr. articles to profl. jours. Mem. APA, Nat. Register Health Svc. Providers, N.J. Psychol. Assn. (bd. dirs., interprofl. rels. com.), Soc. Psychologists in Pvt. Practice (bd. dirs., spkrs. bur. com.). Achievements include founding of OneBrain Integration Psychotherapy Technique. Avocations: travel, reading. Office Phone: 973-762-3149. Personal E-mail: drdevaris@aol.com.

DE VARON, LORNA COOKE, choral conductor; b. Western Springs, Ill., Jan. 17, 1921; d. Vernon Walter and Hazel Mildred (Watts) Cooke; m. Jose de Varon, May 14, 1944; children: David, Joanna, Cristina, Alexander. BA, Wellesley Coll., 1942; MA, Radcliffe Coll., 1945; MusD honoris causa, New Eng. Conservatory, 1988. Asst. condr. Radcliffe Choral Soc., Radcliffe-Harvard Choir, 1942-44; condr. Bryn Mawr Coll. Choir, 1944-47; condr. chorus, chmn. choral dept. New Eng. Conservatory Music, Boston, 1947-88, condr. chorus for concerts with Boston Symphony Orch., 1952-86; concert performer New Eng. Conservatory Chorus, tours in U.S., Europe, Russia, Israel, China; condr. Israel Summer Festival, 1977-79; condr., tchr. choral conducting Tanglewood Festival Chorus, 1952-66; condr. New Eng. Conservatory Camerata, 1989—; prof. emerita New Eng. Conservatory; condr. Longy Chamber Chorus, 1989—2005. Guest condr. Cameron Singers, Israel, 1984, Beijing Radio Chorus and Orch., Beijing, 1987; chmn. Choral Inst. of Composers Conf., 1983-85; mem. choral adv. panel Nat. Endowment for Arts; condr. New Eng. Conservatory Chamber Singers, summers 1982-87, Monadnock Music Festival; founder de Varovistas (small chamber chorus), 2005. Editor, arranger choral works, E.C. Schirmer and Galaxy Pubs., Boston. Mem. Cambridge Arts Council. Recipient medal for Disting. Achievement City of Boston, 1967, medal for Disting. Achievement Radcliffe Grad. Soc., 1972, medal for Disting. Achievement Wellesley Coll., 1978, medal of Israel, 1977, Ludi award New Eng. Conservatory, 1983, Harvard Glee Club medal, 1987. Mem. Am. Choral Condrs. Assn., Pi Kappa Lambda. Home: 94 Lake View Ave Cambridge MA 02138-3326 Personal E-mail: ldevaron@aol.com.

DE VARONA, DONNA, sports reporter, former Olympic swimmer; b. San Diego, Apr. 26, 1947; m. John Pinto; 2 children. BA in polit. sci., UCLA; four doctoral degrees (hon.). On-air analyst, commentator, host, writer ABC Sports, 1965—76, 1983—98, Olympic Coverage NBC, 1976—83; radio host Donna de Varona on Sports. Chair Women's World Cup Soccer Tournament Organizing Com., 1999; served on US Sec. Edn. Commn. on Opportunity in Athletics, 2002—03; founding mem., first pres. Women's Sport Found., 1979—84; served four terms Pres. Coun. Physical Fitness and Sports. Named Most Outstanding Female Athlete World, AP, 1964, United Press Internat. (UPI), 1964; named to US Olympic Hall Fame, Bay Area Hall Fame, San Jose Hall Fame, Woman's Hall Fame, 2003; recipient Internat. Swimming Hall Fame Gold Medallion, Olympia Award for contbn. to Olympic Movement, Olympic Order, Internat. Olympic Com., Susan B. Anthony Trailblazer award, Overcoming Obstacle award, Cmty. Edn. Found., 2002, Theodore Roosevelt (Teddy) award, Nat. Collegiate Athletic Assn. (NCAA), Emmy award for Special Olympics coverage, 1991. Achievements include youngest competitor at 1960 Olympics games; broke 18 world swimming records; won 2 Olympic Gold medals, 400-meter individual medley and 4 by 100 meter relay, 1964 Olympics; won 37 national championships; first female sports broadcaster on network TV, 1965; first woman to do TV commentary on Olympics, 1968; active in passing 1978 Amateur Sports Act by US Congress and 1972 landmark "Title IX" legis.

DEVAUD, JUDITH ANNE See HALVORSON, JUDITH

DEVAUGHN, TARA MARY LEE, mathematics educator; b. Goldsboro, NC, Oct. 2, 1976; d. Gordon and Dona Tuck; m. David DeVaughn, Aug. 7, 1999; children: Payton Michael, Rylee Elizabeth. BE, Mayville State U., ND, 1995—99. Cert. tchr. Alaska, 1999. Math tchr. Fairbanks Northstar Borough Sch. Dist., Eielson AFB, Alaska, 1999—. Curriculum writer Fairbanks Northstar Borough Sch. Dist., 2005—06. Mem.: Nat. Coun. Tchrs. Math.

DEVAULT, KATHY, psychiatric consultant, liaison nurse; b. Bklyn., July 30, 1943; children: David S. IV, Megan. BS in Health Arts, Coll. St. Francis, Joliet, Ill., 1991; MS in Psychiat. Mental Health Nursing, Rush U., Chgo., 1996, DNursing, 1997. RN, N.Y.; cert. clin. specialist. Head nurse Caledonian Hosp., Bklyn., 1966-67, recovery rm. supr., clin. instr., 1967-69; intensive care supr. Arnold Gregory Meml. Hosp., Albion, NY, 1969-72; nurse practitioner in pvt. practice, Albion, 1972-74, Batavia (N.Y.) VA Hosp., 1974-77, Buffalo VA Hosp., 1978-79, Cook County Hosp., Chgo., 1981-98, psychiat. cons.-liaison nurse, 1998—. Mem. Town Coun., Beverly Shores, Ind., 1996—, mem. Plan Commn., 1998—; bd. officer Assn. Beverly Shores Residents, 1988-98. Mem. ANA, AAUW, Am. Psychiat. Nurses Assn., Internat. Soc. Psychiat. Nurses. Avocations: photography, reading.

DEVENISH, NICOLLE See WALLACE, NICOLLE

DEVENY, CHARLOTTE PERRY, musician, educator; b. Maywood, Ill., Apr. 29, 1930; d. Lester Earl Perry and Armede Cooper Draper; m. Glenn Lindquist Harris, Aug. 5, 1950 (div. Apr. 1963); children: Charlotte Armede, Catherine Elizabeth; m. Edwin Rountree Deveny, Feb. 16, 1991. Student Piano Lower Conservatory, Chgo. Mus. Coll., 1936-42; MusB, Northwestern U., 1951. Performer, accompanist, Chgo., 1942—; cellist San Antonio Symphony, 1949; tchr. class piano and strings Park Ridge (Ill.) Sch. Dist., 1951-52; freelance musician various movie, TV, and rec. studios, L.A., 1952-61; cellist Lawrence Welk Orch., L.A., 1961-78; pvt. tchr. piano and cello Palos Verdes, Calif., 1978—; co-dir. Deveny Music Sc., Palos Verdes, 1991—. Recipient over 30 first-pl. medals in piano and cello, Ill., 1936-42. Mem. DAR, Music Tchrs. Nat. Assn., Music Tchrs. Assn. Calif. (pres. South Bay 1983-87, 91-92, 1999-2000). Avocations: reading, writing short stories. Home and Office: PO Box 4328 Palos Verdes Peninsula CA 90274 Office Phone: 310-377-0771. Personal E-mail: devmusch@cox.net.

DEVER, JOYCE, materials engineer; m. Tim Dever; 1 child, Megan. BS in Chemistry, MS in Materials Sci. Materials engr. NASA Lewis Rsch. Ctr. Mem.: Fairview Park Jr. Women's Club. Avocation: aerobics. Office: NASA Glenn Rsch Ctr Bldg 309 Rm 210 Cleveland OH 44135 Business E-Mail: joyce.a.dever.grc.nasa.gov.

DEVERA, GERTRUDE QUENANO, education educator; b. Malasiqui, Pangasinan, Philippines, Dec. 15, 1924; came to U.S., 1950; d. Paulino Castro and Filomena (del Rosario) Magsanoc; m. Perfecto Tamondong DeVera, June 23, 1946 (dec. Sept. 1976). BA, San Francisco State U., 1952; postgrad., U. Calif., Berkeley, 11952-54; MA in English Lit., San Francisco State U., 1956. Calif. tchrs. cert. and life diploma. Tchr. San Francisco Unified Sch. Dist., 1956-88, demonstration tchr., 1958-59; mem. aux. bd. trustees Don Adriano Geslani Montessori Sch., Malasiqui, Luzon, The Philippines, 1997—. Tchr. participant Project Read Behavioral Rsch. Labs., Palo Alto, Calif., 1967-68; cert. demonstrator Astra's Magic Math-Alphaphonics, 1987-88; rschr. in preventive medicine, San Francisco, 1975—. Editing chmn.: Guidelines for Use of the Eudcational Facilities Planning model, 1968 (NDEA award 1968). Summer Inst. grantee NDEA, U. Wash., Seattle, 1968; recipient Hon. Svc. awards Calif. Congress Parents and Tchrs. Inc., Sacramento, 1975, San Francisco 2nd Dist., 1980. Mem. AAUW (legis. interview com. 1970's), Internat. Platform Assn., World Affairs Coun. No. Calif., Libr. of Congress. Democrat. Roman Catholic. Avocations: reading, creative writing, public speaking, attending lectures, various cultural pursuits.

DEVERAUX, JUDE (JUDE GILLIAM WHITE), writer; b. Louisville, Sept. 20, 1947; d. Harold J. and Virgina (Berry) Gilliam; m. Richard G. Sides, 1967 (div. 1969); m. Claude B. White, 1970 (div. 1993). BS Fine Arts, Murray State U., 1970; Cert. in Teaching, Coll. Santa Fe, 1973. Cert. remedial reading tchr. Tchr. elem. sch., Santa Fe, 1970-76; writer, 1976—. Author novels including: The Enchanted Land, 1978, The Black Lyon, 1980, The Velvet Promise, 1981, Casa Grande, 1982, Highland Velvet, 1982, Velvet Song, 1983, Velvet Angel, 1983, Sweetbriar, 1983, Countefeit Lady, 1984, Lost Lady, 1985, River Lady, 1985, Twin of Ice, 1985, Twin of Fire, 1985, The Temptress, 1986, The Raider, 1987, The Princess, 1987, The Maiden, 1988, The Awakening, 1988, The Taming, 1989, A Knight in Shining Armor, 1990, Wishes, 1990, Mountain Laurel, 1990, The Conquest, 1991, The Duchess, 1991, Sweet Liar, 1992, Eternity, 1992, The Invitation, 1993, Remembrance, 1994, Legend, 1996, An Angel for Emily, 1998, The Blessing, 1999, High Tide, 2000, Temptation, 2000, Twin of Fire/Twin of Ice, 2001, The Summerhouse, 2001, A Knight in Shining Armor, 2002, The Mulberry Tree, 2002, Forever, 2002, Wild Orchids, 2003, Forever and Always, 2003, Holly, 2003, Eternity, 2004, The Princess, 2004, Wishes, 2004, River Lady, 2004, Always, 2004. Mem. Costume Soc. Am. Avocations: cooking, computers, travel, collecting books on costume history, reading english history. Office: Pocket Books Simon & Schuster Inc 1230 Avenue Of The Americas New York NY 10020-1586

DEVERE, AMY JO, physical education educator, director; b. Pitts., Oct. 19, 1977; d. James Thomas and Gayle Darlene Devere. BA in Phys. Edn./Athletic Tng., Tusculum Coll., Greeneville, Tenn., 2000; MS in Edn., Va. Poly. Inst. and State U., Blacksburg, 2002. Cert. athletic trainer Nat. Athletic Trainers' Assn. Bd. Certification, 2001, CPR/Automated External Defribrillator profl. rescuer ARC. Grad. asst. athletic trainer Va. Tech, Blacksburg, 2000—02; phys. edn. and health tchr. Georgetown Visitation Prep. Sch., Washington, 2002—, head athletic trainer, 2002—, asst. dir. athletics, 2004—. Mentor Georgetown Visitation Prep. Sch., Washington, 2004—, club moderator student athletic tng. and athletic assn. clubs, 2002—. Mem.: Nat. Athletic Trainers' Assn. (licentiate), Alpha Chi. Roman Catholic. Avocations: travel, golf. Office: Georgetown Visitation Preparatory School 1524 35th St NW Washington DC 20007 Office Phone: 202-337-3350.

DE VERITCH, NINA, musician, educator; b. Montclair, N.J., Aug. 18, 1941; Student, U. So. Calif., 1959-61, Juilliard Sch. Music, 1961-63. Mem. Detroit Symphony Orch., 1968-70; recording artist movies, records, TV, 1971-74; prin. cellist Utah Symphony, 1964-68; mem. faculty U. Utah, 1964-67, Brigham Young U., 1964-68; studio tchr., adjudicator I, master classes, 1980—; freelance cellist, artist tchr. Dallas, 2002—. Vis. assoc. prof. U. Mich., 1990-91; prin. cellist Ann Arbor Chamber Orchestra, 1988-90. Mem.: Michiana Cello Soc. (past sec., bd. dirs.), Mich. Music Tchrs. Assn., Am. Fedn. Musicians, Am. String Tchrs. Assn. Home: 9800 Adolphus Dr Frisco TX 75035-7073

DEVI, AMRITANANDAMAYI (SRI MATA AMRITANANDAMAYI DEVI, AMMA), spiritual leader; b. Kerala, India, Sept. 27, 1953; d. Sugunanandan and Damayanti. Founder Amrita Inst. Med. Scis., Mata Amritanandamayi Mission Trust, Gujarat Earthquake Relief Effort; pres. Centenary Parliament of World Religions, Chgo.; spkr. UN. Subject of film, Darshan — The Embrace, Cannes Film Festival, 2005. Recipient Gandhi-King award for Non-Violence, 2002. Office: Sri Mata Amma Amritapuri PO Kerala Kollum 690525 India also: MA Ctr PO Box 613 San Ramon CA 94583

DEVI, GAYATRI, physician; b. Madras, India, Nov. 2, 1965; d. Tanjore L. and Saraswathy Ramachandran; m. Mike Chou, Apr. 20, 1991; children: Yasmine Ranjini. Grad. advanced levels, U. London, 1983; MD, Grace U., 1987. Bd. cert. neurology, Am. Bd. Neurology and Psychiatry, 1996, psychiatry, 1999. Intern SUNY, 1988-89, resident, 1989-93, chief resident, 1993-94; fellow Columbia U., 1994-95; dir. Long Island Alzheiner's Disease Assistance Ctr. SUNY, Stony Brook, 1995-97, clinical asst. prof. neurology and psychiatry, 1995-97; asst. prof. neurology Columbia U., 1997-99; attending physician dept. medicine and psychiatry Lenox Hill Hosp., 1999—; clin. asst. prof. neurology and psychiatry NYU Sch. Medicine, 2004—. Dir. memory disorders ctr. Columbia Presby.-Eastside, 1997-99; clinical care co-dir. Columbia U. Alzheimer's Disease Rsch. Ctr., 1997-99; dir. N.Y. Memory and Healthy Aging Svcs., 1999—; spkr. in field. Contbr. articles to profl. jours. Grantee Alzheimer's Disease Assistance Ctr. N.Y. State, 1995-97, Pfizer Pharms., 1998. Mem. Am. Psych. Assn., Am. Neurology Assn., Am. Neuropsych. Assn. Republican. Office: NY Memory and Health Aging Svcs 65 E 76th St New York NY 10021-1844 Office Phone: 212-517-6881. E-mail: gd@nymemory.org.

DEVIGNE, KAREN COOKE, retired amateur athletics executive; b. Phila., July 31, 1943; d. Paul and Matilda (Rich) Cooke; m. Jules Lloyd Devigne, June 26, 1965; children: Jules Paul, Denise Paige, Paul Michael. AA, Centenary Coll., Hackettstown, 1963; student, Northwestern U., 1963-65; BA, Ramapo Coll., Mahwah, 1976; MA, Emory U., Atlanta, 1989. Founder GYMSET, Marietta, Ga., 1981—. Cons. Girls Club Am. Marietta, 1989; vol. Cobb County Gymnastic Ctr., Marietta, 1976-95, Ga. Youth Soccer Assn., Atlanta, 1976-95; fundraiser Scottish Rite Children's Hosp., Atlanta, 1989. Recipient recognition awards from various youth groups, Atlanta, 1976—; named Nominee Woman of Yr. ABC News, Atlanta, 1984. Avocations: skiing, tennis, bridge. Home: 4662 Wynmeade Pk NE Marietta GA 30067 also: 7 Sunrise Point Dr Breckenridge CO 80424

DEVILLE, VICKI LYNNE, jewelry manufacturer, commercial real estate broker; b. Portland, Oreg., Sept. 5, 1950; d. Byron Paul and Alice Gertrude (Ely) Brocksen; m. Gary Raymond McGrew, Sept. 11, 1971 (div. 1978); children: Jason Alan, Justin Scott; m. Paul Irving deVille, July 13, 1985; stepchildren: Tricia, Melany, Landon. BS, Portland State U., 1973. Lic. elem. tchr., Oreg. Elem. sch. tchr. Portland Pub. Schs., 1973-75; mortgage loan processor Equitable Savs. and Loan, Portland, 1876-77; adminstrv. asst. The Robert Randall Co., Portland, 1976-79; comml. mktg. mgr. Chgo. Title Ins., Portland, 1979-83; comml. real estate broker Norris, Beggs & Simpson, Portland, 1983-84, Monroe & Friedlander, Honolulu, 1984-87; owner Vicki deVille Earrings Co., Honolulu, 1988—. Recipient Project award Monroe & Friedlander, Inc., 1985 Mem. Nat. Asssn. Realtors, Honolulu Bd. Realtors, Profl. Women's Network, Internat. Pilot Club Honolulu, Ladies Who Invest and Perhaps Speculate (past pres.). Republican. Avocations: skiing, piano playing, gourmet cooking, travel, interior decorating.

DEVINE, BARBARA ARMSTRONG, risk manager; b. Lawrence, Kans., Mar. 2, 1965; BS in Microbiology, U. Ill., 1987; MBA, Lake Forest (Ill.) Grad. Sch., 1997. Cert. purchasing mgr., gen. ins. assoc. in risk mgmt. R & D technician Abbott Labs., Abbott Park, Ill., 1987-90, asst. scientist, 1990-91, assoc. biochemist, 1991-93, purchasing agt., 1993-95, sr. purchasing agt., 1995-96, sect. head med. writing, 1996-97, sr. label editor, 1997-99, labeling group leader, 1999; chem. sales rep. AIC, Inc., Natick, Mass., 1999-2001; sr. purchasing agt. TAP Pharm. Products, Lake Forest, Ill., 2000—02, risk manager, 2002—06; v.p. risk mgmt. Std. Parking Corp., 2006—. Named Outstanding Buyer, Chgo. Minority Bus. Devel. Coun., 1996. Mem. Risk and Ins. Mgmt. Soc., Inst. for Supply Mgmt. Achievements include patents in field. Home: 1942 N Crenshaw Cir Libertyville IL 60061 E-mail: bdevine@standardparking.com.

DEVINE, KATHERINE, environmental scientist, educator; b. Denver, Oct. 15, 1951; BS, Rutgers U., 1973, MS in Econs., 1980; postgrad., U. Md., 1981—82; MS in Elem. Edn., St. Josephs U., 2004. Lab. technician Princeton (N.J.) U., 1974-76; econ. and regulatory affairs analyst, program mgr. U.S. EPA, Washington, 1979-89, cons., 1989-99; exec. dir. Applied BioTreatment Assn., Washington, 1990-91; pres. DEVO Enterprises, Inc., Washington, 1990-99; sr. editor Scientist, Phila., 2000—01; tchr. Phila. Sch. Dist., 2001—04; sci. curriculum specialist Libr. Video Co., Pa., 2004; writer, editor Office of Comm. and Outreach, US Dept. Edn., Washington, 2004—. Chair adv. bd. Applied Bioremediation Conf., 1993; co-chair Environ. Biotech. Conf., 1996, 97, others. Author: N.J. Agricultural Experiment Station of Rutgers University, 1980, Bioremediation Case Studies: An Analysis of Vendor Supplied Data, 1992, Bioremediation Case Studies: Abstracts, 1992; co-author: Biomediation: Field Experiences, 1994, Bioremediation, 1994; founder, pub., editor: (mag.) Biotreatment News, 1990-97; editor: Indsl. Biotech. News, 1998; pub.: The Gold Book, 1994-96; contbr. articles to profl. jours., chpts. to books; co-sponsor over 20 confs. Mem. Women's Coun. on Energy and the Environment, 1991-93. Mem.: AAAS, Am. Chem. Soc., Nat. Assn. Sci. Writers, Futures for Children, Alpha Epsilon Lambda, Alpha Zeta. Personal E-mail: devoinc@aol.com.

DEVINE, LIBBY, art educator, consultant; b. Indpls., Jan. 31, 1952; d. Taylor William and Elizabeth Josephine Jackson; m. Douglas M. Devine, June 12, 1976. BFA, U. Ga., 1974; M of Visual Arts, Ga. State U., 1980. Cert. tchr. Ga., Nat. Bd. Cert. Tchr., 2002, tchr. Early Adolescence through Young Adult. Tchr. art, dept. chair Roswell (Ga.) H.S./Fulton County Schs., 1980—; cons. Ga. Dept. of Edn. Test Devel., Tchr. Cert. Test in Art, 1988—90; sch. arts program coord. Fulton County Dept. of Edn., Fulton County Arts Coun., 1988—, cons. coll. bd., 2002—03; presenter in field. Contbr. articles,; editor curriculum guide. Grantee, Fulton County Arts Coun., 2003—04. Mem.: Profl. Assn. Ga. Educators, Ga. Art Edn. Assn., Nat. Art Edn. Assn. (grant 1991). Office: Roswell HS 11595 King Rd Roswell GA 30075

DEVINE, NANCY, retired postmaster; b. Hyannis, Mass., Feb. 8, 1949; d. Joseph Peter and Rose (Almeida) Cabral; m. Michael G. Devine, Mar. 20, 1971 (div. 1975); 1 child, Paul. Student, U. Mass., 1967—70. Postal clk. U.S. Postal Svc., Centerville, Mass., 1977—80, postmaster West Hyannisport, Mass., 1980—2005; ret., 2005. Affirmative Action planner U.S. Postal Svc., Brockton, Mass., 1979-80, prin. rep./exec. bd., Providence, 1993. Painter in acrylics. Art and Humanities grantee Barnstable Arts Coun., Mass. Art Coun., Nat. Endowment for the Arts. Mem. Nat. Assn. Women Artists, Cape Cod Art Assn., Smithsonian Instn. Home: 20 Delta St Hyannis MA 02601 E-mail: ncdevine@mailcity.com.

DEVITA, M. CHRISTINE, foundation administrator; b. N.Y. BA magna cum laude, Queens Coll., 1977; grad. cum laude, Fordham U., 1980. Bar: N.Y. 1981, U.S. Dist. Ct. (so. dist.) N.Y. 1982, U.S. Supreme Ct. 1986. With legal dept. Reader's Digest Assn., Inc., 1980-87, dep/ gen. counsel, 1984, also bd. dirs.; exec. dir. DeWitt Wallace and Lila Wallace Reader's Digest Funds, N.Y.C., 1987-89, pres., 1989—2002, also bd. dirs.; pres. Wallace Found., 2002—. Editor: Fordham Law Rev. Bd. dirs. Found. Ctr., Reader's Digest Assn., Inc., Queens Coll. Found. Office: Wallace Found 5 Penn Plaza 7th Fl New York NY 10001*

DEVITO, TERESA MARIE, artist; b. Bangoli del Tigino, Italy, June 11, 1920; came to U.S., 1924, naturalized, 1926; d. Bartolomeo and Santo Donatello Cimaglia; m. Americao DeVito; children: Richard (dec.), Sandra Ann DeVito King. BA inEdn., Fairmont State Coll., 1960; MA, W.Va. U., 1964; postgrad., Wagner Coll., 1968; D (hon.), Minsitry Fgn. Affairs of Malta. Tchr. East Fairmont (W.Va.) High Sch., 1960-68, Miller Jr. High Sch., Rivesville, W.Va., 1969-70; instr. art Fairview H.S., 1970-86, Barrockville H.S., Farmington H.S. One-woman shows include Lynn Katler Gallery, NYC, 1975; exhibited at group shows at Morgantown Art Assn. Exhbn., 1960; commd. work includes paintings on cloth at Immaculate Conception Ch., Fairmont, Fairmont Bowling Ctr., 1988, Disney World. Recipient Internat. Statue of Victory, Einstein Peace Medal, Rhodeodendron Festival award, Honoris Causea, Internat. Found., 1987. Mem. AAUW, NEA, Nat. Art Edn. Assn., Tole Painters Am., W.Va. Art Assn., W.Va. Artist and Craftsman Guild, Artists Equity, League Ind. Artists (past v.p.), Village Garden Club, Cath. Daus. Am. (State Ct. of W.Va. award, Nat. Merit award for "Face in a Cloud" entry in poster contest, 2000), Quota Internat. Orgn. Roman Catholic. Home: 417 Newton St Fairmont WV 26554-5218

DEVIVO, ANGE, retired small business owner; b. Bay Shore, NY, Oct. 20, 1925; d. Romeo Zanetti and Karolina (Hodapp) King; m. John Michael DeVivo, Dec. 30, 1950; 1 child, Michael. Student, Washington Sch. for Secs., N.Y.C., 1945-46. Sec. Am. Airlines, N.Y.C., 1946-51; exec. sec. W.C. Holzhauer, N.Y.C., 1951-52; dist. sales mgr. Emmons Jewelers, Inc., Bound Brook, N.J., 1952-53; exec. sec. NJ Rep. State Com., 1960—64; dist. office supr. 19th Decenniel census U.S. Dept. Commerce, Charlotte, NC, 1970; adminstrv. sec. Mercy Hosp., Charlotte, NC, 1973—81; pres. Secs., Plus, Convs., Plus, Charlotte, 1983—91; prin. Ange DeVivo & Assocs., Inc., Charlotte, 1991—92; ret., 1992. Editor: The North Carolina Republican Woman, 2d edit., 1994, 3d edit., 1995; author Precinct Training Manual, 1971. First woman chair Mecklenburg County Rep. Party, 1976; adminstrv. sec. Nat. Broadcast Assn. for Cmty. Affairs, 1987-90; active in local politics, NJ, 1956-64, Conn., 1964-68, NC, 1968-96; active Human Svcs. Coun., Charlotte, 1984-88; conf. mgr., 8th Nat. Recycling Congress, 1989; active Emergency Med. Svc. Adv. Coun., Charlotte, 1981-92, chmn., 1988-90; active Charlotte Women's Polit. Caucus, 1972-96; chair Mecklenburg County Rep. Party, 1976-77; mem. Mecklenburg Evening Rep. Women's Club, Charlotte, 1996-06, pres., 1973-74, 93-94; mem. Mecklenburg County Women's Commn., 1990-96, Women's Roundtable, 1994-95; citizens adv. com. Conv. and Visitors Bur., 1986-90; coord. Women's Equality Day celebration Mecklenburg County Women's Commn., 1990, coord., fin. chair, 1991-92, co-chmn., fin. chair, 1993-96, adv. bd. 1993-96, vice-chair bd., 1995; fundraiser March of Dimes and Leukemia, Ala., 1999, 02, 06; active Rep. Women Today Ala., 1997-01, tel. com., 2001; pres. Cardinal Bus. and Profl. Women's Club, 1979-81; site inspector for spl. events in Jamaica, 1987. Recipient Seal of City of Stamford Mayor of Conn., 1968, Order of Long Leaf Pine award Gov. of N.C., 1974, Cert. Appreciation Cardinal Bus. and Profl. Womens' Club, 1978, Woman of Yr. award, 1982, Entrepreneur of Yr. award Women Bus. Owners, 1987, Cert. Appreciation outstanding leadership and dedicated svc. Charlotte Women's Bus. Owners Assn., 1990-91, Award of Honor in recognition of outstanding svc. Mecklenburg County Women's Com., 1991, Spl. Recognition award for devotion, dedication and untiring efforts Mecklenburg County Women's Commn., 1996, Seal of Mecklenberg County, N.C., 1996; honoree N.C. Fedn. Rep. Women, 1987; nominee Cmty. Svc. award Mecklenburg County Women's Commn., 1994, Hall Fame, N.C. Rep. Party, 1995. Mem.: Rep. Women of the South (mem. telephone com. 2004—06, bd. dirs. 2006, 2006, bd. mem. 2006—). Roman Catholic. Avocations: politics, community service. Personal E-mail: jmdevivo531@cs.com.

DEVLIN, BARBARA JO, school district administrator; b. Milw., 1947; m. John Edward Devlin, 1973; 2 children. BA, Gustavus Adolphus Coll., 1969; MA, U. Mass., 1971; PhD, U. Minn., 1978. Cert. tchr., sch. prin., supt., Minn.; cert. supt., Ill., Minn. Tchr. Worthington (Minn.) High Sch., 1971-75; rsch. assoc. Ednl. R & D, Mpls.-St. Paul, 1975-76, 76-77; coord. edn. svcs. Ednl. Coop. Svc., Mpls.-St. Paul, 1977-79; dir. personnel Minnetonka Pub. Schs., Excelsior, Minn., 1979-85, asst. supt., 1985-87; supt. Sch. Dist. 45, Villa Park, Ill., 1987-95, Ind. Sch. Dist. 280, Richfield, Minn., 1995—. Editor working papers Gov.'s Coun. on Fluctuating Enrollments, St. Paul, 1976. Contbr. articles to ednl. jours. Bd. dir. Richfield Found., 1995—. Named Ill. Supt. of Yr., 1994, Region 9 Adminstr. of Excellence, Minn. Assn. Sch. Adminstrs., 2004; recipient Disting. Alumni award, Gustavus Adolphus Coll., 1994; Ednl. Policy fellow, George Washington U., 1977—78, mem. fellow program, Bush Found. Pub. Schs., 1984—85. Mem. Minn. Assn. Sch. Adminstrs., Rotary Internat. (membership chair Villa Park unit 1989-91, vocat. dir. 1991-92, sec. 1992-93, pres. 1994-95), Optimists Internat. (pres. 2000-2001). Methodist. Office: Richfield Pub Schs 7001 Harriet Ave Richfield MN 55423-3061 Office Phone: 612-798-6010. E-mail: Barbara.Devlin@richfield.k12.mn.us.

DEVLIN, JEAN THERESA, education educator; b. Jamaica, N.Y., Apr. 14, 1947; d. Edward Philip and Frances Margaret (Tillman) Creagh; children: Michael, Bernadette, Patrick. BA magna cum laude, Queens Coll., 1972, postgrad., 1994—95; MA, St. John's U., Jamaica, 1987; PhD, So. Ill. U., 1991. Substitute tchr. Diocese of Bklyn., 1969-75; tchr. St. Gregory's Sch., Bellerose, N.Y., 1975-82; dist. mgr. Creative Expressions, Robesonia, Pa., 1980-83; asst. to dean, adj. instr. workshop supr. Spl. Univ. Program St. John's U., Jamaica, 1983-87, asst. prof. dept. English, 1992; asst. dean St. John's Coll. Liberal Arts, St. Johns U., 1993-94; owner Tara's Tees and Golden Hands Embroidery, 1984-87; from grad. asst. to doctoral fellow English dept. So. Ill. U., Carbondale, 1987-89, storytelling tchr. Continuing Edn., 1992; adj. asst. prof. St. John's U., Jamaica, 1992-94, Poly. U., N.Y., 1995-96, Bayside Acad., N.Y., 1995-97, St. Anthony's H.S., Huntington, N.Y., 1996-99; tchr. SCOPE (gifted and talented program) South Huntington Dist., N.Y., 1999-2000; tchr., asst. prin., tchr. Rambam Mesivta Maimonides H.S., Lawrence, NY, 1999—2001; tchr. Hicksville H.S., 2002, North Shore Hebrew Acad. H.S., 2002—, coord. student spl. svcs., 2006—; asst. prof. L.I. Conservatory, 2002—03; asst. prof. commn. arts Molloy Coll., 1998—. Cons. Family Lit. Project; supr. workshops Popular Culture, 1991-94, Children's Lit. Assn., 1990-92, Midwest Popular Culture, 1991, Wyo. Centennial, 1990; presenter poetry readings, dramatic interpretation, storytelling, including Internat. Rsch. Soc. in Children's Lit., Paris, 1991, Nat. Coun. Tchrs. English Conf., 1992, Ill. Assn. Tchrs. of English, 1990, 91, 92, South Atlantic MLA, 1992, Mid Atlantic Popular/Am. Culture, 1993; speaker Speak Easy Workshop, 1981; showcased Nat. Congress Storytelling, Children's Reading Roundtable, 1990; world-wide storyteller, 1991—; featured spkr. Puppet Guild of L.I., 1997; adj. asst. prof. So. Ill., St. John's U., Polytechnic U., Molloy Coll., 1998—, SUNY, Farmingdale, 2002-03. Author: Gabby Diego, 1992, repub. 1994, Rainbows Stories and Customs from Around the World, 1996; contbr. articles to profl. jours. and children's mags.; contbg. photographer Eye of the Beholder, 2000; actress (videotape and audiocassette) Peter Kagan and the Wind, 1990, 91, played at White House, 1992, Sta. WKTS, 1992-94, Excerpts from Shakespeare, 1999, (videotape) Puppets from A to Z, 2000; performed as storyteller on 5 continents, 1991—; singer with North Shore Hebrew Acad. Choir, CD, Shiriyah, 2003, 04, 05, 06; mem. editl. bd. Habari Gari: A Newsletter for Catholics of African Ancestry, 1999-2000. Den leader Boy Scouts Am., Bayside, N.Y., 1975-80; troop leader Girl Scouts U.S.A., Flushing, N.Y., 1976-78; vol. Elderwise Day Care, Carbondale, Ill., 1992, Alice Wright Day Care Ctr., Carbondale, 1989-92, ABC Quilts (A Pediatric AIDS group), 1991-2000; mem. The Stage Co., Cill Cais Players. Honored for outstanding svc. Boy Scouts Am., 1978; recipient Outstanding Cmty. Svc. award, named Most Admired Woman of the Decade Sta. WPSD-TV, 1991, Internat. Women of Yr., 1993; grantee So. Ill. Art Coun., 1992; named Educator of Excellence, N.Y. State English Coun., 2000, L.I. Lang. Arts Coun., 2001. Mem.: NY State English Coun., Puppet Guild L.I., Nat. Coun. Tchrs. English, Nat. Eng. Hon. Soc., Phi Delta Kappa, Sigma Tau Delta, Alpha Sigma Lambda, Skull and Circle Honor Soc. (St. John's U.). Avocations: needlecrafts, acting, puppetry. Home: 193 W 19th St Huntington Station NY 11746-2118

DE VOE, PAMELA ANN, anthropologist, educator; b. Chgo., Sept. 22, 1946; d. Edward George De Voe and Evelyn Francis De Grave; m. Ronald E. Mertz, Aug. 1971; 1 child, Renée De Voe. BA, U. Wis., 1967; MA, U. Mo., 1971; PhD, U. Ariz., 1979; student, U. Mo., 1980—82. Cons., St. Louis, 1995—99; parent coord. St. Louis Pub. Sch., 1998—99; info. specialist St. Louis CC, 1999—2001; asst. prof. St. Louis U., 2001—; mgr. Cmty. Connections Internat. Inst. St. Louis, 2003—. Adj. faculty Webster U., St. Louis, 2000—, St. Louis C.C., St. Louis, 2000—. Co-prodr.: Refugee Studies Newsletter, 1984—86; editor: Selected Papers in Refugee Issues 1992, 1992; contbr. articles to profl. jours. Fellow Tchg. fellow, U. Ariz., 1976—77, U. Mo., Columbia, 1980—82; grantee HEW Fulbright-Hays grantee, 1977—78, Mo. Humanities Coun., 1989—90. Mem.: Soc. Intercultural Edn. Tng. and Rsch., Assn. Conflict Resolution, Soc. Urban, Nat. and Trans Anthropology, Soc. Anthropology Religion, Soc. Applied Anthropology, Am. Anthropological. Assn. (com. refugee issues 1986, editor CORI 1988—94, bd. dir. gen. anthropology divsn. 1992—96, com. on refugees & immigrants 1994—96, 2000—), Asian Art Soc. (v.p. 1996—98, pres. 1998—99, bd.dir. 1993—2001). Democrat. Avocations: poetry, spinning wool. Home: 165 Bon Chateau Dr Saint Louis MO 63141 Office: Internat Inst St Louis 3654 S Grand Blvd Saint Louis MO 63118 Business E-Mail: devoemertz@sbcglobal.net.

DEVOLITES, JEANNEMARIE ARAGONA, state legislator; b. Swindon, England, Feb. 28, 1956; children: Nichole, Ashley, Cassandra, Alexandra; m. Tom Davis. BA in Math., U. Va., 1978. Mem. Va. State Legis., 1998—, mem. privileges & elections com., mem. transp., gen. laws and rehab. and social svcs. coms. Republican. Roman Catholic. Office: Gen Assembly Bldg PO Box 406 Richmond VA 23218-0406 Office Phone: 703-938-7972. E-mail: jdevolites@aol.com.

DEVONE, DENISE, artist, educator; BFA cum laude, Temple U., 1975; MFA, U. Hawaii, 1978. Instr. Newark Mus., 1990-97; art and music tchr. Holy Cross Sch., Harrison, 1995—. Adj. prof. County Coll. of Morris, Randolph, NJ, 1994—; cons. Donald B. Palmer Mus., Springfield, NJ, 1992-95. Executed murals Kaiser Hosp., Honolulu, 1985, Kaiser Pensacola Clinic, Honolulu, 1986, Distinctive Bodies Fitness, Warren, NJ, 1993, Ambulatory Pediatric Clinic, Overlook Hosp., Summit, NJ, 1994; Sole proprietor of Amalgamated Cocoanuts; one-woman shows include Contemporary Mus., Honolulu, 1992, ETS, Princeton, 1995, Montclair Kimberly Acad., NJ, 1995, 98, ADP Gallery, Roseland, NJ, 1997, Palmyra Gallery, Bound Brook, NJ, 1999; illustrator: Japanese Pilgramage, 1983, The Art of Featherwork in Old Hawaii, 1985. Recipient Purchase awards Hawaii State Found. on Culture and the Arts, 1976, 78, 80, 86, award of merit City and County of Honolulu, 1988; NJ State Coun. on Arts, Dept. State fellow, 1994-95. Mem. Nat. Assn. Women Artists, Inc., Studio Montclair, Inc., City Without Walls, Artists Space. Avocation: piano. Home: 33 Kew Dr Springfield NJ 07081-2530 E-mail: Ddevone@aol.com.

DEVORE, DAUN ALINE, lawyer; b. Ft. Worth; Student, U. Paris IV; BA magna cum laude, U. Calif., Irvine; JD, U. San Francisco; MPA, Harvard U.; postgrad., Oxford U. Bar: Calif., US Ct. Appeals (fed. and 9th cirs.), US Ct. Internat. Trade, US Dist. Ct. (ctrl. dist.) Calif., US Ct. Vets. Appeals. Law clk. US Environ. Protection Agy. Region IX, Constitution Sub-Com., US Senate Jud. Com.; honors clk. civil rights divsn. fed. enforcement US Dept. Justice; summer atty. Office Pub. Defenders for the City and County, San Francisco; lectr. law coll. Seoul Nat. U., Republic of Korea; assoc. Cen. Internat. Law Firm, Seoul; US prin. Othniel H.K. Ltd., Cambridge, Mass., LA, Hong Kong; ptnr. Internat. Bus. Law Firm, Palm Springs, Calif. and Washington. Constitutional law expert; Fulbright fellow judge, Seoul; presenter in field Contbr. articles to profl. jours. City commr. Hist. Site Preservation Bd., Palm Springs, Appeals Bd., Palm Springs; mem. legis. com. San Francisco Commn. on Status of Women. Named America's Miss USA Beauty and Talent Queen, Miss Mass., Miss Palm Springs UN. Mem. ABA (chair internat. law com. gen. practice sect., com. internat. svcs., chmn. subcom. on Asia-Pacific sect. internat. law, internat. law com. gen. practice sect., chmn., mem. standing com. liaison to fgn. and internat. bars.), Internat. Inst. Strategic Studies, Calif. Bar Assn. (com. internat. law), Armed Forces Comm. and Electronic Assn., Harvard Club (bd. dirs. Korea), Toastmasters (numerous speech awards), Phi Delta Phi. Avocations: operatic singer, songwriter, flute. Office Phone: 760-773-2257. Personal E-mail: daundevore@yahoo.com.

DEVORE, KIMBERLY K., healthcare executive; b. Louisville, June 19, 1947; d. Wendell O. and Shirley F. DeV. Student, Xavier U., 1972-76; AA, Coll. Mt. St. Joseph, 1979; BA, Internat. U. Metaphysics, 1999. Patient registration supr. St. Francis Hosp., Cin., 1974-76; cons., bus. mgr. Family Health Care Found., Cin., 1976-77; exec. dir. Hospice of Cin., Inc., 1977-80; pres. Micro Med, 1979-86; v.p. Sycamore Profl. Assn., 1979-86; ptnr. Enchanted House, 1979-86, sec., 1979-80, treas., 1980-83; dist. sales rep. Control-O-Fax, 1986; br. sales mgr., 1987; nat. dealer devel. rep., 1987; nat. computer field sales trainer, 1987-90; pres. U.S. Exec. Leasing and U.S. Med. Leasing, Inc., 1991—2001, Accu Svcs., Inc., 1993—2003, U.S. Med. Mgmt., Inc., 1994-98; ins. agt. United Am. Ins. Co., Orlando, Fla., 2005. Pres. U.S. Med. Mgmt. Ga., Inc., 1996—2006; lic. ins. agt. United Am., 2005—. Pres. Saddle Creek Homeowners Assn., Inc., 1992-95, parliamentarian, 1995-96; chairperson Citizen's Police Adv. Com. City of Roswell, 1997-99; chairperson found. grants Orch. Atlanta, 1998-99, pres., 1999-03, vice-chmn., pres. & CEO, chaplin Unity N. Atlanta, 2000-02, emeritus, 2003; bd. dirs., membership chairperson Smith Plantation City of Roswell, 1996-97; pres. Roswell Citizen's Police Acad., Inc., 1994-95; mem. City of Roswell Med. Devel. Dist. Coun., 1995—; mem. North Fulton Civic League, Inc., 1995-96, 2001-; bd. dirs. Nat. Hospice Orgn., 1979-82, chmn. long-term planning com., fin. com., ann. meeting com., 1979-82, sec., 1980-81, treas., 1981-82; bd. dirs. Hospice of Miami Valley, Inc., 1982-86, also chmn. pers. com., by-laws com.; bd. dirs. Orch. Atlanta, 1998—. Mem. Greater Clin. Soc. Fund Raisers, Better Housing League; mem. service and rehab. com. Hamilton County Unit, Am. Cancer Soc., 1977-78; chair road com. Saddle Creek Homeowners Assn., 1991-92. Mem. Ohio Hospice Assn. (co-founder, state chmn., pres., 1978-83), Nat. League for Nursing, Ohio Hosp. Assn., Nat. Fedn. Bus. and Profl. Women's Clubs, Ohio Fedn. Bus. and Profl. Women's Clubs, Cin. Bus. and Profl. Women's Clubs (pres. 1973-75).

DEVORE, LEIGH ANN, gifted and talented educator, elementary school educator; b. Jacksonville, Fla., June 19, 1969; d. Wayne Kendell Spencer, Sr. and Claudia Parrish Spencer; married, Feb. 20, 1993; children: Richard Dale Jr., James Grey. BS in Edn., Palm Beach Atlantic U., West Palm Beach, Fla., 1991. Cert. elem. edn., spl. edn. NC Dept. Instrn., 2000. Exceptional tchr. Cabarrus County Schs., Concord, NC, 2001—. Home: 3890 Longwood Dr SW Concord NC 28028 Office: Cabarrus County Schools Concord NC 28027

DE VOS, PAULA FRANCESCA, finance company executive, investment advisor, consultant; d. Elliot Adrian and Pauline Francis Mizelle; m. Rene A. de Vos, Apr. 9, 1992; 1 child, Adrian Anthony. Superior Degree- Franch Lang., U. Paris- La Sorbonne, Paris, France, 1981; BA Internat. Economics, U. Calif., Berkeley, Calif., 1982; MBA Fin., U. San Francisco, San Francisco, Calif., 1994. Cert. Financial PlannerTM CFP Bd., 1995. Mgmt. Madrigal Inc., San Francisco; a v.p. JPMorgan Pvt. Bank, San Francisco, 1983—93; v.p. Wells Fargo Pvt. Client Services, Carmel, Calif., 2001—03; pres. Synergist Wealth Advisors LLC, Carmel, Calif., 2003—, Catalyst Wealth Mgmt. LLC, Carmel, Calif., 2003—. Cons. Synergist Wealth Advisors LLC, Carmel, Calif., 2003—. Contbr. articles to profl. jours. Adv. bd. CSUMB Planned Giving Coun., Monterey, Calif., 2003—05; bd. mem. multiple, Carmel, Calif. Mem.: Fin. Planning Assn. Avocations: sports, travel, reading, tennis. Office: Synergist Wealth Advisors LLC PO Box 1844 Carmel CA 93921 Office Phone: 831-626-1442. Business E-Mail: paula@synergistwealth.com.

DEVOS, RENEE NICHOLE, personal trainer, elementary school educator; d. Jacob Cornelius and Helen Ann DeVos. BA, U. NC, Wilmington, 2003. Cert. personal trainer Am. Coun. on Exercise, 1998, lifestyle and weight mgmt. cons. Am. Coun. on Exercise, 1999, group fitness instr. Am. Coun. on Exercise, 1999. Personal trainer and weight rm. mgr. Courts Plus Fitness Ctr., Jacksonville, NC, 1998—2003; tchr. Autism Spectrum Alternative Program, Wilmington, 2003—; phys. edn. and health tchr. Cape Fear Ctr. for Inquiry, Wilmington, 2003—. PTO liaison Cape Fear Ctr. for Inquiry, Wilmington, 2004, phys. edn. program grant cons., 2004—; partnership tchr. Cape Fear Ctr. for Inquiry, U. NC, Wilmington, 2005—. Recipient Outstanding Phys. Edn. Tchr. Intern award, U. NC, Wilmington, 2003; Phys. Edn. Program grantee, 2004—05. Mem.: Alpha Sigma Lambda, Phi Theta Kappa, Phi Kappa Phi. Avocations: photography, surfing, travel, weightlifting. Office: Cape Fear Center for Inquiry 3131B Randall Pkwy Wilmington NC 28403 Office Phone: 910-362-0000.

DEVOUEROIX, CHANNING, interior designer, writer, educator; b. Phila., June 14, 1938; d. William Andrew Anderson and Elsie Lanea Royer; children: Scott Roy, Cindy Burton, Suzanne Varco, Jennifer Slacter. Student, UCLA, 1956—57; BA, Occidental Coll., 1960. Legal sec. Gold, Eggerman and Wapner, Beverly Hills, Calif., 1954—62; elem. tchr. Burbank (Calif.) McKinley Elem., 1960—60, Madison Elem., Colorado Springs, Colo., 1970—72, Penrose Elem., Colorado Springs, 1972—73; owner Sassie Lassie Designs, Colorado Springs and Black Hawk, Calif., 1973—. Owner Llourd and Channing, Coronado, Calif., 1973—. Author poetry. Pres., chmn. ann. tennis tournament Meml. Hosp., Colorado Springs, 1971—80; pres., ball chmn. winter cotillion John Muir Meml. Hosp., Walnut Creek, Calif., 1982—92. Recipient Outstanding Vol., Meml. Hosp., 1974. Mem.: Nat. League Am. Pen Women, Nat. Cathedral, Kappa Kappa Gamma. Avocations: singing, photography.

DEVRIES, LINDA JANE, music educator; b. Conrad, Mont., May 1, 1937; d. Kenneth Paul and Leda Ruth Copley; m. Richard John DeVries, Sept. 11, 1959; children: Allan, Cheryl, Julie, Michelle. B of Music, U. Mont., 1959. Nat. cert. tchr. music. Tchr. piano pvt. practice, Malta, Mont., 1964—2003. Accompanist Malta Pub. Schs., 1974—2003. Mem.: Mont. State Music Tchrs. Assn. (student affiliate chair 1966—70, treas. 1970—82, cert. chair 1982—95, mem. cert. bd. 1995—2003).

DE VRIES, MADELINE, public relations executive; Founder, pres. DeVries Pub. Rels., N.Y.C., 1978—; chmn., CEO DeVries Pub. Rels. (acquired by Interpublic Group), N.Y.C.; public relations dir. Bergdorf Goodman, N.Y.C. Bd. dirs. and trustee Brooklyn Botanic Garden. Named an honoree Matrix Award, New York Women in Communications, 2002. Mem.: Cosmetic Exec. Women (mem. exec. com., chair, mktg. com.). Office: DeVries Public Relations 30 E 60th St New York NY 10022-1008

DE VRIES, MARGARET GARRITSEN, economist; b. Detroit, Feb. 11, 1922; d. John Edward and Margaret Florence (Ruggles) Garritsen; m. Barend A. de Vries, Apr. 5, 1952; children: Christine, Barton. BA in Econs. with honors, U. Mich., 1943; PhD in Econs., MIT, 1946. With IMF, Washington, 1946-87, sr. economist, 1949-52, asst. chief multiple currency pratices div., 1953-57, chief Far Eastern Div., 1957-59, econ. cons., 1963-73, historian, 1973-87. Professorial lectr. econs. George Washington U., 1946-49, 58-63 Author: The International Monetary Fund, 1966-71, The System Under Stress, 2 vols., 1977, The International Monetary Fund, 1972-78, Cooperation on Trial, 3 vols., 1985, The IMF in a Changing World, 1945-85, transl. into Chinese, 1986, Balance of Payments, Adjustment: The IMF Experience, 1945-86, transl. into Chinese, 1989, (with I.S. Friedman) Foreign Economic Policy of the United States in the Postwar, 1947, (with J.K. Horsefield) The International Monetary Fund, 1945-65, Twenty Years of International Monetary Cooperation, 3 vols., 1969; contbr. articles to profl. jours. Recipient Disting. Alumni award U. Mich., 1980, Cert. of Appreciation George Washington U., 1987, Outstanding Washington Women Economist award, 1987; AAUW scholar, 1939-42; U. Mich. Univ. scholar, 1942; Phi Kappa Phi fellow, 1943; MIT fellow, 1943-46; Ford Found. grantee, 1959-62. Mem. Am. Econ. Assn. (CSWEP - Carolyn Shaw Bell award 2002), U. Mich. Alumni Assn., MIT Alumnae Assn., Phi Beta Kappa, Phi Kappa Phi. Mem. United Church of Christ. Home: 10018 Woodhill Rd Bethesda MD 20817-1218 Office Phone: 301-365-0064. Personal E-mail: barmar1022@erols.com.

DE VRIES, ROBBIE RAY PARSONS, writer, illustrator, management consultant; b. Idabel, Okla., Sept. 11, 1929; d. General Forrest Sr. and Jessie Demma (Burch-Oldham) Parsons; m. Douwe de Vries, Apr. 2, 1953; children: Jessica Joan de Vries Kij, Peter Douwe. BS in Bus. Adminstrn. and Journalism, Okla. State U., 1952; postgrad., U. Houston, 1987, 88, Rice U., 1988, 89, U. St. Thomas, 1996, 97. Sec. to mgr. drafting and survey Shell Oil Co., Houston, 1952-53; sub. tchr. Spring Br. Ind. Sch. Dist., Houston, 1989-92; pres., owner Robbie P. de Vries Interests, Houston, 1983—, author, illustrator, pub., internat. cons., 1989—. V.p. Oilfield Systems, Inc., Houston, 1981—, internat. studies dept. U. St. Thomas; bd. dirs. Friends of Okla. State U. Libr., Stillwater; mem. Friends of U. Houston Libr., 1981—; bd. dirs., cons. Ctr. for Internat. Trade, Okla. State U., Stillwater, 1990—; invited guest Peoples Republic of China/U.S. State Dept., China, 1992; bd. assocs. New Internat. Sch. Okla. State U., 1999; lectr. on intercultural comms. Okla. State U., 1999, 2000; cons. Habitat for Humanity Internat.; invited guest to Egypt, Israel and Jordan by U.S. State Dept., 1999. Columnist Conroe, Tex. Daily Courier, 1988-89; editor Idabel Warrior newspaper (Gold medal), 1947, Houston Symphony League newspaper, 1974-75; author, illustrator, pub.: A Cultural Exchange: American and Chinese Weddings, English edit., 1993, Chinese edit., 1995; author, pub.: Regional Study of Russian and the Eurasian States, 1997. Internat. coord. Habitat for Humanity, Philippines, internat. coord. for better housing Egypt, Israel, Jordan; vol. cultural and internat. areas New Orleans, 1960—69, Houston, 1969—; home host internat. youth exch., Netherlands, 1978; grand jury mem. Harris County, Tex., 1986—87; patron Jr. League, Houston, 1970—; docent Mus. Fine Arts, Houston, 1974—; co-chmn. Houston-Baku, Azerbaijan, USSR Sister City, 1979—89; mem. magic cir. Greater Houston Women's Found.; mem. donor Baylor Med. Sch. Devel., 1990—; mem. magic cir. Rep. Women Greater Houston Women's Found., 1989—; bd. dirs. New Orleans C. of C., 1964—69, Houston Symphony Soc. League, 1972, Inst. Internat. Edn., Houston, 1969—, Boy Scouts Am., Houston, 1980—; bd. dirs., chair internat. conf. YWCA, Houston, 1986—87. Recipient Ann. Fund Silver Tray award Houston Symphony League, 1972, Miss Ima Hogg Orchid award Houston Symphony Soc., 1975, Gen. Maurice Hirsch Leaf and Letter award Symphony Soc., 1980, 81, 82, Tex. Mother of Yr., Alpha Delta Pi, 1982, Mayor's award Baku, Azerbaijan USSR, 1979, 83, 87, 89, U.S. State Dept. pin, 1986, 10-Yr. Leadership award Mayor of Baku, 1988, U. Houston Ball Merit/Honor, 1991, Merit award Boy Scouts of Am., 1993, 10-Yr. Svc. award, 1995; named Acting First Lady of Houston for goodwill trip to Baku, Azerbaijan, USSR, by Mayor of Houston Jim McConn, 1979; named Hon. Dep. Sheriff, Harris County Sheriff Johnny Klevenhagen, 1986, Harris County Sheriff Tommy B. Thomas, 1996; feature Honor Villages mag., 1994; certificate of appreciation, Okla. State U. Habitat for Humanity; named hon. lt. gov. of Okla., 2001. Mem.: AAUW (past pres.), Nat. Mus. Women in the Arts (charter), Tex.-Netherlands Bus. Assn., Houston Coun. Writers, Inspirational Writers, Tex. Fine Arts Assn., Nat. Women's Hall of Fame, Forum Club Houston, Tuesday Music Club (yearbook cover designer 1975—78), Étoffe Littéraire (founder, Founder's award 1985), Mu Kappa Tau. Republican. Presbyterian. Avocations: classical music, international entertaining, travel, interior decorating, art. Home and Office: Robbie P de Vries Interests 5100 San Felipe Rd #181E Houston TX 77056-3687 Fax: 713-993-0912. E-mail: robbiedevriesusa@earthlink.net.

DEVRIES SMITH, KATE, lawyer; BS cum laude in Physics, Drake U., 1993; JD cum laude, U. Mich. Law Sch., 1996. Bar: Minn. 1996, US Patent and Trademark Office 1998. Ptnr. Merchant & Gould, Mpls.; co-founder, ptnr. Pauly, DeVries Smith & Deffner, L.L.C., Mpls. Named a Rising Star, Minn. Super Lawyers mag., 2006. Mem.: Minn. Women Lawyers, Minn. Intellectual Property Law Assn., Am. Intellectual Property Law Assn., ABA (mem. intellectual property sect.), Vol. Lawyers Network (bd. dirs., named Vol. Lawyer of Yr. 2005). Office: Pauly DeVries Smith & Defner LLC 900 IDS Ctr 80 S 8th St Minneapolis MN 55402 Office Phone: 612-746-4784. E-mail: kds@pdsdlaw.com.*

DEW, CAROLYN CHRISTINE, health facility administrator, nurse; b. Tarboro, N.C., June 20, 1946; d. Walter Wilson Dew and Vera Louise Edmondson; children: Christina Taylor Ramos, Samuel Allen Taylor. Nursing diploma, Park View Sch. Nursing, Rocky Mount, N.C., 1968; B of Nursing, U. N.C., Chapel Hill, 1982; M of Nursing Adminstrn., U. N.C., Greensboro, 1987. Credentialed clin. nurse specialist in home health, ANA, credentialed nurse adminstr., ANA, credentialed gerontol. nurse, ANA. Home health staff nurse Maria Parham Regional Home Care, Henderson, NC, 1997, Edgecombe Home Care, Tarboro, NC, 1997—98, Maria Parham Reg. Home Care, Henderson, NC, 1998—2003; care team mgr. Tender Loving Care, Durham, NC, 2003; patient care coord. HCR Manorcare - Heartland, Raleigh, NC, 2003—03, dir. profl. svcs., 2003—04; ops. mgr. Liberty Home Care, Raleigh, 2004—. Home health staff nurse Staffbuilders, Henderson, 1995—96; dir. profl. svcs. Home Health Profls., Roxboro, 1994—95; supr. Interim Healthcare, Durham, 1993—94. Contbr. poetry to anthologies. Vol. HCR Manorcare Hospice, Raleigh, 2004. Capt. N.C. State Def. Militia, 1990—92. Republican. Avocations: writing poetry, singing, piano, dance. Home: 7605 Idolbrook Ln Raleigh NC 27615 Office Phone: 919-881-9492, 919-610-2365. Personal E-mail: dewccd142@aol.com.

DEW, JOAN KING, freelance/self-employed writer; b. Columbus, Ga., June 24, 1932; d. Henry Grady and Vivian Pauline (Cook) King; m. Clifford Dew (div.); children: Clifford L. Jr., Michael David; m. Albert Schmitt (div.); 1 child, Christopher Thomas. Student, Fla. State U., 1949—51. Reporter, feature writer Ft. Lauderdale (Fla.) Daily News, 1950—56; editor Nassau (Bahamas) Guardian, 1956—58; stringer UPI, Bahamas, 1956—58; copy chief Art and Publicity, Ltd., Kingston, Jamaica, 1958—60; feature writer, author column Male Call, Valley Times Today, North Hollywood, Calif., 1960—66; freelance writer Hollywood, Calif., 1966—77, Nashville, 1977—88; editor food and wine LA Herald Examiner, 1988—89; exec. editor Ctrl. Coast Adventures, Monterey Peninsula, Calif., 1992—2002; ret., 2002; with Peace Corps, Mozambique, 2003—. Author: Singers and Sweethearts: The Women in Country Music, 1977, Stand By Your Man: The Autobiography of Tammy Wynette, 1978, Minnie Pearl, The Autobiography of Minnie Pearl, 1980, Christmas, 1987; author: (with David Fox) Follow Your Heart, 1988; columnist Nashville Tennessean, 1988; contbr. articles to popular mags. Address: 2112 Calville St #103 Las Vegas NV 89128

DEWAAL, CAROLINE SMITH, education and advocacy organization executive, lawyer; BA in Polit. Sci., U. Vermont, Burlington; JD, Antioch Sch. Law, Washington, DC. Supreme Jud. Ct. Mass.: 1985, US Dist. Ct.: Mass. 1988, US Ct. Appeals, 1st Cir.: 1988. Chief legis. counsel Divsn. Insurance, Commonwealth Mass., Boston, 1985—89; staff atty. Pub. Citzen's Congress Watch, Washington, 1989—91; dir., legal affairs Pub. Voice for Food and Health Policy, Washington, 1991—94; dir., food safety program Ctr. for Sci. in Pub. Interest, Washington, 1994—. Mem., food sect. Transatlantic Consumer Dialogue; task force mem. Coun. for Agrl. Sci. and Tech. Task Force on Foodborne Pathogens: Review of Recommendations; chair, H Thomas Austern Writing award com. Food and Drug Law Inst., 1994—96; mem. Nat. Adv. Com. on Meat and Poultry Inspection, 1997—2000; spkr. in field; provided several congl. testimonies; maintains and annually publishes a listing of foodbourne illness outbreaks, 1999—. Mem. editl. bd. Food and Drug Law Jour., chair adv. bd., 2004—05; contbr. to food safety publications and reports; co-author: Is Our Food Safe? A Consumer's Guide to Protecting Your Health and the Environment, 2002; guest appearances Good Morning America, Today Show, Nightline, Dateline and others. Mem.: Internat. Assn. Food Protection, Mass. Bar. Office: Ctr for Sci in the Pub Interest 1875 Connecticut Ave NW Ste 300 Washington DC 20009 Office Phone: 202-332-9110 ext 366. Business E-Mail: edewaal@cspinet.org.*

DEWAR, LOUISE HELEN, director; b. Trenton, NJ, July 10, 1957; d. Vincent Patrick and Helen Melia Dewar; m. Alfred Channon Morton, Sept. 19, 1981; 1 child, Margaret Helen Morton. BA, Trinity Coll., Hartford, Conn., 1979; MA, Monmouth U., West Long Branch, NJ, 1997. Assoc. registrar, dir. summer sch. Monmouth U., West Long Branch, NJ, 1985—88; tchr. Rutgers Prep. Sch., Somerset, 1997—2001; chair history dept. Ranney Sch., Tinton Falls, 2001—. Trainer Nat. Bd. Profl. Tchg. Stds., Alexandria, Va., 1999—. Mem.: ASCD, Nat. Coun. Social Studies, NJ Coun. History Edn., Am. Hist. Assn. Office Phone: 732-542-4777 130.

DE WEERDT, HILDE GODELIEVE, humanities educator; arrived in US, 1991; d. Fernand Lucien De Weerdt and Marie-Antoinette Emilie Borremans; m. Mary Elizabeth Lucal, July 31, 2005; 1 child, Simon Dean Lucal. BA, MA, KU Leuven, Belgium, 1991; PhD, Harvard U., Cambridge, Mass., 1998. Pub. svcs. libr. Harvard Coll. Libr., Harvard-Yenching Libr., Cambridge, 1999—2002; asst. prof. U. Tenn., Knoxville, 2002—. Author: (scholarly monograph) Competition over Content: Negotiating Standards for the Civil Service Examinations in Imperial China; contbr. articles to profl. jours. Fellow, Belgian Am. Ednl. Found., 1991—92, Am. Coun. Learned Societies, 1996—97, Woodrow Wilson Nat. Fellowship Found., 1997—98, Ctr. for Chinese Studies at U. of Calif., Berkeley, 1998—99, Fairbanks Ctr. for East Asian Rsch., Harvard U., 2004—05, Stanford Humanities Ctr., Stanford U., 2006—07. Mem.: World History Assn., Assn. for Asian Studies, Am. Hist. Assn. Office: U Tenn History Dept 6F Dunford Hall Knoxville TN 37996-4065 Office Phone: 865-974-9867. Office Fax: 865-974-3915. Business E-Mail: hdeweerd@utk.edu.

DEWEESE, ANITA LYNN, medical/surgical nurse; b. Urbana, Ill., Oct. 1, 1963; d. Frank Joseph and Mary Katherine Hartman; m. Richard Allan DeWeese, Feb. 12, 1994; children: Samuel, Jacob. BSN, No. Ill. U., 1986; MSN, INd. U., 1988. RN S.C., cert. neonatal intensive care. Staff nurse ob-gyn. U. Hosp., Indpls., 1986—87; staff/charge nurse neonatal ICU Riley Hosp. for Children, Indpls., 1987—88; clin. nurse specialist Mercy Hosp., Urbana, 1988—89, Palmetto Health Richand, Columbia, SC, 1989—94; obstetric clin. nurse specialist Greenville (S.C.) Hosp. Sys., 1995—2002, obstetric clin. data coord., 2002—. BLS instr. Am. Heart Assn., 1989—. Referee reviewer: Neonatal Network, 1989—. Mem.: Assn. Women's Health Obstetric and Neonatal Nurses (referee reviewer Lifelines 2001—, sect. chair 2002—05), S.C. Perinatal Assn. (membership chair 2000—02), Am. Acad. Pediat. (neonatal resuscitation regional trainer 1988—, mem. steering com. neonatal resuscitation program svcs. 2003—), Sigma Theta Tau. Home: 212 Beagle Run Easley SC 29642 Office: Greenville Meml Hosp 701 Grove Rd Greenville SC 29605

DEWEESE, BARB OAKLEY, secondary school educator; d. John and Helen Oakley; children: Skylar, Darryl. BSCE, U. Ariz., Tucson, 1980. Registered profl. engr., Utah, 2004; cert. tchr. Ariz. Civil engr. U.S. Bur. of Reclamation, Phoenix, 1980—95; tchr. Payson Unified Schs., Ariz., 1996—. Faculty advisor Payson High Key Club, 2003—06. Office Phone: 928-474-2233.

DEWEY, ARIANE, artist, illustrator; b. Chgo., Aug. 17, 1937; d. Charles S. Dewey, Jr. and Marjorie G. Graff; m. Claus Dannasch, Feb. 7, 1976; m. Jose Arugeo, Jan. 27, 1960; 1 child, Juan Dewey Aruego. BA, Sarah Lawrence Coll., 1959. Rsch. and publicity asst. George Nelson, N.Y.C., 1960—62; art editor Harcourt, Brace, Jovanovich, Inc., N.Y.C., 1963—65; freelance artist, illustrator, 1968—. Author, illustrator: Naming Colors, 1995, The Sky, 1993, The Narrow Escapes of Davy Crockett, 1990, The Tea Squall, 1988, Gib Morgan, Oilman, 1987, Febold Feboldson, 1984, Pecos Bill, 1983, Dorin and the Dragon, 1982, The Thunder God's Son, 1981, The Fish Peri, 1979, illustrator: Sally Ann Thunder Ann Whirlwind Crockett, 1985, co-author, co-illustrator: Weird Friends, 2002, Splash, 2000, Rockabye Crocodile, 1988, We Hide, You Seek, 1979, A Crocodile's Tale, 1972, Pilyo the Piranha, 1971, Symbiosis, A Book of Unusual Friendships, 1970, Juan & the Asuangs, 1970, The King and His Friends, 1969, co-illustrator with Jose Aruego: They Thought They Saw Him, by Craig Kee Strete, 1996, The Littlest Wolf, by Larry Dane Brimner, 2002, Gregory the Terrible Eater, by Mitchell Sharmat, 1980, Rum Pum Pum, by Maggie Duff, 1978, Lizard's Home, by George Shannon, 1999, co-illustrator: numerous books, including Where Does the Sun Go At Night?, by Mirra Ginsburg, 1992, Alligators and Others All Year Long, by Cresent Dragonwagon, 1993, Musical Max, by Robert Kraus, 1990, Another Mouse to Feed, by Robert Kraus, 1980, co-illustrator with Jose Aruego: One Duck, Another Duck, by Charlotte Pomerantz, 1984, Runaway Marie Louise, by Natalie Savage Carlson, 1977; other Rosa Reposa by Isabel Campoy, 2002, co-illustrator Antarctic Antics, A Book of Penguin Poems by Judy Sierra, 1998, Safe, Warm and Sung by Stephen R. Swinburne, 1999, How Chipmunk Got His Stripes by Joseph Burchac and James Bruchac, 2001, Turtle's Race with Beaver by Joseph Burchac & James Bruchac, 2003, Lizard's Guest, 2003, Raccoon's Last Race by Joseph Bruchac and James Bruchac, 2004; co-illustrator: Duck, Duck, Goose by Karen Beaumont, 2004. Recipient Goldmedaille, Internat. Buchkunst-Ausstellung, Leipzig, Germany, 1977. Mem.: Soc. Illustrators, PEN, Authors Guild. Avocation: kayaking. E-mail: adewey@mindspring.com.

DEWEY, BARBARA I., librarian, dean; BA, MLS, U. Minn. Head reference and adult svcs. Minn. Valley Regional Libr., Mankato; reference and interlibrary loan libr. Northwestern U. Libr.; dir. admissions Ind. U. Sch. of Libr. and Info. Sci.; dir. info. and rsch. svcs. to interim univ. libr. U. Iowa Librs., 1987—2000; dean of librs., prof. University of Tenn., Knoxville, 2000—. Bd. dirs. New Media Consortium, Knoxville Friends of Literacy, Digital Library Fedn.; mem. Tenn. Coun. on Librs. Author: Achieving Diversity, 2006; contbr. articles to profl. jours. Mem.: Assn. of S.E. Rsch. Librs. (past pres., past chair Diversity Com.). Office: Adminstrv Ste 607 John C Hodges Libr 1015 Volunteer Blvd Knoxville TN 37996 Office Phone: 865-974-4127. E-mail: bdewey@utk.edu.*

DEWEY, ELIZABETH R., lawyer; b. Phoenix, Nov. 29, 1967; Student, Univ. Madrid, Spain, 1989; BA cum laude, Univ. Tulsa, 1990; JD summa cum laude, Am. Univ. of Washington, 1993. Bar: Md. 1993, DC 1995, US Dist. Ct. (DC, Md. dist.), Md. Ct. Appeals, US Ct. Appeals (Fed. cir.). Law clk. Hon. Noel Anketell Kramer DC Superior Ct.; pro bono ptnr. DLA Piper Rudnick Gray Cary, Washington, 1999—. Adj. prof. law Am. Univ. Wash. Coll. of Law. Founder, editorial bd. mem. Journal of Gender and the Law, Am. Univ. of Washington; contbr. articles to profl. jours. Hon. trustee AYUDA Inc. Named co-winner, Young Guns category, Washington Bus. Jour., 2004. Mem.: ABA, DC Women's Bar Assn., Mortar Board, Phi Beta Kappa. Office: DLA Piper Rudnick Gray Cary 1200 Nineteenth St NW Washington DC 20036-2412 Office Phone: 202-861-6218. Office Fax: 202-223-2085. Business E-Mail: elizabeth.dewey@dlapiper.com.

DEWEY, LINDA L., secondary school educator; b. Piedmont, Ala., May 12, 1942; d. Hilton and Nancy Lucille Lawson; m. Allen L. Dewey, June 8, 1990; children from previous marriage: Bradley E. Spear, David A. Spear, William J. Spear. BA, William Carey Coll., Hattiesburg, Miss., 1966. Instr. Southeastern Bapt. Coll., Laurel, Miss., 1966—67; tchr. St. Martin H.S., Biloxi, Miss., 1967—75; substitute tchr. Wichita Falls Ind. Sch. Dist., Tex., 1979—91; tchr. pre-K Kids Corner Day Care, Raleigh, Miss., 1992—96; tchr. Heidelberg H.S., Miss., 1996—. Art dir. Boys and Girls Club, Wichita Falls, 1986—91. Vol. Red Cross, 2005. Baptist. Avocation: quilting. Office: Heidelberg HS Lit Dept PO Box M Heidelberg MS 39439-1012 Business E-Mail: ldewey@eastjasper.k12.ms.us.

DEWEY, PHYLLIS KEEFER, counselor; d. Robert Lloyd Keefer and Alma Adelia Kellogg; m. Ronald David Dewey, June 3, 1967 (div.); children: David Kevin, Christen Anne Dewey Johnson. AA in Social Sci., Erie C.C., 1993; BA, SUNY, Fredonia, 1996; MS in Edn., St. Bonaventure U., 1998. Mgr. Office of Robert J. Meisner, DDS, East Aurora, NY, 1982—85; owner, mgr. Dewey Real Estate Property, Titusville, Pa., 1988—95; mental health therapist Christian Counseling Ministries, West Seneca, NY, 1998—2001; dir. counseling Hilberg Coll., Hamburg, NY, 1999—; mental health therapist, owner Counseling Ctr., Hamburg, 2003—. Spkr. in field. Mem.: Alpha Delta Phi (sec. 1992—93). Office: Counseling Ctr 4250 Southwestern Blvd Hamburg NY 14075

DE WITT, JEANETTE MARIE, physical therapist; d. Dale Frederick and Joan Carol Brandt; m. Joel Eric De Witt, Aug. 6, 2005. BS, Xavier U., Cin., 1996; M.Phys. Therapy, Allegheny U., Phila., 1998. Cert. athletic trainer, core control cert. instr. Phys. therapist TriHealth Pavilion, Cin., 1998—2003, TriHealth Summit Woods, Cin., 2003—05, phys. therapist, supr., 2006—. Adj. prof. Coll. Mt. St. Joseph, Cin., 2003, Xavier U., Cin., 2005—; cons. in field; lead phys. therapist TriHealth-Xavier U. Sportsmedicine, Cin., 2003—. Mem.: Am. Phys. Therapy Assn., Nat. Athletic Trainers Assn. Avocations: running, kayaking, reading, Bible study. Office: TriHealth Physical Therapy at Summit Woods 508 E Business Way Cincinnati OH 45241

DEWITT, KATHARINE CRAMER, museum administrator; BA, Manhattenville Coll. of Sacred Heart. Docent Cin. Art Mus. Co-chair Presdl. Inaugural Com., 2001; mem. Nat. Coun. Arts., Nat. Endowment for Arts, 2002—. Trustee Cin. Children's Hosp. Med. Ctr., Beechwood Home, Stratford Hall Plantation, Va.; co-chmn. Cin. Antiques Festival, 1990, Garden Club of Am., 1995—97. Mem.: Cin. Fine Arts Fund (co-chmn. Individual Gifts 1985, 1993, mem. Allocation Com. 1991—94). Office: Cin Art Mus 953 Eden Park Dr Cincinnati OH 45202 Mailing: Nat Endowment for Arts 1100 Pennsylvania Ave NW Washington DC 20506 Office Phone: 513-721-2787.*

DEWITT, MARY THERESE, forensic specialist, anthropologist, archaeologist, consultant; b. Chgo., Aug. 25, 1948; d. Robert Baldwin and Helen (Rossman) DeW. BA in Anthropology, U. Tex., Arlington, 1995, MA in Interdisciplinary Studies, 1997. Dir. mktg. Homart Devel. Co., Florence, Ky., 1975—76, Melvin Simon & Assocs., Inc., Hurst, Tex., 1976-79; pres. Mary DeWitt Co., Ft. Worth, 1979-85; v.p. mktg. Southmark Comml. Mgmt., Dallas, 1986-87; prin. DeWitt Group and subs. Cat's-Eye Intelligence Svc., Dallas and Ft. Worth, 1988-98; coord. program advisement U. N.Mex., Albuquerque, 1998—. Cons. logistics and documentation one team Internat. Group for Hist. Aircraft Recovery, The Phoenix Group South Pacific, 1989; mem. hist. survey and exhumation team Smithsonian and U. Tex., Giddings, Tex., 1998. Recipient Student Svcs. award, U. N.Mex., 2006. Mem. Am. Coll. of Forensic Examiners, Archaeol. Inst. of Am., Internat. Assn. for Identification, Am. Assn. of Phys. Anthropologists, Nat. Academic Advising Assn., N.Mex. Academic Advising Assn., Lambda Alpha (v.p. 1994-97), Alpha Phi Omega (staff advisor). Home: 612 6th St SW Albuquerque NM 87102-3808 Business E-Mail: mdewitt@unm.edu.

DEWITT-MORETTE, CÉCILE, physicist; b. Paris, Dec. 21, 1922; came to U.S., 1948; d. André and Marie Louise (Ravaudet) Morette; m. Bryce S. DeWitt, Apr. 26, 1951; children: Nicolette, Jan, Chris, Abigail. BS, U. Caen, 1943; PhD, U. Paris, 1947. With Centre Nat. de la Recherche Sci., 1944-65, Maitre de Confs. prof., 1965-88. Mem. Inst. Advanced Studies, Dublin, 1946—47, Copenhagen, 1947—48, Princeton, 1948—50; lectr. U. Calif., Berkeley, 1952—55, U. N.C., Chapel Hill, 1956—71; prof. U. Tex., 1972—93, Jane and Roland Blumberg Centennial prof. physics, 1993—2000, prof. emeritus, 2000—; founder, dir. Ecole d'ete de Physique Theorique, Les Houches, France, 1951—72. Author: Particules Elementaires, 1951, (with Y. Choquet-Bruhat and M. Dillard-Bleick) Analysis, Manifolds and Physics, 1977, rev. edit., 1982, 1996, (with A. Maheshwari, B. Nelson) Path Integration in Non Relativistic Quantum Mechanics, 1979, (with Y. Choquet Bruhat) Analysis, Manifolds and Physics, Part II, 92 Applications, 1989, rev. edit., 2000, (with P. Cartier) Functional Integration, Action and Symmetries, 2006, also articles. Decorated chevalier Ordre Nat. du Mërite, chevalier Ordre des Palmes Acadēmiques; chevalier Ordre Nat. Legion d'Honneur; Rask-Oersted fellow, 1947-48, Prix des Sciences Physiques et Mathematiques (Comite du Rayonnement Français, 1992); recipient (with Bryce DeWitt) Marcel Grossman award, 2000. Fellow Am. Phys. Soc.; mem. Internat. Astron. Union, European Phys. Soc., Inst. Hautes Etudes Scientific (trustee), French Soc. Physics (Membre d'honneur). Home: 2411 Vista Ln Austin TX 78703-2343 Office: U Tex Austin Dept Physics 1 University Station C1600 Austin TX 78712-0268 Office Phone: 512-471-1052. E-mail: cdewitt@physics.utexas.edu.

DEWOLF, JANE EVANS, mathematics educator; d. Franklin J. and Dorothea C. Evans; m. Dennis Keith DeWolf, July 9, 1966; children: Jennifer Jane Steelmon, Wendy Anne Albano, Dennis Keith Jr. BS in Edn., U. Fla., Gainesville, 1996; MA in Edn., Western Carolina U., Cullowhee. Cert. tchr. Nat. Bd. Edn., 2002. Tchr. math. Rockway Jr. H.S., Miami, 1966—71, Highlands Sch., NC, 1976—. Home: PO Box 1296 Highlands NC 28741 Office: Highlands Sch 545 School St Highlands NC 28741 Office Phone: 828-526-2147. Business E-Mail: jane.dewolf@mcsk-12.org.

DEWOLFE, MARTHA, singer, songwriter, publisher, producer; b. Arlington, Tex., Nov. 30, 1959; d. Homer C. and Grace R. DeWolfe. Student, N. Tex. State U., 1978-79, Larimer County Vocat.-Tech., Ft. Collins, Colo., 1983; cert. peace officer, Tarrant County Jr. Coll., Euless, Tex., 1984; student, North Ctrl. Tex. Coun. Govts., 1984-94, Southwestern Law Enforcement Sch. of Police Supervision. Police officer Grand Prairie (Tex.) Police Dept., 1984-94, sgt., 1989-94, supr. crime prevention unit, 1991-92. Mem. Police Employee Rels. Bd., 1990-91; BMI assoc.; established Maui Records, 1992, Midnight Tiger Music, BMI, 1994. Albums include That Flame Keeps Burning, 1992, Take Good Care of My Heart, 1995, Mama Look, 1997; songs include Adrianna, Worse Than Being Lonely, All the Blue, Patsy Come Home, River of Tears, Take Good Care of My Heart, Once a Year, The Drought; acting credits include Paramount's "Denton County Massacre", 1993, and commercials; lead singer Wildcat Canyon Band, 1997—. Sec. Grand Prairie Police Assn., 1985-86. Recipient 1st place Tex. Comml. Art Skill Speed Competition, 1977-78. Mem. Fraternal Order Police, Grand Prairie Police Assn., Tex. Assn. Vet. Police Officers, Country Music Assn., Broadcast Music Internat., Nashville Songwriter's Assn. Internat., No. Calif. Songwriters Assn., Mensa. Avocations: flying, photography. Home: PO Box 266 Martinez CA 94553-0026

DEWOLFE, SUSAN, elementary school educator; b. Beaumont, Tex., Sept. 20, 1948; d. James Borden and Emma Pearl (Gruben) Aubritton; m. Carl Hill DeWolfe, Sept. 15, 1977; children: Katheryn Ann, Elizabeth Susan; m. John Charles Scheifley (div.); children: Steven Lane Scheifley, Brian Allen Scheifley. BS, Lamar U., Tex., 1971. Cert. secondary edn. grades 6-12 Lamar U., 1975. Caseworker Tex. Dept. Pub. Welfare, Angleton, 1976—82; cmty. devel. specialist Tex. Dept. Pub. Welfare, Dept. Human Resources, Protective and Regulatory Svcs., Victoria, 1982—94; permanency planning convener Tex. Protective and Regulatory Svcs., Victoria, 1994—96, case mgr. Houston, 1996—99, CPS supr. Galveston, 1999—2001; sub. tchr. Pearland (Tex.) Ind. Sch. Dist., 2001—. Founding bd. mem. Tex. Coalition Prevention of Child Abuse, Victoria, 1983—86; featured spkr. Govs. Vol. Conf. on Volunteerism, Victoria, Tex., 1980. Contbg. author: Our Fathers Who Art in Heaven, 2006. Founding bd. chair Habitat for Humaity, Victoria, Tex., 1987—88; bd. mem. Victoria (Tex.) Cmty. Theatre, 1980; adv. bd. mem. Food Bank of Victoria (Tex.), 1980. Recipient Svc. to People of Tex. award, Govs. Office, 1985. Avocations: writing, quilting, needlepoint.

DEWOODY, BETH RUDIN, film producer; b. NYC; d. Lewis Rudin; m. Jim DeWoody (div.); children: Carlton, Kyle. Studied Anthropology & Film Studies, U. Calif. Santa Barbara; BA, New Sch. Social Rsch. Pres. May & Samuel Rudin Found. Inc.; exec. v.p. Rudin Mgmt. Co.; contbg. editor Hampton's Cottages & Garden's Mag. Dir.(asst. dir.): (TV series) Born Free; prodn. asst. Annie Hall, The Front, Hair, co-prodr. Enter Juliet. Bd. dir. Creative Time Inc., Whitney Mus. Am. Art, Bklyn. Mus. Am. Art, New Sch. U.; bd. adv. Eos Music Inc. Mailing: Whitney Mus Am Art 945 Madison Ave New York NY 10021*

DEWOSKIN, MARGARET FOGARTY, real estate company executive; Grad., U. Wis. With Hilco Real Estate LLC; v.p. acquisitions Klaff Realty L.P.; exec. v.p. Builders Bank, Chgo.; trans. coord. Orix Real Estate Capital, Inc., Chgo., 2004, sr. v.p., COO. Chair real estate capital investment com. Orix Real Estate Capital, Inc. Named one of Top 40 Under 40, Crain's Chgo. Bus., 2006. Mem.: Wis. Real Estate Alumni Assn. Office: Orix Real Estate Capital Inc 100 N Riverside Plz Ste 1400 Chicago IL 60606 E-mail: margaret.dewoskin@orix.com.*

DEWULF NICKELL, KAROL, editor-in-chief; m. Don Nickell; children: Lauren, Alexander. BA in Journalism, Iowa St. U. Furnishings editor Better Homes and Gardens mag., 1979—87, editor-in-chief, 2001—, Traditional Home mag., 1987—2001, Renovation Style mag., 1995—2000; columnist Country Home mag., 1987—2001. Avocations: gardening, reading, cooking. Office: 1716 Locust St Des Moines IA 50309-3023

DEXTER, CAROL N., mathematics educator; d. Marvin J. and Barbara T. Dexter. BA, Hartwick Coll., Oneonta, N.Y., 1970. Math. tchr. Fulton Jr. H.S., NY, 1971—. Bd. dirs. Friends of History, Fulton, 1978—2006; sec., treas. Upstage Prodns., Fulton, 1998—2006; treas. Friends of Voorhees Pk., Fulton, 2002—06; elder First United Ch., Fulton, 2005—06. Named Tchr. of Yr., Greater Fulton C. of C., 2002—03; recipient Golden Apple, Fulton Tchrs. Assn., 1996. Mem.: Assn. Math. Tchrs. N.Y. State, N.Y. State United Tchrs. (Cmty. Svc. Vol. award 2006). Office: Fulton Jr High Sch 129 Curtis St Fulton NY 13069 Office Phone: 315-593-5440.

DEXTER, DEIRDRE O'NEIL ELIZABETH, lawyer; b. Stillwater, Okla., Apr. 15, 1956; d. Robert N. and Paula E. (Robinson) Maddox; m. Terry E. Dexter, May 14, 1977; children: Daniel M. II, David Maddox. Student, Okla. State U., 1974-77; BS cum laude, Phillips U., 1981; JD with highest honors, U. Okla., 1984. Bar: Okla. 1984, U.S. Dist. Ct. (no. and ea. dists.) Okla. 1985, U.S. Dist. Ct. (we. dist.) Okla. 1987, U.S. Ct. Appeals (10th cir.) 1987; grad. Nat. Inst. Trial Advocacy Advanced Trial seminar. Jud. intern Supreme Ct. Okla., Oklahoma City, summer 1983; assoc. Conner & Winters, Tulsa, 1984-90, ptnr., 1991, shareholder, 1991-2000; mem. dist. judge Tulsa County Dist. Ct., 2000—03; mem. Frederic Dorwart, Lawyers, Tulsa, 2003—. Article editor Okla. U. Law Rev., 1982-84. U. Okla. scholar, 1983. Mem. Okla. Bar Assn. (advising atty. state champion H.S. mock trial team competition 1992), Tulsa County Bar Assn. (bd. dir., budget chair), Order of Barristers, Order of Coif, Am. Inns of Ct. (master emeritus), Delta Theta Phi. Republican. Baptist. Office: Old City Hall 124 E 4th St Tulsa OK 74103 Office Phone: 918-583-9901. Business E-Mail: ddexter@fdlaw.com.

DEXTER, HELEN LOUISE, dermatologist, consultant; b. Cin., July 28, 1908; d. William Jordan and Katharine (Weston) Taylor; m. Morrie W. Dexter, Jan. 27, 1937; children: Katharine, Helen Dexter Dalzell, Elizabeth Taylor, William Taylor. AB, Bryn Mawr Coll., 1930; MD, Columbia U., 1937; postgrad., U. Cin., 1948-50. Intern Jersey City (N.J.) Med. Ctr., 1938-39; internist Cin. Babies Milk Fund Maternal Health Clinic, 1938-45; clinician U. Cin. Med. Sch., 1938-48; lectr. dept. dermatology, 1948-53; practice in medicine specializing in dermatology Clearwater, Fla., 1954—. Dermatology cons. VA, 1955—; investigation of carcinogenic effects of shale oil U.S. Bur.

Mines, Rifle, Colo., 1950. Contbr. articles to profl. jours. Mem. Clearwater Power Squadron Aux.; commr. Town of Belleair, 1980. Recipient Ina Clay trophy Intercollegiate Ski Champion, 1928-30. Mem. AMA, Soc. Investigation Deramtology, Am. Acad. Dermatology, S.E. Dermatol. Assn. (v.p. 1963-65), Fla. Dermatol. Soc., Pan-Am. Dermatol. Soc., Am. Archaeol. Soc., Soc. Tropical Dermatology, Clearwater Yacht Carioue1 Yacht. Presbyterian. Address: 409 Bayview Dr Belleair FL 33756-1409

DEY, CAROL RUTH, secondary school educator; b. N.Y.C., Mar. 9, 1943; d. Robert Lewis Adelson and Anne Millman Adelson Bedell; m. John Peter Dey, Feb. 9, 1968 (div. Feb. 1978). AA, San Bernardino Valley Coll., 1965; BA, Calif. State U., Sacramento, 1969; MBA, Calif. State U., San Bernardino, 1983, postgrad., 1994-95. Sec. U.S. Dept of Interior, USAF, Retail Industry, San Bernardino, Sacramento, Calif., 1960-80; logistics mgr. USAF, San Bernardino, 1980—93; substitute tchr. San Bernardino Unified Sch. Dist., 1994—, Inland Empire Job Corp. Ctr., 1997—. Dancer Coppélia, San Bernardino, Calif., 1984; mem. St. Anne's Ch., San Bernardino, 1978—. Mem. Am. Bus. Women's Assn. (Calif. State Coll. scholar), Smithsonian Inst., AF Assn., Alumni Assn. Calif. State U. San Bernardino. Republican. Roman Catholic. Avocations: ballet, piano, sewing, cooking, singing.

DEY, CHARLOTTE JANE, retired community health nurse; b. Benson, Minn., Dec. 14, 1927; d. Elmer Ellsworth and Charlotte Iona (Eastman) Bowers; m. Thomas A. Dey, June 25, 1948 (dec. Mar. 1973); children: Thomas A. Jr., Scott E. (dec.). Grad., St. Luke's Hosp. Sch. Nursing, 1948; student, Kansas City (Kans.) Jr. Coll., 1968; BS in Nursing with distinction, U. Kans., 1970; MPA, U. Mo., Kansas City, 1975. RN, Mo.; ordained deacon, Episcopal Ch., 1993. Head nurse communicable disease ward St. Luke's Children's Hosp., Kansas City, Mo., 1948-49; head nurse newborn nursery Providence Hosp., Kansas City, Kans., 1949-51; pub. health nurse Johnson County Health Dept., Olathe, Kans., 1951-52, 66-68, pub. health nurse, supr., 1970-72; evening supr. Olathe Community Hosp., 1953-55; office nurse B. Albert Lieberman, Jr., MD, Kansas City, Mo., 1960-66; coord. clin. confs. ANA, Kansas City, 1973-76; chief Bur. Community Health Nursing Mo. Dept. Health, Jefferson City, 1976-93; ret., 1993. Sem. expert panel to review and update criteria to estimate future requirements for nursing pers. div. nursing Dept. Health and Human Svcs., 1984, mem. nat. adv. coun. nursing edn. and practice div. nursing, 1998-2002; chair Mid-Am. Community Health Nursing Leadership Group. Recipient award of merit Assn. State and Territorial Dirs. Nursing, 1992. Mem. ANA (cert. nursing adminstrn. advanced, chairperson exec. com. coun. community health nursing 1989-92), APHA, Nat. League Nursing, Nat. Perinatal Assn., Am. Acad. Health Adminstrn. (pres. Mo. chpt. 1980-82), Mo. State Nurses Assn. (coun. nursing svc. facilitors exec. com. 1983-92), Mo. Pub. Health Assn., Mo. League Nursing, Mo. Perinatal Assn., Kans. State Nurses' Assn. (vice chairperson community health conf. group), Kans. Pub. Health Assn. (legislative com.), Sigma Theta Tau. Mem. Episcopal Ch. Home: 8090 Granite Falls Ct Redmond OR 97756-7389 Personal E-mail: janedey@bendcable.com.

DE ZAFRA ATWELL, DOROTHEA ELIZABETH, retired government agency administrator; b. Rochester, N.Y., Apr. 8, 1942; d. Carlos de Zafra, Jr. and Dorothea Schwartz (Michelsen) de Zafra; m. Wilbur Munroe Atwell, Aug. 11, 2001. BA magna cum laude in Non-Western Civilizations, U. Rochester, N.Y., 1963; M of Pub. and Internat. Affairs, U. Pitts., 1965; diploma in info. resources mgmt., Nat. Def. Univ., Washington, 1994. New Eng. regional exec. World Univ. Svc., N.Y.C., 1965—67; study abroad program asst. CUNY, Queens, 1967—69; mgmt. intern, legis. analyst USPHS, Rockville, Md., 1969—74, privacy act officer, health agys. info. practices analyst, 1974—84, info. sys. security program mgr., 1984—95; sci. edn. program dir. NIH, Nat. Inst. Alcohol Abuse and Alcoholism, Bethesda, Md., 1995—2002; ret. Workgroup chair, author Info. Tech. Security Tng. Regulations: A Role and Performance-Based Model, 1998; archaeology cons., guest instr. gifted and talented enrichment Alexandria City Schs.; mem. diversity coun. NIH; EEO counselor USPHS. Mem. adv. coun. U. Pitts. Alumni Assn. and Internat. Alumni Liason, 2004—06; excavation vol. Alexandria Archaeology, Va., 1990—91, Earthwatch, Nev., 1974, Honduras, 1985—86. Named Fed. 100 award, Fed. Computer Week mag., 1995; recipient Vol. Svc. award, Grad. Sch. Pub. and Internat. Affairs, U. Pitts., 2006, EEO Spl. Achievement award, Nat. Inst. Alcohol Abuse and Alcoholism, 1998, Exemplary Svc. award, Office of Asst. Sec. for Health, U.S. Dept. Health and Human Svcs., 1994, Spl. Recognition award, 1982. Mem.: Computer Security Program Mgrs. Forum (exec. bd. dirs. 1990—93), Fed. Info. Sys. Security Educators Assn. (v.p., pres. 1987—94, Educator of Yr. 1998), Am. Soc. Access Profls. (exec. bd. dirs. 1978—82, editor newsletter), Mensa, Red Hat Soc., Phi Beta Kappa. Democrat. Unitarian Universalist. Avocations: archaeology, history and current events, educational travel. Home: 2020 Cradock St Silver Spring MD 20905

DE ZEGHER, CATHERINE, museum director, curator; b. 1955; Co-founder Kanaal Art Found., Kortrijk, Belgium, 1985, dir., 1987—2000; visiting curator Inst. of Contemporary Art, Boston, 1995—97; exec. dir. Drawing Center, NYC, 2000—06. Lecturer U. of Leeds, Royal Coll. of Art, London, U. of London. Author: Inside the Visible: An Elliptical Traverse of Twentieth Century Art, in, of, and from the Feminine, 1996, The Precarious: Art and Poetry of Cecilia Vicuna and Quipoem, 1997, Mona Hatoum, 1997, Martha Rosler: Rights of Passage, 1997.*

D'HAITI, FELICIA KATHLEEN (FELICIA KATHLEEN MESSINA), fine arts educator; BA, Georgetown U., 1991; MA, Rutgers U., 1995. Cert. Advanced Profl. Md. State Bd. of Edn., nat. bd. cert. tchr. art/early adolescence through young adulthood. Edn. program specialist Smithsonian Office of Edn., Washington, 1995—97; contractor Smithsonian Mag., Washington, 1997—98; fine arts tchr. Prince George's County Pub. Schools, Forestville, Md., 1999—. Recipient Armed Forces Comm. and Electronics Ednl. award, Dept. Def., 1987, Smithsonian Instn. award, 1996, Letter of Commendation, Andrew Jackson Mid. Sch., 2000, 2001; Georgetown U. grantee, 1987-1991, Md. State scholar, 1989, Ralph J. Bunche fellow, Rutgers U., 1992-1994, Trustees fellow, 1994-1995, U. Md. Student Support grantee, 1997-1999, Fulbright Meml. Fund Tchr. Program scholar, 2002. Mem.: ASCD, NEA, Am. Assn. Museums, Am. Ednl. Rsch. Assn., Prince George's County Educators Assn., Md. State Tchrs. Assn., Nat. Art Edn. Assn., Alpha Delta Kappa, Phi Delta Kappa. Independent. Roman Catholic. Avocations: travel, piano, museums, theater. Personal E-mail: fkmdhaiti@aol.com. E-mail: felicia.dhaiti@pgcps.org.

D'HARNONCOURT, ANNE, museum director, museum administrator; m. Joseph J. Rishel, June 19, 1971. BA, Radcliffe Coll., 1965; MA with distinction, Courtauld Inst. Art, U. London, 1967. Curatorial asst. Phila. Mus. Art, 1967-69; asst. curator 20th Century art Art Inst. Chgo., 1969-71; curator 20th Century art Phila. Mus. Art, 1971-82, George D. Widener dir., 1982—. Mem. mus. panel NEA, 1976-78, mem. indemnity panel, 1985-88, mem. mus. program overview panel, 1986-87; mem. Indo-U.S. Subcommn. Edn. and Culture, 1983-87; bd. advs. Ctr. Advanced Study in the Visual Arts Nat. Gallery Art, 1987-89. Organizer: (with McShine) exhbn. Marcel Duchamp, 1973-74, (with others) Philadelphia: Three Centuries of American Art, 1976, Eight Artists, 1978, (with Percy) Violet Oakley, 1979, Futurism and the International Avant-Garde, 1980, (with Sims) John Cage: Scores and Prints, 1982; author: (with Walter Hopps) Etant Donnes. Reflections on a New Work by Marcel Duchamp, 1969, The Cubist Cockatoo: Preliminary Exploration of Joseph Cornell's Hommages to Juan Gris, 1978, John Cage: Paying Attention, 1993, also prefaces for various books. Bd. dirs. Henry Luce Found., Inc., N.Y.C.; trustee Fairmount Park Art Assn. Phila., Georgia O'Keeffe Found.; bd. trustees Japan Soc. N.Y.C.; bd. regents Smithsonian Instn. Fellow AAAS; mem. Am. Philos. Soc., Pa. Coun. Arts, 1992-99, Assn. Art Mus. Dirs. Office: Phila Mus Art Benjamin Franklin Pkwy & 26th St PO Box 7646 Philadelphia PA 19130 Office Phone: 215-684-7701.

DHILLON, JANET L., lawyer; Grad., Occidental Coll., 1984, UCLA, 1991. With Skadden, Arps, Slate, Meagher & Flom LLP, Washington; mng. dir. legal dept. U.S. Airways Group, Inc., Tempe, Ariz., 2004—05, dep. gen. council, 2005—06, sr. v.p., gen. counsel, 2006—. Recipient Order of Coif. Office: US Airways Group Inc 111 W Rio Salado Pkwy Tempe AZ 85281*

DHUE, STEPHANIE, television producer, reporter; BA in Comm., George Mason U. Prodr. The Insiders with Jack Anderson, Fin. News Network; prodr. CNBC, Ft. Lee, N.J.; sr. prodr., reporter Nightly Bus. Report, Washington. Office: NBR 1325 G St NW Ste 1005 Washington DC 20005-3126 Office Phone: 202-682-9029.

DIAL, TAMARA MINIQUE, secondary school educator; b. Charlotte, N.C., May 26, 1978; d. Freddie and Betty Dial. Degree in Social Studies Edn., Fayetteville State U., NC, 2000; MA in History, U. N.C., Charlotte, N.C., 2005. Tchr. Charlotte Mecklenburg Schs., Davidson, NC, 2000—. Mem.: Delta Sigma Theta. Democrat. Avocations: travel, music, reading, shopping. Personal E-mail: honeyglazed@hotmail.com.

DIAL, TERESA, bank executive; BA in Polit. Sci., Northwestern U.; MA, Grad. Sch. of Credit and Fin. Mgmt., Northwestern U. Various positions including pres. & CEO Wells Fargo Bank, San Francisco, 1973—2001; exec. v.p. Wells Fargo & Co., San Francisco, 1998—2001; chmn. LookSmart, San Francisco, 2004—; head, retail div. Lloyds TSB, London, 2005—. Bd. dirs. Onyx Software, Bellevue, Wash., Pinnacle Systems, Mountain View, Calif., NDCHealth Corp. Bd. mem. San Francisco Asian Art Museum, Community Colleges Found. Named one of 25 Women to Watch, US Banker mag., 2005. Office: Lloyds TSB 25 Gresham St London EC2V 7HN England

DIAMANT, ANITA, writer; b. NYC, June 27, 1951; d. Maurice and Helene Diamant; m. James R. Ball, June 11, 1982; 1 child, Emilia. AB, Washington U., St. Louis, 1973; MA, SUNY, Binghamton, 1975. Sr. staff writer Boston Mag., 1986-88; columnist Boston Globe mag., 1988-95; freelance writer, 1988—; columnist Jewishfamily.com., Boston, 1998-99; commentator WBUR-FM, Boston, 1994-96; contbg. editor Parenting Mag., 1994-95. Author: The New Jewish Wedding, 1985, Living a Jewish Life, 1991, The New Jewish Baby Book, 1994, Bible Baby Names, 1996, Choosing a Jewish Life: A Handbook for People Converting to Judaism and Their Family and Friends, 1997, The Red Tent, 1997, Saying Kaddish: How to Mourn as a Jew, 1998, How to be a Jewish Parent, 2000, Good Harbor, 2001, Pitching My Tent, 2003, The Last Days of Dogtown, 2005; editor: Equal Times, 1977—78; contbr. to profl. publs. and mags. Founder, pres. Mayyim Hayyim Living Waters and Cmty. Mikveh and Edn. Ctr., 2000—. Recipient Book of Yr. award Boston Author's Club, 1998, Significant Jewish Book of Yr. award UAHC Reform Judaism Mag., 1999, Booksense Book of Yr. award, 2001. Jewish. E-mail: anitaweb@aol.com.

DIAMOND, DEBORAH LYNN, psychotherapist; b. Lynn, Mass., Jan. 14, 1950; d. George and Mildred (Slipsky) D. BS, Ind. U., 1972, MS, 1977. Lic. mental health counselor, Mass., R.I. Behavioral clinician IV Reception Diagnostic Ctr., Plainfield, Ind., 1978-81, behavioral clinician III, 1981-83, correctional classification specialist, 1983-85; rsch. asst. Brandeis U., Bridgewater, Mass., 1986-88; psychologist Mass. Treatment Ctr., Bridgewater, Mass., 1987-91, Danvers State Hosp., Hathorne, Mass., 1991-92; asst. unit dir. Mass. Treatment Ctr./JRI, Bridgewater, 1992—98, asst. clinical dir. juvenile svcs., 1998—2004; outpatient adult sex offender counseling The Counseling and Psychotherapy Ctr., 1995—; psychotherapist Whitney Acad., Inc., East Freetown, Mass., 2004—. Mem. Am. Counseling Assn., R.I. Assn. Women in Psychology, Assn. for Treatment Sexual Abusers (clin.). Jewish. Avocations: photography, skiing, camping, bicycling, woodworking. Home: 360 Gibbs Ave # 6 Newport RI 02840-3383

DIAMOND, HEIDI JANICE, marketing professional; b. Washington, Dec. 8, 1958; d. Lawrence David and Vicky (Katz) D. BS, U. Md., 1979; postgrad., Boston U., 1976-78; MBA, Am. U., 1989. Account exec. Abramson Assocs., Washington, 1980-82; account exec., media dir. KMD Media, Arlington, Va., 1982-83; mktg. mgr. Hardee's Food Systems, Annapolis, Md., 1983-84, sr. mktg. mgr., 1984-86; dir. field advt. planning and devel. Erols, Inc., Springfield, Va., 1986, dir. advt., planning and devel., 1986-88, dir. mktg., 1988—; sr. v.p. mktg., creative and bus. develop. The Food Network, 1998—2000, sr. v.p. strategic network planning/develop., 2001; exec. v.p. AMC Networks and Rainbow Media, 2001—02; exec. v.p., pres. TV Martha Stewart Living Omnimedia, NYC, 2002—05, cons., 2005—. Named Washington Woman of Yr. Washington Woman Mag., 1986, 87; recipient Viddies award, 1989. Mem. Women in Advt. and Mktg. (bd. dirs. 1983-86). Democrat. Jewish. Office: Martha Stewart Living Omnimedia Inc 11 W 42nd St New York NY 10036

DIAMOND, HELEN, arbitrator, freelance/self-employed mediator; b. N.Y., Feb. 7, 1925; d. Hyman and Eva (Schechter) Weinstein; m. Jerome A. Glasser (div.); children: Alan, Fredda; m. Sidney Max Diamond, Aug. 1987 (div.). BBA, Coll. City N.Y., 1945; MA, Calif. State Coll., 1958; PhD, U. So. Calif., 1968; JD, We. State U., 1990. Bar: Calif. 1990. Tchr. Baldwin Pk. (Calif.) H.S., 1958—64, Citrus Coll., Azusa, Calif., 1964—87; atty. Barber & Bauermeister, Santa Ana, Calif., 1990—96; pvt. practice arbitrator/mediator Laguna Beach, Calif., 1990—. Mem.: Calif. Women Lawyers (chmn. awards 1995—2005, bd. dir. 1995—2005), Calif. Women in Law, Orange County (Calif.) Women's Lawyers (pres. 2004), Pi Lambda Theta (pres.). Democrat. Jewish. Avocations: dance, bridge.

DIAMOND, JACQLYN E., health counselor; b. Chester, Pa., Jan. 15, 1977; cert. conflict mediator, Temple U., 1997; BA in Social Work, West Chester U., 1998, MS in Counseling and Ednl. Psychology, 2005. Cert. student assistance program counselor Pa., STI and HIV counselor Pa., wilderness first aid Pa. Reproductive health counselor Planned Parenthood, Media, Pa., 1999—; youth engagement liaison, prevention specialist, counselor Holcomb Behavioral Health Sys., Media, Pa., 2005—. Dir. Del. County Youth Connection, Holcomb Behavioral Health Sys., Media, 2005—; spkr. in field. Co-founder, pres. outdoor adventure orgn. West Chester U. Mem.: APA, Pi Gamma Mu (assoc.), Chi Alpha Epsilon (assoc.). Avocations: hiking, running, camping, travel, rock climbing. Home: 513 Williamson Cir Media PA 19063 Office: Holcomb Behavioral Health Sys 126 East Baltimore Ave Media PA 19063 Office Phone: 484-444-0412.

DIAMOND, KAREN WALTZER, small business owner, educator; b. N.Y.C., May 20, 1939; d. Bernard and Blanche (Zwillenberg) Waltzer; m. George N. Diamond, Aug. 20, 1960; children: Gary, Deena, Adam. BA, Am. U., 1961. Cert. phys. fitness specialist. Area dir. Eve Nelson Cosmetics, Washington, 1962-63; owner, creative dir. Karen Diamond Sch. Exercise, Bethesda, Md., 1973-84, Karen Diamond Studio, Washington, 1981-84, Diamond Fitness, Inc., Washington, 1985—; mem. com. Idea Found. for Nat. Cert., San Diego, 1984-85; mem. rev. bd. Music in Motion, Alameda, Calif., 1985-86; mem. Md. Gov.'s Commn. Phys. Fitness and Sports, 1979-83; presenter Nat. Industry Conv., Mind/Body Connection, 1985. Author, performer: (exercise audio cassette) Karen Diamond Fitness, 1976; performer, phys. fitness expert ABC TV, Washington, 1976-79, NBC TV, 1976; contbr. articles and revs. to profl. jours., newspapers and mags. Chmn. dance com. Jewish Community Ctr., Washington, 1968-73, bd. dirs. 1972-75. Fellow Am. Coll. Sports Medicine; mem. Met. Dance Assn., Internat. Dance Exercise Assn., Nat. Assn. Women Bus. Owners, Brandeis Women's Com. Avocations: biking, music, travel, cooking, knitting. Home and Office: 4825 Wellington Dr Chevy Chase MD 20815-6249 Office Phone: 301-656-4440. Personal E-mail: karenwdiamond@comcast.net.

DIAMOND, LINDA MANN, social studies educator; b. Chgo., Nov. 28, 1941; d. John and Irene Watkins Mann; m. Darrough Blain Diamond, Aug. 1, 1964; children: Laura Lynn Stillman, Julia True Cox. BA, U. Ill., 1963, MA, 1967; postgrad., Ohio State U. Cert. secondary social studies edn. Fla. Social studies tchr. Pinellas County Schs., Largo, Fla., 1995—. ProEd facilitator Carwise Mid. Sch., Palm Harbor, Fla. Mem.: PEO, Undertakers Adventure Group, Women Watching Wall St., Alpha Delta Pi. Office: Carwise Mid Sch 3301 Bentley Dr Palm Harbor FL 34684 Office Phone: 727-724-1442. E-mail: darrough.1@verizon.net.

DIAMOND, MARIAN CLEEVES, anatomist, educator; b. Glendale, Calif., Nov. 11, 1926; d. Montague and Rosa Marian (Wamphler) Cleeves; m. Richard M. Diamond, Dec. 20, 1950 (div.); m. Arnold B. Scheibel, Sept. 14, 1982; children: Catherine, Richard, Jeffrey, Ann. AB, U. Calif., Berkeley, 1948, MA, 1949, PhD, 1953. With Harvard U., Cambridge, 1952-54, Cornell U., Ithaca, NY, 1954-58, U. Calif., San Francisco, 1959—62, prof. anatomy Berkeley, 1962—. Asst. dean U. Calif., Berkeley, 1967-70, assoc. dean, 1970-73, dir. The Lawrence Hall of Sci., 1990-95, dir. emeritus, 1995—; vis. scholar Australian Nat. U., 1978, Fudan U., Shanghai, China, 1985, U. Nairobi, Kenya, 1988. Author (with J. Hopson): Magic Trees of the Mind, 1998; author: Enriching Heredity, 1989; co-author: The Human Brain Coloring, 1985; editor: Contraceptive Hormones Estrogen and Human Welfare, 1978; contbr. over 155 articles to profl. jours. V.p. County Women Dems., Ithaca, 1957; bd. dirs. Unitarian Ch., Berkeley, 1969. Recipient Calif. Gifted award, 1989, C.A.S.E. Calif. Prof. of Yr. award, Nat. Gold medalist, 1990, Woman of Yr. award Zonta Internat., 1991, U. medal La. Universidad Del Zulia, Maricaibo, Venezuela, 1992, Alumna of the Yr. award U. Calif., Berkeley, 1995; Calif. Acad. Scis. fellow, 1991, Calif. Soc. Biomedical Rsch. Dist. Svc. award, 1998, Alumnae Resources-Women of Achievement Vision and Excellence award, 1999, Benjamin Ide Wheeler award 1999, Achievement award Calif. Child Devel. Adminstrs. Assn., 2001; named Disting. Scholar America, Am. Assn. U. Women, 1997; named to Internat. Educators Hall of Fame, 1999. Fellow AAAS, AAUW (sr.; fellowship chair 1970-85); mem. Am. Assn. Anatomists, Soc. Neurosci., Philos. Soc. Washington, The Faculty Club (Berkeley, v.p. 1979-85, 90-95). Avocations: hiking, sports, painting. Home: 2583 Virginia St Berkeley CA 94709-1108 Office: U Calif Dept Integrative Biology 3060 Valley Life Sciences Bldg Berkeley CA 94720-3116 Office Phone: 510-642-4547. Business E-Mail: diamond@berkeley.edu.

DIAMOND, MARY E(LIZABETH) B(ALDWIN), artist; b. Detroit, Sept. 2, 1951; d. Harold Barber and Evelyn (Glenn) Weaver; m. David Baldwin III, June 24, 1972 (div. Nov. 1982); 1 child, David Damar; m. Robert Proctor Diamond, Oct. 6, 1986; 1 child, Angelique Krista. Freelance artist, cartoonist, photographer Phase II Mag., Detroit, 1981-85; artist Montague Art Galleries Inc., Locust Valley, N.Y., 1989-99; adminstrv. asst., gallery dir. East End Arts and Humanities Coun., Riverhead, N.Y., 1996, 97; gallery dir. East End Arts Coun., Riverhead, 1997. Auditor N.Y. State Coun. on Arts, Huntington, 1995-99, chair decentralization regrant program, Suffolk County, 1999; mem. The Chase Manhattan Smarts Regrant program, Huntington, N.Y., 1999-2001; curator Black History Month exhbn. East Hampton (N.Y.) Artist Alliance, 1999; instr. Parish Art Mus., Southampton, N.Y., 1990-2001; guest spkr. and panelist "African-Am. Artists and Writers", Eastville Hist. Soc., Sag Harbor, N.Y., 1996; guest spkr. L.I. U., Southampton, N.Y., 1995, Jimmy Ernst Artists Alliance, East Hampton, N.Y., 1991, Southampton (N.Y.) Intermediate Sch., 1994, Galerie "Die Treppe", Stuttgart, Germany, "New York, New York" Exhibit, 1995, judge Parrish Art Mus., Southampton, 1993; vis. artist Southampton Adventures in Learning Southampton Elem. Sch., 1996, Adventures in Learning, Southampton Elem. Sch., 1997, internat. exhbn. Galerie "Die Treppe", Reudern, Germany, 1994-97, Salon De Femme Invitational Exbn. Southampton Cultural Ctr., 1997, East End Arts Coun., 1997, Sundance Gallery, Season Opening Invitational Exhbn., 1995, Havre De Grace, Md., 1995, Nat. Jr. Duck Stamp Competition, 1995, Adventures in Learning, Southampton Elem. Sch., 1997-98; bd. dirs. Southampton Cultural and Civic Ctr., 1995; vis. artist Salon at Siena Ctr., Water Hill, N.Y., 1998, What is Kwanzaa, Southampton, 1999, others; guest spkr., presenter, studio tour leader Art Out East, 1997-2001, L.I. Art Tchrs. Assn. Spring Conf., East Hampton, 1997; guest lectr. Studio Tour for Friends of Guild Hall Mus., East Hampton, 1997; judge traveling exhbn. UNICEF, Southampton, 1998; judge Southampton artists student exhbn., N.Y., 2001. Exhbns. include Sundance Gallery, Season Opening Invitational Exhbn., Bridgehampton, N.Y., 1996, Southampton Cultural Ctr., 1995, Clayton & Liberatore Gallery 75th Anniversary Invitational Exhbn., Bridgehampton, N.Y., 1995, Landscape Today; East End Views Guild Hall Mus., East Hampton, N.Y., 1994, 39th Ann. L.I. Artists Juried Exhbn., Hecksher Mus., Huntington, N.Y., 1994, Landscape Observed, Landscape Transformed, Islip Art Mus., East Islip, N.Y., 1992, Nat. League Am. Pen Women, 12th Juried Exhibit, Vanderbilt Mus., Centerport, N.Y., 1992, Art Assn. Harrisburg (Pa.) 66th Ann. Exhibit, 1994, Southampton Cultural Ctr., 1997, Simply Art Gallery, Bklyn., 1997-2001, Shifflett Gallery, L.A., 1999-2001; 2d Place award in oil painting Mather Meml. Hosp. Juried Auction, 1997, 1st Place award in oil painting L.I. Artists Open Juried Art Competition, Brookhaven Cultural Ctr., 1995, Hon. mention North Shore Art Guild Ann. Mems. Exhbn., Brookhaven, 1995, Lynn Shifflett Gallery, L.A., 1995-99, 2000, East End Arts Coun., Riverhead, N.Y., 1997, Elaine Benson Gallery, Bridgehampton, N.Y., 1997-99, Jonkonnu Gallery, Sag Harbor, 1998, Image Gallery, Riverhead, N.Y., 1999, L.I. U., Southampton, 2000. Bd. dirs. Cultural and Civic Ctr., Southampton, N.Y., 1995-2001; trustee Colonial Soc. of Southampton Hist. Soc., 1997-99. Named Outstanding Woman of Eastern L.I., Hero award Southampton Ind. Newspaper, 1996; grantee N.Y. Found. for the Arts, 1994; mem. Southampton Hist. Mus., 1997-2000. Mem. Am. Soc. Portrait Artists, East End Arts Coun., Allied Artists of Am., Southampton Artists Assn. (organized life drawing workshop 1989-94, v.p. 1991, pres. 1992, bd. dirs. 1999-2001, mus. liaison 1999), The Onyx Group (founder, treas., pres. 1992-94), The Artists Alliance of East Hampton, North Shore Art Guild, Guild Hall Mus.

DIAMOND, SHARI SEIDMAN, law professor, psychology professor; b. Chgo., Mar. 17, 1947; d. Leon Harry and Rita (Wolff) S.; m. Stewart Howard Diamond, Nov. 1, 1970; 1 child, Nicole. BA in Psychology, Sociology, U. Mich., 1968; MA in Psychology, Northwestern U., 1970, PhD in Social Psychology, 1972; JD with honors, U. Chgo., 1985. Bar: Ill. 1985. Rsch. assoc. Sch. Law U. Chgo., 1972-73; asst. prof. psychology and criminal justice U. Ill., Chgo., 1973-79, assoc. prof., 1979-90, prof., 1990-2000; assoc. Sidley & Austin, Chgo., 1985-87; sr. rsch. fellow ABF, Chgo., 1987—; lectr. U. Chgo. Law Sch., 1994-96; prof. law and psychology Northwestern U., 1999—. Stanton Clinton sr. rsch. prof., 2000-01, Howard J. Trienens prof. law, 2002—. Cons. govtl. and pub. interests groups including Rsch. Adv. Panel for U.S. Sentencing Commn., 1987-91; acad. visitor dept. law London Sch. Econs., 1981; hon. fellow Ctr. for Urban Affairs Northwestern U., Evanston, Ill., 1973-73; hon. rsch. assoc. U. London, 1970; speaker, lectr. in field; mem. NAS panel on sentencing rsch., 1981-83, panel on forensic DNA evidence, 1994-96. Editor Law and Soc. Rev., 1988-91; past mem. editorial bd. Law and Soc. Rev., 1983-88, Law and Human Behavior, Crime and Justice Annual, Evaluation Rev.; reviewer NSF; contbr. articles to profl. jours. Chair Coll. Edn. Policy Com., 1979-80; dir. tng. grant NIMH Crime and Delinquency, 1979-80. Fellow Northwestern U., 1968-69, NIMH, 1969-71; grantee Spencer Found., 1972-74, disting. scholar, grantee, U. Ill., 1995-98, Law Enforcement Assistance Adminstrn., 1974-76, Ctr. for Crime and Delinquency NIMH, 1976-81, NSF, 1980-83, 90-92, 99—; B. Kenneth West U. scholar, 1995-98. Fellow APA (Award for Disting. Contbns. to Rsch. in Pub. Policy 1991), ABA, Am. Psychol. Soc.; mem. Am. Psychology-Law Soc. (pres. 1987-88), Law and Soc. Assn. (trustee 1979-82). Office: Northwestern U Law Sch 357 E Chicago Ave Chicago IL 60611 Business E-Mail: s-diamond@law.northwestern.edu.

DIAMOND, SUSAN ZEE, management consultant; b. Okla., Aug. 20, 1949; d. Louis Edward and Henrietta (Wood) Diamond; m. Allan T. Devitt, July 27, 1974. AB, U. Chgo., 1970; MBA, DePaul U., 1979. Dir. study guide prodn. Am. Sch. Co., Chgo., 1972—75; supr. publs. Allied Van Lines, Broadview, Ill., 1975—78, sr. account svcs. rep., 1978—79; pres. Diamond Assocs. Ltd., Bensenville, Ill., 1978—. Author: Records Management: A Practical Guide, 3d edit., 1995, Seventeen Steps to Slimness: A Sherlockian Guide to Dieting, 2002; editor: The Serpentine Muse, 1996—, Serpentine Muse-ings, 2004, 2005; condr. seminars Am. Mgmt. Assn., —, Can. Mgmt. Ctr., —. Mem.: Inst. Mgmt. Accts., Baker St. Irregulars, Adventuresses of Sherlock Holmes.

DIAMONSTEIN-SPIELVOGEL, BARBARALEE, writer; b. N.Y.C. d. Rubin Robert and Sally H. Simmons; m. Alan A. Diamonstein, July 22, 1956; m. Carl Spielvogel, Oct. 27, 1981. BA, BC, MA, Doctorate, NYU, 1963; DHL (hon.), Md. Inst. Coll. Art, 1990, Longwood U., 1995. Staff asst. The White House, Washington, 1663—1966; 1st dir. dept. cultural affairs City of New York, 1966—67; dir. of forums McCall Corp., 1967—69; editor spl. supplements, columnist Harper's Bazaar, 1969—71; spl. project dir., guest editor Art News, 1971—93. Columnist Ladies Home Jour., 1979-84; contbr. to Saturday Rev., Vogue, Ms., Partisan Rev., N.Y. Times, Condé Nast, Traveller, House and Garden, others; mem. faculty Hunter Coll., City U. N.Y., 1974-76, New Sch., 1976-84, Duke U. (Inst. Policy Sci.), 1978; arts cons. Sunday Morning CBS-TV, 1978-82; curator Buildings Reborn, Collaborations, Visions and Images, Remaking America, The Landmarks of N.Y. I, II, and III (internat. travelling museum exhibitions.), 1978—, and numerous others. Author: Open Secrets: 94 Women in Touch With Our Time, 1972; editor: Our 200 Years: Tradition and Renewal, 1975; TV interviewer, prodr. About the Arts, WNYC-TV, 1975—79; author: The World of Art, 1902-77, 75 Years of Art News, 1977; Leo Castelli Gallery, 1978; author: Buildings Reborn: New Uses, Old Places, 1978, Inside New York's Art World, 1979; editor: MOMA at 50, 1980; TV interviewer, prodr. ABC-TV Arts, 1980—88, A and E Network, 1980—89; author: Collaboration: Artists and Architects, 1981, Visions and Images: Am. Photographers on Photography, 1981, Interior Design: The New Freedom, 1982, Handmade in Am., 1983; Leo Castelli Gallery, 1984; author: Fashion: The Inside Story, 1985, Am. Architecture Now, 1985, Remaking Am., 1986; Leo Castelli Gallery, 1988; author: The Landmarks of N.Y., 1988, 18 Wonders of the N.Y. World, 1992, The Landmarks of N.Y.: Vol. II, 1993, The Landmarks of N.Y., The Municipal Art Society, 2005; Leo Castelli Gallery, 1994; author: Inside the Art World: Conversations with Barbaralee Diamonstein, 1994, Skills, Values, Dreams, 1995, Singular Voices: Americans Who Make a Difference, 1997, The Landmarks of N. Y.: Vol. III, 1998, Barbaralee's Rules of the Rd.: 59 Simple Ways to Cope with a Complex World, 2001, The Landmarks of New York: An Illustrated Record of the City's Historic Buildings, 2005, The Landmarks of New York, 2006. Nat. juror Vietnam Vet. Meml. Edn. Ctr. Competition, 2004; juror High Line Competition, 2004; bd. advisors Film Anthology Archives, 1969—; mem. Caramoor Ctr. for Music and Arts, 1981—92; Commr. N.Y.C. Landmarks Preservation Commn., 1972—87, N.Y.C. Cultural Commn., 1975—86; vice-chmn. N.Y. Landmarks Conservancy, 1983—87; mem. Pres. coun. Rockefeller U., 1987—; bd. visitors Pub. Policy Inst. Duke U., Durham, NC, 1987—93; mem. U.S. Holocaust Meml. Mus., 1987—93; chmn. N.Y. Landmarks Preservation Found., 1987—95; chair art pub. spaces com. Holocaust Mus., 1987—96; mem. drawing com. Met. Mus. Art, 1990—; Commr. N.Y.C. Arts Commn., 1991—94; trustee Ctrl. Pk. Conservancy, 1993—95; bd. trustee N.Y. Hist. Soc., 1993—95; mem. drawing com. Whitney Mus. Am. Art, 1995—98; mem. U.S. Commn. Fine Arts, 1996—2005; bd. trustees Mus. of Women, the Leadership Ctr., N.Y.C., 1999—; co-chair NGO Assn. Culture Edn. and Comm., 2001—; vice chmn. U.S. Commn. Fine Arts, 2001—02; mem. N.Y. State Travel and Tourism Bd., Caramoor Ctr. for Music and Arts, 1981—92; bd. dir. PEN Am. Ctr., 1980—96, Mcpl. Art Soc., 1973—83, Am. Coun. Arts, 1982—89, N.Y.C. Bicentennial Commn., 1973—77, Bklyn. Acad. Music, 1969—74, N.Y. Landmarks Conservancy, 1973—97, Fresh Air Fund, 1983—, Big Apple Circus, 1989—92, Corcoran Gallery Art, Washington, 1992—99, N.Y. State Hist. Archive's Partnership Trust, 1994—, Whitney Mus. Am. Art, 1995—98, White House Endowment Fund, 1995—98, Friends of the High Line, 2001—; chair Hist. Landmarks Preservation Ctr., 1995—, Nat. Competition for Low Cost Housing, N.Y.C., 2004; mem. Caramoor Ctr. for Music and Arts, 1981—92. Recipient Founder's Day award Pratt Inst., 1994, Outstanding Citizen award Citizen Ctr., 1996, Visionary in Arts award, Mus. Contemporary Crafts, 1996, Heritage Trails award, 1998, Spirit of the City award Women's City Club, 1998, Manhattan award, 1999, New Millenium Humanitarian award HELP, 1999, Gen. Milan R. Stefanik award Slovak Am. Cultural Ctr., 2002, Aging in Am. Humanitarian award, 2003, Gold medal of the Ministry of Fgn. Affairs of Slovakia, 2004, Humanitarian award Jewish Women's Found. N.Y., 2005. Mem.: Nat. Am. Inst. Architects (hon.). Home: 720 Park Ave New York NY 10021-4954

DIANGELO, LINDA MARY, secondary school educator, theater director; d. Frank D. and Frances E. Krenslak; m. Anthony J. DiAngelo, Apr. 7, 1951. Master's, Rowan U., Glassboro, N.J., 2002. Cert. tchr. secondary edn. Glassboro State Coll., 1981. Tchr. Overbrook Regional Sr. HS, Pine Hill, NJ, 1985—2001, Winslow Twp. H.S., Atco, 2001—. Theatre dir. Winslow Twp. H.S., 2001—. Mem.: Internat. Thespian Soc. (sponsor, dir. 1990—2006). Office: Winslow Twp HS 10 Coopers Folly Rd Atco NJ 08004 Office Phone: 856-767-1850. Office Fax: 856-767-5670. Business E-Mail: diangeli@winslow-schools.com.

DIAS, FIONA P., retail executive; m. Floyd Dias. Grad., Harvard U., 1987; MBA, Stanford U. Sr. fin. analyst Merrill Lynch Capital Markets, Inc.; sr. asst. brand mgr. Fixodent and Fasteeth denture adhesives Proctor and Gamble Co., 1996; v.p., corp. develop. Pennzoil Quaker State Co., 1996—99; v.p., mktg. and develop. Frito-Lay Co., 1999—2000; chief mktg. officer Stick Networks, Inc., 2000; sr. v.p., mktg. Circuit City, 2000—05; pres. Circuit City Direct, 2003—; sr. v.p., chief marketing officer Circuit City Stores, Inc., 2005—. Office: Circuit City 9950 Mayland Dr Richmond VA 23233-1464

DIAS, MARI NARDOLILLO, education educator, consultant; b. Providence, July 21, 1952; d. Robert Anthony and Dorothy Ann Nardolillo; m. Raul Dias; children: Lindsay, Adam. BA in Secondary Edn., R.I. Coll., 1974, MA in Vocat. Counseling, 1983; EdD, Johnson & Wales U., 2003—. Cons. Dias & Assocs., N. Kingstown, RI, 1985—; instr. emotional intellingence MotoRing Tech. Tng. Inst., E. Providence, RI, 1995—2000; prof. Johnson & Wales U., Providence, 2000—01; prof. grad. sch. Endicott Coll., Beverly, Maine, 2000—; prof., facilitator Duke U., Durham, NC, 2001. Mentor Feinstein Making a Difference Program, N. Kingstown, 2000—. Actor: (stage play) Talking With, 1996 (Irene Ryan nominee), (musical) The Best Little Whorehouse in Texas, 1996; prodr.: (plays) The Lottery, 1995; dir.: Nicholas Nickelby, 1995, The Monkey's Paw, 1995, James and the Giant Peach, 1997. Patient rep. vol. R.I. Hosp., Providence, 1999—; vol. instr. Odyssey of the Mind; vol. N. Kingstown Sch. Dept. Lights, Camera, Action; vol. performing arts instr. N. Kingstown Recreation Dept.; guest spkr. AIDS Respite Program; vol. cons. R.I. Cambodian Soc.; bd. dirs. St. Mary's Sch., Cranston, RI. Named Outstanding Woman of Yr. in Arts and Edn., Greater Providence YWCA, 2001; recipient Town Hero award, North Kingstown, 1998, Citizen citation, City of Providence, 2001; scholar, Johnson & Wales U., 2000. Mem.: NEA, AAUW (mem. Diversity Task Force, co-author, dir. Reviving the D 1999—, rsch. and projects endowment 2001), Am. Soc. Tng. and Devel., Friends of Oceanography (chair publicity com. 1985—88), Academy Players (bd. dirs. 1992), CCRI Players Club (pres. 1995—96). Avocations: scuba diving, aerobics (cert. instr.), world travel. Personal E-mail: teachdias@home.com. Business E-Mail: MDias@jwu.edu.

DIAS, MICHELE C., primary school educator; b. Ft. Bragg, Calif., Jan. 14, 1949; d. Dana and Jessie Kathryn (Pacini) Coverston; 1 child, Adam Russell. AA, Santa Rosa Jr. Coll., 1970; BA in Spanish, Calif. State U., Sonoma, 1973; clad credential, U. San Diego, 1999. Cert. elem. tchr., Calif. 4th grade tchr. Ft. Bragg Unified Sch. Dist., 1973-74, kindergarten bilingual tchr., 1980—; bilingual tchr. Migrant Edn. Summer Sch., Ft. Bragg, 1988-98. Dist. rep. Nat. Bilingual Edn. Conf., L.A., 1994. Mem. NEA, Calif. Tchrs. Assn., Parents Club (grade level rep. 1999, chair com. 1999). Avocations: music, reading, walking, tutoring, computers. Office: Redwood Elem Sch 324 S Lincoln St Fort Bragg CA 95437-4498

DIAS GRIFFIN, ANNE, investment advisor; MBA, Harvard Bus. Sch.; grad. summa cum laude, Georgetown U. Analyst, Banking Dept. Goldman Sachs; investment analyst Fidelity Investment Ltd., London; analyst & portfolio mgr. Soro Fund Mgmt.; analyst Viking Global Investors; founder, v.p., mng. ptnr. Aragon Global Investors. Trustee Chgo. Symphony Orchestra, Whitney Mus. Am. Art. Named to Top 200 Collectors, ARTnews Mag., 2006. Mailing: c/o Whitney Mus Am Art 945 Madison Ave New York NY 10021*

DIASIO, ILSE WOLFARTSBERGER, volunteer; b. Linz, Austria, Nov. 12, 1946; came to U.S., 1967; d. D.I. Gottfried and Elfriede (Stuchlik) Wolfartsberger; m. Robert B. Diasio, July 4, 1970; children: Christoph, Thomas, Michael. Grad. in Phys. Therapy, U. Vienna, 1967. Phys. therapist Yale-New Haven Hosp., 1968—71, Vis. Nurse Assn., Rochester, NY, 1971—72; symposium coord. dept. pharmacology U. Ala., 1988. Vol. tchr. German, Pemberton Elem. Sch., Richmond, Va., 1980-84, Vestavia Hills Elem. and H.S., 1985-93; organizer student exch. program between Vestavia Hills H.S. and Seebacher Gymnasium, Graz, Austria, 1990, 91, 94. Bd. dirs. Pemberton (Va.) Elem. Sch. PTA, 1979-84, pres., 1982-84; bd. dirs. Va. Commonwealth U. Faculty Woman's Club, 1978-84, Greater Birmingham Ministries, chmn. direct svcs. work group, 1999-2002, Ala. chpt. Fulbright Assn., 1999—; pres. Childrens Svc. League, 1992-93, treas. 1991-92, asst. treas. 1990-91, 2d v.p., rec. sec., 1998-99; vol. Our Lady Queen of the Universe and Sacred Heart of Jesus Cath. Chs., 1988-90; St. Peter's rep. Ala. Arise, diocesan rep., rec. sec., 1988-94; mem. Peace and Justice Commn. of the Cath. Diocese of Birmingham, 1989-95, chair of commn., 1994-95; bd. dirs. Be an Apostle of Christ, vice chair, 2003-06; chair human concerns com. St. Peter's Outreach Commn., 1988-2006; active Direct Svc. Network, 1989—2006, Greater Birmingham Ministries, 1989-2006, treas. Greater Birmingham UNA-USA chpt., 1982-2004, pres., 2005-06, CCD steering com. South Atlantic region rep., 2002—; mem. COMPEER Bd., Birmingham, Ala., 1990-99; active WOC, Call to Action, Bread for the World, CALC, Pax Christi, Amnesty Internat., Nat. Conf. of Cmty. and Justice, Smithsonian Inst., UNICEF, Coalition Against Hate Crimes, 1997—, Birmingham Com. on Fgn. Rels., 1998—; organizer Angel Tree project St. Peter's Cath. Ch., 1988-2006; bd. dirs., sec. World of Opportunity, 2002-06; vol. tchr. for GED preparation. Recipient resolution City of Birmingham, 1999. Mem. AAUW, Nat. Mus. of Women in the Arts, U.S. Holocost Mus., Vereinigung Ehemaliger Körnerschülerinnen, LWV (bd. dirs. Greater Birmingham 1999-2000). Roman Catholic. Avocations: reading, music, skiing, cooking, travel. Home: 1225 Branchwater Ln Birmingham AL 35216-2001 Personal E-mail: idiasio@aol.com.

DIAZ, ANGELA, pediatrician, educator; b. Dominican Republic, Oct. 2, 1954; MD, Columbia Coll. Physicians and Surgeons, 1994. Diplomate Am. Bd. Pediatrics with subspecialty in adolescent medicine. Intern Mt. Sinai Med. Ctr., N.Y.C., 1981—82, resident in pediats., 1982—84, fellow, 1984—85, prof. dept. pediats., 1985—. Mem.: SAM, Am. Acad. Pediats. (Founders of Adolescent Health award 2001). Office: Mount Sinai Med Ctr 320 E 94th St New York NY 10128-5604

DIAZ, ANNE MARIE THERESA, music educator, musician; d. Francis Joseph and Anne Patricia DeMase; m. Carl Anthony Diaz, May 3, 1975 (div. Oct. 2000); children: Christina Bianca Diaz Bailey, Lisa Marie Diaz Gibson. AAS in Music, Onondaga C.C., 1971; student, Carnegie-Mellon U., 1971—73. Sales/mgmt. Bloomingdale's, N.Y.C., 1973—75; owner and designer Sunny Days Creations, Vestal, NY, 1982—85; pvt. tchr. music Seaville, NJ, 1986—90; tchr. spl. edn., art, and music Uppertownship Sch. Sys., Seaville, 1986—90; tchr. music Jennings Music, Marietta, Ga., 1992—96; owner, tchr. music Tchg. Little Fingers to Play, Marietta, 1996—; owner, designer Diadem Creations, 2000—. Musician: Syracuse Civic Light Opera Co., 1970—71, Syracuse Symphony, 1971, Atlanta Wind Symphony, 1998—2000. Pres. Bells Ferry Elem. Sch. PTA, Marietta, 1986—87. Mem.: Music Tchrs. Nat. Assn., Music Educators Nat. Conf., Lexington Home Owners Assn. (pres. 2002—04), Kappa Alpha Theta, Sigma Alpha Iota. Home: 4674 N View Rd Nw Kennesaw GA 30144-1416 Office Phone: 678-982-5141.

DIAZ, CAMERON, actress; b. San Diego, Aug. 30, 1972; d. Emilio and Billie Diaz. Grad. high sch., Long Beach, Calif. Appeared in (films) The Mask, 1994, Feeling Minnesota, 1996, She's the One, 1996, The Last Supper, 1996, Keys to Tulsa, 1996, Head Above Water, 1996, My Best Friend's Wedding, 1997 (Blockbuster Entertainment award), a Life Less Ordinary, 1997, (TV) Space Ghost Coast to Coast, 1994, Very Bad Things, 1998, Fear and Loathing in Las Vegas, 1998, There's Something About Mary (Golden Globe nomination Best Performance by an Actress in a Comedy or Musical Motion Picture), 1998 (N.Y. Film Critics Cir. award, MTV Movie award, Am. Comedy award), Invisible Circus, 1999, Being John Malkovich (Golden Globe nomination Best Supporting Actress in a Motion Picture), 1999, Any Given Sunday, 1999, Charlie's Angels: The Movie, 2000, Things You Can Tell Just by Looking at Her, 2000, Shrek (voice), 2001, Vanilla Sky, 2001, The Sweetest Thing, 2002, Gangs of New York, 2002, Charlie's Angels: Full Throttle, 2003, Shrek 2 (voice), 2004, In Her Shoes, 2005; exec. prodr., host (TV series) Trippin, 2005. Named Female Star of Tomorrow, Nat. Theatre Owners Assn., 1996, Boston Soc. of Film Critics best supporting actress award, 2001, Chicago Film Critics Award for best supporting actress, 2002.

DIAZ, LAURA O., secondary school educator; d. Angel Sanchez and Josephine Rosales Oliva; m. Randolph J. Diaz; children: Cindy Angela, Randolph Matthew. BA, U. Calif., Riverside; MA, U. Redlands, Calif., 2001. Cert. tchr. Calif. Tchr. Colton Joint Unified Sch. Dist., Calif., 1984—95, Redlands Unified Sch. Dist., 1995—. Recipient Tchr. of Year, Redlands Ednl. Partnership, Medal of Honor, Redlands East Valley; Regent scholar, U. Calif., 1978. Mem.: NEA, Nat. Assn. Tchrs. Personal E-mail: lauraodiaz@aol.com.

DIAZ, MARIA G., lawyer; BA, Stanford Univ., 1991; MPP, Harvard Univ., 1994; JD, Stanford Univ. Bar: Calif. Assoc., employment law practice Allred Maroko & Goldberg, LA. Named a Rising Star, So. Calif. Super Lawyers, 2005—06; recipient Wiley W. Manuel award, State Bar Calif., Outstanding Legal Services award, San Diego Volunteer Lawyer Program, Outstanding Service award, US Senator Barbara Boxer; Woodrow Wilson Nat. Fellow. Mem.: Calif. Employment Lawyers Assn., Mexican-Am. Bas Assn. LA, Latina Lawyers Bar Assn. LA, Nat. Employment Lawyers Assn., LA County Bar Assn. Office: Allred Maroko & Goldberg Ste 1500 6300 Wilshire Blvd Los Angeles CA 90048 Office Phone: 323-653-6530. Office Fax: 323-653-1660.*

DIAZ, MARLA J., lawyer; b. Alexandria, Va., Jan. 2, 1975; d. Raymond J. and Elaine M. Diaz. BA in Govt. and Anthropology, Coll. William and Mary, Williamsburg, Va., 1997; JD, Wake Forest U., Winston-Salem, NC, 2001. Bar: Va. 2001, NC 2005. Law clk. Va. Supreme Ct., Richmond, 2001—02; asst. commonwealth atty. City of Norfolk, Va., 2002—04; assoc. Tavss Fletcher, P.C., Norfolk, 2004—. Recipient Buell award, Coll. William and Mary, 1997. Mem.: Va. Beach Bar Assn., Norfolk Portsmouth Bar Assn. Office: Tavss Fletcher PC 555 E Main St 14th Fl Norfolk VA 23510 Office Phone: 757-625-1214. Office Fax: 757-622-7295. Business E-Mail: marla@tavss.com.

DIAZ, SHARON, education administrator; b. Bakersfield, Calif., July 29, 1946; d. Karl C. and Mildred (Lunn) Clark; m. Luis F. Diaz, Oct. 19, 1968; children: Daniel, David. BS, San Jose State U., 1969; MS, U. Calif., San Francisco, 1973; PhD (hon.), St. Mary's Coll. Calif., 1999. Nurse Kaiser Found. Hosp., Redwood City, Calif., 1969-73; lectr. San Jose (Calif.) State U., 1969-70; instr. St. Francis Meml. Hosp. Sch. Nursing, San Francisco, 1970—71; pub. health nurse San Mateo County, 1971—72; instr. Samuel Merritt Hosp. Sch. Nursing, Oakland, Calif., 1973—76, asst. dir., 1976—78, dir., 1978—84; founding pres. Samuel Merritt Coll., Oakland, 1984—; interim pres. Calif. Coll. Podiatric Medicine, 2001. V.p. East Bay Area Health Edn. Ctr., Oakland, 1980-87; mem. adv. com. Calif. Acad. Partnership Program, 1990-92; mem. nat. adv. com. Nursing Outcomes Project; bd. dirs. Calif. Workforce Initiative, U. Calif. San Francisco Ctr. for the Health Professions, 2000--. Bd. dirs. Head Royce Sch., 1990-98, vice chair, 1993-95, chair, 1995-97; bd. dirs. Ladies Home Soc., 1992—, sec. 1994-95, treas., CFO 1995-97, 2nd v.p. 1997-99, pres., 2006; bd. dirs. George Mark Children's House, 2001—; mem. adv. bd. Ethnic Health Inst., 1997—; mem. com. minorities higher edn. Am. Coun. Edn., 1998—. Named Woman of Yr., Oakland YWCA, 1996. Mem. Am. Assn. Pres. Ind. Colls. and Univs., Sigma Theta Tau (bd. dirs. Nu Xi internat. chpt. at-large 2005—, Leadership award Nu Xi chpt. 2001, Philanthropy award 2005). Office: Samuel Merrritt Coll 450 30th St Oakland CA 94609-3302 E-mail: sdiaz@samuelmerritt.edu.

DIAZ, TERESITA PEREZ, chemist; b. Placetas, Las Villas, Cuba, Sept. 2, 1956; arrived in U.S., 1974; d. Pedro Angel and Gladys (Teresita) Perez; m. Luis Diaz, Jr., Sept. 2, 1984; children: Tiffany Marie, Luis III. BS in Chemistry, Monclair U., NJ, 1979. Asst. scientist baby products Johnson & Johnson, Raritan, NJ, 1979—81, assoc. scientist, 1981—84, assoc. scientist toiletries Skillman, NJ, 1984—86, scientist R & D, 1986—96, sr. scientist rsch, devel. and engring., 1996—2001, staff scientist, 2001—02, group leader, 2002—05, mgr., 2006—. Piano tchr., Perth Amboy, NJ, 1975—; coach, trainer Johnson & Johnson Skillman U., 2001—04. Class mother Perth Amboy Cath. Schs., 1989—2003. Recipient Grandview award, Johnson & Johnson, 2000, 2002, 2004, Engring. Excellence award, 2002. Mem.: Nat. Guild Piano Tchrs., Soc. Cosmetic Chemists. Achievements include co-inventor skin toning formulation; co-inventor relaxing personal care composition; co-inventor delivery system for topical skin care agents. Avocations: art, theater, museums, music, films. Office: Johnson and Johnson 199 Grandview Rd Skillman NJ 08558 Office Phone: 908-874-1415. Personal E-mail: tdiaz7@cpcus.jnj.com.

DIAZ MEYER, CHERYL, photojournalist; b. Phillipines; arrived in US, 1981; BA in German, U. Minn., 1990; BA in journalism, Western Ky. U., 1994. Staff photographer Mpls. Star Tribune, 1994—2000; sr. staff photographer Dallas Morning News, 2000—. Named Minn. Photographer Yr., 1999; recipient Pulitzer Prize for breaking news photography, 2004. Office: Dallas Morning News 508 Young St PO Box 655237 Dallas TX 75265-5237

DIBACCO, NADINE LOUISE, retired library director, photographer, writer; b. Biloxi, Miss., Nov. 2, 1952; d. Keith Royce and Ira Jean Allen; m. T. Jay DiBacco, June 1, 1976. AA, Laramie County C.C., 1972; BA in English Edn., U. Wyo., 1974; MS in Mgmt., Regis U., 2000. Cert. pub. librarian, tchr. Nebr. Serials libr. Laramie County C.C., Cheyenne, Wyo., 1974—76; tchr., english St. Agnes Acad., Alliance, Nebr., 1976—77; exec. sec. Gering Police Dept., Nebr., 1977—85; asst. dir. Gering Pub. Libr., Gering, Nebr., 1985—90, libr. dir., 1990—2005; adj. instr. Western Nebr. C.C., Scottsbluff, Nebr., 1991—96. Bd. pres. Panhandle Libr. Sys., Scottsbluff, Nebr., 1991—93, author tour com., 1990—. Com. mem. Scottsbluff/Gering United C. of C., Nebr., 1987—2005, United Way of Scotts Bluff County, Nebr., 1989—90; treas. Mar. of Dimes, Scottsbluff, Nebr., 1983—84; active Nebr. N.G. Civilian Leadership Coun., Lincoln, 2004—05; vice chair, chair-elect pub. libr. sect. Nebr. Libr. Assn., Lincoln, 2005—06. Recipient Individual Devel. Nat. Panel Participant, Bus. and Profl. Women, USA, 1988. Mem.: Soroptimist Internat. of Scotts Bluff County (corr. sec. 2005—06), Nebr. Bus. and Profl. Women (state pres. 2002—03), Soc. for Creative Anachronism (treas. local chpt. 1997—2005, regional pres. 1998—2000, Order of the Pelican 1996). Avocations: photography, music, travel. Office: PO Box 68 Boys Town NE 68010 Office Phone: 402-991-5433. Personal E-mail: nadinedibacco@yahoo.com.

DIBATTISTE, CAROL A., military officer; b. Phila., Dec. 28, 1951; d. Peter Martin DiBattiste and Hilda Yolanda (Battilana) Mignogna. BA magna cum luade, LaSalle U., 1976; JD, Temple U., 1981; LLM, Columbia U., 1986. Bar: Pa. 1982, U.S. Ct. Mil. Appeals 1982, U.S. Supreme Ct. 1985, N.Y. 1989, D.C. 1989, Fla. 1990, U.S. Dist. Ct. (so. dist.) Fla. 1991, U.S. Ct. Appeals (11th cir.) 1991. Commd. 2d lt. USAF, 1976, advanced through grades to maj., 1987, cir. trial counsel Pacific Region, 1982—85; mem. faculty USAF JAG Sch., Maxwell AFB, Ala., 1986—89; chief recruiting atty. Office of Judge Advocate Gen. USAF, Washington, 1989—91; asst. U.S. atty. (So. Dist.) Fla. US Dept. Justice, Miami, 1991—92, dir. Office of Legal Edn., 1992—93; prin. dep. gen. coun. USN, 1993—94; dir. Exec. Office for U.S. Attys., Washington, 1994—98; dep. U.S. atty. (So. Dist.) Fla. US Dept. Justice, Miami, 1998—99; undersec. USAF, Arlington, Va., 1999—2001; ptnr. Holland & Knight, LLP, 2001—03; chief of staff Transp. Security Adminstrn., 2003—04, dep. adminstr., 2004—05; chief credentialing compliance & privacy officer ChoicePoint Inc., McLean, 2005—. Adj. faculty U. Miami Sch. Law Trial Skills, 1998—99; bd. dirs. Alpha Security Group. Editor: The Reporter, Air Force JAG Sch., 1986—87; mem. editl. bd.: Air Force Law Rev., 1984. Bd. visitors Temple U. Sch. Law, 1996-99; trustee USAF JAG Sch. Found., 1993-96, Air Force Falcon Found., 2004—. Mem. ABA (chmn. standing com. on mil. law 1989-91), Fed. Bar Assn. (Young Fed. Lawyer award 1985), Nat. Inst. for Trial Advocacy (faculty 1986-92), USAF Assn. Roman Catholic. Business E-Mail: carol.dibattiste@choicepoint.net.

DIBBLE, SUZANNE LOUISE, nurse, researcher; b. Pittsburg, Calif., June 3, 1947; d. Charles Stanley and Evelyn Virginia (Hansen) D.; m. Myron Bottsford Palmer III, June 12, 1971 (div. July 1974); life ptnr. Jeanne Flyntz DeJoseph, 1984. BSN, U. Del., 1969; MSN, U. Calif., San Francisco, 1971, D Nursing Sci., 1986. RN, Del., Calif. Staff nurse emergency room Stanford (Calif.) U. Hosp., 1969-71, rschr. dept. nursing rsch., 1986-88; instr. med. and surg. nursing Stanford U., 1971-72, renal transplant nurse coord., 1972-73, nurse rschr. dept. diagnostic radiology, 1987-88; staff, charge, head nurse, then supr. Children's Hosp.-Stanford U., 1973-86; mem. faculty stats. dept. U. Phoenix, San Jose, Calif., 1985-92; pres. Data Mgmt. Assocs., San Carlos, Calif., 1985—2000; investigator U. Calif., 1988—; co-dir. Lesbian Health Rsch. Ctr., 1999—, Dibble Cons. Corp., 2006—. Rsch. grant cons. NIH, Oakland, Calif., 1992-94, Loma Linda (Calif.) U., 1995-1999, U. Tex., 2004; manuscript reviewer Oncology Nursing Forum, Pitts., 1993-96, Med.-Surg. Nursing, Pittmn, N.J., 1994—, Jour. of Gay and Lesbian Med. Assn.; editor Culture & Clin. Care, 2005. Editor: Culture and Nursing Care, 1996; contbr. articles to nursing jours. Chmn. task force, mem. NOW, Palo Alto, Calif., 1978—; mem., chmn. Maternal, Child and Adolescent Health Bd., San Mateo County, Calif., 1987-90; mem. strategic planning com. San Mateo County Health Bd., 1989-90. Rsch. grantee Nat. Cancer Inst., 1992-97, 2000—, Nat. Inst. for Nursing Rsch., 1994-99. Mem. ANA, Assn. for Care Children's Health (numerous offices), Oncology Nursing Soc. (numerous offices), Am. Statis. Assn., Sigma Theta Tau (pres. Alpha Eta chpt.). Democrat. Office: U Calif Box 0646 Inst Health & Aging San Francisco CA 94143-0646 E-mail: sue.dibble@ucsf.edu.

DIBELKA, CHARLENE FAY WEBSTER, secondary school educator; b. Melbourne, Victoria, Australia, Jan. 19, 1950; d. George Henry Webster and Charlotte Louise Hutchinson-Webster; m. Albert William Dibelka, Aug. 15, 1985;; children: Angela Danielle, Jeffrey Paul Eddington, Elisa Dawn Eddington-Cacho, Justin Reed Eddington. BA, San Diego State U., 1973, MA, 1982. Cert. tchr. Colo., 1981. Tchr. Uintah Sch. Dist., Vernal, Utah, 1981—83; tech. editor and writer Systems Exploration, Inc., San Diego, 1983—85; tchr. Grossmont Union H.S. Dist., La Mesa, Calif., 1987—91; drama chair/tchr. Sweetwater Union H.S. Dist., Chula Vista, Calif., 1991—. Sponsor Internat. Thespian Soc., Ill., 1991—; county visual and performing arts bd. San Diego County Office Edn., 2002—; dist. visual and performing arts bd. Sweetwater Union H.S. Dist., Chula Vista, 2004—. Dir.: (cmty. and ednl. theatre); actor: (cmty. theatre). Precinct worker Rep. Party, Colorado Springs, Colo.; tchr., leader LDS Ch., Chula Vista, 1983—2006. Finalist Calif. H.S. Educator of Yr., Calif. League High Schs., 2005; recipient Mentor Tchr. Lang. Arts award, Old Globe Theatre and Greater San Diego Tchrs. English, 1994—. Mem.: Ednl. Theatre Assn. (sponsor). Achievements include development of county-wide drama advisory; county awards for theatre instructions. Avocations: tour leader for student travel, singing, swing dance, skiing. Office Phone: 619-628-3007. Business E-Mail: charlene.dibelka@suhsd.k12.ca.us.

DI BENEDETTO, ANN LOUISE, retired accounting administrator; b. Knoxville, Tenn., Jan. 26, 1954; d. William Brown and Louise (Emerson) Nixon; m. Raymond Peters, July 11, 1975 (dec.); m. Robert Di Benedetto, Sept. 22, 2002. BBA, Miami U., Oxford, Ohio, 1976; MBA, Xavier U., 1985. Cert. internal auditor. Acctg. officer Soc. Bank (formerly Citizens Bank), Hamilton, Ohio, 1977—85; internal auditor Procter & Gamble Co., Cin., 1985—86, mgr. audit sect., 1985—88, sr. cost analyst, beauty care, 1985—90; mgr. plant fin. Procter & Gamble Mfg. Co., Phoenix, 1990—92; sr. fin.

analyst, beauty care Procter & Gamble Co., Cin., 1992—93, group mgr., gen. acctg., 1993—96, group mgr. R&D fin., 1996—99, group mgr., global fin., paper divsn., 1999—2002, group mgr. global fin. governance, 2002—03, group mgr., fin., global bus. svcs., 2003—06; ret., 2006. Mem. Inst. Internal Auditors, Inst. Mgmt. Accts. Republican. Congregationalist. Avocations: golf, swimming. Home: 1007 Ann Ave Lady Lake FL 32159

DIBENEDETTO, MICHELLE, finance company executive; 1 child, Katie. Mgr. cmty. lending, grants & tech. assistance programs Citibank, Long Island, 1996—2004, region dir. of cmty. rels. for Long Island and Queens, 2004—. Chair home purchase process initiative Fed. Res. Bank, Long Island. Chair Long Island Arts Coun., New Directions; mem. exec. bd., treas. Long Island Coalition for Fair Broadcasting; treas./sect. Long Island Small Bus. Assistance Corp.; immediate pres. Women's Econ. Developers Long Island; mem. bus. adv. bd. Girl Scouts Am., Nassau County, Black Women Enterprise; sect. Long Island Housing Partnership; bd. dir. Family & Children's Assn.; bd. of campaign Affordable Rental Housing. Mem.: Long Island Women's Agenda (fund raising com.). Office: Citibank NA 180 W Merrick Rd Freeport NY 11520 Business E-Mail: michelle.e.dibenedetto@citigroup.com.

DIBERARDINO, MARIE ANTOINETTE, developmental biologist, educator; b. Phila., May 2, 1926; d. Henry and Adelina (Belfi) DiB. BS in Biology, Chestnut Hill Coll., 1948, JD (hon.), 1990; PhD in Zoology, U. Pa., 1962. Rsch. asst. Fox Chase Cancer Ctr. (formerly Inst. Cancer Rsch.), 1948-58, rsch. assoc., 1960-64, asst. mem., 1964-67; assoc. prof. anatomy Drexel U. Coll. Medicine, Phila., 1967-71, prof. anatomy, 1971-81, prof. physiology, 1981-92, prof. biochemistry, 1992-96, prof. emerita, 1996—. Adv. bd. Internat. Rev. of Cytology, 1976-2000, Differentiation, 1981—, Series: Developmental Biology, A Comprehensive Synthesis, 1982-94; assoc. editor Jour. Exptl. Zoology, 1984-86; Contbr. articles on devel., genetics and cell biology to sci. jours.; contbr. book revs. in field. Mem. NIH Fogarty Internat. Fellowship Study Group, 1984. NSF grantee, NIH grantee; recipient Jean Brachet Meml. award. Fellow AAAS; mem. Am. Soc. Cell Biology (emerita), Soc. for Devel. Biologists (emerita, treas., trustee 1975-78), Internat. Soc. Devel. Biologists, Internat. Soc. of Differentiation (emerita, exec. com. 1978-85, 87-90, bd. dirs. 1980-94). Home: The Quadrangle 7311 3300 Darby Rd Haverford PA 19041 E-mail: mdiberar@drexelmed.edu.

DIBERT, ROSALIE, elementary school educator; Graduate, Calif. U. of Pa., 1964. Tchr. Pitts. Pub. Schs., 1964—2002; coord. Pitts. Initiative, 2002—. Chmn. Exceptional Needs Com.; Gov. at Large for Tchrs. CEC Exec. Bd.; liaison Profl. Standards Com. Finalist Tchr. of Yr., Pa., 1986; named Clarissa Hug Internat. Spec. Educator of Yr., 1990; recipient Bernice Baumgartner Meml. award; Jordan Fundamentals grant, 2000. Mem.: Nat. Coun. for Exceptional Children Com., Pa. Tchrs. Forum, Pa. State Adv. Bd., Western Region Chpt. #104 (pres.), Pa. Fed. Coun. for Exceptional Children, Pa. Chpt. Tchr. of Yr. Chpt. (pres. 1992), Nat. Bd Profl. Tchg. Standards.

DICAMILLO, KATE, writer; b. Phila. Degree, U. Fla., Gainesville, Fla. Author: (children's books) Because of Winn-Dixie, 2000 (named Newbery Honor Book, 2001, Dorothy Canfield Fisher Children's Book award, 2002, NY Times Bestseller, Publishers Weekly Bestseller children's fiction list, 2005), The Tiger Rising, 2001 (Nat. Book award finalist, 2000), The Tale of Despereaux: Being the Story of a Mouse, a Princess, Some Soup, and a Spool of Thread, 2003 (Newbery medal, 2004, NY Times Bestseller, USA Today Bestseller, Book Sense Bestseller, Publishers Weekly Bestseller), Mercy Watson to the Rescue, 2005, The Miraculous Journey of Edward Tulane, 2005. Grantee McKnight Artist fellowship, 1998. Office: Candlewick Press Inc 2067 Massachusetts Ave Cambridge MA 02140

DICANIO, MARGARET BRIEN, freelance writer, former mental health agency administrator; b. Waltham, Mass., Apr. 9, 1929; d. Francis Baxter and Alice (Brown) Brien; m. Vito William DiCanio; Sept. 3, 1951 (div. 1962); 1 child: Frances Alice. BA, Northeastern U., Boston, 1958; MA, Boston U., 1958; PhD, U. Fla., 1971; postdoctoral student, U. Minn., 1975-76. Staff psychologist Danvers State Hosp., Mass., 1958-60; instr., supr. Northeast Airlines, Boston and Miami, Fla., 1960-64; soc. worker Jackson Meml. Hosp., Miami, Fla., 1964-67; asst. prof. sociology Memphis State U., 1970-74; rsch. coord. family medicine U. Tenn. Med. Sch., Memphis, 1974-75; postdoctoral evaluation rsch., dir. cmty. programs Whitehaven Mental Health Agy., Memphis, 1975-76, 76-80; exec. dir. Berkshire Mental Health Agy., Pittsfield, Mass., 1980-81, Region West Mental Health Agy., Newton, Mass., 1981-86; freelance writer Marblehead, Mass., 1986—. Bd. dirs. Health Protection Adv. Coun., Marblehead, 1994-2002; mem. North Shore Violence Prevention Task Force, Salem, Mass., 1994-1998. Author: The Encyclopedia of Marriage, Divorce and the Family, 1989, The Encyclopedia of Violence, 1993; author and editor: The Facts on File Scientific Yearbooks, 1988, 89, 90, 91, The Young Students Learning Library Science Yearbook, 1992, 93. Mem. Women's Vol. Roundtable, Tenn., 1972-74; mem. bd. dirs. Year 2000 com., Lynn, Mass., 1995-96; del. Dem. Nat. Convention, 1972. With U.S. Army, 1948-51. Mem. Mystery Writers of Am. (New Eng. chpt. bd. dirs., treas. 1994-96, regional v.p. 1996-97, mem. juvenile awards com. 1994, tv spls. awards com. 1997, true crime awards com. 1998, true crime columnist for nat. newsletter, fact crime awards com., 2005), Am. Soc. Journalists and Authors, Nat. Assn. Sci. Writers, Soc. Children's Book Writers and Illustrators, Sisters in Crime, ArtSalem, Monday Lunch Club Boston Org. Soc. Svc. Agy. Dirs. (treas. 1986-89). Home: 51 Jersey St Marblehead MA 01945-2463

DICARLO, SUSANNE HELEN, financial analyst; b. Greensburg, Pa., Nov. 24, 1956; d. Wayne Larry and Clara Emogene (Weaver) Gower; m. John Joseph DiCarlo, June 21, 1980; children: Sarah Rose, Kristen Marie. BS in Acctg., Va. Tech., 1978. Auditor U.S. Army Audit Agy., Ft. Monroe, Va., 1978-79; acct. technician Fleet Combat Tng. Ctr., Virginia Beach, Va., 1980-82, supervisory auditor, 1982-83; mgmt. analyst NPDC Human Capital Planning Group, Norfolk, Va., 1983—. Fed. women's program mgr. Fleet Combat Tng. Ctr., 1980—83. Creator newsletter: Fed. Women's Program Mgr., 1980—83. Mem.: Southeastern Assn. Trailriders, Am. Soc. Mil. Comptrollers, Seaside Mountaineers Club (Virginia Beach) (treas. 1986—88). Home: 4013 Dillaway Ct Virginia Beach VA 23456-1257 Office Phone: 757-444-2996 ext. 3917.

DICIACCO, JANIS ANNETTE, psychologist; b. Pueblo, Colo., Sept. 19, 1947; d. Charles DiCiacco and Ruth Isabelle Tearpak. BA in French and Polit. Sci., Colo. State U., Fort Collins, 1969; Diplome, U. Besçanon, France, 1970; MS in Spl. Edn., U. No. Colo., Greeley, 1976; PhD, U. Denver, 1980. Lic. sch. psychologist Colo., 1980, Nat. Assn. Sch. Psychologists, 1984, clin. psychologist Colo., 1986. Spl. edn. tchr. Denver Pub. Schs., 1970—80, sch. psychologist, 1980—2002; clin. psychologist pvt. practice, Denver, 1985—; lectr. in field. Ptnr., pres. Mindful Moods, Inc., Denver, 2005—; lectr. in field. Mem.: APA, Nat. Assn. Sch. Psychologists. Avocations: gardening, golf, tai chi, theater. Office Phone: 303-321-4184.

DICICCO, MARGARET C., lawyer; b. Bklyn., Mar. 22, 1961; d. Vincent Richard and Margaret Josephine (Ciullo) DiCicco; m. James Louis O'Rourke, Sept. 18, 1994. BA in Polit. Sci., Bklyn. Coll., CUNY, 1983; JD, U. Bridgeport, 1987. Bar: N.Y. 1989, U.S. Dist. Ct. (so. dist.) N.Y. 1989, U.S. Dist. Ct. (ea. dist.) N.Y. 1990, Conn. 1994, U.s. Dist. Ct. Conn. 1995, U.S. Supreme Ct. 1998. Assoc. Ginsberg & Caesar, N.Y.C., 1988-89, Abrams & Martin P.C., N.Y.C., 1989-93, Chesney, Murphy & Moran, Westbury, NY, 1993-94, Law Offices of James L. O'Rourke, Stratford, Conn., 1994—. Mem.: ABA, Greater Bridgeport Bar Assn., N.Y. State Bar Assn. Roman Catholic. Home: 221 Nells Rock Rd Shelton CT 06484-3831 Office: Law Offices James L O'Rourke 1825 Barnum Ave Ste 201 Stratford CT 06614-5333 Office Phone: 203-381-9800.

DICK, ANGELA DAWN, elementary school educator; d. Thomas Joseph and LaDonna Faye Harcar; m. Dustin Lee Dick, Dec. 4, 1999; 1 child, Aubrey Marie. AA, Kansas City CC, Kans., 1997; BS in Edn., Emporia State U., Kans., 1999. Kindergarten tchr. Marais des Cygre Valley Schs., Melvern, Kans., 2000—01; tchr. Chase Mid. Sch., Topeka, 2001—05, literacy coach, 2005—. Chair N.Ctrl. Assn. Commn. Accreditation and Sch. Improvement, Topeka, 2004—, title 1 chair, 2005—06, vis. team, 2006—. Author: The Bridge of Dreadful Dreams, 2004, The Other Side of the Wall, 2005. Office: Chase Mid Sch 2250 NE State St Topeka KS 66616

DICK, DANIELLE MARIE, psychology professor, psychiatrist, educator; d. Daniel and Lynn Dick; m. Bryan Salmon, June 2, 1971. BA, U. Va., Charlottesville, 1997; PhD, Ind. U., Bloomington, 2001. Asst. prof. depts. psychiatry and psychology Washington U., St. Louis, 2003—. Faculty assoc. incoming freshman Washington U., St. Louis. Contbr. articles to profl. jours. Fellow, NSF, 1998—2001, NIH, 2001—03; grantee, Nat. Inst. Drug Abuse, 2000—06, Nat. Inst. Alcoholism and Alcohol Abuse, 2004—, 2005—, NIMH, 2005—06, Ctr. Inherited Disease Rsch., 2005—06. Mem.: Soc. Sci. Clin. Psychology, Assn. Psychol. Sci., Rsch. Soc. Alcoholism, Internat. Soc. Psychiat. Genetics, Internat. Soc. Twin Studies, Behavior Genetics Assn. (exec. com. mem. 2003—06, Thompson award 1999). Office: Washington Univ St Louis Psychiatry Box 8134 660 South Euclid Saint Louis MO 63110 Office Phone: 314-286-2297. Office Fax: 314-286-2213. E-mail: dickd@wustl.edu.

DICK, DEBORAH JEAN, elementary school educator; b. Jerome, Idaho, June 27, 1955; d. William Evan and Eleanor June Dick. Assocs. in Edn., Ricks Coll., 1973; BS in Edn., Brigham Young U., 1977; MS in Holistic Nutrition, Clayton Coll., 2001. Cert. profl. tchr. Idaho, Utah. 2nd and 3rd grade tchr. San Juan Sch. Dist., Monticello, Utah, 1977—79; 1st grade tchr. Bear Lake Sch. Dist., Montpelier, Idaho, 1979—80; 1st, 3rd and 6th grade tchr. Madison Sch. Dist., Rexburg, Idaho, 1980—. Mem.: NAFE, Inst. Children's Lit., Internat. Soc. Poets, Delta Kappa Gamma. Office: Madison Middle School 575 W 7th S Rexburg ID 83440-9681

DICKENS, ALICE MCKNIGHT, minister; b. Edgecombe County, N.C., May 6, 1935; d. John and Candis Moore McKnight; m. Ernest Dickens, 1954; children: Ernest Douglas, Ronald, John, Larry, Candice, Mark. Degree in nursing, Edgecombe C.C., 1981. Lic. nurse, N.C. Founder, pastor Ch. of God of Deliverance, Rocky Mount, NC, 1971—; pres. N.C. Dist. Union Apostolic Faith Ch. of God, 1994—. Mem. pastoral staff Apostolic Faith Ch. of God, Franklin, Va., 1982—. Supporter Crisis Ministry/homeless shelter, Rocky Mount; bd. dirs. New Sources, Rocky Mount, NC, 2001—, Meals on Wheels, Rocky Mount, 1998—2000. Recipient hon. mention, Jefferson awards, WTVD-TV, Durham, N.C., 1995, tribute plaque, OIC HIV/AIDS Program, Rocky Mount, 1999. Home: 909 Columbia Ave Rocky Mount NC 27804 Office: Ch of God of Deliverance 900 Columbia Ave Rocky Mount NC 27804

DICKENS, JANIS, media services administrator; b. Des Moines, June 4, 1949; d. M. Wesley and Lenita Bird (Heath) Jordan BS, Iowa State U., 1971; AMLS, U. Mich., 1972. Libr. Monterey (Calif.) Inst. Internat. Studies, 1972-73, Contra Costa Pub. Libr., Pleasant Hill, Calif., 1973-74, L.A. Pub. Libr., 1974-75; br. mgr. San Jose (Calif.) Pub. Libr., 1975-79; head libr. pub. svcs. DeAnza C.C., Cupertino, Calif., 1979-85; dir. libr., instructional svcs. Hartnell C.C., Salinas, Calif., 1985-89; dir. instructional media svcs. U. Calif., Santa Cruz, 1989—2000; dir. U. Calif. Davis, Classroom Tech. Svc., 2000. Pres. Dirs. Edn. Tech. in Calif. Higher Edn., Santa Barbara, 1992-93; bd. dirs. Consortium Coll. and Univ. Media Ctrs., Ames, Iowa, 1995-97. Co-author: (reference book) Classroom Guidelines, 1995; contbr. articles to Coll. and Univ. Media Rev., 1995—. Mem. Fremont Bd. Edn. Task Force on Librs., 1988-91; mem. Alameda County Libr. Commn., Alameda, Calif., 1986-89; mem. People for a Permanent Libr., Fremont, 1987-90. Mem. Am. Libr. Assn., Calif. Libr. Assn., No. Calif. Telecomm. Consortium, Methodist. Avocations: gardening, travel, sports, sailing. Office: U Calif Davis One Shields Ave Davis CA 95616

DICKENS, JOYCE REBECCA, addictions therapist, educator; b. Roanoke Rapids, NC; d. Leslie and Lydia Marie Dickens. M in Addiction Psychology with honors, Capella U., 2000, PhD in Psychology with honors, 2003. Cert. addiction profl. Adj. instr. Broward CC, Ft. Lauderdale, Fla., 1991—; primary therapist addictions Treatment Works, Ft. Lauderdale, 2002—. Mem.: AAUW, Phi Theta Kappa, Alpha Chi. Avocations: tennis, travel, public speaking. Office Phone: 954-258-9829. Personal E-mail: joyced@bellsouth.net. Business E-Mail: JDickens@Broward.edu.

DICKENS-SIMON, NICOLE PEARLENE, language educator; b. Orange, N.J., Mar. 29, 1973; d. Clarence Albert and Alice Naomi Dickens; m. James E. Simon, Jr., Apr. 26, 2000; children: Savion W. Simon, Grace Simon, Serenity Simon. BA in Journalism and Spanish, U. Conn., Storrs, 1995; MA in Edn. Adminstrn., Rider U., Lawrenceville, N.J., 2004; postgrad., Rutgers U., 2005. Cert. std. tchg. N.J., supr. N.J., prin. N.J. Bilingual social worker Conn. Dept. Children and Families, Hartford, 1995—99; tchr. world langs. Abraham Clark H.S., Roselle, NJ, 1999—2000, Union County Magnet H.S., Scotch Plains, NJ, 2000—02, Somerville (N.J.) Pub. Schs., 2002—. Mem. Somerville Mid. Coun., 2004—. Author: (book of poetry) Epiphany, 1997, Mi Abuelita Me Hace una Visita, 2005. Recipient tech. grant, Somerville Edn. Found., 2005. Mem.: ASCD, Am. Assn. Tchrs. Spanish and Portuguese, Fgn. Lang. Educators N.J., Phi Delta Kappa, Alpha Kappa Alpha. Avocations: studying abroad, reading, youth mentor. Office: Somerville Mid Sch 51 W Cliff St Somerville NJ 08876

DICKERMAN, SERAFINA POERIO, real estate broker, consultant; b. Camden, N.J., Sept. 20, 1920; d. Giuseppe Francesco Poerio and Christina Audia; m. John M. Dickerman, Oct. 27, 1956; 1 child, Dorothea Wilhelmina. Attended, Seton Hill Coll., 1938—39, St. Vincent Coll., Latrobe, Pa., 1939—40, Barnard Coll., 1941, Northwestern U., 1943, Strayer Coll., 1951, U. Md., 1971, Am. U., 1953—73. Lic. pvt. pilot, radio operator, meteorologist, radio tel. operator, real estate agt. Md., D.C., Va., N.Y., Fla., Fedn. Internat. Professions Immobilieres, France, cert. internat. property specialist Nat. Assn. Realtors. Mem. Civil Air Patrol Civil Aeronautics Authority, Latrobe, 1939—41; operator control tower radio TWA, Columbus, Ohio, 1941—42; meteorologist Pan Am. Airlines and Colonial Airlines, N.Y.C., 1942—43; stewardess Ea. Airlines, N.Y.C., 1943—45; part-time high fashion model Harry Conover Agy., N.Y.C., 1943—45; negotiator, organizer Airline Stewards and Stewardesses Assn. U.S., Chgo., 1944—46; pres. Dickerman Real Estate/Investment Co., Potomac, Md., 1972—. Participant European Bldg. and Real Estate Study Nat. Assn. Home Builders and European builder orgns., 1963. Contbr. articles to mags. in field. Driver blood mobile, life saver swimmer Nat. Red Cross, Washington, 1955; hostess USO, N.Y.C., 1941; mem. Young Rep. Club, N.Y.C., 1941, Potomac Women's Rep. Club, 1960. First Woman recipient Civil Air Patrol Silver Wings, FAA World War II, 1939—40. Mem.: Nat. Mus. Women in Arts (charter), Italian Culture Soc. Washington, Capital Spkrs. Club (Washington), Women's Golf Assn. of Congl. Country Club, Congl. Country Club (hon. life). Presbyterian. Avocations: music, art, golf, tennis, swimming. Office: Dickerman Real Estate/Investment Co 9030 Bronson Dr Potomac MD 20854 Office Phone: 301-983-2546.

DICKERSON, BETTY, secondary school educator, consultant; b. Warrenton, Va., May 7, 1948; d. Early Columbus Jr. and Mary Elizabeth (Kendrick) Griffith; m. Douglas Jerry Dickerson, Sept. 27, 1991. BS, So. Conn. State U., 1972; MEd, Fla. Atlantic U., Boca Raton, 1978; DDiv (hon.), Word Christianship Ministries, Fresno, Calif., 1993. Cert. tchr., Va., N.C. Home/hosp. tchr. Palm Beach County Pub. Schs., West Palm Beach, Fla., 1978-93; tchr. of the emotionally disturbed Prince William County Pub. Schs., Manassas, Va., 1993-98; substitute tchr. Warren County H.S., Front Royal, Va., 1998-99; math. tchr. Davie County H.S., Mocksville, N.C., 1999—. Contbg. author The Light, 1999. Literacy Missions assoc. Ch. and Cmty. Ministries, So. Bapt. Conf., 1982-99; vol. tutor ESL, Davie County H.S., 1999—. Mem. N.C. Coun. Tchrs. Math. Avocations: horseback riding, writing an ethnographic history of the chickahominy indians, math and logic puzzles, reading. E-mail: bettydickerson@iname.com.

DICKERSON, CLAIRE MOORE, lawyer, educator; b. Boston, Apr. 1, 1950; d. Roger Cleveland and Ines Idelette (Roullet) Moore; m. Thomas Pasquali Dickerson, May 22, 1976; children: Caroline Anne, Susannah Moore. AB, Wellesley Coll., 1971; JD, Columbia U., 1974; LLM in Taxation, NYU, 1981. Bar: N.Y. 1975, U.S. Dist. Ct. (ea. and so. dists.) N.Y. 1975, U.S. Ct. Appeals (2d cir.) 1975, U.S. Supreme Ct. 1980. Assoc. Coudert Brothers, N.Y., 1974-82, ptnr., 1983-86, Schnader, Harrison, Segal & Lewis, N.Y., 1987-88, of counsel N.Y., 1988—; assoc. prof. law St. John's U., Jamaica, N.Y., 1986-88, prof., 1989-2000; prof law Rutgers U., Newark, 2000—. Author: Partnership Law Adviser; contbr. articles to profl. jours. Scholar Arthur L. Dickson scholar. Mem.: ABA, Soc. for Advancement of Socio-Econs., Law and Soc. Assn., Assn. of Bar of City of N.Y., Shenorock Club. Democrat. E-mail: cmdckrsn@rci.rutgers.edu.

DICKERSON, COLLEEN BERNICE PATTON, artist, educator; b. Cleburne, Tex., Sept. 17, 1922; d. Jennings Bryan and Alma Bernice (Clark) Patton; m. Arthur F. Dickerson; children: Sherry M., Chrystal Charmine. BA, Calif. State U., Northridge, 1980; studied with John Pike. Presenter, instr. in field. One-woman shows include Morro Bay Cmty. Bldg., Amandas Interiors, Arroyo Grande, Calif., 1996, Gt. Western Savs., San Luis Obispo, Calif.; exhibited in group shows including Aquarius Show Ctrl. Coast Watercolor Soc., Calif., 2003; represented in permanent collections, including Polk Ins. Co., San Luis Obispo, Med. Ctr. MDM Ins. Co., L.A. Mem. Ctrl. Coast Watercolor Soc. (pres. 1986-87, Svc. award 1998), Art Ctr., Oil Acrylic Pastel Group (chmn., co-chmn. 1989-98, prize Brush Strokes show 1999), Morro Bay Art Assn. (scholarship judge 1998), San Luis Obispo Art Ctr., Valley Watercolor Soc. (co-founder). Avocations: egyptology, chinese painting, art history, forensic anthropology. Home: 245 Hacienda Ave San Luis Obispo CA 93401-7967

DICKERSON, CYNTHIA ROWE, marketing executive, consultant; b. Cin., Apr. 14, 1956; d. Richard Emmett and Frances Jeanette (Ellwanger) Rowe; m. Mark Alan Dickerson, Oct. 24, 1981; children: Shannon Gayle, Meredith Lynne. BSBA, U. So. Calif., 1979. Mgmt. asst. Computer Scis. Corp., Pasadena, Calif., 1974-78; rsch. asst. Dailey & Assocs., L.A., 1978-79; account exec. Young & Rubicam, L.A., 1979-81, Rowley & Linder Advt., Wichita, Kans., 1981-82, Chiat/Day Inc. Advt., San Francisco, 1983-85; product mgr. Sun-Diamond Growers of Calif., Pleasanton, 1985-88; mktg. cons. San Francisco, 1988-90; sr. bus. mgr. Del Monte Foods, San Francisco, 1990-93; dir. mktg. Yorkshire Dried Fruit & Nuts, Inc., San Francisco, 1993-94, Potlatch Corp., 1995-98; dir. category mgmt., dir S. & W. brand bus. unit Tri Valley Growers, 1999-2001; mktg. cons., 2001; v.p. mktg. and sales John Laing Homes, Greenwood Village, Colo., 2002—03, dir. mkt. rsch., 2003—. Named Outstanding Youth Women of Am., Jr. C. of C., 1985. Mem. Am. Mktg. Assn., Soc. Consumer Affairs Profls., Am. Rose Soc., Heritage Rose Group. Republican. Avocations: gardening, youth sports, playing piano, gourmet cooking. Office: John Laing Homes 7979 E Tufts Ave Ste 1150 Denver CO 80237 Office Phone: 720-554-6400. E-mail: cdickerson@johnlainghomes.com.

DICKERSON, NANCY KNEWSTEP, language educator; b. Hampton, Va., Aug. 22, 1943; d. William Edward and Dorothy Marie (Hunt) K.; m. Kenneth J. Stavisky, Sept. 6, 1975 (div. 1996); 1 child, C. Alexandra Stavisky; m. David D. Dickerson, Oct. 11, 1997. BA, Longwood Coll., 1965; MA, Regent U., 1994. Cert. libr. sci. Tchr. Hampton (Va.) City Schs., 1965-77; libr. Gloria Dei Luth. Sch., Hampton, 1984-91; tchr. English Hampton City Schs., 1991-98. Adj. faculty Old Dominion U., 1995-2000; facilitator, tchr. individual student alternative edn. plan Virginia Beach City Pub. Schs., 2000-2005. Exec. bd. mem. Longwood Coll. Found. Bd., Farmville, Va., 1990-96. Mem.: ASCD, Princess Anne Garden Club. Presbyterian. Avocations: rosarian, gardening, rowing, pastel art. Home: 1325 Starling Ct Virginia Beach VA 23451-4953 E-mail: nkdicker@cox.net.

DICKEY, BETTY C., state supreme court justice; b. 1940; m. Jay Dickey, 1960 (div. 1987); 1 adopted child, John 1 foster child, Cindy children: Laura, Ted, Rachel. BA in English, U. Ark., 1962, JD, 1985; attended, Nat. Coll. Dist. Attorneys Executive Program, 1994, FBI Nat. Law Inst., 1994. Former tchr. Pine Bluff High Sch., Ark., Watson Chapel Elementary Sch., Ark.; pvt. practice atty. Pine Bluff, Ark., 1985—86, Little Rock, 1990—91; asst. atty., 1986—90, 1993—94; city atty., 1988—94; atty. State Soil and Water Commn., Ark., 1991—93; prosecutor 11th Jud. Dist., 1995—99; commr. Ark. Pub. Svc., 1999—2003; chief legal counsel Ark. Gov.'s Office, 2003; chief justice Ark. Supreme Ct., 2004, assoc. justice Ark., 2004—. Recipient Atty. Gen.'s Top Prosecutor award, 1997, Top 100 Women in Ark. award, 1998, 1999. Mem.: Jefferson County Bar Assn., Pulaski County Bar Assn., Texas Bar Assn., Ark. Bar Assn. Office: Adminstrv Office of the Cts 625 Marshall St 120 Justice Bldg Little Rock AR 72201 Office Phone: 501-682-6861. E-mail: bcdickey@arkansas.gov.

DICKEY, DEENA LYNNE, music educator, vocalist; b. Lakeland, Fla., June 14, 1962; d. Byron Alfred Dickey and Geraldine Smith Dickey-Curlis. BA in Music Edn. and Vocal Performance, Warren Wilson Coll., Asheville, NC, 1984. Level one cert. Orff Schulwerk, nat. bd. music cert. Music/choral dir. Bethune Acad. Magnet Sch., Haines City, Fla., 1993—95, Polk Ave. Elem. Sch., Lake Wales, Fla., 1996—, McLaughlin Mid. Sch., Lake Wales, 2000—02. Show choir performances Walt Disney World Elem. Showcase, Orlando, Fla., 1993—. Singer: English Chamber Orch. Keener Vocal scholar, 1983. Home: 753 Tartan Loop Lake Wales FL 33853 Office: Polk Avenue Elementary School 110 Polk Ave Lake Wales FL 33853 Office Phone: 863-678-4244. Office Fax: 863-678-4680. Personal E-mail: deemusicclass1@netzero.com. Business E-Mail: deena.dickey@polk-fl.net.

DICKEY, NANCY WILSON, chancellor, physician; b. Watertown, SD, Sept. 10, 1950; m. Franklin Champ; children: Danielle, Wilson, Elizabeth. BA, Stephen F. Austin State U.; MD, U. Tex., 1976. Diplomate Am. Bd. Family Practice. Resident family medicine Meml. Hosp. System, Houston, 1976-79; pres., vice chancellor health affairs TAMUS Health Sci. Ctr.; prof. family medicine TAMUS Coll. Med., College Station, Tex., 1996—, pres., 2006—. Hon. staff Polly Ryon Meml. Hosp., Richmond; active staff Coll. Sta. (Tex.) Med. Ctr., St. Josephs Hosp., Bryan, Tex. Reviewer Jour. of AMA; editl. adv. bd. Patient Care, Med. World News, Med. Ethics Advisor, Archives of Family Medicine. Coach youth soccer, 1986-88; sponsor United Meth. Youth Fellowship, 1991-95; bd. dirs. Hastings Ctr., Office of Early Childhood Devel., Am. Heart Assn.; mem. Christ United Meth. Ch., College Station. Recipient Disting. Alumni award U. Tex. Med. Sch., Citation of Merit Tex. Soc. of Pathologists, 1995. Mem. AMA (pres. elect 1997, pres. 1998, chair bd. trustees 1995-97, vice chair 1994-95, bd. trustees 1989-97, sec. treas. 1993-94, exec. com. 1991, other coms.), Tex. Acad. of Family Physicians, Tex. Med. Assn., Alpha Omega Alpha. Office: 301 Tarrow St #7th Flr College Station TX 77840-7896

DICKEY, TERESA A., secondary school educator; b. L.A., Nov. 4, 1960; d. Jason M. and Amelia A. Dickey; life ptnr. Margaret F. Platis, Oct. 23, 1984. BA, Loyola Marymount U., LA, 1982, MA, 1984. Tchr. St. Francis H.S., Sacramento, 1984—86, Corvallis H.S., LA, 1986—87; tchr./tchr. mentor St. Monica's H.S., Santa Monica, Calif., 1987—93; tchr. Marymount H.S., LA, 1993—. Writing ctr. dir. Marymount H.S., LA, 2003—. Recipient Ind. Study in Japanese Printmaking, Ctr. for Basic Edn., 1991, Internat. Tchr. award, Toyota Motor Co, 2001; fellow Area 3 Writing Project, Calif. Writing Project, 1985, Seminar in Japanese Lit. and Culture, NEH, 1994; Sarah D. Barder Tchr. fellow, Johns Hopkins U., Ctr. for Talented Youth, 2005. Mem.: Calif. Assn. for Tchrs. English (assoc.). Avocations: guitar, golf, Japanese culture, African culture. Office: Marymount High School 10643 Sunset Blvd Los Angeles CA 90077 Office Phone: 310-472-1205. Business E-Mail: tdickey@mhs-la.org.

DICKHUT, KAREN SUE, music educator; b. Springfield, Ill., May 9, 1958; d. Robert William and Russella Mae Hagen; m. Monte Dee Dickhut, June 15, 1985; children: Joel A, Anna K. MusB, MacMurray Coll., 1980; MA Edn., U.

Ill., Springfield, 2004. Tchr. music Southea. Sch. Dist. #337, Augusta, Ill., 1980—87, Ctrl. #3, Camp Pt., Ind., 1996—97, Liberty #2, 2002—. Trustee Camp Pt. Pub. Libr., 1999—. Mem.: Music Educators Nat. Conf., Luth. Women's Missionary League. Luth. Avocations: reading, sewing, gardening. Office: Liberty CUSD #2 505 N Park St Liberty IL 62347

DICKIE, FLORENCE, science educator; b. Cleve., Mar. 4, 1949; d. Ben and Rose Rosolowski; m. Paul Alan Dickie, Aug. 13, 1983; 1 child, Stacy. BS, Baldwin-Wallace Coll., Berea, Ohio, 1970; MAT, Johns Hopkins U., Balt., 1971. Tchr. chemistry Conard H.S., West Hartford, Conn., 1971—. Mem. Newington Jr. Woman's Club, Conn., 1986—2006, Newington Greenways Alliance, 2006. Recipient Chemistry Olympiad award, ACS, 1994, 1995, 1997, 2000, 2004, Outstanding Tchr., Sigma Xi-Quinnipiac Coll., 2005. Mem.: West Hartford Edn. Assn., Conn. Sci. Tchrs. Assn., Am. Chem. Soc. Independent. Avocations: running, bicycling, gardening, woodcarving, travel. Office: Conard HS 110 Beechwood Rd West Hartford CT 06107 Office Phone: 860-231-5931.

DICKINSON, CAROL RITTGERS, art historian, writer; b. Des Moines, Apr. 16, 1933; d. Robert Johnson and Cecil Marjorie (Snyder) Rittgers; m. Donald Ira Dickinson, June 6, 1959; 1 child, Lauren Lucy. BA in English with honors, Drake U., 1954; MA in Art History, U. Hawaii, 1964. Lydia Roberts fellow Columbia U., N.Y.C., 1954-56; instr. Iowa State U., U. Hawaii, Colo Women's Coll., U. Petroleum and Minerals, Dhahran, Saudi Arabia, Colo. Sc. Mines, Golden, 1956-76; dir. pub. programs Denver Art Mus., 1980-83; dir. publicity and edn. Mus. Western Art, Denver, 1985-86; freelance writer, 1979—. Lectr., panelist numerous mus., univs. and profl. groups, Colo., 1980—. Co-editor, contbg. author: Colorado and the American Renaissance, 1980, Walking in Beauty, 1990, The Art of Dean Mitchell, 1999; founding editor Denver Urban Design Forum Newsletter, 1984, 85; contbr. more than 500 articles to nat. and regional newspapers and mags.; art critic Denver Rocky Mountain News, 1990-92. Exec. dir. Foothills Art Ctr., Golden, 1992-2003. Recipient Denver Mayor's Award for Excellence in Arts, 2000, 1st Cultural award, Jefferson Symphony, 2000, medal, Colorado Sch. Mines, 2000, Living Landmarks award, Golden Landmarks Assn., 2005, 1st pl. awards, revs./features, Colo. Press Women; Honoree in naming of The Carol and Don Dickinson Sculpture Garden, Foothills Art Ctr., Golden, Colo., 2005. Mem. Golden Fortnightly Club, Asian Art Assn. Democrat. Episcopalian. Avocations: Asian philosophies and history, Chinese brush painting, films. Home: 1908 Pinal Rd Golden CO 80401-1744 Office Phone: 303-278-1357. Business E-Mail: ddickins@mines.edu.

DICKINSON, ELEANOR CREEKMORE, artist, educator; b. Knoxville, Tenn., Feb. 7, 1931; d. Robert Elmond and Evelyn Louise (Van Gilder) C.; m. Ben Wade Oakes Dickinson, June 12, 1952; children: Mark Wade, Katherine Van Gilder, Peter Somers. BA, U. Tenn., 1952; postgrad., San Francisco Art Inst., 1961—63, Academié de la Grande Chaumière, Paris, 1971; MFA, Calif. Coll. Arts, Crafts, 1982, Golden Gate U., 1984. Cert. Recognition El Consejo Mundial de Artistas Plasticos, 1993. Escrow officer Security Nat. Bank, Santa Monica, Calif., 1953-54; mem. faculty Calif. Coll. of the Arts, Oakland, 1971—2001, assoc. prof. art, 1974—84, prof., 1984-2001, prof. emerita, 2001—, dir. galleries, 1975-85. Artist-in-residence U. Tenn., 1969, Ark. State U., 1993, Fine Arts Mus. of San Francisco, 2000, U. Alaska, 1991; faculty U. Calif. Ext., 1967-70; lectr. U. Calif., Berkeley, 1990—; lectr. in field. Author, illustrator: Elkmont: The Heart of the Great Smoky Mountains National Park, 2005; co-author, illustrator: Revival, 1974, That Old Time Religion, 1975; also mus. catalogs; illustrator: The Complete Fruit Cookbook, 1972, Human Sexuality: A Search for Understanding, 1984, Days Journey, 1985; commissions: U. San Francisco, 1990-2001; solo shows include San Francisco Mus. Modern Art, 1965, 68, Santa Barbara Mus., 1966, Corcoran Gallery Art, Washington, 1970, 74, Fine Arts Mus. San Francisco, 1969, 75, J.B. Speed Art Mus., 1972, Poindexter Gallery, NY, 1972, 74, U. Tenn. Downtown Gallery, 1976 Smithsonian Inst., 1975-81, U. Tenn., 1976, 2005, Galeria de Arte y Libros, Monterrey, Mex., 1978, Oakland Mus., 1979, Interart Ctr., NY, 1980, Tenn. State Mus., 1981-82, Hatley Martin Gallery, San Francisco, 1986, 89, Michael Himovitz Gallery, Sacramento, Calif., 1988-89, 91, 93, 97-98, Gallery 10, Washington, 1989, Diverse Works, Houston, 1990, Ewing Gallery, U. Tenn., 1991, G.T.U. Gallery, U. Calif., Berkeley, 1991, Mus. Contemporary Religious Art, St. Louis, 1995, Coun. Creative Projects, N.Y., 1996, Thacher Gallery, U. San Francisco, 2000, Retrospective U. Tenn, 2005, Tenn. Regional Art Ctr., 2006; represented in permanent collections Nat. Collection Fine Arts, Corcoran Gallery Art, Libr. of Congress, Smithsonian Instn., San Francisco Mus. Modern Art, Butler Inst. Am. Art, Oakland Mus., Santa Barbara Mus., Nat. Mus. Women in Arts, Washington, Achenbach Found. Fine Arts Mus., San Francisco; prodr. (TV) The Art of the Matter-Professional Practices in Fine Arts, 1986—. Bd. dirs. Calif. Confedn. of the Arts, 1983-85; bd. dirs., v.p. Calif. Lawyers for the Arts, 1986—; mem. coun. bd. San Francisco Art Inst., 1966-91, trustee, 1964-67; sec., bd. dirs. YWCA, 1955-62; treas., bd. Westminster Ctr., 1955-59; bd. dirs. Children's Theater Assn., 1958-60, 93-94, Internat. Child Art Ctr., 1958-68. Recipient Disting. Alumni award San Francisco Art Inst., 1983, Master Drawing award Nat. Soc. Arts and Letters, 1983, Pres.'s award Nat. Women's Caucus for Art, 1995, Allgemeines Kunstlerfexidon, 2001, Lifetime Achivement award Nat. Women's Caucus for Art, 2003; grantee Zellerbach Family Fund, 1975, NEH, 1978, 80, 82-85, Thomas F. Stanley Found., 1985, Bay Area Video Coalition, 1988-92, PAS Graphics, 1988, San Francisco Cmty. TV Corp., 1990, Skaggs Found., 1991. Mem.: NOW, Nat. Women's Caucus for Art (nat. Affirmative Action officer 1978—80, nat. bd. dirs. 2000—, Pres.'s award 1995), Arts Advocates, Artists Equity Assn. (nat. v.p., dir. 1978—92), San Francisco Art Assn. (sec., dir. 1964—67), Calif. Lawyers for Arts (v.p. 1986—2004, bd. dirs. 1986—), Calif. Confederation of Arts (bd. dirs. 1983—89), Coll. Art Assn. (chair com. of Women in the Arts 2004—06), Coalition Women's Art Orgns. (dir. 1978—80, v.p. 2000—01), AAUP. Democrat. Episcopalian. Office: Calif Coll of the Arts 1111 8th St San Francisco CA 94107-2247 Personal E-mail: eleanordickinson@mac.com.

DICKINSON, GAIL KREPPS, library science educator; b. Lewistown, Pa., June 10, 1956; d. Harold and Esther (Bourdess) Krepps; m. Willis H. Dickinson, Dec. 22, 1979 (div. 1998); children: Margaret Lee, Elizabeth Ann; m. Michael G. Colson, Sr., June 9, 2003. BS, Millersville U. Pa., 1977; MSLS, U. N.C., 1987; PhD, U. Va., 2000. Libr. Cape Charles (Va.) Pub. Sch., 1977-81, Broadwater Acad., Exmore, Va., 1981-85; instrnl. supervisor Union-Endicott Sch. Dist., Endicott, NY, 1987-96; asst. prof. U. N.C., Greensboro, 2000—04, Old Dominion U., Norfolk, Va., 2004—. Adj. prof. James Madison U., Harrisonburg, Va., 1997-99. Mem. AAUW, ASCD, Am. Ednl. Rsch. Assn., Am. Assn. Sch. Librs. (bd. dirs. 1994-97), N.Y. Libr. Assn. (pres. sch. libr. media sect. 1994), Phi Delta Kappa. Avocations: reading, word and video games.

DICKINSON, JANE W., retired executive secretary, volunteer; b. Sept. 27, 1919; d. Charles Herman and Rachel (Whaler) Wagner; m. E. F. Sherwood Dickinson, Oct. 23, 1943; children: Diane Jane Gray Clem, Carolyn Dickinson Vane. BA, Duke U., 1941; MEd, Goucher Coll., 1965. Exec. sec. Petroleum Industry Com., Balt., 1941-43, Sherwood Feed Mills Inc., Balt., 1943-79. Mem. exec. com. Children's Aid Md., 1960-61; mem. bd. women's aux. Balt. Symphony Orch., 1958-60; dist. chmn. Balt. Cancer Drive, 1957; co-chmn. Balt. United Appeal, 1968; bd. mgrs. Pickersgill Retirement Home. Mem. Three Arts Club (Balt., sec. 1958-60, bd. govs. 1960-64, 67-70, pres. 1970-72), Women's Club of Roland Park (bd. govs. 1960-64, 86-88, 92-94), Cliff Dwellers Garden Club, Alpha Delta Phi Home: Apt 609 1055 W Joppa Rd Baltimore MD 21204-3748

DICKINSON, JEANNE M., secondary school educator; d. William Edward and Patricia Conroy Dickinson. BA, Trinity Coll., Washington, 1981. Tchr., coach Mater Dei H.S., New Monmouth, NJ, 1981—, dean of students, 2002—, math club/seminar moderator, 1995—. Mem.: Assn. of Math Tchrs. N.J., Nat. Coun. Tchrs. Math., N.J. Scholastic Coaches Assn. Avocations: sports, reading. Office: Mater Dei High School 538 Church St New Monmouth NJ 07748

DICKINSON, LINDA MARY, graphics designer, art educator; d. Rudolph Ing Swanson and Esther Marion Fitzsimonds; m. Malvin Earl Dickinson, July 28, 2002; children: Craig, Daniel, Alina. AA with hons., Greenriver CC, 1984; BA with hons., Gonzaga U., 1992; student, Boise State U., Idaho, 1995, student, 1998, U. Idaho, 1996—2002. Cert. tchr. Idaho State Bd. Edn., 1992. Supr., bookkeeper Rainbow Family Ctr., Enumclaw, Wash., 1985; office mgr., bookkeeper Pioneer Med. Clinic, Enumclaw, 1985—88, Counseling Group, Spokane, 1991—93; instr. art and history Lakeland Sch. Dist., Rathdrum, Idaho, 1992—; prin., owner Linkra Design, Rathdrum, 2004—. Spkr. in field; rep. Idaho Idaho Coun. Social Studies, Boise, 1998—2000. Idaho and the American West, 1998. Vol. shelter provider for abused women Police Dept., Enumclaw, 1985—87; mem. steering com. Child Abuse Awareness, Enumclaw, 1985. Fellow, Albertson's Found., 1998. Mem.: NEA, Lakeland (Idaho) Edn. Assn. (mem. com. 2002, mem. exec. bd. 2004—), Kappa Delta Pi, Alpha Sigma Nu (life; officer 1991—92, historian 1991—92). Avocations: art, reading, travel, photography. Office: Linkra Design PO Box 377 Rathdrum ID 83858

DICKINSON, MARGERY ELSIE, missionary, clinical psychologist; b. Petoskey, Mich., Oct. 29, 1940; d. David Eugene and Beryle Mae (Herrington) L.; m. Hugh Dickinson, July 30, 2005. BS with honors, Taylor U., Upland, Ind., 1962; MA with high honors, Wheaton (Ill.) Coll., 1983; student, U. Paris Sorbonne, 1970. Lic. psychologist, Pa., limited lic. psychologist, Mich. Tchr. Waterford (Mich.) Sch. Sys., 1962-65; ednl. missionary, county dir. BCM Internat., Union County, NJ, 1965-69; ednl. missionary BCM Internat. and AIM Internat., Albertville and Paris, France, 1969-70, ednl. missionary, technician Watsa, Democratic Republic of Congo, 1970-81; counselor, therapist BCM Internat./AIM Internat. Amani Counseling Ctr., Nairobi, Kenya, 1983-84; organizer, dir. counseling dept., counselor, cons. BCM Internat., Upper Darby, Pa., 1985-97, psychol. testing and assessment of mission candidates, 1986—95, organizer, dir. mem. care ministries, 1998—2000, mem. care ministries, cons., 2000—. Organizer/facilitator Missions and Mental Health-East, Mt. Bethel, Pa., 1995-97; lectr. in field; spkr. in field. Editor: Commit Thy Way, 1994; author: (Bible study series) Living in Community, 1980, translator (illustrator) Bible lessons from English to Lingala for use in Congo; contbr. articles to profl. jours. Facilitator Bible Club work, Democratic Republic of Congo, 1985—; fundraiser, facilitator printing and distbn. Christian lit., 2001—; leader grief support group First Congl. Ch., Rockford, Mich., 2003; Bible study leader Rockford (Mich.) Bapt. Ch., 2004; cons. Congo Internat. Mission, Grand Rapids, Mich., 2004—. Billy Graham Evangelistic Assn. scholar, 1981-83. Mem.: APA (assoc.), Midwest Mem. Care Network (charter), Christian Therapists Bible Study, Assn. N.Am. Missions, Am. Assn. of Christian Counselors (charter, spkr. regional conf. 1999). Baptist. Avocations: writing, clarinet, walking, weightlifting, swimming. Office: 309 Colonial Dr Box 249 Akron PA 17501-0249 also: BCMI Western Mich 710 Baldwin St Jenison MI 49428-9706 Personal E-mail: worship@rockfordbaptist.com. Business E-Mail: membercare@bcmintl.org.

DICKINSON, MARILYNNE FAY, elementary school educator; b. Bethesda, Md., Feb. 18, 1960; d. Richard and Mary Fay; m. Paul D. Dickinson, Aug. 27, 1983; children: Sean, Kelly. BA, Loyola Coll., Balt., Md., 1982; MA, Loyola Coll., 1987; M in Ednl. leadership, Coll. St. Elizabeth, Clifton, NJ, 2006. Cert. Tchrs. k-8 NJ, Eligibility Prin. NJ, 2006. Tchr. St. Joseph's Sch., West Milford, NJ, 2002—. Ednl. leader and mentor Congressional Youth Leadership Coun., 2005—; yr. book advisor, coord. St. Joseph's Sch., 2003—. Achievements include design of implemented first audio book libr. at St. Joseph's for Cchildren wqith special needs.

DICKINSON, MELINDA S., elementary school educator; b. Lansing, Mich., Dec. 4, 1951; d. William Bentges and Arlene Elizabeth (Gillison) Sharp; m. James Lee Dickinson, July 18, 1997; 1 child from previous marriage, Thomas Nigel Berriman. AA, Lansing CC, Mich., 1972; BA, Mich. State U., East Lansing, 1973, MA. Tchr. Roscommon Mid. Sch., Mich., 1973—74, Highview Elem. Sch., Dearborn Heights, Mich., 1974—76, High St., Walnut and Sheridan Rd. elem. schs., Lansing, 1979—. Creator (game) Econ Around Bingo, 2004; co-author: Teaching' With Beans, 2002. Off-ice ofcl. hockey team Mich. State U., 1995—; docent Mich. Hist. Mus., Lansing, 1997—; Civil War reenactor 7th Mich. Vol. Inf., Co. B, Lansing, 1993—. Mem.: Mich. Edn. Assn., Nat. Coun. Social Studies, Mich. Coun. Econ. Edn. (educator assoc. 2003—, Educator of Yr. 2006), Mich. Coun. Social Studies (exec. bd. 2004—). Avocations: reading, counted cross stitch, knitting, gardening, travel. Office: Sheridan Rd Sch 16900 N Cedar Lansing MI 48906

DICKS, PATRICIA K., legislative staff member; b. Detroit, Nov. 22, 1951; BS, U. Colo., 1973. Sec. Colo. Senate, Denver, 1998—. Office: State Capitol 200 E Colfax Ave Ste 250 Denver CO 80203-1716

DICKSON, ANDREA REBECCA, athletic trainer; b. Rochester, NY, Dec. 1, 1977; BA, Hanover Coll., Ind., 2000; MS, Ea. Ky. U., Richmond, 2001. Cert. athletic trainer Nat. Athletic Trainers' Assn. Bd. Cert., Inc. Asst. athletic trainer, tchr. Meth. Coll., Fayetteville, NC, 2001—03; cert. athletic trainer Jewish Hosp., Frazier Rehah Inst., Louisville, 2003—; ter. sales mgr. SpectraBrace, Louisville, 2004—. Med. support for spl. needs sporting event Jewish Hosp., Frazier Rehab, Louisville, 2003—04. Cert. athletic trainer Louisville Slugfest Quadrapalegic Rugby Tournament, Louisville, Ky., 2003, Bluegrass Wheelchair Tennis Championships, Louisville, Ky., 2003, Bluegrass State Winter Games, Lexington, Ky., 2001; vol. Meth. Coll. Booster Club, Fayetteville, NC, 2003. Scholar, Plattner Family, 1999. Mem.: Nat. Athletic Trainers Assn., Louisville Ski Club, Panhellenic Exec. Bd. (historian 1999—2000), Alpha Delta Pi (philanthropy chair 1997—98, scholarship award). Personal E-mail: dredickson@hotmail.com.

DICKSON, DONNA R., medical/surgical nurse; b. Duluth, Minn., Apr. 19, 1935; d. William James and Ruby R. (Atol) Durfee; m. Martin R. Dickson, Dec. 24, 1958; children: Tracy, Jody, Kelly, Joseph. Diploma, St. Luke's Sch. Nursing, Duluth, 1956; BSN, Coll. of St. Francis, Joliet, Ill., 1983, MS, 1987; postgrad., Roosevelt U., Chgo., 1985-87. RN, Ill.; cert. nurse adminstr.; cert. ACLS, IVT. Head nurse Alexian Bros. Med. Ctr., Elk Grove Village, Ill., coord. operating room patient svcs., nurse clinician ent, 2006—. Contbr. articles to nursing jours. Mem. Acad. Otolaryngoscopy Profl. Assn., Assn. Operating Room Nurses (cert.), Chgo. Thoracic Assn. (cert. ACLS, IVT, clinician operating rm.)Native Am. Profl. Assn. Sci. and Engrs. E-mail: mdickson8909@aol.com.

DICKSON, EVA MAE, credit manager; b. Clarion, Iowa, Jan. 16, 1922; d. James and Ivah Blanche (Breckenridge) Dickson. Grad., Interstate Bus. Coll., Klamath Falls, Oreg., 1943. Reporter Mchts. Credit Svc., Klamath Falls, 1941; with credit dept. Montgomery Ward, Klamath Falls, 1941—42; bookkeeper Heilbronner Fuel Col., Klamath Falls, 1942; stenographer City of Klamath Falls, 1943, bookkeeper, office mgr., 1943—52; owner, operator All Star Bus. Svc., Klamath Falls, 1953—58, Ace Mimeo Svc., Klamath Falls, 1958—73; mgr. Mchts. Credit Svc., 1973—87; customer svc. rep. CBI/Credit N.W., 1987—91. Sec. Klamath Cmty. Concert Assn., 1956—99; treas., memls. chmn. Klamath County chpt. Am. Cancer Soc.; mem. Klamath County Centennial Com., 1982, Unification for Progress Joint Planning Com., 1985; nursing adv. com. Oreg. Inst. Tech., 1982—; mem. Klamath Employment Tng. Adv. Com., 1983—86; sec. Unified City for Progress Task Force, 1983—84, Snowflake Winter Festival, 1984—; sec. First Presbyn. Ch., 1992—2005; bd. dirs. United Way, Klamath Falls, 1980—97; bd. dirs., treas. Hope in Crisis; bd. dirs., sec., treas. Klamath Consumer Coun. Recipient Bronze Leadership award, Assoc. Credit Burs., Inc., 1976. Mem.: Klamath Falls Bus. and Profl. Women's Club (pres. 1966—67, 1976—77, 1996—), Oreg. Fedn. Bus. and Profl. Women's Club (state pres. 1971—72), Nat. Fedn. Bus. and Profl. Women's Club. (nat. fin. com. 1982—83, chmn. nat. fin. com. 1983—84), Klamath County C. of C. (pres. 1979, ambs. com. 1980—), Internat. Consumer Credit Assn., Soc. Cert. Consumer Credit Execs., Klamath Basin Credit Women Internat. (pres. 1976—78), Assoc. Credit Bur. Oreg. (pres. 1978—80), Assoc. Credit Bur. Pacific N.W. (pres. 1981—82), Credit Profls. Internat. (treas. dist. 10 1984—85, 2d v.p. dist. 10 1987—88, 1st v.p. 1988—89, pres. 1989—90, internat. bull. chmn. 1990—), Consumer Credit Assn. Oreg. (pres. 1984—85), Daus. of Am. Colonists (past regent local chpt.), Quota (pres. 1958—59, dist. gov. 1969—70). Republican. Presbyterian. Avocations: painting, travel.

DICKSON, KATHRYN, science educator; PhD in Comparative Animal Physiology, U. Calif., San Diego, 1988. Assoc. prof. biology Calif. State U., Fullerton, 1988—. Recipient award Women in Sci. and Tech., 1999. Achievements include research in development and evolution of endothermy in marine fishes and energetics and morphology associated with locomotion in fishes. Office: U Calif Dept Biology 800 N State College Blvd Fullerton CA 92831-3547

DICKSON-FERRELL, TAMARA L., secondary school educator; d. Jerry B. and Wanda L. Dickinson; m. Joseph Ferrell, Aug. 9, 2002; 1 child, Julia. AA, Cotley Coll., Nevada, Mo., 1985; BA, Iowa State U., Ames, 1988. Educator Roland-Story H.S., Story City, Iowa, 1996—. Mem., del. PEO, Story City, 1984—. Mem.: NCTELA, ISEA, RSEA, NEA. Avocations: reading, theater, movies. Home: 724 W Maple Roland IA 50236 Office: Roland-Story HS 1009 Story St Story City IA 50248

DICKSTEIN, BETH J., lawyer, accountant; b. 1963; BS with highest honors, U. Ill., 1985; JD cum laude, U. Pa., 1988. Bar: Ill. 1988; CPA, Ill. Ptnr. Sidley & Austin, Chgo. Office: Sidley & Austin 1 S First National Plz Chicago IL 60603-2000 Fax: 312-853-7036.

DICLAUDIO, JANET ALBERTA, health information administrator; b. Monroeville, Pa., June 17, 1940; d. Frank and Pearl Alberta (Wolfgang) DiC. Cert. in Med. Rsch. Libr. Sci., Luth Med. Ctr., 1962; BA, Thiel Coll., 1975; MS, SUNY, Buffalo, 1978. Registered record adminstr. Dir. med. records Bashline Hosp., Grove City, Pa., 1962, St. Clair Meml. Hosp., Pitts., 1963-73; asst. prof. Ill. State U., Normal, 1976-81; corp. dir. med. records Buffalo Gen. Hosp., 1981-85; dir. med. records Candler Hosp., Savannah, Ga., 1985-94, med. records analyst, 1994-98; pres. prn Assocs., Savannah, Ga., 1998—. Med. record cons. White Cliff Nursing Home, Greenville, Pa., 1973—75; mgmt. cons. Gifford W. Lorenz MD, Savannah, 1992—94; Medicare compliance officer and coder Health Claims, Inc., Savannah, 1999—2001; mgmt. cons. John D. Northup, Jr., MD, Savannah, 2001—02; auditor, cons. Healthpac Computer Sys., Inc., 2001—. Contbr. articles to periodicals. Bd. dirs. Mid-Ill. Areawide Health Planning Corp., Normal, 1979-81. Mem. Am. Health Info. Mgmt. Assn., Ga. Health Info. Mgmt. Assn., S.E. Ga. Health Info. Mgmt. Assn. Avocations: painting, story telling, dance, reading. Office: Ste 705 PMB 153 7400 Abercorn St Savannah GA 31406 Office Phone: 912-352-8383. E-mail: JDCprn@aol.com.

DICOSIMO, PATRICIA SHIELDS, retired secondary school educator; b. Hartford, Conn., June 27, 1946; d. Richard Nichols and Rose Aimee (Roy) Shields; m. Joseph Anthony DiCosimo, Apr. 18, 1970. BFA in Art Edn. and Printmaking, U. Hartford, 1969; MS in Edn. and Art, Ctrl. Conn. State Coll., 1972; postgrad., Rochester Inst. Tech., 1986-87. Cert. tchr., Conn. Tchr. art Simsbury (Conn.) H.S., 1969—2004; ret., 2004. Tchr. Farmington Valley Art Ctr., Avon, Conn., 1989-95; supr. Nat. Art Honors Soc., Simsbury, 1989-2004; mem. Conn. regional adv. bd. Scholastic Art Awards, 1991, 93—; mem. Conn. Scholastic Arts Awards Com., 1989—, co-chair exhibit, 1994—, prin.'s faculty adv. com., 1969-2004; guest lectr. secondary methods in art edn. Ctrl. Conn. State U., 1994; presenter in field; mem. Conn. Curriculum in Arts, 1995-96, writer, 1995; yearbook advisor U. Hartford, 2005—; alumni com. Hartford Art Sch. (sec., 2006—), U. Hartford Alumni Assn., 2004-05 (v.p., 2005-06); mem. Hartford Art Sch. Inc. 2001-06. One-woman shows include Farmington Woods, 1972, Ellsworth Gallery Simsbury, 1974, Annhurst Coll., 1976, Canaan Nat. Bank, 1991, Terryvill Libr., 1994, Henry James Meml. Gallery, 2004; exhibited in group shows at Ctrl. Conn. State Coll., 1969-72 (Best in Show award 1972), Bristol Chrysanthemum Festival Art Show, 1973-84 (Non-objective award 1973, Graphic award 1975, Mixed Media award 1977, Tracy Driscoll Co. Inc. award 1981, Plymouth Spring award 1983, Dick Blick award 1984), Hartford Ins. Co., 1990, Simsbury Libr. Gallery, 1991-93, Henry James Meml. Gallery, 1992, 2004, Riverview Gallery, 1993, Simsbury Dinner Theater, 1994-2004, Canton Gallery on the Green, 1996, 98 (Best of Conn. Mural Contest 1996), Simsbury Mall Mural, 1999, ENO, 2003, Conn. State Legis. Office Bldg., 2004, Canton Libr. Show, 2005; author: Design as a Catalyst for Learning, 1997 Sec. Greater Bristol (Conn.) Condo Alliance, 1990-95; mem. Family Life & Marriage Enrichment, New Britain, Conn., 1970-77; vol. painter Boundless Playground for Handicapped, Simsbury, Conn., 2002, Turkey Trot Food Dr., Simsbury, Conn., 1993-03, W. Hartford Cow Parade, 2003, Bricks Along the Way Cancer Dr., 2004-05 Named Conn. Art Tchr. of Yr., 1993, Patricia Shields DiCosimo Day in her honor, Town of Simsbury, 1993, Conn. Beginning Educator Support Tchr., Conn. Alliance for Arts Edn. Sch. Dist., 1995—96, Simsbury C. of C. Educator of Yr., 2000; recipient Book award, Hartford Art Sch., 1969, Recycling Cmty. Svc. award, Simsbury, 1999, K-12 Sculpture Tchr. 1st pl., Internat. Sculpture Com. Ctr., 2001, Hon. mention, 2001, 1st prize, 2003, John Nerreal Retired Art Educator award, 2006; grantee, Simsbury Edn. Enhancement Found., 1996—97. Mem. NEA, Nat. Art Edn. Assn., Nat. Art Honor Soc. (advisor 1983-2004), New Eng. Assn. Schs. and Colls. (evaluator 1998-99, 2001, 03), Conn. Art Edn. Assn. (H.S. rep. 1983-85, sec. 1985—, Conn. Art Educator 1993, Conn. Alliance for Arts Edn. award for Simsbury Art and Music 1995), Conn. Art Alliance Assn., Conn. Edn. Assn. (mem. 3-D curriculum project 1995-96, portfolio rev. com. 1999, Goals 2000 edn. project 1999-2004), Conn. Craftsman, Farmington Art Guild (tchr. 1992-95), U. Hartford Alumni Assn. (v.p. 2004-06, sec. 2006—). Roman Catholic. Avocations: jewelry, painting, golf, travel. Home: 19 Hampton Ct Bristol CT 06010-4738 Personal E-mail: pat46art@aol.com.

DIDIER, ELAINE K., library director, educator; m. Gordon Didier. BA, AMLS, PhD, U. Mich., Ann Arbor; studied at, U. Oxford. With U. Mich., Ann Arbor, 1977—99, interim dir. academic outreach, assoc. dean to dean Rackham Sch. Grad. Studies, dir. info. resources Stephen M. Ross Sch. Bus., adj. assoc. prof. Sch. Info., dir. Erasmus/Mich. Master of Bus. Info. Program; dean, prof. Kresge Libr., Oakland U.; dir. Gerald R. Ford Presdl. Libr. and Mus., Ann Arbor, 2005—. Mem. bd. trustees Libr. of Mich., 2001, chair, 2003—04. Mem.: Assn. of Coll. and Rsch. Libraries (exec. bd. mem., rep. to Am. Libr. Assn. Coun.), Mich. Libr. Assn. (past pres.). Office: Gerald R Ford Libr 1000 Beal Ave Ann Arbor MI 48109-2114 Office Phone: 734-205-0566. E-mail: elaine.didier@nara.gov.

DIDION, JOAN, writer; b. Sacramento, Calif., Dec. 5, 1934; d. Frank Reese and Eduene (Jerrett) D.; m. John Gregory Dunne, Jan. 30, 1964 (dec. Dec. 30, 2003); 1 child, Quintana Roo (dec. Aug. 26, 2005). BA, U. Calif., Berkeley, 1956. Assoc. feature editor Vogue mag., 1956-63; former columnist Saturday Evening Post, Life, Esquire; now contbr. The N.Y. Rev. of Books, The New Yorker. Novels include Run River, 1963, Play It As It Lays, 1970, A Book of Common Prayer, 1977, Democracy, 1984, The Last Thing He Wanted, 1996; books of essays: Slouching Towards Bethlehem, 1968, The White Album, 1979, After Henry, 1992; nonfiction Salvador, 1983, Miami, 1987, Political Fictions, 2001, Fixed Ideas, 2003, Where I Was From, 2003, (non-fiction) The Year of Magical Thinking, 2005 (Nat. Book award, nonfiction 2005); co-author: (with John Gregory Dunne) Screenplays for films The Panic in Needle Park, 1971, Play It As It Lays, 1972, A Star Is Born, 1976, True Confessions, 1981, Hills Like White Elephants, 1991, Broken Trust, 1995, Up Close and Personal, 1996. Recipient 1st prize Vogue's Prix de Paris, 1956, Morton Dauwen Zabel prize AAAL, 1978, The Edward MacDowell medal, 1996, Columbia Journalism award, 1999. Mem. Am. Acad. Arts and Letters (Gold medal in Belle Lettres and Criticism, 2005), Am. Acad. Arts and Scis., Coun. Fgn. Rels. Mailing: care Janklow & Nesbit 445 Park Ave New York NY 10022-2606

DIECKGRAFE, INDI, performing arts educator, choreographer; b. Albany, Ga., Jan. 26, 1957; d. Eugene Ralph and Joyce Sheets Dieckgrafe; m. Kevin Christian Dreyer, Dec. 28, 1985; children: Natalie Rae Dreyer, Lydia Grace

Dreyer, Wilhelmena Jean Dreyer. BFA in Dance Performance, Wichita State U., Kans., 1983; MFA in Performance and Choreography, U. Ill., Champaign, 1985. Prof. dance St. Mary's Coll., Notre Dame, Ind., 1985—. Regional leader, cert. in "Interplay" improvisational techniques and prins. Choreographer modern dance, sacred dance, musical theatre. Bd. dirs. United Religious Cmty. Bd., South Bend, Ind., 1996—2005, Conservatory of Dance, South Bend, 2004—06, Ctr. for Women's Intercultural Leadership, St. Mary's Coll., 2001—06. Mem.: Am. Coll. Dance Festival Assn. (state rep. 1989—92). Presbyterian. Avocations: yoga, Volkswagens, massage therapy, pets. Office: Saint Mary's College Dept Communication/Performance 111 Moreau Center for theArts Notre Dame IN 46556

DIEDERICHS, JANET WOOD, public relations executive; b. Libertyville, Ill. BA, Wellesley Coll, 1950. Sales agt. Pan Am. Airways, Chgo., 1951-52; regional mgr. pub. relations Braniff Internat., Chgo., 1953-69; pres. Janet Diederichs & Assocs., Inc.; pub. rels. cons. Chgo., 1970—. Com. mem. Nat. Trust for Historic Preservation, 1975—79, Marshall Scholars (Brit. Govt.), 1975—79; trustee Sherwood Conservatory Music, 2000—04, Northwestern Meml. Hosp., 1985—2005, mem. exec. com., 1995—2000, life trustee; founder Com. of 200; chmn. Field Mus., 2003—, founders coun., 1999—; mem. exec. com. Vatican Art Coun., Chgo., 1981—83; pres. Jr. League Chgo., 1968—69; trustee Fourth Presbyn. Ch., mem. bd. dirs., 1990—93; bd. dirs., mem. exec. com. Chgo. Conv. and Visitors Bur., 1978—87; bd. dirs. Internat. House, U. Chgo., 1978—84; bd. dirs. Latino Inst., 1986—89, Albert Pick Jr. Found. Bd. Trustees. Mem. Chgo. Assn. Commerce and Industry (bd. dirs. 1982-89, exec. com. 1985-88), Internat. Women's Forum, Woman's Athletic Club of Chgo., Comml. Club of Chgo., The Casino Club (Chgo.), Wellesley Coll. Bus. Leadership Coun. Office: Janet Diederichs & Associates 208 S La Salle St Ste 1240 Chicago IL 60604-1111

DIEDRICHS, CAROL PITTS, librarian, dean; b. New Orleans, Mar. 8, 1958; d. Leland Bascom and Mae Nell (Harper) Pitts; m. Frank M. Diedrichs. BA, Baylor U., Waco, Tex., 1980; M of Libr. and Info. Sci., U. Tex., 1981. Serials cataloger U. Houston Librs., 1981-82, head acquisition dept., 1982-87, Ohio State U. Librs., Columbus, 1987-97; asst. dir. for tech. svcs. and collections Ohio State U., Columbus, 1997—2003; dean librs. U. Ky., Lexington, 2003—. Mem. editorial bd. Libr. Collections, Acquisitions and Tech. Svcs., 1989-90, editor-in-chief, 1990-2003; contbr. articles to profl. jours. Chair acquisitions serial control com. OhioLink, asst. dir. for policy devel., 1991-92, chair database mgmt. and stds. com.; mem. OCLC Mems. Council, 2001-03, SOLINET Bd. Dirs., 2005—. Mem. ALA (chairperson discussion group, com. mem., sec. mem.-at-large, chmn. sect., pres., Esther J. Piercy award 1991, Leadership in Acquisitions award 1999), N.Am. Serials Interest Group (mem.-at-large), INNOVATIVE Users' Group (com. mem.), Assoc. Libr. Collections and Tech. Svcs. (pres., mem. scholarly comm. com. 2005-). Office: 1-85 WM T Young Libr U Ky Lexington KY 40506-0456 Office Phone: 859-257-0500 ext. 2087. Business E-Mail: diedrichs@uky.edu.

DIEFFENBACH, LISA M., music educator; b. Pottstown, Pa., Feb. 15, 1967; d. James Clayton and Phyllis Joan Rinehart; m. David Paul Dieffenbach, June 10, 1989; children: Benjamin, Shannon. MusB, Millersville Univ., Millersville, Pa., 1989. Music educator Twin Valley Sch. Dist., Birdsboro, Pa., 1990—. Children's choir dir. Emmanuel Fellowship, Millersville, Pa., 2003; pvt, voice, piano, flute tchr., Birdsboro, Pa., 2002—. Mem.: Music Educator's Nat. Conf. Office: Twin Valley Sch Dist 801 White Bear Rd Birdsboro PA 19508 Personal E-mail: joyfullis@hotmail.com.

DIEHL, DEBORAH HILDA, lawyer; b. Troy, N.Y., Feb. 13, 1951; d. Warren S. and Norma K. (Apple) D.; 1 child, Alexandra Ellen. Student, U. de Rouen, France, 1971-72; BA, St. Lawrence U., 1973; JD, Syracuse U., 1976; postdoctoral, George Washington U., 1978-79. Bar: N.Y. 1977, D.C. 1981, Ohio 1982, Md. 1987. Atty. USDA, Washington, 1976-81; assoc. Thompson, Hine & Flory, Columbus, Ohio, 1981-87, Semmes, Bowen & Semmes, Balt., 1987-90, ptnr., 1990-95, Whiteford, Taylor & Preston, Balt., 1995—. Pres. Mt. Royal Improvement Assn., 1995—97; chair Midtown Cmty. Benefits Dist. Mgmt. Authority, 1998—2000, dir., 1995—2001, Midtown Devel. Corp., 2000—; participant Leadership Md., 1997; mem. U. Md. Baltimore County Tech. Ctr. Adv. Bd., 2001—; mem. vision coun. United Way, 2006—; bd. dirs. Jenkins meml. hist. trust Corpus Christi. Mem.: ABA, Bar Assn. City Balt., Md. State Bar Assn. (bus. law sect. coun. 1998—, chair 2002—03). Avocations: bicycling, travel, economic development. Office Phone: 410-347-8766.

DIEHL, DOLORES, performing company executive; b. Salina, Kans., Dec. 28, 1927; d. William Augustus and Martha (Frank) Diehl. Student pub. schs., Kans. Bus. rep. Southwestern Bell Telephone Co., St. Louis and Kansas City, Mo., 1948-49, Mountain States Telephone Co., Denver, 1949-50; edn. coord. pub. rels. Pacific Telephone/AT&T, L.A. and San Diego, 1950-83; cons. Bus. Magnet High Sch., L.A. Unified Sch. Dist., 1977-79; pres. First Calif. Acad. Decathlon, 1979; owner Community Connection, L.A., 1983—; mgr., dir. DelMar Media Arts, Burbank, Calif., 1985-89; mgr. Susan Blu workshops Blupka Prodns., L.A., 1989—; ptnr., dir. animation and commls. voiceover workshops Elaine Craig Voicecasting, Hollywood, Calif., 1989—; freelance performer, voiceover L.A., 1990—; mgr. Sounds Great Film Looping Workshops, L.A., 1992-93; owner Voiceover Connection, L.A., 1994-95; pres. Voiceover Connection, Inc., L.A., 1995—. V.p. pub. rels. San Diego Inst. Creativity, 1965—67. Pub. rels. dir. Greater San Diego Sci. Fair, 1963—68; mem. exec. com. San Diego's 200th Anniversary Celebration, 1967; mem. Better Bus. Bur. Named one of Seven Top Voiceover Trainer, Animation Mag., 1999; recipient Dedication to Edn. award, Industry Edn. Coun., Calif., 1964. Mem.: Industry Edn. Coun. Calif., L.A. and San Diego (past pres.), Magnet Sch. Consortium Cities (chairperson), L.A. Area C. of C. (bd. dirs. women's coun.), Bus. and Profl. Women's Club, Delta Kappa Gamma (hon.). Republican. Methodist. Home and Office: 691 Irolo St Apt 212 Los Angeles CA 90005-4110 Office Phone: 213-384-9251. E-mail: doloresdiehl@speakeasy.net.

DIEHL, NANCY J., lawyer; b. 1953; d. Robert and Anne Diehl. B, Western Mich. Univ.; JD, Wayne State Univ., 1978. Trial prosecutor Recorder's Ct., Detroit, 1981—84; spl. assignment trial prosecutor Cir. Ct., 1984—87; dir. Child Abuse Unit, 1987—94; dep. chief Child and Family Abuse Bur., 1994—2000; chief projects and tng. divsn. Wayne County Prosecutor's Office, Detroit, 2000—04, chief felony trial divsn., 2004—. Mem. Gov. Task Force on Children's Justice (exec. com.), State Bar Rep. Assembly, 1992—96, 1996—2005. Author, illustrator with Lynda Baker (booklet) It is Good to Tell the Truth, 1988, Kids and Secrets, 1992, author, photographer with Lynda Baker Kids Go to Court, 1988; author (with Lynda Baker): (booklet) Sometimes It Is Sad to Be at Home, What Is a Kid to Do About Domestic Violence, 1997. Recipient Leonard Gilman award, 1999. Mem.: Detroit Met. Bar Assn. (Champion of Justice award 2004), State Bar of Mich. (pres. 2004). Office: Wayne County Prosecutor's Office 1441 St Antoine Detroit MI 48226-2302 Office Phone: 313-224-5742. Business E-Mail: ndiehl@co.wayne.mi.us.

DIEHR, BEVERLY HUNT, lawyer; b. Tampa, Fla., Aug. 19, 1954; d. Carl William Jr. and Helen Fern (Rouse) Hunt; children: Erin Elizabeth, Sara Katherine, Dana Marie. BA with high honors, U. So. Fla., 1975; JD with high honors, U. Fla., 1978. Bar: Fla. 1978, U.S. Dist. Ct. (mid. dist.) Fla. 1979. Staff atty. Three Rivers Legal Svcs. Inc., Gainesville, Fla., 1979-82; assoc. Sessums and McCall, Tampa, 1982-83; asst. dist. legal counsel dist. 6 Fla. Dept. Health and Rehab. Svcs., Tampa, 1983-84; pvt. practice law Tampa, 1984—2004; sr. atty. Fla. Dept. Children and Families, 2004—. Mem. Fla. Bar Assn., Hillsborough County Bar Assn., Fla. Assn. Women Lawyers, Hillsborough Assn. Women Lawyers, Order of Coif. Home: 4301 W Cleveland St Tampa FL 33609-3867 Office: State Fla Dept Children and Families 9393 North Florida Ave Ste 902 Tampa FL 33612 Office Phone: 813-558-5510.

DIEKEMPER, RITA GARBS, landscape company executive; d. Donald Richard and Carol Ann Garbs; m. Gregory Robert Diekemper, Feb. 14, 1987; children: Madelyn Garbs, Thomas Garbs, Grace Rickert. BS in Acctg., U. Mo., 1983. CPA Mo. Auditor Touche Ross & Co., St. Louis, 1983—89, Aslage Kiefer and Co., St. Louis, 1990—95; pres., owner Gardens of Grace LLC, St. Louis, 1995—. Chmn. For Our Future.For Our Kids, St. Louis, 1987—2000; chmn. citizen's adv. com. Mehlville Sch. Dist., St. Louis, 1988—89, bd. dirs., 2001—, pres. bd. dirs., 2005—; chmn. Homes for Holidays Ho. Tour, St. Louis, 2001, 2004; treas. Renew Oakville, St. Louis, St. Mark's Episcopal Ch., St. Louis, 1986—2000, vestry mem., 1986—89, endowment pres., 2000—. Recipient Disting. Svc. award, Mehlville Sch. Dist., 2000. Avocations: gardening, half-marathon runner, triathelete, travel. Home and Office: 2571 Cripple Creek Dr Saint Louis MO 63129 Office Phone: 314-846-3850.

DIEMER, EMMA LOU, composer, educator; b. Kansas City, Mo., Nov. 24, 1927; d. George Willis and Myrtle (Casebolt) D. MusB, Yale U., 1949, MusM, 1950; PhD, Eastman Sch. Music, 1960; LHD (hon.), Ctrl. Mo. State U., 1999. Composer-in-residence Arlington (Va.) Schs., 1959-61; composer, cons. pub. schs., Arlington and Balt., 1964-65; prof. theory and composition U. Md., College Park, 1965-70, U. Calif., Santa Barbara, 1971-91. Organist Ch. of the Reformation, Washington, 1962—71, Ch. of Christ, Santa Barbara, 1973—84, 1st Presbyn. Ch., Santa Barbara, 1984—2001. Composer of over 100 choral and instrumental compositions including Music for Woodwind Quartet, 1976, Four Poems of Alice Meynell for Soprano and Chamber Ensemble, 1977, Symphony No. 2, 1980, Suite for Orchestra, 1981, Suite of Homages, 1985, Church Rock, 1986, Variations for Piano, 4 Hands, 1987, String Quartet No. 1, 1987, Serenade for String Orch., 1988, Concerto for Marimba, 1990, Concerto for Piano, 1991, Sextet, 1992, Four Biblical Settings for Organ, 1992, Fantasy for Piano, 1993, Kyrie for Mixed Chorus, Organ, and Piano - 4 Hands, 1993, Santa Barbara Overture, 1995, Gloria for Mixed Chorus, 2 Pianos and Percussion, 1996, Psalm 122 for Bass Trombone and Organ, Psalm 121 for Organ, Brass and Percussion, Psalms for Flute and Organ, Psalms for Trumpet and Organ, Psalms for Percussion and Organ, 1998, Latin Mass, 2000, Homage to Tschaikovsky, 2000, Piano Trio, 2000, Quartet for Piano and Brass, 2001, Songs for the Earth, 2002, Toccata for Six, 2004, Requiem for woodwind quintet and string quintet, 2004, Chumash Indian Dance Celebration, 2004, Homage to Poulenc, Mozart, and MacDowell, 2004, Oxford Town Hall for organ, 2005; composer-in-residence Santa Barbara Symphony, 1990-92. Fulbright scholar, 1952-53; grantee Ford Found. Young Composers, 1959-61, Kindler Found. Commn., 1963, Nat. Endowment Arts, 1980-81; Kennedy Ctr. Friedheim award, 1992. Mem. ASCAP (ann. awards 1962—), Am. Guild Organists (Composer of Yr. 1995), Internat. Alliance for Women in Music, Am. Music Ctr., Mu Phi Epsilon (award of merit 1995). Democrat. Presbyterian. Avocations: reading, electronic and computer music. E-mail: eldiemer@cox.net.

DIEMER, MADELINE ANN (MADELINE DEMER), psychology educator; b. Toledo, Jan. 31, 1936; d. Milton Lewis, Sr. and Jeanette Wright (Dugan) D.; m. Ian Keith Etherington, Sept. 1953 (div. 1971); children: Lorraine Lee, Kim, Lisa. BA in Psychology, U. S. Fla., 1976, MA in Gerontology, 1980, postgrad. Instr. St. Petersburg (Fla.) Jr. Coll., 1975-77; instr., life skills trainer Pinellas County Schs., St. Petersburg, 1979-84; adminstr., instr. Spiritual Ctr., Largo, Fla., 1984-91; educator, cons. Indep. Projects, Odessa, Fla., 1991—; prof. Fla. Metro Palitan U., 1999—. Author: (book) Journey to Joy: A Guide to Enjoying Your Emotions, 1992, Master of Mansions, 2006; (game) Hearts and Pearls, 1987; contbr. articles to newspapers. Asst. pastor The Spiritual Ctr., Largo, Fla., 2003—06, pastor, 2006—. Republican. Avocations: reading, sewing, design, art, music. Home and Office: 11520 Belmack Blvd N Odessa FL 33556-5102 Personal E-mail: anndiemer@yahoo.com.

DIENER, BETTY JANE, business educator; b. Washington, Sept. 15, 1940; d. Edward George and Minnie (Feild) Diener; m. Robert D. Bell, 1987 (dec. 1993). AB, Wellesley Coll., 1962; MBA, Harvard U., 1964, DBA, 1974. Account exec. Young & Rubicam, Inc., N.Y.C., 1964-70; product mgr. Am. Cyanamid Co., Wayne, NJ, 1970-72; asst. dean Sch. Bus. Case Western Res. U., Cleve., 1974-79; dean Sch. Bus. Adminstrn. Old Dominion U., Norfolk, Va., 1986-87; provost, vice-chancellor acad. affairs U. Mass., Boston, 1987-88, prof. mktg., 1987—2002, spl. asst. to chancellor econ. devel., 1993-94; prof., mgmt. Barry U., Miami Shores, Fla., 2002—. Pres. Environ. Bus. Coun. New Eng., Inc., 1995—97. Contbr. articles to profl. publs. Mem. Citizens Coun. Chesapeake Bay, 1986—87; adviser Jr. League, 1963—64, Plans for Progress, 1968—70, Leadership Met. Richmond, 1980—82; mem. Mass. Gov.'s Adv. Com. Sci. and Tech., 1988—90, Mayor's Task Force Empowerment Zones, 1994; mem. cmty. working group Mass. Mil. Reservation, 1997—2000; pres. Provincetown (Mass.) Repertory Theater, 2002, bd. dirs., 2001—03; commr. Norfolk Indsl. Devel. Authority, 1979—82; bd. dirs. Norfolk Conv. and Visitors Bur., 1979—82, Norfolk C. of C., 1979—82, Greater Norfolk Corp., 1986—87, Va. Orch. Group, 1982—87, Va. Stage Co., 1986—87, Karamu Ho., 1975—79, Woodruff Hosp., 1975—79, Women's City Club Cleve., 1976—79, Coun. Sustainable Fla., 2003—, Bainbridge Grad. Inst., 2003—05; mem. adv. com. state and local govt. programs John F. Kennedy Sch. Govt., Harvard U., 1986—88. Named Outstanding Working Woman, Glamour Mag., 1979; named one of 10 Outstanding Career Women of Decade, 1984; recipient Honor award, Soil Conservation Soc., 1984; Fulbright scholar, 2001. Democrat. Home: 4000 Towerside Terr #1108 Miami FL 33138 Office: Barry Univ Andreas Sch of Business Miami Shores FL 33161 E-mail: bejade@aol.com.

DIENSTAG, CYNTHIA JILL, lawyer; b. NYC, Apr. 17, 1962; d. Jack Jacob Helman and Roni Helene (Turk) Setti; div.; children: Marissa, Allison. AA, Fla. State U., 1981; BS, Fla. Internat. U., 1983; JD, U. Miami, 1988. Bar: Fla. 1989, cert.: (family ct. mediator). Jud. asst. Cir. Ct. Judge Frederick N. Barad, Miami, Fla., 1982—85; assoc. Brenner & Dienstag, P.A., Miami, 1988—90, Weissman & Greenblatt, Ft. Lauderdale, Fla., 1990-91, Elser, Greene & Hodor, Miami, 1991-93; pvt. practice Fla., 1993—. Lectr. in field; mentor US Ct. Appeals (11th cir.); bd. dirs. Fla. Internat. U. Alumni Assn. Named Fla. Legal Elite, Fla. Trend, 2006; recipient Put Something Back award, US Ct. Appeals (11th cir.). Mem.: Broward Profl. Alliance, Broward County and Weston Bar Assns. (co-chair family law sect. sch.'s programs com. & professionalism com.), Miami-Dade County Bar, Fla. Bar (support issues, gen. magistrate and rules com.), First Family Inns of Ct. Office: 326 NE 26th Ter Miami FL 33137 also: Weston Town Ctr 1792 Bell Tower Ln Ste 103 Weston FL 33326 Office Phone: 305-250-4680, 954-315-3672. Personal E-mail: cjpda1@aol.com.

DIENSTAG, ELEANOR FOA, corporate communications consultant; b. Naples, Italy; m. Jerome Dienstag (div. 1978); children: Joshua Foa, Jesse Paul. BA, Smith Coll., Northampton, Mass. Asst. editor Random House/Harper & Row, N.Y.C.; editor/writer Monocle Mag., N.Y.C.; cultural columnist Genesee Valley Newspapers, Rochester, NY; sr. mgr., speechwriter Am. Express, N.Y.C., 1978-83. Freelance journalist, N.Y.C., 1983—; lit. resident Yaddo Y., Va. Ctr. for Creative Arts, 95; lectr., book pub. columnist and reviewer in field. Author: Whither Thou Goest, 1976, In Good Company: 125 Years at the Heinz Table, 1994; contbr. articles, essays and feature stories to N.Y. Times, Harper's, N.Y. Observer, McCalls; columnist New Choices Mag. Recipient Merit award for speechwriting Internat. Assn. Bus. Comm., N.Y., Merit award Am. Express Mgmt. Newsletter, Outstanding Mem. award Women in Comm. Mem. Am. Soc. Journalists and Authors (past pres.). Home and Office: Eleanor Foa Assocs 435 E 79th St New York NY 10021-1034 Office Phone: 212-879-1542. Business E-Mail: efoa@usa.net.

DIERAUF, LESLIE ANN, wildlife veterinarian, conservation biologist, consultant; b. Boston, Feb. 7, 1948; d. Curtis John and Adeline M. (Kirk) D. BS in Microbiology, English cum laude, U. Mass., 1970; VMD, U. Pa., 1974; postdoctoral, U. Calif., Davis, 1974-77. Lic. vet., N.Mex., Calif., DC, Nev., NY, Vt., Va.; cert. community coll. tchr., Calif. Instr. physiology U. Calif., Davis, 1976-77; staff vet. Elk Grove (Calif.) Vet. Clinic, 1977, Midtown Animal Hosp., Sacramento, 1978-79, Marin County Vet. Emergency Clinic, San Rafael, Calif., 1979-87; ind. contractor, 1988-93; staff vet. Calif. Marine Mammal Ctr., Ft. Cronkhite, 1979-82, dir. vet. services, 1982-84, bd. sci. advisors, 1984—; instr. animal health tech. Western Sch. Allied Health Professions, Sacramento, 1977-79; cons. Marine Mammal Cons. Services, Novato, Calif., 1985-90; mem. profl. staff fisheries and wildlife conservation issues, sci. advisor Merchant Marine and Fisheries Com. US Ho. of Reps., 1990-93; policy analyst Assn. Am. Vet. Med. Colls. and Am. Vet. Med. Assn., Washington, 1993; vet Wyoming Animal Hosp., Albuquerque, 1993; worked on the endangered species program for the Southwest US Fish and Wildlife Svc.; dir. Nat. Wildlife Health Ctr., US Geological Soc., Madison, Wis., 2004—. Cons. Nat. Marine Fisheries Svc., Animal and Plant Health Inspectia Svc., Envirovet, 1993—, Naval Ocean Systems Ctr., 1984-90, Calif. Marine Mammal Ctr., 1984—, Pribilof Island Fur Seal Program, 1981-84, San Francisco Zoo, 1979-84, Calif. State U., Hayward, 1979-84; mem. bd. sci. advisors West Quoddy Marine Rsch. Sta., Lubec, Maine, 1979-90; bd. examiners Calif. Dept. Consumer Affairs, 1978-85.; mem. exec. com. Consortium for Conservation Medicine.; mem. coordinating com. US Geological Survey Human Health; mem. US Dept. Interior Partnership and Collaboration Team.; mem. working group Nat. Marine Fisheries Service Marine Mammal Unusual Mortality Editor: Handbook of Marine Mammal Medicine: Health, Disease and Rehabilitation, 1990, 2nd edit. 2001; mem. editorial bd. Diseases of Aquatic Organisms, 1985—; contbr. articles to profl. jours. Mem. com. to Save Squaw Valley Meadow; dir. Calif. Marine Mammal Ctr. Run for Seals; mem. Wildlife Care Assn., Sacramento, Sacramento Jr. Sci. Mus., Sacramento Community Orch., Sacramento Intramural Softball and Volleyball; vol. Belchertown State Hosp., Vet. Assistance, Nicaragua, 1988, Pakistan, 1989; bd. dir. U. Calif. Davis Wildlife Health Ctr. Recipient Erickson Ednl. Found. award 1982-83; Thouron scholar U. Pa., 1974, U. Pa. scholar 1970-73; U. Calif., Davis grantee 1974-76; U. Calif. fellow, 1974-75, Teaching fellow U. Calif., 1975-77. Mem. AAAS (Congl. Sci. Fellow, 1990), Washington, DC, 1990, AVMA (editorial asst. 1986, 88-90, mem. environ. affairs com., Animal Welfare award, 1998), Internat. Assn. Aquatic Animal Medicine (pres. 1986-87, chair sci. govt. com. 1989-91, chair govt. rels. 1991—), Soc. Marine Mammalogy, Am. Assn. Wildlife Vets., Women's Vet. Med. Assn., Wildlife Disease Assn., Calif. Acad. Scis., Marine Mammal Ctr., Friends of Sea Otter, Marine Ecosystem Health SeaDoc Soc. (mem. adv. bd.) US Animal Health Assn. (mem. exec. bd.), Internat. Assn. of Fish and Wildlife Agencies Fish and Wildlife Health Com., Alliance of Veterinarians for the Environment (co-founder, mem.) Democrat. Episcopalian. Avocations: skiing, bicycling, climbing, writing, running. Office: Nat Wildlife Health Ctr 6006 Schroeder Rd Madison WI 53711-6223 Office Phone: 608-270-2401. Business E-Mail: ldierauf@usgs.gov.*

DIERCKS, ELIZABETH GORMAN, elementary school educator; b. Harrisburg, Pa., Aug. 12, 1944; d. Jerome Clement and Martha (Stoll) Gorman; m. Gregory Louis Diercks, July 24, 1982. BS, Pa. State U., University Park, 1966; MEd, U. Md., 1975. Advanced profl. cert. Tchr. Fairfax County (Va.) Pub. Schs., 1966-68, Prince George's County (Md.) Pub. Schs., 1968—, grade level chairperson, 1970-97. Early intervention coord. Ft. Washington Elem. Sch., Prince George's County, 1997-2004. Assoc. Nat. Trust for Historic Preservation, Washington; resident assoc. Smithsonian Assocs., Washington; sustainer The Kennedy Ctr., Washington. Mem. Nat. Pks. Conservation Assn., Pa. State Alumni Assn., Nat. Mus. of the Am. Indian (charter mem.), Nat. Mus. Women in the Arts (charter mem.), Kappa Delta Avocations: travel, hiking, swimming, fitness training, reading.

DIERICKX, CONSTANCE RICKER, psychologist, management consultant; b. Evanston, Ill, June 26, 1952; d. Benjamin Franklin Ricker and Betty June Caldwell; m. Michael James Dierickx; children: Amy Steinlight, April Gambill. PhD, Ga. State U., Atlanta, GA, 1998. Psychologist self employed, Marietta, Ga., 1990—98; cons. RHR Internat.Co., Atlanta, 1998—. Spkr. in field; presenter in field. Vol. Save the Park, Marietta, 2001; member, vol., adv. Ga. Coun. for Hearing Impaired., Atlanta, 1995—98; vol. Citizens to Rescind the Resolution, Marietta; Chair, Selection Com/ Habitat for Humanity, Asheville, NC, 1989—90. Grantee, Undergraduate Research Council - University of North Carolina - Asheville, NC, 1989. Mem.: APA, Soc.for Consulting. Psychology, Bd. Dirs. Network (bd. mem.), National Assn. Corp. Dirs. Unitarian Universalist. Avocations: cooking, reading, walking, boxing fan. Office: RHR Internat Co 1355 Peachtree St Ste 1400 Atlanta GA 30064 Office Phone: 404-870-9160. Business E-Mail: cdierickx@rhrinternational.com.

DIERKES, JUDITH ANN, art educator, artist; b. Memphis, Tenn., Mar. 11, 1955; d. Eugene Victor and Rosalind Barbara Ann (Lerche) D. BFA, U. Tenn., 1976, MS, 1981. Graphic artist Ram Screenprinting, Memphis, 1977-80; comml. artist Bike Athletic, Knoxville, Tenn., 1980-81, Screen Art, Inc., Knoxville, Tenn., 1981-82; adminstrn. asst. Blount Mansion, Knoxville, Tenn., 1982-83; artist-in-residence City of Gatlinburg, Tenn., 1983-87, Sevier County Schs., Sevierville, Tenn., 1987-90; instr. Knox County Schs., Knoxville, Tenn., 1990—97; artist-in-residence Norris (Tenn.) Cmty. Craft Cen., 1993—96. Workshop leader Tenn. Arts Acad., Nashville, 1988, artist-in-residence Tenn. Arts Comm., 1990—, workshop leader, 1990, 91; adj. instr. CArson-Newman Coll., Jefferson City, Tenn., 1992-97, Southwest Tenn. C.C., 1992—, U. Memphis, 1999—, Regents Online Degree Program, 2003—, Dyersburg State C.C., 2004—; instr. Knoxville Coll. Upward Bound, 1993; artist-in-residence Ky. Arts Coun., 2003—, Ark. Arts Coun., 2003—. Exhibited in shows at Art Teachers Exhibit at State Museum, 1992, 94, Electronic Gallery Merit award, 1993; commission Knoxville Airport Skyscape, 1992. Sec. Gatlinburg Art Coun., 1985-86; vol. Knoxville Arts Coun., 1991-94; edn. grants review panel Tenn. Arts Commn., 1993-96. Recipient Outstanding Achievement award UT Coll. Edn., 1981 scholarship Arrowmont Sch. Arts & Crafts, 1987; named Vol. of Week WIZK Radio, 1992, Artist of Month Knoxville Arts Coun., 1993. Mem. Tenn. Art Edn. Assn. (spl. concerns 1991-95), Knoxville Arts Coun., Nat. Art Edn. Assn., NAEA Lifelong Learning Affiliate, NAEA Womens Caucus, Nat. Mus. of Women in Arts. Avocation: reiki 2nd degree. Home and Office: 1541 Dearing Rd Memphis TN 38117-6506 E-mail: jabdart@aol.com.

DIERKING, EMILIE M., secondary school educator; b. Rolla, Mo., May 6, 1955; d. Edward Fritz Carl Dierking and Dorothy Marie (Anderson) Brown; m. Wayne Joyce, April 16, 2006; children: Daniel, Timothy. BA, Coe Coll., Cedar Rapids, Iowa, 1977; MATS, Sch. of Theology, Claremont, Calif., 1983. Religion and social studies educator Pilgrim Sch., LA, 1983-88; social studies educator Immaculate Heart HS, 1988—95; religion instr. Ctrl. Meth. Coll. at Mineral Area Coll., Park Hills, Mo., 1995—97; campus min. Immaculate Heart of Mary HS, Westchester, Ill., 1997—2005; campus min., tchr. theology Guerin Prep HS, River Grove, Ill., 2005—. Interreligious dialogue facilitator Nat. Conf. of Christians and Jews, LA, 1986-87. Mem. AAUW, Nat. Cath. Ednl. Assn., Phi Beta Kappa, Phi Kappa Phi. Mem. Eastern Orthodox. Avocations: music, reading, justice issues, movies. Office: Guerin Prep HS 8001 Belmont Ave River Grove IL 60171 Office Phone: 708-453-6233. Personal E-mail: unefemmechic@yahoo.com.

DIERSING, CAROLYN VIRGINIA, educational administrator; b. Rushville, Ohio, Sept. 13; d. Carl Emerson and Wilma Virginia (Neel) Deyo; m. Robert J. Diersing, Dec. 22, 1962; children: Robert, Timothy, Charles, Sheila, Christina. BA, Ohio State U., 1963; state cert., Ohio Dominican, 1985. Cert. tchr., Ohio. Libr. St. Mary's Sch., Delaware, Ohio, 1979—87; asst. tech. svcs. Beeghly Libr. Ohio Wesleyan U., Delaware, 1987—90, dir. curriculum resource dept. edn., 1990—96; libr. assoc. Westerville Pub. Libr., 1997—. Contbr. poetry to Voices. Mem. ALA, Del. Area Recovery Resources (bd. dirs. 1994-96, treas. 1995, sec. 1996), Ohio Libr. Coun., Franklin County Geneology Soc., Ohio Hist. Soc. Office: Westerville Pub Libr Adult Svcs Dept 126 S State St Westerville OH 43081-2095 Business E-Mail: cdiersin@westervillelibrary.org.

DIESTELHORST, AMY LEA, obstetrician, gynecologist; b. Rockford, Ill., Aug. 30, 1973; d. William Matthew and Valerie Lee Warner; m. Jason Chadwick Diestelhorst; children: Allison, Matthew. BA, Bradley U., 1995;

MD, St. Louis U., 1999. Intern U. South Fla., 1999—2000, resident, 2000—03. Ob-gyn Med. Assoc., 2003—. Fellow: Am. Coll. Ob-Gyn; mem.: AMA. Office: Med Assoc W 180 7950 Town Hall Menomonee Falls WI 53051

DIESTELKAMP, DAWN LEA, government agency administrator; b. Fresno, Calif., Apr. 23, 1954; d. Don and Joy LaVaughn (Davis) Diestelkamp. BS in Microbiology, Calif. State U., Fresno, 1976, MS in Pub. Adminstrn., 1983, cert. in tng. design and mgmt., 1992, MBA, 1995. Lic. clin. lab. technologist, Calif.; cert. clin. lab. dir. Clin. lab. technologist Valley Med. Ctr., Fresno, 1977-82, info. sys. coord., 1983-84, quality control coord., 1984-90, sys. and procedures analyst, 1990-91, Fresno County Superior Ct., 1991-98, ct. info. sys. mgr., 1998—2003, dir. tech., 2003—. Chair mid-level mgrs. edn. com. Jud. Coun. Calif., Ctr. for Jud. Edn. and Rsch., 2000—05; faculty U. Phoenix, 1997; instr. Fresno City Coll. Tng. Inst., 1993—98; faculty Calif. State U., Fresno, 1999—2002; pres. Calif. Ct. Assocs., 2003—06; cons., instr. in field. Mem.: Calif. Ct. Assn., Fresno Met. Mus. Soc. Democrat. Office: 1100 Van Ness Ave Fresno CA 93724-0002 Office Phone: 559-488-2655. Business E-Mail: ddiestelkamp@fresno.courts.ca.gov.

DIETRICH, RENÉE LONG, not-for-profit developer; b. Emerald, Pa., Oct. 10, 1937; d. Emmett A. and Arlene I. (Fenstermaker) Long; m. Bruce L. Dietrich, Nov. 25, 1959; children: Dodson, Katie. BS, Kutztown U., Pa., 1959; MLS, Rutgers U., 1966. Cert. fund raising exec., ednl. specialist. Tchr. history Reading Pub. Schs., Pa., 1959-65, libr. Pa., 1965-69; coord. coop. ed. Reading Area C.C., 1978-81, program adminstr. title III grant, 1982-92, coord. cmty. and legis. rels., 1983-98, dir. instnl. advancement, 1991-98, exec. dir. Found. for Reading, 1986—98; dir. planned giving LUTHERCARE, Lititz, Pa., 1999—. Cons. U.S. Office of Edn., Washington, 1990—2005. Contbr. articles to profl. jours. Bd. dirs. Kutztown U. Found., 1981-90, LWV Pa., 1997-99, Great Valley Coun. Girl Scouts U.S., 1999—2006, Susquehanna Valley Planned Giving Coun., 1999—, sec. 2004-; chair bd. trustees Kutztown U., 1976-81; mem. Berks County Commn. for Women, 1993-96; pres. LWV Berks County, 1995-97. Recipient Disting. Alumni award, Kutztown U., 1981; named to Pa. Honor Roll of Women, 1996. Mem. Assn. Fundraising Profls. (named Outstanding Fundraising Exec. for Ctrl. Pa. 2005), Nat. Planned Giving Coun. Mem. United Ch. of Christ. Avocations: music, reading, politics. Home: 1546 Dauphin Ave Reading PA 19610-2118

DIETRICH, RUTH ROBINSON, chemist, researcher, genealogist; b. Keltonburg, Tenn., Sept. 3, 1922; d. Daniel Lanice Robinson and Sarah Frances Mason; m. John Gordon Dietrich, Aug. 17, 1948 (dec. Aug. 19, 1992); 1 child, Ann Mason. Student, Columbia Tenn. Bus. Coll., 1941; BA, Vanderbilt U., 1945. Rsch. chemist Devoe Raynolds Co., Louisville, 1945—48; office mgr. Norton Psychiat. Clinic, Louisville, 1948—50; substitute tchr. Jefferson Co. Sch. Sys., Louisville, 1958—62; sec. Wilson W. Wyatt Wyatt, Grafton & Sloss, Louisville, 1951—60; staff genealogist Nat. Soc. SAR, Louisville, 1979—87; ret., 1987. Mem. adv. com. Estate and Intangible Taxes Legis. Rsch. Commn., Frankfort, Ky., 1961; class chair Vanderbilt U. Living Endowment, 1964—67, area chair, 1968; del. Tri-State Conf. Strengthening State Legislatures, Cin., 1967; mem. Farmington chpt. Questers, Louisville, 1967—79, pres. Farmington chpt., 1973; del. Ky.-Tenn. Assembly State Legis., Gatlinburg, 1967; trustee City of Devondale, Ky., 1968—74; mem. Mayor's Honest Election Com., Louisville, 1968—70; bd. mem. Jefferson County Govt. Conf., 1968—74; mem. Metro. Area Zoning Com., 1971—74; mem. Citizens Adv. Com. Louisville-Jefferson County Air Bd., 1971—75; dir. Am. Lung Assn., Louisville, 1975—84. Mem.: DAR, LWV (v.p. 1963—65, state coord. 1966, 1968, pres. Ky. chpt. 1969—71), Hon. Order Ky. Cols. (col.), Preservation Ky., Nat. Trust for Hist. Preservation, Colonial Williamsburg, Hist. Buckingham Va., Upper Cumberland Geneal. Assn., Beargrass St. Matthews Hist. Soc., Speed Art Mus. and Alliance (docent 1972—81), Filson Hist. Soc., Vanderbilt U. Alumni Assn. (life; dir. 1971—75), WWII Meml. Soc. (life). Avocations: travel, gardening, music, theater, antiques. Home: 7108 Glen Arbor Rd Louisville KY 40222-6538

DIETRICH, SUZANNE CLAIRE, communications consultant, researcher; b. Granite City, Ill. d. Charles Daniel and Evelyn Blanche (Waters) D. BS in Speech, Northwestern U.; MS in Pub. Comm., Boston U., 1967; postgrad., So. Ill. U., 1973-83. Intern prodn. staff Sta. WGBH-TV, Boston, 1958-59; asst. dir., 1962-64; asst. dir. program invitation to art, 1958; cons. producer dir. dept. instructional tv radio Ill. Office Supt. Pub. Instrn., Springfield, 1969-70; dir. program prodn. and distbn., 1970-72; instr. faculty call staff, speech dept. Sch. Fine Arts So. Ill. U., Edwardsville, 1972-73; grad. asst. for doctoral program office of dean Sch. Edn., 1975-78; rsch. asst. Ill. pub. telecomms. study for Ill. Pub. Broadcasting Coun., 1979-80; cons., rsch. in comm., 1980—. Pub. advisor Bradly Pub., Inc., 1996. Exec. prodr., dir. tv programs Con-Con Countdown, 1970, The Flag Speaks, 1971. Mem. sch. bd. St. Mary's Cath. Sch., Edwardsville, 1991-92; cable tv adv. com. City of Edwardsville, 1994—, co-chair, 1996-98; bd. dirs. Goshen Preservation Alliance, Edwardsville, 1992-94, pres., 1995-97; dir. Madison County Hist. Mus. and Archival Libr., 1999—; mem. Madison County Hist. Soc., bd. dirs., 1997-99; mem. mktg./tourism com. City of Edwardsville, 2005—. Recipient Athena award, Edwardsville/ Glen Carbon C. of C., 2004. Roman Catholic. Home: 1011 Minnesota St Edwardsville IL 62025-1424 Office: 715 N Main St Edwardsville IL 62025-1111 Office Phone: 618-656-7562.

DIETZ, ELIZABETH CAMILLA, investment banker; b. Atlanta, Mar. 11, 1942; d. Harry and Iola (Parker) Dietz. BA, Vanderbilt U., 1964; postgrad., NYU, 1965. Securities analyst Chase Manhattan Bank, N.Y.C., 1964—65; securities sales and rsch. Seiden & deCuevas, N.Y.C., 1966—73; investment banker, exec. v.p., dir. Furman Selz Mager Dietz & Birney, Inc., N.Y.C., 1973—. Mem.: Com. 200, Merchandising Analysts N.Y., Investment Assn. N.Y., N.Y. Soc. Security Analysts, Southampton Bath and Tennis Club, Regency Whist Club, Bond Club N.Y. Home: 116 E 68th St New York NY 10021-5955 Office: Fruman Selz Mager Dirtz & Birney Inc 230 Park Ave Fl 12 New York NY 10169-0011

DIETZ, LAUREL PATRICIA, music educator; b. Portsmouth, Va., June 9, 1978; d. James Alan and Shelia-Gene Dietz. BA in Music, St. Mary's Coll. Md., 2000. Cert. tchr. Md. State Dept. of Edn., 2000. Choral dir. Leonardtown (Md.) H.S., 1998—2000; gen. music tchr. Hollywood (Md.) Elem. Sch., 2000—02, band dir., 2000—02; choral dir. Great Mills (Md.) H.S., 2002—. Asst. marching band dir. Leonardtown H.S. Marching Band, 1999—2000; accompanist St. Mary's Musica, California, Md., 2001—03; asst. marching band dir. Great Mills H.S. Marching Band, 2002—; honor chorus dir. St. Mary's County All County Elem. Sch. Honors Chorus. Recipient Outstanding Tchr. award, LDS Ch., 2000, 2003; grantee in arts edn., Wash. Post, 2000—01. Mem.: Md. Music Educators Assn., Music Educators Nat. Conf. Avocations: tennis, travel, music. Home: 26362 Cherry Ln Hollywood MD 20636 E-mail: dietzlp@yahoo.com.

DIETZ, MARGARET JANE, retired public information director; b. Omaha, Apr. 15, 1924; d. Lawrence Louis and Jeanette Amelia (Meile) Neumann; m. Richard Henry Dietz, May 30, 1949 (dec. July 1971); children: Henry Louis, Frederick Richard, Susan Margaret, John Lawrence. BA, U. Nebr., 1946; MS, Columbia U., 1949. Wire editor Kearney (Nebr.) Daily Hub, 1946-47; state soc. editor Omaha World-Herald, 1947-48; libr. aide Akron (Ohio) Pub. Libr., 1963-66, publicity and display dir., 1966-74; editor Owlet, 1966-74; pub. info. officer Northeastern Ohio Univs. Coll. Medicine, Rootstown, 1974-85, dir. Office Comm., 1985-87, ret., 1987. Writer Ravenna (Ohio) Record-Courier, 1988—92; cons. Kent (Ohio) State U. Sch. Music, 1988—91. Author: Akron's Library: Commemorating Twenty Five Years on Main Street, Silver Reflections: A History of the Northeastern Ohio Universities College of Medicine, 1973-98. Mem. culture and entertainment com. Goals for Greater Akron, 1976; pres. bd. Weathervane Cmty. Playhouse, Akron, 1982-85, sec. to the bd., 1988-93, trustee, 1991-93, historian, 1993—, chair 60th anniversary season, 1994-95; pres. Weathervane Women's Bd., 2005—; trustee Family Svcs. Summit County, Ohio, 1980-84, dist. trustee, 1994—, Am. Heart Assn., Akron dist., 1986-91, Mobile Meals Found., Akron, 1988-91; v.p. Friends of Akron-Summit County Pub. Libr., 1988-94, pres., 1994-95, bd. dirs., 2003—, sec., 2005—; student tutor LEARN Literacy Coun., 1988-94, trustee, 1988-95. Recipient Trustee award Weathervane Cmty. Playhouse, 1985, Family Svcs. Bernard W. Frazier award, 1994, John S. Knight award Soc. Profl. Journalists, 1995. Mem. Women in Comm. (Mary Kerrigan O'Neill award 1995), LWV (edn. found. 1989-92, newsletter editor Akron 1957-60), Coll. Club, Press Club, Akron Women's City Club, Jewish Cmty. Ctr. Home: 887 Canyon Trl Akron OH 44303-2401 Personal E-mail: mjd887@earthlink.net.

DIETZEL, LOUISE ALVERTA, psychologist; b. Canton, Ohio, Nov. 18, 1937; d. Daniel Walter and Velma Irene Bender Miller; m. Cleason Samuel Dietzel, June 18, 1960; children: Laurie Christine, Rebecca Doreen, Beth Ann. BS, Goshen (Ind.) Coll., 1960; MS, St. Michaels Coll., 1976. Lic. psychologist, lic. clin. mental health counselor, Vt. Dir. day care, Mt. Pleasant, Mich., 1965-67, E. Lansing, Mich., 1967-71, Winooski, Vt., 1972-73; sch. cons. Essex Junction (Vt.) Schs., 1976-77; rsch. asst. U. Vt., Burlington, 1976-77; pvt. cons. practice Essex Junction, 1974—. Chair counselor Vt. Clin. Mental Health Counselors, Montpelier, 1989-95, elem. counselor Essex Junction Schs., 1977-94, cons. Head Start, Burlington, Vt., 1992-99; psychology instr. St. Michael's Coll., 1999—. Author: Parenting With Respect and Peacefulness, 1995. Mem. Am. Mental Health Counselors Assoc., Vt. Psychol. Assn., Am. and Vt. Counseling Assn. Avocations: cooking, furniture refinishing, camping, antiqueing. Home: 37 Prospect St Essex Junction VT 05452-3612 Office: Psychol Svcs 6 Hillcrest Rd Essex Junction VT 05452-3611 Office Phone: 802-878-2118. E-mail: louise.dietzel@verizon.net.

DIFABIO, CAROL ANNA, psychotherapist; b. Newark, Aug. 6, 1955; d. Rosario and Antoinette Sarah (Palermo) Nicosia; m. Dante Michael DiFabio, Oct. 13, 1979; 1 child, Nicholas AB, Youngstown State U., 1977, MS, 1979. Lic. profl. clin. counselor. Psychotherapist Cath. Cmty. League, Lisbon, Ohio, 1980—81, Child and Adolescent Svc. Ctr., Canton, Ohio, 1981—88; asst. psychologist Robert Lesowitz, M.D., Inc., Canton, 1987—95; counselor Klein Ind. Sch. Dist., Tex., 1996; psychotherapist North Fulton Psychiat. Care, P.C., Roswell, Ga., 1996—2001; pvt. practice Alpharetta, Ga., 2001—. Mem. ACA, Nat. Bd. Cert. Counselors Roman Catholic. Office: Northfall Counseling Ste 1006 11815 Northfall Ln Alpharetta GA 30004 Office Phone: 770-240-8363.

DIFEDE, JOANN, psychologist; BA, George Washington Univ., 1982; MA, New Sch. for Social Rsch., 1986, PhD, 1992. Assoc. prof. psychology, dept. of psychiatry Weill Cornell Medical Coll., NYC; and assoc. attending psychologist NY Presbyn. Hosp./Weill Cornell Medical Ctr., NYC; also dir., program for anxiety, traumatic stress studies Payne Whitney Clinic, NYC. Cons. NY Presbyn. Hosp. Burn Ctr. Author: (numerous articles, chapters) on assessment, treatment of PTSD. Named one of Best Doctors, NY Mag., 2005; recipient numerous NIH grants; grantee Aaron Diamond Fellowship award, 1992—95. Achievements include publishing first report of successful use of virtual reality tech. for treatment of PTSD following 9/11. Office: Dept Psychiatry & PTSD Program NY Presbyn/Weill Cornell Med Ctr 525 E 68th St New York NY 10021 Office Phone: 212-821-0783. Office Fax: 212-821-0994.*

DIFRANCO, ANI, music executive, musician; b. Buffalo, N.Y., Sept. 23, 1970; Founder Righteous Babe, 1990—. Albums include: Ani DiFranco, 1989, Not So Soft, 1991, Imperfectly, 1992, Puddle Drive, 1993, Out of Range, 1994, Like I Said, 1994, Not A Pretty Girl, 1995, More Joy Less Shame, 1996, Dilate, 1996, Living in Clip, 1997, Little Plastic Castle, 1998, Up, 1999, Little Plastic Remixes, 1999, Fellow Workers, 1999, To the Teeth, 1999, Swing Set, 2000, Revelling/Reckoning, 2001, So Much Shouting, So Much Laughter, 2002, Evolve, 2003, Educated Guess, 2003, Knuckle Down, 2005, Carnegie Hall, 2006, Reprieve, 2006. Office: Righteous Babe Records PO Box 95 Ellicot Sta Buffalo NY 14205-0095 also: c/o Tracy Mann at MG Ltd 6th Fl 355 W 52nd St New York NY 10019

DIGBY, LYNNE A., artist, writer; arrived in U.S., 1962, naturalized, 1975; d. Francis Edwin Beard and Cecily Ida Pankhurst; m. Bruce Raymond Digby-Worsley, Sept. 25, 1954 (dec. Mar. 21, 1957); m. Robert Douglass Burnett, July 23, 1963 (div. Dec. 16, 1982); children: Sarah Candace Burnett, Robert Francis Mucklow Burnett, John Austin Douglass Burnett. Ordinary nat. in mech. engring., Tech. Coll., Gloucester, 1954. Tracer Gloucester Rwy. Carriage Wagon Co., 1951—52; draftsman, tech. illustrator Ordenda Engines, Toronto, Ont., Canada, 1955—57; installation draftsman Gloucester Aircraft Co., 1952—55; market rsch. supr. Toronto, 1960—61; airline reservationist Delta Airlines, N.Y., 1962—63; surface designer Digby Assoc., Goshen, NY, 1983—95, fine artist, writer, designer and poet, 1995—. Author: (collection of poems & sketches) May I Share with You, 2002. Participant, writer MoveOn.org; mem. Common Cause. Recipient Best in Show award for oil painting, Orange County Exhibit, Orange County C.C., 2005, Harness Racing Mus. award, 1995, Best Oil Painting of Yr. award, George McCullough Scholarship, 1958, 1960. Mem.: Woodstock Artist Assn. and Mus. Independent. Office: Digby Assocs 153 Montgomery St Goshen NY 10924 Office Phone: 845-294-6512.

DIGBY, PAMELA ANNETTE, elementary school educator; d. Joe and Annette Tripp; m. William E. Digby, Jan. 2, 1972; children: Donterio, Tamija children: Shaquala Thurman, Tevin. BS, Ga. Coll. and State U., Milledgeville. Cert. middle sch. educator Ga., 1990. 5th grade tchr. Putnam County Elem. Sch., Eatonton, Ga., 1990—. Vacation Bible sch. tchr. Springfield Bapt. Ch., Monticello, Ga., 2002—05; inclusion tchr., 2003—06. Mem.: NEA (assoc.). Home: 9836 Ga Hwy 83 Monticello GA 31064 Office: Putnam County Elementary School 162 Old Glennwood Spring Rd Eatonton GA 31024 Office Phone: 706-485-5141. Business E-Mail: pamtri@yahoo.com.

DIGGLES, PATSY ANN, elementary school educator; b. Jasper, Tex., Sept. 19, 1953; d. Obie and Ophelia Diggles. BS in Edn., Lamar U., Beaumont, Tex., 1975; MEd in Mid-Mgmt. Supervision, SFASU, Nacogdoches, Tex., 1985. Tchr. J.H. Rowe Intermediate, Jasper, Tex., 1976—. Mentor DETCOG (Star), Jasper. Sec. I.W. Norsworthy Scholarship. Recipient Yellow Rose of Tex. award, Gov. Dolph Briscoe, Austin, Tex., 1978. Mem.: NAACP, Tex. State Tchr.'s Assn., VFW Aux. (Tchr. of Yr. award 1994), Elizabeth Ct. Calanthe, Heroine of Jericho (sec.). Democrat. Baptist. Avocations: photography, poetry.

DIGGS, CAROL BETH, marketing professional; b. Lubbock, Tex., Feb. 26, 1949; d. Billy Horace Diggs and Adele Frieda (Krueger) Weinberger. BA with honors, Okla. U., 1970; MA, George Washington U., 1974; postgrad., Johns Hopkins U., 1974—76. Tchr. Norman (Okla.) Pub. Schs., 1970—71; promotion asst. Johns Hopkins U. Press, Balt., 1976—77; tng. asst. 1st Nat. Bank Md., Balt., 1977—78, mktg. coord., 1978—79, br. adminstrn. officer, exec., 1979—83, product mgmt. exec., 1983—85, sr. product mgmt. exec., 1985—87; asst. v.p. Signet Bank Md., Balt., 1987—88; product specialist DISC, Inc., Balt., 1989—91; dir. sales and mktg. svcs. Am. Credit Indemnity divsn. Dun & Bradstreet, 1991—93; v.p. Davis Consulting Group, Balt., 1994—95; pres., mng. dir. Diggs Exec. Search and Bus. Cons., Catonsville, Md., 1995—. Cons. in field. Editor: Tower, Ch. of Messiah, 1982—84. Active Balt. Symphony Chorus, 1976—83, bd. dirs., 1979—81; ch. promotion coord. Md. Bicentennial Fund, Balt., 1983; adv. bd. Md. Ch. News, Bishop Claggett Ctr.; bd. dirs. Am. Red. Cross, Howard County. Fellow, George Washington U., 1972—74, Johns Hopkins U., 1974—76; Eastern Star scholar, Okla. U., 1967, E. K. Gaylord scholar, 1967, 1969. Mem.: MLA, Nat. Assn. Bank Women, Sigma Delta Pi (treas. 1973—74), Alpha Lambda Delta. Republican. Home: 2118 Oak Lodge Rd Baltimore MD 21228-4715 Office: Diggs Exec Search and Bus Cons 2118 Oak Lodge Rd Catonsville MD 21228-4715 Office Phone: 410-455-9978. Personal E-mail: carol.diggs@verizon.net.

DIGHANS, KAY MARIE, elementary school educator, education educator; b. Glendive, Mont., Mar. 16, 1953; d. Kenneth James and Lola Irene (DeWitt) Swenson; m. Rick Dighans, June 5, 1982; children: Nicholas Robert, Kevin Matthew, Eric James. B in Elem. Edn., Mont. State U., 1975; MEd, Lesley Coll., 1993. Kindergarten tchr. Belgrade Pub. Sch., Mont., 1975—81, 3rd grade tchr., 1981—. Adj. prof. Mont. State U., Bozeman, 2004—. Recipient Outstanding Citizen of Belgrade, Belgrade Jaycees, Mont., 1979. Avocations: crafts, football spectator. Office: Ridge View Elem 117 Green Belt Dr Belgrade MT 59714

DI GIACOMO, FRAN, artist; b. Miami, Ariz., Oct. 24, 1944; d. B.J. and LaVenia Marilyn (Beavers) Fain; m. Len DiGiacomo, May 9, 1970; children: Marc, Eric. Student, Scottsdale Artist's Sch., 1985—2000; studied, with David Leffel, with Joe Anna Arnette, with Greg Kreutz, with Howard Terpning. Commissions include portraits of Supreme Court Chief Justice Warren E. Burger, Dist. Atty., 1994, Henry Wade, 1995, Haggar Apparel, Dallas Cowboys' Emmitt Smith, 1993; author: I'd Rather Do Chemo Than Clean Out the Garage, 2003; subject of numerous articles. Recipient 2nd place, 1993, Hon. Mention, 1994, 1st place, 1996, Plano Art Assn.,1st place, 1994, Assoc. Creative Artists, Grumbacher Gold, 1997, 2nd place, 1994, Trinity Arts Guild, 1st place, 1998, 3rd place, 1999, Richardson Civic Art, 3rd place, 1995, Tex. and Neighbors 5 state. Mem. Oil Painters Am. (assoc., signature), Am. Soc. (assoc.), Classical Realism, Portrait Soc. Am., Assoc. Creative Artists (signature). Avocation: tennis.

DIGIAMARINO, MARIAN ELEANOR, retired realty administrator; b. Camden, N.J., July 23, 1947; d. James and Concetta (Biancosino) DiG. BS in Mgmt., Rutgers U., 1978; ThM, Georgian Ct. U., 2004. Clk. stenographer transp. div. Dept. of Navy, Phila., 1965-70, sec., 1970-73, realty asst. Profl. Devel. Ctr. program, 1973-75, realty specialist, 1975-81, supervisory realty specialist, head acquisition and ingrant sect., 1981-85, supervisory realty specialist, mgr. ops. br., 1985-92, spl. asst. for real estate, 1992-99; ret., 1999; pastoral assoc. Ch. of St. Isaac Jogues, Marlton, N.J., 1999—. Instr. USNR, Phila., 1983, 88. Contbr. articles to profl. jours. Mem. AAUW, Soc. Am. Mil. Engrs., Nat. Assn. Female Execs., Phi Chi Theta (pres. Del. Valley chpt. 1984-86, nat. councillor 1984, nat. fundraising com., pres. and corr. sec. (Alpha Omega chpt. 1976-78). Avocations: theater, sports, needlecrafts, reading, beach combing.

DIGIORGIO, SARA AHERN, assistant principal; BS in Biology, U. Va., Charlottesville, 1997; MS in Biomed. Sci., U. Mass., Worcester, 1999; postgrad., U. Mass., Lowell. Sci. tchr. Lynnfield H.S., Mass., 1999—2003, sci. dept. head, 2001—03; dir. of sci. and tech. edn. Shrewsbury H.S., Mass., 2003—06, asst. prin. for student svcs., 2006—. MCAS assessment devel. com. Mass. Dept. Edn., Malden, 2001—05, Title IIB partnership grant reviewer, 2006—. Named Disting. Secondary Educator, Mass. Dept. Edn., 2003, Most Influential Tchr., Mass. Acad. of Math and Sci., 2004, MIT, 2001; fellow, Howard Hughes Med. Inst., 2003; grantee Corning Partners in the Cmty. grantee, Corning Life Sci., 2003, 2005. Mem.: ASCD, Nat. Assn. of Sci. Tchrs., Mass. Secondary Sch. Prins. Assn. Office: Shrewsbury High School 64 Holden St Shrewsbury MA 01545 Office Phone: 508-841-8800.

DIGIOVANNI, JOAN FIMBEL, psychology educator; b. Jersey City, N.J., June 18, 1935; d. Selma Caroline (Kugler) Fimbel; m. Philip DiGiovanni, June 23, 1956; children: Juliet Paula, Portia Jonquil. Student, U. Miss., Europe, 1954; BA in Edn., Fla. So. Coll., 1954; MA in Psychology, Columbia U., 1955; PhD in Psychology, Baylor U., 1961. Lic. psychologist, elem. and sch. psychologist, Mass. Counselor women's residence halls, dean of women's office U. Ill., Champaign, 1955-57; tchg. asst. psychology dept. Baylor U., Waco, Tex., 1958-61; asst. prof. psychology Old Dominion U. (formerly Norfolk Coll. of William and Mary), Norfolk, Va., 1961-63; rsch. asst. U. Mass., Amherst, 1963; asst. prof. psychology, coord. field work svcs. and rehab. Springfield (Mass.) Coll., 1963-65; dir. counseling svc., asst. prof. psychology Western New Eng. Coll., Springfield, 1966-73, prof. psychology, 1973-98, chmn. dept. human studies, 1990-92; vis. prof. psychology U. Ariz., Tucson, 1999—. Adj. prof. psychology Westfield State Coll., 1980—; rsch. assoc. U. Mass., Amherst, 1963; instr. Am. Internat. Coll., Springfield, 1963 vis. scholar Inst. Fine Arts, NYU, 1985, N.Y.U., 1988, U. N. Mex., Albuquerque, 1989; NEH scholar Mex. Colonial Act, U. N. Mex., summer, 1992. Presenter in field. Mem. APA (mem.-at-large div. Psychology of Art 1990—), Am. Soc. Psychopathology of Expression, Am. Assn. Women in Psychology, Mass. Psychol. Assn., New Eng. Psychol. Assn. (steering com. 1993—), Ea. Psychol. Assn., Internat. Coun. Psychologists (area chair), N.Mex. Psychoanalytic Assn., Psi Chi, Alpha Kappa Delta, Phi Theta Kappa. Unitarian Universalist. Avocation: psychobiographer. Office Phone: 520-514-2241. E-mail: jdiartstudio@dakotacom.net.

DIGIUSTO, ELAINE BESSIE, science educator; b. Joliet, Ill., Nov. 1, 1952; d. Phillip and Bessie Frances (Lestina) DiGiusto. BS in Biology, U. St. Francis, Joliet, Ill., 1975; M in Sci. Edn., Olivet Nazarene U., Ill., 1990. 6th grade sci./social studies tchr. Coal City (Ill.) Mid. Sch., 1979—89, 5th grade sci./social studies tchr., 1989—99, 6th grade sci./social studies tchr., coord. 6th grade chemist challenge program, 1999—. Mid. sch. coord. Sch. Improvement Team, Coal City, Ill., 1990—. Mem.: NEA, ASCD, Nat. Middle Sch. Assn., Ill. Edn. Assn., Ill. Sci. Tchrs. Assn., Nat. Coun. Social Studies Tchrs. Roman Catholic. Avocations: reading, travel, crafts. Home: 152 E 1st St Braidwood IL 60408 Office: Coal City Mid Sch 500 S Carbon Hill Rd Coal City IL 60416

DIGNAC, GENY (EUGENIA M. BERMUDEZ), sculptor; b. Buenos Aires, June 8, 1932; came to U.S., 1954; d. Jose Victor Marenco and Margarita Eugenia D.; m. Jose Y. Bermudez, Apr. 7, 1958; children— Alexander, Melanie. Student, U. Buenos Aires, 1952-54. Lectr. in field. Exhibited in one-woman shows at Galeria 22, Caracas, Venezuela, 1967, Michael Berger Gallery, Pitts., 1969, Cinema 2, Caracas, 1971, Pyramid Gallery, Washington, 1971; exhibited in numerous group shows including Corcoran Gallery of Art, Washington, 1958, 59, Inst. Contemporary Arts, Washington, 1967, Bklyn. Mus., 1968, Mus. Modern Art, Buenos Aires, 1971, Mus. Fine Arts, Boston, 1971, Palais des Beaux Arts, Brussels, 1974, Inst. Contemporary Arts, London, 1974; represented in permanent collections including Fundacio Joan Miro, Barcelona, Spain, Palazzo Dei Diamanti, Ferrara, Italy, Museo La Tertulia, Cali, Colombia, Galeria del Banco Central, Guayaquil, Ecuador, The Latinoamerican Art Found., San Juan, P.R., and others in Argentina, Chile, Germany, Italy, Ireland, Spain, U.S. and Venezuela; works include 27 Fire Gestures-, 1970-2000; radio and TV interviews, U.S. and abroad; works with lights, fire and temperatures; subject of profl. articles, films. Recipient prize for light sculpture IX Festival of Art, 1969 Home: 4109 E Via Estrella Phoenix AZ 85028-4515 Office: Osuna Art 7200 Wisconsin Ave Bethesda MD 20814 Office Phone: 602-996-1555. E-mail: gdignac@aol.com.

DIGREGORIO, AMANDA ELIZABETH, medical products executive; b. Boulder, Colo., Dec. 2, 1981; d. Milton Ralph and Beverly Alice DiGregorio. BSc in Athletic Tng., Xavier U., Cin., Ohio, 2004; MSc in Health Adminstrn. and Mgmt., Regis U., Denver, 2005. Cert. athletic trainer Nat. Athletic Tng. Bd. Certification. Asst. athletic trainer Xavier U., Cin., 2000—04; med. asst. sports medicine Colo. U., Boulder, Colo., 2004—05; coord. med. equipment distibn. Colo. Prof. Med., Golden, Colo., 2005—. Med. interpreter Internat. Interpreting, Denver, 2004—; med. translator Wellness Coaches USA, Bluebell, Pa., 2004—; cons. in field. Counselor RAAP, Denver, 2000—. Mem.: Colo. Athletic Trainers Assn., Nat. Athletic Trainers Assn. Avocations: singing, triathlons, volleyball.

DI IORIO, DANIELA, oceanographer, researcher; b. Victoria, B.C., Canada, Feb. 5, 1964; d. Livia and Matthew Di Iorio; m. Donald Newman, June 1995; children: Evan, Marco. BSc in Physics and Astronomy with honors, U. Victoria, 1988, PhD, 1994. Post-doctoral fellow Inst. Ocean Scis., Sidney, B.C., Canada, 1994—95; scientist NATO SACLANT Undersea Rsch. Ctr., La Spezia, Italy, 1995—99; asst. prof. U. Ga., Athens, 1999—. Grantee, NSF, 2005—. Mem.: Acoustical Soc. Am. (corr.; mem. acoustical oceanography tech. steering com. 2002—). Achievements include research in advanced the use of acoustic scintillation to monitor oceanographic flow and turbulence in hydrothermal vent and bottom boundary layer environments. Office Phone: 706-542-7020. Office Fax: 706-542-5888.

DIKET, MARY READ M., academic administrator, educator; b. Oak Ridge, Tenn., Aug. 2, 1944; d. Edmund Warren and Jeanne (Howie) Montgomery; m. Merrill Edward Diket, Feb. 12, 1966; children: Cameron, Melissa, Tally. B in Art Edn., U. Miss., 1965; M in Art Edn., U. So. Miss., 1988; PhD in Art, U. Ga., Athens, 1991. Art and English instr. Murrah High Sch., Jackson, Miss., 1965-66; art instr. St. John's Day Sch., Laurel, Miss., 1971-73, 86; ptnr. Art Assocs. Studio, 1987-89; grad. teaching asst. U. So. Miss., 1987-89, U. Ga., 1989-90, rsch. affiliate, 1991-92; dir. creativity workshop William Carey U., Laurel, Miss., 1992—, dir. honors program, 1992—, prof. art and edn., 1992—. Prodr., instr. workshops U. Ga. Family Housing, 1989; humanities instr. and testing cons. creative scholars program Lamar U., Beaumont, Tex., 1990-93; adj. prof. William Carey Coll., 1992; vis. prof. art dept. U. So. Miss., 1992; reviewer Am. Edn. Rsch. Assn., 1992-, paper presenter, 1992-; dir. Apple Edn. Seed Grant, 1995-96; presenter papers Nat. Art Edn. Assn., 1990-, Fla. State Art History Grad. Symposium, 1991, Nat. Assn. Gifted Children, 1993-96, 2002-06. Co-editor: Trends in Art Education From Diverse Cultures, 1995; editor: Miss. Assn. for Gifted Children, 1993; contbr. articles to profl. jours.; exhbns. U. Miss., 1964-65, Protective Paint Co. Jackson, Miss., 1965, McComb Juried Art Show, 1966, Jones County Jr. Coll., 1987, YWCA, Laurel, Miss., 1988, U. So. Miss., 1988, U. Ga., 1990; costume designer, set designer for 10 plays Laurel Little Theatre, 1981-87; cartoonist: (campus newspaper) Mississippian, 1963. Recipient Nat. Historian award Delta Delta Delta, 1984, Faculty Excellence award William Carey Coll., 1993, Outstanding Humanities Faculty, 1995, Miss. Legis. HEADWAE award for Faculty, 2001, Miss. Alliance for Arts Excellence in Higher Edn., 2002, Nat. Higher Educator of Yr., 2003; grantee Task Force for Edn. Govt. Elect Kirk Fordice, 1991, Lauren Rogers Mus., 1986. Fellow Nat. Art Edn. Assn. (disting.); mem. Internat. Soc. Edn. Through Art, Am. Ednl. Rsch. Assn. (co-chmn. arts and learning 1993, 94, editor arts and learning rsch. 1995, 96), Brain, Neuroscience Edn. (pres. 2002-04), Siminar Rsch. Art Edn. (pres. 1999-2000), Women's Caucus (pres.-elect 2006-), Nat. Art Edn. Assn-.(Manual Barkan award for Pub. of Yr., 2003), Internat. Mind, Brain, Neuroscience Soc. (charter), Miss. Art Edn. Assn., Nat. Assn. for Gifted, Miss. Assn. for Gifted Children, Laurel Arts League, Colonial Dames Am., DAR, Affiliate Garden Clubs Am., Phi Delta Kappa, Alpha Chi (Nat. advisor award 2003). Avocation: theater. Home: 805 N 6th Ave Laurel MS 39440-2710 Office: William Carey Coll 498 Tuscan Ave Hattiesburg MS 39401-5461 E-mail: diketwcc@netdoor.com.

DILALLA, LISABETH ANNE FISHER, developmental psychology researcher, educator; b. Bayshore, N.Y., July 6, 1959; d. David Elemelich and Leila Lois (Katz) Fisher; m. David Louis DiLalla, Aug. 12, 1984; children: Matthew Scott, Shaina Emily. BA, Brandeis U., 1981; PhD, U. Va., 1987. Nat. Inst. Child Health and Human Devel., postdoct. fellow Inst. Behavioral Genetics, U. Colo., Boulder, 1987-90; rsch. assoc. So. Ill. U., Carbondale, 1990-91, rsch. asst. prof., 1991-92, asst. prof. dept. behavioral and social scis., 1992-98, assoc. prof. dept. behavioral and social scis., 1998-99; vis. scholar Brandeis U., 1999, assoc. prof. family cmty. medicine, 1999—. Cons. Joint Legislative Audit and Rev. Com., Richmond, Va., 1984; rsch. cons. Govt. of Bermuda, 1985; statis. cons. U. Va., Charlottesville, 1986-87; cons. Inst. Social Rsch., Boulder, Colo., 1988; workshop leader Women in Sci., Carbondale, 1992-96; tutor for sci. fair Giant City Sch., Carbondale, 1992, 93, 94. Grantee U. Colo. Health Scis., Ctr. Devel. Psychobiology Endowment Fund, 1988, NIH, 1992-95, SIUC, 1993-96; recipient SIUC Spl. Rsch. award, 1993-96, 97-99, SIU Sch. Medicine CRC rsch. grant, 1998-2000, 2002-04, Mensa award, 1991, 98, Shalom award Brandeis U., 1981. Mem. Soc. for Rsch. in Child Devel., Behavior Genetics Assn., Am. Psychol. Soc., Sigma Xi Sci. Honor Soc. (sec., 2002-). Achievements include research on predictors of intelligence from infancy, genetic and environ. influences on aggressive and cooperative play, mother-infant interactions. Office: So Ill U Sch Medicine Dept Family Cmty Medicine Carbondale IL 62901 Business E-Mail: idilalla@siu.edu.

DILEONE, CARMEL MONTANO, retired dental hygienist; b. New Haven, Aug. 24, 1926; d. Nicholas and Martha (Ercolano) M.; m. Eugene Francis Dileone, Jan. 28, 1948; children: Gina, Richard. Dental Hygienist, Temple U., 1945; AA, Albertus Magnus Coll., 1980; BS, U. Bridgeport, 1983; MS, So. Conn. State U., 1985. Registered dental hygienist. Dental hygiene practitioner George M. Montano, DDS, New Haven, 1946-50, George V. Montano, DDS, Orange, 1959-2000, Francis R. Mullen, DDS, West Haven, 1950-55; dental hygiene practioner Herbert Saunders, DDS, Orange, Conn., 1958-63, Children's Dental Assocs., Hamden, 2000—03, Children's Dental Group, New Haven, 2000—; ret., 2006. Instr. Huntington Inst., North Haven, Conn., 1983; adj. assoc. prof. U. Bridgeport, Conn., Fones Sch. Dental Hygiene, 1985-96; adj. faculty U. New Haven, 1994—. Dir., treas. Conn. Hygienists' Polit. Action Com., 1996—2002. Recipient Profl. Recognition award U. New Haven, 1999. Mem.: New Haven Dental Hygienists Assn. (pres. 1949, 1975), Conn. Dental Hygienists Assn. (treas. 1986—88, v.p. 1988—89, pres.-elect 1989—90, pres. 1991, Mabel C. McCarthy award 1983, Pres. award 1994), Am. Dental Hygienists Assn., Am. Soc. Dentistry for Children, Conn. Pub. Health Assn., Sigma Phi Alpha. Roman Catholic.

DILGEN, REGINA MARIE, English educator; b. Bklyn., Feb. 9, 1954; d. John C. and Frances M. (Mollo) D.; m. William A. Tignor, Jan. 8, 1988; children: Mia Stephanie, Francesca Maria. BA, U. Fla., 1976; MA, Fla. Atlantic U., 1985; MA in Libr. Sci., U. South Fla., 1990. Adj. instr. English, Palm Beach C.C., Lake Worth, Fla., 1988-97, assoc. prof., 1997—. Mem. ALA, Nat. Coun. Tchrs. English, Fla. Coll. English Assn. Democrat. Office: Palm Beach CC 4200 Congress Ave Lake Worth FL 33461-4705

DILIBERTI, LARA MARIE, music educator; d. Mark Michael Medvedev and Ludmilla Sokolov; m. Charles Ernest DiLiberti, July 24, 1983 (div.). BS, William Paterson State U., 1980; MA, Columbia U., 1985. Cert. gen. edn. grades K-8. Band dir. Ben Franklin Jr. H.S., Teaneck, NJ, choir dir.; musical dir. Teaneck H.S.; gen. music tchr. Radburn Sch., Fairlawn, NJ; tchr. summer music theatre Fairlawn H.S.; summer vocal dir. Summit (N.J.) H.S., vocal musical dir.; choral dir. Matawan (N.J.) Regional H.S. Mem.: Music Educators Nat. Conf., Am. Choral Dirs. Assn., Adoptees Liberty Movement Assn., Reunited Twins Assn., Kappa Delta Pi. Avocations: writing, running, target shooting. Office Phone: 732-290-2800.

DILL, LAURA LEE, athletic trainer, educator; b. Canton, Ohio, May 28, 1970; d. PerLee Joel and Janine Carol Hartman; m. Douglas Ellis Dill, July 22, 2000; children: Bailey Rose, Hayden Joel. BS, Ohio U., Athens, 1992; MEd, U. Cin., 1994; EdD, Va. Poly. Inst. and State U., Blacksburg, 2006. Athletic trainer U. Calif., Irvine, 1999—2002, Saddleback Coll., Mission Viejo, Calif., 2003—05; athletic trainer, prof. Concordia U., Irvine, 2005—. Mem.: Nat. Athletic Trainers' Assn. (cert.). Avocations: travel, reading. Office: Concordia U 1530 Concordia West Irvine CA 92612 Office Phone: 949-854-8002 1492. Business E-Mail: laura.dill@cui.edu.

DILL, SHERI, publishing executive; With Wichita (Kans.) Eagle, v.p. mktg. Office: The Wichita Eagle PO Box 820 Wichita KS 67201-0820

DILLARD, ANNIE, writer; b. Pitts., Apr. 30, 1945; d. Frank and Pam (Lambert) Doak; m. R.H.W. Dillard, 1965 (div.); m. Gary Clevidence, 1980 (div.); 1 child, Cody Rose; stepchildren: Carin, Shelly; m. Robert D. Richardson, Jr., 1988. BA, Hollins Coll., 1967, MA, 1968. Contbg. editor Harper's Mag., N.Y.C., 1974-81, 83-85; scholar-in-residence Western Wash. U., Bellingham, 1975-78; disting. vis. prof. Wesleyan U., 1979-83, adj. prof., 1983—, writer-in-residence, 1987—98, writer emeritus, 1998—, bd. dirs. Writers Conf., 1984—, chmn., 1991—. Fellow Calhoun Coll., Yale U., New Haven, Conn.; Phi Beta Kappa orator Harvard-Radcliffe U., 1983; mem. U.S. writers del. UCLA US.-Chinese Writers Conf., 1982; mem. U.S. cultural del. to China, 1982; bd. dirs. The New Press, Key West Writers Conf., Wesleyan Writers Conf., Key West Literary Seminars; mem. usage panel Am. Heritage Dictionary. Author (poems): Tickets for a Prayer Wheel, 1974, 3d edit., 2002, Pilgrim at Tinker Creek, 1974 (Pulitzer prize for gen. non-fiction 1975, Best Fgn. Book Pub. in France 1990), Holy the Firm, 1978, Living by Fiction, 1982, Teaching a Stone to Talk, 1982, Encounters with Chinese Writers, 1984, An American Childhood, 1987 (Nat. Book Critics award finalist 1987), The Writing Life, 1989 (English-speaking union Amb. Book award 1990), The Living, 1992, The Annie Dillard Reader, 1994, Mornings Like This, 1995, For the Time Being, 1999 (Maurice Coindreau prize 2001); editor: (with Robert Atwan) Best Essays, 1988; (with Cort Conley) Modern American Memoirs, 1995. Mem. Nat. Com. on U.S.-China Rels., 1982—, St. Mary's Soup Kitchen, Key West, Fla.; bd. dirs. Milton Ctr., Authors League Fund, Key West Literary Seminars, Wesleyan Writers Conf. Recipient N.Y. Presswomen's award for excellence, 1975, Wash. Gov.'s award for contbn. to lit., 1978, Appalachian Gold medallion U. Charleston, 1989, Found. award St. Botolph's Club, 1989, History Maker award Hist. Soc. Western Pa., 1993, Conn. Gov.'s award in the arts, 1993, Milton Ctr. prize, 1994, Campion award Am. Mag., 1994, Am. Acad. Arts and Letters award in Lit., 1998; grantee NEA, 1980-81, Guggenheim Found., 1985-86. Mem. NAACP, Soc. Am. Historians, Authors Guild, Am. Acad. Arts and Letters, Key West Volleyball Assn.,Phi Beta Kappa. Democrat. Address: c/o Timothy Seldes Russell & Volkening 50 W 29th St New York NY 10001-4227*

DILLARD, MARILYN DIANNE, property manager; b. Norfolk, Va., July 7, 1940; d. Thomas Ortman and Sally Ruth (Wallerich) D.; m. James Conner Coons, Nov. 6, 1965 (div. June 1988); 1 child, Adrienne Alexandra Dillard Coons (dec.). Studied with Russian prima ballerina, Alexandra Danilova, 1940's; student with honors at entrance, UCLA, 1958-59; BA in Bus. Adminstrn. with honors, U. Wash., 1962. Modeling-print work Harry Conover, N.Y.C., 1945; ballet instr. Ivan Novikoff Sch. Russian Ballet, 1955; model Elizabeth Leonard Agy., Seattle, 1955-68; mem. fashion bd., retail worker Frederick & Nelson, Seattle, 1962; retail worker I. Magnin & Co., Seattle, 1963-64; property mgr. Kirkland, Wash., 1961—; antique and interior designer John J. Cunningham Antiques, Seattle, 1968-73; owner, interior designer Marilyn Dianne Dillard Interiors, 1973—. Rsch. bd. advisors Am. Biog. Inst., Inc., 1990—. Author: (poetry) Flutterby, 1951, Spring Flowers, 1951; contbr., asst. chmn. (with Jr. League of Seattle) Seattle Classic Cookbook, 1980-83. Charter mem., pres. Children's Med. Ctr., Maude Fox Guild, Seattle, 1965—, Jr. Women's Symphony Assn., 1967-73, "200+1" Org., 1967-70, Virginia Mason Med. Ctr. Soc., 1990—, Nat. Mus. of Am. Indian, Smithsonian Instn., 1992—; mem. Seattle Jr. Club, 1962-65, 97—; mem. Friends of the Pike Place Market (saved the market from demolition), 1971; bd. dirs. Patrons N.W. Civic, Cultural and Charitable Orgns., chmn. various coms., Seattle, 1976—, prodn. chmn., 1977-78, 84-85, auction party chmn., 1983-84, v.p. party/prodn., 1984-85, exec. com., 1984-85, chmn. bd. vols., 1990-91, adv. coun., 1991—; mem. U. Wash. Arboretum Found. Unit, 1966-73, pres., 1969; bd. dirs. Coun. for Prevention Child Abuse-Neglect, Seattle, 1974-75; bd. dirs., v.p., mem. coms. Seattle Children's Theatre, 1984-90, asst. in lighting main stage plays, 1987-93, adv. coun., 1993—2004, asst. in lighting main stage plays Bathhouse Theatre, 1987-90; adv. bd. N.W. Asian Am. Theatre, 1987-2001, Co-Motion Dance Co., 1991—; organizer teen groups Episcopal Ch. of Epiphany, 1965-67; provisional class pres. Jr. League Seattle, 1971-72, next to new shop asst. chmn., 1972-73, bd. dirs., admissions chmn., 1976-77, exec. v.p., exec. com., bd. dirs. 1978-79, sustaining mem., 1984—; charter mem. Jr. Women's Symphony Assn., 1967-73; mem. Seattle Art Mus., 1975-90, Landmark, 1990—, Corp. Coun. for Arts, 1991-2003; founding dir. Adrienne Coons Meml. Fund, 1985, v.p. 1985-92, 95—, pres. 1992-95; mem. steering com. Heart Ball Am. Heart Assn., 1986, 87, auction chmn., 1986; mem. steering com. Bellevue Sch. Dist. Children's Theatre, 1983-85, pub. rels. chair, 1984, asst. stage mgr., 1985; mem. Hist. Seattle Preservation and Devel. Authority, 1997—; mem. Eastlake Cmty. Coun., 1997—; mem. Steamship Virginia V. Found., 1997—; mem. Floating Homes Assn., Seattle, 1999—; mem. Queen Anne Hist. Soc., 2000—; com. chmn. Rep. Precinct, 2000; mem. Kirkland Downtown on the Lake Orgn., 1999—; apptd. City of Kirkland Downtown Strategic Planning Action Com., 2001—; mem. City of Kirkland Transit Ctr. location com., 2001-03. Named Miss Greater Seattle, 1964; honored for leadership in the arts Jr. League of Seattle, 2002; charter mem. Nat. Cowgirl Hall of Fame, 2002. Mem. U. Wash. Alumnae Assn. (life), Pacific N.W. Ballet Assn., Progressive Animal Welfare Soc., Associated Women U. Wash.(student coun. 1962), Husky Honeys (U. Wash. rep. 1961-62, chair fashion bd. U. Wash. 1961-62, Sr. Honor Woman award U. Wash. 1961-62), Acad. Am. Poets, Profl. Rodeo Cowboys Assn. (assoc.), Seattle Tennis Club. Republican. Episcopalian. Avocations: needlepoint, horseback riding, theater, travel, antique restoration. Home and Office: 2053 Minor Ave E Seattle WA 98102-3513 Office Phone: 206-328-0322.

DILLARD, PATRICIA SPRATLING, educational consultant; d. Eugene, Sr. and Maude Morse Spratling; 1 child, John Michael. BS, Ala. State U., Montgomery; MEd, Columbus State U., Ga. Tchr. 2nd grade Rock Mills Elem. Sch., Ala., 1971—72; tchr. 4th and 5th grades reading /lang. arts Matthews Elem. Sch., Columbus, Ga., 1972—74; tchr. 2nd and 3rd grades Balboa Heights and Ft. Gulick Elem. Schs., Pnama, Canan Zone, Panama, 1972—78; instrnl. lead tchr./tchr. support specialist Mucsogee County Sch. Dist., Columbus, Ga., 1978—. Mem. J. W. Darden Found., Opelika, Ala., 2004—06. Nominee Disney Sci. Tchr. of Yr., 2002, 2006. Mem.: NEA, Ct. Apptd. Child Adv., Order of Ea. Star (life; dau. of isis 1991—), Alpha Kappa Alpha Alpha Sorority, Inc. (chairperson track mentoring program 1983—). Office Phone: 706-683-8772. Business E-Mail: dimon@mcsdga.net.

DILLARD, TERESA MARY, school counselor; b. Columbus, Ga., May 12, 1956; d. Francis Joseph and Sadayo (Takabayashi) Luther; m. David Howard Dillard, July 22, 1978; children: Christine Marie, Justin David. BA, U. Md., 1977, MEd, 1981. Cert. guidance counselor, social studies tchr., modern fgn. lang. tchr., Mass., N.C. Asst. to supr. Bur. Govtl. Rsch., U. Md., College Park, 1977-78; tchr. high sch. Montgomery County Pub. Schs., Rockville, Md., 1978-80; substitute tchr. Anne Arundel Pub. Schs., Annapolis, Md., 1981, Bourne County Pub. Schs., Cape Cod, Mass., 1982-84; guidance counselor Camden County Pub. Schs., Camden, NC, 1989-95, Chesapeake (Va.) Pub. Schs., 2003—06. Counselor, advisor U. Md. Relief Ctr., College Park, 1977, tutor Japanese lang., 1977, vol. substitute instr. Japanese lang. dept., 1977; cons. UCNC Radio Talk Show, Elizabeth City, N.C., 1991; program developer Grandy Primary Sch., Camden, N.C., 1989-95. Designer, creator children's clothing. Religious edn. tchr. Ft. Meade (Md.) Chapel Ctr., 1978, St. Bernadette Ch., Severn, Md., 1979-80, Otis Chapel, Otis Air Nat. Guard Base, Mass., 1982-83, coord., dir. religious edn. program, 1983-84, Holy Anolis Ch., Portsmouth, Va., 2004-2006; bd. dirs., tchr. Holy Family Religious Edn. Program, Elizabeth City, N.C., 1989-91; asst. music ministry Holy Family Ch., Elizabeth City, 1991-95 Mem. ACA, Am. Sch. Counselors Assn., U. Md. Alumni Assn., Phi Beta Kappa, Phi Kappa Phi, Alpha Kappa Delta. Roman Catholic. Avocations: sewing, needlecrafts, writing, woodburning, tae kwon do martial arts.

DILLASHAW, EULA CATHERINE, artist, graphics designer; b. Memphis, Feb. 19, 1947; d. John Clemons and Catheryn Livingston (Murdock) Ballew; m. Stanley Neil Williams, July 29, 1968 (div. Sept. 1982); children: John C., Eric N., Heather L.; m. William Alfred Dillashaw, Oct. 22, 1986. Student, Art Instrn. Sch., 1959-63, Memphis State U., 1965-67, Daytona Beach C.C., 1986-89. Exec. sec. Franklin Simon, N.Y.C., 1973-78, Benefit Providers for Local Unions, Memphis, 1979-82; tchr. Eula's Art Studio & Gallery, Lake Helen, 1993—. Tchr. pvt. art classes for children and adults. One-person shows include Daytona Beach Airport, 1996, Daytona Beach Shores City Hall/C. of C., 1997, 00; represented in pvt. collections. Supt. fine arts Volusia County Fair, Deland, 1995—; pres. Lake Helen League of Artists & Crafters, 1994—; supt., bd. dirs. Volusia County Fair Assn. Bd. Recipient Best in Show profl. divsn. Volusia City Fair, 1997. Mem. Lake Helen C. of C. Democrat. Avocations: gourmet cooking, canning, raising pedigree birds, travel. Home: 35 Chardean Ave Ashland MS 38603-6600 Fax: 904 228-0364.

DILLENBURG, CAROLYN EVA LAUER, retired secondary school educator; b. Adair County, Iowa, May 13, 1934; d. Harvey Francis and Lorna Orilda (Gilbert) Lauer; m. Dale Everett Dillenburg, May 29, 1954; children: Candace Dee Brotherton, Shari Sue Eivins, Jeffrey Dale Dillenburg. AA, Creston Jr. Coll., 1954; BS, Iowa State Coll., 1956; MSEd., Drake U., 1968. Cert. secondary tchr. Engr.'s aide GM, Indpls., 1955; math. and sci. tchr. Afton (Iowa) Independent Sch., 1957-58, Runnells (Iowa) Independent Sch., 1958-59; math. and English tchr. Winterset (Iowa) Community Sch., 1959-61; math. and sci. tchr. O-M Community Sch., Orient, Iowa, 1961-63; math. and English tchr. Creston (Iowa) Community Sch., 1964-65; math. tchr. Lenox (Iowa) Community Sch., 1968-94; ret., 1994. Adj. math. tchr. Southwestern C.C., Creston, 1977-81; curriculum coord. Green Valley AEA 14 Schs., 1994-2006. Treas. Iowa Town and Country YWCA, southwest Iowa, 1981-2001; pres. Creston YWCA Coun., 1981—2001; bd. trustees Greater Regional Med. Ctr., 1997—. Mem. NEA (life), S.W. Uniserv (bd. dirs. 1988-92, mem. contract advancement cadre 1992-94, mem. ret. tchrs. cadre 1994—2000), Iowa State Edn. Assn. (life, ret., mem. standing com. for ret. tchrs. 1994—2000), Creston Area Ret. Sch. Personnel Assn., P.E.O., Elzivirs Women's Reading Group, Delta Kappa Gamma, Pi Mu Epsilon, Psi Chi. Mem. United Ch. of Christ. Avocations: antiques, travel. Home: 1392 150th St Creston IA 50801-8406

DILLENKOFFER, JUDITH A., music educator; b. New Orleans, La., 1949; 1 child, Suzanne. B of Music Edn. in Voice, Loyola U., 1971; cert. in drafting and structural, Jefferson Vocational, 1979; cert. auto cad, Jefferson Tech. Inst., 1990. Cert. Notary Public Delgado Jr. Coll., 2004, Teacher State of La. Music ministry organist Archdiocese of New Orleans, 1974—, gen. music tchr., 1972—73, 1977—78; civil and structural drafting J.J. Krebs & Sons, Inc., Metairie, La., 1979—85; survey drafting BFM Corp., Kenner, La., 1985—89; sub. tchr. Jefferson Parish Schools, Metairie, 1987—92; piano tchr. River Ridge Music Sch., La., 1993; owner Music Tutoring by Dillenkoffer, Metairie, 1994—. Composer: Music Compositions Vol. II, 2003, Music Compositions Sept. 11 2001, 2003; poet: A Poet Speaks, 1982. Mem. Nat. Rep. Party, Metairie, 1987—2004; ch. organist; mem. Jefferson Parish Vision 2020, 1999—2003, Airline Pk. Civic Assn., Metairie, 1981—2004. Mem.: Nat. Pastoral Musicians, Music Educators Nat. Conf., Single and Single Again, New Orleans Area Cath. Alumnae Club. Republican. Roman Cath. Avocations: poetry, ceramics, sewing, fishing.

DILLER, ELIZABETH E., architect, educator, artist; b. Poland, 1954; B in Arch., Cooper Union Sch. of Arch., 1979. Ptnr. Diller & Scofidio (now Diller Scofidio & Renfro), NYC, 1979—; assoc. prof. arch. design Princeton U., NJ, 1990—, prof. arch. Works include Inst. of Contemporary Art, Boston, Seagrams, NY, Mus. of Art & Tech., NY, Blur Bldg. (Progressive Architecture Design award), media pavillion for Swiss EXPO 2002, designed viewing platform for Ground Zero, NYC, Brasserie Restaurant, NY (James Beard Found. award for Best New Restaurant Design), Slither, Gifu, Japan, Loophole, Mus. Contemporary Art, Chgo., 1992, Apparatus Drawing, Mus. of Modern Art, NY, 1993, Case#00-17164, New Mus., 1993, Dysfunction, Ctr. d'Art Contemporian de Castres, France, 1993, Desiring Eye, I' dentity and Difference, Triennale, Milan, 1994, Pelts, Thaddeus Ropac Gallery, Paris, France, 1997, Non-Place, San Francisco Mus. Modern Art, 1997, Slow House, At the End of the Century: One Hundred Years of Architecture, Mus. Contemporary Art, LA, 1998, The American Lawn: Surface of Everyday Life, Canadian Centre for Architecture, Montreal, 1998, Public Faces/Private Places, Pusan Internat. Arts Festival, Korea, 1998, His/Her Bathroom, Thomas Healy Gallery, NY, 1998, Dress Code, Landesmuseum, Linz, Austria, 1998, (permanent collections) Travelogues, Internat. Arrivals Terminal 4, JFK Airport, NY, (installation) The Desiring Eye: Reviewing the Slow House, Gallery MA, Tokyo, 1992, Master/Slave, Fondation Cartier, Paris, InterClone Hotel, Ataturk Airport for Istanbul Biennial, 1997, (dance collaborations with the Lyon Ballet Opera of France and Charlerol/Danses of Belgium (touring exhbn.) EJM1:Man Walking at Ordinary Speed and EJM2: Inertia, 1998, (web project) Refresh, Dia Art Found., (video installation) Pageant, Johannesburg Biennial & Rotterdam Film Festival, 1997, (permanent installation) X,Y, Kobe, Japan, 1997, (multi-media work for stage in collaboration with Builders Assn.) Jet Lag, 1998 (Obie award for Creative Achievement), (pub. art commn., permanent video marques) Jump Cuts, United Artists Cineplex, San Jose, Calif., (collaborative dance work with Charlerol/Danses) Moving Target, (collaborative theater work with Dumb Type and Hotel Pro Forma) Business Class, Copenhagen Cultural Capital, (interactive video installation) Indigestion, Barbican Art Gallery, London, Walter Phillips Gallery, Banff, Canada, Biennial Nagoya, Japan, 1997, (electronic project) Subtopia, ICC Gallery, Tokyo, 1997, and several others, installations commissioned by Mus. of Modern Art, Whitney Mus., New Mus. of Contemporary Art, Walker Art Ctr., Minn., Cartier Found., Palais des Beaux-Arts Brussels, and Gallery Ma Tokyo, works are in the permanent collections of Mus. of Modern Art, Mus. Modern Art San Francisco, Fond Nat. d'Art Contemporain, several FRACs in France, Musee de la Mode in Paris, and many private collections, co-pub. with Ricardo Scofidio Back to the Front: Tourisms of War, FRAC Basse-Normandie, 1994, Flesh: Architectural Probes, Princeton Architectural Press, 1995, Blur: The Making of Nothing, Abrams, 2002. Recipient Chrysler award for Innovation in Design, 1988—89, MacArthur Found. award, 1999, Brunner prize in Arch., AAAL, 2003, MacDermott award for Creative Achievement, MIT; Graham Found. Fellowship, 1998—99, Chgo. Inst. for Architecture and Urbanism Fellowship. Office: Princeton U Sch Architecture 5116 Architecture Princeton NJ 08544-0001 Address: Diller Scofidio & Renfro 36 Cooper Sq New York NY 10003 Office Phone: 212-260-7971.

DILLER, PHYLLIS (PHYLLIS ADA DRIVER DILLER), actress, writer; b. Lima, Ohio, July 17, 1917; d. Perry Marcus and Frances Ada (Romshe) Driver; m. Sherwood Anderson Diller, Nov. 4, 1939 (div. Sept. 1965); children: Peter III, Sally, Suzanne Diller Mills, Stephanie Diller Waldron, Perry; m. Warde Donovan, Oct. 7, 1965 (div. July 1975). Student, Sherwood Music Conservatory, Chgo., 1935-37, Bluffton Coll., Ohio, 1938-39; D.H.L., Nat. Christian U., 1973; PhD (hon.), Bluffton Coll., 1993. (Best TV Comedienne award TV Radio Mirror 1965); Author: Phyllis Diller Tells All About Fang, 1963, Phyllis Diller's Housekeeping Hints, 1966, Phyllis Diller's Marriage Manual, The Complete Mother, The Joys of Aging and How to Avoid Them, 1981, (with Richard Buskin) Like A Lampshade in a Whorehouse: My Life in Comedy, 2005; Accompanied Bob Hope entertainment group to South Vietnam, Christmas, 1966, symphony appearances soloing on piano.; Theatrical prodns. include Dark at the Top of the Stairs, 1961, Wonderful Town, 1962, Happy Birthday, 1963, Hello, Dolly!, 1970, Everybody Loves Opal, 1972, What Are We Going to Do With Jenny, 1977, Nunsense, 1989, The Wizard of Oz, 1990-92; numerous appearances TV and radio, concerts, supper clubs and hotels, 1955-; producer, writer: Phyllis Diller Shows, 1963, 64; rec. artist, Verve Records, Columbia Records, pres., BAM Prodns., Ltd., from 1965, PhilDil Prodns., Ltd., 1966-; motion pictures include Eight on the Lam, 1967, The Private Navy of Sergeant O'Farrell, Hungry Reunion, 1981, Pink Motel, 1983, The Nutcracker Prince, 1990, The Boneyard, 1991, The Perfect Man, 1993, The Silence of the Hams, 1994, A Bug's Life (voice), 1998, The Debtors, 1999, Everything's Jake, 2000, The Last Place on Earth, 2002, Hip! Edgy! Quirky!, 2002, West From North Goes South, 2002, Motocross Kids, 2004, West From North Goes South, 2004, Forget About It, 2005; star: TV series The Pruitts of Southampton, 1966-67, Beautiful Phyllis Diller Show, 1968-69 (Recipient honors including Star of Year award Nat. Assn. Theatre Owners), The Bold and the Beautiful (recurring role), 1995-, Titus, 2002; video appearance: How to Have a Moneymaking Garage Sale, 1987. Recipient Minuteman award U.S. Treasury Dept., Disting. Service citation Ladies Aux. VFW, Woman of Year award Variety Club Women Balt.; Golden Apple Hollywood Women's Press Club, 1967, Woman of Year award St. Louis chpt. Nat. Bus. and Profl. Women's Club, 1971; named hon. mayor Brentwood, Calif., 1971; Hon. life mem. San Francisco Press and Union League Club; named Walk of Fame Star on Hollywood Blvd., 1975, Hon. Chair for Outstanding Svc. to Calif. State U. at Los Angeles, Friends of Music Scholarship Auction, 1982; recipient Doctor of Comedy award Kent State U., 1980, AMC Cancer Rsch. Ctr. Humanitarian award, 1981, Child-Help USA Woman of Yr. award, 1989; City of Los

Angeles Proclamation of Phyllis Diller Week Mayor Tom Bradley, 1979; named to Ohio's Hall of Fame, 1981; Commonwealth scholar, 1964. Office: c/o The Sychin Co Ste 208 12747 Riverside Dr Valley Village CA 91607-3303

DILLEY, CAROL, association administrator; b. Ft. Worth; Student, Ft. Worth Sch. Bus., Tarrant County Jr. Coll., Ft. Worth, Tex. Exec. dir. Tex. Longhorn Breeders Assn. Am., Ft. Worth. Office: Tex Longhorn Breeders Assn Am 2315 N Main St Ste 402 Fort Worth TX 76106-8581

DILLINGER, SUSAN ALICE, reading specialist; b. Oyster Bay, June 16, 1950; d. Gerard Thomas and Martha Alice Soper; m. Edwin Thaine Dillinger, Nov. 5, 1988. M Curriculum and Instrn., Kans. State U., 1977, M Spl. Edn., 1986. Tchr.'s lic. Kans. State Dept. Edn. Tchr. 2d-6th grade Unified Sch. Dist. 450 Shawnee Heights, Tecumseh, Kans., 1973—83, tchr. spl. edn., 1983—93; title I reading specialist Unified Sch. Dist. 329 Mill Creek Valley, Alma, Kans., 1993—96; tchr. 4-5th grade lang. arts Unified Sch. Dist. 320, Wamego, Kans., 1996—99; title I reading specialist Unified Sch. Dist. 322, Onaga, Kans., 1999—. Exch. tchr. Washburn U., Topeka, 1992—; conf./ inservice presenter, at-risk coord. Unified Sch. Dist. 322, Onaga, 1999—, dist. chairperson comm. curriculum, 2004—, mem. dist. steering com., 2004—; instr. Kans. State U., Manhattan, 2000—, reading specialist, adj. prof.; trainer Kans. Reading First, 2005—. Membership rep. Jr. League, Topeka, 1989—90, vol. trainer, 1990—91. Named to East Asian Studies Tchr. Program, 2003; recipient Curriculum Devel. in Econs., Kans. Bankers' Assn., 1976. Mem.: Delta Kappa Gamma (rec. sec. 1998—99). Republican. Episcopalian. Avocations: travel, raising, training and showing morgan horses, raising bison, volunteering. Home: 17455 Pauling Run Rd Westmoreland KS 66549 Office: USD 322 400 High St Onaga KS 66521 Office Phone: 785-889-7101. E-mail: lhdmorgan@kansas.net.

DILLITZER, DIANNE RENÉ, sales executive; b. Downey, Ill., Oct. 6, 1956; d. Alvin Lee and Mary Alice (DuVaul) Pollard; m. Ulrich Dillitzer, Oct. 20, 2001. AAS, Coll. St. Catherine, St. Mary's Campus, Mpls., 1991; BA in Applied Behavioral Scis., Nat. Louis U., 1998, MA in Adult Edn., 2000. Word processing operator Debbie Temporaries, Naperville, Ill., 1985-86, Word Processors Personnel-ADIA, Mpls., 1986-88; computer lab. asst. Coll. St. Catherine, St. Mary's Campus, Mpls., 1989-91; adminstrv. asst. First Trust Ctr., St. Paul, 1992-93, Dolphin Temporaries, Mpls., 1993-94; receptionist, adminstrv. asst. Dain Bosworth, Mpls., 1994-96; reading devel. instrnl. asst. Hubble Mid. Sch., 1998-99; computer lab. asst. Franklin Mid. Sch., Wheaton, 1999-2000; inside sales/ednl. materials Scholastic, Inc., St. Charles, Ill., 2002—. Recipient Dirs. award Minn. Inst. Med. & Dental Careers, 1988, Women's Leadership award Abigail Quigley Women's Ctr., 1991, Minority Leadership award U.S. Achievement Acad., 1991, Judson Bemis Visionary award United Negro Coll. Fund, 1995. Mem. NAACP, Nat. Wildlife Fedn., Library of Congress Assocs., Minority Employee Assn. (sec. 1995-96), Smithsonian Assocs. Avocations: reading, working out, gardening, cooking, party planning. Home: 1504 Foxcroft Dr Aurora IL 60506-1267

DILLMAN, KRISTIN WICKER, elementary school educator, musician; b. Ft. Dodge, Iowa, Nov. 7, 1953; d. Winford Lee and Helen Caroline (Brown) Egli; m. Kirk Michael Wicker, Jan. 1, 1982 (dec. June 1982); m. David D. Dillman, Apr. 13, 1990; adopted children: Alek Joseph, Andrew Mikhail. AA, Iowa Ctrl. Coll., 1974; B in Music Edn., Morningside Coll., 1976; M in Mus., U. S.D., 1983. Cert. Tchr. Iowa. Tchr. instrumental music Garrigan Affiliated Schs., Algona, Iowa, 1976-77, Sioux City (Iowa) Community Schs., 1977—. Sr. beauty cons. Mary Kay Cosmetics; pvt. tchr. double bass instr., 2000—. Asst. prin. bassist Sioux City Symphony, 1974-93, 95—, prin. bassist, 1993-95; freelance bassist Sioux City, 1976—; bassist Rockestra, 2003—; pianist and accompanist, St. Mark Luth. Ch., Sioux City, 1996—. Named Tchr. of Yr. Sioux City Community Schs., 1988-89. Mem. NEA, Iowa Edn. Assn., Sioux city Edn. Assn., Sioux City Musicians Assn., Zeta Sigma, Mu Phi Epsilon. Republican. Lutheran. Avocations: golf, walking, gardening, skiing. Office: Crescent Park Elementary School 1114 W 27th St Sioux City IA 51103 Personal E-mail: DunesDave@aol.com.

DILLMAN, LINDA M., retail executive; b. Ft. Wayne, Ind., June 29, 1956; BS, U. Indpls., 1976. With Hewlett-Packard, 1982—87, Wholesale Club (acquired by Wal-Mart Stores, Inc.), Indpls., 1987—91; application devel. mgr. Wal-Mart Stores, Inc., 1991—97, dir. applications devel., 1997—98, v.p. applications devel., 1998—99, v.p. internat. sys., 1999—2002, sr. v.p., CIO info. sys. divsn., 2002—03, exec. v.p., CIO, 2003—06, exec. v.p. risk mgmt. and benefits adminstrn., 2006—. Bd. trustees U. Indpls., 2005—. Bd. dirs. Northwest Ark. Community Coll. Named one of The Top 50 Most Powerful Women in Bus., Fortune mag., 2003, 2004, 2005, Top 50 Most Powerful Women in Bus., 2006. Mem.: Uniform Code Council (bd. mem.). Office: Wal-Mart Stores Inc 702 SW Eighth St Bentonville AR 72716*

DILLON, CAROL K., lawyer; b. Honolulu; BA, Stanford U., 1975; JD, U. Calif. Berkeley, Boalt Hall, 1982. Bar: Calif. 1982. Ptnr. Bingham McCutchen LLP, Palo Alto, chairperson cmml. real estate practice group. Named a No. Calif. Super Lawyer, Law & Politics & SF Magazine, 2004; named one of Silicon Valley Best Lawyers, San Jose Mag., 2002—04; recipient Thelen Marrin Award Outstanding Legal Scholarship. Mem.: Nat. Assn. Coll. & U. Attys., State Bar Calif. Office: Bingham McCutchen LLP 1900 University Ave East Palo Alto CA 94303 Office Phone: 650-849-4812. Business E-Mail: carol.dillon@bingham.com.

DILLON, CAROLYN FRIES, music educator; b. LaGrange, Ill., Mar. 15, 1976; d. Paul Harold and Joanne G. Fries; m. John Patrick Dillon, Aug. 2, 2003; 1 child, Claire Elizabeth. B Music Edn., Ind. U., Bloomington, 1998. Music tchr. Kings Local Schs., Kings Mills, Ohio, 1998—. Adjudicator Lorain County Solo and Ensemble Contest, Ohio, 2003—06. Scholar T.E.A.M., Miami U., 2006. Mem.: Music Educators Nat. Conf. Roman Catholic.

DILLON, DORIS (DORIS DILLON KENOFER), artist, art historian, educator, interior designer; b. Kansas City, Mo., Dec. 1, 1929; d. Joseph Patrick and Geraldine Elizabeth (Galligan) D.; m. Calvin Louis Kenofer, Aug. 25, 1950; children: Wendy Annette Kenofer Barnes, Bruce Patrick Kenofer. BA in Art, U. Denver, 1950, MA in Art History, 1965. Stewardess United Air Lines, 1950-51; founder, chmn. fine arts dept. Regis Coll., Denver, 1970-74; cons. Sarkisian's Oriental Imports, Denver, 1975-93; mus. curator Van Vechten-Lineberry Taos Art, Taos, N.Mex., 1995. Coord. Inter-Relationship Between the Fine Arts and Science Seminars, 1970-74, Colo. Coun. on Arts & Humanities, Denver, 1980, adv. panel, 1981; permanent consular rep. United Cultural Conv., 2004; dep dir. gen. Internat. Biog. Ctr., Eng., 1997-2004; rsch. bd. advisors Am. Biog. Inst., 1997; lectr. Outer Space and Inner Man, Mensa Chpts., Asheville, NC, 2003; permanent US amb. gen. World Forum; lectr. in field. One-woman shows include Heard Mus., Dallas, 1984, El Pueblo Art Gallery/Mus., Colo., 1970, Nelson Rockefeller Collection, N.Y.C., 1984, Amparo Gallery, Denver, 1985, Veerhoff Gallery, Washington, 1986, Colo. Gallery the Arts Mus., Littleton, 1987, Highland Gallery, Atlanta, 1988, The Earth Sci. Mus., Asheville, N.C., 2003, Turchin Ctr. for Visual Arts, Appalachian State U., Boone, N.C., 2005, two-person shows, E Margo Gallery, N.Y.C., 2003, 2006, exhibited in group shows at U. Denver, 1970, Denver Art Mus., 1970, Denver Mus. Natural History, 1976, U. Colo., 1986, Denver C. of C., 1987, Cadme Gallery, Phila., 1987, Internat. Platform Assn., Washington, 1998—2001, Internat. Exhbn. Gallery, Lisbon, 2000, Turchin Ctr. for Visual Arts, Boone, N.C., 2005, exhibitions include St. Johns Coll., Cambridge, Eng., 2001, Vancouver, Can., 2002, 30th Internat. Congress on Sci., Culture and Arts in the 21st Century, Dublin, Ireland, 2003 (Congress Medallion for distinctive participation), Oxford U., Eng., 2006. Named Woman of Yr., ABI, 1998; recipient 1st place drawing award, 4 States Conf. Ctr., Colo., 1960, Salute to Women award, AAUW, 1997, Key award, Excellence Arts, Rsch., Tchg., 1997, Best of Show award, Internat. Platform Assn., Washington, 2001—02, Internat. Visual Artist of the Yr., 2004, Congress medallion, Dublin Congress. Mem.: Denver Art Mus., Asian Art assn. (bd. dirs. 1982—84, treas. 1985), Fine Arts Guild (v.p. 1982), Soc. for Arts, Religion and Contemporary Culture, Nat. Mus. for Women in the Arts (assoc.), Mensa (scholarship juror 1993—94). Avocations: piano, travel, bridge, swimming, hiking. Home and Office: 315 Delphia Dr Brevard NC 28712 Office Phone: 828-883-3623.

DILLON, ELIZABETH DIGGS, medical/surgical nurse; b. Hampton, Va., Dec. 6, 1965; d. Roland Hill and Sharon Ann (Forbes) Diggs. BS magna cum laude, Old Dominion U., Norfolk, Va., 1988. RN, Va., med. surgical cert., 2003. Vol. Hampton (Va.) Gen. Hosp., 1980-86; nurse extern Riverside Hosp., Newport News, Va., 1987; nurse Riverside Regional Med. Ctr., Newport News, 1988—. Mem. Sigma Theta Tau. Home: 77 Shannon Dr Newport News VA 23608-3124

DILLON, JANE ELIZABETH, otolaryngologist; b. Oak Park, Ill., Feb. 22, 1958; MD, U. Ill. Coll. Med., 1983. Cert. Otolaryngology. Resident, surgery U. Ill., Chgo., 1983—84, resident, otolaryngology, 1984—88; staff mem. Good Samaritan Hosp., Downers Grove, Ill., 1988, Hinsdale Hosp., Ill., 1988; instr. Rush Presbyn. St. Lukes Med. Ctr., 1998; staff mem. LaGrange Hosp., Ill., 2003, Edward Hosp., Naperville, Ill., 2003; private practice Hinsdale, Ill. Office: 950 N York Rd Hinsdale IL 60521 Office Phone: 630-654-1391. Office Fax: 630-654-1967.*

DILLON, JOAN KENT, civic worker, volunteer consultant; b. Lafayette, Ind., Apr. 30, 1925; d. Richard and Gladys Kent; m. George Chaffee Dillon, Sept. 11, 1948; children: Kent Chaffee, Courtney Pedersen, Emily Lorillard Berry. BA, Smith Coll., 1947; MA, U. Mo., 1969. Chmn. sales & rental gallery Nelson Art Gallery, Kansas City, Mo., 1956-63; tchr. history Sunset Hill Sch., Kansas City, 1958-69; chmn. Performing Arts Found., 1974-84; pres. Folly Theater Restoration, Kansas City, 1974-85, Kansas City Arts Coun., 1980-82. Active Mo. Adv. Coun. for Hist. Preservation, 1978-81; trustee Nat. Trust for Hist. Preservation, 1978-87; bd. trustees Smith Coll. 1994-99, Smithsonion Nat. Bd. 1993—; bd. dirs. League Historic Am. Theaters, 1975-98, Centerre Bank of Kansas City, 1984-87; active Kansas City Mcpl. Art Commn., 1970-80, Nat. Assn. Schs. of Dance and Theater Accreditation Commn., 1979-81; bd. dirs. Pres.'s Com. Arts and Humanities, 1982-88, Archives of Am. Art, 1983-87, Kansas City Cmty. Found., 1984-87, Ptnrs. for Liveable Communities, 1987-95, Acting Co., 1987-91; bd. commrs. Smithsonian Nat. Portrait Gallery. Mem. Ctr. Exch., Eastward Ho Club. Episcopalian. Avocations: tennis, sailing, reading, travel.

DILLON, KERRIS, social studies educator; d. Carole Jean Helgerson; m. Joseph Michael Dillon, Oct. 5, 2000; children: Sydney Decorah, Gabriel Michael. MEd, U. Phoenix, Ariz., 2006. Cert. tchr. Iowa Dept. Edn. Social studies tchr. Mott H.S., Postville, Iowa, 2002—. Author: (autobiography) The Black Ink Mirror: A Voice from Generation X. Active Allamakee Dems., Waukon, Iowa, 2006. Recipient Recommended Black Belt, Am. Tae Kwon Do Assn., 1997—99. Democrat. Presbyterian. Avocations: writing, travel, scrapbooks. Office Phone: 1-563-864-7652.

DILLON, LORETTA SCHOEN, physical therapist, educator; m. Tim Dillon, May 26, 1984. BS, U. Tex., Dallas, 1983; MS, U. Tex., El Paso, 1994; D in Phys. Therapy, Ariz. U., Mesa, 2006. Lic. phys. therapist Tex., 1983. Staff phys. therapist Providence Meml. Hosp., El Paso, 1989—2006; dir. clin. edn. U. Tex. Coll. Health Scis., El Paso, 1994—. Head lector All Saints Cath. Cmty., El Paso, 2002—06. Academic scholar, Tex. Phys. Therapy Found., 2005. Mem.: Am. Phys. Therapy Assn. (assoc.). Office: U Tex El Paso Coll Health Scis 1101 N Campbell Ave El Paso TX 79902 Business E-Mail: ldillon@utep.edu.

DILLON, PRISCILLA MCAVOY, private school educator; b. Hagerstown, Md., Dec. 11, 1947; d. Rezon Samuel and Rebecca Fox (Fuller) Dillon; children: Rebecca Dillon Reisch, Martha Dillon Reisch. BA, Hollins U., Va., 1970. Educator Wyoming Girls Sch., Wyo., 1981—. Candidate Wyo. State Legislature, 2002, 2004; pub. mem. Wyo. Bd. Medicine, Cheyenne, 2003—06; bd. sec. Sheridan County Pub. Libr., 2005—06.

DILLON, SUSAN, literature and language educator; MA in English, Calif. U., Pa., 1983. Tchr. Calif. Area H.S., Coal Center, Pa., 1976—. Instr. Westmoreland C.C., Youngwood, Pa., 1982. Author: Centennial Bibliography of Thomas Carlyle. Named Tchr. of Yr., Calif. Area Sch. Dist., 2003; recipient Outstanding Am. Tchrs., Nat. Honor Roll Adv. Com., 2005—06, Presdl. Scholar award, Calif. U., Pa., 1975, 1983. Mem.: NEA (nat. edn. dir. 2002), Pa. State Edn. Assn. (life; bd. dirs. 2002). Home: 219 S Allen Ave Donora PA 15033 Home Fax: 724-823-0147. Personal E-mail: dillon.susan@comcast.net. Business E-Mail: dillons@calsd.org.

DILLON, TERRI L., consulting firm executive; b. Winston-Salem, N.C., Sept. 12, 1962; d. Dallas Eugene and Opal Wall Shields; m. Victor Ray Dillon, Apr. 18, 1992; children: Mary Abigail, Leslie Gray, Summer Rae, Dalton Levi. Student, High Point U., 1984-88, Vanderbilt U., 1998, U. N.C., Greensboro, 1999. Proof operator, teller, customer svc. and consumer loan rep. Northwestern Bank (First Union Nat. Bank), Winston-Salem, N.C., 1979-86; adminstrv. asst., grant writer, sr. project mgr. Whitney jones, Inc., Winston-Salem, 1986-97, v.p. fin. and adminstrn., 1997-2001; v.p. adminstrn. Management Recruiters of Greensboro, 2001—. Mem. steering com., chair spkrs. bur. Leave A Legacy of the Triad, Winston-Salem, 1998-99; com. mem. Colfax (N.C.) Inc. Com., 1999; grad. Winston Class of Leadership, Winston-Salem, 2001. Mem. Nat. Ctr. for Non-Profit Bds., Nat. Soc. Fund Raising Execs. (cert., chair 1999 fund-raising day conf. 1999, charter N.C.-Triad chpt., treas. and 1st v.p. 1996-99, pres. 1999-2001), New Garden Moose Lodge, Jr. Achievement N.W. N.C., Inc. (bd. dirs. 1999-2000), Rotary Club of Winston-Salem (sec. 2001). Republican. Methodist.

DILLON, TONI ANN, emotional support educator; b. Point Pleasant, N.J., Jan. 7, 1962; d. Thomas Joseph and Anita Marie Dillon. BA in Edn., Mercyhurst Coll., 1983; M, State Pa., 1991. Cert. elem. educator Pa., tchr. mentally and/or physically handicapped Pa. Emotional support tchr. Sch. Dist. of the City of Erie, Pa., 1983—. Contbr. articles to profl. jours.; author: (1 page in storybook) GoFish! The Offishial Tale, 2001. Leader Penn Lakes Girl Scout Coun., Erie, 1979—. Nominee Disney's Am. Tchr. award, 2000; named Tchr. of Yr., Burton Elem. Sch., 1989, Lincoln Elem. Sch., 1992; recipient St. Elizabeth Ann Seton award, Penn Lakes Girl Scouts, 1990, Outstanding Leader award, 1991, Class Rm. award, Erie Met. Transit Authority, 1997—98, Arts in Edn. award, Lincoln Elem. Parent Tchr. Assn., 1998—99, Bread Box award, Second Harvest Food Bank, 2000. Avocations: photography, gardening, collecting N.Y. Yankee baseball cards, arts and crafts. Personal E-mail: teacherinpink@aol.com. E-mail: tdillon@eriesd.iu5.og.

DILLON RYDMAN, LINDA GAY, nurse, consultant; d. Vanessa Dillon; children: Kate Dillon, Estlin Robert Rydman. BA, BSN, No. Ill. U., DeKalb, Ill., 1973; MS, Univ. Ill. Chgo. Med Cntr., Chgo., 1986. RN Ill., 1973, Mass., 1990; Ccm CCMC, 2001, Cpur McKesson HBOC, 2000, Type 73 Sch. Nursing DuPage County, Ill., 1982, Family Therapist Inst. Juvenile Rsch., 1980. Clin. nursing cons./instr. U. Ill. Med. Ctr., Chgo., 1974—81; dir. of profl. services Home Health of Chgo. South, Inc., Chgo., 1983—85; clin. nurse specialist/staff nurse Loyola U., Maywood, 1985—89; don Linden Oaks Hosp., Naperville, Ill., 1989—90; clin. nurse specialist Ctrl. DuPage Hosp., Behavioral Health, Winfield, Ill., 1992—94; dir. ops. Staff Builders Health Care Svcs., Chgo., 1994—98; utilization mgmt. specialist Marianjoy Rehablink, Wheaton, Ill., 1998—2000; cons. ImageMasters, Clarendon Hills, Ill., 1990—; dir. patient care svcs. Univ. Ill. at Chgo. Med. Cntr., Chicago, Ill., 2001—05. Mem., children's theater bd.,mktg. Theater of Western Springs, Western Springs, Ill., 1994—99. Author (presenter): (monograph) The Affective Disorders Clinic; contbr. presentation, chapters to books. Deacon Cmty. Presbyn. Ch., Clarendon Hills, Ill., 1997—99. Grantee Ann. grant funding Affective Disorders Clinic, Ill. Dept. of Mental Health, 1976-1981. Mem.: Am. Assoc. of Managed Care Nurses, Case Mgmt. Soc. of Am. Office: UNA Hospice of Vt & NH 325 Mt Support Rd Lebanon NH 03766 Home: 79 0224 Ln White River Junction VT 05001 Office Fax: 603-448-1599. Business E-Mail: lrydman@vnavnh.org.

DILLY, MARIAN JEANETTE, humanities educator; b. Vining, Minn., Nov. 7, 1921; d. John Fredolph and Mabel Josephine (Haagenson) Linder; m. Robert Lee Dily, June 22, 1946 (dec. Oct. 1987); children: Ronald Lee, Patricia Jeanette Dilly Vero. Studetn, U. Minn., 1944-45; grad., John R. Powers Finishing Sch., N.Y.C., 1957, Zell McC. Fashion Career Sch., Mpls., 1957, Estelle Compton Models Inst., 1966, Nancy Taylor Charm Sch., N.Y.C., 1967, Patricia Stevens Career Sch., Mpls., 1968; BS in English cum laude, Black Hills State U., Spearfish, S.D., 1975. Instr. Nat. Am. U., Rapid City, S.D., 1966-68; instr., dir. Nancy Taylor Charm Sch., 1966-68; hostess TV shows, 1966-74. Lectr. in personality devel., dir., prodr. beauty and talent pageants, freelance coord. in fashion shows, judge beauty and talent pageants of local, state and nat. levels, 1966—. Actress bit parts Nauman Films Inc., 1970. Active ARC; dir., 1st v.p. Black Hills Girl Scout Coun., 1967-72; chmn. bd. dirs., pres. Luth. Social Svc. Aux., Western S.D. and Eastern Wyo., 1960-65; chmn. women's events Dakota Days and Nat. Premiere, 1968; bd. dirs. YMCA, 1976-81; mem. Dallas Symphony Orch. League, 1987-90, Dallas Mus. of Art League, 1987-90, Women's Club. Dallas County, Tex., Inc., 1987-90. Recipient award Rapid City C. of C., 1968, Fashion awards March of Dimes, 1967-72, Svc. award Black Hills Girl Scout Coun., award of appreciation Yellowstone Internat. Toastmistress Club. Mem. AAUW (sec., mem. exec.b d. 1988-90), Nu Tau Sigma (past advisor), Delta Tau Kappa, Singing Tribe of Wahoo. Avocations: golf, bridge, music, skiing. Address: 1607 Woodward St Erie CO 80516-7529

DIMAGGIO, DEBBI, realtor; b. Oakland, July 14, 1964; d. Vincent S. and Marietta DiMaggio; m. Adam R. Betta, July 25, 1992; children: Bianca Betta, Chase Betta. BS in Polit. Sci., U. Calif., Berkeley, 1987. Realtor Grubb Co., Oakland, 1998—. Bd. dirs. spl. events Children's Support League, Oakland, 1998—; mem. Jr. League Oakland, 2000—. Mem.: Piedmont Baseball & Softball Found. (fundraising chair 2005—). Avocations: tennis, travel, swimming, writing. Office: The Grubb Co 1960 Mountain Blvd Oakland CA 94611 Office Phone: 510-339-0400 227. Business E-Mail: debbi@debbidimaggio.com.

DIMAGGIO, LYNETTE M., physical education educator; d. Donald J. and Esther M. Manchester; m. Anthony T. DiMaggio, Nov. 12, 1977; children: Thomas, Anthony. BA, No. Ill. U., Chgo., 1975; postgrad., Concordia U., River Forest, Ill. Dept. chair phys. edn. Schurz H.S., Chgo., 1992—. Tchr. mem. Schurz H.S., Chgo., 2006, after sch. matters liaison. Mem.: AAHPERD, Ill. Sch. Health Assn., Ill. Assn. Health, Phys. Edn., Recreation, and Dance. Avocations: singing, crafts, painting. Home: 3253 N Newland Ave Hebron IL 60034 Office: Schurz H S 3601 N Milwaukee Ave Chicago IL 60641

DIMAIRA, ANN B., medical/surgical nurse; b. Newark, July 21, 1959; d. Bernard C. and Clair Ellen (Kirchner) Welch; m. Frank C. Dimaira, June 26, 1982; children: Peter Sean, Jennifer Ann, Kathleen Ellen. BSN, Seton Hall U., 1982. Cert. intravenous nurse. Asst. clin. coord. Riverview Med. Ctr., Red Bank, NJ, 1985—90; primary case mgmt. nurse Vis. Nurse Assn. Ctrl. Jersey, Red Bank, 1990—91; asst. to supr. level III MCOSS Nursing Svcs., Red Bank, 1991—92, clin. nursing supr., 1992—95, clin. nurse mgr., 1995—97; staff nurse geriatric care Regency Park Nursing Ctr., 1998—; staff nurse, adminstrv. supr. Riverview Med. Ctr., 2001—. Active in PTA and ch. Recipient State Recognition for Nor'Easter Disaster Care and Coordination, 1992, Galaxy award, Regency Pk. Nursing Ctr., 2005. Personal E-mail: ab721@aol.com.

DI MANNA, MICHELLE ANN, mathematics educator; b. Omaha, Oct. 19, 1970; d. Eugene LeRoy Wollenberg and Clare Marie (Lahowetz) Wollenberg; m. Dominic Lee Di Manna, June 11, 1994; children: Mikala Rose, Matthew Joseph. BA, Met. State Coll. Denver, 1993; M in Edn. Adminstrn., U. Phoenix, Denver, 1997. Lic. tchr. Colo., 1993. Paraprofl. Englewood Pub. Schs., Colo., 1990—92; tchr. math. Columbine H.S., Littleton, 1994—. Mem.: Nat. Coun. Tchrs. Math. Conservative. Roman Catholic. Office: Columbine High School 6201 S Pierce St Littleton CO 80123 Office Phone: 303-982-4484. E-mail: mdimanna@jeffco.k12.co.us.

DI MARCO, BARBARANNE YANUS, principal; b. Jersey City, Nov. 16, 1946; d. Stanley Joseph and Anne Barbara (Dalack) Yanus; m. Charles Benjamin DiMarco, Mar. 15, 1986; 1 child, Charles Garrett. BA in Music Edn., Trenton State Coll., 1968; MA in Spl. Edn., Kean Coll., 1971, elem. edn. cert., 1974, adminstrv. cert., 1976. Cert. elem., music, adminstrn., spl. edn., N.J. Vocal music educator Roselle (N.J.) Bd. Edn., 1968-69, tchr. trainable mentally retarded, 1969-76, tchr. multiple handicapped, 1976—95, tchr. neurologically impaired, 1995—2003; prin. Grace Wilday Jr. H.S., Roselle, 2003—. Color guard instr. Roselle Bd. Edn., 1973—88, elem. tutor, 1976—92, adminstrv. asst. to supt., 1980—85; program dir., sec. Expanded Dimensions in Gifted Edn., Westfield, NJ, 1978—85. Vestryperson St. Luke's Ch., Roselle, 1989-91. Recipient Govs. Tchr. Recognition award, Gov. Florio, N.J., Trenton, 1992-93. Mem. NEA, N.J. Edn. Assn., Roselle Edn. Assn., N.J. Assn. for Retarded Children, Eastern Star (25-yr award 1991), Delta Omicron. Republican. Episcopalian. Avocations: skiing, flying, painting, travel, swimming. Home: 13 Gentore Ct Edison NJ 08820-1029 Office: Grace Wilday Jr HS 400 Brooklawn Ave Roselle NJ 07203 Office Phone: 908-298-2066. Personal E-mail: btdtbarb@aol.com.

DIMEN, MURIEL VERA, psychoanalyst; b. N.Y.C., Sept. 24, 1942; d. Alfred and Dora (Zauzmer) D.; m. Seth L. Schein, Sept. 16, 1965 (div. Aug. 25, 1980). BA, Barnard Coll., 1964; MA, Columbia U., 1966, PhD, 1970; cert., NYU, 1983. Asst. prof. Lehman Coll., Bronx, N.Y., 1970-75, assoc. prof., 1975-81, prof., 1981-88; pvt. practice N.Y.C., 1979—; mem. faculty Nat. Inst. for Psychotherapies, 1989-90; clin. prof. psychology postdoctoral program NYU, 1991—; mem. faculty Derner Inst. Adelphi U., 1993—. Author: The Anthropological Imagination, 1977, Surviving Sexual Contradictions, 1986, Surviving Sexuality, Intimacy, Power, 20003; co-editor: Regional Variation in Modern Greece, 1976, Storms in Her Head: New Clinical and Theoretical Perspectives on Breuer and Freud's Studies on Hysteria, 2001, Gender in Psychoanalytic Space: Between Clinic and Culture, 2002; book rev. editor: Psychoanalytic Dialogues: A Journal of Relational Perspectives; assoc. editor: Studies in Gender and Sexuality. Fellow Am. Anthrop. Assn., N.Y. Inst. for Humanities; mem. APA, Psychoanalytic Soc. Office: 3 E 10th St New York NY 10003-5916 Office Phone: 212-995-9152. E-mail: mdimen@psychoanalyst.net.

DIMENGO, JOSEPHINE, medical/surgical nurse; b. Cleve., Jan. 9, 1954; d. Joseph and Mary (Rihtar) Staric; m. Mark Dimengo, May 25, 1979; children: Cristina, Nicholas, Alexa. Diploma, St. Vincent Charity Hosp., Cleve., 1975; MSN, Frances Payne Bolton Sch., Cleve., 1990. Clinical dir. heart failure Am. Heathways, 2002—. Recipient Helen Lathrope Bunge award. Mem. Heart Failure Soc. Am., Am. Heart Assn., Am. Assn. Heart Failure, Sigma Theta Tau.

DIMENNA, KATHLEEN POLANSKY, special education educator; b. Greensburg, Pa., Mar. 28, 1951; d. John and Agnes Polansky; m. Richard DiMenna, Sept. 14, 1974; children: Allison Maria, Adam Richard. BS in Early Childhood Edn., Drexel U., 1973, MS, 1976. Cert. tchr. Pa. 3rd grade tchr. Sch. Dist. Phila., 1976—79, resource rm. tchr., 1979—88; spl. edn. tchr. St. Katherine Day Sch., Wynnewood, Pa., 1989—97; tchr. students with learning disabilities Archbishop Ryan H.S., Phila., 1997—. Fast For Word coach Sci. Learning, Berkeley, Calif., 2001—. Recipient Pa. High Tech. award, State of Pa., 1985; fellow, Stein Family, 1973; Dolfinger McMahon grantee, 2004. Mem.: Coun. for Exceptional Children. Democrat. Roman

Catholic. Avocations: water aerobics, bicycling, travel. Office: Archbishop Ryan HS 11201 Academy Rd Philadelphia PA 19154 Office Phone: 215-637-1800 273. Personal E-mail: kadimenna@aol.com. Business E-Mail: kdimenna@archbishopryan.com.

DIMITRIOU, DOLORES ENNIS, computer consultant; b. Phila., Apr. 7, 1932; d. Charles Adair and Rubye Stanton (Greene) Ennis; m. John Alexander Dimitriou, Sept. 25, 1954 (div. Aug. 1983); 1 child, Sandra Irene Dimitriou Falor. BS in Math., U. Miami, 1954; MA in Linguistics, U. Tex., 1994. Jet engine supr. GE, Evendale, Ohio, 1954-58; rsch. aide Marine Lab. U. Miami, Coral Gables, 1959-65; supr. tests Weathering Rsch. Svc., Princeton, Fla., 1959-87; income tax preparer H&R Block, Homestead, Fla., 1981-83; small bus. cons., pres., co-founder Facts & Figures Svcs., Homestead, 1983-87; computer cons., trainer Wycliffe Bible Translators, Orlando, Fla., 1987-97. Sec., treas., co-founder Weathering Rsch. Svcs., Princeton, Fla., 1959—95; treas. GILLBT, Ghana, 1994—96. Tax aide Am. Assn. Ret. Persons, 1998—, instr., 2002—; long-term care ombudsman state coun., 2000—01, 2003—05; dist. chmn., 2000—01, 2003—04; ombudsman Fla., 1998—; bd. dirs. Ch. Women United, 1999—2003; ch. rels. Wycliffe Bible Translators, 1998—2003. Named Outstanding Woman in Religion YWCA, U. Miami, 1953-54. Mem.: Cutler Ridge Woman's Club, Mortar Board, Phi Mu Epsilon. Democrat. Avocations: computers, travel, reading, crafts. Home and Office: 10381 SW 209 Ln Miami FL 33189-3612 Personal E-mail: dolores-dimitriou@att.net.

DIMMICK, CAROLYN REABER, federal judge; b. Seattle, Oct. 24, 1929; d. Maurice C. and Margaret T. (Taylor) Reaber; m. Cyrus Allen Dimmick, Sept. 10, 1955; children: Taylor, Dana. BA, U. Wash., 1951, JD, 1953; LLD, Gonzaga U., 1982, CUNY, 1987. Bar: Wash. 1953. Asst. atty. gen. State of Wash., Seattle, 1953-55; pros. atty. King County, Wash., 1955-59, 60-62; sole practice Seattle, 1959-60, 62-65; judge N.E. Dist. Ct. Wash., 1965-75, King County Superior Ct., 1976-80; justice Wash. Supreme Ct., 1981-85; judge U.S. Dist. Ct. (we. dist.) Wash., Seattle, 1985-94, chief judge, 1994-97, sr. judge, 1997—. Chmn. Jud. Resources Com., 1991—94, active, 1987—94. Recipient Matrix Table award, 1981, World Plan Execs. Coun. award, 1981, Vanguard Honor award King County of Wash. Women Lawyers, 1996, Disting. Alumni award U. Wash. Law Sch., 1997, Outstanding Jurist award King County Bar Assn., 2003; named Wash. Women of Yr. Seattle U. Women's Law Caucus, 2004. Mem. ABA, Am. Judges Assn. (gov.), Nat. Assn. Women Judges, World Assn. Judges, Wash. Bar Assn., Am. Judicature Soc., Order of Coif (Wash. chpt.). Office: US Dist Ct 16134 US Courthouse 700 Stewart St Seattle WA 98101 Office Phone: 206-370-8850. E-mail: carolyn_dimmick@wawd.uscourts.gov.

DIMMITT, CORNELIA, psychologist, educator; b. Boston, Mar. 16, 1938; d. Harrison and Martha Fredericka (Read) D.; m. (div.); children: Colin Barclay Church, Jeffrey Harrison Church. BA, Harvard U., 1958; MA, Columbia U., 1966; PhD, Syracuse U., 1970; diplomate, C. G. Jung Inst., Zurich, Switzerland, 1985. Asst. prof. Am. U., Washington, 1970-71; from asst. to assoc. prof. (with tenure) Georgetown U., Washington, 1971-82; pvt. practice Boston, 1985—. Mem. admissions com. Coll. Arts and Scis., Georgetown U., Washington, 1974-76, mem. rank and tenure com., 1977-78; dir. admissions com. C. G. Jung Inst., Boston, 1986-89, pres. tng. bd., 1989-91; pres. NESJA, 1993-97. Author: Classical Hindu Mythology, 1978. NEH fellow, 1979-80. Mem. Am. Oriental Soc., New England Soc. Jungian Analysts, Assn. Grads. in Analytical Psychology (Switzerland), Internat. Assn. for Analytical Psychology. Office: 80 Commonwealth Ave Boston MA 02116-3015

DIMMOCK, VIRGINIA ELLEN, literature and language educator, consultant; d. Howard Gerald and Janet Allen Glabau; m. Donald James Dimmock, Aug. 30, 1985; children: Brett Howard Miller, Ryan Frederick Miller. BA cum laude, Conn. Coll., New London, 1988, MA in Tchg., 1992; 6th-Yr. Cert. in Reading and Lang. Arts, U. Conn., Storrs, 1993. Emergency svcs. dispatcher Waterford (Conn.) Police Dept., 1976—90; tutor lang. arts East Lyme (Conn.) Bd. Edn., 1989—93; cons. lang. arts Chaplin (Conn.) Bd. Edn., 1993—97, Old Saybrook (Conn.) Bd. Edn., 1997—2006, Coventry Bd. Edn., Conn., 2006—. Adj. prof. U. New Haven, New London, Conn., 1999. Comdr. New London (Conn.) Power Squadron, 2000—02, instr. boating safety, 1995—. Fellow: Conn. Writing Project; mem.: Internat. Reading Assn., Conn. Reading Assn. (conf. presenter 1995, cons. 1993—99). Avocations: art, animal rescue, boating, piano. Office: Capt Nathan Hale Mid Sch 1776 Main St Coventry CT 06238

DIMOND, ROBERTA RALSTON, psychology and sociology educator; b. Bakersfield, Calif., Mar. 25, 1940; d. Robert Leroy Vickers and Gail Anderson (Tritch) Ralston; m. James Davis, June 18, 1963 (div. 1970); 1 child, Jamie Amundsen Davis; m. Frederick Henry Dimond, Oct. 20, 1970; children: Frederick Ralston, Robert Vickers (div. 1991). BA in History and English, Stanford U., 1962, MAT in Edn., 1963; MS, U. Pa., 1970, EdD, 1973. Cert. secondary educator, ednl. specialist, counselor, coll. personnel adminstr. Thcr. Kamehameha Sch., Honolulu, 1965-67; asst. to dean of women U. Pa., Phila., 1969-70; asst. prof. Temple U., Ambler, Pa., 1970-87, Montgomery County Coll., Blue Bell, Pa., 1975-80; prof. psychology, speech, sociology Delaware Valley Coll., Doylestown, Pa., 1987—, assoc. prof. liberal arts. Cons. ETS, Princeton, N.J., 1989—; speaker in field; lectr. on sexual responsibilities in the 90s and assertive affirmative action topics; researcher on athletics and aging females syngerism. Author: Gender & RAcial Bias by Vocational Counselors, 1973. Bd. dirs. Concerned Citizens of Upper Dublin, Maple Glen, Pa., 1980-91, Arrowhead Assn., Ambler, Pa., 1990-91. Fellow Newhouse Found., 1960-63; grantee APA, 1969-70. Mem.: MADD, AAUP, APA, Phila. Tennis Assn. (pres.), Stanford Alumni Assn., Phila. Tennis Patrons, U.S. Tennis Assn., Middle States Tennis Assn. (life). Episcopalian. Avocations: tennis (ranked #6 in U.S. in women's 50 and over tennis, # 1 in over 45, # 1 MSTA over 60., duplicate bridge. Office: Delaware Valley Coll Rte 202 Doylestown PA 18901 Home: 48394 Sunburst Dr Lexington Park MD 20653-4588

DIMOPOULOS, LINDA J., food service executive; b. 1951; With Darden Restaurants, Inc., 1982, sr. v.p. fin. ops. Red Lobster, 1993—98, sr. v.p., corp. controller, bus info. sys., 1998—99, sr. v.p., chief info. officer, 1999—2002, chief fin. officer, 2002—.

DI MUCCIO, MARY-JO, retired librarian; b. Hanford, Calif., June 16, 1930; d. Vincent and Theresa (Yovino) DiMuccio. BA, Immaculate Heart Coll., LA, 1953, MA, 1960; PhD, US Internat. U., San Diego, 1970. Tchr. parochial schs., Los Angeles, 1949-54, San Francisco, 1954-58; tchr. Govt. of Can., Victoria, B.C., 1958—60; asst. libr. Immaculate Heart Coll. Libr., Los Angeles, 1960-62, head libr., 1962—72; adminstrv. libr. City of Sunnyvale, Calif., 1972-88; ret., 1988. Instr. Foothill C.C., Los Altos, 1977—95. Mem. exec. bd., past pres. Sunnyvale Cmty. Svcs.; chair for Chefs Who Care, Cmty. Svcs. Agy., 1999— Mem. ICF (past pres.), Cath. Libr. Assn. (past pres.), Sunnyvale Bus. and Profl. Women, Peninsula Dist. Bus. and Profl. Women (past pres.). Home: 736 Muir Dr Mountain View CA 94041-2509 E-mail: JO736@aol.com.

DINA, GWENDOLYN JUDITH, special education educator; b. Evergreen Park, Ill., Feb. 28, 1943; d. Harold Karl and Constance Pauline Doering; m. Michael George Dina, Feb. 29, 1984; 1 child, Daniel Joseph Mathews. BS in Edn., Ea. Ill. U., 1964; MS in Edn., No. Ill. U., 1980. Lic. tchr. of blind and partially sighted State Bd. of Edn., Ill., cert. std. secondary tchr. State Bd. of Edn., Ill., std. elem. tchr. State Bd. of Edn., Ill. Phys. edn. and spl. edn. tchr. Dubuque (Iowa) Sr. H.S., 1967—80; dir. habilitative svcs. Holy Angels Resdl. Facility for Mentally Retarded, Shreveport, La., 1985—92; tchr. of visually impaired Mid-Ctrl. Assn., Peoria, Ill., 1992—96, Spl. Edn. Assn. of Peoria County, Bartonville, Ill., 1996—; early intervention devel. therapist Child and Family Connections, Springfield, Ill., 1998—2002. Author: Mathew's Story: The Early Years of a Child with Asperger's Syndrome, Vision and Hearing Problems, 2001, The Magical Letter L, 2001; editor: Frugal Me: How Teachers Save Their Students and Other Memories, 2002; contbr. articles to profl. jours. Named Educator of Yr., Peoria Assn. Retarded Citizens, 1994; grantee, State of Iowa, 1978, 1979. Mem.: Delta Kappa Gamma (state corr. sec. 2001—03, tchg. scholar 1978, 1979, 1980). Avocations: storytelling, writing, swimming, sewing, knitting. Office: Spl Edn Assn Peoria 6000 S Adams Bartonville IL 61607 Personal E-mail: dina.g198@insightbb.com.

DINATALE, MICHELLE, biology educator; b. Easton, Mass., June 26, 1977; d. Edward and Carol DiNatale. B in Biology, U. Mass. Biology tchr. Nipmuc Regional HS, Upton, Mass., 2001—; rsch. asst. Newton Well. Hosp., Mass. Tchr. advanced placement biology Nipmuc Regional HS, 2002—, student coun. advisor, 2004—, drama club dir., 2004—05; violin tchr., Upton, 2000—. Home: 17 Knowlton Cir Upton MA 01568 Office: Nipmuc Regional HS 90 Pleasant St Upton MA 01568 Office Phone: 508-529-2130. E-mail: mdinatale@mu-regional.k12.ma.us.

DINCECCO, JENNIE ELIZABETH WILLIAMS SWANSON, healthcare administrator, mentor, educator, volunteer; b. Atlanta, Aug. 5, 1932; d. Chester Arthur and Cleo Annie Williams; m. Richard Edward Swanson, Apr. 24, 1954 (dec. 1994); children: Laurel Dee Swanson, Jeffrey Richard Swanson, Scott Edward Swanson; m. Thomas M. Dincecco, Aug. 26, 2000. BS, Northwestern U., 1954; MS, No. Ill. U., 1972, EdD, 1976. Pub. sch. tchr., 1954-69; psycho-ednl. diagnostician, 1969-72; faculty Loyola U., Chgo., 1976-82, asst. prof. ob-gyn and pediat., 1979-82; dir. pre-start project depts. ob-gyn and pediat. Stritch Sch. Medicine, 1978-82; dir. spl. svcs. Cmty. Unit Sch. Dist. 220, 1982-92. Hospice bereavement vol., 1997—; coun. mem., mentor Cong. Unitarian Ch.; antique dealer; mem. Gov. Ill. Com. Preventive Svcs., 1979-80; chair B-3 subcom. First Chance Consortium, 1978-80; chair INTER-ACT, 1979-80; cons. in field Author: Dying With Open Eyes: Alzheimer's Disease, 2005; co-author: Partners in Child Development, 1978; columnist: Woodstock Ind. Newspaper, 2006. Vol. Latino Coalition, Alzheimer's Assn. Grantee HEW, 1973-76, 78-82. Mem.: Ret. Tchrs. McHenry County, Nat. Assn. Edn. Young Child, Nat. Acad. Neuropsychology, Nat. Perinatal Assn., Assn. Maternal and Child Health, Coun. Exceptional Children, Golden Cir., Woodstock Opera House Commn. (chairperson 2001—), Northwestern U. Alumni Assn., Nu Alumni Club, Delta Kappa Gamma (scholar 1974), Delta Delta Delta (life; golden cir.). Unitarian Universalist.

DINEEN, BONNIE R., social studies educator; b. Chgo., Nov. 23, 1946; d. Walter A. and Blanche B. Karpiel; m. Daniel B. Dineen, June 21, 1969; children: Michael, Megan, Kevin. BA in History, No. Ill. U., Dekalb, 1968; postgrad., Northwestern U., Evanston, Ill., U. Ark., Little Rock, 1981—84, U. Colo., Boulder, 1999—2000. Tchr. social studies Sts. Peter & Paul Sch., Naperville, Ill., 1968—69, St. Alexis Sch., Bensenville, 1969—73, Immaculate Conception Sch., North Little Rock, Ark., 1979—88, Immaculate Heart Mary Sch., Maplewood, NJ, 1988—94, Mt. St. Mary Acad. H.S., Little Rock, 1995—97, St. Thomas More H.S., Centennial, Colo., 1997—. Chmn. St. Thomas More H.S., 2002—; mem. diocesan curriculum com. Archdiocese Denver, 2000, tchr. mentor, 1999—. Chair pack com. Boy Scouts Am., Little Rock, 1978—85, asst. com. chair Littleton, Colo., 2005—; mem., sponsor Denver Mus. Nature & Sci., 2000—. Mem.: Nat. Coun. Social Studies, Tchg. East Asia Consortium, Nat. Cath. Edn. Assn., Alpha Omicron Pi. Avocations: travel, reading. Office: St Thomas More Mid Sch 7071 E Otero St Centennial CO 80112-3172

DINERMAN, MIRIAM, social work educator; b. NYC, Apr. 13, 1925; d. Abraham J. and Frances (Shostac) Goldforb; m. Harold Dinerman, June 12, 1951 (dec. June 1976); children: David, Ellen, Ruth. BA with honors, Swarthmore Coll., 1945; MSW, Columbia U., 1949, D of Social Welfare, 1972. Youth dir. Jewish Assn. for Neighborhood Ctrs., N.Y.C., 1949-50, program dir., 1951-54; various social work part time positions, 1955-60; asst. prof. Rutgers U. Grad. Sch. Social Work, New Brunswick, NJ, 1961-72, assoc. prof., 1972-76, prof., 1976-99, asst. dean for acad. planning, 1973-75, assoc. dean, 1975-81, acting dean, 1978, chmn. health care sequence, mem. New Brunswick faculty coun., 1989-93, chair, 1991-92; dir. PhD program Rutgers U. Sch. Social Work, 1992-97, emerita, 1999—. Mem. grants rev. panel Office Human Devel. Svcs., HHS, 1986—90; cons. on health and social svcs. N.J. Legis. Task Force on 21st Century; mem. task force on std. of need N.J. Divsn. Econ. Assistance, 1989—91; manuscript rev. editor Longman's Press, Methuen Press; dir. Ctr. for Internat. and Comparative Social Work, 1977—99; adj. prof. Yeshiva U. Sch. Social Work, 1999—. Editor: Social Work Futures, 1983; mem. editl. bd. Affilia: Jour. Women and Social Work, 1985-94, 95—, book rev. editor., 1995-00, editor-in-chief, 2000-06; contbr. articles to profl. jours., chpts. to books. Bd. dirs. Def. for Children Internat., 1980—88. Grantee NIMH, 1966-67, Rutgers U. Rsch. Coun. and Samuel Silberman Fund, 1979-80. Mem.: NJ AAUP (N.J. task force on health care policy), NASW (chpt. pres. 1984—86, nat. com. on nominations and leadership identification 1988—97, editl. com. 1991—95, NYC steering com. polit. action for candidate election 1996—2001, bd. dirs. N.Y.C. chpt. 1999—2001, sec. bd. dirs. 2003—05, bd. dirs. N.Y.C. chpt. 2003—), Group for Advancement of Doctoral Edn. (sec. steering com. 1990—96), Coun. on Social Work Edn. (program planning com. 1984—89, ednl. policy and planning commn. 1989—94), Internat. Assn. Schs. Social Work (agt. 1988—95, bd. dirs.), Acad. Cert. Social Workers. Home: 353 W 29th St New York NY 10001-4784 Office Phone: 212-960-5289.

DING, AI-YUE, conductor, music educator; b. Beijing, Dec. 17, 1942; arrived in U.S., 1990; d. Depan Ting and Susan Cheng; m. Chenghua Sun, Jan. 17, 1968; children: Tian, Sun. B in Conducting, Conservatory of Music, Shanghai, 1966; M in Sacred Music, So. Meth. U., 1993; postgrad., U. North Tex., 1993—96. Prin. condr. Hunan Symphony Orch., Chang Sha, China, 1967—83, Jiangsu Symphony Orch., Nanjing, China, 1983—90; finding condr. 100 Voice Choir of Ambassadors for Christ, Dallas, 1993—94, Chinese Youth Orch., Dallas, 1995—99, Great Land Choral Soc., Dallas, 1995—2005, life condr., 2005—. Guest condr. Broadcast Symphony Orch., Shanghai, 1996, Symphony Orch of Shanghai Conservatory of Music, Shanghai, 1997, Voice of Change Inc., Dallas, 1998; condr. North Tex. Philharm. Orch., 1997, 2004, United Choir, Dallas, 2000, 1st Dallas Chinese Music Festival, 2004, V-J Day 60th Anniversary Concert, 2005. Named one of Ten Top-Ranked Women Condrs., People's Music Jour., Beijing, 1980; recipient Grand Prize for Condr., 1st Music and Dance Festival, Jiangsu, China, 1987. Mem.: Chinese Musicians Assn., Tex. Music Tchrs. Assn., Music Tchrs. Nat. Assn. Avocations: sports, dance. E-mail: sunding421217@yahoo.com.

DINGER, ANN MONROE, association executive, interior designer; d. Hoke Jefferson and Florence Parsons Monroe; m. Donald Brackett Dinger, Aug. 13, 1960; 1 child, Lynn Ann Dinger Edmonds. BA in Edn. and Art, Mary Washington Coll. U. Va., Fredericksburg, 1958. Cert. tchr. Va. Art tchr. Alexandria (Va.) Pub. Schs., 1958—61; pvt. interior design cons. Alexandria, Charlottesville, Great Falls, Va., 1958—. Docent Robert E. Lee Boyhood Home, Alexandria, 1967—68; chair D.C. Embassy Tour Alexandria Jr. Women's Club, 1967—68; floral chmn. Pres. James Monroe Home, Charlottesville, Va., 1982—86; hospitality chmn. Newcomers Great Falls, 1987—88; dir., pres., adv. bd. mem. Clan Munro Assn., 1992—, mem. Scottish coun., 1992—. Fellowship com. chmn. Immanuel Presbyn. Ch., McLean, Va., 1994—98. Mem.: Clan Munro Assn., Great Falls Hist. Soc., Great Falls Citizens' Assn. Republican. Presbyterian. Avocations: antiques, gardening, travel. Home: 9100 Potomac Woods Ln Great Falls VA 22066

DINGLE, PATRICIA A., education educator, artist; b. Washington, Apr. 19, 1954; d. Asbery and Loretha (Bryant) D. BA, Conn. Coll., 1976; MA in Tchg., RISD, 1977; PhD in Curriculum and Instrn., U. Md., 1996. Cert. art and dance tchr., Md.; ordained to ministry Bapt. Ch., 1998. Instr. dance RISD, Providence, 1976—77; visual artist, dancer R.I. Coun. on Arts, Providence, 1977—78; tchr. art Ctrl. H.S., East Providence, RI, 1978—79, Friendly H.S., Prince Georges County, Md., 1979—82, Prince George's County Pub. Schs., Upper Marlboro, Md., 1987—; chair dept. fine arts High Point H.S., 2000—02; asst. prof. dept. edn. Clarion (Pa.) U., 2002—06. Dir. summer playground Md. Nt. Capital Park and Planning Commn., Prince Georges County, 1999; adj. prof. Western Md. Coll., Westminster, 1999; propr. Ding La Gift Studio, Bowie, Md., 1994—; presenter Md. Art Edn. Assn., Towson, 1997, 98, Nat. Coun. Tchrs. Math., Springfield and Phila., Success 2002 Conf., U. Md.; mem. discussion panel Conn. Coll., New London, 1998; vis. minority scholar/artist U. Wis., Eau Claire, 2000; lectr. Cath. U. Am., summer 2000; mem. Pres. Commn. on the Status of Women, 2003-05, Dept. Rep. Coun., 2004-05; advisor Black Student Union, 2004-05; pres. African Am. Caucus, 2006; presenter in field. Exhibited in solo shows at Office of Cmty. Affairs, New London, Conn., 1973, Parkview Bapt. Ch., Landover, Md., 1975, First Bapt. Ch. in Am., Providence, 1978, Paradise Exhibit, Pa., 2004, others; group shows include Marlborough (Conn.) Arts Festival, 1974, Cummings Art Ctr., New London, 1976, Woods-Gerry Gallery, Providence, 1977, Marlboro Gallery/Prince George's C.C., 1981, Montpelier Mansion, Laurel, Md., 1998, Bowie Arts Expo, Allen Pond, 1999, Electronic Exhibit, N.Y., 2001, NAEA Women's Caucus Womens Artwork, N.Y., 2001, Art Celebrating Women, PA-SSHE Conf., 2002, Main St. Ctr., Clarion, 2004; works represented in permanent collections Carlson Libr. Clarion U.; dir. Young Designers Am. program Ashton-Drake Gallery, 2000. Facilitator youth study circle Prince Georges County Human Rels. Commn., Landover, 1998; mem. grants in cmtys. adv. panel Md. State Arts Coun., 2000-01; mem. mission trip Appalachian Outreach Ctr., Jefferson City, Tenn., 2003; dir. Aesthetic Awareness Day, 2005, Complete Edge Acad. Excellence Project, 2005; assoc. min. Amazing Grace Bapt. Ch., 1998-2002; youth min. Village Bapt. Ch., 2002-03. Sgt. U.S. Army, 1983-87. Recipient 1st Anna Lord Strauss award for cmty. svc., 1976, awards for art; grad. fellow U. Md., 1989, Md. Tech. fellow, 2000; NEH summer seminar faculty profl. devel. project grantee, 2001, 03, faculty profl. devel. grantee, 2003; Social Equity grantee, 2004; Clarion U. Found. grantee, 2005. Mem.: Nat. Art Edn. Assn. (book reviewer 2002—03, 2005). Avocations: research, writing, piano playing, painting. Office: 1412 Perrell Ln Bowie MD 20716 Office Phone: 301-249-1158. E-mail: dingkgift@aol.com.

DINGMAN, JANET SIMPSON, counselor, educator; b. Cin., Apr. 1, 1940; d. Emmett E. and Sydney (Dilworth) Simpson; m. Robert John Wilkinson, Aug. 21, 1965 (div. Sept. 1980); m. Robert Lewis Dingman, Jan. 7, 1984. BS, Wilkes Coll., 1962; MEd, Rutgers U., 1965; EdD, U. Va., 1969. Lic. profl. counselor, Va., W.Va.; cert. clin. mental health counselor, nat. cert. counselor. Tchr., counselor Brick Twp. High Sch., Bricktown, N.J., 1962-67; coord. counseling svcs. Cen. Va. Community Coll., Lynchburg, Va., 1969-84; supr. Children's Svcs. Prestera Ctr. for Mental Health Svcs., Huntington, W.Va., 1984-88, coord. children's and substance abuse svcs., 1988-89; pvt. practice Huntington, 1989-96, Virginia Beach, 1996—. Vocat. expert Social Security Adminstrn., Huntington, 1987-96, Norfolk, 1996—. Bd. dirs. Big Bros./Big Sisters, Huntington, 1984-96, Lynchburg, 1972-84. DuPont fellow U. Va., 1967, 68; named to Lychnos Soc., U. Va., 1969. Mem. ACA, Va. Counseling Assn. (pres. 1977-78), Va. Clin. Counselors Assn., W.Va. Counseling Assn. (pres.-elect 1991-92, pres. 1992-93, Counselor of Yr. 1989), W.Va. Mental Health Counselors Assn. (pres. 1988-89), Am. Mental Health Counselors Assn., Nat. Career Devel. Assn. Episcopalian. Home: 2709 Browning Dr Virginia Beach VA 23456-2533

DINKEY, LAURA LEE, literature and language educator; b. Denver, Dec. 4, 1978; d. George Gerald and Marilyn Betka May Lowe; m. Charles Eugene Dinkey V, Aug. 23, 1997; children: Andrew Darin, Rowan Charles. BA in English, U. No. Colo., Greeley, 2001. English tchr. Westminster HS, Colo., 2002—. Link Crew Leadership coord. Westminster HS, 2002—. Mem.: NEA. Office: Westminster HS 4276 W 68th Ave Westminster CO 80030 Office Phone: 303-428-9541. E-mail: ldinkey@adams50.org.

DINKINS, CAROL EGGERT, lawyer; b. Corpus Christi, Tex., Nov. 9, 1945; d. Edgar H. Jr. and Evelyn S. (Scheel) Eggert; m. Bob Brown; children: Anne, Amy. BS, U. Tex., 1968; JD, U. Houston, 1971. Bar: Tex. 1971. Prin. assoc. Tex. Law Inst. Coastal and Marine Resources, Coll. Law U. Houston, Tex., 1971-73; assoc., ptnr. Vinson & Elkins LLP, Houston, 1973-81, 83-84, 85—, mem. mgmt. com., 1991-96, chair Adminstrv. and Environ. Law practice; asst. atty. gen. environ. and natural resources Dept. Justice, 1981-83, U.S. dep. atty. gen., 1984-85. Chmn. Pres.'s Task Force on Legal Equity for Women, 1981-83; mem. Hawaiian Native Study Commn., 1981-83; dir. Nat. Consumer Coop. Banks Bd., 1981; chair Pres.'s Oversight Bd. on Privacy and Civil Liberties, 2006—. Contbr. articles to profl. jours. Chmn. Gov.'s Conservation Task Force, 2000, Tex. Gov.'s Flood Control Action Group 1980-81; commr. Tex. Parks and Wildlife Dept., 1997-2001; bd. govs. The Nature Conservancy, 1996—, chmn. 2003-04; dir. Oryx Energy Co., 1990-95, U. Houston Law Ctr. Found., 1985-89, 96-98, Environ. and Energy Study Inst., 1986-98, Houston Mus. Natural Sci., 1986-98, 2000—; trustee Tex. Nature Conservancy, 1985—, chmn., 1996-99, mem. exec. com., 2003, bd. dirs., 2003. Mem. ABA (ho. of dels., past chmn. state and local govt. sect., past chair sect. nat. resources, energy, and environ. law, standing com. on fed. judiciary 1997-98, chair 2002—, bd. advisors ABA Jour., chair 2003—, bd. govs. 2005—), Fed. Bar Assn. (bd. dirs. Houston chpt. 1986), State Bar Tex., Houston Bar Assn., Tex. Water Conservation Assn., Houston Law Rev. Assn. (bd. dirs. 1978). Republican. Lutheran. Office: Vinson & Elkins 2300 First City Tower 1001 Fannin St Houston TX 77002-6706 Business E-Mail: cdinkins@velaw.com.

DINKINS, JANE POLING, management consultant, application developer; b. Van Wert, Ohio, Oct. 11, 1928; d. Doyt Carl and Kathryn (Sawyer) Poling. BBA, So. Meth. U., 1974. Stewardess, acting chief stewardess Am. Airlines, 1946—50; exec. sec., adminstrv. asst. Southland Royalty Co., Ft. Worth, 1956—63; exec. sec. Charles E. Seay, Inc., C. W. Goyer Jr., Dallas, 1964—68; sys. analyst, programmer Southland Life Ins. Co., Dallas, 1968—69, 1st Nat. Bank, Dallas, 1969—72, Occidental Life Ins. Co., LA, 1972—73, Pacific Mut. Life Ins. Co., Newport Beach, Calif., 1973—74, mgr. mut. fund subs., 1975; sys. analyst, programmer Info. Svcs. divsn. TRW, Orange, Calif., 1975—79; EDP auditor Union Bank, LA, 1979; sr. EDP auditor Security Pacific Nat. Bank, Glendale, Calif., 1979—80, asst. v.p. LA, 1981; mgmt. cons. Automation Program Office, Fed. Res. Bank, Dallas, 1982—85; pres. Poling & Assocs., Inc., 1985—; adv. auditor Peer Svcs., Inc., Dallas, 1986—88; sr. computer auditor Merabank, Phoenix, 1988—89; quality assurance analyst Am. Airlines, Carrollton, Tex., 1989—91; assoc. DFW Airport, 1991—2001; quality assurance sr. software programmer Experian, Allen, Tex., 1998—99. Vol. Presbyn. Hosp., C.R. Smith Mus. Mem.: Quality Assurance Inst. (Cert. Quality Analyst award), Flight Attendants Lunch Bunch, Kiwi Club (founding mem.), Sigma Kappa. Republican. Methodist. Home and Office: 10019 Regal Park Ln Apt 206 Dallas TX 75230-5543

DINMORE, KATHERINE, principal; b. Harlingen, Tex., Mar. 10, 1960; d. Richard Clayton and Eileen Quinn Dinmore. BS, U. Colo., Boulder, 1983; MS, U. Colo., Denver, 1993; lic. adminstr., U. Denver, 97. Lic. secondary sci. tchr. Colo. Sci. tchr. Gateway HS, Aurora, Colo., 1984—90, Littleton HS, Colo., 1990—99, internat. baccalaureate coord., 1995—99, asst. prin., 2004—05, prin., 2005—; asst. prin. Douglas County HS, Castle Rock, Colo., 1999—2004. Office: Littleton HS 199 E Littleton Blvd Littleton CO 80121-1100

DINSDALE, CAROL ELLEN, special education educator; b. Dallas, May 22, 1953; d. Calvin Anderson Loving and Mims Ellen Brinker; m. Paul Francis Dinsdale, Oct. 19, 1996; children: Kelley Ann Tuggle, Keith Robert Tuggle. Student, George Peabody Coll. for Tchrs., Nashville, 1972; AA in Edn., St. Petersburg Jr. Coll., Clearwater, Fla., 1988; BS in Spl. Edn. magna cum laude, U. South Fla., 1990, MA in Behavior Disorders, 1994. Nat. bd. certification for tchrs.: mid. childhood generalist Nat. Bd. Profl. Tchg. Stds., educator emotional handicaps, specific learning disabilities Fla., educator varying exceptionalities Fla., educator elem. edn. Fla., educator exceptional student edn. Fla., educator English spkrs. of other langs. Fla. Tchr. pre-sch. and kindergarten Highland Pk. Sch., Clearwater, Fla., 1982—88; tchr. of emotionally handicapped students Pinellas County Schs., Mt. Vernon Elem. Sch., St. Petersburg, Fla., 1991—; adj. prof. for spl. edn. U. of South Fla. Coll Edn., St. Petersburg, 2001—. Presenter Internat. Conf. for Adolescents with Behavior Disorders, 1994—; supervising tchr. for interns U. South Fla., St.

Petersburg, 1994—; mentor nat. bd. cert. process State of Fla., 2004—; school-based coord. for minority students Students Targeted for Ednl. Performance, Fla., 1999—; presenter, spkr. Fla. Coun. for Exceptional Children, Fla., 2002—; site-based coach, new tchr. mentor Pinellas County Sch. Bd., Fla., 2001—; presenter, spkr. Fla. Coun. for Children with Behavior Disorders, Fla., 2003—, Fla. Divsn. for Learning Disabilities, Fla., 2004—. Presenter, spkr. Fla. Children's Ministry Conf., St. Petersburg, 2001—; tchr. children's ministry Calvary Chapel, St. Petersburg, 1999—; vol. ministry for children of incarcerated adults Angel Tree through Calvary Chapel, St. Petersburg, 1997—; vol. prison ministry to area correctional facilities Prison Ministry through Calvary Chapel, St. Petersburg, 2004—. Named Marjorie Crick (Fla.) Tchr. of the Yr., Fla. Coun. for Exceptional Children, 2003; recipient Peace Garden School-wide Project award, Radiant Peace, 2001, Tampa Bay's Channel 10, Sci. in the Classroom grant, Pinellas Edn. Found., 2003—04, Grant for Profl. Devel., Increasing Tchg. Competencies, Citigroup Team Mentor Grant, 2003—04, Fla. Watershed Environment grant water resource edn., S.W. Fla. Water Mgmt., 2002—03, Balanced Literacy Grant and Materials, B.A.L.A.N.C.E. Literacy Instrn., Collaborative Consultation Initiative, 1993—94. Mem.: CEC (membership chairperson chpt. 593 1989—90, historian newsletter chpt. 593 1990—91, exec. bd. 2004—, profl. devel. grant 2002—03, Exceptional Student Educator award 2003, grant for profl. devel. 2003—04, grants for classroom, sci., and reading chpt. 176 2003—05, Clarissa Hug Tchr. of Year, USA and Can. 2005), Fla. Coun. Children Behavior Disorders (v.p. 2006), Pinellas Reading Coun., U. of South Fla. Alumni Assn., Internat. Assn. of Spl. Educators, PTA, Phi Kappa Phi, Kappa Delta Phi. Avocations: herpetology, advocating for literacy, gardening. Office: Mount Vernon Elem Sch 4629 13th Ave N Saint Petersburg FL 33713 Office Phone: 727-893-1815.

DINSMORE, ROBERTA JOAN MAIER, library director; b. Phila., Sept. 30, 1934; d. Bert Faust and Emma Baker (Keen) Maier; m. Ray W. Dinsmore, Sr., Oct. 20, 1956; children: Ray Wilson Jr., Jeffrey Maier, Debra Joan, Matthew Bert. BA, Pa. State U., 1956; MLS, Clarion U. Pa., 1990. Proofreader Aluminum Co. Am., Pitts., 1957-60; office mgr. Dinsmore, Lithographer, Punxsutawney, Pa., 1969—; dir. Punxsutawney Meml. Libr., 1978—. Freelance writer Greenburg (Pa.) Tribune Rev., 1980—81; adult edn. tchr. Jeff Tech., Reynoldsville, Pa., 1981—82; freelance writer Punxsutawney Spirit, 2003—. Mem. Jefferson County Constrn. Com., Jefferson County Heritage Com.; mem. sch. dist. strategic planning com.; chair Police Civil Svc. Commn., Punxsutawney; exec. bd. Theatre Arts; ch. libr. Punxsutawney Presbyn. Ch., 1985—; elder Presbyn. Ch.; mem. com. on ministry Kiskiminetas Presbytery; head hostess Welcome Wagon Internat., Memphis, 1976—80; mem. libr. sci. accreditation team Clarion U., Pa.; mem. exec. bd. Punxsutawney Theatre Arts Guild; hospice vol.; tchr. adult discussion class; mem. coun., vice chair Cmty. Action Svc. Corp.; vice chair numerous orgns. Mem.: AAUW (pres., Woman of the Yr. 1987), ALA, Goschenhoppen Historians, Punxsutawney Area Hist. and Geneol. Soc. (charter), Clarion Dist. Libr. Assn. (pres. 1984—86), Pa. Libr. Assn. (past chair pub. libr. divsn.), Punxsutawney Hosp. Aux., Friends of Libr., Pa. Citizens for Better Librs., Irving Club (past pres., v.p.), Garden Club (past pres. Punxsutawney chpt.), PEO. Republican. Avocations: reading, making and selling crafts in small, self-owned business, genealogy. Home: 808 E Mahoning St Punxsutawney PA 15767-2320 Office: Punxsutawney Meml Libr 301 E Mahoning St Punxsutawney PA 15767-2142 Office Phone: 814-938-5020. E-mail: punxlib@adelphia.net.

DINSMORE, SUSAN MARIE, secondary school educator; b. Albia, Iowa, June 11, 1952; d. John Raymond and Kathryn Mae Conway; m. Larry Deane Dinsmore, Apr. 5, 1980 (dec. Dec. 2000); stepchildren: Brook, Jana. AA, Ottumwa (Iowa) Heights, 1972; BA, N.W. Mo. State, 1974; MA, N.E. Mo. State, 1985. Elem. libr. Ottumwa Cmty. Schs., 1974-80, jr. high libr., 1980-84, tchr., 1984—. Mem. Iowa Assn. Mid. Level Edn., Ottumwa Fedn. Tchrs. (sec. 1986—). Roman Catholic. Home: PO Box 286 Fremont IA 52561-0286 Office: Evans Middle Sch 812 Chester Ave Ottumwa IA 52501-4150 E-mail: sdinsmore@iowatelecom.net.

DION, CELINE, musician; b. Charlemagne, Quebec, Can., Mar. 30, 1970; m. Rene Angelil, 1994; 1 child. Singer: (albums) Unison, 1990 (album of the year, 1990), Celine Dion, 1992, Colour of My Love, 1993 (multi-platinum, 1994), Premieres Anees, 1994, Dion Chante Plamondon, 1994, Des Mots Qui Sonnent, 1995, Power of Love, 1995, French Album, 1995, Live A Paris, 1996, Falling Into You, 1997 (Grammy award album of the yr. & best pop album, 1997), C'est Pour Vivre, 1997, The Collection, 1982—88, 1997, Let's Talk About Love, 1997 (Billboard Music award best album, 1998), S'il suffisait d'aimer, 1998, These are Special Times, 1998 (Grammy & Juno awds., 1999), All The Way, 1999, The French Album, 2001, Classique: A Love Collection, 2001, A New Day Has Come, 2002, One Heart, 2003, 1 Fille & 4 Types, 2003, Miracle, 2004, A New Day, 2004, On Ne Change Pas, 2005, Du Soleil au Coeur, 2006, D'Amour Francaise, 2006, (Soundtracks) Real Love, 1979, Beauty & the Beast, 1991 (Grammy award, 1992, best selling single, 1992, Acad. award, 1992), Sleepless in Seattle, 1993, Through the Fire, 1994, Titanic (single My Heart Will Go On), 1999 (Grammy award record of yr., 1999, Grammy award best female pop vocal, 1999, Billboard Music award best soundtrack single, 1998), (shows) The Colosseum, Caesars Palace, Las Vegas, 2003—. Recipient Favorite Female Pop/Rock Artist award, Music awards, 1999, Favorite Adult Contemporary Artist award, Am. Music awards, 1999, Album of Yr. for Titanic, Billboard Music awards, 1999, Album Artist, Billboard Music award, 1999, Adult Contemporary Artist Billboard Music award, 1999.

DIPAOLO, MARCELLA KAY, elementary school educator; b. Wood River, Ill., June 2, 1950; d. William Harvey and Grace Pauline Marie (Highlander) Dorsey; m. Robert Dale DiPaolo, Nov. 29, 1969; children: Tony, Gina, John, Nick. BS, So. Ill. U., Edwardsville, 1980, MS, 1987, Cert. of Math., 1988. Tchr. 3rd, 6th, 7th and 8th grades St. Kevin Sch., East Alton, Ill., 1987—2006; tchr. St. Mary Sch., Alton, Ill., 2006—. Tchr. math. Lewis & Clark Community Coll., Godfrey, Ill., 1989—; coach baseball St. Kevin Sch., 1989—. Roman Catholic. Avocations: reading, swimming, writing. Office: St Kevin Sch 4 Saint Kevins Dr East Alton IL 62024-1872

DI PAOLO, MARIA GRAZIA, language educator, writer; d. Alfredo and Giosina (Di Cicco) Di Paolo; 1 child, Giandomenico Sarolli. BA, Hunter Coll., 1969; MA, Columbia U., 1972, PhD, 1977. Instr. Columbia U., N.Y.C., 1973-77; asst. prof. Vassar Coll., Poughkeepsie, NY, 1977-85, CUNY, N.Y.C., 1985-90, assoc. prof., 1990-94, prof., 1994—, chair dept. langs. & lit. Lehman Coll., 2001—. Mem. pers. & budget com. Lehman Coll. CUNY, N.Y.C., 1986—, pres. Italian Culture Soc., 1996—98; chair Italian rev. panel CUNY Rsch. Found., 1988—89, 1990—91, 1996—97. Author: B. Fenoglio, 1988; translator: Fenoglio's a Private Matter, 1988; mem. editl. bd. Can. Jour. Italian Studies, 1988—; editor: D'Annuzio's Correspondence with Son Veniero, 1994; contbr. articles to various publs. Faculty fellow, Columbia U., 1970—75, Sabattical grantee, Vassar Coll., 1982—83, Rsch. grantee, PSC-CUNY, 1988—89, 1990—91, 2001—. Mem.: MLA, Am. Assn. Tchrs. Italian. Roman Catholic. Avocations: tennis, reading, opera. Business E-Mail: maria-dipaolo@lehman.cuny.edu.

DIPAOLO, SONJA JEAN, retired nurse; b. Campbell, Ohio, June 30, 1938; d. Joseph Koly and Mary Haladay; m. Anthony Mario DiPaolo, Sept. 29, 1962; children: Chiarina Marie Iregui, Mara Lee Bollini. Diploma, St. Elizabeth Hosp. Sch. Nursing, 1959. RN Ohio State Bd. Nursing, 1959. Med./surg. nurse St. Elizabeth Hosp., Youngstown, Ohio, 1959—60; critical care nurse Cleve. Clinic Found., 1960—62; instr. lic. practical nurses Choffin Vocat. Ctr., Youngstown, 1962—64; occupl. health nurse Gen. Fireproofing Fabricating Plant, 1964—66; med. unit nurse Cleve. Clinic Found., 1966—68; obstet. nurse Ind. U., Indpls., 1968—72; occupl. health nurse Fed. Govt., 1976—79; mid. sch. nurse Pky. Sch. Dist., Chesterfield, Mo., 1983—88, health svcs. facilitator, 1988—2000; ret. Cons. to dist. engr. Pky. Sch. Dist., 1997—; presenter confs. in field. Contbr. articles to profl. jours. Bd. dirs. Mo. Concert Ballet, St. Louis, 1982—85; showhouse steering com. St. Louis Symphony, 2002—03; profl. adv. bd. Greater St. Louis Epilepsy Found. Named Suburban Sch. Nurse of Yr., 1997; recipient Pillar of Pky. award, 1997; grantee, Pky. Edn. Found., 1996. Mem.: St. Louis Suburban Sch. Nurses' Assn. (pres. 1997—98, Sch. Nurse of Yr. 1996), Mo. Assn. Sch. Nurses (nominating com. chair 1998—99), Nat. Assn. Sch. Nurses. Roman Catholic. Achievements include development of state of the art school nurses' office for improvement and promotion of a comprehensive school health program; formal orientation program for school nurses; vision and scoliosis screening program; first to enforce blood sugar testing on diabetic students in school. Avocations: travel, reading, antiques, crewing for Susan G. Komen 60 mile race for the cure.

DIPARDO, ANNE, English language educator; BA in English magna cum laude, Calif. State U., Northridge, 1976; MA in English, UCLA, 1977; EdD in Lang. and Literacy, U. Calif., Berkeley, 1991. Assoc. prof. English and edn. U. Iowa, Iowa City, 1991—2002, prof., 2002—. Author: A Kind of Passport, 1993, Teaching in Common, 1998; co-editor Research in the Teaching of English, 2003—; contbr. articles to profl. jours. Recipient Outstanding Scholarship award Nat. Writing Ctrs. Assn., 1993, CEL ELQ Best Article award, 2005; NAE/Spencer postdoctoral fellow, 1995—. Fellow Nat. Conf. Rsch. in Literacy; mem. MLA, Am. Ednl. Rsch. Assn., Nat. Coun. Tchrs. English (Promising Rschr. award 1992, Meade award 2000). Office: U Iowa N246 Linquist Ctr Iowa City IA 52242 Business E-Mail: anne-dipardo@uiowa.edu.

DIPASQUA, AIMEE DORA, physician; d. John M. and Carmen Cortez; m. France Anthony Do Pasqua. BS, SUNY, Cortland; MD, U. Buffalo. Med. resident Vet. Affairs, Buffalo; county health inspector Oneida County Health Dept., Ithaca, NY. Mem.: AMA.

DIPIRRO, JONI MARIE, artist; b. Clarion, Pa., Jan. 7, 1940; d. Edmund Paul and Laura Genevieve (Nietsche) DiP.; children: Paul Edmund Herman, Joni Maria Herman. Student, Acad. of Florence, Italy, 1969-71, U. Buffalo, 1977-78; studied with, Pietro Annigone, Florence, 1969-72. Dir. Sisti Gallery, Buffalo, 1974-76; curator Castellani Art Mus., Lewiston, N.Y., 1979-96. Restored statue at Niagara U., 1975; painted mural at House of Chauncey Stillman, 1979; represented in permanent collection at Castellani Mus., 1978, The White House, Washington, D.C., Womens Hall of Fame, N.Y.; paintings in the Terwilliger Mus., Waterloo, N.Y. Mem. Amherst Soc. Artists, Kenmore Soc. Artists, Societa Delle Belle Arti, Casa di Dante Florence, Art Ctr. Sarasota. Home: 3204 24th Pkwy Sarasota FL 34235-8804 Office Phone: 941-953-4376. Personal E-mail: dipirroart@comcast.net.

DIRLAM, SHARON JOAN, writer; b. Corning, N.Y., Nov. 6, 1940; d. Arthur Clinton and Edith Lorraine (Kirk) Dirlam; m. John D. McCafferty, July 11, 1977; children: Carol Hales, Michael Millern, Cynthia Rokas. Cert. completion, Stanford U., Calif., 1976; Bachelor's degree, Antioch U., Santa Barbara, Calif., 1995; Master's degree, Sch. for Internat. Tng., Brattleboro, Vt., 1996. Profl. journalism fellowship Stanford U., 1976; city editor, reporter Santa Barbara News Press, 1971—78, 2003—05; staff writer L.A. Times, 1979—89; fgn. expert China Daily, Beijing, 1989—90. Author: (book) Beyond Siberia--Two Years in a Forgotten Place, 2004; contbr.: book A Woman's World, 1995. Bd. dirs., mem. Santa Barbara Ret. Peace Corps Vol., 2002—05; vol. U.S. Peace Corps, Birobidjan, Russia, 1996—98, trainer Russia, 1998—2002, Macedonia, Georgia, 1998—2002. Recipient Gold award for best travel story, Pacific Area Travel Assn., 1988. Mem.: ACLU, PEN-USA, Nat. Peace Corps Assn., Womenin Film, Am. Mensa, Sierra Club. Democrat. Avocations: travel, photography, swimming, hiking, reading. Home: 1532 Santa Rosa Ave Santa Barbara CA 93109

DI RUSSO, TERRY, communications educator, writer; b. Trenton, NJ, Nov. 1, 1947; d. Joy (Urban) Rooy; m. Dennis John, June 23, 1973 (div. July 1985); 1 child, Elaine Marie; m. Robert L. DiRusso, Aug. 17, 2002. BS in Comm., Psychology, Edn., Murray State U., 1970, MS in Comm., 1971; postgrad., Cen. Conn. State U., New Britain, 1972. Tchr., teaching asst. Murray (Ky.) State U., Murray, Ky., 1970-71; instr. adult edn. Wincester Bd. of Edn., Winsted, Conn., 1973-76; special lectr. Central Conn. State U., New Britain, Conn., 1975-85; lectr. comm. dept. Tunxis C.C., Farmington, Conn., 1986—; comm. lectr. U. Conn., Waterbury, 1986, Torrington, 1986—; English educator Wincester Bd. of Edn., Conn., 1971—2006. Cons., lectr. Vets. Hosp. Nursing Staff, Meridan, 1981, Bus. and Profl. Women, 1982; faculty cons. Conn. State Conf. Emergency Med. Techs., Hartford, 1988-96; cons. Pvt. Individuals Pub. Speaking Coach, 1976—; comms. lectr. gender comms. and sexual harassment United Techs., E. Hartford, Conn., 1995; presenter in field. Author: (as Terry Finello) Absolute Vengeance, 1999; mem. editl. bd. Elements of Speech Comm., 3rd edit., 1995. Mem. AAUP, NEA, Conn. Edn. Assn., Winsted Edn. Assn., Nat. Coun. Tchrs. English, New Eng. League Mid. Schs., Litchfield County Women's Network, Conn. Assn. Pubs. and Authors. Avocations: tennis, writing. Home: 34 Fawn Hill Dr Burlington CT 06013 Office: Univ Conn University Dr Torrington CT 06790 Business E-Mail: t.dirusso@comcast.net.

DISANTIS, LINDA KATHERINE, lawyer; b. Chgo., Oct. 22, 1946; m. G. Robert Kerr. RN, Luth. Gen. Sch. of Nursing, 1967; BA summa cum laude, Ga. State U., 1985, JD summa cum laude, 1988. Bar: Ga. 1988, U.S. Dist. Ct. (no. dist.) Ga. 1988. RN emergency rm. Cook County Hosp., Chgo., 1967-68; asst. head nurse med. unit Oak Park (Ill.) Hosp., 1968-69; RN neurology unit Case Western Res. Hosp., Cleve., 1970-72; rsch. asst. legis. monitor Ga. Conservancy, Atlanta, 1982-86; intern, researcher Ga. Dept. of Community Affairs, Atlanta, 1986; assoc. Smith, Currie & Hancock, Atlanta, summer 1987, Alston & Bird, Atlanta, 1987—91; environ. coun. UPS, 1991—96, Corp. Compliance Com., 1996—2001, mgr. Corp. Compliance Dept., 2000—01; city atty. Law Dept., Atlanta, 2001—. Contbr. articles to profl. jours. Mem. consumer adv. coun. Ga. Power Co., Atlanta, 1983-86; mem. econ. devel. task force Gov.'s Growth Strategies Commn., Atlanta, 1987-88. Named Woman of Distinction, Com. on Women, State Bar Ga., 2003. Mem. ABA, Ga. Bar Assn., Atlanta Bar Assn., Ga. State U. Alumni Assn. (bd. dirs. 1989—). Avocations: camping, canoeing. Office: Dept of Law 68 Mitchell St Suite 4100 Atlanta GA 30303 Office Phone: 404-330-6400. Office Fax: 404-658-6894. E-mail: lawdepartment@atlantaga.gov.

DISANTO, CAROL L. (CAROL LA CHIUSA), artist; b. Cleve., July 26, 1930; d. Theodore Christian Jenks and Evelyn Mildred Bushnell; m. Salvatore A. Lachiusa, Sept. 14, 1950 (dec. Feb. 1991); children: Drew, Cyd Marie, Dean, Dane; m. Paris Di Santo, June 28, 1992. Student, Cleve. Inst. Art, 1948-50, U. Mexico, Puebla, 1992. Art instr. Grosse Pointe (Mich.) War Meml., 1969-99; watercolor instr. The Art Ctr., Mt. Clemens, Mich., 1988-99, instr., 1988—2002. Host watercolor workshop program Grosse Pointe Cable TV-Comcast, 1986—2002; workshop lectr. Crooked Tree Art Assn., Petoskey, Mich., 1986—87; exhbn. lectr. Kettering U., Flint, Mich., 1999; lectr. various art assns., Mich., 1981—99; artist-in-residence Grosse Pointe War Meml., 1996—98. One-woman shows include Troy Art Gallery, Royal Oak, Mich., 1979, 1984, 1991, 1994, Venice, Italy, 2001, Mich. Women's Hist. Ctr. and Hall of Fame, Lansing, 2002, Remember Mama, 2002, The Art Ctr., Mt. Clemens, Mich., 2003, Grosse Artists Ctr., Mich., 2003, prin. works include Rockport Best of Watercolor, 1997, Encyclopedia of Living Artists, 11th edit., 1998, Am. Artist Mag., 1999, Grace Mag., 1999, Encyclopedia of Living Artists, 12th edit., Grosse Pointe News, 1995—97, exhibited in group shows at Gallery Bai, N.Y., N.Y., 1998, Mich. Watercolor Travelling Show, 2001, Women's Show, Plymouth, Mich., 2003 (1st prize, 03), Great Lakes Juried Show, 2003 (3d prize, 03), Detroit (Mich.) Women Painters and Sculptors, 2003 (1st prize, 03). Co-founder Grosse Pointe Arts Coun., 1993, pres., 1995-97. Mem.: Mich. Coun. Arts and Cultural Affairs, Grosse Pointe Artists Assn. (v.p. 1988—90), Detroit Soc. Women Painters and Sculptors (pres. 1998—2000), Mich. Watercolor Soc., Mich. Assn. Cmty. Arts Agys., Grosse Pointe United Ch. Womens Assn. (bd. 1999—, pres. 2001—). Home: 418 Barclay Rd Grosse Pointe MI 48236-2814

DISBRO, MEGAN BENNER, librarian; b. Adrian, Mich., Mar. 16, 1969; d. William Strand and Andrea Lee Disbro. AA in Liberal Arts with honors, Jamestown C.C., N.Y., 1989; BA in English cum laude, SUNY, Fredonia, 1991; MLS, SUNY, Buffalo, 1995. Cert.: Syracuse U. (legal asst.) 1993; pub. libr.'s profl. cert. State Edn. Dept., N.Y., 1995. Reference libr. James Prendergast Libr. Assn., Jamestown, 1995—2000; tng. libr. Web analyst Chautauqua-Cattaraugus Libr. Sys., Jamestown, 2000—. Trustee, bd. mem. Buffalo free-net libr. complex com. Western NY Libr. Resources Coun., Buffalo; part-time substitute reference libr. Jamestown CC, 2003. Mem. City Dem. Com., Jamestown, 2002—03. Mem.: ALA (assoc.), N.Y. Libr. Assn. (assoc.). Avocations: reading, pilates, writing. Office: Chautauqua-Cattaraugus Libr Sys 106 W 5th St Jamestown NY 14701 Office Phone: 716-484-7135. Office Fax: 716-483-6880. Personal E-mail: mdisbro@yahoo.com. Business E-Mail: mdisbro@cclslib.org.

DISHONG, LINDA S., estate planner; b. Bluffton, Ind., July 2, 1948; d. George William Dishong and Mary Kathryn Randol; children: Loni Marie, Marlou Reneé. Student various schs. for estate and fin. planning, Ind. Cert. estate planning specialist, sr. adv., real estate rep., NASD Series 7 & 63 broker. Pres. estate planning Genesis Projects, Indpls., 1982—89; adminstrn. and customer svc. rep. MR, Inc., Indpls., 1990—99; real estate profl. Coldwell Banker, Indpls., 1998—2000; broker Charles Schwab, Indpls., 2000—01; estate planning, regulation dir. United Fin. Sys. Corp., Indpls., 2001—. Motivational svc. profl., bus. cons. Genesis Projects, Indpls., 1982—89. Mem.: Westfield-Washinton Kiwanis Club, N.W. Kiwanis Club (sec. 1989—95, v.p. 1995—96, pres. 1996—97, Disting. Sec. 1989—95, Disting. Pres. 1996—97). Republican. Avocations: hiking, bicycling, travel, whitewater rafting.

DISHONGH, LISA LYNN, history educator; b. Carlsbad, N.Mex., Oct. 5, 1965; d. Stephen E. Kelly and Cheryl Ann Mladenka; m. Jesus David Luna (div.); 1 child, Sonia R. Luna; m. Nolan Dishongh, Jr., Aug. 31, 1996; 1 child, Kyle Dylan. BA, St. Mary's U., San Antonio, 1988; MA in Am. History, U. Houston, 2006. Cert. tchr. Tex. Store mgr. Naturalizer/Brown Shoes, San Antonio, 1989—92; social studies tchr. Santa Maria ISD, Santa Maria, Tex., 1992—93; history tchr. Channelview ISD, Channelview, Tex., 1993—, history dept. chair, 2001—03, 2005—06. History re-enactor Tex. Army, Washington-on-the-Brazos, 1998—2002; sponsor Jr. Historians, San Jacinto, Tex., 1994—98. Named Tchr. of the Yr., Channelview ISD, 1998; fellow James Madison fellow, James Madison Found., Washington, 2004. Mem.: Va. Hist. Soc., Nat. Coun. for Social Studies. Democrat. Avocations: gardening, reading, hiking, cooking. Home: 1569 County Rd 6763 Dayton TX 77535 Office: Alice Johnson Jr High School 15500 Proctor Channelview TX 77530

DISILVIO, MARILENA, lawyer; b. Vasto, Italy, June 1, 1967; arrived in U.S., 1972; d. Giuseppe and Grazia DiSilvio; m. David A. Young, Jan. 16, 1999; children: Samuel, Alexander. BSN, U. Pa., Phila., 1989; JD, Clev.-Marshall Coll., 1995. Pediat., neonatal nurse Children's Hosp., Phila., 1989—90, Rainbow Batnes Children's Hosp., Cleve., 1990—91; legal nurse cons. Weisman Kennedy, Cleve., 1991—95, atty., 1995—97, Reminger and Reminger, Cleve., 1995—. Contbr. articles to profl. jours. Named one of Ohio's Rising Stars, Cin. Mag., Ohio's Super Lawyer, Inside Bus. Mem.: Inns of Court, Cuyahoga County Bar Assn., Am. Trial Lawyers Assn., Ohio Acad. Trial Lawyers, Cleve. Bar Assn., Ohio Women's Bar Assn., Ohio State Bar Assn., Justinian Forum. Office: Reminger and Reminger 101 Prospect Ave W Ste 1400 Cleveland OH 44115 Office Phone: 216-430-2188. Office Fax: 216-687-1841. Business E-Mail: mdisilvio@reminger.com.

DISMUKES, CAROL JAEHNE, county official; b. Giddings, Tex., July 17, 1938; d. Herbert Emil and Ruby (Alexander) Jaehne; m. Harold Charles Schumann, Feb. 7, 1959 (div. May 1970); children: Timothy, Michael, Keith, Gregory; m. Milton Brown Dismukes, Mar. 19, 1971. Student Tex. Lutheran Coll., 1958. Dep. Lee County Clk., Giddings, Tex., 1970-74, chief dep., 1975-77; accounts receivable clk. Invader Inc., Giddings, 1977-79; prodn. sec. Humble Exploration, Giddings, 1979-80; county clk. Lee County, Giddings, 1980—2006. Mem., Dime Box Ind. Sch. Dist. Trustees, Tex., 1972-80, pres., 1977-80; chmn. Dime Box Homecoming and Mini-Marathon, 1978—2000; chmn. scholar com. Lee Co. Jr. Livestock Show, 1982-2000; v.p. coun. St. John's Luth. Ch., 1982-84, sec., 1986, treas., 1987-89, chmn., 1991-93, 97-99. Mem. County and Dist. Clks Assn. Tex., Dime Box Lions Club (charter, pres. 1996-97, sec. 1999-2003). Democrat. Avocations: reading; sewing. Office: Lee County Clk PO Box 419 Giddings TX 78942-0419 Office Phone: 979-542-3684.

DISMUKES, VALENA GRACE BROUSSARD, photographer, retired physical education educator; b. St. Louis, Feb. 22, 1938; d. Clobert Bernard and Mary Henrietta (Jones) Broussard; m. Martin Ramon Dismukes, June 26, 1965; 1 child, Michael Ramon. AA in Edn., Harris Tchrs. Coll., 1956; BS in Phys. Edn., Washington U., St. Louis, 1958; MA in Phys. Edn., Calif. State U., LA, 1972; BA in TV and Film, Calif. State U., Northridge, 1981. Cert. phys. edn. tchr., std. svc. supr. Phys. edn. tchr., coach St. Louis Pub. Schs., 1958-60, LA Unified Sch. Dist., 1960-84, health and sci. tchr., mentor tchr., 1984-93; coord. gifted and talented program 32d St./U. So. Calif. Magnet Sch., 1993-95, magnet coord., 1995; adminstrv. asst. Ednl. Consortium Ctrl. LA, 1993-95; free-lance photographer, 1970—; owner, bus. cons. Grace Enterprises, 1994-95; owner World Class Images, 1997—. Coord. Chpt. I, 1989—93; mem. sch. based mgmt. team, 1990—93; lectr. on Red Black Connection Dartmouth Coll., 2000, Southwest Coll., 2001, S.E. Mo. State U., 2002. Author: (photography book) As Seen, 1995; editor: parent newsletter, 1975—80; one-woman shows include The Olympic Spirit, 1984, LA-The Ethnic Pl., 1986, Native Am.: Red Black Connection, 1999, Impressions, 1999, Tibet-Photos from the Roof of the World, 2000, Chocolate Women, 2001, The Tarahamara of Copper Canyon, 2001, Homeless on the Street, 2002, Views from West Africa, 2003, Northern Tribes of Thailand, 2005; photo montage: (films) Black Indians: An American Story, 2001; contbr. articles to profl. jours. Mem. adv. coun. Visual Comm., LA, 1980; mem. Cmty. Consortium, LA, 1986—87; mem. adv. com. LA Edn. Partnership, 1986—87; mem. adv. bd. Espo Sports Club, LA, 1994; co-founder Alliance of Native Am. of So. Calif. (ANASCA), 1999; v.p. Alliance of Native Am. of So. Calif., 1999—2003; mem. adv. coun. Ne'ayah, 2001—05; bd. dir. NACHES Found., Inc., LA, 1985—86. Marine Educators fellow, 1992; photography grantee LA Olympic Organizing Com., 1984, See's Candies, 2000, Long Beach Fine Arts, 2001, Tchg. grantee LA Edn. Partnership, 1987-89, Ind. Humanities Coun., 2003-04; recipient Honor award LA-Calif. Assn. Health, Phys. Edn. and Recreation, 1971. Mem. ACLU, NAACP, Urban League, Sierra Club Treepeople. Avocations: travel, collecting dolls and baskets, ethnic art. Home: 3800 Stocker St Apt 1 Los Angeles CA 90008-5119 E-mail: vdismukes@netzero.net.

DISNEY, ANTHEA, publishing executive; b. Dunstable, Eng., Oct. 13, 1946; naturalized, U.S., 1973; d. Alfred Leslie and Elsie (Wale) Disney; m. Peter Robert Howe, Jan. 28, 1984. Ed., Queen's Coll., Eng. Fgn. corr. London Daily Mail, N.Y.C., 1973-75, features editor London, 1975-77, bur. chief N.Y.C., 1977-79; columnist London Daily Express, N.Y.C., 1979-84; dep. mng. editor N.Y. Daily News, N.Y.C., 1984-87; editor Sunday Daily News, 1984-87, US Mag., 1987-88; editor-in-chief Self mag., 1988-89; mag. developer Murdoch Mags., 1989-90; exec. producer Fox TV's A Current Affair, 1990-91; editor-in-chief TV Guide mag., N.Y.C., 1991-95; editorial dir. Murdoch Mags., 1993-95; editor-in-chief I-Guide, Newscorp's Internet Svc., 1995-96; pres., CEO Harper Collins Publishers, 1996-97; chmn., CEO News Am. Pub. Group, N.Y.C., 1997—99, TV Guide, Inc., 1999; exec. v.p. content The News Corp Ltd., N.Y.C., 1999—; exec. chmn. Gemstar-TV Guide International Inc., LA, 2004—. Bd. dirs. Household Internat. Inc., 2001—. Office: The News Corp Ltd Ste 300 1211 Avenue Of The Americas New York NY 10036-8795

DISPENSA-RHOADS, JACLYN MARISA, environmental services administrator; d. Jonathon and Edith Dispensa; m. William Rhoads, Aug. 7, 2005; children: Immanuel Nicolas Rhoads, Isabella Marisa Rhoads. Doctorate, Drexel U., Phila., 2005. Cert. non-profit exec. mgmt. U. Pa., 2005. V.p.

Edifice Rx, Lafayette Hill, Pa., 1997—2005; dir. for conservation policy Pinelands Preservation Alliance, Southampton, NJ, 2004—. Adj. faculty Phila. U., 2004; founder Del. County's Concerned Citizens for Environ. Change, Norwood, Pa., 2005—; organizer, founder First Delaware County Environ. Summit. Active Zoning Task Force, Norwood, Pa., 2006; adv. bd. mem. Environ. Leadership Program, Washington, 2005; mentor Mentor Power, Lawrenceville, NJ, 2005. Scholar, Drexel U., 2001—05. Mem.: Soc. Women Environ. Profls. Green Party. Methodist. Avocations: travel, writing, volunteering. Home Fax: 267-604-0220. Personal E-mail: jdispensa@ecoisp.com.

DISPENZA, MARY CATHERINE, director, educator, photographer; d. Nicholas Joseph Dispenza and Catherine Viola Cox; life ptnr. Mary Ann Woodruff. BA in Art, Loyola Marymount, 1965; MA in Human Behavior, U.S. Internat. U., 1973. Cert. edn. adminstrn. U. Puget Sound, Seattle, 1978, elem. and secondary tchg. credential U. Puget Sound, 1978. Sister in religious cmty. Religious of the Sacred Heart of Mary, L.A., 1958—73; prin. St. Alphonsus Sch., L.A., 1970—73, St. Mary's Sch., Aberdeen, Wash., 1973—84, St. Louise Elem. Sch., Bellevue, Wash., 1985—99; dir. pastoral life svc. dept. Cath. Archdiocese Seattle, 1989—92; dir. Propect Enrichment Presch., Seattle, 1997—2005. Co-founder TEN, Bellevue, Wash., 1993—; exec. bd. mem., co-chair Hands off Wash., Seattle, 1993—98; chair Lesbian and Gay Child Care Task Force, King County, 1993—2005; ednl. cons. Seattle Hebrew Acad., 1994—96; lead rschr. report Our Families, Our Children, 1999; ESL coord. Entre Hermanos, Seattle, 2005—. Illustrated book, Non-Verbal Communication Between Nurse and Patient, LGBT Family Poster Kit for Schools, 2006. Chair br. juvenile jud. sys. Family Conf. Com., Aberdeen, Wash., 1973—79; mem., spkr. Hands off Wash., Seattle, 1993—97; vol. cook, homeless gay youth Lambert Ho., Seattle, 1993—; creator travelling exhibit LGBT Youth, Seattle, 2001—; photographer ann. calendar highlighting LGBT families Lesbian and Gay Child Care Task Force, Seattle, 2001—; editor, continuum Religious of the Sacred Heart of Mary, L.A., 1965—70. Recipient Nat. Disting. Prin., NEA, 1988, Disting. Cath. Sch. Prin., Nat. Cath. Edn. Assn., 1988; grantee, PRIDE Found., 2001—02. Mem.: Nat. Assn. Edn. of Young Children (assoc.). Avocations: photography, art. Office Phone: 425-644-2468. Personal E-mail: mcdispenza@earthlink.net.

DITOMMASO, PHYLLIS BATTIS, special education educator; d. Eleftherios Nicholas and Katherine (Kyriakoula) Battis; m. Anthony Carlo DiTommaso, June 27, 1993. BS in Edn., Ind. U. of Pa., 1979; MEd, W.Va. U., Morgantown, 1981. Cert. tchr. spl. edn., learning disabled, mentally retarded and ED Va. Tchr. Randolph County Bd. Edn., Elkins, W.Va., 1979—86, Norfolk Pub. Schs., Va., 1986—2000, Virginia Beach City Pub. Schs., Va., 2000—. Co-chair Relay for Life, Virginia Beach, 2004; vol. Neptune Festival, Virginia Beach, 2003—, Boardwalk Art Show, Virginia Beach, 2003—. Office: Linkhorn Park Elem Sch 977 First Colonial Rd Virginia Beach VA 23454 Office Phone: 757-496-6870. Office Fax: 757-496-6750. E-mail: phyllis.ditommaso@vbschools.com.

DI TRAPANI, MARCIA A., health facility administrator, community health nurse, educator; b. Madison, Wis., Mar. 7, 1938; d. Alfred H. and Margaret E. Dvorak; m. Anthony R. Di Trapani, Nov. 12, 1960; children: Anthony R. Di Trapani, Jr., Laura M. Clairmont, Nancy A. Erickson. BSN, U. of Wis., 1960; MA, George Mason U., 1994. RN Va., 1974, Wash., DC, 2000. Staff nurse U. Hosps., Madison, Wis., 1960, D.C. Dept. Pub. Health, Washington, 1961—62, Columbia Hosp. for Women, Washington, 1966—68; case mgr. Internat. Rehab. Assn., Inc., Towson, Md., 1976—77; pub. health nurse Arlington (Va.) County Health Dept., 1978—83, Fairfax (Va.) County Health Dept., 1983—90, nursing supr., 1990—95; cmty. health cons. No. Va. C.C., Annandale, Va., 1995—97; exec. v.p., sec., treas. T&MCorp, Reston, Va., 1997—. Profl. practice adv. bd. mem. Va. State Bd. of Nursing, Richmond, Va., 1992—95; nurses leadership planning group mem. Child Devel. Resources, Norge, Va., 1998—2001; instr. George Mason U., Fairfax, 1998—2004. Contbr. articles to profl. jours. Sec. Marjorie F. Hughes Fund for Children, Arlington, Va., 1996—; family assistance coord. Herndon/Reston (Va.) FISH, Inc., 2003; mem. Giving Cir. of Hope, 2004—. Mem.: DAR, ANA (del. to nat. conv. 2001—03), Coalition Va. Nurses, Va. Nurses Assn. (various positions 1994—2003, pres. dist. 8 2001—03, named one of 99 Outstanding Nurses in Va. 1999, Dist 8 Outstanding Nurse award in Nursing Edn. 2000), Va. Pub. Health Assn., Sigma Theta Tau (corr. sec., eta alpha 2002—). Avocations: travel, genealogy, knitting, geocaching. Home: 11500 Drop Forge Lane Reston VA 20191

DITTMER, FRANCES R., curator; m. Thomas Henry Dittmer (div.). Former curator Refco Collection; pvt. cons.; curator of modern & contemporary art Art Inst. Chgo. Bd. dir. Drawing Ctr. Inc., Whitney Mus. Am. Art, NYC; bd. trustees Menil Collection, Dia Art Found., Art Inst. Chgo., 1988—. Named one of Top 200 collectors, ARTnews Mag., 2004. Avocation: Collector of Contemporary Art. Mailing: Art Inst Chicago 111 S Michigan Ave Chicago IL 60603-6110

DITTNER, DEBORAH MARIE, nurse practitioner in family health; b. Apr. 7, 1954; BSN, Western Conn. State U., 1976; student, Albany Med. Coll., 1980; postgrad., Clayton Coll. Natural Health; coaching cert., Adirondack C.C., 1994. RN, N.Y.; cert. primary care nurse practitioner; cert. Reiki. Pvt. practice family nurse practitioner, Saratoga Springs, N.Y., 1981-90; employee health nurse practitioner Samaritan Hosp., Troy, N.Y., 1990-92; pvt. practice ob-gyn. nurse practitioner, Clifton Park, N.Y., 1995-96; pvt. practice family nurse practitioner Bellevue Hosp. Women, Niskayuna, 1996—2001; dir. Wellness Ctr./Health Svcs., Russell Sage Coll., Troy, 1996—; dir. Wellness Ctr./Health Svcs. Sage Coll. of Albany, 2001—; pvt. practice family nurse practitioner Seton Health Sys., Troy, 1997-2000. Reiki master tchr. practitioner Reiki Rm., Saratoga Springs, NY, 2002—. Founder, dir., author, editor newsletter The Baby Umbrella Newsletter, 1987-90. N.Y. state coord. Melpomene Inst. for Women's Health Rsch., St. Paul, 1981-2000; prs. Girls Basketball Booster Club, Saratoga Springs H.S., 1995-98. Mem.: N.Y. State Coll. Health Assn., N.Y. State Coalition of Nurse Practitioners (treas. 1997—99), Am. Coll. Health Assn., Hist. Soc. for the Preservation of the Underground Railroad (treas. 2000—01, v.p. 2001—), Greenfield Hist. Soc. (life; treas. 2000—01, v.p. 2001—), Zonta Club Saratoga County (pub. rels. chair 1985—87). Address: 3149 Route 9N Greenfield Center NY 12833-1713 E-mail: dittnd@sage.edu, dmd7@netzero.net.

DITZ, TOBY LEE, history professor; b. NYC, May 1, 1951; d. Leo M. and Florence B. (Winkler) D.; m. Mark Edward Martin; 1 child, Rebecca. BA, Northwestern U., 1972; MA, Columbia U., 1975, PhD, 1982. Asst. prof. history Johns Hopkins U., Balt., 1982-87, assoc. prof., 1987—, prof., 1994—. Author: Property and Kinship: Inheritance in Early Connecticut, 1750-1820, 1986. Mem. Am. Hist. Assn., Berkshire Conf. Women Historians. Office: Dept History Johns Hopkins U 3400 N Charles S Baltimore MD 21218

DIVINEY, NANCY LYNN, elementary school educator; d. Thomas Peter and Marguerite Lillian Diviney; children: Andrew Thomas DiOrio, Emily Katherine DiOrio. BS in Edn., U. Kans., 1974, MS in Edn., 1988. Cert. elem. tchr. Kans., reading specialist Kans., ESL Kans. Tchr. Sacred Heart Sch., Bonner Springs, Kans., 1974—75, St. Ann's Sch., Prairie Village, Kans., 1975—77, 1984—89, Queen of the Holy Rosary, Overland Park, Kans., 1978—79; substitute tchr. Shawnee Mission (Kans.) Sch. Dist., 1979—84, tchr., 1993—95, reading specialist, 1995—; tchr. Arlington (Tex.) ISD, 1990—92. Ednl. trainer SRA, McGraw Hill, NYC, 1996—; dist. trainer Shawnee Mission Sch. Dist., Kans., 1995—; publr. KC Star, 2004; presenter in field. Vol. Kansas City Hands On, Mo., 2002—; coord. U. Kans. Juniper Garden Grant for Ruston; v.p. Celtic Fringe, Kansas City, Mo., 2004—; vol. Cath. Charities, Kansas City, Kans., 2002—. Nominee Phoebe Apperson Hearst award, Nat. PTA; recipient Dist. Employee Recognition, Shawnee Mission Sch. Dist., 1997, Literacy award, Internat. Reading Assn., Kans., 2000, cert. of appreciation, Kansas. City, 2002, Action Rsch. Project award, Shawnee Mission Sch. Dist., 2002, Project Best Grant award, Emporia State U., 2005; Shawnee Mission Ednl. grantee, 1998, 2000. Mem.: Kans. Reading Assn. (assoc.; conf. presenter 1997, 1998, chmn. READ Week 1999—2000, conf. presenter 2000, 2001, Literacy award 2000), Internat. Reading Assn. (assoc.), Breakfast Reading Club (founder), Alpha Phi (alumna officer 1977—78), Delta Kappa Gamma (assoc.). Avocations: reading, travel, volunteering.

DIVINSKY, MIRIAM, psychotherapist; b. Novosibirsk, Russia, Oct. 14, 1944; came to U.S., 1980; d. Michael and Friderika (Schpatz) Gershman; m. Igor Pesochinsky, Apr. 14, 1982 (div. May 1989); 1 child, Alexander Michael. MS in Linguistics with honors, Kiev (Ukraine) U., 1966; PhD in Cybernetics, Anti-Aircraft Mil. Coll., Kiev, 1978; MA in Psychology, NYU, 1983, ABD in Psychology, 1985. Cert. clin. advanced hypnotherapist. Rschr. Anti-Aircraft Mil. Coll., Kiev, 1967-74; sr. rschr. Moscow U., 1975-76, Moscow Libr. Social Scis., 1976-79; tchg. asst., fellow U. Pa., Phila., 1980-81; rsch. asst., fellow psychology dept. NYU, N.Y.C., 1981-85; sr. cons. Omni Psych, Inc., Stockholm, N.J., 1985-90; dir. Ctr. for Wellnes and Creative Living, Newfoundland, N.J., 1993—. Condr. workshops Experience of Wellness, Past Life, Future Life, Purpose of Life. Contbr. articles to newspapers and profl. jours. Fellow of distinction Kiev (Ukraine) U., 1961-66. Mem. Assn. Past Life Rsch. and Therapies, Internat. Assn. Counselors and Therapists (life), Nat. Assn. Cert. Hypnotherpists. Office: Ctr for Wellness Ste 7A PO Box 615 2713 Rt 23 S Newfoundland NJ 07435 Home: PO Box 1033 Highland Lakes NJ 07422-4033

DIVITA-FROMMERT, ANGELA MARIE, music educator; b. Lewiston, NY, June 28, 1978; d. Michael Louis and Jessie Wrobel DiVita; m. Derek Frommert. B of Music Edn., SUNY, Potsdam, 2000; M in Music Edn., U. Ill., Urbana-Champaign, 2002; MSc in Ednl. Adminstrn. and Supervision, Niagara U., 2005. Cert. K-12 music tchr. Ga., N.Y., pre-K -6 tchr. N.Y., sch. adminstr. N.Y. Freelance clarinet, woodwind tchr., 2000—; music tchr. Niagara Falls (NY) City Schs., 2000—02, 2004—, band dir., 2002—04, Cobb County Sch. Dist., Marietta, Ga., 2002—04. Instrumental adjudicator NY State Sch. Music. Wish coord. Make-A-Wish Found., Marietta, 2002—04; French horn player Cobb Wind Symphony, Marietta, 2002—04. Mem.: N.Y. State Sch. Music Assn. (woodwind judge 2005—), N.Y. State Band Dirs. Assn., N.Y. State Sch. Music Assn. (cert. adjudicator), Music Educators Nat. Conf., Ga. Music Educator's Assn. (chair all-state auditions 2002), Kappa Delta Pi, Sigma Alpha Iota (Eta A Province officer 2006—). Republican. Roman Catholic. Avocations: reading, remodeling homes. Home: 3927 Washington St Niagara Falls NY 14305

DIX, LORAINE H., chemist; b. Cordele, Ga., May 21, 1942; d. D. L. Hardegree and Gladys (Dell) Johnson. BS Chemistry, Emory U., Atlanta, 1964; MBA, Clemson U., Greenville, S.C., 1979. Chemist Am. Cyanamid, Pensacola, Fla., 1964—67; mgr., chemist Phillips Fibers Corp., Greenville, 1967—77; market rschr., planner Phillip Chem., Bartlesville, Okla., 1978—82; dir. corp. budget Philiips Petroleum, Bartlesville, 1982—89, mgr. mktg., 1989—92; ret., 1992. Treas. Regional Girl Scouts U.S.A., Bartlesville; dir. Red Cross Bd., Bartlesville. Democrat. Presbyterian. Avocations: golf, reading. Home: PO Box 39 Genoa NV 89411

DIXON, BONNIE LYNN, lawyer; b. Pitts., Aug. 21, 1955; d. Kenneth Harold and Margaret Louise Dixon. BA, U. Mich., 1978, JD, 1981. Bar: NY 1982, Gaikokuho Jimu Bengoshi, Japan 2002. Fgn. assoc. Nagashima & Ohno, Tokyo, 1981-84; assoc. Mudge, Rose, Guthrie, Alexander & Ferdon, N.Y.C., 1984-89, Breed, Abbott & Morgan, N.Y.C., 1989-91, Schulte, Roth & Zabel LLP, N.Y.C., 1991-94, ptnr., 1995—2001, Morgan, Lewis and Bockius LLP, Tokyo, 2002—03, Dorsey & Whitney LLP, Tokyo, 2004, Atsumi & Ptnrs., Tokyo, 2005—. Adj. prof. U. Mich. Law Sch., 1989-91; founder, pres. Roppongi Bar Assn., Tokyo, 1982-84; founder Japan Women's Profl. Network, 1996. Founder, sec. Internat. Friends Kabuki, Tokyo, 1982-84. Mem. ABA, N.Y. State Bar Assn., Phi Beta Kappa, Zeta Tau Alpha. Avocation: translating japanese kabuki and bunraku drama. Office: Atsumi & Ptnrs Fukoku Seimei Bldg 2-chome, Chiyoda-ku 2-2 Uchisaiwai-cho Tokyo 100-0011 Japan Office Phone: 813-5501-2111. E-mail: b.dixon@apap.gr.jp.

DIXON, CARMEN SUE, science educator; b. Zanesville, Ohio; d. Michael Stephen and Patrica Sue Dixon. BA, Ohio U., 1999. Sci. tchr. East Knox H.S., Howard, Ohio, 2002—. Dept. chair East Knox H.S., Howard, Ohio, 2004, sci. fair coord., 2000—. Recipient State Gov. award, Ohio State U., 2006. Home: P O Box 63 Duncan Falls OH 43739 Office: East Knox HS 23227 Coshocton Rd Howard OH 43028

DIXON, CARRIE J., social studies educator; BA, U. Wash., Seattle, 1992, BA, 1994, MEd, 1996. Cert. profl. educator Wash. Tchr. social studies Bellevue Sch. Dist., Wash., 1996—2003, Edmonds Sch. Dist., Lynnwood, 2003—.

DIXON, DIANE MARIE, biology professor; d. Daniel R. and Gayle P. Moorhead (Stepmother); m. Wayne A. Dixon, June 6, 1987; 1 child, Michael W. BS magna cum laude, SUNY, Geneseo, 1987; PhD in Microbiology, U. Mo., Columbia, 1993. Assoc. prof., chmn. dept. biol. sci. Southeastern Okla. State U., Durant, 1994—. Active children's ministries United Meth. Ch., Durant, 2005—. Recipient Faculty Senate Recognition award for Excellence in Svc., Southeastern Okla. State U., 2004, Faculty Senate Recognition award for Excellence in Tchg., 1997. Mem.: Okla. Acad. Scis. (chmn. microbiology sect. 1999—2000). Democrat. Methodist. Office: Southeastern Okla State U 1405 N 4th Ave PMB 4034 Durant OK 74701 Office Phone: 580-745-2024. Office Fax: 580-745-7459. Business E-Mail: ddixon@sosu.edu.

DIXON, GEORGETTE (GIGI DIXON), bank executive; Grad., Tenn. State U. Mktg. exec. Procter & Gamble, Brown & Williamson Tobacco Corp.; sr. v.p., dir. emerging markets Wachovia Corp., Charlotte, NC, 2002, dr. v.p., dir. nat. partnerships, 2004—. Office: Wachovia 301 South College St, NC 0143 Charlotte NC 28288-0143 Office Phone: 704-715-8579. E-mail: georgette.dixon@wachovia.com.

DIXON, KATHRYN A., social worker; b. Danbury, Conn., Mar. 8, 1966; d. Thaddeus Edward and Mary Kathryn (Mc Ginley) D. BS in Social Work, U. N.H., 1988; MS in Social Work, Fordham U., 1991. Lic. clin. social worker, N.J., N.Y. Psychotherapist pvt. practice, 1991—; staff Rockland Family Shelter, Spring Valley, N.Y., 1990-91; residential social worker St. Christophers Child Care Facility, Dobbs Ferry, N.Y., 1988-90; youth svcs. counselor Bergen County Divsn. Family Guidance, Paramus, NJ, 1991-97; adolescent therapist High Focus Ctrs., Inc., SaddleBrook, N.J., 1997-99; family counseling specialist State of N.J., Hackensack, 1999—2003, drug ct. coord., 2003—. Vol. Girl Scouts USA. Recipient U. Women's award, U. N.H., 1988. Mem. Am. Coll. Forensic Examiners, NASW (past chair Bergen County). Avocations: camping, jewelry making, whitewater rafting.

DIXON, LUGENIA, psychology educator; b. Columbus, Ga., Jan. 20, 1949; d. Sam and Ola (Bowman) Dixon; m. Willie Cornelius Ladner, 1969 (div. Aug. 1973); children: Dexteralan Keith Ladner, Craig Jeffrey Ladner, Olivia Dara Young. Student, Harris Jr. Coll., Meridian, Miss., 1967-68, Columbus (Ga.) Coll., 1971-78; BA in Psychology, U. Ga., 1980, MEd in Early Childhood Edn., 1982, PhD in Ednl. Psychology, 1985; postgrad., Ft. Valley (Ga.) State Coll., 1989; course grad., Art Instrn. Schs., Mpls., 1997. Medicare claims approval clk. Blue Cross/Blue Shield, Columbus, 1969-71, Medicare unit leader, 1975-77; collector Sears, Columbus, 1971-75; substitute tchr. Clarke County Sch. Dist., Athens, Ga., 1981, instrnl. aide, substitute tchr., 1984-85; work/study (rschr.) U. Ga., Athens, 1981-83; substitute tchr. Ga. Retardation Ctr., Athens, 1983-84; asst. prof. psychology Gordon Coll., Barnesville, Ga., 1985-89; assoc. prof. psychology Bainbridge (Ga.) Coll., 1989—2001, prof., 2001, chair CEPO, 2005; E.T.S. reader AP in psychology, 2004—05. Coord. judging Social Sci. Fair, Bainbridge Coll., 1992—, dir., 1997—; coord. minority achievement program Bainbridge Coll., 1992-97; mem. adv. com. on psychology Regents Acad. Co-author: Living Psychology: An Introduction, 1995; co-author: Handbook for Living Psychology: An Introduction, 1995. Sec. Decatur County Artists Guild, 1994, v.p., program chair, 2005—06; mem. Acad. for Learning through Performance Stds. and Assessment, 2005—06. Recipient cmty. svc. cert. Athens Recreation Dept., 1984, internat. scenario writing contest award 5th World Conf. on Children, Youth and Adults, Athens, 1984; mini-grant Bainbridge Coll., 1996;, Regents minority scholar U. Ga., 1983-84; Univ. Sys. Ga. grantee Summer Inst., Brazil. Mem.: Coun. Tchrs. Undergrad. Psychology, Ga. Assn. Educators, AAUW (gender equity liason, Bainbridge br. 1995—96, Ga. Coll. U. rep.). Democrat. Roman Catholic. Avocations: gardening, drawing and painting. Home: 261 Dollar Dr Bainbridge GA 31717-6438 Office: Bainbridge College Hwy 84 Bainbridge GA 31717 Office Phone: 229-248-2571. Business E-Mail: ldixon@bainbridge.edu.

DIXON, MARY, elementary school educator; m. Michael S. Dixon. BA in Phys. Edn., Bethany Coll., W.Va., 1973; MEd in Curriculum & Instrn., Chapman U., San Diego, Calif., 1994. Tchr. Buckeye Local, Dillonvale, Ohio, 1973—74, Lick Wilmerding HS, San Francisco, Calif., 1975—78, St. Pius X Sch., Chula Vista, 1994—96, Tombaugh Elem., Las Cruces, N.Mex., 1997—. Mem.: Internat. Reading Assn., ASCD.

DIXON, PATRICIA ABUD, music educator; b. Santiago, Chile, June 6, 1949; came to U.S., 1967; d. Antonio and America (Cabrera) de Abud; m. Wilbur Lawrence Dixon, Jr., July 28, 1967. BMus, N.C. Sch. of Arts, 1980; MMus, U. N.C., Greensboro, 1986. Instr. of music Wake Forest Univ., Winston-Salem, N.C., 1980—. Artistic dir. Dir. 2nd Am. Classical Guitar Congress, 1989; performer classical guitar in USA, Europe and S. Am., 1985—. Recipient grants Music Mchts. Assn., 1989, Wake Forest U., 1985—, Winston-Salem (N.C.) Arts Coun., 1989, N.C. Humanities Coun., 1992, N.C. Arts Coun., 1992. Mem. The Guitar Found. of Am., The N.C. Sch. of the Arts Alumni Assn., Am. String Tchrs. Assn. Avocations: reading, travel, yoga, hiking, playing guitar. Home: 2868 Wesleyan Ln Winston Salem NC 27106-5848 Office: Wake Forest U Reynolda Rd Winston Salem NC 27109

DIXON, SHEILA, municipal official; married; 2 children. BA, Towson State U., 1976; MS, Johns Hopkins U., 1982. Mem. Dem. State Century Com. Dist 40 City of Balt., 1986-87; city councilwoman Dist 4 Balt. City Coun., 1987—, mem. Drug and Substance Abuse Com., mem. Housing Authority; internat. trade specialist dept. bus. and econ. devel. Md. Office Internat. Bus., Baltimore; pres. Balt. City Coun.; chair Balt. City Bd. of Estimates. Tchr. Stuart Hill Elem. Sch. Recipient Legis. Achievement award Greater Balt. Bd. of Realtors, 1991. Mem. NAACP (Md. State Enolia P. McMillan award 1993), African Am. Women's Caucus, Women Power, Assn. Study Afro-Am. Life and History Inc., Rainbow Coalition, Nat. Forum Black Pub. Adminstrn. Democrat. Office: Balt City Coun 100 N Holliday St Rm 400 Baltimore MD 21202

DIXON, SHIRLEY JUANITA, retired restaurant owner; b. Canton, N.C., June 29, 1935; d. Willard Luther and Bessie Eugenia (Scroggs) Clark; m. Clinton Matthew Dixon, Jan. 3, 1953; children: Elizabeth Swanger, Hugh Monroe III, Cynthia Owen, Sharon Henson. BS, Wayne State U., 1956; postgrad., Mary Baldwin Coll., 1958, U. N.C., 1977. Acct. Standard Oil Co., Detroit, 1955-57; asst. dining room mgr. Statler Hilton, Detroit, 1958-60; bookkeeper Osborne Lumber Co., Canton, N.C., 1960-61; bus. owner, pres. Dixon's Restaurant, Canton, 1961-99; ret. Judge N.C. Assn. Distributive Edn. Assn., state and dist., 1982—; owner Halbert's Family Heritage Ctr., Canton; dir. rep. Avon. Past Pres. Haywood County Assn. Retarded Citizens Bd., 1985-94, past v.p., chmn. bd. dirs.; bd. commrs. Haywood Vocats. Opportunities, 1985-94, treas. bd. dirs.; Haywood Sr. Leadership Council; dist. dir. 11th Congl. Dist. Dem. Women, 1982-85; state Teen-Dem. advisor State Dem. party, 1985-90; del. 1988 Dem. Nat. Conv., Atlanta; alderwoman Town of Canton, N.C.; vice-chair Gov.'s. Adv. Coun. on Aging, State N.C., 1982-89; 1st v.p. crime prevention Community Watch Bd., State N.C., 1985, 86; mem. Criminal Justice Bd., N.C. Assembly on Women and the Economy; chair Western N.C. Epilepsy Assn., Haywood County N.C. Mus. History, 1987—; bd. dirs. W.N.C. Women's Coalition, 1999-2000; co-chair Haywood County Commn. on the Bi-Centennial of Constn., 1987-92; Haywood County Econ. Strategy Commn.; v.p., bd. dirs. Haywood County Retirement Coun., Region A Coun. on Aging; bd. dirs. Haywood County Sr. Housing, C.B.C. United Way (mem. chair); chair bd. Canton Sr. Citizen's Ctr.; mem. Haywood County Ease Retirement Com.; pres., chairwoman bd. Haywood County Assn. Retarded Citizens; bd. dirs. W.N.C Womens Coalition, 1999; pres. N.C. coun. Alzheimer's Disease and Related Disorders Assn.; bd. dirs. Canton Recreation Dept., Western N.C. Alzheimer's Disease and Related Disorders Assn., 1987-91, v.p., C.B; bd. dirs. Haywood Literary Coun., Haywood Sr. Leadership Coun., Haywood County Block Grant Com., W.N.C. Econ. Devel. Com., United Way, 1991—, drive chmn.; mem. legis. subcom. Alzheimer's-State of N.C.; bd. dirs. N.C. Conf. for Social Svcs., 1987-91; v.p. bd. Western N.C. Alzheimer's Assn., 1987-91; pres. State Coun. on Alzheimer's; apptd. mem. Legis. Study Com. on Alzheimer's; apptd. mem. State of N.C. Adv. Bd. on Community Care and Health; mem. Habitat for Humanity Haywood County; bd. chair Pigeon Valley Optimist Club; apptd. by Senate Western N.C. Econ. Devel. Commn.; appointee Haywood County Econ. Devel. Commn., Canton Hist. Commn.; judge U.S. Olympic Torch Bearers; mem. Bd. Mount. Area Resource Ctr., 2004—, Bd. Haywood Cty. Coun. on Aging, 2004—; dist. rep. N.C. Sr. Dems.; pres. Haywood County Sr. Dems. Recipient Outstanding Svc. award Crime Prevention from Gov., 1982, Gov.'s Spl. Vol. award, 1983, Outstanding Svc. award N.C. Cmty. Watch Assn., 1984, Cmty. Svc. award to Handicapped, 1983-84, Outstanding Svc. award ARC, 1988; named Employer of Yr. for Hiring Handicapped N.C. Assn. for Retarded Citizens, 1985, Cmty. Person of Yr. Kiwanis Club, 1991, Citizen of Yr. in Western N.C., 1995, Rec. Outstanding award Haywood Co. Sr. Games, 1992, Roy A. Taylor award for disting. svc., 1999, Smoky Mtn. Mental Health Hero award, 2004, Liston B. Ramsey award, 2005, N.C. Dem. Women Star, 2005; inducted into N.C. Softball Hall of Fame, 1997. Mem. AAUW, NAFE, Women's Polit. Caucus (So. Women's Leadership award 1998), Internat. Platform Assn., Women's Forum N.C., Nat. Bd. Alzheimers Assn. (regional del.), Canton Bus. and Profl. Assn. (pres. 1974-79, Woman of Yr. 1984), Altrusa (Woman of Yr. in N.C. 1989). Democrat. Episcopalian. Avocation: softball club. Home and Office: 104 Skyland Terr Canton NC 28716-3718 E-mail: sjdixon28716@yahoo.com.

DIXON, STEPHANIE BELL, elementary school educator; d. Clarence Marshall and Leola Robinson Bell; m. Bruce Dixon III, June 26, 1993; children: Bruce Justice IV, Braylen Jarrod. MEd, U. NC, Charlotte, 2000. Cert. Nat. Bd. Profl. Tchg. Stds. Tchr. Charlotte-Mecklenburg Schs., 1992—. Dir.: (play) The Christmas Toy Shop. Rep. Kids Voting of Mecklenburg County, Charlotte, 2001—. Named Tchr. of Yr. Mem.: CTA (sch. rep. 2004—06). Democrat. Office: Davidson IB Mid Sch 251 South St PO Box 369 Davidson NC 28036 Office Phone: 980-343-5185. Office Fax: 980-343-5187. Personal E-mail: stephanie.dixon@cms.k12.nc.us. E-mail: bruceandstephanie.dixon@netzero.net.

DIXON-NIELSEN, JUDY E(ARLENE), mortgage banker, marketing professional, consultant; b. Sweetwater, Tex., July 19, 1950; d. Robert E. Stewart and Verna May (Brown) Kirkpatrick; children: Tammy Taylor-Roubik, Tara R. Taylor-Campbell; m. Kenneth L. Nielsen. Cert., U. Houston, 1986; BA in Mktg. and Mgmt. with honors, Ctr. Degree Study, Pa., 1992; postgrad., St. Pauls Theol. Coll. Joined 3d Order Franciscan Order of Divine Compassion. Ops. mgr. Retail Investment Group, Odessa, Tex., 1981-82; sales cons. Rupert Advt., Odessa, Tex., 1982-83; dir. training Paisano Girl Scout Coun., Corpus Christi, Tex., 1979; owner Gingerbread Bakery, Odessa, 1981-83; exec. dir. Nat. Multiple Sclerosis Soc., Midland, Tex., 1983-86; mktg. dir. Melvin, Simin & Assocs., Midland, Tex., 1986-87; exec. dir. West Tex. Rural Health Edn. Ctr., Odessa, 1987-91; owner Creative Svcs., Odessa, 1991—; loan officer M.L. Mortgage. Cons. small bus. mktg., 1984—; mem. ministry to recovering women alcoholics and their families. Editor, pub. West Tex. Health Prospective mag., 1989-90; contbr. articles to profl. jours. Recipient Writing grant Ector County Ind. Sch. Dist., 1990-91, Nat. Vice Chmn.'s award Nat. Multiple Sclerosis Soc., Cmty. Involvement award N.W. Civic League, 1979,

Silver Appreciation award United Way, 1977. Republican. Avocations: poetry, photography, charcoal drawing, image. Home and Office: 5220 W Mescal Glendale AZ 85304 Office Phone: 602-463-8601. Personal E-mail: dixon4849@aol.com.

DIXSON, J. B., communications executive; b. Norwich, N.Y., Oct. 19, 1941; d. William Joseph and Ann Wanda (Teale) Barrett. BS, Syracuse U., 1963; postgrad. in bus. adminstrn., Wayne State U., 1979-81; MBA, Ctrl. Mich. U., 1984. Pub. rels. editl. asst. Am. Mus. Natural History, N.Y.C., 1963-64; writer, prodr. Norman, Navan, Moore & Baird Advt., Grand Rapids, Mich., 1964-67; prin. J.B. Dixson Comm. Cons., Detroit, 1967-74; dir. Pub. Info. Svcs. divsn. Mich. Employment Security Commn., Detroit, 1974-82; news rels. mgr. Burroughs Corp., 1982-83, dir. creative svcs., 1983-85, dir. pub. rels., 1985-86; prin. Dixson Comm., Detroit, 1986-93, Durocher Dixson Werba, LLC, Detroit, 1994—. Lectr., spkr. in field at colls, univs., cmty. orgns. Author: Guidelines for Non-Sexist Verbal and Written Communication, 1976, Sexual Harassment on The Job, 1979, The TV Interview: Good News or Bad?, 1981. Mem. Detroit Mayor's Transition Com. of 100, 1972; mem. bd. mgmt. Detroit YWCA, 1974; chmn. Detroit Women's Equality Day Com., 1975; bd. dirs., founding mem. Feminist Fed. Credit Union, Detroit, 1976; centennial chair Indian Village Assn., 1993-95; founding mem. Mich. Women's Campaign Fund, 1980; active Mich. Task Force on Sexual Harassment in Workplace, Mich. Women's Com. of 100, Mich. Women's Polit. Caucus, Mich. Women's Found. Named Outstanding Sr. Woman in Radio and TV, Syracuse U., 1963; recipient Five Watch award Am. Women in Radio and TV, Mich., 1969, 75, Outstanding Women in Comm. Women's Advt. Club, 1998, cert. of recognition Detroit City Coun., 1976, Feminist of Yr. award NOW, 1977, City of Detroit Human Rights Commn., 1988, Design in Mich. award Mich. Coun. of Arts/Gov. William G. Milliken, 1977, Achievement award U.S. Dept. Labor, 1979, Spirit of Detroit award Detroit City Coun., 1980, PR Casebook, 1983, PR News Case Study, 1986, Pinnacle award Mich. Hosp. Pub. Rels. Assn., 1987, award Nat. Sch. Pub. Rels. Assn., 1992, 21st Century award Corp. Detroit Mag., 1995, Creativity in Advt. award Detroit Newspapers Assn., 2000; subject of Mich. Senate Resolution 412, 1979. Fellow Pub. Rels. Soc. Am. (accredited, pres. chpt. 1983-84, Dist. award and citation 1984, 86, 87, 93, exec. com. corp. sect. 1996-2001, Disting. Svc. award 1999, named to Pub. Rels. Hall Fame 2004), Internat. Assn. Bus. Communicators (Silver Quill award chpt. 1987, 88, 91, 93, dist. 1987, Renaissance award 1988, 91, Mercury award 1987), Nat. Assn. Govt. Communicators (Blue Pencil award 1977, Gold Screen award 1980), Automotive Press Assn., Women's Advt. Club (Top 75 Women in Comm. 1999), Econ. Club Detroit, Maple Grove Gun Club, Detroit Athletic Club. Home: 3000 N Ocean Dr Apt 28b Singer Island FL 33404-3249 Personal E-mail: dixson@ddwpr.com.

DIXSON, JUDY SUE, retired elementary school educator; b. Bell, Calif., Dec. 30, 1944; d. Jack C. and Arlyne J. (Priddy) Parsons; m. Michael Dennis Dixson, Aug. 21, 1965; children: Tiffany Anne, Michael Bradley. BA in Life Sci., Fresno (Calif.) State U., 1966. Cert. tchr., Calif. Tchr. grades 3-5 Fresno Unified Sch. Dist., 1966—2002, mentor tchr., 1985-86; lead tchr. Calif. Sci. Implementarion Network, Fresno, 1993-94; tchr. leader Calif. Elem. Math. Initiative, Sacramento, 1994-95; tchr. Manchester Gifted and Talented Edn. Elem. Sch., Fresno, 1983—2002; ret., 2002. Mem. San Joaquin Valley Math. Project, Fresno, 1992; master tchr. Nat. Tchr. Tng. Inst., Fresno, 1994-95. Writer ednl. materials. Mem.: Calif. Ret. Tchrs. Assn. Avocations: square dancing, round and line dancing, sewing, camping. Home: 4315 E Copper Ave Clovis CA 93619-9560

DIZZIA, MARIA TERESA, actress; b. Elizabeth, NJ, Dec. 29, 1974; d. John Paul and Lorraine Dizzia. BA summa cum laude, Cornell U., Ithaca, N.Y., 1998; MFA, U. Calif., San Diego, 2001. Actor: (plays) Berkeley Repertory, Actors Theatre Louisville, George St. Playhouse, Yale Repertory, Ala. Shakespeare Festival, La Jolla Playhouse, The Civilians, Apparition, 2005, The Wooden Breeks, 2006. Recipient Dean Goodman Award, 2004.*

DJUNG-WONG, IDA I-GIAI, retired pathologist; arrived in U.S., 1949; d. Hsien-Punh Djung and Siu-Ling Siau; m. Philip Shin-Phing Wong, June 6, 1959; children: Lillian Wong, Christopher Wong. BS, U. Shanghai, China, 1932; MD, Women's Christian Med. Coll., Shanghai, 1939; postgrad., Harvard Med. Sch., Boston, 1952. Diplomate Nat. Bd. Med. Examiners, Am. Bd. Pathology. Resident in surgery Lester Chinese Hosp., Shanghai, 1939—41; chief obstetrics, gynecology Hwa-Mei Hosp., Ningpo, China, 1941—49; intern in anesthesia Hosp. Women & Children, Boston, 1949—50, resident in obstetrics, 1950; resident in surgery St. Paul's Hosp., Dallas, 1951; resident in pathology Univ. Hosp., N.Y.C., Mt. Sinai Hosp., N.Y.C., Beth Israel Hosp., N.Y.C., 1952—56; asst. pathologist DC Gen. Hosp., 1956—59, Wadsworth (Ohio) Hosp., 1960—61; pathologist Akron Med. Lab., 1962—89; ret., 1989. Trustee Women's Christian Med. Coll., Shanghai, 1941—44. Recipient cert. of distinction 50 Yrs. in Medicine, Ohio State Med. Assn., 1990. Fellow: Coll. Am. Pathology. Baptist. Avocations: gardening, photography, reading.

DLOTT, SUSAN JUDY, judge, lawyer; b. Dayton, Ohio, Sept. 11, 1949; d. Herman and Mildred (Zemboch) D.; m. Austin E. Knowlton, July 11, 1986 (div. 1988); m. Stanley M. Chesley, Dec. 7, 1991. BA, U. Pa., 1971; JD, Boston U., 1973. Bar: Ohio 1973, U.S. Dist. Ct. (so. dist.) Ohio 1975, U.S. Ct. Appeals (6th cir.) 1976, U.S. Supreme Ct. 1980, U.S. Dist. Ct. (ea. dist.) Ky. 1984, U.S. dist. Ct. (no. dist.) Ohio 1989, Ky. 1990. Law clk. Ohio Ct. of Appeals, Cleve., 1973-74; asst. U.S. atty. U.S. Dist. Ct. (so. dist.) Ohio, Dayton, 1975-79; ptnr. Graydon, Head & Ritchey, Cin., 1979-95; dist. judge U.S. Dist. Ct. for So. Dist. Ohio, Cin., 1995—. Legal reporter Multimedia Program Prodn., Inc., 1982-84; instr. trial advocacy workshop, Harvard Law Sch., 2000. Mem. Ohio Bldg. Authority, 1988-93, vice chmn., 1990-93, Jewish Fedn. Cin., trustee and mem. com. 1979-93, Jewish Cmty. Rels. Coun. Cin., 1980-90, Hamilton County Park Dist. Vol. in Parks, 1985-86 Recipient U.S. Postal Serv. Commendation, 1977, Service award Dayton Bar Assn., 1975-76. Mem. ABA, FBA (asst. treas. 1981-82, treas. 1982-83, sec. 1983-84, v.p. 1984-86), Ohio Bar Assn., Ky. Bar Assn., Cin. Bar Assn., Leadership Cin. Alumni Assn., Queen City Dog Tng. Club, 6th Cir. Jud. Conf. (life), NAACP (life), Hadassah (life), Potter Stewart Inn of Ct. (pres. 1997—), Cavalier King Charles Spaniel Club Jewish. Office: 100 E 5th St Cincinnati OH 45202-3927 Office Phone: 513-564-7630.

DLUHY, DEBORAH HAIGH, dean; b. Summit, NJ, Mar. 4, 1940; d. Richard Hartman Haigh and Elin Frederika Anderson Neumann; m. Robert George Dluhy, June 11, 1962; 1 child, Leonore Alexandra. BA, Wheaton Coll., 1962; postgrad., Boston U., 1962—63, U. Heidelberg, Germany, 1963—65; PhD, Harvard U., 1976. Instr. fine arts Wheaton Coll., Norton, Mass., 1975—76, Radcliffe Coll., Cambridge, Mass., 1977, Boston Coll., Newton, Mass., 1976—78; devel. officer Mus. Fine Arts, Boston, 1978—84, asst. dir. devel., 1984—86; assoc. dean adminstrn. Sch. Mus. Fine Arts, Boston, 1986—87, dean acad. programs and adminstrn., 1987—93, dean, 1993—; dep. dir. Mus. Fine Arts, Boston, 1999—. Trustee Cultural Edn. Collaborative Boston, 1987—90, Wheaton Coll., Norton, Mass., 1988—, mem. exec. com., vice chair fin. and facilities, 2001—02, chair faculty/staff com., mem. governance bd., 2004—, vice chair presdl. search com., 2003—04, chair bd. trustees, 2005—; pres. Wheaton Coll. Alumni Assn., Norton, Mass., 1994—2000; visitor Walnut Hill Sch., Natick, Mass., 1996—; pres. Pro Arts Consortium, 1999—2000; bd. dirs. Boston Arts Acad., 1999—. Fellow, Woodrow Wilson fellow, 1963. Mem.: Assn. Ind. Coll. Art and Design (program com. 1995—2001, bd. dirs., exec. com., chair), Copley Soc. Boston (hon. trustee 1997—), Nat. Assn. Schs. Art and Design (rsch. com. 1990—96, evaluator 1996—, bd. dirs. 1996—, sec. bd. dirs. 2001—, exec. com. 2001—). Office: Sch Mus of Fine Arts 230 Fenway Boston MA 02115-5534 Office Phone: 617-369-3611. Personal E-mail: ddluhy@earthlink.net. E-mail: ddluhy@mfa.org.

DOAK, NANCY ANN, mathematics educator; b. Phila., Feb. 4, 1960; d. Joseph Robert and Marie Florence Doak; 1 child, Michael Christopher. BS in Math/Secondary Edn., Millersville U., Pa., 1982; MA in Edn., Arcadia U., Glenside, 2002. Cert. tchr. N.J., 1984, Pa., 1982. Tchr. math. Lakewood H.S., NJ, 1984—. Creator (power point presentations) Probability and Statistics. Recipient Tchr. of Yr., Lakewood Bd. Edn., 2000. Mem.: N.J. Edn. Assn. Achievements include development of several programs that could help students pass the HSPA. Home: 66 Schoolhouse Rd Chalfont PA 18914 Office: Lakewood HS 855 Somerset Ave Lakewood NJ 08701 Office Phone: 732-905-3525. Personal E-mail: goldeneagle2m@verizon.net. Business E-Mail: ndoak@piners.org.

DOAN, LURITA ALEXIS, federal agency administrator; b. New Orleans, 1958; m. Douglas C. Doan. BA, Vassar Coll.; M in Renaissance Lit., U. Tenn. Knoxville. Founder, pres., CEO New Technology Mgmt., Inc., 1990—2005; adminstr. U.S. Gen. Svcs. Adminstrn., 2006—. Mem. steering com. Women's Majority Network; mem. presdl. search com. Vassar Coll., mem. bd. trustees; mem. Com. of 200, Coun. on Competitiveness, No. Va. Technology Coun. Mem. bd. trustees Shakespeare Theatre. Mem.: Minority Bus. Network, Women in Technology Internat., Nat. Assn. Female Execs., Nat. Assn. Women Bus. Owners. Office: 1800 F St NW Washington DC 20405-0002 Office Phone: 202-501-0800. E-mail: lurita.doan@gsa.gov.*

DOAN, MARY FRANCES, advertising executive; b. Vallejo, Calif., Apr. 16, 1954; d. Larry E. and Dudley (Harbison) D.; m. Timothy Warren Hesselgren, Mar. 19, 1988; children: Edward Latimer, Clinton Robert. BA in Linguistics, U. Calif., Berkeley, 1976; M in Internat. Mgmt., Am. Grad. Sch. Internat. Mgmt., 1980. Trading asst. The Capital Group, L.A., 1980-81; fin. analyst Litton Industries, Beverly Hills, 1981-82; account exec. Grey Advt., San Francisco, L.A., 1982-84, J. Walter Thompson, San Francisco, 1984-85, Lowe Marshalk, 1985-86; account supr. Young & Rubicam, 1986-89; acct. mgr. Saatchi & Saatchi, 1989—95, CEO, pres., 1995—96, worldwide dir. client svc. applications, 1997—98; cons., 1999; v.p. mktg. Roundl, San Francisco, 1999-2000; cons., 2001—02; v.p. mktg. and advt. Good Guys, 2002—04, cons., 2005—. Office Phone: 415-504-6977. Personal E-mail: mfdoan@hotmail.com.

DOANE, EILEEN MALONEY, learning disabilities teacher consultant; b. Welcome, Md., Dec. 5, 1933; d. John Laurence and Lillian Marion (Posey) Maloney; m. Allan Hammond Doane, June 12, 1954; children: Kathleen, Sharon, Elizabeth. BA in Speech Arts, George Washington U., 1955; MA in Edn., Seton Hall U., 1983; postgrad. studies Learning Disabilities, Kean Coll., 1987; PhD, Berne U., 2002. Cert. tchr. of handicapped, speech correction, prin., supr., learning cons., N.J. Mem. child study team Elizabeth (N.J.) Bd. Edn. Spl. Svcs., 1990-95; learning disability tchr. cons., instrnl. supr. Matheny Sch. and Hosp., Peapack, NJ, 1995—; owner, dir. Randolph Denville Ednl. Ctr., Denville. Mem. Outreach Com. St. Peter's Epsicopal Ch., Mountain Lakes, N.J., adult edn. com. Mountain Lakes. Recipient cert. appreciation Vol. Action Ctr., Morristown, N.J, Mental Health Players, Morris County Mental Health Assn., Madison, N.J., 1987, Benefactor award Rotary Found., Evanston, Ill., 1995; named Paul Harris fellow Rotary Found., 1984. Mem. AAUW, N.J. Assn. Learning Cons., Coun. Exceptional Children, Kappa Delta Pi. Democrat. Avocations: bridge, reading, travel. Home: 38 Cobb Rd Mountain Lakes NJ 07046-1143 Office: Randolph Denville Ednl Ctr 3125 Rt 105 Denville NJ 07834 Office Phone: 973-328-8088.

DOANE, MARCIA E., lawyer, food products executive; b. 1941; BA in Music, De Pauw U., Greencastle, Ind., 1963; JD, Loyola U. Sch. of Law, Chicago, 1976. Bar: Ill. 1976. Special asst. atty. gen. Ill., 1978—81; ptnr. Cowen Crowley Nord & Doane; ops. atty. Bestfoods (Corn Products div.), 1989—94, counsel, 1994—96, v.p. legal and regulatory affairs, 1996—97; v.p., gen. counsel, sec. Corn Products Internat., Inc., 1997—. Mem.: ABA, Am. Corp. Counsel Assn., Am. Soc. of Corp. Secretaries, Ill. Women's Bar Assn. (mem. matrimonial law com. 1979—83, mem. trial practice com. 1980—88), Ill. State Bar Assn., Chicago Bar Assn. (mem. probate practice com. 1976—82, mem. real estate com. 1979, 1982, mem. corp. law dept. com. 1995—99). Office: Corn Products Internat Inc PO Box 7100 5 Westbrook Corp Ctr Westchester IL 60154

DOBACK, JOAN M., physician assistant; b. Waterbury, Conn., Nov. 6, 1963; d. James C. and Joan M. McMahon; m. Charles R. Doback, Jr., June 29, 1991; children: Rebecca, Charles III. BS, U. Conn., 1985; M. Health Professions, Northeastern U., 1989. Cert. Physician Asst. Physician asst. Hosp. of St. Raphael, New Haven, Conn., 1989-91, St. Mary's Hosp., Waterbury, Conn., 1991-94, Neurosurgery Assocs. N.W. Conn., P.C., Waterbury, Conn., 1994—. Preceptor of physician asst. students, Waterbury, 1991—. Fellow Am. Acad. Physician Assts. (Conn. chpt.); mem. Assn. Neurosurgical Physician Assts. (sec., treas. 1994-98, co-editor newsletter 1995-98), Am. Assn. Neurologic Surgeons. Avocations: needlecrafts, gardening. Home: 57 Marbern Ln Naugatuck CT 06770-1613 Office: Neurosurgery Assocs of Northwest Ct PC 500 Chase Pkwy Waterbury CT 06708-3346

DOBBS BLACK, LEAH FAYE, elementary school educator; d. William Clabrun Dobbs, Jr. and Betty S. Dobbs; m. Nathan Asbery Black, May 29, 2004; 1 child, Leah Gabriella Black. BS, Samford U., 1996, BA in Spanish, 1996; MEd in ESL, U. Ala., 2002. Asst. to adminstr. Lakeside Bapt. Ch., Birmingham, Ala., 1996—98; tchr. English Secretaria de Educacion Publica, Puebla, Mexico, 1998—99; tchr. ESL and Spanish Blount County Schs., Oneonta, Ala., 1999—2002; tchr. ESL Shelby County Schs., Columbiana, Ala., 2002—04, area specialist ESL Program, 2004—. Recipient John C. Pittman award, Bus. Sch. Samford U., 1996; fellow, U. Ala., 2000—02; scholar, Wal-Mart, 1991, Barber's Dairies, 1994. Mem.: Assn. Supr. and Curriculum Devel., Nat. Edn. Assn., Ala. Edn. Assn., Shelby County Edn. Assn., TESOL, Ala. Assn. ESL (treas. 2002—06), Ala. Assn. Fgn. Lang. Tchrs. (2d v.p. 2004—05, 1st v.p. 2005—06, pres. 2006—), Kappa Delta Pi. Bapt. Office: Shelby County School 410 East College Street Columbiana AL 35051 Office Phone: 205-682-5946.

DOBIS, JOAN PAULINE, academic administrator; b. S.I., NY, Sept. 11, 1944; d. Victor Raymond and Rosanna Elizabeth (Dandignac) Mazza; m. Robert Joseph Dobis, Dec. 21, 1968. BA in History, Notre Dame Coll., S.I., 1966; MS in Advanced Secondary Edn. and Social Studies, Wagner Coll., 1968; profl. diploma in ednl. adminstrn. supervision, Fordham U., 1979, postgrad. Cert. adminstr. and supr. K-12, social studies and math. tchr. K-12, elem., intermediate and jr. high sch. asst. prin., elem., intermediate and junior high sch. prin., N.Y. Tchr. Prall Intermediate Sch., Staten Island, 1966-98, administrv. asst., 1977-82; coord. social studies Dist. 31, Staten Island, NY, 1998—2003; ret., 2003; mentor N.Y.C. Dept. of Edn. Region 7, 2005—. Mem. S.I. Hist. Soc., 1968-, Friends of Down's Syndrome Found., S.I., 1978—, Sister Helen Flynn Scholarship Com., S.I., 1981—, Friends Seaview Hosp. and Home, S.I., 1984—, Friends S.I. Coll., 1979—, Friends Staten Isl. Greenbelt, 1995-, Friends Staten Isl. Botanical Garens, 1995-; adv. bd. Staten Isl. Advance NIE, 1998-. Recipient St. John's U. Pietas medal, 1991; scholar NY State Bd. Regents, 1962, Can. Consulate St. Lawrence U., 1987, Internat. Brotherhood Teamsters U. Calif., 1988, Nat. Geog. Soc. Geography Edn. Program SUNY, Binghamton, 1989, Women in History Program, NY State Coun. for the Humanities, Albany, 1992, Immigration Program, Bard Coll., 1999; Impact II grantee NYC Bd. Edn., 1992, 98. Mem. ASCD, Nat. Coun. Social Studies, N.Y. State Coun. Social Studies, N.Y.C. Coun. Social Studies, S.I. Coun. Social Studies, United Fedn. Tchrs., Am. Fedn. Tchrs., N.Y. State Hist. Soc., Notre Dame Coll. Alumnae Assn. (regent 1978-80, pres. 1982-84), St. John's U. Alumni Fedn. (del. 1980-88, sec. exec. bd. 1988-90, chmn. bd. 1990-94, emeritus 1995—), Phi Delta Kappa (co-founder S.I. chpt., pres. 1985-87, other offices, Tchr. of Yr. award Fordham U. 1993, named Disting. Kappan 1994, Tchr. of Yr. award S.I. chpt. 1998, Kappan of Decade, 1999). Republican. Roman Catholic. Home: 174 Bertha Pl Staten Island NY 10301-3807

DOBLER, JANIS DOLORES, small business owner; b. Dearborn, Mich., June 7, 1946; d. Ralph Orville and DeLoris (Frederick) Yager; m. Gordon John Dobler, June 24, 1977; children Curtis John, Kristin Marie. BS, Wayne State U., 1966. Cert. tchr., Mich. Owner, mgr. Mark Travel, Portage, Mich., 1982—. Grad. asst. Dale Carnegie, Kalamazoo, 1982-84. Bd. dirs. Davenport Coll., Kalamazoo, 1985-87. Named tchr. yr. State of Mich, 1965. Mem. Assn. Retail Travel Agts., Airlines Reporting Corp., Internat. Assn. Travel Agts., Cruise Lines Internat. Assn., Travel Savers, Portage C. of C., Nat. Fedn. Indt. Bus., Better Bus. Bur., Jr. Achievement (bd. dirs. 1985-87). Republican. Roman Catholic. Avocations: knitting, scrapbooks, travel, genealogy. Office: The Mark of Travel 1595 West Center Suite 105 Portage MI 49024-5375 Office Phone: 269-329-2505. E-mail: dobler@rocketmail.com.

DOBRASKO, REBEKAH, cultural organization administrator, historian; b. Akron, Ohio, June 1, 1979; d. Michael and Mary Dobrasko. BA in History, Tulane U., New Orleans, La., 2001; MA in Pub. History, U. S.C., Columbia, S.C., 2005. Edn. asst. Hermann-Grima/Gallier Hist. Houses, New Orleans, 2001—02; intern City of Columbia Planning Dept., Preservation Office, Columbia, SC, 2004—04; info. mgmt. specialist State Hist. Preservation Office, Columbia, 2003—05, rev. and compliance coord., 2005—. Historian/cons. SC. Civil/Human Rights Anthology, Columbia, 2004—. Contbr. archive collection, scientific papers to profl. jour. Hist. preservation vol. Hist. Columbia, Columbia, 2003—06. Fellow, Keepers Preservation Edn. Fund, 2004, Joseph P. Logsdon Fellowship, Amistad Rsch. Ctr., 2000. Mem.: Palmetto Trust Hist. Preservation, Southeastern Soc. Archtl. Historians, S.C. Hist. Assn., Nat. Coun. Pub. History, Nat. Trust Hist. Preservation. Office: SC Dept Archives and History 8301 Parklane Rd Columbia SC 29223 Office Phone: 803-896-6169. Business E-Mail: dobrasko@scdah.state.sc.us.

DOBRIANSKY, PAULA JON, federal agency administrator; b. Sept. 14; d. Lev Eugene and Julia Kusy Dobriansky. BS summa cum laude, Georgetown U., 1977; MA, Harvard U., 1980, PhD, 1991; LHD (hon.), Fairleigh Dickinson U., 2002, Westminster Coll., 2005, Roger Williams U., 2005; LLD (hon.), Flagler Coll., 2003. Adminstrv. aide Dept. Army, Washington, 1973-76; staff asst. Am. Embassy, Rome, 1976; rsch. asst. joint econ. com. U.S. Congress, Washington, 1977-78; NATO analyst Bur. Intelligence and Rsch. US Dept. State, Washington, 1979; staff mem. NSC, White House, Washington, 1980-83, dep. dir. European and Soviet affairs, 1983-84, dir. European and Soviet affairs, 1984-87; dep. asst. sec. of state Human Rights and Humanitarian Affairs, 1987-90; dep. head U.S. Del. to Conf. on Security and Cooperation in Europe, Copenhagen, 1990; assoc. dir. for policy and programs U.S. Info. Agy., 1990-93; co-chair internat. TV coun. Corp. Pub. Broadcasting, 1993-94; sr. internat. affairs and trade advisor Hunton and Williams, Washington, 1994-97; sr. v.p., dir. Washington Office Coun. on Fgn. Rels., 1997—2001; under sec. state for global affairs U.S. Dept. State, 2001—05, under sec. state for democracy and global affairs, 2005—. Commr. U.S. Adv. Commn. on Pub. Diplomacy, 1997-2001; adj. fellow Hudson Inst., 1993-2001. Host: Freedom's Challenge, Nat. Empowerment Television, 1994-96; co-host: Worldwise, 1997. Bd. dirs. Congl. Human Rights Found., 1994-95, Freedom House, 1999-2001, Western NIS Enterprise Fund, 1994-2001, Am. Com. for Aid to Poland, 1994-95, ABA Ctrl./East European Law Initiative, 1994-99; mem. bd. visitors George Mason U., 1994-98; mem. adv. bd. Horton Internat. Inc., 1998-99. Decorated Grand Cross of Comdr. Order of Lithuanian Grand Duke Gediminas, Star of Romania; named Ethnic Woman of Yr., 1990; named one of 10 Most Outstanding Young Women in Am., 1982, 10 Outstanding Working Women of 1990; recipient Georgetown U. Alumni Achievement award, 1986, State Dept. Superior Honor award, 1990, Poland's Highest medal of Merit, 1998, Democracy Svc. medal, Nat. Endowment Democracy, 2002, Dialogue on Diversity Internat. award, 2001; fellow, Rotary Found., 1979, Ford Found., 1980; scholar Fulbright-Hays scholar, 1978. Mem. Internat. Inst. Strategic Studies, Coun. Fgn. Rels., Am. Polit. Sci. Assn., Fulbright Assn., Nat. Endowment for Democracy (bd. dirs. 1993-2001, vice-chmn. 1995-2001), Am. Coun. on Young Polit. Leaders (trustee 1993-2001), U.S. Environ. Tng. Inst. (bd. adv. 1992-93), Harvard Club (bd. dirs. 1982-85), Univ. Club, Phi Beta Kappa, Phi Alpha Theta, Pi Sigma Alpha. Office: US State Dept Washington DC 20520

DOBROF, ROSE WIESMAN, gerontology educator; b. Denver, Nov. 11, 1924; d. Jerome and Mildred (Hornbein) Wiesman; m. Alfred Dobrof, June 8, 1948 (dec. Mar. 2001); children: Marilyn, Joan, Susan, Judy. BA, U. Colo., 1945; MSW, U. Pitts., 1948; DSW, Columbia U., 1976; DHL (hon.), SUNY, 1996, Hunter Coll., 2000, Hebrew Union Coll., 2002. Lect. div. social svcs. Ind. U., Bloomington, 1952-60; dir. group svc. and vol. dept. The Hebrew Home for the Aged at Riverdale, Bronx, N.Y., 1961-63, asst. dir., 1966-70; assoc. prof. Hunter Coll. CUNY, 1975-78, prof. Hunter Coll., 1979-96, Brookdale prof. gerontology N.Y.C., 1979—; exec. dir. Brookdale Ctr. on Aging Hunter Coll., N.Y.C., 1974-93, acting v.p., 1993-94. Doctoral faculty grad. ctr. CUNY, 1979-96; profl. lectr. in cmty. medicine Mt. Sinai Sch. Medicine, 1982—, co-dir. long-term gerontol. ctr., 1979-81, co-dir. geriatric edn. ctr., 1985-96; chair gov.'s task force on long term care in year 2000, 1986; mem. gov.'s task force on older women, 1986-87; adv. com. sr. citizen affairs for Congresswoman Nita M. Lowey, 1990—; mem. N.Y. State Pub. Health Coun., 1991-95, Gov.'s Health Care Adv. Bd., 1991-94; mem. policy com. White Ho. Conf. Aging, 1995, Fed. Coun. on Aging, 1994-96; del. White Ho. Conf. Aging, 2005. Editor-in-chief Jour. Gerontol. Social Work, 1977—. Trustee Jewish Assn. for Svcs. of the Aged, N.Y.C., 1977-83; bd. dirs. N.Y.C. chpt. Nat. Caucus and Ctr. for the Black Aged, 1982—; bd. dirs. New York Found., 1996—, sec., 1999-2002; sr. fellow The Brookdale Found., 1985—; co-chair U.S. Com. for Celebration of UN Yr. of Older Persons, 1997-99; mem. adv. coun. Nat. Inst. Aging, 1998-2002; trustee The Dekay Found., 1999—, Burden Ctr. for the Aged, 1990— Named One of Five Outstanding Alumni, U. Pitts., 1979; recipient Outstanding Alumnus award U. Pitts., 1981, Robert Ray Parks award, 1986, Alice Brophy award The Burden Ctr., 1987, The Gift of Life award Parker Jewish Geriatric Inst., 1989, The Walter M. Beattie Jr. award N.Y. State Assn. Gerontol. Educators Inst., 1989, 1990, The Pres.'s medal Hunter Coll., 1991, Gerontology Educator Merit award, 1991, Merit award Older Women's League Greater N.Y., 1993, Elinor Guggenheimer award Coun. Sr. Ctrs. and Svcs., 1995, Lifetime Achievement award Sr. Action in a Gay Environment, 1997, Lifetime Achievement award Presbyn. Sr. Svcs., 1999, Katherine Engel award Nat. Coun. Jewish Women, 2001, Coalition Leadership award Continuing Care Leadership Coalition, 2004, Burton Blatt Disting. Leadership award Yai Nat. Inst. People with Disabilities, 2004; named to Social Work Hall Fame, Columbia U., 2002 Fellow N.Y. Acad. Medicine; mem. Acad. for the Humanities and Scis., Nat. Assn. Social Workers (Outstanding Leadership award 1983, Social Worker in Aging award 1990, Knee/Whitman award 2002), Nat. Coun. on Aging (Claude Pepper award 2000), N.Y. Acad. Sci., Am. Soc. on Aging (Sr. Achievement award 2000, Lifetime Achievement award 2005), Gerontological Soc., Am. Fedn. Aging Rsch. (bd. dirs. 1996-2004, trustee emerita 2004—), Phi Beta Kappa, Delta Sigma Rho, Pi Gamma Mu Democrat. Jewish. Avocations: bridge, swimming, gardening. Office: Brookdale Ctr on Aging Hunter College 425 E 25th St New York NY 10010 Home: 377 E 33rd St Apt 10H New York NY 10016-9478 Office Phone: 212-481-3780. Business E-Mail: rdobrof@hunter.cuny.edu.

DOBRZYN, JANET ELAINE, quality assurance professional; b. Allentown, Pa., Oct. 9, 1956; d. Frank John and Doris (Ross) D. Diploma, Pottsville Hosp. Sch. Nursing, 1977; AA, L.A. Valley Coll., 1984; BSN, Calif. State Coll., Long Beach, 1985; MSN, Azusa (Calif.) Pacific U., 1991. RN, Calif., Okla., Pa., Ky., Ga.; cert. profl. healthcare quality. Charge nurse evenings Allentown Osteo. hosp., Pa., 1977-80; charge nurse relief Encino Hosp., Calif., 1980-81; registry nurse Profl. Staffing, Northridge, Calif., 1981-82; clin. nurse II pediatric ICU Childrens Hosp. of L.A., 1982-86, clin. info. specialist, 1986-89; quality mgmt. specialist PacifiCare of Calif., Cypress, 1989-91, quality mgmt. spl. projects coord., 1991-92; mgr. quality mgmt. PacifiCare of Okla., Tulsa, 1992-93, sr. project specialist quality mgmt., 1993-95; accreditation facilitator Humana, Louisville, 1995-96; mgr. quality mgmt. Healthwise of Ky., Lexington, 1996-97; mgr. nat. Medicare med. svcs. Prudential Healthcare, Atlanta, 1997-2000; med. affairs assoc. UCB Pharma, Smyrna, Ga., 2000—02; dir. Ctr. for Quality Cobb and Douglas Bds. of Health, 2002—05, privacy officer, 2005—06; clin. quality coord. Cigna Healthcare, Atlanta, 2006—. Adj. faculty Sch. Nursing U. Louisville; guest lectr. Spaulding U.; cons., reviewer of prototype pub. Commerce Clearing House, Inc., Riverwoods, Ill., 1993; mem. ANA/GHAA task force to develop nursing curriculum in managed care for nursing students, 1994; adv. bd. Nurses Book Soc., 2004-06; speaker in field. Camp nurse vol. Forest Home Conf. Ctr., San Bernardino, Calif., 1988; mem. orch. Johnson Ferry Bapt. Ch. Mem. Nat. Assn. for Healthcare Quality, Nat. Assn., Prolife Nurses Assn., Am. Health Info., Am. Soc. for Quality, Mgmt. Assn., Sigma Theta Tau. Republican. Avocations: reading, walking, swimming, videos, music. Home: 889 Lake Hollow Blvd SW Marietta GA 30064 Personal E-mail: changeagent1@bellsouth.net.

DOBRZYNSKI, JUDITH HELEN, journalist, commentator; b. Rochester, N.Y., Mar. 8, 1949; d. Francis Anthony and Theresa (Contino) Dobrzynski. BS cum laude, Syracuse U., 1971. Corr. McGraw-Hill, San Francisco and N.Y.C., 1971—75, Bus. Week, Washington, 1976—79, London, 1979—83, corp. strategies editor, assoc. editor N.Y.C., 1983—88, sr. writer, 1988—91, sr. editor, 1991—94; bus. reporter N.Y. Times, N.Y.C., 1995—97, culture reporter, 1997—2000, dep. bus. editor and editor Sunday Money and Bus. sect., 2000—03; mng. editor CNBC, Englewood Cliffs, NJ, 2003—05, exec. editor, 2005—. Adj. instr. Columbia U. Sch. Journalism, 2002—; mem. New Founds. Corp. Governance Group Harvard U., Boston, 1992—95; adv. panel Corp. Investment Project U.S. Coun. on Competitiveness, Washington, 1990—92. Contbr. articles to profl. jours. and book revs. Trustee CEC Internat. Ptnrs., N.Y.C., 1993—96; bd. dirs. City Lights Youth Theatre, N.Y.C., 1994—96. Recipient Nat. Headliner award 1st Pl. in Bus. and Consumer TV Journalism, 2004, 2005; Knight Found. fellow, Salzburg Seminar, 2002. Mem.: Syracuse U. Newhouse Sch. Alumni Assn. (bd. dirs. 1991—94, pres. 1992—93), Century Assn. Office: CNBC 900 Sylvan Ave Englewood Cliffs NJ 07632 Office Phone: 201-735-3001. E-mail: jhdobrzynski@nyc.rr.com.

DOBSON, BRIDGET MCCOLL HURSLEY, television executive, writer; b. Milw., Sept. 1, 1938; d. Franklin McColl and Doris (Berger) Hursley; m. Jerome John Dobson, June 16, 1961; children: Mary McColl, Andrew Carmichael. BA, Stanford U., 1960, MA, 1964; CBA, Harvard U., 1961. Assoc. writer General Hospital ABC-TV, 1965-73, head writer General Hospital, 1973-75; producer Friendly Road Sta. KIXE-TV, Redding, Calif., 1972; head writer Guiding Light CBS-TV, 1975-80, head writer As the World Turns, 1980-83; creator, co-owner Santa Barbara NBC-TV, 1983—, head writer Santa Barbara, 1983-86, 91, exec. producer Santa Barbara, 1986-87, 91, creative prodn. exec. Santa Barbara, 1990-91; pres. Dobson Global Entertainment, L.A., 1994—. Bd. dirs. Emory U. Carlos Mus.; bd. advisors Atlanta Internat. Sch., 1997-2000. Author, co-lyricist: Slings and Eros, 1993; prodr. Confessions of a Nightingale, 1994; exhibited in gallery show acrylic paintings Swan Coach House, Atlanta, 1997, exhibited oil paintings Raymond Lawrence Gallery, Atlanta, 1999, Fay Gold Gallery, Atlanta, 1999, Tippy Stern Fine Art, Charleston, S.C., 2002; one-woman shows include Mus. S.W., Midland, Tex., 2001, Midwest Mus. Am. Art, Elkhart, Ind., 2001, Charles Allis Art Mus., Milw., 2001, Albrecht-Kemper Mus. Art, St. Joseph, Mo., 2001, Walter Wickiser Gallery, N.Y.C., 2001, Danville (Va.) Mus. Fine Art, 2002, Burroughs-Chapin Art Mus., Myrtle Beach, S.C., 2002, Tippy Stern Fine Art, 2002, Anderson (Ind.) Fine Art Ctr., 2002, Ella Sharp Mus., Jackson, Miss., 2002. Bd. dirs. Carlos Mus., 1998-2001. Walter Wickiser Gallery, N.Y.C., 2003. Recipient Emmy award, 1988. Mem. Nat. Acad. TV Arts and Scis. (com. on substance abuse 1986-88), Writers Guild Am. (award for Guiding Light 1977, for Santa Barbara 1991), Am. Film Inst. (mem. TV com. 1986-88). Office: PO Box 52813 Atlanta GA 30355-0813

DOBSON, DOROTHY LYNN WATTS, retired elementary school educator; b. Santa Monica, Calif., Nov. 29, 1954; d. Seymour Locke and Margaret (Cheeseman) Watts; m. J. Cody Dobson, June 5, 1982; children: Jeremiah, Hannah. BS, Utah State U., 1975; MEd, U. Utah, 1982. Cert. tchr. intellectually handicapped and behaviorally handicapped, elem., Utah. Tchr. San Juan Sch. Dist., Blanding, Utah, 1974-76; behavioral specialist Salt Lake Sch. Dist., Salt Lake City, 1976-77; tchr. Granite Sch. Dist., Salt Lake City, 1977-82; instr. Utah State U., Logan, 1987—2003; tchr. Edith Bowen Lab. Sch., Logan, 1982—2004. Team coord. First Amendment Schs., Bowen Lab. Sch., Logan, 2002—. Author: Utilizing Newspapers in Social Studies, Math. and Science and Language Arts, 1983; also articles. Mem. Nat. Coun. for Social Studies (bd. dirs. 1996-99, Nat. Elem. Tchr. of Yr. 1992, State Farm Good Neighbor award 1993), Utah Coun. for Social Studies (State Elem. Tchr. of Yr. 1991), Nat. Assn. Lab. Schs. Episcopalian. E-mail: dordob@direcway.com.

DOBSON, PARRISH, photographer, educator; d. Peyton Hoge and Parrish Cummings Houston; m. Eugene H. Pool, May 9, 1943; 1 child, Miranda Parrish Pool. BA, Yale U., 1971; MA, Brandeis U., Waltham, Mass., 1980. Dir. careers for girls W.I.S.E., Hanover, NH, 1973—75; dir. women's studies programs Colby-Sawyer Coll., New London, NH, 1975—78; English tchr. Philips Acad., Andover, Mass., 1980—84; photograhy tchr. Buckingham, Browne and Nichols Sch., Cambridge, 1986—. Bd. mem. Kendall Ctr. for Arts, Belmont, Mass., 1996—99; mem. adv. bd. North Haven (Maine) Arts and Enrichment, 1999—; chair arts dept. Buckingham, Browne and Nichols Sch., Cambridge, 2001—. Exhibitions include Cambridge Ctr. for Arts, 1999—2005, The Gallery at 357 Main St., Rockland, Maine, 2003, Botolph Club, 2004. Artist grantee, Mass. Cultural Coun., 1998. Mem.: New Eng. Women in Photography Steering Com., St. Botolph Club (artist assoc. hon. mem.). Avocations: travel, walking, gardening. Home: 263 Payson Rd Belmont MA 02478 Office: Buckingham Browne and Nichols Sch Gerry's Landing Rd Cambridge MA 02138 Studio: 4 Bradley St Somerville MA Office Phone: 617-800-2291.

DOBSON, SUZANNE, science educator; MS in Curriculum Instrn. and Tech., Nova Southeastern U., Ft. Lauderdale, Fla.; MA in Edn., Jacksonville State U., Ala. Tchr. Bartow County Bd. of Edn., Adairsville, Ga., 1991—; tchr. curriculum, sci. Ind. Wesleyn U., Marion, Ind., 2004—. Mem. Nat. Coun. Tchrs. Math. Tutor, lectr. Internat. Dyslexia Assn., Atlanta, 1998—2005. Recipient Tchr. of Promise award, Sci. and Engring. Fair, 1998, grants for innovative programs to be implemented in Adairsville schs., Etowah Edn. Found., 1995, 1996, 1997; scholar NASA Tchr. Enhancement Program, 1999. Fellow: Nat. Sci. Tchrs. Assn.; mem.: Internat. Reading Assn., Ga. Sci. Tchrs. Assn., Internat. Dyslexia Assn. Office: Bartow County Bd Edn 100 College St Adairsville GA 30103

DOBSON, WENDY KATHLEEN, economics professor; BSN, U. B.C., 1963; MPA, Harvard U., 1971, SM, 1972; PhD in Econs., Princeton U., 1979. Pres. C.D. Howe Inst., Toronto, 1981—87; assoc. dep. min. Dept. Fin. Govt. Can., Ottawa, Ont., 1987—89; prof., dir. Inst. Internat. Bus. Rotman Sch. Mgmt. U. Toronto, 1993—. Author: Japan in East Asia: Trade and Investment Strategies, 1993, Multinationals and East Asian Integration, 1997 (Ohira prize, 1998), Financial Services Liberalization in the WTO, 1998, Shaping the Future of North American Economic Space: A Framework for Action, 2002, Taking a Giant's Measure: Canada, NAFTA and an Emergent China, 2004, The Elephant Sheds Its Past, The Implications for Canada, 2006, Governance, Multinationals and Growth, 2005, (chpts.) Bretton Woods: Looking to the Future, 1994, A Part of the Peace, 1994, Trade Technology and Economics: Essays in Honour of Richard G. Lipsey, 1997, Fifty Years After Bretton Woods: The Future of the IMF and the World Bank, 1995, The Growing Importance of the Asia Pacific Region in the World Economy: Implications for Canada, 1997, Trade Technology and Economics, 1997, Whither APEC?, 1997, Prisoners of the Past: Canada's Policy Framework for the Financial Services Sector, 1999; co-editor: Shaping Comparative Advantage, 1987, East Asian Capitalism: Diversity and Dynamism, 1996, Managing U.S. Japanese Trade Disputes, 1996, The People Link, 1997, Fiscal Framework and Financial Systems in East Asia, 1998, East Asia in Transition, 1999; contbr. articles to profl. jours. Steering com. Pacific Trade Devel. Network; adv. com. Inst. Internat. Econs., Washington; mem. Trilateral Commn.; bd. dirs. Toronto-Dominion Bank, TransCan. Pipelines, Can. Pub. Accountability Bd. Office: Rotman Sch Mgmt U Toronto 105 St George St Toronto ON M5S 3E6 Canada Business E-Mail: dobson@rotman.utoronto.ca.

DOBYNS, SUSAN DIANNE, anthropologist, sociologist, educator; Rsch. asst. Ariz. State Mus., Tucson, 1977—78; archaeol. asst. B. P. Bishop Mus., Honolulu, 1979—81; rsch. assoc. U. Ariz., Tucson, 1984—87, rsch. coord. Bur. Applied Rsch. in Anthropology, 1990—94; asst. prof. Rhodes Coll., Memphis, 1989—90; ethnographic asst. Tucson Unified Sch. Dist., 1990—94; adj. faculty Pima C.C., Tucson, 1997—99, instrnl. faculty, 2002—; instr. Pierce Coll. Puyallup, Wash., 1999—2002. Honors program coord. Pima C.C., 2003—; Phi Theta Kappa advisor Pierce Coll. Puyallup, 2000—02. Named Outstanding Young Woman of Am., 1984; recipient award for meritorious peformance in tchg., U. Ariz., 1985, Pride of Puyallup award, Pierce Coll. Puyallup, 2001; grantee Reduce, Reuse & Recycle Program, Ariz. Dept. Environ. Quality, 1992—93; scholar, Wenner-Gren Found. for Anthrop. Rsch., 1996; grad. academic scholar, U. Ariz., 1976—77. Mem.: Soc. for Anthropology in C.C.s, Soc. Applied Anthropology, Am. Anthrop. Assn., Phi Beta Kappa. Office: Pima CC 8181 E Irvington Rd Tucson AZ 85709-4000 Office Phone: 520-206-7784. E-mail: sdobyns@pima.edu.

DOCKERY, LINDA, writer; b. Louisville, Sept. 23, 1952; d. Willie Dockery and Minnie Cotton; m. Roger Lee Schillig. Freelance consulting tchr., Louisville, 1975—2002; spkr. in field; past columnist Banner Gazette. Author: Distant Drums, 1997 (Can.n Fiction award, 1997), Three Little Words, 2002 (Adcott Publishing award Fiction, 2002), Anna Claus: The Woman Behind the Legend, 2003, Cowgirl Up, 2004, Trail of No Return, 2004, An Angel for Christmas, 2003, North Pole Kitchen, 2003, Trusty Steads of Film & TV, 2004, Once Upon A Time, Renegades, Rebels and Rogues of The Old West, 2005, My Book of Thoughts-Poetry From The Heart, 2005, (screenplays) My Special Angel, 1977, Wilderness Love, 1976 (Lippincott award for most promising new screenplay, 1976), Children of Darkness, 1977, Inherit the Devil, 1978 (Sun Burst award Best Screenplay, 1978), Welcome to Hell, 1978, Rain Softly Till Then, 1984, (TV series) A Time for Love, 1981, (film) Inherit the Devil, 1985, (documentary film) For Our Land, 1991, singer country music; contbr. articles to profl. jours.; editor: Pen Works. Named to, Nat. Cowgirl Hall of Fame, Women Who Write the West Hall of Fame, 2002; recipient Faith and Love award Best Christian Short Story, 1980, Golden pen, 1991, Marshal award Poetry, 1992. Mem.: Ind. Film Makers Guild (founding bd. dirs., v.p.), American Film Inst., Ind. Film Inst., Nat. Hist. Soc., Women Writing the West, Women's Writers Guild. Home and Office: 11117 E Old 56 Scottsburg IN 47170 Personal E-mail: dockery2004@aol.com.

DOCKSTADER, DEBORAH RUTH, minister; b. Elmira, NY, Oct. 12, 1948; d. E. Stanley and Ruth Emery Dockstader. BA, Mercyhurst Coll., 1974; MDiv, Princeton Theol. Sem., 1977. Ordained to ministry Presbyn. Ch., 1977. Pastor Lake Champlain Islands Parish, North Hero, Vt., 1977—79, East Greene Presbyn. Ch., Erie, Pa., 1979—84; dir. edn. St. Stephen's Ch., Fairview, 1984—85; assoc. exec. dir. Inter-Ch. Ministries Northwestern Pa, Erie, 1985—93; interim pastor Ross Meml. Presbyn. Ch., Binghamton, NY, 1993—96; pastor Southside Presbyn. Ch., Niles, Ohio, 1997—, First Presbyn. Ch., Girard, 1997—. Perm. jud. commn. Eastminster Presbytery, Youngstown, Ohio, 1999—, mem. com. ministry, 2000—04, mem. comms. com., 2005—; commr. synod assembly Covenant Synod, 1997—2001; vice moderator East Minster Presbytery, 2006; bd. dirs. Emmanuel Cmty. Care Ctr. Bd. dirs. WQLN Pub. TV & Radio, Erie, 1987—90; mem. Erie Tanzania Project Bd., 1987—90, Allegany Nature Pilgrimage Bd., 1988—93; trustee Erie Rotary Club Scholarship Found., 1990—93; sec. bd. dirs. Niles Cmty. Svcs., 1997—; treas. Friends McKinley Libr., 2000—01; mem. Presbyn. Media Mission Bd., 1983—87, Ecumenical Theol. Ctr. Bd., 1987—90; trustee Susquehanna Valley Presbytery, 1994—96; bd. dirs. Manhoning Valley Assn. Chs., 2000—02, Emmanuel Cmty. Care Ctr., 2005—; mem. Presbytery Self Study Com., 2001—02; vice moderator Eastminster Presbytery, 2005—. Mem.: Lions Club. Avocations: reading, birdwatching. Office Phone: 330-505-1192. Personal E-mail: drdockstader@sbcglobal.net.

DOCKSTEADER, KAREN KEMP, marketing professional; b. Salisbury, Md., Feb. 11, 1953; d. Robert George and Laverne (Briggs) Kemp; m. Gerald Hugh Docksteader, Apr. 3, 1997; children from previous marriage: Daniel Richard Arrington IV, James William Arrington. BS, Iowa State U., 1975; MEd, Salisbury U., 1979. Dir. horticultural project Chesapeake Rehab. Ctr., Easton, Md., 1975-76; mgr. greenhouses Bountiful Ridge Nurseries, Inc., Princess Anne, Md., 1976-77; instr. horticulture Dorchester Bd. Edn., Cambridge, Md., 1978-80, Fredrick (Md.) Bd. Edn., 1980-87; instr. agronomy Frederick C.C., 1985; treas. Kemp's Ltd., Inc., Martinsburg, W.Va., 1985-87, pres. Frederick, 1987—2001; mgr. U.S. retail sales Kord Products, Ltd., Brampton, 1995-98; sales and mktg. dir. Angelica Nurseries, Inc., Kennedyville, Md., 2001—; published photographer, author Garden Writers Assn., 2003—. Keynote spkr. Vocat. Counseling Orgn., Md., 1980—88; cons. retail and comml. mktg. groups, 1977—91; dir. Russian-Georgian Rose Project, Tblissi, Georgia, 1993. Editor: (newsletter) The Spreader, 1990; featured narrator: (documentaries) Our Land, Our Future, 1980; exhibitor Assn. Nurserymen, Balt. and King of Prussia, Pa., 1986—2003. Coach 4-H, FFA, NJHA, and other youth orgns., 1977—98; state chair Soil Conservation Poster Competition, Md., 1990—91; judge horticulture county fairs, state and nat. 4-H and FFA activities, 1977—91; co-founder Windows of Opportunity Found., 2000—. Named Conservation Tchr. of the Yr., State Soil and Water Conservation Svc., 1984. Mem.: DAR, Somerset Pa. Hist. Soc., Hackers Creek Hist. Soc., Md. Hist. Soc., New Market Grange, Md. Greenhouse Growers Assn. Avocations: genealogy, writing, needlepoint, gardening, history. Office: Hortgraphics Inc 26875 Mallard Rd Chestertown MD 21620 Business E-Mail: kkemp@hortgraphics.com.

DOCKTER, NANCY JEAN, principal, elementary school educator; b. Bismarck, ND, Aug. 11, 1964; d. Margaret Jane and Arthur Dockter; 1 child, Logan Geovani. BS, Mayville State U., ND, 1986; MA, ND State U., Fargo, 1998. Cert. tchr. ND, elem. prin. ND. 2d grade tchr. McClusky (ND) Pub. Sch., 1987—89; 3rd grade tchr. Burke Ctrl. Pub. Sch., Lignite, ND, 1989—92; 4th grade tchr. Wishek (ND) Pub. Sch., 1992—2006, elem. prin., 1998—. Active PTA, Wishek, 1992—2006, McIntosh County Child Protection Team, Wishek, ND, 2003—. Named Girls' Basketball Coach of Yr., Sch. Dist., 1991, ND Amateur Baseball Woman of Yr., 1987. Mem.: Wishek Edn. Assn. (pres. 1994—95), ND Reading Assn. (assoc.), Wishek Sports Boosters (assoc.), ND Assn. Elem. Prin. (assoc.), ND Assn. Sch. Adminstrs. (assoc.). Office: Wishek Pub Sch Badger St Wishek ND 58495-0247 Office Phone: 701-452-2892.

DODD, ANNE WESCOTT, education educator; b. Bangor, Maine, Apr. 24, 1940; d. Archie H. and Felicia (Ferrara) Wescott; m. James H. Dodd, Feb. 26, 1965; children: Vickie Dodd Gehm, Suzan Dodd de los Heros. BA in History and Govt., U. Maine, 1961, CAS in Ednl. Adminstrn., 1982, EdD, 1994; MA in English, Calif. State U., L.A., 1967. Cert. secondary tchr., Calif., tchr., adminstr., Maine. English tchr. Hallowell (Maine) High Sch., 1961-62; English, social studies and French tchr. Marshall Jr. High Sch., Pasadena, Calif., 1962-67; social studies tchr. Schurr Jr. High Sch., Montebello, Calif., 1967-68; English tchr., chair humanities dept. Machias (Maine) High Sch., 1969-71; English tchr., chair English dept. Wiscasset (Maine) High Sch., 1971-72; English tchr. Brunswick (Maine) High Sch., 1972-77, asst. prin., acting prin., 1977-81; prin. Freeport (Maine) Mid. Sch., 1981-83; adj. faculty in English U. Maine, Augusta, 1983—; sr. lectr. in edn. Bates Coll., Lewiston, Maine, 1984—. Cons. Freeport High Sch., 1992-94; presenter workshops, curriculum writer in field. Author: A Parent's Guide to Innovative Education, 1992 (Excellence award Child mag.), 9 others; editor Jour. Maine Edn., 1991—; contbr. articles to profl. publs. Mem. ASCD, Am. Ednl. Rsch. Assn., Maine Coun. English Lang. Arts (pres. 1986-88, exec. bd. 1984—), Nat. Coun. Tchrs. English, Maine ASCD, Maine Writers and Pubs. Alliance, Soc. Children's Book Writers, Phi Kappa Phi Honor Soc. Avocations: beachcombing, travel. Home: 39 Windemere Rd Brunswick ME 04011-8134 Office: 4 Andrews Rd Lewiston ME 04240

DODD, DARLENE MAE, retired nurse, retired military officer; b. Dowagiac, Mich., Oct. 11, 1935; d. Charles B. and Lila H. Dodd. Diploma in nursing, Borgess Hosp. Sch. Nursing, Kalamazoo, 1957; grad., Air Command and Staff Coll., 1973; BS in Psychology and Gen. Studies, So. Oreg. State Coll., 1987, postgrad., 1987. Commd. 2d lt. USAF, 1959, advanced through grades to lt. col., 1975, staff nurse Randolph AFB, Tex., 1959-60, Ladd AFB, Alaska, 1960-62, Selfridge AFB, Mich., 1962-63, Cam Rahn Bay Air Base, Vietnam, 1966-67, Seymour Johnson AFB, NC, 1967-69, USAF Acad., Colorado Springs, Colo., 1971-72; flight nurse 22d Aeromed. Evacuation, Tenn., 1963-66; chief nurse USAF, Danang Air Base, Vietnam, 1968, flight nurse Yokota AFB, Japan, 1969-71, clin. coord. ob-gyn., flight nurse Elmendorf AFB, Alaska, 1973-76; clin. nurse coord. ob-gyn. and pediatric svcs. USAF Med. Ctr., Keesler AFB, Miss., 1976-79; ret., 1979; with Bear Creek Corp., Medford, Oreg., 1986—2003, ret., 2004. Decorated Bronze Star. Mem. DAV, VFW, Am. Legion (life), Soc. Ret. Air Force Nurses, Ret. Officers Assn., Vietnam Vets. Am., Uniformed Svcs. Disabled Retirees, Air Force Assn., Women of Moose, Psi Chi, Phi Kappa Phi. Home: 712 1st St Phoenix OR 97535-9787

DODD, JAN EVE, lawyer; b. Kansas City, Mo., May 24, 1964; d. Raymond Thomas and Eva Faith (McCorkle) D. BA in Polit. Sci. & Journalism, U. Mo., Columbia, 1985; JD, U. Mo., Kansas City, 1988. Bar: Mo. 1988, Ill. 1989, U.S. Dist. Ct. (so. dist.) Ill. 1989, U.S. Dist. Ct. (ea. dist.) Mo. 1989, U.S. Ct. Appeals (7th cir.) 1991, U.S. Ct. Appeals (8th cir.) 1994. Rsch. asst. Prof. Jack M. Balkin, Kansas City, Mo., 1986-87; jud. law clk. Judge Edward D. Robertson Jr. Mo. Supreme Ct., Jefferson City, Mo., 1988-89; sr. assoc. def. litigation Sandberg, Phoenix & Von Gontard, St. Louis, 1989—; former special state atty gen. State of Mo.; now ptnr., litigation dept. Kaye Scholer, Los Angeles, Calif. Recipient diploma Nat. Inst. for Trial Adv., Mid-Am. Regional, 1994. Mem. Def. Rsch. Inst., Bar Assn. Met. St. Louis, Tower Grove Neighborhood Assn. Office: Kaye Scholer 1999 Ave of Stars Ste 1700 Los Angeles CA 90067 Office Phone: 310-788-1000. Office Fax: 310-788-1200. Business E-Mail: jdodd@kayescholer.com.

DODD, KRISTEN L, social studies educator; b. Des Moines, Iowa, Aug. 25, 1973; d. James R. and Susan D. Lyon; m. Terry P. Dodd, Oct. 14, 2000; 1 child, Zackary L. BS in Edn., SW Mo. State U., 1996; M Curriculum and Instrn., U. Mo., Columbia, 2005. Secondary sch. social studies tchr. Mehlville Sch. Dist., St. Louis, 1998—. Grantee, US Dept. Edn., 2001—02. Mem.: Nat. Coun. Social Studies. Home: 1521 Summer Chase Fenton MO 63026 Office: Mehlville Sr HS 3200 Lemay Ferry Saint Louis MO 63125 Office Phone: 314-467-6000. Business E-Mail: doddk@mehlville.k12.mo.us.

DODD, LOIS, artist, art educator; b. Montclair, NJ, Apr. 22, 1927; d. Lawrence Dodd and Margaret Vanderhoff; m. William Dickey King (div.); 1 child, Eli Benjamin. Student, Cooper Union, 1945-48. Tchr. art Bklyn. Coll., 1971-92. One-woman shows include Tanager Gallery, N.Y.C., 1954—62, Green Mountain Gallery, 1969—76, Fischbach Gallery, 1978—2002, Washington (Conn.) Art Assn., 1977, Cape Split Pl., Maine, 1977—83, N.J. State Mus., Trenton, 1981, Lyman Allyn Mus., Conn., 1980, La. State U., Baton Rouge, 1984, Anne Weber Gallery, Maine, 1987, Caldbeck Gallery, 1990, 1995, 1998, 2001—03, Dartmouth (N.H.) Coll., 1990, 2004, Rider (N.J.) U., 1993, Montclair Art Mus., 1996, Farnsworth Art Mus., Rockland, Maine, 1996, Trenton City Mus., Alexandre Gallery, 2002—, 2004, Bowdoin Coll. Mus., Maine, 2004, Represented in permanent collections Colby Coll. Mus., Cooper Hewitt Mus., Farnsworth Mus., Kalamazoo Art Ctr., Montclair Art Mus., NAD, AT&T, Chase Manhattan Bank, Commerce Bancshares Inc., Met. Life Ins. Co., Readers Digest, R.V. Reynolds Security, Pacific Nat. Bank, First Nat. City Bank, Hood Mus., Dartmouth, Rider U., NJ. Bd. govs. Skowhegan Sch. of Painting and Sculptures, 1980—. Recipient Disting. Alumni citation Cooper Union, 1987; Ingram Merrill Found. grantee, 1971. Mem. NAD, AAAL (award 1986). Office: c/o Alexandre Gallery Fuller Bldg 41 E 57th St New York NY 10022 Office Phone: 212-254-7159.

DODD, VIOLET M., nursing educator, recreational therapist, counselor; b. Zenda, Wis., Nov. 9, 1918; d. Jacob Polyock and Sarah McNeil; m. Jasper Messmore III, Dec. 17, 1943 (dec. Aug. 1944); 1 child, Jasper Messmore IV; m. Ronald Frank Dodd, June 11, 1955. RN, Mercy Sch. Nursing, Janesville, Wis., 1940; BS in Biology, De Paul U., 1948, MA in Edn., 1952; MA in Human Devel., U. Chgo., 1972; MA in Dance/Movement Therapy, Columbia U. Chgo., 1990. RN Ga., Wis.; cert. lic. profl. counselor Ga., registered therapist Acad. Dance Therapy. Head nurse, 2d lt. Army Nurse Corps, Orlando, Fla., 1942—44; clin. instr. St. Xavier Coll., Chgo., 1950—52, dir. edn., 1952—66; instr. psychiat. nursing South Suburban Coll., South Holland, Ill., 1966—87; therapist Dance/Movement Charter Peachford Hosp., Atlanta, 1990—93, Emory Eastside Med. Ctr., Snellville, Ga., 1996—. Adjudicator Nat. Dance Coun. Am., 1966—. Pres. Welcome Wagon Atlanta, 1990—91. Mem.: U.S. Terpsichore Assn., Nat. Assn. Dance Therapy, Imperial Soc. Tchrs. Dance, Freedom Alliance, Sigma Theta Tau. Avocations: reading, gardening, dance, travel, calligraphy. Office: Emory Eastside Med Ctr 1700 Medical Way Snellville GA 30078

DODDS, LINDA CAROL, special education educator; b. Tucson, June 2, 1957; d. George A. and Bette R. (Bell) D. AA, U. Md., 1979; BA, Tex. Tech U., 1982; MBA, Our Lady of the Lake U., 1986, MEd, 2001. Svc. rep. United Svcs. Automobile Assn., San Antonio, 1982-84, portfolio asst. investment mgmt. co., 1984-85, sr. rep., 1985-86, asst. area mgr. Tampa, Fla., 1986-88, area mgr., 1988-92, dist. mgr., 1992-97, San Antonio, 1997-98; reading resource tchr. Boerne Ind. Sch. Dist., Tex., 1999—2002, head spl. edn. dept., 2000—02; resource tchr. N.E. Ind. Sch. Dist., San Antonio, 2002—04; spl. edn. tchr., chmn. Schertz-Cibolo-Universal City Ind. Sch. Dist., 2004—. Treas. Forest Hills Homeowners Assn., Tampa, 1992-93; mem. Tex. Fedn. Rep. Women, San Antonio, 1985; co-chair United Way, 1995-96; active USAA Vol. Corp., Tampa, 1989-1998. Mem.: Soc. CPCU, Delta Mu Delta, Sigma Iota Epsilon.

DODGE, JUDITH C., musician; b. Florence, Ariz., Mar. 15, 1940; d. Natt Noyes and Mildred (Johnson) Dodge; m. David Worthy Breneman, June 10, 1962 (div. Dec. 1992); children: Erica Vernice Breneman, Carleton David Dodge Breneman. BME, U. Colo., 1962; MA, San Francisco State U., 1970; DHL, Va. Theol. Seminary, 2004. Asst. dir. San Francisco Boys Chorus, 1967-70; dir. music, organist St. Columba's Episcopal Ch., Washington, 1972-83; organist, choirmaster St. Lukes Episcopal Ch., Kalamazoo, 1987-889; adj. lectr. music Kalamazoo Coll., 1983-89; music dir., condr. Bach Festival Soc. Kalamazoo, 1985-89; dir. music, organist St. Philips in the Hills Ch., Tucson, 1989-93, St. Columba's Episcopal Ch., Washington, 1993—. Chair music and program bd. Cathedral Choral Soc., Washington, 1996—2003; mem. adv. bd., sacred cirs. Nat. Cathedral, Washington, 1998—; mem. standing commn. liturgy and music Nat. Episc. Ch., 2001—06. Mem. editl. bd. Jour. Assn. Anglican Music; contbr. articles to profl. jours. Mem. task force Kalamazoo Pub. Schs., 1983-84; mem. selection com. New Yrs. Fest, Kalamazoo, 1986; mem. artistic adv. bd., trustee emeritus Gilmore Internat. Keyboard Festival, 1989-94; mem. Standing Commn. on Liturgy and Music of the General Convention of the Episcopal Ch. Named to Outstanding Young Women of Am., 1965. Mem. Am. Choral Dirs. Assn., Am. Guild Organists, Assn. Anglican Musicians (sec., pres., v.p. 1992-95), Royal Sch. Ch. Music, Am. Guild English Handbell Ringers, Kappa Delta Pi, Pi Kappa Lambda, Sigma Alpha Iota. Democrat. Avocations: tennis, opera, golf, travel, theater. Office: St Columba's Episcopal Ch 4201 Albemarle St NW Washington DC 20016-2009

DODGE, LYNN LOUISE, municipal official, librarian; b. Cleve., May 8, 1946; d. Charles Verl and Mary Louise (Wall) D. BA, Meredith Coll., 1968; MS in Libr. Sci., U. N.C., 1969. Br. libr. Henrico County Pub. Libr., Richmond, Va., 1969-74; city libr. Lynchburg (Va.) Pub. Libr., 1974-89; dir. dept. librs. and mus. City of Lynchburg, 1989—. Del. to Gov.'s Conf. Librs. & Info. Sci., Richmond, 1978, 90; mem. State Networking Users Adv. Bd., Richmond, 1986-90; bd. dirs. Greater Lynchburg Transit Co. Mem. adv. coun. continuing edn. U. Va., Lynchburg, 1989-94; mem. adv. coun. Libr. Svcs. and Technology Act, 1999-2004, chair, 2000-2004. Mem. Va. Libr. Assn. (treas. 1982-84). Avocations: travel, reading. Office: Lynchburg Pub Libr 2315 Memorial Ave Lynchburg VA 24501-2650 Office Phone: 434-847-1577. Business E-Mail: lynn.dodge@lynchburg.va.gov.

DODGE, MARCIA MILGROM, director, choreographer; b. Detroit, Apr. 28, 1955; d. Myron L. and Jacqueline (Pushkin) Milgrom; m. Anthony Dodge, Oct. 30, 1980; 1 child, Natasha. BA, U. Mich., 1977. Instr., Collaborative Arts Project 21 NYU, 1996; instr. Marymount Manhattan Coll.; instr., Musical Theatre Dept. Am. Musical and Dramatic Acad., NYC. Assoc. choreographer (Broadway plays) High Society, 1996, co-author with Anthony Dodge & dir. (plays) Sherlock Holmes & The West End Horror, 2002; dir.: (plays) They Shoot Horses, Don't They, Some Enchanted Evening, The Crucifer of Blood, There's One in Every Marriage, Angel Street, Kismet, One Foot on the Floor, Goosebumps Live on Stage, Fit to Print, Accomplice, A Funny Thing Happened on the Way to the Forum, The Second Hurricane, Crimes of the Heart, Thumbs, The Unsinkable Molly Brown, Tell Me On A Sunday, Damn Yankees, Espresso Trasho, 2003; dir. & choreographer (plays) Closer Than Ever, Bye Bye Birdie, On the Town, Off-Key, High Spirits, Sullivan & Gilbert, Radio Gals, Cookin', Hair, Olympus on My Mind, Anything Goes, Ain't Misbehavin', Once on This Island, Finian's Rainbow, Dames at Sea, (academic theatre plays) Merrily We Roll Along, The Mystery of Edwin Drood, Divorce Me Darling, Why Must the Show Go On?, Times Square, Of Thee I Sing, Guys & Dolls; dir.: (plays, NYC) Closer Than Ever, Empty Hearts, The Merry Wives of Windsor Texas, The Music Man, Romance in Hard Times, The Waves, The Loman Family Picnic, High Society, Knight Life: The Girl Who Would Be King, 2005; choreographer (regional plays) Little Shop of Horrors, She Loves Me, In a Pig's Valice, The School for Wives, Company, Another Kind of Hero, Casino Paradise, Velvet Elvis, Book of the Night, Riverview, On the Town, The Three Cuckolds, A Midsummer Night's Dream, ELmer Gantry, Dancing at Lughnasa, Portrait of Jennie, The Little Rascals; dir.: (TV) Sesame Street, Remember Wenn, Elmo's World: Wild Wild West. Mem.: Soc. Stage Dirs. and Choreographers (exec. bd. dir.). Office: c/o Susan Gurman 865 W End Ave New York NY 10025 also: AMDA Musical Theatre Dept 2109 Broadway New York NY 10023*

DODGE, TERESA ANN, elementary school educator; d. Eugene O. and Carol Dockstader; m. Wesly Eugene Dodge, July 11, 1992; children: Alexandria Marie, Samantha Ann, Nicholas Eugene. BA, Boise State U., Idaho, 1992. Tchr. Glenns Ferry (Idaho) Mid. Sch., 1992—. Office: Glenns Ferry Middle School 639 N Bannock Glenns Ferry ID 83623 Office Phone: 208-366-7438. Business E-Mail: dodget@sd192.k12.id.us.

DODSON, ALICEJEAN LEIGH, nursing administrator; b. S.I., N.Y., May 13, 1941; d. Wilbur Thomas Jr. and Beatrice Bertha (Beinert) Leigh; m. Robert Jean Olsen, Dec. 14, 1963 (div. Dec. 1969); 1 child, Aric Robert Olsen; m. Jonathan Boyd Dodson, June 1, 1988; stepchildren: Jacquelyn Nicole, Richard Lewis. BSN, Gustavus Adolphus Coll., 1963; postgrad., U. Puget Sound, 1977-78; M in Nursing, U. Wash., 1979. RN, Minn., Wash., Va. Head nurse ICU, nursing instr. Mary Bridge Children's Hosp., Tacoma, 1967-74; instr. Tacoma C.C., 1974-76, 77-78; instnl. nursing cons. State of Wash., Olympia, 1980-81; head nurse ICU Good Samaritan Hosp., Puyallup, Wash., 1981-83; spl. projects mgr. Puget Sound Hosp., Tacoma, 1983-88; program mgr. Frankfurt (Germany) Mil. Cmty., 1988-90; survey team adminstr. Health Mgmt. Strategies, Alexandria, Va., 1990-92; clin. practice specialist Am. Health Care Assn., Washington, 1992-95; DON Continence Care, Inc., Vienna, Va., 1995-97; project dir. marine new parent support program Quantico/Henderson Hall, 1998—. Reviewer on incontinence Agy. Health Care Policy & Rsch., Washington, 1994-95. Charter mem. Nat. Mus. Women in the Arts; mem. Tacoma Arts Commn., 1987-88; vice chairperson Pub. Arts Task Force, Tacoma, 1986. Lutheran. Avocations: travel, gardening, bicycling. Home: 6707 Kenmont Pl Springfield VA 22152-2424

DODSON, LEISA, music educator; d. Jack L. and Mary Ellen Phillips; m. Bob Dodson, Aug. 5, 1978; 1 child, Jennifer Hodge. BS in Edn., U. Ark., Fayetteville, 1981. Cert. vocal music edn. Ark., 1981. Christian edn. dir. First Christian Ch., Harrison, Ark., 1981—88, music dir., 1981—94; preschool and music tchr. Montessori Children's Schoolhouse, Harrison, 1988—92; elem. music tchr. Harrison Sch. Dist., 1992—. Music dept. chair Harrison Sch. Dist. Actor: (cmty. theater) Sound of Music; Nunsense (Best Actress for Sound of Music; Best Supporting Actress for Nunsense); singer: (soloist in cmty. chorus) Handel's Messiah. Mem., officer Delta Kappa Gamma, Harrison, 1999—2006; mem. Ozark Arts Coun., Harrison; elder First Christian Ch., Harrison, worship leader, 2001—06. Grantee, Harrison Sch. Found., Fulbright Memorial Fund, 2002. Mem.: PEO (rec. sec.), Delta Kappa Gamma (chpt. pres. 2006—). Mem. Disciples Of Christ Ch. Avocations: photography, travel, crossword puzzles. Home: 806 Oriole Harrison AR 72601 Office Phone: 870-741-5043.

DOEBELE, ALEXA C., music educator, director; b. Cambridge, Feb. 28, 1968; d. Don Herrick and Carol McCain Johnson; m. Andy J. Doebele, Jan. 8, 2000. MusB, Washington U., 1990; M in Music Edn., U. Colo., 1993. Lic. Tchr. Colo., 1993. Choir dir. Denver South HS, 1993—95, Panorama Mid. Sch., Colorado Springs, Colo., 1997—98, Harrison HS, Colorado Springs, Colo., 1998—99, Iver C. Ranum HS, Denver, 1999—2003; music tchr. Malley Dr. Elem. Sch., Northglenn, Colo., 1995—97; dir. music Holy Cross Luth. Ch., Wheat Ridge, Colo., 2004—. Grad. instr. U. Colo., Boulder, 2004—. Walter S. Collins scholarship, U. Colo., 2004—05, Freelyn Jeffers fellowship, 2004—. Mem.: Assn. Luth Ch. Musicians, Coll. Music Soc., Music Educators Nat. Conf., Am. Choral Dirs. Assn. (sec. Colo. chpt. 2002—05), Delta Phi Alpha, Pi Kappa Lambda, Phi Beta Kappa. Avocations: movies, computers. Office: U Colo Coll Music CB 301 Boulder CO 80309

DOEBERT, SANDRA L., school system administrator; b. Chicago Heights, Ill., June 5, 1957; d. William Jeremiah Teed and Barbara Ione (Stead) Allen; m. Edward Eugene Doebert, Apr. 20, 1984; children: Jeremiah Eugene, Justin Edward. M in Comm. Studies, No. Ill. U., Dekalb, 1984; cert. advanced studies, Nat. Louis U., Evanston, Ill., 1994; EdS, No. Ill. U., Dekalb, 2002, EdD, 2004. Supt. endorsement Ill., cert. type 75 adminstr. Ill., tchr. Ill. Tchr. Downers Grove (Ill.) South H.S., 1979—85, dean of students, 1985—94; asst. prin. Lemont (Ill.) H.S., 1994—2001, asst. supt. dist. 210, 2001—02, supt. dist. 210, 2002—. Assoc. Sch. Exec. Connect, Highland Park, Ill., 2005—06; pres. Fellowship Ednl. Leadership, DePere, Wis., 2003—06, Three Rivers Edn. for Employment Sys.; bd. dirs. Will County Area Vocat. Ctr. Choir mem. Bethany Luth. Ch., Lemont, 1987—2006. Mem.: Ill. Assn. Sch. Bus. Ofcls., Ill. Assn. Sch. Adminstrs., Ill. H.S. Dist. Orgn. (bd. dirs. 2004—06), S.W. Cook County Coop. Assn. for Spl. Edn. (chairperson), Lemont C. of C., Nat. Assn. Federally Impacted Schs. (bd. dirs. 2003—06), Lemont Jr. Womans Club. Avocations: fitness, singing, travel. Office: Lemont H S Dist 210 800 Porter St Lemont IL 60439

DOERKSEN, MONA DIANE, music educator; b. Moundridge, Kans., Aug. 4, 1966; d. Glen M. and Celia A. Goering; m. Kevin Dale Doerksen, May 30, 1987; children: John Dale, Katharine Diane. MusB Edn., Wichita State U., Kans., 1988, MusM Edn. Lic. tchr. Kans. Band tchr. USD 259, Wichita Pub. Schs., 1989—. Ch. bd. mem. Lorraine Ave. Mennonite Ch., Wichita; vol. soccer coach Derby (Kans.) Recreation Ctr. Mem.: Kans. Music Educators Assn.

DOERRIE, BOBETTE, educational consultant, secondary school educator; b. Albuquerque, June 22, 1944; d. Neill and Dorothy Madelyn (Jones) Patterson; m. Edward Lewis Horton, Aug. 21, 1966 (div. 1990); children: Leah, James, Carol, Neill; m. Jerome Lee Doerrie, July 28, 1991; children: Jennifer, Elena. BA, McMurry Coll., 1966; MEd, DePaul U., 1977. Cert. sec. broadfield sci. Tchr. physics and phys. sci, environ. edn., TAKS Remed. G/T coord. Perryton (Tex.) H.S.; tchr. Summit Sch., Dundee, Ill., 1974-77, Lamesa Middle Sch., 1980-85, Lamesa HS, 1968—69, 1985—91, Perryton HS, 1991—2005; adnl. cons. adult edn. Frank Philipps C.C., 2005—; rsch. dir. Duck Pond Creek Exptl. Farms. Co-dir. Dawson County Sci. Fair, 1981-91; coach Odyssey of the Mind, 1988-91; mem. McMurry U. Ednl. Adv. Bd., 1991-97, engring. team faculty advisor, 1993-2004, sci. olympiad coach, 1998-2000, sci. bowl advisor, 2001-05; instr. astronomy Frank Phillips Coll., 2006—. Bd. dirs. Mus.Dawson County, 1983—90, Libr. Ochiltree County, 1993—95, v.p., 1993—95; bd. dirs. Perrytown Crisis Ctr., 2005—. Recipient Excellence in Teaching award Tex. State Assn. for Physics Tchrs., 1992, Nat. Tchg. award RadioShack, 2001; NSF/Tex. Edn. Assn. Christa McAuliffe grantee, 1993, Outstanding Sci. Educator, Tex. Acad. Sci., 2002, Nat. Tchg. award Health Physics Soc., 2002; named Tchr. of Yr., Region XVI Gifted and Talented Tchrs., 1994, Perryton H.S., 2004. Mem.: Sci. Tchrs. of Tex. (treas. 1998—2001), South Plains Sci. Soc. (pres. 1988, Sharon Christa McAuliffe Tchr. of Yr. 1987), Delta Kamma Gamma (past pres.). Avocations: amateur radio, painting, astronomy, reading, writing. Home: 13925 County Rd B Booker TX 79005-4125 Personal E-mail: bdoerrie@yahoo.com.

DOETSCH, VIRGINIA LAMB, former advertising executive, writer; b. NYC, Oct. 12, 1920; d. Andrew Thomas and Cameola Weeden (Burns) Lamb; m. Gunter H. Doetsch, Oct. 12, 1953 (div. Feb. 1972); 1 child, Hugo. BS, Northwestern U., 1941; postgrad., Columbia U., 1943—44, postgrad., 1946—47. Writer, dir. pub. rels. J. Walter Thompson, Frankfurt, Germany, 1953-56; creative group head, v.p. to ptnr. Tatham-Laird & Kudner (now Euro RSCG), Chgo., 1959—76; v.p. Needham Harper & Steers (now DDB Chgo.), Chgo., 1976-83; free-lance advt. writer and prodr. Chgo., 1983—; writer, rschr. OmniTech Cons. Group now Diamond Tech. Ptnrs., Chgo., 1992-99. Mem. Chgo. Symphony Orch. Women's Assn., 1992—2006; fundraiser, subscription sales Goodman Theatre, Chgo., 2003—; bd. dirs. Better Bus. Bur., Chgo., 1973—76, Jr. Achievement, Chgo., 1973, Chgo. Symphony Orch. Women's Assn., 2002—06. With ARC, 1944—46, China, Burma, India. Decorated Bronze Star; named Woman of Yr., Am. Advt. Fedn., 1973. Mem. Women's Advt. Club Chgo. (Woman of Yr. award 1973), Chgo. Advt. Club (bd. dirs. 1973-76). Home: 400 E Randolph St Apt 828 Chicago IL 60601-7309

DOEZEMA, MARIANNE, art historian, museum director; b. Grand Rapids, Mich., Sept. 8, 1950; d. Charles William and Geraldine Frances (Slopsema) D.; m. Michael Andrew Marlais, Dec. 29, 1977. BA, Mich. State U., 1973; MA, U. Mich., 1975; PhD, Boston U., 1990. Instr. dept. art history and edn. Cleve. Mus. Art, 1976-79, asst. curator, 1990-81; curator edn. Ga. Mus. Art, Athens, 1981-83, assoc. dir., 1983-85; asst. prof. Randolph-Macon Women's Coll., 1992-94; dir. Mt. Holyoke Coll. Art Mus., South Hadley, Mass., 1994—. Author: American Realism and the Industrial Age, 1980, George Bellows and Urban America, 1997; co-editor: Reading American Art, 1998; contbr. articles to profl. jours. Presdl. univ. grad. fellow Boston U., 1985-88, Luce Found., 1987—. Mem. Coll. Art Assn. Am. Office: Mt Holyoke Coll Art Mus Lower Lake Rd South Hadley MA 01075-1499 Office Phone: 413-538-2245. E-mail: mdoezma@mtholyoke.edu.

DOHERTY, SISTER BARBARA, religious institution administrator; b. Chgo., Dec. 2, 1931; d. Martin James and Margaret Eleanor (Noe) D. Student, Rosary Coll., 1949-51; BA in Latin, English and History, St. Mary-of-the-Woods Coll., 1953; MA in Theology, St. Mary's Coll., 1963; PhD in Theology, Fordham U., 1979; LittD (hon.), Ind. State U., 1990; LittD (hon.) (hon.), Dominican U., Ill., 2002. Enter order of the Sisters of Providence. Tchr. Jr. and Sr. High Schs., Ind. and Ill., 1953-63; asst. prof. religion St. Mary-of-the-Woods Coll., Ind., 1963-67, 71-75, pres. Ind., 1984-98; provincial supr. Chgo. Province of Sisters of Providence, 1975-83; dir. Inst. of Religious Formation at Cath. Theol. Union, Chgo., 1999—. Summer faculty NCAIS-KCRCHE, Delhi, India, 1970. Author: I Am What I Do: Contemplation and Human Experience, 1981, Make Yourself an Ark: Beyond the Memorized Responses of Our Corporate Adolescence, 1984; editor: Providence: God's Face Towards the World, 1984; contbr. articles to New Cath. Ency. Vol. XVII, 1982, God and Me, 1988, Dictionary of Catholic Spirituality, 1993. Pres. Leadership Terre Haute, Ind., 1985-86; bd. regents Ind. Acad., 1987-98; bd. dirs. 8th Day Cen. for Justice, Chgo., 1978-83, Family Svcs., Swope Art Mus., Terre Haute, Ind., 1988-98. Arthur J. Schmidt Found. grantee, 1967-71. Mem. Women's Coll. Coalition (nat. bd. dirs. 1984-90), Ind. Colls. Ind., Ind. Colls. Found. (exec. bd.), Ind. Conf. Higher Edn. (chair), Leadership Conf. Women Religious of USA (program chairperson nat. assembly 1982-83, chair Neylan commn. 1993-97), Assn. Am. Colls. and Univs. Democrat. Roman Catholic. Avocations: walking, reading, travel. Office: Cath Theol Union 5401 S Cornell Ave Chicago IL 60615-5664 E-mail: bdoherty@ctu.edu.

DOHERTY, EVELYN MARIE, data processing consultant; b. Phila., Sept. 26, 1941; d. James Robert and Virginia. Diploma, RCA Tech. Inst., Cherry Hill, N.J., 1968. Freelance data processing programmer, NJ, 1978-81; data processing cons. NJ, 1981—. Cons. in main frame & PC field; lectr., mgr. data processing Camden County (NJ) Coll. Contbr. articles to profl. jours.; author: numerous poems. Organizer Earlton South Town Watch; budget com. Cherry Hill Sch. Dist.; adv. for vol. firefighters; vol. tech. lab. learning ctr. Cherry Twp. Libr.; vol. Classroom Computer Learning Ctr. Cherry Hill Schs.; mem. Southhampton Zoning Bd., 2004; mem. bd. edn. Southampton Schs., 2004—05, chairperson cmty. rels.com., 2005—06, bus. and fin. com., 2005—06; mem. bd. edn. Southampton Twp., 2004; founder Babe Didrikson Collingswood Softball Team Women; active Year 2000 Cherry Hill Schs. Tech. Design Com. Mem.: Leisure Towne Singers and Harmonizers, Data Processing Mgmt. Assn. (chmn., mem. ednl. com.). Roman Catholic. Avocations: tennis, bridge, chess, charitable activites.

DOHERTY, KATHERINE MANN, librarian, writer; b. NYC, July 11, 1951; d. Jack Howard Mann and Glenn (Ellis) Andrews; m. Craig A. Doherty, June 16, 1973; 1 child, Meghan Corinne. BA, U. N.Mex., 1973; MSLS, Simmons Coll., 1976. Cataloger Mass. Hist. Soc., Boston, 1976-79; libr. media specialist Zuni (N.Mex.) Pub. Sch.s, 1982-86; libr. dist. Zuni Pub. Schs., 1985-86; unified media specialist Nantucket (Mass.) Elem. Sch., 1986-87; dir. learning resources Fortier Libr., N.H. Cmty. Tech. Coll., Berlin, 1987—. Author: (children's books) Apaches and Navajos, 1989, Iroquois, 1989, (young adult books) Benazir Bhutto, 1990, The Zunis, 1993, Arnold Schwarzenegger, 1993, The Huron, 1994, The Narragansett, 1994, The Chickasaw, 1994, The Ute, 1994, The Chuilla, 1994, The Sioux, 1994, The Golden Gate Bridge, 1995, Hoover Dam, 1995, Mount Rushmore, 1995, Washington Monument, 1995, Gateway Arch, 1995, The Wampanoag, 1995, The Penobscot, 1995, The Astrodome, 1996, The Erie Canal, 1996, the Empire State Building, 1997, The Alaska Pipeline, 1997, Richard I and the Crusades, 2002, New Hampshire, 2005, Massachusetts, 2005, Rhode Island, 2005, others; pub. Field Trial Mag. Office: NH Com Tech Coll Coll Libr 2020 Riverside Dr Berlin NH 03570-3717 Office Phone: 603-752-1113. E-mail: kdoherty@nhctc.edu.

DOHERTY, PATRICIA ANNE, psychologist; b. Ottumwa, Iowa, May 25, 1947; d. Russell S. and Dorotha L. (Moehle) Cadwallader; m. Michael Doherty, Sept.6, 1969; 1 child, David M. BA in History, U. Iowa, 1969, MA, 1974, PhD in Counselor Edn., 1979. Lic. profl. counselor Wis., cert. Nat. counselor. Grad. asst. U. Iowa, Iowa City, 1974-78; counseling intern Colo. State U., Ft. Collins, 1978-79; sr. psychologist U. Wis., Stevens Point, 1979—. Co-author: Women, Power and Relationships; contbr. articles to profl. jour. Mem. Wausau (Wis.) Lyric Choir, 1995—, bd. dir., 1999-2003; ofcl. Wis. Spl. Olympics, Stevens Point, 1989-2005. Mem. ACA, Am. Coll. Pers. Assn., Silvan Tomkins Inst., Nature Conservancy, Phi Delta Kappa, Phi Kappa Phi (exec.com. 2001--), Pi Lambda Theta. Avocations: singing, tennis, swimming, running, skiing. Office: U Wis Stevens Point Counseling Ctr 317 Delzell Hall Stevens Point WI 54481 Home: 9411 Woodland Cir Amherst Junction WI 54407-9169

DOHERTY, PATRICIA MCGINN, psychologist; b. Phila., Apr. 11, 1937; d. Joseph McGinn and Annetta (Dieckhaus) Carr; m. Edward J. Doherty, June 30, 1973. BA, Trinity Coll., 1960; MA, Cath. U., 1964; EdD, Boston U., 1976. Lic. psychologist, Mass., 1973. Faculty, adminstr. Trinity Coll., Washington, 1965-68; counselor Boston U. Counseling Ctr., 1970—73; cons. Human Resource Inst., Brookline, 1973—77; pvt. practice psychologist Boston, 1972—99, Brookline, 1999—. Faculty, adminstr. Boston Inst. Psychotherapy, 1977—83, pres., 1982—90; clin. assoc. Harvard Med. Sch., Cambridge, Mass., 1990—94, 1996—; supr., adminstr. Ctr. Group Psychotherapy, Mass. Gen. Hosp., Cambridge, 1996—; prin. Boston-Threshold Group, 1999—; cons. in field. Contbr. chpts. to books. Pres. Mass. Mental Health Area Bd., Boston, 1986-87. NDEA fellow, 1968-70. Mem.: Mass. Psychol. Assn., NE Soc. Group Psychotherapy (com. chmn., bd. dirs. 1983—), Am. Group Psychotherapy Assn. (com. chmn. 1982—88, bd. dirs. 1988—90, co-chair Inst. subcom. 2003—). Avocations: reading, travel. Office: Psychealth 1415 Beacon St Ste 200 Brookline MA 02446-4812 Office Phone: 617-732-0005. E-mail: patriciadoherty@msn.com.

DOHERTY, RHONDA SUE, mental health services professional; b. Madison, Wis., Sept. 21, 1961; d. Dennis Eugene Doherty and Janet Marie Grignano; 1 child, Amy Therese. BA, U. Wis., Madison, 1989, MS, 1990. Profl. Counselor Wis., 1995. Respite caregiver Family Exch. & Resource Ctr., Madison, 1988—90; intern counselor Tellurian Adolescent Svcs., Madison, 1989, McBurney Disability Ctr., Madison, 1989, Goodwill Cmty. Support, Madison, 1990; vocat. counselor Rock County Cmty. Support, Janesville & Beloit, 1991—93, clin. coord., 1993—. Mem. profl. adv. bd. Beloit Area Cmty. Health Ctr., 2002—05. Mem., sec. Equal Opportunities & Human Rels. Commn., Wis., 1999—2003; deacon First Presbyn. Ch., Beloit, 1998—2000. Mem.: Nat. Alliance for Mentally Ill. Avocations: dance, reading, poetry, creative writing, music. Home: 1823 E Post Rd Beloit WI 53511 Office: Cmty Support Program 64 Beloit Mall Beloit WI 53511

DOHERTY, SHANNEN, actress; b. Memphis, Apr. 12, 1971; d. Tom and Rosa D.; m. Ashley Hamilton, Sept. 24, 1993 (div. 1994); m. Rick Salomon, Jan. 25, 2003 (annulled 2003). Actor TV series Little House: A New Beginning, 1982-83, Our House, 1986-88, Beverly Hills, 90210, 1990-94, Charmed, 1998-2001, Scare Tactics, 2003, North Shore, 2004, Love, Inc., 2005; TV movies The Other Lover, 1985, Robert Kennedy and His Times, 1985, Obsessed, 1992, Rebel Highway: Jailbreakers, Showtime, 1994, A Burning Passion: The Margaret Mitchell Story, 1994, Gone in the Night, 1996, Sleeping with the Devil, 1997, The Ticket, 1997, Satan's School for Girls, 2000, Another Day, 2001, Hell on Heels: The Battle of Mary Kay, 2002, Nightlight, 2003, Category 7: The End of the World, 2005; host Breaking Up With Shannen Doherty, 2006; TV guest appearances include Father Murphy, 1981, Magnum, P.I., 1983, Airwolf, 1984, Highway to Heaven, 1985, 21 Jump Street, 1989, Life Goes On, 1989; films: Night Shift, 1982, (voice) The Secret of Nimh, 1982, Girls Just Want to Have Fun, 1985, Heathers, 1989, Blindfold: Acts of Obsession, 1993, Almost Dead, 1994, Mallrats, 1995, Nowhere, 1997, Striking Poses, 1999, The Rendering, 2002. Baptist.*

DOHMAN, GLORIA ANN, librarian; b. Vermillion, S.D., June 19, 1949; d. Marlyn Doyle and Dorothy Marie (Peterson) Edman; student Ball State U., 1973; B.A., Sioux Falls Coll., 1971; M.S., Tri-Coll. U., 1984; m. Terry L. Dohman, Aug. 16, 1970; children— Robb Quincy, Kristin LeeAnn. Librarian/audio visual coordinator U.S. Dependent Schs., Hahn AFB, W.Ger., 1973-74; library coordinator/dir. Wahpeton (N.D.) Public Schs. and Leach Public Library, Wahpeton, 1974-76; periodicals/media librarian N.D. State Sch. Sci., Wahpeton, 1976—1993, dir. assessment and instl. rsch., 1994—; del. White House Conf. Libraries and Info. Services, 1979; del. N.D. Gov.'s Conf. on Libraries and Info. Services, 1978. Trustee, Leach Public Library, 1977-83, chmn. bd., 1978-80; cons., evaluator C.E. Higher Learning Commn. Mem. ALA, N.D. Library Assn. (sec. acad. sect. 1981-83), LWV (chpt. dir. 1977-79). Lutheran. Home: 1502 14th Ave N Wahpeton ND 58075-5013

DOHMEN, MARY HOLGATE, retired primary school educator; b. Gary, Ind., July 28, 1918; d. Clarence Gibson and Margaret Alexander (Kinnear) Holgate; m. Frederick Hoeger Dohmen, June 27, 1964 (dec. Apr. 2006); children: William Francis, Robert Charles. BS, Milw. State Tchrs. Coll., 1940; M of Philosophy, U. Wis., 1945. Cert. tchr., Wis. Tchr. primary grades Baraboo (Wis.) Pub. Schs., 1940-43, Whitefish Bay (Wis.) Pub. Schs., 1943-64. Contbr. articles, story, poems to various pubs. Bd. dirs. Homestead H.S. chpt. Am. Field Svc., Mequon, Wis., 1970-80; mem. Milw. Aux. VNA, 1975—, 2d v.p., 1983-85, Milw. Pub. Mus. Enrichment Club, 1975—, Boys and Girls Club of Greater Milw., 1986—; vol. Reading is Fun program, 1987—, Milw. Symphony Orch. League, 1960—, Ptnrs. in Conservation, World Wildlife Fund, Washington, 1991—, Milw. Art Mus. Garden Club, 1979—, com. chmn., 1981-86; mem. Chancellor's Soc. U. Wis.-Milw., 1991—; travel lectr. various orgns., 1980—. Mem. AAUW, Milw. Coll. Endowment Assn. (v.p. 1987-90, pres. 1991-93), Bascom Hill Soc. (U. Wis.), Woman's Club Wis., Alpha Phi (pres. Milw. alumnae 1962-64), Pi Lambda Theta (pres. Milw. alumnae 1962-64), Delta Kappa Gamma. Republican. Presbyterian. Avocations: writing, travel, nature.

DOHN, JULIANNE, child protective services specialist; d. William Henry and Geraldine Mae Dohn. BA, SUNY, Buffalo, 1971. Child protective svcs. supr. Erie County Child Protective Svcs., Buffalo, 1974—; coord. Erie County Child Fatality Review Team, Buffalo, 1997—. Cons. in field. Recipient Cert. of Hon. Recognition, Erie County, 1999; grantee, N.Y. State Office of Child and Family Svcs., 1997, 1998. Mem.: U.S. Equestrian Fedn. Avocation: riding and showing horses. Office: PO Box 133 East Aurora NY 14052 Office Phone: 716-998-9202.

DOHONEY, MICHAELA S., lawyer; married. BA summa cum laude, Boston Coll., 1996, JD magna cum laude, 1999. Bar: Mass. Assoc. Corp. Dept. Ropes & Gray LLP, Boston, 2001—. Mem.: Berkshire Bar Assn., Boston Bar Assn., Mass. Bar Assn., ABA. Office: Ropes & Gray LLP One International Place Boston MA 02110-2624 Office Phone: 617-951-7899. Office Fax: 617-951-7050. E-mail: michaela.dohoney@ropesgray.com.*

DOHRN, BERNARDINE, law educator, advocate; BA, U. Chgo., 1963, MA, JD, 1967. Atty. Sidley & Austin, New York, 1984—88; litig. legal assoc. Office of Pub. Guardian, Cook County Juvenile Div., 1988—90; legal rschr. Children's Rights Project, Roger Baldwin Found., ACLU, 1990—91, Legal Assistance Found., Homeless Advocacy Project, 1991; dir. Juvenile Ct. Project Northwestern U. Sch. Law, 1991—92, dir. Children and Family Justice Ctr., 1992—, clin. assoc. prof. Bluhm Legal Clinic, 2000—. Adj. faculty U. Ill./Chgo., Dept. Criminal Justice, 2000—02; vis. law faculty Vrieje U., Amsterdam, 2002—; assoc. prof. Coll. of U. Chgo., 2003, 04; steering com. Ill. Family Violence Coordinating Com., 1994—, Ill. State Ct. Improvement Project, 1996—; adv. bd. Kellogg Sch. Mgmt. Non-Profit Prog., 1997—; mem. Expert Work Group Adoption 2002 Project, U.S. Dept. Health and Human Svcs. Contbr. articles to law jours.; author: Zero Tolerance: Resisting the Drive for Punishment in Our Schools, 2001, A Century of Juvenile Justice, 2002. Mem.: ABA (founding co-chair Task Force on Children 1992—96, adv. com. Immigration Pro Bono Devel. and Bar Activation Prog. 2001—), Human Rights Watch (bd. mem. Children's Rights Project 1995—), Chgo. Reporter (co-chair 1997—, bd. dirs. 1999—). Office: Northwestern U Sch Law 357 E Chicago Ave Chicago IL 60611-3069 E-mail: b-dohrn@law.northwestern.edu.

DOIG, BEVERLY IRENE, retired systems specialist; b. Bozeman, Mont., Oct. 21, 1936; d. James Stuart Doig and Elsie Florence (Andes) Doig Townsend. AA, Graceland Coll., 1956; BA, U. Kans., 1958; MS, U. Wis., 1970; cert. in Interior Design, UCLA, 1993, tng. classes Windows NT oper. sys., 1996, tng. classes in AUTOCAD, 1st level cert. AUTOCAD, 1998. Cert. NCIDQ 2001, lic. interior designer N.Mex., 2002. Aerodynamic technician II Ames Labs.-NACA, Moffett Field, Calif., 1957; real time systems specialist Dept. of Army, White Sands Missile Range, N.Mex., 1958-66; large systems specialist computing ctr. U. Wis., Madison, 1966-70; sr. systems analyst Burroughs, Ltd., Canberra, Australia, 1970-72; systems specialist Tech. Info. Office Burroughs Corp., Detroit, 1973-78; sr. systems specialist Burroughs Gmbh, Munich, 1978-79, Burroughs AB, Stockholm, 1979-80; networking cons. Midland Bank, Ltd., Sheffield, Eng., 1980-83; networking specialist Burroughs Corp. (now UNISYS), Mission Viejo, Calif., 1983-98; ret., 1998. Tchg. asst. Canberra (Australia) Coll., 1972; tchr. Wayne State U. Ext., Detroit, 1976-77; freelance interior designer, 1992-98; with Homeworks Decorating Showroom, Farmington, N.Mex., 1998—; tchr. computer application San Juan Coll., Farmington, 1998—. Vol. youth groups and camps Reorganized LDS Ch., N.Mex., Wis., Australia, Mich., Calif., Germany, U.K.; inner youth worker, Detroit; mentor Saddleback H.S., Santa Ana, Calif.

Scholar Mitchell Math., 1956-58, Watkins Residential, 1956-58. Mem. Assn. Computing Machinery (local chpt. chmn. membership 1969), Lambda Delta Sigma. Avocations: reading, crafts, designing, gardening. Office: Homework Inc 115 W Main St Farmington NM 87401-6242

DOKIC, JELENA, professional tennis player; b. Belgrade, Serbia, Apr. 12, 1983; arrived in Australia, 1994; d. Damir and Liliana Dokic. Profl. tennis player WTA Tour, 1998—. Achievements include Winner 5 career singles titles and 4 career doubles titles, WTA Tour. Avocations: shopping, music, beach. Office: WTA Tour 1 Progress Plz Ste 1500 Saint Petersburg FL 33701-4335

DOLACKY, SUSAN K., music educator; d. Richard T. Davis and Olga E. Johnson; m. David Dolacky, Feb. 26, 1972; children: Jon David, Andrea Sue. BA in Vocal Music Edn., Ctrl. Washington U., 1970; MusM, U. So. Calif., 1972. Prof., head vocal divsn., acad. advisor Shoreline (Wash.) C.C., 1972—, prodr., music dir. opera, Broadway musical, 1972—. Adjudicator Met. Opera Nat. Coun. Dist Auditions. Mem.: Music Educators Nat. (adjudicator), Nat. Assn. Tchrs. Singing (adjudicator). Office: Shoreline CC 16101 Greenwood Ave N Shoreline WA 98133 Office Phone: 206-546-4617. Business E-Mail: sdolacky@shoreline.edu.

DOLAN, ANDREA, secondary school educator; d. Samuel Jerome and Diane Souther Dolan; children: Jillian Owens, E. J. Waggy. BS in Phys. Edn., U. Mary Hardin Baylor, Belton, Tex., 1997. Cert. tchr. Tex. Tchr., coach Killeen Ind. Sch. Dist., Tex., 1997—99; computer tchr., coach Cameron Ind. Sch. Dist., Tex., 1999—2002; computer tchr., volleyball coach Rosebud-Lott Ind. Sch. Dist., Rosebud, Tex., 2002—05; computer tchr., volleyball and softball coach Granger Ind. Sch. Dist., Tex., 2005—. Home: 504 Gloria St Rogers TX 76569-3732

DOLAN, JAN CLARK, former state legislator; b. Akron, Ohio, Jan. 15, 1927; d. Herbert Spencer and Jean Risk Clark; m. Walter John Dolan, Apr. 22, 1950 (dec. July 1986); children: Mark Raymond, Scott Spencer, Gary Clark, Todd Alvin. BA, U. Akron, 1949. Home svc. rep. East Ohio Gas Co., Akron, 1949-50; dietitian Akron City Hosp., 1950-51; tchr. Brecksville (Ohio) Sch. Dist., 1962-66; adminstr. Orchard Hills Adult Day Ctr., West Bloomfield, Mich., 1978-83; mem. Farmington Hills (Mich.) City Coun., 1975-88, Mich. Ho. of Reps., Lansing, 1989-96. Mayor City of Farmington Hills, 1978, 85; elder Presbyn. Ch. Republican. Home: 22587 Gill Rd Farmington Hills MI 48335-4037 Personal E-mail: jcdolan@sbcglobal.net.

DOLAN, JILL S., performing arts educator; b. Pitts., Pa., May 30, 1957; d. Gerald and Cyma Dolan; life ptnr. Stacy E. Wolf. BS, Boston U., Mass., 1975—79; PhD, NYU, 1981—88. Assoc. to asst. prof. U. Wis., Madison, 1988—94; prof., chair, theatre program Grad. Ctr., CUNY, 1994—99; prof., zachary t. scott family chair in drama U. Tex., Austin, 1999—. Exec. dir. Ctr. Gay and Lesbian Studies, N.Y.C., 1996—99. Author: (book) Utopia in Performance: Finding Hope at the Theatre, 2005, Geographies of Learning: Theory and Practice, Activism and Performance, 2001, Presence and Desire: Essays on Gender, Sexuality, Performance, 1993, The Feminist Spectator as Critic, 1988. Named to Acad. of Disting. Tchrs., U. Tex., 2006; recipient Emily Toth award for Best Single-Author Study, Women's Caucus, Popular Culture Assn., 1988, William Kiekhofer Tchg. award, U. Wis., Madison, 1992, Emerging Scholar award, AAUW, 1992, Tchg. Excellence award, U. Tex., Austin, Coll. of Fine Arts, 2002, Crompton-Noll award for Best Essay in Queer Studies, Gay and Lesbian Caucus Modern Languages Assn., 2002. Mem.: MLA (exec. com., drama divsn. 2001—05), Women and Theatre Program (pres. 1990—92), Am. Soc. Theatre Rsch. (nominations com. chair 2004—06), Assn. Theatre in Higher Edn. (pres. 1997—99). Jewish. Avocations: tennis, travel, fiction reading, creative non-fiction writing. Office: Univ Tex 1 University Sta D3900 Austin TX 78712 Office Phone: 512-471-3721. Business E-Mail: jdolan@uts.cc.utexas.edu.

DOLAN, LOUISE ANN, physicist; b. Wilmington, Del., Apr. 5, 1950; BA, Wellesley Coll., 1971; PhD in Physics, MIT, 1976. Jr. fellow in physics Harvard U., 1976-79; asst. prof. physics Rockefeller U., N.Y.C., 1979-82, assoc. prof., 1983-90, lab. head, 1990; prof. physics U. N.C., Chapel Hill, 1990—. Program dir. for theoretical physics NSF, 1995. Recipient Wellesley Alumna Achievement award, 2004; John Simon Guggenheim fellow, 1988. Fellow Am. Phys. Soc. (Maria Goeppert-Mayer award 1987). Office: U NC Dept Physics Chapel Hill NC 27599-0001

DOLAN, REGINA A., security firm executive; BS, St. John's U. With Ernst & Young, 1975—86, ptnr., 1986—92; sr. v.p. fin. and controls Paine Webber Group Inc., 1992—94, CFO, 1994—97, CFO, chief adminstrv. officer, 1997—2001; chief adminstrv. officer pvt. clients and asset mgmt. divsn. UBS Warburg, 2001—02; global head strategic planning and bus. devel. UBS Investment Bank, 2002—. Bd. dirs. Bus. Coun. Southwestern Conn. Office: Paine Webber Group Inc Ste 302 1285 Avenue Of The Americas Fl Sconc New York NY 10019-6096

DOLAN, TERESA A., dean, educator, researcher; MPH, UCLA; BA Zoology, Rutgers U., 1979; DDS, U. Tex., 1983; cert. gen. practice, L.I. Jewish Med. Ctr., 1985; cert. geriatric dentistry, Vets. Adminstrn., 1989; cert. dental pub. health, U. Fla., 1991; grad., Pub. Health Leadership Inst. Fla., 1998; grad. cert., U. Fla., 2001. Diplomate Am. Bd. Dental Pub. Health, 1994. Resident in gen. dentistry dept. dentistry L.I. Jewish Med. Ctr., 1983—84, chief resident in gen. dentistry dept. dentistry, 1984—85; fellow geriatric dentistry Vets. Adminstrn. Med. Ctr., Sepulveda, Calif., 1987—89; asst. prof. U. Fla. Coll. Dentistry, 1989—93, assoc. prof. with tenure, 1993—98, acting assoc. dean acad. affairs, 1996—97, assoc. dean acad. affairs, 1997—2001, prof. with tenure, 1998—, assoc. dean edn., 2001—03, interim dean, 2002—03, dean, 2003—. Rschr., tchr., spkr. in field, lectr. various seminars; vis. asst. prof. U. Calif., 1985—87, adj. asst. prof., 1987—89; faculty discipline com. Fla. Dept. Edn., Statewide Course Numbering Sys., 1998—; reviewer grants in field; participant NIH Summer Inst. Rsh. on Minority Aging, 1991; pres. Am. Bd. of Dental Pub. Health, 2005—06. Contbr. articles to profl. jours.; exec. prodr.: (ednl. satellite videoconf.) Dental Care for the Developmentally Disabled Patient, 1991, Challenges in Geriatrics: Moving on- Rehabilitation After Stroke, 1991, How Much is Enough? Dental Tretament Decisions for Older Adults, 1992; author (dir.): Five Steps to Improving the Oral Health of Your Older Patients: A Guide for Non-dental Health Professionals, 1994. Adv., treating dentist cmty. nursing homes, 1989—96; dentist to low income elderly participants U. Fla. Geriatric Dental Demonstration Project, Jacksonville, 1990—92; dir. dental svcs. to older and medically compromised patients U. Fla. Geriatric Dental Group, 1990—95. Named honorable mention AARP Healthy Older Adults, 2000 Recognition Programs Exemplary Contbns. to Healthy Aging, 1992; recipient numerous grants and awards; fellow Vets. Adminstrn. Geriatric Dentistry; scholar Rsch., Robert Wood Johnson Found. Dental Health Svcs., 1985—87, L.I. U., 1984—85. Mem.: APHA, Am. Coll. Dentists, Phi Beta Kappa, Am. Soc. Geriatric Dentistry (ad hoc reviewer Spl. Care in Dentistry 1992—93, judge Saul Kamen Sci. Report award competition 1993—, chmn. ann. sci. session 1996), Fla. Coun. Aging, Fla. Pub. Health Assn., Am. Assn. Pub. Health Dentistry (abstract reviewer 1987, co-chmn. local arrangements ann. meeting 1992, ad hoc reviewer Jour. Pub. Health Dentistry 1994, session co-chmn. ann. meeting 1996, judge grad. student merit award projects 1997, mem. at large exec. coun. 1997—2000, mem. awards and nominations com. 2000, Pres.'s award 1999), Am. Dental Assn. (com. G Coun. Dental Edn. and Licensure 1999—, Geriatric Dental Care award 1991), Internat. Assn. Dental Rsch. (v.p. abstract reviewer geriat. oral rsch. sect. 1992—93, dir. behavioral sci. and health svcs. rsch. sect. 1992—95, pres.-elect program chmn. geriat. oral rsch. sect. 1993—94, pres. symposium organizer geriat. oral rsch. sect. 1994—95), Am. Assn. Women Dentists (chmn. com. student and component chpts. 1986—88, trustee dist. XIII Calif. 1986—89, contbg. editor Chronicle 1986—91), Acorn Clinic (v.p., acting pres. 1996—97, pres. 1997—99, past pres. 1999—2000), Fla. Coun. Aging (bd. trustees 1993—95), U. Health Sci. Ctr., Edn. Task Force, U. Curriculum Com., Geriatric Rsch., Edn. and Clin. Ctr., ACORN Clinic, Internat. Assn. Dental Rsch. (session co-chmn., abstract reviewer geriat. oral rsch. sect. 1991—92, immediate past-pres., chmn. nominations com. geriat. oral rsch. sect. 1995—96, mem. awards com. geriat. oral rsch. sect. 1996—97, constn. and bylaws com. 1996—), Am. Bd. Dental Pub. Health (dir.-elect 2000—01, pres. 2005—), Am. Dental Edn. Assn. (chair-elect spl. interest group in geriatric dentistry 1991—92, editl. rev. bd. Jour. Dental Edn. 1991—94, chmn. spl. intertest group in geriatric dentistry 1992—93, immediate past chmn. sect. on gerontology and geriat. edn. 1993—94, abstract reviewer ann. session 1998—2000, ann. session planning com. 2002—), Beta Beta Beta, Omicron Kappa Upsilon (Xi Omicron chpt. 1998), Phi Beta Kappa. Office: U Fla Coll Dentistry 1600 SW Archer Rd D 4-6B Box 100405 JHMH Gainesville FL 32610-0405 Office Phone: 352-392-2911. Office Fax: 352-392-3070. E-mail: tdolan@dental.ufl.edu.*

DOLAN-JIMENEZ, MARY F., elementary school educator; b. Chgo., Sept. 19, 1964; d. Sari Rose, adopted d. Shirley Brydon; m. Laurence M. Jimenez (div.); children: Evan Jimenez, Megan Jimenez, Elan Jimenez. BA in Spanish, So. Ill. U., Carbondale, 1988; MS in Counseling, San Diego State U., 1997. Tchr. kindergarten Lexington Elem. Sch,., El Cajon, Calif., 1992—96; tchr. 1st grade Paloma Elem. Sch., Temecula, 1996—2004, tchr. 3d grade, 2004—. V.p. SCEGA Gymnastics Booster Club, Temecula, 2002—. Recipient Silver Apple award, Press Ea. News, Riverside, Calif., 2003; scholar, Calif. Sch. Counseling Assn., 1990—91. Mem.: NEA, Nat. Coun. Social Studies, Calif. Tchr. Assn. Democrat. Home: 43091 Camino Caruna Temecula CA 92592

DOLBER, CAROLE CHRISTOFF, secondary school educator, music educator; d. Francis Russell and Frances Victoria Christoff; m. Paul Christian Dolber, Aug. 30, 1975; 1 child, Trygve Russell Luke. DEd, The Pa. State U., U. Pk., Pa., 1978. Cert. tchr. N.C., 1986. Tchr. music Glenwood Elem. Sch., Chapel Hill, NC, 1986—. Dir. show choir Glenwood Elem. Sch., 1986—. Dir.(founder): Gator Show Choir, 1996. Home: 4107 Thetford Rd Durham NC 27707 Office: Glenwood Elementary Sch 2 Prestwick Rd Chapel Hill NC 27517 Office Phone: 919-968-3473. Personal E-mail: cdolber@nc.rr.com.

DOLBERRY, JEAN MARIE, nursing educator, supervisor; b. Andrews, Tex., May 21, 1954; d. Chester E. Miller and Margie (Wasalee) DeLozier; children: Ashley Micah, Amber Kelly. ADN, Tarleton State U., 1983. RN, Tex. Adminstr. JDJ Health Svcs., Stephenville, Tex.; house supr. rural cmty. hosp.; with Heart of Tex. Meml. Hosp., Brady, Tex., 2005—. Mem. Tex. Rural Health Assn. (senate com. investigating HCFA home health funds adminstrn.), Tex. Nurses Assn. (pres. chpt. 37 1992). Home: 303 Dana Brady TX 76825 Office: CNO Heart of Texas Memorial Hosp Brady TX 76825

DOLE, ELIZABETH HANFORD (LIDDY DOLE), senator, former federal agency administrator; b. Salisbury, NC, July 29, 1936; d. John Van and Mary Ella (Cathey) Hanford; m. Robert Joseph Dole (former U.S. Senator from Kans.), Dec. 6, 1975. BA in Polit. Sci., with honors, Duke U., 1958; postgrad., Oxford U., Eng., summer 1959; MA in Edn. and Govt., Harvard U., 1960, JD, 1965. Bar: DC 1966. Staff asst. to asst. sec. for edn. HEW, Washington, 1966-67; practiced law Washington, 1967-68; assoc. dir. legis. affairs, then exec. dir. Pres.'s Com. for Consumer Interests, Washington, 1968-71; dep. asst. to Pres. The White House, Washington, 1971-73; commr. FTC, Washington, 1973-79; chmn. Voters for Reagan-Bush, 1980; dir. Human Services Group, Office of Exec. Br. Mgmt., Office of Pres.-Elect, 1980; asst. to Pres. for pub. liaison, 1981-83; sec. U.S. Dept. Transp., 1983-87; with Robert Dole Presdl. Campaign, 1987-88; participant 1988 Presdl. and Congl. campaigns; sec. U.S. Dept. Labor, 1989-90; pres. AM. Red Cross, 1991-99; U.S. senator from N.C., 2003—; mem. armed services, banking and aging coms.; chair Nat. Rep. Senatorial Com., 2005—. Mem. nominating com. NC Consumer Coun., 1972; mem. com. armed forces, US Senate, com. banking, housing and urban affairs, spl. com. aging. Author (with Bob Dole Richard Norton Smith and Kerry Tymchuk): (autobiography) Unlimited Partners, 1996; author: Hearts Touched With Fire, 2006. Trustee Duke U., 1974-88; mem. coun. Harvard Law Sch. Assocs., mem. vis. com. Harvard Sch. Pub. Health, 1992-95; mem. bd. overseers Harvard U., 1989-95; hon. chair, Project RoundHouse, 2001. Recipient Arthur S. Flemming award U.S. Govt., 1972, Humanitarian award Nat. Commn. Against Drunk Driving, 1988, Disting. Alumni award Duke U., 1988, N.C. award, 1991, Lifetime Achievement award (Breaking The Glass Ceiling) Women Execs. in State Govt., 1993, North Carolinian of the Yr. award N.C. Press Assn., 1993, Radcliffe medal, 1993, Leadership award LWV, 1994, Maxwell Finland award Nat. Found. Infectious Diseases, 1994, Disting. Svc. award Nat. Safety Coun., 1989, Raoul Wallenberg award for Humanitarian Svc., 1995, Christian Woman of Yr. award, 1996; named one of Am.'s 200 Young Leaders, Time mag., 1974, one of World's 10 Most Admired Women, Gallup Poll, 1988, one of 10 most fascinating people 1996 Barbara Walter's Spl., most inspiring polit. figure 1996 MSNBC, 3rd most admired woman in Am. Good Housekeeping, 1996, 98, one of most powerful women, Forbes mag., 2005; selected for Safety and Health Hall of Fame Internat., 1993; inducted into Nat. Women's Hall of Fame, 1995. Mem. Phi Beta Kappa, Pi Lambda Theta, Pi Sigma Alpha. Republican. Methodist. Office: US Senate 555 Dirksen Office Bldg Washington DC 20510 also: District Office Ste 122 310 New Bern Ave Raleigh NC 27601 Office Phone: 202-224-6342, 919-856-4630. Office Fax: 202-224-1100, 919-856-4053.

DOLE, WANDA VICTORIA, librarian; b. Melrose Park, Ill., Sept. 10, 1942; d. Malburn Sanford and Victoria Bernice (Berner) D.; m. David Richards Helmstadter, May 7, 1966 (div.). BA magna cum laude, Lawrence U., Appleton, Wis., 1964; MA in Classics, Tufts U., 1965; MS, U. Ill., 1975. Asst. editor Scott, Foresman & Co., Glenview, Ill., 1967-68; arch. librarian U. Ky., Lexington, 1976-78; humanities bibliographer U. Ill., Chgo., 1978-80; asst. dir. collection devel. U. Miami, Coral Gables, Fla., 1980-82; reg. sales mgr. Blackwell N. Am./B.H. Blackwell Ltd., Lake Oswego, Oreg., 1982-86; head librarian Pa. State U., Abington, 1986-91; asst. dir. collections, pub. svcs. SUNY, Stony Brook, 1991—99; dean libr. Washburn U., Kans., 1999—. Mem. curriculum adv. com. So. Conn. State U. Sch. Library Sci., New Haven, 1983-85; mem. Ill.-Princeton Expedition to Morgantina, Sicily, 1970. Contbr. articles to profl. jours. Mem. ALA, Art Librs. Soc. N.Am., IFLA (gov. bd., profl. bd.). Episcopalian. Home: 3111 SW 15th St Topeka KS 66604-2515 Office: SUNY Main Libr Stony Brook NY 11794-0001 Business E-Mail: wanda.dole@washburn.edu.

DOLE-RECIO, LECIA, artist; b. San Francisco, 1971; BFA, RI Sch. Design; MFA, Art Ctr. Coll. Design. Exhibited in group shows at Whitney Biennial, Whitney Mus. Am. Art, 2004, one-woman shows include, Richard Telles Fine Art, LA, Adamski Gallery Contemporary Art, Aachen, Germany, Represented in permanent collections, Mus. Contemporary Art, LA, Walker Art Ctr., Mpls., LA County Mus. Art. Mailing: c/o Whitney Museum American Art 945 Madison Ave New York NY 10021

DOLGIN, ELLEN ECKER, English and gender studies professor; b. N.Y.C., June 30, 1951; d. Milton and Esther Ecker; m. James Steven Dolgin, Aug. 10, 1975 (div. June 19, 1990); children: Eva Beth, Andrew Michael. BS in Speech-English Edn., Syracuse U., N.Y., 1973; MA in English, George Peabody Coll. for Tchrs. of Vanderbilt U., Nashville, Tenn., 1975; PhD in English, NYU, 1995. Instr. English Fisk U., Nashville, 1975—77; asst. prof. lit. Ramapo Coll., Mahwah, NJ, 1989—90; lectr. English Bergen C.C., Paramus, NJ, 1991—94. Assoc. prof. English Dominican Coll. of Blauvelt, Orangeburg, NY, 1996—. Author (reviewer): Anna Deavere Smith, Fires in the Mirror, 1994. Mem.: NE Modern Lang. Assn. (women's caucus rep. 2005—06), Modern Lang. Assn. Avocations: amateur theatricals, theater, concerts, museum attendance, cooking/entertaining. Home: 416 Country Club Lane Pomona NY 10970 Office: Dominican Coll of Blauvelt 450 Western Hwy Orangeburg NY 10962 Office Phone: 845-359-7800. Office Fax: 845-359-8025. Personal E-mail: edolgin1@optonline.net. Business E-Mail: ellen.dolgin@dc.edu.

DOLIGOSA, ANNIE LUMAMPAO, elementary school educator, researcher; b. Iloilo, Philippines, June 1, 1949; d. Ananias Balbanido Lumampao and Erlinda Vargas Caliston; m. Luis Doligosa, Dec. 24, 1973; children: Anil, Louie. BS in elem. edn., West Visyas State U., Philippines, 1969; MA in reading edn., West Visayas State U., Philippines, 1994, PhD in curriculum, instrn. and evaluation edn., 2001. Cert. CCT, CCTC-CLAD, CSTE Philippines. Elem. tchr. Banate Elem. Sch., Philippines, 1969—75; master tchr. Barotac Viejo Elem. Sch., Philippines, 1975—82; supr. tchr. West Visayas State U. Lab. Sch., Ibilo City, Philippines, 1982—2001; prof. West Visayas State U., Ibilo City, Philippines, 1989—2001, grad. sch. prof., 1994—2001; second grade tchr. C.P. Kelly Elem. tchr., Compton, Calif., 2002—03; first grade tchr. W.J. Clinton Elem. Sch., Compton, Calif., 2003—. Sch. paper advisor West Visayas State U. Lab. Sch. Pen Blazers, Ibilo City, Philippines, 1996—2001; peer coach CUSD, Clinton Elem. Sch., Compton, Calif., 2004—; support provider Begining Tchr. Support and Assessment, Compton, Calif., 2005—06. Author: (book) Developmental Reading for College Students, 1998, Learning to Write for Grade One, 2000, (articles) Philippine Jour. Edn., 1996. Sec. Kiwanettes, Barotac, Philippines, 1976—77; donor Am. Heart Soc., Calif., 2003, Am. Vets., Calif., 2005, Cancer Soc., Calif., 2005. Recipient Outstanding Nat. Sch. Paper Advisor, Dept. Edn., 1967; grantee Academic Scholarship, West Visayas State U., 1960—68, Faculty Devel. Scholarship, 1993—94, 2000—01. Mem.: Calif. Reading Assn., World Coun. for Curriculum and Instrn., Calif. Tchrs. Assn., Nat. Assn. for Asian and Pacific Am. Edn., Internat. Reading Assn. Roman Catholic. Avocations: reading, music, gardening, writing, poetry.

DOLINICH-MATUSKA, CHRISTINE, artist; b. Elizabeth, N.J., Feb. 24, 1950; d. Anton J. and Irene Marie (Kutay) Dolinich; m. John A. Matuska, Jr., Aug. 14, 1993. Student, Oxford U., England, 1970-71; BA in Studio Art, Rutgers U., 1973; postgrad., Westminster Choir Coll., 1984, 86. Dir. Union County Conservatory, Rahway, N.J., 1987—, Linden (N.J.) Art and Music Studio, 1983-87; critiquer Union County Teen Arts Festival, Union Coll., Cranford, N.J., 1986-94; curator visual arts Merck and Co., Inc., Rahway, 1989; profl. rev. panelist Union County Arts Grants Com., 1990-94. Exhibited in group shows at Los Angeles Women's Ctr., Houston U., Utah U., 1977, Newark Mus., 1982, City Without Walls Gallery, Newark, 1982, 83, 84, 85, 86, Morris Mus., Morristown, N.J., 1987, Merck & Co., Rahway, 1989-93, Douglass Coll.; one-woman shows include Caldwell (N.J.) Coll., 1976, 82, 89, Middlesex Coll. Art Gallery, Edison, N.J., 1985, Douglass Coll. Women Artists Series, 1986-87, Rutgers U., New Brunswick, N.J., 1987, Brookdale Coll, 1988; artists books Rutgers U., U. of Delaware, Newark Library, New Brunswick, 1982-83. Fellow N.J. State Coun. on the Arts, 1984-85; recipient Frist prize Art with Mus. Subjects Cover Contest, Best Mixed Media Work, 1992. Mem. AAUW (radio host Sta. WFMU Women in Music and Art Series 1984-85, lectr., slide and tape presentation Women in Art and Music 1985), Women's Caucus for Art, Music Tchr. Nat. Assn. (1st prize Am. Music Tchr. 1981, 83), Piano Tchrs. Soc. Am. (Genia Robinor Pedagogy award 1989-94, cert. in piano pedagogy). Home: 1348 Pierce St Rahway NJ 07065-3932

DOLINSKY, DIANNE MARIE, secondary school educator; b. Teaneck, N.J., Apr. 10, 1962; BA, Glassboro State Coll., 1984; MS, Fairleigh Dickenson U., 1991. Cert. math tchr. and elem. edn. tchr., N.J. Tchr. math. Clifton Bd. Edn., NJ, 1985—. Mem. NEA, N.J. Edn. Assn., Math. Assn. Am., Passaic County Tchrs. Assn Office: Clifton Bd Edn Clifton High Sch 333 Colfax Ave Clifton NJ 07013-1701

DOLL, LYNNE MARIE, public relations agency executive; b. Glendale, Calif., Aug. 27, 1961; d. George William and Carol Ann (Kennedy) Doll; m. David Jay Lans, Oct. 11, 1986. BA in Journalism, Calif. State U., Northridge, 1983. Freelance writer Austin Pub. Rels. Systems, Glendale, 1978-82; asst. account exec. Berkhemer & Kline, LA, 1982-83; pres., ptnr. Rogers & Assocs., LA, 1983—, head, Mgmt. and Crisis Comm. Practice Group, head, Pub. Sector Dept. Exec. dir. Suzuki Automotive Found. for Life, Brea, Calif., 1986—91; mem., strategic planning com. Gateway to Indian Am. Corp. for Am. Devel., San Francisco, 1988—90. Pub. rels. cons. Rape Treatment Ctr., LA, 1986; regional bd. dir. Nat. Conf. for Cmty. and Justice, LA, nat. bd. dir.; cmty. adv. com. LA Fire Dept.; mem. adv. coun. for pres. Calif. State U., Northridge. Named Pub. Rels. Profl. of Yr.; named one of Women Who Make A Difference, LA Bus. Jour.; recipient Disting. Alumni Award, Calif. State U. Northridge. Mem.: Internat. Motor Press Assn., Pub. Rels. Soc. Am. (Outstanding Profl. (LA chpt.) 1999), Nat. Conf. for Cmty. and Justice (LA region bd. dir. 1996, nat. bd. dir. 2002), So. Calif. Assn. Philanthropy, Coun. on Foundations, Ad Club LA (bd. dir., pres. 1994—95). Democrat. Office: Rogers & Assocs 1875 Century Park E Ste 300 Los Angeles CA 90067-2504 Office Phone: 310-552-6922. Office Fax: 310-552-9052.*

DOLL, PATRICIA MARIE, marketing professional, consultant; b. Bryn Mawr, Pa., Apr. 13, 1960; d. Otello Louis (dec.) and Eleanor Caroline (De Pasquale) De Grandis; m. John Russell Doll, Oct. 5, 1985. BS in Speech Comms., Millersville (Pa.) U., 1982. Lic. radio operator. News reporter, dj, writer, promotions coord. WIXQ and WLAN Radio, Lancaster, Pa., 1978-82; prodr., writer, rschr. WGAL-TV, Lancaster, Pa., 1982; copywriter, advtsg.-mktg. coord. Strawbridge & Clothier, Phila., 1982-87; freelance writer, 1984—; mktg. dir. Rouse & Assocs., Internat. Developer, Phila., Pa., 1987-90; owner Publicity Works, Bowmansville, Pa., 1990—. Contbr. articles to newspapers and trade mags.; producer TV documentary, 1982. Mem. chambers, trade, local orgns.; registered alumni mentor Millersville U.; hospice vol. Named Internat. ATHENA Small Bus. Woman of Yr. award Berks County C. of C., 1996; recipient numerous regional and nat. awards for mktg. and cmty. work, SBA's Women's Bus. Advocate of Yr. award for Ea. Pa., 1997, MS Corp. Achievers award Nat. Multiple Sclerosis Soc., 1999; named 2 awards for outstanding fundraising Am. Heart Assn., 1987, 1 of Top 40 Under 40 Profls. in Ctrl. Pa., 1996, 1 of the Best 50 Women in Bus., Pa., Gov. of Pa., 1997. Mem. Am. Fedn. Musicians, Kappa Delta Phi. Roman Catholic. Avocations: writing, dance, professional violinist, modeling, community service. Business E-Mail: info@publicity-works.com.

DOLLARHIDE, MARY C., lawyer; b. Long Beach, Calif., Jan. 28, 1957; BA with distinction, Occidental Coll., 1979; OTH, Circle Sq. Theatre Sch., N.Y.C., 1981; JD, U. So. Calif., 1988. Bar: Calif. 1988, D.C. 1991, Conn. 1996. Ptnr. Paul, Hastings, Janofsky & Walker LLP, San Diego. Editor-in-chief: So. Calif. Law Rev.; contbr. articles to profl. hours. Mem.: Assn. Am. Trial Lawyers (bd. govs.), ABA. Office: Paul Hastings Janofsky & Walker LLP 3579 Valley Center Dr San Diego CA 92130 Office Phone: 858-720-8660. Office Fax: 858-647-2660. Business E-Mail: marydollarhide@paulhastings.com.

DOLPH, SHARON JEAN, social worker; b. St. Louis, Sept. 22, 1964; d. Raymond Lewis Jr. and Marilyn Grace (Praught) Carpenter; m. James Michael Dolph, May 29, 1993; children: William Lewis, Amanda Grace, John Woodrow, Benjamin Owen BA, Oberlin Coll., 1986; MSW, U. Mich., 1990. Lic. clin. social worker, Mont. Acad. advisor Washington U., St. Louis, 1987—89; social worker Golden Triangle Mental Health Ctr., Havre, Mont., 1991—97; instr. adult edn. Havre Pub. Schs., 1997. Mem. Mental Health Awareness Coun., Havre, 1995-97, Mental Health Network, 1994-97, Stamp Out Suicide Task Force, 1991-94, Critical Incident Stress Debriefing Team, 1992-97; vol. ch. musician, children's ministry, Cub Scouts, Girl Scouts, 4-H Avocations: music, writing, skiing, gardening, sewing. Home: 1015 11th St Havre MT 59501-4625

DOMAN, ELVIRA, retired science administrator; b. NYC; d. Andrew and Lillian (McClary) Hand; m. John H. Holder (div.); children: Paula Holder Simpkins, Rodney M. BA in Chemistry, CUNY, 1955; MA in Biochemistry, Columbia U., 1959; MS in Molecular Biology, NYU, 1960; PhD in Physiology and Biochemistry, Rutgers U., 1965. Jr. tech. U. Hosp. N.Y.U. Bellevue Med. Ctr., 1955; rsch. asst. Coll. Physicians and Surgeons, N.Y.C., 1959-60, Sloan-Kettering Inst. Cancer Rsch., N.Y.C., 1959-60, postdoctoral assoc., postdoctoral fellow, 1965; rsch. assoc. Rockefeller U., N.Y.C., 1965-68; lectr. Douglass Coll. Rutgers U., New Brunswick, N.J., 1970-73; asst. prof. Seton Hall U., South Orange, N.J., 1973-77; assoc. program dir.

NSF, Washington, 1978-92, program dir., 1992-99; ret., 1999. Vis. scientist Rutgers U., 1989; reader Gates Millenium Scholars, Fairfax, Va., 2002—; sci. fair judge pub., pvt. schs., colls. Bd. dirs. Math. Sci., Computer Learning Ctr. of Shiloh Bapt. Ch., Washington, 1989—. Recipient Achievement award NSF, 1986, 92, Outstanding Mentor award U. Md. Balt. County, 2000, 06; grantee Seton Hall U., 1975; elected Hunter Coll. Hall of Fame, 2006. Fellow Am. Inst. Chemists; mem. AAAS, Am. Chem. Soc., Assn. Women Sci., Minority Women Sci., Orgn. Black Sci. (pres. 1990-93).

DOMAN, JANET JOY, professional society administrator; b. Phila., Dec. 16, 1948; d. Glenn J. and Hazel Katie (Massingham) D. Student, U. Hull, England, 1969-70; BA, U. Pa., 1971. Cert. tchr. Clinician Inst. Achievement Human Potential, Phila., 1971-74; dir. English Early Devel. Assn., Tokyo, 1974-75; dir. Evan Thomas Inst. Early Devel., Phila., 1975-77, Inst. Achievement of Intellectual Excellence, 1977-80; vice dir. The Inst. of Achievement and Human Potential, 1980-82, dir., 1982—. Internat. lectr. treatment of brain injured children and superiority. Chair Child Brain Devel., United Steelworkers Am., 1987. Recipient Gold medal Centro Soc. de Reabilitacion Nosa Senhora da Gloria, Rio de Janeiro, 1974, Brit. Star Brit. Inst. Achievement Human Potential, 1976, Sakura Korosho medal Japanese Inst. Achievement Human Potential, 1977, statuette with pedestal Internat. Forum Human Potential, 1980. Office: The Inst of Achievement and Human Potential 8801 Stenton Ave Glenside PA 19038-8319

DOMAN, MARGARET HORN, government policy consultant; b. Portland, Oreg., July 28, 1946; d. Richard Carl and Dorothy May (Teepe) Horn; m. Steve Hamilton Doman, July 12, 1969; children: Jennifer, Kristina, Kathryn. BA, Willamette U., 1968; postgrad., U. Wash., 1968-69, 72. Cert. tchr. Tchr. jr. high Bellevue (Wash.) Sch. Dist., 1969-70, subs. tchr., 1990-91; tchr. jr. high University City (Mo.) Sch. Dist., 1970-71; employment counselor Wash. State Dept. Employment Security, Seattle, 1971; planning commn. mem. City of Redmond, Wash., 1980-83, chmn., 1982-83, city coun. mem., 1983-91, pres., 1990-91; exec. dir. Eastside Human Svcs. Coun., Redmond, Wash., 1992; employment specialist Wash. State Dept. Employment Security, 1993; cons. land use planning & govt. process Redmond, 1993—. Redmond rep. Puget Sound. Coun. of Govt., Seattle, 1984-91, vice chmn., 1988, 90, chmn. transp., 1986-88, exec. bd., 1987, mem. standing com. on transp., 1986-91; bd. dirs., pres. Eastside Human Svcs. Coun., Bellevue, 1983-91, pres., 1990. Mem. state exec. com. Nat. History Day, Olympia, Wash., 1986; vol. Bellevue Sch. Dist., 1977—96; bd. dirs. Redmond YMCA, 1985—86, Youth Eastside Svcs., 1998—2001; bd. dirs. Eastside br. Camp Fire, Bellevue, 1992—94, Redmond Hist. Soc., 1999—2001. Mem. Redmond C. of C. (land use and transp. com. 1994-98), Bellevue Rotary (bd. mem. 2001-05). Republican. Unitarian Universalist. Avocations: skiing, hiking, sailing, world travel. Home: 2104 180th Ct NE Redmond WA 98052-6032 E-mail: domanms@comcast.net.

DOMBRO, MARCIA WINTERS, nurse, academic administrator, educator; b. Clinton, Minn., Dec. 14, 1940; d. Benton Jay and Thelma Elizabeth Winters; m. Roy S. Dombro, Sept. 10, 1967; children: Rayna Lisette, Meryl Elana. BSN, U. Wash., 1963; MS in Adult Edn., Fla. Internat. U., 1976, EdD, 1997. RN. Pub. health nurse Seattle-King County Health Dept., 1964—66, N.Y.C. Dept. Health Bur. Nursing, 1966—67; head nurse home care unit Bellevue Hosp., 1967—68; asst. clin. instr. obstetrics City Hosp. Elmhurst, 1968; clin. instr. obstetrics Miami-Dade C.C., Fla., 1973—74; instr. U. Miami Sch. Nursing, 1976—80; dir. dept. nursing edn. Baptist Hosp. Miami, 1980—92; adj. asst. prof. Sch. Nursing U. Miami, 1984—; chair profl. and cmty. edn. Miami Dade C.C., 1999—2000. Tchr. sex edn. schs., civic groups, parent edn. groups; mem. edtl. bd. Jour. Nursing Staff Devel., 1987—91. Author: Post Partum for the Childbirth Educator-A Programmed Text, 1976, computer program on teen pregnancy, 1986; co-author: rev., 1990; contbr. chapters to books, articles to profl. jours. Mem.: South Fla. Nursing Rsch. Soc. (treas. 1993, pres. 1994—96), Am. Soc. Psychoprophylaxis in Obstetrics (cert. childbirth instr. 1970, coord. South Fla. 1976—81), Nat. League Nursing, Am. Nurses' Assn., Nurses Assn.-Am. Coll. Ob-Gyn. (sec.-treas. Dade County chpt. 1985—89). Jewish. Home: 4530 NE 55th St Seattle WA 98105 Personal E-mail: mdombro@aol.com.

DOMBROWSKI, ANNE WESSELING, retired microbiologist; b. Cin., Jan. 26, 1948; m. Allan Wayne Dombrowski, Apr. 17, 1982; children: Amy, Alicia. BA summa cum laude, Xavier U., 1970; MS, U. Cin., 1972, PhD, 1974. Fellow Scripps Clinic and Rsch. Found., La Jolla, Calif., 1974-76; sr. rsch. microbiologist Merck & Co., Inc., Rahway, NJ, 1976-87, rsch. fellow, 1987-96, sr. rsch. fellow, 1996—2003, ret., 2003. Contbr. articles to profl. jours. Mem.: Am. Soc. Microbiology, Soc. Indsl. Microbiology (sec. 1982—85, dir. 1998—2001). Achievements include patents in field. Avocations: reading, gardening. Home: 51 Landsdowne Rd East Brunswick NJ 08816-4156 Personal E-mail: annewd@aol.com.

DOMENOSKI, ELLEN MARIE, staff nurse; b. Two Rivers, Wis., Jan. 4, 1960; d. Bernard Joseph and Grace Laverne (Lodl) D. Med. asst. diploma, Lakeshore Tech. Sch., 1980; BSN, Marian Coll., 1988. ACLS cert. Staff nurse St. Mary's Hosp., Green Bay Wis., 1989—. Vol. skin cancer screening, 1993-97; active Annual Neilsen Walk for Breast Cancer Awareness, 1993-95. Mem. Wis. Nursing Assn., Nat. League for Nursing. Avocations: reading, crafts, bicycling. Office: St Mary's Hosp 1726 Shawano Ave Green Bay WI 54303-3282

DOMINGO, CORA MARIA CORAZON ENCARNACION, minister; b. Urdaneta City, Philippines, Mar. 25, 1917; arrived in US, 1961, naturalized, 1967; d. Martin Cantaoe and Casimira Agbanlog Echalas; m. Nicanor Barrientos Domingo, Oct. 29, 1950; m. Teofilo Alonzo Manzano, July 8, 1935 (div. Sept. 26, 1950); children: Don Leonardo Manzano, Teddy Teofilo Manzano. BMin. in Practical Theology, Word of Faith Leadership & Bible Inst., Dallas, 1985. Ordained minister Ministry Salvation Ch., 1986. Tchr. Public Sch., Urdaneta City, Philippines, 1939—46; assoc. pastor The Assembly of the First Born, Kahului, Hawaii, 1993—; pres./founder Christ Tabernacle of Praise, Cabuloan, Urdaneta City, Philippines, 1999—; missionary pastor Cabuloan Village Chapel, Cabuloan, Philippines, 1971—99; child evangelist Child Evangelism Fellowship, Honolulu, 1980—92; pastor Maui Evang. Ch., Kahului, Hawaii, 1970—74; landlord and bus. woman Kahului, Hawaii, 1962—. Dir. of Filipino lang. radio program KNUI/KMVI, Kahului, Hawaii. Mem. Friendship Bible com., coord. Maui Christian Women's Club; pres., host Great Commn. Fellowship, 1980—95; mem. Maui Retarded Children's Assn., Big Bros./Big Sisters of Hawaii, Humane Soc.; treas., bd. dirs. Maui Adult Day Care Ctr., 1974—94; pres. Filipino Mins. Fellowship Maui, 1976—98; mem. Maui Christian Mins. Assn.; leader Girls Scout Am. Troop 78, 1953—63; bd. dirs. Status of Women, Com. on Aging, Wailuku, Hawaii. Named one of Maui's Filipino Heroes, 1998; recipient Outstanding Citizen of Filipino Ancestry, Maui Filipino Cmty. Assn., 1965, Milady of the Valley Isle award, 1968, Worthy Matron of Order, Maui Chpt. 5 Order of the Ea. Star of Maui Hawaii, 1975, 1980, 1993, Conservative Patriotic award, Young Am. Found., 2003. Mem.: Maui Filipino Ladies Cir., Bus. & Profl. Women's Club (vp & chmn. 1965—69). Republican. Avocations: reading, sewing, gardening, travel. Home and Office: 739 Iluna Pl Kahului HI 96732

DOMINGO, ESTHER, music educator; b. Havana, Cuba, July 13, 1954; d. Silverio and Esther (Benitez) D. MusB in Music Edn., Mercer U., Atlanta, 1978, MusB in Piano Performance, 1978; MusM in Piano Pedagogy, Ga. State U., 1985. Cert. Yamaha music edn. sys.; cert. Music in Edn. Nat. Tchr. Inst.; cert. ESOL; cert. tchr. grades K-12, Ga. Sec., Spanish/ESOL tchrs. asst. Atlanta Pub. Schs., 1978-81; pvt. piano and Yamah music edn. tchr. Atlanta Music Ctr., 1983-89; piano and music theory tchr. Mercer U., Atlanta, 1980-91; piano and group music classes tchr. The Children's Sch., Atlanta, 1989-92; ESL tchr. Internat. Edn. Ctr., Atlanta, 1991-92; piano, theory and group classes tchr. pvt. home music studio, Atlanta, 1976—; pvt. piano and music theory tchr. Ga. Acad. Music, Atlanta, 1992—; gen. music, choral tchr. Atlanta Pub. Schs., 1992—. Pianist Spanish Mission, Second-Ponce de Leon Bapt. Ch., Atlanta, 1970—; panelist Fulton County Art Coun., 1999; adjudicator for various music festivals in the state. Neighborhood rep. Hispanic cmty. Ga. Power Co., Atlanta, 1978-79; young artist performer DeKalb Coun. for the Arts; panelist Fulton County Arts Coun., 1999; pianist, handbell soloist; mem. handbell choir Second Ponce deLeon Bapt. Ch., 1985—. Recipient Excellence in Edn. award, BellSouth/Braves, 2002; Fine Arts grantee, Atlanta Pub. Schs., 1998. Mem. Music Tchrs. Nat. Assn. (cert.), Atlanta Music Tchrs. Assn. (cert., program chmn. 1990-91, membership chmn. 1991-92, v.p. 1992-93, pres. 1993-94), Ga. Music Tchrs. Assn. (cert.). Baptist. Avocations: handbell performer/choir, swimming, travel. Office: Morningside Elem Sch 1053 E Rock Springs Rd NE Atlanta GA 30306-3099 E-mail: edomingo@atlanta.k12.ga.us.

DOMINGUEZ, ANDREA HOPE, science educator; b. Balt., Md., Nov. 28, 1966; d. Dennis Michael and Iris Myra Frock (Stepmother), Marilyn Joyce Hook; m. Cesar Gregorio Dominguez, Dec. 23, 2005; children: Justin Richard Diggs, Alexandra Brooke Diggs. BS, U. Md., 1988; MS, U. Ala., Birmingham, 1991. Lic. physical therapy Md. State Bd. Phys. Therapy Examiners, cert. tchg. Md. State Dept. Edn., tng. Coll. Notre Dame. Physical therapist asst. program dir. Carroll C.C., Westminster, Md., 1994—98; asst. prof., academic coord. clin. edn. U. Md., Balt., 1998—99; rehab. clin. specialist Johns Hopkins Home Care Group, Balt., 1999—2003; cons. self employed, Lutherville, Md., 2000; sci. tchr. Balt. County Pub. Schs., 2003—. Cons. Capitol Consultants, LLC, Washington, 2000—. Contbr. articles various profl. jours. Philanthropist, Balt., 1996; organizer, fund raising Local Schs., Balt., 2004—06. Mem.: ASCD (assoc.), Md. State Tchrs. Assn. (corr.), Am. Phys. Therapy Assn. (assoc.), Gamma Phi Beta (assoc.; panhellenic del. 1988). Libertarian. Jewish. Avocations: salsa dancing, travel, fitness tng., hiking, reading. Personal E-mail: educator_and_pt@yahoo.com.

DOMINGUEZ, CARI M., federal official; BA, MA, Am. U.; fellow advanced study Program in Pub. Mgmt., MIT; D in Humanitarian Svc. (hon.), Loma Linda U., 2003. Dir. exec. programs Bank Am. Corp.; ptnr. Heidrick & Struggles; dir. Spencer Stuart, San Francisco; prin. Dominguez & Associates, 1999; chair U.S. Equal Employment Opportunity Comm., Washington, 2001—. Named one of 80 Elite Hispanic Women, Hispanic Bus. mag., 100 Most Influential Hispanics in the Country; recipient Eagle Award, Bank America CEO, Award for Excellence, Nat. Image, Inc., 2002, Legacy of Leadership award, Spelman Coll., 2005. Mem.: Human Resources Planning Soc. (bd. mem.), Leadership Found. Internat. Women's Forum (bd. mem.). Office: US Equal Employment Opportunity Comm 1801 L Street NW Washington DC 20507*

DOMINGUEZ, KATHRYN MARY, economist, educator; b. Santa Monica, Calif., Nov. 26, 1960; d. Frederick A. and Margaret M. (McGauren) D. AB, Vassar Coll., 1982; MA, Yale U., 1984, M in Philosophy, 1985, PhD, 1987. Rschr. Congl. Budget Office, Washington, 1984; rsch. scholar bd. of govs. FRS, Washington, 1985—86; asst. prof. pub. policy Kennedy Sch. Govt. Harvard U., Cambridge, Mass., 1987—91, assoc. prof. pub. policy, 1991—97; assoc. prof. pub. policy and econs. U. Mich., Ann Arbor, 1997—2004, prof., 2004—. Rsch. cons IMF, Washington, 1989; vis. asst. prof., asst. dir. internat. fin. sect. dept. econs. Princeton U., 1990-91; Nat. Bur. Econs. Rsch. Olin fellow, 1991-92. Author: (monograph) Oil and Money, 1989; Exchange Rate Efficiency and the Behavior of International Asset Markets, 1992; (with Jeff Frankel) Does Foreign Exchange Intervention Work?, 1993. Mem. Nat. Bur. Econ. Rsch. (rsch. assoc. 2000—), Am. Econ. Assn., Phi Beta Kappa. Democrat. Office: Univ Mich Sch Pub Policy Weill Hall 735 S State St Ann Arbor MI 48109-1220 Office Phone: 734-764-3490.

DOMINI, AMY LEE, portfolio manager; b. N.Y.C., Jan. 25, 1950; d. Enzo Vice and Margaret Cabot (Colt) D.; m. Peter D. Kinder, Sept. 28, 1980 (div.); 1 child, Peter D. CFA. Stockbroker Tucker Anthony & RL Day, Cambridge, Mass., 1975-80, Moseley Securities, Cambridge, 1980-85; portfolio mgr. Franklin R & D Corp., Boston, 1985-87; pvt. trustee Loring, Wolcott & Coolidge, Boston, 1987—. Pres. Domini Social Equity Fund, N.Y.C., 1996—; chair of bd. Linder, Lydenberg, Domini & Co., Cambridge, 1991—; ptnr. Domini Social Investments LLC, Boston, 1997—. Co-author: (books) Ethical Investing, 1984, Challenges of Wealth, Social Investment Almanac, 1992, Investing for Good. Bd. dirs. Social Investment Forum, Washington, 1994—, ch. pension fund Episcopal Ch., N.Y.C., 1994—; governing bd. Interfaith Ctr. on Corp. Responsibility, N.Y.C., 1985-95; mem. social responsibility investments com. Episcopal Ch., N.Y.C., 1985-91. Recipient Accioniste award Accion Internat., 1992, Money's 100 Best Mut. Funds award Money Mag., 1998, SRI Svc. award 1st Affirmative Fin. Network, 1996; named one of World's 100 Most Influential People, Time Mag. 2005. Mem. Nat. Cmty. Capital Assn. (assoc., bd. dirs. 1987-91), Boston Security Analysts Soc., Social Investment Forum, Somerset Club, Cambridge Boat Club. Democrat. Episcopalian. Avocations: day-sailing, gardening. Office: Loring Wolcott & Coolidge 230 Congress St Fl 12 Boston MA 02110-2437

DOMINIAK, GERALDINE FLORENCE, retired accounting educator; b. Detroit, Sept. 28, 1934; d. Benjamin Vincent and Geraldine Esther (Davey) D. BS, U. Detroit, 1954, MBA, 1956; PhD, Mich. State U., 1966. CPA Mich. Audit supr. Coopers & Lybrand, 1958-63; asst. prof. U. Detroit, 1965-68; assoc. prof. Mich. State U., 1968-69; prof. acctg. Tex. Christian U., Ft. Worth, 1969-97, chmn. dept. acctg., 1974-83, prof. emeritus, 1997; Arthur Young prof. acctg. Fla. A&M U., 1977. Author: (with J. Edwards and T. Hedges) Interim Financial Reporting, 1972; (with J. Louderback) Managerial Accounting, 1975, 9th edit., 2000. Ford Found. fellow, 1964-65. Mem. AICPA, Am. Acctg. Assn., Tex. Soc. CPAs, ACLU, Beta Alpha Psi, Beta Gamma Sigma. Roman Catholic. Home: 4401 Cardiff Ave Fort Worth TX 76133-3513

DOMINIC, MAGIE, writer; 1 child, Heather Rose. Actress N.Y.C. Off-off-Broadway movement 1960s; prodr./dir. Children's History Theatre, Woodstock, NY, 1978—84. Assoc. curator Caffe Cino Exhibit, Lincoln Ctr. Libr. for the Performing Arts, N.Y.C., 1985. Author: The Queen Of Peace Room, 2002 (nominated ForeWord Mag. Book of Yr., 2003, nominated Judy Grahn award, 2003, award Can. Women's Studies Assn., 2003); editor, author: Belle Lettres/Beautiful Letters, 1995; author: (anthologies) Outrage, 1993, Pushing the Limits, 1996, Countering the Myths, 1996; Represented in permanent collections St. Vincent's Hosp., N.Y.C., The Malcolm Forbes Collection, prin. works include The Gown of Stillness Installation, Toronto, 1995, N.Y.C., 1996, UN, 1996, The Female Face of Christ: Stations of the Cross; librettist: "Visions of a Wounded Earth", final movement; librettist world premiere, 1997. Recipient Langston Hughes award Clark Ctr., 1968; grantee Dakota Found., Gottlieb Found., Am. The Beautiful Fund, Shaker Found., Artists fellowship New Sch. U. Faculty Devel. Fund. Mem.: Writer's Alliance Newfoundland, League of Can. Poets, Can. Women's Studies Assn.

DOMINICUS, ADELE MARILYN, mathematician, educator; m. Anthony R. Dominicus, Aug. 0, 1994; children: Ariana, Alexis. BS in Elem. Edn., Iona Coll., 1989. Tchr. St. Anthony's Sch., Bronx, 1989—93, Bronx Pub. Schs., 1993—95; chmn. math dept. Melrose Sch., Brewster, NY, 2000—. Mem.: Nat. Coun. Math. Tchrs. Office: Melrose School 120 Federal Hill Rd Brewster NY 10509 Office Phone: 845-279-2406.

DOMMER, SUSAN WAMPLER, music educator; b. Charlottesville, Va., Aug. 3, 1964; d. Leonard Sylvanus and Dorothy Mae (Greaves) Wampler; m. Robert Frederick Dommer, Apr. 7, 1990; children: Justin, Ryan, Lucas. BMed, James Madison U., 1987; MMed, Shenannoah U., 1996. Choral dir. Manassas Pk. Mid. Sch. and HS, Manassas Pk., Va., 1987—89, Parkside and Godwin Mid. Sch., Prince William, Va., 1989—90, Stonewall Mid. Sch., Manassas, 1990—, Manassas Ch. Brethren, Manassas, 1988—. Choir dir. Ch. of the Brethren Annual Conf., 2001; guest conductor Rockingham Dist. Mid. Sch. Chorus, 2004; guest dir. Stafford All-County Mid. Sch. Honors Choir, 2005. Vacation bible sch. co-dir. Manassas Ch. of the Bretheren, Manassas, 2003, vacation bible sch.dir., 2004, kids rap creator, leader, 2002—. Mem.: Va. Educators Assn., Am. Choral Dirs. Assn., Music Educators Nat. Conf. Avocations: scrapbooks, reading. Home: 10184 Ponderosa Pine Ct Manassas VA 20110 Office: Stonewall Mid Sch 10100 Lomand Dr Manassas VA 20109 Office Phone: 703-361-3185. Office Fax: 703-368-1266. E-mail: dommersw@pwcs.edu.

DOMSKI, MARY ANN, philosopher, educator; d. Dieter and Thuan Domski. PhD, Ind. U., Bloomington, IND., 2003; BA in Math. and Philosophy Sci., U. Pa., Phila., 1997; MEd, U.Pa., 1998; MA in the History and Philosophy of Sci., U. Leeds, England, 1999. Cert. secondary edn. Pa., 1998. Asst. prof. Dept. Philosophy Calif. State U., Fresno, Calif., 2003—05, U. N.Mex., Albuquerque, 2005—. Editor: Synthesis and the Growth of Knowledge: Essays at the Intersection of History, Philosophy, Science and Mathematics; contbr. articles to profl. jours. Recipient Norwood Russell Hanson Disting. Grad. Essay award, Dept. History and Philosophy of Sci., Ind. U., 2002, Mikal Lynn Sousa Excellence in Grad. Scholarship award, Coll. Arts and Scis., Ind. U., 2003; fellow, Ind. U., 1999—2004; grantee, NEH, 2004, NSF, 2004; Victor A. Thoren Grad. Student Rsch. fellowship, Dept. History and Philosophy of Sci., Ind. U., 2003. Mem.: North Am. Kant Soc., Philosophy Sci. Assn., Internat. Soc. History of Philosophy of Sci., History Sci. Soc., Am. Philos. Assn. Avocations: travel, movies. Office Phone: 505-277-4139.

DON, AUDREY, clinical psychologist, neuropsychologist, violist, artist; BFA, Columbus Coll. Art and Design, Ohio, 1990; MA, U. Windsor, Ont., 1994, PhD, 1997. Lic. clin. psychologist Wash. Postdoctoral fellow Children's Seashore Ho. of The Children's Hosp. of Phila., 1997—2000; pediat. psychologist, neuropsychologist Children's Therapy Unit, Good Samaritan Hosp., Puyallup, Wash., 2000—03; clin. psychologist, neuropsychologist The Ark Inst. Learning, Tacoma, 2003—; violist Orch. Seattle, 2003—. Exhibitions include Music on Paper paintings, drawings Scio Scio Gallery, Narberth, Pa. Past examiner Wash. State Examining Bd. Psychology. Mem.: APA, Nat. Acad. Neuropsychology, Chamber Music Am. Avocations: viola, chamber music, art. Office: The Ark Inst Learning 1916 S Washington St Tacoma WA 98405

DONADEY, ANNE, humanities educator; PhD, Northwestern U., Evanston, Ill., 1993. Tchr. comparative lit. and women's studies U. of Iowa, Iowa City, 1993—2001; prof. European studies and women's studies San Diego State U., 2001—. Author: Recasting Postcolonialism: Women Writing Between Worlds; editor: Postcolonial Theory and Francophone Literary Studies. Office: San Diego State Univ 5500 Campanile Dr San Diego CA 92182-7704 Office Phone: 619-594-0815.

DONAHE, PEGGY YVONNE, gifted and talented educator, librarian; b. Bismark, ND, May 5, 1940; d. Fred Rottei and Austie Madre Porter; m. Robert Charles Donahe, June 17, 1967; 1 child, Noel Charles. BA in Elem. Edn., U. ND, 1964; MA, Northern U., 1970; bilingual endorsement degree, libr. media degree, Utah State, 1998. Fifth grade tchr. Ashley Sch. Dist., ND, 1964—67; fourth grade tchr. Hesla Sch. Dist., SD, 1967—69; 4th-8th lang. arts tchr. Abercrombee Sch., ND, 1969—89; title I and English tchr. Standing Rocks B/A, Fort Yates, ND, 1989—94; libr., gifted tchr. Aneth Cmty. Sch., Aneth, Utah, 1994—2006; academic dept. head B/A Sch., Skiprock Agy., 2003—05. Pres. ND Reading Assn., Wakpeton, 1977—98; pres. bd. Tao Dine Libr. Assn., Shiprock, ND, 1995—2006; chief fin. leader Aneth Comm. Sch., Utah, 2000—05. Paintings and chalk, displayed at the ND Capital, 1964. Reporter ABC Election, 1981—89. Recipient Educator award, NASA's Educator Program, 2000—06. Mem.: Tao Dine Libr. Assn. Avocations: reading, watercolor painting, knitting, computer design. Home: 1608 N 10th St Wahpeton ND 88075

DONAHOE, MAUREEN ALICE, accounting consultant; b. NYC, June 9, 1959; d. William A. and Alice P. (O'Connor) D. BA in Acctg., Belmont Abbey Coll., 1982; MBA in Fin., Fordham U., 1992. CPA, N.Y.; cert. insolvency and reorgn. advisor. Staff acct. Bankers Trust Co., N.Y.C., 1982-85; sr. auditor Feldman Radin and Co., 1985—87; valuation svcs. mgr. Ernst & Young, 1987-91; sr. mng. dir. FTI Cons., Inc., 1991—2003; founder, ptnr. CCV Restructuring, Rochelle Park, NJ, 2003—. Dir. 417 E. 90th St. Corp., N.Y.C., 1995-2000. Mem. alumni bd. Belmont Abbey Coll., 1994-1997. Mem.: AICPA, Turnaround Mgmt. Assn., Am. Bankruptcy Inst., N.Y. State Soc. CPAs (insolvency and reorgn. com. 1993—94), Assn. Insolvency Accts. Republican. Roman Catholic. Avocation: golf. Home: 12 Upper Mountain Ave Montclair NJ 07042-1814 Office: CCV Restructuring 365 W Passaic St 2d Fl Rochelle Park NJ 07662 Office Phone: 201-518-5601. E-mail: mdonahoe@ccvrestructuring.com.

DONAHOE, PATRICIA KILROY, surgeon; b. Boston, Apr. 12, 1938; MD, Columbia Coll. Physicians and Surgeons, 1964. Diplomate Am. Bd. Surgery with subspecialty in pediat. surgery. Intern Tufts-New Eng. Ctr. Hosp., 1964—65, resident in surgery, 1965—69; resident in pediat. surgery Children's Hosp., Boston, 1969—70, Mass. Gen. Hosp., Boston, 1970—71; pvt. practice in pediat. surgery Boston; chief surgeon Mass. Gen. Hosp. Mem.: Inst. of Medicine of NAS. Office: Massachusetts Gen Hosp Divsn Pediat Surgery 55 Fruit St Boston MA 02114-2696

DONAHUE, AMY STEWART, early childhood education specialist; b. Bridgeport, Conn., Feb. 13, 1977; d. Richard Phillip and Kathleen Mills Long. BA, Chatham Coll., Pitts., 2000; MEd, George Mason U., Fairfax, Va., 2001. Cert. nat. reporting sys. assessor, lic. gen. edn. Va., spl. edn. Va., English as 2d lang. Va. Pub. rels. cons. W.Va. Media Group, Clarksburg, 1997—99; spl. edn. cons., asst. dir., tchr. Easter Seals Child Devel. Ctr., Falls Church, Va., 2000—01; early childhood spl. edn. interventionist Birth to Three Connections, Madison, Wis., 2001—03; curriculum mgr. Rosemount Ctr., Washington, 2003—05; dir. Minnieland Pvt. Day Sch., Woodbridge, Va., 2005—. City coun. appointee Early Childhood Commn., Alexandria, Va., 2005—; mem. Presch. Stds. Workgroup, Washington, 2003—05; trainer for familes and educators on various topics related to early childhood devel. Named Policy Coun. honoree, Rosemount Ctr. Parent's Policy Coun., 2003, 2004, 2005, Mgr. of YR., Rosemount Ctr., 2004; recipient Project Recruit fellowship, George Mason U., 1999—2001. Mem.: Nat. Head Start Assn., Nat. Assn. for Edn. of Young Children. Office: Minnieland at the Glen 4290 Prince William Pkwy Woodbridge VA 22192

DONAHUE, ANN M., television producer; Student, Ohio State U. Legal asst., Century City, Calif.; writer China Beach, Picket Fences, Murder One; prodr. 21 Jump St., Street Justice; writer CSI NBC, LA, 2000—. Author: (plays) Home Fires, (films) Those Beaumont Girls, Three Girls in the Air Force, Three Girls Pose for Playboy. Home: 1412 Warnall Ave Los Angeles CA 90024

DONAHUE, JOAN ELIZABETH, elementary school educator; b. Middlesboro, Ky., Oct. 9, 1954; d. Calvin Coolidge and Cassie Marie (Harville) Whitaker; m. Andrew Lewis Donahue, Aug. 13, 1977; children: Timothy, Laura, Christopher. BS in Home Econs., U. Tenn., 1977; MS Edn., Ouachita Bapt., 1987. Cert. tchr., Ark. Home econs. tchr. Claiborne County Schs., Tazewell, Tenn., 1977-81; 2d grade tchr. Sparkman Schs., Arkadelphia, Sparkman, Ark., 1985, Arkadelphia Schs., 1985-87, Shelby County Schs., Memphis, 1987-89; 3d grade tchr. Mobile (Ala.) County Schs., 1989-91, 4th grade tchr., 1991-92, 3rd grade tchr., 1992-94; 4th grade tchr. Knox County Schs., Knoxville, Tenn., 1994-95, Green Magnet Math and Sci. Acad., Knoxville, 1995-96; 3d grade tchr. Shelby County Schs., Memphis, 1996—. Textbook cons. Walsworth Pub. Co., Marceline, Mo., 1991—; mem. supt. adv. bd. Mobile County Schs., 1991—. Active Woman's Club Am., New Tazewell, Tenn., 1977-81, v.p., 1981, Shelby County Govt. Bd. Commrs. (hon. commr. 1986), Memphis City Coun. (hon. commr. 1986). Classroom Econ. grantee Mobile Jr. League, 1989-90. Fellow Beta Sigma Phi (pres. 1986-878, Woman of Yr. 1987); mem. Joint Coun. on Econ. Edn. (2d place award 1987, 3d place award 1990), Ala. coun. on Econ. Edn. (1st place award 1990, 91, named Ala. Elem. Econs. Tchr. Yr. 1992). Republican. Methodist. Avocations: travel, crafts, basketmaking, antiques, needlecrafts. Home: 625

Kenrose St Collierville TN 38017-3704 Office: Highland Oaks Elem 5252 Annandale Dr Memphis TN 38125-4263 also: Highland Oaks Elem Sch 5252 Annandale Dr Memphis TN 38125-4263

DONAHUE, KATHLEEN FRANCES, elementary school educator; b. Haverhill, Mass., Feb. 25, 1947; d. Robert Gerald and Jane Elizabeth (Roche) Murphy; m. Joseph Walter Donahue, Mar. 15, 1970. BS in Edn., Salem State Coll., 1969; postgrad., Colo. State U., 1981, U. of the V.I., 1985. Elem. educator, Andover, Mass., 1969-73, Methven, Mass., 1973-79; substitute tchr. Poudre R-1 Sch Dist., Fort Collins, Colo., 1981; jr. high tchr. math. V.I. Dept. of Edn., St. Croix, 1982, elem. educator, 1982-88, elem. educator academically talented, 1991—. Chairperson U.S.-V.I. Dept. Edn., St. Croix, 1984, mem. math. task froce, 1985, 86; owner, dir. Kathleen Internat., St. Croix, 1991-94, Kathleen Modeling Agy., 1988-91. Contbr. articles to newspapers and mags. Guest spkr., instr. Good Hope Sch., St. Croix, 1988, Country Day Sch., 1988, V.I. Talented Teen Pageant, 1989, U. V.I. Ext. Svcs., 1993, 94. Recipient Presdl. award for excellence in teaching math. NSF, 1993. Mem. Nat. Coun. Tchrs. Math., Coun. Presdl. Awardees in Math., Coun. for Elem. Sci. Internat., Soc. Indsl. and Applied Math., St. Croix Hotel Assn., Caribbean Hotel Assn. Avocations: lic. pvt. pilot, open water diver.

DONAHUE, LINDA WHEELER, retired English educator, writer; b. Derby, Conn., Nov. 21, 1941; d. Wilson Chatfield and Beatrice (Smith) Wheeler; m. Raymond Maurice Farrell, July 17, 1965 (div. 1977); 1 child, Sarah Elizabeth; m. James John Donahue Jr., Dec. 30, 1977; 1 child, James John III. BS, Nasson Coll., 1963; MS, U. Bridgeport, 1967. Assoc. prof. Mattatuck C.C., Waterbury, Conn., 1968-80; prof. English and humanities Naugatuck Valley C.C., Waterbury, 1980-84, prof. emeritus humanities, 1997—, divsn. dir. arts and humanities, 1988-92. Editor Polio Messenger Newsletter, 1999-2006; contbr. articles to profl. jours. Active Roosevelt Warm Springs (Ga.) Found., 1960—, Gazette Internat. Polio Newworking Inst., St. Louis, 1975—, pres. Polio Outreach of Conn., 2000—, Conn. Coalition Citizens with Disabilities; chair N.W. Activists for Disability Rights; pres. Conn. Union Disability Action Groups, 1998—. Mem. Conn. Heads of English Depts., Nat. Coun. Tchrs. English, NAFE, Assn. Exec. Educators, AAUW, Congress Conn. Cmty. Colls. (pres. 1985), Nat. Orgn. on disability, Am. Rose Soc., Phi Theta Kappa. Congregationalist. Avocations: opera, theater, design, persian cats, gardening. Home: 75 Tallwood Rd Southbury CT 06488-2751 Office: Naugatuck Valley CC Coll Div Arts-Hums 750 Chase Pkwy Waterbury CT 06708-3089 Personal E-mail: poliooutreach@aol.com, linonnline@aol.com.

DONAHUE, MARTHA, retired librarian; b. Danville, Ky., Jan. 5, 1936; d. Thomas E. and Mary Louise (Craig) D. BA, Centre Coll., 1958; MA, Ind. U., 1961; 6th Yr. Specialist's Cert., U. Wis., 1971. Tchr. Pompano Beach (Fla.) Jr. H.S., 1958-60; post libr. U.S. Army, Europe, Bad Tölz, Germany, 1961-65; instr. library Centre Coll., Danville, Ky., 1966-67, U. Wis., Whitewater, 1967-70; assoc. prof. library Mansfield (Pa.) U., 1971-93. Bd. dirs. Mansfield Free Pub. Libr., 1995-97, vol., 1998—; vol. Area Agy. on Aging, Towanda, Pa., 1993—, Sr. Citizen Meals Delivery, 1993—; mem. Parish Coun., Mansfield, 1994-97; bd. dirs. Ctr. Coll. Alumni Bd., 1996-98. Recipient Higher Edn. Act fellowship U. Wis., 1970. Mem. ALA, Pa. Libr. Assn. (chair various coms. 1971—93), Friday Club of Wellsboro, Mansfield Garden Club, Columbia Lit. Exchange, The Book Group, Tioga County Hist. Soc., 1901 Soc. (pres. 2001-02). Roman Catholic. Avocations: reading, gardening, travel, cross country skiing, bicycling. Home: 146 S Main St Mansfield PA 16933-1522

DONALD, AIDA DIPACE, retired publishing executive; d. Victor E. and Bessie DiPace; m. David Herbert Donald; 1 child, Bruce Randall. AB cum laude, Barnard Coll.; MA, Columbia U.; PhD, U. Rochester. Instr. history dept. Columbia U., N.Y.C.; cons. and series editor Hill and Wang Pubs., N.Y.C.; editor Mass. Hist. Soc., Boston, 1960-64, Johns Hopkins U. Press, Balt., 1972-73; social sci. editor Harvard U. Press, Cambridge, Mass., 1973-79, exec. editor, 1979-89, editor in chief, 1989—2000, asst. dir., 1990—2000; ret., 2000. Editor: John F. Kennedy and the New Frontier, 1966, (with David Herbert Donald) Charles Frances Adams Diary, 2 vols., 1965. Pres. Wellfleet Non-Resident Taxpayers Assn., 2005—. Columbia U. Dibblee fellow, 1952-53, U. Rochester fellow, 1955-56, 56-57, Oxford U. Fulbright fellow, 1959-60 Fellow AAUW; mem. Am. Hist. Assn., Orgn. Am. Historians. Avocations: writing, tennis, first editions, antique silver, coins.

DONALD, BERNICE B., judge; b. Miss., Sept. 17, 1951; d. Perry and Willie Bell (Hall) Bowie; m. W. L. Donald, Oct. 9, 1973. BA in Sociology, Memphis State Univ., 1974, JD, 1979; student, Nat. Judicial Coll., 1983, 84. Bar: Tenn. 1979, U.S. Fed. Ct. 1979, U.S. Supreme Ct. 1989. Clk. South Central Bell Telephone Co., 1971-75, mgr., 1975-80; staff atty. Memphis Area Legal Svcs., 1980, Shelby County Public Defenders Office, 1980-82; judge Gen. Sessions Criminal Ct. of Shelby County, Tenn., 1982-88; bankruptcy judge U.S. Bankruptcy Ct. (we. dist.) Tenn., Memphis, 1988-96; U.S. dist. judge U.S. Dist. Ct. (we. dist.) Tenn., 1996—. Mem. adv. com. on bankruptcy rules Jud. Conf., 1996—; faculty mem. Fed. Judicial Ctr., 1991—, Nat. Judicial Coll., 1992—; adj. prof. Shelby State C.C., 1980-84, Cecil C. Humphreys Sch. of Law, 1985-88; lectr., presenter in field. Featured in Essence mag., Ebony mag., Jet mag., Memphis mag., Dollars and Sense mag., Black Enterprise mag. Bd. dirs. Midtown Mental Health, 1990-92, 94-96, Memphis in May, 1994-97, Leadership Memphis, Inc., 1993-96, U. Memphis Alumni Bd., 1994—, Memphis Race Rels. and Diversity Inst., 1994—, Fed. Jud. Ctr.; former bd. dirs. numerous religious and civic orgns. including Calvary St. Ministry, Memphis Literacy Coun., YWCA. Recipient Cmty. Svcs. award Nat. Conf. on Christians and Jews, 1986, Martin Luther King Cmty. Svc. award, Young Careerist award State of Tenn. Raleigh Bureau of Profl. Women, plaques and certs.; named Citizen of Yr. Excelsior Chpt. of Eastern Star, Woman of Yr. Pentecostal Ch. of God in Christ. Mem. ABA (mem. standing com. on Gavel awards 1989-95, mem. adv. com. Ctrl. and Ea. European Law Initiative 1999—, mem. ho. dels. 1993-95, 99—, bd. govs. 1999—, liason labor and employment law sect. 1999—, Law Libr. Congress 1999—, Appellate Judges Conf. 1999-2000, Africa Legal Tech. Assistance Project 2000—, mem. legal opportunity scholarship com. 2000—, Mus.'s bd. dirs. 2000—, numerous jud. adminstrn. divsn. coms.), Nat. Assn. of Women Judges (treas. 1986-87, sec. 1987-88, v.p. 1988-89, pres. elect 1989-90, pres. 1990-91), Am. Judges Assn., Nat. Ctr. for State Cts., Am. Bar Assn., Nat. Bar Assn., Tenn. Bar Assn. (bd. dirs. 1997-98), Memphis County Bar Assn., Shelby County Bar Assn., Am. Trial Lawyers Assn., Assn. of Women Attys. (pres. 1991, bd. dirs.), Nat. Conf. of Bankruptcy Judges (bd. dirs. 1993-96), Nat. Conf. of Women's Bar Assn. (bd. mem.), Nat. Conf. of Spl. Ct. Judges (sec.), Leadership Memphis (pres. 1987, bd. dirs.), Internat. Women's Forum, Memphis Bar Assn. (bd. dirs. 1993), Zeta Phi Beta (Alpha Eta Zeta chpt.). Avocations: reading, crossword puzzles, music, bicycling, walking. Office: Federal Building 167 N Main St Ste 1111 Memphis TN 38103-1831

DONALDSON, EVA G., chemist, writer; b. Henderson, NC, Mar. 19, 1927; d. William and Annie Green; m. Kenneth Donaldson, Feb. 9, 1952 (dec.); children: Sonya D. Bates, Kenneth A., Keith. BS cum laude, Johnson C. Smith U., Charlotte, NC, 1948; MS in Chemistry with honors, Howard U., Washington, 1953; postgrad., U. Washington, Howard U., Cath. U. Am., Am. U., George Washington U., LaSalle U. Coll. Engring., U. Md. Lic. tchr. Washington, 1954. Tchr. chemistry, phys. sci. Spingarn Sr. H.S., Washington, 1954—59; tchr. chemistry, biology and math Dunbar Sr. H.S., 1962—93; author, 1993—; chemist, cancer rschr. NIH. Del., sci. profl. Russia Joint Edn. Conf., St. Petersburg, Russia, 2006—. Author: A Science Incentive Program, A Summer Enrichment Curriculum For Chemistry Students, A Revised Curriculum for the Teaching of Advanced Placement Chemistry. Mem. Howard U. Century Club/U. Capstone Socs. Donors, Washington. Grantee, NSF. Fellow: Wash. Acad. Sci. (Bernice Lamberton award Initiatives Providing Learning Success and Sci. Career Awareness Students); mem.: Washington Nat. Cathedral's Liecracy Program, Nat. Sci. Found., Nat. Profl. Orgn. Devel. Black Chemists and Chem. Engrs. (life), Nat. Sci. Tchrs. Assn., Myers Soc., Legacy Soc., Smithsonian Instn., Kiwanis. Avocations: swimming, ice skating, travel, growing cyrstals.

DONALDSON, KATHLEEN, special education educator; b. Troy, Ohio, Aug. 29, 1950; d. William Butler, Jr. and Dorothy (Polly) Ann Butler; m. David Alan Donaldson, May 17, 1975; children: Ann, Steve. BS in Rehab. Edn., Ea. Ky. U., Richmond, 1976, MA in Learning Behavior Disorders, 2000. Cert. spl. edn. 1992, exceptional edn. learning & behavior disorder 2003, elem., self-contained. Head start tchr. Ky. River Foothills Devel. Coun., Richmond, 1976—78; counselor Berea Hosp. Skilled Nursing Facility, 1978—79; preschool tchr. Ms. Kathy Presch. Playgroups, Richmond, 1984—92; spl. edn. tchr. Paint Lick Elem., Lancaster, 1993—. Team/sch. leader Ky. Instrn. Discipline Schs., Paint Lick, Ky., 2000—, sch.-based spl. edn. liaison, 2000—. Troop coord. Girl Scouts USA, Richmond, Ky., 1986—2000, dist. coord., 1988—92. Mem.: Ky. Nat. Edn. Assn. Office: Paint Lick Elem 6798 Richmond Rd Paint Lick KY 40461 Business E-Mail: kdonalds@garrand.k12.ky.us.

DONALDSON, LISA MILLER, city administrator; b. Tallahassee, Fla., Aug. 8, 1963; d. Charles D. and Virginia Reynolds Miller; m. Gary E. Donaldson, July 24, 1993; 1 child, Haley. AA, Fla. State U., 1984; BA, Fla. Atlantic U., 1996. Asst. to CAO Cen. Corp., Ft. Lauderdale, Fla., 1987-88; planner Broward County Govt., Ft. Lauderdale, 1988-91, equal opportunity compliance analyst, 1991-94; cons. The Donaldson Group, Plantation, Fla., 1996-99, pres., 1999—; spl. projects coord. City of Oakland Park, Fla., 1999-2001; commn. adminstr. Ft. Lauderdale City Commn., 2001—. Chair Census 2000 adv. bd. City of Plantation, 1999. Bd. dirs. 1st United Meth. Ch. Adminstrv. Bd., Ft. Lauderdale, 1999; v.p. El Dorado Homeowners Assn., Plantation, 1998—; mem. fin. bd., bd. dirs. Oakland Park Main St. Orgn.; bd. dirs. Downtown Ft. Lauderdale TMA; trustee 1st United Meth. Ch. Mem. Am. Planning Assn., Am. Polit. Sci. Assn., LEAD Alumni (pres. 1993-94), Plantation Jr. Women's Club, Pi Sigma Alpha. Democrat. Methodist. Avocations: gardening, travel, history. Office: City Ft Lauderdale 100 N Andrews Ave Fort Lauderdale FL 33301 Home: 1645 Eagles Watch Way Tallahassee FL 32312-4064 Fax: (954) 581-6374. E-mail: Donaldsongroup@aol.com.

DONALDSON, MARCIA JEAN, lay worker; b. Wilmington, Del., June 20, 1925; C. Aubrey Smith and Marcia Allen (Hall) Whitman; m. Robert Donald Donaldson, Jan. 8, 1944; children: Robert Gary, Pamela Lynn, David Keith. Student pub. schs., Wilmington. Sunday Sch. tchr., Del., N.J., 1943-70; tchr. Child Evangelism Fellowship, Wilmington, 1943-55, tchr., bd. dirs. NJ, 1955-64, dir. Ocean County, NJ, 1964-73; pres., exec. dir. Christian Children's Assocs., Toms River, NJ, 1964—2005, pres., 2005—. Writer radio and TV syndicated programs worldwide for children; author: (booklet) A 30 Year Adventure; producer, hostess radio and TV program Adventure Pals. Mem. Nat. Religious Broadcasters Assn., Gideons Aux. Office: Christian Children's Assn Inc PO Box 446 Toms River NJ 08754-0446 Office Phone: 732-240-3003. Personal E-mail: adventurepal@juno.com.

DONALDSON, MYRTLE NORMA, music educator, musician; b. Priddy, Tex., Feb. 9, 1923; d. Emil Otto and Brunhilda Eleanore (Riewe) Schneider; m. Fletcher William Donaldson, Feb. 12, 1943; children: Patricia Annette, Rebecca Joyce. BA, U. Ariz., Tucson, 1970; MA, Middle Tenn. State U., Murfreesboro, 1982. Cert. profl. piano tchr. Tenn. Music Tchrs. Assn., profl. piano tchr.'s cert. Nat. Music Tchrs.' Assn. Organist Luth. chs., Aleman and Austin, Tex., 1937-42, 43-50, Kinston, N.C., 1943, Los Alamos, N.Mex., 1951-53; Ft. Worth, 1954-56; organist Tullahoma, Tenn., 1969-81; piano tchr., 1972-2001. Composer: sonata, 1981, theme and variations, 1980. Active Cmty. Concert Bd., Tullahoma, 1973-99, Cmty. Concert Membership Ch., 1974-78, pres., 1978-80, 89-93 Mem. Music Tchrs. Nat. Assn. (cert., com. mem. 1983-99), Mid. Tenn. Music Tchrs. Assn. (sec. Murfreesboro chpt. 1975-77, chair membership state 1977-78, pres. Mid. Tenn. chpt. 1979-81, 87-89, Music Tchr. of Yr. 1992), Delta Phi Alpha. Republican. Lutheran. Avocations: knitting, sewing, creative memories album, national background of grandparents.

DONALDSON, ROBIN FAULK, secondary school educator; b. Mullins, S.C., Jan. 28, 1961; d. Robert Faulk; m. Ricky Slade Donaldson, Dec. 28, 1953; children: Joshua Slade, Timothy Lee. BA in English Lit., Wake Forest U., Winston-Salem, N.C., 1983; MEd, Francis-Marion U., Florence, S.C., 1996; postgrad., Liberty U. Cert. tchr. math and English S.C., 1983. Tchr. Orangeburg Sch. Dist. 3, Holly Hill, 1983—84, Alamance County Schs., Graham, 1988—90, Burlington City Schs., Burlington, NC, 1990—91, Horry County Schs., Conway, 1991—. Tchr. Evergreen Bapt. Ch., NC, 2002—06. Named Tchr. of Yr., Green Sea Floyds H.S., Horry County Sch., 1996, 2006. Mem.: Palmetta Tchrs. Assn. Baptist. Avocations: travel, reading. Home: 196 RL Faulk Lane Tabor City NC 28463 Office: Green Sea Floyds HS 5265 Tulip Lane Green Sea SC 29545 Office Phone: 843-392-3131. Office Fax: 843-392-9805. Business E-Mail: rdonald@gsfh.hcs.k12.sc.us.

DONALDSON, SARAH SUSAN, radiologist; b. Portland, Oreg., Apr. 20, 1939; BS, RN, U. Oreg., 1961; MD, Harvard U., 1968. Intern U. Wash., 1968—69; resident in radiol. therapy Stanford Med. Ctr., Calif., 1969—72; fellow in pediatric oncology Inst. Gustave-Roussy, 1972—73; prof. radiol. oncology Stanford U. Sch. Medicine., 1973—, Catherine and Howard Avery prof., dept. radiation. Recipient Elizabeth Blackwell medal, Am. Med. Women's Assn., 2005. Mem.: NIH. Office: Stanford U Med Ctr Dept Radio/Oncology 875 Blake Wilbur Dr Stanford CA 94305-5847

DONALDSON, WILMA CRANKSHAW, elementary school educator; b. Havre de Grace, Md., Aug. 28, 1942; d. John Hamilton and Wilma Chaffee (Thurlow) Crankshaw; m. James Neill Donaldson, Aug. 5, 1967. BA in Edn. cum laude, Westminster Coll., 1964; MA in Edn., Fairfield U., 1976. Educator Hurlbutt Elem. Sch., Weston, Conn., 1964-78, 92—, Weston Mid. Sch., 1979-91; tchr. Greek Mythology Elem. Sch., 1999—. Team leader Hurlbutt Elem. Sch., 1967—68, 1976—78, sci. rep., 1992—99, developer of curriculum; judge Odyssey of the Mind, Conn., 1995—2001; presenter of photography and Greek myth courses elem. sch., 2002—; tchr. pvt. student art courses; tchr. Music/Lit./Theater Workshop, 1997—; presenter in field; sci. cons. Greenwich Pub. Schs., 2002—. Author: (filmstrip script) Sci. Series, 1972, Metric Math Series, 1973. Chair fine arts New England Sch. Accreditation Com., Weston, 1990-91; trainer Project CHEM, Exxon Corp., 1991—; state planning com., program and site chmn. Conn. Elem. Sci. Day Conf., 1994—; organizer, advisor Student Elem. Sch. Environ. Orgn., 1992-2003, sci. cons. Pub. Schs. Greenwich, Conn., 2002-04; co-organizer, co-founder Elem. Family Sci. Night, Weston, 2000; dir., tchr. Camp Invention, Weston, 2002-04; active Silvermine Arts Enrichment Com. Recipient Faculty Mem. Presdl. Recognition Sch. award U.S. Dept. Edn., 1987-88, Celebration of Excellence award State of Conn., 1989, 92, 95, 98, Laurence Ohmes Meml. award, 1995. Mem. NEA, CEA, Nat. Sci. Tchrs. Assn. (workshop presenter Moscow 1991, NASA-NEWEST award 1997, Laurence P. Ohmes Meml. award 1995), ASCD, Conn. Edn. Assn., Conn. Alliance Arts Edn. (Weston Tchr. of Yr. 1994-95, Conn. Alliance for Art Edn. Disting. Tchr. of Yr. 1995), Coun. Elem. Sci. Internat. (com. chmn. 1991-98), Delta Zeta. Avocations: art, theater, photography, travel.

DONAT, JULIANA SOUTHER, elementary school educator; b. Atlanta, Ga., Dec. 11, 1979; d. Charles Timothy and Cynthia Hill Souther; m. Daniel Seth Donat, Nov. 20, 2004; 1 child, Jacob Seth. BS in Spl. Edn., U. West Ga., Carrollton, Ga., 2003; MEd in Spl. Edn., Brenau U., Gainesville, Ga., 2005. Cert. tchr. Ga. Tchr. Gwinnett County Pub. Schs., Lilburn, Ga., 2003—. Hope Tchr. scholr, State of Ga., 2003—05. Southern Baptist. Avocations: scrapbooks, exercise. Office Phone: 770-921-7707.

DONAT, PATRICIA LYN, education educator, academic administrator; d. Stanley Ray and Phyllis Elizabeth Donat. BA, U. No. Iowa, 1986; MA, U. N.C., 1990, PhD, 1995. Social rsch. asst. Healthy Kids Project, Greensboro, NC, 1990—91, social rsch. assoc., 1991—93, project dir., 1993—95; asst. prof. Miss. U. for Women, Columbus, 1995—2000, divsn. head, edn., and human scis., 1998—99, assoc. prof., dir. gen studies, 2000—03, prof., dir. gen. edn., 2003—05, prof., assoc. v.p. for acad. affairs, 2005—. Consulting editor Psychology of Woman Quar., Cambridge, 2000—; peer evaluator So. Assn. of Colls. and Schs., Atlanta, 2002—; reader AP exams. Ednl. Testing Svc., Princeton, NJ, 2003—04. Author: (instr.'s manual) Instructor's Resource to Accompany A New Psychology of Women, 2005; co-author: (book chpt.) Violence Against Women, 2004; contbr. articles to profl. jours. Mem. Town and Tour, Columbus, 2002—. Mem.: APA, Southeastern Psychol. Assn., Psi Chi. Office: Miss U for Women MUW-1633 1100 College St Columbus MS 39701

DONATH, THERESE, artist, author; b. Hammond, Ind., Dec. 14, 1928; Student, Monticello Coll., 1946-47; BFA, St. Joseph' Coll., 1975; additional study, Oxbow Summer Sch. Painting. Radio/TV personality, 1978-92; interviewer, prodr. Viewpoint Sta. WLNR-FM, Lansing, Ill., 1963-64; reporter, columnist N.W. Ind. Sentinel, 1965; freelance writer Monterey Peninsula Herald, 1981-85; contbg. author Monterey Life mag., 1981-85; asst. dir. Michael Karolyi Found., Vence, France, 1979. Creative cons. Aslan Tours and Travel, 1983-85; instr., lectr. Penland, N.C., 1970, Haystack Mountain Sch., Deer Isle, Maine, 1974, Sheffield Poly., Eng., 1978; bd. dirs., sec. Mental Health Soc. Greater Chgo., 1963-64; exec. dir. Lansing (Ill.) Mental Health Soc., 1963-64. One-woman shows include Palos Verdes (Calif.) Mus., 1974, LA Inst. Contemporary Art, 1978, Mus. Contemporary Art, Chgo., 1975, Calif. State U., Fullerton, 1973, No. Ill. U., DeKalb, 1971, Bellevue (Wash.) Mus. Art, 1986-87; group shows at Gallery-Willis Gray, Decatur, Ala.; represented in permanent collections including Kennedy Gallery, N.Y.C., also pvt. collections; represented in the Mirror Book, 1978, Willis Gray Gallery, Decatur, Ala., 2004—; author, illustrator: Before I Die, A Creative Legacy, 1989; contbr. articles to profl. jours., newspapers; illustrator: Run Computer Run. Recipient awards, No. Ind. Art Mus., 1966, 1970—71, 1973; grantee, Ragdale Found., Lake Forest, Ill., 1982, Michael Karolyi Found., Vence, France, 1980. Business E-Mail: therese@pclnet.net.

DONATO, MICHELE ROSEANNE, lawyer, educator; d. Thomas Donato and Rose Catherine Cardone; m. Peter Weeks, Feb. 22, 1986; 1 child, Jennie. BA, Rutgers U., 1973, JD, 1977. Bar: NJ 1977, (U.S. Supreme Ct.) 1987. Editor Rutgers Law Rev., Newark, 1975—77; law clerk Hon. Merritt Lane, Freehold, NJ, 1977—78; atty. Anschelewitz, Barr, Ansell, and Bonello, Ocean, NJ, 1978—81, Frizell and Pozycki, Metuchen, NJ, 1981—88, Michele R. Donato PA, Lavallette, NJ, 1988—. Adj. prof. Rutgers U., New Brunswick, NJ, 1981—; Assoc. Counsel N.J. Planning Officials, Watchung, 1999—. Contbr. articles in field. Pres., dir. Preservation N.J., Trenton, 1990—99; pro bono atty. Save Barnegat Bay, Ocean, NJ, Coalition Against Oyster Creek Nuclear Station, Ocean, NJ. Mem.: Oxford U. Roundtable, Inst. Gov. Attys., N.J. Planning Officials (Planning award 2003). Avocations: crossword puzzles, sailing, walking. Home: 2202 Oceanfront Lavallette NJ 08735 Office: 106 Grand Ctrl Ave Lavallette NJ 08735 Office Phone: 732-830-0777. Business E-Mail: mdonato@micheledonatoesq.com. E-mail: lawyerlady48@optonline.net.

DONBERGER, KAREN SHEPARD, special education educator, elementary school educator; b. Malcolm Grow, Md., June 7, 1968; d. Ernest A. and Elaine B. Shepard; m. Anthony Paul Donberger, Dec. 18, 1992; children: Allyson, Anthony Jr. BS, U. Md., Coll. Pk., 1991, MEd, 1994. Advanced profl. cert. Md. State Dept. Edn., 2004, postgrad. profl. lic. Commonwealth of Va. Dept. Edn., 2005. Early childhood spl. tchr. Prince George's County Pub. Schs., Upper Marlboro, Md., 1991—97, child find evaluator, 1995—96, infants and toddlers spl. tchr., 1998—99; elem. spl. tchr. Calvert County Pub. Schs., Port Repub., Md., 1997—98; child find tchr. and screener Loudon County Pub. Schs., Ashburn, Va., 1999—. Sub. inclusion specialist The Lt. Joseph P. Kennedy Inst., Washington, 1995—96. Mem.: Coun. Exceptional Children.

DONEGAN, TERESA E., pharmaceutical educator; arrived in US, 1987; d. James Frederick and Ada Donegan. BA in Psychology with honors, U. Waterloo, Ont., 1985; MA in Clin. Psychology, Duquesne U., Pitts., 1988, PhD in Clin. Psychology, 1999. Psychology instr. dept. psychology Duquesne U., Pitts., 1980—90, pre-doctoral tchg. fellow, dept. psychology, 1994—95; psychology instr. dept. psychology Point Pk. Coll., Pitts., 1990, U. Dallas, Irving, 1991—94, Carlow Coll., Pitts., 1995—98; psychology instr. Johns Hopkins' Ctr. Talented Youth Program, Balt., 1995—99; prof. pharmacy U. Pitts., 2001—. Adj. instr. Chatham Coll., Pa., 2003. Mem.: APA, Ctr. Interpretive and Qualitative Rsch., Am. Assn. Coll. Pharmacy. Office Phone: 412-648-9709. Business E-Mail: ted48@pitt.edu.

DONEHEW, PAMELA K., reading specialist; b. Fairmont, W.Va., Sept. 24, 1949; d. Walter Hal Donehew and Eldora Jean (Eddy) Van Tol; m. E. William Ball, Sr., June 1, 1968 (div. Oct. 1993); children: E. William, Jr., Jennifer Catena, Geoffrey J.; m. Lawrence L. Lambert, Feb. 14, 1999; stepchildren: Leslie L., Laura M. AA, Ocean County Coll., Toms River, N.J., 1986; BA in English and Psychology, Monmouth U., 1989, MA, 1991, MSEd, 1992. Cert. reading specialist, tchr. psychology, English tchr., tchr. grades K-12, N.J. Dir. reading ctr. Monmouth U., West Long Branch, N.J., 1989-92; tchr. psychology Manasquan H.S., N.J., 1992-95; reading specialist West Ga. Tech., LaGrange, 1995—. SAT and ACT supr., 1996—. Learning cons. Georgian Ct. Coll., Lakewood, N.J., 1995; reader coll. bds. AP Psychology Exam, 1996—; GRE, GMAT Test administr., 1990-94. Author: Library Handbook, 1996; co-author: Learn to Tutor, 1990. Mem. APA, NEA, Nat. Coun. English Tchrs., Internat. Reading Assn., Phi Delta Kappa.

DONEHEY, MARILYN MOSS, foundation administrator; b. Malad City, Idaho, Sept. 5, 1946; d. Ray Wesley and LaRue Camp Jones; m. Robert David Donehey, Apr. 15, 1966 (div. June 1989); children: Troy Robert, David Ray, Calli-Anne, Suzanne, Erin. AA, Elgin Cmty. Coll., 1987; BA, Judson Coll., 1992. Sec., receptionist Fox Valley Ctr. for Ind. Livng, Elgin, Ill., 1987-88, devel. dir., 1990-91; cmty. outreach specialist Tri-County Ind. Living Ctr., Akron, Ohio, 1993-94; program dir. Soc. of the Blind, Akron, 1997—2002. Subs. tchr. dispatcher, Ill. Sch. Dist. 300, Carpentersville, 1972-81. Precinct com. person Rep. Cen. Com., Kane County, Ill., 1977-90; pres. Consumer Advocacy coun., Akron, 2000-2002.; participant blindness adjustment program La. Ctr. Blind. Mem. Nat. Fedn. of the Blind (vice chair 1997-2001, sec. 2001-2002, scholar 1987). Republican. Mem. Lds Ch. Avocations: music, writing. Office: Soc of the Blind 325 E Market Akron OH 44304 E-mail: mmoss325@aol.com, Lynssom@aol.com.

DONELSON, ROSEMARIE QUIROZ CARVAJAL, human services professional, state official; b. San Antonio, Tex., Sept. 14, 1952; d. Frank Cordero Quiroz and Margaret Carvajal Quiroz; m. Dennis Michael Donelson, Oct. 7, 1972; 1 child, Alexandra (Sasha). Student, U. Tex., San Antonio, San Antonio Coll., 1976—. Assembly line worker Universal Bookbindery, San Antonio, 1971-73; day care instr., office mgr. Madison Sq. Presbyn. Ch., San Antonio, 1973-77; credit analyst Sears Roebuck and Co., San Antonio, 1976-85; adminstrv. tech. Tex. Dept. Human Svcs., San Antonio, 1985—. Video facilitator Pacific Inst., San Antonio, 1999. Active walks/runs Juvenile Diabetes Found., San Antonio, 1997—. Named Outstanding Women in Tex. Govt. Gov.'s Commn. for Women, 1998. Mem. San Antonio Conservation Soc., Nat. Hist. Preservation Soc., Victorian Soc. in Am. Democrat. Roman Catholic. Avocations: reading, antiques, history, exercise. Office: Tex Dept Human Svcs 11307 Roszell St San Antonio TX 78217-2511

DONENFELD, SHARON ETTA, educational and school psychologist; b. Bklyn., Sept. 7, 1948; d. Harry and Elsie (Capp) Kamer; m. Kenneth Jay Donenfeld, June 23, 1968; children— Elissa, Jonathan. Student, Syracuse U., 1968; B.A. (N.Y. State Regents scholar), Hunter Coll., 1969; M.A., New Sch. for Social Research, 1971; postgrad. Yeshiva U., 1971-72, Fordham U., 1974. Cert. sch. psychologist, N.Y., N.J., nat. cert. sch. psychologist; Calif. Research assoc., field team supr. health services mobility study City Univ. Research Found., N.Y.C., 1969-71; psychology intern Coney Island Hosp., Bklyn., 1971-72, psychologist dept. clin. psychology, 1974, staff psychologist dept. child psychiatry, 1978; research assoc. regional med. program Assoc. Med. Schs. Greater N.Y., N.Y.C., 1971-72; sch. psychologist, chmn. child study team Bridgewater-Raritan (N.J.) Schs., 1972-75; sch. psychologist spl. edn.

programs, mem. com. on handicapped Hempstead (N.Y.) Sch. Dist., 1975-77; sch. psychologist Massapequa (N.Y.) Pub. Schs., 1977; pvt. cons. ednl. psychology, Great Neck, N.Y., 1978—; psychologist Kings Park (N.Y.) Schs., 1980—; condr. in-service ednl. programs Hempstead Parochial Schs., 1975-77. Bd. dirs. Saddle Rock Civic Assn., 1975—2001; mem. Womens Am. Orgn. for Rehab. and Tng., 1976—2001. Mem. Nat. Assn. Sch. Psychologists, Am. Psychol. Assn., N.Y. State Psychol. Assn., Nassau County Psychol. Assn., N.J. Assn. Sch. Psychologists, Somerset County Assn. Psychologists. Home and Office: 15 Maplewood Dr Northport NY 11768-3431

DONG, MABEL H, music educator; d. Siu-tong Hau and Yim-ching Chan; m. Tony K Dong, Aug. 10, 1988; 1 child, Vanessa W. MusB, Hong Kong Bapt. U., 1977—81; MusM, SW Tex. State U., 1984—85; DMA in Progress, U. of Colo., 1986—88. Single Subject Tchg. Credential, Music Calif. Teacher's Credential Commn., 1997, Ill. Tchg. Cert., Music Chgo. Bd. of Edn., 1995. Music tchr. Tak Ngai Cath. Sch., Hong Kong, China, 1977—78, Alliance Elem. Sch., Hong Kong, China, 1981—83; job tng. coord. Chinese Mut. Aid Assn., Chgo., 1990—91; music dir. St. Barbara H.S., Chgo., 1991—94; piano/voice instr. Moraine Valley C.C., Palos Hill, Ill., 1992—95; music tchr. Florence Nightingale Sch., Chgo., 1995—96; chinese bilingual tchr. Glenview Elem. Sch., Oakland, Calif., 1996—97; music tchr. Jefferson Sch. Dist., Daly City, Calif., 1997—99, Berkeley Unified Sch. Dist., Berkeley, Calif., 1999—. Com. mem. Berkeley Districtwide Music Curriculum Com., Berkeley, Calif., 2000—; music teacher's workshop presenter Jefferson Sch. Dist., Daly City, Calif., 1997—99. Recipient Second Pl. in Singing (Grad. Divsn.), Nat. Assn. of Teachers Singing, 1985. Mem.: Trinity Coll., London (licentiate LTCL 1983), Associated Bd. of Royal Schools of Music (licentiate LRSM 1981), Internat. Fedn. for Choral Music (assoc.), Chinese Music Tchr. Assn. of No. Calif. (assoc.), Am. Choral Dir. Assn. (assoc.), Music Educator Nat. Conf. (assoc.). Office: Berkeley Unified School District 1500 Derby St Rm 509 Berkeley CA 94704 Personal E-mail: mabelhdong@sbcglobal.net.

DONICK, JULIE K, elementary school educator; m. Michael D. Donick, Jan. 13, 2002. BS, Bucknell U., Lewsiburg, Pa.; M in Tchg., Marygrove Coll., Mich. Cert. tchr. Pa., Mich., Ark. Tchr. Saline Mid. Sch., Mich., 2002—.

DONINI, DINA A., social studies educator; d. Anthony Ortuglio; m. Samuel J. Donini, July 13, 1999. BS in Liberal Arts, Duquesne U., Pitts., MS in Edn. and Info. Tech. Cert. tchr. Pa. Dept. Edn., 2000. Secondary social studies tchr. Shaler Area H.S., Pitts., 2002—. Advanced placement exam reader Coll. Bd., Princeton, NJ, 2005—. Office: Shaler Area High School 381 Wible Run Rd Pittsburgh PA 15219 Office Phone: 412-492-1200 1653.

DONLEY, CORRINE RUSSELL, special education educator, educator; b. East Liverpool, Ohio, Apr. 9, 1936; d. John Louis Russell and Mildred Louise (Shenton) Ziegler; m. Loren Duane Donley, Dec. 28, 1957 (div. Dec. 1989); children: Mark Russell, Kevin Reed, Dana Ryan, Cheryl Ruth. BS, Ohio State U., Columbus, 1958; MEd, Trenton State Coll., N.J., 1981, Tchrs. Coll. Columbia, N.Y., 1989; EdD, Tchrs. Coll. Columbia U., N.Y., 1990. Tcr. Music, Tchr. Handicapped, Supr., N.J. Tchr. of handicapped Pt. Pleasant Schs., Pt, Pleasant, N.J., 1960-63; kindergarten tchr. Pt. Pleasant Beach Schs., Pt. Pleasant Beach, N.J., 1963-64, Howell Township Schs., Howell, N.J., 1967-69, handicapped tchr., 1969-89; supr. Margaret Chapman Sch., Hawthorne, N.Y., 1986-87; asst. prof. spl. edn. Georgian Ct. Coll., Lakewood, N.J., 1989-91; behavior analyst, parent trainer Fred S. Keller Sch., Yonkers, N.Y., 1991-92; asst. prof. spl. edn. U. Wis., Oshkosh, 1992—99, univ. coord. of assessment, 1997—2000; pvt. practice, 2000—. Scribe Georgian Ct. Coll., Ad Hoc Planning Commn., Lakewood, N.J., 1990-91. Asst. dir. music Pt. Pleasant Presbyn. Ch., Pt. Pleasant Beach, N.J., 1970-75; v.p. Assn. Retarded Citizens, Ocean Unit, 1983-85, N.J., 1984-85. Named Tchr. of Yr. Assn. Retarded Citizens, Monmouth, N.J., 1981-82. Mem. NEA, Assn. Applied Behavior Analysis (SIG chair 1990-92), Coun. for Exceptional Children, N.J. Edn. Assn. Presbyterian. Avocation: piano. Business E-Mail: donley@uwosh.edu.

DONLEY, ROSEMARY, university official; Diploma in Nursing, Pitts. Hosp., 1961; BSN summa cum laude, St. Louis U., 1963; M in Nursing Edn., U. Pitts., 1965; postgrad. tng. in psychiatry, U. Pitts., Columbia U., 1967-69; PhD, U. Pitts., 1972; postgrad., Harvard U., 1986; LittD (hon.), Felician Coll., 1981, Villanova U., 1985; LLD (hon.), Loyola U., Chgo., 1988; HHD (hon.), Madonna Coll., 1988; Dr. Pub. Svc. (hon.), R.I. Coll., 1988, La Roche Coll., 1989. Staff nurse St. Mary's Hosp., St. Louis, 1961-63; instr. Pitts. Hosp. Sch. Nursing, 1963-71; cons. Vis. Nurses Assn. Allegheny County, Pitts., 1972; from instr. to assoc. prof. Sch. Nursing U. Pitts., 1971-79; dean and assoc. prof. Sch. Nursing Cath. U. Am., Washington, 1979-86, exec. v.p., 1986—. Bd. dirs. Ea. Mercy Health Care System, Forbes Health Care System, Nursing Econs. Found.; cons. in field; advisor internat. programs, lectr. various colls. and univs. Contbr. articles to profl. jours.; mem. editorial bd. Ednl. Record, 1985—, Jour. Contemporary Health Law and Policy, 1985—. Bd. dirs. Seton Hill Coll., 1991—. Recipient Hon. Recognition award Pa. League for Nursing, 1978, Alumni Merit award St. Louis U., 1980, Woman of Yr. award Pres.'s Commn. on Women, Cath. U. Am., 1984, McGrady award, Cath. Youth Assn. of Pitts. Inc., 1987, Medal of Distinction. U. Pitts., 1987; fellow Robert Wood Johnson Found. and Inst. Medicine, Nat. Acad. Sci., 1977-78; Disting. scholar in nursing NYU, 1994; Alumni fellows award U. Pitts., 1995. Fellow Am. Acad. Nursing; mem. Inst. Medicine, Nat. League for Nursing (pres. 1987-89), Sigma Theta Tau (sr. editor Image Jour. Nursing, 1st v.p. 1971-74, pres. 1975-81). Home: 7004 Riggs Rd Hyattsville MD 20783-2933 Office: Cath U Am Office Of Exec Vp Washington DC 20064-0001

DONLIN, STEPHANIE DARA KALISH, special education educator; b. Teaneck, NJ, Jan. 13, 1957; d. Jack Kalish and Ruth Kalish-Joseph; m. Kenneth Donlin, Aug. 8, 1982; children: Jana, Jared. AA, Mitchell Coll., 1977; BA, U. Hartford, 1979; MA, Ctrl. Conn. State U., 1982. Cert. spl. edn. tchr. Conn. Spl. edn. tchr. Dept. Mental Retardation, West Hartford, Conn., 1979—86; home day care provider Bristol, Conn., 1986—94; spl. edn. tutor Farmington (Conn.) HS, 1994—95; spl. edn. resource tchr. Woodstock Day Treatment, West Hartford, 1995—96; spl. edn. tchr. self-contained classroom Hartford Bd. Edn., 1996—. Mem. steering com. Hartford Bd. Edn., 1999—2000; religious sch. tchr. Beth Israel Temple, Bristol, 1995—96, Congregation B'Nai Sholom, Newington, Conn., 2000—01. Jewish. Avocations: plants, reading, drawing. Home: 399 Ivy Dr Bristol CT 06010

DONLON, CLAUDETTE, performing company executive; Gen. mgr. Am. Ballet Theatre, finance dir.; exec. v.p. Kennedy Center for the Performing Arts. Office: Kennedy Center for the Performing Arts 2700 F St NW Washington DC 20566

DONNALLY, PATRICIA BRODERICK, writer; b. Cheverly, Md., Mar. 11, 1955; d. James Duane and Olga Frances (Duenas) Broderick; m. Robert Andrew Donnally, Dec. 30, 1977; 1 child, Danielle Christine. BS, U. Md., 1977. Fashion editor The Washington Times, 1983-85, The San Francisco Chronicle, 1985-2000; sr. fashion and beauty editor eLuxury.com, 2000; mng. editor PaperCity mag., 2002—04; co-editor Washington Spaces mag., 2004—, editor-in-chief, 2005—. Recipient Atrium award U. Ga., 1984, 87-89, 90, 94-98, 99, Lulu award U. Ga., 1985, 87, award Am. Cancer Soc., 1991, Aldo award, U. Ga., 1994, George A. Hough III award, U. Ga., 1999. Avocation: travel. Office Phone: 703-992-1196. Business E-Mail: tdonnally@washingtonspaces.com.

DONNAN, ROXANNE MARIE, elementary school educator; b. Granite City, Ill., Aug. 29, 1965; d. Otis and Juanita Gault; m. Robert Mack Donnan, Sept. 2, 1995. M in Music Edn., Western Carolina U., Cullowhee, NC, 1989. Cert. tchr. SC, 1989. Tchr. Ellijay Mid. Sch., Ga., 1989—91, Corriher/Lipe Mid. Sch., Landis, NC, 1991—92, Ewing Jr. H.S., Gaffney, SC, 1992—93, St. Paul's Cath. Sch., Spartanburg, SC, 1993—97, Isothermal C.C., Spindale, NC, 1997—99, Spatanburg County Sch. Dist. Two, Spartanburg, SC, 1999—. Home: 682 Wildlife Rd Clinton SC 29325 Office Phone: 864-461-3900. Personal E-mail: rdonnan61@peoplepc.com.

DONNELL, CAROLYN FAYE, music educator; b. Dallas, Tex., Dec. 31, 1949; d. Theodore Sr. and Lena Mae Roberts; m. Larry Donnell, July 6, 1974; children: Larry, Chimeka, Carlena, Lanard. BS in Music, Tex. So. U., Houston, 1976; BS in Secondary Math., U. Tex., Dallas, 1986. Cert. tchr. music all levels Tex. Tchr. music Zumwalt Mid. Sch., Dallas, 1975—76, Boude Storey Mid. Sch., 1976—85, Umphrey Lee Elem. Sch., 1985—. Workshop coord. St. Paul Ch., Dallas, 2001—02. Named Tchr. of Yr., Umphrey Lee Elem. Sch., 1996—97, K104 Tchr. of Yr., Dallas, 2001—03. Mem.: Delta Sigma Theta. Office: Umphrey Lee Elem Sch 7808 Racine Dr Dallas TX 75232-4302

DONNELL, GAYLENE RENEE', special education educator; b. Witchita Falls, Tex., Jan. 14, 1965; d. William Thomas Donnell and Ruby Maxine Collins. MS in Edn., East Ctrl. U., 1999. Cert. educator Tex. Spl. edn. life skills tchr. Sherman (Tex.) I.S.D., 1999—2000; spl. edn. resource tchr. Tyler (Tex.) I.S.D., 2003—04. Lead tchr. Waco (Tex.) I.S.D., 2004—05. Active ch. mem. Crestview Ave. Ch. Christ, Waco, 2005—06. Mem.: Coun. Exceptional Children (assoc.). Office: Waco I S D 805 S 8th St Waco TX 76706 Office Phone: 254-757-3829.

DONNELL, REBEKAH JO, language educator, editor; b. Carrollton, Ga., Apr. 3, 1975; m. Brian Edward Donnell, Dec. 16, 2000; 1 child, Michael Thomas Xander. BA in English, U. West Ga., Carrollton, 1998, MA in English, 2000. Clear Renewable Certificate Ga., 2000. Grad. rsch. asst., writing ctr. tutor U. West Ga., 1998—2000; tchr. English grades 9-12 Crossroads Acad., Carrollton, 2000—. Freelance editor and revision specialist www.prosemaster.com, Carrollton, 2006—. Author: (article) Notes on Contemporary Literature 30.4; editor: (cookbook) Simpkins-Denney Heritage Cookbook and CD. Soloist Rocky Mt. Bapt. Ch., Carrollton, 1985—, asst. libr., 1995—2005, asst. choir dir., 2006—. Named Tchr. of Yr., Crossroads Acad. Mem.: Ga. Assn. Educators. Conservative. Christian. Office: Crossroads Academy 225 E College St Bowdon GA 30108 Office Phone: 770-258-4403. Personal E-mail: caiiiope932000@aol.com. Business E-Mail: rebekah.donnell@carrollcountyschools.com.

DONNELLY, BARBARA SCHETTLER, retired medical technologist; b. Sweetwater, Tenn., Dec. 2, 1933; d. Clarence G. and Irene Elizabeth (Brown) Schettler; children: Linda Ann, Richard Michael. AA, Tenn. Wesleyan Coll., 1952; BS, U. Tenn., 1954; cert. med. tech., Erlanger Hosp. Sch. Med. Tech., 1954; postgrad., So. Meth. U., 1980-81. Med. technologist Erlanger Hosp., Chattanooga, 1953-57, St. Luke's Episcopal Hosp., Tex. Med. Ctr., Houston, 1957-58, 62; engrng. R&D SCI Systems, Inc., Huntsville, Ala., 1974-76; cons. hematology systems Abbott Labs., Dallas, 1976-77; hematology specialist Dallas, Irving, Tex., 1977-81; tech. specialist microbiology systems Irving, Tex., 1981-83; coord. tech. svc. clin. chemistry systems, 1983-84; coord. customer tng. clin. chemistry systems, 1984-87; supr. clin. chemistry tech. svcs., 1987-88; supr. clin. chemistry customer support ctr., 1988-93; supr. clin. chemistry and x-systems customer support ctr., 1993-97; ret., 1997. Contbr. articles on cytology to profl. jours. Mem. Am. Soc. Clin. Pathologists (cert. med. technologist), Am. Soc. Microbiology, Nat. Assn. Female Execs., U. Tenn. Alumni Assn., Chi Omega. Republican. Methodist. Home: 204 Greenbriar Ln Colleyville TX 76034-8616

DONNELLY, LAURA JEAN, science educator; b. Orange, NJ, Feb. 19, 1955; d. Donald Wallace and Loretta Grace Callaway; m. Charles Francis Donnelly, May 24, 1980; children: Lauren Callaway, Charles Francis, Anne Marie, Rachel Jean. BS, U. NH, 1977; MBA, U. NH., 1980; MS, U. Bridgeport, 2000. Cert. profl. State Dept. Edn., Conn. Elem. tchr. New Canaan (Conn.) Pub. Schs., 2001—03; sci. tchr. Greenwich (Conn.) Pub. Schs., 2003—. Advt. exec. Ted Bates Advt., N.Y.C., 1980—90; wildlife biologist, NH, 1977—78. Educator New Canaan Congl. Ch., 2003—06; mem. Nat. Charity League, New Cannan. Mem.: Conn. Sci. Tchrs. Assn. (assoc.), Nat. Sci. Tchr. Assn. (assoc.), Phi Kappa Phi, Alpha Zeta. Independent. Achievements include elected to the electoral coll. for State of Conn. Avocations: swimming, reading, walking. Home: 59 Rural Dr New Canaan CT 06840 Office Phone: 203-637-1744.

DONNELLY, MAVIS J., psychiatrist; d. John Donnelly and Mabel Collins. BA, Princeton U., NJ, 1976; MD, U. Conn., Hartford, 1980. Psychiatrist pvt. practice, Tucson, 1984—; dir. women's program Tucson Psychiat. Inst., 1989—92, Sonora Hosp., 1992—93. Psychiat. expert witness, Tucson, 1990—. Author: The Women's Program, 1990, Dust on the Road, 2005. Pres. Tuscon Animal Assisted Psychotherapy Assocs., 1990—2000. Mem.: AMA, Am. Psychiat. Assn. Office: Gecko Southwest 5650 E 22d St Tucson AZ 85721

DONNELLY, ROSEMARIE, lawyer; b. Dallas, 1956; BA cum laude, Tex. A&M U., 1978; JD, U. Houston, 1988. Bar: Tex. 1988, admitted to practice: US Ct. Appeals (5th Cir.), US Dist. Ct. (No. Dist.) Tex., US Dist. Ct. (So. Dist.) Tex., US Dist. Ct. (Ea. Dist.) Tex., US Dist. Ct. (We. Dist.) Tex. With Andrews Kurth LLP, Houston, 1988—, ptnr., litig. dept. Contbr. articles to profl. jour. Mem.: State Bar Tex., Houston Bar Assn., Order of Barons. Office: Andrews Kurth LLP 600 Travis St Ste 4200 Houston TX 77002-3090 Office Phone: 713-220-4004. Office Fax: 713-238-7253. Business E-Mail: rdonnelly@andrewskurth.com.

DONNEM, SARAH LUND, financial analyst, non-profit consultant, political organization consultant; b. St. Louis, Apr. 10, 1936; d. Joel Y. and Erle Hall (Harsh) Lund; m. Roland W. Donnem, Feb. 18, 1961; children: Elizabeth Prince Donnem Sigety, Sarah Madison Ashe-Donnem. BA, Vassar Coll., 1958. Tech. aide, computer programmer Bell Labs, Whippany, N.J., 1959-60; chmn. placement vol. opportunities N.Y. Jr. League, 1972-73, asst. treas., 1974-75, chmn. urban problems relating to mental health, 1967-69, mem. project rsch. com., 1967-70, chmn., 1973-74, mem. bd. mgrs., 1973-74. Chmn. cmty. rsch. Washington Jr. League, 1970-71, mem. bd. mgrs., 1970-71; mem. Stratford Hall (N.Y.) Com., 1970—; bd. dirs. East Side Settlement House, Bronx, N.Y., 1972-2004, hon., 2005—, v.p., 1975-76, chmn. Nat. Horse Show Benefit, 1976, winter antiques show com., 1994—, co-chmn. adv. com., 1991-94, chmn. VIP Day, 1999—, mem. nominating com., 1990-2000, mem. investment com., 1993-2003, mem. fin. com., 2004-05; bd. dirs. Stanley M. Isaacs Neighborhood Ctr., N.Y.C., 1973-76, v.p., 1975-76; bd. dirs. Presbyn. Home for Aged Women, N.Y.C., 1974-76, v.p., 1976; mem. exec. bd. N.Y. Aux. of Blue Ridge Sch., 1971-75, sec. 1965-67, pres., 1973-75; budget and benevolence com. Brick Presbyn. Ch., N.Y.C., 1973-76, mem. social svc. com., 1973-74, chmn. fgn. students com., 1963-64; bd. dirs. Search and Care, N.Y.C., 1973--76, Project LEARN, Cleve., 1990-96, 2000—, trustee, 2000-06; chmn. Literacy Fund, 1991-95, mem., 1995—; mem. Friends of Project LEARN, 1986—, mem. Fedn. Cmty. Planning, Cleve., coun. on Older Persons, 1978-82, mem. future Planning task Force, 1980-81, commn. on social concerns, 1982-84; trustee Golden Age Ctrs. Greatr cleve., 1979-92, investment com., 1993, 1st v.p., 1980-81, pres. 1981-85, chmn. Western Res. Antiques show, 1979, 80; chmn. cleve. antiques Show Silver Anniv., 2000; mem. women's adv. coun. Westrn Res. Hist. Soc., 1977—, coord. sec., 1978; mem. women's com. Cleve. Orch., 1979-85, Vassar Coll. cleve. sec. 1980-82, v.p., 1983, pres. 1984-86, leadership gift chair 50th reunion; mem. AAVC Club Liaison com., 1986-89, chmn. regional program com., 1987-89; bd. dirs. Cleve. Ballet, 1980-2001, exec. com. 1981, fin. com. 1982-88, 95-98, nominating com., 1988-90, 95-2000, co-chmn. 1997-99; co-chmn. Yale Ball, 1983; bd. advisors Ret. Sr. Vol. Program, 1982, trustee, 1983-90, chmn. long range planning com., 1986, sec. 1987-89; mem. Family Friends Adv. Coun., 1987-89; trustee Fairmount Presbyn. Ch., 1985-88; mem. long range planning com. United Way, Cleve., 1985-87; coord. Friends of Voinovich, 1987-89; womens adv. com. Voinovich for Gov., 1990, Voinovich for Senate, 1997-98, chmn. Voinovich Task Force on Aging, 1990-91, Ohio Adv. Coun. on Aging, 1991-2002, legis. com., 1994-2000; chmn. legis. com. Cuyahoga County Rep. Party, 1994-2000, mem. policy com., mem. fin. com., 1999—, Plain Dealer adv. counsel for elderly coverage, 1991-93; chmn. Johns Hopkins Parents Fund, 1986-88, Project LEARN 15th Anniversary celebration (with Barbara Bush, hon. chmn.), 1989-90; coord. Decorative Arts Trust Cleve. Symposium, 1996; mem. Leadership Cleve. Class 1992; del. White House Conf. on Aging, 1995. Named Vol. of Yr. N.Y. Jr. League, 1975; recipient Sustainer Svc. award Jr. League Cleve., 1990. Mem. Nat. Inst. Social Scis. (membership com. 1972-92, trustee 1984-96), Nat. Soc. Colonial Dames, Colony Club (N.Y.C.), Chevy Chase Club (Washington), Intown club, Vassar Club, Kirtland Club (Cleve.), Historic Charleston Found. (hon. chmn. Internat. Antiques Show, 2004, 2005, 2006) Home (Summer): 2945 Fontenay Rd Shaker Heights OH 44120 Home (Winter): 1 King St Apt 307 Charleston SC 29401

DONNESON, SEENA SAND, artist; b. NYC; d. Max and Ann (Silber) Sand; children: Erika, Lisa. Student, Pratt Inst., Art Students League. Art staff NYU, Nassau County Office Cultural Devel., New Sch. for Social Rsch., N.H. Coll.; guest artist Tamarind Lithography Workshop; vis. artist Clayworks, N.Y.C. One-woman shows include Laruen Rogers Mus. Art, Laurel, Miss., Greenville (N.C.) Mus. Art, Galerie #836, Santa Fe, Lehigh U., Princeton U., Portland (Maine) Mus. Art, Piertrantonio Gallery, N.y.C., U. Calif., LI U., George Washington U., Danville (Va.) Mus. Fine Arts and History, others, exhibited in group shows at SUNY, N.Y.C., Quietude Sculpture Garden, N.J., A.F.A. Pier/92, N.Y.C., Sculpture in Color, Ft. Lauderdale (Fla.) Mus., Norfolk Mus. Arts and Scis., Bklyn. Mus., San Francisco Mus. Art, DeCordova Mus., Alternate Spac, Belgrade Lakes, Maine Mod Art Foundry, N.Y.C., USIS, Mcpl. Art Mus., Tokyo, various, Japan, Musseo de Belles Artes, Buenos Aires, Scotland, Represented in permanent collections Va. Mus. Fine Art, Bklyn. Mus., Doris Freidman Sculpture garden, Albright U., Reading, Pa., Norfolk Mus., USIA Art in Embassies, Los Angeles County Mus. Art, Mus. Modern Art, N.Y.C., Smithsonian Mus., Ft. Lauderdale Mus. Fine Art, Snug Harbor Cultural Ctr., N.Y.C., N.Y. Pub. Libr., Cornell Med. Sch., N.Y.C., others, pvt. collections; contbr. revs. to publs. Recipient numerous art awards; fellow, Edward MacDowell Found.; grantee, Mcpl. Art Soc., N.Y. Art in Pk., 1974, Queens Coun. Arts, 1992; Creative Artists Pub. Svc. grantee, N.Y. State Coun. Arts, 1983—84. Mem.: L.I.C. Artists (bd. dirs.), Nat. Assn. Women Artists (bd. dirs.), Artists Equity. Studio: 20 Sutton Pl S New York NY 10022 Home Fax: 212-753-4967. Personal E-mail: Elaici@aol.com.

DONOGHUE, JOAN E., lawyer; b. Yonkers, NY, Dec. 12, 1956; BA, U. Calif., Berkeley, 1978; JD, U. Calif., Santa Cruz, 1981. Bar: DC 1981. Assoc. Covington & Burling; dep. gen. counsel U.S. Dept. Treasury, Washington; various positions including dep. legal adv. U.S. Dept. State, Washington; assoc. gen. counsel Fed. Home Loan Mortgage Corp. (Freddie Mac), McLean, Va., 2001—04, sr. v.p., prin. dep. gen. counsel, 2004—05, sr. v.p., gen. counsel, 2005—. Adj. prof. Georgetown U.; vis. prof. U. Calif., coun. fgn. rels. internat. affairs fellow. Contbr. articles to profl. jours. Mem.: Am. Soc. Internat. Law (mem. exec. coun.), DC Bar Assn.

DONOGHUE, LINDA, nursing administrator, community health nurse; b. N.Y.C., Feb. 27, 1953; d. Raymond and Mary (McCormack) Carey; m. William Donoghue, June 7, 1975; children: William, Jamie. BSN, Villanova U., 1975; MPA, Am. Internat. Coll., Springfield, Mass., 1986. RN, Mass.; cert. nurse adminstr. cert. home health and hospice care exec. Assoc. dir. nurses Noble Hosp., Westfield, Mass.; adminstr. Tech. Aid Corp., Newton, Mass., 1988-92; exec. dir. Spectrum Home Health, Longmeadow, Mass., 1994—98; COO Jewish Geriat. Svcs., Longmeadow, 1998—. Chair bd. Home Care Risk Mgmt., 1996—99; mem. Instrnl. Conf. Coun., New Eng. Healthcare Assembly; mem. nurse practice adv. com. to Mass. Bd. Registration in Nursing, 1991—93, chair substance abuse task force, 1994—96; mem. adv. task force Home and Health Work Force, 1989—90, home and health care mem. coms., 1989—, others; coord. publ. of stds. of clin. practice in home health care; mem. profl. adv. bd. Bay Path Coll.; apptd. mem. bd. registration in nursing, 1996; vice chair NEHA, 1999—2001, BORN, 1999—2002; bd. dirs., exec. com. Ctr. for Human Devel., Springfield, Mass., 2003—; adj. faculty Sch. Nursing, U. Mass., Amherst. Mem. Am. Coll. Health Care Execs., Am. Soc. Healthcare Risk Mgrs., Nat. Assn. Home Care, Home and Health Care Assn. Mass. (Mgr. of Yr. award for excellence/leadership 1989), Mass. Pub. Health Assn., Villanova U. Nursing Alumni Assn., Sigma Theta Tau. Home: 414 Inverness Ln Longmeadow MA 01106-2826

DONOGHUE, LOUISE I., retired language educator; b. Plainfield, NJ, June 25, 1942; d. Robert Francis Irving and Antoinette Marie Del Vecchie; m. Peter Edward Donoghue, Oct. 29, 1966; children: Eric(dec.), Steven, John. BA, Montclair State Coll., Upper Montclair, NJ, 1964; MA in Latin, Rutgers U., New Brunswick, NJ, 1996. Cert. tchr. NJ. Tchr. Red Bank Regional Sch., 1964—68, Henry Hudson Regional Sch., Highlands, NJ, 1982—2004; ret., 2004. Soprano Highlands Cmty. Singers, 2002—; sec., mem. Shade Tree Commn., Atlantic Highlands, 2004—; tchr. Monmouth County Adult Literacy Program, 2005—06; editor newsletter Donkey Data Dem. Club Monmouth County, 1982—86; pres. Women's Dem. Club Monmouth County, 1984—86; councilwoman Atlantic Highlands Boro Coun., 2001; comitteewoman Boro Atlantic Highlands, 2002—; leader voter registration drives, Atlantic Highlands, NJ; soprano St. Agnes Adult Choir, 1991—. Mem.: Garden Club (v.p. 2006—). Roman Cath. Avocations: reading, gardening, boating, travel. Home: 49 Mount Ave Atlantic Highlands NJ 07716

DONOGHUE, MILDRED RANSDORF, education educator; b. Cleve. d. James and Caroline (Sychra) Ransdorf; m. Charles K. Donoghue (dec.); children: Kathleen, James. EdD, UCLA, 1962; JD, Western State U., 1979. Asst. prof. edn. and reading Calif. State U., Fullerton, 1962-66, assoc. prof., 1966-71, prof., 1971—. Founder, dir. Donoghue Children's Lit. Ctr., Calif. State U., Fullerton, Calif., 2001—. Author: Foreign Languages and the Schools, 1967, Foreign Languages and the Elementary School Child, 1968, The Child and the English Language Arts, 1971, 75, 79, 85, 90, Using Literature Activities to Teach Content Areas to Emergent Readers, 2001; co-author: Second Languages in Primary Education, 1979; contbr. articles to profl. jours. and Ednl. Resources Info. Ctr. U.S. Dept. Edn. Mem. AAUP, AAUW, Nat. Network for Early Lang. Learning, Nat. Coun. Tchrs. English, Nat. Coun. Tchrs. Math., Nat. Coun. Social Studies, Nat. Sci. Tchrs. Assn., Am. Ednl. Rsch. Assn., Nat. Soc. for Study of Edn., Internat. Reading Assn., Nat. Assn. Edn. Young Children, Assn. for Childhood Edn. Internat., Phi Beta Kappa, Phi Kappa Phi, Pi Lambda Theta, Alpha Upsilon Alpha. Address: Calif State U 800 State Coll Blvd Fullerton CA 92834

DONOHOE, CATHRYN MURRAY, journalist; b. Bronx, N.Y. d. Harry and Helen (Crowley) Murray; m. Thomas W. Donohoe. BA cum laude in Am. Lit., Middlebury Coll., 1958; student in Russian lit., Columbia U., 1958—60; student in journalism, American U., 1983—84; cert. in Russian Lang. and Culture, Gornyi Inst., St. Petersburg, Russia, 1993. Rsch. and policy coord. Radio Liberty, N.Y.C., 1963—74; freelance journalist, 1977—84; reporter Potomac Almanac, Potomac, Md., 1985, Washington Times, Washington, 1985—94, deputy editor, features, 1994—. Recipient Nat. Mag. award for pub. svc., 1985. Office: Washington Times 3600 New York Ave NE Washington DC 20002-1996

DONOHOE, VICTORIA, critic, art historian, researcher; b. Phila., Mar. 21, 1929; d. Daniel Joseph and Anne L. (O'Neill) Donohoe. BA, Rosemont Coll., Pa., 1950; MFA, Univ. Pa., Phila., 1952; student, Villa Schifanoia, Florence, Italy, 1952—53; PhD, Villanova Univ., Pa., 1985. Tchr. art history & art studio courses Liberal Arts Coll., Pa., 1950—52, Pa., 1954—55; profl. artist; regular art columnist weekly newspaper, Phila., 1959—62; art critic Phila. Inquirer Met. Newspaper, 1962—. Organizer art exhibits at mus. & galleries. Contbr. numerous anthologies to profl. jour. and encyclopedias. Vol. numerous com. Mem.: Internat. Assn. Art Critics, Lower Merion Conservacy, Lower Merion Hist. Soc., Athenaeum of Phila. Avocations: gardening, walking, public transportation, socializing. Home: 34 Narhook Pk Narberth PA 19072-2124

DONOHUE, ANNE EMLEN, software engineer; b. Rome, N.Y., Mar. 2, 1967; d. Warren Metz and Carol (Taylor) Emlen; m. Brian Patrick Donohue, Sept. 8, 1990; children: Taylor Mae, Catharine Ruth. BA in Computer Sci.,

SUNY, Geseseo, 1989; ME in Software Engring., U. Colo., 1997. Software engr. BDM Internat., Boulder, Colo., 1989-97, Lucent Techs., Westminster, Colo., 1997-99, Level 3 Comm., Broomfield, Colo., 1999—. Mem. IEEE (assoc.), High Pointers Club (Summit of the States). Avocations: greyhounds, hiking.

DONOHUE, CLAIRE P., retired school librarian; b. Glen Cove, NY, Mar. 6, 1941; d. Hubert Aloysius Donohue and Catherine Teresa Scarlett; m. John T. Sexton, Aug. 30, 1975 (div. Apr. 1, 1983). BA, St. John's U., Jamaica, NY, 1965, MA, 1967; MLS, L.I. U., 1974. Cert. secondary English tchr. NY, 1967, sch. libr. media specialist NY, 1974, sch. dist. adminstr. NY, 1995. Tchr. English St. Peter Alcantara Sch., Port Washington, NY, 1966—68; dir. libr. media St. Agnes Acad. H.S., College Point, NY, 1969—77; libr. media specialist Bethpage Union Free Sch. Dist., NY, 1977—91, chair libr. media, 1991—2003; ret., 2003. Adj. instr. N.Y.C. Tech. Coll., Bklyn., 1975—79, Palmer Sch. L.I. U., Greenvale, NY, 1991—95; acting interim dir. Nassau BOCES Sch. Libr. Sys., Massapequa, NY, 2003. Mem.: ALA, Nassau Sch. Libr. Sys. Adv. Coun. (chair 1992—94), L.I. Sch. Media Assn. (bd. mem. 1991—93), N.Y. Libr. Assn. Home: 15 Tojan Dr East Islip NY 11730 Personal E-mail: clairedonohue@optonline.net.

DONOHUE, DIANE FRANCES, artist; b. Waterbury, Conn., Aug. 14, 1946; d. John Magee and Fannie Ada (Dawes) D. Student, New Haven & Hartford Bus. Sch., 1966, New Haven Acad. Bus., 1970, Yale U., 1981, Naugatuck Valley C.C., Waterbury, Conn., 1993-95. From data entry supr. to sys. coord. Data Pack, Inc., Waterbury, 1970-72; from computer operator to programmer Litchfield Farms Shops, Middlebury & Waterbury, 1973-74; from data entry I, II to programm/analyst list State of Conn., Hartford, 1975-77; from programmer to programmer/analyst Ind. Software Consulting, Conn., 1978-82; real estate developer, investor, founder Fanjack Properties, Waterbury, 1982-90; fine artist Artists Attic, Waterbury, 1996—. Cons. artist to student tchr. Western Conn. State U., Danbury, 1972; lectr. Naugatuck Valley Cmty.-Tech. Coll., Waterbury, 1996; restoration artist for pvt. collector, 1996. One-woman show Naugatuck Valley Cmty.-Tech. Coll., 1994; exhibited at Berkshire Mus., Pittsfield, Mass., 1973, others; represented in pvt. collections. Vol. Women's Nat. Polit. Caucus for candidate, Prospect, Conn., 1996, working with elderly and disabled. Recipient 1st pl. ribbon Guilford Fair, Conn., March of Dimes Show, Waterbury, Conn.; hon. mention Bethlehem Fair, Conn., Berkshire Mus., others. Mem. Nat. Mus. Women in the Arts, LWV. Democrat. Roman Catholic. Achievements include writing definitive letters that changed laws for disabled. Avocations: horses, swimming, reading, art, writing. Home and Office: 22 Green Manor Thomaston CT 06787 Office Phone: 860-283-5889.

DONOHUE, EDITH M., human resources specialist, educator; b. Nov. 10, 1938; d. Edward Anthony and Beatrice (Jones) McParland; m. Salvatore R. Donohue, Aug. 23, 1960; children: Kathleen, Deborah. BA, Coll. Notre Dame, Balt., 1960; MS, Johns Hopkins U., 1981; postgrad., CASE (cert. adv. study edn.), 1985; PhD in Human Resources, CASE, 1990. Cert. counselor, national, sr. profl. human resources. Dir. pub. rels. Coll. Notre Dame, Balt., 1970—71, dir. continuing edn., 1981—86; program coord. bus. and industry Catonsville C.C., Balt. County, Md., 1986—88; mgr. tng. and devel. Sheppard Pratt Hosp., Balt., 1988—90; assoc. prof., Sch. Edn. Barry U., 1993—98; cons. in human resources Stuart, Fla., 1985—. Adj. faculty Loyola Coll. Grad. Studies Program, Fla. Inst. Tech., Indian River C. of C. Co-author: Communicate Like a Manager, 1989, Life After Layoff, 2003; contbg. author career devel. workshop manual, 1985; contbr. articles to profl. jours. Pres. Cathedral Sch. Parents Assn., 1972-74; asst. treas., treas. Md. Gen. Hosp. Aux., 1975-78; dir. sect. Exec. Women's Network, Balt., 1983-85; adv. bd. Mayor's Commn. on Aging, 1981-86; bd. dirs. Md. Assn. Higher Edn., 1985-88; vol. trainer United Way Martin County, co-chair campaign, 1994—, strategic planning com., 1998—, bd. dirs., 2004—; steering com. Chautaugua South. Recipient Mayor's Citation, City of Balt. Council, 1985, Woman of Distinction, Martin County, 1999 Mem. AAUW (dir., v.p. 1980-83),, Am. Assn. Tng. and Devel. (bd. dirs.), Am. Counseling Assn., Soc. Human Resources Mgmt., Martin County Personnel Mgt. Assn. (edn. chmn. 1991-94), Martin County Libr. Assn. Inc. (pres. 2001-2003), Martin County C. of C. (edn. com. 1991-94), Friends of Lyric (bd. dirs. chmn., strategic planning, pres.), United Way of Martin County Found. (bd. dirs. 2003—), Martin Meml. Health System (patient safety comr. 2003-), Chi Sigma Iota (pres.), Phi Delta Kappa. Republican. Roman Cath. Avocations: tennis, performing arts, reading, wellness. Home: Apt 3103 144 NE Edgewater Dr Stuart FL 34996-4477 E-mail: edonohue@gate.net.

DONOHUE, JOYCE MORRISSEY, biochemist, toxicologist, dietician, educator; b. Holyoke, Mass., Jan. 27, 1940; d. Richard Charles and Anna Elizabeth (Joyce) Morrissey; m. John Thomas Donohue, Jan. 27, 1973; children: Maura Joyce, John Thomas, Sean Richard, Eric Patrick. BS, Framingham State Coll., Mass., 1961; MS, U. Mass., 1964; PhD, U. NH, 1972. Cert. secondary sch. tchr., Mass.; registered dietitian. Tchr. West Springfield (Mass.) H.S., 1962—66; instr. Framingham State Coll., 1966—68, asst. prof. biochemistry and nutrition, 1971—72, assoc. prof., 1972—73; adj. prof. No. Va. C.C., Annandale, 1974—, Va. Poly. Inst. and State U., Falls Church, 1979—97; health scientist VJ Cicconi & Assocs., Woodbridge, Va., 1981—89; toxicology svc. mgr. Law Environ. Washington Svc. Ctr., Woodbridge, 1989—90; program mgr., toxicologist ICAIR/Life Sys. Inc., Arlington, Va., 1990—94; mgr. toxicology NSF Internat., Washington, 1994—96; lead environ. protection specialist, Office of Water U.S. EPA, Washington, 1996—. Mem. Prince William County Wetlands Bd., 1989—; mem. dietetics program adv. com. James Madison U., Va., 1997—. Recipient Alumni Achievement award, Framingham State Coll., 1986. Mem. AAAS, Am. Dietetic Assn. (cert.), No. Va. Dietetic Assn., Sigma Xi. Home: 11979 William And Mary Cir Woodbridge VA 22192-1314 Office: USEPA 1200 Pennsylvania Ave NW Mail Code 4304T Washington DC 20460 Business E-Mail: donohue.joyce@epa.gov.

DONOHUE, MARY, lieutenant governor; b. Rensselaer County, N.Y. children: Sara, Justin. B.Edn., Coll. New Rochelle, 1968; MS in Edn., Russell Sage Coll., Troy, N.Y., 1973; JD, Union U., 1983. Bar: NY 1983. Tchr. elem., jr. h.s. Rensselaer and Albany County (N.Y.) sch. dists., Albany, 1969-78; law clk., intern U.S. Atty.'s Office, Albany, 1980-83; assoc. O'Connell & Aronowitz, Albany, 1983-88; pvt. practice Troy, 1988-92; asst. county atty. Rensselaer County, 1990-92, dist. atty., 1992-96; justice N.Y. Supreme Ct., 3rd Jud. Dist., 1996-98; lt. gov. State of N.Y., Albany, 1998—. Chair Govs. Task Force on Sch. Violence, 1999—, Task Force on Quality Cmtys., 2000—, Govs. Task Force on Sexual Abuse; chair Capital Dist. Women's Adv. Coun., 1996; mem. Gov.-elect Pataki's Transition Team for Criminal Justice, 1994-96. Republican. Office: Office of Lt Governor State Capitol Rm 246 Albany NY 12224 Office Phone: 518-486-4101. Office Fax: 518-486-4170.*

DONOHUE, PATRICIA CAROL, academic administrator; b. St. Louis, Jan. 11, 1946; d. Carroll and Juanita Donohue; m. James H. Stevens Jr., Aug. 27, 1966 (div. Mar. 1984); children: James H. Stevens III, Carol Janet Stevens. AB, Duke U., 1966; MA, U. Mo., 1974, PhD, 1982. Tchr. math. in secondary schs., Balt., St. Louis and Shawnee Mission, Kans., 1966-71; lectr. U. Mo., Kansas City, 1975-76, rsch. asst. affirmative action, 1976-79, coord. affirmative action, 1979-82, instl. rsch. assoc., 1982-84, acting dir. affirmative action and acad. pers., 1984; dir. instl. rsch. Lakeland C.C., 1984-86; asst. dean acad. affairs, math., engring. and tech. Harrisburg Area C.C., 1986-89, dean sch. bus., engring., and tech., 1989-93, dean Lebanon campus, v.p. cmty. devel. and external affairs, 1993; vice chancellor edn. St. Louis C.C., 1993—2002, acting pres. Florissant Valley campus, 1998-99; pres. Luzerne County C.C., 2002—. Active Pa. Coun. on Vocat. Edn., 1989—93; v.p. St. Louis Sch. to Work, Inc., 1994—96, pres., 1996—2002; chairperson Pa. Occupl. Deans, 1988—93; bd. dirs., chmn. edn. com. Humane Soc. Mo., 1997—2002; cons. evaluator North Ctrl. Assn., 2000—; bd. dirs. Greater Wilkes-Barre Chamber Bus. and Industry, Pa., The Luzerne Found., F.M. Kirby Ctr., Northeastern Pa. Tech. Inst., pres., 2004—05. Bd. dirs., v.p. Am. Cancer Soc. Jackson County, 1975—84; mem. adv. coun. Ben Franklin Partnership, 1988—93; mem. steering com. New Baldwin Corridor Coalition, 1991—93, chair edn. task force, 1992—93; mem. Leadership St. Louis, 1996—97; mem. strategic planning com. Penns Woods Girl Scout Coun., 2003—04, bd. dirs., 2004—; chair pers. com. Penns Woods Girl Scouts Coun., 2005—; bd. dirs. PTA, 1975—77, Cmty. Lebanon Assocs., Ctrl. Pa. Tech. Coun., 1989—93, sec., 1992—93; bd. dirs. Mantec, 1988—93, Delta Gamma Ctr. for Children with Visual Impairments, 2001—03, Osterhout Libr., 2003—, Hemlock coun. Girl Scouts U.S.A., 1987—92. Recipient Outstanding Service and Achievement award U. Mo. Kansas City, 1976, Outstanding Svc. award Ctrl. Pa. Tech. Coun., 1993; Jack C. Coffey grantee, 1978; named Outstanding Woman AAUW, 1989, one of Outstanding Leaders Nat. Inst. Leadership Devel., 1986, Exec. Leadership Inst., 1990, Exec. Leadership Wilkes Barre, 2003, Exec. Leadership Lackawanna, 2004, Cmty. Woman of Yr. Wilkes-Barre, Am. Bus. Women Assn., 2005, Athena award Wilkes-Barre Chamber Bus. and Industry, 2006 Mem.: Assn. Comm. Coll. Trustees (pres. adv. bd. 2005—), Assn. Inst. Rsch., Women's Network, Nat. Assn. Student Pers. Adminstrs., Women's Equity Project, Soc. Mfg. Engrs. (chmn. 1989—90), Am. Assn. Women in Cmty. and Jr. Colls. (Pa. state coord. 1988, bd. dirs. Region 3 1989—91, 2005—06, pres. elect 2006—), Nat. Coun. for Occupl. Edn. (chairperson diversity task force 1991, chairperson job tng. 2000 task force 1992, v.p. programs 1992—93, bd. dirs. 1992—2000, v.p. membership 1993—94, pres. 1995—96, past pres. 1996—97), Am. Assn. Cmty. Colls. (bd. dirs. 1988—91, coun. affiliated chairpersons 1994—2000, commn. on cmty. and workforce devel. 1995—97, chairperson coun. 1996—2000, commn. on cmty. and workforce devel. 1998—2001, acad. pres. 2003—, mem. com. diversity 2006—), Am. Vocat. Assn., Math. Assn. Am., Nat. Coun. Tchrs. of Math., ASCD, Delta Gamma (v.p., del. nat. conv. 1988, pres. 1989-91, bd. dirs. Delta Gamma Ctr. for Children with Visual Impairment 2001-) (del. nat. conv. 1988, pres. 1989—91, v.p., Cream Rose Outstanding Svc. award 1970), Pi Lambda Theta, Phi Kappa Phi, Phi Delta Kappa (pres. 1975, Read fellow 1989). Home: 40 Elmcrest Dr Dallas PA 18612 Office: Luzerne County C C 1333 S Prospect St Nanticoke PA 18634 Office Phone: 570-740-0388. Business E-Mail: pdonohue@luzerne.edu.

DONOHUE, THERESE BRADY, artistic director, choreographer, costume and set designer; b. Wash., Jan. 13, 1937; d. John Bernard and Mary Catherine (Rupert) B.; m. Joseph W. Donohue Jr., June 13, 1959 (div. 1987); children: Sharon Marie, Maura Cathleen (dec.), Sheila Patricia. BA, Coll. of Notre Dame Md., 1958. Cert. tchr. ballet Royal Acad. Dance London. Advt. artist Kronstadt Advt. Agy., Washington, 1958; instr. art The Maret Sch., Washington, 1958-60, Princeton U., NJ, 1967-71; artist dir. Amherst Ballet Centre, Mass., 1971—99, Amherst Ballet Theatre Co., Mass., 1977—2000. Co-dir., founder Pioneer Valley Ballet, Northampton, 1972—77; dancer, tchr. Princeton Ballet, 1962—71; animal masks Charleston (SC) Ballet, 1985—90; choreographer Roanoke (Va.) Ballet theatre, 1983; chair NE Region Craft Choreography Conf., Amherst, 1979; artist, choreographer Nat. Gallery Art, 1986, 88, Guggenheim, 1986, Nat. Mus. Am. Art, 1969, Hirshhorn Mus. and Sculpture Garden, 1993; sch. adminstr. Amherst Ballet, 1999—2004; artist-in-residency programs based on works of Eric Carle, 2006—; artist in-res. Greenwood Elem. Sch., Brookville, Md., 2006. Choreographer (ballets for children) Peter & the Wolf, 1973, One Thousand Cranes, 1974, Punch & Judy, 1975, Amherst Poets, 1977, Uncle Wiggily & the Duck Pond, 1979, (Springfield Symphony) History of Dance, 1983, (Project Opera) Hansel & Gretel, 1983, Sea Study (included in Aberdeen Internat. Youth Festival in Scotland), 1994, Peter Pan Amherst Cmty. Theater, 1995, Aida Commonwealth Opera, 1996, Flower Fairy Ballet, 1997, Ribbon Festival Ballet, 1997; rechoregraphed Matisse's Circus, Dancing with Dubuffet; toured Maui Hawaii Elem. Schs. (Amherst Ballet Theatre Co.), 1996; spl. projects dir. Amherst Ballet, 2003-05; prodr., costumer Eric Carle's The Very Lonely Firefly, 2003, Russian Nat. Dances, 2003, Eric Carle's The Honeybee and the Robber, 2004, The Eric Carle Museum of Picture Book Art; costumer Amherst Ballet's Shim Chung, 2005; ind. prodr.: (puppets and dance) Eric Carle's A House for the Hermit Crab, 2006. Mem. Amherst Arts Coun., 1983-89. Recipient Town of Amherst Arts and Supplemental Edn. award, 1997, Mass. Senate Citation, 2002, C.C. Dakin Medallion award in edn., 2002. Mem. Amherst Club. Avocation: travel. Home and Office: 17 Juniper Ln Amherst MA 01002-1227 Business E-Mail: tbd@crocker.com.

DONOHUE-SMITH, MAUREEN A., medical educator; d. Charles John Donohue and Mary Margaret Griffin; m. Joseph Rounds Smith, May 30, 1984; children: Jonathan Griffin-Smith, Mary Griffin-Smith. BA in English Lit., Pa. State U., State College, 1968; BSN, U. Pa., Phila., 1975; MS, U. Colo., Denver, 1977; PhD, Cornell U., Ithaca, N.Y., 1989. RN N.Y. Psychiat. nurse Mt. Airy Psychiat. Found., Denver, 1976—77; psychiat. nurse psychiat. emergency svc. Denver Gen. Hosp., 1977—78; asst. head nurse Bethesda Psychiat. Found., Denver, 1978—79; instr. Peter Bent Brigham Hosp. Sch. Nursing, Boston, 1979—80; psychiat. nurse Tompkins Cmty. Hosp., Ithaca, 1980—88; instr. psychiat. and mental health nursing Elmira Coll., NY, 1985—88; clin. cons. to nursing svc. Willard Psychiat. Ctr., NY, 1987—88, psychiat. clin. nurse specialist, 1988—90; ext. assoc. IV Family Life Devel. Ctr. Cornell U., Ithaca, 1990—93; rsch. assoc. dept. psychiatry SUNY Health Sci. Ctr., Syracuse Coll. Medicine, 1993—94; asst. prof. Elmira Coll., 1994—. Presenter, and workshop condr. in field. Contbr. articles to profl. jours.; author: Breaker Boy: 1905, 2001 (Catherine Connelly Award for Best in Show poetry contest, 2001). Mem.: Soc. for Rsch. on Child Devel., Am. Psychol. Soc., Sigma Theta Tau.

DONOVAN, ANN BURCHAM, medical office administrator; m. Gary Leonard Donovan, (div. June 1988); children: Leonard Matthew, William Marshall. Student, Baker U., 1970-71; Cert., Kansas City Sch. Med. Assts., 1973. Cert. med. practice exec. Med. asst. Penn Valley Med. Group, Kansas City, Mo., 1973-76, supr. accounts receivable, 1976-82; office adminstr. Heartland Hematology-Oncology Assn., Inc., Kansas City, Mo., 1982—. Cons. on cancer and AIDS patients for med. offices, Kansas City, Mo., 1982-1998 Contbr. articles to profl. jours. Mem. NAFE, Northland Med. Mgrs. Assn., Med. Group Mgrs. Assn., Adminstrs. of Oncology-Hematology Assn., Greater Kansas City Med. Mgrs. Assn. (recognition com.), Kansas City Sci. Fiction and Fantasy Soc. Avocations: painting, horseback riding, fishing, travel. Office: Heartland Hematology Oncology Assn Inc 2000 NE Vivion Rd Kansas City MO 64118-6127

DONOVAN, ANNE, professional basketball coach; b. Ridgewood, N.J., Nov. 1, 1961; Asst. coach Old Dominion U.; head coach women's basketball E. Carolina U., Greenville, 1995-98; head coach Phila. Rage, 1998-99, Indiana Fever, Indianapolis, 1999—. Recipient Naismith Player of Yr. award, 1983, Olympic Team Gold medal, 1984, 88, World Championship Team Gold medal, 1986. Mem. USA Basketball Com. (exec. bd. dirs. 1996—). Achievements include Three time All-Am. selection; led nation in rebounding, 1982; all-time leading scorer, blocker and rebounder Old Dominion Univ.; Olympian, 1980, 84, 88; World Championship team, 1983, 86.

DONOVAN, DIANNE FRANCYS, journalist; b. Houston, Sept. 30, 1948; d. James Henry and Doris Elaine (Simerly) D.; m. Anthony Charles Burba; children: Donovan Anthony, James Donovan. Student, Trinity Coll., Dublin, Ireland, 1969; BA, Spring Hill Coll., 1970; MA, U. Mo., 1975, U. Chgo., 1982. Fgn./nat. copy desk supr. Chgo. Tribune, 1979-80, asst. editor for news/features, 1980-83, lit. editor, 1985-93, mem. editl. bd., 1993-99, sr. editor for recruitment, 2000—02; v.p., editl. page editor The Balt. Sun, 2002—. Vis. prof. U. Oreg. Sch. Journalism, Eugene, 1983-85; adj. faculty Northwestern U. Sch. Journalism, 1980-81, 89-90; bd. dirs. Chgo. Tribune Found. Bd. dirs. Nelson Algren/Heartland lit. awards, Chgo., 1986-93; judge Nat. Headliners' Club Awards, Atlantic City, N.J., 1983. Recipient award for editl. writing Am. Soc. Newspaper Editors, 1999, Media award Chgo. Bar Assn., 1999. Episcopalian. Office: 501 N Calvert St Baltimore MD 21278

DONOVAN, GERALDINE ELLEN, sister; b. Utica, NY, July 28, 1936; d. Gerald Francis and Anne Cecelia (O'Hare) Donovan. BSN, Barry Coll., Miami Shores, Fla., 1960; MS in Nursing Edn. Adminstrn., Boston U., 1967, PhD in Sociology, 1972. RN Fla.; joined Franciscan Sisters of Allegany. Adj. prof., asst. to academic dean Christ the King Sem., East Aurora, NY, 1973—78; adminstr.v. resident, adminstrv. asst. St. Francis Hosp., Miami Beach, Fla., 1978—81; asst. formation directress Franciscan Sisters of Allegany, NY, 1981—83, congregation archivist, 1994—2001, congregation historian, 2001—, v.p. mission and planning St. Petersburg, Fla., 1983—88, v.p. ethics, 1988—90. Trustee, membership corp. St. Francis Hosp., Miami Beach, 1979—85, St. Mary Hosp., West Palm Beach, Fla., 1980—83, St. Anthony Hosp., St. Petersburg, 1981—83. Roman Catholic. Avocations: music, outer space, reading, poetry, singing. Home: St Elizabeth Motherhouse 115 E Main ST Allegany NY 14706-1396 Office: Franciscan Sisters of Allegany PO Box W Saint Bonaventure NY 14778

DONOVAN, HELEN W., newspaper editor; Graduated from, Mount Holyoke Coll., 1969. Exec. editor Boston Globe, 1993—. Adv. bd., Nat. Arts Journalism Program. Office: The Boston Globe PO Box 55819 Boston MA 02205-5819

DONOVAN, KIERSTON FOLEY, science educator; d. Joseph and Mary Foley; m. Sean Donovan, May 20, 2000; 1 child, Joseph. BS in Biology, Tufts U., Medford, Mass., 2000. Cert. life sci. tchr. grades 7-12 Maine Dept. Edn., 2005, phys. sci. tchr. grades 7-12 Maine Dept. Edn., 2005. Sci. tchr. Maine Sch Adminstrn. Dist., Presque Isle, Maine, 2001—. Drama tech. dir. MSAD 1, 2004—. Democrat. Avocations: cooking, exercise, dog training.

DONOVAN, MAUREEN DRISCOLL, lawyer; b. N.Y.C., Dec. 2, 1940; d. Bartholomew and Josephine (Keohane) Driscoll. AB, Coll. of New Rochelle, 1962; LLB with honors, Fordham U., 1966. Bar: N.Y. 1966, U.S. Supreme Ct. 1971, U.S. Ct. Appeals (2d cir.) 1975, U.S. Dist. Ct. (so. dist.) N.Y. 1976. Assoc. White & Case LLP, N.Y.C., 1966-75, ptnr., 1975—. Trustee N.Y. Urban Coalition, N.Y.C., 1990—94, St. Barnabas Hosp., Bronx, NY, 1992—, chair fin. com., 1997—, vice chair bd., 1998—. Mem.: ABA, Englewood (N.J.) Field Club, Coral Beach Club (Paget, Bermuda), Princeton Club (N.Y.). Office: White & Case LLP 1155 Avenue of the Americas New York NY 10036-2787 Office Phone: 212-819-8557. E-mail: mdonovan@whitecase.com.

DONOVAN, SHARON ANN, retired secondary school educator; b. Balt., Feb. 17, 1944; d. Jesse F. and Ruth Elizabeth (Keller) D. BA, U. Md., Balt., 1969. Cert. profl. tchr. Assoc. Coppin-Hopkins Humanities Program, Balt., 1986-91; asst. dean arts and humanities UMBC, Catonsville, Md., 1973-76; asst. to dean fine arts Towson (Md.) State U., 1977-85; tchr. Balt. City Schs., 1986—2005, ret., 2005. Contbr. articles to publs.; founding mem., bd. dirs. The Feminist Press; founder "Herstory" MS Mag., 1976. Grantee Fund for Endl. Excellence. Mem. NCTE, MCTELA, Md. State Conf. on Women's Studies (chairperson, Tchr. of Yr. 1994, 95). Home: 2039 E Lombard St Baltimore MD 21231-1924

DONOVAN, VICKI ANN, elementary school teacher; m. Jack W. Donovan, 1986; children: Brett Cameron, Marissa Leigh (twins). AA in Math. and Sci., Cape Cod (Mass.) C.C., 1979; BS in Elem. and Spl. Edn., Fitchburg (Mass.) State Coll., 1981; MEd in Curriculum and Instrn., Lesley Coll., 1996. 3d grade tchr. Mashpee (Mass.) Elem. Sch., 1982-83; chpt. 1 tchr. Ezra Baker Elem. Sch., Dennis, Mass., 1983-85, 1st grade tchr., 1985-86; 2d grade tchr. Paul Smith Elem. Sch., Franklin, N.H., 1986-87; 5th grade tchr. Belmont (N.H.) Elem. Sch., 1987-94, 4th grade tchr., 1994—. Methods I tchg. mentor, Plymouth State Coll., 1991, 92, 95, 96, 97, 98, student tchr. mentor, 1996, workshop presenter, Math. 1987, Multiple Intelligence's 1998; yearbook advisor Belmont Elem. Sch., 1987—; mem. lang arts curriculum com., 1994—, health fair com., 1997—. Mem. Belmont (N.H.) Civic Pride Orgn., 1993. Belmont Youth and Edn. Com., 1995, Govt. Study Com., 1996; mem. Shaker Regional Edn. com., 1997. Recipient Acad. of Applied Sci. and Ctrl. N.H. Ednl. Collaborative award. 1993; named Outstanding Young Citizen, New Hampshire C. of C., 1998, N.H. Tchr. of Yr., 1998. Mem. NEA (negotiation com. 1988-89). ASCD. Office: Belmont Elem Sch 96 Gilmanton Rd Belmont NH 03220-4220

DONZELL, TARA ELIZABETH, secondary school educator; b. Cadillac, Mich., Dec. 2, 1980; d. Tony Eugene Leggett and Kimberly Sue Wilkinson; m. Christopher Michael Donzell, June 8, 2002; children: Michael Gregory Lowe, Harmony Elizabeth. AA, Northwestern Mich. Coll., Traverse City, 2002; BS in Edn., Ferris State U., Big Rapids, Mich., 2004. Cert. tchr. Mich. English tchr. Cadillac Area Pub. Schs., 2004—. Democrat. Avocations: photography, decorating.

DOODY, BARBARA PETTETT, computer specialist; b. Cin., Sept. 18, 1938; d. Philip Wayne and Virginia Bird (Handley) P.; 1 child, Daniel Frederick Reasor Jr. Attended Sinclair Coll., Tulane U., 1973-74. Owner, mgr. Honeysuckle Pet Shop, Tipp City, Ohio, 1970-76; office mgr. Doody & Doody, CPAs, New Orleans, 1976-77, computer ops. mgr., 1979—; office mgr. San Diego Yacht Club, 1977-79. Owner Hope Chest Linens, Ltd., 1994—2002. Mem. DAR, UDC, Jamestown Soc., Magna Charta, So. Dames, Colonial Dames of 17th Century, Nat. Soc. Daus. of 1812, Daus. Am. Colonists, Dames Ct. Honor, Colonial Order of the Crown, Societe Huguenot Nouvelle-Orleans, Huguenot Soc. Manakin, Soc. Knights of the Garter, Americans of Royal Descent, Plantaget Soc. Republican. Lutheran. Home: 36 Cypress Rd Covington LA 70433-4306 Office Phone: 485-867-5314. E-mail: bdoody@bellsouth.net.

DOODY, MARGARET ANNE, English language educator; b. St. John, N.B., Can., Sept. 21, 1939; came to U.S., 1976; d. Hubert and Anne Ruth (Cornwall) D. BA, Dalhousie U., 1960; BA with 1st class hons., Lady Margaret Hall-Oxford U., 1962, MA, 1965, D.Phil., 1968; LLD (hon.), Dalhousie U., 1985. Instr. English U. Victoria, B.C., Canada, 1962—64, asst. prof. English, 1968—69; lectr. U. Coll. Swansea, Wales, 1969—76; assoc. prof. English U. Calif.-Berkeley, 1976—80; prof. English dept. Princeton U., NJ, 1980—89; Andrew W. Mellon prof. humanities, prof. English Vanderbilt U., Nashville, 1989—99, dir. comparative lit. program, 1992—99; John and Barbara Glyn Family prof. lit. U. Notre Dame, 2000—, dir. PhD in Lit. program, 2001—. Author: A Natural Passion: A Study of the Novels of Samuel Richardson, 1974, The Daring Muse: Augustan Poetry Reconsidered, 1985, Frances Burney: The Life in the Works, 1988, The True Story of the Novel, 1996, (novels) Aristotle Detective, 1978, The Alchemists, 1980, Aristotle e la giustizia poetica, 2000, Aristotle and Poetic Justice, 2002, Poison in Athens, 2004, Mysteries of Eleusis, 2005; author: (with F. Stuber) (play) Clarissa, 1984; editor (with Peter Sabor): Samuel Richardson Tercentenary Essays, 1989; co-editor (with Douglas Murray): Catharine and Other Writings by Jane Austen, 1993; co-editor: (with Wendy Barry and Mary Doody Jones) Anne of Green Gables, 1997. Guggenheim postdoctoral fellow, 1979; recipient Rose Mary Crawshay award Brit. Acad., 1986. Episcopalian. Office: U Notre Dame PhD in Literature Program Notre Dame IN 46556 Office Phone: 574-631-0465. Business E-Mail: mdoody@nd.edu.

DOOLAN, WENDY, professional golfer; b. Sydney, Australia, Dec. 16, 1968; Winner LPGA Champions Classic, 2001, Welch's/Fry's Championships, 2003, Evian Masters, 2004. Competed Futures Tour, Women Profl. Golfers' European Tour, 1992—95, Asian Ladies Tour, 1993—95; rep. Australia seven times internat.; runner-up British Amateur Championships, 1991. Avocations: swimming, tennis. Office: c/o LPGA 100 International Golf Dr Daytona Beach FL 32124-1092

DOOLEY, ANN ELIZABETH, freelance writers cooperative executive, editor; b. Mpls., Feb. 19, 1952; d. Merlyn James and Susan Marie (Hinze) Dooley; m. John M. Dodge, May 8, 1983; children: Christopher Dooley Dodge, Kathryn Dooley Dodge. BA in Journalism, U. Wis., 1974. Free-lance journalist, 1974-75; photo editor C.W. Communications, Newton, Mass., 1975-77, writer, photographer, 1977-79; editor Computerworld O A, Framingham, Mass., 1979-83; editorial dir. Computerworld Focus, Framingham, 1983-92; pres. freelance writers coop. Dooley & Assocs., West

Newbury, Mass., 1992—. Speaker, chmn. mem. editorial adv. bd. various computer confs. Mem. Pub. Relations Soc. Am., Women in Communications (sec. 1982-84). Democrat. Home and Office: 1 Old Parish Way West Newbury MA 01985-1222

DOOLEY, KATHLEEN ANN, elementary school educator; d. Raymond and June Dooley. BA in Edn., We. Wash. U., Bellingham, Wash., 1974; MEd, U. Idaho, Moscow, 1983. Cert. tchr. K-12 Wash., 1974. Tchr. grades 9-12, head coach volleyball, gymnastics and softball Renton H.S., Wash., 1977—91. Healthy sch. leadership project Comprehensive Health Edn. Found., Seattle, 2000—. Site coun. mem. Kulshan Mid. Sch., Bellingham, Wash., 1993—99. Named Wash. State Softball Coach of Yr.; recipient Tchr. Leadership Project grantee, NW ESD 189, 2003. Mem.: Nat. C. Sci. Partnerships (assoc.; tchr. leader 2006—). Avocations: guitar, art, volleyball, badminton. Office: Kulshan Middle School 1250 Kenoyer Dr Bellingham WA 98229 Office Phone: 360-676-4886. Office Fax: 360-647-6892. Business E-Mail: kdooley@bham.wednet.edu.

DOOLEY, SHARON L., obstetrician, gynecologist; b. 1947; MD, U. Va. Mem. faculty Prentice Womens Hosp. Med. Sch. Northwestern U., Chgo., prof., dir. graduate med. edn. Office: Northwestern U Med Sch Prentice Womens Hosp 333 E Superior St Ste 410 Chicago IL 60611-3015

DOOLEY, WENDY BROOKE, vocalist, music educator, administrative assistant; b. Paragould, Ark., Apr. 7, 1976; d. Garry Don and Nina Doris Dooley. MusB, U. Ctrl. Ark., 1999. Lic. tchr. Ark. Dept. Edn., 2000. Clk., employee trainer Crockett Oil Co., Rector, Ark., 1991—97; choral libr. U. Ctrl. Ark., Conway, 1997—99; music tchr. Cabot (Ark.) Jr. High North & South, 1999—2000, Eastside Elem. Sch., Cabot, 2000—01; tchr. Clarkton (Mo.) C-4 Pub. Schs., 2001—; adminstrv. asst. Ark. Govs. Mansion, 2004—. Curriculum devel. com. Cabot Pub. Schs., 2000—01, Clarkton (Mo.) C-4 Pub. Schs., 2001—, cons., 2001—; caterer Simply the Best Catering, Little Rock. Entertainer C. of C., Rector, Ark., 1992—95; mem. Moark Gen. Bapt. Assoc., Campbell, Mo., 1989—2002. Mem.: Ark. Choral Dirs. Assn., Mo. Band Dirs. Assn., Clarkton Tchrs. Assn. (profl. devel. com. mem. 2002—03), Mo. State Tchrs. Assn., Music Educator's Nat. Conf. (sec. collegete chpt. 1998—99). Mem. Assembly Of God. Achievements include first to began a volunteer program to teach children music through the area libraries summer reading programs; started a traveling Vacation Bible School music program. During the summer I travel to different churches and handle all of the music for their VBS. This is a volunteer program without pay; entertain and lead group activities at area retirement centers; entertain at festivals, fair, and other special events. Avocations: travel, singing, reading, gardening. Home: 19 Deerwood Dr Conway AR 72034 Office: Ark Govs Manson 1800 Center St Little Rock AR 72206 E-mail: the_singing_dooley@sbcglobal.net.

DOONE, MICHELE MARIE, chiropractor; b. Oak Park, Ill., Oct. 3, 1942; d. Robert Emmett and Tana Josephine (Alioto) Doone. Cert., Valley Coll. of Med. and Dental Careers, 1962; student, L.A. Valley Coll., 1960-63, Dallas County Community Coll., 1983-84; D in Chiropractic summa cum laude, Parker Coll. of Chiropractic, 1986. Lic. chiropractic, Calif., Tex.; cert. Nat. Bd. Chiropractic Examiners, impairment rater; diplomate Am. Acad. Pain Mgmt., Am. Bd. Disability Analysts. Med. asst. William Orlando M.D., Edwin Crost, M.D., 1962-65; nursing supr., chief radiologic technologist Vanowen Med. Group, North Hollywood, Calif., 1965-76; radiologic technologist/purchasing agt. Lanier-Brown Clinic, Dallas, 1976-83; faculty mem./ chief radiologic technologist Parker Coll. of Chiropractic, Irving, Tex., 1983-85; exam and X-Ray doctor Margolies Chiropractic Ctr., Richardson, Tex., 1986; clinic staff doctor, assoc. prof. Parker Coll. of Chiropractic, Irving, Tex., 1986-87; doctor/ mgr. contractor Accident Ctrs. of Am., Garland, Tex., 1987; clinic dir. Back Pain Chiropractic, Carrollton, Tex., 1988-91; assoc. in group practice Mullican Chiropractic Ctr., Addison, Tex., 1991-97; co-owner, COO, pres. Health North Chiropractic Rehab Ctr PC, Addison, Tex., 1997—2002; assoc. med. dir. Intracorp., Carrolton, 2002—. Adviser health-related matters Inner Devel. Inst., Dallas, 1977—; seminar com. Back Pain Chiropractic, Inc., Metairie, La., 1989-91, clinic dir., 1988-91. Mem.: Parker Chiropractic Rsch. Found., Metroplex Neurospinal Diagnostic Med. and Surg. Group (med. adv. com. 1989—95), Tex. Chiropractic Assn. (chmn. radiology com. 1990—94), Parker Coll. Alumni Assn. (bd. dirs. 1988—90, 1993—94, 1995—2000, 2001—03, Dr. of Yr. 1990), Pi Tau Delta. Home: 11083 Lockshire Dr Frisco TX 75035-3765 Office Phone: 214-763-0412. Business E-Mail: drdoone@comcast.net.

DOORE, CYNTHIA MAY, elementary school educator; b. Haure, Mont., Sept. 13, 1949; d. Victor James Harmon and Sharlene F. (Williams) Harris; m. Roy H. Doore Jr.; children: Roylene May, Ronald Roy. BS in elem. edn., Northern Mont. Coll., 1979, M in elem. edn., 1993. First grade tchr. Sch. Dist. # 9, Browning, Mont., 1979-89, tchr., 1989-93, piloted summer sch. program, 1989, enrichment sci. class, 1990-93, third grade tchr., 1993—. Sec. Blackfeet Cmty. Partnership, Browning, 1992-93; bd. dirs. Blackfeet Cmty. Coll., 1993-95. Recipient Outstanding Contribution Bilingual Edn. award, 1993, Tchr. award NEWEST, N.A.S.A., 1991, Mont. Presdl. award, 1993, Nat. Presdl. award Sci. Teaching Nat. Sci. Found., 1993, Albert Einstein fellowship, 1995. Mem. Am. Fedn. Tchrs., Mont. Sci. Tchrs. Assn. (bd. dirs. 1989—), Nat. Sci. Tchrs. Assn., Delta Kappa Gamma. Mem. Lds Ch. Avocations: raising quarterhorses, paleontology, reading, gardening. Home: PO Box 1380 Browning MT 59417-1380 Office Phone: 406-338-5411 x317. Personal E-mail: cdoore@3rivers.net.

DOORY, ANN MARIE, legislator; married; 2 children. BA in Polit. Sci., Towson State U., 1976; JD, U. Balt., 1979. Bar: Md. Counsel to majority leader Md. State Senate, 1980—81; vol., arbitrator Better Bus. Bur., 1984-86; dep. spkr. pro tem Md. Ho. of Dels., 1999—2003, parliamentarian, 1993—94; mem. Ho. Econ. Matters Com. Md. Gen. Assembly, 1987—94, vice-chair Ho. Judiciary Com., 1995—2003, vice-chair Ho. Econ. Matters Com. Md., 2003—. Mem. Dem. State Ctrl. Com. 43d Legis. Dist., Baltimore City, 1982-86; mem. bd. Ho. of Ruth, 1999-. Named Md.'s Top 100 Women Cir. of Excellence Daily Rec. Mem. Women's Bar Assn., Md. Bar Assn. Democrat. Roman Catholic. also: Md Ho of Dels State Capitol Annapolis MD 21401 Office Fax: 410-841-3558. Business E-Mail: annmarie_doory@house.state.md.us.

DORAND, FREDA J., music educator; b. Waynesboro, Pa., Dec. 7, 1957; d. Verdeen K. and Esther J. Beaver; m. Jeffrey E. Dorand, Aug. 15, 2004; children: John D. Saunders, Isaac R. Saunders, Catherine M. Saunders. BS in Music Edn., Millersville U., Pa., 1979; MA in Ministerial Studies, Gettysburg Luth. Theol. Sem., Pa., 1996. Assoc. in ministry Pa.; cert. level I tchg. Pa., level II tchg. Pa. Organist, pianist United Meth. Chs., Mercersburg, Pa., 1982—87; pvt. music instr. Cumberland Sch. of Music and Dorands Music Studio, Chambersburg, 1982—; organist St. John's Luth. Ch., Mercersburg, 1987—89; dir. music Christ Luth. Ch., Hagerstown, Md., 1989—94; dir. music and youth ministry St. Paul's Luth. Ch., Biglerville, Pa., 1994—2001; music tchr. Fannett-Metal Sch. Dist., Willow Hill, Pa., 1998—; min. ch. music 1st Luth. Ch., Chambersburg, Pa., 2001—. Woodwind clinician James Buchanan H.S. Band, Mercersburg, 1990—2003; instr. woodwind and pit percussion Waynesboro Sr. H.S. Band, Waynesboro, 2001—03. 4-H leader Franklin County 4-H Program, Chambersburg, 1981—89; troop com. mem. Boy Scouts Am., Chambersburg, 2001—04, merit badge counselor music and religion, 1995. Recipient 1-Yr. Svc. pin, Franklin County 4-H Program, 1981, 5-Yr. Svc. pin, 1986. Mem.: Am. Guild English Handbell Ringers (assoc.), Franklin/Fulton County Music Edn. Assn. (assoc.), Fannett-Metal Edn. Assn. (assoc.), Music Educators Nat. Conf. (assoc.), Pa. Music Educators Assn. (assoc.), Am. Guild Organists (assoc.), Lower Susquehanna Synod (assoc.), Phi Lambda Sigma (pres. 1977—79). Evangelical. Avocations: sewing, reading, swimming, travel. Office: Fannett-Metal Sch Dist 14823 Path Valley Rd Willow Hill PA 17271 Office Phone: 717-349-2513. Personal E-mail: fjdorand@pa.net. E-mail: dorandf@fmsd.k12.pa.us.

DORCHAK, GLENDA, electronics company executive; Various positions IBM Canada, 1974—92; dir. sales and svc. AMBRA, 1993; various exec. positions in sales, mktg. and planning IBM US, 1993; pres. Value Am., Inc., Charlottesville, Va., 1998—99, chmn., CEO, 2000; v.p., COO Communications Group Intel Corp., v.p., Desktop Platforms Group, gen. mgr., Consumer Electronics Group. Named one of top 25 execs. of new millennium Computer Reseller News, 1999. Office: Intel Corp 2200 Mission College Blvd Santa Clara CA 95052-8119

DORE, KATHLEEN A., broadcast executive; m. Keith Jepsen. BA in Film and Broadcasting, U. Iowa, 1972, MBA, 1984. Affiliate mktg. mgr. Rainbow Media Holdings, 1982—84, sales dir. Am. Movie Classics, 1984—86, regional dir. Am. Movie Classics, 1986, pres. Bravo Networks, 1996—2002, pres. Ind. Film Channel Cos., 2002—03, pres. Entertainment Svcs., 2003—. Named honoree, Girl Scouts Inc., 2002; named one of Fast 40, Fast Co., 100 Most Powerful Women in Hollywood, Hollywood Reporter, 2003; recipient Lee Salk Goodworks award, Theatreworks/USA, Disting. Alumni Achievement award, U. Iowa, 1998. Mem.: N.Y. Women in Film, Mktg. Soc. for Cable and Telecomm. Industry, Women in Cable and Telecomm. Found. (chair 2001—02, Woman of Yr. 2003). Office: Rainbow Media Holdings 200 Jericho Quadrangle Jericho NY 11753

DORE, PATRICIA ANN, psychologist; b. Chgo., Mar. 2, 1944; d. Robert Patrick Dore and Anne Elizabeth Bruen; m. Peter Ruben Romero, Oct. 16, 1967; 1 child, Peter Anthony Romero. BA Spanish Lang. & Lit., St. Xavier U., 1966; MA in Applied Linguistics, Bilingualism and Math., Northeastern Ill. U., 1977; MS in Psychology, Bilingualism and Lang. Memory, Ill. Inst. Tech., 1981, PhD in Psychology, 1990; postgrad., Oral Roberts U., 2002—. Lic. sch. psychologist State Tchr. Cert. Bd., 1984, cert. Nat. Sch. Psychology Certi. Bd., 1988, sch. psychology State of Calif. Commn. on Tchr. Credentialing, 1987. Primary tchr. Chgo. Pub. Sch., 1968—83, ESL tchr., 1977—83, sch. psychologist internship, 1983—84, bilingual sch. psychologist, 1984—87; bilingual sch. psychologist, counselor San Jose Unified Sch. Dist., 1987—88; bilingual sch. psychologist Palatine (Ill.) Sch. Dist. #15, 1989—99, North Suburban Spl. Edn. Orgn., Arlington Heights, Ill., 1999—2002; ret., 2002. Instr. Vandercook Coll. Music, Chgo., 1979—80; cons. therapist Roth Group, Northbrook, Ill., 1981—93; instr. St. Augustine Coll., Chgo., 1983—85; bilingual sch. psychologist cons. Chgo. Pub. Sch., 1987—2005; bilingual sch. psychologist Glenview (Ill.) Sch. Dist. #34, 1998—, cons., 2001—05, Palatine Sch. Dist. #15, 2002—05, cons. bilingual sch. psychologist, 2002—05; cons. North Suburban Spl. Edn. Orgn., Arlington Heights, 2002—, bilingual sch. psychologist, 2002—05. Singer: Soprano in Gospel Choir. Election judge Election Bd. Chgo., 1990—92; prayer warrior Ptnr. Benny Hinn Min., 2000—. Mayor Daley Youth Found. scholar, City of Chgo., 1962. Mem.: Nat. Assn. Sch. Psychologists (assoc.), Gamma Beta Phi. Achievements include development of language fluency examination for college entrance examination. Avocations: singing, dance, design and decorating, playing organ. Office Phone: 847-702-0321. Home Fax: 847-808-7493. Personal E-mail: pattyann28@comcast.net.

DORF, EVE BUCKLE, artist; b. Oakland, Calif., July 31, 1946; d. John Franklin and Ruth Eva (Kratzer) Buckle; m. Frank Holman, mar. 22, 1970; children: John Buckle Dorf, Frank Lester Dorf. BA, Westminster Coll., 1968; 2d BA, Calif. State U., Sacramento, 1990. Cert. tchr., Calif. Tchr. 2nd grade San Juan Unified Sch. Dist., Carmichael, Calif., 1968-72; docent and internship Crocker Art Mus., Sacramento, 1980-86; children's art instr. Folsom (Calif.) Parks and Recreation, 1987-98. Artist-in-schs. Sacramento Met. Arts Commn., Calif. Artist: Art Auction for Pub. TV, Calif. Juried Shows, 1995-97, Roseville Art Ctr. Juried Shows, 1983-89, 33 group and solo artshows, 1983-98, travelling exhibit Strength from Unity: Expressions from the Island of Ireland and the United States, 2000, Hospice Mask Project, 2002, Thanks for the Mammogram, Sutter Auburn Hosp., 2005, Sandra Craig Women's Clinic, 2005; represented in pub. collections. Vol. art docent Roseville Art Ctr., Calif., 1983-; juror children's art Folsom Sch. Dist., 1994-98; insp. for voting poll place Sacramento County Voter Registration, 1980-98. Recipient Witt Meml. fellowship 1990. Mem. Crocker Art Mus., AAUW (br. photographer 1974-80). Democrat. Episcopalian. Avocations: gardening, cooking, hiking, snowshoeing, picnics. Home: 4400 La Mirada Cir Fair Oaks CA 95628-6664 Personal E-mail: buckledorf@sbcglobal.net.

DORFF, BARBARA L., elementary and secondary school educator; b. Sweetwater, Tex., Feb. 12, 1947; d. Earnest Lee Langley, Jr. and Helen Estelle (Richter) Langley; m. Jim Dorff, Apr. 4, 1975; children: John, Michael. BS in Art Edn., Tex. Tech. U., Lubbock, Tex., 1969; MEd, Tex. A&M U., Commerce, Tex., 1986. Tchr. art Austin Ind. Sch. Dist., 1969—72, Dallas Ind. Sch. Dist., 1972—73, 1975—79, tchr., curriculum specialist, 2001—06; tchr. kindergarten, art Gainesville Ind. Sch. Dist., 1973—75; tchr. McKinney Ind. Sch. Dist., 1995—2001; tchr., curriculum specialist Region 10 Edn. Svc. Ctr., Richardson, Tex., 2006—. Named Tex. Secondary Tchr. of Year, 2002, OELA Rising Star of Year, US Dept. Edn., 2002. Home: 2907 Oakwood Ct Mc Kinney TX 75070 E-mail: barbaradorff@yahoo.com.

DORFMAN, CYNTHIA HEARN, government agency administrator; BA in English with honors, Skidmore Coll., 1970; M in English, Middlebury Coll. Sr. exec. fellow Kennedy Sch. Govt., Harvard U.; dir. OCRI Found.; mgr. Dept. Publs. and Outreach Programs and Projects U.S. Dept. Edn., Washington, dir. media and info. svcs. Office Ednl. Rsch. and Improvement, comm. & develop. dir., Office Innovation and Improvement. Office: US Dept Edn IES Capital Place 555 New Jersey Ave NW Washington DC 20208

DORFMAN, LORRAINE M., clinical psychologist, consultant; b. Bethlehem, Pa., Nov. 9, 1952; d. Richard J. Dorfman and Phyllis L. (Wimmer) Schmidt. BA cum laude, Hunter Coll., 1980; MS, U. Wis., Milw., 1983, PhD, 1986. Lic. psychologist, Pa., N.J. Counselor Stanley M. Isaacs Neighborhood Ctr., Inc., N.Y.C., 1979, YWCA, N.Y.C., 1979-80, U. Wis. Milw. Psychology Clinic, Milw., 1983-84; asst. psychologist De Paul Rehab. Hosp., Milw., 1984; therapist Family Ctr., Columbia Hosp., Milw., 1985, The Counseling Ctr. Milw., Wis., 1985-86; psychologist Bristol-Bensalem Human Svcs. Ctr., 1986-87, Phila. (Pa.) State Hosp., 1986-87, Lehigh U. Counseling Svc., Bethlehem, 1987-88; pvt. practice psychology Allentown, Langhorne, Pa., 1988—. Instr. U. Wis., Milw., 1980-86; cons. Human Svcs. Ctr., Wyncote, Pa., 1988-1997, MBCS Achievement and Guidance Ctrs. Am., Inc., Lawrenceville, N.J., 1988-92, assoc. dir., 1992-93, clin. dir., 1993-94; cons. Hoffmann-LaRoche, Inc., Nutley, N.J., 1990—, CORA Svcs., Inc., Phila., 1991, Plymouth Healthcare Assocs., Plymouth Meeting, Pa., 1990, Operation Par, Inc., St. Petersburg, Fla., 1990—, Bustleton Health Sys., Inc., Huntingdon Valley, Pa., 1991-92, Helpfinders, Fort Washington, Pa., 1989-94, Allegheny Behavioral Health Svcs., 1997, AmeriChoice Behavioral Healthcare, Inc., 1997—, Jefferson Behavioral Health Network, 1997-1999, Magellan Behavioral Health, 1999—, FHC Options/Tricare, 1994-1999, MBC, 1994—, Green Spring, 1997-1999, Penn Behavioral Health Svcs., 1997—, United Behavioral Health, 1997—, United Healthcare Svc. Corp., 1997-, Healthy Edge, 1999-, Horizon, 2000-, Value Options, 2000-; pub. edn. workshops and seminars. Contbr. articles to profl. jours. Vol. con. Human Svc. Ctr., Phila., 1988—. Mem. APA, Nat. Register Health Svc. Providers in Psychology, Phila. Soc. Clin. Psychologists (pub. rels. com. 1990-91), Lehigh Valley Psychol. Assn. (ethics com. chair 1998). Office: One Oxford Valley 2300 E Lincoln Hwy Langhorne PA 19047-1824 also: Cedar Crest Profl Park 1251 S Cedar Crest Blvd Allentown PA 18103-6205 Office Phone: 610-740-0755.

DORIA, MARILYN L., lawyer; b. Boston, Jan. 15, 1944; AB, Brandeis U., 1965; MPA, Syracuse U., 1967; JD, Temple U., 1974. Bar: Pa. 1974, US Dist. Ct. (ea. dist.) Pa. 1974, Tex. 1986, US Dist. Ct. (so. dist.) Tex. 1986, US Ct. Appeals (5th cir.) 1986, US Ct. Appeals (DC cir.) 1986, DC 1993. Dep. asst. to asst. gen. counsel for enforcement FERC, 1980—83, dep. gen. counsel, 1983—85; former ptnr. oil and gas litig. Reynolds Allen & Cook, Houston; now ptnr. Akin, Gump, Strauss, Hauer & Feld, L.L.P., Washington, 1983—, and sect. mgr. energy, land use and environ. practice group. Mem.: Pa. Bar Assn., Tex. Bar Assn., DC Bar Assn., Fed. Energy Bar Assn. Office: Akin Gump Strauss Hauer & Feld Ste 400 1333 New Hampshire Ave NW Washington DC 20036-1564 Office Phone: 202-887-4000. Business E-Mail: mdoria@akingump.com.

DORIGHI, NANCY S., computer engineer; BS in Math., U. San Francisco, 1974; MSEE, Stanford U., 1976. Mgr. air traffic control tower simulator Future Flight Ctrl., Ames Rsch. Ctr. NASA, Moffett Field, Calif., 1976—. Fellow: AIAA (assoc.); mem.: ASME (assoc. editor ASME jour.). Avocations: hiking, skiing, gardening.

DORLEAC, CATHERINE See DENEUVE, CATHERINE

DORLEN, ROSALIND, clinical psychologist, psychoanalyst, medical researcher, educator; MA in Anthropology, Columbia U.; Profl. Diploma in Sch. PSychology, Kean U.; Doctorate in Clin. Psychology, Rutgers U., 1977; post-doctoral cert. in Psychoanalytic Psychotheraphy, Ctr. for Psychoanalytic Tng., NY; post-doctoral cert. in Psychoanalysis, Inst. for Psychoanalysis and Psychotheraphy, NJ. Lic. and bd. cert. Diplomate in Clin. Psychology, cert. school psychologist, psychoanalyst. Pvt. practice, Summit, NJ, 1970—. Pub. edn. chair NJ Working Group on Postpartum Depression, 2005—; bd. dir. Allied Profl. Staff, Overlook Hosp., Summit, NJ, Nat. Register of Health Svc., 1980—; dir. Resilience Project, Overlook Hosp. (sponsored by NJ Psychological Assn.), Summit, NJ; field supervisor Rutgers Grad. Sch. Profl. Psychology; mem. sr. faculty Inst. for Psychoanalysis and Psychotherapy NJ; chairperson adv. bd. for Psychological Well-Being Overlook Hosp., Summit, NJ, mem. adv. bd.; mem. cmty. benefits com. Overlook Adv. Bd., Summit, NJ; psychological health educator and lectr.; spkr. in field; lectured and media appearances about effective parenting, depression, and stress in the workplace. Author: Niche Guide for APA Divsn. 42 (Independent Practice); published and lectured on the subject of strengthening resilience in individuals, children, and communities coping with terrorism, bio-terrorism, and war. Nationally recognized innovator of cmty. initiatives; mem. mcpl. alliance for the Prevention of Drug and Alcohol Abuse; mem. Suburban C. of C., Summit, NJ. Recipient Psychologist Recognition award, NJ Acad. of Psychology, Peterson prize, Rutgers Profl. Sch. Psychology, Disting. Grad. Alumni award, Kean Univ. Dept. of Sch. Psychology. Fellow: APA (mem., Com. for the Advancement of Psychological Practice); mem.: Soc. of Psychologists in Private Practice (past pres.), Am. Bd. Profl. Psychology (fellow in clin. psychology), NJ Psychological Assn. (past pres., mem. ethics com., chairperson, coun. on psychological health, Psychologist of Yr. 2000, Presdl. Citation in Recognition of Outstanding Contribution to Profl. Psychology). Office: 332 Springfield Ave Ste 204 Summit NJ 07901 Office Phone: 908-522-1444. Office Fax: 908-233-9310. Business E-Mail: dorlen@mindspring.com.

DORMAN, JANET LEE VOSPER, elementary school educator; d. Stanley R. and Chester H. Vosper; children: Elizabeth Randolph Worth, Philip Hamilton Worth. BS, Radford Coll., 1969; EdM, Va. Poly. Inst., 1976. Trainer U. Kans., Lawrence, 1991—; sci. lead tchr. Kenmore Mid. Sch., Arlington, Va., 2000—. Ordained elder Old Presbyn. Meeting Ho., Alexandria, Va., 2005—. Named Tchr. of Yr., Chesterfield County H.S., 1999—2000. Mem.: AAUW, Va. Edn. Assn. (bd. dirs., exec. com. 2004—), Arlington Edn. Assn. (exec. bd. 2000—, v.p.), Delta Kappa Gamma. Home: 419 Jackson Pl Alexandria VA 22302 Office: Arlington County Public Schools 200 S Canlin Springs Rd Arlington VA 22204 Office Phone: 703-228-6800. Business E-Mail: lee_dorman@apsva.us.

DORMAN, JO-ANNE, elementary school educator; b. Greenville, Miss. d. Joe Edward and Constance Bonita (Parks) D. BS, Delta State U., 1963. Cert. tchr., Fla. Tchr. Oakcrest Elem. Sch., Pensacola, Fla., 1963-93, 2005—. Traffic sch. instr., 1997—; substitute tchr. Sch. Dist. Escambia County, Pensacola, 1993-200; mem. tech. team Oakrest Sch. Hospitality Com., 2005— Sunday sch. tchr. Methodist Ch., Pensacola, Fla., 1963, 65, 68; voter precinct clk. Escambia County, 1997—; vol. Sr. Friends, 2000—. Named Local Sch. Tchr. of Yr., 1988. Mem.: U. West Fla. Leisure Learners Soc., Pensacola Dog Fanciers Assn., Papillon Club Am., Five Flags Dog Tng. Club. Democrat. Methodist. Avocations: travel, reading, photography, theater. Home: 188 Talladega Trl Pensacola FL 32506-3202 Personal E-mail: jadpaps@yahoo.com.

DORMAN, STEPHANIE, writer; b. Great Bend, Kans., Feb. 9, 1972; d. John Wayne and Marcia Rose (Blank) Keener; m. Lyndel Dorman, Dec. 4, 1988; children: Adele Lynette, Stephan Lawrence. BS in Edn., U. Mo., Columbia, 1994, MS in Ednl. Leadership and Policy Analysis, 2002. Tchr. Columbia Pub. Schs., 1995—2002; adj. prof. U. Mo., Columbia, 2003—05. Co-author: The Kids Book of the 50 Great States, 1998; editor: Mo. Classrooms: Student Successes in Social Studies Jour., 2000—01; featured: (video) Missouri: Our History and Heritage, 2001. Mem. Chuck Graham 19th Dist State Rep., Columbia, Mo., 2004; vol. City of Columbia, 1998—; asst. coach Diamond Coun. Baseball, 2003—. Recipient Eddy award, Mo. Govs. Office, Jefferson City, 1999. Mem.: AAUW, LWV, ASCD, Mo. Coun. Social Studies (rep. 1995—2000), Columbia Chorale (libr. 2005—), Delta Kappa Gamma. Democrat. Avocations: singing, reading, exercise.

DORN, DIANE M., science educator; b. Chilton, Wis., Jan. 11, 1966; d. Dennis and Marian Dorn; m. William Dowell, Feb. 13, 1993. AS in electronics, McHenry C.C., 1990; BS in natural environ. sys., No. Ill., 1994; MEd, Nat. Louis U., 1998. Sci. tchr. Woodstock HS, Woodstock, Ill., 1994—2001, Marian Ctrl. HS, Woodstock, Ill., 2001—. Bd. mem. Ringwood Planning Bd., Ringwood, Ill., 2000—. Recipient monetary award, Earth Watch, 2000. Mem.: Nat. Sci. Tchrs. Assn., Ill. Sci. Tchrs. Assn. Avocations: soccer, snowboarding, bicycling, backpacking, travel. Office: Marian Cath Ctrl HS 1001 McHenry Ave Woodstock IL 60098 Office Phone: 815-338-4220. E-mail: ddorn@marian.com.

DORN, DOLORES, actress; b. Chgo., Mar. 03; d. Edward Dorn Heft and Alice Ellen Eagmin; m. Franchot Tone, May 14, 1966 (dec. 1968); m. Ben Piazza, Aug. 6, 1969 (dec.). Studied with, Uta Hagen, 1964-66, Lee Strasberg, N.Y.C., 1967-82; BFA, Goodman Theater, Chgo., 1962. Pvt. coach to stars, Los Angeles, 1974—; tchr. Am. Film Inst., Los Angeles, 1977-89, Lee Strasberg Theater Inst., Los Angeles, 1983-86; coach Star Search 1984, Los Angeles, 1984. Mem. The Actor's Studio, N.Y.C. Appeared in TV shows Divorce Court, Studio 5B, Family Med. Ctr., Superior Ct., Simon and Simon, Night Cries, Intimate Strangers, Charlie's Angels, Jigsaw John, Tenafly, Girls of Huntington House, Run for Your Life, Strawberry Blonde, Capitol, Sisters, Picket Fences; appeared in motion pictures Tell Me a Riddle, The Stronger, The Candy Snatchers, Thirteen West Street, Underworld U.S.A., The Bounty Hunter, Uncle Vanya (Best Actress award San Francisco Internat. Film Festival 1967), Murders of the Rue Morgue, In the Line of Fire; appeared in Broadway plays The Midnight Sun, Starward Ark, Hide and Seek, (off-Broadway plays) The Pinter Plays, To Damascus, Plays for Bleeker Street, Lime Green Khaki Blue, Between Two Thieves, Uncle Vanya, A Mighty Man Is He, Catch As Catch Can, L.A., Dancing on the Table; contract actress Warner Bros., Columbia Film Studios; dir., playwright On the Telephone at The Actor's Studio, 1995; author (plays) Throw-Away Baby, 1998, Throw-Away Woman, 2001, Throw Away Life, 2002. Mem. Women in Film, Actor's Studio, Am. Film Inst. (hon.). Office: Dale Garrick Internat Agy 1017 N LaCieneqa West Hollywood CA 90069 Office Phone: 310-657-2661.

DORN, JENNIFER LYNN, federal official; b. Grand Island, Nebr., Dec. 7, 1950; d. Harold Clarence and Ethel Agnes D.; 2 children BA, Oreg. State U., 1973; MPA, U. Conn., 1977. Legis. asst. to Senator M. Hatfield US Senate, Washington, 1977-81; com. staff Senate Appropriations, Washington, 1981-83; spl. asst. to Sec. Elizabeth Dole US Dept. Labor, Washington, 1983-84; dir. Comml. Space Transp., Washington, 1984-85; assoc. dep. sec. U.S. Dept. Transp., Washington, 1985-87; asst. sec. policy U.S. Dept. Labor, Washington, 1989-91; sr. v.p. pub. support ARC, Washington, 1991-98; pres. Nat. Health Mus., 1998—2001; adminstr. Fed. Transit Adminstrn. US Dept. Transp., Washington, 2001—05; alt. exec. dir. Internat. Bank for Reconstruction & Devel. (The World Bank), US Dept. Treasury, Washington, 2005—. Mem. Washington Women's Forum, Cosmos Club. Republican. Lutheran. Office: The World Bank 1818 H St NW Rm MC13-525 Washington DC 20433 Office Phone: 202-458-1582. Business E-Mail: jdorn@worldbank.org.

DORN, KATHIE LEE, medical/surgical nurse; b. Dallas, Aug. 8, 1948; d. Gordon Lee and Ruth Mae (Beadle) Cunningham; m. Gordon Lee Dorn, Oct. 30, 1969; Children: Scott Lee, Kelly Lee. Student, So. Methodist U., 1966-68; RN, Elcentro Coll., 1983. ADN, RN, CNOR, CPR Instr., ACLS; cert. plastic surgery nurse. Staff RN Parkland Meml. Hosp., Dallas, 1984-86, Peri-Op. Nurses of Dallas, 1986-87, Barton, Brown & Byrd Plastic Surgeons, Dallas, 1987-88, Mary Shiels Hosp., Dallas, 1988-95; PRN staff RN, CPR instr. Parkland Meml. Hosp., Dallas, 1986-95; scrub nurse, PRN D. Mark Jewell, Plastic Surgery, Eugene, Oreg., 1995-98; recovery room PRN, staff RN Sacred Heart Hosp., Eugene, 1996-97; cruise ship nurse Royal Caribbean Internat., 1998—. Item review bd. mem. Peri-Operative Nurses Inc., Denver, 1994; CPR instr. Dallas Community & Parkland Hosp., 1993-95; v.p. Dorn Microbiological Assocs., Eugene, 1986—. Contbr. various newsletters in field. Vol. Tex. flu step immunizations Tex. Vis. Nurses Assn., 1994, blood drives and fund raising Wadley Blood Bank Guild, 1986-91, clinics Dallas Ind. Sch. Dist., 1982-95, pub. clinics vital signs classes Am. Red Cross, 1980-95, nurse counselor Bolshoi Ballet Acad., Vail, Colo., 1990. Recipient Interlocking Circle of Caring award Delta Airlines, Dallas, 1986. Mem. AORN (nat. and Eugene chpts.), Am. Heart Assn. (mem. sci. coun. 1993—). Republican. Roman Catholic. Avocations: cross country skiing, hiking, weightlifting, interior design, balletomine. Home and Office: 29323 Gimpl Hill Rd Eugene OR 97402-9054

DORN, MARY ANN, retired auditor; b. Overland, Mo., May 1, 1933; d. Bernard J. and Marie (Kunkler) Engler; children: Glennon (dec.), Pat Michael, Michelle; m. Donald Patrick Dorn, June 3, 2002. Student, Fontbonne Coll., 1951-52; AA, Sacramento City Coll., 1975; BS in Bus., Calif. State U., 1981. CPA, Calif.; cert. fraud examiner; cert. govt. fin. mgr. From asst. to acct. Mo. Rsch. Labs., Inc., St. Louis, 1953-55, adminstrv. asst., 1955-60; sec. western region fin. office Gen. Electric Co., St. Louis, 1960-62; credit analyst Crocker Nat. Bank, Sacramento, 1962-72; student tchr. Sacramento County Dept. Edn., 1979-81; acctg. technician East Yolo Community Services Dist., 1983; mgmt. specialist USAF Logistics Command, 1984; auditor Office Insp. Gen. U.S. Dept. Transp., 1984-92; auditor-in-charge Adminstrn. for Children and Families U.S. Dept. Health and Human Svcs., 1992—. Mem. Sacramento Community Commn. for Women, 1978-81, bd. dirs., 1980—; planning bd. Golden Empire Health Systems Agy. Mem. AARP (tax counselor), AAUW (fin. officer 1983—), AICPA, Nat. Assn. Accts. (dir., newsletter editor), Fontbonne Coll. Alumni Assn., Calif. State Alumni Assn., Assn. Govt. Accts. (chpt. officer), Calif. Soc. CPAs, German Geneological Soc. (bd. dirs. 1990—, publicity dir. 1994—), Sun City Lincoln Hills Assn., Beta Gamma Sigma, Beta Alpha Psi. Roman Catholic. Home: 815 Magnolia Ln Lincoln CA 95648-8429

DORN, SUE BRICKER, retired hospital administrator; b. Seattle, Apr. 1, 1934; d. Barney and Frances B. (Schnitzer) Bricker; m. Philip Henry Dorn, Dec. 31, 1955 (dec.); children: Charles, Martha Dorn. BA, Stanford U., Palo Alto, 1955; MA, Bank St. Coll., 1973. Cert. tchr., N.Y. Dir. promotion exec. compensation svc. Am. Mgmt. Assn., N.Y.C., 1956-58; tchr. spl. edn. N.Y.C. Bd. of Edn., 1969-77; assoc. dir. Yale U., New Haven, 1977—79; v.p. Bank St. Coll. of Edn., N.Y.C., 1979-81, Aspen Inst. for Humanistic Studies, N.Y.C., 1981-82; assoc. v.p. Yale U., New Haven, 1982-87; dep. dir. devel. and pub. affairs Mus. of Modern Art, N.Y.C., 1987-94; v.p., vice provost for devel. The N.Y. Hosp.-Cornell Med. Ctr., 1994—98. Mem. maj. gifts com. Stanford U.; cons. in field. Pres. LWV, Warren, Mich., 1962-65, Stanford Alumni Club of N.Y., N.J. and Conn., N.Y.C., 1968-70, 25 East 86th St. Corp., N.Y.C., 1989-93, 95—; mem. dirs. adv. bd. Yale Comprehensive Cancer Ctr., Yale U., 1990-94. Named Citizen of the Yr., Warren C. of C., 1962; recipient Citation, City of Warren, 1963, Gold Spike award and Cert. of Outstanding Achievement, Stanford U., 1976. Mem. Stanford Assocs., Univ. Club. Home: 25 E 86th St New York NY 10028-0553 E-mail: sdorn@nyc.rr.com.

DORNBUSH, RHEA L., psychologist, educator; b. N.Y.C. BA, Queens Coll., 1962, MA, 1963; PhD, CUNY, 1967; MPH, Columbia U., 1981; respecialization clin. neuropsychology, CUNY, 1989. Lic. pychologist, N.Y. Rsch. asst., reseach assoc., teaching fellow Queens Coll., Flushing, N.Y., 1963-65; lectr., asst. prof. Douglass Coll., Rutgers U., New Brunswick, N.J., 1965-68; from asst. prof. to assoc. prof. psychiatry N.Y. Med. Coll., N.Y.C., 1968-76; sr. rsch. scientist Reproductive Biology Research Found., St. Louis, 1976-78; clin. lectr. in med. psychology Washington U. Sch. Medicine, St. Louis, 1976-78; assoc. prof. psychiatry N.Y. Med. Coll., Valhalla, 1978-80, prof. psychiatry, 1980—, prof. neurology, 1994—, dir. neuropsychology svcs., 1990; adj. prof. psychology Queens Coll., CUNY, Flushing, 1983—2004; prof. clin. pub. health Sch. Pub. Health, 2006—. Editor: Chronic Cannabis Use, 1976, Hashish: Studies of Long-Term Use, 1977; contbr. articles to profl. jours. Bd. dirs. Bradford Nat. Corp., 1977-83, Riverdale Sr. Svcs., Inc., Bronx, N.Y., 1984—. NIH Predoctoral fellow, 1964-65; Rsch. grantee NIMH, 1978-80, Rsch. grantee Nat. Fund for Med. Edn., 1984-88, NIH Small Grantee, 1966-68. Mem. Am. Psychol. Assn., Nat. Acad. Neuropsychologists, Internat. Neuropsychology Soc. Office: NY Med Coll Dept Psychiatry Valhalla NY 10595

DORR, AIMEE, dean, education educator; b. LA, Sept. 20, 1942; d. Thomas Osborn and Mary Alice (Perkey) D.; m. Larry John Leifer, Dec. 19, 1962 (div.); 1 child, Simeon Kel Leifer; m. Donald Warren Bremme, Aug. 6, 1977 (div.); 1 child, John Thomas Dorr-Bremme; m. Donald Ross Simpson, Feb. 19, 1989. BS, Stanford U., 1964, MA, 1966, PhD in Psychology, 1970. Acting asst. prof. communication Stanford U., 1967-70, research assoc. in psychiatry and communication, 1970-71, research assoc. in psychiatry, acting asst. prof. communication, childcare policy analyst in Pres.'s Office, 1971-72; asst. prof. edn. Harvard U., Cambridge, Mass., 1972-76, assoc. prof., 1976-78; assoc. prof. communications Annenberg Sch. Communication U. So. Calif., Los Angeles, 1978—81, prof., 1981; prof. edn. UCLA, 1981—, dean Sch. Edn. & Info. Systems, 2005—. Cons. Children's TV Workshop, NBC, KCET, Children's Advt. Rev. Unit, others. Author: Television and Children: A Special Medium for a Special Audience, 1986; editor: (with Edward L. Palmer) Children and the Faces of Television-Teaching, Violence, Selling, 1980, 2d edit., 1981; contbr. articles to profl. jours. Fellow Am. Psychol. Assn., Am. Ednl. Research Assn., Soc. Research in Child Devel., Internat. Communication Assn., Amnesty Internat., Friends Com. on Nat. Legis. Democrat.

DORR, MARJORIE W., healthcare insurance company executive; BBA, U. Iowa; MBA, U. Chgo. Grad. Sch. Bus.; grad., Stanley K. Lacy Exec. Leadership Prog. With SEC, Washington, Algemene Bank Nederland, N.V., Chgo.; v.p. Houlihan, Lokey, Howard & Zukin, Inc., San Francisco; v.p. corp. fin. Anthem, Inc., 1991, CFO Anthem Casualty Ins. Grp., CEO, pres., dir. Prescription Mgmt., 1995—98, COO Blue Cross and Blue Shield Conn. operation, pres. Blue Cross and Blue Shield's East region; pres., CEO N.E. Region SBU Wellpoint, Inc., exec. v.p., chief strategy officer Indpls. Bd. dirs. New Eng. Healthcare Inst. Bd. dirs. Lead Like Jesus. Mem.: CEO Forum, Com. of 200, Young Pres.'s Orgn. Office: Wellpoint Inc 120 Monument Cir Indianapolis IN 46204*

DORR, STEPHANIE TILDEN, psychotherapist; b. Orlando, Fla., Sept. 21, 1950; d. Luther Willis Tilden II and Lillian Murfee (Grace) Owen; m. Darwin Dorr, May 21, 1986. AA, El Camino Coll., 1975; BA, U. N.C., 1985; MA, Western Carolina U., 1991. Lic. clin. psychotherapist State Kans. Behavioral Scis. Regulatory Bd., 2000. Cons. psychologist Sylva (N.C.) Psychol. Assocs., 1991-92; staff psychologist Park Ridge Hosp., Naples, N.C., 1992, Blue Ridge Ctr., Asheville, N.C., 1991-93; pvt. practice psychology Asheville, 1991-93; project mgr. Sedgwick County Dept. Mental Health, Wichita, Kans., 1993-95; pvt. practice psychotherapy and psychol. assessment Counseling and Mediation Ctr., Wichita, Kans., 1995-98; therapist United Meth. Youthville Clinic, Wichita, 1998—2001; clin. therapist Wichita (Kans.) Pub. Schs. Greiffenstein Spl. Edn. Ctr., 2001—. Adj. faculty Kans. Newman Coll., Wichita, 1995—, Butler County (Kans.) Cmty. Coll., 1996-97; Assertive Cmty. Treatment (ACT) team clinician United Meth. Youthville, Wichita, 1997-98; presenter in field. Contbr. articles to profl. publs. Recipient Excellence in Tchg. award Butler County C.C., 1997, Outstanding Faculty Mem. award Butler County C.C., 1998. Mem. APA (assoc.), Psychoanalytic Study Group (sec. 1989-93, award 1993), We. N.C. Psychol. Assn. (mem.-at-large 1985-93, pres.-elect 1993), Kans. Assn. Masters Psychologists (bd. mem. 2005, pres. 2006), Psi Chi, Pi Gamma Mu. Democrat. Episcopalian. Avocations: sewing, rock collecting, gardening. Office: Wichita Pub Schs Greiffenstein Spl Edn Ctr 1221 E Galena Wichita KS 67216 Office Phone: 316-973-6400. Personal E-mail: sdorr@usd259.net, stdorr@cox.net.

DORRILL, MARY SUE VALENTINE, elementary school educator; b. Newton, Miss., Dec. 9, 1944; d. Selmer Louis and Mary Lee (Nelson) Valentine; m. George Lee Dorrill, Aug. 9, 1970; children: Renee Suzanne, John Edward. BS, Miss. State Coll. for Women, 1967; MEd, Miss. State U., 1975. Tchr. Newton (Miss.) Pub. Schs., Jackson (Miss.) Pub. Schs., Kosciusko (Miss.) Pub. Schs., Kosciusko City Schs., Kosciusko; librarian Greenlee Elem. Sch. Mem. Internat. Reading Assn., Miss. Reading Assn., Miss. Profl. Educators. Home: 607 Shadow Wood Dr Kosciusko MS 39090-4723

DORROUGH, VICKI LEE, theater educator; b. Oklahoma City, Mar. 8, 1953; d. Clarence Leroy and Ruby Anne Lewis; m. Bryce Coleman Dorrough, Dec. 23, 1977; children: Matthew Aaron, Kristopher Shawn. BA in Speech Edn., Okla. State U., Stillwater, 1971—75; MA in Ednl. & Cmty. Renewal, U. Okla., Norman, 2003—05. Cert. tchr. Okla. Dept. Edn. Speech/journalism/English tchr. Watonga HS, Okla., 1975—77; speech/acting/stagecrafts tchr. Norman HS, 1977—82; speech & drama tchr. Longfellow Mid. Sch., Norman, 1993—97; speech & acting tchr. Norman N. HS, 1997—99; speech & drama tchr. Whittier Mid. Sch., Norman, 2000—. Internat. thespian troupe Ednl. Theatre Assn., Cin., 1975—; bd. mem., dir. Sooner Theatre, Norman; gifted site goal com. Whittier Mid. Sch., 2000—. Founding mem. IMPACT Okla., Greater Oklahoma City, 2005; mem., former bd. mem. Assistance League of Norman, 1991—; bd. mem. Transition House, Inc., Norman, 2006. Finalist Tchr. of Yr., Whittier Mid. Sch., 2004. Mem.: NEA, Profl. Educators of Norman, Okla. Edn. Assn., S.W. Theatre Conf., Okla. Theatre Edn. Assn. (pres. elect., sec. 1975—82). Methodist. Avocations: gardening, water-skiing, scuba diving, dance, reading. Home: 2023 Morning Dew Trl Norman OK 73072 Office: Whittier Mid Sch 2000 W Brooks Norman OK 73069 E-mail: vickild@cox.net.

DORSEY, DOLORES FLORENCE, retired corporate treasurer, finance company executive; b. Buffalo, May 26, 1928; d. William G. and Florence R. D. BS, Coll. St. Elizabeth, 1950. With Aerojet-Gen. Corp., 1953—, asst. to treas. El Monte, Calif., 1972-74, asst. treas., 1974-79, treas., 1979—2001, ret., 2001. Mem. adv. bd. Scripps Ctr. for Integrative Medicine, 2001—. Mem. Cash Mgmt. Group San Diego (past pres.), Nat. Assn. Corp. Treas., Fin. Execs. Inst. (v.p.). Republican. Roman Catholic.

DORSEY, DONNA BAGLEY, insurance agent; b. Macon, Ga., May 26, 1952; d. Clarence Henry and Sybil Audrey (Phillips) Bagley; m. David M. Lewis, June 14, 1969 (div. May 1979); children: Scott D., Jeffrey A.; m. J. Larry Dorsey, July 1, 1980. Grad. high sch., Macon, Ga. Cert. ins. counselor; cert. profl. ins. woman. Rating clk. Bibb Underwriters Ins., Macon, 1977-80; book-keeper Wilson Typewriter, Macon, 1980-85; customer svc. rep. Ga. Ins. Agy., Macon, 1985; agt., customer svc. rep. Johnson and Johnson Ins., Inc., Macon, 1985—. Recipient Outstanding Customer Svc. Rep. Ga. award Ind. Ins. Agts. Ga., 1993; Ruth Dupree Meml. scholar, 1987, Safeco Ins. Achievement award, 1995, 97; nominee T.J. Mims award of excellence, 1998. Mem. Profl. Ins. Agts. Ga. (bd. dirs. 1990-93, Eagle award 1989), Young Profl. Coun. Ga. (chmn. 1991-92), Ins. Women Macon (treas. 1991-92, v.p. 1992-93, pres. elect 1993-94, pres. 1994-95, Macon Ins. Woman of Yr. 1994, Ga. Ins. Woman of Yr. 1994, President's Vol. award 1994, Macon Ins. Profl. of Yr. 1995, Indivdual Edn. Achievement award 1996). Avocations: reading, water-skiing, swimming. Office: Johnson And Johnson PO Box 4803 Macon GA 31208-4803

DORSEY, HELEN DANNER (JOHNA BLINN), writer, educator; b. Tarentum, Pa., Jan. 18, 1928; d. Frederick William and Harriet (Wiggins) Danner; m. Thomas Brookshier Dorsey, June 30, 1951 (dec.); children: Diana, F. Blinn. BA, U. Iowa, 1949; postgrad., U. Wis., 1950. Food columnist Herald Tribune News Service, N.Y.C., 1956-58; remedial edn. educator U.S. Army, Hoechst, Fed. Republic of Germany, 1954-56; food editor Am. Weekend, Frankfurt, Federal Republic of Germany, 1954-56; with elec. drafting dept. Newport News (Va.) Shipbuilding and Dry Dock Co., 1952-54; tchr. George Wythe Jr. High Sch., Hampton, Va., 1951-52; home econs. tchr. Keokuk (Iowa) High Sch., 1949-51; tchr. Thomas Jefferson Jr. High Sch., Arlington, Va., 1956-57; tchr. home econs. Sr. High Sch., Massapequa, N.Y., 1958-59; contbg. editor Forecast Mag., N.Y.C., 1958-59, 50Plus Mag., N.Y.C., 1958-60; asst. food editor LOOK mag., N.Y.C., 1962-64; celebrity cookbook columnist Newsday Spls. (syndicated), Garden City, N.Y.C., 1964-69, Chgo. Tribune-N.Y. News Syndicate, N.Y.C., 1969-75, Los Angeles Times Syndicate, 1975-87; celebrity foodstyles producer, writer Family Circle mag., N.Y.C., 1985—; contbg. correspondent USA Today & USA Weekend, Arlington, Va., 1985—; contbg. editor The Phila. Inquirer Mag., 1985; celebrity cookbook columnist Celebrity Foodstyle Syndicate, Los Angeles, 1987-88; contract writer for N.Am. The Times of London Syndicates, 1988-89. Columnist Editors Press Svc., Inc., N.Y.C., 1987—; cons. in field. Author: Great performances in the Kitchen, 1988, and 38 cookbooks, 1974-88; contbr. articles to mags. and newspapers. Avocations: swimming, reading.

DORSEY, MARY ELIZABETH, lawyer; b. Florissant, Mo., July 4, 1962; d. Richard Peter Jr. and Dolores Irene (McNamara) D. BA in Acctg., Benedictine Coll., 1984; JD, St. Louis U., 1987. Bar: Mo. 1989, U.S. Dist. Ct. (we. dist.) Mo. 1989, U.S. Dist. Ct. (ea. dist.) Mo. 1990, U.S. Supreme Ct. 1994, U.S. Ct. Appeals (8th cir.) 1997. Rschr. Ind. Legal Rsch., Florissant, 1987-89; atty. assoc. Deeba Sauter Herd, St. Louis, 1989-98; ptnr. Ahlheim & Dorsey, LLC, St. Charles, 1998—. Bd. dirs. North County, Inc.; chair St. Louis Bd. Equalication, 2005—. Merit badge counselor St. Louis Area coun. Boy Scouts Am., 1988—, mem. com. Troop 748, mem. Order of the Arrow, 1992, Brotherhood, 1994; chair Am. Cancer Soc. Relay for Life North County, 2005; corr. sec. Florissant Twp. Open Dem. Club, 1989-91, sgt. at arms, 1991-2000; treas. Friends of Rick Dorsey, St. Louis, 1988, 90, 92, 96; mem. Dem. Com., Florissant Twp., 1996—, 13th State Senate, Mo. Dem. Com., 2004—; legis. amb. Am. Cancer Soc., 2006—. Mem.: ATLA, ABA, St. Charles County Bar Assn., Bar Assn. Met. St. Louis (lectr. law related edn. com. 1988—96), Mo. Assn. Trial Attys., Florissant Ambs., Florissant Valley Jaycees (dir. 1993—94, treas. 1994—95, state dir. 1995—97, v.p. 1997—98), U.S.Jaycees (regional coord. 2002, Nat. Resource Team 2003, sen.), Mo. Jaycees (life; state legal counsel 1997—99, dist. dir. 1998—99, region dir. 2000, membership v.p. 2001, state legal counsel 2002—03), Florissant Rotary Club. Democrat. Roman Catholic. Avocations: golf, camping, theater. Office: Ahlheim & Dorsey LLC 2209 1st Capitol Dr Saint Charles MO 63301-5809 Office Phone: 636-940-8000. Business E-Mail: medorsey@ahlheimdorsey.com.

DORSEY-TYLER, APRIL MELODY, science educator; b. L.A., Oct. 28, 1954; children: Ceri, Alea. BA in Microbiology, So. Ill. U., 1976; PhD in Physiology, U.Birmingham, Eng., 1988. Adj. prof. Ivy Tech. Coll., Kokomo, Ind., 1995—2001; instr. Green River C.C., Auburn, Wash., 1993—94. Home: P O Box 687 Chico CA 95926-9999: PO Box 687 Chico CA 95926

DORSHOW-GORDON, ELLEN, epidemiologist; b. St. Paul, May 16, 1946; d. Bennie and Goldie (Salita) Dorshow; m. Charles Gordon, May 15, 1977; 1 child, Gayle. BS in Med. Tech., U. Minn., 1968, MPH, 1983; postgrad., Western Mich. U., 2002. Infection control coord. Samaritan Health Ctr., Detroit, 1980-83; cons Infection Control Resource Ctr., 1983-84; grad. rsch. asst. Rehab. Inst. Detroit, 1984-85; health and safety/mental health/nutrition coord. Renaissance Head Start, Detroit, 1984-86; infection control market specialist Calgon Vestal Labs., 1986-90; infection control coord. Sinai Hosp., Detroit, 1990-94; dir. quality svcs./infection control Great Lakes Rehab. Hosp., Southfield, Mich., 1994-95; epidemiologist Oakland County Health Divsn. Dept. Human Svcs., Pontiac, Mich., 1995-2000, Kalamazoo County Human Svcs. Dept., 2000—03, Jackson County Health Dept., Independence, Mo., 2003—. Mem. Nat. Sanitation Found. Task Group, 1997-99; mem. S.E. Mich. Epidemiology Com., 1995-2000, Coun. of State and Territorial Epidemiologists; mem. 5th Dist. Med. Response Coalition, 2002-03; presenter in field. Contbr. articles to profl. jours. Vol. B'nai Brith Women Twin Cities Coun., 1973-80, Hadassah, Am. Arab and Jewish Friends, 2002-03. U. Minn. Alumnae Freshman scholar, 1964; recipient Calgon Exec. Dir's. award, 1986, Calgon Vestal Lab. Pacesetter award, 1987. Fellow Mich. Pub. Health Leadership Inst., Wall of Tolerance; mem. NOW, ACLU, AARP, NAFE, Minn. Soc. Med. Tech. (bd. dirs. 1972-75), Minn. Alumnae Assn., Assn. Practitioners Infection Control and Epidemiology (edn. com. chair greater Detroit 1983-85, legis. liason greater Kansas City 2004—, greater Kansas City program com., 2006), Women and AIDS com., Am. Pub. Health Assn., Mo. Pub. Health Assn., So. Poverty Law Ctr, Greater Kansas City TB Coalition, Mid.-Am. Regional Coun. Pub. Health Com., Metro. Ofcl. Health Agys. of Kansas City Area. Avocations: reading, net surfing, volunteering. Office: 313 S Liberty Independence MO 64050 Business E-Mail: ellen.dorshow-gordon@tmcmed.org.

DORTON, TRUDA LOU, medical/surgical nurse, geriatrics nurse; b. Elkhorn Creek, Ky., Aug. 26, 1949; d. Clair Otis Parsons and Joyce Kidd; m. Eugene Anderson, Nov. 26, 1966 (dec. Apr. 1971); children: Gena Lynn, Richard Eugene; m. Leon Dorton, Dec. 15, 1972; children: Leondra Michelle, Jerald Thomas, Jonathan Layne. AS, student, Pikeville Coll., 1993. RN, Ky.; cert. ACLS, PALS. Instr. computer usage Lookout Elem. Sch., Ky., 1983; water/sewage technician McCoy & McCoy Environ. Cons., Pikeville, Ky., 1984; owner Signs of the Times, Elkhorn City, Ky., 1979-89; sec.'s asst. humanities and social scis. divsns. Pikeville Coll., 1989-92; nurse aide Mud Creek Clinic, Grethel, Ky., 1992-93; charge nurse Jenkins Cmty. Hosp., Ky., 1993-94; case mix coord. Parkview Manor Nursing Home, 1994-95, minimum data set and nursing care plan coord., 1995; acute care nurse Harrison Meml. Hosp., Cynthiana, Ky., 1996—2002; dir. nursing Robertson County Health Care Facility, Mt. Olivet, Ky.; long-term care charge nurse Trilogy Health Ctr. at Harrison Meml. Hosp., Cynthiana; med. inpatient svcs. Floyd Meml. Hosp., New Albany, Ind. Vol. nurse aide Mud Creek Clinic, Grethel, 1989-92. Founder free blood pressure clinic H.E.L.P.S. Community Action Program, Hellier, Ky., 1983; co-founder H.E.L.P.S. Community Action Group, Hellier, 1983; mem. Ellis Island Centennial Commn., N.Y., 1986. Appalachian Honors scholar Pikeville Coll., 1989-92. Mem. Nat. Geog. Soc., Ky. Nursing Assn., Order Ky. Cols. (Honorable Ky. Col. 1989), Smithsonian Inst., Nat. Trust Hist. Preservation, World Wildlife Fund, Pikeville Coll. Alumni Assn. Democrat. Mem. Worldwide Ch. of God. Avocations: creating Indian jewelry and wall hangings, classical music, reading. Home: 901 Santa Fe Rd Brooksville KY 41004

DORWARD, JUDITH A., retired business ordering customer service representative; b. Hazleton, Pa., Apr. 16, 1941; d. Eugene Joseph and Dorothy Cecelia (Shields) McNertney; m. Douglas Dean Owens, Apr. 15, 1961 (div. 1968); children: Kevin Patrick Owens, Kelly Shawn Owens; m. Clifford Neal Dorward, July 4, 1969 (div. 1974). AA, Lehigh County Community Coll., 1979; BA, Muhlenberg Coll., 1984; grad. in statis. process control, Process Mgmt. Inst., Inc., Mpls., 1986. Customer svc. clk. Pa. Power & Light Co., Allentown, 1959-61; mgr. Merle Norman Cosmetic Studios, Allentown and Bethlehem, Pa., 1968-70; adminstrv. clk. Pillsbury Co., East Greenville, Pa., 1970-85, ops. prodn. mgr., 1985-87, mgr. distbn. and prodn. control, 1987-93, chair labor rels. com., 1987-91, customer svc., vender liaison mgr., 1993-94; Pillsbury customer svc. rep. Americold Corp., Fogelsville, Pa., 1994-95; exec. field rep. Better Bus. Bureau Ea. Pa., 1996—2001; nat. bus. ordering customer svc. rep. West Corp., Reno, 2001—03. Held various offices Gen. Fedn. Women's Clubs; former voting machine operator Lehigh County, Slatington, Pa. Mem.: Exec. Women Internat. (dir. publs. 1991, dir. membership 1992—93, v.p., pres.-elect 1994, pres. 1995), Phi Beta Kappa. Democrat. Roman Catholic. Avocation: foreign travel. Home: 2830 Linden St Unit 3C Bethlehem PA 18017-3962

DORWART, BONNIE BRICE, historian, retired rheumatologist; b. Petersburg, Va., Jan. 27, 1942; d. Gratien Bertrand and Myrtle Elizabeth (Houser) Brice; m. William Villee Dorwart, Jr., June 22, 1963; children: William Bertrand, Brice Burdan, Michael Walter. AB, Bryn Mawr Coll., 1964; MD, Temple U., 1968. Diplomate Am. Bd. Med. Examiners, Am. Bd. Internal Medicine, Am. Bd. Rheumatology. Intern then resident in internal medicine Lankenau Hosp., Jefferson Med. Coll., Phila., 1968-72; instr. medicine Hosp. U. Pa., Phila., 1972-74; fellow rheumatology U. Pa. Sch. Medicine, Phila., 1974; instr. medicine Jefferson Med. Coll., Phila., 1974-76, asst. prof., 1976-81, assoc. prof., 1981-95, clin. prof., 1995—2003; assoc. investigator divsn. rsch. Lankenau Hosp., Wynnewood, Pa., 1978—88, chief arthritis clinic, 1982—86, chief connective tissue disorders, 1982—97; Civil War med. historian, writer, 2001—. Assoc. dir. Greater Delaware Valley Arthritis Control Program, 1975; mem. Gov.'s adv. bd. on Systemic Lupus Erythematosus, Phila., 1981-88. Author: Carson's Materia Medica of 1851: An Annotation, 2003; contbr. articles to med. jours., chpts. to books. Med. career advisor, active cells workshop Merion Elem. Sch., Pa., 1984-90; fund raiser Arthritis Found., Am. Cancer Soc., Phila., 1974-97; mem. resources com. Bryn Mawr Coll., 1985-90; historian Conf. Ctr. for Med. Edn., Lankenau Hosp., 2006. Named Physician of Yr., 32 Carat Club, Phila., 1986; Janet M. Glasgow scholar Temple U. Sch. Medicine, 1968. Fellow ACP, Coll. Physicians Phila.; mem. AMA, Am. Coll. Rheumatology, Phila. Rheumatism Soc. (pres. 1981-82), Pa. Med. Soc., Philadelphia County Med. Soc. Lutheran. Avocations: cooking, gardening. Home and Office: 124 Maple Ave Bala Cynwyd PA 19004-3031 Office Phone: 610-667-3849. Personal E-mail: dorwart@verizon.net.

DOSS, DELIA L., mathematics educator; d. Norman E. and Mary F. LaPlante; life ptnr. Richard D. Antonio; children: Chasity L. Thornton, Adam L. Thornton. BEd in Secondary Math., BA in History, BS in Math., U. Alaska, Anchorage, 1994; MS in Ednl. Adminstrn., Nat. U., LaJolla, Calif., 2006. Cert. dental hygienist USAF, 1977; driver's lic. hazard material Calif., 1979, secondary math., history tchr. Alaska, 1995. Crosscountry truck driver Tri State, Joplin, Mo., 1979—87; tchr. math., history Matanuska Sch. Dist., Palmer, Alaska, 1991—; adj. prof. Matanuska C.C., Palmer, Alaska, 1997—2001. Advisor, nclb coach Valley Pathways H.S., Palmer, Alaska, 2002—. Sec./treas. Goose Creek Cmty. Ctr., Talkeetna, Alaska, 1989—95; mem. Cmty. Clinic, Talkeetna, Alaska, 1989—91; pres. PTO, Talkeetna, Alaska, 1989—92. Mem.: NEA, MSEA (assoc.; rights com. 1999—2000), Profl. Math. Tchrs. (assoc.). Avocations: motorcycling, hiking, reading, writing. Office Phone: 907-745-2158.

DOSS, JESSICA YARINA, financial analyst; b. Johnstown, Pa., Aug. 1, 1974; d. Robert George and Karen Mastovich Yarina; m. Kenneth E. Doss, May 4, 2003. BA in Sociology, U. Calif., L.A., 1995; postgrad., Pepperdine U., Irvine, Calif., 2004—. Statis. analyst Circuit City Stores, Inc., Walnut, Calif., 1994—99; sr. fin. analyst Roth Staffing Svcs., Inc., Orange, 1999—2004, FileNet Corp., Costa Mesa, 2004—. Mem. com. customer satisfaction Roth Staffing, 1999—2004. Vol. Dem. Nat. Conv., L.A., 2004. Mem.: NOW, Internat. Thespian Soc., Am. Mensa, UCLA Alumni Assn. Independent. Avocations: creative writing, travel, reading.

DOSSEY, NANCY RUTHSTROM, elementary education educator, consultant; b. Houston, Sept. 1, 1947; d. Philip K. and Naomi Ruth (Mason) Ruthstrom; m. Dale A. Dossey, Aug. 3, 1968; children: James Philip, Steven Dale, Sarah Beth. BA, Baylor U., 1968; MEd, U. Houston, 1972. Tchr. 1st grade Austin (Tex.) Ind. Sch. Dist., 1968-69, Spring Branch Ind. Sch. Dist.,

Houston, 1969-72; univ. supr., teaching fellow U. Houston, 1972-73; tchr. English and reading, dept. chair Spring (Tex.) Ind. Sch. Dist., 1973-76; univ. supr. Tex. A&M U., Bryan, 1978-83; per diem cons. Houghton Mifflin Inc., Dallas, 1987; tchr. 2d and 3d grades Conroe (Tex.) Ind. Sch. Dist., 1987—. Mem. Edn. Improvement Coun., Conroe Ind. Sch. Dist., 1994-95; presenter profl. workshops. Mem. April Sound Bd. Govs., Montgomery, Tex., 1989—; mem. park com. April Sound Civic Assn., 1991; adminstr. The Haraldson Found., 1996—; exec. dir. Montogomery County Cmty. Found., 2004—. Mem. ASCD, Internat. Reading Assn., Tex. Classroom Tchrs., Sam Houston Area Reading Coun., Tex. State Tchrs. Reading. Avocations: music, sports. Home: 132 April Breeze St Montgomery TX 77356-5882

DOSSMAN, VIRGINIA GAIL, nurse; b. Houston, Oct. 8, 1958; d. Glen Gale Timmons and Martha Lou (Abbott) Hasse; m. Steve Rudolph Dossman, Jan. 16, 1981; children: Robert Dustin, Steve Nathaniel. Diploma, Goodall Witcher Hosp., 1979; AD, Ctrl. Tex. Coll., 1989; BSN, U. Mary Hardin-Baylor, 1992. Cert. med. surg. cert., Am. Nurses Credentialing Ctr., nursing adminstrn. cert., Am. Nurses Credentialing Ctr., 1993. Staff nurse Goodall Witcher Hosp., Clifton, Tex., 1979-81, Tex. Dept. Corrections, Gatesville, 1981-85, Para Med. Svcs., Waco, Tex., 1984-88, Gatesville Home Health Agy., 1987-88, Coryell Meml. Hosp., Gatesville, 1992-94, head nurse, 1994—. Mem. Coryell County Genealogical Assn. (pres. 1992-93). Democrat. Methodist. Avocations: genealogy, history. Home: 2610 Powell Dr Gatesville TX 76528-1937 Office: Coryell Meml Hosp 1507 W Main St Gatesville TX 76528-1098

DOSTER, SUSAN ELIZABETH, artist; b. Wilmington, Ohio, Nov. 12, 1962; d. Daniel Howard and Barbara Lou (Gibbs) D. BA, Purdue U., 1984; MFA, N.Y. Acad. Art, 1990. Sculptor Sculpture Basis, Bklyn., 1990; instr. Kids Who Can Draw N.Y. Acad. Art, N.Y.C., 1990; mural painter Modeworks, Inc., N.Y.C., 1990-91; decorative painter Horan, Inc., N.Y.C., 1992-93, Elizabeth Whalley, Bklyn., 1995—2000. Instr. figurative sculpture, drawing, painting Greater Lafayette (Ind.) Mus. Art, 1997; instr. founder Southwestern Ohio Atelier, Waynesville, 1997; instr. clay figure Sculpture Ctr., NYC, 1997; instr. in clay portrait sculpture NYU, 1998. One person shows include Purdue U., West Lafayette, Ind., 1996, Watson's Crick Gallery, West Lafayette, 1995, Offices Pennington Post GAllery, Penninging, NJ 2005-06; exhibited in group shows New Figurative Works Group Show, 1990, U. Rochester, 1993, Wilson Art Ctr., Harley Sch., Rochester, 1993, Realistic Painters Group Show, 1995, Sculpture Ctr., NYC, 1997, Grad. Sch. Figurative Art Alumni Assn., NYC, 1997, Schiller Gallery, 2006; exhbns. include: Coryell Gallery, Lambertville, NJ, 2004, 2006, Canal-Frame Gallery, Yardley, Pa., 2005, juror, 2006. Andy Warhol scholar NY Acad. Art, 1987-89; James Wilbur Johnston sculpture finalist, 1990. Home: 9363 New Burlington Rd Waynesville OH 45068-9706

DOTO, IRENE LOUISE, statistician; b. Wilmington, Del., May 7, 1922; d. Antonio and Teresa (Tabasso) D. BA, U. Pa., 1943; MA, Temple U., 1948, Columbia U., 1954; M of Quantitative Sys., Ariz. State U., 1986. Engring. asst. RCA-Victor, 1943-44; rsch. asst. U. Pa., 1944; actuarial clk. Penn Mut. Life Ins. Co., 1944-46; instr. math. Temple U., 1946-53; commd. lt. health svcs. officer USPHS, 1954, advanced through grades to capt., 1963; statistician Communicable Disease Ctr., Atlanta, 1954-55, Kansas City, Kans., 1955-67; chief statis. and publ. svcs., ecol. investigations program Ctr. for Disease Control, Kansas City, 1967-73, chief statis. svcs., divsn. hepatitis and viral enteritis Phoenix, 1973-83; statis. cons., 1984—. Mem. adj. faculty Phoenix Ctr., Ottawa U., 1982-98. Mem. APHA, Am. Statis. Assn., Ariz. Pub. Health Assn., Ariz. Coun. Engring. and Sci. Assn. (officer 1982-90, pres. 1988-89), Primate Found. Ariz. (mem. animal care and use com. 1986—), Bus. and Profl. Women's Club Phoenix, Mil. Officers Assn. Am. (state sec.-treas. 1995-96), Ariz. SPCA (bd. dirs. 2000-01), Sigma Xi, Pi Mu Epsilon. Office: PO Box 22197 Phoenix AZ 85028-0197

DOTSON, DAVINA P., music educator; b. Portland, Ind., Nov. 2, 1966; d. David L. and Diana K. Goodman; m. William B. Dotson, Dec. 17, 1994 (div. Jan. 4, 2006); 1 child, Connor E. BS in Music Edn., U. Indpls., 1989; MS in Music Edn., Butler U., Indpls., 1996. Lic. tchr. Ind., 1989. Instr. music grades 5-12 Union H.S., Dugger, Ind., 1989—90; instr. elem. music SE Fountain Elem., Veedersburg, 1990—. Asst. dir. h.s. marching band Fountain Ctrl. H.S., Veedersburg, Ind., 1990—91; dir. elem. choir SE Fountain Elem., 1991—. Elementary music teacher/sponsor (elementary festival) Circle the State with Song, handbell ringer UMC, choir member/soloist Linden UMC. Mem. Hillsboro Harmony Club, Ind., 1996—2003, pres., 1999—2001. Mem.: Ind. Orff Schulwerk Assoc., Ind. Music Educators Assoc., Music Educators Nat. Conf. Methodist. Avocations: reading, cross stitch, walking, piano, dance. Office: Southeast Fountain Elementary School 780 E US Hwy 136 Veedersburg IN 47987 Office Phone: 765-294-2216 3017. Office Fax: 765-294-3206. Personal E-mail: tigger1966@tds.net. E-mail: dotsond@sefschools.org.

DOTSON, ELIZABETH QUILLEN, speech pathology/audiology services professional; b. Gate City, Va., July 5, 1960; d. Charles Pat and Betty Whited Quillen; m. Leslye W. Dotson, Aug. 20, 1983. BS, Radford U., Va., 1982, MS, 1992. Cert. clin. competence in speech-lang. pathology Am. Speech-Language-Hearing Assn., 1993. Pediatric speech-lang. pathologist Mountain Region Speech and Hearing Ctr., Kingsport, Tenn., 1992—2002, Asheville Speech Assoc., NC, 2002—. Presenter Va. Speech and Hearing Assn., 1992, Tenn. Assn. Audiologists and Speech-Lang. Pathologists, 2001. Narrator: (documentaries) Mountain Children: Speakers and Storytellers, 1992. Mem.: Am. Speech-Language-Hearing Assn. (presenter nat. conf. 2000). Achievements include development of Early Start Child Hearing Services at Mt. Region Speech and Hearing Center: provides intensive aural-oral therapy for children post cochlear implant surgery (only program of its kind in region). Avocations: cooking, reading, herb gardening. Office: Asheville Speech Assoc 1063 Haywood Rd Asheville NC 28806 Office Phone: 828-285-8814. E-mail: moonowl@buncombe.main.nc.us.

DOTSON, STELLA MARIE, nurse; b. Parsons, Kans., Mar. 31, 1953; d. John R. and Rita M. McCall; 1 child, Meghann. ADN, Rogers State Coll., 1990; BSN, Northeastern State U., 1992; MS, U. Okla., 1996. RN, Okla. Legal sec. Thomas H. Williams, Atty., Pryor, Okla., 1970-71; sec. Okla. State U., Stillwater, 1971-72; exec. sec. Jon Douglas Co., Beverly Hills, Calif., 1972-83; confidential sec. Rockwell Internat., Tulsa, 1984-86; exec. sec. Westamerica Mortgage, Denver, 1987; nurse extern St. Francis Hosp., Tulsa, 1989, RN, 1990, Grand Valley Hosp., Pryor, 1990-91; RN emergency dept. Claremore (Okla.) Regional Hosp., 1991, discharge planning-utilization review nurse, 1992; infection control nurse, 1993; employee health nurse, 1994-98; practical nursing instr. N.E. Tech. Ctr., Pryor, Okla., 1998—. Mem. Okla. Nurses Assn. (scholar 1991). Roman Catholic. Avocations: travel, reading. Home: 311 Park Ave Pryor OK 74361-5207 Personal E-mail: sdotson@netechcenters.com.

DOTTERWEICH, LISA JOSETTE, political science professor, researcher; d. Ronald and Linda Dotterweich. BA in Polit. Sci. cum laude, Walsh U., N. Canton, Ohio, 1996—2000; MA in Pub. Policy, Kent State U., Ohio, 2000—05. Grad. asst. Ohio Employee Ownership Ctr., Kent, 2004—05; instr. Kent State U., 2005—. Rsch. asst. Kent State U., 2000—02, tchg. asst., 2002—02, team tchr., 2003—03, tchg. fellow, 2003—04. Contbr. articles to profl. jours., chapters to books. Mem. membership devel. & tng., women of yr. com. Jr. League Canton, Ohio, Inc., 2004—05, mem. admissions/provisional com., 2006—, chair membership devel. & tng. com., 2005—06. Recipient Outstanding Sr. Polit. Sci. award, Walsh U., 2006; David B. Smith Fellowship, Kent State U., 2006, Rsch. grant, 2006. Mem.: Am. Polit. Sci. Assn., Midwest Polit. Sci. Assn., Walsh U. Honor Soc., Pi Sigma Alpha. Roman Catholic. Avocations: reading, writing, travel. Business E-Mail: ldotterw@kent.edu.

DOTY, GRESDNA ANN, theatre historian, educator; b. Oelwein, Iowa, Feb. 22, 1931; d. James William and Gresdna (Wood) D.; m. James G. Traynham, Nov. 28, 1980. AA, Monticello Coll., Alton, Ill., 1951; BA, U. No. Iowa, 1953; MA, U. Fla., 1957; PhD, Ind. U., 1967. Instr. S.W. Tex. State U., San Marcos, 1957—61, asst. prof., 1964—65, La. State U., Baton Rouge, 1967-73, assoc. prof., 1973-79, dir. theatre, 1973-77, 81-91, prof., 1979-84, alumni prof., 1984—, alumni prof. emeritus, 1996—, chair dept. theatre, 1991-93, dean, 2004—. Author: Anne Brunton Merry in the American Theatre, 1971; co-editor: (with Billy J. Harbin) Inside the Royal Court Theatre, 1956-81: Artists Talk, 1990; contbr. articles to profl. jours. Bd. dirs. Arts Coun. Greater Baton Rouge, 1987-92, pres., 1990-91; mem. exec. com. Swine Palace Prodns. Rsch. grantee Nat. Endowment Humanities, 1981, Exxon Edn. Found., 1981. Fellow S.W. Theatre Assn.; mem. Am. Theatre Assn. (bd. dirs. 1977-80), Am. Coll. Theatre Festival (nat. chmn. 1976-79), Am. Soc. Theatre Rsch. (mem. exec. com. 1988-91, v.p. 1994-97), Nat. Theatre Conf. (sec. 1999-02), Coll. Fellows of Am. Theatre (dean-elect 2003-04, dean 2004-06). Home: 122 Highland Trace Baton Rouge LA 70810-5061

DOTY SEWALL, DANA LYNNE, choral director; b. Pitts., Pa., Aug. 18, 1971; d. Delmar Glenn and Virginia Fassett Sewall; m. Mave Roland Albert Doty, Aug. 2, 1997; 1 child, Evan Sewall Doty. BA in Music Edn., Whitworth Coll., Spokane, Wash., 1993; MA in Music Edn., U. St. Thomas, St. Paul, Minn., 2002. Tchr. gen. music K-6 Bethel Sch. Dist., Tacoma, 1993—94; choral dir. 7-12 Central Valley Sch. Dist., Spokane, 1994—98; choral dir. 6-8 Wayzata Mid. Sch., Minn., 1998—2000; choral dir. 10-12 Burnsville H.S., Minn., 2000—01; choral dir. 9-12 Blake Upper Sch., Mpls., 2001—05; choir dir. elem. ch. Plymouth Congl. Ch., Mpls., 2001—05; choral dir. 9-12 Gonzaga Prep. Sch., Spokane, 2005—. Coord. men's honor chorus N.W. Am. Choral Dirs. Assn., Wash., 1996. Supporter, mem. Mercer Island Presbyn. Ch., Mercer Island, Wash., 1992—; supporter March of Dimes, 2004—; advocate Guild Sch., Spokane, 2005—. Mem.: Music Educators Nat. Conf., Am. Choral Dirs. Assn. Democrat. Presbyterian. Avocations: reading, playing games, Sudoku, animals, walking. Office: Gonzaga Prep Sch 1224 E Euclid Ave Spokane WA 99207

DOTZERT, JENNIFER MARIE, special education educator; b. Monroe, Mich., Jan. 16, 1976; d. Carl Frank and Diane Lynn Zortman; m. Scott David Dotzert, Oct. 14, 2000. BS in Edn., Ind. State U., Terre Haute, 1998; MSW, Ind. U., Indpls., 2005. Spl. edn. tchr. Clay Mid. Sch., Carmel, Ind., 1999—. Mem.: NEA, Carmel Clay Edn. Assn., Ind. State Tchrs. Assn. Home: 200 Wintergreen Dr Noblesville IN 46062 Office: Clay Middle School 5150 E 126th St Carmel IN 46033 Office Phone: 317-844-7251. Business E-Mail: jdotzert@ccs.k12.in.us.

DOUCETTE, BETTY, public and community health and geriatrics nurse; b. Mosinee, Wis., Jan. 29, 1924; d. Wenzel and Margretta (Brietenstein) Vavra; m. Nieland R. Doucette, Nov. 12, 1949; children: Tom, Bob, Dan, John, Carol, Bill, Jeanne, Sue, Judy. Diploma, St. Marys Hosp. Sch. Nursing, Wausau, Wis., 1945; student, Nicolet Coll. and Tech. Inst., Rhinelander, Wis., 1971-81, Viterbo Coll., LaCrosse, Wis., 1982. Cert. pub. health nurse. Supr. med. ward St. Marys Hosp., Wausau, 1945-49; indsl. nurse Owens-Ill. Mill, Tomahawk, 1964-69; nurse supr. Golden Age Nursing Home, Tomahawk, Wis., 1969-78; home care nurse Lincoln County Nursing Svcs., Merrill, Wis., 1978-91; RN Lincoln County Health Bd., 1994—; parish nurse, 2000—.

DOUCETTE, MARY-ALYCE, computer company executive; b. Pitts., Feb. 12, 1924; d. Andrew George and Alice Jane (Sloan) Newland; m. Adrian Robert Doucette, Feb. 6, 1945 (dec. June 1983); children: David Robert, Regis Robert. BS cum laude, U. Pitts., 1945. Mgr. Newland Bros., Millvale, Pa., 1946-53; gen. mgr. Newland-Ludlo, Pitts., 1953-72; mgmt. cons. D3 Software, Garden City, NY, 1972-80, sec., corp. officer, 1980—. Fin. sec. Cerebral Palsy Assn., Garden City, Helen Keller Svcs. for Blind, Garden City; mem. Winthrop-U. Hosp. Aux., Mercy League, Friends of Adelphi Univ. Libr., Friends of Hist. St. George Ch. of Hempstead, N.Y., Adv. Coun. for Continuing Edn., Garden City Sch. Dist., 1988—. Mem. AAUW, L.I. Panhellenic, Univ. Club, Nassau County Hist. Soc. (life), Garden City Hist. Soc., Community Club Garden City-Hempstead, Woman's Club Garden City, Alpha Delta Pi, Pi Lambda Theta. Home: 146 Washington Ave Garden City NY 11530-3013 Office: D3 Software PO Box 8051 Garden City NY 11530-8051

DOUCETTE, MICHELLE ANNE, mathematics professor; b. Syracuse, N.Y., June 20, 1956; d. George Albert Doucette, Sr. and Annette Simon Doucette; children: Emily Gelsomin, Ashley Gelsomin, Eric Gelsomin. BS in Secondary Edn., SUNY, Oswego, 1978, MS in Edn., 1981, cert. in secondary math., 1981. Cert. math. tchr. grades 7-12 N.Y. Secondary sch. tchr. Franciscan Acad., Syracuse, NY, 1978—79, Bishop Grimes H.S., East Syracuse, NY, 1979—82; adj. prof. Onondaga C.C., Syracuse, 1986—2000, math. diagnostician, 1991—, assoc. prof. math., 2000—. Pvt. math tutor, North Syracuse, 1996—2000; adj. prof. SUNY, Oswego, 1998—2000. Recipient Trustees Recognition award, Onondaga C.C., 2000—01. Mem.: N.Y. State Math. Assn. Two Yr. Colls., Am. Math. Assn. Two Yr. Colls., Cicero North Syracuse Optimist Club (past v.p., past N.Y. dist. activities chair, past fellowship coord. and caller), Delta Kappa Gamma (legis. chair Beta Kappa chpt. 2003—04). Avocations: running, rollerblading, gardening. Office: Onondaga CC 4941 Onondaga Rd Syracuse NY 13215-2099 Business E-Mail: doucettm@suny.occ.edu.

DOUD, JACQUELINE POWERS, academic administrator; V.p. acad. affairs Woodbury U., L.A., until 1989, pres., 1989—. Office: Woodbury U 7500 N Glenoaks Blvd Burbank CA 91504-1099

DOUDS, VIRGINIA LEE, elementary school educator; b. Pitts., Jan. 17, 1943; d. Leland Ray and Virginia Helen (Dodds) Frazier; m. William Wallace Douds, June 20, 1964; children: William Stewart Douds, Michael Leland Douds. BA in Elem. Edn., Westminster Coll., New Wilmington, Pa., 1964; MA (Master's Equivalency), Dept. Edn., State of Pa., 1990. Cert. elem. tchr., Pa. Elem. tchr./non-graded Good Hope Elem. Sch., Glendale-Riverhills, Wis., 1964-65; elem. tchr./1st grade Carlisle Elem. Sch., Delaware, Ohio, 1965-66; elem. tchr./3rd grade Meml. Elem. Sch., Bethel Park, Pa., 1973-74; elem. tchr./1st and 3rd grades Logan Elem. Sch., Bethel Park, 1974-91; elem. tchr./3rd grade Neil Armstrong Elem. Sch., Bethel Park, 1991-99, Ben Franklin Elem. Sch., Bethel Park, 1999—. Software cons. Coal Kids, U.S. Dept. Mines, 1993; mem. lang. arts, reading com. Bethel Park Schs., 1989-92, cooperating tchr., 1986—, mentor tchr. 1992-93, 95—, mem. instrnl. support team, 1988-91, integrated lang. arts com., 1999-2000; judge Ben Franklin Scholarship Comm., 2001-03; mem. Mid. States Accreditation com., 1993-94, strategic planning com., 1994-95; SIP scholarship com. Bethel Park Fedn. Tchrs., 1973—. Mem. alumni coun. exec. bd. Westminster Coll., 1979-83; mem. exec. bd. Parents Assn., 1985-89. Recipient mini grant/writing, publishing ctr. Bethel Park Schs., 1989, Gift of Time tribute Am. Family Inst., 1990, 91, All Star Educator award U. Pitts./Pitts. Post Gazette, 1996. Mem. Nat. Coun. Tchrs. of English (lang. arts/reading com. 2000-01), Bethel Park Fedn. Tchrs., PTO. Republican. Presbyterian. Avocations: reading, gardening, golf. Home: 2679 Burnsdale Dr Bethel Park PA 15102-2005

DOUGALL-SIDES, LESLIE K., lawyer; b. Washington, Sept. 5, 1953; d. George Malcolm Richardson and Kathleen (Cahill) Dougall; m. Kenneth Jacob Sides, Feb. 19, 1994. BA, New Coll., Sarasota, Fla., 1975; JD cum laude, Florida State U., Tallahassee, 1978. Bar: Fla. 1981, DC 1981, Oreg. 1986, cert.: in city, county and local govt. law 1996, cert. profl. human resources 2001, bar: U.S. Dis. Ct. (middle and southern dist.) Fla., U.S. ct. appeals (11th cir.), U.S. Supreme Ct. Staff atty. Ctrl. Fla. Legal Svcs., Cocoa, 1982—85, dir. atty. Handicapped Law Ctr., 1985—87; asst. city atty., acting city atty. City of Key West (Fla.), 1987—95; asst. city atty. City of Clearwater (Fla.), 1995—; bd. dirs. IRRA, 2000—02; sec. West Ctrl. Fla. Chpt., Indsl. Rels. Rsch. Assn., 2003. Mem.: Indsl. Rels. Rsch. Assn. (sec. West Ctrl. Fla. chpt. 2003, bd. dirs. 2000—02), Soc. Human Resources, Clearwater Bar Assn., ABA. Avocation: sailing. Office: City of Clearwater City Atty's Office PO Box 4748 Clearwater FL 33758 Office Phone: 727-562-4010. Business E-Mail: leslie.dougall-sides@myclearwater.com.

DOUGHERTY, ANDREA M., social studies educator; b. Kingston, NY, Apr. 1, 1947; d. Andrew Joseph Murphy III and June Murphy; m. Vincent M. Dougherty, Jan. 10, 1976; children: Stacy, Courtney. BA, Coll. Mt. St. Vincent, 1968; MA, St. John's U., 1971. Lic. permanent tchg. NY State Edn. Dept. Tchr. St. Raymond's Acad., Bronx, 1970—73; caseworker ULDSS, Kingston, NY, 1973—76; tchr. JA Coleman Cath. HS, Kingston, 1976—78; caseworker UCDSS, Kingston, 1978—86; tchr. Kingston HS, 1986—. Staff mem. Project Capable Law Related Edn. Program, Kingston, 1986—; lead tchr. Social Studies Dept., Kingston HS, 2002—; facilator Kingston HS Jefferson Com., 2002—. Pres. Hurley Rec Swim Bd., Hurley, NY, 1994—96; sch. dist. rep. WWII Commemorative Com., Kingston, 1995—96. Named Outstanding Am. History Tchr., DAR, 2003; recipient Program of Excellence award, Nat. Coun. Social Studies, 1997. Mem.: NY State Coun. Social Studies, Nat. Coun. Social Studies. R-Consevative. Roman Cath. Avocations: travel, reading. Home: 131 Fairway Drive Hurley NY 12443 Office: Kingston HS 403 Broadway Kingston NY 12401 Office Phone: 845-943-1970. Business E-Mail: adougherty@kingstoncityschools.org.

DOUGHERTY, BARBARA LEE, artist, writer; b. L.A., Apr. 25, 1949; d. Cliff and Muriel Tamarra (Rubin) Beck; m. Michael R. Dougherty, Feb. 10, 1970; children: Jessie, Luke, Elvi. BS in Fine Art, N.Y. State Coll., 1975; M of Orgnl. Mgmt., U. Phoenix, 2003; postgrad., Concord Law Sch. Staff writer South Coast Cmty. Newspapers, Santa Barbara, Calif., 1988-90; contbg. editor Art Calendar, Upper Fairmont, Md., 1991—, dir. mktg. Frenchtown, Md., 1993-96, publ., 1997-2001, Art and Info., Westover, Md., 2001—02; exec. dir. Art Inst. and Gallery, Salisbury, Md., 2002—. Instr. art programs, 1975—; mem. City Adv. Bd. on Art, Santa Barbara, 1979-89, chmn., 1991-94; producer KCTV, Santa Barbara, 1990-94; CEO Harvest Am. Publs., 1992-93; judge for art shows Va. Ctr. for the Arts, 1998, Arts Atlantica, 1998, others; pub. Art Calendar, 1997-2001. Author, artist: In Search of a Sunflower, 1992, Harvest California, 1990, Getting the Word Out, 1996, Getting Exposure, 1996; author (book) Art of Conversation, 2005; prodr. 4 videos on art, 1990—; contbr. articles to Mktg. Art, Sunshine Artists, 1996, Art Materials Today, 1999, The Pastel Jour.; contbr. book; one-woman show at Salisbury State U. Galleries, 1994. Fundraiser Boys and Girls Club of Am., Carpinteria, Calif., 1977-93; bd. dirs. Somerset County Art Coun., 1999. Recipient Best of Show award Hosp. Aux., Boulder, Nev., 1991, 1st place award Death Valley 49ers Club, 1989, 2d place award, 1990. Democrat. Roman Catholic. Home and Office: 27528 Fairmount Rd Westover MD 21871-4102 E-mail: barbdoug@dmv.com.

DOUGHERTY, JANE, librarian; b. Hazelton, Pa., Nov. 7, 1953; d. Robert William and Ida Margarete Walker Hogg; m. Michael Aloysius Dougherty, June 28, 1975. BA in French, King's Coll., 1975. Head of pub. svcs. Hazelton (Pa.) Area Pub. Libr., 1975—. Chair, bd. dirs. Leadership Hazelton, 1998—. Mem. AAUW, Am. Libr. Assn., Pa. Libr. Assn. (N.W. chpt. bd. dirs. 1979-87), Agatha Christie Soc. Presbyterian. Home: 42 Hi Tor E Freeland PA 18224-3032 Office: Hazleton Area Pub Libr 55 N Church St Hazleton PA 18201-5857

DOUGHERTY, JANNIESE MARIE, social services administrator, music educator; b. Buffalo, Mar. 20, 1955; d. Ernest P. and Lorraine (Stahl) Rottner; m. William D. Dougherty; children: Michael, Ryan, David. ASME, Alfred (N.Y.) State Coll., 1976; BS in Indsl. Engring., Syracuse (N.Y.) U., 1979; postgrad., Nazareth Coll. Mech. engr. Corning (N.Y.) Glass Works, 1976-78; field maintenance engr. Xerox Corp., Rochester, N.Y., 1979-82; tech. documentation/tng. cons., 1982—93; pvt. piano and music tchr. Penfield, NY; dir. vol. svcs. Shepherd Ho. Comfort Care Home Terminally Ill, 2006—. Mem. marathon team Arthritis Found., 2006; vol. Time Care, Rochester, NY, 2006—. Mem. Nat. Music Tchrs. Assn., Rochester Piano Tchrs. Guild, Alpha Sigma Lambda. Avocations: volunteering, reading, running, knitting. Home: 15 Timus Cir Penfield NY 14526-1118 Office Phone: 585-381-0890. E-mail: jdougherty@rochester.rr.com.

DOUGHERTY, JOCELYN, retired neurologist; b. Topeka, Kans., Oct. 10, 1934; d. Arthur McIntyre and Helen Marie (Olson) Dougherty; m. Fred Herzig. BS in Edn., U. Kans., 1956, MD, 1967. Diplomate Am. Bd. Quality Assurance. Intern Presbyn. Hosp., San Francisco, 1967—68, resident, 1968—70, U. Calif., Davis, Calif., 1970—71, fellow, 1971; fellow in neuro-ophthalmology Columbia Presbyn. Hosp., NY, 1972; neurologist Bronx VA Hosp., Bronx, NY, 1972; cons. Sydenham Hosp., NY, 1973—74, Fairview State Hosp., Calif., 1975—2000; ret., 2000. Cons. St. Barnebes Hosp., Bronx, 1972, Columbia-Presbyn. Harlem Divsn., 1974. Contbr. articles to profl. jours. Mem.: Am. Acad. Neurology. Home: 700 Malabar Dr Corona Del Mar CA 92625-1839

DOUGHERTY, JUNE EILEEN, librarian; b. Union City, NJ, Mar. 27, 1929; d. Robert John and Jane Veronica (Smith) Beyrer; m. Donald E. Dougherty, Dec. 2, 1946; 1 child, Glen Allan. BA in Edn., Paterson State Coll., 1967; postgrad., Rutgers U., 1959—69. With A. B. Dumont, Paterson, N.J., 1950-54; sch. libr. St. Paul's Elem. Sch., Prospect Park, N.J., 1957—. Dir. North Haledon (N.J.) Free Pub. Libr., 1957—92; sec.-treas. Dougherty & Dougherty, Inc., North Haledon, 1968—73. Den mother Boy Scouts Am., 1954—57; mem. Gov. N.J.'s Tercentenary Com., 1962—64. Mem. Am. Libr. Assn., N.J. Libr. Assn., North Haledon Libr. Assn., Cath. Libr. Assn., N.J. Librs. Roundtable, Bergen-Passaic LIbr. Club, Friends N. Haledon Publ. Libr., St. Paul's Social Club. Roman Catholic. Home: 155 Westervelt Ave Haledon NJ 07508-3074 Office: 129 Overlook Ave Haledon NJ 07508

DOUGHERTY, MOLLY IRELAND, organization executive; b. Austin, Tex., Oct. 3, 1949; d. John Chrysostom and Mary Ireland (Graves) D.; m. Richard Pells, Oct. 2, 1999. Student, Stanford U., 1968—71, Grad. Theol. Union, Berkeley, 1976; BA, Antioch U., 1980. Tchr., fundraiser Oakland Cmty. Sch., Calif., 1973-77; assoc. prodr., asst. editor film Nicaragua: These Same Hands, Palo Alto, Calif., 1980; freelance journalist, translator Nicaragua, 1981; exec. dir. Vecinos, Austin, 1984—; cons. Magee & Magee Assocs., 1991—93; English, French and Spanish lang. tutor St. Stephen's Episcopal Sch., Austin, 2003—. Bd. dirs. Nat. Immigration Refugee and Citizenship Forum, Washington, 1985-88; spkr., fundraiser Salvadoran Assn. for Rural Health, 1986—; lectr. St. Stephen's Episcopal Sch., 1989. Office: Vecinos PO Box 4562 Austin TX 78765-4562 Office Phone: 512-476-1608. Personal E-mail: mollydougherty7@gmail.com.

DOUGHERTY, PHYLLIS MARILYN, social worker; b. White Plains, N.Y., Sept. 28, 1944; d. William Morris and Avis Melissa Callman; m. Edward Joseph Dougherty; children: Eric Johansson, Robert Johansson; 1 child, Gregory Booth. BA Douglass Coll., Rutgers U., 1966; MEd, William Paterson U., 1980. Cert. Sch. Social Worker 1978, Prin./Supr. 1984. Trilingual sec. Am. Cyanamid Consumer Products Internat., Wayne, NJ, 1967—68; bilingual caseworker Morris County Welfare Bd., Morristown, NJ, 1968—72; med. social worker Bergen Pines County Hosp., Paramus, NJ, 1977—79; sch. social worker Dover Pub. Sch., NJ, 1979—81, Hardyston Township Sch. Dist., NJ, 1987—2001, Andover Regional Sch., Newton, NJ, 2001—. Sch. social worker Sparta Pub. Sch. Dist., Sparta, NJ, 1987—90. Bd. dirs. in charge of hiring pers. Dover Day Care Ctr., 1970—72. Mem.: Sussex and Warren County Assn. Sch. Psychologists, Sigma Delta Pi, Pi Lambda Theta. Democrat. Lutheran. Avocations: exercise, skiing, reading, aerobics. Office: Andover Regional Sch Dist 707 Limecrest Rd Newton NJ 07860 Personal E-mail: pdougherty@ptd.net.

DOUGHERTY, URSEL THIELBEULE, communications executive, marketing executive; b. Rotenburg, Germany, July 30, 1942; naturalized, US, 1965; d. Hugo and Margarete (Marquardt) Thielbeule; m. Erich A. Eichhorn, Jan. 3, 1979. BA in Polit. Sci. summa cum laude, Cleve. State U., 1971; MA in Polit. Sci., U. Wis., 1972; MBA in Fin., Case Western Res. U., 1982.

Journalist maj. daily, women's mag., Germany, 1962-66; assoc. editor Farm Chems., 1967; publs. mgr. Trabon Sys., 1967-68; rsch. analyst Legis. Coun. State Wis., 1972; pub. rels. adminstr. to mgr. pub. info. Eaton Corp., Cleve., 1972-84; dir. pub. affairs Freightliner/Mercedes Benz Truck Co., Portland, Oreg., 1984-87; v.p. chmn.'s office Daimler Benz N.A. Holding Co., Inc., Washington, 1987-90; v.p. bus. devel., corp. affairs Penske Corp., Cleve., v.p. investor rels., 1990-97. V.p. investor rels. Detroit Diesel Corp., 1998—; founder, prin. USCH Internat. Fin. Comms. Firm; cons. small bus. Trustee Lake Erie coun. Girl Scouts U.S., 1975-82, Sr. Citizen Resources, 1978-81; amb. Jr. Achievement, 1979; steering com. YWCA Career Women of Achievement, 1981; adv. bd. Women's Career Networking, 1980-84; trustee, chair ad hoc planning com. Cleve. Music Sch. Settlement. Office: 1510 Crest Rd Cleveland OH 44121-1722 Personal E-mail: ursel3@ix.netcom.com.

DOUGHERTY BUCHHOLZ, KAREN, communications executive; m. Carl Buchholz; 2 children. BS, Dickinson Collo.; MS, U. Pa. Mem. staff U.S. Sen. John Heinz, Gubernatorial candidate Barbara Hafer, 1990; supr. devel. Pyramid Club, Phila., 1991—93; sales exec. Comcast-Spectacor, 1993—97; pres. Phila. Host com. Rep. Nat. Convention, 1997—2000; v.p. corp. comms. Comcast Corp., Phila., 2000—03, v.p. adminstrn., 2003—. Bd. dirs. Phila. Convention and Vis. Bur.; trustee Crohn's and Colitis Found. Am.; bd. dirs. Millennium Phila.; bd. advisors Dickinson Coll.; bd. govs. Pyramid Club. Named PENJERDEL Coun. Citizen of Yr.; recipient Headliner award, Greater Phila. Hotal Assn., Take the Lead award, Girl Scouts U.S.A. Mem.: Nat. Assn. Women Bus. Owners (hon.). Office: Comcast 1500 Market St Philadelphia PA 19102

DOUGHTEN, MARY KATHERINE (MOLLY DOUGHTEN), retired secondary school educator; b. Belvidere, Ill., Apr. 26, 1923; d. Edwin Albert and Theora Teresa (Tefft) Loop; m. Philip Tedford Doughten, Oct. 15, 1947; children: Deborah Doughten Hellriegel, Susan Doughten Myers, Ann Doughten Fickenscher, Philip Tedford Jr., David, Sarah Doughten Wiggins. BA, DePauw U., 1945; MS, Western Res. U., 1947. Social worker Children's Svcs., Cleve., 1947, San Antonio, 1948-49; tchr. English Indian Valley High Schs., Gradenhutten, Ohio, 1962-66; tchr. English and sociology New Philadelphia (Ohio) High Sch., 1966-86; ret., 1986. Mem. Tuscarawas County Juvenile Judges Citizen's Rev. Bd., 1980—2003, United Way, 1960—67, ARC, PTA, 1955—58, coun. pres., 1960—62, mental health chmn. state bd., 1963—65, libr. chmn., 1966—68; mem. Hospice, 1987—; founding com. Kent State U. Tuscarawas campus, 1961—62; leader Girl Scouts, 1959—68; vol. Ohio Reads, 2000—; vol. Reach for Recovery, Tell a Friend Am. Cancer Soc., 2002—; mem. Tuscarawas Arts Coun.; vol. Tuscarawas County Job and Family Svcs., 2003—; mem. Tuscarawas Philharm. League, Dem. Women, 1986—; bd. dir. Tuscarawas Valley Guidance Ctr., 1950—62, Cmty Mental Health Care, Inc., 1974—82, 1984—92, pres., 1979—81; bd. dir. Alcohol, Drug and Mental Health Svcs. bd., Tuscarawas-Carroll County, 1992—2001, v.p., 1996—98; bd. mem. State CC, 1965—68; founder, bd. dir. Ohio Cmty. Mental Health Svcs., Columbus, Ohio, 1970—80; bd. dir. Mobile Meals, 1992—; bd. dirs. Kent-Tuscounty U. Found., 1996—, pres., 1998—2000, sec., 2006—. Named WJER Woman of the Yr., 2002, Ret. Tchr. of Yr., Quaker Found., 2005; recipient Mental Health award, Cmty. and Profl. Svcs., 1978; Martha Holden Jennings scholar, 1975—76. Mem. AAUW (sec. 1962, v.p. 1996-98), New Philadelphia Edn. Assn., Friends of Libr., Chestnut Soc. (bd. dirs. 1987-89, 2001—), Tuscarawas County Med. Aux. (pres. 1959-60, 86-87, state bd. 1960-64), Union Hosp. Aux. (bd. dirs. 1986-98, editor 1986-98), DAR, Tuscarawas County Ret. Tchrs. Assn. (bd. dirs. 1999—), Coll. Club (scholarship chair 1989-91, 99-2001), Union Country Club, Atwood Yacht Club, Lady Elks, Mortar Bd., Phi Beta Kappa, Alpha Chi Omega, Theta Sigma Phi. Democrat. Presbyterian. Avocations: travel, golf, sailing, reading, photography. Home: 204 Gooding Ave NW New Philadelphia OH 44663-1727 Personal E-mail: philmoll@tusco.net.

DOUGHTY, PAMELA D., education educator; d. Charles J. and Beverly A. Conley; m. Chester E. Jr. Doughty, May 19, 2000; children: Jacob A. Kidd, Raymond E. Kidd. BA in Psychology magna cum laude, Mesa State Coll., Grand Junction, Colo., 1998; MS in Gerontology, Baylor U., Waco, Tex., 2000; PhD in Health Studies, Tex. Woman's U., Denton, 2002. Asst. prof. Tex. A&M U., Kingsville, 2002—. Bd. dirs. Christos Spohn Hosp., Kingsville; presenter in field. Grantee, Adminstrn. on Aging, 2002, Tex. A&M U., Kingsville, 2003—05. Mem.: Soc. for Pub. Health Edn., Am. Soc. on Aging, Tex. Soc. Pub. Health Edn. (bd. dirs. 2003—). Avocations: quilting, water sports. Home: 809 S 24th St Kingsville TX 78363 Office: Tex A&M Univ 700 University MSC 198 Kingsville TX 78363

DOUGHTY, SHANNON SUE, behavior analyst; d. Michael John and Debra Sue Haag; m. Adam Howard Doughty, June 5, 2004. BA in Modern Fgn. Lang., Albright Coll., 1998, BA in Psychology, 1998; MA in Psychology, W.Va. U., 2002, PhD in Psychology, 2004. Therapeutic support staff Holcomb Behavioral Health, Reading, Pa., 1998—2000; tchg. asst. W.Va. U., Morgantown, 2000—01; intern W.Va. U. Hosps., 2001—03; inpatient psychologist Parsons State Hosp., Kans., 2003—05; inpatient svcs. coord. Dual Diagnosis Treatment and Tng. Svcs., Parsons, 2004—05; owner, dir. Carolina Coast Behavioral Svcs., 2005—; behavior-analytic pvt. practice. Psychotropic medication rev. panel Class Ltd., Parsons, 2004—05. Contbr. articles to profl. jours. Mem.: APA, NC Assn. for Behavior Analysis, Southeastern Assn. for Behavior Analysis, Assn. for Behavior Analysis. Office: Carolina Coast Behavioral Svcs PO Box 80901 Charleston SC 29416 E-mail: shannon.doughty@comcast.net.

DOUGHTY-JENKINS, BONNIE-MARIE, middle school educator; b. New Britain, Conn., Mar. 12, 1967; d. Dennis John and Patricia Anne Doughty; m. John C. Jenkins, July 4, 2001. BS in Spl. Edn. and Elem. Edn., St. Joseph Coll., 1989, MA in Spl. Edn., 1995; EdD in Edn. Leadership, Ctrl. Conn. State U., 2005. Tchr. 5th - 8th grades spl. edn. Plymouth Bd. Edn., Terryville, Conn., 1990—99, tchr. 8th grade sci., 1999—. Mem. sch. bd. St. Matthew Sch., Forestville, Conn., 2001—; adminstrv. intern Harry S. Fisher Mid. Sch., Terryville, 2003—04. Mem., scholar com. Harry S. Fisher Mid. Sch. PTA, Terryville, 1990—; mem. Nutmet Artists, Plymouth, 2004—; mem. exec. bd. dirs. Conn. Jr. Women, Inc., 1992—99; mem., chmn. Intersvc. Club Coun., Bristol, 1990—99. Named Jr. Woman of Yr., 1992; named to Subaru Tchr. Hall Fame, 2003; recipient Heart Saver award, Am. Heart Assn., 2003, 2005, Spirit of Am. award, Conn. PTA, 2005; grantee, Shopa Found., 2000, Thomaston Savs. Bank, Conn., 2001, Main St. Cmty. Found., Bristol, 2002. Mem.: ASCD, Plymouth Sch. to Career Action Com., Am. Edn. Rsch. Orgn. Roman Catholic. Avocations: travel, crafts, cooking. Office: Harry S Fisher Mid Sch 79 N Main St Terryville CT 06786

DOUGLAS, ASHANTI SHEQUOIYA See ASHANTI

DOUGLAS, CYNTHIA, academic administrator; b. Park Ridge, Ill., Dec. 27, 1967; d.Lewis C. and Linda Douglas. BA in Econs. and Computer Sci., Northeastern Ill. U., 2001. Office mgr. Douglas Contractors, Chgo., 1985-95; student aid Northeastern Ill. U., Chgo., 1996-97; exec. adminstrv. asst. to pres. Caliber Data Tng., Chgo., 1997—, computer lab. instr., 1998—2001; access svcs. Northwestern Univ. Sch. of Law, Chgo., 2001—. Computer lab. instr., Caliber Data Tng., 1997—. Home: 5500 N Bernard St Chicago IL 60625-4659 E-mail: c-douglas3@law.northwestern.edu.

DOUGLAS, DAISY HOWARD, retired elementary school educator, writer, consultant; b. Morgan City, La., Aug. 12, 1939; d. Linzy John and Julia (Royal) Howard; m. James Allen Douglas, Oct 26, 1963; 1 child, Jewel. BS Elem. Edn., Grambling State U., La., 1962; MA Early Childhood Edn., Va. Commonwealth U., Richmond, 1978; cert, endorsement prin. elem. and mid. sch., Va. Commonwealth U., 1993. Cert. writer Inst. Children's Lit. Hartford, 1989. Tchr. 3d grade Sumpter Williams Elem. Sch., Morgan City, 1962—67; tchr. 5th grade Callao Elem. Sch., Va., 1967—72; tchr. 4th grade Eugene Meyer Elem. Sch., Washington, 1972—76; tchr. kindergarten Cople Elem. Sch., Hague, Va., 1976—85, tchr. 2d grade, 1985—87; tchr. 4th grade Fairfield Elem. Sch., Richmond, 1987—97; ret., 1997. Cons. African culture Richmond City Pub. Schs., 1989—; founder, dir., storyteller Westmoreland County Storytellers, Sandy Point, Va., 1998—; mem. adv. bd. Westmoreland Sch. Sys., Montross, Va., 2004—; bd. dirs. Va. Storytelling Alliance, Richmond. Author: History of St. Paul's Catholic Church, 1977, Jad and Old Annanias, 1997 (Club award, 1998), Daisy's Bayou Tales, 2000 (Club award, 2001), The Descendants of the First Mitchell Wilson of Westmoreland County, Va. 1824-2002, 2002, Africa - My Secret Dream, 2003 (Club award, 2003), China - My Historical Journey, 2003 (Club award, 2003), They Came From Virginia, 2004 (Club award, 2004), Daisy's Delightful Delicacies, 2005. Vol. deliver meals Meals On Wheels Assn., Heathsville, Va., 2000—; judge sci. fair Colonial Beach Sch. Sys., Va., 2000—; amb. Va. State Fair, Richmond, 1998—; leader, life mem. Girl Scouts U.S.; reporter Phi Delta Kappa, 1990—2004, Alpha Kappa Alpha, 1989—97. Named Outstanding Tchr. Am., Fuller and Dees, 1975, Tchr. of Yr., Fairfield Elem. Sch., 1994; recipient Tchr. Excellence award, Va. Edn. Assn., 1989, Svc. award, Alpha Kappa Alpha, 1997, Phi Delta Kappa, 2004. Mem.: NEA, NAACP (life Golden Heritage award). Avocations: reading, travel, cooking, gardening. Home: PO Box 37 Sandy Point VA 22577

DOUGLAS, FRANCES SONIA, minister; b. Stanaford, W.Va., May 12, 1931; d. Frank Gordon and Mary Celia Bradley; m. Paul Alexander Douglas, Jan. 6, 1949 (dec. Mar. 1993); children: Paul Jr., Sonia Paulette, Norton James, Mary Louise, Elizabeth Maria, Naomi Denise, Regina Michele, André(dec.). Doctorate (hon.), Christian Fellowship Ednl. Bible Coll., 1999. Housekeeper, 1955—70; sales rep. Amway Products, Niagara Falls, NY, 1970, Stuart McGuire Shoes, Niagara Falls, 1970, Finelle Products, Niagara Falls, 1980; founder, pastor True Deliverance Temple, Niagara Falls, 1974—2005; overseer True Deliverance, 2005—. Chmn. Cleve. Ave. Sch. Parent Group, Niagara Falls, Harriet F. Abate Sch. Parent Group, Niagara Falls; vice chmn. Niagara Falls Faith Based Collaboration, 2000—01; former treas. Niagara Falls Ministerial Coun.; founder Emmanuel Temple No. 2 Ch., 1952; bd. dirs. Niagara Falls Faith Based Collaboration, 2001—. Recipient Cert. of Appreciation for Outstanding Cmty. Svc., Rainbow Sr. Citizens Inc., 1986. Avocations: embroidery, crocheting, sewing, travel. Office: True Deliverance Temple 1318 Niagara St Niagara Falls NY 14303 Office Phone: 716-282-5587.

DOUGLAS, KIMBERLY, university librarian; MS in libr. sci., Long Island U., Greenvale, NY, 1978. Position at Bigelow Lab. of Ocean Sci., Boothbay Harbor, Maine; dir. Hancock Libr. Biology & Oceanography U. So. Calif., LA, 1982—85, head Sci. & Engring. Libr., 1985—88; libr. staff Calif. Inst. Tech., Pasadena, 1988—, acting libr. dir., 2003—04, univ. libr., 2004—. Libr. adv. coun. IEEE; mem. vis. com. Goddard Space Flight Ctr. Libr. Mem.: Nat. Info. Std. Orgn., Libr. Info. and Tech. Assn. Office: Building 1-43 Calif Inst Tech 1200 E California Blvd Pasadena CA 91125 Office Phone: 626-395-6414. Office Fax: 626-431-2681. E-mail: kdouglas@caltech.edu.*

DOUGLAS, MARJORIE MYERS, writer; b. Oxford, Ohio, Nov. 3, 1911; d. Walter Raleigh and Olinia May (Mattison) Myers; m. Donald Moats Douglas, June 19, 1937; children: Anne Marjorie Brothers, William Walter, Bruce David. BA, U. Minn., Mpls., 1933. Med. social worker Columbia Presbyn. Med. Ctr., N.Y.C., 1934-36; founder med. social work dept. Gillette Hosp. for Crippled Children, 1936-38; social worker Mpls. Pub. Schs., 1960-77. Author: Eggs in the Coffee, Sheep in the Corn, 1994 (Minn. book award), Barefoot on Crane Island, 1998. Named Alumni of Notable Achievement U. Minn., 1999. Home: 4344 Oakdale Ave S Edina MN 55424-1057

DOUGLAS, MARY YOUNGE RILEY, retired secondary school educator; b. St. Louis, Dec. 4, 1930; d. Walter Archibald and Jerdie Lee (Bibb) Younge; m. John Samuel Riley Jr., Apr. 17, 1954 (dec. July 1973); children: John Samuel Riley III, Jerda Marie Riley, Joel Younge Riley; m. Walter Wadsworth Douglas, Jan. 14, 1989. Student, Fisk U., 1947-49; BS, Fontbonne Coll., 1951; Masters, U. Ill., 1953. Tchr. Sumner High Sch., St. Louis, 1953-55, Hadley Tech. Sch., St. Louis, 1956-57; subs. tchr. St. Louis C.C., 1975; tchr. Soldan High Sch., St. Louis, 1975-90, Roosevelt High Sch., St. Louis, 1990-93, Soldan-Internat. High Sch., 1993—2001. Past bd. dirs. Nursery Found., St. Louis, Met. YWCA, St. Louis, Mo. Assn. Social Welfare.

DOUGLAS, ROXANNE GRACE, secondary school educator; b. Orange, N.J., Dec. 17, 1951; d. Joseph Samuel and Mary (Ferro) Battista; m. Richard Joseph Douglas, June 26, 1982; 1 child, Regina Grace. BA cum laude, Montclair State Coll., 1973; student, Sorbonne U., Paris. Cert. French, social studies and elem. sch. tchr., N.J. Tchr. social studies West Orange (N.J.) Bd. Edn., 1973-74, Orange (N.J.) Bd. Edn., 1974-75; substitute tchr. various schs. N.J., 1975-76; supplemental tchr. Irvington (N.J.) Bd. Edn., 1976-80, tchr. govtl. programs, 1980—. Advisor 7th dist. NJSFWC-JM State Bd., 1991-93, 2002-04, membership chmn., 1994-96, 98—, pub. affairs chmn., 1996—, state membership task force, 1999—, edn. chmn., 2000-01, dist. asst., 2001—, 7th dist. v.p., 2002-04, state arts performing chmn., 2004-06, state historian, 2006—, corr. sec. James Caldwell HS HSA, 2003-05, career fair chmn., 2006—. West Caldwell town columnist for local newspaper. V.p. James Caldwell HS Scholarship Com., 2004—; mem. West Caldwell Centennial Com., 2002—; cultural arts chmn. Caldwell/West Caldwell HSA League. Recipient Creative Writing awards NJSFWC-JM, Internat. Vol. of Yr. award, Citizenship award Am. Legion. Mem. Victorian Soc., N.J. Edn. Assn., Nat. French Hon. Soc., Nat. Edn. Hon. Soc., Jr. Women's Club of West Essex (co-pres., liaison internat. affairs chmn., pub. affairs chmn.), Coll. Club Orange-Short Hills, West Essex Women's Club (liaison to jr. woman's club, chmn. internat. affairs and pub. affairs dept. 1st night com. mem., pres., parent adv. coun.-bd. edn., pres., 1994—, internat. affairs chmn., centennial chmn., comm. chmn., performing arts chmn. 1996—), Verona Women's Club (membership chmn., v.p. 1998—, rec. sec. 2000—, twp. centennial com. mem., v.p. 2003-, mem. chmn. 2004-05, corr. sec. 2005—), Willing Hearts and Cultural Arts (chmn.), Hist. Soc. West Caldwell (pres. 1996-). Roman Catholic. Avocations: reading, antiques, walking, writing, travel.

DOUGLAS, VICTORIA JEAN, marketing professional, communications executive, educator; b. Wilmington, Del., Sept. 1, 1972; d. Richard Otto and Genevieve Douglas. Student, U. Caen, France, 1993, Oxford U., Eng., 1995, NYU Paris, 1996; BA in English/French, U. Del., 1996, MA in French Lit., 1999. Dir. comm. Mayor's Office, Wilmington, 1993—2001; mktg. and comm. chief cons. Met. Wilmington Urban League, 2001—; CEO Barracuda Comm., Wilmington, 2000—. Founder, chair Fgn. Lang. and Lit. Assn. Grad. Students, Newark, 1996—97; mem. mktg. com. Dept. Youth and Families, Wilmington, 1999—2000; supporting mem. Del. Ctr. for Contemporary Arts, Wilmington, 2001—; bd. mem. Kuumba Acad., Wilmington, 2001—; curriculum devel. staff, instr. English U. Caen Sch. Law, France, 1997—98; account supr. Saatchi and Saatchi, Rowland, NY, 2001. Organizer Nat. Night Out, Wilmington, 1993—95, Mayor's Breast Cancer Awareness Campaign, Wilmington, 2001; mem. ball com. Am. Diabetes Assn., 2002, mem. leadership coun., 2002—; v.p. sales Wilmington Drama League. Recipient Tomorrow's Leaders Today award, Pub. Allies, 1994, proclamation, City of Wilimington, 2000, Apex Award for Excellence in Mktg. and Pub. Rels. Brochures, 2002, APEX award Design & Layout, 2003, Comm. award, 2003. Mem.: AAUW, Pub. Rels. Soc. Am., Met. Wilmington Urban League, Pi Delta Phi, Golden Key Nat. Honor Soc., Phi Sigma Tau, Sigma Tau Delta.

DOUGLASS, DORRIS CALLICOTT, librarian, historian, genealogist; b. Nashville, Feb. 27, 1941; d. Claude Wilson and Catherine Hardy (Dorris) Callicott; m. George Patton Douglass, Aug. 28, 1965; children: George Archibald, Claudia Dorris Douglass James, Rebecca Rhodes Douglass Johnson. BA, Converse Coll., 1963; MLS, Vanderbilt U., 1965. Collator old newspapers Tenn. State Libr. and Archives, Nashville, 1963—64; cataloger Emory U. Theology Libr., Atlanta, 1965—67; clerical duties Ga. Hist. Commn., Atlanta, 1967; libr. Atlanta Hist. Soc., 1967—69; libr. circulation Columbia State C.C., 1993; asst. Williamson County Archives, 1993—94; libr., substitue in reference and genealogy Williamson County Pub. Libr., Franklin, Tenn., 1989—98, libr., head genealogy, 1998—. Contbr. articles to publs. Mem.: DAR (Tenn. state publicity scrapbook chmn. 1974—76, chpt. chaplain 1984—86), U.S. Daus. War 1812 (chpt. v.p., program chmn. 1985—87, chpt. chaplain 1987—89, chpt. v.p., program chmn. 2003—). Presbyterian. Avocations: collecting pre-1900 school books, travel. Home: 2040 Old Hillsboro Rd Franklin TN 37064 Office: Williamson County Pub Libr 1314 Columbia Ave Franklin TN 37064 Office Phone: 615-595-1246 1.

DOUGLASS, JANE DEMPSEY, retired theology educator; b. Wilmington, Del., Mar. 22, 1933; d. Hazell Brownlie and Ethel Katherine (Smith) Dempsey; m. Gordon Klene Douglass, Aug. 23, 1964; children: Alan Bruce, Anne Lorine, John Gordon. AB, Syracuse U., 1954; postgrad., U. Geneva, Switzerland, 1954-55; AM, Radcliffe Coll., 1961; PhD, Harvard U., 1963; ThD (hon.), U. Geneva, 1994; LHD (hon.), Franklin and Marshall Coll., 1992; DD (hon.), U. St. Andrews, Scotland, 1992; STD (hon.), MacMurray Coll., 2000. Assoc. dir. Presbyn. Student Ctr., Columbia, Mo., 1955-58; teaching fellow Harvard Divinity Sch., Cambridge, Mass., 1959-62; from instr. to prof. Sch. of Theology at Claremont and Claremont Grad. Sch., Claremont, Calif., 1963-85; Hazel Thompson McCord prof. hist. theology Princeton (N.J.) Theol. Sem., 1985-98, emerita, 1998—. Pres. Am. Soc. Ch. History, 1983; v.p. World Alliance of Reformed Chs., 1989-90, pres. 1990-97, hon. mem. exec. com., 1997-2004. Author: Justification in Late Medieval Preaching: A Study of John Geiler of Keisersberg, 1966, 2d edit., 1989, Women, Freedom and Calvin, 1985; editor: (with Jack L. Stotts) To Confess the Faith Today, 1990, (with James F. Kay) Women, Gender and Christian Community, 1997, (with Páraic Réamonn) Partnership in God's Mission in the Middle East, 1998; contbr. articles to profl. jours. Presbyterian.

DOUGLASS, NANCY URE, counselor; b. Pitts., Nov. 14, 1953; d. Robert and Ruth (Jone) Ure; m. Melfard Douglass, Dec. 27, 1975 (dec. June 1994); children: Alexandra Ure, Baily A. BA Sociology, U. Pitts., 1975, MSW, 1989. LCSW, Pa.; cert. home and sch. visitor, Pa. Case worker Children and Youth, Pitts., 1975—78; spl. edn. social worker Allegheny Internat. Unit, Pitts., 1989—91; sch. social worker Woodland Hills Sch., Pitts., 1991—2000; counselor birth parent, infant adoption Children's Home Pitts., 2000—. Cons., spkr. Parental Stress Ctr., Pitts., 1994; keynote spkr. Allegheny Internat. Unit., 1993, 94; spkr. in field V.p. Edgewood (Pa.) Recreation Bd., 1992—; asst. coach Little League Baseball, Edgewood, 1994—; mem. adv. com. Children and Youth Allegheny County, 1994—, Rankin Christian Ctr., 1995— Recipient Cmty. Svc. award Rankin Christian Ctr., Pitts., 1993 Presbyterian. Avocations: travel, reading, exercise. Home: 10 Carmel Ct Pittsburgh PA 15221-3618 Office: 5618 Kentucky Ave Pittsburgh PA 15232

DOUGLASS, SUSAN DANIEL, communications engineer, consultant; b. South Charleston, W.Va., Sept. 17, 1959; d. Charles David and Juliet Sue (Summers) Daniel; m. Michael Watson Douglass, Apr. 5, 1992. BS in Electrical and Electronic Engring., Calif. State U., Sacramento, 1985; MBA, Embry-Riddle Aero. U., 1989; Grad., squadron officer sch., 1988. Radio systems technician USAF, George AFB, Calif., 1978-80, radio systems instr. Keesler AFB, Miss., 1980-82, commd. 2d lt., 1985; advanced through grades to capt., 1989; program mgr. USAF, McClellan AFB, Calif., 1985-86, project engr., 1986-89, project mgr. L.A. AFB, 1989-91, exec. officer, 1991-92; program mgr. Scientific-Atlanta, 1993. Cons., 1993—95. V.p. Bush Hill Elem. PTA, 2000—01; active Va. Run Elem. PTA, Bull Elem. Run PTA; math mentor Bull Run Elem., Centreville, Va., 2003—05; co-chmn. Canterbury Neighborhood Adv. Bd., 1996—98; math and English tutor Dyer-Kelly Elem. Sch., Sacramento, 1985—87. Capt. USAF, 1989. Mem.: Co. Grade Officers Coun. (Officer of Quarter award 1987), Armed Forces Comms. and Electronics Assn., Air Force Assn. Republican. Avocations: dance, computers, golf, horseback riding.

DOUMAS, JUDITH, psychologist, educator; PhD, Union Inst., Cin., 1989. Sr. lectr. Old Dominion U., Norfolk, Va., 1981—89, chief departmental advisor, 1991—. Cons. and lectr., Hampton Roads, Va., 1991—. Bd. dir. Psychopolitical Peace Inst., N.Y.C., 1991—2006. Named Valedictorian, Montclair State U., 1968; recipient Excellence in Teaching award. Avocations: reading, writing, meditation, yoga. Office: Old Dominion Univ Hampton Blve Norfolk VA 23529 Office Phone: 757-683-3000.

DOUSAY, LINDA FAYE, academic administrator; b. Lake Charles, La., Feb. 10, 1951; d. Gervis Clarence and Laura Jeanette (Hamilton) Dousay; children: Michelle Danita Doucett Brown, Laura Jeanette Doucett Smith, Jeremy Layne Doucett, John Donavon Bult. Adminstrv. assoc. Lamar U., Beaumont, Tex., 2001—. Freelance writer, editor, Beaumont, Tex., 1996—; site adminstr. Writer's Voice, Canada, 2004—. Contbr. poetry to lit. publs. (Commemorative award Margaret Reid Contest for Traditional Verse, 2006, Best Poems and Poets of 2005, 2006, 2nd Place Internat. Soc. Poets, 2004, Eleanor Poetry award, 2002, Barnes Poetry award, 2002, Pulse Essay award, 1996). Recipient Tex. Incentive award; Eleanor Perlstein Weinbaum Meml. SCHOLAR, Lamar U., 2004—05. Mem.: Internat. Soc. of Poets (hon.), Tolerance So. Poverty (hon.). Pentecostal. Home: 7487 Shady Ln Beaumont TX 77713 Office: Lamar U PO Box 10024 Beaumont TX 77705 Office Phone: 409-880-8759. Office Fax: 409-880-8121. Personal E-mail: ldousay@yahoo.com. Business E-Mail: linda.dousay@lamar.edu.

DOUT, ANNE JACQUELINE, manufacturing and sales company executive; b. Detroit, Mar. 13, 1955; d. George Edwin and Virginia Irene Boesinger; m. James Edward Dout, July 16, 1977; 1 child, Brian Ross. Student, Macomb C.C., 1972-74; BBA, Western Mich. U., 1976; MBA, Duquesne U., 1982. Cert. cash mgr. Internal auditor Koppers Co. Inc., Pitts., 1976-78, cash analyst, 1978-79, supr. cash ops., 1979-80, mgr. cash ops., 1980-81, mgr. cash ops., asst. treas., 1981-87, dir. treasury svcs., asst. treas., 1987-88; corp. staff v.p., asst. treas. IMCERA Group Inc., Northbrook, Ill., 1988-91; v.p., treas. IMCERA Group, Inc., Northbrook, Ill., 1991-94; exec. v.p., CFO Champion Enterprises, Inc., Auburn Hills, Mich., 1994-98; pres. JJB Enterprises, Inc., Rochester Hills, Mich., 1998—2001; sr. v.p., CFO Pella (Iowa) Corp., 2002—. Bd. dirs. Cavco Industries Inc. Mem. allocations com. United Way, Pitts., 1979-83; bd. dirs. N.E. Lake County Coun. Boy Scouts Am., v.p. adminstrn., 1989-92; bd. dirs. Barat Coll., Lake Forest; Ill., 1992-94, U. Mich. Cancer Found.; bd. visitors Sch. Bus., Oakland U., 1994-2004; devel. com. Mich. Womens Found, 1996-2000. Mem. Treas. Mgmt. Assn. (exec. com. 1988-90, govt. rels. com. 1984-86, bd. dirs. 1986-89, strategic plan com. 1987-90), Gov. Coun. Edu, Fin. Exec. Inst., Mid Am. Com., Econ. Club, Exec. Club, Womens Econ. Club. Protestant. Office: Pella Corp 102 Main St Pella IA 50219

DOUTY, SHEILA, softball player; b. Diamond Bar, Calif., Feb. 26, 1962; Grad., UCLA; master's degree, U. So. Calif. Phys. therapist. Named to, UCLA Athletic Hall of Fame; recipient Silver medal, Pan Am. Games, 1983, Gold medal, Pan. Am. Games, 1987, 1991, 1995, ISF Women's World Championship, 1990, 1994, South Pacific Classic, 1994, Superball Classic, 1995, Atlanta Olympics, 1996, Gold medal, World Championships, 1998, Olympic Games, 2000, Intercontinental Cup, 1993. Office: Amateur Softball Assn Softball Fedn Internat 2801 NE 50th St Oklahoma City OK 73111-7203

DOVAN, CAROL See VAN SCHENKHOF, CAROL

DOVE, JUDY MERRYMAN, theater educator; b. Steubenville, Ohio, Mar. 30, 1956; d. Franklin Thomas and Matsue Kawai Merryman; m. M. Kent Dove, June 28, 1986; children: Joshua Kent, Daniel Franklin, Jennifer Kawai. BA, Capital U., Columbus, Ohio, 1974—78; MA, U. N.C., Chapel Hill, 1980—84. French tchr. Indian Creek Sch. Dist., Wintersville, Ohio, 1978—80; tchg. asst. U. NC, 1980—82; French/theatre arts tchr. Durham County Sch. Sys., NC, 1982—92; theatre arts educator Wake County Pub. Sch. Sys., Raleigh, 1992—. Trainer, tchr. effectiveness tng. Durham County Schs., 1987—92; artistic dir. Meredith Coll. Performing Arts Camp, Raleigh, 2001—; presenter N.C. Theatre Arts Educators, Raleigh, 2000—05; tchr. John Robert Powers, Raleigh, NC, 2000—03; educator Exploris World Cultures Mus., Raleigh, 2004—05; presenter N.C. Sch. Libr. Media Assn., Winston-Salem, 2005; co-founder, co-dir. Children's Harp Theatre. Author: (book review) Literature in Performance, 1981, (play) Undercurrents, 2006; dir.: (cable TV documentary) Viva la France, 1988, (cable TV spl.) A Tribute to

Black History Month, 1990, (musical theatre); actor: (outdoor drama) Trumpet in the Land. Fundraiser Make-a-Wish Found., Raleigh, 1993—2002; den leader - cub scout day camp Occoneechee Coun., Raleigh, 1999—2004; theatre merit badge counselor Boy Scouts Am., Raleigh, 2001—06; asst. den leader Brownie Troop 247, Raleigh, 2003—05; Christian tchr. North Raleigh Presbyn. Ch., Raleigh, 1988—2005, playwright/dir., religious dramas, 2000—06. Recipient Alumni Achievement award, Capital U., Columbus, Ohio, 2006. Mem.: Dramatists Guild of Am., NC Theatre Conf. (assoc. Best Play Mid. Sch. Divsn. 1992—97, Excellence in Directing award 1993—97, K-12 Theatre Educators award 2005), NC Theatre Arts Educators (assoc.; spl. event v.p. 2000—05), Ea. Star (assoc.). Presbyterian. Avocations: harp, playwriting, directing, environmental awareness, baking bread from scratch. Office Phone: 919-881-4970. E-mail: jdove@wcpss.net.

DOVE, RITA FRANCES, poet, language educator; b. Akron, Ohio, Aug. 28, 1952; d. Ray A. and Elvira E. (Hord) Dove; m. Fred Viebahn, Mar. 23, 1979; 1 child, Aviva Chantal Tamu Dove-Viebahn. BA summa cum laude, Miami U., Oxford, Ohio, 1973; postgrad., Universität Tübingen, Fed. Republic Germany, 1974-75; MFA, U. Iowa, 1977; LLD (hon.), Miami U., Oxford, Ohio, 1988, Knox Coll., 1989, Tuskegee U., 1994, U. Miami, Fla., 1994, Washington U., St. Louis, 1994, Case Western Res. U., 1994, U. Akron, 1994, Ariz. State U., 1995, Boston Coll., 1995, Dartmouth Coll., 1995, Spelman Coll., 1996, U. Pa., 1996, U. NC, 1997, U. Notre Dame, 1997, Northeastern U., 1997, Columbia U., 1998, Washington & Lee U., 1999, SUNY, Brockport, 1999; LLD, Pratt Inst., 2001, Howard U., 2001; LLD (hon.), Skidmore Coll., 2004. Asst. prof. English Ariz. State U., Tempe, 1981-84, assoc. prof., 1984-87, prof., 1987-89, U. Va., Charlottesville, 1989-93, Commonwealth prof. English, 1993—; U.S. poet laureate, cons. in poetry Libr. of Congress, Washington, 1993-95, spl. cons. in poetry, 1999-2000; columnist Washington Post, 2000—02; poet laureate Va., 2004—. Writer-in-residence Tuskegee Inst., Ala., 1982; lit. panelist Nat. Endowment for Arts, Washington, 1984-86, chmn. poetry grants panel, 1985; judge Walt Whitman award Acad. Am. Poets, 1990, Pulitzer prize in poetry, 1991, Ruth Lilly prize 1991, Nat. Book award in poetry 1991, 98, Anisfield-Wolf Book awards, 1992—, Shelley Meml. award, 1997, Amy Lowell fellowship, 1997; poetry panel chmn. Pulitzer prize, 1997; final judge Brittingham and Pollack prizes, 1997; juror Christopher Columbus Fellowship Found., 1998-02, Duke Ellington awards, 1999; bd. dirs. Poetry Daily, 2002; chancellor Acad. Am. Poets, 2006-. Author: (poetry) Ten Poems, 1977, The Only Dark Spot in the Sky, 1980, The Yellow House on the Corner, 1980, Mandolin, 1982, Museum, 1983, Thomas and Beulah, 1986 (Pulitzer Prize in poetry 1987), The Other Side of the House, 1988, Grace Notes, 1989 (Ohioana award 1990), Selected Poems, 1993 (Ohioana award 1994), Lady Freedom Among Us, 1994, Mother Love, 1995, Evening Primrose, 1998, On the Bus with Rosa Parks, 1999 (Ohioana award 2000), American Smooth, 2004; (verse drama) The Darker Face of the Earth, 1994 (W. Alton Jones Found. grant 1994, Kennedy Ctr. Fund for New Am. Plays award 1995, Geraldine Dodge Found. grant, 1997), completely rev. 2d edit., 1996, expanded 3d edit., 2000 (first performance Oreg. Shakespeare Festival 1996); (novel) Through the Ivory Gate, 1992 (Va. Coll. Stores Book award 1993); (short stories) Fifth Sunday, 1985 (Callaloo award 1986); (essays) The Poet's World, 1995, (song cycle) Seven for Luck (music by John Williams), 1st performance Boston Symphony Orch., Tanglewood, 1998; mem. editl. bd. Nat. Forum, 1984-89, Iris, 1989—; mem. adv. bd. Ploughshares, 1992—, NC Writers Network, 1992-99, Civilization, 1994-97, Am. Poetry Rev., 2005-; assoc. editor Callaloo, 1986-98; adv. and contbg. editor Gettysburg Rev., 1987—, TriQuarterly, 1988—, Ga. Review, 1994—, Bellingham Rev., 1996—, Internat. Quarterly, 1997—, Callaloo, 1998—, Mid-Am. Rev., 1998—; editor Best Am. Poetry, 2000. Commr. The Schomburg Ctr. for Rsch. in Black Culture, NY Pub. Libr., 1987—; mem. Renaissance Forum Folger Shakespeare Libr., 1993-95, Coun. of Scholars Libr. of Congress, 1994—; mem. nat. launch com. AmeriCorps, 1994; mem. awards coun. Am. Acad. Achievement, 1994-2001; mem. adv. bd. Thomas Jefferson Ctr. Freedom of Expression, 1994—, US Civil War Ctr., 1995-99, Va. Ctr. Creative Arts, 1995—, Student Achievement and Advocacy Svcs., 2002—, DuBois Ctr. Am. History and Culture, 2005-, The Givens Found. for African Am. Lit., 2005-; The Poets Corner elector Cathedral Ch. St. John the Divine, NYC, 1991-2002; bd. govs. Humanities Rsch. Inst. U. Calif., 1996-99; bd. dirs. Poetry Daily, 2004—; chancellor Acad. Am. Poets, 2006—. Presdl. scholar, 1970, Nat. Achievement scholar, 1970-73; Fulbright/Hays fellow, 1974-75, rsch. fellow U. Iowa, 1975, teaching/writing fellow U. Iowa, 1976-77, Guggenheim Found. fellow, 1983-84, Mellon sr. fellow Nat. Humanities Ctr., 1988-89, fellow Ctr. for Advanced Studies, U. Va., 1989-92, fellow Shannon Ctr. for Advanced Studies, U. Va., 1995—; grantee NEA, 1977, 89; recipient Lavan Younger Poet award Acad. Am. Poets, 1986, GE Found. award, 1987, Bellagio residency Rockefeller Found., Italy, 1988, Ohio Gov.'s award 1988, Literary Lion citation NY Pub. Libr., 1991, Women of Yr. award Glamour Mag., 1993, NAACP Great Am. Artist award, 1993, Golden Plate award Am. Acad. Achievement, 1994, Disting. Achievement medal Miami U. Alumni Assn., 1994, Renaissance Forum award for leadership in the literary arts Folger Shakespeare Libr., 1994, Carl Sandburg award Internat. Platform Assn., 1994, Heinz award in arts and humanities, 1996, Charles Frankel prize/Nat. Humanities medal Pres. of US and NEH, 1996; inducted Ohio Women's Hall of Fame, 1991, Nat. Assn. of Women in Edn. Disting. Woman award, 1997, Sara Lee Frontrunner award, 1997, Barnes & Noble Writers for Writers award, 1997, Levinson prize Poetry mag., 1998, John Frederick Nims Translation prize, 1999, Libr. Lion award NY Pub. Libr., 2000, Duke Ellington Lifetime Achievement award, 2001, Emily Couric Women's Leadership award, 2003, Common Wealth award, 2006, Writing Today Grand Master award, 2006; named Phi Beta Kappa poet Harvard U., 1993, Poet Laureate of Commonwealth of Va., 2004-06. Fellow Am. Acad. Arts & Scis.; mem. PEN, ASCAP, Am. Philos. Soc., Poetry Soc. Am., Associated Writing Programs (bd. dirs. 1985-88, pres. 1986-87), Am. Acad. Achievement (mem. golden plate awards coun. 1994—2001), Phi Beta Kappa (senator 1994-2001), Phi Kappa Phi. Office: U Va Dept English 219 Bryan Hall PO Box 400121 Charlottesville VA 22904-4121 Business E-Mail: rfd4b@virginia.edu.

DOVIAK, INGRID ELLINGER, elementary school educator; b. New Britain, Conn., Feb. 10, 1971; d. John Leonard and Marjorie Chain Ellinger; m. Stephen Michael Doviak, June 8, 1996. BS, MA, So. Conn. State U., 1993. Tchr. head dept. enrichment grades k-8 Wntergreen Interdist. Magnet Sch., Hamden, Conn., 1998—. Adj. instr. deptl edn. Sacred Heart U., Fairfield, Conn., 2000—; adj. instr. So. Conn. State U., New Haven, 1998—; presenter Atomic Math Conf., 2001, 02, Conn. Assn. Math. Precocious Youth, 2000, 01, 02, Conn. Assn. Schs.

DOVRING, KARIN ELSA INGEBORG, writer, poet, playwright, media specialist; b. Stenstorp, Sweden, Dec. 5, 1919; arrived in US, 1953, naturalized, 1968; m. Folke Dovring, May 30, 1943. Grad., Coll. Commerce, Gothenburg, Sweden, 1936; MA, Lund U., Sweden, 1943, PhD, 1951; Phil. Licentiate, Gothenburg U., 1947. Journalist several Swedish daily newspapers and weekly mags., 1940-60; tchr. Swedish colls.; rsch. assoc. of Harold Lasswell Yale U., New Haven, 1953-78; fgn. corr. Swedish newspapers, Italy, Switzerland, France and Germany, 1956-60; freelance writer, journalist, 1960—; rsch. prof. comms. and media studies U. Ill., Urbana, 2002. Vis. prof. Internat. U., The Vatican, Rome, 1958-60, Gottingen (W.Ger.) U., 1962; lectr. U.S. Army, Peace Corps, Yale U., U. Wis., McGill U., U. Iowa; rsch. assoc. U. Ill., Urbana, 1968-69, guest lectr., 2001-05; invited contbr. Social Sci. Rsch. Coun., 1988; speaker Conf. Law and Policy, Yale U. Law Sch., 1992-93, 99—; hon. mem. Profl. Women's Adv. Bd. Am. Biograph. Inst., Raleigh, NC, 2003; adv. coun. Internat. Biographical Ctr., Cambridge, Eng.; interviewee radio and TV programs; writer Ill. Alliance to Prevent Nuclear War, radio, theater; prof. comm. and media studies U. Ill. Coll. Comm., 2002—; moderator series U.S.A. Faces the World-Markets in Communications, 2004—; songwriter Hollywood and Nashville; plays for TV movies. Author: Songs of Zion, 1951, Land Reform as a Propaganda Theme, 3d edit., 1965, Road of Propaganda, 1959, Optional Society, 1972, Frontiers of Communication, 1975, English as Lingua Franca: Double Talk in Global Persuasion, 1997, (short stories) No Parking This Side of Heaven, 1982, Harold D. Lasswell: His Communication with a Future, 1987, 2d edit., 1988; (novel) Heart in Escrow, 1990; (poems) Faces in a Mirror, 1995, In the Service of Persuasion: English as Lingua Franca Across the Globe, 2001, Changing Scenery, 2003, Propaganda Is the Poetry of Politics, 2002, Propagandists: The Artists, 2004, (collection of poems) On This and That, 2006; contbr. chpts. to books, articles to mags.; author numerous poems. Named Poet of Yr., Internat. Libr. Poetry, 2000—06; named to, Internat. Poetry Hall of Fame, 1996; recipient Swedish Nat. award for short stories, Bonniers Pub. Ho., Stockholm, 1951. Mem. Soc. Jean Jacques Rousseau of Geneva (hon. life), Acad. Am. Poets. Democrat. Home: 613 W Vermont Ave Urbana IL 61801-4824 Office: U Ill Coll Comm 119 Gregory Hall 810 South Wright St Urbana IL 61801 Office Phone: 217-333-2350.

DOW, LESLIE WRIGHT, communications company executive, photographer, writer; b. NYC, Apr. 28, 1938; d. Charles Leslie Kerr and Margaret Scott (MacArthur) Wright; m. William Arthur Dow, 1987; 1 child, John M. Haywood. AA, Colby-Sawyer Coll., 1957; cert., Katharine Gibbs Sch., 1958. Prodn. asst. Time Inc., N.Y.C., 1958-60; exec. asst. Jefferson-Standard Broadcasting Co., Charlotte, N.C., 1960-68, G.B. Wilkins Inc., Charlotte, 1981—82; pres., pub. relations cons. Wright Comm., Inc., Charlotte, 1982—2006. Contbr. photography to mags. and profl. jours.; contbr. articles to mags. Bd. dirs. Charlotte Symphony Women's Assn., 1964-71, Charlotte Symphony Orch., 1965; mem. Aux. of the Mint Mus., Charlotte, 1965—; trustee Colby-Sawyer Coll., 1997—2006. Mem. NAFE, Am. Soc. Interior Designers (dir. pub. rels. Carolinas chpt. 1984-88), Am. Bus. Women's Assn., Am. Soc. Mag. Photographers, Profl. Photographers N.C., Profl. Photographers Am. Home and Office: 1954 Brawley School Rd Mooresville NC 28117-7083

DOW, LOIS WEYMAN, physician; b. Cin., Mar. 11, 1942; d. Albert Dames and Elsie Marion (Krug) Weyman; m. Alan Wayne Dow, July 23, 1966 (div. Aug. 1979); children: Elizabeth Suzanne, Alan Wayne. BA summa cum laude, Cornell U., 1964; MD cum laude, Harvard U., 1969. Diplomate Am. Bd. Internal Medicine, Am. Bd. Hematology, Am. Bd. Oncology, Am. Bd. Pathology in Hematopathology. Intern Bronx Mcpl. Hosp. Ctr., N.Y.C., 1968—69; resident internal medicine Presbyn. Hosp., N.Y.C., 1969—70; fellow hematology Columbia U. Coll. Physicians and Surgeons, 1970—72; instr., rsch. assoc. U. Tenn., Memphis, 1972—73, asst. prof., 1973—74; rsch. assoc. hematology and oncology St. Jude Children's Rsch. Hosp., Memphis, 1974—77, asst. mem., 1977—80, assoc. mem., 1980—88; assoc. prof. pediat. U. Tenn., Memphis, 1983—88; mem. staff Bapt. Mem. Hosp., Memphis, 1972—88, St. Jude Children's Rsch. Hosp., 1974—88; pvt. practice Newark, 1988—98; mem. staff Med. Ctr. Del. (now Christiana Care Health Ctr.), Wilmington, 1988—98; dir. hematology lab. Med. Ctr. Del. (now Christiana Care Health Ctr.), Newark, Del., 1993—98; mem. staff Alfred I Dupont Inst., 1988—98, St. Francis Hosp., 1996—98. Assoc. prof., Jefferson Med. Coll., Phila., 1988—; cons., Nat. Cancer Inst. Contbr. articles to profl. jours. Fellow ACP; mem. Am. Soc. Clin. Oncology, Am. Fedn. Clin. Rsch., Am. Soc. Hematology, Am. Assn. for Cancer Rsch., Am. Soc. Clin. Pathologists, Cornell Club, Harvard Club. Office: 3917 Heather Dr Wilmington DE 19807-2117

DOW, MARLA, counselor; d. Robert E. and Vonnie L. Summers; m. Richard Dow, Aug. 5, 1989; children: David A., Richard C. AA in Acctg., Diablo Valley Coll., 1984; BA in Bus. Mgmt., St. Mary's Coll., 1986; MA in Marriage & Family Therapy, George Fox U., 1998. Lic. profl. counselor Oreg., 2003, nat. cert. counselor. Counselor Dow Counseling, Lafayette, Oreg., 2003—05; sch. counselor Salem Keizer Sch. Dist., Oreg., 2003—. Vol. Habitat for Humanity, McMinnville, Oreg., 2004—. Grantee Safe & Drug Free Schs. grant, Willamette Valley Edn. Svc. Dist., 2003. Mem.: Oreg. Sch. Counselors Assn. (assoc.), ASCA (assoc.). Avocations: backpacking, bicycling, quilting, gardening. Office: PO Box 1094 Lafayette OR 97127 Business E-Mail: mdow@dowcounseling.com.

DOW, MARTHA ANNE, academic administrator, biology professor; b. Little Rock, Jan. 3, 1939; d. Clarence Edgar and Gretchen Devron (Gable) Eudy; m. Gary Eugene Dow, Aug. 28, 1960; children: Julie, Kevin, Jerilyn. BS in Biology, No. Mont. Coll., 1961; MS in Microbiology, Mont. State U., 1969; PhD in Microbiology, U. Hawaii, 1989. Registered microbiologist. Prof., chair biology No. Mont. Coll., Havre, 1986-90, v.p. acad. affairs, 1990-92; provost Oreg. Inst. Tech., Klamath Falls, Oreg., 1992—98, pres., 1998—. Dir. Mont. Environ. Tng. Ctr., EPA, No. Mont. Coll., 1989; pres. Nat. Environ. Tng. Assn., Phoenix, Oreg., 1990-92. Recipient Disting. Svc. award, Klamath County C. of C., 2000, Candice Richard award, Klamath County Econ. Develop. Corp., 2000. Mem. Am. Assn. for Advancement of Sci., Am. Assn. State Coll. & Univ., Am. Soc. for Engring. Edn., Am. Soc. Microbiology, Am. Water Works Assn., Water Environment Fedn. Methodist. Office: Oreg Inst Tech 3201 Campus Dr Klamath Falls OR 97601-8801

DOW, MARY ALEXIS, auditor; b. South Amboy, N.J., Feb. 19, 1949; d. Alexander and Elizabeth Anne (Reilly) Pawlowski. BS with honors, U. R.I., 1971. CPA Oreg. Staff acct. Deloitte & Touche, Boston, 1971-74; sr. acct. Price Waterhouse, Portland, Oreg., 1974-77, mgr., 1977-81, sr. mgr., 1981-84; CFO Copeland Lumber Yards Inc., Portland, 1984-86; ind. cons. in field, 1986-94; elected auditor Metro, Portland, 1995—. Bd. dirs. Longview Fibre Co., Oreg. Health Sci. U. Med. Group. Past. chmn. bd. dirs., exec. com. Oreg. Trails chpt. N.W. Regional Blood Svcs. ARC; past. bd. dirs., exec. com., treas. Oreg. Mus. Sci. and Industry. Mem.: AICPA, Fin. Execs. Internat. (nat. exec. com., past nat. treas., past pres. Portland chpt., past v.p. western area), Oreg. Soc. CPAs (past bd. dirs.), Am. Woman's Soc. CPAs, Pacific N.W. Intergovtl. Audit Forum (exec. com.), Multnomah Athletic Club (past treas., past trustee), City Club (past bd. govs.). Roman Catholic. Office: Auditor Office Metro 600 NE Grand Ave Portland OR 97232-2736 Office Phone: 503-797-1891. Business E-Mail: dowa@metro.dst.or.us.

DOWBEN, CARLA LURIE, lawyer, educator; b. Chgo., Jan. 22, 1932; d. Harold H. and Gertrude Lurie; m. Robert Dowben, June 20, 1950; children: Peter Arnold, Jonathan Stuart, Susan Laurie. AB, U. Chgo., 1950; JD, Temple U., 1955. Bar: Ill. 1957, Mass. 1963, Tex. 1974, U.S. Surpeme Ct. 1974. Assoc. Conrad and Verges, Chgo., 1957-62; exec. officer MIT, Cambridge, Mass., 1963-64; legal planner Mass. Health Planning Project, Boston, 1964-69; assoc. prof. Life Scis. Inst. Brown U., Providence, 1970-72; asst. prof. health law U. Tex. Health Sci. Ctr., Dallas, 1973-78, assoc. prof., 1978-93; ptnr. Choate & Lilly, Dallas, 1989-92; head health law sect. Looper, Reed, Mark & McGraw, Dallas, 1992-95, of counsel, 1995-99. Adj. assoc. prof. health law U. Tex., 1993-95; cons. to bd. dirs. Mental Health Assn., 1958-86, Ft. Worth Assn. Retarded Citizens, 1980-90, Advocacy, Inc., 1981-85; dir. Nova Health Systems, 1975—, Tockwotton Home, 1994-98. Contbr. articles to profl. jours. Active in drafting helath and mental health legis., agy. regulation in several states and local govts.; bd. dirs. City Providence Retirement Bd., 1996—. Mem. ABA, Tex. Bar Assn., Dallas Bar Assn., Am. Health Lawyers Assn., Hastings Inst. Ethics, Tex. Family Planning Assn. Mem. Soc. Of Friends.

DOWD, FRANCES CONNELLY, retired librarian; b. Newburyport, Mass., Dec. 9, 1918; d. Martin Francis and Nelle Magdalen (Quinn) Connelly; m. James Reynolds Dowd, June 7, 1941 (dec. June 1944); children: James Reynolds Jr., Thomas Henry III. AB, Wellesley Coll., 1941; MLS, Columbia U., 1955. Cataloger Phillips Acad. Libr., Andover, Mass., 1955-57; asst. libr. Wheelock Coll. Libr., Boston, 1957-59; head of circulation U. R.I., Kingston, 1959-62; head libr. Ins. Libr., Boston, 1962-66; head bus. & sci. dept. Providence (R.I.) Pub. Libr., 1966-70; reference libr. Boston U. Libr., 1970-74; head libr. Mass. Horticulture Soc., Boston, 1974-79; reference libr. Haverhill (Mass.) Pub. Libr., 1979-89, Endicott Coll. Libr., Beverly, Mass., 1989—2001; ret., 2001. Lifelong learning instr. No. Essex C.C., 1997—. Editor: Whittier, 1992. Pres. Whittier Home Assn., Amesbury, Mass., 1989-96; treas. Macy-Colby House, 1979—; sec. Amesbury Carriage Mus., 1982—; reunion chmn. Wellesley Coll., 1971, 86. Mem. ALA, Abenaqui Country Club, Wellesley Coll. Club. Republican. Avocations: historic houses and gardens, travel, golf, gardening. Home: 3 Hillside Ave Amesbury MA 01913-2213

DOWD, JANICE LEE, foreign language educator; b. NYC, Jan. 6, 1948; d. Edward H. and Mary A. (Vanek) D. BA, Marietta (Ohio) Coll., 1969; MA, Columbia U., 1971, MEd, 1979, EdD, 1984. Tchr. Teaneck (N.J.) Bd. Edn., 1970-99, supr. world langs., 1999—2002, exec. supr. instrnl. programs, 2002—. Adj. asst. prof. Queens Coll., CUNY, 1984-94, Columbia U., N.Y.C., spring 1988, 93—; N.J. alternate route prof., 1990—; asst. prof. MA TESOL program in China, Changsha, 1986, Shanghai, 1987; SAT program adminstr. Teaneck H.S., 1978-83, yearbook sponsor, 1975-79, newspaper sponsor, 1984-92, co-chair Global/Multicultural Mgmt. Team, 1992-95. Contbr. articles to profl. jours. Mem. program com., v.p., pres. PEO, Teaneck, 1966-, Fulbright-Hayes curriculum specialist Chinese Lang. Assn. Secondary Speakers Summer Study Program, China, 2002, 2004. Fellow, Rockefeller Found., 1988. Mem. Am. Assn. Tchrs. French, Am. Assn. Tchrs. Spanish and Portuguese, Chinese Lang. Assn. for Secondary-Elem. Tchrs., Tchrs. English to Speakers Other Langs., N.Y. State Tchrs. English to Speakers Other Langs., N.J. Tchrs. English to Speakers Other Langs., Am. Assn. Applied Linguists, Am. Coun. Tchrs. Fgn. Langs., Fgn. Lang. Educators N.J., Nat. Assn. Dept. Heads and Suprs. of Fgn. Langs. Home: 56 Boulevard New Milford NJ 07646-1602 Office: Teaneck Pub Sch One Merrison St Teaneck NJ 07666-4798

DOWD, MAUREEN, columnist; b. Washington, Jan. 14, 1952; d. Michael and Peggy D. BA English Lit., Catholic U., Washington D.C., 1973. From editl. asst. to feature writer The Washington Star, 1974-81; from corr. to writer Time mag., 1981-83; metro reporter N.Y. Times, 1983-86, D.C. reporter, 1986-95, opinion-editl. columnist, 1995—. Author: Bushworld: Enter at Your Own Risk, 2004 (Publishers Weekly Bestseller), Are Men Necessary?: When Sexes Collide, 2005. Finalist Pulitzer Prize for nat. reporting, 1992; named one of Glamour's Women of the Yr., 1996; recipient Breakthrough Award, "Women, Men and Media", Columbia U., 1991, Matrix Award, NY Women in Comm., 1994, Pulitzer Prize for commentary, 1999, Damon Runyon Award, Denver Press Club, 2000. Office: NY Times 1627 I St NW Washington DC 20006-4007

DOWDELL, DONNA RENEA, nurse; b. Indpls., Sept. 28, 1968; d. Ollie and Birdie Mae (McClendon) Strong; m. David Lee Dowdell, Jan. 28, 1991. BSN, Ind. U., Indpls., 1990; MS in Holistic Nutrition, Clayton Coll. Natural Health, 1999; PhD in Holistic Nutrition, Clayton Coll. Natural. Health, 2002. RN, Ind.; TB and BLS, Ind.; cert. hypnotherapy, Atwood Inst., 1996; cert. nat. health profl., Nat. Assn. Cert. Natural Health Profls.; cert. care coord; adv. training clin. nutrition, Designs for Health Inst., 1999. Student nurse technician VA Hosp., Indpls., 1988-89; student nurse extern Meth. Hosp., Indpls., 1989-90; staff nurse Riley Hosp., Indpls., 1991; staff home care nurse Pediatric Nursing Specialists, Indpls., 1991-94, Kimberly Quality Care, Indpls., 1992-94; clin. nurse supr. Olsten Kimberly Quality Care, Indpls., 1994, pediatric clin. mgr., 1994-95, case mgr. Las Vegas, 1995; staff RN Sunrise Hosp., Las Vegas, 1995-96; quality coord. Five Star Home Health, Las Vegas, 1997—2000. Pub. health nurse Health Hosp. Corp. Marion County, Indpls., 1992-94; nursing supr. home health Winona Hosp.-Pulse Health Svcs., Indpls., 1994; specialist natural holistic health Health Ministry, 1996—. Vol. Nat. Nurses Day, Indpls., 1992-94. Ind. U. Purdue U. scholar, 1990. Mem. Sigma Theta Tau Internat, Nat. Assn. Cert. Nat. Health Profls. Avocations: singing inspirational music, arts and crafts, reading, watching movie videos, travel.

DOWDELL, SHARONLYN SCOTT, accountant; b. Atlanta, Aug. 25, 1959; d. Joseph Sr. and Artie Bell Scott; m. Michael Grant Dowdell, Apr. 25, 1979 (div. Feb. 1989); children: Michael, Lanecia, Vanita. Tax agt. Dept. Revenue, Atlanta, 1984-95; reimbursement mgr. Dept. Cmty. Health., Atlanta, 1995-2000; owner Dowdell & Assocs, CPAs. Fellow AICPA, Ga. Soc. CPAs, Ga. Fiscal Mgmt. Coun.

DOWDY, ELIZABETH ANN, mathematician, educator; b. Niles, Ohio, Mar. 2, 1977; d. Jake and Francine Elizabeth Dowdy. Bachelors, Mt. Vernon Nazarene U., Ohio, 1999; MA, Ohio State U., Columbus, 2003. Cert. 7-12 math. tchr. Ohio, mid. sch. math. tchr. Ga., gifted edn. tchr. Ga. Tchr. math. Marion Harding H.S., Ohio, 1999—2003, Woodstock Mid. Sch., Ga., 2003—. Coach Marion Harding H.S., Ohio, 1999—2000, Woodstock H.S., Ga., 2003—05; instr. Teen Inst., Marion, Ohio, 2002—03; Jjr. Beta Club advisor Woodstock Mid. Sch., Ga., 2003—. Apt. outreach coord. First Bapt. Ch. of Woodstock, Woodstock, Ga., 2005—06. Office: Woodstock MId Sch 20000 Towne Lake Hills S Dr Woodstock GA 30189 Office Phone: 770-592-3516. Office Fax: 770-591-5054.

DOWDY, HARRIET BRODHEAD, elementary school educator; b. Bklyn., Mar. 16, 1918; d. Nathaniel Boyd Brodhead and Editha Wells Brown; children: Harriet Locklin, Joyce LaPrade. BA, U. Rochester, 1939; MS in Edn., Bank State Coll. Edn., 1970; LHD (hon.), Alderson-Broaddus Coll., 1991. Vol. docent Chapel Car Grace, Am. Bapt. Assembly, Green Lake, Wis., 1995—. Chair ch. rels. Habitat for Humanity, Ripon, Wis., 2002—04; leader Girl Scouts Am., 1950—72. Mem.: AAUW. Baptist. Avocations: reading, travel. Home: 533 W Thorne St Ripon WI 54971

DOWDY, JOANNE KILGOUR, education educator; b. Port of Spain, Trinidad, Nov. 22, 1959; d. Lennox Stanislaus and Kathleen Louise (Armstrong) Kilgour; m. William Harold Dowdy, July 20, 1990 (div. Oct. 1999). BFA, Juilliard Sch., 1987; MA in Tchg., Columbia U., 1989; PhD, U. N.C., 1997. Cert. tchr., N.Y., N.C. Lectr. Shaw U., Wilmington, N.C., 1993; acad. cons. U. N.C., Chapel Hill, 1993-94; instr. N.C. State U., Raleigh, 1994-95; literacy cons. Literacy South, Durham, N.C., 1995-96; lectr. Durham Tech. C.C., 1996-97; asst. dir., asst. prof. Ga. State U., Atlanta, 1997—. Cons. Ga. State U., 1997; bd. dirs. N.C. Equity, Raleigh; mem. adv. bd. Tchrs. for Acad. Support Skills, Cin., 1997. Dir. (video prodn.) Noises in the Attic, 1997, Carmen Montana: A Story of Literacy in Motion, (stage and video prodn.) Brown Blues: Six Women Talk About their Experience of Integration. Recipient Derek Walcott scholarship Nobel Laureate Derek Walcott, 1982/83, Robin Williams award Juilliard Sch., 1994/95, Minority Presence award U. N.C., 1994. Mem. AAUW, NOW, Internat. Reading Assn. Avocations: sewing, correspondence, picture framing.

DOWER GOLD, CATHERINE ANNE, music history educator; b. South Hadley, Mass., May 19, 1924; d. Lawrence Frederick Dower and Marie (Barbieri) Barber; m. Arthur Gold, Mar. 24, 1994 (dec. Oct. 1998). AB, Hamline U., 1945; MA, Smith Coll., 1948; B in Liturgical Music, U. Mont., Gregorian Inst. Am., 1949; PhD, The Cath. U. Am., 1968. Organist St. Theresa Chapel of Little Flower, S. Hadley, Maine, 1937—42; New England rep. Gregorian Inst. Am., Toledo, 1948-49; tchr. music, organist St. Rose Ch. and Sch., Meriden, Conn., 1949-53; supr. music Holyoke Pub. Schs., Mass., 1953-55; instr. music U. Mass., Amherst, 1955-56; prof. music Westfield State Coll., Mass., 1956-90, prof. emerita, 1991—; columnist and freelance writer Holyoke Transcript Telegram, 1991-93. Vis. assoc. prof. music Herbert Lehman Coll. CUNY, 1970—71; concert series presenter Westfield State Coll., 1987—91, rschr. tchr. Author: Puerto Rican Music Following the Spanish American War, 1898-1910, 1983, (monograph) Yella Pessl, 1986, Alfred Einstein on Music, 1991, Yella Pessl: First Lady of the Harpsichord, 1992, Fifty Years of Marching Together, 2001, Las Actividades Musicales en Puerto Rico: despúes de la guerra hispanoamericana 1898-1910, 2006; editor: (newsletter) Westfield State Coll., 2000—; presenter Irish Concert Springfield Symphony Orch., 1981— (plaque, 1982); contbr. numerous articles pub. and poems to anthologies. Pres. Coun. for Human Understanding Holyoke, 1981—83, Friends of Holyoke Pub. Libr., 1990—91; bd. dirs., chmn. nominating com. Holyoke Pub. Libr., 1987—89; bd. dirs. Holyoke Pub. Libr. Corp., 1991—94, Springfield Symphony Orch., 1992—94, Fla. Philharm. Orch., 2000—03, trustee, 2002—03; presiding officer inauguration Dr. Irving Buchman pres. of Westfield State Coll.; mem. ethics com. Holyoke Hosp., 1988—94; sec. Haiti Mission, 1982—94; bd. overseers Mullen U., 1993; hon. mem. bd. Coun. Human Understanding, 1994—; hon. mem. WSC Found., 1994—; co-chair United Jewish Appeal/Jewish Fed. Boca Lago Women's Divsn., South Palm Beach County, 1996—97; mem. St. Patrick's Com., Holyoke, Mass., 1991—; 1st v.p. fin. and adminstrn. Temple Beth El Women in Reformed Judaism, Boca Raton, 1997—99; organist St. Theresa's Ch., South Hadley, 1937—41, St. Michael's Ch., NY, 1945—46. Named Lady Comdr., Equestrian Order of the Holy Sepulchre of Jerusalem, 1987, with star, 1990, Career Woman of Yr., Quota Internat. Holyoke, 1988—, Westfield State Coll. concert series named Catherine A. Dower Performing Arts Series in her honor, 1991; recipient citation, Academia InterAmericana de P.R., 1978, plaque, Mass. Tchrs. Assn., Boston, 1984, medal, Equestrian Order Holy Sepulchre of Jerusalem, Papal Knighthood Soc., Boston, 1984, Performance award, Gov. Dukakis, Mass., 1988, award, P.R. Jour. Al. Margens, 1992, Human Rels. award, Coun. for Human Understanding, Holyoke, 1994, 1st prize, Raddock Eminent Scholar Chair Essay Contest, Fla. Atlantic U., 1996, Internat. Poet of Merit Silver Bowl award, Internat. Libr. Poetry, 2002, 2003, 2004, 2005, 2006, 1st prize, Essay Contest on World Peace by Brotherly Love Press, Mass., 2002, Outstanding Achievement in Poetry award, Internat. Soc. Poets, 2003; vis. scholar, U. So. Calif., 1969. Mem.: Acad. Arts and Scis. PR (medal 1977), Ch. Music Assn. Am. (journalist), Coll. Mus. Soc., Am. Musicol. Soc., Nat. Soc. Arts and Letters (chmn. violin competition 2005, master ceremonies NSAL piano competition 2006, 1st v.p.), Philharm. Assn. Boca (pres. 2002—03), Irish Am. Cultural Inst. (chmn. bd. dirs. 1981—89), Internat. Platform Assn., Lifelong Learning Soc. Fla. Atlantic U. (life; sec. 1994—97, bd. dirs. 1994—98, 2003—), Friends Music Lynn U. (life; bd. dirs., editor music newsletter), Women's Symphony League (life), Friends Holyoke Pub. Libr. (pres. 1990—91), Holyoke Quota (v.p. 1976—79, pres. 1979—81, chmn. speech and hearing com. 1987—94, pres. 1990—92), Westfield State Coll. Found., Univ. Club Fla. Atlantic U. (parliamentarian 2003—05, chmn. bylaws 2005—), B'nai B'rith Boca Lago (sec. bd. dirs. 1994—99, newsletter editor 1999—2000), Phi Beta Kappa. Democrat. Home: 8559 Casa Del Lago Boca Raton FL 33433-2107 Personal E-mail: cathig@juno.com.

DOWEY, ANA L., microbiologist, educator; d. Gilberto Recinos and Esperanza De Recinos; m. Kent W. Dowey, Jan. 4, 1986; children: Erik, Andrew. BSc, San Carlos de Guatemala U., Guatemala, 1983; MS in Microbiology, Calif. State U., Long Beach, Calif., 1987. Lic. med. technologist Harbor U. Calif. Med. Ctr., L.A., 1987. Med. technologist Kaiser Permanente, San Diego, 1989—91, Tri-City Med. Ctr., Oceanside, Calif., 1989—2002; adj. instr. life scis. Palomar C.C., San Marcos, Calif., 2002—. Coord. workshops in field. Grantee, Palomar Coll. Found., 2006, Oceanside Bd. Edn., 2006. Office: Palomar College 1140 West Mission Road San Marcos CA 92069 Office Phone: 760-744-1150 2275. Personal E-mail: adowey@palomar.edu.

DOWLING, CATHERINE LYNN, secondary school educator; b. Houston, Nov. 13, 1954; d. Jimmie Jean and Marvin Woodrow Hunt; m. Fergus Joseph Dowling, June 7, 1946. Degree in vocat. edn., So. Ill. U., Carbondale, 1986; cert. in tchg., Tex. State U., San Marcos, 1996. Enlisted USAF, 1973, spl. agt. and electronics specialist, 1973—93; tchr., coach Seguin (Tex.) H.S., 1996—98, San Marcos (Tex.) H.S., 1998—. With USAF, 1984. Decorated Meritorious Svc., ETC. USAF; recipient Aced. Excellence awards, Tex. State U., San Marcos, 1993—95. Mem.: Assn. Former OSI Agts. (assoc.), Am. Chem. Soc. (assoc.), Am. Running and Fitness Assn. (assoc.), Women in Mil. Svc. for Am. Meml. (assoc.; charter mem.), Am. Legion (assoc.), Kappa Delta Pi (assoc.). Baptist. Avocations: running, reading. Home: 501 Valley View West Dr San Marcos TX 78666 Office: San Marcos High Sch 1301 Highway 123 San Marcos TX 78666 Office Phone: 512-393-6800. Office Fax: 512-392-8927. E-mail: cathy.dowling@smcisd.net.

DOWLING, KATHY, telecommunications industry executive; BS in Acctg. & Mktg., U. Ariz., 1977; MBA, Webster U., St. Louis. With Southwestern Bell Telephone, AT&T, SBC Comms.; mgr., inventory control, dir. oper. Southwestern Bell Wireless, v.p., gen. mgr.; v.p., customer svcs. Cellular One, Chgo., pres., gen. mgr. Boston, 1997—98; regional pres. Cellular One, SNET Wireless; mng. dir., investor rels. and shareowner svcs. SBC Comm. Inc.; exec. v.p., merger integration Cingular Wireless, Atlanta, sr. v.p., customer svc., 2000—. Office: Cingular Wireless Glenridge Highlands Two 5655 Glenridge Connector Atlanta GA 30342

DOWLING, MARY KATHLEEN, elementary school educator; b. Des Moines, July 22, 1950; d. Joseph Patrick and Sadie (Klein) D BA Elem. Edn., Avila Coll., 1972; MA Reading, Clarke Coll., 1983. Joined Sisters of St. Joseph of Carondelet; cert. tchr., Ill., Mich., Mo. Tchr. St. Francis de Sales Sch., Denver, 1972—73, Holy Name Sch., St. Louis, 1975, St. Michael's Sch., Marquette, Mich., 1975—80; tchr., reading coord. Bishop Baraga Sch., Marquette, 1980—84; tchr. sci. Nativity of Our Lord Sch., Chgo., 1984—85; tchr., reading coord. St. Fidelis Sch., Chgo., 1985—90; tchr. St. Philomena Sch., Chgo., 1990—98, asst. prin., 1998—2005; tchr. St. Helen Sch., Chgo., 2005—. Mem. fin. com. St. Aloysius/St. Fidelis Parish, 2005—; vol. Little Bros., Friends of the Elderly. Mem. Internat. Reading Assn., Nat. Cath. Edn. Assn., Ill. Reading Coun., Chgo. Area Reading Assn Home: 2544 W Cortez St 1F Chicago IL 60622-3444 Office: Saint Helen Sch 2347 W Augusta Blvd Chicago IL 60622

DOWNER, ALLISON V., adult, forensic, child and adolescent psychiatrist; b. London, Eng., May 30, 1967; arrived in U.S., 1974; d. Neville Luke and Inez Pearl Downer. MD, N.Y. Med. Coll., Valhalla, 1999. Psychiatrist N.Y. State Office Mental Health, Ossining, NY, 2002—; pvt. practice psychiatry Rye, NY, 2004—; cons. psychiatrist Westchester Jewish Cmty. Svc., Hartsdale, NY, 2005—. Mem.: Am. Acad. Cmty. Psychiatry, Am. Acad. Psychiatry and the Law, Am. Acad. Child and Adolescent Psychiatry, Am. Psychiat. Assn. Home: 39 Hudson Ter Apt 308 Yonkers NY 10701-1995 Office: 35 Purchase St Ste 303 Rye NY 10580

DOWNES, MARIE JEAN, music educator; b. Paterson, NJ, Nov. 28, 1970; d. Nicolas J. and Carol Ann Kronyak; m. Vincent J. Downes, June 24, 1995; 1 child, Kian Patrick. BA, William Paterson U., Wayne, NJ, 1993. Cert. tchr. NJ, 1993. Elem. sch. band dir. Cedar Grove Bd. Edn., NJ, 1993—95; h.s. band dir. MidlandPark Bd. Edn., NJ, 1995—97; elem./mid. sch. band Jersey City Bd. Edn., 1997—. Parishner St. Vincent's Ch., Bayonne, NJ, 2004. Mem.: NEA, Music Educators Nat. Conf., Jersey City Edn. Assn., NJ Edn. Assn. Office: Jersey City Board of Education 325 Claremont Ave Jersey City NJ 07306 Office Phone: 201-306-1635. Business E-Mail: mdownes@jcboe.org.

DOWNES, PATRICIA ANN, minister; b. Sussex, N.J., Dec. 10, 1945; d. Leonard McGill and Violet McCarty; m. Randall Preist Jr., June 21, 1964 (div. May 20, 1988); children: Linda, Randall, Sarah-Elisabeth; m. Donald Downes, Oct. 17, 1992. AA, Brevard C.C., 1986; BSW, U. Ctrl. Fla., 1988; MDiv, Emory U., 1991; postgrad., So. Fla. Ctr. Theol. Studies, 2004—. Lic. practical nurse, Fla., 1965; ordained clergy, cert. in Christian edn. United Meth. Ch. Nurse Holmes Regional Hosp., Melbourne, Fla., 1965—67, therapeutic foster parent, 1967—88; pastor United Meth. Ch., Holly Hill, 1991—94, Miami, 1992—2001, Palm Bay, 2001—. Foster parent trainer Holmes Regional Hosp., Melbourne, 1980—88. Author: Foster Parent Manual, 1983. AIDS counselor, Melbourne, 1985—87; guardian ad litem GAL Program, Brevard County, 1981—86; bd. dirs. YMCA, Melbourne, 1975—79, Miami Urban Ministries, Miami, 1998—2000, Palm Bay Hosp., 2002—; grantwriter Foster Care Cmty. Edn., 1985. Named Child Advocate Yr., Children's Home Soc., 1983; recipient Cmty. Svc. award, Brevard C.C., 1986. Mem.: Dist. Bd. Ordained Ministry. Democrat. United Methodist. Avocations: writing, sewing, reading. Office: Palm Bay United Meth Ch 2100 Port Malabar Blvd Palm Bay FL 32905

DOWNEY, DEBORAH ANN, systems specialist; b. Xenia, Ohio, July 22, 1958; d. Nathan Vernon and Patricia Jaunita (Ward) D. Assoc. in Applied Sci., Sinclair C.C., 1981, student, 1986—91; BA, Capital U., 1994. Jr. programmer, project mgr. Cole-Layer-Trumble Co., Dayton, Ohio, 1981-82; sr. programmer, analyst, project leader Systems Architects Inc., Dayton, 1982-84, Systems and Applied Sci. Corp. (now Computer Sci. Corp.), Dayton, 1984; analyst Unisys, Dayton, 1984-87; systems programmer Computer Sci. Corp., Fairborn, Ohio, 1987—. Cons. computer software M&S Garage/Body Shop, Beavercreek, Ohio, 1986-87. Mem. NAFE, Am. Motorcyclist Assn., Sinclair C. C. Alumni Assn., Cherokee Nation Okla., Cherokee Nat. Hist. Soc. Democrat. Mem. United Ch. Of Christ. Avocations: motorcycles, miniatures, sports, needlecrafts.

DOWNEY, ROMA, actress; b. Northern Ireland, United Kingdom, May 6, 1963; m. David Anspaugh, 1995 (div. 1998); 1 child, Reilly Marie. BA in Fine Arts, Brighton Art Coll., England, 1983; diploma, London Drama Studio, 1985. Actress CBS Television, L.A. Appeared in Irelands Abbey Theatre, U.S. tour The Playboy of the Western World, 1991; on Broadway in The Circle; Off Broadway in Love's Labour's Lost, Tamara, Arms and the Man; TV appearances include A Woman Named Jackie, Touched by an Angel, 1994-2003, Borrowed Hearts, A Child is Missing; appeared in films including (TV series) A Woman Named Jackie, 1991, Devlin, 1992, A Child is Missing, 1995, Borrowed Hearts, 1997, Monday After the Miracle, 1998, A Test of Love, 1999, A Secret Life, 2000, Second Honeymoon, 2000, Sons of Mistletoe, 2001, Hairy Tale, 2003; exec. prodr. Borrowed Hearts, 1997, Monday After the Miracle, 1998, Second Honeymoon, 2000, Hairy Tale, 2003. Nominee Helen Hayes Best Actress award, 1991, Emmy award, 1997, 98, Golden Globe award, 1997-98; recipient TV Guide award for favorite actress in a drama, 1999. Office: Touched by an Angel care CBS/MTM Studios 4020 Radford Ave North Hollywood CA 91604-2101 Address: Gersh Agy 232 N Canon Dr Beverly Hills CA 90210-5302

DOWNING, CAROLINE JANE, art historian, educator, archaeologist; b. Perth, Australia, June 4, 1953; arrived in U.S., 1966; d. Donald Talbot and Flora Agnes Downing; m. Frederick Hemans (div.); children: Adriana Dorothy, Frederick; m. Joseph Alan Hildreth, Sept. 2, 1947; 1 child, Kate. AB cum laude, Boston U., 1976; MA, Ind. U., 1979, PhD, 1987. Assoc. editor Am. Jour. Arch., Boston, 1989—90; prof. art history SUNY, Potsdam, NY, 1990—. Dir. Interdisciplinary Learning Cmtys. Project SUNY, 1992—94, coord. Carnegie Tchg. Project, 1999—, co-developer arch. major, co-developer classical studies minor. Commr. Potsdam (N.Y.) Youth Soccer Assn., 1998—; pres. bd. dirs. SUNY Potsdam (N.Y.) Childcare Ctr., 1993—98. Named Disting. Hons. Prof. of Yr., SUNY, 2004; recipient Excellence in Tchg. award, Pres. SUNY, 2005; grantee, NEH, 1994, 2002. Mem.: Byzantine Studies Conf., Archael. Inst. Am., Phi Kappa Phi, Delta Kappa Gamma. Avocations: painting, reading, hiking. Home: 15 Cedar St Potsdam NY 13676 Office: Art Dept SUNY at Potsdam 44 Pierrepont Ave Potsdam NY 13676 Office Phone: 315-267-2368.

DOWNING, CRYSTAL L., literature and language professor, writer; d. Norris T. and Joy P. Nelson; m. David C. Downing, Aug. 17, 1974. PhD, U. Calif., Santa Barbara, 1986. Prof. English and film studies Messiah Coll., Grantham, Pa., 1994—. Author: (book) Writing Performances: The Stages of Dorothy L. Sayers, 2004, How Postmodernism Serves (my) Faith, 2006; contbr. over 47 essays to film and books (Merit award, 2006), over 42 sci. papers. Vol. Meals on Wheels, York County, Pa., 2000; liturgist, Sunday sch. tchr. Fishing Creek Salem United Meth. Ch., Etters, Pa., 1998—2006. Recipient Outstanding Tchg. Asst. award, U. Calif., Santa Barbara Acad. Senate, 1984, Smith Outstanding Tchg. award, Messiah Coll., 2002; 9 Scholarship Support grants, 1996 - 2006, Clyde S. Kilby Rsch. grant, Marion E. Wade Ctr., 2002. Mem.: MLA. Home: 608 Antler Dr Lewisberry PA 17339-9404 Office: Messiah Col One College Ave Grantham PA 17027 Office Phone: 717-796-1800 7026. Business E-Mail: cdowning@messiah.edu.

DOWNING, FRANCES E., architecture educator; BArch, U. Oreg., 1976, MArch, 1978; PhD, U. Wis., Milw., 1989. Assoc. prof. arch. dept. arch. Tex. A&M U., College Station, assoc. dean faculty, prof. dept. arch. Author: Remembrance and the Design of Place, 2000. Office: A426 Langford A Dept Arch Tex A&M Univ College Station TX 77843-3137

DOWNING, JANE KATHERINE, psychiatric nurse practitioner, lawyer; b. Miami Beach, Fla., Aug. 17, 1944; d. William Edward Cuffe and Mary Eileen McManus. ASN, Palomar Coll., 1973; BS in Law, Western State U., 1981, JD, 1981. Bar: Calif. 1983; RN Tex., 1991. Obstetrics, neonatal and ICU nurse Tri City Hosp., Oceanside, Calif., 1973—79; part-time emergency dept./hosp. nursing supr., 1979—83; part-time cert. law clk. San Diego, 1979—83; pvt. practice atty., 1983—90; emergency dept. nurse San Antonio, 1991—92; disaster health coord. ARC, San Antonio, 1992—94; clin. wound mgmt. cons. Hill-Rom, Inc., Batesville, Ind., 1994—96; psychiat. nurse The Brown Schs., Austin, Tex., 1997—98, Austin State Hosp., 1998—99; part-time nurse case mgr. South Austin Hosp., 2000; nurse case mgr. intermediate trauma care unit Brackenridge Hosp., Austin, 2001; home health nurse Progressive Home Care, Inc., San Antonio, 2002—03; crisis unit charge nurse Ctr. for Health Care Svcs., San Antonio, 2003—04, DON crisis unit, 2005—; charge nurse acute adult psychiat. inpatient admitting unit Laurel Ridge Treatment Ctr., 2005—06. Contbr. articles to publs. Inveterate nursing vol. ARC, San Antonio, 1993—2006. Recipient SW Star award, ARC, 2001. Mem.: Am. Mensa. Democrat. Roman Catholic. Home: 303 Serna Park San Antonio TX 78218 Personal E-mail: jkdrnjd@hotmail.com.

DOWNING, KATHRYN M., former newspaper publishing executive, lawyer; b. Portland, Oreg., Mar. 24, 1953; BA in Econs., Lewis and Clark Coll., 1973; JD, Stanford U., 1979. Various positions Mead Data Ctrl., 1981—90, sr. dir. legal info. pub., 1988; pres., COO Electronic Pub. divsn. Thomson Profl. Pub., 1990—93; pres., CEO Lawyers Coop. Pub. divsn. Thomson Legal Pub., 1993—95, Mathew Bender, 1995—97; pres., CEO Mosby Matthew Bender unit, sr. v.p. Times Mirror, N.Y.C., 1997—99, vice pres., 1996—97, sr. v.p., 1997—98, exec. v.p., 1998—99; pres., CEO L.A. Times, 1998—99, pres., CEO, publisher, 1999—2000; CEO My Potential Inc., Santa Monica, Calif., 2000—01. Bd. dirs. Women's Found. Calif. Mem. Times Mirror Found., Jim Murray Meml. Found.; mem. bd. visitors Sch. Law Stanford U.; trustee Friends of Law Libr. of Congress; bd. visitors UCLA Anderson Sch. Bus.; pres. L.A. Times Fund; bd. trustees Lewis & Clark Coll. Fellow: Broad Urban Supt. Acad.; mem.: Newspaper Assn. Am., Am. Inns of Ct. (past pub. trustee), Am. Assn. Pubs. (bd. dirs.), L.A. C. of C.

DOWNING, MARGARET MARY, newspaper editor; b. Altoona, Pa., June 3, 1952; d. Irvine William and Iva Ann (Regan) D.; m. Gary Beaver; children: Ian Downing-Beaver, Timothy Downing-Beaver, Abby Downing-Beaver. BA magna cum laude, Tex. Christian U., 1974. Reporting intern Corpus Christi Caller Times, 1973; reporter, bur. chief Beaumont (Tex.) Enterprise & Jour., 1974-76, Dallas Times Herald, 1976-80; reporter, asst. city editor, asst. bus., met. editor, mng. editor Houston Post, 1980—93; mng. editor Jackson (Miss.) Clarion-Ledger, 1993-97; editor-in-chief The Houston Press, 1998—. Jurist Pulitzer Prize Awards, 1992, 93; bd. dirs. News Media Credit Union, 1993, Santa's Helpers, 1992-93; mem. membership com. Assn. Alternative Newspapers, 2000- Respite foster parent vol. Harris County Children's Protective Svcs., 1993; chmn. landscape com. Windsor Hills Homeowners Assn.; active Madison Sta. Elem. PTA, 1993—98; coach South Madison County Soccer Orgn., 1997—98, First Colony Soccer Club, 2002—; mem. runners club YMCA, 1994, mem. activities adv. bd., 1994, youth soccer and t-ball coach; coach Quail Valley Soccer Assn., 1999—2005, First Colony Soccer Club, 2005—; vol. Houston Taping for the Blind, 2000—02; vestry Grace Episcopal Ch., 2002—05, mem. children's edn. bd., 2003, mem. worship com., 2005—; bd. dirs. Alvin-Manvel Helping Hands Fund, 2001, Leadership Jackson, 1996—98. Recipient Rick Nelson soccer coaching award, 2001. Mem.: Nat. Soc. Newspaper Columnists, Investigative Reporters and Editors, Inc., Nat. Edn. Writers Assn., Nat. Youth Sports Assn. (cert. coach), Press Club Houston (bd. dirs. 1982—85, pres. 1984, bd. dirs. 2000—04), AP Mng. Editors Assn. (2d v.p. La./Miss. chpt. 1995—96, 1st v.p. 1996—97, pres. 1997—98), Quota Club (bd. dirs. 1996—97). Episcopalian. Home: 3215 Breckenridge Ct Missouri City TX 77459-4907 Office: The Houston Press 1621 Milam St Ste 100 Houston TX 77002-8017 Office Phone: 713-280-2470. Personal E-mail: downingmargaret@yahoo.com. Business E-Mail: margaret.downing@houstonpress.com.

DOWNING, SARAH LINN, application developer; d. Marvin Richard and Brenda Denyse Downing. BS in Math., U. Toledo, 1998. Cert. Microsoft Profl. Wash., Microsoft Application Developer Wash. Programmer,analyst ALN Associates, Inc., South Bend, 1998—99; programmer, analyst Reese Products, Inc., Elkhart, 1999—2002; analyst Tchrs. Credit Union, South Bend, Ind., 2002—04; programmer, analyst Bremen (Ind.) Castings, Inc., 2004—. Mem.: Mensa, DAR. Avocation: sewing.

DOWNS, DOROTHY RIEDER, art historian, consultant, writer; b. Miami, Fla., May 14, 1937; d. William Dustin Rieder and Mary Katherine Thomas; m. R Maurice Downs, July 12, 1955; children: Craig Thomas, Gary Steven. BA, Emory U., 1959; MA in Art History, U. Miami, 1976. Registrar Lowe Art Mus., U. Miami, Coral Gables, Fla., 1977—78; dir. 4 Corners Gallery, Coral Gables, 1978—79, New Gallery, U. Miami, 1986—87; mgr. Ctr. Art Store, Ctr. Fine Arts, Miami, 1982—84; instr. dept. art & art history U. Miami, Coral Gables, 1996; guest curator Lowe Art Mus., U. Miami, Coral Gables, 1999, curatorial cons., 2001—. Cons. Miccosukee Mus., Miami, 1983; instr. art history Fla. Keys CC, Key West, 1995, St. Leo's Coll., Key West, 1995; lectr. in field. Author: Art of the Florida Seminole and Miccosukee Indians, 1995, Patchwork: Seminole & Miccosukee Art and Activities, 2005; prodr., writer: (documentaries) Patterns of Power, 1990. Pres. Tribal Arts Soc. Lowe Art Mus., Coral Gables, 2001—03. Mem.: Native Am. Art Studies Assn.

DOWNS, KARLA J., secondary school educator; d. Bernadette E. Fessler; m. Jerry V. Downs, Oct. 31, 1992; children: Jordy W., Chance J. Degree in Family and Consumer Scis. Edn., Iowa State U., Ames, Iowa, 2000. Tchr. family and consumer scis. Wapsie Valley Schs., Fairbank, Iowa, 2000—01; tchr. family and consumer scis. and health Maquoketa Valley H.S., Delhi, Iowa, 2001—. Mem.: Assn. Career and Tech. Edn. (assoc.). Office: Maquoketa Valley High School 210 South Street Delhi IA 52223 Office Phone: 563-922-2091.

DOWNS, KATHLEEN ANNE, health facility administrator; b. Toledo, Sept. 20, 1951; d. Keith Landis and Cecelia Josephine Babcock; m. Michael Brian Thomas, July 17, 1971 (dec. Oct. 1973); m. David Michael Downs, Aug. 8, 1981. Student, San Diego Mesa Coll., 1968—70; BS, Union Inst., 1989. Cert. profl. med. staff mgmt., provider credentialing specialist, profl. healthcare quality. Sec. Travelodge Internat., Inc., El Cajon, Calif., 1970-73; intermediate stenographer City of El Cajon, 1973-77; adminstrv. asst. MacLellan & Assocs., El Cajon, 1977-78; sr. sec. WESTEC Services, Inc., San Diego, 1978; adminstrv. sec. El Cajon Valley Hosp., 1978-80; asst. med. staff Grossmont Dist. Hosp., La Mesa, Calif., 1980-83, coord. med. staff, 1983-87, mgr., 1987-94; mgr. med. staff Sharp Meml. Hosp., San Diego, 1994; dir. med. staff svcs. Sharp HealthCare, San Diego, 1994-96, sr. specialist med. staff svcs., 1996; dir. med. staff svcs. Alvarado Hosp. Med. Ctr. and San Diego Rehab. Inst., San Diego, 1996-99; mgr. med. staff svcs. Kaiser Permanente Hosp., San Diego, 1999-2001, med. staff svcs. cons., 2001—; dir. med. staff svcs. Paradise Valley Hosp., National City, Calif., 2001—. Tchr. The Vogel Inst., San Diego, 1986; mem. med. staff svcs. adv. com. San Diego C.C. Dist.; adj. faculty Union Inst., 1991-96, Chemeketa C.C., 1991-95; credentials verification orgn. surveyor Nat. Com. Quality Assurance, Washington, 1996—2004. Mem. Nat. Assn. Med. Staff Svcs. (edn. coun. 1989-93, faculty 1990—, chmn. 1991-93, bd. dirs. 1991-93, editl. bd. Over View 1993-96), Calif. Assn. Med. Staff Svcs. (treas. San Diego chpt. 1984-86, pres. 1986-87, state sec. 1999-2001, pres.-elect 2001-03, pres. 2003-05). Avocations: gardening, boating, gourmet cooking, yoga, walking. Business E-Mail: downska@ah.org.

DOWNS, MARY ALANE, lawyer; BA summa cum laude, Mount St. Mary's Coll., 1979; JD, U. Md., 1982. Bar: Md. 1982, U.S. Ct. Appeals, Forth Cir. 1985. Ptnr. Morgan Shelsby Carlo Downs & Everton, P.A., 1985—. Mem. Nat. Moot Ct. Team; faculty mem. Md. Inst. Continuing Profl. Edn. of Lawyers (MICPEL). Mem.: ABA, Md. Assn. Defense Trial Counsel, Defense Rsch. Inst., Baltimore City Bar Assn., Md. State Bar Assn. Office: Morgan Shelsby Carlo Downs Everton 11350 Mccormick Ep 4 Rd Ste 100 Hunt Valley MD 21031-1111 Office Phone: 410-584-2800. E-mail: MADowns@morganshelsby.com.

DOYEL, CINDY M., information technology specialist; b. Stockton, Calif., Dec. 1, 1964; d. Nathan Cameron Doyel and Charlotte Blanche (Epler) Gezi. Student, Calif. State U., Sacramento, 1982-83; AA, MTI Bus. Coll., Sacramento, 1984. Supr. All Am. Mini Storage, Sacramento, 1988-89; mng. contr. The Royce Cos., Roseville, Calif., 1990-93; contr. Calif. Comml., Sacramento, 1993-95; gen. ptnr., operator Sierra Micro, Fair Oaks, Calif., 1995-98; help desk analyst Shared Med. Sys., Sacramento, Calif., 1998-99; info. tech. specialist Legis. Data Ctr., Sacramento, Calif., 1999—. Mem.: NAFE, NOW. Presbyterian. Avocations: writing, reading, waterpolo, swimming, softball. Office: Legis Data Ctr 1100 J Street Ste 110 Sacramento CA 95814-2827

DOYLE, AGNES J, minister; b. New Orleans, La., Jan. 23, 1947; d. Jose Ezequel Johnson and Rita Mae Williams; m. Edward Doyle (dec.); children: Joy Garrison, Jewel Colart. Ordained Pastor 1990. Recruitment and tng. ptnr. Model Neighborhood Programs, 1970—71; asst. personnel dir. Total Cmty. Action, Inc., New Orleans, 1968—71; curriculum instr. New Orleans, 1971—80; sub. tchr. Jefferson Parish Sch. Bd., Gaetna, La., 1990—2002; sr. weapons and tng. dir., 1984—2005; staff min. West Bank Revival Ctr., Terrytown, La., 1985—88; founding pastor Restorative Kingdom Ministry, 1995—2005. Tutor Young Men's Christian's Org., New Orleans. Editor: (periodical) RKM Bulletin. Vol. pastor Grace House of New Orleans, 2000—04. Mem.: Therapist Inst. La., Am. Assn. of Pastoral Counselors. Avocations: writing, poetry, sewing, gardening. Office: Restoration Kingdom Min 1427 Hancock St Gretna LA 70053

DOYLE, CHARLOTTE LACKNER (MRS. JAMES J. DOYLE), psychology educator, writer; b. Vienna, June 25, 1937; came to U.S., 1939, naturalized, 1955; d. George and Mary (Meisel) Lackner; m. James J. Doyle, Aug. 20, 1959. BA summa cum laude (Woodrow Wilson fellow), Temple U., 1959; MA, U. Mich., 1961, PhD in Psychology, 1965. Teaching fellow U. Mich., 1962-64; instr., asst. prof. psychology Cornell U., 1964-66; prof. psychology Sarah Lawrence Coll., Bronxville, N.Y., 1966—. Author: (with W.J. McKeachie) Psychology, 1966,70, (with McKeachie and M. Moffett), 1976, Explorations in Psychology, 1987, Hello Baby, 1989, Freddie's Spaghetti, 1991, Where's Bunny Mommy, 1995, You Can't Catch Me, 1998, Twins!, 2003, Supermarket, 2004, The Bouncing Dancing Galloping ABC, 2006; contbr. articles to profl. pubs. Mem. APA, Assn. for Psychol. Sci., Soc. Children's Book Writers, Phi Beta Kappa. Home: 293 Bronxville Rd Bronxville NY 10708-2801 Office: Sarah Lawrence Coll Dept Psychology Bronxville NY 10708

DOYLE, CHRISTINE ELLEN, museum researcher, educator; b. Jersey City, Oct. 21, 1975; d. Stanley F. and Margaret Rzeczkowski; m. Thomas Doyle, June 11, 2005. BA, Kean U., 1999, MA, 2002. Rsch. cons. Am. Mus. of Natural History, N.Y.C., 1998—; rsch. assoc. Union County Coll., Cranford, NJ, 2001—06; adj. tchr. Kean U., Union, NJ, 2005—. Rsch. cons. to museums, N.Y.C., 1997—; spkr. in field, 2005. Mem.: Grad. Psychology Soc. (v.p. 1999—2000), APA (assoc. Best Master's Thesis of Yr., N.J. chpt. 2002), Psi Chi Honor Soc., Order of Omega, Kappa Delta Tau (pres. 1997—99, Sister of Yr. 1995, 1999).

DOYLE, CONSTANCE TALCOTT JOHNSTON, physician, educator, medical association administrator; b. Mansfield, Ohio, July 8, 1945; d. Frederick Lyman IV and Nancy Jean Bushnell (Johnston) Talcott; children: Ian Frederick Demsky, Zachary Adam Demsky. BS, Ohio U., 1967; MD, Ohio State U., 1971. Diplomate Am. Bd. Emergency Medicine; bd. cert. in emergency crisis response. Intern Riverside Hosp., Columbus, Ohio, 1971—72; resident in internal medicine Hurley Hosp., U. Mich., Flint, 1972—74; emergency physician Oakwood Hosp., Dearborn, Mich., 1974—76, Jackson County Emergency Svcs., Mich., 1975—95; cons. Region II EMS, 1978—79, disaster cons., 1983—95, St. Joseph Mercy Hosp., Ann

Arbor, 1995—, med. flight physician helicopter life support svcs., 1996—2000; core faculty St. Joseph Mercy Hosp./U. Mich. Emergency Residency, Ann Arbor, 1995—; survival flight physician helicopter rescue svc. U. Mich., 1983—91; course dir. advanced cardiac life support and chmn. advanced life support com. W.A. Foote Meml. Hosp., Jackson, 1979—95; dep. dir. emergency svcs. med. ctrl. bd. Washtenaw Livingston County, 2000—; core faculty St. Joseph Mercy Hosp., Ann Arbor, 1996. Clin. instr. emergency svcs., dept. surgery U. Mich., 1981—; faculty combined emergency medicine residency St. Joseph Mercy Hosp.-U. Mich., Ann Arbor, 1995—; asst. med. dir. Region 2 South Biodef. Network, 2002-03, co-med. dir., 2003-05, dep. med. dir., 2005—; instr. EMT refresher courses, Jackson County, Jackson C.C.; MedFlight physician, 1996-99; Washtenaw County Subcom. on Bioterrorism, 2000—; Washtenaw County Local Emergency Planning Com., 1998—; dep. med. dir. Washtenaw/Livingston County Med. Control Authority, 2000—. Contbg. author: Clinical Approach to Poisoning and Toxicology, 1983, 89, 97, May's Textbook of Emergency Medicine, 1991, Schwartz Principles and Practice of Emergency Medicine, 1992, Reisdorff Pediatric Emergency Medicine, 1993; contbr. articles to profl. jours. Served Ground Zero, 2001; mem. Disaster Med. Assistance Team, 2000—; served Ground Zero, 2001, Hurrican Francis, 2004, Hurrican Katrina/Rita, 2005. Fellow Am. Coll. Emergency Physicians (pres. Mich. disaster com. 1987-88, bd. dirs. Mich. 1979-88, chmn. Mich. disaster com. 1979-85, mem. nat. disaster med. svcs. com. 1983-85, chmn. 1987-88, cons. disaster mgmt. course Fed. Emergency Mgmt. Agy. 1982, treas. 1984-85, emergency med. svcs. com. 1985, pres. 1986-87, councillor 1986-87, chair steering com. policy sect., 1994—, mem. disaster sect., 1995—, exec. com. disaster sect. 1997—, chair policy sect. disaster 1995—, vice chair sect. careers in emergency medicine 1997—, chair, 2000-02, past chair 2002-04), Nat. Am. Coll. Emergency Physicians (vice chair sect. of disaster med. svcs. 1990-92, nat. disaster subcom. 1989-90, chair subsect. psychol. rehab. svcs., disaster med. svcs. 1992-94, chair policy and legis. 1994-96, task force on hazardous materials 1993-97, steering com. sect. disaster medicine 1994-2002, exec. com. sect. disaster medicine 1995); mem. ACP, Am. Med. Women's Assn., Am. Assn. Women Emergency Physicians, Mich. Assn. Emergency Med. Technicians (bd. dirs. 1979-80), Mich. State Med. Soc., Washtenaw County Med. Soc., Sierra Club. Jewish. Office: 1251 King George Blvd Ann Arbor MI 48108 also: St Joseph Mercy Hosp Dept Emergency Medicine Ann Arbor MI 48109

DOYLE, DELORES MARIE, retired principal; b. Madison, SD, July 24, 1939; d. Martin N. and Pearl M. (Anderson) Berkelo; m. Patrick J. Doyle; children: Kathleen, Shawn, Tamara, Timothy. AS, Dakota State Coll., Madison, 1959; BS, Mid. Tenn. State U., 1966, MEd, 1968, EdS, 1975; PhD, Peabody/Vanderbilt U., 1980. Cert. career ladder III tchr. Tchr. 4th grade Meriden-Cleghorn Schs., Meriden, Iowa, 1960-62; tchr. 1st grade Hanover (Ill.) Sch., 1963-66; tchr. 2d grade Hobgood Sch., Murfreesboro, Tenn., 1969-70; tchr. 1st grade Reeves-Rogers Sch., Murfreesboro, 1972-80, tchr. 2d grade, 1981-97, prin., 1997-2000; ret., 2000. Cooperating tchr. Mid. Tenn. State U. Student Tchrs., Murfreesboro, 1972—97, mem. task force edn., 1992—93; summer sch. dir. Murfreesboro City Schs., 1986—98; lead project tutor Reeves-Rogers Sch., Murfreesboro, 1987—90. Active Edn. 2000 Com., Murfreesboro C. of C., 1993; trustee Mid Tenn State U. Found., 1995—2001; bd. dirs. Grace Luth. Ch., Murfreesboro, 1991—93, 2001—03, mem. choir, 1975—. Named Career Ladder III Tchr., Dept. Edn., Nashville, 1984; named to Tenn. Tchrs. Hall of Fame, 2001; recipient Tenn. Tchr. of the Yr. award, Dept. Edn., Nashville, 1992, Murfreesboro City Tchr. of the Yr. award, Murfreesboro City Schs., 1991, Mid-Cumberland Dist. Tchr. of the Yr. award, Dist. Dept. Edn., 1991, Trailblazer award, 1995; Creative Tchg. grantee, State Dept. Edn., 1992, 1993. Mem.: Murfreesboro Edn. Assn. (pres. 1981—82), Tenn. Edn. Assn. (Disting. Classroom Tchr. award 1992, Disting. Adminstr. award 2000), Tenn. State Tchr. of Yr. Orgn. (v.p. 2000—), Nat. State Tchr. of Yr. Orgn., Delta Kappa Gamma. Democrat. Avocations: bridge, travel, reading, ballroom dancing. Home: 1710 Sutton Pl Murfreesboro TN 37129-6513 Personal E-mail: pandddoyle@comcast.net.

DOYLE, ENID, art educator; b. Jersey City, N.J., May 22, 1945; d. Abraham and Frieda (Sugarman) Kosowsky; m. John James Doyle, June 4, 1966; children: Robin Marc, Alyse Sara. BA, Jersey City State Coll., 1966; MA, Jersey City State U., 1984. Cert. art tchr., N.J., princ./supr., sch. bus. adminstr., elem., nursery sch. Art tchr. Bayonne (N.J.) Pub. Schs., 1966—. Kindergarten art presenter Jersey City State Coll., 1984. Mem. Bayonne Citizens for Clean Air, 1990—, Mothers Against Drunk Driving, Bayonne, 1988—. Recipient grant Bayonne Bd. Edn., 1988, 90; named Gov.'s Tchr. of Yr., State of N.J., 1987. Mem. NEA, Nat. Art Educators Assn., Art Educators N.J., Art Alliance of N.J., Bayonne Tchrs. Assn. (tchr. rep. 1990—), Rutgers Parents Assn. Avocations: aerobics, painting, drawing. Home: 65 Linnett St Bayonne NJ 07002-4321 Office Phone: 201-558-5824.

DOYLE, EUGENIE FLERI, pediatrician, cardiologist, educator; b. Bklyn., Oct. 19, 1921; d. Paul Charles and Antoinette (Giovannetti) Fleri; m. Joseph Anthony Doyle, Aug. 19, 1944; children: Christopher, Stephen, Eugenie, Jane Marie, Richard. BS, Marymount Coll., Tarrytown, N.Y., 1943, DSc (hon.), 1993; MD, Johns Hopkins U., 1946; DSc (hon.), Coll. New Rochelle, 1975. Intern in pediatrics Johns Hopkins Hosp., Balt., 1946-47; pediatric resident Bellevue Hosp., N.Y.C., 1947-49; fellow pediatric cardiology NYU Med. Ctr., 1949-53, dir. pediatric cardiology, 1958-93; asst. prof. pediatrics NYU Sch. Medicine, 1953-58, assoc. prof., 1959-70, prof., 1970-92, prof. emerita, 1993—, clin. prof. pediatrics, 1994—. Mem. cardiac adv. com. N.Y. State Health Dept., 1983-92; dir. Vis. Nurse Svc., N.Y.C., 1984—. Editor: Pediatric Cardiology, 1985; contbr. articles to profl. jours. Trustee Marymount Coll., 1983-91, vice chair bd., 1988-91. Mem. Am. Acad. Pediatrics, Am. Pediatric Soc., Am. Coll. Cardiology, Am. Heart Assn., N.Y. Heart Assn. (bd. dirs. 1977-84, pres. 1979-81), Cosmopolitan Club. Roman Catholic. Avocations: gardening, travel, ballet. Home: 32 Washington Sq W New York NY 10011-9156 Office: NYU Med Ctr 550 1st Ave New York NY 10016-6402

DOYLE, FIONA MARY, dean, metallurgical engineer, educator; b. Newcastle upon Tyne, Eng., Sept. 27, 1956; came to the U.S., 1983; d. Vincent Thomas and Teresa Mary (Lockey) D.; m. Stephen Craig Blair, Aug. 5, 1990; children: Katherine Nicole Blair, Ian James Blair. BA in Metallurgy and Materials Sci., U. Cambridge, 1978, MA in Natural Sci., 1982; MSc in Extractive Metallurgy, Imperial Coll., 1979, PhD in Metallurgy, 1983. Chartered engr., Great Britain. Grad. trainee metals and minerals div. Davy McKee, Stockton-on-Tees, United Kingdom, 1983; asst. prof. materials sci. and mineral engring. U. Calif., Berkeley, 1983-88, assoc. prof., 1988-94, prof., 1994—, acting assoc. dean coll. engring., 1990, dir. Inst. Environmental Sci. and Engring., 2001—02, chair dept. materials sci. and engring., 2002—05, exec. assoc. dean Coll. Engring., 2005—. Cons. Placer Dome, U.S., San Francisco, 1989-90. Co-editor: Innovations in Materials Processing Using Aqueous Colloids and Surface Chemistry, 1989, Biotechnology in Minerals and Metal Processing, 1989, Mineral Processing and Extractive Metallury Rev., 1990—; editor: Mining and Mineral Processing Wastes, 1990; contbr. articles to profl. jours. Tech. cons. Sierra Club Legal Def. Fund, San Francisco, 1991. Grantee NSF, 1984, U.S. Dept. Interior, 1987, 91, U.S. Dept. Energy, 1990. Mem. Minerals, Metals and Materials Soc., Am. Inst. Mining, Metall. and Petroleum Engrs. (chair aqueous processing com. 1988-90), Instn. Mining and Metallurgy, Electrochem. Soc., Materials Rsch. Soc. Office: U Calif Berkeley Dept Materials Sci 325 Hearst Mining Bldg Berkeley CA 94720-1760 Office Phone: 510-642-7594.

DOYLE, GILLIAN, actress; b. Maidenhead, Berkshire, Eng. came to U.S., 1977; d. John Joseph and Joan (Walker) D. BA in Theatre magna cum laude, Am. U., Washington. Appeared in (off Broadway) Ernest in Love, NYC, 1980; (plays) No Exit, Washington, 1985, Fefu and Her Friends, 1985, The Winters Tale, 1987, A Christmas Carol, 1987, Erpingham Camp, 1989, Turn of the Screw, 1989, Season's Greetings, 1986, Terra Nova, 1987, Mountain, 1990, Old Favorites, 1991, What the Butler Saw, 1993, Fawlty Towers, 1994, Last of the Red Hot Lovers, 1995, The Musical Comedy Murders of 1940, 1996, Move Over Mrs. Markham, 1997, Declarations: Love Letters of the Great Romantics, 1998, Present Laughter, 1999, Two, 1999, U.S.A., 2000, Blithe Spirit, 2002, A Midsummer Night's Dream, 2002, What The Butler Saw, 2003, Homebody/Kabul, 2003, Under Milkwood, 2004, My Boy Jack, 2004, The Fourth Wall, 2005, (play) The Miser, 2006; (musical) The Cradle Will Rock, 2001; (films) Chances Are, 1989, Born Yesterday, 1993, North, 1993, Decade of Love, 1994, Wild Bill, 1994, The Tie That Binds, 1995, Independence Day, 1996, Play Me Again Sam, 1999, Love, 2000, Being Doctor Jack, 2005, In a Different Key, 2005, When Henri Came to Stay, 2005, Seven Shivas, 2006; (TV) Ancient Prophecies III, 1995, Friends, 1995, The Martin Short Show, 1995, Days of Our Lives, 1996, Love's Deadly Triangle: The Texas Cadet Murder, 1996, General Hospital, 1997, Port Charles, 1999, The Man Show, 1999, Titus, 2001, Passions, 2005; (music video) Johnny Sportcoat and the Casuals, 1987; (voiceover) Books on Tape Audio Narrator, 2006; (comml.) United Way, 1988. Mem. SAG, AFTRA, Actors Equity Assn., Phi Kappa Phi. Democrat. Roman Catholic. Avocations: golf, swimming, music, scuba diving. Personal E-mail: gilliandoyle@hotmail.com.

DOYLE, HEATHER SUE, psychologist; b. Warren, Ohio, Apr. 29, 1981; d. John Chuma (Stepfather) and Sue Ann Doyle-Chuma, Russell Lee Doyle. BS magna cum laude, Bethany Coll., W.Va., 2003; MEd, student, Kent State U., Ohio, 2004—. Lic. profl. sch. psychologist Ohio, 2006. Intern art, recreation therapist Fox Run Hosp., St. Clairsville, Ohio, 2001—02; activity asst. The Vista Centre, Lisbon, Ohio, 2002; trainee early intervention childhood specialist Family Child Learning Ctr., Tallmadge, Ohio, 2003—04; trainee behavior intervention specialist Kent (Ohio) State U., 2004—05; sch. psychologist Medina (Ohio) City Schs., 2006—. Tutor preschooler with autism Edwards family, Twinsburg, Ohio, 2004—04; co-facilitator adhd parent group Akron (Ohio) Children's Hosp., 2005—05. Exhibitions include Bethany Coll. Student Art Exhibit, 2002 (Hon. Mention award, 2002, 2003), 2003. Vol. Children's Miracle Network, Wheeling, W.Va., 2000—03. Named Collegiate All-American scholar, U.S. Achievement Acad., 2003; recipient Academic Achievement award, Psi-Chi, 2001—03. Mem.: APA, Student Affiliates Sch. Psychology Kent (Ohio) State U. (social chair 2004—05), Ohio Sch. Psychologists Assn., Nat. Assn. Sch. Psychologists, Dem. Women's Club, Bethany Coll. Psychology Club (pres. 2001—03), Gamma Sigma Kappa, Bethany Coll. Panhellenic Coun. (pres. 2002—03), Beta Nu (exec. coun. 2000—03, panhellenic coun. 2000—03). Democrat. Avocations: tennis, art, reading, animals, music. Home: 3399 E Normandy Park Dr Apt M5 Medina OH 44256 Office Phone: 330-636-4003. Personal E-mail: hdoyle@kent.edu.

DOYLE, IRENE ELIZABETH, electronic sales executive, nurse; b. West Point, Iowa, Oct. 5, 1920; d. Joseph Deidrich and Mary Adelaide Schulte; m. William Joseph Doyle, Feb. 3, 1956. RN, Mercy Hosp., 1941. Courier nurse Santa Fe R.R., Chgo., 1947—50; indsl. nurse Montgomery Ward, Chgo., 1950—54; rep. Hornblower & Weeks, Chgo., 1954—56; v.p. William J. Doyle Co., Chgo., 1956—80, Ormond Beach, Fla., 1980—88. Served with M.C. U.S. Army, 1942—46. Mem.: Electronic Reps. Assn., Oceanside Country Club (Ormond Beach). Republican. Roman Catholic.

DOYLE, JUANITA, medical/surgical nurse; b. Ill., Apr. 18, 1946; d. Raymond Glenn and Claire (Granger) Hayen; m. Robert R. Doyle, June 29, 1968; children: Shawn, Colleen, Kelly, Patrick. Diploma, St. Francis Hosp., Peoria, Ill., 1967; BSN, Lewis U., Romeoville, Ill., 1993. RN Ill. Home health nurse Cmty. Home Health, Joliet; dir. nursing svcs. Cmty. Circle Care, Joliet; recovery and scheduling nurse AmSurg, Joliet; case mgr. med.-surg. dept. Silver Cross Hosp., Joliet. Home: 1524 Mayfield Ave Joliet IL 60435-5730

DOYLE, KRISTENE ANNE, psychologist, educator; b. N.Y.C., Oct. 5, 1972; d. Roger Christopher and Barbara Ann Doyle. BA, McGill U., 1994; MA with Distinction, Hofstra U., 1995, PhD, 1999. Lic. psychologist N.Y. Edn. Dept., 2000. Dir. clin. services Assn. Benefit Children, N.Y.C., 1999—2000; coordl. tng. and devel. Albert Ellis Inst., 2000—, dir. child and family svcs. clinic, 2000—, staff psychologist, 2000—, dir. clin. svcs., 2002—, assoc. exec. dir., 2003—. Adj. asst. prof. St. John's U., Jamaica, NY, 2000—. Author: The Application of Rational Emotive Behavior Therapy In Women's Groups Therapy, My Idiosyncratic Practice of Rational Emotive Behavior Therapy, The Contribution of Social Psychology to Rational Emotive Behavior Therapy; co-author: Achieving Unconditional Self-Acceptance: Rational Emotive Behavior Therapy with a Depressed Woman, Rational Emotive Behavior Therapy and Attention Deficit Psychiatry Disorder, —; mem. editl. bd.: Jour. Rational-Emotive and Cognitive-Behavior Therapy, 2002—. Fellow: Albert Ellis Inst.; mem.: APA, Assn. Behavioral and Cognitive Therapies (chair inst. am. psychol. conv. 2002—05). Office: Albert Ellis Inst 45 East 65th St New York NY 10021 Office Phone: 212-535-0822. Business E-Mail: krisdoyle@albertellis.org.

DOYLE, NANCY HAZLETT, artist; b. Wilmington, Del., July 8, 1947; d. Theodore Jay and Catherine L. (Lynch) Hazlett; m. Michael Doyle, Nov. 20, 1982 (div. 1985). BS in Art Edn., Moore Coll. of Art, 1969; MFA in Painting, Pa. State U., 1975. Tchr. Chester County Juvenile Detention Home, Embreeville, Pa., 1972—73; instr. Pa. State U., State College, 1975—77; artist Chester County Art Assn., West Chester, Pa., 1977—78. One person shows include Pattee Meml. Libr., Pa. State U., University Park, 1974, Cygnet Framing Studio, West Chester, 1986, Va. Lippincott Gallery, Phoenixville, Pa., 1992, Agapè Gallery, Malvern, Pa., 1994; exhibited in group shows Coll. Arts and Arch., Zoller Gallery, Pa. State U., University Park, 1974-75, Erie (Pa.) Art Ctr., 1975, Corcoran Gallery, Washington, 1975, Juniata Coll., Huntingdon, Pa., 1976, Daisy Jamison Soroptimist Ann. Invitational Show, West Chester, 1979-82, Yellow Springs Ann. Art Show, Chester Springs, Pa., 1986-98, Chester County Art Assn. Invitational, 1986-88, Artworks Gallery, Kennett Square, Pa., 1992-95, Main Line Art Ctr., Haverford, Pa., 1994-96, Jun Gallery, Phila., 1994, Leslie Eadeh Art Gallery, Devon, Pa., 1995, Hardcastle Gallery, Wilmington, Del., 1996, Ctr. for Creative Arts, Hockessin, Del., 1997-2000, Del. Ctr. Contemporary Arts, Wilmington, 2001-03, West Chester U., Pa., 2005. Recipient grad. assistantships Pa. State U., 1973-75. Mem.: Del. Ctr. for Contemporary Arts, New Castle County Irish Soc. Democrat. Avocations: photography, crafts, reading, webmaster. Home: 5 Ruth Rd Apt G-5 Wilmington DE 19805 Personal E-mail: ndoylebus@cs.com.

DOYLE, RHONDA GAIL, science educator; d. Albert Leroyce Mongomery and JoAnn Montgomery; m. Ernest Andrew Doyle, Aug. 4, 1978; children: Brian Thomas, Andrea Beth. BS, Northeastern State U., Tahlequah, Okla., 1980. Tchr. secondary sci. Cave Springs H.S., Stilwell, Okla., 1980—82, Stilwell H.S.; acad. facilitator Chewey Christian Acad., Watts, Okla., 1993—97; tchr. secondary sci. Sequoyah H.S., Tahlequah, 1997—2000, Stilwell H.S., 2000—. Spkr. Victim Impact Panel Okla., Stilwell, 2003—06. Recipient H.S. Tchr. Yr., Stilwell H.S., 2003—04. Office: Stilwell High School 1801 W Locust Stilwell OK 74960 Office Phone: 918-696-7275.

DOYLE, VIRGINIA KNEPPER, artist; d. Robert Alexander Steven and Helen Elizabeth Stott; m. William E. Knepper (div.); children: Christopher, Michael; m. John L. Doyle, Jan. 18. BA in English and Psychology, U. Calif., Berkeley, Calif., 1995. Represented in permanent collections Bingham, Osborne, and Scarborough, San Francisco, Calif., The Bendix Corp., Detroit, Mich., Rause and Assocs., Phila., The U.S. Embassy, Luxembourg, Jackson, Cross and Assocs., Washington, D.C., SEVEN, San Francisco, Calif., Strathmore Paper Corp., one-woman shows include Tiburon Heritage and Arts Ctr., Paris, 2004—05, numerous group shows including most recently, exhibited in group shows at Bechtel Internat. Ctr. Stanford U., The Art Angel's Festival, Belvedere, Calif., 2004—05, Escal Winery, Larkspur, Calif., 2004—05, Artisan's Gallery, San Rafael, Calif., 2006, Chico Art Ctr., Calif., Falkirk Cultural Ctr., San Rafael, Calif., exhibitions include Belvedere Libr., Calif., 2004—05, Commonwealth Club, San Francisco, Calif., On-Line Exhibit, Beijing, China, De Young Mus., Sam Francisco, Calif., 2006. Home: 10 Tamalpais Cir Belvedere CA 94920-2488

DOZE, MAUREEN ADELE (MAUREEN ADELE MEE), social studies educator; b. Denver, June 11, 1953; d. James Robert and Mary Louise Mee; m. John Burtis Doze, Mar. 24, 1979; children: Laura Kathryn, Sarah Jocelyn. BA, U. Colo., Boulder, 1976; MA, U. Colo., Denver, 1985. Tchr. mid. sch. social studies Cherry Creek Schs., Englewood, Colo., 1988—. Chief proctor Nat. Evaluation Sys., Conn., 1998—2002. Mem.: Phi Beta Kappa. Avocations: quilting, gardening, reading, travel. Office: Horizon Comty Mid Sch 3981 S Reservoir Rd Aurora CO 80013 Office Phone: 720-886-6100. E-mail: mdoze@cherrycreekschools.org.

DOZIER, ELEANOR CAMERON, computer company executive, writer; b. N.Y.C., May 20, 1939; d. Robert Paul and Marion Gill MacNeil; m. Norman Garlan Dozier, June 23, 1989; children: Karen Gonzales, Robert Bennett, Heidi Bennett, Julia, Ian, Jordan. Rep. to British Isles Max Factor, Inc., Hollywood, Calif., 1966—71; co-owner; also songwriter and poet MacNeil Dozier Pub. Co., Ft. Lauderdale, Fla., 1988—2002; v.p. Computer Dimensions Network Corp., N.Y.C., 1998—. Mktg. dir. Prometheus Devel., San Jose, Calif., 1986—87. Author: (book) O For The Love Of God!, 2003. Recipient commn., Stephen Ministry, Order St. Luke. Episcopalian. Avocations: bicycling, golf, tennis, travel.

DOZIER, KIMBERLY, news correspondent; b. Honolulu, Hawaii, July 6, 1966; BA in Human Rights and Spanish (magna cum laude), Wellesley Coll., 1987; MA in Fgn. Affairs, U. Va., 1993. Washington, DC-based reporter Energy Daily, New Technology Week and Environment Week, Washington, 1988—91; reporter Christian Sci. Monitor, Cairo, 1992—95, Washington Post, Cairo, 1993, CBS News Radio News and Voice of Am., Cairo, 1994—95, San Francisco Chronicle, Cairo, 1995; anchor BBC Radio World Service's, World Update, London, 1996—98; London bur. chief and chief European corr., reporter CBS News, CBS Radio News, London, 1996—2002; chief corr., Middle East Bur. WCBS-TV, NYC, 2002—03; news corr. CBS News, Iraq, 2003—; also reporter CBS Evening News, CBS Evening News (weekend editions), The Early Show and, CBS 24-hour news svc. Recipient Alumnae Travel award, U. Va., 1993, Grand Gracie award, Am. Women in Radio and TV, 2000, Gracie award, 2000, 2001. assignments include the War in Iraq, the War in Afghanistan and the Hunt for Osama bin Laden, the Crisis and Refugee Exodus in the Balkans, Vladimir Putin's election, the Death of Princess Diana, Northern Ireland's Peace Process and the Khobar barracks bombing in Dhahran. Office: CBS TV 51 W 52nd St New York NY 10019-6188*

DRACUP, KATHLEEN ANNE, dean, nursing educator; b. Santa Monica, Calif., Sept. 28, 1942; d. Paul Joseph and Lucy Elizabeth (Milligan) Molloy; children: Jeffrey, Jonathan, Joy, Jan, Brian. BS in Nursing, St. Xavier's Coll., Chgo., 1967; M of Nursing, U. Calif., L.A., 1974; D of Nursing Sci., U. Calif., San Francisco, 1982. Clin. nurse Little Co. of Mary Hosp., Chgo., 1967-70, UCLA Med. Ctr., 1970-74; asst. clin. prof. U. Calif., 1974-78, rsch. fellow dept. medicine, 1979-81, asst. prof. to prof., 1982-99, dean Sch. Nursing San Francisco, 2000—; clin. nurse Sch. Nursing U. Calif. San Francisco Med. Ctr., 1979; pvt. practice psychotherapist, 1980—95. Editor Heart and Lung Jour., 1981-91, Am. Jour. Critical Care, 1991—; editor Critical Care Nursing Series; contbr. chpts. to books, articles to profl. jours. Recipient Eugene Brunwald Acad. Mentorship award Am. Heart Assn., 2003; Disting. Practitioner Nat. Acad., Washington, 1987; Fulbright Sr. scholar, 1995. Fellow Coun. Cardiovascular Nursing, Am. Heart Assn., Am. Assn. Cardiopulmonary Rehab.; mem. Inst. of Medicine, Am. Nurses' Assn., Am. Assn. Critical Care Nurses (life), Sigma Theta Tau. Office: U Calif San Francisco Sch Nursing 2 Koret Way Rm N319 San Francisco CA 94143-0604 Office Phone: 415-476-1805. Business E-Mail: kathydracup@nursing.ucsf.edu.

DRAELOS, ZOE DIANA, dermatologist, consultant; b. Milw., Oct. 13, 1958; d. Dimitri Basil and Lorene June (Legan) Kececioglu; m. Michael Draelos, June 14, 1980; children: Mark, Matthew. BSME, U. Ariz., 1979, MD, 1983. Diplomate Am. Bd. Dermatology. Physician in solo dermatology practice, High Point, NC, 1988—. Cons., owner Dermatology Cons. Svcs., High Point, 1990—. Author: Cosmetics in Dermatology, 1995, Atlas of Cosmetic Dermatology, 2000. Rhodes scholar, Oxford, Eng., 1979. Office: Zoe Diana Draelos MD PA 2444 N Main St High Point NC 27262-7833 Office Phone: 336-841-2040.

DRAGAN, ALEXANDRA, mechanical engineer, consultant, environmental engineer, researcher, engineering educator; d. Ioan and Arety Elena Dragan; 1 child, Miruna Roxanna. BME, MME, U. Bucharest Polytechnica, Romania, 1964; M in Environ. Engring., U. So. Calif., 1993; DEng, U. Constrn., Bucharest, 1998. Registered profl. engr., Calif., N.Y. From engr. to sr. engr. Designing Inst. for Wood Industry, Bucharest, 1967—73; cons. engr. FOREXIM/Technoforest, Bucharest, 1973—76; engr. Jack Stone Engrs., N.Y.C., 1978—81; from sr. engr. to group leader Haines Lundberg Waehler, N.Y.C., 1981—84; from sr. engr. to assoc. Syska and Hennessy, L.A., 1984—86; pvt. practice L.A., Calif., 1984—; chief engr. Donald Dickerson Assoc., L.A., 1986—88; dir. engring. Nat. Air Sys., L.A., 1988; from sr. engr. to supervising mech. engr. III County of L.A. Dept. Pub. Works, Alhambra, Calif., 1988—. Pres. Dragan Engring., L.A., 1984—98; prof. mech. engring. U. Politehnica of Bucharest, 2000—01, prof. emeritus, 2001—. Author: Thermal Processes and Power Generation in Wood Industry, 1973. Recipient Value Engring. award, County of L.A., 1986, Environ. Sci. and Engring. fellow, AAAS and US EPA, 1992. Mem.: ASHRAE (Cert. of Appreciation 1993—94, Symposium Paper award 2001), Internat. Soc. Indoor Air Quality and Climate, Am. Romanian Acad. for Arts and Scis. (exec. com. 2001). Republican. Avocation: singing. Home: 2276 S Beverly Glen Blvd Apt 304 Los Angeles CA 90064-2464 Personal E-mail: draganalexandra@yahoo.com.

DRAGILA, STACY, track and field athlete; b. Auburn, Calif., Mar. 25, 1971; Pole vaulter. Recipient Jesse Owens Award, 2000. Achievements include won Gold Medal, Sydney Olympic Games, 2000; World Champion, 1999; World Indoor Champion, 1997; U.S. Indoor Champion, 1996-2001; U.S. Outdoor Champion, 1996, 97, 99, 2000; 1st and only Women Pole Vault World Champion; 1st and only Women Pole Vault Olympic Gold Medalist. Office: 1 Rca Dome Indianapolis IN 46225-1023

DRAGONETTE, RITA HOEY, public relations executive; b. Chgo., Nov. 4, 1950; d. Louis D. and Edith M. (Finnemann) Hoey; m. Joseph John Dragonette, Sept. 4, 1982 (dec.). BA in English and History, No. Ill. U., 1972. Asst. dir. Nat. Assn. Housing and Human Devel., Chgo., 1975; pub. rels. account exec. Weber Cohn & Riley, Chgo., 1975-76; publicity coord. U.S. Gypsum Co., Chgo., 1976-77; with Daniel J. Edelman, Inc., Chgo., 1977-84, sr. v.p., 1981-84; exec. v.p. Dragonette, Inc., Chgo., 1984-91, pres., 1991-99, GCI Dragonette, Chgo., 1999—2002; prin. Dragonette Cons., 2002—. Home: Ste 422 680 North Lake Shore Dr Chicago IL 60611 E-mail: rmdragonette@ameritech.net.

DRAGOON, VALERIE BALDWIN, art educator; b. Concord, NH, Mar. 26; d. Harley G. and Geraldine H. Baldwin; m. Michael George Dragoon, June 9, 1979; children: George Maxwell, Patrick Chase. Degree, Plymouth State, NH, 1978. Art tchr. k-6 Holy Family Sch., Norwich, NY, 1997—. Rep. Norwich Team Sch. Decision Making, Norwich, NY, 2000—04, City Wide Character Edn. Com., Norwich, NY, 2001—03. Prin. works include Mural Childs Play, 2002. Scholarship chair Norwich PTA, Norwich, NY, 2005—06, pres., 2003—05, v.p., 2003—06. Independent. Roman Catholic. Avocation: skiing. Office: Holy Family Sch 17 Prospect St Norwich NY 13815

DRAGO-SEVERSON, ELEANOR ELIZABETH E., developmental psychologist, educator, researcher; b. N.Y.C., N.Y., Nov. 25, 1961; d. Rosario Philip and Betty Louise (Brisgal) Drago; m. David Irving Severson, Dec. 30, 1989. BA summa cum laude, L.I. U., 1986; EdM, Harvard U., 1989, EdD, 1996. Cert. biology, chemistry tchr., N.Y. Tchr. math. Palm Beach (Fla.) Acad., 1986-87; h.s. tchr. math., basketball coach Hackley Sch., Tarrytown, N.Y., 1987-88; tchr. biology, dir. human devel. Palm Beach Day Sch.,

1990-91, dir. human devel., 1990-91; tchg. fellow Harvard U., Cambridge, Mass., 1993-96, assoc. in edn. Grad. Sch. Edn., 1996—2002, postdoctoral fellow Sch. Edn., 1997-2001, instr., rsch. assoc. Sch. Edn., 1997—2002, lectr. edn. Grad. Sch. Edn., 1998—2005; assoc. prof. edn. Tchrs. Coll. Columbia U., 2005—. Co-dir. J.V. Mara C.Y.O. Sports Camp, Putnam Valley, N.Y., summer 1987. Author: Helping Teachers Learn: Principal Leadership for Adult Growth and Development, 2004 (NSDC Book of Yr. award, 2004), Becoming Adult Learners: Practices and Principles for Effective Development, 2004. Mem. colloquium com. Harvard U., Cambridge, Mass., 1991-92, chair, 1992, mentor to incoming grad. students, 1992-96. Joseph Klingenstein fellow, 1987, tchg. fellow, 1993-96, doctoral fellow, 1994-96; Spencer sm. grant rsch. award, 2000. Mem. ASCD, APA, AAUW, Am. Ednl. Rsch. Assn., Soc. for Rsch. in Adult Devel., Nat. Staff Devel. Coun., Phi Delta Kappa. Roman Catholic. Home: 106 Morningside Dr Apt 73 New York NY 10027

DRAHOS, SANDRA P., retired chemist; b. Chgo., Aug. 3, 1943; d. Berlyn and Elizabeth Anna Pierce; children: David Mark, Elizabeth Anne. BS, U. Wis., 1966. Chemist Ashland Chem., Willow Springs, Ill., 1983—93, Enviropur, McCook, Ill., 1993—95, Chempet, Inc., Addison, Ill., 1995—97, Henkel Adhesives, Eligin, Ill., 1997—2002. Leader, tng. chmn., instr. Boy Scouts of Am., Morris, Ill., 1979—89; leader Girl Scouts of Am., Joliet, Ill., 1983—86; mem. Wee Care, Scottsdale, Ariz., 2002—05, Landscaping Com. for Camello Vista, Scottsdale, 2004—05; vol. Rialto Theatre, Joliet, 1998—2005. Recipient Hobson award, 1999. Mem.: Soc. Tribiologists and Lubricating Engrs. (life; various offices). Achievements include patents for Adhesives for Shoes. Avocations: travel, piano, bridge, art, gardening. Personal E-mail: sdrahos1@msn.com.

DRAKE, ANN M., consumer products company executive; d. James and Mary Lou McIlrath; m. John Drake, II; stepchildren: Joanna, Tracy. B in English, U. Iowa, 1969; MBA, Northwestern U., 1984. Founder, prin. Camwilde Interiors; exec. v.p. DSC Logistics, DesPlaines, Ill., 1990—92, CEO, 1992—. Bus. adv. com. Northwestern U. Transp. Ctr. Mem.: Chgo. Network, Com. of 200. Office: DSC Logistics 1750 S Wolf Rd Des Plaines IL 60018

DRAKE, CAROLYN A., administrative assistant; b. Lockwood, Mo., Jan. 13, 1943; d. Frenk Dirk and Abbie Dean (Cowan) Stolting; m. Stephen Dean Drake, Aug. 15, 1964; children: Eric Chadwick, Rachelle Alene. BS, N.W. Mo. State U., Maryville, 1964; student, U. Wyo., Laramie, Eastern Mich. U., Ypsilanti. Cert. h.s. tchr., Mich.; lic. travel agt. Tchr. King City (Mo.) H.S., 1964-67, Dept. Def. Schs., Clark AFB, Philippines, 1968-69; advt. rep. Seaway Rev., Glen Arbor, Mich., 1981-83; asst. Dennos Museum Ctr., Traverse City, Mich., 1991—. Co-dir. Sci./Math. Inst. Tchr., Traverse City, 1986-89, asst. to dir., 1982-86. Officer, PTO Traverse City; coach Odyssey of the Mind, Trverse City; directoress St. Anne's Altar Guild, Traverse City, 1990—. Recipient Margaret Morse Nice award Wilson Ornithol. Soc., Ann Arbor, Mich., 1988. Episcopalian. Avocations: reading, hiking, wood carving, photography, coin collecting/numismatics.

DRAKE, DIANA ASHLEY, retired financial planner; b. Poughkeepsie, N.Y., Apr. 28, 1937; d. Albert Jackson and Jane Ashley (Ketchum) D.; m. José Akel Abizaid, Dec. 2, 1956 (div. Nov. 1979); children: Cynthia A. Rush, Allison J. Abizaid, Linda A. Wiener, Carol Lynn Abizaid, Amanda Jo Abizaid, Richard Alan Abizaid; m. Sherrill Cleland, Sept. 3, 1988; stepchildren: Ann Cleland Feldmeier, Douglas S. Cleland, Sarah Cleland Allen, Scott C. Cleland. Student, Cornell U., 1955-56, Am. U. of Beirut, Lebanon, 1956-57; BS in Psychology cum laude, Vassar Coll., 1980; CFP, Inst. Fin. Planners, Denver, 1986. CFP. Divorce mediator Fin. Planning Corp. of Va., McLean, 1983-86; investment advisor Cert. Fin. Svc., McLean, 1986; ptnr. Koelz Drake Advisors, Falls Church, Va., 1987-89; pres. Drake Fin. Svcs., Falls Church, 1986-98; bronze distbr. Nikken health and wellness products, prin. Magnetic Living, 1998—2003; ret., 2003. Sec., mem. Bd. Equalization, Falls Church, 1992-94. Contbr. articles to various mags. Elder Falls Church Presbyn. Ch., 1993-96, chair Christian Edn. Com., 1996, planned giving com. 1997-99, revision com. 1997; co-chmn. 100 yrs. aquatics YMCA, New Orleans, 1986. Recipient Disting. Svc. award for 25 Yrs. svcs. Nat. YMCA, 1986. Mem.: DAR, AAUW, Inst. CFPs, No. Va. Inst. Cert. Fin. Planners (sec. 1994—97, bd. dirs. facilities), Sarasota Camera Club, Cornell Club (Sarasota), Zonta (dir. Arlington club 1992—99, cmty. svc. coord.), Cornell Club of Washington (mem. investment and audit com. 1990—99), Meadows Chorus (Sarasota), Vassar Club (Sarasota, Fla.), Highland Oaks Cir. Assn. (bd. dirs., pres. 2003), Delta Gamma. Republican. Avocations: swimming, bridge, writing, photography, travel. Home and Office: 4489 Highland Oaks Cir Sarasota FL 34235 E-mail: dadcleland@aol.com.

DRAKE, ELISABETH MERTZ, chemical engineer, consultant; b. NYC, Dec. 20, 1936; d. John and Ruth (Johnson) Mertz; m. Alvin William Drake, July 31, 1957 (div. 1984); 1 child, Alan Lee. SB in Chem. Engring., MIT, 1958, ScD in Chem. Engring., 1966. Registered profl. engr., Mass. Staff engr. Arthur D. Little Inc., Cambridge, Mass., 1958-64, sr. staff, 1966-76, mgr. risk analysis, 1977-82, v.p. tech. risk mgmt., 1980-82, 86-89, cons., 1990-94; assoc. dir. new tech. MIT Energy Lab., 1990-2000, dir., 1994-95, cons., 2000—; lectr. U. Calif., Berkeley, 1971; vis. prof. MIT, Cambridge, 1973-74; chmn. chem. engring. dept. Northeastern U., Boston, 1982-86. Corp. mgr. MIT, 1981-86; mem. tech. pipeline safety stds. com. U.S. Dept. Transp., 1980-85; mem. mng. bd. AIChE, 1988-90; vice chair com. on rev. and evaluation on army chem. stockpile disposal program NRC, 1993-98, mem., 2002-2004, vice chair com. on chem. demil., 2004—. Contbr. articles to profl. jours.; inventor fractionation method and apparatus, 1972. Fellow AIChE (bd. dirs. 1987-90); mem. AAAS, NAE, Am. Chem. Soc., Sigma Xi. Home: 30F Inman St Cambridge MA 02139-2411 Business E-Mail: edrake@alum.mit.edu.

DRAKE, EVELYN DOWNIE, retired secondary school educator; b. Longmont, Colo., Aug. 23, 1940; d. Milford West and Colette Dorothy (Mraz) Downie; m. Sherman Hoffman Drake, May 18, 1963 (div. 1971); children: Marcella Colette Drake-Bettis, Sherman Downie Drake; m. Robert Dale Mager, July 14, 1975 (div. 1981). BS, U. Wyo., 1962; MA, U. No. Colo., 1980; postgrad., U. Edinburgh, Scotland, 1982, Cambridge U., Eng., 1986. Cert. tchr./vocat. tchr., Colo. Sec./receptionist Barnard Realty, Casper, Wyo., 1959-61, Pure Oil Co. (now UNOCAL), Casper, 1961; coord., tchr. St. Mark's Pre-Sch., Casper, 1965; reporter, feature writer Casper Star-Tribune, Casper, 1970-71; instr., tchr. Casper Coll., 1964-69; tchr. home econs. Kelly Walsh High Sch., 1971-72; tchg. asst. U. No. Colo., Greeley, 1979-80; tchr. of English, journalism, art, home econs. Jefferson County R-1 Schs., Golden, Colo., 1972—97, ret., 1997. Cons., tchr. Casper North Side Ctr., 1969-71. Artist: weaving exhibit, Pub. Libr., Casper, 1968, others. Ctrl. com. Jefferson County Democrats, Lakewood, Colo., 1989—; candidate bd. dirs. Green Mt. Townhouse Corp. #1 Lakewood, 1987; tchr. Lakewood Sister Cities Exch. Program to Miranda, New South Wales, Sutherlandshire, Australia, 1995. Nominated Colo. Tchr. of Yr., Evergreen (Colo.) Jr. High, 1989. Mem. Colo. Lang. Arts Soc., Nat. Coun. Tchrs. of English (planning com. nat. conf. 1989-90), NEA (faculty rep.), Colo. Educators Assn. (faculty rep.), JCEA Edn. Assn. (faculty rep.), Denver Press Club, Phi Delta Kappa (sec. 1995-2006), Delta Kappa Gamma, others. Avocations: art, writing, literature.

DRAKE, GRACE L., retired state senator, cultural organization administrator; b. New London, Conn., May 25, 1926; d. Daniel Harvey and Marion Gertrude (Wiech) Driscoll; m. William Lee Drake, June 9, 1946 (dec.); 1 child, Sandra Drake Sparber. With Am. Photographic Corp., N.Y.C., 1944-72; senator State of Ohio, Columbus, 1984—2001; dir. Ohio Ctr. Advancement Women in Pub. Svc., 2001—. Chair Cuyahoga County Rep. Exec. Commn.; alumnus Leadership Cleve.; active March of Dimes State Bd., HealthSpace Cleve. Bd., Masonic Learning Ctrs. Bd., Positive Edn. Program Bd., Coun. on Older Persons Bd., Northeast Ohio Nursing Initiative Bd. Named Legislator of the Yr., Nat. Rep. Legis.'s Assn., 1988, Grace L. Drake Agrl. Lab. in her honor, Ohio State U., 2003; named to Ohio Women's Hall of Fame, 1995, Pres. James A. Garfield Hall of Fame, 2005; recipient Meritorious Svc. award, Ohio State U., 2001, Ctr. for Health Affairs, 2001, Pub. Affairs award, March of Dimes, 2001. Roman Catholic. Avocations: bridge, golf. Home: 5954 Briardale Ln Solon OH 44139-2302 Office: Cleve State Univ 2121 Euclid Ave UR 140 Cleveland OH 44115 Office Phone: 216-687-4893. Business E-Mail: gdrake@urban.csuohio.edu.

DRAKE, JAYNE KRIBBS, academic administrator, literature educator; b. Oil City, Pa., Aug. 3, 1946; d. A. Merle and Edna May Eisenman Kribbs; m. Jeffrey Richard Drake, Dec. 1, 1984; 1 child, Darren Alexander. BA, Clarion (Pa.) U. of Pa., 1968; MA, Pa. State U., 1969, PhD, 1974. Assoc. dean The Grad. Sch. Temple U., Phila., 1984-91, grad. dean Coll. of Liberal, 1991-96, prof. English, 1975—, dir. tchg. improvement ctr., 1996-99, assoc. dean for student svcs., 1997-98, dir. acad. advising, 1998—2003, vice dean, 1998—2004. Sec. Golden Cradle Bd. Trustees, Cherry Hill, N.J., 1981—; cons. Phila. Sch. Dist., 1990-94. Author: Critical Essays on John Greenleaf Whittier, 1981, American Literary Periodicals, 1978; editor: MLA International Bibliography, 1969-75. Mem. Beagle Club Civic Assn. (v.p. 1994-2000), Nat. Assn. for Acad. Advising (regional rep. 2000-03, chair awards com. 2002-05, chair adminstrv. divsn. 2005—). Avocations: reading, travel, boating. Home: 93 Bunning Dr Kirkwood Voorhees NJ 08043 Office: Dept English Temple U Philadelphia PA 19122 Office Phone: 215-204-4699. Business E-Mail: jayne.drake@temple.edu.

DRAKE, JEANETTE WENIG, communications educator, writer, public relations consultant; b. Marion, OH, Mar. 14, 1963; d. Dwight L. and Mildred D. Wenig; m. Jeffrey P. Drake, Oct., 22, 1994. BA in Advt., Ohio State U., 1985, MA in Journalism, 1993; postgrad., Bowling Green State U., 1999—. cert. in pub. rels., Pub. Rels. Soc. of Am. Dir. advt. and pub. rels. The DeSantis Group, Columbus, OH, 1985-91; dir. comm. YMCA of Ctrl. Ohio, Columbus, 1991-93; co-founder, editor Perimeter Star, Columbus, 1993-95; marketing dir. The Prime Group, Washington C.H., OH, 1993-94; editor, mng. editor Ohio State U., Columbus, OH, 1994-98; asst. prof. U. Findlay, OH, 1998—. Pub. rels. cons., 1994—; bd. mem. Henry Co. Arts Coun., Napoleon, OH, 1999—, Campus Compact, Findlay, OH, 1999—; leader internat. exchange YMCA to Japan, 1992. Regional editor: Dialogue, 1999—; contbr. articles, essays to profl. pubs. Vol. Franklin Co. Children's Svcs., 1994—; cons. Concerned Citizens, OH, 1994—. Recipient Addy award campaign advt. fedn. YMCA, 1991, English award United Way, Columbus, 1993, Savvy award Retail Marketers Assn., 1994, Presdl. Things Gone Right award Ohio State U., 1998, Communicators award, 2001. Mem. Nat. Comm. Assn., Pub. Rels. Soc. of Am. (cert., v.p.), Ctrl. States Comm. Assn., Ohio State Alumni Assn. Avocations: travel, glassblowing, poetry, writing, backpacking. Home: 310 Glendale Ave Findlay OH 45840-5116 E-mail: drake@findlay.edu.

DRAKE, JILL LEAH, elementary school educator; b. Trenton, N.J., Aug. 2, 1954; d. Donald Charles Stoup and Verna Jeanette Stoop; m. Raymond H. Drake, June 26, 1976; children: Christian, Chad, Lindsay. BEd in Early Childhood and Elem. Edn., State Coll. N.H., Trenton, N.J., 1978; MSc in Edn., Nazareth Coll., Pittsford, N.Y., 1997. Tchr. spl. edn. Hebron Ave. Elem. Sch., Glastonbury, Conn., 1988—90, Eastbury Elem. Sch., Glastonbury, 1990—91; tutor spl. edn. Naubauc Elem. Sch., Glastonbury, 1991—92; substitute tchr. Mendon Ctr. and Pk. Rd. Elem. Sch., Pittsford, 1994—96; tchr. Mendon Ctr. Elem. Sch., Pittsford, 1996—. Office: Mendon Center Elem Sch 110 Mendon Ctr Rd Pittsford NY 14534 Business E-Mail: jill_drake@pittsford.monroe.edu.

DRAKE, MIRIAM ANNA, retired librarian, educator, writer, consultant; b. Boston, Dec. 20, 1936; d. Max Frederick and Beatrice Celia (Mitnick) Engleman; m. John Warren Drake, Dec. 19, 1960 (div. Dec. 1985); 1 child, Robert Warren. BS, Simmons Coll., Boston, 1958, MLS, 1971; postgrad., Harvard U., 1959—60; LHD (hon.), Ind. U., 1994; DLS (hon.), Simmons Coll., 1997. Assoc. United Rsch., Cambridge, Mass., 1958-61; with mktg. svcs. Kenyon & Eckhardt, Boston, 1963-65; cons. Boston, 1965-72; head rsch. unit libraries Purdue U., West Lafayette, Ind., 1972-76, asst. dir. libraries, prof. library sci., 1976-84; dean, dir. libraries, prof. Ga. Inst. Tech., Atlanta, 1984-2001, prof. emerita, 2001—; ret., 2001. Trustee Online Computer Libr. Ctr., Inc., 1978-84, chair, 1980-83; trustee Corp. for Rsch. and Edn. Networking, 1991-94, U.S. Depository Libr. Coun., 1991-94, Simmons Coll., 1999-2004; trustee, corporator adv. bd. Engring. Info., 1997—; trustee emerita Simmons Coll., 2004-; bd. dirs. Women's Commerce Club, 2005—. Author: User Fees: A Practical Perspective, 1981, Information Today, 2002; co-author: (with James Matarazzo) Information for Management, 1994; editor: Ency. Libr. Info. Sci., 2nd edit.; mem. editl. bd. Coll. and Rsch. Librs. Jour., 1985-90, Librs. and Microcomputers Jour., 1983-93, Sci. and Tech. Librs., 1989-98, Database, 1989-97; contbr. chpts. to books, articles to profl. jours. and trade mags. Recipient Alumni Achievement award Simmons Coll. Sch. Libr. and Info. Sci., 1985, Kent Meckler Media award U. Pitts., 1994. Fellow: Nat. Fedn. of Abstracting and Indexing Svs. (hon.); mem.: ALA (councilor at large 1985—89, Hugh Atkinson Meml. award 1992), Assn. Info. and Dissemination Ctrs. (pres. 2001—03), Spl. Librs. Assn. (pres.-elect 1992—93, pres. 1993—94, H.W. Wilson award 1983, John Cotton Dana award 2002), Am. Soc. Info. Sci., Am. Mgmt. Assn. Office Phone: 404-636-0154. Business E-Mail: mdrake@bellsouth.net.

DRAKE, PATRICIA ANN GLASSCOCK, psychologist; b. Barbourville, Ky., July 15, 1955; d. Vernon Thomas Glasscock and Neva (Hammons) Kaplan; m. Mark Marvin Drake, Mar. 21, 1987; children: Matthew Marvin, Megan Elizabeth. BA, Marygrove Coll., Detroit, 1977; Ma, U. Detroit, 1978; PhD, Wayne State U., Detroit, 1987. Lic. psychologist, sch. psychologist, Mich. Psychologist Caknipe-Kovach Assoc., Wayne, Mich., 1987-89; sch. psychologist Warren (Mich.) Consol. Schs., 1978—2004; cons. spl. edn. data Wayne Resa, 2004—. Wayne State U. grad. scholar, 1981-87; named to Honorable Order Ky. Cols., 1989. Mem. Nat. Assn. Sch. Psychologists, Macomb-St. Clair Psychol. Assn. (pres. 1991-92). Methodist. Office: Wayne Resa 32500 Van Born Wayne MI 48184

DRAKE, PATRICIA EVELYN, psychologist; b. Lewiston, Maine, Feb. 9, 1946; d. Lewis and Anita (Bilodeau) D.; m. Colin Matthew Fuller, May 13, 1973 (div. Aug. 1983); children: R. Matthew, Meaghan Merry. Diploma, St. Mary's Sch. Nursing, 1967; BS, U. Nev., 1985; MA, Calif. Sch. Profl. Psychology, 1987, PhD, 1989. RN. Nurse Maine Med. Ctr., Portland, 1967-73, U. Calif. Sacramento Med. Ctr., 1973-78, Ben Taub Hosp., Houston, 1978-79; psychology intern Shasta County Mental Health Ctr., Redding, Calif., 1988-89, clin. psychologist, 1989-91, tng. dir., chief psychology, 1991—2005; psychologist pvt. practice, Redding, Calif., 1991—. Mem.: AAUW, APA, Calif. Psychol. Assn., Shasta-Cascade Psychol. Assn., Phi Kappa Phi. Democrat. Roman Catholic. Avocations: swimming, cross country skiing, crafts. Office: 1970 Hartnell Ave Redding CA 96002 Office Phone: 530-225-5980. Business E-Mail: pdrake@co.shasta.ca.us.

DRAKE, PATTI LINN, retired consumer products company executive; b. Cin., June 25, 1925; d. John and Mildred Thyra Linn; m. Melvin Richard Drake, Sept. 15, 1953; 1 child, Julie Ann Daniel. Student, U. Cin., 1946; degree, Art Acad. Cin., 1945; diploma, Cuisine Dieppe, France, 1973. Fashion copy writer Mables, Cin., 1938—45; jewelry design Wadsworth Co., Dayton, Ky., 1945—51; fashion art dir. H&S Pogue Co., Cin., 1951—55; art dir. classified Cin. Enquirer, 1955—60; v.p. fashion promotion Donenfelds, Dayton, Ohio, 1965—95; ret.; art seminar instr. Fairfield Glade, Tenn. Author poetry; mags. Mem.: Fairfield Guild (pres. 1998), Mensa, Oak Ridge Art Ctr. Republican. Episcopalian. E-mail: pldrake@frontiernet.net.

DRAKE, ROBYN RENÉE (ROBYN FIELDER), writer, painter; b. Carroll, Iowa, Jan. 9, 1964; d. Leslie Mac and Fern Marjorie (Schelldorf) Fielder. BA in Painting, Drake U., Des Moines, 1997, BA in Drawing, 1997, BA in Art History, 1997. Artist DeLaurent Fine Arts, Chgo., 1989-90; svc. mgr. Art Shuttle, Inc., Chgo., 1990-94; cons. Rita Bucheit Ltd., Chgo., 1994-96, Feigen Gallery, Chgo., 1995-98; cons., adminstr. Genesis Artists Village, Chgo., 1997—; cons., artist Kozan Studios, Chgo., 1998-99. Guest panelist Capricon Lit. Conv., Oak Brook, Ill., 1997-99, Windycon Lit. Conv., Schaumburg, Ill., 1997-99, World Fantasy Conv., Monterey, Calif., 1998, Providence, R.I., 1999. Author: The Wind at Tres Castillos, 1999; contbg. artist Ency. Living Artists, 11th edit., 1999. Recipient Cert. of Outstanding Achievement NASA, 1979, Open Five Gaited Champion Midwest, 1980, Midwest Saddleseat Equitation Runner-up, 1980. Mem. Degerberg Acad. Martial Arts (savate 1998, 99, Most Fit Female 1998, U.S. Savate Team nominee 2000). Avocations: horses, scuba diving, dance. Office: The Iff Theatre LLC PO Box 25786 Chicago IL 60625-0786 Home: 37375 N Hunt Club Rd Old Mill Creek IL 60083-9693 E-mail: savateuse@aol.com.

DRAKE, SYLVIE (JURRAS DRAKE), theater critic; b. Alexandria, Egypt, Dec. 18, 1930; arrived in U.S., 1949, naturalized, 1952; d. Robert and Simonette (Barda) Franco; m. Kenneth K. Drake, Apr. 29, 1952 (div. Dec. 1972); children: Jessica, Robert I.; m. Ty Jurras, June 16, 1973. M. Theater Arts, Pasadena Playhouse, 1969. Free-lance TV writer, 1962-68; theater critic Canyon Crier, L.A., 1968-72; theater critic, columnist L.A. Times, 1971-91, chief theater critic, 1991-93, theatre critc emeritus, 1993—; lit. dir. Denver Ctr. Theatre Co., 1985; pres. L.A. Drama Critics Circle, 1979-81, free lance travel writer, translator, book reviewer. Mem. Pulitzer Prize Drama Jury, 1994; adv. bd. Nat. Arts Journalism Program, 1994-97. Dir. publs. Denver Ctr. for the Performing Arts, 1994—; artistic assoc. for spl. projects Denver Ctr. Theatre Co., 1994—. Mem.: Am. Theater Critics Assn. Office: Denver Ctr Performing Arts 1101 13th St Denver CO 80204-2100 Office Phone: 303-893-4000. Business E-Mail: sdrake@dcpa.org.

DRAKE, THELMA DAY, congresswoman; b. Elyria, Ohio, Nov. 20, 1949; m. Ted Drake; 2 children. Grad. high sch. Realtor RE/MAX Allegiance Realty, Hampton Roads, Va.; mem. Va. State Ho. Dels. from 87th dist., 1995—2004; chair Va. Housing Commn.; mem. Chesapeake Bay Commn., US Congress from 2nd Va. dist., 2005—, mem. edn. and the workforce com., mem. resources com., mem. armed svcs. com. Bd. mem. Va. Zool. Soc. Named Citizen of Yr., Va. Crime Prevention Assn., Legislator of Yr., YMCA, Commrs. of the Revenue, Va. Cable & Telecom. Assn.; named one of Outstanding Profl. Women of Hampton Roads; recipient John Marshall award, Va. Property Rights Coalition. Republican. United Church Of Christ. Office: US Ho Reps 1208 Longworth Ho Office Bldg Washington DC 20515-4602 Office Phone: 202-225-4215.*

DRAKE-HAMILTON, LILLIE BELLE, retired secondary school educator; b. Coll. Park, Ga., July 15, 1919; d. Charley Grady Drake and Lillie Vesta Gullatt; children: Cynthia Belle, Hilary Phyllis. BA, Agnes Scott Coll., 1940; MA, Middlebury Coll., Vt.; student, U. San Marcos, 1950. Cert. tchr. Fulton County Bd. Edn., 1940. Instr. Spanish Agnes Scott Coll., Decatur, Ga., 1948—51; tchr. Women's Tchr. Tng. Coll., Tripoli, Libya, 1951—53, Glen Burnie Sr. HS, Md., 1957—58, Waterloo Jr. HS, Elkridge, Md., 1958—59, Coll. Park HS, Ga., 1959—81; ret., 1981—. Co-dir. Pan-Am. Student Forum Atlanta (Ga.) Met. Area, 1946—48; mem. governing bd. Nat. Jr. Classical League, 1974; del. congress Am. Classical League, Madrid, 1974. Contbr. articles to profl. jours. Named to Ga. Tchrs. Hall Fame, 1981; recipient Ga. State Achievement award, Key Women Educators, 1996. Mem.: NEA, Spanish Hon. Soc., Fgn. Lang. Assn. Ga. (pres. 1973—75, Lifetime Achievement award for outstanding svc. & contributions to fgn. lang. edn. 2005), Women's Caucus Módern Langs., Vergilian Soc., Classical Assn. Mid. West and South (v.p. Ga.), Am. Classical League, Ga. Assn. Educators (recipient Exceptional Svc. plaque), Am. Assn. Tchrs. Spanish and Portuguese (life; v.p. Ga. chpt. 1960—62, sec., treas. Ga. chpt. 1964—70, pres. Ga. chpt. 1970—72). Democrat. Avocations: travel, gardening. Home: 6201 Roosevelt Hwy PO Box 362 Union City GA 30291

DRAKEMAN, LISA N., biotechnologist; b. Boston, Oct. 30, 1953; d. Paul and Josephine (Covino) Natale; m. Donald L. Drakeman, Aug. 23, 1975. BA, Mt. Holyoke Coll., 1975; MA, Rutgers U., 1983, Princeton U., 1986, PhD, 1988. Chair, v. chair Monclair (N.J.) Redevelopment Agy., 1981-84; vis. scholar Dartmouth Coll., 1988-89; lectr. Princeton U., 1989-92; asst. dir. Alumni Coun. of Princeton U., 1991; dir. administrn. Medarex, Inc., Princeton, NJ, 1991-94, v.p. adminstrn., 1994-96, v.p., 1996-98, sr. v.p., head bus. devel., 1998-2000; CEO Genmab A/S, 1999—. Faculty fellow Grad. Coll. Princeton U., 1991-93, mem. adv. coun. dept. religion, 1996-; bd. dir. Medarex Europe, B.V., GenPharm. Internat., Inc., Biotech. Coun. N.J. Mem. biopharm. adv. coun. Tech. Coun. Greater Phila., 1993-96; mem. Gov.'s Biopharm. Task Force N.J. Econ. Master Plan Commn., Trenton, 1994-95; mem.biotech. adv. com. The Franklin Inst., Phila., 1994-96; commr. Prosperity N.J., 1995-2000; mem. Cancer Inst. N.J. Leadership Coun., 2004—06; bd. dirs., mem. exec. com. Biotechnology Coun. N.J., 2005—. Garden State grad. fellow State of N.J., 1981-85; named to N.J. High Tech. Hall of Fame, 2000. Mem. Soc. Advancement of Women's Health Rsch. (steering com., corp. adv. coun. 1994-97), Biotech. Industry Orgn. (chair nat. capital formation task force 1995-98, Advocate of Yr. award 1995), Biotech. Coun. N.J. (v.p. 1996-2000, Outstanding Industry Woman of Yr. 1996), European Fedn. Pharm. Industries and Assns. (bd. dir. emerging pharm. enterprises sect. 2004-06, v.p. 2006). Home: 49 Rolling Hill Rd Skillman NJ 08558-2319 Office: 457 N Harrison St Princeton NJ 08540 also: Genmab A/S Toldbodgade 33 DK 1253 Copenhagen Denmark

DRAKEOBRIEN, CONSTANCE SUSAN, elementary school educator; b. Phillipsburg, N.J., July 18, 1961; d. James Stanley and Betty J. (Boquist) Drake. BA in Creative and Performing Arts, Franklin Pierce Coll., 1982; N.J. elem. cert., Centenary Coll., 1985. Tchr. lang. arts 7th, 8th grades St. Philip & St. James Sch., Phillipsburg, 1985-86; tchr. math., computers 6th-8th grades, drama 7th-12th grades Cheshire (Conn.) Acad., 1986-88; tchr. math. 7th-8th grades, drama 7th-12th grades Allendale Columbia Sch., Rochester, N.Y., 1988—, computers 6th-8th grades, 1988-92, tutor, 1992—; gifted and talented tchr. Lebanon Borough Sch., NJ, 1997—2001, Greenwich Township Sch. Dist., 2001—. Balloon deliveries Send-a-Smile, Phillipsburg, 1982-84; clown Halena the Clown, Phillipsburg, 1982-84; presenter in field. Mem. Nat. Coun. Tchrs. Math., Nat. Theatre Edn. Assn. Roman Catholic. Office: Greenwich Sch Dist 101 Wyndham Farm Blvd Stewartsville NJ 08886

DRANCE, LISA IACONO, secondary school educator, department chairman; d. John Michael and Josephine Arienti Iacono; m. Daniel Anthony Drance, July 10, 1999. BA, Franklin and Marshall Coll., Lancaster, Pa., 1987; MA, Northwestern U., Evanston, Ill., 1991. Permanent certification English and speech NY, cert. sch. bldg. adminstrn. NY, sch. dist. adminstrn. NY, profl. theater tchr. NY. English and theatre tchr. Babylon (N.Y.) Jr. Sr. H.S., 1997—, dir. English and theatre, 2004—, chmn. English dept., dir. theater program. Dir.: (musicals and plays) Our Town (Babylon Citizens Coun. Arts Best Play award, 2005), The Foreigner (Babylon Citizens Coun. Arts Best Play award, 2006). Mem.: LI Lang. Arts Dirs., LI Lang. Arts Coun., NY State Theatre Edn. Assn. (bd. mem., trustee 1997—), Nat. Coun. Tchrs. English. Office: Babylon Junior Senior High School 50 Railroad Ave Babylon NY 11702 Office Phone: 631-893-7909. Business E-Mail: ldrance@hotmail.com, ldrance@babylonschools.org.

DRANT, SANDRA ELIZABETH, court reporter, educator; b. L.A., July 18, 1939; d. Archie Delbert and Clara Mae DeLane; m. Richard David Drant, Sept. 5, 1959 (div. 1965); m. Richard David Drant, Feb. 3, 1966 (dec. 1996); children: Stacey Allada, Ryan David. AA, Cypress Coll., 1989; BA in English, Chapman U., 1992; MA in Edn., Pepperdine U., 1995; cert. in intermediate reading instrn., Calif. State U., San Bernardino, 2000; cert. in med. transcription, Southeast Regl. Occupl. Prog., 2000. Cert. shorthand reporter, cert. reporting instr. Freelance reporter, Long Beach, Calif., 1960—65; state hearing reporter Calif. Unemployment Ins. Appeals Bd., Long Beach, Workers' Compensation Appeals Bd., Bell Gardens, 1972—82; cert. reporting instr. Cerritos Coll., Norwalk, Calif., 1990—2003, prof. emeritus, 2003—06. Faculty advisor Ct. Reporting Club, 1995-97, 99-2003, ct. reporting dept. co-chair, 1997-2003. Vol. chaperone Mammoth Mountain Ski Edn. Found., Mammoth Lakes, Calif., 1982-84; co-chair Grad-Night com. Mammoth High Sch., Mammoth Lakes, 1988; vol. archaeologist Cypress Coll., 1989-99; apheresis donor ARC, 1994—. Recipient Cert. of Recognition Calif. Legis. Assembly, 1993; named Parent of Yr., Mammoth Mountain Ski

Edn. Found., 1983-84, Outstanding Curricular Advisor, 1995-96, 99-2001. Mem. AAUW, Stanford U. Parents Club (vol. contbr. 1988—). Avocations: field archaeology, skiing, handcrafts, travel, cooking.

DRAPALIK, BETTY R., volunteer, artist, educator; b. Cicero, Ill., July 4, 1932; d. Henry William and Jennie Margaret (Robbins) Degen; m. Joseph James Drapalik, Oct. 30, 1951; children: Betty Jennifer Drapalik Coryell, Joseph Henry. Grad., HS, Cicero. Sec., clk. Gt. Lakes (Ill.) Naval Base, until 1982; sect. to asst. dir. Arden Shore Boys' Home, Lake Bluff, Ill., 1984-87; sub. tchr. art Visual Art Ctr., Waukegan, Ill. One-woman shows include Jack Benny Ctr. Arts, 1995—2004, 2006, Wauconda Area Pub. Libr., 1999, 2002, Invitational First Lady Hearts and Flowers Art Exhbn., Ill., 2001—06 (First Lady award, 2004), GreenBelt Cultural Art Ctr., North Chgo., 2003, Pikes Peak Watercolor Soc. Internat. Watermedia XIII/ Fine Art Ctr., Colo. Springs, 2003, St. Charles Nat. Juried Art Exhbn. and Music Festival, 2005, Lake County Discovery Mus., 2005, exhibited in group shows at Layson Gallery, Waukegan, Ill., 1993, Cmty. Gallery Art, Coll. Lake County, Grayslake, Ill., 1993—99, 2000—06, Women's Works, Old Courthouse Art Ctr., Woodstock, Ill., 1994—2000, 2002, Anderson Art Ctr., Kenosha, Wis., 1994—2005, Hardy Gallery, Ephraim, Wis., 1996—2002 (Purchase award, 1998), North Point Marina, Winthrop Harbor, Ill., 1996—2003 (1st pl. watercolor, 1996, 1999, 2d pl. watercolor, 1997, 1998, Best of Show, 1996, 1997, award of Merit watercolor, 1998, award of Excellence, 1999, 3d pl., 2001, 3d pl. watercolor, 2002), Truman State U., Kirksville, Mo., 1997, Moorehead State U., Minn., 1997, Kenosha Art Assn. and Lake County Art League Combined Art Event, 1997 (Best of Show, 1997), David Adler Cultural Ctr., Libertyville, Ill., 1997—2002, Hawthorne Hollow Art Festival, Kenosha, 1997—98, Deer Path Art League Festival, Lake Forest, 1997, 1999, N.W. N.Mex Arts Coun., Farmington, 1997, Waukegan Visual Arts Ctr., 1998, Zion Chamber Orch. Concert and Art Contest, 1998 (Best of Show, 1st pl.), Kenosha Pub. Mus., 1998 (award of excellence), Spotlight Gallery, Kenosha, 1998—99, Monne's Gallery, 1998, Deilora A. Norris Cultural Ctr., St. Charles, Ill., 1998—2006, 1st ann. Art Discovery Festival, Lake County Discovery Mus. and Lake County Art League, Wauconda, Clausen Art Shop, Wilmette, Ill., 1999, Gull Lake Gallery, Richland, Mich., 1999—2002, Nippersink Gallery, Richmond, Ill., 1999—2001, Deer Path Gallery, Lake Forest, 1999—2003, Wauconda Pub. Libr., 1999, 2002, 2006, Kenosha Art Assn. and Lake County Art League Combined Art Event, 2000 (Best of Show, 2001), Kenosha Art Assn. Art Event, 2001—05 (3d pl., 2002), Green Belt Cultural Ctr., North Chgo., 2000, 2005, City of Zion, Ill., 2001—02, Centennial Days Fine Art Show, 2001, Harring Galleries, Racine, Wis., 2001—05, Guenzel Gallery, Fish Creek, Wis., 2001—02, Jack Benny Ctr. Arts, 2003—06, Colo. Fine Art Ctr., 2003, Cmty. Gallery Art, Coll. Lake County, 2001—05, Western Colo. Watercolor Soc. exhbn., 2004, William M. Scholl Coll. Pediat. Medicine, Rosalind Franklin U. Medicine and Sci., North Chicago, 2005 (2d pl., 2005), Art Wauk, Waukegan, Ill., 2005, 2006, St. Charles Nat. Art Exhbn. and Music Festival, 2005, traveling exhbn., America the Beautiful, 2001—03; work published in Celebrating Door Country's Wild Places, 2001. Former leader, mem. pub. rels. com. Girl Scouts U.S.; visual arts cons. Green Belt Cultural Ctr. Lake County Forest Preserve Dist.; organizer meml. svc. and exhbn. Phil Austin's Life, Waukegan, 2004; leader art program Walkerville (Mich.) Schs., 2003; mem. outreach and evangelism missions bd. First Presbyn. Ch. Waukegan, 2000—02. Recipient Purchase award, Coll. Lake County, Grayslake, 1994, numerous courtesy awards. Mem.: Nat. Mus. Women in the Arts (charter), Bloomin' Artists, N.W. Area Arts Coun., Kenosha Art Assn., Red River Watercolor Soc., Deerpath Art League, Lakes Region Watercolor Guild (past rec. sec., co-program chair, exhibit chair), Lake County Art League (resource person, past pres., various bd. positions, fine arts cons. Green Belt Cultural Ctr. Lake County Forest Preserve), Transparent Watercolor Soc. Am. (life), Internat. Starcraft Camper Club (Ill. chpt. sec./treas. 1975). Evangelical. Avocations: painting, photography, camping, gardening, hiking. Home: 2018 W Grove Ave Waukegan IL 60085-1607 Office Phone: 847-662-2617.

DRAPER, DOROTHY E., middle school mathematics educator; b. Wilmington, Del., June 30, 1954; d. Michael and Mary L. (Kelley) Ferenc; m. Bruce L. Draper, Dec. 27, 1975; children: Alison, Bryn, Catherine. BS in elem. edn., U. Del., 1976; MA in edn., U. N.Mex., 1986, PhD, 1991. Asst. coach women's volleyball Princeton U., NJ, 1976-78; math. instr. St. Mary's Sch., Albuquerque, 1978-80; math. instr., elem. tchr. Our Lady of Fatima Sch., Albuquerque, 1986-89; instr. U. N.Mex., Albuquerque, 1987-89; tchr. La Mesa Elem. Sch., Albuquerque, 1989-93; math. instr. Albuquerque Acad., 2000—. Family Math. coord. La Mesa Elem. Sch., Albuquerque, 1990-92; regional coord. N.Mex. Systemic Initiative in Math/Sci. Edn., 1993-98; Child Find coord. Ctrl. Region Endl. Cooperative, 1998-99; volleyball coach Albuquerque Acad., 2000—. Mem. Nat. Coun. Tchrs. Math., N.Mex. Coun. Tchr. Math. (v.p. 1989-91, pres. 2000-02), Todos, Math. For All, Women Math. Edn., N.Mex. Symphony Guild, Phi Delta Kappa. Home: 8415 Guadalupe Trl NW Albuquerque NM 87114-1124 Office Phone: 505-828-3139. E-mail: draper@aa.edu.

DRAPER, PAMELA DENKERS, elementary school educator; b. Salt Lake City, Nov. 23, 1960; d. Gerrard Bernard and Phyllis Bingham Denkers; m. Jeffery Alan Draper, Sept. 23, 1982; 1 child, Eric Jeffery. BA, U. Utah, Salt Lake City, 2001. Lic. profl. educator level II Utah, 2004. Adminstrv. aide Family History Libr., Salt Lake City, 1982—87. Mentor tchr. to children and teenagers The LDS Ch., Salt Lake City, 1978—2006. Mem. Lds Ch. Office: Oquirrh Hills Middle School 12949 South 2700 West Riverton UT 84065

DRAPER, PENNY KAYE PEKRUL, music educator; b. Lansing, Mich., May 14, 1948; d. Edward Emil Pekrul and June Marie Piche-Fahlen; m. William Burle Draper III, June 13, 1970; children: Paige Lindsley, Josselin Bertrand. BA in Choral Edn. cum laude, Mich. State U., 1970, BA in Applied Piano Pedagogy cum laude, 1971, MA in Musicology, 1983, PhD in Musicology, 1997. Cert. tchr., Mich., continuing edn. tchr., Mich. Choral dir. Williamston (Mich.) H.S., 1970-78; dir. Renaissance Singers, East Lansing, Mich., 1979—, Jr. Renaissance Singers, East Lansing, Mich., 1990—; choral dir. East Lansing Schs., 1993-94; pvt. instruction East Lansing, 1993—. Mem. adj. faculty U. Mich., Flint, 1995—96; choral dir. Youth Choir Plymouth Congl. Ch., 1995—, HOPE Acad., Lansing, Mich., 1996—2002; chair fine arts com. Plymouth Congl. Ch., 1997—2000, chair music sch. com., 1994, mem. organist search com., 2002, chair, dir. music search com.; dir. Plymouth Bell Choir, 2003—. Author program notes MSU Symphony Orch., 1980-83, Lansing Symphony Orch., 1981, Elizabethan Musical Feast, 1983-92; contbr. articles to profl. jours. Mem. Lansing Matinee Musicale, 1997—, chair performing arts students, 2002—; bd. deacons Plymouth Congl. Ch., 2002—03; apptd. humanities profl. Mich. Humanities Coun., 2002—. Piano scholar Mich. State U., 1966-70, Lansing Matinee Musicale, 1965. Mem.: Capital Area Music Tchrs. Assn. (v.p. 1997—99, pres. 1999—2001, Tchr. of Yr. 2003), Mich. Music Tchrs. Assn. (awards chmn. 2002—04, student achievement testing auditions chair 2004—, cert., bd. dirs.), Music Tchrs. Nat. Assn. (local chmn. state convention 2003), Pi Kappa Lambda, Sigma Alpha Iota. Home: 513 Woodland Dr East Lansing MI 48823-3273 Office Phone: 517-351-4632. E-mail: draperpe@msu.edu.

DRAPER, ROBERTA HORNIG, retired journalist; b. Hazelton, Pa., May 20, 1935; d. Carl Orim and Josephine Miriam Hornig; m. Morris Draper, Aug. 15, 1981 (dec.). BS, U. Wis., 1955. Reporter Washington Star, Washinton, DC, 1957—81; congressional prodr. senate NBC News, Washinton, DC, 1981—2001; ret., 2001. Contbg. author (book chpt.) Reporting on Business and The Economy, 1981. Recipient 1st prize, Washington Balt. Newspaper Guild, 1971. Mem.: Nat. Press Club. Home: 3101 New Mexico Ave NW Washington DC 20016

DRATCH, RACHEL, comedienne, actress; b. Lexington, Mass., Feb. 22, 1966; d. Paul and Elaine Dratch. BA in Psychology and Theater, Dartmouth Coll., 1988. Former cast mem. Second City, Chicago, 1992—99; cast mem. Saturday Night Live, 1999—. Actor: (films) Martin & Orloff, 2002, The Hebrew Hammer, 2003, Down with Love, 2003, After School Special, 2003, Dickie Roberts: Former Child Star, 2003, Home of Phobia, 2004, Looking for Kitty, 2004, Her Minor Thing, 2005, Winter Passing, 2005, Click, 2006; (TV series) Game Over, 2004, 30 Rock, 2006; guest appearances include (TV series) Third Watch, 2000, The King of Queens, 2002—04, Kim Possible, 2002, Monk, 2004, Frasier, 2004, O'Grady, 2005, writer, dir., actor (films) The Vagina Monologues Monologues, 2001, writer, actor (two-woman show with Tina Fey) Dratch & Fey, 2000. Office: Saturday Night Live NBC Studios 30 Rockefeller Plz New York NY 10112*

DRAZDOFF, NOLA GAY, psychologist; d. Michael John and LaJuana Joy Drazdoff. BS in Computer Sci. and Bus., U. Puget Sound, WA, 1986; MA in Psychology, Antioch U., Seattle, 1999; Ordained Interfaith Min., One Spirit Interfaith Sem., NY, 2005. Programmer, analyst Weyerhaeuser Real Estate Co., Federal Way, Wash., 1984—88; systems engr. Electronic Data Sys, Southfield, Mich., 1986—87; pres., founder Soundex Info. Sys., Inc., Federal Way, Wash., 1988—90; program mgr. Microsoft, Redmond, Wash., 1990—93; tour leader, counselor Self Employed, Issaquah, Wash., 1999—2000; pres., founder Inspired Path, Inc., Issaquah, Wash., 2001—. Precinct com. officer WA State Dem. Party, Olympia, Wash., 2004—05; bd. adv. Bustan L'Shalom, Jerusalem, 2004—05; bd. dirs. Compassionate Listening Project, Seattle, 2004—05; vol. Friend to Friend: Nursing Home Visitation, Seattle, 1996—2005; vol., fundraiser Child Care Resources, 2003—05. Recipient Proactive Peacemaker award, Season for Non-Violence, Oreg. Chpt., 2002. Mem.: ACA, APA (assoc.), Am. Mental Health Counseling Assn. Avocations: travel, exploring cultures and spiritual tradition, hiking, gardening. Office: Inspired Path Inc 4580 Klahanie Drive SE PMB 434 Issaquah WA 98024 Office Phone: 425-785-5389. Office Fax: 425-222-3543. E-mail: noladr@inspiredpath.com.

DRAZIN, LISA, investment banker, financial consultant; b. Washington, Nov. 26, 1953; d. Sidney and Bernice Ann (Jeweler) D. AB with honors, Wellesley Coll., 1976; MBA, George Washington U., 1980. Chartered fin. analyst. Securities analyst Geico, Inc., Chevy Chase, Md., 1982; mng. prin. Jefferson Securities Ltd., Bethesda, Md., 1983; chmn., CEO Drazin & Co., Inc., Bethesda, 1983-89, Drazin Properties, Inc., Bethesda, 1985-89, Drazin Securities, Inc., Bethesda, 1985-88, Woodmont Asset Mgmt. Inc., 1989—. Affiliate Montgomery County Bd. Realtors; real estate investment banker Restructuring Fed. Deposit Ins. Corp. Founder Ivy Connection, Washington, 1982; bd. dirs. Friends of Tel Aviv U., Jewish Nat. Fund; active Nat. Truste for Historic Preservation, UJA Fedn. of Greater Washington (young leadership divsn., Ruth Heritage Forum), Am. Friends Hebrew U., Jewish Inst. for Nat. Security Affairs, The Israel Project, Nat. Kidney Found., Shakespeare Theatre Guild, Music Ctr. at Strathmere, The Phillips Collection. Fellow Wexner Heritage Found., Renaissance Inst., Friends for Life Benefit, Whitman Walker Clinic, Spiritual Ctr. Am., Assn. for Investment Mgmt. and Rsch., Turnaround Mgmt. Assn.; mem. Nat. Assn. Realtors, Comml. Investment Real Estate Coun., Realtors Nat. Mktg. Inst., CFA Soc. Washington, Inc., Wellesley Club (interns coord., recent grads. rep. 1981-84, Washington), Ben Gurion Club, Beta Gamma Sigma, Tau Zeta Epsilon. Office: Woodmont Asset Mgmt Inc 6403 Kirby Rd Bethesda MD 20817-5523 Office Phone: 301-718-6400. Personal E-mail: lisa.drazin@verizon.net.

DREBEN, RAYA SPIEGEL, judge; b. Vienna, Dec. 3, 1927; came to U.S., 1928, naturalized, 1936; d. Shalom and Rose (Goldschmiedt) Spiegel; children: Elizabeth, Jonathan. AB magna cum laude, Radcliffe Coll., 1949; LL.B. cum laude, Harvard U., 1954. Bar: Mass. 1957, U.S. Supreme Ct. 1960. Law clk. to Judge Bailey Aldrich, U.S. Dist. Ct. for Mass., 1954-55; Bigelow fellow and instr. U. Chgo. Law Sch., 1955-56; asso. Firm Palmer & Dodge, Boston, 1964-71, partner, 1971-79; assoc. justice Mass. Appeals Ct., Boston, 1979—. Lectr. in copyright Harvard U. Law Sch., 1973-76; mem. adv. com. on copyright registration and deposit Libr. of Congress, 1993. Trustee Radcliffe Coll., 1981-89. Recipient 1st prize Nathan Burkan competition Harvard U. Law Sch., 1954, nat. winner, 1954, Haskell Cohen award for disting. jud. svc. Boston Bar Assn., 2004. Mem. ABA (chmn. com. on authors 1977-79), Am. Law Inst. (adv. on restatement, property-donative transactions), Am. Bar Found., Copyright Soc. U.S.A. (trustee 1973-76, editl. bd, bull. 1974-85), Jud. Inst. Mass. Judiciary (chmn. adv. com. 1988-96). Office: Mass Appeals Ct John Adams Courthouse 1 Pemberton Sq Boston MA 02108 Office Phone: 617-725-8556.

DRECHSLER, BEATRICE KRAIN, lawyer; BA magna cum laude, Barnard U., 1984; JD cum laude, Harvard U., 1987. Bar: NY 1988, NY 1988. Ptnr. Real Estate Dept. Kaye Scholer LLP, NYC. Mem.: Internat. Coun. of Shopping Ctrs., Estate Women - NY, Inc., NY Women Execs. in Real Estate. Office: Kaye Scholer LLP 425 Park Ave New York NY 10022 Office Phone: 212-836-8146. E-mail: bdrechsler@kayescholer.com.

DREES, DEDREE ANN, computer graphics designer, educator, artist; b. NY; m. Dana Fisher. BS, Skidmore Coll., Saratoga Springs, NY, 1967; MFA, Pa. State U., Univ. Park, 1970; M of Liberal Arts, Johns Hopkins U., Balt., 1979. Cert. scientific illustration Smithsonian Instn., 1983. Gallery dir. Ferdinand Roten Galleries, Balt., 1970—71; prof. Cmty. Colls. Balt. County, Catonsville, 1971—. Guest curator Balt. Mus. Art, 1977—78. Author and artist: Marbelized Notepaper, designer: Balt. Area Convention and Visitors Assn. Destination and Planning Guide, 2002 (Graphic Design USA brochure award, 2002); exhibitions include Nat. Arboretum, Washington, 1989, Johns Hopkins U. Libr., Balt., 1991, Represented in permanent collections Balt. Washington Internat. Airport. Grantee Interdisciplinary Humanities, NEH, 1974—76, Fulbright Hayes Found., 1977, Internat. Studies Integration Project, U.S. Dept. Edn., 1989—90; scholar, N.Y. State Regents, 1963—67, Comm. Design Program, U. Balt., 2002; MFA Tchg. fellow, Pa. State U., 1968—70. Mem.: Soc. Marblers, Assn. Computing Machinery, Coll. Art Assn., Fulbright Assn. Office: CCs Balt County 800 S Rolling Rd Catonsville MD 21228 Office Phone: 410-455-4423. Business E-Mail: ddrees@ccbcmd.edu.

DREES, DOROTHY E., small business owner, real estate manager; b. Utica, N.Y, Oct. 12, 1953; d. Edward D. and Frances A. (Merritt) Drees; m. Richard D. Hulley. BA in Philosophy, SUNY, 1975; student, Bowman Tech. Sch., 1976, student, 1977. Engraver Appel & Weber, Lancaster, Pa., 1978—81; jeweler Crest Jewel, Fairfield, Iowa, 1982—85; sculptor Zimmerman Studios, Fairfield, 1986; jeweler Americus Diamond, Fairfield, 1987—88; prin., owner Dorothy Drees, Jewelry & Hand Engraving, Fairfield, 1985—; ptnr. Akashic Records & Tapes, Fairfield, 1995—, R&D Real Estate, Fairfield, 1997—. Ptnr.: Richard & Dorothy Jazz Duo, 2000, co-founder: Shakti Lila Band, 2002—. Mem.: Hand Engravers, NRDC, Maharishi U. Mgmt. Town Superradiance, Gen. Soc. Mayflower Descs. Avocations: singing, songwriting, piano, bass, dance. Home and Office: 104 South D St Fairfield IA 52556 Office Phone: 641-472-7524.

DREHER, MARIAM JEAN, education educator; b. Memphis; d. James Ralph and Nina M. (Wells) W.; m. Peter Dreher; 1 child, Silvia. BA, U. Calif., Riverside; MA, PhD, U. Calif. Elem. tchr. Rialto (Calif.) Unified Sch. Dist., reading tchr.; instr. U. Calif., Riverside; prof. U. Md., College Park. Recipient Constance McCullough Rsch. award Calif. Reading Assn., Elva Knight Rsch. grant Internat. Reading Assn. Mem. Internat. Reading Assn., Nat. Conf. Rsch. Lang. and Literacy, Nat. Reading Conf., Soc. Scientific Study Reading, Phi Beta Kappa. Office: U Md Dept Curriculum And Instrn College Park MD 20742-0001

DREIS, MARGARET K., music educator, peer advisor; b. Honolulu, Feb. 9, 1944; d. Henry and Gerturde Aiu Makini; m. David W. Dreis, Dec. 17, 1966; children: Damien K., Francis K., Danielle K. MusB, Fort Wright Coll. Holy Names, 1966; MA in Adminstrn. & Curriculum, Gonzaga U., 1993. Cert. tchg. Ea. Wash. U., 1967. Music tchr. Deer Park Schs., Wash., 1967—69, Spokane Pub. Schs., Wash., 1973—77, music tchr., peer mediation advisor, 1985—. Nominee Equity award, Spokane Pub. Schs., 1997, 1998; recipient Fulbright award, Ea. Wash. U., 2000, Outstanding Educator Yr. award, Washington State U. Music, 2006. Mem.: Exec. Woman's Golf Assn., Ea. Wash. Music Educators (treas. 1999—, Music Educator of Yr. 1993), Downriver 9-Hole Ladies Golf, Sundance 18-Hold Ladies Golf, US Tennis Assn. Avocations: golf, tennis, cooking, crossword puzzles. Home: 6221 S Regal Spokane WA 99223 Office: Spokane Pub Schs N6411 Alberta Spokane WA 99208 E-mail: qualchan@hotmail.com.

DREIZEN, ALISON M., lawyer; b. Bklyn., Sept. 14, 1952; d. Nathan Dreizen and Florence (Morgenstern) Barth. BA, Cornell U., 1974; JD, Harvard U., 1977. Bar: N.Y. State 1978. Assoc. White & Case, N.Y.C., 1977-85, ptnr., 1985-93, 95—, Moscow, 1993-95. Recipient Investment Funds Deal of the Yr., Internat. Hotel Investment Forum, 2002. Office: White & Case 40th Fl 1155 Avenue Of The Americas New York NY 10036-2787

DRELL, PERSIS, physicist; B, Wellesley Coll.; PhD in Atomic Physics, U. Calif., Berkeley, 1983. Postdoctoral rsch. assoc. in high-energy physics Lawrence Berkeley Nat. Lab., 1983—88; asst. prof. physics Cornell U., 1988—97, prof. physics, 1997—, dep. dir., Lab. Nuclear Studies, chair, Synchrotron Radiation Com., Lab. Nuclear Studies; mem. program adv. com. Stanford Linear Accelerator Ctr. (SLAC), Menlo Park, Calif., 1993—95, assoc. dir., 2002—, current chair, scientific policy com. Leader of Cornell Group, Wilson Lab. CLEO (one of the world's most advanced particle detectors), 2000. Named One of the 50 Most Important Women in Science, Discover Mag., 2002. Office: Stanford Linear Accelerator Ctr 2575 Sand Hill Rd Menlo Park CA 94025 Address: Stanford Linear Accelerator Ctr PO Box 20450 Stanford CA 94309 Office Phone: 650-926-3300.

DRENNEN, EILEEN MOIRA, editor; b. Suffern, N.Y., May 27, 1956; d. D.A. and M. Eileen (Connolly) D. AA, Dutchess C.C., N.Y., 1978; BA in English, Fla. State U., 1983. Writer Fla. Flambeau, Tallahassee, 1980-84, editor, 1984-86; features editor Marietta (Ga.) Daily Jour., 1986-87; copy editor Atlanta Jour.-Constn., Atlanta, 1987-89, asst. arts editor, 1989-90, Leisure editor, 1990-93, Weekend Preview editor, asst. features editor, 1993-96, Dixie Living editor, 1997-2000; arts and entertainment editor Atlanta Jour.-Constn., Atlanta, 2000—, dep. features editor, 2001—. Recipient Hon. Mention award Fla. Press Club, 1982, Spotlight award Women in Comm., 1986; AAUW scholar, 1978. Office: Atlanta Jour-Constn Feature Desk 72 Marietta St NW Atlanta GA 30303-2804 Business E-Mail: edrennen@ajc.com.

DRESCHER, FRAN, actress; b. Flushing, N.Y., Sept. 30, 1957; d. Mort and Sylvia D.; m. Peter Marc Jacobson, 1978. Co-creator, writer, prodr., actress in TV series The Nanny, 1993-99; appeared in feature films: Saturday Night Fever, 1977, American Hot Wax, 1978 (Five-Minute Oscar award Esquire mag.), Gorp, 1980, The Hollywood Knights, 1980, Ragtime, 1981, Young Lust, 1981, Dr. Detroit, 1983, This Is Spinal Tap, 1984, The Rosebud Beach Hotel, 1984, UHF, 1989, The Big Picture, 1989, It had to be You, 1989, Cadillac Man, 1990, Wedding Band, 1990, We're Talking Serious Money, 1992, Jack, 1996, Car 54, Where Are You:, 1996, The Beautician and the Beast, 1997 (also exec. prodr.), Picking Up the Pieces, 2000, Kid Quick, 2000; starred in TV series Charmed Lives, 1986, Princesses, 1991, Good Morning Miami, 2003-04; (TV film) Stranger in Our House, 1978, Rock 'n' Roll Mom, 1988, Love and Betrayal, 1989, What's Alan Watching?, 1989, Terror in the Towers, 1993, Beautiful Girl, 2003; actress, exec. prodr. (TV series) Living with Fran, 2005-; guest appearances on TV programs Civil Wars, Alf, Night Court, Nine to Five, Fame, The Tracy Ullman Show; Spokesperson: Old Navy; Author: Enter Whining, 1995, Cancer Schmancer, 2002; (theatre) Some Girl(s), 2006. Recipient Spirit of Life award, City of Hope Cancer Ctr., 2006. Office: Gersh Agy Inc 232 N Canon Dr Beverly Hills CA 90210-5302*

DRESCHER, JUDITH ALTMAN, library director; b. Greensburg, Pa., July 6, 1946; d. Joseph Grier and Sarah Margaret (Hewitt) Altman; m. Robert A. Drescher, Aug. 10, 1968 (div. 1980); m. David G. Lindstrom, Jan. 10, 1981. AB, Grove City Coll., 1968; MLS, U. Pitts., 1971. Tchr. Hempfield Sch. Dist., Greensburg, 1968-71; children's libr. Cin. Pub. Libr., 1971-72, br. mgr., 1972-74; dir. Rolling Meadows (Ill.) Pub. Libr., 1974-79, Champaign (Ill.) Pub. Libr., 1979-85, Memphis/Shelby County Pub. Libr. and Info. Ctr., 1985—. Tenn. del. White House Conf. on Librs. and Info. Svcs. Task Force, 1991-92; mem. Tenn. Sec. of State's Commn. on Tech. and Resource Sharing, 1991, 93, steering com. Tenn. Info. and Infrastructure, 1994-97, nat. adv. panel for assessment of role of sch. and pub. librs. U.S. Dept. Edn., 1995-98. Commn. on 21st century Rhodes Coll., Memphis, 1986-88, presdl. adv. com., 1992-2000; active Leadership Memphis, 1987—, selection com., 1992-96; active Memphis Arts Coun., 1989-94; bd. dirs. Literacy Coun., 1986-91, Memphis NCCJ, 1989-93, Memphis Grants Info. Ctr., 1992-97, sec., 1993-95; bd. dirs. Memphis Literacy Found., 1988-92, v.p., 1989-90; bd. dirs. Goals for Memphis, 1988-93, chair edn. com., 1989-91, chair nominating com., 1992, leadership acad., 1999—; bd. dirs. U. Memphis Soc., 1998-2004; bd. mem. Cmty. Svcs. Agy., 2000-05, fin. com., 2002, bd. dirs., 2002-05, v.p., 2003-05; exec. adv. bd. Children's Mus., 1988-94, exec. adv. coun. U. Memphis, 1989-99; allocations subcom. United Way, 1989-91, allocations com. Memphis Arts Coun., 100 for the Arts, 1989-91, Libr. Self-study Com. U. Memphis; pres. adv. coun. Lemoyne Coll.; search com. for dean librs. U. Memphis, 1999-2001; adv. com. Memphis Symphony Orch., 2003—; v.p. Tennshare, 2004-05, pres., 2005—; bd. mem., treas. Mid South Reads, 2004-06, mem. bd. govs., 2006—. Paul Harris fellow Rotary, Memphis, 2002; recipient Govt. Leader award U. Ill. YWCA, 1981, Communicator of Yr. award Pub. Rels. Soc. Am., 1992, Humanitarian award NCCJ, Memphis, 2003, Charlie Robinson award Pub. Libr. Assn., 2003; named Libr. Coun. Libr. of Yr., 2002-. Mem.: ALA (chmn. intellectual freedom com. 1985—87, mem. coun. 1992—99, mem. nominating com. 2001—02), Assn. Pub. Adminstrs. (midsouth chpt., Adminstr. of Yr. 2002), Pub. Libr. Assn. (v.p., pres. 1994—95), Memphis Libr. Coun., Urban Librs. Coun., Tenn. Libr. Assn., Rotary (bd. dirs. 1992—94, sec. 1993—94, chair membership devel. com. 1994—95, bd. dirs. 2004—06), Beta Phi Mu. Home: 1505 Vance Ave Memphis TN 38104-3810 Office: Memphis Pub Libr & Info Ctr 3030 Poplar Ave Memphis TN 38111 Office Phone: 901-415-2748.

DRESCHHOFF, GISELA AUGUSTE MARIE, physicist, researcher; b. Moenchengladbach, Germany, Sept. 13, 1938; came to U.S., 1967, naturalized, 1976; d. Gustav Julius and Hildegard Friederike (Krug) D. PhD, Tech. U. Braunschweig, Germany, 1972. Staff scientist Fed. Inst. Physics and Tech. Ger., 1965-67; research assoc. Kans. Geol. Survey, Lawrence, 1971-72; vis. asst. prof. physics U. Kans., 1972-74; dep. dir. radiation physics lab. Space Tech. Ctr., 1972-78, assoc. dir., 1979-84, co-dir., 1984-86, dir., 1996—; sr. sci. geology U. Kans., 1991, adj. assoc. prof. physics and astronomy, 1992. Assoc. program mgr. NSF, Washington, 1978-79. Patentee identification markings for gemstones and method of making selective conductive regions in diamond layers. Named to Women's Hall of Fame, U. Kans., 1978; recipient Antarctic Service medal U.S.A., 1979; recipient NASA Group Achievement award, 1983. Fellow Explorers Club; mem. AAAS, Am. Phys. Soc., Am. Geophys. Union, Am. Polar Soc. (pres. 2000-03), Antarctican Soc., Sigma Xi. Home: 2908 W 19th St Lawrence KS 66047-2301 Office: U Kans Dept Physics & Astronomy Lawrence KS 66045-7541 Business E-Mail: giselad@ku.edu.

DRESKIN, JEANET STECKLER, painter, medical artist, educator; b. New Orleans, Sept. 29, 1921; d. William Steckler and Beate Bertha (Burgas) Steckler Gureasko; m. E. Arthur Dreskin, May 9, 1943; children: Richard Burgas, Stephen Charles, Jeanet Dreskin Haig, Rena Dreskin Schoenberg. BFA, Newcomb Coll., 1942; grad. in med. art, Johns Hopkins U., 1943; MFA, Clemson U., 1973; postgrad., Art Students League, N.Y.C., 1946, Art Inst. Chgo., 1946. Cert. med. illustrator. Staff artist Am. Mus. Natural History, N.Y.C., 1943—45, U. Chgo. Med. Sch., 1945—50; mem. faculty Mus. Sch. Art, Greenville, SC, 1950—2005, dir., 1968—75; adj. prof. art U. S.C. at Mus. Sch. Art, 1973—. Mem. faculty Gov.'s Sch. for Arts, Greenville, 1980—; condr. workshops, lectr. in art edn., 1970—2005; mem. arts adv. bd. S.C. State Mus., Columbia, 1984—90; bd. dirs. S.C. Arts Found., 1999—2002; workshop leader art dept. U. Ga., 1985; rep. by Hampton III, Taylors, SC. Exhibited in group shows at Butler Inst. Am. Art, Youngstown, Ohio, 1974, 1983, Chatauqua exhbn. Am. Art, N.Y., 1970, Nat. Mus. Illustrators, N.Y.C., 1986, Represented in permanent collections Smithsonian Nat. Mus. Am. Art, Washington, D.C., S.C. State Art Collection, Columbia,

Ga. Mus. Art, Athens, Greenville County Mus., Guild Hall Mus., East Hampton, N.Y., Gibbes Mus., Charleston, S.C., Columbia Mus. Art, Tex. Fine Art Assn., Sunrise Valley Mus., Charleston, W.Va., Beaufort Mus., S.C., Kate Shipworth Mus. at U. Miss., McDonald Corp. Coll., Chgo., N.C. Nat. Bank Coll., Asheville (N.C.) Mus. Art, Fed. Res. Bank, Richmond, Va., C & S Collection, Columbia, S.C., U. Ala. Mus., Zimmerli Art Mus. (NAWA), Rutgers U., New Brunswick, N.J., Wachovia Bank, SC, NC, exhibitions include Butler Inst. Am. Art, 1974, 1983, Nat. Mus. Ill., 1986, Nat. Print and Drawing, Clemson U., 1987—89, 1993, 9th Internat. Grand Prix, Cannes, France, 1973, Mid-Am. Arts Alliance, Emporia, Kans., 1989—91, 1993—94, Broome St. Gallery, N.Y.C., 1995—96, 2000, 2001, Am. Contemporary Artists, 1994, traveling exhbns. of so. graphics, 1990—, S.C. State Mus., Columbia, 100 years, 100 artists invitational, 2000, "in Depth", Greenville County Mus. of Art, 2005, numerous others; contbr. med. drawings Anatomy of the Gorilla, 1950, med. drawings Surgery of Repair, 1950, med. drawings Williams Obstetrics, 1959, med. drawings Surgical Anatomy, 1990. Mem. Cmty. Found. Greenville, 1968—84, chmn. project coms., 1968—76; historian, hon. mem. Rose Ball, Greenville, 1972—2006; mem. Commn. on the Future Clemson U.; bd. dirs. Charity Ball, Greenville, 1971—, S.C. Arts Found. Recipient Kaplan award, Nat. Assn. Painters in Casein, 1969, 1971, Keenan award, Am. Contemporary Exhbn., Palm Beach, Fla., 1970, Merit award, Internat. Grand Prix, Cannes, 1973, Govs. award for the Arts, Lifetime Achievement, Verner, 2004. Mem.: So. Watercolor Soc. (Mabry award 1981, 1985, 1988, 1997, 2001, 2006), Greenville Artists Guild, Am. Contemporary Artists N.Y.C., Nat. Assn. Med. Illustrators, Nat. Assn. Women Artists (S.C. membership chmn. 1970—), S.C. Watercolor Soc. (pres. 1983—84, bd. dirs. 1985—), Guild S.C. Artists (pres. 1970—71, bd. dirs. 1981—86, pres. 1956—58, 1963, bd. dirs. 1954—83, numerous awards), So. Graphics Coun. (hon.; v.p. 1981 1983, treas. 1988—, invitational exhibits 1975—77, 1988). Avocation: sailing. Home: 60 Lake Forest Dr Greenville SC 29609-5038 E-mail: jeanet@dreskin.net.

DRESSEL, MELANIE, bank executive; m. Bob Dressel; children: Robb, Brent. BS in Polit. Sci., Univ. Wash. With Bank of Calif., 1974—78; dir. private banking Puget Sound Bank; sr. v.p., private banking Columbia Bank, Tacoma, 1993—97, exec. v.p. retail banking, 1997—2000, pres., 2000—; also CEO Columbia Banking System, Inc., Tacoma, 2003—. Chmn. Washington Bankers Assn. Bd. mem. Foss Waterway Devel.; chmn. Exec. Coun. Greater Tacoma; bd. mem. Washington Roundtable, Bellarmine Prep. Sch.; Mary Bridge Children's Found. Tacoma. Named one of 25 Most Powerful Women in Banking, US Banker. Office: Columbia Banking System Ste 800 1301 A St Tacoma WA 98402 Office Phone: 253-305-1900.

DRESSELHAUS, MILDRED SPIEWAK, physics professor, engineering educator; b. Bklyn., Nov. 11, 1930; d. Meyer and Ethel (Teichteil) Spiewak; m. Gene F. Dresselhaus, Aug. 25, 1958; children: Marianne Dresselhaus Cooper, Carl Eric, Paul David, Eliot Michael. BA, Hunter Coll., 1951; DSc (hon.), CUNY, 1982, Hunter Coll., 1982; Fulbright fellow, Cambridge U., Eng., 1951—52; MA, Radcliffe Coll., 1953; PhD in Physics, U. Chgo., 1958; D Engring. (hon.), Worcester Poly. Inst., 1976; DSc (hon.), Smith Coll., 1980, Hunter Coll., 1982, N.J. Inst. Tech., 1984; DHC (hon.), U. Catholique de Louvain, 1988; DSc (hon.), Rutgers U., 1989, U. Conn., 1992, U. Mass., Boston, 1992, Princeton U., 1992; DEngring, Colo. Sch. Mines, 1993; D (hon.), Technion, Israel Inst. Tech., Haifa, 1994; DHC (hon.), Johannes Kepler U., Linz, Austria, 1993; DSc (hon.), Harvard U., 1995, Ohio State U., 1998; PhD (hon.), U. Paris, Sorbonne, 1999; DSc (hon.), Columbia U., 1999; DHC (hon.), Cath. U. Leuven, 2000; DSc (hon.), Northwestern U., 2003, Weizmann Inst., Rehovot, Israel, 2003, U. Mich., 2005, George Washington U., 2005. NSF postdoctoral fellow Cornell U., 1958—60; mem. staff Lincoln Lab., MIT, Lexington, 1960—67; prof. elec. engring. MIT, Cambridge, 1968—, assoc. dept. head elec. engring., 1972—74, Abby Rockefeller Mauze chair, 1973—85, dir. Ctr. for Materials Sci. and Engring., 1977—83, prof. physics, 1983—, Inst. prof., 1985—; dir. Office of Science, U.S. Dept. of Energy, Washington, 2000—01. Vis. prof. dept. physics U. Campinas, Brazil, 1971, Technion, Israel, 1972, 90, Nihon and Aoyama Gakuin Univs., Tokyo, 1973, IVIC, Caracas, Venezuela, 1977; vis. prof. dept. elec. engring. U. Calif., Berkeley, 1983; Graffin lectr. Am. Carbon Soc., 1982; chmn. steering com. on evaluation panels Nat. Bur. Stds., 1978—83; mem. Energy Rsch. Adv. Bd., 1984—90; bd. dirs. Rogers Corp. Contbr. articles to profl. jours. Mem. governing bd. NRC, 1984—87, 1989—90, 1992—96; trustee Calif. Inst. Tech., 1993—2000; overseer Harvard U., 1997—2000; chmn. bd. Am. Inst. Physics, 2003—; bd. govs. Argonne Nat. Lab., 1986—89, Weizmann Inst., Rehovot, Israel, 1999—2000, 2001—. Named to Hunter Coll. Hall of Fame, 1972, Women in Tech. Internat. Hall of Fame, 1998; recipient Alumnae medal, Radcliffe Coll., 1973, Killian Faculty Achievement award, 1986—87, Nat. medal of Sci., 1990, Sigri Great Lakes Carbon award, 1997, Profl. Achievement award, Hunter Coll., CUNY, 1998, Nicholson medal, 2000, Karl T. Compton medal, 2001, Weizmann Woman and Sci. Millennial Lifetime Achievement award, 2000, Nat. Materials Advancement award, Fedn. Materials Socs., 2000, Heinz Award for Tech., the Economy and Employment, 2005, Pender award, U. Pa., 2006. Fellow: AAAS (bd. dirs. 1985—89, pres. 1997—98, chair bd. dirs. 1998—99), IEEE (Founders medal 2004), Am. Carbon Soc. (Achievement medal carbon sci. and tech. 2001), Am. Acad. Arts and Scis., Am. Phys. Soc. (pres. 1984); mem.: NAS (coun. 1987—90, chmn. engring. sect. 1987—90, chmn. class III 1990—93, coun. 1992—96, treas. 1992—96), Am. Philos. Soc., Brazilian Acad. Sci. (corr.), Ioffe Inst., Russian Acad. Scis. (hon.), Engring. Acad. Japan (fgn. assoc. 1993—), Soc. Women Engrs. (Achievement award 1977), Nat. Acad. Engring. (coun. 1981—87). Office: MIT 77 Massachusetts Ave Rm 13-3005 Dept Elec Engring Cambridge MA 02139

DREW, DONNA HOWELL, elementary school educator; b. Lovington, N.Mex., Nov. 3, 1950; d. Howard H. and Jean Howell; m. James Drew, Oct. 26, 1974. B, N.Mex State U., Las Cruces. Tchr. grades 1-4 reading Taft ISD, Tex., 1972; tchr. k-5 reading Tuloso-Midway Ind. Sch. Dist., Corpus Christi, 1975—81, tchr. 2d grade, 1981—91, tchr. 6th grade lang. arts, 1991—. Tchr., mentor, curriculum devel. Tuloso-Midway Ind. Sch. Dist., 1974—. Grantee, Tuloso-Midway Edn. Found., 2005. Mem.: Tex. State Tchrs. Assn. (life). Methodist. Avocations: reading, travel, birdwatching, gardening. Office Phone: 361-903-6600 3305.

DREW, ELIZABETH, commentator, journalist, writer; b. Cin., Nov. 16, 1935; d. William J. and Estelle (Jacobs) Brenner; m. J. Patterson Drew, Apr. 11, 1964 (dec. 1970); m. David Webster, Sept. 26, 1981 (dec. 2003); m. David Felton, Oct. 14, 2004. BA, Wellesley Coll., 1957; LHD, Hood Coll., 1976, Yale U., 1976, Trinity Coll., Washington, 1978, Reed Coll., 1979, Williams Coll., 1981, Georgetown U., 1981, George Washington U., 1994, Trinity Coll., Hartford, 2000. Writer, editor Congl. Quar., 1959-64; freelance writer, 1964-67; Washington editor Atlantic Monthly, 1967-73; host TV interview program Thirty Minutes With, 1971-73; commentator TV program Agronsky and Co. (now Inside Washington), 1973-92; Washington corr. New Yorker Mag., 1973-92; commentator Monitor Radio, 1992—95. Adv. bd. Shorenstein Ctr. on Press and Policies, Harvard U.; adv. coun. Bardeuas Ctr. for Study of Congress, NYU. Author: Washington Jour., 1975, Am. Jour., 1977, Senator, 1979, Portrait of an Election, 1981, Politics and Money, 1983, Campaign Jour., 1985, Election Jour., 1989, On the Edge: The Clinton Presidency, 1994, Showdown: The Struggle Between the Gingrich Congress and the Clinton White House, 1996, Whatever It Takes: The Real Struggle for Political Power in Am., 1997, The Corruption of Am. Politics, 1999, Citizen McCain, 2002; contbr. articles Washington Post, N.Y. Rev. of Books, jours. and periodicals. Recipient award for excellence Soc. Mag. Writers, 1971, Wellesley Alumnae Achievement award, 1973, DuPont award, 1973, Mo. medal, 1979, Sidney Hillman award, 1983, Amb. of Honor award Books Across the Sea, 1984, Lit. Lion award N.Y. Pub. Libr., 1985, Edward Weintal prize, 1988. Home and Office: 5018 Eskridge Ter NW Washington DC 20016 Office Phone: 202-298-6687, 202-342-7131.

DREW, ELIZABETH HEINEMAN, publishing executive; b. Evanston, Ill., Aug. 26, 1940; d. Ben Harlow and Marion Elizabeth (Heineman) D. BA, U. Wis., 1961. With Doubleday & Co., Inc., NYC, 1961-84, prodn. asst., 1961-63, personal asst. to editor-in-chief, 1963-66, adminstrv. asst. to editor-in-chief, 1966-69, editl. asst. to editor-in-chief, 1969-71, assoc. editor, 1971-74, editor, 1974-77, sr. editor, 1977-79, exec. editor, editl. dir., 1979-84; v.p., sr. editor William Morrow and Co., NYC, 1984-92; v.p., pub. Lisa Drew Books/Macmillan Pub. Co., NYC, 1993-94, Lisa Drew Books/Charles Scribner's Sons, NYC, 1994—2006. Tchr. NYU Sch. Continuing Edn., 1981-82. Bd. dirs. Barbara Bush Found. Family Literacy, 1995—, Am. Booksellers Found. for Free Expression, 2004-. Mem.: PEN, Assn. Am. Pubs. (internat. freedom to pub. com. 1978—, freedom to read com. 1988—, chmn. 1990—93, 1994—98, 2004—), Nat. Press Club, Women's Media Group (treas. 1982—84, pres. 1985—86, bd. dirs. 2000—02), First City Club (Savannah, Ga.), Century Assn. (N.Y.). Democrat. Episcopalian.

DREW, INA R., bank executive; BA, Johns Hopkins U., 1978; MA, Columbia U. Floor trader Bank of Tokyo, Manhattan, NY; with Chemical Bank, Springfield, NJ, 1982—96; mng. dir. Global Treasury Divsn. J.P. Morgan Chase & Co., N.Y.C., NY, 1996—. Mem. mgmt. com. J.P. Morgan Chase & Co., 1997—, mem. exec. com., 2003—. Named One of Most Powerful Women in Banking, U.S. Banker Mag., 2003. Office: JP Morgan Chase & Co 270 Park Ave New York NY 10017-2070

DREW, K., financial advisor, management consultant; b. Freeport, N.Y. d. Harry P. and Kathleen (Isdal) Barton; children: Karen, Donna. BA, U. Ga., 1958; postgrad., U. Ill., 1960—61. Dir. YWCA, Corpus Christi, Tex., 1969-72, Dwoskin Nat. Wallcovering Co., Atlanta, 1974-76; dep. asst. fin. presdl. campaign, 1976-77; dir. fin. Presdl. Inaugural, Washington, 1976; dep. adv. for small bus. SBA, Washington, 1977-80, asst. to adminstr., 1980-82; v.p. Alpha Systems, Inc., Washington and Athens, Greece, 1980-85; human resource cons. MBA Mgmt., Inc., McLean, Va., 1982-84; bus. cons. Drew Cons., McLean, 1984—; cons. assoc. Walling, June & Assocs., Old Town Alexandria, Va., 1986-89; fin. advisor The Family Extended, Washington, 1990—; bus. rep. Nikken, Inc., Washington, 1996, KareMor Internat., Inc., Washington, 1996; cons. The B.O.W.L. Group, Washington, 1996—. Fin. advisor SAKA, Inc., Merrifield, Va., 1991—, Warrenton, Va., 1991-92, DeLeand Assocs., McLean, Va., 1991-92; fin. dir. Disting. Environments, Reston, Va., 1992-94. State rep. poverty program and suicide prevention bds. Corpus Christi Bus. Coun., 1969-71; bd. dirs. YWCA, Washington, 1983-85; head speaker's bur. Fairfax Symphony, 1979-85, mem. exec. devel. com., 1979-86; mem. Mental Health Exec. Bd. dirs., Washington, 1983-88; deacon Nat. Presbyn. Ch., Washington, 1988-90; asst. to exec. dir. T. Monk Found., Jazz Sch., Duke U., 1987-89; event dir. Easter Seal Soc., 1990-91; mem. Youth for Tomorrow devel. com. Joe Gibbs Charities, Washington, 1990-98; presdl. campaign team captain Va. and Ga. Inaugural Com., 1993; Ga. Ball host, Washington, 1993; host Presdl. Inaugural Gala, Washington, 1993; In Kind Svc. to White House Advance Office of Pres., 1993—; cons. advisor Battered Spouses & Their Children, Washington, 1995—; campa pres. team, 1996; pres. inaugural host, Washington, D.C., 1996; fin. mgr. Internat. Fellowship Family Extended, Washington, 1993-98; rep. Internat. Fellowship, Washington, 1980—fin., mkgt. adv., mem. new bowl group Urban Prayer Breakfast, Washington, 1997—; job cons. Homeless Bd. and Symposium, Washington, 1997-98; pres. bd. dirs. WAR Against Broken Hearts, Atlanta, 1998—; hostess Christmas at the White House, Washington, 1999; chmn., newspaper editor Rotonda Pet, McLean, Va., 2000; chmn. Urban Prayer Breakfast for Homeless, Washington, 2000; v.p. Rotonda Assn., McLean, 2002-; pres. Su Casa Mi Casa Nat. Home Mgmt., McLean, Va., 2003. Mem. Nat. League Am. Pen Women (v.p., pres. Washington Capital chpt. 1987-89, nat. bd. dirs. 1987-90, nat. roster chmn. 1989—), Bus. and Profl. Women Washington, Nat. Platform Assn., Alpha Gamma Delta. Office: 8350 Greensboro Dr Ste 1-121 Mc Lean VA 22102-3533 Personal E-mail: kdrewjoy@aol.com.

DREW, KATHERINE FISCHER, history professor; b. Houston, Sept. 24, 1923; d. Herbert Herman and Martha (Holloway) Fischer; m. Ronald Farinton Drew, July 27, 1951. BA, Rice Inst., 1944, MA, 1945; PhD, Cornell U., 1950. Asst. history Cornell U., 1948-50; instr. history Rice U., 1946-48, mem. faculty, 1950—, prof. history, 1964—, Harris Masterson, Jr. prof. history, 1983-85, Lynette S. Autrey prof. history, 1985-96, prof. emeritus, 1996—, chmn. dept. history, 1970-80; editor Rice U. (Rice U. Studies), 1967-81, acting dean humanities and social scis., 1973, acting chmn. dept. art and art history, 1996-98. Author: The Burgundian Code, 1949, Studies in Lombard Institutions, 1956, The Lombard Laws, 1973, Law and Society in Early Medieval Europe, 1988, The Laws of the Salian Franks, 1991, Magna Carta, 2004, also articles; editor: Perspectives in Medieval History, 1963, The Barbarian Invasions, 1970; mem. bd. editors Am. Hist. Assn. Guide to Hist. Lit., 1987-94, Am. Hist. Rev. 1982-1985; contbr.: Life and Thought in the Middle Ages, 1967. Guggenheim fellow, 1959, Fulbright scholar, 1965, NEH sr. fellow, 1974—75. Fellow Mediaeval Acad. Am. (coun. 1974-77, 2d v.p. to pres. 1985-87, del. to Am. Coun. Learned Socs. 1977-81); mem. Am. Hist. Assn. (coun. 1983-86), Am. Soc. Legal History, So. Hist. Assn. (vice chair, chair European sect. 1986-88, exec. com. 1989-91), Phi Beta Kappa. Home: 9333 Memorial Dr # 306 Houston TX 77024-5739 Office: Rice U Dept History MS 42 PO Box 1892 Houston TX 77251-1892 E-mail: kdrew@rice.edu.

DREW, SHARON LEE, sociologist; b. L.A., Aug. 11, 1946; d. Hal Bernard and Helen Elizabeth (Hammond) D.; children: Keith, Charmagne. BA, Calif. State U., Long Beach, 1983; postgrad., Calif. State U., Dominguez Hills, 1988—92. Clerical support Compton (Calif.) Unified Sch. Dist., 1967-78; case worker L.A. County Dept. Pub. Social Svcs., 1978—. Den mother Boy Scouts Am., Compton, 1971—72; employee vol. Dominguez Sr. H.S., Compton, 1972—73; project coord. Calif. Tomorrow's Parent Edn. Leadership Devel. Project, 1990; mem. L.A. Caregiver's Network, 1993—94; vol. Calif. State U., Dominguez Hills Older Adult Ctr., 1994, AIDS Project, Long Beach, Calif., 2003; lay min., lay reader St. Lukes Episcopal Ch., Long Beach, 1999—2005. Recipient cert. Calif. Tomorrow-Parent Edn. Leadership Devel. Project, 1990. Mem. Am. Statis. Assn. (So. Calif. chpt.), Internat. Soc. Exploration of Tchg. and Learning, Dominguez Hills Gerontology Assn. (chairperson 1990-91), Alpha Kappa Delta (Xi chpt. treas. 1992-95). Home: 927 N Chester Ave Compton CA 90221-2105 E-mail: msblakcelt@aol.com.

DREWRY, JUNE E., information technology executive; Degree in math., Caldwell Coll. With Mut. Benefit Life Ins. Co., 1978—89; v.p. tech. Aetna Life Ins. and Annuity Co., Hartford, Conn., 1990, pres. of systematized benefits admistrs., 1991—96; sr. v.p. and chief knowlege and tech. officer Lincoln Nat. Corp., 1996—99; exec. v.p. and chief info. officer Aon Corp., Chgo., 2000—. Mem.: Soc. Info. Mgmt. (pres. (N.J. chapt.), at large mem. Internat. Bd. Dir., Internat. pres.). Office: Aon Corp 200 E Randolph St Chicago IL 60601

DREWRY, MARCIA ANN, physician; b. St. Louis, Feb. 15, 1951; d. Owen and Annie Verwell (Smith) Palmer; m. Norman T. Drewry, Sept. 18, 1970 (dec. May 1978); 1 child, Tammy Robbins; m. David W. Worsdell Jr., Dec. 7, 1991. AS with honors, Forest Park Coll., 1989; DO, Kirksville Coll. Osteo. Med., 1993. Diplomate Nat. Bd. Osteo. Med. Examiners; bd. cert. family practice. Intern Riverside Hosp., Wichita, 1993-94; med. transcriptionist Malcolm Bliss Mental Health, St. Louis, 1970-78; asst. adminstr. radiology Incarnate Word Hosp., St. Louis, 1977-79; grant writer molecular virolgoy St. Louis (Mo.) U., 1977-79; med. transcriptionist Neurosurg. Assocs., Inc., St. Louis, 1979-87, Stat Transcription, St. Louis, 1987-88, PRN Transcription, St. Louis, 1988-90; physician Anthony (Kans.) Primary Care Ctr., 1994-96; chief of staff Harper County Hosp. Dist. #6, 1995-96; family practice physician Kiowa (Kans.) Hosp. and Clinic, 1997—2000; staff physician Cen. Fla. Family Health Ctr., Sanford, 2000—; resident Fla. Hosp., East Orlando, 2002—04. Dir. credentials, emergency dept. and med. records Anthony (Kans.) Primary Care Ctr., 1995-96. Capt. Operation Safe St., St. Louis, 1985-89; choir mem. Dover Place Christian Ch., St. Louis, 1986-93; mem. Careers for Homemakers, St. Louis, 1987-89. Mem. Am. Coll. Osteo. Family Physicians, Am. Acad. Osteopathy, Am. Osteo. Assn., Fla. Osteopathic Med. Assn. (Sci. Rsch. award 2004), Kans. Assn. Osteo. Medicine, Bus. and Profl. Women, Beta Sigma Phi, Phi Theta Kappa (pres. 1988-89), Alpha Phi Omega (sec. 1990-91), Theta Psi (promotions asst. 1990-91). Avocations: travel, singing. Home: 2664 Shiprock Ct Deltona FL 32738-8803

DREWS, KRISTINE MAE, secondary school educator; b. Westland, Mich., May 23, 1978; d. Thomas Chester Zedan and Sandra Lee Brandel; m. Jeffrey Drews, July 13, 2001. MA, Walden U., Minn., 2005. Cert. tchr. Mich., 2000. Tchr. sci. Wayne Westland (Mich.) Schs., 2001—. Coord. tutoring Wayne Westland (Mich.) Schs., 2003—; with sales Cornwell Pool and Patio, Plymouth, Mich., 1998—. Scholar, Cornerstone U., 1996—2000. Mem.: Mich. Sci. Tchrs. Assn. Office: John Glenn High School 36105 Marquette Street Westland MI 48185 Office Phone: 734-419-2300.

DREXEL, CAROLYN A., bank executive; b. Manchester, NH; m. Mike Drexel; 1 child, Roy. AA, Wesley Coll., Dover, Del.; BA, Furman U. Teller Bridgehampton Nat. Bank; joined North Fork Bank, Inc., 1979, asst. mgr. Speonk branch, branch mgr. to regional adminstr. South Fork branches, sr. v.p. Branch Network, 1993—97, exec. v.p. Retail Adminstrn. Melville, NY, 1997—. Bd. dirs. Safe Horizon; exec. bd. Friends of Karen. Recipient Disting. Long Islander Award, Epilepsy Found. of Long Island, 1998, 23rd St. Assn. Disting. Citizen Award, Resource Inst. Leadership Award, 2002, La Sallian Medal Award, 2005, AJCongress Fin. Svcs. Industries Awards, 2005. Office: North Fork Bank, Inc 275 Broadhollow Rd Melville NY 11747

DREXLER, JOANNE LEE, art appraiser; b. Washington, Mar. 21, 1944; d. Elias J. and Beatrice Charlotte (Goldberg) D.; m. James R. Cohen, May 31, 1965; children: Terri I., Brett F. Student, Louvre, Paris, 1963-64; BA, Tufts U., 1965; Diamond and Pearl Cert., GIA, N.Y.C., 1974. Tchr. of French Stuyvesant H.S., N.Y.C., 1965-66; decorator, art cons. Joanne Cohen Interiors, Mamaroneck, NY, 1967-69; assoc. prof. Hofstra U., L.I., NY, 1979-80; pres. Esquire Appraisals, N.Y.C. and Larchmont, NY, 1969—. TV appearances include CNN, Sept. 1991; v.p. ASA Manhattan, 2004-05; cons., lectr. in field; art judge various contests, art dealer. Organizer, curator N.C. in N.Y. art show Nat. Arts Club, 1993, African Am. art show Nat. Arts Club, 1994; weekly columnist Gannett chain newspapers, 1980-86; contbr. articles to profl. jours. Mem. Am. Soc. Appraisers (sr., v.p. Hudson Valley White Plains chpt. 1989, bd. dirs. 1997, pres. White Plains chpt. 1993-94, 97-98, sr. v.p. N.Y. chpt. 2004-06, sec. 2006—, v.p. Manhattan chpt. 2004-06), Appraisers' Assn. Am. (cert.), Nat. Arts Club N.Y. (exhbn. com.). Avocations: travel, swimming, horseback riding. Office: Esquire Appraisals Inc 630 1st Ave New York NY 10016-3700 Address: 23 Trudy Ln Bedford NY 10506 Office Phone: 212-889-2580. Business E-Mail: leedrexler@esquireappraisals.com.

DREYER, SHELLY C., lawyer, judge; b. Springfield, Mo., Oct. 31, 1969; d. Robert Thomas and Dorothy Darlene Ross; m. Mark Dreyer, May 27, 2002. BS, Mo. State U., 1992; JD, U. Mo., 1997. Bar: Mo., Ill., Ea. Dist. Mo. Atty. Brown & James, St. Louis, 1997—98; atty./ptnr. James & Dreyer Law Office, St. Peters, Mo., 1998—. Mcpl. judge City Dardenne Prairie, Mo., 2004—. Mem. Big Bros./Big Sisters, St. Louis, 1998—2005. Mem.: Mo. Mcpl. Judge Assn., Mo. Assn. Trial Attys., Assn. Trial Lawyers Am., Rotary Club (vocational chmn. 2002—). Democrat. Avocations: running, boating, tennis. Office: James & Dreyer Law Office 14 Richmond Ctr Ct Saint Peters MO 63376 Business E-Mail: shelly@charliejames.com.

DREYER, SUSAN, orthopedist, educator; b. Chgo., Mar. 7, 1961; MD, U. Ill., 1988. Bd. cert. phys. medicine and rehab. Resident rehab. medicine U. Tex. Health Sci. Ctr., San Antonio, 1988—92; staff mem. Emory U. Hosp., Atlanta, 1996—, Decatur (Ga.) Hosp., 1996—, Crawford Long Hosp., Atlanta, 1996—; asst. prof. orthopedic surgery Emory U. Sch. Medicine, Atlanta, 1996—, asst. prof. phys. medicine and rehab., 1996—97. Recipient Richard and Hilda Rosenthal Found. award for advancement in non-surg. care of low back pain, ACP, 2004. Home: 59 Executive Park South Ne Atlanta GA 30329-2208

DREYFUSS, ROCHELLE COOPER, law educator; b. 1947; BA, Wellesley Coll., 1968; MS, U. Calif., Berkeley, 1970; JD, Columbia U., 1981. Bar: NY 1982. Rsch. chemist Vanderbilt U. Med. Sch., Albert Einstein Med. Sch., Ciba Geigy Corp., 1970—78; law clk. to Hon. Wilfred Feinberg US Ct. Appeals 2nd Cir., NYC, 1981-82; law clk. to Chief Justice Warren E. Burger US Supreme Ct., Washington, 1982-83; asst. prof. NYU Sch. Law, 1983-86, assoc. prof., 1986-88, prof., 1988—, now Pauline Newman prof. law. Cons. Presdl. Commn. on Catastrophic Nuclear Accidents, 1989-90; vis. prof. U. Chgo., 1991; disting. vis. prof. U. Wash., Seattle, 2001. Mem. Am. Law Inst., Phi Beta Kappa, Sigma Xi. Office: NYU Sch Law Vanderbilt Hall Rm 308 40 Washington Sq S New York NY 10012-1099 Office Phone: 212-998-6258. E-mail: dreyfussr@juris.law.nyu.edu.

DRICKEY, RUTH IRENE, elementary school educator; b. Lincoln, Nebr., Dec. 2, 1949; d. Kurt Wolf and Karola Kaufman; children: Daniel Marc Henry, Erin Jessica Kristine. BS, U. Nebr., Lincoln, 1972. Lic. tchr. Va. Tchr. Fairfax County Pub. Schs., Alexandria, Va., 1986—. Trainer Gir. Scout Coun. Nation's Capital, Washington, 1983—, chair, 2004—; instr., trainer ARC, Fairfax County, 1983—. Named Outstanding Vol., Girl Scouts, Washington, 1992; recipient Thanks Badge, 2002. Mem.: AAHPERD, Fairfax County Elem. Phys. Edn., Va. Alliance Health, Phys. Edn., Recreation and Dance. Jewish. Avocations: soccer, reading, cooking. Home: 5806 Helmsdale Ln Alexandria VA 22315 Office: Hayfield Elem 7633 Telegraph Rd Alexandria VA 22315 Office Phone: 703-924-4532. Office Fax: 703-924-4596. E-mail: pig12c2@aol.com.

DRIEMEYER, MARY ALICE, elementary school educator; b. Warner Robbins, Ga., Mar. 18, 1969; d. Daniel Joseph and Catherine Elizabeth Guin; m. Timothy Edward Driemeyer, Nov. 5, 1991; children: Zachary Robert, William Joseph. BS in K-12 Phys. Edn., U. SC, Aiken, 1992; M in Curriculum and Instrn., Nat. Louis U., St. Louis, 1998. Cert. tchr. K-5 phys. edn. tchr. Lindbergh Sch. Dist., St. Louis, Mo., 1993—. Writer health and phys. edn. grade level expectations Mo. Dept. Elem. and Secondary Edn., Jefferson City, 2006; presenter in field. Bldg. coord. United Way, St. Louis, 1997—2006; handler-therapy of unique canine helpers Support Dogs, Inc, St. Louis, 1994—2002. Recipient Shining Star Tchg. award, St. Louis Sci. Ctr., 2004, Blue Ribbon award, Phys. Edn. Ctrl., 2002—05. Mem.: NEA, Lindbergh-Nat. Edn. Assn. (rights and responsibility rep. 1998—), Am. Alliance of Phys. Edn. Recreation and Dance, Nat. Assn. Sport and Phys. Edn., Mo. Staff Devel. Coun., Mo. Alliance of Phys. Edn. Recreation and Dance (St. Louis dist. Phys. Edn. Tchr. of the Yr. 2004—05). Baptist. Avocations: reading, shopping. Home: 6066 Kingsway Dr House Springs MO 63051 Office: Sappington Elem 11011 Gravios Rd Saint Louis MO 63126 Office Phone: 314-729-2460. Office Fax: 314-729-2462. E-mail: mdriemeyer@lindberghschools.ws.

DRIESSEN, CHRISTINE F., broadcast executive; m. Terry Driessen; 2 children. Contr. ESPN, 1985—90, v.p. fin. and planning, 1990—95, sr. v.p. and CFO, 1995—98, exec. v.p. and CFO Bristol, Conn., 1998—. Named one of Top 25 Women in Sports, St. & Smith's Sports Bus. Jour., 1999, Wonder Women in media, Multichannel News, 2003. Office: ESPN 935 Middle St Bristol CT 06010

DRIGGINS, ELAINE EURE, elementary school educator; b. Norfolk, Va., Nov. 24, 1951; d. Lankford Hunter and Ruby Pritchard Eure; m. Billy Joe Driggins, Dec. 3, 1994. BA, Chowan Coll., Murfreesboro, NC, 1973; BS, Campbell Coll., Buies Creek, NC, 1975; MS in Elem. Edn., Old Dominion U., Norfolk, Va., 1991. Elem. edn. tchr. Suffolk (Va.) City Pub. Schs., 1975—. Named Tchr. of Yr., Robertson Elem. Sch., 1996—97. Mem.: Ruritans, Roanoke Chowan Shrinettes, Order of Ea. Star (past matron 1994). Baptist. Home: 006 Corner High Rd Eure NC 27935 Office: Robertson Elem Sch 132 Robertson St Suffolk VA 23438

DRINNON, JANIS BOLTON, artist, poet, volunteer; b. Pineville, Ky., July 28, 1922; d. Clyde Herman and Violet Ethiele (Hendrickson) Bolton; m. Kenneth Cleveland Drinnon, June 13, 1948; 1 child, Dena Daryl. Student, Lincoln Meml. U., Harrogate, Tenn., 1947-48, Newspaper Inst. Am.; comml. art cert., Art Instrn. Sch., Mpls., 1968. Author: (poems) In HIS Care: A Book of Inspirational Poetry, 1998. Organizer, prodr., dir. religious plays drama dept. Alice Bell Bapt. Ch., Knoxville, Tenn.; mem. New Hopewell Bapt. Ch., Knoxville. Named to Internat. Poetry Hall of Fame, 1996; recipient Editors Choice award, Nat. Libr. Poetry. Mem.: Internat. Soc. Poets (disting. mem.). Republican. Avocations: arts, crafts, painting, composing poetry. Home: 7342 Hodges Ferry Rd Knoxville TN 37920-9732 E-mail: kcdrinnon@aol.com.

DRIPPS-PAULSON, MARIA, music educator; b. Chgo., Apr. 14, 1972; d. P. and G. Dripps; m. Timothy Nels Paulson, May 28, 1994; 1 child, Philip Nels Dripps Paulson. BS in Music Edn., U. Ill., Urbana-Champaign, 1990—94; MusM in Music Edn., Northwestern U., Evanston, Ill., 1997—2000; M in Ednl. Leadership, Aurora U., Ill., 2004—06. Cert. Tchr. Ill. Dept. Edn., 1994, Prin. Ill. Dept. Edn., 2005. Asst. band dir. Edwardsville Consol. Unit Sch. Dist. No. 7, 1994—96; dist. wide fine arts tchr. Plano Sch. Dist. No. 88, Ill., 1996—99; band dir. Kaneland Cmty. Unit Sch. Dist. No. 302, Maple Park, 1999—. Mem.: Ill. Assn. Jazz Educators, Music Educators Nat. Conf., Ill. Thespian Assn. (hon.), Nat. Band Assn. (assoc.). Mem.Christian Ch. Home: 42W545 Seavey Rd Sugar Grove IL 60554 Office: Kaneland HS 47W326 Keslinger Rd Maple Park IL 60151 Office Phone: 630-365-5100. Office Fax: 630-365-8421. Business E-Mail: mdripps@kaneland.org.

DRISCOLL, CONSTANCE FITZGERALD, education educator, writer, consultant; b. Lawrence, Mass., Mar. 29, 1926; d. John James and Mary Anne (Leecock) Fitzgerald; m. Francis George Driscoll, Aug. 21, 1948; children: Frances Mary, Martha Anne, Sara Helene, Maribeth Lee. AB, Radcliffe Coll., 1946; postgrad., Harvard U., U. Hartford, U. Bridgeport, U. Mass. Secondary sch. tchr., North Andover, Mass., 1946-48; book reviewer N.Y.C. and Boston pubs., 1955-64; asst. conf. edn. dir. U. Hartford, 1964-68; lectr. Pace U., N.Y.C., 1973-74; edn. commentary Radio WVOX, New Rochelle, N.Y., 1974-75; asst. ednl. adv. Nat. Girl Scouts, 1972-74; pres., owner, dir. Open Corridor Schs. Cons., Inc., Bronxville, N.Y., 1972-84; pres., dir. Open Corridor Schs., Inc., Oxford, Mass., 1984—, Worcester, Mass., 2000—, Sarasota, Jacksonville and Bradenton, Fla., 2003—. Dir. assoc. grad. edn. program with U. Hartford, Bronxville, N.Y., 1975-82; dir. grad. edn. program with U. Bridgeport, Greenwich, Conn., 1975-82; creator in svc. edn. programs pub. schs., Norwalk, Conn., 1983-88; assoc. Worcester State Coll., 1984-85, Fitchburg State Coll., 1986-87; dir. assoc. grad. edn. for tchrs. Anna Maria Coll., Paxton, Mass., 1990-94; assoc. grad. tchr. edn. courses Fitchburg State Coll., 1995-99; English instr. grades 9-12, Bais Chana HS for Girls, Worcester, Mass., 2000—, chair English dept., 2000—; provider long distance learning grad. edn. courses, Antigua and Anguilla, 1997—, U. Bridgeport, Conn., 1995—, assoc. agy. for grad. edn. courses for tchrs., 1995—; profl. devel. points provider Mass. State Dept. Edn., 1995—; tutor, cons. Worcester County Sch. Dists., 1989-95; CEU mgr. for Conn. Dept. Edn. O.C.S., Inc., Conn., 1989—; bi-lingual instr. for Indian and Vietnamese students in grades 5-12, 1988-91; dir. grad. edn. courses for tchrs. Mass. Coll. Liberal Arts, North Adams, 1999—; cons. coll./univ. and grad. sch. placement, admissions procedures, 2000—; adviser, cons. Radcliffe Coll. Admissions Coun., 1946-48; summer dir. swim program ARC, North Andover, Mass., 1942-47; cons. Girl Scouts U.S., health guide multicultural program Greater Lawrence, Mass., 1946-48, holiday radio program, Thanksgiving 1774, Antigua and Barbuda; lectr., series for Girl Guides, Antigua, W.I., 1974. Author numerous poems; contbr. articles to profl. jours., local newspapers. Recipient Educator award Nat. Coun. ARC, Washington, 1985, Edn. award Nipmuc Am. Indian Coun., Webster, Mass., 1985. Office: Open Corridor Schs Inc 212 Lakewood Dr Bradenton FL 34210 also: Open Corridor Schs Inc 1015 Atlantic Blvd Ste 273 Atlantic Beach FL 32233 Personal E-mail: opcorridor@aol.com.

DRISCOLL, GENEVIEVE BOSSON (JEANNE BOSSON DRISCOLL), management and organization development consultant; b. Pitts., Mar. 26, 1937; d. George August and Emma Haling Bleichner; m. John Edwin Bosson, June 17, 1959; 1 child, Matthew Edwin; m. Frederick Driscoll, Oct. 7, 1972; stepchildren: Jennifer Locke, Cynthia Hall, Molly Davis, Julie Ann. BS cum laude, Fla. State U., 1959; postgrad., Nat. Tng. Labs., 1970. Planning asst. Ctr. Planning and Innovation, Dept. Edn. State of N.Y., 1967-71; planning cons. So. Tier Regional Office for Ednl. Planning, Elmira, N.Y., 1971-72; tng. dir. Neusteters, Inc., Denver, 1973-74; orgn. devel. specialist CONNECT, Inc., N.Y.C., 1975-77; cons. Robert H. Schaffer & Assocs., Stamford, Conn., 1977-80; ptnr. Driscoll Cons. Group, Williamstown, Mass., 1980-99; sales tng. mgr. Sheaffer Eaton, Pittsfield, Mass., 1983, mgr. human resources and orgn. devel., 1983-88; dir. human resources Canyon Ranch, Berkshires, 1989-95; dir. The Learning Inst., Bennington, Vt., 1997-99; ret., 1999. Office: 24 Lee Ter Williamstown MA 01267-2039

DRISCOLL, KAREN, communications executive; b. 1970; Dir. mktg. KinderActive; v.p., Nickelodeon brand mktg. Nickelodeon, sr. v.p., mktg. and strategic planning, 2005—. Designer La Casa de Dora campaign (Cable & Telecom. Assn. for Mktg. award). Named one of 40 Executives Under 40, Multichannel News, 2006. Office: Nickelodeon Networks 1515 Broadway 42nd Fl New York NY 10036 Office Phone: 212-258-7500. Office Fax: 212-258-7705.*

DRISCOLL, KIMBERLEE MARIE, lawyer; b. Binghamton, NY, July 17, 1961; d. Patrick Donald and Diane Cecile (Richmond) Lake; m. Matthew Victor Driscoll, Aug. 6, 1983; children: John Patrick, Bennett George. BA, Colgate U., 1983; JD, Union U., 1986. Bar: N.Y. 1987, Mass. 1988. Asst. gen. counsel Oxbow Corp., Dedham, Mass., 1987-90; corp. counsel, sec. Putnam, Hayes & Bartlett, Inc., Cambridge, Mass., 1990-92; v.p., gen. counsel Merrill Internat. Ltd., Cambridge, 1992—2000; gen. counsel Arthur D. Little, Inc., Cambridge, 2000—01; pres. Resolutions Mgmt. Ltd., Houston, 2001—. Mem. ABA (vice chair spl. com. internat. energy law 1993—), Mass. Bar Assn., N.Y. Bar Assn., Turnaround Mgmt. Assn. Office Phone: 781-929-6919. Business E-Mail: kmdriscoll@resolutionsmanagement.com.

DRISCOLL, VIRGILYN MAE (SCHAETZEL), retired art educator, artist, consultant; b. Fond du Lac, Wis., May 14, 1932; d. Edward William and Louise (Heider) Schaetzel; m. Patrick A. Driscoll, Aug. 13, 1955; children: Mark P., Craig A., Chris T. BS in Art Edn., Wis. State Coll., 1954; MS in Art, U. Wis., Milw., 1973. Tchr. elem. art Green Bay (Wis.) Pub. Schs., 1954-55, Elm-Brook Pub. Schs., Elm Grove, Brookfield, Wis., 1955-58, supr. elem. art, 1958-66; tchr. secondary art, dept. chair Greendale (Wis.) Pub. Schs., 1967—93; exec. dir. Wis. Alliance Arts Edn., 1993—2000; dir., co-founder Wis. Champions for Arts Edn. Bus. and Cmty. Advs., Inc., 2002—. Arts Edn. Cons., 2000—; art curriculum task force Wis. Dept. Pub. Instrn., 1981—85; mem. task force Wis. Plan Arts Edn., Arts in Sch.s Basic Edn. Grant, 1986—88; mem. State Supts. Commn. Arts Edn., 1988—89; coord. Student Art Exhibit Wis. Assn. Sch. Bd. Joint Conv., 1988—; mem. steering com. arts edn. Wis. Arts Bd., Wis. Alliance Arts Edn., Dept. Pub. Instrn., 1992—; chmn. Wis. Challenging Content Stds. in Arts, 1994—96; coord., facilitator State Supt.'s Blue Ribbon Commn. Arts Edn., 1999—2000; mem. task force Wis. Dept. Pub. Instrn. Integrated Curriculum Guide, 1999—2000; hon. bd. dirs. Wis. Alliance Arts Edn., 2000—. Mem. editl. bd. Spectrum: Jour. Wis. Art Edn., 1986—87, 1988—90; author: (handbook) National Year of Secondary Art, 1990. Named Educator of the Yr., Beloit (Wis.) Coll., 1986, Wis. Rep. Tchr. Inst., 50th Ann. Nat. Gallery Art, Washington, 1991; recipient Excellence in the Arts award, 2000, cert. of Recognition in the Arts and Art Edn., 2000, Disting. Alumnus award, U. Wis., 2001, Distinction award for Dance Edn., 2002. Mem.: NEA, Milw. Area Tchrs. Art (pres. 1982—83), Wis. Painters and Sculptors, Wis. Alliance Art Edn. (pres. 1991—, bd. dirs.), Wis. Art Edn. Assn. (mem. adv. bd. Young Artists Workshop 1982—99, pres. 1985—87, 1987—89, mem. coun., Wis. Art Educator of the Yr. 1989, Career award 2000—), Nat. Art Edn. Assn. (bd. dirs. 1984—89, secondary divsn. dir., mem. exec. com. 1989—91, We. Region Art Educator of Yr. 1990), U. Wis. Milw. Alunni Assn. (1st v.p. 1966—73, pres. 1968—69, pres., emeritus bd. trustee 1996—2000, emeritus trustee 2000—, co-chair Chancellor's Soc. 2000—03, bd. dirs. womens alumni). Avocation: running. Home: 1161 N Lost Woods Rd Oconomowoc WI 53066-8790

DRISKELL, LUCILE G., artist; b. N.Y.C., Dec. 20, 1924; d. Charles Albert and Clarice Dorothy (Jung) Gall; m. Richard O. Driskell, Sept. 4, 1946; children: Douglas G., Donald A., David O. AA, Finch Coll., 1945; student, La Jolla Art Ctr., Calif., 1956-63, Fratelli Da Prato Foundry, Pietra Santa, Italy, 1973-78, Art Students League, N.Y.C., 1984-88. Artist, San Diego, 1950-63, Cin., 1963-67, Aspen, Colo., 1967-72, Greve in Chianti, Italy, 1972-79, Wellsboro, Pa., 1979—, Phila., 1985—. Represented by Environment Gallery, N.Y.C., 1968—84, Rodger Lapelle Gallery, Phila., 1984—, Agora Gallery, NY, 1993—2002, Amsterdam Whitney Internat. Fine Arts, N.Y.C., 2002—. Paintings, 1995—, sculptures, 1960—, wall reliefs, 1988—, prints, 1956—, Represented in permanent collections Woodmere Art Mus., Phila. Recipient Purchase award, Exxon, N.Y.C., 1978, Wachovia Bank, Wilmington, Del., 1996, Macy's, Washington, 1989, SAS Inst., Inc., Cary, N.C., 2001. Mem.: Nas. Assn. Women Artists, Washington Sculpture Group, Internat. Sculpture Ctr., Art Students League (life). Avocations: hiking, photography, travel. Home: 389 Fischler St Ext Wellsboro PA 16901-8925 E-mail: drisk@epix.net.

DRISKO, CONNIE LEE HASTINGS, dean, dental educator; Degree, Caruth Sch. Dentistry, Baylor Coll. Dentistry, 1961; BS, Baylor Coll. Dentistry, 1975; DDS, U. Mo., Kansas City, 1980. Cert. in periodontics Dept. Vet. Affairs Med. Ctr. Pvt. practice dental hygienist; prof. periodontics U. Louisville Sch. Dentistry, assoc. dean for academic planning, faculty devel., dir. clin. rsch.; dean, Merritt prof. of periodontics Sch. Dentistry, Med. Coll. Ga., 2003—. Bd. dirs. Young Innovations, Inc., 1998. Fellow: Exec. Leadership in Acad. Med. Program for Women, Am. Coll. Dentists. Office: Med Coll Ga Sch Dentistry 1120 15th St Augusta GA 30912*

DRIVER, MARTHA WESTCOTT, literature educator, researcher, writer; b. N.Y.C., Oct. 24; d. Albert Westcott and Martha Louise (Miller) D.; m. Thomas Edward Earl Rhodes, Aug. 4, 2001. BA, Vassar Coll., 1974; MA, U. Pa., 1975, PhD, 1980. Lectr. English Vassar Coll., N.Y.C., 1980-81; from asst. prof. to assoc. prof. Pace U., N.Y.C., 1981-95, prof. English, 1995—2003, Disting. prof. English, 2003—, dir. honors program, 1998-2000. Cons. N.Y. Pub. Libr., 1984; seminar participant Folger Inst., Folger Shakespeare Libr., 1994. Editor: Jour. of the Early Book Soc., 1998—; guest editor: Film & History: The Middle Ages, 1998—99, Literary and Linguistic Computing, 1999; editor: The Medieval Hero on Screen, 2004; author: The Image in Print, 2004; contbr. articles to profl. jours. Mem., lectr. St. John the Divine, N.Y.C., 1995. Recipient Dyson Achievement award, 2003; grantee Rsch. tools grantee, NEH, 1995, travel grantee, Am. Coun. Learned Socs., 1995, NSF, 2001—;, Houghton Libr. Harvard U. fellow, 1996—97. Mem. Early Book Soc. (chair 1988—), Coll. Art Assn., Medieval Acad. Am., Modern Humanities Rsch. Assn. (U.K.), Medieval Club of N.Y. (conf. coord. 1989-94, pres. 1987-89), Internat. Ctr. Medieval Art, Internat. Arthurian Soc., Medieval Feminist Art History Project, New Chaucer Soc. Episcopalian. Avocations: dance, museums, theater, concerts. Office: Pace U English Dept 41 Park Row New York NY 10038-1508 Office Phone: 212-346-1672. Business E-Mail: mdriver@pace.edu.

DRIVER, MINNIE, actress; b. London, Jan. 31, 1970; d. Ronnie and Gaynor Driver. Actress (films) Circle of Friends, 1995, GoldenEye, 1995, Sleepers, 1996, Big Night, 1996, Grosse Pointe Blank, 1997, Mononoke Hime, 1997, Good Will Hunting, 1997, The Governess, 1998, At Sachem Farm, 1998, Hard Rain, 1998, Slow Burn, 1999, An Ideal Husband, 1999, Tarzan, 1999, South Park: Bigger, Longer and Uncut, 1999, Return to Me, 2000, Beautiful, 2000, High Heels and Low Lifes, 2001, Owning Mahowny, 2003, Hope Springs, 2003, Ella Enchanted, 2004, The Phantom of the Opera, 2004; TV appearances include God on the Rocks, 1990, That Sunday, 1994, Cruel Train, 1995; (TV mini-series) Mr. Wroe's Virgins, 1993, The Politician's Wife, 1995; prodr. At Sachem Farm, 1998; TV guest appearances include Lovejoy, 1986, Casualty, 1986, Murder Most Horrid, 1991, Peak Practice, 1993, The Day Today, 1994, Knowing Me, Knowing You with Alan Partridge, 1994,, Will & Grace, 2003, 04; Musician (albums) Everything I've Got in My Pocket, 2004. ShoWest Female Star of Tomorrow award, 1998.

DROKE, EDNA FAYE, retired elementary school educator; b. Sylvester, Tex., Dec. 4, 1932; d. Ira Selle and Faye Emily (Seckinger) Tucker; m. Louis Albert Droke, June 2, 1951; children: Sherman Ray, Lyndon Allen, Lona Faye Droke Cheairs. BEd, Tarleton State U., Stephenville, Tex., 1983. Cert. ESL and 3d-8th lang. arts tchr., Tex. Tchr. ESL and lang. arts Wingate (Tex.) Ind. Sch. Dist., 1983-86; tchr. 2d grade and ESL Collidge (Tex.) Ind. Sch. Dist., 1986-88; tchr. 4th grade and ESL Peaster (Tex.) Ind. Sch. Dist., 1988-89; tchr. Chpt. I in 1st-6th grades, ESL in K-12th grades Ranger (Tex.) Ind. Sch. Dist., 1989-96, tchr. ESL 3d grade, reading recovery tchr., 1996-98, ret., 1998; substitute tchr. I.S.D., Blanket, Tex.; ESL tchr. 220th CSCD, Comanche, Tex., Gustine (Tex.) Ind. Sch. Dist., 2005—06. Tutor Hispanic probationers in English for 220th Dist. Ct., Comanche, Tex., Gustine Ind. Sch. Dist. Reading Improvement, 2000-03; tchr. reading improvement Gustine (Tex.) Ind. Sch. Dist., 2004-05, tchr. ESL, 2004—. Mem. ASCD, Kappa Delta Pi, Alpha Chi. Baptist. Avocations: reading, quilting, knitting, playing piano, painting. Home: 1151 Country Rd 182 Comanche TX 76442 E-mail: edroke@gustine.esc14.net.

DROLL, RUTH LUCILLE, missionary pastor; b. Peoria, Ill., Mar. 13, 1941; d. Elisha John Droll and Beulah Lorene West-Droll; 1 child, Ruth Lucille. BA in bible theology, No. Ctrl. Mpls., 1963. Missionary pastor Assemblies of God, Ariz., 1963—2003. Home: PO Box 3742 Milan NM 87021 Office: Assembly of God PO Box 402 Prewitt NM 87045-0402

DRONET, JUDY LYNN, elementary school educator, librarian; b. Kaplan, La., Dec. 9, 1946; d. Percy Joseph and Zula Mae (Harrington) D. BA in Elem. Edn., McNeese State U., 1968, MEd, 1971. Cert. tchr., libr., adminstr., La. Tchr. Shady Grove High Sch., Rosedale, La., 1968-69, Lake Arthur (La.) Elem. Sch., 1969-86, 88-90, Lake Arthur High Sch., 1986-88, 91-92, 1994-95; libr. Henry Heights Elem. Sch., Lake Charles, La., 1992-93, Welsh Elem. Sch., 1993-94, West End Elm. Sch., 1995-96, Northside Jr. HS, 1996—; state assessor, 1997—; tchr. mentor, 1998—. Univ. supr. McNeese State U., Lake Charles, 1990-91, student tchr. supr.; dir. sch. musical prodns., Lake Arthur, 1976-85; judge sci. and social studies fairs, Lake Arthur, 1985-90, math fair, Jeff Davis Parish, 1993; parish com. Sch. Improvement Plan, 1999—; presenter workshops. Coach girls' softball Lake Arthur Jaycees, 1974; mem. Jeff Davis Parish Arts Coun., Jennings, La., 1990—; mem., hostess Friends of Zigler Mus., Jennings, 1990—; state 1st v.p. Bea Davis Leadership Devel., state com. mem. Mem. La. Assn. Educators, Jeff Davis Parish Assn. Educators (rep.), Calcasieu Parish Assn. Educators, Calcasieu Reading Coun., Women's Libr. Club, Cath. Daus. Am. (sec., regent 1968-93, Dau. of Yr. 1979-80, 93-94), La. Songwriters' Assn. (sec.-treas.), A Block Off Broadway Theater Group (actress, state/props mgr., bd. dirs., choreographer), Delta Kappa Gamma (dist. dir., state chmn., state music rep., state 2nd v.p., Alpha Kappa Golden Apple award, 1999, Epsilon State Achievement award, 2002). Democrat. Roman Catholic. Avocations: painting, needlepoint, songwriting, creative writing, singing. Home: PO Box 214 203 Pleasant St Lake Arthur LA 70549-4513

DROST, MARIANNE, lawyer; b. Waterbury, Conn., Feb. 21, 1950; d. Albin Joseph and Henrietta Jean (Kremski) D. BA, Conn. Coll., 1972; JD, U. Conn., 1975. Bar: Conn. 1975. Assoc. Ritter, Tapper & Totten, Hartford, Conn., 1975-77; sr. atty. GTE Svc. Corp., Stamford, Conn., 1977-84, Chesebrough-Pond's Inc., Greenwich, Conn., 1984-85; corp. sec. GTE Corp., Stamford, Conn., 1985—91; v.p., assoc. gen. counsel fin. GTE Svc. Corp., Stamford, Conn., 1991-97, v.p., dep. gen. counsel, 1997-2000; sr. v.p., dep. gen. counsel, corp. sec. Verizon Comm. Inc., NYC, 2000—. Tutor Lit. Vols., Stamford, 1985-90, bd. dirs. Lit. Vols. Am., 1988-94. Mem. ABA, Am. Soc. Corp. Secs. (former pres., bd. dirs. Fairfield-Westchester chpt.).

DROSTE, CATHERINE JOSEPH, sister; b. Clinton, Iowa, Apr. 21, 1965; d. Leo Clem and Mary Margaret Droste. BA in History, Christendom, 1987; MA in History, Mid. Tenn. State U., 2002; BA in Theology, Angelicum, Italy, 2000. Lic. sacred theology in dogmatic theology Angelicum, Italy, 2002; cert. tchr. Tenn., Adminstr. Va. Tchr. St. Rose Lima Sch., Birmingham, Ala., 1991—92, St. Mary Star Sea Sch., Hampton, Va., 1992—93, Overbrook Sch., Nashville, 1993—96, asst. prin., 1996—97; tchr. St. Cecilia Acad., Nashville; adj. prof. Aquinas Coll., Nashville, 2003—04; sch. adminstr. Our Lady Mt. Carmel Sch., Newport News, Va., 2004—. History dept. chair St. Cecilia Acad., Nashville, 2002—04. Editor: (formation program) St. Cecilia Congregation Ongoing Formation Program; contbr. ecumenical presentation & discussion. Mem. Quality Assessment Bd., Richmond Diocese, 2005—06, Richmond Diocese Strategic Planning Com., Va., 2006. Recipient Tchr. of Yr., Overbrook Sch., 1995. Mem.: Assn. Curriculum & Devel., Nat. Cath. Edn. Assn.

DROZ, ELIZABETH JANE, foundation administrator; b. Aug. 19, 1923; m. John J. Droz, May 26, 1945; 9 children. BS, Cornell U., 1944; M, Syracuse U., 1982. Founder, operator Kitchens by Elizabeth; exec. dir., sec., human resource chair Good News Found. Ctrl. N.Y. Inc., Utica, 1992—. TV comentator and fashion model; owner local real estate firm. Adult edn. advocate Eastern Vicariate, Diocese of Syracuse, N.Y.; pres. several sch. bds.; past mem. Cath. Charities Bd., St. Elizabeth's Hosp. Guild; mem. Fulton Chain of Lakes Assn., Adirondack Mus. Blue Mt. Lake, Arts Guild of Old Forge, Munson Williams Proctor Art Inst.; mem. edn. com. Deacon Cmty. of Syracuse Diocese; eucharistic min. Our Lady of Lourdes; trainer lectors at summer parish St. Bartholomew's Old Forge, lector and eucharistic min. Mem. Ballroom Dance Groups, Found. of Internat. Cooperation. Avocation: travel.

DRUETT, JOAN, writer, maritime historian; b. Nelson, New Zealand, Apr. 11, 1939; came to U.S., 1993; d. Ralph Totten Griffin and Colleen De La Hunt Butcher; m. Ronald John Druett; children: Lindsay, Alastair. BA, Victoria U., Wellington, New Zealand, 1960; tchg. diploma, Christchurch, New Zealand, 1961. Tchr. New Zealand Edn. Dept., 1961-63; actuary Mfrs. Life Ins., Toronto, Can., 1964-65; tchr. Waikato Diocese, New Zealand, 1974-84; freelance writer, 1984—; cons. historian Seafaring Women Project, 1994—; curriculum advisor L.I./Stony Brook (N.Y.) Schs., 1995—. Author: Exotic Intruders, 1984 (Pen award 1985, Hubert Ch. award 1985), Fulbright in New Zealand, 1988, Abigail, 1988, Promise of Gold, 1990, She Was a Sister Sailor, 1991 (Best Book of Am. Maritime History 1992), Petticoat Whalers: Whaling Wives at Sea, 1820-1920, 1992, Hen Frigates, 1999, She Captains, 2000, Rough Medicine, 2000, In the Wake of Madness: The Murderous Voyage of the Whaleship Sharon, 2003, Watery Grave, 2004, Shark Island, 2005. Pres. Waikato Speech Therapy Assn., New Zealand, 1970-74. Mailing: care Laura Langley Agy #3 275 President Street Brooklyn NY 11231

DRUFFEL, ANN BERNICE, researcher, writer; b. Riverside, Calif., Aug. 12, 1926; d. William and Aileen (Walsh) McElroy; m. Charles K. Druffel, Jan. 24, 1953; children: Ellen, Diana, Carolyn, Charlotte, Allis Ann. BA in Sociology, Immaculate Heart Coll.; postgrad., Cath. U. RSW Calif. Family and child welfare worker Cath. Welfare Bur., L.A. and Long Beach, Calif., 1948-53; rschr. Nat. Investigations Com. Aerial Phenomena, Washington, 1957—73, Ctr. UFO Studies, Chgo., 1975—; investigator Mut. UFO Network, Morrison County, Tex., 1973—; rschr., cons. Mobius Soc., L.A., 1986-92. Pub. spkr. on psychic phenomena, UFO's, Native Am. sacred sites at sci. confs., symposia, acad. and civic groups. Author: How to Defend Yourself Against Alien Abductions, 1998, Firestorm!: Dr. James E. McDonald's Fight for UFO Sciences, 2003, Standing in God's Light: In Endtimes, 2006; co-author: (with D. Scott Rogo) The Tujunga Canyon Contracts, 1980, paperback edit., 1989, The Psychic and the Detective, 1983, expanded edit., 1995, (with Armand Marcotte) Past Lives: Future Growth, 1986, 2d edit., 1994, (with Marcotte) Standing in God's Light: In End Times, 2006; contbr. to Ency. of UFOs; (anthology) UFO Abductions, Psychic Pets and Spiritual Animals; contbr. numerous articles to profl. and scientific publs.; cons. Flying Saucer Rev., London, 1980-2005; assoc. editor Mufon UFO Jour., 1978-84; author (filmscript) Dixie North; (TV documentaries) Psychic Detectives, 1989, Report from Unknown, 1990. Named to Am. Libr. Directory. Avocations: hiking, ocean swimming, snorkeling, exploring sacred sites, orchard gardening. E-mail: anndruffel@aol.com.

DRULINER, MARCIA MARIE, education educator; b. Dec. 18, 1946; M in Secondary Edn., U. Nebr., 1974; PhD, Marquette U., 1992. Assoc. prof. edn. Concordia Coll., Bronxville, NY, 1993-95; asst. prof. edn. Northwestern Coll., Orange City, Iowa, 1998-2000; instr. Spanish, Gretna (Nebr.) Pub. Schs., 2000—. Home: 20184 Glenmore Dr Apt 76 Gretna NE 68028 E-mail: mdruliner@cox.net.

DRULLINGER, LEONA PEARL BLAIR, obstetrics nurse; b. Norton, Kans., Aug. 10, 1962; d. Floyd Allen and Frances Marie (Redfield) Blair; m. Richard Lee Drullinger, Aug. 2, 1981; children: Richard Jr., Charity, Kelsy, Brandon. AD in Practical Nursing, Colby C.C., Kans., 1985; ADN, Garden City (C.C., Kans., 1987; BSN, Creighton U., 2003. RN; cert. BLS, ACLS, neonatal advanced life support, inpatient obstetrics. LPN Citizens Med. Ctr., Colby, Kans., 1985—86, Nursing Home, Lakin, Kans., 1986—87; RN labor and delivery staff nurse St. Catherine's Hosp., Garden City, Kans., 1987—88; acting head nurse VA Med. Ctr., Lincoln, Nebr., 1988—90; telemetry nurse Bryan Meml. Hosp., Lincoln, 1990—92; relief staff nurse Nurse Finders, Omaha, 1990—92; contract charge obstetric nurse Hunter Med. Inc., Offutt AFB Hosp., Bellvue, Nebr., 1992—94, Med. Nat. Inc., Offutt AFB Hosp., Bellvue, Nebr., 1994—96; staff nurse Brodstone Meml. Nuckolls County Hosp., Superior, Nebr., 1996—97, Cambridge Meml. Hosp., Nebr., 1997—98; staff relief nurse Olston-KQC Staffing, 1996—; dir. nursing svc. Good Samaritan Ctr., Arapahoe, Nebr., 1998—99; nursing svcs. program coord. Mid-Plains C.C., McCook, Nebr., 2000—02. Relief nurse Olston-KQC Staffing, 1996-2000. Mem. ANA, Nebr. Nurses Assn. Republican. Avocations: reading, crocheting, camping, cooking, sewing. Home: 5521 Spruce St Lincoln NE 68516-1347 E-mail: angelwings32@yahoo.com.

DRUM, ALICE, academic administrator, educator; b. Gettysburg, Pa., June 22, 1935; d. David Wentz and Charlotte Rebecca (Kinzey) McDannell; m. D. Richard Guise, June 15, 1957 (div. Aug. 1975); children: Gregory, Brent, Richard, Robert, Clay; m. Ray Kenneth Drum, Mar. 2, 1979; 1 child, Trevor. BA magna cum laude, Wilson Coll., 1957; PhD, Am. U., 1976. Adj. prof. gen. studies Antioch U., Columbia, Md., 1976-78; adj. asst. prof. English Gettysburg Coll., 1977-80; lectr. gen. studies Georgetown U., Washington, 1980-81; lectr. gen. honors U. Md., College Park, 1980-83; asst. prof. English Hood Coll., Frederick, Md., 1981-85, coord. writing program, 1981-83, assoc. dean acad. affairs, 1983-85; dean freshmen Franklin and Marshall Coll., Lancaster, Pa., 1985-88, v.p., 1988-2001, prof., chair women's studies, 2001—. Team mem. Mid. States Accreditation Assn., 1989-2003; cons. in field. Co-author: Funding A College Education, 1996; contbr. chpts. to books, articles and book revs. to profl. jours. Chair Lancaster County DA Commn., Lancaster, 1990-91; mem. Lancaster County Commn. on Youth Violence, Lancaster, 1990-91; bd. trustees Wilson Coll., 1997—, YWCA, Lancaster. Mellon grantee, 1979; Davison Foreman fellow, 1975-76. Mem. MLA, N.E. MLA, Deans (pres. 1988-89), Coll. English Assn., Phi Beta Kappa (pres. chpt. 1990-91), Phi Kappa Phi. Democrat. Episcopalian. Avocations: hiking, reading, visiting art museums. Office Phone: 717-291-3980. Business E-Mail: alicedrum@fandm.edu.

DRUM, JOAN MARIE MCFARLAND, federal agency administrator, educator; b. Waseca, Minn., Mar. 31, 1932; d. Leo Joseph and Bergetthe (Anderson) McFarland; m. William Merritt Drum, June 13, 1954; children: Melissa, Eric. BA in Journalism, U. Minn., 1962; MEd, Coll. William and Mary, Williamsburg, Va., 1975, postgrad., 1984-85. Govt. ofcl. fgn. claims br. Social Security Adminstrn., Balt., 1962-64; freelance writer Polyndrum Publs., Newport News, Va., 1967-73; tchr. Newport News Pub. Schs., Va., 1975-79; writer, cons. Drum Enterprises, Williamsburg, Va., 1980-82; developer, trainer communicative skills U.S. Army Transp. Sch., Ft. Eustis, Va.,

1982-86; govt. ofcl. test assistance div. U.S. Army Tng. Ctr., Ft. Eustis, 1986, course devel. coord. distributed tng. office, 1992. Adj. faculty English dept. St. Leo Area Coll., Ft. Eustis, 1975-78; del. Communicative Skills Conf., Ft. Leavenworth, Kans., 1983; mem. Army Self-Devel. Test Task Force, 1991-92; task force mem. U.S. Army Tng. FAA; program developer multi-media electronic delivery prototype; tech. tng. facility trainer. Author: Ghosts of Fort Monroe, 1972, Travel for Children in Tidewater, 1974, Galaxy of Ghosts, 1992, Hampton's Haunted Houses, 1998, How to Feed a Ghost, 1998; editor: army newsletter for families, 1968-73, Social Services Resource Reference, 1970; contbr. articles to profl. jours. Chmn. Girl Scouts U.S., Tokyo, 1964-66, Army Cmty. Svc., Ft. Monroe, Va., 1967-68; chmn. publicity Hist. Home Tours, Ft. Monroe, 1971-73; chmn. adv. bd. James City County Social Svcs., 1989-95, chmn. adult svcs., 1989-90; mem. James City County Leadership Devel. Program Bd. Recipient numerous civic awards including North Shore Cmty. Svc. award, Hialeah, Hawaii, 1966, Home Bur. Svc. award, 1975, Svc. award Girl Scouts U.S., Tokyo, 1965, Comdrs. achievement award for civilian svc., 1995, 98. Mem.: Va. Writers Club. Home: 9 Bray Wood Rd Williamsburg VA 23185-5504 Personal E-mail: wmd09@cox.net.

DRUM, SYDNEY MARIA, artist; b. Calgary, Alta., Can., Nov. 20, 1952; d. Ian Mondelet and Dorothy Mary (Weaver) D.; m. Frank DeSalvo, Nov. 7, 1987; 1 child, Christopher. BFA with distinction in art, U. Calgary, 1974; MFA, York U., 1976. Tchr. U. Ill., 1978-83, Govs. State U., 1983-84, Rutgers U., 1984-87. One-woman and 2 person exhibits include Art Gallery Ont., 1978, Condeso/Lawler Gallery, N.Y., 1981, Gallery Pascal, 1983, U. Pitts., 1984, Bau-Xi Gallery, Toronto, 1987, 90, 92, 95, 55 Mercer Gallery, N.Y., 1993, 96, 98, 2000, 2002, 2004, Mus. am Ostwall, Dortmund, Germany, 1994, Hart House-U. Toronto, 1995, Robert Birch Gallery, Toronto, 1999, 2002, Gallery Surge, Tokyo, 1999, Kunsturein Alle Fuerwache, Dresden, 2002, Optisches Mus., Jena, Germany, 2004; represented in pub. collections Can. Coun. Art Bank, U. Toronto, Toronto-Dominion Bank, Petro Can., Mus. Modern Art, N.Y., Phila. Mus. Art, Robert McLaughlin Gallery, Oshawa; commissions include Pope, Ballard, Shepard & Fowle, Chgo., 1983, Zimmerli Mus., Rutgers U., 1990; reviewer art exhibits New Art Examiner, Chgo., 1983-84. Can. Coun. grantee, 1978. Home: 138 W 120th St New York NY 10027-6401

DRUMHELLER, JANET LOUISE, librarian; b. Walton, W. Va., June 23, 1951; d. Nathan Earl and Edna Osial (Dye) Vineyard; m. Fred John Drumheller, Apr. 11, 1971; 1 child, Stephanie Katarina. BS in History, U. Tenn., 1974, MS in Libr. and Info. Scis., 1977. Mgr. Farragut br. Knox County Pub. Librs., Knoxville, Tenn., 1977—81, reference libr., 1983—96, reference svcs. mgr., 1996—. Mem. East Tenn. Homeless Coalition; mem. alumni bd. U. Tenn. Sch. Info. Scis. Mem.: East Tenn. Libr. Assn., Tenn. Libr. Assn. Office: Knox County Libr System 500 W Church Ave Knoxville TN 37902

DRUMMOND, CAROL CRAMER, voice educator, lyricist, writer, artist; b. Indpls., Mar. 5, 1933; adopted d. Burr Ostin and L. Ruth Welch; m. Roscoe Drummond, 1978 (dec. 1983). Student, Butler U., 1951—53; studied voice with Todd Duncan, Frances Yeend, James Benner, Rosa Ponselle, Dr. Peter Herman Adler and John Bullock; studied drama with Adelaide Bishop, Washington, D.C. Original performer Starlite Musicals, Indpls., 1951; singer Am. Light Opera Co., Washington, Seagle Opera Colony, Schroon Lake, NY, 1963, 64; soloist St. John's Episcopal Ch., Lafayette Sq., Washington, 5th Ch. of Christ, Scientist, Washington, 1963-78; performer Concerts in Schs. Program, Washington Performing Arts Soc., 1967—97; soloist with Luke AFB band ofcl. opening Boswell Meml. Hosp, Sun City, Ariz., 1970; painter, artist, 1980—; pvt. tchr. voice Ellsworth H.S., 1986—2006, Mt. Desert Island H.S., 1986—2006, 2006. Soloist numerous oratorio socs.; appearances with symphony orchs. including Nat. Symphony Orch., Fairfax (Va.) Symphony Orch., Buffalo Philharm. Orch., Concerts in the Pk., Arlington Opera Co., Lake George Opera Co., Glens Falls, NY, The Nat. Cathedral, Washington, Noye's Flood, Lufkin, Tex., 1965, Washington Nat. Opera; voiceover radio and TV commls., 1965—84; U.S. Govt. host The Sounding Bd., Sta. WGTS-FM, Washington, 1972—78; dir. ensembles, music/voice cons. Summer Festival of the Arts, S.W. Harbor, Maine, 1992—95, mem. adv. bd., 1986—; dir. Amahl and the Night Visitors, 1992; vocal solo concert The Smithsonian Instn., 1980; pub. svc. announcements 4 Bangor Radio Stas., 2005. Former columnist: Animal Crackers, writer: newspaper and mag. articles and stories; one-woman shows include, Lemon Tree, Bangor, 1995, 1996, Grand Theater, Ellsworth, Maine, 1995, Southwest Harbor (Maine) Pub. Libr., 1997, U. Maine, 1999, Border's, Bangor, 2002; two-woman shows including, Am. Art League, Washington, 1997, two-woman show Cosmos Club, Wash., 1996, Arts Club, 1994, 1995, 1996, artist, owner Dream Come True Notecards, 1997—2006. Bd. dirs. Washington Sch. Ballet, 1978, Animal Rescue Found., Trenton, Maine, 2004—05; aux. bd. Bar Harbor Aux. Music Festival, 2004—; life bd. dirs. Internat. Soundex Reunion Registry, Carson City, Nev. Recipient 1st pl. women's divsn. Internat. Printers Ink Contest, 1951. Mem.: Nat. League Am. Pen Women, Beta Sigma Phi, Kappa Kappa Gamma. Republican. Episcopalian. Avocations: knitting, gardening, reading, travel.

DRUMMOND, PAMELA JOHNSON, mathematics educator; b. Athens, Tenn., Dec. 16, 1946; d. Harry Caldwell Jr. and Mary Elizabeth (Edington) Johnson; m. Joseph Lehman Drummond, Apr. 6, 1979. BA in Math., Converse Coll., Spartanburg, S.C., 1968; MEd, Ga. State U., Atlanta, 1975, EdS, 1976, PhD in Math. Edn., 1988. Math. tchr. Githens Jr. H.S., Durham, 1968-71, Athens Jr. H.S., Athens, Tenn., 1971-72; apt. locator Apt. Reps., Atlanta, 1972-73; math. tchr. Sprayberry H.S., Marietta, Ga., 1973-75, Walton H.S., Marietta, Ga., 1975-88; math. instr. Kennesaw State Coll., Marietta, Ga., 1988—2000, assoc. prof. math. and math. edn., 1993—98, prof. math. and math. edn., 1998—2000, prof. emeritus, 2000—. Cons. in field. Chorus Atlanta Symphony Orch. Recipient Presdl. award for excellence in math. tchg. NSF, 1984, Grammy awards Best Choral Performance, 1996, 98, 2002, 03, Best Classical Album, 1998, 2002; named Outstanding Ga. Educator, Ga. State U., Atlanta, 1984, master tchr., Woodrow Wilson Nat. Fellowship Found., Princeton, N.J., 1987. Mem. Nat. Coun. Tchrs. Math., Math. Assn. Am., Nat. Coun. Supr. Math., Ga. Coun. Supr. Math., Ga. Coun. Tchrs. Math. (v.p. 1986-88), Mu Alpha Theta (nat. pres. 1987-89, regional gov. 1982-86). Democrat. Avocations: cooking, bridge, music, reading.

DRUMMOND, SALLY HAZELET, artist; b. Evanston, Ill., June 4, 1924; d. Craig Potter and Frances (Gillam) Hazlet; m. F. Weichel Drummond, Mar. 25, 1961; 1 child, Craig Potter. Student, Rollins Coll., 1942-44; BS, Columbia U., 1946, postgrad., 1946-48, Inst. Design, Chgo., 1949-50; MA, U. Louisville, 1952. Instr. Skowhegan Sch. Art, 1973. Exhibited in solo shows at, Hadley Gallery, Louisville, 1952, Tanager Gallery, N.Y.C., 1955, 57, 60, Green Gallery, N.Y.C., 1962, Fischbach Gallery, N.Y.C., 1978, Aldrich Mus., Ridgefield, Conn., 1981, Merida Galleries, Louisville, 1982, Artists Space, N.Y.C., 1984, "Surface and Proportion", Margaret Roeder Gallery, N.Y. 1990, Cornell Fine Arts Ctr., Rollins Coll., Winter Park, Fla., 1989, Louisville Visual Arts Assn., 1990, Mitchell Algus Gallery, N.Y.C., 2003; exhibited in group shows at, Am. embassy, Rome, 1953, Fgn. Artists Invitational, Bordighiera, Italy, 1953, Am. Artists Ann., 1960, Whitney Mus., N.Y.C., 1958-59, 64, Green Gallery, 1961, Mus. Modern Art, N.Y.C., 1963, Am. Inst. Arts and Letters, N.Y.C., 1982, L.I. City, N.Y., 1987, Owensboro (Ky.) Mus. Art, 1987, Alexandre Gallery, N.Y.C., 2005; 2 person exhbn.: Springfield (Ohio) Art Ctr., 1988, Urban Callery, N.Y.C., 1989, Hunter Coll., N.Y.C., 2003; retrospective exhbn. at Corcoran Gallery, Washington, 1972; rep. permanent collections at, Mus. Modern Art, Whitney Mus., Met. Mus. Art, N.Y.C., Chase Manhattan Bank, N.Y.C., Ciba-Geigy Corp., Speed Mus., Louisville, U. Iowa Mus. Art, Iowa City, Hirshorn Mus. Art, Washington, Greenwich, Conn., Hudsons Dept. Store, Detroit, AVCO Corp., Citizens Fidelity Bank and Trust Co., Louisville. Recipient Fulbright grant to Venice, 1952-53, Guggenheim grant to France, 1967-68

DRUMMOND, WILLA HENDRICKS, neonatologist, educator, information technology executive; b. Harrisburg, Pa., Dec. 5, 1945; d. George Edson and Leah Clementine (Connelly) Hendricks; m. Thomas Weston Drummond, June 1966 (div. 1978). BA cum laude, Brown U., 1966; MD, U. Pa., 1970; MS in Med. Informatics, U. Utah, 1999. Resident in pediat. Children's Hosp. Phila., 1970-72, cardiology fellow, 1972-74; instr. pediat. U. Pa., Phila., 1973-74; rsch. fellow perinatology U. Oreg., Portland, 1974-75; staff pediatrician Kaiser-Permanente Clinics, Portland, 1975-76; instr. neonatology, fellow Cardiovasc. Rsch. Inst.-U. Calif., San Francisco, 1976-78; asst. prof. pediat. U. Fla., Gainesville, 1978-82, asst. prof. pediat. and physiology, 1981-82, assoc. prof. pediat. physiology and vet. med. scis., 1982-88, prof., 1988—. Cons. Baxter-Travenol Labs., Deerfield, Ill., 1986-88; co-chair Equine Neonatology Study Group, Gainesville, 1981-91; dir. Neonatology Fellowship Program U. Fla., Gainesville, 1981-85; cons., chief med. officer, ICU Data Sys., Inc., Gainesville, 2001-05, interim CEO, exec. v.p. med. affairs, 2004-06, founder, chief med. info. exec., 2006—. Contbr. numerous rsch. papers and abstracts to profl. jours.; poet: Carousel of Progress, 1979. Rsch. grantee (26) including Am. Heart Assn., NIH, Dept. of Def., 1976—; sr. fellow Med. Informatics, 1997-99; named Best Dr. in USA, Best Doctors, Inc., 2005, 06. Mem. Am. Physiologic Soc., Soc. Pediat. Rsch., Am. Pediat. Soc., Am. Acad. Pediat.(exec. steering com. Coun. Clin. Info. Tech. 2005-), Am. Med. Informatics Assn., Am. Heart Assn., So. Soc. Pediat. Rsch., Internat. Soc. Vet. Perinatology (bd. dirs., pres. 1995-97), Internat. Physicians Prevention of Nuc. War (collective Nobel Peace prize 1985), Concerned Scientists, NOW, Sierra Club, Green Peace. Democrat. Office: U Fla Coll Medicine PO Box 100296 Gainesville FL 32610-0296 Office Phone: 352-392-4195. E-mail: DrWilla@peds.ufl.edu.

DRUMMOND BORG, LESLEY MARGARET, geneticist; b. Wellington, New Zealand, Oct. 26, 1948; arrived in U.S., 1986; d. Grant Allen and Yolanda Drummond; m. Kenneth Irvin Borg; children: Marc Borg, Kyle Borg. MBChB, Otago Med. Sch., New Zealand, 1971; MD, Otago Med. Sch., 1983; BSc, Auckland U., New Zealand, 1976. Diplomate Am. Bd. Pediat., Am. Bd. Med. Genetics, cert. clin. geneticist. Fellow clin. genetics U. Auckland Med. Sch., 1974—77, med. geneticist, 1977—79; resident pediat. Hosp. Sick Children, Toronto, Ont., Canada, 1980—82; gen. practitioner ARAMCO, Saudi Arabia, 1983—86; sr. fellow med. genetics U. Wash., Seattle, 1986—88; clin. geneticist Genetic Screening and Counseling Svc., Denton, Tex., 1988—95; dir. genetics divsn. Tex. Dept. Health, Austin, 1995—2004; mgr. health screening unit Tex. Dept. State Health Svcs., Austin, 2004—05, physician cons., 2005—. Clin. asst. prof. Tex. A&M U., College Station, 1991—98; cons. staff Odessa Women's Children's Hosp., Tex., 1991—96, Cook/Ft. Worth Children's Med. Ctr., 1991—98. Contbr. articles to profl. jours. Fellow: Am. Coll. Med. Genetics (founder), Am. Acad. Pediat.; mem.: AMA, Am. Soc. Human Genetics. Avocations: jogging, swimming, hiking. Office: Dept State Health Svcs Health Screening Unit MC1918 1100 W 49th St Austin TX 78756-3160

DRUMMY, KATHLEEN H., lawyer; BA, Univ. Calif., Berkeley, 1973; MA, UCLA, 1974, JD, 1977. Bar: Calif. 1977. Judicial internship Judge Harry Pregerson, US Dist Ct. ctrl dist. Calif., 1976; ptnr. Mucisk Peeler & Garrett LLP, McDermott Will & Emery, Memel Jacobs Pierno Gersh & Ellsworth; ptnr., health law practice Davis Wright Tremaine LLP, LA. Editor (exec.): UCLA Alaska Law Rev.; contbr. articles to profl. jours. Mem.: Am. Health Lawyers Assn., Calif. Bar Assn. Office: Davis Wright Tremaine LLP Ste 2400 865 S Figueroa St Los Angeles CA 90017-2566 Office Phone: 213-633-6800. Office Fax: 213-633-6899. Business E-Mail: kathydrummy@dwt.com.

DRURY, MILDRED BARBARA, evangelist, music educator; b. St. Louis, June 28, 1929; d. Everett Issac and Fiona Lodell Rogers; m. Lotus O.C. Drury, Mar. 25, 1947 (dec.); children: Stephen, James Eugene, Richard Allen. Dance tchr. Bermuda YMCA, St. Louis, 1950—54; min. Leonard Baptist Ch., St. Louis, 1960—80; dir., prison ministry Christian Arts Outreach, St. Louis, 1970—75. Religious tchr. St. Louis City Jail, 1970—82. Singer: UMSL Chorus. Nat. Amb. Goodwill Nat. Assn. Colored Women's Club, Inc.; bd. dir. Lifers Inc., Mo. State Penitentiary. Mem.: Press Club (hon.). Avocation: writing. Home: 1129 Saddlebrook Ct N Saint Charles MO 63304 Office Phone: 636-300-9417.

DRUSEDUM, KIMBERLY BARCLAY, music educator; b. Springfield, Pa., Oct. 15, 1966; d. Robert and Evelyn Knorr Barclay; m. Ward Aaron Drusedum, June 10, 2000. MusB in Choral Edn., U. Nev. Las Vegas, 1990; MS in Ednl. Adminstrn., U. Phoenix, Henderson, Nev., 2001. Dir. of choirs Green Valley H.S., Henderson, Nev., 1991—. Adjudicator Heritage Choral Festivals, Salt Lake City, 2005—; dir. Las Vegas Philharm. Choir, 2003—05; owner So. Nev. Lamplight Carolers, Henderson, 1996—; h.s. choir task force chair Clark County Sch. Dist., Henderson, 2003—. Dir.: (choral performance) Na. Am. Choral Dirs.Assn. Conv. (Only H.S. Choir in Nevad ever selected, 2005). Named Educator of the Yr., Clark County Sch. Dist., 1994—95; recipient Outstanding Alumnus for the Coll. of Fine Arts, U. of Nev. Las Vegas, 2005, Excellence in Edn. Hall of Fame Inductee, Clark County Sch. Dist., 2002. Mem.: Am. Choral Dirs. Assn. (life; chpt. pres. 2005—), Nev. Music Educators Assn. (life; pres.-elect 2005—, Nev. Music Educator of the Yr. 2001—02). Office: Green Valley High School Choir 460 Arroyo Grande Blvd Henderson NV 89014 Office Phone: 702-799-0950. E-mail: kbdrused@interact.ccsd.net.

DRUSHAL, MARY ELLEN, parish administrator, education educator, former academic administrator; b. Peru, Ind., Oct. 24, 1945; d. Herrell Lee and Opal Marie (Boone) Waters; m. J. Michael Drushal, June 12, 1966; children: Lori, Jeff. B of Music Edn., Ashland Coll., 1969; MS, Peabody Coll., 1981; PhD, Vanderbilt U., 1986. Dir. music and spl. ednl. projects Smithville (Ohio) Brethren Ch., 1969-74; tchr. music Orrville (Ohio) Pub. Schs., 1969—70; seminar leader Internat. Ctr. for Learning, Glendale, Calif., 1974-76; dir. Christian edn. First Presbyn. and Christ Presbyn. Ch., Nashville, 1976-84; assoc. prof. Ashland (Ohio) Theol. Sem., 1984-91, acad. dean, 1991-95; provost Ashland U., 1995—2001, prof. edn., 2001—05, prof. emeritus, 2006—; parish adminstr. Peace Luth. Ch., 2006—. Cons. in strategic planning for not-for-profit orgns. Author: On Tablets of Human Hearts: Christian Education with Children, 1991; co-author: Spiritual Formation: A Personal Walk Toward Emmaus, 1990; contbr. articles to profl. jours. Trustee Brethren Care Found., Ashland, 1989-99, Ashland Symphony Orch., 1986-87; pres., fundraiser Habitat for Humanity, Ashland, 1990-94; bd. dirs. JOY Day Care Ctr., 1988-90. Grantee Lilly Endowment Inc., 1991, 93, Brethren Ch. Found., 1989, 90. Mem. Assn. Theol. Schs. (com. underrepresented constituencies 1994-96), Am. Assn. for Higher Edn., Nat. Assn. Ch. Bus. Adminstrs., N.Am. Assn. Profs. of Christian Edn., Assn. Profs. and Rschrs. in Religious Edn., Nat. Assn. Evangelicals, Nat. Assn. Black Evangelical Assns., Epiphany Assn. (bd. dirs. 1994-98). Republican. Lutheran. Avocations: reading, needlepoint. Home: 20041 Sanibel View Cir 102 Fort Myers FL 33908-6991 Personal E-mail: medrushal@sanibelviewfl.com.

DRUSKOFF, BARBARA THERESE, elementary school educator; d. Edward Francis and Helen Sullivan; children: Jennifer Bernier, Mark. Student, Calif. State U., Long Beach, 1980, San Diego State U., 1986; BS in Edn., CUNY, 1966; MEd, Azusa Pacific U., Calif., 1994. Tchr. 1st grade Matawan Sch. Dist., NJ, 1966—67; tchr. elem. sch. Newston Sch. Dist., NJ, 1968—69, Bainbridge Unified Sch. Dist., NY, 1972—74, Lake Elsinore Unified Sch. Dist., Calif., 1987—. Co-chair visual and performing arts Luiseno Elem., Corona, Calif., 1992—, chair math field day, 1999—, provider beginning tchr. support and assessment, 2001—03. Author numerous poems. Mem. Habitat for Humanity, 2003—. Named Tchr. of Yr., Luiseno Elem. and Lake Elsinore Sch. Dist., 1994—95; recipient Best Actress award, North County Cmty. Theater, 1983—86; NY Regents scholar, 1961. Mem.: AAUW (past membership chair 1982—. Scholarship established in her name 1987), Art and Cultural Soc. Fallbrook, Nat. Assn. Educators Am., Nat. Women's History Mus., Mission Conservation Dist. Avocations: acting, the arts, antiques, reading, gardening. Office: Lake Elsinore Unified Sch Dist 545 Chanly st Lake Elsinore CA 92530 Office Phone: 951-674-0750.

DRVAR, MARGARET ADAMS, vocational school educator; b. Morgantown, W.Va., Dec. 22, 1953; d. Lester Morris and Daun Collette (Benson) Adams; m. Marvin Lynn Drvar, July 29, 1978; children: Jacob Elias, Jared Nathaniel. BS in Family Resources, W.Va. U., 1977, MS in Family Resources, 1982. Cert. tchr., vocat. family and consumer scis. tchr., W.Va. Substitute tchr. Monongalia County Bd. Edn., Morgantown, 1983-86; tchr. vocat. family and consumer sci. Clay Battelle Jr.-Sr. H.S., Blacksville, W.Va., 1986-89, 91-92, South Mid. Sch., Morgantown, 1992—, treas. faculty senate, 1997—. Instr. culinary arts Monongalia County Tech. Edn. Ctr., Morgantown, 1989-91; youth group adv. Family, Career, Cmty. Leaders Am. (formerly Future Homemakers of Am.), 1986—. V.p. United Meth. Women, Brookhaven, W.Va., 1985-92; sec. bd. trustees Brookhaven United Meth. Ch., 1989-97; bd. dirs., sec. Morgantown AES Fed. Credit Union, 1989-2006; vol. 4-H leader Brookhaven Bulls 4-H Club, 1992—. Recipient Master Advisor award, Future Homemakers Am. Inc., 1996, Golden Apple Achiever award, Ashland Oil, 1996, Outstanding 4-H Leader Monongalia County award, 1996, Tchr. of Yr. award, W.Va. Family and Consumer Sci. Assn., 2002, Top 10 Tchrs. of the Yr., Am. Assn. of Family and Consumer Scis., 2002, 4-H All Star award for yrs. of cmty. svc., W.Va. 4-H, 2003. Mem.: NEA, Monongalia County 4-H Leaders Assn. (pres. 1998—99, 2001—03), W.Va. Vocat. Assn. (historian family and consumer sci. divsn. 1995—96), Assn. for Career and Tech. Edn., Monongalia County Assn. of Family and Consumer Scis., W.Va.Assn. Family and Consumer Scis. (housing and evniron. divsn. chair 2005—), Monongalia County Edn. Assn., W.Va. Edn. Assn., Am. Assn. Family and Consumer Scis. (cert.) (Top 10 Tchr. of Yr. 2002), Gamma Phi Beta, Alpha Upsilon Omicron. Avocations: travel, camping. Home: 3307 Darrah Ave Morgantown WV 26508-9187 Office: Monongalia County Schs South Mid Sch 500 E Parkway Dr Morgantown WV 26501-6839 Office Phone: 304-291-9340. Business E-Mail: mdrvar@access.k12.wv.us.

DRY, JUDITH KALLEN, dental hygienist, cable producer, writer; b. Chgo., Apr. 5, 1952; d. Irwi Arthur and Marion (Silverman) Kallen; m.Fred Mark Dry, Aug. 14, 1973 (div. May 1985). BA, Northwestern U., 1980, student, 1982. Registered dental hygienist. Dental hygienist A.D.H.A., Chgo., 1982—; freelance dental cons. Chgo., 1982—. Prodr., writer standup comedy HBO, Comic Relief, Second City, Zanies, Politically Incorrect, The Improv; contbr. WGN-AM comedy routines. Avocations: design, dance, cooking, investing. Home: 4250 N Marine Dr Apt 602 Chicago IL 60613-1723

DRYDEN, MARY ELIZABETH, law librarian, writer, actress; b. Chgo., Oct. 18, 1952; d. James Heard and Hazel Anne (Potts) Rule; m. Ian Dryden, Nov. 22, 1975 (div. 1991, dec. 1993); m. Stephen Quadros, Sept. 12, 1992 (div. 1996); m. Larry Borkin, Jan. 3, 2003. Student, U. London, 1969, Bath U., 1970; BA, Scripps Coll., Claremont, Calif., 1971; postgrad., U. Edinburgh, 1971-74. Libr. dir. Hahn, Cazier & Leff, San Diego, 1980, Fredman, Silverberg & Lewis, San Diego, 1980-83, Riordan & McKinzie, L.A., 1985—2003, Paul, Hastings, Janofsky & Walker, L.A., 2004—05, K & R Law Group, L.A., 2005—. Freelance photog. model, 1973-85. Theatrical appearances include Antony and Cleopatra, London, 1984, Table Manners, L.A., 1985, Julius Caesar, L.A., 1986, Witness for the Prosecution, L.A., 1987, Come and Go, L.A., 1988, The Actor's Nightmare, L.A., 1989, The Dresser, L.A., 1989, Absent Friends, Long Beach, Calif., 1990, Run For Your Wife!, Long Beach, 1991, The Hollow, Long Beach, 1992, Cock and Bull Story, Hollywood, 1993, Towards Zero, Long Beach, 1993, Angel Street, L.A., 1994, Bedroom Farce, L.A., 1995, Postmortem, L.A., A Weekend with Sam Beckett, L.A., 1997, Deathtrap, 1998, Angel Street, 1999, Fortinbras, L.A., 1999, Othello, Hollywood, 2000, Sweet Bird of Youth, 2000, Walt Whitman's Song of Myself, Edinburgh Festival, 2000, Richard III, 2002, Ancient Voices, 2004, The Good Doctor, 2005, Footfalls, L.A., 2006, Fatal Attraction, L.A., 2006; (films) Private Collections, 1989, Eye Opener, 1992, A Situation, 1994, Porn Queens of the Seventies, 1994, The Nutty Professor, 1996, The Sophia Replacement, 1996; (TV) War Stories, 2002; Days of Our Lives (NBC), 2003, What Should You Do?, (Lifetime) 2004; also music videos and TV commls.; book critic L.A. Times; contbr. articles to newspapers. Mem. ABA, Brit. Equity, So. Calif. Assn. Law Librs., Brit. Acad. Film and TV Arts, SAG, Mensa, Phi Beta Kappa. Avocations: photography, wine, architecture, fine art, languages.

DRYDEN, SUSAN MEREDITH, secondary school educator; b. Radford, Va., Aug. 4, 1968; d. John Frederick and Shirley Ann (Robbins) D. BS in Sec. Edn., Abuburn U., 1991. English educator Hoover (Ala.) City Schs., 1991—. Fac. honor coun. Hoover High Nat. Honor Soc., 1992-94, internat. baccalaureate fac. Hoover H.S., 1994—. Mem. adv. bd. Jr. High Ranch, Birmingham, Ala., 1994—, vol. Mountain Brook Cmty. Ch., Birmingham, 1994—. Mem. Assoc. of Am. Educators. Republican. Avocations: hiking, white-water rafting, guitar, basketball, reading. Office: Hoover H S 1000 Buccaneer Dr Birmingham AL 35244-4511 Home: 722 Harris Hollow Rd Washington VA 22747-1812

DRYER, BARBARA FERRELL, media specialist, educator; b. Norfolk, Va., July 21, 1948; d. Philip Earl and Bertha Buzzy Ferrell; m. Mark Steven Dryer, Jan. 25, 1968; 1 child, Elizabeth Anne; 1 child, Jeffrey Lawrence. BSEE, Old Dominion U., Norfolk, Va., 1970, postgrad., 1999—. Media specialist Portsmouth Pub. Sch., Va., 1970—79, Norfolk Pub. Sch., 1988—89, Norfolk Collegiate Lower Sch., 1991—. Steering com. Norfolk Collegiate Sch., 2000—, sponsor writing club and newspaper, 1999—. Contbr. articles to profl. jours. Pres. Willard PTA, Norfolk, Va., 1991—93. Recipient Va. Reading Tchr. of Yr., Va. Reading Assn., 1978, Vol. of Yr., Willard Model Sch. PTA, 1989, 1990. Mem.: Va. Ednl. Media Assn. (workshop presenter 2001—), Va. Assn. Ind. Schs., Norfolk Reading Coun., Va. State PTA (life), Friends of the Norfolk Pub. Libr. Democrat. Avocations: reading, gardening, sewing, renovating our historic house. Home: 1514 Maury Cres Norfolk VA 23509 Office: Norfolk Collegiate Sch 5429 Tidewater Dr Norfolk VA 23509

DRZEWIECKI, DARLA RUTH, accountant; b. Pomona, Calif., Apr. 10, 1961; d. James Haywood Dabney, Sr. and Ruth Irene Dabney; m. David Adam Drzewiecki, Jan. 7, 1984; children: Brian Adam, Kenneth James. Posting clk. Scheu Mfg. Co., Upland, Calif., 1979—81; payroll clk. Data Electronics, Inc., San Diego, 1981—83; asst. acct. mgr. Elgar Corp., San Diego, 1983—84, Teledyne Micronetics Inc., San Diego, 1984—85; fin. acct. Teledyne Ryan Electronics, San Diego, 1985—87; sec. and acct. office mgr. Bethany Assembly of God, San Diego, 1990—. Spkr. in field. Youth group leader, Costa Rica, 1984—; vol. homeless teens San Diego, 2002—; youth mission trip Costa Rica, 2002, Bahamas, 2005. Avocations: sports, stamp collecting/philately. Home: 797 Monserate Ave Chula Vista CA 91910 Office: Bethany Assembly God 916 Hollister St San Diego CA 92154 Office Phone: 619-423-0661.

DUANE, JEANNINE MORRISSEY, retired elementary school educator; b. Lancaster, Pa., Dec. 4, 1932; d. Frank Morrissey and Elsie Ebersole; m. W. Richard G. Duane, Jr., Apr. 15, 1963 (dec. 1996). BS in Elem. Edn., Millersville State U., 1954; MEd, Lehigh U., 1979, EdD, 1989. Cert. tchr. N.J., Pa., Hawaii, supr. N.J., supr. elem. tchr. Pa. Tchr. U.S. Dept. Def., Japan, 1959—64, Bermuda, 1970—89, Global Assocs., Kwajalein, Micronesia, 1967—69, Chester (N.J.) Bd. Edn., 1970—89; supr. elem. tchr. interns Lehigh U., Bethlehem, Pa., 1988; ret., 1989. Mem. Washington Twp. N.J. Bd. Edn., 1979—; edn. cons. EdPro Consulting; lectr. NASA, Delta Kappa Gamma Soc. Internat. workshop; rschr. in field. Author: (book) Marshallese-English Phrase Book, 1968, English-Marshallese Cookbook, 1969, The Education of Gifted Children, British and American Schools. Active CAP. Named N.J. nat. Finalist Tchr. in Space, Morris County N.J. Woman of the Yr., 1988. Mem.: NJSBA, ASCD, NEA, N.J. Edn. Assn., N.J. Reading Assn., Challenger Ctr., World Space Found., Lunar Planetary Inst., Phi Delta Kappa. Home: 390 Naughright Rd Long Valley NJ 07853-3847

DUARTE, ROSE MARY R., elementary school educator; b. Carlsbad, N.Mex., Jan. 5, 1948; d. Julian and Lucy R. Ramirez; divorced; children: Clarissa, George, Jeff. BS, Ea. N.Mex. U., Portales, 1979, postgrad., 2000, Coll. S.W., Hobbs, N.Mex., 2006—. Kindergarten tchr. Joe Stanley Smith Sch., Carlsbad, N.Mex., 1980—90, Edison Sch., Carlsbad, 1990—92, Early Childhood Ctr., Carlsbad, 1992—95; tchr. 1st grade Loving Elem., N.Mex.,

1995—2003, kindergarten tchr., 2005—; tchr. 6-7th grade Loving Mid. Sch., 2003—05. Mem.: Am. Legion (sgt. at arms 1988, award 1999). Democrat. Roman Catholic. Avocations: reading, travel. Home: 2607 Davis St Carlsbad NM 88220

DUBARRY, JACQUELINE ANNE, artist, educator; b. Dublin, Jan. 6, 1964; arrived in U.S., 1979; d. James and Marie DuBarry; children: Ashling Anne Fricke, Kyle Robert Fricke. BFA, Sch. Visual Arts, NYC, 1986; MS in Art Edn. with honors, Queens Coll., NYC, 2004. N.Y. State permanent cert. Sculpture instr. Usdan Ctr. for Creative and Performing Arts, NY, 1999—, Hofstra U. Continuing Edn., NY, 2000—03; tchr. grades K-12 Middle County Cen. Sch. Dist., Centereach, NY, 2000—. Curriculum writer elem. and sculpture elective Middle Country Cen. Sch. Dist., Centereach, 2000—; curriculum writer Queens Coll., NY, 2000—03. Faculty art shows, 2000—, exhibited in group shows at Slow Gallery, 2001—. Mem.: Nat. Art Educators Assn. Avocations: painting, sculpting, drawing, yoga. Home: 2540 Chestnut Ave Ronkonkoma NY 11779 Office: Middle County Cen Sch Dist 8-4 3d St Centereach NY 11720

DUBELLE, MOLYNEAU, legal consultant; d. Ainsworth and Yvonne DuBelle. BS, Georgetown U., Washington, 2000, postgrad., 2005—. Pres. The Friendship Store, Palm Coast, Fla., 1991—96; pres., co-founder Flagler Molynium Consulting & Svcs., Arlington, Va., 1999—; paralegal DLA Piper Rudnick Gray Cary, Washington, 2000—03; clin. trial contract negotiator Georgetown U., Washington, 2003—04; legal cons. The World Bank, Washington, 2004—. Author: DuBelle's Dictionary of Patois Words and Expressions. Ct. observer, report contbr. Coun. for Ct. Excellence, Washington, 2001—02. Recipient cert. of achievement, Presdl. Classroom, 1995, Teen Ct. Recognition, 7th Jud. Ct. of Flagler County, Fla., 1995, French and Spanish awards, 1996, award, Internat. Fgn. Lang. Assn., US Achievement Acad. Mem.: Euronet Internat., Mensa (testing coord., proctor 2003—06, Svc. award 2004), Mu Alpha Theta. Avocations: acting, travel, music, fashion, languages. Office: The World Bank 1818 H St NW Washington DC 20433 Office Phone: 202-458-7894.

DUBIN, STACIA, newscaster; b. Milw., Aug. 8, 1972; BA in Journalism and Mass Comm., U. Wis., 1994. Former gen. assignment reporter, cut-in anchor, photojournalist WJFW-TV, Rhinelander, Wis.; former assoc. prodr., weekend assignment editor WMTV, Madison, Wis.; weekend anchor, ct. and crime reporter WKBT-TV, LaCrosse, Wis., 1995—96; weekend morning anchor, reporter WITI-TV, Milw., 1996—2000; freelance reporter, gen. assignment reporter CBS2 Chgo., 2000—02, co-anchor evening news, 2002—.

DUBLON, DINA, former bank executive; b. Brazil, Aug. 1953; BA in Econs. and Math., Hebrew U.; MS, Carnegie Mellon U. Exec. v.p. corp. planning Chase Manhattan Corp., N.Y.C., 1996—2000; CFO, exec. v.p. J.P. Morgan Chase & Co., N.Y.C., 2000—04. Bd. dirs. Accenture, PepsiCo, Inc., Microsoft, 2005—. Trustee Carnegie Mellon U., Global Fund for Women, The Women's Commn. for Refugee Women and Children, Worldlinks. Named Woman of the Year, The Fin. Women's Assn., 2004.

DUBNER, TERYE B., secondary school educator; d. Sidney and Ruth Bock; m. Ronald Allen Dubner, Dec. 26, 1967; children: Cindy W. Hauk, Michael William, Stephen Elliott. MS, So. Meth. U., Dallas, 1969. Cert. math. tchr. Tex. Edn. Assn., 1966. Math. tchr. Centennial H.S., Frisco, Tex., 2003—. Mem.: North Tex. Area Advanced Placement Tchrs. Avocation: gardening. Office Phone: 469-633-5600.

DU BOFF, JILL BONNIE CANDISE, sound effects artist; b. Mamaroneck, N.Y., July 17, 1975; d. Michael Harold and Diane Gail Du Boff. B, New Sch., N.Y.C., 1997. Sound designer Broadway, off-Broadway, Regional Theatre. Nominee Hewes award, Am. Theater Wing, 2005, Drama Desk award, 2005, 2005. Avocations: biking, rock climbing, music. Home: 459 W49th St #2W New York NY 10019 Personal E-mail: jill@jillduboff.com.

DUBOIS, CHRISTINE, writer, educator; b. Richmond Hts., Mo., Dec. 30, 1956; d. Edward N. and Jean Charlotte (Hall) D.; m. Steven E. Bourne, Sept. 16, 1979; children: Lucas, Gabriel. BA in Comm., U. Wash., 1979. Assignment editor Sta. KING-TV, Seattle, 1978-82; editor Olympia Churchman, Seattle, 1983-85; sr. editor Group Health Coop., Seattle, 1986-90; co-owner Turtledove Writers, Bothell, Wash., 1990—. Instr. continuing edn. and writing North Seattle Edmonds Shoreline Cmty. Colls., 1986—; instr. writing Pacific N.W. Writers Conf., Seattle, 1993—, Write On the Sound Conf., Edmonds, 1995—; mem. mgmt. com. FARM, LLC, 1999—. Co-author: (with Steven Bourne) Waiting In Hope, 1993 (Wash. Press Assn. 1st place award 1993); contbr. over 400 articles to jours. Bd. dirs. Mill Creek (Wash.) Coop. Presch., 1998-99, Sacred Heart Shelter, Seattle, 1987-90; active Epis. Ch. Recipient Superior Performance award Wash. Press Assn., 1989, numerous awards from Cath. Press Assn., Soc. Profl. Journalists, Pub. Rels. Soc. Am., others. Mem. Nat. Writers Union, Cath. Press Assn. Avocations: music, sports, cooking. Office: Turtledove Writers PO Box 12777 Mill Creek WA 98082-0777

DU BOISE, KIM REES, artist, photographer, art educator; b. Hattiesburg, Miss., Apr. 7, 1953; d. Samernie and Margaret J. R.; divorced; children: Timothy L., M. Ashley (dec.). BA, U. So. Miss., 1986, M of Art Edn., 1988; postgrad., U. Ala., 1994-95. Art tchr. grades 7-12 Columbia (Miss.) Acad., 1975-76; with prodn./ad design Columbian-Progress/Sunday Mirror (News), Columbia, 1980-81; with advt. design/prodn. Washington Parish ERA-Leader (newspaper), Franklinton, La., 1981; art tchr. grades kindergarten-12 Hattiesburg Prep. Sch., 1984-85; instr. art Pearl River C.C., Poplarville, Miss., 1987-94; artist/photographer Dogwood Studios, 1988-97; artist, photographer PhotoArts Imaging Professionals, 1997—, PhotoArts Imaging Supply. Adj. instr. U. So. Miss., 1996-97, 98-2000; festival coord. Very Spl. Arts Festival, SE Dist., Poplarville, Miss., 1989-94; participant regional round-Table on discipline based art edn. Getty Ctr. for Edn. in Arts, Tulsa, 1988. Ann. Bi-State Competition, 1986, Exhibited in group shows at MSC/JCAIA Art Exhbn., 1991, Miss. Cmty. Jr. Coll. Art, 1991—92, Art by Art Tchrs. MAEA, 1992, Art Student League Exhibit, 1995, photography, U. N.Mex., 1995, So. Miss. Art Assn. Annual Juried Competitions, 1996—98, U. So. Miss., 1998, 2000, Hines C.C., Miss., 2000. Chmn. Troop 21 Dixie Com. Boy Scouts Am., Hattiesburg, 1989-93; mem. Miss. Jaycettes/Marion County Jaycettes, Columbia, 1976-84, U.S. Jaycee Women, 1976-84. Named one of Outstanding Young Women of Am., 1981-84, First Lady #83 (Life Mem.) Miss. Jaycettes, 1982, Winner Speak-Up Competition, Miss. Jaycettes, 1981. Mem. New Orleans Mus. of Art (assoc.), So. Miss. Art Assn., Nat. Mus. of Women in the Arts (charter), Nature Conservancy, U. So. Miss. Alumni Assn. (life), Walter Anderson Mus. Art. Episcopalian. Avocations: fishing, reading. Office: PhotoArts Imaging 1402 Mamie St Hattiesburg MS 39401-6207 Office Phone: 601-582-3686.

DUBOSE, PATRICIA CHAPMAN, science educator, consultant; b. Pensacola, Fla., Dec. 29, 1959; d. Gordon King and Joyce Ann (Belcher) Chapman; m. Ronald Wayne DuBose; 1 child, Sarah Ann. AB in Biology, Wesleyan Coll., Macon, Ga., 1981; EdM in Secondary Sci., U. North Fla., Jacksonville, 1996; EdS in Leadership, Albany State U., Ga., 2004. Quality control tech IV Union Carbide Ag Products, Woodbine, Ga., 1981—85; sci. tchr. Camden County H.S., Kingsland, 1988—2005; sci. specialist Ga. Dept. Edn., Atlanta, 2005—. Mem. supt.'s think tank Camden Bd. Edn., 2002—03; tchr. trainer Ga. Dept. Edn., Kingsland, Ga., 1996—99; author student activities and tchr. resources. Author: Sustainable Seas Tchr. Resources, 2002, 2003. Cookie mgr. Jasmine svc. unit Savannah Coun. Girl Scouts USA, 1996—99, svc. unit mgr., 1999—2001. Named Tchr. of Yr., Camden County H.S., 2003. Mem.: Ga. Assn. Marine Educators (Marine Educator of Yr. 2003), Nat. Assn. Marine Educators, Nat. Sci. Tchrs. Assn., Girl Scouts USA (life Outstanding Leader Jasmine svc. unit, Outstanding Vol. Jasmine svc. unit, Appreciation pin Savannah coun.). Avocations: photography, scrapbooks, fishing. Home: 907 Margaret St Saint Marys GA 31558 Office: Ga Dept Edn 1754 Twin Towers E Atlanta GA 30334 Office Phone: 404-516-1564.

DUBROVSKY, GERTRUDE WISHNICK, journalist, researcher; b. NYC, Mar. 10, 1926; d. Benjamin and Esther Raisa (Katz) Wishnick; m. Jack Dubrovsky, Feb. 24, 1946 (div. Sept. 1975); children: Richard, Steven, Benjamin; m. Sidney Gray, June 13, 1976 (div. June 1997). AB, Georgian Ct. Coll., Lakewood, NJ, 1956; MA, Rutgers U., New Brunswick, NJ, 1959; EdD, Columbia U., N.Y.C., 1974. Tchr. Keyport (N.J.) grammar sch., 1956-57, Point Pleasant (NJ) HS, 1959-61; asst. prof. Trenton (NJ) State Coll., 1964-66; program dir. YIVO Inst. Jewish Rsch., NYC, 1975-81; freelance journalist, writer N.Y. Times, NYC, 1979—; ind. scholar, rschr. Princeton, NJ, 1980—; rschr., writer,asst. to pres. Carnegie Found. Advancement of Tchg., Princeton, 1982-85; Yiddish instr. Ctr. Jewish Life Princeton U., 1974-95. Pres. Documentary III, Princeton, 1980—; specialist in field of Am. Jewish rural history. Author: The Land Was Theirs: Jewish Farmers in the Garden State, 1992, Six From Leipzig, 2004; Editor newsletter: Rural Roots: Jewish Farm History, 1988-95; translator: (poems) Kentucky, 1990 (Jewish Book Club selection); prodr., dir. documentary The Land Was Theirs, 1993 (1st Pl. award Berkeley Film Festival, 1994). Mcpl. committeeperson Dem. Party, Princeton, 1980—, chair, 1982-84; mem. Commn. on Aging, Princeton, 1980—, chair, 1991-93 Fellow Meml. Found. for Jewish Culture, 1975, Oxford (Eng.) Ctr. Hebrew and Jewish Studies, 1994; NEH grantee, 1976, 78; fellow, life mem. Clare Hall, Cambridge U., 2000-01. Mem. Assn. for Jewish Studies, Am. Jewish Hist. Soc., Am. Jewish Archives, Princeton Rsch. Forum. Avocations: swimming, walking, bridge, Scrabble, poetry. Home and Office: 244 Hawthorne Ave Princeton NJ 08540-3826 Office Phone: 609-924-7527. E-mail: gdubrovsky@aol.com.

DUBROW, GAIL LEE, architecture educator; BArch, U. Oreg., 1980; grad. cert. in arch. and urban design, UCLA, 1984, PhD in Urban Planning, 1991. Adj. assoc. prof. history and women's studies; dir. preservation planning and design program, 1990—; prof. depts. arch. and urban design and planning U. Wash., Seattle, assoc. dean for rsch. and computing Coll. Arch. and Urban Planning. Apptd. mem. Seattle Design Commn., 1996—2000; bd. dirs. Vernacular Arch. Forum, 2001—04. Mem. editl. bd.: Jour. Archtl. Edn., 2000—03; author: Asian American Imprints on the Western Landscape, in Preserving Cultural Landscapes in America, 2000; co-editor (with J. Goodman): Restoring Women's History Through Historic Preservation, 2004. Mem.: Assn. Collegiate Schs. Arch. (western regional dir. 2001—04).

DUBROW, HEATHER, literature educator; b. San Antonio, Mar. 5, 1945; d. Hilliard and Helen (Volk) D.; m. Ian Ousby, June 21, 1969 (div. Dec. 1979). BA summa cum laude, Harvard/Radcliffe, 1966; PhD, Harvard U., 1972. Asst. prof. U. Mass., Boston, 1972-73; Leverhulme vis. fellowship U. Kent, Canterbury, Eng., 1973-74; lectr. U. Sussex, Brighton, Eng., 1974-75; from vis. asst. prof. to asst. prof. U. Md., College Park, 1975-80; from assoc. to prof. Carleton Coll., Northfield, Minn., 1980-90; from prof. to John Bascom prof. and Tighe-Evans prof. U. Wis., Madison, 1990—. External rev. team Oberlin Coll., Bryn Mawr Coll. Author: Genre, 1982, Captive Victors, 1987, A Happier Eden, 1990, Echoes of Desire, 1995, Transformation and Repetition, 1997, Shakespeare and Domestic Loss, 1999, Border Crossings, 2001; contbr. articles to profl. jours. Recipient Capt. Jonathan Fay award, Radcliffe Coll., 1966; sr. fellow Nat. Endowment for the Humanities, 1987—88, 2003—04, Guggenheim fellow, 2004. Mem. MLA (mem. editl. bd., exec. coun. 1996-2000), Milton Soc. of Am. (exec. com. 1997-99), Renaissance Soc. Am. (disciplinary rep. 2001-03), Spenser Soc., Phi Beta Kappa. Democrat. Avocations: architecture, art, cooking. Office: U Wis Dept of English 600 N Park St Madison WI 53706-1403 Office Phone: 608-263-2913. Business E-Mail: hdubrow@wisc.edu.

DUBROW, MARSHA ANN, management consultant, musicologist; b. Newark, N.J., Dec. 27, 1948; d. Leo and Rose (Haberman) Dubrow; m. Daniel Leon Chaykin, Jan. 17, 1970 (div. 1985); one child, Alexander; m. David Lorin Rosenberg, July 3, 1988; one step child, Oliver. BA cum laude, U. Pa., 1970; MA, NYU, 1975; MFA, Princeton U., N.J., 1977, PhD, 2001; postgrad., Tufts U., Medford, Mass., 1987, Am. Women's Econ. Devel. Corp. Inst., 1987—88, Leadership Am., 1988, Leadership N.J., 1990, Leadership Inst. for Workforce Devel., 1993. Prodn. coord. Children's TV Workshop, N.Y.C., 1970—73; instr. Princeton U., NJ, 1976—78; mgr. mktg. comm., ops., human resources AT and T Tech., Inc., Morristown, NJ, 1978—80; dir. mktg. and ops. Acadia Comm., N.Y.C., 1980—83; dir. planning and mktg. Access Methods, Inc., N.Y.C., 1984—85; mng. dir. Marsha Dubrow Assoc., Upper Montclair, NJ, 1981—; pres., CEO Technolog, Inc., Upper Montclair, 1985—, Dubrow Group, 2004—. Cantor Congregation B'nai Jacob, Jersey City, 2005—. Bd. dirs. Greater Newark (N.J.) Conservancy. Recipient Theodore Presser Award U. Pa., 1970; fellow Tisch Sch. Arts, 1993-94; named William C. Langley Fellow N.Y. Univ., 1974, Princeton U. fellow, 1976-78, Josephine de Karman Fellow Aerojet Gen. Corp., 1981, Composer's Fellow in Opera Musical Theatre N.J. State Coun. Arts, 1990, Folk Arts Fellow N.J. State Coun. Arts, 1996-98, 2003-05. Mem.: Leadership Found., N.J. Women's Forum (bd. dir., pres.), N.J. Bus. Higher Edn. Forum, Leadership Am. Assn., Dramatists Guild, Internat. Women's Forum (bd. dir.), Women Presidents Orgn., Princeton U. Alumni Coun. (exec. com.), Princeton U. Assn. Princeton Grad. Alumni (governing bd.). Home: 34 Marion Rd Montclair NJ 07043-1932 Office: The Dubrow Group PO Box 43427 Montclair NJ 07043 Personal E-mail: madubrow@comcast.net.

DUBRULLE, FRANÇOISE M., architect, painter, interior designer; b. Orleans, France, May 26, 1929; d. Robert Jean Marie Dubrulle and Madeleine Marie Coutout de Sery. BA in Arch. and arts, Sorbonne/Beaux Arts, Florence; MBA in fine arts and bus., Sorbonne/Beaux Arts, Rome; PhD in History of Arts and Urbanism, Sorbonne/Beaux Arts, Paris. Owner La Bastille Fine Art Gallery, 1972—. Represented in permanent collections in univs. and mus. in U.S. and abroad. Mem.: Art Guild (assoc.; founder). Home: 2748 SE Rood Bridge Dr Hillsboro OR 97123

DUBS, GLORIA L., artist, realtor; b. Hammond, Ind. d. Joseph and Mayme Gish; m. Jack H. Dubs, 1951; children: Jack R., David, Gary. BS, Purdue U., 1951. Lic. realtor, travel agt. Realtor Prudential Realty/Northside Realty, Atlanta. Exhibitions include Ocee Art Ctr., Duluth, Ga., 2001, 2002, 2003. Mem.: Ashford Club. Office Phone: 770-605-2046.

DUBUC, NANCY, communications executive; b. 1969; m. Michael Dubuc; 1 child, Jackson. Grad., Boston U. Worked in World Monitor newsroom; prodr. WGBH, Boston, 1992—95; series prodr. Discover Mag., The Discovery Channel; dir., hist. programming Hist. Channel; v.p., non-fiction and alternative programming A&E Network, 2003—05, sr. v.p., non-fiction programming & new media content, 2005—. Named one of 40 Executives Under 40, Multichannel News, 2006. Office: A&E Television Network 235 E 45th St New York NY 10017 Office Phone: 212-210-1400. Office Fax: 212-850-9370.*

DUBUQUE, AMANDA SUE, mental health services professional; b. Englewood, Colo., June 25, 1980; d. Jerry Alan and Sandra Sue Hull; m. Christopher Lee Dubuque, Oct. 1, 2005. BS in Psychology and Criminal Justice, U. No. Colo., Greeley, 2002; postgrad. in Counseling, U. No. Colo., Denver, 2002—. Human svcs. aid Centennial Developmental Svcs., Evans, Colo., 1999—2001; personal care provider First Choice Home Health, Denver, 2000—01; mental health worker Mount St. Vincent Home, Denver, 2001—. Lutheran. Avocations: sewing, running, camping, fishing, hiking. Home: 17736 E Oxford Pl Aurora CO 80013

DUCHARME, JANICE A., secondary school educator; BA in Psychology, Nichols Coll., Dudley, Mass., 1975. Mgr. Wollberg-Michelson PSL Svc., San Francisco, 1976—81; tchr. Bartlett H.S., Webster, Mass., 1982—. Mem.: Mass. Reading Assn., Webster Edn. Assn., Mass. Tchrs. Assn. Office: Bartlett HS 52 Lake Pky Webster MA 01570 Office Phone: 508-943-8552.

DUCHESNE, CHRISTINA, secondary school educator; MEd, U. Wash., Tacoma, 1995. Cert. tchr. Wash. Biology tchr. Stadium HS, Tacoma, 1993—. Vol. Citizen's for a Healthy Bay, Tacoma, 1992—2006. Office: Stadium High Sch 111 North E St Tacoma WA 98403 Office Phone: 253-571-3063.

DUCK, PATRICIA MARY, librarian; b. Bklyn., Jan. 22, 1951; d. Warren James and Virginia Susan (Noonan) Johnson; m. John Jacob Duck, Feb. 2, 1973; children: Michael, Jennifer, Matthew. BA, George Washington U., 1974; MLS, U. Pitts., 1980, PhD in Libr. Sci., 1992. Libr., serials cataloger U. Pitts., 1980-84, libr., coord., 1984-85, libr., project supr., 1985-86; dir. libr. U. Pitts. Greensburg, 1986—. Facilitator region 10 Gov.'s Conf. Libr. and Info. Svcs., Pitts., 1990. Contbr. articles to profl. jours. Leader troop 47 Girl Scouts U.S., 1990-91; trustee Penn Area Libr., Level Green, Pa., 1989-91. Mem. ALA, Beta Phi Mu. E-mail: pmd1@pitt.edu Avocation: art. Office: U Pitts Greensburg Campus 1150 Mount Pleasant Rd Greensburg PA 15601-5860

DUCKWORTH, TARA ANN, insurance company executive; b. Seattle, June 7, 1956; d. Leonard Douglas and Audrey Lee (Limbeck) Hill; m. Mark L. Duckworth, May 16, 1981; children: Harrison Lee III, Andrew James, Kathryn Anne. AAS, Highline C.C., Seattle, 1976. From acctg. clk. to info. sys. supr. SAFECO Ins. Co., Seattle, 1977-90, rate sys. mgr., 1990-94; sys. mgr. SAFECO Mut. Funds, SAFECO Credit, PNMR, Seattle, 1994-97, mktg. comm. and incentives, quality assurance mgr., 1997-98, dir. comml. lines sys., 1998—2001, dir. quality assurance, 2001—03, dir. personal policy sys., 2003—06. Mem. tech adv. com. for the computer info. svcs. program North Seattle Community Coll., 1984-96, chairperson tech. adv. com., 1988-90. Mem. Star Lake Improvement Club, 1988-94; mem. St. Lukes Luth. Ch., 1986—; mem. Boy Scouts Am., 1996-2003. Mem. NAFE, Nat. Assn. for Ins. Women, Soc. for State Filers, Nat. PTA.

DUCKWORTH, TRACY WELLS, research scientist, educator, biotechnologist; b. Ft. Walton Beach, Fla., Nov. 22, 1965; d. Jim G.C. and Janet Kosko Wells; m. Martin Avery Duckworth, Mar. 24, 1990; children: Madison Wells, Martine Avery Jr. AS in Med. Tech., N.E. Miss. Cmty. Coll., Booneville, 1985; BS in Microbiology and Chemistry, Miss. U. for Women, Columbus, 1987; BS in Med. Tech., Bapt. Med. Ctr., Birmingham, 1988; MAT in Comprehensive Sci., U. W. Ala., Livingston, 2001. Tissue transplant technologist U. Ala., Birmingham, 1988—89; clin. microbiologist Carraway Meth. Medicine, Birmingham, 1987—90; state reference technologist ARC, Birmingham, 1988—90; med. technologist Bryan W. Whitfield Meml. Hosp., Demopolis, Ala., 1990—2002; blood bank specialist Druid City Hosp., Tuscaloosa, Ala., 1991—93; instr. biology U. W. Ala., Livingston, 1991—; sch. adminstr. W. Ala. Preparatory Sch., Demopolis, 2003—05. Cons. ARC, Birmingham, 1988—90; mem. adv. bd. SACS, Montgomery, Ala., 2003—05; recruiting chair U. W. Ala., Livingston, 2006—, creator and chair Labs-To-Go hands on sci., 2005—. Recipient United Meth. Women Spl. Achievement award, First United Meth. Ch., 2001. Mem.: Am. Soc. Microbiologists, Ala. Acad. Scis., Am. Soc. Clin. Pathologists (cert. med. technologist), Beta Beta Beta. Avocations: reading, hiking, canoeing, gardening, nature. Office: U West Alabama Station 7 Livingston AL 35470 Office Phone: 205-652-3732. Business E-Mail: twduckworth@uwa.edu.

DUCLOW, GERALDINE, historian, librarian; b. Chgo., Sept. 20, 1946; d. Steve and Irene (Halat) Hodzima; m. Donald F. Duclow, July 11, 1970. BA in English magna cum laude, DePaul U., 1968; MLS, Rosary Coll. (now Dominican U.), 1969. Reference libr. Chgo. Pub. Libr., 1969-70, Free Libr. Phila., 1970-71, head theatre collection, 1972—, asst. head rare book dept., 2005—. Coord. conf. Preservation Mgmt. for Performing Arts Collections, 1982; cons. Lubin Film Co. exhibit at Nat. Mus. Am.-Jewish History, 1984; cons. and speaker in field. Contbr. articles to profl. jours. Bd. dirs. Theater Alliance Greater Phila., 2000—; bd. trustees Charlotte Cushman Found., 2003—. Recipient Barrymore award for profl. commitment to Phila. Theatre Cmty., 2001. Mem. Am. Soc. for Theatre Rsch., Theatre Libr. Assn. (mem. exec. bd. 1980-95, pres. 1995-98). Avocation: art. Office: Free Libr Phila 1901 Vine St Philadelphia PA 19103-1189

DUCOTE, DEBORAH M., elementary school educator, reading specialist; Elem. tchr. Richardson Mid. Sch., West Monroe, La.; curriculum coord. Richardson H.S., West Monroe. Named La. State Tchr. of Yr., 1993.

DUCRAN, CLAUDETTE DELORIS, retired financial analyst; b. Trinityville, St. Thomas, Jamaica, July 23, 1941; came to U.S., 1962; d. Wellesley Provan and Hilda Maude (Beckford) DuC. Student, Corcoran Sch. Art, Washington, 1967; cert. of diploma, USDA Grad. Sch., Washington, 1972; student, Harvard U., 1976; BBA, George Washington U., 1982; postgrad., Columbia U., 1987. Adminstrv. asst. World Bank, Washington, 1964—75, fin. asst., 1975—85, ops. asst., 1985—88, disbursement asst., 1988—94, disbursement analyst, 1994—96; ret., 1996. Mem. adv. com. Very Spl. Arts Kennedy Ctr., Washington, 1990-93, Hands Across Hemisphere Craft Ctr., Washington, 1991; founder, pres. Let's Learn by Reading, Jamaica, 1990-2000. Author: Exhibitors Guidelines, 1989, 2d edit., 1990. Bd. dirs. Craft Ctr., Washington, 1991-99; panelist Career Week George Washington U., Washington, 1991, Women's Ctr., McLean, Va., 1991; founder, pres. The Claudette D. Ducran Found., Inc., Kingston, Jamaica, W.I., 1995-2001, Eureka Alliance, Inc., Washington, 1995—. Recipient 1st prize Writer's League, Washington, 1967, Internat. Order of Merit, 1994; named Internat. Woman of Yr., 1993-94. Mem.: World Bank 1818 Soc., World Bank Art Soc. (v.p. 1986—88, pres. 1988—93), Jamaica C. of C. (hon. Washington rep. 1997—). Avocations: performing and visual arts, children, travel, working with handicapped, international development. Home: The Brighton 2123 California St NW Apt B1 Washington DC 20008-1804

DUDASH, DEBRA ANN, music educator; b. Mineola, NY, July 15, 1979; d. Frank Michael and Shirley Lynn Dudash. BS, Messiah Coll., Grantham, Pa., 2001; MMus, Five Towns Coll., Dix Hills, NY, 2005; postgrad., SUNY, Stony Brook, 2005—. Tchr. VSCHSD, Valley Stream, NY, 2001—.

DUDASH, LINDA CHRISTINE, insurance company executive; b. Pitts. d. Andrew Daniel and Lillian (Reynolds) D. BA in English, Point Park Coll., 1969. Tech. writer Am. Insts. for Rsch., Pitts., 1968-69; claim svc. rep. Reliance Ins. Co., Pitts., 1969-70, claim rep., 1970-71, claim mgr. Jacksonville, Fla., 1971-73, Harrisburg, Pa., 1973-80, Chgo., 1980-86; maj. case unit mgr. Zurich Ins. Co., Schaumburg, Ill., 1986-88, asst. v.p., mgr. liability claims, 1988-91, asst. v.p., mgr. claims continuous improvement, 1991-92; v.p. dir. field ops. Zurich-Am. Ins., Schaumburg, Ill., 1992-95; sr. v.p. claims Casualty Ins. Co., divsn. Fremont Compensation Ins. Co., Chgo., 1995—2000; sr. v.p., chief claims officer Fremont Compensation Ins. Group, Glendale, Calif., 2000—03. Office: Fremont Compensation Ins Group 500 N Brand Blvd Glendale CA 91203-3392 Address: LC Consulting Dana Point CA 92629 E-mail: linda.dudash@sbcglobal.net.

DUDDY, ETHEL EILEEN (EILEEN DUDDY), accountant; b. Chickasha, Okla., Dec. 28, 1934; d. William John and Minnie Ethel Hunteman; m. Laurence M. Duddy, Dec. 7, 1953; children: Margaret M., Michael L. Student, Okla. Ctrl. U., 1953; AS in Bus., Coll. Marin, 1974; AA in Data Process, Merced Coll., 1974; BA in Bus. Adminstrn./Acctg. with honors, Calif. State U., Stanislaus, 1976. CPA Calif. State Bd. Accountancy. Sec. inst. shop U.S. Civil Svc., Elmendorf AFB, Alaska, 1953-54; dist. office cashier, svc. rep. Mt. States Tel & Tel, Yuma, Ariz., 1956-57; sec. to dist. mgr. Am. Nat. Ins. Corp., Abilene, Tex., 1970—71; staff acct. Holman Accountancy Corp., Atwater, Calif., 1976-79; staff acct., auditor Robert C. Martin Accountancy Corp., Atwater, Modesto, Calif., 1979-80; CPA, staff acct. Ozenbaugh & Smith, CPAs, Merced, Calif., 1981; owner E. Eileen Duddy, Atwater, 1981—. Dir. Calif. Soc. CPAs, Redwood City, 1988-90; founder, chmn. Merced/Atwater CPA Discussion Group, 1982-86. V.p. Merced County Econ. Devel. Corp., 1998—; chmn., bd. dirs. Castle Joint Power Authority, Merced County, 1998-99; mem. City Coun., Atwater, 1996-2000; mem. Calif. State Bd. Accountancy, 1992-97, long range planning com., legis. com., internat. reciprocity com, report quality monitoring com., liason to major case adv.

com.; mem. City of Atwater Audit and Fin. Com.; chmn. City of Atwater Pub. Works Com., coun. liason; vice-chmn., rep. City of Atwater, 1998—; bd. dirs Atwater C. of C., 1996—, past pres. 1987-88, chamber bd. dirs, 1985-91; chmn. Atwater Econ. Devel. com.; mem. legis. com.; mem. Merced County Office Econ. and Strategic Devel. Task Force, 1987-88; alternate Assessment Appeals Bd. Merced County, 1988-91, 91-94, Atwater citizens adv. com., 1994; Atwater Gen. Plan Review Com., 1991-92; active Girl Scouts Am., Brownie troop leader, Jr. troop leader, troop organizer, merit badge cons., 1963-71; den leader Cub Scouts Am., pack com. mem. 1970-72; troop cons. Boy Scouts Am., 1973-78; mem. wives clubs 516th TCW, past pres., Dyess AFB Waiting Wives Club, vol., 1963-71; active AF Handicapped Children's programs, Base Chapel Sunday Sch., tchr. Bible Sch, 1965-68; PTA and sch. vol. Dyess Elem. and Hamilton Elem. Schs., 1963-72; swimming instr. Dyess AFB Red Cross beginners classes, 1968-69. Mem. Am. Cancer Soc. (auditor ann. fund raising auction 1985-97), Am. Inst. CPAs, Calif. Soc. CPAs (bd. dirs., 1988-90, state discussion group com. 1987, past pres. San Joaquin chpt. 1989-90 v.p., chmn. chpt discussion group com. 1982-91, chpt. govt. rels. com. mem. chpt. profl. conduct com., acctg. prins. and auditing stds. com., taxation com., microcomputers user group), Calif. Firefighters Hist. Soc. (bd. dirs, life, treas. 1991—), Soroptimist Internat. Atwater (pres. 1989-90, fin. com. chmn. Sierra Pacific region 1991-92, Soroptomist of Yr., 1992, Woman of Distinction, 1996), Merced Coll. Found (bd. dirs. 1992), Atwater Women's Club, Castle Air Mus. Found (life, Daughters of Air Mus.), Merced Trade Club (dir., bd. dirs. 1998—). Republican. Avocations: computers, home improvement projects, swimming, skiing, art. Office: PO Box 666 Atwater CA 95301-0666 also: 2662 Palm Ave Atwater CA 95301 Office Phone: 209-358-7400. Personal E-mail: lduddy@fire2wire.com.

DUDECK, ANNE LEE, reading specialist; b. Chillicothe, Mo., Aug. 28, 1957; d. John Timothy and Lucy Terry (White) Sanderson; m. Jerry Rodney Daniel, June 4, 1978 (div. Apr., 1985); children: Chris, Ashli; m. David Paul Dudeck, Jan. 4, 1986; 1 child, Matthew. BS in Edn., Mo. Western State Coll., St. Joseph, 1978; M in Reading, N.W. Mo. State U., Maryville, 1995. Cert. elem. tchr., reading specialist, Mo. Kindergarten tchr., remedial reading tchr. Stewartsville C-II Elem., Mo., 1978-80; kindergarten tchr. Sherwood Elem. Sch., St. Joseph, 1980-81, Noyes Elem. Sch., St. Joseph, 1980-81; tchr. 3d grade Humboldt Elem. Sch., St. Joseph, 1981-87, tchr. 4th grade, 1987-93, Chpt. I reading tchr., 1993—97; reading recovery tchr. Webster Elem. Sch., St. Joseph, 1997—. Chmn. Humboldt Spelling Bee, 1992-95; mem. Chpt. 1 reading adv. bd. St. Joseph Sch. Dist., 1993-94; presenter in field (nat. recognition for "in class" chpt. I reading program). Youth leader United Meth. Ch., Oreg., Mo., 1992-95. Mem. Internat. Reading Assn., Mo. State Tchrs. Assn., Internat. Reading Recovery Assn., Webster PTA, Humboldt PTA, Beta Sigma Phi. Avocations: reading, travel, collecing antiques, baskets, gardening. Home: 29636 Hwy 59 Oregon MO 64473-9725

DUDICS-DEAN, SUSAN ELAINE, interior designer; b. Perth Amboy, NJ, Oct. 22, 1950; d. Theodore W. and Joyce M. (Ryals) D.; m. Rick Dean, Apr. 30, 1989; 1 child, Merissa Joyce. BS in Sociology, W.Va. U., 1972; postgrad., Rutgers U., 1975-78, U. Calif., Irvine, 1979-81, Can. Coll., 1981-89. Programmer Prudential Life, Newark, 1972-73; sr. sys. analyst Johnson & Johnson, New Brunswick, N.J., 1978-78, Sperry Univac, Irvine, 1978-80; sr. sys. analyst, project leader Robert A. McNeil, San Mateo, Calif., 1981-83; dist. design dir. TransDesigns, Woodstock, Ga., 1982-93; prin. Celestial Designs, 1980—; cons., dir. So. Living at Home, 2001—. Lectr., spkr. in field. Writer Drapery and Window Coverings, Design Lines, Window Fashions Mag., Designer Lines, Fine Furnishings Internat., Inspired House; guest on TV shows House Doctor, Marketplace Sta. KGO-TV; contbr. articles to profl. jours. High sch. mentor Directions, San Francisco, 1985-95. Recipient awards TransDesigns, Woodstock, 1984-87, 89-91, MoonRise Galleries, 1994-99. Mem. Women Entrepreneurs (membership com., treas. 1983-87), Romance Writers Am., Washington Romance Writers, Ctrl. N.J. Alumni Assn. Delta Gamma (assoc. sec., founder, pres.), Am. Soc. Interior Designers (allied mem. 1989-92), Profl. Bus. Women's Assn., Delta Gamma. Avocations: sewing, scuba diving, ballet, handcrafts. Office Phone: 304-263-3296.

DUDLEY, THORA LOUISE, rehabilitation services professional; b. Ansley, Ala., June 12, 1927; d. Willie Gussie and Henry Dudley. BA, Talladega Coll., 1958; MA in Rehab. Tchg., Hunter Coll., 1959. Cert. Am. Braille Assn. Rehab. tchr. N.Y. Assn. for Blind, N.Y.C., 1959—92; ret. Task force hiv/aids N.Y. Assn. for Blind, N.Y.C., 1992. Singer: (record) My Heavenly Father Watches Over Me. Mem. Lighthouse Choral Group, N.Y.C., 1965—89; performer Tuskegee U., Ala.; pres. chancel choir Butler Meml. United Meth. Ch., Bronx, NY, 1981, lay spkr., 2003, pres. united meth. women, 1986. Recipient Resident of Honor Ho., Talledega Coll., 1954—58, 1st pl., Legendary Apollo Theater, 1970; scholar, Vocat. Rehab. Group, 1958. Mem.: NAACP (life), Little Theater Group (assoc. Key Award 1958), Alpha Kappa Alpha (parliamentarian 1980, charter mem. Eta Omega Omega chpt.). Methodist. Achievements include first black, blind woman to graduate college and graduate school in the state of Alabama; One of the first blind members of Alpha Kappa Alpa. Avocations: singing, reading.

DUDLEY-ESHBACH, JANET, university president; b. Balt. m. Joseph Eshbach; two children. BA in Spanish and Latin Am. Studies, Ind. U.; PhD in Latin Am. Lit., El Colegio de Mexico, Mexico City. Mem. faculty, instr. Spanish Allegheny Coll., Meadville, Pa., 1978-79; asst. prof., then assoc. prof. Spanish and Latin Am. Studies Goucher Coll., Towson, Md., 1979-88; chmn. dept. Modern Langs., then assoc. v.p. Acad. Affairs SUNY, Potsdam, 1988-92, dean Sch. Arts and Scis., then provost, 1992-96; pres. Fairmont (W.Va.) State Coll., 1996—. Mem. Sen. Jay Rockefeller's Trade Mission to Taiwan and Japan, 1997. Mem. MLA, Am. Assn. Higher Edn., Am. Assn. State Colls. and Univs. (internat. studies com.), N.Y. State Assn. Women in Higher Edn., Coun. Colls. of Arts and Scis., Latin Am. Studies Assn., Marion County C. of C., Phi Delta Kappa, Phi Beta Kappa Office: Fairmont State Coll Office of Pres 1201 Locust Ave Fairmont WV 26554-2451

DUDZIAK, EMMA M., cardiac sonographer; b. Buffalo, N.Y., July 27, 1957; d. Norman P. Koneski and Geraldine E. Jans (Queeno); m. Gregory D. Dudziak, Sept. 15, 1979; children: Keith G., Scott G. Diploma, Bryant & Stratton Bus. Inst., Buffalo, N.Y. Registered Diagnostic Cardiac Sonographer Am. Registry of Diagnostic Med. Sonographers, Rockville, Md., 2002. Supr., echo, stress, holter & EKG lab Erie County Med. Ctr., Buffalo, 1982—97; sr. cardiac sonographer Buffalo Heart Group, 1997—. Mem.: Am. Inst. of Ultrasound in Medicine, Soc. of Diagnostic Med. Sonography, ARDMS (assoc.). Roman Catholic. Avocations: travel, bowling, needlepoint, sewing, knitting. Office: Buffalo Heart Group 3435 Bailey Ave Buffalo NY 14215 Office Phone: 716-835-2966. Personal E-mail: thedudz@hotmail.com.

DUDZIAK, MARY LOUISE, law educator; b. Oakland, Calif., June 15, 1956; d. Walter F. Dudziak and Barbara Ann Campbell; 1 child, Alicia. AB in Sociology with highest honors, U. Calif., Berkeley, 1978; JD, Yale Law Sch., 1984; MA, MPhil in Am. Studies, Yale U., 1986, PhD in Am. Studies, 1992. Adminstrv. asst. to dep. dir. Ctr. Ind. Living, Berkeley, 1978-80; law clk., nat. legal staff ACLU, N.Y.C., 1983; law clk. Judge Sam J. Ervin, III Fourth Cir. Ct. Appeals, Morganton, N.C., 1984-85; assoc. prof. coll. law U. Iowa, Iowa City, 1986-90, prof. coll. law, 1990-98. Vis. prof. U. So. Calif., 1997-98, Harvard Law Sch., 2005-; prof. U. So. Calif., 1998-2002, Judge Edward J. and Ruey L. Guirado prof. law and history, 2002-; vis. scholar Kennedy Sch. Govt., Harvard U., 2006-; mem. faculty senate task force on faculty devel. U. Iowa, 1989-90, mem. faculty welfare com., 1990-92, mem. faculty senate task force on faculty spouses and ptnrs., 1991-92, mem. presdl. lecture com., 1992-95; v.p. rsch. adv. com. in social scis., 1992-94; fellow law and pub. affairs program Princeton U., 2002; presenter in field. Author: Cold War Civil Rights: Race and the Image of American Democracy, 2000; editor, co-author: September 11 in History: A Watershed Moment?, 2003; co-editor Legal Borderlands: Law and the Construction of American Borders, 2006, mem. bd. mng. editors Am. Quar., 2003—; contbr. articles to profl. jours. Bd. dirs. Iowa Civil Liberties Union, 1987-88; chairperson office svcs. for persons with disabilities program rev. com., U. Iowa, 1987-88, law sch. ombudsperson, 1991. Charlotte W. Newcombe Doctoral Dissertation fellow Woodrow Wilson Fellowship Found., 1985-86; Old Gold fellow U. Iowa, 1987, 88, 89, Moody Grant Lyndon Baines Johnson Fdn., 1998, Theodore C. Sorenson Fell., JFK Libr. Fdn., 1997, Orgn. Am. Historians-Japanese Assn. for Am. Studies fellow 2000; travel grantee Eisenhower World Affairs Inst., 1993; recipient Scholars Devel. award Harry S. Truman Libr. Inst., 1990. Fellow Am. Coun. on Learned Soc., 2006-, Mem. Am. Soc. Legal History (mem. com. on documentary preservation 1988-2000, mem. program com. for 1988 conf., mem. exec. com., bd. dirs. 1990-92, 95-97, chairperson program com. 1993, mem. nominating com. 1999-2001, chair nominating com. 2001), Am. Hist. Assn. (Littleton-Griswold rsch. grantee 1987), Am. Studies Assn. (mem. nominating com. 1999-2002, chair nominating com. 2002), Assn. Am. Law Schs. (sec.-treas. legal history sect. 1987, vice chair 1988, chair 1989), Law and Soc. Assn. (bd. trustees, 2005-, mem. com., 2004-06, mem. Hurst prize com. 1992), Orgn. Am. Historians, Soc. Am. Law Tchrs., Soc. for Historians Am. Fgn. Rels. Democrat. Office: U So Calif Law Sch Los Angeles CA 90089-0001

DUENAS, LAURENT FLORES, health and nursing consultant; b. Yigo, Guam, Jan. 9, 1947; d. Joaquin Garcia and Maria Acosta (Calvo) Flores; m. Jimmy J. Duenas, Jan. 9, 1971; children: James Richard, Sherry Marie, Kenneth Ray. ADN, U. Guam, 1968; BSN, Mont. State U., 1969; MPH, U. Hawaii, Manao, 1984. RN, Guam, 1968, Mont., 1969; CNA, NLN; cert. SMDP trng., Internat. Pub. Health. Staff nurse Dept. Pub. Health and Social Svc., Guam, 1969—70, nurse supr. I Guam, 1970—71, nurse supr. II Guam, 1972—78, asst. adminstr. Bur. Cmty. Health and Nursing Svc. Guam, 1978—89, detailed adminstr. Guam, 1986—88, adminstr. Guam, 1989—95, ret. Guam, 1995. Health and nursing cons. Guam Legislature and U. Guam, 1996—,"HLATTE" project dir. U. GU, 2003-; adj. faculty health adminstrn., 1999-, bd. dir., chair Pacific Basin Maternal Child Health Resource Ctr., Mangilao, Guam, 1984-96, Pacific Basin MCH coord., Honolulu, 1984-95; mem. State and Territorial Dir. Nursing, 1987-98; mem. Interagy. Leadership Consortium for Individual's with Spl. Needs, 1990-98; mem. Maternal Child Health Task Force, 1996-98, Governor's Vision, 2000; Health Task Force, 1996-2000; chair Nurse Leaders Com., 1995-98, mem., 1998-2000; preceptor nursing students U.Guam, 1995—; bd. dir. Pacific Island Primary Care Assn., 2003-, bd. dir. Pacific Assn. Clin. Tng., 2003-; affiliate mem. Pacific Island Health Officers APNLC, 2003-; presenter in field. Author: Caring for Young Children, modified version, 1998. Recipient Centennial Award Nat. League of Nursing, 1994, Governor's Chief Gadao Disting. Award, 1995. Mem. ANA, APHA, Y'netnon Famaloan Dem. Women Leaders, Am. Pacific Nursing Leaders (coun. pres. 2001-05, treas., 1986-92, vice mem. 1986—), Commn. on Licensure, Guam Bd. Nurses Examiners (bd. dir., chair 1981-90), Guam Nurses Assn. (bd. dir. 1992-94, Leadership Award 1988, Nursing Excellence Award 1990, Guam Nurse of Yr. 1993, Pub. Health Unit Award 1994, Guam Legis. Resolution 1995, 98, CDC Minority Health Champions Health Equity award, 2004), Orgn. Health and Med. Profl. Women (treas. 2003—), Pacific Island Health Officers Assn., Pacific Island Primary Care Assn. (bd. dirs., v.p., 2003), Pacific Assn. Clin. Tng. (bd. dirs., 2003-), Assn. Tchrs. Preventative Medicine. Democrat. Roman Catholic. Avocations: crocheting, collecting recipes, baking, campaign strategies, visiting sick. Home: 3 N Cupa Perez Acres Yigo GU 96929-0142 Office: Univ Guam HLATTE Project UOG Sta Mangilao GU 96923 Business E-Mail: hlatte05@gmail.com.

DUENSING, DOROTHY JEAN, music educator, vocalist; d. George Prescott Duensing I and Patricia Ann (dec.) Gasthoff-Duensing, Catherine Dew-Duensing (Stepmother); m. Michael William Miller, Nov. 9, 1997 (div. Nov. 18, 2004); m. Thomas Andrew Cormie, Oct. 10, 1987 (div. Oct. 3, 1996); 1 child, Mason Andrew Cormie. MusB, Ind. U., 1984; MusM, U. of Mich., 1990. Orff Schulwerk Music-Level I Madonna U., Livonia, Mich., 2001, Orff Schulwerk Music-Level II Madonna U., Livonia, Mich., 2002, Orff Schulwerk Music-Level III Madonna U., Livonia, Mich., 2003. Adj. prof. voice Wayne State U. Dept. Music, Detroit, 1999—; educator, primary music dir. Acad. Sacred Heart, Bloomfield Hills, Mich., 2000—03; dir. mid. sch. vocal music Sherman Mid. Sch., 2004—, Richter Intermediate Sch. Holly Area Schs., Holly, Mich., 2004—. Soprano soloist, sect. leader Christ Episcopal Ch., Dearborn, Mich., 1986—94; part-time voice faculty Ctr. for Creative Studies' Inst. of Music and Dance, Detroit, 1990—2000; alto soloist, sect. leader Temple Israel, West Bloomfield, Mich., 1991—97; artist-in-residence Toledo Opera Co., 1991—99; performing artist Omni Arts in Edn., Southfield, Mich., 1992—; full-time vocal music substitute U. Liggett Mid. and Upper Schools, Grosse Pointe Farms, Mich., 1996; part-time voice, piano faculty Ward Church's Christian Sch. of Fine and Performing Arts, Northville Twp., Mich., 1998—2002; adj. prof. voice William Tyndale Coll., Farmington Hills, Mich., 2001—02; alto soloist, sect. leader Met. United Meth. Ch., Detroit, 2001—02, First Presbyn. Ch., Royal Oak, Mich., 2002—. Choral music dir. Music Study Club, Detroit, 1995—96, Bel Canto Choral Group, Southfield, Mich., 1998—2001; deacon Faith Cmty. Presbyn. Ch., Novi, Mich., 1998—2000; teen choir dir. Faith Cmty. Presbyn., Novi, Mich., 1999—2000. Recipient Hazel Mueller Meml. award, Interlochen Ctr. for the Performing Arts, 1979, 1980, First Pl. Vocalist in the State of Mich., Mich. Schs. Vocal Music Assn., 1980, Dist. Finalist, Met. Opera Assn. (Midwest Dist.), 1991, Second Pl. Winner, Harold Haugh Light Opera Vocal Competition, Ann Arbor, MI, 2001; scholar Interlochen Alumnae Scholarship for Half Tuition at Nat. Music Camp, Interlochen Ctr. for the Performing Arts, 1979, Scholarship, Iota Epsilon Patroness Chpt., Bloomington, IN, 1983, Patricia Brinton-Becirovic Meml. Scholarship, Am. Inst. of Musical Studies, Austria, 1989. Mem.: Livonia Area Piano Tchrs. Forum, Mich. Music Tchrs. Assn., Music Tchrs. Nat. Assn., Detroit Orff Schulwerk Assn., Nat. Orff Schulwerk Assn., Nat. Assn. Tchrs. Singing, Nat. Fedn. Music Clubs' Tuesday Musicale Detroit, PEO Sisterhood, Chpt. FE, Novi, MI (life; chaplain 2001—02), Sigma Alpha Iota (life; Detroit Alumnae chptr. v.p. mem. 2002—). Office: Wayne State U Dept of Music 1321 Old Main Bldg Studio #2315 Detroit MI 48202 Mailing: PO Box 107 Novi MI 48376-0107 Personal E-mail: Divaduensing@aol.com.

DUER, ELLEN ANN DAGON, anesthesiologist, general practitioner; b. Balt., Feb. 3, 1936; d. Emmett Paul and Annie (Sollers) Dagon; m. Lyle Jordan Millan IV, Dec. 21, 1963; children: Lyle Jordan V, Elizabeth Lyle, Ann Sheridan Worthington.; m. T. Marshall Duer, Jr., Aug. 23, 1985. AB, George Washington U., 1959; MD, U. Md., 1964; postgrad., Johns Hopkins U., 1965—68. Intern Union Meml. Hosp., Balt., 1964—65; resident in anesthesiology Johns Hopkins Hosp., Balt., 1965—68, fellow in surgery, 1965—68; practice medicine specializing in anesthesiology Balt., 1968—; faculty Ch. Home and Hosp., Balt., 1969—; attending staff Union Meml. Hosp., Ch. Home and Hosp., Franklin Sq. Hosp., Children's Hosp., James Lawrence Kernan Hosp., Balt., 1982—94; co-chief anesthesiology James Kernan Hosp., 1983—94, med. dir. out-patient surgery dept., 1987—94. Affiliate cons. emergency room Ch. Home and Hosp., Balt., 1969—, med. audit and utilizaions com., 1970-72, mem. emergency and ambulatory care com., 1973-74, chief emergency dept., 1973-74; cons. anesthesiologist Md. State Penitentiary, 1971; fellow in critical care medicine Md. Inst. Emergency Medicine, 1975-76; infection control com. U. Md. Hosp., 1975—; instr. anesthesiology U. Md. Sch. Medicine, 1975—; staff anesthesiologist Mercy Hosp., 1978—, audit com., 1979-80, 82; asst. prof. anesthegiology U. Md. Med. Sch., 1989-94; med. exec. com. Kernan Hosp., 1990-94, v.p. 1990, chief of staff, 1992—; active Tappahannock Family Practice, 1994-96, Rappahannock Gen. Hosp. Family Practice, 1996—, Rappahannock Gen. Hosp., 1996—, ethics com., 1997—; med. examiner No. Neck of Va., 1996—; active Commonwealth of Va. Med. Bd. Mem. AMA, Am. Coll. Emergency Physicians, Am. Acad. Gen. Practitioners, Met. Emergency Dept. Heads Am., Md. Soc. Anesthesiologists, Balt. County Med. Soc., Mid. Peninsula Med. Soc., No. Neck Med. Soc., Med. Soc. Va., Med. and Choir Faculty Med., Chirurg. Soc., Internat. Congress Anaesthesiologists, Internat. Anesthesia Rsch. Soc., Am. L'Hirondelle Club, Annapolis Yacht Club, Chesapeake Bay Yacht Racing Assn., Rappahannock River Yacht Club. Anglican. Address: PO Box 347 White Stone VA 22578-2021 Office Phone: 804-462-5155.

DUERR, DIANNE MARIE, sports medicine consultant, educator; b. Buffalo, July 14, 1945; d. Robert John and Aileen Louise D. BS in Health and Phys. Edn., SUNY, Brockport, 1967; cert., SUNY, Oswego, 1982; postgrad., Canisius Coll., 1970-71. Cert. tchr. NY. Tchr. North Syracuse (NY) Sch. Dist., 1967—2004; project dir. dept. orthop. surgery SUNY Upstate Med. U., Syracuse, 1982—2003; creator Inst. for Human Performance SUNY Health Sci. Ctr., Syracuse, 1988. Coord. scholastic sports injury reporting system project SUNY, 1985-98; mem. com. on scholastic sports-related injuries NIH Inst. Arthritis, Musculoskeletal and Skin Diseases, 1993-96; project dir. dept. orthop. surgery North Syracuse Ctrl. Sch. Dist., 1967-2004. Author: SSIRS Pilot Study Report, 1987, SSIRS Fall Study Report, 1988, SHASIRS Report, 1991; creator Scholastic Sports Injury Reporting System, 1985, Scholastic Head and Spine Injury Reporting System, 1989. Co-chmn. sports medicine USA Amateur Athletic Union, Nat. Jr. Olympic Games, Syracuse, NY, 1987; vol. sports medicine NY State Sr. Games, 1990—95, sports medicine coord., 1990—95, US Roller Skating Nat. Championships, 1995, NY State Womens Lacrosse Championships, 1995, US Nat. Precision Ice Skating Championships, 1997, Youth Basketball of Am., Northeast Regional Tournament, 1999; co-chmn. healthcare, security Empire State Games, Syracuse, 2002; mem. com. sports injury surveillance Ctrs. for Disease Control, 1995; cons. NY Sci., Tech. and Soc. Edn. Project, 1995. Mem. AAUW, NY State AAHPERD (pres. exercise sci. and sports medicine sect., 1994-98), Am. Coll. Sports Medicine, United Univ. Profs., Women's Sports Fedn., Am. Fedn. Tchrs., NY United Tchrs., North Syracuse Tchrs. Assn., Phi Kappa Phi. Avocations: swimming, bicycling, ice skating, reading, photography. Office: 418 Buffington Rd Syracuse NY 13224-2208 Office Phone: 315-449-9509. Personal E-mail: dmduerr@twcny.rr.com.

DUESBERRY, JOELLYN TOLER, artist; b. Richmond, Va., June 30, 1944; d. Arthur Reginald and Joellyn Dean (Toler) D.; m. Dr. Ira Kowal; stepchildren: Rebekah, Jessica. Student, U. Va., 1962-64; BA with distinction, Smith Coll., 1966; MA, NYU, 1967; postgrad., Dartmouth Coll., 1967-68. Instr. in landscape painting Art Students League of Denver, 1989—. One woman shows include Tatistcheff Gallery, N.Y.C., 1979, 81, 83, 85, Gerald Peters Gallery, N.Mex., 1986-2000, Graham Modern Gallery, N.Y.C., 1989-2004, Denver Art Mus., 1992; numerous exhbns.; traveling monotype exhbn. Va. Mus. Fine Arts, 1998-2005, Tremaine Gallery, Hotchkiss, 2005—. Woodrow Wilson fellow NYU Inst. Fine Arts, 1966-67; NEA grantee, 1985. Mem. Phi Beta Kappa. Avocations: helicopter skiing, gardening, xeriscape. Home: 2800 E Willamette Ln Greenwood Village CO 80121-1615 Office: 35 Thimble House Trail Millbrook NY 12545 Office Phone: 303-770-3716. Business E-Mail: studio@joellynduesberry.com.

DUFENDACH, PAULA J., elementary school educator; d. Lyle and Donna Hawkins; m. David Dufendach, May 26, 1979; children: Krisha Smith, Kurt. BS, Calvin Coll., Grand Rapids, 1979; BA, Conerstone U., Grand Rapids, 1979. Lic. tchr. Mich., 1979. Jr. high social studies tchr. Coopersville Area Pub. Sch., Mich., 1994—. Program dir. Brook Cherith Camp, Pierson, Mich., 1998—2002. Children's programming Ravenna (Mich.) Bapt. Ch., 1989—98. Office Phone: 616-997-3442.

DUFF, HILARY ANN, actress, singer; b. Houston, Sept. 28, 1987; d. Bob and Susan Duff. Released own product line Stuff by Hilary Duff. Actor: (TV films) True Women, 1997, Soul Collector, 1999; (TV series) Lizzie McGuire, 2001—03; (films) Human Nature, 2001, Cadet Kelly, 2002, Agent Cody Banks, 2003, The Lizzie McGuire Movie, 2003, Cheaper by the Dozen, 2003, A Cinderella Story, 2004, Raise Your Voice, 2004, The Perfect Man, 2005, Cheaper by the Dozen 2, 2005, Material Girls, 2006, (TV appearances) Chicago Hope, 2000, George Lopez, 2003, American Dreams, 2003, Frasier (voice), 2004; singer: (albums) Lizzie McGuire Television Soundtrack, 2001, Santa Claus Lane, 2002, The Lizzie McGuire Movie Soundtrack, 2003, (debut solo album) Metamorphosis, 2003 (charted #2 on Billboard 200 first week of release);: (albums) Hilary Duff, 2004, Most Wanted, 2005. Internat. spokesperson Kids With A Cause, 1999—. Recipient Nickelodeon Kids Choice Award for Favorite Female Singer, 2004. Office: Pmk Hbh Public Relations 161 Avenue Of The Americas Rm 10r New York NY 10013-1205*

DUFF, PATRICIA, civic activist; b. L.A., Apr. 12, 1954; d. Robert Orr and Mary Williamson; 1 child, Caleigh Sophia Perelman. Student, Internat. Sch. Brussels, 1971, Barnard Coll.; BS in Internat. Econs., Georgetown U., 1976. Spl. asst. to chief counsel house select com. on assassinations U.S. Ho. of Reps., Washington, 1976-78; prodr., writer, researcher John McLaughlin Show-NBC Radio, Washington, 1979-80; asst. rsch. dir. Dem. Nat. Com., Washington, 1980; v.p. Patrick Caddell and Assocs., Washington, 1980-82, Squier, Eskew Assoc., 1982-84; with Mondale for Pres., L.A., 1984, Americans for Hart, L.A., 1984; ind. producer Columbia Pictures, Burbank, Calif.; pres. Revlon Found., 1995-97. Assoc. producer Dem. Nat. Conv., Atlanta, 1988; mem. nat. media adv. bd. Hart for Pres., L.A., 1988 Contbg. editor Vogue Mag., 1989; editor at large Premier Mag., 1995-97; host Duff Talk, Plum TV, 2004—; guest co-host WABC-Radio, 2004-05 Founder Am. Spirit Awards, 1992; chair N.Y. Gov.'s Task Force on Teen Pregnancy, 1994—95, Women Vote Campaign of Emily's List, 1996, Saves Women's Leadership Coun., 1999—2004; mem. platform com. Dem. Nat. Conv., 1984, 1992; mem. Hollywood Women's Polit. Com., 1986; co-chair N.Y. fin. com. Clinton for Pres., 1996; bd. dirs. People for the Am. Way, 1996—2002; mem. bd. councilors Ascus sch. pub. policy and adminstrn. U. So. Calif.; founder, chair bd. dirs. Show Coalition The Common Good, L.A., 1988—; mem. bd. visitors Sch. Fgn. Svc. Georgetown U., 1988—; mem. pvt. sector adv. bd. Inter Am. Devel. Bank; bd. trustees Save the Children, chmn., 2006; bd. dirs. L.A. Colors United, Summer of Svc., Nat. Svc., 1993, L.A. Commn. on Status of Women, 1994—96, Women in Film, 1990—, Lincoln Ctr. Film Soc., 1995—2000; trustee Nat. Pub. Radio, Am. Ballet Theatre, 1995—96; mem. Presdl. Commn. on Libr. of Congress Trust Fund, 1994—2000; founder Families for Justice, 2004. Named one of Rising Young Stars L.A. Times, 1989; named Dem. of Yr. L.A. County, 1989; recipient Women We Love award for polit. activism Esquire Mag., 1990, Women in Film award Women in Film, 1995, Citizen's Achievement award NDD, 1998. Office Phone: 212-722-6390. Personal E-mail: mspduff@aol.com.

DUFFEY, ROSALIE RUTH, elementary school educator; b. Randolph, Mo., July 4, 1938; d. Joseph Anthony and Katherine Ruth Spruytte; m. Robert Lee Duffey, Oct. 20, 1956; children: Susan, Carolyn, Janice, Maryann, Philip, David, Mark. AS in Early Childhood Edn., Ctrl. Mo. State U., 1973, BS in Edn., 1977, MS in Edn., 1980. Cert. tchr. elem. and spl. edn. Mo. Dir. ednl. ops. Head Start West Ctrl. Mo. Rural Devel. Corp., Appleton City, 1966—79; tchr. spl. edn. Butler (Mo.) Elem. Sch., 1979—87; tchr. Parents as Tchrs. Cass RIX Pub. Sch., Harrisonville, Mo., 1987—98; tchr. Marillac Sch., Kansas City, Mo., 1998—99, Trails West State Schs. for Severely Handicapped, Kansas City, 1999—. Mem. policy coun. Head Start, Appleton City; foster parent Divsn. of Family Svcs., Cass and Henry Counties, Mo., 1977—2000. Mem.: Ctrl. Mo. State U. Alumni Assn., Mo. State Ret. Tchrs. Assn., Assn. of Retarded Citizens, Coun. for Exceptional Children, Alpha Phi Delta, Kappa Delta Pi, Phi Kappa Phi, Alpha Phi Sigma. Roman Catholic. Avocations: quilting, gardening, walking.

DUFFY, ANNE M., artist; b. Fairbanks, AK, Sept. 26, 1974; d. Lawrence Kevin and Geraldine Antoinette D. BFA, Univ. Alaska, Fairbanks, AK, 1996; MFA, Pratt Inst., Brooklyn, NY, 1999. Exhibits asst. Univ. Alaska Mus., Fairbanks, AK, 1995-96; lectr. Univ. Alaska, Summer Fine Arts Grp., Fairbanks, AK, 1995, 97-98; advtg. creative cons. Coldwell Banker, Fairbanks, AK, 1996—; editl. asst., pub. rels. Univ. Wash., Seattle, 1999—. Adv. bd. of med., Univ. Wash., Seattle, WA, 1999—, art creative cons., Coldwell Banker, Fairbanks, AK, 1996—. Artist of fine arts, Phylum (show title), 1999, Linum, 1999, Tendere, 1999; contbr. conf. paper in field of libr. and info. sci. Mem. Amnesty Internat., Brooklyn, NY, 1996-99, Fairbanks, AK, 1992-96, Seattle, WA, 1999—. Recipient Bogardus Scholarship, Pratt Inst. Sch. of Libr. & Info. Sci., 1997, 98, 99, rsch. awd., ACRL, Blackwell's Book Svcs., 1999. Mem. Pratt Artists League, 1996—, Golden Key Honor Soc., 1995—, Pratt Inst. Alumni Assn., 1999—, Univ. Alaska Alumni Assn., 1996—, Friends of Univ. of Alaska Mus., 1994—, Phi Kappa Phi, 1996—. Avocations: architecture, writing, travel. Home: care Heather Hayworth 33212 124th St SE Sultan WA 98294-8674 E-mail: aduffy1475@washington.edu.

DUFFY, CHERYL HOFSTETTER, language educator; b. Hill City, Kans., June 23, 1959; d. Paul Louis and Deloris Luhman Hofstetter; m. Robert Edward Duffy, June 5, 1999; m. John Oliver Towns, Aug. 17, 1978 (dec. June 18, 1995); 1 child, Anna Marie Towns. At, Colby C.C., Kans., 1977—78; BSE in English, Emporia State U., Kans., 1981; MA in English, Fort Hays, Kans., 1984; PhD in English, U. Kans., Lawrence, 1996. Writing ctr. tutor Emporia State U., 1978—80; English instr. Colby CC, 1981—86; disabled student svcs. coord. Ft. Hays State U., 1986—88, English instr., 1988—89; curriculum writing specialist Kans. State Dept. Edn., Topeka, 1989—90; gta U. Kans., 1991—92; assoc. prof. English Ft. Hays State U., 1992—, chair English dept., 2004—. Svc.-learning faculty cons. comty. svc. program Kans. State U., 2002—. Author: Teaching Civic Literacy and Research, 2006; contbr. articles to profl. jours. Mem.: Nat. Coun. of Tchrs. of English. Office: Fort Hays State U English Dept 600 Park St Hays KS 67601 Office Phone: 785-628-4285. Business E-Mail: cduffy@fhsu.edu.

DUFFY, NANCY KEOGH, newscaster, broadcast executive; b. Washington, Nov. 24, 1947; d. William Francis and Gertrude K. (Keogh) D.; divorced; children: Peter Patrick, Matthew Michael. Student, St. Mary of the Woods Coll.; AB, Marywood Coll., 1967. News reporter Sta. WHEN TV and Radio, Syracuse, NY, 1967-70; press sec. City of Syracuse, 1970; news reporter Sta. WTVH, Syracuse, 1971-77; news anchorperson Sta. WIXT-TV, Syracuse, 1977—. Talk show host Syracuse New Channels, 1986-87; talk show host, producer Community Connections, 1987-89; instr. Syracuse U. Prodr. TV series Duffy's People, With Steve on Sunday. Founder Syracuse St. Patrick's Parade, 1983, pres., organizer, 1983-2001, hon. pres., 2002-; organizer Cooperstown 50th Ann. Baseball Hall of Fame Parade, 1989, opening ceremonies Empire State Games, 1990; co-organizer Save Our Syracuse Symphony, 1984—; organizer Bark-Out Against Rabies Paws Parade, 1995-98, Artist Eagle Faces Exhibits, 1999-2003; bd. dirs. Syracuse Symphony, 1992-98, The Media Unit, 1977-97; active Project children, Syracuse, YMCA; telethon hostess Muscular Dystrophy Assn.; organizer poetry workshops for children, 1995—; mem. Onondaga County Traffic Safety Bd., 1977-2002, Le Moyne Coll. Pres. Assocs.; honorary chair, Civil War Weekend, Peterborough, NY.; bd. dirs. Native Am. Svc. Agy., 2002. Recipient Nat. Angel award Best Spl. Religion in Media, Post Std. Woman of Achievement award, 1st Downtown award for excellence, 1986, Mayor's Achievement award, 1985, Humanitarian award Project Children, 1993, N.Y. State Senate commendation, 1995; named Woman of Achievement N.Y. State Fair, 1994, YWCA Acad. Diversity Achievers, 2004. Mem. Am. Women in Radio and TV (nat. award 1973), Women in Comms. (Outstanding Communicator award 1985), Syracuse Press Club (bd. dirs. 1987—, v.p. 1990, 97, 98, pres. 1991-92, Bernard and Dorothy Newer Svc. award 1995, lifetime achievement award 2000), Syracuse Rotary (pub. rels. 1989-92), Am. Heart Assn. (hon. co-chair Ctrl. N.Y. 1997). Roman Catholic. Office: Sta WIXT-TV 5904 Bridge St East Syracuse NY 13057-2941 Office Phone: 315-446-9999.

DUFFY, NATALIE W., retired physical education educator; b. Brockton, Mass. d. Henry Joseph and Irene Anderson Willman; m. Philip Edward Duffy; children: Edward, Henry. BS, Tufts U., Medford, Mass.; MS, Syracuse U., N.Y. Instr. Carleton Coll., Northfield, Minn., Beaver Coll., Jenkintown, Pa., Syracuse U., NY; prof. Fairleight Dickinson U., Teaneck, NJ; ret. Dir. Fairleigh Dickinson U. Dance Group, 1982. Author: Modern Dance, 1982. Trustee Silver Bay YMCA, NY, YMCA, Ridgewood, NJ. Home: 56 Burroughs Rd Easton CT 06612

DUFFY, VIRGINIA, minister; b. Cleve., Apr. 10, 1939; d. Paul Daniel and Anna (Nagy) Szaniszlo; 1 child, Steven T. Eisentrout. BA, Elmhurst Coll., Ill., 1962; MA, Oberlin Coll., Ohio, 1965; MDiv, Oberlin Grad. Sch. Theology, Ohio, 1966; MA, Coll. Mount St. Joseph, Cin., 1982. Ordained Min. United Ch. Christ, 1966, cert. Secondary Tchr. Ohio, 1982. Assoc. min. First Congl. United Ch. Christ, Elyria, Ohio, 1965—71, United Ch. in Walpole, Mass., 1971—73; co-min. Mt. Zion St. Paul United Chs. of Christ, New Richmond, Ohio, 1976—83; tchr. West Clermont Local Sch. Dist., Amelia, Ohio, 1984—94; co-min. York St. Congl. United Ch. Christ, Newport, Ky., 1988—90; min., sr. min. Philippus United Ch. Christ, Cin., 1994—2004; interim min., cons. Southwest Ohio No. Ky. Assn., 2005—. Corp. bd. mem. United Ch. Christ, United States, 1996—99; bd. dirs. Religare Assembly Greater Cin. No. Ky., Cin., 1995—99; assoc. coun. Southwest Ch. No. Ky. Assn., Southwest, Ohio, 1977—83. Author of poems, (ednl. resource) The Healthy Life: A Biblical Approach, 1989; co-author: Called tobe Gifted and Giving, 1985. Bd. dirs., chair, vice chair United Ch. Homes, 2000—; bd. trustees IMPACT Over the Rhine, Cin., 1995—2004, Vol. Am., Cin., 1996—2000, Recipient Outstanding Young Women Am., 1971, Excellence Tchg., Cin. Gas and Elec., 1992. Mem.: Delta Kappa Gamma. United Church Of Christ. Avocations: music, reading. Home: 2921 Timberview Dr Cincinnati OH 45211

DUFKA, CORINNE, human rights activist; BA in Social Work, San Francisco State U., 1979; MSW, U. Calif., Berkeley, 1984. Soc. worker, El Salvador; photojournalist Reuters, 1989—99; rschr. Human Rights Watch, Sierra Leone, 1999—2003; rsch. and cons. Chief Investigators and the Prosecutor on the UN-backed Spl. Ct. for Sierra Leone, 2003—; mem. African Div. of Human Rights Watch. Fellow MacArthur Found., 2003. Office: 350 Fifth Ave 34th flr New York NY 10118

DUFNER, DONNA KANE, management information systems, project management educator; b. Greensburg, Pa., July 9, 1948; d. Clarence E. and Marie Anna Daniels; m. John Raymond Kevern, Dec. 23, 1995; 1 child, Kathleen Elizabeth. BA in Sociology cum laude, DePaul U., 1975; MBA, U. Chgo., 1977; MS in Computer and Info. Scis., N.J. Inst. Tech., 1995; PhD in IT Mgmt., Rutgers U., 1995. Cert. project mgmt. profl. 2004. Cons. Planmetrics, Chgo., 1977-79; project mgr. AT&T, U.S. and Ireland, 1979-84; asst. v.p. Chem. N.Y. Corp., 1985-88; wireless networks project mgr. ARDIS (joint venture IBM and Motorola), 1991-94; asst. prof. Poly. U., NY, 1994-96, U. Ill., Springfield, 1996-00, U. Nebr., Omaha, 2000—03, assoc. prof., 2003—. Cons. proj. mgmt. Bell Atlantic/NYNEX, N.J., 1996, ICGS, 1999, Omaha/Douglas County, 2000-03; tchg. fellow Rutgers U., N.J., 1989-90; guest speaker NY Acad. Scis., 1995. Editl. bd. Comm. AIS; contr. articles to profl. jours. Docent Bahai House of Worship, Wilmette, Ill., 1979-82. Recipient Edna True Meritorious Svc. award Bahai Nat. Assembly, 1984, Univ. Scholar award U. Ill., 1998, Outstanding Tchg. award, U. Nebr. Alumni, 2002, Excellence in Tchg. award, 2006. Mem. IEEE (named Outstanding Referee 1998-99, sr. referee, 1998—, Project Mgmt. Profl. Cert.), Assn. Info. Sys., Project Mgmt. Inst., Omaha Women's Leadership Inst. (leadership), Beta Gamma Sigma. Bahai. Avocations: hiking, cross country skiing, cooking, sculpture, pottery. Office: U Nebr Coll Info Sci and Tech Rm 174I Peter Kiewit Inst 110 South 67th St Omaha NE 68182-0392 Business E-Mail: ddufner@mail.unomaha.edu.

DUFRESNE, ELIZABETH JAMISON, retired lawyer; b. Winter Haven, Fla., July 29, 1942; d. John W. and Thelma M. (Kinney) Jamison; 1 child, Brennan. BA, Vanderbilt U., 1964; JD, U. Fla., 1966. Bar: U.S. Dist. Ct. (so. dist.) Fla. 1967, U.S. Dist. Ct. (mid. dist.) Fla. 1968, U.S. Ct. Appeals (5th cir.) 1968, U.S. Supreme Ct. 1969, U.S. Ct. Appeals (11th cir.) 1981. Atty. So. Fla. Migrant Legal Svc., Miami, 1967-69; law reform chief Greater Miami Legal Svc., Miami, 1969-71; assoc. Tobias Simon P.A., Miami, 1971; ptnr. Tobias Simon & Elizabeth duFresne, P.A., Miami, 1971-77; sr. ptnr. duFresne & duFresne, P.A., Miami, 1977-82, duFresne & Bradley, P.A., Miami, 1982-86; equity ptnr. Steel, Hector & Davis, Miami, 1986—2000, bd. dirs., chmn. labor law divsn., ret., 2000. Adj. prof. law U. Miami, Coral Gables, Fla., 1977-93; mem. Civil Justice Adv. Group USDC, S.D. Fla., 1990-2000. Recipient Award of Honor ACLU, Dade, 1969, Award of Merit ACLU, Fla., 1970, 73. Mem. ABA, Fla. Bar Assn. (Pioneer award 1977), Dade County Bar Assn., Fed. Bar Assn., Assn. Trial Lawyers Am., Assn. Trial Lawyers Fla., Fla. Assn. Women Lawyers. Democrat. Roman Catholic. Avocations: cooking, reading, racquetball, bicycling, sailing.

DUGAN, CINDY, music educator, organist; b. Grenada, Miss., Aug. 6, 1953; d. Clovis Jr. and Geraldine McGregor) Harden; children: Dawn Dugan Looney, Clayton Hunter. B Music Edn. cum laude, U. Miss., 1975, M Music Edn., 1993. Pvt. tchr. piano, Grenada, 1975—; tchr. music Kirk Acad., Grenada, 1975—; organist 1st Bapt. Ch., Grenada, 1978—; prof. music Holmes C.C., Grenada, 1993—. Former mem., bd. dirs. Fine Arts Coun., Grenada 1985-90. Mem. Nat. Music Tchrs. Assn. (nat. cert. tchr.), Nat. Piano Guild (piano adjudicator 1992—), Miss. Music Tchrs. Assn. (piano adjudictor 1993—), Former 20th Century Club (membership officer 1999), Phi Kappa Phi. Baptist. Avocations: reading, walking. Home: 94 Semmes Rd Grenada MS 38901-8820

DUGAN, MAUREEN, biology educator, consultant; b. Boston; d. John and Catherine (Cahill) Dugan. BA, Framingham State Coll., Mass., 1971; MEd, Boston Coll., Chestnut Hill, Mass., 1980. Cert. Tchr. Commonwealth Mass., 1971, Nat. Bd. Certification AYA/Sci Nat. Bd. for Profl. Tchg. Stds., 1999. Tchr. sci. Nashoba Regional Sch. Dist., Bolton, Mass., 1971—. Cons. Coll. Bd., N.Y.C., NY, 2001—. Named Outstanding Biology Tchr. Mass., Nat. Assn. Biology Tchrs., 2002; recipient Who's Who Among America's Teachers, 1993. Mem.: Mass. Tchrs. Assn., Mass. Audubon Soc., Appalachian Mountain Club. Roman Catholic. Home: 87 Old County Rd Lancaster MA 01523

DUGGAN, CAROL COOK, research and development company executive; b. Dillon, SC, May 25, 1946; d. Pierce Embree and Lillian Watkins (Eller) Cook; m. Kevin Duggan, Dec. 29, 1973. BA, Columbia Coll., 1968; MS, U. Ky., 1970. Reference asst. Richland County Pub. Libr., Columbia, S.C., 1968-69, asst. to dir., 1970, chief adult svcs., 1971-82; dir. Maris Rsch., Columbia, 1982—. Lectr. Greater Columbia (S.C.) Literacy Coun., 1973—75. Author: A History of the City of Forest Acres, S.C., 1998. Treas. Friends of S.C. Libr., 1995—2003; mem. zoning bd. appeals City of Forest Acres, 1999—; worship com. Washington St. United Meth. Ch., Columbia, SC, 1985—86, 1999—, mem. staff-parish rels. com., 1985—91, 2004—, chmn. staff-parish rels. com., 1993, trustee, 1995—98, mem. adminstr. bd., 1983—86, mem. adminstr. br., 1988—91, mem. adminstr. bd., 1993, mem. ch. coun., 2004—; exec. bd. United Meth. Women, 1983—2001, treas. unit 7, 1989—91, pres. unit 5, 1992—97, treas., 1998—; adminstrv. bd. Washington St. United Meth. Ch., Columbia, SC, 1988—91, 1993; del. S.C. Ann. Conf. of United Meth. Ch., 2004—. Recipient Sternheimer award, Columbia Coll., 1968. Mem.: PEO (pres. 1983—85, chmn. amendments and recommendations com. 1983—85, historian 1986—87, treas. state conv. 1987—88, historian 1990—92, v.p. 1998—99, del. internat. conv. 1999, historian 2002—04), DAR, ALA (chmn. state membership com. 1979—83, councilor 1980—82), S.C. Pub. Libr. Assn. (pres. 1980—81), S.C. Libr. Assn. (sec. 1976, exec. bd. 1976, 1978—82), Columbia Coll. Alumnae Assn. (alumnae coun. spl. events com. 1996—, Columbia Coll. Commn. 150 2003), Beta Phi Mu. Methodist. Home: 2101 Woodmere Dr Columbia SC 29204-4341

DUGGAN, JUANITA D., trade association administrator; BS, Georgetown U., 1982. Spl. asst. to Pres. for pub. liaison Exec. Office of Pres. Ronald Reagan, dir. domestic policy divsn., 1987—88; exec. sec. domestic policy coun. Exec. Office of Pres. George H.W. Bush, 1989, spl. asst. to Pres. for cabinet affairs, 1989—90; exec. v.p. govt. affairs and comm. Nat. Food Processors Assn.; v.p. fed. rels. Philip Morris Corp., Inc., 1996—98; pres., CEO Am. Forest and Paper Assn., 2006—. Pres., CEO Wine & Spirits Wholesalers Am., Inc. Office: Am Forest and Paper Assn 1111 19th St NW Ste 800 Washington DC 20036 Office Phone: 202-463-2700. Office Fax: 202-463-2785.*

DUGGER, MARGUERITE J., retired special education educator; b. Iron River, Mich., Oct. 14, 1916; d. August John Waffen and Ethel May James; m. Clifford Rayson (dec.); 1 child, Suzanne (dec.); m. James A. Dugger; stepchildren: James II, John, Elaine Shaw, Robert. BS, Ea. Mich. U., 1938; MA, Wayne State U., 1952, EdD, 1969. Tchr. physically handicapped Battle Creek Pub. Schs., 1938—51; spl. edn. tchr., summers Syracuse U., 1950—52; prin. Gorman Sch. for Physically Handicapped, Ohio, 1952—55; prin., spl. edn. dir. Kalamazoo Pub. Schs.; edn. dir. Pathway Sch., Phila., 1964; mem. spl. edn. faculty Wayne State U., Detroit, 1965—66; supr. ADHD San Francisco Unified, 1968—72; mem. faculty Western Mich. U., Kalamazoo; coord. spl. edn. Calif. State U., Hayward, 1972—81; ret., 1981. Camping and outdoor activities Battle Creek Pub. Schs., 1941—42. Author: Hands-On Learning in Science, 1982, Adventures and Exceptional Children 1934-1981, 2004. Vol. for homeless, San Francisco, 1992—93; sr. warden St. Andrews Ch., San Bruno, Calif., 1990—93. Recipient Nomads of East Sudan award, Am. Artists for Africa, award, Bd. Edn., Burlingame, Calif.; grantee, Glide Meml. Ch., San Francisco. Mem.: Hamilton Home Owners Assn. (bd. dirs. 1997—99). Democrat. Episcopalian. Home: 555 Byron #102 Palo Alto CA 94301 E-mail: margdugger@aol.com.

DUHAMEL, JUDITH REEDU OLSON, public information officer, former state senator; b. Mitchell, S.D., June 24, 1939; d. John Marvin and Camille (Murphy) Reedy; m. Robert George Olson, Aug. 5, 1961; children: Jeffrey, Jennifer, Jon, Jaime, Jason, Jeremy; m. William F. Duhamel, Aug. 3, 2003. EdB, U. Ariz., Tucson, 1961; MEd, S.D. State U., 1984; postgrad., U. S.D., 1985—. Cert. secondary tchr., edn. adminstrn. Tchr. jr. high sch. Mpls. Pub. Schs., 1961-63; mem. State Bd. Edn., S.D., 1972-83, pres. S.D., 1975-78; dir. S.D. Edn. Policy Seminar, 1975-79; substitute tchr. Rapid City (S.D.) Schs., 1979-81, tchr. adult basic edn., 1979-81, supr. community relations, 1981-88, supr. community edn., pub. info., 1988—95; senator S.D. Legis. (dist. 33), Pierre, SD, 1989—93; edn. dir. Career Learning Center of the Black Hills. Speaker, cons. sch. bds., adminstrs., tchrs., sch. dists., pub. relations, various states, 1972—. Bd. dirs. Black Hills Symphony, 1987—; chair S.D. State Dem. Party, 1998—. Mem. AAUW (Women of Worth award), Rotary, PEO, Delta Kappa Gamma. Democrat. Roman Catholic. Avocations: reading, spectator sports. Office: South Dakota Democratic Party 207 East Capitol Pierre SD 57501-2724 Home: 1106 Hyland Dr Rapid City SD 57701-4456

DUHME, CAROL MCCARTHY, civic worker; b. St. Louis, Apr. 13, 1917; d. Eugene Ross and Louise (Roblee) McCarthy; m. Sheldon Ware, June 12, 1941 (dec. 1944); 1 child, David; m. H. Richard Duhme, Jr., Apr. 9, 1947; children: Benton (dec.), Ann, Warren (dec.). AB, Vassar Coll., 1939; DHL (hon.), Eden Theol. Sem., 2002. Tchr. elem. sch., 1939-41, 42-44; moderator St. Louis Assn. Congl. Chs., 1959—62; trustee 1st Congl. Ch., 1964—66; mem. ch. coun. St. Louis Assn. Congl. Ch., 1974-75, 84-85, 87-89, bd. deaconesses, 1978-81, bd. deacons 1982-85, 92-95, chmn. bd. Christian Edn., 1987-88. Former bd. dirs. Cmty. Music Schs., St. Louis, Cmty. Sch., Ch. Women United, John Burroughs Sch., St. Louis Bicentennial Women's Com., St. Louis Jr. League; pres. St. Louis Vassar Club; pres., bd. dirs. YWCA, St. Louis, 1973-76, chmn. ann. fund, 1989-90; bd. dirs. North Side Team Ministry, 1968-84, Chautauqua (NY) Instn., 1971-79, mem. adv. coun. to bd., 1987—. Mem. adv. coun. Mo. Bapt. Hosp., 1973—89; mem. exec. com. bd. dirs. Eden Theol. Sem., 1981—95, presdl. search com., 1986—87, 1992—93, v.p., bd. dirs., 1991, chmn. 150th ann. com., 1996—2000; sec. bd. dirs. UN Assn., St. Louis, 1976—84, coun. advisors, 1993—, nat. coun., 1995—2001; mem. nat. coun. UN-USA, 1995—2001; pres. bd. dirs. Family and Children's Svc. Greater St. Louis, 1977—79; mem. chancellor's long range planning com. Wash. U., 1980—81, mem. Nat. Coun., Sch. Social Work, 1987—; chmn. Benton Roblee Duhme Scholar Fund; trustee Joseph H. and Florence A. Roblee Found., St. Louis, 1984—, pres., 1984—90; bd. dirs.; chmn. Chautaugua Bell Tower Scholar Fund, 1961—; bd. dirs. Nat. Inland Waterways Libr., St. Louis Merc Libr.; mem. corp. assembly Blue Cross Hosp. Svc. Mo., 1978—86; pres. Joseph H. and Florance A. Roblee Found., 2002. Recipient Mary Alice Messerley award for volunteerism Health and Welfare Coun. St. Louis, 1971, Vol. of Yr. award, YWCA, 1976, Woman of Achievement award St. Louis Globe Democrat, 1980, Outstanding Lay Women nomination Mo. United Ch. of Christ, 1991, Outstanding Alumna award John Burroughs Sch., 1992, Humanitarian award Planned Parenthood St. Louis, 2000. Home: 8 Edgewood Rd Saint Louis MO 63124-1817

DUITMAN, LOIS ROBINSON, artist; b. Green Bay, Wis. m. Rock Duitman; children: Christine M. Bomgardner, Brian R. Plog. Student, Art Student's League, N.Y., Women's U. of The Philippines, Manila, Baylor U., Waco, TX, Orange Coast Coll., Saddleback Coll., CA. Chief copywriter J.C. Penney's, L.A.; asst. editor Calif. Girl Mag., L.A. Tchr. art workshop Pepperdine U., Calif. One woman shows include Spearfish State Teachers' Coll., S. Dak., Roswell Art Mus., State Art Mus. of Santa Fe, Hawaii, 1984, Clearwater, Palm Harbor, Fla., Jacksonville, Dunedin, Sarasota, St. Petersburg, Fla., 1991-97, Rio Rancho (N.Mex.) Country Club, 1997, Albuquerque Little Theatre, 1999; exhibited in group shows at State Art Mus. of Santa Fe, (award), Natl. Art Gallery of The Philippines, Manila, Jehengir Art Gallery, Bombay, Roswell Art Mus., State Art Mus., Santa Fe, N.Mex., Art Encounter Gallery, Las Vegas, Nev., numerous others; painted in Spain, Portugal, France, Aden, Jamaica, The Bahamas, Africa, P.R., Germany, Singapore, Mozambique, others; artist (cookbook covers) Bon Appetit de Las Sandias, 1998, 99. Mem. Internat. Soc. Marine Painters, Fla. Watercolor Soc., West Mesa Woman's Club. Avocations: skiing, tennis, swimming, biking, bowling. Home: 64 Parkside Rd SE Rio Rancho NM 87124-3983

DUJON, DIANE MARIE, director, advocate; b. Boston, Dec. 29, 1946; d. Alfred and Agnes C. (Hall) White; 1 child, Lisa M. Dujon. BA, U. Mass., 1983, MS, 1996. Asst. dir. assessment Coll. Pub. and Cmty. Svc. U. Mass., Boston, 1984-93, co-dir. assessment Coll. Pub. and Cmty. Svc., 1993-97, dir. experiential learning Coll. Pub. and Cmty. Svc., 1997—. Co-editor: For Crying Out Loud: Women's Poverty in U.S., 1996 (Myers Ctr. for the Study of Human Rights in N.Am. Outstanding Book award 1997); prodr. (radio documentary) Workfare: Anatomy of a Policy, 1982 (Alice award 1982), Nat. Commn. on Working Women; alternative radio (NPR) recorded speech, Women, Welfare and Poverty, 1998. V.p. Survivors, Inc., Boston, 1986—. Recipient Earl Douglas award City Mission Soc., 1987, Taking a Stand award Boston Women's Fund, 2004; named Unsung Heroine Rosie's Place, 1997. Mem. NEA, Nat. Welfare Rights Union, Mass. AFL-CIO (mem. exec. women's com. 1997-2001), Mass. Tchrs. Assn., U. Mass. Profl. Staff Union (bd. mem. chpt.), Nat. Edn. Assn., Mass. Tchrs. Assn., Golden Key Internat. Hon. Soc. Baptist. Office: U Mass/Boston 100 Morrissey Blvd Boston MA 02125-3300 Office Phone: 617-287-7126. Business E-Mail: diane.dujon@umb.edu.

DUKAKIS, OLYMPIA, actress; b. Lowell, Mass., June 20, 1931; d. Constantine S. and Alexandra (Christos) D.; m. Louis Zorich; children: Christina, Peter, Stefan. BS, Boston U., 1952, MFA, 1957. Co-founder, artistic dir. Whole Theatre, Montclair, NJ, 1970-90; co-founder Charles Playhouse, Boston; master tchr. NYU, 1970-85. Appeared in over 125 prodns. for regional theatres, N.Y. Shakespeare Theatre, Circle Repertory Theatre, American Place Theatre and numerous Off-Broadway theatres; appearances on stage include A Mother, Mother Courage, The Rose Tattoo, The Cherry Orchard, Three Sisters, The Sea Gull, Long Day's Journey Into Night, Iphegenia in Aulis, Othello, Miss Julie, A Streetcar Named Desire, The Night of the Iguana, King of America, Social Security, Rose, 2005; appearances in film include Lilith, 1964, Twice a Man, 1964, John and Mary, 1969, Made for Each Other, 1971, Death Wish, 1974, Rich Kids, 1979, The Wanderers, 1979, The Idolmaker, 1980, National Lampoon Goes to the Movies, 1982, Flanagan, 1985, Moonstruck, 1988 (Golden Globe, Academy Award Suppporting Actress), Working Girl, 1988, Steel Magnolias, 1988, Look Who's Talking, 1988, Dad, 1989, In the Spirit, 1990, Look Who's Talking II, 1990, Over the Hill, 1992, Look Who's Talking Now, 1993, The Cemetery Club, 1993, I Love Trouble, 1994, Digger, 1994, Jeffrey, 1995, Mighty Aphrodite, 1995, Mr. Holland's Opus, 1996, Dead Badge, 1995, Picture Perfect, 1997, Never Too Late, 1997, Jane Austen's Mafia!, 1998, A Life for a Life, 1998, Better Living, 2000, Brooklyn Sonnet, 2000, The Intended, 2002, The Event, 2003, Charlie's War, 2003, Jesus, Mary and Joey, 2003, The Great New Wonderful, 2005, The Thing About My Folks, 2005, A Mother, A Daughter, And A Gun, 2005; (TV movies) Nicky's World, 1974, The Neighborhood, 1982, The Last Act is a Solo, 1990 (Ace award), Lucky Day, 1991, Fire in the Dark, 1991, Sinatra: The Mini-Series, 1992, Armistead Maupin's Tales of the City, 1994, A Century of Women, 1994, Young at Heart, 1995, A Match Made in Heaven, 1997, Scattering Dad, 1998, The Pentagon Wars, 1998, More Tales of the City (mini-series), 1998, Joan of Arc, 1999, Last of the Blonde Bombshells, 2000, And Never Let Her Go, 2001, Ladies and the Champ, 2001, Further Tales of the City (mini-series), 2001, My Beautiful Son, 2001, Guilty Hearts (mini-series), 2002, Mafia Doctor, 2003, Babycakes, 2003; (TV series) Center of the Universe, 2004. Del. Dem. Nat. Convention, 1988. Recipient 2 Obie awards, Los Angeles Film Critics award, 1988. Mem. Actor's Equity Assn., Screen Actors Guild, Am. Fedn. TV and Radio Artists. Office: William Morris Agy care Parseghian 1325 Avenue Of The Americas Fl 32 New York NY 10019-4702

DUKE, BETSY (ELIZABETH A. DUKE), bank executive; b. July 1952; BFA U. NC, Chapel Hill; MBA, Old Dominion U., Norfolk, VA; grad., Stonier Grad. Sch. Banking, Am. Bankers Assn. Sch. of Bank Investments, Va. Bankers Assn. Sch. Bank Mgmt. Pres., CEO Bank of Tidewater, 1991—2001; sr. v.p. govt. rels. SouthTrust Corp., Va. Beach, Va., 2001—03, exec. v.p. cmty. bank devel., 2003—05; exec. v.p. Merger Project Team Wachovia Bank, Va. Beach, Va., 2005—. Nat. adv. coun. Fannie Mae, 2004—. Named One of 25 Women to Watch, U.S. Banker Mag., 2003. Mem.: Am. Bankers Assn. (chmn.-elect 2003—04, chmn. 2004—05).

DUKE, CAROL MICHIELS, health products executive; b. Alexandria, La., Sept. 2, 1944; d. Leo A. and Elva L. Michiels; m. M. Carey Duke, Apr. 23, 1971; 1 child, Perrianne. Student, Nichols State U., 1974—77; grad., Dale Carnegie Inst., Realtors Inst. Office mgr. Bayou Constrn. Co., Houma, La., 1974—76; mgr. Glynn & Assoc., Houma, 1976—79; owner, broker Century 21 Real Estate One, Houma, 1979—81; v.p., mgmt. cons. Century 21 of Tex. and La., Houston, 1981—82; v.p., gen. mgr. Doyle Stuckey, Houston, 1982—83; broker/mgr. Gary Greene Realtors, Better Homes & Gardens, Houston, 1983—85; regional mgr. Better Homes & Gardens, Des Moines, 1985—95; regional mgr., hearing instrument spec. Miracle Ear, Austin, Tex., 1995—. Dist. mgr. Miracle Ear, Austin, Tex.; seminar condr.; chmn. conv. booth Realtors Nat. Home Builders, Houston, 1983. Editor: Training and Policy Manual, 1982. Chmn. Easter Seal Soc., Houma, 1979. Recipient Top Listing award, numerous Top Quarterly awards, La. Dist. of Century 21, 1980. Mem. Houston Bd. Realtors (edn. com. 1984-85), Tex. Assn. Realtors (realtor/builder, sec. 1983-), Nat. Assn. Realtors, Realtors Nat. Mktg. Inst., Jaycee Jaynes (state bd. dirs. 1976-77, sec. 1977-78). Democrat. Roman Catholic. Home: PO Box 90758 Austin TX 78709-0758 Personal E-mail: hearmeduke@aol.com.

DUKE, CAROLYN, medical/surgical and community health nurse; b. St. Louis, Jan. 24, 1941; d. Frank and Lucille (Herzog) Crowder; m. William Duke, Aug. 29, 1968; children: Jennifer, Laura, Rebecca, Katherine. Diploma, St. John's Hosp., St. Louis, 1962; BSN, St. Louis U., 1964; MSN, U. Calif., San Francisco, 1968. Head nurse St. John's Mercy Med. Ctr., St. Louis, 1964-66; occupational health nurse FMHA, St. Louis, 1984-92; coord. nursing skills lab. St. Louis U., asst. prof. nursing, 1992—2002, nurse rschr. Enternal Feeding Study under Norma Methany PhD, 2003—05, adj. asst. prof. nursing, 2003—. Cons. for mosby Video Skills Series, 1993-94. Author manual for home health aides. Mem. ANA, Sigma Theta Tau. Home: 4532 Beaver Brook Ct Saint Louis MO 63128-3608 Office: St Louis U Sch Nursing 3525 Caroline St Saint Louis MO 63104-1007

DUKE, ELIZABETH M., federal agency administrator; B in polit. sci., Rutgers U.; M in polit. sci., Northwestern U., M in African Studies; PhD in polit. sci., George Washington U. Founder, dir. Govt. Affairs Inst., Office of Exec. and Mgmt. Devel. US Office Pers. Mgmt., 1978—84, dep. asst. dir., dir. policy and systems, Office Training and Devel., 1984—86; prin. dep. sec. Office of Asst. Sec. for Mgmt. and Budget, HHS; dep. asst. sec. adminstrn. Adminstrn. for Children and Families, HHS, 1997—2001; acting adminstr. Health Resources and Services Adminstrn., HHS, 2001—02, adminstr., 2002—. Office: Health Resources and Services Adminstrn Parklawn Bld 5600 Fishers Ln Rockville MD 20857*

DUKE, ELLEN (BEBE DUKE), bank executive; AB, Princeton Univ. Trading positions with Citibank, Lehman Bros., Smith Barney, 1982—95; head market risk mgmt. dept. Smith Barney; head, market risk Solomon Smith Barney; global head market risk mgmt., corp. & investment banking Citigroup Inc., NYC, 2000—03, mng. dir., co-head risk mgmt., mem. mgmt. com., 2003—. Office: Citigroup Inc 399 Park Ave New York NY 10043*

DUKE, ORA ELIZABETH, civic volunteer; b. Dec. 26, 1942; m. D. Mike Duke Sr. (dec.); children: Dawn Elaine, D. Mike Jr. Student, N.Mex. State U., 1963, San Juan Coll., 1969, Yavapai Extension Coll., Page, Ariz., 1975. Asst. reports editor Phys. Sci. Lab., N.Mex. State U., Las Cruces, 1964-67; reservation clk. Del Webb's Wahweap Lodge, Page, Ariz., 1970; asst. instr. arts and crafts Page Ariz. Sch. System, 1971; mem. crew Sanderson Bros. River Expedition, Colo., 1972-75. Mem. John Wesley Powell Mus. Bd., program chmn. 1973-74, The Newcomers Club, 1986-87; wig chmn., Clacasieu Parish Extension Homemakers, 1988—; participant Calif. Conf. on Women, 1986, 87, La. Talent Bank of Women; Page, Ariz. Precinct West Dep. Registrar, Coconino County, 1974-75; sec., Page Recreation Assn., 1970-71, PTA, 1970-71; den mother, pack organizer Cub Scouts Am., 1972; den mother Cub Scout Latter Day Saints, 1971; chmn. Mayor's Commn. Pub. Sch. Expansion Research, Page, Ariz., 1974, Gov.'s com. Waste Disposal Alternatives for No. Ariz., 1975; vol. Titus Country Home Demonstration Office; adv. bd. Internat. Order Rainbow Girls, 1971-75, mother advisor 1974-75. Mem. Cactus Wrens Extension Homemakers Club (pres., organizer 1975-77), Red Sands Extension Homemakers Club (pres. 1973-74), Associated Country Women of the World, Country Women Council, Howard Ruff Discussion Forum (chmn. 1987-88), Nat. Assn. Women in Constrn. (program chmn. 1986-87), Hollywood Extension Homemakers Club (v.p. 1986-87, Vt. mem. 1993, 94), Mich. Extension Homemaker Club, Elks (ladies auxiliary 1999—), Order of the Eastern Star, Habitat for Humanity (nat. reg.) Xi Alpha Kappa (chmn., social chmn., program chmn. 1972-74), Beta Sigma Pi, Xi Beta Phi. Clubs: Lake Powell Yacht (Lake Pals aux., charter); Glen Canyon Golf and Country (social com. 1971-72). Lodges: Order of Eastern Star, Order of The Rainbow for Girls (mother advisor 1974-75, adv. bd. 1971-75). Avocations: antique doll collecting, travel, genealogy. Home: # 760 13618 N 99th Ave Sun City AZ 85351-2813

DUKE, PATTY (ANNA MARIE DUKE), actress; b. N.Y.C., Dec. 14, 1946; d. John P. and Frances (McMahon) Duke; m. John Astin, 1973 (div. 1985); children: Sean, Mackenzie; m. Michael Pierce, March 15, 1986. Grad., Quintano's School for Young Profls. Pres. SAG, 1985-88, lectr. Am. Film Inst., 1988 TV appearances include Armstrong Circle Theatre, 1955, The SS Andrea Doria, The Prince and the Pauper, 1957, Wuthering Heights, 1958, U.S. Steel Hour, 1959, Meet Me in St. Louis, 1959, Swiss Family Robinson, 1958, The Power and the Glory, 1961, All's Fair, 1981-82; (series) The Brighter Day, 1957, Kitty Foyle, 1958, Patty Duke Show, 1963-66, It Takes Two, 1982-83, Hail to the Chief, 1985, Karen's Song, 1987; (TV films) The Big Heist, 1957, My Sweet Charlie, 1970 (Emmy award 1970), Two on a Bench, If Tomorrow Comes, 1971, She Waits, Deadly Harvest, 1972, Nightmare, 1972, Look What's Happened to Rosemary's Baby, 1976, Fire!, 1976, Rosetti and Ryan: Men Who Love Women, Curse of the Black Widow, Killer on Board, The Storyteller, 1977, Having Babies III, Captain and the Kings, 1977 (Emmy award 1977), A Family Upside Down, 1978, Women in White, Hanging by a Thread, Before and After, The Miracle Worker, 1979 (Emmy award 1980), The Women's Room, Mom, The Wolfman and Me, The Babysitter, 1980, Violation of Sarah McDavid, Please, Don't Hit Me Mom, 1981, Something So Right, 1982, September Gun, 1983, Best Dept Secrets, 1984, George Washington: The Forging of a Nation, 1984, A Time to Triumph, 1986, Fight for Life, 1987, Perry Mason: The Case of the Avenging Angel, Fatal Judgement, 1988, Everybody's Baby: The Rescue of Jessica McClure, Amityville: The Evil Escapes, 1989, Call Me Anna, 1990, Always Remember I Love You, 1990, Absolute Strangers, 1991, Last Wish, 1992, Grave Secrets: The Legacy of Hilltop Drive, 1992, A Killer Among Friends, 1992, A Family of Strangers, 1993, Cries From the Heart, 1994, One Woman's Courage, 1994, When the Vows Break, 1995, To Face Her Past, 1996, Race Against Time: The Search for Sarah, 1996, The Disappearing Act, 1997, A Christmas Memory, 1997, When He Didn't Come Home, 1998, A Season For Miracles, 1999, Love Lessons, 2000, Miracle on the Mountain, 2000, Love Lessons, 2000, Little John, 2002, Wrong Turn, 2003, Murder Without Conviction, 2004, Falling in Love with the Girl Next Door, 2006; (theatre) The Miracle Worker, 1959-61, Isle of Children, 1962, Oklahoma!, 2002, Golda's Balcony, 2005; (motion picture appearances) I'll Cry Tomorrow, 1955, The Goddess, 1958, Happy Anniversary, The 4-D Man, 1959, The Miracle Worker, 1962 (Acad. award as best supporting actress 1962), Billie, 1965, Valley of the Dolls, 1967, Me, Natalie, 1969 (Golden Globe award as best actress 1970), the Swarm, 1978, Something Special, 1987, Prelude to a Kiss, 1992, Kimberly, 1999, Bigger Than the Sky, 2005; guest appearances Police Story, 1975, Police Women, 1975, Marcus Welby M.D., 1975, Touched By an Angel, 2003, Judging Amy, 2004 and several others; co-author Surviving Sexual Assalt, 1983, Call Me Anna, 1987, A Brilliant Madness: Living With Manic-Depressive Illness, 1992. Nat. corp. council Muscular Dystrophy Assns. Am. Recipient Emmy Awards, 1964, 69, 76, 79 Mem. AFTRA. Office: William Morris Agy 151 S El Camino Dr Beverly Hills CA 90212-2775*

DUKE, ROBIN CHANDLER TIPPETT, retired public relations executive, former ambassador; b. Balt., Oct. 13, 1923; d. Richard Edgar and Esther (Chandler) Tippett; m. Angier Biddle Duke, May 1962; children: Jeffrey R. Lynn, Letitia Lynn, Angier Biddle Jr. Fashion editor N.Y. Jour. Am., N.Y.C., 1944-46; freelance writer N.Y.C., 1946-50; rep. Orvis Bros., N.Y.C., 1953-58; mem. pub. rels. staff Pepsi Cola Co., Internat., N.Y.C., 1958-62; US amb. to UNESCO US Dept. State, Belgrade, 1980, US amb. to Norway Oslo, 2000—01. Bd. dirs. Am. Home Products, N.Y.C., Internat. Flavors & Fragrances, N.Y.C., East River Bank, New Rochelle, NY; dir. Rockwell Corp., 1977—95; dir. emeritus Inst. Internat. Edn. Co-chmn. Population Action Internat., N.Y.C., 1975-96; Met. Club Washington; bd. dirs. David Packard Found., U.S. Japan Found. Recipient Albert and Mary Lasker Social Svc. award, 1991, Margaret Sanger Woman of Yr. Valor award, 1995. Mem. Coun. on Fgn. Rels., Acad. Arts & Scis., World Affairs Coun. L.I. (co-chmn.), Colony Club, River Club. Democrat. Avocations: skiing, swimming.

DUKE, WANDA K., artist; b. New Castle, Ind., Mar. 19, 1924; d. Raymond Emil and Flemmie (Toppin) Kepner; m. Robert Kerr Duke, Aug. 21, 1945 (div. July 1968); children: Sandra Toppin Hodge, Gregory Hamilton Kerr Duke. Student, So. Meth. U., 1942-43, Purdue U., 1943-44; postgrad., Ariz. State U., 1977. Various positions RCA; med. writer Modern Medicine mag., Mpls., 1969-71; editl. asst., writer The Am. Philatelist, 1975-77; admintrv. asst. in ethnomusicology Ariz. State U. Instr. water media Pima C.C., Green Valley, Ariz., 1993, 95, Green Valley Recreation Assn., 1995, 96; pvt. instr., 1993-97. Exhbns. include N.C. Mus. of Art Exhbn., 1971, Nat. Aqueous, Tubac, Ariz., 1992, 95, 99, Western Fedn. of Water Color Socs., 1990, Nat. Acrylic Painters Assn., Gt. Britain, 1997, Marin Soc. Artists, Ross, Calif., San Francisco Women Artists, Peninsula Art Assn., San Mateo, Calif., Palo Alto Art Group, Calif., Art League, Houston, Walnut Creek Rental Gallery, Calif., Minn. Artists Assn., Mpls., Facet Gallery, Taos, N.Mex., N.C. Mus. of Art, Raleigh, So. Ariz. Water Color Guild, others; work collected in pvt. collections, including L. Boulton, Can., and Neil Armstrong. Active Red Cross Orgn. Recipient numerous painting awards including Best in Show Sonoran Br. Nat. League of Am. Pen Women, 1995, N.C. Mus. of Art Benefit Show, Raleigh, others. Mem. Nat. League of Am. Pen Women (pres., charter mem. Sonoran Desert Br., 1995), Nat. Acrylic Painters Assn. (signature mem.) So. Ariz. Water Color Guild (signature mem.), DAR, Kappa Alpha Theta (bd. dirs.), We. Fedn. Water Color Soc. (signature mem.). Avocations: singing (Augusta Choral Soc., San Francisco Bach Choir), golf, tennis, skiing, table tennis. Home: Apt 28A 5801 Lowell St NE Albuquerque NM 87111-5959 Personal E-mail: juanda3@webtv.net.

DUKERT, BETTY COLE, television producer; b. Muskogee, Okla., May 9, 1927; d. Irvan Dill and Ione (Bowman) Cole; m. Joseph M. Dukert, May 19, 1968 Student, Lindenwood Coll., St. Charles, Mo., 1945-46, Drury Coll., Springfield, Mo., 1946-47; B.J., U. Mo., 1949. With Sta. KICK, Springfield, Mo., 1949-50; adminstrv. asst. Juvenile Office, Green County, Mo., 1950-52; with Sta. WRC-TV-NBC, Washington, 1952-56; assoc. producer Meet the Press, NBC, Washington, 1956-75, producer, 1975—92; sr. producer Meet the Press, NBC News, 1992—. Mem. Robert F. Kennedy Journalism Awards Com., 1978-82, exec. producer, 1997—. Trustee Drury Coll., Springfield, Mo., 1984— Recipient Disting. Alumna award Drury Coll., 1975, Disting. Alumni award U Mo., 1978, Ted Yates award Washington chpt. Nat. Acad. TV Arts and Scis., 1979, Pub. Rels. award for pub. svc. Am. Legion Nat. Comdrs., 1981, Internat. Disting. Svc. Journalism medal U. Mo. Sch. Journalism, 1993, Peter Hackes Meml. award Washington D.C. chpt. Radio/TV News Dirs. Assn., 1995. Mem. Am. Women in Radio and TV, Am. News Women's Club, Radio/TV Corrs. Assn., Women's Forum Washington, Soc. Profl. Journalists (dir. 1983-84, inducted into Hall of Fame 1991), Silver Circle Broadcasting, Nat. Acad. TV Arts and Scis., Nat. Press Club. Office: NBC News 4001 Nebraska Ave NW Washington DC 20016-2733

DUKES, DEIDRA, newscaster; b. Calif. BA in Comm., Calif. State U., Chico. Reporter, anchor Sta. KJEO-TV, Fresno, Calif.; gen. assignment reporter Sta. WPXI--TV, Pitts., 1995—98; reporter, anchor Sta. WSB-TV, Atlanta, 1998—. Bd. dirs. Rainbows, Inc. Hon. adv. bd. minority recruitment program ARC. Mem.: Atlanta Assn. Black Journalists (bd. dirs.), Jr. League Atlanta. Office: Sta WSB-TV 1601 W Peachtree St NE Atlanta GA 30309

DUKES, REBECCA WEATHERS (BECKY DUKES), musician, singer, song writer; b. Durham, N.C., Nov. 21, 1934; d. Elmer Dewey Weathers and Martha Rebecca (Kimbrough) Weathers-Hall; m. Charles Aubrey Dukes Jr., Dec. 20, 1955; children: Aurelia Ann, Charles Weathers, David Lloyd. BA, Duke U., 1956; AA (hon.), Md. Coll. Art and Design, 2003. Lic. elem. sch. tchr. Tchr. Durham City Schs., 1956-57; sec. USMC, Arlington, Va., 1957-58; tchr. Arlington County Schs., 1958-59; office mgr. Dukes and Kooken, Landover, Md., 1976; musical performer Washington and various locations, Va., Md., 1982—. Pres. R.W. Dukes Music Inc. Vocal student Todd Duncan; pianist, vocalist Back Alley Restaurant Lounge, 1982, various hotels, lounges, 1982—; original program, A Life Cycle in Song, presented throughout mid-Atlantic states and Washington; full operatic solo recital, 1983; featured performer benefit for Nat. Symphony Orch., Prince George's Philharmonic; performer Capital Ctr., Cole Field House, George Washington U., Smith Ctr.; operatic solo concert with pianist Glenn Sales, 1985; benefit appearance U. Md. Concert Series, 1986-87; composer over 100 original songs including Between the Lovin' and the Leavin', Covers of My Mind, Gentle Thoughts (lead song Nat. Capitol Area Composers Series), Headin' Home Again, I Would Like to Be Reborn, Miss You, Tears, You Played a Part in My Life, Christmas Memories, Mood Rhapsody, Let Freedom Ring; songwriter, vocalist (album releases-12 songs) Alive, 1992, Rainbow, 1994, Borrow The Sun, 1995, Almost Country, 1999, Rhapsody of Moods, 2000; author: (poems) Pottery, Canyons and Connections, Let the Trees of the Forest Rustle with Praise; contbr. poems to A Question of Balance, 1992, Treasured Poems of America, 1993, Distinguished Poets of 1994. Pres. Nat. Capitol Law League, Washington, 1976-77; pres. women's group, deacon, elder Riverdale Presbyn. Ch., Hyattsville, Md., 1968-94, elder, 1994; chmn. event honoring wives of Supreme Ct. justices, 1981; exec. com. women's com. Nat. Symphony, 1999-2003, bd. dirs.; chmn. awards event Marian Anderson Internat. Vocal Arts Competition, 1991, 95; bd. dirs. Md. Coll. Art and Design; mem. leadership coun. Clarice Smith Performing Arts Ctr. U. Md., 2002-. Recipient Friend of Yr. award Md. Summer Inst. for Creative and Performing Arts, U. Md., 1986, award for Vol. Svcs., Duke U., 1992, Hon. Mention award For the Children of the World Billboard mag., 1996, Billboard Hon. Mention for It's Own Time, 1999; named Hon. trustee Prince George's (Md.) Arts Coun., 1984-96, one of Women of Outstanding Achievement, Prince George's County, 1994. Mem. ASCAP (Popular Music award 1994-2005), Nat. Acad. Recording Arts and Scis., Nashville Songwriters Assn. Internat., Songwriters Assn. Washington, William Preston Few Assn. Duke U. (pres. couns., exec. bd. ann. fund), Internat. Platform Assn., Pres.'s Club U. Md., Univ. Club, Founders Club Duke U. Republican. Home and Office: 7111 Pony Trail Ln Hyattsville MD 20782-1031 Office Fax: 301-927-4073.

DUKES, VANESSA JOHNSON, dietician; b. Charleston, S.C., Aug. 4, 1955; d. Rubin and Christena (Weston) Johnson; m. Warren L. Dukes, May 21, 1983. BS, S.C. State U., 1977, MEd, 1979. Registered and lic. dietitian. Grad. asst. in home econs. S.C. State Coll., Orangeburg, 1977-79; nutritionist Services Council Day Care Ctr., Aiken, S.C., 1980-83; food service supr. III S.C. Dept. Correction, Ridgeville, 1987—; tchr. emotionally handicapped Charleston County Sch. Dist., 1987-97; diet technician, dietitian Sodexho, Des Moines, 1997—; food svc. supr., diet tech., Mariott, Des Moines, 1997—. Dietary asst. S.C. Dept. Health and Environ. Control, Columbia, 1978; substitute tchr. Charleston County Sch. Dist., 1985—; nutritionist Franklin C. Fetter Health Clinic, Charleston, 1988—; companion, homemaker Med. Pers. Pool, Des Moines; asst. food svc. mgr. Fountain West Health Care Ctr., Des Moines, 1995—; hospitality coord. Dietary Dept. BMC, 2004—. Vol. Meals on Wheels, Aiken, 1976, Mercy House Diabetic Clinic, 1999—2004; vol. Project NOW Broadlawns Med. Ctr., 2001; alt. del. S.C. Dem. conv., 1980; voter registrar Aiken, SC, 1980—82. Recipient John H. Cromer Meml. scholarship S.C. Dietetic Assn., 1977. Mem. Am. Dietetic Assn., Ctrl. Iowa Dietetic Assn., Iowa Dietetic Assn., Kappa Omicron Phi. Avocations: reading, creative cooking, gardening, crafts. Home: 4046 Plainview Dr Des Moines IA 50311

DULAC, CATHERINE, biology professor, researcher; Grad., Ecole Normale Supérieure de la rue d'Ulm, Paris; PhD, U. Paris. Rschr. Institut d'Embryologie du Collège de France; postdoctoral fellow Columbia U.; asst. prof. molecular & cellular biology dept. Harvard U., 1996—2000; asst. investigator Howard Hughes Med. Inst., 1997—2002; assoc. prof. molecular & cellular biology dept. Harvard U., 2000—01, prof. molecular & cellular biology, 2001—; investigator Howard Hughes Medical Inst., 2002—. Mem. scientific advisory bd. Senomyx, Inc., Allen Brain Atlas, Max Planck Inst., Friedrich Miescher Inst. Contbr. articles to profl. jours. Recipient Richard Lounsbery award, NAS, 2006. Fellow: AAAS. Achievements include discovery of genes encoding families of pheromone receptors in mammals. Office: Harvard U Rm 4017 16 Divinity Ave Cambridge MA 02138 Office Phone: 617-495-7893. Business E-Mail: dulac@fas.harvard.edu.*

DU LAC, LOIS ARLINE, retired secondary school educator, writer; b. Cleve., July 17, 1920; d. Carl Walter and T. Henrietta Stein; m. Leo Joseph Du Lac, Apr. 20, 1941; children: Arline Du Lac Gerard, Linda Du Lac Jennings, Glen, Carl, Ralph. BA cum laude, UCLA, 1942, MA, 1962; JD, Western State U., Fullerton, Calif., 1982. Tchr. Cornelia Connelly H.S., Anaheim, Calif., 1962-63, Montebello (Calif.) Sch. Dist., 1963, Excelsior/Norwalk (Calif.) Sch. Dist., 1963-64, Garden Grove (Calif.) Unified Sch. Dist., 1964-69; ret., 1969. Creative editor, contbg. author: Constitutional Law, 1981; contbg. author: Murder California Style, 1987, Mord in Kalifornie, 1988; anthology judge, Blood on Their Hands, 2003, Mojave Green for Murder, 2006. Vol. law clk. Cmty. Law Ctr., Santa Ana, Calif., 1982. Mem. Mystery Writers Am. (contbg. author Edgar Ann. 1990, 92), Cath. Press. Assn., Phi Beta Kappa, Alpha Mu Gamma. Avocations: reading, gardening, interior decorating, arranging flowers. Office: PO Box 403301 Hesperia CA 92340-3301 Personal E-mail: loisdulac@verizon.net.

DULANY, ELIZABETH GJELSNESS, editor; b. Charleston, SC, Mar. 11, 1931; d. Rudolph Hjalmar and Ruth Elizabeth (Weaver) Gjelsness; m. Donelson Edwin Dulany, Mar. 19, 1955; 1 son, Christopher Daniel. BA, Bryn Mawr Coll., 1952. Editor, R.R. Bowker Co., 1948-52; med. editor U. Mich. Hosp., Ann Arbor, 1953-54; editorial asst. E.P. Dutton & Co., N.Y.C., 1954-55, U. Ill. Press, Champaign, 1956-59, asst. editor, 1959-67, assoc. editor, 1967-72, mng. editor, 1972-90, asst. dir., 1983-90, assoc. dir., 1990—98, editor, 1998—. Democrat. Episcopalian. Home: 73 Greencroft Dr Champaign IL 61821-5112 Office: U Ill Press 1325 S Oak St Champaign IL 61820-6903 Office Phone: 217-244-0158. Business E-Mail: edulany@uillinois.edu.

DULAS, DEANNE L., lawyer; b. St. Paul, Aug. 29, 1970; BA, U. Minn., 1992; JD, U. Minn. Law Sch., 1995. Bar: Minn. 1995, US Dist. Ct. (dist. Minn.) 1996, US Ct. Appeals (8th cir.) 1996. Shareholder Strandemo, Sheridan & Dulas, P.A., Eagan, Minn. Named a Rising Star, Minn. Super Lawyers mag., 2006. Mem.: Collaborative Law Inst., Minn. Women Lawyers (co-chair jud. elections endorsement com.), Legal Assistance of Dakota County (bd. dirs., pres.), First Dist. Bar Assn., Minn. State Bar Assn. (mem. family law sect.), Dakota County Bar Assn. Office: Strandemo Sheridan & Dulas PA 1380 Corp Ctr Curve Ste 320 Eagan MN 55121 Office Phone: 651-686-8800. E-mail: ddulas@strandemoandsheridan.com.*

DULEY, MARGOT IRIS, historian, educator; b. St. John's, Can., Sept. 15, 1944; d. Cyril Chancey and Florence (Pitcher) Duley; m. Lance Franz Morrow, Aug. 28, 1969 (div. Oct. 1986). BA with 1st class honors, Meml. U. of Newfoundland, 1966; MA, Duke U., Durham, N.C., 1968; PhD, U. London, 1977. Instr. dept. history St. Andrew's Presbyn. Coll., Laurinburg, N.C., 1970-71, Hiram (Ohio) Coll., 1973-75; dir., lectr. pilot program U. Mich., Ann Arbor, 1975-78, dir. law club, 1978-79, assoc. dir. honors program Coll. Lit. Sci. and the Arts, 1979-84; dir. women's studies program, assoc. prof. history Denison U., Granville, Ohio, 1984-89; dir. univ. honors program, assoc. prof. history U. Toledo, 1989-92; prof. dept. history and philosophy Ea. Mich. U., Ypsilanti, 1989—, head dept. history and philosophy, 1992-97, dir. women's studies program, 2000—02, interim assoc. dean Coll. Arts & Scis., 2002—04; dean U. Ill. at Springfield, Coll. of Liberal Arts and Sci., 2004—. Adv. bd. Project on Equal Ednl. Rights, Mich., 1978—82. Editor, chief author: book The Cross Cultural Study of Women, 1986; author: Where Once Our Mothers Stood We Stand, 1993; hist. cons.: films Untold Story, 1999. Mem. Ford Lake Adv. Commn., Ypsilanti, Mich., 1996—2004, chair, 1998—2001, sec., 2001—02; vice-chair Water Conservation Commn., 2003—04. Fellow, Duke U., 1966—67, Lord Rothermere Trust, U. London, 1967—70, Can. Coun., 1971—72, Robert Good, Denison U., 1989; grantee, Nfld. Provincial Adv. Com. on the Status of Women, 1988. Mem.: NOW (chair Mich. ERA task force 1978—80, pres. Mich. conf. 1980—82), Berkshire Conf. Women's History, Can. Hist. Assn., Am. Hist. Assn., Phi Kappa Phi (hon.). Avocations: sailing, hiking, travel, poetry. Office: U Ill Springfield Office Dean Coll Liberal Arts & Scis Univ Hall 3005 One Univ Plz Springfield IL 62703 Office Phone: 217-206-6512.

DUMANDAN, JOY, newscaster; BA in Comm., Montclair State U. Assoc. prodr. Am.'s Talking, CNBC Primetime, Ft. Lee, NJ; reporter Sta. WBRE-TV, Wilkes-Barre/Scranton, Pa., 1996; anchor, reporter Sta. WNYW-TV, N.Y.C.; anchor Sta. WISH-TV, Indpls., 2001—. Mem.: Asian Am. Journalists Assn. Office: WISH-TV 1950 N Meridian St Indianapolis IN 46207

DUMANOSKI, DIANNE, journalist, writer; b. 1944; BA, Vassar Coll.; MA, Yale U. Prodr. WGBH-TV, Boston; staff writer The Boston Phoenix; with Boston Globe, 1979—, environ. journalist, 1983—93; now freelance sci. writer. Lectr. in field; bd. dirs. Environ. Media Svcs.; mem. Ted Scripps Fellowships adv. bd. Author (with Theo Colborn and Pete Myers): (book) Our Stolen Future: How Man-Made Chemicals are Threatening Our Fertility, Intelligence and Survival, 1996. Fellow Ctr. Environ. Journalism, U. Colo., Knight Fellow in Sci. Journalism, 1983—84. E-mail: ddumanoski@earthlink.net.

DUMAS, RHETAUGH ETHELDRA GRAVES, retired university official; b. Natchez, Miss., Nov. 26, 1928; d. Rhetaugh Graves and Josephine (Clemmons) Graves Bell; m. A.W. Dumas, Jr., Dec. 25, 1950; 1 child, Adrienne. BS in Nursing, Dillard U., 1951; MS in Psychiat. Nursing, Yale U., 1961; PhD in Social Psychology, Union Inst. and Univ., 1975; D Pub. Svc. (hon.), Simmons Coll., 1976, U. Cin., 1981; LHD (hon.), Yale U., 1989; LLD (hon.), Dillard U., 1990; LHD (hon.), U. San Diego, 1993, Georgetown U., 1996; D Pub. Svc. (hon.), Fla. Internat. U., Miami, 1996; DSc (hon.), Ind. U., Gary, 1996; LHD (hon.), U. Mass, 1997; JD (hon.), Bethune-Cookman Coll., 1997; LHD (hon.), Regis Coll., 2002. Instr. Dillard U., 1957-59, 61; research asst., instr. Sch. Nursing Yale U., 1962-65, from asst. prof. nursing to assoc. prof., 1965-72, chmn. dept. psychiat. nursing, 1972; dir. nursing Conn. Mental Health Ctr., Yale-New Haven Med. Ctr., 1966-72; chief psychiat. nursing edn. br. Div. Manpower and Tng. Programs, NIMH, Rockville, Md., 1972-76; dep. dir. Div. Manpower and Tng. Programs NIMH, 1976-79, dep. dir. alcohol, drug abuse and mental health adminstrn., 1979-81; dean, prof. U. Mich. Sch. Nursing, 1981-94; vice provost health affairs U. Mich., 1994-97, Lucille Cole prof. sch. nursing, 1994—, vice provost emerita, 1997—, dean emerita, 1997—. Dir. Group Rels. Confs. in Tavistock Model; cons., speaker, panelist in field; fellow Helen Hadley Hall, Yale U., 1972, Branford Coll., 1972; dir. Community Health Care Ctr. Plan, New Haven, 1969-72; mem. U.S. Assessment Team, cons. to Fed. Ministry Health, Nigeria, 1982; mem. adv. com. Health Policy Agenda for the Am. People, AMA, 1983-86; cons. NIH Task Force on Nursing Rsch., 1984; mem. Nat. Commn. on Unemployment and Mental Health, Nat. Mental Health Assn., 1984-85; mem. com. to plan maj. study of nat. long-term care policy Inst. Medicine, 1985; mem. adv. com. to dir. NIH, 1986-87; mem. Sec.'s Nat. Commn. on Future Structure of VA Health Care System, 1990-91; mem. coun. on grad. med. edn. Nat. Adv. Coun. on Nurse Edn. and Practice Workgroup on Primary Care Workforce Projection, Divsn. Nursing, 1994; mem. com. to rev. breast cancer rsch. program U.S. Army Med. Rsch. and Material Command, Inst. of Medicine, 1996-97; mem. Pres.'s Nat. Bioethics Adv. Commn., 1996—. Author profl. monographs; contbr. over 40 articles to profl. publs.; mem. editorial bd. Community Mental Health Rev., 1977-79, Jour. Personality and Social Systems, 1978-81, Advances in Psychiat. Mental Health Nursing, 1981. Bd. dirs. Afro Am. Ctr., Yale U., 1968-72; mem. New Haven Bd. Edn., 1968-71, New Haven City Demonstrations Agy., 1968-70, Human Rels. Coun. New Haven, 1961-63, Nat. Neural Circuitry Database Com., Inst. Medicine, Nat. Acad. Scis., mem. bd. scientific advisors, 1985—; mem. commn. on future structure of vets. health care U.S. Dept. Vets. Affairs, 1990; mem. Pres. Clinton's Nat. Bioethics Adv. Commn., 1996-01. Named Disting. Alumna, Dillard U., 1966; recipient various awards, including cert. Honor NAACP, 1970, Disting. Alumnae award Yale U. Sch. Nursing, 1976, award for outstanding achievement and service in field mental health D.C. chpt. Assn. Black Psychologists, 1980, Pres. 21st Century award The Nat. Women's Hall of Fame, 1994, Lifetime Achievement award, nat. Black Nurses Assn., 2000—. Fellow A.K. Rice Inst., Am. Coll. Mental Health Adminstrs. (founding), Am. Acad. Nursing (charter, pres. 1987-89); mem. Inst. Medicine NAS, Am. Nurses Assn., Nat. Black Nurses Assn., Am. Assn. Colls. Nursing (govtl. affairs com. 1990-93), Am. Pub. Health Assn., Nat. League Nursing (pres. 1997-99), Nat. Bioethics Adv. Commn., Sigma Theta Tau Internat. (mentor award 1989), Delta Sigma Theta. E-mail: rhetaughdumas@sbcglobal.net.

DUMAS, SANDRA KAY, music educator; d. Carroll Willis Formby and Annie Lee Dees; m. Lamah L. Dumas, June 4, 1961 (dec. Jan. 24, 1980); children: Lisa Kay, Stephen Lamah. BA in Edn., La. Tech U., 1963; MusB in Edn., So. Ark. U., 1980. Lang. arts educator Webster Parish Sch. Bd., Cotton Valley, La., 1965—68; music educator Taylor (Ark.) Pub. Schs., 1981—83; pvt. piano/organ tchr., 1983—; elem. music educator White Hall (Ark.) Sch. Dist., 1987—. Organist First Bapt. Ch., Springhill, La., 1975—87, White Hall, 1990—; dir. Moody Singers, White Hall, 1998—. Named Dist. Elem. Tchr. of Yr., 1999; scholar, Sigma Alpha Iota, 1978. Mem.: NEA, Ark. Music Educators Assn., Music Educators Nat. Conf. (pres. So. Ark. U. chpt. 1978—79, Music award 1980), Alpha Chi, Phi Kappa Phi. Baptist. Avocations: writing family history, travel. Home: 604 Rolling Hills Dr White Hall AR 71602 Office: Moody Elem Sch 700 Moody Dr White Hall AR 71602

DUMAS, SANDRA LEE, medical technician, microbiologist; b. Amsterdam, N.Y., Nov. 15, 1949; d. Richard Carl and Eunice Yetive Teschka; children: Stacey Ann Warner, Joseph William Hodlin; m. C. Clifford Jr. A in Clin. Lab. Sci., Empire State Coll., Saratoga Springs, N.Y., 1987, BS in Biology, 1991. Cert. clin. lab. scientist Nat. Cert. Agy. for Med. Lab. Pers. Med. tech. Johnstown (N.Y.) Hosp., 1968-70, Nathan Littauer Hosp., Gloversville, N.Y., 1967-68, med. tech. in microbiology, 1975—. Avocations: painting, golf, boating, photography.

DUMBRAVO, CATHY CROSBY, primary school educator; b. Lake Charles, La., Apr. 9, 1952; d. Elmer Lamont Crosby, Jr. and Lucille Pat (Bradford) Crosby; m. Ben Taylor Johnston, III (div.); m. James Cornell Dumbravo, Feb. 23, 1979; 1 child, Dustin Charles. BS in Elem. Edn., N.E. La. U., Monroe, 1975. Second grade tchr. College St. Elem., Lewisville, Tex., 1992—. Sci. curriculum adv. College St. Elem., Lewisville, 1993—. Bd. mem., v.p. programs PTA, 1996—2006; active children ministry, VBS, SS Lakeland Bapt. Ch., Lewisville, 1997—. Grantee, Lewisville Edn. Found., 2002. Mem.: Lewisville Literacy Coun., Nat. Sci. Tchrs. Assn. Avocations: science education, environmental studies. Home: 1879 Hilltop Dr Lewisville TX 75077 Office: College St Elem Sch 350 W College St Lewisville TX 75057

DUMITRESCU, CRISTINA M., intensive care nurse; b. Bucharest, Romania, Mar. 5, 1960; d. Mircea and Margareta Ispas; m. Gabriel N None, June 6, 1989. Degree in biochem. rsch. mgmt., C.A. Rosetti, Bucharest, 1980, BSc in Biochemistry, 1981; ADN, Walla Walla CC, 1986; BS, U. Wash., 1988. RN Wash., 1986, lic. advance cardiac life support, Medic 7 Dist. Snohomish County, 1996. Biochem. rschr. Pharm. Co. Bucharest, Romania, 1981—82; registry relief nurse Kimberly Quality Care, Seattle, 1986—92; RN/charge nurse Swedish Med. Ctr., Seattle, 1988—93; home care ventilator nurse Nurse's Ho. Call, Seattle, 1989—94; registry relief nurse Amserv Western Med., Seattle, 1990—95; case mgr./mktg. dir. Vis. Nurse Svcs., Seattle, 1991—96; ICCU/CO RN Stevens Med. Ctr., Edmonds, Wash., 1996—. Marketer Vis. Nurse, Seattle, 1991—96; cmty. health care cons. Walla Walla DSHS, 1986; exec. sec./office mgr. Musica Romanica Inc., Seattle, 2000—; property mgmt. Dumitrescu Fourplex, Kent, Wash., 2002—; cmty. svc. dir. Seventh Day Adventist Ch., Seattle, 1992—. Contbr. articles to profl. jours. Dir. allocation of cmty. resources Cmty. Services Ctr., Seattle, 1992; project mgr. Helping Hands of Am., Seattle, 1993—94, Cmty. Services SDA, Snohomish, Wash., 1994—95. Mem.: NAFE (Excellence in Nursing award 2001), Walla Walla Businesswoman's Assn., U. Wash. Alumni Assn., Sigma Theta Tau Internat. Office: Musica Romanica Inc PO Box 5037 Kent WA 98064 Office Phone: 253-859-2870. Office Fax: 253-859-2873. Personal E-mail: xchange60@earthlink.net.

DUMITRU, MIRELA, accountant; b. Constanta, Romania, Dec. 3, 1959; d. Nicolae and Lucia Bradeanu; 1 child, Corina-Luiza. BS, St. Francis Coll., 2003. Acct. Robert Half Internat., Inc., N.Y.C., 1998—2002; acctg. supr. DSi Group, Maspeth, NY, 2002—. Cons. Descendent of Holy Spirit, Ridgewood, NY, 1991—2003. Scholar, St. Francis Coll., 2000. Christian Orthodox. Office: Display Systems PO Box 38 Maspeth NY 11378-0038 Personal E-mail: mireladtru@msn.com.

DUMLER, PATRICIA ANN, critical care nurse; b. San Antonio, Feb. 16, 1960; d. Raymond Lee and Ann Dell (Comer) Dumler; m. David Hastings Smith, Dec. 28, 1985. BSN, U. Md., Balt., 1983; student, James Madison U., Harrisonburg, Va., 1978-81. Staff nurse Bon Secours Hosp., Balt., 1983—85, Rockingham Meml. Hosp., Harrisonburg, Va., 1986—87; clin. nurse II Homewood Hosp. Ctr., Balt., 1987—91; clin. nurse Johns Hopkins Hosp., Balt., 1991—, performance improvement/utilization mgmt. specialist, 1991—.

DUMOVICH, LORETTA, retired real estate company executive, retired transportation executive; b. Kansas City, Kans., Sept. 29, 1930; d. Michael Nicholas and Frances Barbara (Horvat) D. Student public schs., Kansas City. Lic. real estate broker, Kans., Mo. Corp. sec., dir. Riss Internat. Corp., 1950-86, Riss Intermodal Corp., 1969-86, World Leasing Corp., 1969-86; pres., dir. Columbia Properties, Inc., 1969-86; v.p., dir. Republic Industries, 1969-86; corp. sec., dir. Comml. Equipment Co. Inc., Charlotte, N.C., 1980-93; v.p., corp. sec. Commonwealth Gen. Ins. Co., Kansas City, Mo., 1986-93, Heart of Am. Fire & Casualty Co., Kansas City, 1986-93, ret., 1993. Mem. Kansas City (Mo.) Real Estate Bd., Bldg. Owners and Mgrs. Assn. of Kansas City (Mo.), Terminal Properties Exchange (founding mem.), Am. Royal Assn. (gov.) Office: 215 W Pershing Rd Kansas City MO 64108-4317

DUNAWAY, CAMMIE, marketing executive; b. 1962; m. Lendy Dunaway; 1 child, Davis. BS, U. Richmond, 1984; MBA, Harvard U., 1990. Mktg. analyst Martin Agency, Richmond, Va.; account exec. Howard Merrell and Ptnrs., NC; asst. brand mgr. Frito-Lay, Dallas, product mgr., v.p. sales for No. Calif., Wash., Ore., Alaska and Hawaii, head nat. sales force, v.p. for kids and teens mktg., 2001—03; chief mktg. officer Yahoo, Inc., Sunnyvale, Calif., 2003—. Co-founder TravelingChefs; bd. dirs. Brunswick Corp., 2006—. Vol. San Jose Tech Mus.; bd. mem. Jr. Achievement of Silicon Valley. Named one of 100 Top Marketers, Advt. Age Mag. Mem.: Am. Mktg. Assn. Office: Yahoo! Inc 701 First Ave Sunnyvale CA 94089 Office Phone: 408-349-3300. Office Fax: 408-349-3301.*

DUNAWAY, CAROLYN BENNETT, retired sociology professor; b. Atlanta, Mar. 3, 1943; d. Clarence Rhodes and Gay (McKenzie) Bennett; m. William Preston Dunaway, Aug. 26, 1967; 1 child, Robert Bennett Dunaway. BA in Social Scis., Auburn U., 1966, EdD, 1983; MA in Sociology, U. Ala., Tuscaloosa, 1967. Instr. sociology Jefferson State C.C., Birmingham, Ala., 1967-69; prof. Auburn U., Montgomery, Ala., 1970-71; prof. sociology and gerontology dept. Jacksonville (Ala.) State U., 1971-95, prof. emeritus, 1999—. Student counselor Jacksonville State U., Ala., 1971—. Contbd. articles to profl. jours. Cons., trainer Calhoun County Hospice Anniston, Ala., 1983—; presenter Calhoun County Gerontology, Anniston, 1985—; officer Jacksonville Book Club, Ala., 1984; elder, tchr. First Presbyn. Ch., Jacksonville, 1993. Recipient 100 Most Outstanding Women Alumna award Auburn U., 1991, U. Rsch. award Jacksonville State U., 1989. Mem. Ala.-Miss. Sociol. Assn. (v.p. 1975-76, Sociology Club, Inter-Se Study Club, Ala. Fedn. Womens Club (dist. sect.), Phi Kappa Phi, Kappa Delta Pi, Delta Delta Delta, Phi Delta Kappa. Democrat. Presbyn. Avocations: flower arranging, gardening, reading. Home: 902 11th St NE Jacksonville AL 36265-1230 Office Phone: 256-435-3231.

DUNAWAY, CHARJEAN LAUGHLIN, librarian; b. Jennings, La., July 8, 1955; d. John Tillman and Jeannine (Lackey) L.; m. Daryel Dunaway, Aug. 19, 1978. Student, Meridian Jr. Coll., 1972-76; BLS, U. So. Miss., 1980, MLS, 1981. Librarian S.E. Miss. Legal Services Corp., Hattiesburg, 1981, Forrest County Schs., Hattiesburg, 1981-82, St. Andrew's Episcopal Sch., Jackson, Miss., 1982-84; reference librarian Jackson Met. Library System, 1984-86, br. mgr., 1986; asst. dir. Jackson/Hinds Library System, 1986—. Mem. Miss. Paralysis Assn., 1983—, Hinds County Dem. Exec. Com., Jackson, 1984—; staff Mondale/Ferraro Campaign, Miss., 1984. Mem. ALA, Miss. Library Assn., S.E. Library Assn., U. So. Miss. Sci. Alumni Assn. (v.p. 1981-87, pres. 1987-88), NOW (asst. state coordinator 1983-84), Beta Phi Mu. Lodges: Soroptimist. Baptist. Office: Jackson/Hinds Library System 664 S State St Jackson MS 39201-5611

DUNAWAY, FAYE (DOROTHY DUNAWAY), actress; b. Bascom, Fla., Jan. 14, 1941; d. John and Grace D.; m. Peter Wolf, Aug. 7, 1974 (div. 1979); m. Terrence O'Neill, 1983 (div. 1987); 1 child, O'Neill. Student, U. Fla., Boston U. Appearances include as original mem. Lincoln Ctr. Repertory Co., N.Y.C., off-Broadway in Hogan's Goat; also in (play) Curse of the Aching Heart, 1982; motion picture appearances include Bonnie and Clyde, 1967, Hurry Sundown, 1967, Puzzle of a Downfall Child, The Happening, 1967, The Thomas Crown Affair, 1968, A Place For Lovers, 1969, The Arrangement, 1969, The Extraordinary Seaman, 1969, Little Big Man, 1970, The Puzzle of a Downfall Child, 1970, Doc, 1971, La Maison Sous les Arbres, 1971, Oklahoma Crude, 1973, The Three Musketeers, 1973, Chinatown, 1974, The Towering Inferno, 1974, The Four Musketeers, 1975, Three Days of the Condor, 1975, Network, 1976 (Acad. award for Best Actress), The Voyage of the Damned, 1976, The Eyes of Laura Mars, 1978, The Champ, 1979, The First Deadly Sin, 1980, Mommie Dearest, 1981, The Wicked Lady, 1982, Ordeal by Innocence, 1984, Supergirl, 1984, Barfly, 1987, Burning Secret, 1988, La Partita, 1988, Midnight Crossing, 1988, The Gamble, 1989, On a Moonlit Night, 1989, Wait Until Spring, Bandini, 1989, The Handmaid's Tale, 1990, Three Weeks in Jerusalem, 1990, Scorchers, 1990, Arrowtooth Waltz, 1991, Double Edge, 1992, Arizona Dream, 1993, The Temp, 1993, Even Cowgirls Get the Blues, 1994, Don Juan DeMarco, 1995, En brazos de la mujer madura, 1996, The Chamber, 1996, Albino Alligator, 1996, Dunston Checks In, 1996, Twilight of the Golds, 1997, Drunks, 1997, Fanny Hill, 1998 Love Lies Bleeding, 1999, The Messenger: The Story of Joan of Arc, 1999, The Thomas Crown Affair, 1999, The Yards, 2000, Stanley's Gig, 2000, Changing Hearts, 2002, The Rules of Attraction, 2002, Mid-Century, 2002, The Calling, 2002, Blind Horizon, 2004, The Last Goodbye, 2004, El Padrino, 2004, Jennifer's Shadow, 2004, Ghosts Never Sleep, 2004, Love Hollywood Style, 2005; TV movies: Hogan's Goat, 1971, The Woman I Love, 1972, After the Fall, 1974, The Disappearance of Aimee, 1976, Evita Peron, 1981, The Country Girl, 1982, 13 at Dinner, 1985, Beverly Hills Madame, 1986, Raspberry Ripple, 1986, Casanova, 1987, Cold Sassy Tree, (co-exec. prodr.), 1989, Silhouette, 1990 (co-exec. prodr.), Columbo: It's All in the Game (Emmy award for Guest Actress in Drama 1994), Mother Love, 1995, A Family Divided, 1995, The People Next Door, 1996, Rebecca, 1997, Twilight of the Golds, 1997, Gia, 1998, A Will of Their Own, 1998, Running Mates, 2000, The Biographer, 2002, Anonymous Rex, 2004, Back When We Were Grownups, 2004; TV appearances: Seaway, 1965, The Trials of O'Brien, 1966, Road to Avonlea, 1995, Touched By An Angel, 2001, Soul Food, 2002, Alias, 2002, 03; TV miniseries: Ellis Island, 1984, Christopher Columbus, 1985; TV series: It Had To Be You, 1993, A Will of Their Own, 1998, Starlet, 2005-; Acted, dir, prodr. (films): The Yellow Bird, 2001; Author: Looking for Gatsby: My Life, 1995. Recipient Most Promising Newcomer Award Brit. Film Acad., 1968

DUNAWAY, MARSHA LANDRUM, special education educator; b. Roanoke, Va., Feb. 24, 1951; d. John Edward Landrum, Jr. and Diana Smith Landrum; m. Thomas Larry Dunaway, Mar. 17, 1973; children: Larry Scott, Shawn Michael. BS, East Tenn. State U., Johnson, 1973; MS, Radford U., Va., 1982. Postgrad. profl. lic. Va., 1973, cert. swim ofcl. and trainer Va. Swimming Inc., 1990, YMCA Nat., 1982, swim ofcl. Nat. Collegiate Swim Ofcls. Assn., 1990. Spl. edn. tchr. Radford City Schs., 1990—. Dir. Hensel Eckman YMCA, Pulaksi; pres. SWAT Swimming, Radford. Mem.: NEA (life), Radford Edn. Assn. (treas. 1998—2002, pres. 2002—06), Va. Edn. Assn. (pres. New River Uniserv Dist. 3 2005—06, chairwoman PAC New River Uniserv Dist. 3). Office: Radford City Schools 12th St Radford VA 24141 Personal E-mail: mdunaway@rcps.org.

DUNBAR, BONNIE J., engineer, astronaut; b. Sunnyside, Wash., Mar. 3, 1949; d. Robert Dunbar; m. Ronald M. Sega. BS in Ceramic Engring., U. Wash., 1971, MS in Ceramic Engring. cum laude, 1975; PhD in Biomed. Engring., U. Houston, 1983. With Boeing Computer Svcs., 1971-73; sr. rsch. engr. space div. Rockwell Internat., Downey, Calif.; with NASA, 1978—, astronaut, 1981—, mission specialist flight STS 61-8, 1985, mission specialist flight STS-32, 1990, payload commander Shuttle Columbia Flight, 1992, spl. asst. to dep. assoc. adminstr. Washington, 1993, with mission STS-71 Shuttle Atlanis, 1995, with mssion STS-89 Shuttle Endeavour, 1998, asst. dir. univ. rsch. Johnson Space Ctr. Vis. scientist Harwell Labs., Oxford, Eng., 1975; adj. asst. prof. mech. engring. U. Houston, mem. bioengring. adv. group; adj. prof. mech. engring. U. Houston.; bd. dirs. Arnold Air Soc., Angel Flight, Internat. Acad. Astronautics, Exptl. Aircraft Assn., Soc. Women Engrs. Recipient Nat. Engring. award Am. Assn. Engring. Socs., 1992, Engring. Achievement award Design News, 1993, Judith Resnik award IEEE, 1993, Resnik Challenger Medal Soc. Women Engrs., 1993; named to Hall of Fame Women in Tech. Internat., 2000. Mem. AAAS, NSF (engring. adv. bd. 1993-), NAE, Am. Ceramics Soc. (life, Greaves-Walker award 1985, Schwalt Zwalder PACE award 1990, James I. Mueller award, 2000), Soc. Biomed. Engring., Materials Rsch. Soc., Nat. Inst. Ceramic Engrs., Arnold Air Soc. and Angel Flight (bd. dirs.), Keramos, Tau Beta Pi. Achievements include research in ceramics that played a key role in developing the ceramic tiles used in the space shuttle's thermal protection system; first woman assigned to a laboratory mission to operate the Spacelab, its subsystems and experiments.

DUNBAR, DIANA L. (DIANE L. DUNBAR), dancer, choreographer, educator, writer, storyteller, actress; b. Troy, Ala., Mar. 2, 1954; d. Donal Steuben and Sara Lee Dunbar. BA in Fine Arts and Theater, Coll. Charleston, 1979, postgrad., 1979—81; MA in Creative Arts and Performing Arts, NYU, 1990, studied dance and dance history with Lavinia Williams, 1982—89, studied classical East Indian Dance with Indrani Rahman; studied with Mary Anthony, studied with Anna Sokolow. Cert. English tchr. 7-12 grades, spl. edn. tchr. NY. Vol. tchg. asst. classical East Indian Dance for Indrani Rahman NYC; elem. HS tchr. K-12 reading, English lit., writing, tolerance, sci., music, social studies through creative arts NYC Pub. Sch. 106, 1991—2001; elem. HS tchr. K-12 reading, English, writing, tolerance, sci., music, social studies through creative arts NYC Pub. Sch. 94, 2001—02, Hosp. Schs. M, 2002—. Co-pres. Eric & Co. Video, NYC, 1983—2006; tchr., video cons. Youth Can, NYC, 1997—98; dancer, choreographer modern, classical E. Indian, Afro-Haitian, ballroom, hip-hop, world folk dance, jazz, reggae, tap, musical comedy beg. ballet Children's Dance. Actress Hernando DeSoto Conquistador Spain, Hot Springs, Ark., 1979, singer, actress, dancer (musicals) Bound To Rise, NYC, 1979, Shakespeare and Porter, Medicine Show Theatre, 2001; dancer Classical East Indian Dances, 1986—; author, storyteller, dancer Lavinia Williams: The Dancer, NYC, 1989 (Writer's Series Performance award Medicine Show Theater, 1989). Vol. asst. tchr. Classical East Indian Dance NYU, NYC, 1990—; founding sponsor Martin Luther King Jr. Natl. Meml., 2006; active Nat. Arbor Day Found., United Fedn. Tchrs.; leadership coun. So. Poverty Law Ctr., East Village, NY, 2003—; legis. intern Capitol Hill, 1974; worked to save and preserve cmty. gardens and parks NYC, 1997—; mem. Albert's Garden, NYC, 1997—99. Named Outstanding Freshman Girl award, Troy State U., 1972, Oustanding Dancer/Performer Yancey Dance Theatre, NY Times, 1992; named to Wall of Tolerance in Montgomery, Ala., So. Poverty Law Ctr., 2003—; recipient Tchr. award, Children's Creative Writing Fund, 2000. Mem.: LWV, Sacred Dance Guild, Medicine Show Theatre, Smithsonian, GreenGuerillas, Audubon Club, Alpha Gamma Delta Sorority (life Highest GPA Award at Troy State U. for 1972, '73). Avocations: dance, choreographing, writing fiction, nonfiction, and poetry, storytelling, cat rescuing.

DUNBAR, HOLLY JEAN, communications executive, public relations executive; b. Plainfield, NJ, May 15, 1960; d. Robert Kenneth and Marian (DuBets) D. BA, Rutgers U., 1982. Graphic designer Chubb & Son, Inc., Warren, N.J., 1983-86; freelance writer, 1984—; pub. rels. rep., archivist AT&T Bell Labs., Warren, 1987; self-employed graphic designer North Plainfield, N.J., 1987-88; direct response mktg. coord. U.S. and Can. Beneficial Mgmt. Corp. of Am., Peapack, NJ, 1988-94; internal comms. mgr. Beneficial Mgmt. Corp., Peapack, NJ, 1994—98; dir. comms. and mktg. Somerset County United Way, Bridgewater, NJ, 1998—2005; corp. strategy and comm. IEEE, Piscataway, 2006—. Photographer: (survey) Tark Farm Site Monmouth Battlefield, 1982, Ellis Island Restoration, 1988-92; designer: Official Logo and Slogan of Somerset County, NJ, 1985 Recipient Photography award Cook Coll., New Brunswick, NJ, 1981, Chubb & Son, Inc., Warren, 1984, NJ Agrl. Fair, 1994; Outstanding Svc. to 4-H award Somerset County 4-H, Bridgewater, 1996, Outstanding Alumna, 1999, Outstanding Vol., 2000; cited for Distinctive Contbr. NJ Culture and History Am. Studies Dept., Douglass Coll., New Brunswick, 1982, others; Somerset County Bd. Chosen Freeholders award, Somerville, NJ, 1996, 2003. Mem. DAR (nat. vice chmn. pub. rels.-print media 2001-04, dep. rep. Nat. Soc to Vet. Affairs Vol. Svc., 1983-92, state chmn. Am. Heritage-Art NJ Soc. 1989-92, state chmn. NJ Jr. Mem. Centennial Project N.J. Soc. 1991-92, nat. and NJ state page 1983-2000, regent Elizabeth Snyder chpt. 1992-95, registrar, 1991-92, Continental Congress Thatcher award 1992, state chmn. DAR Mag. Advt. NJ Soc. 1992-95, Ad Excellence award, 1993, 94, state corr. sec. NJ soc. 1995-98, state chmn. Conservation NJ Soc., 1998—, Outstanding Jr. Mem. NJ Soc. 1996), N.J. Audubon Soc., N.J. Divsn. Fish and Wildlife-Wildlife Conservation Corps, Internat. Assn. Bus. Communicators, Douglass Coll. Alumnae Assn., Somerset County 4-H Assn., Am. Birding Assn., Clan Dunbar. Avocations: history, genealogy, art, birdwatching, travel. Home: 725 Ayres Ave North Plainfield NJ 07063-1607

DUNBAR, LEILA, antiques appraiser, auction house executive; Graduate in Journalism and Spanish, U. N.C., 1983. Appraiser Dunbar's Gallery, Milford, Mass., 1984—91, pres., 1991—99; regular featured appraiser PBS' Antiques Roadshow, 1996—; sr. v.p., dir. collectibles dept., global dir. online collectibles auctions Sotheby's, N.Y.C., 1999—. Jazz staff mem. WGBH-FM, Boston. Contbr. Downbeat Mag., Reuters News Svc., profl. pubs. including USA Today, AP, N.Y. Times, GQ, N.Y. Daily News, London Standard, New Orleans Picayune, Chgo. Sun-Times, Auction Universe, others; author: Motorcycle Collectibles, 1996, More Motorcycle Collectibles, 1997, Automobilia, 1998. Office: Global Dir Online Collectibles Auctions Sothebys 1334 York Ave New York NY 10021

DUNBAR, LORNA J., special education educator; b. Schnecksville, Pa., Aug. 28, 1970; d. Terrence Arthur and Shirley J. D. BS, Pa. State U., 1992; MEd, Lehigh U., 1997. Cert. elem. and spl. edn. tchr., Pa. Youth care worker Ctrl. Counties Youth Ctr., Bellefonte, Pa., 1989-90; mental health technician/substitute tchr. Meadows Psychiat. Ctr., Centre Hall, Pa., 1992-93; tchr. Pitts. Pub. Schs., 1993-94; therapeutic staff mem. Interim Health Care, Pitts., 1994-95; primary clinician U. Pitts. Med. Ctr., 1994-95; rsch. intern/tchr. Lehigh U., Bethlehem, Pa., 1995-97; spl. edn. tchr. West Shore Dist., New Cumberland, Pa., 1997—; implementation cons. Softmed Sys., Silver Spring, Md., 1999—2005; ind. cons. Brookmeade Healthcare, Atlanta, 2005—. Mem. Coun. for Exceptional Children, Coun. for Children with Behavioral Disorders. Avocations: singing, reading, walking, aerobics. Office: West Shore Sch Dist 507 Fishing Creek Rd New Cumberland PA 17070-3000

DUNBAR, MARY ASMUNDSON, communications executive, public information officer, consultant, investor; b. Sacramento, Calif., Feb. 6, 1942; d. Vigfus Samundur and Aline Mary (McGrath) Asmundson; m. Robert Copeland Dunbar, June 21, 1969; children: Geoffrey Townsend, William Asmundson. BA in English Lit., Smith Coll., 1964; MA in Comm., Stanford U., 1967; MBA in Fin., Case Western Res. U., 1985. Cert. pub. rels. profl. Tchr. Peace Corps, Cameroun, Africa, 1964-66; writer, editor Ednl. Devel. Corp., Palo Alto, Calif., 1967-68, Addison-Wesley, Menlo Park, Calif., 1969-70; freelance writer, editor various cos., Cleve., 1970-85; account exec. Edward Howard & Co., Cleve., 1985-87, Dix & Eaton, Inc., Cleve., 1987-89, sr. account exec., 1990-92, v.p., 1992-96, sr. v.p., 1997—. Author publs. in field. Trustee Cleve. Coun. World Affairs, 1994—99. Smith Coll. scholar, Northampton, Mass., 1960-64; fellowship Stanford Univ., Palo Alto, Calif., 1967; recipient Internat. Assn. Bus. Comm. award, 1987, Women in Comm. award, 1987, Arthur Page award, 1990. Mem. Smith Coll. Club Cleve., Pub. Rels. Soc. Am. (Silver Anvil award 1997), Nat. Investor Rels. Inst. (past pres. Cleve.-No. Ohio chpt., nat. bd. dirs. 2002—, chmn. bd. 2005-06), CFA Soc. Cleve. Republican. Episcopalian. Avocations: yoga, music. Home: 2880 Fairfax Rd Cleveland OH 44118-4014 Office: Dix & Eaton Inc 200 Public Square Ste 1400 Cleveland OH 44114-2316 Office Phone: 216-241-4601. Business E-Mail: mdunbar@dix-eaton.com.

DUNBAR, MARY JUDITH, literature and language professor; PhD, Stanford U., Calif., 1976. Lectr. English U. of London Inst. of Edn., 1970—78; assoc. prof. English Santa Clara U., Calif., 1978—. Co-editor: (book) In Celebration: Anemos. Poems Presented to Denise Levertov; contbr. articles to profl. jours. Recipient Fulbright scholarship, 1961—62, Dreher Internship Grant for Faculty-Student Collaborative Rsch., English Dept., Santa Clara U., 2003—04, Faculty Student Rsch. Asst. Program grant, Santa Clara U., 2005—06, U. Rsch. Grant, 2006—07, Woodrow Wilson fellowship, 1962—63, Univ. Fellowship in Humanities, Stanford U., 1964—65, Leverhulme Fellowship, Univ. Coll., U. of London, 1966—67, NEH grant, NEH with Folger Inst. of Renaissance and 18th-Century Studies, 1982, 1985, 1992, Irvine Curriculum Devel. Grants, Irvine Found. and Santa Clara U., 1992—93, Presdl. Rsch. Grant and Thomas Terry Grants, Santa Clara U., 1979—83, 1986—89, 1995—2006. Mem.: Shakespeare Assn. of Am. Office: Santa Clara Univ English Dept 500 El Camino Real Santa Clara CA 95053 Office Phone: 408-554-4001.

DUNBAR, SHIRLEY EUGENIA-DORIS, small business owner, writer; b. Haverhill, Mass., Apr. 26, 1930; d. Clement and Doris (Riel) Allard; m. Everett Allan Dunbar, Feb. 18, 1967; children: Linda, Andrew, Susan. BA magna cum laude, U. Mass., 1974; MA, U. N.H., 1975; EdD, Nova U., 1979. Cert. gemologist. From instr. to prof. comm. Bunker Hill C.C., Boston, 1975-89, prof. emeritus, 1989—; owner Treasure Coast Gem Lab. Dir. tchg. tng. program, Taipei, Taiwan, 1983—84; owner Dunbar Enterprises, St. Lucie, Fla., 1988—96, Treasure Coast Gem Lab., Port St. Lucie, 1996—; cons. in field. Author: Heisey Glass: The Early Years, 1896-1924, 2000. Dir. Learn to Read, Port St. Lucie County, 1989—91; judge Young Floridian awards St. Lucie County, 1998—. Recipient Pub. Svc. award, Ministry of Edn., Taiwan, 1982—83, citation for outstanding performance, Gov. Michael Dukakis, 1985, Nat. Competition Non-Fiction award, 2001, 1st pl. award, Mid-Adminstrn. Congress, Non-Fiction Pub. Adult Book 1st pl. award, Fla. State, 2001, Best in Show award, Rock and Gem Club, 2003; CAEL fellow, U. Ohio, 1984. Mem.: AAUW (founding br. pres.), Nat. Assn. Jewelry Appraisers, Nat. Assn. Jewelry (cert. appraiser), Nat. League Am. Pen Women, Fla. Women's Consortium. Avocations: silversmithing, goldsmithing, writing. E-mail: shirley400@aol.com.

DUNBAR, SUE, music educator; d. Stanford H. and Sally Q. Hartshorn; m. Bruce C. Dunbar, Nov. 19, 1983; children: Gregory, Cameron. MusB Edn., Heidelberg Coll., Tiffin, Ohio, 1976; EdM in Creative Arts, Lesley U., Cambridge, Mass., 2006. Instrumental music tchr. Amherst (Mass.) Pub. Schs., 1976—. Musician: (flutist) Opera Orchestras, Musicals, Professional Performing Groups. Drum instr. Scots Highland Pipes and Drums, Ashby, Mass., 1997—2006; data technician New Salem Pub. Libr., Mass., 1998—2006; ch. treas. Ctrl. Congl. Ch. New Salem, 2003—06. Home: 25 Millington Rd New Salem MA 01355 Office: Amherst Public Schools 170 Chestnut St Amherst MA 01002 Office Phone: 413-362-1400.

DUNBAR-RICHMAN, ANNE CAMERON, pathologist; b. Bklyn., June 10, 1921; d. Robert Cameron and Alma (Kopriva) Dunbar; m. Robert Richman, July 14, 1950 (div. Apr. 1957); children: Robert Emmett, Carla Jeanne; m. Claude Lee Snider, Oct. 1, 1965 (dec. Dec. 1994). AB in Zoology, George Washington U., 1942; MA in Biology, Colo. Coll., 1944; MD, George Washington U., 1949. Diplomate in pathologic anatomy Am. Bd. Pathology, 1956, in clin. pathology Am. Bd. Pathology, 1959. Intern. Del. Hosp., Wilmington, 1949-50, resident, 1950-51; asst. supt. D.C. Gen. Hosp., Washington, 1952, med. officer pathology svc., 1952-55; assoc. pathologist Drs. A.W. Freshman & Stanley K. Kurland, Denver, 1956-57; pathologist Ball Meml. Hosp., Muncie, Ind., 1958; assoc. pathologist Del. Hosp., 1958-59; jr. pathologist Armed Forces Inst. Pathology, 1959-61; assoc. pathologist Meth. Evang. Hosp., Louisville, 1961-75, 75-76, acting pathologist, 1975, assoc. pathologist, 1976-79, St. Joseph Inmfirmary Audubon Hosp., Louisville, 1976-80, Clin. Pathology Assocs., Louisville, 1977-85; med. dir. lab. Norton S.W. Hosp. (formerly S.W. Hosp.), Louisville, 1980-2001; ret., 2001. Asst. clin. prof. pathology U. Louisville Sch. Medicine, 1965-85, clin. instr., 1961-65; instr. Meth. Evang. Hosp. Sch. Med. Tech., 1963-76; med. dir. med. tech. lab. asst. program Jefferson C.C., 1976-92 Cardiology fellow George Washington U., 1952. Fellow Am. Assn. CLin. Pathologists, Coll. Am. Pathologists; mem. AMA, Ky. Med. Assn., Ky. Soc. Pathologists (pres. 1973, 88), Louisville Soc. Internists (sec.-treas. 1993-94, 1st v.p. 1994-95, pres. 1995-96), Delta Epsilon. Avocations: tennis, gardening, horseback riding. Home: 5502 Hempstead Rd Louisville KY 40207-1251

DUNCAN, ALLYSON K., federal judge; b. Durham, NC, Sept. 5, 1951; BA, Hampton U., 1972; JD, Duke U., 1975. Bar: N.C. 1975, D.C. 1977. Assoc. editor Lawyers Coop. Publ. Co., 1976—77; law clk. to Hon. Julia Cooper Mack DC Ct. Appeals, Washington, 1977—78; appellate atty., asst. to dep. gen. counsel, asst. to chmn. EEOC, 1978—86; assoc. prof. NC Ctrl. U. Sch. Law, 1986—90; assoc. judge NC Ct. Appeals, 1990; commr. NC Utilities Commn., 1991—98; ptnr. Kilpatrick Stockton LLP, Raleigh, NC,

1998—2003; judge US Ct. Appeals (4th cir.), 2003—. Mem.: Wake County Bar Assn. (pres. 2002—03), N.C. Bar Assn. (pres.-elect 2002). Office: Terry Sanford Federal Bldg 310 New Bern Ave Rm 234-A Raleigh NC 27601*

DUNCAN, CHARLOTTE DIANE, retired secondary school educator; b. Princeton, Ky., Nov. 14, 1950; d. Charles M. and Eloise Lisanby; m. Dennis Alan Duncan, Aug. 20, 1971; children: Brian Alan, Katrina Diane. BS, Murray (Ky.) State U., 1972, M, 1982, cert. rank 1 in adminstrn., 1991. Tchr. Hopkins County Bd. Edn., Madisonville, Ky., 1972—76, 1978—2006. Resource tchr. Ky. Intern Program, Madisonville, 1991—2000, Student Tchr. Program, Murray, 2004—05. Mem.: NEA, Hopkins County Edn. Assn., Ky. Edn. Assn. Democrat. Baptist. Avocations: reading, antiques, collecting dishes. Home: 1280 Tippett Rd Hanson KY 42413

DUNCAN, CORINTHA MCKEE, counselor; b. Johnson City, Tenn., Feb. 15, 1955; d. Vestal D. and Goldie Story McKee. B of Bus. Adminstrn., East Tenn. State U., 1994, MEd, 1997. Sales rep., supr. Johnson City Ins. (Tenn.) Agy., Inc., 1980-82; svc. rep., ins. agt. Jonesborough (Tenn.) Ins. Agy., 1982-84; sec. East Tenn. State U., Johnson City, 1984-94, counselor, 1994—; advisor, recruiter, sen. staff senate. Advisor, recruiter East Tenn. State U., Johnson City. Registrar, machine operator Washington County Election Commn., Jonesborough, 1983-89, election officer, 1989—. Mem. Tenn. Assn. Collegiate Registrars and Admissions Officers (chair membership com. 1998—, mem. intercollegiate athletics adv. com. 1997—), Phi Kappa Phi. Republican. Avocations: yard work, crafts, working out, attending athletic events. Home: 608 Franklin St Johnson City TN 37604-6638 Office: East Tenn State U PO Box 70 731 Johnson City TN 37614-0731 Office Phone: 423-439-4213, 800-462-3878. Office Fax: 423-439-4630. Business E-Mail: duncan@etsu.edu.

DUNCAN, CYNTHIA BERYL, university library administrator; b. Madison, Pa., Apr. 26, 1932; d. Andrew and Harriet (Morris) D. BS, California State Coll., Pa., 1953; M.Litt., U. Pitts., 1958; MS, Fla. State U., 1965; PhD (fellow), Ind. U., 1973. Tchr., Gateway Union Sch., Monroeville, Pa., 1953-64; instr. Fla. State U., 1965, spl. librarian, 1966, acting librarian, 1967; asso. prof. library sci., head of reference Mansfield (Pa.) State Coll., 1966-67, Winthrop Coll., Rock Hill, S.C., 1967-70; adj. prof. library sci. Ind. State U., 1972; prof. library sci., dir. Sandel Library, N.E. La. U., 1973-76; dean library services Old Dominion U., Norfolk, Va., 1976—. Adj. lectr. library sci. Cath. U. Am., 1979-80; dir. SOLINET, 1982-85; mem. OCLC Users Council, 1979-81, 85-86 Mem. ALA (chmn. ULS 1984, chmn. sect. rev. com. 1985-86), La. Library Assn., Va. Library Assn. (chmn. coll./univ. sect. 1980-81), Assn. Am. Library Schs. Office: University Library Old Dominion Univ Norfolk VA 23508

DUNCAN, DIANNE WALKER, elementary school educator; b. Altavista, Va., Nov. 15, 1954; d. Robert and Catherine Forte. BS in History and Govt., Longwood Coll., 1977; MEd in Curriculum and Instrn., Va. Commonwealth U., 1993. Cert. tchr. social studies. Social studies tchr. Stonewall Jackson Mid. Sch., Mechanicsville, Va., 1977—98; civics tchr. John Witherspoon Mid. Sch., Princeton, NJ. Cmty. svc. coach John Witherspoon Mid. Sch. Do Something, N.Y.C.; mem. Character Edn. Partnership, Washington, DC; character edn., citizenship presenter N.J. Edn. Assn. Conf., Atlantic City, 2001; mentor jr. level presvc. tchrs. Rider U., Lawrenceville, NJ, Princeton U., NJ. Mem. So. Poverty Law Ctr., Mont., Ala., 2001—; sponsor, coord. of food dr. John Witherspoon and Crisis Ministry Trenton and Princeton, 1999—2003; sponsor, supervise mid. sch. tutors Princeton Young Achievers After Sch. Programs, Princeton, 2000—03; mem. People to People Amb. Programs' Social Studies Edn. Del. to South Africa, 2004. Recipient John Marshall award for excellence in tchg. the Constn., Va. Ctrl. Region, 1995, Best Practices award in citizenship, character edn., N.J., 2000. Mem.: N.J. Edn. Assn., N.J. Coun. Social Studies, Nat. Coun. Social Studies, Assn. Supervision and Curriculum Devel. D-Liberal. Avocations: gardening, reading. Office: Princeton Regional Schs 217 Walnut Ln Princeton NJ 08540 Office Phone: 609-806-4270.

DUNCAN, FRANCES MURPHY, retired special education educator; b. Utica, NY, June 23, 1920; d. Edward Simon and Elizabeth Myers (Stack) Murphy; m. Lee C. Duncan, June 23, 1947 (div. June 1969); children: Lee C., Edward M., Paul H., Elizabeth B., Nancy R., Frances B.(dec.), Richard L.(dec.). BA, Columbia U., 1942; MEd, Auburn U., 1963, EdD, 1969. Head sci. dept. Arnold Jr. H.S., Columbus, Ga., 1960-63; tchr. physiology, Spanish Jordan H.S., Columbus, Ga., 1963-64; tchr. spl. edn. mentally retarded Muscogee County Sch. Sys., Columbus, Ga., 1964-65; instr. spl. edn. Auburn (Ala.) U., 1966-69; assoc. dir. Douglas Sch. for Learning Disabilities, Columbus, 1969-70; prof. edn. and spl. edn. Columbus Coll., 1970-85, ret., 1985. Past dir. Columbus Devel. Ctr.; past sec. exec. bd. Muscular Dystrophy Assn., 1968-70; 73-74; mem. Gov.'s Commn. on Disabled Georgians; past trustee Listening Eyes Sch. for Deaf; past mem. Mayor's Com. on Handicapped; mem. team for evaluation and placement of exceptional children Columbus Pub. Schs.; past pres., Aux., Columbus Med. Ctr. Vol. Med. Ctr. Columbus Regional Healthcare Sys., Ga. Fellow Am. Assn. Mental Retardation; mem. AAUP, AAUW (pres. 1973-75, divsn. rec. sec. 1975—), Coun. Exceptional Children (legis. chmn. 1973-74), Psi Chi, Phi Delta Kappa. Roman Catholic. Home: 100 Spring Harbor Dr #655 Columbus GA 31904 Personal E-mail: duncanf@knology.net.

DUNCAN, GLORIA CELESTINE, elementary school educator, consultant; b. Columbia, S.C., May 31, 1944; d. John Dubois Duncan and Fannie Ruby Batiste; 1 child, Jason Ira. AA, City Coll. San Francisco, 1965; BA, U. Bridgeport, 1968; MA, U. San Francisco, 1984. Presenter Calif. State Dept., Long Beach, 1990; mentor tchr. Alum Rock Sch. Dist., San Jose, 1990—94, educator, 1972—. Adv. bd. San Jose Writing Project, 1993—96; assoc. dir. San Jose State U., 1993—96. Mem. youth adv. bd. Am. Cancer Soc., Santa Clara County, Calif., 1995—, vol., 1985—; mem. edn. com. Kids Voting U.S.A., Silicon Valley, 1994—; sr. warden St. Philip's Episcopal. Ch., San Jose, 1988. Mem.: Informal Computer Using Educators (membership co-chair, mem. adv. bd.), Phi Delta Kappa (Stanford chpt. historian 1995—96, treas. 1996—), Beta Pi Sigma (Soror of Yr. 1996), Delta Kappa Gamma (co-pres. 1996, pres. Gamma Psi chpt. 1998—). Avocations: travel, reading, sewing, knitting, tennis. Office: Mildred Goss Elem Sch 2475 Van Winkle Ln San Jose CA 95116-3758

DUNCAN, GWENDOLYN MCCURRY, elementary school educator; b. Walhalla, SC, Feb. 24, 1943; d. Benjamin Harrison and Lucy Rosa (Quarles) McCurry; m. Harold Edward Duncan, July 29, 1962; children: Gregory Scott, Michael Lane. BA in Elem. Edn., Clemson (S.C.) U., 1984, MA in Elem. Edn., 1999. Cert. tchr. S.C., Nat. Bd. Tchr. Cert., 2002. Tchr. Westminster (S.C.) Elem. Sch., 1984-97, Orchard Park Elem. Sch., Westminster, 1997—2004, James M. Brown Elem. Sch., Walhalla, SC, 2004—. Sunday sch. tchr. Mountain View Bapt. Ch., Walhalla, 1968—; active Westminster Elem. PTA, 1984-97, Orchard Park Elem. PTA, 1997-2004, James M. Brown Elem. PTA, 2004— Mem. NEA, Oconee County Edn. Assn., S.C. Edn. Assn., S.C. Tchrs. of Math., Nat. Coun. of Tchrs. of Math., Kappa Delta Pi. Baptist. Avocations: reading, camping, travel, growing roses. Home: 389 Fowler Rd West Union SC 29696-3122 Office: James M Brown Elem Sch 225 Coffee Rd Walhalla SC 29691

DUNCAN, HOLLY H., foundation executive; b. Cleve., July 8, 1946; d. Martin Luther and Jean Righter Hecht; m. Richard David Duncan, Dec. 23, 1967 (dec. Apr. 19, 2003); children: Darby Hecht, Whitney Duncan Ribonson. BA in Govt. summa cum laude, Ohio U., 1968; MA in Polit. Sci. magna cum laude, Miami U., Ohio, 1970. Grad. asst. Miami U., Oxford, Ohio, 1968-69; jr. officer, polit. sect. U.S. Dept. State, U.S. Fgn. Svc., Bonn, Germany, 1969-70; dir. devel. Fla. Orch., Tampa, 1980-85, Lowry Park Zoo, Tampa, 1985-87; dir. major gifts Eckerd Coll., St. Petersburg, 1987-88; v.p. devel. Ruth Eckerd Hall, Clearwater, 1988-93, Fla. Aquarium, Tampa, 1993-96; pres., CEO Morton Plant Mease Found., Clearwater, 1996—. Panelist Fla. Arts Coun., Tallahassee, 1988—93; pres. Jr. League Clearwater, 1985; chmn. Clearwater Regional C. of C., 2004; pres. Fla. Dance Assn., Tallahassee, 1988—93. Mem.: Assn. Health Philanthropy, Nat. Soc. Fundraising Execs., Bellear Country Club, Countryside Country Club, Phi Beta Kappa, Kappa Kappa Gamma (nat. devel. com. 1988—92). Democrat. Episcopalian. Avocations: current events, sports, wellness consulting. Home: 2724 Burning Tree Ln Clearwater FL 33761-3001 Office: Morton Plant Mease Found 1200 Druid Rd S Clearwater FL 33756-1995 E-mail: holduncan@msn.com.

DUNCAN, JEAN MARIE, language educator; d. Ambrose William and Margaret Jane Naughton; 1 child from previous marriage, Lindsey Nicole. BS in Edn., Truman State U., Kirksville, Mo., 1979; MS in Edn., N.E. Mo. State U., Maryville, 1982. Reading specialist endorsement Harding U., 2006. Spl. edn. tchr. Jefferson C-123 Schs., Conception Junction, Mo., 1979—87, prin., 1982—87; tchr. Decatur Pub. Schs., Ark., 1987—2003, literacy specialist, 2003—. Mem.: Ark. Edn. Assn. Avocations: reading, counted cross stitch, movies. Home: PO Box 432 Gravette AR 72736

DUNCAN, KRISTINA YVONNE, secondary school educator; b. Walla Walla, Wash., May 15, 1978; d. David Sander and Linda Yvonne Schaub; m. William Eugene Duncan, July 5, 1997; children: William David, Molly Rose. Bachelor, Whitman Coll., Walla Walla, 2000; Masters, Ea. Wash. U, Cheney, 2004. Cert. tchr. Wash., 2000. Tchr. Columbia Sch. Dist., Burbank, Wash., 2002—05, Walla Walla Sch. Dist., 2005—. Active P.E.O., Walla Walla, 1996—2006.

DUNCAN, LINDSAY VERE, actress; b. Edinburgh, Scotland, Nov. 7, 1950; m. Hilton McRae; 1 child, Cal. Attended, Ctrl. Sch. Speech and Drama, London. Actor: (films) Loose Connections, 1983, Prick Up Your Ears, 1987, Manifesto, 1988, Body Parts, 1991, The Reflecting Skin, 1991, A Midsummer Night's Dream, 1996, City Hall, 1996, An Ideal Husband, 1999, Mansfield Park, 1999, Star Wars: Episode 1 - The Phantom Menace, 1999, Under the Tuscan Sun, 2003, Afterlife, 2004 (Best Actress award Bratislava Film Festival, Best Actress Bowmore Scottish Screen awards), Starter for Ten, 2006; (TV series) Just William, 1977—78, Reilly Ace of Spies, 1983, Dead Head, 1986, Traffik, 1989 (FIPA Golden award Cannes Internat. Film Festival, 1990), Jake's Progress, 1995, Spooks, 2005, Poirot: The Mystery of the Blue Train, 2005; (TV miniseries) G.B.H., 1991, A Year in Provence, 1993, The Rectors Wife, 1994, The History of Tom Jones, 1997, Oliver Twist, 1999, Shooting the Past, Perfect Strangers, Rome, 2005, Rome 2, 2006; (TV films) Longford, 2006; (Broadway plays) Les Liaisons Dangereuses (Tony award nomination, 1987, Theatre World award, 1987), Top Girls (Obie award, 1982), A Midsummer Night's Dream, Ashes to Ashes, Celebration, The Room, Private Lives (winner Tony award Best Performance Leading Actress in a Play, 2002, Drama Desk Best Actress award, 2002). Office: ICM Oxford House 76 Oxford St London W1D 1B5 England

DUNCAN, LYN M., pathologist, educator; MD, Washington U., 1986. Bd. cert. pathology, dermatopathology. Resident anatomic pathology Barnes Hosp., 1990; fellow dermatopathology Mass. Gen. Hosp., 1991; clin. faculty anatomic pathology; asst. prof. pathology, dir. dermatopathology tng. Harvard Med. Sch. Achievements include research in melanoma, lymphoma, pregnancy associated skin disease, pigmented lesions. Office: Mass Gen Hosp WRN 827 55 Fruit St Boston MA 02114-2696 Fax: 617-726-8711. E-mail: duncan@helix.mgh.harvard.edu.

DUNCAN, MARGARET CAROLINE, physician; b. Salt Lake City, June 9, 1930; d. Donald and Margaret Aileen (Eberts) D.; m. N. Paul Arceneaux, Dec. 26, 1958; children: David Paul, Eleanor Anne, Stephen Louis, Andre. BA, U. Tex., 1952, MD, 1955. Intern Kings County Hosp., Seattle, 1955-56; resident in pediat. John Sealy Hosp., Galveston, Tex., 1956-58; resident in neurology Charity Hosp., New Orleans, 1958-60; fellow child neurology Johns Hopkins Hosp., Balt., 1960-61; mem. faculty La. State U. Med. Ctr., New Orleans, 1961—, prof. neurology and pediat., 1973-2000, prof. neurology emeritus, 2000—. Chmn. La. Com. Epilepsy and Cerebral Palsy, 1976-79. Fellow Am. Acad. Neurology, Am. Acad. Pediat.; mem. Child Neurology Soc., Profs. Child Neurology, Alpha Omega Alpha. Episcopalian. Office: Children's Hosp 200 Henry Clay New Orleans LA 70118

DUNCAN, MARY ELLEN, academic administrator; b. NYC, Aug. 29, 1941; d. Harry and Mary (Laveglia) Fielder; 1 child, Kathryn Mary Dickens. BS, St. John's U., 1963; MA, U. Conn., 1973, PhD, 1982. Grad. rsch. asst. U. Conn., Storrs, 1971-75; instr. English and Latin West Islip Pub. Schs., NYC, 1963-71; instr. Tri-County Tech. Coll., Pendleton, SC, 1975-76, instrnl. assoc. ACCTion Ctr., 1976-82, dir. ea. region, 1980-82, dir. instnl. devel., 1982-83, dean, 1987-88; dean planning and devel. Catonsville Community Coll., Balt., 1988-89, 90-91, interim pres., 1989-90; pres. Tech. Coll. SUNY, Delhi, 1991—98; pres. Howard CC, Columbia, Md., 1998—. Author: Indicators of Institutional Effectiveness, 1989. Recipient Merit award S.C. women in Higher Edn., 1985. Mem. Am. Assn. Community and Jr. Colls. (fed. rels. task force 1990-91, Merit award 1982, John Fry award 1981), Am. Assn. Women Community and Jr. Colls., Nat. Coun. Resource Devel. (legis. liaison 1990—). Avocation: golf. Home: 1236 Crows Foot Rd Marriottsville MD 21104-1445 Office: Howard CC 10901 Little Patuxent Parkway Columbia MD 21044 Office Phone: 410-772-4820. Office Fax: 410-772-4964. E-mail: mduncan@howardcc.edu.

DUNCAN, NANCY CAROL, psychology professor; d. Eugene Joseph and Emma Edna Anaclerio; m. Perry Marshall Duncan, July 18, 1968; 1 child, Scott J. PhD, U. Wash., Seattle. Prof. psychology Hampton U., Va., 1971—. Dir. career opportunities in rsch. scholars program NIMH/Hampton U., 2001—. Author: (articles) Physiology and Behavior; Behavior, Rsch. Instruments and Computers; Jour. Social Psychology; Jour. Physiol. Psychology. Vol. Empower Hampton Rds., Norfolk, Va. Beach, Hampton, 2004—. Grantee, NASA, 1973—75, Dept. Edn., 1996—99, NIMH, 2006—. Mem.: Soc. Computers in Psychology (steering com. 1992—95), Assn. for Psychol. Sci., APA. Unitarian Universalist. Avocations: travel, exercise. Office: Hampton Univ Psychology Dept Hampton VA 23668 Office Phone: 757-727-5347. Personal E-mail: nduncan@infionline.net. Business E-Mail: nancy.duncan@hamptonu.edu.

DUNCAN, PATRICIA, lawyer, broadcast executive; b. LA; m. Winston Peters; children: Collin, Shannon. BA, Pomona Coll., 1979; JD, U. Calif. Berkeley, 1984. Bar: Calif. 1984, U.S. Dist. Ct. (ctrl. dist.) Calif. Assoc. Lillick, McHose & Charles, LA, 1984—86, Dewey Ballantine, LA, 1986—88, Leopold, Petrich & Smith, LA, 1988—92, ptnr., 1992—94; sr. counsel intellectual property and legal affairs Nat. Broadcasting Co., Inc., Burbank, 1994—2000; with NBC-TV, Burbank; assoc. counsel Home Box Office, 2000—02, v.p., sr. counsel west coast programming, 2002—. Mem. Calif. Law Rev., 1982—84. Office: c/o Time Warner Inc One Time Warner Ctr New York NY 10019-8016*

DUNCAN, PEARL ROSE, writer; b. Feb. 24, 1947; AB, Bryn Mawr Coll., Pa., 1969; MPhil, Newton Coll., Mass., 1972. Writer non-fiction books, novels and short stories. Contbg. author Essence mag., N.Y. mag. Recipient Coat of Arms and Letters Patent Nobles in Noblesse Scotland, Ct. of Lord Lyon, 2005. Home: 36H 40 Harrison St New York NY 10013 Mailing: PO Box 18 Church St New York NY 10008 E-mail: pearl@pearlduncan.com.

DUNCAN, SHIRLEY A., portfolio manager; b. Greenville, Ga., Jan. 14, 1949; d. Crawford Lee and Mary Elizabeth Duncan; m. Francis LLoyd Lasenby, Aug. 31, 1968 (div. Oct. 1996); 1 child, Cynthia Diane Lasenby Acosta. Grad., Fla. Bankers Assn. Trust Sch., 1976; student, Fla. C.C., 1982, Jones Coll., 1987—88. Sec. Atlantic Bancorp, Jacksonville, Fla., 1970—82; portfolio mgr. Atlantic Bancorp/First Union, 1982—90, First Union Corp., Tampa, 1990—96; regional investment dir. First Union/Wachovia, Jacksonville, 1996—2003; sr. v.p. Wachovia Corp., Jacksonville, 2003—. Mem.: Assn. Investment Mgmt. & Rsch., Jacksonville Fin. Analysts Soc. (membership chmn. 1986). Avocations: tennis, golf.

DUNCAN, TANYA NICOLE, school athletic trainer; b. Washington, July 16, 1978; d. Sonia Funes and Bryan James Wagner (Stepfather); m. Robert Calvin Duncan, Aug. 13, 2003. BS in Kinesiology, Shenandoah U., Winchester, Va., 2002. Cert. Nat. Athletic Trainers Assn., 2005. Technician weight rm. and aquatics Winchester Phys. Therapy And Sports Medicine, Charlestown, W.Va., 2002—; asst. athletic trainer Shepherd U., Shepherdstown, W.Va., 2005—06. Mem.: Nat. Athletic Trainers Assn. Office: St James Sch 17641 College Rd Saint James MD 21781 Office Phone: 301-733-9330 3041.

DUNCAN-LADD, GEORGIA JONES, elementary school educator; b. Greenwood, Miss., Feb. 9, 1939; d. Siscro F. and Thelma L. (Pounds) Flowers; m. William F. Duncan, June 12, 1964 (div.); m. Roy B. Ladd, Dec. 19, 1982; children: Juan Marcell, Kimberly Michelle. Grad., Practical Nursing Sch., Indpls., 1962; BS in Health Svcs. Edn./Adminstrn., Ind. U., 1981, MPA in Health Systems and Pub. Adminstrn., 1988. RN, Ind. cert. elementary and secondary tchr., Ind. Staff nurse dept. medicine VA Hosp., 1962-67; adminstr. rsch. asst, Krannert Inst. Cardiology Ind. U. Med. Ctr., 1967-82; rsch. technician Wishard Meml. Hosp., 1982-87; tchr. history Thomas Edison Jr. High Sch./Ind. Pub. Schs., 1989-91. Contbr. articles to profl. jours. Vol., recruiter Indie Davis Donor Transplant Program, Calif., 1993. Recipient Olin W. Davis award for Exemplary Teaching of Econs., 1991; Minorities in Teaching scholar State of Ind., 1988; Lilly fellow Ind. U., 1988. Mem. NAACP, Ind. Nurses Assn., Ind. U. Alumni Assn., Sigma Gamma Rho, Inc. (pub. rels. epistoleus 1990—, nat. philo coord. 1992—), Cert. of Disting. Achievement in Edn. 1990), NCNW. Avocations: downhill skiing, racquetball, sewing. Home: 3610 Forest Manor Ave Indianapolis IN 46218-1564

DUNCANSON, PATRICIA ANN, mental health therapist; b. Jersey City, July 5, 1954; d. Thomas George and Thelma Florence Egan; BS in Psychology, David and Elkins Coll., 1976; MS in Counseling, St. Bonaventure U., 1981; m. Gregory S. Duncanson, July 23, 1977; children: Matthew Egan, Michael Stephen. Home tchr. Jamestown (N.Y.) Bd. Edn., 1978-80; client coord. Chautauqua County Resource Center, Jamestown, 1978-80; psychiat. counselor-aide Jamestown Gen. Hosp., 1980-81; program dir. family outreach and crisis intervention Joint Neighborhood Project, Inc., Jamestown, 1981-83; mental health therapist Chautauqua County Mental Health Agy., 1983—; pvt. practice, 1985—, sch. counselor at-risk Jamestown HS, head tchr. Alternative Edn. Program; co-developer Chautauqua County Joint Offender Treatment Program, 1986—; mem. Chautauqua County Child Abuse Com.; support chpt. Parents Anonymous. Mem. Am. Personnel and Guidance Assn., AAUW. Home: 2085 Buffalo St Ext Jamestown NY 14701-2137 Office Phone: 716-483-4209. Business E-Mail: duncanson@madbbs.com.

DUNCAN-WHITE, DYNAH NAOMI JULIETTE, marketing professional; b. Harrogate, York, England, July 18, 1964; arrived in U.S.A., 1967; d. Robert Duncan White and Lesley Marigold Elizabeth Nordyke; m. Arnold Felix Sufalko, Aug. 11, 1990 (div. Oct. 1998). AS, Elgin C.C., Ill., 1993; BS in Bus. Adminstrn., Roosevelt U., Chgo., 1999, MS in Integrated Mktg. and Comm., 2002. Cert. trade show marketer, San Francisco State U.; cert. mgr. of exhibits Trade Show Exhibitors Assn. Office mgr. Ko-Pack Corp. of Am., Bensenville, Ill., 1982—86; midwest rep. LDC Am. divsn. Pioneer Electronics, Rosemont, Ill., 1986—87; sales rep. Contamination Control and Devices, Dundee, Ill., 1987—94; project mgr. Star Displays, Elgin, 1994—95; exhibit mgr. Richardson Electronics, LaFox, Ill., 1995—97; account mgr. exhibit group, Giltspur, Roselle, Ill., 1997—99; sr. corp. account exec. Contempo Design, Libertyville, Ill., 1999; mktg. comm. mgr. Gen. Exhibit and Display, Chgo., 2000, Gen. Exhibits and Design, Inc., Chgo., 2000; promotions dir. Gen. Motors R*Works, Detroit, 2003. Records coord., fin. officer Windy City chpt. Operating Coun. Tradeshow Exhibitors Assn., Chgo.; advisor, rev. com. mem. Cert. Trade Show Marketers Program, Boulder, Colo. Scholastic scholar Roosevelt U., Chgo., 1993-99. Mem. Phi Theta Kappa, Mu Alpha Theta. Republican. Methodist. Avocations: dance, theater, golf, pets. Office: Gen Motors R*Works 535 Griswold Ste 500 Detroit MI 48226 Home: 9034 Newport Way Livonia MI 48150-4170 Office Phone: 313-596-9155.

DUNCKLEY, VICTORIA LYNN, psychiatrist; b. Mountain View, Calif., Apr. 30, 1970; d. James Dunckley and Patricia Von Gruenigen. BSc, U. Calif. San Diego, La Jolla, 1992; MD, Albany Med. Coll., N.Y., 1996. Diplomate Am. Bd. Psychiatry and Neurology, Am. Acad. Child and Adolescent Psychiatry. Resident psychiatry U, Calif., Irvine, 1996—99, chief fellow child and adolescent psychiatry, 1999—2001; adult psychiatrist Advantage Neuropsychiatry, Huntington Beach, 1998—99; cons. psychiatrist OTC Disability Evaluations, Santa Ana, 1999—2001; pvt. practice child adolescent and adult psychiatry Seal Beach, 2000—; child psychiatrist Canyon Acres Residential Treatment Ctr., Anaheim, 2001—; med. dir. Kinship Ctr. Adoption Clinic, Santa Ana, 2001—. Clin. rschr. stuttering medication trials U. Calif. Irvine Med. Ctr., Orange, 2000—01; nutrition com. co-chair Canyon Acres Children's Svcs., Anaheim, 2005. Named All. Am. in 4x100 meter relay, NCAA Divsn. III, 1994, All Am. in 4x100 meter relay, 1995, Outstanding Resident in Child Psychiatry, Am. Acad. Child and Adolescent Psychiatry and Pfizer, 2000; recipient Catch People Caring award, pacific Clinics, 2002; Roy L. Leek Alumni scholar, Albany Med. Coll. Alumni, 1996. Mem.: Assn. Women Psychiatrists, Calif. Med. Assn., Calif. Psychiatric Assn., Am. Psychiatric Assn., Orange County Psychiatric Soc. (councilor 2002—, coun. mem., early career psychiatrist rep. 2002—). Avocations: hiking, tennis, running, reading. Office: Victoria L Dunckley MD Inc Ste 302B 909 Electric Ave Seal Beach CA 90740

DUNCOMBE, PATRICIA WARBURTON, retired social worker; b. London, Jan. 30, 1925; came to U.S., 1940. d. P.G. Eliot and Mary Louise (Thompson) Warburton; m. David S. Duncombe, July 11, 1947 (dec. Apr. 1976); children: Elizabeth, Mari, Edward, David, Peter. BA, Barnard Coll., 1944; MS in Social Work, Columbia U., 1947. Cert. social worker. Social worker YWCA, Chgo., Evanston, Ill., 1947-50, B.I.A., Elko, Nev., 1966-67, Nev. State Welfare Div., Elko, Nev., 1967-69; dir. St. Michael's Youth Residence, Ethete, Wyo., 1970-76; asst. prof. U. Wyo., Laramie, 1976-83; program dir. St. Jude's Ranch, Boulder City, Nev., 1983-85; med. social worker home health agys., Las Vegas, Nev., 1985-95; retired. Author: Within the Circle, 1981, Parish the Thought, 1994, (with Ann Titus) When Death Comes Suddenly, 2000. Mem. Wyo. Commn. for Women, 1971-83, chmn., 1975-77; bd. dirs. SE Wyo. Mental Health, 1980-83; founder Lend-A-Hand Program, Boulder City, 1989 (awarded 700th Point of Light, 1992). Recipient Gov.'s award, 2000. Mem. NASW (chpt. pres. 1979, 81, commn. on women 1977-79, exec. dir. Nev. chpt. 1985-90, Social Work of Yr. award Wyo. chpt. 1980, Nev. chpt. 1989, lifetime achievement award 1992), AAUW (nat. bd. dirs. 1983-85), Mesquite Club (Las Vegas, pres. 1998-99), Phi Theta Kappa. Democrat. Episcopalian. Avocations: gardening, travel, reading, art. Home: 3890 N Buffalo Dr Unit 264 Las Vegas NV 89129-8818

DUNDON, MARGO ELAINE, museum director; b. Cleve., July 3, 1950; d. Elmer Edward and Ruth Ann (Dreger) Buckeye. BS in Comm. cum laude, Ohio U., 1972; postgrad. in Mus. Studies, U. Okla, 1987. Mem. gen. staff Grout Mus. History and Sci., Waterloo, Iowa, 1974—75, coord. edn., 1976—78, co-dir., 1979—87, dir., 1988—90; exec. dir. Mus. Sci. and History, Jacksonville, Fla., 1990—99, pres., 1999—. Apptd. grievance com. Fla. Bar 4th Jud. Cir., 2002—05. Chair Waterloo Hist. Preservation Commn., 1987—88; cultural com. Visitors and Conv. Bur., Waterloo, 1988—90, My Waterloo Days, 1982—83; active Jacksonville Women's Network, Non-Profit Execs. Round Table, 1990—95; appointee Fla. Hist. Commn., Fla., 2006—; bd. dirs. Resource Plus, Waterloo-Cedar Falls, Iowa, 1986—88, CJI, Girls Inc. of Jacksonville, 1994—95, Ritz Theater & LaVilla Mus., 1998—2000, Jacksonville and the Beaches Conv. and Vis. Bur., 2001—, pres., chmn. bd. dirs., 2004—05. Am. Law Inst.-ABA scholar, 1979, 86; recipient Mayor's Vol. Performance award, Waterloo, 1983, Vol. award Gov. of Iowa, 1990. Mem.: Fla. Hist. Commn., Iowa Mus. Assn. (pres. 1984—86), Fla. Attractions Assn. (bd. dirs. 1997—98), Fla. Assn. Mus. (pres. 1995—96, Lifetime Achievement award 2006), Southeast Mus. Conf., Midwest Mus. Conf. (pres. 1988—90), Am. Assn. Mus. (site surveyor mus. assessment program 1982—, site examiner mus. accreditation commn. 1987—, regional councilor 1988—90, Peer Reviewer award 2000), Jacksonville C. of C., Quota Club (pres. 1982), Rotary. Avocations: snorkeling, scuba diving, travel, gardening. Office: Mus Sci & History 1025 Museum Cir Jacksonville FL 32207-9053 Office Phone: 904-396-7062. E-mail: director@themosh.com.

DUNEGAN, JENNIFER LEE, theater educator; b. Alliance, Ohio, Oct. 29, 1950; d. Frank Albert and Elaine Eva Aultz; m. Kenneth Joseph Dunegan, Aug. 4, 1973; children: Abigail, Ian. BS in Edn./Eng., Miami U., Oxford, Ohio, 1968—72, Kent State U., Ohio, 1974—77; MFA in Acting, Case Western Reserve U., Cleve., Ohio, 1979—82; MFA in Directing, U. Cin., Ohio, 1985—87. Eng. tchr. Mayfield City Schs., Mayfield Heights, Ohio, 1972—79, drama coach, 1974—79; co. mem. Ind. Repertory Theater, Indpls., 1982—84, Cleve. Actors Theater Co., 1985—87; instr. U. Cin., 1988; co-founder/prodr. Gt. Works Prodns., Cleve., 1988—96; prof. Ursuline Coll., Pepper Pike, Ohio, 1996—. Bd. dirs. Gt. Works Prodns., 1990—; dir. Ursuline Coll. Theater Program. Playwright: plays In Memory: Anne Frank, 1988, A Civil War Experience, 1990, Lessons in Liberty, 1993, The Belle of Amherst, 1981, touring artist: McGraw-Hill Lit. Theatre, 1984—87. Troop leader Girl Scouts Am., Lake Erie Coun., 2000—; block rep. Kensington Green Assn., S. Russell, Ohio, 1989—; mem. PTO Chagrin Falls Schs., 1998—. Recipient Barclay Leatham award, Case Western Reserve U., 1982, Best Dir., Cin. Enquirer, 1987; grantee fellowship, U. Cin., 1986—87. Mem.: AFTRA, Cleve. Theater Collective, Actors Equity Assn. Avocations: travel, reading, writing, jogging. Home: 62 Potomac Dr Chagrin Falls OH 44022 Office: Ursuline Coll 2550 Lander Rd Pepper Pike OH 44124

DUNEVANT, CAROL DARY, music educator, conductor; b. Wichita Falls, Tex., May 11, 1959; d. David Archie and Carolyn Sue Dary; m. David Lynn Dunevant; 1 child, Cristian Pennington. BMusEd, U. Kans., Lawrence, 1982, MMusEd, 1992—92; Postgrad. studies, U. Cin., 1992—95. Dir. of bands. Chanute (Kans.) H.S., 1984—88; dir. bands. No. Ky. U., Highland Heights, 1995—2002; music dir., condr. Frank Simon Band; conr. Tri-State Chamber Players, 2005. Mgr. festival Ky. Music Educators, Calvert City, 1995—2002. Musician (guest conductor): (music concert) Philharmonic Orch., 2000. Named Outstanding Univ. Tchr., Dist. VI, 1999. Mem.: Internat. Conductors Guild, World Assn. of Symphonic Bands and Ensembles, Women Band Dirs. Internat., Coll. Band Dirs. Assn., Sigma Alpha Iota (advisor 1995—2002), Tau Beta Sigma, Kappa Kappa Psi (hon.), Pi Kappa Lambda. Avocations: boxing, golf, camping, reading. Home: 849 Shawnee Trace Court Cincinnati OH 45255 Office: 849 Shawnee Trace Ct Cincinnati OH 45255 Office Phone: 513-307-5981. Business E-Mail: franksimonband@earthlink.net.

DUNGY, KATHRYN R., humanities educator; b. Stanford, Calif., Sept. 21, 1969; d. Claibourne I. and Madgetta Thornton Dungy; life ptnr. Timothy Voigt. BA magna cum laude, Spelman Coll., Atla., 1991; MA, Duke U., 1993, PhD, 2000. Vis. lectr. U. Vt., Burlington, 1999—2000, asst. prof. Latin Am. and Caribbean history, 2000—04; asst. prof. Latin Am. and Caribbean studies New Coll., Fla., 2004—. Contbg. author: Black Students and Overseas Programs: Broadening the Base of Participation; biographical compiler To Conserve a Legacy: American Art from Historically Black Colleges and Universities; contbr. articles to The So. Friend, Jour. of the NC Friends Hist. Soc. Caribbean Studies. Co-chair Pres.'s Coun. on Racial Equality, 2000—02. Internat. Student Identity Card scholar, CIEE, 1989—90, Fgn. Study scholar, Spelman Coll./Charles A. Merrill Found., 1989—90, Minority fellow, Dana Found., 1989—91, Ford Found. Predoctoral fellow for Minorities, 1991—94, Tinker Found. Summer Rsch. grantee, Duke U., 1993, Latin Am. Studies fellow, 1994—96, George Washington Henderson fellow, U. Vt., 1998—99, Travel grantee, Women's Studies Program, U. Vt., 2001. Mem.: Am. Hist. Assn., Caribbean Studies Assn., Assn. Caribbean Historians, Mortar Bd., Sigma Delta Epsilon (v.p. chpt. 1990—91), Phi Alpha Theta (pres. chpt. 1990—91), Delta Sigma Theta. Avocations: photography, travel. Office: New Coll 5700 Bay Shore Dr Sarasota FL 34243 Office Phone: 941-487-4699. Personal E-mail: kdungy@ncf.edu.

DUNHAM, JOAN ROBERTS, administrative assistant; b. Dayton, Ohio, Jan. 25, 1933; d. Harold Hathaway and Lydia Roberts Dunham. BA, U. Colo., 1954; postgrad., U. Pa., 1959-65, U. Chgo., 1971-72. Office clk. Daniels & Fisher Stores, Denver, 1954-56; clk., stenographer Dept. of State, Madras, India, 1957-59; clk. admissions office Temple Buell Coll., Denver, 1969—71; typist, adminstrv. clk. State of Colo., Denver, 1987-99; ret., 1999. Fgn. lang. fellow U.S. Dept. Health, Edn. and Welfare, U. Pa., 1961-62. Republican. Christian Scientist. Home: 1350 Josephine St Unit 210 Denver CO 80206-2243

DUNHAM, LAURA, elementary school educator; b. Highland Park, Mich., June 2, 1947; d. Clement and Joy C. Harland; m. Roger W. Dunham, Feb. 14, 1969; children: Chad Roger, Craig William. B in Music Edn. cum laude, U. Miami, 1969; BA in Edn. magna cum laude, Fla. Atlantic U., 1979, MEd in Sch. Guidance and Counseling, 2004. Music tchr. grades K-5 Hollywood (Fla.) Park Elem., 1969-70; substitute tchr. grades K-5 Otis AFB Elem. Sch., Falmouth, Mass., 1970-71; music tchr. grades 6-9 Olsen Mid. Sch., Dania, Fla., 1971—74; music tchr. grades 6-12 Westminster Acad., Ft. Lauderdale, Fla., 1979-83; art tchr. Ft. Lauderdale Christian Sch., 1983—2002, chmn. developing tchr. program for new educators, 1993—2002; art tchr. Sunrise Mid. Sch., 2002—03; guidance counselor Broadview Elem. Sch., 2004—. Cons. scholarship and award writer graduating srs. Ft. Lauderdale Christian Sch., 1993-95; sponsor Nat. Art Honor Soc. at Ft. Lauderdale Christian Sch., 1995-2002, Nat. Honor Soc., 2001-02; host Internat. Children's Art Exhbn., 1996; entourage mem. Broward County Ctr. for the Performing Arts, 1996—; com. mem. Broward County Nat. Week of the Ocean, 1996-2002; nat. mem. The Smithsonian Instn., 1998-99; presenter Christian Schs. Fla. Seminar, 1999. Profl. flautist, 1969—. Vol. hosp. surg. suite; Sunday sch. tchr., mem. ch. choirs, handbell choirs, vacation Bible sch. tchr., vol. classroom arts and crafts, deacon, pastor nominating com.; vol. for badges, cub scout leader Boy Scouts Am., 1984—, Habitat for Humanity, 2001-03; active Fla. Rep. Party, 1993—. Named H.S. Tchr. of Yr., Broward County Fair, 1996. Mem. ACA, Nat. Art Edn. Assn., Fla. Art Edn. Assn., Nat. Mus. Women in the Arts, Assn. Ind. Schs. Fla. (accreditation team 1999), Am. Assn. Christian Counselors, Am. Sch. Counseling Assn., U. Miami Alumnae Assn., U. Miami Band of the Hour Club, Mortar Bd., Alpha Tau Omega (little sister), Delta Zeta (alumnae pres., Woman of Yr. Broward County Gold Coast Area Alumnae 1996), U. Miami Alumnae Delta Zeta (area chair), Rho Lambda, Chi Sigma Iota (sec.), Tau Beta Sigma, Alpha Theta Kappa, Sigma Alpha Iota (pres., Province award), Phi Delta Kappa, Phi Kappa Phi, Kappa Delta Pi. Republican. Methodist. Home: 301 Lake Dr Coconut Creek FL 33066-1840 Office: Broadview Elem Sch 1800 SW 62d Ave North Lauderdale FL 33068

DUNHAM, LIZAMARIE BASSIWA, medical technician; b. New Orleans, Nov. 8, 1965; d. Armando Bunag and Concha Alqueza Bassiwa. BS in Med. Tech., U. Md., 1988. Libr. asst. Albin O. Kuhn Libr. and Gallery, Catonsville, Md., 1985-86; customer svc. rep. Army & Air Forch Exch. Svc., Andrews AFB, Md., 1986; med. technologist Prince George's Hosp. Ctr., Cheverly, Md., 1988-89, Georgetown Univ. Hosp., Washington, 1989-90, Walter Reed Army Med. Ctr., Washington, 1989—, R&D team leader, 2002—04, biosafety mgr., 2005—. Stage mgr.: (plays) Liga, 1997; asst. dir. The Acceptance of Sherry Goldstein, 1998. Recipient Outstanding Performance as Med. Technologist award, Dept. Army - Walter Reed, 1993—97, letter of Appreciation, Dept. Army/Dept. Navy, 1999, Commdr.'s award for Civilian Svc., Dept. Army, 2002. Mem.: Am. Soc. Microbiology, Am. Soc. Clin. Pathologists (assoc. cert. microbiology technologist). Avocations: volleyball, dance, cooking, crafts. Office: Walter Reed Army Med Ctr 16th St NW Washington DC 20307-3001

DUNHAM, MARY HELEN, elementary school educator; b. Skiatook, Okla., Dec. 12, 1945; d. Walter and Anna Mae (Escue) Lonsinger; m. Roger Dale Dunham, May 13, 1967; children: Roger Lewis, Carl David. BS in Edn., Northeastern State U., Tahlequah, Okla., 1967. Tchr. elem. sch. Skiatook (Okla.) Marrs Elem. Sch., Vera (Okla.) Sch., Blue Sch., Locust Grove, Okla., St. Paul Sch., Memphis. Mem. Nat. Reading Assn., Okla. Reading Assn., Tulsa Reading Assn., Sigma Epsilon Alpha. Avocations: gardening, outdoor sports, travel. Home: 40301 N 3970 Rd Skiatook OK 74070-4135

DUNHAM, PATRICIA ANN, elementary school educator; b. Jersey City, May 13, 1948; d. Joseph John and Edith Mae (Dayton) Garvey; children: Devon Joseph, Dorie Anne Student, Notre Dame Coll., 1966—67; BA, Jersey City State Coll., 1971; MA Math Edn., N.J. City U., 1996. Clk., typist Nat. Employment Exch. Inc., N.Y.C., 1967—71; tchr. Jersey City Bd. Edn., 1971—. Active Com. Pub. Edn., Jersey City, 1983—; treas. Parents Coun. Jersey City, 1983—95, sec., 1st v.p., 3d v.p.; sec., v.p. Parents Coun. Pub. Sch. 30, Jersey City, 1983-85, pres., 1985-90; adv. com. Confraternity of Christian Doctrine, Our Lady Mercy Ch., Jersey City, 1983-89 Mem. NEA, N.J. Edn. Assn., Jersey City Edn. Assn. (sch. dir., violence and vandalism com. 1980-81), Kappa Delta Pi Democrat. Roman Catholic. Avocations: reading, crocheting, movies. Home: 30 Linden Ave Jersey City NJ 07305-4725 Personal E-mail: pgdunham@comcast.net.

DUNIPHAN, J. P., state legislator, small business owner; b. Aug. 31, 1946; Mem. SD Ho. of Reps., Pierre, 1995—2002, mem. commerce com., judiciary com., chair local govt. com., 1995—2002; mem. SD State Senate, Dist. 33, 2002—. Ptnr. Elks II, 1993—, Quad Investments, 1993—. Republican. Fax: 605-342-6399.

DUNKELMAN, LORETTA, artist; b. Paterson, N.J., June 29, 1937; d. Samuel and Rae (Gutkind) Dunkelman. BA, Rutgers U., 1958; MA, Hunter Coll., 1966. Lectr. Hunter Coll., N.Y.C., 1966-67; vis. artist U. Cin., 1974; asst. prof. U. R.I., Kingston, 1974-75, Cornell U., Ithaca, NY, 1977-80; vis. artist Ohio State U., Columbus, 1984; asst. prof. Va. Commonwealth Univ., Richmond, 1986-88; vis. artist The Sch. of the Art Inst. of Chgo., 1990; vis. prof. art U. Calif., Berkeley, 1993-94. One woman shows include A.I.R. Gallery, N.Y., 1973-74, 78, 81, 83, 87, Douglass Coll., New Brunswick, 1973, U. Cin., 1974, U. R.I., Kingston, 1975, 1708 E. Main Gallery, Richmond, 1987; exhibited in group shows at Whitney Mus. Am. Art, N.Y., 1973, N.Y. Cultural Ctr., N.Y., 1973, Newark Mus., 1973, Cranbrook Acad. Art Mus., Bloomfield Hills, Mich., 1974, Grand Rapids (Mich.) Art Mus., 1974, Johnson Mus., Cornell U., Ithaca, N.Y., 1977, Inst. Art and Urban Resources, Pub. Sch. 1, N.Y.C., 1978, McIntosh/Drysdale Gallery, Washington, 1980, Douglass Coll., Rutgers U., New Brunswick, NJ, 1981, Kulturhuset, Stockholm and Lunds Konsthall, Sweden, 1981-82, Picker Art Gallery, Colgate U., Hamilton, N.Y., 1983, Hopkins Hall Gallery, The Ohio State U., 1984, Kenkeleba Gallery, N.Y., 1985, A.I.R. Gallery, 1985, 91, Bernice Steinbaum Gallery, N.Y., 1986, Anderson Gallery, Va. Commonwealth U., Richmond, Va., 1987, Rabbet Gallery, New Brunswick, N.J., 1989, Michael Walls Gallery, 1989, 148 Duane St., N.Y.C., 1992, Contemporary Art Inst., N.Y.C., 1994, Mason Gross Sch. of the Arts Galleries, Rutgers U., New Brunswick, N.J., 1996, A.I.R. Gallery, N.Y.C., 1997, Kingsborough C.C., Bklyn., 1998, Yaddo Centennial Arts Festival, N.Y.C., 2000, Mabel Smith Douglass Libr., Rutgers U., New Brunswick, 2005; represented in permanent collections Bellevue Med. Ctr., N.Y.C., The Chase Manhattan Bank, N.Y.C., City Univ. Grad. Ctr., N.Y.C., The Picker Art Gallery, Dana Art Ctr., Colgate U., Hamilton, N.Y., U. Cin., Gene Swenson Collection at U. Kansas Art Mus., Lawrence, Bristol-Myers, Squibb, Lawrenceville, N.J., Hunter Coll., N.Y.C. CAPS fellow N.Y. State Coun. Arts, 1975; Visual artist fellow Nat. Endowment for the Arts, 1975, 82, 93, AAUW fellow, 1976-77, Artist fellow N.Y. Found. for the Arts, 1991; grantee Adolph & Esther Gottlieb Found., 1991. Home and Office: 151 Canal St New York NY 10002-5033

DUNKINS, BETTY, small business owner, publishing executive; b. St. Louis, July 16, 1933; d. William and Rose Marie (Vaughn) McPherson; m. Bruce Washington Dunkins, Mar. 19, 1966; children: Bruce, Eric. BS in Med. Record LS, St. Louis U., 1955. Registered med. record adminstr. Med. records adminstr. St. Louis City Govt., 1955-56; chief med. records adminstrn. Good Samaritan Hosp., Dayton, Ohio, 1956-59, HEW-St. Elizabeths Hosp., Washington, 1959-67, pers. staffing specialist, 1967-79; pers. mgmt. specialist HHS, Rockville, Md., 1979-89; owner, mgr. Tying The Knot Wedding Svc., Silver Spring, Md., 1989—; pub. Gray, McPherson Pub. Co., Silver Spring, 1993—. Cons. on weddings to local and nat. TV, Washington and Md., 1990—; advisor on wedding sites to local and nat. TV, Washington and Md., 1994—. Author, editor, pub.: The Perfect Choice, 1994, 98; contbr. numerous articles on weddings to mags. and newspapers. Mem. membership and freedom fund com. NAACP, Washington, 1965-69; cultural chmn. Stonegate Elem. Sch., Silver Springs, 1977-78; mem. membership com. Stonegate Citizen Assn., silver Spring, 1975, area leader, dir. publ., 1976, security officer, 1983-84. Mem. Assn. Bridal Cons. (accredited, honor award 1998), Assn. Wedding Profls. (membership chmn. 1997-98), Alpha Kappa Alpha Sorority (Theta Omega Omega 3rd grade mentor, 1994, 1998-99, Hon. award 1999). Avocations: reading, travel, aerobics.

DUNLAP, CATHERINE MARY, clergywoman; b. Toronto, Ohio, Oct. 28, 1927; d. Michael Nicholas and Lena (Conti) Reale; children: Charles E., Linda Catherine Dunlap Molinaro, Thomas Michael; m. William Freese (dec. Jan. 1980). AS in Bus., Steubenville Bus. Coll., 1946; MA in Christian Edn., Meth. Theol. Sem., Delaware, Ohio, 1983. Ordained diaconal minister United Meth. Ch., 1983. Dir. fin. assistance and ch. rels. Meth. Theol. Sem., 1983-89; diaconal min. Kent United Meth. Ch., Ohio, 1989—2002. Vice pres. bd. diaconal ministry East Ohio Conf., United Meth. Ch., Canton, 1989-92, v.p. NC jurisdictional program com., Detroit, 1988-92, NC jurisdictional bd. ministry, Chgo., 1988-92; pres. East Ohio Conf. United Meth. Women, 1975-79; v.p. bd. publ. United Meth. Ch., 1972-84, mem. bd. higher edn. and ministry, 1984-89. Trustee Ohio No. U., Ada, 1979-89. Recipient Community Svc. award B'nai B'rith, 1967, nat. award United Meth. Women, 1983. Mem. Ch. Women United (pres. 1969-73), Order Ea. Star (chaplain 1969). Avocations: travel, crewel embroidery, reading, walking. Home: 3740 St Andrews Dr Youngstown OH 44505-1670

DUNLAP, CONNIE, librarian; b. Lansing, Mich., Sept. 9, 1924; d. Frederick Arthur and Laura May (Robinson) Robson; m. Robert Bruce Dunlap, Aug. 9, 1947. AB, U. Mich., 1946, AM in Libr. Sci., 1952. Head acquisitions dept., then head grad. library U. Mich. Libr., 1961-75, dep. assoc. dir., 1972-75; univ. libr. Duke U., 1975-80; cons., 1981—. Contbr. articles to publs. in field, chpts. in books. Forewoman Grand Jury U.S. Dist. Ct. 13th Dist. Mich., 1967-68; bd. dirs. U. Mich. Libr. Friends, v.p., 1997-2000, officer at large, 2000-02, bd. dirs. A.B. Bach, 1999—, v.p., 2002, chair, 2003—; treas. Ann Arbor Hist. Found., 1998—. Recipient Disting. Alumnus award U. Mich. Sch Libr. Sci., 1977 Mem. ALA (mem. coun. 1974-83, mem. exec. bd. 1978-83, pres. resources and tech. svcs. divsn. 1972-73), AAUP, Assn. Coll. and Rsch. Librs. (bd. dirs. 1975-78, pres. 1976-77), Assn. Rsch. Librs. (bd. dirs. 1976-80, pres. 1979-80). Address: 1570 Westfield Ave Ann Arbor MI 48103-5740

DUNLAP, ELLEN S., library administrator; b. Nashville, Oct. 12, 1951; d. Arthur Wallace and Elizabeth (Majors) Smith; m. Arthur H. Dunlap, Jr., Dec. 27, 1972 (dec. 1977); m. Frank Armstrong, May 11, 1979; 1 child, Libbie Sarah. BA, U. Tex., Austin, 1972, MLS, 1974. Rsch. assoc. Humanities Rsch. Ctr. U. Tex., Austin, 1973-76, rsch. libr., 1976-83; exec. dir. Rosenbach Mus. and Library, Phila., 1983-92; pres. Am. Antiquarian Soc., Worcester, Mass., 1992—. Dir. 18th Century Short Title Catalogue/N.Am., 1992—. Dir. Worcester Mcpl. Rsch. Bur., 1993—; mem. fin. com. Town of West Boylston, Mass., 1997—, chmn., 2001—05; bd. dir. Greater Worcester Cmty. Found., Mass., 2004—, clerk, 2005—; bd. dir. Mass. Found. for Humanities, 1996—2004, pres., 2002—04; bd. dir. Rare Books Sch. U. Va., 1994—. Mem. Am. Antiquarian Soc., Mass. Hist. Soc., Colonial Soc. Mass., Grolier Club (N.Y.C.), Worcester Club. Office: Am Antiquarian Soc 185 Salisbury St Worcester MA 01609-1636

DUNLAP, KAREN F. BROWN, academic administrator; BA, Mich. State U.; MS, Tenn. State U.; PhD Mass Comm., U. Tenn. Dean reporting, writing and editing faculty The Poynter Inst., St. Petersburg, Fla., pres., 2003—. Bd. trustees Poynter; reporter Nashville Banner, Macon News, St. Petersburgs Times. Co-author: The Effective Editor: How to Lead Your Staff to Better Writing and Better Teamwork, The Editorial Eye. Office: The Poynter Inst 801 3rd St S Saint Petersburg FL 33701

DUNLAP, MARTHA MCKINZIE, retired middle school educator, small business owner; b. Tyler, Tex., Feb. 14, 1947; d. Ned and Jackie Elliott McKinzie; m. Charles R. Moore, Aug. 20, 1966 (div. Dec. 1994); children: C. Brandon Moore, David K. Moore, Matthew Elliott Moore; m. Gerry Randall Dunlap, Jan. 9, 1999; stepchildren: Josh R., Ginger J. BS, Stephen F. Austin State U., 1969, EdM, 1975. Cert. tchr. Tex. 4th grade tchr. Nacogdoches (Tex.) Ind. Sch. Dist., 1969—72; 5th and 7th grade lang. arts tchr. Chapel Hill Ind. Sch. Dist., Tyler, 1987—90; 7th and 8th grade lang. arts tchr. Tyler Ind. Sch. Dist. Moore Middle Sch., 1990—95, 6th grade lang. arts tchr., 1995—2004; ret., 2004; prin., owner Divide & Conquer, Tyler, 2004—. Profl. organizer/owner Divide and Conquer, 2004—. Mem.: AAUW, Nat. Assn. Profl. Organizers, Smith County Ret. Sch. Personnel Assn., Smith County Hist. Soc., Salvation Army Aux., Alzheimr's Alliance Aux., Tyler Woman's Forum, Nat. Women's History Mus. (Washington) (charter mem.), Soc. of Bonner-Whitaker-McClendon House, Heart of Tyler Main St., Historic Tyler, Inc., Delta Kappa Gamma, Alpha Delta Kappa. Republican. Baptist. Avocations: travel, antiques. Personal E-mail: marthadunlap@yahoo.com.

DUNLAP, PATRICIA C., state legislator; b. Rochester, NH, Nov. 6, 1926; Grad. h.s. Mem. N.H. Ho. of Reps., mem. comm., small bus., consumer affairs, econ. devel. coms., also mem. com. environment and agr. Ward clk., Rochester, NH, 1991—92; supr. checklist, 1992; bank customer rels. rep., 90. Treas. Gafney Home for Aged Mgmt. Bd., 1992—; asst. treas. 1st Ch. Congl., 1992-95, fin. sec., 1996—. Mem. DAR (asst. treas. Mary Torr chpt. 1992-94), OWLS (treas. 2001—).

DUNLAVY, COLLEEN A., historian; d. Russell W. and Lillian A. Dunlavy; m. Ronald M. Radano, Mar. 22, 2003. BA in History of Tech., U. Calif., Berkeley, 1980; PhD, MIT, Cambridge, 1988. Lectr. history U. Wis., Madison, 1987—, asst. prof. history, 1988—93, assoc. prof. history, 1993—2000, prof. history, 2000—. Author: Politics and Industrialization: Early Railroads in the United States and Prussia, 1994 (co-winner, Thomas Newcomen award bus. history 1992-1994, 1998). Recipient Vilas Assoc. award, U. Wis., 1995—97, Romnes award, 1997—2002; fellow, Am. Coun. Learned Societies, 1989, German Marshall Fund of U.S., 1997—98, Charles Warren Ctr. Study of Am. History Harvard U., 2004; grantee, Alfred P. Sloan Found., 1999—2000; Vis. fellow, Russell Sage Found., 1998—99. Mem.: Orgn. Am. Historians, Am. Hist. Assn., Soc. History of Tech. (exec. coun. mem. 1995—98), Bus. History Conf. (trustee 1996—99, 2006—). Office: Univ Wis Dept History 455 N Park St Madison WI 53706 Office Phone: 608-263-1854. E-mail: cdunlavy@wisc.edu.

DUNLEAVY, MARA ANNE, science educator; b. New Haven, Conn., Oct. 24, 1956; d. Donald Thomas Dunleavy and Shirley Grace O'Meara. BS in Health Sci., Southern Conn. State Coll., New Haven, 1978; MS in Health Sci., Southern Conn. State Coll., 1984. Science tchr. James Hillhoust HS, New Haven, 1978—. Mentor/master tchr. Conn. Beginning Tchrs. Network Program, 1990—. Mem., relay for life Am. Cancer Soc., Meriden-Wallingford, Conn., 1999—, cmty. coun., 2004—05. Recipient Tchr. Staff Parent award, Bd. Edn., 1995. Mem.: Nat. Sci. Tchrs. Assn., Conn. Sci. Tchrs. Assn., Tradition Golf Club at Wllingford (v.p. 2001—03). Democrat. Roman Catholic. Avocations: reading, exercise. Office: James Hillhoust HS 480 Sherman Pkwy New Haven CT 06511

DUNLEAVY, WILLA GILL, music educator, director; b. Benton, Ill., Feb. 12, 1937; d. Joseph Edward McGovern and Celia Belle Gill/McGovern; m. Kevin Joseph Dunleavy, Mar. 17, 1999; 5 children. AA, William Rainey Harper Coll., 1972; MusM in Edn., MusB in Edn., U. North Tex., 1980, postgrad., 1982. Cert. pub. sch. adminstr. Tex., all level tchr., choral, gen. music K-12 Tex. Organist, choir dir. Presbyn. Synod, Chgo., 1956—73; pvt. tchr. piano, organ; choral dir. Ft. Worth Ind. Sch. Dist., 1974—87, program dir., choral and gen. music k-12, 1987—2002; cons. Macmillan/McGraw Hill, NYC, 2002—; arts edn. cons. Ft. Worth, 2002—. Pres. Youth Orch. Greater Ft. Worth, 2004—; chair, artistic com. Ft. Worth Acad. Fine Arts, 2004—; founding mem. Ft. Worth Arts Edn. Ptnrs., 2002—; past nat. chair and founding mem. Urban Music Leadership Conf., Detroit, 1995—; sec. Nat. Supervisors Music Edn. (Music Educator's Nat. Conf.), Reston, Va., 2001—02; pres. Ft. Worth Administrator's Assn., 1998—99; presenter in field. Author: (music education textbook) Spotlight on Music. Coord. music activities Sister Cities of Ft. Worth, 1987—2002; pres. Palos Twp. Rep. Women, Palos Park, Ill., 1964—67; organist, choir dir. Hickory Hills Presbyn. Ch., 1956—67; pres., founding mem. Urban Music Leadership Conf., Detroit, 1995—2005; sec. Nat. Coun. Supervisors Music Edn., Reston; pres. Youth Orch. Greater Ft. Worth, 1990—2005; chair, artistic com. bd. of directors Ft. Worth Acad. Fine Arts, 2004—; founder, mem. Ft. Worth Arts Edn. Ptnrs., 2002—05; music edn. liaison Imagination Celebration (Kennedy Ctr.), 1986—2002. Mem.: Urban Music Leadership Conf. (assoc.; pres. 1999—2002), Am. Orff Schulwerk Assn. (assoc. Service award), Tex. Choral Dirs. Assn. (assoc.), Tex. Music Educators Assn. (assoc.), Am. Choral Dirs. Assn. (assoc.), Music Educators Nat. Conf. (assoc.), The Ft. Worth Club (assoc.). Conservative. Presbyterian. Avocations: music, writing, travel, reading, theater. Home and Office: 3920 Dawn Dr Fort Worth TX 76116 Home Fax: 817-560-4616. Personal E-mail: willab@swbell.net.

DUNLOP, BECKY NORTON, retired government agency administrator; b. Mpls., Oct. 2, 1951; d. Carl J. and Helen L. (Betow) Norton; m. George S. Dunlop, Sept. 17, 1977. BA, Miami U., Oxford, Ohio, 1973. Polit. dir. Am. Conservative Union, Washington, 1973-77; pres., founder Century Communications Inc., Washington, 1977—; assoc. dep. dir. PPO, The White House, Washington, 1981-82, spl. asst. to pres., 1982-83, dep. asst. to pres., 1983-85; asst. to atty. gen. Dept. Justice, Washington, 1985-87; dep. undersec. Dept. Interior, Washington, 1987-88, asst. sec. Office of Fish and Wildlife and Pks., 1988-89; pres. Century Comms., Inc., 1977—; sec. natural resources Commonwealth of Va., 1994-98; v.p. Heritage Found., Washington, 1998—. Chmn. Fed. Svc. Impasses Panel; bd. sci. advisors CDC, NCEH/ATSDR. Author: Clearing the Air, 2000. Bd. dir. Va. Family Found., Va. Inst. for Pub. Policy, Defenders of Property Rights; bd. govs. Reagan Ranch; mem. adv. com. Landmark Legal Found., Hunters for the Hungry; vice chmn. Women's Ministry, Oakland Bapt. Ch., 2005. Recipient Outstanding Svc. award Federalist Soc., 1988; sr. fellow Atlas Econ. Rsch. Found., Alexis de Tocqueville Inst. Mem. Nat. Wilderness Inst. (bd. dirs.), Am. Conservative Union (bd. dirs.), Assn. Am. Educators (bd. dirs.), Reagan Alumni Assn. (treas. 2002--), CNP (exec. bd.). Republican. Baptist. Avocations: outdoor recreation, reading. Home: 2816 S Joyce St Arlington VA 22202-2249 Office: The Heritage Found 214 Massachusetts Ave NE Washington DC 20002-4958 Office Phone: 202-546-4400. E-mail: dunlopbn@heritage.org.

DUNLOP, KAREN OWEN, lawyer; b. 1966; BS, Georgetown U., 1987; MA, U. Va., 1989, JD, 1992. Bar: Ill. 1992. With Sidley Austin Brown & Wood, Chgo., 1992—, ptnr., 2001—. Mem.: Am. Health Lawyers Assn. (vice chair health sys. transactions com.). Office: Sidley Austin Brown and Wood Bank One Plz 10 S Dearborn St Chicago IL 60603

DUNLOP, MARIANNE, retired language educator; b. Niobrara, Nebr., Mar. 14, 1933; d. Harvey Wesley LaBranche and Karen Sanna Arneson; m. Richard Campbell Dunlop, Apr. 26, 1959; 1 child, Christopher Campbell. BA, Vt. Coll., 1985, MA, 1989. Bd. dir. and bd. mem. The Sargent House Mus., Gloucester, Mass., 1992—96; ESL educator Penasquitos Laubach Literacy Ctr., San Diego, 1999—2002; ret., 2002. Author: (book) Judith Sargent Murray: Champion of Social Justice, 1993; editor: (book) Judith Sargent Murray: Her First 100 Letters, 1995; writer, contbr.: (book) Standing Before Us: Unitarian Universalist Women and Social Reform 1776-1936, 1999; spkr., contbr. (documentary) Judith Sargent Murray: 18th Century Feminist. Officer, bd. dirs. Sargent House Mus., Gloucester, Mass., 1992—96, mem.

adv. bd., 1996—; ESL educator Penasquitos Laubach Literacy Ctr., San Diego, 1999—2002; mem. Sargent House Mus. Mem. Virginia Woolf's Outsider Soc. Unitarian Universalist. Avocation: honoring otherness. Home: 11032 Ipai Ct San Diego CA 92127-1382

DUNMEYER, SARAH LOUISE FISHER, retired health care consultant; b. Ft. Wayne, Ind., Apr. 13, 1935; d. Frederick Law and Jeanette Blose (Stults) Fisher; m. Herbert W. Dunmeyer, Sept. 9, 1967; children: Jodi, Lisa. BS, U. Mich., 1957; MS, Temple U., 1966; EdD, U. San Francisco, 1983. Lic. clin. lab. technologist, Calif. Instr. med. tech. U. Vt., Burlington, 1966-67, Northeastern U., Boston, 1967-68, instr. lab. asst. program, 1968-70; educator, coord. sch. med. tech. Children's Hosp., San Francisco, 1970-73; dir. course devel. for continuing edn. program Pacific Presbyn. Med. Ctr., San Francisco, 1974-82; project mgr., cons. Peabody Mktg. Decisions, San Francisco, 1983-87; sr. rsch. assoc. Inst. for Health and Aging, U. Calif., San Francisco, 1986-89; rsch. analyst student acad. svcs. U. Calif., San Francisco, 1991-94; external cons. Health Care Consulting Svcs., San Francisco, 1986-97; clin. lab. scientist Kaiser Hosp., San Francisco, 1989—2006, ret. Seminar presenter Am. Assn. Blood Banks, San Francisco, 1976, Am. Soc. Clin. Pathologists, Miami Beach, Fla., 1977, Ann. Meeting of Am. Soc. Med. Technology, Atlanta, 1977; site surveyor Nat. Accrediting Agy. for Clin. Lab. Scis., Chgo., 1974-80. Contbr. articles to profl. jours.

DUNN, ANNE EWALD NEFFLEN, retired elementary school educator; b. Elkins, W.Va., Feb. 9, 1935; d. Edgar Lantz and May (Bradley) Nefflen; m. Delma Douglas Dunn, July 20, 1961; children: Susan Bradley Dunn, Robert Cameron, Richard Tullos. BS in Home Econs., U. Md., 1956; student, U. Miami, 1953-54, San Diego State Coll., 1958-60; MEd, U. Ark., 1985. Cert. elem. tchr., reading specialist, gifted and talented, Ark. Tchr. 2d grade San Diego City Schs., 1958-61, Oak Harbor (Wash.) Schs., 1961-63; tchr. 2d and 3d grades Albuquerque Pub. Schs., 1963-65; tchr. 3d grade Prairie Grove (Ark.) Sch. Dist., 1978-85, tchr. gifted and talented, coord., 1985-88, tchr. remedial reading and math., 1988-92, tchr., coord. At-Risk Alternative Edn. 1st grade, 1992-94, chpt. I reading specialist, reading tchr., 1994—2003; ret. Interviewer Navy Relief Soc., Whidbey Island, Wash., 1961-63. Leader 4-H Horse Club, Whidbey Island, 1961-63, 4-H Club, Prairie Grove, 1979-81; leader, trainer Girl Scouts U.S., Prairie Grove, 1975-78; mem. Prairie Grove Libr. Bd., 1980-82; show sec. Nat. Arabian Horse Assn. Show, Albuquerque, 1965. Mem. Phi Delta Kappa. Presbyterian. Avocations: sewing, reading, horseback riding. Home: 22530 Cove Crk S Prairie Grove AR 72753-9230 Office: Prairie Grove Elem Sch 824 N Mock St Prairie Grove AR 72753-2610

DUNN, AUDREY CHRISTINE, speech pathology/audiology services professional; b. New Britain, Conn., May 13, 1976; BA, Our Lady of Elms Coll., Chicopee, Mass., 1998; MS, So. Conn. State U., New Haven, Conn., 2001. Cert. clin. competance Am. Speech-Lang. and Hearing Assn., 2002. Speech-lang. pathologist Meriden (Conn.) Pub. Schs., 2001—. Mem.: Am. Speech Lang. Hearing Assn. (assoc.).

DUNN, DEBRA L., computer company executive; B in Comparative Econs., Brown U., Providence; M in Bus., Harvard U. Exec. devel. mgr. corp. tng. divsn. Hewlett-Packard Co., Palo Alto, Calif., 1983—86, various devel. and mfg. mgmt. positions, 1986—92, mfg. mgr., 1992—93, mktg. mgr., 1993—96, gen. mgr. video comm. divsn., 1996—98, gen. mgr. exec. com., 1998, v.p., 1999—2000, v.p. strategy and corp. ops., 2000—02, sr. v.p. corp. affairs, 2002—. Mem. UN Info. and Comm. Tech. Task Force; bd. dirs. Opportunities Industrialization Ctr. West, BayCat. Office: Hewlett Packard Co 3000 Hanover St Palo Alto CA 94304

DUNN, GLORIA JEAN, artist; b. Detroit, Apr. 21, 1927; d. Donald Stanton and Etta Florence (Barber) Hopkins; m. Eugene Oliver Dunn, Dec. 28, 1944; children: Michael Eugene, Patricia Ann. Student, Wayne County C.C., Taylor, Mich., 1987-90. Instr. arts and crafts YWCA, Wyandotte, Mich., 1963-86; instr. painting and calligraphy, adult edn. Lincoln Park (Mich.) Sch. Sys., 1982-90; owner, mgr. Pen, Brush and Anvil Studio, Southgate, Mich., 1975-95, Gloria Hopkins Dunn Studio of Fine Art, Wyandotte, 1995—; represented by Home Gallery, Taylor, Mich., Swann Gallery, Lincoln Park, Mich., Fuenteo Gallery, Wyandotti. Mem. adv. bd. Wyandotte St. Art Fair, 1962—, organizer, co-chair, 1962-81; art instr. City of Wyandotte Recreation Dept., 2002—. One-woman shows include Taylor (Mich.) Cmty. Libr., Southgate (Mich.) City Hall, Swann Gallery, Detroit, Taylor (Mich.) City Hall, Trenton (Mich.) City Hall. Mem. Southgate Cultural Commn., 1974-82, 91-99. Recipient Cmty. Svc. award City of Southgate, 1978, Hon. Tribute, City of Wyandotte, 1982, 20 Yrs. Dedication to Art award City of Wyandotte, 1991, Salute to Excellence award Downriver Coun. for the Arts, 2003. Mem. Acanthus Art Soc. Wyandotte (pres. 1994-2004), Downriver Arts and Crafts Guild (exhibit chair 1995, 96, 97, 98, 99, 2000, 06, jury chair 2000-01, 06), Art Ambience (historian 1993—, bd. dirs., v.p. 1999—, pres. 2001-02, Downriver Coun. Arts Salute to Excellence award, 2003), Nat. Assn. Fine Arts. Avocations: swimming, photography, gardening, riding. Office: 2930 Biddle St Wyandotte MI 48192-5214

DUNN, JENNIFER BLACKBURN, former congresswoman; b. Seattle, Wash., July 29, 1941; d. John Charles and Helen (Gorton) Blackburn; div.; children: Bryant, Reagan. Student, U. Wash., 1960-62; BA in English Lit., Stanford U., 1963. Sys. engr. IBM, 1964-69; with King County Dept. of Assessments, 1979-80; former chmn. Rep. Party State of Wash., 1981-92; mem. U.S. Congress from 8th Wash. dist., Washington, 1993—2005. Bd. dirs. Nat. Endowment Democracy; mem. ways and means com., homeland sec. com., econ. com.; mem. adv. bd. Internat. Rep. Inst.; participant Preparatory Commn. World Conf. Status of Women, Nairobi, 1985, World Econ. Forum, Davos, Switzerland, 2000. Del. Rep. Nat. Conv., 1980, 84, 88; presdl. apptd. adv. coun. Historic Preservation, adv. coun. volunteerism SBA; apptd. presdl. commn. on debates; N.W. Regional Dir. Met. Operal Regional Auditions; mem. Jr. League of Seattle Named one of 25 Smartest Women in Am., Mirabella mag., one of 10 Most Powerful Women in Wash., Washington Law and Politics mag. Mem. Internat. Women's Forum (Wash. chpt.), Gamma Phi Beta. Republican.

DUNN, JERI L., literature and language educator; b. Mandan, N.D., June 2, 1958; d. Wilbert Arthur Heid and A. Colleen Knudson; m. Colon Lewis Dunn. BS in Secondary Edn., Dickenson State U., N.D., 1980; at, Mary Coll., Bismark, N.D., 1976. Tchr. English and psychology Emmons Ctrl. H.S., Strasburg, ND, Westhope Ctrl. H.S., Beach H.S., Littlesnake River H.S., Baggs, Wyo., Alexander Pub. Sch., Alexander, ND, Hettinger Pub. Sch. Speech and drama coach. Office: Hettinger Pub Sch PO Box 1188 Hettinger ND 58639-1188

DUNN, JERI R., food products executive; Grad., Edinboro State U. With Parker White Metal Co., Curtis Industries; assoc. dir. application systems Stouffer's Hotels; asst. v.p. tech. and standards Nestle SA, Switzerland; v.p., chief info. officer Nestle USA; with Tyson Foods, Inc., Springdale, Ark., 2001—02, sr. v.p., chief info. officer, 2002—. Office: Tyson Foods Inc 2210 W Oaklawn Dr Springdale AR 72762-6999

DUNN, KAREN S., language educator; b. Houston, Nov. 7, 1944; d. Florence John and Annette Freddie Seyer; m. H. Glenn Dunn, June 15, 1968; children: Janet Elizabeth, Michael Glenn. BA, Tex. Christian U., Ft. Worth, 1967. Cert. Spanish, French tchr. Okla. Spanish tchr. Houston Pub. Schs., 1967—68, Ft. Worth Pub. Schs., 1971, Edmond Pub. Schs., Okla., 1996—97; ESL, Spanish and French tchr. Mustang Pub. Schs., Okla., 1997—. Mem.: TESOL, Okla. Fgn. Lang. Tchrs. Assn., Gamma Phi Beta (v.p., philanthropic chmn., asst., Woman of Yr. 2006). Presbyterian. Avocation: handbell choir. Home: 6617 NW 127 Oklahoma City OK 73142 Office: Mustang Pub Schs 906 S Heights Dr Mustang OK 73064

DUNN, LINDA, special education educator; d. David Paul and Irene Davis Lacy; children: Wanda Bond, Douglas, Kimberly Abel, J. Scott, Deirdre Dunham, Ash. BS, U. Tenn., Knoxville, 1971; MA, U. No. Colo., Greeley, 1976. Cert. tchr. Fla. Tchr. spl. edn. Citrus Grove Jr. H.S., Miami, Fla., 1971—78, Citrus Grove Occupl. Tng. Ctr., Miami, Fla., 1979—2003, Citrus Grove Mid. Sch., Miami, Fla., 2003—. Mem.: NEA, Am. Fedn. Tchrs. Office Phone: 305-642-5055. E-mail: tennlinda@hotmail.com.

DUNN, LINDA BAUGH, elementary school educator; b. Richmond, Va., Feb. 18, 1949; d. Haywood Ambrose and Dorothy Johnson Baugh; children: Melinda Dunn Lawson, Rhonda Dunn White, Ashlee Monique Easter, Alyssa Lenee' Easter, Brandon Jamil Easter. Student, John Tyler C.C., Chester, Va., 1968—70; BA, Va. Commonwealth U., Richmond, Va., 1973, MA in Tchg., 1993. Cert. tchr. Va., 1993. Tutor english John Tyler C.C., Chester, Va., 1969—70; photocopy technician Va. Employment Commn., Richmond, 1978—90; rsch. asst. Va. Commonwealth U., Richmond, 1992—93; tchr. Richmond Pub. Schs., 1993—. Writer English curriculum Richmond Pub. Schs., 1996, coord. 21st Century Afternoon Tutorial, 2004—06; presenter in field. Contbr. articles to profl. jours. Nominee Elkhardt Mid. Sch. Tchr. of Yr., Colleagues Elkhardt Mid. Sch., 1995, Ttchr. of Yr., Disney, 1996. Mem.: NEA, Internat. Reading Assn., Nat. Mid. Sch. Assn. Avocations: travel, reading, collecting trinket boxes. Office: Richmond Public Schools Elkhardt Middle 6300 Hull Street Road Richmond VA 23224 Office Phone: 804-745-3600. Office Fax: 804-674-5518. Personal E-mail: ldunn@richmond.k12.va.us.

DUNN, LINDA KAY, physician; b. Grand Rapids, Mich., Jan. 11, 1947; d. Roger John and Mary Kathryn (Bouwer) Kloote; m. Jeffrey Marc Dunn, June 3, 1972; children: David Alan, Kathryn Ann. AB in Chemistry, Hope Coll., 1968; MD, U. Mich., 1972. Diplomate Am. Bd. Ob-Gyn, Am. Bd. Maternal-Fetal Medicine, Am. Bd. Med. Genetics. Resident in ob-gyn. U. Mich., Ann Arbor, 1972-75, fellow in maternal-fetal medicine, 1975-77; hon. rsch. registrar St. Mary's Hosp., London, 1977-78; dir. of perinatology Temple U. Sch. Medicine, Phila., 1978-79, assoc. prof. ob-gyn, 1991-97; dir. subsect. on genetics Pa. Hosp., Phila., 1980-90; pres Medigen, Inc., Phila., 1987-90; dir. maternal-fetal medicine and genetics Abington (Pa.) Meml. Hosp., 1991-97. Med. dir. Comprehensive Maternal and Infant Svcs., Phila., 1987-90; pres. Abington Perinatal Assocs., P.C., 1993-97; dir. maternal-fetal medicine, chair dept. ob-gyn. Allegheny U., 1997-99; pres., CEO Allegheny U. Hosp. at City Ave.; chair dept. ob-gyn. Chestnut Hill Hosp., Phila., 1999—. Fellow Am. Coll. Ob-Gyn.; mem. AMA, Soc. Maternal Fetal Medicine, Am. Soc. Human Genetics, Am. Coll. Med. Genetics, Pa. State Med. Soc., Phila. Obstet. Soc., U. Mich. Med. Ctr. Alumni Soc. (chair 1996), Norman Miller Gynecologic Soc. (pres. 1996). Mem. Soc. Of Friends. Avocations: travel, piano. Office: Chestnut Hill Hosp 8835 Germantown Ave Philadelphia PA 19118-2765 Business E-Mail: linda_dunn@chs.net.

DUNN, MARY ANN, mathematics educator; b. Gadsden, Ala., Dec. 12, 1946; d. Carl Luther and Ruby Frances Coheley; m. James Thomas Dunn, Mar. 30, 1985; 1 child, Rebekah Ann. BS in Secondary Edn., Jacksonville State U., Ala., 1969; MS of Edn., U. of North Fla., Jacksonville, 1974. Math tchr. Robert E. Lee H.S., Jacksonville, 1970—76, Adamson Jr. H.S., Rex, Ga., 1976—82; computer programmer Delta AirLines, Atlanta, 1982—86; math tchr. Louisville H.S., Ga., 1986—89, SE Bulloch H.S., Brooklet, Ga., 1989—91, Harlem H.S., Ga., 1991—93, Manchester H.S., Ga., 1994—2000, Washington County H.S., Sandersville, Ga., 2000—. Nazarene. Avocations: travel, reading, cooking. Home: 614 Park Ave Sandersville GA 31082 Office Phone: 478-552-2324. Personal E-mail: madunn2507@aol.com.

DUNN, MARY MAPLES, academic administrator; b. Sturgeon Bay, Wis., Apr. 6, 1931; d. Frederic Arthur and Eva (Moore) Maples; m. Richard S. Dunn, Sept. 3, 1960; children— Rebecca Cofrin, Cecilia Elizabeth. BA, Coll. William and Mary, 1954, LHD (hon.), 1989; MA, Bryn Mawr Coll., 1956, PhD, 1959; LLD (hon.), Marietta Coll., 1987, Amherst Coll., 1987, Brown U., 1989; LittD (hon.), Lafayette Coll., 1988, Haverford Coll., 1991; LHD (hon.), Transylvania U., 1991, U. Pa., 1995, Mt. Holyok Coll., 1996, Smith Coll., 1998, U. Mass., 1998, U. South, 1999. Faculty Bryn Mawr Coll., 1958-85, prof. history, 1974-85; acting dean Undergrad. Coll. Bryn Mawr (Pa.) Coll., 1978-79, dean, 1980-85; pres. Smith Coll., Northampton, Mass., 1985-95; Carl and Lily Pforzheimer Found. dir. Arthur and Elizabeth Libr. Radcliffe Coll., 1995-99; acting pres., acting dean Inst. for Advanced Study Harvard U., 1999—2000. Author: William Penn: Politics and Conscience, 1967; editor: Political Essay on the Kingdom of New Spain (Alexander von Humboldt), 1972, rev., 1988, (with Richard S. Dunn) Papers of William Penn, vols. I-IV, 1979-87. Trustee The Clark Sch. for the Deaf, 1988-95, Acad. Mus., 1985-95, Hist. Deerfield, Inc., 1986—, Bingham Fund for Teaching Excellence at Transylvania U., 1987—, John Carter Brown Libr., 1994-99, NOW/Legal Def. and Edn. Fund., 1996—, Marlboro Music, 1996—. Recipient Disting. Tchg. award Lindbeck Found., 1969, Radcliffe medal Radcliffe Assn., 2001; fellow Inst. Advanced Study Princeton U., 1974. Mem. Berkshire Conf. Women Historians (pres. 1973-75), Coordinating Com. Women Hist. Profession (pres. 1975-77), Am. Hist. Assn., Am. Philos. Soc. (co-exec. officer 2002—), Inst. Early Am. History and Culture (chmn. adv. council 1977-80), Mass. Hist. Soc., Phi Beta Kappa. Office: American Philosophical Society Exec Office 104 S Fifth St Philadelphia PA 19106-3287

DUNN, MAUREEN H., lawyer; b. Minneola, NY, Aug. 17, 1949; BA, LeMoyne Coll., 1971; JD, Cath. U., 1974. Bar: Tenn., DC. Atty. Tenn. Valley Authority (TVA), Knoxville, 1978—86, asst. gen. counsel, 1986—2001, exec. v.p., gen. counsel, 2001—. Office: Tenn Valley Authority 400 W Summit Hill Dr Knoxville TN 37902-1499 Office Phone: 865-632-2101.

DUNN, NANCY MARABELLA, artist, art educator; b. Shreveport, La., Nov. 22, 1950; d. Sam and Diene Marabella; m. Robby Jack Dunn, Feb. 14, 1986. Student, U. Southwestern LA., 1968—70; BFA, Kansas City Art Inst., 1972. Instr. art Northside Elem. Sch., 1988—99, Broadmoore Lab. Mid. Sch., 1999—2001, So. Hills Elem. Sch., 2001—. Instr. art La. State U. Art Clinic, 1991—, Project Talent, 1995—. Exhibitions include La. State U. Gallery, 1993—, Sanshe, Inc., 1994—, Mmagale Gallery, 1996—, Barnwell Art Ctr., 2003, numerous pvt. and corp. collections. Named Outstanding Young Woman Am., Fedn. Women's Club, 1977, Tchr. of Yr., So. Hills Elem. Sch., 2001.

DUNN, PATRICIA CECILE, investment company executive; b. Burbank, Calif., Mar. 27, 1953; d. Henry and Ruth Marie (Lee) Dunn; m. William W. Jahnke, July 18, 1981; stepchildren: Janai, Jennifer, Michelle, Michael. AB in Journalism and Econ., U. Calif., Berkeley, 1975. V.p. Wells Fargo Investment Advisors, San Francisco, 1983—84, sr. v.p., 1984—85, exec. v.p., 1985—87, chief investment officer, COO, pres., 1987; with Barclays Global Investors, N.A. (formerly Wells Fargo Investment Advisors), San Francisco, 1976—, co-chmn., CEO, 1995—2002, non-exec vice chmn., 2002—06; non-exec. chmn. Hewlett-Packard Co., Palo Alto, Calif., 2005—06. Bd. dirs. Hewlett-Packard Co. 1998-2006 Contbr. articles to profl. jours. Mem. new media bd., U. Calif. Sch. Journalism, Berkeley, adv. bd. U. Calif. Haas Grad. Sch. of Bus., Conf. bd. Global Corp. Governance Rsch. Ctr., dir., mem. exec. com. Larkin St. Youth Svcs., San Francisco. Named one of Most Powerful Women, Forbes mag., 2005; named to Bay Area Coun. Hall of Fame, 2006. Office: Barclays Global Investors 45 Fremont St San Francisco CA 94105-2204*

DUNN, REBECCA M., telecommunications industry executive; b. Selma, Ala. BS in Math., Auburn U., 1970. Asst. engr. South Ctrl. Bell, 1970, engrng. assoc., staff engr., assist. engrng. mgr. costs dist. mgr. capital recovery, 1975, ops. mgr. regulatory, asst. v.p. pub. affairs, 1984, gen. mgr. bus. mktg. for Ala. and Miss. ops., 1987—89; v.p. corp. affairs BellSouth Corp., Atlanta, 1989—91, v.p. human resources and corp. svcs., 1991—99, v.p. shared svcs., sr. v.p. corp. compliance, corp. sec., 2001—. Mem. adv. coun. Coll. of Bus., Auburn U.; vol. United Way; bd. dirs. Atlanta History Ctr., Homeward Inc., Ctrl. Atlanta Progress.

DUNN, SANDRA E., insurance agent; b. Asheville, NC, Mar. 10, 1959; d. Riley Jefferson Wells and Faye (Worley Wells) Bates. Cert. ins. counselor, profl. ins. woman. File clk. then personal ins. sales BB & T Insurance, Asheville, NC, 1977-80, office and agy. mgr., 1980-84, asst. v.p., 1992, v.p., MIS dir., 1996-99, v.p., dir. agy. svcs., 1999—, sr. v.p., 2002—. Computer systems trainer and data conversion specialist BB & T Ins., Charlotte, NC, 1994—96; design rev. and product devel. chair AMS Users Group, 1997—2000, bd. dirs., 2000—05, exec. bd., 2004—05. Mem. Nat. Assn. Insurance Profls., Charlotte Assn. Insurance Women, Cert. Profl. Ins. Women. Avocations: skiing, reading, power walking, golf, baking. Home: 125 Clearwater Ln Mooresville NC 28117-7529 Office: BB & T Insurance Svcs 5925 Carnegie Blvd Ste 400 Charlotte NC 28209-4659 Office Phone: 704-954-3080.

DUNN, VIRGINIA, artist; b. Long Island, NY, Dec. 11, 1951; d. James Joseph and Margaret Virginia Dunn. Student, Marymount Coll., Boca Raton, Fla., Lynn U., 1970—71, SUNY, Purchase, 1972-75, Propersie Sch. of Art, Conn., 1975—76, Silvermine Art Ctr. Nurse's aide St. Joseph's Hosp., Stamford, Conn., 1967-70; with advt. dept. Cuisinart, Greenwich, Conn., 1977-89; tchr. oriental painting Newton Studios. One-woman shows include Greenwich Hosp., 2002, Garden Cafe, Greenwich, 2002, Nathaniel Witheral, exhibitions include Hurlbutt Gallery, Greenwich Libr., various yrs., Conn., Gertrude White Gallery, Greenwich, 1998—2002, Greenwich Garden Ctr., Cos Cob, Conn., 1989—2002 (honorable mention, 2002, 2d place, 2 honorable mentions), Ferguson Libr., Stamford, Conn., 1993—2002 (Koi Fish Chinese Hon Mention, 3d Pl. award, 2001, 2002, 2002, 2003), Hammond Mus. & Japanese Stroll Garden, North Salem, NY, 1993—2006, Whitby Sch., Greenwich, 1994, Rush-Holley House, Cos Cob, 1994, Wilton Libr., Conn., 1995—96, E.C. Potter Gallery, Greenwich, 1996—2002, The Coffee Shoppe, Greenwich Hosp., 1997, Stamford Art Assn., 1999 (3d Pl. award, 2000), Greenwichart, Stamford, 1999, Art Soc. Old Greenwich Sidewalk Shows, 1999—2003, Stamford Art Assn., 2001, Westfield Ct., 2001, Greenwich Libr., Flinn Gallery, 2001, 2002, Landson Park, Katona, NY, 2001—04, Flynn Gallery, Greenwich Libr., 2001—02, Landson Park, Katona, NY, 2002, St. Raphael's Hosp., New Haven, 2002, Hammond Mus., 2002, Circe d'Art Gallery, Rowayton Art Ctr., Hammond Mus., 2002—03, Greenwich Libr., 2003, Riversville Art Show, Gaylordsville, Conn., 2006, Dr. Vincent Carlesi Pain Mgmt., Danbury, Conn. Donator paintings to people and places around the world. Recipient Honorable Mention award Greenwich Art Soc., 1999, other awards for art. Mem. Oriental Brush Artist Guild (mailing com. 1993-2002), Eastern Arts Connection, The Greenwich Art Soc. (mailing com. 1988-89, Second Place award 2000), The Art Soc. of Old Greenwich (hostess 1988-89, 2d place award 2002, numerous honorable mentions), Conn. Graphic Art Ctr., Greenwich Arts Coun., The Stamford Art Assn., The Hammond Mus., Women in the Arts, Rowayton Art Assn. Avocations: music, travel, cats, Bluegrass banjo. Home: 12 Newton Rd Gaylordsville CT 06755

DUNNE, JUDITH DOYLE, information scientist, educator; b. Mineola, NY, Dec. 17, 1962; d. James Macdonnel and Lois Hart Doyle; m. Michael John Dunne, May 28, 1989. BS, North Adams State Coll., 1984. Elem. edn., art tchr. Rosary Acad., Watertown, Mass., 1985—86; 3d and 6th gr. math. tchr. St. Patrick's Sch., Watertown, Mass., 1986—91; art tchr. Holy Name, West Roxbury, Mass., 1991—96; Tech. coord. computer, art and math. tchr. Good Shepherd Sch., Perryville, Md., 1997—. Mem.: Nat. Cath. Edn. Assn. Avocations: crafts, skiing, ice skating, in-line skating. Office: Good Shepherd Sch 810 Aiken Ave Perryville MD 21903

DUNNE, NANCY ANNE, retired social services administrator; b. Ionia, Mich., Aug. 5, 1929; d. Warner Kingsley and Hazel Fern (Allison) McSween; m. James Robert, Oct. 28, 1952; children: James Robert Jr., Stephen Michael. BA, Albion (Mich.) Coll., 1951. Tchr. Oakdale Elem., Grand Rapids, Mich., 1951-53, Lakeside Sch., East Grand Rapids, Mich., 1953; clk. Office of Naval Rsch., Washington, 1954-55; dir. pub. rels. Diocesan Office Health and Social Svcs., Albany, NY, 1971-74; dir. vol. action dept. Coun. of Human Resources, Schenectady, NY, 1974-76; pers. asst. Am. Soc. Assn. Execs., Washington, 1977-78; adminstrv. asst. N.Y. Soc. Cons. Engrs., N.Y.C., 1978-79, Assessment Designs, Inc., Orlando, Fla., 1980-82, Catholic Social Svcs., Orlando, Fla., 1982-84, ret., 1984. Active NY State Comm. Cultural Resources, Albany, 1970-73, Anna Maria Island Cmty. Ctr., 2000-01; bd. dirs. Coalition for the Homeless, Orlando, 1983-87; tutor Anna Maria Island Elem. Sch., Fla.; vol. Blake Hosp., Bradenton, Fla., 1999-2003, Imagine Manatee Task Force, Bradenton, 2003; 1st v.p. Performing arts Downtown Manatee County, Inc., 2003; tutor Anna Maria Island Elem. Sch. Mem. AAUW (pres. Manatee County br. 2001-03), Jr. League of Schenectady (Vol. of Yr. award 1965-66), Schenectady Symphony Orch. (pres. 1969-70), Ladies of Charity (pres. Albany chpt. 1970-72, pres. Orlando chpt. 1984-86, nat. pres. 1990-94, nat. bd. dirs. 2001-02, v.p. internat. 1990-94, bd. dirs. 1994-2000), Women's Club Anna Maria Island (1st v.p. 2004—, pres. 2005-06, rotary club fellowship award, 2003). Roman Catholic. Avocations: reading, travel, golf, bridge, entertaining friends. Home: 6400 Flotilla Dr Apt 31 Holmes Beach FL 34217-1425

DUNNELL, REBECCA, music educator; b. Binghamton, NY; BFA summa cum laude in applied music, Long Island U., 1985; MusM, U. NC, 1993, MusD, 1997. Flutist Lothlorien Inter-Cultural Music, Inc., Huntington, NY, 1980—91; flute prof. Hollins U., Roanoke, Va., 1998—2002; asst. prof. of flute and music hist. Northwest Mo. State U., Maryville, Mo., 2002—. Fellow, Bach Aria Group, 1985; Charles B. Hayes fellowship, U. NC, Greensboro, 1993-1994. Mem.: Nat. Flute Assn., Kansas City Flute Assn. (pres. 2006—, editor newsletter 2003—06). Office: Northwest Missouri State Univ 800 Univ Dr Maryville MO 64468 Business E-Mail: dunnell@nwmissouri.edu.

DUNNING, JEAN, artist; b. Granby, Conn., 1960; MFA, Sch. Art Inst. Chgo., 1985. One-woman shows include, Feature, Chgo., 1987, 1988, Hirshhorn Mus., Washington, 1994, Mus. Contemporary Art, Chgo., 1994, Richard Telles Fine Art, LA, 1995, Galerie Massimo de Carlo, Milan, 1995, Feigen Inc., Chgo., 1996, Feigen Contemporary, 1997, Galleria Massimo de Carlo, Milan, 1998, Malmö Konstmuseum, Sweden, 1999, James Harris Gallery, Seattle, 2000, Bodybuilder & Sportsman Gallery, Chgo., 2001, exhibited in group shows at Changing Views, Feigen Inc., Chgo., 1994, Traces: Body in Contemporary Photog., Bronx Mus. Art, NYC, 1995, Wallflower, Randolph St. Gallery, Chgo., 1995, Up Close & Personal, Phila. Mus. Art, 1996, Slad, Apex Art, NYC, 1997, New Photog. 14, Mus. Modern Art, NYC, 1998, Rapture, MassArt, Boston, 2000, Wanderings of the Mind's Eye: Photographs by Ill. Artists, Mus. Contemporary Art, Chgo., 2004. Grantee, Louis Comfort Tiffany Found., 1993; Individual Artist Fellowship, Ill. Arts Coun., 1992, 1991, Cmty. Arts Assistance Grant, Chgo. Office Fine Arts, 1989, Spl. Assistance Grant, Ill. Art Coun., 1987. Mailing: c/o Museum Contemporary Art 220 East Chicago Ave Chicago IL 60611

DUNN KELLY, RUTH EMMA, management consultant; b. Tuskegee, Ala., Apr. 26, 1945; d. Moses and Annie Virgia Dunn; m. Bernard Kelly, June 2, 2001. BS, Wayne State U., 1985; MS, Ctrl. Mich. U., 1989. Analyst Gen. Motors, Detroit, 1969—99; test adminstr. Aon Cons., Finley, Ohio, 1998—; counselor Macomb County Crisis Ctr., Warren, Mich., 1994—95.

DU NORD, JEANNE, writer, publishing executive; b. June 24, 1939; m. David Arnold Buser, Oct. 10, 2001. BA, Roanoke Coll., 1961; MA, U. Va. Ordained min. Faculty U. Va., Wallops Island, 1964—71; pres. Arcadia Prodns. and Publs., Princess Anne, Md., 1995—, Linden Hill Pub., Md., 1998—. Writing coach Linden Hill Pub., Princess Anne, 2003—; prodr. Chesapeake Celtic Festival, Princess Anne, 1990—; instr. Del. Tech. and C.C., Georgetown, Del., 1993—; guest lectr. and spl. presenter, 1971—. Author: (play) Tides of Time (ArtScape Best Play, 1993), The Green Rocking Chairs (Md. State Arts Coun. Best Play Award, 1999), (non-fiction) The Quest for the Grail, The Celtic Quest, 2004, Beyond Time and Place, 2005, Amazing Cat Tales, 2006. Founder, prodr. The Chesapeake Celtic Festival Furnace Town Living History Mus., Snow Hill, Md.; founder Linden Hill Cultural Found. Recipient Citation for Continuing Excellence in Writing, Gov. Md., 1999; grantee, Somerset Arts Coun., 1995, 1997. Independent. Mem. Celtic Ch. Achievements include development of system of research using forensic linguistics. Avocations: art, design, clothing designer. Office: Arcadia Prodns and Publs 11923 Somerset Ave Princess Anne MD 21853 Office Phone: 410-651-0757. Personal E-mail: LH123@comcast.net.

DUNPHY, MAUREEN MILBIER, literature educator; b. Springfield, Mass., Feb. 25, 1949; d. Donald J. and Mary C. Milbier; m. Terrence Michael Dunphy. BS in Edn., Westfield State Coll., 1971, MEd, 1975, Cert. Advanced Grad. Study, 1988; cert. paralegal, 1996. Tchr. Thornton Burgess Intermediate Sch., Hampden, Mass., 1971-75; reading specialist, reading dept. head West Springfield Jr. H.S., 1975—2002; reading supr. K-12 Westfield (Mass.) Pub. Schs., 2002—. Acting asst. prin. W. Springfield Jr. HS, 1989; cons. Nat. Evaluations Systems, Amherst, Mass. Mem. editl. bd.: MRA Primer, 1999—. Mem. Long Range Bldg. Needs Com., Westfield, 1986-87, 2000-02. Mem. Pioneer Valley Reading Coun. (pres. 1977-79), Mass. Reading Assn. (dir. 1977-81), West Springfield Edn. Assn. (negotiations sec.), Mass. Tchrs. Assn., Hampden County Tchrs. Assn., Internat. Reading Assn. Home: 282 Steiger Dr Westfield MA 01085-4934 Office: North Mid Sch 350 Southampton Rd Westfield MA 01085 Business E-Mail: m.dunphy@mail.ci.westfield.ma.us.

DUNSIRE, DEBORAH, pharmaceutical executive; arrived in US, 1994; MD, U. Witwatersrand, South Africa. Gen. practitioner, South Africa; clinical rschr. Sandoz (now Novartis), 1988, head mktg. and sales of specialty brands, Basel, Switzerland, 1991; head N.Am. oncology ops. Novartis Pharmaceuticals Corp., US pharm. exec. com.; pres., CEO Millennium Pharmaceuticals, Inc., 2005—. Recipient Rising Star award, Health Care Business Women's Assn., 2000, Excalibur Award, Am. Cancer Soc., 2001. Office: Millennium Pharm 40 Landsdowne St Cambridge MA 02139*

DUNST, ISABEL PAULA, lawyer; b. N.Y.C., Feb. 21, 1947; d. Philip R. and Mae F. Dunst. BS, U. Wis., 1967; JD, NYU, 1971; MPH, Harvard U., 1979. Bar: N.Y. 1971, D.C. 1973. Staff atty. Office Gen. Counsel HEW, Washington, 1971-75, sr. aggy., 1975-79, assoc. gen. counsel, 1979—90; ptnr. Hogan & Hartson LLP, Washington, 1990—. Dep. gen. counsel, 1987-90; ptnr. Hogan & Hartson, Washington, 1990—. Bd. dirs. Women's Legal Def. Fund, 1973—75, pres., 1973-74. Mem. ABA, Am. Health Lawyers Assn. Office Phone: 202-637-5818. Office Fax: 202-637-5910. E-mail: ipdunst@hhlaw.com.

DUNST, KIRSTEN, actress; b. Point Pleasant, N.J., Apr. 30, 1982; d. Klaus and Inez Dunst. Appeared in films Bonfire of the Vanities, 1990, High Strung, 1991, Greedy, 1994, Interview with the Vampire, 1994 (Recipient Golden Globe Award nomination for best supporting actress, 1995, Boston Soc. of Film Critics Award for best supporting actress, 1994, Chicago Film Critics Assn. Award for most promising actress, 1994, Best Breakthrough Performance MTV Movie Awards, 1995), Little Women, 1994, Jumanji, 1995, Wag the Dog, 1997, (voice) Anastasia, 1997, Drop Dead Gorgeous, 1999, Dick, 1999, The Virgin Suicides, 1999, Bring It On, 2000, Crazy/Beautiful, 2001, The Cat's Meow, 2001, Spider-Man, 2002 (Best Kiss, Best Female Performance, MTV Movie Awards, 2003), Levity, 2003, Mona Lisa Smile, 2003, Eternal Sunshine of the Spotless Mind, 2004, Spider-Man 2, 2004, Wimbledon, 2004, Elizabethtown, 2005, Marie Antoinette, 2006; TV appearances include ER, 1996, 97, The Outer Limits, 1997. Office: c/o Iris Burton Agy 8916 Ashcrof Ave Los Angeles CA 90069-1327*

DUNSTON-THOMAS, FRANCES JOHNSON, pediatrician, public health official; b. Richmond, Va., Mar. 12, 1943; d. John R. and Ruth E. (Reeves) Johnson; m. George A. Dunston Sr., Aug. 20, 1966 (dec.); m. Gustave R. Thomas, Aug. 16, 1980; children: George Dunston, Karla Dunston. B.A. in Chemistry summa cum laude, Fisk U., 1964; M.S. in Chemistry, Rutgers U., 1972; M.D., Coll. Med. and Dentistry of N.J.-Rutgers Med. Sch., 1978; M.P.H U. N.C., 1985. Diplomate Am. Bd. Pediatrics. Research chemist Am. Cyanamid Corp., Bound Brook, N.J., 1964-71; research chemist Colgate Palmolive Co., Piscataway, N.J., 1972-73; instr. N.J. Med. Sch., Newark, summers 1973-74; resident Med. Coll. Va., Richmond, 1978-81; dep. health dir. Richmond Health Dept., 1981-83, health dir., 1983-; former CEO, NJ Commn. of Health; now prof. community health & preventive medicine and gen. pediatrics, Morehouse Sch. Medicine; Bd. dirs. Richmond YWCA, 1983—, Richmond Urban League, 1982-. Mem. Richmond Acad. Medicine, Richmond Med. Soc., Va. Pub. Health Assn., Richmond Pediatrics Assn., U.S. Conf. Local Health Officers (v.p.), Phi Beta Kappa, Alpha Omega Alpha, Delta Sigma Theta. Clubs: Jack and Jill, Links, Inc. (Richmond). Office: Morehous Schole Medicine 202 Rotherhithe Ln Nw Marietta GA 30066-3492

DUNTON, OUIDA LUEDTKE, secondary school educator, department chairman; d. Robert Earl Luedtke and Melba Jo Whitlock; m. Jason E. Dunton; children: Jessie, Jacque, Zach. BS in Biology, Kennesaw State U., Ga., 1994; MEd, State U. West Ga., Carrollton, Ga., 1998. Tchr. sci. Cobb County Bd. Edn., Marietta, Ga., 1998—2004, Paulding County Bd. Edn., Dallas, Ga., 2004—, chmn. sci. dept., 2005—06. Mem.: Nat. Sci. Tchrs. Assn., Ga. Sci. Tchrs. Assn. (grantee 2006), Nat. Biology Tchrs. Assn. Avocation: quilting. Office: East Paulding High Sch 3320 East Paulding Dr Dallas GA 30157 Office Phone: 770-445-5100.

DUNTON, SUSAN BETH, academic administrator; b. Bayshore, N.Y., Aug. 28, 1955; d. Emerson Waldo and Marjorie Jane (Moore) D. MusB, Ithaca Coll., 1977; MusM, U. S.C., 1980, MEd, 1981; PhD, U. Conn., 1990; postgrad., Harvard U., 1995. Instrumental music tchr. Horseheads (N.Y.) Cen. Sch., 1977-78; residence life coord. Embr-Riddle Aeronautical U., Daytona Beach, Fla., 1981-82; residence dir. Mitchell Coll., New London, Conn., 1982-84, dir. student life, 1984-86; asst. to dean of students U. Conn., Storrs, 1986-89, interim dean students, 1989-91; assoc. dean. acad. svcs. Lindenwood Coll., St. Charles, Mo., 1991, asst. prof., faculty advisor for individualized edn., 1992-93; assoc. acad. dean, asst. prof. Fontbonne Coll., St. Louis, 1993—99; v.p. academic affairs Averett Univ., Danville, Va., 1999—2003; dir. advanced learning and rsch. Inst. for Advanced Learning & Rsch., Danville, Va., 2003—04; asst. dean academic affairs Harvard Divinity Sch., Cambridge, Mass., 2004—. Cons. Student Conduct and Acad. Dismissals Policies, 1991—; presentor Nat. Conf. Co-rschr. Campus Security, 1991. Recipient Tracy R. Teele award ACPA Commn, XV, 1989. Mem. Am. Coll. Pers. Assn., Nat. Assn. Student Pers. Assn., Assn. Student Jud. Affairs. Avocations: crafts, music. Home: 1A Emmons Pl Cambridge MA 02138-3206 Office: Harvard Univ Divinity Sch 45 Francis Ave Cambridge MA 02138 Office Phone: 617-495-3526. Business E-Mail: susan_dunton@harvard.edu.

DUNTON-DOWNER, LESLIE LINAM, writer; b. Washington, Mar. 2, 1961; d. Ronald Kaye Dunton and Elizabeth Earle (Downer) Simpson; 1 child, Jordan Tucker Rountree. AB, Harvard Coll., Cambridge, Mass., 1983; AM, PhD, Harvard U., Cambridge, Mass., 1992. Tchg. fellow Harvard Coll., Cambridge, Mass., 1986-92; lectr. Harvard U., Cambridge, Mass., 1992-93; jr. fellow Harvard Soc. Fellows, Cambridge, Mass., 1993-96. Founding editor Harvard Review, Cambridge, 1984-86; vis. lectr. Tufts U., Medford, Mass., 1988-89. Author (opera libretto) Ligeia, 1994 (Internat. Orpheus prize 1994), (opera libretto) Conquering the Fury of Oblivion, 1995, (opera libretto) Belladonna, 1999; performer (theater) Addresses for Life, 1997, (music theater piece) Into the Flame (Droit dans la flamme; Dar del-e atash), 2001; co-author (with A. Riding) Essential Shakespeare Handbook, 2004, Opera, 2006; prodr. (music CD) Rumi, 2003, Raqs, 2003; co-prodr., commentator (documentary) Aqnazar: A Singer From Badakhshan, 2002; contbr. articles to books and profl. jours. Bd. trustees Internat. Sch. Boston, 2004—. Recipient Sheldon fellowship Harvard U., 1988-89, Rsch. grant Am. Coun. Learned Socs., Eng., 1994, Bellagio Ctr. award Rockefeller Found., Italy, 1997, Ind. Scholar grant Nat. Endowment for the Humanities, 1998-99. Mem. ASCAP, Societe Civile des Auteurs Multimedias, Societe des Auteurs et Compositions, Beta Kappa.

DUNWICH, GERINA, writer, editor; b. Chgo., Dec. 27, 1959; d. W.E. Novotny and Teri Enies (LoMastro) D. Ordained min. Univ. Life Ch., 1998. Freelance writer, 1975—; editor, pub. Golden Isis mag., 1980—. Guest spkr. Craftwise Pagan Gathering, Waterbury, Conn., 1996, The Real Witches' Ball, Columbus, Ohio, 1997, Pagan Day Festival, Westwood, Calif., 2000, West Hollywood, Calif., 2001, 02; spokesperson Wiccan/Neo-Pagan Cmty. Author: Candlelight Spells, 1988, The Magick of Candleburning, 1989, Circle of Shadows, 1990, The Concise Lexicon of the Occult, 1990, Wicca Craft, 1991, Secrets of Love Magick, 1992, The Wicca Spellbook, 1994, The Wicca Book of Days, 1995, The Wicca Garden, 1996, The Wicca Source Book, 1996, Wicca Love Spells, 1996, Wicca Candle Magick, 1996, Everyday Wicca, 1997, A Wiccan's Guide to Prophecy and Divination, 1997, Wicca A to Z, 1997, Magick Potions, 1998, The Wicca Source Book, rev. 2d edit., 1998, Your Magickal Cat: Feline Magick, Lore and Worship, 2000, The Pagan Book of Halloween, 2000, Exploring Spellcraft, 2001, The Cauldron of Dreams, 2002, A Witch's Guide to Ghosts and the Supernatural, 2002, Dunwich's Guide to Gemstone Sorcery, 2003, Phantom Felines and Other Ghostly Animals, 2006; editor, pub. Aquarius Anthology, 1986, The Liberated Voice, 1987, Coven, 1987, Evil Genius Poetry Jour., 1987-88; appeared on numerous radio talk shows across U.S. and Can.; contbr. articles to profl. jours.; contbr.: Circles, Groves and Sanctuaries, 1992, Llewellyn's Witches' Calendar, 1999, 2000, 2001, 2005, Witches' Datebook, 1999, 2000, 2001, 2005, 2006, Llewellyn's Magical Almanac, 1999, 2000, 2001, Llewellyn's Spell-A-Day Calendar, Llewellyn's Herbal Almanac, The Cat Book of Lists, 2001, A Witch Like Me, 2002, Haunted Northern New York, 2002, The Action Hero's Handbook, 2002, The Witch Book, 2002, American Witch, 2003, The Encyclopedia of Haunted Places, 2005. High Priestess and founder Circle of the Old Ways (formerly Coven Mandragora); founder North Country Wicca, 1996; founder Wheel of Wisdom Sch.; bd. adv. Am. Biog. Inst.; founder Paranormal Animal Rsch. Group, 2005. Mem. Pagan Poets Soc. (founder), Circle, The Fellowship of Isis, The Authors Guild, The Authors League Am., Internat. Ghost Hunters Soc. Office: PO Box 234 Stow NY 14785 Business E-Mail: bcollins@publicist.com.

DUNWOODY, SHARON LEE, journalism and communications educator; b. Hamilton, Ohio, Jan. 24, 1947; d. Walter Charles and Fanchon (Kapp) D. MA, Temple U., 1975; PhD, Ind. U., 1978. Asst. prof. journalism Ohio State U., Columbus, 1977-81; from asst. prof. to prof. Sch. Journalism and Mass Comm. U. Wis., Madison, 1981—, dir. Sch. Journalism and Mass Comm., 1998—2003, assoc. dean Grad. Sch., 2003—. Affiliate Inst. Environ. Studies U. Wis., Madison, 1985—, head acad. programs, 1995-98. Co-editor: Scientists and Journalists, 1986, Communicating Uncertainty, 1999. Mem. AAAS (chair sect. on gen. interest in sci. and Eng. 1992-93), Soc. Social Study Sci., Midwest Assn. Pub. Opinion Rsch. (pres. 1989-90), Assn. Edn. in Journalism and Mass Comm. (pres. 2005—). Home: 1306 Seminole Hwy Madison WI 53711-3728 Office: Univ Wis Sch Journalism & Mass Comm 821 University Ave Madison WI 53706-1412 Office Phone: 608-263-3389. Business E-Mail: dunwoody@wisc.edu.

DUONG, ANH, artist, actress; b. Talence, Gironde, France, Oct. 25; came to U.S., 1988; d. Loi and Esther (Tejedor) D. BA, Lycee Evariste Galois, Yvelines, France, 1978; student, Ballet Sch. Acad. Nora Kiss, Paris, 1978-82, U. Beaux Arts, 1979. Ballet dancer various cos., France, 1978-82. Dir. documentary film: El Cuartel Del Carmen, 1988; appeared in films I Shot Andy Warhol, 30, Scent of a Woman, The Mambo Kings, High Art, A Vendre; paintings exhibited in one person shows at Sperone Westwater, N.Y., 1990, Fukuoka, Japan, 1995, Mus. Modern Art PMMK, Belgium, 1997, Gallery Jerome de Noirmont, Paris, 1999, 2001, 2003, Tony Shafrazi Gallery, N.Y., 2000, in group shows at Annina Nosei, N.Y., 1991, Daniel Blau, Munich, 1993; model for numerous mags. including Vogue, Harper's Bazaar, N.Y. Times Mag., Mirabella, Harpers and Queens, Glamour, Donna, Elle, also for numerous runways shows and campaigns for designers, including Donna Karan, Calvin Klein, The Gap, Banana Republic, Christian LaCroix, John Galliano, Isaac Mizrahi, others.*

DUPEY, MICHELE MARY, communications specialist; b. Bronx, NY, Feb. 26, 1953; d. William B. and Sandra Nancy (Raia) D.; m. Daniel Michael Gieser, July 14, 1980 (div. May 1991). BA, Montclair State Coll., 1975; cert. in copywriting, NYU, 1988. Sec. DDB Needham Worldwide Inc. Advt. (formerly Doyle Dane Bernbach Advt. Co.), N.Y.C., 1985—88; asst. pub. info. officer Hudson County (N.J.) Bd. Chosen Freeholders, 1988-2000; media specialist Englewood (NJ) Hosp. and Med. Ctr., 2000—01; freelance copywriter Jersey City, 1988—; pub. info. officer Jersey City Free Pub. Libr., 2004—. Creator ann. Hudson County Women's History Month Program; in-house planning chair 150th Anniversary Celebration of Hudson County; participant Comm. Gay Games IV, N.Y.C., 1991—94; mem. planning com., pub. rels. Hudson County Am. Heritage Festival, 1994—95; program prodr. pub. rels. 1996 Olympic Torch Relay Hudson County, 1996; developer Hudson County ADv. Commn. on Women; developer seminars, prodr. video What is a Freeholder?; spkr. in field. Contbr. articles to profl. publs. Raised pub. awareness of libr. sys. N.J. 2d Largest City. Recipient Gov.'s award, Hudson County Am. Heritage Festival, 1995; fellow Leadership N.J., 1995. Democrat. Roman Catholic. Home and Office: Copy on Target 206 Washington St Apt 3A Jersey City NJ 07302-4566 Office Phone: 201-547-4579. Personal E-mail: wittywoman@aol.com. Business E-Mail: mdupey@jclibrary.org.

DUPLESSIS, AUDREY JOSEPH, school system administrator; b. New Orleans, June 23, 1920; d. Louis Joseph and Sidonie Josephine (DeLaRose) Boyer; m. Norwood Jerome Duplessis, Sr., June 27, 1984. B in Vocat. Edn., So. U., Baton Rouge, 1942; BA, Calif. State U., 1959, MA, 1966. Tchr., dir. Tri State Coll., New Orleans, 1948-50; from elem. tchr. to dir. Magnet Sch. L.A. Unified Schs., 1954—2002, dir. Magnet Sch., 2002—. Playground L.A. Unified Schs., 1956-59, reading resource tchr., 1965-70, curriculum coord., 1972-78, dir. L.A. Unified Magnet Sch., 1978-02; reading tchr. Calif. Lutheran Coll., Thousand Oaks, 1968-70. Mem. United Tchrs. PAC, L.A., 1980-88. Recipient svc. award Congress of Parents, L.A., 1988, spl. recognition U.S. Congress, 1988. Mem. Internat. Assn. Childhood Edn. (state pres. 1987-89, appreciation award 1989), St. Brigid Edn. Com., Delta Sigma Theta. Democrat. Roman Catholic. Avocations: reading, sewing, travel, opera, music.

DUPLESSIS, SANDRA WALSH, librarian, educator; b. N.Y.C., Mar. 14, 1945; d. Maurice David and Helen Rose (Flynn) Walsh; m. Dwight Charles Duplessis, July 11, 1970; children: Anton, Laura, James. BA in Edn., U. La., Monroe, 1966; MLS with honors, La. State U., 1984. Libr., tchr. Chapelle H.S., Metairie, La., West Jefferson H.S., Harvey, La.; libr., cataloger Jefferson Pub. Libr., Metairie, La.; libr., tchr. St. Rita Sch., Harahan, La. Chair Regina Medal Selection Com. Recipient Sister Mary Aquin award/Libr. of the Yr. Mem.: ALA, Greater New Orleans Libr. Assn., La. Libr. Assn., Greater New Orleans Cath. Libr. Assn. (v.p., pres., newsletter editor), Cath. Libr. Assn. (children's sect., mem. at large, sec., v.p., pres.), Beta Phi Mu. Home: 138 Miami Pl Kenner LA 70065

DUPONT, NICOLE, artist; b. Wilmington, Del., July 24, 1957; d. Henry E.I. duPont and Deborah (Eldredge) duPont Hogan. Artist, CEO Visionary Art Studios, Novato, Calif., 1989-93, Creative Light Prodns., Kapa'a, Hawaii, 1993—. Artist; creator Hawaiian Legend Leis; leis collected in museums including Bishop Mus., Honolulu. Adminstrv. for cmty. classes in Hawaiian culture, Kapa'a, 1994-95. Winner 1st Place award Mokihana Festival Lei Contest, 1997, 98. Mem. Kaua'i Soc. Artists, Garden Island Arts Coun., Kaua'i C. of C. Office: Creative Light Prodns 1191 Kuhio Hwy 116 Kapaa HI 96746 E-mail: hnd@aloha.net.

DUPREE, NATHALIE, chef, television personality, writer; b. Dec. 23, 1939; m. Jack Bass. Advanced Cert., Cordon Bleu; D of Culinary Arts, Johnson-Wales U., 2004. Founder Rich's Cooking Sch., Atlanta, 1975; guest PM Mag., Atlanta; host New So. Cooking with Nathalie Dupree, 1986—. Bd. dirs. So. Foodways Alliance, 2000—02. Author: Cooking of the South, 1984, New Southern Cooking, 1986, Natalie Dupree Cooks for Family and Friends, 1988, Nathalie Dupree's Matters of Taste, 1990, Nathalie Dupree Cooks for Family and Friends, 1992, Nathalie Duprees Southern Memorie, 1994 (James Beard award, 1995), Nathalie Dupree Cooks Great Meals for Busy Days, 1994, Nathalie Dupree Cooks Everyday Meals from a Well-Stocked Pantry, 1995, Nathalie Dupree's Quick Meals, 1996, Nathalie Dupree's Comfortable Entertaining: At Home with Ease and Grace, 1998 (James Beard award, 1999). Founder Internat. Assn. Cultural Sch. Recipient Tastemaker award. Fellow: Internat. Assn. Culinary Profls.; mem.: Womens Forum (pres. Atlanta chpt.). Office: 100 Queen St Charleston SC 29401 Office Phone: 843-958-8806. Personal E-mail: nathalieonly@aol.com.

DUPUY, PAMELA MARIE, elementary school educator; b. Inglewood, Calif., Jan. 9, 1957; d. Glen Olan and Pauline Marie (King) DuP. AA, L.A. Community Coll., 1977; BA, Calif. State U., L.A., 1979. Tchr. L.A. Unified Sch. Dist., 1981—. Democrat. Methodist. Office: LA Unified Sch Dist 2611 W 52nd St Los Angeles CA 90043-1917 Office Phone: 213-294-5103. Business E-Mail: msdupuy2123@aol.com.

DUQUESNAY, ANN, actress, singer; Appeared in Broadway plays including Jelly's Last Jam, The Wiz, Blues in the Night; appeared in off-Broadway plays including Spunk; appeared in other plays including Ma Rainey's Black Bottom, House of Flowers, Porgy and Bess, The Outcast, Lady Day, Black Nativity, Bubbling Brown Sugar, Betsey Brown, Hallelujah, Baby!, 2005, (Helen Hayes award, Outstanding Supporting Actress, Resident Musical, 2005) Hot Feet, 2006; appeared on TV shows including PBS' Reading Rainbow, Another World; co-lyricist, co-composer cast album Bring in Da Noise, Bring in Da Funk, 1997 (Grammy nominee). Recipient AUDELCO, San Francisco's Bay Area Theatre Critics Circle award, Best Supporting Actress in a Musical Tony award Bring in Da Noise, Bring in Da Funk, 1996. Address: Ascap One Lincoln Plz New York NY 10023*

DURAN, KARIN JEANINE, librarian; b. Burbank, Calif., Aug. 31, 1948; d. Jose Antonio and Sophia (Cortez) D.; m. Richard Mark Nupoll, Sept. 5, 1971. AA, L.A. Pierce Coll., Woodland Hills, Calif., 1968; BA, Calif. State U., 1970; MLS, U. So. Calif., 1972, PhD, 1986. Libr. Calif. State U., Northridge, 1972—. Lectr. Calif. State U., Northridge, 1977—. Mem. Comision Femenil San Fernando Valley, Calif., 1987-2006. Named Woman of Year Calif. Women Higher Edn., Northridge, 1989, Bicentennial Woman, L.A. Human Rels. Com., 1976; recipient Northridge Extraordinary Svc. Facility award, CSU, 2006, Svc. to Soc. Recognition, 2003. Mem. ALA, Nat. Assn. Chicano Studies, Calif. Libr. Assn., Calif. Acad. Rsch. Librs., REFORMA, Phi Kappa Phi. Avocations: travel, theater, reading. Office: Calif State U Northridge Libr 18111 Nordhoff St Northridge CA 91330-8327 Business E-Mail: karin.duran@csun.edu.

DURBIN, KIRSTEN DAHLMAN, academic administrator; b. Boston, June 15, 1946; d. John Stanley and Lucille Elizabeth (Jacobson) Dahlman; m. William Applebee Durbin Jr., June 14, 1969; children: Alexandra, Adrian, Spencer. BA, U. Mass., 1969. Tchr. elem. sch. N.Y.C. Bd. Edn., 1970-72, Vt. Bd. Edn., Perkinsville, 1972-73; musician Lydian Consort, Needham, Mass., 1974-84; asst. dir. alumni affairs Wheaton Coll., Norton, Mass., 1990-94, major gifts officer, 1995-97; leadership gifts officer, 1997—; jewelry designer, 1992—; owner KLD Designs & Mixed Media, 1997—. Ambassador to Iowa Dukakis Presdl. Campaign, 1987, Ill., 1988; del. Mass. State Dem. Com., 1988-95; mem. town meeting Town of Needham, 1989-96; campaign mgr. several sch. com. races, Needham, 1986-92; campaign field dir. state rep. race, Needham, 1988, campaign mgr., 1994; mem. IMM Investment Group, 2000—. Mem. LWV, Needham Edn. Found. (pres. 1992-94), Women Dems. Metro West (v.p. 1988-90), Women in Devel., Angelica Yaught Club. Avocations: gardening, rollerblading, sculpting, gourmet cooking, music. Home: 301 Nehoiden St Needham MA 02492-2340

DURBIN, MARILYN ANN RAFAL, secondary school educator; d. Henry Antolin and Leonarda Teston Rafal; m. Robert Joseph Durbin, Sept. 5, 1993. BA, Wash. State U., Pullman, 1980. Tchr. Stanfield Sch. Dist., Oreg., 1980—. Sr. project dir., coord. Stanfield Secondary Sch., Oreg., 1983—. Organizer, coord. Site Coun., Stanfield, 2004—06. Avocations: fitness, reading, camping, travel, guitar. Office: Stanfield Secondary School 1200 North Main Stanfield OR 97875 Office Phone: 541-449-3851.

DURDAHL, CAROL LAVAUN, psychiatric nurse; b. Crookston, Minn., Jan. 18, 1933; d. Elmer Oliver and Ovidia (Olson) Durdahl; m. Hans A. Dahl, May 22, 1956 (div. 1983); children: Hana Sorensen-O'Neill, Carla Pederson. RN, St. Lukes Hosp., Duluth, Minn., 1953; BA in Human Svcs., Met. State U., St. Paul, 1982. Staff nurse various hosps., Minn., 1953-59; human svcs. tech. Willmar (Minn.) State Hosp., 1970-74, supplemental tchr., 1974-83; staff nurse Rice Meml. Hosp., Willmar, 1983-86; utilization rev. various nursing homes, Willmar, 1985-86; tchr. Willmar Area Vocat. Tech. Inst., 1986; dir. nurses Glenmore Recovery Ctr., Crookston, Minn., 1986-88; shift supr. Golden Valley (Minn.) Health Ctr., 1988-92; with crisis dept. Hennepin County Med. Ctr., 1988—; managed care of psychiat. and substance abuse MCC Managed Behavioral Care, Mpls., 1992. Contbr. articles to profl. jours. Mem.: AAUW, LWV (pres. and state bd.), Bus. and Profl. Women, Federated Women, Does. Republican. Lutheran. Avocations: reading, walking, crafts. Home: 3720 Independence Ave S Apt 41 Minneapolis MN 55426-3767 Office: Hennepin County Med Ctr 701 Park Ave Minneapolis MN 55415-1623 Personal E-mail: cdurdahl@aol.com.

DUREGGER, KAREN MARIE, health facility administrator; b. Des Moines, Jan. 16, 1952; d. Francis William and Luella Marie (Smith) Moore; m. Michael Steven Duregger, Feb. 26, 1972; children: Chadwick Michael, Joshua William (dec.), Francis Steven. Secretarial diploma, Am. Inst. Bus., Des Moines, 1971; cert. health care adminstr., Des Moines Area Community Coll., 1985. Sec. Harry Rodine Co., Des Moines, 1970, Iowa State Assn. Secondary Sch. Prins., Des Moines, 1971-72; asst. adminstr. Hancock County Care Facility, Garner, 1973-74, adminstr., 1974-89, Duncan Heights, Inc., Garner, 1989—, bd. dirs., recording sec., 1989—. Mem., sec. Mental Health, Mental Retardation and Devel. Disabled Adv. Bd., Garner, 1983-93. Mem. Cmty. Edn. Bd., Garner, 1989-2000; mem. ch. choir, 1993—; mem. Hancock County Little Theatre, 1994—, v.p., 1999—. Mem. County Care Facility Adminstrs. (dist. pres. 1985-87, treas. 1989-91), Human Svcs. Tng. Network, Tng. Planning Group Health Task Force; mem. Bell Choir, 1999. Republican. Lutheran. Avocations: making porcelain and vinyl dolls, remember me dolls, fishing, ballroom and country western dancing, family. Home: 145 W Lyons St Garner IA 50438-1920 Office: 1465 Highway 18 Garner IA 50438-8621

DUREK, DOROTHY MARY, retired language educator; b. Pitts., Jan. 23, 1926; d. Joseph Adam and Helen Barbara (Ondich) D. BS in Edn., Youngstown State U., 1962; MS in Edn., Westminster Coll., 1969. Cert. English tchr., Ohio, comprehensive English cert., Pa. Tchr. English Brookfield (Ohio) Schs., 1962-64, Sharon (Pa.) City Schs., 1964-88. Mem., pres. Coll. Club Sharon, 1993-94. Charter mem., bd. dirs. LWV Mercer County, Pa., 1993—97; docent Butler Inst. Am. Art, Youngstown, 1988—2004, LWV, Montgomery County, Md., 2005—; mem. Shenango Valley Women's Interfaith Coun., Jewish-Christian Dialogue Group, Sharon; charter mem. Mus. Women's Art, Washington, Nat. Mus. of the Am. Indian, Washington; mem., bd. dirs. Christian Assocs. Shenango Valley. Mem.: AAUW (Bethseda-Chevy Chase br.), NEA, Read and Discuss Group, Sharon Lifelong Learning Coun. (bd. dirs. 1995), Sharon Tchrs. Assn., Pa. State Educators Assn., Prospect Heights Lit. Club. Roman Catholic. Personal E-mail: dorothy_durek@yahoo.com.

DURELL, VIVIANE G., psychologist, small business owner; b. Paris, Mar. 22, 1926; d. Andre Di Gioja and Francoise Martinez; m. Jack Durell, May 19, 1955. BSFS, Georgetown U., 1955; MA, George Wash. U., 1958. Cert. Bd. Psychologist, Washington, 1976. Statician IBRD, Washington, 1951—55; rsch. psychologist Gesell Inst. Child Devel., New Haven, 1958—59; psychologist Montgomery Count Bd. Edn., Rockville, Md., 1961—77; cons. psychologist Psychiat. Inst., Washington, 1967—77; group therapist Cmty. Psychiat. Clinic, Bethesda, Md., 1968—73; instr. Montgomery Coll., Takoma Park, 1971—73; pres. Vivianna Inc., McLean, Va., 2002—. Co-author: (book) When Schools Care, Family Therapy Techniques for Problem Behavior of Children and Teenagers. Friends of first ladies Smithsonian Mus. Am.

History, 1990—92; pres. bd. trustees Samaritans of Washington, 1980—96; bd. assocs. mem. Nat. Rehab. Hosp., 1995—. Recipient Lifetime Dedication award, Samaritans of Washington, 1984, Blanch Keith Samaritan of the Yr. award, 1986. Mem.: APA, The Hist. Georgetown Club, Sulgrave Club, Capital Speakers Club (life), Psi Chi (life). Avocations: public speaking, music, travel, languages, cooking. Office Phone: 703-525-6641. Personal E-mail: viviannainc@aol.com.

DURGIN, DIANE, arbitrator, lawyer, mediator; b. Albany, N.Y., May 17, 1946; BA, Wellesley Coll., 1970; JD magna cum laude, Boston Coll., 1974. Assoc. Shearman & Sterling, N.Y.C., 1974-83; corp. sec. Ga.-Pacific Corp., Atlanta, 1983-92, v.p. law, dep. gen. counsel, 1986-89, sr. v.p. law, gen. counsel, 1989-93; arbitrator, mediator Atlanta, 1993—; dep. exec. dir. legal and non-profit affairs Atlanta Housing Authority, 1994-98. Bd. dirs. Atlanta Symphony Orch., 1991-97, Am. Arbitration Assn., 1991-97, Met. Atlanta chpt. ARC, 1988-94, Actor's Express, 2000—, Atlanta Women's Found., 1999—; bd. dirs., mem. exec. com. Alliance Theatre Co., 1985-97; mem. bd. sponsors Georgian Chamber Players, Inc., 1986-92, 97-2002. Mem.: ABA, Am. Law Inst., Ga. State Bar, Bd. Dirs. Network, Nature Conservancy (bd. dirs. Ga. chpt. 1989—96), 191 Club, Order of Coif.

DURGLISHVILI, NANA Z., psychologist, language educator; b. Tbilisi, Rep. of Georgia, Aug. 23, 1963; arrived in US, 1997; d. Zurab Vladimir Durglishvili and Rusudan Noe Tsnobiladzo; m. Jimmy Givi Mukhuradze (div.); 1 child, Zurab J. MA, Ibilisi State U., 1985; BA, Inst. Foreign Lang., 1986; PhD, U. Saarbrucken, 1992. French tchr., asst. prin. Secondary Sch. 91, Tbilisi, Georgia; prof. psychology Tbilisi State U., Tbilisi, Georgia, 1995—97; apt. mgr. MaxMaron, N.Y.C., 1998—2001; asst. psychology Meridian Health Care, Belleville, NJ, 2001—03; French tchr. Matawan Pre-Sch., Matawan, NJ, 2003—04. Pres. France-Georgian Assn., Tbilisi, Georgia, 1992—95; project. mgr. Euro Unions, Tbilisi, Georgia, 1994—97. Author: Defiant Teens, 1993, Personality Disorders in Children, 1999. Avocation: tennis. Home: 55 E 208 St 1H Bronx NY 10467 Personal E-mail: ndurglishv@aol.com.

DURGOM-POWERS, JANE ELLYN, lawyer; b. Denver, Sept. 1, 1948; d. John Albert and Rosemarie (Scordino) Durgom. BSIM in Econs., Purdue U., 1971; JD, Georgetown U., 1974. Bar: N.Y. 1975, U.S. Dist. Ct. (so. dist.) N.Y. 1975, U.S. Ct. Appeals (2d cir.) 1975, U.S. Supreme Ct. 1978, Ill. 1981, D.C. 1987, U.S. Dist. Ct. (no. dist.) Ill. 1989, Wyo. 1994, U.S. Ct. Internat. Trade 2000. Asst. dist. atty., N.Y.C., 1974-76; spl. asst. narcotics prosecutor Office of Spl. Prosecution, N.Y.C., 1976-78; atty. GM Corp., N.Y.C., 1978-81; gen. counsel Genway Corp., Chgo., 1981-83, Nissan Motor Acceptance Corp., Carson, Calif., 1983-87; cons. Nissan Motor Corp., Ltd., Carson, 1987-88; ptnr. Williams and McCarthy law firm, Rockford, Ill., 1988-97; pres., gen. counsel Antel Internat., Inc., 1997-98; pres., CEO Warren Industries LLC, 1998—2001; pres. Internat. Fedn. Family Assns. of Missing Persons From Armed Conflicts, 2001—. Bd. dirs. Internat. Sch. Rock Valley Coll., Rockford. Co-author: (books) Federal Regulation of Consumer Credit, 1981, Jury Instructions for Civil-Criminal RICO Cases. Gen. counsel Nat. League Families POW/MIA in S.E. Asia, Washington, Raoul Wallenberg Humanitarian Inst. Chosen by Rockford mag. as one of city's most interesting people, 1989; recipient cert. Spl. U.S. Congressional Recognition for Outstanding & Invaluable Cmty. Svc., 1995, Nat. Humanitarian Svc. award to Am. MIA's and POW's of the SE Asia War Nat. League of Families, 1995. Mem. ABA (vice chair human rights com. 2000—, chair humanitarian subcom. 2000—), N.Y. Bar Assn., Washington D.C. Bar Assn., Ill. Bar Assn., Rockford C. of C. (bd. dirs.). Avocations: collecting art, antiques. E-mail: jedpll@gmail.com.

DURHAM, BETTY BETHEA, therapist; b. SC, Jan. 27, 1933; d. Liston Fenton and Rosalie (Bracey) Bethea; m. John Lewis Cottrell, June 8, 1952 (div. June 1972); children: John Lewis Jr., Gregory Bethea; m. John I. Durham, Apr. 29, 1988. BS, U.N.C. at Pembroke, 1974; MSW, U. Ga., 1981. Psycho-social specialist Dublinaire Nursing Care, Dublin, Ga., 1979-80; med. social worker C. Vinson V.A. Med. Ctr., Dublin, 1982-86; therapist Raleigh (N.C.) employee's assistance program Raleigh Cmty. Hosp., 1987-88; pastoral counselor Greenwich (Conn.) Bapt. Ch., 1988-94; therapist Big Island, Va., 1995—. Marriage and family counselor Bapt. Ch., Greenwich, 1988-94; supr. grad. studies U. Ga., Fla. State U., Dublin, 1982-86. Editor Hospital Social Svc. manuals, 1982-86. Mem. Laurens County Ga. Mental Health Bd., 1975-76, Ga. Grand Jury and Gov. Com. on Drug Abuse, 1977; survey and coord. of nursing home svcs., Ga., 1982-86 Recipient Citation for Developing Nursing Home Fund Drive Nat. Heart Assn., 1979, Hands and Heart award VA, 1984. Mem. AAUW, Nat. Mus. of Women in the Arts (tour leader Europe and Mid. East 1988—), Nat. Women's History Mus. (charter). Mem. United Meth. Ch. Avocations: needlepoint, painting, horticulture, reading the classics. Home: 1509 Tolley Meadow Rd Big Island VA 24526-2977 Personal E-mail: johnandbettyd@aol.com.

DURHAM, CHRISTINE MEADERS, state supreme court chief justice; b. LA, Aug. 3, 1945; d. William Anderson and Louise (Christensen) Meaders; m. George Homer Durham II, Dec. 29, 1966; children: Jennifer, Meghan, Troy, Melinda, Isaac. AB, Wellesley Coll., 1967; JD, Duke U., 1971. Bar: N.C. 1971, Utah 1974. Sole practice law, Durham, N.C., 1971-73; instr. legal medicine Duke U., Durham, 1971-73; adj. prof. law Brigham Young U., Provo, Utah, 1973-78; ptnr. Johnson, Durham & Moxley, Salt Lake City, 1974-78; judge Utah Dist. Ct., 1978-82; assoc. justice Utah Supreme Ct., 1982—2002, chief justice, 2002—. Pres. Women Judges Fund for Justice, 1987-88. Fellow Am. Bar Found.; mem. ABA (edn. com. appellate judges' conf.), Nat. Assn. Women Judges (pres. 1986-87), Utah Bar Assn., Am. Law Inst. (coun. mem.), Nat. Ctr. State Courts (bd. dirs.), Am. Inns of Ct. Found. (trustee). Office: Utah Supreme Ct PO Box 140210 Salt Lake City UT 84114-0210*

DURHAM, JO ANN FANNING, artist; b. Sulphur Springs, Tex., May 31, 1935; d. William Jeffress and Merle Jo (Barrett) Fanning; m. William E. Durham (dec.); children: William, John Lee (dec.). BS, Tex. A&M U., College Station, 1956; postgrad., U. Tex., Austin, 1953-55, Tex. Woman's U., Denton, Tex., 1953-55; docteur honoris causa in arts, 1994. Exhibited in group shows at Galerie Jean Lammelin, Paris, 1991, Salon D'Automne Grand Palais, 1992—93, Vanderbilt Mus., L.I. VIU, N.Y., 1995, Lever House, VIU, 1995, Pen and Brush Club, 1995, 1996, VIU, N.Y., 1996, Templeton, Ft. Worth Artists and Co., Ft. Worth, 1996, Sumner Art Mus., Washington, 1996, 2004, Belgium Grand Prix, De Paadestallen Van Het Park Van Enghien, Belgium, 1996, Soc. Internat. Des Beaux Arts, Paris, 1996—97, Southwestern Watercolor Soc., D-Art, Dallas, 1996—97, Anthology Art Gallery, Lebanon, 1997, Longboat Key Art Ctr., N. Tex. Health Sci. Ctr., 1997, Atrium Gallery, Ft. Worth, 1998, Laura Knott Gallery, Bradford Coll., Mass., 1998, Lee Scarfone Gallery, U. Tampa, Fla., 1998, Fort Mason, San Francisco, 1998, Yale Med. Sch. Libr., 2000, La Chapelle des Penitents, Gordes, France, 2000, Artist's Mag., 2001, Nautilus Fellowship, Internat. Soc. Exptl. Artists, 2001, Chgo., 2003, Encaustic Works Biennial, 2001, Dennos Mus., Traverse City, 2001, Minetrista Cultural Ctr., Muncie, 2002, Salmagundi Club, N.Y.C., 2002—03, 2005, Columbia U., 2000, Huntsville Mus. Art, Ala., 2001, Beverly Arts Ctr., Chgo., 2003, WALES, Aberdare, 2003—04, Splash 8, 2004, Lee County Alliance of the Arts, Ft. Meyers, Fla., 2004 (Best of Show), The Art Inst., Houston, Tex., 2004, St. David's Hall, Cardiff, Wales, 2005, Salmagund Club, NYC, 2006, Represented in permanent collections 15 paintings Tex. A&M, Tarleton, Ft. Worth Pub. Libr. Downtown. Recipient Gold medal Belgium Grand Prix, 1993, Best of Show, Internat. Soc. of Experimental Artists, 2003, Samuel Leifman Meml. award. Mem. Soc. Watercolor Artists (signature), Internat. Soc. Exptl. Artists (signature; pres. 1999), Soc. Layerists in Multimedia (signature), Allied Artists, Tex. Fine Arts Assn. (past pres., regional dir., exec. bd.), D Art, Dallas Women's Caucus for the Arts, Dallas Artists Rsch. and Exhbn., Southwestern Watercolor Soc. (signature), Tex. Visual Artists Assn., Fort Worth Woman's Club Art Dept., Templeton Art Ctr., Nat. League of Am. Pen Women, Contemporary Art Ctr., Christians in the Visual Arts, Nat. Coll. Soc., Salmagundi Club. Home: 4300 Plantation Dr Fort Worth TX 76116-7607 Office Phone: 817-244-3807. Home Fax: 817-737-6520.

DURHAM, LYNN ELLEN, school psychologist; b. Urbana, Ill., Aug. 10, 1954; d. Leonard and Olga Durham; m. Greydon Anthony Smith, Oct. 31, 1992. BS in Edn., Ea. Ill. U., Charleston, 1975, MA, 1983. Cert. sch. psychologist K-12 Utah State Office of Edn., spl. edn. K-12+ Utah State Office of Edn., early childhood edn. Pre K-3 Utah State Office of Edn., elem. edn. 1-8 Utah State Office of Edn., Nat. cert. sch. psychologist 1989. Tchr. spl. edn. Streator (Ill.) H.S., 1975—78, Sterling (Ill.) H.S., 1978—81; intern sch. psychologist Peoria (Ill.) Sch. Dist., 1982—83; sch. psychologist Uinta Sch. Dist., Vernal, Utah, 1983—84, Jordan Sch. Dist., Sandy, Utah, 1984—. Mem. Jr. League of Salt Lake City, 1997—2005, dir. adv. and strategic planning, 2003—04, dir. project evaluation, 2004—05; vol. Salt Lake Olympic Organizing Com., 2002. Named Educator of the Month, Sandy C. of C., 1987. Mem.: Utah Assn. of Sch. Psychologists (bd. mem. 2004—, treas. 1989—92, membership chair 1996—, pres. 1993—94, Disting. Svc. award 1996). Avocations: stitchery, knitting, miniature houses and interiors, cats. Home: 121 4th Ave Salt Lake City UT 84103 Office: Jordan Sch Dist 9361 South 300 East Sandy UT 84070

DURHAM, MARY SHERRILL, psychologist, writer; b. Covington, Tenn., Nov. 22, 1924; d. Lewis Joseph and Helen (Hardwicke) Sherrill; m. Hugh Durham; children: Thomas, John, Sherry. PhD, U. Md., 1946. Clin. psychologist Va. hosp., 1950—60, DC orgn., 1960—80; pvt. practice Arlington, Va., 1955—. Author: The Therapist's Encounters with Revenge and Foregivenss, 2000, It's All Right to Write: How Famous Authors Overcame the Same Roadblock You Face, 2006. Mem.: New Directions. Democrat. Presbyterian. Avocation: writing. Home and Office: 4508 N 41st St Arlington VA 22207 Office Phone: 703-532-3387. Personal E-mail: msdurham98@aol.com.

DURHAM, NANCY RUTH, elementary school educator, music educator; b. Cushing, Okla., Aug. 28, 1947; d. Edward Fowler and Margaret Mailine Albritton; m. Dale Leonard Durham, Aug. 8, 1970. B in Music Edn., Okla. State U., 1969. Vocal music tchr. grades 3-12 Okeene (Okla.) Pub. Schs., 1969—70; elem. music tchr. grades K-6 Choctaw (Okla.) Pub. Schs., 1970—76; pvt. bus. owner Mayo-Durham Clothing, Wagoner, Okla., 1977—86; bus. owner Bartlesville/Tulsa, Okla., 1986—88; elem. music tchr. Wagoner Pub. Schs., 1988—. Sec. Wagoner Assn. Classroom Tchrs., 1991—93, bldg. rep., 1994—95. Christmas parade chmn. Wagoner C. of C., 1979—80, v.p., 1979—81, pres., 1982; chmn./co-chmn. Tartan Day Celebration State of Okla., 2000—01. Mem.: Okla. Music Educators Assn. (choir dir. grades 5 and 6 elem. choir state honor group 1974, 1976), United Scottish Clans Okla., Scottish Club Tulsa (sec. 1997—2000). Republican. Mem. Ch. Of Christ. Avocations: sewing, embroidery, gardening, exercise, Scottish heritage activities. Home: 1505 Berkley Wagoner OK 74467

DURHAM, SUSAN K., research scientist; b. Stafford, Kans., May 18, 1957; d. Rolla Evern and Betty Florence Durham. BS, Kans. State U., 1979, MS, 1981; PhD, Iowa State U., 1991. Postdoctoral fellow Mayo Clinic, Rochester, Minn., 1991-94, Baylor Coll. Medicine, Houston, 1994-98, rsch. assoc., 1998—; tech. svcs. coord. Diagnostic Systems Lab. Inc., Webster, Tex., 1999—. Mem. Endocrine Soc., Women in Endocrinology (travel award 1993), Am. Soc. Animal Sci. Avocations: reading, antiques, animals. Office: Baylor Coll Medicine 6621 Fannin St Houston TX 77030

DURHAM NORMAN, THENA MONTS, microbiologist, researcher, health facility administrator; b. Bradenton, Fla., July 10, 1945; d. Turner and Silverrene (Taylor) M.; m. Millard Durham, Aug. 30, 1969 (div. 2001); children: Bryce Vincent-Barnard, Brittanie Yvonne; m. Herman H. Norman, August 6, 2005. BS, Fisk U., 1966; MS, Purdue U., 1968. Rsch. microbiologist Ctrs. for Disease Control, Atlanta, 1968-86, assoc. dir. for programs Nat. Ctr. for Prevention Svcs., 1988-95; program analyst Office Dir. Ctr. for Health Promotion and Edn., 1986-88; dir. exec. secretariat Ctrs. for Dis. Control and Prevention, Atlanta, 1995—2001; dep. dir. for policy Nat. Ctr. for HIV, STD, and TB Prevention for CDC, Atlanta, 2001—05; ret., 2005. Cons. FDA; mem. Purdue U. Dept. Biological Scis., alumnae advisory com., pres. coun. Contbr. articles to profl. jours. Mem. NAACP, Neighborhood Planning Unit, SCLC/Women Adv. Coun., So. Christian Leadership Council/Women, Atlanta, 2005; bd. dirs. Cmty. Advanced Practices Nurses, Atlanta, 2004. Recipient Sec.'s award for Disting. Svc. Dept. HHS, 2001. Mem. AAAS, Sci. Rsch. Soc., Am. Soc. Microbiologists, CDC Assn. Exec. Women (founder, co-chmn.), Women in Sci. and Engring., Alumni Adv. Com. Democrat. Office Phone: 404-753-1322, 678-613-6265. Personal E-mail: thena1@bellsouth.net.

DURICK, JOYCE K., elementary school educator; b. Syracuse, Kans., July 14, 1950; d. Harold and Barbara Payne; m. Steven J. Durick, Dec. 19, 1970; children: Scott Dean, Kent John. BS in Edn., Northern State U., Aberdeen, SD, 1986. Paraprofl. Aberdeen Pub. Sch., Aberdeen, SD, 1976—84, tchr. Frederick, SD, 1986—87; tchr., coach Wilmot Sch., SD, 1987—91; tchr. Big Stone City Sch., SD, 1989—90, Milbank Pub. Sch., SD, 1990—2006. Bd. treas. Lockwood Township, SD, 2006—. Mem.: NEA, AAHPERD, Milbank Edn. Assn., Delta Kappa Gamma.

DURKEE, DIANNA, medical/surgical nurse; b. Ft. Worth, June 15, 1958; d. Roy Alfred and Betty Jo (Clement) D. Student, Tex. Woman's U., 1979-81; BSN, U. Tex., Arlington, 1983. Cert. urology nurse, med.-surg. nurse. Charge nurse Scott and White Hosp., Temple, Tex. Mem. Am. Urological Assn. Allied.

DURKIN, DIANE L., retired nurse; b. Youngstown, Ohio, Feb. 1, 1952; d. Harold Henry and Helen Michelle Durkin. Diploma, St. Elizabeth Sch. Nursing, Youngstown, 1973. RN; cert. in neonatal intensive care nursing. Staff nurse St. Christopher Children's Hosp., Phila., 1979-80, Jackson Meml. Hosp., Miami, Fla., 1973-79, 80-81, assoc. head nurse newborn intensive care, 1981—2005, neonatal transport nurse, 1975—79, 1998—2006; ret., 2006. NICU nurse Health Park Hosp., Ft. Myers, Fla., 2005—. Contbr. articles to profl. jours. Mem.: Fla. Neonatal and Pediat. Transport Nurses Assn., S.E. Fla. Assn. Neonatal Nurses (steering com. 1993—94, treas. 1994—96, v.p. 1996—98, pres. 1999, co-founder), Nat. Assn. Neonatal Nurses (NANN pages editor 2000, Central Lines editor 2002—03, chair comms. com., corres. mem. newsletter com., dir.-at-large 2005—). Republican. Roman Catholic. Avocations: reading, walking. Personal E-mail: plemented@aol.com.

DURKIN, DOROTHY ANGELA, university official; b. Glen Cove, NY, June 23, 1945; d. Frank Vincent and Rose Marie Durkin; 1 child, David Francis. BA, SUNY, Stony Brook, 1968; MA, NYU, 1974. Adminstrv. asst. SUNY, Stony Brook, 1965-67; prodn. editor Holt, Rhinehart & Winston, Inc., Stony Brook, 1967-69; editor Hill & Wang Pub., Inc., NYC, 1969-70; asst. dir. pub. info. NYU Sch. Continuing Edn., 1970-72; assoc. dean pub. affairs and student svc. Sch. Continuing and Profl. Studies NYU Sch. Continuing Edn. and Profl. Studies, 1983—2002, assoc. dean strategic devel., 2002—05; co-acting dean NYU Sch. Continuing and Profl. Studies, 2005—. Cons. NYC Ctr. for Lifelong Learning, 1974; prodr. TV series Continuum, Sta. WNYC, 1974; mem. UCEA Commn. on Futures and Markets, 2003-06. Editor: NSF student mag., 1961. Recipient Merit award Andy Advt., 1972, Art Dirs. Club, 1980, Soc. Illustrators, 1980, Big Apple award NY Radio Broadcasters Assn., 1985, Admissions Mktg. Report awards, 1987-88, 98-2001, Catalog Age awards, 1988, 93, Silver and Bronze award in Print Advt., 2004, Gold and Silver award in Print Pub., 2004. Mem. Univ. Continuing Edn. Assn. (chair info. svc. 1980-81, nat. award chair, chair mktg. adv. com. 1989-98, group leader Learn From Success series 1989-90, bd. dir. 1991-93, membership com. 1994-95, mktg. conf. planning com. 1993-00, presenter, Bronze, Silver and Gold awards 1978, 81-2002, Internat. Leadership in Continuing Edn. award 1999, Gold award in publications, 2002, Gold and Bronze award in Electronic Marketing Communications, 2002, Silver award in Mixed Media: Publications, Advertising, PR and Web, mem. commn. on futures and markets, 2003-05), Am. Coll. Pub. Rels. Assn. (nat. award 1973), Coun. for Advancement and Support of Edn. (awards 1982-83, 85-87, 89-90, 92-94), Women in Comms. (job chair), Pub. Rels. Soc. Am. (Am. demographics adv. bd. 1989-90), Direct Mktg. Assn. (Echo Leadership award 1987, 88), Internat. Direct Mktg. Assn., SUNY Alumni Assn. (bd. dir.), The College Bd. (speaker, cons.), Learning Resources Network. Office: NYU Sch Continuing Edn 25 W 4th St Rm 203 New York NY 10003-4475 Business E-Mail: dorothy.durkin@nyu.edu.

DUROCHER, FRANCES A., retired physician, educator; b. Woonsocket, R.I., Mar. 11, 1943; d. Armand D. and Teresa (Leverone) DuRocher. BA with honors, Trinity Coll., 1964; MS, Brown U., 1966; postgrad., Woman's Med. Coll., 1970. Med. resident Phila. VA Hosp. and Med. Coll. Pa., 1971-73; assoc. in internal med. Guthrie Clinic Ltd., Sayre, Pa., 1973-79; assoc. in internal medicine Annandale (Va.) Group Health Assocs., 1979-87; assoc. chair internal medicine Annandale Group Health Assoc., 1986-87; pvt. practice Fairfax, Va., 1987—2004; ret., 2004. Clin. asst. prof. med. and health svcs. George Washington U. Med. Sch., Washington, 1994-2004. Bd. dirs. Fairways of Penderbrook Homeowners Assn., 1993—, sec., 1995-96, pres., 1996—. Mem. AMA, ACP-Am. Soc. Internal Medicine, Am. Med. Women's Assn. (exec. bd. br. I, 1985-91, pres. 1987-88), Med. Soc. Va., Med. Soc. No. Va. Avocations: reading, travel.

DURR, TAMI JOLEEN, mathematics educator; b. West Covena, Calif., July 17, 1970; d. Ronald Gene and Bethel Elaine Long; m. Dean Edward Durr, May 27, 1988; children: Michael Dean, Andrew James. AA, NW Ark. C.C., Bentonville, 2000; BS in Edn. Mid. Level Math/Sci., U. Ark., Fayetteville, 2002, MA in Tchg., 2003. Lic. tchr. Ark. Dept. Edn., 2003. Tchr. math. J.O. Kelly Mid. Sch., Springdale, Ark., 2003—. Mem.: Nat. Coun. Tchrs. of Math. Conservative. Avocation: reading. Home: 2750 Penny Lane Rogers AR 72758 Office: JO Kelly Mid Sch 1879 Robinson Ave Springdale AR 72764 Office Phone: 479-750-8730. Personal E-mail: tdurr@sdale.org.

DURRANT, M. PATRICIA, diplomat; BA, U. W.I., Diploma in Internat. Rels.; Diploma in Overseas Devel. Studies, U. Cambridge, Eng. With Jamaica Fgn. Svc., 1971—, minister, dep. permanent rep. to UN, 1983—87, amb. to Germany, 1987—92, non-resident amb. to Israel, the Netherlands, Switzerland and the Holy See, 1987—92; dir.-gen. Min. of Fgn. Affairs and Fgn. Trade, 1992—95, permanent rep. of Jamaica to UN N.Y.C., 1995—, rep. for Jamaica on Security Coun. UN, 2000—01, vice chair Open-Ended Working Group on the Reform of UN Security Coun.; ombudsman United Nations, N.Y.C. Chair consultative com. UN Devel. Fund for Women; pres. High Level Com. on Tech. Coop. Among Developing Countries, 1999—2001; vice chair preparatory com. spl. session on population and devel. UN Gen. Assembly, 1999. Named Disting. Grad., U. W.I., 1998; recipient Order of Distinction in the rank of Comdr., 1992, Order of Jamaica, 2000, Disting. Achievement award, World Assn. of Former UN Interns and Fellows. Office: Permanent Mission of Jamaica to UN 767 Third Ave 9th Flr New York NY 10017

DURRINGTON, ROSE COLLEEN, education educator, director reading clinic, dean; b. West Fork, Ark., Mar. 23, 1937; d. Loy Lee and Mildred E. (Walker) Stockburger; m. Victor L. Durrington BS Edn., McMurry U., 1972; MEd, Abilene Christian U., 1981; EdD, Tex. Tech U., 1984. Cert. tchr., instrnl. supr., mid-mgmt. adminstr., reading specialist, supt., Tex. Tchr. Hawley Ind. Sch. Dist., Tex., 1972—74, Abilene Ind. Sch. Dist., Tex., 1974—77, supr., 1977—79, lead tchr., 1979—81, prin., 1981—85; asst. prof. Abilene Christian U., 1985—89, assoc. prof., 1989—91, prof., 1991—. Dean Coll. Profl. Studies Abilene Christian U., 1991-93, chair Dept. Edn., 1993-95, dean Coll. Arts and Sci., 1995—; mem. Tex. commn. on Stds. for Tchg. Profession, Austin, 1986-89; chairperson Key City Reading Conf., Abilene, 1990-91; presenter of workshops in reading and remediation Trustee Abilene Ind. Sch. Dist., 1990-96, Taylor County Appraisal Bd., 2000— Recipient Mentor award Student Edn. Assn., Abilene Christian U., 1988 Mem. ASCD, Internat. Reading Assn., Assn. Tchr. Educators, Tex. Profs. Reading (pres. 1991-92), Tex. State Reading Assn., Alpha State Delta Kappa Gamma (state membership com. 1990—), Phi Delta Kappa (past pres.) Republican. Mem. Ch. of Christ. Home: 3010 Salinas Dr Abilene TX 79605-6721 Office: Abilene Christian U PO Box 27915 Abilene TX 79699-0001 Office Phone: 325-674-2209. Business E-Mail: durringtonc@acu.edu.

DURST, CAROL GOLDSMITH, food studies educator; b. Bklyn., Mar. 1, 1952; d. Hyman and Florence (Weisblatt) Goldsmith; m. Marvin Ira Durst, June 18, 1972 (div. Sept. 1977); m. Leslie Mark Wertheim, Apr. 1, 1984; 1 child, William David. BA, Hamilton Kirkland Coll., Clinton, NY, 1973; MA, Columbia U., NYC, 1974; postgrad., Union Inst., Cin., 2000—. Career counselor Hofstra U., Hempstead, N.Y., 1974-75, Ocean County C.C., Toms River, N.J., 1975-76; rsch. assoc. Catalyst, N.Y.C., 1975-77; coord. displaced homemakers program N.Y. State Dept. Labor, N.Y.C., 1977-79; dir. N.Y. restaurant sch. New Sch. Social Rsch., N.Y.C., 1979-83; owner New Am. Catering Corp., N.Y.C., 1983-98; tchr., career counselor Peter Kump's N.Y. Cooking Sch., N.Y.C., 1988-98. Adj. prof. food studies dept. NYU, 1997-2003, Kingsborough CC, 2003, NY City Tech./CUNY, 2004; chmn. dept. hospitality mgmt. Monroe Coll., 2004-05, NY City Tech./CUNY, 2005-06. Author: I Knew You Were Coming So I Baked a Cake, 1997. Mem. AAUW, N.Y. Women's Culinary Alliance (new mem. chmn. 1995-96), Women Chefs and Restaurateurs (chair mentoring program 2003—, bd. dirs. 2005—), Nat. Mus. Women in the Arts, Am. Mus. Natural History, Met. Mus. Art, Internat. Assn. Culinary Profls. (cookbook awards judge 2004-05). Avocations: fine arts, piano, opera, ice skating. Home and Office: PO Box 270 Millwood NY 10546-0270

DURST, JO, artist, educator; b. Wendell, Idaho, Mar. 23, 1948; d. Lewis Cleveland Ross, Ida Mae Ross; m. Robert Wayne Durst, May 26, 1973; children: Tristan, Jefferson. BA, Albertsons Coll., 1970; MA, Idaho State U., 1972. Instr. Miss. State U., Starkville, 1978—. Artist, Starkville, 1998—; dir. performance art Miss. State U., Starkville, 1998—. Mem.: N.Y. Artists Equity Assn., Southeast Theatre Assn., Miss. Alliance for Arts Edn., Miss. Theatre Assn. (Best Dir. 2000), Nat. Oil and Acrylic Painters Soc. Avocations: art, theater, reading, philosophy, women's studies. Home: 799 Pine Cir Starkville MS 39759 Office Phone: 662-325-3205, 662-325-3203. Business E-Mail: bdurst@comm.msstate.edu.

DURST, KAY HORRES, physician; b. Charleston, SC, Feb. 11, 1967; d. George Gardner Durst and Virginia Kay Horres-Durst. Degree (hon.), U. L'Inst. de Tours, France, 1988; student, U. SC, 1989, MD, 1998. Diplomate Am. Bd. Family Medicine. Asst. Durst Family Medicine, Charleston, SC, 1989—90; rsch. asst. MIND Works, Charleston, 1990; tchr. Berlitz Sch. Langs., San Juan, PR, 1991—92; sci. lab. asst. St. John's H.S., San Juan, 1991—92, tchr., 1991—92; intern family medicine U. Fla. Family Medicine, Coral Springs, Fla., 1998—99; resident U. Miami Family Medicine, Miami, Fla., 1999—. Mem.: AMA, Am. Acad. Family Physicians, So. Med. Assn., Philharmonic Assn., Petset, Jr. League. Avocations: sailing, scuba, boating, golf, travel. Home: 2508 NE 21st Ct Fort Lauderdale FL 33305-3516

DUSENBURY, RUTH ELLEN COLE, business owner; b. Balt., June 19, 1929; Social worker Balt. City Welfare Dept., 1950-51; civil rights desk clk. FBI, 1951; asst. buyer, br. store sect. mgr., rsch. supr. Hutzler Bros. Dept. Store, Balt., 1951-58, pub. rels. rep., 1969-72; real estate rep. Robert Knatz Agy., 1969-70; sec., treas., officer mgr., co-owner Speer Cushion Co., Holyoke, Colo., 1974—99; ret., 1999. Active Bus. and Profl. Women's Orgn., 1976—87, Colo. Workforce Devel. Coun., 1999—2001, Rep. Party, 1968—; del. White House Conf. on Small Bus., Washington, 1995; apptd. Congressman Bob Schafer's Bus. Adv. Com., 1998; bd. dirs. Holyoke Cmty. Arts Coun., 1976—2002; charter mem. bd. Colo. Arts. Consortium, chmn., hon. bd. dirs.; pres. Colo. Arts. Coalition; mem. leadership coun. Colo. Nat. Fedn. Ind. Bus., 2002—. Office Phone: 970-854-2204. E-mail: wadusenbury@petelcom.coop.

DUSHENSKY, JACQUELINE AMELIA, banker, educator; b. Albany, N.Y., Jan. 22, 1950; d. Andrew John and Ida Regina; children: George Leon, Andrew John. BS in Med. Tech., Albany Coll. Pharmacy, N.Y., 1972. Registered med. technologist Am. Soc. Clin. Pathologists, 1972. Supr. tchg.

St. Peter's Sch. Med. Tech. St. Peter's Hosp. Albany Coll. Pharmacy, 1972—81, adj. instr. microbiology, 1993—2003; adj. instr. Hudson Valley C.C., Troy, NY, 1983—; mgr. Trustco Bank, Rensselaer, NY, 2003—. Author: Microbiology Lab Manual. Tchr. St. Clare's Ch., Albany. Named Tulip Queen, Albany, 1974; recipient Outstanding Young Women award, 1974, Outstanding Performance award, Trustco Bank, 2005. Mem.: Am. Soc. Clin. Pathology (licentiate). Home: 37 Sunset Blvd Albany NY 12205 Office Phone: 518-479-7233. Personal E-mail: jdushensky@hotmail.com.

DUSKIN, KIMBERLY J, athletic trainer; b. Oklahoma City, Sept. 2, 1979; d. Robert F and Lucy S Duskin. BS, U. Tulsa, 2002. Cert. athletic trainer Nat. Athletic Trainers Assn., 2002. Fellow athletic trainer U.S. Olympic Com., Chula Vista, Calif., 2004—05; asst. athletic trainer Azusa Pacific U., Calif., 2005—. Mem.: Nat. Athletic Trainers Assn. (sec. 2006—). Home: 510 N Wabash Ave Glendora CA 91741 Office: Azusa Pacific University 701 E Foothill Blvd Azusa CA 91702 Office Phone: 626-523-3240. Personal E-mail: kduskin1@yahoo.com. E-mail: kduskin@apu.edu.

DUSSAULT, HEATHER M.B., electrical engineer, researcher; d. Mildred P. Everest; m. Jerry L. Dussault, June 19, 1982. BS in Nuc. Engring., Rensselaer Poly. Inst., Troy, NY, 1980, ME in Nuc. Engring., 1981, PhD, 1995. Nuc. engr. Knolls Atomic Power Lab., Schenectady, NY, 1981—82; electronics engr. USAF, Rome Lab., NY, 1982—95; interim dir. Info. Inst. Air Force Rsch. Lab., Info. Directorate, Rome, 1995—97, tech. advisor info. systems divsn., 1999—2000; program mgr. electronics tech. office Def. Advanced Rsch. Projects Agy., Arlington, Va., 1997—99; asst. prof. computer sci. SUNY Inst. Tech., Utica, 2000—03, asst. prof. elec. engring., 2003—06; tech. focal point DoD Reliability Info. Analysis Ctr., Utica, 2005—. Cons. Quanterion Solutions, Utica, 2003—. Author: (textbook) Evolution and Practical Applications of Failure Modes and Effects Analyses, 1983; contbr. articles to profl. jours. Mem.: IEEE, Assn. Computing Machinery, Am. Soc. Engring. Educators, Am. Nuc. Soc., NY Acad. Scis., Soc. Women Engrs., Tau Beta Pi (pres. NY Gamma 1980—81). Avocations: hiking, gardening. Office: SUNY Institute of Technology Reliability Information Analysis Center Utica NY 13504 Office Phone: 315-351-4203. Office Fax: 315-792-7399. Business E-Mail: dussauh@sunyit.edu.

DUSSAULT, NANCY, actress, singer; b. Pensacola, Fla., June 30, 1936; d. George Adrian and Sarah Isabel (Seitz) D.; m. James D. Travis, Oct. 4, 1958. MusB, Northwestern U., 1957; studies with Alvina Kraus, Lotte Lehmann. Actress: (stage prodns.) Guys and Dolls, 1955, Street Scene, 1959, The Mikado, 1959, The Cradle Will Rock, 1960, Do Re Mi, 1960 (Theatre World award 1960), The Sound of Music, 1962 (Kit Kat Club award), Apollo and Miss Agnes, 1963, What Makes Sammy Run, 1964, Phoebe, 1965, Carousel, 1966, Finian's Rainbow, 1967, Fiorello!, 1968, On a Clear Day You Can See Forever, 1968, South Pacific, 1969, Trelawny of the Wells, 1970, The Last of the Red Hot Lovers, 1972, Detective Story, 1973, Irene, 1975, Winter Interludes, 1976, Side by Side by Sondheim, 1977, (TV series) The New Dick Van Dyke Show, 1971, Too Close for Comfort, 1980-83, (TV spls.) Alan King Looks Back in Anger: A Review of 1972, 1973, Burt and the Girls, 1973, The Many Faces of Comedy, 1973, The Lily Tomlin show, 1973, Night of 100 Stars, II, 1985; solo vocalist Chgo. Symphony Orch., 1957 (Young Artists award Soc. Am. Musicians 1957); other mus. performances include Broadway Answers Selma, 1965, ASCAP Salute, 1967, The Magic of Cole Porter, 1967, The Heyday of Rodgers and Hart, 1969, A Salute of Rudolph Friml, 1969, A Hammerstein Salute, 1972, The Revue of Revues, 1973, A Salute to Jules Styne, 1974; host Good Morning, America, 1975, The Shape of Things, 1982; guest various talk shows including The Tonight Show, The Mike Douglas Show, The Merv Griffin Show. Mem. Actors' Equity Assn., AFTRA, Screen Actors Guild, Am. Guild Mus. Artists, AGVA, Delta Delta Delta. Avocations: needlecrafts, cooking, reading, music.

DUSTMAN, ELIZABETH, art educator, product designer; b. Detroit, June 25, 1919; d. John Anthony and Frances (Brade) Kreuzer; m. Edward Anthony Matula, May 13, 1950 (dec. June 1976); children: Maura, Janet; m. Herman C. Dustman, Aug. 25, 1979 (dec. May 5, 1999); stepchildren: Herman, Karl. BFA, Mundelein Coll., 1940; MEd, Loyola U., Chgo., 1964. Artcraft instr. Chgo. Pk. Dist., 1941-44; art educator Mundelein Coll., Chgo., 1945-46, 1955-81, assoc. prof. emeritus, 1982—; package designer Walgreen Co., Chgo., 1946-51. Instr. U.S. Mil. Recreation Pers. Ind. U., 1942; workship tchr. in field; tchg. painting classes No. Shore Sr. Ctr., Northbrook Pk. Dist. Sr. Ctr. Mem. adv. bd. Northbrook (Ill.) Park Dist., 1983-85; bd. dirs. Northbrook Hist. Soc., 1983-90, North Shore Sr. Ctr., Northfield, 1990—; vol. art tchr. North Shore Sr. Ctr., 1990—, Northbrook Park Dist., 1995— Recipient Outstanding Educator award Outstanding Educators Am., 1972; Am. textiles rsch. grantee Kellogg Found., 1974-75. Avocations: travel, research, lecturing, painting.

DUSTMAN, PATRICIA (JO) ALLEN, elementary school educator, consultant; b. Salem, Ohio, Mar. 22, 1947; d. Alton Davis Allen and Mary Evaline Allen (Iler); m. George Bird Dustman, June 10, 1972; 1 child, Mary Elizabeth Wastchak. BS, Kent State U., 1967—69, MA, 1970—71; EdD, Ariz. State U., 1998. Cert. Teacher AZ. Tchr. Ashtabula City, Ravenna City, N. Ridgeville City Sch. Districts, Ohio, 1969—75; prin. North Ridgeville City Schools, Ohio, 1975—80; asst. supt. Madison Local Schools, Ohio, 1980—82; supt. of schools St. Clairsville-Richland City Schools, Ohio, 1982—85; dist. and bldg. adminstr. Scottsdale Pub. Schools, Ariz., 1985—94; supt. of schools Queen Creek Unified Sch. Dist., Ariz., 1994—98; rschr., cons. SW Interdisciplinary Rsch. Consortium, Ariz. State U., Tempe, Ariz., 1999—; ednl. cons. The Dustman Group, Scottsdale, Ariz., 1999—. Mem. Bel-Tech Adv. Bd., St. Clairsville, Ohio, 1982—85; academic standards design team mem. Ariz. Dept. of Edn., Phoenix, 1996—98; mem. East Valley Think Tank, Mesa, Ariz., 1994—98, Mesa C.C. Adv. Bd., Ariz., 1997—98; mentor SPR-Early Career Preventionist Network, Washington, 2003—; mem., cmty. adv. bd. for student services Osborn Elem. Sch. Dist., Phoenix, 2000—; mem., acad. profls. Sch. of Social Work, Ariz. State U., 2003—. Contbr. articles to profl. jours. Mem. C. of C., St. Clairsville, Ohio, 1982—85; founding mem. and chair Scottsdale Prevention Inst., Ariz., 1985—87; mem. Scottsdale Ednl. Enrichment Services, Ariz., 1985—2003; donor Kent State U. Alumni Assn., The Wilson Conf. of the Coll. of Edn., The Bowman Fellowship Fund, Ariz. State U. Alumni Assn. Founders' Day, 1990—2003. Recipient Key to the City, Mayor and City Coun. of St. Clairsville Ohio, 1985; grantee Key Pers.: Devel. and Implementation Dir.: SW Interdisciplinary Rsch. Consortium, NIH/NIDA, 2002; Tech. grant, Olin Charitable Trust, 1995—98, Saturday Sch., Rural Metro Corp., 1998, Summer Acad. scholarships, MGC Pure Chemicals Am., 1997—98, grant, Key Pers.: Drug Resistance Strategies Project, NIH/NIDA, 1999—. Mem.: Belmont- Harrison Superintendents' Assn. (chair 1983—85), Soc. for Prevention Rsch., Ariz. Sch. Administrators (life), Phi Delta Kappa (program chair 1978—80). Avocations: reading, writing, travel, skiing. Office: Southwest Interdisciplinary Research Con P O Box 873711 Tempe AZ 85287-3711 Office Phone: 480-945-5485. Personal E-mail: dustmangroup@yahoo.com. Business E-Mail: patricia.dustman@asu.edu.

DUSZYNSKI-WALDBILLIG, CYNTHIA, piano educator, performer, adjudicator; b. Milw., Jan. 5, 1958; d. James and Dianne Duszynski; m. Terence Joseph Waldbillig, July 27, 1985; children: Abbey Lynn, Benjamin Jacob. BS, Carroll Coll., 1990. Pvt. tchr. piano C. Duszynski Studio Music, New Berlin, Wis., 1972—. Vocalist Eisenhower Choral Group, New Berlin, 1972-76, Waukesha Choral Union, 1976-77, various solo functions, Milw., 1974—; pianist Bob Hope Talent Search, St. Louis, 1977; pianist, vocalist, dancer Friendship of Ambs., Italy, Austria, Romania, Hungary, 1976; pianist, organist various hotels and chs., Milw., 1972—; adjudicator various music orgns., Milw., 1985—; lectr. various music functions, Chgo., 1990, Milw., 1990—; creator music programs Shared Leadership Program, 1999. Composer: (film music) Go Walk the Hallowed Ground Someday, 1990. Active Youth on Parade, New Berlin Jaycees, 1974; founder, chair LOVE P.A.T.S. Mem.: Milw. Music Tchrs. Assn. (adjudicator 1995—), Wis. Music Tchrs. Nat. Assn. (v.p. 1992—96, judge coord. 1999—2000, v.p. 1999—2001, pres. 2000, Most Outstanding Piano Tchr. award 2000—01, 2002—03, Oustanding Tchr. award 2001—02), Nat. Guild Piano Tchrs. (adjudicator 1994—), Assn. Piano Tchrs. (judge coord. 1999—2000), Nat. Fedn. Music Clubs (adjudicator 1984—), Music Tchrs. Nat. Assn. (lectr. 1990—, state and nationally cert.). Avocations: stained glass, gardening, reading, interior decorating, horseback riding. Home and Office: 5900 S Aberdeen Dr New Berlin WI 53146-5210 Office Phone: 262-679-3575. Business E-Mail: cindy@musicbycindy.com.

DUTCHER, JANICE JEAN PHILLIPS, oncologist; b. Bend, Oreg., Nov. 10, 1950; d. Charles Glen and MayBelle (Fluit) Phillips; m. John Dutcher, Sept. 8, 1971 (div. 1980). BA with honors, U. Utah, 1971; MD, U. Calif., Davis, 1975. Diplomate Am. Bd. Internal Medicine, Am. Bd. Med. Oncology. Intern Rush-Presbyn. St. Luke's Hosp., Chgo., 1975-76, resident, 1976-78; clin. assoc. Balt. Cancer Rsch., Nat. Cancer Inst., 1978-81, sr. investigator, 1981-82; asst. prof. U. Md., Balt., 1982, Albert Einstein Coll. Medicine, N.Y.C., 1983-86, assoc. prof., 1986-92, prof., 1992-98, course co-dir. Advances in Cancer Treatment Rsch. Manhattan, 1984-96; prof. medicine N.Y. Med. Coll., 1998—; assoc. dir. for clin. affairs Comprehensive Cancer Ctr., Our Lady of Mercy Med. Ctr., 1998—. Chmn. biol. response mod. com. Ea. Coop. Oncology Group, Madison, Wis., 1989-95, mem. exec. com., 1995-97, chair renal subcom., 1998—; mem. data safety com. Nat. Heart Lung Blood Inst., Bethesda, Md., 1990-95; mem. biologic response modifier study sect. Nat. Cancer Inst., Bethesda, 1988, 90, 94, 96; mem. NIH Consensus Panel on Early Melanoma, 1992; mem. FDA Oncology Drug Adv. Bd., 1995-99, chair FDA-ODAC, 1996-99, NCI subcom. D for program project rev., 1995-98, mem. subsplty. med. oncology bd. Am. Bd. Internal Medicine, 1997-2003; mem. NCI subcom. A for Cancer Ctrs., 1998-2002; mem. faculty AACR/ASCO Workshop on Clin. Trials Devel., 1996-2002, NIH Progress Rev. Group on Kidney Cancer, 2001. Editor: Handbook of Hematology/Oncology Emergencies, 1987, Modern Transfusion Therapy, 1990; sect. editor: Neoplastic Diseases of the Blood, 3d edit., 1996, 4th edit., 2003; mem. editl. bd. Jour. Immunotherapy, Med. Oncology, Jour. Clin. Oncology, Jour. Clin. Pharm., Ann. Intern. Med.; sect. editor Current Treatment Options in Oncology, 2000-06, Chronic Leukemia, 2000-06; contbr. articles to Blood, Leukemia, Jour. Clin. Oncology, Jour. Immunotherapy, Clin. Cancer Rsch., Soc. Am. Cancer Jour. Recipient Beecham award in Hematology So. Blood Club, 1983, Henry C. Moses Clin. Rsch. award Montefiore Med. Ctr., 1989, Outstanding Alumnus award U. Calif., Davis, 1989; named Outstanding Young Investigator Ea. Coop. Oncology Group, 1993; recipient numerous grants. Internat. Soc. Biol. Therapy (exec. com.). Achievements include findings related to management of alloimmunization to platelet transfusions, intensive maintenance of patients with acute leukemia, studies of new biologic response modifiers as antitumor drugs, management of renal cell cancer, melanoma and breast cancer, study and treatment with biologic antitumor agents, study and treatment of targeted therapies in renal cell cancer and melanoma. Address: Our Lady of Mercy Med Ctr Comprehensive Cancer Ctr 600 E 233rd St Bronx NY 10466-2604 Office Phone: 718-304-7200. Personal E-mail: jpd4401@aol.com.

DUTCHEVICI, SILVIA M., psychotherapist; d. Mihail Ghe. and Lucica Dutchevici. MA, New Sch. U., N.Y., 2001; postgrad., NYU, 2004—. Comm. liason Princess Margarita of Romania Found., Romania, 1991—94; exec. assoc. Ms. Found. for Women, N.Y.C., 1999—2004; psychotherapist Chelsea Psychotherapy, N.Y.C., 2001—; case work supr., program mgr. Arab Am. Family Support Ctr., Bklyn., 2005—. Intern N.Y.C. Freudian Soc., N.Y.C., Parent Child Ctr. of the N.Y. Psychoanalytic Soc., N.Y.C., 2000—01. Contbr. papers to profl. publs. Cons. on Ea. Europe affairs Internat. League for Human Rights, N.Y.C., 1996. Mem.: Nat. Orgn. of Social Workers (assoc.), APA (assoc.). Achievements include research in Tattoos and Sexual Abuse. Office: Chelsea Psychotherapy Assocs Ste 1305 80 8th Ave New York NY 10011 Office Phone: 646-522-4643. E-mail: silvia.dutchevici@gmail.com.

DUTCHOVER, AMY, mathematics educator; b. Livermore, Calif., Feb. 15, 1968; d. David and Leona Walter; m. Brian Dutchover, Mar. 15, 2003. BA in Math., Azusa Pacific U., Calif., 1990, MA in Edn., 1995. Tchr. math. Western Christian H.S., Covina, Calif., 1990—92, Sierra Vista Jr. H.S., 1992—94, Charter Oak H.S., 1994—99, Granada H.S., Livermore, 1999—. Chair math dept. Granada H.S., 2000—04. Conservative. Avocations: travel, scrapbooks. Office: Granada High School 400 Wall Street Livermore CA 94550 Office Phone: 925-606-4800 3537. Office Fax: 925-606-4808. E-mail: adutchover@livermore.k12.ca.us.

DUTTON, CHRISTINA PARKER, interior designer, event planner; b. Washington, Mar. 30, 1968; d. Frederick Gary and Nancy (Hogan) D.; m. Paul Thomas Fucci, Oct. 3, 1998. BA, Occidental Coll., 1991. Spl. asst. Clinton for Pres., Washington, 1992, Inaugural Com., Washington, 1992-93; pres., owner Christina Dutton Interiors, LLC, Washington, 1995—. Cons. spl. events Dem. Nat. Com., Washington, 1992, 96. Mem. Jr. League of Washington. Episcopalian. Office: Christina Dutton Interiors 5017 Tilden St NW Washington DC 20016-2333 Home: 5702 Cricket Pl Mc Lean VA 22101-1817 E-mail: DuttonDC@aol.com.

DUTTON, DIANA CHERYL, lawyer; b. Sherman, Tex., June 27, 1944; d. Roy G. and Monett Dutton; m. Anthony R. Grindl, July 8, 1974. BS, Georgetown U., Washington, D.C., 1967; JD, U. Tex., 1971. Bar: Tex. 1971. Regional counsel U.S. EPA, Dallas, 1975—79, dir. enforcement divsn., 1979—81; ptnr., head firm-wide environ. practice, mem. Dallas practice com. Akin, Gump, Strauss, Hauer & Feld, L.L.P., 1981—. Chair Greater Dallas Chamber Environ. com., 2001; bd. dirs. Girls Inc., 2004—, bd. chair, 2006—; bd. dirs. Mental Health Assn. Dallas, 2005—. Named a Tex. Super Lawyer, Tex. Monthly Mag., 2003—05; named one of Best Lawyers in Am., 1995—, Best Lawyers in Dallas, D Mag., 2001—05, Ams. Leading Bus. Lawyers, Chambers USA, 2003—06, Top 50 Tex. Women Attys., Tex. Monthly Mag., 2003. Mem.: ABA, Dallas Bar Found., Dallas Bar Assn. (chmn. environ. law sect. 1984), Tex. Bar Assn. (chmn. environ. and natural resources law sect. 1985—86). Episcopalian. Office: Akin Gump Strauss Hauer and Feld LLP 1700 Pacific Ave Ste 4100 Dallas TX 75201-4675 Office Phone: 214-969-2855. Office Fax: 214-969-4343. E-mail: ddutton@akingump.com.

DUTTON, JO SARGENT, education educator, researcher, consultant; b. L.A., Calif., Oct. 26, 1940; d. Paul and Jayne (O'Toole) Sargent; m. Ted W. Dutton, Nov. 15, 1979; children: Brooks, Berndan, Mark; step-children: Robert, William, Jeanne, Jerry. BS, U. So. Calif., 1962, MS, 1966; PhD, U. Calif. Riverside, 1996. Cert. elem. tchr., Calif.; corp. paralegal cert.; preliminary adminstrv. svcs. credential. Elem. sch. tchr. 6th grade Lawndale Unified Sch. Dist., 1963-64; reading instr. Culver City (Calif.) Unified Sch. Dist., 1964; prof. edn. U. So. Calif., 1964-65; remedial reading instr. Santa Monica (Calif.) Unified Sch. Dist., 1965-66; dist. remedial reading instr. San Marino Unified Sch. Dist., 1967-70; real estate broker Calif., 1972-96; adj. prof. English Chaffey C. C., Rancho Cucamonga, Calif., 1991-93; rsch. fellowCalif. Ednl. Rsch. Coop. U. Calif., Riverside, 1993-95. Prof. Calif. Bapt. Coll., 1997; dir. rsch. Calif. Virtual U., 1997; dir. devel. U. Calif. Riverside, Sch. Edn., 1997-2000. Contbr. articles to profl. jours. Mem. exec. com. Inland Empire Cultural Found., 1980-83, Sister Cities Internat., Ontario, Calif., 1980-82; chair steering com. San Bernardino County Arts League, 1983-84; commr. San Bernardino County Mus.; mem. bd. Inland Empire Symphony; survey and assessment conductor Calif. Arts Coun. Mem. Am. Ednl. Rsch. Assn., Chaffey Cmty. Arts Assn., Calif. Ednl. Rsch. Assn. Home: PO Box 2960 Blue Jay CA 92317-2960 Office: U Calif Riverside Sch of Edn Riverside CA 92502-9874

DUTTON, SANDRA F., music educator; d. Roy Sanders and Marjorie Rhea Fullen; m. George William Dutton, July 16, 1966; children: Anna Elizabeth Dutton Shaver, John Adam. AS, Va. Intermont Coll., Bristol, 1964; BS, East Tenn. State U., Johnson City, 1966. Cert. Orff Level I and II. Tchr. Smyth County Sch. Dist., Marion, Va., 1966—70; music tchr. Wythe County Sch. Dist., Rural Retreat, Va., 1981—. Pres. MacDowell Music Club, 1996—2002. Mem.: Delta Kappa Gamma. Methodist. Avocations: gardening, genealogy, furniture restoration. Home: 1154 Dutton Hollow Rd Rural Retreat VA 24368-2775

DUVAL, ANNE-GWIN, lawyer; b. Baton Rouge, La., Dec. 19, 1966; BS in Psychology, La. State Univ., 1988, JD, 1991. CPCU 2000; bar: La. 1991. Asst. gen. counsel, risk mgr. Bollinger Shipyards Inc.; counsel Phelps Dunbar LLP, New Orleans. Mem.: Chartered Property Casualty Underwriters Soc., La. State Bar Assn., Phi Delta Phi. Office: Phelps Dunbar Llp 445 North Blvd Ste 701 Baton Rouge LA 70802-5707 Office Phone: 504-584-9294. Office Fax: 504-568-9130. Business E-Mail: anne-gwin.duval@phelps.com.

DUVAL, CYNTHIA, art historian, museum administrator, consultant, curator; b. Port Talbot, South Wales, Oct. 6, 1932; came to U.S., 1972; d. Joseph and Esther (Goldberg) Armstrong; m. Marcel Duval, Aug. 26, 1973; 1 son, Jonathan Armstrong. Degree, Chelsea Sch. Art, London, 1953. Antiques buyer Harrod's, London, 1972-73; gen. appraiser Sotheby's, N.Y., 1973-77; lectr. Ringling Sch. Art, Sarasota, Fla., 1977-79; adminstr. Ringling program Tampa Ringling Mus. Art, Sarasota, 1979-80, sr. curator decorative arts, 1980-86; advisor State Div. of Culture, 1985-86; grants panelist for visual arts Fla., 1985; asst. dir./curator decorative arts Mus. Fine Arts, St. Petersburg, 1989-93; prof. art history St. Petersburg Jr. Coll., 1994—. Cons. curator Bouchelle Ctr. of Decorative Arts Mus. Arts and Scis., Daytona Beach, Fla, 1993-98, cons. to the dir. Wonders cultural program, City of Memphis; liaison to Gov.'s Mansion, Tallahassee, 1984-85; coord. mus. studies program St. Petersburg Coll.; curator Fla. Internat. Mus., 2003—. Author: History of Lighting and Lamps, 1972; Toys of Long Ago, 1972; The Life of a Gentleman, 1972; Love and Marriage, 1972, (catalogs) 500 Years of the Decorative Arts, 1984, Medieval and Renaissance Armor, 1984, Jewelry Through the Ages, 1989, Figures from Life: Porcelain Sculpture from the Metropolitan Museum of Art, 1740-1780, 1992. Recipient Designers Image award Am. Assn. Interior Designers, 1983. Mem. Hist. House Assn., The Decorative Arts Trust, Appraisers Assn. Am. (fine and decorative arts appraiser 1977), Am. Assn. Mus., Internat. Coun. Mus. (mem. internat. exhibitions exchange com.). Avocation: study of social history. Home: 1109 Pinellas Bayway S Apt 303 Saint Petersburg FL 33715-2175 Office: Fla Internat Mus 2d Ave N Saint Petersburg FL 33701 Office Phone: 727-341-7902.

DUVAL, SANDRA, director; d. Jean and Geralde Duval. BA, SUNY, Stony Brook, 1991; MA, Columbia U., NYC, 1994; EdD, George Washington U., 2003. Educator, dir., mentor, vol. NYC Pub. Schs., 1990—94; tchr. English 2d lang. Columbia U., 1992—94; lang. educator, curriculum developer Md. U., College Park; dept. chair DC Pub. Schs., 1994—2000; tchr. edn. program supr. George Washington U., 2003, asst. prof., 2005; program specialist Nat. Assn. Bilingual Edn., 2003—04; staff devel. content specialist Montgomery County Pub. Schs., Germantown, Md., 2004—. Ind. cons. Tezin Inc, Washington, 2001—; adj. prof. Johns Hopkins U., Balt., 2004—05. Prodr.: (documentary) Here There and in Between. Fellow, George Washington U., US Dept. Edn., 1998—2002. Mem.: Alpha Kappa Delta, Phi Delta Kappa (v.p. 2005—06, pres. 2006—). Achievements include development of Toolkits for Afterschool Program Providers. Home: 6600 Luzon Ave NW # 405 Washington DC 20012 Personal E-mail: duval_s@msn.com.

DUVALL, DEBRA, school system administrator; Asst. supt. elem. edn. Mesa Pub. Sch., Ariz., 1987—95, asst. supt. curriculum and instrn., 1987—95, acting assoc. supt., 1995—2000, supt., 2000—. Chair Mesa Cmty. Coll. Commn. on Excellence in Edn., 2001—03. Recipient Disting. Adminstr. award (Supt. Divsn.), Ariz. Sch. Adminstrs. Assn., 2003. Office: Mesa Pub Sch #101 63 E Main St Mesa AZ 85201-7400 Office Phone: 480-472-0000. E-mail: dlduvall@mpsaz.org.

DUVALL, FLORENCE MARIE, software engineer; b. Malden, Mass., Aug. 4, 1953; d. George Perry Jr. and Florence Mary D. BS in Biology-Wildlife Ecology, U. Ariz., 1975; Global MBA, Nat. U., 2000. Chemistry rsch. lab. tech. Burr Brown Rsch. Corp., Tucson, 1975-77; supr. Transamerica Occidental Life, L.A., 1977-79; owner The Post Sta., Tucson, 1980-82; programmer analyst First Capital Life Ins., San Diego, 1982-94; sys. cons. Pacific Life Ins. Co., Newport Beach, Calif., 1994—, Yr. 2000 project mgr., 1996-2000. Vol. cons. patient database genetic counseling dept. Sharps Perinatal Ctr., San Diego, 1993-94; dir. tech. comms. Gospel Light COGIC, 2000—. Webmaster Gospellight Church.org, 1999—. Mem. foster parent program Orange County Social Svc., Orange, Calif., 1999; mem. Gospellight Ch. God in Christ, mem. usher bd. and women's coun., 1999—. Mem. IEEE, Data Processing Mgmt. Asn., Akbash Dogs Internat. (sec. 1998—), Project Mgmt. Inst. Office: Pacific Life Ins Co 700 Newport Center Dr Newport Beach CA 92660-6307 E-mail: fduvall@pacificlife.com.

DUVALL, HOLLIE JEAN, music educator; b. Greensburg, Pa., Dec. 8, 1953; d. William Gilbert Smail and Betty Jane Rygiel; m. Charles Timothy Duvall, Feb. 18, 1977; children: Charles Timothy, Renee Jean. B in Music Edn., Seton Hill Coll., 1995; MA, Ind. U. of Pa., 1997. Pa. instrnl. cert. in music edn. Music dir. Ch. of God (Holiness), Greensburg, Pa., 1970—; wedding and fashion show cons. Greensburg, 1982-98; interior designer, 1982—; freelance pianist, 1985—; instr. piano and voice Pvt. Studio, Greensburg, 1985—; prof. music Westmoreland County CC, Youngwood, Pa., 1996—; music coord., 1998—; prof. music CC of Allegheny County, West Mifflin, Pa., 1999—, Pa. State U., Fayette, Pa., 2002—. Judge-fine arts Keystone Christian Edn. Assn., Pa., 1989—, Ea. Nazarene Regional Div., Greensburg, Pa., 1990, Am. Fedn. Women's Clubs, Greensburg, 1995-97; choral clinician Pa. State Cooperative Ext., 2004. Reviewer in field. Sunday sch. tchr. Ch. of God (Holiness), Greensburg, 1975—. Scholar, AAUW, 1993, PEO Sisterhood, 1994. Mem. Profl. Music Educator's Assn., Armbrust Recreation Assn. (pres. 2006), Alpha Sigma Lambda (Scholarship award 1992). Republican. Avocations: reading, floral arranging, decorating. Office: Westmoreland County CC 400 Armbrust Rd Youngwood PA 15697-1801 Personal E-mail: hollie_duvall@yahoo.com. Business E-Mail: hjd11@psu.edu.

DUVALL, MARJORIE L., English and foreign language educator; b. Lehighton, Pa., Dec. 2, 1958; d. Charles Jacque and Carole Faye (Eckhart) Lusch; m. Glenn Edward Duvall, July 26, 1954. BA in German, Lafayette Coll., 1980; MA in German, U. Fla., 1998; postgrad., East Stroudsburg U., 1982, Ga. So. U., Middlebury Coll., 1988, Augusta State U., U. Pa., 1994, U. S.C., 1993; student, Goethe-Inst., Germany, 2003, Accord Lang. Sch., Paris, France, 2003. German and French tchr. Evans (Ga.) Mid. Sch., 1987-89, Harlem (Ga.) Mid. Sch., 1989-92; ESOL tchr. Lakeside Mid. and H.S.'s, Evans, Ga., 1992-97; ESL tchr. Davidson & Murphy H.S.'s, Mobile, Ala., 1997-99; German tchr. Brookwood H.S., Snellville, Ga., 1999-00; tchr. ESOL and lang. arts for gifted Freedom Middle Sch., Stone Mountain, Ga., 2000—03; tchr. English and German, mem. sch. coun. Dunwoody H.S., Ga., 2003—. Contbr. articles to profl. jours. Recipient scholarship Profl. Assn. Ga. Educators, 1994. Mem.: TESOL, Fgn. Lang. Assn. Ga., Ga. Assn. Gifted Children, Nat. Coun. Tchrs. English, Am. Assn. Tchrs. of French, Am. Assn. Tchrs. of German, Friends of Goethe, DeKalb County Supporters of the Gifted, Mensa (coord. gifted children Ga. chpt.). Episcopalian. Avocations: choral music, piano, swimming, baton twirling, dance. Home: 1587 Old Spring House Lane Dunwoody GA 30338 Office: Dunwoody HS 5035 Vermack Rd Dunwoody GA 30338 Office Phone: 678-874-8574. Personal E-mail: pardette80@aol.com.

DUVAL-PIERRELOUIS, JEANNE-MARIE, educational association executive; b. Chgo., June 5, 1953; d. Paul A. and Virginia (Bertsch) Duval; m. Claude Pierrelouis, Apr. 4, 1982; 1 child, Eryc Pierrelouis. BA, Bryn Mawr Coll., 1977; MEd, Temple U., 1982. Acad. coord. intensive English program Temple U., Phila., 1979-84; asst. dir. coop. grants program Nat. Assn. Fgn. Studnet Affairs, Assn. Internat. Educators, Washington, 1984-86; dir. coop. grants program NAFSA, Assn. Internat. Educators, Washington, 1986-89, sr. dir. ednl. program, 1989-96, assoc. exec. dir., 1996-99; mng. dir. higher edn. programs Am. Couns. Internat. Edn., Washington, 2000—02, v.p. higher edn., 2002—. Cons. Fund Improvement Post Secondary Edn., Washington, 1995-97; mem. exec. com. Alliance Internat. Ednl. and Cultural Exch., Washington, 1997-99. Mem. edn. com. Barrie Sch., Silver Spring, Md., 1998-99. Fulbright grantee Bd. Fgn. Scholarships, 1988. Avocations: weaving, photography. Office: Am Couns Internat Edn ACTR/ACCELS 1776 Mass Ave NW Ste 700 Washington DC 20036 Fax: 202-833-7523.

DUVEEN, ANNETA, artist; b. Bklyn., May 21, 1924; d. Julius and Shirley (Klugman) Applebaum; m. Charles J. Duveen Jr., Dec. 21, 1942 (div. 1954); children: Wendy, Charles III, Peter; m. Benjamin Duveen, Nov. 24, 1976. Student, U. Iowa, 1941, Adelphi Acad., 1941, Columbia U., 1941, 42, 56; HHD, St. Francis Coll., 1986. Founder, pres. Duveen Internat. Ltd., Port Chester, N.Y., 1987—. Lectr. Westchester Arts Coun., White Plains, N.Y., 1993-94. Prin. works exhibited in group and retrospective and one-woman shows including Pacem in Terris Gallery, N.Y.C., 1970, The Signs of God in the World, Santa Croce Basilica Grand Cloister, Florence, Italy, 1985, Marymount Manhattan Coll., 1986, Artiste 86, Rome, 1986; commd. sculptures include heroic meml. busts of Ella T. Grasso, Robert F. Kennedy, St. Maximilian Kolbe and the Papal Family, The Child: Moments in Bronze, Our Lady of the Eucharist, Tabernacle: Our Lady of the Eucharist, many others; also 49 stained glass window designs of St. Anthony; also collage Alas, She Died in Childbirth; co-author, illustrator: Essentials of Astronomy, 1976. Mem. exec. com. Franciscans Internat., Bklyn., 1989-99; internat. rep. for justice, peace and ecology Secular Franciscan Order, Rome, 1990-92; tchr., dir., ednl. specialist, proposal designer, rschr., cons. Fellow Royal Astron. Soc.; mem. AAAS, AAUW, Sede di Dante, N.Y. Acad. Scis., Inst. for Theol. Encounter with Sci. and Tech., Nat. Fedn. Press Women, Portchester Coun. for Arts, Westchester Arts Coun. Home: 23 Tiplady Rd Salem NY 12865-9547

DUVO, MECHELLE LOUISE, oil company executive, consultant; b. East Stroudsburg, Pa., Apr. 25, 1962; d. Nicholas and Arlene Birdie (Mack) D. AS, Lehigh County C.C., 1982. Rehab. counselor Phoenix Project, Bakersfield, Calif., 1982-84; nat. sales mgr. Olympia Advt., L.A., 1984-85; oil exploration cons. Cimmaron Mgmt., Nashville, 1985-86; exec. sec. Pueblo Resources Corp., Bowling Green, Ky., 1986-87; nat. oil cons. El Toro, Inc., Bowling Green, 1986-87; founder, pres. and CEO Majestic Mgmt. Corp., Glasgow, Ky., 1987—; nat. oil cons. Impact Oil, Inc., Glasgow, 1987—. Lease procurator El Toro, Inc., 1986-87; spkr. Nat. Investment Seminars, 1994—. Editor, pub.: (newsletter) The Majestic Field Copy, 1994—. Fundraiser Am. Cancer Soc., LA, 1984-85; vol. Humane Soc., Nashville, 1985-86, Humane Soc., Bowling Green, 1986-87, Boy Scouts Am., 2001-02; counselor Salvation Army, Bakersfield, 1982-84, vol. Kettle and Angel Tree programs, 2001—; vol. mgr. Food Pantry Outreach Program, 1999-2001, Strut Your Mutt, 1999—, Relay for Life, 2001—, Am. Cancer Soc. fundraiser, 2001—, Glasgow chpt. Ky. Assn. for Gifted Edn., 2004—; fundraiser Ky. Assn. for Gifted Edn. Mem. NAFE (exec. program), Internat. Platform Assn. Avocations: house plants, gardening, music, gourmet cooking. Home and Office: Majestic Mgmt Corp 1202 S Green St Glasgow KY 42141-2014 Office Phone: 270-651-3346. E-mail: majesticmgmtcorp@yahoo.com.

DUYCK, KATHLEEN MARIE, poet, musician, retired social worker; b. Portland, Oreg., July 21, 1933; d. Anthony Joseph Dwyer and Edna Elisabeth Hayes; m. Robert Duyck, Feb. 3, 1962; children: Mary Kay Boeyen, Robert Patrick, Anthony Joseph. BS, Oreg. State U., 1954; MSW, U. Wash., 1956. Cert. NASW, Oreg. Adoption worker Cath. Svcs., Portland, 1956-61, Cath. Welfare, San Antonio, 1962; musician Tucson Symphony, 1963-65; prin. cellist Phoenix (Ariz.) Coll. Orch., 1968-78, Scottsdale (Ariz.) Symphony, 1974-80; poet, 1993—. Author: (poetry cassettes) Visions, 1993 (Contemporary Series Poet 1993), Visions II, 1996 (Contemporary Series Poet 1996); author numerous poems. Rep. worker Maricopa County Reps., Phoenix, 1974; mem. Scottsdale Cultural Coun.; NASW bd. Cath. Charities Rep., Portland, 1959-61. Recipient Golden Poet award, World of Poetry, 1991-92, Sec. gift, Phoenix Exec. Bd., 1976, Recognition award, Archbishop Howard, 1961, 5-Yr. Kathleen Duyck award, Cello Congress V, 1996. Mem. Internat. Poetry Hall Fame, Ariz. Cello Soc., Nat. Libr. Poetry (Editor's Choice awards, 1993-2003), Internat. Soc. Poets (Internat. Poet of Merit award, 2003, Outstanding Achievement in Poetry award, 2005, 06), Phoenix Symphony Guild (exec. bd. 1970-80), St. Mary's Alumni Assn., Phoenix Art Mus., Oreg. State U. Alumni Assn., U. Wash. Alumni Assn., Mental Health Guild, Friends Family Svc. Republican. Roman Catholic. Avocations: piano, photography, poetry, music. Home and Office: 4545 E Palomino Rd Phoenix AZ 85018-1719

DUZY, MERRILYN JEANNE, artist, educator; b. L.A., Mar. 29, 1946; d. Berton John and Marva Lorinne (Barrow) D.; m. Howard Bentkower, Sept. 28, 1974. BA, Calif. State U., Northridge, 1974; MFA, Otis Art Inst., L.A., 1988. Tchr. L.A. H.S. for Arts, 1988-90, The Atelier, Chatsworth, Calif. Pvt. tchr., lectr., West Hills, 1991-93; creator slide lecture Walking Through History: Women Artists Past and Present, 1982—; curator Autobiographies, 1977, Erotica '88, 1988, Angeles, Ancestors and Spirit Guides, 1994, Closure invitational Artspace Gallery, 1994, Quarks to Quasars, 1997, Merrilyn Duzy: twenty five years, Mt. San Jacinto Coll., 1998. Lecture, Sex in History: A Pictorial View, 2004. Founder Artists Networking, Woodland Hills, Calif., 1992-93. Mem. Coll. Art Assn., Women's Caucus for Art (pres. So. Calif. chpt. 1980-82, founder, pres. Fla. West Coast chpt. 1983-84, mem. nat. adv. bd.), Group Nine. Home: 8356 Capistrano Ave West Hills CA 91304-3319

DWORIN, MICKI (MAXINE DWORIN), automobile dealership executive; widowed; children: Judy, Diane. V.p. Dworin Chevrolet, Inc., East Harford, Conn., 1955-83, Dworin Auto Leasing. Pres. Eastern Auto Ins., Conn. Chevrolet Dealers Assn., Tarrytown Zone Dealer Coun., Atlantic Coast Region Dealer Coun., Boulevard, Inc. Sec. BBB, Hartford, Conn.; vol. coord. Vol. Broward, 1998-99, Children's Diagnostic and Treatment Ctr., 1996-98, Am. Cancer Soc., 1994-96, Kids in Distress, 1991-95; hon. trustee Hartford Coll. for Women; sec., bd. govs. Point of Am. Condominium; coord. Trinity Coll.; bd. dirs. Combined Health Appeals; chmn. King David Soc., 1995-96. Mem. Advt. Assn. Grtr. Hartford. Fax: 954-522-6770. E-mail: volbrow@safari.net.

DWORIN, MIRIAM JOY, occupational therapist, educator, advocate; b. Columbus, Ohio, Sept. 18, 1938; d. William Evert Burroughs and Elizabeth Sarah Dudley; m. Lowell Dworin, May 20, 1964; children: Nadia Fay Gartner, Daniel William. BA, Houghton Coll., Houghton, NY, 1960; Occupl. Therapist, Austin C.C., Austin, Tex., 1984. Cert. Occupl. Therapist Bd. Cert. Tex. H.S. tchr. Wachung Hill H.S., Wachung Hills, NJ, 1962—64; tchr. Pub. Sch., N.Y.C., 1962—64; libr. U. Tex., Austin, Tex., 1980—84; occupl. therapist Brackenridge Hosp., Austin, Tex., 1984—99, Monte Siesta Rehab. Southwood Care, Austin, 2001—. Exhibited in group shows at Nat. Endowment for Arts, Austin, Tex., 1984 (3d pl. award, 1984). Democrat. Non-Demoninational. Avocations: art, singing, birdwatching.

DWORK, DEBÓRAH, history professor; d. Bernard and Shirley Dwork; m. Kenneth Marek, June 16, 1974; children: Miriam Marek, Hannah Marek. BA, Princeton U., NJ, 1975; MPH, Yale U., New Haven, 1978; PhD, U. Coll., London, 1984. Rose prof. Holocaust history Clark U., Worcester, Mass., 1996—, dir. Strassler Ctr. Holocaust and Genicide Studies, 1996—. Bd.d irs. Jewish Cultural Heritage Found., Stockholm; adv. bd. mem. Facing History and Ourselves, Brookline, Mass.; adv. bd. mem. Internat. Inst. on Jewish Women Brandeis U., Waltham, Mass.; postdoctoral fellow Smithsonian Instn., 1984. Co-author: Holocaust: A History, Auschwitz, 1270 to Present (Nat. Jewish Book Award, Nat. Book Critics list - Germany, Spiro Kostoff Award); author: Children With A Star: Jewish Youth in Nazi Europe, Voices and Views: A History of the Holocaust, War is Good for Babies and other Young Children, monographs in field. Trustee, vice chmn. Jewish Found. for Righteous, NYC, 1995—2006; mem. anti-semitism task force Am. Jewish Com., NYC. Fellow, Wellcome Trust, 1983, 1985, Am. Coun. Learned Socs., 1988; grantee, Lustman Fund, 1991—94, Am. Philos. Soc., 1987, NEH, 1992; Guggenheim fellow, Guggenheim Found., 1993—94, Woodrow Wilson fellow, Woodrow Wilson Internat. Ctr. for Scholars, 1998, Tapper Rsch. grantee, Tapper Charitable Found., 2003—05, Rackham Faculty rsch. grantee, U. Mich., 1988. Mem.: Am. Hist. Assn. Office: Clark U 950 Main St Worcester MA 01610 Office Phone: 508-793-8897.

DWORKIN, IRMA-THERESA, school system administrator, researcher, secondary school educator; b. Busk, Galacia, Poland, May 1, 1942; d. Moses E. and Hedwig (Rappaport) Auerbach; m. Sidney Leonard Dworkin, Aug. 19, 1975 (dec. June 1984); children: Marc Elazar, Meyer Charles, Rebecca Joy. BS in Edn., CCNY, 1964, MS in Ednl. Psychology, 1966, cert. in clin. sch. psychology, 1968; EdD in Reading and Human Devel., Harvard U., 1971. Cert. tchr., reading cons., sch. psychologist, sch. adminstr. Tchr. N.Y.C. Pub. Schs., 1964-66; rsch. asst., lectr. Bd. Higher Edn., N.Y.C., 1966-69; lectr., prof. Haifa (Israel) U., 1971-74; lectr., sr. investigator CUNY, N.Y.C., 1974-76; adminstr., evaluator, proposal and grant writer Bridgeport (Conn.) Pub. Schs., 1984—. Asst. Edn. Clinic CCNY, N.Y.C., 1964—66; Kunin-Lunefeld Found. endouwed prof. chair Haifa U., 1973. Contbr. articles to profl. jours. Vol. Cmty. Closet, Bridgeport, 1991—98; mem. Rep. Town com., Bridgeport, 1992—; bd. dirs. Jewish Bd. Edn., Bridgeport, Jewish Fedn. Greater Bridgeport, chairperson Holocaust edn. com., 1986—89, sec., 1996. Fellow Grolier, Harvard U., 1969—71; grantee fed. and state project. Mem.: Conn. Fedn. Sch. Adminstrs. (sec. 1997—, newsletter editor, website editor 1997—2002), Bridgeport Coun. Adminstrs. and Suprs. (editor, exec. bd. dirs. 1992—98, continuing edn. units mgr. 1993—98, v.p. 1994—98), Conn. Assn. Sch. Psychologists, Conn. Testing Network (newsletter editor). Avocations: reading, physical fitness, painting, writing.

DWORSKY, MARY, interior designer; b. Mpls., Feb. 17, 1948; d. Zollie and Lucille Dworsky. Attended, U. Minn., 1966-71. Cert. interior designer Minn. Interior designer Creative Furniture, Mpls., 1974-79, Mr. Furniture, Mpls., 1980-82, Dorothy Collins Interiors, Edina, Minn., 1982-89, Interior Design Ptnrs., Edina, 1989-92, The Design Studio of Gabberts, Edina, 1992-2000, Mary Dworsky Interior Design Ltd., Mpls. Decorations chair Mpls. Crisis Nursery, 1996, chair Showcase House Cmty. Svc. Mem.: ASID (Minn. chpt. pres. 2000—01, pres. 2000—01, dir., sec., Presdl. Citation 1994, 1996, 1999, 2000, 2002, 2003, 2004), Quota Club Mlps. (bd.mem., v.p.), Rotary (com. chair 1991—99). Home: #121 3720 Independence Ave S Minneapolis MN 55426-3781 Office: Mary Dworsky Interior Design Ltd 275 Market St Ste 451 Minneapolis MN 55405 Office Phone: 612-339-0070.

DWYER, CARRIE ELIZABETH, lawyer; b. San Mateo, Calif., Dec. 19, 1950; d. Robert Harold and Alice Marian (Daley) Dwyer; m. Richard M. Konecky, Feb. 12, 1977; children: Rachel Anne, Philip. BA in English, U. Santa Clara, 1973, JD, 1976. Bar: Calif., NY. Staff atty. Am. Stock Exchange, NYC, 1977-79, exec. asst. to exec. v.p. legal and regulatory affairs, 1979—81, asst. v.p., exec. asst. to pres., 1981—83, v.p., exec. asst. to pres., 1983—85, v.p., assoc. gen. counsel, 1985—87, sr. v.p., gen. counsel, 1987—89; contract lawyer Milbank, Tweed, Hadley & McCoy, NYC; sr. counsel to chmn. Arthur Levitt SEC, 1993—96; exec. v.p. corp. oversight The Charles Schwab Corp., San Francisco, 1996—, gen. counsel, 1998—. Mem. ABA, The Assn. of Bar of City of NY, NY State Bar Assn., Investment Assn. Office: The Charles Schwab Corp 101 Montgomery St San Francisco CA 94104

DWYER, JOHANNA TODD, nutritionist, educator; b. Syracuse, NY, Oct. 20, 1938; d. M. Harold and Frances (Markey) D. BS with distinction, Cornell U., 1960; MSc, U. Wis., 1962; MS, Harvard Sch. Pub. Health, Boston, 1965, DSc, 1969. Asst. prof. Harvard Sch. Pub. Health, 1969-73; home economist Procter & Gamble, Cin., 1962-64; rsch. asst. U. Wis., Madison, 1960-62; assoc. prof. Tufts Med. Sch., 1974, prof. medicine and nutrition, 1984—; sr. scientist human nutrition rsch. USDA, Boston, 1988—, asst. adminstr. for human nutrition Agrl. Rsch. Svc. Washington, 2001—02; sr. nutrition rsch. scientist Office of Dietary Supplements, NIH, 2003—. Dir. Frances Stern Nutrition Ctr., New Eng. Med. Ctr., Boston, 1974—; adj. prof. Harvard Sch. Pub. Health, 1988—. Author 3 books, 1979, 83; editor Nutrition Today, 1995—; contbr. over 450 articles to profl. jours. Mem. Mass. Nutrition Bd., Boston, 1980-2004; cons. Exec. Office of Pres., Washington, 1976; mem. bd. sci. counselors Nat. Cancer Inst., 1985-89; com. mem. and nuitrition work study Am. Cancer Soc., 1990-94; sec. ADA Found., 2004 Robert Wood Johnson Health Policy fellow, 1980-81, John Stalker award Am. Sch. Food Svc. Assn., 1990, Alumni Merit award Harvand Sch. Pub. Health, 2004. Fellow: Am. Soc. Nutrition Scis. (Conrad Elvejhem award for pub. policy 2005), Am. Inst. Nutrition (pres. 1994—95, bd. dirs.), Am. Soc. Clin. Nutrition (sec. 1990—93), Soc. for Nutrition Edn. (bd. dirs. 1975—77, pres. 1976, J. Harvey Wiley award 1983); mem.: APHA (program devel. bd. 1990—92), Dannon Inst. (sci. adv. bd. 2003—), Internat. Life Scis. Inst. (bd. dirs. 1999—, exec. com. 2005—), Food and Drug Law Inst. (bd. dirs. 1980—95), Am. Inst. Food and Wine (bd. dirs. 1991—95), Nutrition Screening Initiative (tech. and sci. rev. com. 1990—2004), Inst. Medicine of NAS (food and nutrition bd. 1990—2000, councilor 2001—03, mil. nutrition com. mem. 2004—, report renew com. 2005), Am. Dietetic Assn. (legis. and pub. policy com. 1998—2004, sec. found. 2005, lectr., bd. mem. ADA Found., Lenna Frances Cooper award 1980, Medallion award 2002), Am. Soc. Parenteral and Enteral Nutrition (adv. bd. 1978—). Office: Tufts New Eng Med Ctr 750 Washington St PO Box 783 Boston MA 02102-0783 Office Phone: 617-636-5273. Personal E-mail: toddyd@msn.com. Business E-Mail: jdwyer1@tufts.nemc.org.

DWYER, JUDITH A., marriage and family therapist; b. Phila., Apr. 15, 1956; d. Arthur William and Virginia Arlene (Courter) Crouthamel; m. John Adam Dwyer, Dec. 15, 1979; children: Allison Michelle, Kimberly Virginia, Matthew John. BS in Elem. Edn., Millersville U., 1978; MA in Pastoral Counseling, La Salle U., 1994. Cert. marriage and family therapist. Intern La Salle Family Studies Clin., Phila., 1992-93, Wayne Counseling Ctr., Wayne, Pa., 1994-95; marriage and family therapist N.E. Career Ctr., Princeton, N.J., 1995-96, Counseling Ctr. at St. Luke U., Glenside, Pa., 1996—. Dir. Support Police Immediate Response Intervention Team, Glenside, Pa., 1996—; vol. Second Alarmes Rescue Squad, Willow Grove, Pa., 1986—. Mem. Am. Assn. Marriage and Family Therapists, Pa. Assn. Marriage and Family Therapists. Republican. Presbyterian. Avocations: church choir, swimming, hiking, reading.

DWYER, KELLY, writer, educator; b. Torrance, Calif., Feb. 28, 1964; d. Richard Stanley and Sharon Arlene (Speigler) D.; m. Louis A. Wenzlow, Jan. 5, 1991. BA, Oberlin Coll., 1987; MFA, U. Iowa, 1990. Teaching asst. U. Iowa, Iowa City, 1988-90; vis. asst. prof. Oberlin (Ohio) Coll., 1994-96. Author: The Tracks of Angels, 1994. James Michener/Paul Engle fellow Iowa Writers' Workshop, 1991-92. Avocations: photography, running, Scrabble.

DWYER, MAUREEN ELLEN, lawyer; BA, Smith Coll., Northampton, Mass., 1973; JD, Cath. U. Am. Columbus Sch. Law, 1978. Bar: DC 1979, US Dist. Ct. (DC), US Ct. Appeals (DC cir.), US Supreme Ct. Shareholder Wilkes Artis, Wash., DC; ptnr. real estate group Pillsbury Winthrop Shaw Pittman, Wash., DC, mng. ptnr. D.C. office. Chmn. adv. bd. Salvation Army; past chmn. Eugene & Agnes Meyer Found. Named one of 100 Most Powerful Women in Wash., Washingtonian mag., 2001. Mem.: Comml. Real Estate Women (past pres.), Fed. City Council, DC C. of C., Urban Land Inst., Greater Wash. Bd. Trade, DC Bldg. Industry Assn., Economic Club. Office: Pillsbury Winthrop Shaw Pittman 2300 N St NW Washington DC 20037-1128 Office Phone: 202-663-8834. Office Fax: 202-663-8007. Business E-Mail: maureen.dwyer@pillsburylaw.com.

DWYER SOUTHERN, KATHY, museum administrator; m. Hugh Southern; 1 child. BA in Mktg., U. Wis., 1968, MA in Arts Adminstrn., 1972. Exec. dir. Nat. Cultural Alliance, 1990—94, Montpelier, Va., 1994—96; pres., CEO Port Discovery, Balt., 1996—2001, Nat. Children's Mus., 2001—. Arts mgmt. prof. Am. U., Va. Commonwealth U., Shenandoah Conservatory Music; bd. dirs. Am. Assn. Mus. Office: Nat Children's Mus 955 L'Enfant Plaza N Ste 5100 Washington DC 20024-2103 Office Phone: 202-675-4120.

DYAL, EDITH COLVIN, retired music educator; b. El Dorado, Ark., Mar. 9, 1928; d. Otis Herbert and Irene (Hammons) Colvin; m. William M. Dyal, May 13, 1950; children: Kathy Dyal Schwab, Deborah Dyal DeMeo, Lisa Dyal Reese. BA, Baylor U., 1949; MA, Columbia U., 1984, MEd, 1985, EdD, 1991. Pvt. piano studio mgr. and tchr. Edith Dyal Studio, Alexandria, Va., 1971-81, Kiawah Island/Charleston, S.C., 1986-94; pvt. piano instr. Panama City, Panamá, 1995-97; ret., 1997. Adj. assoc. prof. music Sch. of the Arts, U. Charleston, 1986-94; cons. Internat. Piano Tchg. Found., N.Y.C., 1986-92. Mem. Music Tchrs. Nat. Assn. (local pres. 1988-90), Nat. Fedn. Music Clubs (local pres. 1991-93). Democrat. Baptist.

DY-ANG, ANITA C., pediatrician; b. Cavite, The Philippines, Feb. 21, 1943; came to U.S., 1970; m. Raymundo Ang., May 1, 1977; children: Aileen Ang, Audrey Ang. MD, U. East Ramon Magsaysay, Quezon City, Philippines, 1967. Diplomate Am. Bd. Pediatrics. Pediat. resident Tulane U. Charity Hosp. New Orleans, 1973; pvt. practice Warsaw, N.Y. Mem. attending staff Wyoming County Cmty. Hosp. Mem. Wyoming County Med. Soc. Office: 78 N Main St Warsaw NY 14569-1329 Office Phone: 585-786-8181.

DYAR, KATHRYN WILKIN, pediatrician; b. Colquitt, Ga., Feb. 20, 1945; d. Patrick McWhorter and Virginia (Wilkin) Dyar; m. James Ansley Patten, Jan. 1, 1985. BS in Biology, Emory U., Decatur, Ga., 1966; MD, Med. Coll. Ga., Augusta, 1970. Resident in pediatrics Eugene Talmadge Meml. Hosp., Augusta, Ga., 1970-72, Georgetown U. Hosp., Washington, 1972-73; pediatrician Children's Clinic, Tifton, Ga., 1973-74, Children and Youth Project, Norfolk, Va., 1974-83, 90-95, dir., 1990-94; pediatrician Hampton (Va.) Health Dept., 1983-90. Fellow: Am. Acad. Pediatrics.

DYAS, ANNA MARIE, gifted and talented educator; b. Ft. Worth, Tex., Apr. 25, 1952; d. Norman Aloysius and Maria Pacheco Smith; m. Fred L Dyas, Nov. 23, 1997; children: Eric Thomas Cowan, Ashley Marie Cowan. BS, U. of Incarnate Word, 1970—74. Professional Educator Tex. Edn. Agy. Tex., 1974. Classroom tchr. St. John's Cath. Sch., San Antonio, Tex., 1975—78, Northside Ind. Sch. Dist., San Antonio, Tex., 1978—81. Classroom tchr. Corpus Christi Ind. Sch. Dist., Corpus Christi, Tex., 1981—87; gifted/enrichment specialist Northside ISD, San Antonio, 1991—. Author: (gifted curriculum writing) Kindergarten Identification Dialogue and Search, A Year of Discovery; co-author: (pep gifted curriculum) Change in the 20th Century. Parishioner Our Lady of Guadalupe, San Antonio, Tex., 1999—2005. Recipient Tchr. of the Yr., Northside ISd, 1998—99, TAGT Gifted Educator of Yr. Region, Tex. Assn. of Gifted Talented, 2000—01, Tex. Assn. of Gifted and Talented, 2000. Mem.: Parent Tchr. Assn., Assn. of Tex. Profl. Educators, Tex. Assn. of Gifted Talented (Region XX Gifted Tchr. of the Yr. 2000, Gifted Tchr. of Yr. 2006). Office: Henry Steubing Elem Sch 11655 Braefield San Antonio TX 78249 Office Phone: 210-397-4350 ext. 3120. Office Fax: 210-706-4374. Business E-Mail: annadyas@nisd.net.

DYBELL, ELIZABETH ANNE SLEDDEN, psychologist; b. Buffalo, Sept. 25, 1958; d. Richard Edward and Angela Brigid Sledden; m. David Joseph Dybell, Nov. 30, 1985. BA in Psychology summa cum laude, U. St. Thomas, Houston, 1980; PhD in Psychology, Tex. Tech. U., 1986. Lic. clin. psychologist, Tex. Rsch. asst. health sci. ctr. Tex. Tech. U., Lubbock, 1983-84, psychol. cons. health sci. ctr. neurology dept., 1982-84; psychology intern U. N.Mex. Med. Sch., Albuquerque, 1984-85; psychotherapist Katz & Assocs. P.C., Houston, 1985-88, Meyer Ctr. for Devel. Pediatrics Tex. Children's Hosp., Houston, 1988-92; pvt. practice Houston, 1990—. Author: (monograph) When Will Life Be Normal?, 1989, Myths of the Super Parent: Finding the Power of Real Parenting, 2003; contbr. articles to numerous publs. Choir mem. St. Thomas More Ch., Houston, 1974-87. Mem. APA, Soc. Pediatric Psychology, Tex. Psychol. Assn., Internat. Dyslexia Assn., Am. Psychol. Soc. (charter). Roman Catholic. Avocations: gardening, horticulture, nature studies. Home and Office: 1770 St James Pl Ste 405 Houston TX 77056-3471

DYBOWSKI, JANE, science educator; b. Fall River, Mass., Nov. 17, 1954; d. Henry and Alexandrina Dybowski; m. Harry A. Proudfoot, Sept. 2, 1989. BS summa cum laude, Bridgewater State Coll., Mass., 1976. Lab technician Morton Hosp., Taunton, Mass., 1976—78; lab instr. Bridgewater State Coll., 1978—80; tchr. sci. Westport H.S., Mass., 1980—. Cons. in field; chmn. Curriculum Com. NEASC, Westport, 1993. Recipient Tchr. Yr., Westport H.S. Nat. Honor Soc., 2004. Mem.: Mass. Fedn. Tchrs., Am. Fedn.Tchrs, Westport Fedn. Tchrs. Avocations: tennis, hiking, cross stitch, reading.

DYBVIG, MARY MCILVAINE, educational consultant, psychologist; b. Chgo., Feb. 23, 1936; d. John Harmon and Mildred Petrina McIlvaine; m. Noel Tyl, June 13, 1958 (div. Apr. 1976); 1 child, Kimberly Tyl; m. Paul Dybvig, Mar. 21, 1978 (div. Feb. 1999); m. Melvin Leonard Sward, Apr. 7, 2002; stepchildren: Alyssa Quanbeck, Mary Eide, Mark Sward, Paul Sward, Natalie Nutting, Carole Sward. BA cum laude, Radcliffe/Harvard U., 1958; MA in Ednl. Psychology, NYU, 1968; PhD in Ednl. Adminstrn., U. Minn., 1992. Tchr. Kinkaid Sch., Houston, 1958—60, Dalton Sch., N.Y.C, 1960—63, Packer Collegiate Inst., Brooklyn, NY, 1963—68, Am. Army Sch., Munich, 1968—69, Düsseldorf (Germany) Internat. Sch., 1969—72, Heinrich-Heine Gymnasium, 1972—73, St. Paul Acad., 1973—77; sch. psychologist St. Paul (Minn.) Schs., 1977—94, prin., 1994—2001; pvt. practice cons./sch. psychologist St. Paul/Mpls., 2001—. Instr. St. Thomas U., St. Paul, 1990—94; cons. in field; presenter in field. Active St. Luke Luth. Ch., St. Paul, 1996—. Mem.: Minn. Assn. Sch. Psychologists, Nat. Assn. Sch. Psychologists, Alpha Delta Kappa. Avocations: travel, golf, cooking. Home: 1640 Mackubin St Saint Paul MN 55117

DYCKMAN, A(LICE) ANN, retired academic administrator; b. Roanoke, Va. d. Dan Henry and Alice May (Austin) Pletta; m. Thomas R. Dyckman, Nov. 14, 1955; children: Daniel Frank, James Richard, Linda Ann, David Lee. MusB, U. Mich., 1955; MA, Cornell U., 1971. Dir. Ithaca Cmty. Sch. Music and Arts, NY, 1971-74; adj. prof. music Thompkins Cortland Community Coll., Dryden, N.Y., 1974-76; exec. staff asst. dept. human devel. and family studies Cornell U., Ithaca, 1976-82, adminstrv. mgr., 1982-86, adminstrv. mgr. Sch. Applied and Engring. Physics, 1986-87; dir. personnel Cornell U. Librs., Ithaca, 1987—2002. Author: (with others) Journal of Library Administration, 1992, The Personnel Manuel: An Outline for Libraries, 1993. Home: 135 Eastlake Rd Ithaca NY 14850-9700 Office: Cornell U Librs 201 Olin Library Ithaca NY 14853-5301

DYCUS, PATRICIA M., education educator, chemical engineer; m. Richard Dycus; children: Megan, Will. MS, Tenn. Tech. Univ., Cookeville, Tenn., 1993, PhD, 1997. Sr. pharm. chemist Schering Plough Inc., Memphis, 1983—88; rsch. assoc. Tenn. Tech. Univ., Cookeville, 1989—91, asst. prof., 1997—2003.

DYE, LANA L., music educator; d. Raymond M. Wieck and Lucille M. Walker; m. Dennis D. Dye, June 22, 2001; children: Gage Alan Michael, Jesse Garrett Dean. MusB, Briar Cliff U., Sioux City, Iowa, 1971; MA, Mankato State U., Minn., 1978. Lic. music tchr. K-14 Iowa, 1971. Tchr. K-12 music Little Rock Cmty. Sch., Iowa, 1971—73; music tchr. Sioux City Cmty. Sch., Iowa, 1973—. Pres., bd. dirs. Siouxland Youth Chorus, Sioux City, 1988—91; mentor Sioux City Cmty. Sch., 2004—, mem. dist. adv. bd. on mentoring, 2005—. Critic reader (textbook) Making Music, 2004. Organist, choir dir., youth leader, tchr. Immanuel Luth. Ch., Sioux City, 1967—, mem. ch. coun., 2004—. Grantee, Best Buy, 2006, Kind World Found., 2006. Mem.: NEA, Siouxland Autism Soc., Tech. Inst. Music Educators, Music Educators Nat. Conf., Sioux City Edn. Assn., Iowa State Edn. Assn. Lutheran. Avocations: music, travel, crafts, computers, camping. Home: 3060 Myrtle Sioux City IA 51103 Office: West Mid Sch 3301 W 19th Sioux City IA 51103 Office Phone: 712-279-6813. E-mail: dyel@sioux-city.ia.us.

DYE, LAURA, physical education educator; EdB, Mo. Western State Coll., St. Joseph, Mo., 1989; MEd, U. of Mo., Columbia, 1993. Phys. edn. tchr. Columbia Pub. Schools, Columbia, Mo., 1989—. Coach and referee Upward Basketball, Columbia, Mo., 2003—06. WIN grant, Women In Sport Network. Mem.: Columbia Cmty. Tchrs. Assn., Mo. State Tchrs. Assn., Mo. Assn. Health, Phys. Edn., Recreation and Dance (Exemplary Phys. Edn. Program award 1996). Office: Columbia Pub Sch 1818 W Worley Columbia MO 65203 Office Phone: 573-214-3400. Business E-Mail: ldye@columbia.k12.mo.us.

DYE, LINDA KAYE, elementary school educator; b. Shelbyville, Tenn., Dec. 26, 1962; d. John William Dye and Adeline Stewart Dye Adams. BS, David Lipscomb Univ., Nashville, 1985; MEd, Tenn. State U., 2004. Title I reading tchr. Bedford County Bd. Edn., Shelbyville, Tenn. Mem. NEA, Tenn. Edn. Assn., Nat. Coun. Tchrs. English, Bedford County Edn. Assn.

DYE, NANCY SCHROM, academic administrator, historian, educator; b. Columbia, Mo., Mar. 11, 1947; d. Ned Stuart and Andrea Elizabeth (Ahrens) Schrom; m. Griffith R. Dye, Aug. 21, 1972; children: Molly, Michael. AB, Vassar Coll., 1969; MA, U. Wis., 1971, PhD, 1974; LittD (hon.), Obirin U., 2005. Asst. prof. U. Ky., Lexington, 1974—80, assoc. prof., 1980—88, prof., 1988, assoc. dean arts and scis., 1984—88; dean faculty Vassar Coll., Poughkeepsie, NY, 1988—92, acting pres., 1992—94; pres. Oberlin Coll., Oberlin, Ohio, 1994—. Author: As Equals And As Sisters, 1981; contbr. articles to profl. jours. Bd. mem. Pomona Coll. Mem.: Coun. Colls. of Art and Scis. (bd. dirs. 1980—91). Office: Oberlin Coll Cox Admin Bldg, Room 201 70 N Professor St Oberlin OH 44074-1090*

DYE, REBECCA FEEMSTER, commissioner; b. Charlotte, N.C., May 8, 1952; BA, U. N.C., 1974, JD, 1977. Spl. counsel Broughton (N.C.) Psychiat. Hosp., 1977-78; atty. project coord. Legal Svcs. N.C., 1978-79; atty. office of chief counsel USCG, 1979-83; law instr. USCG Acad., 1983-85; atty. office of chief counsel Fed. Maritime Adminstrn., 1985-87; minority counsel Com. Merchant Marine & Fisheries, Washington, 1987—95; counsel Coast Guard & Maritime Transp. Subcommittee, Com. on Transp. & Infrastructure, US Ho. Reps., Washington, 1995—2002; commr. Fed. Maritime Commn., Washington, 2002—. Office: Fed Maritime Comm 800 N Capitol St NW Rm 1038 Washington DC 20573 E-mail: rdye@fmc.gov.

DYE, SHARON ELIZABETH HERNDON, speech pathologist; b. Springfield, Mo., June 14, 1952; d. Leonard Leroy and Virginia Louise (Kennard) Herndon; divorced children: Brian Keith Dye, Johnathan Paul Dye, Christopher Shawn Dye. BS, Marquette U., 1973, MS, 1975. Counselor to supr. Career Youth Devel., Milw., 1973—76; speech pathologist Milw. Pub. Schs., 1976-98; head start speech pathologist Peacé Action Milwaukee-Milwaukee, Inc., 1998—; speech pathologist Phillis Wheatley Elem. Sch., Milw., 1999—, Clara Barton, Spotted Eagle H.S., Willowglen Acad., Willowglen Cornerstone, Peace Action, Wis., 2004. Itinerant speech pathologist Wis. Speech Lang. Hearing Assn., 1998-99; speech pathologist North Divn. H.S. PTA, 1998—, mem. spl. edn. com., 2000-02; part-time resident care worker Bell Therapy, Phoenix. Author: (poetry) Wind Riders, 1996; guest host area cable TV program MATA. Vol. House of Correction, Franklin, Wis., 1993, glaucoma screenings, 1995, 96; mem. Jobs for Peace, 1994, 95; past mem. Progressive Milw., Jamie's Club Theatre, featured poet, 1999; mem. spl. edn. com. PTA, 2000-2003; commr. neighborhood perspective com. Fondy Neighborhood Bus. Assn., 2002-2003; mem. In Touch Prayer Ptnrs., 2005-; bd. mem. Wis Edn. Assn. Student Support, 2004-06. Mem. NEA (del. rep. assembly 2000-03), Wis. Speech Lang. Hearing Assn., Wis. Edn. Assn. (del., rep. assembly, student support programs conf. com., 2001-06, student support programs bd. dir., 2003-06), Nat. Assn. Black Speech, Lang. and Hearing, Milw. Tchrs. Edn. Assn. (parent tchr. cmty. partnerships com., speech pathologist alt. bldg. rep., 2006-, spl. edn com., 2004—), Barton Speech Pathologists, Bruce Speech Pathologists, Marquette U. Alumni Assn. Baptist. Avocation: writing inspirational songs and poetry. E-mail: dyese@mail.milwaukee.k12.wi.us.

DYER, ARLENE THELMA, retail company owner; b. Chgo., Oct. 23, 1942; d. Samuel Leo Sr. and Thelma Arlene (Israel) Lewis; m. Don Engle Dyer, July 3, 1965 (div. 1970); 1 child, Artel Terren. Cert. in mgmt. effectiveness, U. So. Calif., 1987; cert. Ryan Designated Subjects, UCLA, 2000. Cmty. resource rep. Calif. State Employment Devel. Dept., LA, 1975-76, spl. projects rep., 1976; employment svcs. rep. Culver City, Calif., 1977; contract writer LA, 1976-80; employment program rep., 1980—; pres. Yabba and Co., LA, 1981-83; pres., designer, cons. Spiritual Ties Custom Neckwear, LA, 1985—; pres. Dyer Custom Shirts, Blouses and Suits, Beverly Hills, Calif., 1988—; contract writer LA Watts Times, 2002; designer Sweet Thoughts & Inspirations, 2003—. Founder self-evaluation seminar, MAMA, 2006; pres. MYSELF, Inc., 1998. Author: Who Are You and What Are You All About?, 1994, Escaping to the Workplace, 1996, I Got the Job!.Now What?, 1998, You Got the Job?.Now What?, 1999, How Was Your Day, 2005, TVGuestpert, 2006; co-author: 101 Great Ways to Improve Your Life, vol. II; exhibited in fashion shows, Calif., 1984—; radio personality, 1995 Vol. Big Sister Gwen Bolden Found., LA, 1986, Juvenile Hall, 1996; mem. Operation PUSH, Chgo., 1983, Mahogany Cowgirls & Co.; program chair Black Advs. in State Svc., 1987—; leader Girl Scouts U.S., LA, 1982, LA Urban League; spirit team leader Calif. Spl. Olympics; mem. Big Sisters of LA. Recipient IRWIN award, 1998; named One of God's Leading Ladies, 2002. Mem. NAACP (Beverly Hills-Hollywood chpt.), Nat. Alliance Homebased Businesswomen (v.p., program chair 1987), NAFE, Nat. Spkrs. Assn. (greater LA chpt.), Calif. State Employees Assn., Greater LA C. of C., Kiwanis Club (dir.), U. So. Calif. Alumni Assn., LA Urban League, Black Women's Forum. Democrat. Avocations: travel, reading, bicycling, roller skating. Office Phone: 323-754-6749. E-mail: arlenedyer@ugotthejob.com, arlene@arlenetdyer.com.

DYER, DENA JANAN, writer; b. Dumas, Tex., July 22, 1970; d. Rayford Allen and Sue Layne Ratliff; m. Carey Wade Dyer, July 8, 1995; children: Jordan, Jackson. BA, Baylor U., Waco, Tex., 1993. Missionary Home Mission Bd., Atlanta, 1993—95; newswriter S.W. Sem., Fort Worth, Tex., 1995—96; freelance writer Granbury, Tex., 1996—. Tchr. drama Granbury (Tex.) Opera Ho., 1998—2001, Fine Arts Acad., Fort Worth, 1999—2000. Actor: Granbury (Tex.) Theater, 1999—2003; author: Grace for the Race, 2004; co-author: The Groovy Chicks Road Trip to Peace, 2006. Mem. women's ministry coun. Lakeside Bapt. Ch., Granbury, 2000—; coord. Mothers of Pre-Schoolers, Granbury, 2004—. Mem.: Advanced Writers and Spkrs. Assn., Writers Info. Network, Christian Humor Writers, Fellowship Christian Writers (online moderator 2002—03). Avocations: reading, scrapbooks, movies, decorating. Home: 1520 Berry Patch Ln Granbury TX 76048 Personal E-mail: denadyer@sbcglobal.net.

DYER, STEPHANIE JO, anesthesiologist; b. Oxnard, Calif., Jan. 25, 1957; d. Donald Eugene and Sharron Lee (Brown) Dyer; m. William J. Carpenter, June 1996 (div. Jan. 2002). BSN, U. N.Mex., 1980; MD, U. Nev., Reno and Las Vegas, 1991. RN, N.Mex., Nev. Intern U. Ariz. Affiliated Hosps.; staff nurse Lovelace Med. Ctr., Albuquerque, 1980-82, U. N.Mex. Hosp., Albuquerque, 1982-83; charge nurse St. Mary's Hosp., Roswell, N.Mex., 1983-84; staff nurse Washoe Med. Ctr., Reno, 1984-91; resident in anesthesiology U. N.Mex., Albuwquerque; assoc. prof. anesthesiology U. Tex. Health Sci. Ctr., San Antonio. Cons. Legis. Com. Health-Health Care, Nev. Legislature, Carson City; rschr. Robert Wood Johnson Found. Study, 1987—88; dir., pres. Armadillo Anes Inc.; v.p. health policy Town Hall Comm., Inc. Author: (proposal) Prevention of Adolescent Pregnancy, 1989. Recipient Don Mello award for Community Svc., 1991. Mem. AMA, Am. Med. Women's Assn. (student coord. Reg. XI 1987-88), Physicians for Social Responsibility (chmn. 1988-89), Am. Soc. Anesthesiologists, Soc. Cardiovasc. Anesthesiologists, Tex. Soc. Anesthesiologists. Republican. Roman Catholic. Avocations: gardening, yoga, running, biking, poetry, writing short fiction stories. Home: 12436 FM 1960 Rd W #164 Houston TX 77065-4809 Office: Alice Regional Hospital 5800 Tennyson Pkwy Plano TX 75024-3548

DYER, SUSAN KRISTINE, editor, librarian; b. Coos Bay, Oreg. d. Stanley Keith and Betty Loray (Jameson) D.; m. Michael E. Gehringer. BA, U. Oreg., 1967, MLS, 1968; MBA, Golden Gate U., 1983. Libr. Morrison & Foerster, San Francisco, 1968-75, info. and gen. svcs. mgr., 1975-80; law libr., records mgr. Thelen, Marrin, Johnson & Bridges, San Francisco, 1980-83; libr. World Bank Sectoral Libr., Washington, 1984-89; ops. mgr. Faxon Co. Fed. Divsn., Herndon, Va., 1989-90, dir., 1990-92, nat. sales mgr. fed., 1992-94; fed. ops. mgr. EBSCO Industries, Springfield, Va., 1994-95, gen. mgr., 1995—2000; sr. editor Am. Assn. of U. Women, Washington, 2000—. Author: Manual of Procedures for Private Law Libraries Supplement, 1984. Bd. dirs. Miriam's Kitchen, Washington, 1986-88. Mem. ALA, Am. Assn. Law Librs. (editor Recruitment Checklist 1974, newsletter editor 1976-79, pres. Western Pacific chpt. 1977-79, exec. bd. 1979-82), N.Am. Serials Interest Group, Spl. Librs. Assn., D.C. Libr. Assn. Office: Am Assn U Women 1111 16th St NW Washington DC 20036

DYER-COLE, PAULINE, school psychologist, educator; b. Methuen, Mass., Aug. 20, 1935; d. E. Dewey and Rose Alma (Des Jardins) Dyer; m. Richard Grey, Aug. 1, 1964 (dec. 1977); children: Douglas Richard, Christopher Lachlan, Heather Judith; m. Malcolm A. Cole, July 23, 1983. BS in Edn. and Music, Lowell State Coll., 1957; MEd, Boston State Coll., 1961; EdD, Clark U., 1991. Lic. ednl. psychologist, Mass.; cert. sch. psychologist, Mass.; nat. cert. sch. psychologist. Supr. music and art Merrimac and W. Newburg (Mass.) Pub. Schs., 1957-59; music editor textbooks Allyn & Bacon, Inc., Boston, 1959-64; prof. music West Pines Coll., Chester, NH, 1969-72; sch. psychologist Nashoba Regional H.S., Bolton, Mass., 1979—2001, chair SPED dept., 1995—2001, dir. SPED dept., 1998—2001; child study dept. Worcester (Mass.) Pub. Schs., 2001—. Vis. lectr., then vis. prof. Framingham (Mass.) State Coll., 1980—; dir. psychol. testing Nashoba Regional Sch. Dist., Bolton, Mass., 1980-94. Author: The Play Game Songbook, 1964; singer (soprano): The Worcester Chorus, 2003—. V.p., bd. dirs. Timberlane Devel. Ctr., Plaistow, N.H., 1970-73; founder Friends of Kimi Nichols Devel. Ctr., Plaistow, N.H., 1973; chmn. human svcs. St. Ann Parish, Southborough, Mass., 1974-77, active, 1973-85; citizen amb. del. People to People, China, 1995; active The Regional Lab., Andover, Mass., 1993-2001. Fellow Frances L. Hyatt fellow, Clark U., 1977—79. Mem. Nat. Assn. Sch. Psychologists (cert.), Mass. Assn. Sch. Psychologists, Mass. Tchrs. Assn., People to People Internat. Roman Catholic. Avocations: music, boating, swimming, reading, creative writing. Home: 43 Crowningshield Dr Paxton MA 01612-1253 Office: Child Study Dept 24 Chatham St Worcester MA 01609 Office Phone: 508-799-3175. Personal E-mail: dyercole@charter.net.

DYER-RAFFLER, JOY ANN, retired special education diagnostician, educator; b. Stiltner, W.Va., Aug. 10, 1935; d. Ralph William and Hazel (Terry) Dyer; m. John William Raffler, Sr., Jan. 1, 1993; 1 child from a previous marriage, Keith Brian DeArmond. BA, U. N.C., Chapel Hill, 1969; MEd in Secondary Edn., U. Ariz., Tucson, 1974, MEd in Spl. Edn., 1976. Cert. spl. edn.-learning disabilities, art edn., spl. edn.-emotionally handicapped. Art educator Tucson Unified Sch. Dist., Tucson, 1970-75, tchr. spl. edn., 1975-89, diagnostician spl. edn., 1989—2003, tchr. exceptional edn., 2003—05; ret., 2005. Den mother Cub Scouts Am., Raleigh, N.C., 1968-69. Recipient grant Tucson Unified Sch. Dist., 1977. Mem.: Ariz. Edn. Assn. Avocations: painting, skiing, birdwatching, weightlifting, jogging. Home: 1781 S Desert Vista Dr Tucson AZ 85748

DYKE, BRENDA JOANN, special education educator; b. Indpls., Apr. 28, 1955; d. Charles Edwin Dyke, Nina JoAnn Dyke. BS in Edn., Ball State U., 1977; MS in Edn., Ind. U., 1987. Cert. spl. edn. tchr. Tchr. John Marshall H.S., 1977—79, IPS #68, 1979—81, Broad Ripple H.S., 1981—83, Valle Vista Hosp., 1983—84, Edinburgh H.S., 1984—85, Indian Creek H.S., 1985—, dept chair Trafalgar, Ind., 1987—. Home: 56 Meadow Ct W Whiteland IN 46184 Office: Indiana Creek High Sch 803 Indian Creek Dr Trafalgar IN 46181-8733 Office Phone: 317-878-2110. Office Fax: 317-878-2112. Business E-Mail: bdyke@nhj.k12.in.us.

DYKEMAN, ALICE MARIE, public relations executive; b. Fremont, Nebr., May 18; d. Cecil Victor and Dorothy Lillian (Sillik) Jansen; divorced; children: David Clair, Cinda Cecille Dykeman Nordgren. Pub. relations dir. Meth. Hosp., Dallas, 1961-72; regional pub. info. officer Small Bus. Adminstrn., Dallas, 1972-74; owner Dykeman Assocs. Inc., Dallas, 1974—. Adj. prof. U. Dallas Grad. Sch. Mgmt., Irving, Tex. 1972-78; guest lectr. numerous Univs., and seminars; mem. pub. rels. com. Dallas/Ft. Worth Fed. Exec. Bd., 1973, mem. minority bus. opportunity com., 1974; mem. Gov.'s Coun. on Small Bus., Tex., 1980-81, 500, Inc., 1982-90; chmn. export coun. pub. affairs task force U.S. Dept. Commerce, 1980-83. Contbr. articles to bus., health care and pub. rels. jours. Mem. fgn. visitors com. Dallas Coun. on World Affairs, 1962-98, Dallas Pub. Health Bd., 1972-74, Dallas Urban Rehab. Stds. Bd., 1981-83, Econ. Devel. Adv. Bd., City of Dallas, 1983-86; pres. Concerned Citizens for Cedar Springs, 1982—; bd. dirs. Oak Lawn Forum, 1983-92; mem. exec. com. Oak Lawn Com., 1983-95. Recipient Matrix award Women in Comm., Dallas, 1968, 88, Lifetime Achievement award Religion Communicators Coun., 1991-04. Fellow Pub. Rels. Soc. Am. (accredited, chmn. S.W. dist. 1971-72, bd. dirs. North Tex. chpt. 1966-72, pres. 1969, assembly del. 1970-73, 91, Norm Teich award for contbns. to pub. rels. 2004); mem. North Dallas Fin. Forum (pres. 1991), Nat. Assn. Women Bus. Owners, North Dallas C. of C. (bd. dirs. 1980-82, chmn. networking skills workshop 1990—), co-founder Breakfast Dallas 1994—), Press Club Dallas (bd. dirs. 1981-83, headliner 4 times), SMU Mustang Club (bd. dirs. 1996-99). United Methodist. Office: Dykeman Assocs Inc 4115 Rawlins St Dallas TX 75219-3661 Office Phone: 214-528-2991. Business E-Mail: adykeman@airmail.net.

DYKEMAN, WILMA, writer, educator; b. Asheville, N.C., May 20, 1920; d. Willard J. and Bonnie (Cole) Dykeman; m. James R. Stokely Jr., Oct. 12, 1940; children: Dykeman Cole, James R. III. BS inSpeech, Northwestern U., 1940; LittD, Maryville Coll., 1974; LHD, Tenn. Wesleyan Coll., 1978; DHL (hon.), U. N.C., Asheville, 1997. Lectr. English dept. U. Tenn., Knoxville, 1975-95, adj. prof., 1985-95; now writer, lectr. Columnist Knoxville News-Sentinel, 1962-99; historian State of Tenn., 1980—; nat. lectr. in field. Author 18 books including: The French Broad: A Rivers of America Volume, 1955, The Tall Woman, 1962, Seeds of Southern Change, 1962, The Far Family, 1966, Return the Innocent Earth, 1973; co-author: Neither Black Nor White, 1957, Tennessee: A Bicentennial History, 1976, Tennessee Women: An Infinite Variety, 1993, Explorations, a collection of essays, 1984, others; contbr. articles to nat. mags. and Ency. Brit. Trustee Berea Coll., 1971-95, Phelps Stokes Fund, 1981-91, U. N.C.-Asheville, 1985-91; active Friends of Great Smokies Nat. Park. Guggenheim fellow, 1956-57, NEH fellow, 1976-77; recipient Hillman award, 1957, Disting. So. Writers award So. Festival of Books, 1989; N.C. Gold medal for Contbn. to Am. letters, 1985. Mem. PEN, Authors Guild, So. Hist. Assn., Cosmos Club, Phi Beta Kappa, Delta Kappa Gamma. Home: 282 Clifton Heights Rd Newport TN 37821-2402 also: 189 Lynn Cove Rd Asheville NC 28804-1910

DYKERS, CAROL REESE, communications educator; b. Cherry Point, N.C., Nov. 30, 1946; d. Charles Lawrence and Eleanor Zahniser Reese; m. Newton Adnair Collyar, Feb. 4, 1968 (div. Dec. 1979); m. John Reginald Dykers Jr., May 12, 1984. BA, U. North Tex., 1968; MA, U. N.C., 1992, PhD, 1995. Advt. copywriter WBEU AM-FM Radio, Beaufort, S.C., 1968; reporter Longview (Tex.) Daily News, 1968-69; tchr. Beaufort H.S., 1970; reporter Savannah (Ga.) Morning News, 1970-73; hist. planning and pub. rels. dir. Lowcountry Coun. Govts., Yemessee, S.C., 1973; editor Hilton Head news Savannah Morning News, 1973-74; editor Longview (Tex.) Morning Jour., 1974-76; editor, then editl. writer Charlotte (N.C.) Observer, 1976-86; asst. metro editor Greensboro (N.C.) News and Record, 1986-88; asst. prof. comms. Salem Coll., Winston-Salem, N.C., 1995—. Contbr. chpt. to book: Assessing Public Journalism, 1998. Mem. Assn. for Edn. in Journalism and Mass Comm. (rsch. chair civic journalism 1997-99), Internat. Comm. Assn. (rsch. paper reader), N.C. Cattlemen's Assn. (past bd. dirs.), Am.-Internat. Charolais Assn., Chatham County Cattlemen's Assn. (past bd. dirs.), Kappa Tau Alpha. Democrat. Episcopalian. Avocations: farming, photography. Home: 1783 Alston Bridge Rd Siler City NC 27344-9581 Office: Salem Coll Main Hall 601 S Church St Winston Salem NC 27101-5318 E-mail: dykers@salem.edu.

DYKES, VIRGINIA CHANDLER, occupational therapist, educator; b. Evanston, Ill., Jan. 10, 1930; d. Daniel Guy and Helen (Schneider) Goodman; children: Ron Lee, Chuch Lee Chandler, james R., Jr. BA in Art and Psychology, So. Meth. U., 1951; postgrad. in occupl. therapy, Tex. Women's U., 1953. Dir. occupl. and recreational therapy Baylor U. Med. Ctr., Dallas, 1956-60, 68-89; pvt. practice Dallas, 1989-92; dir. occupl. and recreational therapy Fla. Hosp., Orlando, 1962-65; staff therapist Parkland meml. Hosp., Dallas, 1965-68. Cons. Arthritis Found., 1974-89, benefactor; Fanny B. Vanderkodi lectr. Tex. Women's U., 1993—. Author: (manual) Lightcast II Splints, 1976; Adult Visual Perceptual Evaluation, 1981; contbr. articles to profl. jours. Sponsor Kimball Art Mus.; mem. bd. regents Tex. Woman's U., 2003—05; mem. coord. bd. allied health adv. com. Tex. Coll. and Univ. Sys., 1980—88; bd. dirs. Tex. Arthritis Found., chmn. patient svcs. com., 1985—89, exec. bd. sec.; bd. dirs. Dallas Opera, also women's bd.; bd. dirs. Dallas Arboretum, Theatre III, Fort Worth Opera, Baylor U. Med. Ctr. Found.; chmn. adv. bd. healing environment program Baylor Med. Ctr.; pres. Diana Dean Head Injury Guild, 1992—93. Named Tex. Occupl. Therapist of Yr., 1985, Chi Omega of Yr., 2006; Ann. Virginia Chandler Dykes Leadership award named in her honor, Tex. Women's U. Mem. Tex. Occupl. Therapy Assn. (life mem. award), World Fedn. Occupl. Therapists (participant 8th Internat. Congress, Hamburg, Germany, 1982, del. to 10th European Congress on Rheumatology, Moscow 1983), Boomerang Club (dir. 1971-88), Les Femmes du Monde, Pierian Lit. Club. Home: 3203 Alderson St Dallas TX 75214-3059

DYKSTRA, GRETCHEN, former foundation administrator; b. Staten Island, NY, Aug. 22, 1948; d. Franz and Jean Dykstra; m. Nathan Leventhal, Feb. 12, 1993. BA, U. Wis.; MEd, PhD, Bank St. Coll. Edn. Founding pres. Times Square Bus. Improvement Dist., NYC, 1992—98; with Rockefeller Found., Edna McConnell Clark Found.; dir. comm. and cmty. rels. NYC Charter Revision Commn.; pres., CEO World Trade Ctr. Meml. Found., 2005—06. Bd. dirs. Save the Children. Office Phone: 212-227-7722. Office Fax: 212-227-7929.*

DYKSTRA LYNCH, MARY ELIZABETH, library and information scientist, educator; b. Phila., May 21, 1939; arrived in Canada, 1964; d. Edward and Marietta R. (Kuiper) Heerema: m. Michael F. Lynch, Aug. 12, 1995; children from previous marriage: Mark Edward, Jeffrey Garth. BA, Calvin Coll., 1960; MLS, Dalhousie U., 1970; PhD, Sheffield U., 1986. Head cataloguer Dalhousie U. Libr., Halifax, Nova Scotia, Canada, 1970—74; asst. prof. Sch. Libr. Svc. Dalhousie U., 1974—78, assoc. prof., 1978—82, assoc. prof. Sch. Libr. and Info. Studies, 1983—86, dir. Sch. Libr. and Info. Studies, 1986—95, prof., 1987—97, prof. emeritus, 1997—. Sr. audiovisual libr. Nat. Film Bd. of Can., Montreal, 1982-83, dir. Sch. info. Mgmt., 1986-1995; mem. adv. bd. Sch. Health Records Sci., Halifax Infirmary, 1984-97, Libr. Technician Programme, Kings Regional Vocat. Sch., N.S., 1987-90; mem. Can. Commn. on Cataloguing, 1986-94; mem. working group on stds. for subject access Nat. Archives of Can., 1987-93; mem. Can. Adv. Com. for Internat. Orgn. for Standardization, Tech. Commn., Info. and Documentation, 1991—; mem. nat. info. highway adv. coun. of Can., 1994-95, 96-97; rsch. officer U. Sheffield (Eng.), 1996-97; cons. in field Author: Access to Film Information, 1977, Precis: A Primer, 1985; editor 2 books, several film catalogues; editl. bd. Film Canadiana, 1982-84, Cataloging and Classification Quar., 1980-86, Expert Sys. for Info. Mgmt., 1990-93, Libr. and Info. Sci. Rsch., 1992-96; series editor, occasional papers Sch. Libr. and Info. Studies Dalhousie U., 1986-94; contbr. articles to profl. jours. Pres. Citadel North Neighbourhood Assn., Halifax, 1988; bd. dirs. CANARIE (Canadian Network for Advancement of Rsch., Industry & Edn.), 1996-98, internat. consultants com. World Info. and Comm. Report, UNESCO, Paris, 1998-99, Biblioteca nazionale centrale, Florence, Italy, 2001. Rsch. grantee Dalhousie U., 1976, 80, 90, 96, Social Scis. and Humanities Rsch. Coun., Ottawa, 1987-90. Mem. Can. Libr. Assn. (rep. Can. com. on cataloguing 1986-94), Nova Knowledge, Internat. Soc. for Knowledge Orgn. Office Phone: 902-494-3656. E-mail: m.lynch@sheffield.ac.uk.

DYLAG, HELEN MARIE, health facility administrator; b. Cleve., Oct. 14, 1950; d. Stanley John and Helen Agnes (Jarkiewicz) D. BSN, St. John Coll., Cleve., 1971; MS, Ohio State U., 1973. RN, Ohio. Nurse V.A. Adminstrn. Hosp., Brecksville, Ohio, 1971-72; clin. specialist, psychiat.-mental health nursing Marymount Hosp./Mental Health Ctr., Garfield Heights, Ohio, 1973-78, dir. consultation and edn. dept., 1978-84, dir. Ctr. for Health Styles, 1984-88; adminstrv. dir. Women's Healthcare Ctr./St. Luke's Hosp., Cleve., 1988-90; adminstrv. dir. dept. of psychiatry MetroHealth Sys, Cleve., 1990-97; CEO FarWest Ctr., Westlake, Ohio, 1997—. Contbg. author: Nursing of Families in Crisis, 1974, Distributive Nursing Practice: A Systems Approach to Community Health, 1977; producer and host "Health Styles" TV Talk Show, 1987-88; contbr. articles to profl. jours. Trustee The Stroke Assn. of Ohio, Cleve., 1990-91; mem. Women of Achievement com., Women's City Club, Cleve., 1989-91; officer, bd. dirs. The Littlest Heroes, Inc., 2000—. Recipient award Greater Cleve. Hosp. Assn., 1981, Innovator award Am. Hosp. Assn./Ctr. for Health Promotion, 1985, Disting. Women Healthcare award Healthcare Monitor and Vis. Nurse Assn. Cleve., 2000, Woodruff prize Excellence Behavioral Health, 2005, Lifetime Achievement award Nat. Coun. for Cmty. Behavioral Healthcare, 2006. Mem. Assn. Mental Health Adminstrs., Am. Coll. Healthcare Execs., Healthcare Adminstrs. Assn. of Northeast Ohio, Sigma Theta Tau. Avocations: interior decorating, gardening, jazz, travel, exercise. Office: FarWest Ctr 29133 Health Campus Dr Cleveland OH 44145-5256

DYNEK, KATHLEEN MARIE, elementary school educator; d. Thomas P. and Mariana Sokalski; m. Christopher Joseph Dynek, June 29, 1991; children: Thomas A., Theodore J., Anthony E. BS in Elem. Edn., No. Ill. U., 1990. Elem. tchr. St. Tarcissus, Chgo., 1991—96, Queen of All Saints, Chgo., 2002—. Contbr. articles to profl. jours. Mem.: ASCD (assoc.), Internat. Reading Assn. (assoc.), Nat. Coun. for Social Studies (assoc.). Home: 8839 Mason Morton Grove IL 60053 Office: Queen of All Saints 6230 N Lemont Chicago IL 60646 Office Phone: 773-736-0567. Personal E-mail: dynek3@comcast.net.

DYRUD, GRACE BEATRICE, psychology professor; b. Red Wing, Minn., Jan. 2, 1935; d. Charles Julius and Viola Margaret Peterson; m. Keith Paul Dyrud, Mar. 19, 1966; children: David, Lara, John, Leah, Lars, Mary. BA, U. Minn., 1957, PhD, 1963. Lic. psychologist, Minn. Faculty mem. River Falls (Wis.) Coll., 1960-62; rsch. scientist Inst. of Child Devel., U. Minn., Mpls., 1958-62; prof. dept. psychology Augsburg Coll., Mpls., 1962—; writer K-12 math-sci. Minnemast, Inst. of Tech., U. Mpls., 1963-68. Author: Developmental Abnormal, 1966; co-editor: (with Keith P. Dyrud) Gates of Hell, 2003; contbr. articles to profl. publs. and confs. Pres. The Park Bugle, St. Paul, 2002. Grad. sch. fellowship dept. psychology U. Minn., 1958-60; faculty-student collaboration grants Augsburg Coll., 1998-2002. Mem. APA, Assn. Psychol. Sci., Midwestern Psychol. Assn. Avocations: art, photography, music, science, outdoor activities. Office: Augsburg Coll 2211 Riverside Ave Minneapolis MN 55454-1350 Office Phone: 612-330-1190.

DYSON, ESTHER, editor-in-chief; b. Zurich, Switzerland, July 14, 1951; d. Freeman John and Verena Esther (Huber) D. BA in economics, Harvard U., 1972. Reporter Forbes Mag., N.Y.C., 1974-77, columnist, 1987—; v.p. New Ct. Securities, N.Y.C., 1977-80, Oppenheimer & Co., N.Y.C., 1980-82; editor Rosen Electronics Letter, 1982; founder, owner, chmn. EDventure Holdings, Inc. (acquired by CNET Networks 2004), 1983—2004; editor at large CNET Networks, 2004—. Founding chmn. ICANN, 1998—2000; bd. dirs. EverNote Corp., 2006—. Author: Release 2.0: A Design for Living in the Digital Age, 1997; columnist Release 3.0, N.Y. Times syndicate; moderator ann. Personal Computer Forum; contbr. articles to profl. jours. Trustee Glasses for Humanity, Nat. Endowment for Democracy. Mem. Women's Forum N.Y., Assn. Data Processing Svc. Orgns., Software Pubs. Assn., ICANN (mem. reform com., 2004). Avocation: swimming. E-mail: edyson@release1-0.com.*

DYTELL, RITA SCHER, health psychology educator, researcher, administra; b. NYC, May 9, 1943; d. Lou and Lisa (Nagel) Scher; m. Robert M. Dytell, Jan. 30, 1965; 1 child, Lorin Beth. BA, CCNY, 1964; PhD, CUNY, 1970. Lectr. CCNY, 1966-68; sr. rsch. scientist Deafness Rsch. and Tng. Ctr. NYU, 1970-71; adj. asst. prof. Bklyn. Coll., John Jay Coll., Marymount Manhattan Coll., NYC, 1972-74; asst. prof. psychology NY Inst. Tech., Old Westbury, 1974-81; analytical rsch. cons., 1981—; mem. grad. adj. faculty dept. communication Iona Coll., NYC, 1984-85; mem. adj. faculty C.W. Post campus LI U., Brookville, NY, 1984—; prof. psychology, dir. Allied Health Studies programs Coll. Mt. St. Vincent, Riverdale, NY, 1985—. Author: (with others) Work and Family: Theory, Research and Application, 1989, Human Stress, vol. 4, 1990; author conf. papers; contbr. articles to profl. jours. Faculty rsch. grantee Am. Assn. Engring. Edn./Naval Health Rsch. Ctr., summers 1989-90. Mem. AAUP, APA, Soc. Behavioral Medicine, Soc. the Psychol. Study Social Issues, Sigma Xi. Office: Allied Health Studies Dept Psychology Riverdale NY 10471 Office Phone: 718-405-3788. E-mail: rita.dytell@mountsaintvincent.edu.

DZIEWANOWSKA, ZOFIA ELIZABETH, pharmaceutical executive; b. Warsaw, Nov. 17, 1939; came to U.S., 1972; d. Stanislaw Kazimierz Dziewanowski and Zofia Danuta (Mieczkowska) Rudowska; m. Krzysztof A. Kunert, Sept. 1, 1961 (div. 1971); 1 child, Martin. MD, U. Warsaw, 1963; PhD, Polish Acad. Sci., 1970. MD recert. U.K., 1972, U.S., 1973. Asst. prof. psychiatry U. Warsaw Med. Sch., 1969—71; sr. house officer St. George's Hosp., U. London, 1971—72; assoc. dir. Merck Sharp & Dohme, Rahway, NJ, 1972—76; vis. assoc. physician Rockefeller U. Hosp., N.Y.C., 1975—76; adj. asst. prof. psychiatry Cornell U. Med. Ctr., N.Y.C., 1978—; v.p., global med. dir. Hoffmann-La Roche, Inc., Nutley, NJ, 1976—94; sr. v.p., dir. global med. affairs Genta Inc., San Diego, 1994—97; sr. v.p. drug devel. and regulatory Cypros Pharms. Corp., Carlsbad, Calif., 1997—99; pres., med. dir. New Drug Assocs., La Jolla, Calif., 1999—; sr. v.p. clin. and regulatory Maxia Pharms, San Diego, 2001—02; v.p. clin. rsch. Ligand Pharm, Inc., San Diego, 2002—. Lectr. in field. Contbr. articles to profl. publs. Bd. dirs Royal Soc. Medicine Found.; mem. alumni coun. Cornell U. Med. Ctr. Recipient TWIN Honoree award for Outstanding Women in Mgmt., Ridgewood (N.J.) YWCA, 1984. Mem. AMA, AAAS, Am. Soc. Pharmacology and Therapeutics, Am. Coll. Neuropsychopharmacology, N.Y. Acad. Scis., PhRMA. (vice chmn. steering com. med. sect., chmn. internat. med. affairs com., head biotech. working group), Royal Soc. Medicine (U.K.), Drug Info. Assn. (Woman of Yr. award 1994), Am. Assn. Pharm. Physicians. Roman Catholic. Achievements include original research on the role of the nervous system in the regulation of respiratory functions, research and development and therapeutic uses of many new drugs, pharmaceutical medicine and biotechnology; molecular biology derived as well as conventional products including antisense, interferon efficacy in cancer, virology and AIDS and drugs useful in cardiovascular, immunological, neuropsychiatric, infectious diseases, and others; impact of different cultures on medical practices and clinical research; drug evaluation and development management strategies of pharmaceutical industries; treatments against cardiac and brain ischemia, cytoprotection.

EADS, PENNI DAUN, music educator; b. Montpelier, Idaho, Oct. 29, 1960; d. Donald J. and Wanda Beth (Densley) Sparks; m. Thomas Andrew Eads, Dec. 21, 1984; children: Michael, Perry, Malena, James, Autumn, Reina, Rey, Joseph, Benjamin, Hyrum, Jonathan. AAS, Ricks Coll., 1981; BMus in Piano Performance, Utah State U., 1983. Piano instr. Ricks Coll., Rexburg, Idaho, 1979-81, Utah State U. Youth Conservatory, Logan, 1981—83; pvt. practice, 1984—; vocal, dance and performance dir. Sunshine Generation, Inc., Dayton, Ohio, 1996—99. Advisor skin, hair care and cosmetics, dir. nutrition and house cleaning products Sunrider Internat., 1987— Missionary LDS Ch., Minn., 1983-84. Scholar Ricks Coll., 1979-81, Utah State U., 1981-83. Mem. Music Tchrs. Nat. Assn., Relief Soc. (tchr. 1979—, pianist 1979—). Avocations: nutrition, reading, walking, gardening, water and dance aerobics. Home: 203 E 1400 S Kaysville UT 84037 Office Phone: 801-451-5482. E-mail: tpeads@gmail.com.

EAGAN, MARIE T. (RIA EAGAN), chiropractor; b. Rockville Ctr., N.Y., June 17, 1952; d. John F. and Mary (Ebner) E. BA, Goddard Coll., 1975; D in Chiropractic Medicine, N.Y. Chiropractic Coll., 1983. Pvt. practice chiropractic medicine, N.Y.C., 1983—. Chiropractic examiner N.Y. State Bd. Chiropractic, 1995. Mem.: Internat. Chiropractic Assn., Am. Chiropractic Assn. Democrat. Office: 20E Vanderventer Ave Ste 100 Port Washington NY 11050 Office Phone: 516-944-9460.

EAGLE, KAREN SUE, special education educator; d. John William and Dorothy May Craig; m. Harold Bradley Eagle, July 26, 1986; children: Kimberly Renee, Brandon Harold, Kelly Lynn. MA in Spl. Edn., Coll. Grad. Studies Inst., W.Va., 1984; MA in Ednl. Adminstrn., Marshall U., W.Va., 1995. Cert. tchr. spl. edn. W.Va., ednl. adminstr. W.Va. Libr. aide Pub. Libr., Jeannette, Pa., 1974—77; group homeworker Westmoreland Group Homes, Greensburg, Pa., 1977—81; spl. edn. tchr. Summers County Sch. Sys., Hinton, W.Va., 1981—2000, prin. elem. sch., 2000—02, spl. edn. specialist, 2006—. Mem. steering com. Summers County Bd. Edn., Hinton, W.Va., 2000—; state trainer SAT W.Va. State Dept. Edn., Charleston, 2001—; mem. Continuing Monitoring Com., Hinton, W.Va., 2004—. Dir. W.Va. Spl. Olympics, Hinton, 1982—87; troop leader, camp counselor Girl Scouts, Hinton, W.Va., 1998—; vol. Summers Co. Energy Express Reading Program, Hinton, W.Va., 2005—06; asst. leader, camp counselor 4-H County Level, Hinton, W.Va., 2005—; Sunday Sch. tchr. St. Patrick's Cath. Ch., Hinton, W.Va., 1981—2000, 2005—. Mem.: W.Va. Edn. Assn. Avocations: landscaping, quilting, reading, camping, hiking. Office: Summers Mid Sch 400 Temple St Hinton WV 25951

EAGLEEYE-LORD, AMY, writer, editor; d. Jack W. and Lynn C. Eagleeye; m. William N. Lord; 1 child, Daisy R. Lord. BA, U. Toledo, 1988—93. Tech. editor Am. Prep. Inst., Killeen, Tex., 1998—2000; medical editor Pro ED Comm., Inc., Beachwood, Ohio, 2001; assoc. writer, editor Am. Greetings Corp., Cleve., 2005—. Office: American Greetings Corp One American Rd Cleveland OH 44144

EAKER, SHERRY ELLEN, editor; b. NYC, Nov. 30, 1949; d. Ira and Lee (Eisenberg) Eaker. BA, Queens Coll., 1971, MS, 1976. Tchr. art, English N.Y.C. Bd. Edn., 1971-76; editor-in-chief Back Stage, The Actor's Resource, N.Y.C., 1977—2006, editor-at-large, 2006—. Editor, compiler Handbook for Performing Artists: The How-to and Who-to-Contact Reference for Actors, Singers, Dancers, 1989, rev. edit., 1991, 1995, 2004, The Cabaret Artist's Handbook-Creating Your Own Act in Today's Liveliest Theatre Setting, 2000. Mem. Drama Desk (sec. 1984-87, v.p. 1987-91), Am. Theatre Critics Assn., Nat. Music Theater Network (bd. dirs.), Nat. Theatre Conf., League Profl. Theatre Women, NY Coalition Profl. Women in Arts and Media (spl. adv.), Inst. Outdoor Drama (adv. coun.), Manhattan Assn. Cabarets, NY Women in Film and TV, Nat. Music Theatre Network (bd. dirs). Avocations: theater, cabaret. Office: Back Stage 770 Broadway New York NY 10003-9595

EALY, CYNTHIA PIKE, artist, real estate agent; b. Eveleth, Minn., Apr. 13, 1932; d. Robert Sheldon Pike and Lila Mary Saari; m. Donald Rae Ealy, Dec. 14, 1952; children: Elizabeth, Dennis, Jonathan, Richard. Student, Coll. of Ams., Mexico City, 1950-52, U. So. Calif., 1952-53. Actress, Mexico City, 1950-52; owner Woodland World Travel, Tarzana, Calif., 1965-70; decorator Ridgewood, NJ, 1970-71; artist, 1972—; realtor, 1987—. Bd. dirs., pres. Rep. Women's club, Woodland Hills, Calif., 1964-69; active Internat. Sch. of Brussels, 1975-80; co-chmn. Reps. Abroad, Europe, 1978-82. Recipient Outstanding Svc. award Am. Women's Club of Brussels, 1984. Mem. Sierra Artists Network, Niguel Art Assn. of Orange County. Avocation: instructing french language and cuisine. also: 27142 Paseo Del Este San Juan Capistrano CA 92675-4927

EANES, JANET TERESA, elementary school educator, music educator; b. Panama City, Fla., Sept. 26, 1955; d. Kenneth O. and Arthalia Claggion Brown; m. Ralph Derwin Eanes, Jr., June 10, 1982; children: Krystle Meggan, Kimberly Miriam. Student, St. Augustine's Coll., 1974—75, Tidewater C.C., Portsmouth, Va., 1975—76; BS in Music, Norfolk State U., 1981. Cert. collegiate profl. edn. K-12 music Va. Piano instr. YMCA, Raleigh, NC, 1974—75; recreation aide Portsmouth (Va.) Pks. and Recreation, 1976—77; youth choir dir. Mt. Calvery Bapt., Portsmouth, 1978—80; pharmacy technician Farmco Pharmacy, Norfolk, 1983—85; adminstrv. asst. Langley AFB, Hampton, Va., 1986—88, Army Corp Engr., Norfolk, 1985; data entry clk. Hampton Social Svcs., 1989—90; pharmacy technician VA Hosp., Hampton, 1990, Revco Pharmacy, Hampton, 1990—91; elem. music tchr. Newport News (Va.) Pub. Sch., 1991—. Sunday sch. tchr. Sixth Mount Zion Bapt., Hampton, 1999. Mem.: NEA (lobbyist 1999—2000), Music Educators Nat. Conf., Alpha Kappa Alpha (rec. sec. 1977—79). Avocations: piano, computers, gardening, cooking, bowling. Office: Newport News Pub Schs Newport News VA 23606

EAPPEN, DEBORAH S., ophthalmologist; b. Chgo., Feb. 28, 1965; d. Jerome Charles and Wilma Marian Spellman; m. Sunil Eappen, June 30, 1990; 4 children. MD, U. Ill. Chgo., 1991. Resident ophthalmology New Eng. Eye Ctr., Tufts U., New Eng. Med. Ctr., Boston, 1992—95; ophthalmologist Harvard Vanguard Med. Assocs., Boston, 1995—. Attending ophthalmologist Mass. Eye and Ear Infirmary, Boston, 1995—. Mem. adv. bd., spokesperson Prevention Shaken Baby Syndrome Am. Acad. Ophthalmology, 1997—; pres. Matty Eappen Found., Chgo., 2005; spokesperson Organ Donation. Recipient Victim Advocate award, State of Mass., 2001, Ophthalmology Resident award, New Eng. Eye Ctr., 1995; scholar, U. Ill. Sch. Medicine, 1991. Mem.: Mass. Soc. Eye Physicians and Surgeons, New Eng. Ophthalmologic Soc. Democrat. Roman Catholic. Avocations: photography, running, nature conservation. Office: Harvard Vanguard Med Assocs 230 Worcester St Wellesley MA 02481

EARHART, EILEEN MAGIE, retired elementary school educator, retired child and family life educator; b. Hamilton, Ohio, Oct. 21, 1928; d. Andrew J. and Martha (Waldorf) Magie; m. Paul G. Earhart; children: Anthony G., Bruce P., Daniel T. BS, Miami U., Oxford, Ohio, 1950; MA in Adminstrn. and Ednl. Services, Mich. State U., 1962, PhD in Edn., 1969; H.H.D. (hon.), Miami U., Oxford, Ohio, 1980. Tchr. home econs. W. Alexandria (Ohio) Schs., 1950-51; elementary tchr. Waterford Twp. Schs., Pontiac, Mich., 1958-65, reading specialist, 1965-67; prof., chmn. family and child ecology dept. Mich. State U., East Lansing, 1968-84; prof., head dept. home and family life Fla. State U., Tallahassee, 1984-89; ret., 1989. Author: Attention and Classification Training Curriculum; co-editor spl. issue of Family Relations, 1984; contbr. chpts. to profl. jours., books. Mem. adv. bd. Lansing Com. on Children's TV, Family/Sch./Cmty. Partnership Project, Tallahassee; bd. dirs. Women's Resource Ctr., Grand Rapids, Mich., Wesley Found., Fla. State U., 1989-99; mem. campus ministries bd. Fla. A&M U., 1995-98; Sunday sch. tchr. Haines City United Meth. Ch., 2001--; mem. Mich. Gov.'s Task Force on Youth. Mem. Nat. Coun. Family Rels. (pres. Assn. of Couns. 1987-88, bd. dirs. 1986-88, chair nat. meeting local arrangements 1992), Fla. Coun. Family Rels. (pres. elect 1985-86, pres. 1986-87), Nat. Assn. Edn. Young Children, Assn. Childhood Edn. Internat., Am. Home Econs. Assn. (named AHEA leader at 75th Ann. of Assn. 1984), Internat. Fedn. Home Econs., Mich. Home Econs. Assn. (pres. 1980-82), Fla. Home Econs. Assn. (chmn. scholarship com. 1986-88, dist. chmn. 1990-91, chmn. nominating com. 1991-92, co-chair ann. meeting 1995), Ednl. Rsch. Assn., Killearn United Meth. Ch., United Meth. Women (cir. chair 1993-97, pres. 1994), Phi Kappa Phi (pres. Fla State U. chpt. 1988-89), Delta Kappa Gamma, Omicron Nu, others. Home (Summer): 22 Oak Tree Ct Franklin NC 28734 Home: 2973 Chickasaw Dr Haines City FL 33844-8419 E-mail: emearhart@aol.com.

EARL, HEATHER JO, food company professional; b. Bridgeport, Conn., June 8, 1971; d. Charles Louis and Josephine Ann Pirozzoli BS, U. Fla., 1992, MS, 1995. Lic. real estate salesperson, Fla.; cert. safety profl. Instr., interim safety specialist U. Fla., Gainesville, 1993—95; supr. safety and tng. Tyson Foods, Jacksonville, Fla., 1995—97, mgr. complex safety Union City, Tenn., 1997—98, mgr. area safety Springdale, Ark., 1998—2000, team leader, 2000—05, mgr. health safety ops., 2005—. Cons. Nat. Ag Safety Database/Conceptual Arts, Gainesville, 1996 Author article and instrnl. videos Bd. dirs. ARC, Union City, 1997-98; vol. Habitat for Humanity, Rogers, Ark., 1998-2000; instr. first aid and CPR, Fla., Tenn., Ark., 1994-2000; mem. Nat. Chicken Coun. Safety and Health Com.; vol. For Pets' Sake, Springdale Workforce Tng. grantee, 1997 Mem. Am. Soc. Safety Engrs. (editor Ark. chpt. newsletter, profl., chpt. sec. 2005-06, v.p. 2006—, Safety Profl. of Yr. award, 2006, NAOSH Champion award 2006), Alpha Zeta. Avocations: antiques, golf. Office: Tyson Foods PO Box 2020 Springdale AR 72765-2020 Business E-Mail: heather.earl@tyson.com.

EARL, LOIS MARIE, medical/surgical and home health nurse; b. Boise, Idaho, Oct. 8, 1951; d. James Edward and Lois Marie (Starr) Perfect; m. Dean O. Earl, Sept. 11, 1982; children: Kelli, Jeremy. Diploma, Boise State Coll., 1972. LPN; cert. in telemetry, intravenous therapy, BCLS. Medivac and flight detachment nurse Idaho N.G., Boise; nurse in stepdown CCU Intermountain Critical Care, Salt Lake City; charge nurse in infection control CareWest Clearfield, Utah; geriatric nurse. With Utah Army N.G., 1973-90. Home: 1521 Owl Ln Brisbane CA 94005-4217

EARL, MARTHA FRANCES, librarian, researcher; b. Washington, Aug. 18, 1956; d. Jefferson Davis Earl, Ruby Smith; m. Walter Robert Gawryla; 1 child, Frank Gawryla; m. Stephen Jack Cobert (div. Aug. 6, 1984). BS, U. Tenn., 1978, MS in Libr. Sci., 1985. Cert. seconary edn. Sci. tchr. First Assembly Christian Sch., Memphis, 1979—80; libr. clk. Memphis State U., 1980—81; sr. libr. asst. U. Tenn., Knoxville, 1981—87; reference libr. Meharry Med. Coll., Nashville, 1987—90; head of reference East Tenn. State U., Coll. Medicine Libr., Johnson City, Tenn., 1990—97; reference coord. U. Tenn. Grad. Sch. Med., Knoxville, 1997—. Cons. Indian Path Hosp., Kingsport, 1990—94, N.E. Tenn. Rehab. Hosp., Johnson City, 1992—97, Morristown Hamblen Hosp., 1993—97, N.E. Tenn. Area Health Edn. Ctr., Greeneville, 1994—98, East Tenn. State U., Johnson City, 2001—; mem. adv. bd. Tenn. Adv. Coun. on Librs., Nashville, 1998—99. Author: (book) Bibkit #9: Managed Care: A Guide to Information Sources, 2000; contbr. chapters to books, revs. to publs., articles to profl. jours. Organizer Tenn. Libr. Legislative Day, 1999—2001; historian Alpha Phi Omega Svc. Fraternity, Knoxville, 1976—78; comm. team Ebenezer United Meth. Ch., Knoxville, 1998—2001, cmty. analysis team, 2006; libr. First United Meth. Ch., Bristol, 1994—97, Holston Chapel United Meth. Ch., Knoxville, 1973—78, Sunday sch. tchr., 1972—78. Grantee Grateful Med. Outreach grant, Nat. Libr. Medicine, 1990—92, Exhibit grant, Nat. Network Librs. Medicine, 1994, 1996, 2003—05, Internet Tng. grant, Nat. Libr. Medicine, 1997—98, Access to Electronic Info. for the Pub. grant, NIH, 2001—02, Physicians Med. Edn. Resource Fund, 2001—04; scholar Nat. Alumni scholar, U. Tenn. Nat. Alumni Found., 1974—78, Roddy Mfg., 1974, 1978, Disting. Alumni scholar, U. Tenn. SIS2006. Mem.: ALA (chpt. rels. coun. 1998—99), Med. Libr. Assn. (Brodman com. for excellence in acad. health scis. libr. 1995—97, So. chpt. rsch. com. chair 1997—98, So. chpt. sec. 1999—2000, program com. leadership and mgmt. sect. 2000—01, R&D and demonstration project jury chair 2000—01, Kronick jury chair 2001—02, So. chpt. comm. com. 2001—, chpt. leadership grant com. 2004—06, chair 2005—, books panel 2006—, Rsch. award South Ctrl. chpt. 2001, 2004, Chpt. award 2004—06), Assn. Coll. and Rsch. Librs. (state affiliate chair 1995—96), Knoxville Area Health Scis. Librs. Consortium (pres. 2001—02), East Tenn. Libr. Assn. (pres. 2003—05), Tenn. Adv. Coun. on Librs. (electronic libr. subcom. 1998—99), Tenn. Health Scis. Librs. Assn. (membership chair 1998—2000), Tri-Cities Health Scis. Librs. Consortium (chair 1994), Tenn. Libr. Assn. (coll. and univ. librs. sect. chair 1996—97, libr. editl. rev. bd. 1996—, pres. 1998—99, conf. com. program chair 1998—2000, assoc. pres. 1999, ad hoc com. on staffing 2000—01, chair strategic planning 2000—03, publs. bd. chair 2003—, Appreciation award 1999, 2002, Centennial award 2002), Tennshare (TELII steering com. 2002—04, chmn. long range planning 2002—04), U. Tenn. Sch. Info. Sci. Alumni Bd. (mentoring subcom. and mem.-at-large 2001—06, chair 2006—, Disting. Alumni award 2006), Pi Lambda Theta, Gamma Beta Phi. Methodist. Avocations: reading, walking, swimming, movies, travel. Office: Univ Tenn Grad Sch Medicine 1924 Alcoa Hwy Knoxville TN 37920 Office Phone: 865-544-9525. Office Fax: 865-544-9527. Personal E-mail: earlmartha@yahoo.com. Business E-Mail: mearl@utk.edu.

EARL, SISTER PATRICIA HELENE, religious studies educator, director; b. Cleve. d. Warren and Helen McLaughlin Earl. BA, Dunbarton Coll. of Holy Cross, Washington, D.C., 1970; MA, Villanova Univ., Villanova, Pa., 1980; PhD, George Mason Univ., Fairfax, Va., 2003. Cert. Advanced Catehist Diocese of Arlington, basic in Catehetics Notre Dame Inst., Arlington, Va.; lic. Supr. Commonwealth of Va., profl. elem. prin., sec. prin., elem. grades pk-8, English7-12 Commonwealth of Va., Instrl. II Pa. Mem. religious cmty. Sisters, Servants of the Immaculate Heart of Mary, Immaculata, Pa., 1974—; dir. religious edn. Our Lady of Lourdes Parish, Arlington, Va., 1983—85; elem. religion, English tchr. Archdiocese of Phila., Diocese of Arlington, Va., asst. supt. of schs., 1990—2003; elem. religion, English tchr. Diocese of Allentown, Pa.; asst. prof., dir. Cath. sch. leadership program Marymount U., Arlington, 2003—. Mem. prin. search com. Diocese of Arlington, 1990—2003; mem. Arlington Diocesan Sch. Bd., 1990—2003, Notre Dame Acad. Sch. Bd., Middleburg, Va., 1990—2003; dir. Cath. Diocesan partnership adv. bd. Marymount Univ., Arlington, 2004—; mem. vis. team-rep. of Va. dept Edn. Mary Washington Coll., Fredericksburg, Va., 2005; speaker in field. Reader for the Prin. of the Yr. award Pvt. Sch. Divsn., Washington Metropolitan area, 1999, 2002. Mem.: Nat. Cath. Edn. Assn., Assn. for Supervision and Curriculm Devel., Nat. Assn. of Secondary Sch. Prin., Nat. Assn. of Elem. Sch. Prin. Roman Cath. Avocations: piano, guitar, reading, writing. Home: 101 N Spring St Falls Church VA 22046 Office: Marymount Univ 2807 N Globe Rd Arlington VA 22207 Office Phone: 703-284-1517. Office Fax: 703-284-1631. Business E-Mail: patricia.earl@marymount.edu.

EARLE, EUGENIA, music educator; b. Birmingham, Ala., May 2, 1922; d. Paul Hamilton Earle and Rosa Munger; m. Jere Butler Faison, Nov. 26, 1969 (dec.). BA, Birmingham So. Coll., 1943; MA, Columbia U., 1956, PhD, 1979. Instr. Mannes Coll. Music, N.Y.C., 1946—63, Union Theol. Sem. Sch. Sacred Music, N.Y.C., 1963—73, Manhattan Sch. Music, N.Y.C., 1963—73; adj. assoc. prof. Columbia U. Tchrs. Coll., N.Y.C., 1969—. Harpsichordist concerts throughout U.S. Composer: Conversation Pieces, 1972, 18th Century Dances: How to Add Melodic Ornamentation, 1973. Mem.: Coll. Music Soc., Am. Bach Soc., Am. Musicol. Soc. Democrat. Presbyterian. Avocations: hiking, attending concerts, theater. Home: 15 W 84st (9D) New York NY 10024

EARLE, JEAN BUIST, finance company executive, computer company executive; b. Newton, N.J., Oct. 5, 1951; d. Richardson and Jean (Mackerly) Buist; m. Terry Dean Earle, Mar. 4, 1989; children: Morgan, Abigail. AB, Cornell U., 1973; MEd, Coll. William and Mary, 1974; MBA, U. Pa., 1987. Mgr. The Korman Corp., Jenkintown, Pa., 1975-77; v.p. ops. Community Assn. Mgmt. Co., Havertown, Pa., 1977-78; adminstrv. asst. Albert Einstein Med. Ctr., Phila., 1978-83; assoc. adminstr. Meml. Hosp. Burlington County, Mt. Holly, NJ, 1983-87; v.p. Overlook Hosp., Summit, NJ, 1987-95; exec. dir. Summit (N.J.) Child Care Ctrs., Inc., 1995-96; owner, ptnr. Elrae, LLP, Chatham, NJ, 1996—; CFO ECLC of N.J., Chatham, 1998—. Past pres. Family Link of Union and Essex Counties, 1994—96; chmn. Kirby Ctr. YMCA Family Coun., 1996—98. Recipient Diana Cuthbertsen award in health, NJ Statewide Parent Advocacy Network, 2003. Fellow Am. Coll. Healthcare Execs; mem. AICPA, Am. Hosp. Assn., U. Pa. Wharton Sch. Alumni Assn., Cornell Club, Ctr. for Enabling Tech. (trustee 1997-2004, treas. 1999-2004), Chatham Assn. for Support in Edn. (founding mem.) Home: 37 Rose Ter Chatham NJ 07928-1826 Office: ECLC NJ 21 Lum Ave Chatham NJ 07928 Office Phone: 973-635-1705. E-mail: jbearle@hotmail.com.

EARLE, MARY MARGARET, marketing executive; b. Newberry, Mich., June 26, 1947; d. William Loren and Naida Theresa (Ward) E. Student, St. Mary's Coll., Notre Dame, Ind., 1965—67. Cert. employment cons. Receptionist Western Girl World, San Francisco, 1968-69; receptionist, sec. Advanced Memory Systems, Sunnyvale, Calif., 1969-71; career cons. Qualified Pers., Madison, Wis., 1972-75; VIP asst. Summit Sports Arena Grand Open, Houston, 1975, S. Petroleum Gp/OTC, Houston, 1976, Astrodomain Assn., Houston, 1976-77; bus. mgr. Mobile Colo TV Prodn., Houston, 1977-80; broadcast bus. affairs dir. G.D.L. & W. Adv., Houston, 1980-90; broadcast talent cons. Willis, Tex., 1990-93; mktg. cons., pvt. practice Marquette, Mich., 1993-95; pres. IXL Creative-Mktg. Excellence, Marquette, 1996—; cable mktg. cons. Bresnan Comm., Marquette, 1998-2000, Charter Media, 2000—02. Modeling judge Page Parks Sch. Modeling, Houston, 1988-91; cons. industry/union rels. AFTRA/SAG, Houston, 1985-92. Houston mem. Fashion Group, 1989-90; sec. Bluebell Estates Assn., Willis, 1991, pres. 1992; pub. rels. vol. Women's Ctr. seminars, Houston, 1984-85; co-chair/treas. Art on the Rocks, 1999—; bd. dirs. Big Bros./Big Sisters; mem. exec. com. domestic Violence Coalition of Marquette County; bd. dirs. Marquette County Humane Soc. Named Disting. Salesman of Yr. Sales and Mktg. Execs., Madison, 1973, 74. Mem. Adminstrv. Mgmt. Soc. (cons. ofcl. panel 1974), Pers. Adminstrs. Soc., Am. Assn. Advt. Agys. (so. broadcast policy com.), Lake Superior Art Assn. (bd. dirs. 1996—), Ishpeming Art Faire Assn. (pres. 2000—), Rotary (pres. Ishpeming, Mich. 2002-03). Avocations: walking, raising dogs. Home and Office: 612 County Road 480 Marquette MI 49855-9411 E-mail: mmearle@chartermi.net.

EARLE, SYLVIA ALICE, research biologist, oceanographer; b. Gibbstown, NJ, Aug. 30, 1935; d. Lewis Reade and Alice Freas (Richie) E. BS, Fla. State U., 1955; MA, Duke U., 1956, PhD, 1966, PhD (hon.), 1993, Monterey Inst. Internat. Studies, 1990, Ball State U., 1991, George Washington U., 1992, U. R.I., 1996, Plymouth State Coll., 1996; DSc (hon.), Ripon Coll., 1994, U. Conn., 1994. Resident dir. Cape Haze Marine Lab., Sarasota, Fla., 1966-67; research scholar Radcliffe Inst., 1967-69; research fellow Farlow Herbarium, Harvard U., 1967-75, researcher, 1975—; research assoc. in botany Natural History Mus. Los Angeles County, 1970-75; research biologist, curator Calif. Acad. Scis., San Francisco, from 1976; research assoc. U. Calif., Berkeley, 1969-75; fellow in botany Natural History Mus., 1989—; chief scientist U.S. NOAA, Washington, 1990-92, advisor to the adminstr., 1992-93; founder, pres., CEO, bd. dirs. Deep Ocean Engrs., Inc., Oakland, Calif., 1981-90; founder, chmn., CEO Deep Ocean Exploration and Rsch., Oakland, 1992—, bd. dirs., 1992—; advisor SeaWeb, 1996—. Bd. dirs. Dresser Industries, Oryx Energy, Inc.; explorer-in-residence Nat. Geog., 1998; dir., Natl. Geographic Suatainable Seas Expedition, 1998—. Author: Exploring the Deep Frontier, 1980, Sea Change, 1995; editor: Scientific Results of the Tektite II Project, 1972-75; contbr. 100 articles to profl. jours. Trustee World Wildlife Fund U.S., 1976-82, mem. coun., 1984—; trustee World Wildlife Fund Internat., 1979-81, mem. coun., 1981-95; trustee Charles A. Lindbergh Fund, pres., 1990-95; trustee Ctr. Marine Conservation, 1992—, Perry Found., chmn., 1993-95; mem. coun. Internat. Union for Conservation of Nature, 1979-81; corp. mem. Woods Hole Oceanographic Inst., trustee, 1996—; mem. Nat. Adv. Com. on Oceans and Atmosphere, 1980-94. Recipient Conservation Svc. award U.S. Dept. Interior, 1970, Boston Sea Rovers award, 1972, 79, Nogi award Underwater Soc. Am., 1976, Conservation Svc. award Calif. Acad. Sci., 1979, Order of Golden Ark Prince Netherlands, 1980, David B. Stone medal New Eng. Aquarium, 1989, Gold medal Soc. Women Geographers, medal Radcliffe Coll., 1990, Pacon Internat. award, 1992, Dirs. award Natural Resources Coun. Am., 1992, Washburn award Boston Mus. Sci., 1995, Charles A. and Ann Morrow Lindbergh award, 1996, Julius Stratton Leadership award, 1997, Kilby award, 1997, Bal de la Mar Found. Sea Keeper award, 1997, Sea Space Environment award, 1997; Environmental Global Zoo Awd., 1998; U.S. Environmental Hew Awd., 1998; named Woman of Yr. L.A. Times, 1970, Scientist of Yr., Calif. Mus. Sci. and Industry, 1981. National Women's Hall of Fame, 2000. Fellow AAAS, Marine Tech. Soc. (Compass award 1997), Calif. Acad. Scis., Calif. Acad. Sci., Explorers Club (hon., bd. dirs. 1989-94, Lowell Thomas award 1980, Explorers medal 1996); mem. Internat. Phycological Soc. (sec. 1974-80), Phycological Soc. Am., Am. Soc. Ichthyologists and Herpetologists, Am. Inst. Biol. Scis., Brit. Phycological Soc., Ecol. Soc. Am., Internat. Soc. Plant Taxonomists. Planted a flag in the seafloor off Hawaii to mark the first solo dive to 1,250 feet without a support vessel, wearing hardened diving suit "JIM"; Set and still holds the depth record for women's solo dive:3,300 feet; designed a manned sub capable of diving to 36,000 feet; lived for two weeks underwater with an all-female crew to test the effects of prolonged subsea habitation. Home and Office: 12812 Skyline Blvd Oakland CA 94619-3125 Personal E-mail: saearle@aol.com.

EARLES, KATHI AMILLE, pediatrician; b. Washington, Aug. 29, 1963; d. Lucius Chism III and Wilma Jean Earles; m. William Alexander Jackson Ross, July 17, 1993; children: William Alexander III Ross, Jordan Nicole Ross, Riley Marie Ross. BA, Howard U., 1986, MD, 1991; MPH, UCLA, 1998. Diplomate Am. Bd. Pediats. Physician CIGNA Healthcare, L.A., 1991—99; asst. clin. prof. Morehouse Sch. Medicine, Atlanta, 1999—, assoc. dir. pediat. residency, 1999—, faculty devel. preceptor, 1999—. Contbr. chpt. to book, article to med. jour. Trustee Zion Hill Bapt. Ch., Atlanta, 2002—. Named Leading African Am. Physician, Black Enterprise mag., 2001; grantee, NIH, Nat. Ctr. for Minority of Health Disparities Rsch., 2001—; scholar, Morehouse Sch. Medicine Dept., 2000—. Mem.: Ga. State Med. Assn., Am. Assn. Pediats., Assn. Pediat. Program Dirs., Atlanta Med. Assn., Nat. Health Execs. Assn., Nat. Med. Assn. (scholar 1992). Democrat. Achievements include research in effects of media on childhood obesity; effects of media on sexual behavior of youth; effects of media on alchol and tobacco consumption on youth; effects of the media violence on youth. Avocations: ceramics, basketball, jazz, reading, cooking.

EARLEY, DEBORAH LORAINE, education educator, researcher; b. Orlando, Fla., Apr. 12, 1970; d. Claris M and Don D Deily (Stepfather), LaVerne M Earley. BA, Fla. Atlantic U., 1990—92, Med, 1994—96, EdD, 1999—2002. Professional Teaching License Fla. Dept. of Edn., 1992. Tchr. Sch. Bd. of St. Lucie County, Ft. Pierce, Fla., 1992—99; adj. faculty Indian River C.C., Ft. Pierce, Fla., 1997—2000; adj. faculty and u. supr. Fla. Atlantic U., 1999—2002, dir., intensive tchr. edn. and devel., 2002—03, dir. of assessment & program evaluation, coll. of edn., 2003—. Program evaluator Fla. Dept. of Edn., 2003—. Contbr. articles to profl. jours. Altar server and lector St. Mark the Evangelist Cath. Ch., 1996—2005. Nominee Disting. Paper, Fla. Edn. Rsch. Assn., 2002, 2003, 2004; grant, Fla. Dept. of Edn., 2004. Mem.: Fla. Assn. of Tchr. Educators, Assn. for Supervision & Curriculum Devel., Internat. Reading Assn. Conservative-R. Catholic. Avocations: golf, boating. Office: Florida Atlantic Univ 500 NW California Blvd CO 116 Port Saint Lucie FL 34986 Office Phone: 772-873-3351. E-mail: dearley@fau.edu.

EARLING, DEBRA MAGPIE, writer, educator; Student, Spokane Falls Cmty. Coll., Univ. Calif., Berkeley; BA, Univ. Washington; MFA in Creative Writing, Cornell Univ., 1991. Assoc. prof., creative writing, Native Am. studies Univ. Mont., Missoula. Author: (novels) Perma Red, 2002 (Am. Book award, 2003, WILLA award, Spur award, Mountains and Plains Bestsellers Assn. award); contbr. chapters to books The Last Best Place: A Montana Anthology, Circle of Women: Anthology of Western Women Writers, Wild Women: Anthology of Women Writers, short stories to Talking Leaves: Contemporary Native American Short Stories. Mem. Confederated Salish and Kootenai Tribes of Mont. Address: Author Mail c/o Penguin USA Publicity 375 Hudson St New York NY 10014 Office Phone: 406-243-4963.*

EARLS, CHRISTINE ROSS, biology professor; d. Donald Joseph and Christine Laforet Ross; m. Richard Theodore Earls, Nov. 21, 1987; children: William, Julie. BS in Biology summa cum laude, Fairfield U., Conn., 1979; MS in Biology, U. Bridgeport, Conn., 1982. Chemist MK Labs., Fairfield, Conn., 1979—80; tchr. sci. Green Farms Acad., 1982—89, dept. chair sci., 1987—89; adj. prof. biology Fairfield U., 1987—2002, vis. instr. biology, 2003—. Contbr. articles to profl. jours. Mem.: Human Anatomy and Physiology Soc., Phi Kappa Phi, Alpha Epsilon Delta. Roman Catholic. Avocations: antiques, reading, piano, painting, drawing. Office: Fairfield U N Benson Rd Fairfield CT 06824-5195

EARLY, BONNIE SUE, piano teacher, music educator; b. Seattle, June 6, 1944; d. Robert Clarence and Arletha Gertrude (Wagner) Berg; m. Kenneth Charles Ko, Aug. 27, 1966 (div. Mar. 1979); children: Eugene H. Ko, Elise Melanie Ko; m. William Wallace Early, Jr., Jan. 11, 1981. Student, Olympic Coll., Bremerton, Wash., 1963-65, U. Wash., Seattle, 1966, U. Utah, 1970-72, West Valley Coll., Saratoga, Calif., 1972-74; BA, Loretto Hts. Coll., Denver, 1982. Comprehensive musicianship cert. Internat. Piano Tchg. Found. Piano tchr. Early Piano Studio, Littleton, Colo., 1981—. Part time tchr. in schs., 1970s and 1980s; adjudicator Nat. Guild Piano Tchrs., 1996—. Ch. musician, accompanying choir, playing keyboard and piano; composer. Bd. dirs. Harvest House for Women, Estes Park, Colo., 1984-94; music coord. Redeemer Temple, 1983-94; chair Littleton/Englewood Piano Guild Ctr., 1999—. Mem. Music Tchrs. Nat. Assn., Colo. State Music Tchrs., Columbina Music Tchrs. Assn. (past pres., v.p.), Foothills Music Tchrs. Assn., Piano Guild, Fedn. Music Clubs, Pacesetters Music Tchrs. Assn. (past pres.). Office: Early Piano Studio 6113 S Cody Way Littleton CO 80123-3286 E-mail: kimamusic@msn.com.

EARLY, DELOREESE PATRICIA See REESE, DELLA

EARNEST-RAHMAN, MICHELLE L., psychologist; b. Peoria, Ill., Apr. 3, 1970; d. Lynn Marie Earnest; m. Muhammed Rezwan Rahman, Nov. 30, 2001; children: Lily Glorious Rahman, Muhammad Sylas Musa Rahman. PsyD, Calif. Sch. Profl. Psychology, Fresno, 2002. Outpatient therapist Valley Child Guidance Clinic, Palmdale, Calif., 2001—03; psychologist Hollygrove Children's Svcs., L.A., 2002—05; therapist Verdugo Hills Autism Project, Calif., 2005—06; psychologist Adolescent Growth Abundant Life, Commerce, 2006—. Consulting psychologist Hollygrove Children's Svcs., L.A., 2002—05; pvt. practice, Santa Clarita, 2005—. Contbr. poetry to anthologies. Mem.: APA, L.A. County Psychol. Assn. Office: Ste 205 27141 Hidaway Ave Santa Clarita CA 91351-4142

EARNEY, MARY K., writer, educator; b. Marfa, Tex., Mar. 2, 1920; d. Hunter Orgain and Fletcher (McKennon) Metcalfe; m. William Harvey Earney (dec. Dec. 1993); children: Craig M., Robert Franklin, John Fletcher, Ann Elizabeth Curtis. BA, U. Tex., 1941; MA, Sal Ross State U., 1969. Clk. West Tex. Utilities, Marfa, 1941, USN, San Diego, 1942-44, O.P.A. Civil Svc., Marfa, 1944-45; newspaper corr., photographer El Paso Times, Ft. Worth Star Telegram, San Angelo Std., El Paso and Ft. Worth, 1953—; tchr. Marfa Ind. Sch. Dist., 1963-73; columnist Big Bead Sentinel, Marfa, 1993-2000. Author: First Find the Courthouse, 1997, Woolgathering, Life in a Little West Texas Town, 2000, For God and Texas, Life of Dr. Francis Asbury Mood, 2001. Mem. NEA, Tex. State Tchrs., Classroom Tchrs. Assn., Retired Tchrs., San Gabriel Writers League, Alpha Phi. Methodist.

EARP, NAOMI CHURCHILL, federal official, lawyer; b. Newport News, Va., Feb. 15, 1950; d. Robert Henry and Naomi (Johnson) Davis; m. Samuel E. Earp, July 19, 1987. BA, Norfolk State U., 1972; MA, Ind. U., 1977; JD, Cath. U., 1982. Bar: Pa. 1985. Social worker City of Norfolk Dept. Welfare, Va., 1972-73, City of Indpls. Employment and Tng., 1973-76; civil rights specialist U.S. Dept. Commerce, Chgo., 1976-79; investigator U.S. Dept. Labor, Washington, 1981-83; pvt. practice as cons. Washington, 1983-85; civil rights specialist U.S. Dept. Navy, Washington, 1985-86; atty. US Equal Employment Opportunity Commn., Washington, 1986-87, vice chmn., 2003—; adminstr. equal opportunity programs USDA, Washington, 1987—. Active Forum Blacks in Agriculture, Washington, 1988, Womens' Action Task Force, Washington, 1988, Nat. Black Rep. Coun. Recipient Am. Jurisprudence award Prepentice Hall, Washington, 1980. Mem. ABA, Pa. Bar Assn., Coun. 100. Republican. Avocations: jogging, biking, dance. Office: US Equal Employment Opportunity Commn 1801 L St NW Washington DC 20507*

EARY, PAMELA HALL, obstetrics nurse, educator; b. Cheverly, Md., Apr. 2, 1967; d. Charles Randall and Lucille B. Hall; children: Glenn, Samuel. BA, U. Va., Charlottesville, 1989; AAS, Piedmont Va. C.C., Charlottesville, 1992; postgrad., Mary Baldwin Coll., Staunton, Va., 2005—. RN Va. Nurse Martha Jefferson Hosp., Charlottesville, 1992—94; instr. Health Occupations Tng. & Devel., Inc., Marion, 1994—97; nurse Wythe County Cmty. Hosp., Wytheville, 1997—99, Va. Ho. Furniture, Atkins, 1999—2000, McKee Foods/Little Debbie, Stuarts Draft, 2000—01, DuPont/DTI, Waynesboro, 2001—03, Augusta Med. Ctr., Fishersville, 2003—. Mem. corp. safety com. Va. Ho. Furniture, 1999—2000. Tutor coord Ulward Bound/Talent Search, Charlottesville, 1986; bd. dirs. Marion Bapt. Ch. Child Devel. Ctr., 1995—96; chmn. student adv. bd. Ulward Bound/Talent Search, Blacksburg, 1984. Mem.: Mensa. Avocations: reading, crafts, water aerobics, interior decorating. Home: 133 Poland St Waynesboro VA 22980

EASLEY, BETSY LEABETH, secondary school educator; b. Wichita, Kans., May 24, 1968; d. Ed E. and Louise Easley (Stepmother). AA, Connors State Coll., Warner, Okla., 1988; BS, Okla. State U., Stillwater, 1993. Cert. tchr. English tchr. Ponca City (Okla.) HS, 1993—. Author: Cargill Consulting's ACT Prep. Youth group asst. St. Mary's Cath. Ch., Ponca City, 2001—06. Mem.: NEA, Ponca City Assn. Classroom Tchrs., Okla. Edn. Assn. Roman Catholic. Office: Ponca City High Sch 927 N 5th Ponca City OK 74604 Office Phone: 580-767-9500 168.

EASLEY, CHERYL EILEEN, nursing educator, department chairman; b. Huntington, W.Va., July 15, 1946; d. Paul Allen and Koneta Seona (Phillips) E. BS, Columbia Union Coll., Takoma Park, Md., 1967; AM, NYU, 1970, PhD, 1989. Pub. health nurse Yonkers (N.Y.) Pub. Health Dept., 1967-68; home care coord. N.Y. Infirmary, N.Y.C., 1969-70; instr. nursing Herbert H. Lehman Coll., CUNY, Bronx, 1971-74; asst. prof. Andrews U., Berrien Springs, Mich., 1974-78, U. Mich. Sch. Nursing, Ann Arbor, 1978-79, interim chmn., grad. program dir. community health nursing, 1980-82, interim asst. dean undergrad. studies, 1983-86; King-Chavez-Parks vis. prof. in women's studies U. Mich., Ann Arbor, 1990; asst. prof. pub. health U. Ill. Coll. Nursing, Chgo., 1989-90; assoc. prof., chmn. dept. community health nursing Coll. Nursing Rush U., Rush-Presbyn. St. Luke's Med. Ctr., Chgo., 1990—, interim assoc. dean ednl. program Coll. Nursing., 1992-93; dir. utilization mgmt. Rush-Presbyn. St. Luke's Med. Ctr., 1993; DON Rush Primary Care Inst., 1994—. Mem. peer rev. panel for advanced nursing edn. program USPHS, Rockville, Md., 1991—; cons. Nat. League for Nursing, N.Y.C., 1988-89. Mem. editorial bd. Jour. Rural Health, 1991-93; contbr. articles to profl. jours., chpts. to books. Chmn. bd. dirs. All Nations Inst. for Social and Econ. Change Inc., Berrien Springs, 1990—; mem. Southwestern Mich. Women's Polit. Coalition, Berrien Springs, 1991—. Grantee HERS Summer Inst. for Women in Higher Edn. Adminstrn., U. Mich., 1981. Mem. APHA (governing coun. pub. health nursing sect. 1980-83, sect. coun. 1986), ANA (cons. 1984-86), Ill. Nurses Assn., Ill. Pub. Health Assn., Sigma Theta Tau, Phi Delta Kappa, Pi Lambda Theta. Adventist. Avocations: reading, handiwork, birding. Office: Rush U Coll Nursing Rush-Presbyn-St Luke's Med Ctr 1743 W Harrison St Chicago IL 60612-3823

EASLEY, JUNE ELLEN PRICE, genealogist; b. Chgo., June 7, 1924; d. Fred E. and Bernadette (Mailloux) Price; m. Raymond Dale Easley, Dec. 24, 1945. Student, McCormack Sch. Commerce, Chgo., 1942—43, Englewood Jr. Coll., 1943—45. Lic. genealogist Assn. Profl. Genealogists. Statis. clk. Arthur Andersen & Co., Chgo., 1968-74; corr. sec. ICG R.R., Chgo., 1974-86; self-employed genealogist-computers Arlington Heights, Ill., 1986-94, Mountain Home, Ark., 1994—2001, Springfield, Mo., 2001—. Editor, typist genealogical books, 1996—. Contbr. religion articles to Daily Herald, 1991; editor romance stories, 1990—, genealogy books, 1996—. Sec. Citizens for Clean Water, Mountain Home, Ark., 1996-98. Mem. AARP (sec. 1997-98), DAR (auditor-treas. Chgo. chpt. 1981-82, rec. sec. Chgo. chpt. 1982-88, Mountain Home ROTC 1995-97, publicity chmn. 1996-97), Huguenot Soc., Nat. Soc. R.R. Bus. Women (newsletter editor 1991-2002), Northwest Suburban Coun. Genealogists (pres. 1988-90, corr. sec. 1990-94), Daus. of War 1812, Daus. of Union Vets. (Civil War). Republican. Avocations: genealogy, writing, antiques, computers, travel. Home and Office: 2315 E Lark St Springfield MO 65804 Office Phone: 417-823-3835. Personal E-mail: juneeasley@alltel.net.

EASLEY, LINDA MARIE, education educator; b. Cottage Grove, Oreg., Mar. 17, 1955; d. Jess C. Easley and Annie M. Gibson; 1 child, Katie. BS in Med. Tech., Northwestern State U. La., Natchitoches, La., 1976; MA in Sci. Edn., La. State U., Baton Rouge, La., 1990, PhD in Curriculum and Instrn., 1992. Tchr. Sunshine H.S., St. Gabriel, La., 1989—91; assoc. prof. Northwestern State U. La., Natchitoches, 1992—2005; tchr. Negreet (La.) H.S., 1998—99; prof. La. State U., Shreveport, La., 2005—. Author: I Have a Story About That: Historical Vignettes to Enhance the Teaching of the Nature of Science, 1992, Physical Science Laboratory Manual, 1992, Living Science, 1995, Cemetary Science, 2005; editor: Soc. Info. Tech. and Tchr. Edn. 2000 Proceedings, 2000, Soc. Info. Tech. and Tchr. Edn. 2001 Proceedings, 2001; contbr. chapters to books, articles to profl. jours. Mem.: La. Sci. Tchrs. Assn., Nat. Sci. Tchrs. Assn., Phi Kappa Phi, Kappa Delta Pi, Phi Delta Kappa. Office: La State Univ Shreveport One University Pl Shreveport LA 71115 Business E-Mail: leasley@lsus.edu.

EASLEY, MARY, retired elementary school educator, state representative; b. Cassville, Mo. m. Truman Easley; children: Michael, Kevin, Lisa Gage. BA in Lang. Arts and Bus., Friends U., Wichita, Kans.; MA, Northeastern Okla. State U., Tahlequah. Rep. Ho. Reps., State of Okla., Okla. City, 1997—. Asst. majority fl. leader Okla. Ho. Reps., Okla. City., 1997—, chair banking and fin. com., 1997—, vice chair subcom. on edn. to appropriations and budget com., 1997—, mem. common edn., energy and utility regulation, and pub, safety and homeland security coms., 1997—. Democrat. Office: 2300 N Lincoln Blvd Rm 302-A Oklahoma City OK 73105 Home and Office: 1360 S 99thE Ave Tulsa OK 74128 E-mail: easleyma@lsb.state.ok.us.

EASLEY, PAULINE MARIE, retired elementary school educator; b. Peoria, Ohio, July 8, 1937; d. Ivan Albert and Helen Margaret (Thompson) Barton; m. Homer Eugene Easley, June 21, 1959; children: David Lynn, Sherryl Lynn Easley Frank. BA in Elem. Edn., Aurora (Ill.) Coll., 1959; MAT, Aurora U., 1987; postgrad., No. Ill. U., 1977-80. Cert. tchr., Ill. Tchr. 2d grade Balt. County Sch. System, 1959-60, Frank Hall Elem./West Aurora Dist., 1960-62; tchr. 1st grade Abraham Lincoln Sch., Aurora, 1962-64; substitute tchr. West Aurora Sch. Dist. 129, Aurora, 1964-65, tchr. 2d grade, 1966-73, tchr. learning ctr., 1973-94; ret., 1994. Adj. instr. Aurora U., 1987-92. Chairperson, deaconess Aurora Advent Christian Ch, 1970, trustee, 1989—94, 1996—98, 2001—02; chair trustee Aurora Advent Christian Ch., 2004—06; libr. Aurora Advent Christian Ch, 2000—; women's fellowship treas. Aurora Advent Christian Ch., Ill., 2000—04; chair mission com. Aurora Advent Christian Ch, 2003—04; co-pres. Aurora Advent Christian Women's Fellowship, 1987—89, treas., 2000—04, mem.-at-large, 2004—; nominating com. Advent Christian Gen. Conf., 2002—; at-large mem. bd. dirs. Women's Home and Fgn. Mission Soc., 1990—95, pres. bd. dirs. (ctrl. region), 1996—2002. Recipient Golden Apple award West Aurora Sch. Dist., 1986. Mem.: West Aurora Edn. Assn. (bldg. rep. 1960—62), Delta Kappa Gamma (2d v.p. Alpha Epsilon chpt. 1992—95, Lambda state orgn. mem. state profl. affairs com. 1993—94, various coms.). Avocations: landscaping, crafts, travel. Home: 82 Raven Dr Aurora IL 60506-4265 Personal E-mail: Pauline@hpeasley.com.

EAST, JANETTE DIANE, marketing consultant; b. Phoenix, Jan. 5, 1950; d. Henry Melvin Clatterbuck and Dorothy (Eakin) Newman; m. John L. East, III, 2003. Student World Campus Afloat, Chapman Coll., 1967-68; BA in Anthropology and Archeology, Ariz. State U., 1972; CNA, Renton Tech. Coll., 1993. Owner, mgr., buyer Walls Galore and Bath Decor, Corvallis, Oreg., 1977-84; mgr., trainer, buyer Bloomingdales, Dallas, 1984-85; mgr. Frederick and Nelson, Seattle, 1986-87; mgr., buyer The Bon Marché, Seattle, 1987-89; mktg. cons. Kinder-Harris, 1989-93; lectr., cons. merchandising and display, 1993—. Intern trainer Oreg. State U., 1981-83. Contbr. articles to profl. jours. Mem. Downtown Mchts. Assn., Corvallis, 1977-84, Oreg. Homebuilders Assn., Corvallis, 1977-84; vol. Make-A-Wish Found., Bailey-Boushay Hospice. Mem. Am. Business Woman's Assn. (Corvallis chpt.); award winning portrait painter. Democrat.

EAST, MARY ANN HILDEGARDE, vocalist; b. Summit, NJ, July 7, 1976; d. Thomas Patrick and Jacqueline Marie McKavitt; m. Joseph Andrew East, Nov. 17, 2001. MusB in Edn., Ind. U., 1999; MusM in Vocal performance, George Mason U., 2005, MusM in Choral Conducting, 2005. Cert. tchr. Va. Gen. music tchr. Sunrise Valley Elem. Sch., Reston, Va., 1999—2000; choral dir. Wash. Irving Mid. Sch., Springfield, Va., 2000—01, George C. Marshall H.S., Falls Church, Va., 2001—, Joyce Kilmer Mid. Sch., 2005—. Sect. leader Washington Women's Chorus, 2002—; mem. Nat. Women's Honor Choir, 2003; conducting intern Wash. Women's Chorus, 2004—05. Mem.: NEA, Chorus Am., Opera Am., Va. Music Educators Assn., Fairfax County Choral Dirs. Assn., Am. Choral Dirs. Assn., Music Educators Nat. Conf., Ind. U. Alumni Assn. (life). Avocation: piano. Office: George C Marshall HS 7731 Leesburg Pike Falls Church VA 22043 Home: 11304 Kessler Pl Manassas VA 20109-7784 Office Phone: 703-714-5452.

EASTER, JEANMARIE, conservator; b. Syracuse, NY, May 11, 1956; d. Stanley Walter and Mary Bonita Kalwara; m. Mark Richard Easter, June 15, 1990. A in Buying and Merchandising, Fashion Inst. Tech., NYC, 1988, BA Restoration of Decorative Objects, 1989. Frame conservator Indpls. Mus. Art, 1989—2001; owner Easter Conservation Svcs. Ltd., Indpls., 2001—. Lectr. Smithsonian Inst., 2006. Contbr. article to profl. jour. Core mem. Meth. Hosp. Task Core, Indpls., 2000—; bd. mem. Friends Herron Sch. Art, Indpls., 2000—, Meridian St. Found., Indpls., 2003—06. Recipient Furniture in France award, Am. Inst. Hist. Artistic Works, France, 2004; Creative Renewal fellowship, Arts Coun. Indpls., London, 2000. Mem.: Contemporary Art Soc., Am. Inst. Conservation Hist. Artistic Works (assoc.; chmn. conservators in pvt. pracice 2003—04). Avocations: gardening, swimming, travel, painting. Office: Easter Conservation Services Ltd 5208 N College Ave Indianapolis IN 46220 Office Phone: 317-396-0885. Personal E-mail: mjeaneaster@aol.com.

EASTER, WANDA DENISE, special education educator; d. Allen Eugene and Marie Nance; m. Mark Howard Easter, July 12, 2003; children: Anthony Terrell Hudson, Lisa Corinne Hudson, Nicholas Bryton Baxter. BS, Western Mich. U., Kalamazoo. Cert. tchr. Tex., 1985. Spl. edn. tchr. Houston ISD, sixth grade tchr., 4th grade tchr., Title I math tchr. Sponsor/mentor Common Bonds, Houston ISD, 2000—06. Recipient Outstanding Educator award, Houston ISD South Region, 1993—2006. Democrat-Npl. Baptist. Avocation: travel. Office Phone: 713-731-5590. Office Fax: 713-731-5598.

EASTERLING, BARBARA J., labor union administrator; Operator Ohio Bell; with Comms. Workers Am. Local 4302, Akron, steward, sec., v.p.; apptd. chief Ohio Labor Divsn., 1970-73; staff rep. Comms. Workers Am., 1973, adminstrv. asst. to v.p. dist. 4, asst. to pres. of union, exec. v.p., 1985, sec.-treas., 1992—, AFL-CIO, 1995—. Mem. exec. com. Union Network Internat., pres. World Women's Commn.; mem. Internat. Conf. Free Trade Unions. Recipient Ohio Women's Hall of Fame award, 1985, award Women's Equity Action League, 1986, Eugene V. Debs award Midwest Labor Press Assn., 1992. Office: Comms Workers Am 501 3rd St NW Washington DC 20001-2760 Fax: 202-434-1481.

EASTMAN, DONNA KELLY, composer; b. Denver, Sept. 26, 1945; d. Donald Lewis and Frances Marie (Smith) Kelly; m. John Bernard Eastman, July 1, 1973; children: Jonathan Kelly, James Alan; stepchildren: Barbara Kathleen, Sally Toye. B in Music Edn., U. Colo., 1967; MA, U. Md., 1973, D in Mus. Arts, 1992. Pvt. studio tchr., coach, 1960—; choral dir. Dept. Def. Overseas Sch., Okinawa, Japan, 1970—72; dir. Choraleers Choral Ensemble, Stuttgart, Germany, 1974—76, Bangkok Music Soc. Ensemble and Madrigal Singers, 1982—84; instr. in music No. Va. C.C., Alexandria, 1986—89. Creator, pianist, vocalist Am. Music Programs for U.S. Mission, Thailand, 1981-84; vis. asst. prof. Ill. Wesleyan U., Bloomington, 1994; vis. composer Sweet Briar (Va.) Coll., 1998, Grinnell (Iowa) Coll., 1999. Composer choral, orchestral, opera, vocal/instrumental solo and chamber, and electronic works; recs. include Capstone Records-Soc. of Composers, Inc. Series CPS 8632, 1996, and New Music for Flute and Piano, CPS 8664, 1999; Living Artist Recs.-Music from the Setting Century Series, Vol. 2, 1996; New Ariel Recordings-Contemporary American Eclectic Music for the Piano Series, AE002, 1996; Columbine Chorale Recs.-European Tour, 1999, Blue House Productions-Alone Into the Crowd, 2002; contbr. to jours. Recipient 6 Internat. Composition awards, Composer Guild, 1991—, Internat. Piano Composition award, Roodeport Internat. Eisteddfod, South Africa, 1991, Glad-Robinson-Youse Composition award, Nat. Fedn. Music Clubs, 1992, Internat. Choral Composition award, Florilège Vocal Tours, France, 1995, Keyboard award, Delius Composition Competition, 1997, Margaret Fairbank Jory Copying Assistance award, Am. Music Ctr., 1999, Nat. Music Composition Competition award, Nat. League of Am. Pen Women, 2000, Miriam Gideon prize for New Music, 2002; fellow, Charles Ives Ctr. for Am. Music, 1990; grantee, 1993, Ragdale Found., 1991, Va. Ctr. for Creative Arts, 1991—2002. Mem. Soc. for Electro-Acoustic Music in the U.S., Internat. Alliance for Women in Music, Soc. of Composers, Inc. (life), Nat. Mus. Women in Arts (charter), Broadcast Music, Inc., Am. Composers Forum, Southeastern Composers League (past pres.), Phi Kappa Phi, Pi Kappa Lambda, Sigma Alpha Iota. Avocations: travel, art glass work, photography. Home: 15253 W Morningtree Dr Surprise AZ 85374-4619 Personal E-mail: dkeastman@cox.net.

EASTMAN, FRANCESCA MARLENE, volunteer, art historian; b. Jamaica Plain, Mass., Jan. 26, 1952; d. Therald Carlton and Martha Jane (Welch) E.; m. Edward Charles Goodstein, Aug. 27, 1989. AB in Art History, Manhattanville Coll., 1972; MA in Art History, Clark Art Inst./Williams Coll., 1974; postgrad., Stanford U., 1976-80. Intern Mus. of Fine Arts, Boston, summers 1971-73; lectr. in art Regis Coll., Weston, Mass., 1974-76; sr. house assoc. Stanford (Calif.) U., 1977-80, tchg. fellow, 1978-79; Stanford student svcs. intern Menlo Coll., Atherton, Calif., 1980-81; now freelance editor. Bd. sec. Trinity Episcopal Sch., Menlo Park, Calif., 1992—96, bd. chair, 1996—98; adv. bd., chair Trinity Sch., 1998; trustee David B. and Edward C. Goodstein Found., L.A., 1995—; vol. scholarship com. Peninsula Cmty. Found., San Mateo, Calif., 1995—; grad. Leadership Redwood City, Calif., 1995—; arts commr., chair Town of Atherton Arts Com., Calif., 1996—, 75th ann. com. leadership coun. Calif., 1998, chair Calif., 1999—; mem. steering com., chair edn. com., founding trustee Episcopal Sch. of the Peninsula, Foster City, Calif., Calif., 1996—; mem. steering com. Arts Coun. San Mateo County Cultural Planning; mem. Menlo Sch. Bd. Fine Arts Com., Atherton, Calif. Mem. Cornell Club (N.Y.C.), Williams Club (N.Y.C.), Pacific Athletic Club. Democrat. Roman Catholic. Avocations: herb gardening, piano.

EASTON, LORY BARSDATE, lawyer; b. 1962; BA in Linguistics summa cum laude, Yale U., 1983, JD, 1988. Bar: Pa. 1990, Conn. 1990, Ill. 1991. Clk. to Jose A. Cabranes, U.S. Dist. Ct. for Conn., 1988-89; clk. to Hon. Ralph K. Winter, U.S. Ct. Appeals for 2d Cir., 1989-90; assoc. Sidley Austin LLP, Chgo., 1990-96, ptnr., 1996—. Mng. editor Yale Law Jour., 1987-88. Office: Sidley Austin LLP One South Dearborn St Chicago IL 60603 Fax: 312-853-7036. Office Phone: 312-853-4601. E-mail: leaston@sidley.com.

EASTON, MICHELLE, foundation executive; b. Phila., Aug. 12, 1950; d. Glenn H. Jr. and Jeanne (Mulhall) Easton; m. Ron Robinson, Sept. 14, 1974; children: Ronald Jr., Daniel, Thomas. AA, BA, Briarcliff Coll., 1972; JD, U. Washington, 1980. Bar: Va. 1981. Asst. to exec. dir. Young Ams. for Freedom, Sterling, Va., 1973-78; asst. to dir. pub. rels. Nat. Right to Work Com., Springfield, Va., 1978; legal asst. Nat. Right to Work Legal Def. Found., 1979; transition team mem. Office of Pres.-Elect, Equal Employment Opportunity Commn., Washington, 1980-81; atty. U.S. Dept. Justice, Washington, 1981; spl. asst. to gen. counsel U.S. Dept. Edn., Washington, 1981-83; pvt. vol. orgns. liaison officer, Africa Bur. Agy. for Internat. Devel., 1984; dir. Missing Children's Program Office of Juvenile Justice and Delinquency Prevention, U.S. Dept. Justice, 1985-87; dir. intergovtl. affairs U.S. Dept. Edn., Washington, 1987-88, dep. under sec. for intergovtl. and interagy. affairs, 1988-91; dir. Office Pvt. Edn., Washington, 1991-93; pres. Clare Boothe Luce Policy Inst., 1993—. Apptd. by Gov. Allen to Va. State Bd. Edn., Richmond, 1994-98, bd. pres. 1996; bd. dirs. The Family Found., Richmond, Va., 1998-99; sec. Nat. Conservative Campaign Fund, 2000—. Mem.: Phila. Soc. (trustee 2000—02). Republican. Episcopalian.

EASTON, SHEENA, rock vocalist, actress; b. Bellshill, Scotland, Apr. 27, 1959; m. Sandy Easton, 1977 (div. 1978); m. Rob Light, 1984 (div. 1986); m. Tim Delarm, July 28, 1997 (div. 1998); children: Jake, Skylar. Grad., Royal Scottish Acad. Music and Drama, 1979. Albums include Take My Time, 1981, You Could Have Been with Me, 1981, Madness, Money and Music, 1982, Best Kept Secret, 1983, A Private Heaven, 1984, The Lover in Me, 1988, Greatest Hits, 1989, My Cherie, 1995, (with Luis Miguel) Me Gustas Tal Como Eres (Grammy award for Mexican-Am. performance 1984), No Strings, 1993, What Comes Naturally, 1991, Freedom, 1997, The Color of Christmas, 1998, Home, 1999, Fabulous, 2000; TV appearances include Miami Vice, 1987, Body Bags, The Highlander, The Adventure of Brisco County Jr., Outer Limits, 1996; Broadway appearances: Man of La Mancha, 1992, Grease; theatre: Joseph and the Amazing Technicolor Dreamcoat, 2005; voiceovers for All Dogs Go to Heaven 2, T.V. Road Rovers. Recipient Grammy award for best new artist, 1981. Office: 18136 Califa St Tarzana CA 91356-1718

EASTON, SUSAN DAWN, biochemist, educator; b. Harvey, Ill., Oct. 8, 1959; d. Dee Charles and Barbara Louise Shaffer. BS in Biol. Scis., Ill. State U., 1981. Med. rsch. technician Washington U. Sch. Medicine, St. Louis, 1981-83; biol. lab. technician VA Med. Ctr., Indpls., 1983-86; rsch. technician Ind. U., Bloomington, 1987-88, rsch. assoc., 1988-92; chemistry, microbiology, validation, document control, quality assurance mgr. Cook Imaging Corp., Bloomington, 1993-96, regulatory affairs mgr., 1996-99, tech. svcs., 1999—2001; tech. svcs. mgr. Baxter Pharm. Solutions, LLC, Bloomington, 2001—05, dir. tech. svcs., 2005—, mem. emergency response team, 2001—. Mem. emergency response team Cook Imaging Corp., Bloomington, 1995-2001; lectr. Ctr. Profl. Advancement, East Brunswick, N.J., 1996—, Internat. Soc. Pharm. Engrs., 2001—; lectr. Internat. Soc. for Pharm. Engrs., 2001. Author: Protein Expression and Purification, 1993. Named one of Outstanding Young Women of Am., 1983. Mem. Internat. Soc. Pharm. Engrs., Parenteral Drug Assn., Phi Sigma. Office: Baxter Pharm Solutions LLC PO Box 3068 Bloomington IN 47402-3068 Home: 3702 Stoney Brook Blvd Bloomington IN 47404 E-mail: susan_easton@baxter.com.

EASTRIDGE, DARLENE F., social worker, dean; d. Robert H. and D. Vaniel Romine; m. Ronnie M. Eastridge, 1978; children: Dana C. Milby, Joshua K. BA in Psychology/Sociology, Campbellsville U., 1986; MA in Edn., Western Ky. U., 1990; MSSW, U Louisville, 1993; PhD, U. Ky., Louisville, 2005. Social worker Ky., 1997. Prof. Campbellsville U., Ky., 1994—, dean Carver Sch. Social Work, 2005—. Site visitor Coun. Social Work Edn., Alexandria, Va., 2006. Author: (national survey) How Social Work Educators Teach Aging in the BSW Curriculum. Bd. dirs. Campbellsville Housing Authority, 2006, Caring Pl., Lebanon, Ky., 2006; chmn. Bluegrass Regional Area Support Svcs., Campbellsville, 1994—2003. Assn. Gerontology in Higher Edn. grantee, U. Pitts., 2000—01, Wilma Dykeman fellow, Appalachian Coll. Assn., 2004—05, China Seminar fellow, 2006. Achievements include research in aging. Avocations: travel, crafts, pets. Office: Campbellsville U #1 University Dr Campbellsville KY 42718 Office Phone: 270-789-5049. Business E-Mail: dfeastridge@campbellsville.edu.

EATON, DORLA DEAN See KEMPER, DORLA

EATON, EMMA PARKER, special education educator; b. Conway, N.C., June 21, 1945; BS in Special Edn., Norfolk State Coll., 1978; MA, Norfolk State U., 1995. Spl. edn. eduator Norfolk Pub. Schs., Va.

EATON, KATHERINE GIRTON, retired library educator; b. St. Paul, Mar. 9, 1924; d. John Frances and Mary Ahleen (Peck) Girton; m. Burt Elliott Eaton, Oct. 18, 1947; children: John Girton, Marilee Eaton Warkentin, David Elliott. BA in Journalism, U. Minn., 1944; MS in Journalism, U. Oreg., Eugene, 1952, MLS, 1968. Reporter Bakersfield Calif., 1945-46; women's editor Rochester Post Bulletin, Minn., 1946-47; legal sec. Broady Law Offices, St. Paul, 1949-51; editor Oreg. State System Higher Edn., Eugene, 1952-53; cons. Oreg. State Libr., Salem, 1968-70; head pub. affairs libr. U. Oreg., Eugene, 1970-85, assoc. prof. emerita, 1985—. Contbr. articles to profl. jours. Chmn. Lane County Mental Health Bd., Eugene, 1964-88, Lane County Libr. Bd., 1981-85, Eugene City Budget Com., 1986-92, Citizens for Lane County Librs., 1980—, Human Resources Planning Project, Lane County, 1986-89; planning and mgmt. coun. Oreg. Mental Health Svcs., 1988-2005, chair, 1996-99, co-chair adv. com., 2005-; founding bd. dirs. Passages, Lane County substance abuse residential program for offenders, 1990-2001; pres. Wilani coun. Camp Fire Inc., 1967-68, nat. bd. dirs., 1966-70, N.W. regional chmn. 1966-70; adv. bd. Oreg. State Mental Health, 1989-2003, chmn. 1999-2003; elections team LWV, Hungary, 1993; mem. U.S. State Dept. Bosnia Elections Supr., 1997, 2000; coord., convener Oreg. Women's Summit, 1996—; Oreg. steering com. Help Am. Vote Act, 2002—. Named Outstanding Young Woman, Eugene Jaycettes, 1956, Outstanding Women of Yr., Lane County Orgns., 1974, Ln. County Vol. Yr., 1989; recipient Gulick, Seaton, Hiitina awards Camp Fire, Inc., 1959, 66, 71, Outstanding Lib. Pub. award The Wilson Co., 1993, U. Oreg. Disting. Svc. award, 1997, Soroptimist Internat. Women of Distinction award, 1998, OASIS Sr. Role Model award, 1998, Adult Vol. of Yr. award J.C. Penney/United Way, 2000. Mem. AAUP (bd. dirs. U. Oreg. 1976-85, pres. 1977-78), ALA (coun. 1976-80), AAUW (del. NGO women's forum Kenya 1985, China 1995), Oreg. Libr. Assn. (hon. life, pres. 1973-74), Nat. Coun. Planning Librs. (pres. 1978-79, 88-89, Disting. Svc. award 1994), Pacific N.W. Libr. Assn. (editor, quar 1985-96, hon. life), Internat. Fedn. Univ. Women (coun. mem. 1983-85), Assn. Oreg. Faculties (state bd. dirs. 1981-89, v.p. 1983-85), AAUW (pres. Oreg. 1975-77, pres. nat. legal adv. fund 1981-85, nat. exec. v.p. 1981-85, Eugene-Lane br. pres. 1962-63), LWV Oreg. (1st v.p. 1989-91, pres. 1991-93, governance coord. 1999-, disting. svc. award 1995), LWV Lane County (pres. 1963-65, 97-99), Oreg. Women's Rights Coalition (pres. 1994-2001, v.p. 2002—), Virginia Gildersleeve Internat. Fund (archival historian, bd. dirs. 1995—, 1st v.p. 1999-2002), Social Order of Beaucean (pres. 1993, 96). Democrat. Presbyterian. Avocations: mystery reading, lobbying, research, editing.

EATON, MAJA CAMPBELL, lawyer; b. 1955; BA, U. Iowa, 1977, JD, 1984. Bar: Ill. 1984, U.S. Dist. Ct. (no. dist.) Ill. 1984, U.S. Dist. Ct. (no. dist.) Calif. 1993. With Sidley Austin Brown & Wood, Chgo., ptnr., 1993—. Former adj. prof. law Chgo.-Kent Coll. Law. Mem.: Def. Rsch. Inst. Office: Sidley Austin Brown and Wood Bank One Plz 10 S Dearborn St Chicago IL 60603

EATON, NANCY RUTH LINTON, librarian, dean; b. Berkeley, Calif., May 2, 1943; d. Don Thomas and Lena Ruth (McClellan) Linton; m. Edward Arthur Eaton III, June 19, 1965 (div. 1980) AB, Stanford U., 1965; MLS, U. Tex., 1968, postgrad., 1969. From cataloger to asst. to dir. U. Tex. Libr., Austin, 1968-74; automation libr. SUNY, Stony Brook, 1974-76; head tech. svcs. Atlanta Pub. Libr., 1976-82; dir. libr. U. Vt., Burlington, 1982-89; dean libr. svcs. Iowa State U., Ames, 1989-97; dean univ. librs. Pa. State U., University Park, Pa., 1997—. Bd. dirs. Ctr. for Rsch. Libr., 1988-92, chair, 1989-90; del. users coun., mem. exec. com. Online Computer Libr. Ctr., Inc., Dublin, Ohio, 1980-82, 86-88, trustee, 1987-02, chair bd. trustees 1992-96; mgr. Nat. Agrl. Text Digitalizing Project, 1986-92; bd. dirs. New Eng. Libr. Network, 1987-89; chair steering com. Digital Libr. Fedn., 2000-02; mem. adv. bd. Nat. Digital Info. Infrastructure and Preservation Program, 2001-02; bd. dirs. Rsch. Librs. Group, 2004-06; co-prin. investigation Mellon Found., 2004—. Co-author: Optical Information Systems: Implementation Issues for Libraries, 1988.; co-editor: A Cataloging Sampler, 1971, Book Selection Policies in American Libraries, 1972; contbr. articles to profl. jours. U.S. Office of Edn. post-master's fellow, 1969; Dept. Edn. Title II-C grantee, 1985, 87-88, Title II-D grantee, 1992-96, Mellon Found. grant. Mem. ALA, Libr. and Info. Tech. Assn. (pres. 1984-85, bd. dirs. 1980-86), Assn. Rsch. Librs. (bd. dirs. 1994-97), Digital Libr. Fedn. (exec. com. 1997-2003), Coalition for Networked Info. (steering com. 1999-2005), Rsch. Librs Group (bd. dirs. 2004—). Democrat. Avocations: tennis, walking. Home: 441 Homan Ave State College PA 16801-6337 Office: Pa State Univ 510 Paterno Library University Park PA 16802-1812 Office Phone: 814-865-0401. E-mail: neaton@psu.edu.

EATON, PAULINE, artist, educator; b. Neptune, N.J., Mar. 20, 1935; d. Paul A. and Florence Elizabeth (Rogers) Friedrich; m. Charles Adams Eaton, June 15, 1957; children: Gregory, Eric, Paul, Joy, Jane(dec.). BA, Dickinson Coll., Carlisle, Pa., 1957; MA, Northwestern U., Evanston, Ill., 1958. Lic. instr. Calif. Instr. Mira Costa Coll., Oceanside, Calif., 1980—82, Idyllwild Sch. Music and Arts, Calif., 1983—; instr. dept. continuing edn. U. N.Mex.; ret., 2006. Juror, demonstrator numerous art socs.; founder, dir. Corrales Art/Studio Tour, 1999—2006; dir., founder Antempo, N.Y.C., 2006. One-woman shows include Nat. Arts Club, NYC, 1977, Designs Recycled Gallery, Fullerton, Calif., 1978, 1980, 1984, San Diego Art Inst., 1980, Spectrum Gallery, San Diego, 1981, San Diego Jung Ctr., 1983, Marin Civic Ctr. Gallery, 1984, R. Mondayi Winery, 1987, exhibited in group shows at Am. Watercolor Soc., 1975, 1977, Butler Inst. Am. Art, Youngstown, Ohio, 1977—79, 1981, NAD, 1978, N.Mex Arts and Crafts Fair, 1994 (Best in Show award), Corrales Bosque Gallery, Art is OK Gallery, Albuquerque, N.Mex., 2004, Represented in permanent collections Butler Inst. Am. Art, St. Mary's Coll., Md., Mercy Hosp., San Diego, Sharp Hosp., Redlands Hosp., Riverside, N.Mex. Women in Arts, Albuquerque Mus.; work featured in: book Watercolor, The Creative Experience, 1978, Creative Seascape Painting, 1980, Painting the Spirit in Nature, 1984, Exploring Painting (Gerald Brommer); author: Crawling to the Light, An Artist in Transition, 1987; author: (with Mary Ann Beckwith) Best of Watercolor Texture, 1997; The Art of Layering: Making Connections, 2004; contbr. chapters to books. Trustee San Diego Art Inst., 1977—78, San Diego Mus. Art, 1982—83. Recipient award, Hollywood (Calif.) Form Arts, 1986, Grumbacker award, Conf. 96 Hill Country Art Ctr., 2d award, Tex. Friends and Neighbors, Irving, 2000, award of excellence, Ariz. Aqueous, 2002, Originals award, N.Mex. Women in Arts, Albuquerque Mus., 2003. Mem.: Soc. Layerists Multi-Media (bd. dirs.), Eastbay Watercolor Soc. (v.p. 1988—90), West Coast Watercolor Soc. (exhbns. chmn. 1983—86, pres. 1989—92), We. Fedn. Watercolor Socs. (chmn. 1983, 3d prize 1982, Grumbacher Gold medal 1983), N.Mex Watercolor Soc. (Grumbacker award, Wingspread award 1999), San Diego Artists Guild (pres. 1982—83), Artists Equity (v.p. San Diego 1979—81), San Diego Watercolor Soc. (pres. 1976—77, workshop dir. 1977—80), Marin Arts Guild (instr. 1984—87), Internat. Soc. Exptl. Artists (Nautilus Merit award 1992, 1998), Watercolor West (Strathmore award 1979, Purchase award 1986), Rocky Mountain Watermedia Soc. (Golden award 1979, Mustard Seed award 1983), Nat. Watercolor Soc., Watercolor USA Soc. (hon. Veloy Vigil Meml. award 1986), Nat. Soc. Painters Acrylic and Casein (hon.). Democrat. Home: 68 Hop Tree Trl Corrales NM 87048-9613 Office Phone: 505-898-1573.

EATON, SHIRLEY M., medical/surgical nurse; d. Benjamin W. Randall Sr. and Rena B. Randall; children: Everett Kennedy, Eran Margret Eaton Parker. MPH, So. Conn. U., 1997. RN Conn. Nursing positions, SC and Conn., 1960—; mem. staff ombudsman program Norwalk (Conn.) Social Svcs., 1996—. Mem. adv. coun. Area of Nursing, Norwalk, 1997—. Author: Handbook for Caregivers to the Elderly, 1998. Deaconess First Presbyn. Ch. of Stamford, Conn. Presbyterian. Avocations: singing, sewing, writing, travel, designing.

EATON ADAMS, ELIZABETH SUSAN, retired middle school educator, jazz musician; b. Norfolk, Va., Apr. 13, 1947; d. Russell Samuel and Miriam Kathleen (Kindermann) E.; m. Robert F. Adams, May 24, 1998. BA, Marquette U., 1970; MS, U. Wis., Milw., 1973; PhD equivalency, Wis. Coll. Conservatory Music, 1979. Cert. tchr. grades 1-6, Wis., reading tchr. grades 1-8, Wis. Reading tchr. grades 1-6 Garfield Elem. Sch., Milw., 1973-77; reading tchr. grades 6-8 King Mid. Sch. Gifted & Talented, Milw., 1979-82; 2d grade tchr. Elm Creative Arts Elem. Sch., Milw., 1983-84; English & social studies tchr., jazz studies tchr. Roosevelt Mid. Sch. Creative Arts, Milw., 1984-89; reading tchr. grades 6-8 Morse Mid. Sch. Gifted & Talented, Milw., 1989-92, English tchr., 1990-94, yoga tchr., 1993-95, reading tchr., 1994-96; asst. to head libr. Marquette U. and Wis. Coll. Conservatory of Music, 1996—2000; English, study skills and curriculum coord. Northshore C.C., 1999, Wellspring House, 1999; reading specialist Rockport (Mass.) Mid. Sch., 2000, ret., 2001. Chmn., advisor Nat. Jr. Honor Soc., Milw., 1991-94; co-dir. Morse Drama Club, 1991-93, advisor, mem., com. mem. Fin Arts Week Morse com., 1991-96. Prodr., vocalist, lyricist, arranger (CD and cassette recs.) It's Time Now, 1995, Lis Adams and Mark French Cape Ann Vocal and Guitar, 2004, others. Trustee Hist. Pabst Theatre, Milw., 1972-79; dir. asst., vol. Summerfest World Festivals, Inc., Milw., 1969-71; vol., fund raiser Sta. WYMS Jazz Radio, 1995; vol. Gibbes Art Mus, Charleston, Symphony League, Charleston, Cape Ann Hist. Mus, Gloucester, Mass., others. Mem. Siddha Yoga, Inc. (ctr. host, 2002, 03), Wis. Arts and Music, Inc., Pi Lambda Theta. Avocations: travel, antiques, genealogy, writing, art. Home: 7 Doctors Run Rockport MA 01966-1357 E-mail: leadams@gis.net.

EAVES, MARIA PERRY, realtor; b. Cluj, Romania; d. Nicholas Brudan and Ema (Filipescu) Perry; m. John Eaves, June 16, 1951; children: Bryan Perry, Susan Eaves Clark. BA, MA, UCLA, 1945; postgrad., Columbia U., 1947-51, U. London, 1953-54. Lic. realtor, Md., Va.; rev. appraiser. Advt. and market analyst Foote, Cone & Belding, N.Y.C., 1948-49; fgn. affairs officer U.S. Dept. State, N.Y.C., 1950-53; dir. rsch. Radio Free Europe Press, N.Y.C., 1955-56; info. officer, media reaction analyst USIA, Washington, 1956-58, rsch. cons., 1958-61; market and pub. opinion cons., Washington, 1969-72; realtor Colquitt Carruthers Inc., Bethesda, Md., 1972-81, Long & Foster Real Estate Inc., Potomac, Md., 1982—. One-woman paintings show at Nicosia, Cyprus; group shows include New Delhi (India), White Plains, N.Y., Bethesda, Md.; also pvt. collections. Vol. Gov. Nelson Rockefeller's Com. to Welcome UN Diplomats, N.Y.C., 1968, 69; mem. World Affairs Coun. Washington; Woodrow Wilson Info. Ctr. for Scholars, Washington; charter mem. Nat. Mus. Women in the Arts, Washington, Nat. Mus. Am. Indian. Mem. NAFE, LWV, AAUW, NARFE, FIAPCI, Internat. Fedn. Realtors, Internat. Real Estate Inst. (registered), Nat. Assn. Realtors, Nat. Assn. Rev. Appraisers and Mortgage Underwriters, Md. Assn. Realtors, No. Va. Assn. Realtors, Women's Coun. Realtors, Greater Capital Area Assn. Realtors, Woman's Nat. Dem. Club (Washington), Tournament Players Club (Potomac, Md.), Diplomatic and Officers Club Ret., Columbia U. Club (Wash.), Mil. Dist. of Washington Club. Democrat. Episcopalian. Avocations: bridge, painting, classical music, reading, computers. Home: 10450 Lottsford Rd Mitchellville MD 20721-2734 Office: Long & Foster Realtors 9812 Falls Rd Potomac MD 20854-3996 Personal E-mail: mariaeaves@erols.com.

EBBERTS, DEANA MARIE, mathematics educator; b. Arkansas City, Kans., July 21, 1970; d. James Dean and Marsha Meire Roe; m. Kelly Gene Ebberts, July 23, 2005; children: William Charles Pennington, Laura Elizabeth Pennington. Bachelors, Southwestern Coll., Kans., 2000. Math. tchr. Pub. Sch., Hamilton, Kans., 2000—. Cheerleading coach Pub. HS, Hamilton, Kans., 2000—; class sponsor 9th-12th Grade Class Sponsor, Hamilton, Kans., 2000—; chairperson Profl. Devel. Com., Hamilton, Kans., 2005—. Pentacostal. Avocations: trumpet, water sports, reading. Office: Hamilton HS 2596 W Rd North Hamilton KS 66853 Office Phone: 620-678-3651. Business E-Mail: debbers@hamilton390.net.

EBELING, VICKI, marriage and family therapist, writer; b. Detroit, Nov. 18, 1948; d. Paul F. and Constance Jean Ebeling; m. James Robert Marchese, 1983; 1 child, Drew Ebeling Marchese. BA, Mich. State U., 1969; M of Sci., Marriage, Family & Child Counseling, Calif. State U., Dominguez Hills, 1990; PhD in Human Behavior, Newport U., 1999. Diplomate Am. Psychotherapy Assn.; cert. youth effectiveness tng. instr.; bd. cert. edn. therapist., Assn. Ednl. Therapists. With various TV and radio prodn. cos., Detroit, Lansing, Mich., 1969-74; TV and film prodn. cos. L.A., 1974-90; psychotherapist/marriage, family and child therapist Torrance, Calif., 1990—; ednl. therapist, 1994—. Pub. Pier Avenue Pub., 2006—. Author: Educating America in the 21st Century, 2002. Counselor South Bay Rape Crisis Ctr., 1988-92; mem. orientation team St. Peter's by Sea Presbyn. Ch., Palos Verdes Estates, Calif., 1993-95; vol. cons. 1736 Family Crisis Ctr., 1988, Calif. Spl. Olympics, 1990-91, pediat. ward UCLA-Harbor Hosp., 1991-92, Child Shelter Care, Los Angeles County Children's Ct., 1992-93, ARC Disaster Svc., 1995—. Named Adult Amateur Horsemanship Champion, Los Serranos Award Circuit, Rolling Hills, Calif., 1993. Mem. Calif. Assn. Marriage and Family Therapists (South Bay newsletter editor 1992-94), Assn. Ednl. Therapists. Office: Vicki Ebeling Phd LMFT BCET 3138 Pacific Coast Hwy Torrance CA 90505-6708

EBENHOLTZ, JEAN MIRIAM, academic administrator; b. N.Y.C., Oct. 24, 1934; m. Sheldon M. Ebenholtz, Jan. 30, 1955; 1 child, Keith H. BA, Adelphi Coll., 1955; MS, U. Wis., 1984. Securities analyst Bank of N.Y., N.Y.C., 1955-60; rsch. asst. Conn. Coll., New London, Conn., 1963-66; income tax cons. H&R Block, Madison, Wis., 1975-76; adminstrv. asst. U. Wis., Madison, 1977-86; acad. coord. N.J. Inst. Tech., Newark, 1986-94, adminstrv. coord., 1994—96; ret. V.p. Neighbors Indeed, 2005—; bd. dirs. Lincoln Hills Found., 2006. Office: NJ Inst Technol Univ Hts Newark NJ 07102 Home: 635 Violet Ln Lincoln CA 95648-8125

EBER, LAURA JEAN, personal trainer; b. Coon Rapids, Minn., Dec. 3, 1973; d. Robert Russell and Linda Ann (Wilkens) Anderson; m. Alan Eber, Aug. 24, 2002; 1 child, David Alan. BA, Coll. St. Catherine, St. Paul, Minn., 1997; MSc, U. Wis., LaCrosse, 2000. Cert. Nat. Athletic Trainers Assn., Nat. Strength & Conditioning Assn., Nat. Acad. Sports Medicine. Aide phys. therapy NovaCare, Mpls., 1999; grad. asst. athletic trainer U. Wis., LaCrosse, 1999—2000; athletic trainer Gundersen Luth. Sports Medicine, LaCrosse, 2000—04, on-call athletic trainer, 2004—. Examiner Nat. Athletic Trainers Assn. Bd. Cert., 2001—; spkr. confs. sport enhancement Gundersen Luth. Sports Medicine, 2001—. Author: (article) Jour. Strength and Conditioning, 2003. Fundraiser bike ride Nat. Multiple Sclerosis Soc., Madison, Wis., 2001—; worship coord. English Luth. Ch., LaCrosse, 2005—. Fellow: Nat. Athletic Trainers Assn.; mem.: Nat. Acad. Sports Medicine, Nat. Strength & Conditioning Assn. Lutheran. Achievements include development of sport enhancement program TOP (Training for Oustanding Performance) at Gundersen Lutheran Sports Medicine. Avocations: scrapbooks, bicycling, hiking, reading. Home: W5353 Norseman Dr La Crosse WI 54601

EBERHARD-NEVEAUX, CHRISTINE, aviation executive, dispute resolution executive; b. Fremont, Ohio, Jan. 12, 1951; d. Richard Lesley and Elva Lucille (Ransom) Eberhard; m. Michael Lee Neveaux, May 24, 1997; stepchildren: Jamie, Stephen, Sarah, Spencer. Student, U. Am., Cholula, Mex., 1972-73; BA in Internat. Studies, Ohio State U., 1973; postgrad., Pepperdine U., 1999. Cert. in dispute resolution; lic. helicopter pilot. Account exec. News-Times Pub. Co., Anaheim, Calif., 1975-76; asst. dir. pub. rels. and devel. Hawthorne Cmty. Hosp., 1977-80; dir. pub. rels. Presbyn. Intercmty. Hosp., Whittier, Calif., 1980-82; pres. CommuniQuest, Simi Valley, Calif., 1982—. Mem. mediation panel Ventura County Superior Ct., Los Angeles County Superior Ct.; contracts with numerous airports and FAA including a contract to teach cmty. involvement course to FAA mgmt. Bd. dirs. L.A. South Bay-Harbor Industry Edn. Coun., 1978-81. Served with USAR, 1975-93. Mem. Res. Officers Assn. (Calif. Outstanding Jr. Officer 1983), Profl. Helicopter Pilots Assn. (past bd. dirs.), L.A. County Commn. on Local Govt. Svcs. (chair air svcs. com. 1994-99), Helicopter Assn. Internat. (past chair heliport promotion and devel. com., chair pub. rels. adv. coun., spl. advisor to bd. dirs. 1991-98), L.A. Internat. Airport C. of C. (bd. dirs. 1983-86), Am. Assn. Airport Execs. (S.W. chpt. bd. dirs. 2002-06, Corp. award Excellence 2001, Pres. award 2006), Internat. Assn. Pub. Participation Practitioners, Whirly-girl Number 766, So. Calif Mediation Assn. (Los Angeles Superior Ct. mediator), Ventura County Dispute Settlement Mediation Panel (mediator). Office: CommuniQuest 2728 Bitternut Cir Simi Valley CA 93065-1315

EBERLEY, HELEN-KAY, opera singer, recording industry executive, poet; b. Sterling, Ill., Aug. 3, 1947; d. William Elliott and P. (Conneely) E. MusB, Northwestern U., 1970, MusM, 1971. Chmn., pres., artistic coord. Eberley Inc., Evanston, Ill., 1973-92; founder H.K.E. Enterprises, 1993—, pres., 1993—; circulation libr. Evanston Pub. Libr., 1995-98; prin., adminstr. The Kidusche Eberley Trust. Founder EB-SKO Prodns., 1976-92, tchr., coach, 1976—; exec. dir., performance cons. E-S Mgmt., 1985-92; featured artist Honors Concert, Northwestern U., 1970, Alumni Concert, 1999, Master Class and guest lectr. various colls. and univs.; host Poetry in Process monthly seminar Barnes & Noble; music lectr. rep. Harvard Club, Chgo.; numerous TV and radio talk show appearances and interviews. Operatic debut in Peter Grimes, Lyric Opera, Chgo., 1974; starred in: Der Rosenkovalier, Cosi Fan Tutte, Le Nozze Di Figaro, Dido and Aeneas, La Boheme, Faust, Tosca, La Traviata, Falstaff, Don Giovanni, Brigadoon, others; jazz appearances with Duke Ellington, Dave Brubeck and Robert Shaw; performing artist Oglebay Opera Inst., Wheeling, W.Va., 1968, WTTW TV/PBS, Chgo., 1968; solo star in: Continental Bank Concerts, 1981-89, United Airlines-Schubert, Schumann, Brahms, Mendelssohn, Faure, Mozart, Duparc/Wolf, Supersta. WFMT Radio, Chgo., 1982-90; featured artist with North Shore Concert Band, 1989; starring artist South Bend Symphony, 1990, Mo. Symphony Soc., 1990, Milw. Symphony, 1990; spl. guest artist New Studios Gala Sta. WFMT, 1995, West Valley Fine Arts Concert Series, Phoenix, 1999; prodr.-annotator Gentlemen Gypsy, 1978, Strauss and Szymanowski, 1979, One Sonata Each: Franck and Szymanowski, 1982; starring artist-exec. prodr. Separate But Equal, 1976, All Brahms, 1977, Opera Lady, 1978, Eberley Sings Strauss, 1980, Helen-Kay Eberley: American Girl, 1983, Helen-Kay Eberley: Opera Lady II, 1984; performed Am. and Can. nat. anthems for Chgo. Cubs Baseball Team, 1977-83, Chgo. Bears Football, 1977; also starred in numerous concert recital and symphony appearances, Europe, Can., U.S.; author: Angel's Song, 1994, The Magdaleva Poems, 1995, ChapelHeart, 1996, Desert Dancing, 1997, Canyon Ridge, 2000, Rivervoice, 2002. Docent, new mem. tour guide Art Inst. Chgo.; spl. events hotline vol. Art Inst. Chgo., Chgo. Christian Indsl. League, St. Joseph's Table of St. Peter's in the Loop, Chgo.; vol., facilitator City Yr. Chgo.-Urban Peace Corps; Chgo. Humanities Festival VIII of Ill. Humanities Coun., Evanston Shelter for Battered Women, Rape Victim Adv., Habitat for Humanity; Midwest Vol. Facilitator 1st Indsl. Realty Trust; mem. Mayor's founding com. Evanston Arts Coun., 1974-75; judge Ice-Skating Competition, Wilmette (Ill.) Park Dist., 1974-77, bd. dirs., 1973-77; bd. dirs. Ctr. for Voice, Chgo., 1994-96; vol. Saints-Usher Corps of Chgo., 1998-99; chmn. fin. Chgo. (Ill.) Youth Symphony. Recipient Creative and Performing Arts award Ind. Jr. Miss. and South Bend Jr. Miss, 1965, Milton J. Cross award Met. Opera Guild, 1968; prize winner Met. Opera. Nat. Auditions, 1968, 1st pl. prize for The Pond, Chicagoland Poetry Contest, 1997, 1st pl. prize and Best of the Best award for The Rose Garden, 1999; F.K. Weyerhauser scholar Met. Opera, 1967. Mem. People for Ethical Treatment of Animals, Am. Soc. for Prevention of Cruelty to Animals, Assisi Animal Found., Am. Guild Mus. Artists, Internat. Platform Assn., Whale Adoption Project, Amnesty Internat., Environ. Def. Fund, Doris Day Animal Found., Poets and Patrons, Humane Soc., Greenpeace, Physicians Com. for Responsible Medicine, Notre Dame Alumni Club, St. Mary's Acad. Alumnae Assn., Delta Gamma. Office: HKE Enterprises 1726 Sherman Ave Evanston IL 60201-5619

EBERLY, RAINA ELAINE, retired psychologist, educator; b. Chambersburg, Pa., Sept. 17, 1952; d. Charles Alton and Betty Jane (Friese) E.; m. Brian Edward Engdahl, July 9, 1977; 1 child, Rebecca Raina. BS in Psychology, U. Pitts., 1973; PhD in Psychology, U. Minn., 1980. Lic. psychologist. Clin. asst. prof. psychology dept. U. Minn., Mpls., 1981-89, clin. assoc. prof., 1990—; psychologist VA Med Ctr., Mpls., 1980—96, tng. dir., 1984-94; psychologist, clin. coord. Vet Ctr., St. Paul, 1996—2006; ret., 2006. Contbr. articles to profl. jours. VA grantee, 1989-90, 90-93. Mem. Internat. Soc. for Traumatic Stress Studies. Achievements include contbn. to understanding of chronic posttraumatic stress disorder and co-morbidity.

EBERSOLE, CHRISTINE, actress; b. Chgo., Feb. 21, 1953; m. Peter Bergman (div.). Student, McMurray Coll., Am. Acad. Dramatic Arts. Actress: (stage prodns.) Angel Street, 1976, Green Pond, 1978, On the Twentieth

Century, 1978, Oklahoma!, 1979, Camelot, 1980, The Three Sisters, 1982, Geniuses, 1983, Harrigan 'n Hart, 1985, Getting Away with Murder, 1996, Gore Vidal's The Best Man, 2000, 42nd Street, 2001 (Tony award, best actress in a musical, 2001), Dinner at Eight, 2002, Steel Magnolias, 2005, Grey Gardens, 2005 (Outer Critics' Cir. award outstanding actress in a musical 2006, OBIE award Village Voice 2006, Drama Desk award outstanding actress in a musical 2006) (feature films) Tootsie, 1982, Amadeus, 1984, Thief of Hearts, 1984, Mac and Me, 1988, (TV movies) The Doll Maker, 1984, Acceptable Risks, 1986, (TV series) The Cavanaughs, 1986; cast mem. Saturday Night Live. Office: William Morris Agy 1350 Avenue Of The Americas New York NY 10019-4702*

EBERT, CAREY DALTON, lawyer; b. 1960; BA in Pub. Policy (cum laude), H. Sophie Newcomb Memorial Coll., 1982; JD, Tex. Tech U., 1985. Bar: 1985, admitted to: US Dist. Ct., No. Dist. Tex., bd. cert. in Consumer Bankruptcy: State Bar Tex., Am. Bankruptcy Bd. Cert. Mem. Ebert Law offices, P.C., Hurst, Tex., 1989—. Panel trustee No. Dist. Tex.; frequent lectr. Debtor Bar Seminars. Mem.: N.E. Tarrant County Bar Assn. (past pres.), Nat. Assn. of Consumer Bankruptcy Attorneys (dir. 2002, past sect., bd. mem., v.p., panelist 1998—), State Bar Coll. Address: Nat Assn of Consumer Bankruptcy Attys 2300 M St Ste 800 Washington DC 20037

EBERT, LESLIE, artist; b. Oregon City, Oreg., Sept. 20, 1962; d. Larry Dwayne Ebert and Carol Kay Bino; m. Paul Ian Boundy, May 2, 1988. BArch, U. Oreg., 1987. Archtl. intern, Portland, Oreg., 1986; studio apprentice Debra Olsen, Portland, 1990—91; owner Leslie Ebert Studio, Portland, 1994—. Exhbn. artist Celebration of Am. Paper Arts, Crane Mus. Papermaking, Mass., 2003, Landmarks in Paper, Friends of Dard Hunter, St. Paul, 2003, Crossing Boundaries, Internat. Symposium of Print Arts, Portland, 2000. Contbr. artwork to book The Artful Greeting, 2003, artwork to mag. Somerset Studio, 2000, artwork Am. Mus. Papermaking, 2003; one-man shows include Wene Gallery, Portland, Ore., 2006, Represented in permanent collections Crane Papermaking Mus., exhibitions include Washington State U. Gallery, 2005, Nat. Coll. Soc. Small Works Exhibit, Cork Gallery, NYC, 2004, SLMM Nat. Exhbn., 2004, Peninsula Fine Arts Ctr., Newport News, Va., 2005, Coos Art Mus., Oreg., 2006, solo exhbns., Wené Gallery, Portland, 2006; curator (exhibitions) Washington State U., 2006, contbg. artist The Art of Layering: Making Connections, 2004. Founding bd. dirs. Art in the Pearl, Portland; mem. curatorial adv. bd. Am. Inst. Archs., Portland, 1992; publicity chair Waterstone Gallery, Portland, 1994; N.W. regional coord. Soc. Layerists in Multi-Media, 2004—. Mem.: Nat. Oil and Acrylic Painters, Internat. Soc. Exptl. Artists, Nat. Coll. Soc., Internat. Assn. Papermakers, Friends of Dard Hunter, N.W. Print Coun., Soc. Layerists in Multimedia (mem. com. 2006). Avocations: travel, photography, gardening, reading. Office: Leslie Ebert Studio PO Box 68604 Portland OR 97268 E-mail: leslie@leslieebert.com.

EBERT, LORETTA CAREN, university librarian; BA, SUNY Binghamton; MA, Colgate U.; MLS, SUNY Geneseo. Past libr. positions U. Rochester, Syracuse U., Mich. State U.; dir. rsch. libraries Rensselaer Poly. Inst., 1994—2006; dir. rsch. libr. NY State Libr., Albany, NY, 2006—. Bd. trustees Troy Pub. Libr., NY. Office: Dir Rsch Libr NY State Libr Cultural Edn Ctr Empire State Plz Albany NY 12230 Office Phone: 518-474-5355.*

EBERT, TRACY, science educator; d. Ernest Ebert and Veronica O'Connell. MA in Biology Edn., U. Ctrl. Fla., Orlando, 1999—2001. Sci. tchr. Hungerford Prep HS, Eatonville, Fla., 2000—. Office: Hungerford Prep HS 100 E Kennedy Blvd Eatonville FL 32715 Office Phone: 407-622-8200 2233.

EBINGER, LINDA ANN, retired nurse; b. North Attleboro, Mass., Apr. 6, 1944; d. Donat Leo Deshetres and Muriel Francis Mumford; m. Carl R. Ebinger, Jr. (dec. Apr. 1994); children: Carl R. III, Eric Edward. Diploma in practical nursing, Lindsay Hopkins Nursing Sch., Miami, 1978. LPN, Fla.; cert. LPN IV therapy. ECG technician Sturdy Meml. Hosp., Attleboro, Mass., 1962-65, with radiology dept., 1968-69; stewardess TWA, 1965; clin. lab. technician Wrentham State Sch., Mass., 1965-71, EKG dept. mgr. Mass., 1965-70; rental property owner, mgr., 1973—; orthop./med.-surg. unit nurse Bapt. Hosp. Miami, 1978-81, oncology unit nurse, 1981-82, ob-gyn. unit, 1982—84, with Joslin Diabetes Care Ctr., 1984-93, orthop./neurol. nurse, 1993-99, nurse short stay overnight unit, 1999—2001, ret., 1961. Vol. Domestic Violence Abuse Ctr., Punta Gorda, Fla., 2002—; mem. Team Punta Gorda. Mem. LWV (sec. Dade County 1995-98, bd. dirs. 1998-2001, pres. Port Charlotte, Fla. chpt. 2004-), Freeman House Soc. (sec. 2002-05), Punta Gorda Isles Yacht Club (co-chair hospitality com.). Republican. Roman Catholic.

EBINGER, MARY RITZMAN, pastoral counselor; b. Reading, Pa., Nov. 23, 1929; d. Michael Erwin and Daisy Mae (Shaeffer) R.; m. Warren Ralph Ebinger, Aug. 11, 1951; children: Lee, Lori, Jonathan. BA, North Cen. Coll., Naperville, Ill., 1951; MS, Loyola Coll., Balt., 1981; grad. student, Wesley Theol. Sem., Washington, 1976, Cath. U., 1977. Cert. nat. counselor Dept. of Md. Health and Mental Hygiene, cert. nat. counselor Am. Assn. Pastoral Counselors; cert. in marriage inventory. Elem. tchr. Naperville Washington Sch., 1952-54; dir. adult work Millian Ch., Rockville, Md., 1974-76; pastoral counselor Washington Pastoral Counselors, 1976-81; assoc. dir. Balt. Washington Conf. Pastoral Care and Counseling, Balt., 1990-95; marriage retreat co-leader. Mem. adj. faculty psychology Frederick C.C., Md., 1982-87, Anne Arnold C.C., Md., 1988-90; pres. Wesley Guild Wesley Theol. Seminary, Washington, 1987-89; del. gen. conf. U. Meth. Ch., 1988, 92; leader marriage retreats and premarriage and marriage inventoppea; marriage and spiritual life retreat co-leader, 1990—. Author: I Was Sick and You Visited Me, 1976, 2d edit., 1995, enlarged and translated into Spanish, 1996, Does Anybody Care, 1978, (with husband Warren) Do-It-Yourself Marriage Enrichment, 1998; contbr. chpt. to book. Growing in Love, 2001, Meditations for Families, 2001, Dimensions for Living, 2001, What? Retire? Past 70, 2004, Running on Empty, 2004. Pres. Ch. Women United, Springfield, Ill., 1969-71; chmn. Episcopacy com. United Meth. Ch., Balt., 1988-90; del. gen. and jurisdictional conf. United Meth. Ch., 1988, 92; chairperson Sharoe Our Strenth, 2004, 05. Recipient Disting. Alumnus award North Cen. Coll., 1990, Loyola Coll., 1991, Two Thousand Women of Achievement award Dartmouth Eng. Mus., 1969. Mem. Am. Assn. Counseling and Devel., Am. Assn. Pastoral Counseling (cert., Atlantic region chmn. theol. and social concerns 1988-92). Avocations: writing, reading, swimming. Home and Office: 407 Russell Ave Apt 4055 Gaithersburg MD 20877-2854 Office Phone: 301-987-6553. Business E-Mail: MREWRE@aol.com.

EBLER, MARILYN ANN, graphic designer, educator; b. Socorro, N.Mex., Mar. 9, 1955; d. Robert Gerald Ebler and Mary Eulala (Castillo) Barber; children: Manuel Anthony Anaya, Josephine Lynn Duke. Cert. Cosmetology, Lea County Beauty Coll., 1977; AAS, N.Mex. Jr. Coll., 1992; BS with honors, Ea. N.Mex. U., 1995; MS in Edn., Capella U., Mpls., 2001. Cosmetologist Glamour House, Hobbs, N.Mex., 1977—85, Linda's Styling Salon, Hobbs, N.Mex., 1985—91; staff graphic arts dept. N.Mex. Jr. Coll., Hobbs, 1991—92; computer lab. asst., office asst. Ea. N.Mex. U., 1993—94; graphic arts asst. N.Mex. Jr. Coll., Hobbs, 1994—95, prof. comml. graphic design, 1995—. Mem. faculty senate N.Mex. Jr. Coll., 1995—; attendee numerous confs. Contbr. graphic designs to profl. jours. Recipient numerous awards. Mem. Vocat. Indsl. Clubs Am. (advisor 1995-97), Kappa Pi (sec. 1993-94). Avocations: photography, water color, cross stitch, walking, crochet.

EBNET, JEANNIE MARIE, enterostomal therapist; b. Port Arthur, Tex., Mar. 2, 1957; d. Alfonce Herman and Deloris Marie (Provost) Honish; m. Michael Joseph Ebnet, Mar. 3, 1979. BSN, U. Tex., Houston, 1979. RN, Tex., Okla.; cert. cmty. health nurse, enterostomal therapy nurse. Staff nurse St. Luke's Episc. Hosp., Houston, 1977-81, Bodimetric Health Svcs., Ft. Worth, 1981-83, Haltom City Hosp., Ft. Worth, 1983-84, North Hills Hosp., Ft. Worth, 1984-87; clin. supr. Osteopathic Home Health, Ft. Worth, 1987-91; br. dir. HealthCor, Inc., Denton, Tex., 1991-92; enterostomal therapist Mother Frances Hosp., Tyler, Tex., 1993—97; clin. supr. Wound Healing Ctr., 1997—98; self-employed, 0198—. Mem. Wound Ostomy, Continence Nurses Soc., Intravenous Nursing Soc., Sigma Theta Tau. Avocations: quilting, crocheting, reading, swimming. Home: PO Box 130012 Tyler TX 75713-0012

EBY, LOIS, artist; b. Tulsa, May 5, 1940; d. Seth Gilman and Mary Nadine E.; m. David W. Budbill; children: Gene, Nadine. BA, Duke U., 1962; MA, Columbia U., 1964. Instr. drawing Cmty. Coll. Vt., Morrisville, 1984-94; adj. faculty art Vt. Coll. of Norwich U., Montpelier, 1994—2001; commentator arts, civil rights and women's issues Vt. Pub. Radio, 1998—. One-person shows at Tribes Gallery, N.Y.C., 1999, Flynn Theatre Gallery Space, Burlington, Vt., 1999, Brown Libr. Gallery, Sterling Coll., Craftsbury Common, Vt., 1997, Julian Scott Meml. Gallery, Johnson State Coll., Vt., 1992; exhibited in group shows at Chaffee Art Ctr., Rutland, Vt., 1995, Helen Day Art Ctr., Stowe, Vt., 1996, Trinity Coll., Burlington, Vt., 1996, T.W. Wood Gallery, Montpelier, Vt. 1999, JVC Jazz Festival, NYC, 2003, Vision Festival, NYC, 2004-2005; represented by West Branch Gallery & Sculpture Pk, Stowe, Vt. E-mail: leby@wildblue.net.

ECCLES, JACQUELYNNE S., psychology educator; BA in Social Psychology, U. Calif. Berkeley, 1966; PhD, U. Calif. Los Angeles, 1974. HS math sci. tchr. US Peace Corps, Ghana, 1966—68; asst. prof. Smith Coll., 1974—76; asst. to assoc. to full prof. U. Mich., 1974—92, asst. v.p. rsch., 1987—88; prof. U. Colo., 1988—92. Chair Internat. Doctorate Program, Life Span Devel. with Max Planck, Berlin, 2002—; mem. Psychology Dept. Exec. Com., U. Mich., 1981—86; Chair U. Mich., Edn., Psychology, 1992—2002; mem. U. Mich., Rackham Exec. Com., 1993—95, Pres. Adv. Com. on Women's Issues, U. Mich., 1993—98; interim chair U. Mich., Dept. Psychology, 1998—99. Mem.: NSF, Nat. Acad. Edn., Pathways to Coll. Network Rsch. Scholars Panel, Adv. Com. for Jossey-Bass Series on new Directions for Youth Devel., Coun. for Soc. for Rsch. Adolescence, Coun. for Soc. for Psycho. Study of Social Issues, Am. Psycho. Assn. Office: U Mich Inst Rsch on Women and Gender 204 S State St Ann Arbor MI 48109 Home: 1109 Pearl St Ypsilanti MI 48197 E-mail: jeccles@umich.edu.

ECHOLS, KARI ELIZABETH, music educator, elementary school educator; b. Dallas, Tex., Apr. 19, 1979; d. Wilburn Oliver Echols, Jr. and Susan Colwell Echols. MusB, Dallas Bapt. U., 2001. Cert. classroom tchr. Tex. State Bd. Edn., 2002. Elem. music tchr. Lone Star Elem. Sch., Keller, Tex., 2002, Bluebonnet Elem. Sch., Fort Worth, 2002—03, Valley Ranch Elem. Sch., Irving, 2003—. Musician: Sideroads Band. Worship leader Northwood Ch., Keller, Tex., 2002—06, mission work Vietnam, 2005. Baptist. Achievements include research in ethnomusicology rsch. in Vietnam. Avocations: travel, music, tennis. Office: Valley Ranch Elem Sch 9800 Rodeo Dr Irving TX 75063 Office Phone: 214-496-8500.

ECHOLS, MARY EVELYN, training services executive, writer; b. LaSalle, Ill., Apr. 5, 1915; d. Francis Ira and Mary Irene (Coleman) Bassett; m. David H. Echols, Aug. 31, 1951 (dec.); children: Susan Echols O'Donnell, William. Grad. St. Mary's Nursing Hosp., Chgo. Founder Internat. Travel Tng. Courses, Inc., Chgo., 1962—; pres. Evelyn Echols Cons. Ltd., 1998, Echols Comms. Ltd., 2004—. Author: Saying Yes to Life. Cons. Harold Washington Coll.'s Hospitality Courses; bd. dirs. Chgo. Conv. and Tourism Bur., Am. Cancer Soc., Gus Giordiano Jazz Dance Chgo., Little Sisters of the Poor; past pres. Pres. Reagan's Adv. Com. for Women's Bus. Ownership; v.p. United Cerebral Palsy Assn.; nat. spokesperson Prevent Blindness in Am.; mem. Women's Internat. Forum. Named Entrepreneur of Yr. Women Bus. Owners N.Y., 1985, Bus. Woman of Yr. Nat. Assn. Women Bus. Owners, 1985, Crain's Chgo. Bus., 1993; named to Chgo.'s Entrepreneurial Hall of Fame, 1992. Mem.: Soc. Am. Travel Agts., Acad. TV Arts and Scis., Chgo. Execs. Club. Office Phone: 773-348-1553. E-mail: evelyn@evelynechols.com.

ECK, MARLA J., special education educator; d. Mary Jane Dixon and P. John Eck, Kathy L. Eck (Stepmother). BA in Psychology, Creighton U., 2002; MEd, U. Kans., 2004. Cert. edn. Kans., spl. edn. Tex. Dining hall discipleship Kids Across Am., Golden, Mo., 1998—99, cook, 2002; ABA therapist Omaha, 2002; child care provider Christ Cmty. Ch., Leawood, Kans., 2002—03; autism tchr. Lansing (Kans.) Elem., 2004—06; autism and comm. tchr. Carrollton, Tex., 2006—. Vol. Spl. Olympics, Omaha, 2002; side walker Heartland Therapeutic Riding Ctr., Stilwell, Kans., 2003—04; small group leader K-Life, Prairie Village, Kans., 2002—04. Scholar Linn scholar, Creighton U., 1998—99, 2000—02; Arts and Scis. Dean's scholar, 1998—99. Mem.: NEA, Autism Soc. Am., Pi Lambda Theta. Avocations: horseback riding, bicycling, writing/editing, guitar.

ECKARD VILARDO, LINDA J., lawyer; Grad., Gettysburg Coll., George Washington U., U. Glasgow. Co-founder, shareholder Roberts & Eckard, PC; ptnr. Davis Wright Tremaine LLP, Washington, DC, 1997; outside counsel Radio One Inc., Lanham, Md., gen. counsel, 1998—, asst. sec., 1999—, v.p., 2001—. Office: Radio One Inc 7th Fl 5900 Princess Garden Parkway Lanham MD 20706 E-mail: lvilardo@radio-one.com.

ECKELS, MARY ELIZABETH, artist; b. Norman, Okla., Sept. 11, 1948; d. Richard Wagner and Beverly (Benjamin) Eckels; m. Robert Earl Wilkinson, Sept. 7, 1967 (div. 1970); m. Robert Dale West Jr., Mar. 30, 1984. BFA, U. Colo., 1984. Registered silversmith. Color separator Lloyd Arkin Advt., L.A., 1968-69; dress maker Benjamins, Albuquerque, 1969; apprentice silversmith Gusterman's Silversmiths, Denver, 1970-71, silversmith, 1971-78, owner, silversmith, 1978—. Featured expert Niederkorn Antiques-Restoration Clinic, Phila., 1989-90, Denver Art Museum, 1983; speaker Denver Pub. Sch. Career Day program, 1975-90. One woman show Gary Bauman's Lewd Jewel Gallery, Denver, 1977; silversmith cruet for Sacrament, Episcopal Ch., Castlerock, Colo., 1981, medals for Telluride Film Festival, 1973—; artist (gospel book cover) Sterling, St. John's Cath. Denver, 1995; gold ring of office for Archbishop of Episc. Diocese, 2005. Com. chmn. Jr. League Denver, 1983-88; mem. Clean Denver Com. Pub. Works, 1982-84; bd. dirs. Womansch. Denver, 1984-86, Larimer Sq. Merchants Adv. Bd., Denver, 1980-90. Recipient 1st place painting award Denver Allied Arts Guild, 1965, art scholarship award Boettcher Found., 1966, 1st Pl. award Platinum Guild Internat. Design Competition, 1998. Mem.: Lower Larimer Arts Assn. (bd. dir. 2002). Republican. Avocations: fly fishing, drawing, sewing, cooking. Office: Gustermans Silversmiths 1418 Larimer Sq Denver CO 80202-1711 Office Phone: 303-629-6927.

ECKERT, JEAN PATRICIA, elementary school educator; b. Pitts., July 22, 1935; d. Homer Mitchel and Berdena Leona (Kessler) Canel; m. William L. Eckert, June 13, 1959; 1 child, Suzanne Mary. BS, Indiana U. Pa., 1957; postgrad., U. Pitts., 1958-59, U. San Diego, 1981. Cert. pub. instrn., Pa. Elem. tchr. Pine-Richland Sch. Dist., Gibsonia, Pa., 1957—60, substitute tchr., 1963—65; elem. tchr. Shaler Twp. Sch. Dist., Glenshaw, Pa., 1965—66, St. Scholastica Sch., Diocese of Pitts., Aspinwall, Pa., 1966—91, substitute tchr., 1991—, tutor, 1991—. Judge election 4th dist. Rep. Party, Aspinwall, 1962-65, 91-98. Mem.: AAUW, Nat. Cath. Edn. Assn., Literacy Vols. Am., Ind. U. (Pa.) Alumni Assn., Delta Zeta (sec. 1955, pres. 1956). Roman Catholic. Avocations: travel, literature. Home: 210 12th St Pittsburgh PA 15215-1600

ECKHARDT, LAUREL ANN, biologist, researcher, educator; b. Palo Alto, Calif., Sept. 4, 1951; d. Joseph Carl Augustus Eckhardt and Ada Jane Williams Smith; m. Michael Warren Young, Dec. 27, 1978; children: Natalie Alice Eckhardt Young, Arissa Caroline Eckhardt Young. BA summa cum laude, U. Tex., 1974; PhD in Genetics, Stanford (Calif.) U., 1980. Damon Runyon-Walter Winchell postdoctoral fellow Albert Einstein Coll. Medicine, Bronx, 1980-83; asst. prof. Dept. Biol. Sci., Columbia U., N.Y.C., 1984-88, assoc. prof., 1989-92; prof. Dept. Biol. Sci., Hunter Coll. of CUNY, 1992—, Marie Hesselbach prof. biology, 1999—. Reviewer immunobiology study sect. Dept. Rsch. Grants, NIH, Bethesda, Md., 1993-96; reviewer grand rev. com. Am. Heart Assn., N.Y.C., 1990-93, sci. rev. Immunological Sciences peer rev. com., Dept. of Def. Breast Cancer Rsch. Program, 1998, 2000, 03, rev. panelist for rsch. tng. fellowships for med. students, Howard Huges Med. Student, Howard Hughes Med. Inst., 2002-04. Assoc. editor Jour. Immunology, 1997-2001; contbr. articles to profl. jours. Rsch. grantee NIH-Inst. Allergy and Infectious Diseases, 1984-90, 90—, Am. Cancer Soc., 1990-95, NIH-Nat. Cancer Inst., 1994-99. Mem. Am. Assn. Immunologists (program com. mem. 1995-99), N.Y. Acad. Scis., Harvey Soc. Democrat. Avocations: tennis, gardening, dance. Office: Hunter College of CUNY Dept Biol Sci 695 Park Ave New York NY 10021-5085

ECKHOFF, SARAH LYNN, music educator; d. David Joseph and Vicki Lee Schroeder; m. Eric Anthony Eckhoff, July 24, 1999. BA in Comms., Ctrl. Meth. Coll., 1999; cert. in Tchg., Ctrl. Mo. State U., 2003; student in Adminstrn., William Woods U., 2005—. Tchr. music Bowling Green R-1 Schs., Mo., 2004—. Musician: Marshall (Mo.) Mcpl. Band, 2000—04, Marshall (Mo.) Philharmonic Orch., 2002—04, Troy (Mo.) Cmty. Concert Band, 2004—. Mem.: Mo. State Tchrs. Assn., Mo. Band Masters Assn., Sigma Alpha Iota. Home: 12869 Hwy VV Bowling Green MO 63334 Office: Bowling Green High School 700 W Adams St Bowling Green MO 63334

ECKLAR, JULIA, freelance writer, novelist; b. Greenville, Ohio, Mar. 14, 1964; d. William T. and Constance Mary (Huffman) E. Grad. parochial sch., St. Martin, Ohio. Temp. word processor Crown Temps. Pers. Pool, Pitts., 1983-85; adminstrv. aide U. Pitts., 1984-87; data entry operator Arthritis Found., Pitts., 1985-86; freelance writer, Monroeville, Pa., 1987—. Condr. seminars Banksville Mid. Gifted Ctr., Pitts., 1990—, Indiana U. Pa., 1992—. Author: Kobayashi Maru, 1989, ReGenesis, 1995; contbr. novellas to mag. Recipient John W. Campbell award World Sci. Fiction Soc., 1991. Mem. Sci. Fiction Writers Am. (Nebula awards jury 1991, Theodore Sturgeon award jury 1991), Pennwriters. Democrat. Avocations: music, animal husbandry, lecturing, sports, native american bead craft.

ECKLUND, CONSTANCE CRYER, French language and literature educator; b. Chgo., Nov. 20, 1938; d. Gilbert and Electra (Papadopoulos) Cryer; m. John E. Ecklund, Mar. 22, 1975. BA magna cum laude, Northwestern U., 1960; PhD, Yale U., 1965. Asst. prof. Ind. U., Bloomington, 1964-66; asst. prof. French, So. Conn. State U., New Haven, 1967-70, assoc. prof., 1970-76, prof., 1976—. Spkr. in field. Contbr. articles to profl. jours. Named Tchr. of Yr., So. Conn. State U., 2002. Mem. AAUP, MLA, Am. Coun. Tchg. Fgn. Langs., Am. Assn. Tchrs. French, Phi Beta Kappa. Republican. Avocations: piano, gardening, cooking, travel, graphic art. Home: 27 Cedar Rd Woodbridge CT 06525-1642

ECKMAN, FERN MARJA, journalist; b. N.Y.C., Aug. 27; d. Isidor Peter and Zara Nettie (Sloate) Friedman; m. Irving Eckman, June 21, 1957. BA, N.Y. U., 1957. Reporter N.Y. Post, 1944-78; assigned to UN, 1945-49, 60-65. Author: The Furious Passage of James Baldwin, 1967; contbg. editor Working Mother, 1981-91; feature writer for nat. publs., 1965-90. Recipient George Polk Meml. award for distinguished met. reporting, 1951, 55; Page One award for community service N.Y. Newspaper Guild, 1955, for best feature reporting, 1961; citation for community service Council Puerto Rican and Spanish-Am. Orgns., 1955; Lasker award for med. journalism, 1960; Front Page award for distinguished feature writing, News Women's Club N.Y., 1949, 51, 56, 64; for distinguished series (co-recipient), 1970; Cultural News award Newspaper Reporters Assn., N.Y.C., 1967; Empire State award for excellence in med. reporting, 1968 Home: 749 W End Ave New York NY 10025-6224

ECKNER, SHANNON F., lawyer; BA in Eng. Lit., U. Cin., 2000, JD, 2003. Bar: Ohio 2003. Law clerk Phyllis G. Bossin Co., L.P.A., Cin., assoc. Mem. Big Sister. Named one of Ohio's Rising Stars, Super Lawyers, 2006. Mem.: ABA, Ohio State Bar Assn. (Family Law Com.), Cin. Bar Assn. (mem, Domestic Rels. Com.), Order of Coif, Phi Beta Kappa. Office: Phyllis G Bossin Co LPA Ste 1210 36 E Fourth St Cincinnati OH 45202 Office Phone: 513-421-4420. Office Fax: 513-421-0691.*

ECKRICH, REGINA, physical education educator, department chairman; d. Joseph and Ann Eckrich. BS, U. Del., Newark, 1977; MS, U. Wyo., Laramie, 1981; PhD, Purdue U., West Lafayette, Ind., 1990. Cert. health fitness instr. Am. Coll. Sports Medicine, 2002. Tchr. and coach Julesburg Sch. Dist., Colo., 1978—79, Sidney Pub. Schs., Nebr., 1979—82; prof. and coach Earlham Coll., Richmond, Ind., 1982—87; grad. asst. Purdue U., West Lafayette, 1987—90; prof. Augustana Coll., Sioux Falls, SD, 1990—95; prof. and dept. chair Colby-Sawyer Coll., New London, NH, 1995—. Chair-elect, chair then past chair Biomechanics Acad., Reston, Va., 2004—. Contbr. chapters to books. Recipient Excellence in Tchg. award, Purdue U., 1989; fellow Wash. Internship Inst., Am. Assn. Colls. and Univs., 2003. Mem.: AAPHERD, Am. Coll. Sports Medicine. Office: Colby Sawyer Coll 541 Main St New London NH 03257 Office Phone: 603-526-3448.

ECKSTEIN, ELAINE CLAIRE, theater educator; b. Cin., Apr. 8, 1945; d. Phyllis Lohr Smolen; m. Eugene Ellsworth Wilson, Sept. 14, 1034; 1 child, Eugene Ellsworth Wilson, Jr. BA, U. Cin., 1967, MFA, 1969. Lead tchr., dance Sch. Creative and Performing Arts, Cin., 1979—; lectr., dance U. Cin.; performer, tchr. Landmark Children's Theatre, Centerville, 2005—06. Bd. trustees Contemporary Dance Theater, Cin., 1984—, Forget-Me-Not Dance Co., 2001—. Prodr.: (mutli-media exhibition) Cincinnati: A Work of Art (Ohio Pub. History award, 2004); (ballet) Showboat Suite, (pbs special, big band new year's eve) Boogie-Woogie Bugle Boy; contbr. arts education standards; (resident choreographer) Various musicals. Mem.: Kappa Delta Pi, Phi Beta. Home: 142 Crestmont Lane Cincinnati OH 45220 Office: School for Creative and Performing Arts 1310 Sycamore Street Cincinnati OH 45202 Office Phone: 513-363-8114. Office Fax: 513-363-8020. E-mail: ecksteе@cpsboe.k12.oh.us.

ECKSTEIN, JULIE, state agency administrator; m. Mark Eckstein; 3 children. BS, Univ. Mo., Columbia; MBA, Washington Univ., St. Louis. Dir. cmty. prog. SSM St. Joseph Health Ctr.; dir. corp. wellness prog. SSM Health Care; exec. dir. Healthy Communities St. Charles County, 2000—05; dir. Mo. Dept. Health & Sr. Svc., Jefferson City, 2005—. Founder CommunityCalendars.net LLC. Mailing: Dept Health & Sr Svc PO Box 570 Jefferson City MO 65102*

ECKSTEIN, MARLENE R., vascular radiologist; b. Poughkeepsie, N.Y., Sept. 6, 1948; d. Marc and Lola (Charm) E. AB, Vassar Coll., 1970; MD, Albert Einstein Coll. Medicine, 1973. Diplomate Nat. Bd. Med. Examiners; cert. Am. Bd. Radiology. Intern in medicine Yale-New Haven Med. Ctr., 1973-74, resident in diagnostic radiology, 1974-77; asst. radiologist, chief vascular radiology sect. South Nassau Cmtys. Hosp., Oceanside, N.Y., 1977-78, assoc. radiologist, chief vascular radiology sect., 1978-81, asst. dir. dept. radiology, chief vascular radiology sect., 1981-83; asst. radiologist Mass. Gen. Hosp., 1983-87, assoc. radiologist, 1987—. Asst. prof. clin. radiology SUNY-Stony Brook Med. Sch., 1980-83; instr. radiology, Harvard Med. Sch., 1983-84, asst. prof., 1984—. Mem. exec. com. and hosp. chmn. United Jewish Appeal of Physicians and Dentists of Nassau County, N.Y., 1981-83. Fellow Am. Coll. Angiology, Soc. Cardiovasc. and Interventional Radiology; mem. AMA, Am. Coll. Radiology, Am. Inst. Ultrasound in Medicine, Am. Assn. Women Radiologists, Am. Med. Women's Assn., Mass. Radiol. Soc., Mass. Med. Soc., New Eng. Soc. Cardiovasc. and Interventional Radiology (pres. 1985-86), Radiol. Soc. N.Am. Achievements include design and development of line of vascular catheters. Home: 141 Fulton Ave Apt 312 Poughkeepsie NY 12603-2841 Office: Mass Gen Hosp Vascular Radiology Sect Boston MA 02114 E-mail: mreckstein@alum.vassar.edu.

ECONOMOS, KATHERINE, oncologist; b. Bklyn., Jan. 4, 1961; MD, State U. NY Bklyn. Health Sci. Ctr., 1986. Cert. ob-gyn 1996, gynecologic oncology 1998. Intern Maimonides Med. Ctr., Bklyn., 1986—87, resident, 1986—90; fellowship U. Tex. Med. Ctr., SW, Dallas, 1990—93; asst. attending physician NY Presbytn. Hosp., N.Y.C., 1993—; assoc. attending physician NY Meth. Hosp., N.Y.C., 1993—2000; asst. prof. to assoc. prof.

Cornell Med. Coll., OB-GYN Dept., N.Y.C., 1993—; assoc. attending physician NY Meth. Hosp., Oncology, Gynecology, N.Y.C., 2000—. Office: Cornell U 525 East 68th St Ste J130 New York NY 10021

ECTON, DONNA R., business executive; b. Kansas City, Mo., May 10, 1947; d. Allen Howard and Marguerite (Page) E.; m. Victor H. Maragni, June 16, 1986; children: Mark, Gregory. BA (Durant Scholar), Wellesley Coll., 1969; MBA, Harvard U., 1971. V.p. Chem. Bank, N.Y.C., 1972-79, Citibank, N.A., N.Y.C., 1979-81; pres. MBA Resources, Inc., N.Y.C., 1981-83; v.p. adminstrn., officer Campbell Soup Co., Camden, NJ, 1983-89; chmn. Triangle Mfg. Corp. subs. Campbell Soup Co., Raleigh, NC, 1984-87; sr. v.p., officer Nutri/System, Inc., Willow Grove, Pa., 1989-91; pres., CEO Van Houten N.Am., Delavan, Wis., 1991-94, Andes Candies Inc., Delavan, 1991-94; chmn., pres., CEO Bus. Mail Express, Inc., Malvern, Pa., 1995-96; bd. dirs. PETsMART, Inc., Phoenix, 1994—98, COO, 1996-98; chmn., pres., CEO EEI Inc., Paradise Valley, 1998—. Bd. dirs. H&R Block, Kansas City, Mo., 1993—, Johns Hopkins' JHPIEGO, Balt., 2004—; commencement spkr. Pa. State U., 1987. Mem. bd. overseers Harvard U., 1984-90; mem. Coun. Fgn. Rels., N.Y.C., 1987—; trustee Inst. for Advancement of Health, 1988-92. Named One of 80 Women to Watch in the 80's, Ms. mag., 1980, One of All Time Top 10 of Last Decade, Glamour mag., 1984, One of 50 Women to Watch, Bus. Week mag., 1987, One of 100 Women to Watch, Bus. Month mag., 1989; recipient Wellesley Alumnae Achievement award, 1987; Fred Sheldon Fund fellow Harvard U., 1971-72; Margaret Rudkin scholar Harvard U., 1969-71. Mem. Harvard Bus. Sch. Assn. (pres. exec. council 1983-84), Harvard Bus. Sch. Club Greater N.Y. (pres. 1979-80, lifetime bd. dir.), Wellesley Coll. Nat. Alumnae Assn. (bd. dirs., 1st v.p. 1977-80). Avocations: public speaking, art, gardening, reading, bicycling.

EDDY, COLETTE ANN, aerial photography studio owner, photographer; b. Sept. 14, 1950; d. William F. and Jeanne (Valeski) Trump; m. Robert K. Eddy, Aug. 21, 1976 (div. Sept. 1992). AA, St. Petersburg (Fla.) Jr. Coll., 1970; BA, U. South Fla., 1973; MS, Nova U., 1988. Yacht caretaker The Sundowner, St. Petersburg, 1972-73; mgr. Aunt Hattie's Restaurant, St. Petersburg, 1973-79, Johnathan Jones, Inc., St. Petersburg, 1979-80; photographer, sales rep. Smith Aerial Photos, Tampa, Fla., 1980—; owner, aerial photographer Aerial Innovations, Inc., Tampa, 1987—; owner Havanna Connection Inc., Carribean. Mem. Tampa Mus. Art. Named Winner Tampa Chamber Small Bus. of Yr., 1998. Mem. Profl. Photographers Am. (30 Merit awards), Fla. Profl. Photographers (22 Merit awards 1987-90), Profl. Aerial Photographers Assn., Tampa C. of C., Emerging Bus. Coun. Republican. Home: 198 Ceylon Ave Tampa FL 33606-3330 Office: Aerial Innovations Inc 3703 W Azeele St Tampa FL 33609-2807

EDDY, DARLENE MATHIS, poet, educator; b. Elkhart, Ind., Mar. 19, 1937; d. William Eugene and Fern (Paulmer) Mathis; m. Spencer Livingston Eddy, Jr., May 23, 1964 (dec. May 1971). BA, Goshen Coll., Ind., 1959; MA, Rutgers U., New Brunswick. NJ, 1961, PhD, 1967. Instr., lectr. Douglass Coll. and Rutgers U., 1962-64, 66-67; asst. prof. English Ball State U., Muncie, Ind., 1967-70, assoc. prof., 1971-75, prof., 1975-99, poet-in-residence, 1989-93, prof. emerita, 1999. Whitinger lectr. Honors Coll., 1998-99; adj. prof. core program and coll. seminar program U. Notre Dame, 2001-; adj. prof. Eng. Goshen Coll., 2002-; cons., presenter in field. Author: The Worlds of King Lear, 1968, Leaf Threads, Wind Rhymes, 1985, Weathering, 1991, Portraits, 1992; poetry editor Forum, 1985-89; contbg. editor Snowy Egret, 1988-89; cons. editor Blue Unicorn, 1995—; founding editor The Hedge Row Press, 1995; contbr. articles to English Lang. Notes, Am. Lit., others; author numerous poems. Mem. commn. on the status of women in the profession, Nat. Coun. of Teachers of English, 1976-79; coord. Women's Studies program, 1976-82. Woodrow Wilson Nat. fellow, 1959-62, Notable Woodrow Wilson fellow, 1991, Rutgers U. grad. honors fellow, 1964-65; recipient numerous rsch., creative teaching and creative arts grants. Mem. AAUW, DAR, Soc. Mayflower Descs., Nat. League Am. Pen Women, League Women Voters. Home: 1840 Cobblestone Blvd Elkhart IN 46514

EDDY, GLADYS LOUISE, educational administrator; b. Castle Rock, Colo., Dec. 25, 1915; d. William Adam and Jessie Louise (Cozens) Shellabarger; m. Willard Oscar Eddy, Aug. 21, 1938; children: Sandra Carol, William Radford. BSBA, U. Denver, 1937. Asst. Colo. State U., Ft. Collins, 1937-42, sect. to pres., 1945-46, instr., 1957-62, 67-79, asst. prof. bus., 1979-84, asst. to dean, Coll. Bus., 1984—; instr. U.S. Army Air Force, Ft. Collins, 1942-43; tchr. Poudre R-1 Sch. Dist., Ft. Collins, 1957-62. Cons. in field; pres., bd. dirs. Colo. Assn. Sch. Bds., Denver, 1973-83; mem. Nat. Adv. Coun. on Vocat. Edn., Washington, 1982-84. Mem. Poudre R-1 Bd. Edn., Ft. Collins, 1971-83, Colo. State Bd. Edn., Denver, 1987-90; bd. dirs. Colo. Parks and Recreation Found., 1984-90; mem. scholar com. Griffin Found., 1996—. Mem. PEO, Mortar Bd. (nat. program dir. 1982), Ft. Collins Country Club, Order Eastern Star, Delta Kappa Gamma, Sigma Kappa. Republican. Episcopalian. Avocation: travel. Home: 509 Remington St Fort Collins CO 80524-3022 Office Phone: 970-491-5325. Business E-Mail: gladys.eddy@colostate.edu.

EDDY, JANET ELIZABETH, retired elementary school educator; b. L.A., Calif., Dec. 23, 1946; d. Raymond Michael Nauroth and Geraldine Cecila Manion; m. Kenneth Leroy Eddy, July 23, 1988; m. Michael William Houston (div.); children: Scott Michael Houston, Molly JoAnne Houston, Katherine Elizabeth Houston. BS Elem. Edn., Dana Coll., Blair, Nebr., 1969. 6th grade North Polk Cmty. Sch., Alleman, Iowa, 1970—72; 5th grade Oakland Cmty. Sch., Oakland, Iowa, 1972—75; 4th grade Dow City Cmty. Sch., Dow City, Iowa, 1977—78, Greenfield Cmty. Sch., Greenfield, Iowa, 1978—2004; ret. Co-pres. Nodaway Valley Edn. Assn., 1999; chair govtl. affairs Nodaway Valley, 1998—2003; bd. dirs. Henry A. Wallace County Life Ctr., 1986—96. Recipient Environ. Educator of the Yr., State of Iowa, 1974, Govs. Vol. award, 1987, 1986. Mem.: St. John's Coun. Cath. Women. Achievements include est. Bilse Ride Around Adair County; est. Miss Adair County Pagent at County Fair. Avocations: reading, antiques, travel, golf.

EDDY, NANCY C., counselor; BS in Elem. Edn., U. Ark., EdM in Sch. Counseling; JD, U. Ark., Little Rock. Counselor Clinton Elem., Sherwood, Ark., 1984—. Treas., bd. dirs. S.W. Ednl. Lab., 2003—. Chmn. Pulaski Fedn. Tchrs. Cmty. Svcs.; co-chmn. Ctrl. Ark. Jobs With Justice; vol. United Way; pres. Ctrl. Ark. Labor Coun., 1999. Office: Clinton Elem 142 Hollywood Ave Sherwood AR 72120

EDDY-JOHNSON, DEANNA M., home health care advocate; b. Bklyn., Aug. 26, 1950; d. Charles Jess and Virginia Fern (Hoelscher) Deck; m. Dennis R. Eddy (div.); children: Denny R. Eddy, Ginger Deann Spillers. Degree in computer programming, Parkland Jr. Coll., Champaign, Ill., 1983; degree in real estate, Parkland Jr. Coll., 1985, nursing cert., 1990. CEO Jenn Swing Co., Urbana, Ill., 1993—97; ptnr. PDC Entertainment Ptnrs., 2006—. Inventor Jenn Swing, 1st full body accessible swing, 1996, The Cubby, toddler swing, 2004; author: Idea to Financial Success, 2003, Patty Panda Joins the Circus, 2005; lyricist I Want to Rock with you Jesus, 2005. Recipient Sec. award, Ambucs Assn., Urbana, 1996. Republican. Baptist. Avocations: walking, bicycling, concerts, plays. Home: 306 Dodson Dr E Urbana IL 61802 E-mail: djohns1105@mchsi.com.

EDEAWO, GALE SKY, publishing company executive, writer; b. Detroit, Mar. 22, 1946; d. John Bryd Martin and Minerva Lee Dubrey; m. Robert Judkins, Jan. 23, 1965 (div. Jan. 1979); children: Consuella Judkins. AA, L.A. City Coll., 1977; student, Calif. State U., L.A., 1977-78. Telecom. PBXtra Placement, L.A., 1979-98; owner, mgr., writer Sky Publs., Savannah, Ga., 1998—; pvt. real estate investor, 2000—. Travel cons. Alwayz Travel, Inglewood, Calif., 1989-92. Peer counselor Rosa Parks Rape Crisis Ctr., L.A., 1990—98, Rape Crisis Ctr., Savannah, Ga., 1999—2001, bd. dirs., 2000—; jail, prison activist, 2000—; AIDS activist, contbg. writer Project Azuka, Savannah, 1998—2000, AIDS Project L.A., 1997—; cmty. outreach, spkr. Alzheimer's Assn., L.A., 1996—97; bd. dirs. Alcoholism Ctr. Women, L.A., 1992—94; leader writer's workshops for youth at risk Dept. Family and Children's Svcs., Savannah, 1999—; founder re-entry program for incarcerated women Project Welcome Home, 2001—; mem. adv. bd. Regional Youth Detention Ctr., 2001—; local storyteller, 2001—; bd. dirs. Interfaith Hospitality Network, 2003—. Mem. Am. Legion Women's Aux. (mem. pub. rels. 1986, historian 2000), Am. Corrections Assn., Nat. Coun. Negro Women, Fraternal Order Police. Democrat. Methodist. Avocations: travel, writing, cats, reading, researching the south. Office: Sky Publs 12511 Largo Dr Savannah GA 31419-2601 Fax: 912-961-9076. Office Phone: 912-920-9411. E-mail: mamasky@aol.com.

EDELBERG, MARY, elementary school educator; BS in Mid. Sch. Edn., Ga. Coll. and State U., Milledgeville, 1996; MS in Edn., Walden U., Mpls., 2004. 7th grade math tchr. Miller Grove Mid. Sch., Ga., 1997—99; 7th grade sci. tchr. Five Forks Mid. Sch., Lawrenceville, Ga., 1999—. Mem. Gwinnett County Teachers As Leaders, Ga., 2004—05. Mem. Atlanta Jaycees, Ga., 2005—06. Mem.: Profl. Assn. of Ga. Educators. Office: Five Forks Middle School 3250 River Rd Lawrenceville GA 30044

EDELMAN, BETSY A. (ELIZABETH EDELMAN), lawyer; b. 1955; BA, Mich. State U.; JD, Emory U. Sch. Law. Bar: Ga. 1980. Gen. counsel RBC Centura Bank, Rocky Mt., NC. Office: Office of General Counsel RBC Centura Bank 1417 Centura Hwy Rocky Mount NC 27804 Office Phone: 404-495-6157. Office Fax: 252-454-4800.

EDELMAN, JUDITH H., architect; b. Bklyn., Sept. 16, 1923; d. Abraham and Frances (Israel) Hochberg; m. Harold Edelman, Dec. 26, 1947; children: Marc, Joshua. Student, Conn. Coll., 1940—41, NYU, 1941—42; BArch, Columbia U., 1946. Designer, drafter Huson Jackson, N.Y.C., 1948-58; Schermerhorn traveling fellow, 1950; pvt. practice, 1958-60; ptnr. Edelman & Salzman, N.Y.C., 1960-79, Edelman Partnership (Archs.), N.Y.C., 1979—2002, Edelman, Sultan, Knox, Wood /Archs. LLP, N.Y.C., 2002—. Adj. prof. Sch. Architecture CUNY, 1972-76, vis. lectr. grad. program in environ. psychology, 1977, 77; vis. lectr. Washington U., St. Louis, 1974, U. Oreg., 1974, MIT, 1975, Pa. State U., 1977, Rensselaer Poly. Inst., 1977, Columbia U., 1979; First Claire Watson Forrest Meml. lectr. U. Oreg., U. Calif., Berkeley, U. So. Calif., 1982. Prin. works include Restoration of St. Mark's Ch. in the Bowery, N.Y.C., 1970-82, Two Bridges Urban Renewal Area Housing, 1970-96, Jennings Hall Sr. Citizens Housing, Bklyn., 1980, Goddard Riverside Elderly Housing and Cmty. Ctr., N.Y.C., 1983, Columbus Green Apartments, N.Y.C., 1987, Chung Pak Bldg., N.Y.C., 1992, Child Care Ctr., Queens, N.Y., 1999. Recipient Bard 1st honor award City Club N.Y., 1969, Bard award of merit, 1975, 82, award for design excellence HUD, 1970, 1st prize Nat. Trust for Hist. Preservation, 1983, award of merit Mcpl. Art Soc. N.Y., 1983, Pub. Svc. award Settlement Housing Fund, 1983, Women of Vision award NOW, 1989, 1st prize for design excellence C. of C., Borough of Queens, N.Y., 1989, Best in Srs.' Housing award Nat. Assn. Home Builders, 1993, Hamilton-Madison House Cmty. Svc. award, 1997. Fellow AIA (dir. N.Y. chpt., chmn. commn. on archtl. edn. 1971-73, chmn. nat. task force on women in architecture 1974-75, v.p. N.Y. chpt. 1975-77, chmn. ethics com. 1975-77, Residential Design award 1969, Pioneer in Housing award 1990, N.Y. State Assn. Archs.-AIA Honor award 1975, Design Merit award N.Y. chpt. 2005); mem. Alliance of Women in Architecture (founding, mem. steering com. 1972-74), Archs. for Social Responsibility (mem. exec. com. 1982-85), Columbia Archtl. Alumni Assn. (bd. dirs. 1968-71). Home: 37 W 12th St New York NY 10011-8502 Office: Edelman Sultan Knox Wood 100 Lafayette St Ste 204 New York NY 10013 Office Phone: 212-431-4901. Personal E-mail: judithedelman@mac.com. Business E-Mail: jedelman@edelmansultan.com.

EDELMAN, LAUREN B., sociologist, law educator; d. Murray J. and Bacia Edelman. JD, Boalt Hall, 1986; PhD, Stanford U., 1986. Asst. to assoc. prof. U. Wis., Madison, 1986—96; prof. U. Calif., Berkeley, 1996—. Fellow, Guggenheim Found., 2000, Ctr. for Advanced Study in the Behavioral Scis., 2003—04. Mem.: Am. Sociol. Assn. (chair, sociology of law sect. 1993—94, Dist. Scholarship award 1995), Law and Soc. Assn. (pres. 2002—03). Achievements include research in analyses of relationship between employment law and organizational governance. Office: JSP Program/ UC Berkeley 2240 Piedmont Ave Berkeley CA 94720-2150 Office Phone: 510-642-4038. Business E-Mail: ledelman@law.berkeley.edu.

EDELMAN, MARIAN WRIGHT, not-for-profit developer, lawyer; b. Bennettsville, SC, June 6, 1939; d. Arthur J. and Maggie (Bowen) Wright; m. Peter B. Edelman, July 14, 1968; children: Joshua, Jonah, Ezra. Merrill scholar, Univs. Paris, Geneva, 1958-59; BA, Spelman Coll., 1960; LLB, Yale U., 1963, LLD (hon.), Smith Coll., 1969, Lowell Tech. U., 1975, Williams Coll., 1978, Columbia U., U. Pa., Amherst Coll., St. Joseph's Coll.; DHL (hon.), Lesley Coll., 1975, Trinity Coll., Washington, Russell Sage Coll., 1978, Syracuse U., Coll. New Rochelle, 1979, Swarthmore Coll., 1980, SUNY Old Westbury, Northeastern U., 1981, Bard Coll., 1982, U. Mass., 1983, Hunter Coll., U. So. Maine, SUNY, Albany, 1984, Bates Coll., Maryville Coll., Bank St., 1986, Claremont Grad Sch., Lincoln U., Georgetown U., Chgo. Theol. Coll., 1987, Wheaton Coll., Tulane U., Grinnell Coll. Brandeis U., Wheelock Coll., Dartmouth Coll., U. S.C., U. N.C., Grad. Ctr. CUNY, U. Wis. Milw., 1988, Interdenom. Theol. Ctr., Hofstra U., Tufts U., Borough Manhattan Community Coll., Wesleyan U., Calif. State U. L.A., Dillard U., U. Md., U. Miami, 1989, Howard U., Beloit Coll., Queens Coll., Am. U., New Sch. of Social Rsch., Coll. of Notre Dame, DePaul U., 1990, Beaver Coll., Fordham U., Simmons Coll., Hamline U., Clark U., Harvard U., Union Coll., 1991, Tuskegee U., Washington U. St. Louis, Hood Coll., Duke U., Mercy Coll., 1992, Princeton U., U. Ill., Calif. State U. San Francisco, Wittenberg Coll., Shaw U., So. Meth. U., 1993, Brown U., U. Balt., Ea. Conn. State U., U. Notre Dame, 1994. Bar: D.C., Miss., Mass. Staff atty. NAACP Legal Def. and Ednl. Fund, Inc., N.Y.C., 1963-64, dir. Jackson, Miss., 1964-68; Congl. and fed. liaison Poor People's Campaign, summer 1968; partner Washington Research Project of So. Center for Pub. Policy, 1968-73; dir. Harvard U. Center for Law and Edn., 1971-73; pres., founder Children's Def. Fund, 1973—. Author: The Measure of Our Success: A Letter To My Children and Yours, 1992, Families in Peril, 1987. Mem. exec. com. Student Non-Violent Coordinating Com., 1961-63; mem. adv. coun. Martin Luther King Jr. Meml. Libr.; mem. adv. bd. Hampshire Coll.; mem. Presdl. Commn. on Missing in Action, 1977, Presdl. Commn. on Internat. Yr. of Child, 1979, Presdl. Commn. on Agenda for 80's, 1980; bd. dirs. NAACP Legal Def. and Ednl. Fund; trustee Spelman Coll., Carnegie Coun. on Children, 1972-77, Martin Luther King Jr. Meml. Ctr.; mem. Yale U. Corp., 1971-77, Aetna Found., Nat. Commn. on Children, 1989—; bd. dirs. Aetna Life Casualty Found., Citizens for Constitutional Concerns, US. com. UNICEF, Robin Hood Found., Aaron Diamond Found., Nat. Alliance Business, City Lights, Leadership Conf. Civil Rights, Skadden Fellowship Found., Parents as Tchrs. Nat. Ctr., Inc.; U.S. rep. UNICEF; active U.S. Olympic Com. Named one of Outstanding Young Women of Am., 1966, 100 Most Influential Black Americans, Ebony mag., 2006; recipient Mademoiselle mag. award, 1965, Louise Waterman Wise award, 1970, Washington of Yr. award, 1979, Whitney M. Young award, 1979, Profl. of Yr. award Black Ent., 1979, Leadership award Nat. Women's Polit. Caucus, 1980, Black Womens Forum award, 1980, medal Columbia Tchrs. Coll., Barnard Coll., 1984, Eliot award Am. Pub. Health Assn., John W. Gardner Leadership award of Ind. Sector, Pub. Svc. Achievement award Common Cause, Compostela award Cathedral St. James, 1987, MacArthur prize fellow, 1985, Albert Schweitzer Humanitarian prize Johns Hopkins U., 1987. Philip Hauge Ahelson award AAAS, 1988, Hubert Humphrey Civil Rights award, AFL-CIO award, 1989, Radcliffe Coll. medal, 1989, Fordham Stein prize, 1989, Gandhi Peace award, 1990, M. Carey Thomas award, Robie award for humanitarianism, Essence award, numerous others; hon. fellow U. Pa. Law Sch. Mem. Phi Beta Kappa (hon.), Inst. Medicine. Office: Children's Def Fund 25 E St NW Washington DC 20001-1522*

EDELMAN, RUTH ROZUMOFF, volunteer; m. Daniel J. Edelman, Sept. 3, 1953; 3 children. Bd. mem. Daniel J. Edelman, Inc., Chgo. Mem. nat. adv. coun. Substance Abuse and Mental Health Svcs. Adminstrn., Ctr. for Mental Health Svcs.; active Commn. Econ. Devel., 1977, Inst. Psychiatry, Northwestern U., Mental Health Assn., Big Bros., Northwestern Meml. Hosp. Citizens Com., Immigrants' Svc. League, Chgo. Hearing Soc., Save the Children Fedn. and Cmty. Devel. Found. Recipient Jan Fawcett Humanitarian award, Depression and Bipolar Support Alliance. Office: Daniel J Edelman Inc Edelman Aon Ctr 200 E Randolph Dr Chicago IL 60601-6436

EDELSBERG, SALLY COMINS, retired physical therapist, educator; b. Rowno, Poland, Aug. 6, 1939; came to U.S., 1949; d. Joseph Luria and Chana (Bebczuk) Comins; m. Warde C. Pierson, Oct. 8, 1968 (div. 1978); m. Paul Edelsberg, Feb. 2, 1979; 1 child, Tema. BS in Phys. Medicine, U. Wis., Madison, 1963; MS, Northwestern U., Evanston, Ill., 1972. Lic. phys. therapist. Staff and supervisory phys. therapist Hines VA Hosp., Maywood, Ill., 1963-67; program dir. Health Careers Council of Ill., Chgo., 1967-70; instr., clin. edn. coord. Programs in Phys. Therapy, Northwestern U. Med. Sch., Chgo., 1970—72, dir., assoc. prof., 1972—99, dir. devel. and alumni rels., 1999—2003. Pres. Phys. Therapy Ltd., Chgo., 1986-95; v.p. World Confedn. Phys. Therapy, 1995-99, exec. com., 1991-95. Mem.: Am. Phys. Therapy Assn. (bd. dirs. 1975—78, 1979—82, Ill. pres. 1972—76, Catherine Worthingham fellow 1999). Personal E-mail: sce1323@sbcglobal.net.

EDELSON, MARY BETH, artist, educator; b. East Chgo. d. Albert Melvin and Mary Lou (Young) Johnson; children: Lynn Switzman, Nick. BA, DePauw U., 1955, DFA (hon.), 1993; MA, NYU, 1959. Atty. Art Inst. Chgo.; instr. Corcoran Sch. Art, Washington, 1970-75; artist in residence U. Ill., Chgo., 1982, 88, U. Tenn., Knoxville, 1983, Ohio U., Columbus, 1984, Md. Inst. Art, Balt., 1985, Kansas City Art Inst., Mo., 1986, Cleve. Art Inst., 1991, U. Colo., 1993, Clemson U., 1994, McMullen Mus. of Art, Boston Coll., 1997, Danish Royal Acad., Copenhagen, 2000—02, Art and Film Sch., Kabelvag, 2004, Yaddo, 2005. Lectr. at various art gatherings. Solo exhbns. include Nicole Klagsburn Gallery, NYC, 1993, A/C Project Rm., NYC, 1993, Creative Time, NYC, 1994, Nicolai Wallner, Copenhagen, Denmark, 1996, Halle für Kunst, Berlin, 1997, Agency Gallery, London, 1998, Malmö Mus., Sweden, 2000, traveling solo exhbn. to 8 sites in US, 2000-02, 30 yr. survey of Edelson's work with 200 page book, full color book, The Art of Mary Beth Edelson, Utopianna, New Harmony Art Ctr., Ind., Retrospective Malmö Konstmuseum, Sweden, 2006; group exhbns. include Feministische Kunst, Stichting de Appel, Amsterdam, The Netherlands, 1980, Mendel Gallery, Mus. du Que., Phillips Gallery, Can., 1986-88, Corcoran Gallery Art, Washington, 1989, Mus. Modern Art, NYC, 1988-89, Walker Art Ctr., Mpls., 1989, W.P.A., Washington, 1989, A.C. Project Room, NYC, 1991-97, Phillippe Rizzo, Paris, 1992, P.P.O.W., NYC, 1992, Fawbush Gallery, NYC, 1992, Amy Lipton Gallery, NYC, 1992, David Zwirner Gallery, NYC, 1993, Turner/Krail Galleries, LA, 1993, Mercer Union, Toronto, 1996, The Agency, London, 1995, Lombard/Freid, NYC, 1995, Linda Kirkland Gallery, NYC, 1996, Boston Mus. Art, McMullen, 1997, Magasin Ctr. National D'Art Contemporain, Grenoble, France, 1997, Dorfman Projects, NYC, 1998, Internat. Ctr. Photography, NYC, 1997, Neuberger Mus., Purchase, NY, 1999, Nicolai Wallner, Copenhagen, 1996, 99, Postmasters, NYC, 1999, New Mus., NYC, 2000, 01, Tate Mus., London, 2001, Gallerie LeLong, NYC, 2002, Guild Hall, East Hampton, 2002; Chelsea Mus., NYC, 2003, ShedHalle Space, Zurick, 2003, Mumok Museum, Vienna, 2003, Internat. Art Festival, Lofoten, Norway, 2004, Tina Kim Fine Arts, NYC, 2005, Remy Toledo Gallery, NYC, 2005, Yaddo Residency, 2005, IASPIS residency, Sweden 2006, Mason Gross Arts Galleries, Rutgers, NJ, 2006, Rutgers U. Traveling Exhbn. to 5 Sites, 2006, Migros Mus., Zurich, 2006; represented in permanent collections: Walker Art Ctr., Nat. Mus. Am. Art, Washington, Nat. Collection, Washington, Nat. Mus. Women in the Arts, Fine Arts Mus. Santa Fe, Seattle Art Mus., Guggenheim Mus. Art, NYC, Mus. Contemporary Art, Chgo., MOMA, NYC, Malmo Mus., Sweden, and others; subject of 15-yr. retrospective travelling to numerous art and ednl. instns. throughout US, 1988-91, Survey of Edelson's Work Rescripting the Story, various locations, 2000-02; author: Seven Cycles: Public Rituals, 1981, To Dance: Painting with Performance in Mind, 1985, Seven Sites, 1988-90, Shape Shifter: Seven Mediums, 1990; author/photographer: Firsthand, 1993, The Art of Mary Beth Edelson, 2002; contbr. articles to profl. jours.; included numerous books including The Power of Feminist Art, 1994, Lone Visions, Crowded Frames, 1994, The Pink Glass Swan, 1995, Art and Propaganda, 1997, Saffrages and She-Devils, 1997, Where is Ana Mendiata, 1999, Picturing the Modern Amazon, 2000, Feminist Art-Theory; An Anthology, 1968-00, Art and Feminism, 2001, The Artists Body, 2000, Sex Politik, 2001, Century City: Art and Culture in the Modern Met., 2001, Alternative Art NY, 2002, The Art of Marybeth Edelson, 2002, The End of Art, 2004, A Well lived Life, 2006. Recipient Visual Arts grant NEA, 1981, 2000, Creative Artists Pub. Svc. grant State of NY, 1982, Andy Warhol Found. grant NEA, Pollack/Krasner Found., Florsheim Found., 2000, Yaddo Residency, 2005, IASPIS Residency in Sweden, 2006. Mem. Conf. Women in Visual Arts (founding mem.), Women's Action Coalition, Heresies Mag. Collective (founding mem.). Home: 110 Mercer St New York NY 10012-3865 Personal E-mail: yourstory@earthlink.net, marybethedelson@gmail.com.

EDELSON, ZELDA SARAH TOLL, retired editor, artist; b. Phila., Oct. 18, 1929; d. Louis David and Rose (Eisenstein) Toll; m. Marshall Edelson, Dec. 27, 1952 (dec. Jan. 16, 2005); children: Jonathan Toll Edelson, Rebecca Jo Edelson, David Edelson Tolchinsky. BA, U. Chgo., 1949, postgrad., 1949-52. Editor-writer Consol. Book Pubs., Chgo., 1953-56; social worker Balt. City Dept. Pub. Welfare, 1956-57; pub. rels. writer Md. Dept. Employment Security, Balt., 1958-59; mus. editor Yale Peabody Mus., New Haven, 1970-76, head publs., 1976-95, editor mus.'s Discovery mag., 1983-95; lectr. in sci. writing Yale U., 1983—84. Author (and illustrator): Apologies for a Nightingale: Images of Turkey, 1997; editor: numerous publs. including The Great Dinosaur Mural at Yale: The Age of Reptiles, 1990. U. Chgo. scholar, 1947-51. E-mail: zeldaedelson@yahoo.com.

EDELSTEIN, BARBARA A., radiologist; b. N.Y.C., 1952; MD, NY Med. Coll., 1977. Cert. diagnostic radiology 1983. Intern Lenox Hill Hosp., N.Y.C., 1977—78; resident Montefiore Hosp., N.Y.C., 1979—82; radiologist Women's Radiology, N.Y.C., 1983—. Office: Womens Radiology 1045 Park Ave New York NY 10028-1030 Office Phone: 212-860-7700. Personal E-mail: b99xray@aol.com. Business E-Mail: barbara@women'sradiology.com.

EDELSTEIN, ROSEMARIE (ROSEMARIE HUBLOU), medical/surgical nurse, educator, geriatrics nurse; b. Drake, ND, Mar. 3, 1935; d. Francis Jerome and Myrtle Josephine (Merbach); m. Harry George Edelstein, June 22, 1957 (div.); children: Julie, Lori, Lynn, Toni Anne. BSN, St. Teresa of Avila Coll., Winona, Minn., 1956; MA in Edn., Holy Names Coll., Oakland, Calif., 1977; EdD, U. San Francisco, 1982, postgrad., 1987, U. Ariz., 1985—; cert. pub. health nurse, U. Calif., Berkeley, 1972. Dir., clin. supr. San Francisco Sch. for Health Professions, 1971-74, Rancho Arroyo Sch. of Vocat. Nursing, Sacramento, 1974-75; intensive care nurse Kaiser-Permanente Hosp., San Rafael, 1976-77; dir. insvc. edn. Ross Hosp., 1977-78; dir. nursing edn. St. Francis Meml. Hosp., San Francisco, 1978-85; med.-surg. staff nurse met. hosps., San Francisco, 1985-90; med.-legal nursing cons., med.-surg. staff nurse St. Luke's Hosp., Duluth, Minn., 1990-91, St. Charles Hosp., New Orleans, 1992, U. Tex. Med. Br., Galveston, Tex., 1992—94; staff nurse St. Anthony of Padua Hosp., Oklahoma City, 1994—95, med.-surg. nurse, 1994-95; nurse Northgate Conv. Hosp., San Rafael, Calif., 1995—, Idaho Falls Care Ctr., 2003—04, Minidoka Mem. Hosp. Extended Care Facility, Idaho, 2004—05, Minidoka Meml. Hosp., 2004—; nurse, charge nurse Ashton (Idaho) Living Ctr., 2005—. Night charge nurse Creekside Conv. Hosp., Santa Rosa, Calif., 1996; charge nurse medications, treatment and Alzheimer's Unit Fallon Conv. Ctr., Nev., 1996; charge nurse Medicare unit White Pine Conv. Ctr., Ely, Nev., 1997; emergency rm., ICU nurse Battle Mt. Gen. Hosp., Nev., 1997; nurse supr. Medicare-Med. Seaview Care Ctr. Sun Corp., Eureka, Calif., 1997—98; mem. staff Walker Post Manor Oxford, NE Lantis Corp., 1998, The Lincoln Ambassador, 1999, Rapid City (S.D.) Care Ctr. Beverly Enterprises, 2000—01, Houghton County Med. Care Facility, Hancock, Mich., 2000—, Norlite Nursing Ctr., Marquette, Mich., 2001—02; mem. staff Medicare unit Everett (Wash.) Rehab. and Care Ctr., 2001—02; mem. staff Whidbey Island Manor, Oak Harbor, Wash.; staff medicare unit St. Joseph Care Ctr., Spokane, 2003; invited mem. people to people nursing edn.

and adminstrn. delegation to Japan, Hong Kong, and China Eisenhower Found. Wayne State U., 1985. Author: The Influence of Motivator and Hygiene Factors in Job Changes by Graduate Registered Nurses, 1977; Effects of Two Educational Methods Upon Retention of Knowledge in Pharmacology, 1981; co-author: (with Jane F. Lee) Acupunture Atlas, 1974. Candidate U.S. Senate Inner Circle, 1988, 89. Lt. col. USAR Med. Res. Mem. Am. Heart Assn., Calif. Nurses Assn., Sigma Theta Tau. Roman Catholic.

EDELSTEIN, TERI J., art educator, art director, consultant; b. Johnstown, Pa., June 23, 1951; d. Robert Morten and Hulda Lois (Friedhoff) E. BA, U. Pa., 1972, MA, 1977, PhD, 1979; cert., NYU, 1984. Lectr. U. Guelph, Ont., 1977-79; asst. dir. for acad. programs Yale Ctr. Brit. Art, New Haven, 1979-83; dir. Mt. Holyoke Coll. Art Mus., South Hadley, Mass., 1983-90, Skinner Mus., 1983-90, mem. faculty dept. art., 1983-90; dir. Smart Mus. Art U. Chgo., 1990-92, sr. lectr. dept. art, 1990-2000; prin., owner Teri J. Edelstein Assocs., Chgo., 1999—. Dep. dir. Art Inst. Chgo., 1992—99; pres. Teri J. Edelstein Assocs. Museum Strategies, 1999—; mem. adv. bd. Sculpture Chgo., 1991—96, Mus. Loan Network, Knight and Pew Founds., 1994—96. Office: 1648 E 50th St # 6B Chicago IL 60615-3207 Fax: 773-241-9992. Office Phone: 773-241-9991. Business E-Mail: tedelstein@tedelstein.com.

EDEN, BARBARA JEAN, actress; b. Tucson, Arizona, Aug. 23, 1934; d. Harrison Connon and Alice Mary (Franklin) Huffman; 1 child, Matthew Michael Ansara; m. Jon Trusdale Eicholtz, Jan. 5, 1991. Student, San Francisco City Coll., San Francisco Conservatory of Music, Elizabeth Holloway Sch. of Theatre. Pres. Mi-Bar Productions; bd. dirs. Security First Nat. Bank of Chgo. Films include Voyage to the Bottom of the Sea, 1961, Five Weeks in a Balloon, 1962, Wonderful World of the Brothers Grimm, 1963, Seven Faces of Dr. Lao, 1964, Harper Valley PTA, 1978, also The Brass Bottle, Ride the Wild Surf, The New Interns, The Girls in the Office, 1979, Condominium, 1980, Return of the Rebels, 1981, Chattanooga Choo Choo, 1984, A Very Brady Sequel, 1996, Mi Casa, Su Casa, 2003, Carolina, 2003; TV debut on series West Point, 1956; numerous other TV appearances; starred in TV series I Dream of Jeannie, 1965-69, Harper Valley P.T.A., 1980-82; appeared in several TV movies including The Feminist and the Fuzz, 1971, A Howling in the Woods, 1971, The Woman Hunter, 1972, Guess Who's Sleeping in My Bed, 1973, The Stranger Within, 1974, Let's Switch, 1975, How to Break Up a Happy Divorce, 1976, Stonestreet: Who Killed the Centerfold Model, 1977, The Stepford Children, I Dream of Jeannie: 15 Years Later, Secret Life of Kathy McCormick, 1989, Your Mother Wears Combat Boots, 1989, Brand New Life, 1989, Her Wicked Ways, 1990, Hell Hath No Fury, 1991, I Still Dream of Jeannie, 1991, Visions of Murder, 1993, Eyes of Terror, 1994, Dead Man's Island, 1995, Nightclub Confindential, 1996, Gentlemen Prefer Blondes, 1998; also stage and club appearances. Office: William Morris Agy c/o Gene Schwam 151 S El Camino Dr Beverly Hills CA 90212-2775

EDEN, F. BROWN, artist; b. Jericho Center, Vt., Oct. 10, 1916; d. Arthur Castle and Eva Merita (Lowrey) Brown; m. Edwin Winfield Eden, Sept. 4, 1937 (dec. 1990); children: Donna Jean, Sandra Elizabeth, Kathy Lynn; m. Allan L. Day, July 11, 1994 (dec.). Student, U. Fla. Extension, 1955—59, U. Mich., 1963. Art instr. Ann Arbor (Mich.) City Club, 1962-63; tchr., oil painting, printmaking Jacksonville (Fla.) Art Mus., 1963-68. One-woman shows include The Fox Galleries, Atlanta, 1986, Harmon Galleries, Sarasota, 1987, 1989—90, 1992—93, Gallery Contemporanea, Jacksonville, Artist Assocs. Gallery, Atlanta, 1965—90, Hodgell Gallery, Sarasota, 1997—, The Center, Ponte Vedra, Fla., 1998, Kent Campus Gallery, Fla. C.C., Jacksonville, 1999, Represented in permanent collections Fed. Res. Bank Atlanta, Bank Am., Coca-Cola, So. Bell, Sheraton Corp., AT&T, Trust Co. Ga., Shell Oil Co., Touche Ross, Cooper and Lybrand, Delta Airlines Crown Rm., 5th Dist. Ct. Appeals Bldg., Daytona Beach, Fla., Edwin and Ruth Kennedy Mus. Am. Art, U. Ohio, Athens, exhibited in group shows at Ala. Nat. Watercolors, exhibitions include Am. Painters in Paris, 1975—76, Painters in Casein and Acrylics, N.Y.C. Chmn. area VI Fla. Artist Group, Jacksonville Mus. Art, 1979—89. Recipient Painting of Yr. award, Mead Co., 1962—63, First award, Fla. Artist Group, 1971, 1979, Fla. Artists, 1969, The Painting award, Maj. Fla. Artists, 1979, others. Mem.: Fla. Crown Treasures, Fla. Artists Jacksonville, Jackson Coalition of Visual Artists, Ala. Watercolor Soc., Ga. Watercolor Soc., Fla. Watercolor Soc. (Signature artist), So. Watercolor Soc., Nat. Mus. of Women in Arts (charter), Am. Women Artists. Avocation: playing organ. Home: 5375 Sanders Rd Jacksonville FL 32277-1333

EDEN-FETZER, DIANNE TONI, health facility administrator; b. Washington, Mar. 1, 1946; d. Lawrence Antonio Laurenzi and Eleanor Charlotte (Sparrough) Watson; m. William Earle Eden, Aug. 5, 1967 (div. 1982); 1 child, Christopher Lance; m. John Thompson Fetzer, Sept. 2, 1987. AA in Nursing, SUNY, Farmingdale, 1978; BS in Nursing, Towson (Md.) State U., 1990; MS in Nursing Informatics, U. Md., 1999. RN, N.Y., Md. Charge nurse dept. neurosurgery U. Md. Hosp., Balt., 1978-79, nurse clincian I, 1979-84, dept. nursing and neurology project coord. Nat. Stroke Data Bank, 1984-90, nursing edn. cons. dept. neurology and neurosurgery, 1984-99, sr. ptnr. neuro intensive care unit, 1990-99; sys. analyst clin. info. sys. Med. Ctr. U. Md., Balt., 1999—2004, lead tech. project clin. info. sys. Med. Ctr., 2004—. Mem. AACN, Am. Heart Assn. (fellow stroke coun.), Sigma Theta Tau. Democrat. Roman Catholic. Office: Univ Md Hosp 22 S Greene St Baltimore MD 21201-1544

EDENS, BETTY JOYCE, reading recovery educator; b. Hillsboro, Tex., Oct. 20, 1944; d. Edward Alton and Mary Alma (Pendley) Harbin; m. Eugene Cliett Edens, May 29, 1964; children: Michael Eugene, Anne-Marie DeWitt, Kristen Babovec. BEd, Ind. U., 1985; MS, Tex. A&M of Commerce, 1995. Cert. elem. tchr., reading tchr., Tex. 1st grade tchr. Monday Primary, Kaufman, Tex., 1986-93, Franklin Elem., Hillsboro, Tex., 1993-96, reading recovery tchr., 1994-98, 99-00, 2nd grade tchr., 1998-99; reading recovery tchr. Hillsboro Elem. Sch., 1999—2005, reading specialist 2d and 3d grades, 2005—. Mem. early literacy com. TSRA, 1998, Susan G. Komen Found. Mem. Reading Recovery Coun. of N.Am., Internat. Reading Assn., Tex. Reading Assn., Heritage League hillsboro. Republican. Mem. Ch. of Christ. Avocations: recreational reading, walking, computers. E-mail: edens@hillsboro.net.

EDENS, ROSEMARY RANDALL, secondary school educator; b. Anderson, Ind., Jan. 15, 1952; d. Ralph E. and Mildred (Hopkins) Randall; m. Dennis R. Edens, July 8, 1972; children: Corie, Abbie, Jill. BS in Edn., Ind. U., 1989, MS in Counseling Edn., 1995. Tchr. sociology and English Jennings County Sch. Corp. Adj. instr. sociology Vincennes U. Mem.: NEA, Nat. Coun. Tchrs. English, Ind. U. Alumni Assn., Ind. State Tchrs. Assn., Jennings County Classroom Assn., Delta Theta Tau, Delta Kappa Gamma.

EDER, ESTHER GARCIA, artist; b. Buenos Aires, Sept. 27, 1931; arrived in U.S., 1951; d. Isaac and Alicia (Aguirre) Garcia; m. Richard Gray Eder, Apr. 21, 1955; children: Maria, Ann, Claire, Michael, Luke, Ben, Jamie. BA, CUNY, 1984; degree in fine arts, Petorutti Acad., Buenos Aires, 1951. Curator Magic Realism Fog Gallery, Vinalhaven, Maine, 1991, also bd. dirs.; curator Childrens Mus. Masks, Boston, 1993, United South End Settlement House, Boston, 1994. Participant First Night Inc., Boston, 1989-94; invited participant 4th Contemporary Art Biennial, Florence, Italy, 2003. One-woman shows include Leverett House Harvard U., Cambridge, Mass., 1991, Alliance Francaise, San Francisco, 1992, Arden Gallery, Boston, 1993-95, 97, 2000, Galerie Esclaramonde, Labaule, France, 1995, J. Hernandez Cultural Ctr., Boston; exhibited in group shows at Musee Adzak, Paris, 1992, 2000, Fog Gallery, Vinalhaven, Mass., 2001, 4th Biennial of Contemporary Art, Florence, Italy, 2003, Latino Arts Ctr., Boston, 2004, Jose Hernandez Cultural Ctr., Boston, 2005, Ctr. Latin Art, Boston, 2005; represented in permanent collections Boston Pub. Libr., Morrisey Libr. U. Calif., Berkeley, Rose Mus. Art, Brandeis U., Waltham, Mass., Vinalhaven, Maine, Musee Adzaak, Paris; pub. collections include Boston Pub. Libr., U. Calif., Berkeley, Rose Mus. Art Brandeis U., Waltham, Mass., Sch. Art and Design, Savannah, Ga.; author: Larchmont Manor Drawings, 1983. Vol. summer art tchr. to local children, Vinalhaven, Maine. First Night Inc. grantee, 1989, 90, 91. Mem.: Boston Artists Guild. Roman Catholic. Avocation: volunteer teacher to local children. Studio: 46 Waltham St #310 Boston MA 02118-2442 Office Phone: 617-869-1224. Personal E-mail: esthergarciaeder@earthlink.net.

EDGAR, RUTH R., retired elementary school educator; b. Great Falls, S.C., Jan. 7, 1930; d. Robert Hamer and Clara Elizabeth (Ellenberg) Rogers AA, Stephens Coll., Columbia, Mo., 1949; BS, So. Meth. U., 1951; MA, Appalachian State U., Boone, N.C., 1977; postgrad., Limestone Coll., Gaffney, S.C., 1971. Lic. real estate salesman, broker. Home economist Lone Star Gas Co., Dallas, 1951—53, So. Union Gas Co., Austin, Tex., 1953—56, Southwe. Pub. Svc. Co., Amarillo, Tex., 1956—57; with Peeler Real Estate, 1970—71, Burns H.S., Lawndale, NC, 1971—73, Ctrl. Cleveland Mid. Sch., Lawndale, 1973—77, Burns Jr. H.S., Lawndale, 1977—88; resource tchr. South Cleveland Elem. Sch., Shelby, NC, 1988—90, Elizabeth Elem. Sch., Shelby, 1990—94, Washington Elem. Sch., Waco, NC, 1990—92; ret., 1994. Mem. supts. adv. coun., Cleveland County, 1971-75, Cleveland County Art Soc., 1972-73, Ctrl. United Meth. Ch Home: 401 Forest Hill Dr Shelby NC 28150-5520

EDGELL, JUDITH CAROL, theater educator; b. Justice, W. Va., Sept. 5, 1946; d. Dallas and Josie Laura Justice; m. Ernest Paul Edgell, Sept. 25, 1971; children: Shanna Catherine Plaster, Benjamin Todd, Joseph Edward. BA, Marshall U., W. Va., 1968; MA, Morehead State U., Ky., 1981. Cert. secondary tchr. Tchr. St. Albans HS, Kanawah, W.Va., 1968—71; children/young adult libr. Tazewell County Pub. Libr., Russell, Va., 1987—89; tchr. Honaker HS, Russell, 1989—97, Richlands HS, Tazewell, Va., 1997—. Coach, forensics, Tazewell County, Russell County, Va., 1988—; cons. Va. Summer Reading Adv. Bd., 1988—89; coach, drama team Va. HS League, Tazewell County, 2003—04. Dir.: (ch. dramatic performance) Cantatas and Live Nativity Scene. Founder, pres. Honeysuckle Garden Club, Justice, W.Va., 1976—77; pres. Cedar Bluff Garden Club, Cedar Bluff, Va., 1986—87; coach, mock trial debate team Boy Scouts Am., Russell County, 1993—95; music dir. Gethsemane Bapt. Ch., Richlands, 2005—06. Mem.: Va. Assn. Speech Drama Debate Coaches. Avocations: golf, sewing, gardening, reading, writing. Office: Richlands HS 138 Tornado Alley Richlands VA 24641

EDGELL, KARIN JANE, special education educator, reading specialist; b. Rockford, Ill., July 17, 1937; d. Donald Rickard and Leona Marquerite (Villard) Williams; m. George Paul Edgell III, May 6, 1960; 1 child, Scott. Student, Rollins Coll., 1955-57; BS, U. Ill., 1960, MEd, 1966; MA, Roosevelt U., 1989; adminstrv. endorsement, U. Va., 2001. Tchr. Alexandria (Va.) City Pub. Schs., 1963-79; asst. to dir. Reading Ctr. George Washington U., Washington, 1979-80; tchr. Winnetka (Ill.) Pub. Schs., 1982-89, Arlington County (Va.) Pub. Schs., 1989—. Mem. NEA, ASCD, Nat. Coun. Tchrs. Eng., Internat. Reading Assn., Va. Edn. Assn., Va. Reading Assn., Coun. Exceptional Children, Phi Delta Kappa Presbyterian. Home: Landmark Mews 6275 Chaucer View Cir Alexandria VA 22304-3546 Office Phone: 703-228-5820. Personal E-mail: karinedgell@mindspring.com.

EDGEMON, CONNIE KAY, director, information management, hospital administrator; b. Edinburg, Tex., Nov. 27, 1947; d. R. P. and Verna Lou (Graham) E.; 1 child, Alexander. Bachelor's degree, Pan Am. U., 1969; MA, Chapman U., 1975. Lic. Psychol. Assoc., profl. counselor; cert. secondary sch. tchr., Tex., Calif. Tchr. Mercedes (Tex.) Ind. Sch. Dist., spring 1968, Corpus Christi (Tex.) Ind. Sch. Dist., 1969-70, Lemoore (Calif.) Unified Sch. Dist., 1971-74, Mission (Tex.) Ind. Sch. Dist., fall 1975; staff psychologist Big Spring (Tex.) State Hosp., 1976-86, psychologist, adminstr., 1986—94, dir. info. mgmt., 1994—. Instr. Howard Coll., Big Spring, 1984-87. Mem. Tex. Pub. Employees Assn. (past pres., past sec.), Beta Sigma Phi (Beta Sigma Phi Pledge of Yr. 1978, Beta Sigma Phi Girl of Yr. 1979, 85, 90, 93, Beta Sigma Phi of Yr. 1982). Avocations: skiing, bridge. Office: Big Spring State Hosp 1901 North Hwy 87 Big Spring TX 79720

EDGEWORTH, EMILY, retired insurance agency executive, retired small business owner; b. Brilliant, Ala., July 12, 1927; d. James Allen and Cara Margie (Mayes) Addison; m. Billy Pate, Oct. 8, 1947 (div. July 1968); m. William Edgeworth, Sept. 24, 1972. Student, Ala. Bus. Coll., 1952; grad. life underwriters tng. coun., U. Ala., 1976. Med. aide, receptionist Office Dr. A.M. Walker, Tuscaloosa, Ala., 1952-58; credit mgr. Busch Jewelry Co., Tuscaloosa, 1958-66; purchasing clk. Avco Fin. Corp., Tuscaloosa, 1966-71; sec. Ala. Farm Bur. Ins. Co., Tuscaloosa, 1971-73; multilines saleswoman Farm Bur. Ins. Co., Tuscaloosa, 1973-76; owner, salesman Emily Edgeworth Ins. Co., Tuscaloosa, 1976-86; owner, mgr. Rural Relics, Tuscaloosa, 1986-89, ret., 1989. Contbr. poetry and short stories to various publs., including Best Poems of 1996 and 1997, Journey of the Mind, 1994, Growing Up on a Two Mule Farm, 1996. Active Heritage Found., Washington, Meals on Wheels, Tuscaloosa, 1980's, Unity Bapt. Ch., Tuscaloosa; active Tuscaloosa Rep. Com., Nat. Rep. Com. Mem. Internat. Soc. Poets (disting. mem.). Avocations: writing poetry and short stories, collecting depression era farm items. Home: 6103 41s St Tuscaloosa AL 35401

EDIDIN, RUTH GLICENSTEIN, mathematics educator; b. Berlin, Apr. 6, 1936; came to U.S., 1964; d. Abraham and Hinda (Lis) Glicenstein; children: Avram, Dan. BSc, Johns Hopkins U., 1971, MEd, 1978, MA, 1980. Tchr. Balt. City Schs., 1977-78; instr. Coppin State Coll., Balt., 1978-80, Goucher Coll., Balt., 1980-84, Morgan State U., Balt., 1984—. Cons. Health Svcs., Balt., 1984-85. Sloan fellow, 1985-86. Mem. Am. Math. Soc., Math. Assn. Am. Jewish. Office: Morgan State U Cold Spring Ln Baltimore MD 21251 Home: 6305 Western Run Dr Baltimore MD 21215-3114

EDLAVITCH, SUSAN T., lawyer; b. Washington, Sept. 29, 1948; BS, Washington U., 1970; JD, Indiana U., 1976; LLM in Taxation with high honors, George Washington U., 1990. Bar: Indiana 1976, DC 1991, Md. 1991, US Tax Ct., US Ct. of Appeals, Fourth Circuit, US Supreme Ct. Law clerk to Judge V. Sue Shields and Judge Patrick D. Sullivan Indiana Ct. of Appeals, 1976—79; atty. Office of Gen. Counsel, FCC, 1980—88, Office of Chief Counsel, IRS, 1988—96; assoc. Venable LLP, Washington, ptnr., federal taxation law, 2000—. Mem. Thompson West Tax Advisory Bd. Author: Tax Management Memorandum, Journal of Real Estate Taxation. Mem.: ABA (mem. tax section, mem. corp. tax and partnership tax com.), DC Women's Bar Assn., Md. State Bar Assn., DC Bar Assn. (mem. corp. tax com.). Office: Venable LLP 575 7th St NW Washington DC 20004 Office Phone: 202-344-4000. Office Fax: 202-344-8300. Business E-Mail: stedlavitch@venable.com.

EDMO, JEAN UMIOKALANI, artist, poet; b. L.A., Apr. 12, 1942; d. Lemuel Kanekikawaiola Cutter and Nancy James Watson; m. Edward McCleary Edmo, Mar. 17, 1984 (dec. Mar. 1996); 8 stepchildren. Grad., Comml. Art Sch., San Francisco, 1963. Author: (poetry) Songs of Life and Love, 2000, rev. edit., 2002, (short stories) Some Passions Never Die, 2002; one-woman shows include nine oil, acrylic and mixed media landscapes., Photographs in One Woman Shows, Chile, 1962; Nat. Photo Book. Nominee Poet of Yr., Internat. Poetry Guild, 2001; recipient Editors award, 2002, Outstanding Achievment cup, Internat. Soc. Poets, Merit Award medal. Green Party. Episcopalian. Avocation: walking, gardening, making craft wreaths, birdwatching.

EDMOND, PENNIE ANNE, science educator; b. Bryan, Ohio, Feb. 2, 1948; d. William T. Bailey and Helen; m. Robin D. Edmond, Oct. 4, 1969; children: Cassandra, John. BS in Chemistry, U. Nev., Las Vegas, 1970, M of Curriculum and Instrn., 1975. Tchr. Clark County Sch. Dist., Las Vegas, 1970—. Mentor to student tchrs. U. Nev., Las Vegas; curriculum cons. Clark County Sch. Dist., Las Vegas. Named Outstanding Physics Tchr., Am. Inst. Physics. Mem.: NEA (local officer 1972—74), Nat. Sci. Tchrs. Assn., Am. Assn. Physics Tchrs. (physics tchr. 1985—). Avocation: ceramics. Home: 6428 Mecham Ave Las Vegas NV 89107

EDMONDS, ANNE CAREY, librarian; b. Penang, Malaysia, Dec. 19, 1924; d. William John and Neil (Carey) E. Student, U. Reading, England, 1942-44; BA, Barnard Coll., 1948; MSLS, Columbia U., 1950; MA, Johns Hopkins U., 1959; postgrad., Western Res. U., 1960-61; LHD, Mount Holyoke Coll., 1994. With War Damage Commn., London, 1944-46; children's asst. Enoch Pratt Free Libr., Balt., 1948-49; reference libr. Sch. Bus. Adminstrn., CCNY, 1950-51; reference libr. then asst. libr. readers' svcs. Goucher Coll., Balt., 1951-60; exchange reference libr. European svcs. libr. BBS, London, 1955; instr. Sch. L.S., Syracuse U., summer 1960; libr. Douglass Coll., Rutgers U., New Brunswick, NJ, 1961-64, instr., summer 1962, fall 1963; libr. Mt. Holyoke Coll., 1964-94. Vis. libr. U. North, Turfloop, South Africa, 1976-77; mem. libr. vis. com. Wheaton Coll., Norton, Mass., 1978-92; mem. local systems adv. group Online Computer Libr. Ctr., Inc., 1984-87, mem. adv. com. on coll. and univ. librs., 1988-89. Author: A Memory Book: Mount Holyoke College, 1834-1987, 1988 (with Gai Carpenter and others) Computing Strategies in Liberal Arts Colleges, 1992. Mem. South Hadley (Mass.) Bicentennial Com., 1975—76; mem. accreditation teams Middle State Assn. Colls. and Secondary Schs., 1963—94, New Eng. Assn. Schs. and Colls., 1986—94; exec. com. New Eng. Libr. Info. Network, 1974—76, 1979—85, chmn., 1982—84; mem. Adv. Commn. Historic Deerfield, 1975—81, 1986—94; trustee Ctr. for Maine Contemporary Art, Rockport, Maine, 2001—; bd. dirs. U.S. Book Exch., 1973—76, 1980—83, Maine Grand Opera, Camden, Conservancy for Camden Harbor Park and Amphiltheatre. Mem. AAUW (bd. dirs. main chpt. 1998—), ALA, Assn. Coll. Rsch. Librs. (pres. 1970-71, chmn. constn. and bylaws com. New Eng. chpt. 1975-76, pres. New Eng. chpt. 1983-84). E-mail: ACE13@midcoast.com.

EDMONDS, BETH, state legislator, lieutenant governor; m. Dan Nickerson. BA, Clark U., 1972; MA, Goddard Coll., 1974. Children's libr. Freeport Cmty. Libr., 1988—; mem. Maine Senate from 23d Dist., Augusta, 2001—, chair labor com., 2001—, mem. marine resources com., 2001—; pres. Maine State Senate, Augusta, 2004—; lt. gov. State of Maine, Augusta, 2004—. Mem. Freeport Housing Trust, 1987-95, chair, 1991-95; chair Freeport Mcpl. Employee Labor Com., 1996-97. Democrat. Home: 122 Hunter Rd Freeport ME 04032 Office: State House 3 State House Sta Augusta ME 04333 Office Phone: 207-287-1500. Office Fax: (207) 287-1585. E-mail: edmonds@gwi.net.

EDMONDS, CRYSTAL D., language educator, distance learning coordinator; d. James and Delores Quick; m. Derek Edmonds, Sept. 6, 1990; children: Daniel, Jewell, Elizabeth. BA, U. NC, Pembroke, 1988, MA, 1997. Admissions counselor U. NC, 1989—99; instr. English Robeson C.C., Lumberton, 2000—, coord. distance learning, 2004—. Recipient Tchr. Yr., Robeson C.C., 2005. Mem.: Robeson C.C. Assn. (assoc.; sec. 2004—05), Robeson C.C. Faculty Assn. (assoc.; pres. 2005—06). Office Phone: 910-272-3700.

EDMONDS, SLIVY, corporate financial executive; b. Norfolk, Va., July 19, 1947; d. Carlton Lee Perkins and Doris Elaine (Edmonds) Dukes. BA in Bus. Mgmt., Marymont Manhattan Coll., N.Y.C., 1977; MBA in Fin., U. Pa., 1979. Flight attendant TWA, N.Y.C., 1970—72, analyst, sr. analyst, 1972—77; sr. analyst Bristol-Meyers Co., N.Y.C., 1979—81, Equitable Life Assurance Soc., N.Y.C., 1981—85, v.p., 1985—86; v.p., CFO Air Atlanta Inc., 1986—. Tutor N.Y.C. Bd. Edn., 1982. Named One of 10 Outstanding Young Working Women, Glamour Mag., 1984. Mem.: Wharton Bus. Sch. Club N.Y. (treas. 1981—84). Democrat.

EDMONDS, TRACEY E., film company executive; b. LA, Feb. 18, 1967; m. Kenneth "Babyface" Edmonds, Sept. 5, 1994 (separated); children: Brandon, Dylan. Attended, Standford U. Pres., CEO Edmonds Entertainment Group, 1996—2006; pres., COO Our Stories Films, 2006—; pres. Yab Yum Entertainment. Actor, exec. prodr.: (films) Hav Plenty, 1997; prodr.: Soul Food, 1997, Light It Up, 1999, Punks, 2000, Josie and the Pussycats, 2001; exec. prodr.: (TV films) Maniac Magee, 2003; actor: (TV series) Soul Food, 2000, College Hill, 2004; exec. prodr.: Lil Kim: Countdown to Lockdown, 2006. Office: Yab Yum Entertainment 1635 N Cahuenga Blvd 6th Fl Los Angeles CA 90028*

EDMONDS, VELMA MCINNIS, nursing educator; b. N.Y.C., Feb. 17, 1940; d. Walter Lee and Eva Doris (Grant) McInnis; children: Stephen Clay, Michelle Louise. Diploma, Charity Hosp. Sch. Nursing, New Orleans, 1961; BSN, Med. Coll. Ga., 1968; MSN, U. Ala., Birmingham, 1980; D of Nursing Sci., La. State U., 2001. Staff nurse Ochsner Found. Hosp., New Orleans, 1961—63, 1987—2002, clin. educator, 1987-89; staff nurse Suburban Hosp., Bethesda, Md., 1963-65; asst. DON svc., dir. staff devel. Providence Hosp., Mobile, Ala., 1967-70; staff nurse MICU U. So. Ala. Med. Ctr., Mobile, 1980-82, clin. nurse specialist, nutrition/metabolic support, 1982-84; instr., coord., BSN completion program Northwestern State U. Coll. Nursing, Pineville, La., 1984-86; head nurse So. Bapt. Hosp., New Orleans, 1986-87; instr. nursing La. State U. Health Sci. Ctr., New Orleans, 1989-91, asst. prof. nursing, 1991—2002; clin. coord. Transitional Hosp. Corp., 1994-95; cons., vis. prof. U. Guam Coll. Nursing and Health Scis., 2002—03. Gov.-apptd. mem. La. Bd. Examiners in Dietetics and Nutrition, 1990—98, sec.-treas., 1996—97; cons., faculty U. Guam, 2002—; co-prin. investigator, project dir. The Recruitment and Retention of Hispanic Nursing Students, U. Tex. El Paso; prin. investigator, vis. rsch. scholar U. Pa. Rsch. Inst., 2005—06; rschr. with recently immigrated Honduran women; rschr. with recently immigrated Mex. women, 2004; presenter in field; reviewer pubs. and grants; cons. in field. Author: publs. in field. Advisor Hispanic C. of C., New Orleans; adv. bd. Cmty. Vietnamese Outreach Program, Meth. Hosp., New Orleans; chmn. Silent Auction, New Orleans Dollars for Scholars Found., 2000; founding bd. dirs., edn. coord. Orgn. Health and Med. Profession Women; mem. ARC Disaster Team. Recipient Excellence in Nursing group award Ochsner Fedn. Hosp., New Orleans, 1987, cert. Merit Tb Assn. Greater New Orleans, 1961; USDA fellow, 2004; fellow Rsch. Inst. U. Pa., 2005—. Mem. ANA, Nat. Soc. Nutrition Edn., La. State Nurses' Assn. (dist. 7), Tex. Nurses Assn., Am. Soc. Parenteral and Enteral Nutrition, La. State Soc. Parenteral and Enteral Nutrition (program and edn. coms.), Mobile Area Nonvolitional Nutrition Support Assn. (past pres.), Transcultural Nursing Soc., Soc. Nutrition Edn., Orgn. Health and Med. Profl. Women (Guam and We. Pacific region founding bd. dirs., edn. coord.), Am. Red Cross Disaster Team, Tex. Nurses Assn., Sigma Theta Tau. Office: U Tex at El Paso Coll Health Scis 1100 N Campbell St El Paso TX 79902 Office Phone: 915-747-7261. Personal E-mail: vmedmonds@hotmail.com. Business E-Mail: vedmonds@utep.edu.

EDMONSON, TRACY K., lawyer; BA, Rice Univ., 1985; JD, Univ. Calif., Berkeley, 1988. Bar: Calif. 1988. Ptnr., corp. fin. Latham & Watkins LLP, San Francisco, chair, San Francisco corp. dept., 2002—, and head, Bay Area Corp. Fin. practice group, 1998—. Frequent public speaker. Named one of Top 20 Under 40, Daily Jour., 2003, No. Calif. Superlawyers, San Francisco Mag., 2004. Office: Latham & Watkins LLP Ste 2000 505 Montgomery St San Francisco CA 94111-2562 Office Phone: 415-391-0600. Office Fax: 415-395-8095. Business E-Mail: tracy.edmonson@lw.com.

EDMONSON-NELSON, GLORIA JEAN, freelance writer; b. Nowata, Okla., Oct. 7, 1938; d. Cornelius Emerson and Virginia (Cole) E.; m. Forest Nelson, Oct. 7, 1996; children: Vincent Ross, Victor Ross, Vernon Ross. AA, Labette C.C., Parsons, Kans., 1959; BS in Mgmt., U. San Francisco, 1979. Adminstr. Far West Lab for Edn. R&D, San Francisco, 1969-81; reporter The Doctor's Co. Med. Malpractice, Emeryville, Calif., 1986-89. Cons. arbitrator NASD, San Francisco, 1992-2000. Author: How to Start a Medical Collecting Agency, 1990, (poetry book) Life Experiences Through Poetry: A Collection of Truths, 1992, Glo's Prose-Reflections of the Soul, 1994, Recognizing Abuse--Reclaiming Your Birthright, 1998, Recognizing Child Abuse and Domestic Violence, 1998, Prayer Works, 2003, (screenplays) What Would God Think?, 2002. Telephone interviewer United Way, 1989-91, voter registrar, 1990-91; skid row ministry West Angeles Ch. of God in Christ, L.A. Recipient various poetry awards. Mem.: NAFE, West Angeles COGIC, Am. Assn. Ret. Persons, Nat. Assn. Securities Dealers. Avocations: poetry, travel, jazz. Address: PO Box 45770 Los Angeles CA 90045-0770 Office Phone: 877-992-2873. E-mail: GEdmon1800@aol.com.

EDMUNDS, JANE CLARA, media consultant; d. John Carson and Clara (Kummerow) Carrigan; m. William T. Dean, Aug. 30, 1947 (div. 1953; dec. July 1984); 1 son, John Charles; Edmund S. Kopacz, Sept. 24, 1955 (div. 1973); children: Christine Ellen, Jan Carson. Student in chemistry and math., Northwestern U. Chemist Mars Inc., Oak Park, Ill., 1942-47; with Cons. Engr. Mag., Maujer Pub. Co., St. Joseph, Mich., 1953-58, 69-74; sr. editor Cons. Engr. Mag. Tech. Pub. Co., Barrington, Ill., 1975-77, exec. editor, 1977-82, editorial dir., 1983-86; asst. editor women's pages rewrite desk News-Palladium, Benton Harbor, Mich., 1967-68; freelance journalist St. Joseph, 1959-68; communications cons. Schaumburg, Ill., 1987—. Chmn. Berrien County (Mich.) Nat. Found. March of Dimes, 1968; mem. campaign com. Rep. Party, 1954. Recipient award Bausch & Lomb, 1940, award Nat. Found. Service, 1969, Silver Hat award Constrn. Writers Assn., 1986, honor mem. 2000, Chmn.'s award Profl. Engrs. in Pvt. Practice div. NSPE, 1987; grantee AID, 1979 Assoc. fellow Soc. Tech. Communication (chmn. St. Joseph chpt. 1972 Disting. Tech. Communication awards); mem. Am. Soc. Bus. Press Editors (past bd. mem.), Constrn. Writers Assn., Smithsonian Instn., Chgo. Art Inst. Assocs., Field Mus. Assocs. Republican. Episcopalian.

EDMUNDS, NANCY GARLOCK, federal judge; b. Detroit, July 10, 1947; m. William C. Edmunds, 1977. BA cum laude, Cornell U., 1969; MA in Teaching, U. Chgo., 1971; JD summa cum laude, Wayne U., 1976. Bar: Mich. 1976. With Plymouth Canton Public Schools, 1971-73; law clk. Barris, Sott, Denn & Driker, 1973-75; law clk. to Hon. Ralph Freeman U.S. Dist. Ct. (ea. dist.) Mich., 1976-78; with Dykema Gossett, Detroit, 1978-84, ptnr. litigation sect., 1984-92; apptd. judge U.S. Dist. Ct. (ea. dist.) Mich., 1992—. Commr. 21st Century Commn. on Cts., 1990; mem. faculty, bd. mem. Fed. Advocacy Inst., 1983-91. Editor in chief Wayne Law Review. Mem. com. of visitors Wayne Law Sch., Detroit; bd. dirs. Mich. Mems. of Stratford Festival; bd. trustees Stratford Shakespearean Festival of Am., Temple Beth El, 1990-97, Hist. Soc. U.S. Dist. Ct. (ea. dist.) Mich., 1993-98. Mem. ABA, FBA (exec. bd. dirs. 1989-92), Am. Judicature Soc., Fed. Judges Assn., State Bar Mich. (chair U.S. cts. com. 1990-91). Avocation: reading. Office: US Dist Ct US Courthouse #211 231 W Lafayette Blvd Detroit MI 48226-2700 E-mail: karen_hillebrand@mied.uscourts.gov.

EDMUNDSON, LORNA DUPHINEY, academic administrator; b. Sept. 6, 1942; MEd, Boston Coll., 1969; EdD, Columbia U. Tchrs. Coll., 1975. Continuing edn. program dir. Am. U. Paris, 1976-77; asst. dean dir. Columbia U., New York, N.Y., 1978-84; acad. v.p. Marymount Coll., Tarrytown, N.Y., 1984-92; acting pres. v.p. Colby Sawyer Coll., New London, N.H., 1993-96; pres. Trinity Coll. Vt., Burlington, Vt., 1996-98, Assoc. Vt. Colls., Shelburne, Vt., 1998—.

EDSFORTH, MAUREEN MCGILL, instructional technology specialist; d. James J. and Marie McGill; m. Wayne H. Edsforth, July 14, 1973; children: Brian P., David J. BS in Elem. Edn., U. Dayton, 1972; MA in Ednl. Tech., Pepperdine U., 2002. Cert. permanent elem. edn. NY, 2002. Sci. tchr. Broward County Pub. Sch., Ft. Lauderdale, Fla., 1972—73; med. libr. Am. Cyanamid, Wayne, NJ, 1973—74; sci., math tchr. Ctrl. Sch., Montville, NJ, 1974—81; math tchr. Kinnelon (NJ) Sch. Dist., 1983—84, St. Mary Sch., Pompton Lakes, NJ, 1986—90; propr. Greenwich (NY) Hardware Antiques, 1991—94; enrichment program coord., tchr. Greenwich Ctrl. Sch. Dist., 1992—94, computer instr., 1994—2002, instrnl. tech. specialist, 2002—. Site mgr. North Hudson Electronic Edn. Empowerment Project, Hudson Falls, NY, 1998—2002; liaison WSWHE BOCES Model Sch., Saratoga Springs, NY, 2002—. Mem., treas. Greenwich Women's Svc. Club, 1990—96; pres. Greater Greenwich C. of C., 1996—97, dir., 1992—2001, 2005—. Mem.: Assn. Supervision and Curriculum and Devel., Internat. Soc. for Tech. in Edn., NY State Assn. Computers and Tech. in Edn. Office: Greenwich Ctrl Sch Dist 10 Gray Ave Greenwich NY 12834 Office Phone: 518-692-9542. E-mail: medsforth@greenwichcsd.org.

EDSON, MARGARET, playwright; b. Washington, July 4, 1961; life ptnr. Linda Merrill. BA, Smith Coll., 1983; MA, Georgetown U., 1992. Tchr., elementary D.C. public schools, 1992—98; tchr. kindergarten John Hope Elem. Sch., Atlanta, 1998—. Author: (play) Wit, 1999. Recipient Drama League of NY playwright award, 1993, LA Drama Critics Circle award, 1996, Berrilla Kerr Found. playwrights award, 1998, Fellowship of Southern Writers drama award, 1999, Pulitzer prize for drama, 1999. Home: 622 Cresthill Ave Ne Atlanta GA 30306-3640

EDSON, MARIAN LOUISE, communications executive; b. Sidney, Mont., Mar. 21, 1940; d. David Ira and Myrtle (Ewing) Drury; m. James Arthur Edson, Oct. 14, 1961; children: Nadine L. Mykins, Jeanine Clare Edson. Student, U. Wash., 1961-62; BS, Mont. State U., 1962; postgrad., SUNY, Binghamton, 1975-76. Cert. tchr. Mont., Wash., N.Y. Lead editor, flight data file Johnson Space Ctr., Houston, 1980-85, coordinator for payload reconfiguration data collection, 1985-86, supr. flight data file, 1986-87; lead technical editor Bell Aerospace/Textron, Buffalo, N.Y., 1987; prodn. mgr. ASYST Software Tech., Rochester, N.Y., 1987-88, publ. mgr., 1988-94; mgr. advanced techs. Ziff-Davis, Rochester, 1997-98; publ. mgr. Raymond Corp., Greene, N.Y., 1994-97, cons., project dir., 1998—2001; owner Doctrina Pub., 2002—. Content writer Ednl. Testing Svc. Edn. com. Bay Area League Women Voters, Houston, 1984-85; assoc. Rochester Women's Network, 1987—; founding mem. Macedon (N.Y.) Reading Ctr., 1968—; bd. dirs. San Antonio League Women Voters, 2005. Fellow Life Office Mgmt. Assn.; mem. AIAA, Soc. Tech. Communicators (pres.), Nat. Mgmt. Assn., Nat. Assn. Purchasing Mgrs., Women in Comm. Inc., Genesee Ornithol. Soc. (newsletter editor), Rochester Acad. Sci., Aububon Soc Avocations: birdwatching, horseback riding, hiking, reading. Office: 14818 River Vista N San Antonio TX 78216 Office Phone: 585-750-2227. Personal E-mail: mdedson@sbcglobal.net.

EDSON, VIRGINIA ELIZABETH, secondary school educator; b. Worcester, Mass., Dec. 21, 1936; d. Theodore Rogers and Beatrice (Manning) E. BS, Framingham (Mass.) State Coll., 1959; MS, Simmons Coll., Boston, 1966. Tchr. Pelham (N.Y.) Meml. High Sch., 1959-61, Wellesley (Mass.) pub. schs., 1961—, head home econ. dept., 1967-76. Bd. dirs. Cath. Social Network, Boston, 1988—. Mem. Am. Home Econs. Assn., Mass. Home Econs. Assn., Ea. Mass. Home Econs. Assn. (bd dirs.), NEA, Mass. Tchrs. Assn., Wellesley Tchrs. Assn. (treas. 1976-79), AAUW, Framingham State U. Alumni Assn., Nat. Soc. DAR, Nat. Soc. Colonial Dames of XVII Century, Nat. Soc. New Eng. Women, Cath. Alumni Club. Avocations: bridge, travel, handcrafts, cooking. Home: 33 Surrey Ln Holden MA 01520-1521

EDWARDS, ANN CONCETTA, human resources director; b. Bklyn., Feb. 15, 1941; d. Joseph T. and Anna R. Lazzarino; m. Andrew F. Edwards, Jan 14, 1967; children: Alison, Jacqueline. BA, U. S.C., 1961; MA, St. John's U., Jamaica, N.Y., 1963. Cert. sr. profl. human resources. From asst. to mgr. human resources Lab-Volt Sys., Inc., Wall Township, N.J., 1982-97, human resources mgr., 1997—2001, human resources dir., 2002—. Author: Putting Your Best Foot Forward, 2004; writer Shore News, Sea Girt, N.J., 1970-75; cons. Edwards Assocs., Sea Girt, 1975-82 Recipient Govs. Certificate of Achievement award N.J. Sch. to Careers Sys., 1997-98. Mem.: NAFE, Jersey Shore Assn. Human Resources (area 1 rep. 1990—92), Soc. for Human Resource Mgmt. (dir. 1994—2006, found. chair 1997—2001, high tech. net 1998—2004, workforce readiness dir. 2002—06). Avocation: writing. Office Phone: 732-938-2000. E-mail: ann.edwardsl@verizon.net.

EDWARDS, ANN LOUISE CORBIN, elementary school educator; b. Warren, Ohio, Dec. 24, 1949; d. Merritt Martin and Ruth (Wright) Corbin; m. Thomas Eugene Edwards Jr., June 20, 1981; children: Thomas E. III, Lauren Wright. BS in Spl. and Elem. Edn., Bowling Green State U., 1972; MEd in Mental Retardation, U. S.C., 1978. Cert. elem. educator, spl. educator for educable mentally handicapped, trainable mentally handicapped, learning disabled, S.C. Tchr. in spl. edn. Washington Ctr., Greenville, S.C., 1972-74; tchr. in learning disabled resource Wade Hampton High Sch., Greenville, 1974-81, also dept. chair in spl. edn., 1974-81; tchr. in learning disabled resource Paris Elem. Sch., Greenville, 1981-87, tchr., 1987—. Coord. sci. fair Paris Elem. Sch., Greenville, 1985—, grants project, 1989—, hist. project, 1989—. Recipient S.C. State Model Classroom award S.C. Dept. Edn., 1975-76; named Outstanding Young Educator of Yr., Taylors Jaycees, Greenville, 1974; State Edn. grantee S.C. Dept. Edn., 1987, 89, 90. Mem. Parent, Tchr., Student Assn. (hon. life, tchr. bd. rep. 1988-90), Audubon Soc. Baptist. Home: 300 Anders Camp Rd Cleveland SC 29635-9684 Office: Furman Univ CS Dept 3300 Poinsett Hwy Greenville SC 29613

EDWARDS, ANNMARIE MONICA, language educator, career coach, entrepreneur; b. Kingston, Jamaica, Jan. 26, 1962; arrived in U.S., 1989; d. Avell George Edwards and Stephanie H. Turner. AA, Fiorello H. LaGuardia C.C., 1991; BS, St. John's U., 1994; MA, Adelphi U., 1996. Cert. RI, 2001, N.E. regional tchg. credential 1996, cert. pub. sch. tchr. NY, 1995, provisional tchg. Mass., 1998. Student tchr. St. John's U., NYC, 1993; tchr. Blanche Cmty. Progress Day Care, Inc. No 2, NYC, 1993—95, Jamaica NAACP Day Care Ctr., NYC, 1995—96; substitute tchr. Portland (Maine) Pub. Sch., 1996, Westbrook (Maine) Sch. Dept., 1996—97, Falmouth (Maine) Sch. Dept., 1996—97, South Portland Pub. Sch., 1996—98; ESL spl. edn. tchr. Judge Rotenburgh Edn. Ctr., Canton, Mass., 1998—98; grade 6 ESL tchr. Providence Pub. Schs., 1998—; CEO, career coach Aria Career Devel. Pres. Rising Star Enterprises, Portland, 1997—98; career cons., workshop presenter Aria Career Devel. Svcs.; cmty. activist Aria Cmty. Devel. Designer (booklets) 50 Ways to Maximize Your Potential, 50 Ways to Maximize Your Job Hunting, 110 Tips for First Time Home Buyers, 50 Tips to Energize Your Workforce, 2006, 50 Proven Strategies to Maximize Your Job Search, 2006, Intuitive Creative Journal, 2006. Tutor Providence Pub. Sch., 2000; transp. coord. Am. Cancer Soc., Portland, 1996—98. Scholar, Carver Fed. Bank, 1991; Howard Meml. scholar, Howard Meml. Fund, 1990—95, Mayor's scholar, City of NY, 1991. Mem.: NAFE, Am. Fedn. Tchrs., Providence Tchrs. Union. Avocations: travel, writing, research, cooking, entertaining. Office Phone: 828-278-0632. Personal E-mail: aria4@charter.net.

EDWARDS, CAROLYN MULLENAX, public relations executive; b. French Camp, Calif., Dec. 3, 1943; d. Charles Harold and Jessie Jewel Mullenax; m. Helton Pressley (div.); m. Dennis D. Edwards, May 29, 1993. BFA, U. Tulsa, 1967; MEd, Ea. N.Mex. U., 1976. Artist Wessels Agy., Spokane, Wash., 1968-70; pub. rels. dir. Spokane (Wash.) Symphony Soc., 1970-72; advt. coord. Crescent Dept. Store, Spokane, 1972-73; art dir., copywriter Sta. KMTY Radio, Clovis, N.Mex., 1976; news editor Clovis News Jour., Clovis, 1976-77; promotion and art dir. Sta. KENW-TV, Portales, N.Mex., 1977-78; coord. alumni affairs and pubs. Ea. N.Mex. U., Portales, 1978-80, dir. pubs., TV and pub. info. Clovis, 1985-90, asst. dir. alumni affairs Portales, 1998-00, dir. pubs., 2000—; devel. and pub. info. dir. Mental Health Resources Inc., Portales, N.Mex., 1980-85; dir. mktg. & pub. info. Clovis Community Coll. (formerly Ea. N.Mex. U.-Clovis), 1990-98; producer pub. affairs program Sta. KMCC-TV, Clovis, 1981-84. Bd. dirs. N.Mex. Outdoor Drama Assn., San Jon, 1986-95, Univ. Symphony League, Clovis, 1984-88. Named N.Mex. Press Women Communicator of Acheivement, 1999. Mem. N.Mex. Press Women (scholarship chair 1994-99, comm. awards 1981-2002, treas. 2000-2001, v.p. 2001—), Nat. Fedn. Press Women (comm. awards 1984-97), Am. Women in Radio and TV, Clovis C. of C. (bd. dirs. 1984-89), Jr. League (Lubbock, Tex.), Coun. for Advancement and Support Edn. (sec.-editor dist. IV 1990-92, design award 1991, 99), Nat. Coun. for Mktg. and Pub. Rels. (dist. IV award 1989-91, 93-97, 99, nat. award 1993-98), Altrusa Club, Nat. Assn. of Vocational and Tech. Edn. (awards 1995-96), Delta Delta Delta (former dist. alumnae officer, chair Delta Century Fund, graphics cons.). Republican. Episcopalian. Avocations: reading, classical music, free lance art, volunteer work, dance. Office: Ea NMex Univ Univ Rels Sta # 6 Portales NM 88130 E-mail: carolyn.edwards@enmu.edu.

EDWARDS, CARYN LOUISE, educational consultant, special education educator; d. Carl Alvar Erickson and Louise Lempe Loven Erickson; m. James Phelps Edwards, Sept. 1, 1966; children: James E., Nicole Anne. BS in Spl. Edn., Wayne State U., 1968; student in Learning Disabilities, Mich. State U., 1969—71. Spl. edn. tchr. Detroit Pub. Sch.; tchr. Okemos Pub. Sch., Mich.; dir., owner Erickson Learning Ctrs., Okemos, adminstr. Jackson, Mich., Lansing, Mich. Presenter in field. Author: Erickson Reader, 2000, Erickson Workbooks, 2000. Mem.: Erickson Learning Found. (exec. cir.), Learning Disabilites Assn. (bd. dirs. 1989—2004, nat. dir. 1996—2003, 2005—). Office: Erickson Learning Ctrs 2043 Hamilton Rd Okemos MI 48864 Office Phone: 517-347-0122. Personal E-mail: carynjpe@aol.com.

EDWARDS, CHARLOTTE ANN, elementary school educator; b. Jasper, Tex., Sept. 16, 1948; d. Delois and geraldine I. (McNeill) Dominy; m. Charles Ray Dorgan, Apr. 5, 1969 (div. Feb. 1985); m. William Lee Edwards, Nov., 1997. BS, Lamar U., 1981; MEd, SFASU, Nacogdoches, Tex., 1991. Lab. technician Tex. Animal Health Commn., Austin, 1968-69; tchr. Brookland (Tex.) Ind. Sch. Dist., 1982-85; tchr. math., sci. and art Jasper (Tex.) Ind. Sch. Dist., 1985—. PTA scholar, 1990. Mem. Tex. Assn. for Advancement of Math. Skills, Conf. Advancement Math. Tech., Tex. Art Edn. Assn., VFW Ladies Aux., Assn. Tex. Profl. Educators (pres. 1989, 91, 93, 97). Ch. of christ. Office: J H Rowe Intermediate Sch 128 Park Ln Jasper TX 75951-3466

EDWARDS, CHERYL L., counselor; d. C.B. and Reva Whitlock; m. Delmar Edwards; children: Daxon, Esti Corcoran, Emberli. Masters, John Brown U., Siloam Springs, 2000. Lic. profl. counselor ACA/Ark., 2002. Lpsw Mercy Behavioral, Fort Smith, Ark., 2003—04; owner Preferred Counseling, Fort Smith, 2004—. Chmn. Camp Compassion, Fort Smith, 2000—. Office: Preferred Counseling 108 N 18th St Fort Smith AR 72902 Office Phone: 479-709-9880. Office Fax: 479-709-9887.

EDWARDS, CHRISTINE E., artist; b. Rockville County, NY, Nov. 10, 1952; d. Charles R. and Virginia Edwards; m. Thomas J. Potter, Apr. 17, 1982; children: Thomas A., Danial Sean; 1 child, Donna Marie. BS in Edn. magna cum laude, U. Tenn., Knoxville, 1975. Exercise rider NY Racing Commn., Belmont, NY, 1968; art tchr. Gatlinburg Pittman HS, Gatlinburg, Tenn., 1975—77, Sch. Arts, St. Thomas, 1980; artist, owner Christy Collection, Suffolk County, NY, 1982—. Artist in residence Mohonk Mountain Ho., New Paltz, NY, 1995; spkr. in field. Robert's Tall Friend, 1984 (commendation Light Island Ho. Preservation Soc.). Leader Married for Life, Islip Town, NY, 2004; mem. adv. coun. Southside Hosp., NY, 1991; mem. adv. bd. Fire Island Light Ho. Soc., NY, 1984—88; pres. South Shore Civic Assn., NY, 1986; v.p. Ocean Beach Ladies Aux., NY, 1977—78. Named to, Bayshore HS Hall of Fame, 2004; recipient cert. of excellence, Islip Town Bd., 2002, Cert. of Honor, South Side Hosp., 1988—93, 1996, Women of 90s award, Cablevision, 1999, Svc. Above Self award, Babylon Rotary, 1984. Mem.: Sons of Norway, Kiwanis. Roman Catholic. Avocations: singing, bicycling, boating, swimming, horses. Home: 7 Maynard Ln East Islip NY 11730 Office: Christy Collection Box 438 Great River NY 11739

EDWARDS, CHRISTINE UTLEY, social services administrator, consultant; b. Key West, Fla., Nov. 12, 1951; d. Samuel Tracy and Shirley (White) Utley; m. Lester G. Edwards, Aug. 11, 1973. B in Eng., U. Southwestern La., Lafayette, 1974; MPA, Syracuse U., 1980. Rsch. asst. So. Mut. Help Assn., Abbeville, La., 1974; dir. women's options Oneida Co. Coop. Extension, New Hartford, N.Y., 1975-76; planning specialist Oneida Co. Community Action, Utica, N.Y., 1980-81; dir. crisis services YWCA, Utica, N.Y., 1981-89; dir. edn. and community affairs Planned Parenthood Mohawk Valley, Utica, N.Y., 1989-95; exec. dir. YWCA Mohawk Valley, 1995-98; mgmt. cons. Computer Connection of Ctrl. N.Y., 1999-2000; exec. dir. Chenango Health Network, 2001—. Mem. com. for rape crisis ctrs. N.Y. State Dept. Health, Albany, 1984-89; cons./trainer Pvt. Devel. Orgn., Domestic and Sexual Violence Related Topics, Ilion, N.Y., 1986-93; adj. faculty mem. Mohawk Valley C.C., Utica, 1989; cons./trainer domestic violence unit N.Y. State Dept. Social Svcs., 1989-92; owner Tiger Lily Antiques, 1995. Founding mem. Rape Crisis Svcs., Utica, 1975; bd. dirs. Mohawk Valley Com. Against Child Abuse, 1985-88; mem. Mt. Markham Family Life Edn. Adv. Com., West Winfield, N.Y., 1988-90; mem. adv. com. rape crisis svcs. YWCA, Herkimer, N.Y., 1989—; bd. dirs. Canine Working Companions, Inc., 1990—, pres. 1993-95; bd. dirs. Metro Utica BPW, sec., 1993-95; master gardener Oneida County Cooperative Extension, 1993-95; mem. N.Y. State AIDS Inst. Statewide Prevention Planning Group, 1994-98; mem. steering com. Cen. N.Y. HIV Care Network, 1993-98; mem. Oneida County Domestic Violence Coalition, 1995-98. Recipient Women of Merit award Mohawk Valley Women's History Project, Utica, N.Y., 1985, Kirkland Art Ctr. Color Photography award, 1989. Mem. N.Y. Coalition Against Sexual Assault (founding mem., pres. 1988-90), Nat. Coalition Against Sexual Assault (bd. dirs. 1985-87). Democrat. Avocations: photographer, cross country skier, hiker, birder, gardener. Home: 140 Elizabethtown Rd Ilion NY 13357-3700

EDWARDS, CYNTHIA (CINDY) CURTIS, mathematics educator; b. Norfolk, Va., June 13, 1961; d. Ellis Wayne and Elizabeth (Betty) Ray Land; m. William Allen Edwards, Nov. 9, 1984; children: Erik Antony, Erin Ashley. BS in Secondary Math., Old Dominion U., Norfolk, Va., 1984. Math tchr. Green Run HS, Virginia Beach, Va., 1984—94, First Colonial HS, Virginia Beach, 1996—97, PA Ctr. for Pregnant Girls, Virginia Beach, 1997—98, Princess Anne HS, Virginia Beach, 1998—. Girls' tennis coach Green Run HS, 1984—88, Princess Anne HS, 1998—2002. Vol. leader Young Life of Virginia Beach, 1980—97; worship leader and singer Beach Fellowship Ch., Virginia Beach, Va., 1988—2006. Recipient Girls' Tennis Coach of the Yr., Va. Beach Sports Club, 2002. Mem.: PTA (licentiate), Nat. Coun. Tchrs. Math. (licentiate). Conservative-R. Christian. Avocations: coed softball, tennis, guitar. Office: Princess Anne HS 4400 Virginia Beach Blvd Virginia Beach VA 23462 Office Phone: 757-473-5000. Office Fax: 757-473-5004. Business E-Mail: cindy.edwards2@vbschools.com.

EDWARDS, CYNTHIA E., principal; d. Melbourne Coogen and Kathleen Adina Shaw; m. Ransford George Edwards, Aug. 20, 2006; children: Sean, Jodi. BS, U. W.I., Jamaica, 1972; Diploma in Edn., U. W.I., 1978, MS, 1982; Advanced Diploma, Bklyn. Coll., N.Y., 1994. Chemistry tchr., dept. head Excelsior H.S., Jamaica, 1972—80; lectr. in sci. edn. Excelsior C.C., Jamaica, 1980—82; jr. prof. sci. edn. U. w.I., Jamaica, 1982—83; sci. tchr. chemistry George Wingate H.S., Bklyn., 1983—88, sci. coord., 1988—91, chmn. sci. dept., 1991—99; prin. Queens Gateway to Health Sci., Jamaica, NY, 1999—. Recipient New Prin.'s Inst. award in leadership devel., 2001; fellow, Cahn Fellows Program, 2005—06. Mem.: ASCD, Am. Ednl. Rsch. Assn., Nat. Assn. Sec. Sch. Prins., Nat. Mid. Sch. Assn. Seventh-Day Adventist. Avocations: piano, voice. Home: 1252 Lynne St Baldwin NY 11510 Office: Queens Gateway to Health Sciences 150-91 87th Rd Jamaica NY 11432

EDWARDS, DONNA HOHMANN, psychologist; b. Denver, Colo., Sept. 1, 1934; d. Lee Kerwith and Irene Hohmann; m. John Edwards, Aug. 15, 1989; children: Marguerite, Suzanne, Rodger, Lee. BA, U. Colo., 1956; EdD, U. No. Colo. Tchr. San Francisco Pub. Sch. Dist., 1959—65; mem. faculty Lamaze Internat., Washington, 1970—; dir. youth svcs. YWCA, Boulder, Colo., 1980—83; teen pregnancy counselor Boulder Pub. Schs., 1980—87; dir. perinatal edn. U. Colo. Health Svcs., Denver, 1983—92; psychologist Colo. Ctr. Biobehavior, Boulder, 2005; family specialist, 1990—. Cons. in field. Author: 113 books on perinatal education, translated into German, Japanese and Spanish. Bd. dirs. Lamaze Internat., Boulder Pub. Schs. Named Outstanding Citizen, Boulder YWCA, 1980, Outstanding Contbr., Lamaze Internat. Home: 4610 Sunshine Canyon Dr Boulder CO 80302

EDWARDS, DORIS PORTER, computer specialist; b. Lambert, Miss., Jan. 18, 1962; d. Willie Morris and Carrie Mae (Tillman) E.; 1 child, Stacy Nicole. AA in Computer Sci., Draughons Coll., Memphis, 1981. Counselor French Riviera Spa, Memphis, 1989-90; pvt. practice, computer application developer Memphis, 1990—; owner, fin. cons., fund locator Developing Processing in Comm., Memphis, 1998—. Bus. owner Developing Processing in Comms.; fin. cons., cream developer. Developer cosmetic cream. Jehovah's Witness. Avocations: mathematics, reading. Home and Office: 5429 Kindle Creek Dr Memphis TN 38141-0543 E-mail: easibis@aol.com.

EDWARDS, GLEITA KAY, primary school educator; b. Chgo., Nov. 27, 1938; d. Leon J. Clemens and Mary Evelyn Palm; children: Ami Brook, Kami Brin. AA, Glendale CC, Ariz., 1983; BA in Edn. magna cum laude, Ariz. State U., Tempe, 1984, MEd in Ednl. Adminstrn., 1987. Tchr. Murphy Sch. Dist., Phoenix, 1985—86, Dysart Dist. Surprise Elem. Sch., 1986—89, Kingswood Elem. Sch., Surprise, Ariz., 1989—. Project coord. Winter Wonderland; sch.-wide coord. Multicultural Fiesta; coord. Kindergarten Parent Orientation/Registration; mem. faculty, adv. com., site coun., grade chair, liaison PTSA. Named Tchr. of Yr., Kingswood Elem. Sch., 2003; recipient Dreammaker Award, Dysart Sch. Dist., 2004. Mem.: Am. Assn. Univ. Women, Internat. Reading Assn., Parent Tchr. Student Assn. Republican. Methodist. Avocations: walking, reading, travel, bicycling. Office: Kingswood Elem Sch 15150 W Mondell Rd Surprise AZ 85374 Office Phone: 623-876-7634. Business E-Mail: gedwards@dysart.org.

EDWARDS, IRENE ELIZABETH (LIBBY EDWARDS), dermatologist, educator, medical researcher; b. Winston-Salem, N.C., Mar. 17, 1950; d. Robert Dixon Edwards and Irene Octavia (Temple) Fisher; m. Clayton Samuel Owens, Apr. 19, 1985; 1 child, Sarah Tay. BS magna cum laude, Wake Forest U., 1972; MD, Bowman Gray Sch. Medicine, 1976; postgrad., N.C. Bapt. Hosp., 1979, U. Ariz., 1981, 84. Diplomate Nat. Bd. Med. Examiners, Am. Bd. Internal Medicine, Am. Bd. Pediatrics, Am. Bd. Dermatology. Intern N.C. Bapt. Hosp., Winston-Salem, 1976-78, resident in pediatrics, 1978-79; resident in internal medicine U. Ariz. Health Scis. Ctr., Tucson, 1979-81, resident in dermatology, 1982-84; instr. dermatology U. Ariz. Coll. Medicine, Tucson, 1984-85, asst. prof. dermatology, 1985-90; clin. rschr., chief sect. dermatology Tucson VA Med. Ctr., 1984-90; chief dermatology Carolinas Med. Ctr., Charlotte, NC, 1990—; clin. assoc. prof. dermatology, clin. rschr. Wake Forest U., Winston-Salem, 1993—, U. N.C., Chapel Hill, 1993—. Nat. lectr. in field. Author: Dermatology in Emergency Care, 1997; co-author: Genital Dermatology, 1994; editor: Genital Dermatology Atlas, 2004; contbr. chpts. to books, numerous articles to profl. jours. Reynolds scholar, 1969-72. Fellow Am. Acad. Dermatology, Am. Acad. Pediatrics; mem. Soc. Pediatric Dermatology, Internat. Soc. Tropical Dermatology, Women's Dermatologic Soc., Internat. Soc. Study Vulvovaginal Disease (pres.), Charlotte Dermatol. Soc., Phi Beta Kappa, Alpha Epsilon Delta. Home: 2409 Cuthbertson Rd Waxhaw NC 28173-8110 Office Phone: 704-367-9777.

EDWARDS, JOSELLE ELIZABETH, performing arts educator; b. Ephrata, Pa., Sept. 17, 1952; d. Luther Jacoby and Betty Jane Epler Edwards. AS in German, York Coll. Pa., 1973; BS in Health and Phys. Edn., Slippery Rock State Coll., 1975; MS in Phys. Edn., Curriculum and Supr., Va. Polytech. Inst. and State U., 1982, MS in Edn., 1989. Instr. Montgomery County Pub. Sch., Harding Elem. Sch., Blacksburg, Va., 1987—99, Montgomery County C.C., Blue Bell, Pa., 1999—. Spkr. in field. Co-author: (album) Figurifics, 1980; contbr. articles to profl. jours. Mentor Big Brothers Big Sisters, Manhattan, Kans., 1987; spkr. Blue Ribbon Commn., Blacksburg, Va., 1996. Recipient Svc. award, Montgomery County C.C., 1999—2004. Mem.: Am. Assn. Health Edn., Pa. Assn. Health Phys. Edn., Recreation and Dance, Nat. Dance Assn., Am. Alliance Health, Phys. Edn., Recreation and Dance. Lutheran. Avocations: travel, dogs, volleyball. Office: Montgomery County Cmty Coll 340 DeKalb Blue Bell PA 19422 Office Phone: 215-641-6517. E-mail: jedwards@mc3.edu.

EDWARDS, JULIE ANN, science researcher; b. Berea, Ohio, Jan. 31, 1945; d. Ralph Frederick and Elsie Marie (Koch) Schmiedlin; m. O. James Edwards; children: J. Patrick, Tommie, Jami. BA in Biology, U. Detroit Mercy, Mich., 1967; postgrad., Murray State U., Ky., 1985, Ea. Mich. U., Ypsilanti, 1988-89. Rschr. VA Hosp., Ann Arbor, Mich., 1969-72, U. Mich., Ann Arbor, 1987—2003; ret., 2003. Contbr. articles to profl. jours. Mem. Sci. Rsch. Club of U. Mich. (sec.), Sigma Xi. Avocations: gardening, sewing, crafts, genealogy.

EDWARDS, JULIE DIANE, women's health nurse; b. Lewiston, Idaho, Jan. 4, 1958; d. William and Shirley Hinkley; adopted by Karl Frank and Margaret Esther (Carver) Stoehr, 1965; m. Raymond LeRoy Murphy, Jr., Mar. 19, 1977 (div. Mar. 1982); 1 child, Raymond LeRoy Murphy III; m. Monte Russell Edwards, Dec. 22, 1984; children: Bryan James, Lindsey Denise. AS with honors, Highline C.C. Coll., Des Moines, Wash., 1982; ADN with honors, Mt. Hood C.C., Gresham, Oreg., 1993. RN, Oreg.; cert. neonatal resuscitation program; cert. ultrasound nurse. Staff nurse maternity unit Woodland Park Hosp., Portland, Oreg., 1993-98; staff on call nurse maternity unit Providence Milwaukie Hosp., Milwaukie, Oreg., 1994-95, 97-99; ultrasound nurse Greater Portland Area Pregnancy Resource Ctrs., 2000—03; ob-gyn staff nurse Family Birth Pl. Adventist Med. Ctr., 2003—. Mem. adv. bd. Adult Basic Edn., Pocatello, Idaho, 1982-85; VISTA vol., 1984-85; vol. Crisis Pregnancy Ctr., Portland, Oreg., 1990-2004; tchr. aide Good Shepherd Sch., 1992-99; Sunday sch. tchr. Good Shepherd Cmty. Ch., 1984-91, 94-99. With U.S. Army, 1976-79. Republican. Christian. Avocations: embroidery, cross country skiing, camping, hiking, scuba diving. Home: 1346 SE Condor Pl Gresham OR 97080-6126

EDWARDS, KASSANDRA BENNETT, psychotherapist, consultant; b. Richmond, Va., June 13, 1944; d. Edward Joseph and Jane Jeffery Stephani; m. Scott Odell Edwards, Nov. 20, 1988; m. Robert Nelson Dills, June 18, 1966 (div. June 1979). BA Psychology, Pitzer Coll., Claremont, Calif., 1966; MA, U. Redlands, Calif., 1982; MSW, San Francisco State U., Calif., 1985. LCSW 1988, lic. marriage, family, and child therapist 1987. Social worker San Mateo County, Calif., 1970—84; counselor, parent edn. instr. Family Svc. Agy., Burlingame, Calif., 1980—86, clin. supr., 1986—93; trainer., cons. Golden Gate Trg., San Francisco, 1986—; oral examiner State of Calif., Bd. Behavioral Sci. Examiners, Sacramento, 1999—2003; subject matter expert State of Calif., Bd. Behavioral Scis., Sacramento, 2002—; psychiat. social worker Kaiser Child Psychiatry Clin., San Francisco, 1996—. Contbr. scientific papers, 2002. Mem.: NASW. Achievements include co-founder San Mateo county's child sexual abuse treatment program; development of intensive outpatient program for treatment of emotionally disturbed adolescents Kaiser SSF child psychiatry clinic. Avocations: travel, bicycling, opera. Office: Kaiser Child Psychiatry Clin 801 Traeger San Bruno CA 94066 Office Phone: 650-742-2746. Business E-Mail: kassandra.edwards@kp.org.

EDWARDS, KATHLEEN, real estate broker, former educator; b. Grundy, Va., Nov. 13, 1929; d. Cornelius and Vallie Mae (Wallace) Lester; m. George Perry Bailey, July 18, 1950; children: Shearer, George, Craig; m. Richard C. Edwards, June 10, 1967; 1 child, Richard Cornelius; stepchildren: Randall, Mark, Ashley. BA, Radford (Va.) U., 1950; MEd, U. Va., 1965. Cert. tchr., Va.; lic. real estate broker. Tchr. pub. elem. schs., Va., 1950-71, N.J., 1971-73; dir., owner Fireside Sch., Va., 1973-81; real estate broker, pres., owner View Properties Inc., Va., 1977—. Mem.: DAR (regent Harmony Hall chpt. 1999—2001), Nat. Assn. Realtors. Avocations: oil and pastel painting, travel. Office Phone: 703-971-7002.

EDWARDS, KATHRYN INEZ, educational consultant; b. LA, Aug. 26, 1947; d. Lloyd and Geraldine E. (Smith) Price; 1 child, Bryan. BA in English, Calif. State U., L.A., 1969; supervision credential, 1974, adminstrn. credential, 1975; MEd in Curriculum, UCLA, 1971; PhD, Claremont Grad. Sch., 1979. Tchr. L.A. Pub. Schs., 1969—78, adv. specially funded programs, 1978—80, advisor librs. and learning-resources program, 1980—81, instructional specialist, 1981—84; cons. instructional media L.A. County Office of Edn., Downey, Calif., 1984-90; coord. ednl. media and tech. Pomona (Calif.) Unified Sch. Dist., 1990-92; cons. edn. tech. Apple Computer, Inc., 1992-96; client mktg. rep. IBM; sales devel. mgr. SUN Microsys., 1999—2000; dir. mktg. Vinendi Universal Interactive Pub., 2000—02; mgr. strategic urban initiatives Apple Computer, 2002—03; nat. measurement cons. Harcourt Assessment, 2003—. Cons. Walt Disney Prodns., Alfred Higgins Prodns., others; mem. distance lng. think tank U.S. Office Edn., 1997. Author: guides and curriculum kits. Apptd. by assembly spkr. Willie Brown Calif. Ednl. Tech. Com., 1990—92; apptd. Calif. State Assembly Resolution from Gwen Moore, 1988, Edn. Coun. Tech. in Learning, 1993—96; mem. spl. com. Cable Access Corp. Co-Owners, 1991—92. Named Outstanding Woman of the Yr., L.A. Sentinel, 1987; recipient cert. commendation, Senator Diane Watson, 1988; Mabel Wilson Richards scholar, 1968, Calif. Congress Parents and Tchrs. scholar, 1968, UCLA fellow, 1968. Mem.: ASCD, Nat. Assn. Media Women, Calif. Media and Libr. Educators Assn. (state conf. co-chair 1989, v.p. legal divsn. 1992—), Calif. Assn. Tchrs. English (conf. del. 1982), L.A. Reading Assn. (pres.), Internat. Reading Assn. (spkr. nat. conv. 1988), Nat. Assn. Minority Polit. Women (Media Woman of the Yr. 1987), Alpha Kappa Alpha. Democrat. Roman Catholic. Avocations: reading, gardening, travel. Office: 6709 LaTyra Blvd # 854 Los Angeles CA 90045-2017 E-mail: kathryne1@comcast.net.

EDWARDS, KRISTINA NELL, elementary school educator; b. Orange, Tex., Nov. 19, 1975; d. George Ollie and Mary Jane Johnson; m. Kerry G. Edwards, July 28, 2005. BS, Lamar State Coll., Beaumont, Tex., 1998. 7th grade sci. tchr. Bridge City Ind. Sch. Dist., Bridge City, Tex., 1999—2003, jr. high and hs coach, 1999—2003; 8th grade sci. tchr. La Porte (Tex.) Jr. High, 2003—. Mem.: Tex. Classroom Tchrs. Assn., Am. Tchr. Fedn., Kappa Delta Pi. Office: La Porte Junior High 401 S Broadway La Porte TX 77571 Office Phone: 281-604-6626. Personal E-mail: kristinanedwards@aol.com.

EDWARDS, LORA BRUNETT, retired property manager; b. Gholson, Miss., Mar. 29, 1915; d. Thomas Morris and Luvenia Augusta Billingsly; m. Marshall Leon Edwards, Apr. 22, 1938 (dec.); children: Billy Eric, Byron Ronald, Thomas Forrest. Sales assoc. J.L Hudson's, Detroit, 1945—55; gen. mgr. Travel Ten Club (Non-Profit), Detroit, 1968—2003. Lt. Mar. of Dimes, Detroit, 1958—68; recruiter and mem. NAACP, Detroit, 1950; motor aide United Cmty. Svcs., Detroit, 1958—68; invitee presdl. inauguration Pres. Jimmy Cater, Washington, 1977—81; nat. steering com. Bill Clinton, Detroit, 1992—2000; contbg. mem. Dem. Nat. Com., Washington, 1992; charter mem. Ams. For Change Presdl. Task Force, Washington, 1993—2000; election pers. City Election Commn., Detroit, 1965—90; mem. philanthropic activities NAACP, Mar. of Dimes, UNCF, Rescue Mission, Feed the Children, So. Poverty Law, Detroit, 1945. Recipient Outstanding Svcs. Membership Campaign, NAACP, 1956, Exemplary Vol. Efforts, Detroit Shopping News, 1968, 5 and 10 Yr. awards-Vol. Motor Aide Transp. of Handicap and Elderly, United Cmty. Svcs. of Met. Detroit, 1973, 1978, Extraordinary Fin. and Moral Support-Democratic Party, Dem. Nat. Com., 1975, Faithful Pub. Svc. award, Detroit City Election Commn., 1990. Mem.: Fitness USA (life), Travel Ten Club (hon.), Stoepel Lite (hon.). Democrat-Npl. Mem. Ch. Of God In Christ. Home: 12632 Stoepel St Detroit MI 48238

EDWARDS, LYNN A., retired school system administrator; b. Cicero, IL, Apr. 1, 1923; d. Calvin S. Yakley and Linda Olson; m. Edward M. Edwards; children: Dean, Dyke, Elizabeth. BA, U. Ill., 1944; MEd, U. Toledo, 1975. Secondary tchr. Sylvania Schs., Sylvania, Ohio, 1968—70, media specialist, 1971—83, sch. adminstr., 1984—86. Named Age Group Ironman Triathlon World Champion, 1992—93; recipient Olympic Distance World Triathlon Champion, Can., 2001, Long Course World Champion, Ind., 1997, numerous championships in marathons and running events.; fellow Fulbright scholar to India, U.S. Congress, 1980 and, 1984. Avocations: participating in numerous running events, teaching fitness class.

EDWARDS, MARIE D., social services administrator; b. Cin., Sept. 17, 1943; d. George Junior Denning and Lola Dortheia Jackson; children: Daniel J., Grayson G.; m. Terrance Anthoney Edwards Sr., July 24, 1982; stepchildren: Terrance A. Edwards, Troy Edwards, Heather Kraus. Owner, mgr. Greendale Grill, Lawrenceburg, Ind., 1980-86, M.E. & Assocs. Realtors, Vevay, Ind., 1986-93; mgr. Coldwell Banker, Lawrenceburg, 1993-98; exec. dir. Dearborn Adult Ctr., Lawrenceburg, 1998—. Bd. dirs. Southea. Ind. Econ. Opportunity Ctr., 1995—, Hist. Landmarks; chairperson I Love Lawrenceburg com., 1999-2000, 2001, 2002, 2003, Bicentennial City of Lawrenceburg, 2001—; chairperson Lawrenceburg Gateway Project, Gateway Ctr. Project. Named Cmty. Leader 2000, Lawrenceburg C. of C., 2001, Cmty. Leader, 2002, 2003, Ofcl. Bell Ringer, City of Lawrenceburg; recipient Dearborn County award for svc. and humanitarian effort, 2001. Mem. Dearborn County C. of C. (gov.'s com. transp., Southea. Women's Network, pres. 2000-2001), Southea. Bd. Realtors (treas. 1990), Order Ea. Star (assoc. matron). Democrat. Methodist. Avocation: gardening. Office: Dearborn Adult Ctr Inc 311 W Tate St Lawrenceburg IN 47025 E-mail: maedwards@seidata.com.

EDWARDS, MJ, lawyer; BS in Chemistry, cum laude, Carleton Coll., 1992; JD magna cum laude, Boston Coll. Law Sch., 2002. Bar: Mass. Bioanalytical chemist Eli Lilly and Co.; assoc. Intellectual Property Dept. Wilmer, Cutler, Pickering, Hale and Dorr LLP, Boston, 2002—. Mem.: Mass. Lesbian and Gay Bar Assn., Order of Coif. Office: Wilmer Cutler Pickering Hale and Dorr LLP 60 State St Boston MA 02109 Office Phone: 617-526-6215. Office Fax: 617-526-5000. E-mail: mj.edwards@wilmerhale.com.*

EDWARDS, PATRICIA BURR, small business owner, consultant; b. Oakland, Calif., Feb. 19, 1918; d. Myron Carlos and Claire Idelle (Laingor) Burr; m. Jackson Edwards, Nov. 14, 1942; children: Jill Forman-Young, Jan Kurzweil. AB, U. So. Calif., 1939, MSEd, 1981. Prin. Constructive Leisure, L.A., 1968—. Spkr. in field; writer, prodr. counseling materials for career, leisure, life planning including computer software, audio cassettes and assessment surveys. Author: You've Got to Find Happiness: It Won't Find You, 1971, Leisure Counseling Techniques: Individual and Group Counseling Step-by-Step, 1975, 3d edit., 1980; (software) Leisure PREF, 1986, Over 50: Needs, Values, Attitudes, 1988, Adapting to Change: The NVAB Program, 1997; contbr. articles to profl. jours., mags. and books. Chmn. L.A. County Foster Families 50th Anniversary, 1962-64, L.A. Jr. League Sustainers, 1964-65, Hollywood Bowl Vols., L.A., 1960-61, Hollywood Bowl Patroness com., 1961—. Mem. Am. Counseling Assn., Calif. Assn. for Counseling and Devel., Nat. Recreation and Park Assn., Assn. for Adult Devel. and Aging, Trojan League, Travellers Aid Soc. L.A., Jr. League L.A., First Century Families of L.A., Delta Gamma. Republican. Episcopalian. Avocations: singing, dance, pets, learning.

EDWARDS, ROBIN MORSE, lawyer; b. Glens Falls, NY, Dec. 9, 1947; d. Daniel and Harriet Morse; m. Richard Charles Edwards, Aug. 30, 1970; children: Michael Alan, Jonathan Philip. BA, Mt. Holyoke Coll., 1969; JD, U. Calif., Berkeley, 1972. Bar: Calif. 1972. Assoc. Donahue, Gallagher, Thomas & Woods, Oakland, Calif., 1972—77, ptnr., 1977—89, Sonnenschein, Nath & Rosenthal, San Francisco, 1989—, mgmt. com., 1998—. Bd. dirs. Temple Sinai, 1997-2002. Mem. ABA, Calif. Bar Assn., Alameda County Bar Assn. (bd. dirs. 1978-84, v.p. 1982, pres. 1983), Alameda County Bar Found. (bd. dirs. 1998-2000). Jewish. Avocations: skiing, cooking. Office: Sonnenschein Nath Rosenthal 525 Market St 26th Fl San Francisco CA 94105-2708 Business E-Mail: redwards@sonnenschein.com.

EDWARDS, SARAH, biology educator; d. K. and P. Edwards. BS Biology, Pre-medicine & Secondary Edn., U. South Fla., Tampa, 1990. Cert. Tchr. N.C., 2002. Tchr. AP biology Davidson County Schools, Lexington, NC, 1998—2002, Pitt County Schools, Greenville, NC, 2002—. Curriculum Grant for Devel. Outside Classroom, N.C. Sci. Tchrs. Assn., 2005. Office: South Central High School 570 W Forlines Rd Winterville NC 28590

EDWARDS, SARAH ANNE, social worker, psychologist; b. Tulsa, Jan. 7, 1943; d. Clyde Elton and Virginia Elizabeth Glandon; m. Paul Robert Edwards, Apr. 24, 1965; 1 son, Jon Scott. BA with distinction, U. Mo., Kansas City, 1965; MSW, U. Kans., 1974; PhD in Applied Ecopsychology, Akamai U., Hilo, Hawaii, 2006. LCSW Calif.; cert. ecopsychologist Inst. Global Edn., 2005. Cmty. rep. OEO, Kans. City Regional Office, 1966-68; social svc./parent involvement and resource specialist Office of Child Devel., HEW, Kansas City, Mo., 1968-73; dir. tng. social svcs. dept., children's rehab. unit U. Affiliated Facility, U. Kans. Med. Ctr., Kansas City, 1975-76; co-dir. Cathexis Inst. S., Glendale, Calif., 1976-77; pvt. practice psychotherapy, tng. and cons. personal and interpersonal, orgnl. behavior, Sierra Madre, Calif., 1973-80; sys. operator CompuServe Info. Svc., 1983-98; faculty mem. grad. dept. applied ecopsychology Inst. Global Edn., 2005—; NGO cons. UNESCO, 2005—. Prodr., co-host radio show Working From Home, on Bus. Talk Radio, 1988-01; co-host radio show Entrepeneur's Home Business Edition, 2003— co-host cable show Working from Home Scripp's Howard Home and Garden Cable TV Network, 1995-97; commentator CNBC, 1996-99, NPR Marketplace, 1996-97; co-host Entrepreneurs Home Bus. Show, WS Radio, 2000—. Columnist for Home Office Computing Mag., 1988-97, Your Home Office, L.A. Times Syndicate, 1997-99, Entrepreneur's Home Office, 1998—, Price CostCo Connection, 1994—, Inc-Com., 2000—; co-author: How to Make Money with Your Personal Computer, 1997, Getting Business to Come to You, 1998, Working From Home, rev. edit., 1999, Secrets of Self-Employment, 1996, Finding Your Perfect Work, 1996, Teaming Up, 1997, Home Businesses You Can Buy, 1997, Cool Careers for Dummies, 1998, Making Money in Cyberspace, 1998, Best Home Business for the 21st Century, 1999, Working From Home, 1999, The Practical Dreamer's Handbook, 2000, Home-Based Business for Dummies, 2000, Changing Directions without Losing Your Way, 2001, Entrepreneurial Parent, 2002, Sitting with the Enemy, A Novel, 2002, Why Aren't You Your Own Boss?, 2003, Best Home Business for People 50+, 2004; mem. editl. bd. Jour. Applied Ecopsychology, 2005—. Dir. nature-guided career counseling and continuing edn. programs Pine Mtn. Inst., 2001—05, Post-Corp. Career Inst., 2006. Address: Box 6775 2624 Teakwood Ct Frazier Park CA 93222 Office Phone: 661-242-2624. Business E-Mail: sedwards@frazmtn.com. E-mail: sarahecopsych@aol.com.

EDWARDS, SHANNON J., science educator; b. Seagraves, Tex., Oct. 6, 1958; d. Doris Lacy; m. Tim Edwards, Aug. 24, 1979; children: Lacy Jo Lusk, Zachary Holland. BS, Tex. Tech U., Lubbock, 1983; MEd, Sul Ross State U., Alpine, Tex., 1997. Lic. secondary sci. Tex. Edn. Agy., 1991, mid-mgmt., adminstr. Tex. Edn. Agy., 1997, cert. supt. Tex. Edn. Agy., 1999. Sci. tchr. Alderson Jr. High, Lubbock, 1991—2000, Dunbar Mid. Sch., Lubbock, 2000—. Avid tchr. Lubbock Ind. Sch. Dist., 1999—2004; web trainer Dunbar Mid. Sch., Lubbock, 2005—. Mem.: Tex. Classroom Tchrs., Lubbock Classroom Tchrs. Office: Dunbar Mid Sch/Lubbock ISD 2010 E 26th St Lubbock TX 79404 Office Phone: 806-766-1300. E-mail: sedwards@lubbockisd.org.

EDWARDS, SHARON JANE, nurse; b. Staten Island, N.Y., Aug. 15, 1967; BSN, Oral Roberts U., 1990; MSN, St. Louis U., 1998, PhD in Nursing, 2002. Nurse extern City of Faith Hosp., Tulsa, 1989-90; nurse Loma Linda (Calif.) U., 1990-93, George Washington U. Med. Ctr., Washington, 1993, Walter Reed Army Med. Ctr., Washington, 1994-96, Jefferson (Mo.). Meml. Hosp., 1997, Belleville Meml. Hosp., Ill., 1997-98; pres. Advanced Practice Nursing Svcs., Inc., St. Louis, 1998—2002; asst. prof. Coll. of Nursing U. South Fla., Tampa, 2002—.

EDWARDS, SHARON MARIE, minister, educator; b. Akron, Ohio, Jan. 28, 1944; d. Michael Robert Batche and Kathleen Marie Austin; m. Ronald Payne Edwards, Apr. 4, 1970; children: Carrie JoAnn, Suzanne Kathleen. BA, Malone U., 1971. Lic. pastor Ohio, 1977, minister Abundant Life Ministries. Pastor Abundant Life Ministries, Akron, Ohio, 1977—78; founder and sr. pastor Harvest Christian Ctrs., Internat., North Canton, Ohio, 1978—. Adv. bd. Living Water Tchg., Internat., Caddo Mills, Tex.; fin. sec. Living Water Ch., Akron; mem. fin. bd. Sherwood Pk. Baptist, Akron; spkr. in field. Author bible studies materials, (corr. course) Foundations Series, 1999—2003. Recipient Voices award, Nat. Campaign Influential Women USA, 2003. Mem.: Women's Missionary Union (mem. state bd. 1972—74). Avocations: travel, bible studies. Office: Harvest Christian Ctrs Internat 116 9th St NW North Canton OH 44720 Office Phone: 330-499-5683.

EDWARDS, SHEILA M., banker, educator; b. Arab, Ala., Aug. 10, 1960; d. Raymond O'Neal and Nellie Marie Moody; children: Melissa LaAnn, Justina Marie. AS, Jefferson State U., Pinson, Ala., 1982; student, Am. Inst. Banking, Birmingham, Ala., 1992, 93. Asst. head teller Leeth Nat. Bank, Cullman, Ala., 1982-83; loan asst. v.p. Regions Bank, Oneonta, Ala., 1987-93; br. mgr. Valley Fin., Guntersville, Ala., 1993-95; adminstrv. mgr. Lowe's, Cullman, 1995-96; comml. lending SouthTrust Bank, Guntersville, 1996-99; v.p. EvaBank, Cullman, 1999—2001; tchr. fin. Am. Inst. Banking-Wallace State, Cullman, 1999—; br. mgr. Colonial Bank, Locust Fork, Ala., 2001—03; v.p., trainer, security officer, sr. project mgr. Cmty. Bank, Blountsville, Ala., 2003—. Career and money coach; spkr. in field. Troop leader Girls Scouts U.S., Blountsville, Ala., coord., 1984—91. Mem.: Bount W Bus. and Profl. Women (pres. 2002—), Cullman Bus. and Profl. Women (pres. 2001—), Ala. Bus. Women (bd. dirs.), Bus. and Profl. Women (v.p. 2000, pres. 2001—), Fin. Women Internat. (pres. Mountain Valley group 1999—2000, state officer 2001—, Ala. v.p. 2002—03, Ala. state officer of edn., tng., state pres. 2003—), C. of C. Office: PO Box 1000 Blountsville AL 35031 Office Phone: 205-429-1001.

EDWARDS, SYLVIA ANN, artist; b. Boston, Jan. 30, 1937; d. Junius Griffiths and Sylvia Emma (Mailloux) E.; m. Sadredin M. Golestaneh (div.); children: Shirin, Nader, Leila. Diploma, Mass. Coll. Art, Boston, 1957, Boston Mus. Fine Arts, 1958; postgrad., Modern Art Studies, London, 1980—81. One-woman shows include Grosvenor Gallery, London, 2003, CCA Gallery, Oxford, Eng., 1996, Munson Gallery, Chatham, Mass., 1992, Jaeshke Gallery, Braunschweig, Germany, 1991, Natalie Knight Gallery, Johannesburg, South Africa, 1991, Bankamura, Tokyo, 1991, Gallery K. Hyazaki Perfecture, 1991, The Berkeley Sq. Gallery, London, 1991, exhibited in group shows at Cadogan Contemporary Art, 1996, Berkeley Sq. Gallery, Korea Art Expo, Seoul, 1996, 2002, N.Y. Art Expo, N.Y.C., 1994, Lond Internat. Contemporary Art Fair, 1989, The Bath Arts Festival, Eng., 1988, Paris Art Salon, 1986, 1987, 1988, Sarasota Visual Art Ctr., Represented in permanent collections Nat. Mus. for Women in the Arts, Washington, Boston U. Spl. Collections, Cape Mus Fine Arts, Dennis, Mass, Mus. Fine Arts, Alexandria, Egypt, Governorate of Alexandria, Mass. Gen. Hosp., Boston, Chelsea Westminster Hosp., London, Midwest Mus. Am. Art, Elkhart, Ind., Tate Gallery, London, publs., Valley of Sils, Lithograph, 1982, N.Mex. Watch, lithograph, 1982, covers, Arts Rev., 1982, 1985, others, numerous, UNICEF cards, Greenpeace publs., World Wildlife/U.K., book covers, reference and art books, others, monographs. Mem. U.K. UNICEF Com. Mem. London Royal Acad., World Watercolor Soc., Chelsea Arts Club/London. Avocations: writing, theater, travel, swimming, reading. Studio: 14 Cadogan Square London SW1X 0JU England

EDWARDS, TERRI LYN WILMOTH, education educator; b. Bremerton, Wash., June 18, 1959; d. Marvin Earl and Beverly Joanne Wilmoth; m. Eddie Lee Edwards, Sr., Nov. 4, 1988; children: Eddie Lee Jr., Clint, Sparky, Jaime. AAS, Rogers State Coll., Claremore, Okla., 1986; BABS in Edn., Langston U., 1988; MEdn., Northeastern State U., Tahlequah, Okla., 1996; postgrad. in Edn. Psychology PhD program, Okla. State U., Stillwater, 1996—. Nat. Bd. Cert. Tchr. Elementary sch. tchr. Coweta (Okla.) Pub. Schs., 1988—2001; Great Expectations instr. Northeastern State U., Tahlequah, 1999—; prof. edn. U. Phoenix, Tulsa, 1999—; instr. COE Northeastern State U., Tahlequah, Okla., 2001—. Spkr. Shurley English, Ark., 1998—2001, Nat. Bd. Profl. Tchg. Stds., 1999—. Named State Sci. Tchr. of Yr., Nat. Conservation Dists., Oklahoma City, 2000; recipient Fulbright Found. award, 2000. Mem.: ASCD, Assn. Childhood Edn. Internat., Nat. Bd. Profl. Tchg. Stds., Delta Kappa Gamma. Democrat. Baptist. Avocation: golf. Home: PO Box 215 Fort Gibson OK 74434 Office: Northeastern State Univ 3100 E New Orleans St Tahlequah OK 74464 Office Phone: 918-449-6596. Business E-Mail: edward22@nsuok.edu. E-mail: terriee_1999@yahoo.com.

EDWARDS, TONYA GREEN, elementary school educator; b. Vidalia, Ga., Feb. 1, 1977; d. Ronnie W. and Brenda Cone Green; m. James Patrick Edwards, Sept. 27, 2003. AS, Brevard Coll., N.C., 1997; B of Health Edn., Ga. Coll. and State U., Milledgeville, 2000; M in Foundations of Edn., Troy U., Augusta, Ga., 2005. Reading/geography tchr. Reidsville Mid. Sch., Ga., 2001—05; lang. arts/geography tchr. JR Trippe Mid. Sch., Vidalia, Ga., 2005—. Participant Glennville 1st Bapt. Ch., Ga., 2003—06. Office Phone: 912-537-3813.

EDWARDS, VIRGINIA DAVIS, music educator, concert pianist; b. Syracuse, N.Y., Jan. 8, 1927; d. Leslie Martz and Elsie (Gannon) Davis; m. William B. Edwards, Jan. 12, 1954. BA magna cum laude, Marshall U., 1948; MusB, MusM, Cin. Conservatory of Music, 1950; postgrad., U. Chgo., 1950-56, U. Calif., Berkeley, 1963. Pianist, young artists series Conservatory of Music, Cin., 1949-50, piano instr. Evanston, Ill., 1955-56; music instr. Harvard Sch. for Boys, Chgo., 1954-55; pianist Opera Studios of Dimitri Onofrei/Bianca Saroya, Chgo., 1957-61; piano instr. Community Music Ctr., San Francisco, 1962-63; v.p. Gold Rush Gun Shop, Benet Arms Co. Imports, San Francisco, 1963-68, Afton, Va., 1968—; pvt. practice Afton, Va., 1978—; instr. piano Mary Baldwin Coll., Staunton, Va., 1988—. Soloist Marshall U. Symphony Orch., 1948, Chgo. Pops Concert Orch., Duluth, Minn., 1961; recitalist Curtis Hall, Chgo., 1961, Legion of Honor, San Francisco, 1966, Sta. WRFK-FM, Richmond, Va., 1979, DAR Constn. Hall, Washington, 2006; prodr., performer Presbyn. Hunger Program series, 1984-87, St. John's Cath. Ch., Waynesboro, Va., 1985, Basic Meth. Ch., 1989, Augusta Hosp. Corp. Benefit, 1989; author: Conspiracy of 30 -- Their Misuse of Music from Aristotle to Onassis, 1994. Mem. AAUW, DAR, Va. Museum Soc. Unitarian Universalist. Office Phone: 540-943-0091.

EDWARDS, WILLARDA V., internist, medical association administrator; MBA, Loyola Coll., Balt.; MD, Univ. Md. Staff Bethesda Naval Hosp.; chief, internal medicine dept. US Navy Hosp., Annapolis; pvt. practice internist Balt., 1984—; pres. Sickle Cell Assn. Am., Balt., 2004—. Recipient Zeta Phi Beta Woman of Yr. in Medicine award, 1997, Md.'s Top 100 Women award, 2003, Girl Scouts Ctrl. Md. award, 2004. Mem.: Nat. Med. Assn., Md. Chpt. (pres. 1996), AMA, Md. Chapt. (pres. 1996). Avocations: bicycling, golf, scuba diving, skiing. Office: Sickle Cell Disease Assn Am Inc Ste 800 231 E Baltimore St Baltimore MD 21202 Office Phone: 410-528-1555.*

EDWARDS DUNCAN, LINDA KAYE, elementary school educator; b. Gaffney, S.C., Mar. 31, 1954; d. Willie Lee and Sarah Ruth (Oglesby) Edwards; m. William L. Duncan. BS, S.C. State U., 1976, MEd, 1981. Cert. tchr. elem. edn., S.C. Reading instr. Mary Bramlett Elem., Gaffney, S.C., 1976-77; spl. edn. instr. Alma Elem. Sch., Gaffney, 1977-79; second-grade instr. Goucher Elem. Sch., Gaffney, 1079-95; summer camp counselor Assn. for Retarded Citizens, Gaffney, 1986-89; after-sch. program coord. and instr. Goucher Elem. Sch., Gaffney, 1993-94, first grade tchr., 1995—. Evaluation team So. Assn. Colls. and Schs., 1991, 94, 95, 97, 98. Vol. Am. Heart Assn., Gaffney, 1994; mem. evaluation team So. Assn. Colls., 1991, 1994—95, 1997—2004, 2005; poll. mgr.; trustee SC State U., 2004—; tutor, choir mem., usher Allen Temple CME Ch., Gaffney, bd. Christian edn., dir. children and youth; ch. sec. Pastor's Aide Soc. Named Goucher Elem. Tchr. of Yr., 1982—83, 2002—03; named one of Outstanding Young Women of Am., 1985, Outstanding Educators of Am., 1998; tchr. incentive grantee, Dept. Edn., Columbia, SC, 1988. Mem. United Teaching Profession (del.), Goucher Sch. Strategic Planning Team, Cherokee County Reading Coun. (v.p. 1987-90), Sigma Gamma Rho (svc. award 1989, treas. 1990-94). Methodist. Avocations: crafts, antiques, reading, interior decorating, desktop publishing. Home: 704 New St Gaffney SC 29340-4258 Office: Goucher Elem Sch 604 Goucher School Rd Gaffney SC 29340-6052 Office Phone: 864-487-1246.

EDWARDS-LEBOEUF, RENEE CAMILLE, public relations executive, protective services official; b. Falls Church, Va., Aug. 6, 1961; d. Walter Thomas and Elizabeth Ann Holt. BS, George Mason U., Fairfax, 1983; MS, Central Mich. U., Merrifield, 1988; grad. program mgmt. course, Def. Systems Mgmt. Coll., 1990. Cert. contracting officer's rep. Logistics analyst The BDM Corp., McLean, Va., 1983-85; deputy program mgr. COMARCO/IBS, Arlington, Va., 1985-88; logistics mgr., speaker, briefer SWL, Inc., Arlington, Va., 1988-89; mem. profl. staff Def. Systems Mgmt. Coll., Ft. Belvoir, Va., 1989-92; dir. computer-aided acquisition and logistics support tng. and edn. Office Asst. Sec. of Def. Prodn. and Logistics, Falls Church, Va., 1992-93; dir. pub. affairs U.S. Dept. Commerce, Nat. Tech. Info.

Svc., Springfield, Va., 1993—. Co-chmn. computer aided acquisition Logistics Systems Rsch. Group. Contbr. articles to profl. jours. Bd. dirs. Woodwalk Condominium, Burke, Va., 1987-96, mem. indsl. tech. adv. com., 1997-99. Named Best Speaker Toastmasters, McLean, 1985, Best Evaluator Toastmasters, McLean, 1985; recipient Excellence award Dept. Def., 1993, Outstanding Svc. award Dept. Commerce, 1996. Mem. Soc. of Logistics Engrs., Pub. Rels. Soc. Am. Republican. Avocations: racquetball, bicycling, embroidery, guitar. Office: US Dept Commerce NTIS 5285 Port Royal Rd Springfield VA 22161-0001

EDWRARDS, KANDACE NECOLE, secondary school educator; b. Rome, Ga., June 27, 1980; MEd in Phys. Edn., Jacksonville State U., Ala. Instr. basketball, tennis Nat. Youth Sports Program, Rome, Ga., 1998—2006; asst. mgr Eckerd Drugs, Cedartown, 2004; tchr., phys. edn, health, coach PVHS, Jacksonville, Ala., 2004—05, Lithis Springs H.S., Ga., 2005—. Mem.: Ga. Educators Assn. Home: 15 Midway School Rd Silver Creek GA 30173

EFFEL, LAURA, lawyer; b. Dallas, May 9, 1945; d. Louis E. and Fay (Lee) Ray; m. Marc J. Patterson, Sept. 19, 1992 (dec. July 30, 2002) m. Robert A. Miltner, Aug. 26, 2006; 1 child, Stephen Patterson. BA, U. Calif., Berkeley, 1971; JD, U. Md., 1975. Bar: N.Y. 1976, U.S. Dist. Ct. (so. and ea. dists.) N.Y. 1976, U.S. Ct. Appeals (2d cir.) 1980, U.S. Supreme Ct. 1980, D.C. 1993, N.C. 1998, Va. 2001; cert. mediator Judicial Coun. Va., 2004. Assoc. Burns Jackson Miller Summit & Jacoby, N.Y.C., 1975-78, Pincus Munzer Bizar & D'Alessandro, N.Y.C., 1978-80; v.p., sr. assoc. counsel Chase Manhattan Bank, N.A., N.Y.C., 1980-96; counsel Baker & McKenzie, N.Y.C., 1996-99; gen. counsel Garban Cos., 1999-2000; counsel LeClair Ryan Flippin Densmore, Roanoke, Va., 2000—02, ptnr., 2002—06, ind. neutral, 2006—. Bd. dirs. Blue Ridge Pub. TV, 2001—; mem. comml. and employment panels Am. Arbitration Assn. Meml. editl. bd.: Alternatives to the High Cost of Litigation. Mem. Workforce Devel. Com., New Century Tech. Coun.; bd. dirs. Bklyn. Legal Svcs. Corp. A, 1992-2000. Named one of Best Lawyers in Am., 2005—06, Va. Legal Elite, 2006. Mem.: ABA (com. pretrial practice 2000—03, litig. sect. co-chair, subcom. atty. client privilege), Roanoke Bar Assn., Va. Bar Assn., N.C. Bar Assn. Office Phone: 415-924-7229. Personal E-mail: laura.effel@earthlink.net.

EFFROS, MICHELLE, electrical engineer, engineering educator; b. NYC, Sept. 7, 1967; d. Richard Matthew and Gail (Hochman) E. BSEE, Stanford U., 1989, MSEE, 1990, PhD, 1994. Elec. engr. Info. Systems Lab., Stanford (Calif.) U.; asst. prof. elec. engring. Calif. Inst. Tech., Pasadena, Calif., 1994—2000, assoc. prof. elec. engring., 2000—05, prof. elec. engring., 2005—, dir. data compression lab. Editor: (newsletter) IEEE Info. Theory Soc., 1995—98. Masters fellow Hughes Aircraft Co., L.A., 1989-90; NSF grad. fellow, Washington, 1990-93; named AT&T Bell Labs. PhD scholar, NJ, 1993, Frederick Emmons Terman Engring. Scholastic award, Stanford u., 1989, NSF Career award, 1995, Charles Lee Powell Found. award, 1997, Richard Feynman-Hughes Fellowship, 1997, named among the World's Top 100 Young Innovators in Tech. and bus. Tech. Review mag, 2002. Mem. Sigma Xi, Phi Beta Kappa, Tau Beta Pi (chpt. pres. 1988-89). Office: M/C 136-93 162A Moore Calif Inst Tech 1200 E California Blvd Pasadena CA 91125

EFIMOVA, ALLA, curator; b. Russia; BA in Liberal Arts, NYU, 1983, MPS, 1986; PhD in Art History and Visual and Cultural Studies, U. Rochester, 1997. Asst. curator photography Visual Studies Workshop, Rochester, NY, 1988—89; instr. dept. art and art history U. Rochester, 1990—92; vis. lectr. dept. art history U. Calif., Irvine, 1995, vis. lectr. art history dept. Santa Cruz, 1996—98; assoc. curator exhbns. U. Calif., Berkeley Art Mus./Pacific Film Archive, 2000—03; curator Judah L. Magnes Mus., Berkeley, 2003—; lectr. art history dept. U. Calif., Berkeley, 2004—. Curator Layers, Fine Arts Gallery, U. Md., Balt., 1995; co-founder, bd. v.p. The Archive: Jewish Immigrant Culture, N.Y.C., 1996—; juror networks exhbn. Calif. Coll. Arts and Craft, 2003; juror memory/loss exhbn. San Francisco State U., 2004. Co-author: Tekstura: Russian Essays on Visual Culture, 1993; co-editor: Heresies 26, 1993. Scholar, Jewish Found. for Edn. Women, 1981, 1982, Internat. Comm. Assn., 1983; grad. fellow, Atari Found., 1984, U. Rochester, 1990—92, Cornell U., 1992—94, Getty Curatorial Rsch. fellow, 2003, Lecture Series grantee, Internat. Group Rsch. grantee, Ctrl. European U., Prague, 1994—96, Rsch. grantee, Woodrow Wilson Ctr., Kennan Inst. for Advanced Russian Studies, 1994, Instrnl. Improvement grantee, U. Calif., Santa Cruz, 1997. Mem.: Soc. for the Historians of East European and Russian Art, Am. Assn. for the Advancement of Slavic Studies, Coll. Art Assn., Am. Assn. Mus. Curators. Office: The Judah L Magnes Mus 2911 Russell St Berkeley CA 94705

EFRON, ROSALYN ESTHER, special education educator; b. Bklyn., Dec. 17, 1927; d. Max and Bessie (Sebold) Schwartz; m. Herman Yale Efron, Sept. 3, 1947; children: Rachel, Adam, Noah. BBA, CCNY, 1949; MA, Kean Coll., Union, N.J., 1966. Intern Garden Sch., 1965-66; spl. edn. tchr. Woodbridge (N.J.) Bd. Edn., 1966-69, Prince George's County Bd. Edn., Upper Marlboro, Md., 1969—. Author: (tng. manual) Teaching Cued Speech, 1985. Recipient Oustanding Cmty. Svc. award KC, Bowie, Md., 1974, Ann. Humanitarian award Prince George's County Sch. Psychologists' Assn., 1993. Mem. Coun. for Exceptional Children (Frances Fuchs award 1994). Home: 909 Brentwood Ln Silver Spring MD 20902-1703

EFROS, ELLEN ANN, lawyer; b. NYC, Jan. 18, 1950; d. Edwin David and Judith (Breitman) E.; m. Fritz R. Kahn, June 26, 1983. BA, Case Western Res. U., 1971; MA, St. John's U., 1973; JD, Hofstra U., 1978. Bar: D.C. 1978, N.Y. 1979, Md. 1990, U.S. Ct. Appeals (5th cir.) 1978, U.S. Ct. Appeals (2d, 7th and D.C. cirs.) 1979, U.S. Ct. Appeals (Fed. cir.) 1993, U.S. Dist. Ct. D.C. 1981, U.S. Ct. Claims 1986, U.S. Supreme Ct. 1989. Trial atty. ICC Gen. Counsel, Washington, 1978-79; assoc. Verner & Liipfert, Washington, 1979-81; ptnr. Vorys, Sater, Seymour & Pease, Washington, 1981-97; hearing officer, office dispute resolution NASD Regulation, Inc., Washington, 1997-2000; ptnr. Rader, Fishman & Grauer, Washington, 2000—05; asst. atty. gen. Dist. of Columbia, Washington, 2005—. Asst. editor Antitrust Law Jour., 1987-90. Mem. ABA (sects. intellectual property and litigation), D.C. Bar Assn., N.Y. Bar Assn., Md. Bar Assn. Office: Office Atty Gen DC 441 4th St NW Flr 6S Washington DC 20001 Office Phone: 202-442-9886. Business E-Mail: ellen.efros@dc.gov.

EFTIMOFF, ANITA KENDALL, educational consultant; b. Granite City, Ill., May 3, 1927; d. David Harlow and Ollie Lorena (Galloway) Kendall; m. Vasil Eftimoff, June 14, 1959; 1 child, James Kendall. BA, Washington U., St. Louis, 1949; MA, So. Ill. U., Edwardsville, 1978, EdD, 1983. Cert. in multiple gen. edn., spl. edn., Ill. Spl. edn. instr. Community Unit 9, Granite City, 1968-83; ednl. cons. Efti Enterprises, Granite City, 1982—; program dir. At-Risk Presch. Grant, Granite City, 1986—. Del. NDEA Conf. Ea. Mich. U., Ypsilanti, 1968, Gifted Edn. Conf. Ill. Office of Edn., Springfield, 1975-77; adminstrv. intern Ill. State Bd. Edn., Springfield, 1981. Editor: Symphony Youth Orch. Newsletter, 1991—, Symphony Vol. Key Notes Newsletter, 1991-93. Bd. dirs. Ill. Gov.'s Adv. Coun. on Women's Affairs, Springfield, Rape Crisis and Sexual Abuse Ctr., So. Ill. U., 1978—, Family Resource Ctr.; chmn. adopt-a-friend St. Louis Ambs., 1982-84, co-chmn. Vets. Day, 1984-86; chmn. St. Louis Symphony Youth Orch., 1985—, St. Louis Symphony Young Artists Competitions, 1993—; mem. aux. St. Louis Children's Hosp., 1980; v.p. mus. activities St. Louis Symphony Vol. Assn.; bd. pres. Ill. Ctr. for Autism, 1993. At-risk presch. grantee Ill. Bd. Edn., 1986—. Mem. AAUW, World Coun. for Gifted and Talented Children, Nat. Assn. for Gifted Children, Assn. for the Gifted, Ill. Council for the Gifted, Asthma and Allergy Found. Southeastern Mo., Am. Lung Assn. St. Louis, Women's Assn. (bd. dirs. 1961—, pres. 1989-91), St. Louis Symphony Women's Assn., St. Louis Art Access (bd. dirs. 2003-04), St. Louis Artist Guild, Nev. Women's Lobby, LWV No. Nev., Progression Leadership Alliance Nev., Washoe County Alliance, Delta Kappa Gamma, Phi Delta Kappa. Lodges: Daus. of Nile, Rotary-Anns. Avocations: performing arts, classical music. Home: 205 E Coyote Dr Carson City NV 89704 Office Phone: 775-849-0567.

EGAN, JAN WENNING, lawyer; b. Centralia, Ill., Feb. 8, 1972; BS in Journalism, with highest honors, U. Ill., 1994; JD cum laude, U. Notre Dame Law Sch., 1997. Bar: Ohio 1997, Mass. 1999. Atty., Cincinnati; assoc. Edwards, Angell, Palmer & Dodge LLP, Boston. Mem.: Mass. Bar Assn., Boston Bar Assn., ABA. Avocations: baseball, reading, golf. Office: Edwards Angell Palmer & Dodge LLP 111 Huntington Ave Boston MA 02199-7613 Office Phone: 617-951-3360. Office Fax: 617-227-4420. E-mail: jegan@eapdlaw.com.*

EGAN, KAREN ESTHER, elementary school educator; b. Elmhurst, Ill., Mar. 2, 1955; d. Lester and Elaine Victoria (Nelson) Madsen; m. Patrick Nelson Egan, June 27, 1987. BA, Luther Coll., 1977; MAT, Nat.-Louis U., 1991. Cert. tchr., Ill. Tchr. elem. phys. edn. Sch. Dist. 44, Lombard, Ill., 1978—92, tchr. elem., 1992—. Coord. jump rope for heart Am. Heart Assn., Lombard, 1978-92; speaker Ill. Kindergarten Conf., 1985, 87, 88, 5th Great Lakes Rd. Coun., 1983. Mem. AAHPERD, NEA, Ill. Edn. Assn., Lombard Edn. Assn., Ill. Reading Coun., Ill. AHPERD (Tchr. of Yr. 1988, speaker convn. 1987). Republican. Lutheran. Avocations: reading, cooking, sewing, crafts, running. Home: 267 N Charlotte St Lombard IL 60148-2035 Office: Hammerschmidt 617 Hammerschmidt Ave Lombard IL 60148-3498 Office Phone: 630-827-4211.

EGAN, LORA RAE, music educator; b. St. Cloud, Minn., Aug. 8, 1973; d. Charles Dean and Wanda Lou Anderson; m. Sean Christopher Egan, Sept. 23, 2000; 1 child, J.J. B Music Edn., S.D. State U., 1997. Dir. instrumental music Marion (S.D.) Pub. Schs., 1998—2002; instrumental dir. Sioux Falls Pub. Schs., 2002—03; pvt. practice Sioux Falls, SD, 2003—. Pvt. percussion instr. Freeman Acad.; dir. Marion City Band, 1999—2002; percussion tchr. Sioux Falls Luth. Sch., 2005; marching percussion specialist area schs., 2004—; percussion clinician SD and Wash., 2006—. Musician (profl. hand drummer, percussionist): Swiss Chorale, Schmeck Fest Pit Orch., 2001—, Sioux Falls Brass Soc., 2002—; with Balleraena Dance Studio, Sioux Falls, SD, 2005—, photographer Sketches of the Eye, 2001. Recipient Outstanding Svc. as an Educator award, Congl. Youth Leadership Coun., 2001. Mem.: Music Educators Nat. Conf., Marion Tchrs. Assn. (pres. 2001—02), Women Band Dirs., Percussive Arts Soc. Avocations: music, tennis, photography. Home and Office: 6601 W Bonnie Ct Sioux Falls SD 57106 Office Phone: 605-361-0650. Personal E-mail: drummergrrl@moose-mail.com.

EGAN, MARTHA AVALEEN, history professor, archivist, consultant, music educator; b. Kingsport, Tenn., Feb. 26, 1956; d. Jack E. and Opal (Pugh) E. BS in Comm., U. Tenn., 1978; MA in History, East Tenn. State U., 1986; postgrad., U. Ky., 1986-89, Milligan Coll., 1990. Cert. tchr., Tenn.; cert. Am. Acad. Cert. Archivists. News reporter, anchor WJCW-AM/WQUT-FM, Johnson City, Tenn., 1980-82; staff asst. 1st Dist. Office U.S. Senator Jim Sasser, Blountville, Tenn., 1982-84; instr. history East Tenn. State U., Johnson City, 1984-86; tchg. asst. dept. history U. Ky., Lexington, 1986-89; rschr./writer history project Eastman Chem. Co., Kingsport, 1991; adj. faculty history and humanities N.E. State Tech. C.C., Blountville, 1992—93, adj. faculty humanities, 2000—03; archivist Kingsport Pub. Libr. and Archives, 1993—2002; adj. asst. prof. history King Coll., Bristol, Tenn., 1994-99; adj. faculty history Emory and Henry Coll., Emory, Va., 2002—; interm faculty social studies dept. Sullivan North H.S. and Sullivan Ctrl. H.S., 2004—05. Author: Images of America: Kingsport, 1998; rschr., writer: Eastman Chemical Company: Years of Glory, Times of Change, 1991; contbr. Ency. of Appalachia, Tenn. Ency. History and Culture, Ency. of the Harlem Renaissance, Ency. of Am. Indsl. History, Dictionary of Am. History. Vice chair Sullivan County Dem. Party, 1992-93; rec. sec. Sullivan County Dem. Women's Club, 1992, corr. sec., 1994; mem. Kingsport Symphony Chorus, sec.-treas, 1994-95; mem. East Tenn. Camerata, Johnson City Civic Chorale. Mem. AAUW (Kingsport chpt.), Orgn. Am. Historians, Appalachian Studies Assoc., Soc. Am. Archivists, Tenn. Archivists, Kingsport Music Club (corr. sec. 1995-97), Sullivan County Hist. Soc. (bd. dirs.), Nat. Flute Assn., Phi Alpha Theta, Pi Gamma Mu, Sigma Delta Chi. Methodist. Avocations: flute, photography. Home: 544 Rambling Rd Kingsport TN 37663

EGAN, MICHELLE D., social sciences educator; b. Chester, Eng. children: Georgina Declan Egan, Georgia. BA, Warwick U.; MA, Va. Poly. Inst. and State U., Blacksburg, 1990, U. Pitts., Pa., 1994; PhD, U. Pitts., 1996. Rsch. asst. CEPS, Brussels, 1991—92; Robert Bosch fellow AICGS, Washington, 1998, Jean Monnet fellow Florence, Italy, 1998—99; rsch. assoc. Atlantic Coun., Washington, 2001—02; asst. prof. Am. U., Washington, 1996—2003, assoc. prof. Sch. Internat. Svc., 2004—. Editor, advisor, bd. dirs. Palgrave EU Series, England, 2005—; rep. Ctr. for Excellence, Washington, 2003—; Jean Monnet chair EU, Brussels, 2004—. Author: Constructing a Single Market, 2001; editor: Creating a Transatlantic Marketplace, 2005. Coord. Europe program SIS/Univ., Washington, 2003—; advisor various scholarships Am. U., Washington, 2000—. Recipient Morton Bender prize, Am. U., 2006, Award for outstanding tchg., Sch. Internat. Svc., Am. U., 1999; fellow, German Marshall Fund, 1999—2000, Howard Found., 2001—02. Mem.: Soc. for Women in Internat. Polit. Economy. Office: American University 4400 Massachusetts Ave Washington DC 20016

EGAN, MOIRA, poet, educator; b. Baltimore, Md., July 21, 1962; d. Michael and Betty Egan. BA, Bryn Mawr Coll., 1980—85; MA, Johns Hopkins U., 1993—94; MFA, Columbia U., 1990—92. Tchr., english & creative writing Catonsville H.S., Catonsville, Md., 2002—; lectr. in english Morgan State U., Balt., 2002—02, Towson U., Towson, Md., 2001—01; instr., ib english Anatolia Coll., Thessaloniki, Greece, 1998—2001; cmty. rels. mgr. Barnes & Noble, NYC, 1997—98; cons. curricular outreach U. Md. Ctr. Visual Arts and Culture, 2003—. Poetry editor Link: A Critical Jour. on the Arts, Balt., 2002—; host, readings for reading benefit series The Learning Bank, Balt., 2002; mem.; contbr. to pedagogical papers sessions Associated Writing Programs, 2001—. Author: (poems) The Garden of Her Choosing (Spl. Merit award, Mayor's Adv. Com. on Arts & Culture, 1994), Poetry, Boulevard, American Letters & Commentary, Laurel Review, Smartish Pace, West Branch, Poems & Plays, Poet Lore, and in numerous other journals., nominated for the Pushcart Prize, 1994, 2002, anthology, Kindled Terraces: American Poets in Greece, Cleave (First Book award, 2004); multi-media visual piece, Elegy. Vol. Com. to Re-elect the Mayor, Balt., 2003. Recipient David Craig Austin Prize, The Writing Divsn., Columbia U., 1992, Campbell Corner Poetry Prize, 2nd Pl., Campbell Corner, 2002; Grad. Writing fellowship, Columbia U., 1990—92, Grad. Tchg. fellowship, Johns Hopkins U., 1993—94. Mem.: Assoc. Writing Programs. Avocations: yoga, travel, reading. Personal E-mail: moirae333@earthlink.net.

EGAN, PATRICIA JANE, foundation administrator, retired director; b. San Francisco, Aug. 7, 1951; 1 child, Kathryn Michele. AB, U. Calif., Berkeley, 1978; postgrad., N.J. Inst. Tech., 1996—. Cert. fund raising exec. Grants officer Mus. Modern Art, N.Y.C., 1979—81; assoc. devel. officer grants Whitney Mus. Am. Art, N.Y.C., 1981—84; assoc. dir. devel. Columbia Bus. Sch., Columbia U., N.Y.C., 1984—86; mgr. major gifts New York Bot. Garden, N.Y.C., 1987—88; dir. devel. N.Y.C. Partnership, 1989—91; dir. devel. Cal Performances U. Calif., Berkeley, 1991—92, instr. bus. and engring. ext. svcs., 2004—. Cons. various cultural and environ. orgns., NY; co-prodr. distance learning course proposal writing N.J. Inst. Tech., 1997—. Prodr., program host Terpischore, Sta. KUSF-FM, 1978—79. Bd. dirs. Universala Esperanto Asocio, NY, 1980—83, Dance Perspectives Found., N.Y.C., 1985—2002, Shakespeare for Kids, 2005—; treas. Dance Perspectives Found., N.Y.C., 1987—91, found. officer, treas.; trustee Riverside Ch., N.Y.C., 1986—87. Fellow, Nat. Endowment Arts, 1977. Mem.: Assn. Tchrs. Tech. Writing, Internat. Assn. Bus. Communicators, Women in Comm., Soc. Tech. Comm. (Bernard J. Goodman Meml. award N.Y. Metro chpt. 1998), Mensa, Esperanto League N.Am., Jr. League San Francisco, Churchill Club, Alpha Epsilon Lambda. Avocations: art, ballet, dance, martial arts. Office: PO Box 194391 San Francisco CA 94119-4391

EGAN, SHIRLEY ANNE, retired nursing educator; b. Haverill, Mass. d. Rush B. and Beatrice (Bengle) Willard. Diploma, St. Joseph's Hosp. Sch. Nursing, Nashua, N.H., 1945; BS in Nursing Edn., Boston U., 1949, MS, 1954. Instr. sci. Sturdy Meml. Hosp. Sch. Nursing, Attleboro, Mass., 1949-51, Peter Bent Brigham Hosp. Sch. Nursing, Boston, 1951-53, ednl. dir., 1953-55, assoc. dir. Sch. Nursing, 1955-59, med. surg. coord., 1971-73, assoc. dir. Sch. Nursing, 1973-79, dir., 1979-85; cons. North Country Hosp., Newport, Vt., 1985-86; infection control practitioner, 1986-87; contract instr. Natchitoches Area Tech. Inst., 1988—90, Sabine Valley Tech Inst., 1990-91; coord. quality assurance Evangeline Health Care Ctr., 1991-92, asst. dir. nursing, 1992-93, coord. quality assurance Natchitoches, La., 1994-96, retired, 1996. Nurse edn. adviser AID (formerly ICA), Karachi, Pakistan, 1959-67; prin. Coll. Nursing, Karachi, 1959-67; dir. Vis. Nurse Service, Nashua, N.H., 1967-70; cons. nursing edn. Pakistan Ministry of Health, Labour and Social Welfare, 1959-67; adviser to editor Pakistan Nursing and Health Rev., 1959-67; exec. bd. Nat. Health Edn. Com., Pakistan; WHO short-term cons. U. W.I., Jamaica, 1970-71; mem. Greater Nashua Health Planning Council. Contbr. articles to profl. publs. Bd. dirs. Matthew Thornton health Ctr., Nashua, Nashua Child Care Ctr.; vol. ombudsman N.H. Council on Aging; mem. Nashua Service League. Served as 1st lt., Army Nurse Corps., 1945-47. Mem. Trained Nurses Assn. Pakistan, Nat. League for Nursing, Assn. for Preservation Hist. Natchitoches, St. Joseph's Sch. Nursing Alumnae Assn., Boston U. Alumnae Assn., Brit. Soc. Health Edn., Cath. Daus. Am. (vice regent ct. Bishop Malloy), Statis. Study Grads. Karachi Coll. Nursing, Sigma Theta Tau. Home: 729 Royal St Natchitoches LA 71457-5716

EGBERT, DONNA, elementary school educator; b. Evansville, Ind., Mar. 3, 1947; d. Arthur Ralph and Helen Daphine E. BME, Murray State U., 1969; MAE, Western Ky. U., 1979. Dir. jr. high sch. band Marion County Public Schs., Lebanon, Ky., 1969-79; tchr. Catholic Schs., Louisville, 1979-85, Breckinridge County Schs., Hardinsburg, Ky., 1988—2005; ret., 2005. Tchr. rep. Site Based Decision Making Coun., Custer, Ky., 1994—2005, elem. academic team Custer Elementary, 1988—2005. Bd. dirs. Voices of Kentuckiana Cmty. Chorus, 2005—. Mem. Honorable Order Ky. Cols., Delta Kappa Gamma Soc. Internat. (2d v.p. 1998—2006), Sigma Alpha Iota (life, chaplain 1968-69). Avocations: walking, singing in choral groups, playing in community band, reading, golf. Home: 4416 Erin Dr Floyds Knobs IN 47119-9301 E-mail: egbertd@excite.com.

EGELSON, PAULINE C., director; b. Geneva, Ill., June 27, 1953; d. Donald and Pauline Wiese Ericson; m. Robert Louis Egelson, Sept. 1, 1979; children: Daniel, Benjamin. BA in Child Devel., Rockford Coll., 1975; MA in Reading Edn., Western Carolina U., 1982; EdD in Ednl. Leadership, U. NC, Greensboro, 1993. Cert. tchr NC, prin. K-12 superintendency NC. Cmty. organizer United Meth. Ch., Asheville, NC, 1975—77; tchr. K-8 Diocese of Charlotte, Asheville, 1977—81; sales staff Dancer's Place, Asheville, 1981—84; reading clinician Western Carolina U., Oteen, NC, 1982—84; tchr. reading Buncombe County Schs., Asheville, 1983—90; ednl. rschr. South Eastern Regional Vision for Edn., Greensboro, NC, 1991—2002, program dir., 2002—05; dir. Ctr. for Partnership to Improve Edn. Coll. Charleston, Sch. Edn., NC, 2006—. Co-author: Formative Teacher Evaluation: Models and Current Findings, 1998, How Class Size Makes a Difference, 2002, Life at Draper Elementary: Taking Small Classes One Step Further, 2002, A Compedium of Senior Project Research, 2003—05, Preliminary Findings: Professional Learning Teams in Elementary Schools, 2004, Intensive Technical Assistance to Rural Low Performing School Districts: Implications for the Field, 2006; co-devel. (video) The Senior Project: Student Work for the Real World, 1999. Named Blue Ribbon Schs. panelist, U.S. Dept. Edn., 2000, 2002; Dropout Prevention grantee, NEA/NFIE, 1989. Mem.: Internat. Reading Assn., Am. Ednl. Rsch. Assn., Jt. Com. Stds. for Evaluation (exec. com. 2001—). Avocations: photography, travel. Office: Ctr for Partnership to Improve Edn Coll Charleston Sch Edn 66 George St Charleston SC 29424 Office Phone: 843-953-7629. E-mail: egelsonp@cofc.edu.

EGELSTON, ROBERTA RIETHMILLER, writer; b. Pitts., Nov. 20, 1946; d. Robert E. and Doris (Bauer) Riethmiller; m. David Michael Egelston, Oct. 10, 1975; 1 child, Brian David. BA in Bus. Administrn., Thiel Coll., 1968; MLS, U. Pitts., 1974; student, Columbia Theol. Sem., 2002—05. Bus. mgr. Pitts. Pastoral Inst., 1968-70; administrv. asst. Coun. Alcoholism and Drug Abuse, Lancaster, Pa., 1970-72; dir. career planning libr. U. Pitts., 1974-78; writer, 1978—; libr. Pitts. Inst. Mortuary Sci., 1991—2001, instr. bus. English, 1992-98; mem. site-based mgmt. team Fox Chapel Area H.S., 1999-2001. Instr. beginning genealogy, 1991-98; book reviewer Coll. Placement Coun., Bethlehem, Pa., 1977-78; cons. State Affiliated Colls. and Univs., 1976; group leader Johns-Norris Assocs., Pitts., 1975-76. Author: Career Planning Materials, 1981, Credits and Careers for Adult Learners, 1985. Bd. dirs. Lauri Ann West Libr., Pitts., 1983-84; active PTA, 1985-88; mem. peace and justice com. Fox Chapel Presbyn. Ch., 1994-2000, deacon, 1995-98, mem. libr. com., 2000-02; mem. spiritual life com. East Liberty Presbyn. Ch., 2002-05, libr. com., 2005 Mem. AAUW (bd. dirs. Fox Chapel Area br. 1980-91, 2001-03, 05—), Les Lauriers (sr. women's hon. at Thiel Coll.), Western Pa. Geneal. Soc. (libr. rsch. com. 1990-94, edn. com. 1992—), Beta Phi Mu. Avocations: hiking, reading, gourmet cooking.

EGEN, MAUREEN MAHON, publishing executive; BA, Trinity Coll., 1964. Editl. trainee and numerous other positions Doubleday & Co., Inc., 1964; mng. dir. Doubleday Book Clubs, 1979, pub., editl. dir., 1981; editor-in-chief Warner Hardcover Books Time Warner Book Group, 1990—98, pres., chief oper. officer NYC, 1998—. Co-chair ann. book fair Goddard Riverside Cmty. Ctr.; mem. diversity steering com. Time Warner Book Group. Bd. dirs. The Ctr. Ind. of Disabled, N.Y.C. Mem.: Assn. Am. Pubs. (mem. freedom to read com.), Women's Media Group. Office: Time Warner Book Group 1271 Ave of Americas New York NY 10020*

EGGEN, BELINDA LAY, education educator; b. Albemarle, NC, Sept. 17, 1952; d. Bobby Grier and Elizabeth White Lay; m. David Paul Eggen, Dec. 31, 1993; children: Jennifer Hackenholt Tillman, Charity Suzanne. BA in English, U. N.C., Charlotte, 1973, MEd in Curriculum and Instrnl. Supervision, 1988; PhD in Edn., U. S.C., Columbia, 2001. Cert. early childhood edn. S.C., 1973, reading recovery 1991, curriculum and instrnl. supervision N.C., 1988, elem. edn. N.C., 1973, elem. prin. S.C., 1989. K-2 multiage classroom tchr. Charlotte-Mecklenburg Schs., Charlotte, 1973—75; instr., advancement studies dept. Ctrl. Piedmont C.C., Charlotte, 1978—81; tchr. grades 4-5 Charlotte Cath. Schs., 1981—83; chpt. 1 reading tchr., grades 2-6 Union County Schs., Monroe, NC, 1984—86; chpt. 1 after sch. coord. Charlotte-Mecklenburg Schs., Charlotte, 1986—88; dist. office math coord. Horry County Schs., Conway, SC, 1988—93, asst. prin. Myrtle Beach, 1993—99; asst. prof. edn. W.Va. State Coll., Institute, 1999—2001; coord. mater of arts in tchg. program U. S.C., Columbia, 1999—2001, program dir., early childhood edn. Beaufort, 2001—, assoc. prof. edn., 2000—. Contbr. articles to profl. jours., chapters to books; reviewer: profl. jours. Fellow: SC Coun. Tchrs. Math. (assoc.; sec. 1996—98), Horry-Georgetown Math. Advancement Coun. (assoc.; pres. 1989—91), Internat. Reading Assn. (assoc.; v.p. 1981—83); mem.: AAUW, AAUP, SC Assn. Edn. Young Children, SC Assn. Tchr. Educators, Reading Recovery Assn., Nat. Coun. Tchrs. English (assoc.), Assn. Am. Colls. Tchr. Edn. (assoc.), Nat. Assn. Edn. of Young Children (assoc.). Roman Catholic. Avocations: boating, African safaris. Office: U SC 801 Carteret St Beaufort SC 29902 Office Phone: 843-521-0856. Office Fax: 843-521-3121. Business E-Mail: bleggenØ@gwm.sc.edu.

EGGERS, MARY LYNN, elementary school educator; b. Lancaster, Pa., Feb. 17, 1952; d. Merle Raymond and Naomi Jones Girvin; m. Charles Frederick Eggers III, June 21, 1975; children: Erica Lynn, Leslie Ann. BS in Edn., Ind. U. Pa., 1974; M in Edn., Millersville U., Pa., 1978. Tchr. first grade Manheim Twp. Sch. Dist., Lancaster, Pa., 1974—82; reading specialist Lampeter-Strasburg Sch. Dist., 1993—. Co-founder, co-dir. Mt. Nebo United Meth. Nursery Sch., Pequea, Pa., 1975—99. Mem.: Lampeter-Strasburg Edn. Assn., Keystone State Reading Assn., Lancaster-Lebanon Reading Coun. Methodist. Avocations: reading, cross stitch, piano, travel. Home: 112 Covered Wagon Drive Willow Street PA 17584 Office: Willow Street Elementary School 9 Main Street Willow Street PA 17584 Office Phone: 717-464-5476. Personal E-mail: marylynn_eggers@l-spioneers.org.

EGGERSMAN, DENISE, computer engineer, educator; b. Orange, Calif., Feb. 22, 1954; d. Arthur Fred and Margaret Frances Eggersman. BS, Kennesaw State U., 1998; MS, U. Phoenix, Ariz., 2002; PhD, Capella U., 2006. Systems adminstrn. Smallwood, Reynolds, Stewart & Stewart, Atlanta, 1983—89; trainer/adminstr. Ctrl. Health, Atlanta, 1989—91; cons. Software Assist, Duluth, Ga., 1991—97; LAN adminstrn. IBM, Atlanta, 1997; project mgmt. Hewlett-Packard, Atlanta, 1998; sales/network engr. Verizon Comm., Alpharetta, Ga., 1999—2001; prof. Chattahoochee Tech. Coll., Marietta, Ga., 2003, Capella U., Mpls., 2003—. South Univ. Online, Pitts., 2004—06, DeVry U. Online, Alpharetta, Ga., 2006—. Vol. Hands on Atlanta, 2003. Mem.: IEEE (assoc.), Am. Intercontinental U., Assn. Computing Machinery. Office: Chattahoochee Tech Coll 980 South Cobb Dr Marietta GA 30066 also: Grad Sch of Tech Capella Univ Minneapolis MN 55402 Home: PO Box 313 Acworth GA 30101 Business E-Mail: denise@drdeniseeggersman.com.

EGGINTON, WYNN MEAGHER, university administrator and program facilitator; b. Portland, Oreg., Oct. 18, 1944; d. George Shaw and Florence Marion (Marriott) Meagher; m. Kendall Watson De Bevoise, Dec. 23, 1966 (div. 1984); children: Jan, Ana, Lyn; m. Everett Egginton, Sept. 27, 1986; 1 stepchild, William Everett. BA, Stanford U., 1966; MA, U. Oreg., 1985; PhD, U. Louisville, 1998. Intern HUD, San Francisco, 1966-68; planning officer Oakland Redevel. Agy., Calif., 1968; Coll. English tchr. US Peace Corps, Thailand, 1969-73; English tchr. Internat. Sch., Santiago, Chile, 1979; instr. English Lane Community Coll., Eugene, Oreg., 1980-81; document analyst U. Oreg., Eugene, 1981-82, coord. communications Coll. Edn., 1982-84; asst. to dean Sch. Edn. U. Louisville, 1984-90, assoc. dir. devel. for major gifts, 1990-92; policy coord. commr.'s office Ky. Dept. Edn., 1992-94; univ. coord. for sch. reform U. Louisville, 1994—98; assoc. v.p. rsch. N.Mex. State U., 2003—. Co-dir. Ctr. of Excellence Sch. Edn., U. Louisville, 1998—; cons., speaker sch. dist./univ. collaboration to various ednl. groups, 1985-2003. Contbr. articles to profl. jours. Mem. Atherton High Sch. Bd., Louisville, 1987-88, choir St. Andrews Episcopal Ch., Louisville, 1986—, U. Louisville Collegium, 1987-88. Recipient Outstanding Svc. award Jefferson County Coun. for Retarded Citizens, 1986, Disting. Achievement award Wash. Edn. Press Assn., 1987. Mem. Am. Ednl. Rsch. Assn. Democrat. Episcopalian. Avocations: contemporary women's literature, piano, gardening, performing arts.

EGGLESTON, REBECCA ANNETTE, maternal/women's health nurse, rehabilitation nurse; b. Searcy, Ark., Dec. 17, 1943; d. William T. and Velda M. (Goodloe) McAfee; m. Richard E. Morris, June 24, 1960 (div. Nov. 1980); children: Terri L. Morris Bomar, Toni L. Morris Carroll; m. Solvin W. Tonkens, Dec. 22, 1986 (dec. June 2002); m. Richard Eggleston, Dec 30, 2003. LPN, Area Vocat. Tech. Sch., Kansas City, Kans., 1973; ADN, Kansas City C.C., 1980; BSN, Webster U., 1992. RN, Kans., Mo. Area Vocat. Tech. Sch.; staff nurse Providence-St. Margaret Hosp., Kansas City, 1973-80; indsl. nurse, office mgr. Kansas City Indsl. Clinic, 1980-81; staff nurse Bethany Med. Ctr., Kansas City, 1981-1999; retired, 1999; outreach nurse specialist Quintiles Phase I Svcs., 2000—; parish nurse St. Francis Parish, 2005—. Active cmty. rels. diabetes unit Bethany Med. Ctr., 1983-86. Officer, v.p., bd. dirs. Cambridge Townhouse Assn., Leawood, Kans., 1989-92; chaperone Rose Bud (Ark.) Band at Presdl. Inauguration, Washington, 1992; mem. adv. bd. Kansas City Kans. C.C. Day Care Ctr.; vol. Habitat for Humanity, Salvation Army, others. Recipient Cert. of Appreciation, Salvation Army, 1994, Korean Am. Sr. Citizen Soc. Kans. City, 2001, Ctrs. for Medicare and Medicaid Svc., 2002, U.S. Dept. Health and Human Svcs., 2002. Mem. ANA, Am. Coll. Occupational and Environ. Medicine (aux.), Mo.-Kans. Assn. Medicine Shoppes, Inc. (flu prevention coord.), Assn. Osteo. Physicians and Surgeons (aux.), Optimist Club. Roman Catholic. Home and Office: 5824 N Kensington Ave Gladstone MO 64119 E-mail: aflunurse@montana.com, Bflunurse@aol.com.

EGIDIO, MARTHA L., real estate broker and salesman; b. Managua, Nicaragua, Feb. 16, 1970; arrived in U.S., 1988; d. Armando Detrinidad and Martha Mendoza; m. John R. Egidio, Feb. 12, 1999; children: Jennifer, Arum, Emily. Studied, So. Nev. Sch. Real Estate, 1997. Real estate agt. Coldwell Banker, Las Vegas, 1997—98, Tailored Mktg., Las Vegas, 1997—98, Properties Plus, Las Vegas, 1998—99, Am. Realty, Las Vegas, 1999—. Office: Am Realty 7331 W Charleston #160 Las Vegas NV 89117 Office Phone: 702-236-7070. Personal E-mail: pastaandbeans@aol.com.

EGLAND, KATHERINE TATUM, educational consultant, director; b. Hattiesburg, Miss., Sept. 3, 1951; d. Felder Tatum and Ardessie Tatum-Eatman; m. William David Egland, Nov. 9, 1979; children: Antonio Karlos Edwards, Yolanda Makeva Egland Wilson, Yolanda Antoniette Edwards, Blanche Nekita Egland Young. Bachelor's, William Carey Coll., Hattiesburg, Miss., 1967, Master's in Edn. and Psychology, 1976. Cert. family life therapy Am. Guidance Coun., 1989. Spl. contbn. fund trustee NAACP, Balt., 1987—, nat. bd. dirs., 1997—. Cons. SPACE, Inc., Gulfport, Miss., 1986—. Author: (play book) SPACE Play for Creative Kids. Civil rights activist NAACP, Balt., 1996. Named to Wall of Tolerance, So. Poverty Law Ctr., 2004. Mem.: AAUW. Catholic. Achievements include development of early childhood education curriculum. Avocations: travel, reading, art. Home: 605 Rosemary Dr Gulfport MS 39507 Office: SPACE Inc 49 Hardy Ct #116 Gulfport MS 39507 Office Phone: 228-617-0891.

EHDE, AVA LOUISE, librarian, educator; b. Buffalo, Feb. 11, 1963; d. Louise and Robert Andrew Kinn (Stepfather), Henry Emil Nonnenberg. BA in History and German cum laude, SUNY, Buffalo, 1995, MLS, 1997. Cert. pub. libr. N.Y. Intern libr. Niagara Falls (N.Y.) Pub. Libr., 1996—97, local history libr., 1997—98; reference libr. Trocaire Coll., Buffalo, 1998—99, libr. dir., 1999; libr. Buffalo & Erie County Pub. Libr., 1999—2002; head reference, sys. coord. D'Youville Coll. Libr., Buffalo, 1999—2002; adj. faculty SUNY Sch. Informatics, Buffalo, 2001—; is. br. supr. Manatee County Pub. Libr. Sys., Bradenton, Fla., 2002—. Co-chair Western N.Y. Reference Discussion Group, Buffalo, 2000—02; mem. Regional Automation Com., Buffalo, 2000—02, TBLC Continuing Edn. Com., 2003—. Co-author: (workshop) Networking and Operating Systems for Librarians, 2001—; author: Implementing New Libr. Technologies, 2003—; book reviewer: Voice of Youth Advocates, 2004—; contbr. Technology Made Simple: an improvement guide for small and medium libraries. Reader Niagara Frontier Radio Reading Svc., Cheektowaga, NY, 1999—2002. Recipient Dr. Marie Ross Wolcott Meml. award, Sch. Info. and Libr. Studies, 1997, yearlong award, Sunshine State Libr. Leadership Inst., 2004—05; grantee, NYLA Reference and Adult Svcs. Sect. Continuing Edn., 2002, Fla. Leadership Summit grantee, Fla. Acad. Mgmt., 2006; Alberta Riggs Meml. scholar, Sch. Info. and Libr. Studies, 1997, Profl. Devel. grantee, Western N.Y. Libr. Resources Coun., 2001, 2002. Mem.: AAUP (v.p., exec. com. 2001—02), ALA, Fla. Libr. Assn., Pub. Librs. Assn., Manatee Young Profls. (amb.), Libr. and Info. Tech. Assn., Beta Phi Mu. Avocations: bicycling, hiking, reading, scuba diving, cooking. Home: 401 Clark Ln Holmes Beach FL 34217 Office: Island Br Libr 5701 Marina Dr Holmes Beach FL 34217 Office Phone: 941-778-1721. Personal E-mail: librarianava@hotmail.com. Business E-Mail: ava.ehde@co.manatee.fl.us.

EHLERS, JOAN, secondary school educator; BS, Coll. William & Mary, Williamsburg, Va., 1976; MS, Wright State U., Fairfax, Ohio, 1983; student, ODU, Norfolk, Va., EVMS. Cert. tchr. Va., 2005, gifted edn. Va. Human anatomy & physiology instr. Hampton City Schs., Va., 1999—.

EHLERS, KATHRYN HAWES (MRS. JAMES D. GABLER), physician; b. Richmond Hill, NY, Aug. 22, 1931; d. Albert and Edna (Hawes) E.; m. James D. Gabler, Dec. 5, 1959; children— Jennifer K., Emily E. AB, Bryn Mawr Coll., 1953; MD, Cornell U.; MD (Hannah E. Longshore Meml. Med. scholar 1953-57, Elsie Strang L'Esperance scholar 1956-57), 1957. Diplomate: Am. Bd. Pediatrics, Am. Bd. Pediatric Cardiology. Intern N.Y. Hosp., 1957-58, asst. resident pediatrics, 1958-60; fellow in pediatric cardiology Cornell U. Med. Coll., N.Y.C., 1960-64, instr. pediatrics, 1964-66, asst. prof., 1966-70, asso. prof. pediatrics, 1970-75, prof., 1975-96, prof. emeritus, 1996—, vice-chmn. pediat., 1988-96; practice medicine specializing in pediat. cardiology N.Y.C., 1958-96. Contbr. articles to profl. jours. Research trainee N.Y. Heart Assn., 1960-62, Am. Heart Assn., 1962-64. Fellow Am. Coll. Cardiology; mem. N.Y. Heart Assn., Am. Heart Assn., Harvey Soc., Am. Pediatric Soc., Am. Acad. Pediatrics, Alpha Omega Alpha.

EHLERT, NANCY LYNNE, elementary school educator; b. Columbus, Ohio, Jan. 25, 1954; d. Ralph E. and Eleanor G. (Seymour) Ater; m. Arthur William Ehlert, Oct. 3, 1987; 1 child, Benjamin Curtis. BA, Bowling Green State U., 1976; MEd, Ohio State U., 1980, postgrad., 1981-92. Tchr. Worthington (Ohio) City Schs., 1976—. Cons. tchr. Ohio State U./NIH Grant Project, Columbus, 1992-93; pilot tchr. BSCS Sci. Curriculum Field Test, Worthington, 1992-93, Soc. Automotive Engrs., Worthington, 1992; strategy for success team Worthington City Schs., 1990; testing software com human growth and devel. grant project NIH, 1995-96; venture capitol grant writing com. Staff Devel. in Restructure our Sch. Environ., 1996. Participant World of Children Town Hall Meetings, 2002—04; vol. designer Del. County Habitat for Humanity. Recipient 1992 Excellence Category Innovation award, 1992. Mem. Nat. Sci. Tchrs. Assn. Theosphist. Avocations: stained glass, sewing, travel.

EHLIG-ECONOMIDES, CHRISTINE A., petroleum engineer; BA cum laude, Rice U., 1971; MAT, U. Kans., 1974, MS in chem. engring., 1976; PhD in petroleum engring., 1979. Rsch. asst. petroleum engring. dept. Stanford U., 1976—78, prog. mgr. geothermal prog., 1979—80, acting asst. prof. petroleum engring, 1979—80; head petroleum engring. dept. U. Alaska, Fairbanks, 1981—83; section head dynamic reservoir description Flopetrol Johnston Schlumberger, Melun, France, 1983—86; section head layered reservoir testing Schlumberger Perforating and Testing, Houston, 1986—88; section mgr. reservoir engring. Schlumberger Well Service, 1988—90; project leader reservoir dynamics Etudes et Productions, Schlumberger, Clamart, France, 1990—92; tech. advisor Schulumberger Internat. Coordination, Houston, 1993—95, Anadrill Schulumberger, Sugar Land, Tex., 1995—96; tech. and mktg. mgr., production enhancement Schulumberger Oilfield Services, 1996—97; area mgr. Latin Am. North Schulumberger Reservoir Tech., Caracas, Venezuela, 1997—99; global account mgr. Schulumberger Global Client Accounts, Houston, 1999—; adj. prof. U. Houston, 2000—. Vis. prof. U. Houston, 1994, Stanford U., 1995. Grantee Standard Oil of Calif. Fellowship, Stanford U. Mem. Soc. Petroleum Engrs. (disting., Europe steering com. 1992, chmn. cultural diversity com. 1993-95, Disting. Achievement award for Petroleum Engring. Faculty, 1982, Formation Evaluation award 1995, Lester C. Uren award 1997, disting. lectr. 1997-98), Phi Kappa Phi, Sigma Xi. Achievements include contributions to analytical models for well-test analysis; development of practical methodology for well-test interpretation, design of testing procedures; evaluation of testing hardware and pressure-transient data quality. Office: Dept Chem Engring U Houston 4800 Calhoun Ave Houston TX 77204-4004 E-mail: ceconomides@uh.edu.

EHLIS, KRISTINE MARIE, music educator; b. Pueblo, Colo., May 23, 1960; d. Janet Lee Sanches. MusB Edn. BME, U. No. Colo., Greeley, Colo., 1982; MusM Suzuki Pedagogy MM, No. Ariz. U., Flagstaff, Ariz., 1987. Tchr. - string specialist Blue Ridge Sch. Dist., Lakeside, Ariz., 1982—86, Mesa Pub. Schs., Mesa, Ariz., 1987—. Dir., nau suzuki inst. N. Ariz. U., Flagstaff, 1999—; treas. Valley of the Sun Suzuki Assn., Mesa, Ariz., 1998—, workshop coord., 1990—. Prinicpal second violin San Marcos Symphony, Chandler, Ariz., 1994—2003. Recipient Disting. Alumni, No. Ariz. U., 1999. Mem.: Valley of the Sun Suzuki Assn. (treas. 1999), Ariz. Suzuki Assn. (treas. 1996—99), Music Educators Nat. Conf., Am. String Tchrs. Assn., Suzuki Assn. of the Am. (life). Democrat-Npl. Avocations: reading, travel, music. Home: 1800 W Elliot Rd #244 Chandler AZ 85224 Office: Mesa Pub Sch 202 N Sycamore Mesa AZ 85201 Office Phone: 602-818-5815. Home Fax: 480-730-2510; Office Fax: 480-472-4888. Personal E-mail: krostomee@cox.net. Business E-Mail: kmehlis@mpsaz.org, suzuki@nau.edu.

EHRENBERG, MIRIAM COLBERT, psychologist; b. N.Y., Mar. 16, 1930; m. Otto Ehrenberg, Sept. 20,1956; children: Ingrid, Erica. BA, Queens Coll.; MA, CUNY; PhD, New Sch. Social Rsch. Psychologist pvt. practice, N.Y., 1970—. Dir. psychotherapy Spence Chapin, N.Y., 1974-84; assoc. dir. Inst. for Human Identity, 1990-94, exec. dir., 1995—; clin. prof. CUNY, 1990—. Author: The Psychotherapy Maze, 1987, Optimum Brain Power, 1985, The Intimate Circle, 1988.

EHRENBERG, SARA JEAN, psychologist; b. Chgo., June 24, 1948; d. Isadore Jack and Marilyn (Millman) E.; m. Jeffrey Kent Tulis, July 16, 1978; children: Elizabeth, Hanna BA Am. History, U. Calif., Santa Cruz, 1970; EdM, Harvard U., 1973; MA Psychology, U. Chgo., 1978, PhD Psychology, 1989. Lic. psychologist, Tex. Tchr. Moss Landing Sch., Watonsville, Calif., 1971—72; adminstrv. asst. Brookline Early Edn. Project, Mass., 1973—75; tchr. Franklin Sch., Lexington, Mass., 1973—74; exec. dir. Westminster Child Care Ctr., Charlottesville, Va., 1978—80; post-doctoral tng. U. Tex., Austin, 1989—91; post-doctoral intern Austin Child Guidance Ctr., Tex., 1991—92; cert. psychologist Balcones Spl. Svcs. Coop., Austin, 1992—93; psychologist Lago Vista Ind. Sch. Dist., Tex., 1993—95, Pflugerville Ind. Sch. Dist., Tex., 1995—97, pvt. practice, Austin, 1997—. Clin. tng. Billings Hosp., U. Chgo., 1975-76; cons. Princeton (N.J.) Ednl. Resources, Inc., 1987, Psychol. Corp., San Antonio, 1989; psychoednl. examiner Learning Abilities Ctr., Austin, 1990-91 Del. Travis County Dem. Ctrl. Com., Austin, 1988, 92; v.p. Congregation Agudas Achim Religious Sch., 1989-90 Recipient NIMH Child Devel. fellowship U. Chgo., 1974-77 Mem. APA, Sch. Psychology Divsn. 16, Tex. Psychol. Assn., Jewish Family Svc. Austin Democrat. Jewish. Office: 4201 Marathon Blvd Ste 305 Austin TX 78756-3410 Office Phone: 512-451-3496.

EHRENFELD, ELLIE (ELVERA EHRENFELD), biologist, researcher; b. Phila., Mar. 1, 1942; m. Donald F. Summers. BA cum laude, Brandeis U., 1962; PhD in Biochemistry, U. Fla., 1967; postdoctoral student, Albert Einstein Coll. Medicine, 1967—74. Asst. to assoc. prof. dept. cell biology Albert Einstein Coll. Med.; from assoc. prof.to prof. biochemistry and biology U. Utah, 1974—92; dean sch. biol. scis. U. Calif., Irvine, 1992—97; dir. Center for Scientific Review, NIH, Bethesda, Md., 1997—2003; chief picornavirus replication, Laboratory of Infectious Diseases NIH, Bethesda, Md., 1997—. Mem. various coms. including rsch. adv. panel Walter Reed Army Inst. Rsch., exptl. virology study sect. NIH; mem. bd. sci. counselors Nat. Inst. Allergy and Infectious Diseases; cons. immunopathology lab. Scripps Inst. Med. Rsch. Recipient Bill Joklik Lectureship award, Am. Soc. Virology; scholar Nat. Sci., Brandeis U. Office: NIAID MSC 6612 6610 Rockledge Dr Bethesda MD 20892-6612

EHRENREICH, BARBARA, writer; b. Butte, Mont., Aug. 26, 1941; d. Ben Howes and Isabelle (Oxley) Alexander; m. John H. Ehrenreich, Aug. 6, 1966; children: Rosa, Benjamin; m. Gary Stevenson, Dec. 10, 1983 BA in Chem. Physics, Reed Coll., 1963; PhD in Biology, Rockefeller U., 1968; D (hon.), Reed College, SUNY, Old Westbury, College of Wooster, Ohio, John Jay College, UMass-Lowell, La Trobe University, Melbourne, Australia. Editor Health Policy Adv. Ctr., NYC, 1969-70; asst. prof. SUNY-Old Westbury, 1971-74; free-lance writer, lectr.; fellow NY Inst. Humanities, NYC, 1980, Inst. Policy Studios, Washington, 1982—; editor Seven Days mag., 1974; columnist Mother Jones mag., 1986-89; essayist Time mag., 1991—97; columnist The Guardian, United Kingdom, 1992—. Author: For Her Own Good: 150 Years of the Experts' Advice to Women, 1978, (with Deirdre English) The American Health Empire, 1970, (with John Ehrenreich) Witches, Midwives and Nurses: A History of Women Healers, 1972, (with D. English) Complaints and Disorders: The Sexual Politics of Sickness, 1973, The Hearts of Men: American Dreams and the Flight from Commitment, (with E. Hess & G. Jacobs) Re-Making Love: The Feminization of Sex, 1986, (with others) The Mean Season: The Attack on the Welfare State, 1987, Fear of Falling: The Inner Life of the Middle Class, 1989, The Worst Years of Our Lives: Irreverent Notes From An Age of Greed, 1990, Kipper's Game, 1993, Blood Rites: Origins and History of the Passions of War, 1997, Nickeled and Dimed: On (Not) Getting by in America, 2001 (Christoper award, 2002, LA Times Book award, 2002, NY Times Bestseller list), Bait and Switch: The (Futile) Pursuit of the American Dream, 2005; contbg. editor: Ms mag., 1981—, Mother Jones mag., 1988—, Leavs mag., 1988—. Recipient Nat. Mag. award, 1980, Ford Found. award for Humanistic Perspectives on Contemporary Issues, 1981; Guggenheim fellow, 1987, Sydney Hillman award for Journalism.

EHRET, JOSEPHINE MARY, microbiologist, researcher; b. Roswell, N.Mex., Feb. 26, 1934; d. Edward and Glenna (Memmer) E. BS, U. N.Mex., 1955. Med. technologist U. Colo. Health Scis. Ctr., Denver, 1956-75, rsch. microbiologist, 1956—, Denver Dept. Health and Hosps., 1980—2004; instr. Sch. Medicine, U. Colo., 1985—. Contbr. articles to profl. publs. Mem. Am. Soc. for Microbiology, Am. Soc. Med. Technologists (cert.), Am. Venereal Disease Assn., Calif. Assn. Continuing Med. Lab. Edn. Democrat. Avocations: reading, birding. Home: 1344 S Eudora St Denver CO 80222-3526 Office: U Colo Sch Medicine Div Inf Dis B168 Dept Medicine 4200 E 9th Ave Denver CO 80262 E-mail: JsphnEhret@aol.com.

EHRET, TERRY, writer; b. San Francisco, Nov. 12, 1955; d. Stephen Henry II and Adelaide Beatrice (O'Connor) E.; m. Donald Nicholas Moe, Apr. 7, 1979; children: Allison, Caitlin, Annelisa. AB in Psychology, Stanford U., 1977; MA in English, San Francisco State U., 1984. English tchr. Notre Dame H.S., Salinas, Calif., 1977-81, Cathedral H.S., San Francisco, 1981-83, Notre Dame H.S., Belmont, Calif., 1984-90; poet, tchr. Calif. Poets in the Schs., San Francisco, 1991—; creative writing tchr. Sonoma State U., Rohnert Park, Calif., 1993-94, San Francisco State U., 1995-97; writer-on-site Poets and Writers Inc., Oakland, Calif., 1997; English tchr. Santa Rosa (Calif.) Jr. Coll., 1991—. Writer-on-site Oakland Mus. of Calif., 1997, Oakland Pub. Libr., 1997; poetry series dir. SRJC Arts and Lectures com., Santa Rosa, 1994—. Author: Suspensions, 1990, Lost Body, 1993 (Nat. Poetry Series 1992, Calif. Commonwealth Club award 1994, (poetry sequence) The Thought She Might: Picasso Portraits (Pable Neruda prize 1995). Founder Sixteen Rivers Press Poetry Publising Collective, Sonoma County Poet Laureate, 2004—06. Mem. Calif. Poets in the Schs., Acad. of Am. Arts. Home: 924 Sunnyslope Rd Petaluma CA 94952-4747 Personal E-mail: tehret99@comcast.net.

EHRITZ, MARIANNE LOUISE, elementary school educator; b. Allentown, Pa., May 6, 1948; d. Joseph Thomas and Gladys Lucille (Legere) Herrity; m. Joseph W. Ehritz, Aug. 7, 1976; children: Kelly, Joseph, Jason. BS in Health and Phys. Edn., East Stroudsburg U., 1976, postgrad., 1976—. Control clk. Call-Chronicle Newspapers, inc., Allentown, 1966-69; mem. office staff Diocesan Mailing System, Allentown, 1969-72; health and phys. edn. tchr. Palmerton (Pa.) High Sch., 1976-80, jr. varsity basketball and head field hockey coach, 1976-80, substitute tchr., 1989-90; health and phys. edn. tchr. St. Thomas More Elem. Sch., Allentown, 1990—. Intramural dir., coach West End Youth Ctr., Allentown, 1985-92; head basketball coach Cathedral Girls C.Y.O. Program, Allentown, 1992-94; asst. coach girls' basketball Keystone Games, 1993, boys' varsity volleyball coach, 1998; head coach St. Thomas More Jr. High Volleyball Teams, 1998— Mem. Cathedral Parish Youth Com., 1985-92, diocesan physical edn. com. 2004-. Named to Atheltic Hall Fame, East Strousburg, 1990. Mem. AAHPERD, Nat. Cath. Ednl. Assn., Allentown Diocesan Lay Tchrs. Assn., Women's Alliance of St. Catharine of Siena. Democrat. Roman Catholic. Avocations: walking, bicycling, hiking. Home: 1938 W Livingston St Allentown PA 18104-3765 Office: St Thomas More Sch 1040 Flexer Ave Unit 2 Allentown PA 18103-5500

EHRLICH, AMY, editor, writer; b. N.Y.C., July 24, 1942; d. Max and Doris (Rubenstein) E.; m. Henry A. Ingraham; 1 son, Joss. Student, Bennington Coll., 1960-63, 64-65. Roving editor Family Cir. Mag., N.Y.C., 1975-76; sr. editor Dial Books for Young Readers, N.Y.C., 1977-82, exec. editor, 1982-85; v.p., editor-in-chief Candlewick Press, Cambridge, Mass., 1991-95, editor at large, 1996—. Author: children's book Zeek Silver Moon, 1972 (named Best Book of Yr. 1972), Leo, Zack and Emmie (named booklist reviewers choice Sch. Libr. Jour. 1981), Leo, Zack and Emmie Together Again, The Snow Queen, 1982, The Random House Book of Fairy Tales, others, (novel) Where It Stops, Nobody Knows, 1988 (ALA booklist Best of the Decade 1989, Dorothy Canfield Fisher award), The Story of Hannukah, Leo Zack and Emmie Together Again, Pome and Peel, 1990, The Dark Card, 1991, Lucy's Winter Tale, 1992, Parents in the Pigpen, Pigs in the Tub, 1993 (Best Youth Picture Book award Booklist 1993), Maggie and Silky and Joe, 1994; editor: When I Was Your Age: Original Stories of Growing Up, Vol. 1, 1996, Vol. 2, 1999, Rachel: The Story of Rachel Carson, 2003.

EHRLICH, AVA, broadcast executive; b. St. Louis, Aug. 14, 1950; d. Norman and Lillian (Gellman) Ehrlich; m. Barry K. Freedman, Mar. 31, 1979; children: Alexander Zev, Maxwell Samuel. BJ, Northwestern U., 1972, MJ, 1973; MA, Occidental Coll., 1976. Reporter, asst. mng. editor Lerner Newspapers, Chgo., 1974-75; reporter, news editor Sta. KMOX, St. Louis, 1976-79; producer Sta. WXYZ, Detroit, 1979-85; exec. producer Sta. KSDK-TV, St. Louis, 1985—. Guest editor Mademoiselle mag., N.Y.C., 1971; freelance writer, coll. prof. Detroit, Chgo., St. Louis, 1987; adj. faculty mem. Washington U., St. Louis, 1994—. Trustee CORO Found., St. Louis, 1976-77, 1986—99, St. Louis Jewish Light, 1999—, Crown Ctr., 2000; bd. dirs. Nat. Kidney Found., St. Louis, 1987, Crown Ctr., 2000—, Hillel Found. of Washington U, 2005—; com. chairperson Crayton H.S. PTO, 2005—. Named Outstanding Woman in Broadcasting, Am. Women in Radio & TV, 1983, Among 18 Most Influential Women in the Region St. Louis Dispatch, 2000; recipient Journalism award Am. Chiropractic Assn., 1989, AP award Ill. UPI, 1989, Illuminator award AMC Cancer Rsch., 1994, Women in Comms. Nat. award, 1988, Emmy award, 1995, Virginia Betts award for Contbns. in Journalism, 1999; CORO Found. fellow in pub. affairs, 1975-76. Mem. NATAS (com. mem. 1986—, bd. dirs. 1994—, 18 local Emmy awards 1986—), Women in Comms., Inc. (sec. 1978-79, Clarion award 1989, Best in Midwest Feature award 1989), Soc. Profl. Journalists. Democrat. Jewish. Home: 8002 Walinca Ter Saint Louis MO 63105-2565 Office: Sta KSDK-TV 1000 Market St Saint Louis MO 63101-2011 Office Phone: 314-444-5120. Business E-Mail: aehrlich@ksdk.gannett.com.

EHRLICH, DONNA M., director, educator; d. Richard A. Anderson and Wanda Aldrich, Rich Aldrich (Stepfather); m. Jeff Ehrlich, June 30, 2000; children: Christine Payton, Amy Payton, Kayla Payton, Beth, Joseph, Rachel. BS in Human Resource Mgmt., Friends U., Wichita, Kans., 1994—96, M in MIS, 2000; postgrad., Nova Southeastern U., Ft. Lauderdale, Fla., 2003—. Data process mgr./office mgr. Nash Finch Co., Liberal, Kans., 1986—96; automation technician Anadarko Petroleum Corp., Liberal, 1997—99; accounts payable staff Seward County C.C., Liberal, 1999—2000; dir. master in health care leadership Friends U., Wichita, 2000—; adj. prof. Wichita State U., 2002—; software engr./fin. DSS Sprint PCS, Overland Park, Kans., 2000—02. Presenter in field. Contbr. articles to profl. jours. Mem.: IEEE (assoc.), Assn. for Info. Systems (corr.), Soc. Case Rsch. (assoc.), Assn. for Computing Machinery (assoc.), Upsilon Pi Epsilon (assoc.). Home: 517 Sagebrush Wichita KS 67230 Office: Friends University 2100 W University St Wichita KS 67213 Office Phone: 316-295-5646. Personal E-mail: jdehrlich@cox.net. Business E-Mail: ehrlichd@friends.edu.

EHRLICH, GERALDINE ELIZABETH, management consultant; d. Joseph Vincent and Agnes Barbara (Campbell) McKenna; m. S. Paul Ehrlich, Jr.; children: Susan Patricia, Paula Jeanne, Jill Marie. BS, Drexel Inst. Tech. Nutrition cons. hypertension rsch. team U. Calif. Micronesia, 1970; regional sales mgr. Marriott Corp., Bethesda, Md., 1976-78; dir. sales and profl. svcs. Coll. and Health Care divsn. Macke Co., Cheverly, Md., 1978-79, v.p. ops. divsn., 1979-80, pres. Health Care divsn., 1980-81; regional v.p. Custom Mgmt. Corp., Alexandria, Va., 1981-83, v.p., 1983-87; v.p. mktg. and healthcare sales Morrison's Custom Mgmt., Mobile, Ala., 1987-88; v.p. sales ARA Svcs., Phila., 1988-93; v.p. bus. devel. ARAMARK, Phila., 1993-95; exec. dir. The Resource Group, Phila., 1995—2001; healthcare mktg. cons., 2001—. Cons. mktg. The Green House, Tokyo, 1987-88; chmn. bd. Mktg. Matrix, Falls Church, Va., 1984—. Mem. Health Systems Agy. No. Va., 1976-77; chmn. Health Care Adv. Bd., Fairfax County, Va., 1973-77; vice chmn. Fairfax County Cmty. Action Com., 1973-77; treas. Fairfax County

Dem. Com., 1969-73; trustee Fairfax Hosp., 1973-77; bd. dirs. Tennis Patrons, Washington, 1984-88, Phila. Singers, 1993-98, Physicians for Peace, 1993-98; mem. adv. bd. Nat. Mus. Women in the Arts, 2000—, mem. bd. Fla. State Com., 2005—. Mem. NAFE, AAUW, Internat. Women's Assn., Am. Mgmt. Assn., Soc. Mktg. Profls., Gulfstream Club, Rotary Club. Home: 1132 Seaspray Ave Delray Beach FL 33483 Office Phone: 561-573-2492. E-mail: gehrlich@profserve.com.

EHRLICH, MARGARET ISABELLA GORLEY, systems engineer, mathematics professor, consultant; b. Eatonton, Ga., Nov. 12, 1950; d. Frank Griffith and Edith Roy (Beall) Gorley; m. Jonathan Steven Ehrlich. BS in Math., U. Ga., 1972; MEd, Ga. State U., 1977, EdS, 1982, PhD, 1987; postgrad., Woodrow Wilson Coll. of Law, 1977-78. Cert. secondary tchr., Ga. Tchr. Dekalb County Bd. Edn., Decatur, Ga., 1972-83; chmn. dept. math. Columbia H.S., Decatur, Ga., 1978-83; with product development Chalkboard Co., Atlanta, 1983-84; math. instr. Ga. State U., Atlanta, 1983-92, lectr., dir. of mentoring, 2001—03; pres. Testing and Tech. Svcs., Atlanta, 1983—; chair dept. math., computer sci. and engring. Ga. Perimeter Coll., Clarkston, 2003—. Course specialist Ga. Pacific Co., Atlanta, 1984-86; sys. engr. Lotus Devel. Corp., 1986-89; rsch. assoc. SUNY-Stony Brook, 1976; modeling instr. Barbizon Modeling Sch., Atlanta, 1991; instr. Ga. State Coll. for Kids, 1984-85; test-taking cons., hon. mem. Comm. Workers of Am. Local 3204, Atlanta, 1985—. Author: (software user manual) Micro Maestro, 1983, Music Math, 1984; (test manual) The Telephone Company Test, 1991, AMI Pro Advanced Courseware, 1992, A Study Guide for the Sales and Service Representative Test, 1993, A Study Guidy for the Technical Services Test, 1995; (book) Philadelphia Methodist Church 1860-90: Members and History, 1998, Mrs. Bell's Mill, 1999; mem. editl. bd. CPA Computer Report, Atlanta, 1984-85. Tchr. St. Phillips Ch. Sch., Atlanta, 1981-88; mem. Atlanta Preservation Soc., 1985, Planned Parenthood, St. Phillips welcome com., 1988-96, drug and alcohol counseling HOPE, 1988-96; sponsor Fair Test 1991—, Ctr. Fair and Open Testing, parish choir St. Phillips Ch., 1995-96; team leader guest svcs. Atlanta Com. Olympic Games, 1996; vol. Atlanta Hist. Soc. Archives and Libr., 2000—/ Named State Tchr. Achievement Recognition Tchr. DeKalb County Bd. Edn., 1979, 80, 81, Most Outstanding Tchr., Barbizon Sch. of Modeling, 1980, Colo. Outward Bound, 1985, Disting. Educator, Ga. State U., 1987; recipient Jefferson Davis Gold Medal, United Daus. of Confederacy, 1999, Exemplary Leader award The Chair Acad., 2006. Mem.: DAR, DeKalb Personal Computer Instr. Assn. (pres. 1984), Assn. Women in Math. (del. to China Sci. and Tech. Exch. 1989—90), Math. Assn. Am., Ga. Coun. Tchrs. Math., Nat. Coun. Tchrs. Math., Math. Assn. Am., Nat. Soc. Colonial Dames XVII Century (recording sec. 2005—), Hamilton Nat. Geneal. Soc. (treas. 1998—), First Families of Ga. (sec.), Ga. Hist. Soc., N.Y.C. Track Club, Atlanta Track Club. Democrat. Episcopalian. Avocations: piano, pilates, fashion, skiing, harp. Home: 240 Cliff Overlook Atlanta GA 30350-2601 Office: Ga Perimeter Coll 555 N Indian Creek Dr Clarkston GA 30021 Office Phone: 678-891-3712.

EHRLICH, MARTHA ANN, elementary school educator; b. Florissant, Mo., Nov. 20, 1961; d. Alvin William and Leanne Margaret Pezdd; m. Evan Drew Erhrlich, Aug. 17, 1984. BS in Edn., U. Mo., St. Louis, 1984; MS, Maryville U., Chesterfield, Mo., 1993. Tchr. St. Catherine of Alexandria, Bellefontaine, Mo., 1984—87, Parkway West Mid. Sch., Chesterfield, 1987—96, Parkway South Mid. Sch., Chesterfield, 1986—. Cons. Steck-Vaughn Pub., Tex., 1993. Named Tchr. of Yr., Parkway South Mic. Sch., 1999, Mid. Sch. Tchr. of Yr., Parkway Sch. Dist., 1999; recipient Excellence in Tchg. award, Emeren Elec. Co., 1999. Mem.: NEA, Orgn. Am. Historians, Parkway Edn. Assn. Avocations: reading, travel, skiing. Home: 610 Rue De Freur Creve Coeur MO 63141

EHRLICH, RISA HIRSCH, artist, educator; d. Sandor Solomon and Sylvia (Duchin) Hirsch; children: Viviana Elizabeth, David Leonardo. MS, Yeshiva U., NYC, 1972. Cert. tchr. NY. Tchr. of English NYC Pub. Schs., 1958—62, tchr. of math., 1966—97. Artist in residence Lookout Sculpture Pk., Lookout Point, Pa., 2005, 06. Exhibitions include Gallery 88, NYC, Suhae Gallery, Ft. Lee, NJ. Co-chair HVG Arts Group, NYC, 1997—2006; active mem. Cmty. Affairs Com. HVG, NYC; active WaHiArts/Uptown Stroll Group, NYC, Transponder Artists Group, NYC. Scholar, Old Ch. Cultural Ctr., 2003. Mem.: Alumni and Friends of LaGuardia. Avocations: square dancing, cooking. Office Phone: 212-740-2136. Personal E-mail: hirschehr@aol.com.

EHRMAN, LEE, geneticist, educator; b. NYC, May 25, 1935; m. Richard Ehrman, 1955; children: Esther, Judith. BS, Queens Coll., 1956; MS, Columbia U., 1957, PhD in Genetics, 1959; DSc (hon.), CUNY, 1989. Mem. faculty Barnard Coll., 1956-58; postdoctoral fellow in genetics Columbia U., N.Y.C., 1959-61, assoc. seminar on population biology, 1981—; mem. faculty SUNY-Purchase, 1970—, prof. div. natural scis., 1972—; Disting. prof. biology SUNY, Purchase, 1995—; mem. spl. study sect. NIH, NIMH, 1979-80. Vis. disting. prof. U. Miami, Coral Gables, Fla., 1981; vis. lectr. U. Puerto Rico, Rio Piedras, 1987; coordinator, panelist workshops, programs in field; mem. panels NIH, 2003—. Author: Behavior Genetics and Evolution, 2nd edit., 1981; assoc. editor Evolution; assoc. editor for genetics and cytology Am. Midland Naturalist; co-editor: Behavior Genetics; assoc. editor, exec. com. Soc. Am. Naturalists, 1977-85, pres.-elect 1990; contbr. more than 500 articles to profl. jours. Recipient Lit. Soc. Found. medal in German, 1956; Shirley Farr postdoctoral fellow, 1961-62; USPHS postdoctoral fellow, 1959-61; faculty exch. scholar, 1974—; NSF grantee, 1979-84; Sr. Scientist awardee Whitehall Found., 1987, 93; NIH gen. med. scis. grantee, 1987—; SUNY travel grantee, 1988, 93, 96; Merck rsch. support grantee, 2000—. Fellow AAAS (Rsch. Support award Merck/AAAS, 2001), Inst. Soc. Ethics and Life Scis; mem. AAUW (life), Am. Soc. Naturalists (pres. 1990), Behavior Genetics Assn. (pres. 1978, Dobzhansky award for lifetime resch. 1988), Soc. for Study of Evolution (exec. council 1986), Phi Beta Kappa, Sigma Xi Home: 2 Jennifer Ln Rye Brook NY 10573-1916 Office: SUNY Div Natural Scis Purchase NY 10577 Office Phone: 914-251-6671. Office Fax: 914-251-6635.

EHRMANN, SUSANNA, language educator, photographer, writer; b. Detroit, Oct. 17, 1944; d. Frederick Michael and Stephanie (Fiala) Ehrmann. Student, Universite Laval, summer 1965; BA, Antioch Coll., 1966; MAT, U. Chgo., 1968. Cert. tchr., Ill., Tex., Va. Tchr. fgn. lang. U. Chgo. Lab. Schs., 1967-74, Maimonides Sch., Brookline, Mass., 1975-76, North Shore Country Day Sch., Winnetka, Ill., 1977-78, Copenhagen Internat. Jr. Sch., 1978-79, Houston C.C., 1979-81, 84, Kinkaid Sch., Houston, 1980-82, Alief Ind. Sch. Dist., Houston, 1982-85, Houston Ind. Sch. Dist., 1990-91; pvt. instr., 1986—; freelance rschr., editor, 1986—; writer, photographer, 1993—. Mem. North Ctrl. evaluating teams, Chgo., Rockford, 1971; mem. MAT coordinating com. on Romance langs., U. Chgo., 1971-74. Creator German Grammar Game, 1982. Reader for the blind, Chgo., 1972-74. NDEA fellow, 1966-68; Goethe Inst. grantee, 1983. Mem. MLA, Am. Assn. Tchrs. of French, Am. Assn. Tchrs. of German. Home: 2422 Potomac Dr Houston TX 77057-4500 Personal E-mail: sfiala2@juno.com.

EICHELBERGER, LISA WRIGHT, academic administrator, nursing educator; b. Columbus, Ga., Sept. 14, 1953; d. George Bruce and Tera (Lee) Wright; m. John Everett Eichelberger, Aug. 29, 1987; children: Matthew, Elizabeth, Tera. BSN, U. Ala., Birmingham, 1975, MSN, 1979, DSN, 1986. Staff nurse Brookwood Hosp., Birmingham, 1975; instr. St. Vincents Hosp. Sch. Nursing, Birmingham, 1975-78; pvt. practice lactation cons. Birmingham, 1978-84; mgr. staff devel. Brookwood Hosp., Birmingham, 1979-80; assoc. dir. St. Vincents Hosp. Sch. Nursing, Birmingham, 1981-84; grad. rsch. fellow U. Ala. Sch. of Nursing, Birmingham, 1984-85; ind. nurse practitioner Auburn (Ala.) Day Care Ctr., 1987-88; asst. dean, asst. prof. Auburn U. Sch. of Nursing, 1985-87; dean, assoc. prof. Miss. Coll. Sch. of Nursing, Clinton, 1988—. Instr. U. Ala. Sch. Nursing, Birmingham, 1980-81; cons., spkr. and presenter in field. Contbr. articles to profl. jours. Mem. Miss. Nurses Assn. (treas. 1990-92, chair fin. com. 1990-92), Miss. Deans and Dirs. Coun. (v.p. 1989-91), Ala. League for Nursing (chmn. state com. on nominations 1978, 80-82, bd. dirs. 1976-82), Nat. League for Nursing, So. Coun. for Collegiate Edn. in Nursing, Sigma Theta Tau. Baptist. Avocations: heirloom sewing, smocking. Home: 403 Berwick S Peachtree City GA 30269-3802

EICHENBERGER GILMORE, JULIE MAE, research scientist; b. New Hampton, Iowa, Aug. 12, 1956; d. Phillip Mathias Eichenberger and Harriette Elizabeth Porter; m. James Cecil Gilmore, Nov. 8, 1986; 1 child, Hallie Jean Gilmore. PhD, U. Iowa, Iowa City, 1998—2001. Registered Dietitian Am. Dietetic Assn., 1987. Dir., food and nutrition U. Iowa Hosps. and Clinics, Iowa City, 1992—96; rsch. scientist U. Iowa Coll. of Dentistry, Iowa City, 1997—. Mem.: Iowa Dietetic Assn. (assoc.; pres. 1998—99, Medallion award 2002), Am. Dietetic Assn. (assoc. Mary P. Huddleson award 2006). Office: Coll of Dentistry Univ of Iowa Iowa City IA 52242 Office Phone: 319-353-5476.

EICHENGER, MARILYNNE KATZEN, museum administrator; children: Ryan, Kara, Julia, Jessica, Talik. BA in Anthropology and Sociology magna cum laude, Boston U., 1965; MA, Mich. State U., 1971. With emergency and outpatient staff Ingham County Mental Health Ctr., 1972; founder, pres., exec. dir. Impression 5 Sci. and Art Mus., Lansing, Mich., 1973-85; pres. Oreg. Mus. Sci. and Industry, Portland, 1985-95; bd. dirs. Portland Visitors Assn., 1985-95; pres. Informal Edn. Products Ltd., 1995—, Portland, 1995—. Bd. dirs. N.W. Regional Edn. Labs., 1991-97; instr. Lansing (Mich.) C.C., 1978; ptnr. Eyrie Studio, 1982-85; condr. numerous workshops in interactive exhibit design, adminstrn. and fund devel. for schs., orgns., profl. socs. Author: (with Jane Mack) Lexington Montessori School Survey, 1969, Manual on the Five Senses, 1974; pub. Mich. edit. Boing mag. Founder Cambridge Montessori Sch., 1964; bd. dirs. Lexington Montessori Sch., 1969, Mid-Mich. South Health Sys. Agy., 1978-81, Cmty. Referral Ctr., 1981-85, Sta. WKAR, 1981-85; active Lansing "Riverfest" Lighted Boat Parade, 1980; mem. state Health Coordinating Coun., 1980-82; mem. pres.'s adv. coun. Portland State U., 1986—90, mem. pres.' adv. bd., 1987-91; bd. dirs. Portland Visitors Assn., 1994-97, Friends of Tryon Creek State Pk., 2001-06. Recipient Diana Cert. Leadership, YWCA, 1976-77, Woman of Achievement award, 1991, Cmty. Svc. award Portland State U., 1992, Cataloguer of Yr. award Catalog Success, 2005. Mem. Am. Assn. Mus., Oreg. Mus. Assn., Assn. Sci. and Tech. Ctrs. (bd. dirs. 1980-84, 88-93), Mus. Store Assn., Direct Mktg. Assn., Zonta Lodge (founder, bd. dirs. East Lansing club 1978), Internat. Women's Forum, Portland C. of C. Office: Informal Edn Products Ltd 2517 SE Mailwell Dr Milwaukie OR 97222 Business E-Mail: sales@museumtour.com.

EICHENLAUB, ROSEMARY WARING, retired music educator; b. Saratoga Springs, N.Y., Dec. 1, 1949; d. Edward Joseph and Marion Hewitt Waring; m. Ed J. Eichenlaub, July 10, 1982; children: Brian, Julie. MusB Cum Laude, Nazareth Coll., 1971, MS Elem. Edn., 1976; Orff cert., Eastman Sch. Music, 1993. Tchr. vocal, gen. music Rochester City Sch. Dist., NY, 1971—2005, ret., 2005. Chairperson Arts Enrichment Com. Sch. 1, 1990—2005; liaison Eastman Sch. Music, 1992; chairperson Character Edn. Program Sch. 1, 1995—2005; music mentor Rochester City Sch. Dist., NY, 1996—2005; presenter All Children Are Children First Conf., 1997; presenter in field; dir., literacy vol., tutor Mozart Chorus Nazareth Coll., 2005—06. Author article in Orff Echo. Com. mem. St. Margaret Mary Ch., Rochester, 1983—. Recipient Outstanding Music Educator award, Rochester Philharmonic Orch., 1998. Mem.: Music Educators Nat. Conf., Greater Rochester Chpt. Am. Orff Schulwerk Assn. (pres. 1990), Am. Orff Schulwerk Conf. (fundraising chair 2000). Roman Catholic. Avocations: reading, theater, skiing, tennis, ballroom dancing. E-mail: eichen35@rochester.rr.com.

EICK-GAMM, KIMBERLY MARIE, social worker; b. Waterloo, Iowa, Sept. 20, 1959; d. Darrell Herbert and Mary Louise (Vela) Eick; m. David William Gamm, July 29, 1995; children: Buckley Alan Necker, Kaleen Christina Necker. AA in Animal Sci., Hawkeye C.C., Waterloo, Iowa, 1995; AA in Human Svc., Kirkwood C.C., Cedar Rapids, Iowa, 1986; BA in Social Work, U. No. Iowa, Cedar Falls, 1998; postgrad. in Counseling, Seton Hall U., South Orange, N.J., 1998—. Cert. substance abuse counselor, lic. social worker Iowa. Shift leader, in-home therapist Four Oaks, Independence and Oelwein, Iowa, 1999—2001; caseworker Tanager Place, Cedar Rapids, 2001—02; in-house therapist Luth. Social Svcs., 2002—03; counselor Substance Abuse Svc. Ctr., 2003—04; caseworker Luth. Svcs. Iowa, Waverly, 2004—. Mem.: ACA. Avocations: golf, horseback riding, walking. Office: Luth Svcs Iowa 106 16th St SW Waverly IA 50677 E-mail: gumbo1@netins.net.

EIDELMAN, SHARON (SHERRY) R., marriage and family therapist; b. Montreal, June 6, 1944; arrived in U.S., 1970; d. Hyman and Lilyan Lipsey; m. Aaron Joshua Eidelman, June 20, 1976; children: Dov, Ilana Eidelman Traube. BA, Coll. of New Rochelle, N.Y., 1987; MA, Columbia U., N.Y.C., 1989; EdM, Columbia U., 1991; MSW, NYU, 1997. LCSW N.Y. Marriage/family therapist Counterforce, Bklyn., 1991—2003, Haverstraw, NY, 2001—. Pet therapist Golden Outreach, Westchester, NY, 1992—95, New Rochelle Humane Soc., 2001—; counselor Y. L. Help Line, Bklyn., 1997—; mem. cmty. adv. bd. Group Home, New Rochelle, 1982—. Mem.: Am. Mental Health Counseling Assn., Kappa Delta Pi. Avocation: gardening. Home: 165 Bon Air Ave New Rochelle NY 10804 Office: 85 New Main St Haverstraw NY 10927 Office Phone: 845-429-6070.

EIFERMAN, SHARON REES, language educator, poet; d. Arthur Rees and Betty Shuster; m. Barry Eiferman (dec.); 1 child, Kenneth Rees. BA, Temple U., Phila., 1969, MA, 1972. Asst. prof. English C.C. Phila., 1974—2006. Contbr. poetry to anthologies; author: (book) Dances in Dialogue, 1991. Mem.: AAUW, N.J. Poetry Soc. (past pres. Wellingboro br.), Cmty. Coll. Humanities Assn. Avocations: walking, dogs. Home: 100 Stratton Ln Mount Laurel NJ 08054 Office: CC of Phila NERC Site Mount Laurel NJ 08054

EIFFERT, CRYSTAL L., lawyer; d. Barry and Betty Eiffert. JD, Nova Southeastern U., Ft. Lauderdale, Fla., 2001. Bar: Fla. 2002. State trooper Va. State Police, Virginia Beach, 1996—99; ptnr. Eiffert & Anthony, P.A., Orlando, Fla., 2002—. Mem.: ATLA. R-Liberal. Office: Eiffert & Anthony PA 122 E Colonial Dr Ste 210 Orlando FL 32801 Office Phone: 407-244-1980. Office Fax: 407-244-1981.

EIGEL, MARCIA DUFFY, editor; b. Denver, July 15, 1936; d. Eugene and Margaret (Foley) Duffy; m. Edwin G. Eigel Jr., May 30, 1959; children: Edwin III, Mary. BA, Webster U., 1958. Editor, writer corp. hdqrs. GE, Fairfield, Conn., 1985-92, copy editor, 1996-2000; dir. comms. Girl Scouts of Housatonic Coun., Bridgeport, Conn., 1994-97; editor Blue Cross of Northeastern Pa., 2001—05, Joint Urban Studies Group, 2005, Jewett Assocs., 2005. Instr. in bus. writing So. Conn. State U., New Haven, 1986, U. Bridgeport, 1990. Writer, editor newsletter Customer Fin. Svcs. News, 1987-92, Woman Traveler, 1990—; contbr. articles and poetry to profl. jours. Bd. trustees Greater Bridgeport (Conn.) Symphony, 1998—. Mem.: AAUW, U. Bridgeport Women's Forum. Home and Office: 33 Pepperbush Ln Fairfield CT 06824-4036

EIGEN, BARBARA GOLDMAN, artist; b. Dayton, Ohio, Jan. 15, 1945; d. Leonard and Lila (Gams) Goldman; m. Eric Franklin Eigen, Sept. 3, 1967; children: Zev, Ron. BA, Cornell U., 1967. Writer Boston U. Dept. Pub. Relations, 1969-71; prof. U. Costa Rica Sch. Fine Arts, San Jose, 1973-76; pres. Eigen Arts, N.Y.C., 1977-89, Jersey City, 1989—. Designer Bellini, Florence, Italy 1983-90, Block China N.Y. 1987-95. Copyrights Ceramic Designs, Melon Tea Set and many others 1977—; participant Designer Tables at Tiffany & Co. 1982; designer dinnerware for Williams-Sonoma, Pottery Barn and Crate & Barrel; lic. designs with Zak designs. Mem. Crafts Council, Hadassah N.Y.C., Ceramic Mfgs. Assn. Democrat. Avocations: reading, swimming. Office: Eigen Arts Inc 150 Bay St Jersey City NJ 07302-2900 Office Phone: 201-798-7310. Personal E-mail: barbara@eigenarts.com.

EIKENBERRY, JILL, actress; b. New Haven, Jan. 21, 1947; m. Michael Tucker; 1 stepchild. Student, Yale U. Actress stage prodns. Saints, 1976, Uncommon Women and Others, 1977, Watch on the Rhine, 1980, Onward Victoria, 1980, Holiday, 1982, Porch, 1984, Fine Line, 1984, Life Under Water, 1985, A Picasso, 2005; feature film appearances include Between the Lines, 1977, An Unmarried Woman, 1977, The End of the World in Our Ususal Bed in a Night Full of Rain, 1978, Rich Kids, 1979, Butch and Sundance: The Early Days, 1979, Hide in Plain Sight, 1980, Arthur, 1981, Grace Quigley, 1985, The Manhattan Project, 1986; TV movie appearances include The Deadliest Season, 1977, Orphan Train, 1979, Swan Song, 1980, Sessions, 1983, Kane and Abel, 1985, Assault and Matrimony, 1987, Family Sins, 1987, A Stoning in Fulham County, 1988, My Boyfriend's Back, 1989, The Diane Martin Story, The Secret Life of Archie's Wife, 1990, An Inconvenient Woman, 1991, Living A Lie, 1991, Doc: The Dennis Littky Story, 1992, Chantilly Lace, 1993, Parallel Lives, 1994, The Other Woman, 1995, My Very Best Friend, 1996, Gone in a Heartbeat, 1996; teleplay Uncommon Women and Others, 1978; regular (TV series) L.A. Law, 1986-94 (Emmy nomination, Supporting Actress - Drama Series, 1994). Office: care William Morris Agency 151 S El Camino Dr Beverly Hills CA 90212-2704

EIKLEBERRY, LOIS SCHILLIE, physician; b. Novinger, Mo., July 19, 1927; d. Frank Carl and Sarah Louise (Gashwiler) Schillie; m. William Francis Eikleberry, June 14, 1952; children: Carol, Linda, Bill Jr.(dec.), Beatrice. BA, William Jewell Coll., Liberty, Mo., 1949; BS in Medicine, Mo. U., Columbia, 1951; MD, State U. Iowa, Iowa City, 1953. Diplomate Am. Bd. Family Practice, 1975. Intern Mercy Hosp., Iowa City, 1954; pvt. practice West Branch, Iowa, 1954—56; physician William Beaumont Army Hosp., El Paso, Tex., 1957—58; pvt. practice Castle Rock, Wash., 1959—61; physician 6th Army Hdqrs., San Francisco, 1962—63; adminstr. Wash. State Dept. Pub. Assistance, Longview, 1963—69; pvt. practice Longview, 1969; with Tri County Health, Denver and Adams County, Colo., 1970—71; pvt. practice Lakewood, Colo., 1972—88; ret., 1988. Author: (biography) A Folk History of Charlie and Nettie Schillie, 1992, A Folk History of J.S. and Maude Gashwiler, 1993. Leader Girl Scouts, 1968. Recipient Citiation of Achievement, William Jewell Coll., 1982. Mem.: P.E.O. Sisterhood (recording sec. 1992—94, treas. 1996—98, pres. 2004—). Avocations: reading, hiking, genealogy, antiques, natural history. Home: 8544 W Illiff Ave Lakewood CO 80227-3030

EIKLENBORG, JOLEEN, education educator, consultant; d. Harold and Isabelle Eiklenborg. BA Edn., U. No. Iowa, Cedar Falls, 1980; MA Edn., U. No. Iowa, 1992. Tchr., instr., coach Grinnell-Newburg Sch. Dist., Iowa, 1986—92; adminstrv. program specialist Tex. Edn. Agy., Austin, 1992—95; health specialist Edn. Svc. Ctr., Region 12, Waco, Tex., 1995—2002; phys. edn. specialist/adminstr. Hallsburg Ind. Sch. Dist., Waco, 2002—06; cps investigator II Tex. DSHS, Waco, 2006—. Catch cons. Tex. U. Houston, Waco, 1998—2006; cons.- sch. health adv. coun. Am. Cancer Soc., Waco, 1998—2006; cons.- driver edn. TEA and ESC 12, Waco, 1992—2002; adj. prof. Tex. State U., San Marcos, 1997—2002. Mem. Robinson Park Com., Waco, 2006—06; chairperson Am. Cancer Soc., Waco, 1995—2006; mem. Am. Heart Assn., Waco, 1995—2006. Named to Whos Who Am. Tchr., Whos Who in Am. Edn., 2006; recipient CATCH Champion, Tex. U. Houston, 2005, Award for Excellence in Tex. Sch. Health, Tex. Dept. of Health, 2006, Tex. Phys. Educator of Month, Tex. Edn. Agy.- Ctr. of Edn. Devel., 2003, Tex. ALL-Well State Planning Team-9 yrs, Am. Cancer Soc. -Tex. Divsn., 1996—2005. Mem.: Iowa Assn. Safety Edn. (pres. 1985, 1993), Am. Driver and Traffic Safety Edn. Assn. (bd. dirs., sec., program chair 1994—2000), Tex. Assn. Health, Phys. Edn., Recreation and Dance (com. and conf. chair 1995—2006, Elem Phys. Edn. Tchr. of Yr. nominee 2006), Tex. Driver and Traffic Safety Edn. Assn. (pres. 2000, 2003, Gene Wilkens Honor Svc. Award 2003), Tex. Sch. Health Assn. (life; pres. 2003, v.p. 2006). Avocations: bicycling, swimming, reading, working with youth. Personal E-mail: joeiklenborg@hotmail.com.

EIL, LOIS HELEN, retired physician; b. Ashland, Wis., Dec. 25, 1920; d. Abraham Isaac Latts and Claire Ida Frindell; m. Harry Meyer Eil, Mar. 12, 1944 (dec.); children: Charles, Alison, Mitchell. BS, U. Minn., Mpls., 1942, MS, 1943, MD, 1946; MPH, Columbia U., N.Y.C., 1967. Diplomate bd. cert. pub. health 1975. Med. dir., supervising physician NYC Health Dept., 1960—65; attending physician, pediatrician Lincoln Hosp., Bronx, 1960—65; med. dir. Am. Pub. Health Assn., NYC, 1968—70; med. dir. regional office NY State Health Dept., White Plains, 1970—83; ret., 1983. Home: 25 Rockledge Ave Apt 903W White Plains NY 10601

EILER, GERTRUDE S., writer; b. Syracuse, N.Y., July 7, 1914; d. Edward Franklin and Gertrude (Van Duyn) Southworth; m. George Phelps, Jan. 4, 1935 (div. 1950); children: William Henry Phelps, George Phelps, James Phelps; m. Edward S. Jay, Dec. 18, 1954 (dec. Aug. 1962); m. George R. Eiler, Aug. 24, 1963 (dec. May 1984); stepchildren: Larry Eiler, Roger Eiler. Student, Wellesley Coll., 1932-33. Asst. sec., treas., v.p. Iroquois Pub. Co., Inc., Syracuse, 1950-60; salesperson Roney Realty Co., Syracuse, 1960-62; registrar Onondaga C.C., Syracuse, 1962-64; asst. editor Singer Pub. Co., 1966-67; propr. Log Cabin Gift Shop, Cuyler, N.Y., 1968-76; freelance editor, typist Syracuse, 1980-90; owner, editor Pine Grove Press, Syracuse, 1990—2002. Mem. Social Art Club Syracuse (sec. 1983-). Avocation: writing. Home: Apt C212 1290 Boyce Rd Pittsburgh PA 15241

EILERS, JENNIFER ANN, special education educator, counseling administrator; b. St. Louis, Oct. 27, 1977; d. Gregory Lee and Carol Ann Barnard; m. Andrew Charles Eilers, July 14, 2001. BFA in Spl. Edn., Webster U., St. Louis, 2000, MA in Tchg. with honors, 2004. Cert. elem. edn. tchr., spl. edn. cross-categorical K-12, in severe devel. disabilities K-12. Applied behavior analysis paratherapist Early Childhood Learning Ctr., St. Louis, 1999—2002; spl. edn. tchr. Spl. Sch. Dist. St. Louis County, 2000—; acad. advisor Webster U., St. Louis, 2004—. Spl. Olympics coach Spl. Sch. Dist., 2003—, mentor tchr., 2003—. Vol. Team Activities for Spl. Kids, St. Louis, 2001—. Named Tchr. of Month, Spl. Sch. Dist., 2003. Avocations: reading, scrapbooks. Office: Sappington Elem Sch 11011 Gravois Rd Saint Louis MO 63126

EIMERS, JERI ANNE, retired counselor; b. Berkeley, Calif., Jan. 20, 1951; d. Alfred D. Wallace and Marjorie E. (Nordheim) Stevens; m. Roy A. Neiman, June 12, 1969 (div. Aug. 1977); children: Lorien, Arwen; m. Richard A. Eimers, Mar. 2, 1996. AA, Palomar Jr. Coll., San Marcos, Calif., 1977; BA in Psychology with distinction, Calif. State U., Long Beach, 1979, MA in Psychology with distinction, 1981; postgrad. Human Sexuality Program, UCLA, 1991-92. Lic. marriage, family, child therapist, Calif.; cert. community coll. instr., counselor; cert. sex therapist. Rsch. asst. Calif. State U., 1978-82; tchr. Artesia (Calif.)-Bellflower-Cerritos Unified Sch. Dist., 1982-83; dir. Am. Learning Corp., Huntington Beach, Calif., 1983-85; social worker Los Angeles County Children's Protective Svcs., Long Beach, 1986-88; sr. social worker Orange County Social Svc. Agy., Orange, Calif., 1988-90; therapist Cypress Mental Health, Cypress, Calif., 1988—, cons., 1990—. Cons., 1990—; group chair, leader Adults Abused as Children, Los Altos Hosp., Long Beach, 1991—, Coll. Hosp., Cerritos, 1993—; speaker, presenter in field. Mem. Child's Sexual Abuse Network, Orange, 1988—; mem. legis. com. Child Abuse Coun. of Orange County, 1988. Women's League scholar, 1980-81. Mem. AAUW, Am. Assn. Marriage, Family Therapists, Calif. Assn. Marriage, Family Therapists, Am. Profl. Soc. for Abused Children, Calif. Profl. Assn. for Abused Children, Phi Kappa Phi, Psi Chi. Republican. Methodist. Avocations: writing, theater, classical and jazz music, swimming. Personal E-mail: eimers@adelphia.net.

EIMON, PAN DODD, artist, writer; b. Union City, Tenn., Mar. 13, 1921; d. Harry Edwin and Pauline Caldwell Dodd; m. Paul Iver Eimon, Nov. 23, 1957. Student in Art, Watkins Inst., 1930—32, Cin. Art Inst., 1932, Chgo. Inst. Art, 1933—34; student, Vanderbilt U., 1938—40, Pan Am. U., 1944; BS in Polit. Sci. and Journalism, U. Tenn., 1952; student, Stanford U., 1962—63. Clk., typist Panama Canal, 1943—45; columnist Panama Star and Herald, Panama, 1943—45; news editor WBIR Radio, Knoxville, Tenn., 1947—49; mng. editor Tenn. Town and City, Knoxville, 1950—58; columnist Am. City Mag.,

N.Y.C., 1950—85; editl. asst. Stanford U. News Svc., Palo Alto, 1961—63; v.p. mktg. Commonwealth Internat., Amarillo, Tex., 1990—2002. Creator Amarillo Internat. Week, 1992—. Author: An American Dream, 1954; co-author: Mining Milestones in Colorado History, 1981; Represented in permanent collections U. South, Sewanee, Tenn., Pa. State U. Mus., State College, one-woman shows include U.S. Embassy, Managua, Nicaragua, 1961, Nat. Gallery, Ulanbator, Mongolia, 1996, Carson County Sq. House Mus., Panhandle, Tex., 2004. Info. dir. St. John's Cath., Denver, 1977—82. Named to Women's Hall of Fame, Women's Forum, 1992; recipient Golden Touch award, C. of C., 1988. Mem.: AAUW (pres. 1994—96, chmn. state conv. 2000, chmn. internat. rels. 2003—06), Art Force (pres. 1989—90), Internat. Club (bd. dir. 1980—). Democrat. Episcopalian. Avocation: community action. Home: 3010 W 16th Ave Amarillo TX 79102 Office Phone: 806-353-7456.

EINIGER, CAROL BLUM, investment company executive; b. Nov. 30, 1949; d. Bernard Michael and Bella (Karff) Blum; m. Roger William Einiger, Dec. 21, 1969; 1 child. BA, U. Pa., 1970; MBA, Columbia U., 1973. With Conde Nast Publs., N.Y.C., 1970-71, Goldman, Sachs & Co., N.Y.C., 1971-72, 1st Boston Corp., N.Y.C., 1973-88, mng. dir., 1982-88, head short-term fin. dept., 1983-88, head capital markets dept., 1985-88; vis. prof., exec.-in-residence Columbia U. Bus. Sch., N.Y.C., 1988-89; mng. dir. Wasserstein Perella & Co. Inc., N.Y.C., 1989-92; CFO, acting pres. Edna McConnell Clark Found., NYC, 1992—96; chief investment officer Rockefeller U., N.Y.C., 1996—. Trustee Horace Mann Sch., 1988-94, U. Pa., 1989-99, mem. audit, budget and fin., investment, external affairs, and student life coms.; bd. overseers Columbia U. Bus. Sch., 1988-, nominating com.; vice chair investment com. Mus. Modern Art, 1994-; mem. adv. bd. Blackstone Alternative Asset Mgmt., 1999-; bd. dirs. Credit Suisse First Boston (U.S.A.), Inc., 2001-02, Boston Properties, Inc., 2004-. Office: Rockefeller Univ 1230 York Ave New York NY 10021-6399

EINREINHOFER, NANCY ANNE, art gallery director; b. Paterson, N.J., Sept. 8, 1944; d. John Edward and Nora (Niland) Gleason; m. Robert Einreinhofer, Nov. 26, 1966; 1 child, Robert. BA in Art, William Paterson Coll., 1976, BA in English, 1977, MA in Visual Arts, 1978; cert. in supervisory mgmt., Rutgers U., 1986; PhD in Mus. Studies, Leicester U., England, 1993. Art critic N.J. News, 1973-76; gallery curator O.K. Harris Works of Art, N.Y.C., 1978; dir. gallery William Paterson U., Wayne, N.J., 1979—. Bd. dirs. Mus. Council of N.J., 1984—; cons. Sussex County Arts Council, N.J., 1987. Author: The American Art Museum: Elitism and Democracy, 1997; contbr. articles to profl. jours. Recipient grant Nat. Endowment for Arts, 1979, NEH, 1984-85, 87-88, N.J State Ccouncil Arts, 1984-85, 85-86, 87-88, 2000—. Mem. Am. Assn. Mus., Internat. Council Mus., Mid Atlantic Assn. Mus., Assn. Coll. and U. Mus. Galleries, Mus. Council of N.J. (exec. bd. 1984-88). Home: 1 Cheyenne Trl Sparta NJ 07871-2924 Office: William Paterson U Ben Shahn Galleries Wayne NJ 07470 Office Phone: 973-720-2654. E-mail: EinreinhoferN@WPUNJ.edu.

EISCHEN, MICHELLE ROBIN, art educator; b. Chgo., Feb. 8, 1972; d. Robert Charles Heinz and Sadie Alice Husko; m. James Patrick Eischen, June 2, 2000. BFA, Sch. Art U. Chgo., Chgo., 1999; MFA, U. S.D., Vermillion, SD, 2004. Vis. prof. S.D. State U., Brookings, SD, 2004—. One-woman shows include Wash. Pavilion Visual Art Mus., 2005, exhibitions include Ritz Gallery, 2006. Mem.: Coll. Art Assn. Democrat. Office: SD State U Visual Arts Dept 106F Grove Hall Brookings SD Business E-Mail: michelle.eischen@sdstate.edu.

EISEL, JEAN ELLEN, educational association administrator; b. Columbus, Ohio, July 18, 1946; d. Joseph Adam and viola Marie (Heintz) E. BA, Coll. St. Francis, 1968; MEd, Boston Coll., 1969. Asst. dir. placement Boston Coll., Chestnut Hill, Mass., 1968-69; dir. counseling and placement Coll. St. Francis, Joliet, Ill., 1970-72; asst. to v.p. student affairs Wittenburg U., Springfield, Ohio, 1972-74, dir. career svcs., 1974-76; asst. dean career svcs. Ohio State U., Columbus, 1976-84; dir. career svcs. Ariz. State U., Tempe, 1984; dir., master's prog. in career mgmt. Fuqua Sch. Bus., Duke U., NC, 2003—; asst. dean corp. and career programs, Sch. Bus. Dominican U., 2004—. Bd. trustees Coll. Placement Coun. Found, Bethlehem, Pa., 1987—, Big Bros./Big Sisters, Tempe, 1990—. Contbr. articles to profl. jours. Chairperson Columbus Area Careers Conf., 1977-79. Mem. Rocky Mt. Coll. Placement Assn. (sec., 1987-89), Midwest Coll. Placement Assn. (v.p. colls., 1980-81), Western Coll. Placement Assn. (regional coord., 1986), Ohio Coopp Ednl. Assn. (exec. com., 1983-84), Tempe C. of C. (com. mem., 1990—). Avocations: sports, theater, travel. Office: Asst Dean-Sch Bus Dominican Univ 7900 W Division St River Forest IL 60305

EISEN, LIZABETHANN R., lawyer; b. Portland, Oreg., June 14, 1972; m. Scott G. Eisen, Sept. 6, 1998. BA magna cum laude, Cornell Univ., 1994; JD, Univ. Pa., 1997. Bar: NY 1998. Assoc. Cravath Swaine & Moore LLP, NYC, 1997—2005, ptnr., corp., 2005—. Contbr. articles to profl. jours. Mem. coun. The Fresh Air Fund. Mem.: ABA, Assn. Bar City N.Y., Woodmont Country Club, Multnomah Athletic Club. Office: Cravath Swaine & Moore LLP Worldwide Plz 825 Eighth Ave New York NY 10019-7475 Office Phone: 212-474-1930. Office Fax: 212-474-3700. Business E-Mail: leisen@cravath.com.

EISEN, MARLENE RUTH, psychologist, educator; b. Chgo., Nov. 23, 1931; d. William and Sophia Maria (Brounwine) Friedlander; m. Lee B. Andalman, Aug. 2, 1963 (dec. July 1974); children: Martin, Dan, Robert; m. Sydney B. Eisen, June 6, 1979. Student, U. Wis., 1948-51; BA, Roosevelt U., Chgo., 1952; MA, U. Chgo., 1967, PhD, 1977. Tchr. Ravinia Nursery Sch., Highland Park, Ill., 1952-56; nursery sch. tchr. Country Schs., North Hollywood, Calif., 1958-61; kindergarten tchr. Sch. Dist. #65, Evanston, Ill., 1962-73; coord. early childhood program U. Chgo., 1974-75; coord. early childhood program, assoc. prof. Harper Coll., Palatine, Ill., 1976-84; pvt. practice cons. ednl. programs Evanston, 1972-86; assoc. faculty Ill. Sch. Profl. Psychology, Chgo., 1982—; pvt. practice psychotherapy Chgo., 1977—; mem. faculty tchr. edn. program Inst. Psychoanalysis, Chgo., 1984-95. Cons. Evanston Sch. Dist. #65, 1967; presenter papers and workshops at various confs., univs., community ctrs., parents groups, ednl. groups and profl. orgns. Contbr. articles to profl. jours. Fellow APA; mem. Soc. Clin. and Exptl. Hypnosis, Am. Soc. Clin. Hypnosis. Avocations: scuba diving, photography, travel, writing. Office: 1604 Chicago Ave Evanston IL 60201

EISENBERG, BARBARA ANNE K., lawyer; b. NYC, Oct. 7, 1945; d. Jerome Comet and Joy Klein; m. Edward Eisenberg, Oct. 20, 1974; 1 child. BA with distinction, Barnard Coll., 1967; JD cum laude, Columbia U., 1970. Bar: NY. Assoc. Kaye, Scholer, Fierman, Hays & Handler, 1970—75; v.p., gen. counsel, corp. sec. Pantasote Inc., Greenwich, Conn., 1978—86; asst. gen. counsel Burlington Industries, Inc., NYC, 1986-88, v.p., assoc. gen. counsel, asst. sec., 1988-93, v.p., assoc. gen. counsel, corp. sec., 1993—98; sr. v.p., gen. counsel, corp. sec. J. Crew Group, Inc., 1998—2001; sr. v.p., gen. counsel, sec. Ann Taylor Stores Corp., NYC, 2001—05, exec. v.p., gen. counsel, corp. sec., 2005—. Pres. Columbia Law Sch. Assn., 2000—02; mem. bd. visitors Columbia Law Sch., 2002—, bd. dirs., Maidenform Brands, 2005—; first v.p. Columbia Law Sch. Assn., 1998—2000; mem. Info. Tech. Law Commn., 2000—01. Mem. ABA, Assn. of Bar of City of N.Y., Corp. Bar Assn. (bd. dirs. 1986-88, vice chmn. SEC-fin. com. 1984-85, chmn. 1985-86), Am. Soc. Corr. Secs. Office: Ann Taylor Stores Corp 7 Times Sq New York NY 10036 Office Phone: 212-536-4229. Office Fax: 212-536-4412. Business E-Mail: barbara_eisenberg@anntaylor.com.

EISENBERG, CAROLA, psychiatrist, educator; b. Buenos Aires, Sept. 15, 1917; came to U.S., 1945; d. Bernardo and Teodora (Kahan) Blitzman; m. Manfred Guttmacher, Oct. 11, 1946 (dec. 1966); m. Leon Eisenberg, Aug. 31, 1967; children: Laurence, Alan. M of Social Work, Liceo de Senoritas; MD, U. Buenos Aires, 1945. Resident in psychiatry U. Md., 1946-48; fellow in child psychiatry Johns Hopkins Hosp., 1948-50, asst. prof. psychiatry and pediatrics Balt., 1960-67; psychiatrist MIT, Boston, 1967-72, dean of students, 1972-78; dean student affairs Harvard Med. Sch., Boston, 1978-90, dir. internat. programs for students, 1990-92, lectr. psychiatry, 1970-92, lectr. social medicine, 1992—; hon. psychiatrist Mass. Gen. Hosp., Boston, 2005. Co-chmn. women in biomed. careers workshop Office on Women's Health, NIH, 1992, mem. adv. com. on rsch. and women's health, 1995-98; mem. com. on human rights ACP; mem. com. on women in sci. and engring. NAS, 1992-95. V.p. Physicians for Human Rights, Boston, 1987-. Recipient Morani Renaissance Woman award, Found. for History of Women in Medicine, 2003. Fellow Am. Psychiat. Assn. (Disting. life fellow 2003, mem. Coun. Internat. Affairs, com. on human rights, Human Rights award 2005), Am. Orthopsychiat. Assn. (life); mem. AAUP. Avocations: travel, music, reading. Home and Office: 9 Clement Cir Cambridge MA 02138-2205 Office Phone: 617-868-0112. Business E-Mail: carola_eisenberg@hms.harvard.edu.

EISENBERG, DOROTHY, federal judge; b. 1929; LLB, Bklyn. Law Sch., 1950. Bar: N.Y. 1951, U.S. Dist. Ct. (ea. and so. dists.) N.Y., U.S. Ct. Appeals (2nd cir.), U.S. Supreme Ct. Assoc. Otterbourg, Stiendler, Houston & Rosen, N.Y.C., 1950-51, Goldman, Horowitz & Cherno, Mineola, NY, 1970-80; pvt. practice Garden City, NY, 1981; ptnr. Shaw, Licitra, Eisenberg, Esernio & Schwartz, P.C., Garden City, 1981-89; bankruptcy judge ea. dist. U.S. Bankruptcy Ct., NY, 1989—. Mem. Com. on Character and Fitness, Appellate divsn., 2nd Dept., 1983-89; panel trustee U.S. Bankruptcy Ct. (so. dist.) N.Y., 1979-89, U.S. Bankruptcy Ct. (ea. dist.) N.Y., 1975-89. Fellow: Am. Bar Found.; mem.: ABA, Fed. Bar Coun. (mem. adv. coun. 2nd cir.), Nassau Suffolk Women's Bar Assn. (former pres.), Bar Assn. Nassau County, Am. Bankruptcy Inst., N.Y. State Women's Bar Assn. (Nassau County chpt.), Nat. Assn. Women Judges. Office: LI Fed Courthouse 290 Federal Plz PO Box 9013 Central Islip NY 11722-4437

EISENBERG, KAREN SUE BYER, nurse; b. Bklyn., Mar. 11, 1954; d. Marvin and Florence (Beck) Byer; m. Howard Eisenberg, May 11, 1974; children: Carly Beth, Mariel Bryn. Diploma, L.I. Coll. Hosp. Sch. Nursing, 1973; BS in Nursing, L.I. U., 1976, M in Profl. Studies, 1977. Nurse recovery room and surg. ICU Downstate Med. Ctr., Bklyn., 1973-75; utilization rev. analyst Bezallel Health Related Facility, Far Rockaway, N.Y., 1975-76; utilization rev. analyst, RN supr. Seagirt Health Related Facility, Far Rockaway, 1976; staff nurse neurosurg. and rehab. nursing Downstate Med. Ctr., Bklyn., 1978, nurse ICU, 1978-79; asst. nursing dir. pathology, clin. rsch. assoc. Rsch. Found., Bklyn., 1979-90; instrl. support specialist pathology SUNY Health Sci Ctr., Bklyn., 1990-92; nurse practitioner pathology SUNY Rsch. Found., Bklyn., 1992-95; nurse rsch. coord. trauma surgery SUNY Health Sci. Ctr./Kings County Hosp. Ctr., Bklyn., 1995—. Clin. rsch. assoc. dept. urology SUNY Health Sci. Ctr., Bklyn., 2001—. Contbr. articles to profl. jours. Mem.: ANA, NY State Nurses Assn., L.I. Coll. Hosp. Alumnae Assn. Office: 450 Clarkson Ave Brooklyn NY 11203 Office Phone: 718-270-3121. E-mail: karenb.eisenberg@verizon.net.

EISENBERG, PATRICIA LEE, medical/surgical nurse; b. Benton, Ky., Aug. 25, 1952; d. James and Katherine (Bolton) Goodman; m. Paul Eisenberg, Apr. 24, 1982; 1 child, Jamie. BSN, Murray (Ky.) State U., 1974; MSN, St. Louis U., 1981. RN; cert. med.-surg. clin. specialist. Charge nurse Mayfield (Ky.) Community Hosp., 1974-75; staff nurse surg. step-down unit Med. U. S.C., Charleston, 1975; charge nurse ICU North Trident Hosp., Charleston; staff nurse ICU VA Hosp., Memphis, 1977-79, staff nurse surg. ICU St. Louis, 1979; staff nurse ICU various hosps., St. Louis, 1979-80; clin. nurse specialist surgery Jewish Hosp. at Washington U., St. Louis, 1981-88, nutritional support clin. nurse specialist, 1989-98; clin. nurse specialist Community Hosp., Indpls., 1998—. Cons. Resource Applications/Mosby Year Book, Inc., 1991-98; cons. Am. Healthcare Inst., Silver Spring, Md., 1990, Sheryl A. Fuetz, Atty., Kansas City, Mo., 1984-86; cons. enteral products Argyle div. Sherwood Med., St. Louis, 1984-2000; clin. faculty Sch. Nursing U. Mo., 1989-93; adj. clin. instr. Grad. Sch. Nursing, St. Louis U., 1982-88; advisor Ross Labs., 1989; adj. grad. faculty Ind. U. Sch. Nursing; contr. NCLEX-RN Exam. Nat. Coun. State Bds. of Nursing, Inc., 1998; adj. grad. faculty Ind. U. Sch. Nursing; speaker in field. Reviewer Concept Media, Inc., 1989-90; reviewer, editor Clin. Specialist Jour., 1986—, Nutrition, 1988, Intravenous Nurses Soc., 1999-; contbr. articles to profl. jours. Vol. Ladue Jr. High Sch., 1987-89, Coun. Girl Scouts, St. Louis, 1984-86, March of Dimes, 1984-85; active children and youth com. Jewish Community Ctr. Assn., 1983-85, Family Fair West County Shopping Ctr., 1984; coord. St. Louis Model Health Fair ARC, 1984, 83, Emerson Electric Health Fair, 1984. Capt. USAR, 1981-87. Recipient Mo. Tribute to Nursing Rsch. award, 1991, Jewish Hosp. Nursing Rsch. award, 1995, Commitment to Evidence-Based Practice Nursing Excellence award, 2003, Comm. Health Network. Mem. ANA (coun. clin. nurse specialist, program planning com. 3d dist. 1984-85, hostess state bd. nursing test 1984, proctor state bd. nursing 1984), Mo. Nurses Assn. (chmn. awards com. 1986-88, dir.-at-large 1988-90, achievement in clin. practice award 1987), Am. Soc. Parenteral and Enteral Nutrition (nat. nurses com. 1986, 87, nursing rep. pub. policy com. 1987-89, nursing rep. 2005-2006), Am. Heart Assn. Coun. Cardiovascular Nursing, Midwest Nursing Rsch. Soc., St. Louis Nursing Rsch. Consortium, Am. Nurses Credentialing Ctr., Clin. Specialist in Med. Surgical Nursing Content Expert Panel, Commn. on Collegiate Nursing Edn., Bd. of Commr. Practicing Nurses Rep., Am. Soc. of Parenteral and Enteral Nutrition Publication Review Bd. (mem. abstract rev. com. 2005-). Personal E-mail: peisenberg@attglobal.net.

EISENBERG, PHYLLIS ROSE, author; b. Chgo., June 26, 1924; d. Lewis Rose and Frances (Remer) Rose Blossom; m. Emanuel M. Eisenberg; 1 child, Bart. BA, UCLA, 1946. Writing instr. L.A. Valley Coll., Van Nuys, Calif., 1975-78, L.A. Pierce Coll., Woodland Hills, Calif., 1983-85, UCLA, 1986; jour. writing instr. Everywoman's Village, Van Nuys, 1987-92; writing instr. Calif. State U., Northridge, 1996—; instr. L.A. Valley Coll., 2003—. Lit. cons., 1975—; instr. writing L.A. Valley Coll., Van Nuys, Calif., 2002-04; presenter in field. Author: A Mitzvah Is Something Special, 1978 (one of 12 outstanding works of fiction of yr. Yearbook Ency. 1979), Don't Tell Me A Ghost Story, 1982 (All Choice Book Internat. Children's Exhbn., Munich 1983), You're My Nikki (NCSS-CBC Notable 1992 Children's Trade Book award, Children's Book of Yr. Bank St. Coll.); contbr. fiction, poetry and non-fiction to numerous newspapers and periodicals; creator Author in the Classroom program, 1986-88. Exec. sec. Founder's Guild of San Fernando Valley Child Guidance Clinic, Studio City, Calif., 1985; writing instr. Sophia Myers Sch. for Visually Handicapped, Van Nuys, 1987; reading instr. remedial program for children YMCA, Van Nuys, 1990; exec. sec. Valley Jewish Cmty. Ctr., North Hollywood, Calif., 1982. Mem. PEN, Soc. Children's Book Writers and Illustrators, Soc. Children's and Young People's Literature. Avocations: folk dancing, textile painting, yoga.

EISENBERG, ROBIN LEDGIN, religious education administrator; b. Passaic, N.J., Jan. 10, 1951; d. Morris and Ruth (Miller) Ledgin. BS, West Chester State U., 1973; M Edn., Kutztown State U., 1977. Administrv. asst. Keneseth Israel, Allentown, Pa., 1973-77; dir. edn. Cong. Schaarai Zedek, Tampa, Fla., 1977-79, Kehilath Israel, Pacific Palisades, Calif., 1979-80, Temple Beth El, Boca Raton, Fla., 1980-99, 2003—, Levis Jewish Cmty. Cen., Boca Raton, 1999—2003. Contbr. Learning Together, 1987, Bar/Bat Mizvah Education: A Sourcebook, 1993, The New Jewish Teachers Handbook, 1994. Chmn. edn. info. Planned Parenthood, Boca Raton Fla. 1989; v.p. for membership Coalition for Advancement of Jewish Edn, 2005- Recipient Kamiker Camp award Nat. Assn. Temple Educators, Pres.'s award for adminstrn., 1990; Mandel fellow in Jewish Edn., Levis Jewish Cmty. Ctr., 2001-2003. Mem. Nat. Assn. Temple Educators (pres. 1990-92, chair UAHC-CCAR-NATE commn. on Jewish edn. 1997-99, accreditation chair 2000—), Coalition Advancement of Jewish Edn. (chair strategic planning com. 2003—, v.p. membership 2005-), Assn. Jewish Ctr. Profls. (Profl. of Yr. award 2003). Avocation: photography. Home: 2428 NW 35th St Boca Raton FL 33431 Office: Temple Beth El 333 SW 4th Ave Boca Raton FL 33432 Office Phone: 561-391-9092. Personal E-mail: robledeise@aol.com. Business E-Mail: reisenberg@bocatemplebethel.org.

EISENBERG, SONJA MIRIAM, artist; b. Berlin, June 10, 1926; arrived in U.S., 1938, naturalized, 1947; d. Adolf and Meta Cecilie (Bettauer) Weinberger; m. Jack Eisenberg, Mar. 31, 1946; children: Ralph, Lynn, Lauren. Student, Queens Coll., Flushing, 1943—46, Middlebury Coll., Vt., 1945, NYU, 1952—54, BA, 1954; postgrad., Nat. Acad. Sch. Fine Arts, 1961. Artist-in-residence Cathedral of St. John the Divine, NYC; apptd. art dir. Hermes Media B.V., Amsterdam, 1992. One-woman shows include Bodley Gallery, N.Y.C., 1970, 1973, 1975, 1980, Galerie Art du Monde, Paris, 1973, Buyways Gallery, Sarasota, Fla., 1973—75, 1978, Galerie de Sfinx, Amsterdam, Netherlands, 1974, Huntsville (Ala.) Mus. Art, 1974, Anglo-Am. Art Mus., Baton Rouge, 1974, Comara Gallery, L.A., 1974, Palm Spring (Calif.) Desert Mus., 1975, Fordham U., N.Y.C., 1976, Omega Inst., New Lebanon, NY, 1979, Am. Mus., Hayden Planetarium, N.Y.C., 1980, Avila Graphics, Ltd., 1981, YWCA, N.Y.C., 1981, Cathedral of St. John the Divine, 1983, 1985, The Millbrook Gallery, NY, 1989, 1994, Christopher Leonard Gallery, N.Y.C., 1993, Park Hotel, Vitznau, Switzerland, 1994, The Burgenstock (Switzerland) Hotels, 1995, Wainscott Gallery, NY, 1997, Galerie Dussmann, Kulturkaufhaus, Berlin, 1998, Horton Gallery, Phila., 2001, exhibited in group shows at Mus. Fine Arts, St. Petersburg, Fla., 1973, Am. Watercolor Soc., 107th, 108th Exhbn., 1974—75, Galerie Frederic Gollong, St. Paul de Vence, France, 1978, Betty Parson's Gallery, N.Y.C., 1981, Foster Harmon Galleries of Am. Art, Sarasota, Fla., 1988, Tokyo Met. Art Mus. 14th Internat. Art Friendship Exhbn., 1989, Galerie Herbert Leidel, Munich, Germany, 1991, Park Ave. Armory, N.Y.C., 1996, Akim-USA, 1996, Represented in permanent collections Archives Am. Art, Smithsonian Inst., Jewish Mus., N.Y.C., Fordham U. Mus., Palm Springs Desert Mus., Omega Inst., Cathedral of St. John the Divine; designer WFUNA cachet for UN Water Power Conf., 1977, UN Internat. Yr. of Disabled Persons, 1981, commd. commemorative painting Crystal Night for Telecom Telefon Karte, Munich, 1993, completed project Seeing the Gospel According to St. John (text and 41 paintings) for Cathedral of St. John, 1987; author: From Here to There and Back Again, 2001, Poems and Paintings, 2002, The Red Painted House, 2002. Regent Cathedral of St. John the Divine, 1990. Recipient Gold medal for artistic merit, Internat. Parliament for Safety and Peace, 1983, Palma D'Oro Europe, 1986. Mem.: Accademia Italia delle Arti e del Lavoro (Gold medal 1981). Home and Office: 1020 Park Ave New York NY 10028-0913 Personal E-mail: sonjaeisenberg@aol.com.

EISENBERG, SUE ANN, music educator; b. Fairfield, Conn., Apr. 7, 1957; d. Marshall and Eleanor Davis Eisenberg; m. John D. Abernathy (div.); m. Glenn Edward Smith, Nov. 25, 2005. BS in Comm., Boston U., 1979; BA in Music Edn. with distinction, George Mason U., Fairfax, Va., 2003, MA in Music Edn. magna cum laude, 2006. Cert. Orff-Schulwerk Levels I-III. Editl. asst. Adweek Mag., Chgo., 1979—83; promotion writer Family Cir., NYC, 1984—87; comm. mgr. BDO Seidman, NYC, 1987—89; promotion mgr. McCalls Mag., NYC, 1989—92; advt. sales exec. Golf for Women, NYC, 1992—94, Mid-Atlantic Media, Washington, 1995—97; gen. music tchr. Fairfax Pub. Schs., 2003—. Mem. Nova Manassas Symphony Orch., 2006. Named Club champion, TPC Golf Club. Mem.: Orff-Schulwerk Assn., Music Educators Nat. Conf. Democrat. Avocations: cello, spinning. Home: 6009 Saint Hubert Ln Centreville VA 20121 Office: Centreville Elem Sch Centreville VA 20121

EISENHARD, JENNIFER LYNN, elementary school educator; b. Allentown, Pa., Jan. 17, 1980; d. Gary Lee and Brenda Darlene Eisenhard. BA, Arcadia U., Glenside, Pa., 2003. Cert. tchr. Pa. Asst. Fox Chase Cancer Ctr. Daycare, Phila., 1999—2000; tchr. McNeil Daycare Ctr., Ft. Washington, Pa., 2000—02; tchr., counselor Northampton C.C., Bethlehem, Pa., 2001—02; case mgr. Big Bros. Big Sisters, Norristown, Pa., 2002; tchr. Sylvan Learning Ctr., Allentown, Pa., 2003—; permanent substitute Bethlehem (Pa.) Area Sch. Dist., 2003—. Substitute Whitehall (Pa.) Coplay Sch. Dist., 2003—04. Home: 3386 Highland Rd Orefield PA 18069

EISENHAUER, CHRISTINE MARIE, community health nurse, educator; b. Yankton, S.D., June 17, 1975; d. Michael Gerald Pinkelman and Janet Marie Kathol; m. Scott Richard Eisenhauer, July 20, 1973. BS, Mt. Marty Coll., Yankton, S.D., 1997; MSN, U. Nebr. Med. Ctr., Omaha, 2003. Cert. cmty. health clin.nurse specialist, ANCC, 2004. Charge nurse Good Samaritan Ctr., Bloomfield, Nebr., 1997—99; pub. health nurse Salvation Army, Omaha, 2000—02; home health / hospice nurse Avera Sacred Heart Hosp., Yankton, SD, 1999—; asst. prof. of nursing Mt. Marty Coll., Yankton, 2002—. Child passenger safety program coord. Mt. Marty Coll., 2003—04, Salvation Army, Omaha, 2001—02; lectr. in field. Contbr. articles to profl. jours. Assoc. Am. Cancer Soc. Coalition; health educator / janitor / ice cream social coord. vol. Lindy Good Sheperd Luth. Ch., Nebr., 1996—2006; adv. bd. Yankton Family Planning. Grantee Injury Prevention Project grantee, Bur. of Indian Affairs, 2001, Mt. Marty Lab. Improvement Project grantee, Benedictine Health Found., 2003, Yankton Cmty. Child Passenger Safety Project grantee, Wellmark Blue Cross Blue Shield, 2003—04, Pub. Health Nursing Project grantee, Nebr. Health Care Cash Fund, 2001—02, Injury Prevention Project grantee, Indian Health Svc.; Pub. Health Br., 2002. Mem.: Sigma Theta Tau (assoc.). Office: Mount Marty College 1105 W 8th Yankton SD 57078 Office Phone: 605-668-1523. Office Fax: 605-668-1607. E-mail: ceisenhauer@mtmc.edu.

EISENHAUER, LINDA ANN, volunteer; b. Logansport, Ind., Dec. 3, 1937; d. Donald Johnson and Isabel Owens (Murdock) Grube; m. Ronald George Eisenhauer, Aug. 12, 1961; 1 child, Donald Johnson. BS, Northwestern U., 1959. Tchr. Devonshire Sch., Skokie, Ill., 1959-61; tchr. 6th grade Atlanta Sch. Dist., 1961-62; tchr. 5th grade Marquette Sch., Gary, Ind., 1962-65. Elected adv. bd. Winfield Twp., Ind., 1987—, sec. adv. bd., pres. 1987—; vol. coun. bd. Am. Symphony Orch. League, Washington, 1975-82; pres. Calumet Parliamentary Unit, 1991-92; bd. dirs. Hospice of Calumet area, 1992—, Northwestern U. Alumnae, 1993—, Legacy Found. Grants, 1994—, Women's Assn. Chgo. Symphony Orchestra, 1999—; founder Greater Gary Heights Arts Coun. and Lake Area Arts Coun.; regional chmn. Indian Advocates for the Arts; bd. dirs. Am. Cancer Soc., chmn. breast cancer clinic. Named Outstanding Young Woman, Ind., 1967; recipient svc. award Northwestern U., 1993. Fellow AAUW (pres. Gary-Merrillville br. 1975-77); mem. N.W. Ind. Symphony (v.p. 1981-85, bd. dirs. 1968—), Women's Assn. N.W. Ind. Symphony (pres. 1972-74, bd. dirs. 1965—), Soc. 600 of Internat. Violin Competition (v.p. 1991, bd. dirs. 1988—), Northwestern U. Alumni Assn. (v.p. 1986-88), Northwestern Alumni Club N.W. Ind. (pres. 1976-96), Kappa Kappa Kappa (pres.), Alpha Chi Omega (pres. alumni chpt.). Republican. Episcopalian. Avocations: travel, golf, health. Address: 1736 Beachview Ct Crown Point IN 46307-9411

EISENSTADT, PAULINE DOREEN BAUMAN, brokerage house executive, state legislator; b. NYC, Dec. 31, 1938; d. Morris and Anne (Lautenberg) Bauman; m. Melvin M. Eisenstadt, Nov. 20, 1960; children: Todd Alan, Keith Mark. BA, U. Fla., 1960; MS, U. Ariz., 1965; postgrad., U. N.Mex. Tchr., Ariz., 1961—65, PR, 1972—73; adminstrv. asst. Inst. Social Rsch. U. N.Mex., 1973—74; founder, 1st exec. dir. Energy Consumers N.Mex., 1977—81; chmn. consumer affairs adv. com. Dept. Energy, 1979—80; v.p. tech. bd. Nat. Ctr. Appropriate Tech., 1980—; pres. Eisenstadt Enterprises, investments, 1983—; mem. N.Mex. Ho. of Reps., 1985—92, chairwoman majority caucus, chair rules com., 1987—, chair sub. com. on children and youth, 1987; mem. N.Mex. State Senate, 1996—2000; Dist. Atty. asst., 2000; mem. senate fin. com., com. higher edn., com. econ. devel., sci. & tech., water & natural resources, electric deregulation com., chair conservation co; mem. senate fin. com., com. higher edn., com. econ. devel., sci. & tech., water & natural resources, electric deregulation com., chair conservation com. Mem. exec. com., vice chair pvt. coun. Nat. Conf. State Legislators, 1987; vice chmn. Sandoval County (N.Mex.) Dem. Party, 1981—; mem. N.Mex. Dem. State Ctrl. Com., 1981—; N.Mex. del. Dem. Nat. Platform Com., 1984, Dem. Nat. Conv., 1984; mem. cmty. adv. bd. Intel Corp., 2004. Dir., host (TV program) Consumer Viewpoint, 1980—82, host N.Mex. Today and Tomorrow, 1992—, exec. prodr., host Tech Talks, 2001—; author: Corrales, Portrait of a Changing Village, 1980; painter (gallery and art show), 2005. Pres. Anti Defamation League, N.Mex., 1994—95; mem. N.Mex. First; pres. Sandoval

County Dem. Women's Assn., 1979—81; vice chmn. N.Mex. Dem. Platform Com., 1984—; mem. Sandoval County Redistricting Task Force, 1983—84, Rio Rancho Ednl. Study Com., 1984—. Named Outstanding Senator, N.Mex. Tech. Showcase, 2000; named to Miami Beach Sr. HS Hall of Fame, 2000; recipient Gov.'s award Outstanding N. Mex. Women, Commn. on the Status of Women and Gov. Bruce King, 1992; grantee, NSF, 1965. Mem.: Rio Rancho Rotary Club (pres. 1995—, Rotarian of Yr. 1995), Kiwanis (1st woman mem. local club). Home: PO Box 658 Corrales NM 87048-0658 E-mail: peisenstadt@aol.com.

EISENSTEIN, ELIZABETH LEWISOHN, historian, educator; b. N.Y.C., Oct. 11, 1923; d. Sam A. and Margaret V. (Seligman) Lewisohn; m. Julian Calvert Eisenstein, May 30, 1948; children: Margaret, John (dec.), Edward. AB, Vassar Coll., 1944; MA, Radcliffe Coll., 1947, PhD, 1953; LittD (hon.), Mt. Holyoke Coll., 1979; LHD (hon.), U. Mich., 2004. From lectr. to adj. prof history Am. U., Washington, 1959-74; Alice Freeman Palmer prof. history U. Mich., Ann Arbor, 1975-88, prof. emerita, 1988—. Scholar-in-residence Rockefeller Found. Ctr., Bellagio, Italy, June 1977; mem. vis. com. dept. history Harvard U., 1975-81, vice-chmn., 1979-81; dir. Ecole des Hautes Etudes en Sciences Sociales, Paris, 1982; guest spkr., participant confs. and seminars; I. Beam vis. prof. U. Iowa, 1980; Mead-Swing lectr. Oberlin Coll., 1980; Stone lectr. U. Glasgow, 1984; Van Leer lectr. Van Leer Fedn., Jerusalem, 1984; Hanes lectr. U. N.C., Chapel Hill, 1985 first resident cons. Ctr. for the Book, Libr. of Congress, Washington, 1979; mem. Coun. Scholars, 1980-88; pres.'s disting. visitor Vassar Coll., 1988; Pforzheimer lectr. N.Y. Pub. Libr., 1989, Lyell lectr. Bodleian Libr., Oxford, 1990, Merle Curti lectr. U. Wis., Madison, 1992, Jantz lectr. Oberlin Coll., 1995, Clifford lectr. Austin, Tex., 1996; vis. fellow Wolfson Coll., Oxford, 1990; sem. dir. Folger Inst., 1999. Author: The First Professional Revolutionist: F. M. Buonarroti, 1959, The Printing Press as an Agent of Change, 1979, 2 vols. paperback edit., 1980 (Phi Beta Kappa Ralph Waldo Emerson prize 1980), The Printing Revolution in Early Modern Europe, 1983 (reissued as Canto Book, 1993), 2d edit., 2005, Grub Street Abroad, 1992; mem. editorial bd. Jour. Modern History, 1973-76, 83-86, Revs. in European History, 1973-86, Jour. Library History, 1979-82, Eighteenth Century Studies, 1981-84; contbr. articles to profl. jours., chpts. to books. Bd. dirs. Folger Shakespeare Libr., 2000—. Belle Skinner fellow Vassar Coll., NEH fellow, 1977, Guggenheim fellow, 1982, fellow Ctr. Advanced Studies in Behavioral Scis., 1982-83, 92-93, Humanities Rsch. Ctr. fellow Australian Nat. U., 1988. Fellow Am. Acad. Arts and Scis., Royal Hist. Soc.; mem. Soc. French Hist. Studies (v.p. 1970, program com. 1974), Am. Soc. 18th Century Studies (nominating com. 1971), Soc. 16th Century Studies, Am. Hist. Assn. (com. on coms. 1970-72, chmn. Modern European sect. 1981, coun. 1982-85, Scholarly Distinction award 2003), Renaissance Soc. Am. (coun. 1973-76, pres. 1986), Am. Antiquarian Soc. (exec. com., adv. bd. 1984-87), Phi Beta Kappa. Office: U Mich Dept History Ann Arbor MI 48109 E-mail: eisenst@mindspring.com.

EISENSTEIN, LINDA, playwright, composer; d. Milan C. and Mildred Brenkus. MA, Cleve. State U., Ohio, 1994. Dir. of new plays Cleve. Pub. Theatre, 1985—94. Dir. of comm. Internat. Ctr. for Women Playwrights, 1996—98. Composer: (musical) Becoming George; composer: (co-author) Discordia (Ohio Arts Coun. Individual Artist Fellowship, 2003, 2004), Star Wares: The Next Generation (Ohio Arts Coun. Individual Artist Fellowship, 1990); author: (play) Three the Hard Way (Ohio Arts Coun. Individual Artist Fellowship, Gilmore Creek Playwriting Award, 1996); author: (composer) (play with music) Rehearsing Cyrano (finalist, Jane Chambers Playwriting Competition, 2001); author: (play) Marla's Devotion (All Eng. Theatre Festival Prize, 1997, All-England Theatre Festival Prize, 1996), The Names of the Beast (Sappho's Symposium Competition, 1996), A Rustle of Wings (West Coast Ten-Minute Play Contest, 2002, West Coast Ten-Minute Play Competition, 1999), Eisenstein's Monster; composer: (musical) A Soldier's Passion, Street Sense (Ohio Arts Coun. New Works Support, 1991), A Soldier's Passion; composer: (co-author) The Last Red Wagon Tent Show in the Land (finalist, No. Ohio Live Achievement Award, 1987, finalist, Midwest Playwrights' Competition). Mem.: ASCAP, Dramatists Guild of Am., Inc., Lit. Managers and Dramaturgs of the Americas (assoc.).

EISENSTEIN, TOBY K., microbiology professor; b. Phila., Sept. 15, 1942; d. Edward and Sylvia (Mandel) Karet; m. Bruce A. Eisenstein, Sept. 8, 1963; children: Eric, Andrew, Ilana. BA, Wellesley Coll., 1964; PhD, Bryn Mawr Coll., 1969. Instr. Med. Sch. Temple U., Phila., 1969-71, asst. prof., 1971-79, assoc. prof. microbiology and immunology Med. Sch., 1979-84, prof., 1984—, acting chair, 1990-92, co-dir. Ctr. Substance Abuse Rsch., 1992—. Mem. bacteriology and mycology study sect. NIH, 1976—80, 1988—92, mem. drugs abuse and AIDS study sect., 1994—2004. Contbr. articles to profl. jours. Recipient Lindback award, Temple U., 1986, Rsch. prize, 2003; NIH fellow, 1965—69, USPHS grantee, 1971—. Fellow: Am. Acad. Microbiology; mem.: AAAS, Coll. Problems Drug Dependence (bd. dirs. 2005—), Psychoneuroimmunology Rsch. Soc., Soc. Neuroimmune Pharmacology (Joseph Wybran award), Internat. Endotoxin and Innate Immunity Soc., Soc. Leukocyte Biology (sec. 1998—2000), Am. Assn. Immunologists, Am. Soc. Microbiology (pres. eastern Pa. br. 1983—86, mem. coun. policy com. 1993—96, chair membership bd. 2003—), Sigma Xi (pres. Temple U. chpt. 1981—83). Office: Temple U Sch Medicine Dept Microbiology and Immunology 3400 N Broad St Philadelphia PA 19140-5104 Office Phone: 215-707-3585. Business E-Mail: tke@temple.edu.

EISER, BARBARA J.A., management consultant; b. Newark; m. Arnold R. Eiser, June 15, 1975; 1 child. BA, Rutgers U., 1973; M in City Planning, Harvard U., 1975; MA in Orgnl. Psychology, Columbia U., 1996. V.p. Bankers Trust Co., N.Y.C., 1985-87; pres. Eiser Learning Sys., Inc., Great Neck, 1987—97; v.p., nat. tng. mgr. No. Trust Co., Chgo., 1998—2000; pres. Paradigm Cons., Inc., 2000—04, Leading Impact, Inc., 2004—. Faculty MBA program Lake Forset Grad. Sch. Mgmt., 2001—04; spkr. in field; presenter in field. Author: Power of Persuasion, 2006; contbr. articles to prof. jours. Bd. dirs. New Trier High Sch. Edn. Found. HUD fellow, 1973-74; EPA fellow, 1974-75. Mem.: Healthcare Bus. Womens Assn., Phila. Human Resource Planning Soc., Human Resources Assn. Chgo. (chair orgn. devel. com.), Harvard Club (Chgo., Long Island chpts. bd. dirs.). Avocations: travel, music, exercise. Home and Office: 1032 Great Springs Rd Bryn Mawr PA 19010 Office Phone: 610-520-0544. Personal E-mail: eiser@leading-impact.com.

EISLER, SUSAN KRAWETZ, advertising executive; b. NYC, Aug. 18, 1946; d. Aaron and Bertha (Platt) Krawetz; m. Howard Irwin Eisler, June 8, 1980; 1 stepchild, Robin Joy; 1 adopted child, Joseph. BA, U. Pitts., 1967; MA, New Sch. for Social Rsch., 1971. Analyst Marplan, Inc., N.Y.C., 1968-69; project dir. Market Facts, Inc., N.Y.C., 1969-70; assoc. rsch. mgr. Gen. Foods, Inc., White Plains, NY, 1970-75, product mgr., 1975-80; rsch. dir. Elizabeth Arden, N.Y.C., 1980-81; v.p., assoc. rsch. dir. Lintas: N.Y. (formerly SSC&B: Lintas Worldwide), N.Y.C., 1981-87, sr. v.p., assoc. rsch. dir., 1987-92, exec. v.p., dir. strategic planning and rsch., 1992-94, Gotham, Inc., 1995—, mng. ptnr., dir. rsch. and info. svcs. Named Woman of Yr., YWCA Acad. Women Achievers, 1989. Mem.: Advt. Rsch. Found. (copy rsch. coun.), Am. Mktg. Assn. Office: Gotham Inc 100 5th Ave Fl 16 New York NY 10011-6996

EISNER, CAROLE SWID, artist; b. N.Y.C., Oct. 30, 1937; d. David and Selma (Claar) Swid; m. Richard Alan Eisner, May 7, 1961; children: Joseph, Susan, Michael, Douglas, Hallie. AB, Syracuse U., 1958; studies with Schwabacher, N.Y.C., 1963; studies with Marge Walzer, Westport, Conn., 1969-78; postgrad., Internat. Sch. Photography, 1976-78. Solo shows include Silvermine (Conn.) Ctr. for Arts, 1977, 84, Lubin House Gallery, N.Y.C., 1979, 82, Segal Gallery, N.Y.C., 1984-85, 86, Jill Youngblood Gallery, L.A., 1985, Jack Gallery, N.Y.C., 1987, 88, First Women's Bank, N.Y.C., 1988, New Inst. of Contemporary Art, London, 1988, David Findlay Galleries, N.Y.C., 1990, Gallery Tanishima, Tokyo, 1992, Gallery Sagan, Tokyo, 1992; group shows include Segal Gallery, N.Y.C., 1985, 86, Guggenheim Mus., N.Y.C., 1986, Images Gallery, Norwalk, Conn., 1986, Jack Gallery, N.Y.C., 1987, Inst. of Contemporary Art, London, 1988, many others; represented in permanent collections at Guggenheim Mus., Syracuse U., Nat. Assocs., Inc., S.E. Banking Corp., Northstar Reins. Co., Knoll Internat., FMC Corp., Skadden, Arps, Meager & Flom, Orion Bank, Ltd., Goldmark Ptnrs., Inc., MBS Multi Mode, Inc., Bill Silver Assocs.; sculptures exhibited at The River Park Atrium, Norwalk, Conn., 1997-98, Chesterwood, Stockbridge, Mass., 1998, Burlington County Coll. Sculpture Garden, Pemberton, N.J., 1998, Veterans Park, Norwalk, 1999, Peninsula Park, Jersey City, 1999, Cranbury Park, Norwalk, 1999, City Hall, Norwalk, 1998-99, Fordham U., 2000, Lock Bldg., Norwalk, 2001, Heritage Park, Norwalk, 2002, Silvermine Guild, Norwalk; created stage design for four Off-Broadway plays at Theater XII, 1978. Recipient Award for Sculpture Merchants Bank and Trust Co., 1975, Champion Internat. Corp., 1980, Rosenthal Award for Outdoor Sculpture, 1978; named among ten outstanding young women Mademoiselle Mag., 1962; finalist Nat. Sculpture Competition, 1980. Home and Office: 1107 5th Ave New York NY 10128-0145 Fax: 212-828-4415.

EISNER, DIANA, pediatrician; b. Houston, May 7, 1951; d. Elmer and Edith (Dubow) E. BA in Biology cum laude, Brandeis U., 1973; MD, Southwestern Med. Sch., 1977. Diplomate Am. Bd. Pediat. Intern, resident Baylor Coll. Medicine, Houston, 1977-80; pvt. practice Houston, 1981—. Chmn. dept. pediat. Meml. N.W. Hosp., Houston, 1990. Recipient Commendation award Children's Protection Com. Tex. Children's Hosp., 1978, Physician's Recognition award AMA, 1983. Mem. Am. Acad. Pediatrics, Tex. Med. Assn., Tex. Pediatric Soc., Houston Pediatric Soc. (treas. 2001-02, sec. 2002-), Harris County Med. Soc. Avocations: ballet, swimming, walking. Office: 2030 North Loop W Ste 125 Houston TX 77018-8132 Office Phone: 713-688-8393. Personal E-mail: dr.diana@sbcglobal.net.

EISNER, EDITH C., adult education educator; b. NYC, Jan. 26, 1925; d. Harry J. and Irenè N. Chelimer; m. Robert Eisner, June 30, 1946 (dec.); children: Mary Eisner Eccles, Emily. BA summa cum laude, Duke U., 1946; MA, Columbia U., 1947. Instr. English U. Md., College Park, 1948—49; tchr., adminstr. Roycemore Sch., Evanston, Ill., 1956—85; docent Block Mus. Art, Northwestern U., Evanston, 1989—. Co-adminstr. Robert Eisner Fellowship Econs. Northwestern U., Evanston; trustee Roycemore Sch., Evanston, 1988—, sponsor Robert Eisner Scholarship; trustee Robert Eisner Trust; benefactor, mem. Dir.'s Cir. Block Mus. Art Northwestern U., Evanston. Mem.: Phi Beta Kappa. Office Phone: 847-869-8557.

EISNER, GAIL ANN, artist, educator; b. Detroit, Oct. 17, 1939; d. Rudolph and Florence (White) Leon; m. Marvin Michael Eisner, June 14, 1959 (dec. Feb. 1993); 1 child, Alan. Student, Art Student League of N.Y.; BFA, Wayne State U. Alan prof. Pace U., NYC; artist-in-residence Farmington Area Arts Commn., Farmington Hills, Mich., 2005—. One-woman shows include The Starkweather Art Cultural Ctr., Romeo, Mich., Shiawassee Arts Ctr., Owosso, Mich., Worthington Art Ctr., Ohio, OK Harris/David Klein Gallery, Birmingham, Mich., Sinclair Coll., LRC Gallery, Dayton, Ohio, U. Mich. Hosps., Ann Arbor, Collin County Coll., Plano, Tex., 1997, Art Ctr. Mt. Clemens, one-woman shows include The City Gallery William Costick Ctr., Farmington Hills, Mich., numerous group shows including most recently, exhibited in group shows at The Art Collector, San Diego, Gwenda Jay Gallery, Chgo., Columbia Greens Coll., Hudson, N.Y., Worthington (Ohio) Art Ctr., Holland Area Arts Coun., Mich., The Art Source, Santa Barbara, Calif., Outside The Line Gallery, Grosse Ile, Mich., Art in the City Halls, Farmington, Farmington Hills, Represented in permanent collections Rabobank, Chgo., Resurrection Hosp., Kanai (Hawaii) Hotel, Jules Joyner Designs, Royal Oak, Mich., The Lumber Store, Chgo., others, also pvt. collections. Recipient Adriana Zahn award Pastel Soc. Am., Heckscher Mus. award, Our Visions: Women in Art award Oakland C.C., 1995, Beatrice G. Epstein meml. award, 1997. Mem. Nat. Assn. Women Artists (Sara Winston Meml. award 1992), N.Y. Artist Equity Assn., Art Student League N.Y. (Sidney Dickinson Meml. award), Birmingham Bloomfield Art Assn. Studio: Ste 108 27600 Farmington Rd Farmington Hills MI 48334-3365 Office Phone: 248-848-9050. Personal E-mail: artstudiofarmington@hotmail.com.

EISNER, REBECCA SUZANNE, lawyer; b. Wheeling, W.Va., Aug. 27, 1962; d. Paul and Marilyn June (Muffeny) Redosh; m. Craig George Eisner, Dec. 30, 1988. BA, Ohio State U., 1984; JD, U. Mich., 1989. Bar: Ill. 1989, Ga. 1993. Pub. rels. and govt. affairs specialist The Dow Chemical Co., Midland, Mich., 1984—86; assoc. Mayer, Brown, Rowe & Maw LLP, Chgo., 1989-92, ptnr., 1996—; assoc. group counsel, asst. v.p. Equifax, Inc., Atlanta, 1993—95. Exec. vol. United Way of Metro Atlanta, 1994; vol. fund raiser Atlanta Women's Fund, 1994. Mem. ABA. Avocations: running, golf. Office: Mayer, Brown, Rowe & Maw LLP 190 S Salle St Chicago IL 60603-3441 Office Phone: 312-701-8577. Office Fax: 312-706-8131. E-mail: reisner@mayerbrownrowe.com.

EIZENBERG, JULIE, architect; BArch, U. Melbourne, Australia, 1978; MArch II, UCLA, 1981. Lic. architect, Calif., reg. architect, Australia. Principal, architect Koning Eizenberg Architecture, Santa Monica, Calif., 1981—. Instr. various courses UCLA, MIT, Harvard U.; lectr. in field; jury member P/A awards. Exhbns. incl. Koning Eizenberg Architecture 3A Garage, San Francisco, 1996, "House Rules" Wexner Ctr., 1994, "The Architect's Dream: Houses for the Next Millenium" The Contemporary Arts Ctr., 1993, "Angels & Franciscans" Gagosian Gallery, 1992, Santa Monica Mus. Art, 1993, "Broadening the Discourse" Calif. Women in Environmental Design, 1992, "Conceptional Drawings by Architects" Bannatyne Gallery, 1991, Exhbn. Koning Eizenberg Projects Grad. Sch. Architecture & Urban Planning UCLA, 1990; prin. works include Digital Domain Renovation and Screening Room, Santa Monica, Lightstorm Entertainment Office Renovation and Screening Room, Santa Monica, Gilmore Bank Addition and Remodel, L.A., 1548-1550 Studios, Santa Monica, (with RTA) Materials Rsch. Lab. at U. Calif., Santa Barbara, Ken Edwards Ctr. Cmty. Svcs., Santa Monica, Peck Park Cmty. Ctr. Gymnasium, San Pedro, Calif., Sepulveda Recreation Ctr., L.A. (Design award AIA San Fernando Valley 1995, Nat. Concrete and Masonry award 1996, AIA Calif. Coun. Honor award 1996, L.A. Bus. Coun. Beautification award 1996, AIA Los Angeles Chpt. Merit Award, 1997), PS # 1 Elem. Sch., Santa Monica, Farmers Market, L.A. Additions and Master Plan (Westside Urban Forum prize 1991), Stage Deli, L.A., Simone Hotel, L.A. (Nat. Honor award AIA 1994), Boyd Hotel, L.A., Cmty. Corp. Santa Monica Housing Projects, 5th St. Family Housing, Santa Monica, St. John's Hosp. Replacement Housing Program, Santa Monica, Liffman Ho., Santa Monica, (with Glenn Erikson) Electric Artblock, Venice (Beautification award L.A. Bus. Coun. 1993), 6th St. Condominiums, Santa Monica, Hollywood Duplex, Hollywood Hills (Record Houses Archtl. Record 1988), California Ave. Duplex, Santa Monica, Tarzana Ho. (Award of Merit L.A. chpt. AIA 1992, AIA Calif. Coun. Merit Award, 1998, Sunset Western home Awards citation 1993-94), 909 Ho., Santa Monica (Award of Merit L.A. chpt. AIA 1991), 31st St. Ho., Santa Monica (Honor award AIACC 1994, Nat. AIA Honor award 1996), others. Recipient 1st award Progressive Architecture, 1987; named one of Domino's Top 30 Architects, 1989. Mem. L.A. County Mus. Art, Westside Urban Forum, Urban Land Inst., Architects and Designers for Social Responsibility, Mus. Contemporary Art, The Nature Conservancy, Sierra Club. Office: Koning Eizenberg Architecture 1454 25th St Santa Monica CA 90404-3008

EKANGER, KARIN L., educational consultant; b. Boise, Idaho, Apr. 8, 1954; d. Bernard Olaf and Mary Louise E.; m. Mitchell Durand, June 3, 1978 (div. Oct., 1980). BA in English with honors, U. Mont., 1976; MEd, Mont. State U., 1983; adminstrv. endorsement, U. Nev. Las Vegas, 1993—98; EdD, Nova Southeastern U., 2003. Cert. K-12 reading splst., 7-12 English, K-12 adminstr. Reading lab tchr. Powell County High Sch., Deer Lodge, Mont., 1976-77; reading lab tutor, substitute tchr. Billings (Mont.) Sch. Dist. # 2, 1977-78; tchr. remedial reading, English Lincoln Jr. High Sch., 1978-79; lang. arts tchr. Castle Rock Jr. High Sch., 1979-84; reading improvement splst. George Dewey High Sch. U.S. Dept. Def. Dependents Schs., Subic Bay, Philippines, 1984-87; reading improvement splst. Grafenwoehr Am. Ele. Sch. Grafenwoehr, Germany, 1987-88; tchr. reading, English Vilseck (Germany) Am. High Sch., 1988-89; reading tchr. Joe Walker Middle Sch. Westside Union Sch. Dist., Lancaster, Calif., 1989-90; tchr. English Highland High Sch. Antelope Valley High Sch. Dist., Palmdale, Calif., 1990-92; reading tchr. J.D. Smith Middle Sch. Clark County Sch. Dist., Las Vegas, 1993-96; tchr. English Las Vegas Acad. Internat. Studies, Performing and Visual Art, 1996-97; tchr. on spl. assignment, 1996—97; tchr. on spl. assignment sys. design, staff devel., 1997; dean of students Valley High Sch., 1998—; adminstr. on spl. assignment Adminstrv. Tng. Dept., 2000—; secondary cons. Pearson Learning Group, Henderson, Nev., 2001—. Summer sch. dean intern Bonanza High Sch., 1997; grant writer; presenter in field; attendee numerous confs. Recipient Cert. Appreciation ARC, 1986-87, Achievement award DoDDS, 1987. Mem. Nat. Coun. Tchrs. English, Internat. Reading Assn., Nev. Assn. Sch. Adminstrs., Clark County Assn. Secondary Sch. Prins., So. Nev. Coun. Tchrs. English and Lang. Arts (exec. bd. dirs. 1997, planner, host Poetry Alive! performance 1997), Assn. Supervision and Curriculum Devel., Phi Delta Kappa. Home: 915 Royal Moon Ave Las Vegas NV 89123-0964

EKANGER, LAURIE, retired state official, consultant; b. Salt Lake City, Mar. 4, 1949; d. Bernard and Mary (Dearth) E.; m. William J. Shupe, Nov. 6, 1973; children: Ben, Robert. BA in English, U. Oreg., 1973. Various pos. Mont. State Employment & Tng. Divsn., Helena, 1975-80, dep. adminstr., 1980-82; adminstr. Mont. State Purchasing Divsn., Helena, 1982-85, Mont. State Personnel Divsn., Helena, 1985-93; labor commr. Mont. Dept. Labor and Ind., Helena, 1993-97; dir. Mont. Dept. Pub. Health and Human Svcs., 1997-2000; rsch., analysis and pers. mgmt. projects, 2000—. Council chair State Employee Group Benefits Coun., 1985-93; bd. dirs. Pub. Employee Retirement Bd., 1988; mem. various state adv. couns. health and human svcs. Home: 80 Pinecrest Rd Clancy MT 59634-9505

EKBATANI, GLAYOL, language educator, director, writer; b. Tehran, Iran; d. Saed and Parvin (Sohai) E. PhD, U. Ill., 1981. Dir., prof. English 2d lang. program U. Maine, Orano, 1987-90; dir. English 2d lang., bilingual programs C.C. Phila., 1990-92; dir., prof. English 2d lang. programs St. John's U., Jamaica, N.Y., 1992—. Rschr. Georgetown U., Washington, 1986-87. Author: Learner Directed Assessment, 1999; contbr. articles to profl. jours. Mem. Nat. Assn. Fgn. Students Washington, Tchrs. English to Spkrs. of Other Langs. (pres. 1991-92). Home: 301 E 79th St Apt 16 New York NY 10021-0951 Office: St John's U 8000 Utopia Pkwy Rm 377 Jamaica NY 11432-1343 Office Phone: 718-990-6097.

ELAM, ELIZABETH L.R., finance educator; b. NY; d. Houston G. and Janet B. Elam; m. Matthew R. E. Romoser; children: Geoffrey Elam Romoser, Katherine Gold Romoser. BS, U. Mass., 1986; MBA, U. Colo., 1988; PhD, U. Wis., 1997. Assoc. prof. mktg. Western New Eng. Coll., Springfield, Mass., 1998—; asst. prof. bus. adminstrn. St. Francis Coll., Fort Wayne, Ind.; asst. prof. mktg. Baruch Coll., N.Y.C. Elder Madison Ave. Presbyn. Ch., N.Y.C., 1994; choir/com. mem. First Congl. Ch., South Hadley, Mass., 1998—. Mem.: Beta Gamma Sigma. Office: Western New England Coll 1215 Wilbraham Rd Springfield MA 01119 Office Phone: 413-782-1391.

ELBERY, KATHLEEN MARIE, lawyer, accountant, cartoonist; b. Boston, Nov. 30, 1959; d. Norman F. and June E. (Ramsay) E. BSBA with high honors, Northeastern U., 1983; JD cum laude, Suffolk U., 1990. Bar: Mass. 1990, U.S. Ct. Appeals (1st cir.) Mass. 1991, U.S. Dist. Ct. Mass. 1991; CPA, Mass, 1986. CPA, supr. Gately & Assocs., P.C., Wellesley, Mass., 1983-87; sr. tax mgr. and multi-state income and franchise tax practice leader KPMG Peat Marwick LLP, Boston, 1988-96; tax mgr. state taxes Arthur Andersen LLP, Boston, 1996—98; pvt. practice Boston, 1998—. Mem. Mass. Dept. Revenue Practitioner Liaison Com.; instr., panel mem. state taxation seminars and profl. devel. courses; spkr. in field. Cartoonist, creator Funny Bone Cartoons, creator Laughter is the Best Medicine - A Collection of Cartoons. Merit scholar Northeastern U., 1978; recipient Outstanding Achievement award in Appellate Brief Writing, 1988. Mem. Mass. Soc. CPAs (chair multi-state tax sub-com. 1996-97), Beta Alpha Psi (rec. sec. 1981-82), Beta Gamma Sigma, Phi Kappa Phi, Phi Delta Phi.

ELCANO, MARY S., lawyer; BA cum laude, Lynchburg Coll., 1971; JD, Cath. U., Washington, 1976. Litigation atty. Balt. Legal Aide Bur., 1976; staff atty. Office Solicitor Dept. Labor, 1979; gen. trial and appellate atty. Office Labor Law U.S. Postal Svc., 1982, exec. dir. Office EEO, 1984, regional dir. human resources N.E. region, 1987, sr. v.p., gen. counsel, 1992-99, exec. v.p., gen. counsel, 1999-2000; ptnr. Sidley Austin Brown & Wood LLP, Washington, 2000—03; gen. counsel, corp. sec. ARC, Washington, 2003—. Office: ARC 430 17th St NW Washington DC 20006 Office Phone: 202-303-5422. Business E-Mail: ElcanoM@usa.redcross.org.

ELCIK, ELIZABETH MABIE, fashion illustrator; b. Bklyn., Sept. 16, 1933; d. Cornelius Peter and Anna Julia (Cunningham) Mabie; m. John Joseph Elcik, Apr. 20, 1963. Grad., Jamesine Franklin Sch. Profl. Arts, N.Y.C., 1954; student in painting, NYU; student life class, Art Students League, N.Y.C., Alliance of Queens Artists, 2003. Fashion illustrator Vogue patterns Conde Nast Publs., 1954-59; freelance illustrator various clients, N.Y.C., 1960-74; fashion illustrator Butterick Fashion Mktg. Co., N.Y.C., 1974-82, McCall Pattern Co., N.Y.C., 1982—2001. Monitor profl. sketch classes, N.Y.C., 1962—79. Exhibitions include Cedar House Gallery, 2004, Alliance Queens Artists, 2005. Scholar N.Y.C Art, 1951, Jamesine Franklin Sch., 1952. Mem.: Women's Studio Ctr. Inc., Nat. Mus. Women in Arts. Roman Catholic. Avocation: travel.

ELDER, DONNA REDD, real estate broker; d. Robert and Geraldine Redd; children: Joshua Mark Griffith, Eric Zane, John Thomas Houston. Accredited staging profl. Staging Profls. Real estate broker RE/MAX Creative Realty, Lexington, Ky., 1988—. Vol. UK Children's Hosp./Mckenna Found., Lexington, 1994; vol. nuturer and cook Habitat for Humanity, Lexington, 1990; vol.mem. adv. bd. Ky. Refugee Ministries, Lexington, 1999; vol. bd. dirs. advisor Faith Cmty. Housing Found., Lexington, 2000; vol. bd. dirs. Realtor Cmty. Housing Found., Lexington, 2000; bd. dirs. food delivery Moveable Feast, Lexington, 1998—2001; vol. food bank mgr. God's Pantry, Lexington, 1996—98; vol. ann. fundraiser Big Brother and Big Sisters, Lexington, 2004. Named Vol. of Yr., Meavable Feast, 1998; named to Platinum Club, RE/MAX Internat., 2003, Hall of Fame, 2003. Mem.: Lexington Bluegrass Assn. Realtors, Ky. Assn. Realtors, Nat. Assn. Realtors (accredited seller rep., cert. consumer real estate cons., cert. new homes specialist, seniors real estate specialist, cert. residential specialist, e-PRO). Episcopalian. Avocations: travel, learning, gardening, volunteering, laughing. Office: RE/MAX creative realty 185 Pasadena Dr #240 Lexington KY 40503 Office Phone: 859-983-9107. Home Fax: 859-278-9192; Office Fax: 859-278-9192. Personal E-mail: donna@donnaelder.com.

ELDER, IRMA, retail executive; b. Xicotencalt, Mex., 1934; m. James Elder, 1963 (dec.); 3 children. Owner, CEO Elder Automotive Group, 1983—. Mem. VIP panel 36th Annual Northwood U. Internat. Auto Show; founder Woman's Automotive Assn. Internat. Bd. dirs. Northwood U., Coll. Creative Studies, Oakland Family Svcs., Econ. Club Detroit. Named Woman Yr., Woman's Automotive Assn. Internat., 2001; named one of 100 Most Influential Women, Crain's Detroit Bus., 100 Leading Women, Automotive News, 2000; recipient Automotive Hall Fame Svc. Citation award, 2000, Pres. award, Ford Motor Co., 2000, 2001, Pride of Jaguar award, 1999, 2000. Achievements include frequently honored for many charitable assn; first woman to own Ford dealership in metropolitan Detroit market; successfully expanded co. from one dealership to eight after death of husband, founder of Elder Automotive; number one Saab dealership in US in volume of automobile sales (Saab of Troy); number one Jaguar dealership in N. Am. in volume of automobile sales (Jaguar of Troy); Elder Automotive consistently ranks top ten of Hispanic Bus. mag. top 500 Hispanic owned co. Office: 777 John R Rd Troy MI 48083 Office Fax: 248-583-0815.

ELDER, JENNIFER ANNE, music educator; b. Memphis, Tenn., Aug. 7, 1980; m. Ronald Leslie Elder, July 12, 2003. B in Music Edn., Murray State U., 2002. Music instr. grades 6-8 Crockett County Mid. Sch., Alamo, Tenn., 2002—03, band dir. grades 7-12, 2003—05; pvt. instr. Fayette Acad., Somerville, Tenn., 2005—, Huntingdon Mid. Sch., Tenn., 2005—, Adamsville Jr./Sr. High, Tenn., 2005—. Ch. pianist Gibson Trinity UMC, 2002—; pianist and clarinet performer Chester County Nursing Home, Henderson, Tenn., 2006. Mem.: Tenn. Educators Assn., Music Educators Nat. Conf., West Tenn. Band and Orch. Assn. Avocations: camping, hiking, travel, reading, cross stitch. Home: 370 Lake Levee Rd Henderson TN 38340

ELDER, MARY LOUISE, librarian; b. Ann Arbor, Mich., Sept. 7, 1937; d. John Dyer and Elsie (Phelps) Elder. BA, St. Louis U., 1959; MA, U. Chgo., 1962; postgrad., U. Calif., Berkeley, 1965-69. Libr. U. Chgo., 1961-63; rare book cataloger U. Kans., Lawrence, 1963-65; rare books libr. St. Louis Pub. Libr., 1969-74; rare book cataloger Duke U., Durham, NC, 1979-84, Smithsonian Inst., Washington, 1984-91, Libr. Congress, Washington, 1991—2002; ret. Mem. ALA, Am. Printing History Assn., Bibliog. Soc., Bibliog. Soc. Am., Cath. Libr. Assn., Soc. History Authorship, Reading and Publishing, Alpha Sigma Nu.

ELDERKIN, HELAINE GRACE, lawyer; b. New Rochelle, N.Y., Sept. 18, 1954; d. EllsworthJay and Madelyn A. (Roberts) E.; m. Stefan Shrier, Feb. 23, 1985. BA, Fla. Atlantic U., 1975; JD, George Mason U., 1985. Bar: Va. 1985, U.S. Ct. Appeals (4th cir.) 1985, U.S. Ct. Fed. Claims 1994. Aide Carter/Mondale Presdl. Campaign Com., Atlanta, 1976, Presdl. Transition Staff, Washington, 1976-77; spl. asst. Agy. Internat. Devel. U.S. Dept. State, Washington, 1977; spl. asst. U.S. Dept. Def., Washington, 1977-79; mem. tech. staff System Planning Corp., Arlington, Va., 1980-83; dir. corp. rsch. Analytics, Inc., McLean, Va., 1983-85, v.p., gen. counsel Fairfax, Va., 1985-91; of counsel Feith and Zell, P.C., Washington, 1986-91; dep. gen. counsel Computer Scis. Corp., 1991—. Mem. Army Sci. Bd., 1994—98. Master: ABA (mem. coun. sect. pub. contract law 2001—05, sect. pub. contract law coun. mem. 2002—); fellow: Mil. Ops. Rsch. Soc. Democrat. Home: 624 1/2 S Pitt St Alexandria VA 22314-4138 Office: Computer Scis Corp 3170 Fairview Park Dr Falls Church VA 22042-4516 Office Phone: 703-641-2532.

ELDERS, JOYCELYN (MINNIE JOCELYN ELDERS, MINNIE JOYCELYN LEE), public health service officer, endocrinologist, former Surgeon General of the United States; b. Schaal, Ark., Aug. 13, 1933; d. Curtis and Haller Jones; m. Oliver B. Elders, Feb. 14, 1960; children: Eric D., Kevin M. BA in Biol., Philander Smith Coll., 1952; MD, U. Ark. Med. Sch., 1960; MS in Biochemistry, U. Ark., 1967. Pediatric intern U. Minn. Hosp., Mpls., 1960-61; pediatric resident U. Ark. Med. Ctr., Little Rock, 1961-63, chief pediatric resident, 1963-64, pediatric rsch. fellow, 1964-67, asst. prof. of pediatrics, 1967-71, assoc. prof. of pediatrics, 1971-76, prof. of pediatrics, 1976-87; dir. Ark. Dept. of Health, Little Rock, 1987-93; pres. Assn. of State & Territorial Health Officers, 1992; surgeon gen. US Dept. Health & Human Services, 1993-94; prof. pediatrics Univ. Ark. Med. Ctr., Little Rock, 1994—98, prof. emeritus, pediatric endocrinology, 1998—; medical dir. Apothecus Pharmaceutical Corp., 2006—. Bd. dirs. Nat. Bank of Ark., North Little Rock, 1979-89. Editorial bd. Jour. Pediatrics, 1981—; contbr. articles on pediatrics to profl. jours. Bd. dirs. Northside YMCA, Little Rock, 1973—; vol. vols. in pub. schs., Little Rock, 1973—. 1st lt. U.S. Army, 1953-56. Recipient NIH Career Devel. award, Worthen Bank's Ark. Profl. Woman of Distinction award, 1987; named one of 100 Women of Ark., 1980, Ark. Dem. Woman of Yr. statewide newspaper, 1988, Presdl. award, Ark. Sociological and Anthropological Assn., 1993. Mem. So. Soc. Pediatrics (rsch. pres. 1979-80), Lawson Wilkins Endocrine Soc. (com. chair 1976), Ark. Sci. and Tech. Commn. (sec. 1975-89), Little Rock C. of C. (bd. dirs. 1980—), Endocrine Soc., Acad. Pediatrics, Am. Pediatric Soc. First African Am. US Surgeon General. Office: U Ark Med Ctr 4301 W Markham # 820 Little Rock AR 72205*

ELDREDGE, LINDA, psychologist; BS, Howard Payne U., 1980; MA, Tex. Woman's U., 1981; EdD, Baylor U., 1989. Lic. psychologist, Tex.; cert. tchr. hearing impaired, sch. counselor, spl. edn. counselor, Tex.; cert. verbal self def. trainer. Tchr. hearing impaired Waco (Tex.) Ind. Sch. Dist., 1982-85, spl. edn. sch. counselor, cons. hearing impaired, 1986-87; doctoral teaching fellow Baylor U., Waco, 1985-87; dir. regional alcohol and drug abuse svcs. Heart of Tex. Coun. Govts., Waco, 1987; psychotherapist Houston, 1989-91; psychologist, 1991—, Tex. Sch. for the Deaf, Austin, Tex., 1993-95. Mem. APA, Am. Deafness and Rehab. Assn., Gentle Art of Verbal Self-Defense Trainers Network, Internat. Soc. for the Study of Subtle Energies and Energy Medicine. Avocations: collecting minerals and seashells, world music, reading, art, water sports. Office: Bldg 4 Ste 200 4601 Spicewood Springs Rd Austin TX 78759

ELDRIDGE, TAMARA LYNN, elementary school educator; b. Kansas City, Mo., Oct. 27, 1961; d. Wayne and Mildred Croy. BS, S.W. Mo. State U., 1984; MA, U. Mo., Kansas City, 1987, EdS, 1992. Cert. tchr., ednl. adminstr., elem. prin., secondary prin., supt., Mo. Adminstrv. intern North Kansas City Sch. Dist., Kansas City, Mo., 1991, elem. tchr., 1985—99; elem. prin. Unified Sch. Dist. 204, Bonner Springs, Mo., 1999—2005; cons., trainer Exceptional Ednl. Cons., Gladstone, Mo., 2005—. Mem. edn. com. United Meth. Ch., Gladstone, Mo., 1993, mem. worship com., 1994; pres. United Meth. Women, 2002-06. Mem. ASCD, NAESP, Nat. Cun. for Social Studies, Tchrs. Approaching Whole Lang. (bd. dirs.), Multi-Age Classroom Group, Am. Slo-Pitch Softball Assn., Mother of Twins Club. Democrat. Avocations: reading, crafts, skiing, softball, travel. Home: 1010 NE 73rd Ter Gladstone MO 64118-2128

ELECTRA, CARMEN (TARA LEIGH PATRICK), actress; b. Sharonville, Ohio, Apr. 20, 1972; m. Dennis Rodman, Nov. 14, 1998 (div. Apr. 6, 1999); m. David Navarro, Nov. 22, 2003 (separated July 2006). Actor(cohost): (TV series) Singled Out, 1997, Baywatch, 1997—98, Hyperion Bay, 1999, BattleBots, 2002, Livin Large, 2002—03, 2003—04, Manhunt, 2004, Tripping the Rift, 2005—; celebrity judge (TV series) Dance Fever, 2003, host Automotive Showcase, 2003, VH1's 100 Greatest Artists of Hard Rock; actor: (TV films) Christmas in Malibu, 1999, Baywatch Hawaiian Wedding, 2003, Lolo's Cafe, 2006; (films) An American Vampire Story, 1997, Starstruck, 1998, The Mating Habits of the Earthbound Human, 1999, Scary Movie, 2000, The Great White Dope, 2000, Sol Goode, 2000, Perfume, 2001, Get Over It, 2001, Whacked!, 2002, Rent Control, 2002, Uptown Girls, 2003, My Boss' Daughter, 2003, Starsky & Hutch, 2004, Max Havoc: Curse of the Dragon, 2004, Dirty Love, 2005, Searching for Bobby D, 2005, Getting Played, 2005, Cheaper by the Dozen 2, 2005, Date Movie, 2006, Scary Movie 4, 2006, Hot Tamale, 2006; voice (TV series) The Simpsons, 2002, King of the Hill, 2003, (video) Lil' Pimp, 2005, American Dad!, 2005, appears in music video for Moby, "We Are All Made of Stars", guest appearance MADtv, 1997, 2000, Just Shoot Me!, 1997, The Drew Carey Show, 2000, The Osbourne Family Christmas Special, 2003, Punk'd, 2004, Monk, 2004, Hope & Faith, 2005, Summerland, 2005, House, M.D., 2005, Stacked, 2005, and several others.*

ELEWSKI, BONI ELIZABETH, dermatologist, educator; b. Cleve., Aug. 7, 1953; d. John Stanley and Alberta (Gulish) E.; married. BA summa cum laude, Miami U., Oxford, Ohio, 1975; MD cum laude, Ohio State U., 1978. Intern U. N.C., Chapel Hill, 1978-79, resident, 1979-82; staff dermatologist Akron (Ohio) Clinic, 1982-88; prof. dermatology Univ. Hosps. of Cleve., Case Western Res. U., 1988-99; prof. U. Alabama, 1999—. Author: (textbook) Differential Diagrams in Dermatology, 2005; editor: Cutaneous Fungal Infections, 1992, 2d edit., 1998; contbr. chpts. to books, articles to profl. jours. Trustee Annenberg Cir., 2006. Fellow Cleve. Dermatology Soc. (sec. bd. dirs., chair skin cancer screening program 1988—, pres. 1994), Am. Acad. Dermatology (bd. dirs. 1996-2000, v.p. elect, 2000, v.p. 2001, pres.-elect 2003-04, pres. 2004); mem. Am. Dermatol. Assn., Women's Dermatology Soc. (sec.-treas., pres.-elect 1999, pres. 2000), Dermatology Found. (trustee 1987-91). Roman Catholic. Home: PO Box 430037 Birmingham AL 35243 Office: U Alabama Birmingham Dept Derm 700 18th St S Birmingham AL 35233-1856 E-mail: BEElewski@aol.com.

ELFMAN, JENNA (JENNIFER MARY BUTALA), actress; b. LA, Sept. 30, 1971; m. Bodhi Rice Elfman, Feb. 18, 1995. Studied with Milton Katselas, LA. Actress in Dharma & Greg Moore Metavoy, L.A., 1997—2002. Actor: (films) include Grosse Point Blank, 1997, Krippendorf's Tribe, Can't Hardly Wait, 1998, (voice only) Dr. Dolittle, 1998, EdTV, 1999, Keeping the Faith, 2000, (voice only) Cyber World, 2000, (voice only) The Tangerine Bear, 2000, Town & Country, 2001, Looney Tunes: Back In Action, 2003, (voice only) Clifford's Really Big Movie, 2004, (voice only) What's Hip, Doc?, 2005, Touched, 2005; TV films) Double Deception, 1993, Her Last Chance, 1996, Obsessed, 2002; (TV series) Townies, 1996, Dharma & Greg 1997-2002, Courting Alex, 2006-; TV appearances include Murder, She Wrote, 1992, Pointman, 1995, The Monroes, 1995, Roseanne, 1995, NYPD Blue, 1995, Murder One, 1995, Almost Perfect, 1996, The Single Guy, 1997, Two and a Half Men, 2004; starred in many music videos including Antrax video for Crossroads Films. Recipient TV Guide award, 1999, 2000, Spirit of the Cmty. award, Assn.for Better Living and Edn., 2005. Avocation: performing ballet. Mailing: c/o Creative Artists Agy 9830 Wilshire Blvd Beverly Hills CA 90212-1825*

ELFTMAN, SUSAN NANCY, physician assistant, childbirth-lactation educator, research director; b. Oakland, Calif., Apr. 3, 1951; d. Arthur Gerhardt Samuel and Ella Johanna (Nelson) E. AA summa cum laude, Chabot Coll., 1971; BA in Zoology, U. Calif., Berkeley, 1973; BS in Med. Sci. magna cum laude, Alderson-Broaddus Coll., 1980; MPH, UCLA, 1990. Bd. cert. physician asst., Calif. Physician asst. So. Calif. Permanente Group, San Diego, 1981-82, Mem. Med. Ctr., Long Beach, Calif., 1982-88, Harriman-Jones Med. Group, Long Beach, 1988-90, Pamela Kushner, MD, Long Beach, 1990—. Spkr. Am. Cancer Soc., Long. Beach, Meml. Med. Ctr., Long Beach, March of Dimes. Fellow Am. Acad. Physician Assts., Calif. Acad. Physician Assts.; mem. Am. Soc. for Psychoprophylaxis in Obstetrics (cert. lactation and childbirth educator). Home: 625 Termino Ave Long Beach CA 90814 Office: Pamela Kushner MD 2865 Atlantic Ave Ste 207 Long Beach CA 90806-1730

ELG, ANNETTE, food products executive; b. Culdesac, Idaho; d. Ralph and Shirley Steigers; m. Brad Elg, 1977; 2 children. B in Acctg., U. Idaho, 1978. With Arthur Andersen LLP; corp. contr. J.R. Simplot Co., Boise, Idaho, 1990, CFO, 2002—. Office: JR Simplot One Capital Ctr 999 Main St PO Box 27 Boise ID 83707-0027

ELGAR, SHARON KAY, science educator; b. Geneseo, Ill., June 27, 1950; BA, Aurora U., Ill., 1972; M in Ednl. Leadership/Adminstrn., Benedictine U., 2006. Lic. EMT Waubonsee Coll.; cert. outdoor edn. and survival tng. courses U. Wis., death and dying, outdoor edn. issues, drugs and society, and gifted edn. courses No. Ill. U., tchr. Ill. Tchr. physics, chemistry, biology Aurora Cen. Cath. H.S., 2001—. Beauty cons. Mary Kay, Inc., Mich.; mem. adv. bd. Kane County Pre-Sch., Geneva; mem. homebound tutoring Kaneland Sch. Dist., Maple Park, Ill. Mem. Town & Country Libr. Dist., Elburn; counselor, aide for grief Conley Outreach Ctr., Elburn. Recipient Gold Ivy Leaf Scholar's honors, Aurora U., 1972. Mem.: Boy Scouts Am. Venture Crew, Am. Girl Scouts Assn., Rockford Cath. Diocese Tchrs. Assn., Ill. Tchrs. Assn. (sec. 1972—), Am. Chem. Soc., Nat. Sci. Tchrs. Assn., St. Peters Women Soc., Elburn Lion's Club, Elburn Legion Aux. Republican. Roman Catholic. Avocations: canoeing, hiking, swimming, exercise, reading. Home: 200 Oak Dr Elburn IL 60119 Office: Aurora Cen Cath H S 1255 N Edgelawn Dr Aurora IL 60506 Office Phone: 630-907-0095.

ELGAVISH, ADA, molecular and cellular biologist; b. Cluj, Romania, Jan. 23, 1946; came to U.S. 1979; d. David and Malca (Neuman) Simchas; m. Gabriel A. Elgavish, Dec. 28, 1968; children: Rotem, Eynav. BSc, Tel-Aviv U., 1969, MSc, 1972; PhD, Weizmann Inst. Sci., Rehovot, Israel, 1978. Postdoctoral vis. fellow NIH, Balt., 1979-81; instr. U. Ala. Sch. Medicine, Birmingham, 1981-82, rsch. assoc., 1982-84, rsch. asst. prof. pharmacology, 1984-89, asst. prof. comparative medicine, 1989—92, assoc. prof. comparative medicine, 1992—2002, assoc. prof. genetics, 2002—. Scientist Cell Adhesion and Matrix Rsch. Ctr., Birmingham, 1995—, Clin. Nutrition Rsch. Ctr., 2001—, Ctr. Metabolic Bone Disease, Ctr. for Aging, 1996; mem. Cancer Ctr.; founder Diacell, Inc., 1998. Grantee Cystic Fibrosis Found., 1986—90, Am. Lung Assn., 1987—92, NIH, 1989—2000, Interstitial Cystitis Assn., 1998, Am. Inst. Cancer Rsch., 2000, Pfizer, 2000—03. Mem.: Am. Assn. Cancer Rsch., Soc. for Basic Urol. Rsch., Am. Physiol. Soc., Sigma Xi. Office: U Ala Sch Medicine Dept Genetics Birmingham AL 35294-0024 Office Phone: 205-934-6547. Business E-Mail: aelgavis@uab.edu.

ELGIN, SARAH CARLISLE ROBERTS, biology researcher and educator; b. Washington, July 16, 1945; d. Carlisle Bishop and Lorene (West) Roberts; m. Robert Lawrence Elgin, June 9, 1967; children: Benjamin Carlisle, Thomas James. BA in Chemistry, Pomona Coll., 1967; PhD in Biochemistry, Calif. Inst. Tech., 1971. Research fellow Calif. Inst. Tech., Pasadena, 1971-73; asst. prof. biochemistry and molecular biology Harvard U., Cambridge, Mass., 1973-77, assoc. prof., 1977-81; assoc. prof. biology Washington U., St. Louis, 1981-84, prof., 1984—, prof. edn., 2001, prof. genetics, 2003; mem. Nat. Com. on Sci. Edn. Stds. and Assessment, NAS/NRC, 1992. Mem. editl. bd. Jour. Cell Biology, NYC, 1980-82, Jour. Biol. Chemistry, 1985-88, Molecular Cellular Biology, 1989-; exec. editor Nucleic Acids Rsch., 1983-88; assoc. editor Molecular Cell, 1998-, Bio Med Net; co-editor-in-chief Cell Biology Edn., 2002-05; contbr. papers in field. Mem. molecular biology study sect. NIH, 1986-89. Recipient Prof.'s award Howard Hughes Med. Inst., 2002, 2006; rsch. grantee NIH, 1987, 88, 91, 93, 98, 99, 2003, 05, NSF, 1986. Fellow AAAS (sect. on biol. scis. 1991—); mem. Am. Soc. Biol. Chemists (program com. 1984), Am. Soc. Cell Biology (coun. 1983-85, 92-94, publs. com. 1989-91, edn. com. 1992-2005), Genetics Soc. Am. Office: Washington U Biology Dept CB 1229 One Brookings Dr Saint Louis MO 63130-4899 Office Phone: 314-935-5348. Office Fax: 314-935-5125. Business E-Mail: selgin@biology.wustl.edu.

ELIAS, SARAH DAVIS, retired English language educator; b. Chgo., Aug. 9, 1934; d. Calvin Paul and Julia Elizabeth (Bush) Davis; m. Antoine Jack Elias, Aug. 28, 1960. BA, Roosevelt U., 1957; MA, Morgan State U., 1973; MS, Johns Hopkins U., 1983. Cert. tchr., Ill., Calif., Md. Elem. tchr. Chgo. Pub. Schs., 1958-62, Palo Alto (Calif.) Unified Sch. Dist., 1969-70; tchr. Balt. City Schs., 1969—92, chmn. reading dept., 1978-81, English tchr., 1982-92; supervising tchr. Coppin State Coll., Balt., 1973-75; instr. history Morgan State U., Balt., 1992—93, advisor Academic Devel. Ctr., 1992—. Resource coord., tutor Johns Hopkins Tutorial Projects, Balt., 1968; social studies text cons. Harcourt, Brace, Jovanovich Pub., Balt., 1972; lectr. English and reading, Morgan State U., 1999-2003; bd. dirs. Charms Inc., 2000-03. Author: An Account of the Longview: Texas Riot of July 11, 1919, 2004. Mem. Mayor's Task Force on Edn., Balt., 1967-69, Mayor's Bicentennial Com., 1974-76. Am. Fedn. Tchrs.-Cornell U. fellow, 1967. Mem. Balt. Tchrs. Union (contract negotiator 1967-69), Herbert M. Frisbey Hist. Soc., NAACP (life), Delta Sigma Theta (life), Clubs: Chums (bd. dirs. 1992-94). Democrat. Baptist. Home: 20 Olmstead Green Ct Baltimore MD 21210-1508 Office: Acad Devel Ctr 1700 E Coldspring Ln Baltimore MD 21251 Office Phone: 443-885-2055.

ELIASON, ARLENE F., mathematician, educator; b. Kanawha, Iowa, June 14, 1949; d. Harold C. Eliason and Berneice J. Lein. AA, Waldorf Coll., Forest City, Iowa, 1969; BA, Concordia Coll., Moorhead, Minn., 1970; MA in Tchg. of Math., Minot State U., ND, 1997. Cert. tchr. ND, 1973. Instr. Minot Pub. Schs., ND, 1970—2001, Rasmussen Coll., Eagan, Minn., 2001—05, Minn. Sch. Bus., Shakopee, 2005—. Recipient Instl. Svc. award, Rasmussen Coll., 2005. Mem.: Math. Assn. Am. Home: 17250 Barberry Circle Eden Prairie MN 55346 Office: Minnesota School of Business - Shakopee 1200 Town Square Shakopee MN 55379 Office Phone: 952-345-1200. E-mail: aeliason@msbcollege.edu.

ELIASON, BONNIE MAE, county treasurer; b. Stanley, N.D., Jan. 10, 1947; d. Melvin Otis and Mabel Isabel (Borst) Howell; m. Murrey Allen Eliason, June 23, 1971; 1 child, Christal Medora. BA, Minot State Coll., 1970. Clk. N.D. Personal Property Tax Collector, Bismarck, 1965, Mountrail County Auditor, Stanley, 1970—74; dep. Mountrail County Treas., Stanley, 1974—77, treas., 1979—. Vice pres., mem. Am. Legion Aux., Stanley, 1980. Mem. Stanley Women's Bowling League (sec., treas. 1973-74, v.p. 1976-77, pres. 1977-78), Stanley Women's Bowling Assn. Presbyterian. Avocations: reading, crossword puzzles, sewing. Home: 7915 70th NW Stanley ND 58784-9013 Office: PO Box 69 Stanley ND 58784-0069

ELISHA, LARISA, musician, performer, educator; b. Baku, Russia, Jan. 12, 1963; d. Vladimir Chumakov and Mariya Chumakova; m. Steven Kenneth Elisha, May 19, 2002; 1 child, Patrick A. BA, A. Lunatcharsky Conservatory of Music, Minsk, Belarus, 1986, MMus, 1987—89; D in Violin performance, K. Lipinski Acad. Music, Wroclaw, Poland, 1996—97; cert. in chamber music, U. Wis., Milw., 1997—99. Prof., violin M. Glinka Coll. Music, Minsk, Belarus, 1985—89, A. Lunatcharsky Conservatory of Music, Minsk, Belarus, 1987—89, K. Szymanowski Coll. of Music, Wroclaw, Poland, 1989—97, K. Lipinski Acad. Music, Wroclaw, Poland, 1989—97, prof., strings methodology, 1996—97, Inst. U. Wis., Milw., 1997—99; prof., violin Wis. Conservatory of Music, Milw., 1998—99; violinist artist in residence Washburn U., Topeka, 1999—. Concertmaster State Witold Lutaslawski Philharm. Symphony Orch., Wroclaw, Poland, 1989—97, Topeka Symphony Orch., 1999—, Wichita Grand Opera, 2002—; prin. violin Chamber Orch. Leopoldinum, Wroclaw, Poland, 1990—93; first violinist, artistic dir. String Quartet Wratislavia of Philharm. Hall, Wroclaw, Poland, 1995—97; violinist, Piano Trio U. Wis. Inst. Chamber Music, Milw., 1997—99; assoc. concertmaster Green Bay Symphony Orch., Waukesha, Wis., 1997—99; co-founder, violinist Elaris Duo, 2000—, Chamber Music Series, Elaris String Academy, 2004—. Author: The Russian Violin School's Traditions, 1986, Methodology of Teaching Violin Players, 1986; musician (violinist): (soloist) Musica Polonica Nova, 1989, Acad. Music Concert Hall, 1990, Chamber Music Festival, 1991, State Witold Lutoslawski Philharm. Symphony Orch., 1991, Koszalin Philharm. Orch., 1991, Leopoldinum, 1992, K. Lipinski Acad. Music Concert Hall, 1993, Gioventi Musicale d'Italia Festival, 1993, Wieniawski Festival, 1993, Theater Hall Acad. Music, 1997, Topeka Symphony, 1999—2000, 2003, 2005, Pittsburg State U., 2001—03, Lawrence Chamber Orch., 2005, Sunflower Chamber Orch., 2005, (recitals) Elaris Duo, Washburn U., 2000—04, Sunflower Music Festival, 2000—, Miss. Symphony Orch., 2003, Colo. Music Festival, 2000—01, Bergen Internat. Festival, 2004 (Musician Yr., Kans. Fedn. Music Clubs (KFMC), 2003), Koncertgebouw Hall, Warsaw Nat. Philharmony Hall, World Famous Concert Halls, Karajan Hall, (CD) Elaris Duo, 2005—. Named to Kans. Touring Program. Mem.: Chamber Music Am., Am. String Tchrs. Assn., Coll. Music Soc., Northeast Kans. Music Tchrs. Assn., Music Tchrs. Nat. Assn. Office Phone: 785-670-1891. E-mail: elarisduo@cox.net.

ELIZABETH, MARY, science educator, consultant; b. Stockton, Calif., June 1960; d. Joann Lee Haines Meays. BS in Microbiology, Ind. U., Bloomington; MS in Biology, U. Pacific, Stockton, Calif., 1991; MS Hydrologic Sci., U. Calif., Davis, 2001. Student tchr., rsch. assoc. U. Pacific, Sacramento, 1986—91; sr. registered environ. health specialist Environ. Health, San Joaquin County, Stockton, 1991—98; tchg. asst., rsch. assoc. U. Calif., Davis, 1998—2001; scientist Ecologic Engring., Rocklin, 2001—06; tchr. sci. Inderkum H.S., Natomas Unified Sch. Dist., Sacramento, 2004—06, MLK, JHS, Grant Joint Union H.S. Dist., 2005—. Recipient Adv. of Yr., Stockton Bicycle Club, 1994. Mem.: Nat. Sci. Tchrs. Assn., Calif. Sci. Tchrs. Assn. (life), Sierra Club (Delta Sierra group, mother lode chpt. exec. com. chair 1992—98), Ind. U. Alumni Assn. (life). Conservative. Roman Catholic. Avocations: kayaking, gardening, bicycling, travel. Home: PO Box 160442 Sacramento CA 95816 Office Phone: 916-286-4766.

ELIZABETH, , II, (ELIZABETH ALEXANDRA MARY), By the Grace of God of the United Kingdom of Great Britain and Northern Ireland and of Her Other Realms and Territories Queen, Head of the Commonwealth, Defender of the Faith; b. London, Apr. 21, 1926; d. King George VI (formerly Duke of York) and Queen Elizabeth (formerly Duchess of York); m. Prince Philip Mountbatten, Duke of Edinburgh, Nov. 20, 1947; children: Charles Philip Arthur George (now The Prince of Wales), 1948, Anne Elizabeth Alice Louise (now The Princess Royal), 1950, Andrew Albert Christian Edward (now The Duke of York), 1960, Edward Antony Richard Louis (now The Earl of Wessex), 1964. Succeeded to throne following death of father, Feb. 6, 1952; crowned Queen, June 2, 1953. Achievements include fluent speaker of French. Avocations: photography, horseback riding. Address: Buckingham Palace London SW1A 1AA England

ELIZONDO, PATRICIA, sales executive; B in Fin., Ind. Univ.; MBA, Univ. Notre Dame. Internal auditor Xerox Corp., 1981, various mgmt. positions to v.p., gen. mgr., Md./Va. customer bus. unit and sr. v.p. fin./professional and health care industry sales ops., now sr. v.p. major accts. Named one of 50 Most Important Hispanics in Tech. & Bus., Hispanic Engr. & Info. Tech. mag., 2005. Office: Xerox Corp 100 Long Ridge Rd Stamford CT 06904 Office Phone: 203-968-3000.*

ELKIN, CAROLE KAINE, retired educational diagnostician; b. Kewanee, Ill., Jan. 15, 1949; d. Francis Bernard and Julie Ann Kaine; 1 child, Jody Elkin Mackey. BA in Edn., Baylor U., Waco, Tex., 1971, MS in Edn., 1977. Tchr. St. Mary's Cath. Sch. West, Tex., 1972—73, Whitney Ind. Sch. Dist., Tex., 1973—80, Hillsboro (Tex.) Ind. Sch. Dist., 1980—94; ednl. diagnostician Hill County Spl. Edn. Coop., Hillsboro, 1994—96, Mexia (Tex.) Ind. Sch. Dist., 1996—97, Shepherd (Tex.) Ind. Sch. Dist., 1997—2000, Alvarado (Tex.) Ind. Sch. Dist., 2000—01, Cleburne (Tex.) Ind. Sch. Dist., 2001—06; ret., 2006. Lead diagnostician Shepherd (Tex.) Ind. Sch. Dist., 1997—2000. Named Outstanding Young Women of Am., 1975. Mem.: Metro West Tex. Ednl. Diagnostician Assn. (pres. elect 2005—06, pres. 2006—), Episcopal Alter Soc., Daus. of the King, Delta Kappa Gamma (chmn. newsletter 1979—). Episc. Avocations: reading, computer games, swimming, basketball, playing bunco. Home: 1407 Alford Dr Hillsboro TX 76645 Personal E-mail: kano92820@sbcglobal.net.

ELKIN, JUDITH, lawyer; b. NYC, Jan. 1, 1956; BA with honors in Am. History, summa cum laude, SUNY at Binghamton, 1978; JD cum laude, U. Wis., 1981. Bar: Wis. 1981, Tex. 1982, NY 2004, admitted to practice: Tex. Supreme Ct., US Supreme Ct., US Ct. Appeals (5th Cir.), US Ct. Appeals (6th Cir.), US Ct. Appeals (10th Cir.), US Ct. Appeals (11th Cir.), US Dist. Ct. (No. Dist.) Tex., US Dist. Ct. (So. Dist.) Tex., US Dist. Ct. (Ea. Dist.) Tex., US Dist. Ct. (We. Dist.) Tex. Ptnr., Bus. Reorganization & Bankruptcy Practice Group Haynes and Boone LLP, Dallas, co-chair, Fin. Sect. Spkr. in field. Bd. dir., exec. bd., sec. Dallas Zoological Soc., 1998—2004. Mem.: Internat. Women's Insolvency and Restructuring Confederation (IWIRC) (sec./trea. 2002—06), COMBAR (Hon. N. Am. Mem., Comml. Bar Assn. United Kingdom), Am. Bankruptcy Inst., Internat. Bar Assn. (com. J, Internat. Insolvency), ABA (cohmn. bankruptcy and insolvency litig. com., Litig. Sect. 1997—2001, bus. bankruptcy com., Bus. Law Sect.), Phi Beta Kappa. Office: Haynes And Boone Attorneys 153 E 53rd St Rm 4900 New York NY 10022-4636 Office Phone: 212-659-4968. Office Fax: 212-884-8228. Business E-Mail: judith.elkin@haynesboone.com.

ELKIN, LOIS SHANMAN, business systems company executive; b. Cin., Oct. 31, 1937; d. Jerome David and Mildred Louise (Bloch) Shanman; m. Alan I. Elkin, May 6, 1962; children: Karen A., Jeffrey R. BA in Math., Goucher Coll., 1959. Sys. engr. ea. region IBM, Balt. and Columbia, S.C., 1959-61, mgr. Computer Test Ctr. ea. region, 1961-64; exec. v.p. Advance Bus. Sys., Balt., 1964—, A&L Real Estate, Balt., 1970—; pres. Our World Gallery, Inc., Balt., 1995—. Mentor for math. and bus. Goucher Coll., Balt., 1982—86; co-owner ATMS, Balt., 1994—2002; guest lectr. MBA program Loyola Coll. Md., Balt., 1993—94, Towson U., 1999; steering com. Loyola Ctr. Closely Held Cos., Balt., 1993—; conducted seminars Towson U. Leadership Group, 1999; bd. dirs. Hunt Valley Bus. Forum, Balt.; mng. dir.

Enable Technologies, Balt., 2001—; bd. dirs. Soshana S. Cardin Jewish Cmty. H.S., 2005—; judge Md. Entrepreneur of Yr. Awards by Ernst Young, 2006. Vol. House of Ruth, Balt., 1990—, Image Recovery Ctr., Union Meml. Hosp., Balt., 1995—96; exec. bd. dirs. Pride of Balt. II, 1994—2000; co-chair Multiple Sclerosis Class of '98 fundraiser, 1998; exec. bd. Md. chpt. Nat. Multiple Sclerosis Soc., 2000—05; sponsor maj. fundraising event Johns Hopkins Children's Ctr., Balt., 2002; chair Gala, Balt. Zoomerang!, 2004; bd. dirs. Hearing and Speech Agy., Balt., 1996—2001. Named Md. Entrepreneur of Yr., Ernst & Young, 2001; named to, Circle of Excellence, 2004; recipient AAA Torch award for ethics in bus., 1997, Champion of Children award, Casey Cares Found., 2004, Bravo! Entrepreneur award, SmartWoman Mag., 2005, honoree, Chimes Ann. Hall of Fame Tribute, 2002. Mem.: Women's Bus. Club (founder 2002—), Nat. Assn. Women Bus. Owners (Woman of the Yr. award Balt. chpt. 1985). Avocation: collecting art. Office: Advance Bus Sys 10755 York Rd Cockeysville Hunt Valley MD 21030-2114

ELKINS, CAROLINE M., history professor, writer; b. NJ, 1969; m. Brent Elkins; children: Andy, Jake. BA in African History, Princeton U., 1991; AM, Harvard U., 1996, PhD, 2001; Fellow, Radcliffe Inst., 2003—04. Asst. prof. history Harvard U., Hugo K. Foster assoc. prof. African studies. Author: Imperial Reckoning: The Untold Story of Britain's Gulag in Kenya, 2005 (Pulitzer Prize for nonfiction, 2006); co-editor (with Susan Pedersen): Settler Colonialism in the Twentieth Century, 2005. Conversant in Swahili, Kikuyu; subject of 2002 BBC documentary, Kenya: White Terror. Office: Harvard U CGIS S Bldg Rm S432 University Hall Cambridge MA 02138 Office Phone: 617-495-2568. Business E-Mail: elkins@fas.harvard.edu.*

ELKINS, JENI L. MCINTOSH, systems support specialist; b. Chgo., Sept. 23, 1967; d. Glen Reed McIntosh and Cherie Lee Whybrew; m. Robert Lloyd Elkins Jr., Apr. 23, 1994. BA Orgnizational Comm. & Spanish, Ind. U., 1991, MBA Mktg., 1998. Sr. libr. asst. Ind. U., Gary, 1994—97, webmaster, 1997; mgr. Net Nitco, Hebron, 1997—98; webmaster Citizens Fin. Svcs., Munster, 1999—2003, Valparaiso U., Valparaiso, 2004—. Author: Bub's Glasses, 1998. Vol. instr. ESL Gavit High Sch., Hammond, Ind., 1993; founding mem. AUSA, Ind., 1990—91; pres., alumni bd. Ind. U. NW, 2001—02; exec. coun. mem. Ind. U., 2002—. Lutheran. E-mail: jelkins@alumni.indiana.edu.

ELKINS, KATHERINE MARIE, elementary school educator; b. Denver, Mo., Apr. 13, 1942; d. Eugene Forrest and Erma Louise (Wasson) Huber; m. Robert Wayne Ferguson, May 15, 1965 (dec. Apr. 1977); 1 child, Michael Harve. BS in Edn., Mo. Western Coll., 1972; MEd, Kans. State U., 1985. Cert. tchr., Mo., Kans. Proofreader St. Joseph (Mo.) News Press, 1961-68; tchr. spl. edn. North Platte Sch. Dist., Camden Point, Mo., 1972-75; tchr. Troy (Kans.) Elem. Sch., 1981-85, Unified Sch. Dist. 406, Wathena, Kans., 1985—. Mem. Kans. Reading Assn. (v.p., pres. 1984-88), Wathena Edn. Assn. (sec. 1986-88, 90-91), VFW Aux., Delta Kappa Gamma (sec. 1988-90). Independent. Mem. Christian Ch. Avocations: reading, ceramics, gardening, travel. Home: PO Box 65 Troy KS 66087-0065 Office: Unified Sch Dist 406 705 Jessie Wathena KS 66090

ELKINS, KATHRYN MARIE, alcohol/drug abuse services professional, recreational therapist; b. Peckville, Pa., Mar. 19, 1967; d. Thomas Cyril and Kathryn Theresa Berta; children: Korey Alan, Thomas Elkins. AA, U. Scranton, 2000, BA in Human Svcs. and Liberal Studies, 2003. Compact disc printer op. Time-Warner, Olyphant, Pa., 1985—96; therapist self employed, Scranton, Pa., 1996—2004; art therapist Women's Halfway House, Lake Ariel, Pa., 1998—2004, drug and alcohol counselor, 2002—04. Art residency programs Everhart Mus., Scranton, Pa., 1998—2003. TV health cast, Dealing with Chronic Pain, 1999; contbr. articles to profl. jours. V.p. Dexter Hanley Student Govt., Scranton, Pa., 1994—96, ores., 1996—2003; den mother helper Boy Scouts of Am., Clifford, Pa., 1997—2001. Recipient Alumni Svc. award, Scranton. Republican. Roman Catholic. Avocations: art, travel, sports, gardening, photography. Home: 50 Main St Clifford PA 18413

ELKINS, TONI MARCUS, artist, art association administrator; b. Tifton, Ga., Feb. 22, 1946; m. Samuel M. Elkins, 1968; children: Stephanie Elkins Sims, Eric Marcus. Student, Boston U., 1965; ABJ, U. Ga., 1968; postgrad., Columbia (S.C.) Coll., Athens, 1980-82; postgrad. photography/silk screening, Columbia (S.C.) Coll. Owner, designer Designs by Elkins, Columbia, 1986—. Water color artist, 1983—; supt. fine art S.C. State Fair Art Exhbn., 1987-96. Auction chair The Elegant Egg McKissick Mus., Columbia, 1994; bd. dirs. Trustus Theatre, 1994-96; chmn. S.C. Playwright's Festival, 1994—. Recipient Best of Show award 18th Internat. Dogwood Festival, 1991, So. Water Color Assn. Pres.'s award, 1992, Purchase award Anderson County Arts Coun. 17th Ann. Exhibit, 1992, Meyer Hardware award Rocky Mountain National, 1992, Howard B. Smith award S.C. Watercolor Ann., 1992, Women of Distinction award Girl Scouts of Congaree Area, Inc., 2000, Tex. Watercolor Soc. Camlin award, So. Watercolor Soc. Cheap Joe's award, Trenholm Artists Guild Pres. award. Mem. Nat. Watercolor Soc. (1st v.p. 2003—), Watercolor U.S.A., S.C. Watercolor Soc., Nat. Watercolor Okla., Penn. Watercolor Soc., Ga. Watercolor Soc., Rocky Mountain Nat. Watercolor Soc., Cultural Coun. of Richland & Lexington Counties (exec. bd. sec. 1990-93), Ctrl. Carolina Cmty. Found. (chmn. devel. 2000—, chmn. nominations 2004-2005), Southeastern Art and Craft Expn. (adv. bd. 1993-94, Elizabeth O'Neill Verner award 1999), Columbia Coll. Com. of 150, Women in Philanthropy (founder 2002). Avocations: reading, swimming, art, rare books. Home: 1511 Adger Rd Columbia SC 29205-1407 Office Phone: 803-206-8492. Business E-Mail: telkins@ksbellc.com.

ELLEDGE, GLENNA ELLEN TUELL, journalist; b. Welch, W.Va., Aug. 2, 1931; d. William Jackson and Ellen Annabelle (Jackson) Tuell; div.; children: Carl Gene, Jerry Elwood, Ernest Everett. Certificate in comptometer, Capital City Coll., 1949; student, Wytheville (Va.) C.C., S.W. Va. C.C., Richlands, Va. Intermont Coll. Accounts clk. Household Fin. Corp., Charleston, W.Va., 1951-52; with incest divsn. FBI, Washington, 1953; asst. bookkeeper and acctg. clk. Ft. McNair Officers Open Mess, Washington, 1953-54; stat. analyst Office Strategic Intelligence, Washington, 1954-55; stock control 836th Supply Squadron, Langley AFB, Va., 1957-59; acct., office asst. Comml. Contracting, Troy, Mich., 1970-71; office svcs. asst. Southwestern State Hosp., Marion, Va., 1971-95; staff writer, photographer Saltville (Va.) Progress, 1977-81, Saltville News-Messenger, 1981-93, Family Cmty. Newspapers, Marion, 1993-2000, Saltville Progress, 2000—. Fire brigade Southwestern State Hosp., Marion, 1986-93, instr. CPR, 1986-89, adv. bd., 1986-93. Editor, keyboardist Grandma's Favorite Recipes, 2000, Lucy's Secret, 2001-02. Vol. Air Force Family Svcs., 1956-69, den mother Cub. Scouts Am., 1962-67; bd. dirs. Smyth County Crisis Ctr., Marion, 1971-81; sec., pres. Smyth Coun. Santa's Elves, Marion, 1974-78, Family Oriented Group Home parent Group Home Juveniles 28th Juvenile Domestic Rels. Ct., Abingdon, Va., 1978-81; EMT, instr. Am. Heart Assn., Smyth, Wise, Grayson Counties, 1986-89; mem. and former sunday sch. tchr., supr. Laural Springs United Meth. Ch.; chairperson Mayor's promotional com., Marion, 1994-95; mem. Surry County (N.C.) Hist. Soc., Grayson County (Va.) Hist. Soc. Mem. Nat. Fedn. Press Women (del. 1978, awards), Va. Press Women (del. 1978, awards), Va. Press Assn. (awards), Nat. Press Assn., Nat. Soc. DAR, Nat. Soc. Col. Dames XVII Century. Jamestowne Soc. Republican. Avocations: writing, reading, travel. Office: PO Box 901 Marion VA 24354-0901 Personal E-mail: ellglen@hotmail.com.

ELLEMAN, BARBARA, editor; b. Coloma, Wis., Oct. 20, 1934; d. Donald and Evelyn (Kissinger) Koplein; m. Don W. Elleman, Nov. 14, 1970. BS in Edn., Wis. State U., 1956; MA in Librarianship, U. Denver, 1964. Sch. libr. media specialist Port Washington (Wis.) High Sch., 1956-59, Homestead High Sch., Thiensville-Mequon, Wis., 1959-64; children's libr. Denver Pub. Libr., 1964-65; sch. libr. media specialist Cherry Creek Schs., Denver, 1965-70, Henry Clay Sch., Whitefish Bay, Wis., 1971-75; children's reviewer ALA, Chgo., 1975-82, children's editor, 1982-90, editor Book Links, 1990-96. Vis. lectr. U. Wis., 1974-75, 81-82, U. Ill., Circle Campus, 1983-85; Disting. scholar children's lit., Marquette U., 1996—; cons. H.W. Wilson Co., 1969-75; mem. Libr. Congress Adv. Com. on selection for children's books for blind and physically handicapped, 1980-88, Caldecott Calendar Com., 1986; judge The Am. Book Awards, 1982, Golden Kite, 1987, Boston Globe/Horn Book, 1990; mem. faculty Highlights for Children Writers Conf., 1985-90; mem. orgn. com. MidWest Conf. Soc. Children's Books Writers, 1974-76; chair Hans Christian Andersen Com., 1987-88; advisor Reading Rainbow, 1986-96, Ind. R.E.A.P. project, 1987-93; jury mem. VI Catalonia Premi Children's Book Exbhn., Barcelona, Spain, 1994; adv. bd. Parent's Choice, Cobblestone Publ., Georgia Pub. TV's 2000, The New Advocate mag., 20th Century Children's Writers, Encyclopedia of Children's Literature, Cooperative Children's Book Ctr., U. Wis., Madison, Riverbank Rev., 1998—, Ency. of Children's Lit., 1998—; lang. arts com. NCTE Notable Books, 1997—; spkr. in field. Author: Reading in a Media Age, 1975, 20th Century Children's Writers, 1979, rev. edit., 1984, What Else Can You Do With a Library Degree?, 1980, Popular Reading for Children, 1981, Popular Reading II, 1986, Children's Books of International Interest, 1984, Tomie dePaola, His Art and His Stories, 1999, Holiday House: It's First 65 Years, 2000, Virginia Lee Burton: A Life in Art, 2002; contbr. articles to profl. jours. Publicity chair Internat. Bd. Books for Young People Congress, Williamsburg, Va., 1990; bd. trustees Eric Carle Mus. Picture Book Art, 2004-. Recipient Jeremiah Ludington award Ednl. Paperback Assn., 1996, Hope S. Dean award Found. Children's Lit., 1996. Mem. ALA (2000 Caldecott Com. 1999—), Soc. Children's Book Writers (mem. orgn. com. MidWest Conf. 1974-76), Internat. Bd. Books for Young People (U.S. assoc. editor Bookbird 1978-86, chair nominating com., 1985, bd. dirs. 1990-92), Children's Reading Round Table Chgo. (award 1987), Nat. Coun. Tchrs. English (bd. dirs. children's lit. assembly 1986-88, mem. editl. adv. bd. CLA bull. 1989-91, mem. using nonfiction in classroom com. 1990-96, 2000 Caldecott com., Laura I. Wilder com. 2001--). Address: 20 Bayon Dr Apt 5 South Hadley MA 01075

ELLEN, JANE, composer, music educator, researcher; b. San Pedro, Calif., May 11, 1956; BA, U. N.Mex., 1992, postgrad., 1992-93. Cert. music tchr., N.Mex. Freelance composer, Albuquerque, 1986—. Parish organist Our Lady of Annunciation, Albuquerque, 1994—98; nat. dir. Composers Bur. Signa Alpha Iota Am., 1999—; contract prof. ElderHostel, U. N.Mex., 1996—2001; resident instr. OASIS, 1996—. Composer (more than 300 works including): Dancing in Deep Heaven for chamber orch., 1991; composer: Elegy for the Children of Sarajevo, woodwind quintet, 1992; composer: (with text by Ann Cragg) Phantom Lost for voice, oboe and piano, 1999; composer: Images of Rome for piano, 2000; composer: (with text by Claire Roth) The Eternal Ring for SATB choir, 2001;: commns. include NEA/NMAD; composer: MTNA state composer New Music Across Am., Canossian Daus. of Charity, Am. Guild Organists Dist. VII Conf., 1993, 2003, N.Mex. Quincentenary Commn., N.Mex. Women Composers Guild, (with text by Roth) Per La Grazia di Dio for SATB choir, 2001, (with text by Roth) Hearts and Hands United for SATB choir, 2002. Recipient 1st place award Nat. League Am. Pen Women, 1996, 1st, 2d and 3d place awards, 1998. Mem. ASCAP (grantee 1990—), Music Tchrs. Nat. Assn. (profl. cert.), Phi Beta Kappa, Phi Kappa Phi, Sigma Alpha Iota (Ruby Sword of Honour award 1992, Ring of Excellence award, 2006). Roman Catholic. Avocations: reading, studying italian, writing poetry and prose, watching old films, researching civil war music. Home: 2226 B Wyoming NE 182 Albuquerque NM 87112-2620 Personal E-mail: Jane@JaneEllen.com.

ELLENBERGER, DIANE MARIE, nurse, consultant; b. St. Louis, Oct. 5, 1946; d. Charles Ernst and Celeste Loraine (Neudecker) E. RN, Barnes Hosp., St. Louis, 1970; BSN, St. Louis U., 1976; MSN, U. Colo., 1977. Bd. cert. legal nurse cons.; cert. clin. nurse specialist. Staff nurse hosps., clin. nurse, St. Louis, 1973-76; nurse clinician Sedalia, Mo., 1977-78; nurse clinician, educator Bothwell Hosp., Sedalia, 1977-78; clin. nurse specialist, coord. perinatal outreach edn. Cardinal Glennon Meml. Hosp. Children, St. Louis, 1978-80; instr. McKendree Coll., Lebanon, Ill., 1980; asst. prof. Maryville Coll., St. Louis, 1982-85; nurse cons. Carr, Korein, Tillery, Attys. at Law, East St. Louis, Ill., 1986—97; owner, nurse cons. The Med-Legal Advantage, San Anselmo, Calif., 1997—. Owner, operator Diane Designs Needlepoint, St. Louis, 1981-96. Contbr. articles to profl. jours. Mem. Divine Sci. Ch. With Nurse Corps, USAF, 1970-72. Mem. ANA (Calif. affiliate bd. dirs. 1998-2002), AACN, Am. Assn. Legal Nurse Cons. (Bay Area bd. dirs. 1999-2003), Nat. Perinatal Assn., Assn. Women's Health, Obstetric and Neonatal Nurses, Mo. Nurses Assn. (bd. dirs. 1995-97, bylaws chair 1990-2001, del. to ANA 1996, 3d dist. pres. 1993-96), Mo. Perinatal Assn. (v.p. 1980), Sigma Theta Tau. Office: PO Box 1638 San Anselmo CA 94979-1638 E-mail: mladvntg@pacbell.net.

ELLENBERGER, KATHLEEN SUE BOWMAN, special education educator; b. San Francisco, Feb. 17, 1950; d. John Francis and Patricia Ann (Bofinger) Bowman; m. Dearld Lynn Ellenberger, July 16, 1977; children: Emily Jane, Renden Ray. AA, American River Jr. Coll., 1970; AB with honors, U. Calif.-Berkeley, 1972. Cert. tchr. elem., early childhood, learning handicapped. First grade tchr. Big Valley Unified Sch. Dist., Adin, Calif., 1974—79; spl. edn. tchr. (learning handicapped) Lassen County Schs., Adin, 1981—2001. Active leader 4-H, Drug and Alcohol Abuse Prevention, Integrating Arts in the Curriculum, Sch. Improvement Program, Big Valley Primary Sch., 1979—84; mem. Early Childhood Edn. Com., 1977—79; organizer Mothers Are People Too Club, 1979. Mem.: Calif. Tchrs. Assn., NEA. Home: 616 Main St PO Box 196 Adin CA 96006-0196

ELLENBOGEN, ELISABETH ALICE, retired accountant; b. Lemberg, Ukraine, Sept. 10, 1940; d. Joseph and Leah Karolina (Wiener) Ellenbogen. B in Humanities, Pa. State U., cert. in acctg.; student, Elizabethtown Coll. Cert. civil servant. Buyer McCrory Corp., York, Pa., 1959-65; account mgr. WT Grant Co., York, Pa., 1965-70; various acctg. civil svc. positions Commonwealth of Pa., Harrisburg, 1970-89. Contract mgr. health and human svcs. Commonwealth of Pa., 1989—99. Author: Bill of Rights for Citizens Facing the End of Life, 1997, (bulletin) Out Cry!, 1975, (policies/procedures) Constitutional Rights for Handicapped Citizens, 1975—. Bd. dirs. ACLU, Pa., 1978—2003, disability rights adv. Pa., 1978—; convenor Ecumenical Coalition to Abolish the Penalty of Death, Pa., 1985—2003; activist Harrisburg Rape Crisis, 1973—77; counselor Women's Ctr., Harrisburg, 1975—79. Mem.: NOW, Prime Time Group (mem. women's consciousness raising support 1973—77). Democrat. Jewish. Home and Office: 298 Colonial Rd # 4 Harrisburg PA 17109-1556 Personal E-mail: billofrights@hotmail.com.

ELLENBOGEN, MARJORIE, retired elementary school educator; b. N.Y.C., Oct. 28, 1936; d. Franklyn and Molly (Berman) E. BA, Vassar Coll., 1958; MA, Columbia U., 1959. Cert. elem. tchr., N.Y. Tchr. Bd. Edn. N.Y.C. Allen-Stevenson Sch., N.Y.C., 1959-60, Ethical Culture Sch., N.Y.C., 1960-65, Columbia Grammar Sch., N.Y.C., 1965-67, UN Internat. Sch., N.Y.C., 1967—97. Vol. Lighthouse Internat., 1997—. Avocations: swimming, travel. Home: 45 Sutton Pl S New York NY 10022-2444

ELLENBROOK, CAROLYN KAY, religious organization administrator; b. Denton, Tex., Sept. 2, 1943; d. Herman and Winnie Louise (Garrett) Baker; m. Edward Charles Ellenbrook, Jr., Apr. 13, 1968; 1 child, Margaret. A, Cameron Jr. Coll., 1963; BS in Edn., Okla. State U., 1965. Child welfare caseworker State of Okla., Lawton, 1965—68; religious edn. sec. Comancho-Cotton Bapt. Assn., Lawton, 1981—. Contbr. chapters to books Heart Call-The Call to Prayer, 1998; co-author: (book) Comanche-Cotton Baptist Association A Centennial History, 1902-2002, 2002. Area adv. City PTA, Lawton, 1977—80, mem., 1973—86; treas. Eisenhower H.S. PTA, 1984—86; pres. So. Bapt. Women's Missionary Union, Okla., 1993—98. Named Ch. Women of Yr., DAR, 2000. Mem.: Nat. So. Bapt. Sec. Orgn., Okla. So. Bapt. Sec. Orgn., So. Bapt. Assoc. Religious Educators (pres. 2002). Avocations: hiking, history, writing, travel, working with children. Home: 1603 Keystone Dr Lawton OK 73505 Office: Comanche-Cotton Baptist Assoc 2612 E Ave Lawton OK 73505 Personal E-mail: ecebrook@sirinet.net.

ELLENWOOD, HEATHER SKY, music educator; d. Steven Louis Ellenwood and Kelly Lynne Morgan. MusB in Music Edn., Mich. State U., East Lansing, 2003. Music tchr. Walton Charter Acad., Pontiac, Mich., 2003—04; dir. of bands Merrill Cmty. Schs., 2005—. Pvt. trumpet instr., Merrill, 2000—. Recipient Crystal Apple award, Saginaw News, 2006. Mem.: Gordon Inst. Learning, Internat. Trumpet Guild, Music Educator's Nat. Conf., Mich. Sch. Band & Orch. Assn., Phi Kappa Phi, Nat. Soc. Collegiate Scholars, Golden Key. Avocations: scuba diving, travel, cooking, egyptology. Office: Merrill Cmty Schs 755 W Alice St Merrill MI 48637

ELLER, KAREN KREIMANN, elementary school educator; d. Gladwin Glenn and Jacqueline Kreimann; m. N. H. (Bud) Eller, Apr. 14, 1984. BA in Bibl. Edn., Columbia Internat. U., SC, 1975; M in Elem. Edn., Ga. State U., Atlanta, 1977. Tchr. gifted Tyrone Elem. Sch., Ga., 1992—95; tchr. fifth grade Spring Hill Elem., Fayetteville, 1995—. Tchr. Flat Creek Bapt. Ch., Fayetteville, Ga., 1993—2006. Recipient Tchr. Yr., Huddleston Elem. Sch., 1986, Spring Hill Elem. Sch., 2006. Mem.: Ga. Coun. Social Studies, Pa. Ga. Educators. Baptist. Office: Spring Hill Elementary 100 Bradford Square Fayetteville GA 30215 Office Phone: 770-460-3432.

ELLERBEE, LINDA (LINDA JANE SMITH), reporter; b. Bryan, Tex., Aug. 15, 1944; m. Mac Smith, 1964 (div. 1966), m. Van Veselka, 1968 (div. 1971), children: Vanessa, Joshua, m. Tom Ellerbee, 1973 (div. 1974). Student, Vanderbilt U., Nashville, 1962—64. Newscaster, disc jockey Sta. WVON, Chgo., 1964-67; program dir. Sta. KSJO, San Francisco, 1967-68; reporter Sta. KJNO and AP, Juneau, Alaska, 1969-72; news writer AP, Dallas, 1972; TV reporter KHOU, Houston, 1972—73; gen. assignment reporter Sta. WCBS-TV, N.Y.C., 1973-76; Washington corr. NBC News, 1976—78; co-anchor Weekend, NBC News, NBC-TV, 1978—79; corr. NBC Nightly News, 1979—82; co-anchor NBC News Overnight, 1982-84, Summer Sunday, 1984; corr., reporter Today Show, NBC-TV, 1984—86; reporter Good Morning America, 1986; writer, anchor Our World, ABC-TV, 1986—87; prodr., writer, host Nick News, Nickelodeon Network, 1993—; founder, pres. Lucky Duck Prodns., N.Y.C., 1987—; commentator Cable News Network, 1989; writer, host On the Record, Microsoft online, 1996—. Author: And So It Goes: Adventures in Television, 1986, Move On: Adventures in the Real World, 1991, Take Big Bites: Adventures Around the World and Across the Table, 2005; exec. prod. (TV spls.) A Conversation with Magic (Cable ACE award 1992), It's Only Television (Peabody award 1992); exec. prod., writer, host (news/mag. program) Nick News (Columbia duPont award 1993, Parents' Choice Found. Gold TV award); writer, anchor, Our World (Emmy for best writing 1986); weekly syndicated columnist King Features, N.Y.; (narrator) Baby Boom, 1987, Addicted, 1997 (also exec. prodr., writer, filmography prodr.); filmography prodr. (miniseries) Oh What a Time It Was, 1999; exec. prodr. (TV) several Intimate Portraits 1998-2003, Feeding the Beast: The 24-Hour News Revolution, 2004; prodr. (TV mini series) Oh What a Time It Was, 1999; exec. prodr. (TV series) When I Was a Girl, 2001; prodr. Inside TV Land: Primetime Politics, 2004 (also writer), Inside TV Land: Tickled Pink, 2005; guest appearances Murphy Brown, 1989, 1993, Ellen, 1998, The Fight to be Fit, Nick News, 2005. Office: Lucky Duck Prodns 96 Morton St Fl 4 New York NY 10014-3326*

ELLERMAN, PAIGE L., lawyer; b. Covington, Ky., May 11, 1974; BA, U. Ky., 1995; JD, Salmon P. Chase Coll. Law, 1999. Bar: Ohio 1999, Ky. 2000, Ind. 2001, US Dist. Ct. Southern Dist. Ohio, US Dist. Ct. Eastern Dist. Ky., US Dist. Ct. Western Dist. Ky., US Supreme Ct. Assoc. Taft, Stettinius & Hollister LLP, Cin. Mem. Profl. Women's Resource Grp. Pres. The Yearlings, Inc.; mem., Ann. Support Com. Elizabeth Med. Ctr. Found., chair, Benefactor Drive, 2006—. Named one of Ohio's Rising Stars, Super Lawyers, 2005, 2006. Mem.: Salmon P. Chase Coll. Law Alumni Assn. (pres., Bd. Govenors), FBA, Cin. Bar Assn. Office: Taft Stettinius & Hollister LLP 425 Walnut St Ste 1800 Cincinnati OH 45202-3957 Office Phone: 513-381-2838. Office Fax: 513-381-0205.*

ELLETT, LINDA MICK, special education educator; b. Des Moines, Iowa, Dec. 26, 1947; d. LeRoy and Ardith (Jennings) Mick; m. Thomas Charles Ellett, June 12, 1971. BA, U. No. Iowa, 1970; postgrad., U. Minn., 1975-83; MA, San Diego State U., 1991. Tchr. Benton Community Sch. Dist., Van Horne, Iowa, 1970-73, Robbinsdale Sch. Dist. # 281, Mpls., 1973-75, Osseo (Minn.) Sch. Dist. # 279, 1975-83; mktg. analyst ShareCom, Mpls., 1983-84; wellness presentor Healthy Eating Lifestyles, Mpls., 1984-85; resource specialist Poway (Calif.) Unified Sch. Dist., 1987—, tchr. cons., 2000—03. Mentor tchr. Poway Unified Sch. Dist., 1993—. Presentor Minn. Coun. on Health, Mpls., 1983-85, Minn. Coun. of Health Promotion and Wellness, Mpls., 1983-85; program com. Minn. Women's Network, Mpls., 1983-85; mem. Poway Unified Sch. Dist. Lang. Arts Coun., 2004-06 Named Vol. of Yr. Minn. Coun. on Health, 1985. Mem. Coun. for Exceptional Children, Learning Disabilities Assn., Pi Lambda Theta (Beta Beta chpt. 1st v.p. 1993-94, pres. 1994-95, Region V co-pres. 1996-97). Avocations: cooking, sewing, weaving, yoga.

ELLICKSON, JUDITH A., literature and language educator; b. Dubuque, Iowa, Feb. 9, 1954; d. Neil P. and Mary Theresa Gallagher; m. Jack Howard Ellickson, Feb. 28, 1976; children: Jessica, Jamie Mowry, Joe, Jennifer Barton. BS, U. Wis., Platteville; MS, MSCI, U. Wis., Whitewater; MS, Viterbo U., LaCrosse, Wis. Cert. adminstrn. and edn. Reading specialist Johnson Creek (Wis.) Schs., coord. gifted and talented; cons. Inst. Acad. Excellence, Madison, Wis., Harcourt & Brace, Madison; reading specialist Sun Prairie (Wis.) Sch.; reading coord. Omega Sch., Madison; reading specialist Title I Middleton (Wis.) Cross Plain. Pres. Rushford (Minn.) JC, 1980—82. Mem.: WTGT, AWSA, ASCD, Madison Area Reading Coun. (pres.-elect 1997—2006), Wis. State Reading Assn. (mem. leadership com. 1997—2006, mem. network com.), Internat. Reading Assn. (field leader 2004—06), Federated Womans Club (pres. 1980—84), Gamma Phi Beta (pres. 1974—78). Home: 1813 Sunrise Ct Stoughton WI 53589

ELLICKSON, PHYLLIS LYNN, political scientist; b. Springfield, Mass., Apr. 22, 1942; d. Frank Walter Rutter and Winifred Annette Grayston; m. Bryan Carl Ellickson, June 19, 1965; 1 child, Paul Bryan. BA, Mount Holyoke Coll., 1963; PhD, MIT, 1973. Rschr. Arthur D. Little Inc., Cambridge, Mass., 1964—66; asst. prof. UCLA, 1973—74; social scientist Rand, Santa Monica, Calif., 1974—85, sr. behavioral scientist, 1985—. Mem. ednl. adv. bd. The Best Found., L.A., 1994—; mem. nat. adv. bd. Monitoring the Future, Ann Arbor, Mich., 1998—; expert panel mem. Dept. Edn., Washington, 1998—2000. Contbr. articles to profl. jours. Adv. bd. Partnership for a Drug Free Am., N.Y.C., 2002—. Mem.: Soc. for Prevention Rsch., Phi Beta Kappa. Achievements include development of award-winning drug prevention program Project ALERT. Avocations: travel, opera. Home: 18409 Wakecrest Dr Malibu CA 90265 Office: Rand 1776 Main St Santa Monica CA 90407 Business E-Mail: phyllis_ellickson@rand.org.

ELLINGSEN, BARBARA JOYCE, music educator; b. Oak Park, Ill., Apr. 27, 1955; d. John Franklin and Joyce (Smith) Johnson; children: Jeremy James, Andrew Daniel, Nathan Samuel. AA, Coll. of DuPage, 1975; MusB, Elmhurst Coll., 2002; M in music edn., VanderCook Coll. Music, Chgo., 2006. Elem. music tchr. Hannum Elem. Sch., Oak Lawn, 2002—. Recipient Meta Grace Keebler scholarship, Keebler Corp., 2001, Sherratt scholarship in mMusic, Elmhurst Coll., 2001. Mem.: Ill. Music Educators Assn., Music Educators Nat. Conf., Lambda Sigma Psi, Kappa Delta Pi, Phi Kappa Phi. Republican. Avocations: playing clarinet, bicycling, arts and crafts, gardening. Home: 418 S Monterey Ave Villa Park IL 60181 Office Phone: 708-423-1690. Personal E-mail: clarinet1955@earthlink.net.

ELLINGSON, MARY, b. Carroll, Iowa, Oct. 8, 1938; d. Raymond William and Mildred Ressa Leonard; m. William Arthur Ellingson, June 11, 1960; children: Mary, Anne BS honors, Iowa State U., 1961; MS, George Williams Coll., 1983. Tchr. various schs., 1967—; councilman City of Naperville, Ill., 1995—. Rsch. cons., 1988-95 Co-author: The Baby Book: A Resource Manual of Services for Children Under 3 Years Old, 1990, YMCA Infant/Toddler Child Care, 1990; contbr. articles to profl. jours Mem. Nat. Child Task Force YMCA, Chgo., 1980-83, rsch. assoc., 1983-88; mem. edn. adv. com. 13th Congl. Dist., 1990-97; co-chmn. Celebration 2000, Naperville, 1996-2001; bd. dirs. Citizen Appreciate Police, Naperville, Naperville Cmty. Outreach, 1998-2004, Naper Settlement Mus.; co-chair tourist bur. Naperville

Devel. Partnership, 1999—; sec. Sunriser Rotary Club Naperville Recipient Leadership award Celebration 2000, 1999, Disting. Svc. award Jaycees, 2000, Suburban Pk. & Recreation award Pk. Dist., 2000; named Citizen of Yr. Am. Legion, 2000 Mem. Nat. Flute Assn., Naperville C. of C., Chgo. Flute Assn., Kappa Omicron Nu, Phi Kappa Phi Avocations: gardening, walking. Office: 400 S Eagle St Naperville IL 60540-5279

ELLINGTON, JANE ELIZABETH, experimental psychologist; b. Little Rock, Jan. 23, 1946; d. Julian Buril and Dorothy (Davidson) Priddy; m. Edward Lee Stephens, May 22, 1982. AB, Washington U., St. Louis, 1968; MA, Abilene Christian U., 1971; PhD, U. North Tex., 1984. Staff psychologist West Tex. Rehab. Ctr., Abilene, 1971-75; tchg. fellow U. North Tex., Denton, 1981-84; asst. prof. psychology Austin Coll., Sherman, Tex., 1987-92, assoc. prof. psychology, 1992—, chair dept. psychology, sociology & anthropology, 1995-2000. Mem. APA, Am. Name Soc., Southwestern Psychol. Assn. Mem. Ch. of Christ. Avocation: quilting.

ELLINGTON, KAREN RENAE, school system administrator; b. Turlock, Calif., Oct. 19, 1965; d. Edward Ray and Barbara Janet (Rafatti) E. BS, Calif. Poly., 1989; postgrad., Chapman U., 1994-96. Tchg. credentials include multiple subject, agr., bus., spl. edn.-learning handicapped; cert. resource specialist; cert. crosscultural, lang. and acad. devel. specialist. Asst. mgr. House of Fabrics, San Luis Obispo, Calif., 1985-88, Macy's, Sacramento, 1988-90; clk. Raley's, Modesto, Calif., 1990-93; substitute tchr. Merced & Stanislaus Counties, Calif., 1993; resource specialist Los Banos (Calif.) H.S., 1994—. Computer instr. ARBOR, Modesto and Merced, 1994-97. Leader 4-H, Merced County, 1990—, dir. 1998—; mem. Calif. State Citizenship Coun., 1999—. Mem. NEA, Calif. Tchrs. Assn., Los Banos Tchrs. Assn., Coun. for Exceptional Children, Calif. Ag. Tchrs. Assn. (assoc.), Internat. Dyslexia Assn. Avocations: travel, stitchery, photography, athletics. Office: Los Banos HS 1966 S 11th St Los Banos CA 93635-4812 E-mail: karenellington@hotmail.com, kellington@losbanosusd.k12.ca.us.

ELLINGTON, MILDRED L., librarian; b. Marion, Ohio, June 7, 1921; d. Edward J. and Julia Ellen (Oiler) E. BA, Olivet Nazarene Coll., Kankakee, Ill., 1943; MA in French, Ohio State U., 1952; MA in English, Bowling Green (Ohio) U., 1964; MLS, Rosary Coll., River Forest, Ill., 1976. English and French tchr. Morral (Ohio) High Sch., 1944-49, Reddick (Ill.) High Sch., 1949-55; English tchr. Bremen Community High Sch., Midlothian, Ill., 1955-58, Bloom Twp. High Sch., Chicago Heights, Ill., 1958-60, Willowbrook High Sch., Villa Park, Ill., 1960-66; English tchr., then libr. dir. Addison Trail High Sch., Ill., 1966-82; reference librarian Maywood Pub. Library, Ill., 1982—2006. Sunday sch. supt. Elgin (Ill.) Ch. of the Nazarene, 1985-92. Mem. Ill. Library Assn. Democrat. Mem. Ch. of the Nazarene. Avocations: opera, singing, genealogy, travel.

ELLINGWOOD, SUSAN, editor; BA, Dickinson Coll.; grad. study, St. Antony's Coll., Oxford. Researcher The New Yorker Mag., Washington; asst. mng. editor The New Republic mag.; news editor, fgn. desk Wall St. Jour., 1997—2000; sr. editor, fin., internat., polit. news Brill's Content; editl. dir. Com. to Protect Journalists; staff editor, Op-Ed desk NY Times, 2004—. Served with USAR. Office: Op-Ed Page NY Times 229 W 43rd St New York NY 10036 Office Phone: 212-556-8435. Office Fax: 212-556-4100, 212-556-3690. Business E-Mail: opedcity@nytimes.com.

ELLINWOOD, JANICE GREENBERG, art educator; b. Hartford, Conn., July 4, 1952; d. Bennett and Hilda (Podnetsky) Greenberg; m. Edward Scott Rosenthal, Nov. 11, 1978 (div. Dec. 1991); children: Amy Dawn Rosenthal, Lindsey Jean Rosenthal, Samantha Robyn Rosenthal; m. James John III McCoart, Aug. 20, 1995 (div. Apr. 2003); m. Jamie Brian Ellinwood, Aug. 17, 2004. BS, Skidmore Coll., Saratoga Springs, N.Y., 1974; MFA, George Washington U., 1986. Buyer, visual presentation dir. Blake's Dept. Stores, Springfield, Mass., 1974—77; instr. bus. Bay Path Coll., Longmeadow, Mass., 1977—78; from lectr. to prof. fine and applied arts, chmn. dept. Marymount U., Arlington, Va., 1980—, chair fashion design, fashion merchandising. Cons. to exhibit "Between a Rock and a Hard Place: A Dialogue on Sweatshops, 1820 to the Present Smithsonian Instn., Washington, 1998; organizer, grantee Contemporary Bulgarian Art Exhibit Marymount U., 2002; cons. Fashion Industry Forum U.S. Dept. Labor, Washington, 1996; conf. chair An Acad. Search for Sweatshop Solutions Marymount Coll., 1997. Editor: (conf. proc.) An Academic Search for Sweatshop Solutions, 1997; contbr. articles to profl. jours. Sr. Scholar grantee, Fulbright Scholarship Bd., 2001—02. Mem.: Internat. Textile and Apparel Assn., Costume Soc. Am., Coll. Art Assn. Am., So. Assn. of Colls. and Schs. Commn. on Colls. Office: Marymount Univ 2807 N Glebe Rd Arlington VA 22207 E-mail: janice.ellinwood@marymount.edu.

ELLIOT, ALEXANDRA, special education educator, real estate agent; BS in Psychology, Santa Clara U., Santa Clara, Calif., 1995; MS in Spl. Edn., Calif. State U., Hayward, Calif., 2005; MS, Calif. State U., 2005. Cert. Reading Specialist Tex., Spl. Edn. Tchr., Reading Tchr. Calif., Spl. Edn. Calif. Tchr. MSD, Calif., 1996—99; reading specialist SRVUSD, Calif., 1999—2002; spl. edn. tchr. CVUSD, Calif., 2002—05. Mem. calif. Assn. Resource Specialists, Calif., 2002—05, Austin Bd. Realtors, Austin, Tex., Tex. Bd. Realtors, Austin, Tex. Author: (manual) Teaching Word Identification Skills to Students with Learning Disabilities. Voter registration vol., Calif. Avocations: gardening, cooking, hiking, nature.

ELLIOT, JANET LEE, occupational therapist; b. Hannibal, Mo., Aug. 6, 1955; d. Bobby Neal and Mary Elizabeth (Ford) Vandiver; m. Roger Larry Elliot, July 26, 1986. Student, U. Mo., 1979, MD, 1981; MPH, Med. Coll. Wis., 1999. Lic. family practitioner, surgeon, breath alcohol tech.; diplomate Am. Acad. Pain Mgmt., Am. Bd. Forensic Examiners. Resident Truman Med. Ctr., Kansas City, Mo.; with occupational gen. Landmark Med. Ctr., Kansas City, Mo., 1982-84, North Indsl. Clinic, Kansas City, 1984-88; aviation med. examiner N.J., 1985; with mini residency occupational medicine Robert Wood Johnson Med. Sch., U. of Medicine and Dentistry of N.J., 1987; dir. of occupational medicine Suburban Heights Med. Ctr., Chicago Heights, Ill., 1988—. Mem. Am. Occupational Medicine Assn., Am. Acad. Family Practice, Am. Assn. Ry. Surgeons, Norfolk and Western Ry. Assn., Am. Coll. Forensic Examiners, Am. Acad. Pain Mgmt., VFW. Republican. Roman Catholic. Avocations: skiing, football, dance, movies.

ELLIOT, KATHLEEN ANN, school system administrator; b. Kew Gardens, N.Y., Sept. 27, 1942; d. Thomas Peter Jr. and Ann D'oilé (Jenkins) Rothwell; m. Lee Elliot, May 23, 1980 (div. Feb. 1999); 1 child, Laurie Ann. BFA, Syracuse (N.Y.) U., 1964. Tchr. N.Y. Pub. Sch. Sys., Seaford, 1964-65; advt. account exec., supr. various agys., N.Y.C., 1966-86; tchr. N.Y. Pub. Sch. Sys., Cornwall, 1986-90; dir. recreation Pine Lakes C.C., North Ft. Myers, Fla., 1991-94, Seven Lakes Assocs., Ft. Myers, Fla., 1994—99, S.W. Fla. Coll., 2002—. Sec. bd. dirs. Country Pines Condominium Assn. North Ft. Myers 1997-98. Mem. AAUW (sec. 1997—), Syracuse U. Alumni Club Ft. Myers, Resort and Comml. Recreation Assn. Republican. Roman Catholic. Avocations: reading, recreational writing, swimming, boating. Home: 1200 Hall Rd Fort Myers FL 33903-5718

ELLIOTT, CANDICE K., interior designer; b. Cedar Rapids, Iowa, Aug. 29, 1949; d. Charles H. and Eunice A. (Long) Goodrich; m. John William Jr. Elliott, Jan. 27, 1973 (div.); 1 child, Brandon Christian; m. Timothy G. Kling, Sept. 14, 2002; 3 stepchildren, John William III, Timothy Andrew, Nathan David. BA, U. Iowa, 1971. Interior designer Dayton's, Mpls., 1971-76, Candice Interior Space Planning and Design, Guilford, Conn., 1981-87; owner, interior designer Sofa Works, King of Prussia, Pa., 1987-90; interior designer Jerrehians's Home Furnishings, West Chester, Pa., 1990-92; dir. sales and visual merchandising Sheffield Furniture, Malvern, Pa., 1992-95; owner Candice Interior Space Planning and Design, Wayne, Pa., 1996-97, Mt. Vernon, Iowa, 1997-2000, Kill Devil Hills, NC, 2000—01, Kitty Hawk, NC, 2001—. Bd. dirs. The Old Capitol Restoration Com., Iowa City, 1970-76; curator Guilford Keeping Soc., 1983-88; cons. Zion Episcopal Ch., North Branford, Conn., 1985-88; mem. planning and zoning bd. City of Mt. Vernon, Iowa, 1997-99; cons. design commn. Duck Woods Country Club, 2004-05 Mem. Am. Soc. Interior Designers (bd. dirs. Conn. chpt., profl. mem.), Duck Woods Country Club, Roanoke Island Garden Club (pres. 2005—). Republican. Avocations: golf, needlepoint, gardening. Home and Office: 1016 Creek Rd Kitty Hawk NC 27949

ELLIOTT, CAROLYN COLE, secondary school educator, department chairman; b. South Boston, Va., July 7, 1943; d. Raleigh Newmsn Cole and Gladys Ruth Newcomb; m. Clyde Clifton Elliott; children: Natalie Elaine, Mark Landon. AA, Averett Coll., Danville, Va., 1964; BS, Longwood U., Farmville, Va., 1966; MEd, U. NC, Charlotte, 1999. Cert. tchr. NC. Tchr. Halifax County Sch., Halifax, Va., 1966—77, Granville County Schs., Oxford, NC, 1977—80, Allenstown Schs., NH, 1980—85, Manchester City Schs., NH, 1985—88, Iredell-Statesville Sch., Statesville, NC, 1988—, chmn. sci. dept., 2003—. Regional judge Exploravision/Nat. Sci. Teachers Assn., Arlington, Va., 2006—; master tchr. NCTeach, Charlotte, NC, 2000—05, SciLink, Raleigh, NC, 1994—2004, NC Leadership Network Earth Sci. Tchr., Charlotte, 1996—99; textbook reviewer Glencoe Pub., Columbus, Ohio, 2004—; presenter in field. Contbr. North Carolina Support Documents; contbr.: Support Document for Honors Physical Science, Resourse Guide for Oceanography and Coastal Processes. Pres. South Boston Bus. Women Club, Va.; oxford's jr. womens club Oxford, NC. Named Tchr. of Yr., South Iredell HS, 2000; recipient State Presidential award for Excellence in Math. and Sci. Tchg., NSF, 2000—01, Nat. Tchr. award, Radioshack, 1999—2000, Dist. Tchr. of the Yr., Iredell-Statesville Sch. Sys., 2000-2001, Ben Craig Outstanding Educator award, First Union Bank, 2001. Mem.: Nat. Sci. Tchr. Assn. (awards and recognition com. 2005—, state coord. Bldg. Presence in Sci. program 2005—, dist. Outstanding Tchg. award 1995), NC Sci. Tchr. Assn. (life; dist. 7 dir., v.p., pres., past pres. 2004), Delta Kappa Gamma (1st v.p., 2d v.p. 1985—95), Phi Kappa Phi (assoc.), Kappa Delta Pi (assoc.). Office: South Iredell HS 299 Old Mountain Rd Statesville NC 28677 Office Phone: 704-528-4536. Business E-Mail: celliott@iss.k12.nc.us.

ELLIOTT, CAROLYN ELIZABETH, educator, writer; b. Eureka, Kans., Apr. 18, 1952; d. William Hill and Janice Elizabeth (Crouch) Elliott; 1 child, Marissa Elizabeth. BA, U. Northern Colo., 1974, MA, 1977. Lic. tchr., Colo. Tchr. Bozeman (Mont.) Pub. Schs., 1974, Boulder (Colo.) Valley Pub. Schs., 1977—2005, ret., 2005. Editor Boulder-Westminster (Colo.) tchr. newspaper, 1984-85. Chmn. Broomfield (Colo.) High program for gifted, 1980-88; mem., presenter Colo. Dept. Edn. Instrnl. Design Cadre, 1986-88. Recipient Exemplary Tchr. of Yr. award KCNC Channel 4 News, Denver, 1991. Best Shot Tchr. award Centaurus High Sch., Colo. Nuggets, Denver Post, Lafayette and Denver, Colo., 1992. Mem. Nat. Edn. Assn. (life, Colo. chpt., Boulder Valley chpt.). Avocations: reading, writing, music. Home: 708 Homestead St Lafayette CO 80026 Office Phone: 303-604-1836. Personal E-mail: carolyneelliott@comcast.net.

ELLIOTT, CAROLYN SAYRE, librarian, educator; d. William Mulford Sayre and Margery Adams Conrad; m. David Lindsey Elliott, Aug. 8, 1970; children: Matthew Thomas, Gregory Richard. BA cum laude, Syracuse U., 1970, MA, 1973; MLIS, SUNY, Albany, 1991. Asst. slide curator Bird Libr., Syracuse U., NY, 1973—76; reference asst. Bartle Libr., SUNY, Binghamton, 1993—94; asst. clk. Miller Libr., KC, LaPlume, Pa., 1977—91, dir., 1994—99; head libr. Lackawanna Trail H.S., Factoryville, Pa., 1999—. Part-time lectr. Keystone Coll., LaPlume, 1976—. Author: Love in Vain, 1973, NREN Update, 1993; contbr. articles to profl. jours. Pres. Lithia Valley Food Co-op, Factoryville, 1983—85; mem. North Branch Friends, Overcare Com., Forty-Fort, 1999—2001. Mem.: ALA, Theta Alpha Kappa, Beta Phi Mu. Quaker. Avocations: reading, travel, knitting, camping. Home: 40 Highland Ave Factoryville PA 18419 Business E-Mail: celliott@epix.net.

ELLIOTT, DONNA LOUISE, artist; b. Oak Park, Ill., Sept. 2, 1931; d. Carl and Sarah Louise (Shelton) Reinecke; m. Gerald Morris Elliott, June 24, 1950. BS in Art Edn., U. Wis., Milw., 1966. Art tchr. Grafton H.S., Wis., 1969—70; instr. art Cardinal Stritch U., Fox Pt., Wis., 1990—95; leader workshop Wauwatosa Woman's Club, Wauwatosa, Wis., 1996; instr. workshop West Bend Art Mus., Wis., 1999, Peninsula Sch. Fine Arts, Fish Creek, Wis., 2002—03; leader Watercolor Workshop Enrichment Ctr., Bonita Springs, Fla., 2004; instr. Art League Bonita Springs, 2004—05. One-woman shows include Firehouse Gallery, Cedarburg, Wis., 1972, Milw. Athletic Club, 1974, 1982, 1993, Sistermoon Gallery, Milw., 1978, Marine Bank, Fox Pt., 1987, Concordia Coll. Gallery, 1988, Firestation Gallery, Milw., 1989, Alexian Village Gallery, 1994, Metrix Co., Waukesha, Wis., 1997, The Andersen Arts Ctr., Kenosha, Wis., 1999, exhibitions include League of Milw. Artists Show, 1970—2003 (Best of Show, 1982, 1994), Wis. Watercolor Soc., 1989—2003, Wis. Women in Arts, Milw., 1990 (award of Excellence, 1982), Wis. Painters and Sculptors (various shows), 1995—2003 (1st place, 1998, Exhbn. award, 1999), Wustum Mus., Racine, Wis., 2002—03, Midwest Biennial New Visions Gallery, 2003, Art League of Bonita Springs, Fla., 2004, 2005, Represented in permanent collections Am. Internat. Supply Co., Tex., SBC-Wis. Telephone Co., Coopers & Lybrand, Milw., Northwestern Mutual Ins. Co. Vol. watercolor instr. North Shore Sch. Srs., United Meth. Sch., Whitefish Bay, Wis., 2001. Mem.: Naples Art Assn., Wis. Artists in All Media/Wis. Painters and Sculptors (chair S.E. chpt. 2001—03), Transparent Watercolor Soc. Am., Art League of Bonita Springs (life). Methodist. Avocations: weightlifting, walking, swimming, travel. Home: 9102 Windswept Dr Bonita Springs FL 34135-8187

ELLIOTT, DOROTHY GAIL, music educator, writer; b. Kennard, Ind., Oct. 23, 1918; d. Clyde Harrison and Hazel Uvah (Houk) Copeland; m. Robert E. Elliott, Aug. 22, 1948 (dec. Mar. 1997); children: R. Bruce, Marla Beth, John H. BS in Edn., Ball State Tchrs. Coll., 1940; student Chgo. Theol. Sem., U. Chgo., 1944—47. Tchr. music and math. New Castle (Ind.) Jr. H.S., 1940-43; dir. religious edn. Bethany Union Ch., Chgo., 1945-47; dir. youth activities Hillfields Congl. Ch., Coventry, Eng., 1947-48; music tchr. grades 4, 5, 6 and 7 Silberstein Elem. Sch., Dallas, 1967-70; dir. H.S. choir Singapore Am. Sch., 1970-71; music tchr. grades 4, 5, 6 and 7 Degolyer Elem. Sch., Dallas, 1971-72; music edn. writer J. Weston Walch, Pub., Portland, Maine, 1973—; proprietor Noteman Press, Dallas, 1982—. Author: Harmonious Recorder, 1969, ZOUNDS!, 1973, Sight-Singing for Young Teens, 1981, Rediscovered Songs, 1991, (play) G.T.T. (Gone to Texas), 1984; author, editor: JUBILEE!, 1987, Dancing with Cancer, 1995; contbg. author: Music and You, 1991; editor, pub. Dancing With Cancer, 2006. Named Music Alumni of Yr., Ball State U., Muncie, Ind., 1979. Mem. Am. Recorder Soc., Music Educators Nat. Conf., Am. Orff-Schulwerk Assn. Democrat. Avocations: gardening, crafts, theater, concerts. Home and Office: 2603 Andrea Ln Dallas TX 75228-3503 Office Phone: 214-327-4466. Personal E-mail: dorothyell@aol.com.

ELLIOTT, ELEANOR THOMAS, foundation executive, volunteer; b. N.Y.C., Apr. 26, 1926; d. James A. and Dorothy Q. (Read) Thomas; m. John Elliott, Jr., July 27, 1956. BA, Barnard Coll., 1948; DHL (hon.), Duke U., 2002. Assoc. editor Vogue mag., 1948-52; asst. dir. research and speech writing div. N.Y. State Republican Com., 1952; social sec. to Sec. of State and Mrs. John Foster Dulles, 1952-55; dir. James Weldon Johnson Community Centers, N.Y.C., 1955-60; bd. dirs. Celanese Corp., 1974-87, CIT Fin. Corp., 1978-81, INA Life Ins. Co. of N.Y., 1983-1998. Author: Glamour Magazine Party Book, 1966. Trustee Barnard Coll., 1959—, chmn. bd., 1973-76; bd. dirs. Maternity Center Assn., 1960-70, pres., 1965-69; bd. govs. N.Y. Hosp., 1972—, v.p., 1979—; bd. dirs. Found. for Child Devel., N.Y.C., 1969—, chmn., 1972-79, 1973—; bd. dirs. United Way Greater N.Y., 1977-86, NOW Legal Def. and Edn. Fund, 1983-90, Catalyst Inc., 1978-83, Am. Women's Econ. Devel. Corp., 1980-86, Woodrow Wilson Nat. Fellowship Found, 1983—, chmn. 1993-1999, co-chair, Nat. Adv. Coun., 2000—, Edna McConnell Clark Found., 1984-93, Coun. on Women's Studies, Duke U.; overseer Cornell U. Med. Coll., 1995—. Recipient Alumni medal, Columbia U., 1977, medal of distinction, Barnard Coll., 1979, Red Cross Humanitarian award, 1986, Extraordinary Woman of Achievement award, NCCJ, 1978, Disting. Trustee award, United Hosp. Fund., 1991, Disting. Cmty. Svc. award, 1994, award for disting. svc. to City of New York, St. Nicholas Soc., 2002. Mem.: Colony Club of N.Y.C. Episcopalian. Home: 1035 5th Ave New York NY 10028-0135 Fax: 212-472-6506.

ELLIOTT, ERIC S, insurance company executive; B in mgmt. and fin., Temple U., MBA. Sr. v.p. managed care/pharmacy services Rite Aid Corp., 1989; CEO Eagle Managed Care (Rite Aid); with Mellon Bank; sr. v.p. pharmacy mgmt. CIGNA, 2000—03; sr. v.p. bus. mgmt. PCS Health Systems; v.p. pharmacy mgmt. Aetna Inc., 2003—. Office: Aetna Inc 151 Farmington Ave Hartford CT 06156

ELLIOTT, INGER MCCABE, apparel designer, consultant, textiles executive; b. Feb. 23, 1933; arrived in U.S., 1941, naturalized, 1946; d. David and Lova (Katz) Abrahamsen; m. Osborn Elliott, Oct. 20, 1973; children from previous marriage: Kari McCabe, Alexander McCabe, Marit McCabe. AB in History with honors, Cornell U., 1954; postgrad., Harvard U., 1955; AM, Radcliffe Coll., 1957. Photographer Photo Rschrs., 1960—98; pres. China Seas, Inc., N.Y.C., 1972—91, Gifted Textile Collection to L.A. County Mus. Art, 1991—. Textile Exhibit L.A. County Mus. Art, 1996—96; cons. Sotheby's Inc., 1992—; mem. Coun. Fgn. Rels. Author: A Week in Amy's World, A Week in Henry's World, Exteriors, 1992; contbr.: photographic essays to Esquire, Vogue, Life, Newsweek, N.Y. Times, Infinity, House & Garden; author: Batik: Fabled Cloth of Java, 1985, 2004. Mem. East Asia vis. com. Harvard U.; trustee The Asia Soc., Am. Scandinavian Found. Recipient Roscoe awards, 1978—91. Mem.: Am. Soc. Mag. Photographers, Trust Historic Preservation, Com. of 200, Ellis Island Yacht Club (lt. comdr.), Cosmopolitan Club, Phi Beta Kappa. Home: 84 Water St Stonington CT 06378

ELLIOTT, JEAN ANN, retired library director; b. Martinsburg, W.Va., Jan. 18, 1933; d. Howard Hoffman and Dorothy Jean (Horn) E. AB in edn., Shepherd U., 1954; MS in libr. sci., Syracuse U., 1957; MS, Shippensburg (Pa.) U., 1974. Asst. libr. Fairmont U., W.Va., 1957-60; reference asst. U. Pitts., 1960-61; acting libr. Shepherd U., 1961-62, coord. libr. sci., 1962-97. Compiler Jefferson County Hist. mag., 1990. Nat. treas. Palatines of Am., Columbus, Ohio, 1986-88. Mem. ALA, AAUW, DAR (W.Va. treas. 1980-83, 86-89, 95-98, state regent 1998-2001, hon. state regent 2001—), W.Va. Libr. Assn. (election chmn. 1988-90), Jefferson County Hist. Soc., Nat. Soc. Daus. Am. Colonies (nat. libr. 1991-94, hon. state regent 1991—), Nat. Soc. Daus. 1812 (nat. libr. 1994-96), W.Va. Soc. Daus. 1812 (state pres. 1991-94, hon. state pres. 1994—), Nat. Soc. Daus. Colonial Wars (state pres. 2001—), Alpha Beta Alpha (nat. exec. sec. 1968-76), Phi Kappa Phi. Presbyterian. Avocations: genealogy, travel, knitting, computers. Home: PO Box 1649 Shepherdstown WV 25443-1649 E-mail: jaelliot@ix.netcom.com.

ELLIOTT, JOANN ROSE, retired elementary school educator; d. Earl Alvin Elliott and Martha Reed. BS, U. Wis., Oshkosh, 1965, MS, 1972. Tchr. 1st grade Nicolet Elem. Sch., Kaukauna, Wis., 1964—66; tchr. Electa Quinney Elem. Sch., Kaukauna, 1966—88, Park Elem. Sch., Kaukauna, 1988—95, Dr. H.B. Tanner Elem. Sch., Kaukauna, 1995—98, ret., 1998.

ELLIOTT, MARGARET S., science educator; d. Craig and Susan Elliott. BA in Zoology, Calif. State U., Fresno, Calif., 1994; Tchg. Credential, Chapman U., Concord, Calif., 1998; MS in Ednl. Tech. Leadership, Calif. State U., Hayward, Calif., 2005. Sci. tchr. Mt. Diablo Unified Sch. Dist., Concord, Calif., 1998—. Tech. integration leader Mt. Diablo Unified Sch. Dist., Concord, Calif., 1998—. Web master - exec. bd. Mt. Diablo Edn. Tchrs. Assn., Concord, Calif., 2002—05. Recipient Tchr. Recognition for Exemplary Use of Tech., CTAP Region IV, 2003, Silver Award for Web Design, World Wide Web Awards, 2003, Award for Execellence for Edn. Web Site, Tchrs. Corner, 2003, SIlver Award for Web Design, Am. Assn. of Web Masters, 2003, Golden Web Award, 2000. Mem.: NSF, Calif. Sci. Tchrs. Assn. Office: Foothill Mid Sch 2775 Cedro Ln Walnut Creek CA 94598 Office Phone: 925-939-8600. Office Fax: 925-256-4281. Business E-Mail: sylvan_beach@mac.com.

ELLIOTT, MARIAN KAY, real estate manager; b. Wheatland, Wyo., Aug. 29, 1950; d. James Beal Jr. and Marian L. Angle; m. William Paul Elliott, June 1, 1978; children: Kenneth James Judd, L.R. Dedee Judd, William Paul, Joseph G., Christina Hope, Denise Faith. Cert. Mont. Comml. Credit Mgmt. Assn.; therapeutic foster parenting Dept. Family Svcs.; lic. real estate agt. Wyo. Comml. credit mgr. Pacific Steel, Mills, Wyo., 1978—79; mgr. investment real estate Casper, Wyo., 1981—; real estate assoc. Associated Brokers, Casper, 1982—85. Local reporter National Voter; editor: (newsletter) Wyoming Recycler. Chair fundraising com. Casper Jaycee Jinx, 1974—76; Wyo. scholastic pageant judge Casper Jaycees, 1993; amb. Casper Area C. of C., 1995—96; guardian Youth in Crisis and Mentally Disabled Adults, Casper, 1996—2002; ct. apptd. spl. advocate for abused and neglected children CASA of Natrona County, Casper, 2002—05; vol. Blue Envelope Health/ Elem. Strep Prevention Program, Casper, 1975—78; vol. resource class aide Elem. Sch., Casper, 1975—76, PTA bd. mem., 1979—83; foster parent Dept. Family Svcs., Casper, 1986—96, spkr. new foster parent tng., 1987—98; advocate, lobbyist foster children's rights Foster Parents of Natrona County, Casper, 1989—91; v.p. St. Christopher's Presch. Guild, Casper, 1976; confirmation class tchr. St. Mark's Episcopal Ch., Casper, 1975—78. Mem.: Hat Club/ Resources for Women in Spl. Circumstances (pres. 1997—2001), Big Bros./ Big Sisters Ctrl. Wyo. (adv. coun. 2002—03). Democrat. Achievements include sued for and won the right to sue elected officials in the State of Wyoming; helped change Wyoming laws to allow earlier adoption of foster children. Avocations: gardening, fine arts. Home: 1434 S Beech St Casper WY 82601 Personal E-mail: chadelliott1@msn.com.

ELLIOTT, MEAGAN BYRNE, elementary school educator; b. Tarzana, Calif., Aug. 24, 1979; d. Patrick Stephen and Denise Jean Byrne; m. Rob Earl Elliott, Aug. 2, 2001; 1 child, Kalyn Byrne. BS, No. Ariz. U., 2001, MEd, 2004. Cert. tchr. elem. edn. Ariz. Bd. Edn., 2001. Tchr. St. Mary's Cath. Sch., Flagstaff, Ariz., 2001—, head Dept. Math. and Sci., 2001—. Mem.: Nat. Coun. Tchrs. English (life), Nat. Coun. Tchrs. Math. (life). Office Phone: 928-779-1337.

ELLIOTT, MISSY (MELISSA ARNETTE ELLIOT), musician; b. Portsmouth, Va., July 1, 1971; d. Ronnie and Pat Elliott. Grad., Manor H.S., Portsmouth, 1990. With Elektra Entertainment, 1996—; owner Gold Mind. Musician: Supa Dupa Fly, 1997 (Platinum), Da Real World, 1999 (Platinum), Miss E.So Addictive, 2001 (Platinum), Under Construction, 2002 (2 times Platinum), This Is Not A Test!, 2003, The Cookbook, 2005. Nominee 3 Grammy awards, 2002, 2 Grammy awards, 2003; named Best Female Hip-Hop Artist, BET, 2002, 15th of 50 Greatest Hip Hop Artists, VH1, 2003; recipient Best Video of Yr. for The Rain, Rolling Stone, 1997, Soul Train Lady of Soul award for Best R&B/Soul or Rap Music Video for Get Ur Freak On, 2001, Grammy award for Best Rap Solo for Get Ur Freak On, 2002, Soul Train Lady of Soul award for Best R&B/Soul or Rap Music Video for One Minute Man, 2002, Grammy award for Best Female Rap Solo Performance for Scream aka Itchin, 2003, Soul Train Music award for Best R&B/Soul or Rap Music Video for Work It, 2003, Soul Train Lady of Soul awards for Best Song and Best Music Video for Work It, 2003, Video of Yr., Best Hip Hop Video for Work It, 2003, Favorite Female Hip-Hop Artist, Am. Music Awards, 2003, 2005, Best Female Hip Hop award, Black Entertainment TV (BET), 2006, Video Spl. Effects award for We Run This, MTV Video Music Awards, 2006. Office: Elektra Entertainment 75 Rockefeller Plz New York NY 10019*

ELLIOTT, SUSAN AUGUSTE, psychologist, psychotherapist, consultant; b. Mt. Shasta, Calif., Aug. 24, 1951; d. Cecil Edwin and Edith Ruth (Holland) E.; m. Richard Martinez, 1973 (div. 1975); 1 child, Lorin Wade Alder; m. Mark Johnson, 1999. AB, U. Calif., Berkeley, 1973; postgrad., Calif. State U., San Francisco, 1975-76, Towson (Md.) State U., 1984-85; MA, Goddard Coll., 1988; doctoral student, Fielding Inst., 2000—. Lic. psychologist-master, Vt. Co-founder, crisis worker, fundraiser, project dir. Humboldt

Women for Shelter and Umbrella Project, Arcata, Calif., 1976-81; devel. coord. House of Ruth, Balt., 1984; orgnl. cons., Balt., 1984-85; counselor Tri-County Youth Svcs., Charlotte Hall, Md., 1985-86; sexual assault clinician Walden Counseling Ctr., California, Md., 1986-87; coord., organizer SAFELINE, Chelsea, Vt., 1987-88; clinician Orange County Mental Health Svcs., Randolph, Vt., 1988-92; psychologist, psychotherapist, Montpelier & Barre, Vt., 1989—. Founding co-dir. Our House, Barre, Vt., 1989; conf. coord. Women and Therapy, Plainfield, Vt., 1988; supr., trainer Vt. Dept. Corrections, Vt. Dept. Mental Health, 1988-91, World Congress Mental Health, Washington, 1983; dir. programs Prevent Child Abuse-Vt., 1998-99; clin. supr. family support program and Allenbrook Homes for Youth, Easter Seals, 1993—; creator outdoor retreats for sexually abused and abusive youth, 1997—; bd. dirs. Vt. Partnership for Abuse Free State, 1993-99. Contbg. author: Politics of the Heart, 1987; guest reviewer Women and Therapy, 1987; co-editor Vt. Psychologist, 1990; author sexual abuse-free environment for teans curriculum for jr. high schs. Lobbyist Md. Food Com., Balt., 1982. Recipient appreciation award Humboldt Easter Seal Soc., 1981, Svc. to Children and Families award Ct. Vt. Social Workers Assn., 1991; grantee Reader's Digest, 1976, Jenny McKean Moore Fund for Writers, 1984; Charlotte Newcombe scholar Towson State U., 1985. Mem. APA (assoc.), Assn. for Treatment and Tng. in the Attachment of Children, Intenat. Soc. for Traumatic Stress Studies. Avocations: gardening, swimming, cross country skiing, writing. Address: RR 1 Box 152 East Calais VT 05650-9513 E-mail: sabinpond@aol.com.

ELLIOTT, SUSAN SPOEHRER, information technology executive; b. St. Louis, May 4, 1937; d. Charles Henry and Jane Elizabeth (Baur) Spoehrer; m. Howard Elliott Jr., Sept. 2, 1961; children: Kathryn Elliott Love, Elizabeth Elliott Niedringhaus. AB, Smith Coll., 1958. Systems engr. IBM, St. Louis, 1958-66; founder, chmn., CEO, SSE (Sys. Svc. Enterprises, Inc.), St. Louis, 1966—; systems analyst Mo. State Dept. Edn., Jefferson City, Mo., 1967-70; systems coord. Bank of Am. (formerly Boatmen's Nat. Bank), St. Louis, 1979-83. Bd. dirs., exec. com. Mo. Automobile Club; class C dir., dep. chmn. Fed. Res. Bd., St. Louis, 1996-98, chmn., 1999-2000; bd. dirs. Ameren Corp., Angelica Corp., Regional Bus. Coun., St. Louis Regional Commerce and Growth Assn., sec. bd. dirs., 1991-94; bd. dirs. AAA Mo. Trustee, vice-chmn. Mary Inst., St. Louis, 1976-89, Webster U., 1987-96; commr., vice-chmn. St. Louis Civil Svc. Commn., 1985-86, Mo. Lottery Commn., Jefferson City, 1985-87; bd. dirs. St. Louis Zoo, 1990-96, St. Louis Sci. Ctr., 1995-2004, 2006—; mem. pres.'s adv. coun. area coun., tech. com. Girl Scouts U.S.; chair women bus. owner's com. United Way, 1996-97. Mem. Internat. Women's Forum. Republican. Presbyterian. Avocations: golf, exercise. Office: SSE (Sys Svc Enterprises Inc) 77 West Port Plz Ste 500 Saint Louis MO 63146-3126 Office Phone: 314-439-4701. Business E-Mail: sselliott@SSEinc.com.

ELLIOTT, TAMMY JO, chemistry educator; d. Shirley Marlene and Clair Robert Smith; m. William Joseph Elliott, July 29, 2000; children: Gunnar Emerson, Colton Robert. BS in Chemistry, U. Pitts., 1989. Cert. Secondary Edn. Seton Hill Coll., Pa., 1997. Analytical chemist Eli Lilly, Indpls., 1989—95; chemistry tchr. Greensburg Salem HS, Pa., 1998—. Mem.: Am. Chem. Soc. Office: Grensburg Salem HS 65 Mennel Dr Greensburg PA 15601 Office Phone: 724-832-2960. Business E-Mail: telliott@wiu.k12.pa.us.

ELLIOTT, TERI MICHELLE, elementary school educator; b. Biloxi, Miss., Mar. 24, 1981; d. Charles Wayne and Edith Ann Peterson; m. Jeremy Shea Elliott, May 31, 2003; 1 child, Grace Ann. BS in Early Childhood Edn., State U. West Ga., Carrollton, Ga., 2003. Cert. tchr. early childhood edn. Ga., 2003. Tchr. Temple (Ga.) Elem. Sch., 2003—. Co-capt. relay for life Temple (Ga.) Elem. Sch., 2003—, sponsor academic team, 2004—05, sponsor honor club, 2005—. Recipient Tchr. of Month award, Temple (Ga.) Elem. Sch. Faculty, 2005. Republican. Bapt. Avocations: reading, scrapbooks, hiking. Office: Temple Elementary School 95 Otis Street Temple GA 30179 Office Phone: 770-562-3076. Business E-Mail: teri.elliott@carrollcountyschools.com.

ELLIOTT, VIRGINIA F. HARRISON, retired anatomist, publisher, educator, investment advisor, kinesiologist, philanthropist; b. St. Louis, Mar. 15, 1918; d. George Benjamin and Florence Gertrude (McManus) H.; m. William Hector Marsh, Dec. 1, 1963 (dec. Dec. 1986); m. George William Elliott, Oct. 27, 1991; stepchildren: Carolyn Frances Roberts, George William II, Robert Bonner (dec. Apr. 1995), Cathrine Susan Dimino. BS, U. Wis., 1940, PhD, 1959; MA, Columbia U., 1944. Lectr. Columbia U., NYC, 1943-46; asst. prof. Mary Washington U., Fredericksburg, Va., 1946—48, Oreg. State U., Corvallis, 1948-50, assoc. prof., 1950-59; instr. Army Med. Acad./Brooks Army Med. Ctr., San Antonio, 1959-60, assoc. prof., 1960-64; lectr. Hadassah Med. Sch., Hebrew U. of Jerusalem, 1965; pvt. practice Washington, 1969—87; ret., 1987. Fashion model, 1936-47, with John Robert Powers Schs., Phila., Pitts., NYC, 1943-47; cons. U. Tex. Med. Sch., 1962-64, U.S. Pentathlon Team, San Antonio, 1960-64, Dentists for Treatment of Pain from Muscular Tension, San Antonio, 1960-64; vis. prof. grad. sch. U. Wash., Seattle, 1961; lectr. in field Contbr. articles to profl. jours. Bd. visitors Sch. Edn., U. Wis., Madison, 1992-95, now emeritus; mem. Washington com. Nat. Coun. on Women's Giving. Recipient Civilian Meritorious Svc. award U.S. Civil Svc., 1965; Amy Morris Homans fellow, 1958; hon. fellow U. Wis., 1956, 58, 59. Fellow AAHPERD, Tex. Acad. Sci.; mem. Am. Alliance Health, Phys. Edn., Recreation and Dance, Am. Assn. Anatomists divsns. Fedn. Am. Socs. for Exptl. Biology (emeritus), Cosmos Club (emeritus). Presbyterian. Avocations: designing clothing, furniture, landscaping and boats, sculpting, painting. Home: 6333 Cavalier Corridor Falls Church VA 22044-1301

ELLIOTT-ZAHORIK, BONNIE, nurse, administrator; b. Algona, Iowa; AAS, Coll. Lake County, Grayslake, Ill., 1979; student, U. Iowa, Iowa City; BS, U. St. Francis, Joliet, Ill., 1988; MS, Nat. Louis U., Evanston, Ill., 1989; grad., Kellogg Inst. Mgmt., 2001. Bd. cert. nurse adminstr.-advanced, critical incident stress debriefing provider, ACLS provider. Chair coordinating coun. Vista Health, Waukegan, Ill., 1998, chair managerial coun., 1998, 2002; dir. med./surg. oncology, inpatient pediat., adolescent and outpatient units across the life span Vista Health/Victory Meml. Hosp., 2000—04, nursing adminstrn. mgr., 2004. Preceptor/mentor Graceland U., Parkside and St. Xavier U.; fellow doctorate program adminstrn. Walden U., 1995—96. Contbr. articles to profl. jours. Mem. combined appeal com., vol. Am. Heart Assn., 1995—2003; co-chair Victory Healthcare Svcs. Combined Appeal Campaign, 1997; mem. Ill. Gov. Blagojevich's Workforce Met. Chgo. Health Care Coun., 2004—, Workforce Coun. Health Care Leadership Critical Skills Shortage Initiative, 2004—; mem. healthcare adv. bd. Ill. Inst. Tech., 2004—06. Mem.: AACN, Ill. Orgn. Nurse Leaders (bd. dirs. 1991—, pres. 1998, past pres., state chmn. bylaws com. 1998—99, pres. 2000, strategic planning com. 2000—, pres. IONL region 2-B 2001), Ill. Coalition Nursing Resources (exec. bd. dir. 2000—05, legis. funding com. 2001—, pres. 2004), Ill. Coun. Nurse Mgrs. (past pres. Region 2B), Orgn. Nurse Leaders (chair gen. provisions/intro.info. task force).

ELLIS, ANNE ELIZABETH, fundraiser; b. Orngestad, Aruba, Aug. 21, 1945; d. Thomas Albert and Anne Elizabeth (Belis) Wolfe; m. Earl Edward Ellis, Feb. 14, 1970. BS, La. State U., 1967. Fashion coord., Baton Rouge, 1962-67; textile researcher La. State U., Baton Rouge, 1965-67; buyer I.H. Rubensteins., Baton Rouge, 1967-68; fashion distbr. J.C. Penney, Inc., Arlington, Tex., 1969-70, asst. buyer Dallas, 1970-73; exec. dir. Nassau County Mus. Fine Art Assn., Roslyn, NY, 1985-88. Speaker C.W. Post U., Greenvale, N.Y., 1988—; cons. in field. Chmn., editor: (cookbook) Specialities of the House, 1981-83. Bd. dirs., com. chmn. Congregational Ch., Manhasset, N.Y., 1975-96; exec. v.p., bd. dirs., com. chmn. Jr. League Internat.; benefit gala chmn., com. chmn. Grenville Baker Boys & Girls Club, Locust Valley, N.Y., 1983-91; pres. bd., vice-chmn. cmty. outreach, benefit gala chmn. Tilles Performing Art Ctr. L.I. U., Greenvale, N.Y., 1985—; bd. dirs., benefit co-chmn. Nassau County Family Assn. Svcs., Hempstead, 1988-96; benefit vice-chmn. Glen Cove/North Shore Cmty. Hosp., 1989-93; mem. exec. bd., exec. v.p., trustee WLIW, L.I. Pub. TV, 1990-2001, chmn. bd. dirs., 1997-99; trustee Cmty. Found. of Oyster Bay, 1991-94; trustee Dowling Coll., Oakdale, N.Y., 1993-98, exec. bd., 1997-98; adv. bd. Westbury (N.Y.) Gardens, 1993-97; chmn. adv. bd. Long Island chpt. Save the Children, 1995-2001; trustee L.I. U., 1998—. Recipient Vol. of Yr. award Jr. League L.I., 1984, 85, Outstanding Vol. Svcs. and Commitment award County of Nassau, 1989, Juliette Low award Nassau County Girl Scouts, L.I., 1991, Disting. Leadership award, L.I., 1991, Outstanding Community Vol. award Jr. League of L.I., 1991-92, Disting. Svc. medal L.I. State Parks Found., 1999, Women of Achievement award Jr. League L.I., 2000. Mem. P.E.O. (pres. 1985-87), The Creek Inc., Meadowbrook Club Inc., Nat. Arts Club, Lost Tree Club, Forest Creek Club, Kappa Kappa Gamma (alumna pres. 1971-72). Republican. Congregationalist. Avocations: golf, gardening, needlepoint.

ELLIS, BERNICE, financial planner, investment advisor; b. Bklyn. d. Samuel and Clara H.; m. Seymour Scott Ellis; children: Michele, Wayne. BA, Bklyn. Coll., N.Y.; MS, Queens Coll., N.Y., 1970. Cert. fin. planner NY, 1987, elem. educator NYC. Tchr. elem. L.I. Sch. Dists., Merrick, NY; tchr. reading N.Y.C. Bd. of Edn., Bklyn., 1972—73; coord. Reading is Fundamental, Lawrence, NY, 1973—75; pres., founder N.Y. State Assn. for Gifted and Talented, Valley Stream, NY, 1974—87; pres. Ellis Planning, Valley Stream, 1984—. Cons. Nassau County Bd. Coop. Ednl. Svcs., Westbury, N.Y., 1973-74; adminstrv. intern region II U.S. Office Edn., 1977-78; adj. asst. prof. Nassau C.C., Garden City, N.Y., 1975-91, adj. assoc. prof., 1991-94, adj. full prof., 1995—; fin. commentator Money Talk radio program WHPC FM; arbitrator NASD, 1996. Contbr. articles to profl. jours and fin. newsletters. Mem. adv. com. Ams. for Ams. for Hope, Growth and Opportunity, 1998; mem. Nat. Rep. Party, Valley Stream Rep. Party, N.Y. State Rep. Party. Recipient Ednl. Professions Devel. Act fellow CUNY Inst. for Remediations Skills for Coll. Pers., Queensborough C.C., 1970-73; named Business Person of Yr. Nat. Rep. Congl. Com., 2003. Mem. AAUW (North Shore bd., chmn. Money Talk 1991—), Nat. Assn. Securities Dealers (arbitrator 1996), Nat. Alliance of Sales Execs., Inst. for CFP, Inst. for CFP L.I. (bd. dirs.), Internat. Assn. Fin. Planners (legis. com. L.I. chpt. 1986-87), N.Y. State Reading Assn., Adj. Faculty Assn. Nassau C.C., L.I. C. of C., Rotary, Womens Nat. Republic Club. Avocations: reading, swimming. Office: Ellis Planning Inc 628 Golf Dr Valley Stream NY 11581-3594

ELLIS, CAROL OSTER, rehabilitation physician; b. Vermillion, S.D., July 11, 1940; d. John and Florence Ogden Manter; m. Thomas Harlow (div.); children: Thomas Harlow, Elaine Harlow Higuera; m. William R. Ellis, May 25, 1991. BA, U. Ga., 1962; MD, Med. Coll. Va., 1967. Cert. Am. Bd. Preventative Medicine. Intern Bon Secours Hosp., Grosse Pointe, Mich.; resident St. Johns Hosp., Detroit; staff physician Pan Am., Kennedy Space Ctr., Fla., 1969—81; med. dir. AT&T, N.Y.C., 1981—96; assoc. Downtown Family Medicine, N.Y.C., 1996—2000; med. dir. Natural Medicine and Rehab., Bridgewater, NJ, 2002—. Fellow: NY Occupl. Med. Assn. (pres. 1998—99); mem.: Atlanta Women's Med. Assn. (pres. 1990—91), NY Med. Assn. (asst. treas. 2001—02), Alpha Xi Delta, Alpha Omega Alpha, Phi Beta Kappa. Avocations: scuba diving, pilates, tai chi. Home: 19 Colony Rd Edgewater NJ 07020-1505 Office Phone: 908-252-0242. Personal E-mail: weillisc@attglobal.net.

ELLIS, CAROLYN TERRY, lawyer; b. N.Y.C., Apr. 20, 1949; D. Francis Martin and Sarah Baker (Ames) E. m. H. Lake Wise, Feb. 27, 1982; children: Carolyn Campbell Wise, Burke Ames. BA, U. Chgo., 1971; JD, NYU, 1974. Bar: N.Y. 1975. Rsch. analyst Dept. Justice, N.Y.C., 1973-74; from assoc. to ptnr. Lord, Day & Lord, N.Y.C., 1974-86; ptnr. Coudert Bros., N.Y.C., 1986-98; pres., gen. counsel Bklyn. (N.Y.) Cmty. Housing & Svcs., Inc., 1998—2003; asst. atty. gen. Charities Bur. N.Y. State Office Atty. Gen., 2003—. Instr. Bklyn. Law Sch., 1980-82. Mem. Assn. of Bar of City of N.Y. (antitrust and trade regulation com. 1989-92, internat. trade com. 1993-95).

ELLIS, CYNTHIA BUEKER, musician, educator; b. Santa Monica, Calif., Dec. 3, 1958; d. Robert Arthur and Patricia June Bueker; m. Tony Lyle Ellis, June 18, 1983. B Music, Calif. State U., 1981, M Music, 1983. 2nd flutist Pasadena (Calif.) Chamber Orch., 1981—84; piccoloist Pacific Symphony Orch., Santa Ana, Calif., 1979—; prin. flutist Opera Pacific Orch., Costa Mesa, Calif., 1995—; lectr. Calif. State U., Fullerton, 1985—; applied flute instr. Pomona Coll., Claremont, Calif., 1990—92. Adj. faculty Claremont Grad. Sch., 1996—97; mem. faculty Pacific Symphony Inst., 1993—; flute instr. Pomona Coll., 1990—92. Contbr. articles to profl. jours.; musician: (songs) (for motion pictures) Twilight, 1998, Kissing a Fool, 1998, Pentagon Wars, 1998, She's So Lovely, 1997, First Time Felon, 1997, Campfire Tales, 1996, Breaking Commandments, 1996, Baby's Day Out, 1994, Pochahontas, 1994, Stayed Tuned, 1992, Wind, 1992; numerous others. Family coord. Southern Calif. Labrador Retriever Rescue, 1999—. Mem.: Music Tchrs. Assn. Calif., Nat. Flute Assn. (chamber music competition 1st place award 2000), Mu Phi Epsilon, Phi Kappa Phi, Pi Kappa Lambda. Republican. Methodist. Avocations: exercise, cooking. Home: 1192 Beechwood Dr Brea CA 92821

ELLIS, DEBORAH MARIE, art educator; d. Deborah Marie Ellis. Minor Spanish, Universidad de Alcala de Henares, Spain, 1997; BFA in Art Edn., Bowling Green State U., 1998; MA in Art Edn., Kent State U., 2003. Cert. K-12 visual art edn. Ohio. Visual art tchr. Cleve. Mcpl. Sch. Dist., 1998—. Aux. police officer Lakewood City Police, Ohio, 2001—; mem. reunion com. Lakewood H.S., 2002—. Recipient Power of Art award, Robert Raushenburg Soc., 1995; grantee, ICARE, 1999—2002. Mem.: Ohio Art Edn. Assn., Nat. Art Edn. Assn., Westshore Orchid Soc., Phi Delta Kappa. Avocations: growing orchids, art. Home: 1477 Westwood Lakewood OH 44107 E-mail: dellis19@juno.com.

ELLIS, DIANE DEANE, dental hygienist, educator; d. Russell L. and Lillian F. Deane; m. Gordan E. Ellis, Nov. 1973; children: Ryan D., Lyndsey D. AS, West Liberty State, W.Va., 1971; BS, U. Bridgeport, Conn., 1977; MS, Ctrl. Conn. State Coll., New Britain, 1991. Registered dental hygienist Mass., Conn., R.I. Pvt. practice dental hygienist, Greenfield, Mass., 1971—88, New Haven, 1971—88, Hamden, Conn., 1971—88, Providence, 1971—88; instr. dental hygiene CC of R.I., 1988—90; prof. allied health Tunxis CC, Farmington, Conn., 1990—. Adv. bd. allied dental program Tunxis CC, Farmington, Conn., 1998—. Mem.: Am. Dental Hygiene Assn. Office: Tunxis CC 271 Scott Swamp Rd Farmington CT 06032 Business E-Mail: dellis@commnet.edu.

ELLIS, E. SUSAN, library director, lay minister; b. Louisville, Sept. 22, 1954; d. William Stanley and Elizabeth Mae Ellis. B Music in Vocal Performance, Eastern Ky. U., Richmond, 1977; MS in LS, U. Ky., 1988. Lic. lay minister Christian Ch. Disciples of Christ. Libr. faculty Ky. State U., Frankfort, 1988-91; libr. dir. Cynthiana-Harrison County Pub. Libr., Cynthiana, Ky., 1991—; music dir. Rep. Christian Ch. Disciples of Christ, Cynthiana, 1997—2000. Mem. ALA, Ky. Libr. Assn. Office: Cynthiana-Harrison County Pub Libr 104 N Main St Cynthiana KY 41031-1205 E-mail: sellis@harrisonlibrary.org.

ELLIS, HARRIETTE ROTHSTEIN, editor; b. Memphis, Feb. 29, 1924; d. Samuel and Edith (Brodsky) Rothstein; m. Manuel J. Kaplan, June 1, 1944 (div. Jan. 1970); children: Deborah Elise Kaplan-Wyckoff, Claire Naomi Kaplan Miller, Amelia Stephanie Kaplan Parker; m. Theodore J. Ellis, 1991 (div. Jan. 1992); m. Oscar U. Burlin, 1995. Student, Memphis State U., 1941—43, Memphis Art Acad., 1940-43; BA, U. Ala., Tuscaloosa, 1944; postgrad., UCLA, 1949—50, Chouinard Art Inst., L.A., 1948. Advt. art/copy retail industry, New Orleans, Albuquerque, L.A., 1944—49; writer, graphic artist for newspapers and mags., L.A., 1944—49; editor Jewish Fedn. News, Long Beach, Calif., 1969—81; dir. corp. comm. Startel Corp., Irvine, Calif., 1981—82; editor, writer Calif. Fashion Publs., L.A., 1982—86; editor Valley Mag., Granada Hills, Calif., 1997; pub. rels. Joan Luther & Assocs., Beverly Hills, Calif., 1988—90; editor Jewish Cmty. Chronicle, Long Beach, 1990—2006; contbg. editor Orange County Jewish Life, 2006—. Mem. com. implementation flouridation city water sys., Long Beach; cmty. interfaith com.; bd. dirs. Hillel, Camp Komaroff, 1994—2001, Jewish Cmty. Ctr., Long Beach, Temple Israel, Long Beach. Named Woman of Yr., Temple Israel, Pioneer Women; recipient awards, Coun. Jewish Fedn. Mem.: AAUW, Am. Jewish Press Assn. (exec. com.), So. Calif. Media Profls. (pres. 1997—2002, bd. dirs., treas., v.p., Newspaper awards), Women of Reform Judaism (bd. dirs.), Nat. Fedn. Press Women (Newspaper awards), Sierra Club. Avocations: theater, music, travel, archaeology.

ELLIS, JANICE RIDER, nursing educator, consultant; BSN, U. Iowa, 1960; MN, U. Wash., 1971; Phd, U. Tex., 1990. RN, Wash. Staff nurse various hosps., Wash., Oreg., Iowa; prof., dir. nursing edn. Shoreline C.C., Seattle. Rschr. in field.; nursing edn. cons., Seattle Author textbooks; contbr. to profl. jours.; cons. in field. Mem. ANA, Nat. League Nursing, Wash. State Nurses Assn., Sigma Theta Tau, Phi Kappa Delta.

ELLIS, JOANNE HAMMONDS, computer consultant; b. Rome, Ga., Aug. 15, 1946; d. James Randolph and Louise Hammonds; m. James H. Ellis Jr.; 1 child, Stephanie Louise Cantrell Ellis. BS, AB, Jacksonville State U., Ala., 1968; MBA, Ga. State U., Atlanta, 1979, MPA, 1981. Computer sys. analyst GSA, 1983—91; dir. info. resources mgmt. NARDAC, 1991—94, Food and Nutrition Svcs. USDA, Alexandria, Va., 1994—2001; dir. info. resources mgmt. divsn. Nat Fin. Ctr. USDA, New Orleans, 2001—05; mktg. cons. Centre, Ala., 2005—; v.p. Alpha Ten Techs., Inc. Mem. Office Mgmt. & Budget's Info. Tech. Resources Bd.; dir. Info. Resources Mgmt. Coun.; computer cons. Contbr. articles to profl. jours. Named Fed. Exec. of Yr, New Orleans Fed. Exec. Bd., 1998; recipient Meritorious Svc. medal, USN, 1991. Mem. Assn. Women in Computing, Federally Employed Women, Atlanta Assn. Fed. Execs., NAFE, Dept. of Def. Exec. Leadership Devel. Program, Beta Sigma Phi. Methodist. Home: PO Box 208 Centre AL 35960 E-mail: ellisjho@tds.net.

ELLIS, JOYCE K., writer, educator; b. St. Louis, Mo., Aug. 31, 1950; d. Edward William Krohne, Jr. and Eunice Anna Krohne; m. Steven W. Ellis, Nov. 29, 1969; children: Gregory, Sharie Thoelke, Maryanne Doerfler. BA summa cum laude in English, Northwestern Coll., 1991—94. Free-lance writer, Mpls., 1970—; free-lance book editor, 1984—; writing mentor Jerry B. Jenkins Christian Writers Guild corr. course, Black Forest, Colo., 2002—; asst. editor Evang. Beacon mag., Pursuit mag., Mpls., 1994—97; writing instr. various confs. around country, 1980—; lectr. in field, 1982—. Asst. dir. Write-to-Publish Conf., Wheaton, Ill., 2002—; conv. chair Evang. Press Assn., Mpls., 2003—04. Author: Wee Pause, 1977, Overnight Mountain, 1979, The Big Split, 1979, Snowmobile Trap, 1981, Plug Into God's Rainbow, 1984, 30 Ways to Enrich Your Family Fun, 1993, Tiffany, 1986, 2d edit., 1996, The 500 Hats of a Modern-Day Woman, 1999; co-author: Bible Bees, 1981, Tell Me a Story, Lord Jesus, 1981, When the Kids Are Home from School, 1991; co-author, editor: Post-Abortion Trauma and Nine Steps to Recovery, 1991, Learning to Trust Again, 1999; editor: The One-Minute Bible for Kids, 1993 (Gold Medallion award, Evang. Christian Publishers Assn., 1994), The One-Minute Children's Bible (published in U.K.), 1995, One-Minute Bible Devotions for Kids (revision of The One-Minute Bible for Kids, new publisher), 1998; contbr. articles to numerous mags. and jours. Sunday sch. tchr. Good News Bible Ctr., Mpls., 1968—77; choir mem. Wooddale Ch., Richfield and Eden Prairie, 1977—95, Pioneer Girls leader Richfield, 1978—81; soloist and worship team leader Westwood Cmty. Ch., Chanhassen, 1995—98, Edinbrook Ch., Brooklyn Park, 1999—. Mem.: Minn. Christian Writers Guild (pres.), Nat. League Am. Penwomen, Evang. Press Assn. (assoc.), Sigma Tau Delta. Avocations: travel, photography, reading, crafts, needlecrafts. Personal E-mail: joyce@joycekellis.com.

ELLIS, JULIET S., bank executive; b. Washington, Ind., Feb. 23, 1959; d. John Topping Simpson; widowed; children: Christian, John. BA, Ind. U., 1981. CPA; chartered fin. analyst. Field cons. Merrill Lynch, Houston, 1981-87; sr. v.p. investment mgmt. group, sr. portfolio mgr. Chase Bank, Houston, 1987—. Methodist. Office: Chase Asset Mgmt 600 Travis St Houston TX 77002-3002

ELLIS, LAURA RENEE, music educator; b. Albert Lea, Minn., Dec. 11, 1963; d. Leon Ray and Annette leNoir (Christianson) E. BA, Luther Coll., 1986; MusM, U. Kans., 1989, D Musical Arts, 1991. Asst. prof. U. of the Ozarks, Clarksville, Ark., 1991-96; prof. music McMurry U., Abilene, Tex., 1996—2003; assoc. prof. music U. Fla., Gainesville, 2003—. Parish organist Ch. of the Heavenly Rest, Abilene, 1996-2003. Performer CD recording Legacy: Laura Ellis Plays Organ Works of Jeanne Demessieux, 1996. Dial Corp. faculty enrichment grantee, 1994; winner Gruenstein Meml. Organ Competition, Chgo. Club of Women Organists, 1988. Mem. Am. Guild Organists (dean), Music Tchrs. Nat. Assn., Fla. Music Educators, Phi Beta Kappa, Pi Kappa Lambda. Lutheran. Avocation: golf. Home: 4609 NW 20th Dr Gainesville FL 32605-1335 Office: U Fla Sch Music PO BOX 117900 Gainesville FL 32611

ELLIS, LESLIE ELAINE, psychologist; d. Ira Milton and Evelyn Fogel Marks; m. Clyde Arthur Ellis, Jr., Feb. 16, 1969; children: David Michael, Eric Arthur. BA in Psychology, U. Fla., 1969, MA in Rehab. Counseling, 1972; PhD in Theatre, Fla. State U., 1982; MA in Psychology, Fielding Grad. Inst., 2002, PhD in Clin. Psychology, 2004. Cert. Rehab. Counselor Commn. Rehab. Counselor Certification, Rolling Meadows, Ill., Clin. Supr. Fla., lic. Mental Health Counselor. Instr. acting Fla. State U., 1982; instr. speech North Fla. Jr. Coll., Madison, Fla., 1983; dir. academic svcs. Profl. Employment Tng. Inc., Svcs., Clearwater, Fla., 1988—91; intern rehab. counseling Cognitive Rehab. Inst., Tampa, Fla., 1994—95; pvt. practice counselor, 1995—2003; intern clin. counseling Bay Area Psychol. Svcs., St. Petersburg, Fla., 1996—98; with Wein Ctr. Memory Disorders Mt. Sinai Hosp., Miami, Fla., 2001; intern neuropsychology Rehab. Solutions, Tampa, 2002—03; intern clin. psychology Counseling Ctr. U. South Fla., 2002—03; clin. dir. Genesis Behavioral Healthcare, Tampa, 2004—. Adj. instr. St. Petersburg (Fla.) Coll., 1991—94; adj. faculty Argosy U., Tampa, 2004—; mem. com. Nat. Rehab. Counselors Cert. Exam, Princeton, NJ, 2002, Princeton, 04; cons. in field; presenter in field. Author: Lose Weight By Surgery, 1974, Nutrition Guide to Brand Name Baby Foods, 1977, Teacher's Guide to Dramatic Techniques for Use with Handicapped Students, 1982; actor(dancer): (plays) Desire Under the Elms, 1979; author (dir.): (films) Teenaged and Pregnant, 1982, (plays) Merfel's Magic Wand, 1982; dir.: (plays) Ghost of Canterville Hall, 1984; author: (songs) Theme Song Leon County Spl. Olympics, 1983; co-author: (plays) The Trial of Ruby McCollum, 2003 (Honorable Mention award Sundance, 2003); contbr. articles to profl. jours., newspapers, mags. Mem. spl. events com. Fla. State Spl. Olympics, 1980—83; adv. bd. Thomas County Schs., 1985—86; adv. com. Career Devel. Ctr. Thomas Area Tech. Sch., 1985; chmn. pubs. Am. Theatre Assn., 1982—83. Recipient Disting. Performance Design Spl. Needs Program, Nat. Alliance Bus., 1987, Outstanding Performance award, Gov. Ga., 1987, Gov. Fla., 1989. Mem.: APA (student sci. com. 1999—2003), Phi Kappa Phi, Eta Rho Pi. Democrat. Jewish. Achievements include patents for book hanging device. Office: National Ednl Training Sys Inc 16116 No Florida Ave Lutz FL 33549 Office Phone: 727-365-8522. Personal E-mail: lesliee@tampabay.rr.com.

ELLIS, LOREN ELIZABETH, artist, educator; b. Binghamton, N.Y., Dec. 12, 1953; d. William Thomas and Ann (Dyshuk) E. BA, U. South Fla., 1974; MFA, Fla. State U., 1977. Instr. Fla. State U., Tallahassee, 1976—77, U. South Fla., Tampa, 1978—81, Parsons Sch. Design, N.Y.C., 1990—. Curator 14 artists Unique Visions, Great Neck Art Ctr., NY; founder Art for Healing N.Y.C. website. One-woman shows include Lotos Club, NYC, A.G. Ludwick Gallery, Tampa, Gallery Saireido, NYC, County Ctr. Bldg., Tampa, Park Ave Bank, NYC, Mus. of Morelia, Mex., 2005, Represented in permanent collections Santa Barbara Mus. Art, Calif.; author: Photographs and Thoughts, 1977; video documentary A Tiny Voice. Fellow Fla. State U., 1977, Fla. Arts Coun., 1977, Tampa/Hillsborough Arts Coun., 1991, Puffin Found., 1994; grantee Lower Manhattan Cultural Coun., 2006. Avocations: tennis, sailing. Office: 2350 Broadway New York NY 10024-3200 Office Phone: 212-946-1160. E-mail: loren@lorenellisart.com.

ELLIS, MARIA VANESSA, dance educator; b. Utica, NY, Mar. 25, 1980; d. Arthur William and Phyllis Dontino Ellis; m. Shaun Robert Nave. B in Dance Tchg. and Choreography, Mercyhurst Coll., Erie, Pa., 2002; MBA, Everglades U., Sarasota, Fla., 2006. Ballet mistress and dancer Mohawk Valley Ballet, Utica, NY, 1994—98; dancer Mercyhurst Coll., Erie, 1998—2002; grant reviewer Erie Arts Coun., Erie, Pa., 2002; ballet dancer Tracees Dancing Starz, Naples, Fla., 2002—06; owner Dance Arts by Maria, Naples, 2006. Dancer Liturgical Dance Com., Erie, 1998—2002. Independent. Cath. Avocations: dance, reading, crafts. Home: 17152 Antigua Rd Fort Myers FL 33912

ELLIS, MARY LOUISE HELGESON, information technology company executive; b. Albert Lea, Minn., May 29, 1943; d. Stanley Orville and Neoma Lois (Guthier) Helgeson; m. David Readinger, Nov. 5, 1994; children from previous marriage: Christopher, Tracy. BS in Pharmacy, U. Iowa, 1966; MA in Pub. Adminstrn., Iowa State U., 1982, postgrad., 1982—83. Faculty Duquesne U., Pitts., 1977; cons. in pharmacy Colville, Wash., 1978—79; dir. pharmacy Mt. Carmel Hosp., Colville, 1978—79; clin. pharmacist Iowa Vets. Home, Marshalltown, 1980—81; instr. Iowa Valley C.C., Marshalltown, 1981—83; dir. Iowa Dept. Substance Abuse, Des Moines, 1983—86, State of Iowa Pub. Health, Iowa Dept. Pub. Health, Des Moines, 1986—90; spl. cons. health affairs Blue Cross/Blue Shield of Iowa, 1990—91; v.p. Blue Cross/Blue Shield of Iowa and S.D., 1991—2000; ret., 2000; bus. cons., 2001—05; v.p. Medicare, Affiliated Computer Svcs., 2005—. Chair Iowa Health Data Commn., Des Moines, 1986—90; bd. dirs. Health Policy Corp. Iowa, 1986—90; adj. asst. prof. U. Iowa, Iowa City, 1984—; commd. officer U.S. FDA, 1989—90; mem. alumnae bd. dirs. U. Iowa Coll. of Pharmacy, 1989—; chair Nat. Commn. Accreditation of Ambulance Svcs., 1992—97; commencement spkr. U. Iowa, Coll. Pharmacy, Iowa City, 2003. Mem. Iowa State Bd. Health, 1981—83, v.p., 1982—83; mem. adv. coun. Iowa Valley C.C., 1983—85. Named Alumnae of Yr., U. Iowa Coll. Pharmacy, 2005; recipient Woman of Achievement award, Des Moines YWCA, 1988. Mem.: APHA, Iowa Pub. Health Assn. (bd. dirs., Henry Albert award 1990), Iowa Pharmacists Assn., Pi Sigma Alpha, Phi Kappa Phi, Alpha Xi Delta. Republican. Home: 2912 Caulder Ave Des Moines IA 50321-2637

ELLIS, MISSIE LYNNE, music educator; b. Pitts., July 22, 1975; d. Gary Edward and Linda Clymer Ellis. B in Music Edn., Fla. So. Coll., 1998. Dir. bands Meadowbrook Mid. Sch., Orlando, Fla., 1998—2001, Lakeview Mid. Sch., Winter Garden, Fla., 2001—. Dir. all-county honors band Orange County Pub. Schs., 2005—. Deacon Wekiva Presbyn. Ch., Longwood, Fla., 2005—. Named Tchr. of Yr. at Meadowbrook Mid. Sch., Orange County Pub. Schs., 2002. Mem.: Nat. Assn. for Music Edn., Fla. Music Educators Assn., Fla. Band Masters Assn. Republican. Presbyterian. Avocations: golf, walking, reading, shopping, computers. Office: Lakeview Mid Sch 1200 W Bay St Winter Garden FL 34787 Home: 502 Lake Bridge Ln #1617 Apopka FL 32703 Office Phone: 407-877-5010 ext 275. Office Fax: 407-877-5019. Business E-Mail: ellism4@ocps.net.

ELLIS, NANCY KEMPTON, adult education educator; b. Chgo., Nov. 3, 1943; d. Robert Lawrence and Mildred Elizabeth (Kitcher) Kempton; m. William Grenville Ellis, Dec. 30, 1963; children: William Grenville Jr., Bradford Graham. AA, Endicott Coll., 1963; BA, Castleton State Coll., 1970; MA, Marian Coll., 1989. Tutor remedial reading Waterville (Maine) Pub. Schs., 1975-79, migrant tutor, 1980, tchr. 1st grade, 1980-81; tchr. 4th grade Vassalboro (Maine) Pub. Schs., 1981-82; dir. study skills Wayland Acad., Beaver Dam, Wis., 1983-89, chair ednl. support, 1989-91, dir. spl. programs, 1993-95, co-pres., 1982-95. Chair Wis. Ind. Sch. Educators, 1985-89, conf. co-chair, 1988; active Wis. Fellowship of Poets, 1993-95; wildlife presenter Beaver Dam Pub. Schs., 1994-95; adj. faculty Grad. Sch., Concordia U. Wis., Mequon, 1997-2003; presenter in field. Editor Marshland Monarch, 1984-88, Spouse News. Bd. dirs., festival dir. Beaver Dam Arts Assn., 1990-93; bd. dirs. AAUW Beaver Dam, 1992-95; coord. Beaver Dam Cmty. Forum on Health Care. Avocations: walking, writing poetry, bonsai, herb gardens. Office: 8655 N Regent Rd Fox Point WI 53217-2362

ELLIS, PATRICIA, primary school educator; d. Victor and Della Roddy Staudaher; m. Frank Willis Ellis, June 9, 1962; children: Robert George, Mechelle Ellis Vandervert. BA, U. Idaho, 1961. Cert. tchr. Idaho, Wash. 1st and 2d grade tchr. American Falls (Idaho) schs., Pocatello (Idaho) schs.; 2d-3d grade multigraded tchr., 1st-3d grade tchr., 1st-6th grade gifted progam tchr. Richland (Wash.) schs. Recipient Crystal Apple award, Richland C. of C., 2003—04, Autism Tchr. award, 2003—04, award, Pacific NW Assn. Geosci. Tchrs., 2004—05. Home: 1838 Birch Richland WA 99354

ELLIS, PATRICIA WEATHERS, retired small business owner, computer technician; b. Shelby, N.C., June 21, 1941; d. William Roy and Lucille Elzora (Allen) Weathers; m. Donald Eugene Ellis, Nov. 16, 1957; children: Dana Michelle, Lisa Maria. Student, Gaston Coll., Gastonia, NC, 1970, student, 1982. Tel. operator So. Bell, Greensboro, N.C., 1959-61, Gastonia, N.C., 1961-63, dial clk., 1963-68, frame technician, 1968-79, test technician, 1980-84, maintenance adminstr., 1984-85, toll test technician, 1985-87; electronic technician BellSouth, Gastonia, 1987-91, Charlotte, N.C., 1991-2000, electronic technician toll rm. Gastonia, 2000—02; store mgr. Ellis Carpet and Floor Ctr., Inc., 2002—, 2002—. Store mgr. Ellis-Bowen Carpet Svc., Gastonia, 1969—70. Commr. Gaston County, Gastonia, 1992-96; bd. dirs. Gaston County Health Dept., Airport Com., Gaston Mus. Art and History, 1992-96, Gaston County Dept. Social Svcs.; alt. Ctrl. Lina Coun. Govts., 1994-95; mem. dedication com. Gaston Good Neighbor; com. mem. Right-Sizing County Govt Named Ky. Col., 2002. Mem. Tel. Pioneers Am., Home Builders Assn. Gaston County, Inc., Woman's Aux. Fedn. Postal Clks. (charter; pres. Gastonia 1966, State v.p. 1966-69), The Garden Soc., Daniel Stowe Botanical Gardens, Gaston C. of C Republican. Avocations: art, writing poems and songs, collecting dolls and stamps. Office Phone: 704-867-8337.

ELLIS, PHYLLIS SIMERLY, elementary educator, reading specialist; b. Banner Elk, N.C., Sept. 10, 1935; d. William McKinley and Mary Alice (Graybeal) Simerly; m. George Mark Ellis, Dec. 26, 1956; children: Suzanne Melissa Ellis Mikkelson, Jennifer Lynn Huff. BS, East Tenn. State U., 1957, MA in Reading, 1959. Cert. prin., N.C., reading specialist, N.C., Tenn. Teaching fellow East Tenn. State U., Johnson City, 1957-59; tchr. Roanoke Va. City Schs., 1960-62, Burlington (N.C.) City Schs., 1962-64, Gaston County Schs., Cherryville, N.C., 1964-70, Granville County Schs., Oxford, N.C., 1970-74, Guilford Primary Sch., Greensboro, N.C., 1974-92. Lead tchr. Kids Save the Eatrh Club. Vol. Am. Heart Assn., Greensboro, 1980—. Nat. Multiple Sclerosis Soc., High Point, N.C., 1982—; pres. Classroom Tchrs. Assn., Gaston County, 1968-69; animal adoption endangered species; adopted acreage S. Am. rain forest. N.C. Ctr. Advancment Teaching fellow, 1988; Named Sci. Tchr. of Yr. Guilford County Schs., N.C. Sci. Tchrs. Assn., Greensboro, 1989; recipient Sci. Playwright award N.C. State U., 1987. Mem. Environ. Def. Fund, Internat. Reading Assn. (pres.-elect. 1991—), Assn. Childhood Edn. Internat. (pres. 1969-70), N.C. Sci. Tchrs. Assn., N.C. Math Tchrs. Assn., Greater Guilford Sci. Assn., Greater Greensboro Reading Assn. (pres. elect 1993), Delta Kappa Gamma, Phi Delta Kappa. Methodist. Avocations: antiques, interior decorating. Home: 1714 Scarborough Rd High Point NC 27265-2420

ELLIS, RHONDA LYN, history educator; b. Fairbanks, Alaska, July 20, 1970; d. Charles Robert and Bobbie Jane Ellis. MA magna cum laude in History, West Chester U., Pa., 1995. Cert. tchr. social studies Pa., 1995. Tchr. history and psychology Coatesville (Pa.) H.S., 1997—2004; tchr. history Downingtown East H.S., Exton, Pa., 2004—. Co-advisor students against drunk driving club Coatesville (Pa.) H.S., 1999—2004; co-advisor history club Downingtown H.S., 2005—. Democrat. Avocations: travel, reading. Office Phone: 610-363-6400.

ELLIS, ROSEMARY, editor-in-chief; Sr. editl. positions Working Woman, Self, Travel & Leisure; exec. editor Time Inc. Interactive, Time Inc. New Media; web site dir, exec. editor Expedia Travels; cons. Real Simple, AOL Web Properties divsn.; sr. v.p., editl. dir. Prevention Mag., 2003—06; editor-in-chief Good Housekeeping, 2006—. Office: Good Housekeeping Hearst Corp 300 W 57th St New York NY 10019-5288 Office Phone: 212-649-2200.*

ELLIS, ROSS, non-profit organization executive; Co-owner Visions & Images; pres. Elegant Events; v.p., dir. corp. affairs and events pharm. comm. co.; dir. resource devel. child abuse prevention group; founder, CEO Love Our Children, USA, 1999—. Active with Starlight Children's Found.; mem Phillip Morris Domestic Violence Coun. Mem.: NY Entertainment Publicists Soc. (bd. dirs.), NY Women's Agenda, NY Women in Comm. (bd. dirs.). Achievements include created and ran Dreams Come True program at Mt. Sinai Med. Ctr. Office: Love Our Children USA 220 E 57th St New York NY 10022 Office Phone: 888-347-5437. Business E-Mail: info@loveourchildrenusa.org.

ELLIS, YVONNE, mathematics professor; life ptnr. David Harris; 1 child, Ketsia. MS magna cum laude, U. Calif., Riverside. Prof. San Bernardino Valley Coll., Calif., 1997—. Office: 701 S Mt Vernon Ave San Bernardino CA 92401 Office Phone: 909-384-8520.

ELLISON, BETTY D., retired elementary school educator; b. Meriwether County, Ga., Jan. 28, 1950; d. Haywood Sr. and Mary Susan (Green) Daniel; m. Darthus Ellison, Jr., June 25, 1972; children: Darthus III, Keith Brandon. BA, Morris Brown Coll., 1972; MA, Atlanta U., 1975. Cert. tchr. Tchr. Meriwether County Bd. Edn., Greenville, Ga.; reading specialist Talbot County Bd. Edn., Talbotton, Ga. Advisor Nat. Jr. Honor Soc.; owner, operator Ellison's Tutorial Svc. Ga. State Tchrs. scholar; named County Star Tchr., 1991. Mem. NEA, Internat. Reading Assn., Ga. Assn. Educators, Zeta Phi Beta, Pi Delta Phi.

ELLISON, CATHY WALKER, history educator, literature and language educator, educational consultant; b. Murfreesboro, Tenn., Dec. 9, 1969; d. James Nelson and Betty Jane Copeland Walker; m. Tim Fred Ellison, June 10, 1989; children: Loretta Ann, Eli Damon, Keith Warren. BS, Troy U., Ala., 1991, MEd, 1993. English and history tchr. Dixie Acad., Louisville, Ala., 1991—93; substitute tchr. Enterprise (Ala.) City Sch., 1993—95, alter. English tchr., 1995—96; English and history tchr. Geneva (Ala.) City Sch., 1996—. Mem.: Pilot Club (youth coord. 1995—), Delta Kappa Gamma (pres. 2006). Office: Geneva City Sch 505 Panther Dr Geneva AL 36340 Office Phone: 334-684-9379. Business E-Mail: policeteacher@entercomp.com.

ELLISON, LOIS TAYLOR, internist, educator, medical association administrator; b. Fort Valley, Ga., Oct. 28, 1923; d. Robert James and Annie Maude (Anderson) Taylor; m. Robert Gordon Ellison, Feb. 11, 1945; children: Robert Gordon, Gregory Taylor, Mark Frederick, James Walton, John Charles. BS, U. Ga., 1943; MD, Med. Coll. Ga., 1950. Fellow, Univ. Hosp., Augusta, Ga., 1950-51; mem. faculty Med. Coll. Ga., Augusta, 1951—, prof. medicine and surgery, 1971—2000, assoc. dean, 1974-75, provost, 1975-84, assoc. v.p. planning (hosps. and clins.), 1984—2000, prof. emeritus medicine and surgery, 2000, med. historian, provost emeritus, 2000—. Attending VA Med. Ctr., Augusta; civilian cons. Eisenhower Army Med. Ctr., Fort Gordon, Ga.; mem. coal mine health research adv. council Nat. Inst. Occupational Safety and Health, 1972-75; bd. dirs. East Central Ga. Health Systems Agy., 1975-79, treas., 1979—; bd. dirs. Oak Ridge Associated Univs., 1978-84; mem. adv. council Univ. Systems Ga., 1975-84; mem. exec. com. Ga. Health Coordinating Council, 1980 Contbr. numerous articles to profl. jours. Bd. dirs. United Way Greater Augusta, 1975-78, chair div. hosp. and health, 1978, chair div. colls. and univs., 1980; mem. adminstrv. bd. Trinity-on-the-Hill United Methodist Ch., Augusta, 1974-77, mem. pastor-parish com., 1978— NIH grantee, 1963-68; included in NIH Nat. Libr. Medicine exhbn., 2003. Fellow Am. Coll. Chest Physicians; mem. Am. Physiol. Soc., Am. Med. Women's Assn., AMA, Assn. Am. Med. Colls., Am. Lung Assn. (dir. 1967—, sec. 1982-85, pres.-elect 1985-86, pres. 1986-87), Am. Heart Assn. (pres. Ga. affiliate chpt. 1982-83, dir. 1979—), So. Soc. Clin. Investigation, Am. Lung Assn. of Ga. (pres. 1984-85), Ga. Heart Assn. Office: Med Coll Ga 1120 15th St AE-3055 Augusta GA 30912 Office Phone: 706-721-4013. Business E-Mail: ellisonl@mcg.edu.

ELLIS-SCRUGGS, JAN, theater arts educator; b. Phila., Apr. 7, 1951; d. Roger C. and Greta M. Ellis; m. William Marquis Scruggs, Aug. 8, 1970; children: William Marcus Jr., Christopher Michael. BA, Cheyney U., 1987; MS in Adult and Continuing Edn., Cheyney U., Pa., 2006; MA, Villanova U., 1991. Lectr., instr. U. Conn., Storrs, 1989-90; theatre arts instr. Delaware County C.C., Media, Pa., 1994-95; asst. prof. theatre arts Cheyney (Pa.) U., 1993-94, 97—; actor, singer, dir., theater educator, adminstr. U.S. and London. Assoc. prodr., Citeaux, Inc., London, 1979-83; dir. Cheyney U., 1997—. Mem. editl. adv. bd., Collegiate Press, San Diego, 1999—. Missionary, Mother Bethel African Meth. Episc. Ch., Phila., 1994—. Recipient Charles and Mary Lindback Disting. Tchg. award, 2005—06. Mem. AFTRA, SAG (Screen Actors Guild), Actors Equity Assn., Alpha Psi Omega. Home: 7942 Cedarbrook Ave Philadelphia PA 19150 Office: Cheyney U of Pa Marian Anderson Music Ctr Cheyney PA 19319 Business E-Mail: jellis-scruggs@cheyney.edu. E-mail: jebs267@aol.com.

ELLMANN, SHEILA FRENKEL, investment company executive; b. Detroit, June 8, 1931; d. Joseph and Rose (Neback) Frenkel; m. William M. Ellmann, Nov. 1, 1953 (dec. Jan. 16, 2002); children: Douglas Stanley, Carol Elizabeth, Robert Lawrence. BA in English, U. Mich., 1953. Dir. Advance Glove Mfg. Co., Detroit, 1954—78; v.p. Frome Investment Co., Detroit, 1980—96, pres., 1996—. Mem.: U. Mich. Alumni Assn., Nat. Trust Hist. Preservation, VFW Aux. Home: 28000 Weymouth Dr Farmington Hills MI 48334 Personal E-mail: sheilaellmann@yahoo.com.

ELLNER, CAROLYN LIPTON, non-profit organization executive, dean, consultant; b. Jan. 17, 1932; d. Robert Mitchell and Rose (Pearlman) Lipton; m. Richard Ellner, June 21, 1953; children: D. Lipton, Alison Lipton. AB cum laude, Mt. Holyoke Coll., 1953; AM, Columbia Tchrs. Coll., 1957; PhD with distinction, UCLA, 1968. Tchr., prof., adminstr. N.Y. and Md., 1957-62; prof. dir. tchr. edn., assoc. dean Claremont Grad. Sch., Calif., 1967-82; prof., dean sch. edn. Calif. State U., Northridge, 1982-98, dean emerita, 1998—. Pres., CEO On-the-Job Parenting. Co-author: Schoolmaking, 1977, Studies of College Teaching, 1983 (Orange County Authors award 1984). Trustee Ctr. for Early Edn., L.A., 1968-71, Oakwood Sch., L.A., 1972-78, Mt. Holyoke Coll., South Hadley, Mass., 1979-84, Pacific Oaks Coll. and Children's Sch., 2004—; commr. Economy and Efficiency com., L.A., 1974-82, Calif. Commn. Tchr. Credentialing, 1987-90, 93—, vice chair, 1995-96, chair, 1996-98; bd. dirs. Found. for Effective Govt., L.A., 1982, Calif. Coalition for Pub. Edn., 1985-88, Valley Hosp. Found., 1992-94, Mt. Holyoke Alumnae Assn. Bd., 1993-96; founding dir. Decade of Edn., 1990; assoc. dir. New Devel. in Sci. Project NSF, 1985-94; bd. dirs., chair edn. com. Valley Industry and Commerce Assn., 1990-93, v.p. 1993-94; co-prin. dir. Mid South Calif. Arts Project, 1991-98; mem. coun., trustees L.A. Alliance for Restructing Now (LEARN), 1992-2000; bd. dirs. Inner City Arts Found., 1993-96; involved with L.A. Annenberg Met. Project (LAAMP); exec. bd. DELTA, 1995—, Calif. Subject Matter Projects, 1998—. Ford Found. fellow 1964-67, fellow Ednl. Policy Fellowship Program, 1989-90; recipient Office of Edn. award U.S. Office of Edn., 1969-72, Alumnae medal of honor Mt. Holyoke Coll., 1998; W.M. Keck Found. grantee, 1983, 94. Mem. ASCD, Am. Edn. Rsch. Assn., Am. Assn. Colls. for Tchr. Edn., Nat. Soc. for Study of Edn. Home and Office: 1205 S Oak Knoll Ave Pasadena CA 91106-4442 E-mail: ellner@otjp.org.

ELLNER, RUTH H., realtor; b. Jerusalem, Feb. 27, 1945; arrived in US, 1981; d. Shalom and Yona Avishi Morchi (Mizrahi) Toby; m. Paul Hatchett; m. Larry Ellner (div.); m. Alfred Santo, July 30, 2002; 1 child; 1 child from previous marriage. Diploma, HS, Israel. Realtor Keyes Co., Miami, Fla., 1997—2003, Ocean View, Miami, Fla., 2003—; singer, songwriter, screen playwright self employed. Author: Incest to Where?, 2005. Served with Israeli Air Force. Home: 19001 NE 14 Ave 111 Miami FL 33179 Home Fax: 305-354-4085. Personal E-mail: ruthellner@hotmail.com.

ELLSTROM, ANNETTE, research consultant; b. Duluth, Minn., Dec. 19, 1952; d. Raymond Charles Ellstrom and Ruth Elaine (Bloomquist) Larson; m. Jeffrey Ellstrom-Calder, July 30, 1982; children: Hannah, Ian. BA in Social Work, Psychology, Sociology, Concordia Coll., 1974; MSW, U. Wis., 1978. Group therapist N.D. State Indsl. Sch., 1973; social worker Fergus Falls (Minn.) State Hosp., 1974, Jackson County Dept. Social Services, Black River Falls, Wis., 1975-77; sr. clin. social worker U. Wis. Hosp., Madison, 1979-90, clin. instr. medicine, 1989—; mktg. mgr. Med. Media Assocs., Madison, 1990-97. Cons. Waupun (Wis.) Meml. Hosp., 1979-84, lectr. grad. sch. social work U. Wis., Madison, 1979-82, prin. investigator in rsch. U. Wis. Hosp., Madison, 1985—. Editor: A Guide to Patients and Families, 1984; mem. editl. bd. Advances in Renal Replacement Therapy; contbr. articles to profl. jours. Del. trustee, bd. dirs. Nat. Kidney Found., N.Y.C., 1983-91, chmn. bd. dirs., Milw., 1985-87, vice chmn., 1983-85, sec., 1982-83, chmn. patient svcs. com., 1981-82, bd. dirs., 1981—, chmn. nat. tng. and edn. com., mem. nat. patient svcs. com., N.Y.C., 1987-91, mem. pers. com., bd. dirs. Madison chpt., 1979-80; bd. dirs. Combined Health Appeal Wis., 1990-97, sec., 1992-97; mem. nat. rsch. com. Am. Assn. Spinal Cord Injury Psychologists and Social Workers, N.Y.C., 1988-95; bd. dirs. Wisc. Conf United Ch. of Christ, 2001—, chmn bd. 2006—. Recipient Health Advancement award Nat. Kidney Found. Wis., 1985, Vol. Yr. award Nat. Kidney Found. Wis., 1984, Vol. Service award Nat. Kidney Found. Wis., 1983, Nat. Nephrology Social Worker of Yr. Merit award Nat. Kidney Found. and Council of Nephrology Social Workers, 1987; hon. adoptee Winnebago Indian Tribe, 1978; named Outstanding Young Wisconsinite Wisc. Jaycees, 1988. Mem. Council Nephrology Social Workers (nat. v.p. 1984-86, nat. exec. com. 1984-86, Nat. Nephrology Social Worker Yr. award 1987, mem. Nat. Rsch. Rev. com. 1996—), Nat. Assn. Social Workers, Pi Gamma Mu. Democrat. Avocations: travel, camping, skiing, gardening, swimming.

ELLSWEIG, PHYLLIS LEAH, retired psychotherapist; b. Irvington, N.J., Apr. 19, 1927; d. Sumar and Jeanette (Geffner) Schwartz; m. Martin Richard Ellsweig, Dec. 25, 1947; children: Bruce, Steven. BS, East Stroudsburg U., Pa., 1947; EdM, Lehigh U., 1966, EdD, 1972. Tchr. Stroud Union High Sch., 1963-66; guidance counselor East Stroudsburg (Pa.) Schs., 1966-68; asst. prof. edn. East Stroudsburg U., 1968; staff psychologist, outpatient supr. Mental Health Center Carbon, Monroe and Pike Counties, Stroudsburg, Pa., 1968-80; pvt. practice in psychotherapy and clin. hypnosis Stroudsburg, 1969-87. Mem. staff Pocono Hosp., 1968—80; pub. spkr. in field; cons. to schs. and pvt. orgns.; tchr. adult edn., Palm Beach County, Fla. Mem. Am. Soc. Clin. Hypnosis, Internat. Soc. Hypnosis, NOW (profl. cons. 1973—). Home: 2584 NW 12th St Delray Beach FL 33445-1353

ELLSWORTH, LAURA E., lawyer; b. NYC; BA, Princeton Univ., 1980; JD magna cum laude, Univ. Pitts., 1983. Bar: Pa. 1983. Ptnr.-in-charge Pitts. office Jones Day. Adv. com. for study of rules and practices US Dist. Ct., Western Dist. of Pa., 2003; adj. prof. law Univ. Pitts. Sch. of Law. Named a Leader in the Law, Legal Intelligencer, 2004; named one of the top female litigators in Pa., Pa. Law Weekly, 2004; recipient President's award, Pa. Bar Assn., 2002. Fellow: Am. Bar Assn.; mem.: Acad. of Trial Lawyers of Allegheny County, Pa. Bar Assn. (bd. mem.), Order of Coif. Office: Jones Day One Mellon Bank Ctr 31st Fl 500 Grant St Pittsburgh PA 15219 Office Phone: 412-394-7929. Office Fax: 412-394-7959. Business E-Mail: leellsworth@jonesday.com.

ELLSWORTH, PHOEBE CLEMENCIA, psychology professor; b. Hartford, Conn., Jan. 22, 1944; d. John Stoughton and Edith (Noble) E.; m. Samuel Raymond Gross, Nov. 7, 1979; children: Alexandra Ellsworth, Emma Beth Ellsworth. AB, Harvard U., 1966; PhD, Stanford U., 1970. Asst. prof. Yale U., New Haven, 1971-75, assoc. prof., 1975-79, prof., 1979-81, Stanford U., 1981-87; prof. psychology and law U. Mich., Ann Arbor, 1987—, Frank Murphy Disting. U. Prof. law and psychology, 2003—. Assoc. editor JESP, 1977-80; mem. social sci. rev. com. NIMH, 1973-77, com. on law and social sci. SSRC, 1975-84, rev. panel on law and social sci. NSF, 1983-85; mem. rev. bd. Am. Bar Found., 1987-91; bd. trustees Russell Sage Found., 1992-2002. Author: (with others) Emotions in the Human Face: Guidelines for Research And a Review of the Findings, Methods of Research in Social Psychology, Person Perception; contbr. articles to profl. jours. Fellow APA, Am. Acad. Arts and Scis.; mem. Soc. Exptl. Social Psychology, Am. Psychology Law Assn., Internat. Soc. Research on Emotion (charter)., Law and Soc. Assn. Home: 442 Huntington Pl Ann Arbor MI 48104-1800 Office: U Mich Sch Law 970 Legal Rsch 625 S State St Ann Arbor MI 48109-1215 Office Phone: 734-763-5781. E-mail: pce@umich.edu.

ELLSWORTH, TINA MARIE, elementary school educator, social studies educator; b. Kansas City, Mo., Oct. 5, 1978; d. Michael William and Deborah Michelle Johns; m. Jeremy Ryan Ellsworth, June 17, 2000. BS in Edn., Ctrl. Mo. State U., Warrensburg, 2003. Tchr. social studies Harrisonville Cass R-9 Sch. Dist., Mo., 2003—. Recipient Educator of Month, Harrisonville Cass R-9 Sch. Dist., 2004. Office: Harrisonville High School 1504 East Elm Harrisonville MO 64701 Personal E-mail: callmetj@aol.com. E-mail: ellsworth@harrisonville.k12.mo.us.

ELLYN, LYNNE, energy executive; Degree in computer sci. and mgmt., Oakland U., 1979; MBA, Mich. State U. Various positions to mgr. advanced tech. devel. Chrysler Corp.; dir. bus. systems devel., acting v.p. global systems deployment Xerox Corp., 1993-96; v.p. bus. applications Netscape Comm. Corp., 1996-98; named v.p. info. systems orgn. Detroit Edison Co., 1998; now sr. v.p., chief info. officer DTE Energy Co., Detroit. Fellow Cutter Bus. Tech. Coun. Mem. dean's adv. bd. Oakland U. Decision and Info. Sciences Sch. Named one of 100 Most Influential Women Bus. Leaders, Crain's Detroit Bus., 2002, Top Mich. Women in Computing, Assn. for Women in Computing, 2003, Premier 100 IT Leaders, Computerworld, 2005. Office: DTE Energy Co 2000 2nd Ave Detroit MI 48226-1279*

EL MALLAKH, DOROTHEA HENDRY, editor, publishing executive; b. Emmett, Idaho, July 16, 1938; d. David Lovell Parker and Lygia Teressa (Dalton) Hendry; m. Ragaei William El Mallakh, Aug. 26, 1962 (dec. Mar. 19, 1987); children: Helen Alise, Nadia Irene. BA in Modern Langs., Lewis and Clark Coll., 1960; MA in History, U. Colo., 1962, PhD in History, 1972; postgrad., Georgetown U., 1962-63. Exec. adminstr., treas. Internat. Rsch. Ctr. Energy & Econ. Devel., Boulder, Colo., 1973-87, exec. dir., 1987—. Assoc. editor Jour. Energy & Devel., Boulder, 1975-87, mng. editor, 1987—; bd. dirs. Rocky Mountain Eye Found., Boulder. Author: The Slovak Autonomy Movement, 1979; author (with others): The Genius of Arab Civilization, 1983, Gulf Oil in the Aftermath of the Iraq War: Strategies and Policies, 2005; editor: The Energy Watchers I-IX, 1990-98; author and editor: Saudi Arabia, 1982. Perrine Meml. fellow, U. Colo., 1960-61, Rare Lang. fellow, U.S. Govt., U. Colo., 1961-62, Rotary Internat. fellow, Boise, Idaho, 1962. Mem. Internat. Assn. Energy Econs. (v.p. internat. affairs 1989-91, sec. 1988-89). Office: ICEED 850 Willowbrook Rd Boulder CO 80302-7439 Office Phone: 303-442-4014. Business E-Mail: iceed@colorado.edu.

ELMAN, NAOMI GEIST, artist, theater producer; b. Chgo. d. Harry and Rita (Goldstein) Geist; m. Murray Elman, May 29, 1946 (dec. Dec. 1965); 1 child, Margaret (Peggy) Gillespie. Student, Hamilton Inst. for Girls, Nat. Acad. of Design, Art Students League. Personal mgr. in performing arts, prodr. concerts in, N.Y.C. and Hawaii, N.Y., Hawaii, 1968-80. One-woman shows include Churchill Gallery, 1962, Pen and Brush Club, 1986, Neuwirth Gallery, Phoenix, 1994; exhibited in group shows; represented in a permanent collection Tchrs. Coll. N.Y.C. Alumni Assn. Vol. nurses aid pvt. and army hosps., ARC, 1939-45; v.p. N.Y. Diabetes Assn., 1955-58; mcpl. chmn. Dem. Club, Tenafly, N.J., 1958; Dem. com. woman, 1959-61; bd. dirs. Nat.

Children's Cardiac Home, N.Y.C., 1940-49, Bergen County Dem. Club, 1958-60. Recipient Margareet Sussman award, 1985, Salamagundi award, 1987, Julia Lucille award, 1988. Mem. Internat. Platform Assn., Soc. Mil. Widows, Retired Officers Club (life), Disabled Am. Vets., Artists Equity, Kent Art Assn. Democrat. Address: PO Box 1278 Amherst MA 01004-1278

ELMENDORF-LANDGRAF, MARY LINDSAY, retired anthropologist; b. Ruby, S.C., Apr. 13, 1917; d. James Calvin Lindsay and Ana Eugenia MacGregor; m. John van Gaasbeek Elmendorf, Dec. 27, 1937 (dec. Feb. 1980); children: Calvin Lindsay, Susan Elmendorf Roberts; m. John L. Landgraf, Nov. 27, 1981. AB in Psychology, U. N.C., Chapel Hill, 1937, MA in Social Work and Pub. Adminstrn., 1940; PhD in Anthropology, Union Grad. Sch., 1972, U. N.C., Chapel Hill, 1987, PhD (hon.), 1994. Rsch. fellow Ford Found., N.Y.C., Mex., 1972-73; anthropologist World Bank, Washington, 1975—95, USAID, Washington, 1980-85, Internat. Devel. Rsch. Ctr., Ottawa, Calif., 1980-90; ret., 1996. Instr. Putney (Vt.) Sch., 1941—43; dir. AFSC Spanish Refugee Program, France, 1945—46; dir. CARE de Mex., 1952—60; coord. off-campus studies Brown U., 1962—65; coord. off-campus studies New Coll. U. Fla., 1965—69, adj. prof. anthropology, 1992—2000; vis. assoc. prof. anthropology Hampshire Coll., Amherst, Mass., 1973, Semester at Sea, 1974—75; mem. part-time faculty Goddard Coll., Vt., 1973—75; mentor New Coll. Fla., 1987—; advisor Union Inst., 1990—; lectr. in field; cons. in field. Author: The Mayan Woman and Change, 1972, La Mujer Maya y el Cambio, 1973, Nine Mayan Women: A Village Faces Change, 1976, The Socio-Cultural Aspects of Excreta Disposal, 1980, The International Drinking Water and Sanitation Decade and Women's Involvement, 1990, Priorities, Challenges and Strategies: A Feminine Perspective, Women, Water and UNIFEM, 2001, Water is Life at Hannover, Germany, 2002, Rights, Resources, Culture and Conservation in the Land of the of Yucatan, Mexico: Studies Inspired by the Work of Mary Elmendorf, 2004; contbr. numerous articles to profl. jours.; collection papers Smathers Libr., U. Fla., Nat. Anthrop. Archives, Smithsonian Instn. Recipient with other Quaker vols. Nobel Peace Prize, 1947; recipient Margaret Mead award, 1982, Disting. Alumna award U. N.C., 1993, Lifetime Achievement award 2006, Humanitarian award 2006; Ford Found. fellow, 1972-73. Fellow: Soc. Applied Anthropology, Am. Anthrop. Assn.; mem.: UNIFEM (founding bd. mem. 1965), AAAS, AAUW, Sister Cities, UN Assn. USA, Planned Parenthood (bd. mem. Fla. ho. 1975—78), Internat. Drinking Water Commn. (ad hoc com. 2003—). Democrat. Mem. Soc. Of Friends. Achievements include 1st anthropologist invited to join World Bank staff, 1975. Avocations: painting, enjoying grandchildren. Home: 700 John Ringling Blvd Apt 2305 Sarasota FL 34236-1551 also: San Miguel Allende Mexico Personal E-mail: maryelmendorf17@aol.com.

ELMER, MARILYN ANN, education educator, author; b. Marlette, Mich., Nov. 14, 1931; d. Kent J. and Hazel Fern (Smith) Hager; m. Joseph Nathaniel Elmer, Aug. 22, 1954; children: Melissa, Kent. BS, Bob Jones U., 1953; MS, Fla. State U., 1961. Elem. tchr. Saginaw (Mich.) Pub. Schs., 1953-54; tchr. jr. high sch. Bob Jones Acad., Greenville, S.C., 1954-56, 60-62; elem. tchr. Brent Christian Sch., Pensacola, Fla., 1956-60; coll. tchr. dept. edn. Bob Jones U., Greenville, 1962—. Workshop speaker Greenville Pub. Schs., 1970-73, nationwide Christian Sch. conventions, 1973—. Author, editor elem. sch. textbooks.

ELMORE, BETH ROBINSON, science educator; b. Statesville, N.C., Mar. 10, 1967; m. Jeffrey Paul Elmore, May 17, 1989; children: Julia, Laura. BS in Biology, Wake Forest U., Winston-Salem, 1989. Tchr. Mill Creek Mid. Sch., Claremont, NC, 1999—. Office: Mill Creek Middle School 1041 Shiloh Rd Claremont NC 28610 Office Phone: 828-241-2711. E-mail: beth_elmore@catawba.k12.nc.us.

ELMORE, CENIETH CATHERINE, music educator; b. Wilson, NC, July 4, 1930; d. Thomas Onestrus Elmore and Effie Lee Morris. MusB in Theory, U. N.C., Greensboro, 1953; MusM in Composition, U. N.C., 1962, MA in Musicology, 1963, PhD in Musicology, 1972. Piano tchr. pub. sch., Fuquay Springs, NC, 1953—57, Louisburg, NC, 1957—60; grad. asst. piano tchr. U. N.C., Chapel Hill, 1960—63; music prof. Campbell U., Buies Creek, NC, 1963—94, prof. emeritus, 1994—. Lectr. in field; pvt. piano tchr., 1998—. Author. Active Franklin County Arts Coun., Louisburg, NC, 1970—, Franklin County Person Place Preservation Soc., Louisburg, 1980—, Perry's Chapel Bapt. Ch., Franklinton, NC, 1948—. Named Artist of Yr., Franklin County Arts Coun., 1995. Mem.: N.C. Music Tchrs. Assn. (bd. dirs., chair arts awareness and advocacy 2006—), Am. Musicological Soc., Raleigh Piano Tchrs. Assn. (first v.p. 1996—98, 2000—02, pres. 2002—04, chair young artist auditions composition competition 2004—). Republican. Achievements include research in a structural analysis of Schoenberg's 15 Gedichte aus "Das Buch Der Hargenden Garten" von Stefan George; stylistic considerations in the piano sonatas of Nicholai Medtner. Avocations: painting, reading, gardening, travel, internet. Home: 981 Perry's Chapel Church Rd Franklinton NC 27525-8263 Personal E-mail: ceniethelmore@aol.com.

EL-MOSLIMANY, ANN PAXTON, paleoecologist, educator, writer; b. Fullerton, Calif., Aug. 2, 1937; d. Donald Dorn and Sarah Frances (Turman) Paxton; m. Mohammed Ahmad El-Moslimany, May 31, 1962 (dec.); children: Samia, Ramsey, Rasheed. BS, N.Mex. State U., 1959; MS, Am. U., Beirut, 1961; PhD, U. Wash., 1983. Tchr. various schs., 1959-83, Kuwait U., 1984—86, Seattle Ctrl. C.C., 1986-90; prin., tchr. Islamic Sch. Seattle, 1989-99, curriculum coord., 1999—. Paleoecological rschr. Palynological Consultants, 1987—; founding dir. Islamic Sch. of Seattle; adv. bd. Islamic Sch. League Am. Author: Zaki's Ramadan Fast, 1994; contbr. articles to sci. jours.; mem. adv. bd. Aziah mag. Speaker Children of Abraham Organization. Mem. Amnesty Internat., Am. Quaternary Assn., Islamic Sch. League. Moslem. Avocations: travel, literature, history. Office: Islamic Sch Seattle 720 25th Ave Seattle WA 98122-4902 Mailing: PO Box 367 Seahurst WA 98062 E-mail: annelmoslimany@yahoo.com.

ELPERS, KIMBERLY KAY, science educator, consultant; d. Larry Gene and Beverley Diana Georges; m. Roger Lee Elpers, June 16, 1979; children: Rachel Michelle, Blake Matthew, Paige Diane. M Edn.with Sci. Endorsement, Ind. State U., Terre Haute, 1984. Tchr. k-5 sci. Sts. Peter and Paul Sch., Haubstadt, Ind., 1981—. Sci. cons. Ind. Soybean Bd., Indpls., 2006—, Ind. Dept. Sci. Edn., Indpls., 2004—; patient cons. DePuy Spine - Johnson & Johnson Co., Raynham, Mass., 2004—06. Finalist Presdl. award Sci. Tchg., NSF, 2006; recipient Tchr. of Yr., Diocese Evansville, 2004. Mem.: NSTA (assoc.; reviewer 1992—2006, web watcher 2004), Evansville Area Reading Coun. (assoc.), Hoosier Assn. Sci. Tchrs. Inc. (assoc.). Office: Sts Peter and Paul School 210 N Vine St Haubstadt IN 47639 Personal E-mail: kelpers77@hotmail.com.

ELROD, DEBORAH LEE, special education educator; b. Bradford, Pa., June 27, 1952; d. Richard Irving McKelvey and Betty Jean Slingerland McCarty; m. Allen Wayne Elrod, Dec. 17, 1978. BS in Edn., Stephen F. Austin State U., 1974; MEd, Sam Houston State U., 1985. Cert. profl. reading specialist, provisional elem. edn., provisional elem. reading, provisional lang. and/or learning disabilities, provisional physically handicapped. Resource tchr. spl. edn. Newton (Tex.) Ind. Sch. Dist.; spl. edn. resource tchr. Aldine Ind. Sch. Dist., Houston; tchr. Hoffman Mid. Sch., 2000—. Instr. (part-time) No. Harris County Coll., Houston, 1990-92; coord. dyslexia program Hoffman Mid. Sch., 2001— Named Tchr. of Yr. Carmichael Elem. Sch., 1993. Mem. Internat. Reading Assn., Tex. State Reading Assn., Greater Houston Area Reading Coun., Delta Kappa Gamma Avocation: figure skating. Office Phone: 713-613-7670. Personal E-mail: debonice@msn.com.

ELROD, JOY CHEEK, nurse; b. Ft. Gordon, Ga., Dec. 16, 1955; d. Alton Waldo and Peggy Jim (Hewin) Cheek; children: Dana Maria, Zacharia Daniel. AA, Emmanuel Coll., 1984; BSN, Med. Coll. Ga., 1986. Coord. Wellness Systems Inc., Athens, Ga., 1986-87; staff nurse Athens Regional Med. Ctr., 1987-90, Ty Cobb Health Care System, Royston, Ga., 1990—, healthy beginnings coord., 1991—2005. Med. outreach tng. amb. Ty Cobb Health Care System, Ga. Hosp. Assn., Royston, 1991-92; instr. Neonatal Resusitation Providers, 1996—. Mem. No. Jud. Dist. Task Force for Family Violence, 1994-1999, Cmty. Adv. Bd. Safehouse Ministries, Inc., 1995-2000; bd. mem. N.E. Ga. Coun. Domestic Violence, 2000—; art and Franklin Counties Family Outreach, Franklin County Commn. for Children and Youth, 1994-2000. Baptist. Home: 1038 W Main St Bowersville GA 30516-1225

ELROD, KERI LYNN, athletic trainer; d. Kenny and Sally Elrod. BS in Sports Medicine and Athletic Tng., BS in Edn., Mo. State U., Springfield, 2001; MA in Edn., Western Carolina U., Cullowhee, N.C., 2003. Cert. athletic trainer Nat. Athletic Tng. Assn. Bd. of Certification, 2000; strength and conditioning specialist Nat. Strength and Conditioning Assn., 2004. Coord. of fitness and athletic tng. Mo. State U., West Plains, 2003—. Mem.: Nat. Strength and Conditioning Assn., Nat. Athletic Tng. Assn. Office: Mo State Univ 128 Garfield Ave West Plains MO 65775 Office Phone: 417-255-7936. E-mail: kerielrod@missouristate.edu.

ELROD, LINDA DIANE HENRY, lawyer, educator; b. Topeka, Kans., Mar. 6, 1947; d. Lyndus Arthur Henry and Marjorie Jane (Hammel) Allen; divorced; children: Carson Douglas, Bree Elizabeth. BA in English with honors, Washburn U., 1969, JD cum laude, 1971. Bar: Kans. 1972, U.S. Supreme Ct. 2004, cert.: U.S. Supreme Ct. (domestic mediator) 1999. Instr. U. S.D., Topeka, 1970-71; research atty. Kans. Jud. Council, Topeka, 1972-74; asst. prof. Washburn U., Topeka, 1974-78, assoc. prof., 1978-82, prof. law, 1982-93, disting. prof., 1993—, dir. Children and Family Law Ctr., 2001—. Vis. prof. law U. San Diego, Paris Summer Inst., 1988, 90, Washington U. Sch. Law, St. Louis, 1990, 98, summer 1991, 93, Fla. State U. Law Sch., spring, 2000. Author: Kansas Family Law Handbook, 1983, rev. edit., 1990, supplement, 1993, Child Custody Practice and Procedure, 1993, supplements, 1994-2005; co-author: Principles of Family Law, 1999, 5th edit., 2003, Kansas Family Law Guide, 1999, supplements, 2000-06; editor Family Law Quar., 1992—; mem. NCCUSL joint editl. bd. on uniform family law; reporter Uniform Child Abduction Prevention Act, 2004-; contbr. articles to profl. jours. Pres. YWCA, Topeka, 1982-83; vice-chair Kans. Commn. on Child Support, 1984-87, Supreme Ct. Commn. on Child Support, 1987—; chair Kans. Cmty. Svc. Orgn., 1986-87; adv. bd. CASA, 1997—; bd. dirs. Appleseed, 2000-05; elder Westminster Presbyn. Ch., 2006—. Recipient Disting. Svc. award Washburn Law Sch. Assn., 1986, Washburn Alumni Assn., 2005; named YWCA Woman of Distinction, 1997; Woman of the Yr. scholar Am. Bus. Women's Assn., 2006. Mem. ABA (coun. family law sect. 1988, sec. 1998, vice-chair, 1999, chair 2000-01, chair Schwab Meml. Grant Implementation 1984-87, co-chair Amicus Curiae com. 1987-92, co-chair pro bono child custody project adv. bd. 2001-2005), steering com. on unmet legal needs of children 2002-2005), Topeka Bar Assn. (sec. 1981-85, v.p. 1985-86, pres. 1986-87), Kans. Child Support Enforcement Assn. (bd. dirs. 1988—, Child Support Hall of Fame 1990), Kans. Bar Assn. (sec.-treas. 1988-89, com. ops. and fin. 1988, pres. family law sect. 1984-86, Disting. Svc. award 1985), NONOSO, Phi Kappa Phi, Phi Alpha Delta Alumni Assn. (justice 1976-77), Phi Beta Delta, Kappa Alpha Theta (pres. alumnae chpt. 1995-97). Presbyterian. Avocations: bridge, reading, quilting. Office: Washburn U Law Sch 17th and College Topeka KS 66621 E-mail: linda.elrod@washburn.edu.

ELROD, LU, retired music educator, actress; b. Chattanooga, Apr. 23, 1935; d. John C. Elrod and Helen Pauline (Kohn). MusB, Ga. State U., 1960; M in Music Edn., U. Ga., 1970, EdD, 1971; PhD, U. London, 1975. Prof. music, music coach U. Md., Balt., 1972-78, Calif. State U., L.A., 1978—2004, now prof. emerita. Singer with Dallas Opera, 1957. Appeared in movies Charly, 1969, Brewster's Millions, 1986, Major Pettigrew and Me, 1976, Seduction of Joe Tynan, 1977, Atlanta Child Murders, 1985, Children Don't Tell, 1986, For Love or Money, 1986, High School High, 1996, Wag the Dog, 1997, The Big Lebowski, 1998, Primary Colors, 1998, Lloyd the Ugly Kid, 1999, Beautiful, 1999, Glory Days, 2001, Freaky Friday, 2004, Kicking and Screaming, 2005; appeared on TV in Lazarus Syndrome, 1980, Hill Street Blues (Emmy award), 1988, Superior Court, 1988, TV Bloopers, 1989, Beakman's World (Emmy award), Dream On, 1993, Misery Loves Company, 1995, Caroline in the City, 1995, Louie, 1996, George and Alana, 1996, Maggie, 1998, Two Guys and a Girl, 2000, Glory Days, 2001, I Love the 90's, 2004; appeared in TV commls Recipient Gold medal, Silver medal swimming Am. Atheletic Union, 1955, Leadership Devel. award Ford Found., 1967, Leadership Fellows award Ford Found., 1968; Tift Coll. voice scholar, 1953, Baylor U. voice scholar, 1956; Lu Elrod scholarship named at Calif. State U., LA, 1989; named to Calif. State U., L.A. Wall of Fame, 1993; named Disting. Prof. Arts and Letters, 1993. Mem. AAUP, AFTRA, SAG, Am. Guild Variety Artists, Calif. Faculty Assn., Coll. Music Soc. Achievements include established 32 music, theatre, communication studies scholarships through fund-raising activities, collective bargaining, social work, and athletes 1978-2006. Office: Calif State Univ 5151 State University Dr Los Angeles CA 90032-4226 Business E-Mail: lelrod@calstatela.edu.

ELSE, CAROLYN JOAN, retired library director; b. Mpls., Jan. 31, 1934; d. Elmer Oscar and Irma Carolyn (Seibert) Wahlberg; m. Floyd Warren Else, 1962 (div. 1968); children: Stephen Alexander, Catherine Elizabeth. BS, Stanford U., 1956; MLS, U. Wash., 1957. Cert. profl. libr. Wash. Libr. Queens Borough Pub. Libr., N.Y.C., 1957—59, U.S. Army Spl. Svcs., France, Germany, 1959—62; info. libr. Bennett Martin Libr., Lincoln, Nebr., 1962—63; br. libr. Pierce County Libr., Tacoma, 1963—65, dir., 1965—94; ret., 1994. Wellness cons. Nikken, Inc., 1994—. Mem. Higher Edn. Coun., South Puget Sound, 1988—92; bd. dirs. Tacoma Philharmonic, 2005—; mem. distbn. com. Greater Tacoma Cmty. Found., 2005—; mem. study commn. Wash. State Local Governance, 1985—88; bd. dirs. Campfire, Tacoma, 1984—92, Cmty. Health Care, 1997—2003. Mem.: Pacific N.W. Libr. Assn. (sec. 1969—71), Wash. Libr. Assn. (v.p. 1969—71), ALA, Tacoma Rotary #8 Club (bd. dirs. 1995—97), City Club (Tacoma). Personal E-mail: carolyn.else@stanfordalumni.org. E-mail: cjelse@harbornet.com.

ELSEA, CHRISTINE E., music educator; b. St. Joseph, Mo., Feb. 27, 1971; d. Thomas Edwin and Suzanne Miles Schneider, Thomas Edwin and Suzanne Miles Schneider; m. Edward Madison Elsea, III, June 29, 1996. Student, Oberlin Conservatory, Ohio, 1989; BS in Edn., U. Mo., Columbia, Mo., 1996. Music educator Kirkwood H.S., Mo., 1995, St. James H.S., Mo., 1995—96, Rolla Mid. Sch., Mo., 1996—99, Oak Grove Elem. Sch., Poplar Bluff, Mo., 1999—2001, Northwest Elem. Sch., Houstonia, Mo., 2002—04, Santa Fe H.S., Alma, Mo., 2004—06, Lebanon Jr. H.S., Mo., 2006—. Fellow, Fulbright Meml. Fund, 2004. Mem.: Mo. Music Educators Assn., Mo. Choral Dirs. Assn., Pi Kappa Phi. Democrat. Roman Cath. Home: 108 Bluebird Ln Lebanon MO 65536-2073

ELSHTAIN, JEAN BETHKE, social sciences educator; b. Windsor, Colo., Jan. 6, 1941; d. Paul G. and Helen L. Bethke; m. Errol L. Elshtain, Sept. 3, 1965; 1 adopted child, Bobby Bethke children: Sheri, Heidi, Jenny, Eric. BA in History, Colo. State U., 1963; MA in History, U. Colo., 1965; PhD in Politics, Brandeis U., 1973; LLD (hon.), Gonzaga U., 1996; DHL (hon.), Valparaiso U., 1996, Grinell Coll., 1997, Maryville U., 1997, Messiah Coll., 1999, Carthage Coll., 2000, Lake Forest Coll., 2001, Siena Coll., 2002, North Park Coll., 2002, U. West Timisoara, Romania, 2005. Prof. polit. sci. U. Mass., Amherst, 1973-88, Vanderbilt U., Nashville, 1988-94; vis. prof. Harvard U., Cambridge, Mass., 1994; prof. ethics U. Chgo., 1995—. Lectr. in field. Author: Public Man, Private Woman: Women in Social and Political Thought, 1982, 2d edit., 1992 (Top Choice Acad. Book), Czech transl., 1999, Ukranian transl., 2002, Women and War, 1987, Japanese transl., 1994, Power Trips and Other Journeys, Essays on Feminism as Civic Discourse, 1990, Meditations on Modern Political Thought: Masculine/Feminine Theme Luther to Arendt, 1992, Democracy on Trial, 1995 (N.Y. Times Notable Book, 1995), Augustine and the Limits of Politics, 1996; co-author: But Was It Just? Reflections on the Morality of the Gulf War, 1992; editor: The Family in Political Thought, 1982, Just War Theory, 1991, The Jane Addams Reader, 2002, Just War Against Terror: The Burden of American Power, 2003 (One of the Best Non-Fiction Books of 2003 Pub. Weekly); co-editor: Women, Militarism and War, 1990, Politics and the Human Body, 1995, Promise to Keep, Decline and Renewal of Marriage in America, 1996, Real Politics, Political Theory and Everyday Life, 1997, New Wine in Old Bottles: International Politics and Ethical Discourse, 1998 (Top Choice Acad. Book), Who are We? Critical Reflection, Hopeful Possibilities, 2000 (Best Acad. Book Am. Theol. Booksellers Assn., 2000), Jane Addams and the Dream of American Democracy, 2002, Just War Against Terror: The Burden of American Power in a Violent World, 2004 (Named One of Top Non-Fiction Book of Yr. Pubs. Weekly). Bd. dirs. Nat. Endowment Democracy, 2002—; trustee Inst. Advanced Study, 1994—99, Nat. Humanities Ctr., NC, 1996—2005; chair Coun. Civil Soc., NYC, Chgo., 1995—, Coun. Families Am., N.Y.C., 1995—; apptd. Coun. of Nat. Endowment for Humanties, 2006—. Recipient award for Disting. Lifetime Contbn. to Faith and Scholarship, C.S. Lewis Soc., 2005, Jane Addams medal for lifetime scholarly achievement, Rockford Coll., 2005, Ind. Humanties award, 2006. Fellow: AAAS; mem.: Am. Soc. Polit. and Legal Philosophy (v.p. 1996—97), Am. Polit. Sci. Assn. (v.p. 1998—99, Maguire chair ethics Libr. Congress 2003—04, Goodnow award for Lifetime Svc. 2002, Gifford lectr. 2006). Avocations: movies, reading. Home: 4010 Wallace Ln Nashville TN 37215-2308 Office: U Chgo Div Sch 1025 E 58th St Chicago IL 60637-1509 Office Phone: 773-702-7252. Business E-Mail: jbelshta@uchicago.edu.

ELSOM, MARGARET STRIPLIN, elementary school educator; b. Richmond, Va., Sept. 18; d. Norman D. and Shirley B. Striplin; m. David M. Elsom, Aug. 2, 2000; children: Jeremy David, Megan Sarah Volk. BS in Elem. Edn., Chadron State U., Nebr., 1985; MA in Curriculum and Instrn., Lesley U., Cambridge, Mass., 2005. Cert. tchr. of sci., social studies, and English S.D. Dept. Edn. Mid. sch. tchr. Newell Mid. Sch. Tchr., SD, 2001—04, Belle Fourche Mid. Sch., 2004—. Mem.: NEA, S.D. Edn. Assn., Delta Kappa Gamma, Alpha Delta Kappa. Office: Belle Fourche Mid Sch 2305 13th Ave Spearfish SD 57783 Office Phone: 605-723-3367.

ELSON, SUZANNE GOODMAN, social services administrator; b. Memphis, Oct. 17, 1937; d. Charles F. and Isabel (Ehrlich) Goodman; m. Edward Elliott Elson, Aug. 24, 1957; children: Charles Myer, Louis Goodman, Harry II. Student, Randolph-Macon Women's Coll., Lynchburg, Va.; BA, Agnes Scott Coll., 1959. Sec. Nat. Coun. Jewish Women, N.Y.C., 1977-79; pres. Nat. Mental Health Assn., 1980-82; trustee emeritus Randolph Macon Women's Coll., 1988-98, 99. Chmn. Am. Craft Coun., 1989-92, hon. chmn., 1992-94, hon. trustee, 1994-; bd. dirs. Rosalynn Carter Inst., 1990-, Nat. Coun. Medicine Emory U., 1990-95; trustee Va. Mus. of Fine Art., 1992-96, High Mus. Fine Art, 1972-92, Am. Craft Mus., 1999-; bd. regents U. System of Ga., 1993-97; adv. bd. Breast Cancer Rsch. Found., 1998-; bd. dirs. Friends of Art and Preservation in Embassies, 1999- (trustee 1998); bd. govs. Mus. of Art and Design, 1998-; trustee Soc. for the Four Arts, 2003-, Preservation Soc. of Palm Beach, 2004- Home: 180 Cocoanut Row Palm Beach FL 33480-4121

ELSTON, JOAN WILMA, adult education educator, real estate agent; b. Kansas City, Mo., Sept. 20, 1938; d. William Hamilton Elston and Alyce Jean (Clark) Elston, Jones; m. Paul Wesley Sweeney, Sept. 10, 1968 (div.). BS, U. Kans., Lawrence, 1960; MS, U. So. Calif., L.A., 1972. Cert. spiritual practitioner United Ch. of Religious Sci., 2000; tchr. Calif., 1960, reading tchr. Calif., 1968, C.C. student personnel worker Calif., 1976, C.C. instr. Calif., 1976, supr. Calif., 1976, adminstr. Calif., 1978, lic. real estate agt. Calif., 1989. Tchr. Compton Unified Sch. Dist., Calif., 1960—80; instrnl. designer DeJean Designs, Norwalk, Calif., 1985—90; instr. Cerritos C.C., Calif., 1989—90, Nat. U., Irvine, Calif., 1989—90; realtor Remax Real Estate Specialist, Long Beach, Calif., 1992—2000; tchr. Lynwood Unified Sch. Dist., Calif., 1996—2004; realtor Main St. Realtors, Long Beach, Calif., 2000—; instrnl. facilitator U. of Transformational Studies and Leadership, Culver City, Calif., 2000—. V.p. Compton Edn. Assn., Calif., 1969—70; treas. Mid-Cities chpt. Internat. Reading Assn., Compton, Calif., 1973—74; conv. del. NEA, Dallas, 1979; mem. leadership team Mark Twain Elem. Sch., Lynwood, Calif., 2001—04; mem. supt.'s adv. bd. Lynwood Unified Sch. Dist., Calif., 2001. Contbr. articles to profl. jours. Pres. Mid-Cities Schs. Credit Union, Compton, Calif., 1973—80. Named to Pres.'s Club, Re/Max Real Estate Internat., 1994. Mem.: Calif. Assn. of Realtors, Nat. Assn. Realtors (assoc.), Calif. Tchr.'s Assn. (life), Am. Contract Bridge League (assoc. Jr. Master 2005-2006). Achievements include development of a Reading Instructional guide for K-6, 1967; design of multi-media presentation that was used to instruct graduate students @ University of Southern California, 1971 & presented at a National Educational Conference, 1972; conducted workshops for The Loyola Television Conference, 1972 and for The California Teacher's Association, 1978; chaired a committee charged with reforming Math Instructional methods, 1977; created and implemented a homework program where students made 1.5 months growth for each month of instruction on The California Test of Basic Skills, 1975-1976; produced A Multi-Media Programmed Module That When Field Tested, Students Showed Significant Growth In Their Ability To Select And Sequencially Organize The Main Ideas Of A Story, 1971. Avocations: traveling, swimming, playing bridge, writing, reading. Office: Main Street Realtors 244 Redondo Ave Long Beach CA 90803 Office Phone: 562-719-2311. Home Fax: 562-438-5560; Office Fax: 562-719-2211. Personal E-mail: realgodjw@yahoo.com.

ELTO, ERIN K., psychologist; b. Detroit, Aug. 27, 1946; d. Edwin Edward and Alice Leota E. AA, Stephens Coll., 1966; AB, Webster Coll., 1970; MA, Mich. State U., 1973; advanced cert., CCNY, 1988; PsyD, Yeshiva U., 1994. Cert. psychologist. Social worker Shiawassee Intermediate Sch. Dist., Corunna, Mich., 1973-77, Lamphere Pub. Schs., Madison Heights, Mich., 1977-79; mgmt. trainee Prudential Ins. Co., Milburn, N.J., 1979-81; social worker Katzenbach Sch. for Deaf, W. Trenton, N.J., 1981-84; social worker-counselor J-47 Sch. for Deaf, N.Y.C., 1984-88; psychologist Office Hearing Handicapped, Visually Impaired, N.Y.C., 1989—; clin. psychologist intern Ctr. for Preventive Psychiatry, White Plains, N.Y. Assertive Discipline Program, Katzenbach Sch. for Deaf; prin. designee Suicide Prevention/Child Abuse Reporting IS 131, N.Y.C., 1986-89; parent group leader Katzenbach Sch. for Deaf, West Trenton, 1986-87. Vol. N.Y. Assn. for Child Abuse, 1990. Grantee Chancellor's Shepherd's Program N.Y.C. Bd. Edn. and Rudin Found. 1988-90. Mem. APA, NASP, N.Y. Assn. Sch. Psychologists. Office: NYC Bd Edn 400 1st Ave Fl 7 New York NY 10010-4004

ELVIDGE, CHRISTINA MARIE, director; d. John and Rose Ann Elvidge. MA, U. Scranton, Pa., 1995; student, Ind. U. Pa., Indiana, Pa., 1998—. Lectr. English dept. Luzerne County CC, 1995—97; lectr. English Marywood U., Scranton, Pa., 1997—, dir. hons. and fellowships, 2004—. Advisor Kappa Gamma Pi, Nat. Cath. Coll. Grad. Honor Soc., Scranton, Pa., 2004. Mem.: Pa. Coll. English Assn. (pres. 2004—05), Kappa Gamma Pi (adv. 2004—). Democrat. Avocations: reading, writing. Office: Marywood University 2300 Adams Avenue Scranton PA 18509 Office Phone: 570-348-6211. Business E-Mail: elvidge@marywood.edu.

ELWELL, BARBARA LOIS DOW, foundation administrator; b. Purcell, Okla., Feb. 15, 1933; d. Henry Kenneth and Leah Maude (Caldwell) Dow; m. Robert G. Elwell, Apr. 7, 1956 (div. July 1977); children: David Robert, Kenneth Dow. Student, Endicott Coll., 1950-51, Jackson Von Ladau Sch. Design, 1952-54. Sec. to adv. fgn. students MIT, Cambridge, Mass., 1954—60; founder and dir. Alternative House, Inc., Lowell, Mass., 1976-84; mem. staff Encode Tech., Inc., Nashua, NH, 1984-87; staff asst. Harvard Smithsonian Ctr. Astrophys., Cambridge, Mass., 1987-99; pvt. asst. Smithsonian Astrophys. Obs., 1999—2006. Founder Alternative House, Lowell, 1978; founding mem. Mass Coalition of Battered Women Svc. Groups, Boston, 1976, steering com., 1976-84, adv. bd. 1978-80. Recipient Outstanding Achievement award, Mass. Coalition of Battered Women Svc. Groups, 1976. Avocations: woodworking, antique collecting, miniatures, gardening, painting. Home: 142 Graniteville Rd Chelmsford MA 01824-1122 Personal E-mail: belwell@netway.com.

ELWELL, ELLEN BANKS, music educator, writer; b. Chgo., Sept. 24, 1952; d. Robert Arthur and Elizabeth Carolyn Banks; m. James F. Elwell, June 8, 1974; children: Chad, Nathan, Jordan. Diploma, Moody Bible Inst., Chgo., 1974; BMus, Am. Conservatory of Music, 1976. Piano instr., Wheaton, Ill., 1974—. Mem. bd. Ch. Pianists Inst., Wheaton. Author:

Toddlers Songbook, 1994; author: (video), 1995; author: Beginner Praise, 1992, Piano Praise, 1993, Beginner Praise II, 1994, Piano Praise II, 1996, The Christian Mom's Idea Book, 1997, Beginner Praise for Violin, 1998, Beginner Praise for Christmas, 1999, Quiet Moments of Hope for Moms, 1999, Quiet Moments of Faith for Moms, 1999, Quiet Moments of Wisdom for Moms, 1999, Quiet Moments of Encouragement for Moms, 1999, Beginner Praise III, 2000, When There's Not Enough of Me to Go Around, 2001, Intermediate Praise, 2002, Primer Praise, 2004, Primer Praise II, 2006, One Year Book of Devotions for Moms, 2005, One Year Mini for Moms, 2006. Mem.: Nat. Music Tchrs. Assn. (v.p. for programs 1999—2001). Republican. Avocations: jogging, reading. Home: 2067 Hallmark Ct Wheaton IL 60187

ELWOOD, PATRICIA COWAN, state official, political scientist, consultant, educational consultant; b. Haverhill, Mass., Oct. 22, 1941; d. Raymond Bernard and Florence Eva Cowan; children: Robert Michael, Douglas Matthew. BS, Tufts U., 1963; MS in Edn., Boston U., 1965; PhD, U. Md., 2008. Tchr./trainer Boston Pub. Schs., 1964-67; dir. Head Start Program, various cities, Mass., 1968; adminstrv. asst. dept. child study Tufts U., Medford, Mass., 1967-68; diagnostician, tchr./counselor Program for Hearing Impaired Richmond (Calif.) Pub. Schs., 1968-69, supr., 1970-73; asst. to dir. Berkeley (Calif.) Profl. Studies Abroad Program, New Delhi, 1969-70; curriculum writer Prince Georges County Pub. Schs., Upper Marlboro, Md., 1974, learning problems and hearing specialist, 1976—2005; chief of protocol, sec. DC Govt., 2005—. Lectr. Trinity Coll., Washington, 1980-84; cons. Pan Am. Health Orgn., Caribbean, 1978-80; coord. state conf. early childhood edn., grad. asst., 1978; cons. in field. Author: From a Professional Parent's Prospective, 1994; co-author: Social and Emotional Development of Young Children, 1968, Alameda County California Public Schools Health Curriculum, 1969, Piaget's Theory as It Relates to Early Childhood Curricula, 1979; co-editor: Parent-Centered Programs for Young Hearing Impaired Students, 1976; implemented approved self-authored grant for one of first Parent-Infant Programs in the U.S.; contbr. articles to profl. jours. Apptd. mem. Inst. for Dist. Affairs, U. DC, 1981-82; fin. com. Sidwell Friends Sch., 1985-90; elected mem. Dem. State Com., Washington, 1985—, fin. chmn., 1988-90; parent bd. St. Albans Sch., 1993-94; 1st vice chmn. Ward III Dem. Com., Washington, 1988-91, 95—, fin. sec., 1994-95, treas., 1986-88; past fin. and policy com. presdl., senate, ho. reps., gubernatorial campaigns; campaign co-chmn., ward chmn. steering com. DC and Greater Washington area polit. candidate campaigns, 1980—; co-founder DC Soccer, 1978, DC Baseball Connection, 1994-95; head com. to bring Am. Legion Baseball to DC, 1994-95; bd. dirs. Babe Ruth League, Little League and Boys and Girls Club, 1986-91, Nat. Child Rsch. Ctr., 1977-82, Washington Hearing and Speech Ctr., 1982-87, Washington Tufts Alliance, co-chair, 1986-88, vice-chair, 1985-86, treas., 1988—, chair interviewing com., 1990—; apptd. Coun. Govts. Task Force Com. on Growth and Transp., 1990-92; commr. Mayoral Appointee, Nat. Capital Planning Commn., 1987—, exec. com., 1993—, vice chair, 1995—; nominating com., trustee U. DC, 1988-92; presdl. appointee Selective Svc. Bd., 1988-91, 2004-06; bd. dirs. Ft. Myer Swim Team, 1983-85, 89-90; elected mem. alumni coun. Tufts U., 1988—, chair interviewing com.; bd. trustees City Lights Sch., 1993-97, soccer adv. com., 1995-96; bd. dirs. DC Mental Health Assn., Anacostia Coord. Com., African-Am. Mus.; adv. coun. Hist. Soc. Washington, 1998; adv. com. Y-Care 2000 Found.; adv. bd. Hist. Preservation Soc., 1998-2001; active DC Agenda; founding mem. DC Baseball PAC, 2004-05. Named Outstanding Young Woman in Am., 1966. Mem. Nat. Assn. for Edn. Young Children, World Affairs Coun., Nat. Trust for Historic Preservation, Internat. Bus. Coun. (bd. dirs.), Citizens Against Gun Violence, Nat. ASsn. State Secs., Nat. Protocol Assn., Tufts U. Alumnae Assn. Democrat. Avocations: politics, swimming, walking, baseball. Office: Office Dist Sec 1350 Pennsylvania Ave NW Ste 419 Washington DC 20004 Office Phone: 202-727-6306. E-mail: patricia.elwood@dc.gov.

ELWOOD-AKERS, VIRGINIA EDYTHE, librarian, retired archivist; b. L.A., Nov. 9, 1938; d. George Henry and Eileen Edythe Elwood; m. Roy Stanley Akers, Apr. 12, 1980 (widowed May 2003). BA, UCLA, 1964; MLS, U. Oreg., 1972; MA in Mass. Comm., Calif. State U., Northridge, 1981. Editor UCLA, L.A., 1970-71, writer, 1971-72; libr., archivist Calif. State U., Northridge, 1972—2001, ret., 2001. Reader Huntington Libr., San Marino, Calif., 1990—. Author: Women War Correspondents in the Vietnam War, 1988; contbr. articles to profl. jours. Calif. State U. Found. grantee, Northridge, Calif. State U. Libr. grantee. Mem. Western Assn. Women Historians, Soc. Calif. Archivists. Democrat. Episcopalian. Avocations: travel, musical theater. E-mail: virgoea@aol.com.

ELY, DEBORAH D., elementary school educator; b. Boston, May 17, 1953; d. John Merton Gardner and Elsie Mable Hilyard; m. David Marion Ely, Sept. 24, 1977; 1 child, Ryan David. AA in christian edn., Eastern Nazarene Coll., 1974, BS in edn., 1976; M, Mich. State, 1983. Tchr. Airport Cmty. Sch., 1979—2006. Chmn., sch. improvement team Airport AIMS, Carleton, Mich.; team MEAP coord. Airport Cmty. Sch., Carleton, 2001—03. Ch. pianist Bapt. Ch. Recipient Whole Apple award, Monroe Intermediate Sch., 1993, 1998. Republican. Baptist. Avocations: painting, camping, piano, crafts. Home: 147 W Newburg Rd Carleton MI 48117 Office Phone: 734-654-6205. Business E-Mail: dely@airport.k12.mi.us.

ELY-RAPHEL, NANCY, diplomat; b. NYC, Feb. 4, 1937; d. Thomas Clarkson and Margaret (Merritt) Halliday; widowed; children: John Duff Ely, Robert Duff Ely, Stephanie Joyce Raphel. AB, Syracuse U., 1957; JD, U. San Diego, 1968. Bar: Calif. 1968, U.S. Supreme Ct. 1976. Dep. city atty. City of San Diego, 1969—70; asst. U.S. atty. So. Dist. Calif., 1970—71; assoc. Tyler, Cooper, Grant, Bowerman and Keefe, New Haven, 1971—72; from asst. to assoc. dean Sch. Law Boston U., 1972—75; atty.-advisor U.S. Dept. State, Washington, 1975—77; spl. atty. Boston Strike Force U.S. Dept. Justice, 1977—78; asst. legal advisor African Affairs U.S. Dept. State, Washington, 1978—87, asst. legal advisor Nuclear Affairs, 1988—89; dep. asst. Sec. of State Bur. Democracy, Human Rights and Labor Affairs, Washington, 1878—83, prin. dep. asst., 1993—95; Balkan coord. Bur. European and Can. Affairs, Washington, 1995—98; U.S. amb. to Slovenia, Am. Embassy, Ljubljana, 1998—2001, sr. advisor to sec., 2001—03; counselor on internat. law, 2003; v.p. Save the Children, Washington, 2003—. Mem. Coun. on Fgn. Rels., 1990—. Recipient Outstanding Alumni award U. San Diego Law Sch., 1979, Superior Honor award U.S. Dept. State, Washington, 1983, 84, Presdl. Meritorious Svc. award U.S. Govt., Washington, 1986, 94, 98, Presdl. Disting. Svc. award, 1992, Author Hughes Career Achievement award, 2001, U.S. Dept. State Dir. Gen.'s Cup, 2004. Home: 1304 30th St NW Washington DC 20007-3343 E-mail: nancyelyraphel@earthlink.net.

EMANUEL, GLORIA PAGE, retired secondary school educator; b. Dallas, Apr. 5, 1947; d. Daniel and Leola (Green) Page; m. Lawrence Ray Emanuel, Oct. 2, 1971; children: Lawrence Ray Jr., Kevin Lawrence. Student, Paul Quinn Coll., 1966—67; BS, Ea. Tex. State U., 1970; MEd, Prairie View A&M U., 1975. Cert. tchr. Tex., profl. counselor Tex. Tchr. social studies Waco (Tex.) H.S., 1971—82, Univ. Mid. Sch., Waco, 1982—2004, ret., 2004. Chairperson solcial studies, block leader, 1985—93; assn. rep. Univ. Mid. Sch., 1985—93, coord. Adopt-a-Sch., 1992—, coord. Ptnrs. in Edn., 2003—04; mem. Campus Action Com., 1985, Campus Adv. Coun., 1990—91, Supt. Adv. Coun. for Social Studies, 1991—92. Mem. North Tex. Min. Wives, Waco-Temple, 1971—; asst. sec. area II Waco-Temple Missionary Soc.; mem. Joshua Chapel AME Ch., Waxahachie, Tex.; historiographer Gloria Emanuel Unit AME, 1985. Mem.: NAFE, NEA, Heart of Tex. Counselors Assn., Tex. State Tchrs. Assn., Order Ea. Star, Sigma Gamma Rho. Avocations: travel, photography, collecting historical stamps, collecting scenic post cards, collecting scenic slides. Home: 2024 King Cole Dr Waco TX 76705-2749

EMANUEL-SMITH, ROBIN LESLEY, special education educator; m. Allen Weston Smith, Apr. 14, 1983; children: David, Ariel, Weston. BS in Engring., U.S. Mil. Acad., 1981; BS in Health-Phys. Edn. summa cum laude, Cameron U., Lawton, Okla., 1992; M Spl. Edn., Coll. of St. Rose, Albany, 1995. Cert. spl. edn., health and phys. edn. tchr., N.Y. Enlisted U.S. Army, 1974-76, commd. 2nd lt., 1981, advanced through grades to capt., 1984, resigned, 1990; tchr. spl. edn. Ulster County Bd. Coop. Edn1. Svcs., Port Ewen, NY, 1992—. Roman Catholic. Avocations: weightlifting, coaching and officiating youth soccer, softball and baseball. Office: Ulster County Bd Coop Ednl Svs Rt 32 New Paltz NY 12561 Personal E-mail: prteacher@msn.com.

EMBER, CAROL R., anthropology educator, writer; b. Bklyn., July 7, 1943; d. Hy and Elsie (Kardonsky) Ruchlis; m. Lawrence Baldwin, 1963 (div. 1969); m. Melvin Ember, Mar. 21, 1970; children: Katherine Ann, Julie Beth. BA, Antioch Coll., 1965; postgrad., Cornell U., 1965-66; PhD, Harvard, 1971. Lectr. Hunter Coll. CUNY, 1970-71; from asst. prof. to assoc. prof. CUNY, 1971-80; prof. Hunter Coll., 1981-97; exec. dir. Human Rels. Area Files Yale U., New Haven, 1997—. First author: Anthropology, 1973, Cultural Anthropology, 1973, first author: 12th edit., 2007, Anthropology: A Brief Introduction, 1991, 4th edit., 2000, Cross-Cultural Research Methods, 2001, first editor: Cross-Cultural Research for Social Science, 1998, Research Frontiers in Anthropology, 1998, New Directions in Anthropology, 2004, Encyclopedia of Medical Anthropology, 2004, Encyclopedia of Sex and Gender, 2004; co-author (with M. Ember): Marriage, Family and Kinship: Comparative Studies of Social Organization, 1983; co-author: (with Burton Pastemak and M. Ember) Sex, Gender and Kinship: A Cross-Cultural Perspective, 1997; co-editor: Portraits of Culture, 1998, Countries and Their Cultures, 2001, Encyclopedia of Diasporas, 2005. Woodrow Wilson Fellow, 1965-66, predoctoral fellow NIMH, 1969-70; rsch. grantee NSF, 1983-84, 86-98, U.S. Inst. Peace, 1990-92. Mem.: Human Behavior and Evolution Soc., Soc. for Psychol. Anthropology, Soc. for Cross-Cultural Rsch. (pres. 1985), Am. Anthrop. Assn. Office: Yale U Human Rels Area Files 755 Prospect St New Haven CT 06511-1225

EMBRY, JESSIE L., historian, researcher; d. Bertis L. and Anna E.C. Embry. BA magna cum laude, Brigham Young U., Provo, Utah, 1973, MA, 1974. Oral historian LDS Ch., Salt Lake City, 1976; historian preservation intern Utah State Hist. Soc., Salt Lake City, 1976—79; coord. heritage conservation program Am. studies Brigham Young U., Provo, 1979—84, oral history program dir. Charles Redd Ctr. for Western Studies, 1979—94, instr. history dept., 1982—, asst./assoc. dir. Charles Redd Ctr. for Western Studies, 1994—, acting dir. Charles Redd Ctr. for Western Studies, 2001, 2002. Presenter and cons. in field. Author: Richardson Family History: An Oral History Study, 1982, After 150 Years: The Latter-day Saints in Sesquicentennial Prespective, 1983, La Sal Reflections: A Redd Family Journal, 1984, Community Development in the American West: Past and Present Nineteenth and Twentieth Century Frontiers, 1985, Mormon Polygamous Families: Life in the Principle, 1987, Black Saints in a White Church: Contemporary African American Mormons, 1994, Wasatch County History, 1996, In Their Own Language: Mormon Spanish Speaking Congregations in the United States, 1997, Asian American Mormons: Bridging Cultures, 1999, North Logan Town, 1934-1970, 2000, Mormon Wards as Community, 2001; co-author (with James B. Allen): Hearts to the Fathers: History of the Genealogical Society of the LDS Church, 1993; co-author: (with James B. Allen and Kahlile Mehr) Hearts Turned to the Fathers, 1995; mem. editl. bd.: Mormon Hist. Studies, 2003—; contbr. articles to profl. jours. Mem. adv. bd. Utah History Fair, 1990—93; docent LDS Mus. Ch. History and Art, 1991—; active Provo Landmarks Commn., 1995—2002, 2006—. Recipient Friend of the Humanities award, Utah Humanities Coun., 2002, Leonard J. Arrington award, 2004. Mem.: Utah Valley hist. Soc. (pres. elect 2000—01, pres. 2001—02, past pres. 2002—03), Mormon Social Sci. Assn. (coun. mem. 1995—99), Western History Assn. (bd. editor Western Hist. Quarterly 1998—2001), Coalition Western Women Historians (program com. 1984, 1987, roving reporter 1990—92), John Whitmer Hist. Assn. (nominating com. 1989—90, coun. mem. 1990—92, v.p./pres. elect 1993 1994, pres. 1994—96, program chair 1995—97, jour. editor 1997—2000, book rev. editor 2001—04), Assn. Utah Historians (coun. mem. 1988—89), Am. Hist. Assn. (co-program chair Pacific Coast Br. 2001—02), Orgn. Am. Historians, Western Assn. Women Historians, Nat. Coun. for Preservation Edn. (NW region coun. mem. 1981—84), Utah Women's History Assn. (coun. mem. 1979—81, v.p./pres. elect 1981—82, pres. 1982—83, coun. mem. 1983—84), Utah State Hist. Soc. (program com. 1990), NW Oral History Assn. (Utah rep. 1985—94, newsletter editor 1999—2000), Mormon History Assn. (exec. sec. 1983—87, program com. 1987, newsletter editor 1987—90, awards com. 1989—90, exec. sec. 1990—94, newsletter reporter 1990—94, program com. 1992—94, local arrangements com. 1992—2993, local arrangements chair 1994, program chair 1995, newsletter editor 1997—2001, local arrangements chair 2004, program com. 2004, Leonard J. Arrington award 2004), Phi Kappa Phi, Phi Alpha Theta (nominating com. 2001—04). Avocations: reading, embroidery, cooking, writing, research. Office: Charles Redd Ctr for Western Studies Brigham Young Univ 366 SWRT Provo UT 84602

EMEK, SHARON HELENE, risk management consultant; b. Bklyn., Oct. 23, 1945; d. Hyman Sampson and Cynthia Gertrude (Roth) Rabinowitz; children: Aleeza Judith, Joshua Michael, Elana Yael. BA, CCNY, 1967; MA, Bklyn. Coll., 1970; EdD, Rutgers U., 1977. Cert. ins. counselor. Dir. preliminary program for small coll. Bklyn. Coll., 1969—71, 1973—74; dir. Am. Ctr. Reading Skills, Tel Aviv, 1972; asst. prof. Brookdale C.C., Lincroft, NJ, 1975—77, Rutgers U., New Brunswick, NJ, 1977—82; pres. Emek Group, Inc., N.Y.C., 1980—98, CEO Metro Ptnrs., Inc., N.Y.C., 1998—2001; ptnr. CBS Coverage Group, Inc., 2001—. Spkr. profl. meetings. Author: Answers for Managers, 1986, Dealing Successfully with Key Management Issues, 1986; contbr. articles to profl. jours. Mem. Mayor's Small Bus. Adv. Bd., N.Y.C., 1998—2001, Small Bus. Rsch. and Tech. Adv. Coun. IBM, 1998—2000; bd. dirs. Ctr. Women's Bus. Rsch., 2006—; mem. adv. coun. Women's Fin. Network Siebert, 2000—02; founding bd. dirs. Nat. Mus. Women's History, 1997—2002; mem. bd. Ctr. Women's Bus. Rsch., 2000—; bd. dirs. Family Bus. Coun. Greater N.Y., 1997—98, Women's Econ. Devel. Task Force, N.Y.C., 1999—2001; bd. dirs., v.p. N.Y. Women's Agenda, 2000—04; vice chair bd. dirs. Inst. Student Achievement, 1999—; mem. adv. bd. Women's Leadership Exch., 2002—; chmn. Ind. Ins. Agents & Brokers, NY, 2006—, bd. dirs., 2003—. Recipient Promising Rsch. award, Nat. Coun. Tchrs. English, 1978, Woman of Power and Influence award, NOW, 1999. Mem.: Ind. Ins. Agts. and Brokers N.Y., Coun. Ins. Brokers Greater N.Y., Women's Pres. Orgn., Assn. Profl. Ins. Women, Nat. Assn. Ins. Women (Helen Garvin Outstanding Achiever in Ins. Industry award 1999), Coun. Ins. Brokers Greater N.Y., Nat. Assn. Women Bus. Owners (bd. dirs., pres. 1997—98, Mem. of Yr. 1997), Profl. Ins. Agts. Assn., Ind. Ins. Agts. and Brokers Am. (chair elect bd. dirs.), Emily List (majority coun.). Avocations: writing, reading, jogging, tennis, travel. Office Phone: 212-684-5670 x 101. Business E-Mail: semek@cbsinsurance.com.

EMERICK, JOYCE JEAN, elementary school educator; b. Patton Township, Pa., June 19, 1938; d. George Charles and Rosena A. (Duncan) Martin; m. Charles Wayne Emerick, Mar. 31, 1988. BS in Edn., Indiana U. of Pa., 1960, MEd, 1967; postgrad., U. Hawaii, 1966, Pa. State U., 1963. Cert. elem. tchr., Pa. Supr. student tchrs. Gateway Sch. Dist., Monroeville, Pa., 1963—96, tchr., 1960—96; ret., 1996. Active Christian Missionary Alliance Ch., 1967—; coach Girls Softball Team, Murrysville, Pa., 1964; classroom vol. Gateway Sch. Dist., 1996-2004, Fla. Charter Sch., 2006-; substitute tchr. C.C. Allegheny County Child Dev. Ctr., 1997-2004. Mem. NEA, Pa. State Edn. Assn., Gateway Edn. Assn. (sec. 1962), Indiana U. Pa. Alumni Assn., Order Eastern Star. Avocations: reading, crafts, swimming, travel, golf. Office: Gateway Sch Dist Moss Side Blvd Monroeville PA 15146

EMERLING, CAROL G., management consultant; b. Cleve., Sept. 13, 1930; d. Bernard and Florence A. Greenbaum; m. Norton Harvey Noll, Oct. 1, 1950 (dec. July 1951); m. Stanley Justin Emerling, May 2, 1953 (div. Aug. 1971); children— Keith S., Susan C.; m. Jerrold A. Fadem, Aug. 24, 1974 (div. Oct. 1977). Student, Vassar Coll., 1948-49, Case Western Res. U., 1949-50; LL.B. summa cum laude, Cleve. State U., 1955. Bar: Ohio 1955, Calif. 1975, N.Y. 1982, U.S. Supreme Ct. 1975. Instr. Cleve. Coll., 1956-59; from staff atty. to atty.-in-charge Legal Aid Defenders Office, Cleve., 1962-70; regional dir. FTC, Cleve., 1970-74, L.A., 1974-78; sec. Am. Home Products Corp., N.Y.C., 1978-96; chmn. bd. Global Health Coun., 1998—2002. Adv. com. criminal rules Supreme Ct. Ohio, 1970-73; chmn. Cleve. Fed. Exec. Bd., 1973; internat. health policy cons.; mem. nat. adv. com. Cleve. State U. Law Sch. Co-author: The Allergy Cookbook, 1969; contbr. articles to legal jours. Founder Pepper Pike (Ohio) Civic League, 1959; sec. Pepper Pike Charter Commn., 1966. Recipient Claude E. Clarke award Legal Aid Soc., 1967, Disting. Service award FTC, 1972. Mem. State Bar Calif., State Bar Ohio, State Bar N.Y. Personal E-mail: cgemerling@earthlink.net.

EMERSON, ALICE FREY, political scientist, educator emerita; b. Durham, N.C., Oct. 26, 1931; d. Alexander Hamilton and Alice (Hubbard) Frey; divorced; children: Rebecca, Peter. AB, Vassar Coll., 1953; PhD, Bryn Mawr Coll., 1964; LLD (hon.), Wheaton Coll., 1986, Middlebury Coll., 1998; DHL (hon.), Trinity Coll., 1992. Tchr., Newton (Mass.) High Sch., 1956-58; mem. faculty Bryn Mawr (Pa.) Coll., 1961-64, U. Pa., Phila., 1966-75, asst. prof. polit. sci., 1966-75, dean of women, 1966-69, dean of students, 1969-75; pres. Wheaton Coll., Norton, Mass., 1975-91, pres. emerita, 1991—; sr. fellow Andrew Mellon Found., N.Y.C., 1991-98, sr. advisor, 1998—2002. Bd. dirs. AES Corp.; mem. bd. Edna McConnell Clark Found., HERS Mid-Am. Mem. World Resources Inst., Szburg Seminar, Nantucket Hist. Assn., MGH-IHP.

EMERSON, ANNE DEVEREUX, museum administrator; b. Boston, Oct. 6, 1946; d. Kendall and Margaret (Drew) E.; (div. 1980); children: Josephine, Hannah; m. Peter Alexander Altman, 1992. BA magna cum laude, Brown U., 1968; MA, Fletcher Sch. Law and Diplomacy, Tufts U., 1969; MBA, Boston U., 1990. Exec. asst. to v.p. adminstrn. Boston U., 1977—85, dir. adminstrn., program devel., 1985—88; exec. dir. Ctr. for Internat. Affairs Harvard U., Cambridge, 1988—98, acting exec. dir. David Rockefeller Ctr. for L.Am. Studies, 1995—96; pres. Bostonian Soc., Boston, 1998—2002; exec. dir. The Boston History Ctr. and Mus., Inc., 1999—, pres., 2004—. Bd. dirs. Integrated Foster Care, Cambridge, 1985-89; trustee Winsor Sch., 1989-91, Internat. Honors Program, 1995-2003; bd. dirs. World Affairs Coun., Boston, 1991-94, Urban Edge, 2003-; mem. exec. com. Boston Com. Fgn. Affairs, 1997-99. Mem.: Phi Beta Kappa. Office: The Boston Mus Project 55 Court St Boston MA 02108

EMERSON, CLAUDIA, poet, language professor; b. Chatham, Va., 1957; d. Claude and Mollie E.; m. Kent Ippolito, 2000. BA in English, U. Va., 1979; MFA in Creative Writing, U. NC, Greensboro, 1991. Acad. dean Chatham Hall, Chatham, Va., 1996—98; assoc. prof. English U. Mary Washington, Fredericksburg, Va., 1998—. Bd. trustees Chatham Hall, Chatham, Va., 1998—2004. Contbg. adv. editor Shenandoah, guest editor Visions Internat.; author: (poetry collections) Pharaoh, Pharaoh, 1997 (Pulitzer Prize nomination), Pinion, An Elegy, 2002, Late Wife, 2005 (Pulitzer Prize for poetry, 2006). Recipient Associated Writing Program's Intro award, 1991, Acad. of Am. Poets Prize, 1991, Mary Washington Coll. Alumni Assn. Outstanding Young Faculty award, 2003; grantee Nat. Endowment for Arts fellowship, 1994, Va. Commn. for Arts Individual Artist Fellowship in Poetry, 1995, 2002, Witter Bynner Found. fellowship in poetry, Libr. of Congress, 2005.*

EMERSON, HARRIETT ANNE, small business owner; b. Corsicana, Tex., Apr. 28, 1925; d. Harold Ralph and Willie Pearl (Richey) E. BME, U. Tex., 1945, MusM, 1947. Concert violinist, N.Y.C., 1949-64; founder Emerson Travel, Inc., N.Y.C., 1964--; mgr. and ptnr. Emerson & Emerson, Cattle, Farms and Real Estate, Powell, Tex., 1990—2000; pvt. practice Powell, 2000—; developer Pearl Valley Estates Gated Cmty., Powell, Tex., 2000—. Bd. dirs. Am. Soc. Travel Agents, Wash. 1981-87; bd. adv. travel and tourism N.Y. State, Albany 1985—. Composer: Violin Solo, Cowboy Dance 1957. Recipient Disting. Achievement award U. Tex., 1975, Austrian Gold Medal award Austria Tourist Office, Vienna 1977, Tourism award Irish Tourist Office, N.Y.C. 1977, Sean Moses award N.Y. A.S.T.A. 1977. Mem. Daughters Am. Revolution, Am. Soc. Composers Authors and Publishers, 41-74 Club N.Y.C., U. Tex. Alumni N.Y.C., Am. Soc. Travel Agents. Home and Office: PO Box 204 Powell TX 75153-0204

EMERSON, JO ANN H., congresswoman; b. Washington, Sept. 16, 1950; d. Ab and Sylvia Hermann; m. Bill Emerson, 1975 (dec.); children: Victoria, Katharine; m. Ron Gladney, 2000; stepchildren: Elizabeth, Abigail, Alison, Jessica, Stephanie, Sam. BA in Polit. Sci., Ohio Wesleyan U., 1972; DHL (hon.), Westminster Coll., Fulton, Mo. Mem. US Congress from 8th Mo. dist., 1996—; mem. appropriations com., 1998—. Sr. v.p. pub. affairs Am. Ins. Assn.; dir. state rels. and grassroots progs. Nat. Restaurant Assn.; dep. dir. comm. Nat. Rep. Congl. Com. Mem. PEO Womens's Svc. Grp. (FY chpt.), Cape Girardeau; mem. adv. bd. Arneson Inst. Practical Politics and Pub. Affairs, Ohio Wesleyan U.; co-chair Congl. Hunger Ctr.; bd. dirs. Bread for the World; hon. and life trustee Westminster Coll.; bd. dirs. Presbyn. Children's Home, Farmington, Mo. Recipient Rural Housing Legislator of Yr., Nat. Assn. Home Builders, 2001, Schwarz Pharma Leadership in Pharmacy award, Nat. Assn. Chain Drug Stores, 2002, Ground Water Protector award, Nat. Ground Water Assn., 2005. Mem.: Copper Dome Soc., S.E. Mo. State U. Republican. Presbyn. Office: US Ho Reps 2440 Rayburn Ho Office Bldg Washington DC 20515-2508 Office Phone: 202-225-4404.*

EMERSON, KATHY, writer; b. Liberty, N.Y., Oct. 25, 1947; d. William Russell Gorton and Theresa Marie Coburg; m. Sanford M. Emerson, May 10, 1969l AB, Bates Coll., 1969; MA, Old Dominion U., 1972. Freelance writer, Wilton, Maine, 1976—. Author: Writer's Guide to Everyday Life in Renaissance Eng., 1996, Face Down series, 1997—, Diana Spaulding Mysteries, 2003—, others, —. Mem.: Sisters in Crime, Novelists Inc., Am. Crime Writer's League. Home: PO Box 156 Wilton ME 04294-0156 E-mail: emerson@megalink.net.

EMERSON, KIRK, government agency administrator; BA in Psychology, Princeton U.; M in City Planning, Mass. Inst. Tech.; PhD, Indiana U. Dir. U.S. Inst. for Environmental Conflict Resolution, 1998—. Mem.: Am. Political Science Assoc. (William Anderson Award 1998), Am. Inst. of Certified Planners, Am. Planning Assoc., Am. Arbitration Assoc., Arizona's Dispute Resolution Assoc., Am. Bar Assoc. Dispute Resolution Sec., Assoc. for Conflict Resolution. Office: 130 S Scott Ave Tucson AZ 85701-1922

EMERSON, NORENE ROGERS, music educator; b. Ogden, Utah, May 14, 1931; d. Cecil Clay Rogers and Idella Ethel Carter; m. Raymond Maurice Emerson, Sept. 17, 1954. BA with high honors, U. Utah, 1953. Pvt. piano tchr., Salt Lake City, 1946—. Piano soloist Utah Artist, Utah Concerts Coun., Salt Lake City, 1963—64. Mem. Temple Sq. Concert Series Com., Salt Lake City, 1996—; organizer downtown outdoor concert series, Salt Lake City; bd. trustees Gina Bachauer Internat. Piano Found. Recipient Piano Tchr. Recognition award, Keith Jorgensen Music Co., Salt Lake City, 1992. Mem.: Music Circle, Utah Music Tchrs. Assn., Nat. Fedn. Music Clubs, Piano Club, Mu Phi Epsilon Internat., Phi Beta Kappa. Republican. Mem. Lds Ch. Avocation: photography. Home and Studio: 3543 Monte Verde Dr Salt Lake City UT 84109 Personal E-mail: norbird70@aol.com.

EMERY, CAROLYN VERA, civilian military employee, retired noncommissioned officer; d. Earl Woodrow Emery. AA, Ctrl. Tex. Coll., 1988. Commd. 2d. lt. U.S. Army, 1982, advanced through ranks to master sgt., 2000, noncommissioned officer in charge force protection br. HHC U.S. Army Pacific Fort Shafter, Hawaii, 1999—2003; retired, 2003; force protection program mgr. Dept. Def. U.S. Army, Alaska, 2003—06, mgr. antiterrorism program Dept. Def. Ft. McPherson, Ga., 2006—. Decorated Bronze Order of the Marechaussee. Office: Fort Mcpherson GA 30330 Home: PO Box 134 Winston GA 30182

EMERY, CECILIA RUTH, learning disability educator; b. Prague, Okla., Sept. 11, 1950; d. Francis Riley and Minnie (Sekera) E. AS, St. Gregory Coll., 1970; BEd, East Ctrl. State U., 1972, M i Learning Disabilities, 1976, M in Counseling Psychology, 1981. Cert. elem. tchr., learning disabilities tchr., emotional distrubance, sch. psychologist, sch. psychometrist. Elem. tchr.

Prague (Okla.) Pub. Schs., 1972-75, learning disability tchr., 1975-78, 85—; sch. psychometrist State of Dept., Oklahoma City, 1978-79; ednl. coord. Boley (Okla.) Sch. for Boys, 1979-81, 81-83; psychol. asst. Dept. of Corrections, Boley, 1983-85. Mem. North Ctrl. Edn. Accrediation Team, 1990, 93. Mem. NEA, Okla. Edn. Assn., Learning Disability Assn. Home: RR 3 Box 129 Prague OK 74864-9802

EMERY, DAWN WEBBER, lawyer; b. Fairfax, Va. d. Daniel Cotton and Marie Irene Webber; m. John James Emery, Aug. 12, 1998. BS in Sales and Mktg., Weber State U., Ogden, Utah, 1997; JD cum laude, Gonzaga U. Law Sch., Spokane, Wash., 2003; AA in Paralegal Studies with honors, Mountain-west Coll., Salt Lake City, 2003; CLE, 2004—05. Bar: Wash., Utah, U.S. Dist. Ct. Wash. Vol. legal intern Salt Lake City Prosecutor's Office, Salt Lake City, 2001; intern then ind. contractor C. Raymond Eberle, Attorney and Counselor at Law, Spokane, Wash., 2001—06; extern Spokane County Prosecutor's Office, 2003; instr. legal rsch. and writing Moutain West Coll., Salt Lake City, 2005; attornet Dunn & Dunn, 2005; owner D. Emery Esq. Law Offices, Holliday, Utah, 2006—. Sailboat on Sound, 2004 (First Pl.). Vol. lawyer wills and trusts Tuesday Nite Bar; voter registration agt., 2004; election judge, 2004. Recipient Highest Grade Comparative Law and Advanced Evidence award, Gonzaga Law Sch., 2002; scholar, Miss Hispanic Utah, 1993, Weber State U., 1995—97, Miss Petite Utah, 1999, Judge's scholar, Gonzaga U. Law, 2001—03. Mem.: Women Lawyers of Utah (bd. mem. 2005—06, newsletter editor), Utah Law Enforcement Credit Union, Christian Legal Soc., White Maple Pl. Homeowners Assn. (pres. 2004—06). Episcopalian. Avocations: photography, reading. Office: D Emery Esq Law Offices #534 #760 S Highland Dr Salt Lake City UT 84106

EMERY, NANCY BETH, lawyer; b. Shawnee, Okla., July 9, 1952; d. Paul Dodd Finefrock and Kathryn Jo (Saling) Hutchens; m. Lee Monroe Emery, May 18, 1974. BA with highest honors, U. Okla., 1974; JD, Harvard U., 1977. Bar: D.C. 1981. Atty. advisor Office Gen. counsel, USDA, Washington, 1977-79; legal advisor Fed. Energy Regulatory Commr. Matthew Holden, Jr., Washington, 1979-81; assoc. Pierson, Ball & Dowd and predecessor Sullivan & Beauregard, Washington, 1981-83, Paul Hastings, Janofsky & Walker, Washington, 1983-87, ptnr., 1987-93, Sutherland, Asbill & Brennan, Washington, 1993-97; v.p., gen. counsel, corp. sec. Calif. Ind. Sys. Operator Corp., 1997-99; ptnr. Hopkins & Sutter, Washington, 1999-2001, Ballard, Spahr, Andrews & Ingersoll, LLP, Washington, 2001—03; sr. v.p., gen. counsel, corp. sec. CPS Energy, San Antonio, 2003—. Nat. adv. bd. USAID Tng. Program, 1994—98. Bd. dirs., sec. Park Place Condominium Assn., Inc., Washington, 1982—84; page Continental Congress DAR, 1978—82, chpt. del., 1981, 1984; bd. dirs. New Hope Housing, Inc., Alexandria, Va., 2001—03, chmn. strategic planning com., 2002—03, exec. com., 2003; bd. dirs. Carver Cultural Arts Ctr. Devel. Bd., 2005—. Mem.: ABA (natural resources energy and eviron. law sect. 1990—98, bd. editors Natural Resources & Environment 1990—98, pub. utility law sect., vice chmn. electricity com. 1998—, chmn. program com. 2000—01, chmn. mem. com. 2001—02, chmn. strategic planning com. 2001—02, mem. coun. 2002—, chmn. cmty. involvment 2002—04), Soc. Profl. Journalists, Fed. Energy Bar Assn. (chair tax com. 1986—87, chair FERC ops. and adminstrn. com. 1991—93, chair elec. utility regulation com. 1995—97, chair program com. 1997—98), Mortar Bd., Phi Beta Kappa. Democrat. Office: CPS Energy PO Box 1771 San Antonio TX 78296-1771 Office Phone: 210-353-2406. Business E-Mail: nbemery@cpsenergy.com.

EMERY, VIRGINIA OLGA BEATTIE, psychologist, researcher; b. Cleve., Apr. 9, 1938; d. W. Joseph P. and Antoinette Pauline (Misjak) Kennick; m. Paul Hamilton Beattie Sr., 1960 (div. 1975); children: Tamsan Beattie Tharin, Paul Hamilton Beattie Jr.; m. Paul E. Emery, 1979. BA, U. Chgo., 1962, PhD, 1982; MA, Ind. U., 1973. Diplomate Am. Bd. Disability Analysts, Am. Acad. Traumatic Stress; lic. psychologist, NH, Ohio; cert. brief therapist Nat. Acad. Brief Therapists; cert. cognitive therapist Nat. Bd. Behavioral Therapists, cert. domestic violence counselor endorsement; cert. expert traumatic stress, cognitive therapist. Asst. prof. psychology Case Western Res. U., Cleve., 1986—89, asst. clin. prof. psychiatry, 1986—89; sr. faculty assoc. Ctr. on Aging and Health, Concord and Hanover, NH, 1986—89, dir., 1989—; adj. clin. asst. prof. psychiatry Dartmouth Med. Sch., Lebanon, NH, 1983—85, clin. assoc. prof., 1989—. Mem. com. human devel. NIMH, Adult Devel. and Aging Traineeship, U. Chgo., 1974-76; sub-project dir. Case Western Res. U. Sch. Medicine, 1986-90; sec. women's faculty assn. Case Western Res. U., 1987-89; cons. Vets. Affairs Med. Ctr., Manchester, NH, 1989—; sub-project dir. NIMH Mental Health Clin. Rsch. Ctr. Grant, Case Western Res. U. Sch. Medicine, 1986-90; mem. Dartmouth Coll. and Dartmouth Med. Sch. Neurosci. Group, 1990—; Dunaway-Burnham vis. scientist Dartmouth Med. Sch., 2005; Paul Janssen lectr. U. Goteberg, Sweden, 1997; Dunaway-Burnham vis. scientist Dartmouth Med. Sch., 2005; lectr. in field. Author: Language and Aging, 1985, Pseudodementia: A Theoretical and Empirical Discussion, 1988, Language Impairment in Dementia of the Alzheimer Type: A Hierarchical Decline, 2000, Interface between Vascular Dementia and Alzheimer Syndrome: Nosologic Redefinition, 2000, Retrophylogenesis of Memory in Dementia of the Alzheimer Type: A New Evolutionary Memory Framework, 2003, Noninfarct Vascular Dementia and Alzheimer Syndrome Spectrum, 2005; editor: Dementia: Presentations, Differential Diagnosis, and Nosology, 1994, 2d edit., 2003; contbr. chapters to books, articles to profl. jours. Bd. dirs. Frontiers of Knowledge Civic Trust, Concord, 1990—, pres. 1990-95. Recipient Adult Devel. and Aging grant, traineeship NIH/NIMH, 1974-76, Rsch. prize Am. Aging Assn., 1983, Havighurst prize for aging rsch. U. Chgo., 1984, NH Hosp. award for outstanding rsch. in dementia, 2003; named Frontiers of Knowledge Atlee Zellers lectr., 1994, Paul Janssen Med. Inst. lectr., 1997; rsch. grantee Western Res. Coll., 1986-87, NIMH Mental Health Clin. rsch. grantee, 1986-89. Fellow Gerontol. Soc. Am. (Disting Creative Contbn. award 1989; clin. medicine membership com. state liaison 1998—; lectr. Boston 2002), Am. Psychol. Assn., NH Psychol. Assn. (bd. dirs. 1991-93, chair com. acad. rsch. interests 1992-94, sec. 1994—, Riggs Disting. Contbn. award 1991, chmn. Women and Minorities com. 2001—), APA (student rsch. award 1984), Am. Acad. Experts in Traumatic Stress; mem. AAAS, AAUW, Internat. Psychiat. Rsch. Soc., Internat. Psychogeriatric Assn. (Pfizer lectr. 1997, 2d place award for rsch. paper 1995, 2nd Pl. Rsch. award in psychogeriatrics for paper 1995, IPA/Bayer Rsch. award in psychogeriat. 1995), Boston Soc. Gerontol. Psychiatry, Acad. Psychosomatic Medicine, NY Acad. Scis., Am. Acad. Experts in Traumatic Stress, Assn. Alzheimer's Disease Scientists, Am. Mensa Ltd. Home: 15 Buckingham Dr Bow NH 03304-5207 Office: Dartmouth Med Sch Dept Psychiatry Box HB 7750 Lebanon NH 03756 Personal E-mail: vobemeryphd@aol.com. Business E-Mail: v.olga.emery@dartmouth.edu.

EMIG, CAROL A., music educator, musician; d. Clifford R. Sterner and Violet E. Knechel; children: Elizabeth A., Andrew T. BS in Music Edn., Mansfield U., Pa., 1978; MusM in Music Edn., West Chester U., Pa., 2003. Instrnl. cert. II Pa. Dept. Edn. Organist, choir dir. Little Zion Luth. Ch., Telford, Pa., 1985—97; dir. vocal music freshman ctr. Quakertown Cmty. Sch. Dist., 1998—. Piano accompanist coach. Mem.: Am. Guild Organists, Am. Choral Dirs. Assn., Nat. Assn. Music Edn. Avocation: travel. Home: 22 Longview Rd Perkasie PA 18944 Office: Quakertown HS Freshman Ctr 349 S 9th St Quakertown PA 18951 E-mail: cemig@qcsd.org.

EMME, (EMME ARONSON), model, apparel designer; b. NYC; Degree in speech comm., Syracuse U. Reporter, Flagstaff, Ariz.; morning anchor NBC affiliate Sta. KNAZ-TV; spokesperson Revlon and numerous fashion houses; clothing designer Emme; supermodel. Lectr. in body image and self-esteem at h.s. and univs.; first model invited to speak to a congressional subcom. on eating and body-image disorders, Washington. Host Fashion Emergency, E! Entertainment TV; author: True Beauty-Positive Attitudes & Practical Tips from the World's Leading Plus Size Model, Life's Little Emergencies, 2003; columnist: Ask Emme. Hon. bd. dirs. Eating Disorders & Awareness Prevention, Am. Anorexia & Bulimia Assn.; ambassadors Mutiple Sclerosis Soc. Named Woman of Yr., Glamour Mag., 1997; named one of 50 Most Beautiful People, People Mag., 1994, 1999, Most Fascinating Woman of Yr., Ladies Home Jour., 1997, Most Important Women in Am., 1999; named to Orange Plus Hall of Fame, Syracuse U.; scholar Full athletic scholar, Syracuse U., Rowing Team. Studio: William Morris Agency Brian Dubin 1325 Ave of Americas Flr 15 New York NY 10019*

EMMERICH, KAROL DENISE, foundation executive, daylily hybridizer, former retail executive; b. St. Louis, Nov. 21, 1948; d. George Robert and Dorothy (May) Van Houten; m. Richard James, Oct. 18, 1969; 1 son, James Andrew. BA, Northwestern U., 1969; MBA, Stanford U., 1971. Nat. divsn. account officer Bank of Am., San Francisco, 1971-72; fin. analyst Dayton Hudson Corp., Mpls., 1972-73, sr. fin. analyst, 1973-74, mgr. short term financing, 1974-76, asst. treas., 1976-79, treas., 1979—, v.p., 1980-93; exec. fellow U. St. Thomas Grad. Sch. Bus., 1993—; pres. Emmerich Found., Edina, Minn., 1993—. Bd. dirs. Slumberland; co-owner Springwood Gardens. Bd. dirs. Hemerocallis Soc. Minn. Mem. Minn. Women's Econ. Roundtable. Home and Office: 7302 Claredon Dr Edina MN 55439-1722

EMMERING, ADRIENNE NOELLE, artist, graphics designer; b. Glendale, Calif., Dec. 21, 1952; d. John Glenn Hartis and Gabrielle Adrienne Matelen; m. Robert Thoms Emmering, Mar. 27, 1991. BFA, UCLA, 1995. Cert. Illustrator Otis/Parsons, LA, 1991. Owner Design of All Kinds, Fairfield, Calif., 1995—. Bd. mem. Vacaville Art League, 1996—2006; art critic for local news pubs.; coord. vol. activities for local art groups. Vol. Fairfield Visiting Arts Assn., 1994—2006; mem., editor-newsletter NOW, Santa Rosa, 1994—96. Grantee, Antelope Valley Arts Assn., Lancaster, Calif., 1970. Mem.: Vacaville Art League (bd. mem. 1996—). Avocations: languages, reading, painting, photography, philosophy. Home: 1148 Illinois Fairfield CA 94533

EMMETT, RITA, professional speaker; b. Chgo., Apr. 12, 1943; d. Thomas Henry Dorney and Helen Fischer; m. Bruce Karder, May 21, 1994; children: Robb Sean, Kerry Shannon. BA in English, Northeastern Ill. U., 1979; MS in Adult and Cont. Edn, Nat. Louis U., Evanston, Ill., 1985. Coord. edn. programs Leyden Family Svc., Franklin Park, Ill., 1977-95; pres. Emmett Enterprises, Inc., Des Plaines, 1994—. Adj. faculty Triton Coll., River Grove, Ill., 1977-99, Wright Coll., Chgo., 1985-99; presenter in field. Author: The Procrastinator's Handbook: Mastering the Art of Doing It Now, 2000; The Procrastinating Child: Helping Your Child Do It Now!, 2002, The Clutter-Busting Handbook, 2005, Great Speakers Anthology; contbr. articles to newspapers and mags. Pres. Parent's Club, River Grove, 1987-88; keynote spkr. Gov.'s Mansion, Springfield, Ill. Mem. Bus. and Profl. Women (Achievement award 1986), Assn. Consultation and Edn. (sec.), Ill. Prevention Network, Century Club, Nat. Spkrs. Assn., Profl. Spkr.'s of Ill. (bd. dirs. 1995-96, 2002-03). Roman Catholic. Avocations: reading, writing, travel. Office Phone: 847-699-9950. E-mail: rita@ritaemmett.com.

EMMONS, MARY K., history educator; d. Vincent A. Kulik and Joan A. Ulrich; m. Richard A. Emmons; children: Kevin, Brian, Meghan. BA in Elem. Edn., Kean U., Union, N.J., 2000, postgrad., 2005—. Asst. mgr. Investors Savings Bank, Hillside, NJ, 1984—90; clk. Pathmark, Gerwood, NJ, 1990—97; youth minister St. Joseph's Parish, Maplewood, NJ, 1996—2000; tchr. Lincoln Sch., Garwood, NJ, 2000—. Youth minister vol. St. Anne's Ch., Garwood, NJ, 2004—06. Named Tchr. of Yr., Garwood Bd. of Edn., 2002, 2003. Mem.: Garwood Edn. Assn., N.J. Edn. Assn., Phi Kappa Phi. Avocations: travel, softball, volleyball, boating. Business E-Mail: memmons@garwoodschools.org.

EMOLA, SHAUNA, athletic trainer; b. Bryan, Tex., Jan. 10, 1980; BS, Nicholls State U., Thibodaux, La., 2003. Cert. athletic trainer LATA, 2003. Athletic trainer South Lafourche H.S., Galliano, La., 2003—05, Huntsville H.S., Tex., 2005—06. Home: 2527 Clarks Ln Bryan TX 77808 Personal E-mail: shaunaemola@yahoo.com.

EMONET, SHEILA LEBLANC, elementary school educator; b. Opelousas, La., July 29, 1947; d. Kirtley Paul and Charlene Marie LeBlanc; m. Charles Emonet, Apr. 1, 1967; children: Mark Todd, Scott Michael. BS, La. State U., 1985, MEd, 1995. Cert. elem. tchr., La. 7th, 8th grade social studies tchr. Brusley (La.) Mid. Sch., 1986; 3rd, 4th grade tchr. Melrose Elem. Sch., Baton Rouge, La., 1986-90; 4th grade math., sci. tchr. Lanier Elem. Sch., Baton Rouge, 1990—. STARLAB instr., 1990-95; tchr. Chgo. Math. Project, 1994-95. Recipient Presdl. award for Excellence in Sci. NSF, 1994, South Ctrl. Bell mini grant, 1990, Tchr. of Dow Kit grant, 1993-95, NSF (La. State U.) grant, 1990-92. Mem. Nat. Coun. Tchrs. Math., Nat. Sci. Tchrs. Assn., Assn. Profl. Educators (v.p. 1989-90). Roman Catholic. Avocations: travel, nature study, needlecrafts, reading. Office: Lanier Elem Sch 4705 Lanier Dr Baton Rouge LA 70812-4020

EMRICH, JEANNE ANN, poet, artist, publishing executive; b. Mpls. d. George Jacob Emrich and Janis Virginia (Elstone) Emrich Erickson; m. Glenn Merle Eriksen, Jan. 17, 1981 (div. Dec. 27, 2004); children: Thielen NaRyan, Anthony. BA in Art History, U. Minn., 1969. Pub., founder Lone Egret Press, Mpls., 1996—2005; founder. first editor HAIGA Online, Mpls., 1998—2001; tchr. The Loft Lit. Ctr., Mpls., 1998—2000. Author, editor: The Haiku Habit, 1996, Barely Dawn, 1999, Berries and Cream: Contemporary Haiga in North America, 2000, Reeds: Contemporary Haiga, 2003—; actor(playwright): Coming Home, 2004,: Second Chance, 2005, Fallen Grasses, 2006. Bd. dirs. Bloomington Art Ctr., 1994—98. Recipient H.G. Henderson award, Haiku Soc. Am., 1995, 2001, 1st place award, San Francisco Internat. Tanka Competition, 2005. Mem.: Nat. League of Am. Penwomen (pres. br. and state assn. Minn. chpt. 1998-2000), Minn. Artists Assn. (pres. 1988-90), Minn. Watercolor Soc. (founder, first pres. 1983-86), Tanka Soc. Am. (v.p. 2005, Anthology guest editor 2005), Minn. Haiku Soc. (co-founder 2003), Rendezvous Minn. (co-founder, first pres. 1993-94). Avocations: nature study, painting, book arts. E-mail: jemrich@aol.com.

ENAYA, MAYSAA ASAD, chemistry educator, physics educator; arrived in U.S., 1994; d. Asad Yousef and Mai Dawood Enaya; m. Haroon Rashid Abdoh, Sept. 6, 1994; children: Omar Haroon Abdoh, Yousef Haroon Abdoh, Rashid Haroon Abdoh. BA in Chemistry, Jordan U., Amman, 1995; postgrad., U. Tex., Dallas, 2004—. Cert. in tchg. U. Tex., 2003. Tchr. Brighter Horizons, Baton Rouge, 1998—2001, Brighter Horizons Acad., Garland, Tex., 2001—, basketball coach, 2004—05. Mem.: NSTA. Home: 2802 Champlin Ct Richardson TX 75082 Office: Brighter Horizons Acad 3145 Medical Plz Dr Garland TX 75044 Office Fax: 972-675-2063. Business E-Mail: menaya@brighterhorizons.org.

END, LAUREL JEAN, psychologist, educator; b. Milw., May 15, 1956; d. Edgar Matthew and Audrey Rose (Plant) E.; m. Frederick Daniel Franklin, May 19, 1984. BA, U. Wis., 1978; MA, Kent State U., 1982, PhD, 1984. Teaching fellow Kent (Ohio) State U., 1981-84; asst. prof. psychology, acad. advisor Psychology Honor Soc. Salve Regina Coll., Newport, R.I., 1984—. Contbr. chpts., abstracts to profl. pubs. Mem. AAAS, Ea. Psychol. Assn., Am. Psychol. Assn., Sigma Xi. Roman Catholic. Avocations: travel, hiking, reading.

ENDAHL, ETHELWYN MAE, elementary education educator, consultant; b. Duluth, Minn., May 27, 1922; d. Herman and Florence Jenny (Mattson) Johnson; m. John Charles Endahl Sr., Nov. 27, 1943; children: Merrilee Jean, Marsha Louise, John Charles Jr., Kimberly Ann. BS in Library Science, U. Minn., Mpls., 1943; MA in Edn., Fairfield U., 1978; attended, Elmhurst (Ill.) Coll., 1966-68, U. Bridgeport, Conn., 1981-83, Northeastern U., Martha's Vineyard, Mass., 1982-85, U. Conn., 1971. Cert. Tchr. Conn. Librarian children's hosp. Davenport (Iowa) Pub. Library, 1943-44; librarian Omaha (Nebr.) Pub. Library, 1944; tchr. 4th gr. Center Elem. Sch., New Canaan, Conn., 1968-81, writing coord., 1981-83; staff devel. Dept. Edn. State of Conn., 1986-88; writing coord. East Elem. Sch., New Canaan, 1986-88; instr. Grad. Sch. Edn. Simmons Coll., Boston, 1989. Leader Reminiscence Writing Courtland Gardens Nursing Home, Stamford, Conn., 1985-86; leader adult writing group Charlotte Hobbs Library, Lovell, Maine, 1987-89; leader writing process-children's group Cmty. Ctr., Boca Grande, Fla., 1994; cons. writing process Banyan Elem. Sch., Sunrise, Fla., 1995-96; writing tchr. John Knox Village Retirement Ctr. Mem. AAUW, Nat. League of Pen Women, Older Women's League. Democrat. Quaker. Avocations: women's studies, reading, writing, hiking. Home: 528 Village Dr Pompano Beach FL 33060-7718 Personal E-mail: ettaend@aol.com.

ENDER, PAULINE LOUISE, painter; d. Henry and Helen M. Lodewyck; m. Paul Peter Ender, Feb. 9, 1957; children: Mara, Victoria, Leah, Elese, Norman. Student, Wayne State U., 1952—53. Fashion artist Winkleman Bros., Detroit, 1952—53; artist Reidel Advt., 1953—55; fashion artist, advt. J.L. Hudson Co., 1955—57; artist Rossi Advt., East Detroit, 1986—89. Painting demonstrations Progressive Artist Club, St. Clair Shores, Mich., 2000—05, Wayne County. C.C., Belleville, 2004; slide presentation West Bloomfield High Sch., 2003. Prin. commd. works include, 8 paintings Orch. Pl., Detroit, 1997, 6 paintings Greektown Casino, 2000, 48 paintings Detroit Pub. Schs., 2001—05, 16 paintings Cobo Conv. Ctr., Detroit, 2004. Mem.: Detroit Soc. Women Painters & Sculptors (bd. dirs. 1992—2005), Art Serve, The Scarab Club (bd. dirs. 1994—2005, Gold medal 1992). Avocations: travel, sketching, photography, reading.

ENDERS, ELIZABETH MCGUIRE, artist; b. New London, Conn., Feb. 18, 1939; d. Francis Foran and Helen Cuseck (Connolly) McGuire; m. Anthony Talcott Enders, June 9, 1962; children: Charles Talcott, Alexandra Eustis, Camilla, Ostrom II. BA, Conn. Coll., 1962; MA, NYU, 1987. Trustee Artists Space, NYC, 1986-95, Conn. Coll., New London, 1988-93; assoc. dept. prints and illustrated books Mus. Modern Art, 1993—, Lyman Allyn Art Mus., 1994—. One-woman shows include Paul Schuster Gallery, Cambridge, Mass., 1966, Ulysses Gallery, NYC, 1992, 1994, Lyman Allyn Art Mus., New London, Conn., 1994, Charles Cowles Gallery, NYC, 1995, Norbert Considine Gallery, Princeton, NJ, 1997, Artists Space, NYC, 2001, Charles Shain Libr., Conn. Coll., 2004, 2006, Alua Gallery, New London, 2006, Represented in permanent collections Wadsworth Atheneum, Hartford, Conn., exhibited in group shows at Boston Symphony Orch., 1982, NYU, 1983, Conn. Coll., 1988, Bronx Coun. on Arts, 1990—91, Addison Gallery Am. Art, 1993, Angel Art, LA, 1993, Lyman Allyn Art Mus., New London, Conn., 1994—95, 1998, 1999, one-woman shows include Real Art Ways, Hartford, Conn., 2004, 2006, exhibited in group shows at So. Allegheinies Mus. Art, Loretto, Pa., 1994, Artists Space Multiple, 1995, New Mus. Contemporary Art, NYC, 1995, Denise Bibro Fine Art, 1995, 1998, NY Studio Sch., 1995, 2002, Divine Design '95, LA, Spring Benefit Raffle, Sculpture Ctr., NYC, 1996, 1997, 1998, 2000, 2003, 2004, 2005, Charles Cowles Gallery, 1996, 1998, 2000, 2001, 2002, 2003, 2005, Fax Art Week, Copenhagen, Assn. Danish Graphic Artists, 1996, Open Studio, Downtown Arts Festival, NYC, 1997, 1998, Dieu Donne Papermill, 1997, 1999, 2001, Robert Brown Gallery, Wash., DC, 1999, 2001, 2002, 2003, 2004, NY Acad. of Art Benefit Auction, 1999, Cooley Gallery, Old Lyme, Conn., 1999, 2002, (Benefit for the Nature Conservancy), Nielsen Gallery, Boston, 2001, Artwalk, Coalition for the Homeless, 2001, Pfizer Inc., 2004, 2005, traveling group show Artists Space, 1992, 1994, Southeastern Ctr. Contemporary Art, Winston-Salem, N.C., 1993, Allentown Art Mus., Pa., 1994, Cleve. Ctr. Contemporary Art, 1994, Salt Lake Art Ctr., Salt Lake City, 1995, Kemper Ctr. Contemporary Art and Design, Kansas City, Mo., 1996, Bass Mus. of Art, Miami Beach, Fla., 1997, Flint Inst. Arts, Mich., 1998, Blaffer Gallery, U. Houston, Tex., 1998, Contemporary Art Ctr., Va. Beach, 1998, Tampa Mus. of Art, 1998—99, Art Mus. of Southeast Tex., 1999, Fresno Metropolitan Mus., Calif., 2000, www.sfnbotanicalart.com, 2003, 2004, 2005, Represented in permanent collections, Addison Gallery of Am. Art, Andover, Mass., Florence Griswold Mus., Old Lyme, Graham Gund, Cambridge, Dow Jones, NYC, Agnes Gund, Lyman Allyn Art Mus., Conn. Coll., New London, Pfizer Inc. Recipient Citation of Appreciation, Conn. Coll., 1990, medal, 1993. Mem. The Bklyn. Mus., Contemporary Art Coun., The Century Assn. Home: 530 E 86th St New York NY 10028-7535

ENDICO, MARY ANTOINETTE, artist; b. Bronx, N.Y., June 13, 1954; d. Felix and Katherine (Gluck) E.; m. Robert W. Fugett. BFA, Boston U., 1976. Artist cons. D'Arches Fine Art Paper, France, 1983; demonstrator, lectr. art groups N.Y. State, 1980-97; sec. Sugarloaf (N.Y.) Guild, 1980-88. Self-employed artist, Sugar Loaf, 1977—; group shows include Art of Orange and Rockland N.Y. Invitational, 1986, Aqueous Annual, Ky., 1987, 88, 89, 94, Nat. Exhibit Am. Watercolors, N.Y., 1989, 90, 91, N.E. Watercolor Annual, N.Y., 1991, Nat. Watercolor Soc., Calif., 1992, 2001, San Diego Internat., 1997, Am. Watercolor Soc., 2006, Am. Watercolor Soc., 139th Annual; permanent collections include Del Monte Corp., N.Y., IBM Corp., N.Y., The Ambra Found., N.H., Ashville (N.C.) Mus., Ky. Mus., Bowling Green. Mem. Nat. Watercolor Soc. (signature), Northeast Watercolor Soc. (co-founder 1991), Knickerbocker Artists, Orange County Watercolor Soc., Salmagundi Club, Ky. Watercolor Soc.(signature mem.) Avocation: road cycling. Office: Endico Watercolor Originals PO Box 31 1386 Kings Hwy Sugar Loaf NY 10981 Office Phone: 845-469-9272.

ENDICOTT, JENNIFER JANE REYNOLDS, education educator; b. Oklahoma City, Oct. 17, 1947; d. M. Ector and Jessie Ruth (Carter) Reynolds; m. William George Endicott, June 2, 1969 (dec. Sept. 1976); 1 child, Andrea A. BA History, U. Okla., 1969, MEd Adminstrn., 1975, PhD, 1987. Cert. secondary edn. tchr.: history, govt., geography, econs., adminstr., Okla. Mid. sch. tchr. Norman (Okla.) Pub. Schs., 1970-77, adminstr. elem. edn., 1977-80; grad. asst. U. Okla., Norman, 1984-88; adj. lectr. U. Ctrl. Okla., Edmond, 1988-90, asst. prof., 1990-94, assoc. prof., 1995-98, prof., 1999—. Mem. adv. bd. The Annual Editions Series, Guilford, Conn., 1994—; editor Okla. Assn. Tchr. Educators Jour., 1997-2001, mem. editl. bd., 2002—; reviewer Action in Teacher Education ATE Jour.; contbr. articles to profl. jours. Bd. dirs. Cleveland County Hist. Soc., Norman, 1980-88, Arts and Humanities Coun., Norman, 1982-88; bd. dirs. Jr. League, Inc., Norman, 1982-90; bd. dirs. Assistance League, Norman, 1982-90, pres. 1988-89. Recipient Harriet Harvey Meml. award U. Okla. Found., 1984, Edn. and Profl. Svcs. Diversity award, 2006; named Norman Cmty. Family of the Yr. Finalist, LDS Ch., Norman, 1985; named to The Educator's Leadership Acad., The Outstanding Profs. Acad., 1999-2000. Mem. ASCD, Okla. Assn. for Supervision and Curriculum Devel., Okla. Assn. Tchr. Educators (bd. dirs. 1994-2003, pres. 1996-97, exec. sec. 2001-03), Am. Assn. Tchr. Educators, Soc. for Philosophy and History of Edn., Nat. Soc. Study of Edn., Am. Ednl. Rsch. Assn., Philosophy of Edn. Soc., Kappa Delta Pi (univ. sponsor 1991-96), Phi Delta Kappa (bd. dirs. Mid. State chpt. 1993-99, v.p. 1997-99, Svc. Key 1998). E-mail: jendicott@ucok.edu.

ENDLICH, LILI, psychotherapist; b. Paris, Apr. 4, 1936; d. Lazar and Anne (Schnitkind) Gurwith; m. Harold Louis Endlich, Dec. 22, 1955 (div. Dec. 1983); children: Lisa, Eric, Keith; m. Robert Arthur Holtzman, July 6, 1986. BA in Zoology, Washington U., St. Louis, 1956; MA in Sociology, Phillips Grad. Inst., 1978; PhD in Psychology, Internat. Coll., 1985. Lic. marriage family child counselor Calif. Bd. Behavioral Scis. Tchr. Everywoman's Village, 1979—99; counselor San Fernando Valley Counseling Ctr., 1977-79, clin. dir., 1983-85, supr., 1985—; pvt. practice Sherman Oaks, Calif., 1992—; tchr. Calif. State U., Northridge, 1998—. Tchr. Pierce Coll. Cmty. Svcs., 1986-90, North Valley Jewish Cmty. Ctr., 1979-82, L.A. Valley Coll. Cmty. Svcs., 1972-89; tchr. grad. program for tchrs. U. Phoenix, 1988—; cons., tchr. stress mgmt. Granada Hills Hosp., 1979-85; spkr. in field. Endowed internat. fellow AAUW; recipient award of merit L.A. Human Rels. Commn., L.A. County Dept. Mental Health. Mem. Am. Assn. Marriage and Family Therapy (clin.), Calif. Assn. Marriage and Family Therapists, Obsessive-Compulsive Disorders Found. (clin.), Anxiety Disorders Assn. Avocations: bicycling, travel, reading, creating new workshops. Home and Office: 3901 Kingswood Rd Sherman Oaks CA 91403 Office Phone: 818-783-2004. E-mail: Lendlich@msn.com.

ENDRES, ELEANOR ESTELLE, speech pathology/audiology services professional; b. Balt., Dec. 11, 1953; d. Thomas Edward and Elizabeth Jane Donatt; m. Charles Jeffrey Knickman, Feb. 1974 (div. Mar. 1981); m. Gregory Scott Endres, Apr. 1119; children: Meghan, Graciela, Daniel. BS, Towson State U., Md., 1976; MS, Towson State U., 1989. Speech pathologist Anne Arundel Pub. Schs./Infant Toddlers Program, Glen Burnie, Md., 1989—.

Asst. county exec. campaign TAAAC, 2001; religious edn. tchr. Holy Trinity Ch./Archdiocese of Balt., Glenn Burnie, 1998—. Recipient ACE award, Am. Speech and Hearing Assn., 2003. Mem.: Speech and Lang. Assn. of Anne Arundel County (exec. bd. 1999), Md. Speech and Hearing Assn. (exec. bd. 2000—, Svc. award 2000). Democrat. Roman Catholic. Avocation: dogs. Home: 17 Proctor Ave Glen Burnie MD 21061 Office: AACO Infant Toddlers Program Point Pleasant Elem Sch Glen Burnie MD 21060

ENEGUESS, ANN CAVANAUGH, social services administrator; b. Evanston, Ill., Sept. 27, 1924; d. Matthew Patrick and Mary Ethel (Kelleher) Cavanaugh; m. Daniel Francis Eneguess, July 29, 1950 (dec.); children: David Michael (dec.), Katharine Ann Given, Daniel Francis, John Matthew (dec.). B.A., Regis Coll., Weston, Mass., 1946. Field dir. So. Nassau Girl Scout Council, Freeport, N.Y., 1946-49; exec. dir. Wellesley Girl Scout Council, Mass., 1949-51; reporter, feature writer Keene Evening Sentinel, N.H., 1957-64; owner, operator Deer Run Day Camp, Deer Run No. White Water, Peterborough, N.H., 1958-68, 70—; field exec., edn. dir. Swift Water Girl Scout Council, Manchester, N.H., 1962-84, fund devel dir., 1984-87; state pres. Gen. Fedn. Women's Clubs, N.H., 1993—. Pres., Monadnock Chorus & Orch., Peterborough, 1985, chmn. 250th Celebration of Peterborough, 1989. Recipient Thanks Badge Swift Water Girl Scout Council, 1954, St. Ann's award Diocese of Manchester, 1978; Named Career Girl of USA Internat. Friendship League, 1947, Named Outstanding Woman of Yr., Beta Sigma Phi, 1983-85. Mem. Assn. Girl Scout Exec. Staff (v.p. 1964-66, sec. 1978-80), AAUW (pres. 1965-67, state pres. N.H., pres. Green Valley Ariz. br. 1998-99), Audubon Soc., Soc. Protection N.H. Forest, Hist. Soc. Peterborough, Hist. Soc. Tubac, Woman's Club. Republican. Roman Catholic. Avocations: skiing, chorus, community service. Home: PO Box 135 Peterborough NH 03458-0135 Personal E-mail: aceneguess@juno.com.

ENG, CATHERINE, health facility administrator, physician; b. Hong Kong, May 20, 1950; came to U.S., 1953; d. Doi Kwong and Alice (Yee) E.; m. Daniel Charles Chan; 1 child, Michael B. BA, Wellesley Coll., 1972; MD, Columbia U., 1976. Diplomate Am. Bd. Internal Medicine, Am. Bd. Gastroenterology; cert. added qualifications geriat. Intern in internal medicine Presbyterian Hosp./Columbia U., Presbyterian Med. Ctr., 1976-77, resident in internal medicine, 1977-79; fellow in gastroenterology/hepatology N.Y. Hosp./Cornell U. Med. Coll., 1979-81; instr. medicine Cornell U. Coll. Medicine, NYC, 1980-81; staff physician On Lok Sr. Health Svcs., San Francisco, 1981-86, supervising physician, 1986-91, med. dir., 1992—. Asst. clin. prof. dept. family and cmty. medicine U. Calif., San Francisco, 1986-95, asst. clin. prof. dept. medicine, 1992-95, assoc. clin. prof. dept. medicine, 1995-2001, clin. prof. medicine, 2001—; primary care specialist Program of All-inclusive Care for the Elderly, San Francisco, 1987-94; asst. chief dept. medicine Chinese Hosp., San Francisco, 1993-98, chmn. com. credentials, 1994—. Instr. BLS Am. Heart Assn., San Francisco, 1988-92; mem. nominating com. YWCA of Marin, San Francisco, San Mateo, 1991-95; mem. mgmt. com. YWCA-Chinatown/North Beach, San Francisco, 1989-95; bd. dirs. Chinatown Cmty. Children's Ctr., San Francisco, 1987-90. Durant scholar Wellesley Coll., 1972. Fellow ACP; mem. Am. Geriat. Soc., Am. Soc. Aging, Am. Gastroent. Assn., Calif. Med. Assn. (assoc.), San Francisco Med. Soc. (assoc.), Sigma Xi, Alpha Omega Alpha. Avocations: reading, hiking. Home: 130 Dorchester Way San Francisco CA 94127-1110 Office: On Lok Sr Health Scvs 1333 Bush St San Francisco CA 94109-5691 Office Phone: 415-292-8886. E-mail: cathy@onlok.org.

ENG, HOLLY S.A., lawyer; b. 1966; BA in English & Econ., St. Cloud State Univ., 1989; JD, Georgetown Univ., 1993. Bar: Minn. 1993. Atty. Dorsey & Whitney LLP, Mpls., 1993—2001, ptnr., labor, employment practice group, 2001—; spl. assignment Mpls. City Atty. Off., 1997. Guardian ad Litem Minn. Guardian ad Litem Program; instr. Univ. St. Thomas Grad. Sch. Bus., 1999—2001. Grantee Nat. Lawyer's Guild Fellowship, Georgetown Univ. Mem.: Minn. Women Lawyers. Office: Dorsey & Whitney LLP Ste 1500 50 S Sixth St Minneapolis MN 55402-1498 Office Phone: 612-343-2164. Office Fax: 612-340-2868. Business E-Mail: eng.holly@dorsey.com.

ENGEL, AMY J., corporate financial executive; BS in Bus., SUNY, Buffalo, 1977, MBA in Fin., 1978. Treasury analyst Kennecott Cooper, Stamford, Conn., Perkin Elmer, Tinton Falls, NJ, Carborundum Co., Niagara Falls, NY; with Philip Morris Internat., 1981, supr. treas. ops., mgr. fin. planning and analysis, asst. treas.; dir. corp. financing Philip Morris Mgmt. Corp., 1990, asst. treas. corp. financing, mng. dir. global corp. fin., mng. dir. global risk mgmt., 1999; v.p., treas. Altria Grp., Inc., 2002—. Office: Altria Grp Inc 120 Park Ave New York NY 10017*

ENGEL, CAROL LOUISE, music educator; b. Tracy, Minn., Sept. 1, 1948; d. Elmer Roy Johnson, Frances Lucille Johnson; m. John Robert Engel; children: Christopher, Benjamin. BS in Music, Minn. U.-Mankato, 1970. Pianist, organist, Balaton, Minn., 1962—66, East Grand Forks, Minn., 1975—; supr. United Day Nursery, Grand Forks, ND, 1977—92; tchr. piano East Grand Forks, Minn., 1980—97; accompanist musicals, ensembles, solos, concerts East Grand Forks Pub. Schs. #595, 1987—; pianist Valley Meml. Homes, Grand Forks, ND, 1991—; tchr. elem. music East Grand Forks Pub. Schs. #595, 1992—. Accompanist Cmty. Theaters, Grand Forks, ND, 1975—80. Musician (CD): Piano by Carol, 1991, Piano by Carol 2, 1994, Forever Yours, 2000, In My Heart There Rings A Melody, 2001, Sacred Songs for the Soul, 2005. Pianist, entertainer VFW Conv., Grand Forks, 2001, First Night, Grand Forks, 1992—97. Mem.: Music Boosters, Music Educators Nat. Conf., Sigma Alpha Iota (life; President - local chapter 1968—69). Republican. Lutheran. Avocations: painting, reading, travel, crafts. Home: 616 8th St SE East Grand Forks MN 56721 Office: East Grand Forks Public Schools - #595 1900 13th St SE East Grand Forks MN 56721 Office Phone: 218-773-2911. Personal E-mail: cengel@gra.midco.net. Business E-Mail: cengel@egf.k12.mn.us.

ENGEL, TALA, lawyer; b. N.Y.C. d. Volodia Vladimir Boris and Risia (Modelevska) E.; m. James Colias, Nov. 22, 1981 (dec. Nov. 1989). AA, U. Fla., 1952; BA in Russian and Spanish, U. Miami, 1954; JD, U. Miami, Coral Gables, 1957; postgrad., Middlebury Coll., 1953. Bar: Fla. 1957, Ill. 1962, D.C. 1982, U.S. Dist. Ct. (so. dist.) Fla. 1957, U.S. Dist. Ct. (no. dist.) Ill. 1962, U.S. Supreme Ct., 1965. Pvt. practice in immigration law, Miami, Fla., 1957—61, Chgo., 1966—86, Washington, 1987—89, Chgo., 1990—93, Washington, 1993—2002, Miami, Fla., 2002—. Atty. Immigration and Naturalization Svc., Chgo., 1961-62; parole agt. Ill. Youth Commn., Chgo., 1963-66. Editor The Lawyer, 1956; mem. editl. bd. Miami Law Quar., 1955-57, 10 ML Q 110 Criminal Law, 10 ML Q 608 Ins. Law, 1955-56. Bd. dirs. Cordi-Marian Settlement, Chgo., 1977-93. Mem.: Fla. Bar Assn., Fed. Bar Assn., Chgo. Bar Assn. (entertainment com. 1971—72, devel. of law com. 1985—87), Ill. Bar Assn. (gen. assembly 1984—86), Fla. Bar Found. (life), Chgo. Bar Found. (life), Nu Beta Epsilon, Alpha Lambda Delta. Avocations: theater, singing, computers, Russian and Spanish languages, travel in 99 countries. Home: 601 Three Islands Blvd #215 Hallandale Beach FL 33009 Office Phone: 954-455-7044. Personal E-mail: talaengel@aol.com.

ENGEL, WALBURGA See VON RAFFLER-ENGEL, WALBURGA

ENGEL-ARIELI, SUSAN LEE, physician; b. Chgo., Oct. 7, 1954; d. Thaddeus S. Dziengiel and Marion L. (Carpenter) Kasper; m. Udi Arieli. BA, Northwestern U., 1975; MD, Chgo. Med. Sch., 1982. Diplomate Am. Bd. Gen. Practice, Am. Bd. Ambulatory Medicine. Med. technician G.D. Searle, Skokie, Ill., 1972, 73, assoc. dir., 1983-84, dir. U.S. Regional Clin. Support, 1984-86; rsch. editorial asst. U. Chgo., 1974; rsch. assoc. Loyola U., Maywood, Ill., 1977-78; intern Rush Presbyn. St. Lukes Hosp., Chgo., 1982-83; resident U. Chgo., 1983; mgr. hosp. products div. Abbott Labs., Abbott Park, Ill., 1986-87. Bd. govs., dep. gov. Am. Biog. Inst. Rsch. Assn., 1988; vis. prof. Rush Presbyn.-St. Luke's Hosp., Chgo., 1985, faculty assoc., 1985; assoc. investigator, asst. prof. medicine King Drew Med. Ctr., UCLA, 1985-90; practical cardiology panel experts, 1988; Med. World News Rev. panel, 1988; bd. dirs. Am. Soc. Handicapped Physicians, acting v.p.; bd. dirs. fundraising, chmn. Vestibular Disorders Assn. Author: How Your Body Works, 1994, C-D Rom version, 1995; contbr. articles to profl. and scholarly jours. Bd. govs. Art Inst. Chgo., 1985—, mem. aux. bd., 1988—, mem. multiple benefit coms., 1984—, vice chmn. Capital Campaign, 1984-85; mem. pres. com. Landmark Preservation Coun., Chgo., 1984-90, chmn. multiple coms. polit. candidates, 1986; bd. dirs. Marshall unit Chgo. Boys Clubs, 1984—; mem. benefit com. Hubbard St. Dance Co. 10th Gala, 1988, Victory Garden's Theatre Ann. Benefit, 1988. Recipient Gold award, 1995, Nat. Health Info. award, 1995; Internat. Coll. Surgeons fellow, 1982. Mem. AMA, ACP, Am. Fedn. for Clin. Rsch., Southern Med. Assn., Ill. State Med. Soc., Chgo. Med. Soc., Am. Acad. Med. Dirs., Nat. Acad. Arts and Scis., Am. Soc. Handicapped Physicians (bd. dirs., v.p.), Vestibular Disorders Assn. (bd. dirs., pub. rels. com., co-chmn. fundraising). Avocations: german language, organ playing, composing music, writing.

ENGELBERG, ELAINE A., retired secondary school educator; b. N.Y.C., Mar. 18, 1930; d. Hyman and Anna (Fried) Rosen; m. Edward Engelberg, July 27, 1950; children: Stephen Paul, Michael Joseph, Elizabeth Joyce. BA, Bklyn. Coll., 1951; postgrad., London Sch. Econs., 1975-76; MA, Boston U., 1981; PhD in Social Psychology, Brandeis U., 1994. Personnel asst. USES, Eugene, Oreg., 1951-52; statis. asst. Dept. Army, Madison, Wis., 1952-55, Cavendish Lab., Cambridge, Eng., 1956-57; rsch. asst. U. Mich., Ann Arbor, 1959-60; tchr. Lexington (Mass.) High Sch., 1968—2006; master tchr. in charge curriculum and student tchrs., 1988-89; ret. On sabbatical leave on gender issues Brandeis U., 1982-83 Recipient Outstanding Tchr. award U. Chgo., 1983, Tchr. of Global Issues award Clark U., 1989. Mem. Mass. Coun. Social Studies, Am. Psychol. Assn. (high sch. affiliate), Edn. for Living in Nuclear Age, Educators for Social Responsibility (organizer), NOW, MADD, Phi Beta Kappa, Pi Lambda Theta. Jewish. Avocations: hiking, dance, ballet, art, gardening. Home: 1300 NE 16th Ave Portland OR 97232 E-mail: eengelberg@comcast.net.

ENGELBERG, GAIL MAY, fine arts patron; m. Alfred B. Engelberg, May 5, 1990. Trustee Engelberg Charitable Found.; bd. trustee Solomon R. Guggenheim Mus., NYC; bd. dir. Jazz at Lincoln Ctr., NYC. Office: Guggenheim Mus Trustees 1071 Fifth Ave New York NY 10128-0173 also: The Engelberg Foundation 1050 N Lake Way Palm Beach FL 33480-3252 Office Phone: 212-877-4050.

ENGELBREIT, MARY, art licensing entrepreneur; b. St. Louis, 1952; m. Phil Delano, 1977; 2 children. Illustrator greeting card cos., 1983; founder, pres. Mary Engelbreit Studios Retail and Pub. Cos., St. Louis, 1983—; founder, head The Mary Engelbreit Store; founder, creator Mary Engelbreit's Home Companion mag., 1996—. Illustrator The Snow Queen, 1993, The Night Before Christmas, 2001. Office Phone: 314-726-5646.

ENGELHARDT, REGINA, cosmetologist, artist, small business owner; b. Kiwerce, Poland, Oct. 1, 1928; came to U.S., 1949; d. Marian and Maria (Wardach) Engelhardt; m. Gerard Edward Twardon, May 30, 1953 (div. 1961); children: Miriam Teresa Twardon Bielski, Elizabeth Maria Twardon Israel, Renee Marie Twardon Gilchrist. Grad., Laski Inst. Tech., 1951; lic. cosmetologist, Hamtramck Beauty Sch., 1960; art student, Mercy Ctr., 1980-84. Sec. Am. Savs., Detroit, 1950-55; cosmetologist Magic Touch Salon, Oak Park, Mich., 1960—. Owner Regina's Fine Arts, Detroit, 1986—, Art Restorations, 1986—; art tchr. Farmington Activity Ctr., Farmington Hills, Mich., 1993—; spkr. in field. Artist lithographs; represented in permanent collection at Althorp Mus., Eng., 1998, also pvt. collections in U.S., Can., Poland, Eng., India, The Philippines. Mem. Dem. Nat. Com., 1996—; mem. nat. com. to preserve social security and medicare, 1993—. Recipient Gold and Silver medals Internat. Art Challenge, 1987-88, 90, Kubinski award Friends of Polish Arts, 1989, First and Fourth awards Mich. State Exhibit, 1988. Mem. Sculptores Guild of Mich., Four Octave Club, Farmington Artists Club (6 Popular Vote awards 1985, 86, 97, merit award local art exhibit 1997, two merit awards 1998), Sierra Club, Nature Conservancy. Roman Catholic. Avocations: music, needlecrafts, dance, reading. Home: 17345 Wildemere St Detroit MI 48221-2722 Office Phone: 313-864-0895.

ENGELKER, LYNSEY L., athletic trainer, professional athletics manager; b. Denver, May 4, 1978; d. Herman L. and Karen L. Engelker. AS, Northeastern Jr. Coll., Sterling, Colo., 1998; BS, U. Nebr., Kearney, 2000; MS, Ariz. State U., Tempe, 2003. Cert. athletic trainer Nat. Athletic Trainers Assn., 2001, strength & conditioning specialist Nat. Strength & Conditioning Assn., 2000, first aid/CPR/AED Am. Heart Assn., 2005. Athletic tng. internship Nokia Sugar Bowl, Coral Gables, Fla., 2000—01, U. Miami, Coral Gables, 2000—01; grad. asst. athletic trainer Ariz. State U., Tempe, 2001—03; head athletic trainer Greek Softball Fedn., Athens, Greece, 2002—04; clin. athletic trainer & HS head athletic trainer SW Sports Medicine & Rehab., Mesa, Ariz., 2003—04; account mgr. RS Med., Phoenix, 2004—. Participant Women's NCAA Coll. World Series, Oklahoma City, 2001—02; head athletic trainer European championships Greek Softball Fedn., Saronno, Italy, 2002—03, head athletic trainer U.S. cup women's softball, Honolulu, 2002—03, head athletic trainer and med. dir. summer Olympics, Athens, Greece, 2002—04, head athletic trainer Greece cup, 2002—03. Home: 9020 S 4th St Phoenix AZ 85042 Office: RS Medical 14001 SE First St Vancouver WA 98684 Office Phone: 866-849-6160. Home Fax: 602-243-1978; Office Fax: 602-243-1978. Personal E-mail: lengelker@yahoo.com. Business E-Mail: lengelke@rsmedical.com.

ENGELMAN, CYLINDA ANDERSON, elementary school educator; b. Dodge City, Kans., Apr. 11, 1956; d. Tom and Janey Anderson; m. Daniel Engelman, Oct. 15, 1984; children: Zach, Jake. BS, Kans. State U., Manhattan, 1979. Cert. secondary edn. Colo. Dept. Edn., 1980. 7th grade life sci. tchr. Lewis Palmer Mid. Sch., Monument, Colo., 1995—. Scholar, Kans. State U., 1978—79. Achievements include 1990 winner of Pikes Peak Marathon; 1986 winner of Colorado Governors Cup 10K road race; 1986 State TAC womens champion 1/2 marathon road race. Avocations: yoga, running, hiking, gardening, bicycling. Home: 370 Largo Palmer Lake CO 80133 Office: Lewis Palmer Middle School 1776 Woodmoor Dr Monument CO 80132 Office Phone: 719-488-4776. Personal E-mail: cdengelman@adelphia.net. Business E-Mail: cengelman@lewispalmer.org.

ENGELMAN, ELIZABETH, playwright, trade association administrator; b. Balt., Jan. 27, 1970; d. William Hillard and Frances Lee (Hoffenberg) Engelman; m. Michael Bigelow Dixon, July 1, 2006. BA, Brown U., Providence, 1992; MFA, Columbia U., NYC, 1996. Asst. lit. mgr., dramaturg Agpus Theater Louisville, 1995—97; lit. mgr., dramaturg Intiman Theatre, Seattle, 1997—98; dramaturg, dir. new play devel. ACT Theatre, Seattle, 1998—2001; lit. dir. McCarter Theatre, Princeton, NJ, 2001—04; pres. Lit. Mgrs. & Dramaturgs Ams., NYC, Mpls., 2004—, chmn. bd. dirs., 2006—. Adv. bd. Emigrant Theatre, Mpls., 2005—; cons. Playwrights Ctr., Mpls., 2004—. Co-editor: Humona Festival: The Complete Plays, 1996—97, New Monologues for Women by Women, 2004—05, The Best 10 Minute Plays, 2004. Mem. Minn. Citizens for Arts, Mpls., 2006. Named Outstanding Dramaturgy, Columbia U., 1999. Mem.: Internat. Theatre Inst.

ENGELMAN, MARJORIE JECKEL, retired higher education administrator; b. Delavan, Ill., Oct. 9, 1927; d. John B. and Reka M. (Hellman) Jeckel; m. Kenneth L. Engelman, Mar. 26, 1949; children: Ann K., Barth B. BA, Ill. Wesleyan U., 1945-49; MA, Northwestern U., 1953; MS, U. Wis., 1965, PhD, 1977. Dir. outreach/ext. U. Wis., Green Bay, 1973-85, dir. equal opportunity, 1974-79; asst. to chancellor affirmative action U. Wis. ext., Madison, 1985-89. Part-time instr. U. Wis., Madison, 1991-93. Author: Aerobics of the Mind: Keeping the Mind Active in Aging, 1996, Mental Fitness Cards, 100 Exercises for Healthy Brain, 2004; contbr. articles to publs. Bd. trustees Garrett-Evangel. Sem., Northwestern U., Evanston, Ill., 1975-96; bd. Meriter Retirement Svcs., Meriter Health, Madison, 1985-96; bd. dirs. Madison Campus Ministry, 1994-96; del. to White House Conf. on Aging, 1995. Kramer Fund grantee, 1985, Wis. Humanities grantee, 1980. Mem. Assn. Aging Groups in Wis., Am. Soc. Aging, Phi Delta Kappa, Phi Kappa Phi. Democrat. Unitarian. Avocations: hiking, canoeing, reading, bicycling, textile arts. Home: 738 Seneca Pl Madison WI 53711-2918 Office Phone: 608-238-9707. Business E-Mail: engelman@wisc.edu.

ENGELMAN, ROSALYN ACKERMAN, artist, marketing executive; b. Liberty, N.Y., Jan. 2, 1938; d. Nathan and Lillie (Schultz) Ackerman; m. Irwin Engelman, Nov. 24, 1956; children: Madeleine Florence, Marianne Leslie. BA, CCNY, 1958; MS, U. Rochester, 1978. Tchr. art, N.Y.C., 1958, N.J., 1964-66; lectr., fund raiser, docent Meml. Art Gallery, Rochester, N.Y., 1972-74; rschr. Meml. Arts Gallery, Rochester, 1975-78; co-chair arts Westport (Conn.) Bicentennial Com., 1975-76; mem. Met. Arts Resources Com., Rochester, 1977-78; pres. Westport-Weston Arts Coun., 1980-81; devel. officer Conn. Pub. TV, 1982-83; v.p. mktg. Praxis Media, 1984—. Exhbns. include regional N.J. galleries, Gronsky Gallery, Kravetz Gallery, Rochester, Temple Israel, N.Y.C., 1997, T-Zart Gallery, N.Y.C., 1994, Baruch Coll., N.Y.C., 1998, Nigerian Embassy, 1998, Nat. Arts Club, N.Y.C., 1999, Adelphi Univ. Gallery, 1999, Masters Mystery Show, Fla. Internat. U., 2004, Norwalk (Conn.) Symphony, 2004; one woman shows: Nat. Arts Club, 1999, Mishkin Gallery Baruch Coll., 2001, Nico Gallery Seattle, 2001, All Commemorative Show NAC NY, 2002, Earthplace Westport, 2003, Thomas Walsh Art Gallery Fairfield U., 2003, Barbara Gillman Gallery, Miami, Fla., 2004, Art Miami Fla., 2004, Caelum Gallery, N.Y.C., 2004, 05-, Masters Mystery Show, Miami, 2004, Art Miami Gillman Gallery, 2005, Queensborough C.C. Art Gallery, Bayside, NY, 2005, Phthalo Gallery, Bay Harbor, Fla., 2005, Etra Fine Arts, Gallery, Miami, 2005-2006, Compton Goethals Gallery, N.Y.C., 2006; commns.: Substantive and Procedural Aspects of Internat. Criminal Law, The Hague Netherlands, 2000. Bd. dirs. Long Wharf Theatre, 1980-83, Performers Conn., 1980-84, Mus. Art Sci. and Industry, Bridgeport, Conn., 1990; chair bd. dirs. Westport-Weston Arts Coun., 1982—; bd. dirs. Nat. Corp. Theatre Fund, 1981-88, treas., 1982, pres., 1984. Recipient citation Town of Westport, 1981, Gold medal Grumbacher award, 1998. Mem. Alumni Assn. U. Rochester, Nat. Arts Club. Office Phone: 212-213-1569. Personal E-mail: ra936@aol.com.

ENGELMANN, MARY LYNN, nursing educator; d. Marilyn Johanna Hoover; m. Gary Engelmann, May 29, 1976; children: Christina Lynne, Brett Warren, Elliot Lawrence. EdD, No. Ill. U., DeKalb, 2002. RN Ill., 1977. Prof. nursing Coll. of DuPage, Glen Ellyn, Ill., 1994—. Author: (books for nursing educators) Teaching Nursing: The Art and Science. Mem.: Nat. Assn. Assoc. Degree Nurses, Nat. League Nursing (mem. editl. bd., mem. task force for excellence in nursing edn. 2005—), Phi Kappa Phi, Sigma Tau Delta. Office: College of DuPage 425 Fawell Blvd Glen Ellyn IL 60137 Office Phone: 630-942-2538. Business E-Mail: engelman@cod.edu.

ENGELS, BEATRICE ANN, artist, poet, retired real estate company executive; b. N.Y.C., Oct. 1, 1925; d. Sydney and Marguerite Agnes (Carroll) Jonap; m. James J. Engels, May 10, 1944 (dec.); children: James J. Jr.(dec.), Edward R., Marguerite Mary McHale. Brokers degree, Dowling Coll., 1970. Agt. real estate sales Kathleen Hart Real Estate, Bayport, NY, 1969—70; pres., real estate broker Beatrice A. Engels Realty, Patchogue, NY, 1970—76, Blue Point, NY, 1976—95; dir., pres. Beatrice A. Engels Art Gallery, Patchogue, 1970—76, Petite Pallette Art Gallery, Bayport, 1989—91; ret., 1995. Mem. real estate bd. Suffolk County, 1970—80; ecology adv., Blue Point, 1974—94; columnist LI Advance, Patchogue, NY, 1971—75, Suffolk County News, Sayville, NY, 1971—75. Author: Morning Song, 1996 (Editor's Choice award, 1996), Sea Sonnets and Other Poems, 1997, Endless Skies of Blue (Editor's Choice award, 1997), Best Poems of 1997, Celebration of Poets, 1997, Outstanding Poets of 1998 (Editor's Choice award, 1998), Best Poems of 1998; author: (compiled by Famous Poets Press) Our 100 Most Famous Poets, 2004; author, illustrator: Marguerite, The Story of a Dolly, 2003; author: (songs) Best Christmas Present, 1998. Mem. Blue Point Rep. Club, 1970—88. Mem.: Famous Poets Soc., Rosary Soc. (pres.), Internat. Soc. Poets (life), Wet Paints Studio Group (life). Roman Catholic. Achievements include ecological efforts that helped to save the wetlands near Blue Point, N.Y. E-mail: beabysea@bellsouth.net.

ENGER, LINDA, mathematics educator, consultant; d. Herschell and Mary Wilbanks; m. William Enger; children: Scott, Jennifer. BS, Okla. State U., Stillwater, 1972, MS, 1976. Tchr. math. Eureka Jr. High, Mo., 1972—73, Bristow Jr. High, Okla., 1973—75, Sapulpa Jr. High, Okla., 1975—76, Athens H.S., Tex., 1981—94, Pine Tree H.S., Longview, Tex., 1994—97, Cross Roads H.S., Tex., 1997—98, Athens H.S., Tex., 1998—. High school pre-calculus (lessons for teachers) Vectors and Parametric Equations, H.S. algebra 1 (lessons using cartoon characters) Quadratics and Direct Variation, fundamental math. course -internet (lessons). Mem.: Nat. Coun. Tchrs. Math. Home: 10672 County Rd 3909 Athens TX 75752-3863 Office: Athens High School 708 E College Athens TX 75751 Office Phone: 903-677-6920.

ENGERRAND, DORIS DIESKOW, retired business educator; b. Chgo., Aug. 7, 1925; d. William Jacob and Alma Louise Wilhelmina (Cords) Dieskow; m. Gabriel H. Engerrand,Oct. 26, 1946 (dec. June 1987); children: Steven, Kenneth, Jeannine. BS in Bus. Adminstrn., N. Ga. Coll., 1958, BS in Elementary Edn., 1959; M. Bus. Edn., Ga. State U., 1966, PhD, 1970. Tchr., dept. chmn. Lumpkin County H.S., Dahlonega, Ga., 1960-63, 65-68; tchr. Gainesville, Ga., 1965; asst. prof. Troy (Ala.) State U., 1969-71; asst. prof. bus. Ga. Coll. and State U., Milledgeville, 1971-74, assoc. prof., 1974-78, prof., 1978-90, chmn. dept. info. sys. and comms., 1978-89; retired, 1990. Contbr. articles on bus. edn. to profl. publs. Named Outstanding Tchr. Lumpkin County Pub. Schs., 1963, 66; Outstanding Educator bus. faculty Ga. Coll., 1975, Exec. of Yr. award, 1983. Fellow Assn. for Bus. Communication (v.p. S.E. 1978-80, 81-84, 89-92, bd. dirs.), Nat. Bus. Edn. Assn., Ga. Bus. Edn. Assn. (Postsecondary Tchr. of Yr. award 10th dist. 1983, Postsecondary Tchr. of Yr. award 1984), Am. Vocat. Assn., Ga. Vocat. Assn. (Educator of Yr. award 1984, Parker Liles award 1989), Profl. Secs. Internat. (pres. Milledgeville chpt. 1996-97), Ninety-nines Internat. (chmn. N. Ga. chpt. 1975-76, named Pilot of Yr. N. Ga. chpt. 1973). Methodist. Home: 1674 Pine Valley Rd Milledgeville GA 31061-2465

ENGGAS, GRACE FALCETTA, academic administrator; b. Hartford, Conn., May 25, 1946; d. Giacomo and Frances Catanzaro Falcetta; m. David Hirsh Enggas, Mar. 16, 1974. BA, U. Conn., 1971; MA, Ohio State U., 1973; grad., New Eng. mgmt. Inst., Wellesley, Mass., 1995. Cert. in Myers Briggs Type Inventory, 1987. Contract underwriter Travelers Ins. Cos., Hartford, 1965-71; asst. mgr., Jones Grad. Twr. Ohio State U., Columbus, 1972-73; resident counselor Worcester (Mass.) State Coll., 1974-77; area coord. Ea. Conn. State U., Willimantic, 1977-78, assoc. dir. housing, 1978-87, dir. housing, 1987—2002, coord. scholarship and fin. aid counseling, 2002—. Bd. dirs. and v.p. Literacy Vols. of NECT, 1990-2006; treas. Charter Cable Adv. Bd., 1989—. Mem. Nat. Assn. Student Pers. Adminstrs., Assn. Coll. and Univ. Housing Officers, State U. Adminstrv. Faculty/Am. Fedn. State, County and Mcpl. Employees local #2836 Collective Bargaining Unit (treas. 1978, sec. 1986-92, v.p. 1992—, del. 1992, sec. Local 2836 1998—). Democrat. Home: 58 Mountain Rd Mansfield Center CT 06250-1211 Office: Ea Conn State Univ 83 Windham St Willimantic CT 06226-2211 Office Phone: 860-465-5369. Business E-Mail: enggas@easternct.edu.

ENGH, ANNA P., lawyer; BA cum laude, Davidson Coll., 1981; MEd, U. Va., 1982; JD first in class, Coll. William & Mary, 1989. Bar: Va. 1989, DC 1991. Law clk. for Judge John Butzner US Ct. Appeals (4th cir.); ptnr., Litig. Practice Group Covington & Burling, Washington, mem. mgmt. com. Mem.: Order of Coif. Office: Covington & Burling 1201 Pennsylvania Ave NW Washington DC 20004-2401 Office Phone: 202-662-5221. Office Fax: 202-662-6291. Business E-Mail: aengh@cov.com.

ENGISCH, TOSCA MARIANNE, artist, educator, social worker; b. N.Y.C., Sept. 5, 1943; d. Nickolas Grable and Mary Ann Messina; m. Alan Charles Engisch, Dec. 15, 1962; children: Kathrin Lin, Nicole Ann, Petra Marie, David Alan. At, County Coll. Morris, Randolph, N.J., 1970—79; BA in Art and Gerontology, Coll. St. Elizabeth, Convent Sta., N.J., 1986; MA in Painting, U. Dallas, Irving, Tex., 2004. Bd. cert. gerontol. social worker N.J. Display mgr. Kresge's Dept. Store, Newark, 1961—62; instr. drawing and painting Jefferson Twp. Schs. Continuing Edn., NJ, 1977—78; recreation staff State Psychiat. Hosp., Greystone Park, 1977—79; activities dir. Adult Day Care Ctr., Morris, 1986—89; social worker Morris County Social Svcs., 1989—95; instr. children's art Tarrant Arts Coun., Bedford, Tex., 2001—02; instr. continuing edn. art U. Tex., Arlington, 2005—. Reviewer arts grants and awards Tarrant Area Arts Coun., Tex., 2000—; painter; photographer. Organizer child day care ctr. Star of Sea Cath. Ch., NJ, 1975, mem. social justice com. NJ, 1975; membership com. LWV, NJ, 1970—78, mem. publicity com. NJ, 1970—78; mem. bd. summer recreation program Jefferson PTA, NJ, 1974, 1975, 1980; bd. mem. Tarrant County Arts Coun., Tex., 1997—99. Grantee, Arts Ala Carte, 1980, Dover Arts Assn., 1980; scholar, St. Elizabeth's Coll., 1985, U. Dallas, Irving, 2002—04. Mem.: Am. Portrait Soc., Trinity Art Guild (pres. 2006—), Christians in Visual Arts. Roman Catholic. Avocations: hiking, photography, classical guitar. Home: 6205 Cascade Cir Watauga TX 76148-2128

ENGLAND, LYNNE LIPTON, lawyer, pathologist; b. Youngstown, Ohio, Apr. 11, 1949; d. Sanford Y. and Sally (Kentor) Lipton; m. Richard E. England, Mar. 5, 1977. BA, U. Mich., 1970; MA, Temple U., 1972; JD, Tulane U., 1981. Bar: Fla. 1982, U.S. Dist. Ct. (mid. dist.) Fla. 1982, U.S. Ct. Appeals (11th cir.) 1982; cert. clin. competence in speech pathology and audiology. Speech pathologist Rockland Children's Hosp., N.Y., 1972-74, Jefferson Parish Sch., Gretna, La., 1977-81; audiologist Rehab. Inst. Chgo., 1974-76; assoc. Trenam, Simmons, Kemker, Scharf, Barkin, Frye & O'Neill, Tampa, Fla., 1981-84; asst. U.S. atty. for Middle Dist. Fla. Tampa, 1984-87; asst. U.S. trustee, 1987-91; ptnr. Stearns, Weaver, Miller, Weissler, Alhadeff & Sitterson, P.A., 1991-94, Prevatt, England & Taylor, Tampa, Fla., 1994-99; pvt. practice Brandon, Fla., 1999—. Editor Fla. Bankruptcy Casenotes, 1983. Recipient clin. assistantship Temple U., 1972-74. Mem. Comml. Law League, Am. Speech and Hearing Assn., Tampa Bay Bankruptcy Bar Assn. (dir. 1990-95), Am. Bankruptcy Inst., Fla. Bar Assn., Hillsborough County Bar Assn., Order of Coif. Jewish. Avocations: tennis, golf, playing french horn and piano. Office: 1463 Oakfield Dr Ste 125 Brandon FL 33511-0802 Office Phone: 813-661-6464. Business E-Mail: englandlawoffice@aol.com.

ENGLE, CAROLE RUTH, aquaculture economics professor; b. Harrisburg, Pa., July 7, 1952; d. Morris Mumma Engle and Mildred Evelyn (Orris) Wambold; m. Nathan Mayhew Stone, May 30, 1981; children: Reina, Eric, Cody. BA, Friends World Coll., 1975; MS, Auburn U., 1978, PhD, 1981. Vis. prof. U. Centroamericana, Managua, Nicaragua, 1981-83; fisheries economist Inter-Am. Devel. Bank, Santiago, Panama, 1984-85; asst. prof. econs. Auburn U., Montgomery, Ala., 1985-88; assoc. prof. aquaculture econs. U. Ark., Pine Bluff, 1988-94, prof., 1994—; dir., Aguacultural Fisheries Ctr., U. Ark., Pine Bluff, 1989—. Aquaculture coord. U. Ark., Pine Bluff, 1989—; cons. FAO, Rome, 1986, 88. Contbr. articles to profl. jours.; editor conf. proceedings. Mem. World Aquaculture Soc., Am. Fisheries Soc., Am. Assn. Agriculture Econs., So. Agriculture Econs. Assn., Ark. Acad. Scis. Avocations: gardening, reading, swimming. Office: U Ark PO Box 108 1200 University Dr Pine Bluff AR 71601-2799 Business E-Mail: cengle@uaex.edu.

ENGLE, JANE, research nurse, artist, chaplain; b. L.A., June 15, 1942; d. John Dean and Florence (Updike) E. BA with honors, U. N.C., Chapel Hill, 1965; BSN, Cornell U., Ithaca, N.Y., 1970; MS in Nursing, U. Ill., Chgo., 1974; MDiv magna cum laude, Wesley Theol. Sem., 1988. RN Md. Tchr., vol., trainer Peace Corps, Afghanistan, 1965—68; pub. health nurse Tufts Delta Health Ctr., Mound Bayou, Miss., 1969; coord. pub. health nursing Ill. Cmty. Clinic, Chgo., 1970—72; nursing cons. rsch. edn. Dept. Pub. Health, Chgo., 1974—78; rsch. nurse AIDS, NIH, Bethesda, Md., 1989—97; abstract artist and paper maker, 1997—; hosp. chaplain, 2002—. Mem. AIDS task force Interfaith Conf. Met. Washington, 1988-90. Author: Outcome Measures in Home Care, 1987, Immune-Based Therapy for HIV, 1996; contbr. article to profl. jours. Vol. homeless agys.; v.p. women's bd. Episcopal Ch., Washington, 1981—82; mem. bd. deacons Nat. Presbyn. Ch., Washington, 1982—86; mem. Mayor's Task Force on Standards, Washington, 1985—87, Foundry Gallery, Washington, 2001. Wesley Theol. Sem. Biblical scholar, 1988; named Person of Week Washington Times, 1992; recipient award for excellence in painting, 2000, The Ethel Lorraine Bernstein Meml. award for excellence in painting Corcoran Coll. Art and Design, 2000. Mem. ANA (pres. local chpt. 1976-78), Assn. Nurses in AIDS Care, Phi Beta Kappa, Sigma Theta Tau. Democrat.

ENGLE, JEANNETTE CRANFILL, medical technician; b. Davie County, N.C., July 7, 1941; d. Gurney Nathaniel and Versie Emmaline (Reavis) Cranfill; m. William Sherman Engle (div. 1970); children: Phillip William, Lisa Kaye. Diploma, Dell Sch. Med. Tech., 1960; BA, U. N.C., Asheville, 1976; MS in Biomed. Sci.-Genetics, Marshall U., 1999. Instr. Dell Sch. Med. Tech., Asheville, 1960-67; rotating technologist Meml. Mission Hosp., Asheville, 1967-68, asst. supr. hematology, 1968-71; supr. Damon Subs. Pvt. Clinic Lab., Asheville, 1971-73; chemistry technologist VA Med. Ctr., Durham, N.C., 1973-74, 75-76, supr., 1974-75, asst. supr. microbiology Salem, Va., 1976-79; supr. rsch. Med. Svc. Lab., Salem, 1979-90; flow cytometrist VA Med. Ctr., Huntington, W.Va., 1990-92, cons. to clin. lab. flow cytometry dept., 1992—. Reviewer Jour. Club, Roanoke-Salem, Va., 1980-90. Author: (poem) Reflections on a Comet, 1984; contbr. numerous articles and abstracts on med. tech. to profl. jours., 1982—. Mem. The Acting Co. Ensemble. Democrat. Episcopalian. Avocations: reading, flower arranging, interior design, art, music. Home: 4775 Green Valley Rd Huntington WV 25701-9793 E-mail: jeaengle@aol.com.

ENGLE, KATHLEEN FAYE, elementary education educator; b. Rapid City, SD, July 8, 1958; d. Frank Denton and Marie Lucille (Coffield) Packard; m. Steven S. Engle, June 1, 1984; children: Kirstin Marie, Kalin Kathleen. BS in Edn., Black Hill State Coll., 1980. Tchr. physical edn. Campbell County Sch. Dist., Gillette, Wyo., 1980-84, Weston County Sch. Dist., Newcastle, Wyo., 1985—. Mem. evaluatin team Conestiga Rep., Gillette, 1982-83; mem. adv. team Newcastle Mid. Sch., 1981—, evaluation team, 1992—. Middle Sch. Physical Edn. Teacher or the Year, Nat. Assn. for Sport & Phys. Edn., 1995. Mem. Wyo. Edn. Assn., Wyo. Alliance Physical Edn. Health Recreation and Dance, Wyo. Coaching Assn., Newcastle Edn. Assn., Delta Kappa Gamma. Avocations: aerobics, weightlifting. Office: Newcastle Mid Sch 116 Casper Ave Newcastle WY 82701-2705

ENGLE, MARY ALLEN ENGLISH, retired physician; b. Madill, Okla., Jan. 26, 1922; d. Russell C. and Vera (Apperson) English; m. Ralph Landis Engle, Jr., June 7, 1945 (dec. Oct. 2000); children: Ralph Landis III (dec.), Marilyn Elizabeth. AB cum laude, Baylor U., Waco, Tex., 1942; MD, Johns Hopkins U., Balt., 1945; D.Sc. (hon.), Iona Coll., New Rochelle, N.Y., 1982. Diplomate: in pediatric cardiology Am. Bd. Pediatrics. Intern pediatrics Johns Hopkins Hosp., 1945-46, asst. dir. pediatrics out-patient dept., 1946-47, fellow pediatric cardiology, 1947-48; instr. pediatrics Johns Hopkins U., 1946-48; asst. resident Sydenham Hosp. Contagious Diseases, Balt., 1946, N.Y. Hosp., 1948-49, asst. attending pediatrician, 1952-60, assoc. attending pediatrician, 1960-62, attending pediatrician, 1962-92, hon. staff, 1992—; fellow in pediatrics Cornell U., N.Y.C., 1949-50, mem. faculty, 1950-92, prof., 1969-92, prof. emeritus, 1992—, Stavros S. Niarchos prof. pediatric cardiology, 1979-92, emeritus, 1992—. Med. dir. Insts. in Care Premature Infant, 1952-55, dir. pediatric cardiology, 1963-92. Recipient Spence-Chapin award for contbns. to pediatrics, 1958, award of merit Philoptochos Soc. N. and S. Am., 1978, Woman of Conscience award Nat. Council Women, 1979, citation Nat. Bd. Med. Coll. Pa., 1979, Disting. Achievement award Baylor U., 1981, Disting. Alumna award Baylor U., 1988, Maurice Greenberg Disting. Svc. award N.Y. Hosp.-Cornell Med. Ctr., 1991; hon. fellow Cornell U. Med. Coll. Alumni, 1984; Mary Allen Engle Div. Pediatric Cardiology, N.Y. Hosp.-Cornell U. Med. Coll. dedicated in her honor, 1992, Johns Hopkins U. Soc. Scholars award, 1992, Alumni Assoc. Detlev Bronk award, 1993, Disting. Alumna award, 2002. Mem. Am. Acad. Pediat. (charter mem. sect. cardiology, Founder's award cardiology sect. 1983), Am. Clin. and Climatological Assn. (recorder 1992-2000, pres. 2003-04), Am. Heart Assn. (bd. dirs. 1975-78, award of merit 1975, Helen B. Taussig award 1976), N.Y. Heart Assn. (bd. dirs. 1980-86), N.Y. Acad. Medicine, N.E. Pediatric Cardiology Soc., Harvey Soc., Soc. Pediatric Rsch., Assn. European Pediatric Cardiologists (corr.), Royal Soc. Medicine (bd. dirs. Found. 1983-92, hon. bd. dirs. 1992-2000), Am. Coll. Cardiology (master tchr. 1969, 73, 76, trustee 1974-79, bd. govs. 1990-94, pres. N.Y. State chpt. 1991-92, Theodore and Susan Cummings Humanitarian award 1973, 76), Am. Pediatric Soc., Pediatric Cardiology Soc. Greater N.Y., N.Y. Cardiology Soc. (bd. dirs., pres. 1986-87), Soc. Scholars, Phi Beta Kappa, Alpha Omega Alpha. Presbyterian.

ENGLE, SANDRA LOUISE, management consultant; b. Grand Haven, Mich., Aug. 5, 1949; d. J. Edward and Ethel Caroline (Westerhouse) E. AA, Muskegon Community Coll., 1969; BA in Bus. Adminstrn., Mich. State U., E. Lansing, 1971; postgrad., Mich. State U., 1984-86. Cert. project mgmt. profl. Clk. and dept. mgr. Meijers Inc., Muskegon, Grand Haven, Grand Rapids, Mich., 1971-74; ins. agt. Prudential Ins. Co., Muskegon, 1974; bookkeeper Muskegon Correctional Facility, 1974-75; bus. office mgr. Kent County Dept. of Social Svcs., Grand Rapids, Mich., 1975-76; budget and fin. dir. Mich. Dept. of Licensing and Regulation, Lansing, 1976-86; mgmt. svcs. div. dir. Mich. Dept. of State, Lansing, 1986-87; dept. svcs. area dir. Mich. Dept. of Edn., Lansing, 1987; dep. bur. dir. Mich. Dept. of Labor, Lansing, 1987-89; asst. treas. Mich. Employment Security Commn., Detroit, 1989-90; dir. adm. svcs. Mich. Dept. Labor, Lansing, 1990-93; dir. budget devel. and info. Mich. Dept. Mgmt. and Budget, Lansing, 1993-98; sr. mgr. info. tech. Spectrum-Mazimus divsn. Maximus, Inc., Austin, Tex., 1998—. Bd. dirs. R.E. Olds Transp. Mus., 1989. Mem. Humane Soc. of U.S., World Wildlife Fund. Avocations: autocross, gardening. Home: 2533 E Ellis Rd Muskegon MI 49444-8703 Office: Maximus Inc 2800 S IH Ste 160 Austin TX 78704 E-mail: sandraengle@mazimus.com.

ENGLEMAN CONNORS, ELLEN G., federal agency administrator; b. Indpls., Sept. 21, 1959; BA in Eng. and Comm., Ind. U., 1983, JD, 1987; MPA, Harvard U., 1994. Bar: Ind. 1987, U.S. Dist. Ct. (no. and so. dists.) 1987. Pub. affairs exec. GTE, 1987—92; pres., CEO Electricore, Ind., 1994—2001; adminstr. rsch. and spl. programs adminstrn. U.S. Dept. Transp., Washington, 2001—03; mem. Nat. Transp. Safety Bd. (NTSB), Washington, 2003—, chmn., 2003—05. Dir. Corporate & Govt. Affairs, Direct Relief Internat., 1993—94. Bd. dirs. Direct Relief Internat., dir. corp. & govt. affairs. Lt. USNR, 1999—. Recipient Disting. Pub. Svc. award, USCG, 9/11 medal, U.S. Dept. Transp., 2003 Laurel, Aviation Week. Mem.: Pub. Rels. Soc. Am. (cert. pub. rels.). Office: NTSB Headquarters 490 L'Enfant Plaza SW Washington DC 20594

ENGLER, DEANNA K., science educator; b. Long Island, N.Y., Apr. 2, 1965; d. Robert J. and Verne L. Healy; m. Scott D. Engler, May 16, 2004; 1 child, Zachary Robert. BS in Biology, Seton Hall U., N.J., 1987; MS in Marine Sci., U. S.C., Columbia, 1990. Assoc. prof. Fla. Keys C.C., Tavernier, Fla., 1986—; asst. dir. edn. Marine Resources Devel. Found., Key Largo, 1993—99; tchr. Coral Shores H.S., Tavernier, 1999—. Recipient Monroe County Inclusion Tchr. of Yr., 2001, Coral Shores H.S. Inclusion Tchr. of Yr., 2001, 2005. Office: Coral Shores HS 89901 Old Hwy Tavernier FL 33070 Office Phone: 305-853-3222.

ENGLER, EVA KAY, dental and veterinary products company executive; b. Czechoslovakia, May 7, 1927; m. Alfred Engler (dec. 1979); children: Raya, Michael David. Pres., founder med. and dental mfg. co. Engler Engring. Corp., Hialeah, Fla., 1964—. Avocations: languages, painting. Office: Engler Engring Corp 1099 E 47th St Hialeah FL 33013-2139 Office Phone: 305-688-8581. Office Fax: 305-685-7671. Personal E-mail: eengler@bellsouth.net.

ENGLER, JENNIFER A., theater educator; b. Wichita, Kans., Aug. 14, 1973; d. Earl R. and Rhonda K. Carra; m. Paul W. Engler, Apr. 29, 2000; 1 child, Grant V. Associates, Butler County C.C., Kans., 1993; BFA, Emporia State U., Kans., 1995; MFA, Mich. State U., E. Lansing, 1998. Dance tchr. Young World Dance Studio, Wichita, 1989—95; grad. asst. Mich. State U., East Lansing, Mich., 1995—98; tchr. YMCA - Physical Therapy, Mpls., 1998—2000; prof. Minn. State U., Mankato, 2000—03, Tex. Christian U., Ft. Worth, 2003—. Selection com. mem. Kennedy Ctr. Am. Coll. Theatre Festival, 2000—03. Dir.: (plays, over 30 U. productions); (plays, profl. and regional theaters). Faculty senate mem. Tex. Christian U., Fort Worth, 2005—. Edinburgh Fringe Festival grant, Tex. Christian U., 2006. Mem.: Assn. Theatre in Higher Edn. Roman Cath. Avocations: knitting, jogging, puzzles, dance. Office: Tex Christian Univ Box 297510 Fort Worth TX 76129 Office Phone: 817-257-5043. Office Fax: 817-257-7344. Business E-Mail: j.engler@tcu.edu.

ENGLER, SHERRIE LEE, artist, illustrator; b. Paducah, Ky., July 9, 1962; d. Randell Ralph Teitloff and Patricia Frances Hobgood; m. Eric Andrew Engler, Oct. 11, 1996; 1 child, Chelsey Patrice. BS in Graphic Design, Ark. State U., Jonesboro, 1985. Equine artist Headed West, Greenfield, Tenn., 1985—. Equine illustration, Photos & Drawings for Equine Conformation &Anatomy, True Horse Stories Equine Research, Inc. Art scholar, Ark. State U., 1981—85. Master: Equine Arts Protection League (life; founder 2004—); mem.: Equine Art Guild (assoc.), N.Am. Artists Blue Book (life), Nat. Mus. Women in the Arts (assoc.). Home: 2797 Stafford Store Rd Greenfield TN 38230 Office: Headed West 2797 Stafford Store Rd Greenfield TN 38230 Office Phone: 731-235-3373. Business E-Mail: sales@horseartandgifts.com.

ENGLISH, CANDACE ALLEN, assistant principal; d. Paul Mills and Norma Petre Allen; m. Barry Gene English, May 12, 1997; 1 child, David Lloyd Lash. BA in Drama, U. Ga., Athens, 1980; MEd in Ednl. Adminstrn., Ga. State U., Atlanta, 1992, PhD in Ednl. Adminstrn., 2000. T-4 Cert. in English (grades 7-12) Ga. Bd. Edn., L-7 Leadership Cert. in Edn. Ga. Bd. Edn., 2000. Advt. sales KBIC Radio, Alice, Tex., 1983—84; purchasing supr. Hammond Industries, Huntsville, Ala., 1984—86; lead tchr., 9th grade Pebblebrook HS, Mableton, Ga., 1990—99; asst. prin. Griffin Mid. Sch., Smyrna, 1999—. Presenter/facilitator, paws discipline program Cobb County Schs., Marietta, 2005—. Contbr. articles to profl. jours. Sponsor, student leadership team (student coun.) Griffin Mid. Sch., 2000—. Grantee Dr. Kay Crouch scholarship, Kappa Delta Pi, Ga. State U., 1992—93, Henry H. Hill Laureate Doctoral scholarship, 1993. Mem.: Assn. Supervision and Curriculum Devel., Kiwanis, Phi Delta Kappa. Democrat. Roman Catholic. Avocations: hiking, reading, volunteer work. Office: Griffin Mid Sch 4010 King Springs Rd Smyrna GA 30082

ENGLISH, ERIN, secondary school educator; b. Bellflower, Calif., Jan. 18, 1977; d. William English, Jr. and Phyllis English. Student, Concordia U., Irvine, Calif., 1994—98. Single subject profl. clear tchg. credential life sci. Calif. Commn. on Tchr. Credentialling, 2001. Substitute tchr. Ctrl. Unified Sch. Dist., Fresno, Calif., 1999, h.s. sci. tchr., 1999—, dept. chair, 2004—. Bible class tchr. Clovis (Calif.) Ch. of Christ, 1999—2006. Recipient Hon. Chpt. FFA Degree, Nat. FFA Orgn., 2003. Office: Central Unified School District 2045 N Dickenson Ave Fresno CA 93722 Office Phone: 559-276-5276 225. Business E-Mail: eenglish@centralusd.k12.ca.us.

ENGLISH, EVONNE KLUDAS, artist; b. Cherokee, Iowa, Dec. 31, 1934; d. Earl Philip and Ruby Jacqueline (Whiting) Kludas; m. John Cammel English, July 29, 1966. BFA, Drake U., 1957; postgrad., U. No. Iowa, 1958—59; MFA, U. Iowa, 1962. Instr. h.s. & jr. h.s. art Sycamore Cmty. Unit Sch. Dist. 427, Sycamore, Ill., 1959-61; instr. art Wis. State U., Whitewater, 1962-63; asst. prof. art Stephen F. Austin State U., Nacogdoches, Tex., 1963-66. Instr. adult edn. Lawrence (Kans.) Arts Ctr., 1976; presenter in field. One woman shows include Sanford Mus., Cherokee, 1958, Cmty. Ctr., Cherokee, 1966, Baker U., Baldwin, Kans., 1971, 76, 7 East 7th Gallery, Lawrence, 1975-79, Unitarian Gallery, Kansas City, Mo., 1980, Kansas City Kans. Pub. Libr., 1984, Kans. U. Med. Ctr. Gallery of Art, Kansas City, Kansas, 1986, Lawrence Pub. Libr., 1986, 91, Baldwin State Bank, 1988, Lawrence C. of C., 1988, Galesburg (Ill.) Civic Art Ctr., 1988, Park Coll., Parkville, Mo., 1991, Sta. KSHB-TV, Kansas City, Mo., 1993, Art Affair, Baldwin, 1997; group exhbts. include Santa Fe Connection, Kansas City, 1979, Baker U., 1980, Kansas City Kansas Pub. Libr., 1995, Iowa Art Salon, 1957-59, 61-62, 65, Gallery Arkep, N.Y.C., 1965, George Walter Vincent Smith Art Mus., Springfield, Mass., 1965, Soc. Am. Graphic Artists, 1966, Galesburg Civic Art Ctr., 1983, Lawrence Arts Ctr., 1983, 97, Carrier Fine Arts Show, Belle Mead, N.J., 1984-85, 88, 90, 92, Gallery Lawrence, 1986, Hays (Kans.) Arts Coun., 1990, Hunterdon Art Ctr., Clinton, N.J., 1991, Wis. State U., Whitewater, 1962, Park Ctrl. Gallery, Springfield, Mo., 1976, Crown Ctr., Kansas City, Mo., 1979, Kellas Gallery, Lawrence, 1980-82, 84, Santa Fe Depot Ctr., 1985, Baldwin City Pub. Libr., 1993-95, Art Affair, Baldwin, 1996-98, 2002-06, Carnegie Ctr. for Arts, Dodge City, Kans., 2001, Carnegie Bldg., Lawrence, Kans., 2002, others; represented in permanent collections at Baker U., Baldwin, Spencer Mus. Art, U. Kans., others; designer bicentennial plate Baldwin City ofcl. seal, 1976. Panelist Spencer Mus. Art, Lawrence, 1978. Grantee State Wis. Bd. Regents State Colls., 1963, Lawrence Lithography Workshop 1988; recipient award Atchison Art Assn., 1997. Mem. Baldwin Cmty. Arts Coun. (sec. 1988-90, exhibit com. chair 1988-90), Delta Phi Delta. Unitarian Universalist. Avocation: photography. Studio: PO Box 537 Baldwin City KS 66006-0537

ENGLISH, MARLENE CABRAL, management consultant; b. Lawrence, Mass., Apr. 28, 1954; d. Amick John and Mary Rose (Vasconcelos) Cabral; m. Richard Gayle English, June 24, 1978. BBA, U. Mass., 1976. Acct. mgr. Revlon, Inc., N.Y.C., 1977—79; tech. rep. Rapidata, Inc., N.Y.C., 1979—80; mgr. acctg. sys. group Pannell, Kerr, Forster, Dallas, 1980—83; mgmt. cons. Blythe/Nelson, Dallas, 1983—84, Prism Cons., Arlington, Tex., 1984—. Sec., treas. Highland-Avery Industries, Inc., Dallas, 1988-95. Author: And God Created Woman, 1995. Tech. sys. procurement & installation Rep. Nat. Conv., Dallas, 1984; dir. Faith Harvest Ministries, Inc., Dallas, 1990-95; sys. cons. Van Cliburn Internat. Piano Competition, Ft. Worth, 1985 Roman Catholic. Avocations: history, antique linen restoration, gardening, writing, classical music. Home and Office: Prism Cons 4320 Rambling Creek Dr Arlington TX 76016-3418 Personal E-mail: jicky@sbcglobal.net.

ENGLISH, MILDRED OSWALT, retired nurse supervisor; b. Moberly, Mo., May 28, 1916; d. Oscar and Lulu (Street) Oswalt; m. Deaver English, Apr. 9, 1955. RN, Jewish Hosp. St. Louis Sch. Nursing, 1942; BS, U. N.C., 1952. RN, Tex. Pub. health nurse supr. Mo. Div. Health, Jefferson City, Mo., 1946-56; supervising pub. health nurse L.A. County Health Dept., 1957-67; sch. nurse Bonita Unified Sch. Dist., San Dimas, Calif., 1967-72; quality assurance coord. Moberly (Mo.) Regional Med. ctr., 1973-83; ret., 1983. Cmdr. Nurse Corps, USNR Ret., active duty 1943-46.

ENGLUND, GAGE BUSH, dancer, educator; b. Sept. 7, 1931; d. Morris Williams and Margaret Wallace (Gage) Bush; m. Richard Bernard Englund, Dec. 1, 1959; children: Alixandra Gage, Rachel Rutherford. Student, Sch. Am. Ballet, 1960. Founder Birmingham Civic Ballet, 1952; mem. Robert Joffrey Ballet, N.Y.C., 1957-60, soloist, 1959-60; mem. Am. Ballet Theatre, N.Y.C., 1960-63, Huntington Dance Ensemble, L.I., N.Y., 1968-69; soloist Dance Repertory Co., 1969-72; tchr. ballet, assoc. chmn. Friends of Am. Ballet Theatre, N.Y.C., 1972—. Dir. Ala. By-Products Corp., 1971—77; rehearsal coach Am. Ballet Theatre II, 1973—85; mem. scholarship com. Am. Ballet Theatre Sch., N.Y.C., 1974—; rehearsal coach Joffrey Ballet II, 1985—95, Am. Ballet Theatre Studio Co., 1995—. Trustee Ballet Theatre Found., 1974—87, v.p., 1980—81; trustee Chapin Sch., 1982—2003, Animal Med. Ctr., N.Y.C., 1982—, Cancer Rsch. Inst., 1984—, Episcpoal Sch. N.Y., 1979—83; bd. dirs. Children's Hosp. Clinic, Birmingham, 1955—57, Spoleto Festival, U.S.A., 1980—83, Ala. State Ballet, 1967—, Birmingham Civic Ballet, 1952—67. Named Queen, Birmingham Festival Arts, 1957; recipient Silver Bowl award, 1957, Lucia Chase award for svcs. to Am. Ballet Theatre, Soc. Fine Arts U. Ala., 2001, Patron of the Arts award, 2002; Ford Found. scholar, 1960. Mem.: Am. Guild Mus. Artists, Jr. League N.Y.C., Colonial Dames Ala., Colony Club, Lakewood Country Club. Episcopalian. Home: PO Box 469 17367 Scenic Hwy 98 Point Clear AL 36564

ENGOLIO, ELIZABETH ANN, lawyer; b. Baton Rouge, Feb. 4, 1979; d. Edward Nathaniel Engolio, Jr. and Beverly Labbe Engolio. BA magna cum laude, U. La., Lafayette, 2001; JD, So. U., Baton Rouge, La., 2004. Bar: La. 2005. Law clk. Edward N. Engolio, Atty. at Law, Plaquemine, La., 2003—05; law clk. dist. mgr.'s office' 18th Jud. Dist., Plaquemine, La., 2004—05; atty. Elizabeth A. Engolio, Atty. at Law, Plaquemine, La., 2005—; asst. dist. atty. Dist. Atty.'s Office, 18th Jud. Dist., Plaquemine, La., 2005—. Mem. leadership team St. John Youth Ministry, Plaquemine, La.; mem. evangelization team St. John the Evangelist Cath. Ch., Plaquemine, La., 2005—. Mem.: La. State Bar Assn., 18th Jud. Dist. Bar Assn. (scholarship 2002). Democrat. Roman Catholic. Office: Elizabeth A Engolio Atty at Law 23716 Railroad Ave Plaquemine LA 70764 Home: 23716 Railroad Ave Plaquemine LA 70764-3301 Office Phone: 225-687-8988. Office Fax: 225-687-1802. E-mail: elizabethengolio@yahoo.com.

ENGSTROM, JEAN, medical/surgical nurse; b. N.Y., Sept. 21, 1952; d. Elmer Eric and Gloria Ellen (Cote) E. AAS, Helene Fuld Sch. Nursing, 1978; BSN magna cum laude, Lehman Coll., Bronx, 1997. LPN Westchester County Med. Ctr., Valhalla, NY, 1971—77; RN Burke Rehab., White Plains, NY, 1978—80; staff nurse Bronx VA Med. Ctr., NY, 1980—83; with Thera Care Agy., NYC, 1997; sch. nurse PS 138 Bronx Dept. Edn., 1997—.

ENGSTROM, STEPHANIE CLOES, artist, small business owner; b. L.A., Nov. 1, 1943; d. John Augustus Cloes and Margaret Virginia Gerlach; m. Jean-Claude Louis Engstrom, Sept. 1, 1962 (div. 1967); children: Dominique Yvette Lubow, Denise Collette Engstrom. Student, UCLA, U. Md., USDA Grad. Sch. Broadband licensee, 1983—. Adminstrv. mgr. Microband Corp. Am., Washington, 1972-74; sr. mgmt. cons. various, 1976—. Tchr. Fairfax County Adult Edn., Vienna, Va., 1991-92, creativity workshop Guild Natural Sci. Illustrators Internat. Conf., Evora U., Portugal, 2000, Coll. of the Atlantic, Bar Harbor, Maine, 2001, Palos Verdes (Calif.) Art Ctr., 2001-04, Univ. Kans., Lawrence, 2002, Guild of Natural Sci. Illustrators; cofacilitator Artist's Way Sems. Borders Books & Music, Torrance, Calif., 1998. Cover artist: (book) International Studbook, Cheetah, Acinonyx jubatus, 1988; artist, writer Endangered Species Note Cards, 1986-90, Internat. Wildlife Rancher, 1989; juried group show Palos Verdes Art Ctr., 2000, 01, 02, 03, 04 (Artists Open Group People's Choice award 2000); solo show, The Distinctive Edge, 2001. Pres. PTA, Hermosa Beach, Calif., 1971-72; vol. Smithsonian, Washington, 1982-94; keeper aide Nat. Zool. Pk., Washington, 1985-90. Mem. Guild Nat. Sci. Illustrators (artist, writer newsletter 1988-89, 99—, pres. So. Calif. chpt. 2000-02, pres., 1999), Artists Open Group Palos Verdes Art Ctr. (prior v.p., pres. 2005—). Avocations: amateur naturalist, amateur animal behaviorist, writing poetry. Home and Office: 500 Avenue G Apt 25 Redondo Beach CA 90277-6002 Office Phone: 310-540-9867. E-mail: stephengstrom@yahoo.com.

ENOCHS, LORI M., science educator, department chairman; b. Orange, Calif., Feb. 7, 1969; d. Bob and Addie Jameson; m. James M. Enochs, July 28, 2001. BS, Azusa Pacific U., Calif., 1992. Cert. EMT LA County, Calif.; tchr. Calif., tchg. credential Assn. Christian Schs. Internat. Dept. mgr. Zee Med. Svc. Co., Ontario, Calif., 1986—97; care ptnr. UCLA Med. Ctr., Westwood, Calif., 1992—94; EMT, care ptnr. Western Med. Ctr. Anaheim, Anaheim, 1995—96; edn. dept. sec. Whittier (Calif.) Hosp. Med. Ctr., 1997—2000; sci. dept. chair Whittier Christian H.S., La Habra, Calif., 2000—. Hurdles coach Whittier Christian H.S., 2000—, EMT, 2000—, sr. class advisor, 2001—. Grantee, So. Calif. Credit Union, 2004. Mem.: Nat. Sci. Tchr. Assn., Calif. Sci. Tchr. Assn. (assoc.). Conservative. Methodist. Avocation: scrapbooks. Office: Whittier Christian HS 501 N Beach Blvd La Habra CA 90631 Office Phone: 562-694-3803. E-mail: lenochs@wchs.com.

ENOS, MINDY See PARSONS, MINDY

ENRIGHT, CYNTHIA LEE, illustrator; b. Denver, July 6, 1950; d. Darrel Lee and Iris Arlene (Flodquist) E. BA in Elem. Edn., U. No. Colo., Greeley, 1972; student, Minn. Sch. Art and Design, Mpls., 1975-76. Tchr. 3d grade Littleton Sch. Dist., Colo., 1972-75; graphics artist Sta. KCNC TV, Denver, 1978-79; illustrator No Coast Graphics, Denver, 1979-87; editorial artist The Denver Post, 1987—. Illustrator, editor "Tiny Tales" The Denver Post, 1991-94. Recipient Print mag. Regional Design Ann. awards, 1984, 85, 87, Phoenix Art Mus. Biannual award, 1979, third pl. Best of the West award for illustration, 2004. Mem. Mensa. Democrat. Home: 1210 Ivanhoe St Denver CO 80220-2640 Office: The Denver Post 101 W Colfax Ave Denver CO 80202-5177

ENRIGHT, STEPHANIE VESELICH, investment company executive, financial consultant; b. LA, Mar. 24, 1934; d. Stephen P. and Violet (Guthrie) Veselich; m. Robert James Enright (dec. Sept. 1982); children: Craig James, Brent Stephen, Erin Suzanne, Kyle Stephen. BA, U. So. Calif., LA, 1952, MS, 1975. Fin. and engring. cons. Orange County, Santa Ana, Calif., 1976—79; fin. cons. The Sim-Ehrflo Group, Newport Beach, Calif., 1979—81; pres. Enright Premier Wealth Advisors, Torrance, Calif., 1981—; fin. columnist Copley/Daily Breeze Newspaper, Torrance, Calif., 1982—. Adj. faculty mem. UCLA, U. So. Calif.; pres. Pacific Home Builders. Author: Family Wealth Counseling: Getting to the Heart of the Matter, 1999, Strictly Business, 2001; contbr. articles to profl. jours. Mem. Com. Assn. of the Peninsula, Palos Verdes, Calif., 1986; found. dir. Little Co. of Mary Hosp., Torrance; dir. endowment com. Pa. Art Assn.; adv. bd. Assistance League; bd. dirs. Pa. Symphony Soc., 1991, El Camino Coll. Found., Torrace Libr. Found.; adv. bd. Switzer Ctr. Bloombergs Top Wealth Mgnr., 2002-06. Mem. Fin. Planning Assn. (bd. dirs., officer 1982-84, Planner of Month award 1984), Nat. Assn. Women Owners, Nat. Assn. Fin. Edn., Registry Profl. Planners, Fin. Planning Assn., Torrance C. of C., Assistance League (bd. dirs. South Bay), Women in Constrn., Trojan Club and League (bd. dirs. 1978-79, 91—). Republican. Avocations: travel, writing. Office: 21515 Hawthorne Blvd Ste 1200 Torrance CA 90503-6517 Office Phone: 310-543-4559. Business E-Mail: senright@enrightpremier.com.

ENROTH-CUGELL, CHRISTINA ALMA ELISABETH, neurophysiologist, educator; b. Helsingfors, Finland, Aug. 27, 1919; came to US, 1956, naturalized, 1962; d. Emil and Maja (Syren) Enroth; m. David W. Cugell, Sept. 5, 1955. MD, Karolinska Inst., 1948, PhD, 1952; Hon. Doctors Degree, U. Helsinki, Finland, 1994. Resident in ophthalmology Karolinska Sjukhuset, 1949-52; intern Passavant Meml. Hosp., 1956-57; with Northwestern U., Evanston, Ill., 1959-91, prof. emeritus, 1991—, prof. dept. neurobiology and physiology and dept. biomed. engring., 1074—1978; mem. vision rsch. program com. Nat. Eye Inst., 1974-78, mem. nat. adv. eye coun., 1980-84. Contbr. articles to profl. jours. Recipient Ludwig von Sallman award Internat. Assn. Rsch. in Vision and Ophthalmology, 1982. Fellow Am. Inst. Med. and Biol. Engring., Am. Acad. Arts and Sci.; mem. Am. Assn. Rsch. in Vision and Ophthalmology (co-recipient Friedenwald award 1983, recipient W.H. Helmerich III award 1992), Soc. Neurosci., Am. Physiol. Soc., Physiol. Soc. (U.K.) Office: Northwestern U McCormick Sch Engring Technl Inst 2145 Sheridan Rd Evanston IL 60208-0834 Business E-Mail: enroth@northwestern.edu.

ENSIGN, JACQUELINE, social worker; b. Oakland, Calif., Sept. 14, 1931; d. John A. and Helene A. (Symons) London; m. Ernest F. Ensign, Nov. 28, 1957; children: Jane Ann, Susan Amy. BA, U. Calif., Berkeley, 1953, MSW, 1956. Social worker Jewish Family and Children's Service, Phoenix, 1963-70, St. Luke's Hosp., Phoenix, 1970-72; coordinator social services Boswell Hosp., Sun City, Ariz., 1976-84; case mgr. Sun City Area Agy. on Aging, 1985-86; pvt. practice social work Tempe, 1986—. Chmn. social work sub-com. Am. Cancer Soc., Phoenix, 1984-86. Mem. Berkeley Path Wanders Assn. (founder). Democrat. Avocations: swimming, hiking, gardening. Home: 1023 Shattuck Ave Berkeley CA 94707-2625

ENSLER, EVE, playwright, actress; b. NYC, May 25, 1953; m. Richard McDermott, 1978 (div. 1988); adopted stepson Dylan McDermott; life ptnr. Ariel Orr Jordan. BA, Middlebury Coll., Vt., 1975; LittD (hon.), Middlebury Coll., 2003. Founder V-Day, 1998; leader writing group Beford Hills Correctional Facility for Women, 1998—; faculty mem. Omega Inst. Playwright Coming From Nothing, The Vagina Monologues, 1997 (Obie Award, 1997), Necessary Targets, 2002, Conviction, Lemonade, The Depot, Floating Rhoda and the Glue Man, Extraordinary Measures, The Good Body, 2004, The Treatment, 2006; exec. prodr.: (documentaries) What I Want My Words to Do to You: Voices From Inside a Women's Maximum Security Prison, 2003; author: Vagina Warriors, 2005. Trustee PEN Am. Ctr., chair, Women's Com. Recipient Berrilla-Kerr Award playwriting, Elliot Norton Award outstanding solo performance, Jury Award theater, US Comedy Arts Festival, Media Spotlight Award for leadership, Amnesty Internat., 2002, Matrix Award, 2002; Guggenheim Fellowship in playwriting. Vagina Monologues has been translated into over 35 languages & enlists many celebrities as performers/activists. Mailing: PEN American Ctr 588 Broadway Ste 303 New York NY 10012 also: Omega Institute 150 Lake Dr Rhinebeck NY 12572*

ENSMINGER, MARGARET E., sociologist, researcher; b. Roanoke, Ala., July 5, 1942; d. Ross E. and Margaret Goodhue Ensminger; m. Sheppard G. Kellam, July 10, 1976. PhD, U. Chgo., 1978; BA, Earlham Coll., Richmond, Ind., 1964; MA, U. Nebraska, Omaha, 1972. Asst. prof. Ill. Inst. Tech., Chgo., 1978—82, Johns Hopkins U., Sch. Hygiene and Pub. Health, Balt., 1983—90, assoc. prof., 1991—98; prof. Johns Hopkins U., Bloomberg Sch. Pub. Health, 1999—. Contbr. articles to profl. jours. Bd. mem. Health Care All, Balt., 2005—06. Fellow: Coll. Problems Drug Dependence (life; bd. mem. 2001—05); mem.: Am. Sociol. Assn. Achievements include following a cohort of first grade students from 1966 to 2003. Office: The Johns Hopkins U 624 N Broadway Baltimore MD 21205-1900 Office Phone: 410-955-2308. E-mail: mensming@jhsph.edu.

ENTZI, KAREN RUSSELL, orchestra educator; d. John A. and Angeline Noe Russell; m. John A. Entzi, Jan. 4, 1989; 1 child, Angeline Lorraine Bumgardner. MusB, U. NC, Greensboro, 1973; MS in Tchg., N.W. Mo. State U., 1995. Tchr. Richland Dist. I and II, Columbia, SC; orch. tchr. Charlotte (NC) Mecklenburg Sch.; tchr. Lexington (SC) Sch. Dist. #2, Lancaster (SC) County Sch.; orch. tchr. Johnston County Sch., Smithfield, NC, 2002—, Cumberland County Schs., Fayetteville, NC. Condr. Johnston County Youth Orch., Smithfield, NC, 2003—; adj. tchr. violin U. NC, Pembroke. Musician: various profl. performances. Mem.: NC Music Educators Assn., Am. String Tchrs. Assn., Nat. String Orch. Assn. Home: 27 Due West Dr Leicester NC 28748 Office Phone: 919-345-6702. Personal E-mail: karenentzi@hotmail.com.

EPEL, LIDIA MARMUREK, dentist; b. Buenos Aires, Sept. 30, 1941; came to U.S., 1966; d. Israel and Ita Rosa (Sonabend) Marmurek; children: Diana, Bryan. BS, Buenos Aires U., 1959, DDS, 1964. Lic. dentist, N.Y. Gen. practice dentistry, Argentina, 1965-66, Long Beach, NY, 1967-70, Lynbrook, 1970—, Rockville Centre, 1973—. Bd. dirs. Rosa Lee Young Childhood Ctr., Rockville Centre, 1982-94, Rockville Centre Edn. Found., 1990—; mem. adv. com. on HIV/AIDS Bd. Edn. Rockville Centre Pub. Schs., 1994—; past pres. Queens-L.I. Women's Dental Study Group. Fellow Internat. Coll. Dentists, Pierre Fauchard Acad., Am. Coll. Dentistry, L.I. Acad. Odontology; mem. ADA (ho. of dels. 1996—, coun. membership 2002—, com. internat. programs of devel.), Fedn. Dentaire Internat., Nassau County Dental Soc. (bd. dirs., chair com. on pub. and profl. rels. 1990-96, chair com. on health, 1989-92, chair membership com. 1993, treas. exec. com. 1993, sec. exec. com. 1994, v.p. 1995, mem. membership task force 1994-95, pres-elect 1996, pres. 1997, dir. Greater L.I. dental meeting, chair, 2004), Overseas Dentist Assn. (pres. NY chpt. 1968-72), Dental Soc. of State of NY (coun. for pub. and profl. rels. 1990—, chair children's dental health month campaign 1991, chair mem. recruitment and retention 1995—, bd. govs. 1998—, chair reference com. 1998, mem. coun. on nominations 1998, coun. on constitutional by-laws 1999), NY State Dental Assn. (bd. govs. 1996—, exec. com. 2005), Coalition Against Domestic Violence (bd. dirs. 2000—), Hadassah (bd. dirs. Rockville Ctr. 1983-84, 92-93). Democrat. Jewish. Avocations: painting, travel. Office: 165 N Village Ave Rockville Centre NY 11570-3761 Office Phone: 516-766-6430.

EPHRON, NORA, writer; b. NYC, May 19, 1941; d. Henry and Phoebe (Wolkind) E.; m. Dan Greenburg (div.); m. Carl Bernstein (div.); children: Jacob, Max; m. Nicholas Pileggi. BA, Wellesley Coll., 1962. Reporter N.Y. Post, 1963-68; free-lance writer, 1968—; contbg. editor, columnist Esquire mag., 1972-73, sr. editor, columnist, 1974-78; contbg. editor N.Y. mag., 1973-74. Author: Wallflower at the Orgy, 1970, Crazy Salad, 1975, Scribble Scribble, 1978, Heartburn, 1983, Nora Ephron Collected, 1991, I Feel Bad About My Neck: And Other Thoughts on Being a Woman, 2006; screenwriter: (with Alice Arlen) Silkwood (nominated Acad. award for best original screenplay), 1983, Heartburn, 1986, Cookie, 1989, When Harry Met Sally (nominated Acad. award, BAFTA award for best screenplay), 1989, My Blue Heaven, 1990; dir., screenwriter (with Delia Ephron) This Is My Life, 1992, Mixed Nuts, 1994, Michael, 1996, You've Got Mail, 1998; co-screenwriter, dir. Sleepless in Seattle (nominated Acad. award for best original screenplay), 1993; prodr., dir. Lucky Numbers, 2000; screenwriter, prodr. Hanging Up, 2000; playwright Imaginary Friends, 2002; screenwriter, dir., Bewitched, 2005. Mem. Writers Guild Am., Authors Guild, Dirs. Guild of Am., Acad. Motion Picture Arts and Scis.*

EPP, DIANNE NAOMI, secondary school educator; b. Yankton, S.D., Oct. 1, 1939; d. Willard H. and Florence A. (Leigh) Waltner; m. Anthony R. Epp, Aug. 18, 1964; children: Alain-René Epp Weaver, Rachel Epp Buller. BA in Chemistry, Bethel Coll., 1961; MA, U. Mo., 1963; cert. etudes, L'Ecole d'Administration, Brussels, 1965. Chemistry instr. Bethel Coll., North Newton, Kans., 1963-64; sci. tchr. Ecole Secondaire, Sundi-Lutete, Zaire, 1965-67; rsch. chemist FMC Glass Lab., Golden, Colo., 1967-70; vis. instr. Nebr. Wesleyan U., Lincoln, 1973-74, 77-79, 1980-81; chemistry tchr. East High Sch., Lincoln, 1982—93, 1994—2005; vis. scholar Miami U., Oxford, Ohio, 1993-94. Cons. NSF Doing Chemistry Videodisc, 1988; cons. small scale CD ROM Synapse Corp., Lincoln, 1993. Author: Chemical Manfacturing: The Process of Mixing, 2000, Experimental Design: The Chemistry of Adhesives, 1998, Product Testing: The Chemistry of Ice Cream, 1998; cons. editor: Starting at Ground Zero, 1989; author: (monograph series) A Palette of Color, 1995; contbr. articles to profl. jours. Recipient Excellence in Teaching award Cooper Found., 1990, Excellence in High Sch. Chemistry Teaching award Am. Chem. Soc., 1990, 91, Presdl. award for Excellence in Sci. and Math. Teaching NSF, 1994, Kiewit Found. Tchg. award, 1997, 01, Christa McAuliffe award, 2005. E-mail: depp@huskeraccess.com.

EPPERSON, STELLA MARIE, artist; b. Oakland, Calif., Nov. 6, 1920; d. Walter Peter and Martha Josephine (Schmitt) Ross; m. John Cray Epperson, May 10, 1941; children: Therese, John, Peter. Student, Calif. Coll. Arts & Crafts, 1939, 40-41, 56; postgrad., Art Inst., San Miguel d'Allende, Mex., 1972. Portrait artist Oakland Art Assn., 1956—, San Francisco Women Artists, 1962—, Marin Soc. Artists, Ross, Calif., 1971—. Art docent Oakland Mus., 1969-71, mem. women's bd., 1971—, art chmn. fund raiser, 1971-89, art guild chmn., 1965-69, chmn. exhbt. Japanese artists in Brazil, Kaiser Ctr., Oakland, for honoring artist Xavier Martinez, event honoring Neil Armstrong, Calif. Coll. Arts and Crafts. One-woman shows include Oakland Mus. Auction, 1993, Univ. Club, San Francisco, 1994; exhbns. include Women's Art Gallery, San Francisco, Kaiser Ctr., St. Mary's Coll. Hearst Gallery, numerous others; commd. portrait Mrs. Evangelina Macapagal, Malacalang Palace. Recipient San Francisco Women Artists, 1989, Oakland Art Assn., 1991, 1997, 2000, Marin Soc. Artists, 1992, Figurative Subject First award, Oakland Art Assn. Mem. Oakland Art Assn. (1st award in small format show 1998, 1999 Artistic award in Kaiser Ctr. Gallery Exhibit, Merit award 2000, Artistic award 2001), San Francisco Women Artists, Marin Art Assn., U. Calif. Berkeley Faculty Club, Orinda Country Club. Republican. Roman Catholic. Avocations: dress design, gourmet cooking, tennis. Home: 31 Valley View Rd Orinda CA 94563-1432

EPPICH, LOIS KATHLEEN, science educator; b. Morristown, NJ, June 22, 1952; m. John Henry Eppich; children: Katherine, John Edward. BS in elem. edn., Ft. Hays State U., 1974; MS in geosciences, Miss. State U., 2004. Tchr. Unified Sch. Dist., Goodland, Kans., 1977, Miami Sch., Amoret, Mo., 1980—82, Unified Sch. Dist., Cunningham, Kans., 1982—84, Dodge City Cmty. Coll., 1988; sci. tchr. St. Peter and Paul Sch., Seneca, Kans., 1988—. Brownie and jr. leader Girl Scouts Am., 1985—90; cub scout asst. with badge work Boy Scouts Am., 1990—. Mem.: Kans. Assn. Tchrs. of Sci., Nat. Sci. Tchrs. Assn., Delta Kappa Gamma. Avocations: reading, crocheting, hiking. Office: 401 Pioneer St Seneca KS 66538

EPPLEY, FRANCES FIELDEN, secondary school educator, writer; b. Knoxville, Tenn., July 18, 1921; d. Chester Earl and Beulah Magnolia (Wells) Fielden; m. Gordon Talmage Cougle, July 25, 1942; children: Russell Gordon Eppley, Carolyn Eppley Horseman; m. Fred Coan Eppley, Mar. 8, 1953; 1 child, Charlene Eppley Sellers. BA in English, Carson Newman Coll., 1942; MA, Winthrop U., 1963. Tchr. East Corinth (Maine) Acad., 1942-43, pub. schs., Charlotte, NC, 1950-53, 59-83, Greenville, SC, 1954-56, Spartanburg, SC, 1957-58; Head Start tchr., summers 1964-68. Author: First Baptist Church: Its Heritage, 1982, Flint Hill Church, 1984, Religion and Astrology, 1991, Astrology and Prophecy, 1992, Sammy's Song, Jericho, Aunt Lillian's Sea Foam Candy, The First Astrologer, 1993, The Story of William Fielden, 1998, Search for an Ancestor, 1999, Christmas Magnus, Stella and the Sitting Stone, Messiah, An Immediate Family, 1999, The Signs of Your Life, 2000, Another Mary, 2000, The Winter Solstice, 2001, Of Course Your Child Can Read!, 2002, Columbus: The Race Home, 2003, Canada Trilogy, 2003;: To A Japanese Friend, 2002, Wacky Kings and Mystic Things, 2003, The Yellow River, 2003, To A Japanese Friend, 2004. Mem. hist. com. N.C. Bapt. Conv., 1985-88. Alpha Delta Kappa Grantee, 1970. Mem. NEA, N.C. Social Studies Conf., Writers Assn., Alpha Delta Kappa, Pi Kappa Delta, Alpha Psi Omega. Baptist. Mailing: 1421 Delane Ave Apt 5N Charlotte NC 28211

EPPOLITO, MARY, assistant principal, educator; b. Bklyn., Feb. 10, 1975; d. Nicholas Joseph and Maria Silecchia; m. Joseph Eppolito Jr., Aug. 5, 2000. BA in Elem. Edn. magna cum laude, Bklyn. Coll., 1997; MS in Reading, Adelphi U., 1999; profl. diploma, L.I. U., 2003. Cert. sch. adminstr. N.Y., 2003, elem. edn. N.Y., 1997, reading specialist N.Y., 1999. Reading specialist Monroe-Woodbury Ctrl. Sch. Dist., Central Valley, NY, 2000—03; elem. asst. prin. Minisink Valley Ctrl. Sch. Dist., Slate Hill, 2003—05; asst. prin. Monroe-Woodbury Sch. Dist., 2005—. Adj. prof. SUNY, New Paltz, 2003—04, Rockland Tchrs. Ctr., 2004—. Mem.: Golden Key Honor Soc., Kappa Delti Pi (life Honors in Edn. 1997). Roman Catholic. Avocation: travel.

EPPS, ANNA CHERRIE, immunologist, educator, dean; b. New Orleans, July 8, 1930; d. Ernest and Anna L. (Johnson) Cherrie; m. Joseph M. Epps, Sr., Nov. 23, 1968. BS, Howard U., 1951, PhD, 1966; MS, Loyola U., New Orleans, 1959. Technologist clin. lab. dept. Our Lady of Mercy Hosp., Cin., 1953-54; asst. prof., acting chmn. dept. med. tech. Xavier U., New Orleans, 1954-60; technologist dept. medicine La. State U. Sch. Medicine, New Orleans, 1954-60; asst. prof. microbiology Coll. Medicine Howard U., Washington, 1961-69; fellow dept. medicine Sch. Medicine Johns Hopkins U., Balt., 1969; asst. prof., USPHS faculty fellow dept. medicine Tulane U. Sch. Medicine, New Orleans, 1969-71, assoc. prof., 1971-75, prof., 1975—97, assoc. dean student svcs., 1970—97; dir. med. edn. reinforcement and enrichment program Tulane U. Med. Ctr., New Orleans, 1969—97; acting dean, v.p. acad. affairs Meharry Med. Coll., Nashville, 1994—96, dean sch. med., sr. v.p. acad. affairs, 1997—2002, dean emerita, sr. advisor to pres., 2002—. Co-author: Medrep, Tulane U.; co-editor: Medical Education: Responses to a Challenge; mem. editorial bd. Jour. Med. Edn., 1980—; contbr. articles to med. jours. Trustee Children's Hosp., New Orleans, 1977-79; regent Georgetown U., Washington, 1975—; bd. dirs. Diabetes Assn. Greater New Orleans, 1978; mem. La. Bd. Health and Rehab. Svcs., 1972; adv. mem. Kellogg Nat. Fellowship Program, 1981. Recipient award for meritorious rsch. Interstate Postgrad. Med. Assn. N.Am., 1966, Scroll of Merit, Nat. Med. Assn., 1980, Herbert W. Nickens award, AAMC, 2003. Mem. Am. Soc. Clin. Pathologists (cert. in med. tech. and blood banking), Am. Soc. Med. Technologists, Am. Assn. Blood Banks (cert. in blood banking), Am. Soc. Tropical Medicine and Hygiene, AAUP, Musser-Burch Soc., Albertus Magnus Guild, Washington Helminthol. Soc., Am. Soc. Bacteriologists, Sigma Xi. Home: 769 Sinclair Cir Brentwood TN 37027-2921 Office: Meharry Med Coll 1005 D B Todd Blvd Nashville TN 37208 Office Phone: 615-327-5935. Business E-Mail: acepps@mmc.edu.

EPPS, MISCHA BUFORD, lawyer; b. El Reno, Okla., 1969; BA cum laude, Washington U.; JD, U. Austin, 1994. Bar: Mo. 1994, US Dist. Ct., We. Dist. of Mo., Kans. 1999, US Dist. Ct., Dist. of Kans. Ptnr. Shook, Hardy & Bacon LLP, Kansas City, Mo. Bd. dirs. Legal Aid of Western Mo., JCBA Found., Cleveland Ave. Bapt. Ch. Mem.: Kans. Bar Assn., Jackson County Bar Assn., Nat. Bar Assn. (President's Award 2003), Kansas City Met. Bar Assn. (Young Lawyer of Yr. 2003). Office: Shook, Hardy & Bacon LLP 2555 Grand Blvd Kansas City MO 64108 Office Phone: 816-559-2500. Office Fax: 816-421-5547. E-mail: mepps@shb.com.

EPPS, ROSELYN ELIZABETH PAYNE, pediatrician, educator; b. Little Rock, Dec. 11, 1930; d. William Kenneth and Mattie Elizabeth (Beverly) Payne; m. Charles Harry Epps, Jr., June 25, 1955; children: Charles Harry III (dec.), Kenneth Carter, Roselyn Elizabeth, Howard Robert. BS, Howard U., 1951, MD, 1955; MPH, Johns Hopkins U., 1973; MA, Am. U., 1981. Intern Freedmen's Hosp., Howard U., Washington, 1955-56, pediatric resident, 1956-59, chief resident, 1958-59; practice medicine specializing in pediatrics Washington, 1960; med. officer, pediatrics D.C. Dept. Pub. Health, Washington, 1961-64, dir. Clinic for Retarded Children, 1964-67, chief Infant and Pre-Sch. div., 1967-71, dir. children and youth project, 1970-71, dir. maternal and crippled children services, 1971-75; chief Bur. Clin. Services D.C. Dept. Human Services, Washington, 1975-80, acting commr. pub. health, 1980; instr., asst. research investigator Howard U. Coll. Medicine, Washington, 1960-61, prof. Dept. Pediatrics and Child Health, 1980-98, chief divsn. child devel., dir., 1985-89, dir. Child Devel. Ctr., 1985-89; rsch. assoc., vis. scientist smoking tobacco and cancer program, div. cancer prevention and control Nat. Cancer Inst. NIH, Washington, 1989-91; expert Nat. Cancer Inst. NIH, Pub. Health Applications Br., Bethesda, Md., 1991-97; scientific program adminstr. Nat. Cancer Inst. Pub. Health Applications Branch, Bethesda, Md., 1997-98; med. pub. hlth cons., 1998—; sr. program advisor for women's health programs Women's Health Inst., Howard U., Wash., 1999—. Chmn. task force to prepare comprehensive child care plan for D.C. Dept. Human Services, 1973-74; mem. nat. task force on pediatric hypertension Heart, Lung and Blood Inst., NIH, 1975; chmn. rsch. grants rev. com. maternal and child health and crippled children's svcs. HEW, Rockville, Md., 1978-80; sec. Commn. Licensure to Practice Healing Arts, Washington, 1980; trustee med. svc. D.C. Blue Shield Plan Nat. Capital Area, 1980; chmn. sec.'s adv. com. on rights and responsibilities of women HEW, Washington, 1981; dir. high-risk young people's project Howard U. Hosp., 1981-85; Washington coord. Know Your Body Program Am. Health Found., N.Y.C., 1982-91; mem. bd. advs. Coll. Home Econs. Ohio State U., Columbus, Ohio, 1983-87; adv. com. Nat. Ctr. for Edn. in Maternal and Child Health Georgetown U., Washington, 1983-89; nat. steering com., subcom. chmn. Healthy Mothers, Healthy Babies Coalition, Washington, 1983-90, mem. nominating com., 1991; cons. sickle cell disease NIH, 1984-88, Govt. Liberia and World Bank, 1984, UN Fund for Population Activities, N.Y. and Caribbean, 1984, filmstrip Miriam Berg Varian/Parents Mag. Films, 1978; bd. dirs. Vis. Nurse Assn., Inc., Washington, 1983-89; pres. bd. dirs. Hosp. for Sick Children, Washington, 1986-90, bd. dirs., 1984-94; frequent guest lectr. Weekly columnist Your Child's Health, Afro-Am. Newspaper, Washington, 1960-63; contbr. articles syndicated column Nat. Newspaper Pubs. Assn., 1982, Nat. Newspaper Assn., 1986-87; co-author audiocassettes; exhibitor sci. program; exhibit: Women Chage the Faces of Medicine; contbr. more than 90 articles to profl. jours. US trustee Children's Internat. Summer Villages, Casstown, Ohio, 1969—76, pres., 1974—75; trustee nat. bd. Palmer Meml. Inst., Sedalia, NC, 1969—71, Ford's Theater, Washington, 1973—79; bd. mgrs. YWCA of DC, 1970—83, vice chmn., 1975—76; v.p. Jack and Jill of Am., Inc., Washington, 1970—71; nat. bd. dir. Ctr. Population Options, Washington, 1980—86, Alexander Graham Bell Assn. for Deaf, Washington, 1974—78; bd. dir. Washington Performing Arts Soc., 1971—81, v.p., 1979—81, hon. dir., 1981—. Recipient Leadership and Meritorious Service in Medicine award Palmer Meml. Inst., 1968, 14th Ann. Fed. Women's award CSC, Washington, 1974, Superior Performance award D.C. Govt., 1975, Meritorious Community Service award Howard U. Sch. Social Work Alumni Assns. and vis. com., 1980, Cert. Commendation Mayor of DC, 1981, Roselyn Payne Epps M.D. Recognition Resolution of 1983 Council DC, 1983, Disting. Vol. Leadership award March of Dimes Birth Defects Found., 1984, Community Svc. award DC Hosp. Assn., 1990, Physician of Yr. award Women's Med. Assn. N.Y.C., 1990, 91; named Outstanding Vol. in Leadership category YWCA Nat. Capital Area, 1983; inducted into DC Women's Hall of Fame DC Commn. for Women, 1990, Hall of Fame, DC, 2005; grantee Robert Wood Johnson Found., Princeton, N.J., 1982, dir. maternal and child health HHS, Rockville, Md., 1986; honored Tribute Resolution of 1981 declaring Feb. 14 Dr. Roselyn Payne Epps Day, Council of D.C., 1981; recipient Ophelia Settle Egypt award Planned Parenthood of Met. Washington, 1991, Advocacy award Soc. Advancement Women's Health, 1996, Horizon award Nat. Assn. Negro Bus. and Profl. Women's Clubs, 1999, Dorothy I Height award, Nat. Coun. of Negro Women, 2001, Lifetime Achievement award, Girls Inc., 2003. Fellow Am. Acad. Pediatrics (alt. state chmn. D.C. 1973-75, exec. com. D.C. chpt. 1983-94, pres. D.C. chpt. 1988-91, sec. cmty. pediatrics sect. 1973-75, cert. appreciation 1979, mem. coun. of child and adolescent health, cmty. and internat. health sect., charter mem., exec. com. 1992-94); mem. Acad. Medicine, AMA (alt. del. Nat. Med. Assn. 1983-85), Am. Med. Women's Assn. (chmn. pub. health com. 1973-75, pres. br. 1 1974-76, sec. 1988, v.p. 1989, pres-elect nat. 1990, pres. 1991, found. founding pres. 1992, bd. dirs. 1992-97, chmn. nominating com. 1993, Physician of Yr. award 1991, Cmty. Svc. award 1990, Elizabeth Blackwell award 1992), Women's Forum Washington, Med. Soc. D.C. (exec. bd. 1990, sec. 1990, pres.-elect 1991, pres. 1992, chair exec. bd. 1993, ann. Cmty. Svc. award 1982), Am. Pediatric Soc., D.C. Hosp. Assn. (Cmty. Svc. award 1990), Am. Pub. Health Assn. (action bd. 1977-79, joint policy com. 1978-79, gov. council 1978-81), Met. Washington Pub. Health Assn. (gov. council 1975-78, 81-83, ann. award 1981), Nat. Med. Assn. (chmn. pediatric sect. 1977-79, Ross Labs. award 1979, Outstanding Svcs. to Children during Internat. Yr. of Child award 1979, Meritorious Service Appreciation award 1979, W.M. Cobb co-lectr. 1985, mem. Coun. on Maternal and Child Health, 1974-92, chmn. 1979-89, ann. Roselyn Payne Epps Symposium 1994—, Grace Marilyn James award for Disting svc. Pediatric sect. 1991, Achievement award 1993, ann. Roselyn Payne Epps symposium 1994—), Am. Hosp. Assn. (maternal and child health sect. governing coun. 1989, 1992-94, maternal and child health nominating com. 1991), Soc. for the Advancement of Women's Health Rsch. (award for advocacy 1996), The Women's Forum of Washington, Alpha Omega Alpha, Delta Omega, Alpha Kappa Alpha. Mem. United Ch. of Christ. Clubs: Pearls (pres. 1984-86), Carrousels (corr. sec. 1978-80), Links (pres. Met. chpt. 1986-89) (Washington), Cosmos. Lodge: Zonta, Internat. Women's Forum. Home and Office: 1775 N Portal Dr NW Washington DC 20012-1014

EPSTEIN, BARBARA MYRNA ROBBIN, retired language educator; b. Chgo., Oct. 15, 1939; d. Jack M. and Angeline Delores (Benzuly) Robbin; m. Erwin Howard Epstein, Sept. 3, 1961; children: Jack R., Eric M., M. Avi. BS, U. Wis., 1961; MA, U. Chgo., 1964. Bilingual assessment, transitional bilingual, secondary English, elem. tchr. Ill. Tchr. Sch. Dist. 65, Evanston, Ill., 1963—64, Waynesville R-IV Schs., Ft. Leonard Wood, Mo., 1980—82, Am. Sch. Found., Monterrey, Mexico, 1982—83; instr. U. P.R., Rio Piedras, 1964; cons., tchr. Colegio Ingles, Monterrey, 1979—80; English tchr. Rolla Pub. Schs., Mo., 1983—92, Pickerington Local Schs., Ohio, 1992—98; bilingual tchr. Schaumburg Sch. Dist., Ill., 1998—2006, bilingual assessment liaison, 2003—06; ret., 2006. Pres. Rolla Cmty. Tchrs. Assn., 1991—92; pres. Ozarks chpt. Phi Delta Kappa, Rolla, 1986; state pres. Ptnrs. of the Americas (Brazil-U.S.), Mo., 1987—88; bd. dirs. South Ctrl. Mo. Arts Coun.,

1991—92. Recipient Kemper Knapp scholarship, U. Wis., 1957—61, humanities fellowship, U. Chgo., 1962—64, tchr. recognition, U. Kans., 1991. Mem.: NEA, AAUW (sec. Glenview chpt. 2001—04, pres. 2004—, pres. Glenview Br. 2004—), Ill. Assn. Multilingual-Multicultural Educators, Nat. Coun. Tchrs. of English, Nat. Assn. Bilingual Educators, Hadassah of Chgo. Jewish. Avocations: movies, theater, reading, travel, cooking. Home: 135 Rutgers Ct Glenview IL 60026 Office Phone: 847-357-5073. E-mail: bmepstein@ameritech.net.

EPSTEIN, BROOKE C., lawyer; 2 children. BA, Columbia U. Barnard Coll., 1992; JD, So. Meth. U., 1998. Bar: Tex. 1998. Assoc. gen. counsel Barrett, Burke, Wilson, Castle, Daffin & Frappier, L.L.P., Addison, Tex. Named a Rising Star, Tex. Super Lawyers mag., 2006. Mem.: ABA, Dallas Bar Assn. Office: Barrett Burke Wilson Castle Daffin & Frappier LLP 15000 Surveyor Blvd Ste 100 Addison TX 75001 Office Phone: 972-386-5040.*

EPSTEIN, CYNTHIA FUCHS, sociology educator, writer; BA in Polit. Sci., Antioch Coll., 1955; postgrad., U. Chgo. Law Sch., 1955—56; MA in Sociology, New Sch. Social Rsch., 1960; PhD, Columbia U., 1968. Instr. anthropology Finch Coll., 1961—62; assoc. in sociology Columbia U., 1964—65, instr. Barnard Coll., 1965; instr. sociology Queens Coll., N.Y.C., 1966—67, asst. prof., 1968—70, assoc. prof., 1971—74, prof., 1974—84; prof. grad. ctr. CUNY, 1974, Disting. prof. Grad. Ctr., 1990; resident scholar Russell Sage Found., 1982—88; co-dir. Program in Sex Roles and Social Change Ctr. Social Scis., Columbia U., 1977—82, co-dir. NIMH tng. grant on sociology and econs. of women and work Grad. Ctr., disting. prof. Grad. Ctr., 1990—. Vis. prof. Health Sci. Ctr. SUNY, Stony Brook, 1975, Stanford Law Sch., 1997; vis. fellow, 2002; vis. scholar Stanford U., 1991, Columbia Law Sch., 2004, Phi Beta Kappa, 1991-92; com. on women's employment and related social issues NRC-NAS, 1981-88; adv. com. on econ. role of women Pres.' Coun. Econ. Advisers, 1973-74; cons., lectr. and spkr. in field. Author: Woman's Place: Options and Limits in Professional Careers, 1970, Women in Law, 1981, 2d edit., 1993, Deceptive Distinctions: Sex, Gender and the Social Order, 1988, The Part-time Paradox: Time Norms, Professional Life, Family and Gender, 1999; editor: (with William J. Goode) The Other Half: Roads to Women's Equality, 1971; (with Rose Laub Coser) Access to Power: Cross-National Studies of Women and Elites, 1981, (with A. Kalleberg) Fighting for Time, 2004, Shifting Boundaries of Work and Social Life, 2004; mem. editl. bds. Signs, Women's Studies, Internat. Jour. Work and Occupations, Sociol. Focus, Women 1974, Dissent, Am. Jour. Sociology, CUNY Mag., Gender and Soc.; contbr. chpts. to books, articles to profl. jours. Trustee Antioch U., 1984—97. Recipient Award for Disting. Contbn. to Study of Sex and Gender, ASAN, 1994, Rebecca Rice award Antioch Coll., 1997; grantee Inst. Life Ins., 1974, Ford Found., 1975-77, Rsch. Found. City of N.Y., 1974-76, 90-93, Guggenheim Meml. Found., 1976-77, Ctr. Advanced Study in Behavioral Scis., 1977-78, 2005, Russell Sage Found., 1982-90, Sloan Found., 1995—; fellow NIH, 1963-66, MacDowell Colony, 1973, 74, 77, 80, Guggenheim Found., 1976-77, Ctr. Advanced Study in Behavioral Sci., 1977-78, Va. Ctr. Creative Arts, 1984. Mem. AAAS, Ea. Sociol. Soc. (v.p. 1977-79, exec. coun. 1973-74, pres. 1983-84, I Peter Gellman award, Outstanding Contbn. to Discipline Merit award 2004), Am. Sociol. Assn. (coun. 1974-77, com. exec. office and budget 1978-81, chmn. sect. on orgns. and occupations, chmn. sect. on sociology of sex roles 1973-74, chair culture sect. 2000-01, pres.-elect, 2004-05, pres. 2006—, Jessie Bernard award 2003), Social Rsch. Assn., Internat. Sci. Commn. on Family. Office: CUNY Grad Ctr 365 5th Ave New York NY 10016-4309 Business E-Mail: cepstein@gc.cuny.edu.

EPSTEIN, ELAINE MAY, lawyer; b. Phila., May 29, 1947; d. Sidney and Helen (Brill) Epstein; m. James A. Krachey, July 25, 1987; stepchildren: Ross Krachey, Anna Krachey. BA, U. Pa., 1968; MA, Yale U., 1971; JD, Northeastern U., 1976. Assoc. Law Offices of P.J. Piscitelli, Brockton, Mass., 1975-78; ptnr. LoDolce & Epstein, Brockton, 1978-94, Todd & Weld, Boston, 1994—. Mem. Bd. Bar Overseers, Boston, 1984-88; trustee Mass. Continuing Legal Edn., Boston, 1991-93. Mem. editl. bd. Mass. Lawyers Weekly, 1993-98. Fellow Mass. Bar Found. (trustee 1993-98); mem. ABA, Mass. Bar Assn. (pres. 1992-93), Women's Bar Assn. (pres. 1979-80). Democrat. Jewish. Home: 4 Manns Hill Cres Sharon MA 02067-2267 Office: Todd & Weld 28 State St Fl 31 Boston MA 02109-1775

EPSTEIN, LEE JOAN, political science professor, law educator; b. NYC, Mar. 17, 1958; d. Kenneth Maurice and Ann (Buxbaum) Spole BA with high honors, Emory U., Atlanta, 1980, MA, 1982, PhD, 1983. Mallinckrodt Disting. Univ. prof. polit. sci. Washington U., St. Louis, 1998—2006, prof. law, 2000—06; Beatrice Kuhn prof. law Northwestern U., 2006—. Author: Conservatives in Court, 1985; co-author: Supreme Court and Legal Change, 1992, The Choices Justices Make, 1998, The Supreme Court Compendium, 2003, Constitutional Law for a Changing America, 2004, Advise and Consent, 2005; contbr. articles to profl. jours., chpts. in books. Fellow Am. Acad. Polit. and Social Sci., Am. Acad. Arts and Scis.; mem. Am. Polit. Sci. Assn., Midwest Polit. Sci. Assn., Law and Soc. Assn., Pi Sigma Alpha, Alpha Epsilon Phi. Jewish. Avocations: skiing, tennis. Office: Northwestern U Sch Law 357 E Chgo Ave Chicago IL 60611-3069 Office Phone: 312-503-1838. Business E-Mail: lee-epstein@northwestern.edu.

EPSTEIN, MARSHA ANN, public health service officer, physician; b. Chgo., Feb. 4, 1945; 1 child, Lee Rashad Mahmood. BA, Reed Coll., 1965; MD, U. Calif., San Francisco, 1969; MPH, U. Calif., Berkeley, 1971. Diplomate Am. Bd. Preventive Medicine. Intern French Hosp., San Francisco, 1969-70; resident in preventive medicine Sch. Pub. Health, U. Calif., Berkeley, 1971-73; fellow in family planning dept. ob-gyn. UCLA, 1973-74; med. dir. Herself Health Clinic, LA, 1974-79; pvt. adult gen. practitioner LA, 1978-82; dist. health officer Los Angeles County Pub. Health, LA, 1982—2001, area med. dir., 2001—. Part-time physician U. Calif. Student Health, Berkeley, 1970—73; co-med. dir. Monsenior Oscar Romero Free Clinic, LA, 1992—93. Mem.: APHA, Calif. Acad. Preventive Medicine, So. Calif. Pub. Health Assn., LA-Am. Med. Women's Assn., Am. Med. Women's Assn., Am. Coll. Physician Execs. Democrat. Jewish. Avocations: dance, native plants, meditation. Office: Tucker Health Ctr 123 W Manchester Blvd Inglewood CA 90301 Office Phone: 310-419-5301. Business E-Mail: mepstein@ph.lacounty.gov.

EPSTEIN, SUSAN BAERG, librarian, consultant; b. Chgo., Feb. 28, 1938; d. Philip William and Alice (Mackenzie) Ruppert; m. William Baerg, 1960 (div. 1971); children: Elisabeth Baerg, William Philip Baerg, Sara Margaret Baerg; m. A. H. Epstein, 1977 (div. 1981). BA in Econs., Wellesley Coll., 1960; MLS, Immaculate Heart Coll., 1972. Sys. analyst IBM, San Jose, Calif., 1960-63, Control Data Corp., Palo Alto, Calif., 1963-64; dir. tech. and automation svcs. Huntington Beach (Calif.) Pub. Libr., 1972-74, asst. city libr., 1974-78; spl. asst. to county libr. Los Angeles County Pub. Libr., L.A., 1978-81, chief tech. svcs., 1979-81; pres. Susan Baerg Epstein, Ltd., Costa Mesa, Calif., 1981—. Columnist: Libr. Jour., 1984—. Mem.: ALA (chair com.), Calif. Libr. Assn. (councilor 1973—80). Office: 1992 Lemnos Dr Costa Mesa CA 92626-3534 Office Phone: 714-754-1559. Personal E-mail: sbepstein@aol.com.

EPSTEIN-SHEPHERD, BEE, coach, hypnotist, educator; b. Tubingen, Germany, July 14, 1937; arrived in U.S., 1940, naturalized, 1945; d. Paul and Milly (Stern) Singer; m. Leonard Epstein, June 14, 1959 (div. 1982); children: Bettina, Nicole, Seth; m. Frank Shepherd, 1991 (dec. 1992). Student, Reed Coll., 1954—57; BA, U. Calif., Berkeley, 1958; MA, Goddard Coll., 1976; PhD, Internat. Coll., 1982; DCH, Am. Inst. Hypnotherapy, 1999. Bus. instr. Monterey Peninsula Coll., Calif., 1975—85; owner, mgr. Bee Epstein Assocs., Calif., 1977—; cons. to mgmt. Carmel, Calif., 1977—; pres. Success Tours, Inc., Carmel, 1981—; founder, prin. Monterey Profl. Spkrs., 1982. Instr. Monterey Peninsula Coll., Golden Gate U., U. Calif., Santa Cruz, Am. Inst. Banking, Inst. Ednl. Leadership, Calif. State Fire Acad., U. Calif., Berkeley, Foothill Coll., U. Alaska; pres. Becoming Media, Inc., 2002. Author: 5 Days to Less Stress, 1983, How to Create Balance at Work, at Home, in Your Life, 1988, Stress First Aid for the Working Woman, 1991, Free Yourself from Diets, 1994, Mental Management for Great Golf, 1996, Building Champions. A Guide for Parents of Junior Golfers, 2005, Mental Mastery System, 2001; developer Mind Power Technology, 2004; contbr. articles to newspapers and trade mag. Rsch. grantee, 1976. Mem.: Nat. Guild Hypnotists, Peninsula Profl. Women's Network, Nat. Spkrs. Assn. Democrat. Jewish. Office: PO Box 221383 Carmel CA 93922-1383 Office Phone: 831-625-3188. Personal E-mail: drbeeMM@aol.com.

ERB, BETTY JANE, retired real estate agent; b. Balt., July 10, 1930; d. Edgar Smith Shanks and Delora Hickman Cockrum; m. William Cornelius Smith, Oct. 14, 1950 (div. Aug. 11, 1966); children: Stephen Cole Smith, Scott Douglas Smith, Cindy Lynn Smith; m. George Lewis Erb, Apr. 30, 1982. Mainframe computer operator Svc. Bur. Corp., Balt., 1974—86; real estate agt. Carroll County Assn. Realtors, Westminster, Md., 1988—2002. Contbr. articles to various pubs. Mem.: Carroll County Coin Club (pres., v.p., sec., bd. dirs.). Baptist. Home: 402 Barnes Ave Westminster MD 21157

ERBACHER, KATHY, writer, editor, marketing consultant; b. Kansas City, Mo., 1947; d. Philip Erbacher and Thelma Lillian Erbacher Sammon BS in English Theater Edn., U. Kans., Lawrence, 1970; BA magna cum laude in Art, Met. State Coll. of Denver, Denver, 1983. Reporter Kansas City Star (Mo.), 1970-72; newswriter, publicist Washington U., St. Louis, 1972-76; copy editor Kansas City Star-Times (Mo.), 1976-79; corp. comm. mgr., editor Petro-Lewis Corp., Denver, 1979-82; assoc. editor arts and travel editor Denver Mag., 1984-86; owner Arts Internat., 1987—; internat. editor, sr. writer Gates Rubber Co., Denver, 1987-90; feature writer/editor Rocky Mountain News, 1998-2001; creative svcs. writer Denver Newspaper Agy., 2001—02; pres. Erbacher Creative, LLC, 2003—. Creative dir. TV shorts for contemporary art collection Denver Art Mus., 1983-84. Bd. dirs. Met. State Coll. Alumni Assn., 1986-87, co-chair 1987 Met. State Coll. Alumni Awards Dinner, Denver; bd. govs. Met. State Coll. Found., 1986-87; mem. program com. Colo. Bus. Com. for the Arts, 1989-90; mem. pub. affairs adv. com. Denver Ctr. for Performing Arts, 1989-98; active Denver Art Mus. Alliance for Contemporary Art, 1984—; Colo. Trade Mission del. to Japan, 1994. Recipient nat. and regional award for arts writing Denver Partnership, 1986, award for Artbeat column in Denver mag. Colo. MAC News, 1986, also award for spl. fashion sect.; co-recipient award for Gates Rubber Co. Global Comm. Bus./Profl. Advt. Assn., 1988; 1st pl. award for best advt. sect. Rocky Mountain News, Cherry Creek Arts Festival, Colo. Press Assn., 1999, 1st place Gold Pinnacle award for 2000 Rocky Mountain News Cherry Creek Arts Festival advt. sect., Internat. Festivals and Events Assn., 2000. Mem. Denver Art Mus., Museo de las Ams., Colorado Springs Fine Arts Ctr., Denver Bot. Gardens. Avocations: visual art, theater, films, travel, Spanish language. E-mail: er_bac1@earthlink.net.

ERBE, CHANTELL VAN, artist; b. Jersey City, Dec. 31, 1968; d. Gary Thomas Erbe and Edny Lourdes Gualtieri. Lender James A. Michener Mus., Doylestown, Pa., 2004—. Exhibitions include Nat. Arts Club, N.Y.C., 1995—2003, Butler Inst. Am. Art, Youngstown, Ohio, 2000, Mus. Tex. Tech. U., Lubbock, 2003, J. Wayne Stark Gallery, College Sta., Tex., 2003, Pen and Brush Galleries, N.Y.C., 2004, Danville (Va.) Mus. Fine Arts and History, 2004, The Broome St. Gallery Soho, N.Y., 2004, Bergstrom-Mahler Mus., Neenah, Wisc., 2004, Huntsville (Ala.) Mus. Art, 2004, Mcallen (Tex.) Internat. Mus., 2005, Woodbury Gallery, Orem, Utah, 2005, Krasl Art Ctr., St. Joseph, Mich., 2005, Turtle Bay Exploration Mus., Redding, Calif., 2005, McInich Art Gallery, Manchester, NH, 2006, in various publs. Recipient Art award for Most Creative Artist, Ramapo Coll., 1987, Strathmore award, Strathmore Paper Co., N.Y.C., 1996, Am. Biog. award for Outstanding Work in Colored Pencil, 2000, 2d Pl award, Sharon Arts Ctr., Peterborough, NH, 2004. Mem.: Colored Pencil Soc Am., Allied Artists Am. (bd. dirs. 1996—2004, Salmagundi award for graphics 2001), Catharine Lorillard Wolfe Art Club. Avocations: colored pencil art, mixed media art, photography, poetry, literature. E-mail: info@chantellvanerbe.com.

ERDELY, DIANE LOUISE, educator; b. Greene County, Pa., Feb. 24, 1945; d. Ernest Leon and Mary Louise (Forquer) Warnick; m. Daniel Charles Erdely, Apr. 12, 1969. BM, W.Va. U., 1967; MEd, Temple U., 1969. Cert. learning disabilities tchr., cons. Tchr. educable mentally retarded Jefferson Sch., Phila., 1967-69; tchr. trainable mentally retarded Thomas Paine Sch., Cherry Hill, N.J., 1969-88, cast mem. Walt Disney World, 2004—; learning disbalities tchr., cons.; vol. NJ Audubon. Office: Cherry Hill Pub Schs Cen Adminstrn Heritage Sch PO Box 5015 Cherry Hill NJ 08034-0391 Home: 591 Russ Pond Dr Kissimmee FL 34759-3280

ERDMAN, BARBARA, visual artist; b. N.Y.C., Jan. 30, 1936; d. Isidore and Julia (Burstein) E. Postgrad., Chinese Inst., 1959-60; BFA, Cornell U., 1956. Visual artist, Santa Fe, 1977—. Guest critic Studio Arte Centro Internat., Florence, Italy, 1986; guest lectr. Austin Coll. Sherman, Tex., 1986; mem. Oracle Conf. Polaroid Corp., nationwide, 1986-88. One-woman shows include Aspen Inst., Baca, Colo., 1981, Scottsdale (Ariz.) Ctr. for Arts, 1988, AAAS, Washington, 1994, Farrell/Fischoff Gallery, Santa Fe, N.Mex., 2005; exhibited in group shows, 1959—, including AAAS, 1994, Wichita Falls Art Mus., Tex., 1996, San Bernardino County Mus., 1998; represented in permanent collections N.Mex. Mus. Fine Arts, Santa Fe, IBM, N.Y.C.; author: New Mexico USA, 1985. Bd. dirs. N.Mex. Right to Choose, Santa Fe, 1981-87, Santa Fe Ctr. for Photography, 1983, pres. bd. 1985-89; mem. N.Mex. Mus. Found., Albuquerque Mus. Found. Mem. Art Student's League (life), Soc. for Photographic Edn. (guest lectr. 1987), Santa Fe Ctr. for Photography (pres., bd. dirs. 1984-89), Am. Coun. Arts. Avocations: ceramics, textiles, cats. Home and Office: 1070 Calle Largo Santa Fe NM 87501-1090

ERDOES, MARY CALLAHAN, investment banker; m. Philip Erdoes. BS in Math., Georgetown Univ.; MBA, Harvard Univ., 1993. With Bankers Trust; portfolio mgr. Meredith, Martin & Kaye; head, fixed income group, JPMorgan Flemming Investment Mgmt Divsn. JPMorgan Private Bank, 1996—2002, mng. dir., global head, investments, 2002, now CEO. Bd. dir. UNICEF, 2005—. Named one of 100 Most Powerful Women in World, Forbes mag., 2005. Office: JP Morgan Pvt Banking 345 Park Ave New York NY 10154 E-mail: mary.erdoes@jpmorgan.com.*

ERDOS, JOANNA E., school counselor, secondary school educator; d. Paul Thomas and Eva Judith Erdos. AA in Theatre Arts, LA City Coll., 1973; BA in Theatre Arts, UCLA, 1975; MSc in Counseling and Guidance, Calif. Luth. U., 2001. Cert. Secondary Edn. Tchr. UCLA, 1975, English Tchr. UCLA, 1976, in Cross Cultural Lang. and Academic Devel. LA Unified Sch. Dist., 1994, Pupil Pers. Svcs. Credential Calif. Luth. U., 2001. Substitute tchr. LA Unified Sch. Dist., 1976—77, mentor tchr., 1997—99, all dist. speech tournament founder, dir., academic decathlon judge, newspaper editor, asst. proofreader, textbook selection com. mem., write test reader; tchr. John Marshall HS, 1977—2003, master tchr., 1992—95, counselor, 2003—, asst. coach speech and debate team, 1979—80, coach speech and debate team, 1980—92, co-chairperson performing arts, 1995—97, stds. based assessment coord., 1999—2000, accreditation com., focus group leader, sec. booster club, mem. 50th anniversary organizing com., chairperson 65th anniversary organizing com., chairperson 70th anniversary organizing com., co-chairperson 75th anniversary organizing com. Restructuring team leader Coalition Essential Schs.; tutor in field. Supporting mem. LA Conservancy, 1988—; chaperone LA Olympics Amateur Athletics Assn.; mem. Los Feliz Improvement Assn., Cultural Heritage Found., Nat. Trust Hist. Preservation. Nominee Tch. of Yr., John Marshall HS, 1988; named Outstanding Young Educator LA, Bayanihan Jaycees, 1986; recipient Appreciation award, Masonic Lodge, 1977, Lions Club, 1981, 1982, 1983, 1984, 1985, 1986, 1989, 1991, 1992, 1994, Cheerleaders Spirit award, John Marshall HS, 1984, Baseball Team Appreciation award, 1984, Basketball Team Appreciation award, 1985, Student Coun. Cmty. Svc. award, 1985, 1986, 1987, 1988, Academic Decathlon Appreciation cert., 1990, Nat. Excellence in Speech award, Nat. Forensic League, 1984, Degree Spl. Distinction, 1986, Degree Outstanding Distinction, 1991, Diamond Coach award, 1993, Outstanding Young Educator Calif., Calif. Jr. C. of C., 1987, Fellowship award, Am. Legion Freedoms Found., 1988. Mem.: NEA, Western Assn. Coll. Admissions Counselors, LA City Coll. Theatre Alumni and Assocs. (charter mem., bd. dirs., sec.), Theatre West, Internat. Thespian Soc., Drama Tchrs. Assn. So. Calif., Nat. Coun. Tchrs. English, English Coun. LA (workshop presenter), Calif. Tchrs. Assn., John Marshall HS Faculty Assn. (pres., sec.), Nat. Forensic League (dist. tournament ofcl.), Calif. HS Speech Assn. (state coun. mem., area chairperson, state tournament ofcl.), United Tchrs. LA, Western Bay Forensic League (pres., sec.), Sr. High Assn. Speech Educators (pres., co-founder), John Marshall Parent Tchr. Student Assn. (Hon. Svc. award 1990, Appreciation cert. 1983), John Marshall HS Alumni Assn. (founding mem. 1979—, v.p. faculty liaison 1979—, variety show prodr. and performer, newsletter editor), LA City Coll. Theatre Alumni Assn. (bd. mem. 1993), Culinary Historians So. Calif. (membership com. co-chair), UCLA Alumni Assn. (life), Sigma Tau Sigma, Pi Lambda theta. Avocations: reading, travel, Scrabble, history, cooking. Office: John Marshall HS 3939 Tracy St Los Angeles CA 90027

ERDRICH, LOUISE (KAREN ERDRICH), writer, poet; b. Wahpeton, ND, June 7, 1954; d. Ralph Louis and Rita Joanne (Gourneau) E.; m. Michael Anthony Dorris, Oct. 10, 1981 (dec. Apr. 1997); children: Abel (dec.), Sava, Madeline, Persia, Pallas, Aza. BA, Dartmouth Coll., 1976; MA, Johns Hopkins U., 1979. Vis. poet, tchr. ND State Arts Coun., 1977-78; tchr. writing Johns Hopkins U., Balt., 1978-79; communications dir., editor Circle-Boston Indian Council, 1979-80; textbook writer Charles Merrill Co., 1980; owner BirchBark Books and Native Arts, Mpls., 2000—; founder BirchBark Books Press, Mpls. Author: (textbook) Imagination, 1981; (poetry) Jacklight, 1984, Baptism of Desire, 1989; (novels) Love Medicine, 1984 (Nat. Book Critics Circle award for fiction 1984, Virgina McCormick Scully prize 1984, LA Times award for best novel 1985, Sue Kaufman prize for first fiction Am Acad. and Inst. of Arts and Letters 1985), The Beet Queen, 1986, Tracks, 1988, (with Michael Dorris) The Crown of Columbus, 1991, (with Dorris) Route 2, 1991, The Bingo Palace, 1994, The Blue Jay's Dance: A Writer's Year with Baby, 1995, Tales of Burning Love, 1996, The Antelope Wife, 1998, Last Report on the Miracles at Little No Horse, 2001, The Master Butchers Singing Club, 2003, Four Souls, 2004, The Painted Drum, 2005; (children's) Grandmother's Pigeon, 1997, The Birchbark House, 1999 (Am. Indian Youth Lit. award, 2006), Game of Silence, 2005; contbr. short stories, essays and poems to popular mags., other publs. Johns Hopkins U. teaching fellow, 1979; Macdowell Colony fellow, 1980; Yaddo Colony fellow, 1981; vis. fellow Dartmouth Coll., 1981; Guggenheim fellow, 1985-86; recipient numerous awards for profl. excellence including Nelson Algren award, 1982, Pushcart prize, 1983, Nat. Mag. Fiction award, 1983, 87, First prize O. Henry awards, 1987. Mem. PEN (exec. bd. 1985-90), Am. Acad. Arts and Letters, Authors Guild, Western Lit. Assn. Address: c/o Wylie Aitken & Stone Inc 250 W 57th St Ste 2114 New York NY 10107-2199 Office: Birchbark Books and Native Arts 2115 W 21st St Minneapolis MN 55405*

EREKSEN, CHRISTA ANN, social worker, marriage and family therapist; b. Manville, N.J., Oct. 19, 1973; d. Paul Erek Ereksen and Chris Anntoinette Bladzinski; m. Marshall Chandler McCoy, July 2, 1996 (div. Jan. 2001). Cosmetology lic., Richards Beauty Coll., San Bernardino, Calif., 1994; A in Liberal Arts, Victor Valley Coll., 1999; B in Psychology, Calif. State U., San Bernardino, 2002; postgrad., Calif. Bapt. U., 2004; postgrad, Walden U. Cosmetologist Fantastic Sams, Apple Valley, Calif., 1995—99; eligibility worker San Bernardino County, 1999—2000, social worker II, 2000—04. Intern marriage and family therapy Foothills AIDS Project, San Bernardino, 2003—04, MFI Recovery, Riverside, Calif., 2003—04; dist. social worker Calif. Dept. Corrections, Parole and Cmty. Services Divsn., 2004—. Mem.: APA, Calif. Assn. Marriage and Family Therapists, Calif. State Alumni Assn., Phi Kappa Phi. Democrat. Roman Catholic. Avocations: reading, writing, poetry. Office: 303 W 5th St San Bernardino CA 92401 Office Phone: 909-383-4694 2045.

EREM, SUZAN, writer; b. Hackensack, N.J., Sept. 13, 1963; d. Nejat Hussein Erem and Elaine Gloria Dinallo; m. Robert Timothy Yeager, Apr. 25, 1987 (div. Dec. 1997); 1 child, Ayshe Rezan. B in Journalism/English, U. Iowa, 1985. Field mgr. Ill. Pub. Action Coun., Rock Island, 1985-86; union rep. Iowa United Profls., Des Moines, 1987-89; editl. asst. The Town Jour., Saddle River, N.J., 1989; organizer Local 32B-32J Svc. Employees Internat. Union, N.Y.C., 1989-90; rsch. asst. Labor Coalition on Pub. Utilities, Chgo., 1991; comms. dir. Local 73 Svc. Employees Internat. Union, Chgo., 1993-2000. Mem. adv. com. U. Ill. Labor Edn. Program, Chgo., 1999. Author: Labor Pains: Stories from Inside America's New Union, 2001; contbr. articles to Am. Anthropologist, Sojourners Mag., N.Am. Review, Iowa Woman; editor/designer The Jour., 1993-2000. Field organizer Jesse Jackson for Pres., Cedar Rapids, Iowa, 1988; founding mem. Rainbow Coalition of Iowa, Des Moines, 1989; area coord. Jesus Garcia for Sen., Chgo., 1992; steering com. mem. Oak Park Cmty. Action, Oak Park, Ill., 1991-93; del. Chgo. Fedn. of Labour, 1993-2000; co-chair Nat. Writers Union Local 12, 1999, nat. del., 1999, 2001. Mem. Ill. State Labor Press Assn. (v.p. 1998-99). Avocations: hiking, travel, rollerblading. Home: 1114 Outer Dr State College PA 16801-8239

ERHART, SUE A., lawyer; b. Cin., Oct. 6, 1971; BS, Xavier U., 1993; JD, U. Cin. Coll. Law, 1996. Bar: Ohio 1996, Ind. 1999. Law clerk Hon. Robert L. Miller, Jr., US Dist. Ct. Northern Dist. Ind., Hon. David A. Nelson, US Ct. of Appeals Sixth Cir.; ptnr. Keating, Muething & Klekamp PLL, Cin. Named one of Ohio's Rising Stars, Super Lawyers, 2005, 2006. Fellow: Cin. Acad. Leadership for Lawyers; mem.: Potter Stewart Am. Inn of Ct., Ind. State Bar Assn., Ohio State Bar Assn., FBA, Cin. Bar Assn. Office: Keating Muething &Klekamp PLL One E Fourth St Ste 1400 Cincinnati OH 45202 Office Phone: 513-579-6400. Office Fax: 513-579-6457.*

ERICKSON, CAROL JEAN, literature and language professor; b. St. Cloud, Minn., Dec. 25, 1943; d. Clarence Joseph and Lucille Frances Reiter; m. Eric Bruce Erickson, Aug. 13, 1966 (dec. July 2004); children: Holly Lynn, Kirk Adam. BS in English, St. Cloud State U., Minn., 1962—66; MA in Tchg. and Learning, St. Mary's U. Minn., Winona, 1996—98. Lang. arts educator Sch. Dist. 728, Elk River, Minn., 1966—. Speech coach Vandenberge Jr. High, Elk River, Minn., 1966—2000, lang. arts chair, 1968—85, site coun. chair, 2000—03; past sec., faculty rep., and parliamentarian Elk River Edn. Assn., Minn., 1968—78; lang. arts dist. 728 curriculum com. Dist. 728, Elk River, Minn., 2001—03. State v.p. Jaycee Women, Minn., 1975—76; founder, past chair, bd. mem. Rivers of Hope, Monticello, Minn., 1989—2005. Nominee Tchr. of Yr., Elk River Edn. Assn., 1980; recipient Key Woman, Minn. Jaycee Women, 1977, Minn. Tchr. Excellence, Minn. Edn. Assn., 1983. Mem.: NEA, Edn. Minn., Elk River Edn. Assn., Delta Kappa Gamma (past chair, past parliamentarian, current mem.). Roman Catholic. Avocations: gardening, reading, travel. Office Phone: 763-241-3400.

ERICKSON, DONNA JOY, writer; b. Boston, June 8, 1955; d. Samuel Jacob and Lillian Doris (Koven) Gilman; m. Jeffrey W. Erickson, Oct. 26, 1975; 1 child, Ryan S. Assoc. in Bus. with high honors, Massasoit C.C., Brockton, Mass., 1979. Asst. to meteorologist, pub. rels. coord. New Eng. Weather Sci., Hull, Mass., 1986-88; freelance feature writer South Shore News, Rockland, Mass., 1988-91; staff feature writer Abington/Rockland Mariner, Marshfield, Mass., 1992-94; staff writer South Shore Baby Jour., Kingston, Mass., 1992-98; owner A Flair For Writing, 1989—. Author hist. essay, 1989; radio Job Hour Program gues WMSX Radio AM, Brockton, Mass., 1992. Facilitator Alliance for Mentally Ill-Sibling/Adult Children Group, Brockton, Mass., 1986. Recipient South Shore Baby Jour. award, 1995. Mem. Nat. Writers Union, Cassel Comm. Network Writers and Panel Experts, South Shore Ad Club (mem. bd. dir. 1992-94, newsletter editor 1992-94). Avocations: walking, meditation, alternative therapies. Personal E-mail: donna@aflairforwriting.com.

ERICKSON, ELAINE MAE, composer, educator, poet; b. Des Moines, Iowa, Apr. 22, 1941; d. Iver Carl and Ruth Eloise (Johnson) Erickson. MusB, Wheaton Coll., 1964; MusM, Drake U., 1967. Pvt. piano tchr., Des Moines, 1964—; music libr. Main Pub. Library, Des Moines, 1965-67; composer-in-residence Ford Found. Fellowship, Ft. Lauderdale, Fla., 1967-68; tchr. piano music theory Drake U., Des Moines, 1969-72; pianist Ctr. for New Music State U. Iowa, Iowa City, 1974-76; piano tchr. Waxter Ctr., Balt., 1988-89,

Church Lane Elem. Sch., Balt., 1989-90; tchr. music composition Ctrl. Coll., Pella, Iowa, 1993-96; composer-in-residence Charles Ives Ctr. Am. Music, New Milford, Conn., 1981—83, 1993. Guest composer Meet the Composer, Saranac Lake, NY, 1987; touring artist Very Spl. Arts Iowa, 1994—. Author (poetry) Separate Trains, 1988, A Visit Home, 1990, Solo Drive, 1992, Portraits and Selected Poems, 1994, The Cottage, 2001, Summer Evening, 2004; writer 5 operas, 3 performed at Peabody Conservatory, Balt., 1986-91; contbr. poetry to numerous jours. Pianist various retirement homes, Balt., Des Moines, 1978—, music appreciation tchr., Balt., 1991-93, Des Moines, 1993—; organist Divinity Luth. Ch., Towson, Md., 1987-88. Recipient Pyle Commn. award Iowa Composers Forum, Des Moines, 1997, composition award Nat. League Am. Pen Women, 1992; touring grantee Iowa Arts Coun., 1974-75, 81-82. Democrat. Avocation: photography. Home and Office: 3700 Hillsdale Dr Des Moines IA 50322-3947 Office Phone: 515-252-7662.

ERICKSON, LINDA E., retired academic administrator; b. Longview, Wash., Sept. 20, 1940; d. John Emil and Hazel Rydberg Erickson. BA in Music and Psychology with honors, Lewis and Clark Coll., 1962; MA in Student Pers. Adminstrn., Syracuse U., 1964; MusM in Piano Pedagogy, U. South Fla., 1970. Resident instr. U. South Fla., Tampa, 1964-65, instr., asst. prof., 1964-72, asst. dean of women, 1965-71, asst. to v.p. for student affairs, 1971-73, dir. new student rels., 1973-81, dir. admissions, 1981-86, asst. v.p., univ. registrar, 1986-96; ret., 1996. 1st pres., founding mem. Fla. Assn. Women Educators, 1966-73; founding mem., 2d pres. Fla. Coll. Pers. Assn., 1975-78; bd. dirs., nat. cons. Nat. Orientation Dirs. Assn., 1977-81; exec. com., sec., pres. Fla. ACT Coun., 1981-96; guardian ad litem Guardian Ad Litem Program, 13th Jud. Cir. Ct., Fla., 1996-2001; vol. neonatal ICU St. Joseph's Women's Hosp., Tampa, 1997-2001. Recipient Dist. Alumnus award, Lewis and Clark Coll., 1977. Mem. Mortar Bd., Mu Phi Epsilon, Phi Kappa Phi, Delta Delta Delta. Avocations: music, travel, genealogy, physical fitness, reading. Home: 10217 Devonshire Lake Dr Tampa FL 33647

ERICKSON, LINDA RAE, elementary school educator; b. Huron, S.D., Aug. 17, 1948; d. Robert Emil and Esther (Schorzman) E. BS, U. Nebr., 1966; MA, U. No. Colo., Greeley, 1970; cert., U. Denver, 1990. Cert. elem. tchr., adminstr., prin. Spl. edn. resource tchr., Ignacio, Colo., 1983-85; elem. tchr. Woodland Park, Colo., 1985-86; tutor spl. edn. Am. Sch. London, 1987; elem. tchr. Borough of Brent, London, 1987, Internat. Sch. Hampstead, London, 1987-88; tchr. spl. edn. Carronhill Sch. for Handicapped, Stonehaven, Scotland, 1988-89; elem. tchr. Littleton (Colo.) Pub. Schs., 1970-83, 89-01; staff developer Pub. Edn. Bus. Coalition, 2001—; affiliate faculty Regis U., 2001—. Enrichment program coord. Sandburg Sch., 1991; co-chair Alternative Authentic Assessment Com., 1991—2001, Sandburg Parent Adv. Com., 1993—96; facilitator Littleton Pub. Schs., 1977—83, 1990—2001; workshop presenter Nat. Coun. Tchrs. English, Nat. Coun. Social Studies, WNET-TV Sta.; mem. Littleton Dist. Assessment Com., 1997—2001; chair Mother/Daughter Book Club, 1997—; affiliate faculty, supr. student tchrs. Regis U., 2001—; presenter in field. Active Fawcett Soc., London, 1987-89, NEA-Colo. Edn. Assn. Women's Caucus, 1979-01; mem. Sandburg Sch. mother/daughter book club, 1996—; founder mother/son book club, 1999-2000. Woman of Yr. nominee Littleton Jaycees, 1982; fed. grantee Use of Group Paperbacks in the Elem. Classroom, 1978. Mem. ASCD, NEA (women's leadership tng. cadre 1978-85), NOW, Colo. Edn. Assn., Littleton Edn. Assn. (bd. dirs., chair unit-bargaining team 1976-85), Internat. Reading Assn. (chair Pikes Peak 1986, Colo. coun. children's books award com. 1993-97, workshop presenter, reader meets writer com. co-coun. 1996—, tutor comitis crisis ctr. for homeless 1995-97, conf. presenter), Nat. Coun. Tchrs. English (co-lang. arts soc. exec. bd. dirs. 1995-97, co-chair storytelling contest 1997-98, mem. editl. bd. 1997-2001, presenter state conf. 1997), Planned Parenthood, Sierra Club, Alpha Delta Kappa, Phi Delta Kappa. Democrat. Lutheran. Avocations: skiing, water-skiing, scuba diving, mountain biking, gardening. Home: 439 Saddlewood Cir Highlands Ranch CO 80126-2284

ERICKSON, MARY ANN, athletic trainer, educator; d. Theodore Morris and Mary Ann Sprague; m. Joseph John Erickson, Mar. 24, 1984; children: Charles Henry, Andrew Lavery. BS, Ithaca Coll., N.Y., 1978; MS, Ind. State U., Terre Haute, 1980; PhD, U. N.Mex, Albuquerque, 1998. Cert. athletic trainer Nat. Athletic Trainers' Assn. Bd. of Certification. Tchr., athletic trainer El Paso Ind. Sch. Dist., Tex., 1980—85, Ysleta Ind. Sch. Dist., El Paso, 1985—86; fitness cons. YMCA, Corning, NY, 1986—88; athletic trainer Santa Fe Pub. Schs., 1988—96; part-time instr. U. N.Mex, Albuquerque, 1996—98; assoc. prof. exericise sci. Ft. Lewis Coll., Albuquerque, 1998—. Chmn. N.Mex Athletic Trainers' Practice bd. State of N.Mex, Santa Fe, 1995—98; chmn. instl. rev. bd. Ft. Lewis Coll., Durango, Colo., 2005—. Contbr. articles to profl. jours. Recipient Faculty Devel. Grant, Ft. Lewis Coll., 2000; grantee, Nat. Athletic Trainers Assn. Rsch. and Edn. Found., 1998. Mem.: N.Am. Soc. for Psychology of Sport and Phys. Activity, Nat. Athletic Trainers' Assn. (accreditation site visitor joint rev. com. 2003—). Avocations: rowing/sculling, bicycling, running, swimming, rafting. Office: Fort Lewis Coll 1000 Rim Dr Durango CO 81301 Office Phone: 970-247-7694. Personal E-mail: ericosn_m@fortlewis.edu. Business E-Mail: erickson_m@fortlewis.edu.

ERICKSON, PATRICIA ANN, physical therapist, educator; b. Holton, Kans., Jan. 29, 1955; m. Alan Erik Erickson, June 7, 1980; children: Christopher Erik, Erika Marie, Elizabeth Ann. BS in Phys. Therapy, U. Kans., Lawrence, 1977; DPT in Phys. Therapy, Creighton U., Omaha, 2003. Lic. phys. therapist Kans. Bd. of Healing Arts, 1977. Phys. therapist Levy and Assoc. Phys. Therapy, Denver, 1984—89; dir. phys. therapist asst. program Colby C.C., Kans., 1989—. Phys. therapist asst. program site visitor Commn. Accreditation in Phys. Therapy Edn., Alexandria, Va., 2000—. Treas. Colby Wellness Com., Kans., 1989—; leader Thomas County 4-H, 1994—2004; co-leader to leader Sunflower coun. Girl Scouts USA, 1994—2002; dir. religious edn. Sacred Heart Cath. Ch., 1997—2004, lector, cantor and eucharistic min., 1989—2006. Recipient Academic Excellence award, Kans. Phys. Therapy Assn., 1998, Tangeman award, Colby C.C. Endowment Assn., 1998. Mem.: AAUW (pres. 2004—06), NEA, Kans. Edn. Assn., Kans. Phys. Therapy Assn. (com. chairperson 2000—06), Am. Phys. Therapy Assn. Roman Catholic. Avocations: cooking, reading, gardening. Office: Colby CC 1255 S Range Ave Colby KS 67701 Office Phone: 785-462-3984 ext. 327. Business E-Mail: pat.erickson@colbycc.edu.

ERICKSON, RUTH ALICE, poet, artist; b. Green Bay, Wis., Apr. 9, 1933; d. Walter Byron and Verona Ann (Giese) Kottke; m. Clyde Gordan Hansen, Oct. 15, 1949 (dec. Dec. 1965); children: Gary Hansen, Gloria Hansen, Debora Hansen, Dale Hansen; m. Norton M. Erickson, July 31, 1977. Nursing asst., Nursing Acad. Green Bay, 1966. Choir dir. St. John's Luth. Ch., Green Bay, 1954—66; nurse Nursing Home, Hosp., DePere, Wis., 1966—79; poet Green Bay, 2001—. Author: Spiritual Lyrics and Poems, 2001, Hidden Haven, 2003, (chapbook) Its for the Berries, 2004, A Christmas Journey in Poetry, 2004, (poetry) A Kaleidoscope of Poetry, 2005. Mem. Leadership Coun. on Human Rights. Recipient Merit Silver Bowl award, Internat. Soc. Poets, 2002, Two Bronze Medallions, 2003, Silver Cup award, 2003. Home: 2139 Packerland Dr Green Bay WI 54304 Personal E-mail: Ruthae92@msn.com.

ERICKSON, SUE ALICE, health educator, consultant, nurse; b. Sailor Springs, Ill., Feb. 3, 1938; d. Charles Ashby and Myra Estella (McPherson) Inskeep; m. Dale Gilbert Erickson, Sept. 25, 1959; children: Erin Erickson Fonken, Kelly, Sean B. Diploma in Profl. Nursing, St. Luke's Hosp., 1959; BA, Stephens Coll., 1981; MS in Community Health Edn., U. N.Mex., 1987, Phd in Community Health Edn., 1992. RN; cert. health edn. specialist. Nurse, health educator Sandia Nat. Labs., Albuquerque, 1985-88; cons. Cuidandos Los Ninos, Albuquerque, 1988-90; cons., bd. dirs., speaker Pioneer Bible Translators, Duncanville, Tex., 1983—95, vice chmn. bd. dirs., 1993—94; owner SAE Health Comms., LLC, 1993—. Asst. matron, health educator Chidamoyo Christian Hosp., Karoi, Rhodesia, 1968-70, vol. nurse tchr., Zimbabwe, 1991; instr. Pioneer Missions Inst., 1982-94; vis. lectr. dept. medicine U. Zimbabwe, 1995, 97-00, 01, 04; adj. health instr. Equip, Inc., 1994-04; adj. prof. health edn. U. N.Mex., 2001; adj. prof. bioethics Lincoln (Ill.) Christian Sem., 1996, 01, 03, Hope Internat. U., Fullerton, Calif., 1997; bd. dirs. Best Choice Edn. Svc.; mem. adv. com. abstinence in edn. State of N.Mex., 2004—; mem. N.Mex. Abstinence Edn. Coalition, 2003—; pres. TTL Care Assessment and Edn., 2006—; instr. primary health care Pioneer Bible Translators, Ducanville, Tex. 2005—; nurse tng. cons., provider Aegin Place Home Care, Footprints Homecare, Albuquerque 2005—; instr. primary health care Pioneer Bible Translators, Dallas, 2005, 06; pres. TTL Care Assessment and Edn., LLC, 2006-. Author: (course for HS students/pregnancy crisis ctrs.) After Abstinence, 2005. Vol. nurse educator New Heart, Inc., Albuquerque, 1975-80; mem. bd. dirs. Covenant Christian Fellowship, Albuquerque, 1984-88; dir. Christian Edn., Hts. Christian Ch., 1992-96; adv. Boy Scouts Am., 1978-86; organize dir. Fibromyalgia Support Group Albuquerque, 1989-95. St. Luke's Hosp. Sch. Nursing scholar, 1959; named Disting. Alumnus, Mt. Vernon Township H.S., 2006. Mem. ACA, AAHPERD, Christian Med. and Dental Assn. Republican. Avocations: backpacking, running, biking, skiing, music. Home: 2904 Calle Grande NW Albuquerque NM 87104-3146 Office Phone: 505-344-3570. Personal E-mail: saede2@cs.com.

ERICSON, ELIZABETH (ZIBBY), architect; Prin., chair sci. practice Shepley Bulfinch Richardson & Abbott, Boston, 1981—. Peer reviewer Gen. Svcs. Adminstrn.; KECK/PKAL cons.; overseer Boston Archtl. Ctr.; lectr. in field. Prin. works include Beth Israel Deaconess Hosp., Healthcare Replacement campus at Bronson Meth. Hosp., Sci. and Engring. Bldg., Case Western U., Knight Libr., U. Oreg. Fellow: AIA. Office: Shepley Bulfinch Richardson & Abbott 40 Broad St Boston MA 02109-4306

ERICSON, RUTH ANN, retired psychiatrist; b. Assaria, Kans., May 15; d. William Albert and Anna Mathilda (Almquist) E. Student, So. Meth. U., 1945—47; BS, Bethany Coll., 1949; MD, U. Tex., 1951. Intern Calif. Hosp., L.A., 1951-52; resident in psychiatry U. Tex. Med. Br., Galveston, 1952-55; psychiatrist Child Guidance Clinic, Dallas, 1955-63; clin. instr. Southwestern Med. Sch., Dallas, 1955-72; practice medicine specializing in psychiatry Dallas, 1955-2000; ret., 2002. Cons. Dallas Intertribal Coun. Clinic, 1974-81, Dallas Ind. Sch. Dist., U.S. Army, Welfare Dept., Tribal Concerns, Alcoholism, Adv. Bd. Intertribal Coun. Pres. U. Tex. Women's Athletic Assn., 1951—52. Recipient Disting. Svc. award, Am. Med. Women's Assn., 1999, Alumni award of merit, Bethany Coll., Lindsborg, Kans., 2000, Recognition award 5 State Regional Sci. Fair, Dallas Morning News, 2001. Fellow Am. Geriat. Assn., Royal Soc. Medicine; mem. So. Med. Assn. (life), Tex. Med. Assn. (life), Dallas Med. Assns. (life), Am. Psychiat. Assn. (life), Tex. Psychiat. Assn., North Tex. Psychiat. Assn., Am. Med. Women's Assn. (Disting. Svc. award 1999), Dallas Area Women Psychiatrists, Alumni Assn. U. Tex. (Med. Br.), Navy League (life), Air Force Assn., Tex. Archaeol. Soc. (life, 45 Yr. Recognition award 2002), Dallas Archaeol. Soc. (hon. life, pres. 1972-73, 82-84, 89-91, 97-99, archival rschr., pres. 1997-99, historian 1997—), South Tex. Archaeol. Soc., Tarrant County Archeol. Soc., El Paso Archeol. Soc., N.Mex. Archaeol. Soc., Paleopathology Soc., Internat. Psychogeriatric Assn. (Famous Women of the 20th Century), VASA Lodge, Alpha Omega Alpha, Delta Psi Omega, Alpha Psi Omega, Pi Gamma Mu, Lambda Sigma, Alpha Epsilon Iota, Mu Delta. Lutheran. Home: 6436 Rivervater Trl Fort Worth TX 76179-3783

ERICSSON, APRILLE, aerospace engineer; b. Bklyn. BS in Aeronautical/Astronautical Engring, MIT; MSEE, Howard U., PhD in Mech. Engring. Aerospace Option. Aerospace engr. in Guidance Navigation and Control Ctr. NASA Goddard Space Flight Ctr., Greenbelt, Md. Adj. prof. math. dept. Bowie State U.; adj. prof. mech. engring. dept. Howard U. Recipient Top 50 Minority Women in Sci. and Engring. Nat. Tech. Assn., 1996, 97, Women in Sci. and Engring. award, 1998, Spl. Recognition award Black Engrs. award Conf., 1998, Cmty. Svc. award Fed. Exec. Bur. Md., 1999, Giant in Sci. award Quality Edn. for Minorities, 2000. Mem. NASA Goddard Space Flight Ctr. Spkrs. Bur., Women of NASA. Avocations: football, basketball, softball, bicycling, tennis. Office: NASA Code 556 Inst Sys Branch Goddard Space Flight Ctr Greenbelt MD 20771-0001

ERICSSON, SALLY CLAIRE, not-for-profit official; b. Madison, Wis., Jan. 16, 1953; d. William H. and JoAnn (Finnell) Ericsson; m. Thomas A. Garwin, Oct. 7, 1979; children: Rachel Garwin, Benjamin Garwin. B in Urban and Regional Planning, U. Ill., 1976; M in Pub. Policy, Harvard U., 1981. Legis. analyst Dem. Steering and Policy Com, Washington, 1982-87; adminstr. asst. Rep. Sam Geidenson U.S. Ho. Reps., Washington, 1987-89; legis. asst. to Sen. John F. Kerry U.S. Senate, Washington, 1989-90; asst. to pres. for policy and exec. Svc. Employees Internat. Union, Washington, 1990-93; assoc. under sec. for econ. affairs U.S. Dept. Commerce, Washington, 1993-96, dep. chief of staff, 1996-97; assoc. dir. natural resources Coun. Environ. Quality, Exec. Office of the Pres., 1997-99; dir. outreach Pew Ctr. Global Climate Change, Arlington, Va., 1999—2005. Home: 1805 Monroe St NW Washington DC 20010-1014

ERIKSEN, BARBARA ANN, writer, researcher; b. Mason City, Iowa, Sept. 13, 1931; d. Arthur Charles Beckel and Katherine Irma Konvalinka; m. Charles Walter Eriksen, Apr. 3, 1971; 1 stepchild, Kathy; m. Wesley Clemence Becker (div.); children: Jill, Jeffrey, Linda, James. BA, U. Ill., 1970, MA, 1972. Rsch. asst. dept. psychology U. Ill., Champaign-Urbana, 1968—72, rsch. assoc. dept. psychology, 1972—87; author Harlequin Romances, 1988—93. Editor: Perception and Psychophysics, 1975—87; author: The Practical Princess, 1980, 15 Romance Novels, 1985—93 (named Best Harlequin Romance for Cinderella Wife, Romantic Times Mag., 86); contbr. articles to profl. jours. Dir. mktg. Oakland (Ill.) Econ. Devel. Found., 1980. Recipient ranked 9th nationally, Jr. Ladies US Lawn Tennis Assn., 1949. Mem.: Ladies Aux. Oakland VFW, United Meth. Women, Oakland Lions Club. Avocations: gardening, tennis, cooking, painting, birdwatching. Home: 22485 State Hwy 133 Oakland IL 61943-6812 Personal E-mail: erikbarb@consolidated.net.

ERKENBRACK, LORI JEAN, county official; b. Fort Dodge, Iowa, Feb. 19, 1958; d. Donald Gene and Zola Rae Schoop; m. Gene Lester Erkenbrack, May 20, 1989; children: Eugene Eldred Erkenbrack II, Donald Jean, Dellie Gene, Marae Helen. AA in Christian Edn., Nebr. Christian Coll., 1991, AA in Ch. Music, 1991. Motor vehicle dep. Calhoun County Treas., Rockwell City, Iowa, 1978—85; sec. Hunt Truck Lines, Roseville, Minn., 1986—87; tchr. vocal music grades k-8 Norfolk Country Sch., Nebr., 1987—88; sec. for dir. devel. Nebr. Christian Coll., 1988—89, music dept. sec., 1988—89; with motor vehicle dep. Calhoun County, Rockwell City, Iowa, 1997—99, treas., 1999—. Leader Girl Scouts, Rockwell City, 2003—05; asst. cub master and treas. Pack 94 Cub Scouts, 2004—05; sec. Rockwell City/Lytton Fine Arts Boosters, 2002—05; mem. Calhoun County Rep. Women, 1997—2005; christian edn. dir./sunday sch. supt./ch. pianist Rockwell City Ch. of Christ, 1996—2005. Mem.: Iowa State County Treas. Assn. (assoc.), Studebaker Drivers Club (assoc.), Order Ea. Star (assoc.; past matron 1981, 1982, 1986, Grand Organist 1985). Conservative. Avocation: camping. Home: 729 Lake St Rockwell City IA 50579 Office: Calhoun County 416 4th St Ste 2 Rockwell City IA 50579 Office Phone: 712-297-7111. Office Fax: 712-297-7479. Personal E-mail: sonny@iowatelecom.net. E-mail: lerkenbrack@calhouncountyiowa.com.

ERKKILA-RICKER, BARBARA HOWELL, writer, photographer; b. Boston, July 11, 1918; d. John William and Adelia Parsons (Jones) Howell; m. Onni R. Erkkila, Apr. 27, 1941 (dec. 1981); children: John W., Kathleen L., Marjorie A.; m. G. Ashton Ricker, FEb. 5, 2000. Student, Boston U. Evening Coll., 1959—62. Corr. Gloucester (Mas.) Daily Times, 1936-53, feature writer, 1953—, women's editor, 1967-72, cmty. news editor, 1972-74. Editor weekly mag. Essex County Newspapers, Gloucester, 1973, editl. asst., 1974-85, writer, photographer, 1970—; tchr. Russian, Ipswich (Mass.) Pub. Schs., evenings, 1962-63; jewelry designer; quarry historian. Author: Hammers on Stone, 1981, Village at Lane's Cove, 1989; editor Lane's Cove Cook Book, 1954; contbr. articles to popular mags. Asst. traffic mgr. Lepage's, Inc., 1936-40; mem. price panel OPA, 1944-46; mem. ARC nurse's aide class Addison Gilbert Hosp., 1942-43; mem. Gloucester Hist. Commn., 1967-69, 93-2000; formerly active Girl Scouts U.S.A.; sec. Lanesville C.C., 1957-94; apptd. granite industry cons. Cape Ann (Mass.) Hist. Assn. Mus., 1997. Recipient 2d prize for feature writing UPI, 1970, historian award Town of Rockport, 1978, First Walker Hancock award City of Gloucester, 1999. Mem. Sandy Bay Hist. Soc., Ohio Geneal. Soc., Westford Hist. Soc., Cape Ann Hist. Assn., North Shore Rock and Mineral (charter), North Shore Button Club. Congregationalist. Home and Office: 7 School St North Chelmsford MA 01863-2109 Office Phone: 978-251-3578. E-mail: barickgran@aol.com.

ERLA, KAREN, artist, painter, collagist, printmaker; b. Pitts., Nov. 17, 1942; d. Jack and Lenore (Kamons) Franklin; children: Stephanie, Joan. BFA, George Washington U., 1965; postgrad., Parsons Sch. Design, 1979-81, Carnegie Inst., 1958-59, Boston U., 1960-62, Pratt Inst., 1980-82, NYU, 1981. Solo exhbns. include Phoenix Gallery, N.Y.C., 1985, E.L. Stark Gallery, N.Y.C., 1988, Bertha Urdang Gallery, N.Y.C., 1986, Bennett and Siegel Gallery, 1989, 90, U. of South, Sewanee, Tenn., Manhattanville Coll., Purchase, N.Y., 1982, Printmaking Council of N.J., 1982, Bennet Siegel Gallery, N.Y.C., 1990, Bryant Gallery, N.Y.C., 1990, Queens Coll., N.Y.C., 1991; group shows include Herbert Johnson Mus. Art, Atlanta Coll. Art, Van Straaten Gallery, Chgo., Greene Gallery, Guilford, Conn., Nat. Mus. of Am. Art, Washington, D.C., Fine Arts Museum of L.I., N.Y., Zimmerli Mus., New Brunswick, N.J., Printmaking Council of N.J., Somerstown Studios and Gallery, Somers, N.Y., Cork Exhbn. in Lincoln Ctr., Fay Gold Gallery, Atlanta, 1984, Boston Printmakers 37th Nat. Exhbn., 1985, The Print Club's 61st Internat. Juried Exhbn., Phila., Schering-Plough Corp. Gallery, Madison, N.J., New Brunswick, N.J., Australian Nat. Gallery, 1989, E.L. Stark Exhbn., 1990, Am. Embassy, 1990, others; represented in permanent collections at Balt. Mus. of Art, Herbert F. Johnson Mus., Cornell U., Bklyn. Mus. Art, Huntsville Mus. Art, Ala., L.A. County Mus. Art, Met. Mus. Art, N.Y., Nat. Museum Am. Art, Australian Nat. Gallery, Smithsonian Inst., New Orleans Mus. Art, Phila. Mus. Art, Tampa Mus., Fla.; featured in Monograph of Karen Erla (text by Ronnie Cohen) 1988, Monoprints Karen Erla (text by Dr. Mary Lee Thompson), Paintings: Karen Erla (text by Bertha Urdang and E.L. Stark); featured in Newsday as New Yorker mag.; solo exhibitions E.L. Stark Gallery, Bertha Urdang Gallery, N.Y.C. Harrison Library, Harrison, N.Y. Manhattanville Coll., Purchase, N.Y., Sound Shore Gallery, N.Y.C., The Print Club 62d Internat., Phila. Recipient Nat. Art award, Pa., 1959, award Herbert F. Johnson Mus., Cornell U., award Mamroneck Artists Guild, 1983, Outstanding Svc. award N.Y. State Assembly, 2004, Outstanding Svc. award Westchester County Bd. Legislators, 2004, Outstanding Svc. award White Plains Bd. Legislators, 2004, Outstanding Svc. award N.Y. Bd. Legislators, 2004. Mem. World Print Council, Printmaking Council N.J., Artists Equity, Pratt Graphic Ctr., L.A. Printmaking Soc. Avocations: music, reading, travel. Address: PO Box 202 North White Plains NY 10603-0202

ERLEBACHER, ARLENE CERNIK, retired lawyer; b. Chgo., Oct. 3, 1946; d. Laddie J. and Gertrude V. (Kurdys) Cernik; m. Albert Erlebacher, June 14, 1968; children: Annette Doherty, Jacqueline McCarthy. BA, Northwestern U., 1967, JD, 1973. Bar: Ill. 1974, U.S. Dist. Ct. (no. dist.) Ill. 1974, U.S. Ct. Appeals (7th cir.) 1974, Fed. Trial Bar 1983, U.S. Supreme Ct. 1985. Assoc. Sidley & Austin, Chgo., 1974-80, ptnr., 1980-95, ret., 1996. Fellow Am. Bar Found.; mem. Order of Coif.

ERLEBACHER, MARTHA MAYER, artist, educator; b. Jersey City, Nov. 21, 1937; d. Desiderius and Mary Mayer; m. Walter Erlebacher, June 26, 1961 (dec. Aug. 1991); children: Adrian Immanuel, Jonah Daedalus. Student, Gettysburg (Pa.) Coll., 1955-56; B of Indsl. Design, Pratt Inst., 1960, MFA, 1963; DFA (hon.), NY Acad. Art, 2006. Indsl. designer, illustrator Arthur Wagner Assocs., N.Y.C., 1956-61; tchr. anatomy and figure drawing U. of Arts, Phila., 1978-94. Tchr. Phila. Coll. Art, 1966-68, 78-94; tchr. anatomical drawing and painting Grad. Sch. Figurative Art, N.Y. Acad. Art, N.Y.C., 1992—, others; guest lectr. Grad. Sch. Art Yale U., 1974, Vassar Coll., Poughkeepsie, N.Y., 1975, Phila. Coll. Art, 1976, U. Conn., Storrs, 1977, Tyler Sch. Art Temple U., 1978, Med. Coll. Pa., Phila., 1987, N.Y. Acad. Art, 1990, others; vis. artist colls. and univs. including U. Wis., Oshkosh, 1979, Syracuse U., 1986-87, U. Mich., 1988, Calif. State U., 1989, 91, Tulane U., New Orleans, 1992, Kalamazoo Inst. Arts, 1989; panelist arts shows, 1978—; juror U. Del., 1979, N.Y. Statewide Bi-Annual, Trenton, 1984, Moss Rehab. Hosp., Phila., 1985, Tex. Nat. '98, Nacogdoches. Exhibited in one-person shows at Robert Schoelkopf Gallery, N.Y.C., 1973, 75, 78, 80, 82, 85, Dart Gallery, Chgo., 1976, 78, 83, Koplin Gallery, L.A., 1989, 91, Kalamazoo Inst. Arts, 1989, Fischbach Gallery, N.Y.C., 1993, 95, The More Gallery, Phila., 1993, 97, 2000, Hackett-Freedman Gallery, San Francisco, 1999, 2002, Arnot Mus., Elmira, NY, 2001, Forum Gallery, N.Y.C., 2003, Seraphin Gallery, Phila., 2005, others; exhibited in group shows Bklyn. Mus., 1960, Phila. Art Alliance, 1967, Suffolk Mus., Stony Brook, N.Y., 1971, Pratt Manhattan Ctr., 1971, Am. Acad. Arts and Letters, N.Y.C., 1973, 76, 87, Yale U. Art Gallery, 1973, Phila. Civic Ctr., 1974, Mus. Art, Penn. State U., 1974, 76, N.Y. Cultural Ctr., 1975, Libr. Congress, 1975, U. Notre Dame, 1976, Ringling Mus. Art, Sarasota, Fla., 1976, Fogg Art Mus. Harvard U., Cambridge, Mass., 1976, Art Gallery Boston U., 1977, Penn. Acad. Fine Arts, 1978, 81, 82, Phila. Mus. Art, 1979, Centro Colombo Americano, Bogota, Colombia, 1979, Fendrick Gallery, Washington, 1980, Print Club, Phila., 1980, 88, Albright-Knox Gallery, Buffalo, 1981, Woodmere Art Gallery, Phila., 1982, Univ. Art Mus., Santa Barbara, Calif., 1983, N.J. State Mus., Trenton, 1984, Hudson River Mus., Yonkers, N.Y., 1986, Sch. Fine Arts Gallery Ind. U., 1987, Sherry French Gallery, N.Y.C., 1988, 91, 92, Jack Wright Gallery, Palm Beach, Fla., 1992, Contemporary Realist Gallery, San Francisco, 1993, 94, Gerald Peters Gallery, Sante Fe, 1993, Fletcher Gallery, Sante Fe, 1994, Arnot Mus., Elmira, 2000, So. Allegheny Mus. Fine Art, Altoona, Pa., many others; represented in pvt. and pub. collections including Cleve. Mus. Art, Ball State U., Muncie, Ind., AT&T Co., Inc., Chgo., U. Notre Dame, Art Inst. Chgo., Fogg Mus. of Art, Fed. Reserve Bank, N.Y.C., Penn. Acad. Fine Arts, Phila., Valparaiso U., Phila. Mus. Art, Libr. Congress, Flint Inst. Arts, N.J. State Mus., others. Recipient Bertha Shay award Cheltenham Art Ctr., 1967, Netsky-Sernaker Meml. prize, 1973, Vivian and Meyer P. Potamkin prize, 1974; Yaddo fellow, 1966, 73, sr. fellow Nat. Endowment for Arts, 1982, fellow Pa. Coun. on Arts, 1988; grantee Ingram Merrill Found., 1978, Mellon Venture Fund, 1987; also other grants and awards. Home: 7733 Mill Rd Elkins Park PA 19027-2708 Personal E-mail: mmayererlebacher@aol.com.

ERLENMEYER-KIMLING, L., psychiatrist, researcher; b. Princeton, NJ; d. Floyd M. and Dorothy F. (Dirst) Erlenmeyer; m. Carl F. E. Kimling. BS magna cum laude, Columbia U., 1957, PhD, 1961; DSc (hon.), SUNY, Purchase, 1997. Sr. rsch. scientist N.Y. State Psychiat. Inst., N.Y.C., 1960-69, assoc. rsch. scientist, 1969-75, prin. rsch. scientist, 1975-78, dir. div. devel. behavioral studies, 1978—, chief med. genetics, 1991—; asst. in psychiatry Columbia U., 1962-66, rsch. assoc., 1966-70, from asst. prof. to assoc. prof. psychiatry and genetics, 1970—78, prof., 1978—. Adj. prof. psychology New Sch. Social Rsch., 1971—97; mem. peer rev. group NIH, 1976—80; mem. work group guidance and counseling Congl. Commn. Hungtinton's Disease, 1976—77; mem. task force intervention Pres.'s Commn. Mental Health, 1977—78; mem. initial rev. group NIMH, 1981—85; mem. adv. bd. Croatian Inst. Brain Rsch., 1991—93. Editor: Life-Span Research in Psychopathology, 1986; issue editor: Differential Reproduction, Social Biology, 1971, Genetics and Mental Disorders, Internat. Jour. Mental Health, 1972, Genetics and Gene Expression in Mental Illness, Jour. Psychiat. Rsch., 1992, Measuring Liability to Schizophrenia: Progress Report, 1994; mem. editl. bd. Social Biology, 1970—79, Schizophrenia Bull., 1978—2004; issue editor: Schizophrenia Bull., 1994; mem. editl. bd. Jour. Preventive Psychiatry, 1980—84, Croatian Med. Jour., 1991—, Neurology/Psychiatry/Brain Rsch., 1991—97, Am. Jour. Med. Genetics: Neuropsychiat. Genetics, 1992—. Recipient Merit award, NIMH, 1989—96, William K. Warren Schizophrenia Rsch. award, Internat. Congress Schizophrenia Rsch., 1995, Disting. Investigator award, Nat. Alliance Rsch. on Schizophrenia and Depression, 1996, Lifetime Achievement award, Internat. Soc. of Psychiatric Genetics, 2002; grantee, NIMH, 1966—69, 1971—, Scottish Rite Com. Schizophrenia, 1970—74, 1984—87, 1989—94, W. T. Grant Found., 1978—86, MacArthur Found., 1981, Stanley Found., 1995—2001, Nat. Alliance Rsch. on Schizophrenia and Depression,

1996—2000. Fellow: APA, Am. Psychol. Soc., Am. Psychopath. Assn. (Joseph Zubin award 2005); mem.: ACLU, AAAS, Soc. Study Social Biology (bd. dirs. 1969—84, sec. 1972—75, pres. 1975—78, bd. dirs. 1992—96), N.Y. Acad. Scis., Internat. Soc. Psychiat. Genetics (Lifetime Achievement award 2002), Behavior Genetics Assn. (mem.-at-large 1972—74, Theodosius Dobzhansky award 1985), Am. Soc. Human Genetics, Nat. Resources Defense Coun. (pres. 2006—), Emily's List (majority coun. 2002—), NY Presbyterian Hosp., Earth Justice, Animal Legal Def. Fund, Animals and Soc. Inst. (bd. dirs. 2005—), Planned Parenthood, John Lennox Soc., People for Am. Way (pres. coun. 2006—), Greenpeace, Interfaith Alliance, Union Concerned Scientists, Defenders of Wildlife (pres.'s coun. 2003—), Earth Island, Environ. Def., Sierra Club, Sigma Xi, Phi Beta Kappa. Office: NY State Psychiat Inst Dept Med Genetics 1051 Riverside Dr Mail Unit 6 New York NY 10032-2603 Business E-Mail: le4@columbia.edu.

ERLER, MARY FRANCES, art educator; d. Robert Philip and Floy Lee Feser; m. Paul William Erler, Apr. 5, 1975; children: Jonathan, Emilie. BS, Colo. State U., Ft. Collins, 1974; M of Music Edn., Concordia U., River Forest, Ill., 1998. Leader youth crew US Youth Conservation Corps, Ft. Collins, Colo., 1973—74; rsch. asst. Colo. State U., 1974—76; tchr. sci. Heritage Christian Sch., 1975—76; dist. receptionist Ashton Ranger Dist., Idaho, 1977—79; sci. reporter, columnist Tobacco Valley News, Eureka, Mont., 1985—89; substitute tchr. Tawas Area Schs., Mich., 1990—96; tchr. fine arts, music Holy Family Sch., East Tawas, 1994—2006; environ. ednl. cons. Loon Lake Luth. Retreat Ctr., Hale, Mich., 2006—. Tchr. Sunday sch. Zion Luth. Ch., Ashton, 1976—79; tchr. Sunday sch., choir dir. Holy Cross Luth. Ch., Eureka, 1988—89; choir dir., tchr. Zion Luth. Ch., Tawas City, 1989—2000. Scholar, Nat. Merit Scholar Assn., 1970, Colo. State U., 1974. Avocations: painting, music, hiking, camping.

ERLICH, RUTH L., artist; b. Phila., Jan. 8, 1918; children: Reese, Janyce Erlich-Moss. Student, U. So. Calif., L.A., UCLA. One-woman shows include Westwood Art Assn., 1961, LA Art Corps, 2003, exhibitions include L.A. County Mus. Art, Portland Mus. Art, San Francisco Legion of Honor, San Francisco Mus. Art, Palm Springs Mus. Art, Racine Mus. Art, Wis. Mem.: Westwood Art Assn. (pres. 1961—62), Nat. Water Color Soc. (v.p. 1980). Home: PO Box 19261 Oakland CA 94619 Personal E-mail: rerlich@pacbell.net.

ERLICHSON, MIRIAM, fundraiser, writer; b. Bronx, NY, July 26, 1948; d. Jack and Bess (Hyatt) E.; m. Walter Forman, Sept. 26, 1970 (div. 1975); m. Victor Petrusewicz, July 17, 1980. BA in English, CCNY, 1969, MA in English, 1976; postgrad., Hunter Coll., 1970-71; JD, Pace U., 1993. Cert. secondary tchr., N.Y. Tchr. English Intermediate Sch. 84, Bronx, 1972-78; coord. ann. and planned giving N.Y. Hosp.-Cornell Med. Ctr., N.Y.C., 1979-90; sr. devel. assoc. I.H. Found., Inc., N.Y.C., 1996-98, assoc. dir. N.E. region, 1998—2002; devel. comms. mgr. G.H. Ednl. Found., Inc., N.Y.C., 2002—03. Mem. Jane Austen Soc. (Eng.), N.Y.S. Bar, Phi Beta Kappa.

ERNSBERGER, PHYLLIS W., musician; b. Nashville, Tenn., Dec. 4, 1950; d. John Thomas and Ruth Marita West; m. John David Ernsberger, June 13, 1976; children: Rebecca, Karl, Deanna. BA in Music, U. Wash., Seattle, 1974; MA in Ch. Music, Westminster Choir Coll., Princeton, N.J., 1977. Organist Milwaukie (Oreg.) 1st Bapt., 1984—2000, Portland (Oreg.) 1st Bapt., 2000—05; dir. music, organist St. Andrew Luth., Vancouver, 2005—. Precinctwoman GOP, Portland, 1990—. Mem.: Am. Choral Dirs. Assn., Am. Guild Organist (sub-dean 2000, program chair 2000—02, dean 2002, coord. 2007 regional conv. 2004—). Avocations: languages, gardening, dance, Celtic fiddling. Office: St Andrew Luth Ch 5607 NE Gher Rd Vancouver WA 98662 Office Phone: 360-892-7160. E-mail: erns@hevanet.com.

ERNST, SUZANNE, academic administrator, educator; d. Leslie Rudolph Schwartz and Bernice Mary Sheridan; m. William R. Ernst, Aug. 25, 1957 (div.); children: Dawn L., Mark H., Erin R.(dec.), Lori S. Ernst-Furtmann, Paul W. BS, U. Nev., Reno, 1958; MEd, U. Nev., 1974. Asso. in Social Work Nev. State Bd. Examiners for Social Workers, 1988; cert. retirement planner U. So. Calif., Percy Andrus Gerontology Ctr., 1981, jr. h.s. tchr. Nev. State Bd. Edn., 1958. Tchr. Washoe County Sch. Dist., Reno, 1958—59, Burlingame Sch. Dist., Millbrae, Calif., 1959—60, San Rafael Sch. Dist., Vallecito, Calif., 1960—61; sr. svcs. dir., sr. nutrition program Cath. Charities So. Nev., Las Vegas, 1974—77; field rep. State of Nev., Divsn. for Aging Svcs., Las Vegas, 1977—82, dep. adminstr., 1982—88, adminstr., 1988—96; dep. to chancellor Nev. Sys. Higher Edn., Las Vegas, 1996—99, chief adminstrv. officer, 1999—2005, spl. asst. to chancellor, 2006—. Columnist Sr. World and Sr. Spectrum, Las Vegas, 1980—96; prodr., host, action srs. KVBC, Las Vegas, 1982—89; bd. dirs. Nat. Assn. State Units on Aging, Washington, 1990—96; del. White Ho. Coun. on Aging, Washington, 1995. Commr. City of Las Vegas Housing Authority, Las Vegas, Nev., 1989—93; bd. mem. Nev. Bd. of Examiners for Long-Term Care Adminstr., Las Vegas, Nev., 1990—96, Cmty. Housing Resource Bd., Las Vegas, Nev., 1986—88, State of Nev. Employee Mgmt. Com., Nev., 1986—2002, Clark County, City of Las Vegas Citizens' Govt. Efficiency Com., Las Vegas, Nev., 1992—92, Clark County Cmty. Devel. Adv. Com., Las Vegas, Nev., 1989—2006, Nev. Pub. Health Found., Inc., Las Vegas, Nev., 1996—2005; grand jury mem. Fore-Person Fed. Grand Jury on Organized Crime, Las Vegas, Nev., 1987—89. Named Outstanding Alum, Gamma Phi Beta Alumni, U. Nev., Reno, 1970, Outstanding Citizen, B'nai B'rith, 1989, Disting. Woman So. Nev., 1989—, Mother of Yr., Nev. Silver State, 1993, Outstanding Alumnus, U. Nev., Las Vegas, Coll. Edn., 1998; recipient Cmty. Achievement award, Adminstrn. on Aging, 1989; grantee, Fleishman Found., 1976. Mem.: Phi Kappa Phi. Democrat. Roman Catholic. Avocations: travel, reading. Office: Nev Sys Higher Edn 5550 W Flamingo Rd Ste C-1 Las Vegas NV 89103 Office Phone: 702-889-8426. Business E-Mail: ernsts@nevada.edu.

ERNSTOFF, RAINA MARCIA, neurologist; b. N.Y.C., Sept. 12, 1944; d. David and Rose (Fleischmann) E.; m. Sandy Hansell; children: Saul, Jenny, Amy. MD, Wayne State U., 1970; BA, Wheaton Coll., Mass. Diplomate Am. Bd. Psychiatry and Neurology. Dir. Myasthenia Gravis Treatment Ctr., Royal Oak, Mich., 1978—; assoc. clin. prof. Wayne State U.; clin. dir. Myasthenia Treatment Ctr., Beaumont Hosp., Mich. Instr. dept. neurology Wayne State U., Detroit, asst. clin. prof.; med. adv. com. mem. Greater Detroit Alzheimer's Assn.; pres. Myasthenia Gravis Found. of Am. Contbr. articles to profl. jours. Bd. dirs. Nat. Myesthenia Gravis Found. Am. Fellow: ACP, Am. Acad. Neurology. Office: 747 Beaumont Med Bldg 3535 W 13 Mile Rd Royal Oak MI 48073-6710 Office Phone: 248-435-5700.

ERON, MADELINE MARCUS, psychologist; b. New Brunswick, N.J., Sept. 8, 1919; d. Israel and Rae (Becker) Marcus; m. Leonard David Eron, May 21, 1950; children: Joni Eron Hobson, Don Marcus, Barbara Faye. Student, U. Mich., 1937-39; BA, NYU, 1941; MA, Columbia U., 1942. Lic. psychologist, Ill., N.Y.; nat. cert. Sch. Psychologist. Intern in psychology Phila. State Hosp., 1942-43; psychology extern Neurol. Inst. Columbia Presbyn. Med. Ctr., N.Y.C., 1943-44; sr. clin. psychologist Inst. Crippled and Disabled, N.Y.C., 1944-51; cons. psychologist New Haven, 1951-55; clin. psychologist Rip Van Winkle Clinic and Found., Hudson, N.Y., 1958-62; chief psychologist Berkshire Farm for Boys, Canaan, N.Y., 1961-62; pvt. practice psychology specializing in retng. the brain injured Iowa City, 1962-63; cons. Cedar Rapids (Iowa) Community Sch. Dist., 1963-67; dir. psychol. svcs. Comprehensive Evaluation-Rehab. Ctr., U. Iowa Med. Sch., Iowa City, 1968-69; sch. psychologist Winnetka, Glencoe and Skokie (Ill.) Elem. Sch. Dists., 1969-72, Evanston (Ill.) Twp. High Sch., 1972-90. Bd. dirs. Lincoln Ctr. Clin. Services, Highland Park, Ill. Mem. Am. Psychol. Assn. (div. sch. psychology, rehab. psychology, child and youth service), Iowa Psychol. Assn. (sec. 1965-67), Midwestern Psychol. Assn., Nat. Assn. Sch. Psychologists (charter), Ill. Sch. Psychologists Assn. (charter), Assn. Advancement Psychology, N.Y. State Psychol. Assn., Psi Chi. Home: 1075 E Victory Dr Ste 241 Lindenhurst IL 60046-7911

ERRECART, JOYCE, lawyer; b. Vergennes, Vt., July 1, 1950; d. Lloyd Maurice and Lillian Adela (Jay) Hier; m. Michael Terry Errecart, Mar. 30, 1971; children: Michael Jay, Jacqueline Marie. BA, Wellesley Coll., 1972; JD, Am. U., 1976; LLM in Taxation, Georgetown U., 1981. Bar: Md. 1976, U.S. Tax Ct. 1977, Vt. 1984, U.S. Dist. Ct. Vt. 1984. Law clk. to spl. trial judge U.S. Tax Ct., Washington, 1975-76; trial atty. dist. counsel IRS, Washington, 1976-83; assoc. Dinse, Erdmann & Clapp, Burlington, Vt., 1983-86; sole practice Burlington, 1986-91; commr. Vt. Dept. of Taxes, Montpelier, Vt., 1991—. Mem. ABA (tax sect.), Vt. Bar Assn. (tax sect.). Republican. Avocation: quilting. Office: Vt Dept Taxes Pavilion Office Bldg Montpelier VT 05602

ERSAY, MOLLY ANN, counselor, consultant; b. Washington, N.C., Oct. 22, 1940; d. Albert Henry and Arnette M. Ross; married, Dec. 17, 1973. BS, U. So. Miss., Hattiesburg, 1954. Commd 2d lt. USAF, psychologist; dir. manpower rsch. and testing Chrysler Automotive Corp., Detroit; dir. quality assurance Dept. Children and Families, Miami, Fla.; cons.; clin. lic. mental health counselor Key West, Fla. Avocations: reading, cooking, travel, sailing. Office: Counseling Ctr Key West Inc 1111 12th St Ste 206 Key West FL 33040 Office Phone: 305-294-8777. Office Fax: 305-294-8298. Personal E-mail: reemae@aol.com.

ERSKINE, KALI (WENDY COLMAN), psychoanalyst; b. Flushing, N.Y., July 6, 1950; d. Leo M. and Ray (Fine) Colman BS, Tufts U., Medford, Mass., 1972; MA, NYU, 1977, PhD in Occupl. Therapy, 1984; postgrad., Phila. Sch. of Psychoanalysis, 1988—92. Cert. psychoanalyst. Occupational therapist Extended Family Ctr., San Francisco, 1973-74; cons. child abuse San Francisco, 1974-75; sr. occupational therapist Roosevelt Hosp., N.Y.C., 1975-77; adj. instr. occupational therapy dept. NYU, N.Y.C., 1977-80; asst. prof. occupational therapy dept. Boston U., 1980-83; dir. grad. edn. occupational therapy, dept. assoc. prof. Temple U., Phila., 1984-87; cons. curriculum design Kean Coll. N.J., Union, 1985-88; cons. spl. projects, vice provost for rsch.- grad. studies Temple U., Phila., 1987-88; evaluation rsch. coord. Nat. Inst. Adolescent Pregnancy, Phila., 1986-90; pvt. practice psychotherapy and psychoanalysis, 1988—. Tng. and supervising analyst Phila. Sch. of Psychoanalysis, Editor VAPS Aviso newsletter, 1998-2000; contbr. articles to profl. jours. and texts in occupl. therapy and psychoanalysis (under names Wendy Colman and Kali Erskine). Fellow Am. Occupl. Therapy Assn.; mem. APA (Divsn. psychoanalysis), Nat. Assn. Advancement Psychoanalysis, Vt. Assn. for Psychoanalytic Studies, Soc. Phila. Sch. Psychoanalysis. Achievements include being first person to earn doctorate in occupational therapy. Office: Montpelier Psychoanalytic Group 201 Kildrummy Way Montpelier VT 05602 Office Phone: 802-223-6465. Business E-Mail: kalispack@madriver.com.

ERVA, KAREN THERESE, elementary school educator; b. Hancock, Mich., May 27, 1957; d. Earl Raymond and Nancy Ann Erva. Student, Mich. Technol. U., Houghton, 1975—77; BS, No. Mich. U., Marquette, 1979, MED, 1985. Tchr. Bark River-Harris Elem. Sch., Harris, Mich., 1979—. Sec. Bark River-Harris PTO. Recipient Treetop award for outstanding educator, MEAD Edn. Fund, 2000. Mem.: Bark River-Harris Edn. Assn. (v.p. 2005—06), Delta Kappa Gamma. Office: Bark River-Harris Sch PO Box 350 Harris MI 49845

ERWIN, BARBARA F., school system administrator; b. Chgo. married; 2 children. BS in Spl. Edn., Ind. U., Bloomington; MS in Sch. Adminstrn., Purdue U., West Lafayette, Ind.; PhD in Sch. Adminstrn., Ind. U., Bloomington. Mid. sch. spl. needs tchr.; Title IV-C cons. Ind. Dept. Pub. Instrn.; spl. edn. diagnostician; tchr.; elem. sch. prin.; supt. Ind., Tex., Allen (Tex.) Ind. Sch. Dist., 1994—2000, Scottsdale (Ariz.) Pub. Sch., 2000—. Nominee Nat. Supt. of Yr., 1999; named Supt. of Yr., Tex. Assn. of Sch. Bds., 1997, Tex. Assn. Sch. Adminstrs., 1998; recipient Top Suburban Supt. Leadership Learning award, Am. Assn. of Sch. Adminstrs., 1996. Office: Scottsdale Pub Sch Edn Ctr 3811 N 44th St Phoenix AZ 85018-5420

ERWIN, BETTY, bank executive; b. Charlotte, N.C., Nov. 11, 1945; d. John and Lula Bell Erwin; children: Wanda E. Dae, Johnny Maurice. BTh, Teamers Sch. of religion, 1989; BD, Teamers Sch. of Religion, 1991; BA, Shaw U., 1996; M in Christian Edn., Pheiffer U., 1998; Doctorate of Min., New Life Theol. Sem., 2000. Asst. buyer First Union, Charlotte, NC, 1986—97; courier specialist First Union Nat. Bank, Charlotte, 1997—2001; tchr. Charlotte-Mecklenburg Sch. Sys., 2002—; min. Antioch Bapt. Ch. Bible instr., Leadership tchr., facilitator women's ministry and singles ministry, asst. dir. Christian edn. Antioch Bapt. Ch. Mem.: Alpha Chi. Home: 3045 La Salle St Charlotte NC 28216 Office Phone: 704-333-2312. E-mail: drb1@bellsouth.net.

ERWIN, JOAN LENORE, artist, educator; b. Berkeley, Calif., Feb. 12, 1932; d. Ralph Albert and Dorothy Christine (Wuhrman) Potter; m. Byron W. Crider, Jan. 28, 1956 (div. May 1975); children: Susan Lynne Crider Adams, Gayle Leann Crider; m. Joseph G. Erwin Jr., May 28, 1976; children: Terry, Ray, Steve, Tim. BS, U. So. Calif., 1954; MS in Sch. Adminstrn., Pepperdine U., 1975. Cert. tchr., Calif.; registered occupational therapist, Calif. Occupational therapist Calif. State Hosp., Camarillo, 1955-56, Harlan Shoemaker Sch., San Pedro, Calif., 1956-57; tchr. Norwalk (Calif.) Sch. Dist., 1957-59, Tustin (Calif.) Sch. Dist., 1966-68, Garden Grove (Calif.) Sch. Dist., 1968-92; freelance artist Phelan, Calif., 1976—; comml. artist Morningstar Creations, Fullerton, Calif., 1982-92; substitute tchr. Snowline Sch. Dist., Phelan, Calif., 1994—; owner, artist Plumfrog Creations, Phelan, 2000—03. Artist Y.U.G.O., Los Alamitos, 1977-87; organizer 34th Annual Open Internat. Exbhn. Art, San Bernardino County Mus., 1999; resident artist High Desert Ctr. for the Arts, Victorville, 2000-2004; pvt. tchr. art, tutor, 1994—. One-woman shows include Victorville C. of C., 2004, Redlands Art Gallery, 2005, exhibited in group shows at San Bernardino County Mus., Redlands, Calif., Riverside Art Mus., Wildlife Artist Assn., American West Art Show, Norco, Calif., 2004—06 (premiere artist, 2004, 2005); pet portrait artist, U.S. and Eng., 1978—85, author, artist Biblical coloring books, 1985—90. Bd. dirs. San Bernardino County Mus., Fine Arts Inst.; juror county fair San Bernardino, Calif., 2003— Named Premier Artist, City of Norco Annual Show, 2004, 2005; grantee, Ford Found., 1957—58, Mentor Tchr. Program, 1986; Calif. Elks scholar, 1952—53. Republican. Baptist. Avocations: gardening, travel. Home: 10080 Monte Vista Rd Phelan CA 92371-8371 Personal E-mail: jaybird92371@yahoo.com.

ERWIN, LINDA MCINTOSH, retired librarian; b. Austin, Tex., June 22, 1939; d. William Erwin and Martha (Ferguson) McIntosh; m. Kenneth James Erwin, June 7, 1962 (div. Feb. 1986); 1 child, Jason Emerson. BA magna cum laude, U. Tex., 1961, MLS, 1968. Tchr. Spanish, Victoria (Tex.) H.S., 1961-62, El Campo (Tex.) H.S., 1962-63, Del Valle (Tex.) H.S., 1963-66; libr. U. Tex., Austin, 1968-69, Corpus Christi Pub. Librs., 1981-89; cons. South Tex. Libr. Sys., Corpus Christi, 1989-99, asst. coord., 1999—2006; ret., 2006. Ford Found. scholar, 1966-67. Mem. Tex. Libr. Assn., Phi Beta Kappa, Alpha Phi, Sigma Delta Pi.

ERWIN, NICOLE RENEE, pharmacist; b. Belleville, Ill., Aug. 19, 1972; d. Kenneth and Beverley Ann (Kaiser) E. BS cum laude, St. Louis Coll. Pharmacy, 1995. Registered pharmacist, Ill. Student pharmacist Walgreen's, Fairview Heights, Ill., 1992-95; pharmacist Schnuck's, Centralia, Ill., 1995—. Mem. Am. Pharmacist's Assn., Ill. Pharmacist's Assn., Met. East Pharmacists Assn., Am. Mensa Soc., Rho Chi. Home: 13980 Locust Ln Aviston IL 62293 Office: Schnuck's Pharmacy 1075 W Broadway Centralia IL 62801-5309

ERWIN, SANDRA KAY, music educator; b. DuQuoin, Ill., Mar. 15, 1958; d. Samuel Louis and Maryln Kay Erwin. BA in Music Edn., Mont. State U., 1981; MS in Music Edn., U. Ill., 1985; cert. in edn. adminstrn., U. South Ala., 2001. Tchr., asst. dir. bands Laurel (Mont.) Pub. Schs., 1981—84; tchr., band dir. Champaign (Ill.) Pub. Schs., 1985—91; music dept. instr. U. South Ala., Mobile, 1991—94; tchr., band dir. Mobile County Pub. Sch. Sys., 1994—. Chmn. K-12 music curriculum com., Champaign, 1985—87; scr5ibe Bldg. Leadership Team, Chickasaw, 1998—2001; chmn. Acad. Achievement Com., Chickasaw, 2002—05. Vol. Stone St. Bapt. Ch., Mobile, Ala., 2004; musical coord. Music & Me Drug Free Schs., Mobile, 1992—94; troop leader Girls Scouts of Deep South, Mobile, 2003—. Recipient Excellence in Edn. award, U.S. Dept. Edn., 1987—88. Mem.: NEA, Music Educators Nat. Conf. Avocations: reading, music, sports, movies. Home: 5712 Longmeadow Ct Mobile AL 36609 Office: Clark Magnet Sch 50 12th Ave Chickasaw AL 36611

ERZINGER, KATHY MCCLAM, nursing educator; b. Lake City, S.C., July 14, 1951; d. Curtis Brown and Parneace Ora (Timmons) McClam; m. Dennis Eugene Erzinger, Sr., June 22, 1974; children: Amberlyn Marie, Dennis Eugene Jr. AA, Brevard C.C., 1971; BS in Vocat. Edn., Carson-Newman Coll., 1974; degree in Vocat. Nursing, Simi Valley Adult Sch., 1997. Lic. vocat. nurse, cert. intravenous therapy and blood withdrawal; staff devel. Tchr. First Bapt. Acad., Thousand Oaks, Calif., 1988—90, Hillcrest Christian Sch., Thousand Oaks, 1990—93; charge nurse Victoria Care Ctr., Ventura, Calif., 1997—98; per diem charge nurse Thousand Oaks (Calif.) Health Care, 1995—; dir. staff devel. Westlake Healthcare Ctr., Westlake Village, Calif., 2001—02; instr. Simi Valley Adult Sch., Simi Valley, Calif., 2000—. Vol. Am. Cancer Assn., Simi Valley, 2003. Mem.: NEA, Calif. Vocat. Educators, Calif. Coun. for Adult Edn., Simi Educators Assn., Calif. Tchrs. Assn., Health Occupations Students of Am. Republican. Avocations: painting, baking, walking, music, gardening. Office: Simi Valley Adult School 3192 Los Angeles Ave Simi Valley CA 93065 E-mail: erzingerk@msn.com.

ESCALLÓN, ANA MARÍA, writer; b. Columbia; With Art Mus. Ams., Orgn. Am. States, Washington, 1996—2004. Author: Gerchman, 1994, Mejia-Guinand, 2002; 18 sculptures by Colombian artist Fernando Botero positioned along Constitution Ave in Washington, DC, 1996, An Architect of Surrealism, works by Roberto Matta, Mus. of the Americas, 2004, Sculpture in Four Dimensions, 2004.

ESCARRA, VICKI B., retired airline company executive; b. Atlanta; married; 2 children. Grad., Ga. State U.; exec. mgmt. program, Columbia U.; exec. leadership program, Harvard U. Joined, in-flight svc. div. Delta Airlines Inc., Atlanta, 1973—92, dir. in-flight svc. ops., 1992—94, v.p. reservation sales, 1994-96, v.p. reservation sales and distribution planning, 1996, v.p. airport customer svc. to sr. v.p. airport customer svc., 1996—98, exec. v.p., chief customer svc. officer, 1998—2001, exec. v.p., chief mktg. officer, 2001—04. Serves on Women Build Steering Coun. of Habitat for Humanity, Internat.; bd. dirs. AG Edwards, Atlanta C. of C., Woodward Acad., Atlanta Convention and Visitors Bur., chair elect, 2003—05; bd. visitors Emory Univ. Named Women of Year, Women Looking Ahead mag.; named one of 200 Most Powerful Women in Travel, Travel Agent mag., 1997, 1999, 2000, 2001; recipient Nat. Aviation and Space Exploration Wall of Honor certificate, Nat. Air & Space Mus. of Smithsonian Institution, 2000, YWCA Women of Achievement award, 2002. Mem.: Com. of 200, Internat. Women's Forum, Wings Club, Women in Aviation Internat., Atlanta Rotary Club.

ESCHETE, MARY LOUISE, internist; b. Houma, La., Feb. 8, 1949; d. Marshall John and Louise Esther (Davis) E.; m. Lorphy Joseph Bourque, July 7, 1979. BS, La. State U., 1970; MD, La. State U. Med. Ctr., Shreveport, 1974. Diplomate, Am. Bd. Internal Medicine. Resident in internal medicine La. State U. Med. Ctr., Shreveport, 1974-77, staff instr., 1979, fellow in infectious disease, 1979; pvt. practice Houma, 1980-83; staff, dept. internal medicine South La. Med. Assocs., Houma, 1983—. Chmn. infection control Terrebonne Gen. Hosp., 1981—2000, 2002—, mem. performance improvement, 2000—, vice chief staff, 2005—; chmn. infection control S. La. Med. Ctr., 1983—; pub. health dir. Region III, 1993—98, pub. health infectious disease cons., 1998—. Contbr. articles to med. jours. Bd. dirs. Houma Battered Women's Shelter, 1983-87, Houma YWCA, 1987-94; mem. Roche Nat. AIDS Adv. Bd., 1993; Triparish vol. activist, 1994. Named Citizen of Yr. Regional and State Social Workers, 1992, Outstanding Dr. in South East. Mem. ACP, AAAS, AMA, Infectious Disease Soc., Am. Soc. Microbiology, So. Med. Assn. (grantee 1978), N.Y. Acad. Sci., La. State Med. Soc., Terrebonne Parish Med. Soc. (sec. 1982-83, treas. 1988-89, 98—, v.p. 1993-94, pres. 1994-95), Krewe of Hyachinthians (pres. 1989-90, 94-95, bd. dirs. 1990-96), Houma Jr. Women's Club (reporter 1988-89, rec. sec. 1989—, pres.-elect 1991-93, pres. 1993-95, chaplain 1998—2002), Alpha Epsilon Delta. Democrat. Roman Catholic. Avocation: gardening. Home: 3984 Highway 311 Houma LA 70360-8115 Office: Chabert Med Ctr 1978 Industrial Blvd Houma LA 70363-7055 Office Phone: 985-873-5130, 985-873-1800.

ESCOBAR, DEBORAH ANN, gifted and talented educator; b. Schenectady, NY, Aug. 21, 1952; d. Richard H. and Rose Marie (Denny) Quay; m. Jorge Escobar, Oct. 25, 1975; children: Rosana, Michael, Jorge R. AA, Schenectady County C.C., NY, 1988; BA, Russell Sage Coll., Troy, NY, 1990; MA, State Univ. Albany, NY, 1995. Lic. tchr. social studies, secondary, gifted and talented edn. NY. Asst. editor, legis. liaison Internat. Assn. Fire Chiefs, Washington, 1972-76; tchr. gifted and talented Guilderland Sch. Dist., NY, 1991—. Author: Answering the Call, 1993, Teaching the History of the Albany Internat. Airport, 2000, Creating Hist. Documentaries, 2001, From Africa to NY: Slavery in NY State, 2001, (website) NYS Archives Legacies, 2003. Named Outstanding New Tchr. Sally Mae and Am. Assn. Sch. Adminstrs., Washington, 1992, NYS Hist. Day Tchr. of the Yr., 2001; Nat. Hist. Day Richard T. Ferrell Tchr. of Merit, 2001, Bruce W. Dearstyne Ann. Archives award, 2004. Mem. NY State Coun. Social Studies, Capital Dist. Coun. Social Studies, Phi Alpha Theta, Phi Kappa Phi, Phi Theta Kappa. Democrat. Avocations: writing, dance, genealogy. Office: Farnsworth Mid Sch State Farm Rd Guilderland NY 12084

ESCOBAR, MARISOL See MARISOL

ESCOBEDO CABRAL, ANNA, federal official; m. Victor Cabral; children: Raquel, Viana, Catalina, Victor Christopher. BA, UCLA, 1987; MPA, Harvard U., 1990; JD, George Mason U. Exec. staff dir. U.S. Rep. Task Force on Hispanic Affairs, Washington, 1991—99; dep. staff dir. U.S. Senate Com. on Judiciary, Washington, 1993—99; pres., CEO Hispanic Assn. on Corp. Responsibility, Washington, 1999—2003; U.S. treasurer US Dept. Treasury, Washington, 2004—. Dir. Smithsonian Ctr. for Latin Initiatives Smithsonian Inst., 2003—; gov., bd. mem. Am. Red Cross. Office: Dept of Treasury 1500 Pennsylvania Ave NW Rm 2134 Washington DC 20220 Office Phone: 202-622-0100. Office Fax: 202-622-2258.

ESCOTT, SHOOLAH HOPE, microbiologist; b. Stamford, Conn., May 20, 1952; d. Robert R. and Fanny (Levy) E.; m. Joseph J. Sulmar, Sept. 6, 1992. Cert. med. tech., St. Vincent's Hosp., Bridgeport, Conn., 1974; BS, U. Conn., 1974; MS, Northeastern U., Boston, 1985. Cert. med. technologist. Clin. lab. scientist NCA, 1976; med. technologist St. Elizabeth's Hosp., Boston, 1976, Harvard U. Health Svcs., Cambridge, Mass., 1976-79; med. technologist microbiology lab. New Eng. Deaconess Hosp., Boston, 1979-84; supr. microbiology Norwood (Mass.) Hosp., 1984-87; adminstrv. supr. microbiology labs. Med. Ctr. Ctrl. Mass., Worcester, 1991-96; supr. microbiology lab. Worcester Meml. Hosp., Worcester, 1987-91; mgr. microbiology Meml. Hosp., 1996-98; regional coord. northeast office Nat. Lab. Tng. Network, Boston, 1998—2001, CDC tng. advisor N.E. office, 2001—. Named Nat. Merit Scholar, 1970; grantee, 1970. Mem. Am. Soc. Clin. Pathologists, Am. Soc. for Microbiology, Am. Soc. for Microbiology, N.E. Assn. for Clin. Microbiology and Infectious Disease (bd. dirs. Mass. chpt. 1989-91, 99-2000, treas. 1991-93, pres.-elect 1993-94, pres. 1994-95, past pres. 1995-96). Achievements include study of parasites of South East Asian refugees; the culturing of genital mycoplasmas in low birth weight neonates and poster at Nat. ASM on C.Difficile toxin detection, poster at Nat. ASM on premier EHEC Kit for shiga-toxin producing e-coli. Address: 3 Viles Rd Lexington MA 02421-5515

ESFANDIARY, MARY S., physicial scientist, operations consultant; b. Passaic, N.J., June 27, 1929; d. Peter J. and Veronica R. (Kida) Nieradka; m. Mohsen S. Esfandiary; children: Homayoun Austin, Dara S. BS in Chemistry,

St. John's U., 1951; postgrad., Polytechnic Inst. N.Y., 1955-56. Research chemist Picatinny Arsenal, Dover, N.J., 1951-56; supr. phys. sci. Bur. Mines, Washington, 1956-61; asst. to dir. research Nat. Iranian Oil Co., Tehran, 1961-64; lectr. U. Tehran and Aryamehr Inst. Tech., Tehran, 1961-64, 69-73; dir. internat. affairs Acad. of Scis., Tehran, 1977-79; chief geog. names br. Def. Mapping Agy., Washington, 1981-86, chief prodn. mgmt. office, 1986-87, chief support div., chief inventory mgmt. div., 1987-90, chief product mgmt. dept., 1990-92, dep. dir. distbn. mgmt. ops. Combat Support Ctr., 1993, chief, co-prodn. mgmt. divsn., 1993-94, chief divsn. internat. ops. coprodn. mgmt., 1993-96; ops. mgmt., 1996; dir. MS svcs. Washington, 1997—. Contbr. papers and articles to tech. jours., 1952-78. Pres. UN Delegations Women's Club, N.Y.C., 1967-69, v.p., program dir., 1964-67; pres. Diplomatic Corps. Com. for Red Cross, Bangkok, Thailand, 1974-76; v.p., bd. dirs. Found. for Blind of Thailand, Bangkok, 1973-77. Recipient Badge of Honor for Social Service, Thailand, 1975, 1st Class medal Red Cross, Thailand, 1976. Home and Office: 4401 Sedgewick St NW Washington DC 20016-2713

ESHEL, HANNA M., sculptor, painter, photographer; b. Jerusalem, Isreal, Sept. 5, 1926; arrived in U.S., 1978; d. Pinchas Baltinester and Dina Friedman; 1 child, Ory. Student in art, Bezalel, Jerusalem, 1944—46; student in painting, Ecoze de la Grande Chaumiere, Paris, 1953—54, Academie de la Grande Chaumiere. Painter, sculptor, photography, Europe, Israel, US, 1959—2005. Author: Michelangelo and Me, Six Years in My Carrara Haven, 1996; pub. (DVD) 4 Lives of Hanna Eshel-A Portrait of an Artist, 2005; exhibitions include numerous thoughout Europe, Israel, US. Second lt. Israeli Air Force, 1947—51. Avocations: reading, theater, travel, music, art history.

ESHELMAN, GEORGIA LEE, music educator; b. Canton, Ohio, Aug. 10, 1945; d. Roy D. Carrothers and Leona E. Teufel-Carrothers; m. Jack J. Eshelman, Nov. 23, 1979; 1 child, John R. BS, Kent State U., Ohio, 1968, MA, 1974; PhD, U. Akron, Ohio, 1999. Cert. elem. tchr. Ohio. Instr. Wayne Coll., U. Akron, Orrville, Ohio, 1999, Malone Coll., Canton, Ohio, 1999—. Rschr., writer Stark Fed. Credit Union, Canton, 2004—06. Musician: (CD) Simple Life, 2002, God's Own Peace be With You, 2003. Instr. St. Barbara's Sch., Massillon, Ohio, 2005—06. Recipient Attendance Improvement and Writing Process award, Canton City Schools, 1994; grantee, 1992. Roman Catholic. Avocations: reading, gardening, music, travel. Home: PO Box 266 Greentown OH 44630 Office: Malone Coll 515 - 25th NW Canton OH 44709 Office Phone: 330-471-8200. Home Fax: 330-833-5340. Business E-Mail: geshelman@malone.edu.

ESHETU, GWENDELBERT LEWIS, retired social worker; b. Cairo, Ill., Mar. 22, 1940; d. Rassie A. and Naomi (Briggs) Lewis; m. Frederick O. Carr (div. 1976); 1 child, Melisande Caprice; m. Fisseha Eshetu, Feb. 17, 1984 (div. 1990). BA, U. Wis., Milw., 1966, MS, 1972. Caseworker Milw. County Dept. Social Services, 1966-70; social worker Ill. Dept. Children and Family Services, Cairo, 1971, Milw. Pub. Schs., 1972—97; ret., 1997. Instr. field placement for grad. students, Milw. Pub. Schs. and U. Wis., Milw., 1973-75. Mem. Nat. Assn. Social Workers, Nat. Assn. Black Social Workers, Milw. Sch. Social Workers Assn., Wis. Assn. Black Social Workers (office holder), Acad. Cert. Social Workers, NAACP (life), Mensa (life), Eta Phi Beta. Democrat. Avocation: writing fiction. Home: 3019 N 55th St Milwaukee WI 53210-1564

ESHLEMAN, DIANE VARRIN, bank executive; b. Jan. 1956; d. Robert D. Varrin; m. Gregory V. Eshleman, Sept. 6, 1980. Grad., Princeton U., 1978. With Chemical Banking Corp.; exec. v.p. Chase Manhattan bank; mng. dir., chief procurement officer info. tech. JP Morgan Chase, N.Y.C. Named one of 25 Women to Watch, US Banker Mag., 2003. Office: JP Morgan Chase 270 Park Ave New York NY 10017-2070

ESHOO, ANNA GEORGES, congresswoman; b. New Britain, Conn., Dec. 13, 1942; d. Fred and Alice Alexandre Georges; children: Karen Elizabeth, Paul Frederick. AA with honors, Canada Coll., 1975. Chmn. San Mateo County Dem. Ctrl. Com., Calif., 1978-82; chair Human Rels. Com., 1979-82; mem. U.S. Congress from 14th Calif. dist., 1993—; at-large minority whip; mem. energy and commerce com., intelligence com. Chief of staff Calif. Assembly Spkr. Leo McCarthy, 1981; regional majority whip No. Calif., 1993-94. Co-founder Women's Hall of Fame; chair San Mateo County (Calif.) Dem. Party, 1980; active San Mateo County Bd. Suprs., 1982-92, pres., 1986; pres. Bay Area Air Quality Mgmt. Dist., 1982-92; mem. San Francisco Bay Conservation Devel. Commn., 1982-92; chair San Mateo County Gen. Hosp. Bd. Dirs. Democrat. Roman Catholic. Office: US House Reps 205 Cannon Ho Office Bldg Washington DC 20515-0514

ESHOO, BARBARA ANNE RUDOLPH, non-profit administrator; b. Worcester, Mass., Sept. 27, 1946; d. Charles Leighton and Irene Isabella (Wheeler) Rudolph; divorced: l child, Melissa Clinton; m. Robert Pius Eshoo, July ll, l98l. Student, Morehead State U., 1964-66, U. N.H., 1974, 75; BA, New England Coll., l976. Asst. to dir. Currier Gallery Art, Manchester, NH, 1976-78, coord. pub. rels., 1979-82; dir. pub. rels. Daniel Webster Coll., Nashua, NH, 1982-87, chief advancement officer, 1988-95; v.p. instnl. advancement Ea. Conn. State U., Willimantic, 1995—2004; sr. v.p. Assn. Advancement YMCA Greater Hartford, Conn., 2004—. Mem. faculty Currier Art Ctr., Manchester, 1977-79; bd. advisers New Eng. Coll. Art Gallery, Henniker, N.H., 1989-91. Advisor on planned giving United Way, Nashua, 1989-90; com. mem. Manchester Mayor's Task force on Youth Affairs, 1986-88, Manchester Bd. of Sch. Commn., 1986-90; del. N.H. Sch. Bds. Assn., 1988-90; trustee, bd. sec. Manchester Hist. Assn., 1990-95; mem. Mayor's Com. on Leadership, Manchester, 1988-91; bd. dirs. Swiftwater coun. Girl Scouts U.S., 1990-95; chairperson parents com. Bennington Coll.; mem. N.Am. devel. orgn. YMCA, 2004— Mem.: N.Am. YMCA Devel. Officers Orgn., Middlesex County C. of C., Assn. Fundraising Profls., Coun. Advancement and Support of Edn., Assn. Governing Bds. Univs. and Colls. (facilitator 1995—2003, planning com.), Conn. Com. on Planned Giving, Nat. Com. on Planned Giving, Am. Coun. on Edn. (state of Conn. rep. Office Women in Higher Edn.), Conn. Women in Higher Edn., Nat. Soc. Fundraising Execs. (bd. dirs., v.p. pub. affairs N.H./Vt. chpt. to 1995), Newcomen Soc. Conn., Rotary (Nashua West chpt. 1990—95), Advt. Club N.H. (bd. dirs., v.p. 1980—82). Avocation: performing and visual arts. Office: YMCA Metrop Offices 241 Trumbull St 2d Fl Hartford CT 06103 Office Phone: 860-522-9622 ext. 2308. Business E-Mail: barbara.eshoo@ghymca.org.

ESKEW, DOROTHY, art educator; b. Atlanta, Dec. 9, 1949; d. John Hardin and Dorothy Cortez McGarity Eskew; 1 child, Briana Dennis Long. BFA in Graphic Design, U. Ga., 1973. Cert. art edn. K-12 Ga. Graphic designer, office mgr. Crown Printing Co., Forest Park, Ga., 1973—98; art tchr. Henry County Bd. Edn., McDonough, Ga., 1998—. Mem.: Profl. Assn. Ga. Educators, Ga. Art Edn. Assn., Nat. Art Edn. Assn., Delta Kappa Gamma. Avocations: writing, poetry, drawing, painting, photography. Office: Ola High Sch 357 N Ola Rd Mcdonough GA 30252

ESKIN, CATHERINE R., language educator; b. Phila., Aug. 8, 1966; d. Bernard A. and Debra Lynn Eskin; children: Theophila Mathilda, Hunter Emanuel. PhD, U. Tex., Austin, 1995. Asst. prof. Norwegian U. Sci. and Tech., Trondheim, Norway, 1995—97; vis. asst. prof. Drexel U., Phila., 1997—99; assoc. prof. English Fla. So. Coll., Lakeland, 1999—. Program dir. Hadassah, Polk County Fla., Lakeland, 2006; mem. bd. Temple Emanuel, Lakeland, 2003—. Mem.: MLA, Renaissance Soc. Am., Sixteenth Century Soc., Shakespeare Assn. Am. Office: Fla So Coll 111 Lake Hollingsworth Drive Lakeland FL 33801 Office Fax: 863-680-4117.

ESKRIDGE, JUDITH ANN, retired secondary school educator; b. Tuscola, Ill., July 15, 1941; d. Reed Warren and Marjorie May (Reeder) Blain; m. Donald R. Henderson, July 10, 1966 (div. Dec. 1977); m. Howard Dean Eskridge, June 29, 1986; children: Kendra Eskridge Chriss, Jodi Henderson Samsa. BA, MacMurray Coll., 1963; MEd, U. Ill., 1968. Title I tchr., dir. Arcola (Ill.) Cmty. Unit #306, 1978—2004; ret., 2004. Tchr. Arcola Elem. Sch., 2004—. Chair Keal scholarship com. Meth. Ch.; trustee Arcola United Meth. Ch., 2006—. Recipient Cert. of Appreciation Ea. Ill. Area Spl. Edn., 1988, Education is Key award, 2004; Keal scholar, 2004—. Mem.: Ill. Ret. Tchrs. Assn., Douglas County Ret. Tchrs. Methodist. Avocations: reading, gardening, exercising, travel. Home: 424E E County Road 1250 N Tuscola IL 61953-7074 Personal E-mail: judy.eskridge@netcare-il.com.

ESLINGER, DENISE MARIE, social worker; b. Pitts., July 22, 1954; d. Miron and Sophia Juba; m. Kenneth Nelson Eslinger, July 22, 1979 BS Biology cum laude, Baldwin Wallace Coll., 1978; MA Counselor, Human Svcs., John Carroll U., 1985, cert. sch. psychologist, 1987; cert. supt., asst. supt., prin., Ashland U., 1995; PhD, Ind. State U., 2006. LCSW; cert. web designer 2005, cognitive therapy 2003, sports counselor 2003, supt, Ohio, 2002, asst. supt. Ohio, 1995, elem. prin. Ohio, 1995, lic. profl. clin. counselor LPCC, 1997, Diplomate Nat. Bd. Cert. Clin. Hypnotherapist, 1990, cert. tchr. biology, gen. sci., psychology, social psychology grades 7-12 Baldwin-Wallace Coll., 1978. Sch. psychologist, psychometrist MetroHealth Med. Ctr., Cleve., 1987—90; asst. to prin., sch. psychologist, computer advisor Midview Local Sch. Dist., Grafton, Ohio, 1990—96; rsch. and tchg. asst. Early Child and Elem. Edn. Ind. State U., Terre Haute, 1996—97; coord. tech., sch. psychologist Midview Local Sch. Dist., Grafton, 1997—98, dir. curriculum and tech., 1998—2004, sch. psychologist, 2005—. Adj. faculty Elyria campus Ashland U., Ohio, 1997—. Fellow, NASA Rsch. Ctr., Lewis Rsch. Ctr., 1994—97. Mem. Nat. Assn. Sch. Psychologists (cert. 1989), Ohio Sch. Psychologists Assn. (cert, 1987, com. 1989-90), Cleve. Assn. Sch. Psychologists, Greenpeace, World Wildlife Fedn., Audubon Soc., Phi Kappa Phi, Kappa Delta Pi, Pi Lambda Theta Avocations: racquetball, jogging, photography. Home: 10312 Elliman Rd Mantua OH 44255-9482 Office Phone: 440-748-1233. E-mail: deslin@leeca.org.

ESPADAS, ELIZABETH ANNE, language educator; d. Leroy and Anna G. Qualls; m. Juan de la Cruz Espadas, June 18, 1966; children: Juan, Carlos. PhD, U. Ill., Urbana-Champaign, 1971. Tchg. and rsch. asst. U. of Ill., Urbana-Champaign, 1966—69; instr. of Spanish U. of Del., Newark, 1970—71, asst. prof. of Spanish, 1971—78; vis. prof. Franklin and Marshall Coll., Lancaster, Pa., 1978—79; vis. prof. Spanish Lincoln U., Lincoln University, Pa., 1979—81; prof. of modern lang. Wesley Coll., Dover, Del., 1981—. Author: (bibliographic guide) A lo largo de una escritura: Ramón J. Sender; contbr. articles to profl. jours. Pres., bd. mem. Mid. Atlantic Coun. for Latin Am. Studies, Asociacion Internacional de Letras Femeninas Hispánicas, 1975—2006. Fellow Summer Seminars and Inst. fellow, NEH, 1977, 1980, 1987, 1994, 1998, Dissertation fellow, U. of Ill., 1969—70; grantee Rsch. grantee, Spain's Ministry of Culture, 1993, Del. Humanities Forum, 1988, Grant-in-Aid, Instituto de Estudios Altoaragoneses, Huesca, Spain, 2001. Mem.: MLA. Avocation: travel. Office: Wesley College 120 N State St Dover DE 19901 Office Phone: 302-736-2359. E-mail: espadael@wesley.edu.

ESPARZA, KACIE LYNNE, military officer; b. Atlantic, Iowa, June 27, 1980; d. Stanton Farrell Campbell and Lisa Luanne Flowers; m. Andrew Arthur Esparza, II, Nov. 3, 2001; 1 child, Andrew Arthur III. Student, CC Air Force, Davis-Monthan AFB, Ariz., 2000—. Asst. mgr. Hy-Vee Food Stores, Souix Falls, SD, 1999—2000; enlisted USAF, 2000; maintenance prodn. mgr. 358 Amu 355 Amxs 355 Wing, Davis-Monthan AFB, 2001—. Dormitory coun. pres. 355 Wing, Davis-Monthan Air Force Base, Ariz., 2001. Republican. Lutheran. Avocations: writing, vocal music, art, softball, dance. Personal E-mail: kacie.esparza@americanamicable.com. Business E-Mail: kacie.esparza@dm.af.mil.

ESPARZA, KAREN ANN, history educator; b. Orange, Calif., Mar. 5, 1954; d. William Lee and Jeanette Nadine Whitaker; children: Jacob Oldrich, Joseph William. BA, U. Calif., LA, 1977. Ride operator Disneyland, Anaheim, Calif., 1972—78; tchr. Orange Unified Sch. Dist., 1977—2000, 2000—. Recipient Tchr. Yr., Masonic Lodge Yorba Linda, 2004; grantee, NEH Landmark Am. History Program, 2005; scholar, Gilder Lehrman Inst. Am. HIstory, 2004. Mem.: NEA (life), Freedom Found. (grantee 1995, 2002, 2003), Calif. Coun. Social Studies, Calif. Teachers Assn. (life). Democrat. Avocations: travel, yoga, running. Office: Travis Ranch Middle School 5200 Via de la Escuela Yorba Linda CA 92887 Office Phone: 714-777-0584. Office Fax: 714-777-1769.

ESPENOZA, CECELIA M., lawyer, law educator; b. Murray, Utah, July 28, 1958; d. Benney and Ruth Gable (Jimenez) E.; m. Michael Sheehan, Apr. 25, 1992. BA in Pol. Sci. with honors, U. Utah, 1979, JD, 1982. Bar: Utah 1982, Colo. 1992, U.S. Dist. Ct. Utah 1982, Tex. 1997. Dir. migrant unit Utah Legal Svcs., Inc., Salt Lake City, 1982-84; city prosecutor Sandy City, Utah, 1984-86; spl. asst. to U.S. atty./ city prosecutor Salt Lake City, 1986-90; law prof. CLEO program Ariz. State U., 1989; assoc. prof. law U. Denver, 1990-97; vis. prof., assoc. prof. St. Mary's U. Ctr. for Legal and Social Justice, San Antonio, 1997—2000; sr. assoc. gen. counsel Exec. Office for Immigration Rev. US Dept. Justice, 2003—. Mem., bd. Immigration Appeals, 2000-03. Contbr. articles to profl. jours. Judge Pro Tempore Salt Lake City Small Claims Ct., 1985-89; bd. dirs. Salt Lake Legal Aid Found., 1986-89, Hispanic Youth Ministry Com., Denver, 1991-93; chmn. rules com. State Dem. Party, Salt Lake City, 1988; ind. candidate Arlington County Sch. Bd., 2005; appointed to Va. Latino Adv. Commn. Bd., 2004—. Leary scholar U. Utah, 1979-82. Mem. ABA (mem. immigration coord. com. 1989-95, mem. pro bono devel. bd Ford Found. 1990-97), Am. Bar Assn. Young Lawyers (dist. rep. ABA-YLD 1984-86, chairperson immigration assistance 1987-89, minorities in the profession 1989-90), Hispanic Nat. Bar Assn. (regional pres. 1988-89), Utah State Bar, Utah Hispanic Bar Assn. (v.p. 1985-87, pres. 1987-89); Fellow, Nat. Hispanic Leadership Inst., 2003. Office: US Dept Justice Exec Office for Immigration Rev 5107 Leesburg Pike Ste 2600 Falls Church VA 22041

ESPER, SUSAN, diversified financial services company executive; BS in Acctg., Providence Coll., Rhode Island. CPA Mass. Ptnr., fin. svcs. industry practice Deloitte & Touche, Boston. Vol. Big Sister Assn. Greater Boston; mem. women's leadership com. United Way; corp. adv. bd. Commonwealth Inst. Mem.: Nat. Investment Co. Svc. Assn. Office: Deloitte Consulting 200 Clarendon St Boston MA 02116*

ESPEUT, CAMILLE COTTRELL, retired art educator; b. Washington, Dec. 11, 1924; d. Camille James and Mary Ellen (Craft) Cottrell; m. LeRoi Espeut. BA, Vassar Coll., N.Y., 1944; MA in Art Edn., Cath. U., DC, 1953. Art tchr. DC Pub. Schs., Washington, 1947, Kelly Miller Jr. High, Washington, 1948—55; art tchr., head dept. Eastern Sr. High, Washington, 1955—64; pvt. summer sch. tchr. Patio Sch., Washington, 1953—63; art tchr., head dept. Cardoza Sr. High, Washington, 1964—78; ret., 1978. Vol. D.C. Ret. Tchrs. Assn., 1978—; vol. fundraiser Urban League, 1960—70; art work advertising Vassar Booksale, Washington, 1960—70, salesperson, 1988—99. Mem.: Alumni Assn. of Vassar Coll., Smithsonian RAP Program, D.C. Vassar Club. Democrat. Episcopal. Home: 4506 17th St NW Washington DC 20011 Address: Riderwood Village 3156 Gracefield Rd #507 Silver Springs MD 20904

ESPINOSA, CAROLE JO, counselor, educator; b. El Paso, Tex., Oct. 18, 1955; d. Joe Espinosa and Ann Diaz-Espinosa. BS, U. Tex., El Paso, 1999; MA in Clin. Psychology, Sul Ross State U., Alpine, Tex., 2001, MEd in Counseling, 2003; postgrad. in Clin. Psychology, Fielding Grad. U., Santa Barbara, Calif., 2004—06. Owner Mont. Vista Svcs., El Paso, Tex., 2000—03, Summit Consulting Group, 2003—. Adj. prof. El Paso C.C., 2001—, Webster Grad. U., Ft. Bliss, 2005—, U. Tex., 2006—. Mem. Spl. Olympics, Area 19, El Paso, 1985—86. Mem.: APA (assoc.), Psi Chi. E-mail: cespinosa1@elp.rr.com.

ESPINOSA, NANCY SWEET, artist, anthropologist; b. Jackson, Mich., Feb. 21, 1956; d. Harland Guy and Genevieve Kathryn Sweet; m. John P. Espinosa, 1978 (div. 1998). BFA in Two-Dimensional Art, BS in Anthropology, Ea. N.Mex. U., 1998, BS in Anthropology, 1998, MA in Anthropology, 2002. Comm. operator III N.Mex. State Police, Roswell, N.Mex., 1980—88; emergency comm. operator Roswell Police Dept., 1989—96; fellow Ea. N.Mex. U., 1999—2002, archaeol. collections mgr., 2000—02; curator Salmon Ruins Mus. and Rsch. Libr., Bloomfield, N.Mex., 2003—04, curator, edn. coord., 2004—. Exhibited in group shows at Clovis C.C./Ea. N.Mex. U., 1996, BFA Gallery, 1998. Home: 3105 Stanford Ave Farmington NM 87402-8845 Office Phone: 505-632-2013. Personal E-mail: espnart@hotmail.com.

ESPINOZA, LINDA, elementary school educator; b. Montebello, Calif., Oct. 1, 1947; d. George Morse Burns and Betty Lou Asbjeld. BA in English, Calif. State U., Fullerton, 1970. Tchg. credential Calif., 1971. Tchr. grades 5 and 6 Lone Hill Mid. Sch., San Dimas, Calif., 1971—73; tchr. grade 6 Shull Elem. Sch., 1973—76; tchr. reading and English grade 6 Ramona Mid. Sch., La Verne, 1976—86, tchr. social studies grade 7, 1986—91, tchr. social studies grade 8, 1991—. Rep. Bonita Unified Tchrs. Assn., La Verne, Calif., 1972—, exec. bd. mem., 1991—2005, negotiator, 1997—. Named Tchr. of Yr., Ramona Mid. Sch., 2000—01; recipient WHO award, Calif. Tchrs. Assn., 2004—05. Home: 35998 Donny Cir Palm Desert CA 92211 Office: Ramona Mid Sch 3490 Ramona Ave La Verne CA 91750 Office Phone: 909-971-8260.

ESPIRICUETA, SYLVIA, counseling administrator; b. Chgo., June 17, 1960; d. Zeferino Sáenz and Maria Delua; m. Valentine Espiricueta, July 26, 1986; 1 child, Valentine IV. BS in Edn. magna cum laude, Pan Am. U., Edinburg, Tex., 1983; MS in Edn., Counseling, Guidance, U. North Tex., 1990. Cert. counselor Tex., tchr. Tex. Bilingual tchr. Mission Sch. Dist., Tex., Austin Ind. Sch. Dist., Tex., Irving Ind. Sch. Dist., Tex.; tchr. Spanish Mesquite Ind. Sch. Dist., Tex.; binlingual psychotherapist MHMR, Dallas, Galaxy Ctr., Garland, Tex.; elem. sch. counselor Grand Prairie Ind. Sch. Dist., Tex., Arlington Ind. Sch. Dist., Tex. Whole brain tutor, Dallas, Ft. Worth, 1998—; lectr. in field; bilingual storyteller Arlington Pub. Libr., 2002. Singer (songwriter): (CD) After the Rain Comes the Sun, 2003; author: Positive Choices, 1996, Teach to Reach, 2002, Choosing to Learn to Climb, 2002. Internat. singer, songwriter. Finalist, Festival Cancion Latin Am., Calif., 2003; recipient 2d pl. singer/songwriter, Festival de la Cancion, 2004, Song of Yr., 2005. Mem.: ASCAP, L.A. Music Network, Ft. Worth Songwriters Assn. Office Phone: 682-365-2894. Personal E-mail: espiricuetasylvia@hotmail.com.

ESPIRITU, ANTONINA, economics professor; b. Philippines; d. Filomeno and Bienvenida Espiritu. BS in Applied Econs., De La Salle U., Manila, Philippines, 1982; MA in Econs., U. Hawaii-Manoa, Honolulu, 1989; PhD in Econs., U. Nebr., Lincoln, 1998. Staff asst. to the pres. Pacific Activated Carbon Co., Inc., Manila, 1983—85; lectr. De La Salle U., Manila, 1984—85; rsch. asst. Yokohama Nat. U., Japan, 1986—87; lectr. U. Nebr., Lincoln, 1995—97; asst. prof. Hawaii Pacific U., Honolulu, 1998—2002, assoc. prof., 2002—. Econ. rsch. staff cons. Asian Devel. Bank, Manila, 1992. Author: articles in profl. jours. Recipient Econs. Rsch. scholarship, Ministry Edn. Japan, 1985—87, scholarship, East-West Ctr., 1988—89, Econs. Edn. Grad. scholarship, NSF, 1994—96, Grad. Tchg. scholarship, U. Nebr., 1996—97; fellow Mcconnell Dissertation, U. Nebr. Dept. Econs., 1997—98.

ESSA, LISA BETH, elementary school educator; b. Nov. 19, 1955; d. Mark Newyla and Elizabeth (Warda) Essa. BA, U. Pacific-Stockton, 1977, MA in Curriculum and Instrn. Reading, 1980. Cert. tchr. elem., multiple subject and reading specialist Calif., master tchr. 2000. Libr. media specialist Delhi (Calif.) Elem. Sch. Dist., 1978-80; reading clinic tutor San Joaquin Delta C.C., Stockton, Calif., 1980; libr. media specialist Hayward (Calif.) Unified Sch. Dist., 1980—. Chair curriculum coun. Hayward Unified Sch. Dist., 2000—01; support provider Beginning Tchr. Support Provider, 2000—01, 2004—05. Supr. San Francisco host com. Dem. Nat. Conv., 1984. Recipient Hon. Svc. award, 1999. Mem.: Hayward Unified Tchrs. Assn., Calif. Tchrs. Assn., Jr. League San Francisco. Episcopalian. E-mail: lessa@husd.k12.ca.us.

ESSANDOH, HILDA BRATHWAITE, primary school educator; b. N.Y.C., Feb. 19, 1925; d. Charles Christopher and Millicent Marian (Boxill) Brathwaite; m. Samuel O. Essandoh, June 11, 1959; children: Millicent Efua, Yvonne Araba, Dorothy Esi. BA, Hunter Coll., 1959; MS, Bank Street Coll. Edn., 1976, profl. diploma in supervision-adminstrn., 1980. Cert. nursery, kindergarten, 1st-6th grades, sch. adminstrn. and supervision. Tchr. kindergarten N.Y.C. Bd. Edn., 1962-91. Recipient Ely Trachtenberg award. Home: 548 W 165th St New York NY 10032-4942

ESSELSTEIN, RACHEL, mathematician, educator; d. James Esselstein and Barbara Springer. BA in Math., U. Calif. San Diego, La Jolla, 2002; MA in Math., Dartmouth Coll., Hanover, N.H., 2004. Tchr. Summerbridge San Diego, La Jolla, Calif., 2000; grad. advisor Dartmouth Coll., 2005—. Recipient Dean's Leadership award, Muir Coll.- U. Calif. San Diego, 2002; fellow GAAN Fellowship, Dartmouth Coll., 2005—06. Mem.: Assn. Women in Math., Am. Math. Soc., Math. Assn. Am.

ESSERMAN, SUSAN GAYLE, lawyer; b. Chgo., June 20, 1952; d. Ronald and Charlene (Cohen) E.; m. Andrew H. Marks, Aug. 3, 1975; children: Stephen Matthew, Clifford Michael, Michael David. Student, Williams Coll., 1972-73; BA, Wellesley Coll., 1974; JD, U. Mich., 1977. Bar: D.C 1977, Fla. 1977. Jud. clk. to Hon. Oliver Gasch U.S. Dist. Ct. D.C., Washington, 1977-78; assoc. Steptoe & Johnson, Washington, 1978-84, ptnr., 1985-93, ptnr., chair Internat. Dept.; asst. sec. commerce for import adminstrn. U.S. Dept. of Commerce, Washington, 1994-96, acting gen. counsel, 1996; gen. counsel, 1997-98; dep. US trade rep. Office of the US Trade Rep., Washington, 1998. Co-author: (book chpt.) United States Regulation of International Trade, 1986. Mem. ABA (editor-in-chief Internat. Law News 1988-91); mem. Nat. Women's Law Ctr. Network, D.C. Bar (chair internat. law sect. 1988-89), Fla. Bar Assn., Women's Legal Def. Fund. Democrat. Home: 9513 Brooke Dr Bethesda MD 20817-2207 Office: Steptoe & Johnson LLP 1330 Connecticut Ave, NW Washington DC 20036 Office Phone: 202-429-6753. Office Fax: 202-429-3902. E-mail: sesserman@steptoe.com.

ESSICK, CAROL EASTERLING, elementary school educator; d. Woodrow Wilson and Laura Byrd Easterling; m. Irving Louis Essick, Mar. 26, 1994. MusB, Berry Coll., 1980. Cert. performance based tchr. Ga. Profl. Stds. Commn. Elem. music specialist McDuffie County Schs., Thomson, Ga., 1980—81, Waycross (Ga.) City Schs., 1981—93, Ware County Schs., Waycross, 1993—98, Glynn County Schs., Brunswick, 1998—. Vice-chairperson Goodyear Elem. Sch. Coun., Brunswick, 2001—02, sec., 2002—. Mem.: NEA, Music Educators Nat. Conf., Sigma Alpha Iota (life Sword of Honor 1979). Methodist. Avocations: golf, photography, coin collecting/numismatics. Office: Goodyear Elem Sch 3000 Roxboro Rd Brunswick GA 31520 Personal E-mail: cessick@adelphia.net. Business E-Mail: cessick@glynn.k12.ga.us.

ESSIG, KATHLEEN SUSAN, academic administrator, consultant, management consultant; b. Denver, July 5, 1956; d. Robert and Ethel Essig. BS in BA, Colo. State U., 1979, MS, 1987. CPA, Colo. Personal fin. planner, v.p. fin. Successful Money Mgmt., Ft. Collins, Colo., 1987-88; accts. payable technician Colo. State U., Ft. Collins, 1980-81, supr. comml. accts. receivable, 1981-83, gen. acct. II, 1983-85, supr. student loans, 1985-87, supr. accts. receivable, acct. II, 1988-89, cost acct. III, 1989-94, univ. ofcl., contr., 1994; univ. mgmt. cons. KPMG Peat Marwick, Denver, 1994-97, U.K., 1995-97; mgr. prin. cons. Oracle Corp., Redwood Shores, Calif., 1998—. Mem. Am. Bus. Women's Assn. (v.p. 1985, Woman of Yr. 1985), Nat. Assn. Accts. Avocations: photography, golf, skiing, scuba diving.

ESSIG, LINDA, lighting designer, director; b. Suffern, NY, 1964; BFA, NYU, 1984, MFA, 1985. Chair dept. theatre U. Wis., Madison, 2002—04, Ariz. State U., Tempe, 2004—05, dir. Sch. Theatre and Film, 2005—. Lighting designer in field. Author: Lighting and the Design Idea, The Speed of Light: Dialogues on Lighting Design and Technological Change. Grant panelist Ariz. Commn. on the Arts; dir. Univ. Resident Theatre Assn., 2004—05. Grantee, Nat. Endowment for the Arts, 2006. Mem.: Internat.

Assn. Lighting Designers, Assn. Theatre in Higher Edn., US Inst. Theatre Tech., United Scenic Artists. Office: Ariz State Univ School Theatre and Film PO Box 872002 Tempe AZ 85287-2002 Office Phone: 480-965-5337. Office Fax: 480-965-5351.

ESSINGER, SUSAN JANE, special education educator; b. Paris, Ill., Oct. 7, 1952; d. Rex Milburn and Virginia Ellen (White) E. BS in Edn., Ea. Ill. U., Charleston, 1973; MS in Edn., Ind. State U., 1981, postgrad. Cert. learning disabilities, elem., educationally mentally handicapped with early childhood endorsement. Elem. tchr. Havana (Ill.) Sch. Dist., 1973-74; tchr. early childhood spl. edn. Paris Sch. Dist. 95, 1974—. Mem. APA, NEA, IDEC, CEC, Assn. for Edn. Young Children, Ill. Edn. Assn., Paris Tchrs. Assn. Avocations: dollmaking, gardening, collecting coins and stamps. Home: 1104 S Main St Paris IL 61944-2823 Office: Paris Sch Dist 95 S Main St Paris IL 61944 E-mail: sessinger@comwares.net.

ESTABROOK, ALISON, surgeon, educator; b. NYC, Oct. 29, 1951; d. Edwin Burke and Shirley (Butler) E.; m. William Harrington, June 12, 1982. BA, Barnard Coll., 1974; MD, NYU, 1978. Resident in surgery Columbia-Presbyn. Med. Ctr., N.Y.C., 1978-81, 82-84, fellow in surgery, onocology, 1981-82, asst. prof. surgery, 1984—, dir. Breast Clinic, 1985—97, Florence Irving asst. prof., 1989-92, chief breast surgery, 1991-97, assoc. prof. surgery, 1992-95, prof. clin. surgery, 1995—; chief breast surgery St. Luke's Roosevelt Hosp., N.Y.C., 1998—. Mem.: Am. Soc. Breast Disease (bd. dirs. 1996—2001), Soc. Surg. Oncology, N.Y. Surg. Soc., N.Y. Met. Breast Group, Assn. Women Surgeons, Am. Soc. Clin. Oncology, Sigma Xi (Kappa chpt.). Office: St Lukes Roosevelt Hosp 425 W 59th St New York NY 10019-1104 Office Phone: 212-523-7500. Business E-Mail: ae9@columbia.edu.

ESTE, YOLANDA DENISE, philosopher, educator; b. Winchester, Ky., Mar. 25, 1962; d. Charles Ogden and Sandi Elaine Estes; m. Timothy Wayne Hunter, Jan. 3, 1990; children: Francisco Estes, Andre Estes. BA in Philosophy, U. Ky., Lexington, 1990, MA in Philosophy, 1993, PhD in Philosophy, 1997. Gaines fellow U. Ky., Lexington, 1987—90, instr., 1990—97; vis. asst. prof. U. Colo., Boulder, 1997—98; asst. prof. Miss. State U., 1998—2004, assoc. prof., 2004—. Vis. scholar U. Ky., 2005, Maisei Daigaku, Tokyo, 2006—; invited lectr. various univs. Editor (with A. Lorenzo Farr, P. Smith, C. Smyth): (book) Marginal Group and Mainstream American Culture, 2000; author: book chpts., jour. articles, encyclopedia entries, internat. and nat. conf. papers. Host semi-weekly student dinners for free discussion of philosophy, ethics and culture, 1998—. Grantee stipend for Interdisciplinary Study at Universitat Regensberg, Germany, DAAD, 1990, Rsch. in Christian Religion, Criss Endowment, 1998—2004. Mem.: Miss. Philo. Assn. (v.p., pres. 2000—01), Am. Philo. Assn., North Am. Fichte Soc. Independent. Avocations: creative writing, gardening, language study. Office: Dept Philosophy and Religion Miss State Univ PO Drawer JS Mississippi State MS 39762 Business E-Mail: yde1@ra.msstate.edu.

ESTEFAN, GLORIA MARIA (GLORIA MARIA MILAGROSA FAJARDO), singer, lyricist; b. Havana, Cuba, Sept. 1, 1957; came to US, 1959; d. Jose Manuel and Gloria G. (Garcia) Fajardo; m. Emilio Estefan, Jr., Sept. 2, 1978; children: Nayib Emil, Emily Maria. BA in Psychology, U. Miami, Fla., 1978, MusD (hon.), 1993. Co-owner Bongos Cuban Cafe, Orlando, 1997—, Miami, 2000—, Larios on the Beach, Cafe Cardozo, Cabana Beach Resort (formerly Palm Court Resort Hotel), Vero Beach, The Cardozo, Miami. Member group Miami Sound Machine, 1975-; singer: (albums) Otra Vez, 1981, Rio, 1982, A Toda Maquina, 1984, Eyes of Innocence, 1984, Primitive Love, 1985, Let It Loose, 1987, Cuts Both Ways, 1989, Into The Light, 1991, Greatest Hits, 1992, Mi Tierra, 1993 (Grammy Award for Best Tropical Latin Album, 1994), Christmas Through Your Eyes, 1993, Hold Me, Thrill Me, Kiss Me, 1994, Abriendo Puertas, 1995 (Grammy Award for Best Tropical Latin Performance, 1996), Destiny, 1996, Gloria Estefan: The Evolution Tour Live in Miami, 1997, gloria!, 1998, Everlasting Gloria, 1999, Alma Caribena, 2000 (Grammy Award for Best Traditional Tropical Latin Album, 2001), No Me Dejes De Querer, 2000, Greatest Hits Volume II, 2001, Que Siga La Tradicion, 2001, Live in Atlantis, 2002, Unwrapped, 2003, Live & Unwrapped, 2004; author: (children's books) The Magically Mysterious Adventures of Noelle the Bulldog, 2005. Achievements include The Miami Sound Machine's single, Conga, being the first to crack the pop, dance, Black and Latin charts simultaneously.*

ESTELL, DORA LUCILE, retired educational administrator; b. Ft. Worth, Mar. 3, 1930; d. Hugh and Hattie Lucile (Poole) E. BA, East Tex. Bapt. U., 1951; MA, U. North Tex., 1959; EdD, East Tex. State U., 1988. Tchr. Mission (Tex.) Ind. Sch. Dist., 1951-53; tchr., adminstr. Marshall (Tex.) Ind. Sch. Dist., 1953-68; dep. dir. Region VII Edn. Svc. Ctr., Kilgore, Tex., 1968-94, ret., 1994. Contbr. articles to profl. jours. Bd. dir. South Milan County United Way, Richards Meml. Hosp. Named Rockdale Citizen of Yr., 2001. Mem. Rockdale C. of C. (bd. dirs.), Phi Delta Kappa. Baptist. Avocations: photography, gardening. Home: 611 W Bell Ave Rockdale TX 76567-2809 E-mail: lucile-estell@sbcglobal.net.

ESTELL, MARY ESTHER, music educator, emergency medical technician, protective services official; d. William Henry and Judith Rae Estell. BME, Wheaton Coll., 1999. Cert. EMT Ill.; firefighter II Ill. Dir. bands Donovan Sch., Ill., 1999—2000, Earlville CUSD #9, 2000—. EMT, firefighter Mendota Fire Dept., Ill., 2001—. Office: Earlville CUSD #9 415 West Union St Earlville IL 60518

ESTERLY, NANCY BURTON, retired physician; b. N.Y.C., Apr. 14, 1935; d. Paul R. and Tanya (Pasahow) Burton; m. John R. Esterly, June 16, 1957; children: Sarah Burton, Anne Beidler, John Snyder, II, Henry Clark, II. AB, Smith Coll., 1956; MD, Johns Hopkins U., 1960. Intern, then resident in pediatrics Johns Hopkins Hosp., 1960-63, resident in dermatology, 1964-67; instr. pediatrics Johns Hopkins U. Med. Sch., 1967-68; instr., trainee La Rabida U. Chgo. Inst.; also dept. pediatrics U. Chgo. Med. Sch., 1968-69; asst. prof. Pritzker Sch. Medicine, U. Chgo., 1969-70, assoc. prof., 1973-78; asst. prof. dermatology Abraham Lincoln Sch. Medicine, U. Ill., 1970-72, assoc. prof. dermatology and pediatrics, 1972-73; dir. div. dermatology, dept. pediatrics Michael Reese Hosp. and Med. Ctr., Chgo., 1973-78; prof. pediatrics and dermatology Northwestern U. Med. Sch., 1978; head div. dermatology, dept. pediatrics Children's Meml. Hosp., Chgo., 1978-87; prof. pediatrics and dermatology Med. Coll. Wis., Milw., 1987—2004, prof. emeritus dermatology, 2005—; head div. dermatology, dept. pediatrics Children's Hosp. Wis., Milw., 1987—2004; ret., 2004. Editor-in-chief Pediatric Dermatology, 1983—; contbr. numberous articles to profl. jours. Recipient David Martin Carter award, Am. Skin Assn., 2002, Lifetime Career Educator award, Dermatology Found., 2002, Disting. Svc. award, Med. Coll. Wis., 2004. Mem.: Wis. Pediat. Soc., Women's Dermatol. Soc. (Rose Hirschler award), Soc. Pediat. Dermatology (1st Lifetime Achievement award 1998), Soc. Pediat. Rsch., Am. Acad. Pediatrics, Soc. Investigative Dermatology, Wis. Dermatol. Soc., Am. Dermatol. Assn., Am. Acad. Dermatology, Internat. Soc. Pediat. Dermatology, Sigma Xi. Personal E-mail: nesterly@comcast.net.

ESTES, CARROLL LYNN, sociologist, educator; b. Fort Worth, May 30, 1938; d. Joe Ewing and Carroll (Cox) E.; 1 child, Duskie Lynn Gelfand Estes. AB, STanford U., 1959; MA, So. Meth. U., 1961; PhD, U. Calif., San Diego, 1972; DHL (hon.), Russell Sage Coll., 1986. Rsch. asst., asst. study dir. Brandeis U. Social Welfare Rsch. Ctr., 1962-63, rsch. assoc., 1964-65, project dir., 1965-67; vis. lectr. Florence Heller Grad. Sch., 1964-65; rsch. dir. Simmons Coll., 1963-64; asst. prof. social work San Diego State Coll., 1967-72; asst. prof. in residence dept. psychiatry U. Calif., San Francisco, 1972-75, assoc. prof. dept. social and behavioral scis., 1975-79, prof., 1979-92, chair dept. social and behavioral scis., 1981-93, coord. human devel. tng. program, 1974-75; dir. Aging Health Policy Rsch. Ctr., 1979-85, Inst. for Health and Aging, 1985-99. Faculty rsch. lectr. U. Calif., 1993; LaSor lectr. Oreg. Health Scis. U, 2005; co-founder Concerned Scientists in Aging, 2005. Author: The Decision-Makers: The Power Structure of Dallas, 1963; co-author: Protective Services for Older People, 1972, U.S. Senate Special Committee on Aging Report, Paperwork and the Older Americans Act, 1978, The Aging Enterprise, 1979 Fiscal Austerity and Aging, 1983, Long Term Care of the Elderly, 1985, Political Economy, Health and Aging, 1984, The Long Term Care Crisis, 1993, The Nation's Health, 2001, 7th edit., 2003, Critical Gerontology, 1999, Social Policy and Aging, 2001, Social Theory, Social Policy and Aging, 2003, Health Policy, 4th edit., 2004; contbr. articles to profl. jours. Mem. Calif. Commn. on Aging, 1974-77; cons. U.S. Senate Spl. Com. on Aging from 1976, Notch Commn. U.S. Commn. Social Security, 1993-94; bd. dirs. Nat. Com. to Preserve Social Security and Medicare, 2002—. Recipient Matrix award Theta Sigma Phi, 1964, award for contbns. to lives of older Californians, Calif. Commn. on Aging, 1977, Helen Nahm Rsch. award U. Calif., San Francisco, 1986, Woman Who Would Be Pres. League of Women Voters, 1998. Mem. Inst. Medicine of NAS, ACLU, Am. Sociol. Assn. (Disting. Scholar award Aging and Life Course 2000), Assn. Gerontology in Higher Edn. (pres. 1980-81, recipient Beverly award 1993, Tibbitts award 2000), Am. Soc. on Aging (pres. 1982-84, Leadership award 1986), Geronotol. Soc. Am. (Kent award 1992, pres. 1995-96), Older Women's League (v.p. 1994-97), Soc. Study Social Problems, Alpha Kappa Delta, Pi Beta Phi. Office: U Calif San Francisco Inst Health & Aging 3333 California St Ste 340 San Francisco CA 94118-1944 E-mail: carroll.estes@ucsf.edu.

ESTÉS, CLARISSA PINKOLA, psychoanalyst, poet, writer; Author: Women Who Run With the Wolves, 1992, The Gift of Story, 1993.

ESTES, ELAINE ROSE GRAHAM, retired librarian; b. Springfield, Mo., Nov. 24, 1931; d. James McKinley and Zelma Mae (Smith) Graham; m. John Melvin Estes, Dec. 29, 1953. BSBA, Drake U., 1953, tchg. cert., 1956; MSLS, U. Ill., 1960. With Pub. Libr. Des Moines, 1956-95, coord. ext. svcs., 1977-78, dir., 1978-95, ret., 1995. Lectr. antiques, hist. architecture, librs.; mem. conservation planning com. for disaster preparedness for librs. Author bibliographies of books on antiques; contbr. articles to profl. jours. Mem. State of Iowa Cultural Affairs Adv. Coun., 1986—94, Nat. Commn. on Future of Drake U., 1987—88; chmn. Des Moines Mayor's Hist. Dist. Commn.; mem. nominations review com. Iowa State Nat. Hist. Register, 1983—89; chmn. hist. subcom. Des Moines Sesquecentennial Com., 1993, Iowa Sister State Commn., 1993—95; mem. com. 40th Anniversary Drake U. Alumni Weekend, 50 Yr. Drake Alumni Weekend, 2003; mem. July 4 com. Iowa Sesquecentennial; nat. exch. dir. Friendship Force, 1997; mem. nat. adv. bd. Cowles Libr., 1998—; mem. Gov.'s Iowa Centennial Meml. Found., 2003—; mem. acquisition com. Salisbury House, 2003; mem. cultural ctr. task force African Am. Hist. Mus., 1999—2003; mem. Iowa author com. Pub. Libr. Des Moines Found., 2001—; mem. Terrace Hill Commn., 2001—; bd. dirs. Des Moines Art Ctr., 1972—83, hon. mem., 1983—; bd. dirs. Friends of Libr. USA, 1986—92, Henry Wallace House Found., Iowa Libr. Centennial Com., 1990—91, Wagner Hall Preservation Project, 2004—. Recipient Recognition award Greater Des Moines, YWCA, 1975, Disting. Alumni award Drake U., 1979, Woman of Achievement award YWCA, 1989, Excellence in Hist. Preservation award City of Des Moines, 1994, Contbn. to Cmty. award Connect Found., 1995, Friend of Literacy award Pub. Libr. of Des Moines Found., 2003; named Tassel Honoree in her honor, Forest Libr., 2002; named to Wall of Fame, YWCA, 2003. Mem.: ALA (30th Anniversary Honor Roll for Intellectual Freedom 1999), Iowa Soc. Preservation Hist. Landmarks (bd. dirs. 1969—97), Libr. Assn. Greater Des Moines Metro Area (chmn. 1992, pres.), Iowa Urban Pub. Libr. Assn., Iowa Libr. Assn. (life; pres. 1978—79), Iowa Antique Assn., Terrace Hill (Gov.'s Mansion) Soc. (bd. dirs. 1972—. v.p. 1991—93, pres. 1993—96), Links Inc. (40th ann. com. 1997), Drake U. 50 Yr. Club, Questers Inc. Club (pres. 1982, state 2d v.p. 1984—86, 1st v.p. 1990—2000, pres. 1997, state pres. 2000—03, pres. 2001—03), Rotary (history com. 2001—06), Proteus Club (pres. 2003—04).

ESTES, MARY K., virologist; PhD, U. NC. Prof. molecular virology, microbiology, & medicine Baylor Coll. Medicine, Houston. Adv. bd. Virology Jour., Burroughs Wellcome Fund; bd. dirs. Gulf Coast Consortia. Editor: (books) Viral Gastoenteritis (One Nation), 1997. Adv. com. Admin. Ctr. Biologistics Evaluation and Rsch. FDA, 1998—. Fellow, AAAS, 1999. Mem.: AAAS (chmn. med. scis. 1999—2001), Inst. Medicine. Achievements include cloning Norwalk virus & developing vaccine. Office: Baylor College of Medicine 1 Baylor Plz Houston TX 77030 Office Phone: 713-798-3585. Office Fax: 713-789-3586. E-mail: mestes@bcm.edu.

ESTES, PAMELA JEAN, pastor; b. Topeka, Oct. 14, 1953; d. Jack E. and Bonita A. (Hatfield) E. BA in music edn., Ouachita U., 1974, M in music edn., 1976; MLS, Vanderbilt U., 1983; MDiv, Boston U., 1988, MST, 1989. Tchr. Thayer (Mo.) Schs., 1976-79; libr. Pochontas (Ark.) H.S., 1979-82; libr. intern Vanderbilt U., 1982-83, libr., 1983-85; cataloger Boston U. Sch. Theology, 1985-89; pastor Union Congl. Ch., Walpole, Mass., 1987-88; pianist East Walpole (Mass.) United Meth. Ch., 1988-89; pastor First United Meth. Ch., Camden, Ark., 1989-92, Stamps (Ark.) Charge, 1992-93, St. James United Meth., Little Rock, 1993-96, St. Luke United Meth. Ch., Little Rock, 1996—2000, First United Meth. Ch., Blytheville, Ark., 2000—. Pvt. musician, 1970—; cataloger Ouachita, 1976-82; chair Commn. on the Status and Role of Women, 1989-95, Ark. Del. to White House Conf. on Librs., 1991, Sexual Harrassment Task Force United Meth. Ch., Ark., 1992-95. Editor: United Methodist Women's Day Reference, 1991; author numerous poems. Debate moderator LWV, Camden, Ark., 1989-92; vol. Friends of the Libr., Little Rock, 1993-95; trustee Hendrix Coll., 2004—. Oxnam scholar Boston U. Sch. Theology. Mem. DAR (Charlevoix Chpt.), P.E.O., Nat. Music Club, Rotary (Paul Harris fellow), Blytheville Gosnell C. of C. (bd. dirs.), Ark. Conf. Bd. Pensions, Orphans Music Club, Blytheville/Gosnell C. of C. (bd. dirs.), Sigma Alpha Iota, Delta Kappa Gamma. Democrat. Avocations: music, reading, children, poetry, travel. Home: 608 Ridgeway N Blytheville AR 72315 Office: First United Meth Ch 701 W Main Blytheville AR 72315 Office Phone: 870-763-3351. E-mail: pjestes@missconet.com.

ESTÉS, RUTH ANN, art educator; b. Hillsboro, Ohio, Sept. 30, 1966; d. Ernest Herman and Mary Imogene (Gall) Parker; m. Jesse Brunner Estes Jr., Nov. 18, 1988; children, Amanda Nicole, Mary Kassidy. BS in Edn., Wright State U., 1988, EdM, 1997. Cert. tchr., Ohio. Substitute tchr. Tri-County North Sch. Dist., Lewisburg, Ohio, 1988-91, Preble Shawnee Sch. Dist., Camden, Ohio, 1988-90, C.R. Coblentz Sch. Dist., New Paris, Ohio, 1988-90, West Alexandria (Ohio) Sch. Dist., 1988-89; grad. asst. in micro-computer lab. Wright State U., Dayton, Ohio, 1989-90; art instr. for severely behavioral handicapped C.R. Coblents Mid. Sch., West Manchester, Ohio, 1991; tchr. art Corpus Christi Elem. Sch., Dayton, 1989-94; tchr. art and gifted Bradford Elem. Sch., 1994—2005, Bradford H.S., 2005—. Asst. supt. fine arts dept. Highland County Fair, Hillsboro, Ohio, 1982-84; freelance artist. Merit Badge counselor Miami Valley coun. Boy Scouts Am., 1992—. Named We. Ohio Art Tchr. of Yr., 2005. Mem. Nat. Art Edn. Assn., Ohio Art Edn. Assn. (Darke County connector), Ohio Cath. Edn. Assn., Ohio Edn. Assn. Avocations: fine arts, sewing, interior decorating. Home: 5139 Folkerth Rd Greenville OH 45331-7708

ESTEVEZ, ANNE-MARIE, psychologist, lawyer; b. Hiaieah, Fla., Jan. 3, 1968; d. Antonio Jesus and Linda Francis (Murphy) E. BA in Psychology cum laude, U. Miami, 1990. Acct. asst. Project Advisors Corp., Miami, Fla., 1986-87, bookkeeper, 1987-88, asst. to the pres., 1989-90. Author: (ethnographic rsch.) World-War II Vet--Buster Murphy, 1989 (preserved in U. Miami Libr.). Vol. fundraiser and polit. conv. worker for Democrats. Mem. Women in Communications, Inc., Female Execs. of Am., Phi Kappa Phi, Psi Chi, Phi Kappa Alpha (little sister). Roman Catholic. Avocations: scuba diving, volunteer work.*

ESTILETTE, KATHLEEN C., music educator; b. Ft. Worth, Oct. 6, 1955; d. Thomas William and Norma Dean Crenshaw; m. Randall Bryan Harper, Oct. 1973 (div. 1980); children: Thomas Randall Harper, Stephen Bryan Harper; m. Michael Estilette, Mar. 31, 1989 (div. Apr. 2001). Grad., Jasper (Tex.) H.S., 1973; student in Piano Studies, 1996—. Sec. Jasper Meml. Hosp., 1980—83, Jasper Title and Abstract, 1983—86, Lawyers Title, Carrollton, Tex., 1986—89, Richard Jackson and Assoc., Dallas, 1989—92; sec., office mgr. Law Firm of Bill Reppeto, Dallas, 1992—96; owner, tchr. Piano Studio, Carrollton, 1995—. Asst. tchr. Piano Studio of Dr. Mary Humm, McKinney, Tex., 1997—98; singer and composer Step By Step, Dallas. Editor (scale book): Scale Technique, 1998. Mem., sponsor James Group-A Christ Centered 12-Step Program, Dallas, 1988—. Mem.: Carrollton Music Tchrs. Assn. (pres. 1999—2000, Tchr. of Yr. 1999—2000). Ch. Of Christ. Avocations: piano playing, singing, reading, cross stitching. Home: 3139 Barton Rd Carrollton TX 75007

ESTIN-KLEIN, LIBBYADA, advertising executive, writer; b. Newark, July 13, 1937; d. Barney and Florence B. (Tenkin) Straver; m. Harvey M. Klein, Sept. 9, 1984. Student, Syracuse U., 1955-57; BS, Columbia, 1960; RN, Columbia-Presbyn. Med. Ctr., 1960; cert., N.Y. Sch. Interior Design, 1962. Med. rsch. tech. writer, N.Y.C., 1960-62; pres. Libbyada Estin Interiors, N.Y.C., 1962-65; v.p. advt. and pub. relations Behrman/Estin Inc., N.Y.C., 1965-67; account exec., dir. pub. rels. J.S. Fullerton, Inc., N.Y.C., 1968-69, Kallir Philips Ross Inc., N.Y.C., 1969-71; copy supr. William Douglas McAdams Inc., N.Y.C., 1971-75, Sudler & Hennessey Inc., N.Y.C., 1975-80; v.p., exec. adminstr., creative dir. Grey Med. Advt. Inc., N.Y.C., 1980-84; founder, ptnr. Estin Sandler Comm. Inc., N.Y.C., 1984; v.p. Barnum Comm. Inc., N.Y.C., 1984-86; sr. v.p. ICE Comm., Inc., Rochester, N.Y., 1986-87; sr. cons. Nelson Comms., Inc., Sudler & Hennessy Inc., Worldwide Healthcare Comms., N.Y.C., 1998—2003; pres. Estin-Klein Comm. Inc., Rochester and Pittsford, NY, 1987—2005, Ellicott City, Md., 2005—. Dir. health group Robert Comm., Inc., East Rochester, NY, 1993-95; bd. dirs., Perinatal Network of Monroe County, Pathways to Health. mem. PRSA Health Acad.; sr. cons. Nelson Comms., Ind., Sudler & Hennessy Inc., Worldwide Healthcare Comms. Inc., NYC, 1993-2004. Mem. Pub. Rels. Soc. Am., Advt. Women N.Y., Am. Advt. Fedn., Advt. Coun. of Rochester, Rochester Sales and Mktg. Execs. Club, Mktg. Communicators of Rochester, Am. Med. Writers Assn., Women in Comm., Healthcare Mktg. and Comms. Coun., Healthcare Bus. Women's Assn., Am. Nurses Assn., Allied Bd. Trade, Columbia-Presbyn. Hosp. Alumnae Assn., Columbia U. Alumnae Assn., Syracuse U. Alumnae Assn., Sigma Theta Tau, Delta Phi Epsilon. Office: Estin-Klein Comms 2769 Westminster Rd Ellicott City MD 21043 Office Phone: 410-480-4380. Personal E-mail: libbyada@aol.com.

ESTLUND, CYNTHIA, law educator; BA summa cum laude, Lawrence U., 1978; JD, Yale U., 1983. Law clk. to Juege Patricia Wald US Ct. Appeals (DC Cir.), 1983—84; assoc. Bredhoff & Kaiser, Washington, DC, 1985—89; asst. prof. law U. Tex. Sch. Law, 1989—93, prof., 1993—99, Leroy G. Denman, Jr., regents prof. law, 1994, assoc. dean academic affairs, 1995—98; Samuel J. Rubin vis. prof. law Columbia Law Sch., NYC, 1998, prof., 1999—2006, Isidor and Seville Sulzbacher prof. law, 2004—06, vice dean rsch., 2004; vis. prof. law NYU Sch. Law, 2005—06, Catherine A. Rein prof. law, 2006—. Contbr. articles to law jours. Office: NYU Sch Law 40 Washington Sq S, 314G New York NY 10012 Office Phone: 212-998-6184. Office Fax: 212-995-4881. E-mail: cynthia.estlund@nyu.edu.*

ESTRIN, ALEJANDRA AUDREY, science educator; b. Mpls., Mar. 23, 1973; d. Jorge Alberto and Leonilda Edith Estrin. BA in Biology, Gustavus Adolphus Coll., 1995; MS in Biol. Scis., Minn. State U., 1998; post grad. in Anthropology, U. Wis.Milw., 2001—. Tchg. asst. Minn. State U., Mankato, 1997—98, 2000—01; adj. instr. Inver Hills C.C., St. Paul, 1998—2001, Normandale C.C., St. Paul, 1998—2001, Met. State U., St. Paul, 1998—2001; lectr., tchg. asst., tutor U. Wis., 2001—; lectr. U. Wis, Green Bay, 2002—03; instr. Cardinal Stritch U., Milw., 2004—. Vol. Sixteenth St. Cmty. Health Ctr., Milw., 2004—05, Esperanza Unida, Milw., 2004—05, CORE/El Centro, Milw., 2005—. Evolution edn. advocacy U. Wis., Milw., 2005—06. Recipient Ctr. Latin Am., Caribbean Studies Undergrad., Grad. Student Travel award, U. Wis., 2005, Roberto Hernandez Ctr. Applied Rsch. award, 2006; Grants-in-Aid of Rsch., Sigma Xi, 2006. Mem.: Am. Anthrop. Assn. (assoc.), Nat. Orgn. for Women (assoc.), Sigma Delta Epsilon (assoc.), Sigma Xi (assoc.), Alpha Phi Omega (life). Jewish. Office: U Wis Sabin Hall 110 3413 N Downer Ave Milwaukee WI 53211 Office Phone: 414-229-3196. Business E-Mail: aaestrin@uwm.edu.

ESTRIN, JUDITH, computer company executive; m. Bill Carrico. BS in Maths. and Computer Sci., UCLA; MSEE, Stanford U. Co-founder Bridge Comms.; pres., CEO Network Computing Devices; chief tech. officer, sr. v.p. Cisco Sys., Inc., San Jose; chmn. Packet Design, Palo Alto, 2002—. Bd. dirs. Fed. Express, Sun Microsystems, Walt Disney Co. Named to, Women in Tech. Internat. Hall Fame. Office: Packet Design Inc 3400 Hillview Ave Bldg 3 Palo Alto CA 94304 Fax: 408-526-4100.*

ETEFIA, FLORENCE VICTORIA, retired school psychologist; b. Alton, Ill., Feb. 13, 1946; d. Esau and Pearl (Taylor) Anthony. BA, Mich. State U., 1968; MAT, Oakland U., Rochester, Mich., 1972; EdS, Wayne State U., 1977, MA, 1987, postgrad. Cert. tchr. mentally impaired, Mich.; spl. edn. supr., Mich.; cert. tchr. mentally impaired, learning disabled, K-8 gen. edn., psychology, Mich. Spl. edn. tchr. Sch. Dist. of Pontiac, Mich. Mem. NEA, Mich. Edn. Assn., Pontiac Edn. Assn., Delta Sigma Theta. Home: 3035 Debra Ct Auburn Hills MI 48326-2044

ETEROVICH MAGUIRE, KAREN ANN, actress, writer; b. Cleve., Feb. 24, 1961; d. Anthony William and Alice (Troyan) Eterovich; m. John Gordon Maguire. BA, U. Akron, Ohio, 1983; MFA, U. S.C., Columbia, 1989. Actress ArtReach Touring Theatre, Cin., 1983—85; actress, office mgr. Indpls. Shakespeare Co., 1984—86; grad. tchg. asst. U. S.C., Columbia, 1986—89; acting intern Shakespeare Theatre, Washington, 1987—88; resident profl. tchg. assoc. Cornell U., Ithaca, NY, 1991—92; actress Ind. Repertory Theater, Indpls., 1993; actress, producer, dir. Love Arm'd Productions, N.Y.C., 1993—. Producer Cosmic Leopard Productions, N.Y.C., 1994—2002; publicity cons. Fertile Ground Inc., N.Y.C., 1995—97. Actor: (Multi-Media Play) Love Arm'd, Aphra Behn & Her Pen, 1997 (Listed in Grants & Awards). Recipient Juliet Hardtner Endowment for Women in the Arts, McNeese State U., 2000, NEH Endowment for Faculty Devel., Albertson Coll.of Idaho, 2000, N.Y. State Coun. on the Arts Decentralization Program, Keuka Coll., 2001; grantee, La. Endowment for the Humanities, 2005. Avocations: skiing, swimming, tennis. Office: Love Arm'd Productions P O Box 2668 Times Sq Station New York NY 10108-2668 Office Phone: 212-967-7711 x4667. Business E-Mail: karen_eterovich@hotmail.com.

ETHAN, CAROL BAEHR, psychotherapist, psychoanalyst; b. N.Y.C., May 30, 1920; d. Irving and Sadie (Goldman) Baehr; m. Sy Ethan, Mar. 18, 1955; children: Willa Capraro, Barbara Capraro Ethan. Trained, Greenwich Inst. Psychoanalytic Studies, 1965-70; BA in Psychology with honors, NYU, 1978; MA in Psychology, New Sch. Social Rsch., 1981. Tchr. Queens Coll., 1956-57; consumer psychology rschr., cons., 1950-70; staff psychotherapist Fifth Ave. Ctr. Counseling & Psychotherapy, 1965-70; psychotherapist-psychoanalyst pvt. practice, N.Y.C., 1967—. Writer: Irvington (N.J.) Herald, 1946, Walt Framer Prodns., 1949—50, columnist: Rhinebeck Gazette-Advertiser, 1981—86. Vol. social rehab. program Queens County Mental Health Soc., 1965—66; Dem. committeewoman Queens County, 1960. Recipient Founders Day award, NYU, 1978; fellow Internat. Coun. Sex Edn. and Parenthood, Am. U. Fellow: Am. Orthopsychiat. Assn.; mem.: APA, Am. Counselors Assn., Nat. Assn. Advancement of Psychoanalysis (cert. psychoanalyst), Am. Psychotherapy Assn. (cert. diplomate), N.Am. Assn. Masters in Psychology (cert.), Internat. Acad. Behavioral Medicine, Counseling and Psychotherapy (clin. mem.), Family and Divorce Mediation Coun. N.Y., Am. Mental Health Counselors Assn., N.Y. State Assn. Practising Psychotherapists (cert.). Address: 235 W 76th St New York NY 10023-8217 Office Phone: 212-595-4657. E-mail: cethan@nyc.rr.com.

ETHERIDGE, DIANA CAROL, internet business executive; b. Nebr., Mar. 18, 1940; d. Elvon Lynn and Enola Nadene Howe; m. Brian Newman Etheridge, May 30, 1940; children: Melissa Ann, Juliana Lynn Student, U. Geneva, Switzerland, 1960-61; BA, U. Denver., 1962; MA, Simmons Coll.,

1981. Cert. tchr., Colo., Fla.; real estate lic., Fla., 1995. Tchr. French, science, English Denver Pub. Schs., 1962-63, 64-68; tchr. 7th grade, French tchr. preK-7th grade St. Anne's Episcopal Sch., Denver, 1974—76; tchr. 6th grade, French tchr. k-8th grade, co-founder Collegiate Sch., Denver, 1976—80; real estate broker Merrill Lynch, Prudential, Long & Foster, Treder Realty, Potomac, Md. and Titusville, Fla., 1982—, Vincent Keenan Realtors, Cape Canaveral, Fla. Mem. No. Va. Coun. Comml. Realtors, Fairfax, Va., 1993—95, Govtl. Internat. and Info. Svcs. Coms., Fairfax, Internat. Real Estate Inst., Alexandria, Minn., 1996—2006, World Trade Ctr. Inst., Balt., 1995; cert. internat. property specialist Nat. Assn. Realtors, 1994—2000, judge Who is Today's Realtor, 1995; pres., founder EDEA, Inc., Merritt Island, Fla., 1997—, Cybernastics, Inc., Merritt Island, 1999—, Flexystema/Flexhome, Merritt Island, 2000—. Editor: My Hawaii (by Jane Thomas). House bill proofreader Colo. State Legislature, Denver, 1970; campaign staff mem. U.S. Congressman Dave Weldon, Melbourne, Fla., 1996, 1998, 2000; hon. chmn. Fla. bus. adv. coun. Nat. Rep. Congl. Com., 2003. Recipient Lifetime award Prudential Preferred Properties, 1990 Mem.: Meridian Internat., Md. Assn. Realtors, Fla. Bus. Adv. Coun., Montgomery Assn. Realtors (Lifetime award), Nat. Assn. Realtors, Nat. Assn. Home Builders, Nat. Assn. Women in Constrn., Meridian Internat., Hospitality and Info. Svcs. Internat. Club, Optimists Club (past pres. Capital City), Brevard County Newcomer's Club, Welcome to Washington Internat. Club, Long and Foster Pres.'s Club (life), Phi Beta Kappa, Pi Beta Phi. Achievements include patents for building construction; tensioned building system. Avocations: skiing, swimming, scuba diving, hiking, aerobics. Office Phone: 321-453-7665. E-mail: diana_etheridge@yahoo.com, info@edea.com.

ETHERIDGE, MELISSA LOU, singer, lyricist; b. Leavenworth, Kans., May 29, 1961; d. John and Elizabeth Etheridge; m. Tammy Lynn Michaels, Sept. 22, 2003; children: Bailey, Beckett. Student, Berklee Coll. of Music, Boston, 1970. Wrote songs for the film, Weeds; albums include Melissa Etheridge, 1988, Brave and Crazy, 1989, Never Enough, 1992, Yes I Am, 1993, Your Little Secret, 1995, Breakdown, 1999, Skin, 2001, Lucky, 2004, Greatest Hits: The Road Less Traveled, 2005. Named Entertainer of Year Can. Acad. Recording Arts and Scis., 1990; Grammy award, Best Female Rock Vocal for "Aint It Heavy," 1993, Female Rock Vocal Performance for "Come to My Window," 1994; named one of 100 Most Influential People, Time Mag., 2005. Address: MEIN PO Box 884563 San Francisco CA 94188-4563

ETHERIDGE, SUSAN B., social worker; b. Dallas, May 30, 1945; d. William Bernard Dougherty and Eva Sue Lemmons; m. Jimmy Coleman Etheridge, June 6, 1970; children: Stephani, Catherine, Jamie, Alex, Marti. BS in Edn., U. North Tex., 1967; MS in Social Work, U. Tex., 1993. Lic. master social worker Tex. Dir. counseling Crisis Pregnancy Ctr., Dallas, 1982—84; child protective svcs. specialist Child Protective Svcs., Dallas, 1984—88, child protective svcs. supr., 1988—95; psychotherapist Cmty. Psychotherapy Ctr., Inc., Dallas, 1992—95; program dir. Child Protective Svcs., Plano, Tex., 1995—99, program adminstr. Dallas, 1999—2004; exec. dir. Collin County Children's Advocacy Ctr., 2004—. Mem. Regional Tng. Acad. Adv. Bd.; mem. planning com. Guardian Ad Litem Tng. Conf., Tarrant County Jr. Coll. Annual Sexual Abuse Conf.; co-leader group treatment program TDHS; mem. steering com. Target: Kids in Ct.; former bd. chair Cmty. Psychotherapy Ctr.; spkr. in field. Author: Resource Curriculum for Mother's of Incest Victim Group, 1994, Permanent Planning Team Protocol, 1996, A Guide to Child Abuse Investigations for Drug Exposed Infants, 1997. Former bd. dirs. Collin County Children's Advocacy Ctr.; former bd. mem. Tex. Assn. Infant Mental Health. Named Caseworker of Yr., Collin County Advocacy Ctr., Plano, Tex., 1998; recipient Team Excellence award, Advocacy Ctr. Tex., Austin, Tex., 1999. Home: 331 Crosscreek Dr Wylie TX 75098-6983 Office: 2205 Los Rios Plano TX 75074 Office Phone: 972-633-6601.

ETHERINGTON, CAROL A., medical association administrator; b. Tenn. married. MSN in Psychology and Mental Health. RN Tenn. With Internat. Med. Corps, Bosnia-Herzegovina, 1994; pres., bd. dirs. U.S. sect. Doctors Without Borders, 1999—; asst. prof. nursing Vanderbilt U. Med. Ctr., Nashville. Founder Victims Intervention Program, Nashville Police Dept., 1975—95; mem. internat. com. ARC, 1980, vol. for disaster relief. Recipient Internat. Achievement award, Florence Nightingale Internat. Found., Geneva, 2003, Florence Nightingale medal, Internat. Red Cross, 1997—98. Office: Vanderbilt Univ 336 First Hall 461 21st Ave S Nashville TN 37240

ETHERTON, JANE, retired sales executive, marketing professional; b. Sevierville, Tenn., Oct. 11, 1953; d. Arthur B. (Jack) and Grace Etherton; m. Randy King, Aug. 18, 1974; 1 child, Kevin King. Student, Abbey Dale Grange, Eng., 1971-72, U. Tenn., 1972-74, U. South, 1994-98, Tusculum Coll., 1999—. Lic. funeral dir. Funeral dir. Holly Hills Funeral Home, Knoxville, Tenn., 1973-86; pre-arrangement trust dir. Berry's Morticians, Knoxville, 1987-89; gen. mgr. Southpointe Mortgage Co., Sevierville, 1989-91; dir. ops. Southpointe Fin. Svcs., Knoxville, 1991-92; pres., chief profl. officer United Way of Sevier County, Sevierville, 1993-2000; dir. sales and mktg. Collier Foods, Knoxville, Tenn., 2000—01, Aberdeen Mktg., Sevierville, Tenn., 2001—. Recipient Pres. citation Sevier Sunrise Rotary 1995. Mem. Smoky Mountain Hist. Soc., Smoky Mountain Toastmasters (v.p. pub. rels. 1996-99). Episcopalian. Home: 1208 Tara Ln Sevierville TN 37862-2963 Office: Aberdeen Mktg Sevierville TN 37862

ETIENNE, MICHELE, financial consultant; b. Cap Haitien, Haiti, Oct. 16, 1946; d. Raymond and Claudia (Prophete) Kersaint; m. Ernst Etienne, Mar. 2, 1967; children: Patrick, Bernard. BBA, Baruch Coll., 1976. Dir. fin. Martha Graham Ctr., N.Y., 1973-98; fin. adv. Lee Strasberg Theatrical Inst., N.Y., 1999—. Pres. Primevere Club; mem. Casegha. Home: 84-15 168th St Jamaica NY 11432 Office: Lee Strasberg Theatrical Inst 115 E 15th St New York NY 10003-2188 E-mail: metienne16@aol.com.

ETKIN, ALEXANDRA, physician; b. Donetsk, Russia, Oct. 7, 1970; came to U.S., 1993; d. Victor and Asye Tsarevskiy; m. Edward Etkin, Aug. 4, 1995. MD, Donetsk St. Gorky Med. Inst., Ukraine, 1993, Brooklyn Hosp. Ctr., 1995-98. Resident Bklyn. Hosp. Ctr., 1995-98. Mem. AMA. Office: Med P C 2015 Bath Ave Brooklyn NY 11214-4857

ETTENGER, DEBORAH JEAN, music educator; b. Denver, Sept. 7, 1947; d. John Richard and Grace Spencer Bond; m. James Francis Ettenger, July 14, 1984; 1 child, Devon Christopher. BA in Music Edn., U. Wyo., 1970; BA in Gen. Edn., Loretto Heights Coll., Denver, 1988. Lic. gen. music tchr. K-12 Colo., instrumental music tchr. 3-12 Colo., classroom tchr. K-6 Colo., cert. Carl Orff method tchg. music. Gen. music tchr. grades 7-9 Harrison Sch. Dist. # 2, Colorado Springs, Colo., 1971—72; gen. music tchr. grades K-5 Aurora (Colo.) Pub. Schs., 1972—. Mem.: Rocky Mountain Orff Schulwork Assn., Colo. Music Educators Assn., Music Educators Nat. Conf., Colo. Hunter-Jumper Assn., Delta Omicron, Gamma Phi Beta. Methodist. Avocations: gardening, singing in church choir, singing in musicals and light opera, Boy Scouts, competing in horse shows.

ETTER, DELORES M., civilian military employee; Student, Okla. State U., U. Tex., Arlington; BS in Math., Wright State U., Dayton, Ohio, 1970, MS in Math., 1972; PhD in Elec. Engring., U. New Mex., 1979. Mem. faculty dept. elec. and computer engring. U. N.Mex., 1979-89, assoc. chair dept., 1987-89, assoc. v.p. acad. affairs, 1989; prof. elec. and computer engring. U. Colo., Boulder, 1990-98; dep. under sec. for sci. and tech. US Dept. Def., Washington, 1998—2001; disting. chair sci. & tech. office naval rsch. U.S. Naval Acad., 2001—05; asst. sec. for rsch. devel., & acquisition, USN US Dept. Def., Washington, 2005—. Mem. Naval Rsch. Adv. Com., 1991-97, chmn. 1995-97; vis. prof. info. sys. lab.Stanford U., 1983-84; bd. dirs. Def. Sci. Bd., 1995-98, Nat. Sci. Bd., 2002-2005; prin. U.S. rep. NATO rsch. and tech. bd., tech. cooperation program; mem. bd. vis. Nat. Def. U.; panel mem. numerous studies. Recipient Pub. Svc. award Dept. Navy, 1998, Fed. Women in Sci. and Engring. Lifetime Achievement award. Fellow IEEE (pres., acoustics, speech and signal processing soc. 1988-89, editor in chief Transactions on Signal Processing jour. 1993-95, Disting. lectr. 1996-97, Harriet Rigas award 1998), AAAS, Am. Soc. Engring. Edn.; mem. NAE. Office: US Dept Def 1000 Navy Pentagon Rm 4E739 Washington DC 20350*

ETTER, FAYE MADALYN, interior design company executive; b. Boston, Dec. 19, 1951; d. Charles Gaines and Rosemarie (Verlinde) E. BS in Design and Merchandising, Drexel U., 1973, MS in Interior Design, 1987. Staff designer Bloomingdale's, Jenkintown, Pa., 1980-83, design dir. Chestnut Hill, Mass., 1983-85; pres. Etter Interiors, Newton, Mass., 1985—. Contbr. articles to interior design mags. Mem. Am. Soc. Interior Designers (sec. 1988, chair designers auction 1990, bd. dirs. 1988, 90, 91, Presdl. Citation 1988, 90). Office: Etter Interiors 8 Varick Rd Waban MA 02468-1319

ETTINGER, PENNY A., medical/surgical nurse; b. Ft. Worth, Apr. 23, 1965; d. Donna Lou (Pollock) Tuck; children: Chandler Wayne, Zachary Stephen, Shaylin Rose. BSN, U. Tex., El Paso, 1987; MBA, Webster U., 2005. RN, Calif., Tex., Ark. Charge nurse Driftwood Convalescent Home, Salinas, Calif., 1988; staff nurse med./surg. unit Natividad Med. Ctr., Salinas, 1988; unit dir. orthopedics-neurology Sun Towers Hosp., El Paso, 1989-94; nurse mgr. med./surg. ICU, orthopedics clinic Drew Meml. Hosp., Monticello, Ark., 1994—99; emergency rm nurse Munroe Regional Med. Ctr., Ocala, Fla., 1999—, ED quality coord., 2005—. Home: 2217 NE 35th St Ocala FL 34479-2964 Office: Munroe Regional Med Ctr Emergency Dept Ocala FL Office Phone: 352-402-5171.

ETZEL, RUTH ANN, pediatrician, epidemiologist, educator; b. Milw., Apr. 6, 1954; d. Raymond Arthur and Marian Dorothy Etzel. Student, St. Olaf Coll., 1972-73; BA in Biology summa cum laude, U. Minn., 1976; MD, U. Wis., 1980; PhD, U. N.C., 1985. Bd. cert. Am. Bd. Pediat., Am. Bd. Preventive Medicine. Resident in pediat. N.C. Meml. Hosp., Chapel Hill, 1980-83; adj. asst. prof. pediat. Emory U. Sch. Medicine, Atlanta, 1985-87; epidemic intelligence svc. officer Ctr. Environ. Health Ctrs. Disease Control, Atlanta, 1985-87, med. epidemiologist Ctr. Environ. Health and Injury Control, 1987-90, chief air pollution and respiratory health br., 1991-96, asst. dir. preventive medicine residency program, 1992-97; dir. divsn. epidemiology and risk assessment Office Pub. Health and Sci., Food Safety and Inspection Svc., USDA, Washington, 1998—2001; adj. prof. environ. and occupl. health George Washington U., Washington, 2000—. Mem. preventive medicine and pub. health test com. Nat. Bd. Med. Examiners, 1992—94; mem. US Med. Licensing Exam. Step 2 Preventive Medicine and Pub. Health Test Material Devel. Com., 1992—94; mem., trustee Am. Bd. Preventive Medicine, 1992—2001, vice chair pub. health and preventive medicine, 1997—2001; commissioned officer US Pub. Health Svc, 1985—2005. Editor: Am. Acad. Pediat., Pediat. Environ. Health, 1999—; assoc. editor: Current Problems in Pediatrics and Adolescent Healthcare, 2005—; contbr. articles to profl. publs. Recipient Arthur S. Flemming award, DC Jaycees, 1991; Robert Wood Johnson Clin. scholar, U. N.C., 1983—85, MacPherson scholar, 1972. Fellow: Am. Coll. Preventive Medicine, Am. Acad. Pediats. (Ctrs. Disease Control and Prevention liaison 1986—94, chmn. sect. epidemiology 1988—92, ex-officio 1993—94, chmn. com. environ. health 1995—99, mem. com. on native Am. child health 2003—, mem. exec. com. sect. epidemiology 2005—); mem.: Internat. Soc. Environ. Epidemiology, Ambulatory Pediatric Assn. (mem. rsch. com. 1987—, comms. dir. 2002—05), Delta Omega, Phi Beta Kappa. Personal E-mail: retzel@earthlink.net.

ETZKORN, SUSAN, elementary school educator, small business owner; d. Jim and Betty Bolin; m. Rick Etzkorn, Mar. 25, 1982; children: Kaley, Gunnar. MEd, U. Ark., Fayetteville, 1987. Cert. elem. tchr. Ark. Tchr. Barling Elem. Sch., Ark., 1982—86, Ind. St. Elem., Pine Bluff, 1986—88, Demonstration Sch., Columbus, Miss., 1988—90, Hudson PEP Elem., Longview, Tex., 1990—91, Haines City Elem., Fla., 1991—92, Brigham Acad., Winter Haven, 1992—94, Raymond F. Orr Elem., Fort Smith, Ark., 2000—. Owner Learning Oasis, Fort Smith, Ark., 1995—. Author: Teacher Tested Reading Tips, 1990. Leader Girl Scouts USA, Fort Smith, Ark., 2003—06, AWANA's, 2003—04. Grantee, Ark. Sci. and Tech. Found., 2004. Mem.: National Sch Supply and Equipment Assn. (assoc.). Baptist. Avocations: travel, camping. Office Phone: 479-646-3711.

EU, MARCH FONG, ambassador; b. Oakdale, Calif., Mar. 29, 1929; d. Yuen and Shiu (Shee) Kong; children by previous marriage: Matthew Kipling Fong, Marchesa Suyin Fong; m. Henry Eu, Aug. 31, 1973; stepchildren: Henry, Adeline, Yvonne, Conroy, Alaric. Student, Salinas Jr. Coll.; BS, U. Calif.-Berkeley, 1943; MEd, Mills Coll., 1947; EdD, Stanford U., 1956; postgrad., Columbia U., Calif. State Coll.-Hayward; LLD, Lincoln U., 1984; LLB (hon.), Western U., 1985; DHL (hon.), Northrup Coll., 1991; LLB (hon.), Pepperdine U., 1993. Chmn. divsn. dental hygiene U. Calif. Med. Center, San Francisco, 1948-56; dental hygienist Oakland (Calif.) Pub. Schs., 1948-56; supr. dental health edn. Alameda County (Calif.) Schs.; lectr. health edn. Mills Coll., Oakland; mem. Calif. Legislature, 1966-74, chmn. select com. on agr., foods and nutrition, 1973-74; mem. com. natural resources and conservation, com. commerce and pub. utilities, select com. med. malpractice; chief of protocol State of Calif., 1975-83, sec. of state, 1975-94; amb. to Federated States of Micronesia, Am. Embassy, Pohnpei, 1994—. Chmn. Calif. State World Trade Commn., 1983-87; ex-officio mem. Calif. State World Trade Commn., 1987—; spl. cons. Bur. Intergroup Relations, Calif. Dept. Edn.; ednl., legis. cons. Sausalito (Calif.) Pub. Schs., Santa Clara County Office Edn., Jefferson Elementary Union Sch. Dist., Santa Clara H.S. Dist., Santa Clara Elementary Sch. Dist., Live Oak Union H.S. Dist.; mem. Alameda County Bd. Edn., 1956-66, pres., 1961-62, legis. adv., 1963, Assembly Retirment Com., Assembly Com. on Govtl. Quality Com., Assembly Com. on Pub. Health; pres. Alameda County Sch. Bds. Assn., others; U.S. advisor Shenzhen Internat. Ent. Co., Ltd., Shenzhen, Guangzhou, China, 1997; internat. hon. advisor 4th World Chinese Entrepreneurs Conv., Vancouver, B.C., 1997; hon. chmn. Sino-Am. Inst. Human Resources, L.A., 1997; U.S. advisor Internat. Hort Exposition for 1999, Kunming, Yunnan, 1997; exec. adv. bd. Asian Am. Policy Rev. Bd., Washington, 1998, others; adj. prof. on regional and continuing edn. Calif. State U., Sacramento, 2000; S.E. Asia advisor Startec Global Telecomm., Inc.; bd. dirs. East L.A. Coll. Found.; adv. bd. for canonization of Blessed Junipero Serra, Santa Barbara, Calif., 2000-01; hon. advisor Internat. Leadership Found., Sacramento, Calif., 2000; adj. prof., sr. adv. Calif. State U. Coll. Continuing & Regional Edn., Sacramento, 2000; sr. advisor S.E. Asia, Startec Global Oper. Co., Bethesda, Md., 2000; bd. regents presdl. adv. com. So. Calif. U. Health Scis., Whittier, Calif., 2002. Mem. adv. bd. for canonization of Father Junipero Sierra, Franciscan Fathers, Santa Barbara, Calif., Internat. Leadership Found. Recipient Cmty. Svc. award Coll. of San Mateo, Ann. Humanitarian award Women's Ctr., Coll. of Law, San Diego, Asian Am. on the Move award for politics L.A. City Employees Asian Am. Assn., Outstanding Svc. to Cmty. award Irish-Israeli Italian Soc. San Francisco, Disting. C.C. Alumni award Calif. C.C. and Jr. Coll. Assn., Outstanding Woman award Nat. Women's Polit. Caucus, Daisy award Calif. Landscape Contrs. Assn., 1980, Milton Shoong Hall of Fame Humanitarian award, 1981, Citizen of the Yr. award Coun. for Civic Unity of San Francisco Bay Area, 1982, Woman of the Yr., Dems. United, San Bernardino, 1986, Woman of Achievement Award of Distinction, San Gabriel Valley YWCA, 1987, Disting. svc. award Rep. of Honduras, 1987, Woman of the Yr. award Santa Barbara County Girls Club Coalition, 1987, Polit. Achievement award Calif. Dem. Party, Black Caucus, 1988, 1989, JFK Am. Leadership award Santa Ana Dem. Club, 1989, Cmty. Leadership award Torat-Haijun Hebrew Acad., 1990, Citizen of Yr. award Chinese-Am. United for Self Employment, 1996, Govt. Svc. award friends of Mus. of Chinese Am. History, L.A., 1997,Mother of the Yr. award No. Am. TV Corp., 1999, Lifetime Achievement award Orgn. Chinese Ams. Inc., 1999, Outstanding Overseas Chinese award San Francisco Chinese Benevolent Assn. and Chinese Consol. Women's Assn. San Francisco, 2001, Outstanding Citizen award Chinese Am. Citizens Alliance, 2002, Spirit of Am. award Chinese Am. Citizen's Alliance, 2003, numerous others; March Fong Eu ann. achievement award named in her honor Nat. Notary Pub. Assn.; named Remarkable Woman of Calif., Gov. Calif., 2004. Fellow Internat. Coll. Dentists; mem. Navy League (life), Am. Dental Hygienists Assn. (pres. 1956-57), No. Calif. Dental Hygienists Assn., Oakland LWV, AAUW (area rep. in edn. Oakland br.), Calif. Tchrs. Assn., Calif. Agrl. Aircraft Assn. (hon.), Calif. Sch. Bd. Assn., Alameda County Sch. Bd. Assn. (pres. 1965), Alameda County Mental Health Assn., Calif. Pub. Health Assn. Northern Divsn. (hon.), So. Calif. Dental Assn. (hon.), Bus. and Profl. Women's Club, Soroptimist (hon.), Hadassah (life), Ebell Club (L.A.), Chinese Retail Food Markets Assn. (hon.), Chinese Women's Assn. Singapore, Am. Assn. Singapore, Pilot Club Internat., Clara Barton Soc. Am. Red Cross (L.A. chpt.), Delta Kappa Gamma, Phi Alpha Delta (hon.), Phi Delta Gamma (hon.), others. Democrat. Avocation: painting.

EUBANK, PIPER, psychiatrist; d. Harvest and adopted d. Foster Eubank. BA in Psychology, U. Calif., Irvine, 1989; MD, Drexel U., Phila., 1996. Resident adult psychiatry Oreg. Health Scis. U., Portland, 1996—99; fellow child psychiatry U. Calif., Irvine, 1999—2001; child and adolescent psychiatrist County of Orange, Health Care Agy., Costa Mesa, Calif., 2002—. Mem. physician content rev. bd. Healthcasts/Profl. TV Network, N.Y.C., 2005—. Author poetry. Mem. Universalist-Unitarian Ch., Laguna Beach, Calif., 2006. Finalist Flute Competition, Calif. Music Tchrs. Assn.; recipient Youth Leadership award, Hugh O'Brien Found.; scholar, Mills Coll., U. Calif., Irvine; Rock Sleyster scholar for Outstanding Med. Student Performance in Psychiatry, AMA. Mem.: Physician's Com. For Responsible Medicine, Am. Psychiat. Assn., Am. Acad. Child and Adolescent Psychiatry, Internat. Libr. Poetry (hon.; Am. amb. poetry), Phi Beta Kappa, Psi Chi. Universalist-Unitarian. Avocations: music/art therapy (flute/poetry), movement therapy (dance/yoga), animal-assisted therapy (canine). Personal E-mail: piper121@msn.com.

EUBANKS, SHARON Y., former federal agency administrator; b. Mount Olive, Miss., Sept. 1955; BA, Miss. State U.; JD, Georgetown U. With U.S. Dept. Justice, Civil Divsn., 1983—2005, dep. dir. comml. litig., 1995—99, dep. dir. tobacco litig. team, 1999—2000, dir. tobacco litig. team, 2000—05.

EUBANKS, SONIA MELISA, education educator; b. Baton Rouge, La., May 27, 1974; d. Donald R. and Adele Ledoux Eubanks. BS, So. U. & A&M Coll., Baton Rouge, 1995, MS, 1999, MS, 2005. Prof. Ctrl. Tex. Coll., Seattle, 2000—06, Baton Rouge C.C., Baton Rouge, 2002—. Author: Legalization of Gambling: A Political Odyssey. Mem.: Alpha Kappa Alpha (mem. assistance team for Katrina hurricane victims). Democrat. Roman Catholic. Office: Baton Rouge CC 5310 Florida Blvd Baton Rouge LA 70806 Office Phone: 225-216-8165. Personal E-mail: eubankss@mybr.cc.

EUBANKS-POPE, SHARON G., real estate company executive, entrepreneur; b. Chgo., Aug. 26, 1943; d. Walter Franklyn and Thelma Octavia (Watkins) Gibson; m. Larry Hudson Eubanks, Dec. 20, 1970 (dec. Jan. 1976); children: Rebekah, Aimée; m. Otis Eliot Pope, June 7, 1977; children: O. Eliot Jr., Adrienne. BS in Edn., Chgo. Tchrs. Coll., 1965; postgrad., Ill. Inst. Tech., 1967, John Marshall Law Sch., 1970, Governor's State U., 1975-76. Educator, parent coord. Chgo. Bd. Edn., 1965-77; owner, ptnr. Redel Rentals, Chgo., 1977—. Realtor, 1990—. Adminstrv. bd. St. Mark United Meth. Ch., Chgo., 1967, bd. trustees, 1988; com. chair Englewood Urban Progress Ctr., Chgo., 1973; coord., educator LWV, 1975-76; chair comms. Marian Cath. HS, 1999-2005, adv. bd.; mem. Cottage Grove Tax Increment Financing Bd., 2005—. Named Outstanding Sch. Parent Vol., Chgo. Bd. Edn., 1977; recipient Outstanding Cmty. Law Class award LWV, 1975-76, Christian Leadership award United Meth. Women, Chgo., 1985. Mem.: NAACP, NAFE, Nat. Assn. Realtors, Am. Soc. Profl. and Exec. Women, St. Mark Cmty. Devel. Corp. (v.p. 2003—), Links, Inc., Jack and Jill Am., Inc. (Chgo. chpt. journalist 1989—91, parliamentarian 1991, founder Parents for Parity in Edn. 1992, pres. Eubanks-Pope Devel. Co., Inc. 1993, Midwestern region sec.-treas. 1993—95, nat. treas. 1998—2000, Midwestern regional dir. 1995—97), Alpha Beta Gamma (female exec. del. to China People to People Amb. program 1998). Office: Redel Rentals 4338 S Drexel Blvd Chicago IL 60653-3536

EUCHARISTA, SISTER MARY, sister, educational association administrator, secondary school educator; b. Arcadia, Calif., Feb. 13, 1960; d. Carl Anthony and Mary Dolores Mazurik. BE, Whitworth, Spokane, Wash., 2001. Tchr. St. Michaels Acad., Spokane, Wash., 1984—, adminstr., 1996—; alto Singing Nuns, Spokane, Wash., 1982—. Mem. adv. bd. NIWP, Moscow, 1997—2005, Singing Nuns, Spokane, 2000—. Avocations: writing, skiing, reading, horseback riding, travel. Office Phone: 509-462-4335.

EUGENI, MICHELLE L., academic administrator; d. Carl Eugeni and Sharon Cathey; m. David Geilhufe. BA, U. Calif., Santa Cruz, 1993; MA in Tchg., Boston U., 1994; postgrad., U. Houston. Asst. editor NSTA, Arlington, Va., 1994—97; tchr., dept. chair Almaden Country Sch., San Jose, Calif., 1997—2003; tchg. asst. Dept of Ednl. Leadership and Cultural Studies, Houston, 2004—05; rsch. asst. Inst. for Urban Edn., Houston, 2005—. Recipient Oberholtzer Award for Outstanding Doctoral Student, Dept of Ednl. Leadership and Cultural Studies, U. of Houston, 2005—06, Cowell Coll. Svc. award, Cowell Coll., UC Santa Cruz, 1993; scholar Coll. of Edn. Alumni Assn. scholar, Coll. of Edn. Alumni Assn., U. of Houston, 2006—, Sch. of Edn. scholar, Boston U., 1993—94. Mem.: ASCD, Nat. Coun. for the Social Studies, Am. Ednl. Rsch. Assn. Office: Univ of Houston College of Education 4800 Calhoun Rd 401 Farish Hall Houston TX 77204-5031 Personal E-mail: mleugeni@uh.edu.

EURICH, JUDITH, art appraiser, printmaker; Tchr. Acad. Art Coll., Hearst Art Gallery, St. Mary's Coll., Moranga, Calif., Univ. Calif. Ext., San Francisco; curatorial asst., asst. curator, curator, prints, drawings, 19th century photogs. San Francisco Mus. Achenbach Found. for Graphic Arts, 1981—92; specialist to dir., print dept. Butterfield & Butterfield (now Bonhams & Butterfields), San Francisco, 1995—. Lectr. in field. Office: Bonhams & Butterfields 220 San Bruno Ave San Francisco CA 94103 Office Phone: 415-503-3259. Office Fax: 415-861-8951. Business E-Mail: judith.eurich@bonhams.com.

EURICH, NELL P., education educator; b. Norwood, Ohio, July 28, 1919; d. Clayton W. and Adah (Palmer) Plopper; m. Alvin C. Eurich, Mar. 15, 1953 (dec. 1987); children: Juliet Ann, Donald Alan; m. Maurice Lazarus, 1988. AA, Stephens Coll., 1939; BA, Stanford U., 1941, MA, 1943; PhD, Columbia U., 1959. Dir. student union U. Tex., 1942-43; resident counselor Barnard Coll., 1944-46; asst. to pres. Woman's Found., 1947-49; officer charge pub. relations State U. N.Y., 1949- 52; acting pres. Stephens Coll., 1953-54; asst. prof. English NYU, 1959-64; academic dean New Coll., Sarasota, Fla., 1965; dir. project to reorganize curriculum Aspen (Colo.) Pub. High Sch., 1966; dean faculty, prof. English Vassar Coll., 1967-70; provost, dean faculty, prof. English, v.p. acad. affairs Manhattanville Coll., NY, 1971-75; sr. cons. Internat. Council for Ednl. Devel., 1975-82, Acad. for Ednl. Devel., 1982-88. Mem. nat. selection com., chmn. Rocky Mountain regional com. Nat. Endowment Humanities, 1966-67, cons., 1970-71; mem. Middle States commn. Marshall Scholarships, 1967-68; chmn. Northeastern region, 1969-71; mem. U.S. Commn. on Ednl. Tech., HEW, 1968-69; mem. overseer's vis. com. on summer sch. and univ. extension Harvard, 1969-75; mem. panel of judge's Fed. Woman's award, 1969; cons. Acad. for Ednl. Devel., 1970-71; mem. career minister rev. bd. U.S. Dept. State, 1972; participant Ditchley Conf. V, 1973; mem. Rhodes Scholarship Selection Com., 1976; moderator exec. seminar Aspen Inst. for Humanistic Studies, 1977, 79, 80; dir. Adult Learning Project Carnegie Found. for Advancement Teaching, 1985-90; advisor Nat. Acad. of Engring., 1987-88; vis. com. Neuro Scis., Mass. Gen. Hosp. Author: Science in Utopia, 1967, Higher Education in Twelve Countries: A Comparative View, 1981, (with B. Schwenkmeyer) Great Britain's Open University, 1971, Corporate Classrooms, 1985, The Learning Industry, 1991; contbg. author: (Alvin Toffler) Learning for Tomorrow, 1974, From Parnassus: Essays for Jacques Barzun, 1976; contbr. articles to profl. jours. Past trustee Bank Street Coll., Salisbury Sch., Hudson Guild Neighborhood House, Colo. Rocky Mountain Sch., Bennington Coll.; trustee Carnegie Coun. on Policy Studies in Higher Edn., 1977—80, Carnegie Found. for Advancement of Teaching, 1978—84; trustee emeritus New Coll.

Found., 1964—2001. Mem. MLA, Am. Assn. Colls. (spl. com. on liberal studies 1966-70), World Soc. Ekistics, Nat. Coun. Women (hon.), Century Assn. N.Y.C. Home: 144 Brattle St Cambridge MA 02138-2202

EUSTER, JOANNE REED, retired librarian; b. Grants Pass, Oreg., Apr. 7, 1936; d. Robert Lewis and Mabel Louise (Jones) Reed; m. Stephen L. Gerhardt, May 14, 1977; children: Sharon L., Carol L., Lisa J. Student, Lewis and Clark Coll., 1953-56; BA, Portland State Coll., 1965; MLibrarianship, U. Wash., 1968, MBA, 1977; PhD, U. Calif., Berkeley, 1986. Asst. libr. Edmonds C.C., Lynnwood, Wash., 1968-73, dir. libr.-media ctr., 1973-77; libr. Loyola U., New Orleans, 1977-80; libr. dir. J. Paul Leonard Libr., San Francisco State U., 1980-86, Rutgers State U. N.J., New Brunswick, 1986-89, v.p. info. svcs., 1989-91, v.p. univ. librs., 1991-92; libr. dir. U. Calif., Irvine, 1992-97; ret., 1997. Mem. adv. coun. Hong Kong U. Sci. and Tech. Librs., Princeton U. Libr., U. B.C., Can.; cons. in field Author: Changing Patterns of Internal Communication in Large Academic Libraries, 1981, The Academic Library Director, Management Activities and Effectiveness, 1987; columnist Wilson Libr. Bull., 1993-95; contbr. articles to profl. jours. Pres. Seattle Repertory Orgn.; trustee Seattle Repertory Theatre. Mem. ALA, Calif. Libr. Assn., Assn. Coll. and Rsch. Librs. (pres.), Rsch. Librs. Group (chair bd. dirs.).

EUSTIS, JOANNE D., university librarian; BA in English lit., Ind. U., 1974, MLS, 1974, MA in English lit., 1979. Various libr. positions Va. Poly. Inst. and State U., 1974—98, interim libr. dir., 1992—94; univ. libr. Case Western Res. U., Cleve., 1998—. Office: Kelvin Smith Libr Case Western Res U 11055 Euclid Ave Cleveland OH 44106-7151 Office Phone: 216-368-2992. E-mail: joanne.eustis@case.edu.*

EVANOFF-MCGEORGE, MARNIE HUBBELL, elementary school educator; b. Erie, Pa., Oct. 5, 1950; d. Michael Lawrence and Anne Hubbell Evanoff; 1 child, R. Hubbell McGeorge. B of Elem. Edn., Edinboro State U., Pa., 1972, MEd, 1975. Tchr. City of Erie Sch. Dist., Pa., 1972—88, 1993—. Author: Manners for Everyday/A Coloring Book, 1993. Mem. Jr. League, 1984—2005, PEO Sisterhood chpt. X, 1971—; elder 1st Presbyn. Ch. Covenant, Erie, 1993—; bd. dirs. Stonegate Assn., 2005—, Am. Dream Inst. Pa. State. Mem.: ASCD, DAR, NEA, Nat. Coun. Social Studies. Republican. Presbyterian. Avocations: travel, sewing, reading, walking, swimming. Home: 420 Sandstone Ct Erie PA 16505 Office: Roosevelt Mid Sch 2300 Cranberry St Erie PA 16502

EVANOVICH, JANET, writer; Attended, Douglass Coll. Author: (Stephanie Plum series) One For the Money, 1994, Two For the Dough, 1996, Three to Get Deadly, 1997, Four to Score, 1998, High Five, 1999, Hot Six, 2000, Seven Up, 2001, Hard Eight, 2002, Visions of Sugar Plums, 2002, To the Nines, 2003, Ten Big Ones, 2004 (Publishers Weekly Bestseller list, 2004), Eleven on Top, 2005 (No. 1 NY Times Bestseller hardcover fiction list, 2005, No. 1 Publishers Weekly Bestseller hardcover fiction list, 2005, Quills award for mystery/suspense/thriller, 2005), (Romance novels written under pseudonym Steffie Hall) Hero at Large, 1987, Foul Play, 1989, (Romance novels) The Grand Finale, 1988, Thanksgiving, 1988, Manhunt, 1988, Ivan Takes a Wife, 1989, Back to the Bedroom, 1989, 2005, Wife for Hire, 1990, Smitten, 1990, The Rocky Road to Romance, 1991, Naughty Neighbor, 1992, Metro Girl, 2004, (novels) Twelve Sharp, 2006 (The Quill award for Mystery/Suspense/Thriller, 2006); co-author (with Charlotte Hughes): (Full series) Full House, 2002, Full Speed, 2003, Full Tilt, 2003, Full Blast, 2004, Full Bloom, 2005. Mem.: Mystery Writers Am. (pres. 2006). Address: c/o Robert Gottleib Trident Media Group 36th Fl 41 Madison Ave New York NY 10010*

EVANS, AUDREY ELIZABETH, physician, educator; b. York, Eng., Mar. 6, 1925; came to U.S., 1957, naturalized, 1962; d. Leonard Llewellyn and Phyllis Mary (Miller) E. Licentiate Sch. Medicine, Royal Coll. Surgeons, Edinburgh, 1950. Intern Royal Infirmary, Edinburgh, 1950-52; physician tumor therapy Children's Hosp., Boston, 1957-65; instr. pediatrics Harvard U. Med. Sch., 1961-65; asst. prof. pediatric hematologist U. Chgo., 1965-69; prof. pediatrics U. Pa., 1969—, now emeritus. Dir. oncology Children's Hosp., Phila., 1969-89. Home: 2010 Spruce St Philadelphia PA 19103-6569 Office: Children's Hosp ARB 902 324 S 34th St Philadelphia PA 19104-4399

EVANS, B. PAIGE, artistic director; b. NYC, Nov. 12, 1962; d. Thomas William and Lois Logan Evans; m. Ariel Diaz, Jan. 6, 1999 (div. June 2000); 1 child, Tyler Evans Diaz. BA, Harvard Coll., 1984. Arts editor Internat. Courier, Rome, 1985—86; tchr. lit. St. Stephen's Sch., Rome, 1986—89; lit. mgr. Manhattan Theatre Club, NYC, 1990—97, dir. artistic devel., 2001—; adj. prof. NYU, 1995—96; writing fellow Inst. Current World Affairs, Havana, Cuba, 1998—2000. Playwriting resident MacDowell Colony, 1996—98. Author: (off-Broadway play) Mind Above All, 1996. Mem.: 454 15th St Owners Corp. (treas. 1995—). Democrat. Avocations: triathlete, playwriting, teaching. Office: Manhattan Theatre Club 311 W 43rd St New York NY 10036

EVANS, BARBARA, art educator; b. El Paso, Tex., Aug. 12, 1955; d. August Edward and Claudine Heidi Munich; m. William Martin Evans, June 12, 1982; children: Rory, Shane. BA in Art, SUNY, Stony Brook, 1978; MS in Secondary Edn., Dowling Coll., NY. Cert. art tchr. NY, primary edn. tchr. NY. HS art tchr. Roosevelt Sch. Dist., Roosevelt, NY, 1998—. Mem.: Nat. Art Tchrs. Assn., NY State Tchrs. Assn. Avocations: painting, gardening. Office Phone: 516-867-8666.

EVANS, BETTY VAUGHN, minister; b. Campbell, Ala., Sept. 3, 1954; children: Robert, Rochelle, James. D in Ministry, Victory Bible Coll., 2003. Ordained evangelist Ch. God in Christ, 1985, ordained minister Ch. God in Christ, 1986, ordained pastor Whole Lifw Christian Ch./TX, 1995, cert. restorative therapist Faith Based Counselor Tng. Inst. Tex., 2000. Pastor Storehouse Ministry Fellowship, Inc., San Antonio, 1995—. Spkr. in field. Chmn. bus. adv. coun. Tex. chpt. Nat. Rep. Congl. Com., 2005—. Nominee Black Achievement award, San Antonio, Tex., 2003; named Pioneer Woman Pastor, San Antonio Express News, 2003. Office: Storehouse Ministry Fellowship Inc 14100 Nacogdoches Rd San Antonio TX 78247 Office Phone: 210-599-8136. E-mail: storehousemf.org.

EVANS, BONITA DIANNE, education educator; b. N.Y.C., Jan. 14, 1940; d. Roy Simon and Verna (Ashton) Evans; m. Robert John Watts, Aug. 1981 (div. 1996); 1 child, Helena Watts. BA, U. Canberra, Australia, 1990; MDS, Monash U., Melbourne, Australia, 1992; PhD, Walden U., Minn., 1996. With Middle East Bureau UN, 1974—; mem. diplomatic mission, Namibia, 1978, peacekeeping forces Israeli Egyptian border, 1979—80; with dept. prime min. and cabinet Australian Dept. Fgn. Affairs, Canberra, Australia, 1986—87; devel. rsch. officer Aboriginal Hostels, Canberra, Australia, 1987—88; cultural affairs asst. US Embassy, Canberra, Australia, 1988—90; adj. prof. English Montclair State U., NJ, 1996—2000; vis. prof. Rutgers U., Newark, 1999—2000; prof. history, women's studies William Paterson U., 1998—; faculty, Global Studies Monmouth U. Author: Youth in Foster Care, 1997, Kijani, 2002, New Hope Rising, 2002. Recipient cert. Congressional Recognition for Invaluable and Outstanding Svc. to Cmty., NJ State and Gen. Assembly, 2005, letter of appreciation for recognition of outstanding contributions to edn., NJ State Governors Office, 2005.

EVANS, CAROL ANN, reading specialist; b. Meridian, Miss., Aug. 1, 1947; d. Charles and Anne Bishop Easterling; m. Robert David Evans, Aug. 23, 1969; children: Kelly Sinclair, David Robert. BS in Edn., Miss. State U., Starkville, 1969, MA in Edn., 1970. Cert. elem. tchr. Ariz., reading specialist Ariz. Tchr. Lowndes County Elem. Sch., 1969—71, Miss. Pub. Sch. Sys., 1973—74, Olive Tree Day Sch., 1974—75, Palo Alto Presch., 1975—80, U. Nev., Las Vegas, 1979—80, Clark County Pub. Schs., 1980—83, Dept. of Def. Sch., 1983—84, Saudi Arabia Internat. Sch., 1984—86, Village Meadows Elem., 1986—87, New River Elem. Sch., 1987—94, Desert Mountain Sch., 1994—. Coord. ann. fund drive Am. Kidney Found.; officer PTA, Gene Ward Elem. Sch., Las Vegas. Recipient award, Phoenix Ednl. Trust, 1997, Mid. Sch. Educator of Yr. award, Desert Mountain Mid. Sch., 1999, Pride award, Deer Valley Unified Sch. Dist., 2006; grantee, Wells Fargo Bank, 1997, 1999; Lit. Classroom grant, Phoenix West Feading Coun., 1999. Mem.: Ariz. Assn. Curriculum Devel., Ctrl. Ariz. Mid. Level Assn., Phoenix West Reading Assn., Nat. Coun. Tchrs. of English, Internat. Reading Assn., Ariz. Desert Land Trust Coun. Republican. Methodist. Avocations: travel, reading, child advocacy projects, art council. Home: 11002 E Lovingtree Ln Scottsdale AZ 85262 Office: Desert Mountain Sch 35959 N 7th Ave Desert Hills AZ 85086 Office Phone: 623-445-3549. E-mail: Carol.Evans@dm.dvusd.org.

EVANS, CARRIE L., state legislative lawyer; b. Regina, Sask., Can., Aug. 15, 1970; d. Karen A. Evans and William K. Forshner, Samuel E. Evans (Stepfather); life ptnr. Pamela R. Bennett. BA, Minot State U., ND, 1990; MA, So. Ill. U., Carbondale, 1994; LLB, Osgoode Hall Law Sch., North York, Ont., Can., 1997. Dir. direct svcs. Battered Women's Program, Baton Rouge, 1998—2001; state legis. lawyer Nat. Gay and Lesbian Task Force, Washington, 2001—03, Human Rights Campaign, Washington, 2003—05, state legis. dir., 2005—. Bd. advisors ann. rev. issue Georgetown Jour. Gender and the Law, 2004—. Recipient Blaney, McMurtry, Stappells, Friedman prize in 1st Nations and the Law/Rights of Indigenous Peoples, Osgoode Hall Law Sch., 1996, Helen Grossman, Q.C. award for outstanding svc. to cmty. and Legal Aid Svcs. Program, 1997. Personal E-mail: carevans@gmail.com.

EVANS, CHARLOTTE MORTIMER, communications consultant, writer; b. Newton, NJ, Nov. 26, 1933; d. Karl Otto and Wilhelmina (Otterbach) Pfau; m. John Atterbury Mortimer, Nov. 20, 1964; children: Meredith Elizabeth, Mandy Leigh; m. G. Robert Evans, Sept. 4, 1982. Student, Douglass Coll., 1952—54; BS, RN, Columbia U. Presby. Hosp., 1957; postgrad., Columbia U. Presbyn. Hosp., 1957—59, NYU, 1959—60; MPA, Coll. of Notre Dame, 1979. Spl. assignment nurse Columbia-Presbyn. Med. Center, N.Y.C., 1957—59; med. advt. copywriter Paul Klemtner & Co., N.Y.C., 1959—61, William Douglas McAdams Agy., N.Y.C., 1961—62; account exec. Arndt, Preston, Chapin, Lamb & Keen, N.Y.C., 1962—63; Rocky Mountain corr. Med. World News, Denver, 1963—64; owner Publicite, Denver; gen. mgr. Center Mktg. Assn., Palo Alto, Calif., 1964—66; freelance writer, pub. rels. and mgmt. cons. Woodside, Calif., 1966—85; pres. Communications for Youth, 1979—. Mem. Palo Alto-Stanford Hosp. Aux., 1968—72; pub. rels. assistance Peninsula Children's Ctr., Palo Alto, 1968—73, Triton Mus. Art, San Jose, Calif., 1966—70; health component Early Childhood Com. Woodside Elem. Sch. Dist.; past chair, mem., bd. dirs. ct.-apptd. spl. advocate program CASA-Kane County, 1989—96; mem. San Mateo County Mental Health Adv. Bd., Friends of Woodside Libr. Bd., 1983—85, Nat. CASA advocate program, 1989; vol. Nat. Com. for Prevention Child Abuse and Neglect, 1987—96; acting chair, founder Chicagoland Media & Children Com., 1993—96; adv. com Our Children's Place, Kane County, 1995—98; mem. Rep. Senatorial Inner Cir., 1982—86; chmn. citizens adv. com. San Mateo County Juvenile Social Svcs.; mem. adv. com. South County Youth and Family Svcs. Program; mem. Statewide Citizens Adv. Com. on Child Abuse and Neglect, Ill. Dept. Children and Family Svcs., 1987-1999, 1987—99; chair adv. com. to Congressman Dennis Hastert on Family and Child Legis., 1990—92; bd. dirs. N.J. Jr. C. of C./UNICEF/African Project, 1960—61, Natividad Ranch, first-time offenders program, 2001—, Friends of the Monterey Symphony, 2000—.

EVANS, CLAIRE (MARY EVANS), painter, educator; b. Augusta, Ga., Aug. 8, 1929; d. John Franklin Patrick and Mary Viola Dowling; m. Charles Lane Evans, Oct. 18, 1951; children: Joel Lane, Ellen Claire. BA, Converse Coll., 1951. Tchr., lectr. Rocky Mountain Coll. Art and Design, Denver, 1979—. One-woman shows include Foothills Art Ctr., Golden, Colo., 1978, UMC Gallery, U. Colo., Boulder, 1979, Jack Meier Gallery, Houston, 1988, Zaplin-Lampert Gallery, Santa Fe, 1988; group shows include West '82 Art and the Law, St. Paul, 1982, Joslyn Biennial, Omaha, 1984, Foothills Art Ctr., 1984, Colo. Springs Biennial, 1985, Boulder Art Ctr., 1987; represented in corp. collections including United Bank, Amoco Prodns., Petrolewis Corp., ARCO, Sohio, Am. Exploration; represented in permanent collection The Art Collector Gallery, San Diego. Studio: 2810 Wilderness Pl Ste E Boulder CO 80301-5453

EVANS, CYNTHIA MAE, music educator; d. George Lovic Evans, Jr. and Shirley Price Evans. BA in Music Composition, Va. Commonwealth U., Richmond, 1984. Cert. tchr., choral & elem. music. Va. Dept. Edn. Choral & photojournalism tchr. Bluestone Sr. High, Skipwith, Va., 1991—95; kindergarten music tchr. Clarksville Elem., 1994—95; music tchr. Chase City Elem., 1995—, Buckhorn Elem., South Hill, 1995—. Composer (singer): (song (recorded with 5th grade class) Songs Around Us, 2002 (Congl. & Presdl. letters, 2003). Office: Buckhorn Elem 500 Gordon Lake Rd South Hill VA 23970 Office Fax: 434-447-3075. Business E-Mail: cevans@meck.k12.va.us.

EVANS, EILEEN, music educator; b. Rochester, N.Y., Apr. 12, 1960; d. Helmut Kurt and Ingrid Elisabeth Jung; m. Ken Davis Evans, July 30, 1980; children: Jennifer, Jason, Jesse. AA, Wstn. Wyo. C.C., 1984; BMus, Brigham Young U., 1998. Pvt. piano tchr., Green River, Wyo., 1980—. Mem. Nat. Wyo. Music Tchr. Assn., Nat. Guild Piano Tchrs. Mem. Lds Ch. Home: 1590 Nebraska St Green River WY 82935-5953

EVANS, ELIZABETH ANN WEST, retired real estate agent; b. Xenia, Ohio, Mar. 28, 1933; d. Millard Stanley and Elizabeth Denver (Johns) West. BA, Ohio U., Athens, 1966, MA, 1968. Cert. GRI, 1993. Sec. various orgns., Ohio, 1952-61; tchr. Ohio U., Athens, 1966-67, Zanesville, 1968-72, Collier County Pub. Schs., Naples, Fla., 1972-77; sales Helen's Hang Ups, Naples, 1978-79; mgr. pvt. practice Wilmington, Ohio, 1979-87; adminstrv. asst. Powell Assocs., Cambridge, Mass., 1987-90; real estate agt. Bill Evans Realty, Inc., Naples, 1989-90, Howard Hanna Real Estate Svcs., Naples, 1991—93, Downing-Frye Realty, Inc., Naples, 1993—97, Downing-Frye Referral Network Realty Inc., Naples, 1997—2002; ret., 2002. Cape May resident rep. to Ohio Presbyn. Retirement Svcs., 2004—. Fellow: Phi Beta Kappa; mem.: DAR (chaplain 1988—90, chmn. Motion, Picture, Radio and TV 1992—94, asst. chaplain 1994—96, chaplain 2000—01, chmn. pub. rels. 2003—05), Kappa Alpha Theta (50-yr. mem.), Phi Kappa Phi, Phi Sigma Iota. Republican. Presbyterian. Home: 182 Cape May Dr Wilmington OH 45177

EVANS, FAITH, singer; b. Fla., June 10, 1973; m. Christopher Wallace (The Notorious B.I.G.), 1995 (dec.); 1 child, Christopher Wallace Jr., 1996. Student, Fordham U. Singer: (albums) Faith, 1995, Keep The Faith, 1998 (Grammy award for best rap performance, 1998), Faithfully, 2001, The First Lady, 2005; singer: (background vocals) (Mary J. Blige) My Life, 1994, Ballads, 2001, (Hi-Five) Keep it Goin On, 1992, (Frankie) My Heart Belongs to You, 1997, (The Notorious B.I.G.) Life After Death, 1997, (Eric Benet) Day in the Life, 1999, (Jon B.) Pleasures U Like, 2001, (Kelly Price) Priceless, 2003, and others; singer: (background vocals, assoc. prodr.) (LSG) Levert, Sweat, Gill, 1997. Office: c/o Bad Boy Records 1440 Broadway, 16th Fl New York NY 10018

EVANS, HELEN RUTH, music educator, pianist; b. Grant City, Mo., May 26, 1913; d. John Larkin and Inez (Florea) Hall; m. Donald Maurice Mathias, Oct. 7, 1934 (div.); m. Thomas Claude Evans, Sept. 1. Grad., No. Colo. U. Piano tchr., Colo., 1940-50, N.Mex., 1950-96; ret., 1996. Mem. AAUW, N.Mex. Music Tchrs. Assn., Delta Kappa Gamma. Republican. Presbyterian. Avocations: pianist, reading, cooking.

EVANS, JANET, publishing executive; b. Raleigh, N.C., Sept. 16, 1956; d. Leonard Odell and Sue J Mills. Mktg. advisor Evans & Wade Advt. Ltd., Raleigh, 1977—79; pres. Ivy Ho. Pub. Group, Raleigh, 1993—. Bd. dirs. Found. Internat. Meetings. Editor various organizational newsletters. Mem. Raleigh C. of C., NC, 1980—2002. Mem.: Pubs. Assn. of the South. Republican. Baptist. Avocations: reading, travel, walking. Home: 5527 Golden Arrow Ln Raleigh NC 27613 Home Fax: 919-781-9042. Business E-Mail: janetevans@ivyhousebooks.com.

EVANS, JO BURT, communications executive, rancher; b. Kimble County, Tex., Dec. 18, 1928; d. John Fred and Sadie (Oliver) Burt; m. Charles Wayne Evans II, Apr. 17, 1949; children: Charles Wayne III, John Burt, Elizabeth Wisart. BA, Mary Hardin-Baylor Coll., 1948; MA, Trinity U., 1967. Owner, mgr. Sta. KMBL, Junction, Tex., 1959-61; real estate broker Junction, 1965-74; staff economist, adv. on 21st Congl. Dist., polit. campaign Nelson Wolff, 1974-75; asst. mgr., bookkepper family owned ranches/rental property Junction, 1948—; gen. mgr. TV Translator Corp., Junction, 1968—, sec.-treas., 1980—. Treas., asst. to coord. Citizens for Tex., 1972; historian Kimble Hist. Soc.; mem. Com. of Conservation Soc. to Save the Edwards Aquifer, San Antonio, 1973; homecoming chmn. Sesquicentennial Yr., Junction; treas., asst. coord. New Consitution, San Antonio, 1974; legis. chair Hill Country Women, Kimble County, 1990—; cashier Texan Theatre; campaign chmn. for Challenge U. Mary Hardin, Baylor, 2000; curator Tex. Tech. U. Herbarium, 2006. Named an outstanding Texan, Tex. Senate, 1973. Mem. AAUW (scholarship named in honor 1973), Nat. Translator Assn., Daus. Republic Tex., Tex. Sheriffs Assn., Nat. Cattlewomens Assn., Internat. Platform Assn., Bus. and Profl. Women (pres. 1981-82), Edwards Plateau Tex. Master Naturalists. Republican. Mem. Unity Ch. Home: PO Box 283 Junction TX 76849-0283 Office: 618 Main St Junction TX 76849-4635 Office Phone: 325-446-3407.

EVANS, JOY, foundation administrator; b. Waterbury, Conn., Feb. 15, 1940; 4 children. Student, Hartford Coll. for Women, 1959. Weekly radio personality Young Stars on Parade Sta. WBRY, Waterbury, 1951-58; exec. sec. dir.'s office Discover Am. Travel Orgns., Washington, 1962-71; exec. sec. adminstr.'s office Nat. Ctr. for Housing Mgmt., Washington, 1971-72; exec. sec. mgr.'s office Nat. Visitor's Ctr. Nat. Park Svc. Dept. Interior, 1972-73; staff asst. divsn. pub. programs NEH, Washington, 1973-81, pub. info. officer, office of the chair, 1981—. Founding chair fed. woman's com. NEH, 1980-82, liaison White House task force on the humanities and arts 1981-82; spkr. commencement address Nat. Coll. Bus. and Tech., Charlottesville, Va., 2002, 04. Staff newsletter editor Not Hardcopy Newsletter, 1996-98. Mem. Annandale Homeowner's Assn. (pres. Terrace Townhouses 1989-92, TTA newsletter editor 1988-92), Soc. Govt. Meeting Planners (D.C. chpt. 1991-92). Roman Catholic. Avocations: music, art, dance, photography, theater, feng shui. Office: Nat Endowment for Humanities Rm 402 1100 Pennsylvania Ave NW Washington DC 20506-0001 Office Phone: 202-606-8446. Business E-Mail: jevans@neh.gov.

EVANS, JUDITH P., music educator; b. Akron, Ohio, May 29, 1945; d. Clyde J. and Margie M. Petersen; m. Frederick F.D. Evans, Dec. 27, 1969. B in Music Edn., Baldwin Wallace Coll., 1967; M in Music Edn., Fla. Atlantic U., 1974. Elem. string tchr. Alliance (Ohio) Pub. Schs., 1967—68, Fremont (Ohio) Pub. Schs., 1968—70; orch. dir. Margate (Fla.) Mid. Sch., 1970—79, Pine Ridge Mid. and Barron Collier High, Naples, Fla., 1979—2006. Pres. Fla. Am. String Tchrs. Assn., 1976; clinician United Musical Instruments, Elkhart, Ill., 1982—; chair Acad. Tchrs. Edn. Found., Naples, 1998. Editor: (mag.) Nat. Sch. Orch. Assn. Bull., 1990—95. Dir. Collier County Chamber Strings, Naples, 1998—. Named Fla. Music Educator of Yr., Fla. Music Edn. Assn., 1994—95; recipient Golden Apple award, Edn. Found. Collier County, 1996, Alumni Achievement award, Baldwin Wallace Coll., 1997. Mem.: Collier County Music Tchrs. Assn. (pres. 1984—86, treas.), Fla. Orch. Assn. (pres. 1981—83), Am. String Tchrs. Assn. (nat. sec. 1994—96, Svc. award 1996, named Fla. Educator of Yr. 2004). Home: 191 Oakwood Ct Naples FL 34110-1145

EVANS, JULIE ROBIN, lawyer; b. Forest Hills, N.Y., Feb. 25, 1961; d. Theodore and Sally (Klein) Kuschner; m. John Robert Evans, Sept. 7, 1987. BA, SUNY, Albany, 1983; JD, Hofstra U., 1986. Bar: NY 1987, Mass. 1987, US Dist. Ct. (so. and ea. dists.) NY 1988. Asoc. Wilson, Elser, Moskowitz, Edelman & Dicker LLP, NYC, 1986—, ptnr. Editorial staff, Hofstra Law Rev., 1985-86. Mem. ABA, NY Bar Assn. Office: Wilson, Elser, Moskowitz, Edelman & Dicker LLP 23rd Fl 150 E 42nd St New York NY 10017-5639 Office Phone: 212-490-3000 2668. Office Fax: 212-490-3038. E-mail: evansj@wemed.com.

EVANS, LARA ADELE, elementary school educator; BA in Elem. Edn., U. Pitts., 1990; M in Reading Specialization K-12, Duquesne U., Pitts., 1996. Tchr. Pitts. Pub. Schs., 1990—. Mem. Parent-Sch. Comty. Coun., Pitts., 1996—; mgr. Tutoring Program, Pitts., 2000. Recipient Gold Star for Leadership in Edn., Pitts. Coun. on Pub. Edn., 2002, Greenfield Svc. award in edn., Greenfield C.C., 1996. Avocations: reading, exercise.

EVANS, LAURIE, library director; MLS, U. North Tex., 1973. Libr. children's section Dallas Pub. Libr., interim dir. librs., 2004—05, dir. librs., 2005—. Mem.: ALA. Office: Dallas Pub Libr 1515 Young St Dallas TX 75201 E-mail: director@dallaslibrary.org.*

EVANS, LINDA KAY, publishing executive; b. Tipton, Ind., June 16, 1945; d. Walter K. and Ruth S. (Fakes) E. BA in English, Purdue U., Lafayette, 1968. Asst. to mng. editor Random House Pubs., N.Y.C., 1969-71; asst. to dir. editorial svcs. Sch. div. McGraw-Hill Book Co., N.Y.C., 1971-75, mgr. state contracts and inventory dept., 1975-88; bookstore owner, pres. The Literary Bookshop, N.Y.C., 1988-93; prodn. mgr. trade div. Simon & Schuster, N.Y.C., 1994—2004, sr. prodn. mgr. trade div., 2004—. Pub. cons. for sch. textbooks Prentice-Hall Book Co., Englewood Cliffs, N.J., 1992-93. Recipient Holiday Window Display award to Lit. Bookshop, Greenwich Village C. of C., 1990. Avocations: reading, travel, antiques. Office: Simon & Schuster Trade Div 1230 Ave of the Americas New York NY 10020-1586 Office Phone: 212-698-7237.

EVANS, LOUISE, investor, retired psychologist; b. San Antonio; d. Henry Daniel and Adela (Pariser) E.; m. Thomas Ross Gambrell, Feb. 23, 1960. BS, Northwestern U., 1949; MS in Clin. Psychology, Purdue U., 1952, PhD in Clin. Psychology, 1955. Lic. marriage, family and child counselor Calif.; Nat. Register of Health Svc. Providers in Psychology; lic. psychologist, Calif., N.Y. (inactive); diplomate Clin. Psychology, Am. Bd. Profl. Psychology. Intern clin. psychology Menninger Found. Topeka (Kans.) State Hosp., 1952-53; postdoctoral fellow clin. child psychology Menninger Clinic, Topeka, 1955-56; staff psychologist Kankakee (Ill.) State Hosp., 1954-55; head staff psychologist child guidance clinic Kings County Hosp., Bklyn., 1957-58; dir. psychology clinic Barnes-Renard Hosp.; instr. med. psychology Sch. Medicine Washington U., 1959-60; clin. rsch. cons. Episc. City Diocese, St. Louis, 1959-60; pvt. practice Fullerton, Calif., 1960—93; fellow Internat. Coun. Sex Edn. and Parenthood, 1984, Am. U., Washington. Psychol. cons. Fullerton Cmty. Hosp., 1961-81; staff cons. clin. psychology Martin Luther Hosp., Anaheim, Calif., 1963-70; chair, participant psychol. symposiums, 1956—; spkr., lectr. in field. Contbr. articles on clin. psychology to profl. publs. Elected to Hall of Fame Ctrl. H.S., Evansville, Ind., 1966; recipient Svc. award Yuma County (Ariz.) Head Start Program, 1972, Statue of Victory Personality of Yr. award Centro Studi E. Ricerche Delle Nazioni, Italy, 1985, Alumni Merit award Northwestern U. Coll. Arts and Scis., 1997; named Miss Heritage, Heritage Publs., 1965. Fellow AAAS (emeritus), APA, Soc. Clin. Psychology, Soc. for the Psychology of Women Psychotherapy Divsn., Soc. Consulting Psychology (dir. exec. bd. 1976-79, Internat. Psychology Lifelong Contbns. Advancement of Psychology Internat. Recognition award 2002), Acad. Clin. Psychology, Am. Assn. Applied and Preventive Psychology (charter), Royal Soc. for the Promotion of Health Eng. (emeritus), Internat. Coun. Psychologists (dir. 1977-79, sec. 1962-64, 73-76, 2 awards 2003, recognition for pioneering leadership in internat. psychology, named amb. for life award 2003), Am. Orthopsychiat. Assn. (life), World Wide Acad. Scholars of N.Z. (life), Assn. Psychol. Sci. (charter), LA Soc. Clin. Psychologists (exec. bd. 1966-67), Internat. Coun. Psychologists; mem. AAUP (emeritus), Calif. Psychol. Assn. (life, ins. com. 1961-65), LA County Psychol. Assn. (emeritus), Orange County Psychol. Assn. (charter founder, exec. bd. 1961-62), Am. Pub. Health Assn. (emeritus), Internat. Platform Assn., N.Y. Acad. Scis. (emeritus), Purdue U. Alumni Assn. (life, past pres. coun., mem. dean's club, Citizenship award 1975, Disting. Alumni award 1993, Old Master 1993), Northwestern U. Past 1851 Soc. (Coll. Arts and Scis. Merit award

1997), Ctr. Study Presidency, Soc. Jewelry Historians USA (charter), Alumni Assn. Menninger Sch. Psychiatry, Sigma Xi (emeritus). Achievements include development of innovative theories and techniques of clinical practice; acknowledged pioneer in development of psychology as science and profession both nationally and internationally, and in marital and family therapy, and in consulting to hospitals and clinics. Office: PO Box 6067 Beverly Hills CA 90212-1067 Office Phone: 310-474-1361. Office Fax: 310-474-1361.

EVANS, MARCIA K., school system administrator; b. Boston, Feb. 23, 1948; m. J. Brian Evans, Aug. 23, 1974; children: Megan, Rebecca, Tristan. BSEd, Lesley Coll., 1970; MEd, Boston Coll., 1976; EdD, Boston U., 1990. Tchr. Breen Sch., Lawrence, Mass., 1970-73; guidance counselor Town of Dartmouth, Mass., 1976-81; supr. student tchrs. Boston U., 1984-87; prin. Stockbridge (Vt.) Ctrl. Sch., 1992—. Home: RR 2 Box 448 Bethel VT 05032-9338

EVANS, MARGARET A., volunteer; b. N.Y.C., Jan. 20, 1924; d. Bernard J. and Katherine (Walsh) Markey; m. John Cullen Evans, Jr., Nov. 24, 1951. BA, Coll. Mt. St. Vincent, 1944; postgrad., Columbia U. Rep. N.Y. Telephone Co., 1944; pers. office Sak's 34th, N.Y.C., 1944-45, tng. supr. selling and non-selling depts., 1945-49, spl. assignment for store mgr., 1949-50; non-selling tng. supr. Gimbel Bros. and Saks 5th Inc., 1950-51; rep. Gimbels and Sak's 34th at NCCJ Retail Group meeting, 1949-50; instr. textile painting for ARC Chelsea Navy Hosp., 1952-54. ARC vol., 1980-92. Bd. dirs. Marblehead Hosp. Aid Assn., 1954, pres. 1955-58; sec. Mass. Hosp. Assn. Coun. of Hosp. Auxilliaries, 1957-59, chmn. North Shore region, 1959-61, chmn.-elect 1961-62, state chmn., 1962-64; exofficio trustee Salem Hosp.; trustee Mary A. Alley Hosp., 1956-79, chmn. bd. 1974-79; mem. Welcome Wagon of Fairfield/Easton (Conn.), 1979-83; chmn. Fairfield/Easton Theatre Group, Fifth Wheel Club of Fairfield, 1983-85. Mem. Alumnae Assn. Coll. Mt. Saint Vincent, Arrangers of Marblehead (chmn. garden therapy 1967-79), Marblehead Women's Newcomers (pres. 1953). Home: 108 Cedarwood Ln Fairfield CT 06825-1308

EVANS, MARGARET ANN, human resources administrator, business owner; b. Great Bend, Kans., Dec. 26, 1947; d. Freddy Florence and Peggy (Hawkins) Green; children: Carl André, Christopher Dion. B in Psychology, U. Mo., 1971, MPA, 1972. Pers. specialist Met. Jr. Coll., Kansas City, Mo., 1972-73; employee rels. specialist Amoco Oil Co., Kansas City, 1973-74; classification specialist Richards-Gebaur AFB, Mo., 1974-75; employee rels. officer Govt. Employee Hosp. Assn., Kansas City, 1977-84, mgr. pers., 1984-87, dir. human resources, 1987—. Mem. pers. com. Sta. KKFI, Kansas City, 1989—; mem. cert. bd. Human Resource Inst., exam devel. dir., 1994-95, sec.-treas., 1995-96. Sec. and v.p. Booster Club, Hickman Mills High Sch., Kansas City, 1989—; bd. dirs. Saturday Scholars, 2000-02. Ford Found. fellow U. Mo., 1971; recipient Contbr. of Yr. award Human Resource Mgmt. Assn., 1992, Pres. award 1993, 1995; named One of Kansas City's 100 Most Influential Kansas Citians KC Globe Most Influential African Ams. of Kansas City, 1993, 95, 96, 97. Mem. NAFE, Soc. Human Resources Mgmt. (pers. rsch. com. Kansas City chpt. 1989—, nat. com. 1990—, sec.-treas. Mo. state coun. 1992-93, bd. dirs., v.p. at large 1999-2000, v.p. Area IV 2001, 02, 03), Pers. Mgmt. Assn. (co-chmn. coll. rels. 1981), Urban League, NAACP, Links, Inc., ASTD, Alpha Kappa Alpha (chair midwestern regional conf., 1996, Outstanding Grad. Soror). Home: 10216 E 96th St Kansas City MO 64134-2309 Office: Govt Employee Hosp Assn 17306 E US Highway 24 Independence MO 64056-1808

EVANS, MARGARET PATSOS, photographer, photography educator; b. Syracuse, N.Y., June 4, 1947; d. James George and Margaret Eileen (Jones) Patsos; m. Arnold Jay Berman, Aug. 12, 1989. BA, Goddard Coll., 1977; MFA, Rochester (N.Y.) Inst. Tech., 1989. Tchr. Seoul (Republic of Korea) Fgn. Sch., 1974-75; photographer Coop. Ext. Assn., Rochester, 1977-78; freelance photographer Rochester, 1978-84; asst. coord., acad. advisor Coll. Liberal Arts Rochester Inst. Tech., 1984-86, with scheduling & registration office Coll. Arts/Photograhy, 1986-87, coord. acad. advisors Ctr. for Imaging Sci., 1987-90, vis. mem. faculty, 1992-93; mem. faculty Mohawk Valley C.C., Utica, N.Y., 1990-92, Shippensburg (Pa.) U., 1995—. Photographer Metro. Forum, Rochester, 1994; artist residency, Artists' Mus., Lodz, Poland. Exhibited in group shows including Upstairs Room, N.Y.C., 1994, others. Program dir. Returned Peace Corps Vols., Rochester, 1986; artist mem. artist adv. panel Pyramid Arts Ctr., Inc., Rochester, 1980-90; mem. edn. com. S.E. Area Coalition Vision 2000 Project, Rochester, 1994; bd. mem. Shape Gallery, Shippensburg, Pa. Recipient Charles Rand Penny award Meml. Art Gallery, 1986, Best of Exhbn. award Digital Photography '94, Peoria (Ill.) Art Guild, 1994, Ernst Haas award Maine Photographic Workshop, 1995. Mem. Soc. Photographic Educators. Avocations: hiking, gardening. Office: Dept Comm/Journalism Shippensburg U Shippensburg PA 17257 E-mail: mpevan@ship.edu.

EVANS, MARGARET UTZ, secondary school educator; b. Gladwyne, Pa. d. Joseph H. and Marion Irwin (Laughead) Utz; m. James Irvin Evans. BA, King's Coll., Briarcliff Manor, N.Y.; MA, Ea. Bapt. Theol. Sem., Wynneword, Pa. Tchr. Menaul High Sch., Albuquerque, Haverford Sch. Dist., Havertown, Pa., Penn-Delco Sch. Dist., Aston, Pa. Recipient Wilbor T. Elmore prize in history, James A. Barkley award in history. Mem. NEA.

EVANS, MARSHA JOHNSON, former non-profit association administrator, retired military officer; b. Springfield, Ill., Aug. 12, 1947; d. Walter Edward Johnson and Alice Anne Field; m. Gerard Riendeau Evans, June 30, 1979. AB, Occidental Coll., 1968; MA, Fletcher Sch., 1977, MA in Law & Diplomacy, 1977; postgrad., Nat. War Coll., 1988-89. Commd. ensign USN, 1968, advanced through grades to rear admiral, 1993; mideast policy officer Commander-in-Chief, U.S. Naval Forces, Europe, London, 1977-79; spl. asst. to sec. US Dept. Treasury, Washington, 1979-80; staff analyst Office of Chief Naval Ops., Washington, 1980-81; dep. dir. Pres. Commn. on White House Fellowships, Washington, 1981-82; exec. officer Recruit Tng. Command, San Diego, 1982-84; commanding officer Naval Tech. Tng. Ctr., San Francisco, 1984-86; battalion officer, sr. lectr. polit. sci. U.S. Naval Acad., Annapolis, Md., 1986-88; chief of staff San Francisco Naval Base, 1989-91, U.S. Naval Acad., Annapolis, Md., 1991-92; exec. dir. of the standing com. on mil. and civilian women Dept. Navy, 1992-93; comdr. Navy Recruiting Command, Washington, 1993-95; supt. Naval Postgrad. Sch., Monterey, Calif., 1995-97; CEO, nat. exec. dir. Girl Scouts U.S.A., NYC, 1998—2002; pres. ARC, Washington, 2002—05. Presidential appointee bd. visitors, U.S. Military Academy at West Point; interim dir. George C. Marshall European Ctr. Security Studies, Garmisch Partenkirchen, Germany, 1996-97; bd. dirs. Lehman Brothers Holdings, Inc., May Dept. Stores Co., AutoZone, Inc., Weight Watchers Internat., Inc., Huntsman Corp., Office Depot, 2006-Advisory bd. Pew Partnership for Civic Change Pew Charitable Trusts; dir. Naval Academy Found. White House fellow, 1979; Chief Naval Ops. scholar, 1976. Mem. Mortar Bd., Phi Beta Kappa.

EVANS, MARY See EVANS, CLAIRE

EVANS, MARY MAGEE, secondary school educator, language educator; b. Humboldt, Tenn., Dec. 31, 1949; d. Robert C. and Julia B. Magee; m. Robert F. Evans, Jr., Aug. 30, 1969; children: Adam, Eric, Jane. BA, Tenn. Tech. U., 1971; MS, No. Ariz. U., 2005. Tchr. Smith County Schs., Carthage, Tenn., 1972—73, Clarksville (Tenn.)-Montgomery County Schs., 1973—77, Lydia Patterson Inst., El Paso, Tex., 1977—79; tchr., instnl. specialist Mesa (Ariz.) Pub. Schs., 1993—. Named Tchr. of Yr., Stapley Jr. H.S., 1998, Master Tchr., Mesa Pub. Schs., 2002. Avocations: reading, travel. Home: 2946 E Menlo St Mesa AZ 85213 Office: Stapley Jr HS 3250 E Hermosa Vista Mesa AZ 85213

EVANS, MARY MELINDA, special education educator; b. Phillipsburg, NJ, Mar. 7, 1957; d. Peter H. DeBoer and Flora L. Gargiulo; m. Richard W. Evans, Feb. 19, 1983; children: William R., Thomas J., Lauren F., Ainslie S. BA in Psychology, Arcadia U., Glenside, Pa.; EdM, Harvard U., Cambridge, Mass.; Cert. of Completion, U. Copenhagen, 1980. Tchr. NY, 1988, cert. therapeutic crisis intervention trainer Cornell U., 2002. Asst. dir. learning ctr. SUNY, Farmingdale, 1982—84; adj. faculty Finger Lakes CC, Canandaigua, NY, 1984—85; spl. edn. instr. Wayne-Finger Lakes Bd. Coop. Ednl. Svcs., Newark, NY, 1988—, therapeutic crisis intervention trainer, 2003—. Bd. edn. Marcus Whitman Ctrl. Schs., Rushville, NY, 2001. Home: 3839 Kearney Rd Stanley NY 14561 Office: Wayne Finger Lakes Board Cooperative Educational Services 4120 Baldwin Rd Rushville NY 14544 Personal E-mail: mevans@wflboces.org.

EVANS, MERYL K., writer; b. Fort Worth, Tex., Jan. 20, 1970; d. Alvin D. and Karen Kaplan; m. Paul A Evans; 3 children. BA, Am. U., Washington, 1992. Cert. Internet Tech. NYU, 2000. Program analyst FAA, Washington, 1992—95; IT cons. CIBER, Inc., Dallas, 1995—97; bus. analyst GTE, Irving, Tex., 1997—98; process analyst, tech. writer SBC Svcs., Inc., Richardson, Tex., 1998—2005; writer, editor, rschr. meryl.net, Plano, Tex., 2000—. E-mail: merylk@gmail.com.

EVANS, MICHELLE T., county official; b. Elizabeth City, N.C., June 4, 1959; d. Kirby Lee and Carrol (Owens) Tillett; m. George Hunter Evans, June 19, 1977; 1 child, Stella Asia. Grad., Manteo (N.C.) H.S., 1977. Gift buyer Fearings Inc., Manteo, 1977-79; dental asst. Randal Latta, DDS, Manteo, 1979-80; with Dare County, Manteo, 1984—, tax collector, 1993—. Bd. dirs. Munis Computer Group, Raleigh, N.C., 1999—. Vol., Dept. Social Svcs., Manteo. Mem. N.C. County and Mcpl. Tax Collectors (dir. Dist. I, 1999—). Democrat. Avocations: running, biking, swimming. Office: Dare County Tax Dept 211 Budleigh St Manteo NC 27954

EVANS, NANCY PELTIER, behavioral specialist, educator; d. Frenchy M. and Barbara Anne (Williams) Peltier; m. Geoffrey David Evans, Aug. 14, 1983; children: Keith Donald, Laura Anne. BA in Tchg., Sam Houston State U., Huntsville, Tex., 1974. Cert. tchr. Tex., 1974. Tchr., coach Coldspring Ind. Sch. Dist., Tex., 1975—81, Waller Ind. Sch. Dist., Tex., 1981—85, behavioral specialist, 1995—. Named Favorite Tchr. of Yr., Waller Jr. High, 1985. Mem.: Assn. Tex. Profl. Educators (life), Waller Women's Club (social dir. 2002—06). Independent. Roman Catholic. Avocation: travel. Home: 31814 Cypress Cir Waller TX 77484 Office: Waller Ind Sch Dist 2202 Waller Waller TX 77484 Office Phone: 936-372-4112. Personal E-mail: nevans46@yahoo.com. Business E-Mail: nevans@waller.isd.esc4.net.

EVANS, ORINDA D., federal judge; b. Savannah, Ga., Apr. 23, 1943; d. Thomas and Virginia Elizabeth (Grieco) E.; m. Roberts O. Bennett, Apr. 12, 1975; children: Wells Cooper, Elizabeth Thomas. BA, Duke U., 1965; JD with distinction, Emory U., 1968. Bar: Ga. 1968. Assoc. Fisher & Phillips, Altanta, 1968-69, Alston, Miller & Gaines, Atlanta, 1969-74, ptnr., 1974-79; judge US Dist Ct. (No. Dist.) Ga., Atlanta, 1979—, chief judge. Adj. prof. Emory U. Law Sch., 1974-77; counsel Atlanta Crime Commn., 1970-71 Recipient Disting. award BBB, 1972. Mem. Atlanta Bar Assn. (dir. 1979) Democrat. Episcopalian. Office: US Dist Courthouse 1988 US Courthouse 75 Spring St SW Atlanta GA 30303-3309

EVANS, PAMELA H., secondary school educator; b. Youngstown, Ohio, Dec. 15, 1959; d. William Edward and Lois Eileen Godward; m. John I. Evans, June 21, 2003. B of Secondary Edn., Ariz. State U., Tempe, 1982. Tchr. Scottsdale Unified Sch. Dist., Ariz., 1985—; coach, choreographer Ariz. Sunrays, Phoenix, 1997—. Cons. Ariz. Dept. Edn., Phoenix, 2001—; gymnastics judging officer Nat. Assn. Women Judges, 1984—. Dist. liaison Scottsdale Unified Schs., 1997—. Named Adapted Phys. Edn. Tchr. of Yr., Southwest Region, 2005, Choeographer of Yr., Ariz., 2003, 2004, Mid. Sch. Tchr. of Yr., Mayor of Scottsdale, Ariz, 2004. Mem.: Ariz. Assn. Health, Phys. Edn. and Recreation, Nat. Assn. Gymnastics Judges, US Assn. Gymnastics. Avocations: running, weightlifting, dance, hiking. Home: 8030 E Avalon Dr Scottsdale AZ 85251 Office: Scottsdale Unified Sch Dist 3811 N 44th St Phoenix AZ 85018 Office Phone: 480-484-3600 5107. E-mail: pevans@susd.org.

EVANS, PAT, mayor; b. Abilene, Tex., Feb. 12, 1943; m. Chuck Evans, 1964; 3 children. BA, U. Tex., Austin, 1964; JD, So. Meth. U., 1991. Atty. Gay & McCall, Inc., 1991—95; family law instr. Southeastern Paralegal Inst., 1996—97; atty., 1991—; dep. mayor pro-tem Plano, Tex., 2000; mayor, 2002—. Tchr. Richardson Ind. Sch. Dist., 1964—70; owner landscape design co. Exec. bd. North Tex. Coun. Govts.; exec. com. Dallas REgional Mobility Coun.; mem. Plano Econ. Devel. Exec. Bd.; past. pres. Jr. League, Plano; mem. Metroplex Mayor's Coun., Collin County Mayor's Coun. Office: City of Plano 1520 Avenue K Plano TX 75074

EVANS, PATRICIA MARIE, sales executive; d. Frank and Evelyn Francis Logandice; m. Larry Earl Evans, Feb. 19, 1971; children: Dana Lynn, Kim Marie Evans-Meyer. Student, Riverside CC, Calif., 1993. Cert. new home sales Profl. Bldg. Industry Assn., 1996. Loan officer RP Fin. Svcs., Riverside, 1993—94; hostess Pacific Greystone Homes, Corona, Calif., 1994—95; jr. sales asst., sr. sales agt. Lewis Homes Mgmt. Corp., Upland, Calif., 1995—99; sr. sales agt. Lennar Homes/U.S. Home, Anaheim, Calif., 1999—2002, Citation Homes, Irvine, Calif., 2002—03, Centex Homes, Corona, 2003—. Mem. adv. com. Lennar Homes, Anaheim, 2002. Recipient three Outstanding Sales Achievement plaques, Nat. Assn. Homebuilders, 1997. Mem.: Sales and Mktg. Coun. Orange County, Inland Empire. Republican. Avocations: gardening, cooking, wine tasting, travel, reading.

EVANS, PATTI RENEE, art director; b. Clarksville, Tenn., Oct. 26, 1964; d. Milton David Evans and Lula Alberta evans. BSc, Austin Peay State U., Clarksville, 1987, Mid. Tenn. State U., Murfreesboro, Tenn., 2003—. Graphic designer CPS Corp., Franklin, Tenn., 1988—97; sr. graphic designer C.R. Gibson, Nashville, 1997—2000; sr. art dir. Thomas Nelson, Inc., Nashville, 2001—. Vol. Samoritans Purse, Nashville, 2003—05, Red Cross, Nashville, 2005. Petty officer 2nd class USNR, 2000—. Decorated Navy and Marine achievement medal Navy Reserve. Avocations: flying, motorcycling, running. Office: Thomas Nelson 501 Nelson Pl Nashville TN 37214

EVANS, PAULA LEMMERMANN, educational association administrator; b. Springfield, Ill. d. Merle Edward and Betty Louise Evans. BS, Univ. Mo., Rolla, Mo., 1982; MA, Univ. Mo., Kans. City, Mo., 1990; MAT, Univ. Fla., Gainsville, Fla., 1992. Chair, math, computer sci., econ. Harvard Westlake Sch., N. Hollywood, Calif. Office: Harvard Westlake Sch 3700 Coldwater Cayon North Hollywood CA 91604 Office Phone: 818-487-6544.

EVANS, R. MARLENE, county agency administrator; b. Riverside, Calif., Apr. 15, 1950; d. Donald R. Evans and Minnie L. Taylor; m. David Franklin Eldridge, Jr., June 23, 1987 (div. June 1992); children: Kymberlie Renee Neal, Kahshanna Almani Evans. BA in Sociology, Calif. State U., San Bernardino, 1987, MSW, 1996; PhD, LaSalle U., Mandeville, La., 1999. Eligibility worker San Bernardino County Transitional Assistance Dept., Redlands, Calif., 1986-88; assessment and referral counselor United Way, Inc., Ontario, Calif., 1988-90; intake assessment and referral counselor Charter Hosp., Redlands, 1990-91; eligibility worker DPSS, Redlands, 1991—96; social svc. practitioner San Bernardino County CPS, San Bernardino, 1996-97, San Bernardino County Adoptions, San Bernardino, 1997-99, supervising social svc. practitioner, 1999—. Kaiser Found. grantee, 1995. Mem.: NASW, AAUW (Career Devel. grantee 1993), North Rubidoux Women's Club (sec., v.p., pres.). Democrat. Roman Catholic. Avocations: sewing, contemporary jazz, reading, mentoring. Home: PO Box 6941 San Bernardino CA 92412-6941 Office: San Bernardino County Dept Children's Svcs San Bernardino CA 92415-913

EVANS, ROBYN V., science educator; b. Mobile, Ala., Nov. 25, 1979; d. Robert L. Simpson and Edith M. Evans-Simpson. BS in Biology, Fla. A&M U., Tallahassee, 2002; MS in Biology, Ga. State U., Atlanta, 2004. Asst. to tchr. anatomy and physiolgy Ga. State U., Atlanta, 2002—04; instr. human anatomy and physiology Ga. Perimeter Coll., Clarkston, 2005—. Recipient Disting. Scholars award, Flordia A&M U., 1998. Mem.: The Order of Ea. Star, Alpha Epsilon Delta. Personal E-mail: robynvevans@hotmail.com.

EVANS, ROSEMARY HALL, civic worker; b. Lenox, Mass., Mar. 25, 1925; d. Alfred A. and Rosamond (Morse) Hall; m. Richard Morse Colgate, Jan. 1, 1949; children: Jessie Morse, Margaret Auchincloss, Pamela Morse; m. James H. Evans, July 1, 1972 (div. 1984). Trustee Menninger Found., Topeka, Princeton (N.J.) Theol. Sem.; founding mem., life trustee Nat. Recreation and Park Assn., Washington; past dir. Nat. Audubon Soc., N.Y.C.; former collaborator Nat. Park Svc. Mem.: Colony Club (N.Y.C.), Lenox (Mass.) Club, Profile Club (Sugar Hill, N.H.). Avocations: walking, gardening, reading, farming, bird watching. E-mail: rhe@ncia.net.

EVANS, SARA, country singer, songwriter; b. Mo., Feb. 5, 1971; m. Craig Schelske; children: Avery, Olivia, Audrey. Signed contract with RCA, Nashville, 1996; performer with group Sara Evans & North Santiam. Singer: (albums) Three Clouds and the Truth, 1997, No Place That Far, 1998, Girls' Night Out, 1999, Born to Fly, 2000, Restless, 2003, Real Fine Place, 2005, (singles) True Lies, 1997, Three Clouds and the Truth, 1997, Shame About That, 1997, Cryin' Game, 1998, No Place That Far, 1998, Born to Fly, 2000 (Video Yr., Country Music Assn., 2001); background singer: songs "I Never Really Knew You", Key, 1994; singer "Almost New", Clay Pigeon (Original Soundtrack), 1998, "That's the Beat of a Heart", Where the Heart Is (Original Soundtrack), 2000, "Mary of the Wild Moor", Songcatcher (Original Soundtrack), 2001. Office: RCA Record Group 1400 18th Ave S Nashville TN 37212 Office Phone: 615-301-4300.*

EVANS, SHEILA S., secondary school educator; b. Newport, Tenn., July 31, 1955; d. Austin and Doris Caldwell Metcalf; m. Allen Evans, Sept. 10, 1983; 1 child from previous marriage, Anthony Jacob Stokely. MS Curriculum and Instrn, U. Tenn., Knoxville, 1985. Tchr. Jefferson County Sch. Sys., Dandridge, Tenn., 1985—. Cons. dance coach U. Tenn., Knoxville. Mem. ednl. bd. Discover Life in Am.; vol. The Great Smoky Mt. Nat. Park. Named Wal-Mart Tchr. of Ur., 2006; recipient Disney Tchr. award, 2006. Mem.: Tenn. Assn. Dance, West Point Parents Club East Tenn., Nat. Trust Hist. Preservation, Assn. Preservation Tenn. Antiquities, Gt. Smoky Mountains Assn., Nat. Pks. Conservation Assn. Avocation: antiques. Home: 869 Lakewood Dr Jefferson City TN 37760 Office: Jefferson County HS 115 W Dumplin Valley Rd Dandridge TN 37725

EVANS, SHERRIE LEA, secondary school educator; b. Stephenville, Tex., Jan. 15, 1958; d. James Dalton and Mildred Pauline Cleghorn; m. J. Scott Evans, Dec. 28, 1980; children: James Van, Jay Dalton. MEd, Tarleton State U., Stephenville, 1976. Dance tchr. Stephenville Ind. Sch. Dist., 1982—. Office Phone: 254-968-4141.

EVANS, STEPHANIE E., theater producer; b. Lowell, Mass., Aug. 5, 1977; d. Steven Higgins and Higgins M. Martha; m. Daniel A. Higgins, Oct. 29, 2005. MPA, Seton Hall U., South Orange, N.J., 2006. House mgr. Shakespeare Theatre of N.J., Madison, 2002—04; office mgr. N.J. Theatre Alliance, Morristown, 2005—. Scholar, Non-Profit Endowment Fund, 2004—06. Mem.: Pi Alpha Alpha. Office Phone: 973-540-0515 11. Personal E-mail: stephigg@yahoo.com. E-mail: sevans@njtheatrealliance.org.

EVANS, SUSAN A., chemist; Postdoctoral and rsch. fellow Edsel B. Ford Inst. for Med. Rsch. and dept. pathology Henry Ford Hosp., Detroit; v.p. rsch., devel. and engring. LifeScane, Inc., a Johnson and Johnson Co., Milpitas, Calif. Fellow: Nat. Acad. Clin. Biochemistry; mem.: NCCLS (fin. com., nominating com., strategic planning com., area com. on clin. chemistry and toxicology), Internat. Fedn. Clin. Chemistry (sec. and corp. rep. edn. and mgmt. divsn.), Am. Assn. Clin. Chemistry (sec. 2002—, exec. com. bd. dirs., fin. com., ex-officio mem. ho. of dels. steering com., chair program coord. commn., sec., chair, councilor Fla. sect., vice chair San Diego sect. 1993, recording sec. Chgo. sect. 1997, founding mem., treas. industry divsn., mem. long range planning com. 1985—89, mem. coun. steering com. 1987—88, co-chair ann. meeting 1988). Achievements include research in has focused on immunodiagnostic methods.

EVANS, THELMA JEAN MATHIS, internist; b. East St. Louis, Ill., Jan. 29, 1944; d. Clemmie and Catherine (Rose) Mathis; m. Timothy Charles Evans, June 29, 1968; children: Cynthia Marie, Catherine Elizabeth (twins). BS in Zoology with honors, U. Ill., 1967; MD, U. Ill., Chgo., 1969. Intern, then resident U. Ill. Hosp., Chgo., 1969-71, fellow in pulmonary medicine, 1971-73; med. dir., acute care unit Presbyn.-St. Luke's Hosp., Chgo., 1973-75, asst. to dir. emergency svcs., 1975-77; staff physician Health Specialists, S.C., Chgo., 1977-80, AT&T (Western Electric), Cicero, Ill., 1980-85, Health First, Inc., Chgo., 1985-89, Michael Reese Health Plan, Chgo., 1989-98; mem. adv. bd. Advocate Profl. Group, Chgo., 1998—; bd. dirs. Advocate Health Care Network, Chgo., 2000—. Instr., Rush Med. Coll., Chgo., 1973-84; tuberculosis control officer, infectious disease sect. Chgo. Dept. Health, 1976-77. V.p., Com. to Elect Timothy C. Evans, Chgo., 1989. Grantee, Chgo. Lung Assn., 1972-73. Fellow: ACP; mem.: AMA, AMWA, NAACP. Democrat. African Methodist Episcopal. Avocations: photography, gardening, collecting thimbles, bells and music boxes. Office: Advocate Health Ctrs 9831 S Western Ave Chicago IL 60643-1791 Office Phone: 777-445-3500. Office Fax: 773-445-3500.

EVANS, TRESE, psychometrist, psychotherapist; b. Greenwood, Miss., Aug. 5, 1956; d. Edgar and Ruby Evans. BA, U. Miss., University, 1978, MA, 1984. Psychotherapist, psychometrist Region VI Mental Health Ctr., Greenwood, Miss., 1984-86; psychometrist State Dept. Edn., Cleveland, Miss., 1986-88, Jackson, Miss., 1988-92; psychometrist, case mgr. Rankin County Sch. Dist., Brandon, Miss., 1992—97; dir., psychometrist, psychotherapist Miss. Dept. Edn. Spl. Edn. Office, 1997—. Mem. Am. Psychol. Assn. (assoc.), Alpha Kappa Alpha. Mem. Ch. of Christ. Avocations: walking, piano, singing, reading. Home: 5390 Cedar Park Dr Jackson MS 39206-4122 Office: Rankin County Sch Dist 1220 Apple Park Pl Brandon MS 39042-4498 Office Phone: 601-359-3498.

EVANS, ZOE O'QUINN, elementary school educator; d. James A. and Ann Lane O'Quinn; m. Christopher Lee Evans, Mar. 20, 1993; children: Quinn Elise, Kenneth James. BS, West Ga. Coll., Carrollton, GA; M, U. West Ga., Carrollton, GA; EdS, U. West Ga. National Board Certified Teacher (Science/Early Adolescence) Nat. Bd. for Profl. Tchg. Stds., 2004. 8th grade sci. tchr. Madras Mid. Sch., Newnan, Ga., 1997—2001; 7th grade sci. tchr. Ctrl. Mid. Sch., Carrollton, Ga., 2001—. Various children's ministries Tabernacle Bapt. Ch., Carrollton, Ga. Recipient Tchr. of Yr., Ctrl. Mid. Sch., 2006, Madras Mid. Sch. Tchr. of Yr., Madras Mid. Sch., Finalist Presidental Award of Excellence in Math. and Sci. Tchg., NSF, 2005. Mem.: PA of Ga. Educators, NSTA, Ga. Sci. Teachers Assn., Chi Omega. Office Phone: 770-832-8114.

EVANSON, BARBARA JEAN, middle school education educator; b. Grand Forks, N.D., Aug. 15, 1944; d. Robert John and Jean Elizabeth (Lommen) Gibbons; m. Bruce Carlyle Evanson, Dec. 27, 1965; children: Tracey, John, Kelly. AA, Bismarck State Coll., 1964; BS in Spl. and Elem. Edn., U. N.D., 1966. Tchr. spl. edn. Winship Sch., Grand Forks, 1966-67, Simle Jr. High, Bismarck, 1967-70; tchr. Northridge Elem. Sch., Bismarck, 1980-86, Wachter Middle Sch., Bismarck, 1986—. Cons. Dept. Pub. Instrn., Bismarck, 1988—, Chpt. I, Bismarck, 1989—, McRel for Drug Free Schs., Denver, 1990-95. Co-founder The Big People, Bismarck, 1978-95; mem. task force Children's Trust Fund, N.D., 1984; senator N.D. Legislature, Bismarck, 1989-94; mem. N.D. Bridges Adv. Bd., 1991-97, DPI English Adv. Com., 1993—; co-facilitator Lead Mid. Sch. for Carnegie, 1994-97, N.D. Health Adv. Coun., 1993-94, N.D. Tchr.'s Fund for Retirement, State Investment Bd. 1996—; co-founder, bd. dirs. Neighbors Network, 1983—. Recipient Gold Award Bismark Norwest Bank, 1985; named Tchr. of Yr., N.D. Dept. Pub. Instrn., 1989, Legislator of Yr., Children's Caucus, 1991, Outstanding Alumnae,

Bismarck State Coll., 1991, Milken Nat. Tchr. of Yr., 1995-96, KX Golden Apple award, 1999. Mem. N.D. Reading Assn., N.D. Coun. of Tchrs. of English., NEA, N.D. Edn. Assn., Bismarck Edn. Assn. Avocations: walking, reading, travel, remodeling. Office: Wachter Middle Sch 1107 S 7th St Bismarck ND 58504-6533

EVANS SNOWDEN, AUDRA LYNN, counselor; b. Flint, Mich., July 16, 1976; d. Frances Anne Howard and William Edward Evans; m. Eugene Russell Snowden, Jr., July 21, 2001. BA Comm., Mich. State U., 1997; MEd in Ednl. Leadership, Saginaw Valley State U., 2002; MA in counseling, Oakland U., 2003—05. Nat. bd. cert. counselor, tchr. Mich. 7th grade sci. tchr. Sherman Mid. Sch., Holly, Mich., 2000—04; sch. counselor Richter Intermediate Sch., Holly, Mich., 2004—. Mem. exec. bd. Holly Area Youth Coalition, Mich., 2001—. Named Asset Builder, Holly Area Youth Coalition, 2001; Alpha Gamma Delta scholar, 1997. Mem.: Genessee Area Counseling Assn. (assoc.), Assn. Mich. Sch. Counselors (assoc.), Mich. Counseling Assn. (assoc.), Mich. Sch. Counselor Assn. (assoc.), Phi Beta Delta (assoc.), Golden Key (assoc.), Kappa Delta Pi (assoc.), Chi Sigma Iota (assoc.), Alpha Gamma Delta (life; scholarship chair 1995—96, Scholarship Key 1997). Avocations: scrapbooks, rubber stamping, reading, exercise, travel. Office: Richter Intermediate Sch 920 East Baird St Holly MI 48442 Office Phone: 248-328-3037. Office Fax: 248-328-3034. E-mail: audra.snowden@holly.k12.mi.us.

EVANS-TRANUMN, SHELIA, commissioner, former literature and language educator; b. Durham, NC, Aug. 19, 1951; Grad., NC Central U.; MA, Long Island U. Former English teacher, NYC; dir. auxiliary svcs. for high schools NY Ed. Dept., 1989—93, with, 1993—, assoc. commissioner of ed. Host Ed. Dialogue, WNYE TV25. Trustee Casey Family Programs, 2003—; bd. mem. New Visions, Middle Schools Initiative. Recipient Disting. Svc. award, NY Urban League. Office: NY Ed Dept 55 Hanson Pl Brooklyn NY 11217*

EVARTS, MARY H., mathematics educator; d. Harry J. and Mary V. Brown; children: John C., Suzanne M., Brian M., James B. BA, Immaculata Coll., Pa., 1967; Masters Equivelants Edn., Cabrini Coll., Radnor, Pa., 1988. Cert. secondary sch. tchr. Pa., 1967. Sci. computer programmer GE Missile and Space Vehicle Dept, Valley Forge, Pa., 1967—69; substitute tchr. Haverford Twp. Sch. Dist., Havertown, Pa., 1969—75, tchr. math., 1984—; tchr. St. Norbert Sch., Paoli, Pa., 1981—84. Scheduler Haverford Mid. Sch., 1986—. Mem.: NEA, Haverford Twp. Edn. Assn., Pa. State Edn. Assn. Office: Haverford Twp Sch District 1701 Darby Rd Havertown PA 19083

EVDOKIMOVA, EVA, prima ballerina assoluta, director, producer, consultant, actress; b. Geneva, Dec. 1, 1948; parents Am. citizens; m. Michael Gregori, 1982. Student, Munich State Opera Ballet Sch., Royal Ballet Sch., London; studied privately with Maria Fay (London), Vera Volkova (Copenhagen), Natalia Dudinskaya (Leningrad), 1964-66; student in Music Studies, Guild Hall Sch. Music, London, 1964—66; student in Drama Studies, H.B. Studio, N.Y.C., 1997—2000. Pres. of jury Rudolf Nureyev Internat. Ballet Competition, Budapest, 1994, 96, 98; chm. Jury Varna Internat. Ballet Competition, Bulgaria, 1996; ballet mistress Boston Ballet, 2002-03; ballet coach; drama performances 5 off offBroadway drama prodns., 1997-2002; contemporary dance performances created for her by Igal Perry, Henning Rübsam, Angela Jones; simultaneous translation and interpretation between English, French, German, Russian, Italian, Danish. Latin Studies. Debut Royal Danish Ballet, Copenhagen, 1966; Prima Ballerina Assoluta, Deutsche Oper Berlin, 1969-90; frequent guest artist with numerous major ballet cos. worldwide including London Festival Ballet, English Nat. Ballet, Am. Ballet Theatre, Paris Opera Ballet, La Scala, Kirov Ballet, Tokyo Ballet, Teatro Colon, Nat. Ballet of Can., Stuttgart Ballet, Royal Danish Ballet, and all other major nat. ballet cos.; premiered roles in Rudolf Nureyev's classical ballet prodns., ptnr., 1971-86; appeared in over 16 classical and modern ballets with Rudolf Nureyev across the world; repertoire of more than 130 roles includes Swan Lake, Giselle, La Sylphide, Sleeping Beauty, Romeo and Juliet, Don Quixote, La Bayadere, Onegin, Raymonda; created roles in many contemporary ballets for stage, film and TV; film appearances include The Nutcracker, La Sylphide, Cinderella, A Family Portrait, The Romantic Era, Invitation to the Dance, Portrait of Eva Evdokimova, and others. Recipient Diploma, Internat. Ballet Competition, Moscow, 1969; winner Gold medal Varna Internat. Ballet competition, 1970; awarded title Prima Ballerina Assoluta, Berlin Senate, 1973, Berlin Critic's Prize, 1974; first fgn. mem. Royal Danish Ballet, first Am. and Westerner to win any internat. ballet competition, first Am. to perform with Kirov Ballet, 1976, first Am. to perform in Peking after the Cultural Revolution, 1978, first and only Am. dancer with portrait in permanent collection, Mus. Drama and Dance, Leningrad, St. Petersburg, Russia, only Am. performer ever to be honored in a German opera house, Grand Défilé ceremony, 1990 Deutsche Oper Berlin; recipient letter for meritorious svc. from Pres. Bush, 1990, numerous other awards; holder world record for 67 curtain calls with 40 minute standing ovation, Berlin, 1990. Achievements include world record performing in two different Giselles, two full length Prokofiev Ballets and eight other works with three companies; at Lincoln Center, New York, in three debuts with three different companies within a three month period.

EVE, (EVE JIHAN JEFFERS), rap artist, actress; b. Phila., Nov. 10, 1978; Formed female rap duo EDGP; former mem. DMX's Ruff Ryders posse; signed one-yr. deal with DMX's new label Aftermath. Performer: (albums) Let There Be Eve.Ruff Rider's First Lady, 1999, Scorpion, 2001, Eve-Olution, 2002; musician: (songs) "Eve of Destruction", 1998; musician: (with Gwen Stefani) "Let Me Blow Ya Mind", 2001 (Grammy award best rap/sung collaboration, 2001); musician: (with The Roots) "You Got Me"; musician: (with Blackstreet & Janet Jackson) "Girlfriend/Boyfriend"; musician: (with Missy Elliott) "Hot Boyz"; actor: (films) XXX, 2002, Barbershop, 2002, The Woodsman, 2003, Barbershop 2: Back in Business, 2004; (TV series) Eve, 2003; co-exec. prodr. (TV series) Eve, 2003, actor guest appearances Third Watch, 2003, One on One, 2004, actor, voice over (video game) XIII, 2003. Office: Interscope Records 2220 Colorado Ave Santa Monica CA 90404

EVELETH, JANET STIDMAN, law association administrator; b. Balt., Sept. 6, 1950; d. John Charles and Edith Janet (Scales) Stidman; m. Donald P. Eveleth, May 11, 1974. BA, Washington Coll., 1972; MS, Johns Hopkins U., 1973. Counselor Office of Mayor, Balt., 1973-75; asst. dir. Gov. Commn. on Children, Balt., 1975-78; lobbyist Balt., 1978-80; comm. specialist Med. Soc., Balt., 1980-81; dir. pub. affairs Mid-Atlantic Food Dealers, Balt., 1981-84; dir. comm. Home Builders Assn., Balt., 1984-87, Md. Bar Assn., Balt., 1987—. Contbr. articles to profl. jours. Recipient Gov. citation State of Md., 1993, Citizen citation City of Balt., 1993. Mem.: NAFE, Nat. Assn. Bar Execs. (chmn. pub. rels. sect. 1994—95, Achievement award 1995, E.A. Wally Richter award 1997, Luminary award 1999, 2001, 2003), Md. Soc. Assn. Execs. (pres. 1992—93), Am. Soc. Profl. Women, Pi Lambda Theta, Alpha Chi Omega. Office: Md Bar Assn 520 W Fayette St Baltimore MD 21201-1781 Office Phone: 410-685-7878 ext. 3025. E-mail: jeveleth@msba.org.

EVELYN, BALL LOVE, mathematics educator, department chairman; b. York, S.C., July 9, 1963; d. Hugh M. and Catherine G. Love; m. Jonathon H. Ball. BA, Clemson U., S.C., 1985. Cert. tchr., secondary math. S.C. Dept. Edn. Tchr. Greenwood HS, SC, 1985—86, York Comprehensive HS, 1986—87, W. Henderson HS, Hendersonville, NC, 1987—97; tchr., dept. chair Hunter Huss HS, Gastonia, NC, 1990—. Named to Nat. Honor Roll of Tchrs., 2006; recipient Tchr. of Yr. award, Hunter Huss HS. Office: Hunter Huss HS 1518 Edgefield Ave Gastonia NC 28052

EVELYN, PHYLLIS, minister; d. Aaron K Redcay and Phyllis M Noble, Donald Noble (Stepfather) and Barbara Pfeiffer Redcay (Stepmother); m. Frank C. Templin, Aug. 23, 1963 (div.); children: Charles R Templin, Afton M Templin. BA, Northwestern U., 1960—64; MDiv, Eden Theol. Sem., 1999—2002. Ordained into United Church of Christ Ea. Assn. MO Conf. UCC, 2002. Sales adminstr. for copy products Eastman Kodak Co., Rochester, NY, 1977—84; owner Gulf Island Marine, Cedar Key, Fla., 1984—86; investment exec. Paine Webber, Bakersfield, Calif., 1987—90; fin. advisor Am. Express Fin. Advisors, St. Louis Mo., Mo., 1997—99; settled pastor First Congl. Ch. of Shelburne, UCC, Mass., 2002—. Pres. Bd. of Ministerial Aid, MA-UCC, Framingham, Mass., 2005—; exec. coun. mem. at large Franklin Assn., MA UCC, Greenfield, Mass., 2003—05; ex-officio bd. mem. Hilltown Churches Food Pantry, Ashfield, Mass., 2002—. Publisher (book) American Dream Business Park. Bd. dirs. Pioneer Valley Habitat for Humanity, Florence, Mass., 2003—05, grant writer, liaison to faith cmty. rels. com., 2002—05. Recipient Top Midwest Regional Sales Rep. 7th Period, Eastman Kodak Co., Copy Products Div., 1980, Blinder President's Club Top Sales Position, Blinder Robinson Inc., 1987. Democrat-Npl. United Ch. Of Christ. Achievements include development of copy products to market and opening of a new copy products office for Kodak Company in Anchorage, Alaska, 1984. Avocations: travel, flying, sailing. Home: 22 Common Rd Shelburne Falls MA 01370 Office: First Congregational Ch 22 Common Rd Shelburne Falls MA 01370 Business E-Mail: phylevelyn@comcast.net.

EVENS, LUCIE ANN, music educator; b. Pittsfield, Ill., Sept. 28, 1949; d. Mildred Eloise and Walter Orin Cook; m. Mark Evens, Aug. 18, 1974; children: Sarah Rachel, Emily Caroline Moughan, Joshua Adam. BS in music edn., NYU, 1969—74; MS in edn. environ. sci., CUNY, 1989—92. Permanent Music Teacher, Grades PreK-12 NYC & NY State, 1974, Permanent Teacher of Common Branches NYC & NY State, 1987, Certified Reading Specialist NY State, 1987. Kindergarten tchr. P.S. 164Q, Flushing, NY, 1984—86, 4th grade tchr., 1986—89, P.S. 219Q, 1989—90; music tchr. & choral dir. P.S. 164Q, Flushing, NY, 1990—; founding dir. SUNY Maritime Coll. Chorale, Bronx, 2002—; musical dir. Sullivan County Dramatic Workshop, Hurleyville, 2004—. Mem. United U. Professions, Albany, NY, 2003—. Singer: (TV musical documentary) Illinois Sings; actor: (musical) Annie Get Your Gun; musician (also costume designer): (musical) Pippin; dir.: (environmental program) NYC Sanitation Dept. Team Up To Clean Up. Recipient Choral Performance, Pres. of the USA (Bill Clinton), 1993, Dem. Party (Hillary Rodham Clinton), 1992; Molly Parnis award, Molly Parnis, 1990, Bette Midler's Rose award, NYC Dept. of Sanitation, 2001. Mem.: Am. Choral Directors' Assn., Am. Fedn. of Teachers, United Fedn. of Teachers, Music Educators' Assn. of NYC, United U. Professions, Nat. Choral Directors' Assn., Sigma Alpha Iota, Kappa Delta Pi. Am. Independent. Avocations: gardening, singing, antiques. Home: 147-28 77th Road Flushing NY 11367 Office: PS 164Q Queens Valley School 138-01 77th Avenue Flushing NY 11367 Office Phone: 718-544-0630.

EVENSKI, ANDREA JEAN, orthopedist; d. Linda Jean Kiraly and Robert Edward Evenski. BS, U. Conn., Storrs, 1996; MD, Brody Sch. of Medicine, Greenville, N.C., 2003. Rsch. chemist Nat. Inst. of Environ. Health Scis., Research Triangle Park, NC, 1997—99; resident in orthopaedics Akron Gen. Med. Ctr., Ohio, 2003—. Ho. officer treas. Akron Gen. Med. Ctr., Ohio, 2004—05. Office: Akron Gen Med Ctr 400 Wabash Ave Akron OH 44303 Office Phone: 330-344-6000.

EVERETT, CHERYL ANN, music educator, pianist; b. Crawfordsville, Ind., July 7, 1945; d. Howard Dennis and Thelma Louise (Rutledge) P. Student, DePauw U., 1975. Church organist Christian Sci. Ch., Methodist Ch., Presbyn. Ch., Crawfordsvill, Ind., 1958—; celeste player Indpls. Philharmonic Orch., 1994—; accompanist Wabash Coll. Glee Club, Crawfordsville, 1997—; adj. instr. piano Wabash Coll., 2003—. Chmn. Ind. Jr. Festival Nat. Fedn. Music Clubs, 1984-94, Indpls Jr. Festival Nat. Fedn. Music Clubs, 1984-94, Indpls. West Festival, 2000—; chmn. Indpls. West Festival, 2000—; performed in recitals and master classes of Internat. Workshops in Italy, Eng., France, Can., Switzerland, 1986-89, with Internat. String Orch. in workshops in Eisenstadt, Austria, 1989; adjudicator Tippecanoe Piano Tchrs. Lafayette, Ind, 1993-97, Logansport (Ind.) Piano Tchrs., 1993-97, Stickley Meml. Competition, South Bend, Ind., 1989, Ind. State Fair Young Hoosier Pianists Competition; accompanist U. Indpls., 2006. Founder, dir. Presbyn. Artists Concert Series, Crawfordsville, 1991; founder, organizer Montgomery County Multi-keyboard Extavaganza featuring 170 players, Crawfordsville, 1995-97; hon. life mem. Presbyn. Ch. USA. Chosen 15 times Ideal Lady, Sunshine Soc. Girls, 1977-97. Mem. Indiana Music Tchrs. Assn. (chair monster concert 1998, Tchr. of Yr. 1999), Nat. Music Tchrs., Indpls. Piano Tchrs. (pres. 1986-88), Nat. Guild of Piano Tchrs., Crawfordsville Music Club (pres. 1989), Ind. Fedn. Music Clubs, Nat. Fedn. Music Clubs. Avocations: sewing, needlecrafts, quilting. Home: 207 S Water St Crawfordsville IN 47933-2536 E-mail: ceverett@link2000.net.

EVERETT, CLAUDIA KELLAM, retired special education educator; b. Mobile, Ala., Dec. 28, 1933; d. Claude M. and Minnie L. Kellam; m. Thomas Sherwood Everett Sr., June 18, 1953; children: Thomas Sherwood Jr., Sherilisa Ann. BA magna cum laude, Roberts Wesleyan Coll., 1958; MS summa cum laude, Barry U., 1988. Cert. English, spl. edn. tchr. Fla., N.Y. Tchr. Dade County Pub. Schs., Miami, Fla., 1959-67, Carol City Elem. Sch., Miami, 1967-77; pers. mgr., payroll supr. Harrington Cos., Miami, 1977-81; honors English tchr. Citrus Grove Jr. HS, Miami, 1981-87; spl. edn. tchr. Citrus Grove Mid. Sch., Miami, 1987-90; tchr. severely emotionally disturbed children Hilton (N.Y.) HS, 1990-91; tchr. emotionally disturbed and mentally retarded, learning disabled Hill Elem. Sch., Brockport, NY, 1991-92; tchr. emotionally/learning disabled, mentally retarded Oliver Mid. Sch., Brockport, 1991—2001; ret., 2001. Cons. cmty. benevolent agys., Miami, 1969—83; pvt. tutor, 2001—. Author: numerous poems. Youth dir. Ctrl. Alliance Youth, Miami, 1960—80; cmty. advisor youth affairs Carol City, Miami, 1970—87; founder, pres. Tchr.-Parent Study Group, Miami, 1970—80; 1st v.p., sec., treas. PTA Carol City, 1967—77; pres. Teens to S.Am. Christian Missionary Alliance, Miami, 1978—80, cons. tech. action, 1980—90. Recipient Svc. award, Christian Missionary Alliance Cmty., 1980, Youth in Action award, S.Am. Missions, 1978. Mem.: S.E. Edn. Opportunities Handicapped, Coun. Exceptional Children (mem. divsn. learning disabilities 1989—, mem. divsn. mentally retarded 1989—, mem. divsn. emotionally handicapped 1989—). Republican. Avocations: reading, photography, tutoring, writing for children, visiting elderly in nursing homes. Home: 2355 Westside Dr Rochester NY 14624-1933

EVERETT, DONNA RANEY, finance educator; b. Corpus Christi, Tex., May 30, 1939; d. Donald Wayne and Zora Lee (Wynne) Raney; div.; 1 child, Donna Melinda. BA, Phillips U., Enid, Okla., 1961; MS, U. Houston, 1983, EdD, 1988. Various positions various orgns., Tex., 1965-80; adj. prof. U. Houston, 1983-88; asst. prof. bus. Tex. Tech U., Lubbock, 1988-89, Lamar U., Beaumont, Tex., 1989-90; asst. prof. bus. edn. Tex. Tech U., Lubbock, 1990-93; assoc. prof. bus. and mktg. edn. Ea. N.Mex. U., Portales, 1993-94; asst. prof. bus. edn. U. Mo., Columbia, 1994-96, Morehead State U., Morehead, Ky., 1996—. Sponsor Zeta Kappa chpt. Pi Omega Pi, Phi Beta Lambda; co-sponsor Gamma Chi, Delta Pi Epsilon; undergrad. mentor, 1996. Troop leader Girl Scouts U.S., Ft. Worth and Lake Jackson, Tex., 1964-80, dir. tng. Lake Jackson coun., 1980-82. Recipient curriculum devel. award Tex. Higher Edn. Coordinating Bd., 1987-88, outstanding article award Nat. Assn. Bus. Tchrs. Edn. Rev., 1992, Outstanding Paper award Orgn. Systems Rsch. Assn., 1997, Dean's Excellence in Tchg. award Coll. Bus./Morehead State U., 1999; named Outstanding Faculty Mem., Tex. Tech U., 1991. Mem. Am. Ednl. Rsch. Assn. (bus. edn. and inf. sys. spl. interest group), Internat. Soc. Tech. in Edn., Tex. Bus. Edn. Assn. (editor 1988-93, Collegiate Bus. Tchr. of Yr. dist. 4 1988, dist. 17 1992), Nat. Bus. Edn. Assn. (mem. computer enrichment task force), Tex. Computer Edn. Assn., Ky. Bus. Edn. Assn., S.W. Fedn. Adminstrv. Disciplines (Disting. Paper award 1989, 93, 2000), Am. Vocat. Assn. (com. mem. 1990-95), Delta Pi Epsilon (pres. Alpha Gamma chpt. 1988-89), Phi Delta Kappa (sec. Alpha Mu chpt.). Avocations: travel, reading.

EVERETT, KAREN JOAN, retired librarian, genealogist, educator; b. Cin., Dec. 12, 1926; d. Leonard Kelly and Kletis V. (Wade) Wheatley; m. Wilbur Mason Everett, Sept. 25, 1950; children: Karen, Jan, Jeffrey, Jon, Kathleen, Kerry, Kelly, Shannon. BS in Edn. magna cum laude, U. Cin., 1976, postgrad., 1982-85, Coll. Mt. St. Joseph, 1981-86, Xavier U., Cin., 1985-87, U. Cin., 1982-85, Miami U., 1987. Libr. S.W. Local Schs., Harrison, Ohio, 1967-97, dist. media coord., 1980-97, dist. vol. dir., 1980-97, ret., 1997; instr. genealogy U. Cin., 1998—. Tchr. genealogy U. Cin., 1997—; cons. in field; bd. dirs. U. Cin. ILR; lectr. in field. Contbr. articles to profl. jours. Pres. Citizens Adv. Coun., Harrison, Ohio, 1981-84, 88—, Citizens Adv. Coun., 1989; state chmn. supervisory div. Ohio Ednl. Libr./Media Assn.; mem. Ohio Ambulance Licensing Bd., 1991—. Named Woman of the Yr., Cin. Enquirer, 1978, Xi Eta Iota, 1979; named PTA Educator of the Yr., 1981, others. Mem. NEA, Ohio Ednl. Libr./Media Assn. (chair supervisory div. 1990—, bd. dirs. 1993-94), Ohio Edn. Assn., S.W. Local Classroom Tchrs. Assn., Hamilton County Geneal. Soc. (bd. dirs. 1992—). Avocations: flying, travel, genealogy. Personal E-mail: karywib@aol.com.

EVERETT, KATHERINE MILTON, special education educator; b. McComb, Miss., July 9, 1953; d. Lloyd Elder and Julia Gertrude (Martin) M.; m. James Pittman Everett, Aug. 14, 1976; children: James Pittman Jr., Julia Rea. AA, S.W. Jr. Coll., 1973; BS, Miss. State U., 1975; MEd, U. So. Miss., 1986. Cert. spl. edn. tchr., spl. subjects supr., Miss. Spl. edn. tchr. McComb Sch. Dist., 1975-87, head tchr., 1987-90, curriculum/tech. specialist, 1999, tech. coord., dist. MSIS contact person, 2002; dir. spl. svcs. Stone County Sch. Dist., Wiggins, Miss., 1990—91; tchr. spl. edn. McComb Sch. Dist., 1991—. Mem. com. So. Edn. Consortium, Hattiesburg, Miss., 1990. Mem. coun. McComb PTA, 1989-90; mem. Coun. on Ministries, Meth. Ch., McComb, 1987-93, mem. Childrne's Coun., 1990, mem. adminstrv. coun., 1987-93. Travelers Orgn. scholar, 1987. Mem. Coun. for Exceptional Children, Miss. Orgn. for Spl. Edn. Svcs. Home: 611 Pennsylvania Ave Mccomb MS 39648-4740 Office Phone: 601-684-4661, 601-248-2938. E-mail: everettk@mde.k12.ms.us.

EVERETT-THORP, KATE, digital marketing executive; Grad. in Journalism, San Diego State U., 1991. TV reporter; media planner J. Walter Thompson U.S.A., San Francisco; v.p.-crusader advt. programs CNET, 1993; chmn. media measurement task force Internet Advt. Bur.; pres., CEO Lot21, San Francisco, 1998; chmn. Carat Interactive, 2002. Office: 548 4th St San Francisco CA 94107-1621

EVERHART, ANGIE, model; b. Akron, Ohio, 1969; d. Bobby and Ginnie E. Model Seventeen, 1985—. Appeared in Glamour, Sports Illustrated Swimsuit Edition, (film) The Last Action Hero, 1993, Bordello of Blood, Jade.

EVERHART, GLORIA ELAINE, music educator; d. Thomas and Catherine Rosalie Oland; m. Frederick Everhart, Apr. 13, 1974; 1 child, April. MusB, Peabody Conservatory Music, 1967; postgrad., U. Ill., Towson State U. Tchr. piano, voice, music theory Everhart Piano Studio, Columbia, Md., 1960—; tchr. vocal music Howard County Pub. Schls., 1967—74, tchr. h.s. vocal music, 1984—86; long term substitute music tchr. Glenelg Country Sch., 2002—02. Music dir. The Alleluias, Inc., Columbia, 1987—2004. Dir.: (choral performances) The Alleluias in Concert. Sec., treas. bd. dirs. Everhart Animal Hosp., Inc., 1975—91; music dir. The Alleluias, Inc., Columbia, Md., 1987—2005, Bethany Ln. Bapt. Ch., Ellicott City, Md., 1968—75; min. music and worship Rolling Hills Bapt. ch., Clarksville, 2002—; music min. Bethel Bapt. Ch., Ellicott City, 1997—2002. Mem.: Am. Choral Dirs. Assn. (assoc.). Avocations: reading, internet studies, ethnomusicology, jumble word puzzles, Scrabble.

EVERHART, VELMA VIZEDOM, retired home economics educator, retired real estate agent; b. Hamilton, Ohio, May 26, 1916; d. Jacob Frederick and Edna (Stewart) Vizedom; m. Herbert Marion Everhart, June 1, 1940 (dec.). BSc in Home Econs., Ohio State U., 1938, MSc in Home Econs., 1954. Cert. tchr. Ohio. Tchr. New Madison (Ohio) Village Sch., 1938—41, St. Joseph's Acad., Columbus, Ohio, 1941—43, Columbus City Schs., 1954—56; cafeteria supr. Mt. Carmel Hosp., Columbus, 1943—44; rsch. asst. home econs. Ohio State U., Columbus, 1945—54, assoc. prof. home econs., 1956—78; sales assoc. Heiskell Realtors, Circleville, Ohio, 1979—89. Bd. dirs. Ohio Presbyn. Retirement Ctr., Columbus, 1998—2001, 2005—; pres.-elect. Forum - Thurber Towers, Columbus, 1997—99, bd. dirs., 1999—; mem. Presbyn. life com. Scioto Valley Presbytery, Columbus, 1998—2004; advisor steering com. scholarships Ohio State U., Columbus, 1969—75; mem. Nat. and Ohio Rep. Party; elder, clk. of session Presbyn. Ch., Circleville, 1984—90, trustee, 1993—95. Recipient Alfred J. Wright svc. to students award, Ohio State U., 1964, Student Appreciation award, 1974, Meritorious Svc. award, 2005. Mem.: Coll. Human Ecology Alumni Soc. (sec. 1998—2004), Ohio State U. Alumni Soc., Phi Upsilon Omicron (local chmn. 1964, nat. pres-elect 1972—74, nat. pres. 1974—76, chmn. bd. dirs. ednl. found. 1976—84). Achievements include research in work counter surface finishes. Avocations: golf, football, quilting. Home: 645 Neil Ave # 208 Columbus OH 43215

EVERITT, ALICE LUBIN, labor arbitrator; b. Dec. 13, 1936; d. Isador and Alice (Berliner) Lubin. BA, Columbia U., 1968, JD, 1971. Assoc. Amen, Weisman & Butler, N.Y.C., 1971-78; spl. asst. to dir. Fed. Mediation and Conciliation Svc., Washington, 1978-81; pvt. practice labor arbitration Washington, N.Y.C., 1981-87, Petersburg, Va., 1987—. Mem. various nat. mediation and arbitration panels including Fed. Mediation and Conciliation Svc., U.S. Steel and United Steelworkers, Am. Arbitration Assn. Editor: Dept. Labor publ., 1979. Treas., bd. mem. Petersburg Libr. Found., Inc.; mem. planning commn. City Petersburg. Mem. Am. Arbitration Assn., Soc. Profls. Dispute Resolution, Indsl. Rels. Rsch. Assn., Civil War Roundtable of Richmond Office: 541 High St Petersburg VA 23803-3859

EVERSOLE, BARBARA LOUISE, administrative assistant; b. Ukiah, Calif., Dec. 25, 1926; d. Clarence and Alta Anita (Eldred) Ballou; m. Walter Robert Eversole, Dec. 16, 1945; children: Ronald Edward, Richard Walter. AA, Armstrong Coll., Berkeley, Calif., 1945. Pvt. sec. Mendocino County Farm Adminstrn., Ukiah, 1945—46, U.S. VA, Ukiah, 1946—48; sec. Eversole Mortuary, Ukiah, 1955—75. Designer, supr. constrn. Hudson-Carpenter Park, Ukiah. Vol. fundraiser, worker Beautification of McGarvey Park, Ukiah; mem. revitalization of downtown com. C. of C., Ukiah; chmn. Cultural Arts Commn., Ukiah; sec. Mendocino County Grand Jury; chmn. bd. trustees Sun House Guild, pres., grant writer. Named Woman of Achievement, Soroptimist Internat., 1981, Outstanding Citizen of Yr., Ukiah C. of C., 1984; recipient award for beautification of McGarvey Park, City of Ukiah, Calif. Parks and Recreation award, 1978, recognition for outstanding hist. preservation, Mendocino County Hist. Soc. and City of Ukiah, 1981. Mem.: Order Eastern Star (life). Avocations: gardening, writing, travel, landscape design. Home (Winter): 47350 Via Florence La Quinta CA 92253 Home (Summer): 180 Barbara St Ukiah CA 95482 E-mail: beversole@saber.net.

EVERSON, JEAN WATKINS DOLORES, librarian, media consultant, educator; b. Forest City, N.C., Feb. 14, 1938; d. J.D. Watkins and Hermie Roberta (Dizard) Watkins; children: Curtis Bryon, Vincent Keith. BS Elem. Edn., U. Cin., 1971, M Secondary Edn., 1973. Cert. X-ray technician. Educator Cin. Pub. Schs., Cin., 1965—2002, classroom tchr., parent/school coord., 1965—2002; work study coord. Butler County Edn. Ctr., Fairfield, Ohio, 1997—98; long term sub. Brown County -Georgetown Sch. Sys., Gerogetown, Ohio, 1993; sr. staff asst., cpc/alcohol substance abuse, inc. Cin. Pub. Schs., Cin., 1992—93; libr. tech. media; libr. media tech. asst. langsam libr. University of Cin.cinnati-Langsam Library, Cincinnati. Dir. and coord. tutoring program So. Baptist Ch., Cincinnati, 1990—91. Author: (booklet) Gospel Music: Copywrite Laws, 1987 (1987). Prodr./dir./coord. city music festival in music hall Cin. Pub. Schs., 1972—77. Mem.: Ohio Assn. Suprs. and Work Study Coords., Music Educator Nat. Conf. Baptist. Avocations: travel, walking. Home: PO Box 8337 West Chester OH 45069 Office: Cin City Pub Schs-Woodward 7001 Reading Rd Cincinnati OH 45237 Home Fax: 513-858-6880; Office Fax: 513-758-1279. Personal E-mail: jeanwatkinseverson@msn.com. Business E-Mail: eversoj@cpsboe.k12.oh.us.

EVERS-WILLIAMS, MYRLIE BEASLEY, advocate, cultural organization administrator; b. Vicksburg, Miss., Mar. 17, 1933; m. Medgar Evers (dec. June 11, 1963); 3 children; m. Walter Edward Williams 1975 (dec. 1995). Student, Alcorn State U.; BA in Sociology, Pomona Coll., 1968, Doctorate (hon.); cert., Simmons Coll.; Doctorate (hon.), Medgar Evers Coll., Spelman Coll., Columbia Coll., Chgo., Bennett Coll., Tougaloo Coll., Willamette U. Mem. staff, sec. NAACP; asst. dir. planning Claremont (Calif.) Colls., 1968—70; v.p. advt. & publicity Seligman & Latz, N.Y.C., 1973-75; dir. consumer affairs Atlantic Richfield Co.; commr. Pub. Works Bd., L.A., 1987-95; chairwoman NAACP, 1995-98. Civil rights leader, lectr. Author: For Us the Living, 1967, Watch Me Fly, 1999; co-author (with Steven Kasher) The Civil Rights Movement, 1996, (with Harriet Jacobs) Incidents in the Life of a Slave Girl, 2000, (with Russell J. Rickford) Betty Shabazz, 2003, editor: (with Manning Marable)The Autobiography of Medgar Evers, 2005; contbg. editor Ladies Home Jour. Candidate for Congress in Calif., 1970; candidate for L.A. City Coun., 1987; head So. Calif. Dem. Women's Divsn.; convener Nat. Women's Polit. Caucus; founder, chmn. Medgar Evers Inst.; mem. adv. bd. Boys & Girls Clubs Ams. Youth for Unity and Allstate Found., 2004. Named Woman of Yr., Glamour Mag., 1995, Ms. Mag., 1995, one of Women of Yr., Ladies Home Jour., 1996, one of 200 most influential women, Vanity Fair mag., Jan. 1999; recipient Mary Church Terrell award Delta Sigma Theta, 1996, Althea T.L. Simmons Social Action award, 1998, Spingarn award, NAACP, Atlanta, 1998, Trumpeter's award, Nat. Consumers League, New Orleans, 1998, U.S. Congl. Black Caucus Achievement award, Woman of Honor award LWV, Image award for civil rights NAACP, Woman of the Yr. award State of Calif. Mem.: NAACP (chmn. emeritus, nat. bd. dirs.). Office: MEW Assocs Inc 15 SW Colorado Ave Bend OR 97702-1150

EVERT, HEATHER LYNN, dance instructor; b. Cin., Ohio, Oct. 24, 1977; d. Richard Rodney and Karen Inez (Musser) Evert. BFA, U. Akron, Ohio, 2000; BS, U. Akron, 2001; student, Malone Coll. Dancer Met. Classical Ballet Co., Cin., 1992—96, Ohio Ballet, Akron, 1997; dance tchr. Tanze Performing Arts Studio, Fairfield, Ohio, 2001—02; dancer Hamilton Ballet Theater, Ohio, 2001; dance tchr. YMCA, Orrville, Ohio, 2002—. Choir mem. High St. Christian Ch., Akron, 1996—2006; outreach performer YMCA, 2002—06; actor, performer Mill St. Players, Dalton, 2002—06. Recipient German Book award, U. Cin., 1996; Margaret Hall O'Brien scholarship, Soc. of DAR, 2006, grant, Women's PEO, 2006. Mem.: Ohio House Rabbit Soc. Republican. Disciples Of Christ. Avocations: music, reading, sewing, gardening, genealogy. Home: 10495 Black Diamond Rd Marshallville OH 44645 Office Phone: 330-631-7378.

EVERT, MARGARET JANE, principal; b. Chgo., July 27, 1947; d. George and Margaret Mary (Hussey) Brown; m. Robert Lawrence Evert, Oct. 4, 1969; 1 child, Elizabeth Anne; m. Christopher Deutscher, May 30, 1997. BA in Elem. Edn., Northeastern U., 1969; MA in Ednl. Adminstrn., Dominican U., 1997. Cert. elem. tchr., elem. adminstr., Ill. Tchr. St. Leonard Sch., Berwyn, Ill., 1969-70, St. Edmund Sch., Oak Park, Ill., 1971-93, acting prin., 1993-96, prin., 1996—2004, St. Joseph Sch., Addison, 2004—. Mem. adv. bd. I Search Program, Oak Park, 1993—. Bd. dirs. Rochetta-Wessies Scholarship Found., 1993—; mem. MADD. Mem. ASCD, NAESP, Nat. Cath. Edn. Assn. Avocations: piano, travel, reading. Office: St Joseph Sch 330 E Fullerton Addison IL 60101 Office Phone: 630-279-4211. E-mail: office@stjosephschooladdison.org.

EVIATAR, LYDIA, pediatrician, neurologist; b. Bucharest, Romania, Apr. 7, 1936; came to U.S., 1966; d. Joseph and Ghitea (Scheinberg) Tamir; m. Abraham Eviatar, Oct. 9, 1956; children: Joseph, Daphne. BSc, Faculte des Scis., Strasbourg, 1954; MD, Hadassah Hebrew U., Jerusalem, 1961. Diplomate Am. Bd. Pediatrics, Am. Bd. Neurology with spl. competence in child neurology. Intern and resident Tel Hashoner Hosp., Tel Aviv, 1961-65; U.C.P. fellow UCLA, 1966-67, fellow in pediatric neurology, 1967-69; pediatric neurologist Bronx (N.Y.) Lebanon Hosp., 1970-79; resident in neurology Montefiore Hosp. Med. Ctr., Bronx, 1973-75; pediatric neurologist L.I. Jewish Med. Ctr., 1979-86; chief pediatric neurology Schneider Children's Hosp., New Hyde Park, NY, 1986-99; from assoc. prof. to prof. pediatrics and neurology Albert Einstein Coll. Medicine, Bronx, NY, 1989-99, chief emeritus Pediat. Neurology Sch., 1999—. Co-author: (with others) Pediatric Neurology, 1988, 2004. Grantee Nat. Inst. Neurol. Disease and Blindness, 1970-77, Acad. Cerebral Palsy, 1980-81, Richmond award, 1981; recipient teaching award Am. Acad. Otolaryngology, 1983. Fellow Am. Acad. Pediatrics, Am. Acad. Neurology (cert. neurologist, child neurologist); mem. Epilepsy Soc., Child Neurological Soc. Office Phone: 718-470-3450. Business E-Mail: eviatar@lij.edu.

EWALD, ROBERTA GRANT, artist, writer; b. Mpls., Aug. 25, 1915; d. Oscar and Hanna Theolinda (Johannson) Grant; m. Henry C. Ewald, Sept. 7, 1946; 1 child, Grant Christian. Student, U. Minn., Calif. Sch. Fine Arts, Coll. San Mateo, Golden Gate Coll. Asst. various firms, San Francisco, 1946—64; owner, artist Travers Art Gallery, South San Francisco, 1973—86; owner, adminstr. Ewald Travel Svc., South San Francisco and San Bruno, Calif., 1967—86; founder, pres. Keyboard Prodns., 1990—. Cons. Capuchino Cmty. Theater, 1984; creator, curator WestWing Art Gallery at Sanchez Art Ctr., Pacifica, 1996—2000. Lead role, author: (musical) The Wanderers, 1978; co-producer revision, 1982, 1992; poetry, I'm All I Know, 1983; co-producer: (TV show) Pacifica, 1982; dir.: children's choirs, music events; songwriter, singer, actress, musician (piano and guitar):; writer, illustrator: poetry My View; writer, prodr., lead: (musicals) Madam Bella's Saloon, 1983; Coastside Bowl, 1988; We Meant Well, 1989; prodr.: Moving Matters, 1991, Annual Producer's Showcase, 1993—. Founder Seaside Music Acad., San Francisco State U., 1999. Recipient Merit award, Capuchino Cmty. Theater, 1983, 1984, Lifetime Achievement in Arts, City of Pacifica, 1998, numerous awards for paintings, San Francisco and Calif. art exhibits, Lifetime Achievement award, City of Pacifica. Mem.: Crystal Springs Creative Writers, Citizens Against Waste, Pacific Art Connections, Pacifica Spindrift Players (named Outstanding Mem. 1980), Art Guild, Kiwanis.

EWALD, WENDY TAYLOR, photographer, writer, educator; b. Detroit, June 28, 1951; d. Henry Theodore and Carolyn Davison (Taylor) E.; m. Thomas Joseph McDonough, Oct. 21,1990; 1 child, Michael German. BA, Antioch Coll., 1974. Founder, dir. Camera Work, London, 1971-73, Mountain Photography Workshop, Whitesburg, Ky., 1975-81; tchr. photography Self-Employed Women's Assn., Raquira, Colombia, 1982-84, Gujarat, India, 1988-89; edn. cons. Fotofest, Houston, 1989-91; sr. rsch. assoc. Duke U., Durham, NC, 1991—. Artist-in-residence Ky. Arts Coun., Whitesburg, 1976-80; asst. dir., scriptwriter Cine-Mujer, Bogota, 1986; vis. assoc. prof. photography Bard Coll., Annandale, N.Y., 1996; sr. fellow Vera List Ctr. for Art and Politics New Sch. U., 2001-04. Author, editor: Appalachia: A Self-Portrait, 1978; author: Portraits and Dreams, 1985, Magic Eyes, 1992, I Dreamed I Had A Girl In My Pocket, 1996, Secret Games: Collaborations with Children, 1969-99, 2000, I Wanna Take Me a Picture: Teaching Writing and Photography to Children, 2001, The Best Part of Me: Childen Talk About Their Bodies, 2001. Recipient prize Lyndhurst Found., 1986; Fulbright fellow, fellow Nat. Endowment for Arts, 1988, non-fiction fellow N.Y. Found. for Arts, 1990, MacArthur fellow, 1992. Home: PO Box 582 Rhinebeck NY 12572-0582

EWART, CLAIRE LYNN, author, illustrator; b. Holland, Mich., June 15, 1958; d. John Adamson Ewart and Caryl Jane (Curtis) Van Houten; m. Thomas Andrew Herr, Aug. 31, 1l985; 1 child, Celeste Juliana. Student, Oberlin Coll., 1976-77; BFA, RISD, 1980. Animator, acting art dir. WSJV-TV and Pub. TV, Elkhart and South Bend, Ind., 1977-79; art dir. Computer Creations, South Bend, 1981-85; freelance courtroom illustrator, 1985-92; freelance illustrator Ft. Wayne, 1985-94; freelance author, illustrator Harper Collins, Putnam, Clarion, N.Y.C., 1989—. CEO Agricor, Marion, Ind. Author: One Cold Night, 1992, The Giant 2003, Fossil, 2004; illustrator: Time Train, 1991, Sister Yessa's Story, 1992, The Legend of the Persian Carpet, 1993, The Dwarf, The Giant, and the Unicorn, 1996, The Biggest Horse I Ever Did See, 1997, Torch in the Darkness, 2000, The Mystery of the Grindlecat, 2003; books featured on PBS: Reading Rainbow and Storytime; Ilustrator Children's Writers and Illustrators Market; represented in permanent collections. Vol. anti-toxic dump orgns., Ft. Wayne, 1992-93. Recipient ADI awards in computer animation, 1984-85, Women of Achievement in Advt. award Women in Comms., 1985, ADDY Citation of Excellence, 1989, Celibrate Literacy award Internat. Reading Assn., 1992, Woman of Achievement award YWCA, Ft. Wayne, 1996. Mem. Soc. Children's Book Writers and Illustrators, Designer/Craftsmen Guild (pres. 2006—). Avocations: gardening, hiking.

EWEN, PAMELA BINNINGS, retired lawyer; b. Mar. 22, 1944; d. Walter James and Barbara (Perkins) Binnings; m. Jerome Francis Ayers, Aug. 22, 1965 (div. July 1974); 1 child, Scott Dylan Ayers; m. John Alexander Ewen, Dec. 13, 1974 (div. Feb. 2003); m. James Craft Lott, Dec. 27, 2003. BA, Tulane U., 1977; JD cum laude, U. Houston, 1979. Bar: Tex. 79, U.S. Dist. Ct. (so. dist.) Tex. 81, U.S. Ct. Appeals (5th cir.) 81. Law clk. Harris, Cook, Browning & Barker, Corpus Christi, Tex., 1977—79; assoc. Kleberg, Dyer, Redford & Weil, Corpus Christi, 1979—80; atty. law dept. Gulf Oil Corp., Houston, 1980—84; assoc. Baker & Botts, L.L.P., Houston, 1980—84, ptnr., 1988—2004; ret. Author: Faith On Trial, 1999, Walk Back the Cat, 2006. La. Legis. scholar, New Orleans, 1976—77. Mem.: ABA (forum com. on franchising 1983—85, law practice mgmt. sect., subcom. Women Rainmakers Assn.), Tex. Assn. Bank Coun., Tex. State Bar (bd. dirs. 1994—97), Am. Petroleum Inst. (com. on product liability 1982—85, spl. subcom. to gen. com. on law), Order of Barons, Jr. Achievement S.E. Tex. (bd. dirs. 1997—2001, bd. dirs. Inprint, Inc. 2002—04). Home: 715 Kiskatom Ln Mandeville LA 70471 Personal E-mail: pamelaewen@bellsouth.net.

EWERS, ANNE, opera company director; BA in Theatre, Frontbonne Coll., MusB; MusM in Opera Prodn., U. Tex. Gen. dir. Boston Lyric Opera, 1984—89, Utah Opera, Salt Lake City, 1990—2005; CEO Utah Symphony & Opera, Salt Lake City, 2002—. Bd. trustees OPERA Am.; panelist NEA. Dir.: (60 productions for more than 25 opera cos.); (Operas) Dreamkeepers, The Seven Deadly Sins of the Petite Bourgeoisie, 2003, Pierrot humare, 2005. Founder Utah Opera Young Artist Program, 1992; hon. trustee Big Bros./Big Sisters, 1999—; bd. advisors Opera Boston, 1998—, Salt Lake City Downtown Alliance, 1999—2002; mem. auditions adv. bd. Met. Opera, Utah, 1999—2004; cons., panelist NEA, 1987—; bd. trustees Salt Lake Conv. & Visitors Bur., 1995—2002; hon. chair Muscular Ddystrophy Found., Salt Lake City, 1994. Mem.: Utah Women's Forum (mem.-at-large 1997—2002), Internat. Women's Forum (mem.-at-large 1995—). Office: Utah Symphony & Opera 123 W South Temple Salt Lake City UT 84101-1403 Office Phone: 801-533-5626. Business E-Mail: aewers@utahsymphonyopera.org.

EWERS, DENISE YVONNE, music educator; d. Herbert George and Wanda June Lent; m. Todd Patrick Ewers, July 27, 1991; children: Deidre, Jocelyn. BME, Ill. Wesleyan U., 1988; MME, Ill. State U., 1990. Music tchr. Milledgeville Sch. Dist., Ill., 1988—89; gen. music tchr. Princeton Elem. Sch. Dist., Princeton, Ill., 1990—93; choral dir. Dixon Publ. Schs., Ill., 1993—. Mem.: America Choral Dirs. Assn., Ill. Music Educators Assn. (dist. VIII rep. 1998—2002), Sigma Alpha Iota. Avocations: boating, reading, theater, acting. Home: PO Box 93 501 N Cochran Ave Milledgeville IL 61051 Office: Dixon HS Lincoln Statue Dr Dixon IL 61021 Office Phone: 815-284-7723.

EWERS, MARLA ROUSE, voice educator; b. Charleston, Ill., Dec. 11, 1952; m. John M. Ewers; children: John Robert, Meridith Anne. MusB, Ea. Ill. U., 1975; MS in Edn., U. Ill., 1995, EdD, 2004. Music specialist grades K-8 Decatur (Ill.) Pub. Schs., 1979—94, 1997—98; grad. asst. U. Ill., Urbana, 1994—97; choral dir. Stephen Decatur H.S., 1998—2000, Eisenhower H.S., Decatur, 2000—04, Stephen Decatur Mid. Sch., 2004—, MacArthur H.S., 2006—. Adjudicator Ill. H.S. Assn., Bloomington, 1993—. Mem.: Music Educators Nat. Conf., Assn. Supervision and Curriculum Devel., Am. Choral Directors Assn., Phi Delta Kappa, Sigma Alpha Iota (treas. 1988—92, Sword of Honor 1993). Home: 881 S Oakland Ave Forsyth IL 62535 Office: Stephen Decatur Mid Sch One Educational Park Decatur IL 62526 Office Phone: 217-424-3156. E-mail: mewers@dps61.org.

EWERSEN, MARY VIRGINIA, retired school system administrator, poet; b. Van Wert County, Ohio, June 7, 1922; m. Herbert Ewersen (dec.); 2 children. BS in Elem. Edn., Bowling Green, 1966, Toledo and Ohio State U. Cert. tchr. K-12, reading, Ohio. Remedial reading tchr. Port Clinton (Ohio) City Schs., 1966-70, reading tchr. chpt. I/coord., 1970-94; ret. Lyrics writer Hilltop Records. Author: Keepsakes and Celebrations!, 1997, (activity card set) From Hyperactive to Happy-Active in Limited Spaces, 1979, The Lures of Pan, 2001, of poems. Mem. Internat. Reading Assn., Sandusky Choral Soc., Acad. Am. Poets, Internat. Soc. Poets, Kappa Delta Pi. Home: 1786 S Hickory Grove Rd Port Clinton OH 43452-9637 Office: 431 Portage Dr Port Clinton OH 43452-1724

EWERT, JENNIFER KRISTIN, counselor; d. Wilbert Thomas and Christine J. Ewert; m. Joshua Douglas Lee, Aug. 11, 2001. BS in Psychology with honors, Valparaiso U., 1998; MA, Marquette U., 2000. Lic. clin. profl. counselor Ill., nat. cert. counselor. Team leader Segue, Inc., Jackson, Mich., 2000—03; therapist Maine Ctr., Pk. Ridge, Ill., 2003—06, Thresholds Young Adult Program, Chgo., 2006—. Chmn. spl. interest group Cmty. Behavoiral Healthcare Assn., Chgo., 2004—06. Named Employee of Yr., Segue, Inc., 2003. Mem.: ACA, Ill. Counseling Assn., Alpha Xi Epsilon Alumnus Assn. (treas. 2004—). Office: Thresholds Young Adult Program 4219 N Lincoln Ave Chicago IL 60618

EWING, ANNA M., stock exchange executive; Mng. dir., electronic commerce CIBC World Markets; sr. v.p., systems engring. NASDAQ Stock Market, Inc., Conn., 2000—05, exec. v.p. ops., chief information officer, 2005—. Office: NASDAQ Stock Market Inc 80 Merritt Blvd Trumbull CT 06611 also: NASDAQ Stock Market Inc 1 Liberty Plz New York NY 10006

EWING, ELISABETH ANNE ROONEY, priest; b. San Bernardino, Calif. m. James E. Ewing. Student, Mt. San Antonio Coll., 1978. Ordained priest Communion Evang. Episcopal Ch., 1998, ordained to ministry Meth. Ch. Pastor, gen. overseers, CEO St. Matthew's Nationwide Chs., N.Y.C. Mem. Rand Rsch. Corp.; mem. diplomat cir. L.A. World Affairs Coun. Co-editor: (book) Church History, 1996—98, The Church Visible, 1996—98, Life After Death, 1996—98, Bible Lessons, 1996—98; head pub. rels., assoc. editor Pinnacle Today Internat. Mag.; assoc. editor: St. Matthew Tribune. Recipient St. Augustine cross, Archbishop of Canterbury. Mem.: Knights of Malta (dame).

EWING, MARILYN, English educator; b. Rochester, N.H., Oct. 19, 1940; d. Thomas Kirby and Ida Maryann (Scala) McKee; m. Richard Edwin Ewing, June 29, 1963 (div. Nov. 1974); 1 child, Julie E. BA cum laude, U. N.H., 1962; MA, U. No. Colo., 1974; PhD, U. Colo., 1982. Tchr. Portsmouth (N.H.) H.S., 1962-63, Green Springs (Ohio) Local Sch., 1964-66; tchg. asst. U. No. Colo., Greeley, 1973-77; tchg. asst., part-time instr. U. Colo., Boulder, 1977-82; from asst. prof. to assoc. prof. English, Eastern Oreg. U., La Grande, 1982—. Translator poems by Pablo Neruda, Colo.-North Rev., 1976; columnist The Longmont (Colo.) Ledger, 1971; author essays and articles; editor: Wine for the Plains, 2005 Recipient Svc. award Oreg. Women in Higher Edn., 1999. Mem. NOW, MLA, Nat. Coun. Tchrs. English, Oreg. Writing Project (mem. steering com. 1994—), Lambda Pi. Office: Eastern Oreg U 1 University Blvd La Grande OR 97850-2807 Office Phone: 541-962-3360. Business E-Mail: mewing@eou.edu.

EWING BROWNE, SHEILA, chemistry professor, physical organic chemist; BS, U. Tenn., 1971; PhD, U. Calif., Berkeley, 1974. Joined Mt. Holyoke Coll., S. Hadley, Mass., 1976—, Bertha Phillips Rodger prof. chemistry. Mentors students with independent rsch. projects; mentor New England Bd. of Higher Education's Sci. and Engring. Academic Support Network; co-founder Sistahs in Sci., 1994—. Recipient Presdl. award for Excellence in Sci., Math. and Engring. Mentoring, NSF, 1998, 2005 AAAS Mentor award for Lifetime Achievement, 2006. Office: Chemistry Dept Mt Holyoke Coll Rm GO2B Carr Lab 50 College St South Hadley MA 01075-6407 Office Phone: 413-538-2020. Business E-Mail: sbrowne@mtholyoke.edu.

EWING-MULLIGAN, MARY, food products executive; Pres. Internat. Wine Ctr., NYC, Inst. Masters of Wine North Am.; exec. dir. Wine & Spirit Edn. Trust, London. Chief judge Critics Challenge, 2004—. Co-author: Wine For Dummies, Red Wine For Dummies, White Wine For Dummies, French Wine For Dummies, Italian Wine For Dummies, Wine Style; contbr. columns in newspapers The Daily News,; featured in Food & Wine mag., NY Times, The Wine Spectator, Newsday, Gourmet mag. Achievements include being the first woman in America to achieve Master of Wine title. Office: International Wine Center 350 7th Ave Ste 1201 New York NY 10001 Office Phone: 212-239-3055. Office Fax: 212-239-3051.*

EWINS, MAXIE STAEDTLER, librarian; b. Germany, Sept. 13, 1936; came to U.S., 1959; m. George D. Ewins; children— Lini, Katrine, Franzi, Fritz MA, Free U., Berlin, 1959; MS, Pratt Inst., 1978. Library dir. Montvale Pub. Library, N.J., 1975-78; library dir. Fletcher Free Library, Burlington, Vt., 1979—. Bd. govs. Med. Ctr. Vt., Burlington, 1983—, trustee, 1988—. Mem. ALA, Vt. Library Assn. (past. pres.) Office: Fletcher Free Libr 235 College St Burlington VT 05401-8317

EXUM, STEPHANIE ROXANNE, medical educator; MD, East Carolina U., 2000; BS in Biology and Pre-Med., Xavier U., New Orleans, 1996. Residency in internal medicine, psychiatry Rush U. Med. Ctr., Chgo., 2000—05; instr. Loyola U. Med. Ctr., Maywood, Ill., 2005—, dir. women's mental health program, 2005—, dir. women's mental health program dept. psychiatry, 2005—; instr. psychiatry. Stritch Sch. Medicine, Maywood, 2005—. Mem.: AMA.

EYERMAN, CHARLOTTE, curator, art historian; BA in English, cum laude, Holy Cross Coll., 1987; PhD in History of Art, U. Calif. Berkeley, 1997. Asst. curator paintings J. Paul Getty Mus., LA, 2002—05; curator modern art St. Louis Art Mus., Mo., 2005—. Lectr. impressionism in context So. Meth. U., 1993; tchr. art history U. So. Calif., LA, Art Ctr. Coll. Design, Pasadena; vis. instr. Union Coll., Schenectady, NY, 1994—96, asst. prof. Visual Arts Dept., 1996—2001, John D. and Catherine T. MacArthur asst. prof., 1996—97; Flagship Forum lectr. Smithsonian Associates, 2000; lectr. in field; founder elucidART, Inc. Contbr. articles to profl. jour. Office: Saint Louis Art Mus Forest Park One Fine Arts Drive Saint Louis MO 63110-1380*

EYRE, HEIDI L., psychology professor; d. Ralph M. Eyre, Jr. and Deborah L. Eyre. PhD, U. Ky., Lexington, 2004. Asst. prof. psychology Delta State U., Cleveland, Miss., 2004—06, Jacksonville State U., Ala., 2006—. Mem.: Assn. Psychol. Sci., Soc. Tchg. Psychology, Soc. Personality and Social Psychology, Assn. Behavior Analysis (assoc.). Office: Jacksonville State University 700 Pelham Road North Jacksonville AL 36265 Office Phone: 256-782-5895. E-mail: heyre@jsu.edu.

EYRE, PAMELA CATHERINE, retired career officer; b. Chgo., Nov. 3, 1948; d. Francis Thomas and Jane (Burd) E. BA, Ctrl. State U. Okla., 1972; MPA, U. Okla., 1976; postgrad., U. Tex., 1998—. Commd. 2d lt. U.S. Army, 1973, advanced through grades to lt. col., 1991, test and evaluation officer Ft. Gordon, Ga., 1982-85, R&D coord. Ft. Monmouth, N.J., 1985-88, with army gen. staff Pentagon Washington, 1988-91, acquisition policy staff officer Army Secretariat Pentagon, 1991-94, asst. project mgr. Def. Telecom. Svc., 1994-95, test and evaluation officer Army Secretariat Pentagon, 1995-96; ret., 1996; program mgr. unmanned aerial vehicles Mission Techs., Inc., San Antonio, 2000—02. Home: 3103 N Bentsen Palm Dr Mission TX 78574 E-mail: pceyre@gmail.com.

EYRES, BETH KATHLEEN, literature educator; d. Robert and Loree Eyres; life ptnr. H. K. Batsell. BA in Secondary Edn. and English, Ariz. State U., Tempe, 1988; MA in English with distinction, No. Ariz. U., Flagstaff, 2005. Tchr. Deer Valley H.S., Glendale, Ariz., 1991—. Mem. Ariz. Academic Decathlon, Gilbert, 2000—03, state essay coord., 2001—04. Exhbn., South Mountain CC, 1998. Named Honored Educator, U. Ariz., 1997, Most Influential Tchr., Ariz. State U., 2002. Mem.: Phi Kappa Phi. Home: 1339 E Mulberry Phoenix AZ 85014 Office: Deer Valley High School 18424 N 51st Ave Glendale AZ 85308 Office Phone: 602-467-6857. Personal E-mail: ap_arama@yahoo.com.

EYRING, MAXINE LOUISE, small business owner, esthetician; d. William Charles Whippo and Catherine Marie Bennett; m. William John Eyring (div.). Student, Catonsville C.C., Baltimore, 1964. Lic. estetician Md., 1979. Owner Maxime's Skin and Nail Care, Annapolis, Md., 1980—88; with Salon West, Annapolis, 1988—89, Lord's and Lady's Salon, Annapolis, 1989—91; esthetician Robert Andrew Day Spa, Gambills, Md., 1991—97, Vincent's Masterpiece Internat. Day Spa, Annapolis, 1997—2000, Rumors of Annapolis, 2000—02; mgr. Esthencian Vincent's Masterpiece Internat. Day Spa, 2002—. Democrat. Lutheran.

EYSTER, MARY ELAINE, hematologist, educator; m. Robert E. Dye, Jan. 2, 1965; children: Robert E. Dye, Charles Dye. AB, Duke U., 1956, MD, 1960. Intern. N.Y. Hosp.-Cornell Med. Coll., N.Y.C., 1960-61, resident in medicine, 1961-63, fellow in hematology, 1963-66, instr. medicine, 1966-67, asst. prof. medicine, 1967-70; asst. prof. medicine Milton S. Hershey Med. Ctr. Pa. State U., Hershey, 1970-73, assoc. prof. Milton S. Hershey Med. Ctr., 1973-82, prof. Milton S. Hershey Med. Ctr., 1982—, chief hematology divsn., dept. medicine Coll. Medicine, 1973-96. Bd. dirs. Hemophilia Ctr. Cen. Pa., 1973—, AIDS Clin. Trials Unit Pa. State U., 1987—; faculty rsch. assoc. Am. Cancer Soc., 1966-71; mem. State Hemophilia Adv. Com, 1973—, chmn., 1977-79, 1988-90; mem. policy bd. Coop. F VII inhibitor study Nat. Heart, Lung and Blood Inst., 1975-79; mem. med. and sci. adv. counc. Nat. Hemophilia Found., 1976-77, 83-89, chmn. med. adv. com. Del. Valley chpt., 1979-82; co-investigator, mem. multi-agy. task force on AIDS HHS, 1982-83; mem. blood products adv. com. FDA, 1985-89; exec. com. NIH-NIAID Clin. Trials, 1988-90; mem. forum on blood safety and availability Inst. of Med., 1993-95. USPHS grantee, 1976-95. Fellow ACP; mem. Am. Fedn. Clin. Rsch., World Fedn. Hemophilia, Am. Soc. Hematology, Internat. Soc. Thrombosis and Haemostasis, Insternat. Soc. Hematology, Pa. Soc. Hematology and Oncology (bd. dirs. 1982-85), Am. Assn. for Study of Liver Diseases, Phi Beta Kappa, Alpha Omega Alpha. Office: Milton S Hershey Med Ctr PO Box 850 Hershey PA 17033-0850 Office Phone: 717-531-8399. E-mail: eeyster@psu.edu.

EZAKI-YAMAGUCHI, JOYCE YAYOI, dietician; b. Kingsburg, Calif., Mar. 18, 1947; d. Toshikatsu and Aiko (Ogata) Ezaki; m. Kent Takao Yamaguchi, Oct. 28, 1972; children: Kent Takao, Jr., Toshia Ann. AA, Reedley Coll., 1967; BS in Foods and Nutrition, U. Calif., Davis, 1969. Dietetic intern Henry Ford Hosp., Detroit, 1969-70, staff dietitian, 1970-71; renal dietitian Sutter Meml. Hosp., Sacramento, 1971-72; therapeutic dietitian Mt. Sinai Hosp., Beverly Hills, Calif., 1972-73; clin. dietitian Pacific Hosp., Long Beach, Calif., 1973-77; consulting dietitian Doctor's Hosp., Lakewood, Calif., 1976-77; clin. dietitian Mass. Gen. Hosp., Boston, 1977-78, Winona Meml. Hosp., Indpls., 1978-80; renal dietitian Fresno (Calif.) Community Hosp., Calif., 1980—. Author: (computer program) Dialysis Tracker, 1987; author: (with others) Cultural Foods and Renal Diets for the Dietitian, 1988, Standards of Practice Guidlines for the Practice of Clinical Dietetics, 1991. Religious chair Fresno Dharma Sch. Fresno Betsuin Buddhist Temple, 1994—; sec. Japanese Lang. Sch., 1997-01. Mem. Nat. Kidney Found. (exec. com. coun. renal nutrition 1991-98, region V rep., nutrition editor, chair patient and pub. edn. com. 1992-93, chair elect comms. chair 1994-95, chair 1995-96, past chair 1997-98, chair nominations com., chair rsch. grant com., Disting. Svc. award 1996, Nat. Kidney Found./Coun. on Renal Nutrition Recognized Renal Dietitian award 1999), Am. Dietetic Assn. (bd. cert. renal nutrition specialist, renal practice group 1993-98, renal practice group nominating com. chair 1999), No. Calif/No. Nev. chpt. Nat. Kidney Found.

(disting. achievement award coun. on renal nutrition 1993, co-chair-elect 1993-94, co-chair 1994-95, co-past chair 1995-96, treas., corr. sec.). Buddhist. Avocations: computers, cross stitch.

EZELL, KIMBERLY HARDISON, educator; b. Savannah, Ga., June 5, 1957; d. Bobby West and Sarah Anne (Ledford) Hardison; m. Guilford Dudley Ezell, July 24, 2005; children: James Dewitt Eddins, Joel Isaac, Joseph Dudley. BS, Mid. Tenn. State, Murfeesboro, 1978; MEd, Ga. State, Atlanta, 1984, EdS, 1987. Cert. profl. sch. counselor ACA, 1984. Tchr. Cobb County Schs., Marietta, Ga., 1979; tchr. and counselor Greater Atlanta Christian Schs., 1979—91, Cobb County Schs., Marietta, 1991—92; counselor and tchr. Williamson County Schs., Franklin, Tenn., 1993—. Mid. sch. mentor counselor Williamson County Schs., Franklin, Tenn., 1996—. Vol. Habitat Humanity; active mem. 4th Ave. Ch. of Christ, Franklin, Tenn., 1993—. Named Tchr. of Yr., Greater Atlanta Christian Schs., 1984. Mem.: ACA. Home: 1500 Volunteer Pkwy Franklin TN 37069 Office: Woodland Mid Sch Brentwood TN 37027 Office Phone: 615-472-4931 ext. 1403. E-mail: kimberlyezell@comcast.net.

EZELL, MARGARET M., language educator; John Paul Abbott prof. of liberal arts Tex. A&M U., College Sta., 1997—. Author: The Patriarch's Wife: Literary Evidence and the History of the Family, Writing Women's Literary History, Social Authorship and the Advent of Print; editor: (series) Women Writers in English, 1350-1830. Fellow, John Simon Guggenheim Meml. Found., 2003. Office: Tex A&M U Dept English 243D Blocker Bldg (MS 4227) College Station TX 77843

EZENWA, JOSEPHINE NWABUOKU, social worker; b. Oct. 20, 1959; d. H.M. Eze-Igwe Silas O. and H.R.H. Veronica Ezenwa; children: Bryan, Brenda, Sean. BA in Psychology and Human Svc. (hon.), Fontbonne Coll., St. Louis, 1980; MSW, Washington Univ., St. Louis, 1981; postgrad., St. Louis U., 1991—93. Diplomate Am. Coll. Profl. Mental Health Practitioners, 2002. Rsch. dir. Nat. Benevolent Assn., St. Louis, 1981-89; tchr. U. City Sch. Dist., St. Louis, 1989-94; therapist Presbyn. Children's Home, St. Louis, 1994-95; social worker St. Louis Regional Med. Ctr., 1995-97; founder, chair St. Louis Regional Med. Ctr. Dialysis Support Group, 1995-97; social worker St. Louis U. Hosp., 1997; CEO, pres. BBS Care U.S.A., Inc., St. Louis, 1997—; pres. BBS Charities, Inc., St. Louis, 2000—; chair Bus. Adv. Coun. Nat Rep. Congl. Com., St. Louis, 2002—. Founder and chair St. Louis Regional Med. Ctr. Dialysis Support Group, 1995-97; chair long range planning com. Washington U.; co-chair Bus. Adv. Coun., 2002; presenter in field. Chair bus. adv. coun. Nat. Rep. Congl. Com., 2002—. Named Businesswoman of Yr., Nat. Rep. Congl. Com., 2003; recipient Nat. Leadership award, St. Louis Regional Med. Ctr. Dialysis Support Group, 2002, Gold Medal award, Nat. Rep. Congl. Com., 2003. Mem. NASW, NAFE, Coun. Nephrology Social Workers; Nat. Assn. Forensic Counselors; Nat. Assn. Cognitive Behavioral Therapists, Washington U. Sch. Social Work Alumni Assn. (bd. dir.); Creve Coeur-Olive C. of C.; Lions Club. Avocations: choreography, fashion cons., event coord., design, travel. Office: St Louis U Hosp 3536 Vista Grand Saint Louis MO 63110 also: BBS Care USA Inc 7151-7155 Olive Blvd Saint Louis MO 63130 Office Phone: 314-725-7733.

EZOE, MAGDALENA, music educator, composer, musician; arrived in US, 1951; MusM in Piano, U. Mich., Ann Arbor, 1968. Tchr. Dominican H.S., Detroit, 1954—65; asst. prof. music St. Dominic Coll., St. Charles, Ill., 1965—68; assoc. prof. music Siena Heights U., Adrian, Mich., 1968—. Music tchr. Internat. Sch. of the Sacred Heart, Tokyo, 1970—73. Liturgical music dir., cantor Dominican Sisters Adrian, Mich., 1973—2006; mem. Adrian Symphony, Mich., 1981—89. Recipient Creative Arts award, Dominican Sisters Adrian, 1976, Sr. Eileen K. Rice Outstanding Tchg. award, Siena Heights U., 2004—05, Fred Smith Champion award, 2006. Mem.: Coll. Music Soc. (corr.). Roman Catholic. Avocations: travel, japanese crafts, japanese calligraphy, japanese painting. Office Phone: 517-264-7898.

FAATZ, JEANNE RYAN, councilman; b. Cumberland, Md., July 30, 1941; d. Charles Keith and Elizabeth (McIntyre) Ryan; children: Kristin, Susan. BS, U. Ill., 1962; postgrad.; MA, U. Colo., Denver, 1985. Instr. speech dept. Met. State Coll., Denver, 1985-98; sec. to majority leader Colo. Senate, 1976-78; mem. Colo. Ho. Reps. from Dist. 1, 1979-98; dir. Colo. Sch.-to-Career, 1999—2001; councilwoman City of Denver, 2003—. Former ho. asst. majority leader. Past pres. S.W. Denver YWCA Adult Edn. Club; former mem. bd. mgrs. S.W. Denver YMCA; past pres. Harvey Park (Colo.) Homeowners Assn. Gates fellow, Harvard U., 1984. Home: 2903 S Quitman St Denver CO 80236-2208 Office Phone: 303-763-8562. E-mail: jeanne.faatz@ci.denver.co.us.

FABBRI, ANNE R., critic, curator; b. Norristown, Pa. d. Remo and Anna Wild (Butterworth) F.; m. Joseph Henry Butera (div.); children: Virginia, Remo, Joseph F. (Jay). AB cum laude, Radcliffe Coll.; MA in Art History, Bryn Mawr Coll., 1971. Art lectr. Villanova U., Pa., 1971-73, Drexel U., Phila., 1974-76; art critic, art editor The Drummer, Phila., 1976-79; art critic The Bulletin, Phila., 1978-80; dir. Alfred O. Deshong Mus., Widener U., Chester, Pa., 1980-82, The Noyes Mus., Oceanville, NJ, 1982-91; dir. Paley Design Ctr. Phila. U., 1991-2001; art critic Phila. Daily News, Art in Am., Art Matters, The Art Newspaper, Am. Artist, 1998—, Phila. Style mag., 2002—; lectr. arts adminstrn. Rosemont Coll., 2000—03, lectr. humanities, 2001—03. Bd. dirs. Phila. Vol. Lawyers for the arts, 2001-03; mem. adv. com. Main Line Art Ctr.; chair adv. com. Art in City Hall, Phila., 1999-2003; chair New Visions, Phila. Furniture Exhbn., 1998-2004. Chair, mem. adv. com. Art in City Hall, 1999—. Vis. NEH fellow U. Calif.-Berkeley, 1980, Princeton U., 1981; recipient John Cotton Dana award Mus. N.J. Assn. Mus., 1991. Mem. Am. Assn. Museums, Coll. Art Assn., Internat. Assn. Art Critics. Home and Office: 642 Valley View Ln Wayne PA 19087-2024 Office Phone: 610-989-0588. Personal E-mail: arfabbri@aol.com.

FABE, DANA ANDERSON, state supreme court justice; b. Cin., Mar. 29, 1951; d. George and Mary Lawrence (Van Antwerp) F.; m. Randall Gene Simpson, Jan. 1, 1983; 1 child, Amelia Fabe Simpson. BA, Cornell U., 1973; JD, Northeastern U., 1976. Bar: Alaska 1977, U.S. Supreme Ct. 1981. Law clk. to justice Alaska Supreme Ct., 1976-77; staff atty. pub. defenders State of Alaska, 1977-81; dir. Alaska Pub. Defender Agy., Anchorage, 1981—88; judge Superior Ct., Anchorage, 1988—92; deputy presiding judge Third Judicial Dist., 1992—95; justice Alaska Supreme Ct., Anchorage, 1996—, chief justice, 2000—03. Chair Alaska Supreme Ct. Civil Rules Com., Alaska Supreme Ct. Judicial Outreach Commn., Alaska Ct. System Law Day Steering Comm., Alaska Teaching Justice Network. Named alumna of yr. Northeastern Sch. Law, 1983; recipient Northeastern Sch. Law Alumni Pub. Svc. award, 1991. Mem.: Am. Judicature Soc. (bd. dirs.), Alaska Bar Assoc. (bd. govs. 1987—88, co-chair Gender Equality Sect.). Office: Alaska Supreme Ct 303 K St Fl 5 Anchorage AK 99501-2013 Office Phone: 907-264-0622.*

FABEND, FIRTH HARING, writer; b. Tappan, NY, Aug. 12, 1937; d. James Firth and Elizabeth Haring; m. Ernest Carl Fabend, Feb. 12, 1966; children: Caroline Firth Bartlett, Lydia Elizabeth Fabend. BA, Barnard Coll., 1959; MA, Montclair State Coll., 1980; PhD, NYU, 1988. Editorial asst. Nat. Bur. Econ. Rsch., N.Y.C., 1959-61; copy editor Harcourt, Brace, N.Y.C., 1961-65; spl. projects editor Harper & Row, N.Y.C., 1965-73; writer, historian, editor Montclair, N.J., 1973—. Author: The Best of Intentions, 1968, Three Women, 1972, A Perfect Stranger, 1973, The Woman Who Went Away, 1981, Greek Revival, 1985, A Dutch Family in the Middle Colonies, 1989; editor: Tappan: 300 Years, 1988, Zion on the Hudson: Dutch New York and New Jersey in the Age of Revivals, 2000, A Catch of Grandmothers, 2004; contbr. articles to profl. jours. Recipient Hendricks MS prize New Netherland Project, 1989, Ann. Book award N.Y. State Hist. Assn., 1989; fellow New Netherland Inst., 1996. Fellow The Holland Soc. N.Y., Authors Guild. Democrat. Mem. United Ch. of Christ. Avocations: reading, gardening, walking, cooking, travel. Home and Office: 54 Elston Rd Montclair NJ 07043-1956

FABER, SANDRA MOORE, astronomer, educator; b. Boston, Dec. 28, 1944; d. Donald Edwin and Elizabeth Mackenzie (Borwick) Moore; m. Andrew L. Faber, June 9, 1967; children: Robin, Holly. BA, Swarthmore Coll., 1966, DSc (hon.), 1986; PhD, Harvard U., 1972; DSc (hon.), Williams Coll., 1996. Asst. prof., astronomer Lick Obs., U. Calif., Santa Cruz, 1972-77, assoc. prof., astronomer, 1977-79, prof., astronomer, 1979—; Univ. Prof. U. Calif., Santa Cruz, 1996—. Mem. astronomy adv. panel NSF, 1975-77; vis. prof. Princeton U., 1978, U. Hawaii, 1983, Ariz. State U., 1985; Phillips visitor Haverford Coll., 1982; Feshbach lectr. MIT, Cambridge, Mass., 1990; Darwin lectr. Royal Astron. Soc., 1991; Marker lectr. Pa. State U., 1992; Bunyan lectr. Stanford U., 1992; Tomkins lectr. U. Calif., San Francisco, 1992; Mohler lectr. U. Mich., 1994; mem. Nat. Acad. Astronomy Survey Panel, 1979-81Nfat. Acad. Com. on Astronomy and Astrophysics 1993-1995; chmn. vis. com. Space Telescope Sci. Inst., 1983-84; co-chmn. sci. steering com. Keck Obs., 1987-92, leader DEIMOS spectrograph team, 1993—; mem. Wide Field Camera team Hubble Space Telescope, 1985-97, user's com., 1990-92, mem. advanced radial camera selection team, 1995,co-chmn. TAC review comm., 2002; mem. treas. pgm. advis. comm. 2002-; mem. Calif. Coun. on Sci. and Tech., 1989-94,; Com. on Future Smithsonian Instn., 1994-95; mem. White House Space Sci. Workshop, 1996, Waterman Awards Com., NSF, 1997-99, Nat. Medal of Sci. selection com., 1999-2001; mem. Plumian Prof. selection com. Cambridge U., 1998—. Assoc. editor: Astrophys. Jour. Letters, 1982-87; editorial bd.: Ann. Revs. Astronomy and Astrophysics, 1982-87; contbr. articles to profl. jours. Trustee Carnegie Instn., Washington, 1985—; bd. dirs. Ann. Revs., 1989—, SETI Inst., 1997—; editl. affairs com. Ann. Revs., 1996—; exec. com. Ann. Revs., 1998—; Scripps Instn. Oceanography Coun., 2000--; bd. overseers Fermilab, 2002--. Recipient Bart J. Bok prize Harvard U., 1978, Director's Distinguished Lectr. award Livermore Nat. Lab., 1986; NASA Group Achievement award, 1993, DeVaucouleurs medal U. Tex., 1997; Carnegie Lectr. Carnegie Inst. Washington, 1988, 99; NSF fellow, 1966-71; Woodrow Wilson fellow, 1966-71; Alfred P. Sloan fellow, 1977-81; listed among 100 best Am. scientists under 40, Sci. Digest, 1984, listed among 50 best Am. Women scientists, Discover Mag., 2002; Tetelman fellow, Yale U., 1987. Fellow Calif. Coun. on Sci. and Tech.; mem. NAS (vice chair adv. panel on cosmology 1993, rsch. in astronomy commn. on orgn. and mgmt. astrophysics 2001, co-chmn. TAC rev. commn. 2002, mem. treas. program adv. commn. 2002--), Am. Philos. Soc. Am. Acad. Arts and Scis., Calif. Acad. Scis., 1998—, Am. Astron. Soc. (councilor 1982-84, Dannie Heineman prize 1986), Internat. Astron. Union, Am. Philos. Soc., Phi Beta Kappa, Sigma Xi. Office: U Calif Lick Obs Santa Cruz CA 95064 E-mail: faber@ucolick.org.

FABIAN, JANE, former ballet company executive; Mng. dir. Nashville Ballet. Mem.: Tenn. Assn. Dance (pres. bd. dirs. 2000—06). Office: Nashville Ballet 3630 Redmon Dr Nashville TN 37209-4827 E-mail: janefabian@aol.com.

FABIAN, KELLY JEAN, physical therapist; b. Honolulu, Nov. 25, 1974; d. Juan Galvan, Jr. and Valerie Ann Comeau; m. Joshua Regar Fabian, Dec. 16, 2000; children: Joshua Regar Fabian, Jr., Jacob Tyler. BS in Movement Sci., U. Pitts., 1997, MS in Phys. Therapy, 1999. Cert. athletic trainer. Phys. therapist North Hills Orthop. Sports Therapy, Sewickley, Pa., 1999—2000, Rushmore Phys. Therapy, Delean, NJ, 2001—. Lectr. in field., EATA scholar, 1997. Mem.: Nat. Athletic Trainers Assn. Avocations: reading, swimming, crocheting.

FABING, SUZANNAH, museum director; b. Cin., Oct. 1, 1942; d. Howard Douglas John and Esther Clare (Marting) F.; m. Peter B. Doeringer, June 19, 1965 (div. June 1981); 1 child, Eric Atchley; m. James Alexander Muspratt, Aug. 21, 1993. AB in Art History with hons., Wellesley Coll., 1964; AM, Harvard U., 1965. Asst. to curator of Ancient art to dep. dir. mus. Fogg Art Mus./Harvard U., 1965-83; curator of records Nat. Gallery of Art, Washington, 1983-84, mng. curator of records and loans, 1984-91, head Divsn. of Rsch. on Collections, 1991-92; dir., chief curator Smith Coll. Mus. of Art, Northampton, Mass., 1992—2005. Overview panel NEA, 1993-94; reviewer NEH, 1992-94; surveyor AAM Mus. Assessment Program, 1991—; mem. Art Info. Task Force, Getty Art Info. Program, 1990-94; vis. com. Wellesley Coll. Mus., 1988—, Fitchburg Art Mus., chmn. 1983-88, others; trustee Fitchburg Art Mus., 1975-82, Revels, Inc., 1981-82, 88-92), others. Contbr. articles to profl. jours. Mem. New Eng. Mus. Assn. (panelist), Mus. Computer Network (bd. dirs. 1984-90, sec. 1988, v.p. 1988-89, pres. 1989-90), Phi Beta Kappa. Avocation: languages. Office: Hillyer Hall Smith Coll Northampton MA 01063-0001 E-mail: sfabing@smith.edu.

FABJ, VALERIA, education educator; b. Cremona, Italy, Dec. 22, 1962; d. Olga Malaguti and Giancarlo Fabj; m. Thomas Williams, June 9, 1985; children: Stephanie Vittoria Williams, Michael Thomas Willliams. PhD, Northwestern U., Evanston, Ill., 1989. Prof. Emerson Coll., Boston, 1989—2000, No. Ill. U., DeKalb, Ill., 2000—01, Lynn U., Boca Raton, Fla., 2001—. Contbr. articles to profl. jour. Mem.: Am. Forensic Assn., Nat. Comm. Assn. Office: Lynn U 3601 North Mil Trl Boca Raton FL 33431 Office Phone: 561-237-7794. Business E-Mail: vfabj@lynn.edu.

FABRE, NIZA ELSIE, African studies and Hispanic literature educator; b. Guayaquil, Guayas, Ecuador; BA, CUNY, 1980, MA, 1982, MPhil, 1989, PhD, 1991. Assoc. prof. Ramapo Coll. N.J., Mahwah, 1992—. Author: Americanismos, Indigenismos, Neologismos y Creación Léxica en la Obra de Jorge Icaza, 1993, Blacks in Central America (English transl.), 2006; contbr. articles to profl. jours. Mem. MLA, N.E. MLA, Circulo de Cultura Panamericano, Circulo de Escritores y Poetas Iberoamericanos, Assn. Ecuadorianists in N.Am., Popular Culture Assn., Soc. Renaissance and Barque Hispanic Poetry.

FABRICATORE, CAROL DIANE, artist, educator; d. Sandy and Marilyn Fabricatore; m. David Robert Giroux, May 24, 1986; 1 child, Chloe. AA, Farmingdale U., 1978; BFA, Parsons Sch. Design, 1983; MFA, Sch. Visual Arts, 1992. Asst. dir. art Foote, Cone & Belding/Leber Katz, N.Y.C., 1984—87; freelance illustrator Briarcliff Manor, NY, 1987—. Illustrator The N.Y. Times, N.Y.C., 1992—; prof. Sch. Visual Arts, N.Y.C., 1994—. Contbr. artwork to jours., newspapers and mags.; illustrator: The Black Book, 2004 (Best of Show award, 2004); Exhibited in group shows at 407 Gallery, Chelsea, N.Y., 1996, The San Francisco (Calif.) Show, 2000 (Gold Winner award, 2000), No. Westchester (N.Y.) Ctr. Arts, 2000 (Best of Show award, 2000), SUNY Westchester C.C., 2002, Chung-Cheng Gallery St. John's U., 2004; selected for book and show: Graphis Annual Reports 9, 2005. Avocations: horseback riding, running. Personal E-mail: carol.fabricatore@att.net.

FABRY, MARILYN SUE, mathematician, educator; b. McAlester, Okla., June 13, 1953; d. Arthur and Laura Quadracci; children: Stephanie Renee, Andrew Michael. BS, Okla. State U., Stillwater, 1975. Math tchr. Carney Pub. Schs., Okla., 1975—79, Azle ISD, Tex., 1979—84, Crowley ISD, Tex., 1984—87, Grapevine-Colleyville ISD, Grapevine, Tex., 1987—93, Los Alamos Pub. Schs., N.Mex., 1994—. After sch. tutor/coord. Los Alamos Pub. Schs., 2003—06. Pianist White Rock Bapt. Ch., Los Alamos, 1994—99. Office Phone: 505-663-2549.

FABRY, VICTORIA JOAN, biology professor; BA in Biology, U. Calif., Santa Barbara, 1976, MA in Biology, 1983, PhD in Biology, 1988. Postdoctoral investigator chemistry dept. Woods Hole Oceanog. Instn., 1988—90; biogeochemist Marine Environment Lab. IAEA, Monaco, 1990—92; asst. prof. dept. biol. scis. Calif. State U., San Marcos, 1993—97, assoc. prof., 1997—2002, prof., 2002—. Chair dept. biol. scis. Calif. State U., San Marcos, 2000—02. Contbr. articles to profl. jours. Vol. fisheries dept. Peace Corps-Smithsonian Instn. Environ. Prog., Sabah, Malaysia, 1977—79. Recipient President's award, Innovation in Tchg., 2001, President's award, Scholarship and Creative Activity, 2006; grantee Nat. Sea Grant John Knauss Congressional fellowship, US Senate Commerce Com., 1984. Office: Dept Biol Scis Calif State U San Marcos 333 S Twin Oaks Valley Rd San Marcos CA 92096-0001 E-mail: fabry@csusm.edu.*

FACCIPONTI, LAURA LYNNE, theater educator; b. Easton, Pa., Mar. 9, 1964; d. Anthony Charles and Patricia Anne Facciponti. BFA in Related Arts, Kutztown U. Pa., 1986; MFA in Directing/Acting, Syracuse U., N.Y., 1991. CL4 cert. Alba Emoting instr. 2005. Asst. prof. theatre E. Stroudsburg U., Pa., 1995—98; assoc. prof. drama U. N.C., Asheville, 1998—. Adj. prof. Northampton C.C., Bethlehem, Pa., 1992—95. Author: (plays) The Place of the Great Turtle's Back, Birds of a Feather; actor: (plays) Boston Marriage, At the Black Pig's Dyke, The Seagull; dir.: Cloud Nine, How I Learned to Drive, Dancing At Lughnasa, The Shape of Things, Come Back to the Five and Dime, As You Like It, Free to Be You and Me, Wind of a Thousand Tales, Picnic, others. Mem.: Actor's Equity Assn. (life). Avocations: singing, art, travel. Office: U NC CPO # 1700 One University Heights Asheville NC 28804 Office Phone: 828-232-2992. Business E-Mail: lfacciponti@unca.edu.

FACKLER, ELIZABETH, writer; b. Lansing, Mich., May 23, 1947; d. Edward John and Mabel Marion (Jackson) Fackler; m. Michael Stoner Sinkovitz, Mar. 2, 1985. BA in Sociology cum laude, U. Calif., San Diego, 1977. Pub. Western Star Books. Author: (novels) Arson, 1984, Barbed Wire, 1986, Blood Kin, 1992, Backtrail, 1993, Road From Betrayal, 1994, Legend of El Chivato, 1995, Badlands, 1996, Texas Lily, 1997, Breaking Even, 1998, Patricide, 2000, When Kindness Fails, 2003, Endless River, 2005, Bone Justice, 2006, short stories, poetry. Mem.: Capitan Women's Club (pres.). Avocation: southwest history. E-mail: elizasin@trailnet.com.

FADDEN, SISTER R. PATRICIA, academic administrator, nun; b. Canonsburg, Pa. d. Gerald and Ruth Fadden. AB in Math., Immaculata Coll.; MA in Edn., Ohio State U.; EdD in Edn., Immaculata Coll. Tchr. elem. sch., 1960—68; tchr. West Cath. H.S. Girls, 1968—77; dir. of studies Cardinal O'Hara H.S., 1977—85; prin. Archbishop Prendergast H.S., Upper Darby, Pa., 1985—90; dir. secondary curriculum and instr. Office of Edn. Archdiocese of Phila., 1991—99; prin. Villa Maria Acad., Malvern, Pa., 1999—2002; pres. Immaculata U., Immaculata, Pa., 2002—. Mem. bd. trustees Immaculata Coll., 1991—2000, adj. faculty, 1991—2000; vice chair exec. com. Commn. on Secondary Schs. Mid. States Assn., mem. strategic planning com., mem. com. on instn.-wide accreditation, mem. com. to restructure; chair IHM Profl. Devel. Com., 1995—2000. Office: Immaculata Coll 1145 King Rd Immaculata PA 19345

FADER, SHIRLEY SLOAN, writer; b. Paterson, N.J. d. Samuel Louis and Miriam (Marcus) Sloan; m. Seymour J. Fader; children: Susan Deborah, Steven Micah Kimchi. BS, MS, U. Pa. Writer, journalist, author, Paramus, NJ. Chmn., coord. ann. writers seminar Bergen C.C., 1973-76. Author: (books) The Princess Who Grew Down, 1968, From Kitchen to Career, 1977, Jobmanship, 1978, Successfully Ever After, 1982 (Brit. edit. 1985), Wait a Minute: You Can Have It All, 1993, paperback edit., 1994; (columns) Jobmanship, People and You, Family Weekly mag., 1971-82, How to Get More From Your Job, Glamour mag., 1978-81, Start Here, Working Woman mag., 1980-88, Work Strategies, Working Mother mag., 1987-88, Women Getting Ahead, Ladies Home Jour., 1980-90, How Would You Handle It, New Idea mag., 1984—, Moving Up, Woman mag., 1989-90, Career Expert "Ask the Experts", Woman's World mag., 1992-95; contbg. editor Family Weekly, 1971-82, Glamour mag., 1978-81, Working Woman mag., 1980-88, Working Mother mag., 1987-88, Ladies Home Jour., 1980-90, Woman mag., 1989-90; contbr.: (book) Foundations of English, 2002; contbr. articles on career, relationships and travel to mags. worldwide. Mem. Authors Guild, Am. Soc. Journalists and Authors (moderator ann. writer's conf. 1971-2000, nat. v.p. 1976-77, mem.-at-large nat. exec. coun. 1976-78, 83-86, nat. sec., mem. exec. coun. 1995-96), Nat. Press Club, Newswomen of N.Y. Address: 377 Mckinley Blvd Paramus NJ 07652-4725

FADIMAN, ANNE, writer, educator; b. NYC, Aug. 7, 1953; d. Clifton and Annalee Whitmore (Jacoby) F.; m. George Howe Colt, Mar. 4, 1989; children: Susannah, Henry. BA, Harvard U., 1975. Contbr. editor Harvard Magazine, Cambridge, Mass., 1973-75; instr. Nat. Outdoor Leadership Sch., Lander, Wyo., 1975-76; columnist Country Journal, Manchester, N.H., 1978-79; asst. sci. editor Life, N.Y.C., 1979-81, columnist, 1986-87, staff writer, 1981-88; columnist, editor-at-large Civilization, Washington, 1994—97; editor The Am. Scholar, Washington, 1997—2004; Francis writer-in-residence Yale U., New Haven, 2005—. Bd. incorporators Harvard Magazine, Cambridge, Mass., 1985— (bd. dirs., 1985-91), vis. lectr. Smith Coll., 2000-02. Author: The Spirit Catches You and You Fall Down, 1997 (Nat. Book Critics Circle award for nonfiction, 1997, LA Times Book Prize for Current Interest, 1997, Ann Rea Jewell Non-Fiction Prize, Boston Book Rev., 1997), Ex Libris: Confessions of a Common Reader, 1998; editor: Best American Essays, 2003, Rereadings, 2005. Recipient Nat. Magazine award for Reporting, Am. Soc. Magazine Editors, 1987, Nat. Mag. award for essays, 2003; named John S. Knight fellow in Journalism Stanford (Calif.) U., 1991-92. Mem. Phi Beta Kappa (hon.).

FADLEY, ANN MILLER, language educator, literature educator; b. Ft. Worden, Wash., Nov. 22, 1933; d. Albert Delmar and Helen Elizabeth (Bush) Miller; m. Mit Rowley White, June 19, 1953 (div. Apr. 1977); children: Don M., Sharon L. White, Barbara A. White Salzman, Brian A.; m. John Lewis Fadley, Oct. 13, 1979 (dec. Jan., 1996). Student, Denison U., 1951-53; BA cum laude, Ohio State U., 1974, MA, 1976, PhD, 1986. Lectr. Ohio State U., Columbus, 1981-84; instr. Ohio Dominican Coll., Columbus, 1984-87; asst. prof. English, Marshall U., Huntington, W.Va., 1987-88; assoc. prof. English, Fla. So. Coll., Lakeland, 1988-99; ret., 1999. Adj. prof. Ohio U., Ironton, 1988; panelist pub. TV, Columbus, 1985; chmn. Nat. Poetry Day, 1991-97; chmn. vis. creative writers Fla. So. Coll., Lakeland, 1990-99. Author: (fiction and poetry) Onionhead, 1989, 95, (poetry) Birmingham Poetry Review, 1992, Heartbeat, 1994, pre-concert lecture for Nat. Shakespeare Co.'s As You Like It, Fla. So. Coll. Festival of Arts, Feb. 18, 1997; poetry readings Lakeland Choral Soc. Concert, Apr., 1997, Nat. Humanities Ctr., 1998, and many others; also articles and lit. criticisms; asst. editor Ohio Jour., 1975-76; founder, editor Cantilever Jours., 1989-96; vis. poet Fla. So. Coll., 1998, guest poet Cantilevers, 1999. Organizer, pres. Tri-Village Jr. C. of C. Wives Club, Columbus, 1959-60; awards chmn. Young Musician's competition; chair Ruth Flower Brown Scholarship, Huntington, 1988; contest supr., mem. com. SCORE, 1988; judge VFW Voice of Democracy contest, Lakeland, 1990, 91, Fla. state judge, 1992; trustee Christ United Meth. Ch., Lakeland, 1991-96, sec. trustees, 1991-93, 95, mem. bldg. com., organ fund task force, 1993-94, chairperson status and role of women, 1996-98, adminstrv. bd., 1996-98, women's exec. com., 2003—, pastor parish com., 2005-06, sec. com., 2005-06, lay mem. meth. conf., 2005-06, c0-chmn. Care Ministry, 2006; judge short fiction contest Nat. League Am. Pen Women Fla. State Assn. 1996, 98, short fiction and poetry contest, 1997, creative writing Polk County Citrus Festival, 1993, poetry contest Nat. League Am. Pen Women, Lakeland, Fla., 2000. Grantee Fla. Endowment Humanities, 1991, Jessie Ball duPont Found.Nat. Humanities Ctr., 1998; recipient Merit award Fla. Poets Competition, WORDART Soc., 1990, 96, 98, Distinction award, 1991, 97, recipient hon. mention Nat. League Am. Pen Women, Lakeland, 1993, 94, award hanging poetry Arts in the Park, Lakeland, 1993, 94, hanging poetry display Lake Morton Libr., 1994. Mem. Delta Delta Delta Republican. Avocations: gardening, swimming, fishing, decorating, travel.

FAGADAU, JEANNE MALKOFF, art dealer; d. Morris L. and Sally Malkoff; m. Sanford Payne Fagadau, Aug. 28, 1949; children: Warren, Leslie Newman, Thomas. BE, OH State U., 1950. Art dealer Fagadau and Wolens, Jeanne Fagadau Fine Art, 1980—95. Vol. bd. Nat. Sch. Vol. Program, 1972—75. Vol. coord. Dallas Ind. Sch. Dist., Dallas, 1970—80; pres. Southwest Family Inst., 1982—84; chmn. and mem. adv. bd. Arts Magnet HS, 1983—85; chair Magnet Sch. Edn.; mem. adv. bd. Arts and Humanities, U. Tex., Dallas. Mem.: Nat. Coun. Jewish Women (pres. Greater Dallas sect. 1968—70), Planned Parenthood, Dallas Mus. Art (Women's Coun. award 2003, Humanitarian award, Hannah Solomon award), Dallas Symphony (bd. mem. 1999—2006). Democrat. Jewish. Avocations: music, art, reading, walking, politics. Business E-Mail: Fagadauart@aol.com.

FAGER, HEATHER ELAINE, language educator; d. Jerre Edward and Barbara Lee Fager. BA in English, Mont. State U., Bozeman, 2001. Wilderness instr. Alternative Youth Adventures, Boulder, Mont., 2002—02; tchr. Eek Sch., Lower Kuskokwim Sch. Dist., Eek, Alaska, 2004—. Advisor student govt. Eek Student Governmetn, 2004—06. Trail crew vol. mem. Mont. Conservation Corps, Helena, 2001. Named Greek Woman Yr., MSU Panhellinic Coun., 1998. Mem.: Alpha Omicron Pi (pres. 1994—98). Avocations: painting, swimming, running, camping. Home: PO Box 8 Eek AK 99578 Office: Eek School PO Box 50 Eek AK 99578 Office Phone: 907-536-5228. Personal E-mail: heatherfager@mac.com. E-mail: heather_fager@lksd.org.

FAGIN, CLAIRE MINTZER, nursing educator, nursing administrator; b. NYC; d. Harry and Mae (Slatin) Mintzer; m. Samuel Fagin, Feb. 17, 1952; children: Joshua, Charles. BS, Wagner Coll., 1948; MA, Tchrs. Coll. Columbia, 1951; PhD, NYU, 1964; DSc (hon.), Lycoming Coll., 1983, Cedar Crest Coll., 1987, U. Rochester, 1987, Med. Coll. Pa., 1989, U. Md., 1993, Wagner Coll., 1993, Loyola U., 1996, Case Western Res. U., 2002; LLD (hon.), U. Pa., 1994, U. Toronto, 2004; DHL (hon.), Hunter Coll., 1993, Rush U., 1996, Johns Hopkins U., 2003. Staff nurse, clin. instr. Sea View Hosp., S.I., NY; clin. instr. Bellevue Hosp., N.Y.C.; psychiat. nurse cons. Nat. League for Nursing, N.Y.C.; asst. chief psychiat. nursing svc. clin. ctr. NIH; rsch. project coord. dept. psychiatry Children's Hosp., Washington; instr., assoc. prof. psychiat.-mental health nursing NYU, N.Y.C., dir. grad. programs in psychiat. mental health nursing, 1965—69; chmn. nursing dept., prof. Herbert H. Lehman Coll., CUNY, N.Y.C., 1969—77; dir. Health Professions Inst., Montefiore Hosp. and Med. Ctr., 1975—77; Margaret Bond Simon dean sch. of nursing U. Pa., Phila., 1977—92, Leadership chair prof., 1992—96, interim pres., 1993—94, dean emeritus, prof. emeritus, 1996—. Bd. dirs. Provident Mut. Ins. Co., 1988—96, chmn. audit com., 1985—96, exec. com., 1986—96, adv. com., 1996—2003; bd. dirs., mem. audit com. Salomon, Inc., 1994—97; bd. dirs., compensation Radian Inc., 1994—2002; bd. dirs. Vis. Nurse Soc., NY, Van Ameringen Found., 1996—2004, Nat. Sr. Citizens Law Ctr.; dir. program bldg. acad. geriatric nursing John A. Hartford Found., 2000—05; spkr., cons. in field. Contbr. articles to profl. jours. Named Disting. Dau. Pa., 1994; recipient Achievement award, Wagner Coll., 1956, Tchrs. Coll., 1975, Disting. Alumna award, NYU, 1979, Founders award, Sigma Theta Tau, 1981, Hon. Recognition award, ANA, 1988, Woman of Courage award, Women's Way, 1990, Alumni Merit award, U. Pa., 1991, First Leadership award, Trustee Coun. Pa. Women First, 1991, Caring award, Phila. Vis. Nurses Assn., 1994, Lillian Wald award, N.Y. Vis. Nurses Assn., 1994, Hildegard Peplau award outstanding contbn. psych-nursing, 1994, Pres. medal, NYU, 1998, Nightingale Lamp award, Am. Nurses Found., 2002; disting. scholar, 1984, hon. fellow, Royal Coll. Nursing, 2002. Mem.: Nat. League for Nursing (pres. 1991—93), Am. Orthopsychiat. Assn. (bd. dirs. 1972—75, exec. com. bd. dirs. 1973—75, pres. 1985—86), Am. Acad. Nursing (governing coun. 1976—78, Living Legend award 1998, Civitas award 2005, 2005), Inst. Medicine of NAS (governing coun. 1981—83, chmn. bd. health promotion and disease prevention 1991—94, mem./chair Lienhard Com. 1999—2004). Address: 200 Central Park S Apt 12E New York NY 10019-1415 Personal E-mail: cfagin@att.net.

FAGUNDO, ANA MARIA, language educator; b. Santa Cruz de Tenerife, Spain, Mar. 13, 1938; came to U.S., 1958; d. Ramón Fagundo and Candelaria Guerra de Fagundo. BA in English and Spanish, U. Redlands, 1962; MA in Spanish, U. Wash., 1964, PhD in Comparative Lit., 1967. Prof. contemporary lit. of Spain and creative writing U. Calif., Riverside, 1967—. Vis. lectr. Occidental Coll., Calif., 1967; vis. prof. Stanford U., 1984. Author 11 books of poetry including Invention de la Luz, 1977 (Carbala de Oro Poetry prize Barcelona 1977), Obra Poetica: 1965-90, 1990, Isla En Si., 1992, Antologia, 1994, El Sol, La Sombra En El Instante, 1994, La Miriada de Los Sonambulos, 1994, Trasterrado Marzo, 1999, Pacabras Sobre Las Dias, 2004, The Poetry of Ana Maria Fagundo: A Bilingual Anthology, 2005; founder, editor Alaluz, 1969—. Grantee Creative Arts Inst., 1970-71, Humanities Inst., 1973-74; Summer faculty fellow U. Calif., 1968, 77; Humanities fellow, 1969. Mem. Am. Assn. Tchrs. Spanish and Portuguese, Sociedad Gen. de Autores de Espana. Roman Catholic. Avocations: tennis, jogging, walking. Office: U Calif Spanish Dept Riverside CA 92521-0001 Home: Valdevarnes 13 5o D 28039 Madrid Spain

FAHEY, BARBARA STEWART DOE, public agency administrator; b. Chgo., Aug. 9, 1950; d. William Bethel and Doris (Charn) Doe. BA, U. Colo., 1972; MA, Sangamon State U., 1975. Dir. Wilderness Study Project, Springfield, Ill., 1973-75, Environ. Ctr., Boulder, Colo., 1976-79; natural resource specialist U.S. Bur. Reclamation, Denver, 1977-78; rsch. assoc. Nat. Conf. State Legislatures, Denver, 1979-80; asst. to transp. dir. City of Boulder, 1980-81, project mgr., 1981-85, parking coord., 1985-90, open space planner, 1991-92; interpretive park naturalist Jefferson County, Golden, Colo., 1992, adminstr. Nature Ctr., 1993-95; county dir. Colo. State U. Coop. Extension in Jefferson County, 1995—. Vice chmn. Boulder County Energy Adv. Com., Boulder, 1987; bd. mem. County Bd. Rev., Boulder, 1984-86, Historic Boulder, 1991-92. Bd. mem. Colo. Open Space Coun., Denver, 1979-80; mem. Leadership Boulder C. of C., 1986. Named Young Career Woman Colo. Bus. and Profl. Women's Fedn., Denver, 1981; recipient Innovation award Denver Coun. Govts., 1985, State Dir.'s Merit award, 1997, Nat. Program Leadership award Assn. Natural Resources Ext. Profls., 2002, State Program Excellence award Colo. Alliance for Environ. Edn., 2004. Mem. Nat. Assn. Interpretation, Denver Botanic Gardens, Denver Mus. Sci. and Nature, Colo. Native Plant Soc., Boulder Bus. and Profl. Women (treas. 1983-84, v.p. 1987-88, pres. 1989-90, winner speech contest 1985), Sierra Club (bd. mem. Sangamon Valley Group 1973-75). Avocations: cross country skiing, backpacking, hiking, classical and folk music. Office: 15200 W 6th Ave Ste C Golden CO 80401-6588 Office Phone: 303-271-6620. Business E-Mail: bfahey@co.jefferson.co.us.

FAHMIE, DEBORAH, music educator; b. Newark, Mar. 12, 1955; m. Anthony Fahmie, Feb. 25, 1978; children: Tara Ann, Christopher. B in Music Edn., Coll. N.J., 1977; MA in Music Edn., U. Ctrl. Fla., 2006. Cert. Music Education K-12 Fla. Music tchr. Osceola Dist. Schs., Kissimmee, Fla., 1988—; trainer Nat. Bds. Profl. Tchg. Stds., Arlington, Va., 2002—. Author Silver Burdett Pub. Co., 2001—03, Warner Bros. Publs., 2002—03. Author: (curriculum project) The Rainforest Project (Fla. Music Educator's Innovative Project of the Yr. award, 2004), (project developer) Falcon's Feast Dinner Theater (Sch. to Work, Best Practices award, 2000), (project development) Children's LitARTure. Working Artistically with Children's Literature (Disney Teacheriffic award, 1999), (project developer) Music and Movement Playtime for the Developing Brain (Disney Teacheriffic Award, 2002). Dir. Holy Redeemer Contemporary Choir, Kissimmee, Fla., 1983—2005; pres. Osceola Ctr. Arts, Kissimmee, Fla., 2000—03, Phi Delta Kappa, Osceola County, Fla., 2000—04; founder, pres. Arts for a Complete Edn. Coalition, Fla., 1995—2005; pres. Fla. Elem. Music Educators Assn., Fla., 2005—. Recipient United Arts Educator of the Yr. award, United Arts of Ctrl. Fl., 2001, ACE/FAAE Educator Yr., Arts for a Complete Edn., Fla. Alliance for Arts Edn., 2001; grantee FGrant funded project, Fla. Elem. Music Educators Assn., 1996, Arts for a Complete Edn. Tchr. Incentive Grant, Arts for a Complete Edn., 1998, 2001, 2002; scholar Am. Orff Schulwerk Assn. Nat. Scholarship Program, Am. Orff Schulwerk Assn., 1996; grant funded project, Osceola Found. for Edn. Grant, 1995, 1998, 2000. 2002, Chpt. VI from the Dept. of Edn., 1993, 1996, 2000. Mem.: Fla. Music Mentors Assn., Fla. League of Arts Tchrs., Ctrl. Fla. Orff Chpt. (sec. 1998—2001), Am. Orff Schulwerk Assn., Fla. Elem. Music Educator's Assn. (pres. 2000—05), Phi Delta Kappa (past pres. 1998—2005). Achievements include development of AmeriCorp Arts Project for the Boys and Girls Clubs of Greater Tampa Bay; Writing team for Grade level expectations in music education; Task force and writing team for Florida Music Assessment Project; Music subtest development committee for Institute for Instructional Research and Practice; Team building for Disney Executive Team Retreats. Home: 958 Florida Pkwy Kissimmee FL 34743 Office: Cypress Elem 2251 Lakeside Dr Kissimmee FL 34743 Office Phone: 407-344-5000. Home Fax: 407-344-5006; Office Fax: 407-344-5006. E-mail: fahmied@osceola.k12.fl.us.

FAHMY HUDOME, RANDA, lawyer; b. Syracuse, N.Y., Feb. 4, 1964; d. Mahmoud Hussein and Irandukht (Vahidi) F.; m. Michael Hudome; 1 child, Alexandria. BA summa cum laude, Wilkes U., 1986; JD, Georgetown U., 1990. Fin. dir. Holtzman for Congress, Wilkes-Barre, Pa., 1986; lobbyist Citizens for Am., Washington, 1987; legal asst. Hamlin Blaszkow, Washington, 1987; with Koonz, McKenney & Johnson, Washington, 1988, Willkie, Farr & Gallagher, Washington, 1989-90, assoc., 1990—94; fgn. policy counsel to Sen. Spencer Abraham U.S. Senate, 1994—2001; assoc. dep. sec. energy Pres. George W. Bush, 2002—03; pres. Fahmy Hudome Internat., 2004—. Apptd. Md. Comm. for Women; dir. Muslim Women Lawyers for Human Rights. Adminstrv. editor Law and Policy in Internat. Bus., 1989-90. Mem. Rep. Nat. Lawyers Assn., Washington, 1990—. Mem. Internat. Law Soc. Georgetown U. Law Sch. (bd. dirs. Washington chpt. 1988-89), Md. Bar Assn., DC Bar Assn., U.S. Ct. Internat. Trade. Office: Fahmy Hudome Internat LLC 815 Connecticut Ave NW #200 Washington DC 20006 Office Phone: 202-429-5566. Office Fax: 202-429-5577. E-mail: randa@fahmyhudome.com.

FAHNESTOCK, JEAN HOWE, retired civil engineer; b. Pitts., May 22, 1930; d. James Murray and Hazel Margaret (Alberts) F. AA, Stephens, 1950; BS in Civil Engring., Carnegie-Mellon, 1955. Registered profl. engr., Ill., Mich., Iowa. Sr. project mgr. De Leuw, Cather & Co., Chgo., 1955-92; ret. Design mgr. De Leuw, Cather & Co., Kuwait, 1978-81, Abu Dhabi, 1981-85, Kennedy Expy. and Elgin-O'Hare Expy., Chgo., 1985-92. Fellow ASCE (life); mem. NSPE, Ill. Soc. Profl. Engrs. (life). Republican. Presbyterian. Avocations: bridge, travel, politics. Home: 4606 W Bryn Mawr Ave Chicago IL 60646-6632 Personal E-mail: jhf4606@comcast.net.

FAHRBACH, RUTH C., state legislator; b. NYC; Grad. high sch., East Meadow, N.Y. Mem. Dist. 61 Conn. Ho. of Reps., 1981—, minority whip, mem. appropriations com., pub. health com., legis. mgmt. com., select com. of inquiry. Active Windsor Rep. Town Com.; mem. Windsor Bd. Edn., 1977-81, v.p., 1979-80; bd. dirs. Celebrate Windsor, Inc., 2001-04, 05—; local emergency planning com. mem., 2003-. Mem. First Dist. Rep. Womens Club, Fedn. Rep. Women, Civitan Club Windsor (past pres), Nat. Order of Women Legislators, Conn. Order of Women Legislators (sec.), Conn. Fedn. of Rep. Women, Nat. Fedn. of Republican Women, St. Casimir's Lithuanian Club Women's Aux. Home: 592 Poquonock Ave Windsor CT 06095-2204 Office: Legis Office Bldg Rm 4200 Hartford CT 06106-1591 Business E-Mail: ruth.fahrbach@housegop.po.state.ct.us.

FAHRENWALD, NANCY LYNN, nursing educator, researcher; b. Huron; m. Carl R. Fahrenwald. PhD, U. Nebr., Omaha, 2002. RN SD. Nursing faculty mem. SD State U., Brookings, 1995—. Office: South Dakota State University Box 2275 Brookings SD 57007 Office Phone: 605-688-4098.

FAHRINGER, CATHERINE HEWSON, retired savings and loan association executive; b. Phila., Aug. 1, 1922; d. George Francis and Catherine Gertrude (Magee) Hewson; m. Edward F. Fahringer, July 8, 1961 (dec.); 1 child, Francis George Beckett. Grad. diploma, Inst. Fin. Edn., 1965. Notary pub. Fla. With Centrust Bank (formerly Dade Savs. and Loan Assn.), Miami, 1958—85; v.p. Centrust Bank, Miami, 1967—74, sr. v.p., 1974—82, sec., 1975—79, head savs. pers. and mktg. divsn., 1979—83, exec. v.p. office of chmn., 1984, dir., 1984—90, co-chmn. audit com. of bd. dirs., 1990; referral assoc. Referral Network Inc. subs. Coldwell Banker, 1990—. Pub. arbitrator NASD, 1999-2005. Contbr. articles to profl. jours. Trustee United Way of Dade County (Fla.), 1980-87, chmn. audit com. 1982-84, trustee, Pub. Health Trust, Dade County, 1974-84, sec. 1976, vice chmn., 1977-78, chmn. bd., 1978-81; mem. adv. coun. Women's Bus. Devel. Ctr., Fla. Internat. U., 1993-95; mem. spl. steering com. Breast Cancer Task Force, Jackson Meml. Hosp., 1991; hon. bd. govs. U. Miami, Soc. for Rsch. in Med. Edn.; trustee South Fla. Blood Svc., Miami, 1979-84, vice chmn., 1980, chmn., 1981-84; trustee Dade County Vocat. Found., 1977-81; trustee Fla. Internat. U. Found., 1976-90; trustee emeritus, 1990, v.p. bd., 1978-81, pres. 1982-84; bd. dirs. Sta. WPBT-TV, 1984-2002, founding lifetime dir., 1995, chmn. budget and fin. com., 1986, mem. exec. com. 1985-92, sec. 1987, investment com., 1988-90, vice chmn. 1988-92, mem. fin. com., 1992, chmn. audit and control com., 1994, 2000, 2001, mem., 1997-98; bd. dirs., mem. nominating com. Girl Scout Coun., Tropical Fla., 1985-89, chmn. 1988-89, mem. long range planning com., 1986-88; citizens oversight com. Dade County Pub. Sch. System, 1986-90, chmn. 1988-90; bd. dirs. New World Sch. of Arts, 1987-90, chmn. devel. com., 1987-90, chair New World Sch. of Arts Gala, 1990; mem. Disaster Relief Com., chair Hurricane Disaster Relief Distbn. Ctr., 1992; mem. fin. commn., chmn. capital improvement fund com. Coral Gables Congrl. Ch., summer concert series com., chmn. refreshement sub-com.; commd. Stephen min., 1995—; mem. grievance com. 11th Jud. Cir. Fla. Bar, 1988-92; bd. trustees United Protestant Appeal, 1994-96; mem. parking adv. bd. City of Coral Gables, 1997-98, bd. of adjustments, 1998—, vice chmn., 2001—2003, chmn.2003—; mem., 3rd v.p. Bush chpt. Women's Cancer Assn. U. Miami, 1997-99, 2nd v.p., treas. and parliamentarian, 1999-2001, chmn. meml. fund, 1998-2003, 3rd v.p., 2002-03. Named Women of Yr. in fin., Zonta Internat., 1975, amb., Air Def. Arty., 1970, U.S. Army Air Def. Command, 1970, Woman of Yr. in Sports, Links Club, 1986, First Lady of Athletics, Fla. Internat. U., 2003; recipient Trail Blazer award, Women's Coun. of 100, 1977, Cmty. Headliner award, Women in Comm., 1983, Outstanding Citizen of Dade County award, 1984, Honors and Recognition award, Golden Panthers Club of Fla. Internat. U., 1989, Disting. Svc. and Leadership award, Fla. Internat. U., 1991, apprecation, New World Sch. of the Arts, 1990, Meritorious Pub. Svc. award, Fla. Bar, 1991, Outstanding Svc. award, Country Club Coral Gables, 2001, hon. BA, U. Hard Knocks Alderson-Broaddus Coll., 1987, Key to City of Coral Gables for Cmty. Svc., 2000, Dedicated Svc. award, Women's Cancer Assn. of U. Miami, 2001, Outstanding Svc. Award, 2001, Woman's Day Disting. Woman of Svc. Recognition, Coral Gables Congregational Ch., 2006. Mem.: LWV, Women's Union Russia, Fla. Women's Alliance (bd. dirs. 1983—91, pres. 1987—89), Internat. Women's Alliance, Savs. and Loan Pers. Soc. South Fla., Savs. and Loan Mktg. Soc. South Fla. (past pres.), Inst. Fin. Edn. (life; nat. dir., past pres. Local Greater Miami chpt.), Greater Miami Women's Golf Assn. (social dir. 1999—2001), Greenway Women's Golf Assn. (treas. 1988—89), Balt. Women's Golf Assn., Fla. Internat. U. Athletics Club, Golden Panther Club (bd. dirs. 1988—, v.p. 1991, pres. 1992—94), Links Fla. Internat. U. Club (v.p. 1992, bd. dirs., sec.), Country Club Coral Gables (treas. women's golf assn 1988—89, sec., bd. dirs., found. trustee 1993, v.p. bd. dirs. 1994, pres. 1995, chmn. bldg. restoration, capital improvement and maintenance com. 1995—99, bd. advisor 1996—99, liaison City of Coral Gables 1997—99, rear commodore, vice commodore, historian, adv., chair The Fleet 1998, commodore 1999, publicity chmn. woman's bd. 2000—01, pres. women's golf assn. 2001—02, mem. adv. bd. dirs. 2002—, golf adv., directory chair 2003—06), Dade Bus. and Profl. Women's Club (past pres.). Democrat.

FAIGAO, WENDY KALAYAAN, musician, music company executive; b. N.Y., N.Y., Jan. 26, 1971; d. Bataan Go and Jane Greeley Faigao. Freelance musician, Boulder, Colo., 1992—; engr., prodr. Sky Trail Studio, Boulder, 1997—2000; prin., owner WooMusic, Inc., Denver, 2004—. Tchr. music Naropa U., Boulder, 2002, 04, Swallow Hill, Denver, 2004—05; cons. in field. Musician (prodr.): (albums) Wide Awake & Dreaming, 1999, Ecolalia, 2000 (Best Album award Westword Mag., 2000, named to Best Colo. CDs of Yr. list), Gonna Wear Red, 2002 (named to Best Colo. CDs of Yr. list), Walking The Skyline, 2004, Angels Laughing, 2005; musician: (TV films) Uncommon Goals, 1999, Mountain of Dreams, 2003, (TV series) FoodNation with Bobby Flay, Good Day Colo. theme song. Named Best Singer Songwriter, Denver's (Colo.) Westword Mag., 1998, 1999, 2002, 2003, 2004, Winner, Lillith Fair Talent Search, 1999, Ind. Artist of Yr., Hapi Skratch Entertainment, 2003, Best Boulder Musician, The Boulder (Colo.) Weekly, 2004, Best Singer/Songwriter, The Boulder (Colo.) Daily Camera, Best Local Artist, Colo. Daily. Avocations: gardening, walking, hiking, running, rollerblading. Office: WooMusic Inc PO Box 18818 Denver CO 80218

FAIKS, JAN OGOZALEK, lobbyist; b. Nov. 17, 1945; d. Edmund Frank and Anna Marie (Chupella) Ogozalek. BA, Fla. State U., 1967. Tchr. Anchorage (Alaska) Sch. Dist., 1968—76, counselor, 1976—78; owner, mgr. Green Connection, Anchorage, 1978—81; mem. Alaska State Senate, Alaska, 1982, pres., 1982; now lobbyist, v.p., govt. affairs Pharm. Rsch. and Mfrs. Assn. Am. (PhRMA), Washington, 2004—. Author: Llama Training-Who's In Charge, 1981; editor: course devel. in career math., 1976. Rsch. chmn., v.p. Common Sense for Alaska, 1980—82; bd. dirs. People Against State Income Tax, 1979—, Common Sense for Alaska, 1980—, Anchorage (Alaska) Symphony, 1984, Alaska Spl. Olympics. Named Outstanding Secondary Tchr., Anchorage Sch. Dist., 1977; recipient First Lady vol. award, Gov. of Alaska, 1981, Pres.'s award, Common Sense for Alaska, 1981. Mem.: Nat. Coun. State Legislators, Anchorage (Alaska) Symphony Women's League (pres. 1980—81), Anchorage (Alaska) C. of C. (legis. chmn. 1980—82, exec. com. 1981—82, bd. dirs. 1981—), Gen. Fedn. Women's Club (legis. chmn. 1979—82), Phi Beta Phi (pres. 1974—76). Republican. Presbyn. Avocations: backpacking, fishing, llamas. Office: PhRMA 1100 Fifteenth St NW Washington DC 20005

FAIN, CHERYL ANN, translator, editor; b. Providence, May 16, 1953; d. Harry and Pearl (Friedman) F. Student, U. Salzburg, Austria, 1973-74; BA with high distinction, U. R.I., 1975; MA, postgrad. cert. Eng.-German Transl., Monterey Inst. Internat. Studies, 1978. Cert. translator German-English, French-English Am. Translators Assn. Freelance German and French transl. various govt. agys., transl. burs., record co., pvt. clients, Washington, Balt. and Monterey, Calif., 1976—; in-house German and French med. translator Social Security Adminstrn., Balt., 1984-94; German/French trans. Embassy of Switzerland, Washington, 1994—, sci. and tech. specialist, 1994—2003; U.S. policy analyst, 2003—. Mem. Swiss delegation to the European Space Agy. Internat. Space Sta. Working Group, Washington, 1994-2003. Translator: Perspectives on Mozart, 1978, also various articles and liner notes, program notes, U.S., Switzerland; contbr. articles to popular mags. and jours. Mem.: Nat. Capital Area Transl.'s Assn. (spkr. Translating for Foreign Governments seminar 2004), Am. Translators Assn., Sci. Diplomats' Club of Washington, Phi Kappa Phi. Avocations: international travel, performance in operas, choral concerts and plays. Home: 2401 Calvert St NW Apt 421 Washington DC 20008-2667 Office: Embassy of Switzerland 2900 Cathedral Ave NW Washington DC 20008-3499 Business E-Mail: cheryl.fain@eda.admin.ch.

FAIN, NICOLE M., elementary school educator; b. Park Ridge, Ill., Apr. 1, 1981; d. Ronald and Linda Fain. BA in History and Secondary Edn., Northeastern Ill. U., Chgo., 2003; postgrad., Aurora U., Williams Bay, Wis. Tchr. Northwood Mid. Sch., Woodstock, Ill., 2004—. Home: 6315 Ojibwa Ln Mchenry IL 60050 Office: Northwood Mid Sch 2121 N Seminary Ave Woodstock IL 60098 Office Phone: 815-338-4900. Personal E-mail: nfain@d200.mchenry.k12.il.us.

FAIR, JEAN EVERHARD, retired education educator; b. Evanston, Ill., July 21, 1917; d. Drury Hampton and Bess Marion (Everhard) F. BA, U. Ill., 1938; MA, U. Chgo., 1939, PhD, 1953. Tchr. Evanston (Ill.) Twp. High Sch., 1940-48, 1954-58; tchr. U. Minn. High Sch., 1948-49, U. Ill. High Sch., 1951-53; prof. edn. Wayne State U., Detroit, 1958-82, now prof. emeritus. Cons. in edn.; cons. Mich. Ednl. Goals, Objectives and Assessment in Social Studies; reviewer of position statements for teaching and learning, standards, assessment and other manuscripts for Nat. Coun. Social Studies. Contbr. articles to profl. jours. Mem. AAUW, Nat. Council for Social Studies (pres. 1972, dir. 1958-61, 73-75), Assn. for Supervision and Curriculum Devel., Social Sci. Edn. Consortium, LWV, Phi Beta Kappa. Mem. United Ch. Christ.

FAIR, KATHLEEN MARGARET, elementary school educator; b. Pitts., Oct. 15, 1946; d. Norman Morgan and SueBeth (Archer) F. BA, Coll. Wooster, 1968; MA, Brown U., 1970, postgrad., Washington U., St. Louis, U. R.I., Salve Regina. Tchr. Wheeler Sch., Providence, R.I., 1969-75, Friends Acad., Dartmouth, Mass., 1975—. Contbr. articles to profl. jours. Mem. Dartmouth Hist. Commn., 1979—2002; mem. Dartmouth Town Meeting, 1988—; bd. dirs. Waterfront Area League, New Bedford, Mass., 1992, Big Sister Program, New Bedford, 1990-92. Mem. Nat. Coun. Social Studies. Avocations: needlecrafts, minatures, reading. Office: Friends Acad Tucker Rd North Dartmouth MA 02747

FAIRBAIRN, BARBARA JEAN, university administrator; b. N.Y.C., May 31, 1950; d. Desmond Noble and Anne Elizabeth (Fisher) F. BA, Stetson U., 1972; MS, W.Va. U., 1976. Dir. svcs. for students with disabilities SUNY, Binghamton, NY, 1977—. Bd. dirs. Sheltered Workshop for Disabled, Inc., Binghamton; elder Conklin Presbyn. Ch.; lay preacher Susquehanna Valley Presbytery. Named Woman of Achievement, Soroptimists at Broome County Status of Women Coun., 1985. Mem. Assn. for Higher Edn. and Disability. Avocations: acting, singing, travel. Office Phone: 607-777-2686. Business E-Mail: bjfair@binghamton.edu.

FAIRBAIRN, JOYCE, Canadian government official; b. Lethbridge, Alta., Can., Nov. 6, 1939; m. Michael Gillan (dec.). BA in English, U. Alta., 1960; B Journalism, Carleton U., 1961. Mem. news staff Ottawa (Ont., Can.) Jour., 1961; mem. staff parliamentary press gallery UPI, Ottawa, 1962-64; mem. staff parliamentary bur. F.P. Publs., 1964-70; legis. asst., sr. legis. advisor Prime Minister of Can. Pierre Elliott Trudeau, 1970-84, comms. coord., 1981-83; mem. Senate for Province of Alta., 1984—, appt. to privy coun., leader govt., 1993-97, minister with spl. responsibility for literacy, 1993-97, spl. advisor for literacy, 1997. Mem. Spl. Senate Com. on Youth, Senate Standing Coms. on Transp. and Comm., Legal and Constl. Affairs, Fgn. Affairs, Agr. and Forestry, mem. senate social affairs com.; founding mem. standing com. on Aboriginal peoples; chair spl. com. on Anti-Terrorism, 2001, 05; vice chair Nat. Liberal Caucus and Western and No. Liberal Caucus, 1984-91; co-chair nat. campaign com. Liberal Party of Can., 1991. Past mem. senate U. Lethbridge; inducted into Kainai Chieftanship, Blood Nation, pres., 2004—; chmn. Friends of Can. Paralympics, 1998-2003; chmn. bd. dirs. Can. Paralympic Found., 2003—. Named hon. col. 18th Air Def. Regt., Royal Can. Army. Office: Can Senate 571-S Centre Block Ottawa ON Canada K1A 0A4 Office Phone: 613-996-4382. E-mail: fairbj@sen.parl.gc.ca.

FAIRBAIRN, URSULA FARRELL, human resources executive; b. Newark, Feb. 5, 1943; d. Henry C. and Clara J. (Ziefle) Otte; m. William Todd Fairbairn III, May 14, 1978; children: W. Todd, Mary, Joyce Sjoberg. BA, Upsala Coll., 1965; MAT in Math., Harvard U., 1966. Instr., numerous mktg. positions IBM, N.Y.C., 1966-78; exec. asst. to sec., White House fellow U.S. Treasury Dept., Washington, 1973-74; exec. asst. to chmn. bd., group dir. IBM, Armonk, N.Y., 1978-79, v.p. mgmt. svcs., then v.p. mktg. ops. west, 1980-84, dir. pers. resources, 1984-87, dir. bus. and mgmt. edn., 1987, dir. edn., 1987-89, dir. edn. and mgmt. devel., 1989-90; sr. v.p. human resources Union Pacific Corp., Bethlehem, Pa., 1990-96; exec. v.p. human resources and quality Am. Express Co., N.Y.C., 1996—2005; pres. CEO Fairbairn Group, LLC, 2005—. Bd. dirs. VF Corp., Greensboro, N.C., Air Products Corp., Allentown, Pa., Sunoco Corp., Phila., Circuit City Stores, Inc., Richmond, Centex Corp., Dallas. Contbg. author: Managing Human Resources in the Information Age, 1991. Mem. Com. of 200, Catalyst, N.Y.C.; vice-chair Nat. Acad.-HR; chair Pers. Round Table. Mem. Bus. Roundtable, Employee Rels. Com., Labor Policy Assn. Avocations: gardening, art, reading, walking, travel. Office: Centex Corp 2728 N Harwood St Dallas TX 75201-1516 Office Phone: 214-981-5000. Office Fax: 214-981-6859.

FAIRBANKS, CYNTHIA, secondary school educator; b. Houston, Nov. 6, 1957; d. Hardy Ewald Fairbanks and Doris Eby. BA, Houston Bapt. U., 1980; MEd, U. of Tex., Austin, 1984. Cert. tchr. Tex. Edn. Agy., 1980. Dept. chair/social studies Sharpstown H.S., Houston, 2000—, instrnl. coach, 2006—. Project mgr. social studies curriculum Region IV, Houston. Musician West U. Bapt. Ch., Houston, 1975—2006. Mem.: Houston Coun. for Social Studies. Christian. Avocations: golf, music, sports, reading. Office Phone: 713-771-7215.

FAIRCHILD, DORCAS SEXTON, language educator; b. Persia, Tenn., June 21, 1938; d. Philip Riley Sr. and Eula Kate (Robinette) Sexton; m. Joe Elmer Fairchild, Apr. 2, 1969. BS, East Tenn. State U., 1960. Cert. secondary English and social studies tchr., Tenn. English tchr. Rogersville (Tenn.) H.S., 1960-80, Cherokee Comprehensive H.S., Rogersville, 1980—, chmn. English dept., 1993—. Sponsor Beta Club, Rogersville, 1984—. Stock Market Game, Rogersville, 1989—. Sunday sch. tchr. Marion Robinette Meml. Ch., Rogersville, 1975—. Mem. NEA, Tenn. Edn. Assn., East Tenn. Edn. Assn., Hawkins County Edn. Assn., Nat. Coun. Tchrs. of English, Tenn. Coun. Tchrs. of English, Delta Kappa Gamma (pres. 1972-74). Republican. Avocations: reading, walking, crocheting. Home: 110 Par 3 Cir Rogersville TN 37857-3916 Office: Cherokee Comprehensive HS 2927 Highway 66 S Rogersville TN 37857-5169

FAIRCHILD, PHYLLIS ELAINE, school counselor; b. Franklin, La., Feb. 23, 1927; d. Joseph Virgil and Georgiana (Bourgeois) F. BS in Chemistry and Biology, U. Southwestern La., 1946; postgrad., La. State U., 1949-50, MEd in Guidance, 1966. Cert. chemistry, biology, gen. sci., Spanish and social studies tchr., counselor, La. Tchr. sci. St. Mary Parish Sch. Bd., Franklin, 1952—58, counselor, 1977—82; tchr. sci. Am. Dependent Schs., Yokohama, Japan, 1958—60, London, Lakenheath, England, 1960—61, Ramey AFB, PR, 1961—62, Norfolk City Schs., Va., 1962—63, Iberville Parish Sch. Bd., Plaquemine, La., 1963—66; tchr. sci., counselor East Baton Rouge Parish Sch. Bd., Baton Rouge, 1966—77; counselor Hanson Sch. Bd., Franklin, 1982—94, 1996—98; ret., 1998. Mem. adv. com. La. Dept. Edn., Baton Rouge, 1976, 78. Mem. DAR (regent Attakapas chpt. 2003—, dir. 6th Dist. 2004—), Coun. on Aging Bd., La. Landmarks Soc., Cath. Daus. Am. (co-chmn. religious litergy 1992-94), Fortnightly Lit. Club (pres. 1982-83), Sigma Delta Pi, Pi Gamma Mu, Kappa Kappa Gamma, Delta Kappa Gamma (chmn. membership, scholarship, profl. affairs 1971-77, parliamentarian 1996-98). Avocations: reading, walking, piano, writing. Home: 214 Morris St Franklin LA 70538-6127 Personal E-mail: Phyllis@teche.net.

FAIRCLOTH, MARY WILLIAMS, minister, educator; d. Willie Sylvester and Katie Ruth Williams; m. Alonzo Vernon Faircloth, Nov. 23, 1978. BS in Mgmt., Rutgers U., 1978; MDiv, New Brunswick Theol. Sem., 1995. Mgmt. staff Port Authority N.Y. and N.J., N.Y.C., 1967—95, adminstrv. asst., 1978—84; clin. chaplain Ctr. for Hope, Linden, NJ, 1995—96, Dobbs Youth Devel. Ctr., Kinston, NC, 1997—2000; pastor Anderson Chapel AME Ch. AME Ch., Inc., Greenville, NC, 1998—; prof. ethics/religion/philosophy Shaw U., Raleigh/Greenville, NC. Ch. growth and devel. AME Ch., Greenville, 1999—. Tchr., organizer, youth leader Dobbs Youth Devel. Ctr., Kinston, 1998—2002. Recipient Cert. of Achievement, Pitt County Meml. Hosp., 1997, 1998, 1999. Mem.: Assn. Seminarians (life; pres./v.p. 1992—94, Cert. of Achievement 1995). Methodist. Avocations: travel, reading, writing, antiques, cooking. Home: 208 Buckingham Dr Winterville NC 28590-9418 Office: Anderson Chapel AME Church PO Box 30791 3788 Ivan Harris Rd Greenville NC 27833 Office Phone: 252-746-8427. Personal E-mail: andersonchapame@aol.com.

FAIRFIELD, PAULA KATHLEEN, sound recording engineer; b. Halifax, N.S., Can., Sept. 17, 1961; d. Henry Alfred and Sylvia Kathleen Fairfield; life ptnr. Carla Mary Murray. BFA, N.S. Coll. of Art and Design, Halifax, 1984. Freelance sound editor, Toronto, Ont., Canada, 1987—97; freelance picture editor, 1987—96; gen. mgr. Charles St. Video, Toronto, Ont., Canada, 1987—94; sec. treas. Pandora Pictures Inc, Toronto, Ont., Canada, 1987—98; pres. MHz Sound Design Inc, Toronto, Ont., Canada, 1997—2000, L.A., 1998—. Cons., design arts Ont. Arts Coun., Toronto, 1992; sr. tech. wirer CTV Networks, Network Relocation and Olympic installation, Toronto, 1994—95; instr., post prodn. sound Ont. Coll. of Art and Design, Toronto, 1997; sound supr., sound designer The Black Dahlia. Dir.: (electronic media installation) MIRAGE, (short film) Screamers, Livewires, Fragments; sound effects editor and sound designer (feature film) Sin City, sound supervisor and sound designer (television series) La femme Nikita, sound effects editor and sound designer Due South, artist (exhibition group) Retrospective of Canadian Film and Video, George Pompidou Centre, Paris, Anteneo Femista De Madrid, Madrid, sound supr. and sound designer (feature film) Assault on Precinct 13, artist (exhibition group) Olympic Musem, Sarajevo, Museum of Modern Art, Zagreb, Croatia, Bienal De La Imagen En Movimento, Madrid, Infermental 10: There-Between-Here, Osnabruck, sound effects editor (feature film) A Love Song for Bobby Long, sound effects editor and sound designer Terminator 3: Rise of the Machines, Spy Kids 3D: Game Over; sound editor, designer: (feature film) The Black Dahlin, 2006; Lucky Number Slevin, 2006. Jury mem. and adjudicator Can. Coun. for the Arts, Ottawa, 1989—97, Toronto Arts Coun., Toronto, 1989—97, Ont. Arts Coun., Toronto, Ontario, 1990—97. Recipient B award, Can. Coun. for the Arts, 1992, Gemini Award for Achievement in Sound Editing: Due South, Acad. of Can. Cinema and TV, 1996, Can. Musicvideo VideoFACT Award, 1994; grantee audio prodn. grantee, Can. Coun. for the Arts, 1990, Explorations grantee, Can. Coun. for the Art, 1990, Video Prodn. grantee, 1989, 1987, Photography grantee, 1986, Film Prodn. grantee, Ont. Arts Coun., 1993, Video Prodn. grantee, 1992, Audio Prodn. grantee, Can. Coun. for the Arts, 1999, 1992, Film Prodn. grantee, 1994. Mem.: Am. Film Inst., Women in Film, L.A., Am. Working Malinois Assn., United Schutzhund Clubs of Am., Audio Engring. Soc., Soc. of Motion Picture and TV Engrs., Motion Picture Editors Guild, Internat. Alliance of Theatrical Stage Emplyees, Moving Picture Technicians, Artists and Allied Crafts, Profl. Orgn. of Women in Entertainment Reaching Up (founding mem. 2000—03), S.W. Working Dog Assn. Office Phone: 818-980-0306.

FAIRHURST, MARY E., state supreme court justice; b. 1957; BA in Polit. Sci. cum laude, Gonzaga U., 1979, JD magna cum laude, 1984. Bar: Wash. 1984. Jud. clk. to Hon. William H. Williams Wash. Supreme Ct., 1984, jud. clk. to Hon. William C. Goodloe, 1986; chief revenue, bankruptcy and collections divsn. Wash. Atty. Gen.'s Office, 1986—2002; justice Wash. Supreme Ct., Olympia, 2003—. Mem. Wash. Supreme Ct. Gender and Justice Commn., Access to Justice Bd. Com. Established Lawyers and Students Engaged in Resolution Program; mem. Girl Scouts Bd. of Pacific Peak Council; mem. bd. advisors Gonzaga Law Sch. Recipient Steward of Justice award, 1998, Allies for Justice award, LEGALS, P.S., 1999. Mem.: Wash. Women Lawyers (past pres., Passing the Torch award 1999), Wash. State Bar Assn. (past. pres., mem. bd. govs.). Office: Wash Supreme Ct PO Box 40929 415 12th Ave SW Olympia WA 98504-0929 Business E-Mail: J_M_Fairhurst@courts.wa.gov.*

FAIRLIE, CAROL HUNTER, artist, art educator; b. White Plains, NY, Dec. 14, 1952; d. Robert Fairlie; m. Jiri Dolezal, Sept. 18, 1988. MFA, U. North Tex., 1990—93. Four Year Cert., Painting Penn. Acad. Fine Arts, 1974. Lectr. U. North Tex., SOVA, Denton, Tex., 1993; assoc. prof. art Sul Ross State U., Alpine, Tex., 1996—. Newsletter editor, Nat. Watercolor Soc., Los Angeles, Calif., 2002—04. Exhibitions include Glass-Scapes, Houston, Plate Glass, West Tex. Signature Watercolor Exhbn., Nat. Competition, FAC Contemporary Artists, Nat. Competition, Laredo Internat. Watercolor Exhbn., Ariz. Aqueous, IX/94, Nat. Competition, WASH Internat. Juried Exhbn., Watercolor USA, Nat. Competition, Pa. Acad. Fellowship Exhbn., Pa. Watercolor Soc. Nat. Exhbn., Noyes Museum, Oceanville, NJ, Side By Side NWS/PWCS Watercolor Exhbn. (Barnett Meml. Award, 2002), Watercolor Mo. Nat. Works on Paper Exhbn., La. Nat. Watercolor Exhbn., Western Colo. Watercolor Exhbn., Krasdale Gallery Corp. Exhbn., Krasdale Galleries, Pa. Watercolor Soc., Nat. Competition, Pa. Acad. Fellowship Exhbn., Nat. Watercolor Soc./ Phila. Watercolor Soc., 2004—05, one-woman shows include Enclosure, Irving Arts Assn., Brno-Dallas Sister City Exch., Ivancice Cultural Ctr., Laredo Ctr. for the Arts, Alpine Gallery Night, Salon 109, North Harris Coll., exhibitions include Kansas Watercolor Soc. Great 8, 2005. Co dir. Desert Islander Tahitian Dance Troupe, Alpine, Tex., 1996—2003; costume and programs Big Bend Players, Theatrical Group, Alpine, Tex., 2002—03; juror Region 18 H.S. Art programs, All area, west Tex., Tex., 1999—2006; treas. Alpine Family Crisis Ctr., Alpine, Tex., 2001—06, Alpine Pub. Libr., Alpine, Tex., 1998—2006; v.p. Purple Sage Women's Club, Alpine, Tex., 2000—02; treas. Alpine Women's Club, Alpine, Tex., 1998—99. Fellow: Pa. Acad. Fine Arts; mem.: Big Bend Arts Coun. (pres. 2004—06), Phila. Watercolor Assn., Pa. Watercolor Soc. (signature), Nat. Watercolor Assn. (assoc.), Watercolor Art Soc., Houston (assoc.), Midland Arts Assn., Mid Am. Print Alliance. Office: Dept of Fine Arts & Comm SRSU Box C-90 Alpine TX 79832

FAIRSTEIN, LINDA A., prosecutor, writer; b. Westchester County, NY, May 5, 1947; m. Justin N. Feldman BA in English Lit., Vassar Coll.; JD, Univ. Va. Joined Manhattan District Atty.'s Office, 1972, chief sex crimes unit, 1976—. Author: (non-fiction) Sexual Violence, 1994 (NY Times notable book, 1994), (novels) (Alexandra Cooper series) Final Jeopardy, 1996, Likely to Die, 1997, Cold Hit, 1999, The Dead House, 2001, The Bone Vault, 2003, The Kills, 2004, Entombed, 2005, Death Dance, 2006. Active in human-rights and legal organizations. Fellow: Am. Coll. Trial Lawyers. Office: Office Dist Atty Sex Crimes/Spl Victims Bur 210 Joralemon St Brooklyn NY 11201-3745 Mailing: PO Box 226 New York NY 10021-0014*

FAISON, LUGENIA MARION, special education educator; b. Bklyn., Apr. 17, 1954; d. Jerry Faison and Marion Braxton-Faison. BA in Elem. Edn., U. V.I., St. Croix, 1982; MA in Learning Disabilities and Reading, U. Fla., Coral Gables, 1989; MA in Counseling and Guidance, Point Loma Nazarene U., 2002. Profl. clear multiple tchg. credential, profl. clear spl. edn. credential, profl. clear pupil pers. svcs. credential. Elem. tchr., St. Croix, 1976—93; spl. edn. tchr. Pasadena, Calif., 1994—. Mem.: ASCD, NAACP. Democrat.

FAIT, GRACE WALD, writer, retired language educator; d. Samuel and Evelyn Ragosin Wald; m. Jerome Myles Portman (div.); m. Irwin Fait, Sept. 10, 1966 (dec.). AA, Miami-Dade C.C., 1982. Self-employed home developer, Delray Beach, Fla., 1958—68; officer mgr., legal sec. Milton Grusmark, Miami Beach, 1968—70; exec. legal sec. Courshon & Courshon, Miami Beach, Fla., 1972—77; exec. sec. to pres. Funding, Inc., North Miami Beach, Fla., 1970—72; ESL tchr. Broward C.C., Coconut Creek, Fla., 1983—99; ret., 1999. Liaison Broward C.C./Voice of Wynmoor, Coconut Creek, 2001—04. Asst. editor, staff reporter: Voice of Wynmoor, 1983—2004; contbr. articles, revs., poems to profl. publs. Pub. rels. vol., advisor Friends of North Regional Libr., Coconut Creek, 2003—. Avocations: piano, reading, writing. Home: 3403 Bimini Ln A2 Coconut Creek FL 33066 Office: Voice of Wynmoor 3403 Bimini Ln A2 Coconut Creek FL 33066

FAITH, RUTH L., retired mathematician; b. Blairsville, Pa., Mar. 13, 1929; d. Harry S. and Ruth H. Faith. BS, Indiana U. of Pa., 1950; MBA, U. South Fla., Tampa, 1983. E.A. (inactive), IRS, 1975. Math. U.S. Geol. Survey, Washington, 1950, Douglas Aircraft, El Segundo, Calif., 1955—56; aerodynamist Singer Corp., White Oak, Md., 1956—70; tax acct. self employed, Cape Coral, Fla., 1970—77; sec. treas. Source, Inc., Cape Coral, Fla., 1978—91, ret. N. Ft. Myers, Fla., 1991. Dir. Source Inc., Cape Coral, Fla., 1980—. Contbr. articles pub. to profl. jour. Ruth Faith Endowed scholarship fund Fla. Gulf Coast Univ., 2001. Mem.: Am. Bus. Women's Assn. (pres. 1971). Achievements include patent for bar code reader, 1968-69. Home: 2525 E 1st St Apt 1809 Fort Myers FL 33901

FAIZ, ALEXANDRIA, researcher, writer; d. Robert Lee and Eileen Helen (Wagner) F. BA in English and Biology with honors, Fairfield U., 1993; postgrad., Columbia U., 1993-94. Nat. outreach coord. Thirteen/Sta. WNET, NYC, 1996—98; rsch. cons. SCIENS Pub. Rels., 1999—2000; sr. rsch. mgr. Studley, Inc., 1999—. Mem. editl. bd. Columbia: A Magazine of Poetry and Prose, 1993; author, editor: In Honor of the Earth, 1997. Founding mem. Alumnae Forum, Fairfield, 1995; co-founder student adv. coun., literacy vols. Southeastern Fairfield County, 2002-2004; trustee Alfred Adler Inst. N.Y., 1997—. Recipient Outstanding Women of Conn., 2003. Mem.: PEN (mem. freedom to write com.), Nat. Writers Union (asst. nat. grievance officer 2002—04), History of Sci. Soc., Philosophy of Sci. Assn., U.N. Assn. U.S. (chmn. UNA YPIC), Gt. Books Found., Nature Conservancy, Toastmasters, Am. Mus. Natural History. Roman Catholic. Avocations: issues concerning intellectual property and freedom of expression, professional ethics, foreign policy. Office Phone: 203-947-2497, 203-947-2497. E-mail: afprofessional@hotmail.com.

FAJARDO, SARAH ELIZABETH JOHNSON, financial consultant; b. Montgomery, Ala., July 27, 1956; d. Robert Kellogg and Mary Loretta (Franks) Johnson; m. Thomas Ronald Fajardo, Sept. 5, 1987; children: Emilia Katherine, Roberto Thomas. BA in Anthropology, U. Ariz., 1979; postgrad., Inst. Fin. Edn., Tucson, 1985-87. Resident advisor Tucson Job Corps, 1980-81; felony release specialist Pretrial Release of Pima County, Tucson, 1981-82; dir. retention counseling Tucson Coll. Bus., 1982-84; teller, new account rep. Western Savs., Tucson, 1984-86; stockbroker Western Savs./Invest, Tucson, 1986-87; fin. planner Boucher, Oehmke & Quinn, Tucson, 1987-89, Consolidated Investment Svcs., 1989-92; registered rep. Plan Am., 1992—93; designed and developed investment dept. Nat. Bank Ariz., 1993—95; fin. cons. pvt. client svcs. Wells Fargo Investment (formerly Norwest), 1995—. Mgr. telemarketing dept. Ariz. Theatre Co., Tucson, 1988-89. Contbr. articles to profl. jours. Mem. com. Tucson Tomorrow, 1988; founding mem. Brewster Ctr. for Victims of Family Violence, Tucson, 1982-86; vol. Peace Corps, Senegal, Africa, 1979; chair ann. awards banquet events YWCA Women on the Move, 1991, grad. leadership tng. program, 1990; mem. investment adv. and fin. com. So. Ariz. Ctr. Against Sexual Assault, 2002-03; bd. dirs. Ariz. Children's Assn., 1999—; chair fin. com. Planned Parenthood So. Ariz., 1993-2005, bd. dirs., 2001-2005. Mem. Resources for Women (group leader of money talks 1987), NAFE, Successful Bus. Referral Club, Indsl. Recreation Coun. (treas. 1986-87), Greater Tucson Econ. Coun. (small bus. task force 1992-93). Democrat. Avocations: gourmet cooking, bicycling, weightlifting, running, gardening. Office: Wells Fargo Investments Wells Fargo Pvt Client Svcs 2195 E River Rd Ste 105 Tucson AZ 85718 Office Phone: 520-529-5937. Business E-Mail: fajardse@wellsfargo.com.

FAJT, KAREN ELAINE, art educator; d. E. Albert and Angeline Louise DeLuca; m. Henry Gervase Fajt, Jr., June 22, 1974; children: Merritt Lynn, Holly Elizabeth. BA, Seton Hill U., 1970; MEd, U. Pitts., 1973. Art educator Hempfield Area Sch. Dist., Greensburg, 1970—. Bd. trustees Laurel Ballet Theatre, Greensburg, 1989—93; mem. St. Lucy's Aux. to the Blind., Pitts., 1994—, Frick Art and Hist. Ctr., 2001—, Westmoreland Mus. Am. Art, 1985—; bd. dirs. Lawyers' Aux., Greensburg, 1978—. Recipient Sullivan award, Seton Hill U., 1970. Mem.: NEA, Hempfield Area Edn. Assn., Pa. State Edn. Assn., Nat. Art Edn. Assn., Greensburg Coll. Club (bd. trustees 1970—, parliamentarian 1970—, chmn. scholarship com.), Univ. Club. Avocations: painting, travel, reading, gardening, shopping. Office: Hempfield Area School Dist RD # 6 Greensburg PA 15601 Personal E-mail: kartger@aol.com.

FALANGA-LIVEROTTI, SHAUNA MARIE, secondary school educator; b. Stoughton, Mass., Dec. 23, 1977; m. Gianni Liverotti. BA in History, BSc in Secondary Edn., Salve Regina U., Newport, R.I., 1995—99; MA in Modern European History, U. Manchester, Eng., 2000—01. Cert. Tchr. Fla. Dept. Edn. Social studies tchr. Diocese of Orlando, Fla., 2002—04; social studies dept. chair Eustis HS, Fla., 2004—. Educator Discovery Ednl. Network, 2005—; student coun. sponsor Eustis HS, 2005—06, founder, sponsor, panthers of the past history club. Recipient Rookie Tchr. of Yr., Lake County Sch. Board-Eustis HS, 2005—06. Home: 3317 Indian Trl Eustis FL 32726 Office: Eustis HS 1300 E Washington Ave Eustis FL 32726 Office Phone: 352-357-4147. Business E-Mail: liverottis@lake.k12.fl.us.

FALCO, EDIE, actress; b. Northport, NY, July 5, 1963; d. Frank Falco and Judith M. Anderson; 1 adopted child, Anderson. BFA, SUNY, Purchase, NY, 1986. Appeared in films Sweet Lorraine, 1987, The Unbelievable Truth, 1990, Trust, 1990, Time Expired, 1992, Laws of Gravity, 1992, I Was on Mars, 1992, Bullets Over Broadway, 1994, Backfire!, 1995, The Addiction, 1995, Layin' Low, 1996, The Funeral, 1996, Breathing Room, 1996, Firehouse, 1997, Cost of Living, 1997, Cop Land, 1997, Trouble on the Corner, 1997, A Price Above Rubies, 1998, Hurrican Streets, 1998, Judy Berlin, 1999, Random Hearts, 1999, Overnight Sensation, 2000, Death of a Dog, 2000, Sunshine State, 2002 (Best Supporting Acress award LA Film Critics Assn. 2002, Golden Satellite award best supporting actress 2003), Family of the Year, 2004, The Girl from Monday, 2005, The Great New Wonderful, 2005, The Quiet, 2005, Freedomland, 2006; appeared in TV movies The Sunshine Boys, 1995, Jenifer, 2001, Fargo, 2003; appeared in TV series Oz, 1997-99, The Sopranos, 1999- (Golden Globe award best actress in a drama 2000, 03, Emmy for best actress 1999, 2001, 2003, Actor of Yr., Am. Film Inst. 2001, Golden Satellite award 2002, SAG award 2003); TV guest appearances include Homicide: Life on the Street, 1993-94, 97, Law & Order, 1993-94, 97, New York Undercover, 1995; film dir. Rift, 1993; TV prodr. Stringer, 1999; theater appearances include Side Man, 2000, The Vagina Monologues, 2001, Frankie and Johnny in the Clair de Lune, 2002. Office: c/o Sandra Marsh Mgmt 9150 Wilshire Blvd Ste 220 Beverly Hills CA 90212-3429*

FALCO, JULIA FAYE, secondary school educator; b. Fitzgerald, Ga., Apr. 24, 1947; d. Robert B. and Laura (Brown) Wilcox; m. James Anthony Falco, Aug. 24, 1968; children: Valencia Angelique, Tiffany Nicole. AA, Miami Dade Jr. Coll., Fla., 1967; BS in Elem. Edn., Fla. Meml. Coll., 1971; MS in Elem. Edn., Nova U., 1977. Tchr. Dade County Schs., Miami, 1973—, dir., mgr. after sch. care, 1983-86. Mem. Fla. Meml. Coll. Alumni Assn., Coconut Grove Village West Home Homeowners Assn., Coconut Grove Negro Women's Club, Inc., Alpha Kappa Alpha. Lodges: Young Matrons (Sunday Sch. tchr.). Baptist. Avocations: reading, sewing, cooking, interior decorating. Home and Office: 3421 Florida Ave Miami FL 33133-5066 Office Phone: 305-445-3587. E-mail: jf@dadeschools.net.

FALCO, MARIA JOSEPHINE, political scientist; b. Wildwood, NJ, July 7, 1932; d. John J. and Mafalda M. (Barbieri) F. AB, Immaculata Coll., Pa., 1954; student, U. Florence, Italy, 1954-55; MA, Fordham U., 1958; PhD, Bryn Mawr Coll., Pa., 1963; postdoctoral rsch. fellow, Yale, 1965-66; quantitative data analysis, U. Mich., 1968; mgmt. program, Carnegie-Mellon U., 1983. Instr., then asst. prof. history and polit. sci. Immaculata Coll., Pa., 1957-63; asst. prof. polit. sci. Washington Coll., Chestertown, Md., 1963-64; rsch. asst. Genevieve Blatt; candidate for U.S. Senator from Pa., 1964-65; asst. prof., then assoc. prof. polit. sci. Le Moyne Coll., Syracuse, NY, 1966-73, chmn. polit. sci. dept., 1967-73; prof. polit. sci. Stockton State Coll., Pomona, NJ, 1973-76; chmn. social and behavioral scis. faculty U. Tulsa, 1976-79; dean Coll. Arts and Scis., Loyola U., New Orleans, 1979-85; prof. polit. sci. Loyola U., New Orleans, 1985-86; v.p. acad. affairs DePauw U., Greencastle, Ind., 1986-88, prof. polit. sci., 1988-93, prof. emerita, 1993—. Speaker in field; adj. prof. polit. sci. Tulane U., New Orleans, 1996-97. Author: Truth and Meaning in Political Science: An Introduction to Political Inquiry, 1973, Bigotry: Ethnic, Machine and Sexual Politics in a Senatorial Election, 1980; editor: Through the Looking Glass: Epistemology and the Conduct of Political Inquiry: An Anthology, 1979, Feminism and Epistemology: Approaches to Research in Women and Politics, 1987, Feminist Interpretations of Mary Wollstonecraft, 1996, Feminist Interpretations of Niccolo Machiavelli, 2004; cons. editor Political Parties and the Civic Action Groups; contbr. articles and book revs. to profl. jours Mem. Mayor's Task Force on Future of New Orleans, 1983-85, Women's Equity Action League, 1979-81, LWV, 1960-63, 82-84; bd. dirs. Inst. for Human Rels., Loyola U., Inst. Human Understanding, New Orleans, 1985-86; pres. Syracuse chpt. New Dem. Coalition, 1970-71; mem. pres.'s coun. Loyola U., New Orleans, 1997-2000, mem. Ars Dean's coun., 2000-06. Fulbright scholar U. Florence, Italy, 1954-55; faculty fellow in state and local politics Nat. Ctr. for Edn. in Politics, 1964. Mem. AAUP (v.p. LeMoyne chpt. 1971-72), Womens Caucus Polit. Sci. (pres. 1976, named Mentor of Distinction 1989), Am. Polit. Sci. Assn. (Benjamin Evans Lippincott award com. 1976, chmn. sect. program com. 1975, com. acad. freedom and profl. ethics, chair com. for outstanding conv. paper award women and politics rsch. sect. 1990-91), Midwestern Polit. Sci. Assn. (com. status of women), Northeastern Polit. Sci. Assn., S.W. Polit. Sci. Assn. (outstanding conv. paper com.), Founds. Polit. Theory Group, Common Cause, Great Lakes Coll. Assn. (dean's coun. 1986-88), Assn. Jesuit Colls. and Univs. (dean's coun. 1979-85), Assn. Am. Colls. (coun. for liberal learning 1985-87), Western Polit. Sci. Assn., Ind. Polit. Sci. Assn. (pres., chair 1992-93), Ind. Social Sci. Assn., So. Polit. Sci. Assn., Jefferson Parish LWV (bd. dirs. 1999—, pres. 2001-02), Jefferson Parish Bus. and Profl. Women (1st v.p. 2002-04, pres. 2004-05) Roman Catholic. Home: 4709 Tartan Dr Metairie LA 70003 Business E-Mail: falco@loyno.edu.

FALCON, KIMBERLY SUE, science educator; b. East Palestine, Ohio, Nov. 16, 1972; d. Fran and Sue Falcon. BS in EDn., Youngstown State U., Ohio, 1998; post grad., Walden U., Mpls., 2005—. Sci. tchr. Whitehall City Schs., Whitehall, Ohio, 1998—. Sci. dept. chair Whitehall City Schs., Whitehall, Ohio, 2000—, mentor coord., 2002—. Scholar, Martha Holden Jennings Found., 2002. Mem.: Sci. Edn. Coun. Ohio (assoc.). Office: Whitehall City Schs Whitehall OH

FALCONER, KAREN ANN See DAVIS, KAREN

FALCONES, ETTA Z., mathematician, math and computer science education and administration; b. Tupelo, Miss. AB in Math., Fisk U., 1953; MS, U. Wis., 1954; PhD, Emory U., 1969. Instr. Okolona Coll., 1954—63; tchr. Chattanooga Sch. Sys., 1963—64; asst. prof. Spelman Coll., Atlanta, 1964—71, assoc. prof. math., 1972—90, Calloway Prof. Math., 1990—. Asst. prof. math. Norfolk State U., 1971—72; founder NASA Women in Sci. Program, 1987, NASA Undergrad. Sci. Rsch. Program, 1987; assoc. provost for sci. programs and policy Spelman Coll., Atlanta, 1990—. Recipient AWM Louise Hay award, 1995. Mem.: AAAS, Atlanta Minority Women in Sci. Network, Am. Math. Soc., Nat. Assn. Mathematicians (founder). Office: Spelman Coll Math Dept Box 953 350 Spelman Ln SW Atlanta GA 30314-4399

FALES, LISA JOSE, lawyer; b. Indpls., Apr. 3, 1962; BA, U. Md., 1984; JD, U. Balt., 1990. Bar: Md. 1990, DC 1992, US Dist. Ct., Md. 1992. Legislative specialist, consumer protection div. Md. Atty. Gen. Office, 1983—89; summer assoc. Venable LLP, Balt., 1989; ptnr., govt. antitrust practice group Howrey Simon Arnold & White LLP, Washington; ptnr., regulatory practice group Venable LLP, Washington, 2004—. Co-chair, moderator & presenter Nat. Inst. for Women Corp. Counsel conference, 2003. Bd. dirs. Women's Law Ctr. for Md.; mem. benefits com. NOW Legal Defense and Education Fund. Mem.: ABA (mem. antitrust section), DC Bar Assn. (chair consumer affairs com. 1994—96, mem. steering com. 1996—97, mem. antitrust section), Md. Bar Assn. (mem. antitrust section). Office: Venable LLP 575 7th St NW Washington DC 20004 Office Phone: 202-344-4349. Office Fax: 202-344-8300. Business E-Mail: ljfales@venable.com.

FALK, BARBARA HIGINBOTHAM, music educator; b. Grindstone, Pa., May 22, 1950; d. Warren Charles and Erma Lou (Randolph) Higinbotham; m. Helmut Falk, July 7, 1973; children: Gregory Brock, Jennifer Arlene. BA in Music Edn., Western Ky. U., 1972; postgrad., Jersey City State Coll., 1974, postgrad., 1997, Montclair State Coll., 1990—91, Yale U., 1993; MA in Creative Arts Edn., Rutgers U., 1994; postgrad., Caldwell Coll., 1996, St. Peter's Coll., Jersey City, 1996—98. Cert. music tchr. N.J., Orff cert. tchr. N.J. Band dir. Bridgeton (N.J.) Jr. H.S., 1972—73; instrumental music tchr. Hopewell Twp. Sch., Bridgeton, 1972—73; gen. music tchr. Marlboro (N.J.) Twp. Schs., 1973—79; music dir. S. Br. Ref. Ch. Nursery Sch., Somerville, NJ, 1987; vocal and gen. music tchr. Washington Twp. Schs., Long Valley, NJ, 1988—. Youth choir dir. First Bapt. Ch., Freehold, NJ, 1981—83, Bridgewater Bapt. Ch., 1987—89; mem. master tchr. governing com. N.J. Symphony Orch., 1993—; cons. to N.J. Dept. Edn. State Arts Curriculum Framework Writer, Trenton, NJ, 1997; mem. Morris County profl. devel. bd. N.J. Dept. Edn., 1999—; chair Morris County Profl. Devel. Bd., 2002—03; presenter in field. Bible sch. music dir. Jackson (N.J.) Bapt. Ch., 1977—79, 1st Bapt. Ch., Bridgeton, 1980—86. Recipient Master Tchr. award, N.J. Symphony Orch. and Dodge Found., 1993; grantee Creating Original Opera grant, N.Y. Met. Opera Guild, 1993. Mem.: N.J. Edn. Assn. (profl. devel. bd. 2001—), Music Educators Nat. Conf., Washington Twp. Edn. Assn. (exec. com. 1993—, pres. 2001—), Kappa Delta Pi. Baptist. Avocations: golf, gardening. Office: Old

Farmers Rd Sch 51 Old Farmers Rd Long Valley NJ 07853 Home (Summer): 30 Garfield Pl Ocean City NJ 08226 Home: 327 Scully Ct Belle Mead NJ 08502 Office Phone: 908-876-3919. E-mail: bhfalk@patmedia.net.

FALK, BARBARA MARIE, psychologist; b. Nov. 16, 1940; PhD, U. Ill., 1972. Asst. prof. U. Ill., Champaign-Urbana, 1972-73; staff psychologist St. Louis Juvenile Ct., 1973-74, supr. psychologist, 1974-80; pvt. practice Chesterfield, Mo., 1977—2003. Pres. Cmty. H.S. Dist. 218 Tchrs. Assn., Blue Island, Ill., 1969. Office: 14443 Bantry Ln Unit 15 Chesterfield MO 63017-5740 Personal E-mail: barbarafalk@earthlink.net.

FALK, DIANE M., research information specialist, librarian, writer, editor, director; b. NYC; d. Leon H.E. Falk and J. Constance Moorehead (Lilienthal) Stephenson. BA in English and World Lit., Columbia U., 1973, MLS, 1979. Text editor, bibliog. enhancement N.Y. Times Info. Svc., Inc., N.Y.C., 1980—; rsch. libr., documents analyst Atlantis Energy and Minerals, N.Y.C., 1980-81; project coord. legal dept. GAF Corp., N.Y.C., 1981-82; cataloger Exxon Edn. Found., N.Y.C., 1982; indexer, fact-checker H. W. Wilson & Co., Bronx, N.Y., 1982; bibliog. orgn. The Rockefeller Found., N.Y.C., 1983; rsch. info. specialist Harkavy Info. Svc., N.Y.C., 1983-84, Newsworld Comm., N.Y.C., 1985, features writer, 1977—78, rsch. libr., 1985; dir. rsch., head libr., editl. rsch. specialist The World & I: The Mag. for Lifelong Learners, Washington, 1986—. Copy editor, rsch. mgr. HSA-UWC, N.Y.C. and Washington, 1974-75, 86; reference asst. Lehman Libr., Columbia U., N.Y.C., 1978; rsch. libr., documents analyst UN Ctr. for Transnational Corps., 1979; coord., conf. participant Ambs. for Peace, 2001—, Svc. for Peace; cons. in field Editor-in-chief FOCUS, 1979-80; editor website jour., e-jour. and conf. planner, World Media Assn.; contbr. articles to profl. jours. English and comms. prof., vol. United to Serve Am., Washington Saturday Coll., Howard U., Washington, 1992-94; ofcl. lectr./tour guide Washington Times Found. and Corp.; conf. coord. Internat. Acad. Arts, World Media Assn., Literary, Bus., Legal and Polit. Groups and Issues, 1991—; instr., conf. demonstrator for internet and other knowledge mgmt. tech. rsch. resources; vol. Ambs. for Peace Seminars, 2001-03; sponsor, participant Svc. for Peace, 2002. Recipient Corp. award Washington Times Corp., 1997, Cert. of Appreciation, Intellectual Freedom Com. D.C. Libr. Assn., 1996-97, 2002-03, Amb. of Peace Lifetime Achievement award Ambs. Svc. for Peace, 2005, Cert. of Honor, Amb. of Peace award, Interreligious and Internat. Fedn. for World Peace and Interreligous Internat. Peace Coun., 2006. Mem. ALA, World Media Assn. (editor e-jour.), Spl. Librs. Assn., D.C. Libr. Assn. (cert. of appreciation chair Intellectual Freedom com., 2002-03), Intellectual Freedom Interest Group (chairperson 1996-97, com. chair 2002-03), Rsch. and Reference Interest Group, Women's Fedn. for World Peace (sec. D.C. chpt. 1993—), Internat. Leadership Seminars (staff vol. 1991—), Internat. Fedn. for World Peace (signature campaign staff 1990-91, vol. 1990—, acting sec. 1993—), The Prosperity Coun. (editor newsletter 1991), Inst. Mus. and Libr. Svcs., World Assn. Non-Govtl. Orgns., Purestyle, Inc. (first membership chair 2006—). Avocations: photography, arts, travel, writing. Home: 508 Columbia Rd NW Washington DC 20001-2904 Office Phone: 202-635-4059. Personal E-mail: dianemfalk@yahoo.com. E-mail: dfalk@wmassociation.com.

FALK, ELLEN STEIN, media specialist, educator; b. Mobile, Ala., Aug. 19, 1942; d. Louis James and Elizabeth Jeffers Stein; m. Michael Marc Falk, July 3, 1968; 1 child, Rachel Mara. BS in Fine Arts, Spring Hill Coll., 1964; student, St. Thomas Aquinas, 1981—85; MEd, William Paterson U., 2005. Cert. tchr. N.J., 1986. Flight attendant United Airlines, N.Y.C., 1965—68, flight ops. office Newark, 1968—73; tchr. Meml. Sch., Montvale, NJ, 1986—2001, media specialist, 2001—. Del. People To People Amb. Program, China, 1994, New Zealand, Australia, 2001. Named Tchr. of Yr., Govs. Tchr. Recognition Program, 1994. Mem.: Montvale Tchrs. Assn. (negotiation com.), Nat. Assn. Sch. Librs., Nat. Coun. Tchrs. English, Internat. Reading Assn., Friends of Libr., Parent Tchr. Orgn., Kappa Delta Pi, Pi Lambda Theta. Home: 77 Akers Ave Montvale NJ 07645 Office: Memorial School 53 West Grand Avenue Montvale NJ 07645 Office Phone: 201-391-2900 503. Business E-Mail: efalk@mail.montvale.k12.nj.us.

FALK, URSULA ADLER, psychotherapist; b. Bad Mergentheim, Germany, Dec. 17; came to U.S., 1939; d. Albert and Sophie (Neubauer) Adler; m. Gerhard Falk, Jan. 8, 1949; children: Cynthia, Daniel, Clifford. BA, Ohio U., 1951; MSW, Bryn Mawr Coll., 1953; EdD, U. Buffalo, 1976. LCSW. Caseworker Norristown (Pa.) State Hosp., 1952-55, Cuyahoga Child Welfare, Cleve., 1955-57, Booth Meml. Hosp., Buffalo, 1958-62; dir. social svcs. Meth. Home for Children, Williamsville, N.Y., 1962-71; cons. Newfane (N.Y.) Health Facility, 1971—; pvt. practice Kenmore, Niagara Falls, N.Y., 1989—. Social worker Jewish Ctr., Buffalo, 1972-78; instr. SUNY, Buffalo, 1978-83, dir. social svcs. Presbyn. Home, 1983-89, cons. 1978-83. Author: Nursing Home Dilemma/Who Cares, 1976, Aging in America and Other Cultures, 1981, On Our Own, 1989, American Nursing Home/Final Solution, 1991, Interviews with Patients in Psychotherapy, 1994, Grandparents, 2002, Youth Culture and the Generation Gap, 2005, Deviant Nurses, 2006; contbr. articles to profl jours. Mem. NASW, N.Y. State Bd. Nursing (bd. dirs.). Jewish. Avocations: swimming, reading, bicycling, ping pong/table tennis, writing. Home: 109 Louvaine Dr Buffalo NY 14223-2743 Office Phone: 716-284-5785.

FALKEY, MARY E., finance educator; b. San Jose, Calif., Jan. 18, 1949; d. Archie Robert and Florence Beckett Furr; m. Mark Steven Falkey, May 14, 1977; children: Mark Falkey, Jr., Elizabeth, John. BA, San Jose State U., 1972; MA, Nat. U. San Diego, 1980; MS, Va. Tech., 2003. Personnel coord. Host Internat., Inc., Santa Monica, Calif., 1972—74; mgr. human resources IVAC Corp., San Diego, 1974—76; dir. human resources Napp Sys., San Marcos, Calif., 1976—78; prof. Prince George's CC, Largo, Md., 1997—; adj. instr. Ctrl. Tex. Coll., Vallencia C.C., Prince Georges C.C., 1978—97. Site coord. Vol. Income Tax Assistance Program, Largo, 2003, 2004. Mem.: Am. Assn. Cmty. Colls., Md. Soc. Accts., Am. Assn. U. Profs., Tchrs. Acctg. Two Yr. Colls. Office: Prince Georges CC 301 Largo Rd Largo MD 20774 Office Phone: 301-322-0769. Business E-Mail: falkeymx@pgcc.edu.

FALKOFF, GAIL GOLDSTEIN, mathematics educator, department chairman; d. Maurice and Ruth Celia Goldstein; m. Barry Jay Falkoff, June 22, 1969; children: Michelle Susan, David Seth, Marissa Joy. BA, Simmons Coll., Boston, 1969; MEd, Lesley U., Cambridge, Mass., 1991. Math. tchr. Lincoln Jr. H.S., Malden, Mass., 1969—70, Malden H.S., 1970—73, Peabody Veterans Meml. H.S., 1985—. Head math. dept. Peabody Veterans Meml. H.S., Mass., 2001—; bd. mem. Salem State Coll. Collaborative Math. and Sci., 2001—; mem. North Shore Math. Dept. Heads, Lynnfield, 2003—. Mem.: Nat. Coun. Tchrs. Math. Avocations: travel, knitting, reading. Home: 2 Terri Rd Peabody MA 01960 Office: Peabody Veterans Meml HS 485 Lowell St Peabody MA 01960 Office Phone: 978-536-4519. E-mail: falkoffg@peabody.k12.ma.us.

FALKOWSKI, BRENDA LISLE, retail buyer, director; b. Lexington, Ky., July 2, 1943; d. Edward Spencer and Evelyn (Wright) Lisle; m. Edward John Falkowski, Oct. 19, 1963; children: Brenda June Falkowski-Ashway, Richard Spencer, Lance Edward. AA in Liberal Studies, Neumann Coll., Aston, Pa., 1994, BS in Liberal Studies, 1998. Pres., v.p. Tokyo Am. Club Women's Group, Tokyo, 1981-85; assoc. Webb Jewelers and Silversmiths, West Chester, Pa., 1986-89; realtor Fox and Lazo Realtors/Prudential Preferred Properties, West Chester, 1990-92; internat. cons. corp. svcs. Fox and Lazo Relocation Mgmt., Paoli, Pa., 1993-95; pres. Touch of Glass Inc., Mt. Pleasant, SC, 1993—2000; v.p. Brenlan Assocs. Inc., Mt. Pleasant, 1995—; exclusive buyers agt. The Real Buyers Agt., Mt. Pleasant, SC, 2001—. Bd. govs. Tokyo Am. Club, 1981—85; cons. cross-cultural relocation, West Chester, Pa., 1996—98; internat. cons. Chamness Relocation, Mt. Pleasant, SC, 2002—. Monthly contbr. newspaper column The Tokyo Am., 1983-95. Membership chair Reps. Abroad, Tokyo, 1984; neighborhood vol. Am. Cancer Soc., Am. Heart Assn., Am. Kidney Found. Mem.: NAFE, AAUW, Nat. Assn. of Exclusive Buyers Agts., Nat. Assn. Realtors, Nat. Assn. Bus. Coaches (E. Cooper Prof. Women), Adult Women's Network, Internat. Women's Club. Methodist. Avocations: breeding of rare dogs, personal fitness training, retirement home pet therapy. Home: 3527 Stockton Dr Mount Pleasant SC 29466-6990

FALKOWSKI, THERESA GAE, chemistry educator; b. El Paso, Tex., Mar. 19, 1958; d. Chester Doan and Patricia Ann Harman; m. Henry Steven Falkowski, May 16, 1981. AA, Potomac State Coll., 1978; BA, W.Va. U., 1980. Lab. asst. Potomac State Coll., Keyser, W.Va., 1977-78, gen. chem. prep rm. mgr., 1986—, chem. lab. instr., 1995-99; chem. lab. tchg. asst. W.Va. U., Morgantown, 1981-83, chem. lab. tech., 1981-85, adj. instr. chemistry, 1999—. Cons. USS N.C. Battleship Meml., Wilmington, 1981—; mem. haz-mat response team Potomac State Coll., 1993—. Author: Clark Hall of Chemistry: A Pictorial History, 1996, Laboratory Manual for Chemistry 112, 1996; illustrator: Laboratory Manual for Chemistry 115/116, 1991. Mem. Am. Chem. Soc., W.Va. Acad. Sci., Carnegie Mus. Natural History and Sci. Ctr., The Nat. Maritime Ctr., The N.C. Aquarium Soc., The Mote Marine Lab. Avocations: model building, world war ii history, aircraft identification, science fiction. Office: Potomac State Coll Fort Ave Keyser WV 26726

FALL, DOROTHY, artist, writer, art director, art association administrator; b. Rochester, N.Y., Apr. 7, 1930; d. Isadore and Esther Paula (Rudman) Winer; m. Bernard B. Fall (dec. Feb. 1967); children: Nicole Francoise, Elisabeth Anne, Patricia Madeleine Marcelle. BFA, Syracuse U., 1952; postgrad., Am. U., 1956-58, 66; student, Acad. de la Grande Chaumiere, Paris, 1961, Acad. Julian, 1965. Dep. art dir. AMERIKA Mag. U.S. Info. Agy., Washington, 1956-80; owner, art dir. Fall Design Comms., Washington, 1980-88; dir. Gallery 10, Washington, 1994—2001. Bd. dirs. Pyramid Atlantic, Riverdale, Md. Author: Bernard Fall: Memories of a Soldier-Scholar, 2006; editor: Last Reflections on a War, 1967, 2d edit., 2000; art dir., designer Space Science Comes of Age, 1981; one-woman shows include Mickelson Gallery, Washington, 1969, 73,79, 84, Plum Gallery, Kensington, Md., 1989, O St. Studio, Washington, 1989, 92, AVA Gallery, Lebanon, N.H., 1990, Covington & Burling, Washington, 1990, Am. Hort. Soc., Alexandria, Va., 1993, Gallery 10, Washington, 1996, 2000, Cosmos Club, 2000, Galerie Internationale, N.Y.C., 1968, Maison de France, Phnom Penh, Cambodia, 1962; group shows include Hanoi (Vietnam) Fine Arts Coll., 2000, Assioma Gallery, Prato, Italy, 2000, 01, Marino Marini Mus., 2001, Pistoia, Italy, Venezia Viva, Venice, 2001, UN, N.Y.C., 2001; represented in permanent collections and by Verve Art Gallery, Leuven, Belgium, Gallery 10, Washington, AVA Gallery, Lebanon, N.H., Aries East, Brewster, Mass. Recipient gold medal award Art Dirs. Club of Met. Washington Exhibits, 1965, 66, 69, 79, distinctive merit Art Dirs. Club of N.Y. Exhibits, 1969, 74, 77, 78, 79, 81, 82, 83, silver medal N.Y. Soc. Illustrators, 1969. Mem. Women's Caucus on Arts, Washington Sculptors Group, Artists Equity, Cosmos Club. Home: 4535 31st St NW Washington DC 20008-2130 E-mail: dofall@aol.com.

FALL, MARIJANE EATON, counselor educator; b. Sanford, Maine, Oct. 4, 1940; d. Harold Vincent and Estella Anne (Prescott) Eaton; m. David William Fall (div. 1985); children: David Gregory, Gretchen, Amy. BA, Nasson Coll., 1963; MS, U. So. Maine, 1986; EdD, U. Maine, 1991. Lic. profl. counselor, Maine; lic. mental health counselor, Iowa; nat. cert. counselor. Counselor Wiscasset and Damariscotta (Maine) Pub. Schs., 1986—89; pvt. practice Westport Island, Maine, 1987—92, Iowa City, 1993—95, Gorham, Maine, 1995—; lectr. II counseling U. So. Maine, Gorham, 1991—92, prof., 1995—; asst. prof. U. Iowa, Iowa City, 1992—95. Mem. adj. faculty U. Maine, Orono, 1990; cons. Big Bros. and Big. Sisters, Damarcocotta, Maine, 1989-92, Iowa Test of Basic Skills, Iowa City, 1993—; supr. play therapists, Maine, then Iowa, 1992—. Co-author: (with John M Sutton Jr.) Clinical Supervision: A Handbook for Practitioners, 2004; mem. editl. bd. Sch. Counselor, 1993—; contbr. articles to profl. publs., chpts. to books. Troop leader, cons. Girl Scouts U.S., Sanford, Maine, 1978-84; pres. bd. dirs. Sanford Young Men's Christian Assn., 1981—, hon. life mem., 1983. George Nasson scholar Nasson Coll., Springvale, Maine, 1963. Mem. ACA (cert.), North Cen. Assn. Counselor Edn. Suprs., Play Therapy Assn., N. Atlantic Regoin Assn. Counselor Edn. (pres. 1999-2000), Assn. Counselor Edn. (exec. bd. 1999-2000), Maine Assn. Play Therapy (founder 1999, bd. dirs. 1999—, pres. 2005—). Mem. Soc. Of Friends. Avocations: walking, writing, reading. Office: U So Maine 400 Bailey Hall Gorham ME 04038 Office Phone: 207-780-5472. E-mail: mjfall@usm.maine.edu.

FALLCREEK, STEPHANIE JEAN, non-profit organization executive; b. Springfield, Mo., May 6, 1950; d. Martha Jean (Barton) Wertz; m. Jerry R. Tillman, 1987; children: Ernest, Daniel, Christopher, Joseph; stepchildren: Shannon, Tiffanie. AB in History, U. Okla., 1972; MSW in Social Welfare, U. Calif., Berkeley, 1974, DSW in Social Welfare, 1984. Dir. Inst. for Geron. Research and Edn., N.Mex. State U., Las Cruces, 1983-87, N.Mex. State Agy. on Aging, Santa Fe, 1987-91; dir. Office of Planning N.Mex. Dept. of Health, 1991-92; dir. div. long term care N.Mex. Dept. Health, Albuquerque, 1992; exec. dir. Fairhill Ctr. for Aging, Cleve., 1992—2006; pres., CEO Fairhill Ctr. (formerly known as Fairhill Ctr. for Aging), 2006—. Pres. Fallcreek & Assocs., Cleve., 1982—; sr. assoc. Age Wave Inc., Emeryville, Calif., 1985-87; cons. various hosps. and health care orgns.; speaker confs. and trade shows; guest radio and TV programs on aging. Author: (with others) A Healthy Old Age: A Sourcebook for Health Promotion with Older Adults, Health Promotion and Aging: Strategies for Action, Health Promotion and Aging: A National Resource of Selected Programs; also articles and book chpts.; mem. editl. bd. Generations, 1999-2002. Bd. dirs. Am. Soc. on Aging, 1992-1995, Nat. Assn. State Units of Aging, 1987-91, S.W. Soc. on Aging, 1992-97, Goodwill Industries Cleve., 1999-2004; moderator First Bapt. Ch. of Greater Cleve., 1997-98; treas., fin. chair Laurel Lake Retirement Cmty., 1999-2004, 06—; bd. dirs. RSVP Greater Cleve., 2002—05, chmn. governance com., 2004—. Danforth fellow, 1972-78; named to Women of Note, Crains Cleve. Bus., 2004. Mem. AAUW, Nat. Coun. on the Aging (policy com. 2004-05), Soc. for Values in Higher Edn., Nat. Assn. Social Workers, Am. Soc. on Aging., Nat. Coun. on Aging (pub. policy com. 2004—). Office: Fairhill Ctr 12200 Fairhill Rd Cleveland OH 44120-1013 Office Phone: 216-421-1350. E-mail: sfallcreek@aol.com, sfc@fairhillcenter.org.

FALLER, RHODA, lawyer; b. NYC, Dec. 21, 1946; d. Benjamin and Marion (Mediasky) Sragg; m. Stanley Grossberg, Apr. 12, 1973 (div. Oct. 1983); children: Joseph Seth, Daniel Benjamin; m. Bernard Martin Faller, May 31, 1987. BS, SUNY, Stony Brook, 1967; MS, Pace U., 1973; JD, NY Law Sch., 1978. Bar: N.Y. 1979, N.J. 1979, U.S. Dist. Ct. N.J. 1979, Fla. 1980, U.S. Dist. Ct. (ea. and so. dists.) N.Y. 1982, Ky. 1996, U.S. Dist. Ct. (ea. dist.) Ky. 1997. Assoc. Fuchsberg & Fuchsberg, N.Y.C., 1982-91, DeBlasio & Alton, P.C., N.Y.C., 1991-95, Rhoda Grossberg Faller, Esq., Teaneck, 1995-96, Becker Law Office, Louisville, Ky., 1997-2000; pvt. practice Louisville, 2000—. Mem.: Women Lawyers Assn., Louisville Bar Assn., Fla. Bar Assn., N.Y. State Bar Assn., Ky. Bar Assn., Ky. Acad. Trial Attys., Nat. Assn. Women Bus. Owners, Assn. Trial Lawyers Am., Million Dollar Advocates Forum. Democrat. Jewish. Home: 213 Mockingbird Gardens Dr Louisville KY 40207-5718 Office: Law Office of Rhoda Faller PLLC 455 S 4th St Ste 310 Louisville KY 40202 Office Phone: 502-582-2212. Business E-Mail: rfaller@fallerlaw.com.

FALLER, SUSAN GROGAN, lawyer; b. Cin., Mar. 1, 1950; d. William M. and Jane (Eagen) Grogan; m. Kenneth R. Faller, June 8, 1973; children: Susan Elisabeth, Maura Christine, Julie Kathleen. BA, U. Cin., 1972; JD, U. Mich., 1975. Bar: Ohio 1975, Ky. 1989, U.S. Dist. Ct. (so. dist.) Ohio 1975, U.S. Ct. Claims 1982, U.S. Ct. Appeals (6th cir.) 1982, U.S. Supreme Ct. 1982, U.S. Tax Ct. 1984, U.S. Dist. Ct. (ea. dist.) Ky., 1991. Assoc. Frost & Jacobs, Cin., 1975-82; ptnr. Frost & Jacobs LLP, Cin., 1982-2000; mem. Frost Brown Todd LLC, Cin., 2000—. Chmn. first amendment, media and advt. practice group Frost Brown Todd LLC, 2001—, co-chmn. India cons. group, 2006—. Assoc. editor Mich. Law Rev., 1974-75; contbg. author: MLRC 50-State Survey of Media Libel and Privacy Law, 1982-93, MLRC 50-State Survey of Media Libel Law, 1999-, MLRC State Survey of Employment Libel and Privacy Law, 1999-. Bd. dirs. Summit Alumni Coun., Cin., 1983-85; trustee Newman Found., Cin., 1980-86, Cath. Social Svc., Cin., 1984-93, nominating com., 1985-88, sec., 1990; mem. Class XVII Leadership Cin., 1993-94; mem. exec. com., def. counsel sect. Media Law Resource Ctr., 1998-2002, chmn. membership com., 2003—; pres., def. counsel sect. Libel Def. Resource Ctr., 2001; mem. parish coun. St. Monica-St. George Ch., 1996-2000. Recipient Career Women of Achievement award YWCA, 1990. Mem. ABA (co-editor newsletter media litig. 1993-97), FBA, Ky. Bar Assn., No. Ky. Bar Assn., No. Ky. Women's Bar Assn., Ohio Bar Assn. (chair media law com. 2001-02), Cin. Bar Assn. (com. mem.), Potter Stewart Inn of Ct., U. Cin. Alumni Assn., Arts & Scis. Alumni Assn. (bd. govs. U. Cin. Coll. 1988-2000), U. Mich. Alumni Assn., Mortar Bd., Leland Yacht Club, Coll. Club, Clifton Meadows Club, Phi Beta Kappa, Theta Phi Alpha. Roman Catholic. Home: 5 Belsaw Pl Cincinnati OH 45220-1104 Office: Frost Brown Todd LLC 2200 PNC Ctr 201 E 5th St Cincinnati OH 45202-4182 Office Phone: 513-651-6941. Business E-Mail: sfaller@fbtlaw.com.

FALLETTA, JO ANN, conductor; b. NYC, Feb. 27, 1954; d. John Edward and Mary Lucy (Raciopp) F.; m. Robert Alemany, Aug. 24, 1986. BA in Music, Mannes Coll. Music, N.Y.C., 1976; MA in Music, Juilliard Sch., N.Y.C., 1983, PhD in Musical Arts, 1989; doctorate (hon.), Marian Coll., Wis., 1988, Old Dominion U., 1996, Canisius Coll., 2000. Music dir. Queens Philharmonic, NYC, 1978-91, Den. Chamber Orch., Colo., 1983-92; assoc. condr. Milw. Symphony, Wis., 1985-88; music dir. Women's Philharmonic, San Francisco, 1986-96; music dir., condr. Long Beach Symphony, Calif., 1989-00; music dir. Va. Symphony, Norfolk, 1991—, Buffalo Philharm., 1999—. Over 30 recordings with the London Symphony, the Buffalo Philharmonic, the Virginia Symphony, the English Chamber Orchestra, the New Zealand Symphony, the Long Beach Symphony, the Czech National Symphony and the Women's Philharmonic. Stokowski Conducting Competition, Toscanini Conducting award, John S. Edwards Award, Am. Symphony Orchestra League, Seaver/Nat. Endowment for the Arts Conductors Award, 2002. Office: c/o Genevieve Spielberg Inc 12 Princeton St Summit NJ 07901

FALLIN, MARY COPELAND, lieutenant governor; b. Warrensburg, Mo., Dec. 9, 1954; d. Joseph Newton and Mary (Duggan) Copeland; children: Christina, Price. BS, Okla. State U., 1977. Bus. mgr. Okla. Dept. Securities, Oklahoma City, 1979-81; state travel coord. Okla. Dept. of Tourism, Oklahoma City, 1981-82; sales rep. Associated Petroleum, Oklahoma City, 1982-83; mktg. dir. Brian Head (Utah) Hotel & Ski Resort, 1983-84; dir. sales Residence Inn Hotel, Oklahoma City, 1984-87; dist. mgr. Lexington Hotel Suites, Oklahoma City, 1988-90; real estate assoc. Pippin Properties, Inc., Oklahoma City, 1990-94; state rep. Okla. Ho. of Reps., Oklahoma City, 1990-94; lt. gov. State of Okla., Oklahoma City, 1995—. Chmn. Nat. Conf. Lt. Govs. Mem., del. Okla. Fedn. Rep. Women; mem. Am. Legis. Exch. Coun., Nat. Conf. State Legislatures; former bd. mem. United Way Oklahoma City, YWCA; mem. adv. bd. Trail of Tears; former hon. chair Organ Donor Network; former hon. co-chair Indian Territory Arts and Humanities Coun.; former co-chair Festival of Hope; active Crossings Cmty. Ch. Named Woman of Yr., Ladies in Comm., 1998, Girl Scouts Am., 1998, Nat. Legislator of Yr., Okla. Ladies in the News, Disting. Former Student, U. Ctrl. Okla.; recipient Bi-liner award, 1997, Guardian of Small Bus. award, Small Bus. Adv. award, Nat. Fedn. Ind. Small Bus., Women in the News award, Women in Comm. Mem.: Aerospace States Assn. (chmn. 2003—05). Republican. Office: Office Lt Governor Oklahoma State Capitol 2300 N Lincoln Blvd Rm211 Oklahoma City OK 73105 Office Phone: 405-521-2161. Office Fax: 405-525-2702. Business E-Mail: mary.fallin@ltgov.state.ok.us.*

FALLON, BARBARA G., oncologist; b. Cambridge, Mass., Sept. 26, 1952; d. Henry Patrick and Kathleen Elizabeth Fallon; m. Bennett Jay Bernblum; children: Daniel, Alyssa. BA, Trinity Coll., 1975. Cert. Am. Bd. Internal Medicine, 1983, Medical Oncologist 1985. Attending physician Grove Hill Med. Ctr., New Britain, Conn., 2004—, New Britain Gen. Hosp., 1993—; asst. prof. medicine U. Conn. Med. Sch., 1988—; med. dir. Wolfson Pallative Care Program, 2000—04. Chmn. Conn. Cancer Pain Initiative, 1994—95, mem., 1995—. Vol., lectr. Am. Cancer Soc., Meriden, Conn., 1995—. Recipient Career Develop. award, Am. Cancer Soc., 1983—86. Fellow: Am. Coll. Physicians; mem.: AMA, Am. Soc. Clin. Oncology, Am. Coll. Physicians. Avocations: sailing, skiing. Home: 9 Cutler Rd Old Lyme CT 06371 Office: Grovehill Med Ctr 300 Kensington Ave New Britain CT 06051

FALLON, RAE MARY, psychology professor, educational consultant; b. N.Y.C., Apr. 13, 1947; d. Frank J. and Santa A. T.; m. John J. Fallon, 1972; children: Sean, Christopher. BA, CUNY, 1968, MA, 1971; PhD, Fordham U., 2001. Cert. N-6 tchr., spl. edn. tchr., N.Y. Elem. tchr. Pub. Sch. 1, Bronx, NY, 1968—72; pre-sch. tchr. Valley Nursery Sch., Walden, NY, 1972—73; tchr. spl. edn. Orange-Ulster Bd. Coop. Edn. Svcs., Goshen, NY, 1973—75, early childhood specialist, 1982—89; instr. edn. Mt. St. Mary Coll., Newburgh, NY, 1989—93, asst. prof., 1993—2001, assoc. prof. psychology, 2001—. Early childhood cons., Montgomery, N.Y., 1989—; mem. early childhood com. Valley Ctrl. Sch. Sys., Montgomery, 1994. Mem. West Street Sch. Cmty. Sch. Bd., Newburgh, 1990—; mem. early intervention com. Orange County Health Dept., Goshen, 1993—; chmn. program com. Montgomery Rep. Club, 1990-94. Mem. ASCD, Coun. for Exceptional Children, Assn. for Edn. Young Children (regional coord. 1991-92), Kiwanis, Delta Kappa Gamma (pres. Alpha chpt. 2002-06), Phi Delta Kappa Roman Catholic. Office: Mt St Mary Coll 330 Powell Ave Newburgh NY 12550-3412 Office Phone: 845-569-3169.

FALLON, SALLY, writer; b. Santa Monica, Calif., June 22, 1948; d. Harry Herman and Margaret Kirkpatrick Wetzel Jr.; m. William Byron Holt, May 19, 1970 (dec. Sept. 1970); m. John B. Fallon, Mar. 24, 1972; children: Sarah, Nicholas, James, Davidson. BA in English with honors, Stanford U., 1970; MA in English with high honors, UCLA, 1972. Pres. Weston A. Price Found., Washington, 1999—. Author: Nourishing Traditions, 1996; editor jour. Price Pottenger Nutritional Found., 1997-98; contbr. articles on nutrition and health to profl. publs. V.p. Price Pottenger Nutrition Found., San Diego, 1997-98; founder A Campaign for Real Milk, Washington, 1997. Office: Weston A Price Found PBM 106-380 4200 Wisconsin Ave NW Washington DC 20016-2143 E-mail: safallon@aol.com.

FALLS, KATHLEENE JOYCE, photographer; b. Detroit, July 3, 1949; d. Edgar John and Acelia Olive (Young) Haley; m. Donald David Falls, June 15, 1974; children: Daniel John, David James. Student, Oakland Community Coll., 1969-73, Winona Sch. Profl. Photography, 1973-80. Lic. amateur radio-technician class, cert. photog. specialist Profl. Photographers Am., 1988, photog. craftsman Profl. Photographers Am., 1990, cert. electronic imaging Profl. Photographers Am., 1990, master artist Profl. Photographers Am., 1990, profl. photographer Profl. Photographers Am., 2004, master electronic imaging Profl. Photographers Am., 2004. Printer Guardian Photo, Novi, Mich., 1967-69; printer, supr. quality control N.Am. Photo, Livonia, 1969—76; free lance photographer, 1969—76; owner, pres. Kathy Falls, Inc., Camden, 1976—2001; ptnr. Taking Better Pictures, 2006—. Instr. continuing edn. Monroe County (Mich.) C.C., 1981—83, instr. digital imaging, 1994—95; instr. Internat. Photography and Art Sch., Indpls., 2004; nat. artisan judge Congl. H.S. Art Competition, 1985—2000; owner Picture Perfect, Carlton, Mich., 1987; co-owner Haleys Gift Shoppe, Dundee, 1989; pub. info. officer Am. Radio Relay League, 1998—2000. Author: (booklet) Emergency Photo-Retouching for Photographers, 1988; photographer (represented in spl. categories) Profl. Photographers Am. Nat. Loan Collection, 1980, 1981, 1983, 1987, 2002, 2004—05, (permanent collections) Monroe County Hist. Mus., Archives Notre Dame; editor: The Hertzian Herald, 1998; contbr. articles to profl. jours. Active Big Bros. and Big Sisters, Monroe, 1986—87; corr. sec. Monroe Women's Ctr., 1986—88; mem. Amateur Radio Emergency Svc.; pres. Our Lady of Knock divsn. Laoh Adrian, Laoh State Bd., 2001—03; pres. Artworks Hillsdale County Arts Coun., 2006; Catechist St. Parick's Ch., Carleton, 1984—87, mem. parish coun., 1998—2000; bd. dirs. Ladies Ancient Order of Hibernians. Mem.: NAFE, Nat. Orgn. Women Bus. Owners, Monroe C. of C. (chmn. council women bus. owners), Monroe County Fine Arts Coun., Am. Photog. Artisans Guild (bd. dir. 1987—, Photog. Artisan degree 1989, Artisan Laurel degree 1991, pres. 1992, editor Palette Page 2001—04, exec. sec. 2001—, exec. dir. 2002, coun. mem., Fuji

Masterpiece award 2005), Profl. Photographers Am., Profl. Photographers Mich. (artisan chair 1982—83, bd. dir. 2000—, dir. 2001—02, Best of Show award 1976, Artist of Yr. 1980, Best of Show award 1981, Artist of Yr. 1991, Best of Show award 2001), Detroit Profl. Photographers Assn. (artisan chmn. 1981—82, bd. dir. 1987—, Best of Show award 1981, 1983), Am. Soc. Photographers, Hillsdale Art Guild, Toastmasters, Monroe County Radio Comms. Assn., Ladies Ancient Order of Hibernians (bd. dir. 1998—99), Monroe Camera, Hillsdale County Amateur Radio Club, Scarab Club Detroit, Internat. Club. Republican. Roman Catholic. Avocations: guitar, piano, drawing, travel, camping. Home and Office: 14940 Carpenter Rd Camden MI 49232 Office Phone: 517-368-4995. Personal E-mail: katfalls@tdi.net. Business E-Mail: info@takingbetterpictures.com.

FALMAGNE, RACHEL JOFFE, psychologist, educator; PhD in Psychology, Univ. Brussels. Faculty Clark Univ., Worcester, Mass., 1973—, now prof., dept. psychology. Co-editor: Mind and Social Practice: Selected Writings by Sylvia Scribner, 1997, Representing Reason: Feminist Theory and Formal Logic, 2003; author: Language as a Constitutive Factor in Logical Knowledge, 1988. Mem.: Internat. Soc. Theoretical Psychology (pres. 2005). Office: Dept Psychology Clark Univ 950 Main St Worcester MA 01610-1477 Office Phone: 508-793-7262. Business E-Mail: rfalmagne@clark.edu.*

FALZANO, COLLEEN, special education educator; b. Glens Falls, NY, Oct. 9, 1962; d. Richard Joseph and Patricia Anne (Sheridan) F. AA, Ulster County C.C.; BA in Psychology, SUNY, New Paltz; MS in Edn., SUNY, Brockport; diploma with honors, St. John's U., 2001, EdD, 2003, cert. in instrnl. leadership, 2003. Substitute tchr. Kendall (N.Y.) Ctrl. Sch. Dist., 1986-87, Holley (N.Y.) Ctrl. Sch. Dist., 1986-87, Albion (N.Y.) Sch. Dist., 1986-87; tchr. spl. edn. Children's Home Kingston, N.Y., 1987-90, New Paltz Ctrl. Sch. Dist., 1990-91, Saugerties (N.Y.) Ctrl. Sch. Dist., 1991-93; tchr. resource room, cons. Kingston City Sch. Dist., 1993—. Recipient Gappy Gurrison award, 1981, Dean's award for acad. excellence St. John's U. Mem. ASCD, Internat. Soc. Tech. Edn., NY Mid. Sch. Assn., Nat. Coun. Tchrs. Math., Nat. Sci. Tchrs. Assn., Mid-Hudson Field Hockey Ofcls. Assn. (pres.), Phi Delta Kappa. Avocations: mountain biking, hiking, writing, jogging. Home: 5 Boxwood Ct Saugerties NY 12477-2009 E-mail: drfalz@yahoo.com.

FAM, HANAA, psychiatrist; b. Alexandria, Egypt, Mar. 25, 1963; arrived in U.S., 1989; d. Wadie Zaki Bassily-Ayad and Evyleen Iskander Attia; m. Raout Michael Fam; children: Abraam Raout, Maiam Raout. MD, Alexandria U., Egypt, 1988. Diplomate Am. Bd. Neurology and Psychiatry. Faculty and staff psychiatrist Cedars Sinai Med. Ctr., L.A., 2003—; staff psychiatrist St. Joseph Hosp., Orange, 2005—. Med. dir. St. Mariam Med. Clinic, Inc., Costa Mesa, Calif., 2003—; sec. Child and Adolescent Psychiat. Soc., L.A., 2006. Mem.: Orange County Psychiat. Soc. Mem. Coptic Ch. Egypt. Avocation: cooking. Office: St Mariam Med Clinic 1901 Newport Blvd Costa Mesa CA 92627

FANGEROW, KAY ELIZABETH, nurse; b. Thomas, Okla., June 27, 1952; d. Byron Frederick and Wilma Jean (Bickford) Mayfield; children: David Andrew, Sarah Elizabeth. Student, Oral Roberts U., 1970-71; BS in Nursing magna cum laude, Calif. State U., Long Beach, 1975; MS in Health Care Adminstrn., U. LaVerne, 1991. RN, Calif.; cert. pub. health nurse. Staff nurse pediatrics service Long Beach Meml. Hosp., 1974-75, Riverside (Calif.) Community Hosp., 1975-76, Parkview Community Hosp., Riverside, 1982-84; supervising pub. health nurse County Health Dept., San Bernardino, Calif., 1976—, coord. sch. based and sch. linked health care svcs., 1994—; dir. Westside Park Sch. Based Health Ctr. FQHC Clinic, 2002; grant writer County Health Dept., San Bernardino, Calif., 1994—. Cons. Am. Home Health, Santa Ana, Calif., 1986—2000. Instr. Inland Counties chpt. Am. Cancer Soc., Riverside, 1977—; mem. cmty. action coun. San Bernardino County Youth Justice Ctr., 1999—; chair child death rev. team San Bernardino County, 2005—. Mem. Am. Pub. Health Assn. (co-author abstract 1986, 87, 89, coordinator hypertension worksite project, diabetes control project, pub. health nursing homeless project, presenter ann. meeting 1986, 87, 89), Pub. Health Nurse Group (chmn. 1977-78, vice chmn. profl. performance com. 1978, sec. peer rev. com. 1978), San Bernardino County Asthma Coalition, Sigma Theta Tau (Gamma Alpha chpt., honoree for child abuse prevention supervising pub. health nurse of yr. 2002) San Bernardino County Child Death Review Team (chair, 2005). Democrat. Home: 555 Oak Hill St Ontario CA 91761 Office Phone: 909-388-0479. Business E-Mail: kfangerow@dph.sbcounty.gov.

FANN, MARGARET ANN, counselor; b. Pasco, Wash., July 16, 1942; d. Joseph Albert David and Clarice Mable (Deaver) Rivard; m. Jerry Lee Fann, June 13, 1986; children: Brenda Heupel, Scott Sherman, Kristin Johnson, Robert Lack III. AA, Big Bend C.C., Moses Lake, Wash., 1976; BA in Applied Psychology magna cum laude, Ea. Wash. U., 1977, MS in Psychology, 1978. Cert. mental health counselor, Wash.; cert. chem. dependency counselor II, nat. cert. addictions counselor II, cert. in chronic psychiat. disability. Intern counselor Linker House Drug Rehab., Spokane, Wash., 1976-78; drug counselor The House drug program, Tacoma, Wash., 1978-80; exec. dir. Walla Walla (Wash.) Commn. Alcohol, 1980-82; dir. Cmty. Alcohol Svcs. Assn., Kennewick, Wash., 1982-86; primary care coord. Carondelet Psychiat. Care Ctr., Richland, Wash., 1986-90; part-time instr. Ea. Wash. U., Cheney, 1981-88; instr. Columbia Basin Coll., Pasco, 1990-93; adminstr. Action Chem. Dependency Ctr., Kennewick, 1993—. Bd. dirs. Benton-Franklin County Substance Abuse Coalition, Pasco, Kennewick, Richland, 1990—. Vol. Pat Hale for Senator, Kennewick, 1994. Mem. Am. Counselors Assn., Nat. Mental Health Counselors Assn., Wash. State Mental Health Counselors Assn., Tri-Cities Counselors Assn., Phi Theta Kappa. Avocations: swimming, bicycling, running. Office: Action Chem Dependency Ctr 552 N Colorado St Ste 5525 Kennewick WA 99336-7779 also: Benton-Franklin County MICA Detoxification Ctr 1020 E 7th Ave Kennewick WA 99336-5936

FANNIN, JOSEPHINE JEWELL, social services administrator; b. W.Va., Feb. 12, 1944; Student, Davis Coll., Am. Inst. Banking, L.A., 1962-65, Nat. Floral Inst., 1966-68; lic., Bucks Coll., Newtown, Pa., 1984; AAS in Human Svcs., Ariz. Western Coll., 1994; MA in human svc., U. of Wexford, 2000, PhD in Human Svc. Leadership Mgmt., 2004. Women's program dir. for Europe, USN, Rota, Spain, 1976-77; with mktg. svcs. dept. Bank of Am., Fairfield, Calif., 1962-65; comml. accounts specialist Commerce Bank, St. Charles, Mo., 1970-73, 75-76, comml. accounts rep., 80-82, Pa. Nat. Bank, Phila., 1978-81; info. and referral field nurse Upjohn Health Care, Newtown, 1982-85, info. and referral specialist Jacksonville, Fla., 1985-89; dir. vol. and ret. sr. vol. program Western Ariz. Coun. Govts., Yuma, 1992-94; sr. program adminstr. Mid East Area Agy. on Aging, Brentwood, Mo., 1994-99; exec. dir. Hosp. Hospitality Ho., Huntington, W.Va., 1999—. Spkr. Internat. Platform Assn., 1985-95. Bd. dirs. Ch. Women United, Bucks County, Pa., 1980-85, Yuma Regional Med. Ctr., 1992-94; bd. dirs., mem. fin. com. Jacksonville and Yuma hospices, 1985-94; ombudsman adv. Western Ariz. Coun. Govts., 1989-94; mem. adv. bd. vol. clearing house and human svcs. program St. Charles C.C., 1995, bd. dirs., 1997; exec. dir. Hosp. Hospitality House, 1999—; bd. dirs. St. Charles Cmty. Coun., 1997, City of Huntington Found., 2000. Recipient Outstanding Employee award Western Coun. Govts., 1994. Mem. AAUW, Assn. Fundraising Profls., Nat. Soc. Fund Raising Execs., Zonta (past bd. dirs. and program dir. Yuma), Rotary Internat. (bd. dirs.), Phi Theta Kappa (Alumni award 1994). Avocations: travel, writing, speaking on current events and senior advocacy and volunteer programs. Office: Hosp Hospitality House 2801 S Staunton Rd Huntington WV 25702 Home: 1661 Washington Blvd Huntington WV 25701 E-mail: huntingtonhhh@aol.com.

FANNING, DAKOTA, actress; b. Conyers, Ga., Feb. 23, 1994; d. Steve and Joy Fanning. Actor: (films) Tomcats, 2001, I Am Sam, 2001 (Best Young Actor/Actress award Broadcast Film Critics Assn.), Father Xmas, 2001, Trapped, 2002, Sweet Home Alabama, 2002, Hansel & Gretel, 2002, Uptown Girls, 2003, The Cat in the Hat, 2003, Man on Fire, 2004, Hide and Seek, 2005, Nine Lives, 2005, War of the Worlds, 2005 (Best Young Actress, Broadcast Film Critics Assn., 2006), Dreamer: Inspired by a True Story, 2005, (voice): (TV films) Kim Possible: A Stitch in Time, 2003,: (TV miniseries) Taken, 2002, (guest appearances): (TV series) ER, 2000, Ally McBeal, 2000, Strong Medicine, 2000, CSI: Crime Scene Investigation, 2000, The Practice, 2000, Spin City, 2000, Malcolm in the Middle, 2001, The Fighting Fitzgeralds, 2001, The Ellen Show, 2001, Friends, 2004, (guest appearances, voice) Family Guy, 2001. Named one of The 10 Most Fascinating People of 2005, Barbara Walters Special. Office: Osbrink Talent Agy 4343 Lankershim Blvd Ste 100 North Hollywood CA 91602 Office Phone: 818-760-2488.

FANNING, ELLEN, biology professor, research scientist; BS in Chemistry, U. Wis.-Madison; PhD in Virology, U. Cologne, Germany, 1977. Asst. prof. Univ. Konstanz, Germany; prof. and acting chair Inst. for Biochemistry Univ. Munich; now Stevenson Prof. Molecular Biology, Dept. Biological Sciences Vanderbilt Univ., Nashville. Vis. prof. Dept. Genetics Harvard Med. Sch.; mem. editl. bd. Jour. of Virology; assoc. dir. Nat. Inst. Health Tng. Grant of Viruses, Nucleic Acids and Cancer; prof. Howard Hughes Med. Inst. Mem.: German Science Found. Peer Review Bd., Milwaukee Found. Corp. (Shaw Scholar Sci. Adv. Bd.), European Molecular Biology Orgn. Office: Vanderbilt U 2325 Stevenson Ctr 1161 21st Ave S Nashville TN 37235 Office Phone: 615-343-5677. Office Fax: 615-343-6707. E-mail: ellen.h.fanning@Vanderbilt.Edu.

FANOS, KATHLEEN HILAIRE, osteopathic physician, podiatrist; b. Bremerhaven, Germany, Aug. 18, 1956; came to U.S., 1957; d. Homer Dantangelo and Ilse Helmar (Ochs) F. AAS in Music, Nassau C.C., Garden City, N.Y., 1976; BS in Music Edn., Hofstra U., 1978, postgrad., 1978-79; D Podiatric Medicine, Coll. Podiatric Med. and Surgery, Des Moines, 1987, DO, 1994. Diplomate Am. Bd. Internal Medicine. Tchr. music McKenna Jr. HS and Eastlake Elem. Sch., Massapequa, NY, 1978—79; musician numerous profl. orgns., NY, 1979—, Iowa, 1979—; preceptorship in podiatry Bayshore, NY, 1987-88; pvt. practice podiatry Hyde Park, West Roxbury and Brookline, Mass., 1988-91; resident in internal medicine Winthrop U. Hosp., Mineola, NY, 1994-97; internist Cmty. Med. Assocs., Jackson, NJ, 1997-2000, Ocean County Family Care, Jackson, NJ, 2000—03, Hinds Internal Medicine, Jackson, Miss., 2003—. Ins. med. examiner Portamedic, Burlington, Mass., 1988-91. Mem. AMA, ACP, Am. Bd. Internal Medicine, Am. Soc. Internal. Medicine, Am. Osteo. Assn., Am. Coll. Osteo. Family Physicians, N.Y. State Internal Medicine Soc., Phi Theta Kappa, Pi Kappa Lambda, Sigma Sigma Phi, Phi Delta Epsilon. Avocations: music, tennis, bowling, skiing, travel. Office Phone: 601-376-2115. Personal E-mail: kfanos@jam.rr.com.

FANSELOW, JULIE RUTH, writer; b. Springfield, Ill., July 26, 1961; d. Byron and Ruth Leona (Neumann) F.; m. Bruce Edward Whiting, Apr. 25, 1992; 1 child, Natalie BS in Journalism, Ohio U., Athens, 1982. Reporter Salem News, Ohio, 1982—85; editor Vindicator, Youngstown, Ohio, 1985—89; reporter Times-News, Twin Falls, Idaho, 1989—91; pvt. practice writer Boise, Idaho, 1991—. Co-founder Guidebookwriters.com Author: (book) Traveling the Oregon Trail, 1993, 2002, Idaho Off the Beaten Path, 1998, 2006, Texas (Lonely Planet), 1999, 2002, British Columbia (Lonely Planet), 2001; contbr. articles to nat. publs. Recipient 1st pl. for mag. writing Idaho Press Club, 1992, 1st pl. for guidebook Nat. Assn. Interpretation, 1993 Mem. Am. Soc. Journalists and Authors, Lewis and Clark Trail Heritage Found., Oreg.-Calif. Trail Assn. Unitarian Universalist. Avocations: kayaking, travel, reading, arts, hiking. Home: 1504 Columbus St Boise ID 83705-2509 Personal E-mail: juliewrites@yahoo.com.

FANSLOW, MARY FRANCES, information scientist; b. Kingsport, Tenn. d. Robert Francis and Malinda C. Fanslow. BA in Chemistry and Biology, U. Tenn., Knoxville, 1982; MLA in Libr. and Info. Mgmt., Emory U., Atlanta, 1983; MA in History, East Tenn. State U., Johnson City, 2004. Asst. prof. of med. bibliography Mercer Univ. Sch. Medicine Libr., Macon, Ga., 1983—84; info. scientist Eastman Chem. Co., Kingsport, Tenn., 1984—. Leader Girl Scouts Am., Kingsport, Tenn., 1998; bd. dirs. Bridge Refugee Svcs., 2005—; trustee So. Appalachian Highlands Conservancy, 2001—; instr. Jr. Achievement, Kingsport, 1995—. Recipient Outstanding Arts/Humanities Thesis award, East Tenn. State U., 2005. Home: 1413 Brightridge Dr Kingsport TN 37664

FANTASIA, (FANTASIA MONIQUE BARRINO), singer; b. High Point, NC, June 30, 1984; 1 child: Zion Quari Barrino. Contestant American Idol, 2004; singer J Records, 2004—. Singer: (songs) I Believe, 2004 (Top Selling Single of Yr., Billboard Music Awards, 2004, Top Selling R&B/Hip-Hop Single of Yr., Billboard Music Awards, 2004), Summertime, 2004, Chain of Fools, 2004, (albums) Free Yourself, 2004; author: Life Is Not a Fairy Tale, 2005; actor: (TV films) Life Is Not a Fairytale: The Fantasia Barrino Story, 2006; numerous TV guest appearances. Recipient Image award for Outstanding Female Artist, NAACP, 2005. Winner, American Idol, 2004. Office: c/o J Records 745 Fifth Ave New York NY 10151

FANTOZZI, JANET ROSEN, music educator; d. Joseph and Philomena Rosen; m. Donald Robert Fantozzi, Jr., Mar. 27, 1957; children: Danielle, Donald. EdM, Pa. State U., State College, 1982. Cert. music tchr. Conn., 1984. String tchr. Enloe Gifted and Talented H.S., Raleigh, NC, 1977—83, Appleton H.S. East, Wis., 1983—84, Fairfield H.S., Conn., 1984—90; suzuki string tchr. Union Sch., Unionville, Conn., 1992—. Mem.: Suzuki Assn. of the Ams. Congregationalist. Avocations: opera, reading, writing, travel, violin. Home: 107 Woodlawn Dr Torrington CT 06790 Office: Union School 173 School St Unionville CT 06085 Office Phone: 860-673-2575. Personal E-mail: dfantozz@optonline.net. Business E-Mail: fantozzij@fpsct.org.

FANTOZZI, PEGGY RYONE, geologist, environmental planner; b. Providence, Feb. 2, 1948; d. Eugene Baker and Cynthia (Bragg) Ryone; m. Thomas Allen Collins, Jan. 4, 1969 (div. 1985); children: Christin, Cindi; m. Thomas Edward Fantozzi, Mar. 22, 1985 (div. 1989); 1 child, Amy. BA in Earth Scis., Bridgewater State Coll., 1969; MS in Geology, Franklin and Marshall Coll., 1971. Registered sanitarian, Mass.; cert. wastewater treatment operator grade 4-M; cert. soil evaluator. Project mgr. Coastal Zone Mgmt. Grant, Eastham, Mass., 1980—81; geologist, project mgr. BSC Group/Cape Cod, Barnstable Village, Mass., 1982—88; sr. environ. scientist A.M. Wilson Assocs., Osterville, 1988—94, Daylor Consulting Group, Braintree, Mass., 1994—97. Instr. earth scis. and geology Bridgewater (Mass.) State Coll., 1972-74, Cape Cod C.C., West Barnstable, Mass., 1979-82; cons. conservation and health bds. Town of Bourne, Mass., 1984-85; mem., chair State Comm. for the Conservation of Soil, Water and Related Resources, 1996—; mem. Nat. Resources Conservation and Devel. Coun., 1998. Bd. dirs., v.p. Assn. for Preservation of Cape Cod, Orleans, Mass., 1979-85; trustee Cape Cod Mus. Natural History, Brewster, 1982-85; advisor Barnstable County Marine Resources program, 1980-82; chmn. Eastham Conservation Comm., 1978-82, Selectmen's Task Force on Local Pollution, Bourne, 1985-87; del. Barnstable County Water Resources Adv. Coun., 1979-89, Bourne Shore and Harbor Com., 1989-92; rep. Tri-Town Septage treatment Facilities Planning Commn., Eastham, Orleans, citizen's adv. com. groundwater discharge program Mass. Dept. EPA, 1987-88, Surface Water Quality, 1990, 93, Mass. Bays Program Citizen Adv. Steering Com., 1992—; pres. Mass. Assn. Conservation Dists., 1995-98; chair Mass. State Commn. for the Conservation of Soil, Water and Related Resources, 1998—; mem. Cape Cod Water Protection Collaborative, 2006—, mem. steering com., 2006—. Grantee USDA-Natural Resources Conservation Svc., 1997-98. Mem. Nat. Assn. Conservation Dists. (dir.), Mass. Health Officers Assn., Mass. Water Works Assn., Monument Beach Civic Assn. Home: 25 Shore Rd Buzzards Bay MA 02532-5425 Office: Land Use Permitting 25 Shore Rd Bourne MA 02532-5425

FANTZ, JANET NELSEN, school psychologist; b. Chgo., July 29, 1943; d. Harold Frederick and Louise (Maurer) Nelsen; m. Paul Richard Fantz, July 31, 1965; children: Deborah Fantz Clay, Susan Fantz Gibbs, Paul William. BS in Edn., So. Ill. U., Carbondale, 1965, MS in Edn., 1968; post grad. studies, NC State U., Raleigh, 1981—82. Nat. cert. sch. psychologist Nat. Assn. Sch. Psychologists, lic. psychol. assoc. NC State Bd. Examiners Practicing Psychology. Tchr. Mehlville Sch. Dist., Mo., 1965—69, sub. tchr., 1969—71; homebound tchr. Spl. Sch. Dist., St. Louis, 1971—72; sch. psychologist Alachua County Sch. Dist., Gainesville, Fla., 1973—78, Dade County Sch. Dist., Miami, 1979, Wake County Sch. Dist., Raleigh, 1980—. Mentor psychologist Wake County Sch. System, Raleigh, 1990—, mem. assessment com., 1996—2006, chairperson assessment com., 1996—99, learning disabilities com., 2003—05. Vol. March of Dimes Mothers March, 2006; vol. Kids for Christ Woodhaven Baptist Ch., Holly Springs, NC, 2002—03, preschool com. mem., 2005. Mem.: Nat. Assn. Sch. Psychologists, NC Sch. Psychology Assn., Psi Chi, Kappa Delta Pi, Pi Lambda Theta. Baptist. Avocations: travel, bridge, reading. Home: 2002 Ambrose Park Ln Cary NC 27518 Office: Wake County Sch System 3600 Wake Forest Rd Raleigh NC 27611 Office Phone: 919-387-4408. E-mail: jfantz@wcpss.net.

FANUS, PAULINE RIFE, librarian; b. New Oxford, Pa., Feb. 14, 1925; d. Maurice Diehl and Bernice Edna (Gable) Rife; m. William Edward Fanus, June 20, 1944; children: Irene Weaver, Larry William, Daniel Diehl. BS, Pa. State U., 1945; MLS, Villanova U., 1961; postgrad., Temple U., 1986—. Periodical libr. Tex. Coll. Arts Industries, Kingville, 1945; tchr. nursery sch. Studio Sch., Wayne, Pa., 1953-55; libr. circulation, reference Franklin Inst., Phila., 1963-66; asst. libr. Ursinus Coll., Collegeville, Pa., 1966; catalog libr., instr. Eastern Coll., St. Davids, Pa., 1967-71; head libr. Agnes Irwin Sch., Rosemont, Pa., 1971-93, head libr. emeritus, 1993—. Book reviewer The Book Report. Mem. AAUP (chpt. sec. Eastern Coll. 1970-71). Home: 78 Holly Dr New Holland PA 17557-9476

FARAG, MAUREEN ANN, assistant principal; b. Boston, June 19, 1948; d. William McCarthy and Elizabeth Marie Crimmins; m. Robert David Farag, Apr. 8, 1972; children: Jessica Ann Farag Waters, Regan Marie. BA in Art Edn., Madonna Coll., Livonia, Mich., 1970; MS in Art Edn., Purdue Calumet U., Hammond, Ind., 1974; postgrad., Ind. U., Gary, 1987. Tchr. art Highland Mid. Sch., Ind., 1970—2003, asst. prin., 2003—. Mem.: ASCD, Nat. Assn. Secondary Sch. Prins., Ind. Assn. Prins., Art Edn. Assn. Ind. (mem. exec. bd. 1992—). Avocations: reading, gardening. Home: 1161 St Joseph St Gary IN 46403 Office: Highland Mid Sch 2941 41st St Highland IN 46322

FARAN, ELLEN WEBSTER, publishing executive; b. Cambridge, Mass., June 17, 1951; d. James John and Ellen (Gallishaw) F. BA, Radcliffe Coll., 1973; MBA, Harvard U., 1981. Editl. asst. Folger Shakespeare Libr., Washington, 1974-77; editl. assoc. Internat. City Mgmt. Assn., Washington, 1977-79; gen. mgr. David R. Godine Pub., Boston, 1980-82; cons. Nat. Acad. Press, Washington, 1982-83; assoc. pub. Harper & Row, NYC, 1983-90; chief fin. officer Farrar, Straus & Giroux, NYC, 1990; v.p., dir., fin., plan. devel., trade, reference divsn. Houghton; dir. MIT Press, Mass., 2003—. Adj. faculty NYU Sch. of Continuing Edn., 1992—; speaker pub. course Radcliffe Coll., 1989—, bd. adv. Beacon Press (chair). Office: MIT Press Mass Inst Tech Cambridge MA 02138

FARBER, ROSANN ALEXANDER, geneticist, educator; b. Charlotte, N.C., Nov. 21, 1944; d. J. Wilson Jr. and June Adell (Childs) Alexander; m. Gerald Lee Farber, July 28, 1966 (div. Jan. 1969); m. Thomas Douglas Petes, July 20, 1973; children: Laura Elizabeth Petes, Diana Christine Petes. AB in Biology, Oberlin Coll., 1966; postgrad., U. Pitts., 1967-68, Albert Einstein Coll. Medicine, 1969; PhD in Genetics, U. Wash., 1973. Diplomate in clin. cytogenetics and clin. molecular genetics Am. Bd. Med. Genetics. Postdoctoral fellow Nat. Inst. for Med. Rsch., London, 1973-75; rsch. assoc. Children's Hosp. Med. Ctr., Boston, 1975-77; from asst. prof. to assoc. prof. U. Chgo., 1977-88; assoc. prof. dept. pathology and lab. medicine, program molecular biology and biotechnology, curriculum genetics and molecular biology U. N.C., Chapel Hill, 1988-97, prof., 1997—, prof. dept. genetics, 2001—. Mem. U. N.C. Lineberger Comprehensive Cancer Ctr., 1996—. Contbr. articles to profl. jours. NIH grantee, 1978—. Mem. AAAS, Am. Soc. Human Genetics. Achievements include research in human molecular genetics, somatic cell genetics, cancer genetics. Home: 612 Morgan Creek Rd Chapel Hill NC 27517-4928 Office: U NC CB 7525 Brinkhous-Bullitt Bldg Chapel Hill NC 27599 Office Phone: 919-966-6920. E-mail: rfarber@med.nc.edu.

FARBER, ROSELEE CORA, counselor; d. Wayne Cunningham and Margaret Cora Farber. B, U. Tex, Edinburg, 1991; M in Counseling, Liberty U., Lunchburg, Va., 1995. Missionary, tchr. Child Evangelism Fellowship, Argentina, 1960—65, Nicaragua, 1966—72, Mexico, 1973—75, World Evangelism, Brownsville, Tex., 1973—77, Fellowship Internat. Mission, 1977—; counselor South Tex. Family Counseling, Rio Grande Valley, 2001—. Tchr. Rio Grande Bible Inst., Edinburg, Tex., 1985—. Mem.: Am. Assn. Christian Edn., Play Therapy Assn., Am. Counseling Assn. Republican. Baptist. Office: South Tex Family Counseling 4300 S Bus Hwy 281 Edinburg TX 78539 Office Phone: 956-342-1876. E-mail: msrosalei@sbcglobal.net.

FARBER, ZULIMA V., former state attorney general, lawyer; b. El Caney, Oriente, Cuba, Sept. 21, 1944; BA, Montclair State Coll., 1968, MA, 1970; JD, Rutgers U., 1974. Bar: NJ 1974, US Supreme Ct. 1983. Asst. prosecutor Bergen County, NJ, 1975—78; asst. counsel to Gov. Brendan Byrne State of NJ, Trenton, 1978—81, pub. advocate, pub. defender Cabinet of Gov. James J. Florio, 1992—94; assoc. Lowenstein Sandler PC, Roseland, NJ, 1981—85, ptnr. litig., 1986—92, 1994—2006; atty. gen. State of NJ, Trenton, 2006. Mem. Com. on Criminal Rules, Com. on Evidence Rules, Com. on Character NJ State Supreme Ct., 1986—92, mem. Adv. Com. on Ethics, 1994—; mem. NJ State Adv. Com. US Commn. on Civil Rights, 1987—, chairperson, 1990—94; vis. assoc. Eagleton Inst., Rutgers U., 1994—. Contbr. articles to law jours. Trustee Fairleigh Dickinson U., 1994—; chair bd. trustees Jersey City Med. Ctr., 1982—92, 1994—96. Named one of 25 Women of Influence in NJ, NJBiz Mag., Most Influential Black Americans, Ebony mag., 2006. Fellow: Am. Bar Found.; mem.: Nat. Abortion Rights Action League, NJ Chap. (pres.). Democrat.*

FARDY, LYDIA J., educator; b. Boston, June 17, 1949; d. William MacIntyre and Barbara Dailey Jewell; m. Richard Wiley Fardy, Aug. 7, 1971; children: James Reed, Lisa Jewell, Jonathan Richard. AA, Lasell Jr. Coll., 1969. Lic. childcare provider Mass. Kindergarten lead tchr. Robert's Day Sch., Cambridge, Mass., 1969-71; lead tchr. 4 year olds Kendall Sch., Belmont, Mass., 1972-73; asst. dir., head tchr. KinderCare, Billerica, Mass., 1981-82; co-dir. Abundant Life Christian Sch. and Learning Ctr., Wilmington, Mass., 1983-84; family childcare provider Lydia's Country Nursery Family Day Care, Billerica, 1984-2000; head tchr. Kendall Sch., Belmont, Mass., 1989-90; lead tchr. KinderCare Learning Ctrs., Inc., Burlington, Mass., 2000—. Ind. ednl. cons. Discovery Toys, Billerica, 1984-85; beauty cons. Mary Kay, Billerica, 1993-97. Bicentennial mem. Libr. of Congress, 1999—. Mem. Family Childcare Assn. (co-pres. 1987-88, chair comms. 1980's), Assn. Childhood Edn. Internat., Adult and Children's Alliance. Avocations: interior decorating, gardening, music, embroidery, cooking.

FARELLA, ANGELINA, pediatrician, educator; MD, Rose U., 1995. Cert. car seat techician. Intern pediatrics U. Tex. Med. Br., 1995—96, resident, 1996—98; chair, Dept. Pediatrics Clear Lake Regional Med. Ctr.; pediatrician A Brighter Tomorrow Pediatrics. Recipient Leadership award (Young Physician), AMA Found., 2005. Mem.: Am. Acad. Pediatrics, Bay Area Pediatrics Soc. (pres.). Office: A Brighter Tomorrow Pediatrics 425 Henrietta St Webster TX 77598 Office Phone: 281-332-0500.*

FARENGA, JUSTINE-LOUISE PORTER, music educator; b. Danbury, Conn., Feb. 28, 1981; d. Angelo Farenga and Louise Porter-Hahn. MusB, U. N.H., 2003; MusM, postgrad., Ariz. State U., 2006—. Cert. music tchr. grades K-12 choral, instrumental and gen. Conn., 2003, Maine, 2003. Choral and gen. music tchr. Woodstock (Conn.) Mid. Sch., 2003—05; grad. asst. choral dept. Ariz. State U., Tempe, 2005—; choir dir. grades 6-8 Higley Unified Sch. Dist., Ariz., 2006—; choir dir. Ocatillo Springs United Meth. Ch., Chandler, Ariz., 2006—. Children's choir dir. U. Presbyn. Ch., Tempe, 2005—06. Recipient Music Talent award, Ariz. State U. Choral Dept., 2005, 2006.

Mem.: Music Educators Nat. Conf., Am. Choral Dirs. Assn. (treas. Airz. chpt.), Golden Key. Home: Apt # 2148 875 W Pecos Rd Chandler AZ 85225 Personal E-mail: justine_farenga@hotmail.com.

FARENTHOLD, FRANCES TARLTON, lawyer; b. Corpus Christi, Tex., Oct. 2, 1926; d. Benjamin Dudley and Catherine (Bluntzer) Tarlton; children: Dudley Tarlton, George Edward, Emilie, James Dougherty, Vincent Bluntzer (dec.). AB, Vassar Coll., 1946; JD, U. Tex., 1949; LLD, Hood Coll., 1973, Boston U., 1973, Regis Coll., 1976, Lake Erie Coll., 1979, Elmira Coll., 1981, Coll. Santa Fe, 1985. Bar: Tex. 1949. Pvt. practice, 1949-65, 67-76, 80—; mem. Tex. Ho. of Reps., 1968-72; dir. legal aid Nueces County, 1965-67; pres. Wells Coll., Aurora, NY, 1976-80; asst. prof. law Tex. So. U., Houston, Thurgood Marshall disting. vis. prof., 1994-95. Lawyer; b. Corpus Christi, Tex., Oct. 2, 1926; d. Benjamin Dudley and Catherine (Bluntzer) Tarlton; children: Dudley Tarlton, George Edward, Emilie, James Dougherty, Vincent Bluntzer (dec.). AB, Vassar Coll., 1946; JD, U. Tex., 1949; LLD, Hood Coll., 1973, Boston U., 1973, Regis Coll., 1976, Lake Erie Coll., 1979, Elmira Coll., 1981, Coll. of Santa Fe, 1985. Bar: Tex. 1949. Pvt. practice, 1949-65, 67-76, 80—; mem. Tex. Ho. of Reps., 1968-72; dir. legal aide Nueces County, 1965-67; asst. prof. law Tex. So. U., Houston; pres. Wells Coll., Aurora, N.Y., 1976-80; disting. vis. prof. Thurgood Marshall Tex. So. U., Houston, 1994-95. Mem. Human Relations Com., Corpus Christi, 1963-68, Corpus Christi Citizen's Com. Community Improvement, 1966-68; mem. Tex. adv. com. to U.S. Commn. on Civil Rights, 1968-76; mem. nat. adv. council ACLU; mem. Orgn. for Preservation Unblemished Shoreline, 1964—; Dem. candidate for Gov. of Tex., 1972; del. Dem. Nat. Conv., 1972, 1st woman nominated to be candidate v.p. U.S., 1972; nat. co-chmn. Citizens to Elect McGovern-Shriver, 1972; chmn. Nat. Women's Polit. Caucus, 1973-75; mem. Dem. platform com., 1988; trustee Vassar Coll., 1975-83; bd. dirs. Fund for Constl. Govt., Ctr. for Devel. Policy, 1983—, Mexican Am. Legal Def. and Ednl. Fund, 1980-83; chmn. Inst. for Policy Studies, 1986-91; mem. bd. dirs. Rothko Chapel, 1997—. Recipient Lyndon B. Johnson Woman of Year award, 1973. Mem. State Bar Tex. Mem. Human Rels. Com., Corpus Christi, 1963-68, Corpus Christi Citizens Com. Cmty. Improvement, 1966-68; mem. Tex. adv. com. to U.S. Commn. on Civil Rights, 1968-76; mem. nat. adv. coun. ACLU; mem. Orgn. for Preservation Unblemished Shoreline, 1964—; Dem. candidate for Gov. of Tex., 1972; del. Dem. Nat. Conv., 1972, 1st woman nominated to be candidate v.p. U.S., 1972; nat. co-chair Citizens to elect McGovern-Shriver, 1972; chmn. Nat. Women's Polit. Caucus, 1973-75; mem. Dem. Platform Com., 1988; trustee Vassar Coll., 1975-83; bd. dirs. Fund for Constl. Govt., Ctr. for Devel. Policy, 1983—, Mexican Am. Legal Def. and Ednl. Fund, 198--83; chmn. Inst. for Policy Studies, 1986-91; bd. dirs. Rothko Chapel, 1997—, chmn., 2001—. Recipient Lyndon B. Johnson Woman of Yr. award, 1973, Lifetime Svc. award, Dem. Party of Tex., 1998. Mem. State Bar Tex. Home: 2929 Buffalo Speedway Apt 1813 Houston TX 77098-1710 Personal E-mail: emailsissy@aol.com.

FARGASON, PATRICIA J., psychologist; b. Gainesville, Ga., Feb. 9, 1946; d. William Leslie and Mauryce Harrison Fargason; m. Tom O Massey, Dec. 3, 1953. BA, Brenau Coll., Gainesville, Ga., 1968; MEd, U. of Ga., 1972, PhD, 1975. Cert. addiction specialist Am. Acad. of Healthcare Providers, 1996. Program dir. Bradford Adolescent Unit, Birmingham, Ala., 1989; clin. dir. COPAC, Brandon, Miss., 1990—. Program dir. Five Oaks RTC, Houston, 1988—89. Sec. NCSAC, Atlanta, 1994—2000. Mem.: APA. Office: COPAC 3949 Hwy 43 N Brandon MS 39047 Office Phone: 800-446-9727. Office Fax: 601-829-4278. E-mail: patsyf@copacms.com.

FARGO, HEATHER, mayor; b. Oakland, Ca, Dec. 12, 1952; m. Alan Moll. BS in environmental planning and mgmt., U. Cal-Davis, 1975. Mem. Sacramento City Coun., 1989—98; mayor City of Sacramento, Calif., 2001—. Office: City Hall 5th Fl 915 I St Sacramento CA 95814 Business E-Mail: hfargo@cityofsacramento.org.*

FARHAT-HOLZMAN, LAINA, writer, editor; b. Rochester, N.Y., Sept. 9, 1932; d. Saul H. Chazan and Sara A. Minkin; m. Edward Henry Holzman, Feb. 23, 1997; m. Hormoz Farhat (div.); children: Kameron, Katherine Ariana. BA, UCLA, 1957; MA, U. So. Calif., L.A., 1969, PhD, 1973. Editor GTE Sylvania, Sunnyvale, Calif., 1975—79, Westinghouse, 1979—86; editor-in-chief Sci. and Tech. Mag. and Jour. C3I, Mountain View, 1986—90; asst. prof. Golden Gate U., San Francisco, 1990—95; columnist Santa Cruz Sentinel, 1998—, Watsonville Pajaronian, 2005—. Dir. U.N. Assn., San Francisco, 1990—95; lectr. great decisions programs World Affairs Coun. (San Francisco and Monterey chpts.) and AAUW. Author: Strange Birds from Zoroaster's Nest, 2005, God's Law or Man's Law, 2005, The Slave Who Lied, 2006. Mem.: World Affairs Coun. (v.p. programs Monterey chpt. 1999—2002), Internat. Soc. Comparative Study of Civilizations (jour. editor and v.p. 2000—). Home: 170 Tiburon Ct Aptos CA 95003-5833 Personal E-mail: lfarhat102@aol.com.

FARINA, MARIANNE, theology studies educator, consultant; b. Bronx, N.Y., Nov. 27, 1952; d. Frank Christopher Farina and Catherine Josephine Lombardo; life ptnr. Sisters of the Holy Cross, Jan. 15, 1976. BFA in Comm. Design, Parsons Sch. and New Sch. Rsch. U., NY, 1974; MA in Pastoral Theology, Santa Clara U., Calif., 1996; PhD in Theol. Ethics, Boston Coll., Mass., 2003. Tchr. Holy Cross Sch., Rockville, Md., 1978—81; dean students St. Mary's Acad., Alexandria, Va., 1981—83; tchr. Holy Cross Sch., Dhaka, Bangladesh, 1983—87; pastoral dir. edn. Diocese Mymensingh, Bangladesh, 1987—94; dir. rsch. and scholarship Ctr. Intercultural Leadership St. Mary's Coll., Notre Dame, Ind., 2003—05; asst. prof. Dominican Sch. Philosophy and Theology, Berkeley, Calif., 2005—. Adj. prof. Pacific Sch. Religion, Berkeley, Calif., 1998—2002, campus minister Newman Ctr., 1998—2001; mem. Islamic studies task force Grad. Theology Union, Berkeley, 2003—06. Author: Deveolping National Catechetical Plans, 2003; contbr. chapters to books, articles to profl. jours. Mem. Sisters of the Holy Cross, Notre Dame, 1976; v.p. Compassionate Listening Project, Bainbridge, Wash., 2005; trustee St. Mary's Coll., Notre Dame, Ind., 2006. Recipient Women Making a Difference award, YWCA, 2005. Mem.: Am. Acad. Religions (assoc.), Am. Assn. Muslim Social Scientists (assoc.), Soc. Christian Ethics (assoc.), Cath. Theologica Soc. Am. (assoc.). Office: Dominican School of Philsophy and Theolo 2301 Vine Street Berkeley CA 94708 Office Fax: 519-883-1372. Business E-Mail: mfarina@dspt.edu.

FARINELLI, JEAN L., management consultant; b. Phila., July 26, 1946; d. Albert J. and Edith M. (Falini) F. BA, Am. U., Washington, 1968; MA, Ohio State U., Columbus, 1969. Asst. pub. relations dir. Dow Jones & Co., Inc., N.Y.C., 1969-71; account exec. Carl Byoir & Assocs., Inc., N.Y.C., 1972-74, v.p., 1974-80, sr. v.p., 1980-82; pres. Tracy-Locke/BBDO Pub. Relations, Dallas, 1982-87, Creamer Dickson Basford, Inc., N.Y.C., 1987-88, chmn., chief exec. officer, 1988-98; pres., chief exec. officer Eurocom Corp. & PR (U.S.), 1991, Corp. Graphics, Inc., 1992; pres. Farinelli Cons. Group, LLC, 1999—, 20 Sutton Pl. South, Inc., 2003—. Dir. The Cologne Life Reinsurance Co., 1997-99. Recipient PR CaseBook, PR Reporter, N.H., 1984, Silver Spur, Tex. Pub. Rels. Assn., Dallas, 1985, Matrix award Women in Comms., 1993. Mem.: Nat. Found. for Infectious Diseases (former trustee), Arthur W. Page Soc. (treas., v.p. adminstrn. and fin.), Internat. Pub. Rels. Assn. (pub. rels. seminar), Nat. Investor Rels. Inst., The Women's Forum (bd. dirs.), Women in Comms. (chmn. 1995, dir. 1999—, Matrix award 1993), Pub. Rels. Soc. Am. (Silver Anvil awards chmn. 1987, acad. exec. bd. 1990—91, trustee found., Silver Anvil award 1980—81, 1985, Excalibur award Houston chpt. 1985, Best of Show Silver Anvil award 1998). Office: 20 Sutton Pl S New York NY 10022-4165

FARKAS, RHONDA DAWN, principal, education educator; b. Bklyn., Nov. 26, 1959; d. Max and Sylvia Farkas. BA, Bklyn. Coll., N.Y., 1981, MS, 1982, Advanced Certificate, 1985; EdD, St. John's U., Queens, N.Y., 2002. Cert. trainer learning styles N.Y., 2000. Asst. prin. PS 206 Dist. 22, Bklyn., 1998—2001; supr. Extended Sch. Day Program and Academic Intervention Svcs. grades K-5 PS 152 Dist. 22, Bklyn., 2001—, prin., 2001—. Magnet curriculum writer grades K-6 PS 206 Dist. 22, 1999; rep. Mentor Tchr. Internship Program Dist. 22, Bklyn., 2002—; mem. tchr. edn. adv. panel Bklyn. Coll., 2003—; mem. New Visions Prins. Mentoring Program N.Y.C. Leadership Acad., 2004—05. Contbr. chapters to books, articles to profl. jours. Mem. hon. commn. Congrl. Youth Leadership Coun., 2005. Recipient All-American Scholar award, U.S. Achievement Acad., 2001, Nat. Collegiate Edn. award, 2001, Excellence in Rsch. award, St. John's U., 2002, Certificate of Excellence, 2002, Honary Commn. award, Congl. Youth Leadership Coun., 2005, Cmty. Partnership award, N.Y. State Assemby, 2006. Mem.: Nat. Elem. Sch. Prins. Assn., Assn. Supervision and Curriculum Devel., Phi Delta Kappa, Kappa Delta Pi. Avocations: writing, travel, gardening. Personal E-mail: RhondaDawn@aol.com.

FARLEY, BARBARA L., elementary school educator; b. Chicago Heights, Ill., July 13, 1957; d. George Jacob and Bette Jane Resnik; m. Mark Alan Farley, June 27, 1981; children: Beth Michelle, Jessica Claire. BA in Edn., U. NC, Chapel Hill, 1979; M Math. Edn., U. Houston, 1983. Cert. tchr. NC. 6th grade tchr. Beth Yeshuran Day Sch., Houston, 1979—83; 7th grade math. tchr. Alief Mid. Sch., Tex., 1983—88; evening sch. tchr. math. Alief Evening Sch., 1988—92; 6th/7th grade math. tchr. I Weiner Secondary Sch. (name now Emery Weiner Sch.), Houston, 1995—. Jewish. Office: Emery Weiner Sch 9825 Stella Link Houston TX 77025

FARLEY, CAROLE, soprano; b. Le Mars, Iowa, Nov. 29, 1946; d. Melvin and Irene (Reid) Farley; m. Jose Serebrier, Mar. 29, 1969; 1 child, Lara Adriana Francesca. MusB, Ind. U., 1968. Fulbright scholar Hochschule für Musik, Munich, 1968-69. (Musician of Month, Musical Am./Hi Fidelity 1977), Am. debut at Town Hall, N.Y.C., 1969, Paris debut, Nat. Orch., 1975, London debut, Royal Philharmonic Soc., 1975, S.Am. debut, Teatro Colon, Philharmonic Orch., Buenos Aires, 1975; soloist with, major Am. and European symphony orchs., 1970—. soloist, Welsh Nat. Opera, 1971, 72, Cologne Opera, 1972-75, Phila. Lyric Opera, 1974, Brussels Opera, 1972, Lyon Opera, 1976, 77, Strasbourg Opera, 1975, Linz Opera, 1969, N.Y.C. Opera, 1976, New Orleans Opera, 1977, Cin. Opera, 1977, Met. Opera Co., N.Y.C., 1977—, Zurich Opera, 1979, Chgo. Lyric Opera, 1981, Can. Opera Co., 1980, Düsseldorf Opera, 1980, 81, 84, Palm Beach Opera, 1982, Theatre Mcpl. Paris, 1983, Theatre Royale dela Monnaie Brussels, 1983, Teatro Regio, Turin, Italy, 1983, Nice Opera (France), 1984, 86, 87, 88, Cologne Opera, 1985, Teatro Comunale, Florence, Italy, 1985, BBC Opera, 1987, TeatroColon, Buenos Aires, 1987, 88, 89, Opera de Montpellier (France), 1988, 94, Theatre des Champs Elysees, Paris, 1988, Helsinki Festival, 1989, Tchaikovsky Opera Arias Pickwick/IMP Records, 1993, Met. Opera Premiere Shostakovich Opera Lady Macbeth of Mtzensk, 1994, Theatre Capitole de Toulouse Wozzeck, 1994, internat. tour with Nat. Chamber Orchestra of Toolouse, 2003; on New Zealand Broadcasting Commn. Orchestral Tour, 1986; TV film for ABC Australia La Voix Humaine, also co-producer compact disc and video for BBC, London, 1990; co-producer compact disc and video The Telephone, 1990; recorded compact disc Weill, 1992, Metro. Opera Shostakovich: "Lady Macbeth", 1994, Strausslieder with Czech Philharmonic, 1995, Les Soldats Morts, 1995 (Grand Prix du Disque); recorded for Deutsche Gramophone (Diapason d'or prize 1997), Chandos, CBS, BBC, ASV, RCA, Ricercar and Varese-Sarabande records, London/Decca Records, IMP Masters, Pickwick; new CD Naxos: Selected Songs Ned Rorem, 2001, The Songs of Ernesto Lecuona For Bis Records, 2003; Argentine premier Bomarzo by Alberto Ginastera, Teatro Colón Buenos Aires, 2003, Bolcom Songs for Naxos, 2005. Recipient Abiati prize for her role as Lulu, Italy, 1984, Deutsche Schallplatten award for recording Carole Farley Sings French Songs, 1988, Editor's Choice award, Gramophone Mag., 2005, Editor's Choice award for DVD of Month, Gramophone Mag., 2006; named Alumni of Year, U. Ind., 1976; two-time Grammy nominee, 2004, 2006. Mem.: Am. Guild Mus. Artists. Home: 270 Riverside Dr New York NY 10025-5209 E-mail: caspi123@aol.com.

FARLEY, CAROLYN JUANITA, music educator; b. Cleve., Oct. 25, 1963; d. Christopher and Minnie (Zell) Phillips; m. Sam Winkfield, Nov. 27, 1987 (div. July 15, 1992); m. Michael Alan Farley, June 22, 1996; children: Marilyn, Michael Alan Jr.; 1 stepchild, Arline. MusB, Cleve. State U., 1988, MusM in Choral Conducting, 1994. Cert. tchr. music K-12 Ohio, Orff I music tchr., Kodaly I music tchr. Piano tchr. Rainey Inst. Music, Cleve., 1977—96, Murtis Taylor, Cleve., 1982—90, E. End Neighborhood House Settlement Music Sch., Cleve., 1988—95; music tchr. K-6 Elyria (Ohio) Bd. Edn., 1989—90; minister of music Cornerstone Bapt. Ch., Cleve.; coord. music Mt. Pleasant United Meth. Ch., Cleve., 2000—; music tchr. 7-12, k-3 Beachwood (Ohio) Bd. Edn., 1990—. Workshop clinician Annointed Ministries, Cleve., 1990—94. Composer: (songs) Prince of Peace, 1994 (Anointed, 1994). Mem. Dem. Nat. Com., 1990—2000. Recipient Creative award, Annointed Ministries, 1994. Mem.: Kindermusik Internat., Musicians United to Stay in Contact, Black Gospel Musicians' Exchange (birthday coord. 1999—). Democrat. Methodist. Avocations: guitar, bass, flute, composing. Home: 2782 Richmond Rd Beachwood OH 44122 Office: Beachwood Bd Edn 24601 Fairmont Blvd Beachwood OH 44122 E-mail: cjf@bw.beachwood.k-12.ohio.us.

FARLEY, DOROTHY BIEBER, artist, educator; b. St. Louis, May 27, 1927; d. Ralph Paul and Ida (Parker) Bieber; m. Donald Gene Farley, June 16, 1951; children: Dale Ellen Greulich, Ronald Wesley. BFA Art Edn., U. Ill., 1949. Tchr. secondary sch. art, Ferguson, Mo., 1949—51, Normandy, Mo., 1955—57; dir. art gallery Craft Alliance, St. Louis, 1970—81; city clk. Crystal Lake Park, Mo., 1981—89; clk. senate budget and taxation com. Md. State Assembly, 1991—2002. Exhbn. juror, lectr., cons., 1977—87; treas. Craft Alliance, 1967—68, pres., 1968; tchr., enamel artist, 1955—89. Cmty. chmn. March of Dimes, Creve Coeur, Mo., 1963; mem. adv. commn. University City Loop Spl. Bus. Dist., 1981; bd. dirs. Holistic Health Ctr. St. Louis, 1983—86; vol. St. John's Mercy Hosp. Med. Ctr., 1986—89; vol. craftshop YWCA, Anne Arundel County, Md., 1990—95; vol. Tawes Garden Gift Shop, 1995—; mem., treas., bd. dirs. Friends Quiet Waters Park, 1991—99; treas. Bay Ridge Home and Garden Club, 2001—. Mem.: DAR, Nat. Mus. Am. Indian (Wellspring Soc.). Home: 60 Hull Ave Annapolis MD 21403-4505

FARLEY, KATHERINE G., real estate company executive; b. 1950; m. Jerry I. Speyer, 1991; 1 child. Grad., Brown U., 1971; MA in Architecture, Harvard Grad. Sch. of Design, 1976. Mgr. bus. devel. for E. Asia Turner Construction; sr. mng. dir. Latin Am. and Global Corp. Mktg. Tishman Speyer Properties, N.Y.C., 1984—. Exec. com. mem. Internat. Rescue Com.; chmn. emeritus Women In Need; exec. com. mem. NY Philharmonic, Brearley Sch.; bd. mem. Lincoln Center for the Performing Arts, Lincoln Center Theater, Alvin Ailey Dance Co. Named one of Top 200 Collectors, ARTnews Mag., 2004, 2005, 2006. Avocation: Collector of Contemporary Art. Office: Tishmanspeyer Properties 45 Rockefeller Plz Fl 12 New York NY 10111-1299 Office Phone: 212-715-0300.*

FARLEY, MONICA M., medical educator; BA/MD with distinction, U. Mo., Kansas City. Cert. Am. Bd. Internal Medicine, 1983, DEA Certificate 1981, lic. Ga. Med. 1981, diplomate Subspecialty of Infectious Diseases 1986. Intern, internal medicine Emory U. Hosp., 1980—81, resident, internal medicine, 1981—83, fellow, infectious disease, 1983—85; rsch. fellow, pub. health svc. tng. grant, dept. microbiology Emory U. Sch. Medicine, 1985—86, sr. assoc., dept. medicine, 1986—88, asst. prof. medicine, dept. medicine, 1988—93, assoc. prof. medicine, dept. medicine, 1993—99, acting dir., divsn. infectious disease, dept. medicine, 1999—2000, adj. asst. prof. microbiology and immunology, 1994—, prof. medicine, dept. medicine, 1999—, assoc. dir., divsn. infectious diseases, dept. medicine, 2000—; assoc. investigator VA Hosp., Atlanta, 1986—88; rsch. assoc. VA Med. Ctr., Atlanta, 1989—93, staff physician, 1989—; dir. Ga. Emerging Infectious Program, 1996—. Mem., State Med. Adv. Bd. Group B Streptococcus Assn., 1994—99, mem. Nat. Med. Adv. Bd., 1995—99; mem. adv. bd. Pfizer Postdoctoral Fellowship Program in Infectious Diseases, 2002—. Mem. editl. bd. Am. Jour. Med. Sciences, guest editor Am. Jour. Med. Sciences, Emerging Microbial Threats, 1996, reviewer in field; contbr. articles to profl. jours., chapters to books. Recipient Investigator award, Med. Rsch. Svc., VA, 1986, Rsch. Assoc. award, Med. Rsch. Svc., 1989, Alumni Achievement award, U. Mo. Kansas City Sch. Medicine, 1994, James H. Nakano Citations for Outstanding Scientific Papers published in 1995, Ctr. for Disease Control, 1996, James H. Nakano Citations for Outstanding Scientific Papers published in 1997, 1998, James H. Nakano Citations for two Outstanding Scientific Papers published in 2000, 2001, Dept. Health and Human Services Secretary's award for Disting. Svc. (FoodNet Surveillance Team), 1998. Fellow: Infectious Diseases Soc. Am. (mem. women's com. 1993—96, mem. program planning com. 2000—03); mem.: Am. Soc. for Microbiology, Infectious Diseases Soc. Ga. (pres. 2003—), Am. Fedn. for Med. Rsch. (AFMR) (pres. elect 1997—98, pres. 1998—99, pres. AFMR Found. 1999—2000), So. Soc. for Clin. Investigation (councilor 1996—2000), Am. Fedn. Clin. Rsch. (AFCR), now Am. Fedn. Med. Rsch. (AFMR) (councilor, So. sect. 1993—94, chair-elect, So. sect. 1994—95, nat. coun. 1994—, chair, So. sect. 1995—96, co-chair, pub. policy com. 1995—, pres. elect 1997—98, pres. 1998—99), Alpha Omega Alpha. Office: VA Med Ctr (Atlanta) Rsch-Infectious Disease 1670 Clairmont Rd Decatur GA 30033 Office Phone: 404-728-7688. Office Fax: 404-329-2210. Business E-Mail: mfarley@emory.edu.*

FARLEY, PEGGY ANN, finance company executive; b. Phila., Mar. 12, 1947; d. Harry E. and Ruth (Lloyd) F.; m. Reid McIntyre, Dec. 31, 1985 (div.); 1 child, Margaret Ruth Farley. AB, Barnard Coll., 1970; MA with high honors, Columbia U., 1972. Admissions officer Barnard Coll., N.Y.C., 1973-76; adminstr. Citibank NA, Athens, Greece, 1976-77; cons. Orgn. Resources Counselors, N.Y.C., 1977-78; sr. assoc. Morgan Stanley and Co. Inc., N.Y.C., 1978-84; mng. dir., CEO AMAS Securities Inc., N.Y.C., 1984-98; also bd. dirs. AMAS Securities, Inc., N.Y.C.; pres., CEO Ascent Asset Mgmt. Adv. Svc., Inc., N.Y.C., 1998-99. Pres., CEO, bd. dirs. Ascent/Meredith Asset Mgmt. Inc., N.Y.C., 1999-2006, Ascent/Meredith Portfolio Mgmt. Inc., N.Y.C., 1999-2004, Robert R. Meredith & Co. Inc., N.Y.C., 1999-2004, Ascent Capital Mgmt., Inc., 2004—, Ascent Securities, Inc., 2004—; partner Ascent Med. Tech. Fund, 1999—; mng. dir. Ascent Pvt. Equilty, 1999—, Ascent Capital Adv., 2001—. Author: The Place Of The Yankee And Euro Bond Markets In A Financing Program For The People's Republic of China, 1982, Ascent Quar. Rev. Mem. Columbia U. Seminar on China-U.S. Bus. Mem. China Inst., Fgn. Policy Assn., Met. Club, Econ. Club of N.Y. Republican. Presbyterian. Avocations: gardening, films, swimming. Home: 908 Owassa Rd Newton NJ 07860-4015 Office: Ascent Capital Management Inc 1160 Fifth Ave New York NY 10029 Personal E-mail: peggyfarley@hotmail.com.

FARLEY, WENDY LEE, lay worker, educator; b. Greencastle, Ind., Apr. 13, 1958; d. William Edward and Doris June (Kimbel) F.; m. Clifford Allen Grabhorn, Oct. 11, 1987; 1 child, Emma Elizabeth. BA, U. N.H., 1981; MA, Vanderbilt U., 1987, PhD, 1988. Sunday sch. tchr. North Decatur (Ga.) Presbyn. Ch., 1989—; assoc. prof. religion Emory U., Atlanta, 1988—. Author: Tragic Vision and Divine Compassion: A Contemporary Theodicy, 1990, Eros for the Other: Retaining Truth in a Pluralistic World, 1996, The Wounding and Healing of Desire, 2005. Vol. Amnesty Internat. Mid-East Coordination Group, 1986—, Bread for the World, 1986—. Mem. Am. Acad. Religion, Soc. of Phenomenology and Existential Philosophy. Office: Dept Religion-Callaway S214 Emory Univ 537 Kilgo Cir Atlanta GA 30322-0001*

FARMER, CHERYL CHRISTINE, internist, industrial hygienist; b. Detroit, Sept. 15, 1946; d. Donald Richard and Dorothy Ruth Farmer; m. Dennis Michael Mukai, Aug. 3, 1968 (div. Sept. 1977). BA in Edn., Mich. State U., 1968; BS in Biology, Wright State U., 1974; MS in Indsl. Hygiene, U. Mich., 1978; MD, Mich. State U., 1982. Tchr. art Five Points Elem. Sch., Fairborn, Ohio, 1968-70; real estate saleswoman Dawson Realty, 1970; sanitarian trainee Dayton Health Dept., Dayton, 1973; acting chief air pollution control southwest dist. Ohio EPA, 1975, data analyst Columbus, 1976; intern St. Joseph Mercy Hosp., Ann Arbor, Mich., 1982-83, resident medicine, 1983-85; internist Winton Hills Med. Ctr., Cin., 1985-87; pvt. practice Ann Arbor, Mich., 1988—. Internist, Elm St. Med. Ctr., Cin., 1987-88; mem. peer rev. com. Magnacare Health Maintenance Orgn., Cin., 1988; mem. membership com. St. Joseph Mercy Hosp., 1990-94; mem. ethics com. Huron Valley Physicians Assn., 1996—; mem. bioethics com. Mich. State Med. Soc., 1994—; past com. mem. Washtenaw County Med. Soc., 1992-94; commr. city charter City of Ypsilanti, 1993-94. Co-chmn. Citizens for Clean Air Com., Dayton, 1970-74, Miami Valley Citizens for Transfer, Fairborn, 1974; mayor of Ypsilanti, Mich., 1995—. Named Woman Physician of the Yr., Mich. State Med. Soc., 2002, one of Washtenaw County's Most Influential Women of 2003, Business Direct Weekly, 2003; recipient Athena award, Ypsilanti area C. of C., 1996, Liberty Bell award, Wash. County Bar Assn., 1998, Bill Steude award for ethics in govt., Mich. Assn. Municipal Atty.'s, 2002, Martin Luther King Jr. Humanitarian award, Eastern Mich. Univ., 2003. Mem. AMA, ACP, Am. Med. Womens' Assn., Acad. Medicine Cin. (mem. steering com. women in medicine 1986-88, co-chmn. networking and mentoring subcom. 1986-88), LWV, NOW, Sierra Club, Phi Kappa Phi, Kappa Delta Pi, Alpha Kappa Delta (hon.). Democrat. Avocations: sailing, gardening, victorian home restoration. Office: 1950 Manchester Rd Ann Arbor MI 48104-4916 Office Phone: 734-973-4800.

FARMER, CORNELIA GRIFFIN, lawyer, consultant, county hearings official; b. NYC, Mar. 3, 1945; d. John Bastin and Elizabeth McCue (Sussman) Griffin; m. William Paul Farmer, Jan. 8, 1972; children: Suzanne Elizabeth, John Paul. BA, Mt. Holyoke Coll., 1967; M in Regional Planning, Cornell U., 1970; JD, Marquette U., 1978. Bar: Wis. 1978, Pa. 1981, Minn. 1996, Oreg. 1999, Ill. 2002. Planner Frederick P. Clark Assocs., Rye, NY, 1970-71, Tri State Regional Planning Com., N.Y.C., 1971-72, State of Wis. and City of Milw., 1973-75; assoc. Friebert & Finerty, Milw., 1978-80, Baskin & Sears, Pitts., 1981-82; cons. County of Allegheny, Pitts., 1983; adj. faculty U. Pitts., 1986-94; jud. law clk. Commonwealth Ct. of Pa., Pitts., 1992-95; pvt. practice Mpls., 1996—99; staff atty., hearings ofcl. Lane Coun. Govts., Eugene, Oreg., 1999—2001. Vic-chmn. loan monitoring com. Pitts. Countywide Corp., 1981—87; child adv. Allegheny County Pro Bono Program, Pitts., 1986—92; mediator Dispute Resolution Ctr., St. Paul, 1998—99; adj. faculty U. Wis., Milw., 1978—79. Book reviewer, referee books and articles. Vol. polit. campaigns Milw., Pitts., Mpls., Chgo., and Eugene, 1972-2004; trustee Falk Sch. Fund; v.p. PTA Falk Lab. Sch. U. Pitts., 1985-89; ct. monitor abuse cases WATCH, Mpls., 1996-99; vol. WITS tutoring and mentoring program, 2002-, Start Making A Reader Today, Eugene, Oreg.; mem. Ill. Adv. Coun. of Midwest Eye-Banks, 2004—; head class agent Mt. Holyoke Coll., 2002—, chair reunion gift com.; mem. classes and reunions com. Mt. Holyoke Coll. Alumnae Assn., 2006—; vol. Cabrini Green Legal Aid Clinic, Chgo., 2005—; lector Holy Name Cathedral, Chgo., 2004—. Mem. ABA, APA, Chgo. Bar Assn., Silver Bay Assn. Coun., Mt. Holyoke Club Pitts. (past pres., treas.).

FARMER, JANENE ELIZABETH, artist, educator; b. Albuquerque, Oct. 16, 1946; d. Charles John Watt and Regina Mortimere (Brown) Kruger; m. Michael Hugh Bolton, Apr. 1965 (div.); m. Frank Urban Farmer, May 1972 (div.). BA in Art, San Diego State U., 1969; postgrad., U. San Diego, San Diego State U., U. Calif., San Diego, 1983—85. Owner, operator Iron Walrus Pottery, 1972-79. Tchr. Cath. schs., San Diego, 1983—86, Ramona Unified Sch. Dist., 1986—, mentor tchr., 1994—98, cons. tchr., 2001—03; tchr. environ. art San Diego Natural History Mus., 1996—97, San Diego Wild Animal Park, 1996, U. Calif., San Diego, 2003. Exhibited in group shows at San Diego Mus. Art, San Diego City Adminstrn. Bldg., Univ. City Libr., San Diego, Art Scene Gallery, Kauai, Hawaii, Am. Soc. Interior Designers, San Diego, Sierra Club Bookstore, Quail Bot. Gardens, Encinitas, Calif., Art Ctr./Old Forge, Arts Guild Old Forge, N.Y., 2004. Mem. Coronado Arts and Humanities Coun., 1979—81; mem. edn. adv. com. La Jolla (Calif.) Playhouse, 1996; mem. edn. com. Calif. Wolf Ctr., 1999—2001. Grantee, Calif. Arts Coun., 1980—81. Roman Catholic. Home: 4435 Nobel Dr #35 San Diego CA 92122-1559 Personal E-mail: janenefarmer@sbcglobal.net.

FARMER, JOY A., literature educator; d. Barney Oldfield Farmer and Josie Irene Craig. BA, Agnes Scott Coll., Decatur, Ga., 1972; MA, U. Va., Charlottesville, 1973, PhD, 1977. Asst. prof. of English Kennesaw State U., Ga., 1991—93; prof. of English Reinhardt Coll., Waleska, 1993—. Author:

(literary criticism & original poetry) Flannery O'Connor Review, Tex. Review, Studies in Short Fiction, Humanities in the South, Kennesaw Review, Poem, Lucidity, Manna, Parnussus, Lit. Jour. Grassroots organizer Howard Dean and John Kerry presdl. campaigns, Kennesaw, 2003—04. Mem.: MLA, Soc. for Study of So. Lit., Phi Beta Kappa. Democrat. Avocations: showing dogs, editing. Office: Reinhardt Coll 7300 Reinhardt Coll Cir Waleska GA 30183 Office Phone: 770-720-5633. Office Fax: 770-720-5602. Business E-Mail: jaf@reinhardt.edu.

FARMER, LAUREL ANN, elementary school educator; d. Harry H. Sr. and Ruth A. Jasperson; m. Eric W. Farmer, July 17, 1993; children: Brandyn C., Baylee A. Grad. in elem. edn., Southwestern Coll., Phoenix, 1995. Tchr. Andalucia Mid. Sch., Phoenix, 1996—98, 2001—, Granada Primary Sch., Phoenix, 1998—2001. Praise team vocalist New Life Cmty. Ch., Peoria, Ariz., 2005—06, women's ministry tchr., worship leader, 2005—06. Republican.

FARMER, MARTHA LOUISE, retired academic administrator; b. Cin. d. William S. and Genevieve (Fye) Farmer. BA, Wheaton Coll., 1935; postgrad., Wellesley Coll., 1936; MA, Columbia U., 1937, EdD, 1956. Assoc. prof. Manhattanville Coll. Sacred Heart, 1936-43, 46-48; adminstr. dept. student life City Coll., CUNY, 1948-69, prof., coord. dept. student pers. svcs., 1969-75, cons. student pers. svcs. for adults in higher edn., 1975—. Vis. prof. Grad. Sch. Edn., N.Y. U., 1967-69; cons. student personnel services for adults in higher edn., 1975—. Editor: Student Pers. Svcs. For Adults in Higher Edn., 1967, Counseling Svcs. for Adults in Higher Edn., 1971. Mem. mgmt. com. Emma Ransom YWCA, N.Y.C., 1958, mem. resident com., 1956-58; mem. jr. high teens com. YWCA, Ridgewood, N.J., 1962-75; mem. N.J. com. U.S. Commn. on Civil Rights, trustee Hispanic Commn. on Alcoholism in N.J. Served as lt. USNR (W), 1943-46. Recipient Bernard Reed award, 1963, 85-86, Winifred Fisher award, 1974. Mem. Am. Coll. Pers. Assn. (program com. 1960-62, mem. com. I, 1963-65, chmn. Com. XIII 1965-67, mem. Com. IV 1968-72), Am. Pers. and Guidance Assn., Assn. U. Evening Colls. (coms. 1961-72), U.S. Assn. Evening Students (chmn. bd. trustees 1970-71, hon. life trustee 1975—), Evening Student Pers. Assn. (pres. 1962-63), Adult Student Pers. Assn. (chmn. bd. trustees 1968-71, hon. life trustee 1975—). Home: 800 Bestgate RD Annapolis MD 21401-3016

FARMER, MARY BAUDER, artist; b. San Diego, Nov. 30, 1953; d. Chester Robert and Dixie Bauder; m. L. Michael Dowling, July 1990. BS, Auburn U., Ala., 1986; ind. study with Joan Snyder; BFA, Ga. State U., Atlanta, 2002; BFA in studio Arts, Atlanta Coll. Art, 2003. Exec. dir. Birmingham Woman's Med. Clinic, Ala., 1975-80; pres. Beacon Clinic, Montgomery, Ala., 1980-83; ptnr. Hill, Rose and Farmer, Atlanta, 1988-90; owner, mgr. Studio M. Farmer, San Rafael, Calif., 1990—; creative dir., pres. Twin Studios, Inc., Atlanta, 1995-97; pres. Resource for Visual Artists, 2005—. V.p. Global Interests Inc., 1990—. Author, pub.: The Landlord's Primer for Georgia: A Self-Help Guide for Inexperienced Landlords. Mem. pub. rels. com. Project Open Hand, Ga. Citizens for Arts; mem. Bus. Com. for Arts. Mem. LWV, Ga. Women's Agenda (founder), West Coast Encaustic Artists (founder), Art League Norther Calif., ACLU, Omicron Delta Kappa. Democrat. Studio: 501 Palm Dr 4 Novato CA Home: 531 D St San Rafael CA 94901 Office Phone: 415-302-4348.

FARMER, NANCY, state official; b. Jacksonville, Ill., 1956; m. Darrell Hartke. Grad., Ill. Coll., 1979. Exec. dir. Skinker-DeBaliviere Cmty. Coun.; state rep. dist. 64 Mo. Ho. of Reps., 1993—2001; asst. treas. State of Mo., 1997—2001, treas., 2001—. Mem. Woman's Polit. Caucus Mo. Ho. of Reps.; dir. intergovernmental affairs City of St. Louis, 1997. Active Woman's Com. Forest Park, Roseadale Neighborhood Assn., mem. exec. com.; active West End Arts Coun.; cand. for Mo. U.S. Senator, 2004. Mem. Ctrl. West End Assn., Women Legislators Mo. Office: PO Box 210 Jefferson City MO 65102

FARMER, SUSAN LAWSON, retired broadcast executive, former secretary of state; b. Boston, May 29, 1942; d. Ralph and Margaret (Tyng) Lawson; m. Malcolm Farmer, III, Apr. 6, 1968; children: Heidi Benson, Stephanie Lawson. Student, Garland Jr. Coll., 1960-61, Brown U., 1961-62; LHD, Bryant Coll., 2004. Mem. Providence Home Rule Charter Commn., 1979-80; sec. of state State of R.I., Providence, 1983-87; pres., CEO Sta. WSBE-TV R.I. PBS, Providence, 1987—2004. Spl. adv. R.I. Family Ct., 1978-83; mem. nat. voting stds. panel Fed. Election Commn. co-chmn. Nat. Voter Edn. Project; mem. electoral coll., 1984; chmn. Gov.'s Com. on Ethics in Govt., 1985-86; mem. tchg. facility and adv. panel Internat. Ctr. on Election Law and Adminstrn.; mem. nat. edn. adv. com. Pub. Broadcasting System, 1987-89; trustee Eastern Ednl. TV Network, 1987-95; mem. R.I. Task Force on Tech., 1995-04, R.I. Info. Mgmt. Commn., 1997; bd. dirs., mem. exec. com. Program Resources Group, 1993-01; mem. Gov.'s Telecom. Task Force, 2000-04; mem. nat. media adv. com. WomenFuture, 2002-04. Bd. dirs. Justice Resources Corp., R.I. Council Alcoholism, R.I. Hist. Soc., Planned Parenthood (R.I. chpt.), R.I. Rape Crisis Ctr., The Newport Inst., Marathon House, Inc., chmn.; mem. Mayor's Task Force on Child Abuse, R.I. Film Commn.; v.p. Miriam Hosp. Found.; mem. adv. com. Women in Polit. and Govtl. Careers Program, U. R.I., 1985-95; mem. adv. bd. Com. for Study of Am. Electorate-Ford Found. Project-Efficacy in State Voting Laws, 1986; mem. Commn. to Study Length of Election Process, 1985-87; steering com. Nat. Fund for America's Future, Project Vote R.I.; bd. dirs. Dawn for Children Tng. Thru Placement; pres. R.I. PBS Found.; bd. dirs. R.I. Anti-Drug Coalition Exec. Com., Nat. Forum for Pub. TV Execs., 1998-2004, chmn., 1999; mem. corp. Butler Hosp. Named Woman of Yr., Nat. Women's Polit. Caucus, 1980; recipient Nat. Advocacy award Assn. Pub. TV Stas., 2004. Mem. LWV, NATAS (bd. govs. New Eng. chpt. 1995—), N.E. Assn. Schs. and Colls. (com. on tech. and course instns.), So. Ednl. Comms. Assn. (bd. dirs. 1993-96), R.I. Women's Polit. Caucus (Woman of Yr. 1980), Bus. and Profl. Women (Woman of Yr. 1984), Common Cause, Save the Bay, Providence Preservation Soc., Orgn. State Broadcasting Execs, Agawam Hunt Club, Mill Reef Club (Antigua, West Indies), Nat. Assn. of Ams. Pub. TV Stas. (trustee 1996-2002, Nat. Advocacy award, 2004), Nat. Acad. TV Arts and Scis. (bd. govs. N.E. chpt. 1995-2001), Nat. Ednl. Telecomms. Assn. (bd. dirs. 1997-2004, Nat. Forum Pub. TV Execs. (bd. dirs. 1998-2004, chmn. 1999). Home: 190 Upton Ave Providence RI 02906-1552 Personal E-mail: sfarmer10@cox.net.

FARMER RATZ, KATHY ANN, secondary school educator; b. Chattanooga, Oct. 17, 1956; d. Stanley James and Katherine Louise (Phillips) Farmer; m. William Ray Ward, Apr. 6, 1979 (div. Mar. 1989); m. Leo Thomas Ratz. BS, Mid. Tenn. State U., 1977, MEd, 1978, MEd in Spl. Edn. Vision Disabilities, 2005, EdS, 1980. Tchr. Queensland (Australia) Dept. Edn., Brisbane, 1989; with Ahlstrom Filtration Inc., 1992—2000; tchr. Hamilton County Dept. Edn., Chattanooga, 1977—. Group leader to Japan and Australia, World Learning, Inc. (formerly Experiment in Internat. Living), Brattleboro, Vt., summers, 1985-88. Vol. Am. Heart Assn., Chattanooga, 1989—; apptd. col. aide de camp Gov's. staff State of Tenn., 1991. Recipient Lyndhurst Tchrs. award, 1988; named Tenn. Amb. Good Will, 2004; grantee Jr. League Chattanooga, Inc., 1991, grantee Pub. Edn. Found., Chattanooga, 1999. Mem. AAUW (bd. dirs. election found. 1987-88), Delta Kappa Gamma (chmn. rsch. com. 1983, chmn. high sch. essay contest 1993). Democrat. Methodist. Avocations: foreign travel, camping, hiking, water sports, skiing. Home: 334 Shadow Ridge Dr Chattanooga TN 37421-5359 Office: Ooltewah Middle Sch 5100 Ooltewah Ringgold Rd Ooltewah TN 37363-8613

FARNAM, JENNIFER M., elementary school educator; b. Brainerd, Del., Apr. 22, 1952; d. Virgil and Ruth Eibes; m. Dale L. Eibes, Apr. 27, 1991; 1 child, Lewis. BS, St. Cloud State U., Minn., 1974. Cert. tchr. Minn. Tchr. Menahga (Minn.) Pub. Sch., 1980—. Fin. sec., PPRC chair, Sunday sch. tchr. Pine River (Minn.) United Meth. Ch. Named Tchr. of Yr., Edn. Minn., Menahga. Office: Menahga Pub Sch 216 Aspen Ave SE Box 160 Menahga MN 56464 Office Phone: 218-564-4141. E-mail: jfarnam@menahga.k12.mn.us.

FARNAN, BETTY LYNNE, secondary school educator; b. Smithville, Mo., July 18, 1949; d. David Guthrie Cockrill and Joyce Lillian Henton; m. Philip Eugene Farnan, June 7, 1969; children: Tina Michelle, Joshua Philip. BA in English, U. Mo., Kansas City, 1973. Cert. English tchr. grades 7-12 Mo., 1973. English tchr. Our Lady of the Angels, Kansas City, 1989—2004, Westport H.S., Kansas City, 2005—. Office: Westport High School 315 E 39th Kansas City MO 64111-1530

FARNER, DARLA A., artist; b. East Chgo., Ind., Mar. 13, 1959; d. Richard Calvin Vickery and Charlene Elizabeth Cornett; m. Randy Dean Farner, Aug. 25, 1988. Degree equivalent in Med. Office, MTI Food C.C., Gresham, Oreg., 1989. Web artist WaterColorInMotion.com, Portland, 1999—. Office: WaterColorInMotion.com 1024 NE 195th Portland OR 97230 Office Phone: 503-666-2804. Business E-Mail: darla.farner@comcast.net.

FARNEY, CHARLOTTE EUGENIA, musician, educator; b. Long Beach, Calif., Jan. 06; d. Charles Thomas and Eugenia Moody (Fisher) Dalton; m. John Nathan Pierce, Aug. 1972 (div. 1978); m. Raymond C. Farney, June 30, 1990; stepchildren: Anna Louise, Paul Jerrod. AA, Orange Coast Coll., Costa Mesa, Calif., 1959; MusB, U. Redlands, 1962; MusM, Yale U., 1966; D of Musical Arts, U. Ariz., 1983. Std. secondary cert. tchg. music K-12 and Spanish Ariz. Cellist Denver Symphony Orch., 1966—69; instr., mem. faculty trio West Tex. State U., Canyon, 1969—71; grad. tchg. asst. cello U. Ariz., Tucson, 1977—81; string orch./gen. music tchr. Tucson Unified Sch. Dist., 1979—90; string orch. tchr. Scottsdale (Ariz.) Unified Sch. Dist., 1995—2001, Washington Elem. Sch. Dist., Phoenix, 2001—; cellist Tucson Symphony Orch., 1977—90, West Valley Symphony, Sun City, Ariz., 1990—2005, String Sounds, Phoenix, 1994—99. Pvt. cello tchr., Denver, 1966—69, Scottsdale, Ariz., 2002—; prin. first chair cellist Amarillo Symphony, Tex., 1969—71; cellist Symphony Orch., Toluca, Mexico, 1974—77; cello soloist Tucson Civic Orch., 1982, Chaparral Christian Ch., 1998—; cons. in field. Author music revs. Asst. Sunday sch. tchr. Scholar, Yale U., 1963—66, Denver Symphony Guild, 1968, Tchrs. Performance Inst./Oberlin Coll., 1969, Blossom Music Sch., 1970. Mem.: Music Educators Nat. Conf., Am. String Tchrs. Assn. with NSOA (coach String Fling Phoenix chpt. 2000—02, coach Cellobration 2001—03), Sigma Alpha Iota (chaplain U. Redlands chpt 1960—61, v.p. mem., program chmn. Phoenix Alumni chpt. 1996—2000, 2004—06, Sword of Honor 1998, Rose of Honor 2000). Avocations: travel, chamber music. Home: 6202 E Aster Dr Scottsdale AZ 85254 Personal E-mail: charcello1@cox.net.

FARNGALO, ROSEMARIE MERRITT, school psychologist; d. Ormond StClair and Elaine Louis Merritt; children: Aisha Ferngalo, Zuri Ferngalo. BS in Criminal Justice, CUNY, 1980, MEd in Sch. Psychology, 1993; PhD in Guidance and Counseling, Union Inst. & U., 2004. Cert. sch. psychologist Ga. Instr. Interborn Inst., NYC, 1980—81; health rschr. WHO, Trinidad and Tobago, 1981—84; educator NYC Bd. Edn., Bklyn., 1984—93; sch. psychologist Dekalb County Schs., Decatur, Ga., 1995—. Behavior cons. DPCH, Decatur, 2004—; cons. United Way, Atlanta, 2005—. Named Outstanding Presenter, Peer Helpers Dekalb County, 2004, Unity Cmty. Coalition, Ga., 2004. Mem.: Nat. Assn. Sch. Psychologists, Order Ea. Star (chaplain 2002—04), Zeta Phi Beta (Outstanding Presenter 2003). Democrat. Avocations: travel, music, reading. Office: Deklab County Schs 5839 Meml Dr Stone Mountain GA 30083 Office Phone: 678-676-1930. E-mail: rfarngalo@comcast.net.

FARNHAM, KATHERINE A, music educator, vocalist; d. Dean A and Betty L Farnham; m. Pamir Kiciman. MusB summa cum laude, Berklee Coll. of Music, 1993—96; MusB, U. of Cin. Coll.-Conservatory of Music, 1991—93; MusM, U. of Miami Sch. of Music, 2002. Voice & piano faculty Boston Music Co., 1997, Sdoia-Satz Music Inst., Miami, Fla., 1997—2000; voice faculty Creative Workshops, Aventura, Fla., 2000—01; music theatre voice faculty New World Sch. of the Arts, Miami, Fla., 2001—03; dir. The Miracles of Hope Sch. for the Performing & Healing Arts, Hollywood, Fla., 2003—. Songwriter (albums) For the Love of it All, Songs from the Troubadour; singer (also songwriter and co-producer): (original words & music) Mosaic, Miami's theme song; songwriter (original words & music) Destiny (South Fla. Songwriter of the Yr., 2003); composer (producer): (contemporary musical) Age of the Jaguar. Recipient Performer/Songwriter Competition Winner, Berklee Coll. of Music, 1995; Mortar Bd. Scholarship for Leadership, U. of Cin. Coll.-Conservatory of Music, 1993. Mem.: Nat. Acad. of Rec. Arts & Sciences, NAFE, Am. Soc. of Composers, Authors & Publishers. Christian. Avocations: reading, movies, swimming, yoga, travel. Home: Ste 323 740 S Burnside Ave Los Angeles CA 90036 Office Phone: 305-609-7464. Personal E-mail: kathfarnham@earthlink.net.

FARNHAM-DIGGORY, SYLVIA, psychologist, educator; b. Lynchburg, Va., Aug. 16, 1927; d. Albert Ayrton and Lola Marshall F.; children—Matthew, Jonathan. Ph.B., U. Chgo., 1946; PhD in Psychology, U. Pa., 1961. Asst. prof. psychology Carnegie-Mellon U., Pitts., 1966-70, asso. prof., 1970-75; prof. U. Tex., Dallas, 1975-76, head programs in psychology and human devel., 1975-76; H. Rodney Sharp prof. ednl. studies and psychology U. Del., Newark, 1976—, dir. acad. studies assistance program, 1986—. Author: Cognitive Processes in Education, 1972, Learning Disabilities, 1978, Schooling, 1990; contbr. articles to profl. jours. Fellow Nat. Inst. Edn., 1976 Mem. Am. Psychol. Soc., Cognitive Sci. Soc., Soc. of Friends. Democrat.

FARNSLEY, GAIL, information technology executive; BS in Computer Sci., Bowling Green State U.; MBA, Purdue U. With Pub. Svc. Indiana, Emery Air Freight; various tech. and mgmt. positions Georgia-Pacific Corp.; internal cons., sales, mktg. & distbn., Corp. Info. Tech. Divsn. Cummins, Inc., 1997—99, leader Ctrl. Area Info. Tech., 1999, leader Power Generation Info. Tech., 2000, chief info. officer, 2002—, v.p., 2005—. Steering com. Columbus Connected Cmty. Partnership; Dean's exec. coun. Purdue Sch. Tech.; v.p. bd. dir. Dancer's Studio, Inc. Mem.: Soc. for Info. Mgmt., Women & Hi Tech. Office: Cummins Inc 500 Jackson St Columbus IN 47201*

FARNSWORTH, ELIZABETH, broadcast journalist; b. Mpls., Dec. 23, 1943; d. H. Bernerd and Jane (Mills) Fink; m. Charles E. Farnsworth, June 20, 1966; children: Jennifer Farnsworth Fellows, Samuel. BA, Middlebury Coll., 1965; MA in History, Stanford U., 1966; LLD (hon.), Colby Coll., 2002. Reporter, panelist PBS World Press, KQED, San Francisco, 1975-77; reporter InterNews, Berkeley, Calif., 1977-80; freelance TV and print reporter, San Francisco, 1980-91; fgn. corr. MacNeil/Lehrer News Hour, San Francisco, 1991-95; chief corr., prin. substitute anchor News Hour with Jim Lehrer, Arlington, Va., 1995-97, San Francisco, 1997-99, sr. corr., 1999—2004, spl. corr., 2005—. Co-author: El Bloqueo Invisible, 1974; prodr., dir. documentary Thanh's War, 1991 (Cine Golden Eagle award); contbr. articles to various publs. Mem. adv. bd. Berkeley Edn. Found., 1990-95, U. Calif. Sch. Journalism, Berkeley; mem. nat. adv. bd. Ctr. Investigative Reporting, 2001-; bd. dirs. Data Ctr., Oakland, Calif., 1993-95. Recipient Golden Gate award San Francisco Film Festival, 1984, Best Investigative Reporting award No. Calif. Radio, TV News Dirs.' Assn., 1986, Blue Ribbon, Am. Film and Video Festival, 1991, Silver World medal N.Y. Film Festivals, 2001; nominee Emmy award, 2002. Mem. AFTRA, NATAS, World Affairs Coun. No. Calif. (bd. dirs. 1998-2004), Nat. Adv. Writers Corps, Phi Beta Kappa. Presbyterian. Avocations: gardening, hiking, poetry.

FARON, FAY CHERYL, private investigator, writer; b. Kansas City, Mo. d. Albert David and Geraldine Fay (Morgan) F. Student, Glendale (Ariz.) C.C., 1967-68, Ariz. State U., 1968-71, U. Ariz., 1971-72. Lic. pvt. investigator, Calif. Owner Monogramation, San Francisco, 1976-80; assoc. prodr. Sta. KGO-TV, San Francisco, 1980-81, Power/Rector, San Francisco, 1982-83; owner Office in the City, San Francisco, 1982-83, The Rat Dog Dick Detective Agy., San Francisco, 1983—. Lectr., spkr. San Francisco U., 1984—, San Francisco Assn. Legal Assts., 1984—, Commonwealth Club San Francisco, 1987, Calif. Collectors Coun., San Francisco, 1992—. Book Passage Mystery Writers Conf., 1997-99. Author: A Private Eye's Guide to Collecting a Bad Debt, 1991, Missing Persons, 1997; author/editor: The Instant National Locator Guide, 1991, 2nd edit., 1993, 3rd edit, 1996, Rip-Off, 1998; columnist Ask Rat Dog, 1993—; host, writer: (Court TV Crime Story Spl.) Rip-Offs and Scams, 2000. Co-founder, pres. bd. ElderAngels, San Francisco. Subject of Jack Olsen's book, Hastened to the Grave, 1998. Mem. Nat. Assn. Investigative Specialists, Nat. Assn. Bunco Investigators (asst.), Profls. Against Confidence Crimes (asst.), Sisters in Crime. Avocations: biking, camping, horseback riding, river rafting, travel.

FARQUHAR, MARILYN GIST, cell biologist, pathologist, educator; b. Tulare, Calif., July 11, 1928; d. Brooks DeWitt and Alta (Green) Gist; m. John W. Farquhar, June 4, 1952; children: Bruce, Douglas (div. 1968); m. George Palade, June 7, 1970. AB, U. Calif., Berkeley, 1949, MA, 1952, PhD, 1955. Asst. rsch. pathologist Sch. Medicine U. Calif., San Francisco, 1956—58, assoc. rsch. pathologist, 1962—64, assoc. prof., 1964—68, prof. pathology, 1968—70; rsch. assoc. Rockefeller U., N.Y.C., 1958—62, prof. cell biology, 1970—73, Sch. Medicine Yale U., New Haven, 1973—87, Sterling prof. cell biology and pathology, 1987—90; prof. pathology cell molecular medicine U. Calif., San Diego, 1990—, chair divsn. cellular and molecular medicine, 1991—99, prof. cellular & molecular medicine, chair dept. cellular & molecular medicine, 1999—. Mem. editorial bd. numerous sci. jours.; contbr. articles to profl. jours. Recipient Career Devel. award NIH, 1968-73, Disting. Sci. medal Electron Microscope Soc., 1987, Gomori medal Histochem. Soc., 1999, A.N. Richards award Internat. Soc. Nephrology, 2003, FASAB Excellence Sci. award, 2006. Mem.: NAS, Internat. Soc. Nephrology (A.N. Richards award 2003), Am. Soc. Nephrology (Homer Smith award 1988, Gottschalk award 2002), Am. Assn. Investigative Pathology (Rous Whipple award 2001), Am. Soc. Cell Biology (pres. 1981—82, E.B. Wilson medal 1987), Am. Acad. Arts and Scis. Home and Office: U Calif San Diego Sch Med 12894 Via Latina Del Mar CA 92014-3730

FARQUHAR, MICHELE C., lawyer; b. De Ridder, La., May 29, 1957; BA magna cum laude, Duke U., 1979; JD, U. Va., 1984. Bar: Calif. 1984, D.C. 1985. Mem. USA Today Launch Team Gannett Co.; staff White House Press Office; law clk. Judge John M. Shaw, U.S. Dist. Ct., W. Dist. Louisiana, 1984—85; acting dep. asst. sec. & chief staff Nat. Telecom. & Info. Adminstrn., U.S. Dept. Justice; chief Wireless Telecom. Bur., FCC; ptnr. Hogan & Hartson LLP, Washington, co-chmn. comm. practice group. Mem.: Fed. Comm. Bar Assn. (sec., exec. com., found. chmn. 1996—97, Distinguished Svc. Award 1991, 2000), D.C. Bar, State Bar Calif., Duke U. Bd. Trustees (mem. 1997—99), Duke U. Alumni Assn. (pres. 1997—98). Office: Hogan & Hartson LLP Columbia Sq 555 Thirteenth St NW Washington DC 20004-1109 Office Phone: 202-637-5663. Office Fax: 202-637-5910. Business E-Mail: mcfarquhar@hhlaw.com.

FARR, BARBARA F., minister; d. Claude H. Wesley and Margaret H. Waters; m. Cletis G. Smith (dec.); m. Terry F. Farr, Oct. 20, 1993; children: Lourie A. Hargis, James W. Harris. Pastor, pres. Full Gospel Lighthouse Ministries, Muncie, Ind. Fellow: Wings for Women. Pentecostal. Avocations: reading, fishing, travel. Home: 1909 S Biltmore Muncie IN 47302 Office: Full Gospel Lighthouse Ministries 1600 W 15th Muncie IN 47302 Office Phone: 765-284-9539.

FARR, JUDITH BANZER, retired literature educator, writer; b. NYC, Mar. 13, 1936; d. Russell John and Frances Anna (Wissell) Banzer; m. George F. Farr, Jr., June 30, 1962; 1 child, Alec Winfield. BA, Marymount Manhattan Coll., 1957, LHD, 1992; MA, Yale U., 1959, PhD, 1965. Instr. in English Vassar Coll., Poughkeepsie, NY, 1961-63; asst. prof. St. Mary's Coll., Moraga, Calif., 1964-68; assoc. prof. SUNY, New Paltz, 1968-77, Georgetown U., Washington, 1978-90, prof. of English and Am. Lit., 1990-99, prof. emerita, 1999—. Vis. assoc. prof. Georgetown U., 1977—78. Author: The Life and Art of Elinor Wylie, 1983, The Passion of Emily Dickinson, 1992, I Never Came to You in White: A Novel, 1996, The Gardens of Emily Dickinson, 2004 (Crayshaw award of the Byron, Keats and Shelley Meml. Trust Brit. Acad., 2005); editor: Twentieth Century Interpretations of Sons and Lovers, 1970, New Century Views: Emily Dickinson, 1995; contbr. articles, poems, short stories to profl. and comml. publs. Recipient Alumnae award for Distinction in Arts and Letters, Marymount Manhattan Coll., NYC, 1976, Alpha Sigma Nu Best Book award, 1993, Alumnae award for scholarly distinction, Mary Louis Acad., 2001, Rose Mary Crawshay prize, Byron, Keats and Shelley Meml. Trust, The Brit. Acad., 2005; grantee, NY State Rsch. Found., 1974, Am. Coun. Learned Socs., 1984, 1986, Georgetown U. Ctr. German Studies, 1992; Morgan-Porter fellow, Yale U., 1960—61, Am. Philos. Soc. fellow, 1983. Mem. Authors' Guild, Emily Dickinson Internat. Soc., Cosmos Club. Avocations: antiques, gardening, art. Home: 5064 Lowell St NW Washington DC 20016-2616

FARRAND, LOIS BARBARA, pharmaceutical company administrator; b. Chgo., Oct. 5, 1935; d. Harold Everett Peel, Ethel Barbara Rizer; m. Michael MacNaughton Farrand, June 12, 1954; children: David Everett, Jill, Jon Michael. Student, U. Colo., 1953—55, Western Mich. U., 1961—62; AA, LaSalle U., Chgo., 1969. Ins. agt. Ins. Investors Diversified, Kalamazoo, 1971—73; floor covering salesperson, mgr. Montgomery Ward, Kalamazoo, 1973—82; real estate agt. Perry Realtors, Kalamazoo, 1982—83; floor covering salesperson, office mgr. N.Y. Carpet World, Portage, 1982—2000; sec. Quantum Resources, Portage, 2001—. Mem.: UN, DAR (vice regent 2001—), Schoolcraft Hist. Soc. Democrat. Avocations: genealogy, music, presenting historical programs. Home: 6600 Constitution Blvd Apt 216 Portage MI 49024-8900

FARRAR, DONNA BEATRICE, health facility administrator; b. Ayer, Mass., Feb. 4, 1950; d. Raymond H. and Shirley E. (Perham) F. B Music Edn., U. Mass., Lowell, 1971; MDiv, Bangor Theol. Sem., 1979; D Ministry, Christian Theol. Sem., 1987; M Family Studies, U. Ky., 1997. Tchr. music Billerica (Mass.) Pub. Schs., 1971-76; chaplain intern various hosps., Bangor, Maine, 1979; assoc. pastor Emanuel United Ch., Hales Corners, Wis., 1980-82; chaplain resident Ind. U & Meth. Hosp., Indpls., 1982-85; assoc. chaplain Ohio State U. Hosps., Columbus, 1985-87; assoc. dir., dir. Ind. U. Med. Ctr., Indpls., 1987-92; dept. dir. U. Ky. Hosps., Lexington, 1992—. Mem.: Am. Assn. Marriage and Family Therapists (lic. marriage family therapist). Democrat. Mem. Christian Ch. Avocations: reading, felines, dance, travel, art. Office: U Ky 800 Rose St # H-118 Lexington KY 40536-0293

FARRAR, ELAINE WILLARDSON, artist; b. L.A. d. Eldon and Gladys Elsie (Larsen) Willardson; children: Steve, Mark, Gregory, JanLeslie, Monty, Susan. BA, Ariz. State U., 1967, MA, 1969, PhD, 1990. Tchr. Camelback Desert Sch., Paradise Valley, Ariz., 1966-69; mem. faculty Yavapai Coll., Prescott, Ariz., 1970-92, chmn. dept. art, 1973-78, instr. art in watercolor, oil, acrylic painting, intaglio, 1971-92, instr. art relief intaglio and monoprints, 1971-92; grad. advisor Prescott Coll. Master of Arts Program, 1993-97, 2004—. One-woman shows include R.P. Moffat's, Scottsdale, Ariz., 1969, Art Ctr., Battlecreek, Mich., 1969, The Woodpeddler, Costa Mesa, Calif., 1979, numerous group shows including most recently, exhibited in group shows at Prescott Fine Arts Assn., 1999, 2001, 2002, Prescott Fine Art Assn., 2006, The Elements, 2001, Collage & Works on Paper, 2002, Faces & Forms To The Edge, 2004. Mem., curator Prescott Fine Arts Visual Arts com., 1992-97, Works on Paper, 2002; mem. exec. com., 1996-98; bd. dirs. Prescott Fine Arts Assn., 1995-98, Friends Y.C. Art Gallery Bd., 1992-97. Mem. Northern Ariz. Watercolor Assn., Mountain Artists Guild (past pres.), Women's Nat. Mus. (charter Washington chpt.), mus. of North Ariz. and Phoenix Art Mus., Kappa Delta Pi.

FARRELL, DEBBIE L., elementary school educator, media specialist; b. Suffern, NY, May 26, 1962; d. John A. and Elizabeth F. Golden; m. Tom M. Farrell, Dec. 29, 1984; children: Jennifer Lynn, Megan Elizabeth. B, U. Memphis. Cert. tchr./media specialist NC, 2003. Media specialist Brawley Mid. Sch., Mooresville, NC, 2003—.

FARRELL, DONNA MARIE, photographer, graphics designer; b. Hackensack, N.J., Jan. 24, 1968; d. Raymond Patrick and Rosemarie Farrell; m. Paul David Levy. BFA, Va. Commonwealth U., 1991. Freelance artist Murals in Motion, 1991—; photographer/graphic artist McFarlane Design Group, Bloomingdale, NJ, 1999—2005; supr. after sch. program St. Mary's Parish, Pompton Lakes, NJ, 2006. Capt. The Rave, Montclair, NJ, 1998—2002; photographer Goodwill Games, New York, 1998—98, Paraylmic Games, Atlanta, 1996—96; adj. prof. William Paterson U., Wayne, NJ, 1991—92; athlete Sportfriends Soccer Club, Wayne, NJ, 2000—; athlete, quarterback N.Y. Dazzels, Women's Profl. Football League, L.I., NY, 2004. Prin. works include mural Olympic Athlete Commemorative Mural Project. Vol., photographer Revlon Run/Walk, New York, 2002—02, Goals for Life, Montclair, 2000—02; vol., photographer, mem. WISE (Women in Sports and Events), N.Y.C., 2003. Named Women of Distinction World of Art, Lenni Lenape Girl Scout Coun., 1993; recipient Gold medal, Ga. Games, 1994, 1995, 1997; grantee Art & Photography grant, Summer Olympics, 1992, 1996, Winter Olympics, 1994, 1998. Mem.: N.J. Club Printing Ho. Craftsmen, Nat. Mus. Women in Arts, U.S. Soccer Found., Women's Sport Found., Women in Sports and Events, Sportfriends Soccer Club. Roman Catholic. Office: Murals in Motion 31 Walnut St Oakland NJ 07436 Office Phone: 973-727-8339. E-mail: dmfmim@yahoo.com.

FARRELL, ELIZABETH ANN, secondary school educator; b. Phila., May 3, 1980; d. Theodore Joseph and Eileen Ann Farrell. BA in Info. Sys. Mgmt., U. of Md., Balt., 2003. Tchr. secondary edn. Anne Arundel County Pub. Schs., Annapolis, Md., 2003—, coach h.s. varsity soccer Pasadena, Md., 2004—, coach h.s. varsity lacrosse, 2004—; coach under-9 girls soccer Balt. Bays, Balt., 2005—. Office Phone: 410-255-9600 239. Personal E-mail: efarrell@aacps.org.

FARRELL, KAREN F., school nurse practitioner; d. James P. Dunn and Helen Marie Lynch; m. Paul R. Farrell, Apr. 20, 1974; children: Heather, Michael, Lauren, Thomas, Kevin. AAS, Middlesex County Coll., Edison, NJ, 1972; BSN, Stockton State Coll., 1986; sch. nurse cert., Trenton State Coll., 1989, MEd, 1996. Cert. sch. nurse, ANCC. Staff nurse Georgetown Univ. Hosp., Washington, 1972—74; sch. nurse Belmar Elem. Sch., NJ, 1990—91, Neptune Bd. Edn., NJ, 1991—92, Wall Twp. Bd. Edn., NJ, 1992—. Faculty mem. Nat. Assn. Sch. Nurses, Colo., 2003—. Mem.: Monmouth County Sch. Nurses Assn. (sec., pres.-elect, pres., program chair, Sch. Nurse of Yr. 1997), NJ State Sch. Nurses Assn. (parlimentarian 2004—05), Nat. Sch. Nurses Assn., Women of Irish Heritage-Jersey Shore, Irish-Am. Culture Inst., Sigma Theta Tau. Roman Catholic. Avocation: genealogy. Home: 2502 Emerson Ave Spring Lake NJ 07762 Office: Wall Twp Bd Edn W Belmar Sch 925 17th Ave Belmar NJ 07719 Office Phone: 732-556-2573, 732-974-1551.

FARRELL, KIMBERLY H., music educator; d. Edmund M. and Judith G. Scheiber; m. Timothy P. Farrell, Aug. 10, 1996; children: Kathryn Judith, Ryan Gene. BMus in Edn. with distinction, U. Maine, Orono, 1989; MMus, U. Oreg., Eugene, 1996. Cert. tchr. Colo., 2001. Tchr. choral music Lin-Wood Sch., Lincoln, NH, 1990—94; tchr. elem. music Mapleton Sch., Mapleton, ND, 1997—99; tchr. choir & orch. Durango Sch. Dist., Colo., 1999—; ind. beauty cons. Mary Kay Cosmetics, 2000—. Mem., sect. leader Durango Choral Soc., 1999—; singer Santa Fe Desert Chorale, 2004—; adj. prof. music Valley City State U., ND, 1996—99; singer Robert Shaw Carnegie Hall Choral Workshop, 1994, 97. Mem.: Music Educators Nat. Conf., Am. Choral Dirs. Assn., Delta Zeta. Avocations: skiing, reading, Broadway shows. Home: 102 Long Hollow Lane Durango CO 81301 Office: Miller Middle School 2608 Junction St Durango CO 81301 Office Phone: 970-247-1418. Personal E-mail: kfarrell1@marykay.com. E-mail: kfarrell@durango.k12.co.us.

FARRELL, MARGARET DAWSON, lawyer; b. Bellingham, Wash., July 23, 1949; d. Sterling Jacob and Irene Hegg; m. David S. Farrell, June 10, 1972; children: Lindsay S., Charles D. BA cum laude, Smith Coll., 1971; postgrad., Georgetown U., 1971-72; JD, U. Cin., 1974. Bar: Ohio 1974, U.S. Dist. Ct. (so. dist.) Ohio 1974, R.I. 1976, U.S. Dist. Ct. R.I. 1976. Assoc. Frost & Jacobs, Cin., 1974-76; from assoc. to ptnr. Tillinghast, Collins & Graham, Providence, 1976—81; ptnr. Hinckley, Allen & Snyder LLP, Providence, 1981—. Lectr. Bryant Coll., 1979-80; dir., sec. Bank R.I., 1996—, Bancorp R.I., Inc., 2000—. Trustee Women and Infants Hosp., Providence, 1981—, sec., 1982-96, vice chair, 1996—2003, chair 2004—; bd. dirs. Women and Infants Corp., Providence, 1989—2003, chair 2004—, sec., 1989-96, vice chair, 1996-2003, chair, 2004—; trustee, sec. Providence Preservation Soc. Revolving Fund, 1982-88; trustee Butler Hosp., 1995—, Care New England Health Sys., 1996—, R.I. Hist. Soc., 1980-85, Gordon Sch., East Providence, R.I., 1990-95; trustee Hosp. Assn. R.I., 1989-2003, mem. exec. coun., 1998-2003; trustee, sec., pres. Found. for Repertory Theatre, R.I., 1978-84; R.I. del. Am. Hosp. Assn. Congress Hosp. Trustees, 1993-98; mem. R.I. Bd. Regents for Elem. and Secondary Edn., 1987-90. Mem. ABA, R.I. Bar Assn. Avocations: golf, sailing, skiing, horseback riding. Office: Hinckley Allen & Snyder LLP 50 Kennedy Plz Ste 1500 Providence RI 02903 Office Phone: 401-274-2000.

FARRELL, MARY COONEY, securities analyst; b. Hartford, Conn., Dec. 8, 1949; d. Garrett Francis and Agnes Dwyer (Cooney) Farrell; m. James Andrew Rahl, Jr., Jan. 25, 1975; children: Katherine, Stephen. BA in Econs., Manhattanville Coll., 1971; MBA in Fin., NYU, 1976. Security analyst Pershing & Co., Inc., N.Y.C., 1971—74, Smith Barney, Harris Upham & Co., Inc., N.Y.C., 1976—78, Merrill Lynch, Pierce Fenner & Smith, N.Y.C., 1978—80, Bean Murray, Foster Securities, Inc., N.Y.C., 1980—82; portfolio mgr. Marine Midland Bank, N.Y.C., 1974—76; security analyst, v.p. Paine Webber Mitchell Hutchins, Inc., N.Y.C., 1982—2000; mng. dir., chief investment strategist UBS, NYC, 2000—05, co-head wealth mgmt. investment strategy & rsch. group. Panelist Wall Street Week, PBS; bd. dir. W.R. Berkley Corp., 2006—. Author: Mary Farrell's Beyond the Basics: How to Invest Your Money, Now That You Know a Thing or Two. Past trustee NYU; mem. bd. overseers Stern Sch. Bus. NYU. Recipient Disting. svc. award, Nat. Assn. Investment Clubs, 1982, Woman of the Yr., Manhattanville Coll., 1999, Laura A. Johnson Woman of the Yr., Univ. Hartford, 2001. Fellow: Fin. Analysts Fedn.; mem.: Fin. Women's Assn. (civic affairs chmn. 1982—83, dir. 1977—79,, Private Sector Woman of the Yr. 2002), N.Y. Soc. Security Analysts. Mailing: WR Berkley Corp Board of Directors 475 Steamboat Rd Greenwich CT 06830

FARRELL, PAMELA CHRISTINE, secondary school educator; b. Cin., Jan. 5, 1965; d. Thomas Harry and Barbara Jane Farrell; children: Thomas Patrick Farrell-Turner, Ronald Bryan Farrell-Creed. M, U. Dayton, Ohio, 1998. Cert. Comprehensive Math. and Sci. Tchr. State of Ohio, 1985. Tchr. Ripley-Union-Lewis-Huntington H.S., Ohio, 1985—94, Milford Exempted Village Schs., Ohio, 1994—97, Princeton City Schs., Cin., 1997—. Tchr. Brown County Schs., Georgetown, Ohio, 1987—93, So. State C.C., Fincastle, Ohio, 1988—90. Tchr. catechism St. Michael Ch., Sharonville, Ohio, 2003—. Named Tchr. of Yr., Radio Shack, 2000; recipient Tchr. Achievement award, Ashland, 1996, Commendation award, Sci. Edn. Coun. Ohio, 2000; Martha Holden Jennings scholar, U. Dayton, 1989. R-Consevative. Roman Catholic. Achievements include patents pending for Static Magic or PONAM. Avocations: travel, bicycling, hiking, sports, Special Olympics. Home: 11004 Main Street Cincinnati OH 45241 Office: Princeton High School 11080 Chester Road Cincinnati OH 45246 Office Phone: 513-552-8410. Personal E-mail: suavenus@aol.com. E-mail: pfarrell@princeton.k12.oh.us.

FARRELL, PATRICIA ANN, psychologist, educator, writer; b. NYC; d. Joseph and Pauline Farrell. BA, Queens Coll.; MA, PhD, NYU. Lic. psychologist, NJ, Fla.; cert. online computer instr. Assoc. editor Pubs. Weekly Mag., NYC; editor Bestsellers Mag., NYC; assoc. editor King Features Syndicate, NYC; staff psychologist, intake coord. Mid-Bergen Cmty. Mental Health Ctr., Paramus, NJ; instr. Bergen C.C., Paramus, 1978-94; prof. clin. psychology Walden U., 1995—2001. Resident clin. psychology Am. Inst. for Counseling, NJ, 1990-91; cons. Family Counseling Svc. of Ridgewood, NJ, 1984; clin. psychology intern Marlboro (NJ) Psychiat. Hosp., 1984-85, staff psychologist, 1985-87; rsch. analyst Mt. Sinai Sch. Medicine, 1987-88; account exec., sr. med. writer Manning, Selvage and Lee, NYC, 1988-90; sr. clin. psychologist, mem. med. staff Greystone Pk. (NJ) Psychiat. Hosp., 1990-96; pvt. practice psychology, Englewood Cliffs, NJ; health sci. editor Time Warner Cable, Channel 10 News, 1995-2000; med. specialist NJ Divsn. Disability Determination, 1997—; police surgeon Boro Ft. Lee, NJ, 1998—; psychiatry preceptor U. Medicine and Dentistry NJ Med. Sch.; cons. pharm. clin. protocols; psychologist, expert moderator on anxiety and panic WebMD, 2000—. Guest radio and TV shows including The Today Show, Crier Live, Nat. Geog. TV, MSNBC, The Abrams Report, The Big Idea, Ron Reagan's Connections, Hollywood at Large, The View, The O'Reilly Factor, ABC Sports Spl., VH1, E!, ABC World News with Anderson Cooper, Court TV, Rapid Fire, CNN Radio, Geraldo Rivera Show, Newsweek-on-Air, Voice of Am., Family Talk, Up Front Tonight, Buchanon & Press, Pros and Cons, Local Live, USA Radio Network, Ken Hamblin Show, KNU Radio, Fox Beyond the News, Real Talk, Jay Thomas Radio Show, Sally Jessy Raphael, Montel Williams, Gordon Elliott Show, Inside Edit., Am. Jour., Joan Rivers Show, Fox Cable News, Good Day NY, Mark Walberg, Am. After Hours, Dini, The Shirley Show, Camilla Scott, USA Live, Alive and Wellness with Carol Martin, News Talk, Maury Povich, Caucus NJ, It's Your Call, One-on-One, The Carnie Wilson Show, AP Newswire, Judge for Yourself TV Show, NYC 10 O'Clock News, Cosmo, Redbook, Self, Shape, Fitness, Latina, Maxim, Good Housekeeping, AARP, Cooking Light, Smart Money, Ct. TV Investigative Reports, In Touch, Woman's World, Achieve Solutions, All You, First for Women, Washington Post, Fox & Friends, Eyewitness News, Reuters TV, Timeout NY, Detroit News, Knight-Ridder News, Chgo. Tribune, Home Office Computing, Working Woman, NY Post, Boston Globe, NY Daily News, NY Times, Chateleine, New Woman, Phila. Enquirer, WPIX-TV, NY, UPN 9 News, WWOR-TV News, WNRR-TV, In Your Interest, LTV, Channel 10 News, On Campus, Sta WTTM, WSNJ, WHSI-TV, Bloomberg News, UPI News, KGAB, WSAR, Don Weeks Show, Common Concerns, WHSE-TV, Alan Nathan's Battle Lines, Dirk Van NBC radio, Ruth Koscielak Show, Voice of Am., WTOP, Redbook, Ramp, Eyewitness News, Cork Talks Back, TalkSport, The Week, Pink, Life & Style, Ladies Home Jour., Reuters TV, Bev Smith Show, Fitness, Shape, Prevention, In Touch, More, The Oregonian, Arnie Arneson Show, Talk Am., Real Simple, Quick and Simple, Marie Claire, Seventeen, Parents, Shape, Prevention, AARP Bull., Women's Health, Inside TV, Baby Talk, Family Circle, Women's Day, Metro NY, Physical, Wall St. Jour. Radio, Christian Single, Mental Health Law Report; author: (manual) Alzheimer's Disease Assessment Scale test, How To Be Your Own Therapist, 2004; contbr. chpts. Fifty Things to Do When You Turn Fifty, 2005; contbr. articles to Writer's Digest, Real World, Postgrad. Medicine, newspapers. Bd. dirs., chmn. med. liaison com. liaison to dept. psychiatry Bergen Pines County Hosp., Paramus, 1994-95. McDonald's rsch. grantee, 1994-95; recipient Sci. award Rotary Club. Avocations: exercise, racquetball, kite-flying, film making. Office: PO Box 1525 Englewood Cliffs NJ 07632-0283 Personal E-mail: pfarrell@ix.netcom.com.

FARRELL, SUZANNE (ROBERTA SUE FICKER), ballerina; b. Cin., Aug. 16, 1945; d. Robert Ficker and Donna (Von Holle) Holly; m. Paul Mejia, Feb. 21, 1969 (div. 1997). Studies with Marian LaCour, Cin. Conservatory Music; student, Sch. Am. Ballet, 1960—61; LHD (hon.), Georgetown U., 1984, Fordham U., 1987; DFA (hon.), Yale U., 1988; LLD (hon.), U. Notre Dame, 1990; D of Performing Arts (hon.), U. Cin., 1990; ArtsD (hon.), Middlebury Coll., 1992; LHD (hon.), Coll. Mt. St. Vincent, 1995; Doctorate (hon.), Harvard U., 2004. With Maurice Bejart's Ballet of the 20th Century, Brussels, 1969, NYC Ballet, 1961—69, 1975—89, became featured dancer, 1962, prin. dancer, 1965—69, 1975—89; program creator, Exploring Ballet with Suzanne Farrell Kennedy Ctr., Washington, 1993—; artistic dir. The Suzanne Farrell Ballet, 2000—. Hon. lectr. dance U. Cin.; guest tchr. Sch. Am. Ballet, Kennedy Ctr. for Performing Arts; prof. dance Fla. State U., 2000—, Francis Eppes Chair in Arts. Appeared in film version Midsummer Night's Dream, Bejart Ballet of 20th Century, Brussels, 1971—75, appeared as Juliet in Romeo and Juliet, appeared with NYC Ballet in New Ravel Festival, Tzigane, in G Major, 1976, (documentary) Elusive Muse, 1996, created roles in other ballets Ah, Vous Dirais Je, Maman?, the young girl in Rose in Nijinsky, Clown of God, 1971, Laura in I Trionfi, (NYC Ballet) Chaconne, Mozartiana, Diamonds, featured in TV show Balanchine Dance in Am., Parts I-IV, featured in Exploring Ballet with Suzanne Farrell at the Kennedy Ctr., 1993—; author: (autobiography) Holding on to the Air, 1990; repetiteur George Balanchine Trust. Mem. sr. adv. bd. NY chpt. Arthritis Found.; mem. arts adv. bd. Princess Grace Found.-USA; mem. NY State Coun. on Arts; pres. bd. Profl. Children's Sch. Recipient Merit award, Mademoiselle mag., 1965, Dance mag. award, 1976, Award of Honor for Arts and Culture, NYC, 1979, Spirit Achievement award, Albert Einstein Coll. Medicine, 1980, Merit award, Brandeis U., Emmy award, 1985, Golden Plate award, Am. Acad. of Achievement, 1987, Arts award, Gov. of NY State, 1988, Nat. Medal of Arts, 2003, Capezio Dance Award, 2005, Kennedy Ctr. Honor, John F. Kennedy Ctr. for Performing Arts, 2005.*

FARREN, ANN LOUISE, chemist, information scientist, educator; b. Portage, Pa., Dec. 5, 1926; dJ. Edward and Ann (Conrad) F AB, U. Pa., 1948. Biochemist Jefferson Med. Coll./Valley Forge Hosp., Phila./Phoenixville, 1948—52; organic chemist Smith, Kline & French Labs., Phila., 1952—53; chemist Rohm & Haas Co., Phila., 1953—56; head info. office Am. Chem. Soc. News Svc., N.Y.C., 1956—59; with BIOSIS, Phila., 1959—, profl. rels. officer, 1962-74, mgr. edn. bur., 1974-78, sr. edn. specialist, 1978-95, lead database specialist, 1996-98, ret., 1998, ednl cons., 1998—. Profl. rels. officer BIOSIS, Phila., 1962—74, mgr. edn. bur., 1974—78, sr. edn. specialist, 1978—95, lead database specialist, 1996—98. Bd. dirs. Delaware Valley Sci. Coun., 1972— Fellow AAAS; mem. Am. Chem. Soc. (Ullyot award 1993), Nat. Assn. Sci. Writers Home: 5720 Wissahickon Ave Apt D19 Philadelphia PA 19144-5610 E-mail: alf12@aol.com.

FARRER, CLAIRE ANNE RAFFERTY, anthropologist, educator; b. NYC, Dec. 26, 1936; d. Francis Michael and Clara Anna (Guerra) Rafferty; 1 child, Suzanne Claire. BA in Anthropology, U. Calif., Berkeley, 1970; MA in Anthropology and Folklore, U. Tex., 1974, PhD in Anthropology and Folklore, 1977. Various positions, 1953-73; fellow Whitney M. Young Jr. Meml. Found., NYC, 1974-75; arts specialist, grant adminstr. Nat. Endowment for Arts, Washington, 1976-77; Weatherhead resident fellow Sch. Am. Rsch., Santa Fe, 1977-78; asst. prof. anthropology U. Ill., Urbana, 1978-85; assoc. prof., coord. applied anthropology Calif. State U., Chico, 1985-89, prof., 1989—2001, prof. emerita, 2002—, dir. Multicultural and Gender Studies, 1994. Cons. in field, 1974—; mem. film and video adv. panel Ill. Arts Coun., 1980-82; mem. Ill. Humanities Coun., 1980-82; vis. prof. U. Ghent, Belgium, 1990; vis. prof. Southwestern studies Colo. Coll., Colorado Springs, 2002-06, Hulbert chair in Southwestern studies, 1997; bus. mgr. Calif. Folklore Soc., 1994-99; NEH and Harry J. Gray disting. vis. prof. in humanities U. Hartford, Conn., 2002-03. Author: Play and Inter-Ethnic Communication, 1990, Living Life's Circle: Mescalero Apache Cosmovision, 1991, Thunder Rides a Black Horse: Mescalero Apaches and the Mythic Present, 1994, 96, others; co-founder, co-editor Folklore Women's Commn., 1972; editor spl. issue Jour. Am. Folklore, 1975, 1st rev. edit., 1986; co-editor: Forms of Play of Native North Americans, 1979, Earth and Sky: Visions of the Cosmos in Native North American Folklore, 1992; contbr. numerous articles to profl. jours., mags. and newspapers, chpts. to books. Recipient J. Gordon prize in S.W. Studies, Colo.Coll.; numerous fellowships and grants. Fellow Am. Anthrop. Assn.; mem. Authors Guild, Am. Ethnol. Soc., Am. Folklore Soc., Am. Soc. Ethnohistory, Astronomy in Culture. Home: PO Box 50293 Colorado Springs CO 80949-0293 Personal E-mail: clairerfarrer@aol.com.

FARRER-BORNARTH, SYLVIA, writer, artist; b. Rochester, N.Y., Dec. 11, 1935; d. Arthur and Anne (Hendricks) Farrer; m. Philip William Bornarth, June 15, 1963; children: Daniel, Ian. AAS, Rochester Inst. Technology, 1957, BFA, 1963, MFA, 1967. Painter, printmaker, artist hist. decoration Genesee County Mus., Mumford, NY, 1975—88; exec. dir. Seneca Falls (N.Y.) Hist. Soc., 1988-92; artist, writer, assoc. editor Genesee Country Mag., Geneseo, N.Y., 1992-95; writer, rschr. Seaway Trail Mag., Sackets Harbor, N.Y., 1992—. With Hist. Gardens Rev., London, 2000-03. Mem. Bookbinder, Gardens Book Restoration. Avocations: photography, orchids, roses, water gardens. Home: 7831 Jay St Pultneyville NY 14538 E-mail: sfbornarth@aol.com.

FARRIGAN, JULIA ANN, retired small business owner, educator; b. Albany, N.Y., July 19, 1943; d. Charles Gerald and Julia Tryon (Shepherd) F. BS in Elem. Edn., SUNY, Plattsburgh, 1965; MS in Curriculum Planning and Devel., SUNY, Albany, 1973, U. Manchester, Eng., 1973; postgrad. in adminstrv. svcs., Calif. State U., Fresno, 1976-78. With Monroe-Woodbury Ctrl. Sch. Dist., Monroe, N.Y., 1965-90; dist. coord. gifted programs The Pine Tree Sch., 1979-90; ptnr. Baskets Plain and Fancy, Jackson, Ga., 1994—2000; owner The Basket House. Adj. prof. Gifted Edn. Contbr. articles to profl. jours. Vol. Jackson United Meth. Ch. Mem. DAR (registrar William McIntosh chpt., Robert Daniell chpt.), AFT, ASCD, N.Y. United Fedn. Tchrs., Nat. Assn. for Gifted Children, Coun. Exceptional Children, Monroe-Woodbury Tchrs. Assn., Kiwanis (officer), Colonial Dames 17th Century (Thomas Johnson chpt.), Daus. Am. Colonists (Gov. Robert Danell chpt.), Basket Weavers Guild Ga., Delta Kappa Gamma (officer Upsilon chpt., state editor). Democrat. Methodist.

FARRINGTON, BERTHA LOUISE, retired nursing administrator; b. Poteet, Tex., Jan. 20, 1937; d. Leonard Gilbert and Janie (Hernandez) Lozano; m. James Charles Farrington, Jan. 30, 1965; children: Mark Hiram, Robert Lee. BSN, Tex. Women's U., 1960; NP, U. Tex., 1984. RN, Tex. Charge nurse emergency rm. Parkland Meml. Hosp., Dallas; head nurse emergency rm./day surgery Bapt. Meml. Hosp., Pensacola, Fla.; asst. dir. health svcs. U. Tex. Southwestern Med. Ctr., Dallas, dir. student health svcs., ret., 2002. Cons. Student Health Com. E-mail: j.bfarrington@sbcglobal.net.

FARRINGTON, HELEN AGNES, personnel director; b. Queens, NY, Dec. 1, 1945; d. Joseph Christopher and Therese Marie (Breazzano) F AS, Interboro Inst., N.Y.C., 1965; AA, Ohio State U., 1983, BS Human Resource Mgmt., 1987; Mgmt. cert., U. Mich., 1980. Pers. adminstr. Am. Electric Power Co., N.Y.C., 1974—79, supr. human resources Ohio Power divsn. Newark, 1979—87; dir. human resources Citizens Utilities Co., Stamford, Conn., 1987—88; mgr., exec. search firm Arthur Lyle Assocs., Norwalk, Conn., 1988—89; dir. human resources CaroLee Designs, Inc., Greenwich, Conn., 1990—92, ind. human resources cons., 1992—95; dir. human resources Gartner Group, Stamford, 1993—95; prin., CPO HFA Resources LLC, Niwot, Colo., 1996—; pres. Helen Farrington Group, Niwot, 2005—. Bd. dirs. emeritus Boulder Cmty. Hosp.; former bd. dirs.-at-large MARC, Lakewood, Colo. Mem.: Consultants Forum, Boulder Area Human Resources Assn., Colo. Human Resources Assn., Soc. Human Resources Mgmt. (cons. forum), Boulder C. of C. Office: PO Box 438 Niwot CO 80544-0438 Office Phone: 303-417-9025. Personal E-mail: helenfarrington@msn.com.

FARRIOR, HELEN HOOKS, retired assistant principal; b. Duplin County, N.C. d. Matthew Clark Hooks and Canary Jane Brown-Hooks; m. Willie Albert Farrior, Sept. 30, 1962 (dec.). BA in Edn., Shaw U., 1958; MEd, N.C. Ctrl. U., 1966. Cert. notary pub. N.C., realtor N.C. Tchr., asst. prin. Washington Dr. Jr. H.S., 1958—66; asst. prin., coord. curriculum Hillcrest Mid. Sch., 1967—90; asst. prin. E.E. Smith Sr. H.S., 1990—94, ret., 1994. Mem. regional screening com. N.C. Tchg. Fellows Scholarship Program; bd. dirs. Ft. Bragg Fed. Credit Union Adv. Bd. State Employees. Mem. redevelopment commn. Fayetteville, 1988—93, vice chmn. redevelopment commn., 1993; numerous other positions; chmn. precinct 16 Cumberland County Dem. Party, 1985—93, vice chmn. precinct 16, 2005—, del. to conventions, 1987—; trustee First Bapt. Ch., Fayetteville, NC; bd. dir. Cumberland County Sch. Bd., 2000—. Democrat. Bapt. Home: 1707 Eldridge St Fayetteville NC 28301

FARRIS, CHARLYE OLA, lawyer; b. Wichita Falls, Tex., 1930; d. James and Roberta Farris. Bachelor's Degree, Prairie View A&M Coll.; postgrad., U. Denver; JD, Howard U., 1953. Bar: Tex. 1953. Pvt. practice, Wichita Falls, 1955—. Office: 921 7th St Wichita Falls TX 76301

FARRIS, ERIN ANDERSON, lawyer; b. Kings Mountain, NC, Nov. 17, 1977; d. Teresa Gail Anderson; m. Timothy Dean Farris, Mar. 20, 2004. BA, Wake Forest U., Winston Salem, NC, 2000; JD, U. Tex., Austin, 2003. Bar: Tex. 2003. Assoc. Baron & Budd, P.C., Dallas, 2003—. Bd. mem. Mothers Against Teen Violence, Dallas, 2005—06. Mem.: Am. Trial Lawyers Assn. Avocations: cooking, scrapbooks, reading. Office: Baron & Budd PC 3102 Oak Lawn Avenue Dallas TX 75219 Office Phone: 214-521-3605.

FARROW, MARGARET ANN, former lieutenant governor; b. Kenosha, Wis., Nov. 28, 1934; d. William Charles and Margaret Ann (Horan) Nemitz; m. John Harvey Farrow, Dec. 29, 1956; children: John, William, Peter, Paul, Mark. Student, Rosary Coll., 1952-53; BS in Polit. Sci. and Edn., Marquette U., 1956, postgrad., 1975-77. Tchr. Archdiocese of Milw., 1956-57; trustee Elm Grove Village, Wis., 1976-81, pres. Wis., 1981-86; mem. Wis. Assembly, Madison, 1986-89, Wis. Senate from 33rd dist., Madison, 1989—2001; lt. gov. State of Wis., 2001—03; dir. local govt. affairs Whyte Hirshboeck Dudek Govt. Affairs, 2003—. Chair govt. effectiveness, 1998-2001, asst. majority leader, 1998; mem. joint com. on audit, 1993-97, mem. joint survey com. on tax exemptions, 1993-97, chair Wis. women's coun., 1991—, Rep. caucus chair, 1996, 99, mem. coun. on workforce excellence, 1995—, mem. Wis. glass ceiling commn., 1993—; mem. Senate Com. on edn., 1999, Senate com. on labor, 1999. Republican. Home: W 262 # 2402 Deer Haven Dr Pewaukee WI 53072-4572

FARSHEE, MARLENA W., title company executive; b. Prattville, Ala., Sept. 30, 1964; d. Albert G. Wallace Jr. and Mary Margaret Gray; m. Charles Morgan King, Feb. 6, 1981 (dec. Jan. 1985); 1 child, Candice King; m. William B. Farshee, Jr., Aug. 8, 1999; children: Carly, Anna, William. Legal sec. Sasser & Littleton, PC, Mont., Ala., 1992—94; mgr. Closing Assocs., Prattville, 1994—98; pres. Flagship Closing Svcs., Mont., 1998—2004; owner Advantage Closing, LLC, Mont., 2004—. Mem.: Greater Montgomery Homebuilders Assn. (assoc. com. chair 2001—02, Assoc. of Yr. 2002), Women's Coun. Realtors, Real Estate Assn. Ala. (affiliate com. 2000—03). Republican. Methodist. Avocations: gardening, reading, boating. Home: 120 Huckleberry Dr Deatsville AL 36022 Office: Advantage Closing LLC 6767 Taylor Cir Montgomery AL 36117 Office Phone: 334-558-0166. Office Fax: 334-558-0213.

FARSI, CARLA EMILIA, mathematics professor; b. Florence, Italy, July 18, 1959; d. Carlino and Margherita Farsi. Laureate, U. Florence, Italy, 1983; PhD, U. Md., 1989. Tchg. asst. U. Md., 1985—87, rsch. asst., 1987—88; post-doctoral fellow U. Toronto, 1989—91; asst. prof. U. Colo., 1991—97, assoc. prof., 1997—. Avocations: mountain climbing, skiing. Office: U Colo Dept Math 395 UCB Boulder CO 80309-0395 Office Phone: 303-492-7422. Office Fax: 303-492-7707. Business E-Mail: farsi@uclid.colorado.edu.

FARVER, CINDY L., elementary school educator; b. Pitts., Dec. 14, 1952; d. William John Hilton, Sr. and Eleanor Jacquline Hilton; m. Newberry C. Farver; 1 child, Katherine ELizabeth. Psychology & Counseling, Newberry Coll., S.C., 1970—73; Elem. Edn., Akron U., Ohio, 1974—79; M, Marygrove Coll., Mich., 2002—04. Cert. Tchr. Ohio Dept. Edn., 1979. 7th grade geography tchr. Medina City Schs., Ohio, 1979—2000, 8th grade history tchr., 2000—. Many positions Jr. Women's Civic Club, Akron, Ohio, 1987—2006. Recipient Excellence in Tchg. award, Medina City Sch. Found., 2002. Mem.: NEA. Home: 645 Kovack Cove Wadsworth OH 44281 Office: Medina City Schs 420 E Union St Medina OH 44256 Office Phone: 330-636-3601. Personal E-mail: c_farver@hotmail.com.

FARVER, JANE, museum director; Dir. Lehman Coll. Art Gallery, CUNY, 1989—92; dir. exhbns. Queens Mus. Art, 1992—97; dir. List Visual Arts Ctr., MIT, 1999—. Curator Global Conceptualism: Points of Origin, 1950s-1980s. Office: List Visual Arts Ctr 20 Ames St Bldg E15 Cambridge MA 02139 E-mail: jfarver@mit.edu.

FARWELL, NANCY LARRAINE, public relations executive; b. Sellersville, Pa., May 2, 1944; d. Warren Gregory and Mary Rita (Zaniboni) F. BA, Pa. State U., 1966. Asst. TV rep. H.R. TV Reps., Phila., 1966-68; various positions Hawthorne Advt. Inc., Phila., 1968-73; dir. employee rels. Colonial Penn Group, Inc., Phila., 1973-75, mgr. press rels., 1976-78, mgr. pub. rels., 1978-82; dir. comm. Provident Mut. Life Ins. Co., Phila., 1982-83, asst. v.p., comm., 1983-87; pres. Nancy Farwell Assocs., Phila., 1987-90; v.p. Anne Klein & Assocs., Inc., Mt. Laurel, NJ, 1990-92, sr. v.p., 1992-97, sr. v.p., COO, 1998-2001, sr. v.p. strategic planning, 2001—03, sr. councilor, 2003—. Adv. bd. City of Phila. Century IV Tall Ships, 1982. Author: (photo essay) Philadelphia, 1976; contbr. chpt. to home health care mktg. book. Founder, co-chair Portico Row Neighborhood Assn., Phila., 1989-92; bd. dirs. Washington Sq. West Project Area Com., Phila., 1990-92, Boys and Girls Clubs of Metro Phila. Adv. Coun., 1991—; adv. com. Phila. 6th Police Dist., 1990-92. Mem. Pub. Rels. Soc. Am. (10 Pepperpot awards, 2 Awards of Excellence, Silver Anvil award of Excellence), Phila. Pub. Rels. Assn. Office: Anne Klein and Assoc Inc 401 Route 73 N Ste 108 Marlton NJ 08053-3429 Office Phone: 856-988-6560.

FARY, SANDRA SUZANNE, science educator; b. Fremont, Calif., July 20, 1968; d. Richard Clovis Fary and Virginia Ann McNulty; m. Michelle Annette Pinaud, July 12, 2003; children: Cooper Davis Pinaud, Owen Fischer Pinaud. BA, U. Calif., Davis, 1993; MEd, St. Michael's Coll., Colchester, Vt., 2003. Sci. tchr. Manchester (Vt.) Mid. Sch., 1997—98, Camels Hump Mid. Sch., Richmond, Vt., 1998—. Environ. tchr. U. Vt., Burlington, 1998—2003; writer, designer Landscape Change Project curriculum, 2006. Interpretive trl. map project ccoord. Richmond Rivershore Preserve, 2002—04. Nominee Vt. Sci. Tchr. of Yr., 2005; recipient Gov.'s award for environ. excellence in edn., State of Vt., 2005. Mem.: NEA, Nat. Tennis Assn. Avocations: cross-country skiing, painting, tennis. Home: 5 Tourin Rd Jericho VT 05465 Office: Camels Hump Mid Sch 173 School St Richmond VT 05477 Office Phone: 802-434-2188. E-mail: sandra.fary@cesu.k12.vt.us.

FASEL, IDA, literature and language professor, writer; b. Portland, Maine, May 9, 1909; d. I.E. Drapkin and Lilian Rose Harwich; m. Oscar A. Fasel, Dec. 24, 1946 (dec. Apr. 1973). BA in English Lang. and Lit. with distinction, Boston U., 1931, MA, 1945; PhD, U. Denver, 1963. Mem. faculty English U. Conn., New London, Midwestern U., Wichita Falls, Tex., Colo. Woman's Coll., Denver; prof. English U. Colo., Denver, 1962-77, prof. emerita of English, 1977. Presenter in field; contest judge. Transl. from French and Italian, editl. cons.: Renaissance and Baroque Lyrics, 1962; author (poetry): On the Meanings of Cleave, 1979 (Nortex Press Publ. award), Where Is the Center of the World?: Selections From Seven Chapbooks, 1981-1991, 1998 (U. West Fla. and Before the Rapture Press prize chapbooks), All Real Living Is Meeting, 1999 (Colo. Book award finalist, 2000), The Difficult Inch, 2000, Journey of a Hundred Years, 2002, Air, Angels and Us, 2002, Waking to Light, 2002 (Best Chapbook Angels Without Wings Found., 2003), Aureoles, 2002 (Best in Small Chapbook Class), The True Purpose of Planes, 2004; author: (poetry) Leafy as a Locust Tree, 2005 (Colo. Book award finalist, 2006), We Were Not Falling but Rising, 2006, In the Heart of the Heartland, 2006; contbr., editl. cons.: The Study and Writing of Poetry, 1983; contbr. articles to profl. jours., chpts. to books, poetry to anthologies and jours. Recipient Disting. Alumni honor Boston U., 1979, Alumni Poetry prize, 1983, 85, Before the Rapture Chapbook prize, 1985, Colo. Poet Honor, Friends of Denver Pub. Libr., 1991, Panhandler Chapbook prize, U. West Fla., 1991, Prize Poems award Colo. Authors League, 1993, 94, Nortex Press award, 1998, Juniper Press award, 2002, finalist Colo. Book award, 2000, 03, 06; named Poet Laureate, Colo. Woman's Coll.; Faculty Rsch. fellow U. Colo., 1979. Mem. Milton Soc. Am. (life), Friends of Milton's Cottage (charter), Assn. Literary Scholars and Critics, Conf. on Christianity and Lit., Poetry Soc. Tex., Colo. Endowment for the Humanities, Denver Woman's Press Club, Phi Beta Kappa. Avocations: ballet, Star Trek, collecting angels, piano, translating French poetry. Home: 165 Ivy St Denver CO 80220-5846

FASH, VICTORIA R., business executive; Sr. v.p. bus. strategy Dun & Bradstreet Corp., 1995-96; exec. v.p., CFO Cognizant, 1996—; exec. v.p., chmn., CEO IMS Internat., Westport, Conn., 1999—. Bd. dirs. Orion Capital Corp. Office: IMS Health Inc 1499 Post Rd Fairfield CT 06430-5940

FASICK, ADELE MONGAN, library and information scientist, educator; b. N.Y.C., Mar. 18, 1930; d. Stephen Leo and Florence (Geary) Mongan; m. Frank Fasick, Aug. 14, 1955 (div. 1986); children: Pamela, Laura, Julia. BA, Cornell U., 1951; MA, Columbia U., 1954, MSLS, 1956; PhD, Case Western Reserve U., 1970. Libr. N.Y. Pub. Libr., 1955-56, L.I.U., Bklyn., 1956-58; asst. prof. Rosary Coll., River Forest, Ill., 1970-71; prof. U. Toronto, 1971-96, dean Faculty of Libr. and Info. Sci., 1990-95. Adj. prof. San Jose State U., 1999—, U.C., 2002—. Author: Managing Children Services in Public Libraries, 1991, 2d edit., 1998, Beauty Who Would Not Spin, 1987; co-author: ChildView, 1987; editor: Lands of Pleasure, 1990; editor International Research Abstracts: Youth Library Services, 1993—. Mem.: ALA (com. on accreditation 1990—92), Assn. Librs. and Info. Sci. Edn. (pres. 1992), Internat. Fedn. Libr. Assn. (sec./treas. sect. on reading 1997—2003), Assn. Libr. Svc. to Children (exec. bd. 1980—84). E-mail: amfasick@earthlink.net.

FASKE, DONNA See KARAN, DONNA

FASMAN, MARJORIE LESSER, artist, writer; b. San Francisco, Dec. 1, 1916; d. Sol Leonard and Fay (Grunauer) Lesser; m. Morris Pfaelzer II, Apr. 12, 1938 (div. 1959); children: Fay Ellen Pfaelzer Abrams, Betty Pfaelzer Rauch; m. Michael J. Fasman, Mar. 30, 1961. Student, Wellesley Coll., 1934-37; BA, U. Penna. Designer for Mercado and cmty. events L.A. Music Ctr., 1946-48. Author: The Diary of Henry Fitzwilliam Darcy, 1998. Vol. Physicians for Social Responsibility, L.A.; founder (with others) Venice Family Clinic, 1985, UCLA Med. Ctr. Auxiliary (bd. dirs.). Recipient Corit Kent Peace award Immaculate Heart Coll., 1992. Mem. Women of L.A. (Hope is a Woman award 1998). Democrat. Jewish. Avocation: writing.

FASNACHT, HEIDE ANN, artist, educator; b. Cleve., Jan. 12, 1951; BFA, R.I. Sch. Design, 1973; MA in Studio Art, NYU, 1981. Vis. artist Bennington Coll., Vt., 1980, 1983, Cranbrook Acad., Bloomfield Hills, Mich., 1984, Cleve. Art Inst., 1981; asst. prof. art SUNY-Purchase, 1981—87; art instr. Parson's Sch. Design; vis. artist R.I. Sch. Design, 1985, Md. Inst. Coll. Art, 1985; asst. prof. dept. visual and environ. studies Harvard U., Cambridge, Mass., 1993—94, Pilchuck artist-in-residence, 2004. One-woman shows include New Gallery of Contemporary Art, Cleve., 1981, Vanderwoudel/Tananbaum Gallery, N.Y.C., 1983, 1985, Hill Gallery, Birmingham, Mich., 1984, 1986, Germans van Eck Gallery, N.Y.C., 1988, Yale U. Art Gallery, 2002, Kent Gallery, N.Y.C., 2003, 2005, Galeria Trama, Barcelona, 2003, Galerie les Filles du Calvaire, Paris and Brussels, 2005, Bernard Toale Gallery, Boston, 2005, Represented in permanent collections Bklyn. Mus. Art, Dallas Mus. Art, Columbus Mus. Art, Norton Gallery of Art, Santa Barbara Mus. Art, Yale Art Gallery, Phila. Mus. Art, Mus. Fine Arts, Boston, Hammer Mus., UCLA, Yale Art Gallery, Fogg Mus.; contbr. articles to profl. jours. Fellow, MacDowell Colony, 1981, 1983, 2005, Yaddo, 1980, 1985, Hand Hollow Found., 1983, Rockefeller Found., 2003, Lucas Vusual Arts Program, Montalvo; grantee, NEA, 1979, 1994, Athena Found., 1983, Louis Comfort Tiffany Found., 1986, Guggenheim Mus., 1991, Adolph and Esther Gottlieb Found. Home: 4 White St Apt 4A New York NY 10013-2469 Personal E-mail: heidestudio@earthlink.net.

FASNACHT, JUDY ANN, science educator, small business owner; b. Harrisburg, Pa., Apr. 5, 1953; d. William Stanley and Anna Jane Collier; m. Donald Arthur Fasnacht, July 26, 1975; 1 child, Joelle Alayne. BSc in Edn., Bloomsburg U., 1975; MSc in Edn., Temple U., 1980. Cert. permanent tchg. Pa. Tchr. sci. Halifax Area Sch. Dist., Pa., 1975—. Advisor sci. fair Halifax Sch. Dist., 1984—94; co-owner Robert Leshers Meats, Elizabethville, Pa., 1994—; mem. educators adv. coun. Whitaker Ctr. for Sci. and Arts, Harrisburg, Pa., 2002—; mem. edn. com. Ned Smith Ctr. for Nature and Art, Millersburg, Pa., 2002—. Mem., recording sec. Ctrl. Pa. Sci. Ctr., Harrisburg, 1984—87; advisor Phi Delta Sorority, 1987—91. Recipient Exemplary Program award, Shippensburg U., 1998—99; grantee energy grant, Family Sci. Festival, Pa. Dept. Edn., 1991. Mem.: Pa. Sci. Tchrs. Assn., Am. Bus. Women's Assn. (recording sec. 1980—81, v.p., pres. 1999—2000, ednl. spkr. local chpts., Woman of Yr. 1987). Avocations: reading, swimming, antiques. Home: 608 Lentz Ave Millersburg PA 17061 Office: Halifax Area Middle Sch 3940 Peters Mountain Rd Halifax PA 17032-9505 E-mail: dafjaf@epix.net.

FASSLER, KERIN IRENE, accountant; b. Vallejo, Calif., Jan. 4, 1948; d. Robert Wayne and Leila Jean Hall; m. Micheal Joseph Fassler, June 3, 1993; children: Michelle Ann Garcia, Preston Daniel; m. David Michael Mayugba, Oct. 24, 1966 (div.); children: Christina Denise Mayugba, Jennifer Irene Mayugba. AA, Am. River Jr Coll., Sacramento, Calif., 1989; BS, Regents Coll., Albany, NY, 1995; MA, Webster U., St. Louis, 1999. Farm laborer, Dixon, Calif., 1968—71; various govt. positions Sacramento, 1972—78; realtor assoc. Red Carpet, Sacramento, 1978—82; bus. owner Kerin's RV Rentals, Sacramento, 1986—90; budget analyst Various Govn't Agencies, 1986—97; mgmt./program analyst DOD, 1997—2005; sys. acct. US Army Corps Engrs., Anchorage, 2002—. Chmn. Red Carpet Realtors Associate's Com., Sacramento, 1980—80; bd. dirs. Info. and Referral Program United Way, Sacramento, 1988—91; pres. Internat. Tng. in Comm., Sacramento, 1989—89. Decorated Achievement Medal for Civilian Svc. US Army, Commander's Award for Civilian Svc.; recipient Presdl. Recognition, Pres. Ronald Reagan, 1988. Mem.: Am. Soc. of Mil. Comptrollers (assoc.; v.p. Denali chpt. 1996), Intertel (assoc.), Mensa (assoc.). Republican. Roman Catholic. Avocations: crocheting, scuba diving, skiing, sewing, crafts. Office: US Army Corps of Engrs 2204 3rd St Elmendorf Afb AK 99506 Office Phone: 907-753-2894. Personal E-mail: kifmjf@earthlink.net.

FAST, NAOMI MAE, retired physician; b. Fairview, Okla., May 4, 1929; d. John Martin Hein and Lydia Fruechting; m. Wilmer Dean Fast, July 25, 1948; children: Mary Kay, Charles David Kimmel. BA, Phillips U., Enid, Okla., 1950; DO, Kans. City Coll. of Osteopathic Surgery, 1959. Staff mem. Enid Meml. Hosp., Okla., 1963—88; ret., 1988. Mem. hosp. bd. Enid Meml. Hosp., 1975—80; chmn. sch. bd. Hennessey Sch., Okla., 1977, mem. sch. bd., 1974—79. Mem.: Okla. Osteopathic Assn., Am. Osteopathic Assn. (life). Republican. Evangelical Free Ch. Avocations: farming, travel. Home: 507 Manning Dr Hennessey OK 73742

FATONE, GINA ANDREA, music educator; d. Anthony Fatone and Betty Marie Rose Fatone; 1 child, John-Antonio Havika. BA in Music (Keyboard Performance), U. Conn., Storrs, 1984; MusM in Music Performance (harpsichord), New Eng. Conservatory, Boston, 1987; MA in Music (ethnomusicology), U. Calif., Santa Cruz, 1992; PhD in Ethnomusicology, UCLA, 2002. Postdoctoral fellow U. Calif., Santa Cruz, 2002—03; asst. prof. music Bates Coll., Lewiston, Maine, 2003—. Dir. Bates Coll. Gamelan Orch.; ch. organist; performer of S.E. and Ea. Asian music; field rschr. in cross-cultural music learning; dir. ann. world music weekend Bates Coll. Contbr. chapters to books. Multicultural music educator, Maine, 2004—. Fellow Chancellor's Dissertation fellowship, UCLA, 2001—02, Regent's fellowship, U. Calif., 1989—90; grantee Tanaka grantee for Asian Study, Freeman Found. Com. of Bates Coll., 2004—06, Humanities grantee, Mellon Found., Grad. Student fellowship, Internat. Coun. for Can. Studies, 2000; scholar Wilma Elias scholar for acad. achievement, U. of Conn., 1984. Mem.: Coll. Music Soc., Soc. for Ethnomusicology. Independent. Unitarian Universalist. Avocations: travel in Asia, wilderness hiking, gardening. Home: 71 Wellman St Lewiston ME 04240 Office: Bates College Olin Arts Center 75 Russell St Lewiston ME 04240 Office Phone: 207-753-9693. Personal E-mail: gfatone@bates.edu.

FATTORI, RUTH A., human resources specialist, electronics executive; BS, Cornell U. Advanced mfg. engr., various human resources positions Xerox Corp.; mng. dir. European ops., v.p., chief quality officer GE Capital, London; sr. v.p. human resources Siemans Corp., Siemans AG, Asea Brown Boveri; exec. v.p. process and productivity Conseco, Inc.; sr. v.p. human resources, comm. productivity and quality global tech. infrastructure group JPMorgan Chase & Co.; exec. v.p. human resources Motorla, Inc., Schaumburg, Ill., 2004—. Bd. trustees Polytechnic U., Trinity Pawling Sch. Office: Motorola Inc 1303 E Algonquin Rd Schaumburg IL 60196 Office Phone: 847-576-5000. Office Fax: 847-576-5372.

FAUCETTE, MERILON COOPER, retired secondary school educator; b. Washington, Ark., Oct. 17, 1931; d. Andrew and Narciss (Tyus) Cooper; m. Clarence William Faucette, Jr., May 17, 1958 (dec. 1982); children: Billie Reneé, Gwenevere Yvetta. BS, Ark. Bapt. Coll., Little Rock, 1953; MEd, Henderson State U., Arkadelphi, Ark., 1975. Tchr. Searcy (Ark.) Sch. Dist., 1953-61, Pulaski County Spl. Sch. Dist., Searcy, 1961-86; ret., 1986. Mem.: Telephone Pioneers Am. (assoc.).

FAUGHT, BRENDA DORMAN, health sciences educator; m. Jesse Albert Faught. AA, Phoenix Coll., 1970—73. Master Tchr. Tex. State PTA, 1998. Testing clk. Midland Coll., Tex., 1998—2000, health sciences continuing edn. specialist, 2002—. Tchr., kids coll. Midland Coll., Tex., 1992—97; store mgr. Connie's Fashion, Midland, Tex., 1993—94; owner Party Pizazz, Midland, Tex., 1993—95; substitute tchr. Midland Ind. Sch. Dist., 1994—95; part-time testing clk. Midland Coll., Tex., 1995—98. Pres. Volunteers In Pub. Schools, Midland, Tex., 1988—89, Midland City Coun. of PTA, Tex., 1989—90, Goddard Jr. H.S., Midland, Tex., 1990—91, Midland Freshman H.S., Tex., 1991—92, Midland H.S. PTA, Tex., 1993—94; mem. Midland Symphony Guild, Tex., 1992—99; parade of homes chmn./treas. Jr. Woman's Club, Midland, Tex., 1985—90; pres. Opportunity Ctr. Aux., Midland, Tex., 1983—84, Santa Rita Elem. Sch. Parent, Tchr. Assn., Midland, Tex., 1986—87; by-laws com. mem. Alamo Heights Bapt. Ch., Midland, Tex., 1990—93, spl. events com. chmn., 1989—92, vacation bible sch. chmn., 1989—90, parliamentarian, 1998—99; pres. & mem. Youth Centers, Midland, Tex., 1992—93; pres., treas. Greater Midland Football Cheerleader Bd., Tex., 1989—92; mem. Midland Coll. 25th Anniversary, Tex., 1998—99; pres. Cert. Pub. Accountants Wives Club, Midland, Tex., 1975—81. Recipient Nat. Dean's List, Ednl. Comm., Inc., 1997—98, 1998—99. Mem.: Tex. Administrators of Continuing Edn. for Cmty./Jr. Colleges (assoc.), Tex. PTA (hon.; life mem.), Phi Theta Kappa Hono Soc. (life), Sigma Kappa Nat. Social Sorority (life; pres. of Midland alumnae 1975—80, Ernstine Duncan Collins Pearl Ct. Award 1989). R-Consevative. Southern Bapt. Avocations: ceramics, party decorating, needlecrafts, crewel, tennis. Office: Midland Coll 3600 N Garfield - DHS #228 Midland TX 79705 Personal E-mail: bdfmidtx@aol.com. E-mail: bfaught@midland.edu.

FAUL, MAUREEN PATRICIA, health facility administrator; d. Michael M and Margaret A Faul; life ptnr. Stacey Citrin. BSN, Wheeling Jesuit U., W.Va., 1983. RN Pa., 1983. V.p. Heart Ctr. of Excellence North Broward Hosp. Dist., Ft. Lauderdale, Fla., 1998—2003; pres. The Resh Group, Inc, Coral Springs, Fla., 2003—05; CEO, Pulmonary Physicians of South Fla., LLC, Miami, 2005—. Bd. dirs. Am. Heart Assn., Ft. Lauderdale, Fla., 1998—2003. Office: Pulmonary Physicians of South Fla LLC 3625 NW 82d Ave # 408 Miami FL 33166 Personal E-mail: mpfaul@bellsouth.net.

FAULDS, ROXANNE M., media and technology educator; b. Oak Park, Ill. d. Wesley Robert and Helen J. Elkins; m. John Douglas III Faulds. MA in ednl. adminstrn., Dominican U., Ill., 2000; B in Philosophy, Grand Valley State U., Mich., 1980. Elem. tchr. Am. Sch. Guatemala, Guatemala City, 1980, Berwyn North Dist. 98, Ill., 1982—98, mid. sch. tchr., 1998—2000, media/tech. specialist, 2001—. Pres. North Berwyn Edn. Assn., Ill., 1996—. Vice chair Ill. Edn. Assn., Lombard, Ill., 2003—06; vol. Habitat for Humanity, Zambia, 2006. Recipient Educator of Yr., Local Unit PTA, Ill., 1996. Mem.: NEA, Ill. Edn. Assn., Ill. Sch. Libr. Media Assn., Am. Libr. Assn.

FAULES, BARBARA RUTH, retired elementary school educator; b. Austin, Tex., Mar. 10, 1940; d. Milton Friedrich Hausmann and Ruth Elizabeth Hornbuckle; m. John Wilson Faules, May 30, 1967. BA cum laude, Harding U., 1962; MA in Curriculum and Instrn., U. Mo., Kansas City, 1995. Cert. elem. tchr., Mo. Tchr. 4th grade Searcy Grammar Sch., Ark., 1962—64, Pulaski County Spl. Sch., Little Rock AFB Elem., Jacksonville, Ark., 1964—67; tchr. grades 3, 4, and 6 Butcher Greene Elem. Consol. Sch. Dist. #4, Grandview, Mo., 1967—98, ret., 1998. Contbr. (poetry) Sunrise and Soft Mist, 1999 (Editor's Choice 1999). Mem. Nat. Congress Parents and Tchr. (hon. life mem.). Mem. Ch. of Christ. Avocations: freelance photography, writing, gardening, reading, travel. Home: 9131 Big Bethel Dr San Antonio TX 78240-2852 Personal E-mail: tchow1101@sbcglobal.net.

FAULK, BETTY PRICE, elementary school educator; b. Whiteville, N.C., Oct. 23, 1954; d. Ralph Lee and Velma Mae (Williams) Price; m. Stanley Cecil Faulk, Jr., Mar. 18, 1977; children: Eric Michael, Jason Matthew. BS in Bus. Adminstrn., U. N.C., Wilmington, 1976; MEd, Chapman Coll., 1991. Cert. elem. tchr. Substitute tchr. Nassau Sch. Dist., Hilliard, Fla., 1984-86, Palmdale (Calif.) Sch. Dist., 1986-88; tchr. Cactus Sch., 1988—2003, chair student study team, coun. rep., 1991-95; 3rd grade tchr. Golden Poppy SCh., 2003—. Chair site com. Cactus Sch., 1992-93. Mem.: Palmdale Elem. Tchrs. Assn., Calif. Tchrs. Assn., NEA. Avocations: visiting museums, camping, travel, collecting handpainted birds. Office: Palmdale Sch Dist 37230 37th St E Palmdale CA 93550 Home: 29606 Highway 9 Tecumseh OK 74873-5614 Personal E-mail: sbfaulk@yahoo.com.

FAULK, TANYA WILLIAMS, school disciplinarian; b. Norfolk, Va., Oct. 8, 1963; d. Joseph H. and Joan C. Williams. BS, Old Dominion U., Norfolk, Va., 1987; MEd, Regent U., Virginia Beach, Va., 1997; postgrad., Nova Southeastern U., Ft. Lauderdale, Fla. Cert. tchr. Va. Note ops. adminstr. Crestar Bank, Norfolk, 1985—95; tchr. Norfolk Pub. Schs., 1995—2001, orientation coord., 2001—02, safe schs. coord., 2002—03, dean of students, 2003—. Pres. Enoch Youth Assn., Norfolk, 2001—. Mem.: VASSAP, Norfolk Fedn. Tchrs., Ednl. Leader Assn. Democrat. Baptist. Avocations: reading, sewing, singing. Office: Norfolk Pub Schs Lafayette Winona Middle Sch 1701 Alsace Ave Norfolk VA 23509

FAULKNER, FRANCES MAYHEW, retired federal agency administrator; b. Englewood, NJ, Feb. 21, 1930; d. Benjamin Alan and Laura Sanford Mayhew; m. Douglas Albert Faulkner, Sept. 1949 (dec.); children: June E., Lee A., Glen A. Student, Brown U., Providence, 1947—48. Postmaster US Postal Svc., New Kingston, NY, 1987—2005; ret. Mem.: NY State Hist. Assn., Del. County Hist. Assn. (Merit award 2005), Nat. Assn. Postmasters US, Hist. Soc. Middletown, New Kingston Valley Assn. Democrat. Avocations: travel, reading, gardening, antiques.

FAULKNER, JULIA ELLEN, opera singer; b. St. Louis, Nov. 1, 1957; d. Seldon and Dona Leah (Clark) F. MusB cum laude, Ind. U., 1980, MusM, 1983. Instr. voice No. Ariz. U., Flagstaff, 1984, Iowa State U., 1984-85; studio voice tchr., 1998—2002; asst. prof. U. Wis. Sch. Music, 2003—. Master tchr. young artist program Lamusica Linica, 2004—; master tchr. Top Opera, 2005—. Solo performances with opera cos. and theaters at La Scala, Carnegie Hall, NYC, San Francisco Opera Ctr., 1985-86, Woldftrap Opera Co., Vienna, Va., 1986, Bavarian State Opera, Munich, 1987-91, Vienna State Opera, Austria, 1991-97, Met. Opera, NYC, 1997—, LA Philharm., San Francisco Philharm., also in Miami Fla., Berlin, Hamburg, Germany, Lyon, Jerusalem, Bordeau, Stockholm, Amsterdam and Genoa; dir. Oklahoma and Old Maid and the Thief, Flagstaff, 1984; rec. artist Elektra, 1990, Der Rosenkavalier, 1991, Rossini, Semiramide, Schumann, Genoveva; recorded Pergolese Stabat Mater Deutsche Grammophone Das Paradis und die Peri, Verdi's Falstaff Recipient award Met. Opera, N.Y.C., 1985, 3d prize Whitaker Internat. Voice Competition, 1985, Festspiel prize Bavarian State Opera, 1988. Democrat. Office: Sch of Music Univ Wis Madison WI 53703 Office Phone: 608-263-1922. E-mail: juliafaulkner@charter.net, jfaulkner2@wisc.edu.

FAULKNER, KRISTINE, communications executive; b. 1968; Bus. devel. mgr. Digital City Hampton Roads, gen. mgr.; dir., internet pub. Daily Press, Va.; sr. product mgr., Web Hosting Services Cox Comm., Atlanta, 2000—04, v.p., Product Devel. and Mgmt., 2004—. Named one of 40 Executives Under 40, Multichannel News, 2006. Office: Cox Communications 1400 Lake Hearn Dr Atlanta GA 30319 Office Phone: 404-843-5000. Office Fax: 404-843-5975.*

FAULKNER, LAURA R., lawyer; b. Columbus, Ohio, Aug. 18, 1974; BA in Polit. Sci., Miami U., 1996, BA in Eng. Lit., 1996; JD, U. Dayton, 1999. Bar: Ohio 1999, US Dist. Ct. Southern Dist. Ohio 2000, US Dist. Ct. Northern Dist. Ohio 2001. Assoc. Weltman, Weinberg & Reis Co., L.P.A., Cin. Named one of Ohio's Rising Stars, Super Lawyers, 2006. Mem.: Am. Bankruptcy Law Forum, Cin. Bar Assn., Ohio State Bar Assn. Office: Weltman, Weinberg & Reis Co LPA 525 Vine St Ste 800 Cincinnati OH 45202 Office Phone: 513-723-2200. Office Fax: 513-723-2239.*

FAULKNER, MARTYE LEANNE, mathematician, educator; d. Elgia Leroy and Linda J. Link; m. Brian Thomasa Faulkner, Aug. 2, 1997; 1 child, Jordan Elijah. BS, Tenn. Technol. U., 1993, MSc, 1995; PhD, U. Ky., 1999. Asst. prof. math. Ky. Wesleyan Coll., Owensboro, Ky., 2000—. Foster parent Cabinet for Children and Families, Owensboro, Ky., 2002—06. Mem.: Math. Assn. Am. Office Phone: 270-926-3111.

FAULKNER, MELANIE E., music educator; d. Miles and Erin Mauldin; m. Rick Faulkner; 1 child, Lindsey Meadows. MusB in Edn., Lee U., Cleveland, Tenn., 1978. Cert. tchr. Music tchr. Lexington County Sch. Dist. 5, Columbia, SC, 1978—84, Gwinnett County Schs., Lawrenceville, Ga.; music specialist Hillsborough County Schs., Fla., 1989—. Pres. Hillsborough County Elem. Music Educators Coun., Tampa, Fla. Named Tchr. of the Yr., N.W. Elem., Tampa, FL, 1997, Hunter's Green Elem., Tampa, FL, 2003. Mem.: Hillsborough County Elem. Music Educators Coun., Fla. Elem. Music Educators Assn., Fla. Music Educators Assn., Music Educators Nat. Conf. Mem. Ch. Of God. Avocations: gardening, piano. Office: Hillsborough County Schs Tampa FL E-mail: melanie.faulkner@sdhc.k12.fl.us.

FAULKNER, REBECCA CLAY, reading educator; b. Greenville, S.C., Jan. 26, 1948; d. Charles Richard Jr. and Rebecca Evelyn (Tinsley) Clay; m. Thomas Green Faulkner III, June 29, 1979; children: Andrew Thomas, Joshua David, Charles James. BA, Furman U., 1969; MEd, Clemson U., 1973; EdD, Nova Southeastern U., 1997. Cert. elem. tchr., adminstr., supr., reading dir./coord. early childhood, S.C. Classroom tchr. Sch. Dist. Greenville, SC, 1969—73, reading specialist, 1973—91, reading recovery tchr. leader, 1991—98, asst. adminstr., 1998—2000; asst. prof. and chair dept. elem. edn. North Greenville U., SC, 2000—02; prof. U. S.C. Upstate, Spartanburg, 2003—. Cons. Nat. Urban Assn.; pres. Genesis Assoc. Ednl. Cons. Co. Mem. ASCD, AAUW, Internat. Reading Assn., Nat. Assn. Edn. Young Children, Rotary Episcopalian. Avocations: reading, travel, camping, sewing, gardening. Home: 119 Blue Water Trl Taylors SC 29687-5947 Office: 800 Univ Way Spartanburg SC 29303 Office Phone: 864-503-5516. E-mail: drgenesis@charter.net.

FAUNCE, SARAH CUSHING, retired curator; b. Tulsa, Aug. 19, 1929; d. George Jr. and Helen Pauline (Colwell) F. BA, Wellesley Coll., 1951; MA, Washington U., St. Louis, 1959; postgrad., Columbia U., 1960-63. Tchr. history Hartridge Sch., Plainfield, NJ, 1954-56; tchr. art Mary C. Wheeler Sch., Providence, 1958-59; instr. art history Barnard Coll., N.Y.C., 1962-64; sec. adv. council art history Columbia U., 1963-70, registrar, curator,

1965-70; exhbn. cons. Jewish Mus., N.Y.C., 1968-70; curator paintings and sculpture Bklyn. Mus. Art, 1970-98, curator emeritus, project dir. Courbet Catalogue Raisonné project, 1998—. Author: Courbet, 1993; exhbn. catalog author: Anne Ryan Collages, 1974, Carl Larsson, 1982; author, editor: Belgian Art 1880-1914, 1980, Courbet Reconsidered, 1988, In the Light of Italy: Corot and Early Plein Air Painting, 1996; editor: Northern Light: Realism and Symbolism in Scandinavian Painting 1880-1910, 1982. Travel grantee Columbia U., 1963 Mem. AAM-ICOM, Coll. Art Assn., Phi Beta Kappa. Democrat. Office Phone: 646-878-2707. E-mail: faunce.courbet@mindspring.com.

FAUNTLEROY, ANGELA COLLEEN, music educator; b. Phila., Dec. 16, 1956; d. Rudolph Simmons and Marlyn Fauntleroy. MusB in Applied Piano, Boston Conservatory Music, 1978; MusB in Music Edn., U. of the Arts, 1989; MusM in Edn. Adminstrn., Cheyney U., 1994. Cert. secondary educator Pa., 1996. Music tchr. Sch. Dist. of Phila., 1980—. Mem.: Nat. Assoc. Female Execs., The Schoolmen's Club of Phila., Sigma Alpha Iota, Kappa Delta Pi, Nu Theta Chpt., Internat. Honor Soc. in Edn. Avocations: travel, dance. Home: 4533 Sansom St Philadelphia PA 19139-3624 Office Phone: 215-299-7000. E-mail: afauntleroy@phila.k12.pa.us.

FAUST, AMY KAY, elementary school educator; b. Brainerd, Minn., Apr. 17, 1975; d. Carl William and Susan Kay Faust. BA in Elem. Edn., Coll. St. Benedict, St. Joseph, Minn., 1997; MA in Elem. Edn. (hon.), Calif. State U., Long Beach, 2005. Cert. reading specialist Calif. Esl tchr., interpreter Ind. Shcool Dist. 740, Melrose, Minn., 1997—98; elem. tchr. Garden Grove (Calif.) Unified Sch. Dist., 1998—. Mem.: Internat. Reading Assn., Phi Kappa Phi, Phi Lambda Theta. Home: 1380 Village Way Apt F204 Costa Mesa CA 92626 Office: Garden Grove Unified Sch Dist 12871 Estock Ave Garden Grove CA Office Phone: 714-663-6331. E-mail: aimsfaust@yahoo.com.

FAUST, DIANA JEAN, religious studies educator; b. McCook, Nebr., May 24, 1953; d. Wayne Eugene Naugle and Delores Elaine (Larsen) Leff; m. Harlan Ray Faust, Jan. 4, 1975; children: Katrina Marie, Jennifer Elaine BS, U. Nebr., 1975. Cert. elem. and spl. edn. tchr., Nebr; cert. Christian Edn., St. Paul Sch. Theology, Kansas City, 2004. Tchr. spl. edn. Ft. Calhoun (Nebr.) Community Schs., 1975-78; owner, ptnr. Faust Investments, Inc., Omaha, 1980-84; dir. discipling ministries St. Andrew's United Meth. Ch., Omaha, 2004—. Mem. Millard Bd. Edn., 1991-98, sec., 1992-93, 95-96, pres., 1993-94, 97. Mem. Greater Omaha Geneal. Soc., Phi Lambda Theta. Avocations: genealogy, crafts. Home: 4275 S 173rd St Omaha NE 68135-2634 Office: St Andrew's United METH CH 15050 W Maple Rd Omaha NE 68116 Office Phone: 402-431-8560 ext. 31. Business E-Mail: dfaust@standrewsomaha.net.

FAUST, DREW GILPIN, historian, educator; b. NYC, Sept. 18, 1947; d. McGhee Tyson and Catharine (Mellick) G.; m. Stephen Faust, Dec. 28, 1968 (div. 1976); m. Charles E. Rosenberg, June 7, 1980; 1 child, Jessica Rosenberg. BA magna cum laude, Bryn Mawr Coll., 1968; MA, U. Pa., Phila., 1971, PhD, 1975. Asst. prof. Am. civilization U. Pa., Phila., 1976-80, assoc. prof., 1980-84, prof., 1984-89, Stanley I. Sheerr prof. history, 1988-89, Annenberg prof. history, 1989—2000; dean Radcliffe Inst. for Advanced Study at Harvard U., 2000—; Lincoln prof. history Harvard U., 2001—. Walter Lynwood Fleming lectr. La. State U., 1987; mem. ednl. adv. bd. Guggenheim Found., 1988—; cons. Before Freedom Came: African American Life in the Antebellum South, exhbn. at Mus. Confederacy, 1988-91; NEH panel Interpretive Rsch. Program, 1987; mem. Pulitzer Prize History Jury, 1986, 90; lectr. various colls. and univs. Author: A Sacred Circle: The Dilemma of the Intellectual inthe Old South, 1977, paperback edit., 1986, James Henry Hammond and the Old South: A Design for Mastery, 1982, The Creation of Confederate Nationalism: Ideology and Identity in the Civil War South, 1988, Southern Stories: Slaveholders in Peace and War, 1992, Mothers of Invention: Women of the Slaveholding South in the American Civil War, 1996 (Avery Craven prize 1996, Honoarble metion annual awards, Asn. Am. Pub., 1997, Francis Parkman prize, 1997, mem. editl. bd. Jour. Am. History, 1991—, Pa. Mag. History and Biography, 1986-89, Jour. So. History, 1981-86; contbr. articles to profl. jours. Trustee Andrew Mellon Found. Recipient Jules F. Landry award James Henry Hammond and the Old South, 1982, Charles Sydnor award, Prize Soc. Historians of Early Am. Republic, 1983, article prize Berkshire Conf. Women's Historians, 1991; U. Pa. Rsch. Found. grantee, 1982; assoc. fellow Stanford Humanities Ctr., Stanford U., 1983-84, Am. Coun. Learned Socs. fellow, 1986, Guggenheim fellow, 1987, Mass. Hist. Soc. fellow, 2002, Elizabeth Hall fellow Concord Acad., 2003. Mem. So. Hist. Assn. (chair nominating com. 1993, exec. coun. 1987-90, Frank L. Owsley prize com. 1987, pres. 1999-2000), Am. Hist. Assn. (v.p. profl. divsn. 1992-95, coun. mem. 1992—), Orgn. Am. Historians (chair Avery Craven Prize Com. 1991, 97, chair program com. 1987, mem. coun. 1999-2002), Am. Studies Assn. (mem. coun. 1988-90, Honoable metion Hope Franklin award, 1997), Hist. Soc. Pa. (mem. bd. 1988-91), So. Assn. Women Historians (membership com. 1988-, pres. 1998-99), Am. Acad. Arts & Scis., Am. Philosophical Soc. Office: Radcliffe Inst Adv Study Harvard Univ Cambridge MA 02139

FAUST, NAOMI FLOWE, education educator; b. Salisbury, N.C. d. Christopher Leroy and Ada Luella (Graham) Flowe; m. Roy Malcolm Faust, Aug. 16, 1948. AB, Bennett Coll., Greensboro, N.C.; MA, U. Mich., 1945; PhD, NYU, 1963. Tchr. elem. Pub. Schs. Gaffney, SC; tchr. English, French, phys. edn. Atkins H.S., Winston-Salem; instr. English Bennett Coll. and So. U., Scotlandville, La., 1944—46; prof. English Morgan State Coll., Balt., 1946—48; tchr. English Greensboro Pub. Schs., NC, 1948—51, N.Y.C. Pub. Schs., 1954—63; prof. edn. Queens Coll. of CUNY, Flushing, 1964—82; writer, lectr., poetry readings, 1982—. Lectr. in field. Author: Discipline and the Classroom Teacher, 1977; (poetry) Speaking in Verse, 1974, All Beautiful Things, 1983, And I Travel by Rhythms and Words, 1990; contbr. poetry to jours. Named Tchr.-Author of 1979, Tchr.-Writer; recipient Cert. of Merit for Poem Cooper Hill Writers Conf., 1970, Achievement award L.I. br. AAUW, 1985, Poet of the Millennium award Internat. Poets Acad., Excellence in World Poetry award Internat. Poets Acad., 2002; named Internat. Eminent Poet, Internat. Poets Acad. Mem. AAUP, AAUW, Acad. Am. Poets, Nat. Coun. Tchrs. English, Nat. Women's Book Assn., Nat. Assn. Univ. Women (L.I. br.), World Poetry Soc. Intercontinental, N.Y. Poetry Forum, Poetry Soc. Am., NAACP, United Negro Coll. Fund, Alpha Kappa Alpha, Alpha Kappa Mu., Alpha Epsilon. Home: 11201 175th St Jamaica NY 11433-4135

FAVARO, MARY KAYE ASPERHEIM, pediatrician, writer; b. Edgerton, Wis., Sept. 30, 1934; d. Harold Wilbur and Genevieve Catherine (Hyland) Asperheim; m. Biagino Philip Favaro, May 31, 1969; children: Justin Peter, Gina Sue. BS, U. Wis., 1956; MS, St. Louis Coll. Pharmacy, 1965; MD, U. Wis., 1969. Instr. pharmacology St. Louis U. and St. Mary's Hosp. Sch. Practical Nurses, 1959-64; staff pharmacist U. Hosps., Madison, Wis., 1964-65; intern Albany (N.Y.) Med. Center, 1969-70; resident, 1970-71; resident in pediatrics U. S.C., Charleston, 1971-72, asst. prof. pediatrics, 1973-75; pvt. practice pediatrics, 1974-99; ret. Author: Pharmacology, an Introductory Text, 2005; The Pharmacologic Basis of Patient Care, 1985. Mem.: AMA. Roman Catholic. Home: 1407 Southwood Dr Surfside Beach SC 29575 Office Phone: 843-267-6879. Personal E-mail: maryfav@aol.com.

FAVERO, MICHELE MAREE, music educator, musician; b. Omaha, June 6, 1970; d. Valentino Reno and Caryl June (O'Brien) F.; m. Thomas Rex Kluge, June 13, 1998. B in Music, So. Meth. U., 1993; M in Music, U. Nebr., 1997; diploma, Royal Acad. Music, London, Eng., 1994, Liszt Acad. Music, Budapest, Hungary, 1995. Freelance pianist, Budapest, Hungary, 1994-95; pvt. piano instr., 1994-95; accompanist Omaha Pub. Schs., 1997-98; freelance pianist, 1995—; pvt. piano instr., 1995—2000, 2004—; chmn. piano dept., exec. dir. Omaha Conservatory Music, 2000—04. Mem. Mu Phi Epsilon. Republican. Roman Catholic. Avocations: reading, studying languages, drawing, exercising, cooking. Office Phone: 402-397-1597.

FAVOR-HAMILTON, SUZANNE MARIE, track and field athlete, Olympian; b. Stevens Point, Wis., Aug. 8, 1968; m. Mark Hamilton, May 1991. BS, U. Wis., 1991. Track and field athlete Nike. Winner 4 indoor NCAA mile titles, 4 outdoor 1,500m titles; winner 9 NCAA titles and 21 individual Big Ten championships, 6 time nat. champaion; 3 time Olympian; former Am. record holder 1,000 meters; current Am. record holder in indoor 800 meters. Achievements include Am. Record Holder in 1,000m 1995 and indoor 800m, 1999.

FAVORULE, DENISE, publishing executive; Advt. dir. Stagebill Mag., 1993—96; advt. mgr. Prevention Mag., 1996—98, nat. advt. dir., 1998—99, assoc. pub., 1999—2000, v.p., pub., 2000—. Office: Rondale Press Inc 33 E Minor St Emmaus PA 18098-0099 Office Phone: 212-573-0379. Office Fax: 610-967-7726. E-mail: denise.favorule@rodale.com.*

FAWCETT, FARRAH LENI, actress, model; b. Corpus Christi, Tex., Feb. 2, 1947; d. James William and Pauline Alice (Evans) F.; m. Lee Majors, July 28, 1973 (div. 1982); 1 son, Redmond James. Student, U. Tex. at Austin. Works as model. Movie debut in Myra Breckenridge, 1970; other film appearances include Love is a Funny Thing, 1970, Logan's Run, 1976, Somebody Killed Her Husband, 1978, Sunburn, 1979, Saturn 3, 1980, Cannonball Run, 1981, Extremities, 1986, See You in the Morning, 1989, Man ofthe House, 1995, The Apostle, 1997, The Love Master, 2000, Dr. T and the Women, 2000; TV movie appearances include Charlie's Angels, 1976, Murder in Texas, 1981, The Red Light Sting, 1984, The Burning Bed, 1984, Between Two Women, 1986, Nazi Hunter: The Beate Klarsfeld Story, 1986, Margaret Bourke-White, 1989, The Substitute Wife, 1994, Dalva, 1996, Silk Hope, 1999, Baby, 2000, Jewel, 2001, Hollywood Wives, 2003; regular on TV series Charlie's Angels, 1976-77, Good Sports, 1991, Spin City, 2001, The Guardian, 2001-02; other TV appearances include Harry O, McCloud, The Six Million Dollar Man, Marcus Welby, M.D., Apple's Way; N.Y.C. Stage debut (off-Broadway) Extremities, 1983; TV miniseries appearances include Poor Little Rich Girl: The Barbara Hutton Story, 1987, Small Sacrifices, 1989, Children of the Dust, 1995; Posed for Playboy, 1995. Mem. Delta Delta Delta.

FAWCETT, GAYLE P., bank executive; m. Ken Fawcett; 2 children. Degree, Mass. Sch. Fin. Studies; student in Fin. Studies, Fairfield U. Cert. para-planner. Joined Berkshire Bank, Pittsfield, Mass., 1977, sr. v.p. Retail Banking and Ops. Bd. dirs. EastPoint Tech. Users Group. Bd. dirs. St.Mark's Ch. Fin. Com. Named One of 25 Women to Watch, U.S. Bankers Mag., 2003. Office: Berkshire Bank 24 North St PPO Box 1308 Pittsfield MA 01202-1308

FAWCETT, JOY LYNN, retired professional soccer player; b. Inglewood, Calif., Feb. 8, 1968; m. Walter Fawcett; children: Katelyn Rose, Carli, Madilyn Rae. Degree in phys. edn., U. Calif., Berkeley, 1990. Women's soccer coach UCLA, 1993-97, 1993—97; mem. U.S. Nat. Women's Soccer Team, 1987—2004; profl. soccer player San Diego Spirit, 2001—03. Named 3-time All-Am., 1987—89, Most Valuable Player, So. Calif., L.A. Times, 1987, World Cup Champion, 1991, 1999, MVP, WUSA, 2002, Defender of Yr., 2002; named to, U. Calif. Berkeley Hall of Fame, 1997; recipient Silver medal, Sydney Olympics, 2000. Achievements include 1995 FIFA World Cup, Sweden; 1994 CONCACAF Qualifying Championship, Montreal; U.S. Olympic Festival, Denver, 1995; FIFA Women's World Cup, Sweden, 1995; gold medal U.S. Women's Soccer Team, Atlanta Olympic Games, 1996, Athens Olympic Games, 2004; mem. Ajax of Manhattan Beach Club Soccer Team (champions U.S. Women's Amateur Nat. Cup, 1992, 93). Office: US Soccer Fedn 1801-1811 S Prairie Ave Chicago IL 60616

FAWCETT-YESKE, MAXINE ANN, music educator; m. Robert Yeske. BS in Music, U. Colo., Denver, 1985; MS in Music, U. Nebr., Omaha, 1987; PhD in Music, U. Colo., Boulder, 1997. Asst. prof. music Truman State U., Kirksville, Mo., 1997—99; assoc. prof. music Nebr. Wesleyan U., Lincoln, 1999—. Office: Nebraska Wesleyan University 5000 Saint Paul Ave Lincoln NE 68504 Office Phone: 402-465-2291. Business E-Mail: mfy@nebrwesleyan.edu.

FAWSETT, PATRICIA COMBS, federal judge; b. 1943; BA, U. Fla., 1965, MAT, 1966, JD, 1973. Pvt. practice law Akerman, Senterfitt & Edison, Orlando, Fla., 1973-86; commr. 9th Cir. Jud. Nominating Commn, 1973-75, Greater Orlando Crime Prevention Assn., 1983-86; judge US Dist. Ct. (Mid. Dist.) Fla., Orlando, 1986—, chief judge. Trustee Legal Aid Soc., 1977-81, Loch Haven Art Ctr., Inc., Orlando, 1980-84, U. Fla. Law Sch., 2001—; hon. trustee Reago Spiritual Scholarship Found., 1999—; commr. Orlando Housing Authority, 1976-80, Winter Park (Fla.) Sidewalk Festival, 1973-75; bd. dirs. Greater Orlando Area C. of C., 1982-85. Mem. ABA (trial lawyers sect., real estate probate sect.), Am. Judicaturs Soc., Assn. Trial Lawyers Am., Fla. Bar Found. (bd. dirs. grants com.), Commn. on Access to Cts., Fla. Coun. Bar Assn. Pres.'s (pres., bd. dirs. 9th cir. grievance com.) Osceola County Bar Assn., Fla. Bar (bd. govs. 1983-86, budget com., disciplinary rev. com., integration rule and bylaws com., com. on access to legal system, bd. of cert., designation and advt., jud. adminstrn., selection and tenure com., jud. nominating procedures com., pub. rels. com., ann. meeting com., appellate rules com., spl. com. on judiciary-trial lawyer rels., chairperson midyr. conv. com., bd. dirs. trial lawyers sect.), Orange County Bar Assn. (exec. coun. 1977-83, pres. 1981-82), Order of Coif, Phi Beta Kappa. Office: US Dist Ct Federal Bldg 80 N Hughey Ave Ste 611 Orlando FL 32801-2231

FAY, LAUREL ANN, marriage and family therapist; b. Port Jefferson, NY, Sept. 25, 1973; d. Vincent Joseph Sydlansky and Ann Louise Rackoff; m. Robert Alan Fay, Sept. 9, 2000; children: Isabel Ann, Emily Taylor. BA, Syracuse U., 1995; MSc, U. Md., College Park, 1999. Lic. Clin. Marriage Family Therapist Md., 2001. Staff therapist, divorce edn. coord. Ctr. Children, LaPlata, Md., 1999—2001; pvt. practice Silver Spring, Md., 2001—; program dir., staff therapist COSD Ctr., Columbia, Md., 2002—03. Adj. faculty supr. U. Md., College Park, 2003—05; cons. Bowie Counseling Svcs., Md., 2004—05; marriage and family therapist approved supr., 2003—; spkr. in field. Mem.: Am. Assn. Marriage and Family Therapy (clin. mem. 2001—), Stepfamily Assn. Am. (assoc.). Avocations: reading, writing, painting, theater. Office: 9525 Georgia Ave Ste 203 Silver Spring MD 20910 Office Phone: 301-588-5861. Personal E-mail: laurel@laurelfay.com.

FAY, MARY ANNE, retail executive; m. Mark A. Fay. Jr. exec. program, Allied Dept. Stores, 1955; exec. program, Federated Dept. Stores, 1970; grad. in retail, U. Minn. V.p. gen. mdse. mgr. Levy's, Federated Dept. Stores, Tucson, 1974—83, regional v.p. stores, 1981—83; v.p. divsnl. mdse. mgr. Mainstreet, Federated Dept. Stores, Chgo., 1983—86, Alexander's Inc., NYC, 1986—92. Pvt. practice retail cons., Tucson, 1992—. Lifetime trustee Carondelet, Tucson, 1994—2005; chair Ariz. Cancer Ctr., Tucson, 1998—2002; bd. dirs. Tucson Symphony Women's Assn., 2001—05, ARC. Achievements include one of the first vice presidents in my field at Federated Dept. Stores. Home: 5421 N Paseo Soria Tucson AZ 85718

FAY, SAMANTHA C., mathematics educator; b. Fargo, ND, Sept. 10, 1977; d. James P. and Meredith J. Fay. BS, U. Ill., 1999; MA, U. Ctrl. Ark., 2003. Vol. Peace Corps, Kamabi, Guinea, 1999—2000; tchr. Oregon (Wis.) H.S., 2001—03; instr. U. Ctrl. Ark., Conway, 2003—. Instr. Upward Bound, Conway, 2005. Mem.: Math. Assn. Am., Soc. for Creative Anachronisms. Avocations: archery, hiking, historical re-creation. Office: Univ Central Arkansas 201 Donaghey Ave Conway AR 72035 Office Phone: 501-450-5684. Business E-Mail: sfay@uca.edu.

FAY, TONI GEORGETTE, communications executive; b. NYC, Apr. 25, 1947; d. George E. and Allie C. (Smith) Fay. BA, Duquesne U., Pitts., 1968; MSW, U. Pitts., 1972, MEd, 1973. Caseworker N.Y.C. Dept. Welfare, 1968-70; regional commr. Gov. Pa. Coun. Drugs and Alcohol, 1973-76; dir. social svcs. Pitts. Drug Abuse Ctr., 1972-73; dir. planning and devel. Nat. Coun. Negro Women, 1977-79; exec. v.p. D. Parke Gibson Assocs., 1979-82; mgr. cmty. rels. Time Inc. (now Time-Warner Inc.), N.Y.C., 1982-83, dir. corp. cmty. rels. and affirmative action, 1983-93, v.p., corp. officer, 1993-2001; pres. TGF Assocs., Englewood, NJ, 2001—. Bd. dirs. UNICEF, Congl. Black Caucus Found., NAACP Legal Def. Fund Bd., Franklin and Eleanor Inst., Apollo Theatre Found.; apptd. bd. advs. Nat. Inst. Literacy, 1996—, Nat. and Cmty. Svc., 2000. Named Woman of the Yr., Pitts. YWCA, 1975, N.Y. Women's Forum; named one of 100 Top Women in Bus., Dollars and Sense Mag., 1986; recipient Twin award, YWCA U.S.A., 1987. Office: TGF Assocs 233 W Hudson Ave Englewood NJ 07631 Personal E-mail: tonigfay@aol.com.

FAYE, THALIA GARIN, retired microbiologist, educator; b. Jerusalem, June 9, 1938; came to U.S., 1965; d. Joseph and Esther (Wengroviz) Garin; m. Allan Faye, Aug. 17, 1967; children: Howard, Scott. BSc, Tel-Aviv U., 1960, MSc, 1962. Specialist in clin. microbiology and pub. health. Microbiologist pediat. rsch. Kaplan Hosp., Rehovot, Israel, 1962-64, Biosci. Lab., Van Nuys, Calif., 1966-69; supr. microbiologist Biochem. Lab. Procedure, North Hollywood, Calif., 1969-76; mgr., microbiologist Olive View Med. Ctr., Sylmar, Calif., 1977—2003; ret., 2003—. Mem. NA'AMAT USA (life mem., club pres. 1976-78, coun. pres. 1982-84, nat. bd. dirs. 1987-93, coord. Western area 1997-2001), Am. Soc. Microbiology. Democrat. Jewish. Avocations: reading, computing, solving crossword puzzles. Office: Olive View Med Ctr 14445 Olive View Dr Sylmar CA 91342-1437

FAZIO, EVELYN M., publisher, writer, agent, editor; b. Hackensack, N.J. BA in History, U. Bridgeport, 1975; MA in History, U. Conn., 1977. Cert. social studies tchr. NJ. Tchr. social studies Cedar Grove (N.J.) High Sch., 1977-79; prodn. editor Prentice-Hall, Inc., Englewood Cliffs, NJ, 1980-82, devel. editor, 1982-83, acquisitions editor, 1983-85; sr. acquisitions editor P-H/Simon & Schuster, Inc., Englewood Cliffs, 1985-88; mng. editor Random House, Inc., N.Y.C., 1988—; exec. editor polit. sci., internat. rels. and policy studies Paragon House Pubs., Inc., N.Y.C., 1989-91; editorial dir. Marshall Cavendish Pubs., N. Bellmore, NY, 1992-95; v.p., pub. M.E. Sharpe, Armonk, NY, 1995—2001; v.p. e-content acquisition Baker & Taylor, Bridgewater, NJ, 2001—03; dir. EMF Agy., Hackensack, NJ, 2003—; ptnr. Internat. Lit. Arts, LLC, Hackensack, NJ, 2004—, Moscow, Pa., 2004—. Co-author: (series) Staying Sane When Your Family Comes to Visit, Staying Sane When You're Dieting, Staying Sane When You Quit Smoking, Staying Sane When You're Planning Your Wedding, Staying Sane When You're Buying or Selling Your Home, Staying Sane When You're Going Through Menopause, Girls Night Out:Poker.

FEAL, GISELE CATHERINE, foreign language educator; b. Froges, France, July 5, 1939; arrived in U.S., 1965; PhD in Spanish, U. Paris, 1964; PhD in French, U. Mich., 1973. Instr. Ea. Mich. U., Ypsilanti; lectr. U. Mich., Ann Arbor; asst. prof. SUNY Coll., Buffalo, 1974-80, chair dept., 1977-80, assoc. prof., 1980—92, assoc. v.p., 1983—88, prof., 1992—2002. Author: Le Théâtre de Crommelynck, 1976, La Mythologie Matriarcale, 1993, Ionesco. Un Theatre Onirique, 2001. Mem. Alliance Française de Buffalo (bd. dirs. 1980-93). E-mail: fealgc@gmail.com.

FEARN, HEIDI, physicist, researcher; b. Sutton-in-Ashfield, Eng., Aug. 21, 1965; came to U.S., 1989; d. Lawrence Leonard and Erika Hanna Elfrede (Kröger) F. BS Theol. Physics honors, Essex U., Colchester, Eng., 1986; PhD Theol. Quantum Optics, Essex U., 1989. Grad. lab. demonstrator Essex U., 1986—89; postdoctoral rsch. asst. Max Planck Inst. Quantum Optics, Garching, Germany, 1989; rsch. assoc. U. N.Mex., Albuquerque, 1989—91; lectr. physics Calif. State U., Fullerton, 1991—92, asst. prof. physics, 1992—95, assoc. prof. physics, 1995—97, prof. physics, 1997—. Vis. scholar U. Ariz., Tucson, 1989-91; cons. Los Alamos (N.Mex.) Nat. Lab., 1994—Kavli Inst. Theoretical Physics scholar, 2003—05. Mem. AAAS, Am. Assn. Physics Tchrs., Optical Soc. Am., Am. Phys. Soc. Office: Calif State U Physics Dept 800 N State College Blvd Fullerton CA 92831-3547 Business E-Mail: hfearn@fullerton.edu.

FEARON, CHARLENE O'BRIEN, special education educator; b. Worcester, Mass., Feb. 17, 1952; d. Robert Joseph and Christine Rita O'Brien; m. Laurence William Fearon, July 6, 1990; 1 child, Caitlin. BA in Edn., St. Joseph Coll., West Hartford, Conn., 1974, MA in Edn., 1977; postgrad., Fairfield U., Conn., 1985—89. Spl. edn. tchr. Worcester Pub. Schs., 1974—75, Regional Dist. # 4, Deep River, Conn., 1975—. Adj. faculty mem. Ctrl. Conn. State Coll., New Britain, Conn., 1979, St. Joseph Coll., West Hartford, Conn., 1979—86; cons. adv. com. Conn. State Dept. Edn., Hartford, 1986—99. Trustee United Ch. of Chester, Conn., 2004—. Avocations: photography, reading, drawing, walking. Personal E-mail: Fearun@aol.com.

FEARS, BELLE DECORMIS, retired physician; b. Accomac, Va., Feb. 5, 1921; d. Joseph LeCenne and Mabel (Lewis) DeCormis; m. William Earl Fears; children: Barbara Fears Haynes, Richard Bradford. BA, Duke U., Durham, NC, 1942; MD, Med. Coll. Va., Richmond, 1945. Internship Med. Coll. Va. Hosp., 1945—46; pvt. gen. practice medicine Accomac, 1950—65; health dir. Ea. Shore Health Dist., Accomac and Nassawadox, Va., 1965—83; ret., 1983. Belle D. Fears Health Ctr. named in her honor. Home: 23610 N St E5 Onancock VA 23417-2024

FEASEL, MANDY SESSUMS, literature educator; b. Union, Miss., Dec. 12, 1974; d. Noah Maxwell and Linda Gayle Sessums; m. Jamie Wade Feasel, July 24, 1998; 1 child, Rpwan Gayle. AA in Liberal Arts, East Ctrl. C.C., Decatur, Miss.; BA in English, U. So. Miss., Hattiesburg, 1997, MA in English, 2002. Cert. tchr. Nat. Bd., 2004. Tchr. English Union Pub. Schs., Miss., 1998—. Sponsor jr. class Union Pub. Schs., 1998—, sponsor drama club, 2002—. Tchr. Sunday sch. FBC, Union, 2005—. Recipient Lindwood Orange award, U. So. Miss. English dept., 2001—02, Star Tchr., 2004—05. Southern Baptist. Avocations: gardening, reading. Office: Union Pub Schs 101 Forest St Union MS 39365

FEATHER, NANCY JOANNE, lawyer, educator; BS in Journalism, BA in English, W.Va. U., Morgantown, 1985; MS in Edn., Duquesne U., Pitts., Pa., 1992, JD, 1997. Bar: Pa. 1997; cert. tchr. Pa., 1992. Mgr. Trau & Loevner, Inc., Pitts., 1988—96; from law clk. to atty. Beroes Law Ctr., Pitts., 1996—99; instr. Pitts. Tech. Inst., Oakdale, 1999—2006. Lt. (j.g.) USN, 1985—88. Mem.: Am. Criminal Justice Assn., Allegheny County Bar Assn., So. Poverty Law Ctr., ACLU, Delta Delta Delta (Pott Found. scholar 1980). Office: Pitts Tech Inst 1111 McKee Rd Oakdale PA 15071 Office Phone: 412-809-5399 4737.

FEATHERMAN, SANDRA, retired academic administrator, political science professor; b. Phila., Apr. 14, 1934; d. Albert N. and Rebe (Burd) Green; m. Bernard Featherman, Mar. 29, 1958; children: Andrew Charles, John James. BA, U. Pa., 1955, MA, PhD, U. Pa., 1978. Asst. prof. dept. polit. sci. Temple U., Phila., 1978-84, assoc. prof., 1984-91, asst. to pres., 1986-89, pres. faculty senate, 1985-86, dir. Ctr. Pub. Policy, 1986-91; vice chancellor acad. adminstrn., prof. polit. sci. U. Minn., Duluth, 1991-95; pres. U. New Eng., Biddeford, Maine, 1995—2006; pres. emeritus, 2006—. Mem. New Eng. Assn. Schs. and Coll. Higher Edn. Commn., 2002—06; mem. commn. women in higher edn. Am. Coun. Edn., 2005—. Author: Jews, Black and Ethnics, 1979, Race and Politics at the Millenium, 2000; contbr. articles to profl. jours. Nat. bd. Girls Inc., 1971—74; pres. Pa. Fedn. C.C., Girls Inc.; sec. Maine Women's Forum, 2002—, pres., 2005—; bd. Maine Compact Higher Edn., 2003—06, exec. bd., 2003—06; commr. Am. Coun. on Edn. Commn. on Women in Higher Edn., 2005—06; chair Maine Jud. Compensation Commn., 2005—, Maine Commn. on Jud. Compensation, 2005—; chair ethics comm. State of Maine, 2006—; chair Gov.'s Blue Ribbon Commn. on Health Care, Maine, 2006—, Maine, 2006; bur. osteo. edn. Am. Osteo. Assn., 2004—06; nat. bd. dirs. Women and Founds.-Corp. Philanthropy, 1986—91; bd. dirs. Citizens Com. Pub. Edn. Phila., 1977—89, pres., 1979—81; trustee C.C. Phila., 1970—92, chmn. bd. trustees, 1984—86; life trustee, v.p. Samuel Fels Found., 1978—; bd. dirs. United Way SE Pa., 1977—89, United Way Pa., 1981—84, U. New Eng., Gulf of Maine Aquarium, Kennebec Girl Scout Coun., Virginia Gildeslove Internat. Fund.,

2003—, Vis. Nurse Assn., 2002—03; chair Assembly Pres. Am. Assoc. Coll. Osteopathic Medicine; chmn. Maine Commn. on the State Ceiling on Tax-exempt Bonds, 1999—2000; bd. dirs. Maine Cmty. Found., 2006—. Named Disting. Daughter Pa., State Pa., 2004; recipient Brooks Graves award, Pa. Polit. Sci. Assn., 1982, Cmty. Svc. award, City of Phila., 1984, Women's Achievement award, YWCA, 1989, Adminstr. of Yr. award, Minn. Women in Higher Edn., 1994, Champion of Econ. Growth award, Maine Devel. Found., 2002, Women Who Make a Difference award, Internat. Women's Forum, 2004, Women of Distinction award, 2004. Mem.: AAUW (bd. dirs. Phila. chpt. 1975—78, 1980—91, pres. 1984—86, nat. chair internat. fellowships panel 1987—91, nat bd. dirs. 1993—, Outstanding Woman award 1986), Am. Coun. Edn. (commn. on advancement racial and ethnic equality 2001—, commn. women higher edn. 2005—06), Maine Ind. Colls. Assn. (pres. 1998—2000), Greater Portland Alliance Colls. and Univs. (pres. 1997—98), Nat. Assn. Ind. Colls & Univs. (com. policy analysis & pub. rels. 2001—), Am. Polit. Sci. Assn., Maine Ind. Colls. Assn. Office: U New Eng PO Box 428A Kennebunkport ME 04046 Office Phone: 207-602-2306. Business E-Mail: sfeatherman@une.edu.

FEATHERS, GAIL M. WRATNY, social worker; b. Gowanda, NY, Nov. 19, 1958; d. Frank John and Elinor Louise (Miller) Wratny; m. Donald James Feathers, May 24, 1980; children: Ryan James, David John, Rachel Marie. BA in English, SUNY, Geneseo, 1982; MSW, Syracuse U., 1992. Cert. social worker. Staff U. Rochester (N.Y.) Med. Ctr., 1992; social worker cmty. of caring program Cath. Family Ctr., Rochester, 1993-95, Cath. Charities of Livingston County, Mt. Morris, N.Y., 1995-97; dir. social work Nicholas H. Noyes Meml. Hosp., Dansville, N.Y., 1997—. Social svcs. adv. com. Livingston County Dept. Social Svcs., Mt. Morris, 1993—, chair, 2000—01; social worker early intervention program Livingston County Dept. Health, 1996—2000; mem. Livingston County Teen Pregnancy Prevention Task Force, Mt. Morris, 1993—99, Livingston County Cmty. Resource Network, Mt. Morris, 1993—, chair, 1994—98; family and consumer edn. com. Cornell Coop. Ext., 1999—2002, bd. dirs.; mem. Wayland Cmty. Chest, 1997—2003, sec., 2001—03. Mem. Livingston-Wyoming Assn. Retarded Citizens, 1986—96, bd. dirs., 1987—96, chairperson advocacy com., 1988—92, children's svcs. com., 1988—91; organizer, mem. parents panel on children who have disabilities SUNY Geneseo and Livingston-Wyoming-Steuben Bd. Coop. Ednl. Svcs., 1988—94; mem. adv. coun. N.Y. State Senate Select Com. for the Disabled, NY, 1990—92; mem. Rochester Sch. Deaf Task Force, 1996; mem. deaf awareness panel SUNY Geneseo and Nat. Tech. Inst. for the Deaf, 1998—99. Mem.: NASW. Avocations: golf, reading. E-mail: gfeathers@noyes-hospital.org, rdfthr3307@aol.com.

FEATHERSTONE, DIANE L., utilities executive; B in Econs. and History, Towson U.; M in Econs., U. Va. CPA. Joined Constellation, 1976; pres. Constellation Energy Source; v.p. mgmt. consulting and auditing Constellation Energy Group, Balt.; v.p., gen. auditor Edison Internat., Rosemead, Calif., 2002—, v.p., gen. auditor So. Calif. Edison subs., 2002—. Office: Edison Internat 2244 Walnut Grove Ave Rosemead CA 91770

FEBER, JANE BOXER, elementary school educator; b. Ellenville, N.Y., Apr. 17, 1951; d. Nathan and Lee Boxer; m. Daniel Adam Feber, Apr. 27, 1973; 1 child, Adam H. BA, Jacksonville U., 1973; MEd, U. North Fla., 1977. Tchr. Duval County Pub. Schs., Jacksonville, Fla. Author: Creative Book Reports, 2004. Named Tchr. of Yr., Duval County Sch. Bd., 1987; recipient Gladys Prior award for tchg. excellence, U. North Fla., 2002. Mem.: Internat. Reading Coun., Nat. Coun. Tchrs. English (Edwin Am. Hoey award 2006), Fla. Coun. Tchrs. English (chmn. conf. registration 2001—, pres. elect, Tchr. of Yr. 2003). Avocations: reading, travel, gardening. Office: Mandarin Mid Sch 5100 Hood Rd Jacksonville FL 32257 E-mail: janefeber@hotmail.com.

FEBREY, THERESA M., assistant principal; b. Rochester, NY, 1959; d. Philip Anthony and Shirley Ann Febrey. BE summa cum laude, SUNY, Cortland, 1982; ME summa cum laude, Ithaca Coll., NY, 1989; CAS, SUNY, Brockport. Cert. tchr. N.Y. State Edn. Dept., sch. adminstr. N.Y. State Edn. Dept., sch. dist. adminstr. N.Y. State Edn. Dept. Tchr. Wayne Ctrl. Schs., Ontario, NY, 1985—98; tchr. and coach Rush-Henrietta Ctrl. Schs., Henrietta, 1998—2000, Rochester City Schs., 2000—02; asst. prin. Churchville Chili Ctrl. Schs., Churchville, 2002—03, Penfield Ctrl. Schs., 2003—. Dept. chair Wayne Ctrl. Schs., Ontario, NY, dist. coord., team leader and state edn. cons., turnkey coach, co-creator character edn. curriculum elem. and mid. schs., 1997; assoc. prof. and coach SUNY, Stony Brook, 1983—84; instr. and coach Babson Coll., Wellesley, Mass., 1984—85. Bd. mem. United Meth. Ch. Day Care Ctr., Rochester, 1985; capt. U.S. Select Soccer Team Europe Tour. Named 1st Team All-American, Nat. Soccer Coaches Assn. NCAA. Mem.: ASCD, Nat. Assn. Secondary Sch. Prins. Achievements include development of system for implementation and communication, academic intervention for failing students; capt. first women's national tournament champion soccer team; first woman to win Broderick award in college soccer. Avocations: soccer, volleyball, boating, music.

FECHHELM, JANICE, science educator, researcher, illustrator; b. East Orange, N.J., Jan. 15, 1954; d. John Frances and Mary Catherine Drukten; m. Robert George Fechhelm, June 24, 1977; children: Lauren, Kristen. MS in Wildlife and Fisheries Sci., Tex. A&M U., College Station, 1981. Cert. secondary sci. tchr. Tex. Edn. Assn., 1991. Pub. sch. tchr. Coll. Sta. Sch. Dist., Tex., 1991—. Rsch. field tech. LGL Ecol. Rsch. Assoc., Bryan, Tex., 1996—2006; dir. distance learning cmty. Tex. A&M U., College Station, 2002—. Co-author, illustrator Fishes of the Gulf of Mexico, 1998, revised edit., 2005. Bd. dir. Brazos Valley Mus., Bryan, Tex., 2006. Recipient Tchr. of Yr., Coll. Sta. Ind. Sch. Dist., 1998, 2005. Mem.: Nat. Sci. Tchrs. Assn. (assoc.). Achievements include research in larval fish of the Cape Fear Estuary. Home: 8722 Bent Tree Dr College Station TX 77845 Office: Cypress Grove Intermediate Sch 900 Graham Rd College Station TX 77845 Personal E-mail: jfechhelm@csisd.org.

FEDDERSEN STEWARD, MARYANN ODILIA, psychotherapist; b. Wilmington, Del., Nov. 17, 1945; d. Charles Martin and Ann Catherine F.; m. Fred A. Steward; children: Sarah Catherine, Anna Marie. B.A., Duquesne U., 1967; M.Ed., U. Pitts., 1970, Ph.D., 1975. Counselor, group leader Neighborhood Youth Corps, Pitts., 1967-68; ednl. coordinator Community Action of Pitts., 1968-71; ednl. facilitator Mon-Yough Council on Drug Abuse, McKeesport, Pa., 1971-73; counselor cons. Allegheny Intermediate Unit Pitts., 1973-75; child and family therapist No. Communities Mental Health Program, Pitts., 1974-85; psychologist FosterGrandParents/Home Visitor Program, Pitts., 1976-80; pvt. practice, 1977—; cons., trainer Washington-Green Co. (Pa.) Head Start, 1979-82; trainer Title XX programs, Pa., 1979-81. Mem. adv. council North Side Pitts. Salvation Army, 1983-2000; bd. dirs. Pitts. Cancer Guidance Inst., 1988-93. Recipient recognition award Foster Grandparent Program, 1980. Mem. Assn. Counseling and Devel., Am. Mental Health Counselors Assn. Clubs: Moraine Sailing (sec. 1982-88), U.S. Internat. Fireball Assn. (dist. 4 commodore 1984-89), Am. Assn. Univ. Women (Fox Chapel Area br. gourmet lunch com. 2004—), Western Pa. Family Ctr. Home and Office: 309 N Pasadena Dr Pittsburgh PA 15215-1832

FEDELI, SHIRLEY ANN MARTIGNONI, retired secondary school educator; b. Rockford, Ill., Aug. 19, 1935; d. Peter William and Catherine Gertrude (Domino) Martignoni; m. Eugene Anthony Fedeli, Oct. 24, 1959; 1 child, Lisa Marie. BA in Child Devel., Rockford Coll., 1957. Elem. tchr. Bloom Sch., Rockford, 1957-68; social studies chair St. Peter Cathedral Sch., Rockford, 1980—. Spkr. in field. Founder Pappagallo--Italian Culture News, 1995—. Tour dir. Columbus Day com., Rockford, 1992, 1994, 1995, 1999, 2002, 2006; founder, dir. Amici Italiani-Folk Dancers Adult and Youth, 1986—; chair St. Joseph Italian tradition and folklore Graham-Ginestra Hist. Home, 1980—99; initiation bd. Outdoor Edn. Pub. Atwood, city of Rockford Schs. Program, 1958—68; founder Club La Vita Italiana, 1995—; culture, edn. chmn. Italians in N.W. Ill., 1980—; source vol. Rockford City Schs., 1999, SOURCE vol., 2000—03; mem. Golden Apple selection com. Rockford Pub. Schs.; chair Ethnic Village Fundraiser; mem. Rockford Hist. Soc.; mem. school program Leonardo Da Vinci Burpee Nat. Hist. Mus.; supporter Rockford's Millennium; emcee Gourmet Alley, Rockford, coord., On the Waterfront Event, 1998—2004; hist. tour guide River Dist.; mem. Rockford Sesquicentennial Interfaith City program; spkr. civic and religious orgns.; mem. Winnebago County Vision Project; intergenerational com. Rock Valley Coll.; tchr. leader Rock Valley Coll. Ctr. Learning in Retirement; spkr. Youth Vol. Svcs. Panel, 2006; mem. Multi-Cultural Svc. Com. Bd. of Mental Health, Springfield, 1997—, Rock River Valley Green Communities. Environ. Com.; apptd. Rockford Diocese Social Studies Curriculum Devel., 1998—2000, Corpus Christi Cath. of St. Peter; mem. Columbus spl. event com. Klehm Arboretum; bd. dir. and v.p. Ethnic Heritage Mus., Rockford, 1987—2006, pres.; mem. World Peace Day Ethnic Dance Com.; mem. steering com. Rockford Sister City in Italy, 2005—. Recipient Bishop O'Neill award Diocese of Rockford, 1986, Studs Terkel Humanities Svc. award, 2002, Futurists award Rockford Sesquicentennial, 2002, Lifescape Comty. Svc. award, 2002, United Way Rock River Valley Vol. Ctr. award, 2005, Comty. Svc. award Rockford Park Dist., 2005, Rockford Coll. Golden Grads Woman's award, 2005; inducted in Italian Am. Hall of Fame, 1996; named Outstanding Social Studies Tchr. State of Ill., 1989; recognition in Rockford Register Star newspaper, Rockford Pub. Libr. Newsletter; nominee Excalibur award, 2003, 2004, Veritas award, 2002, Woman of Yr. award St. Peter Cathedral, 2004, Rockford Park Dist. Cmty. Vol. award, 2005; nominee Sr. Ill. Hall of Fame, 2005; Vol. of Yr. award United Way, 2005, RSVP Pres. Gold Vol. Svc. award, 2005. Mem.: DAR, Nat. Women in Am. History, Italian Folk Art Fedn. Am. (bd. dirs.), Nat. Cath. Soc. Foresters (v.p., youth leader), Delta Kappa Gamma Internat. Hon. Tchg. Soc. (1st v.p., 2d v.p., sec., coms.). Roman Catholic. Avocations: touring italy/europe, volunteering, reading.

FEDER, JUDITH, dean; BA in Polit. sci., Brandeis U., 1968; MA in Polit. sci., Harvard U., 1970, PhD in Polit. sci., 1977. Rsch. fellow Brookings Inst., Washington, 1972—73; rsch. assoc. Spectrum Rsch., Inc., Denver, 1974—75; health policy analyst Govt. Rsch. Corp., Washington, 1975—76; sci. fellow Nat. Ctr. Health Svcs. Rsch., Dept. Health, Ed. & Welfare, 1976—77; sr. rsch. assoc. The Urban Inst., 1977—84; co-dir. Ctr. Health Policy Studies Georgetown U. Sch. Medicine, 1984—92; acting asst. sec. planning & evaluation US Dept. HHS, 1993—95; rsch. prof. pub. policy Georgetown U., 1995—98, prof., dean policy studies, 1999—. Author: Medicare: The Politics of Federal Hospital Insurance, 1977; co-author: Financing Health Care for the Elderly: Medicare, Medicaid and Private Health Insurance, 1979, Insuring the Nation's Health: Market Competition, Catastrophic and Comprehensive Approaches, 1981; editor (with John Holahan and Theodore Marmor): National Health Insurance: Conflicting Goals and Policy Choices, 1980; editor: (with Diane Rowland and Anita Salganicoff) Medicaid Financing Crisis: Balancing Responsibilities, Priorities and Dollars, 1993; contbr. articles to profl. jours., chapters to books. Sr. advisor Kaiser Family Found. commn. on Medicaid & the Uninsured; staff dir. US Congress Pepper Commn., 1989—91. Mem.: Nat. Acad. Soc. Ins., Nat. Acad. Pub. Adminstrn., Inst. Medicine. Office: Georgetown Pub Policy Inst 3600 N St NW Ste 200 Washington DC 20007*

FEDERICO, JOSEPHINE A.M., music educator; b. Syracuse, N.Y., June 14, 1942; d. Matthew Frank and Mary Jane (Calcagno) Sindoni; m. Carmine Federico, June 20, 1964; children: Carmen J., Joanna M. Federico Cox. MusB in Music Edn., Marywood U., Scranton, 1964; MusM in Music Edn., Syracuse U., 1970; postgrad., Eastman Sch. Music, Rochester, N.Y., 1987, U. Buffalo, E. Stroudsburg U., Pa. Vocal music tchr. North Syracuse Ctrl. Schs., NY, 1964—68; pvt. music tchr. Liverpool, NY, 1964—; music dir. St. Margarets Ch., Mattydale, NY, 1979—84; choir dir. St. Rose of Lima Ch., North Syracuse, 1983—84; music tchr. Solvay Sch. Dist., NY, 1986—89, Diocese of Syracuse/St. Rose Lima Sch., North Syracuse, 1989—. Dir. Italian Choraliers of Syracuse, 1980—; accompanist N.Y. State convs. of Order Sons of Italy in Am., 1980—; adjudicator N.Y. State Sch. Music Assn., 1984—; diocesan rep. Onondaga County Music Educators Assn., 1989—. Com. mem. Onondaga County Columbus Quincentennial Commn., 1990—92. Recipient Outstanding Music Educator award, Syracuse Symphony Orch., 2000. Mem.: Onondaga County Music Edn. Assn. (bd. dirs.), Onondaga County Music Educators Assn., Pastoral Musicians Assn., Ctrl. N.Y. Assn. Music Tchrs., N.Y. State Sch. Music Assn., Music Educators Nat. Conf., Marywood Coll. Alumni Assn. (pres. 1980—81), Order Sons of Italy in Am. (v.p. state scholarship commn. 1980—, state trustee 1984—88, Progresso lodge pres. 1998—, trustee 2006—). Roman Catholic. Home: 4966 Driftwood Dr Liverpool NY 13088 Office: Saint Rose of Lima School 411 S Main St North Syracuse NY 13212

FEDERMAN, CINDY B., science educator, retail executive; b. Phila. BA, Rutgers U., New Brunswick, N.J., 1992; MA, Arcadia U., Glens Mills, Pa., 2000. Cert. tchr. biology grades 9-12 Dept. Edn., N.J., 1993. Sci. tchr. Voorhees Pub. Schs., NJ, 2001—; retail sales mgr. Mt. Holly Bicycles. Author: (curriculum guide) Teacher's Guide to the Birds of Hog Island, Maine. Vol. and supportor Humane Soc. of US, 1990—2006; vol. Humane Edn. Soc. of US, 1993—2005; vol. and supporter Women's Sports Found., 1998—2002; participant bike-a-thons ALS Soc., Phila., 2000—05; pres. Rutgers Environ. Action, New Brunswick, 1988—91. Recipient cholarship, Cherry Hill Bd. Edn., 1987; grantee, PSE&G, 1994, Balance Bar, Inc., 2006. Mem.: N.J. Sci. Tchrs. Assn., Outdoors Club of NJ. Avocations: hiking, bicycling, kayaking. Office Phone: 856-795-2025.

FEDOCK, BARBARA C., primary school educator, consultant; D, Western Carolina U., 1999—2003. Superintendent NC Dept. of Pub. Instrn., 2003, Principal NC Dept. of Pub. Instrn., 2003, Master's Degree in Middle School Language Arts NC Dept. of Pub. Instrn., 1998, BA English 9-12 NC Dept. of Pub. Instrn., Reading K-12 NC Dept. of Pub. Instrn., 1990, Mathematics Mars Hill Coll., 1998, Academically Gifted Education U. of NC at Charlotte, 1997. High sch./mid. sch. math. and english cons., NC Dept. of Pub. Instrn., 2001—03; curriculum specialist Buncombe County Schools, Asheville, NC, 2003—; online prof. Western Internat. U. Online. Edn. cons., Asheville, NC, 2001—; profl. learning cmty. coach, 2004—; end-of-grade reading test item writer and reviewer NC Dept. of Pub. Instrn., 1999—, writing test com. mem., 2003—; reading cons., NC, 2001—; math., english, lang. arts, writing, ged, and sat cons., Statewide, NC, 2001—; tchr. expectation of student achievement trainer, NC, 2001—; multicultural and diversity trainer, NC, 2001—; hispanic cultural trainer, NC, 2001—; paideia coach, Asheville, NC, 2001—05. Care ptnr. Hospice, Asheville, NC, 2003—05. Fellow Dist. Tchr. of the Yr., Buncombe County Sch. Bd.; fellow, Mountain Area Writer's Project, 1998, Internat. Comm. and Technol. Advancement for Global Understanding at Duke U., 1996—99, NC Dept. of Media Comm., 1997—98. Fellow: Nat. Reading Assn. (life); mem.: Assn. for Supr. and Curriculum Devel., Nat. Counsel of English Teachers, NC English Teachers, Nat. Mid. Sch. Assn. Home: 106 Bull Mountain Rd Asheville NC 28805 Personal E-mail: bfedock@juno.com.

FEDOROFF, NINA VSEVOLOD, research scientist, consultant, educator; b. Cleve., Apr. 9, 1942; d. Vsevolod N. Fedoroff and Olga S. (Snegireff) Stacy; children: Natasha, Kyr, James. BS, Syracuse U., 1966; PhD, Rockefeller U., 1972. Asst. mgr. transl. bur. Biol. Abstracts, Phila., 1962-63; flutist Syracuse (N.Y.) Symphony Orch., 1964-66; acting asst. prof. UCLA, 1972-74; postdoctoral fellow UCLA and Carnegie Inst. Washington, Los Angeles and Balt., 1974-78; staff scientist Carnegie Inst. Washington, Balt., 1978-95; dir. Biotechnol. Inst., Pa. State U., 1995—, Willaman prof. of life scis., 1995—, Evan Pugh prof., 2002—; external prof. Santa Fe Inst., 2003—. Dir. Life Scis. Consortium, Pa. State U., 1996—2002; prof. dept. biology John Hopkins U., 1979-95; mem. devel. biology panel NSF, Washington, 1979-80; sci. adv. panel Office of Tech. Assessment, Congress, Washington, 1979-80; recombinant DNA adv. com. NIH, Bethesda, Md., 1980-84; sci. adv. com. Japanese Human Frontier Sci., 1988; sci adv. com. Competitive Rsch. Grants Office, USDA; mem. commn. on life scis., basic biology bd. NRC, NAS, 1984-90; bd. dirs. Genetics Soc. Am.; mem. bd. overseers Harvard U., 1988-91; trustee BIOSIS, Phila., 1990-96; mem. NAS Coun., 1991-94; dir. Internat. Sci. Found., 1992-93; mem. adv. com. Directorate for Biol. Scis., 1994-97; bd. dirs. Sigma-Aldrich Corp., 1996—; mem. nat. sci. bd. NSF, 2000-06. Editor: Gene, 1981—84, Perspectives in Biology and Medicine, 1991—2001, Procs. Nat. Acad. Sci., 1996—2000; editor, bd. rev. editors: Sci., 1985, mem. sci. adv. bd.: The Plant Jour., 1991—98, book editor: various publs.; contbr. chapters to books articles to profl. jours. Recipient Merit award, NIH, 1990, Howard Taylor Ricketts award, U. Chgo., 1990, Arents Pioneer award, Syracuse U., 2003; grantee, NSF and USDA, 1979—84, NIH, 1984—99, NSF, 1992—, NASA, 1997—2000. Mem.: AAAS, NAS (editor procs. 1995—), AAAS (bd. dirs. 2000—03), European Acad. Scis., Am. Acad. Arts and Scis., Nat. Sci. Bd., Sigma Xi (McGovern Sci. and Soc. medal 1997), Phi Beta Kappa (vis. scholar 1984—85, vis. scholar 1984—85). Avocations: choral music, gardening, tango. Home: 2398 Shagbark Ct State College PA 16803-3367 Office: Huck Insts Life Scis Pa State U University Park PA 16802

FEE, ELIZABETH, medical historian, administrator; b. Belfast, Northern Ireland, Dec. 11, 1946; d. John Alexander and Deirdre (Carson) F. BA, Cambridge U., Eng., 1968, MA, 1972; PhD, Princeton U., 1978. came to U.S., 1968. Prof. history and health policy Johns Hopkins U., Balt., 1978—; chief history of medicine divsn. Nat. Libr. of Medicine, Bethesda, Md., 1995—. Author: Women and Health: The Politics of Sex in Medicine, 1983, Disease and Discovery: A History of the Johns Hopkins School of Hygiene and Public Health, 1916-1939, 1987, (with Daniel M. Fox) AIDS: The Burdens of History, 1988 (with Linda Shopes and Linda Zeidman) The Baltimore Book: New Views of Local History, 1991, (with Roy M. Acheson) A History of Education in Public Health: Health That Mocks the Doctors' Rules, 1991, (with Daniel M. Fox) AIDS: The Making of a Chronic Disease, 1992, (with Nancy Krieger) Women's Health, Politcs, and Power: Essays on Sex/Gender, Medicine, and Public Health, 1994, (with Steven H. Corey) Garbage! The History and Politics of Trash in New York City, 1994, (with Esther M. Sternberg, Anne Harrington, Thedore Brown) Emotions and Disease: An Exhibition at the National Library of Medicine, 1997, (with Theodore M. Brown) Making Medical History: The Life and Times of Henry E. Sigerist, 1997, (with Theodore M. Brown) The APHA: 125 Years Old--and Approaching the Millennium, 1997, (with Theodore M. Brown) American Public Health Association. Conflict and Controversy: From Medical Care Policy to the Politics of Environmental Health, 1998, (with Charles S. Marwick) Breath of Life: An Exhibition That Examines the History of Asthma, the Experiences of People with Asthma, and Contemporary Efforts to Understand and Manage the Disease, 2001, (with Susan E. Lederer and Patricia Tuohy) Frankenstein: Penetrating the Secrets of Nature: An Exhibition by the National Library of Medicine, 2002; contbr. monographs to profl. jours. Recipient Kellogg Nat. fellowship, Kellogg Found., 1984-87, Golden Apple award, Johns Hopkins U., 1991, NCM Regents award for scholarship, 2000. Mem. Am. Pub. Health Assn. (Viseltear award 1997), Sigerist Circle (chair), Am. Assn. History of Medicine. Avocations: gardening, hiking, theater. Office: Nat Libr Medicine 8600 Rockville Pike Bethesda MD 20894-0001 Office Phone: 301-496-5406. E-mail: elizabeth_fee@nlm.nih.gov.

FEEBACK, LORETA DOTALINE KREEGER, artist; b. Omaha, July 7, 1938; BFA, Kansas City Art Inst., 1960; MA, U. Mo., Kansas City, 1993. Sales/designer Keeshan's Frame & Gallery, Kansas City, Mo., 1991—95; sales cons. Keith Coldsnow Artist Materials, Overland Park, Kans., 1995—98; art tchr. Johnson Co. C.C., Overland Park, 1998—2001, Johnson County Parks and Recreation, Overland Park, 1992—; mem. Image Art Gallery, Kansas City, Mo., 2005—. Pastel Artist Internat., 1999, book, The Best of Pastels, 1996, mag., Pastel Artist Internat., 2001; actor:; exhibitions include Albrecht-Kemper Mus. Recipient Patron award, Kans. Pastel Soc., 1988—89, Juror's award, Degas Pastel Soc., 1990, Nat. Art Competition, City of Merriam, Kans., 1998—2003. Mem.: Greater Kans. City Art Assn. (former pres.), Nat. Oil and Acrylic Painters Soc., MidAm. Pastel Soc. (founding pres. and founder).

FEENEY, JOAN N., judge; BA in French and Govt., Conn. Coll., 1975; MA, Amherst Coll.; JD, Suffolk Univ. Law Sch., 1978. Law clk. to Judge Harold Lavien U.S. Bankruptcy Ct. Mass., 1978-79, law clk. to Judge James N. Gabriel, 1978-79, 82-86; assoc. Feeney & Freeley, Boston, 1979-82; assoc., then ptnr. Hanify & King P.C., Boston, 1986-92; bankruptcy judge U.S. Bankruptcy Ct. Mass., Boston, 1992—. Mem. Suffolk Univ. Law Review, 1976-78; editor Suffolk Transnational Journal, 1977-78, Suffolk Voluntary Defenders, 1977-78, Volunteer Lawyer's Project. Mem. Mass. Assn. of Women Lawyers, Am. Bankruptcy Inst. Office: Thomas O'Neill Federal Bldg 10 Causeway St Rm 1101 Boston MA 02222-1009

FEENEY, MARYANN MCHUGH, not-for profit professional; b. Bklyn., July 9, 1948; d. Michael Daniel and Mary Bridget (Hourican) McH.; m. Brian Francis Feeney, Sept. 21, 1974 (dec. Mar. 1992); 1 child, Michael. BA, Marymount Manhattan Coll., 1980; MA, Bklyn. Coll., 2002. Human resources mgr. Muir Cornelius Moore, Inc., NYC, 1977-84; human resources dir. Statue of Liberty-Ellis Island Found., NYC, 1984—88; pres. The Taft Inst., NYC, 1988—97; dir. nat. fundraising Girls Scouts U.S.A., NYC, 1997—99; exec. dir. Bklyn. Tech. H.S. Alumni Assn., 2003—05; dir. instnl. advancement Bishop Loughlin Meml. H.S., 2005—. Exec. prodr. Your Vote Video, 1991 (nominated ACE and Emmy awards 1991). Bd. dirs. Bklyn. Conservatory of Music, 1992-94, SFX-Prospect Park Baseball, Bklyn., 1986-2006; pres. emeritus, trustee The Taft Inst. at Queens Coll., 1997—. Recipient Cmty. Svc. award SFX-Prospect Park Baseball, 1992, 95, 97. Mem. Ireland House at NYU, Park Slope Civic Coun. (trustee). Democrat. Roman Catholic. Avocations: reading, history, gardening. Office Phone: 718-857-2700. Personal E-mail: mfeeney3@aol.com. Business E-Mail: mfeeney@blmhs.org.

FEES, NANCY FARDELIUS, special education educator; b. Santa Monica, Calif., Mar. 25, 1950; d. Carl August and Dodi Emma (Hedenschau) Fardelius; m. Paul Rodger Fees, June 4, 1971; children: Evelyn Wyoming, Nelson August. BS, Mills Coll., 1971; MA in Edn., Idaho State U., 1975. Cert. tchr., Calif., Idaho, Wyo., R.I. Specialist curriculum mgmt. Barrington (R.I.) High Sch., 1975-81; coordinator learning skills ctr. Northwest Community Coll., Powell, Wyo., 1982-84, instr., 1985—. Pres. Children's Resource Ctr., 1985-89, bd. dirs., 1983-89, 91-2002. Editor (with others) The Great Entertainer, 1984. Vol. Buffalo Bill Hist. Ctr., Cody, Wyo., 1981-1992; mem. Centennial Com., Cody, 1983; mem. parent's adv. com. Livingston Sch., 1989-92, chmn., 1991-92; dir. Christian Edn. Christ Episcopal Ch., 1995-2004, dir. peace camp 1999-2003; mgr. Math. Tutoring Ctr., Northwest Coll., 2004—. Mem. Council Exceptional Children. Democrat. Episcopalian. Home: 1718 Wyoming Ave Cody WY 82414-3320

FEESE, SUZANNE, lawyer; b. Danville, Ky. BA with honors, Agnes Scott Col., 1984; JD, Yale Univ., 1987. Bar: Ga. 1988. Law clk. Judge R. Lanier Anderson III, US Ct. Appeals 11th Cir.; ptnr., Tax Practice Group & hiring ptnr., Atlanta King & Spalding, LLP, Atlanta. Trustee Agnes Scott Coll.; mem. Chair Council Atlanta Women's Found.; past chairwoman Ga. Ctr. for Children. Mem.: ABA, State Bar Ga. Office: King & Spalding LLP 191 Peachtree St Atlanta GA 30303 Office Phone: 404-572-3566. Office Fax: 404-572-5100. Business E-Mail: sfeese@kslaw.com.

FEESLER, MOLLY J., secondary school educator; b. Columbus, Ohio, May 13, 1964; BS in Edn., Rio Grande Coll., Rio Grande, Ohio, 1986; MS in Edn., Ohio U., Athens, 1990—90; Adminstrv. Cert., Ashland U., Ashland, Ohio, 0200. Cert. tchr. Ohio, 1986. Tchr. Columbus City Schs., Ohio, 1988—89, St. Francis DeSales H.S., Columbus, 1989—95, asst. prin. and athletic dir., 1995—2000; tchr. and coach Pickerington North H.S., Pickerington, Ohio, 2000—. Head softball coach Pickerington North H.S., 2000—; softball coach St. Francis DeSales H.S., Columbus, 1990—2000. Mem.: Ohio H.S. Softball Coaches Assn. (pres. 2003—05). Office: Pickerington North High School 7800 Refugee Rd Pickerington OH 43147 Office Phone: 614-830-2700. E-mail: molly_feesler@fc.pickerington.k12.oh.us.

FEGRAEUS, SUSIE A., principal; d. Johnnie Edward and Betty Raye Brezik; m. Eric Robert Fegraeus, Nov. 23, 1974; children: Jason, Jacob. BS in Elem. Edn., U. North Tex., 1974, MA in Edn., 1979; EdD in Ednl.

Adminstrn., Tex. A&M U., 1999. Cert. tchr., supr., mid-mgmt. Tchr. Dallas Ind. Sch. Dist., 1974—84, Garland (Tex.) Ind. Sch. Dist., 1984—89, asst. prin., 1989—2000, prin., 2000—. Mem.: TASSP, ASCD. Avocation: sports. Office: North Garland High Sch 2109 Buckingham Garland TX 75042 Office Phone: 972-675-3120. E-mail: safegrae@garlandisd.net.

FEHL, PATRICIA KATHERINE, retired physical education educator; b. Cin., May 29, 1927; d. Norman and Gertrude (Morris) F.; A.B. cum laude, DePauw U., 1949; M.S., Ind. U., 1955, Ed.D., 1966. Tchr., Crawfordsville Schs., Ind., 1950-52; critic tchr., lab. sch., coll. methods instr. Ind. U., Bloomington, 1952-62; assoc. prof. health, phys. edn. and recreation U. Cin., 1962-73; prof., chmn. dept. gen. program Sch. Phys. Edn., W.Va. U., Morgantown, 1973-89, prof. emerita, 1989—; vis. com. W.Va. U., 1991-94. Kennedy Found. grantee, 1966; named to DePauw U. Athletic Hall of Fame, 1994, W.Va. Hall of Fame, 1988. Fellow Am. Sch. Health Assn.; mem. Am. Alliance for Health, Phys. Edn., Recreation and Dance (Honor award 1986, v.p. recreation 1973-75, chmn. nominating com. 1985, 88-90), Midwest Dist. AAHPERD (historian, 1974-78, pres. 1978-80, Pres.'s award 1976, Honor award 1983, Meritorious award 1986, parliamentarian 1973, 76, 87-88, 91, 93), Ohio Assn. Health, Phys. Edn. and Recreation (hon. life, v.p., chmn. divsn. girls and women's sports 1970-72, parliamentarian 1992-93, trustee 1992-94, Meritorious award 1973), W.Va. Assn. Health, Phys. Edn. and Recreation (v.p. recreation 1975, Honor award 1978, Ray O. Duncan award 1987), W.Va. Recreation and Parks Assn. (bd. dirs. 1978-81, treas. 1983, pres. 1982-84; profl. cert. 1980), Ohio Parks and Recreation Assn. (pres. 1972; Meritorious award 1974), Midwest Assn. Phys. Edn. for Coll. Women (governing bd.), Nat. Recreation and Park Assn., U.S. Power Squadron, Pro Cin. Squadron (Outstanding Mem. 1992, Chapman award 1994), Phi Delta Kappa, Pi Lambda Theta, Delta Kappa Gamma. Contbr. articles to jours.; contbr. to Ohio Secondary Girls Phys. Edn. Curriculum Guide Address: 314 Harvard Ave Terrace Park OH 45174-1114

FEHR, LOLA MAE, health facility administrator; b. Hastings, Nebr., Sept. 29, 1936; d. Leland R. and Edith (Wunderlich) Gaymon; m. Harry E. Fehr, Aug. 15, 1972; children: Dawn, Cheryl, Michael. RN, St. Luke's Hosp., Denver, 1958; BSN magna cum laude, U. Denver, 1959; MS, U. Colo., Boulder, 1975. Dir. staff devel. Weld County Gen. Hosp., Greeley, Colo., 1972-76, dir. nursing, 1976-80; exec. dir. Colo. Nurses Assn., Denver, 1980-89; dir. membership Assn. Oper. Rm. Nurses, Inc., Denver, 1989-90, exec. dir., 1990-99; pres. Fehr Cons. Resources, 1999—; exec. dir. Am. Soc. Bariatric Physicians, 2000—01; program dir. Colo. Ctr. for Nursing Excellence, 2003; exec. dir. N.Y. State Nurses Assn., 2003—. Editor: Colo. Nurse, 1980—89. Recipient U. Colo. Alumni award, Colo. Nurses Assn. Profl. Nurse of Yr. award. Mem. Am. Acad. Nursing, Nat. Assn. Parliamentarians, Am. Soc. Assn. Execs., N.Y. State Nurses Assn., Sigma Theta Tau. Office Phone: 518-782-9400 ext. 201. Business E-Mail: lolafehr@gmail.com.

FEIDNER, MARY P., retired speech and language pathologist; b. Cin., Jan. 24, 1933; d. Paul Francis and Rosemary (Witte) Thesing; m. Edward Joseph Feidner, Aug. 27, 1955; children: Julie Marie, Elizabeth Ann, David Mark, Eric Joseph, Jon Edward. BS in Secondary Edn., U. Dayton, 1954; MS in Speech Pathology, U. Vt., 1971; cert. advanced grad. study, St. Michael's Coll., 1987. Elem. tchr. Holy Angels Sch., Dayton, Ohio, 1954-55, Norfolk (Va.) Sch. Dist., 1955-56; speech instr. U. Vt., Burlington, 1965-66; speech therapist Ctr. for Disorders of Comm., Burlington, 1966-69; speech-lang. pathologist So. Burlington (Vt.) Sch. Dist., 1971-95. Clin. supr. U. Vt., Burlington, 1990-95. Lister Town of Hinesburg, Vt., 1995-2000; coord. Friends of Families, Hinesburg, 1998—2000 project dir. Vt. Coun. Humanities, Hinesburg, 1999-2000; chmn. Hinesburg Dem. Com., 1997-2000; docent Park-McCullough Historic House, North Bennington, Vt. Mem. Am. Speech, Lang., and Hearing Assn., Vt. Speech, Lang., and Hearing Assn., Lions, Delta Kappa Gamma (state pres. 1999-2001, pres. chpt. 2001-03). Democrat. Avocations: piano, reading, attending plays and concerts, playreading group, writing group. Home: 26 College Rd North Bennington VT 05257 E-mail: maryfeidner@earthlink.net.

FEIG, BARBARA KRANE, elementary school educator, author; b. Mitchell, S.D., Nov. 8, 1937; d. Peter Abraham and Sally (Gorchow) Krane; m. Jerome Feig, June 8, 1963; children: Patricia Lynn, Lizabeth Ann. Student, Washington U., St. Louis, 1955-58; BE, Nat. Coll. Edn., 1960; postgrad., Northeastern Ill. U. Tchr. various schs., 1960-68, Anshe Emet Day Sch., Chgo., 1966-68, Sacred Heart, Chgo., 1982—, New City Day Sch., Chgo., 1983-90, Chgo. Pub. Schs., 1990—. Pres. J.B. Pal & Co., Inc., Chgo., 1975—; bd. dirs. Barclee Cosmetics, Inc., Chgo., Media Merchandising, Chgo.; meeting planner Ismes, Bergamo, Italy, 1987—, Tecnica, Chgo., 1987—, Meeting Network, Chgo., 1987—. Author: Now You're Cooking: A Guide to Cooking For Boys and Girls, 1975, The Parents' Guide to Weight Control For Children, 1980; mem. editorial staff Other Voices, 1985—; developer edml. toy, 1985. Mem. womens bd. Francis Parker Sch., Chgo., 1972—; trustee Chgo. Inst. for Psychoanalysis, 1975—; bd. dirs. Juvenile Diabetes Found., Chgo., 1976—. Mem. Women of the Professions and Trades, Jewish Fedn. Avocations: skydiving, scuba diving, mountain climbing, skiing, marathons. Home: 1340 N Astor St Apt 2906 Chicago IL 60610-8438

FEIGEN, IRENE, artist, educator; b. Bklyn., Aug. 13, 1944; d. Max and Jean (Weingarten) Marder; m. Daniel Feigen, Mar. 29, 1963; children: Erik, Nicole, Ross. BFA, Bklyn. Coll., 1964; MFA, CCNY, 1965; cert. Printmaking, NYU, 1985. Lic. tchr., N.Y.; cert. printmaker, N.Y. Tchr. fine arts N.Y.C. Bd. Edn., 1962-65; prof. fine arts Fairleigh Dickinson U., Madison, N.J., 1980-87; freelance artist, art educator Art Expo N.Y., 1980-90. Artist in residence, Livingston Home and Sch. Assn., 1980—, Riker Hill Art Park, Livingston, N.J., B'nai Abraham, Livingston, 1987. Exhbns. include Robert Ward Galleries, N.Y.C., Korby Gallery, Cedar Grove, N.J., Bergen Mus., Paramus, N.J., Morris Mus., Morristown, N.J., Montclair Mus., Hebrew Home for Aged, Riverdale, N.Y., The Nese Gallery, Irvine, Calif., Newark Mus., Papermill Playhouse Gallery, Millburn, N.J., Straleys Gallery, Livingston, N.J., Whichcraft Studio, South Orange, Long Beach Island, N.J., The Key Gallery, N.Y.C., Art 3 Assocs., Livingston, Art 3 of Ft. Lee, N.J., MCI, SONY, Lewis Internat., Clifton Radiology Ctr., among others; creator Livingston Loveletters poster Township of Livingston, 1999; artist participant ArtRageous Edwin Gould Svcs., 2004. Mem. Allied Bd. Trade; bd. dirs. Arts Coun. Livingston, 1990, 92, pres. 1999, 2000. Recipient numerous artistic awards, including 1st prize Art at the Oval, Livingston, 1999, Woman Yr., Township Livingston, 2005. Mem. Internat. Soc. Arts, West Essex Watercolor Soc., Essex County Arts Soc. (bd. dirs. 1980-85), Livingston Arts Assn. (v.p. 1977-85, bd. dirs. 1970-85), The Printmakers Coun., Mus. Contemporary Crafts, Artists Equity, Livingston Arts Coun. (pres., 2006—). Home: 48 Blackstone Dr Livingston NJ 07039-1843

FEIGENBAUM, JOAN, computer scientist, mathematician; b. Bklyn., Sept. 19, 1958; d. Harry and Joyce Leslie (Gildersleeve) F.; m. Jeffrey Nussbaum. BA in Math. magna cum laude, Harvard U., 1981; PhD in Computer Sci., Stanford U., 1986; MA (Privatum), Yale U., 2001. Prin. mem. tech. staff AT&T Bell Labs., Murray Hill, NJ, 1986—95; head, algorithms and distributed data AT&T Labs-Rsch., Florham Park, NJ, 1998—99, mem. rsch. staff, 1996—2000; prof. computers sci. dept. Yale U., New Haven, 2000—05; Henry Ford II prof. computer sci., 2006—. Program chair CRYPTO-91, Santa Barbara, Calif., 1991; mem. program com. STOC-91, New Orleans, 1991, STOC-94, Montreal, Can., STOC-99, Atlanta; panel mem., Grace Hopper Celebration of Women in Computing, Sci. Policy, 1994; co-chair DIMACS Workshops, 1989, 90, 96; program com. chair Crypto, 1991, IEEE Conf. on Computational Complexity, 1998; program com. mem. Crypto, 1989, 1993, 1996, Eurocrypt, 1992, 1999, IEEE Conf. on Computation Complexity, 1993, Internat. Computing and Combinators Conf., 1998, Financial Cryptography, 1999, 2000, workshop on Internet and Network Economics, 2005; NSF, mem. eight proposal-evaluation panel, 1993-2005; steering-com. mem., DIMACS Special Focus on Computation and the Socio-Economic Sciences, 2004-; session organizer, chair, Info. Security: Principles and Pub. Policy, AAAS, 1995, Incentive Compatibility in Internet Computation, AAAS, 2003; mem., NAS Computer Sci. and Telecommunications Bd., 2002-; bd. dir. Inst. Math. and Its Applications, 1999-2002; adv. bd. mem., John Hopkins U. Computer Sci., 1999-2002; steering com. mem., DIMACS spl. year on massive data sets, 1997-98; co-chair DIMACS spl. focus on Next Generation networks, 2000-2003; NRC panel mem., Intellectual Property Protection in the Emerging Information Infrastructure, 1998-99; steering com. mem., conf. on computational complexity, 1994-97, DIMACS spl. yr. on logic and algorithms, 1995-96; project com. chair, DIMACS, 1994-96; participant, NAS Frontiers of Sci. Symposium, 1995; session organizer, chair, Security and Privacy in the Information Economy, NAS Frontiers in Sci. Symposium, 1996; panel mem., Past, Present, and Future Challenges, NSF Conf. on Women in Sci., 1995; speaker various colls., univs. and confs. Mem. editl. bd. Jour. Algorithms, 1992-96, SIAM Jour. on Computing, 1993-2002; guest editor, 1989-90, Jour. Cryptology, mem. editl. bd. 1990-96, editor-in-chief, 1997-2002; area editor Comm. of Assn. for Computing Machinery, 1988-89; guest editor Jour. Computer and Sys. Scis., 1991, 1998, IEEE Trans. on Information Theory, 1996; adv. bd. mem. Jour. Privacy Tech., 2004-;contbr. articles to profl. jours. Invited spkr. Internat. Congress of Mathematicians, Berlin, 1998. Math. Scis. Postdoctoral fellow NSF, 1986, Xerox Corp. Grad. fellow, 1984. Fellow Assn. Computing Machinery (guest editor, Communication of the ACM, 1988-89; program com. mem. symposium on theory of computing, 1991, 1994, 1999, 2001, conf. on computer and communications security, 1993, 1994, 2005, ACM/SIAM symposium on discrete algorithms, 1999, workshop on security and privacy in digital rights mgmt., 2001, symposium on principals of distrubuted computing, 2004; Sigecom vice-chair, 2005-2007, Sigact exec. com. mem., 2005-2007; program com. chair, workshop on digital rights mgmt., 2002; co-chair conf. on electric commerce, 2004; gen. chair conf. on electronic commerce, 2006); charter mem., Computing Rsch. Assn. Com. on the Status of Women, 1991-96; mem. Am. Math. Soc., Assn. for Women in Math.(mem.-at-large, 2000-04; tutorial co-chair, conf. on electronics commerce, 2003; gen. co-chair, workshop on digital rights mgmt., 2003; selection com. mem., Grace Murray Hopper award, 2001-), Internat. Assn. Cryptologic Rsch. (program com. CRYPT089 conf. 1989, CRYPTO93 conf. 1993, Eurocrypt92 conf. 1992, Eurocrypt 99 conf. 1999, COCCS93 conf. 1993, COCCS94 conf. 1994, fellows selection com., 2003-), Phi Beta Kappa. Democrat. Jewish. Home: 148 W 23rd St Apt 2A New York NY 10011-2447 Office: Yale U Dept Computer Sci PO Box 208285 New Haven CT 06520-8285 Office Phone: 203-432-6432. Office Fax: 203-432-6373. Business E-Mail: jf@cs.yale.edu.*

FEIGIN, BARBARA SOMMER, marketing consultant; b. Berlin, Nov. 16, 1937; arrived in US, 1940, naturalized, 1949; d. Eric Daniel and Charlotte Martha (Demmer) Sommer; m. James Feigin, Sept. 17, 1961; children: Michael, Peter, Daniel. BA in Polit. Sci., Whitman Coll., 1959; cert. of Bus. Adminstrn., Harvard-Radcliffe Program Bus. Adminstrn., 1960. Mktg. rsch. asst. Richardson-Vick Co., Wilton, Conn., 1960-61; market rsch. analyst SCM Corp., N.Y.C., 1961-62; group rsch. supr. Benton & Bowles, Inc., N.Y.C., 1963-67; assoc. rsch. dir. Marplan Rsch. Co., N.Y.C., 1968-69; exec. v.p. worldwide strategic svcs., mem. agy. policy coun. Grey Advt. Inc., N.Y.C., 1969-99. Bd. dirs. VF Corp., Circuit City Stores, Inc.; past chmn. Advert Rsch. Found. Contbr. articles to profl jours. Overseer emeritus Whitman Col; past bd advisors Catalyst. Recipient Women Achievers Award, YWCA, 1987. Mem.: Mkt. Rsch. Hall of Fame.

FEIGIN, JUDITH ZOBEL, educational psychologist; b. N.Y.C., Mar. 17, 1941; d. Isador and Regina (Schwechter) Zobel; m. Ralph David Feigin, June 26, 1960; children: Susan M., Michael E., Debra F. BS, Hunter Coll., N.Y.C., 1960; MA in Edn., St. Louis U., 1977; EdD, U. Houston, 1987. Tchr. Boston pub. schs., 1960-63; spl. tchr. Briarwood Sch., Houston, 1979-81; instr. U. Houston, 1983-84, Pearland Ind. Sch. Dist., Tex., 1986-87; dir. learning support ctr. Tex. Children's Hosp., Houston, 1986—2006; assoc. prof. child psychology program Baylor Coll. Medicine, Sch,. Allied health Scis., 2006—. Psychometrician St. Louis Children's Hosp., 1975-76; cons. in field. Author: Development of Social Skills, 1987, Language Arts/Social Skills: A Temperament-based Curriculum, 1986; co-author: Educational Development of Child with Turner's Syndrome, 1985. Mem. Mental Health/Mental Retardation Authority of Harris County, Houston, 1981-84; v.p. Orton Dyslexia Soc., Houston, 1980-82. Mem. Am. Psychol. Assn., Tex. Assn. for Children with Learning Disabilities, Coun. for Exceptional Children, Coun. for Learning Disabilities, Phi Delta Kappa. Office: Baylor Coll Medicine Sch Allied Health Scis 1 Baylor Plz Houston TX 77030 Office Phone: 832-822-3700. E-mail: jzfeigin@texaschildrenshospital.org.

FEIGL, DOROTHY MARIE, chemistry professor, academic administrator; b. Evanston, Ill., Feb. 25, 1938; d. Francis Philip and Marie Agnes (Jacques) F. BS, Loyola U., Chgo., 1961; PhD, Stanford U., 1966; postdoctoral fellow, N.C. State U., 1965-66. Asst. prof. chemistry St. Mary's Coll., Notre Dame, Ind., 1966-69, assoc. prof., 1969-75, prof., 1975—, chmn. dept. chemistry and physics, 1977-85, bd. regents, 1976-82, acting v.p., dean faculty, 1985-87, v.p., dean faculty, 1987-99, Denise DeBartolo York prof. of chemistry, 2003—. Author: (with John Hill and Erwin Boschmann) General Organic and Biological Chemistry, 1991, (with John Hill and Stuart Baum) Chemistry and Life, 1997; contbr. articles to chem. jours., chpts. to texts. Recipient Spes Unica award St. Mary's Coll., 1973, Maria Pieta award, 1977 Mem. Am. Chem. Soc., Royal Soc. Chemistry, Internat. Union Pure and Applied Chemistry, Sigma Xi, Iota Sigma Pi. Democrat. Roman Catholic. Office: Dept Chemistry Saint Mary's College Notre Dame IN 46556

FEIGON, JUDITH TOVA, ophthalmologist, educator, surgeon; b. Galveston, Tex., Dec. 2, 1947; d. Louis and Ethel Feigon; m. Nathan C. Goldman; children: Michael G., Miriam G. AB, Barnard Coll., Columbia U., 1970; postgrad., Rice U., U. Houston, 1970-71; MD, U. Tex., San Antonio, 1976. Diplomate Am. Bd. Ophthalmology. Intern Mt. Auburn Hosp., Cambridge, Mass.; intern, clin. tchg. fellow Harvard U. Med. Sch., 1976-77; resident in ophthalmology Baylor Coll. Medicine, Houston, 1977-80, fellow in retina, 1980-82, clin. faculty, 1982-95; asst. prof. ophthalmology U. Tex. Med. Br., Galveston, 1982-85, clin. asst. prof., 1985-91, clin. assoc. prof., 1992—; pvt. practice medicine specializing ophthalmology, vitreoretinal diseases, surgery, Houston, 1983—. Physician advisor to Houston br. Tex. Soc. to Prevent Blindness, 1987-89, also bd. dirs., mem. staff Meth., St. Lukes, Tex. Children's, St. Joseph's Hosp., Twelve Oaks Hosp.; clin. faculty Baylor Coll. Medicine, 1982-95. Contbr. articles to profl. publs. Mem. Assn. Am. Physicians and Surgeons, Am. Acad. Ophthalmology, Tex. Med. Assn. Houston Ophthal. Soc., Harris County Med. Soc., U. Tex. San Antonio Alumni Assn., Am. Soc. Retina Specialists, Tex. Ophthalmol. Assn., Houston Ophthal. Soc. (exec. bd. 2000-03). Office: 7515 Main St Ste 650 Houston TX 77030-4599 Office Phone: 713-799-1737.

FEILER, JO ALISON, artist; b. LA, Apr. 16, 1951; d. Alfred Martin and Leatrice Lucille Feiler. Student, UCLA, 1969, Art Ctr. Coll. Design, LA, 1970—72; BFA, Calif. Inst. Arts, 1973, MFA, 1975. Asst. dir. Frank Perls Gallery, Beverly Hills, Calif., 1969-70; photography editor Coast Environ. mag., LA, 1970-72; art dir. Log/An Inc., LA, 1975-82. One-woman shows include Inst. Contemporary Art, London, 1975, Calif. Inst. Arts, Valencia, 1975, NUAGE, LA, 1978, Susan Harder Gallery, N.Y.C., 1984, exhibited in numerous group shows, 1975—, Represented in permanent collections Nat. Portrait Gallery, London, Victoria and Albert Mus., Met. Mus. Art, N.Y.C., Mus. Modern Art, Los Angeles County Mus. Art, Internat. Mus. Photography, Rochester, N.Y., Santa Barbara Mus. Art, Oakland Mus., Mus. Fine Arts, Houston, Biblioteque Nat., Paris, Musee D'Art Moderne de la Ville de Paris, Fondation Vincent Van Gogh, Arles, France, others. Recipient cert. art excellence, Los Angeles County Mus. Art, 1968, award, Laguna Beach Mus. Art, 1976; Calif. Inst. Arts scholar, 1974. Mem.: Royal Photog. Soc. Gt. Britain. Democrat. Avocations: cross country skiing, tennis, collecting art and books, music. Address: Manoir de Clairefontaine Chemin Fontaine Marie 14910 Benerville-Sur-Mer France

FEIN, LINDA ANN, nurse anesthetist, consultant; b. Cin., Dec. 10, 1949; d. Joseph and Elizabeth P. (Kannady) Stofle; m. Thomas Paul Fein, Dec. 11, 1971. Nursing diploma, Miami Vly. Hosp. Sch. Nursing, Dayton, Ohio, 1971, Wright State U., 1969; postgrad., U. Cin. Med. Ctr., 1978. Nursing asst. Miami Valley Hosp, 1969-71; staff nurse operating rm. Cin. Children's Hosp. and Med. Ctr., 1971, 73, Peninsula Hosp., Burlingame, Calif., 1972-73; staff nurse operating rm., emergency rm. Doctors Hosp., San Diego, 1972; staff nurse emergency rm. Ohio State U. Hosps., Columbus, 1973-75, head nurse operating rm., 1975-76; staff nurse anesthetist Bethesda Hosps., Cin., 1978-86, 2006—, Mercy Hosp. Fairfield, Cin., 1986-95; locum tenens anesthetist Fort Hamilton-Hughes Hosp., Hamilton, Ohio, 1994—95, staff anesthetist, 1995—2006, Butler County Surgery Ctr., Hamilton, 2000—06, Bethesda Hosp., Cin., 2006—. Childbirth educator psychoprophylactic method, 1975—; critical care nursing cons. Med. Communicators & Assocs., Salt Lake City, 1985-89; ind. nursing cons., 1989—; co-owner Exec. Shops, Cin., 1982-85; spkr. in field. Search com. Cin. Gen. Hosp. Sch. Anesthesia for Nurses, 1981-82; bd. dirs. YWCA, 1988-91, Children's Diagnostic Ctr., 1989-95, pres. bd. dirs., 1994, Planned Parenthood, 1992-95. Recipient recognition award for profl. excellence First Nurse Anesthesia Faculty Assocs., 1982, Florence Nightingale awards, 1995. Mem. Miami Vly. Hosp. Sch. Nursing Alumni Assn., Cin. Gen. Hosp. Sch. Anesthesia for Nurses Alumni Assn., Nurse Anesthetists Greater Cin., Ohio Assn. Nurse Anesthetists, Am. Assn. Nurse Anesthetists, Am. Assn. Critical Care Nurses, Nat. Registry Cert. Nurses in Advanced Practice (cert.), Ohio Coalition Nurses with Specialty Cert., Am. Soc. Critical Care Medicine, Am. Trauma Soc., NAFE, Altrusa Internat. (officer 1985-92), Order Eastern Star. Republican. Methodist. Avocations: antiques, gourmet cooking, african violets, roses, swimming. Home: 650 History Bridge Ln Hamilton OH 45013-3659

FEIN, SHEILA CAROL, artist; b. N.Y.C., Jan. 16, 1956; d. Saul Israel and Mae (Libsky) Eisenberg; married; children: Jenna, Kara, Caitlin and Amanda (twins). BS in Graphic Design, SUNY, Buffalo, 1977. Comml. artist, instr. C.E.T.A. Program N.Y. C. of C., Schenectady, 1977-78; freelance illustrator & design, 1978-83; fine artist Gallery Assns., N.Y., Pa., Washington, Rome, Conn., L.A., 1983—; art dir. Bob Gail Orch. & Entertainment, Beverly Hills, Calif., 1994—. Painter (portraits) Pres. Clinton, 5 Marx Bros., prominent mems. L.A. cmty. Mem.Thousand Oaks Art Assn. Avocations: poetry, sketching, family, crafts.

FEIN, SUSANNA GREER, literature educator; b. Des Moines, Dec. 26, 1950; d. Martin Luther and Martha Morrison Greer; m. Joshua Ben Fein, June 9, 1973; children: Elizabeth May, Carolyn Molly; m. David Raybin, Mar. 21, 1989; 1 child, Jonathan Greer Raybin. BA in English with honors, U. Chgo., 1973; MA in English, U. Va., 1974; MA in English and Am. Lang. & Lit., Harvard U., 1980, PhD in English and Am. Lang. & Lit., 1985. Asst. prof. English dept. Kent State U., Ohio, 1985—91, assoc. prof. English dept., 1991—98, coord. undergrad. studies English dept., 1991—94, prof. English dept., 1998—, chair English dept., 2000—04, coord. ancient, medieval and renaissance studies, 2001—, coord. comparative lit., 2004—. Mem. editl. bd. Kent State U. Press, 1988—90, 1996—2000; trustee found. bd. Kent State U. Found., 2002—06. Author: Moral Love Songs and Laments, 1998; editor: Rebels and Rivals: The Contestive Spirit in the Canterbury Tales, 1991, Studies in the Harley Manuscript, 2000, The Chaucer Rev.: A Jour. of Medieval Studies and Lit. Criticism, 2001—; mem. editl. bd.: Jour. The Early Book Soc., 2005—. Grantee, Ohio Humanities Coun., 1991, NEH, 1997—98. Mem.: Early Book Soc., New Chaucer Soc., Inst. Bibliography and Editing. Office: Kent State U English Dept PO Box 5190 Kent OH 44242-0001 E-mail: sfein@kent.edu.

FEIN, SYLVIA, author, painter; b. Milw., Nov. 20, 1919; d. Alfred E. and Elizabeth (Routt) F.; B.S., U. Wis., Madison, 1942; M.A., U. Calif., Berkeley, 1951; m. William K. Scheuber, May 30, 1942; 1 dau., Heidi. One-woman exhbns. include: U. Wis. Meml. Union Gallery, 1942, Milw. Art Inst., 1942, Perls Galleries, N.Y.C., 1946, Feingarten Galleries, San Francisco, 1957, 59, Carmel, Calif., 1959, N.Y.C., 1961, Sagittarius Gallery, N.Y.C., 1958, St. Mary's Coll., Moraga, Calif., 1960, Kunstkabinett, Frankfurt, W.Ger., 1960, Mills Coll. Art Gallery, Oakland, Calif., 1962, Ruthermore Galleries, Oakland, 1962, Maxwell Galleries, San Francisco, 1963, Nicole of Berkeley (Calif.), 1965, Bresler Galleries, Milw., 1966, Oshkosh (Wis.) Pub. Mus., 1967; numerous group exhbns., 1941—, latest being 5th Winter invitational Calif. Palace Legion of Honor, 1964, Art of Landscape, San Francisco Art Inst. travelling exhibit, 1964-65, Three Painters, St. Mary's Coll., 1964, Magic and Fantastic Art, Walnut Creek (Calif.) Library, 1968; author: Heidi's Horse, 1976, First Drawings: Genesis of Visual Thinking, 1993; owner, pub. Exelrod Press, 1975—; chmn. Archtl. Rev. Comm., Pleasant Hill, Calif., 1975. Mem. bldg. com. Pleasant Hill City Hall and Downtown Redevel., conflict resolution panel Contra Costa County. Home: 190 Rolling Ridge Way Martinez CA 94553-9655

FEINBERG, GLENDA JOYCE, retail executive; b. Louisville, Feb. 8, 1948; d. Harold and Winnie Esther (McIntosh) F.; divorced; 1 child, Anthony John. Student, Purdue U., 1967-68, Ind. U., 1977-79. Cert. in restaurant and personnel mgmt. Beverage mgr. Don Ce Sar Beach Hotel, St. Petersburg Beach, Fla., 1979-80; catering dir. Best Western-Skyway Inn, St. Petersburg, Fla., 1980-83; gen. mgr. Village, Inc., St. Petersburg Beach, 1983-86; banquet mgr. Tradewinds Resort Hotel, St. Petersburg Beach, 1986-87; exec. mgr. Ponderosa, Inc., Clearwater, Fla., 1987-90; food and beverage dir. Days Inn Island Beach Resort, St. Petersburg Beach, 1990-92; owner, mgmt. cons., pvt. caterer G.F. Sans Inc., 1992—. Bd. dirs. AIDS Coalitions Pinellas, 1990. Mem. NOW, World Wildlife Fedn., Nat. Geog. Soc., Greenpeace, Amnesty Internat., Environ. Def. Fund, Nat. Audubon Soc., Nat. Arbor Day Found. Democrat.

FEINBERG, WENDIE, television producer; BS in Journalism, U. Fla.; MS in Journalism, Boston U. Sr. prodr. Nightly Bus. Report, Miami, Fla. Recipient of three local Emmy Awards for Best Newscast, Best Investigative Reporting, and Best Pub. Affairs Programming, Best News Series/Documentary, Radio & TV News Directors Assn., 1990. Office: NBR Enterprises 14901 NE 20th Ave Miami FL 33181-1121

FEINER, ARLENE MARIE, librarian, researcher, consultant; b. Spring Green, Wis., Mar. 23, 1937; d. Herman Joseph and Cecelia Margaret (Meixelsperger) F. BA in History, Alverno Coll., 1959; MA in Libr. Sci., Rosary Coll., 1971; MA in Orgnl. Devel., Loyola U., Chgo., 1985. Gen. office worker USIA, Washington, 1959-60; adminstrv. sec. Nat. Coun. Cath. Women, Washington, 1960-62; asst. libr. U. Md., Munich, 1962-64; preliminary cataloger, 1st editor MARC Pilot Project Libr. of Congress, Washington, 1965-67; head libr. Acad. Holy Cross, Kensington, Md., 1967-70, Jesuit Sch. Theology Libr., Chgo., 1971-79; coord. serial activities, women's studies bibliographer Loyola U., Chgo., 1979-86; tech. svcs., collection devel. cons. DuPage Libr. Sys., Ill., 1986-91; contract adminstr. Wabash Nat. Fin., Arlington Heights, Ill., 1992-99; founder, dir. Women's Inst. and Gallery, New Harmony, Ind., 2000—. Editor: (bibliography) Current Serials, 1980-85; compiler: (bibliography) Guide to Women's Studies Sources, 1985; author poems; contbr. articles to profl. jours. Bd. dirs. Women's World Ctr., Chgo., 1985—88. Grantee Assn. Theol. Schs. in U.S. and Can., 1976. Mem. ALA, Nat. Mus. Women in Arts, C.G. Jung Inst. Chgo. Roman Catholic. Avocations: poetry, hiking, music. Home: PO Box 373 New Harmony IN 47631-0373

FEINER, FRANCINE, art educator, photographer; b. Bklyn., Nov. 12, 1946; d. Robert and Sarah Shirley Miller; children: Jason Ivan, Gail Arlene. BFA in edn., Pratt Inst., Bklyn., 1968; MS in spl. edn. and elem. edn., Hofstra U., N.Y., 1979. Art dir. Leadership Inst., Hempstead, NY, 1979—87; liason officer students and sch. dist., tchr. art, math. in group homes Juvenile Detention Ctr., Westbury, NY, 1979—87; art educator Uniondale Sch. Dist., NY, 1987—2006; art, math., title I English educator Leadership Tng. Inst., Uniondale Sch. Dist., NY, 1997—2006. Photographer Uniondale Sch. Dist., NY, 1990—2006; team leader Staff Devel. Dept., Uniondale, NY, 2003. Exhibitions include C.W. Post Coll. All County Art Exhibit, African American Mus., Town Hall in Hempstead. Fundraiser Toys for Tots (Marines), Nassau County, 1990—2001; mentor Promoting Positive Self Image, Uniondale, NY, 1999—2001; com. mem. Box Tops for Edn., Uniondale, NY, 2000—06;

fundraiser Victims of Hurricane Katrina, Uniondale, NY, 2005; creator backdrops Uniondale Sch. Dist., NY, 2001—06. Recipient Peace Posters Hon. award, Lion's Club. Mem.: NEA. Avocations: photography, museums, art.

FEINSTEIN, DIANNE, senator; b. San Francisco, June 22, 1933; d. Leon and Betty (Rosenburg) Goldman; m. Bertram Feinstein, Nov. 11, 1962 (dec.); 1 child, Katherine Anne; m. Richard C. Blum, Jan. 20, 1980. BA History, Stanford U., 1955; LLB (hon.), Golden Gate U., 1977; D Pub. Adminstrn. (hon.), U. Manila, 1981; D Pub. Service (hon.), U. Santa Clara, 1981; JD (hon.), Antioch U., 1983, Mills Coll., 1985; LHD (hon.), U. San Francisco, 1988. Fellow Coro Found., San Francisco, 1955-56; with Calif. Women's Bd. Terms and Parole, 1960-66; mem. Mayor's com. on crime, chmn. adv. com. Adult Detention, 1967-69; mem. Bd. Suprs., San Francisco, 1970-78, pres., 1970-71, 74-75, 78; mayor City of San Francisco, 1978-88; US Senator from Calif., 1992—. Mem. exec. com. U.S. Conf. of Mayors, 1983-88; Dem. nominee for Gov. of Calif., 1990; mem. Nat. Com. on U.S.-China Rels.; mem. judiciary com., appropriations com., rules and adminstrn. Com., energy and natural resources com; mem. Coun. Foreign Rels. Mem. Bay Area Conservation and Devel. Commn., 1973-78; mem. Senate Fgn. Rels. Com. Recipient Woman of Achievement award Bus. and Profl. Women's Clubs San Francisco, 1970, Disting. Woman award San Francisco Examiner, 1970, Coro Found. award, 1979, Scopus award Am. Friends Hebrew U., 1981, French Legion of Honor, 1984, Brotherhood/Sisterhood award NCCJ, 1986, Comdr.'s award U.S. Army, 1986, Disting. Civilian award USN, 1987, Coro Leadership award, 1988, Pres. medal U. Calif., San Francisco, 1988, Lifetime Achievement award, Nat. AIDS Found., 1993, Awareness Achievement award, Bd. of Sponsors Breast Cancer Awareness, 1995, Donald Santarelli award, Nat. Orgn. for Victims Assistance, 1996, Congl. Excellence award, MADD, 1997, Paul E. Tsongas award, Lymphoma Rsch. Assn. of Am., 1997, Abraham Lincoln award, Ill. Coun. Against Handgun Violence, 1998, Congl. award, Nat. Assn. Police Orgn., 1999, Celebration of Courage award, Handgun Control, Inc., 1999, Congl. Champion award, Coalition Cancer Rsch., 1999, Winning Spirit award, Women's Info. Network Against Breast Cancer, 2000, Recognition award, Susan G. Komen Breast Cancer Found., 2000, Woodrow Wilson award, Woodrow Wilson Internat. Ctr. Scholars, 2001, Torch of Liberty award, Anti-Defamation League, 2002, Dr. Nathan Davis award, AMA, 2002, Pub. Svc. award, Am. Soc. Hematology, 2003, Leadership award, Alta Med Health Svcs. Corp., 2004, Pat Brown Legacy award, 2004, Lifetime of Idealism award, City Yr., 2004, Legislator of Yr. award, Calif. Sch. Resource Officer's Assn., 2004, Nat. Disting. Advocacy award, Am. Cancer Soc., 2004, Women of Achievement award, Century City Chamber of Commerce, 2004, Friend of Watershed award, Ventura County Assn. of Water Agencies, 2004, Outstanding Mem. US Senate award, Nat. Narcotic Officers Assn. Coalition, 2005; named Number One Mayor All-Pro City Mgmt. Team City and State Mag., 1987, Person of Yr., Nat. Guard Assn. Calif., 1995, Funding Hero, Breast Cancer Rsch. Found., 2004; named one of Congl. Quarterly's Top 50 Mem. of Congress, 2000, Most Powerful Women, Forbes mag., 2005. Mem. Trilateral Commn., Japan Soc. of No. Calif. (pres. 1988-89), Inter-Am. Dialogue, Nat. Com. on U.S.-China Rels. Democrat. Jewish. Office: US Senate 331 Hart Senate Office Bldg Washington DC 20510-0001 also: District Office Ste 2450 One Post Street San Francisco CA 94104 Office Phone: 202-224-3841, 415-393-0707. Office Fax: 202-228-3954, 415-393-0710.*

FEIR, DOROTHY JEAN, entomologist, educator, physiologist; b. St. Louis, Jan. 29, 1929; d. Alex R. and Lillian (Smith) F. BS, U. Mich., 1950; MS, U. Wyo., 1956; PhD, U. Wis., 1960. Instr. biology U. Buffalo, 1960-61; mem. faculty St. Louis U., 1961—, prof. biology, 1967-99, prof. biology emeritus, 1999—. Mem. tropical medicine and parasitology study sect. NIH, 1980-84 Editor Environ. Entomology, 1977-84; mem. editl. bd. Jour. Med. Entomology, 1995-99, chair editl. bd., 1999. Fellow Entomol. Soc. Am. (pres.-elect 1987-88, pres. 1988-89, Riley Achievement award north ctrl. br. 1993), Mo. Acad. Sci. (v.p. 1987-88, pres.-elect 1988-89, pres. 1989-90, Most Disting. Scientist award 1995); mem. AAAS, Am. Physiol. Soc., N.Y. Acad. Sci., Phi Beta Kappa, Sigma Xi. E-mail: feirdj@slu.edu.

FEISTHAMMEL, AUDREY MARIE, museum director, educator; d. William Feisthammel and Amelia Sophia Stein. Master's degree, Western State Coll., Gunnison, Colo., 1953. Cert. profl. acceptance NEA, Calif., prof. emeritus Emeritus Inst. Tchr. Barr H.S. Grand Island (Nebr.) Sch. Dist., 1947—50; tchr. Downey (Calif.) H.S. Downey Sch. Dist., 1955—56; tchr., dist. supr. Earl Warren H.S., Downey, 1956—68; prof. Orange Coast Coll., Costa Mesa, Calif., 1968—86; dir. Grace Dee Mays Mus., LA, 2004—. Dist. supr. home econs. Downey Unified Sch. Dist., 1966—67, devel. trailer concept for vocat. foods occupations, 1968; dir. vocat. edn. Orange Coast Coll., Costa Mesa, 1978—86; author career-related booklets Coast C.C. Dist., Costa Mesa, 1980—86; dir. trailer concept for vocat. edn. occupations Orange Coast Coll., Costa Mesa, 1980—86. Author: (biography) Tribute of Respect Unlock The Past - Improve The Future, (career-related booklets) Educational: In the Home-Energy Matters, Income Tax Incentives, In College - Money Matters, Food Service Training, Safety Manuels, Classroom Instruction Manuals.; contbr. hist. rsch.; author: (book of poems) Tribute. Donator Halstead family home Hist. Soc., Kans., 1988; donator art Grace Dee Mays Mus., Inc., L.A., 2004—06. Recipient Home Beautification award, City of Garden Grove, 1983—2006. Mem.: Nat. Women's History Mus., Nat. Mus. Women in the Arts, Nat. Geographic, Smithsonian Nat. Mus. of the Am. Indian, Order of Amaranth (life; royal matron 1990—91), Lambda Delta Lambda, Order of Ea. Star (life; worthy matron 1984—85). Achievements include development of Power Sewing Vocational Program; design of Vocational Foods Occupations Trailer Concept; development of Vocational Training Program Commercial Food Services. Avocations: collecting, research, photography, writing, poetry.

FEITLOWITZ, MARGUERITE, writer, literary translator; b. Hagerstown, Md., July 14, 1953; d. Robert Daniel and Virginia (Giancola) F.; m. David L. Anderson, Feb. 19, 1984. Student, U. Dijon, France, 1974; BA, Colgate U., 1975. Preceptor expository writing program Harvard U., Cambridge, Mass., 1993-99; prof. lit. Bennington (Vt.) Coll., 2002—. Author: A Lexicon of Terror: Argentina and the Legacies of Torture, 1998; editor, translator: Information for Foreigners: Three Plays by Griselda Gambaro, 1992; translator: Theatre Pieces: An Anthology by Liliane Atlan, 1985; contbr. articles to newspapers, mags. and profl. jours. Mary Ingram Bunting fellow, 1992-93; Fulbright scholar, Argentina, 1990, 98-99; grantee Marion and Jasper Whiting award, Boston, 1995; Fulbright Sr. Scholar, Argentina, 1999; Harvard Faculty Rsch. grantee, 1998. Mem. PEN, Authors Guild, Am. Literary Translators Assn., Latin Am. Studies Assn., Amnesty Internat. Democrat. Jewish. Office: Bennington Coll One Coll Dr Bennington VT 05201 Office Phone: 802-760-7574. Business E-Mail: mfeitlowitz@bennington.edu.

FELD, CAROLE LESLIE, marketing executive; b. L.A., Nov. 12, 1955; d. Harold Brenman and Phyllis Pearl (Fishman) F.; m. David C. Levy; 1 child, Alexander Wolf Levy. BA, U. Calif., Berkeley, 1979; MBA, U. So. Calif., 1982. Mgr. rsch. Columbia Pictures, L.A., 1982—83; dir. promotion and field pub. Tri-Star Pictures, N.Y.C., 1983—86; dir. promotion and retention mktg. Home Box Office, N.Y.C., 1987—92; v.p. promotion and advt. Pub. Broadcasting Svc., Washington, 1992—97, sr. v.p. advt., promotion and corp. comm., 1995—99, sr. v.p. comm. and brand mgmt., 1999—2000; v.p. brand mktg. The Motley Fool, Washington, 2000—01, mktg. cons., 2002—03; prin. Giving Tree Group, Washington, 2003—. Pres. CINE; cons. New Sch. Beacons in Jazz Program, N.Y.C., 1990—. Named one of Mktgs. Top 100 Advertising Age, 1995. Achievements include creator "PBS Kids" brand. Avocations: skiing, travel, art, films. Office Phone: 202-415-2669. Business E-Mail: carole@givingtreegroup.com.

FELD, KAREN IRMA, columnist, journalist, commentator, speech professional; b. Washington, Aug. 23; d. Irvin and Adele Ruth (Schwartz) F. BA, Am. U., 1969. Columnist, reporter Roll Call Newspaper, Washington; coord. nat. pub. rels. Ringling Bros./Barnum & Bailey Circus, Washington; publicist Twentieth Century Fox, L.A.; pub. rels. account exec. Harshe, Rotman & Druck, L.A.; freelance writer, broadcaster; corr. People mag., Washington, 1980—85; adj. instr. Polit. Campaign Mgmt. Inst. Kent State U., 1981; broadcaster Voice Am., 1984; columnist, contbg. editor Capitol Hill mag., Washington, 1980—89; columnist Washington Times, 1986—87, Universal Press Syndicate, 1988—89, Creators Syndicate, 1989—90; syndicated columnist Capital Connections, 1990—; Prodigy polit. columnist, 1990—93. Radio/TV commentator syndicated radio segment Radio America, 1993-04; syndicated columnist Nat. Post, 1998-99; Washington editor Delta Shuttle Sheet, 2000-05; columnist Washington Examiner, 2005-06; lectr. in field, 1990—. Contbr. articles to Parade mag., People mag., Money mag., Time mag., Vogue mag., George, USA Weekend, Family Circle, others. Recipient Health Journalism award Am. Chiropractic Assn., 1991. Mem. AFTRA/SAG, Nat. Fedn. Press Women (Excellence in Journalism award 1984-06), Capital Press Women (v.p. 1985-91, Excellence in Journalism award 1984-05), Am. Soc. Journalists and Authors (award), N.Am. Travel Journalists Assn. (Best Mag. Feature award 2003), Nat. Press Club, Capitol Hill Club, Woodmont Country Club (Rockville, Md.), U.S. Senate Press Gallery, White House Corr. Assn., Soc. Profl. Journalists (bd. dirs., v.p. chpt., Editl. Writing award 2004), SDX Found. (bd. dirs.) Jewish. Office: 1698 32nd St NW Washington DC 20007-2969 Office Phone: 202-337-2044. Personal E-mail: news@karenfeld.com.

FELDEN, TAMARA, German language educator, translator; b. Niederdorfelden, Hesse, Fed. Republic of Germany, Dec. 23, 1953; came to U.S., 1977; d. Franz Joseph and Maria Josepha (Weiand) Noha; m. David John Archibald, 1975 (div. 1995); children: David Alexander, Mark Allan, Natalie Ann. AA, Steilacoom Community Coll., 1980; BA, U. Md., 1983, MA, 1984, PhD, 1990. Cert. translator. Grad. teaching asst. U. Md., College Park, 1983-85; instr. Allan Hancock Coll., Santa Maria, Calif., 1987-89; asst. prof. Augustana Coll., Rock Island, Ill., 1990-97; internat. student program coord. Black Hawk Coll., Moline, Ill., 1997—2005; dir. internat. affairs U. Chgo., 2003—. Author: Frauen Reisen, 1990; contbr. articles to profl. jours. Co-founder, v.p. local chpt. NOW, Lompoc, Calif., 1989-90; mem. NAACP, NOW, Amnesty Internat. and others. Recipient Faculty Rsch. grants Augustana Coll., 1991, 96, Augustana Rsch. Found. grant, 1993. Mem. MLA, Am. Assn. Tchrs. German, Coalition of Women in German, N.Am. Heine Soc., Soc. for German-Am. Studies, German Studies Assn., Midwest MLA. Democrat. Avocations: reading, gardening, restoring antique furniture, travel, discussions with friends and students. Office: U Chgo Office Internat Affairs 1414 East 59th St Chicago IL 60637

FELDER-HOEHNE, FELICIA HARRIS, librarian, researcher; b. Knoxville, Tenn. d. Henry Thomas and Luvilla Tate Harris. BS in English, Knoxville Coll., 1958; MS in Libr. Sci., Atlanta U., 1966; postgrad., U. Tenn., 1972—78. English tchr. McMinn County Schs., J.L. Cook Sch., Athens, Tenn., 1958—60; adminstrv. asst. Knoxville (Tenn.) Coll., 1960—63, adminstrv. asst. to the dir. pub. rels., 1963—65; grad. libr. asst. Trevor Arnett Libr., Atlanta U., 1965—66; head circulation and reserve svcs. Alumni Libr. Knoxville Coll., 1966—69; tchr., libr. summer study skills program United Presbyn. Ch., Bd. Nat. Missions, Knoxville Coll., 1967—68; prof., reference libr. John C. Hodges Libr. U. Tenn., Knoxville, 1969—. Founder, dir. LARKS: Librs. Linking with At-Risk Students, Knoxville, 1997—; prin. rschr. The George Washington Carver DVD Project, 2003. Author: A Subject Guide to Basic Reference Books in Black Studies; co-author: (online ency.) Project TAPP: Tennesse Authors Past and Present, 1999—; contbr. Notable Black American Women, Book I, Notable Black American Women, Book II, Behavioral & Social Sciences Librarian;, author poems; contbr. articles to profl. jours. Adv. bd. Mentoring Acad. for Boys, Knoxville, 1997—; sec. to bd. Ctr. for Neighborhood Devel., Knoxville, 2000—02; dir. pub. rels. Concerned Assn. Residents East, Knoxville, 1988—90; active Tenn. Valley Energy Coalition, Knoxville, 1988—90, Town Hall East, Knoxville, 1988—, Save Our Cumberland Mountains, Tenn., 1988—; religious task force World's Fair, Knoxville Internat. Energy Exposition, 1982; pres. Spring Place Neighborhood Assn., Knoxville, 1980—; pk. vol. Knox County Pk. Vol. Corps., 2003—; land devel. com. Knoxville Farmer's Mkt., 2004—05; cmty. action com. Leadership Class 2005; active West End Acad. Outreach, 1989—, Solutions to Issues of Concern to Knoxvillians, 1999—, Tribe One, 2000—, Safety City Outreach of Knoxville PD, 2004—, Cmty. Action Com. Leadership Class, 2005, Teen Challenge, 1985—; bd. dirs. Knoxville-Knox County Libr., 1971—77, sec. to bd., 1972—77; bd. dirs. Ctr. for Neighborhood Devel., Knoxville, 1998—2002, UT Fed. Credit Union, Knoxville, 1984—89; adv. bd. dirs. Knox County Parks and Recreation, 2004—; adv. bd. dirs. Bd. Probation and Parole State of Tenn., Knoxville, 2003—; mem. YWCA, YMCA. Named Citizen of Yr., Order of Ea. Star, 2004, in her honor Dedicated Svc. Meml. Pk. Bench, Knox County Pks. and Recreation Dept., Mayor Mike Ragsdale, 2006; named one of Outstanding Young Women of Am., 1967; named to U. Tenn. African Am. Hall Fame, 1994; recipient Cert. of Merit for Contbns. to Edn., Jack and Jill, Inc., 1976, Plaque of Appreciation, Interdenominational Concert Choir, 1976, Religious Svc. award, NCCJ, 1976, Citizen of the Yr. award, Order of the Ea. Star Prince Hall Masons, 1979, Cert. of Appreciation, Knoxville's Internat. Energy Exposition, 1982, Pub. Svc. award, U. Tenn. Nat. Alumni Assn., 1984, Habitat for Humanity award, 1992, Merit award for outstanding achievement, City of Knoxville, Mayor Ashe, 1994, The Humanitarian Libr. Spirit award, 1994, Spl. Svc. commendation, Mayor Victor Ashe, 1994, Spirit award, The Miles 500 Libr., 1994, 1999, 2005, Citation for Svc., Knoxville Police Dept., 1998, Cmty. Cornerstone award, Knoxville News-Sentinel, 1998, Harold B. Love Outstanding Cmty. Involvement award, Tenn. Higher Edn. Commn., 2003, The Vol. Spirit award, U. Tenn., 2003, Plaque of Appreciation, U. Tenn. Fed. Credit Union, 2004, Sincerity Disting. Libr. award, Daily Beacon, 2004, Hardy Liston Symbol of Hope award, U. Tenn., 2006. Mem.: LWV, NAACP, ALA, Nat. Mus. Women in the Arts (charter), East Tenn. Libr. Assn., Tenn. Libr. Assn., Knoxville Opera Guild, Met. Opera Guild, Knoxville Opera Co. (bd. dirs. 1999—2005), Character Counts Orgn., Dogwood Arts Festival (charter), Beck Cultural Exch. Ctr. (charter), Citizens Police Acad. Alumni Assn., Alpha Kappa Alpha. Achievements include first to first African American librarian hired at the University of Tennesse campus and faculty. Avocations: community service, music, poetry, theater. Office: 152M John C Hodges Libr 1015 Volunteer Blvd Knoxville TN 37996-1000 Office Phone: 865-974-0018. Business E-Mail: ffelder@utk.edu.

FELDERMAN, LENORA I., physician; b. N.Y.C., July 17, 1952; d. Ephraim Jacob and Sylvia (Farber) F.; children: Alexandra Danielle, Johnathan Reed MD, N.Y. Med. Coll., 1981. Diplomate Am. Bd. Dermatology. Resident in dermatology Albert Einstein Med. Ctr., Bronx, 1982-85; resident in internal medicine Montefiore Hosp., Bronx, N.Y., 1981-82, assoc. attending dermatologist, 1985-97, Lenox Hill Hosp., N.Y.C., 1985—; asst. prof. medicine/dermatology Albert Einstein Coll. Medicine, N.Y.C., 1985-97, Cornell U. Med. Coll., 1998—. Speaker on dermatology and skin care. Contbr. articles to profl. jours. Bd. dirs. Variety Children's Charity. Recipient Am. Women's Med. Assn. award, 1985, Pathology award N.Y. Med. Coll., 1985. Fellow Am. Acad. Dermatology, Internat. Soc. Dermatology, Soc. Pediatric Dermatology; mem. AMA, Dermatology Soc. Greater N.Y., Med. Soc. State N.Y., New York County Med. Soc., Alpha Omega Alpha. Avocations: reading, design, skiing, dance, bicycling. Office: 1317 3rd Ave New York NY 10021-2995 Office Phone: 212-734-0091.

FELDHAMER, THELMA LEAH, architect; b. Bklyn., May 10, 1925; d. Frank and Anna Pearl (Shapiro) Sitzer; m. Carl Feldhamer, Aug. 27, 1950 (dec. Apr. 1990); children: Raquel Alexander, Mark David. BArch, Cooper Union for Advancement, Sci. and Arts, 1978. Registered architect, Colo. Prin. Thelma Feldhamer, P.C. Aia Architect, Denver, 1980—. Active Pres. Council of Denver; pres.-elect to Colo. State Drafting Tech. Com. State Bd. Community Colls. and Occupational Edn., City and County of Denver Dept. Pub. Works Affirmative Action Office and Goals com. Lt. col., pers. officer Colo. Wing, CAP, Lowry AFB, 1979—. Lt. col., pers. officer Colo. Wing, CAP, Lowry AFB, 1979—. Mem. adv. bd. Emily Griffith Opportunity Sch.; vol. Denver Dumb Friend League, 1994—; pres. nat. women's com. Brandeis U., 1998—; treas. Denver chpt. Hadassah, 1996—. Mem. AIA, Women in Architecture (Denver chpt.), Bus. and Profl. Women's Club, Denver, Inc. (pres. 1974-76, 89-90, treas. 1987-89, 91—), Denver C. of C., Altrusa Club (wd v.p., bd. dirs. Denver 1984), El Mejdel Temple, Daus. of Nile. Democrat. Jewish.

FELDHUSEN, HAZEL JEANETTE, elementary school educator; b. Camp Douglas, Wis., Feb. 20, 1928; d. Vincent O. and Helen (Johnson) Artz; m. John F. Feldhusen, Dec. 18, 1954; children: Jeanne V., Anne M. B, U. Wis., 1965; M, Purdue U., 1968; postgrad., U. Wis. Tchr. Suldal Sch., Mauston, Wis., 1947-50, Lake Geneva (Wis.) Schs., 1950-55, West Lafayette (Ind.) Schs., 1965-91. Presenter World Conf., Hamburg, 1985, Juneau (Alaska) Schs., 1986, Vancouver (B.C., Can.) Schs., 1990, Norfolk (Va.) Schs., 1991, Taiwan Nat. U., 1992, U. New South Wales, Sydney, Australia, 1993, New Zealand Schs., Auckland, 1993; 2d Nat. Conf. Gifted, Taiwan, 1992, Sarasota, Fla., 1998. Author: Individualized Teaching of the Gifted, 1993, 2d edit., 1997; contbr. chpts. to books, articles to profl. jours. Mem. Tchr. of Yr. Com., West Lafayette, 1988. Recipient Outstanding Tchr. award Tchrs. Am., 1974, Appreciation award U. Stellenbosch, 1984, Appreciation award Australian Assn. for the Gifted, 1987; winner Golden Apple Tchg. award Greater Lafayette C. of C., 1989, Disting. Alumnus award Purdue U., 1996. Mem. NEA, Ind. State Tchrs. Assn., West Lafayette Edn. Assn. (Outstanding Achievement award 1984), Phi Delta Kappa, Delta Kappa Gamma (v.p 1983-85). Avocations: reading, interior decorating. Home: Sarasota Bay Club 1301 N Tamiami Apt 205 Sarasota FL 34236 Personal E-mail: feldhusenjf@aol.com.

FELDMAN, ARLENE BUTLER, aviation industry executive; BA cum laude in Polit. Sci., U. Colo., 1975; JD, Temple U. Sch. Law, 1978. Supervising atty. U.S. Railway Assn., Phila., 1977-82; dir. divsn. aeronautics N.J. Dept. Transp., Trenton, 1982-84; from acting dir. to dep. dir. tech. ctr. FAA, Atlantic City, N.J., 1984-86, dep. dir. Western-Pacific region Exec. Sch. L.A., 1986-87, dep. dir. Western-Pacific region, 1986-87, regional adminstr. N.Eng. Region Burlington, Mass., 1988-94, exec. sch., 1986-87, eastern regional adminstr. Jamaica, N.Y., 1994—. Panelist, guest spkr. Women in Aviation Conf., 1992, 93; vice-chair N.Y. Fed. Exec. Bd.; chairperson regional airport sys. planning adv. com. Delaware Valley Regional Planning Commn.; founder rotorcraft R&D forum FAA. Chairwoman Boston Federal Exec. Bd. Saving Bond, 1993; mem. adv. bd. U. So. Calif. Recipient Presdl. Meritorius Rank award Sr. Exec. Svc., Disting. Svc. award N.J. Aviation Hall of Fame, Amelia Earhart medal; inducted N.J. Aviation Hall of Fame, 1997. Mem. ABA, Ninety-Nines Internat. Orgn. (Earhart medal), Lawyer/Pilot Bar Assn., Air Traffic Control Assn. (dir., exec. bd., conf. panel moderator 1993, 91, spkr. 1993, chmn. bd. 1996, chmn. elect 1997), Am. Assn. Airport Execs., Am. Assn. State Hwy. and Transp. Ofcls., Am. Helicopter Soc., Helicopter Assn. Internat. (hon.), Nat. Assn. State Aviation Ofcls., Nat. Coun. Women in Aviation Aerospce, Internat. Aviation Women's Assn., Profl. Women Contrs., Inc. (1st hon. mem.), Wings Club N.Y.C. (bd. govs. 1996), Pi Sigma Alpha. Office: FAA 1 Aviation Plz Jamaica NY 11434

FELDMAN, CECILE ARLENE, dean, dental educator; b. NYC, Oct. 8, 1959; d. Melvin and Claire (Halpern) F.; m. Harry Kenneth Zohn, Aug. 19, 1984. BA, U. Pa., 1980, DMD, 1984, MBA, 1985. Asst. prof. U. Pa. Sch. Medicine, 1985—88, NJ Dental School, U. Medicine & Dentistry NJ, Newark, 1988—98, prof. dept. gen. dentistry and cmty. health, 1998—, acting to interim dean, 1999—2001, dean, 2001—. Cons., author in field; leadership inst. fellow Am. Dental Edn. Assn., 1988; adj. prof. dept. dental care systems U. Pa., sr. adj. fellow Leonard Davis Inst. Health Econs., Wharton Sch. Fellow Acad. Gen. Dentistry, Internat. Coll. Dentists, Am. Coll. Dentists; mem. ADA, Am. Assn. Dental Schs., Internat. Assn. Dental Rsch., Am. Assn. Pub. Health Dentistry, Am. Med. Informatics Assn., N.J. Dental Assn. Office: NJ Dental Sch 110 Bergen St Newark NJ 07103-2400 Office Phone: 973-972-4634. Office Fax: 973-972-3689. Business E-Mail: feldman@umdnj.edu.*

FELDMAN, CLARICE ROCHELLE, lawyer; b. Milw., Dec. 2, 1941; d. Harry and Beatrice (Hiken) Wagan; m. Howard J. Feldman, July 11, 1965; 1 child, David Lewis. BS, U. Wis., 1963, LL.B., 1965. Bar: Wis. 1965, D.C. 1969, Md. 1984. Appellate atty. NLRB, Washington, 1965—69; co-counsel to Joseph A. Yablonski, Washington, 1969; atty. Washington research project Clark Coll., 1970-72; asso. gen. counsel United Mine Workers Am., Washington, 1972-74; partner Becker, Channell, Becker & Feldman, Washington, 1974-76, Becker & Feldman, 1976-77; gen. counsel Ams. for Energy Independence, Washington, 1978-80; atty. Office of Spl. Investigations, Dept. Justice, 1980-84; pvt. practice law Washington, 1984-98; atty. pro bono, 1999—. Trustee Washington Internat. Sch., 1987-98; advisor Assn. Union Democracy. Mem. Wis., D.C., Md. bar assns. Republican. Jewish. Home: 4455 29th St NW Washington DC 20008-2307

FELDMAN, ELAINE BOSSAK, medical nutritionist, educator; b. NYC, Dec. 9, 1926; d. Solomon and Frances Helen (Fania) Nevler Bossak; m. Herman Black, Dec. 23, 1951 (div. 1957); 1 child, Mitchell Evan; m. Daniel S. Feldman, July 19, 1957 (dec. June 2005); children: Susan, Daniel S. Jr. AB magna cum laude, NYU, 1945, MS, 1948, MD, 1951. Diplomate Am. Bd. Internal Medicine, Nat. Bd. Med. Examiners; cert. in Clin. Nutrition. Rotating intern Mt. Sinai Hosp., N.Y.C., 1951-52, resident in pathology, 1952, asst. resident, 1953, fellow in medicine, resident in metabolism, 1954-55, rsch. asst. in medicine, 1955-58, clin. asst. physician Diabetes Clinic, 1957; asst. vis. physician Kings County Hosp., Bklyn., 1958-66, assoc. vis. physician, 1966-72; asst. attending physician Maimonides Hosp., Bklyn., 1960-68; spl. fellow USPHS Dept. of Physiol. Chemistry U. of Lund, Sweden, 1964-65; attending physician Eugene Talmadge Meml. Hosp., Augusta, Ga., 1972-92, Univ. Hosp., Augusta, 1972-92, cons., 1973; prof. medicine Med. Coll. Ga., Augusta, 1972-92, prof. emeritus, 1992—, chief sect. of nutrition, 1977-92, chief emeritus, 1992—, acting chief sect. of metabolic/endocrine disease, 1980-81, prof. physiology and endocrinology, 1988-92, prof. emeritus physiology and endocrinology, 1992—; instr. medicine SUNY Downstate Med. Ctr., 1957-59, asst. prof. medicine, 1959-68, assoc. prof. medicine, 1968-72. Tchg. fellow dept. zoology U. Wis. Grad. Sch., 1945-46, dept. biology NYU Grad. Sch., 1946-47; cons. N.Y.-N.J. Regional Ctr. for Clin. Nutrition Edn., 1983-92; vis. prof. and Harvey lectr. Northeastern Ohio Sch. Medicine, Youngstown, 1985; cons., vis. prof. U. Nev. Sch. Medicine (NCI grant), 1989-94; mem. nat. adv. com. nutrition fellowship program Nat. Med. Fellowship Inc., 1988-95; dir. Ga. Inst. Human Nutrition, 1978-92, dir. emeritus, 1992—; dir. Clin. Nutrition Rsch. Unit, 1980-86; mem. med. nutrition curriculum initiative adv. bd. U. N.C., Chapel Hill, 1992-2001; advisor ednl. materials Am. Inst. Cancer Rsch., 1997—. Author: Essentials of Clinical Nutrition, 1988; (with others) Conference on Biological Activities of Steroids in Relation to Cancer, 1969, Nicotinic Acid, 1964, The Menopausal Syndrome, 1974, Hyperlipidemia, Medcom Special Studies, 1974, Medcom Famous Teaching in Modern Medicine, 1979, Harrison's Principles of Internal Medicine, 1980, Health Promotion: Principles and Clinical Applications, 1982, The Encyclopedic Handbook of Alcoholism, 1982, The Climacteric in Perspective, 1986, Selenium in Biology and Medicine, Part A., 1987, Medicine for the Practicing Physician, 1988, Clinical Chemistry of Laboratory Animals, 1989, Ency. Human Biology, 1991, Laboratory Medicine: The Selection and Interpretation of Clinical Laboratory Studies, 1993, Modern Nutrition in Health and Diseases, 1994, Nutrition Assessment-A Comprehensive Guide for Planning Intervention, 1995, The Women's Complete Healthbook, 1995, The American Medical Women's Association's Guide to Nutrition and Wellness, 1996, Normal Nutrition and Therapeutics, 1996, Handbook of Nutrition and Food, 2001; editor: Nutrition and Cardiovascular Disease, 1976, Nutrition in the Middle and Later Years, 1983 (paperback edit. 1986), Nutrition and Heart Disease, 1983, Handbook of Nutrition and Food, 2001, 2nd edit., 2006, Human Nutrient Needs in the Life Cycle, 2001; mem. editl. adv. bd. Contemporary Issues in Clin. Nutrition, 1980-92; mem. edit. bd. Am. Jour. Clin. Nutrition, 1983-91, 92-98, Jour. Clin. Endocrinology and Metabolism, 1984-88, MidPoint: Counseling Women through Menopause, 1984-85, Jour. Nutrition, 1985-89; cons. editor Jour. Am. Coll. Nutrition, 1982-94; mem. edit. bd. Complementary Med. for the Physician, 1996-2000; contbg. editor Nutrition Rev., 1997-2002; mem. editl. bd. Nutrition Today, 1999—;

reviewer Jour. Lipid Rsch., Biochm. Pharmacology, Sci., The Physiologist, Jour. Am. Acad. Dermatology, Israel Jour. Med. Scis., N.Y. State Jour. Medicine, Jour. of Nutrition Edn., Jour. Am. Dietetic Assn., Am. Jour. Medicine, Am. Jour. Med. Sci., So. Med. Jour., Jour. AMA, Jour. NCI; contbr. more than 175 articles to profl. jours; presenter in field. Mem. tech. adv. com. for sci. and edn. Rsch. Grants Program, Human Nutrition Grants Peer Panel, USDA, 1982, mem. bd. sci. counselors human nutrition; Community Svc. Block Grant Discretionary Program Panel; vice chmn. Urban and Rural Econ. Devel. Panel, Dept. HHS, 1982, grant reviewer, 1983; mem ad hoc and spl. rev. coms. and groups NIH, 1979-93, mem. nutrition study sect., 1976-80; mem. Rev. Panel Nat. Nutrition Objectives, Life Scis. Rev. Office, Fed. Am. Socs. Exptl. Biology, 1985-86; mem. subcom. Women's Health Trial Nat. Cancer Inst., 1987, mem. bd. sci. counselors cancer prevention and control program, 1990-94; mem. adv. com. Clin. Nutrition Rsch. Unit, U. Ala., 1986-94, Ga. Nutrition Steering Com., 1974-75, Ctrl. Savannah River Area Nutrition Project Coun. 1974-75, ednl. adv. com. Health Central, 1980; mem. geriatrics and gerontology rev. com. Nat. Inst. on Aging, 1986-90; breast cancer initiative peer rev. Dept. of Def., 1997, 98. N.Y. Heart Assn. rsch. fellow, 1955—57. Fellow Am. Heart Assn. Coun. on Atherosclerosis (nominating com. 1978, chmn. nominating com., mem. exec. com. 1979-80, Spl. Recognition award 1995), Am. Inst. Nutrition (grad. nutrition edn. com. 1980-83, 89-93); mem. Am. Coll. Nutrition (chmn. com. pub. affairs), Am. Soc. for Clin. Nutrition (com. on nutrition edn. 1982, chmn. subcom. on nutrition edn. in med. schs. 1983-84, chmn. com. on med./dental residency edn., 1985-87, com. on subsplty. tng. 1988-92, nominating com. 1982, 90, chair nominating com. 1994, com. on clin. practice issues in health and disease 1989-92, Nat. Dairy Coun. award 1991, rep. coun. acad. socs. 1990-96, membership com. 1996-2005, chair 1999, 2000), Fedn. Am. Socs. Exptl. Biology. Am. Oil Chemists Soc., Am. Physiol. Soc., Endocrine Soc., Soc. Exptl. Biology and Medicine, So. Soc. Clin. Investigation, Am. Diabetes Assn., Am. Fedn. Clin. Rsch., Am. Gastroent. Assn., AMA (Joseph B. Goldberger award 1990), Am. Med. Women's Assn. (profl. resources com. 1975-76, med. edn. and rsch. fund com. 1976-79, chmn. 1978-90, chmn. student liaison subcom. of membership com. 1981-84, pres. Br. 51, Augusta 1977-80, treas. 1980-97, Calcium Nutrition Edn. award 1991, CSRA Girl Scout Women of Excellence award 1994), Am. Soc. Parenteral and Enteral Nutrition, Am. Heart Assn. (Ga. affiliate, nutrition com., chmn. sci. session for nutritionists, 1978, chmn. nutrition com. 1979-90, mem. long range planning com. 1980-81, rsch. com. 1980-83, bd. dirs. 1987-90, profl. edn. task force, 1988-89), Richmond Country Med. Assn., Augusta Opera Assn. (bd. dirs. 1973-2002, 06-, recording sec. 1973-74, pres. 1974-75, coord. audience devel. 1975-77, at-large exec. com. 1994-96, chair nominating com. 1994-96, corr. sec. 1998-99, 1st v.p. 1999-2000, chair search com., gen. dir. 2002), Augusta Sailing Club (women's com. 1973), Greater Augusta Arts Coun. (Arts Festival Collage 1982 chmn. promotion and publicity com., Festival coms. 1983-86, 89-93, 95, 96, 98, 99, bd. dirs. 1984-94, Vol. of the Yr., 2001), Gertrude Herbert Inst. Art (bd. dirs. 1987-92), Authors Club Augusta, Philomathic Club (sec. 1999-2001), Phi Beta Kappa, Sigma Xi (chpt. sec. 1982-83, pres. elect 1983-84, pres. 1984-85), Alpha Omega Alpha. Avocations: opera, wine tasting, travel. Home: 4275 Owens Rd Apt 1222 Evans GA 30809 Personal E-mail: efeldman17@comcast.net.

FELDMAN, ELISE, lawyer; b. Wilmington, Del., Mar. 27, 1973; BA, Columbia U., N.Y.C., 1995; JD, NYU, N.Y.C., 2000. Bar: N.Y. 2001. Asst. to the pres. ACLU, N.Y.C., 1995—96; Americorps Vista staff Cmty. Impact, N.Y.C., 1996—97; jud. clk. Chambers of Hon. Elliott Wilk, N.Y.C., 2000—01; assoc. Friedman & Wolf, N.Y.C., 2001—. Singer: (choral singing) St. Cecilia Chorus. Vol. 20s/ 30s com., Congregation Beth Simchat Torah, N.Y.C., 2003—06. Grantee Pub. Interest grantee, NYU Sch. of Law, 1999; scholar Root-Tilden-Kern scholar, 1997—2000, Paul Rapoport Meml. scholar, Lesbian Bisexual Gay Cmty. Svcs. Ctr., 1997. Mem.: ABA. Avocations: rock climbing, travel, rugby. Office: Friedman & Wolf 1500 Broadway Ste 2300 New York NY 10036 Office Phone: 212-354-4500.

FELDMAN, EVA LUCILLE, neurology educator; b. N.Y.C., Mar. 30, 1952; d. George Franklin and Margherita Enriceta (Cafiero) F.; children: Laurel, Scott, John Jr. BA in Biology and Chemistry, Earlham Coll., 1973; MS in Zoology, U. Notre Dame, 1975; PhD in Neurosci., U. Mich., 1979, MD, 1983. Diplomate Am. Bd. Neurology; lic. med. practitioner, Mich. Instr. dept. neurology U. Mich., Ann Arbor, 1987-88, asst. prof. neurology, 1988-94, mem. faculty Cancer Ctr., 1992-2000, assoc. prof. neurology, 1994-2000, prof., 2000—, Russell N. DeJong prof. neurology, 2004—. Mem. faculty neurosci. program U. Mich., Mich. Diabetes Rsch. and Tng., Ann Arbor, 1988—; dir. JDRF Ctr. for the Study of Complications in Diabetes. Contbr. chpts. to books, articles to profl. jours. Grantee, NIH, 1989, 1994, 1997, 1998, 2001, 2003, Juvenile Diabetes Rsch. Found., 1994, 1997, 1999, 2001, Am. Diabetes Assn., 2005. Achievements include research on the elucidation of the role of growth factors in the pathogenesis of human disease. Office Phone: 734-763-7274.

FELDMAN, FRANCES, retired social worker; b. Hudson, N.Y., May 22, 1932; d. Abraham and Anna (Bendit) Finkelstein; m. Albert Feldman, Feb. 20, 1955 (dec.); children: Jeffrey, Randy, Debra, David. BA, Syracuse U., 1953; MSW, Wurzweiler Sch. of Social Work, N.Y.C., 1984. Cert. social worker. Group worker Jewish Community Ctr./Essex County, Newark, N.J., 1953-55; dir. social work Peekskill (N.Y.) Community Hosp., 1971—99; ret., 1999. Pres. 1st Hebrew Congregation, Peekskill, 1984-86.

FELDMAN, HELAINE, editor, public relations associate; b. Bklyn., June 22, 1937; d. Joseph H. and Ruth Levine; m. Chester Feldman, Aug. 6, 1961; children: Jeffrey, David. BS, Syracuse Univ., Syracuse, NY, 1958. Assoc. editor Dick Moore & Assoc., Inc., New York, NY, 1966—, sr. assoc., 1966—. Contbg. editor: (newsletter) Equity News, 1975, Aftra Mag., 1990. Mem.: Drama Desk, Coalition of Profl. Women in the Arts & Media, League of Profl. Theatre Women. Home: 144-09 Coolidge Ave Briarwood NY 11435 Office: Dick Moore & Assoc 165 W 46th St New York NY 10036 Office Phone: 212-719-9570. E-mail: helfel22@aol.com.

FELDMAN, JACQUELINE, retired small business owner; b. Bklyn., May 21, 1936; d. Emanuel L. and Tillie Rappon; m. Gerald D. Feldman (dec.); children: Bruce G., Lee A. Owner Sweet Stop Inc., Staten Is., NY, 1978—86; purchasing agent Va. Med. Ctr., Bklyn., 1971—78. Mem. arts and culture bd. City of Pembroke Pines, Fla., 1990—94; vol., bd. mem. Deborah Heart, Pembrooke Pines, 1999—2006. Mem.: Half Century Club (pres., founder 1993—2000). Democrat. Jewish. Home: 1151 SW 128 Ter #D405 Pembroke Pines FL 33027

FELDMAN, JACQUELINE MAUS, psychiatrist, educator; b. Omaha, Dec. 29, 1953; 2 children. BS, U. Iowa, Iowa City, 1976; student in Psychology and Behavioral Genetics, U. Tex., Austin, 1976—79; MD, U. Tex., Houston, 1983. Lic. physician N.C. Bd. Med. Examiners, 1985, diplomate Am. Bd. Psychiatry and Neurology, 1988, lic. physician Ala., 1990. Resident psychiatry Duke U. Med. Ctr., Durham, NC, 1983—87, chief resident Duke Inpatient Psychiatry, 1986—87, exec. chief resident psychiatry, 1986—87; psychiatric cons. Mental Health Clinic VA Med. Ctr., Durham, NC, 1987—90; dir. Emergency Psychiatry Svcs. Duke U. Med. Ctr., Durham, 1987—90, med. dir. Gen. Open Adult Psychiatric Unit, 1987—90, clin. assoc. psychiatry, 1987—90; from asst. prof. to prof. psychiatry U. Ala., 1990—2000, Patrick H. Linton prof. psychiatry, 2000—, med. dir. Cmty. Psychiatry Program, 1990—, dir. Divsn. Pub. Psychiatry, 1991—, exec. dir. Comprehensive Cmty. Mental Health Ctr., 1991—. Emergency physician Guilford County Mental Health Ctr., Greensboro, NC, 1985—89; bd. dirs. Ctr. Rsch. Women's Health U. Ala., mem. numerous coms.; adv. com. Ala. Dept. Corrections, 1995—; reviewer jours. in field; cons. in field. Contbr. articles to profl. jours. Named Outstanding Pub. Sector Psychiatrist, Ala. Alliance Mentally Ill, 1998, Outstanding Psychiatry Faculty, U. Ala., 2005; named one of Best Doctors in Am., 1998, 2004; fellow, Hedwig van Amerigen Exec. Leadership Medicine Program, 2001; grantee, Civitan Internat. Rsch., 1992—94, Cmty. Mental Health Svcs., 1993—97, Abbott Labs., 1993—95, Zeneca Pharm., 1995—96, Aetna Academic Forum, 1998—2000, Johnson & Johnson, 2002—. Mem.: So. Psychiat. Assn., Nat. Alliance Mentally Ill, Group Advancement Psychiatry (com. psychiatry and the cmty.), Birmingham (Ala.) Psychiat. Soc. (pres. 1995—96), Birmingham (Ala.) AllianceMentally Ill, Assn. Women Psychiatrists, Am. Psychiat. Assn. (com. comml. support 1999—2003), Am. Assn. Psychiat. Adminstrs., Am. Assn. Cmty. Psychiatrists (nat. bd. dirs. 1996—, pres. 2000—04, past pres. 2004—), Ala. Psychiat. Soc., Ala. Coun. Mental Health Bds., Am. Psychiat. Found. (bd. dirs. 2001—). Office: Cmty Psychiatry Program Univ Ala 908 20th St S 4 CCB Birmingham AL 35294-2050

FELDMAN, JANIE LYNN, psychologist; b. Perth Amboy, N.J., Apr. 9, 1964; d. Nicholas and Mae Feldman; m. Michael Brian Lehner, June 11, 1989; children: Samantha Fay Lehner, Nicole Melanie Lehner, Rachel Lee Lehner. BA, U. Del., Newark, Del., 1986; MA, Yeshiva U., Bronx, N.Y., 1992, D Psychology, 1992. Lic. Psychologist NJ Bd. of Psychol. Examiners, cert. Sch.Psychologist NJ Dept. of Edn. Psychotherapist Newark Beth Israel Med. Ctr., Newark; sch. psychologist Bernards Twp. Pub. Schs., Basking Ridge, NJ; psychologist Watchung Psychol. Associates, Watchung, NJ, 1992—2002; psychologist in pvt. practice Warren, NJ, 2002—; dir., psychologist in pvt. practice Mountain Psychol. Group, Warren, NJ, 2004—. Cable tv show guest appearances Real Life With Mary Amoroso, Union, NJ. Special guest appearance (live cable TV talk show) Real Life With Mary Amoroso: Terrorist Attack, Sept. 11, 2001, (live cable television talk show) Real Life With Mary Amoroso: Surviving the Affair, Real Life With Mary Amoroso: Are You Raising a Brat?, Real Life With Mary Amoroso: Women's Aggression/Women Trashing Women. Mem. AAUW, Warren, NJ. Mem.: APA, NJ. Psychol. Assn. Achievements include Established pvt. psychol. practice without accepting med.ins. Avocations: skiing, photography, bicycling. Office: Mountain Psychol Group 27 Mountain Bvld Ste 1 Warren NJ 07059 Office Phone: 908-222-1099. Office Fax: 908-222-9970. Business E-Mail: drjanie@yahoo.com.

FELDMAN, KAYWIN, museum director, curator; BA, U. Mich.; MA in mus. mgmt. and art hist., U. London. Ednl. curator British Mus. Art; dir. Fresno Met. Mus. Art, Hist. and Sci., Calif., 1996—99, Memphis Brooks Mus. Art, Tenn., 1999—. Curator It's Only Rock and Roll. Recipient Ctrl. Calif. Excellence in Bus. award, 1996. Office: Memphis Brooks Mus Art Overton Park 1934 Poplar Ave Memphis TN 38104

FELDMAN, LILLIAN MALTZ, educational consultant; b. N.Y.C. d. Jacob and Ida (Burko) Maltz; m. Harry A. Feldman (dec. Jan. 1985); children: Ronald, Donna Feldman Weisman, Jeffrey, Robert. AB, George Washington U., 1937, MA, 1939; EdD in Early Childhood Edn., Syracuse U., 1987; HLD (hon.), SUNY, 1993. Cert. tchr., guidance counselor, sch. adminstr., N.Y. Elem. sch. guidance counselor Syracuse (N.Y.) Sch. Dist., 1963-65, Kindergarten tchr., 1957-63, dir. early children edn., 1965-83; dir. Syracuse Head Start, summers 1968-70; cons. early childhood edn. Syracuse, 1985—. Adj. instr. child, family and community studies Syracuse U., 1988-89, adj. prof. child and family studies, 1990-91. Author invited papers in early child devel. and care, 1988, 89, 95, 96. Adv. com. network adv. bd. Dr. Martin Luther King Jr. Cmty. Sch., Syracuse, 1988—. Named Woman of Achievement in Edn., Post-Standard, Syracuse, 1969; recipient Hannah G. Solomon Award Nat. Coun. Jewish Women, Syracuse, 1979, Honoree Na'amat USA 1988, Friend of Children award Women's Commn. Task Force on Children, 1992. Mem. Syracuse Assn. for Edn. Young Children (Outstanding Early Childhood Educator award 1984), Consortium for Children's Svcs. (Silver Dove award 1985, Friend of Family award 1992), Onondaga County Child Care Coun. (Community Svc. award 1983, Friend of Children award 1992), Delta Kappa Gamma, Phi Delta Kappa. Democrat.

FELDMAN, MARTHA SUE, political scientist, educator; b. Oak Ridge, Tenn., Mar. 31, 1953; d. Melvin J. and Nancy Ann (McCarty) F.; m. Hobart Taylor III, Oct. 30, 1993; 1 child, Bruce Alexander Feldman Taylor. BA in Polit. Sci., U. Wash., 1976; MA in Polit. Sci., Stanford U., 1980, PhD in Polit. Sci., 1983. Asst. prof. dept. polit. sci., asst. rsch. sci. Inst. Pub. Policy Studies U. Mich., Ann Arbor, 1983—89, assoc. prof. dept. polit. sci., 1989—2001, assoc. prof. Sch. Pub. Policy, 1995—2001, prof. polit. sci. and pub. policy, 2001—03, assoc. dean Ford Sch. Pub. Policy, 2001—03; prof., Johnson chair for civic governance and pub. mgmt., dept. policy, planning and design Sch. Social Ecology, U. Calif. Irvine, 2003—. Health svcs. rschr. U. Wash., Seattle, 1975—76; cons. to Com. on Ability Testing NAS, Washington, 1980; regulatory impact analyst for fossil fuels Dept. Energy, Washington, 1980—81; vis. scholar Stanford (Calif.) U. Ctr. Orgns. Rsch., 1990—91; vis. prof. Luigi Bocconi U., Milan, 1991, Swedish Sch. Econs., Helsinki, Finland, 1992, U. Bergen, Norway, 2002. Author: Order Without Design: Information Production and Policy Making, 1989, Strategies for Interpreting Qualitative Data, 1994; co-author: Reconstructing Reality in the Courtroom, 1981, Gaining Access, 2003; editor: Orgn. Sci., 2006—; contbr. articles to profl. jours. Ameritech fellow, 1986, Rackham Faculty Rsch. grantee, 1984-85, Brookings Instn. Rsch. fellow, 1979-80, NIMH fellow, 1978-79, others. Office: U Calif Irvine Dept Policy Planning and Design 226G Social Ecology I Irvine CA 92697-7075 E-mail: feldmanm@uci.edu.

FELDMAN, NANCY E., social worker; d. Seymour S. Kolten and Eva J. Moskovitz; m. Edward Howard Feldman; 1 child, Joshua. MSW, Loyola U., Chgo., 1995. Social worker pvt. practice, Merrillville, Ind.; co-owner Phaze 1 Day Spa, Highland. Mem.: NASW. Home: 1912 Lambert Ln Munster IN 46321 Office: Phaze 1 Day Spa 2449 45th St Highland IN 46322

FELDMAN, NANCY JANE, insurance company executive; b. Green Bay, Wis., July 6, 1946; d. Benjamin J. and Ellen M. Naze; m. Robert P. Feldman, Aug. 24, 1968; 1 child, Sara J. BA, U. Wis., 1969, MS, 1974. Supr. EPSDT program Minn. Dept. Human Svcs., St. Paul, 1974-80, supr. healthcare programs, 1980-84; team leader human resources budget Minn. Dept. Fin., St. Paul, 1984-87; asst. commr. Minn. Dept. Health, St. Paul, 1987-91; team leader CORE program Minn. Dept. Adminstrn., St. Paul, 1991-93; dir. state pub. programs Medica, Allina Health Sys., Mpls., 1993-95; CEO UCare Minn., St. Paul, 1995—. Bd. chair Minn. Coun. Health Plans, Mpls., 1995—; bd. dir. Stratis Health. Bd. dirs Vols. Am. Health Nat. Svcs., 1994—; vice chair bd. dir. Ctr. for Victims of Torture, 1997-2003, chair, 2004. Mem. Women's Health Leadership Trust, Nat. Inst. Health Policy. Avocations: distance swimming, bicycling, travel. Office: UCare Minn PO Box 52 Minneapolis MN 55440-0052 Home: 4822 Folwell Dr Minneapolis MN 55406 E-mail: nfeldman@ucare.org.

FELDMAN, SARI, library director; b. May 29, 1953; Dep. dir. Cleve. Pub. Libr.; exec. dir. Cuyahoga County Pub. Libr., Ohio, 2003—. Mem. WebJunction E-Learning Adv. Com. Office: Cuyahoga County Pub Libr 2111 Snow Rd Parma OH 44134 Office Phone: 216-749-9419.*

FELDMANN, JUDITH GAIL, language professional, educator; b. Grenora, ND, Jan. 10, 1938; d. Jule and Evelyn (Hagen) F.; children: Robert, Carole Elizabeth. BA magna cum laude, Minot State Tchrs. Coll., 1962; MA, Mich. State U., 1971; postgrad, U. Oslo, 1980, U. London, 1982, 85; postgrad., Western Mich. U., 1987, Eastern Mich. U., 1992-93, Harvard U., 1994. Cert. tchr., secondary adminstrn., Mich. English tchr. Minot Pub. Schs., ND, 1961, Charlotte Pub. Schs., Mich., 1962; grad. asst. instr. Mich. State U., East Lansing, 1996; reading specialist, English educator Jackson (Mich.) Pub. Schs., 1964—2005. English educator, 1964—2005. Mem. ASCD, Internat. Reading Assn., Mich. Reading Assn. (presenter Grand Rapids 1995), Jackson Edn. Assn. (v.p.). Home: 2791 Brookside Blvd Jackson MI 49203-5532 Office Phone: 517-841-3828. Personal E-mail: judithfeldmann@comcast.net.

FELDSHUH, TOVAH S., actress; b. N.Y.C., Dec. 27, 1952; d. Sidney and Lillian (Kaplan) F.; m. Andrew Harris-Levy, Mar. 20, 1977; children: Garson Brandon, Amanda. BA, Sarah Lawrence Coll., Bronxville, N.Y.; McKnight fellow, Guthrie Theatre-U. Minn. Broadway debut in: Cyrano de Bergerac, 1973; starring role in Yentl, N.Y.C., 1974, Yentl Goes to Broadway, 1975; leading lady Am. Shakespeare Festival, Stratford, Conn., 1976, 80, 81; off-Broadway appearance in Three Sisters, 1977; nat. tour in Peter Pan, 1978; starring role in Broadway musicals Sarava, 1978, Lend Me A Tenor, 1989, Golda's Balcony, 2003 (Tony nom. best actress in a play, 2004), Hello, Dolly!, 2006; one-woman show, Guthrie Theater, 1980, 81; actor (films) Nunzio, 1978, The Idolmaker, 1980, Cheaper to Keep Her, 1980, Daniel, 1983, Brewster's Millions, 1985, Silver Bullet, 1985 (voice), Blue Iguana, 1988, Saying Kaddish, 1991, A Day in October, 1992, Trouble, 1995, Comfortably Numb, 1995, Aaron's Magic Village, 1995, Hudson River Blues, 1997, Montana, 1998, Charlie Hoboken, 1998, A Walk on the Moon, 1999, The Corruptor, 1999, Happy Accidents, 2000, The 3 Little Wolf's, 2001, The Believer, 2001, Kissing Jessica Stein, 2001, Friends and Family, 2001, Noon Blue Apples 2002, The End of the Bar, 2002, Tollbooth, 2004, Life on the Ledge, 2005, The Reality Trap, 2005, Alchemy, 2005, A House Divided, 2006, O Jerusalem, 2006, Just My Luck, 2006, Lady in the Water, 2006; (TV films) Scream Peggy Scream, 1973, The Amazing Howard Hughes, 1977, The World of Darkness, 1977, Terror Out of the Sky, 1978, The Triangle Factory Fire Scandal, 1979, Thief Beggarman, 1979, The Women's Room, 1980, Sexual Considerations, 1991, Citizen Cohn, 1992, Love and Betrayal: The Mia Farrow Story, 1995; (TV series) Ryan's Hope, 1976, Murder Inc, 1981, Mariah, 1987, L.A. Law, 1987, As The World Turns, 1994; (TV mini series) Holocaust, 1978, A Will of Their Own, 1998; guest appearances include Serpico, 1976, The Bob Newhart Show, 1977, Barnaby Jones, 1977, The Love Boat, 1977, 1984, Airwolf, 1984, Law & Order, 1991, 1992, 1994, 1995, 1996, 1998, 2000, 2001, 2002, & 2004, All My Children, 1997, Cosby, 1999, The Education of Max Bickford, 2002 and several others. Recipient Theatre World award, Outer Critics Circle award, Drama Desk award, Israeli Govt. Friendship award, Eleanor Roosevelt Humanitarian award.*

FELDT, GLORIA A., social services administrator; b. Temple, Tex., Apr. 13, 1942; m. Alex Barbanell; 3 children; 3 stepchildren. BA in Sociology and Speech with honors, U. Tex. Permian Basin, 1974; postgrad., Ariz. State U., Western Behavioral Scis. Inst., La Jolla, Calif. Broadcast operator Sta. KOIP-FM, Odessa, Tex., 1965-67; substitute tchr. Ector County Ind. Sch. Dist., Odessa, Tex., 1967-68; tchr., spl. projects dir. head start Greater Opportunities of the Permian Basin, Odessa, Tex., 1968-73; exec. dir. Planned Parenthood of West Tex., Odessa, 1974-78; exec. dir., CEO Planned Parenthood Ctrl. and Northern Ariz., Phoenix, 1978-96; pres. Planned Parenthood Fedn. Am., Planned Parenthood Action Fund, N.Y.C., 1996—2005; also bd. dirs. Planned Parenthood Fedn. Am. Mem. steering com. Pro-Choice Ariz.; founder Planned Parenthood Fedn. Am. Leadership Inst.; cons. in leadership and strategic planning for non-profit orgns. Spkr. in field; Author: Behind Every Choice Is a Story, 2003, The War on Choice:The Right-Wing Attack on Women's Rights and How to Fight Back, 2004. Mem. exec. bd. Ariz. Affordable Health Care Found.; bd. dirs. Pro-Choice Resource Ctr., Hospice of the Valley; mem. cmty. adv. bd. Jr. League of Phoenix; mem. adv. bd. UN Assn.; charter mem. Ariz. Women's Town Hall; active Charter 100, World Affairs Coun., Ariz. Acad. Town Halls. Recipient Women of Achievement award, 1987, Ruth Green award Nat. Exec. Dirs. Coun., 1990, award Women Helping Women, 1989, 94, Golden Apple award Sun City chpt. NOW, 1995, City of Phoenix Martin Luther King, Jr. Living the Dream award City of Phoenix Human Rels. Commn., 1996. Mem. APHA, Nat. Family Planning and Reproductive Health Assn., Ariz. Pub. Health Assn.

FELIOUS, ODETTA, vocalist; b. Ala., Dec. 31, 1930; d. Reuben and Flora (Sanders) Holmes; m. Don Gordon (div. 1959); m. Gary Shead, 1960; m. Iversen Minter, 1977. Degree in Classical Music/Musical Comedy, L.A. City Coll. Singer Turnabout Theater, Hollywood, Calif. Recs.: Odetta Live at Blue Angel, 1953, Ballas and Blues, 1956, Live at Gate of Horn, 1957; recs. My Eyes Have Seen, Newport Folk Festival, Ballad for American, 1959, Odetta at Carnegie Hall, Odetta Sings Christmas Spirituals, 1960, Odetta and the Blues, Odetta at Town Hall, Sometimes I Feel Like Crying, 1962, Odetta Sings Folk Songs, Odetta, Fantasy, One Grain of Sand, 1963, It's A Mighty World, Odetta Sings of Many Things, 1964, Odetta Sings Ballads and Blues, Odetta Sings Dylan, 1965, Odetta in Japan, At the Gate of Horn, 1966, Odetta at Carnegie Hall, 1967, Odetta Sings the Blues, 1968, The Essential Odetta, 1973, Odetta, Verve/Folkways, Odetta, Archive of Folk and Jazz, 1974, Ballad for American/Lonesome Train, 1976, Odetta and the Blues, Movin' It On, 1987, Christmas Special, 1998, To Ella, Best of the Vanguard Years, Blues Everywhere I Go, 1999; recs.: Gonna Let it Shine, 2005; appeared Carnegie Hall, Newport Folk Festival, New Orleans Jazz Festival, Ann Arbor Folk Festival; performer: (films) Cinerama Holiday, Sanctuary, Ballad of Rambling Jack, (TV series) including The Autobiography of Miss Jane Pittman; recs.: Lookin' For a Home, 2001. Recipient Sylvania award for excellence, 1959, Key to the City of Birmingham, Ala., 1965, Presdl. Nat. Medal of Arts, 1999; Duke Ellington fellow Yale U. Office: Douglas A Yeager Prodns 300 W 55th St # 15 New York NY 10019-5138 Office Phone: 212-245-0240. Fax: 212-245-6576. E-mail: yeagerprod@aol.com.

FELISKY, BARBARA ROSBE, artist; b. Chgo., Mar. 24, 1938; d. Robert Lee and Margaret (Black) Rosbe; m. Timothy Felisky, Oct. 6, 1962; children: Kendra, Marc, Kyra. BA in Edn., U. Mich., 1960. Tchr. Peekskill (N.Y.) Sch. Dist., 1960-61; asst. to edn. dir. Simplicity Pattern Co., N.Y.C.; tchr. Anaheim (Calif.) Sch. Dist. Contbr. articles to mags. Bd. guilds Orange County Performing Arts Ctr., Costa Mesa, Calif., 1983-85. Mem. Laguna Beach Art Mus., L.A. County Mus. Art, Gamma Phi Beta, Calif. Art Club. Avocations: travel, photography. Home: 2942 E Lake Hill Dr Orange CA 92867-1910

FELIX, PATRICIA JEAN, retired steel company purchasing professional; b. Baptistown, N.J., Dec. 13, 1941; d. Dmitri and Rosalia (Hryckowian) F. Student, Pratt Inst., 1960-61, Moravian Coll., Bethlehem, Pa., 1961-63. Cert. purchasing mgr. Pricing analyst Riegel Paper Corp., N.Y.C., 1966-69; placement mgr. Gardner Assocs., N.Y.C., 1969-72; buyer Bethlehem Steel Corp., 1973-78, buyer exempt, 1978-84, sr. buyer, 1984, purchasing supr., 1984-94, raw materials team, 1994-97, sr. sourcing specialist, 1997—2003, ret., 2003. Sec. coun. St. Nicholas Russian Orthodox Ch., Bethlehem, 1982-85, mem. coun., 1985-91, bldg. com., 1992-93, 97, icon com., 1996-97, bldg. com. 1998—; mem. coun. Bethlehem-Tondabayashi Sister City Commn., 2003—, v.p. coun., 2004— sec., 1989-90, chmn., 1991-93. Mem. Nat. Assn. Purchasing Mgrs. Home: 1721 Millard St Bethlehem PA 18017-5142

FELKER, OUIDA JEANETTE WEISSINGER, special education educator; b. Vicksburg, Miss., Oct. 31, 1931; d. Eugene Liddell and Alice Byron (Cato) Weissinger; m. George Hugh Boyd Jr., Feb. 5, 1958 (div. 1968); children: James Eugene, Ouida Ann Boyd Baldwin, Alice Emelyn Boyd Dewey, Rosalie Jeanette, George Hugh III; m. Paul Henry Felker Jr., Mar. 4, 1983 (dec.). BS, U. Tenn., 1952; MA, U. South Fla., 1974, EdS, 1985; EdD, U. Sarasota, 1987; grad. gemologist, Gemological Inst. Am., 1993. Cert. ins. appraiser. Tchr. health, phys. edn. South HS, Knoxville, Tenn., 1953; founder, exec. dir. Happyland Kindergarten, Clayton, Ga., 1955-56; tchr. spl. edn. Laurel Student Ctr., Fla., 1968-72; tchr. spl. edn., vocat. coord. Sarasota County Student Ctr., Fla., 1972-78, tchr., 1985-88; founder, exec. dir. Exceptional Industries, Venice, Fla., 1979-82; staffing specialist Nokomis Elem. Sch., Fla., 1988-90, Englewood Elem. Sch., Fla., 1990—97, Taylor Ranch Elem. Sch., Venice, Fla., 1990—97; ret. Tchr. of handicapped Venice Area Rotary Clubs, Fla., Rio de Janeiro, 1982; liaison for exception student edn. Ideal Alternative HS and Life Program, 1990-97; owner Jewelery by Appointment, 1989-, Weddings by Ouida in a Tropical Setting. Bd. dirs. St. Mark's Day Sch., Venice, 1986-89; mem. St. Mark's Choir; past pres. Episcopal Ch. Women, Venice Area Coll. Club. Mem. Fla. Rehab. Assn. (past chpt. treas. and pres.), Suncoast Gesneriad Soc. (v.p. 1987-91), Accredited Gemologist Assn. (cert. 1992—), Nat. Assn. Jewelry Appraisers, Nat. Jewelry Appraisal Registry, Phi Mu Alumnae Assn. (treas. 1992-93, v.p. 1994-95, pres. 1995—). Republican. Episcopalian. Avocations: gemology, gardening, ethnic cooking. Home: 729 Apalachicola Rd Venice FL 34285-1605 Personal E-mail: ouida.jba@verizon.net.

FELL, ELIZABETH P., education educator; d. Alvin Curtis and Annie Mae Paul; m. Ray Fell, Dec. 18, 1965; children: Ashley, Allison, Kirk. BS in Edn., Livingston U, 1964, ME, 1968; EdD in Elem. Edn., U. Ala. Birmingham, 1985. Cert. Elem. Edn. 1975. Elem tchr. elem. sch., Ga., Fla., Ala., 1964—81;

asst. prof. Mobile Coll., Ala., 1981—89; prof., chair, Curriculum and Instrn. Troy U., Dothan, Ala., 1989—2005; ret. Nat. Scholastic Judge Am. Jr. Miss, Mobile, 1986—89; SACS Facilitator and Review Chmn. So. Assn. of Coll. and Sch. Ala. Elem. and Middle Sch. Vol. Ret. Seniors Vol. Program, Grandparents Raising Grandchildren, Vols. in Police Svc., Habitat for Humanity Assessment. Named Ms. Flaming Glow/Ms. Congeniality, Ms. Sr. Sweetheart of Am., 2004. Mem.: AACTE, Nat. Council for the Social Studies, Nat. Council for Tchr. of English, Alpha Delta Kappa (state bd., state corr. sec.), Phi Delta Kappa (hon.), Kappa Delta Pi (Counselor). E-mail: gfell@ala.net.

FELL, M. ANN, publishing executive; BA in Comm., Boston U., 1980; graduate pub. program, N.Y.U., 1982. Asst. mktg. mgr. Time Warner Inc., N.Y.C., 1981-83; mktg. rsch. mgr. Conde Nast Inc., N.Y.C., 1983-86; sales rep. Spy Mag., N.Y.C., 1986-87, Forbes Mag., N.Y.C., 1987-88, Venture Mag., N.Y.C., 1988-90; pres., group pub. SCENE Pub. Inc., N.Y.C., 1990—. Office: SCENE Publishing Inc 930 5th Ave New York NY 10021-2651

FELLENSTEIN, CORA ELLEN MULLIKIN, retired credit union executive; b. Edwardsville, Ill., June 2, 1930; d. Russell K. and Elberta Mable (Rheude) Mullikin; m. Charles Frederick Fellenstein, Feb. 24, 1951; children: Keith David, Kimberly Diane. Student, Cmty. Coll., 1980-83. Teller, loan officer, office mgr. Credit Union of Johnson County, Olathe, Kans., 1976-84, 1st. v.p., supr. lending, collection and Mastercard depts. Lenexa, Kans., 1984-86, exec. v.p., 1987-94. Vol. Cerebral Palsey, 1957—66, Olathe Cmty. Hosp., 1976—92, Shawnee Mission (Kans.) Med. Ctr., 1986—90, Caring For Others, Amigos de Los Ninos de Mexico, 1996—, Mex. Children's Refuge, 1998—2004, HOSTS (Help One Student to Succeed) Program, San Juan, Tex., 1995—2004; Precinct committeewoman Johnson County Reps., Olathe, Kans., 1976—92; mem. First Christian Ch.; bd. dirs. Consumer Credit Counseling Svc., Kansas City, Mo., 1992—94. Mem. NAFE, Internat. Assn. Credit Card Investigators, Internat. Credit Assn., Kans. Credit Assn., Credit Profls. (dir. 1983-92, Exec. of Yr. Johnson county chpt.), DAR (treas. 1966-86), Daus. Am. Colonists (treas. 1976-86), Friends of Historic Mahaffie Farmstead, Soroptomist Internat., Beta Sigma Phi. Mem. Christian Ch. Avocations: genealogy, camping, travel.

FELLER, CANDI P., counselor; b. Tenarkana, Tex., Dec. 21, 1947; d. Marvin and Sara Pauline Pynes; children: Michelle Wilde, Jennifer Parchem, Melissa Kostecki. BA, U. Houston, 1969; MEd, U. Mo., 1980. Lic. profl. counselor Nat. Bd. Certified Counselors, cert. secondary tchg. Tex., Mo. Tchr. Pearce Jr. H.S., Tex., 1969—70, Splendora (Tex.) Pub. Schs., 1973—74, Humble (Tex.) H.S., 1974; counselor St. Louis CC, 1981—. Contbr. articles to profl. jours. Mem. advisory bd. Pathways to Independence, St. Louis, 1995—, Logos Sch., St. Louis, 1995—. Mem.: Mo. Assn. Higher Edn. & Disabilities (v.p. 2004, treas. 2005—). Office: St Louis CC 11333 Big Bend Kirkwood MO 63122 Office Phone: 314-984-7582. Business E-Mail: cfeller@slcc.edu.

FELLER, LORETTA ANNE, elementary school educator; b. Youngstown, Ohio, Dec. 13, 1946; d. Joseph and Julia Loretta (Bednar) Kolesar; m. Thomas Joseph Feller, Aug. 19, 1972; children: Jonathan Joseph, Jeffrey Thomas. BS in Elem. Edn., Youngstown U., 1964-69; postgrad., U. Ill., Champaign, 1982-84, Wright State U., 1990-94, Antioch U., 1994—96, U. Dayton, 1996—2003. Elem. tchr. St. Luke Sch., Boardman, Ohio, 1967-69, St. Nicholas Sch., Struthers, Ohio, 1969-70, Reed Middle Sch., Hubbard, Ohio, 1970-72, Reynoldsburg (Ohio) Middle Sch., 1972-73, St. Pius X Sch., Reynoldsburg, 1973-74, St. Alphonsus Sch., Grand Rapids, Mich., 1974-76; dir. rel. edn. Holy Redeemer, Jenison, Mich., 1976-78; elem. tchr. St. Matthew Sch., Champaign, Ill., 1982-90, St. Luke Sch., Beavercreek, Ohio, 1990—, sci. dept. chair, 1998—. Com. mem. edn. commn. St. Luke Sch., Beavercreek, 1992-93; yearbook adv. St. Matthew Sch., Champaign, 1984-90; rep. edn. commn. Holy Redeemer Parish Coun., Jenison, 1976-78. Mem. Jr. Womens Club, Champaign, 1982-90, YMCA Wives Club, 1972-94; mem. Rotaryanns, Beavercreek, 1990-94, chmn. sci. dept., 1995—; pres. Miami Valley Coun. Cath. Musicians and Nat. Pastoral Musicians, 1995—; mem. Archdiocesan Worship Com. of Cin Named Outstanding Young Educator, Reynoldsburg Jaycees, 1974; recipient Contribution to Cath. Edn. award Peoria (Ill.) Diocese, 1987, Tchr. Excellence in Edn. award Miami Valley Coun. Cath. Edn., 1998. Mem. Nat. Cath. Edn. Assn. (nominee Outstanding Tchr. 1993), Ohio Cath. Edn. Assn., Ohio Edn. Assn., Slovak Cath. Sokols. Roman Catholic. Avocations: music, sewing, travel. Home: 1378 Cowman Ct Beavercreek OH 45434-6714 Office: St Luke Sch 1442 N Fairfield Rd Beavercreek OH 45432-2697

FELLER, MIMI A. (MILLICENT FELLER), newspaper publishing executive; BA cum laude, Creighton U., 1970; JD, Georgetown U. Asst. dir. congl. rels. Gen. Svcs. Adminstrn., 1975-77; legis. asst. Environ. and Pub. Works Com. US Senate, 1977-81; from legis. dir. to Washington chief of staff Sen. John Chafee (Rep.), R.I., 1981-83; dep. asst. sec. legis. affairs US Dept. Treasury, 1983-85; from v.p. to sr. v.p. pub. affairs and govt. rels. Gannett Broadcasting, Inc., 1985—. Bd. dirs. Nat. Ct. Apptd. Spl. Advs. Assn. Bd. dirs. Creighton U. Recipient Distinq. Alumnus award Creighton U., 1987. Office: Gannett Co Inc 7950 Jones Branch Dr Mc Lean VA 22107

FELLIN, OCTAVIA ANTOINETTE, retired librarian, historical researcher; b. Santa Monica, Calif. d. Otto P. and Librada (Montoya) F. Student, U. N.Mex., 1937—39; BA, U. Denver, 1941; BS in L.S., Dominican U., River Forest, Ill., 1942. Asst. libr. instr., libr. sci. St. Mary-of-Woods Coll., Terre Haute, Ind., 1942-44; libr. U.S. Army, Bruns Gen. Hosp., Santa Fe, 1944-46, Gallup (N.Mex.) Pub. Libr., 1947-90; post libr. Camp McQuaide, Calif., 1947; freelance writer, 1950—. Libr. cons.; N.Mex. del. White House Pre-conf. on Librs. & Inof. Svcs., 1978; dir. Nat. Libr. week for N.Mex., 1959. Author: Yahweh the Voice that Beautifies the Land, 1975; A Chronicle of Mileposts a Brief History of the University of New Mexico, Gallup Campus, 1968. Chmn. Gallup St. Naming Com., 1958—59; organizer Gt. Decision Discussion groups, 1963—85; chmn. Aging Com., 1964—68, Gallup Mus. Indian Arts and Crafts, 1964—78, Gallup Sr. Citizens Ctr., 1965—68; publicity com. Gallup Inter-Tribal Indian Ceremonial Assn., 1966—68; active Gov.'s Com. 100 on Aging, 1967—70; bd. dirs., sec., co-organizer Gallup Area Arts Coun., 1970—78; bd. dirs. Gallup Opera Guild, 1970—74; chmn. adv. bd. Gallup Sr. Citizens, 1971—73; active N.Mex. Libr. Adv. Coun., 1971—75, vice chmn., 1974—75; mem. Eccles. Conciliation and Arbitration Bd., Province of Santa Fe, 1974; chmn. pledge campaign Rancho del Nino San Huberto Empalme, Mexico, 1975—80; chmn. hist. com. Gallup Diocese Bicentennial, 1975, steering com., 1975—78; active Cathedral Parish Coun., 1980—83, v.p., 1981; cmty. edn. adv. coun. U. N.Mex., Gallup, 1981—82; pres. Rehoboth McKinley Christian Hosp. Aux., 1983; chmn. Red Mesa Art Ctr., 1984—88; Diocese of Gallup rep. to nat. convocation on laity concerns with Pope John Paul II, San Francisco, 1987; pres. Gallup Area Arts Coun., 1988; century com. Western Health Found., 1988; cultural bd. Gallup Multi-Model Cultural Com., 1988—95; chmn. aux. scholarship com. Rehoboth McKinley Christian Hosp. Aux., 1989—; co-organizer, v.p. chair fund raising com. Gallup Pub. Radio com., 1989—95; active McKinley County Recycling Com., 1990—; local art selection com. N.Mex. Art Dirs., 1990; N.Mex. organizing chmn. Rehoboth McKinley Christian Hosp. Aux., chmn. cmty. edn. loan selection com., 1990—; com. mem. Rio Grande Hist. Collection, NMSU, 1991—96; bd. dirs., corr. sec. Rehoboth McKinley Christian Hosp. Aux., 1991—94; chmn. Trick or Treat for UNICEF, Gallup, 1972-77, Artists Coop, 1985-89; active Network: Nat. Cath. Social Justice Lobby; mem. N.Mex. Humanities Coun., 1979, Gallup Centennial Com., 1980-81; 35th anniversary com. U. N.Mex., Gallup, 2001—02; mem. mural project Gallup, N.Mex., 2005—06; mem. coalition to repeal death penalty Gallup (N.Mex.) Group, 2001—; fund devel. cons. Cath. Indian Ctr., 2001—03; active N.Mex. ACLU, 2001—; mem. adv. coun. to U.S. Cath. Bishops, 1969—74; chmn. Gallup (N.Mex.) Sr. Citizen Ctr., 1974—77. Recipient Dorothy Canfield Fisher Libr. award, 1961, Outstanding Cmty. Svc. award Gallup C. of C., 1968, 70, Outstanding Citizen award, 1974, Benemerenti medal Pope Paul VI, 1977, Celibrate Literarcy award Gallup Internat. Reading Assn., 1983-84, Woman of Distinction award Soroptimists, 1985, N.Mex. Disting. Pub. Svc. award, 1987, Edgar L. Hewitt award Hist. Soc. N.Mex., 1992, Gov.'s award as Outstanding N.Mex. Woman, 1988, Cmty. Svc. award U. N.Mex., 1993; Octavia Fellin Pub. Libr. named in her honor, 1990. Mem.: NAACP, LWV (v.p. 1953—56), AAUW (co-organizer Gallup br. 1969—94, v.p. co-organizer Gallup br., chmn. com. on women), ALA, N.Mex. Gallup Film Soc. (v.p. 1950—58, co-organizer), N.Mex. Mcpl. League (pres. libr.'s divsn. 1979), Gallup C. of C. (organizing chmn. women's div. 1972, v.p. 1972—73), N.Mex Archtl. Found., Plateau Scis. Soc., N.Mex. Libr. Assn. (hon.; chmn. hist. materials com. 1964—66, pres. 1965—66, chmn. com. to extend libr. svcs. 1969—73, chmn. local and regional history roundtable 1978, v.p., sec., salary and tenure com., nat. coord. N.Mex. Legis. com., Libr. of Yr. award 1975, life, Cmty. Achievement award 1983, Lifetime Membership award 1994), Nat. New Deal Preservation Assn. (bd. mem. N.Mex. chpt.), Habitat for Humanity, Call to Action Nat. Ca. Renewal Org., Pax Christi U.S.A., Hist. Soc. N.Mex. (bd. dirs. 1980—83), Gallup Hist. Soc., Women's Ordination Conf. Network, N.Mex. Women's Polit. Caucus, N.Mex. Foklore Soc. (pres. 1958), Alpha Delta Kappa (hon.). Roman Catholic. Home and Office: 513 E Mesa Ave Gallup NM 87301-6021

FELLINGER-BUZBY, LINDA, interior and industrial designer; b. Altoona, Pa., Oct. 1, 1952; d. John and Louise (Reighard) Fellinger; m. Gordon Buzby, June 21, 1975 (div. 1987); 1 child, Sarah. BFA, Moore Coll. Art and Design, Phila., 1975; M Indsl. Design, Domus Acad., Milan, 1990. Project mgr., designer Interspace Inc., Phila., 1972-78; cons. interior residential design and indsl. pub. design Smith Kline Corp., Phila., 1978-79; interior designer, Phila., 1979—; prof. interior design Moore Coll. Art and Design, Phila., 1986-90; prof. interior design and architecture Phila. Coll. of Textile and Sci., Phila., 1996-98. Mem. Am. Soc. Interior Designers, Interior Design Council (exec. com. 1987—), Phila. Mus. Art (collaborative com.). Republican. Episcopalian. Achievements include patents for modular wall washer light fixture with moveable lens, environmentally sensitive postcard Earthly Greetings, portable pocket phones for personal communications system, Dupont corianbathroom sink design, eyeglasses, child's safety vest. Home: 703 Polo Cir Bryn Mawr PA 19010-3841

FELLOWS, ALICE COMBS, artist; b. Atlanta, Sept. 14, 1935; d. Andrew Grafton III and Wilhelmina Drummond (Jackson) Combs; m. Robert Ellis Fellows Jr., Aug. 20, 1957 (div. 1978); children: Ariadne Elisabeth Fellows-Mannion, Kara Suzanne Fellows. BFA, Syracuse U., 1957; M in Clin. Psychology, Antioch U., 1992. Guest artist Yaddo, Saratoga Springs, N.Y., 1991; artist-in-residence Dorland Colony, Temecula, Calif., 1983; guest lectr. psychology seminar UCLA, 1990. Exhibited works in numerous group and one-woman shows including The True Artist, di Rosa Preserve, Napa, 2004, Shakespeare As Muse, Schneider Mus., Ashland, Oreg., 2004, di Rosa Preserve, Napa, 2003, 04, Hiromi Gallery, Santa Monica, Otis Gallery, Otis Coll. Art and Design, L.A., 2000, L.A. Mcpl. Art Gallery, C.O.L.A. Fellows Exhbn., 1998, El Camino Coll., 1997, Hunsaker-Schlesinger Gallery, 1996, The Armory Ctr. at Pasadena, 1996, Barnsdall Mcpl. Gallery, 1995, Claremont Grad. Sch. Gallery, 1991, Saxon-Lee Gallery, L.A., 1989, Santa Monica Coll. Gallery Art, 1988, J. Rosenthal Gallery, Chgo., 1986, The Biennial at the Hirshhorn Mus. and Sculpture Garden, Washington, 1986, Kirk de Gooyer Gallery, L.A., 1984, 85, many others; works represented in numerous collections including The Norton Collection, Santa Monica, Broad Found., Santa Monica, Mint Mus., Charlotte, N.C., N.C. Mus. Raleigh, N.C., Security Pacific Corp., L.A., Ft. Lauderdale Mus.; others. Arts commr. City of Santa Monica Arts Commn., 1995—99; mem. Pub. Art Com., Santa Monica, 1996—2000; mem. artists adv. bd. L.A. Mcpl. Art Gallery at Bransdall, 1998—2001. Recipient Durfee Found. award; grantee Dale Chihuly grant for Srs. Making Art Workshops, 1996; painting fellow Western States Arts Fedn./NEA, 1990, painting fellow Getty Trust, 1990, NEA fellow in painting, 1991, City of L.A. Individual Artist's fellow, 1998. Home: 18880 Melvin Ave Sonoma CA 95476 E-mail: alice@alicefellows.com.

FELLOWS, ESTHER ELIZABETH, musician, music educator; b. Miami, Ariz., Nov. 5, 1952; d. John Wilmont and Flora Elizabeth (Eyestone) Walker; m. James Michael Fellows, Aug. 20, 1976; children: Joy Christine, Rachel Lindsay, Daniel Matthew, Jessica Grace. B in Music Edn., U. Colo., 1975. Co-dir. Children's Piano Lab. U. Colo., Boulder, 1975-76; instr. So. Calif. Conservatory Music, Sun City, 1976-78; pvt. instr. Ft. Lauderdale, 1978-84; instr. Ft. Lauderdale Christian Sch., 1981-83; sect. violinist Signature Symphony Tulsa Ballet, 1984—; prin. 2nd violin Bartlesville Symphony, Okla., 1990—; pvt. instr. Broken Arrow, Okla., 1984—, Mounds, Okla. Pvt. instr. Ft. Lauderdale, 1978-84. Mem. Music Tchrs. Nat. Assn. (cert. piano, violin and viola), Am. String Tchrs. Assn., Am. Viola Soc., Okla. Music Tchr. Assn., Suzuki Assn. Am., Hyechka Music Club Tulsa, Tulsa Accredited Music Tchrs. Assn. (chmn. scholarship com., past pres., now parliamentarian, chmn. dist. achievement auditions); chmn. OMTA Dist. Achievement Auditions, Parliamentarian of TAMTA. Avocation: biking. Home: 19821 S Harvard Ave Mounds OK 74047-5049 E-mail: jefellows@juno.com.

FELSTED, CARLA MARTINDELL, librarian, writer, editor; b. Barksdale Field, La., June 21, 1947; d. David Aldenderfer Martindell and Dorthe (Hetland) Horton; m. Robert Earl Luna, Aug. 24, 1968, (div. 1972); m. Hugh Herbert Felsted, Nov. 2, 1974. BA in English, So. Meth. U., 1968, MA in History, 1974; MLS, Tex. Woman's U., 1978. Cert. secondary tchr., Tex.; cert. learning resources specialist, Tex. Tchr. Bishop Lynch High Sch., Dallas, 1968-72, Lake Highlands Jr. High Sch., Richardson, Tex., 1973-75; instr. Richland Coll., Richardson, Tex., 1973-76; library asst. So. Meth. U., Dallas, 1977-78; librarian Tracy-Locke Advt., Dallas, 1978-79; corp. librarian Am. Airlines, Inc., Ft. Worth, 1979-84; research librarian McKinsey & Co., Dallas, 1984-85; reference librarian St. Edward's U., Austin, Tex., 1985—2002, assoc. prof., 1994—2002; libr. Sedona (Ariz.) Pub. Libr., 2003—. Ptnr. Southwind Info. Svcs. and Southwind Bed-Breakfast, Wimberley, Tex., 1985-92. Editor, compiler: Youth and Alcohol Abuse, 1986; co-editor Mexican Meanderings, 1991-99; contbr. Frommer's travel guides, 1991-96. Mem. adv. bd. Sch. Libr. and Info. Scis., Tex. Women's U., Denton, 1982-84; mem. curriculum com. Wimberley Ind. Sch. Dist., 1986; bd. dirs. Hays-Caldwell Coun. on Alcohol and Drug Abuse, San Marcos, Tex., 1986-88, Inst. Cultures for Wimberley Valley, 1989-91, Tex. Alliance Human Needs, 1992-96; Tex. Team Survivor, Danskin Triathlon, 1995-2002, co-capt. 1997-99; vol. Breast Cancer Resource Ctr., 1998-2000, Sedona Cultural Pk., 2003-04, Sedona Pub. Libr., 2003, Sedona Gt Decisions, 2003-; dem. party precinct comm., 2004-06 Grantee St. Edward's U., 1986-89, 96. Mem. ALA, Tex. Libr. Assn. (dist. program com., membership com. 1986-88, Tex.-Mex. rels. com. 1992-2002), REFORMA, Wimberley C. of C. (bd. dirs. 1987-88). Unitarian Universalist. Avocations: health issues research and advocacy, regional and ethnic cooking, physical fitness, art history, travel.

FELSTINER, MARY LOWENTHAL, history professor; b. Pitts., Feb. 19, 1941; d. Alexander and Anne Lowenthal; m. John Felstiner, Feb. 19, 1966; children: Sarah Alexandra, Aleksandr. BA, Harvard U., 1963; MA, Columbia U., 1966; PhD, Stanford U., 1971. Prof. history San Francisco State U., 1972—2006. Author: To Paint Her Life, 1994, Out of Joint, 2005. Recipient prize in women's history, Am. Hist. Assn., 1995. Mem.: Phi Beta Kappa. Office: San Francisco State Univ History Dept 1600 Holloway Ave San Francisco CA 94132-1722

FELT, JULIA KAY, lawyer; b. Wooster, Ohio, Apr. 8, 1941; d. George Willard and Betty Virginia F.; m. Lawrence Roger Van Til, May 31, 1969. BA, Northwestern U., 1963; JD, U. Mich., 1967. Bar: Ohio 1967, Mich. 1968. Tchr. Triway Local H.S., Wooster, Ohio, 1963-64; assoc. Dykema, Gossett, PLLC, Detroit, 1967-75, ptnr., 1975—; adj. asst. prof. dept. cmty. medicine Wayne State U., Detroit, 1974-05. Contbr. articles to profl. jours., chpts. to books. Trustee Rehab. Inst., Detroit, 1971-01, sec., 1974-77, 91—99, vice chmn., 1978-83, 85-90, chmn. bd., 1983-85; trustee Detroit Med. Ctr. Corp. 1984-85; bd. dirs. Travelers Aid Soc., Detroit, 1974—90, v.p., 1978-81, United Way Cmty. Svc. Detroit, bd. dirs., 1981-2005; vis. com. U. Mich. Law Sch., Ann Arbor, 1972-06, nat. vice chmn. law sch. fund, 1984-86, bd. dirs. Detroit Assn. U. Mich. Women, 1968-72, pres., 1971-72, Mich. Women's Found., trustee, 1993-02, bd. dirs. Med. Ethics Resource Network of Mich., 2002-05 Planned Giving Round table Southeastern Mich., chmn., 1993-94; chmn. Leave a Legacy Southeastern Mich., 1996-98. Campbell Competition winner U. Mich. Law Sch., 1967; recipient Svc. award Mich. League Nursing, 1977, Alumna-in-Residence U. Mich. Alumnae Coun., 1986, Disting. Svc. award Mich. Bus. and Profl. Assn., 1998. Fellow Am. Bar Found., Mich. Bar Found., Am. Health Lawyers, Mich. Hospice and Palliative Care Orgn. (Educator of Yr. award 2002), Am. Acad. Health Care Attys. of Am. Health Lawyers(pres. 1985-86, bd. dirs. 1980-87); mem. Mich. Soc. Hosp. Attys. (pres. 1975-76, bd. dirs. 1975-77), Cath. Health Assn. U.S. (legal services adv. com. 1980-84), Gov's. Commn. on End Life Care, 1999-02, Adv. Com. Pain and Symptom Mgmt. 1999-02, ABA, Ohio State Bar Assn., State Bar Mich. (com. medicolegal problems 1973-81, adminstrv. rule making com. 1978-79, awards com. chmn. 1989-99, disabilities com. Open Justice Commn., 1999-04, Equal Assn. Initiatives 2004-), Detroit Bar Assn., Women Lawyers Mich., Am. Soc. Law and Medicine. Presbyterian. Office: Dykema Gossett PLLC 400 Renaissance Ctr Detroit MI 48243-1668 Office Phone: 313-568-6700.

FELTENSTEIN, MARTHA, lawyer; b. Kansas City, Mo., 1954; BA, Princeton U., 1975; MPhil, U. London, 1977; JD, Columbia U., 1981. Bar: N.Y. 1982. Ptnr. Skadden, Arps, Slate, Meagher & Flom, N.Y.C. Office: Skadden Arps Slate Meagher & Flom 4 Times Sq Fl 24 New York NY 10036-6595

FELTER, JUNE MARIE, artist; b. Oakland, Calif., Oct. 19, 1919; m. Richard Henry Felter, Feb. 7, 1943; children: Susan, Tom. Student, San Francisco Art Inst., 1960, student, 1961, Oakland Art Inst., 1937—40. Instr. San Francisco Mus. Art, 1965—78, San Francisco State U., 1970—78, U. Calif., 1979—80, Santa Rosa Jr. Coll., Calif., 1981, Elaine Badgley-Arnoux Sch. Art, San Francisco, 1982, Elaine Badgley-Amoux Sch. Art, San Francisco, 1983, U. Calif., San Francisco, 1979—80, 1984—85. One-woman shows include Kennedy Gallery, 2001, Holy Names U., Oakland, 2001, Gumps Gallery, San Francisco, 1965-66, Linda Ferris Gallery, Seattle, 1971, Richmond Art Gallery, 1971-74, Dana Reich Gallery, San Francisco, 1978, 80-81, Susan & June Felter 871 Fine Arts Gallery, San Francisco, 1987, 89, 90, 92, 1999, 2006; exhibited in group shows at San Francisco Mus. Art., 1960-79, Civic Arts Gallery, Walnut Creek, Calif., 1983, U.S. Art, San Francisco, 1990, Oakland Art Mus., 1991, Wiegand Gallery, 1992, Jack London Square Oakland, 1993, U.S. Embassy, Vienna, Austria, 1995; group show include: Sanzhez Art Ctr., Pacifica, Calif., 2006, 871 Dine Art Gallery, San Franciso, 2006; represented in permanent collections at Nat. Mus. Art, Washington, Oakland Mus. Calif. Art, San Jose (Calif.) Mus. Art, Achenbach Found. Mus. Fine Arts, San Francisco, Yale U. Art Gallery, New Haven. Home and Office: 1046 Amito Dr Berkeley CA 94705-1502

FELTNER, JEANNE LOU, mathematics educator; b. Festy, Ky., Nov. 25, 1948; d. Kelly and Melissa Ritchie; m. Corbett Brown Feltner, June 20, 1970; children: Tonya Lou Williams, Alison Rae. BA in Math., Berea Coll., Ky., 1970; MEd, Morehead State U., Ky., 1979. Std. tchg. cert. Tchr. Cordia HS, Hazard, Ky., 1973—2004, Perry County Ctrl. HS, Hazard, 2005—. Coach acad. team, Hazard, 1996—2004. Mem.: Phi Kappa Phi. Home: 1114 Cockrells Trace Rd Hazard KY 41701

FELTON, HELEN MARTIN, retired adult education educator, writer; d. George Burnie Martin, Sr. and Mabel Benjamin Martin; m. Samuel Page Felton, Dec. 31, 1955; 1 child, Samuel Page Jr. BA in Speech and Drama, Miami U., Oxford, Ohio, 1949; MA in Drama, U. Wash., 1952. Instr. and cons. Adult Edn. Supervision and Mgmt. Program's Interpersonal Comm. for Suprs. South Seattle C.C., 1971—90; team tchr. interpersonal comm. ext. program U. Wash., Seattle, 1973—80; adj. instr. speech comm., drama and creative dramatics Shoreline (Wash.) C.C., 1974—84; mem. grad. com. Antioch U., Seattle, 1995—98. Box office staff Penthouse Theatre Drama Dept. U. Wash., Seattle, 1951—51, sec. creative drama office, 1951—52; camp councilor Girl Scouts, L.A., 1952—52; asst. field exec. Girl Scout Coun., L.A., 1953—53, dist. dir. and program tng. advisor, Seattle, 1955—60; customer contact rep. Gas Co., Seattle, 1954—55; presenter in field. Dir.(writer): (plays) Alaska Hawaii and Japan, (asst. dir.) Thurber Carnival, (music dir.): (Operas) Threepenny Opera; contbr. Together: Communicating Interpersonally, 1st edit., 1975, 2nd edit., 1980. Mem.: Internat. Assn. Theatre for Children and Young People U.S. Ctr., Am. Assn. Theatre Educators, Theatre Comm. Group. Avocations: drama, music, international relations.

FELTON, SANDRA HALEY, special education educator; b. Memphis, Aug. 5, 1935; d. Louis Andrew and Seco (Wilson) Haley; m. Ivan Emerson Felton, June 22, 1957; children: Lucretia, Peter, Douglas. BA in Bibl. Edn., Columbia Internat. U., 1957; MEd, U. Miami, 1968. Cert. spl. edn. tchr., Fla. Edn. therapist Ednl. Guidance Svc., Miami, 1969-73; tchr. Miami Christian Sch., Miami, 1974-85, Hialeah High Sch., Miami, 1985—98. Pres., founder Messies Anonymous, Miami, 1980-91. Author: The Messies Manual, 1981, The Messies Superguide, 1985, Messie No More, 1988, Meditations for Messies, 1992, When You Live with a Messie, 1994, Messie Motivator, 2000., Neat Mom, Messie Kids, 2002, Smart Organizing, 2005, Organizing Magic, 2006. Republican. Baptist. Home and Office: 5025 SW 114th Ave Miami FL 33165-6012

FELTS, JOAN APRIL, retired elementary school educator; b. Tulsa, Apr. 8, 1940; d. John Hickland and Dorris Retha (Finley) Matlock; m. Wayne Keith Felts, Aug. 19, 1962; children: David Wayne, Michael Scott, Steven Doyle BS Edn., Northea. State U., Tahlequah, Okla., 1962. Cert. tchr., Okla. Tchr. Ruby Ray Swift Elem. Sch., Arlington, Tex., 1962—64; co-owner Felts Family Shoe Store, Muskogee, Okla., 1966—89; tchr. Hilldale Elem. Sch., Muskogee, 1979—2000; ret., 2000. Leader Neosho dist. Boy Scouts Am., 1969-78, trainer, 1978-88 Recipient Dist. Merit award Boy Scouts Am., 1982, Wood Badge tng. award Nat. coun., 1983, Silver Beaver award Tulsa coun., 1985; named Tchr. of Yr. Hilldale Ind. Schs., 1988 Mem. Hill Assn. Classroom Tchrs. (chmn. staff devel. 1985-89, newsletter editor 1988-90), Northea. State U. Alumni Assn (bd. dirs. 1976-95, pres.-elect 1990-91, pres. 1991-93), Beta Sigma Phi (pres. Xi Zeta Zeta chpt. 1993-95, named Woman of Yr. Muskogee chpt. 1987), Kappa Kappa Iota Republican. Methodist. Avocations: writing, reading, sewing, trivia. Home: 109 Grandview Blvd Muskogee OK 74403-8608

FENBY, BARBARA LOU, social worker; b. N.Y.C., Apr. 29, 1938; d. Rudolph Louis Fessler and Lucie McRea (Koppel) Divona; m. George Fenby, June 25, 1960 (div. 1985); children: Heather, Derek. AB, U. Rochester, N.Y., 1960; MSW, UCLA, 1962; PhD of Social Work, Boston Coll., 1992. Lic. social worker, Mass. Social worker Calif. Youth Authority, Norwalk, 1962-63, Lichfield (Eng.) Child Guidance Clinic, 1964-66, Luzerne County Child Welfare, Wilkes-Barre, Pa., 1966-68, Manchester (Conn.) Hosp., 1968-70, Worcester (Mass.) Youth Guidance Ctr., 1970-75; dir. clin. svcs. Cmty. Mental Health Ctr., Schohaire, NY, 1976-80; mental health coord. Mass. Dept. Mental Health, Concord, 1980-86, assoc. area dir., 1986-88, mental health dir., mental health dept., 1988—, site dir. case mgmt., 1990, dep. area dir., 1995—2000; dir. cmty. svcs. Dept Mental Health Metro. Suburban, Westorough, Mass., 2000—. Teaching consultation Profl. Edn. Programs, Marlborough, Mass., 1981-84, 83—. Contbr. articles to profl. jours. Trustee Bd. Library Trustees, Leicester, Mass., 1973-75; mem. City of Marlborough Planning Commn., 1989—, Midstate Trail Com., Mass., 1988—. Hon. Mention, Bernart Competition, 1969. Mem. Nat. Assn. Social Workers, Am. Group Psychotherapy Assn., Assn. Women in Social Work, Nat. Register Clin. Social Workers. Democrat. Avocations: hiking, backpacking, tennis. Office: Mass Dept Mental Health Box 288 Lyman St Westborough MA 01581

FENDER, ALLISON JEAN, physical therapist, personal trainer; b. Asheville, NC, Nov. 16, 1979; d. Allan Douglas and Peggy Boone Fender. BS, Mars Hill Coll., NC, 2001; MS, Western Carolina U., Cullowhee, NC, 2003; postgrad., U. Md., Balt., 2006—. Phys. therapist Patricia Neal Outpatient, Harriman, Tenn., 2003—04, HQM, Rockwood, Tenn., 2004—06; lead phys. therapist Nat. Neuro, Knoxville, Tenn., 2006—. Co-pres. Roane

County Stroke Club, Kingston, Tenn., 2003—05. Mem.: Nat. Strength Conditioning Assn., Nat. Athletic Trainers Assn., Am. Phys. Therapy Assn., Delta Zeta. Baptist. Avocations: horseback riding, hiking, mountain biking, softball, adaptive sports. Home: 114 Old Holderford Rd Kingston TN 37763 Office: Nat Neuro Ste 301 11440 Parkside Dr Knoxville TN

FENDER, KIMBER L., library director; MLS, U. Ky., 1983. Reference libr. Boone County Pub. Libr.; mgr. info. svcs. ATE Mgmt. and Svcs. Co.; head pub. svcs. Campbell County Pub. Libr.; libr. Institutions/Books-by-Mail Dept. Pub. Libr. of Cin. & Hamilton County, 1988, libr. Deputy Libr.'s Office-Main Libr. Svcs., 1993, asst. to dir., 1995, head info. sys., 1998—99, exec. dir., 1999—. Pres. S.W. Ohio and Neighboring Librs. Bd.; chair Ohio Pub. Libr. Info. Network Bd. Mem. Workforce Investment Bd., LSTA Adv. Coun., Kent State U. Pub. Librs. Core Constituency Adv. Team, U. of Ky. Sch. of Libr. and Info. Sci. Adv. Coun. Recipient Profl. Achievement Award, No. Kentucky U., 1999. Office: Pub Libr of Cin and Hamilton County 800 Vine St Cincinnati OH 45202-2009*

FENDERSON, CAROLINE HOUSTON, psychotherapist; b. East Orange, N.J., June 17, 1932; d. George Cochran and Mary Bullard (Saunders) Houston; m. Kendrick Elwell Fenderson, Jr.; 1 child, Karen Sibley. BA, Vassar Coll., 1954; MA, U. So. Fla., 1973. Lic. mental health counselor, Fla.; diplomate Am. Bd. Cert. Managed Care Providers, diplomate Am. Psychotherapy Assn.; cert. Nat. Bd. for Cert. Clin. Hypnotherapists, Inc.; cert. trainer, devel. of human capacities Found. for Mind Rsch.; cert. Eye Movement Desensitization and Reprocessing therapist; ordained to ministry of edn. Unitarian Universalist. Dir. religious edn. Unitarian Universalist Ch., St. Petersburg, Fla., 1960—80, min. religious edn. Clearwater, Fla., 1981—83; cons. counselor and staff devel. Pinellas County Schs., Fla., 1973—83; pvt. practice Clearwater and Palm Harbor, 1983—. Author: Life Journey, 1988; (with Kendrick Fenderson Jr.) Magnets, 1961, Southern Shores, 1964; (with others) Man the Culture Builder, 1970, U.U. Identity, 1979; contbr. articles to profl. jours. Pub. affairs chmn. St. Petersburg Jr. League, 1960; founder Childbirth and Parent Edn. League of Pinellas County, 1960-70, pres., v.p., com. chair, tchr.; v.p. Child Guidance Clinic, St. Petersburg, 1960. Mem. ACA, Eye Movement Desensitization and Reprocessing Internat. Assn., Liberal Religious Edn. Dirs. Assn. (v.p. 1980-81), Assn. Transpersonal Psychology, Assn. Humanistic Psychology, Internat. Transpersonal Assn., Unitarian Universalist Assn. (com. 1975-79), Phi Beta Kappa, Kappa Delta Pi. Home: 29 Freshwater Dr Palm Harbor FL 34684-1106 Office: 25 400 US 19 N Ste 172 Clearwater FL 33763 Office Phone: 727-797-7211.

FENDRICH, JEAN, elementary school educator; b. Harrisburg, Pa., Mar. 9, 1950; d. John and Josephine Dalton; children: Krista, Andrew, Alan, Carolyn. BS, Elizabethtown Coll., Pa., 1972; MS in Edn., Lebanon Valley Coll., Annville, Pa., 2000. Tchr. 4th grade Ctrl. Dauphin Sch. Dist., Harrisburg, Pa., 1972—78; tchr. 7th grade sci. Milton Hershey Sch., 1992—2000; tchr. 8th grade phys. sci. Tredyffrin/Easttown Sch. Dist., Berwyn, 2000—02; tchr. 8th grade sci. Carlisle Area Sch. Dist., 2002—. Dir., troop leader Girl Scouts of Am., Harrisburg, 1976—90; cub scout chmn., den mother Boy Scouts of Am., 1984—88. Mem.: NEA, Carlisle Area Edn. Assn., Nat. Sci. Tchrs. Assn. Conservative. Roman Catholic. Avocations: running, hiking, birdwatching, bicycling, canoeing. Home: 913 Forbes Rd Carlisle PA 17013 Office: Carlisle Area School District 623 West Penn St Carlisle PA 17013 Office Phone: 727-240-6773. Personal E-mail: fendrichj@carlisleschools.org.

FENIGER, SUSAN, chef, television personality, writer; Former mem. staff Le Perroquet, Chgo., Ma Maison, L.A., L'Oasis, France; formerly chef, co-owner City Cafe, L.A.; chef, co-owner CITY, L.A., 1985—94, Border Grill, L.A., 1985—91, Santa Monica, 1990—. Co-host (TV series) Too Hot Tamales, 1995—, Tamales' World Tour, (radio show) Good Food; co-author: City Cuisine, 1989, Mesa Mexicana, 1994, Cantina, 1996, Cooking with Too Hot Tamales, 1997; guest appearances (TV series) Oprah Winfrey Show, Maury Povich, Today Show, Sabrina the Teenage Witch, featured in USA Today, People Mag., Entertainment Weekly. Active Scleroderma Rsch. Found. Named Chef of Yr., Calif. Restaurant Writers, 1993. Mem.: Chef's Collaborative 2000, Women Chefs and Restaurateurs. Office: Border Grill 1445 4th St Santa Monica CA 90401*

FENN, SANDRA ANN, programmer, analyst; b. Sugar Land, Tex., Oct. 31, 1953; d. William Charles and Helen Maxine (Kyle) F.; m. Jimmie Dan Watts, May 21, 1973 (div. June 1988); children: Gabriel Nathaniel Watts, Lindsay Nichelle Garza. AA in Gen. Studies summa cum laude, Alvin (Tex.) C.C., 1994; BS in Computer Info. Sys., U. Houston, Clear Lake, 2000. Shampoo asst. LaVonne's Salon of Beauty, Houston, 1972-73; coding clk. Prudential Ins. Co., Houston, 1974-75; word processing operator MacGregor Med. Assn., Houston, 1983-85; computer applications analyst Computer Scis. Corp., Houston, 1987-92; program support adminstr. Sci. Applications Internat. Corp., Houston, 1992-95, programmer/analyst, 1995-98; software developer astronaut office Johnson Space Ctr., 1998-2000; info. tech. analyst El Paso Corp., Houston, 2000—03; discovery interviewer Williams Bailey Law Firm, Houston, 2003—. Ind. cons. Arbonne Internat., 2005—. Mem. Am. Bus. Women's Assn. (newsletter chair 1995-2001, 1999 Woman of Excellence), Phi Theta Kappa. Avocations: horseback riding, camping, biking, volleyball, reading. Home: 1619 Newcomb Way Houston TX 77058-2264

FENNELL, DIANE MARIE, marketing professional, process engineer; b. Panama, Iowa, Dec. 11, 1944; d. Urban William and Marcella Mae (Leytham) Schechinger; m. Leonard E. Fennell, Aug. 19, 1967; children: David, Denise, Mark. BS, Creighton U., Omaha, 1966. Process engr. Tex. Instruments, Richardson, 1974-79; sr. process engr. Signetics Corp., Santa Clara, Calif., 1979-82; demo lab. mgr. Airco Temescal, Berkeley, Calif., 1982-84; field process engr. Applied Materials, Santa Clara, 1984-87; mgr. product mktg. Lam Rsch., Fremont, Calif., 1987-90; dir. sales and mktg. Ion & Plasma Equipment, Fremont, Calif., 1990-91; pres. FAI, Half Moon Bay, Calif., 1990-96; v.p. mktg. Tegal Corp., Petaluma, Calif., 1997-99; v.p. mktg. and sales Semicaps, Inc., Santa Clara, Calif., 1999—2001; exec. dir. Ctr. for Internat. Devel., Santa Clara, 2001—03; pres. World Info., Menlo Park, Calif., 2003—. Founder, coord. chmn. Plasma Etch User's Group, Santa Clara, 1984-87; tchr. computer course Adult Edn., Half Moon Bay, Calif., 1982-83. Founder, bd. dirs. Birth to Three program Mental Retardation Ctr., Denison, Tex., 1974-75; fund raiser local sch. band, Half Moon Bay, 1981-89; community rep. local sch. bd., Half Moon Bay, 1982-83. Mem. Am. Vacuum Soc., Soc. Photo Instrumentation Engrs., Soc. Women Engrs., Material Rsch. Soc., Commonwealth Club. Avocations: hiking, reading, gardening. Home: 441 Alameda Ave Half Moon Bay CA 94019-5337

FENNELL, TERESA ANN, psychologist; b. Feb. 18, 1955; d. Robert Wallace and Patricia Louise (Riley) Fennell; m. Duncan Marshall, Nov. 11, 1978 (div.). BA in Spanish, Erskine Coll., 1976; MA in Counseling Psychology, U. Pacific, 1982. Registered marriage,family, child counselor. Intern Calif. Counselor Valley Cmty. Counseling Svcs., Stockton, Calif., 1981—84; exec. dir. Parents Anonymous Ala., Inc., Anniston, Ala., 1984. Mem.: Assn. Specialists in Group Work, Assn. Religious and Value Issues in Counseling, Nat. Vocat. Guidance Assn., Ala. Network Victim Svcs., Am. Assn. Counseling and Devel., Am. Mental Health Counselors Assn., Assn. Measurement and Evaluation in Guidance, Internat. Platform Assn. Democrat. Presbyn.

FENNELL ROBBINS, SALLY, writer; b. Greensburg, Pa., Feb. 17, 1950; d. Clifford Seanor and Charlotte Louise (Hoffman) Fennell; m. John W. Robbins, Sept. 22, 1984. BS in Journalism cum laude, Ohio U., 1972; MA in Journalism magna cum laude, Marshall U., 1974. Intern, reporter Tribune-Rev., Greensburg, Pa., 1972; prodn. asst. Harper's Bazaar, N.Y.C., 1972; reporter UPI, Birmingham, Ala., 1972-73; reporter, dept. editor Home Furnishings Daily, Fairchild Pubs., N.Y.C., 1974-77; acct. exec. supr., client svc. mgr., v.p. Burson-Marsteller, N.Y.C., 1977-83; group mgr., v.p. pub. rels. divsn. Ketchum Comm., 1983-84; freelance writer, editor, 1984-89; dir. comm. Deloitte & Touche Retail Svcs. Group, NY, 1989-93; writer and author, 1993—; grad. teaching asst. Sch. Journalism/Reporting, Marshall U., Huntington, W.Va., 1973-74. Home and Office: 237 E 20th St New York NY 10003-1805 E-mail: sally.robbins@att.net.

FENNELLY, JANE COREY, lawyer; b. NYC, Dec. 12, 1942; d. Joseph and Josephine (Corey) F. BA, Cornell U., 1964; MLS, UCLA, 1968; JD, Loyola U., L.A., 1974. Bar: Calif. 1974, U.S. Dist. Ct. (ctrl. and so. dists.) Calif. 1974, U.S. Dist. Ct. (ea. dist.) Calif. 1977, U.S. Dist. Ct. (no. dist.) Calif. 1980, N.Y. 1982, Colo. 1993, Ariz. 1995. Ptnr. Graham & James, 1976-83; with legal dept. Bank of Am., L.A., 1973-76, Wyman, Bautzer, Kuchel & Silbert, L.A., 1983-87, Dennis, Shafer, Fennelly & Creim (merged with Bronson & McKinnon), L.A., 1987-96; with Squire, Sanders & Dempsey, Phoenix, 1996—98; prin. Jane C. Fennelly, P.C., Phoenix, 1998—; of counsel Creim, Macias & Koenig LLP, L.A., 1999—. Mem. ABA, Am. Bankruptcy Inst., Calif. Bankruptcy Forum, L.A. County Bar Assn. (bd. dirs., mem. exec. com. comml. law and bankruptcy sect. 1989-92), Maricopa County Bar Assn., Fin. Lawyers Conf. (pres. bd. dirs. 1983-84, mem. bd. govs. 1984—). Home: 15356 W Pasadena Dr Surprise AZ 85374 Office: #610 Ste 101 15508 W Bell Rd Surprise AZ 85374 Office Phone: 602-909-1855. E-mail: jane.fennelly@azbar.org.

FENNER, SUZAN ELLEN, lawyer; b. Grand Junction, Colo., Dec. 5, 1947; d. Harry J. and Louise (Bain) Shaw; m. Michael Lee Riddle, Apr. 24, 1969 (div. Feb. 1976); m. Peter R. Fenner, Nov. 24, 1978; children: Laura Elizabeth, Adam Kyle. BA, Tex. Tech U., 1969, JD, 1971. Bar: Tex. 1972, U.S. Dist. Ct. (no. dist.) Tex. 1972. Assoc. Smith & Baker, Lubbock, Tex., 1971-72; law clk. to presiding judge U.S. Dist. Ct., Dallas, 1972-73; assoc. Gardere Wynne Sewell LLP, Dallas, 1973-78, ptnr., 1978—, chair retirement com., 1973—, chair tax practice., 2001—, mem. ptnrs. bd., 1991—94. Bd. dirs. Tex. Lawyers Ins. Exch., 1983—, S.W. Benefits Assn. (formerly S.W. Pension Conf.), 1987—92, pres., 1990—91. Bd. dirs. East Dallas Devel. Ctr., 1982—91; Lone Star coun. Camp Fire USA, 1995—2001, v.p. outdoor programs, 1996—98, pres.-elect, 1997, pres., 1998—2000; bd. dirs. Episcopal Ch. Women of the Diocese of Dallas, 1992—2002, pres., 1996—2000; del. to triennial nat. conv. Episcopal Diocese of Dallas, 1994, 1997, 2000, asst. chancellor, 1994—2004, exec. coun., 1995—2000, standing com., 2001—04; pres. Episcopal Ch. Women for Episcopal Ch. of Ascension, 1992, bd. dirs., 1992—94; pres. Province VII Episcopal Ch. Women, bd. dirs., 1999—2002; exec. coun. Province VII of the Episcopal Ch., 1999—2002; mem. vestry Episcopal Ch. of the Ascension, 1996—99, 2005—; bd. dirs. High Adventure Treks for Dads and Daus., 2005—. Mem. ABA, Tex. Bar Assn. (chmn. bar. jour. com. 1982-88), Dallas Bar Assn. (treas. employee benefits com. 1998, sec. 1999, v.p. 2000, pres. 2001), Dallas Bus. League (pres. 1986). Avocation: sailing. Home: 600 Goodwin Dr Richardson TX 75081-5603 Office: Gardere Wynne Sewell LLP 1601 Elm St Ste 3000 Dallas TX 75201-4761 Office Phone: 214-999-4576. E-mail: sfenner@gardere.com.

FENNEY, LINDA, pharmaceutical executive; MD, Charing Cross Med. Sch. U. London. Resident in internal medicine Stanford U. Med. Ctr.; fellow in cardiology Veterans Adminstrn. Med. Ctr., Palo Alto, Calif.; various positions including dir. safety and surveillance and assoc. med. dir. cardiovasc. therapy Roche Pharm.; clin. faculty Stanford U. Dept. Cardiology; v.p. med. affairs Eclipse Surgical Technologies; pres., v.p., clin. rsch./govt. programs Ischemia Rsch. and Edn. Found.; sr. v.p. rsch., product devel. and regulatory affairs Connetics, 2001—. Office: Connetics Corporation 3160 Porter Dr Palo Alto CA 94304-1212

FENNING, LISA HILL, lawyer, mediator, retired judge; b. Chgo., Feb. 22, 1952; d. Ivan Byron and Joan (Hennigar) Hill; m. Alan Mark Fenning, Apr. 3, 1977; 4 children. BA with honors, Wellesley Coll., 1971; JD, Yale U., 1974. Bar: Ill. 1975, Calif. 1979, U.S. Dist. Ct. (no. dist.) Ill., U.S. Dist. Ct. (no., ea., so. & cen. dists.) Calif., U.S. Ct. Appeals (6th, 7th & 9th cirs.), U.S. Supreme Ct. 1989. Law clk. U.S. Ct. Appeals 7th cir., Chgo., 1974-75; assoc. Jenner and Block, Chgo., 1975-77, O'Melveny and Myers, L.A., 1977-85; judge U.S. Bankruptcy Ct. Cen. Dist. Calif., L.A., 1985-2000; mediator JAMS, Orange, Calif., 2000-01; ptnr. Dewey Ballantine LLP, L.A., 2001—. Bd. govs. Nat. Conf. Bankruptcy Judges, 1989-92; pres. Nat. Conf. of Women's Bar Assns., N.C., 1987-88, pres.-elect, 1986-87, v.p., 1985-86, bd. dirs.; lectr., program coord. in field; bd. govs. Nat. Conf. Bankruptcy Judges Endowment for Edn., 1992-97, Am. Bankruptcy Inst., 1994-2000; mem., bd. advisors Nat. Jud. Edn. Program to Promote Equality for Women and Men in the Cts., 1994—. Mem., bd. advisors: Lawyer Hiring & Training Report, 1985-87; contbr. articles to profl. jours. Durant scholar Wellesley Coll., 1971; named one of Am's. 100 Most Important Women Ladies Home Jour., 1988, one of L.A.'s 50 Most Powerful Women Lawyers, L.A. Bus. Jour., 1998, named one of So. Calif. Superlawyers, L.A. Mag., 2005. Fellow Am. Bar Found., Am. Coll. Bankruptcy (bd. regents 1995-98); mem. ABA (standing com. on fed. jud. improvements 1995-98, mem. commn. on women in the profession 1987-91), Individual Rights and Responsibilities sect. 1984—, bus. law sect. 1986—, bus. bankruptcy com.), Nat. Assn. Women Judges (nat. task force gender bias in the cts. 1986-87, 93-94), Nat. Conf. Bankruptcy Judges (chair endowment edn. bd. 1994-95), Am. Bankruptcy Inst. (nominating com. 1994-95, bd. steering com. stats. project 1994-96), Calif. State Bar Assn. (chair com. on women in law 1986-87), Women Lawyers' Assn. L.A. (ex officio mem., bd. dirs., chmn., founder com. on status of women lawyers 1984-85, officer nominating com. 1986, founder, mem. Do-It-Yourself Mentor Network 1986-96), Phi Beta Kappa. Democrat. Office: Dewey Ballantine LLP 333 S Grand Ave 26th Fl Los Angeles CA 90071 Office Phone: 213-621-6000. Business E-Mail: Lfenning@deweyballantine.com, lfenning@dbllp.com.

FENOGLIO-PREISER, CECILIA METTLER, retired pathologist, educator; b. NYC, Nov. 28, 1943; d. Frederick Albert and Cecilia Charlotte (Asper) Mettler; m. John Fenoglio Jr., May 27, 1967 (div. 1977); 1 child, Timothy; stepchildren: Johanna, Andreas, Nicholas; m. Wolfgang F.E. Preiser, Feb. 16, 1985. Ach, Coll. St. Elizabeth, 1965; MD, Georgetown U., 1969. Diplomate Am. Bd. Pathology. Intern Presbyn. Hosp., NYC, 1969-70; dir. Ctrl. Tissue Facility Columbia-Presbyn. Med. Ctr., NYC, 1976-83; co-dir. div. surg. pathology Presbyn. Hosp., NYC, 1978-82, div. dir. surg. pathology, 1982-83; dir. Electron Microscop. Lab. Internat. Inst. Human Reprodn., 1978-85; assoc. prof. pathology Coll. Physicians and Surgeons, Columbia U., 1981-82, prof., 1982-83, attending pathologist, 1982-83; dir. lab. services Albuquerque VA Med. Ctr., 1983-90; prof. pathology U. N.Mex. Sch. Medicine, Albuquerque, 1983-90, also vice-chmn. dept. pathology; MacKenzie prof., chmn. dept. pathology and lab. medicine U. Cin. Sch. Medicine, 1990—2005, dir. Cancer Ctr., 2001—05; ret., 2005. Mem. com. gastrointestine cancer WHO. Author: General Pathology, 1983, Gastrointestinal Pathology, An Atlas and Text, 1999, 2nd edit., 1999, Tumors of the Large and Small Intestine, 1990; editor: Advances in Pathobiology Cell Membranes, 1988-92, Advances in Pathobiology: Aging and Neoplasia, 1976, Progress in Surgical Pathology, vols. I-XIV, 1980-87, Advances in Pathology, vols. I-V, 1988-89. Grantee NIH, 1973, 79-82, 84-87, 85-2005, Cancer Rsch. Ctr., 1975-83, Population Coun., 1973-83, Nat. Ileitis and Colitis Found., 1979-80, Am. Cancer Soc., 1987-94. Fellow AAAS (life); mem. U.S. and Can. Acad. Pathology (edn. com. 1980-85, coun. 1984-87, exec. com. 1987-91, v.p. 1987, pres.-elect 1988, pres. 1989, fin. com. 1998-2001), Internat. Acad. Pathology (N.Am. v.p. 1990-94, pres. 1996-98, exec. com. 1990-2000, edn. com. 1998—), Nat. Surg. Adj. Breast Project (sci. adv. bd.), Am. Assn. Pathologists, Armed Forces Inst. Pathology (sci. adv. bd. 1990—), N.Y. Acad. Sci., N.Y. Acad. Medicine, Fedn. Am. Scientists for Exptl. Biology, Gastrointestinal Pathologist Group (founding mem. edn. com. 1983-85, sec.-treas. 1993-96, pres.-elect 1996, pres. 1997), S.W. Oncology Group (chmn. GI tumor biology com., chmn. pathology com., chmn. correlative sci. com.), Arthur Purdy Stout Soc. (coun. 1987-90). Personal E-mail: cecilia.fenogliopreiser@uc.edu.

FENSELAU, CATHERINE CLARKE, chemistry professor; b. York, Nebr., Apr. 15, 1939; d. Lee Keckley and Muriel (Thomas) Clarke; m. Allan Herman Fenselau, 1962 (div. 1980); children: Andrew Clarke, Thomas Stewart; m. Robert James Cotter, 1984. AB, Bryn Mawr Coll., 1961; PhD, Stanford U., 1965. Research scientist U. Calif.-Berkeley, 1965-67; instr. to prof. Johns Hopkins U., Balt., 1967-87; chmn. chemistry, biochemistry U. Md., Balt. County, 1987-98, prof. dept. chemistry and biochemistry College Park, 1998—; chmn. dept. chemistry and biochemistry, 1998-2000. Cons. NIH, NSF, USDA, U.S. Army, FDA, others. Editor: Biomed. Environ. Mass Spectrometry, 1973—89; editor: (assoc. editor) Analytical Chemistry, 1990—; contbr. articles to profl. jours. Recipient Hillebrand prize, Chem. Soc. Washington, 2005. Fellow: AAAS; mem.: U.S. Human Proteomic Orgn. (pres. 2004—06), Am. Soc. Pharmacology and Exptl. Therapeutics, Am. Chem. Soc. (Garvan medal 1985, Md. Chemist award Md. sect. 1989), Am. Soc. Mass Spectrometry (pres. 1980—82). Office: U Md Dept Chemistry Biochemistry College Park MD 20742-0001

FENSTERMACHER, JOYCE DORIS, real estate agent, real estate appraiser; b. Scranton, Pa., Feb. 25, 1932; d. Brenton Luellen and Doris Baer; m. J. Gordon Fenstermacher, Dec. 10, 1955; children: Karen, Peter, Christopher. BA, U. Miami, 1953. Lic. real estate broker Pa., cert. residential appraiser. Real estate agt. Fried Realty, Harrisburg, Pa., 1972, Doucherty & Twigg, Harrisburg, Pa., 1973—77, Jack Gerghen Realty, Harrisburg, Pa., 1977—82, Coldwell Banker Realty, Harrisburg, Pa., 1982—91, Re/Max Realty Profls., Harrisburg, Pa., 2001—05; appraiser Robert Jones Appraisers, Harrisburg, Pa., 1991—2001. Singer, actress Harrisburg Cmty. Theater; lead singer York (Pa.) Cmty. Theater; founder Harrisburg Opera Soc.; elder Faith Presbyn. Ch., 1989—91, pres. corp., 1991. Named one of Business Women of Yr., Patriot News, Harrisburg, 1990. Mem.: Harrisburg Bd. Realtors (mem. ethics com. 1985—91, mem. legis. com. 2003—05). Republican. Avocations: golf, singing. Home: 4427 Avon Dr Harrisburg PA 17112 Office: Re/Max Realty Profls Inc 1250 N Mountain Rd Harrisburg PA 17112

FENTON, KATHRYN MARIE, lawyer; b. Bridgeport, Conn., July 24, 1953; d. George Joseph and Josephine Marie (Barron) F.; m. William Evan Kovacic, May 18, 1985. BA summa cum laude, Fairfield Univ., 1975; JD cum laude, Georgetown U., 1978. Bar: D.C. 1978. Law clk. to Hon. Oliver Gasch U.S. Dist Ct. D.C. dist., Washington, 1978-79; atty. bur. competition FTC, Washington, 1979-83, atty. advisor to chmn. James C. Miller III, 1983-84; assoc. Jones, Day, Reavis & Pogue, Washington, 1984-88, ptnr., antitrust & govt. regulation practices, 1989—. Editor in chief, Georgetown Law Jour.; contbr. articles to law jours. and profl. publs.; editl. chair Antitrust Law Jour. 1992-97. Mem. ABA (antitrust, adminstrv. law sects.). Roman Catholic. Avocations: antiques, quilting. Office: Jones Day 51 Louisiana Ave NW Washington DC 20001-2113 Office Phone: 202-879-3746. Office Fax: 202-626-1700. Business E-Mail: kmfenton@jonesday.com.

FENTON, MARY CATHERINE, literature educator; d. Gerald Paul and Stephanie Coleman Fenton; m. Anthony Andrew Hickey, July 2, 1999; children: Ellie Norton, Gracie Norton, Thomas Hickey. BA, U. Wyo., Laramie, 1980, MA, 1982; PhD, U. Ky., Lexington, 1990. Assoc. prof. of english Western Carolina U., Cullowhee, NC, 1992—. Recipient U. Scholar award, Western Carolina U., 2005—06, U. of NC Bd. of Governors' award for Excellence in Tchg., U. of NC, 2004, Chancellor's Disting. Tchg. award, Western Carolina U., 2003, Coll. of Arts & Sciences Tchg. award, 2003, Excellence in Grad. Student Mentoring: Faculty award, 2001, Chancellor's award for Outstanding Tchg. Assistants, U. of Ky., 1990, Ellershaw award for Outstanding Ph.D. Student, 1990. Mem.: Milton Soc. of Am. (exec. com. 2006—). Home: 242 Wren Lane Whittier NC 28789 Office: Western Carolina Univ 424 Coulter Bldg Cullowhee NC 28723 Office Phone: 828-227-3934. Business E-Mail: mfenton@wcu.edu.

FENTON, MONICA, retired biomedical researcher; b. Elizabeth, NJ, Mar. 2, 1944; d. Edward B. and Veronica (Kryszczuk) Zacharczyk; m. C. Gerald Bischoff (div. 1971); m. Roger A. Fenton, July 30, 1983 (dec. Jan. 1995). Student, Union Coll., Cranford, N.J., 1962-66. Sr. rsch. tech. Bristol-Myers Co., Hillside, N.J., 1963-75; tech. adminstr., electron microscopist Albert Einstein Coll. Medicine, Bronx, N.Y., 1975-88; asst. to dir. Ctr. Rsch. Occupational & Environ. Toxicology Oreg. Health Sci. U., 1988—2000; ret., 2000. Mng. editor Third World Med. Rsch. Found., N.Y.C., 1987-95, editorial cons., 1990—; corr. & devel. editor Experimental and Clinical Neurotoxicology, 1992-2000; copy editor (proc.) The Grass Pea: Threat and Promise, 1989, Nutrition, Neurotoxins and Lathyrism, 1994, (transcripts) Toxicity of Cycads, 1988; contbr. articles to profl. jours. Mem. Electron Microscopy Soc. Am. Avocations: skiing, biking, gourmet cooking. Home: PO Box 880321 Steamboat Springs CO 80488-0321

FERBER, LINDA S., museum director; BA cum laude, Barnard Coll., 1966; MA, Columbia U., 1968, PhD in Art History, 1980. Curator Am. Painting and Sculpture The Bklyn. Mus., 1970-97, chief curator, 1985-99, Andrew W. Mellon curator Am. Art, 1997—2005; v.p., dir. NY Hist. Soc. Mus., 2005—. Author: William Trost Richards (1833-1905): American Landscape and Marine Painter, 1980, Tokens of a Friendship: Miniature Watercolors by William T. Richards, 1982, (with others) The New Path: Ruskin and the American Pre-Raphaelites, 1985, Never at Fault: The Drawings of William T. Richards, 1986, (with others) Albert Bierstadt: Art and Enterprise, 1991, (with others) Masters of Color and Light: Homer, Sargent and the American Watercolor Movement, 1998, Pastoral Interlude: William T. Richards in Chester County, 2001, (with others) In Search of a National Landscape: William T. Richards in the Adirondacks, 2002; contbr. articles on 19th and 20th century Am. art history. Wyeth Endowment for Am. Art fellow, 1976-77; recipient Disting. Alumna award Barnard Coll., 2001, Fleischman award Smithsonian Archives of Am. Art, 2002. Mem. Coll. Art Assn., Am. Assn. Mus., Am. Studies Assn., Assn. Art Mus. Curators, Century Assn., Orgn. Am. Historians, Assn. for State and Local History, Cosmopolitan Club, Phi Beta Kappa. Office: NY Hist Soc 170 Ctrl Pk W New York NY 10024 Office Phone: 212-873-3400 259. Business E-Mail: lferber@nyhistory.org.

FERENCZ, CHARLOTTE, pediatrician, epidemiologist, preventive medicine physician, educator; b. Budapest, Hungary, Oct. 28, 1921; came to U.S., 1954; d. Paul Ferencz and Livia deFekete. BSc, McGill U., 1944, MD, CM, 1945; MPH, Johns Hopkins U., 1970. Cert. pediatrics Royal Coll. Physicians and Surgeons, Can., pediatric cardiology Am. Bd. Pediatrics. Demonstrator McGill U., Montreal, 1952-54; asst. prof. pediatrics Johns Hopkins U., Balt., 1954-58, U. Cin., 1959-60; asst. prof. SUNY, Buffalo, 1960-66, assoc. prof., 1966-73; assoc. prof. epidemiology and preventive medicine U. Md. Sch. Medicine, Balt., 1973-74, prof., 1974-98, prof. pediatrics, 1985—, prof. emeritus, 1998—. Prin. investigator population based study Etiology of Congenital Heart Disease, 1981-89; mem. epidemiology and disease control study sect. NIH, 1984-88; pres. Delta Omage Alpha chpt. Pub. Health Soc., 1990-92. Recipient M.E.S. Abbott scholarship McGill U., 1943-45, M.E.R.I.T. award Nat. Heart, Lung & Blood Inst., 1987, Fogarty Internat. Ctr. Health Sci. Exchange award NIH, 1988, Helen B. Taussig award Am. Heart Assn. Md. Affiliate, 1991, Achievement award Univ. Ctr. Life Scis., Balt., 1993, Johns Hopkins U. Disting. Alumnus award, 2001. Fellow Am. Acad. Pediatrics (Spl. Achievement award Md. chpt. 1994), Am. Coll. Cardiology; mem. Teratology Soc. Democrat. Office: U Md Sch Medicine 660 W Redwood St Baltimore MD 21201-1541

FERENTINO, SHEILA CONNOLLY, psychologist, consultant; d. John Francis Connolly and Mabel Rose McCabe; 1 child, James. BA, Hunter Coll. CUNY; MS in Spl. Edn., CUNY, 1963; profl. diploma in Psychology, St. John's U., 1973; PhD in Psychology, Hofstra U., 1991. Cert. tchr. blind and partially sighted NYS, 1962, braillist Libr. Congress, 1964, sch. psychologist NY, 1972, lic. psychologist NY, 1993. Tchr. elem. sch. Nassau County Sch. Dist., NYC, 1960—61; tchr. blind Nassau Bd. Cooperative Edn. Svcs. Spl. Edn., NY, 1961—72, psychologist, 1972—2004; child psychologist, children with disabilities pvt. practice, Freeport, NY, 2005—. Tchr. Summer Headstart, Hollis, NY, 1968—69, dir., 1970; adj. prof. Hunter Coll. CUNY, NYC, 1963—65; asst. dir. after sch. activities for blind Bd. Cooperative Edn. Svcs., 1965—70. Contbr. articles to profl. jours. Chmn. mus. trips com. Helen Keller Svcs. for Blind, Nassau County, 1961—70; contbr. Evaluation Measures for Handicapped Pre-Schoolers. Grantee, NY State Dept. Edn., 1980, 1989, Vanderbilt U., 1988. Mem.: APA, Nat. Assn. Prevention Blindness, Nassau Couny Psychol. Assn., NY State Psychol. Assn., Sigmund Freud Soc., Orton

Soc. Avocations: classical music, opera, travel, wildlife conservation, maritime museums. Home: 18-05 215 St Apt 2B Bayside NY 11360 Office: 110 Garfield St Freeport NY 11520 Office Phone: 917-655-5691. Personal E-mail: posone@verizon.net.

FERGIE, (STACY ANN FERGUSON), singer; b. Whittier, Calif., Mar. 27, 1975; d. Terri and Pat Ferguson. Band mem. Wild Orchid, 1996—2002, Black Eyed Peas, 2003—. Singer: (albums) (with Wild Orchid) Wild Orchid, 1997, Oxygen, 1998, Fire, 2001, (with Black Eyed Peas) Elephunk, 2003, Monkey Business, 2005, (solo albums) The Dutchess, 2006, (songs) (with Wild Orchid) At Night I Pray, 1996, Talk to Me, 1997, Supernatural, 1997, Be Mine, 1998, Stuttering (Don't Say), 2001, (with Black Eyed Peas) Where is the Love?, 2003, Shut Up, 2003, Let's Get It Started, 2004 (Grammy, Best Rap Performance, 2005), Hey Mama, 2004 (MTV Music Video Award), Don't Phunk with My Heart, 2005 (Grammy award, Best Rap Group Performance, 2006), Don't Lie, 2005, My Humps, 2005 (MTV Video Music award for Best Hip-Hop Video, 2006), (as solo artist) London Bridge, 2006; actor: (films) Be Cool, 2005, Poseidon, 2006; (TV series) Kids Incorporated, 1984—89, The Charlie Brown & Snoopy Show, 1984—85, Great Pretenders, 1999. Named one of 50 Most Beautiful People in the World, People mag., 2004; recipient MTV Europe award for Best Pop Act (with Black Eyed Peas), 2004, 2005, Favorite Pop Group & Rap Group, Am. Music Awards, 2005. Studio: A&M Recording Studios 1416 North La Brea Hollywood CA 90028 Office Phone: 323-469-5181. Office Fax: 213-856-2712.

FERGUS, KATHERINE YOUNG, lawyer; b. Bangor, Maine, Mar. 3, 1972; BA, Bowdoin Coll., 1994; JD magna cum laude, Suffolk U., 1997. Bar: Mass. 1997, Maine 1997, US Dist. Ct. (Dist. Mass.). Assoc. Willcox, Pirozzolo & McCarthy, PC, Boston, 1997—99, Duane Morris LLP, Boston, 2000—. Mem.: Women's Bar Assn. Mass., Nat. Assn. Women Lawyers, Boston Bar Assn., Mass. Bar Assn., ABA. Office: Duane Morris LLP Ste 500 470 Atlantic Ave Boston MA 02210 Office Phone: 617-289-9253. Office Fax: 617-289-9201. E-mail: KYFergus@duanemorris.com.*

FERGUS, PATRICIA MARGUERITA, language educator, writer, editor; b. Mpls., Oct. 26, 1918; d. Golden Maughan and Mary Adella (Smith) Fergus. BS, U. Minn., 1939, MA, 1941, PhD, 1960. Various pers. and editing positions U.S. Govt., 1943-59; mem. faculty U. Minn., Mpls., 1964-79, asst. prof. English, 1972-79, coord. writing program conf. on writing, 1975, dir. writing centre, 1975-77; prof. English and writing, dir. writing ctr., assoc. dean Coll. Mt. St. Mary's Coll., Emmitsburg, Md., 1979-81; dir. writing seminars Mack Truck, Inc., Hagerstown, Md., 1979-81; writer, 1964—. Editor, 1997—; vocal soloist, 1997—; editl. asst. to pres. Met. State U., St. Paul, 1984—85; coord. creative writing, writer program notes for Coffee Concerts The Kenwood, 1992—94; dir. Kenwood Scribes Presentation, 1994; spkr., cons. in field; dir. 510 Groveland Assocs.; bus. mgr. Eitel Hosp. Gift Shop; freelance manuscript editor, 1997—99; writer, reviewer Whittier Pubs., Long Beach, NY, 1997; instr. Elderlearning Inst., 1999—2000, Univ. Coll., U. Minn., 1999—2000; poetry and prose reading, retirement cmtys., 2002—06; pres., resident coun. Walker Tree Tops, Mpls., 2003—04, spl. events dir., master of ceremonies, dir., spkr., 2003—06. Author: Spelling Improvement, 5th edit., 1991; contbr. to Downtown Cath. Voice, Mpls., Mountaineer Briefing, ABI Digest, Women in the Arts The Penletter; contbr. poems to Minn. English Jour., Women in the Arts, Decatur Area Arts Coun. Newsletter, Mpls. Muse, The Moccasin, Heartsong and Northstar Gold, The Pen Woman, Midwest Chaparral, Rhyme Time, The Best of Rhyme Time, 1998, Fantasy, 1998; contbr. short stories to anthologies, including Seeking the Muses, Inspired Works of Creativity, 2000; musical works performed at St. Olaf Ch., 1997, Nat. League Am. Pen Women, 1998. Mem. spl. vocal octet St. Olaf Ch. Choir, 1977-79, 81-92, St. Olaf Parish Adv. Bd., 1982-84, Windmore Found. for the Arts., 1996. Recipient Outstanding Contbn. award U. Minn. Twin Cities Student Assembly, 1975, Horace T. Morse-Amoco Found. award, 1976; Golden Poet award World of Poetry, 1992; Ednl. Devel. grant U. Minn., 1975-76, Mt. St. Mary's Coll. grant, 1980; 3d prize vocal-choral category Nat. Music Composition Contest, Nat. League Am. Pen Women, poetry prize No. Dist. Women's Club, Va., 1996. Mem.: Midwest Fedn. Chaparral Poets (poetry judge, numerous poetry prizes including 1st prize 1998, 1999, 2001, 2003), Mpls. Poetry Soc. (pres. 2000—02, numerous poetry prizes including 1st prize 1999, 2d prize 2003, 1st prize 2006), World Lit. Acad., Nat. League Am. Pen Women (Minn. br. and state past pres., 1st pl. Haiku nat. poetry contest 1992), Minn. Coun. Tchrs. English (chmn. career and job opportunities comm., spl. com. tchr. licensure, sec. legis. com.), Nat. Coun. Tchrs. English (regional judge 1974, 1976—77, state coord. 1977—79), Mpls. Woman's Club (critic writers group). Roman Catholic. Home and Office: 1509 10th Ave S 319 Minneapolis MN 55404-1752 Office Phone: 612-827-4867.

FERGUS, VICTORIA J., art and education educator; b. Dayton, Ohio, Aug. 22, 1952; d. Joseph Lester Jr. and Mary Jean (James) F. BA in Art Edn., George Peabody Coll. Tchr., 1974, MA in Art, 1976; PhD in Edn. and Art, Purdue U., 1987. Grad. teaching asst. George Peabody Coll. for Tchrs., Nashville, 1974-75; instr. La. State U., Eunice, 1975-77; art tchr. Morton Elem. Sch., West Lafayette, Ind., 1978-79; grad. teaching fellow Purdue U., West Lafayette, Ind., 1977-81; artist, designer, owner Artwear, 1981—; instr., head tchr. outreach programs Dulin Gallery of Art, 1981-83; asst. prof. W.Va. U., Morgantown, 1983-89, assoc. prof., 1989—. Art instr. summer art series Tullahoma (Tenn.) Fine Arts Ctr., 1971; artist in residence La. State U., Eunice, 1975-76; presenter at workshops in field; mem. Gov.'s Task Force for Arts in Basic Edn.; mem. Arts in Edn. Task Force, 1990—; mem. evaluation com. Arts in Edn. Program, Ind., 1977-79; mem. ARts Advocacy Com. of W.Va. One woman show at La. State U., 1975, W.Va. U., 1989; exhibited in group shows at W.Va. U., 1984, 85, 86, 87, 89, 91, Butler Inst. Am. Art, 1986, 91, Touchstone Ctr. for Crafts, Pa., 1986, Dupont Galleries, Mary Washington Coll., Fredricksburg, Va., 1987, Monongalia Arts Ctr., Morgantown, 1988, Trumbell Art Gallery, Warren, Ohio, 1988, Lebel Gallery, 1989, Electronic Gallery, Atlanta, 1988, 89, 91, others; contbr. book revs. to profl. publs. Judge poster show U.S. Dept. Energy, 1989, Tullahoma Fine Arts and Crafts Show, 1985, South Jr. High Sch., Morgantown, 1987, 18th Ann. Tullahoma Fine Arts and Crafts Fair, Tenn., 1987, poster contest Am. Lung Assn., W.Va. Girl Scouts Am., 1985, Monongalia Art Ctr., 1984, Youth Art Month, 1985, Tenn. Valley Student Art Show, 1982, others. Named West Va. Art Educator of Yr., 1990-91; mem. 2000 Women of Achievement, 1992; grantee W.Va. Arts and Humanities, 1991, NEA, W.Va. Dept. Edn., 1991, others. Mem. ASCD, Nat. Art Edn. Assn. (H.E. divsn. dir., 1998-2000, student chapters nat. advisor, 2000-05,Art Tchr. of Yr. ea. region 1987, Presdl. Citation award 1993, Presdl. Achievement award 1993), W.Va. Art Edn. Assn. (dir. higher edn. div. 1985-90, pres. 1987-89), Nat. Am. Crafts Coun., Nat. Mus. for Women in Arts, Arts Advocacy W.Va., W.Va. Humanities Ctr., W.Va. Artists Guild, Nat. Am. Crafts Coun., U.S. Soc. for Edn. in Arts, Phi Kappa Phi. Methodist. Avocations: hiking, travel, water-skiing. Home: 410 Lewis St Morgantown WV 26505-3716 Office: W Va U PO Box 6111 Morgantown WV 26506-6111

FERGUSON, BENETTA N., secondary school educator; b. Columbus, Ohio, Apr. 11, 1979; d. Ronald K. and Jacquelyn M. Ferguson. BS, Ohio State U., Columbus, 2002; MS, U. SC, Columbia, 2004. Tchr., athletic trainer Lexington H.S., SC, 2004—. Athletic trainer Providence Hosp., Columbia, 2006—. Office: Lexington High School 2463 Augusta Highway Lexington SC 29072 Office Phone: 803-359-5565.

FERGUSON, CATHLEEN MICHELE, elementary school educator; b. Teaneck, N.J., Jan. 4, 1977; d. Edward John and Diane Patricia Ferguson. BS, U. Miami, Coral Gables, Fla., 1999; MA in Edn., St. Peter's Coll., Jersey City, N.J., 2001. Cert. tchr. biol. sci. N.J. Bd. Edn., 2000, supr. N.J. Bd. Edn., 2001. Tchr. Secaucus (N.J.) Mid. Sch., 1999—. Asst. dir. day camp spl. needs Secaucus (N.J.) Recreation Dept., 1999. Mem.: N.J. Edn. Assn. (assoc.). Office: Secaucus Middle School 11 Mill Ridge Road Secaucus NJ 07094 Office Phone: 210-974-2022.

FERGUSON, DIANA S., food products executive; b. 1963; M in Mgmt., Northwestern U.; Bachelor's, Yale U. With Eaton, Fannie Mae, First Nat. Bank Chgo., IBM, US Fort James Corp.; v.p., treas. Sara Lee Corp., 2001—. Fellow: Leadership Greater Chgo. Office: Sara Lee Corp 3 First Nat Plaza Chicago IL 60602-4260

FERGUSON, LISA BERYL, accountant; b. L.A., Apr. 17, 1958; d. Harry Alfred Abramson and Dolores Gloria Cohen; m. Jeffrey Monroe Ferguson, June 23, 1984 (div. Oct. 1992); children: Kate Emily, Colin James; m. Michael Jonathan Miqdadi, May 17, 2003. BSBA, U. Phoenix, 1997. CPA Calif., 2000; notary pub. Calif., 1979. Acct. Neal Levin and Co., Beverly Hills, Calif., 1978—2002; acct., mng. ptnr. Premier Bus. Mgmt. Group, 2003—. Democrat. Office: Premier Bus Mgmt Group 15260 Ventura Blvd # 1700 Sherman Oaks CA 91403 Office Phone: 818-933-2600.

FERGUSON, MARGARET ANN, tax specialist, consultant; b. Steuben County, Ind., Mar. 24, 1933; d. Leo C. and Ruth Virginia (Engle) Wolf; m. Billy Hugh Ferguson, Feb. 15, 1955 (dec. Oct. 1971); children: Theresa Ruth, Scott Earl, Wade Leo, Luke, Angela, Cynthia, Brenda. AA in Psychology/Social Svs., Palomar Coll., San Marcos, Calif., 1977; BA in Behavioral Sci., Nat. U., Vista, Calif., 1980. Enrolled agt. Office mgr., adminstr. asst. Better Bus. Bur., San Diego, 1979-82; tax technician IRS, Oceanside, Calif., 1982-84, problem resolution tax specialist, 1985-87, revenue agt., 1987-90; pvt. cons. Vista, Calif., 1991—. Instr. adult edn. Vista Unified Sch. Dist., 1990-99; mem. adv. com. of nat. cemetery sys. Dept. Vet. Affairs, 1991-98; adv. coun. IRS, 1999-2001, mem. taxpayer advocate panel, 2005—. Mem. AAUW (treas.), Calif. Assn. Ind. Accts., Calif. Soc. Enrolled Agts. (dir. Palomar chpt. 1993-95, 2000-01, 1st v.p. 1998-2000), Inland Soc. Tax Cons., Assn. Homebased Bus., Gold Star Wives Am., Inc. (regional pres. 1989-90, chpt. pres. 1992-93, 96-97, nat. pres. 1993-95, chmn. nat. bd. dirs. 2004-06). Avocations: lace making, needle work, gardening, writing. Home and Office: 1161 Tower Dr Vista CA 92083-7144 Personal E-mail: gswtax@aol.com.

FERGUSON, MARGARET GENEVA, writer, publisher, real estate broker; d. James B. and Dollie (McCloud) F. Student, Kansas City Jr. Coll., 1949, YMCA Real Estate Inst., 1960, Bryant and Stratton Bus. Coll., 1962, Ill. Inst. Tech., 1969, 70, 72; postgrad. in sociology, Chgo. State U. pub. spkr. Sec. Cook County Grand Jury, 1979; acting mgr. internal svc. dept. Xerox Corp., 1985-86, fin. specialist, 1984-87. Tutor reading and math., 1988; instr. sociology Chgo. State U., 2001-2002; host Black Image Prodn. Cable 19, 1989; interviewed on various TV shows, including PM Mag., 1983; active pub. rels. newspapers, Chgo., Detroit, Kansas City, St. Louis, 1970-91; conductor workshops in field; participant Pan Meth. Pilgrimage to Eng., 1984, World Meth. Conf., Nairobi, Kenya, 1986; spkr. in field. Author, pub.: The History of St. Paul CME Church 1907-1988, 1989, Books in Print, 1989-90, This Is Your Life Dr. Owens, 1991. Co-treas. fund raiser Citizens for Mayor Harold Washington, Chgo., 1987; treas. St. Paul Mortgage Fund, 1984; vol. Am. Cancer Soc., Salvation Army, Lighthouse for the Blind, 1982, Dem. Nat. Conv., 1996, Olympic Torch, Nat. Coun. State Legis.; dist. pres. Christian Methodist Episcopal Ch. Nat. Women's League, 1980-86, nat. fin. sec., 1980-92; officer St. Paul Christian Methodist Episcopal Ch., 1983—; v.p. lay ministry, 1987-92, pres. 1992-99; 2d v.p. Ann. Conf. Lay Ministry, 1996-99; sec. Christian Methodist Episcopal Long Range Planning Commn., 1982-86; mem. Chgo. State Street Women's Coun.; judge Chgo. City Elections Bur., 1997; mem. State Street Woman's Coun., 1976, Du Sable Mus., 1990. Recipient PUSH Person Min. award, 1970, Vol. of Yr. award Chgo. Lighthouse, 1982, Gold Coaster award Kiwanis Club, 1983, Black on Black Love award, 1988, History Writing award Christian Meth. Episcopal Ch., 1990, 1st Lady award V-103FM, 1991, Key to City, Ft. Smith, Ark., 1992, Lifetime Achievement Culture Ctr. award, Citizens award V-103FM, 1994, Bishop's award C.M.E. Ch., 1996; named to Cultural Citizens Found. Hall of Fame, 1990. Mem. NAACP, Nat. Coun. Negro Women, People United to Serve Humanity (prison ministry award 1991, Fred Davis award 1994, Steward of Yr. award 1999), Chgo. Bd. Realtors, S.W. Suburban Bd. Realtors, Hyde Park Co-op Soc. (bd. dirs. 1994-95), Internat. Platform Assn., Am. Assn. Ret. Persons (55 Alive instr. 1996—), DuSable Mus., Lambda Kappa Mu.

FERGUSON, NANCY L., psychotherapist, social worker; b. Milw., Jan. 8, 1947; d. Earl Wayne and LaVerne Caroline Ferguson; children: Nathan J. Rosnow, Katherine Ann Rosnow. BA, U. Wis., Madison, 1971; MSW, U. Wis., Milw., 1983. Lic. clin. social worker; cert. alcohol and drug counselor. Adminstr. McMahon Residential Ctr., Milw., 1973-79; children's program coord. Horizon House, Milw., 1980-84; family therapist Elmbrook Meml. Hosp., Brookfield, Wis., 1984-97; sch. social worker Greendale (Wis.) Schs., 1987—2002; psychiat. social worker Greenbriar Hosp., Milw., 1991-95; psychotherapist Acacia Clinic, White-Leonard Clinic, Lighthouse Clinic, Milw., 1993—; asst. prof. Cardinal Stritch U., Milw., 1997—2005. Cons., trainer, spkr. Nancy L. Ferguson & Assocs., LLC, Milw., 1997—. Co-author: Community Living Guide, 1976; author: Adolescent Post-Treatment Support: A High School Substance Recovery Course, 2001. Mem. NASW. Unitarian Universalist. Office: 2577 N Downer Ave #215 Milwaukee WI 53211 Office Phone: 414-964-9200 216. Business E-Mail: nfergus@execpc.com.

FERGUSON, PAMELA SANTAVICCA, language educator, department chairman; b. Plainfield, N.J., Apr. 15, 1949; d. Russell L. and Laura Esther (Telander) Ferguson; children: Daniel, Elizabeth. BA, Douglass Coll., 1971; MEd, Rutgers U., 1972. Cert. elem. tchr., N.J. Tchr. Orchard Road Sch., Montgomery Twp., N.J., 1972-84; county coord. Congrl. Campaign, Centre County, Pa., 1986; dir. Christian edn. St. Andrews Ch., State College, Pa., 1987-88; exec. dir. Food Bank State Coll., 1992—2000; devel. dir. Strawberry Fields Inc., 2002; English dept. chair South Hills Sch. of Bus. and Tech., State College, Pa., 2002—, chmn. Dept. English, 2005—. Interfaith Mission, State College, 1992-2000. Committeewoman State Coll. Bd. Dems., 1986-2000; vestry mem. St. Andrews Episcopal Ch., 1988-95, 2005, reader, chalice bearer, 1992—, chair capital campaign, 1998; founder Cmty. Safety Net, 1996; bd. dirs. Vol. Centre, 1997-99, bd. dirs. Centre County United Way, Meals on Wheels, 2004—. Recipient Cmty. Leadership award Nat. Assn. Cmty. Leadership, 1998; named Citizen of Yr., 1997. Mem. Leadersip Ctr. County, Rotary Internat. (group study exch. 1996—), Meals on Wheels (bd. dirs.). Democrat. Episcopalian. Avocations: hiking, reading, travel. Home: 2322 Oak Leaf Dr State College PA 16803 Office: South Hills Sch of Bus and Technology 480 Waupelani Dr State College PA 16801

FERGUSON, RENEE, news correspondent, reporter; b. Oklahoma City, Aug. 22, 1949; d. Eugene and Mary Ferguson; m. Ken Smikle; 1 child, Jason. BS in journalism, Ind. U., 1971. With Sta. WLWI-TV, Indpls.; reporter Sta. WBBM-TV, Chgo., 1977—81; news corr. CBS Network, NYC, Atlanta; gen. assignment reporter Sta. WMAQ-TV, Chgo., 1987—, investigative reporter, 1997—. Recipient 7 Chgo. Emmy awards, 5 Assoc. Press awards, AWRT Gracie Allen award, Columbia-duPont award, Studs Terkel Media award, 2006; fellow Benton fellowship in Journalism, U. Chgo., 1991, Criminal Justice fellow, Univ. S. Calif. Annenberg Inst. Justice & Journalism, Nieman fellow, Harvard U., 2006—07. Mem.: Investigative Reporters & Editors (mem. bd. 2006—). Office: NBC5 Chgo WMAQ 454 N Columbus Dr Chicago IL 60611*

FERGUSON, SARAH, The Duchess of York; b. London, Oct. 15, 1959; d. Ronald Ivor Ferguson and Susan Mary (Fitzherbert Wright) Barrantes; m. Andrew, Duke of York, July 23, 1986 (div. 1996); children: Beatrice Elizabeth Mary, Eugenie Victoria Helena. Student, Hurst Lodge, Sunningdale, Eng., Queen's Secretarial Coll., London. Spokeswoman Weight Watchers Internat., 1997—. Author: Budgie the Little Helicopter, 1989, Budgie at Bendick's Point, 1989, Budgie Goes to Sea, 1991, Budgie and the Blizzard, 1991, Victoria and Albert-Life at Osborne House, 1991, Travels with Queen Victoria, 1993, My Story, 1996, Dining with the Duchess, 1998, Winning the Weight Game, 2000, Dieting With the Duchess, 2000, What I Know Now, 2003, Little Red, 2003, Little Red's Christmas, 2004. Recipient Mother Hale award, 1996. Address: Simon & Schuster Publicity Dept Ste C3A 1230 Avenue Of The Americas Fl Concl New York NY 10020-1586

FERGUSON, STACY ANN See **FERGIE**

FERGUSON MCGINNIS, KATHRYN JOAN (KATHY FERGUSON MCGINNIS), flight attendant; b. Toledo, Ohio, Oct. 7, 1947; d. Donald E. and Alice I. (Hart) Ferguson; m. Michael E. McGinnis Sr., Aug. 6, 1988; 1 child, Gary Alan McGinnis stepchildren: Michael E. McGinnis Jr., Patrick McGinnis, Thomas McGinnis, Kathleen McGinnis. BS in Chemistry, U. Toledo, Ohio, 1969; post grad. in Chemistry and Edn. Cert. gen. and comprehensive sci. U. Toledo, tchr. Ohio, 2002. Flight attendant United Airlines, Chgo., 1970—; substitute tchr. Toledo Pub. Schs., 1988—2004; student tchr. Waite HS, 2000—01; substitute tchr. St. Thomas Sch., 2001; student field tchg. Sylvania (Ohio) Southview, 2000—01; GED tutoring Women Blessing Women, Toledo, 2002—; substitute tchr. Oregon City Schs., Oregon, Ohio, 2003—05; long term substitute Ctrl. Cath. High, Toledo, 2005; religious edn. St. Thomas Ch., Toledo; long term substitute DeVilbiss HS, Toledo; substitute tchr. Dioceses of Toledo; undergrad asst. U. Toledo. Contbr. articles various profl. jours. Co-chair, mem. Path to Life, Maternity Housing and Outreach; co-team leader CANA II Diocesan Remarriage Assistance, 1995—2005; com. mem. Justice and Peace Group Emmaus Cluster; youth group dir. St. Ann's Ch., 1976—77; vol. aide Connecting Point Runaway Shelter, 1977—80; team group mem. Cath. Alumni Club. Mem.: Assn. Flight Attendents. Roman Catholic. Avocations: swimming, travel, gardening.

FERGUSON-WHITEHEAD, WENDY SANDRA, elementary school educator, art educator, artist; d. Keith Melville and Carol Lane; m. Alan Robert Whitehead, Dec. 28, 1999. Diploma in edn., Monash U., Melbourne, Griffith U., Queensland. Tchr. art East Oakleigh Primary Sch., Victoria, Australia, 1977—89, Springvale West Primary Sch., 1989—94, Burleigh Heads Primary Sch., Queensland, 1995—98; lectr. art Griffith U., 1998; tchr. Manning Elem. Sch., Roanoke, NC, 1999—2000, Weldon Elem. Sch., 2000—01; tchr. art, sci., lead tchr. art Swift Creek Elem. Sch., Whittakers, 2001—06. Author of poems. Mem.: Wilson Active Artists, Nat. Art Educators Assn., Internat. Reading Assn. Avocations: travel, reading, sewing, quilting.

FERGUSSON, FRANCES DALY, former academic administrator; b. Boston, Oct. 3, 1944; d. Francis Joseph and Alice (Storrow) Daly. BA in Art History, Wellesley Coll., 1965; MA in Art History, Harvard U., 1966, PhD in Art History, 1973; DLitt, U. Hartford, 2000, U. London, 2001, Bard Coll., 2006. Asst. prof. art Newton Coll., Mass., 1969—75; assoc. prof. art U. Mass., Boston, 1974—82, asst. chancellor, 1980—82; provost, v.p. acad. affairs, prof. art Bucknell U., Lewisburg, Pa., 1982—86; pres. Vassar Coll., Poughkeepsie, NY, 1986—2006. Bd. dirs. HSBC Bank USA, Wyeth Pharms., 2005—, Mattel, Inc., 2006—; trustee Mayo Found., 1988—2002, chmn., 1998—2002; trustee Ford Found., 1989—2001, Hist. Hudson, 1990—99. Bd. overseers Harvard U., 2002—; bd. dirs. Noguchi Found., 2004—, Fgn. Policy Assn., 2003—, Found. Contemporary Arts, 2006—, Nat. Humanities Ctr., 2006—, Second Stage Theater, 2006—. Recipient Founder's award, Soc. Archtl. Historians, 1973, Eleanor Roosevelt at Val-Kill medal, 1998, Centennial medal, Harvard Grad. Sch. of Arts and Scis., 1999, Alumni award, Wellesley Coll., 2001; fellow Am. Acad. Arts & Sciences, 2002. Avocation: piano.

FERHOLT, J. DEBORAH LOTT, pediatrician; b. New Rochelle, NY, Aug. 27, 1942; d. Sidney and Rose Lott; m. Julian Ferholt, June 19, 1963; children: Beth, Sarah. BS in Biology, U. Rochester, 1963, MD, 1967. Diplomate Am. Bd. Pediat. From instr. to assoc. prof. Yale Sch. Nursing, New Haven, 1969-90, lectr., 1990—2001, clin. assoc. prof. pediatrics, 1987—2003; pvt. practice pediatrics New Haven, 1982—. Author: (book) Health Assessment of Children, 1980 (Best Pediatric Book award 1981). Fellow Am. Acad. Pediatrics. Office: 303 Whitney Ave New Haven CT 06511-7204 Office Phone: 203-776-1243.

FERLAND, BRENDA L., state representative; b. Lebanon, N.H., Oct. 23, 1949; d. Wilbur Fred Snelling and Lorraine Latouche; m. Daniel Edward Ferland; children: Lisa Marie, James Daniel. State rep. N.H. Ho. of Reps., Concord, 1997-98, 2001—. Treas. Charlestown (N.H.) Econ. Assn. Tourism, 1996-, Jesse Farwell Sch. Trust, 1990-95; mem. Charlestown Bd. of Select, 2000—, N.H. Traffic Safety Commn., 1998-, VFW Ladies Aux., 1999. Office: NH State Legis State House Concord NH 03301

FERLAND, DARLENE FRANCES, management consultant; b. Pawtucket, R.I., Feb. 11, 1955; d. Stephen William and Frances Grace (Masterson) Regula; m. Edward Oscar Ferland, Nov. 22, 1973; 1 child, Francesgrace. AS in Criminal Justice, Salve Regina U., 1975, BA in History and Polit. Sci., 1976; MA in History, Providence Coll., 1980; PhD in Human Resource Mgmt., Clayton U., 1991. Dir. Barbizon Sch. R.I., Providence, 1979-82, Barbizon Agy. R.I., Providence, 1980-81; tchr. Bay View Acad., Riverside, R.I., 1982-84; v.p. Edward Ferland Constrn. Co., Pawtucket, R.I., 1983—; pres. Enterprising Images Inc., Pawtucket, 1985—. Guest lectr. Providence Coll., 1980—. Nat. judge numerous scholarship pageants, 1978—. Mem. Bay View Alumnae Assn. (pres. 1981-84, Outstanding Alumna award 1983, 94), Arrive Alive Am. (nat. bd. 1986—), Salve Regina Alumni Assn. (pres. 1986—), AAUW (Providence chpt. pres. v.p. 1983-86, legis. chair 1982-83). Democrat. Roman Catholic. Avocations: reading, travel, music, theater, voluntary services. Home and Office: 225 Greenslitt Ave Pawtucket RI 02861-3231 also: Cabrita Point St Thomas VI 00802 also: Swan's Nest 34 Dory Ct Wakefield RI 02879-5922

FERNANDES, JANE K., academic administrator, educational consultant, sign language professional; b. Worcester, MA, Aug. 21, 1956; d. Richard Paul and Mary Kathleen (Cosgrove) Kelleher; m. James John Fernandes; children: Sean William, Erin Frances. BA comparative lit., Trinity Coll., Hartford, CT, 1978; MA comparative lit., U of Iowa, Iowa City, IA, 1980, PhD comparative lit., 1986. Acting dir. (ASL prog.) Northeastern U., Boston, 1986—87; chmn. (sign comm.) Gallaudet U., Wash., DC, 1987; coord. (interp. tng.) Kapiolani C.C., Honolulu, 1988—90; dir. Statewide Ctr., Dept. of Ed., Honolulu, 1990—95; v.p. Gallaudet U, Wash., DC, 1995—2000, provost, 2000—06. Edit. rev. bd. Perspectives in Ed. & Deafness, Wash., DC, 1994—97. Co-author: (novels) Signs of Eloquence, 2003. Chair State Commn. Persons with Disabilities, Honolulu, 1993—95, mem., 1988—95; mem. (bd. of dir.) Goodwill Indust. of Honolulu, Honolulu, 1992—95; joint com. Am. Annuls of the Deaf, 2005—. Recipient Alice Cogswell, Gallaudet U, 1993; fellow alumni, U. Iowa, 2001. Mem.: Nat. Assoc. of the Deaf.

FERNANDES, KATHLEEN, scientist; b. Hayward, Calif., Jan. 2, 1946; d. Edward Daniel and Lillian May (Silva) F. BA, U. Calif., Santa Barbara, 1967; MA, San Jose State U., 1969; PhD, Stanford U., 1974. Mem. project staff San Jose (Calif.) State U., 1969-71; rsch. asst. Stanford (Calif.) U., 1971-73; assoc. rsch. scientist Am. Inst. Rsch., Washington, 1973-79; rsch. assoc. Ctr. Study Evaluation, L.A., 1979; supr. personnel rsch. psychologist Navy Personnel Rsch. and Devel. Ctr., San Diego, 1979-88; scientist Space and Naval Warfare Systems Ctr., San Diego, 1988—. Cons. Navy Sci. Assistance Program, Pearl Harbor, Hawaii, 1985-86; expert user interface design. Author design specifications for mil. command and control systems. Mem. Human Factors and Ergonomics Soc. (sec.-treas. San Diego chpt. 1985-86). Home: 3146 Old Kettle Rd San Diego CA 92111-7710 Office: Space and Naval Warfare Systems Ctr Code 24225 San Diego CA 92152 Business E-Mail: kfernandes@san.rr.com.

FERNANDEZ, AMY, artist, illustrator, writer, educator; b. Queens, N.Y., Sept. 16, 1956; d. Albert David and Mary Louise Fernandez. BA, Syracuse U., 1978. Editor The Xolo News, N.Y.C., 1987—; columnist Top Notch Toys, Lakeland, Fla., 2002—, Dogs In Rev., Santa Barbara, Calif., 2004—; feature writer Dog World Mag. Author: Dog Breeding As A Fine Art (DWAA Presdl. award Excellence, 2003), Hairless Dogs- The Naked Truth, The Xoloitzcuintli Handbook (Ellsworth Howell award, 2004). Recipient award Merit, Illustration, Salmagundi Club, 1980, award Merit, Watercolor Painting, Soc. Illustrators, 1982; scholar, Pastel Soc. Am., 1981. Mem.: Dog Writers Assn. Am.

(bd. mem. 1999—2003), Xoloitzcuintli Club Am. (pres. 1998—2004). Avocations: photography, dog training, printmaking, dog breeding. Office: Snappyprints PO Box 754152 Forest Hills NY 11375 Personal E-mail: snappyprints@aol.com.

FERNANDEZ, GISELLE, newscaster, journalist; b. Mex. Former student, Sacramento State U. Past journalist, Pueblo, Colo.; past anchor WCIX-TV, Miami; past anchor Today (weekend edit.), NBC Nightly News (Sunday edit.) NBC-TV, co-host Access Hollywood; anchor KTLA Morning News. Guest anchor CBS This Morning, CBS Evening News, CBS Weekend News; contbr. (TV) Eye On America, CBS Sunday Morning News, Face the Nation, 48 Hours. Prodr.: (films) Our Story, 2004; author (children's book): Gigi and the Birthday Ring, 2004. Recipient 5 Emmy awards. Avocations: hiking, running. Home: 620 S Rossmore Ave Los Angeles CA 90005-3845

FERNANDEZ, HAPPY CRAVEN (GLADYS FERNANDEZ), academic administrator; b. Scranton, Pa., Mar. 3, 1939; d. Orvin William and Florence (Waite) Craven; m. Richard Ritter Fernandez, June 10, 1961; children: John Ritter, David Craven, Richard William. BA, Wellesley Coll., 1961; MA in Teaching, Harvard U., 1962; MA, U. Pa., Phila., 1970; EdD, Temple U., 1984. Social studies tchr. various pub. schs., 1961-64; from vis. asst. prof. to prof. Sch. Social Adminstrn. Temple U., Phila., 1974—92; exec. dir. Parents Union for Pub. Sch., Phila., 1980-82; dir. The Child Care and Family Policy Inst., Phila., 1988-92; city councilwoman Phila., 1992-98; candidate for mayor City Phila., 1998-99; pres. Moore Coll. of Art and Design, Phila., 1999—. Cons. Nat. Com. for Citizens in Edn., Columbia, Md., 1982—87, Phila. Youth Study Ctr., 1988—90; commr. Phila. Gas Commn, 1992—97; trustee Edn. Law Ctr., Phila., 1983—2005; bd. dirs. Cultural Fund, 1996—98; chair Select Com. on Bus. Taxes, 1992—98, Select com. on Land Reuse, 1997—98; pres. Delaware Valley Child Care Coun., 1988—90. Author: Parents Organizing to Improve Schools, 1976, The Child Advocacy Handbook, 1980, Elder Care and Child Care Policies of Philadelphia Area Businesses, 1991. Chair bd. dirs. Am. for Dem. Action, Phila., 1980—92; chair Children's Coalition, 1982—86; bd. dirs. Phila. Citizens for Children and Youth, 1986—93; founder Parents Union for Pub. Schs., 1972—, chair Phila., 1972—75, 1978—80; trustee Phila. Award, 2003—; del. Dem. Nat. Conv., 1988, 1992, 1996; bd. dirs. Greater Phila. Cultural Alliance, 2000—, chmn. bd., 2004—, Pa. Women's Forum, 2000—. Recipient Women in Edn. award Women's Way, 1989, Pub. Citizen of Yr. award NASW, 1991, Local Elected Ofcl. award Pa. Citizens for Better Librs., 1993, Pub. Svc. award Homeowners Assn. Phila., 1994 Phila. Op. Smile award, 1999, Woman of Yr.-Ivy Willis award, 2000, Fleisher Art Meml. Founders award 2001, Woman of Achievement award AAUW, 2005; named Outstanding Advisor, Health Promotions Coun., 1994, 2002, Disting. Dau. of Pa., 2002—; Wellesley Coll. scholar, 1961. Mem.: Nat. Assn. Ind. Colls. and Univs. (bd. dirs. 2003—), Assn. Ind. Schs. of Art and Design (nat. sec. 2001—04, vice chmn. nat. bd. dirs. 2004—). Mem. United Church Of Christ. Avocation: tennis. Home: 3400 Baring St Philadelphia PA 19104-2076 Office: Moore College 20th & Parkway 4 Philadelphia PA 19103 Office Phone: 215-568-4515 x1100. Business E-Mail: hfernandez@moore.edu.

FERNANDEZ, KATHLEEN M., cultural organization administrator; b. Dayton, Ohio, Oct. 8, 1949; d. Norbert Katzen and Yenema Vermeda (Bermingham) F.; m. James Robert Hillibish, Oct. 1, 1977. BA, Otterbein Coll., 1971. Edn. asst. Ohio Hist. Soc., Columbus, 1971, vol. coord., 1971-74, interpretive specialist Zoar, 1975-88; site mgr. Village State Meml., Zoar, 1988—2004; freelance mus. cons. Canton, Ohio, 2004—05; exec. dir. North Canton Heritage Soc., 2006—. Author: A Singular People: Images of Zoar, 2003. Bd. dirs., newsletter editor Ohio & Erie Canal Corridor Coalition, Akron, 1989—. Mem. Am. Assn. State and Local History, Nat. Trust Hist. Preservation, Zoar Cmty. Assn., Communal Studies Assn. (pres. 1981, editor newsletter 1981-86, 1997-2004, bd. dirs. 1995—, exec. dir. 2004—), Am. Assn. Mus. (surveyor mus. assistance program 1999—). Office: 221 18th St NW Canton OH 44703

FERNANDEZ, LISA, softball player; b. Long Beach, Calif., Feb. 27, 1971; m. Mike Lujan. Grad., UCLA, 1995. Mem. Calif. Commotion Amateur Softball Assn.; pitching and hitting coach UCLA Softball Team, 1995—. Pitcher U.S. Olympic Softball Team, Atlanta, 1996, Sydney, 2000, Athens, 04. Recipient Gold medal Pan Am. Games, 1991, 1999, ISF Women's World Championship, 1990, 94, 1998, 2002, Women's World Challenger Cup, 1992, Intercontinental Cup, 1993, South Pacific Classic, 1994, Superball Classic, 1995, Atlanta Olympics, 1996, Sydney Olympic Games, 2000, Athens Olympic Games, 2004, Honda award, 1991-93; named All-Am. Amateur Softball Assn., 1990-1993, 1995-1999, Sports Woman of Yr., 1991-92, MVP ASA Women's Major National, 1992, 1996-1999, mem. ASA Women's Major National Championship teams, 1990-92, 1996-99, NCAA Championship teams, 1990, 1992 Office: USA Softball 2801 NE 50th St Oklahoma City OK 73111-7203 also: TPS Hdqs care Lisa Fernandez PO Box 35700 Louisville KY 40232-5700

FERNANDEZ, SUZANNE LYN, elementary school educator, music educator; b. Elizabeth, NJ, Feb. 13, 1975; d. Wayne and Joanne Lucas; m. William Fernandez, July 28, 2001. B of Early Childhood Edn., West Chester U., Pa., 1997; M in Curriculum and Instrn., U. Phoenix, 2005. Cert. elem. tchr. Ariz., 2001. Tchr. gen. music DW Higgens, Tempe, Ariz., 2001—02, Joseph Zito Sch., Phoenix, 2002—. Dir., condr. ann. sch. concerts Joseph Zito Sch., 2002—. Mem.: Ariz. Kodaly Assn., Ariz. Orff Assn. Office Phone: 602-455-2500.

FERNÁNDEZ, TERESITA, sculptor; b. Miami, 1968; BFA, Fla. Internat. U., 1990; MFA, Va. Commonwealth U., 1992. Artist-in-residence ArtPace, San Antonio, 1998; fellow Am. Acad. in Rome, 1999; artist-in-residence The Fabric Workshop and Mus., Phila., 2005. Represented by Lehmann Maupin Gallery, NYC. Exhibitions include Real/More Real, Mus. Contemporary Art, Miami, 1995, South Fla. Cultural Consortium, Boca Raton Mus. Art, 1995, Defining the Nineties, Mus. Contemporary Art, Miami, 1996, Container 96, Copenhagen Cultural Capital, 1996, Enclosures, New Mus. Contemporary Art, NYC, 1996, Corcoran Gallery Art, Washington, DC, 1997, X-Site, Contemporary Mus., Balt., 1997, The Crystal Stopper, Lehmann Maupin Gallery, 1997, Seamless, De Appel, Amsterdam, 1998, Threshold, The Power Plant, Toronto, 1998, Borrowed Landscape, Deitch Projects, NYC, 1999, Luminous Mischief, Yokohama Portside Gallery, Japan, 1999, Deja-vu, Miami Art Fair, 2000, not seeing, Doug Lawing Gallery, Houstin, 2000, Reading the Museum, Nat. Mus. Modern Art, Tokyo, 2001, Off the Grid, Lehmann Maupin Gallery, 2002, Marie Walsh Sharpe Art Found. Show, Ace Gallery, NYC, 2002, The Young Latins, Nassau County Mus. Art, NY, 2002, Helga de Alvear, Madrid, 2003, In Situ: Installations and Large-Scale Works, 2004, Lehmann Maupin Gallery, 2005. Named a MacArthur Fellow, John D. and Catherine T. MacArthur Found., 2005; recipient Louis Comfort Tiffany Biennial award, 1999; Individual Artist's Grant, Visual Arts, NEA, 1994, Cintas Fellow, 1994, CAVA Fellow, Nat. Found. Advancement in Arts, 1995, Metro-Dade Cultural Consortium Grant, 1995. Mailing: c/o Lehmann Maupin Gallery 540 West 26th St New York NY 10001-5504

FERNBERGER, MARILYN FRIEDMAN, not-for-profit developer, consultant, volunteer; b. Phila., Aug. 13, 1927; d. David and Edith (Rosen) Friedman; m. Edward Fernberger, June 21, 1947; children: Edward Jr., Ellen, James. BA, U. Pa., 1948. Promoter, developer, executor major events for cmty. orgns. and instns. on local, nat. and internat. basis. Co-chmn. US Pro Indoor Tennis Championships, 1967-92; co-chmn. Phila. Women's Tennis Championships, 1970-79; cons. tennis promoters throughout US, creates new events and expands markets for existing events; staged profl. women's tennis tournament, Phila., 1970-79; cons. Internat. Mgmt. Group for Advanta Women's Tennis Championships; cons. on fundraising and art adminstrn.; former event coord. U. Pa. Inaugural Centenary Tennis Hall of Fame dinner; bd. dirs. Phila. Internat. Indoor Tennis Corp., Nat. Jr. Tennis League, Am. Tennis Assn., Phila. Tennis Patrons Assn., Phila. Youth Tennis & Edn. Benefit, Arthur Ashe Youth Tennis and Edn. Bd.; bd. dirs. Group of Four representing Wimbledon Mus., London, Roland Garros Mus., Paris, Tennis Australia Mus., Melbourne, and Internat. Tennis Hall of Fame, Newport, RI; lifetime trustee Internat. Tennis Hall of Fame; v.p. Middle States Patrons Assn.; chmn. Middle States Devel. Com., chmn. membership com.; chmn. Nat. Arthur Ashe Day; publ. com. U.S. Tennis Assn.; mem. Phila. Women's Interclub Bd.; founder, mgr. Ea. Pa. Boy's Championships; active Phila. Gold Cup; founder, chmn. People to People Sports Jr. Exhbns. Contbr. to nat. and internat. publs., including World Tennis mag., Tennis South Africa, Tennis Italiano, Tenis Espanol, Algeman Dagblad, Royal Tennis, Japan, Tennis Australia, Tennis de France, Brit. Lawn Tennis Jour. of Lawn Tennis Assn., Eng. Trustee Phila. Mus. Art; lifetime bd. mem., mem. adv. com. Phila. Mus. Art Assocs.; past pres. Rodin Mus., mem. bd. or officer United Way, Nat. Coun. Jewish Women, Fairmount Park Assn. for Hist. Sites, Phila. Sports Congress, Nat. Art Mus. Sport, Internat. Tennis Hall of Fame and Mus.; sec. treas. Tennis N.Am., Internat. Tennis Tournamet Dirs. Assn.; pres., Women's Tournament Dirs. Assn.; active Pa. Ballet, Emergency Aid, Albert Einstein Med. Ctr., Drama Guild, Ctr. for Internat. Visitors, Festival Theatre New Plays, U. Arts, Inst. Contemporary Art; mem. assocs. com., past chmn., life mem., pres. Rodin Mus.; bd. dirs. Phila. Mus. Art; life trustee Internat. Tennis Hall of Fame and Mus.; mem. mus. devel. gala 2004 50th anniversary celebration, mus. com. dir., long range planning com., accreditation com., ann. fund com.; chmn. Phila. City of Yr. 1996 Dinner, Internat. Tennis Hall of Fame, mem. gala com. 1980-, lifetime trustee 2005. Recipient Marlboro award, Humanitarian Svc. award Phila. Bd. Edn., Kelly award Pa. Parks and Recreation Commn., Cmty. Svc. award Big Bros.-Big Sisters, Police Athletic League, Coren award Nat. Jr. Tennis League Phila., YWCA, Phila., Mangan Svc. award USTA/Mid. States, Pub. Svc. award City of Phila., 8 times, Appreciation award Orange Bowl Com. Rotary Club, Phila., Phila. Bd. Edn., Chmn.'s award Internat. Tennis Hall of Fame and Mus., Pres.'s award Internat. Tennis Hall of Fame, 2002; named to USTA/Mid. States Hall of Fame, 1999; enshrined in Phila. Jewish Sports Hall of Fame, 2005, Major Wingfield Soc. of USTA, 2006. Mem. US Tennis Writers Assn. (bd., officer), Internat. Tennis Tournament Dirs. Assn. (bd., officer), Assn. Tournament Dirs. (bd., officer), U. Pa. Alumni Assn. (bd., officer), Internat. Tennis Club USA (hon., Olympic planning com.). Home and Office: 1112 Penmore Pl Rydal PA 19046-1239 Home Fax: 215-886-4230.

FERRACO REDINGER, ANDREA, biology educator; b. Pitts., Pa., Apr. 26, 1979; d. Samuel Gene Ferraco, Jr. and Maria Seppi Ferraco; m. David Vincent Redinger, Nov. 26, 2005. BS in Biology, St. Vincent Coll., Latrobe, Pa., 2001; MS in Edn., Duquesne U., Pitts., Pa., 2002. Cert. tchr. Pa., 2002. Tchr. biology Greensburg (Pa.) Salem H.S., 2003—. Asst. biotechnology outreach St. Vincent Coll., Latrobe, 2004—. Fellow, Duquesne U., 2003. Mem.: Pa. Sci. Tchrs. Assn. (McIllwaine Sci. Tchg. award 2004), Nat. Assn. Biology Tchrs. (named Outstanding New Biology Tchr. of Yr. 2005). Office: Greensburg Salem High School 65 Mennel Drive Greensburg PA 15601 Office Phone: 724-832-2960.

FERRÁEZ-MCKENZIE, MARIE ANTOINETA, literature and language professor, real estate agent; b. Laredo, Tex., Oct. 23, 1950; d. Jesus Antonio Ferraez and Maria Belia Vela; 1 child, Ana Marie. BS in edn., U Tex., Austin, 1976; MA in English, U. Tex., Brownsville, 1998. English tchr. Brownsville Ind. Sch. Dist., Tex., 1976—; English adj. tchr. U. Tex., Brownsville, 1999—. Office: Homer Hanna HS 2615 E Price Rd Brownsville TX 78521-2430

FERRAIOLO, KATHLEEN MARY, political science professor; d. Stephen A. and Regina Ann (Bowler) Grammatico; m. James Mark Ferraiolo, Aug. 24, 2002. BA in Polit. Sci. magna cum laude, Coll. Holy Cross, Worcester, Mass., 1998; MA in Govt., U. Va., Charlottesville, 2001, PhD in Govt., 2004. Tchg. asst. Phillips Acad., Andover, Mass., 1998; tchr. Choate Rosemary Hall Sch., Wallingford, Conn., 1999; instr., tchg. asst. U. Va., Charlottesville, 1999—2003; vis. asst. prof. James Madison U., Harrisonburg, Va., 2004—05, asst. prof., 2005—. Cons. Pew Partnership for Civic Change, Charlottesville, 2001—; co-advisor political sci. dept., student adv. group James Madison U. Editor: New Directions in Civic Engagement: University Avenue Meets Main Street, 2004; co-editor: Inventing Civic Solutions: A How-To Guide on Launching and Sustaining Successful Community Programs, 2005; contbr. articles to profl. jours. Student vol. U. Va., Charlottesville, 1999—2003; alumni interviewer admissions office Coll. Holy Cross, Worcester, Mass., 2000—; vol. baker St. Thomas Aquinas Ch.-Salvation Army, Charlottesville, 2004—. Recipient Outstanding Tchg. award, Delta Delta Delta, 2005; fellow Miller Ctr. Pub. Affairs, U. Va., Charlottesville, 2003—04; Dana scholar, Coll. Holy Cross, 1996—98. Mem.: So. Polit. Sci. Assn., Am. Polit. Sci. Assn., Alpha Sigma Nu, Pi Sigma Alpha, Phi Beta Kappa. Roman Catholic. Avocations: photography, scrapbooks, reading, counted cross stitch. Office: James Madison Univ Dept Polit Sci MSC 1101 Harrisonburg VA 22807 Office Phone: 540-568-7369. Office Fax: 540-568-8021.

FERRANTE, OLIVIA ANN, retired secondary school educator, consultant; b. Revere, Mass., Nov. 9, 1948; d. Guy and Mary Carmella (Prizio) F. BA, Regis Coll., 1970; MEd, Boston Coll., 1971, postgrad., 1977-81, Middlebury Coll., 1974, Lesley Coll., 1982. Cert. history tchr., tchr. of blind. Chmn. Braille dept. Nat. Braille Press, Boston, 1971-74; tchr. of visually impaired, spl. needs dept. Revere H.S., 1974-92; ret., 1992. Steven J. Rich scholarship com., 1993—; cons. Revere PTA, 1984—. Contbr. articles to profl. jours. Vol. Morgan Meml., Boston, 1983—, tchr. braille, 1993—, tchr. literacy program, 1993—; mem. Revere Com. for Handicapped Affairs, 1985—, Everett (Mass.) Chorus, 1974-76, Adult Music Ministry, 1989, Revere First Com., 1993, publicist; soloist Revere Music Makers, 1977-79; mem. partnership com. Internat. Year Disabled, 1980-81; mem. adult choir Immaculate Conception Ch., 1966—, lectr., 1995—, cantor, 1997; publicist Revere Commn. on Disabilities, 1985—, Revere Hist. Commn., 1996—, Cath. Daus., SHARE, 1995—, A Woman's Concern, 1996; mem. adv. bd. Mass. Commn. of Blind, 1988—, governing bd. on ind. living, 1989; access monitor Mass. Orgn. on Disability, 1988—; mem. adv. bd. Radio Reading Svc. for Blind, 1989; mentor Nat. Braille Literacy Project, 1992, Braille Lib., 1995—; mem. Friends of the Sick Children's Trust, 1992; vol. Birthright, 1992, ProLife Office, 1992; active Arts Coun. Coop, 1992—; mentor Vision Found., 1993—; friend Wang Ctr., 1993—, Boston Pub. Garden and Common, 1993—, Boston Pops, 1992—; mem. mobility adv. bd. Mass. Com. for Blind, 1994—; mem. Historic Mass., 1994—, Cath. League, 1994—; friend Paul Revere House, 1994—; mem. Peregrine Fund, 1994—, Ctr. for Marine Preservation, 1994—; sponsor Rite of Cath. Initiation for Adults, 1995—; publicist Next Door Theater Group, 1996, Animal Umbrella Cat Shelter, 2003—; mem. access task force Revere Pub. Libr., 1996; mem. Revere 2000 Com., 1998-99. Mem. NEA, Internat. Soc. for Endangered Cats, Mass. Tchrs. Assn. Revere Tchrs. Assn., Nat. Space Soc., Nat. Cath. Assn. for Persons with Visual Impairment, Cath. Daus. of Am. (publicist), Soc. Bl. Kateri Tekakwitha, 1997, Friends of Revere Pub. Libr., Friends of Librs. for Blind, Friends of Boston Symphony Orch., Nat. Writers Union, Amnesty Internat., Soc. Creative Anachronism, Women Affirming Life, Michael Crawford Internat. Fan Assn., Revere Soc. for Cultural and Hist. Preservation (publicist, life mem., v.p. 1998—, chmn. grants com. 1998, 2000 com., 1998), Chelsea Hist. Soc., Mass. Aviation Hist. Soc., Brian Boitano Fan Club, Barry Manilow Fan Club, Michael Feinstein Fan Club, Feregrine Fund, Paul Revere House, Greater Lynn Arts and Crafts Soc. Roman Catholic. Avocations: travel, music, swimming, ice skating, crafts. Home: 115 Reservoir Ave Revere MA 02151-5825 Office: Revere High Sch Spl Needs Dept 101 School St Revere MA 02151-3099

FERRARA, ANNETTE, editor, educator; MA in Modern Art History, Theory and Criticism, Sch. of the Art Inst. Chgo. Rsch. asst. The Andy Warhol Catalogue Raisonné Project; dir. Alan Koppel Gallery, Chgo.; asst. dir. The Arts Club Chgo.; founding editor, writer TENbyTEN, Chgo., 1999—. Guest lectr. Columbia Coll., DePaul, SAIC; tchr. contemporary art history Mus. of Contemporary Art, Chgo. Co-author: Xtreme Interiors, 2003; contbr. writings to Artforum, Book Forum, Zingmagazine, Provincetown Arts. Mem.: Chgo. Art Critics Assn. Office: TENbyTEN 222 S Morgan 3E Chicago IL 60607 Office Phone: 312-421-0480. Office Fax: 312-421-0491. Business E-Mail: contact@tenbyten.net.*

FERRARI, L. KATHERINE, speech professional, consultant, entrepreneur; b. Chgo. d. August and Aurora (Lenzi) Puccinelli; m. Charles Wasserman; children: Michael John, Alexandra Marie; m. Gordon Wharton Holt Jr. MA in Architecture, Stanford (Calif.) U., 1972, MS in Engring., 1972; BA in Polit. Sci., Northwestern U.; M in Hypnotism, Hypnotism Tng. Sch. L.A., 1989. Educator Moreland Sch. Dist., San Jose, Calif., 1961-65; pres. Ferrari Design, Los Gatos, Calif., 1970—; project dir. AIA Energy Conservation Retrofit, San Jose, Calif., 1978—81, AIA/N.A.S.A. tech. house of future, Moffet Field, 1982—85; pres. Internat. Laughter Soc. Inc., Los Gatos, 1983—, Ferrari Communications, Los Gatos, 1989—. Bd. dirs. Pacific We. Bank, San Jose; bldg. cons. & design in field; product designer Internat. Laughter Soc. Inc., Los Gatos, 1983—; trainer non-profit groups. Contbr. articles to profl. jours. Mem. Advanced Tech. Advancement Com., Moffett Field, Calif., 1977-89; pres., v.p. League of Eastfield Children's Ctr., Campbell, Calif., 1964-66; pres., treas. Triton Mus. of Art, Santa Clara, Calif., 1979-81; bd. dirs. Coun. Environ. & Econ. Improvement, San Jose, Calif., 1976-79. Art Inst. scholar. Mem. AIA (hon. assoc., bd. dirs. San Jose chpt.), A.S.I.D., Nat. Speakers Assn., Am. Coun. Hypnotists, Nat. Guild Hypnotists. Avocations: travel, reading. Office: Ferrari Communications 16000 Glen Una Dr Los Gatos CA 95030-2911

FERRARI, LINDA GALE, art educator; d. Carlin Maxwell Felter and Emily Elizabeth Smith. Student in English, Butler U., Indpls., Inc., 1962; student in Fine Arts, Inst. Chgo., Ill.; student in Art History, U. Chgo., Ill., 1963—67; student in Edn., U. Calif., Berkeley, 1970—73. Cert. tchr. Calif. Asst. registrar Art Inst. Chgo., 1964—66; fin. aid counselor U. Calif., Berkeley, 1968—73, personnel rep., 1967—73; tchr. English, art Oakland Sch. Dist., Calif., 1974—75; tchr. ceramics Pacific Grove Sch. Dist., Calif., 1975—84; instr. Ferrari of Carmel Gallery, Calif., 1985—97; illustrating artist McGraw Hill Publs., Monterey, Calif., 1998—2003. Tchr. graphic arts Calif. Dept. Corrections, Soledad, 2001—. Democrat. Avocations: art, painting, reading, writing. Home and Office: PO Box 3273 Carmel CA 93921 E-mail: ferrariofcarmel1@earthlink.net.

FERRARO, BETTY ANN, retired state senator; b. Newport, Vt., Mar. 3, 1925; d. Clarence John and Mauretta Rowena (Potter) Morse; m. Dominic Thomas Ferraro, Oct. 8, 1964; children: Deborah, David, Susan, Barbara. Student, Mary Hitchcock Hosp. Sch. Nursing, Coll. St. Joseph, Rutland, Vt. Exec. sec. to asst. treas. Ctrl. Vt. Pub. Svc. Corp., Rutland, 1943-44; sec. to dean N.Y. Med. Coll., N.Y.C., 1944-46; model G. Fox Co., Hartford, Conn., 1947; corp. sec., office mgr. John Russell Corp., Rutland, 1970-80; exec. dir. Rutland Area Coordinated Child Care Com., Washington, 1977-79; adminstrv. asst. Hilinex of Vt., Rutland, 1981-83; owner Classic Connection Gift Shop, Rutland, 1983-87; adminstr. Vicon Recovery Sys., Inc., Rutland, 1987-90. Owner, operator nursery sch., 1973—77; mgr. Day Care Ctr., 1978—80; mem. Rutland City Bd. Aldermen, 1984—86, 2001—03; resource dir. Rutland City Emergency Mgmt. Team for State of Vt., 1984—90; mem. Vt. State Cmty. Devel. Commn., 1986. Chmn. Rutland City Rep. Com., 1991-93; county committeewoman State Rep. Com., 1984-86, rep.; rep. Rutland County Rep. Com.; state del. Rep. Nat. Conv., 1992; Rep. campaign coord. State of Vt., 1997-98; county co-chair Jim Douglas for Gov., 2001-02; mem. Vt. Ho. Reps., 1990-92; mem. Vt. Senate, 1992-94, 95-97; mem. jud. nominating bd. Human Resource Investment Com., 1995-96, Vt. Student Assistance Corp. Bd.; mem. Amtrak Study Commn., 1995-96; bd. dirs. Vt. Physicians Coun., 1997—, Coll. St. Joseph, 1996-2000, Marble Valley Transit, 1996—, sec. bd. dirs.; mem. adv. bd. Paramount Theatre, 1997-2000; sec., receptionist Orton Family Found., 1999-2000; sec., receptionist Eddy Enterprises, Inc., 2000-01; county co-chair Jim Douglas for Gov., 2002; hon. chair Kevin Mullin for Sen. Campaign, 2004—; mem. Vt. State Transp. Bd, 2003-05; devel. coord. Neighbor Works We. Vt., 2002-2005. Fleming Inst. fellow, 1995; named Woman of Yr. Green Mt. Coun. of Boy Scouts Am. Mem. Nat. Assn. Women in Constrn. (chartered, past pres.), Rutland County Rep. Women. Republican. Roman Catholic. Avocation: flower arranging. Home and Office: Condo 17 155 Dorr Dr Rutland VT 05701-3853 E-mail: b.m.ferraro@verizon.net.

FERRARO, GERALDINE ANNE, lawyer, former congresswoman; b. Newburgh, NY, Aug. 26, 1935; d. Dominick and Antonetta L. (Corrieri) F.; m. John Zaccaro, 1960; children: Donna, John, Laura. BA, Marymount Manhattan Coll., 1956; JD, Fordham U., 1960; postgrad., NYU Law Sch., 1978; degree (hon.), Marymount Manhattan Coll., 1982, NYU Law Sch., 1984, Hunter Coll., 1985, Plattsburgh Coll., 1985, Coll. Boca Raton, 1989, Va. State U., 1989, Muhlenberg Coll., 1990, Briarcliffe Coll. for Bus., 1990, Potsdam Coll., 1991. Bar: N.Y. 1961, U.S. Supreme Ct. 1978. Atty. pvt. practice, NYC, 1961-74; asst. dist. atty. Queens County, NY, 1974-78; chief spl. victims bur., 1977-78; mem. 96th-98th Congresses from 9th NY Dist., 1979—85; sec. House Democratic Caucus; 1st woman vice presdl. nominee on Democratic ticket, 1984; fellow Harvard Inst. of Politics, Cambridge, Mass., 1988—92; mng. ptnr. Keck Mahin Cate & Koether, NYC, 1993-94. Appointed Amb. to UN Human Rights Commn., 1994-95; co-host Crossfire, CNN, 1996-97; pres. G&L Strategies Golin Harris Internat., 1999—, Fox News Nightly, 1999—. Author: Ferraro, My Story, 1985, Changing History: Women, Power, and Politics, 1993, Framing a Life, 1998. Chair Dem. Platform Com., Bertarelli Found.; Dem. candidate U.S. Senate, 1992, 98; U.S. President Clinton's appointee to UN Human Rights Commn. Conf., Geneva, 1993, World Conf., Vienna, Austria, 1993, World Conf. on Women, 1995; bd. dirs. Fordham Law Sch. Bd. Visitors; bd. advocates Planned Parenthood Fedn. Am.; bd. dir. Nat. Women's Health Rsch. Ctr., Nat. Dem. Inst. Mem. Queens County Women's Bar Assn. (past pres.), Coun. Fgn. Rels., Internat. Inst. Women's Polit. Leadership (former pres.). Roman Catholic.

FERRARO, MARGARET LOUISE (PEG FERRARO), elementary school educator; b. Apr. 9, 1939; BS Edn., Kutstown State U., 1961. Tchr. Abington Sch. Dist., Pa., 1961—64; tchr. secondary sch. Nazareth Area Sch. Dist., Pa., 1978—2001. Chmn. zoning bd. Upper Nazareth Twp., 1970, sec. planning commn., 1968, treas., 1986, 1st woman elected to bd. suprs., 1986; bd. dirs., chair edn. com. Lehigh Valley Chamber Orch., 1982-2001; 1st Rep. woman elected countywide Northampton County Coun., 1989-97, 3d term, 2001-05, v.p., 2002-05; chmn. Northampton County Rep. Com., 1998-2002; mem. Northampton County Indsl. Devel. Authority, 2003—, Northampton County Housing Authority, 2003—; mem. adv. bd. Excellence In Pub. Svc., Inc., 2006— Recipient Nazareth Area H.S. Disting. Alumni award, 1994 Republican. Home: 339 Schoeneck Ave Nazareth PA 18064-1224

FERRARO, MARIE, dental hygienist; b. Jamaica, West Indies, Mar. 12, 1937; arrived in U.S., 1964; d. Louis Ezekel and Uta Doreen Ferraro; m. Lionel Cunningham, Dec. 13, 1957; children: Sonia Francis, Karel. AS, N.Y.C. Tech. Coll., 1970; BS, Lehman Coll., 1986; MS, Columbia U., 1988. Registered dental hygienist N.Y. Dental hygienist Montefiore Med. Ctr., Bronx, NY, 1970—. Dental health coord. N.Y.C. Pub. Schs., Bronx, 1970—87. Mem.: Am. Dental Hygienists Assn., Columbia Alumni Assn. Democrat. Baptist. Home: PO Box 343801 Homestead FL 33034-0801 Office Phone: 786-243-2530. Personal E-mail: mfernet@bellsouth.net.

FERREE, CAROLYN RUTH, radiation oncologist, educator; b. Liberty, NC, Jan. 29, 1944; d. Numer Floyd and Mary Isabel (Glass) Black; m. Richard C. Sanders, June 5, 1999. BA, U. N.C., Greensboro, 1966, DSc (hon.), 1998; MD, Bowman Gray Coll., Winston-Salem, N.C., 1970. Diplomate Am. Bd. Radiation Oncology. Intern medicine N.C. Bapt. Hosp., Winston-Salem, 1970-71, resident in radiation oncology, 1971-74; instr. radiation oncology Bowman Gray Sch. Medicine, Winston-Salem, 1974-75, asst. prof., 1975-80, assoc. prof., 1980-87, prof., 1987—. Contbr. articles to profl. jours. Mem., v.p. County Bd. of Pub. Health, Winston-Salem, 1985-92; bd. dirs. U. N.C.-Greensboro Excellence Found., 1988-94; med. dir. Forsyth County chpt. Am. Cancer Soc., 1975-90; bd. dirs. Hospice, 1998—; trustee U. N.C.-Greensboro, 2005—. Recipient Disting. Svc. award U. N.C.-G Alumni, 1997, Disting. Achievement award Wake Forest U. Sch. Medicine, 1999; named Disting. Woman of N.C. in Professions, Gov.'s award, 1998, Patient Advocate award Cancer Svcs., 2002, Outstanding Oncologist award So. Assn. Oncology, 2005; voted Top Dr. by peers, 2000-05. Fellow Am. Coll.

Radiology; mem. AMA (N.C. del. to AMA), Pediat. Oncology Group (radiotherapy coord.), N.C. Med. Soc. (2d v.p. 1990-91, sec.-treas. 1991-95, pres.-elect 1996, pres. 1997), Am. Soc. Therapeutic Radiologists Orgn. Office: Wake Forest U Sch Medicine Med Center Blvd Winston Salem NC 27157-0001 Office Phone: 336-713-3600. Business E-Mail: cferree@wfubmc.edu.

FERREE, PATRICIA ANN, quality assurance professional; b. Middletown, N.Y., Oct. 5, 1947; d. William Harry and Florence Arlene (Sarr) Krenrich; m. Daniel Milton Ferree, Feb. 13, 1972; children: Patricia Ann, Daniel Milton Jr. AS, Ctrl. Fla. C.C., Ocala, 1969; BS in Nursing, Va. Commonwealth U., 1985. Cert. cardiac nurse therapist. Critical care nurse Fla. Hosp., Orlando, 1969-76, cardiac nurse therapist, 1976-80, head nurse cardiac rehab., 1980-82; nurse adminstrn., rsch. nurse Va. Heart Inst., Richmond, 1982-86; coord. health care cost containment Cir. City Stores, Inc., Richmond, 1986, mgr. health and safety, 1986-89, corp. mgr. workers' compensation and safety, 1989-94, corp. sr. analyst for managed care unit in risk mgmt. dept., 1994-97; training quality assurance auditor Concentra Health Svcs., 1997—98, nurse case mgr., 1998—2003, case mgmt. specialist, 2004, nat. quality training specialist, 2004—. Choir dir. Courthouse Rd. Seventh-Day Adventist Ch., Richmond, 1983-89, min. music, 1989-94; curriculum com. Richmond Acad. Home and Sch. Leader; chmn. cardiovascular task force Am. Heart Assn., 1984-85; youth leader Tampa 1st Seventh-Day Adventist Ch., 1998—. Recipient svc. plaque cardiology dept. Fla. Hosp., 1982; Peggy Gibson Meml. nursing scholar, 1967, Fla. Bd. Edn. nursing scholar, 1967-69. Mem. NAFE, Am. Assn. Occupational Health Nurses, Am. Soc. Safety Engrs., Soc. Nursing Profls., Am. Assn. for Cardiovascular and Pulmonary Rehab. (founding), Richmond Met. Soc. for Cardiac Rehab. (founding), West Coast Regional Case Mgmt. Assn., Phi Kappa Phi, Sigma Zeta. Republican. Avocations: music, computer art. Office: Concentra 5130 Eisenhower Blvd Tampa FL 33634 Office Phone: 813-806-2526.

FERRELL, CATHERINE K., sculptor, painter; b. Detroit, Apr. 27, 1947; d. Robert Byron and Elizabeth (Crapo) Klemann; m. William Barksdale Ferrell Jr., Nov. 4, 1987; children: Adrienne Elizabeth, Peter Klemann. Student, U. Mich., 1966-67; BA in Sculpture, Fla. Atlantic U., 1969; MA in Sculpture, U. Miami, Fla., 1972. Asst. to sculptor Luis Montoya Montoya Art Studios, West Palm Beach, Fla., 1983; pres., sculptor Art Equities, Inc., Vero Beach, Fla., 1986—. One-woman shows include Musee Universale, Montreal, Can., 1985, Elliott Mus., Stuart, Fla., 1985, Lighthouse Gallery Inc., 1991, J. Sexton Gallery, Vero Beach, Fla., 1996, McCreeless Fine Arts Gallery, Asbury Coll., Lexington, Ky., 1996, U. Mich., Flint, Mich., 1996, Cornell Mus., Delray Beach, Fla., 1999, Pen Brush, Inc., NY, 2002, Pen and Brush Inc., NYC, 2002, Cheryl Newby Gallery, SC, 2003; represented in permanent collections: Norton Mus. Art, West Palm Beach, Fla., Bennex Internat., Oslo, Norway, Brevard Mus. Art, Melbourne, Fla., Gunter Schultz-Franke, Arch., Osnabruch, West Germany, dr. Paul Gingras, Palm Beach, Fla.; numerous pvt. collections Recipient Silver medal, Audubon Artists Am. Fellow Nat. Sculpture Soc. (colleague), Am. Artists Profl. League; mem. Am. Soc. Marine Artists, Am. Acad. Women Artists, Knickerbocker Artists, Allied Artists (assoc.), Profl. Artists Guild, Artists Forum, Pen and Brush, Inc., S.E. Sculptors Assn., Catherine Lorillard Wolfe Art Club, Salmagundi Club (Cert. of Merit, Elliot Liskin Meml. award 1993, Pres. award 1994) Home: 12546 Highway A1A Vero Beach FL 32963-9411 Office Phone: 772-589-1552. Personal E-mail: tcferrell@aol.com.

FERRELL, ELIZABETH ANN, lawyer; b. Morgantown, W.Va., Feb. 10, 1957; BA magna cum laude, U. SC, 1979, JD, 1982. Bar: SC 1982, DC 1985. Law clk. to Hon. Sol Blatt, Jr. US Dist. Ct. Dist. SC, 1982—84; assoc. Pierson Ball & Dowd, Washington, Piper & Marbury, Washington, 1988—91, ptnr., 1991; ptnr., govt. contracts group Sonnenschein Nath & Rosenthal LLP, Washington, 1991—. Office: Sonnenschein Nath & Rosenthal LLP Ste 600, E Tower 1301 K St NW Washington DC 20005 Office Phone: 202-408-6420. Office Fax: 202-408-6399. Business E-Mail: eferrell@sonnenschein.com.

FERRELL, JUDY ANN, elementary school educator; b. Tulsa, Dec. 21, 1947; d. Fred Ellis Hansen and Elouise Frances Wade; m. Dennis Richard Ferrell, June 12, 1971; children: Jennifer Rebecca, Karen Elizabeth, Brian Vernon. BS, Okla. State U., Stillwater, 1971; MS, Okla. State U., 2002; Cert., U. Md., College Park, 1988, Charles County C.C., LaPlata, Md., 1989; postgrad., Trinity Coll., Washington, 1989—92. Cert. tchr. Okla., Md. 1st-6th grade phys. edn. tchr. Del Roy Woods Elem. Sch., Monterey, Calif.; substitute math/spl. edn. tchr. Sullivan's Elem. Sch., Vokosuka, Japan; 5th grade tchr. James Craik Elem. Sch., Waldorf, Md.; students-at-risk 6th-12th and substitute tchr. K-12th Stillwater Pub. Schs.; 5th grade tchr. Sangre Ridge Elem. Sch., Stillwater. Mentor student tchrs. Stillwater Pub. Schs., tchr. trainer sci.; testing reviewer Okla. Dept. Edn., Oklahoma City. Fundraiser United Way, Stillwater; coord. collection of toys Toys for Tots, Stillwater; coord. fundraising Kenyan Orphanage, Stillwater; vol. Outdoor Environ. Ctr., Stillwater. Comdr. USN, 1970—93. Named Outstanding Tchr., Charles County, Md., 1993, Elem. Math. Tchr. of Yr., Profl. Math. Assn., Norman, Okla., 2003. Mem.: ASCD, Nat. Sci. Tchrs. Assn., Nat. Coun. social Studies, Nat. Coun. Tchrs. Math., Phi Kappa Phi. Democrat. Presbyterian. Avocations: gardening, tennis, counted cross stitch, travel. Home: 2523 S Range Rd Stillwater OK 74074 Office: Sangre Ridge Elementary School 2500 S Sangre Rd Stillwater OK 74074

FERRELL, MARCIE A., elementary school educator; b. Harvey, Ill., Feb. 28, 1972; d. Fred and Bettye Ferrell. BEd, Chgo. State U., 2000. Tchr. Dist. 150, South Holland, Ill., Dist. 152.5, Marlcham, Ill.; dir. day care Discovery Learning Ctr., Tinley Pk., Ill. Mem.: ASCD. Avocation: singing. Home: 18205 Morgan St Ste 5B Homewood IL 60430 Office: Sch Dist 150 Greenwood 16800 Greenwood St South Holland IL 60473

FERRERA, VINITA, lawyer; BA magna cum laude, U. Colo., 1992; JD cum laude, NYU, 1995. Bar: Mass., NY. Joined Wilmer, Cutler, Pickering, Hale and Dorr LLP, Boston, 1996, ptnr. Intellectual Property Litig. Practice Group; spl. asst. dist. atty. Middlesex County Dist. Atty.'s Office, Mass., 1999. Mem.: Am. Intellectual Property Law Assn., Boston Bar Assn., ABA. Office: Wilmer Cutler Pickering Hale and Dorr LLP 60 State St Boston MA 02109 Office Phone: 617-526-6208. Office Fax: 617-526-5000. E-mail: vinita.ferrera@wilmerhale.com.*

FERRERE, RITA L., band director, music educator; b. Grove City, Pa., Feb. 19, 1965; d. Regis R. and Anna F. Ferrere. BS summa cum laude in Edn., Clarion U., 1987; M in Music Edn., Dana Sch. Music, Youngstown State U., 1992. Cert. instrnl. level II tchg. Pa., 1991. Instrumental music /band tchr. Elk County Christian H.S., St. Marys, Pa., 1988—94; instrumental music/band dir. Kane Area Sch. Dist., 1994—95, Brookville Area H.S., Pa., 1995—2001; instrumental music tchr. Chartiers Valley Intermediate Sch., Pitts., 2001—02; instrumental music/band dir. Moniteau Sch. Dist., West Sunbury, Pa., 2002—. Jazz band dir./founder Jazz Transitions Big Band, Pa., 1990—95; band dir. Harrisville Cmty. Band, Pa., 1994—98. Recipient Band Dir. Distinction award, Fiesta-Val Band Festival, Va. Beach, 2001. Mem.: Phi Beta Mu (Nu chpt.), Pa. Music Educators Assn. (life), Women Band Director's Internat. Assn. (life), Music Educators Nat. Conf. (life). Avocation: music. Home: 272 Boyers Rd PO Box 55 Forestville PA 16035 Office: Moniteau HS 1810 West Sunbury Rd West Sunbury PA 16061 Personal E-mail: rferrere@moniteau.k12.pa.us.

FERRI, KAREN LYNN, lawyer; b. McKeesport, Pa., Aug. 15, 1956; d. Edward James and Carole Elizabeth (Petterson) Ferri. BA, Duquesne U., 1977, JD, 1981. Bar: Pa. 1981, U.S. Dist. Ct. (we. dist.) Pa. 1981, U.S. Supreme Ct. 1986. Law clk. Weiler & Dolfi, Pitts., 1980-81, assoc., 1981-84; of counsel Stokes, Lurie & Cole, Pitts., 1984-90; sole practice Murrysville and Pitts., 1984—. Weekend mgr. Ferri Supermarkets Inc., Murrysville, Pa., 1977-90; atty. Ferri Enterprises, 1981-96. Bd. dirs. Crisis Ctr. North, Pitts., 1986-89, vol., 1986-2001; bd. dirs. planned parenthood, 1998-2005. Recipient Sr. Leaders award Duquesne U., 1977, Am. Jurisprudence award Joint Pubs. Total Client-Service Library Pitts., 1978-79. Mem.: ABA (family law com. Bar Found. 2003—), Allegheny County Bar Assn. (mem. family law com.), Pa. Bar Found., Pa. Bar Assn. (family law sect.), Duquesne U. Alumni Assn., Am. Inns of Ct. (Pitts. chpt. 1992—95), Westmoreland County Bar Assn. (family law com., fee dispute com.), Women's Bar Assn. Roman Catholic. Home: 3319 Carriage Cir Export PA 15632-9214 Office: 3950 William Penn Hwy Ste 2 Murrysville PA 15668 Office Phone: 724-733-4666.

FERRIERO, DONNA M., pediatric neurologist; B., M., Rutgers U.; MD, U. Calif. San Francisco, 1979. Prof. neurology & pediatrics U. Calif. San Francisco, 1987—, chief of Child Neurology; vice dean U. Calif. San Francisco Sch. Medicine, 2005—; dir. Neonatal Brain Disorders Ctr., U. Calif. San Francisco. Chmn. Chancellor's Comm. on Status of Women U. Calif. San Francisco, mem. Chancellor's Coun. on Faculty Life; editorial bd. Jour. Cerebral Blood Flow & Metabolism; adv. bd. Neurophyxia. Contbr. scientific papers; editor: (books) Developmental Neuroscience: Developmental Brain Injury, 2005, Pediatric Neurology: Principles & Practice, 2006. Mem. Soc. Pediat. Rsch. Coun.; bd. dirs. Child Neurology Found., 2000—05, Child Neurology Soc., 2005—. Recipient Disting. Teaching award, Academic Senate, Chancellor's award for the Advancement of Women, U. Calif. San Francisco, 2000, Sidney Carter award, Am. Acad. Neurology. Mem.: Am. Neurol. Assoc., Inst. Medicine. Office: UCSF Depts of Neurology & Pediatrics 521 Parnassus Ave San Francisco CA 94143 Office Phone: 415-502-1099. Office Fax: 415-502-5821. E-mail: ferrierod@neuropeds.ucsf.edu.

FERRIGNO, HELEN FRANCES, librarian, musician, educator; b. Trenton, N.J., Aug. 25, 1937; d. Joseph John and Frances (Leniart) Klidzia; m. Maurice Ferrigno, Oct. 3, 1964; children— Lisa, Nina. Student Hartt Coll. Music, Hartford, Conn., 1962-64; B.A., Rivier Coll., Nashua, N.H., 1977-80; M.L.S., Simmons Coll., 1982. Pvt. music tchr., Conn. and N.H., 1965—; free-lance flutist and piccoloist, 1974—; co-owner/mgr. Ancus Books, Nashua, 1974—; cataloger/info. cons./systems analyst Digital Equipment Corp., Merrimack, N.H., 1984—; librarian Daniel Webster Coll., Nashua, 1982-84, chmn. lecture series, 1982-83; flutist Nashua Symphony Orch., 1975-77. Mem. parents adv. bd. New Eng. Conservatory Prep. Sch., Boston, 1981-82; vol. Am. Heart Assn. Mem. ALA, Assn. Coll. and Research Libraries, Library and Info. Tech. Assn., New Eng. Library Assn., Beta Phi Mu. Roman Catholic. Home: 76 Manchester St Nashua NH 03064-6218

FERRINGER-BURDICK, SUSAN, elementary school educator; d. R. and D. Ferringer; m. Douglas Burdick, Sept. 13, 1980; children: Andrew, Benjamin, Jonathan. BA in Elem. Edn., Grove City Coll., 1981. Cert. exercise instr. Pub. Found., Erie, Pa., 1998. Asst. dir. Cambridge Springs (Pa.) Pub. Libr., 1990—91; tchr. Union City Area Sch. Dist., Pa., 2001—03. State contact NTL Healthcare Found., Washington, 1998—. Sec., past prodr. Cmty. Theatre, Cambridge Springs, 1978—. Mem.: French Creek Valley Cmty. Theatre.

FERRIS, GINGER LEIGH, education educator, consultant; d. James H. and Sarah A. Ferris. BS in Elem. Edn., Old Dominion Coll., Norfolk, Va., 1968; MEd, U. Va., Charlottesville, 1973. Postgrad. profl. lic. Va. Lead tchr. early childhood program at Child Study Ctr. Old Dominion U., instr. elem. edn., 1973—76; mental health educator Comprehensive Mental Health Svcs., Virginia Beach, Va., 1977—84; asst. prof. edn. Va. Wesleyan Coll., Norfolk, 1985—. Edn. cons., 1995—. Trainer Head Start, Va., NC, 1967—70; advisor early childhood edn. Tidewater (Va.) C.C., 2000—. Office: Va Wesleyan Coll 1584 Wesleyan Dr Norfolk VA 23502 Fax: 757-466-8283. Office Phone: 757-455-3236. E-mail: gferris@vwc.edu.

FERRIS, RITA BERNADETTE, social worker; b. New Haven, Conn., Aug. 9, 1918; d. John B. and Olympia (D'Orio) Affinito; m. Edward A. Ferris, Aug. 8, 1942 (dec. Jan. 1987); 1 child, Miles. AB, Albertus Magnus Coll., 1940; postgrad., McGill U., 1940—41; MS, Fordham U., 1942; postgrad., Yale U., 1945. Caseworker Cath. Family Agy., Norfolk, Va., 1944, sr. caseworker New Haven, 1944-46, 50-52; social worker Psychiat. Clinic VA, Hartford, Conn., 1947-48; case workers, sr. citizen coord. Asnuntuck C.C., Enfield, Conn., 1978-79; tutor young children primary grades Broward County, Fla., 1983—. Vol. adult handicapped and retarded, 1986; v.p. Rep. Women's Club, Suffield, Conn., 1985, Ch. Guild Orgn., Suffield, 1986, Newcomers Club; pres. Coll. Alumnae, Milford, Conn., 1970; chief checker polls, Suffield, Conn.; vol. I'm a Listener program. Mem.: NASW, AAUW (v.p. Fla. Broward county 1992—), Bocci Club (bd. dirs., sec.), All War Vets. Club. Republican. Roman Catholic. Avocations: singing in a choral group, western line dancing, bocci, art courses, political discussion groups. Home: Garfield Bldg A208 1601 SW 128th Ter Pembroke Pines FL 33027-2149

FERRIS-WAKS, ARLENE SUSAN, compliance officer; b. N.Y.C., Apr. 4, 1954; d. Jack Charles and Marcia (Berman) Ferris; m. Robert Gilman Waks, Sept. 20, 1981; 1 child, Jason Lowell. BA cum laude, SUNY, Buffalo, 1977; M. of Libr. and Info. Sci., CUNY, 1981. Rsch. analyst Zimmerman & Assocs., Washington, 1981-83; sr. mkt. analyst Am. Stock Exch., N.Y.C., 1983-84; prin. market analyst N.Y. Stock Exch., N.Y.C., 1984-97; sr. compliance officer First Union, Boca Raton, Fla., 1996-99; assoc. dir. compliance Dalton Kent Securities Group, Inc., N.Y.C., 1999—2001; fin. advisor Morgan Stanley Dean Witter, 2003—04; supervisory investigator N.J. Bur. of Securities, 2004—. Lectr./demonstrator N.Y. Stock Exch., 1989-96; cons. independent compliance, Westfield, NJ. Mem. Nat. Soc. Compliance Profls. Home: 601 Kensington Dr Westfield NJ 07090-3604 Office: Office Atty Gen NJ Bur of Securities PO Box 47029 Newark NJ 07101 Office Phone: 973-504-3627. Personal E-mail: afwaks@lycos.com.

FERRON, JENNIFER, marketing executive; BA in Communications, Boston Coll. Acct. exec. Arnold Publ. Relations, Boston; with Kraft Sports Mgmt. Group (New England Patriots and Foxboro Stadium), 1997—, v.p. mktg. ops., 2006—. Media planner FIFA Women's World Cup. Named one of 40 Under 40, Boston Bus. Jour., 2006. Office: New England Patriots Kraft Sports Mgmt One Patriot Pl Foxboro MA 02035-1388*

FERRY, JOAN EVANS, school counselor; b. Summit, N.J., Aug. 20, 1941; d. John Stiger and Margaret Darling (Evans) F. BS, U. Pa., 1964; cert., Coll. of Preceptors, London, 1966; EdM, Temple U., 1967; postgrad., Villanova U., 1981. Cert. elem. sch. tchr., elem. sch. counselor; cert. vol. Dale Carnegie; cert. cash flow cons. Indsl. photographer Bucksco Mfg. Co., Inc., Quakertown, Pa., 1958-59; math. and German tutor St. Lawrence U., Canton, NY, 1959-61; research asst. U. Pa., Phila., 1963; tchr. elem. sch. Pennridge Schs., Perkasie, Pa., 1964—77, elem. sch. counselor, 1981—2001; pvt. practice counselor, real estate partnership Perkasie, 1981—; chair child study team Perkasie Elem. Sch., 1988-94; editor Princeton Pub. Group, NJ, 2000—; owner Capitial Funding Solutions, 2003—; self-employed as cash flow cons., 2004—. Tutor math., German, St. Lawrence U., Canton, N.Y., 1959-61; supervisory tchr. East Stroudsburg U., Pennridge Schs., 1971-74; research asst. U. Pa., Phila., 1963; mem. acad. coms. for Pennridge Schs.; adj. faculty Bucks County Community Coll., 1983—; instr. Am. Inst. Banking, 1982—; notary pub., 1986—; mcpl. auditor, sec. bd. auditors, 1984-90, mcpl. auditor 1990—, chmn. bd. auditors 1990—; cons. in field. Author (with others) Life-Time Sports for the College Student: A Behavioral Objective Approach, 1971, 3d rev. edit. 1978, Elementary Social Studies as a Learning System, 1976. Vol. elem. sch. counselor Perkasie, 1979-81; mem. Hilltown Civic Assn., 1965-70, 92—; chair exec. com. Hilltown PTO, 1965-73; soloist Good Shepherd Episcopal Ch. Choir, Hilltown, 1964-77, mem. choir, 2000—; mem. steering com. Perkasie Sch., 1989-95; poll watcher, 1993; med. vol. Olympics, Atlanta, 1996; vol. Dublin Ambulance Squad, 1996—, House Rabbit Soc., Chadds Ford, Pa., 1998—, Spl. Olympics World Games, Summer, N.C., 1999, Silverdale Quick Response Med. Svc., 1999-2001, Chalfont Ambulance Squad, 2000—; mem. Dublin Vol. Fire and Ambulance Co., Silverdale (Pa.) Fire Co.; mem. prin.'s round table Perkasie (Pa.) Sch., 1997; vol. House Rabbit Soc. Southeastern Pa./Del. Foster Home and Sanctuary, Chadds Ford, Pa., 1998—; vol. marshal First Union US Pro Championship Cycling Race, Phila., 1999-2005; vol. spl. driver Bush Family and Friends at Rep. Nat. Conv., Phila., 2000, Bucks County Crisis Response Team, 2001—; mem. Chalfont Chem. Fire Engine Co. No. 1; mem. Nat. Arbor Day Found., Best Friends Animal Sanctuary. NSF grantee, Washington, 1972-73, Philanthropic Edn. Orgn. grantee, Doylestown, Pa., 1982; recipient Judith Netzky Meml. Fellowship award B'nai B'rith, Phila., 1979; Durning scholar Delta Delta Delta, Arlington, Tex., 1981, Am. Mgmt. Assns. scholar, N.Y.C., 1983, Achievement award Women's Inner Circle, 1990, Golden Acad. award for lifetime achievement, 1991; named to Women's Internat. Hall of Fame, 2003, Internat. Tennis Hall of Fame, 2000, Cmty. Leaders of Am. Hall of Fame, 1990, Internat. Bus. and Profl. Women's Hall of Fame, 1994, Millennium Hall of Fame, 1999; recipient Lifetime Achievement Acad. Humane Soc. U.S., Internat. Honor Soc. In Edn., Cert. of appreciation Atlanta Olympics Med. Team, 1997, Hon. Educator cert. St. Joseph's Indian Sch., 1996, ARC, 1986, Cert. Achievement in Recognition of Contbn. as Med. Svcs. Vol. at Centennial Olympic Games, 1996, Honor Award for Svc. to Edn. and Tchg. Profession, 1996, 99, award for Outstanding Svc. to Edn. Pennridge Schs., 1999, Cert. of appreciation Spl. Olympics World Summer Games, 1999, World Lifetime Achievement award, Raleigh, 2003, 21st Century award for Achievement, Internat. Bio. Ctr., 2004. Mem. AAUW, NEA, NAFE, Humane Soc. U.S., Pa. State Edn. Assn. (polit. action com. for edn., chair Pennridge Schs. 1986—, del. leadership conf. 1987, 89, Honor award for svc. to edn. and tchg. profession, 1996, 99), Pennridge Edn. Assn. (faculty rep. 1986-88, exec. coun. 1986—, negotiations resource com. 1987-89, 1990-93, steering com. Perkasie Sch. 1989-95, chair Child Study Team, 1988-94, Instructional Support Team, 1992—), Am. Inst. Banking (chair 1987), U.S. Tennis Assn. (hon. life), Pa. and Mid. States Tennis Assn. (hon. life), U.S. Profl. Tennis Registry, Mid. States Profl. Tennis Registry, Women's Internat. Tennis Assn., Nat. Ski Patrol (Svc. Recognition award 1994, 2004), Spring Mountain Ski Patrol(Outstanding Aux.), Pa. Elected Women's Assn., Bucks County Assn. Twp. Ofcls., Bucks County Sch. Counselors Assn., Pa. Sch. Counselors Assn., Pa. Assn. Notaries, Am. Soc. Notaries, Am. Cash Flow Assn., Internat. Fedn. Univ. Women, Internat. Platform Assn.(pes. task force on small bus. issues 2005—), Rails-to-Trails Conservancy, World Wildlife Fund, Bucks County Sch. Counselors Assn., Highpoint Athletic Club, Pennridge Cmty. Rep. Club. (rec. sec. 1986-91, publicity chmn. 1991-92, Pen care chmn. 1992—), Assn. Tennis Profls. Tour Tennis Ptnrs., Sierra Club, The Nature Conservancy, Nat. Wildlife Fedn., John Wayne Found., Nat. Fedn. Indep. Bus., Mediterranean Club, Phila. Sports Club, Delaware Valley Jaguar Club, Jaguar Clubs N.Am., Nockamixon Boat Club, Peace Valley Yacht Club, Kappa Delta Pi. Episcopalian. Avocations: land and water sports, flying, music, parasailing, photography. Home and Office: 834 Rickert Rd Perkasie PA 18944

FERSHTMAN, JULIE ILENE, lawyer; b. Detroit, Apr. 3, 1961; d. Sidney and Judith Joyce (Stoll) F.; m. Robert S. Bick, Mar. 4, 1990. Student, Mich. State U., 1979-81, James Madison Coll., 1979-81; BA in Philosophy and Polit. Sci., Emory U., 1983, JD, 1986. Bar: Mich. 1986, U.S. Dist. Ct. (ea. dist.) Mich. 1986, U.S. Ct. Appeals (6th cir.) 1987, U.S. Dist. Ct. (we. dist.) Mich. 1993. Assoc. Miller, Canfield, Paddock and Stone, Detroit, 1986-89; assoc. Miro, Miro & Weiner P.C., Bloomfield Hills, Mich., 1989-92; pvt. practice, Bingham Farms, Mich., 1992—; of counsel Zausmer, Kaufman August & Caldwell, P.C., Farmington Hills, Mich., 2002—. Adj. prof. Schoolcraft Coll., Livonia, Mich., 1994—; lectr. in field. Author: Equine Law & Horse Sense, 1996, More Equine Law and Horse Sense, 2000 Bd. dirs. Franklin Cmty. Assn., 1989-92, sec., 1991-92; mem. Franklin Planning Commn., 1993-94; bd. dirs. Am. Youth Horse Coun., 2003—. Recipient Nat. Ptnr. in Safety award Assn. for Horsemanship Safety and Edn., 1997, Outstanding Achievement award Am. Riding Instrs. Assn., 1998, Catalyst award, 2002; named one of 40 Bus. Leaders Under 40, Crain's Detroit Bus., 1996. Mem. ABA (planning bd. litigation sect. young lawyers divsn., vice chair ABA/TIPS animal ins. law 2005—), FBA (courthouse tours com. Detroit chpt., featured in Barrister mag. in 21 Young Lawyers Leading US into 21st Century 1995), State Bar Mich. (exec. coun. young lawyers sect. 1989-96, chmn. 1995-96, bd. commrs. 1994-96, 99—, grievance com. 1997-99, structure and governance com. 1997-98, strategic planning action group 2001, rep. assn. 1997-2002, chmn. rep. assembly 2001-02, exec. com. 2006-), Oakland County Bar Assn. (profl. com. 1995—, chmn. 1998-99 Inns of Ct. com. 1995—, chair 1998-99, bd. dirs. 2001—, Professionalism award 2000), Mich. State Bar Found. (trustee 2003—), Markel Equestrian Safety Bd., Women Lawyers Assn., Soc. Coll. Journalists, Phi Alpha Delta, Omicron Delta Kappa, Phi Sigma Tau, Pi Sigma Alpha. Avocations: horse showing, writing, music, art. Office: 31700 Middlebelt Rd Ste 150 Farmington Hills MI 48334 Home: 31700 Briarcliff Franklin MI 48025 Office Phone: 248-851-4111. Personal E-mail: fershtman@aol.com.

FERSTANDIG ARNOLD, GAIL, research scientist, educator; m. Edward Arnold, 1981; children: Elizabeth, Emily. PhD, Purdue U., 1987. Sr. rsch. scientist Rutgers U., Ctr. of Advanced Biotechnology and Medicine, Piscataway, NJ, 1987—. Partnered (with husband Edward Arnold) in 1987 to form laboratory at Rutgers University, Center of Advanced Biotechnology and Medicine that is working with a 20 member research team to develop and apply structure-based drug and vaccine designs for the treatment and prevention of serious human diseases, most notably AIDS. Co-directs (with husband Edward Arnold) an effort to develop chimeric human rhinoviruses as potential vaccines for HIV/AIDS. Office: Rutgers U Ctr Advanced Biotechnology & Medicine 679 Hoes Ln Rm 020 Piscataway NJ 08854 Office Phone: 732-235-4343. Office Fax: 732-235-5788. Business E-Mail: gfarnold@cabm.rutgers.edu.

FERTITTA, ANGELA, dean; BFA, MFA, U. Colo. Dean academic affairs Art Inst. Boston at Lesley U., Boston, adj. prof. drawing & painting/foundation. Exhibitions include Faculty Honorarium Exhbn. Office: Art Institute of Boston at Lesley University 700 Beacon St Boston MA 02215-2598 Office Fax: 617-585-6600.

FESHBACH, NORMA DEITCH, psychologist, educator; b. N.Y.C., Sept. 5, 1926; m. Seymour Feshbach; children: Jonathan Stephan, Laura Elizabeth, Andrew David. BS in Psychology, CCNY, 1947, MS in Ednl. Psychology, 1949; PhD in Clin. Psychology, U. Pa., 1956. Diplomate Am. Bd. Prof. Psychology; cert. in clin. psychology, Phila.; lic. clin. and ednl. psychologist, Calif. Tchr. Betsy Ross Nursery Sch., Yale U., 1947-48; clin. psychologist Yale U. Med. Sch., 1948; teaching asst. dept. psychology Yale U., 1948-51; research asst. human resources research office George Washington U., Washington, 1951-52; psychology intern Phila. Gen. Hosp., 1955-56; research assoc. dept. psychology U. Pa., 1959-61; research assoc. Inst. Behavioral Sci. U. Colo., 1963-64; assoc. research psychologist dept. psychology UCLA, 1964-65; clin. psychologist II UCLA Neuropsychiat. Inst., 1965; prof. Grad. Sch. Edn. UCLA, 1965—, prof. psychology dept., 1975-92, chmn. dept. edn., 1985-90, interim dean Grad. Sch. Edn., 1991-92, acting dir. Corinne A. Seeds Univ. Elem. Sch., 1985-89. Fulbright sr. lectr./researcher U. Rome, 1988; lectr. Jr. Coll. Phys. Therapy, New Haven, Conn., 1948-49, dept. psychology, U. Pa., 1956-57, UCLA Neuropsychiat. Inst., Calif. Dept. Mental Hygiene, Los Angeles, 1966-69; vis. asst. prof. Stanford U. dept. psychology, 1961-62, U. Calif. Berkeley, 1962-63; vis. scholar dept. exptl. psychology Oxford U., 1980-81; co-prin. investigator various projects and programs; co-prin. dir. and investigator NIMH Tng. Program in Applied Human Devel., 1986-91, co-dir. tng. grant in applied human devel., 1991—; clin. and research cons. Youth Services, Inc., Phila., 1955-61; also cons. various media orgns.; head program in Early Childhood and Devel. Studies, 1968-80; dir. NIMH Tng. Prog. in Early Childhood and Devel. Studies, 1972-82; prog. dir. Ctr. for Study of Evaluation, UCLA Grad. Sch. Edn., 1966-69; co-dir. UCLA Bush Found. Tng. Prog. in Child Devel. and Social Policy, 1978-82; chair grad. faculty UCLA Grad. Sch. Edn., 1979-80. Editorial cons., mem. editorial bd. psychology and ednl. research revs., contbr. numerous articles on child psychology to profl. jours. Mem. adv. coun. of Women's Clinic, Los Angeles, 1974-76; mem. adv. bd. Nat. Com. to Abolish Corporal Punishment in Schs., 1972-80, Nat. Ctr. for Study of Corporal Punishment and Alternatives in the Schs., 1976—; mem. profl. adv. com. on Child Care, Los Angeles Unified Sch. Dist., 1978-80; trustee EVAN-G Com. to End Violence Against the Next Generation, 1972-80; exec.

bd. Internat. Soc. for Research in Agression, 1982-84. Recipient James McKeen Cattell Fund Sabbatical award, 1980, 81, Townsend Harris Medal, Disting. Alumnus award CCNY, 1982, Disting. Sci. Achievement in Psychology award Calif. Psychol. Assn., 1983, Achievements in Psychology award CUNY, 1989, GSE Faculty award Harold A. and Lois Haytin Found., 1991; named Faculty Mem. Woman of Yr. Nat. Acad. Profl. Psychologists, Los Angeles, 1973; U.S. Pub. Health Tng. fellow, 1953-56; rsch. grantee NIMH, 1972-77 (co-principal with D. Stipek), 77-82, 1986—, Hilton Found., 1985-86, Spencer Found. 1984-85, Child Help, USA, 1982-84 (co-principal with C. Howes), UCLA Acad. Senate, 1981—, Bush Found., 1978-83, 79-80, 80-81, 81-82, 82-83 (co-dir. with J.I. Goodlad), Adminstrn. for Children, Youth and Families, 1981-82 (co-dir. with J.I. Goodlad), NSF, 1976-77, 77-78, 78-80 (co-prin. with S. Feshbach), Com. on Internat. and Comparative Studies, 1973-74, 77-78. Fellow Am. Psychol. Assn. (officer var. coms., Disting. Contbn. Psychology and Media, Divsn. 42, 1992); mem. Assn. Advancement Psychology, AAAS, AAUP, Am. Bd. Profl. Psychologists, Am. Ednl. Research Assn., Calif. Assn. for Edn. Young Children, Nat. Assn for Edn. Young Children, Internat. Assn. Applied Psychology, Internat. Soc. for Research on Aggression, Internat. Soc. Study of Behavioral Devel., Internat. Soc. Prevention Child Abuse and Neglect, Nat. Register of Health Services Providers in Psychology, Soc. for Research in Child Devel., Western Psychol. Assn. (pres. 1979-80); Sigma Xi, Delta Phi Upsilon.

FESKO, COLLEENE, art appraiser; B, Bucknell Univ. Tchr., art hist. Mount Ida Coll.; appraiser Childs Gallery, Boston; cons. Vespi Corp.; joined Skinner, Inc., Boston, 1987, now v.p., and dir., Am., European paintings & prints dept. Appraiser Antiques Roadshow, WGBH-PBS; founder, Firewall Gallery Skinner, Inc. Lectr., writer in field. Mem.: Art Table women in arts orgn. Office: Skinner Inc 63 Park Plz Boston MA 02116 Office Phone: 617-350-5400. Office Fax: 617-350-5429. Business E-Mail: tvappraisers@skinnerinc.com.

FESLER, ELIZABETH, educator, psychologist; b. Youngstown, Ohio, Nov. 5, 1930; d. Raymond and Mary (Theodore) Cosetti; married, July 8, 1953; 1 child, Kim. BS, Kent State U., 1952, MS, 1981, PhD, 1974. Tchr. Buchtel H.S., Perkins H.S., 1952—62; counselor Akron, Ohio, 1962—70; psychologist Akron Pub. Schs., 1970—76, coord. spl. needs, 1976—78; prin. Goodrich Jr. H.S., Akron, 1978—80; dir. spl. edn. Akron Pub. Schs., 1980—89; asst. dir., dir. Gilmour Acad., Gates Mills, Ohio, 1989—2003, dean academics, curriculum and profl. devel., 2003—. Pres. Support, Inc., mem. suicide prevention com.; bd. dirs. Planned Parenthood Assn., chmn. edn. divsn.; v.p. bd. dirs. Mental Health Assn.; mem. women's aux. bd. Summit County Juvenile Ct.; mem. Children's Transitionals Svcs. Bd. Cmty. advisor Jr. League. Scholar, Kent State U. Mem.: APA, Akron Assn. Secondary Sch. Prins., Akron Assn. Psychologists, Ohio Assn. Secondary Sch. Prins., Ohio Assn. Psychologists, Nat. Assn. Sch. Psychologists, Am. Assn. Secondary Sch. Prins., Alpha Xi Delta. Home: 65 N Wheaton Rd Akron OH 44313-3969 Office: Gilmour Academy Gates Mills OH 44040

FESTIN, FE ERLITA DIOLAZO, psychiatrist, director; arrived in U.S., 1986; m. Nestor P. Festin, Oct. 27, 1984; children: Ingrid, Shannon. BS, U. Philippines, Manila, 1975, MD, 1979. Lic. physician Mass., diplomate Am. Bd. Psychiatry and Neurology. Staff psychiatrist acute psychiatry VA Boston Healthcare Sys., Brockton, Mass., 1990—, med. dir. acute psychiatry inpatient svc., 2006—. Assoc. dir. Harvard South Shore Residency, Brockton, Mass., 1998—. Mailing: 940 Belmont St Brockton MA 02301-5596

FETRIDGE, BONNIE-JEAN CLARK (MRS. WILLIAM HARRISON FETRIDGE), civic volunteer; b. Chgo., Feb. 3, 1915; d. Sheldon and Bonnie (Carrington) Clark; m. William Harrison Fetridge, June 27, 1941; children: Blakely (Mrs. Harvey H. Bundy III), Clark Worthington. Student, Girls Latin Sch., Chgo., The Masters Sch., Dobbs Ferry, N.Y., Finch Coll., N.Y.C. Bd. dirs. region VII com. Girl Scouts U.S.A., 1939-43, nat. program com., 1966-69, nat. adv. bd., 1972-85, internat. commr.'s adv. panel, 1973-76, Nat. Juliette Low Birthplace Com., 1966-69; bd. dirs. Girl Scouts Chgo., 1936-51, 59-69, sec., 1936-38, v.p., 1946-49, 61-65, chmn. Juliette Low world friendship com., 1959-67, 71-72; mem. Friends Our Cabana Com. World Assn. Girl Guides and Girl Scouts, Cuernavaca, Mexico, 1969—, vice chmn., 1982-87; founder, pres. Olave Baden-Powell Soc. of World Assn. Girl Guides and Girl Scouts, London, 1984-93, bd. dirs., 1984—, hon. assoc., 1987; asst. sec. Dartnell Corp, Chgo., 1981-91, sec., 1991-98, bd. dirs. 1989-98; vice chmn. Dartnell Found., 1990-2000, Ravenswood Found., 2001—; bd. dirs. Jr. League of Chgo., 1937-40, Vis. Nurse Assn. Chgo., 1951-58, 61-63, asst. treas., 1962-63; women's bd. dirs. Children's meml. Hosp., 1946-50; v.p. parents coun. Latin Sch. Chgo., 1952-54, bd. dirs. alumni assn., 1964-69; Fidelitas Soc., 1979, 96; mem. women's bd. U.S.O., 1965-75, treas., 1969-71, v.p., 1971-73; mem. women's svc. bd. Chgo. Area coun. Boy Scouts Am., 1964-70, mem. nat. exploring com., 1973-76; staff aide and ARC Motor Corps, World War II. Recipient Citation of Merit Sta. WAIT, Chgo., 1971, Juliette Low World Friendship medal Girl Scouts U.S.A., 1989; 1st recipient Medal of Recognition World Assn.Girl Guides and Girl Scouts, London, 1993; Baden-Powell fellow World Scout Found., Geneva, 1983. Mem. Nat. Soc. Colonial Dames Am. (life, Ill. bd. mgrs. 1962-65, 69-76, 78-82, v.p. 1970-72, corr. sec. 1978-80, 1st v.p. 1980-84, state chmn. geneal. info. svcs. com. 1972-76, corr. sec. 1978-80, hist. activities com. 1979-83, mus. house com. 1980-83, house gov. 1981-82), Chgo. Dobbs Alumnae Assn. (past pres.), Nat. Soc. DAR, Conn. Soc. Genealogists, New Eng. Hist. Geneal. Soc., N.Y. Geneal. and Biog. Soc., Newberry Libr. Assocs., Chgo. Hist. Soc. (life), Casino Club, The Racquet Club Chgo., Onwentsia Club, Union League Club. Republican. Episcopalian. Home: 1100 Pembridge Dr Apt 215 Lake Forest IL 60045

FETTERLY, BARBARA LOUISE, artist; b. Painesville, Ohio, May 28, 1930; d. Ralph Frances and Claire Louise (Marquis) Fetterly; m. Henry Joseph Hargis Jr., June 4, 1955 (dec.); children: Ben William, William John, Glenn D. AA, Citrus Coll., 1985. Artist Art Gallery, La Puente, Calif., 1984-94; gallery owner Hargis Chim Gregg Art Gallery, Pomona, Calif., 1994—. Grantee Millenn Prodn., Pomona, Calif., 1994-97. Mem. Carlsbad Oceanside Art League (life), DA Gallery Non Profit, Pomona Valley Art (dir. 1988, life), Corona Art Assn. (life), Women in Arts Mus. (charter mem.), Covina Arts and Crafts, Parks and Recreation (life). Republican. Baptist. Avocations: amateur radio, tennis, swimming, sewing, pool. Studio: BHUA El Cerrito CA 92881 Office: Gallery SoHo 300 A South Thomas St Pomona CA 91766 Office Phone: 951-340-1060. E-mail: FINEART28@aol.com.

FETTERLY, MARY E., counseling administrator; b. Wenatchee, Wash., Aug. 9, 1960; d. Jesus Gonzalez Pliego, Anita Maria Castillo; m. Roger Dale Fetterly, Aug. 14, 1982 (div. Nov. 20, 2000). Grad. H.S., Burien, Wash. Cert. completion fgn. credentials analysis. Internat. admissions evaluator U. Wash. Office Grad. Admissions, Seattle, 1980—91, internat. admissions counseling svcs. coord., 1991—. Recipient Cert. Appreciation to Region 1 Conf., Nat. Assn. for Fgn. Student Affairs, 1997. Mem.: Nat. Assn. for Fgn. Student Affairs (nat. com. on edn. and tng. 2001—), Nat. Assn. Grad. Admissions Profls., Assn. Wash. State Internat. Student Affairs, Seattle Athletic Club. Roman Catholic. Avocations: Karate, travel, collecting thimbles, bicycling, skiing. Office: U Wash Grad Admissions #301 Loew Hall Box 352191 Seattle WA 98195-2191 Home: Apt B 4124 214th St SW Mountlake Terrace WA 98043-6517

FETTNER, MARILYN, management consultant; b. Chgo. MA in Human Resources Devel., Webster U., St. Louis, Mo., 1994. Qualified MBTI User Gainsville, Fla., 2000, cert. leadership devel. instr. Dir. profl. devel. North Shore Bd. Realtors, Northbrook, Ill., 1990—96; br. sales mgr. Coldwell Banker, Libertyville, Ill., 1996—97; mgr. tng. and devel. McCormick Pl./Navy Pier, Chgo., 1997—98; prin., career cons. Fettner Career Consulting, Highland Park, Ill., 1998—. Cert. assoc. Lee Hecht Harrison, Chgo., 2001. Author (spkr.): (seminar presentation) What's Your Best Fit? How to Make Career Choices Based on the Real You, 2002—04, Human Capital: Your Organization's Most Powerful Competitive Advantage, 2003, How to Get the Job, 2006; guest career cons. (TV appearance) Starting Over, NBC, 2004. Vol. career cons. CARA, Chgo., 2006. Mem.: ACA, Assn. Career Profls. Internat., Nat. Career Devel. Assn. Avocations: reading, travel, running, movies, writing. Office: Fettner Career Consulting 910 Skokie Blvd 213 Northbrook IL 60062 Office Phone: 847-831-0079. Business E-Mail: marilyn@fettnercareerconsulting.com.

FEUERBORN, RITA KAZLAUSKAS, music educator, musician; b. Waukegan, Ill., Sept. 4, 1971; d. Kaz and Terese Kazlauskas; m. Andrew D. Feuerborn, Mar. 27, 1999; children: Grace L., Benjamin K. MusB in Performance, DePaul U., Chgo., MusB in Music Edn., MusM in Performance. Suzuki trained Ill., 1995. Orch. tchr. Rotolo Mid. Sch., Batavia, Ill., 1996—. Violinist Rockford Symphony Orch., Ill., 1995—2000; substitute violinist Elgin Symphony Orch., Ill., 1997—2002; violin instr. Blue Lake Fine Arts Camp, 1997; guest condr. U-46 Festival Orch., 2006; free-lance musician, Ill. Grantee, Ill. Arts Coun., 2002. Mem.: Am. String Tchrs. Assn. (assoc.). Office: Rotolo Middle School 1501 S Raddant Rd Batavia IL 60510 Office Phone: 630-406-6306. Business E-Mail: rita.feuerborn@bps101.net.

FEUERHELM, HEATHER M., language arts educator; b. Lake City, Iowa, Oct. 10, 1967; d. Harry W. and Barbara S. Merrick; m. Randall L. Feuerhelm, June 27, 1992; children: Benjamin Andrew, Elijah Warren. MA in Tchg. of English in the Secondary Schs., U. No. Iowa, Cedar Falls, 2000. Cert. master educator Iowa. Tchr., coach Jefferson H.S., Cedar Rapids, 1991—2006, Grant Wood AEA Literacy Cons., Cedar Rapids, 2006—; adj. prof. Mt. Mercy Coll., Cedar Rapids, 2006—. Reading cons., staff devel. specialist Jefferson HS, 2004—. Contbr. poetry, journal article, research writing, poetry to jours., articles to profl. jours. Tchr., com. mem., musician Gloria Dei Luth. Ch., Cedar Rapids, 1992—. Named to Jefferson Hall of Fame, Jefferson HS, 1996; recipient Spl. Tchr. award, Cedar Rapids C. of C., 1996. Mem.: NEA, Iowa State Edn. Assn., Iowa Coun. Tchrs. English, Nat. Coun. Tchrs. English. Avocations: reading, swimming, travel, fine arts. Office: Jefferson HS 4401 6th St SW Cedar Rapids IA 52404

FEUERSTEIN, PENNY, artist; b. Chgo. d. Charles Gustin and Edith Reich; m. Jay Feuerstein; children: Lina, Alexa. BS, So. Ill. U., 1982; MFA, Sch. Art Inst. Chgo., 1999. Keyline design Feldkamp Malloy, Chgo., 1983-84; package design Lipson & Assocs., Northbrook, Ill., 1984-86; freelance textile designer, artist Chgo., 1986—. Mem. Leukemia Rsch. Found., 1985—. Mem. Comtemporary Art Soc.

FEUERSTEIN, SANDRA JEANNE, judge; b. NYC, Jan. 21, 1946; m. Albert Feuerstein, June 5, 1966; children: Adam, Seth. BS, U. Vt., 1966; JD, Benjamin Cardozo U., 1979. Bar: N.Y. 1980, U.S. Dist. Ct. (so. and ea. dists.) N.Y. 1983, U.S. Ct. Mil. Appeals, 1988, U.S. Tax Ct. 1988, U.S. Supreme Ct. 1988. Sr. law asst. NY State Supreme Ct., Mineola, 1980-86, matrimonial referee, 1985-86; judge Nassau County Dist. Ct., Hempstead, NY, 1987—93; assoc. justice NY State Supreme Ct. (10th judicial dist.), 1994—99, NY State Supreme Ct. (Appellate div., 2d dept.), 1999—2003; judge U.S. Dist. Ct. (ea. dist.) NY, 2003—. Law sec. to adminstrv. judge Leo J. McGinity, Mineola, 1985-87; lectr. Trial Def. Bar of Nassau County, 1984, Town and Village Justice Continuing Jud. Edn., 1987; mem. discovery oversight com. U.S. Dist. Ct. (ea. dist.) N.Y., 1983-86; mem. Nassau County Exec.'s Blue Ribbon Panel on Domestic Violence, 1989; mem. com. on civil litigation U.S. Dist. Ct. (ea. dist.) N.Y. 1989-91. Assoc. editor Nassau Lawyer, 1984-87, editor, 1987-89; contbr. numerous articles to profl. jours. Counsel Merrick Sr. Citizens Ctr., 1980-87; life mem. Hadassah, Long Beach Meml. Hosp. Aux.; bd. dirs. L.I. Arts Coun.; life mem., bd. dirs. Am. Cancer Soc.; dir., Benjamin N. Cardozo Sch. Law, Yeshiva U. Recipient Mesivta Torah award, 1985. Mem. Women's Bar Assn. of N.Y. State (v.p. 1990, pres. Nassau County chpt. 1988-89, founder pro bono project, judiciary com., spl. matrimonial com. 1985-86, v.p. 1986-87, 87-88, 90, chmn. judiciary com. 1984), Nassau County Bar Assn. (bd. dirs. 1988, Pro Bono Recognition award 1990), Franklin D. Roosevelt Inns of Ct. (master), Bus. and Profl. Women of Nassau County, L.I. Ctr. for Bus. and Profl. Women, Yeshiva U. Alumni Assn. (founding bd. dirs.), Acad. of Law (pub. edn. com.). Office: Dist Ct 1014 Federal Plaza Central Islip NY 11722

FEUSS, LINDA ANNE UPSALL, lawyer; b. White Plains, NY, Dec. 9, 1956; d. Herbert Charles and Edna May (Hart) Upsall; m. Charles E. Feuss, Aug. 16, 1980; children: Charles Herbert, Anne Hart. BA in French lit., Colgate U., 1978; JD, Emory U., 1981. Bar: Ga. 1981, SC 1981, Minn. 2000. Assoc. Rainey, Britton, Gibbes & Clarkson, Greenville, SC, 1981-83; counsel Siemens Energy & Automation, Atlanta, 1983-91, Siemens Corp., Atlanta, 1991-93, sr. counsel, 1993-94, assoc. gen. counsel, 1994-98; v.p., gen. counsel Pillsbury Co., Mpls., 1998-2000; v.p., gen. counsel to exec. v.p. legal and human resources PEMSTAR Inc., Rochester, Minn., 2001—03; v.p., gen. counsel, sec. C.H. Robinson Worldwide Inc., Eden Prairie, Minn., 2003—. Rep. law coun. II Mfr.'s Alliance, Washington, 1995-98; rep. law com. Nat. Elec. Mfr.'s Assn., Washington, 1995-98; bd. govs. St. Thomas U. Sch. Law, 2006—; mem. adv. bd. PACER, 2005—. Bd. dirs. Am. Heart Assn., Greenville, 1981-83, Success with Children, 1999, CityLights, 1999; mem. leadership com. Woodruff Arts Ctr. Campaign, Atlanta, 1985-90; vol. High Mus. Art, Atlanta, 1993-99, Ga. 100 Mentor Exch., 1998. Mem. ABA, Am. Corp. Coun. Assn. (dir. Ga. chpt. 1995-98, v.p. Ga. chpt. 1996, pres. 1997), State Bar Ga., SC Bar, Minn. Bar Assn., Colgate Club Atlanta (pres. 1986-88, bd. dirs. 1989-98). Office: CH Robinson Worldwide Inc 8100 Mitchell Rd Eden Prairie MN 55344-2248

FEY, TINA, actress; b. Upper Darby, Penn., May 18, 1970; m. Jeff Richmond, June 3, 2001; 1 child, Alice. BA in drama, U. Va., 1992. Writer: TV series Saturday Night Live: 25th Anniversary, 1999, The Colin Quinn Show, 2002, NBC 75th Anniversary Special, 2002, writer, composer: films Mean Girls, 2004; actor: (films) Mean Girls, 2004, Man of the Year, 2006; writer Saturday Night Live, 1997—2006, head writer, 1999—2006; actor: (TV series) Saturday Night Live, 2000—06; actor, writer, co-prodr.: 30 Rock, 2006—; actor guest appearances (TV series) Upright Citizens Brigade, 1999, The Real World/Road Rules Extreme Challenge, 2001, Film 72, 2004, 60 Minutes, 2004. Named Entertainer of Yr., Entertainment Weekly, 2001. Mailing: 3 Arts c/o David Miner 9460 Wilshire Blvd 7th Fl Beverly Hills CA 90212*

FEY, VICKI PETERSON, church musician; b. Homestead, Fla., Aug. 2, 1954; m. Stephen H. Fey, May 25, 1979; children: Alan J., Jordan M. MusB, Stetson U., Deland, Fla., 1976; MusM, North Tex. State U., Denton, 1982. Staff accompanist Southwestern Bapt. Theol. Sem., Ft. Worth, 1981—83; co-dir. music First Presbyn. Ch., Vero Beach, Fla., 1983—94, dir. music ministry Kingwood, Tex., 1994—99, Bristol, Tenn., 1999—. Adj. instr. applied organ King Coll., Bristol, Tenn., 1981—. Mem.: Presbyn. Assn. Musicians (pres. exec. bd. 2004—06). Presbyterian. Home: 509 Cedar Valley Rd Bristol TN 37620 Office: First Presbyterian Church 701 Florida Ave Bristol TN 37620 Office Phone: 423-764-7176. Home Fax: 423-764-5836. Personal E-mail: vpfey@yahoo.com. E-mail: svfey@fpcbristol.org.

FIACCO, BARBARA A., lawyer; AB in Govt., magna cum laude, Dartmouth Coll., 1991; JD cum laude, Harvard U., 1996. Bar: Mass. 1997, US Dist. Ct. (Dist. Mass.), US Ct. Appeals (Fed. Cir.), US Ct. Appeals (1st Cir.). Law clk. to Hon. Richard J. Cardamone US Ct. Appeals (2nd Cir.); ptnr. Foley Hoag LLP, Boston. Mem.: Am. Intellectual Property Law Assn. (vice chair membership com.), Fed. Cir. Bar Assn., Boston Patent Law Assn., Women's Bar Assn., Boston Bar Assn., ABA, Phi Beta Kappa. Office: Foley Hoag LLP Seaport World Trade Center West 155 Seaport Blvd Boston MA 02110 Office Phone: 617-832-1227. Office Fax: 617-832-7000. E-mail: bfiacco@foleyhoag.com.*

FIALKA, DEBORAH RIDGELY, writer; b. Cambridge, Md., Mar. 8, 1941; d. James Rogers and Catherine (Ridgely) Sollers; m. John Joseph Fialka, Oct. 14, 1967; children: Benjamin Barnett, Jennifer Wren, Joseph Aram. BA, St. John's Coll., 1963; postgrad., U. Va., 1963. Garden writer Washingtonian Mag., Garden Design Mag., Washington, 1981—94; landscape designer, garden tchr., 1979—92; organic farmer, 1992—2002; rural planner Calvert County Md. Dept. Planning and Zoning, Prince Frederick, 1998—2003. Mem. Fairfax County Agrl. and Forestal Dists. Adv. Bd., Fairfax County, Va., 1989—. Author, editor: Washington Star Garden Book, 1988, 2d edit., 1993. Co-founder McLean Farmers Mkt., Fairfax County, 1989; bd. dirs., co-founder Md. Organic Growers Coop., Jessup; bd. dirs. Washington Youth Gardens, 1982—. Recipient Poetry prize, Atlantic Monthly, 1957. Mem.: Am. Chestnut Found., Nature Conservancy, Md. Organic Food and Farming Assn. Roman Catholic. Avocations: reading, travel, dance, poetry. Office: Farview Farm Lusby MD Personal E-mail: drfarview@hotmail.com.

FICCA, RHONDA LEE, music educator; b. Rochester, Pa., Sept. 9, 1959; d. Alfred and Filamena (Sarracino) Ficca. B of Music Edn., Wittenberg U., Springfield, Ohio, 1981; masters equivalent, Dept. Edn., Harrisburg, Pa., 1992. Music tchr./choral dir./coach Ansonia (Ohio) Area Sch. Dist., 1981—82; music tchr./choral dir. New Carlisle (Ohio) Mid. Sch., 1982—86; elem. music tchr./choral dir. New Brighton (Pa.) Area Sch. Dist., 1986—; cloral dir. United Hosanna Min., 1996—98. In-svc. presenter New Brighton Area Sch. Dist., 1995—, Beaver Valley Intermediate Unit, Aliquippa, Pa., 2000—; cooperating tchr. Geneva Coll. Edn. Dept., Beaver Falls, Pa., 1991—; grade chair practical and fine arts depts. New Brighton Elem. Sch., 1986—; co-chair New Brighton Caring Team for Children, 1996—. Dir. music New Brighton Adult Cmty. Choir, 1997—; mem. New Brighton PTA; pres. Dorcas Women's Ministries Beaver Falls Christian Assembly, 1991—, choir dir., 1986—, bd. mem., sec., 2000—, sound sys. mgr., 2000—, children's ch. tchr., 1986—. Recipient Founder's Day award, New Brighton PTA, 1995, Random Acts of Kindness award, Blue Cross/Blue Shield of We. Pa., 2000, Beaver County Peace Links award, 2001, Beaver County Sheriff's Dept. award, 2003, Lee Canter'r Assertive award, 1995—. Mem.: NEA, Pa. Music Educator's Assn., Music Educator's Nat. Conf., New Brighton Edn. Assn. (sec., pub. rels. chair 1991—), Pa. State Edn. Assn., Beaver Valley Cmty. Concert Assn. (vol. 1995—), Delta Kappa Gamma (music chair 2000—02, social chair 2002—, Woman of Distinction award 2000, 2001, ATHENA award nominee 2002). Home: 617 21st St Beaver Falls PA 15010 Office: New Brighton Elem Sch 3200 43rd St New Brighton PA 15066 Office Phone: 724-843-1194 161. Personal E-mail: rficca@access995.com. Business E-Mail: rficca@nbsd.k12.pa.us.

FICEK, DEBRA L., secondary school educator; b. Minn. d. Donald D. and Hilda G. Grosklags; m. Myron A. Ficek; children: Grant, Kent. BA, Bethel U., St. Paul, Minn., 1977. Tchr. English Brandon H.S., Minn., 1977—81; tchr. pre-sch. Spicer Sunshine Presch., Minn., 1982—94; tchr. English Paynesville H.S., Minn., 1994—. Author: various children's stories. Pres. Green Lake Preservation Soc., Spicer, 2000—02. Named Nat. Honor Roll Outstanding Am. Tchr., 2005—06; recipient scholarship, Reader's Digest, 1976. Mem.: Edn. Minn. Paynesville Assn. Avocations: gardening, reading, writing, bicycling.

FICHTHORN, FONDA GAY, retired principal; b. Jamestown, Ohio, Sept. 4, 1949; d. Robert William and Evelyn Elizabeth (Schmitt) Fichthorn. BS, Otterbein Coll., 1970; MEd, Wright State U., 1983. Cert. tchr., prin., supr., elem. music, gifted edn. Ohio. Elem. tchr. Groveport (Ohio) Madison Schs., 1970-71, Miami Trace Schs., Washington Court House, Ohio, 1971-92, prin., 1992-2000; ret., 2000. Part-time gifted coord. Clark County Schs., Ohio, 2000-05; part-time dist. value added specialist Miami Trace Schs., Ohio, 2003-05; part-time coord. gifted students Springfield City Schs., Ohio; part-time core subject specialist Miami Trace Local Schs., 2005-06. Bd. dirs. Scioto Paint Valley Mental Health Ctr., crisis vol. Recipient Class Act award Sta. WDTN-TV, 1990. Mem. AAUW, Phi Delta Kappa, Delta Kappa Gamma. Republican. Avocations: piano, flute, travel, gardening. Home: 7313 State Route 729 NW Washington Court House OH 43160-9526 Office Phone: 937-505-2836. E-mail: fondagf@erinet.com.

FICHTNER, MARGARIA, journalist; b. Lakeland, Fla., May 4, 1944; d. August Albert and Margaret Louise (Kelly) Fichtner. BA, Fla. So. Coll., 1966. Feature writer, fashion editor Miami Herald, 1968—92, book editor, 1992—2001, book critic, 2001—03, sr. feature writer, 2003—. Recipient First Pl. Criticism award, Am. Assn. Sunday and Feature Editors, 1996, Fla. Soc. Newspaper Editors, 1997, First Pl. Criticism Green Eyeshade award, Soc. Profl. Journalists, 2000, First Pl. Critical Writing Sunshine State award, 2003. Office: The Miami Herald Pub Co One Herald Plz Miami FL 33132-1693 Office Phone: 305-376-3630. Business E-Mail: mfichtner@miamiherald.com.

FICK, DENISE, elementary school educator; d. Hubert J. and Sharon J. Fick. BS, Tex. Tech U., Lubbock, 1981; postgrad., East Tex. State U., Commerce, 1986, Tex. A & M U., 1991. Cert. tchr. Tex. Sci. educator Richardson Ind. Sch. Dist., Tex., 1985—, sci. dept. chair, 2001—05. Author: (screenplays) Brown Shoes, The Dark Side Of Normal. Philanthroist, fundraiser San Francisco AIDS Found., 1997—2006. Mem.: NSTA (assoc.). Avocations: cycling, swimming, travel, photography, writing. Office Phone: 4690593-8026.

FICKENSCHER, DOROTHY (DEBBIE) E.B., secondary school educator; d. Wesley Evans and Mary Clifton Buchanan; children: Louis Evans, Elaine Clifton. BA, Smith Coll., 1967; MA in Tchg. History, Brown U., 1971; student, George Washington U., 1970—80. Cert. tchr. Md., secondary prin. and supr. Md. Tchr. Montgomery Pub. Schs., Rockville, Md., 1971—96, tchr. resources Seneca Valley H.S., 1996—2001, cons. tchr. Office Staff Devel., 2001—04, lead tchr. literacy Blair H.S., 2004—. Mgr. 10 pin bowling team Spl. Olympics, Montgomery County, Md., 1999—. Recipient Above and Beyond the Call of Duty award, PTSA. Mem.: Delta Kappa Gamma (1st v.p. 2004—06). Home: 13604 Hopkins Rd Germantown MD 20874 Office: Blair HS 51 University Blvd E Silver Spring MD 20901

FICKER, ROBERTA SUE See FARRELL, SUZANNE

FICKES, KELLY ANN, personal trainer; b. Leonardtown, Md., Feb. 28, 1979; d. Carrie and Vic Fickes. BS, Salisbury U., Md., 2002; MEd, Kutztown U., Pa., 2003. Athletic trainer Kutztown U., 2002—03; phys. edn. instr. Fairfax County (Va.) Pub. Sch., 2003—05, head athletic trainer, 2003—. Mem.: Nat. Athletic Trainer's Assn. (cert.).

FICKES, LYNDA LURHAE, elementary school educator; b. Lincoln, Nebr., Oct. 9, 1948; d. Jesse Allen and Ina Rosella Scheuneman; m. Robert Russell Fickes, July 8, 1973; children: Kevin, Shannon, Robyn, Chad. Bachelor, U. Nebr., Lincoln, 1970; Masters, Doane Coll., Crete, Nebr., 1995. Tchr. 1st grade Grand Island Pub. Sch., Nebr., 1970—. Office: Howard Elem 502 W 9 Grand Island NE 68801 Office Phone: 308-385-5916. E-mail: lfickes@gips.org.

FICKLER, ARLENE, lawyer; b. Phila., Apr. 21, 1951; BA cum laude, U. Pa., 1971, JD cum laude, 1974. Bar: Pa. 1974, D.C. 1980, U.S. Supreme Ct. 1989. Ptnr. Hoyle Fickler Herschel & Mathes LLP, Phila. Staff atty. Commn. on Revision of Fed. Ct. Appellate System, 1974-75; exec. asst. Bicentennial Com. Jud. Conf. of U.S., 1975-76. Comment editor U. Pa. Law Rev., 1973-74; co-reporter American College of Trial Lawyers Mass Tort Litigation Manual; contbr. chpt. to book and articles to law jours. Pres. U. Pa. Law Sch. Alumni Bd. Mgrs., 1997-99; trustee Jewish Fedn. of Greater Phila., 1981-88, 89-93, 94-98, 99—, Phila. Bar Found., 1993-98, Jewish Cmty. Rels. Coun. Greater Phila., 1983-94, 98-2000; trustee Jewish Cmty. Ctrs. of Phila., 1997—, chair, 2003—06; trustee HIAS Immigration Svcs. Phila., 1998—, treas., 1999-2003; mem. United Jewish Appeal Nat. Young Women's Leadership Cabinet, 1982-87; v.p. Phila. chpt. Am. Jewish Congress, 1995-2001; co-chmn. Phila. Jewish Cmty. Ctr. Maccabi Games, 2001; dir. Jewish Cmty. Ctr Assn., 2006—. Recipient Mrs. Isidore Kohn Young Leadership award Jewish Fedn. Greater Phila., 1981, Next Generation Leadership award Jewish Cmty. Ctrs. Assn., 2000, award of merit U. Pa. Law Sch. Alumni, 2001. Mem. ABA, Am. Law Inst., Am. Bar Found., Pa. Bar Assn., D.C. Bar, Phila. Bar

Assn. (chmn. fed. cts. com. 1992), Fed. Bar Coun. of Second Cir., U. Pa. Am. Inn of Ct. Office: Hoyle Fickler Herschel & Mathes LLP One South Broad St 1500 Philadelphia PA 19103 Office Phone: 215-981-5850. Business E-Mail: afickler@hoylelawfirm.com.

FIDEL, RAYA, information science educator; b. Tel Aviv, Jan. 18, 1945; came to U.S., 1977; BSc, Tel Aviv U., 1970; MLS, Hebrew U., Jerusalem, 1976; PhD, U. Md., 1982. Tchr. Adult Edn. Ctr., Jerusalem, 1971-72; br. libr. Hebrew U., Jerusalem, 1972-77; asst. prof. libr. sci. U. Wash., Seattle, 1982-87, assoc. prof. libr. sci., 1987-2000, prof. Info. Sch., 2000—, head Ctr. Human-Info. Interaction The Info. Sch., 2003—. Vis. libr. Duke U. Libr., Durham, N.C., 1992-93. Author: Database Design, 1987; editor Advances in Classification, 1991-94 (award 1992-94); contbr. articles to profl. publs. Recipient Research award Am. Society for Information Science, 1994 Mem. AAUP (chair U. Wash. chpt. 1990-92, pres. state conf. 1992-97), Assn. Computing Machinery, Am. Soc. Info. Sci. (dir.-at-large 2000-02). Home: 5801 Phinney Ave N Seattle WA 98103-5862

FIDLER, SUSAN, recreation director; BS, Ind. State U., 1992, MS, 2000. Cert. recreational sports specialist Nat. Intramural Recreational Sports Assn., pool operator Nat. Swimming Pool Found., water safety instr. ARC, scuba diver Nat. Assn. Underwater Instr. Secondary math. tchr. Logansport (Ind.) Cmty. Schs., 1992—95, Cloverdale (Ind.) Cmty. Schs., 1995—98; asst. dir. sports, recreation facilities Rose-Hulman Inst. Tech., Terre Haute, Ind., 1998—2001; asst. dir. informal recreation, facility mgr. slaughter recreation ctr. U. Va., Charlottesville, 2001—02, dir. recreation instrn., club sports, 2002—. Head volleyball, asst. varsity track coach, girls' jr. varsity basketball coach Cloverdale Cmty. Schs., 1996—98; head volleyball coach, girls' basketball coach Logansport Cmty. Schs., 1993—95. Volleyball official Va. HS League, Charlottesville, 2001—06; vol. coach Charlottesville Area Volleyball Club, 2004—06. Mem.: AAHPERD, Nat. Fedn. Officals Assn., Learning Resource Network, Nat. Intramural Recreational Sports Assn., Charlottesville Tennis Patrons Assn.

FIDONE, LAURA PEEBLES, social worker; b. Little Rock, Nov. 30, 1962; d. L.M. and Tish (Maynard) Peebles; m. Jeff W. Fidone, Sept. 9, 1989. BA, Harding U., 1985, MSW, 1987. Lic. social worker, Ark., Tex., lic. cert. social worker, bd. cert. social worker., advanced clin. practitioner. Intern Ark. State Dept. Health, Little Rock, 1985-86; social worker intern Youth Home Inc., Little Rock, 1986-87; med. social worker VA Med. Ctr., Little Rock, 1987-91, Shreveport, 1991-94; med. social worker, discharge planning team leader Specialty Hosp., Tyler, Tex., 1994-97. Co-chair Nat. Celebration of Social Work Monty, Little Rock, 1988, 91, co-chair enrichment com., 1989-91; co-chair La. Celebration of Social Work Monty, 1991, group therapist Cancer Support Group, 1990-91, Intensive Care Support Group, 1988-89, neurology multidisciplinary team leader, 1989-91, acute care medicine multidisciplinary team leader, 1991-94, vol. and student supr., 1991-94. Vol. bereavement group therapist Shiloh Ch. of Christ, tchr. boundaries and parenting seminars, motherhood seminar, 2000, group leader woman's Bible class and women's ministries, 2001—. Fellow NASW; mem. Tex. Med. Alliance, Smith County Med. Alliance Soc. Mem. Ch. Christ.

FIEDLER, LOIS JEAN, psychologist, educator; b. Park Falls, Wis., July 4, 1938; d. Herbert W. and Ethel (Newman) F.; m. Harold John LeVesconte, Jan. 31, 1986 BS, U. Wis., 1960; MS, Purdue U., 1963; PhD, Mich. State U., 1970. Lic. psychologist, Calif., Minn. Tchr. Wausau Bd. Edn., Wis., 1960—62; counselor Counseling Ctr. and Housing Wis. State U., Oshkosh, 1963—66; advisor, asst. dir. Mich. State U., East Lansing, 1966—69, instr., asst., 1968—70; psychologist, asst. prof., acting dir. student counseling bur. womens studies U. Minn., Mpls., 1970—86; asst. dir. counseling svcs. San Jose State U., Calif., 1986—88; clin. dir. Growth Leadership Ctr., Mountain View, Calif., 1992—95; pvt. practice, cons., 1992—98; coord. Millpond Emergency, 1995—. Contbr. numerous profl. articles Co-founder, officer New Communities, Mpls., 1971-75, Psyche, Inc., Mpls., 1973-80; bd. dirs. Alcohol and Other Drug Abuse Programming, Minn., 1980-83, Nat. Coun. on Alcoholism, Santa Clara County, 1993-97, pres., 1995-97 Named Vol. of Yr., San Jose Emergency, 2004. Mem. APA, Am. Coll. Pers. Assn. (exec. coun. 1978-81, pres. Minn. 1974-75, Diamond Honoree 2006) Home: 577 Mill Pond Dr San Jose CA 95125-1418

FIEL, MAXINE LUCILLE, journalist, behavior analyst, educator; Student in psychology and humanities, NYU. Nat. columnist, contbg. editor Mademoiselle Mag., NYC, 1972—2001; nat. columnist Women's World, Englewood, NJ, 1979-89; contbg. editor Overseas Promotions, NYC, 1979—; articles and features editor Japanese Overseas Press, 1976—; feature editor N.Y. Now, NYC, 1980-91; contbg. editor Woman's World mag., 1979-89, Bella mag., England, 1987-89; nat. columnist First mag. for women, 1989-91; founder Starcast Astrological Svcs., Floral Park, NY, 1993—; columnist Borderland Mag., Japan, 1995—2000, IM Mag., Japan, 1997—2000; pres. GemEssence Co., 2002—. Cons. legal profession jury selection, 1984—; mktg. cons. Imperial Enterprises, Tokyo and Princeton, NJ, 1983—; cons. spokesperson Rowland Co., NYC, 1972-81, Allied Chem. Co., NYC, 1972-75; lectr., cons. Atlanta and Fla. Bar Assns., 1986—; creator Touch Game Parker Bros., Salem, Mass., 1971-76; behavior analyst and comm. advisor multi-nat. bus. corps.; cons. Chesebrough-Ponds, Footwear Coun., Grand Marnier Liquor; founder Starcast Astrological Svcs., 1993; pres. Interglobal Mktg. Co., 1999. Pioneer field of polit. body lang., 1969; author: Lovescopes, 1998, The Little Book of Body Language, 1998; contbr. articles to Wireless News Flash, News Am., LA Times, Newhouse News Svc., Newspaper Enterprise Assocs., King Features, Borderland Mag., Glamour, Redbook, Cosmopolitan, others; adv. bd. mem. Writers Digest Mag., 2002; TV appearances on morning and afternoon shows including A Current Affair, The Regis Philbin Show, Eyewitness News, Cable News Networks, Tonight Show, Today Show, Good Morning Am., Joan Rivers Show, Jenny Jones, Entertainment Tonight, Hard Copy, Inside Edition, BBC Breakfast Show, Good Morning Japan, Fox News Channel, MSNBC, many others; appears in daily segment Good Morning Japan; own daily TV show on Nippon Network, Japan, 1989-2004. Active Sister Cities, Tokyo and NYC; charter mem. Elem. Sch. Cultural Exch., Toyko and NYC, Ctr. Environ. Edn.; bd. dirs. Periwinkle Prodns. Anti-Drug Abuse, NYC, Adirondacks Save-A-Stray. Recipient Achievement award field behavioral sci. and photojournalism, Tokyo, 1974, Outstanding Rsch. award field psychology of gesture, Tokyo, 1976, Outstanding Achievement award Internat. Conf. Soc. Para-Psychology, 1974-75, award for contbn. to Asand Inst. for Humanistic Psychology; honored guest at award dinner for involvement and support in the merging of Eye Rsch. Inst. Boston and Harvard Med. Sch., 1991. Mem. AFTRA, Internat. Found. Behavioral Rsch. (past v.p.), Nat. Writers Assn. (profl.), Profl. Writers Assn., Authors Guild, Authors League, World Wildlife Fund, Whale Protection Fund, Environ. Def. Soc., Nature Conservancy, Greenpeace, People for Ethical Treatment Animals, Humane Assn. U.S., Sea Shepherd Conservation Soc., Defenders of Wildlife, Guiding Eyes for Blind, Braille Camps for Blind Children, Save the Children, Lotos Club (NYC), East End Yacht Club (Freeport, NY). Office: 338 Northern Blvd Ste 3 Great Neck NY 11021-4808 Office Phone: 516-482-3700. Personal E-mail: fiel5megavisions@aol.com. E-mail: interglobal@verizon.net.

FIELD, ANDREA BEAR, lawyer; b. New London, Conn., Nov. 30, 1949; d Geurson Donald and Lorraine (Solomon) Silverberg; m. Thornton Withers Field, May 17, 1984; children: Benjamin, Geoffrey. Student, Wellesley Coll., 1967-69; BA, Yale U., 1971; JD, U. Va., 1974. Bar: Va. 1974, D.C. 1978, U.S. Ct. Appeals (3d, 4th, 5th, 7th, 8th and D.C. cirs.). Assoc. Hunton & Williams LLP, Washington and Richmond, Va., DC, 1974-81, ptnr. Washington, 1991—, mng. ptnr., resources, regulatory & environ. law, and mem. exec. com. Mem. ABA (chair sect. natural resources, energy and environ. law 1989-90, coun. 1984-87, 90-91, chair com. air quality 1982-84, vice chair teleconf. com. 1990—, environ. controls bus. law sect. 1990-91, vice chair com. environ. law, real property, probate and trust law sect. 1990-91; chair standing com. on natural conf. groups 1993-94, nat. conf. lawyers and scientists 1990-93, sect. ad hoc com. nat. insts. 1989-90, coun. sect. sci. and tech. 1991-92), Va. Bar, DC Bar. Office: Hunton & Williams 1900 K St NW Washington DC 20006-1109 Office Phone: 202-955-1558. Office Fax: 202-778-2201. Business E-Mail: afield@hunton.com.

FIELD, BARBARA STEPHENSON, small business owner; b. San Raphael, Calif., Dec. 10, 1958; d. Thomas David and Shirley Anne (Rowe) Stephenson; m. Frederick W. Field, Nov. 25, 1985 (div. Sept. 1987); 1 child, Chantelle Nicole. Student, Grossmont C.C., La Jolla, Calif., Bishops Coll., La Jolla. Internet retail exec. Have2Have.com, L.A., 1998—. Active supporter of missing children and terminal illness charities. Democrat. Home and Office: 6456 Lunita Rd #119 Malibu CA 90265-2629 E-mail: barbarafield4@yahoo.com.

FIELD, CHARLOTTE, communications executive; BS in Elec. Engring., Mich. Tech. Univ.; MBA, Farleigh Dickinson Univ., NJ; grad., INSEAD Exec. Mgmt. Program, Harvard Advanced Mgmt. Program. Grad. intern AT&T Bell Labs., NJ; mgr., integration broadband phone ops. Comcast Cable Co., sr. v.p., nat. comm. engring. Named to Walk of Fame, Rocky Mt. Chpt. Women in Cable & Telecom., 2004; recipient Women in Tech. award, Soc. Cable Telecom. Engrs., Cable-Tec Expo Awards, 2005. Office: Comcast Cable Co 1500 Market St Philadelphia PA 19102-2148 Office Fax: 215-981-7790.*

FIELD, DOROTHY MASLIN, minister; b. Port Chester, N.Y., June 10, 1925; d. Walter Adrian and Dorothy Hepworth Maslin; m. David Meredith Field, Sept. 14, 1946 (div. Oct. 16, 1976); children: Nancy Jean, Michael Maslin, Susan Field Nelson, Jeffrey David. BA, Douglass Coll., 1946; MS, U. Pa., 1961; MDiv, Drew U., 1982. Pastor Packard Meml. United Meth. Ch., Media, Pa., 1980—81, Kedron United Meth. Ch., Morton, Pa., 1981—84; v.p. for resident svcs. Cornwall (Pa.) Manor, 1984—86; pastor Chestnut St. and Ranshaw United Meth. Chs., Shamokin, Pa., 1986—92; pastor (serving in retirement) Crozerville United Meth. Ch., Aston, Pa., 1992—. Dir. Shamokin area ministry Ea. Pa. Conf. of the United Meth. Ch., Valley Forge, Pa., 1988—92. Pres., v.p. LWV, Delaware County, Pa., 1996, pres. Swarthmore, Pa., 1994—96; sec. Kiwanis Club, Chester, Pa., 1999; treas. Women's Internat. League for Peace and Freedom, Swarthmore, 1995—2003. Named Swarthmore Citizen of the Yr., Lions Club Swarthmore, 1994. Mem.: Lions Club Swarthmore, Order of St. Luke (life), Pi Lambda Theta, Phi Beta Kappa Assn. of the Del. Valley (life). Methodist. Avocations: reading, walking, travel. Home: 100 Rutgers Ave 8 PO Box 379 Swarthmore PA 19081-0379 Office Phone: 610-543-8015. Personal E-mail: dotf1@aol.com.

FIELD, JUDITH JUDY, librarian; b. Bucyrus, Ohio, Sept. 30, 1939; d. William Harrison and Eva Gertrude (Miller) Judy; m. Nathaniel Lamson Field III, Jan. 25, 1959. BBA, U. Mich., 1961, M.L.S., 1963, MBA, 1969. Library mgr. Western Electric Bell Telephone Labs., Indpls., 1962-65; asst. librarian Natural Sci. Library, Ann Arbor, Mich., 1965-66; assoc. librarian Sch. Bus. Adminstrn., Ann Arbor, 1966-69; library mgr. Inst. Internat. Commerce, Ann Arbor, 1969-71, research assoc., 1971-72; head gen. reference Flint Pub. Library, Mich., 1972-86; dir. Legis. Ref. Libr., St. Paul, 1987; mgmt. cons., 1988—; sr. lectr. libr. and info. sci. Wayne State U., 1989—. Pres. Mich. Interorgn. Council on Continuing Library Edn., Lansing, Mich., 1983-85; bd. dirs. Continuing Library Edn. Network and Exchange, Washington, 1979-81. Editor: International Finance Bibliography, 1971, Apprentice and Training Program, 1972, Beginning Positions and Training Program, 1973, Michigan Legal Literature, 1991; editl. bd. The One-Person Lib. Mem. LVA. Mem. ALA (com. accreditation 1993-97, task force adv. com. White House Conf. 1990-92), Friends of Detroit Pub. Libr., Spl. Librs. Assn. (dep. conf. chmn. 1983, chmn. libr. mgmt. divsn. 1983-84, pres. Mich. chpt. 1981-82, bd. dirs. 1975-77, 86-89, 96-99, pres. 1997-98, conf. chair 1994), Am. Soc. Info. Sci. (pres. Mich. chpt. 1991-93, honors fellow 1996), ARMA Internat. Edn. Found. (bd. trustees 1998-2002), Internat. Fedn. Libr. Assn. (edn. and tng. 1999-2003, svc. sci. 2003-05, knowledge mgmt. 2005—, sec. 2005-06, chair 2006-). Republican. Avocations: archaeology, backgammon. Home: 20500 Clement Rd Northville MI 48167-1334 Office: Wayne State U 106 Kresge Lib Detroit MI 48202 Office Phone: 313-577-8539. Business E-Mail: aa4101@wayne.edu.

FIELD, JULIA ALLEN, futurist, strategist, environmentalist; b. Boston, Jan. 5, 1937; d. Howard Locke and Julia Wright Allen. BA cum laude, Harvard U., 1960; postgrad., Harvard Grad. Sch. Design, 1964-65, Pius XII Grad. Art Inst., Florence, Italy, 1961—62; MA, PhD fellow, Walden U. Inst. Adv. Studies, 1983-89. With Joint Harvard-Karachi Univ. Expdn. to Baluchistan, Pakistan, 1957, Survey USSR zoos for IUCN, Morges, Switzerland, 1964; cons. Walter Gropius for Baghdad Project, 1960, Sasaki, Dawson & Demay, Architects for St. Louis Zoo and Nat. Zoo, Washington, DC, 1964—65; Amazon Wildlife report for Nature editor Life Mag., 1968; cons. Forestry Dept. of Simla, India, 1969—70; founder, v.p. Black Grove, Inc., Miami, Fla., 1970-80; founder, pres. Amazonia 2000, Bogota, Colombia, 1970—79; leader Task Force Amazonia 2000, DAINCO, 1977-78; elected pres. New Found. Amazonia 2000 in Gen. Assembly, Leticia, Colombia, 1979—, Acad. Arts and Scis. of the Ams., Miami, Fla., 1979—. Adv. Techno-Update Jour., New Delhi, 1969-70; mem. Presdl. Com. on Innovative Tech. Devel. Group of Yr. 2000, Colombia, 1971-74; mem. survey U.S.S.R. Zoos for Internat. Union for Conservation of Nature, Morges, Switzerland, 1964; advisor Techno-Update Jour., Simla, 1969-70; man and biosphere com. UNESCO, Colombia, 1972-78; mem. Task Force on Colonization Report to Pres. of Colombia, 1973; Hon. Nat. Insp. resources and environment Republic of Colombia, 1982—; bd. visitors Duke U. Primate Ctr., 1979-82; keynote spkr. World Jungle Conf., U. Sci. Ctr. Penang, Malaysia, Dec. 1979, HSUS Nat. Leadership Conf. Wildlife Exploitation, Saddlebrook, N.J., 1968, II symposium and forum tropical biology, Leticia, Amazonas, Republic of Colombia, 1969; participant Only One Earth Forum, UN Environ. Programme, Rene Dubos Ctr., N.Y.C., 1987, internat. seminar econ. coop. future Amazon Basin, Leticia, 1970; cons., spkr., lectr. in field Author: Man and Nature, the Integral Concept, 1965, Amazonia 2000, 1978, Amazonia as a World Model, 1972; (film) Man Against Nature, 1966; editor Man and Nature Series, 1969-73, Game and Wildlife Preserves in U.S.S.R., 1969, Conservation in the USSR, 1972, Amazon Wildlife Exploitation Report for Nature Editor, Life Mag., 1968; created exhbn. Writing on the Wall for internat. conf., Cities in Context U. Notre Dame, 1968; dir. (film) Man Against Nature; contbr. articles to profl. jours and popular mags. including Nature, Life. Mem. City of Miami Bicentennial Com., 1975-76; coord. Cmty. of Man Task Force, Miami, 1975-76; mem. Blueprint for Miami 2000, 1982-85; founder Amacayacu Nat. Park, Amazonia, Colombia, 1975; co-creator, builder Villa Ciencia, Rio Cotuhe, Colombia, 1975 Fellow Royal Geog. Soc. (London) (life); mem. Internat. Hydrogen Energy Assn., EarthJustice Legal Def. Fund, The Nature Conservancy, Friends of Earth, Friends of Worldwatch, Nat. Resources Def. Coun. Home and Office: 9450 Old Cutler Rd Miami FL 33156-2242 Fax: 305-663-5600.

FIELD, KAREN ANN (KAREN ANN SCHAFFNER), real estate broker; b. New Haven, Conn., Jan. 27, 1936; d. Abraham Terry and Ida (Smith) Rogovin; m. Barry S. Crown, 1954 (div. 1969); children: Laurie Jayne, Donna Lynn, Bruce Alan, Bradley David; m. Michael Lehmann Field, 1969 (div. 1977); m. Ronald E. Schaffner, Apr., 1998. Student, Vassar Coll., 1953-54, Harrington Inst. Interior Design, 1973-74, Roosevelt U., 1987—. Cert. residential specialist. Owner Karen Field Interiors, Chgo., 1970-86, Karen Field & Assocs. Realtors, Chgo., 1980-81; pres., ptnr. Field-Pels & Assocs. Realtors, Chgo., 1981-86; with top sales volume Sudler-Marling, Inc., Chgo., 1989; sales broker Koenig & Strey GMAC, Chgo., 1992—. Mem. Women's Coun. Camp Henry Horner, Chgo., 1960; bd. dirs., treas. Winnetka Pub. Sch. Nursery (Ill.), 1961-63; pres. Jr. Aux. U. Chgo. Cancer Rsch. Found., 1960-66, mem. exec. com. women's bd., 1965-66, co-chair Grand Auction; bd. dirs., sec. United Charities, Chgo., 1966-68, Victory Gardens Theatre, Chgo., 1979; co-founder, pres. Re-Entry Ctr., Wilmette, Ill., 1978-80; mem. br. Child Abuse Svcs., Chgo., 1981-89, Stop AIDS Real Estate Divsn., 1988, AIDS Walkathon Com., 1990; bd. dirs. The Chgo. Ctr. for Self-Taught Art, 1993-96. Recipient Servian award Jr. Aux. of U. Chgo. Cancer Rsch. Found., 1966, Margarite Wolf award Women's Bd., U. Chgo. Cancer Rsch. Found., 1967, Founder's award, 1997, WAIT Woman of Day. Mem. Chgo. Real Estate Bd., Chgo. Assn. Realtors, English Speaking Union (jr. bd. 1958-59), Art Inst. Chgo., Field Mus., Union League Club, Pres.'s Club, Founders Club, Confrerie de la Chaine des Rotisseurs (Dame de la Chaine), Fulton River Dist. Assn., Friends of the River. Office: Koenig & Strey GMAC 900 N Michigan Ave Chicago IL 60611-1514

FIELD, LINDA G., secondary school educator; b. Sanford, Maine, Jan. 31, 1953; d. Donald G. and Rita Y. Bourque; m. Steven Marshall Field, June 4, 1976; children: Steven Marshall Jr., David Justin. BS, U. of So. Maine, Gorham, 1976. Cert. classroom tchr. Maine State Dept. of Edn. Classroom tchr. Sanford Sch. Dept., 1989—. Reading vol. Volunteers of Am., Wells, Maine, 1989—90; mem. support team Sanford Sch. Dept., 2001—. Contbr. articles to newspapers. Mem.: Am. Fedn. Tchrs. Office: Sanford School Dept 668 Main St Sanford ME 04073 Office Phone: 207-324-8454.

FIELD, MARTHA AMANDA, law educator; b. Boston, Aug. 20, 1943; d. Donald T. and Adelaide (Anderson) Field; children: Maria Adelaide, Gabriel Hartry, Lucas Anthony. BA in Chinese History, Radcliffe Coll., 1965; JD, U. Chgo., 1968. Bar: DC 1969. Law clk. to Justice Abe Fortas, US Supreme Ct., 1968-69; asst. prof. U. Pa. Law Sch., Phila., 1969—72, prof., 1973—78; prof. law Harvard Law Sch., Cambridge, Mass., 1979—, Langdell prof. law, 1998—. Vis. prof. law Harvard Law Sch., 1978—79. Author: Surrogate Motherhood, 1991; co-author: Equal Treatment for People with Mental Retardation, 2000, Legal Reform in Central America: Dispute Resolution and Property Systems, 2001. Office: Harvard Law Sch 1563 Massachusetts Ave Cambridge MA 02138 Office Phone: 617-495-2962. Office Fax: 617-496-4947. Business E-Mail: mfield@law.harvard.edu.

FIELD, PATRICIA, apparel designer; Fashion designer. Costume designer (TV series) Crime Story, 1986, L.A. Takedown, 1989, Spin City, 1996—2002, Sex and the City, 1998—2004, Big City Blues, 1999. Recipient Award for Excellence for Costume Design for TV (contemporary), Sex in the City, Costume Designers Guild, 2000, 2004, Emmy Award for Outstanding Costumes for Series, Sex and the City, 2002. Office: Hotel Venus 382 W Broadway New York NY 10012

FIELD, SALLY MARGARET, actress; b. Pasadena, Calif., Nov. 6, 1946; m. Steven Craig, Sept. 16, 1968 (div. 1975); children: Peter, Eli; m. Alan Greisman, Dec. 15, 1984 (div. 1993); 1 son, Samuel. Student, Actor's Studio, 1973-75. Starred in TV series Gidget, 1965, The Flying Nun, 1967-70, The Girl With Something Extra, 1973, The Court, 2002, Brothers & Sisters, 2006-; film appearances include The Way West, 1967, Stay Hungry, 1976, Heroes, 1977, Smokey and the Bandit, 1977, Hooper, 1978, The End, 1978, Norma Rae, 1979 (Cannes Film Festival Best Actress award 1979, Acad. award 1980), Beyond the Poseidon Adventure, 1979, Smokey and the Bandit II, 1980, Back Roads, 1981, Absence of Malice, 1981, Kiss Me Goodbye, 1982, Places in the Heart, 1984 (Acad. award for best actress 1984), Murphy's Romance (also exec. producer), 1985, Surrender, 1987, Punchline, 1987 (also prodr.), Steel Magnolias, 1989, Soapdish, 1991, Not Without My Daughter, 1991, Homeward Bound: The Incredible Journey, 1993 (voice), Mrs. Doubtfire, 1993, Forrest Gump, 1994, Homeward Bound II: Lost in San Francisco, 1996 (voice)(also prodr.), Eye for an Eye, 1996 (also prodr.), Where the Heart Is, 2000, Say It Isn't So, 2001, Legally Blonde 2: Red, White & Blonde, 2003; TV movies include Maybe I'll Come Home In the Spring, 1971, Marriage: Year One, 1971, Home for the Holidays, 1972, Bridger, 1976, Sybil, 1976 (Emmy award 1977), All the Way Home, 1981, Merry Christmas George Bailey, 1997 (also prodr.), A Cooler Climate, 1999 (also prodr.), David Copperfield, 2000; TV mini series David Copperfield, 1986, A Women of Independent Means, 1995 (also exec. prodr.), From the Earth to the Moon, 1998 (also dir.); exec. prodr. The Christmas Tree, 1996 (also writer, dir.), The Lost Children of Berlin, 1997; prodr. Dying Young, 1991; dir. Beautiful, 2000; guest appearances include The Hollywood Squares, 1966, Rowan & Martin's Laugh-In, 1968, Carol Burnett & Co., 1979, Saturday Night Live, 1993, King of Hill (voice), 1997, Murphy Brown, 1998, ER, 2000-2003 (several episodes), and several others.*

FIELD-HALEY, BETTY, artist, art educator; b. Albany, Ga., Jan. 4, 1936; d. Charles Heard Field and Martha Lowery Hale; m. John Edward Haley, Oct. 26, 1966; children: Holly Anne Haley, Michael Shannon Haley. BFA, U. Ariz., Tucson, 1958; cert. art, Ind. U., Bloomington, 1969; MA in Art History, Ariz. State U., Tempe, 1965; postgrad., U. Calif., Santa Barbara, 1980—81. Art cert. Ind. U., Bloomington, 1969, cert. drawing & painting Art Students League, N.Y., 1965, Art Students League, N.Y., 1966. Tchg. asst. Ariz. State U., Tempe, 1960—63; instr. St. Paul Coll., Lawrenceville, Va., 1963; art instr. adult edn. U. Oreg., Eugene, 1984—85; art instr. Calif. Poly. U. Ext., San Luis Obispo, 2001—03, San Luis Obispo Art Ctr., 2002—04, San Luis Obispo Pub. Access TV, 2000—. Bd. dirs. San Luis Obispo Art Ctr., 1995—2000, San Luis Obispo Arts Coun., 1995—2000; owner, dir. Field Fine Arts Gallery, Los Osos, Calif., 1995—. Represented in permanent collections Art Students League, N.Y.C., exhibitions include Yuma Fine Arts Assn. Gallery, Ariz., 1964, Woodstock St. Gregory's Ctr., N.Y., 1967, U. Calif. Women's Ctr. Gallery, Santa Barbara, 1975, 1977, 1978, U. Greenhouse Gallery, U. Calif., 1982, U. Oreg. EMU Gallery, Eugene, 1984, U. Oreg. Koinonia Ctr., 1985, Nat. Wildlife Fedn. Gallery, Vienna, Va., 1988, Nat. Geologic Survery Gallery, Reston, Va., 1989, Gt. Falls Art Ctr. Gallery, Va., 1991, George Mason U., Fairfax, Va., 1992, Borders Book and Music, Wash., 1994, Cal Poly U. Union Art Gallery, 1997, Sylvester Winery Gallery, Paso Robles, Calif., 2006, photos of paintings, N.Y. Daily News, Santa Barbara News Press, Wash. Post, San Luis Obispo New Times, others. Tchr. Sunday sch. St. Benedict's Episcopal Ch., 1996—2006. Recipient Painting prize, Topedo Factory Art Ctr., 1993, drawing prizes. Democrat. Episcopalian. Avocations: walking, camping, swimming. Home and Office: Field Fine Arts Gallery 1600 4th St Los Osos CA 93402

FIELDING, ELIZABETH BROWN, education educator; b. Ligonier, Ind., Feb. 17, 1918; d. Herbert Benjamin and Roberta (Franklin) B.; m. Frederick Allan Fielding, May 23, 1942 (wid. July 1962); children: Elizabeth Enndriss Fielding, Frederick Allan Fielding, Jr. BA, Smith Coll., 1939; MA, U. San Francisco, 1975. Cert. tchr. com. colls., Calif. Field staff mem. San Francisco Bay Girl Scout Assn., 1963-69; exec. dir. Tri-City Project on Aging, Rodeo, Calif., 1970-73; tchr., cons. various univs., 1974—. Mem. curriculum com. U. Calif., Berkeley, 1979-80; chair edn. programs Diablo Valley Found. on Aging, Walnut Creek, Calif., 1980s. Author: The Memory Manual: 10 Simple Things You Can Do to Improve Your Memory After 50, 1999, Teacher's Guide to The Memory Manual, 2000; contbr. articles to profl. jours. Chair Mental Health Task Force, County Coun. for Aging, Contra Costa County, 1974-76; mem. Sr. Svcs. Commn., City of Lafayette, Calif., 1981-2003; pres. bd. dirs. Calif. Specialists on Aging, Calif., 1976-79. Mem. Western Gerontol. Assn. (now Am. Soc. on Aging), Authors Guild, Calif. Writers Club. Avocations: writing, genealogy, art, birdwatching. Home: 1824 Stanley Dollar Dr 4A Walnut Creek CA 94595

FIELDING, ELIZABETH M(AY), public relations executive, writer; b. New London, Conn., May 16, 1917; d. Frederick James and Elizabeth (Martin) F. AB, Conn. Coll. for Women, 1938; MA in Pub. Adminstrn., Am. U., 1944. Dollar-a-year cons. Census Bur., 1938-39; rsch. writer Rep. Nat. Com., Washington, 1940, acting dir. rsch., 1944, asst. dir. rsch., 1948-53; govt. statistician, personnel clk., economist, 1941-42; civil def. dir. South Woodley, Va., 1943-46; rsch. writer Rep. Nat. Com., 1942-48; staff writer, spl. cons. to several U.S. congressmen, 1944-52; exec. sec., legis. asst. to Senator Alexander Wiley of Wis., 1953-54; assoc. dir. rsch. Rep. Nat. Com., 1954-57; rschr., speech writer, 1960-61; staff aide Rep. Nat. Platform Coms., 1944, 48, 52, 56, 60; legis. analyst, newsletter editor Nat. Assn. Electric Cos., 1957-60; pub. rels. dir. Nat. Fedn. Rep. Women, 1961-68; spl. asst. to asst. postmaster gen. U.S. Post Office Dept., 1969-71; pub. affairs dir. Pres.'s Coun. on Youth Opportunity, 1970-71; asst. adminstr. for pub. affairs Nat. Credit Union Adminstrn., 1971-75; pres. Profl. Enterprises, 1975—; editl. asst. U.S. Ho. of Reps., 1976-82. Author numerous party publs. including: A History of the Republican Party, 1854-1944. Editor Rep. Clubwoman, 1961-68; dir. spl. activities women's div. United Citizens for Nixon-Agnew, 1968; fin. coordinator Inaugural Com., 1968-69; Grievance Commn., State of Md., 1980-89; auxiliary policewoman Met. Police Dept., Washington, 1942-45. Recipient Achievement medal for outstanding govt. service Conn. Coll., 1971; Disting. Service award Nat. Fedn. Rep. Women, 1964, 67; named Hon. Citizen, several U.S. cities. Mem. AAAS, NAFE, Am. Polit. Sci. Assn., Am. Acad. Polit. and Social Sci., Am. Soc. for Socio-Econs., Soc. for Scholarly Pub., Nat. Press Found., Washington Ind. Writers, Soc. for Tech. Communication, Nat. Mus. of Women in Arts, Nat. Fedn. Press Women, HALT-Ams. for Legal Reform, Pemaquid Watershed Assn., Treasure Cove Citizens Assn. (pres. 1976-78, 92-93), Washington Nat. Cathedral, Phi Beta Kappa. Clubs: Nat. Press, Am. News Women's, Capital Press Women, Capitol Hill, Congl. Staff, Senate Staff, Antique Auto of Am. Home: 1312 Thornton Pkwy Fort Washington MD 20744-6869

FIELDING, HELEN, writer; b. Yorkshire, Eng., Feb. 19, 1958; 2 children. BA English, St. Anne's Coll., U. Oxford, Eng., 1979. Prodr. BBC-TV, England, 1979—89; freelance writer, 1989—; former columnist The Daily Telegraph; columnist The Independent of London, 2005—. Columnist London Ind., 1995—. Author: (novels) Cause Celeb, 1995, Bridget Jones's Diary, 1996, Bridget Jones: The Edge of Reason, 1999, Bridget Jones's Guide to Life, 2001, Olivia Joules and the Overactive Imagination, 2004; exec. prodr., screenwriter: (films) Bridget Jones's Diary, 2001 (London Critics Circle Film award for best screenwriter, 2002, Evening Standard British Film award for best screenplay, 2002); Bridget Jones: The Edge of Reason, 2004. Avocations: hiking, swimming, reading, movies. Office: c/o Viking Publicity 375 Hudson St New York NY 10014*

FIELDING, PEGGY LOU MOSS, writer; b. Davenport, Okla., Oct. 28, 1928; d. John Richard and Hazel (Matlock) Moss; B.S., Central State U., 1949, M.A., U. Santo Tomás, 1971. Tchr. various U.S. govt. overseas schs., Japan, Cuba and Philippines, 1955-71; owner Partners in Pub., Tulsa, 1975—; instr. writing Tulsa C.C., 1976 Mem. Okla. Writers Fedn., Tulsa Night Writers Club, Romance Writers Am. Democrat. Baptist. Office: PO Box 50347 Tulsa OK 74150-0347

FIELDS, C. VIRGINIA, city manager; b. Birmingham, Ala., Aug. 4, 1946; d. Peter and Lucille (Chappel) Clark; div. BA, Knoxville Coll., 1967; MSW, Ind. U., 1969; grad., NYU. Adminstr. social services Children's Aid Soc., 1971; supr. NYC Work Release Program; chair Cmty. Bd. 10, 1981-83; dist. leader 70th AD, Part C; city councilwoman Dist. 9, NYC, 1990-97; borough pres. Manhattan, NY, 1997—. Bd. mem., mem. Homeland Security Working Group Nat. League of Cities. Mem. NY State Coun. Black Elected Dems., NYC Coun. Black and Hispanic Caucus, Harlem Urban Devel. Corp., NY Urban League, Manhattan, Black Leadership Commn. on AIDS; bd. dirs. Morningside Daycare and Headstart Program; bd. mem. Jazz at Lincoln Ctr., Am. Mus. of Natural History, Mus. of City of NY, el Museo del barrio, Mus. of Art and Design. Mem. Ea. Star, Alpha Kappa Alpha, LINKS. Office: Mcpl Bldg 1 Centre St Fl 19 New York NY 10007-1602*

FIELDS, DAISY BRESLEY, human resources specialist, writer; b. Bklyn., 1915; m. Victor Fields, Aug. 2, 1936; 1 child, Barbara Fields Ochsman. Student, Hunter Coll., 1932-35, Am. U., 1949-53. Pers. officer USAF Base, Norfolk, Va., 1942-45; asst. pers. officer Dept. Agr., Phila., 1945-47; asst. dir. pers. Smithsonian Instn., Washington, 1954-60; chief spl. programs NASA, Washington, 1960-67; spl. asst. Fed. Womans Program VA, Washington, 1967-70; sr. program assoc. Nat. Civil Svc. League, 1971-72; cons. Equal Employment Opportunity/Affirmative Action, 1978—90; exec. dir. Federally Employed Women, Washington, 1975-77. Pres. Fields Assocs., Silver Spring, Md., 1978—2000; exec. dir. The Womens Inst., Am. U.; instr. Mt. Vernon Coll., 1979-80, Am. U., 1982; cons. USAID, 1990-93; freelance writer. Author: A Woman's Guide to Moving Up in Business and Government, 1983; editor: Winds of Change: Korean Women in America, 1991; contbr. articles to profl. jours. Chair Montgomery County (Md.) Pers. Bd., 1972-78; chair legis. com. Comm. for Women in Pub. Adminstrn., 1976-79; commr. Md. Commn. for Women, 1973-77, commr. Montgomery County Commmn. for Women, 1979-82; editor newsletter, past pres. Clearinghouse on Womens Issues; v.p., mng. editor Womens Inst. Press; bd. dirs. Nat. Womans Party, 1989-97. Reciipent UN Assn. U.S.A. award, 1980, Vet. Feminists Am. medal, 1998. Mem. NAFE, Nat. Coun. Career Women, Womens Equity Action League (pres. Md. 1972-74, award 1978), Federally Employed Women (pres. 1969-71, editor newsletter 1972-77, award 1974, 78), Nat. Press Club, Am. News Womens Club, Internat. Womens Writing Guild, Washington Ind. Writers, Capital Press Women, Fedn. Orgns. Profl. Women (exec. coun. 1976-77, 80-82), Nat. Assn. Women Bus. Owners, Freelance writer. Home and Office: #404 3005 S Leisure World Blvd Silver Spring MD 20906-8305 Personal E-mail: dbresley@aol.com.

FIELDS, DEBBI (DEBRA FIELDS ROSE), cookie franchise executive; b. Oakland, Calif. m. Randy Fields (div.); children: Jessica, Jenessa, Jennifer, Ashley, McKenzie; m. Michael Rose, Nov. 29, 1997. Profl. water-skier Marine World; founder Mrs. Fields Chocolate Chippery (now Mrs. Fields Inc.), Palo Alto, 1977, Mrs. Fields Inc., Park City, Utah, 1978—, pres., CEO, 1977—93. Bd. dirs. Outback Steakhouse, 1996—, WKNO, The Orpheum Theater. Author: (cookbook) 100 Recipes from the Kitchen of Debbi Fields, I Love Chocolate, 1994, Debbi Fields Great American Desserts, (autobiography) One Smart Cookie. Mem.: Soc. Entrepreneurs. Office: Mrs Fields Original Cookies 2855 Cottonwood Pkwy Ste 400 Salt Lake City UT 84121-7050*

FIELDS, EMILY JILL, secondary school educator; MA, Mich. State U., East Lansing, 2001. Cert. tchr. Colo., 1999. Tchr. Adams 50, Westminster, Colo., 2000—.

FIELDS, FELICIA P., actress; b. Chgo. Actress (plays) Jammin' With Pops, Showboat, Lincolnshire Theatre, Carousel, Damn Yankees, Big River, Dreamgirls, The Wiz, Hot Mikado, Ain't Misbehavin', Hello Dolly!, Sophisticated Ladies (Joseph Jefferson award best actress in a musical), The Rose Tattoo, Goodman Theater, The Amen Corner, A Christmas Carol, Ties That Bind, Ma Rainev's Black Bottom, (Broadway plays) The Color Purple, 2005 (Theatre World award, 2006, Clarence Derwent award, Actors' Equity Found., 2006). Mailing: c/o Broadway Theatre 1681 Broadway New York NY 10019-5827*

FIELDS, HARRIET GARDIN, counseling administrator, educator; b. Pasco, Wash., Feb. 25, 1944; d. Harry C. and Ethel Jenell (Rochelle) Gardin; m. Avery C. Fields; 1 child, Avery C. BS in Edn., S.C. State U., Orangeburg, 1966; MEd, U. S.C., 1974. Lic. profl. counselor and supr.; nat. bd. cert. counselor and career counselor. Tchr. Richaldn Sch. Dist., Columbia, S.C., 1966-67 73-76; counselor supr. S.C. Dept. Corrections, Columbia, 1971-73; counselor Techinal Edn. System, West Columbia, S.C., 1967-70; exec. dir. Bethlehem Community Ctr., Columbia, 1976-79; human rels. cons. Calhoun County Schs., St. Matthews, S.C., 1979-82; admission counselor Allen U., Columbia, 1982-83; pres., cons. H.G. Fields Assn., Columbia, 1973—. Exec. dir. Big Bros./Big Sisters, Columbia, 1984-87 Mem. Richland County Coun., Columbia, 1989-97, chair, 1993, 94, 95, 96, 97; 2d vice chair Richland County Dem. Party, Columbia, 1984-88; sec. Statewide Reapportionment Com., 1990-97; mem. Richland Lexington Immunization Com., Hope for Kids, The Lifeline: Mission to Families; bd. commrs. Midlands Tech. Coll., 2001—, mem. enterprise campus authority. Recipient inaugural Woodrow Wilson award Greater Columbia C. of C., 1994, Pres.'s Disting. Svc. award Nat. Orgn. Black County Ofcls., 1996, numerous human rels. and outstanding svc. awards. Mem. ACA (resolutions chair So. br. 1993-94, parlimentarian 1998, 99-2000, mem. governing coun.), SC Counseling Assn. (chair govt. rels. 1985-97, 98-99, pres. 1982-83), Assn. Multicultural Counseling Devel. (v.p. for African Am. concerns 1999-2000, rep. to Am. governing coun. 2000-2003), SC Coalition Pub. Health, Nat. Assn. Counties (d. dir. 1996, bylaws and election cm. 1996, 97, employment steering com. 1997), Nat. Assn. Counties (employment steering com. 1993-97, chair youth subcom. employment steering 1995-97, vice chair 1993-94), Am. Bus. Women's Assn. (pres. Midlands chpt. 1998-99), Columbia C. of C. Democrat. Methodist. Avocations: travel, reading. Home and Office: HG Fields and Assocs 412 Juniper St Columbia SC 29203-5055

FIELDS, JANICE L., food service executive; m. Doug Wilkins; 2 children. From crew mem. to regional v.p. Pitts. McDonald's Corp., 1978—94; v.p Pitts. region McDonald's USA, 1994—2000; v.p. Great Lakes divsn. McDonald's Corp., 2000; sr. v.p. SE divsn. McDonald's USA, sr. v.p. ctrl. divsn., 2000—03, pres. ctrl. divsn., 2003—06, exec. v.p., COO, 2006—. Bd. dirs. Ronald McDonald House Charities, Urban League. Recipient WON award, Women's Operator Network, 1988, Women's Leadership award, Women's Network, 2002. Office: McDonald's Corp 2111 McDonald's Dr Oak Brook IL 60523*

FIELDS, JERRI LYNN, foundation administrator; b. Sept. 1965; d. Larry and Janice Fields; m. David Burgess. B in English, Western Ill. U., M in Coll. Student Pers. Adminstrn. Positions at De Paul U., Chicago; dir. youth svcs. Horizons Cmty. Svcs., Chicago, anti-violence project dir., dir. programs; exec. dir. Rape Victim Adv., Chicago, 1998—2001; devel. and comm. dir. Fund for City of N.Y., 2001, V-Day: Until the Violence Stops, N.Y.C., 2001—02, exec. dir., 2002—. Past pres. Ill. Coalition Against Sexual Assault; mem. leadership com. Rape Victim Advs.; mem. adv. coun. RAINN Nat. Sexual Assault Hotline.

FIELDS, LAURIE, psychologist, educator; b. Havre de Grace, Md., Oct. 26, 1959; d. Charles Bleefield and Kathryn Ann McGlaughlin. BA in psychology magna cum laude, U. Md., 1988—92; PhD, U. SC, 1992—98. Lic. Psychologist Calif., 2000, cert. group psychotherapist 2005. Asst. clin. prof. dept. psychiatry and behavioral sci. U. Calif., Davis, 2000—05, asst. clin. prof. dept. psychiatry San Francisco, 2006—. Cons. Children's Workforce Needs Task Force S.C. Dept. Mental Health, 1996—97; mem. med. staff wellness com. U. Calif Davis Med. Ctr., 2003—. Contbr. chapters to books, articles to profl. jours. Recipient Donald K. Freedheim Develop. award, APA Psychotherapy Divsn., 1995, Outstanding Grad Student award, U. SC, 1997; Merrill Dow fellow, Nat. Inst. Drug Abuse, Addictions Rsch. Ctr., 1990, Outstanding Dissertation fellow, U. SC, 1997. Mem.: APA, Am. Group Psychotherapy Assn. (clin. mem.). Democrat. Office: U Calif San Francisco Dept Psychiatry 1001 Potrero Ave Ste 7M San Francisco CA 94110 Office Phone: 415-437-3037. E-mail: laurie.fields@ucsf.edu.

FIELDS, RUTH KINNIEBREW, secondary and elementary educator, consultant; b. Notasulga, Ala. d. Lee Wesley and Olivia S. (Scruggs) Kinniebrew; m. Benjamin Belton Fields, Dec. 24, 1950; children: Ivan W., Benjamin B. Jr. BS, Tuskegee Inst., 1949, MEd, 1954, postgrad., 1971—75. Cert. vocat. home econs. tchr., Ala.; cert. supt. edn., Ala. Prin., tchr. Choctaw County Bd. Edn., Butler, Ala., 1950-56; dietician, tchr. home econs. Hale County Bd. Edn., Greensboro, Ala., 1957-62; prin., tchr. Tuscaloosa (Ala.) County Bd. Edn., 1962-64, tchr. home econs., 1964-67, home sch. worker, 1967-76, tchr. kindergarten, early childhood edn., 1976-85. Supervising tchr. of students Ala. A&M U., Normal, U. Ala., Tuscaloosa, 1976-85; sec./treas. Dist. II Attendance Suprs., Ala., 1974-75. Bd. dirs. ARC, Tuscaloosa, 1967-73, Girl Scouts, Tuscaloosa, 1967-73, ARC, Tuscaloosa, 1968-74, LWV, Tuscaloosa, Black Warrior coun. Boy Scouts Am.; treas. Planned Parenthood, Tuscaloosa, 1967-76, Cmty. Svc. Programs, Tuscaloosa, 1968-74, Tuscaloosa City Bd. Edn.; advisor Chpt. 2/Title II Adv. Coun., Tuscaloosa, 1985-89. Recipient Presdl. Assoc. award Tuskegee U., 1990; named to Nat. Women's Hall of Fame, 1995. Mem. NEA, AAUW, LWV (dir. Greater Tuscaloosa chpt. 2003), Ala. Edn. Assn. (Excellence in Edn. 1982), Tuscaloosa County Edn. Assn., Nat. Women's History Mus., The Links, Inc., Delta Kappa Gamma, Alpha Kappa Alpha, Gamma Sigma Sigma. Democrat. Baptist. Avocations: reading, working puzzles, walking, cooking, travel. Home: PO Box 1755 Tuscaloosa AL 35403-1755

FIELDS, SARA A., travel company executive; With Boeing Aircraft, Renton, Wash.; flight attendant UAL Corp., Elk Grove Village, Ill., 1963, various positions including mgr. flight attendant training, mgr. indsl. rels., dir. inflight svc internat., dir. employee rels., 1963—94, sr. v.p. onboard svc., 1994—. Office: UAL Corp 1200 E Algonquin Rd Arlington Heights IL 60005-4712 also: PO Box 66100 Chicago IL 60666-0100 Fax: 847-700-4899.

FIELDS, SHEILA CRAIN, elementary school educator; b. Big Sandy, Tex., Jan. 8, 1953; d. James Daniel and Janet Crain; m. Jerry Dale Fields, July 13, 1973; children: Carrie Fields Lentz, Angie. BS in Elem. Edn., Tex. A&M U., 1975. Tchr. Bryan (Tex.) Ind. Sch. Dist., 1975—. Commr. Bryan (Tex.) Hist. Landmark Commn., 2005; vol. March of Dimes, Bryan, 2005, 2006, Am. Cancer Soc., Bryan, 2005, 2006. Named Tchr. of Yr., Fannin Elem. Sch., 2005. Mem.: PTA (parliamentarian 2004—05), Assn. Tex. Profl. Educators (treas. 1999—2000, state sec. 2000—01, state v.p. 2001—02, state pres. 2002—03, William B. Travis award 2002, Harvey Mitchell Cmty. Heritage award 1998), Delta Kappa Gamma (treas. 2004—06). Meth. Home: 3106 Red Robin Loop Bryan TX 77802 Office: Fannin Elem 1200 Baker St Bryan TX 77803 Office Phone: 979-209-3800.

FIELDS, SUZANNE BREGMAN, syndicated columnist; b. Washington, Mar. 7, 1936; d. Samuel Holiday and Sadie (Hurwitz) Bregman; m. Theodore Martin Fields, June 16, 1957; children: Alexandra, Miriamne, Tobias. BA, George Washington U., 1957, MA, 1964; PhD, Cath. U., 1971. Freelance writer, Washington, 1965-71; editor Innovations Mag., Washington, 1971-79; columnist Vogue mag., Washington, 1982; author Like Father, Like Daughter (Little Brown), 1983; columnist Washington Times, 1984—; syndicated columnist L.A. Times Syndicate, Washington, 1988-2001, Chgo. Tribune Media Svcs., 2001—05, Creators Syndicate, 2005—. TV commentator, regular panelist CNN & Co. Mem. Phi Beta Kappa. Jewish. Home: 1934 Biltmore St NW Washington DC 20009-1510 Office: The Washington Times 3600 New York Ave NE Washington DC 20002-1996

FIELDS, TINA RAE, artist, ecopsychologist; b. Paradise, Calif., Dec. 29, 1960; adopted d. Henry C. Fields and Tilla M. Fields (Jacobs). BA in Humanities and Arts with honors, Old Coll., 1985; PhD, East-West Psychology, Calif. Inst. Integral Studies, 2001. Cert. CMT Ralston Sch. Massage, 1998, FSS Shamanism and Shamanic Healing, 1990. Field faculty Lesley U., Audubon Expdn. Inst., Cambridge, Mass., 1999—2004, Belfast, Maine, 1999—2004; core MA faculty New Coll. Calif., North Bay Campus for Culture, Ecology, and Sustainable Cmty., 2004—, program co-dir., 2005—. Artist-in-residence Douglas Co. Sch. Dist., Nev., 1986, Alpine Co. Arts Commn., Calif., 1986—88; artistic dir., songleader EnChantMent, 2005—. Author: (articles publ.) The Celtic Connection, 1994, Tricycle the Buddhist Review, 1999, Proceedings of the N.Am. Assn. of Environ. Edn., 2002, Shamanism = An Encyclopedia of World Beliefs, Practices and Cultures (vol. 1), 2004, (art publ.) Jour. for Anthropology of Consciousness, Mythlore, 2006. Social and environ. justice: Food Not Bombs, San Francisco; vol. GE-Free Sonoma County, 2005—; nuc. test site activist Russian River Creekkeeper, Nev., 2005—. Recipient Author's Choice award, Mythopoeic Soc., 1988; fellow Calif. Grad., 1994—99; scholar Imagery in Healing Invitational scholar, Washoe Med. Ctr., Reno NV, 1988, CIIS, 1997—98. Mem.: Enchantment (artistic dir. 2005—), Anthropology of Consciousness (mem. exec. bd. 1998—2001). Green Party. Avocations: music, contradance, guerrilla ontology. Office: 99 Sixth St Santa Rosa CA 95401 Office Phone: 707-568-2558 2.

FIELDS, VELMA ARCHIE, medical/surgical nurse; d. Charles and Ella Ruth Archie; m. Herrell Lee Fields Sr., July 29, 1972; children: Sherri Debnam, Herrell Jr., LaShonda Hairston. BSN, Winston-Salem State U., 1968. Cert. N. C. State Bd. Nursing. Nurse, oper. rm. nurse N.C. Bapt. Hosp., Winston-Salem, 1969—90; nursing instr. Forsyth Tech. Coll., Winston-Salem, 1990—93; client coord. Sr. Svcs. Meals-on-Wheels, Winston-Salem, 1993—96; nurse Nursefinders, Winston-Salem, 1997—. Segment based on story of Velma Field's hat and her daddy (off-Broadway play) Crowns, 2002—03. Vol. cardiopulmonary instr. ARC, Winston-Salem, NC, 1980; vol. Nurse Database for Bioterrorism Response Team Forsyth County Dept. Pub. Health, 2003—; vol. nightingale Nat. Black Theatre Festival, 2005; deacon Emmanuel Bapt. Ch., Winston-Salem, NC. Recipient Race Progress Promotors Achievement award in healthcare, Effort Club, New Bethel Bapt. Ch., Winston-Salem, N.C., 2001, Cert. Appreciation, NC Dept. Health and Human Svcs. Baptist. Office Phone: 336-995-8372.

FIELDS, WENDY LYNN, lawyer; b. NYC, Sept. 22, 1946; d. Sidney and Helen (Silverstein) F. BA, George Washington U., 1968, JD, 1976. Bar: D.C. 1976. Assoc. Arent, Fox, Kintner, Plotkin & Kahn, Washington, 1976-78; ptnr. Weissbard & Fields, Washington, 1978-83, Wilkes, Artis, Hedrick & Lane, Washington, 1983-86, Foley & Lardner, Washington, 1986-97, Katten Muchin Zavis Rosenman, Washington, 1997—. Mem. George Washington Law Rev., 1973-75. Mem. D.C. Bar. Assn. Office: Katten Muchin Zavis Rosenman 1025 T Jefferson St NW East Lobb Ste 700 Washington DC 20007-5214 Office Phone: 202-625-3800.

FIELDS-GOLD, ANITA, retired dean; b. Amarillo, Tex., Oct. 29, 1940; d. Dera and Mamie Maureen (Craig) Bates; m. Maurice Gold; 1 child, William Kyle. Grad. nursing, Jefferson Davis Hosp., 1962; BSN, Tex. Christian U., 1966; MSN, Northwestern State U. La., 1974; PhD, Tex. Women's U., 1980. C.E. coord., asst. prof. Northwestern State U., Shreveport; prof., dean McNeese State U., Lake Charles, La.; ret., 2000. Gov.'s appointee, chmn. S.W. La. Hosp. Dist. Commn., 1989—91; vice chair Region 5 Healthcare Reform Consortium. Mem. allocations com. and loaned exec. United Way, 1991—92, Am. Heart Assn.; Am. Cancer Soc.; ARC; vice chmn. Region 5 Health Care Reform Consortium, 2005. Recipient Ben Taub award, 1962, Ann Magnussen award, ARC, 1977. Mem.: ANA (del.), Lake Charles Dist. Nurses Assn. (bd. dirs., Nurse of Yr. award 1972, 1980), La. Nurses Assn. (past pres. and 1st v.p., Spl. Recognition award 1993, Nightingale Hall of Fame award 2002), Phi Kappa Phi, Delta Kappa Gamma, Sigma Theta Tau (Image of Nursing award 1993). Home: 2339 21st St Lake Charles LA 70601-7946 Personal E-mail: amgold@cox-internet.com.

FIELDS-JENKINS, DELORIS JEAN, elementary school educator; b. Tupelo, Miss., Feb. 27, 1955; d. Phillip, Sr. and Dollie Bell Fields. BS, Miss. Valley State U., Itta Bena, 1978; postgrad., U. Miss., Oxford, 1992—94, U. So. Miss., Hattiesburg, 1996—98. Cert. tchr. Miss. 6th grade math tchr. Lawndale Elem. Sch., Tupelo, Miss., 1983—. Fund raiser coord. St. Jude Rsch. Hosp., Tupelo, 1992—. Named Tchr. of Distinction, Create, 2002—03. Mem.: NAACP, Delta Sigma Theta (life). Home: 2000 Bella Vista Tupelo MS 38801 Office: Tupelo Pub Sch 72 South Green St Tupelo MS 38804 Office Phone: 662-841-8890.

FIELO, MURIEL BRYANT, interior designer; b. Bklyn., Dec. 11, 1921; d. Harry and Minnie (Dick) Bryant; m. Julius Fielo, June 17; one child, Michael Kenneth. Student, Rutgers U., 1965—69; cert., N.Y. Sch. Interior Design, 1970. Gen. mgr. Fidelity Discount Corp., Irvington, NJ; advt. supr. Lincoln Loan Co., Essex County, NJ, 1941—49; interior designer Alex Fielo Interior Decorators, Newark, 1942—49, prin., 1949—69, owner, 1969—. Designer, cons., space engr. Mudge Interior Design Studios, East Orange, N.J., 1969-; mem. adv. panel Interior Design mag., 1977-. Clk. Essex County Bd. Freeholders, 1972-76; commr. East Orange Bus. Devel. Authority, 1977-86; mem. U.S. adv. coun. SBA-Region II, 1980-811 active LWV, 1950-55; organizer, first pres. South Orange chpt. Women's Am. ORT, 1952-54, mem. nat. speakers bur., 1952-65, parliamentarian No. N.J. coun., 1955-65; pres. Amity chpt. B'nai B'rith, Newark, 1946-48, v.p. No. N.J. coun., 1948-49, various nat. and state positions, 1948-80; mem. nat. com. on sect. fund raising Nat. Coun. Jewish Women, 1979-81, nat. tour chmn., 1979-81; trustee cmty. svc. coun. Oranges and Maplewood, United Way Essex and West Hudson, 1981-83; bd. dir. East Orange Ctrl. Ave. Mall Assn., 1979-83, chmn. new voter registration drive East Orange 2d Ward, 1955, entire city, 1969; pres. East Orange Dem. Club, 1957-58, campaign coord. for Dem. mayoral candidate, 1969; calendar coord. Essex County Dem. Com., 1970-76; mem. N.J. Bipartisan Coalition for Women's Appointments, 1981. Named Outstanding Entrepreneur of 1984, Gov. of N.J., Outstanding Orgn. Pres., Kean Coll. Profl. Women's Assn., 1985, Wonder Woman of 1986, Bus. Jour. N.J., One of Eight Women To Watch, Jersey Woman mag., 1987, Bus. Person of Yr., East Orange C. of C., 1988; recipient various awards for civic svc. Mem. Internat. Soc. Interior Designers (bd. dir. 1981-85), Nat. Home Fashions League (N.J. membership chmn. N.Y. chpt. 1981-82), Interior Design Soc., Internat. Interior Design Assn. (charter), N.J. Assn. Women Bus. Owners (state bd. dir. 1979-82), Women Entrepreneurs N.J. (pres. 1981-85, CEO 1987—), N.J. Home Furnishings Assn. (bd. dir. 1981-84, 86—), Constrn. Specifications Inst., N.J. Soc. AIA profl. affiliate), Guild Designer Woodworkers, Women Bus. Ownership Ednl. Coalition (N.J. pres. 1985-87, CEO 1987—, mem. steering com. interior designers for licensing in N.Y. 1985—), East Orange C. of C. (bd. dir. 1977—, v.p. 1981-85), Bus. and Profl. Women's Club Oranges (bd. dir. 1958-66). Jewish. Home and Office: Mudge Interior Design Studio 185 S Clinton St East Orange NJ 07018-3099 Office Phone: 973-673-6008. Office Fax: 973-672-7287. Business E-Mail: mbfielo@erols.com.

FIERMAN, ELLA YENSEN, retired psychotherapist; b. Cleve., June 20, 1922; d. Cecil Hoy and Dorthea Carolina Yensen; m. Chandler Garner Screven (div.); m. Louis B. Fierman, Sept. 25, 1947; children: Daniel B., Lauren C. BS, Case Western Res. U., 1944; MA, State U. Iowa, 1947; postgrad., Yale U., 1969—71; PhD, Saybrook Inst., 1982. Clin. psychiat. intern. Cleve. State Receiving Hosp., 1947—48; kindergarten tchr. US Army Dependents Sch., Fukuoka, Japan, 1948—49; clin. psychologist Mental Hygiene Clinic, Hartford (Conn.) Hosp., 1950—51; office adminstr. pub. health rsch. Yale U., New Haven, 1952—53, rsch. asst. psychiatry dept., 1953—55; psychotherapist Psychotherapy Assocs., New Haven, 1968—2002, adminstr., 1969—72, exec. dir., 1972—2002; ret., 2002. Cons. in field; trainer encounter groups Jewish Cmty. Ctr., New Haven, 1970—72; chmn. bd. dirs. Human Resource Ctr. Conn., New Haven, 1973—75. Author: The Role of Cues in Stuttering, 1955; co-author: Bibliotherapy in Psychiatry, 1947, 2d edit., 1978, Human Anxiety, 1956, 2d edit. Leader Girl Scouts US, Woodbridge, Conn., 1964—67. Recipient citation, State of Conn., 2005; grantee, Western Res. U., 1940—44. Mem.: APA, New England Psychol. Assn., Conn. Psychol. Assn. Avocations: gardening, birds, alternative medicine.

FIERO-MAZA, LORRAINE DORIS, music educator; d. Joseph Martin and Doris Lorraine Rodrigues; m. David Alfonzo Maza, Feb. 14, 2006; 1 child, André Rodrigo Trosan. MS in Music Edn., Ctrl. Conn. State U., New Britain, 1996; postgrad., Hartt Sch. Music, West Hartford, Conn. Tchr. music Pub. Sch. Sys., Fairfield, Conn., 1986—. Mentor best tng. Fairfield Pub. Schs., 1997—. Mem. PETA, Southbury, Conn., 2006; agt. Keeping Kids Safe Network, 2004. Grantee, Conn. Assn. Adminstrs., 2000. Mem.: NEA. Liberal. Roman Catholic. Avocations: travel, writing, exercise, reading, music. Office Phone: 203-255-8316. Personal E-mail: boccabella@sbcglobal.net.

FIERRO, MARCELLA FARINELLI, forensic pathologist, educator; b. Buffalo, May 24, 1941; d. Marcello Francis and Lena Louise (Luppino) Farinelli; m. Robert J. Fierro, May 30, 1966. BA in Biology (cum laude), D'Youville Coll., NY, 1962; MD in Forensic Pathology, SUNY, Buffalo, 1966. Cert. Am. Bd. Pathology. Intern, resident Ottawa Civic Hosp., Ontario, Canada; resident, pathology Cleve. Clinic Ednl. Found., Ohio, 1973—74, Va. Commonwealth Univ., 1973—74; chief resident, pathology with fellowship in forensic pathology, dept. legal medicine Med. Coll. Va./Va. Commonwealth Univ., Richmond, Va., 1973—74; deputy chief med. examiner, city med. examiner State of Va., Richmond, 1975-92; staff pathologist Richmond Med. Coll. Va. Hosp., 1975—92; clin. prof., pathology Univ. Va., Charlottesville, 1983—92, 1999—2002; prof. pathology East Carolina Sch. Medicine, Greenville, NC, 1992—94; designated med. exam. and forensic pathologist Med. Exam Sys., NC, 1992-94; chief med. examiner State of Va., Richmond, 1994—. Chmn. forensic pathology com. CAP, 1996-2001; co-dir. Vir. Inst. of Forensic Sci. and Medicine; cons. FBI task force on Nat. Crime Investigation Ctr., unidentified Persons and Missing Person Files, Washington, DC, 1983-; presenter and lectr. for profl. orgns. Bd. editors, reviewer Am.

Journal of Forensic Medicine and Pathology, 1979—; contbr. articles to peer-reviewed jours.; guest appearances (TV series) New Detectives, Discovery Channel, BBC. Recipient Lifetime Achievement award, Sch. Medicine and Biomedical Scis. Med. Alumni Assn., State Univ., Buffalo, 2001. Mem. AMA, Internat. Assn. for Identification, Am. Med. Women's Assn., Med. Soc. Va., Richmond Acad. Medicine, Va. Soc. Pathology, Nat. Assn. Med. Examiners (bd. dirs. 1993-95, mem. exec. com. 1995, pres. 1991), Am. Acad. Forensic Sci., Coll. Am. Pathologist; fellow Am. Soc. Clin. Pathologist (mem. forensic pathology coun. 1992-96). Office: Office Chief Med Examiner 400 E Jackson St Richmond VA 23219

FIESER, CHERIE ROSE, editor, curator; b. Hazleton, Pa., Jan. 2, 1954; d. Louis H. and Edith L. Luchi; m. Stephen Carl Fieser, Dec. 9, 1978. BA in Humanities summa cum laude, Pa. State U., Harrisburg, 1997, MA in Am. Studies summa cum laude, 2002. Lic. Real Estate Broker Commonwealth Pa., 1983. Assoc., office mgr. Pecora Real Estate, West Hazleton, Pa., 1972—78; editl. work, book prodn. spl. event projects adminstr. Christian Publ., Inc., Camp Hill, Pa., 1979—82, dir. advt. and mktg., 1982—91; broker Century 21, Harrisburg, Pa., 1981—90; editor Harrisburg, 1985—; asst. to dir., Murray Libr. Messiah Coll., Grantham, 1991—, curator book arts Murray Libr., 2004—. Notary pub., West Hazleton, 1975—79; invited paper presenter Pearl S. Buck Internat. Symposium, Zhenjiang, China, 2005. Co-editor (book) Citizen Extraordinaire: The Diplomatic Diaries of Vance McCormick in London & Paris, 1917-1919, With Other Documents from a High-Minded American Life, co-curator (exhibition) Richard Koontz: Art, Design, Invention, initiator/curator (permanent collection) Ruth E. Engle Memorial Collection of Original Children's Book Illustration, contributor/editor (book manuscript) Dictionary of the Holocaust: Biography, Geography, Terminology. Recipient Best Student Paper award, Humanities Divsn., Pa. State U., 1995. Mem.: Nat. Mus. Women in Arts, Hershey Pub. Libr., Susquehanna Art Mus., Hist. Harrisburg Assn., Friends Murray Libr. (bd. dirs., steering com.), Friends Midtown (chair bylaws com.), Habitat for Humanity, Capital Area Greenbelt Assn., Phi Kappa Phi. Independent. Judeo-Christian. Avocations: Holocaust studies, book collecting, bicycling, Chinese history and culture. Office: Messiah College One College Avenue Grantham PA 17027 Office Phone: 717-691-6006 7181. Office Fax: 717-691-6042. E-mail: cfieser@messiah.edu.

FIESSINGER, BETTINA A., mental health counselor, educator; b. Newark, Nov. 21, 1946; d. Benjamin Robert and Myrle Elizabeth Vitale; m. David Warren Fiessinger, Nov. 27, 1965; children: David Warren, Scott Thomas. AA, Palm Beach C.C., Palm Beach Gardens, Fla., 1993; BA, Fla. Atlantic U., 1995; MS in Psychology, Nova Southeastern U., 1997, D in Sch. Psychology, 2006—. Lic. mental health counselor. Customer svc. mgr. Intelcom Info. Systems, West Palm Beach, Fla., 1983-86; dir. customer svcs. for State of Fla., Cellular One, West Palm Beach, 1986-88; dist. adminstr. Milner Bus. Products, West Palm Beach, 1988-89; sales mgr., store mgr. Cellular Trading Co., Miami, Fla., 1989-93; accounts payable/receivable The Mobile Phone Co., Boca Raton, Fla., 1993-97; substitute tchr. Palm Beach County Dist. Schs., 1995-97; adolescent, child and family therapist Sandy Pines Hosp., Tequesta, Fla., 1997—. Bd. dirs. Vacation Village, Clermont, Fla., 1996, v.p., 1994, pres., 1995; counselor Life Line/Cath. Charities, Palm Beach Gardens, 1993-97; coord., head Eucharistic mins. Cathedral of St. Ignatius, 1995—; bd. dirs. Kid Sanctuary, 2006—. Mem. APA (assoc.), ACA (profl.). Roman Catholic. Home: 5340 Edenwood Ln Palm Beach Gardens FL 33418-7843 Office Phone: 561-745-1750.

FIESTER, ELIZABETH ANN, secondary school educator; b. Sunland, Calif., Mar. 5, 1958; d. Richard David and Shirley Jean Fiester. BA in Theatre, Calif. State U., Fresno, 1981, MA in Theatre, 1987. Box office mgr. Good Co. Players, Fresno, Calif., 1983—95; tchr. Clovis West H.S., 1995—. Dir. Good Co. Players, 1983—; adj. faculty Fresno City Coll., 1988—94. Home: 1552 N College Ave Fresno CA 93728 Office: Clovis West High School 1070 E Teague Fresno CA 93720 Office Phone: 559-327-2000. Office Fax: 559-327-2293. Personal E-mail: efiester@prodigy.net. E-mail: elizabethfiester@cusd.com.

FIFELSKI, THERESE YOLANDE, microbiologist; b. Highland Park, Mich., May 18, 1933; d. Edmond Joseph LaVallee and Noella Marie Desrosiers-LaVallee; m. Richard Joseph Fifelski; children: Michael, Patrick, Anne-Therese, Christopher, James. BA, Marygrove Coll., Detroit, 1954. Microbiologist rschr. Parke Davis, Detroit, 1954—62. Vol. Jackson Symphony Guild; pres., vol. Woman's Club of Jackson; vol. Jr. Dorcas, mem. choir St. Rita's Ch.; bd. dirs. Jackson Chorale, Mich., 1980—, Clarke Lake Players, Jackson, 2000, Jackson Civic Theatre, 2000, Ctr. Stage Jackson, 2000—06. Scholarship named in her honor, AAUW, Jackson. Home: 6128 Brown's Lake Rd Jackson MI 49203

FIFER CANBY, SUSAN MELINDA, library administrator; b. Stockton, Calif., Jan. 23, 1948; d. Reginald Dekovan and Shirley Rae (Canaday) Fifer; m. Thomas Yellott Canby, Oct. 9, 1982. BS, U. Nebr., 1970; MLS, U. Md., 1974. Circulating libr. Nat. Geog. Soc., Washington, 1975-81, asst. libr., 1981-83, dir. libr., 1983-94, dir. libr. & indexing, 1994-99, dir. librs., 1999—, v.p. librs. and info. svcs., 2002—. Mem. mems. coun. OCLC, Dublin, Ohio, 1997-2003; literacy tutor; bd. dirs. Washington Lit. Coun., 1999-2001. Bd. dirs. tech. com. D.C. Coun. Govts., 1985-88, D.C. Libr. Coun., 1997-2003, Capital Area Libr. Network, 1989-95, 98—, chair, 1994-95; v.p. bd. dirs. Sandy Spring Mus., 2002—. Named Alumna of Yr., U. Md., 2004; Knight fellow, Salzburg Seminar, 2004, Freeman fellow, 2005. Mem.: ALA (John Cotton Dana award 1985, 1989), Spl. Librs. Assn. (pres. DC Spl. Librs. 2003—04, Innovations and Tech. award 2001, Factiva Leadership award 2005). Avocations: gardening, reading. Home: 6855 Haviland Mill Rd Clarksville MD 21029-1308 Office: Nat Geog Soc Libr 1145 17th St NW Washington DC 20036-4701 Office Phone: 202-857-7787. Business E-Mail: sfiferca@ngs.org.

FIFFIE PROCTOR, JOANN, media and technology specialist; b. New Orleans; d. Joseph Paul Sr. and Elouise Marie Fiffie. BA in Comm., U. Southwestern, Lafayette, La., 1980; EdM, Minot State U., 1992; M of Libr. and Info. Sci., U. So. Miss., 1997. Tchr. St. James Sch. Bd., Lutcher, La., 1992-93, tchr. computers, 1994-96; spl. edn. tchr. Calif. Sch. Dist., Sacramento, 1993-94; instr. Southwestern U., Lafayette, La., 1997-98; media/tech. specialist St. John Sch. Bd., Reserve, La., 1998—; rschr. Lyndon Baines Johnson Presdl. Libr., 1996—2000. Dir. sta. WJLO-TV Magnet Sch., LaPlace, La., 2000. Founder mag. Tender Times, 2000. Active Parent-Tchr., St. James, La., 1994-96; pres./CEO House Hands & Hugs, Vacherie, La.; mem. adv. bd. Big Brothers & Sisters, Lafayette. Houma-Terabone grantee, 1998; Metrovision Sch.-To-Career grantee, 2002. Mem. ALA, AAUW, NEA, Libr. Info. Tech. Assn., Nat. Assn. Female Execs., Mothers of 21st Century Leaders. Office: John L Ory Magnet Sch 182 W 5th St La Place LA 70068-4501

FIFIELD, LILLENE H., psychotherapist, educator; b. L.A., Oct. 1941; d. Howard Charles Fifield and Esther Shana Goldstein; life ptnr. Margaret Marshall. BA with honors, Calif. State U., L.A., 1971; MSW with honors, U. So. Calif., L.A., 1973. Acad. Cert. Social Worker 1979, LCSW 1980, Qualified Clin. Social Worker 1993, bd. cert. diplomat Nat. Assn. Social Worker, 1993, cert. Nat. Cert. Social Worker. Rsch. assoc. Regional Rsch. Inst. in Social Welfare, U. So. Calif., L.A., 1972—75; lectr. Calif. State U., Fullerton, 1975—79; pvt. practice psychotherapist L.A., 1976—; psychiat. social worker Douglas County Health Dept., Roseburg, Oreg., 1980—83; dir./site coord. distance edn. MSW program Calif. State U., Long Beach, Calif., 1998—2001; dir. mental health L.A. Ctr. for Edn. Rsch., 2001—04. Cons./lectr. in menatl health field, L.A., 1973—; bd. pres., trainer Calif. Alcoholism Found., L.A., 1974—76; psychiat. trainer Oreg. State Bd. Mental Health Examiners, Salem, 1982. Author: On My Way to Nowhere, Alienated: Isolated & Drunk, Alcoholism in the Gay Community, 1979. Bd. mem. L.A. County Alcohol Adv. Bd., 1974—77; foundering mem., bd. dirs. L.A. Gay & Lesbian Ctr., 1971—75; founding mem., bd. dirs., 1st co-chair Calif. Women's Commn. on Alcoholism, 1976; del. Internat. Women's Year, 1977. Named Woman of Yr., L.A. Gay and Lesbian Cmty., 1978; recipient Cert. of Recognition, Calif. Legis., 2001, Cert. Commendation for Profl. Adv. and Mental Health of Gay and Lesbian People, City of West Hollywood, Calif., 2002. Mem.: NOW, NASW, Glendale Area Mental Health Assn., L.A. Gay and Lesbian Psychotherapy Assn. (bd. mem., collegue, treas. 1999—2003, Cmty. Svc. award 2002), Circle of Life L.A. Gay and Lesbian Ctr. (founder, Honorable Placque 1998). Democrat. Jewish. Avocations: travel, reading, snorkeling, hiking, history. Office: Lillene Fifield 4444 W Riverside Dr Ste 205 Burbank CA 91505-4048

FIFKOVA, EVA, behavioral neuroscience educator; b. Prague, Czechoslovakia, May 21, 1932; came to U.S., 1968; d. Ivan and Maria Fifka. MD, Charles U., Prague, 1957; PhD, Inst. Physiology Czechoslovakia Acad. Scis., Prague, 1963. Lectr. Charles U., 1954-60; mem. staff Czechosolvakia Acad. Scis., 1960-68; research assoc. Calif. Inst. Tech., Pasadena, 1968-74; asst. prof. behavioral neurosci. U. Colo., Boulder, 1974-75, assoc. prof., 1975-78, prof., 1978—. Mem. neurobiology adv. panel NSF, Washington, 1982-85; alcohol biomed. rsch. rev. com. Nat. Inst. Alcohol Abuse and Alcoholism, 1988-89; mem. neurology study sect. NIH, 1990-94; mem. rev. bd. Bionat. Sci. Found., 1992—. Contbr. numerous articles to profl. jours. U. Colo. Faculty fellow, Boulder, 1979, 84; research grantee Nat. Inst. Aging, Bethesda, Md., 1984—, Nat. Inst. Alcohol, 1983—, Nat. Inst. Mental Health, 1988—. Mem. AAAS, Am. Physiol. Soc., Soc. Neurosci., Am. Assn. Anatomists, Electron Microscopy Soc. Am., Inst. Brain Rsch. Orgn. Clubs: Cajal (Denver). Office: U Colo Dept Psychology PO Box 345 Boulder CO 80309-0345

FIKE, DOROTHY JEAN, science educator; d. Oliver Michael and Dorothy Elizabeth (Spanagel) Fike. BS, Capital U., Columbus, Ohio, 1967; MS in Biology, Cleve. State U., 1972; postgrad. in human genetics, U. Mich., Ann Arbor, 1981; postgrad. in exptl. pathology, Va. Commonwealth U., Richmond, 1984—91. Cert. med. tech. Miami Valley Hosp. Staff technologist Euclid (Ohio) Gen. Hosp., Euclid, 1967—72, asst. chief technologist, 1972—73, ednl. coord., 1973—74; from instr. to asst. prof. U. Vt., Burlington, 1974—81; asst. prof. Va. Commonwealth U., Richmond, 1982—90; supr. blood bank/immunology/seratology Kaiser Permanente, Cleve., 1991—94; prof., chair, program dir. clin. lab. sci. Marshall U., Huntington, W.Va., 1995—. Contbg. author: chpts. to book Sheehan Clinical Immunology, 1990, 1997; co-author: (instr.'s manual) McKenzie Clinical Hematology, 2003. Mem.: W.Va. Soc. Clin. Lab. Sci. (pres. 1998—99), Ea. Cabell County Humanities Orgn. (bd. dirs. 1999—2002, sec. 2002—04, pres. 2005—06), Am. Soc. Clin. Lab. Sci. (mem. consumer response panel 2002—, Sherwood Prof. Achievement award 2005). Avocations: reading, gardening, hiking, walking. Home: 3675 Henry White Ona WV 25545 Office: Marshall U 1 John Marshall Dr Huntington WV 25755-0003

FIKE, HOLLY RENEE, music educator; b. Oklahoma City, July 1, 1974; d. George Dennis and Wynemia Lorene Fike. B of Music Edn., Southwestern Okla. State U., Weathrford, 1997; MusM, Southwestern Okla. State U., Weatherford, 1998. Cert. Instrumental/Vocal Tchr. k-12 Okla. Bd. Edn., 1999. Grad. asst. Southwestern Okla. State U., 1997—98; band/vocal tchr. Waurika Pub. Schs., 1998—2001; k-6 music tchr. Richardson Ind. Sch. Dist., Tex., 2001—02; band tchr. Duncan Pub. Schs., Okla., 2002—. Tchr. Southwestern Okla. State U. Band Camps, 2003—. Actor: Chisolm Trail Hist. Mus., 1999, 2004—06. Mem.: Okla. Secondary Sch. Activities Assn., Southwestern Band Dir.'s Assn., Okla. Bandmasters Assn., Music Educators Nat. Conf. Avocations: reading, exercise, home improvement. Office: Duncan Pub Schs PO Box 1548 Duncan OK 73534

FILARDO, TAMRA L., social studies educator; b. Dodgeville, Wis., Dec. 10, 1971; d. James and Lettie Wehrle; m. Nick Filardo, Nov. 24, 2000; 1 child, Luke; children: Joah, Koby. BS, U. Wis., Platteville, 1994; MA in Tchg., Marycrest U., Davenport, Iowa, 1998. Cert. 7-12 social studies, psychology, history, political sci. Wis. Dept. Pub. Instrn., 2001. Social studies tchr. Argyle H.S., Wis., Dodgeville H.S., Wis., 2001—. Student coun. advisor; mock trial advisor, Dodgeville; volleyball coach, Dodgeville; class advisor Argyle H.S. Mem.: Wis. Edn. Assn. Coun., Nat. Edn. Assn., Tchrs. of Psychology in Secondary Schs., Legion Aux. (assoc.). Home: 511 Washington St Mineral Point WI 53565 Office: Dodgeville High School 912 W Chapel St Dodgeville WI 53533 Office Phone: 608-935-3307. Business E-Mail: tfilardo@dsd.k12.wi.us.

FILARSKI HASSELBECK, ELIZABETH, television host/personality; b. Cranston, RI, May 28, 1977; d. Kenneth J. Filarski and Elizabeth A. DelPadre; m. Tim Hasselbeck, July 6, 2002. Degree in Art, Boston Coll., 1999. Tchr., Belize, 1997; contestant, finished fourth Survior: The Australian Outback, 2001; judge Miss Teen USA Pageant, 2001; shoe designer Puma; host The Look for Less, The Style Network, 2001—; co-host The View, ABC, 2003—. Office: The View ABC 320 W 66th St New York NY 10023-6304 also: Babette Perry Internat Creative Mgmt 8942 Wilshire Blvd Beverly Hills CA 90211

FILBERT, ELEANOR JANE, special education educator; b. McCall Creek, Miss., July 26, 1949; d. Ervin Erastus and Hellon Ruth (Palmer) Fleming; m. Robert Morris Filbert Jr., Sept. 27, 1969; children: Robert III, Eleanor, Hellon, Michael, Paul, Paula. Student, S.W. C.C., Summit, Miss., 1991-92, Copiah-Lincoln C.C., 1992; BS in Elem. Edn., U. So. Miss., 1994; MEd, Alcorn U., 1999; postgrad., Capella U. Cert. tchr., Miss. Justowriter Enterprise Jour., McComb, Miss., 1967-69; tchr. asst. Valpraiso (Fla.) Elem. Sch., 1975-76; computer operator Enterprise Jour., McComb, 1983-86; tchr. spl. edn. Amite County HS, Liberty, Miss., 1994—98; tchr. Mobile County Pub. Schs., 1998—2003; tchr. spl. edn. Franklin County Schs., Meadville, Miss., 2003—; tchr. EMD Alice Birney Mid. Sch., Charleston, SC, 2004—. Mem. CEC (sponsor 1994-95), Miss. Assn. Educators. Republican. Baptist. Avocations: travel, camping, sewing, music, sports. Office: Amite County H S Liberty MS 39645 Home: 230B Miami St Ladson SC 29456 Office Phone: 843-764-2212. E-mail: memaw99@hotmail.com.

FILBERT-ZACHER, LAURA MARGARET, research and development company executive; b. Columbia, Mo., Nov. 27, 1953; d. Garvin Preston and Marlene Lillian (Gorsuch) Filbert; m. Terry Wayne Vaughan (div.); m. James Richard Johnston (div.); 1 child, Damien Isaac Johnston; m. John Andrew Zacher, May 27, 1995. BS in Recreation, Parks & Tourism, U. Mo., Columbia, MS in Cmty. Devel. Rsch. technician Environ. Trace Substances Rsch. Ctr. U. Mo., Mo., 1984—91; rsch. specialist U. Mo., Rural Policy Rsch. Inst., 1991—94; programs specialist Mo. Dept. Econ. Devel., Jefferson, 1994—96; ops. mgr. City Portsmouth, Va., 1996—98; spl. projects mgr. St. Louis Devel. Corp., 1999—2004; sr. project mgr. Econ. Development Resources, St. Louis, 2004—. Contbr. articles to profl. jours. Contbr. So. Poverty Law Ctr., Natural Resources Def. Coun. Fellow, Farm Found., 1992. Mem.: Mo. Cmty. Devel. Soc. (pres.-elect, pres.), Cmty. Devel. Soc. (dir. 2003—). Liberal. Unitarian. Avocations: painting, reading, films, travel, camping. Office: Econ Devel Resources 200 South Hanley Ste 601 Saint Louis MO 63105 Office Fax: 314-727-5544. Business E-Mail: lfzacher@edr-consulting.com.

FILCHOCK, ETHEL, education educator; BS in Edn., Kent State U. Tchr. Cleve. Pub. Schs.; with EFC Creations, Solon, Ohio. Author: Voices in Poetics: Vol. 1, 1985 (Merit award), Hall of Fame, Ethel Filchock, Vol. 1, 1991, (book of poetry) Softer Memories Across a Lifetime, 1989, (poetry chapbook) A Glimpse of Love, 1991; composer: Praise God, The Lord is Coming; lyricist (numerous songs including most recently) (Harmonious Honor award, Award for Excellence, 2000), (songs) Beautiful Lady of Medugorje, 1993, This Holy Morning, 1998, Theatre of the Mind, 2003, Only The Faces Change, 2003, Amerecord, 2003, My Beautiful America, 2003, this Holy Child, 2003, What About Tomorrow, 2003, Rolling On For Freedom, 2003, Something About You, 2003, Santa's Ho-Ho-Ho, 2003, Hilltop, 2003, Holiday Blues Circle of Life, 2003 (named into Nat. Lib. Poetry, 03). Chmn. sch. United Way, 1985-86. Recipient Cert. of Achievement N.Y. Profl./Amateur Song Jubilee, 1986, Editor's Choice award Disting. Poets of Am., Outstanding Achievement in Poetry, Nat. Libr. Poetry, 1993, Outstanding Poets of 1994, Interregnum Nat. Libr. Poetry, Best Poets of 1995, Transformation, Nat. Libr. of Poetry, Editor's Choice award Outstanding Achievement in Poetry, 1996, 2000-02, Nat. Libr. Poetry, 1995-96, 2001, Outstanding Poets of 1998 for Magnanimous Beauty, Nat. Libr. Poetry, 1998, Editor's Choice award, 1998. Mem. NAFE, Am. Fedn. Tchrs. Clubs: Akron Manuscript. Roman Catholic. Avocations: painting, travel, dance, fishing.

FILER, EMILY SYMINGTON HARKINS, retired foundation administrator, writer, non-profit consultant; b. Balt., May 12, 1936; d. Frank Fife and Grace (Cover) Symington; m. George Archer Harkins, June 21, 1958 (div. 1982); children: Montgomery Fox, Emily Harrison (dec. Apr. 1978); m. Robert Hoagland Filer, June 24, 1989. Degree, Villa Julie Med. Sec. Sch., Balt., 1955; CPE, Sentara Norfolk Gen. Hosp., Va., 2002—03. Cert. vol. adminstr., 1985; CPE Levell, CPE cert., Sentara Norfolk Gen. Hosp., 2003. Registrar Johns Hopkins Hosp., Balt., 1955-57, sec. hearing and speech ctr., 1957-58; pres. Distaff Wives, San Francisco, Boston, 1958-63; v.p., bd. dirs. The Planning Council, Tidewater, Va., 1969-78; pres. Jr. League of Norfolk (Va.)-Virginia Beach, 1972-74; founder, coord. Lee's Friends, Norfolk, 1978-86, exec. dir., 1986-2001; ret., 2001; dir. devel. YWCA S Hampton Rds., 2004—06; assoc. chaplain Sentara Norfolk Gen. Hosp., 2006—. Chmn. Tidewater dist. Va. Council Soc. Welfare, 1985-87, Va. Council Social Welfare, 1988; bd. dirs. Va. Wesleyan Coll., Norfolk, 1979-2001, Olde Huntersville Devel., Norfolk, 1985-87; mem. Glennan Geriat. Clerkship Faculty Ea. Va. Med. Sch., 1996-2001; nat. cons., trainer, vis. instr. Norfolk State U., Old Dominion U., Regent U., Tidewater C.C., Va. Wesleyan Coll. Lic. pastoral caregiver, lay reader The Ch. of Good Shepherd, 1992—, instr. adult Sunday sch., 1998, group leader Alpha program, 1999-2000, co-leader lay pastoral care, 2000-2004, lay eucharistic visitor, lay eucharist visitor; chair, Pastoral Care Coun., 2003-2004; bd. dirs., sec., exec. com. Westminster Canterbury of Virginia Beach, 1993-2001; mem. Mayor's Commn. on Aging, Virginia Beach, 1996-2000, vice chair, 1997-2000, chair, 1999-2001, mem. mayor's Census 2000 com.; bd. trustees Va. Wesleyan Coll., 1979-2001; mem., past pres. Tidewater dist. Va. Coun. on Social Welfare; steering com. Hampton Rds. Leadership Prayer Luncheon, 1999, co-chair prayer luncheon, 2001—; del. Episcopal Diocese of So. Va., 1999-2000, co-chair Diocese Gala, 2001; mem. profl. adv. group Clin. Pastoral Edn., 2001—, co-chair, 2001-2003, self study group 2004-2005; vol. assoc. chaplain Westminster Canterbury, 2003; sec., Tidewater Pastoral Counseling Svc. Bd., 2006-. Named Gt. Citizen of Hampton Roads, 1987, Va. Vol. Adminstr. of Yr., Internat. Assn. for Vol. Adminstrn. Va. affiliates, 1992; recipient Women in Transition award YWCA of South Hampton Roads, 1989, Spl. award Outstanding Profl. Women of Hampton Roads, 1989, Disting. Merit citation NCCJ, 1992, Outstanding Cmty. Svc. award Delta Sigma Theta Norfolk Alumae chpt., 1997, Pub. Citizen of Yr. award NASW, Va. chpt., 1999, Jefferson award, WAVY 10, Cmty. Svc., 2003, First Woman in Bus. Achievement award, Inside Bus., 2004, Vol. Hampton Rds. Cmty. Achievement award, Lee's Friends Found., 2004, Leading Edge Adopter award YWCA So. Hampton Roads and Emily Filer, 2005. Mem. Internat. Assn. for Vol. Adminstrs. (cert. liaison, region IV 1986, profl. devel. liaison assn. 1987-88, region IV 1987-88, 93-94, recertification chair 1990-92, exec. planning com. Internat. Conf. on Vol. Adminstrn. 1997, chair subcom. peer assessment 2000-02), Southeastern Va. Assn. for Vol. Adminstrs. (dep. sec. 1986-87, pres. 1987-89), Tidewater Cancer Network (assoc. 1986), Nat. Hospice Orgn. (profl.), Va. Assn. for Hospice Orgn. (assoc.), Jr. League of Norfolk-Va. Beach (hon., sustainer, past pres., 1st Outstanding Sustainer award 1981), Assn. for Jr. Leagues Internat. (Disting. Vol. Centennial Cookbook profile 1996), Assn. for Fund Raising Profl. (Hampton Roads bd. 2005-06), Hampton Rds. C. of C. (co-chmn. bus. dist. forum 2006), CVA peer assessment, 2001-. Episcopalian. Avocations: reading, walking, gardening, cooking, painting. Personal E-mail: emilyfiler@yahoo.com.

FILER, NALENE TAI, literature and language educator; b. New Kensington, Pa., Jan. 14, 1978; d. Gilbert James and Ruth Elizabeth Filer. BA, Grove City Coll., Pa., 2000; MEd, U. Va., Charlottesville, 2003. Cert. instr. I in English and comm. Pa. English tchr., drama dir. William Monroe HS, Stanardsville, Va., 2000—04; English tchr. Hatboro-Horsham HS, Pa., 2004—. Forensics team coach William Monroe HS, 2000—04. Keyboardist, praise team Calvary Ch., Sauderton, Pa., 2004—, mem. Katrina relief team, 2005; pianist, praise team Maple Grove Christian Ch., Charlottesville, 2001—04. Republican. Avocations: volleyball, travel. E-mail: nfiler@hatboro-horsham.org.

FILEWICZ-COCHRAN, RENATTA T., parliamentarian; b. Chgo., Ill. d. Frank and Frances Angeline Filewicz; children: Renatta C. Holt, Krista Cochran Zimny. BS, Fla. So. U., Lakeland. Profl. registration Nat. Assn. Parliamentarians. Parliamentarian City of Largo, Fla. Pres. Jr. League, Royalty Theatre Co. Mem.: Nat. Assn. Parliamentarians (sec.), Fla. State Assn. Parliamentarians (pres. 1973—75), Alpha Chi Omega, Delta Delta Delta.

FILI, PATRICIA KEVENA, social welfare administrator, poet, playwright; b. Portland, Oreg., Mar. 17, 1951; d. James Theodore and Elizabeth Frances Feely. BA in English, Portland State U., 1981; MA in Comm., U. Portland, 1986; MDiv, Pacific Sch. Religion, 1992. Tng. and quality mgr. Share Svcs. for Non-Profits, San Francisco, 1997—99; dir. devel. and comm. AIDS Project East Bay, Oakland, Calif., 2000—; exec. dir. Lighthouse Cmty. Ctr., Hayward, Calif., 2006—. Cmty. co-chair HIV Prevention Planning Coun. Alameda County, Calif., 2000—03. Contbr. book; actor: (ritual theater) Oracles of the Living Tarot; playwright: plays Thread; prodr.: (performance event) Gender Art; author: (poetry) Inspiration; dir.: Thread for Magical Acts Ritual Theatre Play/Rites Festival. Adv. bd. mem. Nat. Ctr. for Transgender Equality, Washington, 2005; diversity del. Green Party of the U.S., 2006; host com. co-chair for creating change conf. Nat. Gay and Lesbian Task Force, Washington, 2005—05; mem. roundtable City of Oakland, Calif., 2003; steering com. mem. Out in Oakland, 2004; nat. religious leadership roundtable Nat. Gay and Lesbian Task Force, Washington, 2006. Sgt. USAF, 1970—73. Recipient Cmty. Ptnr. award, Transgender Law Ctr., 2005. Green Party. Wicca. Achievements include facilitated non-discrimination legislative protections in the areas of gender identity and expression in Oakland and Alameda County in Northern California. Avocations: activism, writing, performing, spiritual practice, music. Home: 1461 Alice St #311 Oakland CA 94612 Office: Lighthouse Community Center 1217 A St Hayward CA 94543 Office Phone: 510-881-8167. Personal E-mail: pkcelticwitch@yahoo.com.

FILI-KRUSHEL, PATRICIA, media company executive; b. Nov. 12, 1953; BA, St. John's U., Jamaica, NY, 1975; MBA, Fordham U., Bronx, NY, 1982. Various positions including prog. contr. ABC Sports ABC, 1975—79; dir. sports adminstrn. HBO, 1979—80, dir. sports and spls. prog. budgeting, 1980—81, dir. of prodn., 1981—83, v.p. bus. affairs, 1984—88; sr. v.p. programming & prodn. Lifetime TV, 1988—89; grp. v.p. Hearts/ABC-Viacom Entertainment Svcs., 1990—93; pres. of ABC Daytime Walt Disney Co., 1993—98, pres., ABC TV, 1998-2000; pres., CEO Web MD Health, 2000—01; exec. v.p., adminstrn. AOL Time Warner Inc. (now Time Warner Inc.), 2001—. Bd. dirs. Oxygen Media, Inc. Co-chair child care initiative Mayor Bloomberg's Commn. on Women's Issues; trustee Pub. Theatre; bd. dirs. Ctrl. Pk. Conservancy; bd. comm., trustee Fordham U. Named Woman of Yr., Police Athletic League; named one of 50 Most Powerful Women, Fortune mag., 1998; recipient Muse award, Women in Film, 1993, Vision award, 1996, Women of Achievement award, Women's Project and Prodns., 1999, Matrix award, NY Women in Comm., Inc., Crystal Apple award, City of NY. Mem.: Acad. TV Arts and Scis. (exec. com., bd. govs.), NY Women in Film (past pres.). Office: Time Warner Inc One Time Warner Ctr Rm 12-235 New York NY 10019-8016

FILIPPELLI MARANDOLA, LINDA PATRICIA, school psychologist; d. Louis and Virginia Rose (Giannamore) Filippelli; m. Thomas Domenic Marandola, III, Apr. 17, 1988; children: Marissa Lindsay Marandola, Julianna Rose Marandola. BA summa cum laude, Providence Coll., 1984; MA, R.I.

Coll., 1986, CAGS, 1987. Cert. nat. cert. sch. psychologist 1991, lic. ednl. psychologist Mass., 1988, cert. sch. psychologist R.I., 1987, Mass., 1987. Sch. psychologist Dighton-Rehoboth Sch. Sys., Dighton, Mass., 1987—88; early childhood sch. psychologist North Attleboro Sch. Sys., North Attleboro, Mass., 1988—91; sch. psychologist Johnston Pub. Schs., Johnston, RI, 1991—. Adj. prof. in ednl. psychology R.I. Coll., Providence, 1986—99. Mem.: Mass. Assn. Sch. Psychologists, RI Assn. Sch. Psychologists, Nat. Assn. Sch. Psychologists. Avocations: reading, sewing, crafts.

FILKINS, SUSAN ESTHER, small business owner; b. McCloud, Calif., Dec. 21, 1958; d. Donald Gene Ragan and Sandra Esther (Lange) Heron; m. Timothy John Filkins, Oct. 10, 1987; children: Erin Sue, Ann Lauren, Eric Timothy. Degree in Office Adminstrn., Moore's Bus. Coll., Sacramento, 1978; AS in Studio Art and Design summa cum laude, Cayuga C.C., Auburn, N.Y., 2001. Lic. real estate, broker. Adminstrv. asst. Sacramento Blood Ctr., 1979—83; convention coord. Calif. State Blood Banking Sys., Sacramento, 1982; supr. radiology Mercy Gen. Hosp., Sacramento, 1983—87; owner, pres. Rose Sparrows Agy., Skaneateles, NY, 1988—. Radiology computer software specialist Mercy Gen. Hosp., Sacramento, 1986; cons. Syracuse U. Ctr. Career Svcs., 2002—03. Photographer N.Y. State Fair Exhbn., 1996, 1997, 2002. Mem. planning bd. Village of Elbridge, 1990—91; team leader Jordan-Elbridge Site-Base Mgmt. Jordan-Elbridge Ctrl. Sch. Dist., 1993—; mem. Cayuga County Arts Coun., 2000—; alumni program coord. Syracuse U.; com. person Rep. Com., Elbridge, NY, 1998—. Mem.: Phi Theta Kappa. Baptist. Avocations: theater, writing, photography. Office: Rose Sparrows Agy PO Box 645 Skaneateles NY 13152

FILLIAT, ELIZABETH HARTLEY, retired secondary school educator; b. Albany, Ga., Oct. 8, 1942; d. Shell Elbert and Mary (Deese) Hartley; m. Ronald Wardall, June 6, 1963 (div. Jan. 15, 1971); 1 child, Thomas Ronald Wardall (dec.); m. Roland Paul Filliat, July 7, 1979; 1 child, Annette Elizabeth. BA, The City Coll., CUNY, 1970; MEd, Ga. State U., 1973. Cert. tchg. in reading specialist T-5 Ga. Dept. Edn., 2005, leadership in instrnl. supervision - reading L-5 Ga. Dept. Edn., 2005, svc. in data collector S-5 Ga. Dept. Edn., 2005. Jr. HS tchr. English Lowndes County Sch. Sys., Valdosta, Ga., 1970—71; HS tchr. English DeKalb County Sch. Sys., Decatur, Ga., 1971—73, reading specialist - elem. sch., 1973—78, instrnl. lead tchr., 1978—84, HS reading tchr. and reading dept. chair, 1984—2000; ongoing substitute tchr. Fulton County Sch. Sys., Atlanta, 2001—. Secondary reading adv. com. mem. Ga. Dept. Edn., Atlanta, 1987. Mem. northside adv. com. Atlanta Jour. Constn., 2004—05; mem. writer's group North Fulton Dem. Party, Atlanta, 2004—05. Nominee Honor Tchr. award, Atlanta Jour. Constn., 1998; recipient Tchr. of Quarter, Ga. Power Co., DeKalb County's So. Dist., 1986, Citizenship award, Kiwanis Club South DeKalb County, 1989, Cert. of Merit, W.D. Clowdis chpt. Nat. Beta Club, 1994, Wal-Mart Tchr. of Yr., Wal-Mart Found., 1998. Mem.: NEA (life), Ga. Assn. Reading, Orgn. Dekalb Educators (life), Ga. PTA (life), Ga. Assn. Educators (life), Kappa Delta, Alpha Psi Omega. Democrat. Episcopalian. Avocations: writing, reading, travel, theater. Home: 580 S Riversong Lane Alpharetta GA 30022-1800 Personal E-mail: efilliat@aol.com.

FILLION, MARY L., history educator; b. Dodgeville, Wis., Sept. 5, 1952; d. Gordon Walter and Carol Maxine Christiansen; m. Richard Touchton, Mar. 26, 1994; children: Carol Fillion Vollmer, Victor John. BA, U. Wis., Platteville, 1974, MS, 1986. Cert. tchr. Fla. Tachr. Union Bapt. Excel Inst., Denver, 1986—87; tchr. Marion County Pub. Schs., 1987—2006, West Port H.S., Ocala, Fla., 2002—06. Recipient Golden Apple Tchr., Found. for Pub. Edn., 2004. Mem.: NEA. Office: West Port HS 3733 SW 80th Ave Ocala FL

FILLMAN, MICHELE RENEE, nurse; b. Pottstown, Pa., Mar. 26, 1963; d. Bruce Rodney Mauger and Barbara Gertrude (Sassani) McKim; m. Dennis Craig Fillman, Sept. 30, 1989; children: Seth Michael, Zachary Paul, Abigail Renee. Diploma, The Reading Hosp. Sch. Nursing, 1987; student, Kutztown U., 1990—. RN Pa. Staff nurse The Reading Hosp. & Med. Ctr., Pa., 1987-88, 2000—04, Vis. Nurse Assn. Pottstown and Vicinity, Pa., 1988-92, asst. nursing supr. home health, 1992—96, staff nurse, 1996—2000, per diem nurse, 2004—; staff nurse performance improvement dept. Home Health Care Mgmt., Pa., 2005—. Tchr. Sunday sch. Hopewell Mennonite Ch., Pottstown, 1989—. Recipient George W. Kehl Fund award, Reading Hosp. Sch. Nursing, 1987, James W. Rentschler and Laura A. Rentschler Fund award, 1987. Mem. Alumni Assn. Reading Hosp. Sch. Nursing, Phi Kappa Phi. Republican. Avocations: photography, travel. Office: The Vis Nurse Assn Pottstown and Vicinity 1610 Med Dr Pottstown PA 19464 Home: 329 Fancy Hill Rd Boyertown PA 19512-8153

FILSHIE, MICHELE ANN, editor; b. Hartford, Conn., Mar. 5, 1964; d. Joseph James Fitzgibbons and Judith Ann (Bennett) Small; m. Glenn Filshie, May 24, 1986 (div. 1997). BA in English, U. Western Ont., London, 1986. Asst. to the pub. Black Sparrow Press, Santa Rosa, Calif., 1991—2002. Pres., bd. dirs. Sonoma County People for Econ. Opportunity, Santa Rosa, Calif., 1999-2001; candidate West Sonoma County Union H.S. Dist. Sch. Bd., 1998, elected trustee, 2000. Recipient Write Women Back into History award Nat. Women's History Project, Windsor, Calif., 1995. Mem. NOW (pres. Sonoma County chpt. 1994-96), Nat. Women's Polit. Caucus, Sebastopol C. of C., Rotary Club of Sebastopol Sunrise (past dir.). Democrat. Avocation: dance. Home: 8020 Hill Dr Sebastopol CA 95472-2733

FINAN, JANE, zoologist, educator; d. Ernest and June Finan; children: Elizabeth Bechinski, Amanda Bechinski. BS in Zoology, U. R.I., Kingston, 1977; MS in Zoology, Iowa State U., Ames, 1981. Asst. prof. Coll. So. Idaho, Twin Falls, 1982—86; adj. instr. SUNY, Cortland, 1987, Tompkins Cortland C.C., Dryden, NY, 1988—89; instr. Lewis-Clark State Coll., Lewiston, Idaho, 1990—. Leader Girls Scouts Am., Moscow, Idaho, 1992—94; pres. Moscow Day Sch., 1990—92; coach Odyssey of the Minds, Moscow, 1994—96. Recipient Excellence in Tchg. by Adj. Instr. award, Lewis-Clark State Coll., 1997, President's award for Outstanding Tchg., 2001, Excellence in Tchg. award, Naval ROTC, 1999. Mem.: Sigma Xi. Office: Lewis-Clark State College 500 8th Ave Lewiston ID 83501 Office Phone: 208-792-2407.

FINAURI, GRACIELA MARIA, foreign service official; b. Buenos Aires, June 18, 1956; d. Gerardo and Norma Mercedes (Burich) F. Student in law, Cath. U. Buenos Aires, 1985. Adminstr. protocol dept. Ministry of Fgn. Affairs, Buenos Aires, 1979-85, pvt. sec. min., 1985-87; pvt. sec. amb. Embassy of Argentina, Rome, 1987-91; pvt. sec. min. Ministry of Internal Affairs, Buenos Aires, 1993-95; chief of protocol Senate of Argentina, Buenos Aires, 1995-98; pvt. sec. to v.p. Argentine Republic, Buenos Aires, 1995-98; attaché Mission of Argentina to UN, N.Y.C., 1998—2003; consular agt. Consulate Gen. and Promotion Ctr. Argentine Republic in N.Y., N.Y.C., 2003—05; asst. exec. sec. Am. Min. Fgn. Affairs, Argentina, 2005, min. fgn. affairs, under sec. fgn. policy, 2006—. Named Cavalier of Hon. and Merit, Haiti Republic, 1983, Officer of Order of Merit, Italian Republic, 1985; recipient Insignia award, Mex. Order of Aztec Eagle, 1984. Roman Catholic. Office Phone: 5411 4819 7452. Business E-Mail: gmf@mrecic.gov.ar.

FINBERG, MELINDA C., theater educator; b. Phila., Mar. 6, 1956; d. Raymond H. and Doris W. Finberg; m. Raymond D. Agran, June 8, 1986; children: Alexander Everett Agran, Meredith Bronwyn Agran. BA in Brit. Lang. and Lit. cum laude, Yale U., New Haven, Conn., 1978; MA in English, Princeton U., N.J., 1986, PhD in English, 2001. Editor, N.Y.C., 1980—84; tchr., lectr. Princeton U., NJ, 1986—91; writer and editor Newtown, Pa., 1993—; exec. dir., instr. Shakespeare without Fear, Newtown, Pa., 2003—; dramaturg Newtown, Pa., 2003—; guest dramaturg Oreg. Shakespeare Festival, Ashland, 2005. Editor: (anthology) Eighteenth-Century Women Dramatists (Oxford University Press); author: (multimedia educational pilot) The Shakespeare Project; dramaturg (play) The Belle's Stratagem (Elliot Hayes Award in Dramaturgy from the Lit. Managers and Dramaturgs of the Americas (LMDA), 2006). Facilitator Shir Ami/Newtown Presbyn. Interfaith Discussion Group, Newtown, Pa., 2004—06; mem. Yale Alumni Schs. Com., Phila., 2002—06. Scholarship, Nat. Merit Scholarship Bd., 1978, fellowship, Princeton U., 1984 -1988, Assn. of Princeton Grad. Alumni, 1988, Rsch. grant, Princeton U. Women's Studies' Program, 1988. Mem.: MLA, Soc. of Children's Book Writers and Illustrators, Assn. for Theater in Higher Edn., Am. Soc. for Eighteenth-Century Studies, Lit. Mgrs. and Dramaturgs of the Americas. Home: 27 Amaryllis Ln Newtown PA 18940 Personal E-mail: wordsmith78@verizon.net.

FINCH, ALBERTA MAY, retired pediatrician; b. Port Jervis, N.Y., Jan. 27, 1926; d. Herbert LeRoy Finch and Bertha May Funzell; m. Otto Roy Weber, July 12, 1952; children: Lawrence, Charles, Kathy, Phillip, Jeffrey. BS, Pa. State U., 1946; MD, Temple U., 1950. Diplomate Am. Bd. Family Practice. Pvt. practice pediatrics, Linglestown, Pa., 1952—62; pvt. practice family medicine Stroudsburg, Pa., 1962—85; pediatrician United Meth. Ch., Zaire, 1985—90, Pocono Med. Ctr., East Stroudsburg, Pa., 1993—99; sch. physician East Stroudsburg U., 1990—93; ret., 1999. Mem. exec. bd. Pocono Med. Ctr., East Stroudsburg U., 1971—75. Sec./treas. Torch, 1990—; mem. Health Cmty. Alliance; bd. dirs. Children and Youth Svcs. Monroe County, Stroudsburg, 1971—77, 1980—86, 1996—2002; bd. dirs., treas., v.p., pres. Monroe County Planned Parenthood, Stroudsburg, 1965—74; child health physician Monroe County, 1962—85, 1991—92; mem. com. United Way of Monroe County, Tannersville, Pa., 1989—94; mem. PMC Cmty. Health Assessment Steering Com., East Stroudsburg, 1993—98, Health Cmtys. Alliance, Stroudsburg, 1992—, pres., 1995—96, 1998—, Ch. Women United, 2000—03; Sunday sch. tchr. Stroudsburg United Meth. Ch., 1963—70, 1972—85, 2002—; mem. Stroudsburg Coun. Chs., 1992—, pres., 2000—02; bd. dirs. Home Health Svcs. Monroe County, East Stroudsburg, 1971—78, Cmty. Coalition for Improvement of Maternal and Chila Health, East Stroudsburg, 1982—98. Named Lady of Yr., Beta Sigma Phi, Stroudsburg, 1978, Alberta Finch Children's Endowment Fund in her honor, 1997, Paul Harris fellow, Rotary Found., 1999, Humanitarian of Yr., Pocono Mountains C. of C., 2000, Woman of Distinction, East Stroudsburg U., 2001; recipient Mission Recognition award, Stroudsburg United Meth. Ch., 1986, Liberty Bell award, Monroe County Law Assn., 1983, Health Promotion award, Monroe County C. of C., 1983, Svc. Above Self award, Rotary, 1999, Gold medal, Pocono Med. Ctr., 1999, Eugenia S. Eden award, Pocono Svcs. Family and Children, 2005. Mem.: DAR, Torch (pres. 1995—96, sec./treas. 1998—), Quiet Valley Hist. Assn. (bd. dirs. 1992—98). Republican. Avocations: camping, travel, medical antiques, doll collecting, dollhouses. Home: RD # 5 Box 5106 Stroudsburg PA 18360 E-mail: 20web@epix.net.

FINCH, EVELYN VORISE, financial planner; b. Marietta, Ohio, Jan. 20, 1930; d. Richard Raymon Juantzee and Oreatha Fay (Carnes) Metcalf; m. Herman Frederick Ahrens, May 13, 1948 (dec. Apr. 2006); children: Erick K.F. Ahrens, Hilda Kate Ahrens(dec.), Nicole Schwartz; m. James Derwood Finch, June 29, 1973 (dec. Oct. 1993). BS in Music Edn., Concord U., Athens, W.Va., 1961; postgrad., U. Md., Coll. Park, Am. U., Wash., Northeastern U., Boston, 1990. Registered Health Underwriter, Boston. Music tchr. Prince George's County Pub. Schs., 1961—72; pvt. piano tchr. Washington, 1961—73; sales rep. china and crystal Quality Products Co., Washington, 1973—80; ins. agt. Mut. of Omaha Cos., Washington, 1980—92, Memphis, 1992—94; pvt. practice Alamo, Tenn., 1994—; tax specialist H&R Block Inc., Jackson, Tenn., 2002—06. Ind. assoc. Pre-Paid Legal Svcs., Inc., 2000—. Supporting mem. Nat. Mus. Women in Arts, Washington, 1990—, Women's Philharm., San Francisco, 1993—. Mem.: LWV (Memphis br.), AAUW (br. pres. 1994—96, Tenn. chmn. ednl. found. 1996—98, mem. Nat. Diversity Resource Team 1997—2000), Internat. Assn. Fin. Planners, Nat. Assn. Health Underwriters (registered health underwriter), Nat. Assn. Ret. Fed. Employees, Chesapeake Bay Yacht Clubs Assn. (commodore 1982), Prince George's Yacht Club (commodore 1978), Potomas River Yacht Clubs Assn. (legis. chair 1978-87), Nat. Boating Fedn. (pres. 1985—87), Kappa Delta Pi, Pi Mu. Home and Office: 208 Finch Rd Alamo TN 38001-5923 Office Phone: 731-656-2002. Personal E-mail: evelynfinch@msn.com.

FINCH, JULIA LAURA, counselor; b. Lubbock, Tex., Oct. 14, 1974; d. Jill Lynette Blackstock; m. Bruce Finch, Oct. 14, 2005; 1 child, Braylen Lee. BS, Tex. Tech. U., Lubbock, 1999, MEd in Counseling with honors, 2005. Lic. profl. counselor intern Tex.; nat. cert. counselor. Caseworker and investigator Child Protective Svcs., Lubbock, Tex., 2000—04; counselor South Plains Coll., 2004—06, Lubbock County Ct. Residential Treatment, 2006—. Mem. Spl. Svcs. Adv. Bd., Lubbock, Tex., 2004—06, Lubbock Housing Authority, 2004—06. Mem.: West Tex. Counseling Assn., Am. Counseling Soc., Phi Kappa Phi, Chi Sigma Iota (v.p. 1999—2006).

FINCH, SHEILA, writer; b. London, 1935; 3 children. Postgrad., Ind. U. Faculty creative writing El Camino Coll., Torrance, Calif. Author: (novels) Infinity's Web, 1985, Triad, 1986, The Garden of the Shaped, 1987, Shaper's Legacy, 1988, Shaping the Dawn, 1989, Tiger in the Sky, 1999, Reading the Bones, 2003, Birds, 2004, (short fiction including) The Confession of Melakos, 1977, The Man Who Lived On The Queen Mary, 1983, Babel Interface, 1988, Rembrandts of Things Past, 1989, Firstborn Seaborn, 1995, The Falcon and the Falconer, 1997, Nor Unbuild the Cage, 2000, Forkpoints, 2002, Reach, 2003, Confessional, 2004. Winner 1998 Nebula award for short fiction: Reading the Bones. Avocations: travel, tai chi, hiking, 4-wheeling in the desert. Office: c/o Avon Books Harper Collins 10 E 53rd St New York NY 10022-5244

FINCHER, MARGARET ANN, librarian, educator; b. Harrodsburg, Ky., June 2, 1934; d. Henry Alexander and Minnie Bee (White) Cathey; m. Willie John Fincher, Jr., Apr. 1, 1955; children: John Richard, Joseph Michael, Judy Darlene, James Andrew. BS in Bus. Edn., Auburn U., 1955; MEd, U. New Orleans, 1978. Bookkeeper, Markle's Drug Store, Auburn, Ala., 1952-54; asst. to dir. Auburn U. Library, 1955; elem. tchr., Birmingham, Ala., 1958-64; bus. edn. tchr. Abramson HS, New Orleans, 1964-01; ret., 2001; owner, mgr. craft shop Fanci Krafts, New Orleans, 1977-78; asst. supr. Shaklee Corp., 1979-85; libr., media ctr. dept. chmn. Abramson Sr. High Sch. Orleans Parish Sch. Bd., 1984-99, libr. media cons. Faith Christian Acad., 2004—. Supr. adult Bible tng. dept. Word of Faith Temple, 1982-94, cons. library devel., 1982, tchr., 1975-80, deaconess, 1983—; bd. dirs. Lamb Day Care Center, 1979-81; sustaining mem. Meth. Hosp. Aux., 1967—; adv./sponsor Christian Life on Campus Club. Recipient Am. Legion citation of appreciation, 1981; Future Bus. Leaders Am., award of Appreciation, 1976. Mem. ALA, Donna Villa Improvement Assn., Metro. Ednl. Media Orgn., Ch. and Synagogue Library Assn., So. Bus. Edn. Assn., Nat. Bus. Edn. Assn., La. Assn. Bus. Edn., La. Library Assn., La. Vocat. Assn., United Tchrs. New Orleans, Policemen's Assn. New Orleans (hon.), Tamaron Homeowners Assn. (treas. 1992—), Abramson Libr. Media Club (sponsor 1986-01), Phi Delta Kappa. Republican. Mem. Christian Ch. Home: 211 Lake Sabine Ct Slidell LA 70461

FINCHER, NORMA BEEBY, music educator, elementary school educator; b. Phila., Aug. 12, 1954; d. Robert Thomas and Mary Adams Beeby; children: Mark Wesley, David George. Attended, Fla. Bible Coll., 1972—74, Luther Rice Seminary, 2002—06. Asst. Florence Coun. Aging, SC, 1974—75; tchr. kindergarten Florence Christian Sch., 1975—81, Mid-Way Bapt. Ch., Raleigh, NC, 1988—89, ch. pianist & organist, 1988—2000; elem. & string tchr. Wake Christian Acad., Raleigh, 1989—. Ch. pianist Pleasant Grove Bapt. Ch., Fuquay Varina, NC, 2002—05; founder, dir. string program Wake Christian Acad. Named Tchr. of Yr., Wake Christian Acad., 2004. Mem.: Music Educators Nat. Conf. Republican. Baptist. Avocations: antiques, art. Home: 8508 Crowder Rd Raleigh NC 27603 Office: Wake Christian Acad 5500 Academy Lane Raleigh NC 27603 E-mail: normafincher@yahoo.com.

FINCHER, RUTH MARIE EDLA, medical educator, dean; b. Hartford, Conn., Dec. 16, 1949; d. Wilber Roe and Hannah Camilla (Andersen) Griswold; m. Michael Edward Fincher, June 26, 1977. BA, Colby Coll., 1972; BMS, Dartmouth U., 1974; MD, Emory U., 1976. Diplomate Am. Bd. Internal Medicine. Intern then resident internal medicine Emory Hosps., Atlanta, 1976-79; practicing internist Pub. Health Svc., Ludowici, Ga., 1979-81; pvt. practice internal medicine Hinesville, Ga., 1981-82; staff physician Am. Lake VA Med. Ctr., Tacoma, Wash., 1982-84; asst. prof. medicine Med. Coll. Ga., Augusta, 1984-89, assoc. prof., 1989-94, prof. medicine, 1994—, vice dean acad. affairs, 1994—. Pres. Clerkship Dirs. in Internal Medicine, Washington, 1992—93; com. chair Nat. Bd. Med. Examiners, Phila., 1995—96, bd. mem., 2005—; co-chair rsch. in med. edn. com. Assn. Am. Med. Colls., Washington, 1995—96, chair group on ednl. affairs, 1996—97. Co-editor: Clinical Medicine 2nd Edit., 1995; contbr. articles to profl. jours.; editl. bd. Am. Jour. Medicine, Birmingham, Ala., 1994-98, Jour. Gen. Internal Medicine, 1998—. Bd. mem. Nat. Bd. Medical Examiners at Large, 2005—. Named award in her honor. Fellow: ACP (gov. Ga. chpt. 2003—, bd. dirs. ACP Found., J. Willis Hurst Tchg. award 1994, Disting. Tchg. award 1996); mem.: Assn. Am. Med. Colls. (Ednl. Affiars Career scholarship So. Group 2006), Alpha Omega Alpha (bd. dirs. 2003—, Robert J. Glaser Disting. Tchg. award 1996, Daniel S. Tostesen award for leadership in med. edn. 2003, Inaugural inductee U. Sys. Ga. Hall of Fame 2004). Avocations: woodworking, gardening, running. Office: Med Coll Ga CB 1843 1457 Laney Walker Blvd Augusta GA 30912 Office Phone: 706-721-3529. Business E-Mail: rfincher@mail.mcg.edu.

FINCHUM, SHERRY SORRELLS, school system administrator; d. George Fred Sorrells and Freddie Loretta Ingle; m. William Mark Finchum, May 7, 1993; children: Brent Emory McAfee, Eric Dayton McAfee, Katie Ingle McAfee. BS in Vocat. Home Econ., Carson Newman Coll., Jefferson City, Tenn., 1980; MS, U. Tenn., Knoxville, 2002. Cert. tchr. kindergarten Carson Newman Coll., 1980, tchr. elem. East Tenn. State U., 1980, career ladder I Tenn. Dept. Edn. Tchr. kindergarten DeBusk Elem. Sch. Greene County Schs., Tenn., 1980—81; ednl. asst. grade 1 East View Elem. Sch. Greenville City Schs., 1985—86; tchr. vocat. home econ. West Greene HS Greene County Schs., 1986—87; tchr. kindergarten DeBusk Elem. Sch. Greene County Schs., 1987; tchr. lang. arts and sci. grade 2 Tusculum View Elem. Sch. Greeneville City Schs., 1992—93, tchr. kindergarten, 1993—94, Jefferson County Schs., Dandridge, 1994—2003, dir. curriculum and accountability, 2003—. Mem. choir New Market Bapt. Ch., Tenn., chmn. pers. com., 2003—. Named Jefferson County Tchr. of Yr. K-4, Jefferson County Schs., 2001. Mem.: NEA, Jefferson County Kindergarten Tchrs. (chairperson 1994—2002), Nat. Assn. Elem. Sch. Prins., Tenn. Assn. Elem. and Mid. Sch. Prins., Tenn. Coun. Social Studies, Tenn. Edn. Assn., Jefferson County Edn. Assn., Knoxville Area Assn. Edn. Young Children, Tenn. Assn. Edn. Young Children, Nat. Assn. Edn. Young Children (assoc.), Jefferson County Historical Soc., Phi Kappa Phi. Home: 1291 Ashwood Dr Jefferson City TN 37760-5350 Office: Jefferson County Schools PO Box 190 Dandridge TN 37725 Office Phone: 865-397-3194. Office Fax: 865-397-3301. Business E-Mail: finchums@k12tn.net.

FINDER, JOAN BORNHOLDT, academic administrator; b. St. Louis, Feb. 19, 1954; d. Michael and Charlotte E. (Barisic) Bornholdt; m. Kevin Gerard Finder, Oct. 6, 1984; children: Elizabeth Mara, Julia Katherine. BA in Theatre summa cum laude, Fontbonne Coll., 1976; MA in Media Communication, Webster U., 1987. Cert. secondary speech tchr., drama tchr., English tchr., Mo. Drama and English tchr. Valle High Sch., Ste. Genevieve, Mo., 1976-79; asst. dir. admission Fontbonne Coll., St. Louis, 1979-83; assoc. dir. Webster U., St. Louis, 1983—. Presenter at internat. convs.; freelance theatre dir., St. Louis, 1976-85. Vol. theatrical cons. Borgia High Sch., Washington, Mo., 1990—; producer, dir. The Company Theatre, St. Louis, 1978-86; chairperson liturgy commn. Seven Holy Founders Ch., 1993—, commr. parish coun., 1993—, sch. bd. officer, 2001-04 Mem. Mo. Assn. Coll. Admission Counselors bd. dirs. 2001—), Mo. Assn. Collegiate Registrars and Admission Counselors, Mo. Assn. Cmty. and Jr. Colls. Roman Catholic. Avocations: theater, singing, ballooning. Home: 7213 General Sherman Ln Saint Louis MO 63123-2317 Office: Webster U 470 E Lockwood Ave Saint Louis MO 63119-3194

FINDLEY, KATHRYN E.C., psychologist; b. Detroit, Feb. 23, 1944; d. Oliver Clare Garwood and Elsie Madeline Everson-Garwood; m. J. D. Findley, Apr. 7, 1989; children: Raymond, Regina, Jaccata, Jason; m. Ralph Edward Cadger (div.); children: Steven Cadger, Karen Cadger, Rhonda Dauryn Cadger Soltysiak. Diploma, Harper Hosp. Sch. Nursing, 1965; BA in Health Edn., Ottawa U., 1990; MA in Psychology, Forest Inst. Profl. Psychology, 2001, PsyD, 2003. RN. Owner, operator Sweetwater Ranch & Retreat, Edwards, Mo., 1986—; owner, pres. Sweetwater Therapeutics, Inc., 1986—; nurse mgr. Royal Oaks Hosp., Windsor, 1988—95; mental health nurse adminstr. Soleas Home Care, 1995—2002; staff nurse Lakeland Regional Hosp., Springfield, 2001—02; intern/resident Pointe Terre Wellness Ctr., Bolivar, 2002—04. Bd. dirs. Alternative Health Sys., Inc., Clinton, Mo., sec., 1997—; presenter in field; adj. prof. Forrest Inst., Springfield, Mont., 2004—. Author: Whole in One, 1995. Foster parent, 1992—97; amb. Warsaw C. of C., Warsaw, Mo., 1996—2001; commr. Warsaw City Airport Commn., 1999—2002; bd. dirs. Redlands YMCA, 1982—85; costume designer The Great Y Chorus, 1981—85. Mem.: APA (sec. divsn. 55 2004—), Mo. Psychol. Assn. Avocations: farming, gardening, sewing. Home and Office: 33292 Knabby Creek Ln Edwards MO 65326 E-mail: drkathrynf@yahoo.com.

FINDLEY, MILLA JEAN, nutritionist; b. Dallas, Aug. 14, 1934; d. Houston Henry and Juanita Imogene (Lisenbe) Shaw; m. Jack Stacy, may 29, 1952; children: Jere, David. Diploma, Rutherford Bus. Sch., Dallas, 1959; student, Mountain View C.C., 1978, El Centro C.C., 1976, Cedar Valley C.C., 1985. Tchrs. Aid diploma Stratford Career Inst., D.C., 2002, Early Childhood Edn. diploma Stratford Career Inst., D.C., 2002. File clk. Texaco Oil Co., Dallas, 1952-53; sales assoc. Toys R Us and Sears, Dallas, 1970s; nutrition specialist Cedar Hill Ind. Sch. Dist., Tex., 1983-87, Duncanville Ind. Sch. Dist., Tex., 1996—. Active cradle roll Cedar Hill Ch. of Christ, 1996. Recipient nutrition award Tex. Sch. Food Svcs. Assocs., Lewisville Ind. Sch. Dist., 1987. Mem. NAFE, Assn. Tex. Profl. Educators. Avocations: foods, church, parks, books. Home: 510 Meadow Ridge Dr Cedar Hill TX 75104-1977

FINE, ANNE, writer; b. Leicester, Eng., Dec. 7, 1947; d. Brian and Eileen Mary (Baker) Laker; m. Kit Fine, Aug. 3, 1968 (div. 1991); children: Ione, Cordelia. BA with honors, U. Warwick, Eng., 1968. Tchr. Cardinal Wiseman Secondary Sch., Coventry, U.K., 1968-69; info. officer Oxfam, Oxford, England, 1969-71; tchr. Saughton Prison, Edinburgh, Scotland, 1971-72. Author: (children's fiction) The Summer-House Loon, 1978, The Other Darker Ned, 1979, The Stone Menagerie, 1980, Round Behind the Ice House, 1981, The Granny Project, 1983, Scaredy-Cat, 1984, Anneli the Art Hater, 1986, Madame Doubtfire, 1987, Crummy Mummy an Me, 1987, A Pack of Liars, 1988, Goggle-Eyes, 1989, Bill's New Frock, 1989, The Book of the Banshee, 1991, Flour Babies, 1992, Step By Wicked Step, 1995, The Tulip Touch, 1996, Charm School, 1999, Bad Dreams, 2000, Up on Cloud Nine, 2002, Stories of Jamie and Angus, 2002, The True Story of Christmas, 2003, Frozen Billy, 2004, The Road of Bones, 2006, others; (adult fiction) The Killjoy, 1986, Taking the Devil's Advice, 1990, In Cold Domain, 1994, Telling Liddy, 1998, All Bones and Lies, 2001, Raking the Ashes, 2005. Decorated Order Brit. Empire; named Children's Author of Yr., Brit. Book Awards, 1990, 1993, U.K. nominee for Hans Christian Andersen Author award, 1998, Children's Laureate, 2001—03; recipient Children's Lit. award, The Guardian, 1990, Carnegie medal, Brit. Libr. Assn., 1990, 1993, Whitbread Children's Novel award, 1993, 1996, Horn Book award, Boston Globe, 2003; fellow, Royal Soc. Lit., 2003. Avocations: reading, walking. Office: David Higham Assocs 5-8 Lower John St Golden Sq London W1R 4HA England

FINE, DEBORAH, Internet company executive, former apparel executive; V.p., advt. dir. Family Cir. Mag., 1991—93; v.p., assoc. pub. Mary Emmerling's Country, 1993—94; advt. dir. Glamour mag., 1994—95, assoc. pub., 1995—96, v.p., pub., 1999—2001; pub. Bride's Mag., 1996—99; pres. Teen Bus. Avon Products, Inc., 2001—05; CEO, Victoria Secret, Pink Brand Limited Brands, Inc., 2005—06; CEO, iVillage, Inc. NBC Universal, NYC, 2006—. Office: iVillage Inc 500 7th Ave 14th Ave New York NY 10018*

FINE, JANE MADELINE, visual artist; b. N.Y.C., Sept. 25, 1958; d. Arnold and Cecile (Glassen) F. BA, Harvard U., 1980; MA, Tufts U., 1982; postgrad., Skowhegan Sch. Painting, 1989. One-woman show Casey M. Kaplan, N.Y., 1995; exhibited in group shows at Bard Coll., 1991, Marymount Coll., 1990,

PS 122 Gallery, 1989, The Drawing Ctr., 1988, Soho Ctr. for Visual Artists, 1988, White Columns, N.Y., 1992, Jack Tilton Gallery, N.Y., 1993, Leo Tony Gallery, N.H., 1994, Art in Gen., N.Y., 1994, Petzel/Borgmann Gallery, N.Y., 1994, Marymount Manhattan Coll., 1995, Arena, Bklyn., 1995, E.S. Vandam, N.Y., 1995, PPOW Gallery, New York, 1999, 2000, Hunterdon Mus Art, Clinton, NJ, 2000. Fellow Millay Colony for the Arts, 1990, Yaddo, 1990, NEA, 1989, Visual Artists fellow N.Y. Found. for the Arts, 1994.

FINE, MARJORIE LYNN, lawyer; b. Bklyn., Aug. 14, 1950; m. John Kent Markley, May 6, 1979; children: Jessica Paige Markley, Laura Anne Markley. BA, Smith Coll., 1972; JD, U. Calif., 1977. Bar: Calif. 1977. Assoc. to ptnr. Donahue Gallagher Woods, Oakland, Calif., 1977-87; sr. counsel Bank of Am., San Francisco, 1987-89; assoc., gen. counsel Shaklee Corp., San Francisco, 1989-90; gen. counsel, v.p. Shaklee U.S., Inc., San Francisco, 1990-94, Shaklee U.S., Shaklee Technica, 1995-99, Yamanouchi Pharma Techs., Inc., 1999-2001; gen. counsel, sr. v.p. Shaklee Corp., 2001—05, gen. counsel, exec. v.p., sec., 2005—. Judge pro tem Oakland Piedmont Emeryville Mcpl. Ct., 1982-89; fee arbitrator Alameda Co. Bar Assn., 1980-87. Mem. ABA, Calif. Bar Assn., Calif. Employment Law Coun. (bd. dirs. 1993-03, 05—). Jewish. Office: Shaklee Corp 4747 Willow Rd Pleasanton CA 94588-2740

FINE, PAMELA B., newspaper editor; Grad., U. Fla. Reporter Daytona Beach News, 1979; several editl. positions with Atlanta Journal-Constitution, 1982—94; mng. editor, v.p. Mpls. Star Tribune, 1994—2002; mng. editor The Indianapolis Star, 2003—. Nat. conf. chair Associated Press Mng. Editors Assn., 2000; juror for Pulitzer Prize. Office: The Indianapolis Star PO Box 145 Indianapolis IN 46206-0145 Office Phone: 317-444-6168. Business E-Mail: pam.fine@indystar.com.

FINE, RANA ARNOLD, chemical and physical oceanographer; d. Joseph and Etta (Kreisman) Arnold; m. Shalle Stephen Fine, June 20, 1965 (div. 1979); m. James Stewart Mattson, Jan. 5, 1983. BA, NYU, 1965; MA, U. Miami, 1973, PhD, 1975. Systems analyst Svc. Bur. Corp. subs. IBM, Miami, 1965-69; rsch. assoc. Rosenstiel Sch. U. Miami, 1976-77, rsch. asst. prof., 1977-80, rsch. assoc. prof., 1980-84, assoc. prof., 1984-90, prof. marine and atmospheric chemistry, 1990—, chair divsn. marine and atmospheric chemistry, 1990-94; assoc. program dir. NSF, Washington, 1981-83. Mem. div. polar programs adv. com. NSF, Washington, 1987-90, geophys. study com. NAS, Washington, 1989-92, ocean studies bd., 1992-98, adv. panel Tropical Ocean/Global Atmosphere Program, 1990-93, chair adv. panel major ocean programs, 1996-98; bd. trustees UCAR 2005—, Inter-Am. Inst. Global Ch. SSC, 2004— Contbr. articles to profl. jours. Vol. guide Vizcaya Mus., Miami, 1967-78, adv. panel mem. methane hydrade rev. 2003-04. Grantee NSF, 1977—, NOAA, 1986—, Office of Naval Rsch., 1983-88, NASA, 1990-97. Fellow: AAAS (chair-elect atm and hydrospheric sci. sect. 2001—04), Am. Meteorol. Soc. (coun. mem. 2001—04), Am. Geophys. Union (sec. oceanography sect. 1986—88, pres.-elect oceanography sect. 1994—96, pres. 1996—98); mem.: Oceanography Soc. Avocations: sailing, scuba diving, fishing, tennis, reading. Office: RSMAS/MAC/U Miami 4600 Rickenbacker Cswy Miami FL 33149-1031 Business E-Mail: rfine@rsmas.miami.edu.

FINE, SALLY SOLFISBURG, artist, educator; b. Aurora, Ill., July 20, 1948; d. Roy John Jr. and Edith Warrick (Squires) Solfisburg; m. Philip Clark Fine, May 5, 1973 (div. 1997); children: Alexander, Arielle. BFA, Ohio U., 1970; postgrad., Boston U., 1978-82, MFA, 1985. Graphic designer Mus. of Sci., Boston, 1970-72; teaching fellow Boston U., 1980-81; instr., lectr. U. Mass., North Dartmouth, 1993-95; sr. lectr. Bradford Coll., 1995-96, asst. prof., 1996-2000; assoc. prof. art. Regis Coll., Weston, Mass., 2000—. Prin. S.S. Fine Design, Boston, 1970—. Solo shows include Viridian Gallery, N.Y.C., Bradford Coll., Chapel Gallery; exhibited in group shows at DeCordova Mus., Lincoln, Mass., Danforth Mus. of Art., Framingham, Mass., Brockton (Mass.) Fuller Mus. Art, Brockton (Mass), Art Mus., Newport (R.I.) Art Mus., A.I.R. Gallery, N.Y.C., Cité Internationale Gallerie, Paris. Bd. dirs. Kendall Ctr. for the Arts, 1983-86. Visual Artists grantee Mass. Coun. for the Arts, 1995, Sculpture fellow New Eng., Found. for the Arts, 1995, others. Mem. AAUP, Coll. Art Assn. Avocations: swimming, gardening, biking. E-mail: sallyfine@comcast.net.

FINE, TERRI SUSAN, political science professor; b. Buffalo, N.Y., Sept. 9, 1962; d. Morris and Gloria Fine; m. Barry Wick (div.). BA, U. Albany, N.Y., 1983, MA, 1985; PhD, U. Conn., Storrs, 1989. Grad. asst. U. Albany, 1983—85; adj. lectr. U. Conn., Storrs, 1986—89; asst. prof. U. Cen. Fla., Orlando, 1989—94, assoc. prof., 1994—. Participant Summer Inst. for Israel Studies, Boston, 2006. Contbr. articles to profl. jours. Bd. dirs. Summit Charter Sch., Maitland, Fla., 1997—, Jewish Fedn., Maitland, 2005—; guardian ad litem Sanford, Fla., 2002—. Recipient several tchg. and svc. awards, Excellence in Tchg. award, U. Cen. Fla., 2006. Mem.: Fla. Polit. Sci. Assn. (pres. 2000—02), So. Polit. Sci. Assn., Am. Polit. Sci. Assn. Office: U Cen Fla 4000 Central Florida Blvd Orlando FL 32816-1356

FINE, VIRGINIA O., psychologist; b. Great Falls, Mont., Apr. 18, 1921; d. Jesse Thomas and Helen (Hanner) Owens; m. Robert D. Kemble, Oct. 29, 1944 (div. 1968); children: Stephen B. Kemble; Brian S. Kemble, David B. Kemble, Maricia J. Kemble, Janet Kemble Onopa; m. Jules Fine, July 6, 1969 (dec. 1983). BA, Okla. A & M, 1943; postgrad., Columbia U., 1945; MEd, U. Hawaii, 1964, PhD, 1975. Lic. psychologist, Hawaii. Psychologist U. Hawaii, Honolulu, 1964-74; pvt. practice Honolulu, 1974—, Kailua, Hawaii, 1994—. Cons. Family Ct., Honolulu, 1978-85, Dept. of Edn., Honolulu, 1994-95. Mem. APA, Hawaii Psychol. Assn., Assn. Humanistic Psychology, Assn. for Transpersonal Psychology, Assn. for Advancement of Psychology. Democrat. Unitarian Universalist. Avocations: bed and breakfasts, lace making. Home: 1042 Maunawili Loop Kailua HI 96734-4621 E-mail: finev001@hawaii.rr.com.

FINEBURG, AMY C., social studies educator; b. Buffalo, July 10, 1972; d. Donald Richard Cheek and Carolyn Thede Decker; m. Amy C. Cheek, June 11, 1994; 1 child, Micah S. BA, Samford U., Birmingham, Ala., 1994, MA, 2000. Tchr. psychology, English Homewood H.S., Ala., 1995—2003; chair social studies dept. Spain Pk. H.S., Hoover, 2003—. Chair Tchrs. Psychology Secondary Schs., Washington, 2004—06. Recipient Secondary Tchr. Yr., Hoover City Schs., 2005, Presdl. citation, APA, 2005; grantee, Homewood City Schs. Found., 1999, Mayerson Found., 2003, Hoover City Schs., 2004. Mem.: Ala. Edn. Assn., Am. Ednl. Rsch. Assn., Nat. Coun. Social Studies, Tchrs. Psychology Secondary Schs. (mem.-at-large, chair 2000—06), Nat. Forensic League (coach 1996—2006, Degree of Distinction 1998). Office: Spain Park High School 4700 Jaguar Drive Hoover AL 35242 Office Phone: 205-439-1400. E-mail: afineburg@hoover.k12.al.us.

FINEMAN, GERALDINE GOTTESMAN, artist; b. Phila., Mar. 8, 1920; d. Harry and Bessie Gottesman; m. Al I. Fineman, Nov. 28, 1943 (dec. Nov. 2002); children: Samuel, Lawrence. BS in Edn., N.J. State Tchrs. Coll., 1941; MEd, Temple U., 1949. Tchr. elem., Blackwood, NJ, 1941—43, Phila., 1943—45; tchr. deaf, 1960—70; watercolorist, 1970—. Vol. tchr. sign lang., Boca Raton, Fla., 2000—. Represented in permanent collections Gallaudet U., Kellogg, Battle Creek, Mich., Nat. Deaf Inst., Fla. Mem. bd. assocs. Jewish Found. for Group Homes, Rockville, Md., 1992—; aux. mem. bd. assocs. Gallaudet U., Washington, 1985—2002; vol. sec. Rogers East Condominium Assn., 1989—; established program for developmentally disabled deaf adults Rockville. Recipient Betty Lehr Meml. award, Abingdon Art Ctr., Pa., 2003, Alan R. Chiara Meml. award, Golden Artist Colors, 2005. Fellow: Artist Guild Boca Mus., Palm Beach Watercolor Soc. (honorable mention, Judge's Recognition, Orchid Show prize), Women in Visual Arts; mem.: Fla. Watercolor Soc. (signature mem. 2005, 3rd pl., honorable mention). Avocations: swimming, sewing, travel, reading. Home: 900 NE Spanish River Blvd Boca Raton FL 33431 E-mail: jerrigf@aol.com.

FINEMAN, JEANETTE KRULEVITZ, retired artist; b. Balt., Apr. 21, 1919; d. Jacob and Ruth Irene Krulevitz; m. Jerome Fineman, Jan. 4, 1947 (dec. Jan. 1978); children: David, Elliott, Mary. Accreditation in med. illustration, U. Md., 1940; BFA cum laude, Md. Inst. Coll. Art, 1970, MFA, 1972. Med. illustrator Sinai Hosp., Balt., 1940, Charleston (W.Va.) Gen. Hosp., 1941-43; head art dept. St. Timothy's Sch., Stevenson, Md., 1973-79; ret., 1979. One-woman shows include Johns Hopkins U., Balt., Villa Julie Coll., Balt., Oheb Shalom Temple, Balt., Balt. Hebrew Cong.; exhibited in group shows at Corcoran Gallery Art, Washington, Balt. Mus., Peale Mus., Balt. (prize), NY Acad. Design (prize); contbr. illustrations to profl. jours. Mem. Oakland (Calif.) Mus. Home: St Pauls Towers 100 Bay Pl Oakland CA 94610

FINESTONE, SHEILA, senator, retired legislator; b. Montreal, Que., Can., Jan. 28, 1927; d. Monroe and Minnie Abbey; m. Alan Finestone, June 9, 1947; children: David, Peter, Maxwell, Stephen. BS in Edn., McGill U. M.P. to Ho. of Commons for Mount Royal, 1984, 1988, 1993—99; critic for commn. and culture, 1985—93; Sec. of State Multiculturalism and the Status of Women, 1993—96; appt. Senate of Can., Ottawa, Ont., Canada, 1999—. Advisor to Parliament on eliminating anti-personal land mines; mem. transp. and comm., statutes and regulations; vice chair human rights; mem. spl. com. custody and access in divorce, constitution amendments edn.; past pres. La Fed. des Femmes du Quebec; mem. Quebec Referendum Organizer Les Yvettes, 1980; vice chair Amendment Equality Rights Can. Constn., 1985; min. of state Status of Women; leader Can. Delegation to Beijing World Conf. on Women's Rights, 1995; mem. exec. com. Can. Assn. Former Parliamentarians, Can. Land Mines Found., Adopt a Minefield Can. Pres. (hon.) Young Men and Young Women's Hebrew Assn.; ret. sec. Parliamentarian Assoc.; guide Canadian Mus. of Civilization; exec. World Exec. of Inter Parliamentary Union; mem. Nat. Coun. Jewish Women; hon. gov. Jewish Gen. Hosp.; mem. exec. com. Orgn. Jewish Parliament; bd. mem. Nat. Collection Fund, Mus. Civilization, 2005—. Named Person of the Yr., McGill U., 2001; recipient Jackie Robinson Leadership award, 1996, Samuel Bronfinan Leadership award, 1995, O.R.T. Sophie Benett award, 1996. Mem. Orgn. Rehab. and Tng. Liberal.

FINGERHUT, MARILYN ANN, federal agency administrator; b. Bklyn., Oct. 3, 1940; d. Robert Vincent and Marion (Carroll) F.; m. David W. Haartz, May 14, 1988; children: Margot, D. Bradley. BS in Cell Biology, Coll. of St. Elizabeth, Convent Station, N.J., 1964; PhD in Cell Biology, Cath. U. Am., 1970; MS in Occupational Health, Harvard U., Boston, 1981. Tchr. elem. schs., Jersey City, 1961-62, East Orange, N.J., 1964-65; instr. Coll. of St. Elizabeth, 1970-71; rsch. assoc. N.J. Coll. Medicine and Dentistry, Newark, 1971-72; asst. prof. to assoc. prof. St. Peter's Coll., Jersey City, 1973-80; researcher St. Joseph Med. Ctr., Paterson, N.J., 1977-80; predoctoral fellow USPHS, 1966-69, commd. capt., 1989; epidemiologist Nat. Inst. for Occupational Safety and Health, Cin., 1981-88, br. chief, 1988-94, sr. scientist office of dir. Washington, 1994-95, asst. dir. ops., 1995-96, chief staff, 1996—99; coord. occup. and environ. health WHO, Geneva, 2000—02; internat. coord. NIOSH, Washington, 2003—. Contbr. articles to sci. jours. Founding mem. Women's R&D Ctr., Cin., 1987-95; v.p. Internat. Commn. on Occupl. Health, 2006—. Recipient disting. svc. medal, 2000, commendation medal USPHS, 1989, 92. Mem. APHA, Soc. for Epidemiologic Rsch. Democrat. Roman Catholic. Office: NIOSH 200 Independence Ave SW Washington DC 20201 Business E-Mail: mfingerhut@cdc.gov.

FINK, ALMA, retired elementary school educator; b. Missoula, Mont., Sept. 2, 1934; d. Frederick James and Annabelle (Pearson) Gariepy; m. Millard Allen Fink, June 18, 1955 (dec. Sept. 1980); children: Melanie Ann, Laurie Jean. Diploma, Western Mont. Coll., Dillon, 1954; BA, U. Mont., 1968, MA, 1992. Cert. elem. and reading tchr., Mont. Tchr. 1st grade Granite County Elem. Sch., Phillipsburg, Mont., 1954-55, Missoula County Pub. Schs., Missoula, 1955-56, 68-99; ret. Mem. Five Valleys Reading Coun., MIssoula. Editor state newsletter Chit Chat. Named Gold Star Tchr., KECI-TV, 1998. Mem. NEA (life), Missoula Elem. Edn. Assn. (polit. action com. for educators, mem. exec. bd.), Alpha Delta Kappa (Mont. state pres. 1988-90, pres. chpt., regional chmn., Violet award). Roman Catholic. Avocations: sewing, crafts, sports, reading, travel. E-mail: fink@rigsky.net.

FINK, CATHY DEVITO, small business owner; b. Jacksonville, Fla., Dec. 23, 1957; d. Pasquale and Kay Francis (Mentry) DeVito; m. Robert Thomas Fink, May 5, 1984; 1 child, Christopher DeVito Fink. AAS, Canton (N.Y.) Agrl. & Tech., 1978. Adminstv. asst. MPR Assocs., Washington, 1978-84; owner, dir. CDF Svcs., Falls Church, Va., 1984—. PAC mgr. Neece, Cator & Assocs., Inc., Washington, 1987—. Tchr. computers Haycock Elem. Sch., Fairfax, Va., 1986-87, pres. PTA; v.p. Capital Boys Hockey Club, Washington, 1987-89; bus. mgr. Women in Housing and Fin. Mem. NAFE, Nat. Economists Club (bus. mgr. 1988—), Nat. Economists Ednl. Found. (bus. mgr. 1988—), Bus. Network Internat. (pres. Falls Church chpt.). Republican. Roman Catholic. Avocations: raquetball, computer technology, bicycling, teaching children, business management. Office: CDF Svcs 6712 Fisher Ave Falls Church VA 22046-1820

FINK, ELOISE BRADLEY, art director; b. Decatur, Ill., Mar. 13, 1927; d. Keith and Eileen Bradley; m. John Fink, Aug. 8, 1949 (div.); children: Sara, Joel, Alison. BA in English with honors, U. Ill., 1949; student, Colo. Coll., 1951. Cert. tchr., Ill. Tchr. English, social studies Paxton, Decatur and Arlington Heights, Ill., 1949-56; freelance Scott Foresman, Ency. Brit. and SRA, 1956-80; dir. pub. rels. Rehab. Inst. Chgo., 1980-82; instr. creative writing and poetry Loyola U., Water Tower campus, Chgo., 1983-90; artist-in-residence Ill. Arts Coun., 1984-93; facilitator workshops in poetry, fiction and nonfiction New Trier Ext., 1974—2004. Founder, editor, pres. Thorntree Press, Winnetka, Ill., 1985—. Author: The Girl in the Empty Nightgown, 1986, Lincoln and the Prairie After, 1999. Poetry contest judge U. S.C. Writers, 2005. Recipient Friends of Lits. awards (2), Gwendolyn Brooks award for Twenty Significant Ill. Poets; Breadloaf Writing Conf. fellow, 1986. Mem. Acad. Am. Poets, Poetry Soc. Am. Home: 804 Kings Lake Ct Virginia Beach VA 23452-4643

FINK, RUTH GARVEY, diversified financial services company executive; b. Colby, Kans., Apr. 26, 1917; d. Ray Hugh and Olive Hill (White) Garvey; m. Richard Lloyd Cochener, Feb. 17, 1942 (dec. 1954); children: Bruce Garvey Cochener, Diana Broze, Caroline Bonesteel; m. Harry Bernerd Fink, Mar. 31, 1955. BA, U. Ill., 1938; postgrad., U. Kans., 1940—41; HHD (hon.), Washburn U., 1981. Mng. ptnr. C & G Grain Co., Topeka, 1954—55; v.p., dir. CGF Grain Co., Topeka, 1957—84; pres., dir. Midwest Industries, Inc., Topeka, 1972—83, CGF Industries, Inc., Topeka, 1983—97, Freedom Family LC, 1997—. Bd. dirs. Garvey, Inc., Wichita; past bd. dirs. Stauffer Comm., Inc., Topeka. Trustee Washburn Endowment Assn., Topeka, 1960—, active com. tornado reconstrn., 1966—68; chmn. Washburn Coll. Bible, 1979—; Kans. regent Gunston Hall, Lorton, Va., 1965—79; trustee Hoover Presdl. Libr., West Branch, Iowa, 1983—88; mem. electoral coll. State of Kans., 2004. Named Disting. Kansan, Native Sons and Daughters of Kans., 2004; named to Topeka Bus. Hall of Fame, Jr. Achievement of N.E. Kans., 2003; recipient Cmty. Leader award, Topeka Panhellenic Coun., 1981, Monroe award, Washburn Alumni Assn., 1991, N.E. Kans. Leadership award, Washburn U., 2002; Paul Harris Fellow, Rotary Internat., 2004. Mem.: PEO, Nat. Soc. Colonial Dames in Kans. (Roll of Honor 1980), Delta Gamma (Cable award 1965, Shield award 1970). Republican. Congregationalist. Office: Ste 805 534 S Kansas Ave Topeka KS 66603-3430

FINKEL, MARION JUDITH, internist, pharmaceutical administrator; b. N.Y.C., Nov. 2, 1929; d. Israel and Bella (Stillman) Finkel; m. Simon V. Manson, Sept. 12, 1954. Student, L.I. U., 1945-48; MD (Howard Sloan Meml. scholar), Chgo. Med. Sch., 1952. Intern Jersey City Med. Ctr., 1952-53; resident in internal medicine Bellevue Hosp., N.Y.C., 1954-56; med. editor Merck and Co., 1957-61; pvt. practice specializing in internal medicine, N.Y.C., 1956-57, NJ, 1961-63; with FDA, 1963-85, dir. divsn. metabolic and endocrine drugs, 1966-70, dep. dir. bur. drugs, 1970-71, 72-74, dir. office new drug evaluation, 1971-72, 74-82, dir. office orphan products devel., 1982-85; exec. dir. R&D Berlex Labs., Inc., 1985-88; v.p. drug registration and regulatory affairs Sandoz Pharms., Inc., 1988-94, v.p. corp. regulatory compliance, 1994-95, cons. regulatory affairs, clin. R&D, 1995—. Contbr. chpts. to books, numerous articles to profl. jours. Recipient award of merit FDA, 1972, Superior Svc. award USPHS, 1976, 84, Fed. Woman's award Fed. Govt., 1976, Meritorious Exec. award, 1980; named Disting. Alumnus, Chgo. Med. Sch., 1977, L.I. U., 1980. Office: 21 Squirrel Run Morristown NJ 07960-6411

FINKELMAN COX, PENNEY, film producer; b. Ardmore, Pa., July 5, 1951; d. Jayne Miriam (Isaacs) Finkelman; m. James Douglas Cox, Feb. 9, 1986. BA, Barnard Coll., 1973. Exec. DreamWorks; exec. v.p. Sony Pictures Animation, 2002—. Asst. dir. (TV films) Skokie, 1981, co-prodr. (films) Terms of Endearment, 1983, Broadcast News, 1987; prodr.: (films) Honey, I Shrunk the Kids, 1989, Welcome Home, Roxy Carmichael, 1990, 'Til There Was You, 1997, The Prince of Egypt, 1998; exec. prodr. V.I. Warshawski, 1991, I'll Do Anything, 1994, Joseph: King of Dreams, 2000, Shrek, 2001; exec. prodr.: (films) Snakes on a Plane, 2006. Office: Sony Pictures Animation 10202 West Washington Blvd Culver City CA 90232*

FINKELSTEIN, BARBARA, education educator; b. Bklyn., Mar. 22, 1937; d. Joseph and Helene (Gutter) Eisenberg; m. James D. Finkelstein; children: Donna Ilene, Laura Helene. BA, Barnard Coll., 1959; MA, Columbia U., 1960, EdD, 1970. Asst. prof. U. Md., College Park, 1970-74, assoc. prof., 1974-83, dir. Internat. Ctr. for Study of Edn., Policy and Human Values, 1979—, mem. East Asian com., 1980—, prof. edn., 1983—. Dir. Mid-Atlantic Region Japan-in-the-Schs. Program, 1985—, Nat. Intercultural Edn. Leadership Inst., Internat. Ctr. for Trausullal Edn. Author, editor: Regulated Children, Liberated Children, 1979 (Critic's Choice award 1981), Governing the Young: Teacher Behavior in Primary Schools in Nineteenth-Century United States, 1988, Experiencing Education and Culture inJapan: Transcending Stereotypes, 1990, Discovering Culture in Education: An Approach to Program Design and Evaluation, Education Historians as Mythmakers, 1992, A Crucible of Contradictions: Historical Roots of Violence Against Children, 2001, Is Adolescence Here to Stay? 2002; editor Reflective History series Tchrs. Coll. Press; exec. editor Pedagogica historica, Jour. Edn. Policy; contbr. articles to profl. jours. Recipient Oredr of the Rising Sun, Japan, 2005, Disting. Scholar Tchr., U. Md., 2005—06; grantee U.S.-Japan Found., 1985—88; NEH fellow, 1976—77, fellow U. Tokyo, 1992. Mem. Am. Ednl. Studies Assn. (pres. 1979-82), History of Edn. Soc. (bd. dirs. 1980-82, v.p. 1998, pres. 1998-99), Am. Ednl. Rsch. Assn. (v.p. 1989—). Home: 3916 Garrison St NW Washington DC 20016-4220 Office: U Md Dept Edn Policy College Park MD 20742-0001 E-mail: bf6@umail.umd.edu.

FINKELSTEIN, CLAIRE, law educator; BA magna cum laude, Harvard U., 1986; MA in Philosophy, U. Paris, Sorbonne, 1987; JD, Yale U., 1993; PhD in Philosophy, U. Pitts., 1996. Acting prof. law U. Calif., Berkeley, 1995—2000, prof., 2000—01; vis. faculty U. Pa. Law Sch., Phila., 2000—01, prof. law and philosophy, 2001—, dir. Inst. for Law and Philosophy, 2003—04. Contbr. articles to law jours. Office: U Pa Law Sch 3400 Chestnut St Philadelphia PA 19104 Office Phone: 215-898-5798. Office Fax: 215-573-2025. E-mail: cfinkels@law.upenn.edu.

FINKELSTEIN, HONORA MOORE, writer, editor, consultant; b. Midwest, Wyo., July 18, 1941; d. Stanley and Gladys Beatrice (Parker) Moore; m. Thomas Norton Lynch, May 16, 1964 (div. Feb. 1980); children: Aileen Marie, Kathleen Bernadette, Bridget Colleen; m. Jay Laurence Finkelstein, Mar. 15, 1980; 1 child, Michael Marcus. BA in English, Rice U., 1963; MA in English, U. Tex., 1970; PhD in English, U. Houston, 1976; grad. pub. course, Rice U., 1977. Ordained minister of Wholistic Healing, 1991. Publs. editor Ctr. Mgmt. Studies Johnson Space Ctr., 1974-75; asst. prof. Houston Bapt. U., 1975-79; instr. U. Tex., El Paso, 1979-80; owner, operator Communications Unltd., Houston and El Paso, 1976-80, Communications, Ink, Reston, Va., 1980-93; editor lifestyle sect. Times Newspaper, Arundel Orgn., No. Va., 1987-88. Workshop dir. Internat. Women's Writing Guild, NY, 1986—, Peacemakers' First Internat. Women's Peace Conf., Dallas, 1988, Consciousness Frontiers, 1990, 93, 95, Women in Comm., 1990, White Shell Woman, 1991, Silva Mind Control, 1993, 95; owner El Amarna Mall, Grayville, Ill., 1995; adj. prof. U. So. Ind., 1999-2005, U. Evansville, 2004-05. Author: (book) A Very Short Guide to Style, 1975, (novel) Magicians, 1994; co-author: (books) Car Buyer Beware, 1977, Beautiful Skin, 1985, The Chef Who Died Sautéing, 2006; producer, host: (TV talk show) Kaleidoscope for Tomorrow, 1991-98; contbr. numerous articles, presentations, revs. to profl. jours. Participant RESULTS Lobby, No. Va., 1987; founder Sunweavers, Inc., 1993; co-founder Sunweavers Ctr. for Whole Life Edn., 1995, Grayville Mus. Assn., 1996. Served with USN, 1963-64. Grantee Nat. Soc. Arts & Letters, 1970; named Faculty Woman of Yr. Assn. Women Students Houston Bapt. U., 1979; recipient 1st place award for best presentation of a spl. holiday, 2nd place award for best lifestyle section Suburban Newspapers of Am. Assn., 1987, 1st place award Va. Press Assn., 1988. Mem. Internat. Women's Writing Guild, Nat. League Am. Pen Women, Earthstewards Network, Network of Light (bd. dirs.), Washington Manx Soc. (bd. dirs.), Assn. Philippine-Am. Women, Grad. English Soc. (pres. 1974-75), Phi Kappa Phi. Avocations: peacemaking and conflict resolution, psychic studies, psychology studies, health and healing. Home: 121 E South St Grayville IL 62844-1635

FINKEN, TRACY ANN, lawyer; b. Easton, Pa., Nov. 14, 1971; BA, Bloomsburg U., 1993; JD cum laude, Widener U., 1998. Bar: Pa. 1998, NJ 1998. Assoc. Anapol, Schwartz, Weiss, Cohan, Feldman & Smalley, PC, Phila. Arbitrator Phila. County Arbitration Program. Mem.: Pa. Trial Lawyers Assn., Pa. Bar Assn., Phila. Bar Assn., Nat. Order of Barristers. Office: Anapol, Schwartz, Weiss, Cohan, Feldman & Smalley 1710 Spruce St Philadelphia PA 19103 Office Phone: 215-735-0773. Office Fax: 215-875-7731. E-mail: tfinken@anapolschwartz.com.*

FINLAND, CHRISTINE ELAINE, school counselor; b. Sturgis, Mich., Oct. 23, 1948; d. Charles Hartford and JoAnn Eloise (Grady) Cross; m. Thomas Francis Finland, Jr., Dec. 19, 1986; children: Teresa, Jason, Javon, Jaime and Jennifer. BS in Edn., Ind. U., Ft. Wayne, 1973; MS in Edn., St. Francis Coll., Ft. Wayne, 1975; MS in Counseling and Guidance, Valdosta State U., GA., 1993. Hosp. and homebound tchr. Marion County Schs., Buena Vista, Ga., 1978-79; tchr. spl. edn. Ochlocknee (Ga.) Children's Ctr., 1979-80, Comprhensive Psychoednl. Ctr., Valdosta, 1985-86; tchr. self-contained behavioral disorders Valdosta Jr. High Sch., 1986-88; tchr. behavioral disorders Valdosta City Schs., 1980-85, tchr. emotional behavioral disorders, 1988-94; guidance counselor S.L. Mason Elem. Sch., Valdosta, 1994-97; sch. counselor Berrien Elem. Sch., Nashville, 1997—2002, Pelham City Mid. Sch., 2002—. Named Tchr. of Yr., Valdosta City Schs., 1982. Mem. ACA, Coun. for Exceptional Children, Ga. Assn. Sch. Counselors. Democrat. Lutheran. Home: 15 Banner Hill Dr Thomasville GA 31757-2971

FINLAYSON-PITTS, BARBARA JEAN, chemistry professor; b. Ottawa, Ont., Can., Apr. 4, 1948; d. James Colin and Jean Burwell (Moore) Finlayson; m. James N. Pitts Jr., May 27, 1976. BSc (Hons.) in Chemistry, Trent U., Ont., Can., 1970; MS in Chemistry, U. Calif., Riverside, 1971, PhD in Chemistry, 1973. Rsch. asst., then postdoctoral rsch. chemist U. Calif., Riverside, 1970-74; asst. prof. chemistry Calif. State U., Fullerton, 1974-77, assoc. prof., 1977-81, prof. chemistry, 1981-94, U. Calif., Irvine, 1994—. Mem. grants rev. panel EPA, 1980-86; mem. rsch. screening com. Calif. Air Resources Bd.; mem. editl. bd. Revista Internacional de Contaminacion Ambientel; mem. com. on tropospheric ozone NAS, 1989-91, com. atmospheric chemistry, 1989-92; mem. awards program adv. com. Rsch. Corp., 1993-95. Author: Atmospheric Chemistry: Fundamentals and Experimental Techniques, 1986, Chemistry of the Upper and Lower Atmosphere, 2000; mem. editl. bd. Rsch. on Chem. Intermediates, 1995—, Atmospheric Environ., 1996—, Internat. Jour. Chem. Kinet., 1996-2000, Jour. Environ. Sci. Health, 1996-97, Jour. Phys. Chemistry, 1998—; contbr. numerous articles to refereed jours. Fellow AAAS, NAS, Am. Acad. Arts and Sciences; mem. Am. Chem. Soc. (award for creative advances in environ. sci. 2004), Am. Geophys. Union, Am. Women in Sci., Iota Sigma Pi. Episcopalian. Avocation: fly fishing. Office: U Calif 328 Rowland Hall Mail Code 2025 Irvine CA 92697-0001

FINLEY, CHARLENE P., elementary school educator; children: Sarah, David. AA, Nassau C.C., Garden City, N.Y., 1970; BA, Thomas Edison Coll., Trenton, N.J., 1999. Cert. tchr. N.J. Tchr. Our Lady Grace Sch., Somerdale, NJ, 1988—2001; sci. tchr. Magnolia Pub. Sch., NJ, 2002—. Mem. steering com. mid. states accreditation Our Lady Grace Sch., 1996—98, coord. sci. curriculum, 1996—2001; coord. sci. curriculum Jr. HS Magnolia Pub. Sch., 2002—. Adv., moderator youth week Borough Magnolia, 2001—. Named South Jersey All-Star Tchr., Newspapers in Edn., 1998, 2000, 2004; recipient Outstanding Achievement in Edn. award, Scientific Am., 2006. Mem.: N.J. Edn. Assn. Avocations: yoga, gardening. Office: Magnolia Elem Sch 420 Warwick Rd N Magnolia NJ 08049-1399

FINLEY, EMMA ROSEMARY, science educator; b. Gulfport, Miss., Sept. 23, 1935; d. Frank Ransom and Rosemary Blackmarr; m. Chester William Finley, Aug. 8, 1954; children: Margaret Finley Hase, Chester Lawrence, Robert Stacy. Ednl. Specialist, U. of So. Miss., 1995—2001; BS, U. of NC, 1968—70; MS, U. of So. Miss., 1971—75. Master Teacher Nat. Bd. for Profl. Tchg. Standards, 2001. Sci. educator Long Beach Sch. Dist., Miss., 1970—73, Harrison County Sch. Dist., Gulfport, Miss., 1973—. Sci. fair sponsor Harrison County Sch. Dist., Gulfport, Miss., 1973—; art fair sponsor North Woolmarket Sch. Parent Tchr. Student Assn., Biloxi, Miss., 1998—2002; candidates' mentor Nat. Bd. for Profl. Tchg. Standards, Long Beach, Miss., 2002—. Illustrator (resource guides) Oceanography and Coastal Processes, 1998, Global Awareness, Global Environmental Education, 1996. Mem. Gulf Coast Federated Women's Club, Gulfport, Miss., 2002—06; vol. Friends of the Libr., Gulfport, Miss., 2000—06; endowed Finley scholarship Miss. Gulf Coast C.C. Found., Perkinston, Miss., 2003—06. Named Tchr. of Yr., d'Iberville Mid. Sch., 1990, Woolmarket Sch., 1993, Ageless Hero for Love of Learning, Blue Cross/ Blue Shield of Miss., 2003; recipient Outstanding Instrn. in Marine Sci. award, Miss.-Ala. Sea Grant Consortium, 1991, 1994; Nature Trail grantee, BellSouth, Butterfly Garden grantee, 2001—03. Mem.: AAUW, NEA, Miss. Assn. Educators, Nat. Marine Educators' Assn., Nat. Sci. Teachers' Assn., Miss. Sci. Teachers' Assn. (v.p. and pres. 1988—90, Miss. Outstanding Elem. Sci. Educator 1980, Exemplary Mid. Sch. Sci. Tchr. 2002), Phi Delta Kappa. Episcopalian. Avocations: nature artist, gardening, reading, conservationist. Office: West Wortham Middle Sch 20199 West Wortham Rd Saucier MS 39574 Office Phone: 228-831-1276. Office Fax: 228-539-5962. Business E-Mail: rfinley@harrison.k12.ms.us.

FINLEY, GLENNA, writer; b. Puyallup, Wash., June 12, 1925; d. John Ford and Gladys De Ferris (Winters) F.; m. Donald MacLeod Witte, May 19, 1951; 1 child, Duncan MacLeod. BA cum laude, Stanford U., Calif., 1945. Prodr. internat. divsn. NBC, 1945-49; film libr. March of Time, 1949; with news bur. Life Mag., 1950; publicity and radio writer Seattle, 1950-51; freelance writer, 1951-57; contract writer New Am. Libr. Inc., N.Y.C., 1970—. Author numerous books including Master of Love, 1978, Beware My Heart, 1978, The Marriage Merger, 1978, Wildfire of Love, 1979, Timed for Love, 1979, Love's Temptation, 1979, Stateroom for Two, 1980, Affairs of Love, 1980, A Business Affair, 1983, Wanted for Love, 1983, A Weekend for Love, 1984, Love's Waiting Game, 1985, A Touch of Love, 1985, Diamonds for My Love, 1986, Secret of Love, 1987, The Marrying Kind, 1988, Island Rendezvous, 1990, Stowaway for Love, 1992, The Temporary Bride, 1993. Named Matrix Table Woman of Achievement, 1976. Mem.: Women's Univ. Club (Seattle). Republican. Anglican. Home: 7868-F Rea Rd Charlotte NC 28277

FINLEY, JULIE HAMM, ambassador, former political party official; Nat. co-chmn. Fin. Dole for Pres., 1995—96; asst. secy. 1996 Rep. Nat. Conv.; co-chmn. D.C. Republican Party, Team 100, 1997—2005; nat. committee-woman D.C. Republican Com., 1999—2005; US amb. to Orgn. for Security & Cooperation in Europe, 2005—. Founding bd. mem. US Com. on NATO. Office: Orgn for Security & Cooperation in Europe Kaerntner Ring 5-7 1010 Austria

FINLEY, KATHERINE MANDUSIC, professional society administrator; b. Mansfield, Ohio, Nov. 8, 1954; d. Sam and Ann Julia (Konves) Mandusic; m. Edwin D. McDonell, Aug. 18, 1979 (div. Dec. 1994); m. Jeffrey A. Finley, June 12, 1999. BA, Ohio Wesleyan U.; MA in History and Mus. Studies, Case Western Res.; MBA, Ind. U. Rschr. Conner Prairie Mus., Fishers, Ind., 1978-82; exec. dir., rsch. historian Ind. Med. History Mus./Ind. Hist. Soc., Indpls., 1982-91; asst. dir. comm. and mktg. Ind. U. Ctr. Philanthropy, 1991-93; exec. dir. Roller Skating Assn. Internat., Indpls., 1993-2000, Assn. Rsch. Nonprofit Orgns. and Voluntary Action, 2000—05; mem. faculty philanthropic studies Ind. U.-Purdue U., Indpls., 2001—; rsch. dir. William E. Smith Inst. for Assn. Rsch., 2004—05; dir. Am. Coll. Sports Medicine Found., Indpls., 2005—. Author: (book) The Journals of William A. Lindsay, 1989; contbg. editor: The Encyclopedia of Indianapolis, 1994; contbr. articles to profl. jours. Pres. Altrusa Internat. Indpls., 1995—97, treas., 1998—99, chmn. svc. com., 1999—2000; pres. Altrusa Found. Indpls., 2001—03; bd. dirs. Nat. Mus. Roller Skating, Lincoln, 1994—2000. Mem.: Assn. Fund Raising Profls. (bd. dirs. Ind. chpt. 2003—), Ind. Soc. Assn. Execs. (chair edn. com. 1997—98, chair conv. com. 1999—2000, bd. dirs. 1999—2001, chair found. 2000), Nat. Soc. Fund Raising Execs. (cert.), Am. Soc. Assn. Execs. (mem. ethics com. 2004—, Assn. Exec. of Yr. 2002, cert. meeting planner 2003), MINI Cooper Car Club Ind. (club advisor 2003—04), Toastmasters (v.p. edn. 1998—99, v.p. pub. rels. 2000, v.p. edn. 2000—02, gov. area 18 2001—02, v.p. edn. 2006—), Rotary Internat. of Indpls., Phi Beta Kappa, Sigma Iota Epsilon, Beta Gamma Sigma. Avocations: reading, walking, gourmet cooking. Office: ACSM Found 401 W Michigan St Indianapolis IN 46202 Business E-Mail: kfinley@acsm.org.

FINLEY, KATHLEEN MARIE, marriage and family therapist, educator; b. Aberdeen, Wash., Nov. 12, 1947; d. Maurice Burke and Geraldine Jeanette Hickey; m. Mitchel B. Finley, Mar. 9, 1974; children: Sean Thomas, Patrick Daniel, Kevin Andrew. BA with honors, Gonzaga U., Spokane, Wash., 1970, MA in Counseling Psychology, 1990; MA in Religious Edn., Fordham U., Bronx, N.Y., 1972. Assoc. dir. family life office Cath. Diocese of Spokane, 1977—81; dir. of formation Mater Dei Ministry Inst., Spokane, 1995—97; marriage preparation counselor St. Aloysius Parish, Spokane, 1993—. Presenter marriage preparation weekends Cath. Diocese of Spokane, 1977—; adj. instr. religious studies dept. Gonzaga U., Spokane, 1981—. Author: Building Christian Families (Thomas More Press medal, 1984), Amen: Prayers for Families With Children, Our Family Book of Days: A Record Through the Years, Building a Christian Marriage: Eleven Essential Skills, The Liturgy of Motherhood (2nd Pl. award Family Life, Cath. Press Assn., 2005), Savoring God: Praying With All Our Senses, Welcome: Prayers for New and Pregnant Parents, Prayers for the Newly Married. Mem. Nat. Assn. of Cath. Family Mins., 1980—2004. Recipient Nat. Merit Scholarship semifinalist, 1966. Roman Catholic. Avocations: reading, travel. Office: Gonzaga Univ Religious Studies Dept AD Box 57 Spokane WA 99258 Office Phone: 509-323-6770. Business E-Mail: finley@gonzaga.edu.

FINLEY, MARGARET MAVIS, retired elementary school educator; b. Jackson, Mich., Dec. 2, 1927; d. Allen Aaron and Minnie Mavis (Graham) Lincoln; m. Duane Douglas Finley, Aug. 23, 1952; 1 child, Linda Louise. BS, Ea. Mich. U., 1960; postgrad., Pepperdine U., 1968-72. Cert. tchr., Mich., Calif. Tchr. Jackson (Mich.) Sch. Dist., 1960-67, Pomona (Calif.) Sch. Dist., 1967-88; ret., 1988. Contbr. poetry and articles to profl. jours. Mem.: NEA, DAR (sch. liaison chair (Los Cerritos chpt.)), Calif. Tchrs. Assn., Calif. Ret. Tchrs. Assn. (resource chair divsn. 82). Avocations: writing, reading, hiking, travel, theater. Home: 1072 Cypress Point Dr Banning CA 92220-5404

FINLEY, MARLYNN HOLT, elementary educator consultant; b. Columbia, Mo., Oct. 19, 1936; d. Robert McDonnell and Lorraine Isabelle (Miller) Holt; husband dec. BS in Edn., U. Mo., 1958, MS in Edn., 1965, PhD in Spl. Edn., 1978. Cert. elem. educator, elem. adminstr., spl. educator. Elem. tchr. Ferguson (Mo.)/Florissant Schs., 1958-59, 60-61; elem., jr. high tchr. Anniston (Ala.) Schs., 1959-60; univ. instr. U. Mo., Columbia, 1961-64; elem. tchr. Riverview (Mo.) Gardens Schs., 1964-65; lang. arts cons. St. Charles (Mo.) Schs., 1966-69, Parkway Schs., Chesterfield, Mo., 1969-73, reading specialist, 1973-95; ednl. cons. self-employed Town & Country, Mo., 1995—. Jefferson Club trustee chmn. Devel. Coun., U. Mo., Columbia, 1991—. Grantee, 1967-69, 70-71. Alumni adv. chmn. Coll. Edn. Alumni, U. Mo., 1969-89; Sunday sch. tchr. Ladue Chapel Presbyn., St. Louis, 1960-61, deacon, 1999—. Recipient Carter award U. Mo., 1965, Life Saving award, 1980. Mem. AAUW, Internat. Reading Assn. (treas. 1970-72), St. Louis Suburban Reading Assn. (Svc. award 1982), Order of Ea. Star (grand rep. of B.C. and Yukon 1999-00, assoc. conductress 1982, conductress 1983, assoc. matron 1984, worthy matron 1985, 00, sec. 1987-95), PEO, Pi Lambda Theta, Zeta Tau Alpha. Republican. Avocations: reading, swimming, walking, skating, bridge, travel. Home: 378 Shetland Valley Ct Chesterfield MO 63005-4839

FINLEY, PATRICIA ANN, psychologist, artist; b. Phoenix, Oct. 30, 1936; d. Richard Edward and Ethel Buck Finley; m. William M. Larson, Aug. 31, 1957 (div. June 5, 1978); children: Sabin Lynne Larson, Shura Lee McGraw, Sean William Larson. BFA Graphic Design, Univ. Ariz., Tucson, Ariz., 1958; MS Art Edn., Univ. Oreg., Eugene, Oreg., 1981, PhD Art Edn., 1984; PhD Psychology, Walden Univ., Mpls., 2002. Cert. basic tchg. Oreg., 1982, lifetime tchg. in C.C. Ariz., 1987. Coll. instr. Ariz. State Univ./Columbia Coll., Phoenix, 1985—95; psychotherapist Sexual Assault Recovery Inst., Phoenix, 1990—94, Westside Social Svc., Phoenix, 1994—97; clin. specialist ProtoCall Crisis Line, Portland, 1997—2000; sex offender therapist New Horizons Wellness Svc., Portland, Oreg., 2000—01; Psychologist, owner, dir. Lake Oswego (Oreg.) Counsel Ctr., 2001—. Exec. dir. Phoenix Festivals, Phoenix, 1987—90; bd. cert. expert Am. Acad. Trauma Svc., Portland, Oreg., 1997—. Media coord. John Denver Ariz. Windstar Connection Group, Phoenix, 1989; mem., planning com. Very Spl. Arts, Scottsdale, Ariz., 1993. Fellow: Kappa Kappa Gamma; mem.: Milton H. Erickson Found., Eye Movment Desensitisation & Reprocessing, Am. Psychol. Assn., Am. Mental Health Assn. (Oreg. chpt.), Psi Chi. Independent. Unitarian. Avocations: running, swimming, reading, cooking, antiques. Office: Lake Oswego Counseling Ctr Inc 15110 SW Boones Ferry Rd #248 Lake Oswego OR 97035 Office Phone: 503-675-2830.

FINLEY, SARA CREWS, medical geneticist, educator; b. Lineville, Ala., Feb. 26, 1930; m. Wayne H. Finley; children: Randall Wayne, Sara Jane. BS in Biology, U. Ala., 1951, MD, 1955. Diplomate Am. Bd. Med. Genetics; cert. clin. geneticist; cert. clin. cytogeneticist. Intern Lloyd Noland Hosp., Fairfield, Ala., 1955-56; NIH fellow in pediatrics U. Ala. Med. Sch., Birmingham, 1956-60; NIH trainee in med. genetics Inst. Med. Genetics, U. Uppsala, Sweden, 1961-62; mem. faculty U. Ala. Med. Sch., 1960-96, co-dir. lab. med. genetics, 1966-96, prof. pediatrics, 1975-96, occupant Wayne H. and Sara Crews Finley chair med. genetics, 1986-96, prof. emeritus, 1996—; Disting. Faculty lectr. Med. Ctr., U. Ala. at Birmingham, 1983; mem. staff U. Ala. Hosp., Children's Hosp. Ala. Mem. ad hoc com. genetic counseling Children's Bur., HEW, 1966; mem. ad hoc rev. panel for genetic disease and sickle cell testing and counseling programs, 1980; mem. genetic diseases program objective rev. panel Bur. Maternal and Child Health and Resources Div., HHS, 1989, mem. adv. group on lab. quality assurance, 1989. Birmingham Author papers on clin. cytogenetics, human congenital malformations, human growth and devel. Mem. White House Conf. Health, 1965; mem. rsch. manpower rev. com. Nat. Cancer Inst., 1977-81; mem. Sickle Cell Disease Adv. Com., NIH, 1983-87; chairperson physician's campaign bd. dirs. United Way, 1993-95. Recipient Disting. Alumna award U. Ala. Sch. Medicine Alumni Assn., 1989, Med. award Ala. Assn. for Retarded Children, 1969, Turlington award Planned Parenthood of Ala., 1982, Nat. Outstanding Alumnae award Zeta Tau Alpha, 1992, Disting. Alumna award U. Ala. Nat. Alumni Assn., 1994, Brother Bryan Prayer Point award Birmingham Women's Com. of 100, 2001, Gardner award Ala. Acad. Sci., 2002, Local Legend award Am. Med. Women's Assn. Nat. Libr. Medicine, 2004, Lifetime Achievement award Birmingham Bus. Jour., 2003, So. Women of Dist. award So. Women's Ctr., 2005; co-recipient Will Holmes award Children's Aid Soc. Birmingham, 1999; named Top Ten Women in Birmingham, 1989, Top 31 Most Outstanding Alumnae U. Ala., Tuscaloosa, 1993, Ala. Healthcare Hall of Fame, 2001; Finley-Compass Bank Genetics Conf. Ctr. with portrait opened, 2001. Fellow AMA (founding), Am. Coll. Med. Genetics; mem. Am. Soc. Human Genetics, Med. Assn. Ala. (Samuel Buford Word award 2003, Fifty Year Club 2005), Ala. Assn. Retarded Children (Ann. Med. awad 1969), Ala. Acad. Sci., Jefferson County Med. Soc. (pres. 1990), Jefferson County Pediatric Soc., So. Med. Assn., NY Acad. Sci., Caduceus Club, Rotary Club of Birmingham, Phi Beta Kappa, Sigma Xi, Alpha Omega Alpha, Alpha Epsilon Delta, Omicron Delta Kappa, Phi Kappa Phi, Zeta Tau Alpha. Office: U Ala Kaul Bldg 210E Birmingham AL 35294 E-mail: scfinley@webtv.net.

FINLEY, SARAH MAUDE MERRITT, retired social worker; b. Atlanta, Nov. 19, 1946; d. Genius and Willie Maude (Wright) Merritt; m. Craig Wayne Finley, Aug. 10, 1968; children: Craig Wayne Jr., Jarret Lee. BA, Spelman Coll., 1968; postgrad., Atlanta U., 1968-69. Cert. GPS/MAPP leader 2001. Job placement advisor Marsh Draughton Bus. Coll., Atlanta, 1971-72; child attendant Fulton County Juvenile Ct., Atlanta, 1972; social worker Fulton County Dept. Family and Children Svcs., Atlanta, 1972-2000, casework supr., 1976-98, Title VI customer svc. coord. Ctrl. City/North Area office, 1990-98, ret., 1998; counselor/asst. to the project dir. Right Way Home Project N.W. Area Office, 1998-99; social svcs. case mgr. Placement Resource Devel. N.W. Area Office, 2000; social worker Dept. Family and Children Svcs. Clayton County, Jonesboro, Ga., 2000—05, ret., 2005. Supr. Count on Me video Ga. Dept. Human Resources, 1987; mem. Spelman's Team of Alumni Recruiters, Spelman Coll. Vol. coord. family support program Family Support Group of Atlanta Detachment of 2d Army Maneuver Tng. Command.; vol. family support coun. 87th Maneuver Area Command (now 4th Brigade, 87th Divsn.), 1991-93; del. Ft. McPherson (Ga.) Army Family Symposium, 1992, 3d ann. worldwide USAR Family Support Conf., St. Louis, 1992 Mem.: Fulton County Ret. Employees Assn., Ga. County Welfare Assn., Nat. Alumnae Assn. Spelman Coll., Womens Aux. Ga. VFW. Baptist. Avocations: poetry, reading, volunteer work, stress mgmt. Personal E-mail: maudngen@aol.com.

FINLEY, SUSIE QUANSTROM, energy executive, retired elementary school educator; b. Kewanee, Ill., Mar. 3, 1950; d. Melvin Dale and Annamae (Kubelius) Quanstrom; m. Dana J. Finley, July 12, 1980; 1 child, Tiffany Nicole. BS in Edn., North Tex. State U., 1972; cert. in bus. and legal secretarial, Draughan's Bus. Coll., Albuquerque, 1973; cert. in English lit., U. N.Mex., 1975; cert. in pub. rels., N.Mex. Jr. Coll., 1985. Owner, dealer Solar Age Industries, Hobbs, N.Mex., 1982—, v.p. advt. and pub. rels. Albuquerque, 1986—94; tchr. Edgewood (N.Mex.) Elem. Sch., 1994—2002, ret., 2002; mktg. and purchasing mgr. Cherriwyn Gift Shop, St. James Tearoom, Albuquerque, 2005—. Lobbyist N.Mex. Solar Energy Inst., 1985-86. Named Employee of Yr., Camp Fire Boys and Girls, 1992; recipient Christian Bros. Tchg. award, Coll. Santa Fe, 1994. Mem. NAFE, N.Mex. Solar Energy Inst. Republican. Avocations: camping, reading, travel, antebellum southern history. Home: 13412 Circulo Largo NE Albuquerque NM 87112-3764

FINLEY-MORIN, KIMBERLEY K., secondary school educator; b. San Angelo, Tex., Nov. 23, 1954; d. James Griffith Jr. and Imogene (Powers) Finley; m. Michael Morin, Feb. 15, 1986. BA cum laude, Pan Am. U., 1982; MA, Endicott Coll., 2004. Cert. Acupressuriest. Tchr. Dallas Theatre Ctr., Greenfield (Mass.) Child Care Ctr.; site coord., tchr. Greenfield Girls Club; tchr. theatre/acting Shea Theatre, Turners Falls, Mass.; prof. theatre/speech Greenfield Com. Coll., 1996—. Resident dir. Fellowship Players of South Deerfield, 1996—. Pres. Arena Civic Theatre, 1992—. With USN, 1976-80. Mem. Tex. Ednl. Theatre Assn., Alpha Omega. Home: 62 High St Turners Falls MA 01376-1709 Office Phone: morin@gcc.mass.edu, 413-775-1278.

FINN, CHARLOTTE KAYE, interior designer; b. NYC, May 11; d. Edward and Florence (Karp) Kaye; m. Allen Charles Finn (dec. Oct. 2000); children: Andrew, Richard, Gregg. BA cum laude, Hunter Coll. Cert. Braille transcriber, Libr. of Congress. Apprentice designer J.H. Harvey, 1958-64; pvt. practice interior design White Plains, NY, 1965. Design cons. R.H. Macy's, 1977-78; product designer H.J. Stotter, George Kovacs, Grindley-of-Stoke, Sigma Marketing, Smith & Weigler. Work featured in publs. including House Beautiful, Interior Design, Residential Interiors, N.Y. Times, Palm Beach Life, Palm Beach Daily News, Home Furnishings Daily, The Designer, Home Environment, Sensuous Interiors, Prentice Hall; author Planning, Designing and Decorating a Room-Step by Step A How to Manual for Anyone, 2005. Recipient S.H. Hexter award, Burlington House award. Mem.: NOW, LVW, Phi Beta Kappa.

FINN, FRANCES MARY, biochemist, researcher; b. Pitts., May 6, 1937; d. Stephen B. and Geraldine H. (Weber) F.; m. Klaus Hofmann, Feb. 26, 1965 (dec. Dec. 25, 1995); m. Eric Reichl, July 19, 1999. BS in Chemistry, U. Pitts., 1959, MS in Biochemistry, 1961, PhD in Biochemistry, 1964. Asst. rsch. prof. biochemistry U. Pitts., 1969-73, assoc. rsch. prof., 1973-80, assoc. prof. medicine, 1980-88, prof., 1988-99, prof. emerita, 1999—. Mem.: Am. Chem. Soc., Endocrine Soc., Am. Soc. for Biochemistry and Molecular Biology, Am. Peptide Soc., Protein Soc. Home: 150 Brooks Bnd Princeton NJ 08540-7545 E-mail: ffreichl537@yahoo.com.

FINN, NITA ANN, social worker; b. N.Y.C., Jan. 2, 1936; m. Jerold G. Finn, Aug. 27, 1955; children: Bruce L., Betsy Finn-Dicarlo. BA in Psychology, Brandeis U., 1957; MSW, Simmons Coll., 1971. Lic. ind. clin. social worker. Co-dir. Families Extended, Family Counseling Svc., Newton, Mass., 1973-74; child and family psychotherapist Boston Childrens Svcs., 1975-76; project supr. adolescent and family svcs. Justice Resource Inst., Boston, 1976-77; social worker City of Newton, Mass., 1977-79; project dir. Dare Cape Cod, 1979-80; supr. of intake Dept. Social Svcs. Commonwealth of Mass., Cape Cod, 1980-82; pvt. practice, South Harwich, Mass., 1983—. Clin. cons. group facilitator Women's Empowerment Through Cape Area Networking, Harwich Port, Mass., 2001—. Home: PO Box 145 South Harwich MA 02661-0145 Office: 2 Brettwood Rd South Harwich MA 02661-0145 Personal E-mail: nitafinn@comcast.net.

FINNBERG, ELAINE AGNES, psychologist, editor; b. Bklyn., Mar. 2, 1948; d. Benjamin and Agnes Montgomery (Evans) Finnberg; m. Rodney Lee Herndon, Mar. 1, 1981; 1 child, Andrew Marshal Herndon. BA in Psychology, L.I. U., 1969; MA in Psychology, New Sch. for Social Rsch., 1973; PhD in Psychology, Calif. Sch. Profl. Psychology, 1981. Diplomate Am. Bd. Forensic Examiners, Am. Bd. Forensic Medicine, Am. Bd. Med. Psychotherapists and Psychodiagnosticians, Am. Bd. Disability Analysts (profl. adv. coun.), Am. Bd. Psychol. Specialties, Prescribing Psychologists Register (fellow), lic. psychologist Calif. Rsch. asst. med. sociology Cornell U. Med. Coll., NYC, 1969-70; med. abstractor USV Pharm. Corp., Tuckahoe, NY, 1970-71, Coun. Tobacco Rsch., NYC, 1971-77; editor, writer Found. Thanatology Columbia U., NYC, 1971-76, 1973-74; dir. grief psychology and bereavement counseling San Francisco Coll. Mortuary Scis., 1977-81; rsch. assoc. dept. epidemiology and internat. health U. Calif., San Francisco, 1979-81, asst. clin. prof. dept. family and cmty. medicine, 1985-93, assoc. clin. prof., dept. family and cmty. medicine, 1993—; active med. staff Natividad Med. Ctr., Salinas, Calif., 1984—2002, 2004—, chief psychologist, 1984—96. Asst. chief psychiatry svc. Natividad Med. Ctr., 1985—96, acting chief psychiatry, 1988—89, vice-chair medicine dept., 1991—93, sec.-treas. med. staff, 1992—94; cons. med. staff Salinas Valley Meml. Hosp., 1991—2003, Mee Meml. Hosp., 1996—97; dir. tng. Monterey Psychiat. Health Facility, 1996—97, chief clin. staff, 1996—97; expert cons. Calif. Bd. Psychology; cons. psychologist Calif. Forensic Med. Group, 1984—, Calif. Dept. Mental Health Sexually Violent Predator Program, 1996—. Editor: Jour. Thanatology, 1972—76, Cahtexis, 1976—81, Calif. Psychologist, 1988—95. Mem. Gov.'s adv. bd. Agnews Devel. Ctr., San Jose, Calif., 1988—96, chair, 1989—91, 1994—95. Mem.: APA, Internat. Soc. Police Surgeons, Internat. Rorschach Soc., Soc. Personality Assessment, Assn. Treatment Sexual Abuses, Am. Med. Writers Assn., Assn. Advancement Behavior Therapy, Western Psychol. Assn., Forensic Mental Health Assn. Calif., Mid-Coast Psychol. Assn. (sec. 1985, treas. 1986, pres. 1987, Disting. Svc. to Psychology award 1993), Soc. Behavioral Medicine, Calif. Psychol. Assn. (Disting. Svc. award 1989), Nat. Register Health Svc. Providers Psychology. Personal E-mail: finnberg@sbcglobal.net.

FINNEGAN, JENNIFER MICHELLE, veterinarian; b. Manhattan, Kans., Sept. 14, 1974; d. Michael John and Barbara Jean Finnegan. BS, U. Kans., 1997; DVM, Kans. State U., 2003. Assoc. vet. St. Francis, Holt Rd. Pet Hosp., Indpls., 2003—06; vet. Well Pets Economy Clinics, Indpls., 2003—; relief vet. Self-Employed, Indpls., 2006—. Cons. vet. Morgan County Humane Soc., Martinsville, Ind., 2004—. Contbr. articles various profl. jours., scientific papers. Mem.: AVMA, Kans. Vet. Med. Assn., Ind. Vet. Med. Assn., Chesapeake Bay Retriever Relief, Rescue.

FINNEGAN, MARGARET MARY, school librarian; b. Dell Rapids, SD, Jan. 3, 1944; d. Peter A. and Mary M. Klein; m. Eugene G. Finnegan; 1 child, Joy. Degree in edn., Presentation Coll., 1964; BS in edn., Mount Senario Coll., 1969. Tchr. St. Jerome's Sch., St. Paul, 1964—66, 1967—69, Our Lady of Sorrows Sch., Ladysmith, Wis., 1966—67, Our Lady Gate of Heaven Sch., Chgo., 1971—73, St. Lawrence O'Toole Sch., Matteson, Ill., 1975—2004, Infant Jesus of Prague Sch., Flossmoor, Ill., 2004—05, libr., 2005—. Bd. dirs. Matteson Libr., 1977. Named Star of Sch., St. Lawrence O'Toole Sch., 1985. Mem.: NSTA, Ill. Reading Coun., Ill. Sci. Tchrs. Assn. (paper chmn. 1990—91). Democrat. Roman Catholic.

FINNEGAN, SARA ANNE (SARA F. LYCETT), publisher; b. Balt., Aug. 1, 1939; d. Lawrence Winfield and Rosina Elva (Huber) F.; m. Isaac C. Lycett, Jr., Aug. 31, 1974. BA, Sweet Briar Coll., 1961; MLA, Johns Hopkins U., 1965; exec. program, U. Va. Grad. Sch. Bus., 1977. Tchr., chmn. history dept. Hannah More Acad., Reisterstown, Md., 1961-65; redactor Williams & Wilkins Co., Balt., 1965-66, asst. head redactory, 1966-71, editor book div., 1971-75, assoc. editor-in-chief, 1975-77, v.p., editor-in-chief, 1977-81, pres. book div., 1981-88, group pres., 1988-94; editor Kalends, 1973-78, 89-92; exec. sponsor jour. Histochemistry and Cytochemistry, 1973-77. Dir. Passano Found., 1979—91. Editor: Visions, Friends of Art of Sweet Briar Coll. Mag., 2001—03. Trustee St. Timothy's Sch., Stevenson, Md., 1974—83; mem. adv. bd. Balt. Ind. Schs. Scholarship Fund, 1977—81; mem. adv. coun. grad. study Coll. Notre Dame of Md., 1983; mem. bd. overseers Sweet Briar Coll., 1987—88, bd. dirs., 1988—2000, chmn.-elect, 1994, chmn., 1995—2000, dir. emerita, 2003—; docent The Walters Art Mus., 1994—; v.p. The Walters Art Mus. Docents, 2000—01, pres., 2001—02; bd. trustees The Walters Art Mus., 2001—02; bd. dirs. The Woman's Indsl. Exch., Balt., 1997—2000, v.p., 1998—2000; bd. dirs. Friends of Art of Sweet Briar Coll., 2000—06, The Hamilton St. Club, 2003—06, The Art Seminar Group, 2004—. Mem. Assn. Am. Pubs. (exec. coun. prof. and scholarly pub. divsn. 1984-85), Internat. Sci., Tech. and Med. Pubs. Assn. (group exec. 1986-93, chmn.-elect 1988, chmn. 1989-92). Republican. Lutheran.

FINNERAN, KATIE (KATHLEEN FINNERAN), actress; b. Chgo., Jan. 22, 1971; Actor: (Broadway plays) On Borrowed Time, 1991—92, Two Shakespearean Actors, 1992, My Favorite Year, 1992—93, In the Summer House, 1993, The Heiress, 1995, Neil Simon's Proposals, 1997—98, The Iceman Cometh, 1999, Cabaret, 2000—01, Noises Off, 2001—02 (Tony award for Best Performance by a Featured Actor in a Play, 2002, Outer Critics Circle award, Drama Desk award nomination), (off-Broadway) Pig Farm, 2006; (films) Night of the Living Dead, 1990, You've Got Mail, 1998, Liberty Heights, 1999, Live at Five, 2005, Bewitched, 2005; (TV films) Plainsong, 2004; (TV series) Bram and Alice, 2002, Wonderfalls, 2003, The Inside, 2005—, (guest appearance) Sex and the City, 1998, Frasier, 1999, All My Children, 1999, Oz, 2001.*

FINNERTY, FRANCES MARTIN, medical administrator; b. Asheville, N.C., Dec. 23, 1936; d. Robert James and Elizabeth Howerton (Babbitt) Martin; m. Richard Phillip Caputo, Sept. 23, 1961 (div. 1974); m. Frank A. Finnerty Jr., July 26, 1975; children: Jonathan, Robert, Richard. Student, Mary Washington Coll., 1954-55, Croft Coll., 1955-57. Dist. mgr. Bus. Census Dept. Commerce, Suitland, Md., 1969-71; program coord. Georgetown U. D.C. Gen. Hosp., Washington, 1972-76; clin. mgr. Hypertension Ctr. Washington, 1976-82; project dir. PharmaKinetic Clin. Rsch. Labs., Balt., 1983; dir. mktg. Classic Glass, Alexandra, Va., 1984-86; office adminstr. Frank A. Finnerty Jr., M.D., Washington, 1987—. Cons. U.S. Census, U.S. Army, The Pentagon, Washington, 1969-70; cons. mapping ops. U.S. Census, Prince Georges County, Md., 1970; cons. paramedics pers. Merck Sharpe & Dohme, West Point, Pa., 1974. Contbr. articles to profl. jours. Recipient Cmty. Svc. award Dist. of Columbia, 1980. Mem. Am. Art League (Disting. Artist award 1993), Nat. Assn. Women in Arts, Dist. Med. Soc. Wives. Avocations: artist, landscape artist, reading. Home: 5 Eagle Circle Brevard NC 28712-4205 Office Phone: 828-883-8407.

FINNERTY, ISOBEL, Canadian senator; b. Timmins, ON, Can., July 15, 1930; m. Leslie Finnerty; children: Lorne, John. Grad., Timmins Bus. Coll., 1948. Med. sec., Timmins, 1948—58; internat. trainer Nat. Dem. Inst. for Internat. Affairs, Benin, 1994; senator The Senate of Can., Ottawa, 1999—. Bd. dirs. YMCA, Stratford, 1970—72; mem. fundraising com. Burlington Art Ctr. Liberal.

FINNERTY, LOUISE HOPPE, food products executive; b. Alexandria, Va., Jan. 19, 1949; d. William G. and Ruth A. (Ehren) Hoppe; m. John D. Finnerty, May 21, 1988; 1 child, William Patrick Taylor. BA, Va. Commonwealth U., 1971; postgrad., Am. U., 1972—73. Staff asst. to Dr. Henry Kissinger NSC, Washington, 1971-73; adminstrv. asst. Nat. Petroleum Coun., Washington, 1973-75; profl. staff mem. Senate Armed Svc. Com., Washington, 1976-81; spl. asst. Office Legis. Affairs, U.S. Dept. State, Washington, 1981-84, dep. asst. sec. of state, 1984-88; mgr. govt. affairs PepsiCo, Inc., Purchase, NY, 1988-91; dir. govt. affairs PepsiCo Foods and Beverages Internat., Somers, NY, 1991-95; v.p. internat. govt. affairs PepsiCo., Inc., Purchase, 1995—2003, v.p. global health and wellness policy, 2004—. Mem. Spring Lake Bath and Tennis Club, Coveleigh Club. Republican. Lutheran. Avocations: reading, gardening, cooking. Home: 400 Park Ave Rye NY 10580-1213 also: 506 2nd Ave Spring Lake NJ 07762-1107 Office: PepsiCo Inc 700 Anderson Hill Rd Purchase NY 10577-1444 Business E-Mail: louise.finnerty@pepsi.com.

FINNERTY, MADELINE FRANCES, consulting firm owner; b. Stockbridge, Mass., Jan. 3, 1949; d. John James and Frances Finnerty. BA cum laude, Newton Coll. of Sacred Heart, Newton, Mass., 1971; MBA, Ashland U., 1984; PhD Human and Orgn. Sys., Fielding Inst., Santa Barbara, 1999. From plant staff to gen. employee involvement mgr. Sprint United Tel. Co., Mansfield, Ohio, 1977-92; tng. and orgn. devel. mgr. Nat. Exch. Carrier Assn., Whippany, NJ, 1984-87; pres. Finnerty Internat., Ashland, Ohio, 1992—. Rotary Club Ashland, Ashland Women's Assn., Ashland Area Chorus, Ashland Cmty. Arts Ctr. Bd., 2000-03, United Way Ashland Bd., 2004-, Mem. ASTD (pres. Mohican Valley chpt. 1984, regional coord. 1986-89, dir. women's network 1990-91, nat. nominating com. 1992-94, quality symposia adv. com. 1992-94, Internat. Conf. Expn. Proposal rev. com., 2004), AAUW (program chair 1995-97), North Ctrl. Ohio Employee Participation Coun., Ashland Area C. of C. Office: Finnerty Internat 1046 Oak Hill Cir Ashland OH 44805-2947

FINNEY, FANNIE D., minister, educator; b. Weldon, N.C., Dec. 08; d. Walter P. and Corinthian H. Daniels; m. Walter M. Finney; 1 child, Ava Finney Hurdle. BA, Strayer U., 1974; degree, Norfolk State U., Va., 1975; PhD in Holistic Health Sci., Clayton U., 2003; PhD (hon.), Weldon Theol. Seminary, NC, 1975. CLU Va.; lic. cosmetologist Va. Ind. assoc. PrePaid Legal Svcs. Va., Norfolk; prin., owner Fannie D. Finney Ministries, Norfolk. Covenant elder Worldwide Ministries, San Diego, 2003—05; adv. rsch. Nat. Biog. Inst., 1999. Mem. amb. coun. Morris Cervellow Dr., San Diego, 1996; mem. commonwealth coun. State Va., 1998—99; pres. Nat. Senatorial Conv., Washington, 1994; mem. task force The Heritage Found., 1994. Named Woman of Yr., Nat. Bibliog. Soc., 1995, Most Influential Woman of Yr., Nat. Biog. Inst., 1998; recipient Patrick Henry award, Gov. James Gilmore, 1999. Mem.: Concerned Women Am., Pinewood Garden Club, Tidewater Street Garden Club. Republican. Presbyn. Avocations: bowling, reading. Home and Office: 2722 Westminster Ave Norfolk VA 23504-4528

FINNEY, LEE, retired social worker; b. Balt., Feb. 25, 1943; d. E. William and Mildred Lee (Refo) Carr; m. James Nathaniel Finney, Feb. 25, 1967 (div. Aug. 1970); 1 child, Karen Elizabeth. Student, Sweet Briar Coll., 1961-63; BA in Govt., George Washington U., 1965; MS in Counseling, Calif. State U., Hayward, 1986. Caseworker N.Y.C. Welfare Dept., 1966-68; probation officer N.Y.C. Probation Dept., 1968-74; dep. probation officer Alameda County Probation Dept., Oakland, Calif., 1974-78, child welfare social worker, 1979-80; children's svcs. social worker Contra Costa County Dept. Social Svcs., Richmond, Calif., 1980-87, social work supr. Antioch, Calif., 1987-88, dir. staff devel. Martinez, Calif., 1989-90; pay equity analyst Contra Costa County Pers. Dept., Martinez, 1988-89; labor rels. cons. Indsl. Employers and Distributors Assn., Emeryville, Calif., 1990—2005. Instr. edn. psychology dept. Calif. State U., Hayward, 1987-89; mem. exec. bd. Contra Costa Ctrl. Labor Coun., Martinez, 1987-89; no. v.p., chief negotiator Svc. Employees Internat. Union Local 535, Oakland, 1983-88; chair Coalition for Children and Families, Richmond, Calif., 1986-88. Author booklet: First Steps to Identifying Sex and Race Based Inequities in a workplace: A Guide to Achieving Pay Equity, 1989. Bd. dirs. YWCA, Contra Costa County, 1989-91; pres., acting dir. Comparable Worth Project, Inc., Oakland, 1984-87; mem. Adv. Com. on Employment and Econ. Status for Women Contra Costa, 1984-89, chair, 1987-89. Recipient Cmty. Svc. award Vocare Found., 1976, Golden Nike award Emeryville Bus. and Profl. Women, 1986, Woman of Yr. award Todos Santos Bus. and Profl. Women, 1989, Women Who Have Made a Difference award Coalition of Labor Union Women, 1989. Democrat. Avocations: sailing, travel, natural history. Office: IDEA 2200 Powell St Ste 1000 Emeryville CA 94608-1869 Home: 670 Americana Dr Apt 16 Annapolis MD 21403-3121 E-mail: lee.finney@worldnet.att.net.

FINNEY, LILA D., school system administrator; d. Gabriel Milton and Juanita Mae Daspit; 1 child, Jennifer Finney Mullins. BS, Centenary Coll., Shreveport, La., 1972; MEd, Va. State U., Petersburg, 1977; PhD, La. State U., Baton Rouge, 1997. Tchr. elem. sch. gifted Caddo Parish Schs., Shreveport, 1984—90; program evaluator La. State Dept. Edn., Baton Rouge, 1990—91, mgr. effective schs. program Bossier City, 1991—96, dir. region VII svc. ctr., 1997—98; supr. testing Caddo Parish Pub. Schs., 1998—2001, dir. profl. devel., 2001—. Adj. prof. La. State U., Shreveport, 1986—; mem. steering com. fin. planning team La. Ins. Consortium, 1998—; mem. adv. edn. com. Alliance Edn., 1999—. Mem.: Nat. Staff Devel. Coun., Phi Delta Kappa, Delta Kappa Gamma (sec. 2002—). Episcopalian. Avocations: travel, reading, gardening. Office: Caddo Parish Pub Schs 3908 Joplin Ave Shreveport LA 71108

FINNEY, SARA JANE, psychologist, educator; b. Neillsville, Wis., Jan. 13, 1972; d. Michael H. and Mary J. Finney; m. Steven M Hinrichs, June 14, 2003. BA, U. Wis., Eau Claire, 1994; MA, U. Nebr., Lincoln, 1997; PhD, U. Nebr., 2001. Asst. prof. James Madison U., Harrisonburg, Va., 2001—. Assessment specialist Ctr. for Assessment-James Madison U., Harrisonburg, Va., 2001—. Contbr. articles to profl. jours., chapters to books. Named Outstanding Jr. Faculty in Grad. Psychology Dept., James Madison U., 2003; recipient Outstanding Faculty in Psychology award, 2003. Mem.: Assn. of Psychol. Sci. (assoc.), Am. Ednl. Rsch. Assn. (assoc.), Structural Equation Modeling Spl. Interest Group (assoc.; treas. 2003—06). Democrat-Npl. Office: James Madison University Center for Assessment-MSC 6806 Harrisonburg VA 22807 Office Phone: 540-568-6757. Personal E-mail: finneysj@jmu.edu.

FINNIE, DORIS GOULD, investment company executive; b. Mpls., Sept. 2, 1919; d. Earl Chester and Marie Ethelee (McGulpin) Gould; m. Donald Johnstone Finnie, May 23, 1939 (dec. 2003); children: Dianne Elaine Boggess, Denise Finnie-Pascento; m. Harry W. Shade, Jan. 1, 2004. BA in Journalism, U. Denver, 1941. Office mgr. K&P, Inc., Golden, Colo., 1965-82; exec. dir. Rocky Mountain Coal Mining Inst., Lakewood, 1982—2000; conf. coord. Colo. Mining Assn., 2000—. Editor Procs. of Rocky Mountain Coal Mining Inst., 1982-2000. Founder City of Lakewood, 1968; dir. Alzheimer and Kidney Found., Denver, 1970-72. Recipient Ernest Thompson Seton award Camp Fire, Inc., 1963, St. Barbara's Day medal Colo. Mining Assn., 1999; named Woman of Yr. Denver Area Panhellenic, 1977; Paul Harris fellow Rotary Internat., 1998. Mem. Colo. Soc. Assn. Execs., Meeting Planners Internat. (Humanitarian award 1992), Profl. Conv. Mgmt. Assn., Mortar Board (Disting. Lifetime Mem. Achievement award 2001), Kappa Delta (Outstanding Alumnae award 1959, 74, Order of Emerald 1987, Order of Pearl 1995). Avocations: gourmet cooking, playing bridge. Office: 11701 W 21st Pl Lakewood CO 80215-1101

FINNIE, JOAN, adult education educator; b. Helena, Mont., Aug. 21, 1937; d. Phillip William and Esther Bowman Roth; m. John McCorkindale (dec.); children: Carrie McCorkindale, Kathryn McCorkindale Croxdale; m. Iain Finnie, July 28, 1969. BS with distinction, U. Minn., 1959. Tchr. Palo Alto Sch. Dist., Calif., 1960—61, Orinda Sch. Dist., Calif., 1961—62, Acalanes Adult Sch., Lafayette, Calif., 1981—83. Bd. mem., sec. Berkeley Repertory Theatre, 1976—90; bd. mem., founder Backstages Rep. Theatre, 1976—90; bd. mem. Am. Diabetes Assn., Oakland, Calif., 1977—86; bd. mem., alumni assn. Ecole Bilingue de Berkeley, 2004—05; bd. mem. Junior League of Oakland-East Bay, 1972—. Mem.: Sogetsu (corr. sec. 2003—05), Ikebana Internat. (v.p. 2000—03, bd. mem.), U. Calif. Berkeley Sect. Club (hon.; bd. mem. 1987—, pres. 1990—91, arranger/event planner, open house 2004, arranger/event planner, winter dinner 2005), Claremont (Calif.) Book Club (pres. 1981—82), Omicron Nu, Phi Upsilon Omicron, Prytanean Honor Soc. (sec. 2003—05, bd. mem.). Avocation: ihebana flower arranging. Home: 2901 Avalon Ave Berkeley CA 94705 E-mail: finnie@me.berkeley.edu.

FINOCCHIARO, PENNY MORRIS, secondary school educator; b. Glendale, Calif., Sept. 30, 1949; d. C. Harold and Margaret (Nelson) Morris; m. Paul D. Finocchiaro, Apr. 9, 1996; children from previous marriage: E. Pierce III, Hailey M. BA in Speech and English, Muskingum Coll., New Concord, Ohio, 1971; MA in Edn., Nat. U., Sacramento, 1991. Cert. multiple and single subject tchr. Assoc. prodr. Alhecama Players, Santa Barbara (Calif.) C.C. Dist., 1972-86; docent Santa Barbara Mus. Art, 1975-86; importer Cambridge Place Corp., Santa Barbara, 1974-86; promotions and fund raising Stewart-Bergman Assocs., Nevada City, Calif., 1986-89; travel columnist The Union, Grass Valley, Calif., 1987-90; tchr. drama and English Bear River H.S., Grass Valley, 1991-98, dept. chair visual and performing arts, 1993-98; tchr. English lit. Lyçee Français La Perouse, San Francisco, 1999—, chair dept. English, 2001—. Art docent coord. Deer Creek Sch., Nevada City, 1986-90, pres. Parent Tchr. Club, 1987-88. Recipient award for valuable contbn. to schs. Nevada City Sch. Dist., 1990, Dir.'s award Santa Barbara C.C., 1982, Tchrs. Who Make a Difference award Assn. of Calif. Sch. Adminstrs., 1998. Mem.: No. Calif. Ednl. Theatre Assn., Calif. Ednl. Theatre Assn., Ednl. Theatre Assn., Calif. Assn. Tchrs. English, Nat. Coun. Tchrs. of English. Avocations: art and antique collecting, rollerblading, travel, biking, swimming, theater. Home: 226 Francisco St San Francisco CA 94133 Office: Lycee Francais Internat 755 Ashbury St San Francisco CA 94117-4013 Office Phone: 415-661-5232 315. Business E-Mail: pfinocchiaro@lelycee.org.

FINQUE, SUSAN BETH, theatre artist, theater director; b. LA, Aug. 27, 1957; d. Burton William Fink and Diana Goss; m. Maria Elena Martinez, Nov. 1, 2002. BA, U. Calif., 1981; MFA, Yale Sch. Drama, 2003. Vis. prof. U. Wis., Mlkw.; artistic dir. Alice B. Theatre, Seattle, 1986—94; vis. dir. Cornish Coll. Arts, 1988—94, U. Wash., 1989—91; vis. prof. Antioch Coll., Yellow Springs, Ohio, 1994—97; assoc. artistic dir. Group Theatre, 1998—99; freelance dir., actor, educator, 1975—. Bd. mem. Evansville Arts Coun., Wis., 2004—. Dir.: (theatre performance) (L)imitations of Life; author: (play) Portraits Of Iowa; dir.(creator): (theatre performance) Sudden Transfers: A New Theatrework On Women In Prison, (conceiver) T/S Crossing: A New Theatrework On Transexuality, (creator) Governing Bodies, Contents Under Pressure; co-creator, dir.: Professor Marvel's Miracle Pandemonium Review And Side Show; actor(co-creator): (theatre company) Caught In The Act: A Theatre Collective Of Four Short Women; dir.: (numerous Shakespeare) Comedy of Errors, As You Like It, MacBeth, Taming Of The Shrew, Hamlet, Midsummer Nights Dream, (co-creator) (theatre performance) Unkle Tomm's Kabin: A Deconstruction Of The Novel By Harriet Beecher Stowe, (musical) Kiss of the Spider Woman, 2006 (Joseph Jefferson's award for Best Dir., 2006). Dir., educator for at-risk youth Am. Friends Svc. Com., Seattle, 1989—94; co. mem. Bathouse Theatre, 1985—86. Recipient Milton Kaufman Dirs. award, Yale Sch. Drama, 2003, Career Acknowledgement prize, Nat. Fund For Lesbian And Gay Artists, 1995; grantee Rsch. grant, Larry Kramer Fund For Rsch., 2003; grant for new work, Seattle Arts Commn., 1988, 1990, Individual Artist grant, King Country Arts Commn., 1992, grant for new work, Wash. State Arts Commn., 1990, Dirs. fellow, Theatre Comm. Group, Nat. Endowment For The Arts, 2000. Home: 443 South First St Evansville WI 53536 Office: Real Coffee 18 E Main St Evansville WI 53536 Office Phone: 206-898-0919.

FINTA, FRANCES MICKNA, secondary school educator; b. Stafford Springs, Conn., June 17, 1927; d. John Joseph Mickna and Mary Frances Breslin; m. Quinn Finta, Aug. 21, 1951; children: John Wright, Susan Frances Finta Phillips. BA in Math., Boston U., 1949; postgrad., U. Va., 1963—69, Prince George's C.C., Largo, Md., 1982, No. Va. C.C., Alexandria, 1982—84, postgrad., 1994, U. Va., Fairfax, 1988—89; MEd in Guidance and Counseling, George Mason U., 1975. Cert. tchr. Va. Food prodn. mgr., dining rm. mgr., waitress, field ops. rep., liaison to airlines Marriott Corp., Marriott In-Flight Svcs., Inc., Washington, 1950—62; tchr. math, Arlington (Va.) Pub. Schs., 1963—72, 1963—. Substitute tchr. Fairfax (Va.) Pub. Schs., 1972—73; substitute tchr. Arlington (Va.) County Pub. Schs., 1972—. Mem. Arlington County Scholarship Fund for Tchrs., Inc., 1995—, sec., 1996—2001, treas., 2002—; mem. Friends of Arlington Parks, 1995—, Maywood Cmty. Assn., 1966—; treas. Washington-Lee H.S. Band Booster Club, 1979—81, Evelyn Staples for County Bd., 1991; vol. coord. David Foster for Sch. Bd., 1994, 2003; mem. Arlingtonians for a Better County, 1999—2003; Maywood del. Arlington County Civic Fedn., 1982—, nominating com., 2006—, mem. awards com., 2005—06, exec. com., 1995—, chmn. exec. com., 1995—97, treas., 2000—06, v.p., 2006—; mem. Arlington County Rep. Com., 1994—, chmn. hdqrs., 2000—, mem. fin. com., 1994—95, canvass chmn., 2000, 2000, 2002, 2004, 2006, chmn. nominations com., 2000—01, chmn. credentials com., 2006; mem. steering com. John Hager for Gov., 2000; del. to state conv. Rep. Party Va., 1996, 1998, 2000, Va. Fedn. Rep. Women, 1996—; mem. credential com. Va. 8th Dist. Rep. Conv., 1998; sec.'s adv. com. Commonwealth of Va., 1998—2002; mem. Organized Women Voters of Arlington, 1997—2004, mem. nominating com., 2000, treas., 2000—04. Recipient Hon. Guardian of Srs.' Rights award, 60 Plus Assn., 1999, Vol. Svc. award, Arlington County Rep. Com., 1995—99, Hilda Griffith Lifetime Achievement award, 1999, Leon Delyannis Cmty. Involvement award, 1997, award of Excellence, 2004, Cert. of Appreciation, Arlington County Civic Fedn., 1988, 1997, Jour. Newspapers trophy, 2001, Parent Vol. award, Washington-Lee H.S. Band Boosters Club, 1979, Appreciation award, 1981, Parent Vol. award, Woodmont Elem. Sch., 1975, Patrick Henry award, Commonwealth of Va., 2001, Disting. Meritorious Svc. award, Arlington County Civic Fedn., 2003, Vol. Svc. award, Arlington County Rep. Com., 2003, Cert. of Appreciation, Arlington County Voters in Partnership Program, 2001. Mem.: AAUW (del. to Arlington County Civic Fedn. 1994—, co-1st v.p. programs 2001—03, exec. com. 2001—, 1st v.p. programs 2002—03, policy chair 2003—05, co-policy chair 2005—), NEA, Arlington Ret. Tchrs. Assn. (1st v.p. programs 2004—, exec. com. 2004—, v.p. programs 2004—06, pres. 2006—), Arlington Edn. Assn., Va. Edn. Assn., Va. Ret. Tchrs. Assn. (life), Arlington County Civic Fedn. (mem. exec. com. 1995—, mem. awards com. 2005—06, treas. 1998—2006, v.p. 2006—), Maywood Cmty. Assn. (delegate 1982—, nominating com. 2006), Arlington County Taxpayers' Assn., Arlington Rep. Women's Club (auditor 1996, asst. treas. 1997, pres. 1998—99, newsletter editor 1998—99, exec. bd. 1998—, chmn. achievement awards 2000, chmn. bylaws com. 2000, chmn. Barbara Bush literacy com. 2000, dir. 2000—01, auditor 2002—03, chair fin. com. 2002—). Republican. Roman Catholic. Avocations: civic and political activities, reading. Home: 3317 23d St N Arlington VA 22201-4310

FINUCANE, ANNE M., communications executive, marketing executive; married; 4 children. BA with honors, U. N.H. Pub. info. officer Mayor of City of Boston; dir. creative svcs. Sta. WBZ-TV, Boston; head creative svcs. Hill, Holliday, Connors, Cosmopulos, Inc., Boston, dir. account mgmt., dir. corp. devel.; prin. Anne Finucane Mktg. and Telecomm., Boston; sr. v.p., dir. corp. mktg. and comm. Fleet Fin. Group, Boston, 1995—. Bd. dirs. Internat. Ctr. for Journalists. Bd. dirs. Urban Improv, Emerson Coll., New Eng. Coun., Mass. Women's Forum; co-chmn. tech. divsn. United Way of Mass. Bay Campaign, 1995, 96; mem. adv. coun. Children's Defense Fund, Washington, Conservation Law Found. Office: Fleet Fin Group Corp Mktg & Comm One Federal St Boston MA 02110 Fax: 617-346-4740.

FINUCANE, MELISSA LUCILLE, psychologist, researcher; d. Anthony and Veronica Finucane. BS with honors, U. Western Australia, Perth, 1991, M of Psychology, 1998, PhD, 1997. Lic. Psychologist Western Australia. Rsch. scientist Decision Sci. Rsch. Inst., Eugene, Oreg., 1997—2001; rsch. investigator Ctr. for Health Rsch., Hawaii, Kaiser Permanente Hawaii, Honolulu, 2001—. Recipient Australian Skeptics Eureka prize, 1999; grantee, NSF, 2000—, Nat. Inst. on Aging, 2001—. Mem.: AAAS, APA, Am. Psychol. Soc., Soc. Risk Analysis, Soc. Judgement and Decision Making. Achievements include research in affect heuristic, risk perception and decision-making competence. Office: Ctr Health Rsch Hawaii Kaiser Permanente Hawaii 501 Alakawa St Honolulu HI 96817 Office Phone: 808-432-4754. Office Fax: 808-432-4785. Business E-Mail: melissa.l.finucane@kp.org.

FIOCK, SHARI LEE, marketing professional, consultant; b. Weed, Calif., Oct. 25, 1941; d. Webster Bruce and Olevia May (Pruett) Fiock; children from previous marriage: Webster Clinton Pfingsten, Sterling Curtis. Cert., Art Instrn. Sch., Mpls., 1964. Copywriter Darron Assocs., Eugene, Oreg., 1964—68; staff artist Oreg. Holidays, Springfield, 1966—69, 1971; co-owner, designer Artre Enterprises, Eugene, 1969—74; design entrepreneur Shari & Assocs., Yreka, Calif., 1974—99; exec. dir. Siskiyou County Econ. Devel. Coun., Yreka, 1999—2005; gen. mgr. Jefferson State Trailer Works Divsn. R.T. Shanahan, Inc., 2006—. Cons., devel. sec. Cascade World Four Season Resort, Siskiyou County, 1980—86; owner Coyote Pub., 1991—99; adminstrv. asst., coord. regional catalog Gt. No. Corp. U.S. Dept. Commerce and Econ. Devel., 1994—96; local cons. CalEnergy Co., Inc., 1998—99. 5 ton chain saw sculpture, Oreg. Beaver, 1967, Holiday Fun Book, 1978; author, illustrator: Family Reunions and Clan Gatherings, 1991, Blue Goose Legend, 1995, 1998; editor: Choo and Moo Cookbook, 1998. Counselor Boy Scouts Am., 1983—91; mem. steering com. counties exhibits Calif. State Fair, coord. Siskiyou County booth, 2006; mem. leadership program Ford Family Found., 2005, mem. Ford Inst. Leadership, 2005; mem. Leadership Siskiyou County, 2001; co-creator Klamath Nat. Forest Interpretive Mus., 1979—91; rschr. Beaver Ofcl. State Animal, Eugene, 1965—71; residential capt. United Way, Eugene, 1972. Mem.: Classic-Hist. Vehicle Assn.-Siskiyou Region (editor/pub. Rust Bucket 2003—), Siskiyou Writers Club (co-founder, past pres.). Home and Office: 406 Walters Ln Yreka CA 96097-9704 Office Phone: 530-842-7279. E-mail: sharifiock@snowcrest.net.

FIOL MATTA, LIANA, judge; Grad., Trinity Coll.; M., Columbia U., 1988, JSD, 1996; JD, U. P.R. Prof. Inter-Am. U., 1978—88, Pontifical Catholic U.; judge PR Ct. of Appeals, 1992—2003; justice PR Supreme Ct., 2004—. Author numerous articles in professional journals. Mem.: P.R. Bar Assn. Office: PR Supreme Ct PO Box 9022392 San Juan PR 00902-2392*

FIORI, PAMELA, publishing executive, writer; b. Newark, Feb. 26, 1944; d. Edward and Rita (Rascati) F.; m. Colton Givner. BA cum laude, Jersey City State Coll., 1966. Tchr. English Gov. Livingston High Sch., Berkeley Heights, NJ, 1966-67; assoc. editor Holiday Mag., NYC, 1968-71, Travel & Leisure Mag., NYC, 1971-74, sr. editor, 1974-75, editor-in-chief, 1975-80; editor-in-chief, exec. v.p. Am. Express Pub. Corp. (Travel & Leisure/Food & Wine), NYC, 1980-89, editorial dir., exec. v.p., 1989-93; editor-in-chief Town & Country, NYC, 1993—. Columnist: Travel & Leisure, 1976—89, Town & Country, 1993—; contbr. articles to periodicals. Founding chmn. UNICEF Snowflake Project; bd. trustees US Fund for UNICEF. Recipient Chevalier de l'Ordre du Merite, 1985, Melva C. Pederson award for disting. travel journalism Am. Soc. Travel Afts., 1992, Outstanding Woman of the 90s award Found. for Neurosurg. Rsch., 1994, Bus. award Nat. Italian Am. Found., 1996, Fashion Oracle of Yr., Coun. Fashion Designers, 2004, Audrey Hepburn Humanitarian award UNICEF, 2005. Office: Town & Country 300 W 57th St New York NY 10019-3794 Office Phone: 212-903-5334.

FIORINA, CARLY (CARA CARLETON SNEED FIORINA), former computer company executive; b. Austin, Tex., Sept. 6, 1954; d. Joseph and Madelon Sneed; m. Frank J. Fiorina; 2 stepchildren BA in Medieval History and Philosophy, Stanford U., 1976; MBA, Robert H. Smith Sch. Bus. U. Md., College Park, Md., 1980; MSc in Mgmt., MIT, 1989; postgrad., UCLA. Account exec. Long Lines AT&T, 1980, sr. v.p. Global Mktg., pres., AT&T network systems, N. Am., 1994—95; exec. v.p. corp. ops. Lucent Technologies, Murray Hill, NJ, 1995—96, pres., consumer products bus., 1996—97, group pres. Global Svc. Provider bus., 1997—99; pres. Hewlett-Packard Co., Palo Alto, 1999—2000, CEO, 1999—2005, chmn., 2000—05. Bd. dirs., PowerUp, Hewlett-Packard, 1999-2005, Merck & Co. Inc., 1999-2001, Revolution Healthcare Group, 2005-, Cybertrust, 2005-, MIT, Taiwan Semiconductor Mfg. Co., 2006-; mem., US China Bd. Trade., 1999-, US Space Commn., 2004- Author: Tough Choices: A Memoir, 2006. Named one of Fortune Mag. Most Powerful Women in Am. Bus., Top 50 Women To Watch, Wall St. Jour., 2005; recipient Appeal of Conscience award, 2002, Concern Worldwide Seeds of Hope award, 2003, Leadership award, Private Sector Coun., 2004; grantee Hon. Fellow, London Bus. Sch., 2001. Business E-Mail: csfiorina@sbcglobal.net.*

FIORITO, REBECCA, elementary school educator; b. Lewisburg, Pa., June 21, 1974; d. Willie Edward and Marie Elizabeth Jones; m. Eric Fiorito, May 28, 1999; children: Morgan Jane, Jenna Marie, Regan Jacqueline. BA, Kutztown U., Pa., 1992—96; MEd, Wilkes U., Wilkes-Barre, Pa., 2001—05. Cert. Tchr. Pa. Dept. Edn., 1999, Tchr., Secondary Edn., Social Studies Pa. Dept. Edn., 2000. Dept. chaiperson WSD, Ambler, Pa., 2005—. Home: 2067 Fruitville Rd East Greenville PA 18041 Office: Wissahickon Mid Sch 500 Houston Rd Ambler PA 19002 Office Phone: 215-619-8110. Business E-Mail: rfiorito@wsd.k12.pa.us.

FIOTI, JEAN K., pharmacist; b. Wilkes-Barre, Pa., Dec. 4, 1959; d. William Raymond and Jean (Welebob) Kustis; m. Vito Joseph Fioti, Oct. 24, 1987; children: Christoper Joseph, Maria Celesta. BS in Pharmacy, Duquesne U., 1982; PharmD, U. Md. at Baltimore, 2000. Registered Pharmacist, 1982. Pharmacy mgr. Rite Aid Corp., Wilkes-Barre, Pa., 1982—90; cons. pharmacist Beverly Enterprises, Wilkes-Barre, 1995; v.p. Precision Mgmt. Cons., Inc., Wilkes-Barre, 1995—97; pharmaceutical sales rep. Bayer, Inc., West Haven, Conn., 1990—95; market devel. assoc. Merck, Inc., West Point, Pa., 1995—96; sr. clin. hosp. rep. Genentech, Inc., S. San Francisco, 1996—98; mid-atlantic regional cons. cardiology svcs. Schering-Plough, Kenilworth, NJ, 1998—99; immunology specialist Centocor, Inc., Malvern, Pa., 1999—2001, clin. info. scientist, med. affairs-immunology, 2001—. Instr. SAT Princeton Review, 1996-98. Mem. Lackawanna Co. Pharmaceutical Assn. (v.p. 1996-97). Avocations: music, archaeology, tutoring. Office: Centocor Inc 550 Lantern Hill Rd Shavertown PA 18708-9451

FIRCHOW, EVELYN SCHERABON, German language and literature educator, writer; b. Vienna; arrived in US, 1951, naturalized, 1964; d. Raimund and Hildegard (Nickl) Scherabon; m. Peter E. Firchow, 1969; children: Felicity (dec. 1988), Pamina. BA, U. Tex., 1956; MA, U. Man., 1957; PhD, Harvard U., 1963. Instr. coll. math. Balmoral Hall Sch., Winnipeg, Man., Canada, 1953—55; tchg. fellow in German Harvard U., Cambridge, Mass., 1957—58, 1961—62; lectr. German U. Md. in Munich, 1961; instr. German U. Wis., Madison, 1962—63, asst. prof., 1963—65; assoc. prof. German U. Minn., Mpls., 1965—69, prof. German and Germanic philology, 1969—, McKnight rsch. prof., 2004—; vis. prof. U. Fla., Gainesville, 1973; Fulbright rsch. prof. Iceland, 1966—67, 1980, 1984; vis. rsch. prof. Nat. Cheng Kung U., Tainan, Taiwan, 1982—83; permanent vis. prof. Jilin U., Changchun, China, 1987—. Vis. prof. U. Graz, Austria, 1989, Austria, 91, Austria, 2002—03, U. Vienna, Austria, 1995, U. Bonn, 1996, Nat. U. Costa Rica, 2000. Editor and author: (under name E.S. Coleman) Taylor Starck-Festschrift, 1964, Stimmen aus dem Stundenglas, 1968, (under name E.S. Firchow) Studies by Einar Haugen, 1972, Studies for Einar Haugen, 1972, Was Deutsche lesen, 1973, Deutung und Bedeutung, 1973, Elucidarius in Old Norse Translation, 1989, The Old Norse Elucidarius: Original Text and English Translation, 1992, Notker der Deutsche von St. Gallen: De interpretatione, 1995, Categoriae, 2 Vols., 1996, De nuptiis Philologiae et Mercurii, 2 Vols., 1999, Notker der Deutsche von St. Gallen (950-1022): Ausführliche Bibliographie, 2000, De consolatione Philosophiae, 3 vols., 2003, Reluctant Modernists, Festschrift Peter Firchow, 2002, Gottfried von Strassburg: Tristan und Isolde, 2004; translator: Einhard: Vita Caroli Magni, Das Leben Karls des Grossen, 1968, 84, 95, Einhard: Vita Caroli Magni, The Life of Charlemagne, 1972, 85, Icelandic Short Stories, 1974, 87, East German Short Stories, 1979, (with P.E. Firchow) Alois Brandstetter, The Abbey, 1998; dir., editor Computer Clearing-House Project for German and Medieval Scandinavian, to 2000; assoc. editor Germanic Notes and Revs., Am. Linguistics, Germanic Linguistics; contbr. articles and book revs. to profl. jours. Fulbright scholar Tex., 1951-52; fellow Alexander von Humboldt-Stiftung, Munich, 1960-61, Tuebingen, 1974, Marburg, 1981, Goettingen, 1985, Tokyo, 1991, Marburg and Berlin, 1993, Bonn, 2001, Fulbright Found., Iceland, 1967-68, 80, 94, Austrian Govt., 1977, NEH, 1980-81, Am. Inst. Indian Studies, 1988, BUSH fellow, 1989, Thor Thors fellow, 1994, Faculty summer fellow and Mc Knight summer fellow, 1995, 96, 99, 2004, Deutscher Akademischer Austausdienst (DAAD) rsch. fellow, 2000; elected hon. mem. Multilingual Rsch. Ctr., Brussels, 1986. Mem. AAUP, MLA (chmn. divsn. German lit. to 1700 1979-80, 93-96, vice chmn. pedagogical seminar for Germanic philology 1979-86, 91-93, chair 1994), Medieval Acad. Am., Soc. German-Am. Studies (chair Linguistics I 1992), Internat. Comparative Lit. Assn., Soc. for Advancement Scandinavian Studies (chmn. Germanic philology 1979, text editing 1980, linguistics 1984, computers and Old Norse 1985), Assn. for Lang. and Linguistic Computing (founding mem.), Am. Comparative Lit. Assn., Midwest Modern Lang. Assn. (chmn. German I 1965-66, chmn. Scandinavian 1979), Am. Assn. Tchrs. German, Mediävisten Verband, Soc. for Germanic Philology, Österreichische Germanisten-Gesellschaft, Assn. Lit. Scholars and Critics. Office: U Minn 205 Folwell Hall 9 Pleasant St SE Minneapolis MN 55455 Business E-Mail: firch001@umn.edu.

FIREBAUGH, FRANCILLE MALOCH, academic administrator; b. El Dorado, Ark., July 15, 1933; d. Delton Verdis and Dorothy Lucille (Measeles) Maloch; m. John David Firebaugh, Dec. 28, 1970. BS, U. Ark., 1955; MS, U. Tenn., 1956; PhD, Cornell U., 1962. Instr. U. Tex., Austin, 1956-58; asst. prof. home econs. Ohio State U., Columbus, 1962-65, assoc. prof., 1965-69, prof., 1969-88; dir. Sch. Home Econs., 1973-82; acting v.p. agrl. adminstrn.; exec. dean of agr., home econs., natural resources, 1982-83; assoc. provost Office Acad. Affairs, 1983-84; vice provost for internat. affairs, 1984-88; acting provost, v.p. acad. affairs, 1985-86; dean coll. human ecology Cornell U., Ithaca, NY, 1988-99, dir. spl. projects office of pres. and provost, 2000—01, vice provost for land grant affairs, spl. asst. to the pres., 2001—05, sr. consultant to provost, 2005—. Mem. joint com. on agrl. research and devel. Bd. Internat. Food and Agr., 1982-87. Author: Home Management: Context and Concepts, 1975, Family Resource Management, 1981, 88. Bd. dirs. Columbus Coun. on World Affairs, 1987-88, Boyce Thompson Inst. for Plant Rsch., 1991-97; moderator First Baptist Ch., 1981-83; bd. dirs. Cayuga Med. Ctr., 1992-2001, Panamerican Agr. Sch., Zamorano, Honduras, 1994—, Kendal at Ithaca, 1995-2003; Families and Work Inst., N.Y.C., 1995—; trustee Ithaca (N.Y.) Coll., 2000—, Cmty. Found. of Tompkins County, 2000-02. Mem. Nat. Coun. Family Rels., AAAS, Am. Home Econs. Found. (bd. dirs. 1987-90), Am. Assn. of Family and Consumer Scis., Ohio State U. Faculty Club (pres. 1988), Assn. Women in Devel. (sec. 1988-89), Sigma Xi, Sigma Delta Epsilon, Kappa Omicron Nu, Phi Upsilon Omicron, Gamma Sigma Delta, Phi Kappa Phi, Epsilon Sigma Phi. Office: Cornell U Office of Provost 449 Day Hall Ithaca NY 14853-2801 Business E-Mail: fmf1@cornell.edu.

FIREHOCK, BARBARA A., interior designer; b. Alexandria, Va., Feb. 2, 1944; d. George W. Jr. and Geraldine Tinsley (Wallin) Sickler; m. Scott Walton Ripley, Dec. 27, 1966 (div.); m. Raymond B. Firehock, Jr.; 1 child, Christopher Francis. BA, U. N. Tex., 1966; postgrad., U. Md., 1976-77. Vol. Peace Corps, Colombia, 1967-69; owner Walnut Hill Interiors, 1981—, Staunton, Va.; instr. in interior design Charles County C.C., 1990; site supr./interior design internship U. Md., College Park, 1992. Program com. Matawoman Creek Arts Ctr., Charles County, Md., 1995-96; fundraiser The Gallery Com. of Charles County, 1988-94; interior designer Fredericksburg Area Svc. League Decorator Showhouse, 1997—, So. Md. Decorator Showhouse, 1998. Design work featured in Town and Country, 1997, Community Carousel Weekly Show/Prestige Cable, Fredericksburg, The Maryland Independent, 1991, The Maryland House and Garden Pilgrimage, 1995-96, Traditional Home, 1999. Spl. events chair Charles County Garden Club of Md.; charter mem. Blackfriars Theater, Staunton, Hist. Staunton Found.; area rep. Ctr. for Cultural Interchange, 2005—; chair Christ Ch. Concert Series, LaPlata, 1995. Named Woman of Yr., Bus. and Profl. Women, Charles County, 1982; recipient Residential Restoration award, Hist. Staunton Found., 2003. Fellow Nat. Trust for Hist. Preservation (nat. capitol area fellow, design assoc.); mem. ASID, Interior Design Soc. (pres. Md. chpt.), AAUW (pres., v.p., cultural chair Charles County chpt.), Chi Omega (rush info. chair for So. Md. 1993-98). Democrat. Episcopalian. Avocations: horseback riding, gardening, needlecrafts, genealogy. Home and Office: 330 Vine St Staunton VA 24401-4354 E-mail: whidesign@aol.com.

FIRESTONE, NANCY B., federal judge; b. Manchester, N.H., Oct. 17, 1951; d. Albert and Bernice (Brown) F. BA, Washington U., St. Louis, 1973; JD, U. Mo., 1977. Bar: Mo. 1977, U.S. Ct. Appeals (2nd, 4th, 5th, 6th, 9th, 8th and 10th cirs.). Trial atty. U.S. Dept. Justice, Washington, 1977-84, asst. chief, 1984-85, dep. chief environ. enforcement, 1985-89, dept. asst. atty. gen., environment & natural resources div., 1995—98; assoc. dep. adminstr. EPA, 1989-92, adminstrv. judge, 1992-95; judge US Ct. of Fed. Claims, 1998—. Adj. prof. Georgetown U. Law Ctr., 1986—. Mem. ABA.

FIRESTONE, SUSAN PAUL, artist; b. Madison, Wis., Nov. 13, 1946; d. John Robertson and Sue Hadaway Paul; m. John D. Firestone, Nov. 30, 1943 (div.); children: Mary, Lucy. BA, Mary Baldwin Coll., 1968; MFA, Am. U., 1972; MA in Art Therapy, NYU, 2002. Child and adolescent psychotherapist Inst. Psychoanalytic Tng. and Rsch., registered art therapist, master of arts board cert. Mem. Art Table, N.Y.C., Mus. bd. Corcoran Gallery, Washington; trustee Skowhegan Sch., N.Y.C.; mem. faculty Corcoran Coll. Art & Design; adj. faculty Corcoran Coll. Art and Design; artist, art therapist Red Cross 9/11 Recovery Program. Artist/author: Armour-Amour, 1992; solo exhbns. include Gallery K, Washington, 1983-95, Harmony Hall, Washington, Md., 1993, NIH, Bethesda, Md., 1992, Peat Marwick Inaugural Show, Washington, 1988, Covington and Burling, Washington, 1985, others; group exhbns. Inst. of Contemporary Art, Boston, 1995, San Diego Art Inst., 1995, Nat. Mus. of Women in Arts, 1994, Drawing Ctr., NY, 1993, Ctr. for Visual Arts, U. Toledo, 1993, Coll. of Notre Dame, Md., 1993, Minot (N.D.) Art Gallery, 1993, Art Works Gallery, Green Bay, Wis., 1993, Arlington Cemetary Women's Meml., 2005, Retrospective Exhbition 2006, Mary Baldwin Coll., 2006 others; various pub. and pvt. collections. Resident Pyramid Atlantic, Riverdale, Md., 1993; cultural exch. student USIS/Morocco, 1994. Office: Redstone Studio 59 Wooster St New York NY 10012-4349 E-mail: rubilite@aol.com.

FIRMSTONE, KRISTAL, elementary school educator; b. Mt. Pleasant, Pa., Feb. 22; d. Richard and Bonnie Hutchinson. MA in Edn., California U. Pa., 1995. Elem. tchr. Frederick County Pub. Schools, Winchester, Va., 1997—98; mid. sch. tchr. Yough Mid. Sch., Ruffsdale, Pa., 1999—. Behavioral specialist cons. WJS Psychol., Uniontown, Pa., 1998—. Active Internat. Order Rainbow, Scottdale, Pa., 1986—2006. Ednl. fellow, California U. Pa., 1993—95. Mem.: NEA.

FIRSTENBERG, JEAN PICKER, film institute executive; b. NYC, Mar. 13, 1936; d. Eugene and Sylvia (Moses) Picker; m. Paul Firstenberg, Aug. 9, 1956 (div. July 1980); children: Debra, Douglas BS summa cum laude, Boston U., 1958. Asst. producer Altman Prodns., Washington, 1965-66; media advisor J. Walter Thompson, N.Y.C., 1969-72; asst. for spl. projects Princeton U., NJ, 1972-74, dir. publs. NJ, 1974-76; program officer John and Mary R. Markle Found., N.Y.C., 1976—80; CEO Am. Film Inst., L.A., Washington, 1980—; mem. Citizens' Stamp Advisory Com. U.S. Postal Svc., 2002—. Bd. dirs. Trans-Lux Corp.; former chmn. nat. adv. bd. Peabody Broadcasting Awards; bd. dirs. Trans-Lux Corp. Former trustee Boston U.; mem. adv. bd. Will Rogers Inst., N.Y.C.; chmn., bd. advisors Film Dept. N.C. Sch. of Arts. Recipient Alumni award for disting. service to profession Boston U., 1982; seminar and prodn. chairs at directing workshop for women named in her honor Am. Film Inst., 1986 Mem. Women in Film (Crystal award 1990), Trusteeship for Betterment of Women, Acad. Motion Picture Arts and Scis. Office: Am Film Inst 2021 N Western Ave Los Angeles CA 90027-1657 Office Phone: 323-856-7677.

FISCHBACH, RUTH LINDA, ethics educator, social scientist, researcher; b. NYC, June 7, 1940; d. Edward Joseph and Bess (Wolsk) Zeitlin; m. Gerald David Fischbach, July 8, 1962; children: Elissa, Peter, Mark and Neal (twins). Student, Mt. Holyoke Coll., 1958—60; BS, RN, Cornell U., 1963; MS, Boston U., 1975, PhD, 1983; MPE, Washington U., 1990. Dir. patient edn. Beth Israel Hosp., Boston, 1978-80; postdoctoral fellow Washington U. Sch. Medicine, St. Louis, 1983-86, asst. rsch. prof., 1986-90, asst. dean, 1989-90; asst. prof. Harvard Med. Sch., Boston, 1990-98; sr. advisor for biomed. ethics Office of Dir. for Extramural Rsch./NIH, Bethesda, Md., 1998—2001; prof. bioethics Coll. Physicians and Surgeons, Mailman Sch. Pub. Health Columbia U., NYC, 2001—, dir. Ctr. Bioethics, 2001—. Dir. Program for Humanities in Medicine Washington U. Sch. Medicine, 1988—90, Program in Practice of Sci. Investigation Harvard Med. Sch., 1990—98; bd. dir. Pub. Responsibility in Med. and Rsch., Boston, 1992—; reviewer Univ.-wide AIDS Rsch. Program State Calif., 1995; adv. bd. Beth Israel Clin. Investigator Tng. Program, Boston, 1995—; vice chmn. bd. dirs. Pub. Responsibility in Med. and Rsch., Boston, 2002—. Producer: (dramatization) Miss Evers' Boys, 1993; editl. bd. Sci. & Engring. Ethics, 1994—; contbr. articles to profl. jours., chpts. to books. Pres. Lincoln Sch. PTA, Brookline, Mass., 1978—80; vol. Mass. Coalition of Battered Women Svc. Groups, Boston, 1993—98; trustee Penzance Point, 1998—, Parc Somerset Condo., Chevy Chase, Md., Morris Jumel Mansion, 2002—; med. and profl. adv. coun. Gold Found., 2002—; bd. dirs. Joint Com. on Status of Women, Boston, 1990—97. Fellow Exec. Inst. of Advanced Study, St. Louis, 1988; recipient Disting. Alumna award Cornell U., 2003. Mem. Applied Rsch. Ethics Nat. Assn. (bd. dirs. 1994—), Mass. Bioethics Forum (bd. dirs. 1994—), Md. Mothers of Twins (pres. 1969-70), Bioethics Consortium of Ukraine (adv. bd. 2005—), Sigma Theta Tau. Avocations: horticulture, travel, music. Home: 100 Riverside Dr # 3A New York NY 10024 Office Phone: 212-305-8387.

FISCHBARG, ZULEMA F., pediatrician; b. Buenos Aires, Mar. 22, 1937; arrived in U.S., 1962; d. Naun and Esther (Pollner) Fridman; m. Jorge Fischbarg; children: Gabriel Julian, Victor Ernesto. MD, U. Buenos Aires, 1960. Pediatric intern Children's Hosp., Louisville, 1962-63, resident in pediatrics, 1963, chief resident in pediatrics, 1964; fellow hematology Michael Reese Med. Ctr., Chgo., 1964-66, Presbyn. St. Lukes Hosp., Chgo., 1966-67; fellow pediatric hematology Children's Meml. Hosp., Chgo., 1967-68; asst. clin. pediatrician U. Chgo., 1968-69; instr. in pediatrics Cornell U. Med. Sch., N.Y.C., 1970-72, asst. prof. in pediatrics, 1972-76; assoc. prof. clin. pediatrics Weil Med. Coll., Cornell U., N.Y.C., 1978—; emeritus assoc. attending pediatrician N.Y. Hosp., Queens; med. specialist, sch. health dept. Health, N.Y.C., 1994—. Assoc. in pediat. Lenox Hill Hosp., N.Y.C.; instr. in medicine Ill. U., Chgo., 1967—68; assoc. attending physician N.Y. Hosp., N.Y.C., 1972—. Fellow: Am. Acad. Pediat. Democrat. Jewish. Home: 530 E 72d St Apt 17B New York NY 10021 E-mail: zule@nyc.rr.com.

FISCHER, DALE SUSAN, judge; b. Orange, N.J., Oct. 17, 1951; d. Edward L. and Audrey (Tenner) F.D. Student, Dickinson Coll., 1969-70; BA magna cum laude, U. So. Fla., 1977; JD, Harvard U., 1980. Bar: Calif. 1980. Ptnr. Kindel & Anderson L.L.P., L.A., 1980-96; spl. counsel Heller Ehrman White & McAuliffe, L.A., 1996-97; judge L.A. Mcpl. Ct., 1997, L.A. Superior Ct., 2000; dist. judge U.S. Dist. Ct. Ctrl. Dist. Calif., L.A., 2003—. Faculty Nat. Inst. Trial Advocacy; lawyer in classroom Constl. Rights Found.; moderator, panelist How to Win Your Case with Depositions. Recipient Lawyer in Classroom award Constl. Rights Found. Mem. Nat. Assn. Women Judges, Am. Judicature Soc., So. Calif. Bus. Litigation Inn of Ct. (past pres.). Office: US Dist Ct 255 E Temple St Rm 830 Los Angeles CA 90012 Office Phone: 213-894-7115.

FISCHER, DEBORAH LYNN, school nurse practitioner; b. Bloomington, Ind., May 4, 1949; d. Merle J. and Joy A. Kendall; m. Leroy O. Fischer, Dec. 26, 1970; children: Troy B., Lance P. BS in Nursing, Ind. State U., 1972; MS in Nursing, U. Evansville, 1976. RN Ind., 1972; Ind. Teacher Cert., Sch. Svc. Pers. 1976. Staff nurse St. Joseph's Hosp., Huntingburg, Ind., 1972; sch. nurse North Spencer Sch. Corp., Lincoln City, 1972—. Presenter various workshops, programs, Indpls.; faculty mem. sch. nurse Emergency Svc. for Children, Indpls., 1999—; bd. mem. Spencer County Child Protective Team, Rockport, Ind. Bd. dir. North Spencer Cmty. Action Ctr., Dale, 1993—. Mem.: Ind. State Teachers Assn., Nat. Assn. Sch. Nurses, Ind. Assn. Sch. Nurses, Lambda Sigma Theta Tau Internat. Hon. Soc. Nursing. Roman Catholic. Home: 12255 E St Rd 62 Saint Meinrad IN 47577 Office: North Spencer Sch Corp 3720 E St Rd 162 Lincoln City IN 47552 Office Phone: 812-937-2400. Business E-Mail: dfischer@mail.nspencer.k12.in.us.

FISCHER, DEBRA LYNNE, music educator; d. Maxine Sene Fischer. B Music Edn., Wartburg Coll. Cert. music tchr. Iowa. Mid. and HS vocal and band tchr. Goldfield (Iowa) Cmty. Sch. Dist., 1984—86; K-12 vocal music tchr. Twin Rivers Cmty. Schs., Bode, Iowa, 1986—87; K-8 vocal tchr., 5-8 band tchr. Meservey/Thornton/Sheffield/Chapin Schs., Thornton, Iowa, 1987—95; 7-12 vocal music tchr. Creston (Iowa) Cmty. Sch. Dist., 1995—. Recipient Youth Plus Excellence In Edn. award, Union County Youth Plus, 2000, Excellence In Edn. award, Dekko Found., 2001. Mem.: Iowa Choral Dirs. Assn., Beta Sigma Phi (Pi Beta Xi Chpt.), Delta Kappa Gamma (Pi Chpt.). Avocations: travel, music. Office: Creston HS 601 W Townline St Creston IA 50801

FISCHER, GAYLE, elementary school educator; b. Fort Worth, Mar. 27, 1950; d. Noble Eugene and Myrtle Mildred (Aycock) Chandler; m. Roger William Harlin, May 23, 1979 (div. 1987); children: Jesse Chandler Harlin, Laura Claire Harlin; m. Terry Wayne Fischer, Mar. 18, 1990. BS in Edn., U. Ga., 1973; MS in Edn., U. Okla., 1990, PhD in Ednl. Psychology, 1998. Cert. tchr., Nat. Bd. Tchrs., 2002, Tex., Okla.; cert. elem. prin., spl. edn., Okla. Tchr. Cobb County Dist., Marietta, Ga., 1973-75; tchr. of emotionally disturbed Spring Br. Acad., Houston, 1976-78; 4th grade tchr. Aldine Sch. Dist., Houston, 1979-81; tchr. of emotionally disturbed Mid-Del Schs., Midwest City, Okla., 1979-81; 3d grade tchr. Mid Del Schs., Midwest City, Okla., 1989-99; 6th and 8th grade tchr. Norman (Okla.) Sch. Dist., 1988-89; spl. edn. tchr. Norman Pub. Schs., 1999—. Trainer behavioral mgmt. Mid-Del Schs., 1990-95; chmn. adminstrv. com. Okla. Commn. on Tchr. Preparation, Oklahoma City, 1991-95; adj. instr. Coll. Edn., U. Okla., Norman, 1999—; appointed to program accreditation com. Okla. Commn. for Tchr. Preparation, 2001; mem. profl. accreditation com. Okla., 2000-03. Mem. NEA, ASCD, Coun. for Exceptional Children, Coun. for Children with Behavioral Disorders, Coun. Adminstrs. in Spl. Edn., Nat. Coun. for Accreditation of Tchr. Edn., Okla. Assn. Colls. Tchr. Edn. (presenter winter conf. 1993), Assn. Classroom Tchrs., Okla. Edn. Assn. (mem. task force to develop competencies for licensure and cert. 1996-97, credentials com. del. assembly 1996-97, nat. bd. cert. 2002). Avocations: writing, research, boating. Home: 6028 SE 104th St Oklahoma City OK 73165-9606

FISCHER, JOYCE FAYE, engineering educator; b. Dayton, Ohio, May 24, 1945; d. Otis Crawford and Dorothy Margaret Brown; m. Robert Allen Fischer, Apr. 11, 1966; children: Robert Bryan, Jason Allen. PhD, U. Tex., Austin, 1995. Engring. tech. GE, Cin., 1966—68; asst. prof. Tex. State U., San Marcos, Tex., 2004—. Tchg., rsch., grant dir., cons. Tex. State U., San Marcos, 1990—; spkr. in field. Contbr. articles to profl. jours. Educator, rschr. Tex. State U, San Marcos, 1988—2005. Grantee, Tex. Edn. Agy., 2004. Mem.: Nat. Mus. Am. Indian (assoc. Cert. of Merit 2004), Kappa Delta Pi (assoc.), Nat. Honor Soc. (assoc.), Alpha Chi (assoc.), Phi Kappa Phi (life). Achievements include development of teacher curriculum and pedagogy workshops for preservice and inservice teachers. Home: 600 Dale Dr San Marcos TX 78666 Office: Tex State U 601 U Dr Math Bldg Rm 470 San Marcos TX 78666 Office Phone: 512-245-8023. Office Fax: 512-245-3425. E-mail: jf10@txstate.edu.

FISCHER, KAREN A., librarian; b. St. Paul; BA in History, Hamline University, St. Paul, Minn., 1969; MLS, University of Minnesota, Minneapolis MN, 1969—71; MA in Hist. of Sci., Mont. State U., 1980. Cataloger U. Iowa, Iowa City, 1971—73; head tech. svcs. Coll. St. Benedict, St. Joseph, Minn., 1973—76; cataloger and reference libr. Mont. State U., Bozeman, 1976—86; dir. libr. Ctrl. Oreg. C.C., Bend, 1986—93, U. Minn. Morris Campus, 1993—2000; head reference and instrn. Gould Libr., Carleton Coll., Northfield, Minn., 2000—03; dir. libr. U. Puget Sound, 2003—. Mem.: ALA, Assn. Coll. and Rsch. Librs. Office: Libr U Puget Sound 1500 N Warner St Tacoma WA 98416 Home: 1208 Buena Vista Ave Fircrest WA 98466

FISCHER, LINDA DEMOSS, charter boat company executive; b. Saginaw, Mich., Jan. 8, 1951; d. Duane LaGene and Esther Ella (Rine) DeMoss; m. Jerry Lewis Bowles, Nov. 17, 1967 (div. 1969); 1 dau., Christie Jenean; m. 2d, Ronald Louis Fischer, July 4, 1981; 1 son, Ryan Louis. Student pub. schs., Satellite Beach, Fla. Bookkeeper Patrick AFB (Fla.) Officers Club, 1966-70; sec. Virginia Constrn. Co., Cocoa Beach, Fla., 1973-74; hostess, waitress Bernard's Surf, Cocoa Beach, 1974-79; cocktail waitress, waitress Pelican Point Inn, Cocoa Beach, 1979-81; owner, mgr. Fischer's Harbor Sea Foods, Port Canaveral, Fla., 1982—95; owner, mgr. Canaveral Charter Boats, Inc., Port Canaveral, 1981—95; broadcaster, author radio program Angler's Angle, Sta. WEZY, 1983-86; corp. officer Sea Fresh Products, Inc., 1981—. Mem. Port Canaveral Tenants Assn., Southeastern Fisheries Assn., Organized Fisherman of Fla., Cocoa Beach C. of C., Astron. Soc. Pacific, Am. Soc. Notaries, Fla. Animal Hosp., Internat. Fund for Animal Welfare, Humane Soc. U.S. Home: 2570 Newfound Harbor Dr Merritt Island FL 32952-2869

FISCHER, MARSHA LEIGH, retired civil engineer; b. San Antonio, May 9, 1955; d. Joe Henry and Ellen Joyce (Flake) F. BSCE, Tex. A&M U., 1977. Engrng. asst. Tex. Dept. Hwys. and Transp., Dallas, 1977-79; dist. mgr., local provisioning application Bell Comm. Rsch., Piscataway, NJ, 1988-91; outside plant engr. AT&T (formerly Southwestern Bell Tel. Co.), Dallas, 1979-82; staff mgr. for budgets Southwestern Bell Tel. Co., Dallas, 1982-84, area mgr., engrng. design Wichita Falls, Tex., 1984-86, area mgr. Ft. Worth, 1986-88, dist. mgr. engring., 1992-94, dir. customer svcs., 1994-95, dir. network engring., 1996-99, dir. outside plant planning, 1999—2000, regional mgr. constrn., 2000—02, exec. dir. constrn. engring., 2002—05. Named one of Outstanding Women of Am., 1987. Mem. NSPE, Tex. Soc. Profl. Engrs., Tex. Soc. Civil Engrs., Profl. Engrs. in Industry, Tex. A&M Assn. Former Students. Republican. Avocations: tennis, travel, reading, bicycling. Home: 4711 Ridge Dove San Antonio TX 78230-1192

FISCHER, MARY E., special education educator; b. Kansas City, Mo., July 7, 1948; d. Tom Earl and Sue Turner (Fitts) Walker; m. Timothy Montgomery Fischer, Sept. 4, 1971; children: Ethan David, Elizabeth Louise. AB, U. Mo., 1971; MSE, Cen. Mo. State U., Warrensburg, 1981; PhD, U. Wash., 1997. Occupl. therapy asst. Children's Therapy Ctr., 1971-73, tchr., 1976-78, psychometrist, 1978-79; program coord. United Cerebral Palsy, Camp Wonderland, Lake of the Ozarks, Mo., 1983; developmental presch. tchr. Children's Therapy Ctr., 1979-84, 75-76; project assoc. Early Childhood Follow Along Study, U. Wash., 1985-87; rsch. assoc. U. Wash., 1987-88; project assoc. Rsch. and Evaluation Network, U. Wash., 1989; project mgr. ChildFind project, Child Devel./Mental Retardation Ctr., Seattle, 1989-90; project coord. N.W. Insvc. Coop. for Transdisciplinary Teams U. Wash., Seattle, 1990-93; project coord. Choices, 1992-95; coord. Wash. Statewide Sys. Change Project, 1993-94; regional dir. Ctr. for Supportive Edn., Seattle, 1994-97; elem/early childhood spl. edn. and readiness to learn coord. Olympic Ednl. Svc. Dist. 114, Bremerton, Wash., 1997—2005; ednl. specialist Bethel Sch. Dist., 2005—. Adj. prof. Western Wash. U., 1999-2001; instr. Seattle Pacific U. Contbr. articles to profl. jours. Active Kitsap Infant Mental Health Coalition, Kitsap County Commn. on Children and Youth, 2002—; family resource coord. tng. project; chair It's Time for Kitsap Kids Devel. Assets Initiative, 2003—05; mem. KCR Spl. Quest Team, 2003—; dir. children's choir Lake City Presbyn. Ch., 1999—2002. Mem.: ASCD, Assn. for Persons with Severe Handicaps, Coun. for Exceptional Children (sec. divsn. for early childhood 2001—03, bd. dirs. 2001—), Nat. Assn. Edn. Young Children, Soc. Creative Anachronism, Bremerton Kiwanis Club, Pi Lambda Theta (Outstanding Mem. 1990), Phi Kappa Phi. Avocations: singing, camping, crafts. Home: 1514 N Montgomery Bremerton WA 98312 Personal E-mail: maryfischer@hotmail.com.

FISCHER, MICHELLE K., lawyer; BA in Econs. magna cum laude with distinction, Yale U., 1986; JD with honors, U. Chgo., 1989. Bar: Ohio 1989, D.C. 1991. With Jones Day, Cleve., 1989—, ptnr., 1999—. Mem.: ABA (antitrust law sect.), Ohio State Bar Assn. (bd. govs. antitrust law sect.). Office: Jones Day North Point 901 Lakeside Ave Cleveland OH 44114-1190

FISCHER, NANCY, secondary school educator; BS in Edn., SE Mo. State U., Cape Girardeau, 1983, M in Natural Sci., 2003. Cert. secondary tchr. Mo., 1983. Secondary tchr. Valle Cath. H.S., Ste. Genevieve, Mo., 1983—; faculty mem. Mo. Scholars Acad., Columbia, 1998—. Workshop presenter SuccessLink, Jefferson City, Mo., 2001—. Sec. Ste. Genevieve Mcpl. Band, 1990—2006. Recipient Presdl. award for Excellence in Sci. Tchg., NSF, 1999, Commrs. award, Mo. Dept. Edn., 1999, award for Excellence in Sci. Tchg., Monsanto, 1999, Subaru Midwest Sci. Tchg. award, Subaru, 2001. Mem.: NSTA, Mo. Track and Cross Country Coaches Assn., Mo. H.S. Volleyball Coaches Assn., St. Louis Area Physics Tchrs., Sci. Tchrs. Mo. Office: Valle Cath High Sch 40 N Fourth St Sainte Genevieve MO 63670 Office Phone: 573-883-7496. Office Fax: 573-883-9142.

FISCHER, NORA BARRY, lawyer; b. Pitts., June 13, 1951; d. Michael T. and Olga G. (Stipetich) Barry; m. Donald R. Fischer, Jan. 3, 1976; children: Erin, Lauren, Adam. BA magna cum laude, St. Mary's Coll., Notre Dame, Ind., 1973; JD, U. Notre Dame, 1976. Bar: Ill. 1976, Pa. 1977, U.S. Dist. Ct. (no. dist.) Ill. 1977, U.S. Dist. Ct. (we. dist.) Pa. 1977, U.S. Ct. Appeals (3rd cir.) 1981, U.S. Supreme Ct. 1982, W.Va. 1990, U.S. Dist. Ct. (so. dist.) W.Va. 1990, U.S. Dist. Ct. (no dist.) W.Va. 2002. Legal editor Callaghan's, Chgo., 1976-77; assoc. Meyer, Darragh, Buckler, Bebenek & Eck, Pitts., 1977-80, jr. ptnr., 1980-82, ptnr., 1983-92, mem. exec. com., 1987-89; ptnr. Pietragallo Bosick & Gordon, Pitts., 1992—, mem. practice mgmt. com., 1996—. Pratice group leader Def. Litig. Group, 2002—. Mem. Pitts. Allegheny Co. Pvt. Industry Coun., 1982-84. Mem.: ABA, Acad. Trial Lawyers (past pres.), Allegheny County Bar Assn. Found., Exec. Womens Coun., Ins. Women

Pitts., Allegheny County Bar Assn, (med.-legal com. 1984—89, interprofl. code com. 1985—86, judiciary com. 1985—88, health law sect. 1990—92, civil litigation com. 1990—93, health law sect. vice chair 1992—93, health law sect chair 1994, bd. govs., women in law com., edn. subcom., mem. fellows com.), Pa. Bar Assn. (civil litigation com. 1985—87, ins. and surety law com. 1991), Am. Inns of Court (pres. 1999—2001). Democrat. Roman Catholic. Office: Pietragallo Bosick & Gordon 3800 The Oxford Ctr Pittsburgh PA 15219 Office Phone: 412-263-1821. Business E-Mail: NBF@PBandG.com.

FISCHER, PAMELA SHADEL, public relations executive; b. Harrisburg, Pa., Feb. 28, 1959; d. Richard Lee and Pauline Louise (Nies) S.; m. Charles J. Fischer Jr., June 11, 1983; 1 child, Zachary Joseph. BA in English, Lebanon Valley Coll., Annville, Pa., 1981; AMP, U. Pa., 2005. Cert. child passenger safety technician AAA. Pub. rels. coord. Pa. Optometric Assn., Harrisburg, 1981-83; pub. rels. dir. Morris Ctr. YMCA, Cedar Knolls, NJ, 1983-85; pub. rels. coord. Delta Dental Plan of N.J., Parsippany, 1985-86; pub. rels. mgr. AAA N.J. Automobile Club, Florham Park, NJ, 1986-91, mgr. mem. svcs. and pub. affairs, 1991-94, asst. v.p. pub. rels. & safety, 1994-96, asst. v.p. pub. affairs and fin. svcs., 1996—2002, v.p. pub. affairs and fin. svcs., 2002—. Corp. capt. United Way of Morris County, Cedar Knolls, 1985—90, chmn. publs. com., 1989—90, chmn. mktg. com., 1991—95, v.p. mktg., 1996, mem. women's leadership initiative exec. com., 1999—, vice chmn., 2002—03, chmn., 2003—04; career counselor Lebanon Valley Coll., 1983—90, alumni amb., 2004—; mem. hwy. traffic safety policy adv. com. Gov.'s Office, 1998—; chair legis. com. Gateway Tourism Coun., 1997—2000; mem. Driver Edn. Commn. N.J., 1999—2005; bd. dirs. First Night of Morris County, 1999—2002, chmn., 2004; mem. NJ Motor Vehicle Commn., 2003—, vice chmn., 2004—05; mem. N.J. Child Passenger Safety Coalition, 2003—; mem. corp. leadership coun. Family Svc. Morris County, NJ, 2005—; trustee Trans Options, 2005—; co-chmn. Gov.-elect Jon Corzine's Transp. Transition Team, 2005—06; bd. dirs. Morris Ctr. YMCA, 1992—94, Hist. Morris County Visitors Ctr., 1999—, bd. pres., 2001—04. Rotary Found. scholar, 1981; recipient Gold award United Way of Morris County, 1988, Traffic Safety award Gov.'s rep., 2004, Salute to the Policy Maker award Exec. Women of N.J., 2006. Mem. Pub. Rels. Soc. Am. (bd. dirs. 1995), N.J. Press Assn., N.J. Travel Industry Assn., N.J. Comm. Regional Plan Assn., Internat. Assn. Bus Communicators, Y's Club of Cedar Knoll (pres. 1986-91), Long Valley Ice Hockey Club (dir. media rels. 2003—). Republican. Roman Catholic. Avocations: reading, writing, photography, skiing, hockey. Office: AAA NJ Automobile Club 1 Hanover Rd Florham Park NJ 07932-1888 Office Phone: 973-245-4858. Personal E-mail: aaanjacpr@aol.com.

FISCHER, VIOLETA PÈREZ CUBILLAS, Spanish literature and linguistics educator; b. Havana, Cuba, Nov. 20, 1923; came to U.S., 1959; d. Josè M. and Carmen (Reyes Pizey) Pèrez Cubillas; m. Rolando F. Fischer, Dec. 27, 1947 (dec. May 1994); 1 child, Violet Fischer Pack. PhD in Law, U. Havana, 1949; postgrad., U. N.C., 1967-68, MA in Romance Langs., 1975. Prin. Spl. Ctr. for English Teaching, Havana, Cuba, 1945—59; lawyer Havana, Cuba, 1949—59; asst. prof. East Carolina U., Greenville, NC, 1962—66; prof. Spanish lit. and linguistics Coastal Carolina Community Coll., Jacksonville, NC, 1970—96; ret., 1996. Speaker various civic, mil., ednl. assns., and community colls., 1963—. Bd. dirs. Onslow County Community Concerts, Jacksonville, N.C., 1987; chmn. CCCC Women's Assn., 1972-73. Recipient Josè de la Luz y Caballero award Cruzada Educativa Cubana Assn., 1987, Juan J. Remos award Cruzada Educativa Cubana, 1987, N.C. State Svc. award for 30 yrs. of svc., 1994; Paul Harris fellow Rotary Internat., 1996. Mem. MLA, Nat. Assn. Cuban Lawyers, Havana Bar Assn. in Exile, Nat. Cuban Tchrs. Assn., Nat. Assn. Cuban-Am. Educators, Count of Galvez Hist. Soc., Sigma Delta Mu (co-founder, state rep.), Delta Kappa Gamma (chmn. world fellowship com. 1982-84, 96-98, Wreath of Excellence ednl. award 1989, 2d v.p. Upsilon chpt. Jacksonville 1994-96). Roman Catholic. Home: 2107 Perry Dr Jacksonville NC 28546-1642

FISCHLER, BARBARA BRAND, librarian; b. Pitts., May 24, 1930; d. Carl Frederick and Emma Georgia (Piltz) Brand; m. Drake Anthony Fischler, June 3, 1961 (div., Oct. 1995); 1 child, Owen Wesley. AB cum laude, Wilson Coll., Chambersburg, Pa., 1952; MM with distinction, Ind. U., 1954, AMLS, 1964. Asst. reference librarian Ind. U., Bloomington, 1958-61, asst. librarian undergrad. library, 1961-63, acting librarian, 1963; circulation librarian Ind. U.-Purdue U., Indpls., 1970-76, pub. services librarian Univ. Library, sci., engring. and tech. unit, 1976-81, acting dir. univ. libraries, 1981-82, dir. univ. libraries, 1982-95; retired, 1995; dir. Sch. Libr. and Info. Sci. Ind. U.-Purdue U., Indpls., 1995—. Vis. and assoc. prof. (part-time) Sch. Libr. and Info. Sci. Ind. U., Bloomington, 1972-95, counselor-coord., Indpls., 1974-82, dir. sch. libr. and info. sci. campus Ind. U.-Purdue U., Indpls., 1995—; resource aide adv. com. Ind. Voc. Tech. Coll., Indpls., 1974-86; adv. com. Area Libr. Svcs. Authority, Indpls., 1976-79; mem. core com., chmn. program com. Ind. Gov.'s Conf. on Librs. and Info. Svcs., Indpls., 1976-78, mem. governance com., del. to conf., 1990; mem. Ind. State Libr. Adv. Coun., 1985-91; cons. in field. Contbr. articles to profl. jours. Fund-raiser Indpls. Mus. Art, 1971, Am. Cancer Soc., Indpls., 1975; vol. tchr. St. Thomas Aquinas Sch., Indpls., 1974-75; fund-raiser Am. Heart Assn., Indpls., 1985; bd. dirs., treas. Historic Amusement Found., Inc., Indpls., 1984-91; bd. advisors N.Am. Wildlife Park Found., Inc., Battle Ground, Ind., 1985-91, bd. dirs., 1991—; mem. adv. bd. Ind. U. Ctr. on Philanthropy, 1987-90. Recipient Outstanding Svc. award Ctrl. Ind. Area Libr. Svc. Authority, 1979, Outstanding Libr. award Ind. Libr.-Ind. Libr. Trustee Assn., 1988, Louise Maxwell award for Outstanding Achievement, 1989, William Jenkins award for Outstanding Svc. to Ind. U. Libr. and the Libr. Profession, 1996. Mem. ALA, Libr. Adminstrn. and Mgmt. Assn. (vice chair and chair elect fund raising and fin. devel. sect. 1991-92), Ind. State Libr. Adv. Coun., Midwest Fedn. Libr. Assns. (chmn. local arrangements for conf. 1986-87, sec. 1987—, bd. dirs. 1987-91), Ind. Libr. Assn. (chmn. coll. and univ. div. 1977-78, chmn. libr. edn. div. 1981-82, treas. 1984-86), German Shepherd Dog Club of Cen. Ind. (pres. 1978-79, treas. 1988-89, v.p. 1989-90, pres. 1990-93, bd. dirs. 1993—), Wabash Valley German Shepherd Dog Club (pres. 1982-83), Cen. Ind. Kennel Club (bd. dirs. 1984-86), Pi Kappa Lambda, Beta Phi Mu. Republican. Presbyterian. Avocations: ethology, horseback riding. Home: 735 Lexington Ave Apt 3 Indianapolis IN 46203-1000 Office: Ind-Purdue U 755 W Michigan St Indianapolis IN 46202-5195

FISCHLER, SANDY LYNN, charitable and informational organization executive; b. Anchorage, Alaska, Dec. 28, 1962; d. Joseph Michael Fischler and Sharon Leigh (Blodgett) Smith. Student, U. Alaska, 1980-83, Circle in Square Theatre Sch., 1983. Spl. event coord. Universal Studios Fla., Orlando, 1993-95; prodn. mgr. Headdress Ball, Orlando, 1994; assoc. prodr. Nickelodeon "Guts", Orlando, 1994; event mgr. First Night Providence, 1995; prodr. bike stunt segment 1997 Holiday Bowl Halftime Show, San Diego, 1997; event prodr. ESPN X Games, San Diego, 1995-98; ptnr. Avalanche Events Group, 1998—; owner 4th Wall Events, 1998—; event mgr. NFL Experience, Super Bowl XXXIII, 1999; broadcast mgr. NFL Experience, Super Bowl XXXIV, XXXV, XXXVI, XXXVII; exec. dir., founder The Pilonidal Support Alliance, 2005—. Vol. Feral Cat Coalition, San Diego, 1998, Kisses for Kats Pet Rescue, 2000-01, Cat's Meow Cat Rescue, 2002--. Mem. Women in Sports and Events, Internat. Festival and Events Assn., Calfest, Nat. Sports Mktg. Network. Avocations: gardening, stained glass. Home: 5911 Cerritos Ave Long Beach CA 90805

FISCHMAN, JANE ANN VOGEL, retired secondary school educator; b. Buffalo, July 29, 1939; d. Henry Eugene and Rosalind Pearl (Garten) Vogel; m. Stuart Lee Fischman, June 25, 1960; children: Lisa Anne, Everett Hal (dec.) BS English, Edn., Simmons Coll., 1961; MEd English, Remedial Reading, SUNY, Buffalo, 1965, diploma computers in edn., 1988, PhD English Edn., 1996. Cert. reading, N.Y., English, N.Y., Mass. Tchr. English Riverside H.S., Buffalo, 1961—65; tchr. spl. remedial program San Juan Sch., PR, 1974; tchr. secular faculty, mid. sch., lang. arts, reading, libr. Kadimah Sch. Buffalo, 1974—85; vis. faculty English dept. Hebrew U., Jerusalem, 1989; summer fellow We. N.Y. Writing Project, 1989—90, rsch. cons., 1991; doctoral intern SUNY, Buffalo, 1990; ret., 1991. Adj. faculty Niagara County C.C., Hilbert Coll., Canisius Coll.; presenter in field Contbr. articles to profl. jours Chair Buffalo Jewish Coalition for Lit.; bd. dirs. Jewish Fedn. Buffalo. Mem. Bur. Jewish Edn., Pi Lambda Theta, Phi Delta Kappa Home: 255 Louvaine Dr Buffalo NY 14223-2757

FISCHMAN, MYRNA LEAH, accountant, educator; d. Isidore and Sally (Goldstein) Fischman. BS, Coll. City NY, 1960, MS, 1964; PhD, NYU, 1976. CPA N.Y. Asst. to contr. Sam Goody, Inc., N.Y.C.; tchr. accounting Ctr. Comml. H.S., N.Y.C., 1960—63, vicat. adviser, 1963—66; instr. acctg. Borough of Manhattan C.C., N.Y.C., 1963—66; self-employed acct. N.Y.C., 1960—; chief acct. investigator rackets Office Queens Dist. Atty., 1969—70, cmty. fels. coord., 1970—71; adv. prof. L.I. U., 1970—79, prof. acctg. taxation and law, 1979—, coord. grad. capstone courses, 1982—86, dir. Sch. Profl. Accountancy Bklyn. Campus, 1984—, dir. Ctr. Acctg. and Tax Edn., 1986—, chmn. acctg. dept. Editor: Ea. Bus. Educators Jour., 1988. Rsch. cons. pre-tech. program N.Y.C. Bd. Edn., mem., 1992—; acct.-advisor Inst. for Advancement of Criminal Justice; acct.-cons. Coalition Devel. Corp., Interracial Coun. for Bus. Opportunities; treas. Breakfree Inc., Lower East Side Prep. Sch.; mem. ednl. task force Am. Jewish Com., 1972—; mem. Chancellor Com. Against Discrimination in Edn., 1976—97; chmn. supervisory com. Fed. Credit Union # 1532, N.Y.C., 1983—; chmn. consumer coun. Astoria Med. Ctr., 1980—92; mem. subcom. on bus. edn. to the econ. devel. and mktg. com. Bklyn. C. of C., 1984—; mem. adv. bd. acctg. dept. burough of Manhattan C.C., 1997—; mem. Bus. Edn. Adv. Coun.; mem. steering com., youth div. N.Y. Dem. County Com., 1967—68; del. to Nat. Conv. Young Dems. Am., 1967, rep. assigned to women's activities com., 1967; mem. legis. adv. bd. N.Y. State Assemblyman Dennis Butler, 1979—97. Recipient award for meritorious svc., Cmty. Svc. Soc., 1969, Lifetime Achievement award, Soroptimist Internat. Bklyn., 1997. Mem.: NEA (bus. edn. assns.), AAUP, AICPA, Inst. Mgmt. Accts. (dir. N.Y. chpt. 1983—, dir. profl. devel. 1986—87, dir. pub. rels. 1987—88, dir. manuscripts 1991—92, dir. univ. rels. 1993—94), Tax Inst. L.I. U. (dir. Blyn. chpg. 1984—), N.Y. State Soc. CPAs (mem. com. on recruitment for CPA careers 1981—, auditing com. 1991—, gen. com. on edn. in colls. and univs. 1991—, pub. rels. com. 1992—, pres. Bklyn. chpt. 2001—02, bd. dirs. 2005—, Dr. Emanuel Saxe Outstanding CPA in Edn. award 1994—95), Fed. Credit Union (chmn. supervisory com. # 1532 n.Y.C. 1983—, bd. dirs. 1989—), Young Alumni Assn., Am. Assn. Jr. Colls., Doctorate Assn. N.Y. Educators (v.p. 1975—97), Assn. Govt. Accts. (dir. N.Y. chpg. 1983—, pres. elect n.Y. chpg. 1989—90, pres. N.Y. chpt. 1990—91), Fin. Execs. Inst., Grad. Students Orgn. NYU (treas. 1971—73), Internat. Soc. Bus. Edn., Nat. Eastern (co-chmn. ann. meeting 1967), Am. Acctg. Assn., Govt. Accts. (v.p. 1973—74, dir. rsch. and manuscripts 1985—, pres. elect N.Y. chpt. 1989—90, pres. 1990—91, bd. dirs. N.Y. chpt. 1994—), Emanu-El League Congregation Emanu-El, N.Y. (chmn. cmty. svcs. com. 1967—68), Jewish Guild for Blind, Jewish Braille Inst., Cmty. Welfare Com. Assn., Friends Met. Mus. Art, Friends Am. Ballet Theatre, Women's City Club (N.Y.), Delta Pi Epsilon (treas. 1976). Democrat. Jewish. Achievements include development of new bus. machine course and curriculum Borough Manhattan Bus. C.C. Office: LI U Sch Bus Rm H700 1 University Plz Rm 700 Brooklyn NY 11201-5301 Office Phone: 718-488-1157. Business E-Mail: myrnafischman@liu.edu.

FISH, BARBARA JOAN, investor, small business owner; b. Seattle, June 12, 1936; d. George Francis Linehan and Maureece Shirley (Frederick) McCullough; m. Ralph Edwin Fish, July 14, 1956 (dec. Nov. 1986). Grad. high sch., Portland, Oreg. Owner Sea and Sand R.V. Park, Depoe Bay, Oreg., 1977—; real estate investor State of Oreg. Active St. Augustine's Ch. Mem. Lincoln City C. of C., Depoe Bay C. of C., Oreg. Sheriff's Assn. (hon.). Republican. Roman Catholic. Avocations: travel, gardening. Home and Office: Sea and Sand RV Park 4985 N Highway 101 Depoe Bay OR 97341-9740 Office Phone: 541-764-2313.

FISH, JANET ISOBEL, artist; b. Boston, May 18, 1938; d. Peter and Florence (Voorhees) F. BA, Smith Coll., 1960; postgrad., Skowhegan Art Sch., 1961; BFA, MFA, Yale U., 1963; DFA (hon.), Lyme Acad., 2000. Represented by D.C. Moore Gallery, N.Y.C. One-woman shows D.C. Moore Gallery, N.Y.C., Columbus (Ga.) Mus., Ogunquit Mus. Am. Art, Maine, also others; traveling exhbn. Yellowstone Art Ctr., Billings, Mont., 1995-97; represented in permanent collections Whitney Mus. Am. Art, N.Y.C., Met. Mus. Art, N.Y.C., Cleve. Mus. Art, Dallas Mus. Fine Arts, Am. Fedn. Arts, Am. Acad. Inst. Arts and Letters, Art Inst. Chgo., Kemper Mus., Kansas City, Albright-Knox Gallery, Buffalo, N.Y., Newark Mus., Mpls. Mus. of Art, Nat. Gallery of Victoria, Melbourne, Australia, Powers Inst., Sydney, Australia, Colby Coll., Waterville, Maine, Mus. of Fine Arts, Houston Art Ctr., RISD, Providence, Mus. Art, Providence, Va. Mus. Fine Arts, Richmond, Yale U., New Haven, Smith Coll. Mus. Art, Northampton, Mass., Albrecht Art Mus., St. Joseph, Mo., Milw. Art Mus., Hunter Mus. Art, Chattanooga, others. Bd. govs. Skowhegan Sch. Painting and Sculpture, Marie Walsh Sharpe Art Found. Recipient Harris award Chgo. Bienale award, 1974, Outstanding Woman Artist award Aspen Mus., 1992; MacDowell fellow, 1968, 70, 72; Yale scholar, Australian Coun. for Arts grantee, 1975. Mem. NAD (Henry Ward Ranger Purchase prize 2001, William A. Paton watercolor prize 2005, elected nat. academician 1994), Am. Acad. Arts and Letters (award 1994) Office Phone: 212-966-0616. Personal E-mail: jfcp1@earthlink.net.

FISH, JEANNE SPENCER, artist, retired lawyer; b. Sedan, Ks., Jan. 15, 1921; d. Charles William and Lena (Hall) Spencer; m. Robert Irwin Fish, Jan. 6, 1947. BA, U. Kans., Lawrence, 1942, JD, 1945; BA in Art, Humboldt State U., Arcata, Calif., 1974. Bar: Ks. 1945. Assoc. C.W. Spencer, Atty. at Law, Sedan, 1945-47; city atty. City of Sedan, 1947; asst. gen. counsel Ks. State Corp. Commn., Topeka, 1948-51; artist Eureka, Calif., 1974—. One-woman shows include oil paintings, 1977, 1986, 2004 Mem. AAUW (pres. local chpt. 1964-65), P.E.O. (pres. local chpt. 1972-73, 95-96, 99-01, pres. Humboldt Reciprocity Bur. 1996), Redwood Art Assn. (pres. 1979-81, Best of Show award 1973), Humboldt Docent Coun. (pres. 1977-79), Humboldt Arts Coun. (pres. 1982-83), Humboldt Sponsors, Phi Kappa Phi. Republican. Episcopalian. Avocations: flute, music, golf, travel.

FISH, MARY MARTHA, economics professor; b. Albert Lea, Minn., July 17, 1930; d. Charles H. and Olga (Stennes) Thomassen; m. Donald C. Fish, Oct. 1954 (dec.); children: Jill S., Lynn M., Jason M BBA, U. Minn., 1951; MBA Econs, Tex. Tech. Coll., 1957; PhD, U. Okla., 1963. Statis. asst. Iowa Bd. Control, 1951—53; pub. health analyst State of Calif., 1953—54; analytical statistician 46th Med. Gen. Lab., U.S. Army Forces, Tokyo, 1954—57; instr. econs. and bus. Odessa Coll., Tex., 1957—58; asst. prof., then assoc. prof. West Tex. State U., 1961—66; prof. econs. U. Ala., 1966—99, prof. emeritus, 1999—. Prof. econs. Landegg Internat. U., Wienacht, Switzerland, 2000-02; Fulbright lectr. U. Liberia, 1974-75, Gambian Govt., 1978-79; cons. in field Co-author: Convicts, Codes and Contraband, 1974; contbr. articles to profl. jours Founding mem. Nat. Campaign for Tolerance; mem. So. Poverty Tolerance Program, 1995. Grantee U. Ala., 1967-68, 87-89, Dept. Labor, 1978-79; Fulbright rsch. fellow, Taiwan, 1995; Phifer Faculty Scholar, 1998, fellow AAUW, 1960 Mem. Am. Econ. Assn., So. Econ. Assn Mem. Baha'i faith. Home: 1405 High Forest Dr N Tuscaloosa AL 35406-2153 Business E-Mail: mfish@cba.ua.edu.

FISHBEIN, ESTELLE ACKERMAN, lawyer; BA in Polit. Sci. magna cum laude, Hunter Coll., 1955; LLB, Yale U., 1958. Bar: U.S. Dist. Ct. D.C. 1959, U.S. Ct. Appeals (D.C. cir.) 1959, U.S. Supreme Ct. 1968, Md. 1968, U.S. Ct. Appeals (4th cir.) 1973. Staff atty. office gen. counsel div. old age and survivors ins. HEW, 1959-64, sr. staff atty. div. Medicare, 1965-68, editorial asst. to Md. Constl. Conv. Commn. (on leave from fed. employment), 1965-68; spl. asst. atty. gen. U. Md., 1968-75; gen. counsel Johns Hopkins U., Balt., 1975-91, v.p., gen. counsel, 1991—2003; v.p., gen. counsel emerita, 2004—. Speaker various orgns., colls., univs.; mem. character com. Ct. Appeals Md. 8th jud. cir., 1972-89, chmn., 1980-89. Contbr. articles to profl. jours. Active EEO task force Am. Coun. on Edn., 1972-74; trustee Lafayette Coll., 1988-91, Tchrs. Ins. Annuity Assn., 1988—2005; dir. Med. Ctr. Ins. Co., 1995—2003; mem. Sec.'s Adv. Com. on Sci. Integrity, U.S. Dept. HHS. Named to Hall of Fame Hunter Coll. Alumni Assn., 1974. Mem. Nat. Assn. Coll. and Univ. Attys. (exec. bd. 1971-73, sec.-treas. 1973-75, 2d v.p. 1977-78, 1st v.p. and program chmn. 1978-79, pres.-elect 1979-80, pres. 1980-81. Home: 7005 Rue de Marquis Naples FL 34108

FISHBONE, VIVIAN MANPERL, artist; b. N.Y.C., July 13, 1926; d. Isidore and Rose (Kovner) Manperl; m. Stanley E. Zeeman, June 21, 1947 (div. July 1966); children: Susan Rogers, Wendy Blom; m. Herbert Fishbone, Oct. 23, 1966. AB, Skidmore Coll., 1946; postgrad., Lehigh U., 1964-66, Art Students League, N.Y.C., 1966-70. Rsch. asst. Rockefeller Inst., N.Y.C., 1946, Jefferson Med. Coll., Phila., 1947-50; rsch. asst. dept. phys. medicine U. Pa., Phila., 1947; tchr. Pennridge Jr. High Sch., Perkasie, Pa., 1965-66. Vis. artist Lafayette Coll., 2001. One-woman shows, 1978—, including Kemerer Mus., Bethlehem, Pa., 1986, Four Corners Gallery, Lambertville, N.J., 1987, 89, Touchstone Theater, Bethlehem, 1992, Wired Gallery, Bethlehem, Pa., MCS Gallery, Easton, Pa., many others; exhibited in group shows, 1978—, including Allentown (Pa.) Art Mus., 1978, 81, 89, Lehigh U., Bethlehem, 1980, Hunterdon Art Ctr., Clinton, N.J., 1981, 84, 86, 88, 89, Lehigh Art Alliance, Allentown, 1982, 84, Kemerer Mus., 1985, Muhlenberg Coll., Allentown, 1984, 86, 93, New Arts Program, Kutztown, Pa., 1993-2006; represented by Connefions Gallery, Easton, Pa. Winner Easton (Pa.) Ctr. Square Show, 1979; recipient best of show award Easton Area Artists, 1971, 1st prize for portraiture, 1975; purchase prize Easton Pub. Libr., 1972, 1st prize for oil or acrylic Cmty. Art League, Easton, 1979, 1st prize Juried Mems. Show, Hunterdon Art Ctr., Clinton, N.J., 1994. Mem. ACE Art Cmty. Easton, Lehigh Valley Arts Coun., Lehigh Art Alliance (bd. dirs. 1970-75, floating award 1982), Women in Arts, Art Students League (life), New Arts Program. Home: 580 Village Dr Bethlehem PA 18018-6351

FISHBURN, JANET FORSYTHE, dean; m. Peter Clingerman Fishburn, 1958; children: Susan, Katherine, Sally. BA magna cum laude, Monmouth Coll., 1958, LHD (hon.), 1984; PhD, Pa. State U., 1978. Ordained to ministry Presbyn. Ch., US, 1988. Dir. Christian edn. 1st United Presbyn. Ch., Cleveland Heights, Ohio, 1958-60; lectr. Pa. State U., 1977-78; asst. prof. Christian edn. Theol. Sch., Drew U., Madison, NJ, 1978-83, assoc. prof., 1983-90, asst. prof. Am. ch. history, 1982-83, assoc. prof., 1983-95, prof. tchg. ministry, 1990-95, prof. emeritus, 1995—, acting dean Theol. Sch., 1994-95. Parish assoc. Mt. Freedom Presbyn. Ch., 1991—94; manuscript reviewer Scholars Press, Fairleigh Dickinson Press, U. Pa. Press; lectr. in field, 1982—; panelist, spkr. profl. confs. and religious orgns.; cons. Books for Pastors Series Abingdon Press, 1987; mem. social justice com. Newton Presbytery, 1989—95, mem. coun., 1995—2001, 2004—, mem. com. on ministry, 2001—04, chmn. personnel com., 2005—. Author: (book) The Fatherhood of God and the Victorian Family: The Social Gospel in America, 1982, Confronting the Idolatry of Family: A New Vision for the Household of God, 1991, Parenting is for Everyone: Living Out Our Baptismal Covenant, 1996; editor: Drew Gateway, 1989—93; contbr. articles and revs. to profl. jours., clergy jours. and encys; editor: People of a Compassionate God: Creating Welcoming Congregations, 2003. Leader weekly bible study Madison Presbyn. Ch., 1985—89, mem. chancel choir, 1982—90, Morristown United Meth. Ch., 1992—96, co-leader spiritual growth group, 1990—; spkr. clergy confs.; tchr. adult edn. Mem.: Am. Soc. Ch. History, Presbyn. Profs. Social Witness Policy (panel coord. 1994, 2006), United Meth. Assn. Scholars Christian Edn. (chmn. rsch. com. 1995—97). Avocation: genealogy. Office Phone: 908-630-8787. Business E-Mail: jfishbur@drew.edu.

FISHENFELD, GRACE, artist, educator; b. Bklyn., July 31, 1932; d. Joseph and Jean (Lipofsky) Goldberg; m. Bernard Fishenfeld, May 28, 1953; children: Keith, Randi. AAS, N.Y. State U. Applied Arts, 1952; BS, Molloy Coll., 1972; MA, CW Post, 1976. Cert. art tchr., N.Y. Layout advt. designer Denhardt & Stewart, N.Y.C., 1952-53; art dir. Mid Island YMYWHA, Wantagh, N.Y., 1964-72; art tchr. Brentwood (N.Y.) H.S., 1972-92. Pub. rels. chmn., edn. chmn., designer, organizer Wonderful World of Art Tchg. Manual, 1996. Exhibited one-woman show at Coral Springs (Fla.) Mus. Art, 2005; group shows include Natan D. Rosen Art Gallery and Mus., 1992 (Best in Show award), Artist Guild of Norton Gallery, Fla., 1995 (award of distinctive merit), Lake Worth (Fla.) Art League, 1997 (1st prize for graphic image, Best in Show award 1999), Coral Springs Mus. Art., Fla., 2004-05, Butler Inst. Art, Ohio, 2005-06, Cornell Mus. History and Art, Delray Bach, Fla. Dir. spring celebration of H.S. art exhbn., Palm Beach County, Fla., 1996-97. Named One of 8 Emerging Women Artists, Rosen Gallery Nat. Search, Boca Raton, Fla., 1993; recipient Award Coral Springs Mus., 1999; recipient Best in Show award, Great Neck Ctr. Arts nat. art competition, 1999, 1st prize in painting, Fla. Art Show, 2000. Mem. Women in Visual Arts (bd. dirs., pub. rels. com. 1992—, edn. chmn. 1996-98, Life Achievement award 2004), Profl. Artist Guild of Boca Raton Mus., Nat. Assn. Women Artists (Sara Winston award 1996), Women in Visual Arts (bd. dirs. 1993-95, fundraiser 1997-2006, chmn. vol. art program 1997-98, Best in Holiday Art Show competition award 1998, scholar 2006). Avocations: jazz and classical music. Home: 6875 Willow Wood Dr Boca Raton FL 33434-3527 also: 75 Knightsbridge Rd Apt 1C Great Neck NY 11021 also: 4410 NE 15th Terr Oakland Park FL 33334 E-mail: fishenfeld@aol.com.

FISHER, ALICE S., federal agency administrator, lawyer; b. Louisville, 1967; BA, Vanderbilt U., 1989; JD, Catholic U., 1992. Bar: DC 1993. Assoc. Sullivan & Cromwell LLP; dep. spl. counsel US Senate Spl. Com. to Investigate Whitewater Devel. & Related Matters, 1995—96; ptnr. Latham & Watkins, LLP, Washington, 1996—2001, 2003—05; dep. asst. atty. gen. criminal divsn. US Dept. Justice, Washington, 2001—03, asst. atty. gen. criminal divsn., 2005—. Named one of Top 40 Lawyers Under 40, Nat. Law Jour., 2005. Office: US Dept Justice Robert F Kennedy Bldg Tenth St & Constitution Ave NW Rm 2107 Washington DC 20530 Office Phone: 202-637-2148. Office Fax: 202-637-2201.

FISHER, ANITA JEANNE (KIT FISHER), retired language educator; b. Atlanta, Oct. 22, 1937; d. Paul Benjamin and Cora Ozella (Wadsworth) Chappelear; m. Kirby Lynn Fisher, Aug. 6, 1983; 1 child from previous marriage, Tracy Ann. Postgrad., Stetson U., 1961, postgrad., 1987; BA, Bob Jones U., 1959; postgrad., U. Fla., 1963, 87, 90; MAT, Rollins Coll., 1969; PhD in Am. Lit., Fla. State U., 1975; postgrad., U. Ctrl. Fla., 1978, NEH Inst., 1979, U. Ctrl. Fla., 1987, Disney U./U. Ctrl. Fla., 1996, Jacksonville U., 1996, Agnes Scot Coll. AP Inst., 1998, Duke U., 1999. Cert. English, gifted and adminstrn. supr., in ESOL. Chairperson basic learning improvement program secondary sch. Orange County, Orlando, Fla., 1964-65; chmn. composition Winter Park (Fla.) HS, 1978-80; chmn. English depts. Orange County Pub. Schs., Fla., 1962, 71; reading tchr. Woodland Hall Acad., Reading Rsch. Inst., Tallahassee, 1976; instr. edn., journalism, reading, Spanish, thesis writing Bapt. Bible Coll., Springfield, Mo., 1976-77; prof. English S.W. Mo. State U., Springfield, 1980-84, instr. continuing edn. music and creative writing, 1981-82, editor LAD Leaf; tchr. Volusia County Schs., Fla., 1984-88, 95-97, gifted students Fla., 1986-88; tchr. Lee County Schs., 1988-95; gifted students Lake Mary HS, 1997; tchr. Seminole Pub. Schs., 1997—2004; ret., 2004. Instr. Seminole CC; adj. prof. Edison CC, 1989—95, U. So. Fla., 1990—95, Barry U., 1993; steering com. So. Assn. Colls. and Schs.; active Fla. Coun. Tchrs. English; assessor tchr. performance Nat. Bd. Profl. Tchg. Stds.; panel mem. PSAT/NMSQT Descriptive Score Report Ednl. Testing Svc.; chair advanced placement vertical team Lake Mary HS, 2000—01, chair dept. English, chair vertical team curriculum implementation, from 2001; spkr., presenter in field. Co-editor: Fla. English Jour., 1998—2000; contbr. articles to profl. jours. Vol. Green County Action Com., 1977, Heart Fund, 1982; book reviewer Voice Youth Advs. Writing Program fellow U. Ctrl. Fla., 1978; mem. Rep. Nat. Com., from 1994; active Rep. Presdl. Task Force, 1998—2000. Named Lee County Tchr. of Distinction, 1994—95. Mem.: Seminole County Tchrs. English (chartered, pres. 1998—2000), Volusia Coun. Tchrs. English (pres. 1997), Fla. Coun. Tchrs. English (chair commn. ESL 1997—99, sch. adv. coun.), Nat. Count. Tchrs. English, Phi Delta Kappa (historian). Presbyterian. Home: Eustis, Fla. Died Aug. 21, 2006.

FISHER, ANN BAILEN, lawyer; b. N.Y.C., Oct. 15, 1951; d. Eliot and Elise (Thompson) Bailen; m. John C. Fisher, Apr. 6, 1980. BA magna cum laude, Radcliffe Coll., 1973; JD, Harvard U., 1976. Bar: N.Y. 1977. Assoc. Sullivan

& Cromwell, N.Y.C., 1976-80, 82-84, ptnr., 1984—, assoc. Paris, 1980-82. Mem. ABA, N.Y. State Bar Assn. Clubs: Cosmopolitan, Harvard (N.Y.C.). Episcopalian. Office: Sullivan & Cromwell 125 Broad St Fl 32 New York NY 10004-2400

FISHER, BARBARA A., former broadcast executive; b. 1954; m. Michael Scott; children: Kyle, Zachary. BA, Oberlin Coll., Ohio. Publicist A&M Records; prodr. Dave Bell Assoc.; v.p. creative affairs New World Pictures, MCA TV Entertainment; dir. movies and miniseries Universal TV Entertainment, 1987—91, pres., 1991—99; exec. v.p. Lifetime Entertainment Svcs., 2002—04.

FISHER, CARLYN FELDMAN, artist, writer; b. Atlanta, Nov. 5, 1923; d. Abrom Lewis and Jennie (Saul) Feldman; m. Ted V. Fisher, 1944 (div. 1972); m. Morris Berthold Abram, Jan. 22, 1975 (div. May 1987); 1 child, Eve Fisher Shulmister. BS in Fine Art, Skidmore Coll., 1945; postgrad., Atelier 17, Paris, 1964, Pembroke Coll., Oxford, Eng., 1984. Founder, pub. Abstract Arts Festival of Atlanta, 1955-67; art editor Atlanta Mag., 1966-72; dir., writer, rschr. NEA, 1967-68; writer, dir. TV documentaries PBS, Channel 8, 1974-75; exec. prodr. Cape Cod/Sta. WGBH, Cape Cod, Boston, 1986-87. Co-founder, exec. Arts Festival Atlanta, 1953-62; chair bd. Hambidge Ctr., Rabun Gap, Ga., 1992-96; trustee adv. bd. Mus. Art, U. Ga., Athens, 1983—; artist-in-residence Hambidge Ctr. for Arts and Scis., Rabun Gap, 1987, 92-95, Mishkenot Sha'ananim, Jerusalem, 1987. One-person shows include Alexander Gallery, Atlanta, 1965, Heath Gallery, Atlanta, 1971, 88, Oglethorpe Gallery, Atlanta, 1973, Elaine Starkman Gallery, N.Y.C., 1982, Signature Shop Gallery, 1990, Dorothy Berge Gallery of Contemporary Art, Stillwater, Minn., 1993, Studio Exhbn., Atlanta, 1995; exhibited in group shows Atlanta High Mus. Art Shop, 1962, Ga. Artists Exhbn., 1967, Skidmore Coll., Saratoga Springs, N.Y., 1970, Lighting Assocs., Inc., N.Y.C., 1977, Ga. Artists Working in N.Y., N.Y.C., 1982, Cape Mus. Fine Arts, Dennis, Mass., 1985, Sen. Wyche Fowler Jr. Ga. Exhbn., Washington, 1991, Trinity Gallery, Atlanta, 1992; commd. murals installed Cobb Galleria Conv. Ctr., Atlanta, 1994; included in Exhbn. of Ga. Artists, Washington, 1992-93, The Great Frame Up Gallery, 1998; commd. sculpture installed in front of The Jewish Comty. Ctr., Atlanta, 1989; murals at the Westin Hotel Ballroom, Savannah, 1999,designer, executor commemorative poster for Piedmont Park Centennial Celebration, 1995; rschr., author: The Arts in Georgia, 1967-68; writer, co-dir. (TV documentaries) The Image Makers, 1974 (Emmy award); exec. prodr. (TV documentary) Art In Its Soul, 1987 (Silver Apple award). Bd. dirs. Richard Allen Ctr., N.Y.C., 1977-79; bd. dirs., exec. com. Ga. chpt. Nat. Mus. Women, Washington, 1987-95. Grantee Nat. Endowment for Arts, 1967-68; Ga. Women in the Visual Arts award State of Ga., 1997. Mem. Mensa, bd. mem. U. Georgia, Georgia Mus. Art, Atlanta History Ctr. Archives Avocations: travel, swimming, hiking, mountain climbing, teaching art. Home: 62 Forrest Pl NE Atlanta GA 30328-4868

FISHER, CARRIE FRANCES, actress, writer; b. Beverly Hills, CA, Oct. 21, 1956; d. Eddie Fisher and Debbie Reynolds; m. Paul Simon, 1983 (div. 1984); 1 child, Billie Catherine. Ed. high sch., Beverly Hills, Calif.; student, London Cen. Sch. Speech and Drama. Mem. chorus in Broadway musical Irene, 1972, also in Broadway prodn. Censored Scenes from King Kong; appeared in films Shampoo, 1975, Star Wars, 1977, Mr. Mike's Mondo Video, 1979, The Blues Brothers, 1980, The Empire Strikes Back, 1980, Under the Rainbow, 1981, Return of the Jedi, 1983, Garbo Talks, 1984, The Man with One Red Shoe, 1985, Hannah and Her Sisters, 1986, Hollywood Vice Squad, 1986, Amazon Women on the Moon, 1987, Appointment With Death, 1988, When Harry Met Sally., 1989, The 'Burbs, 1989, Loverboy, 1989, She's Back, 1989, Sibling Rivalry, 1990, Drop Dead Fred, 1991, Soapdish, 1991, This Is My Life, 1992, Austin Powers: International Man Of Mystery, 1997, Scream 3, 2000, Famous, 2000; TV movies include Come Back, Little Sheba, (spl.) 1977, Leave Yesterday Behind, 1978, Liberty, Sunday Drive, 1986, Sweet Revenge, 1990; TV series Leaving L.A., 1997; author: Postcards from the Edge, 1987, (also screenplay, 1990), Surrender the Pink, 1990, Delusions of Grandma, 1994.

FISHER, CHRISTINE S., music educator; BA cum laude, Pembroke State U., 1975; M in Music Edn., U. S.C., 1980. Tchr. 10-12 Dillon H.S., 1975-78; K-6 music tchr., band tchr. McKenzie, Timrod, Bonaire & TansBay Elem., 1978-84; tchr. 7-8 Southside Mid. Sch., 1984-97; 7-8 grade band tchr. Southside Mis. Sch., 1998—. Clarinet Florence Symph. Orch., bd. dirs.; bd. dirs. Cmty. Concert Assn., S.C. Arts Alliance; chairperson Pee Dee Tchr. Forum. Named S.C. Tchr. of Yr., 1998, State Honor Roll Tchr. 1993; recipient numerous grants. Mem. Palmetto State Tchrs. Assn., Music Educators Nat. Conf., S.C. Music Educators Assn., S.C. Band Dirs. Assn., Pi Beta Mu. Avocations: playing clarinet, travel. Home: 1918 Effies Ln Florence SC 29505-2921

FISHER, COLLEEN M., trade association administrator; b. Pitts., Sept. 29, 1954; d. C. Francis and Dolores Rita (Darby) Fisher. BA, Georgetown U., 1976; MA, George Washington U., 1980. Legis. asst. Senator Richard S. Schweiker, Washington, 1976-81; profl. staff mem. U.S. Senate Appropriations Com., Washington, 1981-83; sr. v.p. govt. rels. Nat. Apt. Assn., Washington, 1983-91; indsl. rels. mgr. Resolution Trust Corp., Washington, 1991-95; exec. dir. Coun. for Affordable and Rural Housing, Alexandria, Va., 1996—; ptnr. Stuart-Fisher Meeting Mgmt. LLC, Fredericksburg, Va., 1999—. Mem. Fredericksburg Rep. Com., 1995—. Roman Catholic. Home: 803 Sylvania Ave Fredericksburg VA 22401-4736 Office: CARH 1112 King St Alexandria VA 22314-3022 Office Phone: 703-837-9001.

FISHER, CONNIE MARIE, physical therapist; b. Johnstown, Pa., Dec. 29, 1972; d. James Michael and Janet Fisher. BS with honors in Athletic Tng. and Sports Medicine, Calif. U. of Pa., California, Pa., 1995; MA in Phys. Therapy, St. Francis U., Loretto, Pa., 2002. Cert. in phys. therapy Am. Phys. Therapy Assn., 2003, athletic trainer Nat. Athletic Tng. Bd. Certification, Nebr., 2004. Student athletic trainer The U. Notre Dame, Ind., 1994; phys. therapist, athletic trainer Conemaugh Health Sys., Johnstown, Pa., 1996—. Athletic trainer Vantage Phys. Therapy, Johnstown, Pa., 2004—05; phys. therapist Phoenix Rehab., Cresson, Pa., 2006. Recipient Clin. Excellence award, St. Francis, Q.P.A. award, Calif. U. of Pa., WOW award, Conemaugh Health Sys.; Presdl. scholar, Calif. U. of Pa. Mem.: Nat. Athletic Tng. Assn. (licentiate), Am. Phys. Therapy Assn. (licentiate). Roman Cath. Achievements include selected as first female trainer for men's basketball team at California University of Pennsylvania. Avocations: walking, swimming, reading, football. Home: 1513 Jefferson Ave Portage PA 15946 Office: Conemaugh Health System Franklin St Johnstown PA 15901 Office Phone: 814-242-9881. Personal E-mail: conkey3@verizon.net.

FISHER, DEBRA A., communications executive, educator; b. Muncie, Ind., May 23, 1957; d. David A. Hampton and Janet L. Valencia; 1 child, Amy Lynn. BA summa cum laude, Grand Canyon U., Phoenix, Ariz., 2002. Devel. dir. Sojourner Ctr., Phoenix, 1991—95; prin. Bapt. Mgmt. Svcs., Phoenix; pres., owner Vision Treks Cons., Phoenix, 1998—2002, Castle Bridge Comms., Phoenix, 2002—. Editor Canyon Inst. Advanced Studies, Phoenix, 2000—. Mem. Ariz. Town Hall, Phoenix, 2001—03; bd. dirs. Cancer Ctr. Phoenix Children's Hosp., 1989—91, founder Michael Fisher Meml. Fund, 1984. Ray-Maben scholar, Grand Canyon Univ., 2002. Mem.: Sholan Consortium, Alpha Chi (chpt. pres. 2001—02), Pi Lambda Theta. Avocations: hiking, travel, reading. Office: Castle Bridge Comms 4949 W Wescott Dr Glendale AZ 85308

FISHER, DEENA KAYE, social studies education administrator; b. Elk City, Okla., Dec. 20, 1950; d. Earl Dean and Rosa Lee (Stone) Music; m. Mike Fleck, May 29, 1970 (div. June 1988); children: DeeAnna Michelle, Carrie Denise, William Michael; m. Tom Fisher, Nov. 13, 1993; 1 stepchild, Eleni. BA in Edn.-Social Sci., Southwestern Okla. State U., 1979, MEd in Social Sci., 1983, MEd in Sch. Counseling, 1987; EdD, Okla. State U., 2004. Instr. in social sci. Cordell (Okla.) H.S., 1979-85, El Reno (Okla.) C.C., 1985-88, Upward Bound guidance and career counselor, instr., 1987-89; instr. Am. History Yukon (Okla.) H.S., 1986-87; instr. polit. sci. and Am. history Southwestern Okla. State U., 1987-89; chair dept. Am. history, instr. Am. govt. Woodward (Okla.) H.S., 1989-96; instr. social studies Northwestern Okla. State U., Alva, 1989—, assoc. prof., 2004; dean Northwestern Okla. State U., Woodward Campus, 2002—. Author ednl. materials in field. Del. Dem. Nat. Conv., Okla. Dem. Party, Chgo., 1996; law day coord. Okla. Bar Assn., Woodward, 1990-96; regional coord. Citizen Bee, Tulsa World, 1994-97; panelist U.S. History Nat. Assessment of Ednl. Progress, St. Louis, 1994. Recipient Outstanding Am. History Tchr. award Okla. Soc. DAR, 1993, Tchr. of Yr. award Okla. Supreme Ct., 1992; Bill of Rights Edn. Collaborative grantee, 1991. Mem. Nat. Coun. for Social Studies (ho. dels., co-chmn. resolution com. 1996), Okla. Social Studies Suprs.' Assn. (membership bd. 1997), Okla. Coun. for Social Studies (del.-at-large 1996, pres. 1994-96), Woodward Edn. Assn. (pres. 1996), Woodward C. of C. (mem. edn. com. 1997), Delta Kappa Gamma (pres. Psi chpt. 1996-98), Phi Delta Kappa. Mem. Christian Ch. (Disciples Of Christ). Avocations: reading, chess. Home: 3308 Bent Creek Dr Woodward OK 73801-6931 Office: Northwestern Okla State U Woodward Campus PO Box 1046 Woodward OK 73802-1046 Office Phone: 580-256-0047.

FISHER, DORIS, retail executive; m. Donald G. Fisher; 1 child, Robert J. Co-founder Gap, Inc., 1969, merchandiser, 1969—2003, bd. dir., 1969—. Trustee Stanford U. Named one of most powerful women, Forbes mag., 2005. Office: Gap Inc Two Folsom St San Francisco CA 94105 Office Phone: 650-952-4400.*

FISHER, ERIN, psychology professor; b. Rockford, Ill. m. Chris Fisher. MS, No. Ill. U., DeKalb, 1995. Asst. prof. Rock Valley Coll., Rockford, 1995—. Actor: (theater performance) The Vagina Monologues. Adviser Coll. Dems., Rockford, 1999—2003. Named Most Enthusiastic Instr., Rock Valley Coll. Student Commn., 2001, Adviser of the Yr., 2002; recipient Excellence in Innovation in Tchg. award, 2001. Democrat. Office: Rock Valley Coll 3301 N Mulford Rd Rockford IL 61114 Office Phone: 815-921-3386.

FISHER, FRANCES, actress; b. Milford-on-Sea, Eng., May 11, 1952; d. William I. and Olga (Moen) F.; 1 child, Francesca Ruth Fisher-Eastwood. Student, Lee Strasberg, Stella Adler, Marilyn Fried, Sandra Seacat, HB Studios. Appearances include (films) Can She Bake a Cherry Pie?, 1985, Tough Guys Don't Dance, 1986, Patty Hearst, 1987, Lost Angels, 1988, Pink Cadillac, 1989, Welcome Home Roxy Carmichael, 1989, L.A. Story, 1991, Unforgiven, 1992, Baby Fever, 1992, The Stars Fell on Henrietta, 1994, Molly and Gina, 1992, Female Perversions, 1993, Striptease, 1995, Wild America, 1996, Titanic, 1997, True Crime, 1998, The Big Tease, 1998, The Rising Place, 2002, Gone in 60 Seconds, 2000, (TV) Elysian Fields, 1987, Sudie & Simpson, 1988, Cold Sassy Tree, 1989, Promises to Keep, 1990, Lucy & Desi: Before the Laughter, 1991, Devlin, 1987, Crime and Punishment, 1989, Law and Order, 1990, Praying Mantis, 1992, Attack of the 50 Foot Woman, 1993, The Other Mother, 1994, Strange Luck, 1995, Becker, 2000, Audrey Hepburn, 1999, Titus, 2001, Jackie, 2000, Glory Days, 2001, (theater) Cat on a Hot Tin Roof, 1981, Hay Fever, 1981, The Chain, 1983, Desire Under the Elems, 1982, Still Life, 1983, Ruffian on the Stair, 1979, A Midsummer Night's Dream, 1981, Hunchback of Notre Dame, 1981, Orpheus Descending, 1986, The Hitchhikers, 1985, Crackwalker, 1987, Fool for Love, 1985, Three More Sleepless Nights, (Drama Logue award 1996), 1996, 1984, 1984, Jammed, 1997. Mem. Actors Studio. Office: Nevin Dolcefino Innovative Artists 1505 10th St Santa Monica CA 90401

FISHER, HEIDI ALICE, librarian; b. Quakertown, Pa., Mar. 31, 1963; d. David Allen and Martha Catherine (Breisch) F. BA in Latin, St. Olaf Coll., 1985; MS, Drexel U., 1987. Grad. asst. Drexel U. Hagerty Libr., Phila., 1985-87; asst. order libr. LI order divsn. Princeton (N.J.) U., 1987-90, asst. order libr. LII Firestone Libr., 1990-95, asst. order libr. LIII order divsn., 1995—. Mem. N.Am. Serials Interest Group. Avocations: crocheting, gardening, reading, model trains. Home: 574 Doloro Dr Morrisville PA 19067-6833 Office: Princeton U Libr 1 Washington Rd Princeton NJ 08544-2002 Office Phone: 609-258-5415.

FISHER, IRENE B., lawyer; b. Odessa, Russia, July 20, 1965; BA summa cum laude, Yale U., 1987; JD cum laude, Harvard U., 1990. Bar: N.Y. 1990. Assoc. Milbank, Tweed, Hadley & McCloy, 1990—94; v.p., assoc. gen. counsel Triarc Co., Inc., 1994—96; dep. gen. counsel Big Flower Holdings, Inc., 1996—2002; gen. counsel Lane Capital LLC, 1996—2002, NBTY Inc., 2002—. Mem.: Phi Beta Kappa. Office: Nbty PO Box 9001 Bohemia NY 11716-9001 Office Phone: 631-567-9500.

FISHER, JANET WARNER, secondary school educator; b. San Angelo, Tex., July 7, 1929; d. Robert Montell and Louise (Buckley) Warner; m. Jarek Prochazka Fisher, Oct. 17, 1956 (div. May 1974); children: Barbara Zlata Harper, Lev Prochazka, Monte Prochazka. BA, So. Meth. U., 1950, M of Liberal Arts, 1982; student various including, Columbia U., U. Dallas, U. Colo., U. London and others. Cert. English, German and ESL tchr., K-12, Tex., N.Y. Bd. dirs., sec. Masaryk Inst., N.Y.C., 1968-71; with orphan sect. Displaced Persons Commn., Washington, 1950; fgn. editor Current Digest of the Soviet Press, N.Y.C., 1953-55; cable desk clk. Time, Inc., N.Y.C., 1955-56; tchr. of English and reading, langs. Houston Ind. Sch. Dist., 1975-80; tchr. Carmine Ind. Sch. Dist., Round Top, Tex., 1980-82; tchr. German Region IV Interactive TV, 1983-85; adj. prof. English U. Houston, 1983-87; tchr. Royal Ind. Sch. Dist., Brookshire, Tex., 1989-92, Hempstead Ind. Sch. Dist., Waller County, Tex., 1992-94. Adj. prof. English, U. Houston, Houston C.C., 1983-87, 1997—; tchr. Amnesty Program, Houston, 1988-90; adj. prof. English Blinn Coll., Brenham, Tex., 1995-97. Candidate sch. bd., South Orangetown, N.Y., 1962, state rep., Houston, 1980; del. Houston Tchrs. Assn., 1975-80; officer LWV, Nyack, N.Y., 1960-62; trustee, chair adminstrn. bd. Shepherd Drive United Meth. Ch., Houston, 1994-2003; del. Tex. ann. conf. United Meth. Ch., 1994-2001; del. Tex. State Dem. Conv., 1996, 2000, 02. Recipient award for Svc. to Missions, United Meth. Ch., Houston, 1985. Mem. AAUW, NOW, WILPF, Harris County Women's Polit. Caucus. Avocations: Russian and German literature, real estate development.

FISHER, JEWEL TANNER (MARY FISHER), retired construction company executive; b. Port Lavaca, Tex., Oct. 31, 1918; d. Thomas M. and Minnie Frances (Dunks) Tanner; m. King Fisher, Aug. 13, 1937; children: Ann Fisher Boyd, Linda Fisher LaQuay. A in Bus., Tex. Luth. Coll., 1937. Sec. treas. King Fisher Marine Svc., Inc., Port Lavaca, 1959-82, dir., cons., 1958-98; artist, poet. Trustee Meml. Med. Ctr., 1976-81, 90-94, Golden Crescent Coun. Govts., 1980-81, Crisis Hotline Calhoun County, 1985-93; pres. bd. trustees Meml. Med. Ctr., 1992-93; trustee Golden Crescent Coun. Govts., 1980-81. Lic. pvt. pilot. Mem. DAR (regent Guadalupe Victoria chpt. 1986-88), Daus. Republic Tex., 99's, Internat. Orgn. Women Pilots. Home: PO Box 166 Port Lavaca TX 77979-0166

FISHER, JO ANN, television technical director; b. Mpls., Sept. 14, 1957; d. Philip and Rita Blossom (Joss) F.; m. Steven William Koeln, Oct. 29, 1983; children: Nathan Ross Fisher-Koeln, Gertrude Rose Fisher-Koeln. BA, U. Minn., 1981. Floor dir. KSTP-TV, Mpls., 1979-82, duty dir., 1982-85, tech. dir., 1985-88, occasional dir., 1987-88; freelance dir., tech. dir. IDS/Amex Fin. Advisors, Mpls., 1987—, Met. Sports Commn., Mpls., 1989—, IVL Post, Mpls., 1990—, KTCA Pub. TV, St. Paul, 1990—, ESPN, 1993—, Juntunen Media Group, 1995—, Juntunen Mobile TV, 1998—, N.W. Mobile TV, 1992-99. Owner jewelry bus. Mem. com. J.C.C. Childcare, St. Paul, 1989-93; vol. St. Paul Pub. Schs., 1991—; mem. com. Shir Tikvah Synagogue, Mpls., 1992-93, chair com., 1994-95. Recipient I.D.E.A. award, 1993. Democrat. Jewish. Avocation: reading mysteries. Personal E-mail: fisherjoni@msn.com.

FISHER, JOELY, actress; b. Burbank, Calif., Oct. 29, 1967; d. Eddie Fisher and Connie Stevens; m. Christopher Duddy, 1996; 2 children. Student, Univ. Paris, Emerson Coll. Actor: (films) I'll Do Anything, 1994, The Mask, 1994, Mixed Nuts, 1994, Family Plan, 1998, Inspector Gadget, 1999, Nostradamus, 2000, Slingshot, 2005; (TV films) Dedicated to the One I Love, 1991, Jitters, 1997, Seduction in a Small Town, 1997, Icebergs: The Secret Life of a Refrigerator, 1998, Perfect Prey, 1998, Thirst, 1998, Coming Unglued, 1999, Kidnapped in Paradise, 1999, (TV series) In the Loop, 1998, Ellen, 1994-98, Normal, Ohio, 2000-01, Baby Bob, 2002-03, Til Death, 2006, (Broadway plays) Grease; performed with Connie Stevens and Bob Hope overseas during Persian Gulf War; sang before Pres. and Mrs. Bush at Kennedy Ctr. Office: c/o Fox Entertainment Group Inc 1211 Avenue of the Americas Ste 302 New York NY 10036*

FISHER, KATHRYN PATTILLO, education educator, department chairman; b. Decatur, Ga., Jan. 16, 1968; d. David Jonathan and Emily Roquemore Pattillo; m. Jeremy Eleazer Fisher, Aug. 31, 1996; children: William Ross, Samuel Todd, Emily Grace. BA, Agnes Scott Coll., Decatur, Ga., 1990; MEd, Auburn U., Ala., 1994, EdD, 1998. Cert. tchr. N.C. Tchr. Pace Acad., Atlanta, 1990—93; housing & residence life coord. Auburn U., 1994—97; dir. pub. programs Catawba Sci. Ctr., Hickory, NC, 1998—2002; asst. prof., chair Sch. Edn. Lenoir-Rhyne Coll., Hickory, 2002—. Cons. Catawba Sci. Ctr., Hickory, 2002—. Driver, delivery Meals on Wheels, Hickory, 2003—. Mem.: Nat. Sci. Tchrs. Assn., Rotary, Alpha Lambda Delta (hon.). Democrat. Lutheran. Avocations: tennis, walking. Office: Lenoire Rhyne Coll Campus Box 7203 625 7th Ave NE Hickory NC 28603

FISHER, KIM, artist; b. 1973; BFA, UCLA, 1996; MFA, Otis Coll. Art & Design, 1998. One-woman shows include, China Art Objects, LA, 1999, 2001, Midway Contemporary Art, St. Paul, 2003, John Connelly Presents, NYC, 2004, Shane Campbell, Oak Park, Ill., 2004, Modern Inst., London, 2005, exhibited in group shows at LA-LV-LA, Donna Beam Fine Art Gallery, U. Nev., 1997, The Comestible Compost, Gallery 207, West Hollywood, Calif., 1998, Young & Dumb, ACME, LA, 2000, Platypus, Lawrence Rubin Greenberg Van Doren Fine Art, NY, 2001, Selections, Bolsky Gallery, Otis Coll. Art & Design, LA, 2001, Cancelled Art Fair!, China Art Objects, LA, 2001, The Stray Show, boom, Chgo., 2002, 21 Paintings from LA, Robert V. Fullerton Art Mus., San Bernardino, Calif., 2002, Fair, Royal Coll. Art, London, 2002, Works for Giovanni, China Art Objects, LA, 2003, Still or Sparkling?, John Connelly Presents, NY, 2003, A Red Letter Day, Fredericks Freiser Gallery, NY, 2003, such things I do just to make myself more attractive to you, Peres Projects, LA, 2004, Whitney Biennial, Whitney Mus. Am. Art, 2004.

FISHER, LINDA R., science educator, department chairman; b. Oklahoma City, Oct. 27, 1951; 1 child, Avery Katherine. M, Oklahoma City U., 2002. Sci. tchr., chair Thackerville Pub. Schs., Okla., 1995—2000; chair sci. dept, tchr. Ardmore City Schs., Okla., 2000—. Group leader United Meth. Women, Ardmore, 1995—2000. Named Tchr. of Yr., Ardmore City Schs., 2000. Mem.: Nat. Sci. Tchrs (assoc.). Avocations: writing, reading. Office: Ardmore City Schs 701 Veterans Blvd Ardmore OK 73401 Office Phone: 580-226-7680. Personal E-mail: lindafisher1027@hotmail.com.

FISHER, LISA GRAY, English language educator; d. J. Glenn and Ursula A. Gray; m. Richard C. Fisher, Mar. 21, 1974; children: Kristina, Eliot. BA in English, Pomona Coll., Claremont, Calif., 1970; MA in Edn., Coll. Santa Fe, N.Mex., 1994. Instr. English U. N.Mex., Penaso, 1974—76; editor Houghton Mifflin Co., Boston, 1976—80; instr. English Santa Fe (N.Mex.) C.C., 1988—95; chair English dept., tchr. Santa Fe Prep. Sch., 1993—. Contbr. poetry, nonfiction, and short fiction to various publs. Adviser to students serving as tchg. assts. Headstart, other local prep. schs., Santa Fe, 1995—. Recipient Youth grant, NEH, 1973—74. Mem.: Nat. Coun. Tchrs. of English. Avocations: writing, travel, swimming. Office: Santa Fe Prep Sch 1101 Camino Cruz Blanca Santa Fe NM 87505

FISHER, LUCY, film producer; b. NYC, Oct. 2, 1949; d. Arthur Bertram and Naomi (Kislak) F.; m. Douglas Z. Wick, Feb. 16, 1986; children: Sarah, Julia, Tessa. BA in English, cum laude, Harvard U., 1971. Reader United Artists; v.p. prodn. 20th Century Fox, L.A., 1979-80; v.p. worldwide prodns. Zoetrope Studios, Burbank, Calif., 1980-81; v.p., sr. prodn. exec. Warner Bros. Pictures, Burbank, 1981-87, sr. v.p., 1987-89, exec. v.p. prodn., 1989-96; vice chmn. Columbia Tristar Motion Picture Co., Culver City, Calif., 1996-2000; prodr. Red Wagon Productions, Culver City, Calif., 2000—, pres. Prodr.: (films) Stuart Little 2, 2002, Peter Pan, 2003, Win a Date with Tad Hamilton!, 2004, Bewitched, 2005, Jarhead, 2005, Memoirs of a Geisha, 2005, Stuart Little 3: Call of the Wild, 2005; exec. prodr.: (TV series) Stuart Little, 2003. Recipient Crystal award, 1998. Office: Red Wagon Entertainment Hepburn West 10202 Washington Blvd Culver City CA 90232-3119*

FISHER, MICHELE RENEE, lawyer; b. Champlin, Minn., May 29, 1974; BA in Criminal Justice and Spanish, St. Cloud U., 1997; JD, William Mitchell Coll. Law, 2000. Bar: Minn. 2000, US Dist. Ct. (dist. Colo.), US Dist. Ct. (dist. Minn.), Minn. Supreme Ct. Assoc., mem. nat. wage and hour litig. team Nichols, Kaster & Anderson, P.L.L.P., Mpls. Named a Rising Star, Minn. Super Lawyers mag., 2006. Mem.: Assn. Trial Lawyers of Am., Fed. Bar Assn., Minn. Women Lawyers, ABA, Minn. State Bar Assn., Hennepin County Bar Assn., Nat. Employment Lawyers Assn. Office: Nichols Kaster & Anderson PLLP 4600 IDS Ctr 80 S 8th St Minneapolis MN 55402 Office Phone: 612-256-3229. E-mail: fisher@nka.com.*

FISHER, NANCY, writer, producer, director; b. Oct. 21; d. Seymour and Tema Fisher; 1 child, Sarah Olivia. BA, Barnard Coll. Head creative group Doyle, Dane, Bernbach Advt., London; creative group head Benton & Bowles Advt., London, McCann Erickson Advt., N.Y.C.; creative dir. Norman, Craig & Kummel Advt., N.Y.C.; pres. Nancy Fisher Inc., N.Y.C., 1981—2002, Creative Programming Inc., N.Y.C., 1981-89. Author: Vital Parts, 1993, Side Effects, 1994, Special Treatment, 1996, Code Red, 1998, Code Blue, 2000; creator, writer, prodr. (TV series) Womanwatch, 1982—89, Celebrity Chefs, 1983—89, (numerous home video cassettes including) Look Mom, I'm Fishing (Parents Choice award), The Annapolis Book of Seamanship Video Series (Cindy award), The Christmas Carol Video, Video Dog, Video Cat, Video Baby; prodr.: (TV series) The Real Bottom Line. Sr. v.p., dir. comm. The Ch. Pension Group, N.Y.C., 2000—. Recipient 5 broadcast awards Network Documentary Series. Mem. Dirs. Guild Am., Authors Guild.

FISHER, NANCY DEBUTTS, library director; b. Pitts., Apr. 10, 1945; d. Jacob John DeButts and Marie Christine Grills; m. Bruce C. Fisher, May 29, 1971. BS, Cleve. State U., 1968; MSLS, Case Western Res. U., 1973. Reference libr. Cleveland Heights-University Heights Pub. Libr., 1968-79; mgr. Beachwood (Ohio) br. Cuyahoga County Pub. Libr., 1980-90; dir. Wickliffe (Ohio) Pub. Libr., 1990—. Mem. adv. coun. Wickliffe United Way, 1991—2001; key communicator Wickliffe City Schs., 1992; mem. comm. com. Lake County United Way, 2002—, mem. cabinet, 2003—04; mem. Wickliffe Cmty. Adv. Panel, 1995—; grad. Leadership Lake County, 2003; bd. dirs. Wickliffe Civic Ctr., Inc., 1999—, pres. bd. dirs., 2004—; mem. adv. com. Holden Aboretum Warren H. Corning Libr., 1999—2002; mem. alumni planning com. Case Western Res. U. Libr. Sci., 1997—; mem. Lake Hosp. Sys., women's health adv. bd., 1999—. Mem.: ALA, Cleve. Area Met. Libr. Sys. (bd. dirs. 1994—96, mem. pers. com. 2003—), Ohio Libr. Coun., Lake County C. of C. Bd., Wickliffe C. of C. (v.p. 1998—99, pres. 2001—03, Civic Leader of Yr. 1999), Rotary (pres. 1992—94, chair charity ball 2002—03). Home: 939 Stuart Dr South Euclid OH 44121-3425 Office: Wickliffe Pub Libr 1713 Lincoln Rd Wickliffe OH 44092-2499 Office Phone: 440-944-6010. Business E-Mail: nfisher@wickliffe.lib.oh.us.

FISHER, NANCY LOUISE, pediatrician, geneticist, retired nurse; b. Cleve., July 4, 1944; d. Nelson Leopold and Catherine (Harris) F.; m. Larry William Larson, May 30, 1976 (div. Oct. 2000); 1 child, Jonathan Raymond. Student, Notre Dame Coll., Cleve., 1962-64; BSN, Wayne State U., 1967; postgrad., Calif. State U., Hayward, 1971-72; MD, Baylor Coll. of Medicine, 1976; M in Pub. Health, U. Wash., 1982, certificate in ethics, 1993. Diplomate Am. Bd. Pediatrics, Am. Bd. Med. Genetics. RN coronary care unit and med. intensive care unit Highland Gen. Hosp., Oakland, Calif., 1970-72; RN coronary care unit Alameda (Calif.) Hosp., 1972-73; intern in pediatrics Baylor Coll. of

Medicine, Houston, 1976-77, resident in pediatrics, 1977-78; attending physician, pediatric clinic Harborview Med. Ctr., Seattle, 1980-81; staff physician children and adolescent health care clinic Columbia Health Ctr., Seattle, 1981-87, founder, dir. of med. genetics clinic, 1984-89; maternal child health policy cons. King County div. Seattle King County Dept Pub. Health, 1983-85; dir. genetic svcs. Va. Mason Clinic, 1986-89; dir. med. genetic svcs. Swedish Hosp., 1989-94; pvt. practice Seattle, 1994-97; med. cons. supr. office of managed care Wash. State Dept. Social and Health Svcs., Olympia, 1996-97; med. dir. Medicaid Dept. of Social and Health Svcs., Wash., 1997-99; assoc. med. dir. Govt. Programs Regence Blue Shield, 1999; med. dir. Regence Blue Shield, 2000—02; chief med. officer Wash. State Health Care Authority, 2003—. Nurses aide psychiatry Sinai Hosp., Detroit, 1966—67; charge nurse Women's Hosp., Cleve., 1967; rsch. asst. to Dr. Shelly Liss, 76; with Baylor Housestaff Assn., Baylor Coll. Medicine, 1980—81; clin. asst. prof. grad. sch. nursing U. Wash., Seattle, 1981—85, clin. asst. prof. dept. pediat., 1982—92, clin. assoc. prof. dept. pediat., 1992—; com. appointments include Seattle CCS Cleft Palate Panel, 1984—97; bd. dirs., first v.p. King County Assn. Sickle Cell Disease, 1985—86, acting pres., 1986, pres., 1986—87; hosp. affiliation include Childrens Orthopedic Hosp. and Med. Ctr., Seattle, 1981—, Virginia Mason Hosp., Seattle, 1985—89, Harborview Hosp., Seattle, 1986—89; mem. Wash. State Steering Coun. Stroke and Heart Disease, 2006—, Wash. State Vaccine Adv. Com., 2006—. Contbr. articles to profl. jours. Active Seattle Urban League, 1982-96, 101 Black Women, 1986-94; bd. dirs. Seattle Sickle Cell Affected Family Assn., 1984-85, Am. Heart Assn., 2001—, March of Dimes 2002—; mem. People to Citizen Ambassador Group; sec. Health and Human Svcs. Com. on Infant Mortality, 1993—2003; mem. Twins Com. Inst. of Medicine, 1995-2000; Evaluation, Rsch. and Planning Group Ethical Legal and Social Implications Nat. Human Gerome Rsch. Inst., 1997-2000. Served to lt. USN Nurse Corps, 1966-70; mem. State Steering Com. on Heart Disease and Stroke, 2005—. Fellow Am. Coll. Medicine Genetics (founder); mem. AMA, APHA, Am. Heart Assn. (bd. dirs. King County 2001—, Pacific NW affiliate bd. 2006—, Physician of Yr.), Am. Acad. Physician Execs., Student Governing Body and Graduating Policy Com. Baylor Coll. Medicine (founding mem. 1973-76), Loans and Scholarship Com. Baylor Coll. Medicine (voting mem. 1973-76), Am. Med. Student Assn., Student Nat. Med. Assn., Admission Com. Baylor Coll. Medicine (voting mem. 1974-76), Am. Med. Women's Assn., Am. Acad. Pediatrics, Am. Soc. Human Genetics, Nat. Spkrs. Assn., Nat. Quality Found. (steering com.), Wash. State Assn. Black Providers of Health Care, Soc. Health and Human Values, Wash. State Soc. Pediatrics, Wash. State Med. Assn. (women in medicine com., interspilty. coun., fin. com.), Seattle C. of C. (mem. Leadership Tomorrow 1988—), Sigma Gamma Rho, Phi Delta Epsilon. Office: Wash State HCA 676 Woodland Sq Loop SE MS-42701 Olympia WA 98504-2701 Office Phone: 360-923-2709. Business E-Mail: nancy.fischer@hca.wa.gov.

FISHER, ORA T., lawyer; BS in Econ., Univ. Pa., 1984; JD cum laude, Univ. Mich., 1991. Bar: Calif. 1991. Internal cons. and public fin. banking officer JPMorgan, NYC; atty. Latham & Watkins LLP, San Francisco, 1991—97, atty., Silicon Valley office Menlo Park, 1997—2004, mng. ptnr. Silicon Valley office, 2004—, and co-chair, venture & tech. practice group. Mem.: ABA, San Francisco Bar Assn., State Bar of Calif. Office: Latham & Watkins LLP Silicon Valley Office 135 Commonwealth Dr Menlo Park CA 94025

FISHER, REBECCA RHODA, lawyer; b. Milw., 1971; BA in Polit. Sci., U. Minn., Mpls., 1993; JD, William Mitchell Coll. Law, St. Paul, 1999. Bar: Minn. 1999, US Dist. Ct. (dist. Minn.) 2000, Wis. 2005. Law clk. criminal appeals Office of Minn. Atty. Gen., 1998—99; assoc. Ramsey & DeVore, 1999—2003; atty. Law Office of Rebecca Rhoda Fisher, P.L.L.C., Roseville, Minn. Contbr. articles to profl. publs. Named a Rising Star, Minn. Super Lawyers mag., 2006; named one of Up and Coming Attys., Minn. Lawyer, 2004. Mem.: Nat. Assn. Criminal Def. Lawyers, Minn. Assn. Criminal Def. Lawyers, Minn. Soc. Criminal Justice, ABA, Minn. Women Lawyers, Warren E. Burger Inn of Ct., Ramsey County Bar Assn., Minn. State Bar Assn. (chair criminal law sect. 2006—, vice chair criminal law sect. 2005—06, sec., treas. criminal law sect. 2003—05, chair new lawyers sect. 2005—06, vice chair new lawyers sect. 2004—05, sect. new lawyers sect. 2003—04). Office: Law Office of Rebecca Rhoda Fisher PLLC 2589 Hamline Ave North Ste B Roseville MN 55113 Office Phone: 651-251-3838. E-mail: rebecca@rrflaw.com.*

FISHER, SHARON SUE, music educator; d. Reid Kenneth and Velma Alice Atchley; m. Hunter Lee Fisher, Dec. 11, 1987; 1 child, Ryan Howard Perry. BS in Edn., Ea. N.Mex U., Portales, 1968. Elem. tchr. James Bickley Sch., Clovis, N.Mex., 1968—70, Wash. Ave. Elem. Sch., Roswell, N.Mex., 1970—87; 1st grade tchr. Mabank Primary Sch., Tex., 1991—96; elem. music tchr. Lakeview Elem. Sch., Gun Barrel City, Tex., 1996—. Founding dir. PALS Elem. Performing Arts Group, Gun Barrel City, 2004—05; asst. direc. elem. honor choir, Mabank, 2005—. Named Lakeview Elem. Tchr. of Yr., Lakeview Elem., 1996, Miss Southeastern N.Mex, Jaycees/Miss New Mex. Pageant, 1965, Miss Roswell N.Mex, Jaycees/Miss Roswell Pageant, 1965. Mem.: Tex. Music Educators Assn., Assn. Tex. Profl. Educators. Office Phone: 903-880-1600.

FISHER, SHERRY M., secondary school educator; d. John and Susan Metcalfe; m. Dean Fisher; children: Cody, Kyle. BA, Ithaca Coll., N.Y.; MS in Edn., U. of Bridgeport, Conn. Cert. tchr. English grade 7-12 N.Y. Tchr. Webutuck H.S., Amenia, NY, 1996—. Office Phone: 845-373-4106.

FISHER, STEPHANY, newscaster; b. Tex. m. Rick Fisher; 1 child. Degree in Comm., Wash. State U. Anchor, reporter Sta. KNDO-TV, Yakima, Wash., Sta. WYFF-TV, Greenville, SC; anchor Sta. KPTV-TV, Portland, 2000—03, Sta. WGCL-TV, Atlanta, 2003—. Recipient Talent of Yr. award, Wash. State U. Edward R. Murrow Sch. Comm., 1991. Office: Sta WGCL-TV 425 14th St NW Atlanta GA 30377

FISHER, TERESA MARIE, psychologist, forensic specialist; b. Canyon Country, Calif., Feb. 23, 1975; d. Robert Alstrand and Susan Jeanne Fisher. BA, U. Calif., Irvine, 1996; MA, Calif. Sch. Profl. Psychology, 1998, PhD in Psychology, 2000. Lic. psychologist Calif., 2002. Intern psychology Alliance Healthcare Corp., Sun Valley, Calif., 1998—99, Dorothy Kirby Detention Ctr., L.A., 1999—2000; postdoctoral fellow Northeast Valley Health Corp., San Fernando, Calif., 2000—01; postdoctoral resident Job Corps Ctr., Long Beach, Calif., 2000—01; staff psychologist Calif. Instn. Men, Chino, Calif., 2001—. Adj. prof. Argosy U., Costa Mesa, Calif., 2004; evaluator San Bernardino (Calif.) County Ct., 2002—; coord. Developmental Disabilities Program Calif. Instn. Men, 2004—06. Author: Psychological Violence: A Handbook for Assisting Stalking Victims, 1999. Mem.: APA, Am. Psychology-Law Assn., Am. Assn. Correctional and Forensic Psychology, Calif. Correctional Psychology Assn., Mensa, Psi Chi. Avocations: fencing, golf, theater, basketball, art museums. Home: 17887 Lone Ranger Trail Chino Hills CA 91709 Office: PMB 121 4200 Chino Hills Pkwy Ste 820 Chino Hills CA 91709

FISHER, TERRI LYNN, emergency nurse practitioner; b. Ames, Iowa, Apr. 7, 1970; d. Steven Carl and Paula Ann (Mayernick) F. BSN, Humboldt State U., Arcata, Calif., 1992; MSN, Calif. State U., Sacramento, 2005. RN, CNS Calif., Colo.; cert. BLS, ACLS, PALS. Staff nurse shock-trauma ICU Mercy Med. Ctr., Redding, Calif., 1993-96; ICU nurse Nursefinders, San Jose, Calif., 1996-97; nurse, case mgr. Amador Home Health, Rocklin, Calif., 1997-98; adminstr. nursing supr., trauma/neuro ICU nurse Sutter Roseville Med. Ctr., Roseville, Calif., 1998—2003; critical care divsn educator St. Joseph's Hosp., Denver, 2003—05; flight nurse Air Ambulance Specialists Inc., Denver, 2005—. Republican. Christian. Home: 2807 W 98th Cir Federal Heights CO 80260-6102

FISHER-BISHOP, KELLY MARIE, literature educator, department chairman; b. Omaha, July 17, 1977; d. Stephen Charles and Christine Marie Fisher; m. Joseph William Bishop, July 22, 2000; 1 child, Stella Marie Bishop. BA in English and Edn., St. Louis U., Mo., 1999. Cert. tchr. English grades 9-12 Mo. Tchr. St. John the Bapt. H.S., St. Louis, 2000—. Coord. advanced placement St. John the Bapt. H.S., 2003—, advisor prom com., 2003—; coord. Shakespeare competition English Speaking Union, 2005—. Recipient Poetic Achievement award, Creative Comm., 2006; grantee, 2004. Mem.: Nat. Coun. Tchrs. of English. Office: St John the Bapt HS 5021 Adkins Ave Saint Louis MO 63116

FISHGRAB, BARBARA JEANNE, school psychologist, mental health services professional; b. Fredonia, Kans., Dec. 13, 1950; d. William Jr. and Geraldine Lee (Dalton) Parks; m. Donald Ray Fishgrab, Aug. 9, 1974 (div. Nov. 1990); children: Philip, Charity, Tabitha. BS in Elem. Edn., Baptist Bible Coll., 1975; MA in Psychol. Counseling, Liberty U., 1991, BS in Multidisciplinary Studies, 2000; MA in Psychology, Argosy U., Phoenix, 2005. Cert. crisis prevention trainer. Elem. sch. tchr. Hilltop Christian Sch., Tse Bonito, N.Mex., 1986-88, Gallup- McKinley County Schs., Gallup, N.Mex., 1990-91, guidance counselor, 1991-92, student assistance counselor, 1992-94, sch. psychologist, 1994—2001; mental health counselor Mesilla Valley Four Corners Resource Ctr., Gallup, N.Mex., 1994-95, Our Lady Mt. Carmel Home for Girls, Gallup, N.Mex., 1995—2001; sch. psychologist Deer Valley Sch. Dist., Phoenix, 2001—02, Saddle Mountain Sch. Dist., 2002—05, Washington Elem. Sch. Dist., 2005—06; pre-doctorate psychology intern Miss. State Hosp., Whitfield, Miss., 2006—. Mem. adv. bd. Drug Free Schs., Gallup-McKinley, 1995—2001. Mem.: ACA, Ariz. Psycholog. Assn. (student affiliate), Am. Psycholog. Assn. (student affiliate), Am. Counseling Assn., Am. Assn. Christian Counselors, Nat. Assn. Sch. Psychologists, World Congress Martial Artists Assn., Phi Delta Kappa. Avocations: swimming, hiking, racquet ball, tae-kwondo. Office: Was Elem Sch Dist 8033 N 27th Ave Phoenix AZ 85051 Personal E-mail: brunettestarfish@cox.net.

FISH-KALLAND, YVONNE J., language educator; d. Marilyn Knapp and P. Glenford Fish; m. Paul Kalland, Dec. 19, 1998. MA, SUNY Albany, 2006. Lectr. SUNY Cortland, 2000—02; assoc. prof. English Onondaga CC, Syracuse, NY, 2002—. Recipient Excellence in Tchg. Award, NISOD, 2004, Tchr. Recognition, Who's Who Am. Tchrs., 2004, Advisor Appreciation Award, Alpha Sigma Zeta Chpt. of Phi Theta Kappa, 2005—06. Avocations: hiking, skiing, art. Office: Onondaga Community College 4941 Onondaga Road Syracuse NY 13215 Office Phone: 315-498-2637. E-mail: fishkayv@sunyocc.edu.

FISHKIN, ANNE SONYA, retired special education educator; b. Bklyn., N.Y., Nov. 25, 1938; d. Harry Aaron and Judith Esther Pollack; m. F. William Kroesser, Oct. 26, 1996; children: Ruth Ellen, Amy Lynne Caplan. AB, Shimer Coll., 1958; MA in Psychology, U. Colo., 1970; PhD in Applied Behavioral Studies in Edn., Okla. State U., 1989. Cert. sch. psychologist Okla. Dept. Edn. Enrichment tchr. Guthrie (Okla.) Pub. Schs., 1975—76, Millwood Pub. Schs., Oklahoma City, 1976—78; enrichment tchr./sch. psychologist Edmond (Okla.) Pub. Schs., 1978—90; asst. prof. Marshall U. Grad. Coll., South Charleston, W.Va., 1990—94, assoc. prof. spl. edn. of gifted edn., 1994—97, rsch. specialist, 1997—2000; ret. Parent edn. coord. for family judge cir. W.Va. Supreme Ct. Appeals, Charleston, 1998—2002, parent edn. evaluator, 1998—2002; dir. Eastman Acad. Summer Sch., 2006. Editor: Investigating Creativity in Youth: Research and Methods, 1999; contbr. chapters to books, articles to profl. jours. Chair social action com. Congregation B'nai Israel, Charleston, W.Va., 2003—; active Commn. on Social Action, Union Reform Judaism, 2006—; v.p. Okla. Odyssey of the Mind, 1982—89; vice-chair W.Va. Odyssey of the Mind, 1992—98, W.Va. Creative Adventures Network (Destination Imagination), 1999—. Recipient Hon. Mention for outstanding rsch. article, Rsch. and Evaluation Divsn. of the Nat. Assn. for Gifted Children, 1994; grantee, W.Va. Grad. Coll. and GMI Engring. and Mgmt. Inst., 1991, Summer Tng. Inst., Educating Gifted Students with Learning Disabilities, Albuquerque, 1995, Parent Edn. Project Evaluator, W.Va. Supreme Ct. of Appeals, 1998, 1999, 2000, 2002, The Greater Kanawha Valley Found., 2006; grant, Mission W.Va., 2005. Mem.: Okla. Assn. for Gifted/Creative/Talented (v.p. 1989—90), W.Va. Assn. for Gifted and Talented (pres., newsletter editor 1995—96), Creativity Divsn. Nat. Assn. for Gifted Children (Guest (Issue) Editor of Creativity Divsn. Newsletter 1990, 1993, 2001), Nat. Assn. for Gifted Children (chair creativity divsn. 1990—91), Am. Mensa (gifted children's adv. com. 1987—90), Ctrl. Okla. Mensa (scholarship chair, proctor, gifted children's coord. 1982—89), Vandalia Mensa (scholarship chair, proctor coord. 1991—). Home: 813 Whispering Way South Charleston WV 25303 Personal E-mail: anne_fishkin@hotmail.com.

FISHMAN, HELENE BETH, social worker; b. Portchester, N.Y., Oct. 23, 1937; d. Henry William and Hortense (Baumblatt) Sandground; B.A., Mt. Holyoke Coll., 1959; M.S. in Social Work, Columbia U., 1961; m. Bernard Fishman, Feb. 14, 1959; children: Kara Jo, Charles Lee. Psychiat. social worker Children's Village, Dobbs Ferry, N.Y., 1961, 1965-66; asst. dir. Afro-Am. Cultural Found., White Plains, N.Y., 1968-78; mental health technician tchr., White Plains, 1970-71; cons. social worker, Hartsdale, N.Y., 1978—; cons. edn./research Oceanic Soc., Stamford, Conn., 1985-86. Chmn. cottage program Greenburgh Dist. 7; active PTA. Mem. Assn. for Children with Learning Disabilities (chmn. dist. 7). Jewish. Home: 6 Old Farm Ln Hartsdale NY 10530-2204

FISK, CATHERINE LAURA, law educator, lawyer; m. Erwin Chemerinsky. AB summa cum laude, Princeton Univ., 1983; JD, Univ. Calif., Berkeley, 1986; LLM, Univ. Wis., Madison, 1995. Bar: Calif. 1986, D.C. 1988. Staff atty. U.S. Ct. Appeals 9th cir., San Francisco, 1986—87, law clerk, 1987—88; assoc. Rogovin Huge & Schiller, Washington, 1988—90; atty. Appellate Staff, Civil Div., U.S. Dept. of Just., Washington, 1990—91; lectr. Univ. Wis. Law Sch., Madison, 1991; assoc. prof. Loyola Marymount Univ., 1992—96, prof., 1996—2003; vis. prof. Univ. Calif., Los Angeles, 1997—2002, Duke Univ., 2002; prof. Univ. Calif., Los Angeles, 2003—04, Duke Univ., 2004—. Contbr. articles prof. law jour. Vice-chair spec. comm. Investigative Oversight, City of Los Angeles, 1998; bd. dir. ACLU So. Calif., 1996—2004, exec. comm., 1998—2000, 2003—04, v.p., 2000—04; mem. nat. comm. commercial speech ACLU, 2003—; chair Willard Hurst Prize comm., Law & Society Assn., 2003—04. Recipient Pro Bono Svc. award, ACLU So. Calif., 2004, Distinguished Law Prof., 2003, Excellence in Education award, Indsl. Relations Rsch. Assn., 2000. Mem.: Am. Soc. Legal Hist. (mem. comm. membership 1997—99), Labor Law Group. Office: Duke Univ Sch Law Sci Dr & Towerview Rd Durham NC 27708-0360

FISK, DORIS ROSALIE SCANLAN, volunteer; b. Mpls., Aug. 20, 1915; d. Arthur William and Lea Marie (Beauchaine) Scanlan; m. Ellsworth William Fisk, Aug. 31, 1942; children: Gregory, Janine, Marilyn, Kathleen. Student, Mpls. Bus. Coll., 1935, U. Minn., 1940, San Antonio Jr. Coll., 1964. Hosp. vol. ARC, 1940-71; vol. Audie Murphy Vets. Hosp., 1972—; med. transcriber Radiology Assocs., San Antonio, 1962-64; nurse office mgr. for surgeon San Antonio, 1964-77; vol. Sr. Svc. Orgn., San Antonio, 1970—; vol., fund raiser Vis. Nurse Assn. S.W. San Antonio, 1992-97; vol. Quantum Brookhollow Med. Ctr., 1999—. Sec. vol. Demo-Ne Demos, San Antonio, 1960-64; pres. YWCA Wives, San Antonio, 1964-65, Espada Mission Aux., San Antonio, 1965-66; chair March of Dimes, San Antonio, ARC, 1940-1971, chmn. of vols.; vol. usher and seamstress Harlequin Theatre, from 1971; treas. altar soc. St. Mary's Cath.Ch., 1984-92; pres. flu shot prog. VNA, vol. Brookhollow Libr., 1995-96; chmn. Brooke Gen. Hosp. Vols. Recipient Golden Globe award Vol. Vis. Nurse of the Yr., San Antonio, 1993, Gold Key ring J.C. Penney; Letter of Congratulation, Pres. Clinton. Mem. AAUW, La Société Francaise Canadian, Ret. Sr. Vols. (bd. mem. 1970—), Officers Wives Club (tour guide 1996-97, tel. chairperson 1999-2000, 2000-2001), Smithsonian Instn., Williamsburg, Met. Mus., Beta Sigma Phi (life), Kappa Kappa Gamma. Democrat. Roman Catholic. Avocations: travel, reading, sewing. Home: 109 Timaaron Ct Weatherford TX 76085-3025

FISK, LOIS L., secondary school educator; b. Evanston, Ill., Jan. 12, 1944; d. James C. and Lois M. Sprague; m. Robert D. Fisk, Aug. 14, 1964; children: Lisa Ellison, Julie LaMatte, James. Attended, MacMurray Coll., 1962—64; BA, Carhage Coll., 1966; Masters degree, N.Mex. State U., 1984. Tchr. English, Alamagordo Pub. Schs., N.Mex., 1984—89, choral tchr., 1989—2000, Ruidoso Pub. Schs., N.Mex., 2000—. Music tchr. New Mex. State U. Active Tiger Music Theatre, 1995—2000; dir. edn. 1st Meth. Ch., DeKalb, Ill., 1974—77. Mem.: N.Mex. Music Educators Assn. Avocations: gardening, reading, travel, physical fitness.

FISKE, SANDRA RAPPAPORT, psychologist, educator; b. Syracuse, N.Y., Sept. 25, 1946; d. Sidney Saul and Helen (Lapides) Rappaport; m. Jordan J. Fiske, June 22, 1974. BS, Cornell U., 1968; MEd, Tufts U., 1969; MA, Columbia U., 1971, PhD, 1974. Supervising sch. psychologist St. Elizabeth's Sch., N.Y.C., 1971—76; instr. clin. psychology Columbia Tchrs. Coll., N.Y.C., 1973; clin. asst. dept. psychology Columbia, N.Y.C., 1975—76; adj. prof. Syracuse U., 1976; sch. psychologist Syracuse Bd. Edn., 1976—77; prof. psychology Onondaga C.C., Syracuse, 1976—87, prof., 1989—, chair social sci. dept., 1993—99; pvt. practice psychology Syracuse, 1976—. NIMH fellow, 1969-72. Mem. APA, Ctrl. N.Y. Psychol. Assn., Sigma Xi, Psi Chi. Home: 2 Signal Hill Rd Fayetteville NY 13066-9674 Office: Onondaga Community Coll Dept Psychology Syracuse NY 13215 Office Phone: 315-498-2100. Business E-Mail: fiskes@sunyocc.edu.

FITCH, BLAKE, museum director, photographer, curator; b. Greensboro, NC, 1971; BFA, Pratt Inst., 1994; attended, Art Inst. Chgo., 1998; MS in arts adminstrn., Boston U., 2001. Exec. dir. Griffin Museum of Photography, Winchester, Mass. Curator Photobooth, Jan Staller: A Retrospective. Office: Griffin Mus Photography 67 Shore Rd Winchester MA 01890 E-mail: blake@griffincenter.org.

FITCH, DARLENE, elementary school educator; b. Dallas, Jan. 14, 1946; d. James and Faye Snyder; 1 child, Derek. B of Edn., East Tex. State U., Commerce, 1968; postgrad., Nazareth Coll. Tchr. Pittsford Ctrl. Schs., NY, 1968—2006. Cons. McGraw Hill, reviewer math book; bldg. chmn., treas. Park Rd. Sch.; part-time gardener Wayside Gardens, Macedon. Mem. Tchr. Ctr. Policy Bd., Pittsford, NY; tchr. Sunday sch. Fairport Meth. C. Mem.: Rochester Alumnae Panhellenic Assn. (pres.), Lakeside Country Cloggers (treas. 2004—06), Delta Kappa Gamma, Kappa Delta (treasury advisor U. Rochester chpt.). Avocations: gardening, dance, painting, reading, travel. Home: 1 Parkland Dr Fairport NY 14450

FITCH, JANET, writer; b. L.A. Grad., Reed Coll. Mng. editor Am. Film mag.; editor The Mancos Times Tribune; book reviewer Speak mag., San Francisco. Author: (novels) Kicks, 1996, White Oleander, 1999, Paint It Black, 2006, short stories. Office: c/o Heather Rizzo Little Brown and Co 1271 Avenue of the Americas New York NY 10020*

FITCH, LINDA BAUMAN, retired elementary school educator; b. Elmira, NY, Jan. 6, 1947; d. Floyd Theodore Bauman and Wilma Mildred Rennie; m. H. Taylor Fitch, Feb. 15, 1969; children: Trevor Andrew, Matthew Taylor. BS, Keuka Coll., Keuka Park, 1969. Elem. tchr. Penn Yan (N.Y.) Ctrl. Sch. Dist., 1972-73, tchg. asst. K-5, 1999—2005; computer coord. Fitch Auto Supply, Penn Yan, 1973-99. Com. chmn. troop 48 Boy Scouts Am., Branchport, N.Y., 1986-92; v.p. Penn Yan Cen. Sch. Bd., 1984-92, 95-97, pres., 1992-95; chmn. pub. rels. Yates Day Care Ctr., Penn Yan, 1980-82; mem. Bd. Coop. Ednl. Svcs., 1992-99. Mem. Nat. Sch. Bds. Assn. (fed. rels. network 1988-99), N.Y. State Sch. Bds. Assn. (state legis. network 1991-99), Four County Sch. Bds. Assn. (legis. chmn., 2d v.p., 1st v.p., pres., mem. commr.'s adv. coun. sch. bd. mems. 1995). Republican. Presbyterian. Avocations: needlecrafts, reading, swimming. Home: 3120 Kinneys Corners Rd Bluff Point NY 14478-9752 Personal E-mail: tnlfitch@adelphia.net.

FITCH, NANCY ELIZABETH, historian, educator; b. White Plains, N.Y., June 17, 1947; d. Robert Franklin and Nancy Elizabeth (Harvey) F. BA in Polit. Sci./English Lit., Oakland U., Rochester, Mich., 1969; MA in History, U. Mich., 1971, PhD in History, 1981. Danforth tchg. intern dept. history U. Mich., Ann Arbor, 1970; asst. prof. history and lit. Sangamon State U., Springfield, Ill., 1972-74; sr. social sci. rsch. analyst The Congl. Rsch. Svc. of Libr. of Congress, Washington, 1975-78; asst. to the chmn./historian U.S. EEO Commn., Washington, 1982-89; asst. prof. history Lynchburg Coll. of Va., 1989-91; asst. prof. African Am. studies Temple U., Phila., 1991-92; Jesse Ball Dupont vis. scholar Randolph-Macon Woman's Coll., Lynchburg, Va., 1992-93; assoc. prof. history U. N.C. at Asheville, 1993-95; assoc. prof. history and English Coll. New Rochelle, NY, 1995—, chair dept. NY, 1999—2003. Chmn.'s rep. White House Inst. on Hist. Black Colls. and Univs., U.S. Dept. Edn., 1985-89, EEO com.; pub. rels. vol. S. Africa Exhibit Project, Washington, 1986-88; mem. adv. com. DuPont Vis. Scholars Project, Va. Found. Ind. Colls., 1990-91; adj. prof. in history Shaw U., Asheville, 1994; lectr. Jesse Ball DuPont Found. Coll. Confs. on Diversity, The Aspen Inst., Queenstown, Md., 1995, 96; participating historian, spkr. Schomburg Ctr. for Rsch. in Black Culture, N.Y.C., 1994, Booker T. Washington Jr. Anniversary Commemoration. Anthology Editor: How Sweet the Sound: The Spirit of African American History, 1999; editl. assoc.: Jour. South Asian Lit., 1969-79; co-editor: Diversity: A Jour. of Multicultural Issues, 1995-98; mem. editl. adv. bd. Kente Cloth: African Am. Voices in Tex.; contbr. book reviews to Jours.; author: (series) Essays on Liberty, 1988; contbr. articles to profl. jours. Organizer, producer Ann. Dr. Martin Luther King Jr. Celebration prog., Washington, 1986-88; guest lectr. on history of Am. music Blue Ridge Music Festival, Lynchburg, 1991; participant Radio America African-Am. contbrs. to art and lit., 1990; vol./cons. The Holiday Project, Washington, 1986-88; mem. Widening Horizons Prog. of D.C. Pub. Schs., 1986-88; trustee Sister to Sister Internat, 2004. Recipient Achievement award Mt. Vernon Day Care Ctr., 1983, Spl. Commendation, U.S. EEO Commn., 1985-89, Ft. Drum Sgt. Maj.'s medal for svc. 10th Mountain div. Light Inf., Ft. Drum, N.Y., 1992; fellow Ford Found., 1971-72, Nat. Def. Fgn. Lang., 1970, U. Mich., 1970-71, 78-79, John Hay Whitney Found., 1969-70; Faculty summer seminar fellowship Nat. Endowment for the Humanities, U. Kans., Lawrence, 1996; Alden B. Dow creativity fellow Northwood U., 1998; Millennium writer Westchester Libr. Sys. Inc., 2000. Fellow Soc. Values in Higher Edn.; mem. Assn. for Study African Am. Life and History, Orgn. Am. Hists., Phi Alpha Theta (faculty advisor 1990-91). Republican. Episcopalian/Buddhist. Avocation: photography. Home: 267 Bedford Ave Mount Vernon NY 10553-1517 Office: Coll New Rochelle 29 Castle Pl New Rochelle NY 10805-2338

FITCH, RACHEL FARR, health policy analyst; b. July 27, 1933; d. Allen Edward and Rosie Leola (Jones) Farr; m. Coy Dean Fitch, Mar. 31, 1956; children: Julia Anne, Jaquelyn Kay. Student, Little Rock U., 1965-67; BS, St. Louis U., 1974, MS, 1976, PhD, 1983. RN, Mo. Psychiat. staff nurse VA Ft. Root Hosp., North Little Rock, Ark., 1954-57; surg.-med. staff nurse St. Vincent Infirmary, Little Rock, Ark., 1957-65; acute care nurse Georgetown U. Hosp., Washington, 1968-69; pub. health nurse to adminstr. South office Vis. Nurse Assn. Greater St. Louis, 1970-73; cons. in edn. St. Louis City Health Dept., 1977-80; rsch. specialist Sen. John C. Danforth, St. Louis, 1980; owner RFF Assocs., 1983-86. Project dir. study of infant mortality in city of St. Louis, 1978. Mem. community health edn. com. Am. Heart Assn., 1977-87; bd. dirs. LWV of Mo., 1984-2001, editor newspaper, 1984-87, dir. health issues, 1987-99, 1st v.p. 1999-2001, 2003—; chmn. Mo. Consumer Health Care WATCH, 1996-2002; mem. adv. com. Mo. Medicaid Consumer, 1996-97; mem. Mo. Welfare Coord. Com., 1997-99; mem. healthcare mgmt. and policy adv. com. Maryville U., 2002—04; mem. Mo. Found. for Health Advocates steering com., 2003—04; sec. St. Louis U. Hosp. Aux. Mem. APHA, Acad. Polit. Sci., Grand Jury Assn. St. Louis (bd. dirs.), Woman's Club St. Louis U. Sch. Medicine (past pres., bd. dirs. 2004—), Jr. League St. Louis, Sigma Theta Tau. Address: 23 Lenox Pl Saint Louis MO 63108-1901 Office Phone: 314-961-6869. Personal E-mail: rachel.farr.fitch@sbcglobal.net.

FITCHETT, TAYLOR, law librarian; b. 1947; BA, Kans. State U., 1970; MLS, U. Ala., 1979. Acting dir., Law Libr. U. Ala., 1981—83; assoc. libr., Law Libr. Tulane U., 1983—86; dir., Law Libr. U. Cin., 1986—98; assoc. libr., Law Libr. U. Va., 1998—2000, dir. Law Libr. and Lectr. Gen. Faculty,

2000—. Mem.: Va. Assn. Law Libr. (chmn., publications com.), Am. Libr. Assn., Am. Assn. Law Libr. Office: Office of Law Libr Dir U Va 580 Massie Rd Charlottesville VA 22903-1789 Office Phone: 434-924-7725. Business E-Mail: tf2u@virginia.edu.

FITTS, CATHERINE AUSTIN, investment advisor; b. Phila., Dec. 24, 1950; d. William Thomas Jr. and Barbara Kinsey (Willits) Fitts. AA, Bennett Coll., 1970; student, Chinese U., Hong Kong, 1971; BA, U. Pa., 1974, MBA, 1978; postgrad., MIT. With Dillon, Read & Co., Inc., N.Y.C., 1978-89, sr. v.p., 1984-86, mng. dir., 1986-89, also bd. dirs.; asst. sec. housing, urban devel., fed. housing commr. HUD, Washington, 1989-90; pres., chmn. Hamilton Securities Group, Inc., Washington, 1990-97, Solari, Inc., Tenn., 1998—. Adv. bd. Fedn. Nat. Mortgage Assn. Fannie Mae, 1992—93; emerging markets adv. com. SEC, 1990—93; mem. Gold Anti-Trust Action Com. Columnist: Mapping the Real Deal, Scoop Media. Bd. dir. Student Loan Mktg. Assn. Sallie Mae, 1991—94; mem. grad. adv. bd. Wharton Sch., U. Pa., Phila., 1986—95. Office Phone: 731-764-2515. Business E-Mail: catherine@solari.com.

FITZ-CARTER, ALEANE, retired elementary school educator, composer; b. Council Bluffs, Iowa, July 24, 1929; d. Andrew Wilburt and Beatrice Mildred (Maddox) Fitz; m. James Benny Carter, Dec. 10, 1958 (wid. Aug. 1964); children: Angel Beatrix, Angel Sherrie. BSEd, U. Nebr., 1956. Elem. sch. tchr. Omaha Pub. Schs., 1956—69; instr. Black history and music U. Nebr., Omaha, 1970—74; nat. faculty mem. Gospel Music Workshop Am. Inc., 1986—2005; tchr. music Ascension Luth. Sch., L.A., 1990—94; min. music Messiah Luth. Ch., L.A., 1996—2003; ch. musician Tamarind Seventh Day Adventist Ch., Compton, Calif., 1997—2003; performing artist Nebr. Arts Coun., Omaha, 1980—, Iowa Arts Coun., Des Moines, 1998—; tchr. adult edn. L.A. Unified Schs., 1998—; ednl. cons. Torrance Unified Schs., Calif., 1997—99; ret., 2005. Min. music Olivet Luth. Ch., Hawthorne, 2003-05; program prodr. KETV TV, Omaha, 1970-73; talk show host, Radio Sta. KOWH, Omaha, 1973-74; comm. cons. Mayor's Human Rels. Bd., Omaha, 1970-73; midwest bd. rep. Nat. Black Media Coalition, Washington, 1973-76, others; tchr. Black Awareness Opportunities Industrialization Ctr., 1969-74; instr. history of jazz, Oasis, L.A., 1997-2001; arranger, librettist, lyricist, elocutionist, storyteller, lectr. in field Recs. include I Love Jesus, 1965, A Mighty Fortress, 1986; performer: (one-woman show) Rosa Parks, 1979—, Omaha Junior Theater, 1980—85; actress: I Elvis; Hard Copy, 1992; Ice Cube video Dead Homie MTV, 1990; (films) A Man Apart, 2003; music dir. (stage) One Last Look, Marla Gibbs Theater, 1990; contbr. articles to profl. jours.; composer: One Child, 1993, (sacred hymns) Psalm 91, 1993—97, Children's TV workshop, Strawberry Square II: Take Time, NETV, 1983; performer: South African Chs. of KwaZulu Natal and African Enterprises, 1995. Presentation Visiting With Huell Howser, KCET; rschr. soul food history and cooking; amb. storytelling programs Dwight D. Eisenhower's People to People, to South Africa, 2004. Nominee Best Supporting actress, Great White Hope Ctr. Stage, Omaha, Nebr., 1982; recipient Comty. Christian Leadership award, Salem Baptist Ch., Omaha, Nebr., 1987, Woman in Fine Arts award, Alyce Wilson Womens Ctr., Omaha, 1987, 5 yr. ACT-SO award, NAACP, Omaha, 1986, Outstanding Songwriter award, 1987—88, Psalm 91 Song of Yr. award, Thurston Frazier Chorale, 1987, Nebr. Chpt. Gospel Music Workshop of America Inc. award, 1987—88, Fine Arts award, Bethesda Seventh Day Adventist Ch., 1988, Comty. Guest Day, Bethesda Seventh Day Ch., Omaha, Nebr., 1988, Outstanding Svc. award, L.A. Union Seventh Day Acad., 1992, Creativity in music award, Thurston Frazier Chorale, Gospel Music Workshop Am., 1993, Svc. comty. award, Salem Baptist Mission, Norfolk, Nebr., 1995; grantee, L.A. Dept. of Cultural Affairs. Mem.: ASCAP, SAG, Nat. Storytelling Network, Rec. Acad., Profl. Musicians Union - Local 47, Nebr. Congress of Parents and Tchrs. (hon. life), Gold Star Wives Am., L.A. Pianist Club, VFW Ladies Aux., Sigma Gamma Rho (Gamma Beta Sigma chpt.). Adventist. Avocations: walking, swimming, cooking. Mailing: PO Box 90087 Los Angeles CA 90009 Home: 200 E Hyde Pk Blvd 1 Inglewood CA 90302 Personal E-mail: Psalm91@mymailstation.com.

FITZGERALD, ADELAIDE YVONNE, occupational child care educator; b. West Point, Miss., July 19, 1964; d. Arvied Edward and Pauline (Robertson) Wilson; m. John William Fitzgerald, Jr., June 15, 1985; 1 child, Ninna Ruth. Student, Miss. U. for Women, 1985. Presch. dir. Presbyn. Ch., Columbus, Miss., 1985-86; kindergarten tchr. St. Mary Sch., Columbus, 1986-90; occupational child care instr. East Miss. Community Coll., Mayhew, 1990—; kindergarten tchr. Annunication Cath. Sch., 1992—94, Mitchell Elem., 1994—. Mem. Nat. Employment and Tng. Assn., Am. Vocat. Assn., Miss. Assn. Vocat. Edn., Miss. Assn. Children Under Six, 4-Miss. Assn. Children Under Six (rep. 1991-92). Baptist.

FITZGERALD, ANGELA MICHELLE, special education educator; d. Phyllis Karen Goodpaster and Thomas Lee Manino, Terry Eugene Goodpaster (Stepfather); m. Anthony James Fitzgerald Jr., June 26, 2004; 1 stepchild, Jordan Tyler 1 child, Ryland Michael. AA, Parkland Coll., Champaign, Ill., 2000; BS in Spl. Edn., U. Ill., Urbana-Champaign, Ill., 2003. Cert. LBS 1 - Tchg. Ill., 2003. Comm. ptnr. Provena Covenant Med. Ctr., Urbana, Ill., 1996—2003; spl. edn. tchr. Unity West Elem. Sch., Tolono, 2003—. Summer camp dir. Champaign-Urbana Spl. Recreation, Champaign, 2004—05. Scholar William E. Albin and Charlotte C. Young Scholar, U. Ill., 2002, David Debolt Tchr. Shortage Scholarship, State of Ill., 2002-2003. Mem.: Kappa Delta Pi (assoc.), Phi Theta Kappa (assoc.). Avocations: reading, scrapbooks. Office Phone: 217-485-3918.

FITZGERALD, CATHLEEN MARIE, medical and surgical intensive care nurse; b. Buffalo, July 19, 1969; d. Paul Walter and Cathleen Ann (Farrell) Schulz; m. James John Fitzgerald, Aug. 13, 1993; children: Jessica Lynn, Meghan Rose, Nicole Ann, Matthew James. BSN, SUNY, Buffalo, 1992. RN, N.Y. Nurse in charge Harris Hill Nursing Facility, Cheektowaga, N.Y., 1992; nurse med. and surg. ICU, Erie County Med. Ctr., Buffalo, 1992—. Democrat. Roman Catholic. Avocations: camping, reading, crafts. Home: 137 Theresa Ct West Seneca NY 14224-4743 Office: Erie County Med Ctr 462 Grider St Buffalo NY 14215-3021

FITZGERALD, CHRISTINE ELIZABETH, school psychologist; b. Ann Arbor, Mich., Jan. 25, 1965; d. Michael Alan Robson and Lucinda Delphine Brandzel; m. Scott Terence Fitzgerald, Apr. 18, 1992; children: Kelsey Christine, Scott Patrick. BA, Dominican U., 1988; MA in Sociology, Loyola U., Chgo., 1992, EdM in Sch. Psychology, 1997, PhD in Psychology, 1998. Nat. cert. sch. psychologist. Adminstrv. asst. Copia Internat. Ltd., Wheaton, Ill., 1991—95; counselor Sarah's Inn Domestic Violence Agy., Oak Park, Ill., 1995—98; sch. psychologist J. Sterling Marton H.S., Cicero, Ill., 1997—98, Carol Stream (Ill.) Sch. Dist., 1998—99, Elmhurst (Ill.) Sch. Dist., 1999—. Cons. Everyone is Welcome, St. Charles, Ill., 1998—, Children Count, Elmhurst, 2005. Recipient Outstanding Psychology Student award, Rosary Coll., 1987—88. Mem.: Ill. Sch. Psychology Assn., Nat. Assn. Sch. Psychology. Avocations: circus aerial arts, magic. Home: 542 S Michigan Ave Villa Park IL 60181

FITZGERALD, JANET ANNE, philosophy educator, academic administrator; b. Woodside, N.Y., Sept. 4, 1935; d. Robert W. and Lillian H. (Shannon) F. BA magna cum laude, St. John's U., 1965, MA, 1967, PhD, 1971, LLD (hon.), 1982. Joined Sisters of St. Dominic of Amityville, Roman Catholic Ch., 1953; NSF postdoctoral fellow Cath. U. Am., summer 1971; prof. philosophy Molloy Coll., Rockville Centre, NY, 1969—, pres., 1972-96, pres. emerita, 1996—. Trustee L.I. Regional Adv. Coun. on Higher Edn., 1972-96, chmn., 1981-84; trustee Commn. on Ind. Colls. and Univs., 1981-84, 89-92, Cath. Charities, Diocese of Rockville Centre, 1979-82; trustee Fellowship of Cath. Scholars, 1977—, v.p., 1977-80; invited expert peritus Vatican Internat. Conf. on Cath. Higher Edn., Rome, 1989; prof. St. John Neumann, Archdiocese of N.Y.; invited auditor St. Thomas Aquinas Pontifical U., Rome, 1999. Author: Alfred North Whitehead's Early Philosophy of Space and Time, 1979. Mem. bd. advisors Sem. of Immaculate Conception, 1975-80; mem. adv. bd. pre-theology program Dunwoodie Sem., Archdiocese of N.Y.; mem. pub. policy com. N.Y. State Cath. Conf., 1992-94; mem. N.Y. State Edn. Dept.-Blue Ribbon Panel on Cath. Schs., 1992-93; 1st woman grand marshal St. Patrick's Day Parade, Glen Cove, 1992. Recipient Disting. Leadership award L.I. Bus. News, 1988, plaque of recognition L.I. Women's Coun. for Equal Edn. Tng. and Employment, 1989, Pathfinder award Town of Hempstead, 1990, Disting. Long Islander in Edn. award Epilepsy Found. L.I., 1991, Educator of Yr. award Assn. Tchrs. N.Y., 1980, Spl. award for arts in edn. L.I. Arts Coun., 1994; honored by L.I. Cath. League for Religious and Civil Rights, 1989; named L.I.'s 100 Influentials, L.I. Bus. News, 1992, 93, 94, 95, 96. Mem. Soc. Cath. Social Scis. (bd. advisors). Office: Molloy College PO Box 5002 Rockville Centre NY 11571-5002 Office Phone: 516-678-5000 6362. Business E-Mail: jfitzgerald@molloy.edu.

FITZGERALD, JOAN V., artist; b. Batavia, NY, Jan. 24, 1930; d. Russell Edward Voyer and Marian Ruth Voyer Montague; children: Remy C. Orffeo, Jerome P. Orffeo, Andres Orffeo. BS in Art Edn., Buffalo State Coll., 1963, MS in Art Edn., 1968. Tchr. art Hamburg Ctrl. Schs., NY, 1964—85; asst. prof. Erie C.C., Buffalo, 1985—92, acting asst. acad. dean, 1989—90, instr. fine arts, 1992—98. Author: The Magic Lunch Box, 2003, Not Another Christmas!, 2004, The Iris House, 2006, numerous poems; Exhibited in group shows at Period Gallery, 2000—05 (Spl. Recognition award), exhibitions include Broome St. Gallery, NYC, Somarts Gallery, San Francisco, Indigo Gallery, Norfolk, Va., Gallery 219, Decatur, Ill., Afif Gallery, Phila., Main St. Gallery, Groton, NY, Viridian Gallery, NYC, Schoharie Nat. Small Works, Cobleskill, NY, 2004 (Dirs. Choice award), Boise State Women's Ctr., NJ Ctr. for the Visual Arts, First Frontier Collage Soc., Austin, The Stage Gallery, Merrick, NY, Art West Gallery, Jackson, Wyo., Brand Exhbn. Ctr., Glendale, Calif., Nat. Collage Soc., Hudson, Ohio, Cork Gallery, Lincoln Ctr. for Performing Arts, NY Cuyahoga Art Ctr., Cuyahoga Falls, Ohio, Butler Inst. Am. Art, Salem, Ohio, Nat. Arts Club, NYC, Meml. Art Gallery, Rochester, NY, Ceres Gallery, NY, New Century Gallery, NYC, North East Collage and Assemblage Soc., Burlington, Vt., Springfield Mus. Art, Chautauqua Inst. Art, NY, Cooperstown Nat. Exhbn., DelMar Nat. Drawings and Sculpture Exhibit, Corpus Christi, Tex., Spar Nat., Shreveport, La., Assn. for Cult. Alternatives, NYC, Wind River Nat., Utah, Boise Art Ctr., Las Vegas Mus. Art, Impact Gallery Nat., Buffalo, Carnegie Art Ctr., North Tonawanda, NY. Co-chair Environ. Conservation Commn., Hamburg, 1990—92; mem. People for Parks, 2001—05. Recipient Dir.'s Choice award, Main St. Gallery Small Works Exhbn., Eight Spl. Recognition awards, Period Gallery Internat. Internet Exhbns., award, Buffalo Soc. Artists, Pres.'s award, Erie C.C., Buffalo, others. Mem.: Nat. Collage Soc., Western NY Artists Group (bd. dirs. 2000—06, chmn. 2002), Buffalo Soc. Artists (pres. 1980).

FITZGERALD, JUDITH KLASWICK, federal judge; b. Spangler, Pa., May 10, 1948; d. Julius Francis and Regina Marie (Pregno) Klaswick; m. June 5, 1971 (div. Dec. 1982); 1 child; m. Barry Robert Fitzgerald, Sept. 20, 1986; 1 child. BSBA, U. Pitts., 1970, JD, 1973. Legal rschr. Assocs. Fin., Pitts., 1972-73; law clk. to pres. judge Beaver County (Pa.) Ct. Common Pleas, 1973-74; law clk. to judge Pa. Superior Ct., Pitts., 1974-75; asst. U.S. atty. U.S. Dist. Ct. (we. dist.) Pa., Pitts. and Erie, 1976-87, U.S. bankruptcy judge Pitts., Erie and Johnstown, 1987—, U.S. Dist. Ct. (ea. dist.) Pa., U.S. Dist. Ct. U.S. V.I., U.S. Dist. Ct. Del. Adj. prof. law U. Pitts., 2003-2004, 2005-2006. Co-author: Bankruptcy and Divorce, Support and Property Division, 1991; editor: Pennsylvania Law of Juvenile Delinquency and Deprivation, 1976; contbr. articles to profl. jours. Mem. Pitts. Camerata, 1978-80, Allegheny County Polit.-Legal Edn. Project, 1980, Mendelssohn Choir Pitts., 1982—; mem. coun. Program to Aid Citizen Enterprise, 1985-87. Recipient Spl. Achievement awards Dept. Justice, Spl. Recognition award Pittsburgh mag., Operation Exodus Outstanding Performance award Dept. Commerce, 1986. Mem. Internat. Women's Insolvency and Restructuring Conf., Allegheny County Bar Assn., Women's Bar Assn. of Western Pa., Nat. Conf. Bankruptcy Judges, Am. Bankruptcy Inst., Nat. Conf. Bankruptcy Clks., Comml. Law League of Am., Fed. Criminal Investigators Assn. (Spl. Svc. award 1988), Zonta. Republican. Lutheran. Avocations: singing, reading, travel. Office: US Bankruptcy Ct 600 Grant St Ste 5490 Pittsburgh PA 15219-2805

FITZGERALD, KATHY, health and physical education educator; d. Thomas Joseph Fitzgerald and Dolores Regina Cain; life ptnr. Lisa A. Gourley. AS in Edn., Cmty. Coll. of Beaver County, Monaca, Pa., 1981; BS in Edn., Indiana U. Pa., 1983; postgrad., Duquesne U., Pitts., 1997. Cert. tchr. K-12 health and phys. edn. Tchr. St. James Cath. Sch., Pitts., 1983—86, Savannah/Chatham County Schs., Savannah, Ga., 1986—91, Laural Sch. Dist., New Castle, Pa., 1994—95, Hopewell Sch. Dist., Aliquippa, Pa., 1995—96, Pitts. Pub. Schs., 1996—. Avocations: boating, gardening, skiing.

FITZGERALD, MARILYN HICKS, health science association administrator; b. Danville, Ill., Nov. 4, 1946; d. Sheldon and Chrystine Belle (Brown) Hicks; m. Michael P. Fitzgerald; 1 child, Dennis McSorley. BA, Randolph Macon Woman's Coll., 1968. Admissions recruiter Randolph-Macon Woman's Coll., Lynchburg, Va., 1968—69; accreditation dir. Am. Assn. Mus., DC, 1969—75; realtor Jackson Properties, McLean, Va., 1975—77; sr. v.p. Am. Acad. Physician Assts., Alexandria, 1977—. Author: (book) Museum Accreditation: A Report to the Profession, 1970. Vol. Arlington Food Assistance Ctr., Va., 1994—; bd. mem. Women's Home Arlington, 1996—; mem. McLean Planning Com., McLean, 1999—2002. Mem.: Woman's Nat. Democratic Club. Democrat. Protestant. Avocations: photography, interior design, Feng Shui. Home: 1526 Poplar Pl Mc Lean VA 22101 Office: Am Acad Physician Assts 950 N Washington St Alexandria VA 22314 Office Phone: 703-836-2272. Business E-Mail: marilyn@aapa.org.

FITZGERALD, MARY IRENE, retired school psychologist; b. Hartford, Conn., Dec. 11, 1929; d. Daniel Thomas and Margaret (Queenin) Fitzgerald. AA, U. Hartford, 1949; AB in English Lit., Smith Coll., Northampton, Mass., 1951; MA in Guidance, U. Conn., 1960, cert. in advanced grad. study, 1962. Permanent cert. tchr. K-8 Conn., secondary cert. English Conn., cert. guidance counselor Conn., sch. psychologist Conn. Tchr. Conn. Pub. Schs., East Hartford, 1952—61; guidance counselor Old Saybrook (Conn.) Jr.-Sr. HS, 1961—62, Staples HS, Westport, Conn., 1962—64; sch. psychologist Windham Pub. Schs., Willimantic, Conn., 1964—90; ret., 1990. Vol. counselor Police Athletic League, Manchester, Conn., 1994—98; trustee Lutz Children's Mus., Manchester, 2003—05; mem. Manchester Land Conservation, 1970—, Dem. Aux. Town Com., Manchester, 1953—55. Mem.: NOW, Conn. Assn. Sch. Psychologists, Am. Contract Bridge League, Alumnae Assn. Smith Coll., Mensa, Hartford Smith Coll. Club, Manchester Country Club (sec., bd. govs. 1986—), Delta Kappa Gamma. Roman Catholic. Avocations: golf, bridge. Home: 12 Garth Rd Manchester CT 06040

FITZGERALD-HUBER, LOUISA G., education educator, researcher; b. Balt., July 17, 1940; d. Charles Galt and Ida (Noon) Fitzgerald; m Horst Wolfram Huber, July 11, 1969. BA, Goucher Coll., 1962; MA, Harvard U., 1965, PhD, 1974. Asst. prof. Harvard U., Cambridge, Mass., 1975-80; lectr. Harvard U. Ext., Cambridge, Mass., 1987-91; assoc. rschr. Fairbank Ctr. Harvard U., Cambridge, Mass., 1984—; lectr. Wellesley (Mass.) Coll., 1995—. Vis. prof. U. Heidelberg, Germany, 1981-82, 87. Contbr. articles to profl. jours. Woodrow Wilson fellow, 1962-63. Mem. Phi Beta Kappa. Avocations: swimming, figure skating. Home: 20 Prescott St Cambridge MA 02138-3935 Office: Fairbank Ctr Harvard Univ CG15 South S138 1730 Cambridge St Cambridge MA 02138

FITZGERALD-VERBONITZ, DIANNE ELIZABETH, not-for-profit developer; b. Tampa, Fla., July 11, 1943; d. James Gerald and Bernice Elizabeth (Creel) F.; children: Deborah Elizabeth Guilbault Starr, Fred Anthony Guilbault Jr. AA, Montgomery Coll., 1979; BS in Health Svcs. summa cum laude, No. Ariz. U., 1985, MEd, 1987. Nurse in Washington Internship, Advanced Internship. Pvt. practice counselor, Phoenix; mem. faculty C.V. Mosby Co., St. Louis; nurse clinician in orthopedics; mgr. orthopedic program Kimberly Quality Care; adminstr. Staff Builders Health Svcs., Phoenix, Cypress Health Care Svcs.; now exec. dir. Ariz. Psychol. Assn., Scottsdale. Bd. dirs. Valley of Sun Sch. and Rehab. Ctr., Arthritis Found.; mem. Am. Vol. Med. Team; med. vol. Habitat for Humanity. Named one of Top Ten Bus. Women in Managed Health Care, Today's Ariz. Woman, 1998. Mem.: State and Provincial Psychol. Assns., Am./Ariz. Soc. Assn. Execs. (bd. dirs.), Nat. Assn. Orthopedic Nurses (pres. 1989—90), Phi Kappa Phi (life).

FITZGIBBON, KATHERINE LENORE, conductor, music educator; b. Indpls., July 25, 1976; d. Joan Meltzer and Daniel Harvey FitzGibbon. BA in Music, Princeton U., 1998; MusM in Conducting, U. Mich., 2002. Dir. choirs Duxbury Schs., Mass., 2002—; chorusmaster Windsor Symphony Orch., Ont., Canada, 1999—2002; choral condr. U. Mich., Ann Arbor, 1999—2002; dir. vocal music Noble and Greenough Sch., Dedham, Mass., 1998—99; voice and conducting faculty Berkshire Choral Festival, Sheffield, Mass., 2001—, head faculty, 2003—; soprano, asst. condr. Boston Secession, 2002—; dir. choral activities Clark U., Worcester, Mass., 2003—; asst. condr. Radcliffe Choral Soc., Harvard U., 2003—04; choral dir. Boston U., 2005; condr. Cornell U. Chorale, 2006—07; asst. dir. choirs Cornell U., 2006—. Conducting fellowship, U. of Mich., 1999—2001. Mem.: Nat. Collegiate Choral Orgn., Boston Singers Resource, Coll. Music Soc., Am. Choral Dirs. Assn., Phi Beta Kappa. Home: 27 Bradbury St Allston MA 02134-1404

FITZNER, KATHRYN ETHRIDGE, psychotherapist; b. Winder, Ga., June 20, 1953; d. L. Clifford and M. Jeanne (Sexton) E.; m. John A. Fitzner Jr., Aug. 21, 1971 (div. 1979); 1 child, John A. Fitzner III. BS cum laude, Ga. So. U., 1975; MSW, U. Ga., 1984. Caseworker, prin. Dept. Family & Children Svcs., Augusta, Ga., 1980-84; social worker Northside Hosp., Atlanta, 1984-85, Scottish Rite Children's Hosp., Atlanta, 1985-87; psychotherapist Rapha, Inc., Atlanta, 1987-92; ret., 1992. Cons. Northside Hosp. Aux., Atlanta, 1985, Outward Bound students Paine Coll., Augusta, 1984. Initiator Community Task Force Child Sexual Abuse, Augusta, 1984; advisor, tchr. Mt. Paran Ch. of God, Atlanta, 1985-86. Mem. Acad. Cert. Social Workers (lic. clin. social worker), Nat. Assn. Social Workers, Ga. Soc. for Hosp. Social Workers (treas. 1986-87), Nat. Assn. Clin. Social Workers, Delta Zeta (scholar 1970-71, chmn.). Republican. Avocation: poetry. Home: 2202 Country Park Dr Smyrna GA 30080-8270

FITZPATRICK, JANE, entrepreneur; b. Cuttingsville, Vt., Nov. 18, 1923; m. John H. Fitzpatrick, Sept. 7, 1944; children: Nancy Jane, JoAnn Fitzpatrick Brown. HHD (hon.), N. Adams State Coll., Mass., 1978; LHD (hon.), U. Mass., 1987, Am. Internat. Coll., Springfield, Mass., 1994. Co-founder, chmn. bd. Country Curtains, Stockbridge, Mass., 1956—. Life trustee Boston Symphony Orch., trustee, 1982—96; trustee emerita The Norman Rockwell Mus., Stockbridge, Mass. Chmn. Berkshire Theatre Festival, Stockbridge, Mass, (bd. pres. 1977-98). Office: PO Box 954 Stockbridge MA 01262-0955

FITZPATRICK, KATRINA S., band director; b. Peoria, Ill., Sept. 18, 1979; d. Thomas P. and Elizabeth Marie Shipley; m. Craig Andrew Fitzpatrick, June 22, 2002. B in Music Edn., Bradley U., 2001; MA in Music Edn., Ill. State U., 2003—. Band dir. Morton Unit Sch. Dist., Ill., 2002—. Mem.: Fed. Musicians Union, Music Educator Assn., Nat. Bandmaster Assn., Sigma Alpha Iota (v.p. 1998—2001).

FITZPATRICK, LOIS ANN, library administrator; b. Yonkers, NY, Mar. 27, 1952; d. Thomas Joseph and Dorothy Ann (Nealy) Sullivan; m. William George Fitzpatrick, Jr., Dec. 1, 1973; children: Jennifer Ann, Amy Ann. BS in Sociology, Mercy Coll., 1974; MLS, Pratt Inst., 1975. Clk. Yonkers Pub. Libr., 1970-73, libr. trainee, 1973-75, libr. I, 1975-76; reference libr. Carroll Coll. Libr., Helena, Mont., 1976-79, acting dir., 1979, dir., 1980—; asst. prof. Carroll Coll., Helena, 1979-89, assoc. prof., 1989-99, prof., 2000—. Bd. dirs. Mont. Shares 2000-; chmn. arrangements Mont. Gov.'s Pre White House Conf. on Libraries, Helena, 1977-78; mem. steering com. Reference Point coop. program for librs., 1991; mem. adv. com. Helena Coll. of Tech. Libr., 1994—; adv. coun. Mont. Libr. Svcs., 1996-2000; mem. Networking Task Force, 1998-2003, Laws Revision Task Force, 1998-2001, Not Ready for Prime Time Freedom Fighters, 2004-; pres. elect Helena Area Health Sci. Libraries Cons., 1979-84, pres., 1984-88; bd. dirs. Mont. FAXNET; mem. cancer comprehensive cancer plan State Mont., 2004—. Co-chmn. interst group OCLC; chmn. local arrangements Mont. Gov.'s Pre White House Conf.; mem. Mont. Race for the Cure, 1998-2004; bd. dirs. ACLU-MT, 2000—, pres., 2005-2007; mem. adv. com. Am. Cancer Soc. Lewis and Clark County. Mem. Mont. Libr. Assn. (task force for White House conf. 1991, chair govt. affairs com. 1997-2003, 2005-, EdLINK-MT 1997-99, 2000-01), Soroptimist Internat. of Helena (2d v.p. 1984-85, pres. 1986-87), Am. Cancer Soc. (mem. lapel program, 2005—, mem. Cancer Advocacy Network program, 2005—). Home: 1308 Shirley Rd Helena MT 59602-6635 Office: Carroll Coll Jack & Sallie Corette Libr 1601 N Benton Ave Helena MT 59625-0001 Office Phone: 406-447-4341. Business E-Mail: lfitzpat@carroll.edu.

FITZPATRICK, NANCY HECHT, editor; b. Dec. 29, 1942; d. Ira Youngwood and Bettie Jane (Van Cleave) Hecht; m. Alan Rush Fitzpatrick, Dec. 15, 1973 (dec.); m. Thomas H. Gervais, May 17, 2003. Student, Upsala Coll., 1960-62, New Sch. Social Rsch., 1962-64, Johns Hopkins U., summer 1987, Bennington Coll., summer 1988; MFA in writing, Union Inst., 2005. Asst. copy editor Am. Home mag., N.Y.C., 1964-68; v.p. Creative Comms. Assocs., Newark, 1968-70; sr. editor Family Circle mag., N.Y.C., 1970-77; corp. sec., v.p. mktg. Alternative Telecom. Corp., N.Y.C., 1977-92; exec. editor Meeting News mag., N.Y.C., 1993-95; assoc. news editor, book and art reviewer The Vineyard Gazette, 1997—2001; archivist and publs. editor Wampanoag Tribe of Gay Head/Aquinnah, 2002—04; editor Spice Arts and Entertainment Guide, 2005—. Editor various publs. Mem.: LWV, NOW, Lower Adirondack Regional Arts Coun. (adv. bd.), Eastern Bedford Environ. Assn. (treas.), Empire women in Telecom. (pres.), N.Y. Women in Comms.

FITZROY, NANCY DELOYE, engineering executive, mechanical engineer; b. Pittsfield, Mass., Oct. 5, 1927; d. Jules Emile and Mabel Winifred (Burr) deLoye; m. Roland Victor Fitzroy, Jr., Mar. 24, 1951. BChemE, Rensselaer Poly. Inst., Troy, 1949; DEng (hon.), Rensselaer Poly. Inst., 1990; DSc (hon.), N.J. Inst. Tech., 1987. Registered profl. engr., N.Y. Heat transfer engr. corp. R & D GE, Schenectady, NY, 1950-71, mgr. heat transfer consulting, 1971-74, strategy planner, 1974-76, mgr. program devel. gas turbine divsn., 1976-82, mgr. energy and environ. program, 1982-87. Dir. West Hill Devel. Corp., Rotterdam, NY, 1955—65; mem. adv. com. rsch. NSF, Washington, 1972—75; mem. transp. rsch. bd. coordinating com. rsch. and tech. NRC, 1996—99; cons. in field; bd. dirs. ASME Found., 1989—95, 1997—, trustee, 1998—. Author, editor: book Heat Transfer and Fluid Flow, Data Books, 1955—75. Charter mem. Rensselaer Poly. Inst. Coun., 1972—. Named to Rensselaer Poly. Inst. Hall of Fame, 1999; recipient Demers medal, Rensselaer Poly. Inst., 1975, Achievement award, Fedn. Profl. Women, 1984, Disting. Alumna medal, Rensselaer Poly. Inst., 1996. Fellow: ASME (1st woman nat. pres. 1986—87, trustee Gear Rsch. Inst. 1987—89), Soc. Women Engrs. (Outstanding Achievement award 1972), Instn. Mech. Engrs. London (hon.); mem.: Assn. Engrngs. Socs. (gov. 1987—89), Nat. Acad. Engrng., Coral Ridge Yacht Club (Ft. Lauderdale, Fla.), Mohawk Golf Club, Whirly-Girls Club, Ninety-Nines Club. Republican. Episcopalian. Achievements include patents in field.

FITZSIMMONS, BECKY BARLOW, lawyer; b. Princeton, NJ, Apr. 2, 1968; BA, Western Md. Coll., 1990; JD, U. Md. at Baltimore, 2000. Bar: Ohio 2000. Assoc. Dinsmore & Shohl LLP, Cin. Named one of Ohio's Rising Stars, Super Lawyers, 2006. Mem.: Ohio State Bar Assn., Cin. Bar Assn., ABA. Office: Dinsmore & Shohl LLP 255 E Fifth St Ste1900 Cincinnati OH 45202-4700 Office Phone: 513-977-8200. Office Fax: 513-977-8141.*

FITZSIMONDS, CAROL STRAUSE, artist, art gallery director; b. Richmond, Va., Mar. 13, 1951; d. Bernard Halle Strause and Elizabeth Curry; m. James Russell Fitzsimonds, June 8, 1974; 1 child, Christopher Lee. BFA, Hollins Coll., 1973. Ptnr. Torpedo Factory Printmakers Inc., Alexandria, Va., 1986—88, 1993—2001; instr. printmaking and bookbinding Newport (RI)

Art Mus. Sch., 2002; instr. printmaking Providence Art Club, Providence, 2002—; instr. bookbinding Providence Handicraft Club, Providence, 2003; dir. Green River Gallery, Bristol, RI, 2005—. Address: 251 Water St Portsmouth RI 02871-4139 Personal E-mail: fitsimjc@cox.net.

FITZSIMONS, MARJORIE KITCHEN, art consultant; b. Cin., Apr. 8, 1946; d. John Milton and Jane Rauch Kitchen; m. Michael John FitzSimons, Aug. 8, 1970; children: Kelly, Colin, Ellie, Libby. BA, Wellesley Coll., 1967; MAT, Harvard U., 1970. Cert. women bus. owner Majority Bus. Initiative. Rschr. Frick Art Reference Libr., N.Y.C., 1968-69; tchr. Univ. Liggett Sch., Grosse Pointe, Mich., 1980-85; corp. cons. Joy Emery Gallery, Grosse Pointe, 1988-90; art cons., owner Art Cons. Svcs., Grosse Pointe, 1991—. Vol. Detroit Artists Market, 1980-99; mem. Altar Guild, Christ Ch., Grosse Pointe, 1985—; bd. dirs. Garden Club Mich., Grosse Pointe, 1989—, Friends Modern Art, Detroit Inst. Arts, 1997—. Mem. Women's Dist. Golf Assn., Women's Econ. Club. Episcopalian. Avocations: golf, sailing. Home and Office: 2727 N Ocean Blvd #6 Gulf Stream FL 33483-7357

FITZSIMONS, MAUREEN See O'HARA, MAUREEN

FITZSIMONS, NANCY MARIE, social work educator; b. St. Paul, Mar. 29, 1963; d. Robert Thomas and Norma Theresa Fitzsimons. BS in Social Work, Mankato (Minn.) State U., 1985; MSW, U. Ill., Chgo., 1991, PhD, 1997. Cmty. worker Ada S. McKinley, Chgo., 1986—88; program coord. Little City Found., Palatine, Ill., 1988—90; family therapist Krejci Acad., Naperville, Ill., 1991—93; sr. rsch. specialist U. Ill., Chgo., 1995—99, rsch. asst. prof., 1999—2001; asst. prof. Minn. State U., Mankato, 2001—06, assoc. prof., 2006—. Author: (online curriculum and workbook) Shadow Victims: Crimes Against People with Disabilities, (tng. curriculum) Disability Awareness for Law Enforcement, Taking Charge: Responding to Abuse, Neglect and Financial Exploitation, Abuse, Neglect & Exploitation: Recognition, Reporting & Prevention for Direct Support Persons, Abuse, Neglect & Exploitation: Recognition, Reporting and Prevention for QMRPs, Abuse, Neglect & Exploitation: Recognition, Reporting & Prevention for Administrative Personnel. Mem. steering com. Mankato Area Healthy Youth, 2004—. Named Outstanding Advisor, Coll. Social and Behavioral Scis., Minn. State U. Mankato, 2006, Disting. Tchr., 2004, Social Work Alumna of Yr. dept. social work, Mankato State U., 1997; grantee, Office of Violence Against Women, US Dept. Justice, 2003—05, Adminstrn. of Devel. Disabilities, HHS, 1998—2001, Nat. Inst. on Disability and Rehab. Rsch., US Dept. Edn., 1999—2000, Office of Devel. Disabilities, Ill. Dept. Human Svcs., 1999—2000, Insp. Gen. of Ill. Dept. Children and Family Svcs., 2000—01; scholar, Minn. State U. Mankato, 2006. Mem.: NASW, Minn. Social Svcs. Assn., Am. Assn. Mental Retardation, Assn. Baccalaureate Social Work Program Dirs., Coun. on Social Work Edn. Office: Minn State U Mankato 358 Trafton Sci Ctr N Mankato MN 56001 Office Phone: 507-389-1287. E-mail: nancy.fitzsimons@mnsu.edu.

FITZSIMONS, SHARON RUSSELL, international consumer goods, financial and treasury executive; b. Toronto, Ont., Can., June 25, 1945; d. Leslie and Winifred; m. John Henry Fitzsimons, Jan. 4, 1969; children: Luke, Michael. BA, U. So. Calif., 1968; MA, Calif. State U., 1971; MS in Bus. Adminstrn., U. Calif., Irvine, 1978; grad. internat. bus. ISMP program, Harvard Bus. Sch., 1990. Mgr. rsch. William Pereira Assocs., Newport Beach, Calif., 1970-71; asst. mgr. interior design Concept Environment Inc. subs. Ford Motor Co., Orange County, Calif., 1971-72; v.p. Urban Interface Group, Orange County, 1972-74; cons. in field, 1975-76; mgr. strategic planning Mission Viejo Co., Orange County, 1976-80; mgr. fin. Philip Morris Internat., N.Y.C., 1980-82, asst. treas., 1983-84, ops., strategic mktg. and logistics exec. PM Australia Ltd., Melbourne, 1984-86, dir. U.S. export logistics and customer svc., N.Y.C., 1987-90, internat. fin. dir. treas., N.Y.C., 1990—; chmn., CEO, Internat. Intrigues, 1997—, pres., CEO, co-trustee Pamco Historic Property Mgmt. Co., Phoenix, Ariz. CEO trustee Mem. Harvard Women's Alumnae Network Assn. (bd. dirs.), Women in Mgmt., Harvard Club Greater N.Y., The Internat. Alliance.

FIX, IRENE M., music educator; b. Phila., Mar. 26, 1935; d. Werner Frederick Mueller and Marie Anna Westermann; m. David W. Fix (div.); children: Paul David, Sybil. Studied with Jose Echaniz; MusB cum laude, U. Rochester, NY, 1956. Performers cert. Eastman Sch. Music, U. Rochester, 1956. Mem. staff piano dept. Eastman Sch. Music Prep. Sch., Rochester, 1956—57; piano instr. St. Anne's Sch., Charlottesville, Va., 1958—60, Neighborhood Music Sch., New Haven, 1960—62, Music Arts Sch., Highland Park, Ill., 1962—68, Collegium Musicale, Montepulciano, Italy, 1974—79, Nazareth Schs., Rochester, 1991—2003; pvt. piano instr. Chgo., 1968—71, Rochester, 1980—90, Westchester, Pa., 2004—. Pianist, collaborator Accedemia Chigiana, Siena, Italy, 1976—80. Musician: Reading Symphony Orch., Eastman-Rochester Symphony, (solo recitals) Nat. Gallery, U. Va., others. Avocations: cooking, gardening, tennis, cats. Home: 671 Fairview Rd PO Box 224 Glenmoore PA 19343

FJELSTED, MAE FRANCIS, retired psychologist; b. Unionville, Mich., Mar. 7, 1939; d. Cyril Howard MacKenzie and Elizibeth Theresa Koepf; m. Lyle Gradon Fjelsted, Sept. 6, 1958; 1 child, Mark Thomas. AA in Art, San Antonio Coll., 1975; BA in Psychology, U. Tex., San Antonio, 1977; MEd in Sch. Psychology with honors, S.W. Tex. State U., San Marcos, 1988. Lic. nat. cert. sch. psychologist, psychol. assoc., specialist in sch. psychology Tex. Activity technician Villa Rosa Psychiat. Hosp., San Antonio, 1982—85; case mgr. Bexar County Mental Health Mental Retardation, San Antonio, 1985—86; learning disabilities specialist St. Phillips Coll., San Antonio, 1988—91, St. Mary's U., San Antonio, 1991; ednl. diagnostician Pearsall (Tex.) Ind. Sch. Dist., 1992—93; assoc. sch. psychologist Uvalde (Tex.) Consol. Sch. Dist., 1993—95; lic. specialist in sch. pay San Antonio Ind. Sch. Dist., 1995—2005; ret. Edn. cons., mem. adv. bd. Tex. Interparter Fellowship, San Antonio, 1995—2005. Den mother Cub Scouts Am., N.Y.C., 1971—73; coord., welcome chair USAF Family Svcs., Andrews AFB, 1966—70; com. mem. Interagy. Child Abuse Network, San Antonio, 1987—94. With USAF, 1958—60. Named Airman of Month, 544th Reconizon Squadron, 1989. Mem.: Tex. Irlen Assn. (edn. chair), Tex. Assn. Sch. Psychologists (area V rep, membership chair, awards and honors chair, Outstanding Sch. Psychologist award 1995, Lifetime Achievement award 2005), Nat. Assn. Sch. Psychologists, Psi Chi. Avocations: painting, reading, sewing. Home: 1148 Blackberry Cir Baker FL 32531

FLACK, DORA DUTSON, writer, performing artist, lecturer; b. Kimberly, Idaho, July 9, 1919; d. Alonzo Edmund and Iona (James) Dutson; m. A. LeGrand Flack, Jan. 7, 1946; children: Marc Douglas, Lane LeGrand, Kent Dutson, Marlane, Karen, Marie. Exec. sec. Utah State Nat. Bank, Salt Lake City, 1938-46. Mem. lit. panel Utah Arts Council, 1979-81; mem. faculty Brigham Young U. Edn. Week, 1976-83; mem. faculty World Conf. on Records, Salt Lake City, 1980. Author: (with Vernice G. Rosenvall and Mabel H. Miller) Wheat for Man.Why and How, 1952; England's First Mormon Convert, 1957; (with Louise Nielson) Dutson Family History, 1957, 2d rev. edit., 1998; What About Christmas?, 1971; Fun with Fruit Preservation, 1972; (with others) The Joy of Being a Woman, 1972; (with Lula P. Betenson) Butch Cassidy, My Brother, 1975; Dry and Save, 1976 (U.S. Info. Service selection for Internat. Book Fair, Cairo, 1978); (with Janice T. Dixon) Preserving Your Past, 1977; Christmas Magic, 1977; Testimony in Bronze, 1980; (with Karla C. Erickson) Gifts Only You Can Give, 1984; Bread Baking Made Easy, 1984; (with others) Flood Fighters, 1984, (with others) Celebration of Christmas, 1988, Christmas Magic All Year Long, 1991, Bountiful Centennial Cemetery Historical Walking Tour, 1992, Centennial Contest Collection, 1992, Dwellings--90 Homes in Bountiful Built Before 1900, 1992; History of Bountiful Centennial, 1995; History of League of Utah Writers, 1996, (with others) The Gifts of Christmas, 1999; contbr. numerous articles, stories to hist., religious and homemaking mags.; performing artist western U.S.; TV and radio appearances. Mem. Utah Gov.'s Com. on Employment Handicapped, 1975-81. Recipient numerous state and nat. writing awards, including Utah Arts Coun., 1969, 73-75, 77, 80, 84, Bountiful Total Citizen award Utah C. of C., 1993; named Bountiful's Citizen of Yr. BPOE Elks Lodge 2442, 1998. Mem. League Utah Writers (Writer of Yr. award 1982), Nat. League Am. Pen Women, Daus. Utah Pioneers. Republican. Mem. Lds Ch. Home and Office: 448 E 775 N Bountiful UT 84010-3538

FLACK, ROBERTA, singer; b. Black Mountain, N.C., Feb. 10, 1939; d. Laron and Irene F.; m. Stephen Novosel, 1966 (div. 1972). BA in Music Edn., Howard U., 1958. Tchr. music and English lit. pub. schs., Farmville, N.C., Washington, 1959-67; rec. artist Atlantic Records, 1968—. Star ABC TV spl. The First Time Ever, 1973; composer: (with Jesse Jackson and Joel Dorn) Go Up, Moses; albums include: First Take, 1969, Chapter Two, 1970, Quiet Fire, 1971, Killing Me Softly, 1973, Feel Like Makin' Love, 1975, Blue Lights In The Basement, 1977, Roberta Flack, 1978, The Best of Roberta Flack, 1981, I'm The One, 1982, Born To Love, 1983, Hits and History, 1984, Roberta Flack, 1985, Oasis, 1989, Set the Night to Music, 1991, Roberta, 1994; writer TV theme song Valerie. Recipient Gold Record for The First Time Ever I Saw Your Face, 1972; Grammy awards for best record, best song (The First Time Ever I Saw Your Face), 1972, best record, best female vocalist (Killing Me Softly With His Song), 1973, best pop vocal duo (Where Is The Love), 1972, Star on the Hollywood Walk of Fame, 2000; winner Downbeat's reader poll as best female vocalist, 1971-73; City of Washington celebrated Roberta Flack Human Kindness Day, 1972. Mem. Sigma Delta Chi. Office: care Atlantic Records 75 Rockefeller Plz New York NY 10019-6908

FLACKE, JOAN WAREHAM, physician, anesthesiologist, educator; b. Evanston, Ill., Dec. 16, 1931; d. Loyal Delbert and Alice (Cummings) Wareham; m. Werner E. Flacke, Aug. 7, 1957; children: Christopher, Gary, Timothy. BA, Scripps Coll., 1953; MD, Harvard U., 1959. Rsch. fellow Med. Sch., Harvard U., Boston, 1964-67, rsch. assoc., 1967-69, instr., 1969-70; asst. prof. med. sci. U. Ark., 1972-75, assoc. prof. med. sci., 1975-76; adj. assoc. prof. UCLA, 1977-82, adj. prof., 1982-89, prof.-in-residence, 1989-95, prof. emeritus, 1995—. Cons. to FDA, 1989-93; assoc. examiner Am. Bd. Anesthesiology, L.A., 1974-76; program chmn. Anesthesia Ednl. Found., La.A., 1986-91; dir. cardiovascular anesthesiology UCLA Hosp., 1990-91. Contbr. numerous articles to profl. jours. Mem. Am. Soc. Anesthesiologists, Assn. Univ. Anesthesiologists, Internat. Anesthesia Rsch. Soc., Soc. Cardiovascular Anesthesiologists, Calif. Soc. Anesthesiologists, Mass. Med. Soc. Roman Catholic. Avocations: reading, skiing, needlecrafts, horseback riding. Home and Office: PO Box 308 Wolcott CO 81655-0308 E-mail: flacke@colorado.net.

FLADELAND, BETTY, historian, educator; b. Grygla, Minn., Jan. 18, 1919; d. Arne O. and Bertha (Nygaard) F. BS, Duluth State Coll., 1940; MA, U. Minn., 1944; PhD (Rackham fellow), U. Mich., 1952. Mem. faculty Wells Coll., Aurora, N.Y., 1952-55, Central Mich. U., 1956-59, Central Mo. State Coll., 1959-62; mem. faculty So. Ill. U., Carbondale, 1962—, prof. history, 1968—, disting. prof., 1985, disting. prof. emerita, 1986—. Vis. prof. U. Ill., summer 1966 Author: James Gillespie Birney: Slaveholder to Abolitionist, 1955, Men and Brothers: Anglo-American Antislavery Cooperation, 1972, Abolitionists and Working Class Problems in the Age of Industrialization, 1984, also articles. Recipient Anisfield-Wolf award in race relations, 1972, Queen award, 1984; grantee Am. Philos. Soc., 1963, 75, Lilly Found., 1962; NEH teaching grantee, 1984 Mem. Am. Hist. Assn., So. Hist. Assn. (exec. council), Orgn. Am. Historians (exec. bd.), Assn. Study Afro-Am. Life and History, Norwegian-Am. Hist. Soc., Soc. Historians Early Am. Republic (adv. bd., bd. editors, pres.), ACLU, NAACP, Phi Beta Kappa, Phi Kappa Phi. Home: Liberty Village 2950 West Ridge Pl #230 Carbondale IL 62901-7135 Office: So Ill Univ Dept Of History Carbondale IL 62901

FLAGG, MARY KAY, mathematics educator; d. Fred and Rita Kramer; m. James N. Flagg, Jr., June 22, 1985; children: Joshua, David. BS, Rice U., Houston, 1984; MS, Calif. Inst. Tech., Pasadena, 1986, U. Houston, 2003, PhD, 2006. Tutor Alvin Elem. Sch., Alvin, Tex., 2004; grad. tchg. fellow U. Houston, 2004—06, lectr., 2006—. Chmn. children's edn. com. First United Meth. Ch. of Alvin, Tex., 2005—06; dir. edn. Lake Houston United Meth. Ch., Huffman, Tex., 1999—2003. Recipient Magna Cum Laude, Rice U., 1984; Nat. Merit scholar, 1980—84, Brown Engring. scholar, Brown Found., 1980—84, Grad. Student fellow, NSF, 1984—86. Mem.: Math. Assn. of Am., Americal Math. Soc., Phi Beta Kappa, Phi Bata Delta, Sigma Xi (assoc.). Methodist. Avocations: English handbells, decorative painting, math tutoring, clarinet. Office: U Houston 609 Philip G Hoffman Hall Houston TX 77204-3008 Business E-Mail: mflagg@math.uh.edu.

FLAHERTY, CYNTHIA MEAD, music educator; b. Silver Creek, NY, Jan. 29, 1957; d. Lewis Stephen and Carol D. Mead; children: Travis Martin, Meghan Grace. MusB magna cum laude, SUNY, Fredonia, 1979, MusM summa cum laude, 1982. Elem. music tchr. Dunkirk City Schs., NY, 1979—99, workshop leader BOCES, 1981—, mid. sch. music tchr., 1999—, creator music instrn. music program, writer, arranger; workshop leader SUNY (Fredonia Sch. Music), 1981—, music tchr., 1999—. Dir. Marauder Steel Drum Band, Dunkirk, 1999—, Dunkirk Mid. Sch. Musicals, 2001—. Composer: (songs) Escape, 2001. Vol. various local charities, Dunkirk, Fredonia, 1999—; vol. United Way, 2005—06, Humane Soc., 2004. Scholar, Fulbright Meml. Fund, Japan, 2001. Mem.: NY State Union Tchrs. and United U. Profs., Dunkirk Tchrs. Assn., Chautau County Music Tchrs. Assn., Am. Fedn. Tchrs. Avocations: kayaking, swimming, cross country skiing, canoeing, rollerblading. Office: Dunkirk Mid Sch 525 Eagle St Dunkirk NY 14048 Office Fax: 716-366-9357. Business E-Mail: cynthia.flaherty@fredonia.edu.

FLAHERTY, KATHLEEN RUTH, telecommunications industry executive; b. Boston, May 19, 1951; d. John P. and Annette (Baker) Flaherty; m. Kenneth D. Davis, Dec. 30, 1973. BA, Northwestern U., 1973, MS, 1975, PhD in Indsl. Engring., 1979. Policy analyst US Dept. Commerce, Gaithersburg, Md., 1976-79; sr. mgr. sales programs Gen. Electric Info. Services Co., Rockville, Md., 1979-80; sr. mgr. network planning MCI, Washington, 1981-82, dir. network engring., 1982-84, v.p. fin. ops., 1984-86; v.p. communications network services MCI N.E., Rye Brook, NY, 1986—90; v.p. product mktg. MCI, 1990, named sr. v.p., 1993; sr. v.p. worldwide sales & mktg. Concert Services (joint venture of MCI & Brit. Telecom), 1993—95; sr. v.p., marketing dir. nat. bus. communications Brit. Telecom, 1995—97; sr. v.p. global product architecture MCI, 1997—98; pres., COO WinStar Europe SA, 1998—99, WinStar Internat., 1999—2001; chief mktg. officer AT&T bus. services AT&T Corp., 2004—. Dir. CMS Energy Corp., 1995—2004; mem. Industry Adv. Coun. McCormick Sch. Engring., Northwestern U. Coordinator Cmty. Garden Program, Washington, 1983; treas. Woodbine Condominium Assn., Washington, 1979-81. Named one of Outstanding Young Women of Am., Jaycees, 1982; Walter P. Murphy Fellow, 1973. Mem. Sigma Xi. Avocations: reading, camping, gardening, swimming. Office: AT&T Bus Services One AT&T Way Bedminster NJ 07921

FLAHERTY, LOIS TALBOT, editor, psychiatrist, educator; b. Nashville, Apr. 28, 1942; BA, Wellesley Coll., 1963; MD, Duke U., 1968. Diplomate Nat. Bd. Med. Examiners. Intern D.C. Gen. Hosp., 1968-69; resident in psychiatry Georgetown U. Hosp., 1969-71; resident in child psychiatry Johns Hopkins Hosp., 1971-73; pvt. practice Cross Keys, Md., 1973-81; dir. tng. divsn. child and adolescent psychiatry U. Md., 1981-89, assoc. prof. med. sch. divsn. child and adolescent psychiatry, 1982-93, dir. divsn. child and adolescent psychiatry, 1984-92, adj. assoc. prof., 1994—; clin. assoc. prof. psychiatry U. Pa., 1997-2000; pvt. practice Blue Bell, Pa., 1994-99; editor Adolescent Psychiatry, 2000—. Instr. depts. psychiatry and pediatrics Johns Hopkins U. Sch. Medicine, 1973-92; attending staff psychiatrist family, child and adolescent divsn. Sinai Hosp. Balt., 1974-77; staff child psychiatrist Walter P. Carter Ctr., 1977-78, dir. child and adolescent svcs., 1978-92, acting dir. inpatient adolescent unit, 1979-80; clin. asst. prof. U. Md., 1977-81; lectr. psychiatry Harvard U., 2002—; cons. Northwest Drug Alert Sinai Hosp. Balt., 1971-72, St. Vincent's Child Care Ctr., 1973-78, Children's Guild, Inc., 1975-82, SSA, Balt., 1985, many others. Contbr. chpts. to books, articles and book revs. to profl. jours. NIMH grantee, 1983-86. Fellow: Am. Soc. for Adolescent Psychiatry, Am. Psychiat. Assn. (disting.); mem.: Group for Advancement of Psychiatry, Am. Coll. Psychiatrists, Am. Acad. Child Psychiatry. Office: 4 Charlesgate East #605 Boston MA 02215-2369 Personal E-mail: lflaher770@aol.com.

FLAHERTY, PAMELA POTTER, bank executive; b. Jefferson City, Mo., July 1, 1944; d. Reese H. and Mary Jane (Stagg) Potter; m. Peter A. Flaherty, Nov. 28, 1970; children: Jonathan Peter, David Alexander. BA, Smith Coll., 1966; MA in internat. rels., Johns Hopkins U., 1968. Various positions internat. banking Citicorp, N.Y.C., 1968-76, various position consumer banking, 1976-85, head of human resources, 1985-89, head of consumer banking in N.E., 1989—95, senior v.p., dir. community rels., 1995—98; senior v.p., global community rels. Citigroup Inc. (formerly Citicorp), N.Y.C., 1998—. Bd. dirs. Rockefeller Fin. Svcs., Inc., N.Y.C.; mem. adv. coun. Bass plc U.S., 1990—; bd. dirs., mem. exec. com. Am. Women's Econ. Devel. Corp., N.Y.C., 1987—. Bd. mem. Johns Hopkins Medicine, 2000—; trustee Johns Hopkins Univ., Colonial Williamsburg Found. Named one of Women Who Make a Difference by Smith Coll. Club of N.Y., 1991. Mem. Com. of 200. Office: Citigroup 399 Park Ave New York NY 10043*

FLAHERTY, SERGINA MARIA, ophthalmic medical technologist; b. Düsseldorf, Germany, Nov. 22, 1958; came to U.S., 1962; d. Austin W. and Evelyn (Kähl) F. Cert. ophthalmic med. technologist. Ophthalmic asst. U.S. Army, Ft. Rucker, Ala., 1978-82; ophthalmic technician Wiregrass Total Eye Care Clinic, Enterprise, Ala., 1983-86, Straub Hosp. and Clinic, Honolulu, 1986-90; ophthalmic technologist Eye Cons. of San Antonio, San Antonio, 1993-96, Stone Oak Ophthalmology, San Antonio, 1996—. Founder, owner, CEO Ophthalmic Seminars of San Antonio, 1996—. Mem. Assn. Tech. Pers. in Ophthalmology, Ophthalmic Photographer Soc., Hawaii Ophthalmic Assts. Soc. (founding mem., sec. 1987-89, pres. 1989-90), Ophthalmic Pers. Soc. San Antonio (program dir. 1994-95, 2001—, pres. 1996-2000). Avocation: shin shin toitsu aikido. Office: Stone Oak Ophthalmology Ste 100 325 Sonterra Blvd San Antonio TX 78258-3932 Office Phone: 210-490-6759. E-mail: ophthsem@gvtc.com.

FLAHERTY, TINA SANTI, corporate communications specialist, writer; b. Memphis; d. Clement Alexander and Dale (Pendergrast) Santi; m. William Edward Flaherty, Feb. 22, 1975. BA, U. Memphis; doctorate (hon.), St. John's U., Balt. Commentator host interview program Sta. WMC-TV, Memphis; newscaster, commentator Sta. WHER, Memphis; cmty. rels. specialist Western Electric Co., N.Y.C.; v.p. pub. rels. divsn. Grey Advt., N.Y.C.; dep. dir. corp. rels. Colgate-Palmolive Co., N.Y.C., dir. corp. rels., corp. v.p., v.p. in charge of communications; v.p. pub. affairs GTE Corp., Stamford, Conn.; pres., chief exec. officer Image Mktg. Internat., N.Y.C. Author: The Savvy Woman's Success Bible, 1997 (one of Top Motivational Books of Yr., Books for a Better Life 1997), Talk Your Way to the Top, 1999, What Jackie Taught Us: Lessons from the Remarkable Life of Jacqueline Kennedy Onassis, 2004. Former chmn. Bus. Coun. of UN Decade for Women; bd. dirs. Nat. Jr. Achievement; mem. The White House Pub. Affairs Advisors; nat. bd. dirs. Animal Med. Ctr. Recipient Jr. Achievement Meml. award; named One of N.Y.C.'s Outstanding Women of Achievement, NCCJ, One of 100 Top Corp. Women, Bus. Week, One of 73 Women Ready to Run Corp. Am., Working Woman, Woman of Distinction, Birmingham So. Coll., One of 100 Amazing Ams., Am.'s Elite, 2000. Mem. DAR, Com. of 200, Internat. Women's Forum, Daughters of the American Revolution (DAR). Home and Office: Image Mktg Internat 1040 Fifth Ave New York NY 10028-0137 Office Phone: 212-535-0025. Personal E-mail: imi1040@aol.com.

FLAITZ, CATHERINE M., dean, dental educator; BA in Psychology, Creighton U., DDS; MS in Pediat. Dentistry, U. Iowa. Bd. cert. oral and maxillofacial pathology. With Creighton U., U. Iowa, U. Colo.; pvt. practice pediat. dentistry Denver; prof., chair diagnostic sci. Dental Branch, U. Tex., Houston, dir. oral and maxillofacial pathology residency program, 2001—02, interim dean, 2002—04, dean, 2004—. Prof. pediat. dentistry Dental Branch, U. Tex., 1992; mem. editl. bd. Pediat. Dentistry, Jour. Dentistry Children, Am. Jour. Dentistry; cons. commn. dental accreditation advanced specialty edn. programs ADA; bd. mem. Friends of the Nat. Inst. of Dental and Craniofacial Rsch., 2005—. Mem. editl. bd.: Archives of Pathology and Laboratory Medicine. Named Tex. Dentist of Yr., Tex. Acad. Gen. Dentistry, 2005; recipient George W. Teuscher Silver Pen award, Jour. Dentistry Children, 2001. Fellow: Am. Acad. Pediat. Dentistry (mem. grants and fellowship com., mem. pres. circle); mem.: ADA, Internat. Coll. Dentists, Omicron Kappa Upsilon, Tex. Dental Assn., Internat. Assn. Dental Rsch., Am. Assn. Dental Rsch., Am. Acad. Oral Medicine (mem. clinical investigation and abstract com.), Greater Houston Dental Soc., Am. Acad. Oral and Maxillofacial Pathology (exec. coun.), Am. Dental Edn. Assn., Am. Coll. Dentists. Office: Univ Tex Health Sci Ctr Dental Branch 6516 MD Anderson Blvd Rm 147 Houston TX 77225-0068 Office Phone: 713-500-4021. Office Fax: 713-500-4089. Business E-Mail: catherine.m.flaitz@uth.tmc.edu.

FLAKE, LEONE ELIZABETH, special education educator; b. New Orleans, Jan. 12, 1938; d. Alfred Charles and Ione (Mills) Ittmann; m. Allen Oliver Flake, July 25, 1959; children: Diana Lee, Alan Mark, Wendy Lynn BA, St. Mary's Dominican, New Orleans, 1973; MEd, U. New Orleans, 1979, postgrad., 1980. Cert. elem. tchr., learning disabled, social maladjusted, emotionally disturbed, kindergarten, mild moderate, severe profound, computer literacy, La. Tchr. grade 2 Jefferson Parish Sch. Board, Metairie, La., 1973-74, tchr. grade 3, 1974-75, tchr. grade 1, 1975-79, tchr. spl. edn., emotionally disturbed, 1979—87, generic tchr., spl. edn., 1987—, tchr. spl. edn., exptl. tchr., 1991—. Substitute prin. Marie Riviere Elem., Metairie, 1992— Chair spl. edn. Marie Riviere Elem., 1987—, sch. rep., 1987—, sch. dir. very spl. arts., 1987—, tchr. spl. needs, 1991—, elem. discipline com., 1987—, sch. bldg. level com. for project read, 1992—, elem. safety com., 1987—, sch. effectiveness action plan com., 1987—, sch. bldg. level com., 1987—, spl. program to upgrade reading task force, 1984-85; counselor, At Risk Students for Project Charlie, 1991— Recipient Merit cert.Jefferson Parish Coun. Of Charitable Involvement, 1985, Key to City Jefferson Parish, 1985, Outstanding Tchr. award Am. Petroleum Inst., 1992-93 Mem. The Orton Dyslexic Soc., Internat. Reading Assn., La. Reading Assn., Coun. for Exceptional Children (Appreciation cert. 1991), Children and Adults with Attention Deficit Disorders, J.C. Ellis Coop. Club (v.p. 1984-84), Phi Delta Kappa, Kappa Delta Pi, Beta Sigma Phi (internat., preceptor 1973—) Avocations: travel, painting, reading. Home: 3701 Wanda Lynn Dr Metairie LA 70002-4523

FLAKES, SUSAN, playwright, scriptwriter, theater director; b. San Diego, July 9, 1943; d. Herbert Franklin and Dorothy Jean (Loafman) Barrows; m. Donald Lewis Flakes, Dec. 31, 1964; 1 child, Daniel Keith. BA, U. N.Mex., Albuquerque, 1965; MA, San Diego State U., 1969; PhD, U. Minn., 1973. Asst., then assoc. prof. Tisch Sch. Arts N.Y. U., N.Y.C., 1973-76, dept. chair Tisch Sch. Arts, 1973-76; founder, artistic dir. Blue Tower Theatre, Stockholm, 1977-80, Strindberg's Intima Teater, Stockholm, 1981-83, Source Prodns., N.Y.C., 1984-90. Instr. U.S. Internat. Univ., San Diego, 1972-73; founder, artistic dir. 1st Strindberg Festival, Stockholm, 1977; mem. Women's Project and Prodns., N.Y.C., 1984-90; v.p. Ibsen Soc. Am., N.Y.C., 1986-99; coord. writers unit W. Coast Ensemble Theatre, Hollywood, Calif., 1991-93. Author: (plays) The Woman Will Play Strindberg's Christina, Laura, Silent Star, And Immortality, Marilyn's Rose, Portrait of Psyche, Daddy's Eyes, To Take Arms, Cafe L.A., Café Heaven, (with Shirl Hendryx) 4F; (libretto with Galt MacDermot) Take It Higher, Maid of Lorraine; (with Gabe Green) Any Saints Out There?, It Girls; (screenplays) To Take Arms, Stand the Storm, Hometown, Inc., Café L.A., Café Heaven, Francois Poet/Thief, Lifetime Achievement, Immortality, The Sacred Garden; (with Stephane Haskell) Immortalité: Daddy's Eyes, The Sacred Garden, The Acting Teacher, The Acting Lesson; dir. Hughie, 1989, Mother Love, 1994; contbr. articles to profl. jours., chpts. to books; creator Exptl. Theatre Wing, U.G. Drama Tisch Sch. Arts, NYU, 1975-76; contbr. (play) And Immortality to Baltic Seasons Mag., Russia, 2003; author 2 screenplays (1st Pl. award, 2d Pl award, Screenwriting Competition winner Film Industry Network, 2005). Ensign

USN, 1965-67. Recipient winner 10-minute play festival, Fire Rose Productions, 2004, Fullerton Coll. Playwriting Festival, Resident Theater Co., 2004, Alliance of L.A. Playwrights New Works Lab 2004 at the Co. of Angels, LA, Lamia Ink Internat. competition, 1991; fellow Am. Film Inst., 1990; grantee Nat. Endowment for Arts, 1972, Travel grantee Am. Scandinavian Found., Norwegian and Swedish Govts., 1985-86, 89, 94, 2001. Mem. Dramatists Guild, Actor's Studio (playwright/dirs. unit), Am. Film Inst. (finalist directing workshop for women 2003), Alliance L.A. Playwrights, Phi Beta Kappa. Address: 7552 Amazon Dr #1 Huntington Beach CA 92647 Personal E-mail: sflakes@socal.rr.com.

FLANAGAN, BARBARA, journalist; b. Des Moines; d. John Merrill and Marie (Barnes) F.; m. Earl S. Sanford, 1966. Student, Drake U., 1942-43. With promotion dept. Mpls. Times, 1945-47; reporter Mpls. Tribune, 1947-58; women's editor, spl. writer Mpls. Star and Tribune, 1958-65; columnist Mpls. Star, 1965—. Author: Ovation, Minneapolis. Active Junior League Mpls., Womans Club Mpls. Mem. Mpls. Soc. Fine Arts (life), Mpls. Inst. Arts (founding mem. Minn. Arts Forum), Mpls. Club, Minikahda Club, Kappa Alpha Theta, Sigma Delta Chi. Episcopalian. Office: Mpls Star Tribune 5th And Portland Sts Minneapolis MN 55488-0001

FLANAGAN, DEBORAH MARY, lawyer; b. Hackensack, N.J., Sept. 17, 1956; d. Joseph Francis and Mary Agnes (Fitzsimmons) F.; m. Glen H. Koch, Aug. 27, 1983. BA summa cum laude, Fordham U., 1978, JD, 1981; LLM in Taxation, NYU, 1987. Bar: N.Y. 1982 and U.S. Dist. Ct. 1988. V.p., assoc. tax counsel The McGraw-Hill Inc. Cos., N.Y.C., 1981—. Mem. Assn. Bar City N.Y., Fordham U. Law Alumni Assn., NYU Law Alumni Assn. Home: 268 E Saddle River Rd Saddle River NJ 07458-2812 Office: The McGraw-Hill Companies 1221 Avenue Of The Americas 48th Fl New York NY 10020-1095

FLANAGAN, DIANE L., property claims professional; b. Tampa, Fla., Apr. 3, 1960; d. Robert and Jean Beale Deertrick; m. Shawn P. Flanagan, Oct. 24, 1981; children: Kevin R., Andrew. AIC, IIA, Malvern, Pa., 1985; degree in bus. mgmt. devel., Ea. Mennonite U., Harrisburg, Va., 2003. Claims property profl. Donegal Mut., Maytown, Pa., 1978—89; claims profl. Harrisburg, Pa., 1989—93; with claims dept. USFG / St. Paul / Met. Ins., Lancaster, Pa., 1993—2001; property claims profl. Nationwide Ins., Lancaster, 2001—05, Donegal Mut. Ins., Maytown, 2005—. Leader Boy Scouts Am., Maytown, 2002—04, Cub Scouts leader, 1995—98. Recipient Customer Svc. award, 2004, Integrity award, 2004. Mem.: Soc. Ins. Trainers. Avocation: volleyball. Office: Donegal Mut Ins Box 302 Maytown PA 17550

FLANAGAN, FIONNULA MANON, actress, writer, theater director; b. Dublin; came to U.S., 1968; d. Terence Niall and Rosanna (McGuirk) F.; m. Garrett O'Connor, Nov. 26, 1972; 2 stepchildren. C.I.H.E., U. Fribourg, Switzerland, 1962; student, Abbey Theatre Sch., Dublin, 1964-66. Pres. The Rejoycing Co., 1978—. Stage appearances include: Ulysses in Nighttown, N.Y.C., 1974, Lovers, 1968, Ghosts, 1989, Happy Days, 1991, Unfinished Stories, 1992, Countess Cathleen, 1992, Summerhouse, 1994; author, actress one-woman shows: James Joyce's Women, 1977 (L.A. Drama Critics award, San Francisco Theatre Critics award, Drama-Logue award); films include: Ulysses, 1967, In the Region of Ice, 1980, Mr. Patman, 1980, James Joyce's Women, 1984, Reflections, 1984, Chain Reaction, 1985, Death Dreams, 1992, Mad at the Moon, 1992, Money for Nothing, 1993, Some Mother's Son, 1996, Waking Ned Devine, 1998, With or Without You, 1999, The Others, 2000, Divine Secrets of the Ya-Ya Sisterhood, 2002, Tears of the Sun, 2003, One of the Oldest Con Games, 2004, Blessed, 2004, Man About Dog, 2004, Transamerica, 2005, Four Brothers, 2005; TV appearances include: The Picture of Dorian Gray, 1973, The Legend of Lizzie Borden, 1975, Rich Man Poor Man, 1976 (Emmy award for most outstanding support role 1976), How the West Was Won, 1977-79 (Emmy nominee 1978), A Winner Never Quits, 1986, White Mile, 1994, Kings in Grass Castles, 1998, To Have and To Hold, 1998, For Love or Country: The Arturo Sandoval Story, 2000, Murder She Wrote: The Celtic Riddle, 2003, Revelations, 2005; dir. Freedom of the City, Theatre West L.A., 1988 (Dramalogue award), Faith Healer, 1989, Away Alone, Court Theatre, L.A., 1991, Abbey Theatre, Dublin, 1992, A Secret Affair, 1999, Havana Nocturne, 2000; TV guest appearances include: Chicago Hope, 1999, Enterprise, 2002, Law & Order: Special Victims Unit, 2003, Nip/Tuck, 2004. Mem. AFTRA, SAG, Actors' Equity, Irish Actors Equity. Office: Don Buchwald & Assocs 6500 Wilshire Blvd Ste 2200 Los Angeles CA 90048-4942*

FLANAGAN, JUDY, director, special events consultant; b. Lubbock, Tex., Apr. 28, 1950; d. James Joseph II and Jean (Breckenridge) F. BS in Edn., Memphis State U., Tenn., 1972; postgrad., Disney U., Orlando, Fla., 1975—81, Valencia C.C., 1977—79, Rollins Coll., Winter Park, Fla., 1979; MS in Comm., U. Tenn., Knoxville, 2004. Area/parade supr. entertainment divsn. Walt Disney World, Orlando, Fla., 1972—81; parade dir. Gatlinburg C. of C., Tenn., 1981-85; entertainment prodn. mgr. The 1982 World's Fair, Knoxville, 1982; cons. Judy Flanagan Prodns./Spl. Events, Gatlinburg, 1982—, Miss U.S.A. Pageant, Knoxville, 1983; prodn. coord. Nashville Network, 1983; dir. sales River Terr. Resort, Gatlinburg, 1985-86; account exec. Park Vista Hotel, Gatlinburg, 1986-88; project coord. Universal Studios, Fla., 1988-90; dir. spl. events U. Tenn., Knoxville, 1990—2006; creative cons. for spl. events, parades, 2006—. Dir. Neyland Stadium Expansion Dedication, 1996—; U. Tenn. Bicentennial Events, 1994, 21st Century Campaign Major Events; prodn. mgr. 1984 World's Fair Parades and Spl. Events, New Orleans, Neil Sedaka rock video, Days of Our Lives daytime soap opera. Extraordinary eucharistic minister, lectr. Cath. Ch. Recipient Gatlinburg Homecoming award, 1986, World Lifetime Achievement award, 1993. Mem.: ASPCA, Nat. Women's History Mus. (charter mem.), Nat. Wildlife Found., Ocean Conservancy, African Wildlife Found., Natural Resources Defence Council, Tenn. Festivals and Events Assn. (bd. dirs.), Internat. Festivals and Events Assn. (cert. festival and events exec., found. bd.), Internat. Spl. Events Soc., The Ocean Conservancy, Return Wild Horses to Freedom, World Wildlife Fund, Defenders of Wildlife, Humane Soc. U.S., Doris Day Animal League, Sierra Club, U. Tenn. Soc. Pres. Club. Roman Catholic. Home: 835 Breckenridge Ln Savannah TN 38372

FLANAGAN, LOUISE W., federal judge; b. Richmond, Va., June 26, 1962; married; 2 children. Ba magna cum laude, Wake Forest U., 1984; JD, U. Va. Law Sch., 1988. Bar: NC 1988, DC 1989. Law clk. to Hon. Malcolm J. Howard US Dist. Ct. (Ea. Dist.) NC, 1988—89; assoc. Sonnenschein, Nath & Rosenthal, 1989—90, Ward & Smith, 1990—93, ptnr., 1994—99; magistrate judge (part-time) US Dist. Ct. (Ea. Dist.) NC, 1995—2003, dist. judge, 2004—, chief judge. Mem.: NC Bar Assn. (dispute resolution coun.).

FLANAGAN, MARIANNE, music educator; d. William James and Catherine Theresa Flanagan. B in Music Edn., N.E. La. U., 1984; M in Music Edn., U. So. Miss., 1998. Cert. Nat. Bd. Cert. Tchr. Early and Young Adolscent Music, 2000. Band dir. Bastrop (La.) Jr. HS, 1988—89; dir. band Bastrop HS, 1989—91, Lakeview Mid. Sch., Winter Garden, Fla., 1991—92, Colonial HS, Orlando, Fla., 1992—. Mem.: Internat. Assn. Jazz Educators, Music Educators Nat. Conf., Fla. Bandmasters Assn. (adjudicator 1995—, mem. profl. resource com. 1996—). Office: Colonial HS 6100 Oleander Dr Orlando FL 32807 Business E-Mail: flanagan@ocps.net.

FLANAGAN, MARTHA LANG, publishing executive; BS in Fine Arts, U. Cin., 1978. Various exec. secretarial positions, 1960—73; corp. sec., asst. to pres. Cin. Enquirer, 1973—. Mem. adv. com. to Cin. Police Chief, 1976-85; mem. Cin. Music Hall Centennial Com., 1976-78; mem. adv. bd. U. Cin. Coll. Design, Art, Architecture and Planning, 1988-91; trustee Neediest Kids of All, 1980—, Women's Fund Greater Cin. Found., 2000—, St. Ursula Acad., 2002—05. Office: The Cincinnati Enquirer 312 Elm St Fl 20 Cincinnati OH 45202-2739 Business E-Mail: mflanagan@enquirer.com.

FLANAGAN, SUSAN MARIE, special education educator; d. John Bresnahan Flanagan and Marguarite McKenna; m. Norman Christian Kristoff, 1981 (div. 1983). MS, Johns Hopkins U., 2001; BS, Wheelock Coll., 1979. Meyers Briggs Cert. Md., 1990, cert. State Dept. Edn. Md., 1997, Pvt. Pilot Fla., 1995. Dir. pediat. play therapist Dartmouth Hitchcock Med. Ctr., Hanover, NH, 1979—81; pediat. play therapist Meml. Sloan Kettering Hosp., New York City, 1981—83. Recruiter Cosmopolitan, New York, 1983—88; real estate developer Foxmoore Assocs. Ltd. Partnership, Annapolis, Md., 1988—97; child adv.- entreprenuer Susan Flanagan, M.S., LLC, Annapolis, 1997. Author (designer): Phlanagan Phonics Reading Program (Amb. Award, 2003). Bd. mem. Jr. League of Annapolis, 1988—2003. Clara E. Cade Scholarship, Quincy Sch., 1974. Mem.: Learning Disabilities Assn., Coun. For Exceptional Children, Johns Hopkins Alumni Assn., Pvt. Pilots Assn. (pvt. pilot). Achievements include design of Created a remedial reading program for students with disabilities. Avocations: collector of movie memorabilla, fitness training, long distance runner, gourmet cooking. Office: Susan Flanagan MS LLC 2315 Forest Drive Annapolis MD 21401

FLANAGAN KELLY, ANNE MARIE, academic administrator; b. North Kingstown, RI, Apr. 13, 1954; d. John James Flanagan and Margaret Mary Ortstein; children: Timothy Kelly, Brigid Kelly. Cert. advanced studies, SUNY, BA; MEd, Pa. State U. Cert. sch. dist. adminstr., sch. adminstrv. supr., nursery, kindergarten and grades 1-6, spl. edn. K-12. Grade 4 tchr. Narrowsburgh Ctrl. Sch. Dist., Narrowsburgh, NY, 1976; spl. edn. tchr. Tompkins-Seneca-Tioga BOCES, Ithaca, NY, 1977—80; learning disabilities specialist Ithaca City Sch. Dist., Ithaca, NY, 1980—81; head tchr. Adolescent Day Sch./Cmty. Treatment Ctr., Worcester, Mass., 1981—83; resource/cons./remedial tchr. Onteora Ctrl. Sch. Dist., Boiceville, NY, 1986—93; supr. spl. edn. Ulster BOCES, New Paltz, NY, 1993—. Adv. bd. 21st Century Grant- Ulster BOCES and Ellenville CSD, New Paltz, NY, 2001—; mem. NY State Coun. of Admstrs. Spl. Edn., NY; student success mgr. SUNY-Ulster, Stone Ridge; lectr., presenter in field. Contbr. articles to profl. jours. Religious edn. tchr. St. Joseph's Ch., Kingston, NY, 1989—2000, eucharistic min., 1996—2003; merit badge counselor Boy Scouts of Am. Troop 20, Hurley, NY, 1999—2003; mem. Kingston H.S. Alumni Choir, 2002—, St. Joseph's Music Ministry, Kingston. Fellow Spl. Edn., US Office Edn., 1976-1977; grantee VATEA, NY State Edn. Dept., 1995—97. Mem.: Regional Bd. N.Y. State Parent Tchr. Assn. (scholarship chairperson 1993—95, Hudson Valley chpt.), N.Y. State United Tchrs., SUNY Cortland Alumni Assn., SUNY New Paltz Alumni Assn., Penn State U. Alumni Assn., Coun. for Exceptional Children, Assn. Supervision and Curriculum Devel. Roman Catholic. Avocations: reading, singing, church activities, athletic events. Home: 28 Village Ct Kingston NY 12401 Office: Ulster BOCES 175 Route 32 N New Paltz NY 12561 Personal E-mail: kellya@sunyulster.edu. Business E-Mail: akelly@mhric.org.

FLANDERS, ELEANOR CARLSON, community volunteer; b. Spearville, Kans., Mar. 27, 1916; d. Carl Edward and Laura Rebecca (Pine) Carlson; m. Laurence Burdette Flanders, Jr., June 6, 1941; children: Laurel F. Umile, John C., Lynette F. Moyer, Paul L. BA, cert. journalism, U. Colo., 1938; family inst. cert., Vassar Coll., 1958. Examiner of credits U. Colo., Boulder, 1938-41; stock market analyst trust dept. First Nat. Bank, Longmont, Colo., 1970-85; landlady Historic Library Hall Apt. House. V.p. St. Vrain Valley Sch. Bd., 1978—84. Contbr. articles to profl. jours. Mem. PEO Sisterhood, 1948—; nat. treas. Am. Mothers NY, 1988—90; club leader 4-H Boulder County, 1947—63; pres., charter mem. Boulder County Mental Health Clinic, 1947—60; N. Colo. area rep. Am. Field Svc., Longmont, 1965—70; coord. tutoring program Boulder County Juvenile Ct., 1965—81; trustee, farm mgr. Carl and laura Carlson trust, Oberlin, Kans., 1971—85; trustee, dir. Colo. 4-H Youth Fund, Ft. Collins, 1973—86; trustee, investment counsel Am. Mothers Endowment Fund, NYC, 1979—90; founder, pres. St. Vrain Edn. Found. Endowment Fund, Longmont, 1985—2004; trustee, bd. dirs. Longmont Cable Trust, 1986—89; dir. St. Vrain Valley Sch. Bd., 1978—86; active Boulder County Ext. Svc. Com., 1985—90; precinct worker, del. Reps., Longmont, Boulder, 1941—; trustee, investment com. 1st Congl. Ch., Longmont, 1960—2001. Mem.: AAUW (charter), St. Vrain Hist. Soc. (dir., pres. 1970—), Sunshine Club, U. Colo. Alumni Assn. (dir., sec. 1950—58), Delta Kappa Gamma (hon.). Avocations: gardening, travel, duplicate bridge, reading, writing. Home: Covenant Village 9153 Yarrow St #1418 Broomfield CO 80021

FLANIGEN, EDITH MARIE, materials scientist, consultant; BA in Chemistry magna cum laude, D'Youville Coll., 1950; MS in Inorganic Physical Chemistry, Syracuse U., 1953; DSc (hon.), D'Youville Coll., 1983. Rsch. chemist Union-Carbide Corp., 1952—56, researcher, molecular sieve group, 1956—73, corp. rsch. fellow, 1973—82, sr. corp. rsch. fellow, 1982—88; sr. rsch. fellow materials sci. UOP Tarrytown Tech. Ctr., NY, 1988—91, UOP fellow, 1991—94, ret. NY, 1994; cons. White Plains, NY, 1994—. Has served as Amb. World for Zeolites, lectr.; mem. of a group of inventors and educators to brainstorm for ideas for new math and sci. sch. at Inventors Hall of Fame. Named to Nat. Inventors Hall of Fame, 2004; recipient Disting. Svc. award, Am. Chem. Soc. (Western NY Sect.), 1990, Chemical Pioneer award, Am. Inst. Chemists, 1991, Perkin medal (first women to win this award), Soc. Chem. Ind. (Am. Sect.), 1992, Francis P. Garvan-John M. Olin medal, Am. Chem. Soc., 1993, Internat. Zeolite Assn. award, 1994, Outstanding Women Scientist, NY Acad. Sciences, 1996, Achievement award, Indsl. Rsch. Inst., 2004, Lemelson-MIT Lifetime Achievement award, 2004. Achievements include patents in field. Home: 502 Woodland Hills Rd White Plains NY 10603-3136

FLANNELLY, LAURA T., mental health nurse, nursing educator, researcher; b. Bklyn., Nov. 7, 1952; d. George A. Adams and Eleanor (Barragry) Mulhearn; m. Kevin J. Flannelly, Jan. 10, 1981. BS in Nursing, Hunter Coll., 1974; MSN, U. Hawaii, 1984, PhD in Ednl. Psychology, 1996. RN, N.Y., Hawaii. Psychiat. nurse Bellevue Hosp., N.Y.C., 1975, asst. head nurse, 1975-77; psychiat. nurse White Plains (N.Y.) Med. Ctr., 1978-79; community mental health nurse South Beach Psychiat. Ctr., N.Y.C., 1979-81; psychiat. nurse The Queen's Med. Ctr., Honolulu, 1981-83; crisis worker Crisis Response Systems Project, Honolulu, 1983-86; instr. nursing U. Hawaii, Honolulu, 1985-92, asst. prof., 1992—, assoc. grad. faculty, 1998—; adj. instr. nursing Hawaii Loa Coll., Honolulu, 1988; assoc. prof. Am. Samoa Community Coll., Honolulu, 2000—, adj. instr. nursing, 1987, 89, 90. Mem. adv. bd., planning com. Psychiat. Day Hosp. of The Queen's Med. Ctr., Honolulu, 1981-82; program coord. Premenstrual Tension Syndrome Conf., Honolulu, 1984; dir. Ctr. Psychosocial Rsch., Honolulu, 1987—; program moderator 1st U.S-Japan Health Behavioral Conf., Honolulu, 1988; faculty Ctr. for Asia-Pacific Exch., 1995-99, Internat. Conf. on Transcultural Nursing, Honolulu, 1990; mem. bd. dirs. U. Hawaii Profl. Assembly, 1994-97; mem. Hawaii State Coun. Mental Health, 1997—. Contbr. articles to profl. jours. N.Y. State Bd. Regents scholar, 1970-74; NIH nursing trainee, 1983-84; grantee U. Hawaii, 1986, 91, Hawaii Dept. Health, 1990. Fellow Internat. Soc. Rsch. on Aggression; mem. AAAS, APA, Am. Ednl. Rsch. Assn., Am. Psychol. Soc., Am. Psychiat. Nurses Assn., Am. Statis. Assn., Nat. League for Nursing, N.Y. Acad. Scis., Sigma Theta Tau (rec. sec. chpt. 1995-97). Achievements include research on aggressive behavior, educational testing, learning styles, problem-based learning, cross-cultural differences, statistical modeling.

FLANNERY, BERNITA L., music educator; b. Aberdeen, SD, May 15, 1955; d. Elmer and LaVina Hopf; m. James A. Flannery, May 26, 1979; children: Corey, Nathaniel, Rachel. BSc in Music, No. State U., Aberdeen, S.D., 1977. Music tchr. Bridgewater, Emery Schs., SD, 1977—79, Hosmer, SD, 1983—90, Roscoe, SD, 1990—94, Edmunds Ctrl. Sch., Roscoe, SD, 1994—; elem. music tchr. St. Marys Elem. Sch., Salem, SD, 1979—80. Ch. organist St. Thomas, Roscoe, 1990—; dir. cmty. choir, Roscoe, 1990—. Mem.: Phi Beta Mu. Office: Edmunds Ctrl Sch PO Box 317 Roscoe SD 57471

FLANNERY, ELLEN JOANNE, lawyer; b. Bklyn., Dec. 13, 1951; d. William Rowan and Mary Jane (Hamilla) Flannery. AB cum laude, Mount Holyoke Coll., 1973; JD cum laude, Boston U., 1978. Bar: Mass. 1978, DC 1979, U.S. Ct. Appeals (DC cir.) 1979, U.S. Dist. Ct. DC 1980, U.S. Ct. Appeals (4th cir.) 1981, U.S. Supreme Ct. 1983. Spl. asst. to commr. of health Mass. Dept. Pub. Health, Boston, 1973—75; law clk. U.S. Ct. Appeals DC cir., Washington, 1978—79; assoc. Covington & Burling LLP, Washington, 1979—86, ptnr., 1986—, co-chmn. Food & Drug Regulatory Practice Group. Lectr. ins. U. Va. Sch. Law, 1984—90, Boston U. Sch. Law, 1993, bd. visitors, 1995—; lectr. ins. U. Md. Sch. Law, 1994; mem. Nat. Conf. Lawyers and Scientists, AAAS-ABA, 1989—92; chair Fellows Adv. Rsch. Commn., 2002—06. Contbr. articles to profl. jour. Fellow: Am. Bar Found. (chair fellows adv. rsch. com. 2002—, sec. fellows 2005—06, chair elect fellows 2006—); mem.: ABA (chmn. life scis. divsn. 1982—84, chmn. com. med. practice 1987—88, chmn. life scis. divsn. 1988—91, vice chair food and drug law com. 1991—97, chmn. sect. sci. and tech. 1992—93, del. of sci. and tech. sect. to ho. of dels. 1993—, chmn. coordinating group on bioethics and the law 1998—2000, vice chair Ho. Tech. Com. 2002—04, chmn. conf. sect. and divsn. dels. 2003—), Cosmos Club. Office: Covington & Burling LLP 1201 Pennsylvania Ave NW Washington DC 20004-2401 Office Phone: 202-662-5484. Office Fax: 202-662-6291. Business E-Mail: eflannery@cov.com.

FLANNERY, REBECCA R., harpist; b. Hartford, Conn., Jan. 27, 1952; MusB, SUNY, Stony Brook, 1975; MusM, Yale U., 1978; cert., Am. Ctr. for the Alexander Technique Tchr. Tng., 1987. Mem. N.Y. Harp Ensemble, tours U.S., Can. and Europe, 1970-73; mem. flute and harp duo Chrysolith, tours U.S. and Can., 1976—. 2nd harp New Haven Symphony; instr. harp Hartt Sch. Music, U. Hartford, U. Conn.; founder Conn. Harp Festival. Rec. artist (album) Dreams and Fantasies, (CD) This Son So Young. Recipient Sprague-Woolsey Hall Competition award, 1978; named one of Outstanding Young Women in Am., 1981. Mem. Am. Harp Soc. (pres. Conn. chpt.). E-mail: rflanner@concentric.net.

FLANNERY, SUSAN MARIE, library administrator; b. Newark, Feb. 18, 1953; d. John Patrick Flannery and Assunta (Lardieri) Ege; m. Stephen A. Coren, Oct. 6, 1984. BA in History of Art, U. Pa., 1974; MLS, Simmons Coll., 1975. Dir. of libr. Newton Country Day, 1975-77, Am. Sch. in Switzerland, Montagnola, 1977-78; young adult libr. Somerville (Mass.) Pub. Libr., 1979-81; reference libr. Cary Meml. Libr., Lexington, Mass., 1981-83; asst. dir. Lucius Beebe Libr., Wakefield, Mass., 1983-87; dir. Reading (Mass.) Pub. Libr., 1987-91; assoc. dir. Cambridge (Mass.) Pub. Libr., 1991-1993, dir., 1993—. Steering com. Mass. delegation to White Ho. Conf. on Librs., 1990; corporator East Cambridge Savs. Bank. Reviewer Sch. Libr. Jour.; contbr. articles to profl. jours. Incorporator Cambridge (Mass.) Family YMCA, 1991—93; bd. dirs. Guidance Ctr., Inc., Cambridge, 1994—2000, sec., 2001—. Recipient Friend to Writers award, PEN New Eng., 2004, Leading Role award, Cambridge Cmty. TV, 2005. Mem. ALA (Mass. councilor 1993-97, John Cotton Dana award 1989, Outstanding Libr. Adv. 20th Century 2000), ACLU Mass. (adv. bd. 1994-96, bd. dirs. 1996—2004), Mass. Libr. Assn. (pres. 1985-87, v.p. 1983-85), Rotary (bd. dirs. Cambridge 1993-99, v.p. 1995-96, pres. 1997-98, pres. Reading club). Office: Cambridge Pub Libr 359 Broadway Cambridge MA 02139 Office Phone: 617-349-4032. E-mail: sflannery@cambridgema.gov.

FLATO, GWYNDOLYNN SUE, fine art educator; b. El Paso, Tex., Sept. 27, 1959; d. Fountain Edward and Martha Lou (Lackey) Stitt; m. Tomas Chavez, Aug. 2, 1980 (div. July 1988); 1 child, Renee Rochelle Chavez; m. Steven David Flato, Sept. 28, 1991. MusB in Theory and Composition, U. Tex., El Paso, 1981, cert. music tchr., 1991, cert. classroom tchr., 1993. Pvt. piano tchr., El Paso, 1977—; instrumental music dir. Radford Sch., El Paso, 1982-84, music dir., 1984-92; rotating drama tchr. Ysleta Sch. Dist., El Paso, 1992-93; fine arts tchr. Ysleta Elem. Sch., El Paso, 1993-95, East Point Sch., El Paso, 1995—. Choir dir. East Point Sch., El Paso, 1996—; sch. pianist Radford Sch., El Paso, 1982-92, class sponsor, 1988, 90, 91; composer, pianist, El Paso, 1975—. Contbr. poetry to anthologies; composer, pianist, performer Gwyndolynn Stitt Chavez in Concert, 1985; performer Margie Adams in Concert, 1983. Facilitator Div. Recovery Care Class Harvest Christian Ctr., 2003—06. Mem. Nat. Music Tchrs. Assn., Tex. Music Tchrs. Assn., El Paso Music Tchrs. Assn. (chmn. composition contest 1990—, condr. piano ensemble state conv. 1990, 91, Tchr. of Yr. East Point Sch. 1996-97). Avocations: composing, art, writing, gardening.

FLATTAU, PAMELA EBERT, research psychologist, consultant; b. Chgo., Dec. 24, 1946; d. Raymond Clarence and Sylvia Anne (Jones) E.; m. Edward Samuel Flattau, Feb. 1, 1977; children: Jeremy Paul, Victoria Celeste. BSc with honors, U. Leeds, Eng., 1969; MS, U. Ga., 1972, PhD, 1974. Congrl. sci. fellow AAAS-APA, Washington, 1974-75; staff officer NAS/NRC, Washington, 1975-81, sr. staff officer, 1985-90, unit dir., 1990-95; policy analyst NSF, Washington, 1981-85; mgr. Flattau Assocs. LLC, Washington, 1995—; mem. rsch. staff STPI, Inst. for Def. Analyses, Washington, 2003—. Mem. exec. com. Coun. Profl. Assns. for Fed. Stats., Washington, 1986-87. Editor: Research Doctorate Programs in U.S., 1995; author, editor series Biomed and Behavioral Research Personnel 1975-80, 1994; author, contbr.: Science and Engineering Indicators Series, 1981-85. Bd. dirs. Assn. Advancement Psychology, Washington, 1980-82. Mem. AAAS, APA (NSF travel grantee 1992, 2000, Young Psychologist travel award 1976), Am. Psychol. Soc., Soc. for Social Studies of Sci., Human Resources Planning Soc., Sigma Xi. Office: Flattau Assocs LLC 5335 Wisconsin Ave NW Ste 440 Washington DC 20015-2052 E-mail: p.flattau@att.net.

FLAUCHER-FALCK, VELMA RUTH, retired special education educator; b. Hazleton, Iowa, Feb. 10, 1935; d. Amos Burdette and Florence Ella (Short) Flaucher; m. Kenneth Elgin Bienfang, Nov. 26, 1958 (div. Oct. 1975); children: Kende Sue Wynn, Victor Nolan Bienfang, Rodney Dean Bienfang; m. James Leo Falck, July 30, 1994. BA, U. No. Iowa, 1973, MA, 1977. Tchr. kindergarten Orange Ctr. Elem. Sch., Waterloo, Iowa, 1954—59; tchr. Van Eaton Elem. Sch., Waterloo, 1962; tchr. Headstart Exceptional Persons, Waterloo, 1967—68; tchr. kindergarten Hudson Sch. Dist., Hudson, Iowa, 1969—71; dir. activities Friendship Village, Waterloo, 1973—74; tchr. resource AEA7 Spl. Edn., Cedar Falls, Iowa, 1975—94; ret., 1994. Author: Whatever Became of LuAnn?, 2002, Where Did Sally Go?, 2004, Have You Seen Hannah?, 2004, Christina's House, 2004; contbr. poems to Internat. Libr. Poetry. Mem.: Iowa Ret. Sch. Pers., Tues. Tourists Book Club of Oelwein. Avocations: writing, reading, music, painting. Home: 1111 1st St NE Oelwein IA 50662

FLAVIN, SONJA, artist; b. Southampton, NY, Sept. 25, 1936; m. Daniel N. Flavin Jr., Oct. 28, 1961; 1 child, Stephen Conor. MFA in Weaving and Textile Design, Rochester Inst. Tech., 1982; BA in Art History, Washington Sq. Coll., 1978. Advisor Dan Flavin Catalogue Raisonné, 1998—. One-woman shows include San Juan Capistrano Libr. Gallery, 1997; group shows include Elaine Benson Gallery, Bridgehampton, N.Y., 1990, Internat. Textile Fair Exhbn., Kyoto, Japan, 1994, Craft Art Western N.Y., Burchfield-Penney Art Ctr., Buffalo, N.Y., 1996-97, Chamot Gallery, Jersey City, N.J., 1998; co-curator Weltge Exhbn., 1987, Bauhaus Weaving Workshop, Phila. Catalogued George Eastman archives, Rochester, N.Y., 1981-82, Bauhaus textiles, Busch-Reisinger Mus./Harvard U., Cambridge, 1980; workshops for L.A. Unified Sch. Sys. Park Program, 1996. Recipient Grand Prize 3rd Am. Crafts awards, N.Y., 1990, fellowship N.Y. Found. Arts, 1986.

FLEAGLE, CYNTHIA LYNN, art educator; b. Des Moines, Iowa, Apr. 16, 1966; d. George Marvin Richards and Joyce Ann Baker; m. Matthew Vernon Fleagle, June 28, 2003; 1 child, Grace Allana Crabb. BA, Grand View Coll., Des Moines, 1988; MA in Tchg., Drake U., Des Moines, 1989. Graphic artist Norwest Mortgage, West Des Moines, Iowa, 1989—94; graphic designer Value Mktg., Des Moines, 1994—2000; asst. prof. art Grand View Coll., Des Moines, 2000—. Faculty grantee, Iowa Coll. Found., 2002—03. Mem.: Digital Arts Group. Democrat. Home: 3846 3rd St Des Moines IA 50313-3512 Office: Grand View College 1200 Grandview Ave Des Moines IA 50316 Office Phone: 515-263-2893. Home Fax: 515-282-6661. Business E-Mail: cfleagle@gvc.edu.

FLECHNER, ROBERTA FAY, graphics designer; b. N.Y.C., June 7, 1949; d. Abraham Julius and Evelyn (Medwin) F. BA, CCNY, 1970; MA, NYU, 1972; cert., Printing Industries Met., N.Y., N.Y., 1974, 75, 79. Researcher, asst. editor Arno Press, N.Y.C., 1970-73; free-lance editor Random House, N.Y.C., 1973-74, graphic designer/compositor coll. dept., 1984-88; graphic designer Core Communications in Health, N.Y.C., 1974-76; prodn. mgr. Heights-Inwood News, N.Y.C., 1976-77; art dir., graphic designer Jour. Advt. Research, N.Y.C., 1976-81; prin., graphic designer/compositor W.W. Norton & Co., Inc., N.Y.C., 1977—, McGraw Hill, Inc., N.Y.C., 1990-94, 2000—; graphic design, layout artist, compositor R. Flechner Graphics, 1976—. Graphic designer, layout artist, compositor R. Flechner Graphics, 1976—; mech. artist Fawcett, N.Y.C., 1979-80; graphic designer Avon Internat., N.Y.C., 1982; art dir., compositor, layout artist Source: Notes in the History of Art, N.Y.C., 1982—; graphic designer John Wiley & Sons, Inc., N.Y.C., 1985. Designer stationery, 1979 (Art Direction mag., Creativity-cert. distinction 1979). Art dir. enviroNews, N.Y. State Atty. Gen.'s Environ. Protection Bur., N.Y.C., 1977-78. Mem. Graphic Artists Guild, NOW, Women's Nat. Book Assn. (cons.), NAFE, Women's Caucus for Art, Am. Inst. Graphic Arts, CCNY Alumni Assn., NYU Alumni Assn. Office: 10615 Queens Blvd Flushing NY 11375-4365 E-mail: rflechner@aol.com.

FLEESLER, FAITH B., writer; b. N.Y.C., June 13, 1973; d. Zachary and Barbara F. BA in English, Binghamton, U., 1995; MA in English, Carnegie Mellon U., 1996; postgrad., Tchrs. Coll., Columbia U. Libr., Binghamton, N.Y., 1991-95; instr. 92nd St. YM-YWHA, N.Y.C., 1993-97, 2000—; teaching asst. Binghamton U., 1994-95; instr., tutor Tchrs. Coll., Columbia U. Writing Skills Ctr., N.Y.C., 1996-98; corp. comm. & technical writer CSI Complex Syss., N.Y.C., 1997-98; product coord., technical writer Info. Builders, Inc., N.Y.C., 1998—. Adj. prof. Hofstra U., Hempstead, N.Y., 1996-97; story coord. King World Prodns., N.Y.C., 1997; mem. Rhetoric Colloqium, Pitts., 1995-96; mentor, instr. Pitts. Cmty. Literacy Ctr., 1995; rsch. asst. profl. writing project English dept. Carnegie Mellon U., Pitts., 1995; participant in program for future faculty Carnegie Mellon U. Teaching Ctr., Pitts., 1995. Co-developer/co-editor: (textbook) Rhetoric 242 Handbook: Writing and Discourse, 1994, (manual) Rhetoric 242 Teaching Assistant Manual, 1995; co-editor, staffwriter mag. Wordplay: Mag. Creative Nonfiction, 1994, Tchr.'s Coll. Columbia U.: Non-fiction Workshop Mag., 1996; asst. editor Offcl. Jour. Conf. English Edn., 1997; staff writer mag. World: Bristol-Meyers Squibb Co., 1997. Carnegie Mellon U. scholar, 1995-96. Mem. Soc. Technical Comm. Avocations: travel, exercise, waterskiing, theater, movies. Home: 350 1st Ave Apt11c New York NY 10010-4905

FLEETWOOD, M. FREILE, psychiatrist, educator; b. Valparaiso, Chile, Nov. 20, 1915; d. Alfonso Larrea and Berta (Cordovez) Freile; children: Harvey Blake, Francis Freile. MD, U. Chile, 1941; PhD, Pedagogic Inst., Santiago, Chile, 1947; MD, U. of State of N.Y., 1950. Instr. biochemistry to asst. in pub. emergencies U. Chile, Santiago, 1937-41, resident in neurology at neurol. clinic, 1941-42, head of rsch. lab. in psychiatry, 1944-48; resident in psychiatry Henry Phipps Clinic, John Hopkins U., Balt., 1942-44; provisional asst. in psychiatry to out-patient psychiatrist N.Y. Hosp., N.Y.C., 1948-61; attending psychiatrist Gracie Square Hosp., N.Y.C., 1961—; clin. asst. prof. psychiatry Cornell Univ., N.Y. Hosp., N.Y.C., 1970-88, emeritus status, 1988—. Instr. psychiatry, Payne Whitney Clinic, Cornell U., N.Y. Hosp., N.Y.C., 1950-63; cons. Family Svc. of Patterson, N.J., 1955-56, East Harlem Project Community Svc. Soc., N.Y.C., 1960-61, Manhattan Family Svc. Ctr. Community Svc. Soc., N.Y.C., 1960-61; asst. psychiatrist NYU, U. Hosp., Bellevue Med. Ctr., N.Y.C., 1954, psychiatrist 1954-55, and others. Contbr. articles to profl. publs. Recipient Rockefeller Found. grantee, 1942-43, 43-44, 44-45, Sagin Fund grantee, 1952-53, Squibb Fund grant, 1952-53. Mem. AAAS, Med. Soc. State and County of N.Y., Am. Med. Soc. on Alcoholism and Other Drug Dependencies, Am. Psychiat. Assn. (N.Y. county dist. br.), N.Y. Acad. Sci., Spanish Am. Med. Soc., Pan Am. Med. Soc., N.Y. Soc. for Adolescent Psychiatry, The N.Y. County Review Orgn., Women's Med. Assn. N.Y., Am. Med. Women's Assn. Office: PO Box 1955 28 Central Ave Amagansett NY 11930 Home: 5 West 86th St 12E New York NY 10024

FLEEZANIS, JORJA KAY, musician, educator; b. Detroit, Mar. 19, 1952; d. Parios Nicholas and Kaliope (Karageorge) F.; m. Michael Steinberg, July 3, 1983. Student, Cleve. Inst. Music, 1969-72, Cin. Coll.-Conservatory Music, 1972-75. Violinist Chgo. Symphony Orch., 1975-76; concertmaster Cin. Chamber Orch., 1976-80; violinist Trio D'Accordo, Cin., 1976-80; asst. prin. 2d violinist San Francisco Symphony Orch., 1980-81; assoc. concertmaster San Francisco Sympony Orch., 1980-89; acting concertmaster Minn. Orch., Mpls., 1988-89, concertmaster, 1989—; violinist Fleezanis-Ohlsson-Grebanier Piano Trio, San Francisco, 1984—; faculty mem. San Francisco Conservatory of Music, 1983-89, U. Minn., 1989—. Founder Chamber Music Sundaes, San Francisco, 1980-89, The Am. String Project, 2002; radio host St. Paul Sunday Show, Minn. Pub. Radio, 1998-2000; guest concertmaster, London Classical Players, L.A. Philharmonic, Sydney Symphony, Balt. Symphony; vis. prof. Ind. U., 2003—. Performer World Premiere John Adams Violin Concerto with Minn. Orch., 1994, Nicholas Maw, Sonata for Solo Violin, commd. by Minn. Pub. Radio, 1997, Sir John Tavener's Ikon of Eros, commd. for her by Minn. Orch., 2002; commd. by Pub. Radio Internat. and Minn. Pub. Radio for world premiere of Nicholas Maw Sonata for Solo Violin, 1998; soloist Am. premier Benjamin Britten Double Concerto, 1998; rec. artist Reference CRI, Koch, Cypre's Records. Democrat. Avocations: photography, cooking. Office: Minn Orch 1111 Nicollet Mall Minneapolis MN 55403-2406 Office Phone: 612-371-5653. E-mail: fleeberg@earthlink.net.

FLEHARTY, MARY SUE, government agency administrator; b. Lincoln, Nebr., Aug. 13, 1962; d. Joseph Patrick and Joy Lou (Harnish) Huntley; m. Bradley Daryle Osborne, Mar. 26, 1983 (div. June 1988); m. Terry Lester Fleharty, Aug. 13, 1990. Student, Lincoln Sch. Commerce, 1996-97; student in sign lang., S.E. C.C., 2003—. Cert. EMT. Loan processor Am. Charter Fed. Savings and Loan, Lincoln, 1981-84; pub. broadcast exchange operator, sec. Lincoln Clinic, P.C., 1989-91; PBX operator, sec. Woods Park Med. Mgmt. Inc., Lincoln, 1991-93; data reporting asst. Harris Tech. Group, Lincoln, 1993; lease coord. Progressive Lease, Inc., Lincoln, 1993; PBX comms. specialist Branker Buick, Lincoln, 1994-97; sec., receptionist Reel Quick, Inc., Lincoln, 1997-98; case mgmt. sec. Madonna Rehab. Hosp., Lincoln, 1998-2000; exec. adminstrv. asst. Nebr. Heart Inst., Lincoln, 2000; office clk. Nebr. Dept. Labor, Lincoln, 2000—01, staff asst. I, 2001—. Sec. Lincoln Police Citizen Acad., 2001—03. Vol. ARC, Lincoln, 1977—, chmn., 1983-84, pres. Lincoln Fire Dept. Aux., 1993. Named Outstanding Vol. ARC, 1985. Mem. NAFE, Benevolent Patriotic Order of Does (inner guard 1999, sec. 2000-01, chaplain 2000-02, flag bearer 2003—), Lancaster County Emergency Mgmt., Internat. Assn. Workforce Profls. (state chpt. pres. 2004-06). Republican. Presbyterian. Avocations: handbell ringing, shuffleboard, pool, bowling, gardening. Office: Nebr Dept Labor 550 S 16th St Lincoln NE 68508 Office Phone: 402-471-9962. Personal E-mail: msfleharty@gmail.com.

FLEISCHER, AMY, mechanical engineer, educator; b. Charleton Heights, W.Va., 1969; m. Paul Fleischer, 1992; 1 child, Katherine. PhD in Mech. Engring., U. Minn., 2000. Assoc. prof. mech. engring. Villanova U., Pa., 2000—. Office: Villanova University 800 Lancaster Ave Villanova PA 19085 Office Phone: 610-519-4996.

FLEISCHHAKER, KARIN, insurance agent; b. Warren, Minn., Oct. 8, 1947; d. William Valentine and Margaret Mary (Staloch) Gerszewski; 1 child, Tamara Lynn. Student Gen. Bus., U. Minn., St. Paul, 1988. CPCU Ins. Inst. Am., 1987. V.p. comml. mktg. Lee F. Murphy, Inc., St. Paul/ Mpls., 1979—84; account exec. Corroon & Black of Minn., Mpls., 1984—86; mktg. rep comml. lines The Drew Agy., Inc., St. Paul, 1986—89; producer, inst. First Am. Ins. Agy., Crookston, Minn., 1989—90; comml. mktg. rep. Hendrickson Agy/Bus. Ins. Brokers, Bloomington, Minn., 1990—94; large acct. mktg. rep. A and H Ins., Inc., Reno, 1995—98; comml. and personal lines agt. Farmers Ins. Group, Sparks, Nev., 1998—2000; comml. acct. mgr., contract specialist A and H Ins. Inc./ Western Ins. Co., Reno, 2000—04; welding robot operator Artic Cat Inc., Thief River Falls, Minn., 2004—. Comml. lines underwriter, artist, rschr. Minn. Mutual Fire and Casualty Co., Mpls., 1965—74; loss prevention engring. clk. The St. Paul Cos., 1974—75; dept. mgr. personal lines. Alexander & Alexander, St. Paul, 1975—79. Author (Pen Name Kathryn Weiss): (novels) The Dance of a Lifetime. Vol. Mpls. Aquatenniel, 1979—86; chmn, Crookston Ox Cart Days, 1989—90. Avocations: painting, sculpting. Office: Artic Cat Inc 601 Brooks Ave Thief River Falls MN 56701

FLEISCHMAN, FRANCINE D., secondary school educator; b. Bklyn., N.Y., Jan. 28, 1951; d. Alvin and Lillian Rachel Moskowitz; m. Herman Israel Fleischman, Feb. 3, 1973; children: Meredith, Brandon, Gary. BS, West Conn. State U., 1973; MS, CUNY, 1975. Tchr. Bd. Edn., Bklyn., 1973—. Prof. Nassau C.C., Garden City, NY, 1994—; v.p. United Mutual Industries, Inc., Merrick, NY, 1987—. Home: 2970 Hewlett Ave Merrick NY 11566

FLEISHER, BETTY, artist, educator; b. Bklyn., June 7, 1932; d. Simon and Sadie Ellis; m. Harvey A. Fleisher, Oct. 30, 1955; children: Stephanie, Margaret. AA, Miami Dade C.C., 1972; BFA, Fla. Internat. U., 1974; MA, Goddard Coll., 1978. Adj. prof. Miami (Fla.) Dade C.C., 1974-76, Fla. Internat. U., Miami, 1978-88; instr. art Art Ctr. of South Fla., Miami. Lectr. in art Brandeis Women, Hollywood, Fla., 1985, Elders Inst. Fla. Internat. U., Miami, 1980. Exhibited in group shows at Soc. of the Four Arts, Palm Beach, Fla., 1974, 1976, 1987, Fla. Internat. U. Faculty Exhbn., 1983, Hollywood (Fla.) Art and Culture Ctr., 1987, Mus. Contemporary Art, North Miami, Fla., 1990, Art 800, Miami, Fla., 1997, 1998, 2000, 2002, Miami Beach Conv. Ctr., 2004, Art Miami, Miami Beach Conv. Ctr., 2004, Represented in permanent collections Neiman Marcus, Coral Gables, Fla., Boca Raton, Fla. Mem. panel Art in Pub. Places, Broward and Ft. Lauderdale, Fla., 1996-98. Mem. Nat. Assn. Women Artists. Jewish. Avocations: gourmet cooking, designing. Home: 21150 Point Pl Apt 1605 Miami FL 33180-4038 Office Phone: 305-332-0640. Personal E-mail: bettyfleisher@bellsouth.net.

FLEISHMAN, SUSAN NAHLEY, entertainment company executive; b. Charlottesville, Va., Sept. 26, 1960; d. Richard and Mary Daniels Nahley; m. Eric Philip Fleishman, Dec. 28, 1995; 1 child, Henry Richard. BA in Am. Lit., Middlebury Coll., 1982. Copywriter Macy's, N.Y.C., 1984—86; dir. Interbrand, N.Y.C., 1986—87; asst. v.p. Continental Ins., N.Y.C., 1987—93; dir., pub. affairs Sony Corp. Am., N.Y.C., 1993—95; v.p. corp. comm. and pub. affairs Universal Studios, L.A., 1995—2000, sr. v.p. corp. comm. & pub. affairs Los Angeles, Calif., 2000—05; exec. v.p. corp. comm. Warner Bros. Entertainment Inc., Burbank, Calif., 2005—. Bd. dirs. Workplace, Hollywood, L.A., 2001—, St. Joseph's Hosp., Burbank, Calif., 2002—; trustee The Cantry Sch., Valley Village, Calif. Office: Warner Bros Entertainment Inc 4000 Warner Blvd Burbank CA 91522

FLEISZIG, SUZANNE MARIANE JANETE, optometry educator; b. Melbourne, Australia, Sept. 5, 1960; came to U.S., 1990; d. Kornel Fleiszig and Judith Mary (Falus) Fleiszig-Farkas. BSc in Optometry, U. Melbourne, 1983, MSc in Optometry, 1985, PhD, 1990. Lic. optometrist, Victoria, Australia. Postdoc. fellow Harvard U. Med. Sch., Boston, 1990-93, instr., 1993-94; prof. optometry U. Calif., Berkeley, 1994—, assoc. dean rsch., 2003—. Cons. to contact lens industry, 1993—. Mem. editl. bd. Eye and Contact Lens. The Ocular Surface Jour.; contbr. articles to Investigtive Ophthalmology and Vision Sci., Jour. Clin. Microbiology, Infection and Immunity. Postdoctoral fellow Nat. Soc. To Prevent Blindness, 1991, C.J. Martin fellow Nat. Health and Med. Rsch. Coun. Australia, 1992; rsch. grantee NIH, 1995—, 2005—; recipient Borish award, 1997, Glenn A. Fry award, 2005. Mem. Am. Soc. for Microbiology, Assn. for Rsch. in Vision and Ophthalmology, Internat. Soc. for Contact Lens Rsch. (pres. 2005), Tear Film and Ocular Surface Soc. (governing bd. 2005—). Achievements include discovery that contact lens wear enhances bacterial binding to human corneal cells, discovered that Pseudomonas aeruginosa invades epithelial cells. Office: U Calif 688 Minor Hall Optometry Berkeley CA 94720-0001 Office Phone: 510-643-0990.

FLEKSHER, CASSANDRA C., psychology and research rehabilitation professional; b. NJ, 1975; d. Daphne T. Berger; m. Mark Fleksher, 2002; 1 child, Dillon. BA in Psychology and Criminal Justice Studies, Alfred U., 1997; MA in Forensic Psychology, John Jay Coll. Criminal Justice, 2000. Neuropsychology RA II neuropsychology and neurosci. lab. Kessler Med. Rehab. Rsch. & Edn. Corp., West Orange, NJ, 2001—03, rsch. coord. II rehab. engring. analysis lab., 2003—04, neuropsychology rsch. coord. II virtual reality lab, 2004—. Author (researcher): (journal abstract) Archives of Clinical Neuropsychology, Archives of Physical Medicine & Rehab.; author: (research assistant) Jour. Internat. Neuropsychological Soc.; research coordinator (cognitive research): Examining the Demands of Driving in Multiple Sclerosis; research assistant II Assessment & Rehabilitation of Cognitive Symptoms of Multiple Sclerosis. Mem.: APA, Nat. Acad. Neuropsychology. Personal E-mail: cfleksher@gmail.com.

FLEMING, ALICE CAREW MULCAHEY, writer; b. New Haven, Dec. 21, 1928; d. Albert Leo and Agnes (Foley) Mulcahey; m. Thomas J. Fleming, Jan. 19, 1951; children: Alice, Thomas, David, Richard. BA, Trinity Coll., Washington, 1950; MA, Columbia U., 1951. Author: The Key to New York, 1960, A Son of Liberty, 1961, Doctors in Petticoats, 1964, Great Women Teachers, 1965, The Senator from Maine: Margaret Chase Smith, 1969, Alice Freeman Palmer: Pioneer College President, 1970, Reporters At War, 1970, General's Lady, 1971, Highways into History, 1971, Pioneers in Print, 1971, Ida Tarbell, The First of the Muckrakers, 1971, Nine Months, 1972, Psychiatry, What's it All About?, 1972, The Moviemakers, 1973, Trials that Made Headlines, 1974, Contraception, Abortion, Pregnancy, 1974, New on the Beat, 1975, Alcohol: The Delightful Poison, 1975, Something for Nothing, 1978, The Mysteries of ESP, 1980, What to Say When you Don't Know What to Say, 1982, The King of Prussia and a Peanut Butter Sandwich, 1988, George Washington Wasn't Always Old, 1991, What, Me Worry?, 1992, P.T. Barnum: The World's Greatest Showman, 1993, A Century of Service, 1997, Frederick Douglass From Slave to Statesman, 2003; editor: Hosannah the Home Run!, 1972, America Is Not all Traffic Lights, 1976; contbr. articles to mags. Nat. bd. dirs. Medic Alert Found. U.S., 1991-97, vice chmn., 1996-97, past chmn. N.Y. regional bd.; mem. pres.'s coun. United Hosp. Fund. Recipient Nat. Media award, Family Svc. Assn. Am., 1973, Alumnae Achievement award, Trinity Coll., 1979, Nat. Vol. of Yr. award, Medic Alert Found., 1991, 1993. Mem. PEN, Authors Guild. Address: 315 E 72nd St New York NY 10021-4625 E-mail: Fleming315@aol.com.

FLEMING, BLANCHE MILES, educational association administrator; d. William Alford and Mary Blanche (Cottman) Miles; m. Daniel Edward Fleming II, Apr. 12, 1952 (dec. Mar. 1970); 1 child, Daniel Edward III. BS, Del. U., 1939; MA, Columbia U., 1947; PhD, Union Grad. Sch., Yellow Springs, Ohio, 1976. Cert. profl. edn., Del.; lic. bus. cert., Del. Tchr. English Wilmington (Del.) Bd. Edn., prin. Bayard Jr. H.S., supr. social studies, intern to supt. of schs., 1974-75; coord. undergrads. Del. State U., Dover, 1971; exec. dir. Nat. Tchr. Corps U. Del., Newark, 1970-72; dir. secondary edn. Del. Bd. Edn., Wilmington, 1980-83; pres. B.M. Fleming & Assocs. Charter mem. Helping Hands Cmty. Svc., Inc., Wilmington, 1996—; bd. dirs. Common Cause of Del., Wilmington, 1984—, Housing Opportunity of No. Del., Wilmington, 1987—, Del. state adv. com. U.S. Commn. on Civil Rights, Washington, 1991—; chair housing com. LWV, Wilmington, 1997—. Recipient Legacy from Del. Women award Chesapeake Bay Girl Scouts, Wilmington, 1987. Mem. Nat. Assn. Univ. Women (pres. 1990-94, cert. of appreciation 1994), Wilmington Women in Bus. (bd. dirs. 1983-85), Delta Kappa Gamma Internat. (corr. sec. 1991-93), Phi Delta Kappa, Kappa Delta Pi, Pi Beta Lambda. Avocations: photography, painting, poetry. Office: Fleming & Assocs 2806 W 5th St Wilmington DE 19805-1824

FLEMING, CHERYL DIANE, realtor; b. Tupelo, Miss., Oct. 28, 1951; d. John Garland and Wilma Doris Robbins; m. Wilber Ray Fleming, Nov. 8, 1980; 1 child, Elizabeth Ann. Cert. Relocation Assoc. Tenn. Realtor Roch Ford and Assoc., Memphis, 1985—86, Menke & Assoc., Germantown, Tenn., 1986—95, Pyramid Realtors, Germantown, Tenn., 1995—98, Cnue-Leike Realtors, Germantown, Tenn., 1998—. League leader La Leche League, Memphis, 1982—99. Recipient Million Dollar Provider, Pyramid realtors, 1997—98. Mem.: Am. Bus. Women's Assn. (pres. 1995—2005), 19th Century Club. Presbyn. Avocations: gardening, reading, interior decorating, tennis, pets.

FLEMING, DARIEN K.S., lawyer; BA summa cum laude, Boston Coll., 1999, JD magna cum laude, 2002. Bar: Mass. 2002. Assoc. estate planning Bingham McCuthcen LLP, Boston; assoc. Kirkpatrick & Lockhart Nicholson Graham, LLP, Boston, 2006—. Mem.: Women's Bar Assn. Mass. (bd. dirs.), Boston Bar Assn., Phi Beta Kappa. Office: Kirkpatrick & Lockhart Nicholson Graham LLP State Street Financial Center One Lincoln St Boston MA 02111-2950 Office Phone: 617-951-9071. Office Fax: 617-261-3175. E-mail: dfleming@klng.com.*

FLEMING, DIANE PRICE, academic administrator; b. Rocky Mount, N.C., Dec. 29, 1939; d. Jack and Christine (Vester) Price; children: Susannah Price Fleming Hughes, Robert Bloomer Fleming (dec.). BA, Atlantic Christian Coll., Wilson, N.C., 1963; MA, East Carolina U., Greenville, N.C., 1995; EdD, Nova Southeastern U., Fort Lauderdale, Fla., 2004; EdS, East Carolina U., Greenville, N.C., 2004. From tchr. to dir. elem. edn. Franklin County Schs., Louisburg, NC, 1978—2003; ret., 2003; instr. English Louisburg Coll., 2005—. Dist. rep. N.C. Assn. Compensatory Edn., 1997—; chmn. bd. dirs. Franklin County Partnership for Children, Louisburg, 1993—; guardian ad litem N.C. Judicial Sys., 1991—. Mem. N.C. History Mus. Assocs. (local chmn.), Franklin County Arts Coun. (bd. dirs. 1984-88, 97—), Person Place Preservation Soc. (bd. dirs.). Democrat. Episcopal. Avocations: gardening, reading, playing bridge, travel.

FLEMING, GINA MARIE, music educator; b. Aurora, Ill., Nov. 28, 1977; d. Lynn Allen and Linda Louise Pehlke. B in Music Performance, Ill. State U., Normal, 2000, B in Music Edn. magna cum laude, 2002. Cert. tchr. Ill. Tchr. music Adventures in Learning, Naperville, Ill., 2003, Newark Grade Sch., Ill., 2003—06, Richland Grade Sch., 2006—. Mem. venture crew 402 com. Boy Scouts Am. Mem.: NEA, Percussive Arts Soc., Music Educators Nat. Conf., Tau Beta Sigma (pres. 1999—2001). Republican. Roman Catholic. Avocations: figure skating, sewing, crafts.

FLEMING, GLORIA ELAINE, retired physician; b. Ganado, Tex., Oct. 10, 1925; d. Owen Samual and Nellie Faye Rogers; m. James Mantooth, Sr. (dec.); children: Deborah Ann Mantooth Stricklin, James Mantooth, Jr.; m. George Fleming (dec.). BS cum laude, Tex. A&M, Kingsville; MD, U. Tex., Galveston. Family practice physicisian, Dickinson, Tex., 1969—86; physician emergency medicine Galveston County Meml. Hosp., LaMarquez, Tex., 1989—91; ret., 1991. Chief of staff Galveston County Meml. Hosp., Texas City. Mem.: Galveston County Med. Soc. (pres.). Republican. Roman Catholic. Home: 1900 Darryknoll Ln Houston TX 77024

FLEMING, JANE WILLIAMS, retired elementary school educator, writer; b. Bethlehem, Pa., May 26, 1926; d. James Robert and Marion Pauline (Melloy) Groman; m. George Elliott Williams, July 2, 1955 (div. July 1965); children: Rhett Dorman, Santee Stuart, Timothy Cooper; m. Jerome Thomas Fleming, Sept. 25, 1980 (dec. 2002). BS, UCLA, 1951; MA, Calif. State U., Long Beach, 1969. Tchr. San Diego Unified Sch Dist., 1951-55, Costa Mesa (Calif.) Sch. Dist., 1955-56, Long Beach (Calif.) Sch. Dist., 1956-58, 62-87, 90-92; ret. Author: Why Janey Can't Teach, 2001. Mem. Phi Kappa Phi, Ret. Tchrs. Assn., UCLA Alumni Assn., Planetary Soc. (charter), Red Hat Soc., Mus. of Tolerance. Avocations: theater, travel. Address: PO Box 13053 Long Beach CA 90803-8053 Personal E-mail: jwilli5687@aol.com.

FLEMING, JUANITA WILSON, nursing educator, academic administrator; BS, Hampton Inst., 1957; MA, U. Chgo., 1959; PhD, Cath. U. Am., 1969; D Pub. Svc., Berea Coll., 1994. From staff nurse to head nurse med.-surg. pediat. unit Children's Hosp., Washington, 1957-58; pub. health nurse Bur. Pub. Health Nursing, 1959-60; instr. nursing children Sch. Nursing Freedmen's Hosp., Washington, 1962-65; cons. pub. health nursing dept. pediat. Child Devel. Clin., Howard U., 1965-66; from asst. prof. to assoc. prof. U. Ky. Coll. Nursing, Lexington, 1969-73; prof. U. Ky., Lexington, 1973—, spl. asst. to pres. for acad. affairs, 1991—2001, prof. emeritus, 2001—06; provost v.p. acad. affairs Ky. State U., Frankfort, 2003—. Mem. grad. faculty Coll. Nursing, U. Ky, 1971—, asst. dean grad. edn., 1975-81, assoc. dean, dir. grad. edn., 1982-86; prof. Coll. Edn. Edpt. Edn. Policy Studies and Evaln., 1979—; assoc. vice-chancellor acad. affairs Med. Ctr., 1984-91; prin. investigator nursing care high risk infants State Maternal and Child Health Divsn., 1972; project dir. advanced nurse tng. grant divsn. nursing Dept. Health Edn. and Welfare, 1977-80, prin. investigator high tech home care chronically ill children Bur. Maternal Child Health, 1989-93; prin. investigator healthcare and devel. status Children and Their Families MIRT Fogarty Ctr., 2001-2002; vis. prof. Case We. Res. U., Cleve., 1984, West Chester U., 1997; Martin Luther King/Rosa Parks/Cesar Chavez vis. prof. U. Mich., Ann Arbor, 1989, Elizabeth Carnegie endowed vis. prof. Howard U., 1995; Houston Endowed Minority Health and Rsch. Disting. vis. prof. Prairie View U., 1998; prin. investigator Am. Nurses Found., 1970-71; Faville lectr. Wayne State U., 1998. Recipient Ky. Nurses Assn. award, Marion E. McKenna leadership award, 1988, Disting. Svc. award ANA, 1994; Olhson scholar U. Ill., 1999, Robert A. Zumwinkle Student Rights award U. Ky. Student Govt. Assn., 2001, U. Ky. Pres. Diversity award, 2004, Diversity award, U. Ky. Inst. Medicine, 2005; named Living Legend, Am. Acad. Nursing, 2004, U. Ky. Sch. Pub. Health Hall of Fame, 2006. Mem.: NAS, Ky. Inst. Medicine, Inst. Medicine. Office: Provost Ky State Univ Frankfort KY 40601 Office Phone: 502-597-6395. Business E-Mail: juanita.fleming@kysu.edu.

FLEMING, LEE VIRGINIA, writer, art critic, curator; b. Phila., Jan. 26, 1952; d. Ralph Daniel and Helen Haymond (Wolfe) F. B.A. in English Lit., Yale U., 1972; M.A. in English Lit., U. Toronto, 1974. Visual arts editor Washington Rev., 1979—; Washington corr. ARTnews, N.Y.C., 1982—, Washingtonian, 1980—; galleries art critic, Washington Post; writer Washington Art Review; freelance writer; contbr. Beaux Arts mag., Paris, Smithsonian Mag., Images & Issues, 1980—; reporter visual arts Nat. Pub. Radio (WAMV) morning edit., Washington, 1985, WETA TV show 'Around Town"; curator, organizer, cons., lectr. to schs. and mus. including R.I. Sch. Design, Corcoran Sch. Art, Balt. Mus., Md. Inst., Washington Project for Arts, Md. Art Place, 1979. Author: Someone Special, 1983. Scriptwriter for performance arts, 1981. Author art catalogues, 1981. Contbr. articles and revs. to numerous cultural publs. D.C. Commn. Arts fellow, 1981, 84; UCross Found. resident, 1985. Mem. Washington Rev. of Arts (trustee 1980-85, sec. 1981). Club: Elizabethan (Yale U.). Home and Office: 1924 Park Rd NW Washington DC 20010-1021 Address: WETA TV 2775 S Quincy St Arlington VA 22206

FLEMING, MARGARET A., adoption advocate, adoption service director; 5 children. Former teacher, substance abuse counselor, clin. social worker; founder, dir. Adoption-Link, Chgo., 1993—; founder, co-dir. Chances by Choice, Chgo., 2002—. Named one of Chicago's 100 Most Influential Women, Crain's Chicago Business mag., 2004. Office: Adoption Link Inc 1113 South Blvd # W2 Oak Park IL 60302-2840

FLEMING, MARION PARKER, education educator; b. Branchville, Va., Aug. 19, 1931; d. Theodore Roosevelt and Theresa Harris Parker; m. LeRoy Fleming, July 18, 1954; children: Cheryl, Patricia Sapp, Sandra. BS, Hampton Inst., Va., 1952; MA, Hofstra U., Hempstead, NY, 1968. Cert. adminstr. NY. Tchr. Huntington HS, Newport News, Va., 1952—55, US Army Edn. Ctr., Straubing, Germany, 1957—58, IC Norcom HS, Portsmouth, Va., 1958—59, North Jr. HS, Brentwood, NY, 1961—65, Roosevelt Jr.-Sr. HS, NY, 1965—68, chmn. English dept., 1969—82, adminstrv. supr., 1983—87, asst. prin., 1987—90; prof. Five Towns Coll., Dix Hills, NY, 1990—99, Nassau CC, Garden City, NY, 1999—. Organizer, facilitator Awakenings civil rights program, 2002—05. Named Outstanding Educator, Roosevelt Sch. Dist., Most Amazing Vol., AARP, Nassau County, 2005; recipient Sojourner Truth award, Bus. and Profl. Women's Club, Ednl. award, NAACP, Cmty. Svc. award, 100 Black Women, Garden City, 2005, NY State United Tchrs., 2006. Mem.: LWV (chmn. voter svcs. 2003—), Nat. Coun. Tchrs. English, Alpha Kappa Alpha. Avocations: reading, travel, gardening, scrapbooks. Home: 91 Nassau Pkwy Hempstead NY 11550

FLEMING, MARJORIE FOSTER, freelance writer, artist; b. Phila., Sept. 12, 1920; d. Major Bronson and Helen Margaret (Vertner) Foster; m. John Joseph Hundermark, Sept. 24, 1949 (div. Sept. 1955); children: John Foster Hundermark, David Laurence Hundermark; m. Paul Stewart Fleming, May 6, 1961. BA, Ursinus Coll., 1942; studied painting with Morris Blackburn, Pa. Acad. Fine Arts and Cheltenham Ctr. for Arts; with Robert Goldman, Cheltenham Twp. Ctr. Arts; studied painting with Paul Wieghardt, Chgo. Art Inst. and Cheltenham Twp. Ctr. for Arts. Cert. tchr. Cost acct. Philco Corp., Phila., 1942-43; asst. bank auditor Liberty Title and Trust, Phila., 1943-44; asst. dept. spl. events Phila. Evening Bulletin, 1945-47; asst. stage TV and radio show prodr. Phila., 1947-49. Appeared on Wit's End (live pilot TV show), 1948, guest Poetry Today, Sta. WRTN radio, N.Y.C., 1997. Author: Whispers of Escaped Thoughts, 2003; Whispers of Escaped Thoughts, 2003; contbr. poetry to local newspapers. Vol. occupl. therapist ARC; spl. duty hostess for Purple Heart and Stage Door Canteen, WWII. Mem. Internat. Poetry Mus., Internat. Libr. Poetry, Internat. Soc. Poets (inducted into Hall of Fame Mus.), Poetry Guild, Am. Diabetes Assn., Cheltenham Ctr. Arts, Kappa Chi Delta, Omega Chi. Republican. Methodist. Avocations: sculpture, photography, creative needlework, pianist, collecting sheet music, art, creative writing. Home: 82 Holly Dr Crystal Lake IL 60014-5022

FLEMING, PATRICIA STUBBS (PATSY FLEMING), artist; b. Phila., Mar. 17, 1936; d. Fredrick Douglass Stubbs and Marion Turner Stubbs Thomas; m. Harold S. Fleming, June 1958 (div. Feb. 1971); children: Douglass, Craig, Gordon. BA, Vassar Coll., 1957; postgrad., NYU, 1958-60, U. Pa., 1957-58, Pa. Acad. Fine Arts, 1957-58. Legis. asst. to reps. U.S. Ho. of Reps., Washington, 1971-77; asst. to sec. HEW, Washington, 1977-78, dir. intergovtl. and legis. affairs Office Civil Rights, 1979-80; asst. to sec. U.S. Dept. Edn., Washington, 1979-80, dep. asst. sec. legis., 1980-81; sr. pub. policy assoc. James H. Lowry & Assocs., Washington, 1981-83; chief staff Rep. Ted Weiss U.S. Ho. of Reps., Washington, 1983-86, profl. staff mem. subcom. human resources & intergovtl. rels, 1986-93; spl. asst. to sec. HHS, Washington, 1993-94; dir. Office Nat. AIDS Policy The White House, Washington, 1994-97, cons. on govt. rels. and AIDS policy and programs, 1997—2000; freelance artist Bethesda, Md., 2006—. Washington rep. Joint Co-sponsored UN Programme on HIV/AIDS, 1997-99; mem. bd. Prevention Works: Needle Exch. Program in the Nation's Capitol. One-person shows include NYU, Foundry Gallery, Washington, Anne C. Fisher Gallery, Washington; exhbns. include NYC, Washington and St. Petersberg, Russia, New Delhi, Cairo and numerous others. Democrat. Episcopalian. Avocations: travel, music, reading. Home and Studio: 6009 Massachusetts Ave Bethesda MD 20816-2041 Office Phone: 301-320-5420. E-mail: pfleming@erols.com.

FLEMING, RENÉE L., opera singer; b. Indiana, Pa., Feb. 14, 1959; d. Edwin Davis Fleming and Patricia (Seymour) Alexander; m. Richard Lee Ross, Sept. 23, 1989 (div. 2000). BM in Music Edn., Potsdam State U., 1981; MM, Eastman Sch. Music, 1983; student, Juilliard Am. Opera Ctr., N.Y.C., 1983—84, Juilliard Am. Opera Ctr., 1985—87; PhD (hon.), Juilliard, 2003. Exclusive rec. artist Decca Records, London, 1995—. Debut engagements include Spoleto Festival, Charleston and Italy, 1986-90, Houston Grand Opera & N.Y.C. Opera, 1988, 89, San Francisco Opera, 1991, Met. Opera, Paris Opera at the Bastille, 1991, Covent Garden, London, 1989, Teatro Colon Buenos Aires, 1991, Vienna State Opera, 1993, La Scala, 1993, Lyric Opera of Chgo., 1993, Paris Opera at Palais Garnier, 1996; author: The Inner Voice (also German, Japanese, French and U.K. publs.), 2004. Bd. trustees Carnegie Hall Corp., 2004—; mem. adv. bd. White Nights Found. Am., 2005—, Louise T. Blouin Found., 2005—. Decorated Chevalier de la Légion d'Honneur, 2005; winner Met. Opera Nat. Auditions, 1988; recipient George London prize, 1988, Richard Tucker award, 1990, Solti prize l'Acad. du Disque Lyrique, 1996, Prix Maria Callas, Academie due Disque Lyrique, 1997, Prize l'Acad. du Disque Lyrique, 1998, Lotos Medal of Merit, 2005; Fulbright scholar, Frankfurt, Germany, 1984-85, Classical Brits award for outstanding contbn. to music, 2004; named Vocalist of Yr. Mus. Am., 1997, Female Artist of the Yr., Classic Brits Awards, 2003, Prix Maria Callas, Acad. du Disque Lyrique, 2005; nominated 9 Grammy awards, 1997-2006; recipient 2 Grammy awards, 1999, 2003; 3 gramophone awards, 1999, Record of yr., Opera award, Recital award, Gift of Music award Orch. of St. Luke's, 2000; named one of top 10 classical singers of the 90s, AP, 2000; La Diva Renée dessert named in her honor by chef Daniel Boulud, 1999; Commandeur de l'Ordre des Arts et des Lettres, France, 2002; Renee Fleming iris introduced, 2004. Mem.: Royal Acad. Music (hon.). Office: care ML Falcone Pub Rels 155 W 68th St Apt 1114 New York NY 10023-5817

FLEMING, RHONDA, actress, singer; b. L.A. d. Harold Cheverton and Effie (Graham) Louis; m. Darol W. Carlson; 1 child, Kent Lane. Student, pub. and pvt. schs., L.A., Beverly Hills. Appeared in 40 motion pictures, including Spellbound, 1945, Spiral Staircase, 1945, Out of the Past, 1947, A Connecticut Yankee in King Arthur's Court, 1949, The Great Lover, 1949, The Eagle and the Hawk, 1950, Cry Danger, 1951, Last Outpost, 1951, Hong Kong, 1952, Tropic Zone, 1953, Tennessee's Partner, 1955, Gunfight at OK Corral, 1956, Slightly Scarlett, 1956, Home Before Dark, 1958, Pony Express, 1953, The Nude Bomb, 1980; Broadway debut in The Women, 1973; appeared in musical and plays, including The Boyfriend, 1975, Marriage Go Round, 1960, Bell, Book and Candle, 1962, Kismet at Music Center, 1976; sang Gershwin concert in; 10-week tour, 1963; starred in Las Vegas, Nev., 1959, one-woman concert at Hollywood Bowl, 1964, numerous guest appearances on TV series and talk shows including MacMillan and Wife, Love Boat; TV movies include The Last Hours Before Morning, 1975; NBC's Legends of the Screen, 1980, Metromedia Spl. Road to Hollywood, 1983, Wildest West Show of the Stars, 1986. Founder Rhonda Fleming Mann Clinic and Resource Ctr. for Women's Comprehensive Care at UCLA, PATH (People Assisting the Homeless) Rhonda Fleming Family Ctr.; benefactor Music Ctr.; supporter Childhelp USA, Achievement Rewards Coll. Scientists; life assoc. Pepperdine U.; founding mem. French Found. for Alzheimer Rsch.; adv. bd. Olive Crest Treatment Ctrs. for Abused Children; supporter Freedoms Found. at Valley Forge, City of Hope, Excellence in Media, SPCA, Humane Soc. USA; patron of the arts Music Ctr. Blue Ribbon; bd. dirs. World Opportunities Internat., St. John's Med. Ctr.; mem. nat. adv. cabinet Guideposts. Recipient award NCCJ, Gold Angel award Excellence in Media, Woman of the World award Childhelp, USA, Eve award Mannequins of the Assistance League, 1986, Our Lady of Perpetual Inspiration award; named Woman of Year City of Hope, Oper. Children, 1991, honoree of the Music Ctr. Club 100, 1992, UCLA Alumni Assn. Disting. Contbns. award to UCLA Cmty., 2000; Rhonda Fleming Rsch. fellowship for women's cancer established at City of Hope, 2000.

FLEMING, SUZANNE MARIE, academic administrator, freelance/self-employed writer; b. Detroit, Feb. 4, 1927; d. Albert T. and Rose E. (Smiley) F. BS, Marygrove Coll., 1957; MS, U. Mich., 1960, PhD, 1963. Joined Congregation of Sisters Servants of Immaculate Heart of Mary, Roman Catholic Commn., 1945. Chmn. natural sci. div. Marygrove Coll., Detroit, 1970-75, v.p., dean, 1975-78, acad. v.p., 1978-80; asst. v.p. acad. affairs Eastern Mich. U., Ypsilanti, 1980-82, acting assoc. v.p. acad. affairs, 1982-83; provost, acad. v.p. Western Ill. U., Macomb, 1983-86; vice chancellor U. Wis., Eau Claire, 1986-89; freelance writer, 1989—. Vis. scholar U. Mich., 1989-2001; pres. Mich. Coll. Chemistry Tchrs. Assn., 1975; councilor Mich. Inst. Chemists, 1973-77; bd. dirs. Nat. Ctr. for Rsch. to Improve Postsecondary Teaching and Learning, 1988-90. Contbr. articles to profl. pubs. NIH rsch. grantee, 1966—69. Home and Office: 2888 Cascade Dr Ann Arbor MI 48104-6659

FLESHER, GAIL A., lawyer; b. 1960; BA, Wharton Sch., U. Pa., 1983; JD, Hastings Coll. Law, 1988. Bar: N.Y. 1989, Conn. 1989. Assoc. Davis, Polk & Wardwell, N.Y.C., 1988—96, pntr., 1996—, hiring ptnr. & mem. firm recruitment com. Mem.: NALP Found. Law Career Research & Edn. (chmn. 2000—02, bd. trustees 1992—), ABA. Office: Davis Polk & Wardwell 450 Lexington Ave New York NY 10017 Office Phone: 212-450-4469. Office Fax: 212-450-3469. Business E-Mail: gail.flesher@dpw.com.

FLESHER, MARGARET COVINGTON, communications consultant, writer; b. San Angelo, Tex., July 29, 1944; d. Charles C. and Helen Irene (Little) F.; m. Alexander Ribaroff, Dec. 11, 1976 (div. June 1988). BA in Polit. Sci., Vassar Coll., 1966. Assoc. editor Harcourt Brace Inc., N.Y.C., 1966-74; prodr. Guidance Assocs. subsidiary of Harcourt Brace, N.Y.C., 1974-76; freelance writer, editor London, 1976-81; sr. editor Franklin Watts, Inc., N.Y.C., 1981-85; pres. The Westport (Conn.) Pub. Group, 1985-89; coord. cmty. rels. Texaco Inc., White Plains, N.Y., 1989-91, sr. coord. media rels., 1991-93, contbg. editor, 1993-97; pursuit. cons. Deloitte & Touche, Wilton, Conn., 1998—2005, sr. mgr. strategic client svcs. devel. group, 2005—. Author: Mexico and the United States Today: Issues Between Neighbors, 1985, New Leaves: A Journal for the Suddenly Single, 1987. Mem.: Internat. Women's Writing Guild, Fairfield County Pub. Rels. Assn. (bd. dirs. 1991—92), The Assn. for Women in Comm. (Fairfield County chpt. pres. 1986—88, v.p. profl. devel. 1994—95, Westchester chpt. bd. dirs., Clarion award 1995), Conn. Women's Forum (chair comm. com., sec. 2003—06), Conn. Press Club (v.p. programs 1998—99). Avocations: hiking, yoga, photography, gardening. Office: Deloitte & Touche 10 Westport Rd Wilton CT 06897-4522

FLESKES, CAROL LYNN, environmental engineer; b. Yakima, Wash., Aug. 4, 1946; d. Victor Leo and Margaret Ann (O'Neill) Rabung; m. Hubert William Fleskes, Oct. 24, 1972; children: Susan Carol, Brett William. BSCE, U. Wash., 1969. Registered profl. engr., Wash., Oreg., Calif. City engr. City of Albany, Oreg., 1970-72; design engr. John Sharrah & Assocs., Red Bluff, Calif., 1973-74; solid waste engr. Butte Co., Oroville, Calif., 1974-75; project engr. Ringel & Assocs., Oroville, 1975-77; environ. engr. Wash. Dept. Ecology, Olympia, 1978-88, program mgr. toxic cleanup program, 1988-94, program mgr. water resources, 1994-97, adminstrv. svcs. mgr., 1997—. Bd. mem Bd. of Registration for Profl. Engrs. and Land Surveyors, 1993-2003; chair Town of Bucoda (Wash.) Planning Commn., 1983-93; vol. firefighter Town of Bucoda, 1978-85; emergency med. technician Town of Bucoda Fire Dept., 1979-83. Recipient Disting. Mgrs. award Gov. of Wash., 1991. Mem. NSPE, Wash. Soc. Profl. Engrs. (Environ. Engr. of Yr. award 1991). Avocations: camping, crafts. Home: 502 S Wright St Bucoda WA 98530 Office: Wash Dept Ecology PO Box 47600 Olympia WA 98504-7600 Fax: (360) 407-6989. E-mail: cfle461@ecy.wa.gov.

FLETCHALL, SANDRA KAY, occupational therapist; b. Aug. 18, 1952; BS in Occupl. Therapy, U. Mo., 1974; M in Pub. Health Adminstr., U. Memphis, 1982. Dir. U. Tenn. Med. Group, Memphis, 1987-93; cert. hand therapist Hand & Rehab. Splsts., Greensboro, N.C., 1994; sr. therapist Spicer Contract Svcs., Memphis, 1995-98; owner, therapist Functions by Fletchall, Memphis, 1998—. Apptd. clin. faculty occupl. and phys. therapy U. Tenn., Memphis, 1996—. Prodr. (video) Functional I Will Be, 1999, When I'm Back on My Feet, 1999; contbr. articles to profl. jours. Recipient Award of Excellence Tenn. Occupl. Therapy Assn., 1999, Recognition of Achievement award for advancing occupl. therapy in burn, prosthetic rehab. Am. Occupl. Therapy Assn., 2000. Home: 7180 Helene Dr Millington TN 38053-4753

FLETCHER, (MARTHA) ANN MESSERSMITH, retired counselor, educator; b. Indpls., June 9, 1935; d. Lloyd Lowell and Fae Elizabeth (Houston) Messersmith; m. Lindsay Bruce Smith, Dec. 28, 1957 (div. 1974); children: Montgomery Bruce, Jean Elizabeth; m. Robert Rolph Fletcher, May 16, 1976; 1 dau., Nancy Roberta. B.A., DePauw U., 1956; M.Ed., U. Houston, 1967. Cert. tchr., Tex., Ind.; lic., cert. profl. counselor, Tex.; cert. mediator; lic. family mediator. Coordinator elem. phys. edn. programs Cities of Clarendon Hills and Hinsdale (Ill.), 1957-61; tchr., speech therapist Tex. Sch. for Cerebral Palsied, Galveston, 1961-64; developer, dir. social services Moody House, Galveston, 1962-67; missionary Global Missions Methodist Ch., LaPaz, Bolivia, 1968-74; coordinator, instr., trainer ednl. paraprofls. program Mountain View Coll., Dallas, 1974-82, counselor, 1982-2006; marriage enrichment workshops, Africa, U.S., Nepal, Tonga, Philippines, Can., 2000—. Recipient Innovator of Yr. award, 1982, Student Devel. award, 1995. Mem. adv. bd. Dallas C.C., Ministry; tchr., advisor Highland Park United Meth. Ch. Mem. Tex. Educators Ednl. Paraprofls. (state dir. 1982-83). Contbr. articles to profl. jours. Home: 6112 E Lovers Ln Dallas TX 75214-2028 Personal E-mail: amf6320@sbcglobal.net.

FLETCHER, BETTY BINNS, federal judge; b. Tacoma, Mar. 29, 1923; BA, Stanford U., 1943; LLB, U. Wash., 1956. Bar: Wash. 1956. Mem. firm Preston, Thorgrimson, Ellis, Holman & Fletcher, Seattle, 1956—79; judge U.S. Ct. Appeals (9th cir.), Seattle, 1979—, sr. judge, 1998—. Mem.: ABA (Margaret Brent award 1992), Fed. Judges Assn. (past pres.), Am. Law Inst., Wash. State Bar Assn., Phi Beta Kappa, Order of Coif. Office: US Ct Appeals 9th Cir 1200 6th Ave 21st Fl Seattle WA 98101*

FLETCHER, CARRIE J., lawyer; BA in Polit. Sci., with distinction, U. Mich., 1993, JD, 1995. Bar: Ill. 1996, US Dist. Ct. (No. Dist. Ill.) 1996, Mass. 1999, US Dist. Ct. (Dist. Mass.) 1999. Assoc. Epstein Becker & Green PC; sr. counsel Gen. Comml. Litig. Practice Group Foley & Lardner LLP, Boston. Mem.: Women's Bar Assn., Ill. State Bar Assn., Mass. Bar Assn. Office: Foleg & Lardner LLP 111 Huntington Ave Boston MA 02199 Office Phone: 617-342-4066. Office Fax: 617-342-4001. E-mail: cfletcher@foley.com.*

FLETCHER, DENISE KOEN, strategic and financial consultant; b. Istanbul, Turkey, Aug. 31, 1948; came to U.S., 1967, naturalized, 1976; d. Moris and Kety (Barkey) Koen; m. Robert B. Fletcher, Nov. 11, 1969; children— David, Kate. AB (Coll. scholar), Wellesley Coll., 1969; M in City Planning, Harvard U., 1972. Analyst Ea. div. Getty Oil Co., N.Y.C., 1972-73, sr. analyst, 1973-74, cash mgmt. and bldg. supr., 1974-76, Getty Oil Co. (Eastern), 1976; asst. treas. N.Y. Times Co., N.Y.C., 1976-80, treas., 1980-88; pres. Fletcher Assocs. Inc., Larchmont, NY, 1988-96; CEO Comm. Venture Group, Ltd., N.Y.C., NY, 1989-90; v.p., CFO Bowne & Co., 1996-98, sr. v.p., CFO, 1998—2000; exec. v.p., CFO Mastercard, 2000—03; sr. v.p., CFO Davita, Inc., 2004—05; CFO, exec. v.p. fin. Vulcan Inc., 2005—. Bd. dirs. Unisys Corp. Bd. dirs. Overseas Edn. Found. Internat., 1989-90, Boy Scouts Am., Exploring, 1991-93; bd. dirs., trustee and v.p. bd. dirs., exec. com. YWCA, N.Y., 1987-2002, Girl Scouts USA, 2000-02; mem. budget com. City of Larchmont, N.Y., 1981-83, chmn. zoning bd. appeals, 1987—, mem. selection com., 1985-87; mem. alumni exec. coun. Harvard U. Sch. Govt., 1982-87. Mellon scholar, 1970 Mem. Academy of Women Achievers, The Business Leadership Coun., Fin. Execs. Internat., Fin. Women's Assn., Women's Forum, Treasurers Club N.Y., Harvard Club (N.Y.C.), Phi Beta Kappa.

FLETCHER, DONNA ANGELLA, secondary school educator; b. Spanish Town, St. Catherine, Jamaica, Jan. 17, 1973; d. Melvin Fletcher and Beverly Vinnetta Thaxter, Cebert Glenn (Stepfather) and Audrey Fletcher (Stepmother). BA, SUNY, Stony Brook, 1995; MA, EdM, Columbia U., NYC, 2000. Cert. 7-12 English tchr. NY, 1999, 7-12 social studies tchr. NY, 2003. Classroom tchr. NYC Bd. of Edn., 1997—2004; mentor tchr. NYC Dept. of Edn., 2004—. Home instrn. tchr. NYC Bd. of Edn., NYC, 2000—04. Mem. Rainbow PUSH Coalition, NYC, 2005—06; master guide, tchr. Adventist Youth/Pathfinder, Bronx, NY, 2001—03; mem. Faithful Youth Challengers, Roosevelt, NY, 2003—06. Mem.: Nat. Coun. Social Studies, Nat. Coun. Tchrs. English, Schomburg Ctr., Kappa Delta Pi. Democrat. Seventh Day Adventist. Avocations: writing, reading, travel, opera, theater. Home: 276 Tudor St Waterbury CT 06704 Office: NYC Dept Edn Brooklyn NY 11201 Personal E-mail: dnnfletcher@aol.com.

FLETCHER, DOROTHY JEAN, hospital administrator, educator; b. Cleve., May 14, 1932; d. Melvin Albert Heidloff and Dorothy Florence Geiger; m. Archibald Eaton Fletcher, Jr., Oct. 9, 1932; children: David Jeffrey, Sally, Thomas Eaton. Degree in Nursing, St. Luke's Hosp., Cleve., 1953; BS in Health Studies, Barat Coll., Lake Forest, Ill., 1981; MA in Human Resource Devel., Webster U., St. Louis, 1986. RN Ill., cert. addictions counselor, Ill., addictions nurse, Ill.; ordained Presbyn. Ch., 1999. From staff nurse to discharge planning RN Ctrl. DuPage Hosp., Winfield, Ill., 1972—75, discharge planning RN, 1975—76; dir. nursing Nursing Home, Waukegan, Ill., 1981—82; from staff nurse to case mgr. behavioral svcs. Highland Pk. Hosp., Ill., 1982—94, case mgr. behavioral svcs., 1992—94. Mem. long range planning com. Sch. Dist. 65, Lake Bluff, 2003—. Vol. Lake County Forest Preserves, Ill., 1994—97; elder Presbyn. Ch., Lake Forest, 1999, chmn. program, 1995—2003; bd. dirs. Lake Bluff Libr., Ill., 1985—90. Recipient Outstanding Alumni award, Barat Coll., 2003, Mother Burke award, 2003. Mem.: LWV (chmn. voting com. 2004—05), Shields Township Dems. (observer sch. dist. voting 2002—), Lake Forest Lake Bluff Arts (assoc.), Botanic Gardens (docent 1995—). Democrat. Presbyn. Avocations: history, genealogy, reading, baseball, gardening. Home: 323 Park Ln Lake Bluff IL 60044

FLETCHER, JEAN STOUT, retired special education educator; b. Abington, Pa., July 18, 1935; d. H. Stratton and Margaret Engle (Slaughter) Stout; m. Alan J. Fletcher, Aug. 23, 1958; children: Bruce Alan, Lynne Margaret O'Brien, Amy Jean Eichhorst. BS, Beaver Coll., 1957; postgrad., U. R.I., 1957; MA, Montclair State Coll., 1976. Cert. tchr. regular edn.K-8, spl. edn. ages 3-21, learning disability tchr. cons. 4th grade tchr. Glenside (Pa.) Elem. Sch., 1957-58; 1st grade tchr. Mt. Pleasant Elem. Sch., West Orange, N.J., 1958-60; supplemental instr. Riker Hill Elem. Sch., Livingston, N.J., 1969-73, 2d grade tchr., 1973-75; 4th grade tchr. Lake Hiawatha Elem. Sch., Parsippany, N.J., 1975-76, intermediate neurologically impaired tchr., 1976-82; perceptually impaired tchr. Brooklawn Jr. High Sch., Parsippany, 1982-86, Cen. Jr. High Sch., Parsippany, 1986-88; 6th grade resource tchr. Cen. Middle Sch., Parsippany, 1988—2000; ret., 2000. Sci. standing com. mem. Parsippany Sch. Dist., 1976-82, on-site mgmt. com., 1990-91; bd. dirs. Vista Info. Group, Inc., Morristown, N.J.; rep. to Par-Troy Hill Curriculum Planning Com., Ctrl. Mid. Sch., 1993-95. Pres. Livingston Womens Club, 1972-74; co-campaign mgr. Town Coun. Campaign, Livingston, 1972; dist. commr. Am. Cancer Soc., Basking Ridge, N.J., 1988-92; solicitor March of Dimes, 1994; vol. YMCA, Somerset Hills, 1993-96, fundraiser office of advancement Arcadia U., 2000—, Paige Whitney Babies Ctr., Basking, N.J., 2002—, North Collier Hosp., Naples, 2005—. Recipient Tchr. of Yr., Parsippany Troy Hills award, 2000, Alumni award for outstanding svc., Arcadia U., 2002. Mem. NEA, N.J. Edn. Assn., Parsippany/Troy Hills Edn. Assn., Beaver Coll. Alumni Assn. (dir. No. N.J. chpt., recruiter, coll. night rep. 1988—), Morris County Ret. Educators Assn., Montville Rep. Club, Friends of the Libr., Alpha Delta Kappa (Mu chpt. treas. 1990-92, budget chmn., corr. sec. 1994—). Presbyterian. Home (Summer): 54 Eugene Dr Montville NJ 07045-9193 Office: Central Middle Sch Rt 46 Parsippany NJ 07054 Home (Winter): 1680 Winding Oaks Way 202 Naples FL

FLETCHER, KEYANA JAMES, small business owner, performing company executive; b. New Orleans, Dec. 11, 1977; d. John David and Joyce Hardy James; m. Gregory Michael Fletcher, Oct. 27, 2001; children: Kingsley Jordan children: Joshua Gregory. BFA, Howard U., Washington, 2000. Owner and dir. Dance Upon A Dream Studios, Potomac, Md., 1995—. Co-founder, bd. dirs. Petite Soc. Washington, Bethesda, Md., 2002—04. Office: PO Box 6268 Washington DC 20015 Office Phone: 202-545-0976. E-mail: danceuponadream@hotmail.com.

FLETCHER, LOUISE, actress; b. Birmingham, Ala., 1936; d. Robert Capers F. BA, U. N.C., 1957; student acting with Jeff Corey; LHD (hon.), Gallaudet U., 1982, Western Md. Coll., 1986. Films include Thieves Like Us, 1973, Russian Roulette, 1974, One Flew Over the Cuckoo's Nest, 1975 (Acad. award as best actress), Exorcist II: The Heretic, 1976, The Cheap Detective, 1977, The Magician, 1978, Natural Enemies, 1979, The Lucky Star, 1979, The Lady in Red, 1979, Strange Behavior, 1980, Brainstorm, 1981, Strange Invaders, 1982, Once Upon a Time in America, 1982, Firestarter, 1983, Overnight Sensation, 1983, Invaders from Mars, 1985, The Boy Who Could Fly, 1985, Nobody's Fool, 1986, Flowers in the Attic, 1987, Two Moon Junction, 1987, Blue Steel, 1988, Best of the Best, 1989, Shadowzone, 1989, Blind Vision, 1990, The Player, 1991, Return to Two Moon Junction, 1993, Tollbooth, 1993, Virtuosity, 1995, Mulholland Falls, 1995, 2 Days in the Valley, 1995, Edie & Pen, 1995, High School High, 1995, Girl Gets Moe, 1996, Heartless, 1996, Love Kills, 1998, A Map of the World, 1999, More Dogs than Bones, 1999, Cruel Inventions, 1999, Time Served, 1999, Very Mean Men, 2000, Silver Man, 2000, Seeing in the Dark, 2000, Big Eden, 2000; TV appearances include Maverick, Wagon Train, The Law-Man, Playhouse 90, The Millionaire, Alfred Hitchcock, Thou Shalt Not Commit Adultery, 1978, A Summer to Remember, 1984, Island, 1984, Second Serve, 1985, Hoover, 1986, The Karen Carpenter Story, 1988, Nightmare on the 13th Floor, 1988, Twilight Zone, 1988, Final Notice, 1989, The Hitchhiker, 1990, Tales from the Crypt, 1991, In a Child's Name, 1991, Boys of Twilight, 1991, The Fire Next Time, 1992, Civil Wars, 1993, Deep Space Nine, 1994, 95, 96, 97, 98, 99, The Hawunting of Cliff House, Dream On, 1994, Someone Else's Child, 1994, VR5, 1994, 95, Picket Fences, 1996, Stepford Husbands, 1996, Twisted Path, 1997, Breastmen, 1997, Married to a Stranger, 1997, Profiler, 1997, The Practice, 1998, Brimstone, 1998, Devil's Arithmetic, 1999. Bd. dirs. Deafness Rsch. Found., 1980—. Mem. Nat. Inst. Deafness and Other Communicable Disorders (adv. bd.).

FLETCHER, MARIS, literature educator; b. Ark., Aug. 10; d. C. W. and Annie Tolbert; m. Orville Fletcher; children: Ken, Mark. MA in English, Sul Ross State U., 1980; MA in Comp. Lit., U. Ark., 1995, PhD in Comp. Lit., 1996. Instr. for master gardeners. Instr. U. Ozarks, Clarksville, Ark., 1980—90, U. Ark., Fayetteville, Ark., 1990—97; assoc. prof. Ark. State U., Beebe, Ark., 1997—, tchr. French and humanities, travel coord., dir. cultural film svcs. Instr. Upward Bound, Fayetteville, 1990—97. Contbr. columns in newspapers. Judge White County Creative Writers, Searcy, Ark., 1998—. Methodist. Avocation: gardening. Office: Ark State Univ 1000 Iowa St Beebe AR 72012 Home: 221 N Cypress Beebe AR 72012 Office Phone: 501-882-8321. E-mail: mjfletcher@asub.edu.

FLETCHER, MARJORIE AMOS, librarian; b. Easton, Pa., July 10, 1923; d. Alexander Robert and Margaret Ashton (Arnold) Amos; A.B., Bryn Mawr Coll., 1946; m. Charles Mann Fletcher, May 14, 1949; children: Robert Amos, Elizabeth Ashton, Anne Kennard. Asst. to dir. rsch., then rsch. asst. to pres. Penn Mut. Life Ins. Co., 1946-49; officer A.R. Amos Co., Phila., 1949-66; part-time tchr., 1965-68; librarian Am. Coll., Bryn Mawr, Pa., 1968-77, archivist, 1973—, dir. oral history collection, 1975—, lectr. on archives, 1975—, asst. prof. edn., 1973-87, dir. archives and oral history, 1977—; curator art collection Am. Coll., 1981-; pres. pub. rels. MAF Enterprises, 1987—. Author articles in field. Recipient awards Phila. Flower Show, 1965—; bd. dirs. Emergency Aid Found. Mem. Spl. Librs. Assn. (pres. Phila. 1977-78), Soc. Am. Archivists (chairperson oral history sect. 1981-87, award of merit 1987), Oral History Assn., Hist. Soc. Pa., U.S. Pony Club, D.A.R., Nat. Soc. Colonial Dames in Commonwealth of Pa., Emergency Aid Pa. Found., Phila. Skating Club, Davis Creek Yacht Club, Bridlewild Pony Club (sponsor), Bridlewild Trails Club (Gladwyne). Republican. Episcopalian. Home: 1135 Norsam Rd Gladwyne PA 19035-1419 Office: Am Coll Bryn Mawr PA 19010 Office Phone: 610-526-1452. Business E-Mail: marge.fletcher@theamericancollege.edu.

FLETCHER, MARTHA JANE, elementary school educator; b. Henderson, Tex., Mar. 12, 1951; d. Ben Hardy and Winnie B. Bearden; m. Charles Ray Fletcher, Nov. 25, 1976; children: Jennifer Kaye, Rebecca May. BS in Elem. and Secondary Edn., Stephen F. Austin State U., Tex., 1973. Elem. tchr. Jasper ISD, Tex., 1975—76; jr. high social studies tchr. Woden ISD, Tex., 1986—. Methodist. Avocations: fishing, swimming, cooking. Home: 121 Pine Nacogdoches TX 75965 Office: Woden ISD PO Box 100 Woden TX Office Phone: (936)564-7903.

FLETCHER, RITA R., social studies educator; d. Burnett VanDorn and Gertrude Cabaniss Russell. BA in History, George Mason U., 1972; M in Elem. Edn., Winthrop U., 1986. Cert. tchr. S.C., 1981. Stds./variance cost acct. Cone Mills, Carlisle, SC, 1976—81; social studies tchr. Union (S.C.) County Schs., 1981—. Pres. Union County Edn. Assn., 2002—05. Min. music Lockhart (S.C.) First Bapt. Ch., 1991—95. Named Tchr. of Yr., Achievement Academy, 2005. Mem.: NEA (assoc.), Nat. Coun. Social Studies, S.C. Edn. Assn. Democrat. Baptist. Avocations: reading, travel, music. Office Phone: 864-429-2101. E-mail: rrftchr@earthlink.net.

FLETCHER, ROBIN MARY, health facility administrator; b. Waco, Tex., May 24, 1952; d. Arthur Hale Fletcher and Bersha Pauline (King) Gardner; 1 child, Jonathon Potter. AAS in Nursing, Tarrant County Jr. Coll., 1973; B of Liberal Studies in healthcare adminstrn. summa cum laude, St. Edwards U., 1996; M of Pub. Health in Cmty. Health, U. Tex., Houston, 1997. Staff/charge RN St. Joseph Hosp., Ft. Worth, 1973-75; staff RN/asst. head nurse Tarrant County Hosp. Dist., Fort Worth, Tex., 1975-76; staff/charge RN/asst. patient care coord. Med. Plaza Hosp., Ft. Worth, 1977-80; home health nurse Upjohn Health Care and Med. Pers. Pool, Fort Worth, 1981; med. care analyst, rev. supr. and mgr., dir. rev. Tex. Med. Found., Austin, 1981-83, 84-96; TQI coord. VA North Tex. Health Care Sys., Dallas, 1998-99; project dir. Tex. Med. Found., Austin, 1999—2002, dir. physician and hosp. quality improvement, 2002—. Bd. dirs., adv. bd. for med. record program Tex. Women's U., Dallas, 1989-90. Mem. ANA, Tex. Nurses Assn., Tex. Pub. Health Assn., Am. Diabetes Assn. (bd. dirs. local chpt. 1996-98), Health Care Compliance Assn., Alpha Sigma Lambda Nat. Honor Soc. Avocations: antiques, jogging, volkssports, rollerblading, travel. Office: Tex Med Found Barton Oaks Plz Two 901 Mopac Expy S Ste 200 Austin TX 78746

FLETCHER, SUSANN (SUSANN RENEE SMITH), actress, playwright; b. Wilmington, Del., Sept. 7, 1955; d. LaVergne MaGill and Lola Mae (Seymore) Smith; life ptnr. Susan K. Jester. BS, Longwood Coll., 1977. Broadway and nat. tour theater appearances include How to Succeed in Business Without Really Trying, 1996-97, Guys and Dolls, 1995, The Goodbye Girl, 1993, Jerome Robbins' Broadway, 1988-91, My One & Only, 1986, Raggedy Ann, 1985, Do Black Patent Leather Shoes Really Reflect Up?, 1984, The Best Little Whorehouse in Texas, 1980-82; also appearances in film and TV; performer (cast albums) The Goodbye Girl, Jerome Robbins' Broadway, Do Black Patent Leather Shoes Really Reflect Up?; author, dir., choreographer (club act) Susann Fletcher in Girl!, 1986; playwright A Girl Called Dusty, 2005. Facilitator AIDS Mastery Workshop, internat., 1988—. Mem. AFTRA, SAG, Actors Equity Assn. Office: PO Box 324 Edgewater NJ 07020-0324

FLETCHER, SUZANNE WRIGHT, epidemiologist, medical educator, editor; b. Jacksonville, Fla., Nov. 14, 1940; d. Robert Dean and Helen (Selmer) Wright; m. Robert H. Fletcher; children: John Wright, Grant Selmer. BA, Swarthmore Coll., 1962; MD, Harvard Med. Sch., 1966; MSc, Johns Hopkins U., 1973. Diplomate Nat. Bd. Med. Examiners, Am. Bd. Internal Medicine. Intern Stanford (Calif.) U. Med. Ctr., 1966—67, resident, 1967—68; physician 22nd med. detachment U.S. Army, New Ulm, Germany, 1969—70; asst. prof. epidemiology and health Mc Gill U., Montreal, Canada, 1974—77, assoc. prof., 1977—78, asst. prof. medicine, 1973—78; dir. med. clinic dept. medicine NC Meml. Hosp., 1978—82; assoc. prof. medicine U. NC, 1978—83, co-chief divsn. gen. medicine and clin. epidemiology dept. medicine, 1978—86, rsch. assoc. health svcs. rsch. ctr., 1978—90, vice chmn. clin. svcs., 1981—90, prof. medicine, clin. prof. epidemiology, 1983—90, program dir. faculty devel. gen. medicine and gen. pediatrics, 1985—90, co-dir. internat. clin. epidemiology network program Rockefeller Found., 1986—90; prof. ambulatory care and prevention Harvard Med. Sch., 1994—; editor Annals of Internal Medicine, Phila., 1990—93. Adj. prof. medicine U. Pa., Phila., 1990—93, Jefferson Med. Coll., 1991—93, U. NC, 1994—; physician internal medicine; chmn. NIH Tech. Assessment Conf., 1992, Nat. Cancer Inst. Internat. Workshop, 1993; active World Bank Seminar on Preventive Strategies in Med. Edn., Hangzhou, China, 1986, Ad Hoc NCI Com. on BSE Cancer Detection Rsch. and Applications, 1986. Author: Clinical Epidemiology—The Essentials, 1982, 4t edit., 2005; contbr. chapters to books, articles to profl. jours. Named rsch. grantee, Conseil de la Recherche en Sante du Quebec, 1975—77; recipient Can. Nat. Health Rsch. Scholar award, Can. Govt., 1975—78; grantee, Health and Welfare Can., 1976—78, Robert Wood Johnson Teaching Hosp. Gen. Medicine Group Practice Program, 1980—84, Nat. Ctr. Health Scis. Rsch. and Health Tech., 1985—89, Rockefeller Found. Clin. Epidemiology Resource and Tng. Ctr., 1986—90, NIH, 1987—90, 1997—. Master: ACP (med. knowledge self assessment program 1984—85, clin. practice subcom. 1987, pub. policy subcom. 1988—89); fellow: Coll. Physicians Phila., Am. Coll. Epidemiology (bd. dirs. 1990—93, chmn. pub. com. 1992—94); mem.: APHA, Am. Bd. Internal Medicine (bd. govs. 1981—87), NCI Bd. Sci. Advisors, World Assn. Med. Editors (v.p. 1997—2001), Internat. Clin. Epidemiology Network (bd. dirs.), Inst. Medicine (coun. 1993—96, exec. com. 1993—96), Soc. Gen. Internal Medicine (counsellor 1978—81, pres.-elect 1982—83, pres. 1983—84, co-editor Jour. Gen. Internal Medicine 1984—89, mem. publs. com. 1990—, chmn. Glaser award com. 1991). Unitarian Universalist. Office: 208 Boulder Bluff Chapel Hill NC 27516 Business E-Mail: Suzanne_Fletcher@hms.harvard.edu.

FLETCHER, WINONA LEE, theater educator; b. Nov. 25, 1926; m. Joseph Grant; 1 child, Betty. BA, Johnson C. Smith U., 1947; MA, U. Iowa, 1951; PhD, Ind. U., 1968. Prof. speech and theatre Ky. State U., Frankfort, 1951-78; prof. theatre and afro-Am. studies Ind. U., Bloomington, 1978-94, prof. emeritus, 1994; assoc. dean COAS, 1981-84. Costumer, dir. summer theatre, U. Mo., Lincoln, 1952-60, 69. Sr. editor: Community Memories: A Glimpse of African American Life in Frankfort, Ky., 2003. Recipient Lifetime Achievement award, 1993; Am. Theatre fellow, 1979. Mem. Am. Theatre for Higher Edn., Black Theatre Network, Ky. Hist. Soc., Nat. Assn. Dramatic and Speech Arts, Nat. Theatre Conf., Alpha Kappa Alpha. Home: 317 Cold Harbor Dr Frankfort KY 40601-3011

FLETTNER, MARIANNE, opera administrator; b. Frankfurt, Germany, Aug. 9, 1933; d. Bernhard J. and Kaethe E. (Halbritter) F. Bus. diploma, Hessel Bus. Coll., 1953. Sec. various cos., 1953-61, Pontiac Motor Div., Burlingame, Calif., 1961-63, Met. Opera, NY, 1963-74, asst. co. mgr. NY, 1974-79; artistic adminstr. San Diego Opera, 1979—. Avocations: travel, hiking, swimming, cooking. Home: 4015 Crown Point Dr San Diego CA 92109-6270 Office: San Diego Opera 1200 Third Ave 18th Fl San Diego CA 92101-4112 Office Phone: 619-232-7636, 619-533-7004. Business E-Mail: marianne.flettner@sdopera.com.

FLEXNER, JOSEPHINE MONCURE, musician, educator; b. Marion, Va., Oct. 11, 1919; d. Walter Raleigh Daniel and Harriet Ashby (Ogburn) Moncure; m. Kurt Fisher Flexner, Dec. 20, 1942; children: Thomas Moncure, Peter Wallace. BA, Univ. Richmond, 1941; tchr. cert. in piano, Peabody Conservatory, 1945; MS in piano, Juilliard Sch. Music, 1950. Class piano tchr. Balt. Pub. Sch., 1945-46; mem. piano faculty Peabody Conservatory Prep., Balt., 1945-46, Pius X Sch. Manhatanville Coll. Sacred Heart, N.Y.C., 1946-50, Henry Street Settlement Sch., N.Y.C., 1949-50; piano tchr. Bronxville, N.Y., 1950-54; mem. piano faculty Rhodes Coll., Memphis, Tenn., 1970-82; piano tchr. St. Mary's Episcopal Sch., Memphis, 1982-87. Judge for Tenn. piano auditions, 1980—85; judge Tenn. Nat. Guild Auditions, 1983—84. Contbr. articles to profl. jours. Den mother Boy Scouts Am., 1963-65, vice chmn., 1964-65; precinct worker, capt. Nat. Elections, Memphis, 1972, 74; mem. Memphis Arts Coun., 1977-79; area chmn. Westchester Soc. Performing Arts, 1964-66, chmn. cultural activities Sch. No. 8, Yonkers, N.Y., 1963-66; vice chmn. music dept. Bronxville Women's Club, 1964-66; pres. chancel choir Dutch Reformed Ch., Bronxville, 1963-66; program chmn. Seoul Internat. Women's Assn., Seoul, Korea, 1967-68, chmn. cultural activities Seoul Am. Schs., 1966-68, chmn. culutral seminars Am. Women's Club, Seoul, 1967-68; treas., pres. Greater Memphis Music Tchrs. Assn., 1975-79; bd. dirs. Young Peoples Piano Concerto Competition, 1979-85, Tenn. Music Tchrs. Assn., 1977-79. Named Tchr. of Yr., Greater Memphis Music, 1983, Tenn. Music Tchrs. Assn., 1985. Democrat. Presbyterian. Avocations: writing, reading, playing piano. Home: The Fountains at Millbrook 17 Crestview Rd Millbrook NY 12545

FLICK, CAROL J., middle school educator; b. Denver, Dec. 13, 1944; d. David Marshall and Eleanore Francis (Jones) Brewer; m. Leland Gene Johnson, Aug. 4, 1965 (div. Feb. 1975); children: Teri Lynn Johnson Flick Key, Troy Lee Johnson; m. Wayne A. Flick, Mar. 29, 1975; children: Patrick Allen, Pamela Kay. BA, Mesa State Coll., Grand Junction, Colo., 1976; MA, U. No. Colo., Greeley, 1990; postgrad., Colo. State U., 2000—. Cert. tchr., Colo. Asst. mgr. Safeway Stores, Grand Junction, 1975-84; tchr. Sch. Dist. 51, Grand Junction, 1989—. Assessment liaison Sch. Dist. 51, 1996—. Mem. Nat. Staff Devel. Coun., Nat. Coun. Tchrs. English, Colo. Edn. Assn., Colo. Staff Devel. Coun., Mesa Valley Edn. Assn. (area dir. 1989-99, polit. action com. 1995-99, Outstanding Tchr. 1995-96), Beta Sigma Phi, Phi Delta Kappa (Outstanding Tchr. award 1995), Delta Kappa Gamma (v.p. 1995-99). Avocations: reading, continuing education, singing, writing, hiking. Home: 3026 Cline Ct Grand Junction CO 81504-5612

FLICK, CONNIE RUTH, real estate agent, real estate broker; d. Hugh D and Lenore Violet Myers; children: Kendra A Merriman, Tonya L Moore, Charity I Risley. Lic. Ind. Real Estate Broker Ind. Profl. Licensing Agy., 1968. Plant mgr. USPS, Terre Haute, Ind., 1993—, quality specialist Lafayette, Ind., 1986—93; owner, realtor, broker Flick Realty, Crawfordsville, Ind., 1968—; ins. agt. Met. Ins. Co., Lafayette, Ind., 1981—82; supr. mail processing USPS, Lafayette, Ind., 1985—86; hq test team mem. USPS, Equipment Devel., Merrifield, Va., 1989—92. Priority mail improvement team USPS, Indpls., 1995—96, activation coord., Inpls., Ind., 2000—02, mgr., air mail facility, 1995—96, acting postmaster (officer in charge), Lafayette, Ind., 1995—96, internat. svc. ctr. activation coord., Chgo., 1999—2000. Mem. Sch. Bd. Nominating Com., Crawfordsville, Ind., 1983—85; fund raising chmn. Hose PTO, Crawfordsville, Ind., 1980—81; vice precinct committeeman Rep. Party, Crawfordsville, Ind., 1980—85. Recipient Gold Sales award, Met. Ins. Co., 1981, Cert. of Appreciation, US Postal Svc., 1991, U.S. Postal Svc., 2001. Mem.: MIBOR, Past Presidents Bus. and Profl. Women (pres. 1979—80), Nat. Assn. of Realtors, Montgomery County Bd. of Realtors (sec. 1969—72), Ind. Realtors Assn., Ea. Star, Fatermal Order of Women of the Eagles, Women of the Moose. Independent-Republican. Baptist (Brownsvalley Missionary Baptist Church). Avocations: swimming, reading, birdwatching, puzzles, genealogy. Home: 300 Covington St Crawfordsville IN 47933-1332 Office: United States Postal Service 150 West Margaret Dr Terre Haute IN 47802-9997 Office Phone: 812-231-4011. Personal E-mail: connier.flick@usps.gov. E-mail: cflick@usps.gov.

FLIEGER, VERLYN B., literature educator; b. Hanover, Pa., Feb. 24, 1933; PhD, Cath. U. Am., Washington, D.C., 1968—77. Prof., dept. English U. Md., College Park, 1997—. Author: (novel) Pig Tale, Splintered Light, A Question of Time, Interrupted Music. Office: Univ Md College Park MD 20742 Office Phone: 301-405-3836. Personal E-mail: verlyn@mythus.com.

FLINK, ELISHEVA H., orthopedic surgeon; m. Chaim Isaac Flink; children: Yisrael Meir, Moishe. BS, Rensselaer Poly. Inst., Troy, N.Y., 1974; MD, U. Mich., Ann Arbor, 1979. Bd. cert. orthopedic surgeon Am. Bd. Orthopedic Surgery. Asst. attending Mt. Sinai Med. Svcs. at Queens and Elmhurst Hosps., Jamaica, NY, 1999—. Named Resident of Yr., Harrington Arthur Rsch. Ctr., 1990. Fellow: Am. Acad. Orthop.Surgeons. Office: Queens Hosp 8268 164th St Jamaica NY 11415

FLINSPACH, URSULA R., pharmacist, mathematics professor; b. Washington, Pa., Jan. 22, 1950; d. Albert M. Sr. and Rose K. Jackson; m. Donald A. Flinspach, Jr., May 20, 1972; 1 child, Donald A. III. BS in Math., So. Ill. U., Carbondale, 1975; AA in computer sci., John Wood C.C., Quincy, Ill., 1985; cert. in pharmacy tech., Harcourt Learning Direct, 2001. Cert. tchr. math., sci., computer sci. Ill., 1974, Mo., 1975, pharmacy technician Ill., 1997, Nat. Bd. Pharmacy Technician Cert., 1998, Mo., 2000. Math. instr. Highland HS, Ewing, Mo., 1975—76; math. and computer sci. instr. Notre Dame HS, Quincy, Ill., 1977—85; math. instr. Homer HS, 1986—88; math./physics instr. Mt Zion HS, 1989—92; math. instr. Routt HS, Jacksonville, 1993—95, Unity HS, Mendon, 1995—98; cert. pharmacy technician ShopKo Stores, Inc., Quincy, 1998—. Golf coach Notre Dame HS, Quincy, Ill., 1978—85; coach Mt Zion HS, 1989—92, Unity H.S., Mendon, 1996—98. Neighborhood chairperson Mother's Mar. of Dimes, Quincy, Ill., 2003—03; vol. runner Hannibal Regional Hosp., Hannibal, Mo., 1996—2003; vol. coach Little People's Golf Tournament, Quincy, 1979—85; team leader Shopko store #2139 United Way, 1999—99; mayoral candidate Ind. Party, Quincy, Ill., 1995—96. Tradevman 2d class WAVES USN, 1969—72. Decorated Nat. Def. Medal USN; nominee Hero of the Year award, Champaign County, 1989; recipient Above and Beyond Tchg., Homer Cmty. Consol. Sch. Bd., 1986—88, 5-10k Bronze medal, Hannibal Regional Hosp., 2001. Mem.: Quincy Soc. Fine Arts, Pharmacy Technician Certification Bd., Am. Pharmacists Assn. Roman Catholic. Achievements include first female from 1967 Trinity High School to enlist in the military WAVES during Vietnam; first female Mayoral candidate Quincy Illinois. Avocations: reading, continued education, walking/hiking, music, biking. Home: 1608 Madison Quincy IL 62301 Office: ShopKo Stores Inc 3200 Broadway Quincy IL 62301 Personal E-mail: uflin@hotmail.com.

FLINT, LAURA A., elementary school educator; b. Danville, Ill., July 4, 1964; d. Charles E. Dubois and Karen S. Nixon; m. Terry G. Flint, Jan. 1, 2000; children: Jordan, Chelsea, Cameron; m. Howard G. Berg, Dec. 19, 1987 (div. Oct. 27, 1998); children: Alexander, Aidan. AS, Danville Area CC, Ill., 1984; BA, Western Ill. U., Macomb, 1986. Cert. tchr., K-9 lang. arts and history Ill., 1989. Tutor Sylvan Learning Ctr., Champagne, Ill., 1991—95; 2nd & 6th grade tchr., basketball coach Rantoul City Schs., 1990—93; teen reach coord. Project Success, Danville, 1999—2000; jr. high lit. tchr. Rossville-Alvin Schs., Rossville, 2000—. Peer mediation coord. Rossville-Alvin Schs., 2001—; mem. PTO. Mem., coun. on adm./grad./academic stds. Western Ill. U., Sociology Dept., 1986; vol. Project Read/ESL, Champagne, 1989. Mem.: Rossville-Alvin Edn. Assn., Phi Kappa Phi, Kappa Delta Pi. Presbyterian. Avocations: reading, poetry, travel, films.

(HARRISON) FLINT, NANCY ELIZABETH, retired medical association administrator; b. Worcester, Mass., Feb. 24, 1941; d. Dorothy Stearns (Pickett) Gallagher and Thornton Webster (Gallagher) Pickett; m. Albert Gordon Flint, June 20, 1992; m. George Couper Harrison, Dec. 23, 1961; children: David George Harrison, Susan Elizabeth Fothergill Harrison, Paul Richard Harrison. Degree, Lasell Coll., Auburndale, Mass., 1961. Adminstr. of continuing med. edn. courses for Harvard Med. Sch. tchg. hosp. Mass. Gen. Hosp., Boston, 1980—96. Mem. Bus. & Profl. Womens Assn., Downtown Boston Chapter, Mass.; notary pub. Notary Law Inst., Commonweath of Mass. & State of Fla.; secret security clearance The Mitre Corp., Bedford, Mass.; chpt. pres. Profl. Sec. Internat., Boston; state cert. tchr. of med. assisting & med. office mgmt. The Bryman Sch., Brookline, Mass.; tchr. of med. terminology Div. of Cont. Ed., Marian Ct. Jr. Coll., Swamscott, Mass. Mem. Air Response Team of SW Fla, Cape Coral, Fla.; vol. officer Cape Coral Police Dept., Cape Coral, Fla.; officer Grand Chpt. of Mass., Order of the Ea. Star, Newton, Mass.; elected dir. Ea. Star of Mass. Charitable Found. Inc., Newton, Mass., Ednl. Found. of the Grand Chpt. of Mass., Newton, Mass., Woodcrest Assn., Chelmsford, Mass.; worthy matron, puritan chpt. Order of the Ea. Star of Mass., Lowell, Mass., worthy Matron, Laurel Hill Chpt. Newburyport, Mass. Master: Colonial Dames of the XVII Century, Daughters of the Am. Colonists (regent, state officer); mem.: DAR (regent, state chmn.). R-Conservative. Congregational Protestant. Home: 3827 S E 2nd Place Cape Coral FL 33904-4816 Personal E-mail: nanphf@aol.com.

FLIPPO, KAREN FRANCINE, social welfare administrator; b. Chgo., Nov. 19, 1947; d. Irving Albert and Ruth Goldie Feuerstadt; m. Charles Wayne Flippo, Aug. 6, 1978; 1 child, Ian David. BA in Govt., Am. U., 1969; M in Rehab. Adminstrn., U. San Francisco, 1981. Legis. aide Calif. Senate Subcom. on the Disabled, San Francisco, 1980-81; membership svcs. coord. Calif. Life Underwriters Assn., Oakland, 1981-84; project dir. U. San Francisco, 1984-90; sr. rsch. analyst InfoUSE, Berkeley, Calif., 1990-91, 2000; tng. assoc. Va. Commonwealth U., Richmond, 1991-96; dir. best practice initiative United Cerebral Palsy Assn., Washington, 1996-99, COO, 1999; rehab. program specialist Nat. Inst. on Disability and Rehab. Rsch., Dept. Edn., Washington, 2000; v.p. Brain Injury Assn., Alexandria, Va., 2001—03; exec. dir. Nat. Assn. Couns. on Devel. Disabilities, Washington, 2003—. Adv. bd. mem. InfoLines, St. Augustine, Fla., 1995—; bd. dir. CQL; dir. spl. projects Assn. for Persons in Supported Employment, Richmond, 1997-98. Lead editor: Assistive Technology: A Resource for School, Home and Community, 1995. Mem. Rehab. Engring. and Assistive Tech. Soc. N.Am., Assn. for Persons in Supported Employment (v.p. bd. dirs. 1993-95). Avocations: travel, reading, golf, community service. Office: Assn Couns on Devel Disabilities 225 Reinekers Lane Alexandria VA 22314 E-mail: kfflippo@aol.com.

FLISS, JULIA WADE, elementary school educator, poet; b. Elk Grove Village, Ill., Sept. 9, 1974; d. Carolyn Antoinette (Stoner) and Robert Charles Fliss. MA, U. Phoenix, Denver, 2005. Cert. tchr. Colo. Tchr. Denver Pub. Schools, 1997—. Cmty. svc. liason Denver Arts and Svc. Cmty., 1997—. Mem.: PETA, Greenpeace, Slowfood, Odyssey Inst., PeaceJam. Home: 31144 Snowshoe Rd Evergreen CO 80439 Office: Denver Pub Schs 900 Grant St Denver CO 80204 Office Phone: 720-424-5652. Personal E-mail: julia_fliss@dpsk12.org.

FLOCKHART, CALISTA, actress; b. Freeport, Ill., Nov. 11, 1964; d. Ronald and Kay Flockhart; 1 adopted child, Liam BFA, Rutgers U., 1988. Actress Ally McBeal Twentieth Century Fox, L.A. Appeared in Broadway plays, including The Glass Menagerie, The Three Sisters; actress (films) Quiz Show, 1994, Getting In, 1994, Naked in New York, 1994, Pictures of Baby Jane Doe, 1996, The Birdcage, 1996, Milk and Money, 1997, Drunks, 1997, Telling Lies in America, 1997, A Midsummer Night's Dream, 1999, Like a Hole in the Head, 1999, Jane Doe, 1999, Things You Can Tell Just By Looking at Her, 2000 The Last Shot, 2004, Fragiles, 2005; (TV movies) Darrow, 1991, Lifestories: Families in Crisis-The Secret Life of Mary Margaret: Portrait of a Bulimic, 1992, Bash: Latter Day Plays, 2001; (TV series) Guiding Light, 1989, Ally McBeal, 1997-2002, Brothers and Sisters, 2006-; (TV appearances) The Practice, 1998, (voice only) Happily Ever After: Fairy Tales for Every Child (Rip Van Winkle episode), 1999. Recipient Golden Globe award for Best Actress award, 1998 Office: Internat Ceative Mgmt Inc 8942 Wilshire Blvd Beverly Hills CA 90211*

FLOECKHER, LOUISE BYRNE WELDON, volunteer; b. NY, NY, July 28, 1928; d. Arthur Cornelius Byrne and Mary Elizabeth Colton; m. Peter Wren Floeckher (dec.). Student, Finch Jr. Coll., NY, 1946. Vol. N.Y. Presbyn. Hosp., 1962—75, prof. dir., vol. svcs., 1975—85. Mem.: Soc. of the Four Arts, Nat. Croquet Ctr., Colony Club. Avocations: croquet, travel. Home: 225 Everglade Ave #7 Palm Beach FL 33480

FLOERSCH, SHIRLEY PATTEN, dietician, consultant; b. Fayette, Ala., Mar. 22, 1924; d. Thomas Warren and Virgie Lee (Shirley) Patten; m. Joseph Paul Floersch, Aug. 5, 1950; children; Shirley Anne, Mary Jo, Paula. BS in Home Econs., Miss. State Coll. for Women, 1946. Cert. dietitian. Dietetic intern Vanderbilt U., Nashville, 1947; asst. adminstrv. dietitian St. Thomas Hosp., Nashville, 1947-48; adminstrv. dietitian Midstate Bapt. Hosp., Nashville, 1948-51; clin. dietitian St. Elizabeth's Hosp., Washington, 1953-56, VA Hosp., Houston, 1956; therapeutic dietitian Our Lady of the Lake Hosp., Baton Rouge, 1956-59; clin. dietitian USPHS, New Orleans, 1961-78; cons. dietitian New Orleans Home and Rehab. Ctr., 1980-92; retired. Recipient, Dan Forth fellow, 1945, Sr. Citizen Cert. of Merit, Archdiocese of New Orleans, 1998. Mem. Am. Dietetic Assn., 1947—, La. Dietetic Assn., New Orleans Dietetic Assn. (past. pres., treas, com. chmn. 1961—), Nutrition Today Soc., Nat. Assn. Retired Federal Employees (pres.), pres. St. Ann. Over Fifty CLub, 1995-97. Clubs: Chapelle Parents (Metaine, La.) (corr. sec., parliamentarian 1982—). Democrat. Roman Catholic. Avocation: sewing. Home: 8680 Jefferson Hwy Apt 227 Baton Rouge LA 70809-2266

FLOETER, VALERIE ANN, music educator; b. Davenport, Iowa; d. Russell Michael Krebs and Jean Antonia Luerman; m. Alan Dale Floeter, Aug. 21, 1976; children: Sean, Jessi. BA in Math., Alverno Coll., 1976; MusM, Concordia U., 2002. Computer programmer Northwestern Mut. Life, Milw., 1976; software engr. Midwest Analog & Digital, New Berlin, 1977—78, GE Corp., Waukesha, 1978—81; freelance cons., 1981—98; organist Mt. Calvary Luth. Ch., Waukesha, 1986—; tchr. piano pvt. practice, 1989—. Adj. prof. music Wis. Luth. Coll., Milw., 1998—; pres. Software Experience, Waukesha, 1985—; treas. Soli Deo Gloria Inst. Arts, 2003—. Musician: (albums) In the Fullness of Time, 1998, In Three Days, 1999, In Joyful Hope, 2000, In Our Hearts, 2003, (music books) Hymnprovisions, 2004, 12 Sacred Solos for Piano, 2005. Mem.: Hymn Soc., Assn. Luth. Ch. Musicians. Avocation: genealogy. Home: S33 W30212 St David Dr Waukesha WI 53189

FLOOD, ANGELA, interior designer, artist; b. NYC, Jan. 22, 1945; d. Americo Montes and Carmen M. Hansen; m. Oscar William Rocafort, June 2, 1963 (div.); 1 child, Angélique Rocafort-Ward; m. Steven Arthur Flood, June 12, 1988. Student, NYU, 1965—66, Pace U., 1973—76; AAS, Suffolk C.C., 1992. Artist, curator F.O.R.E., Bedford, NY, 1976—86; owner, designer A&S Interiors, Westhampton Beach, NY, 1992—; owner design and art exhbns. Exhibitions include Easthampton (NY) Town Hall, 2001, 2006, Westhampton Beach Libr., 2002, 2006, Southampton RML Gallery, 2003, Easthampton Guild Hall Mus., 2004, 2005, 2006, Easthampton Artist Alliance Hall, 2005, 2006, L.I. Maritime Mus., 2006. Counselor ARC, White Plains, NY, 1974—77. Republican. Avocations: horseback riding, kayaking, canoeing, sailing, skiing. Office: A&S Interiors PO Box 413 Westhampton Beach NY 11978 Personal E-mail: lilly11967@yahoo.com.

FLOOD, DOROTHY GARNETT, neuroscientist; m. Paul David Coleman, Feb. 26, 1983 (div. 2006). BA cum laude, Lawrence U., 1973; student, U. Ill., 1972-73; MS, PhD, U. Rochester, N.Y., 1980. Sr. instr. in anatomy U. Rochester, 1980-83, asst. prof. neurology, neurobiology and anatomy, 1984-90, assoc. prof. neurology, neurobiology and anatomy, 1990-94; sr. sci. Cephalon, Inc., West Chester, Pa., 1994—. Contbr. to book chpts. and articles in field; mem. editl. bd. Neurobiology of Aging, 1989—. Recipient Fenn award U. Rochester, 1980; grantee NSF, NIH, Office of Naval Rsch., 1979-94. Mem. Soc. Neurosci. Office: Cephalon Inc 145 Brandywine Pkwy West Chester PA 19380-4249 Business E-Mail: dflood@cephalon.com.

FLOOD, H. GAY (HULDA GAY FLOOD), editor, consultant; b. Plainfield, N.J., Aug. 14, 1935; d. William Edward and Lucy (Dycker) Flood. BA, Smith Coll., 1957. With picture dept. Sports Illustrated, Time Inc., N.Y.C., 1957-58, with letters dept., 1958-59, reporter, 1959-60, writer-reporter, 1960-71; assoc. editor, 1971-85, sr. editor, 1985-90. Mem. Greater Consistory First Reformed Ch., Nyack, NY; assoc. mem. The Ch. of the Pilgrimage, Plymouth, Mass. Mem.: Smith Coll. Students Aid Soc., Alumnae Assn. Smith Coll., Boston Smith Coll. Club, Garden Club Nyack (chair cmty. flower show 2001), Smith Coll. Club N.Y. Office: 7 Sampson Commons Plymouth MA 02360

FLOOD, JOAN MOORE, paralegal; b. Hampton, Va., Oct. 10, 1941; d. Harold W. and Estalena (Fancher) M.; 1 child by former marriage, Angelique. B.Mus., North Tex. State U., 1963; postgrad., So. Meth. U., 1967-68, Tex. Women's U., 1978-79, U. Dallas, 1985-86. Clk. Criminal Dist. Ct. Number 2, Dallas County, Tex., 1972-75; reins. libr. Scor Reins. Co., Dallas, 1975-80; corp. ins. paralegal Assocs. Inc. Group, 1980-83; corp. securities paralegal Akin, Gump, Strauss, Hauer & Feld, 1983-89; asst. sec. Knoll Internat. Holdings Inc., Saddle Brook, N.J., 1989-90, 21 Internat. Holdings, Inc., N.Y.C., 1990-92; dir. compliance Am. Svc. Life Ins. Co., Ft. Worth, 1992-93; v.p., sec. Express Comm., Inc., Dallas, 1993-94; fin. transactions paralegal Thompson & Knight, Dallas, 1994-96; corp. transactions paralegal Jones,

Day, Reavis & Pogue, Dallas, 1996-97, Weil, Gotshal & Manges, LLP, 1998—99; corp. paralegal PennCorp. Fin. Group, Inc., Dallas, 1999-2001; debt trade mgr. Patton Boggs LLP, 2001—03, sr. paralegal bus. transactions, 2003; corp. paralegal Carrington, Coleman, Sloman & Blumenthal, LLP, Dallas, 2003—05. Mem. ABA, Tex. Bar Assn. Home and Office: PO Box 190165 Dallas TX 75219-0165 Personal E-mail: jmfdallas@msn.com.

FLOOD, SANDRA WASKO, artist, educator; b. N.Y.C., Mar. 12, 1943; d. Peter Edmund Wasko and Margaret Dalores Kubek; m. Michael Timothy Flood, June 28, 1969. BA in English, UCLA, 1965; postgrad., Museo de Arte Moderno, Rio de Janeiro, 1970-73, U. Wis., 1977-78. Std. secondary tchg. credential L.A. State Coll., 1966. English, journalism instr. Nobel Jr. High, Northridge, Calif., 1967-69; ESL instr. U.S.-Brazil Inst., Rio de Janeiro, 1972-73; pvt. practice printmaking instr. Alexandria, Va., 1979—. Pub. rels. dir. Washington Women's Art Ctr., 1980; artist-in-residence U. Md., College Park, 1984; printmaking instr. St. Mary's Coll., St. Mary's City, Md., 1985; workshop coord. Lee Arts Ctr., Arlington (Va.) County Cultural Affairs, 1989—97; v.p. Gallery 10, Washington, 1995—97; program chair Women's Caucus for Art D.C. Chpt., 1998—99; founder, dir. Living Labyrinths for Peace, 2005. One-woman shows include Sch. 33 Installation Space, Balt., 1996, St. Peter's Ch., N.Y.C., 1989, Montpelier Cultural Arts Ctr., Laurel, Md., 1992, Gallery 10, Washington, D.C., 1994, 1996, exhibited in group shows at Peninsula Fine Arts Ctr., Newport News, Va., 1995, The Nat. Mus. Women in the Arts, Washington, 1996, Phillips Collection, 1988, Bookchamber Internat., Moscow, 1990, Corcoran Gallery Art, Washington, 1999, Charles Sumner Sch. Mus., 2000, Millennium Ctr., 2001, Rockville (Md.) Arts Pl., 2002. Mem. Ylem Artists Using Sci. and Tech., San Francisco, 2002—06, Art Sci. Collaborative Inc., N.Y.C., 2002—06. Named Best of Show, Artists Equity D.C., Washington, 1997; Individual Artists fellow Va. Commn. for the Arts, Richmond, 1994; grantee Friends of the Torpedo Factory, Alexandria, Va., 1989. Mem.: The Labyrinth Soc., Washington Project for the Arts/Corcoran, Md. Printmakers, N.Am. Print Alliance, Women's Caucus for Art (program chair 1998—99), Washington Sculptor's Group. Avocations: creative writing, classical music, hiking. Studio: 57 N St NW Washington DC 20001-1254 Home: 2229 Lake Ave Baltimore MD 21213 Office Phone: 703-217-6706. E-mail: waskoart@comcast.net.

FLOOD, TAMELA MICHELLE, elementary school educator; b. Memphis, Dec. 14, 1975; d. Evelyn Virigina Frison and Robert Lee Bridges, James Townsel (Stepfather); m. James Arthur Flood, May 18, 2002; 1 child, Reginald James. M in Sch. Counseling, Freed Hardeman U., 2005. 8th grade math. tchr. Memphis City Sch., 1999—. Home: 4250 Riche Ave Memphis TN 38128 Office: Memphis City Schl Havenview Middle 1481 Hester Rd Memphis TN 38116 Personal E-mail: tfrison1975@yahoo.com.

FLOR, HERTA, psychology professor; b. Schnaittenbach, Germany, Apr. 23, 1954; d. Georg and Maria (Reitinger) F. BS, U. Würzburg, Germany, 1977; diploma, U. Tübingen, Germany, 1981, PhD, 1984. Postdoctoral fellow Yale U., New Haven, 1983-84; asst. prof. U. Bonn, Germany, 1984-85; vis. asst. prof. U. Pitts., 1985—87; asst. prof. U. Tübingen, 1987—90; vis. prof. U. Marburg, Germany, 1990-91; Heisenberg fellowship U. Tübingen, 1991-93; assoc. prof. Humboldt U., Berlin, 1993-94, prof., 1995; prof. neurosci. U. Heidelberg Ctrl. Inst. Mental Health, Mannheim, Germany, 2000—. Author: Psychobiology of Pain, 1991. Recipient Pain Rsch. prize German Pain Soc., 1992, 2000, prize for clin. rsch., Smithkline Beecham Found., 1996, Sertürner award for pain rsch., 1999, Max-Planck Rsch. prize, 2000, Muscle Pain Rsch. award, 2001, German Psychology prize, 2002, Basic Rsch. award German Fed. State Baden-Württemberg, 2004; fellow Deutsche Forschungsgemeinschaft, 1987-90. Mem. AAAS, Internat. Assn. Study of Pain, Soc. for Psychophysiol. Rsch., Soc. for Neurosci. Achievements include research in psychophysiology and behavioral treatments of chronic pain; role of cortical reorganiztion in chronic pain, especially phantom limb pain. Office: U Heidelberg Dept Neuropsy & Clin Psych Ctrl Inst Mental Health J5 68159 Mannheim Germany Business E-Mail: flor@zi-mannheim.de.

FLORA, CORNELIA BUTLER, sociologist, educator; b. Santa Monica, Calif., Aug. 5, 1943; d. Carroll Woodward and May Fleming (Darnall) Butler; m. Jan Leighton Flora, Aug. 22, 1967; children: Gabriela Catalina, Natasha Pilar. BA, U. Calif., Berkeley, 1965; MS, Cornell U., 1966, PhD, 1970. Asst. to full prof. Kans. State U., Manhattan, 1970-89, dir. population rsch. lab., 1970-78, univ. disting. prof., 1988-89; program adviser Ford Found., Bogota, Colombia, 1978-80; prof., head dept. sociology Va. Poly. Inst. and State U., Blacksburg, 1989-94, univ. disting. prof., 2001—; dir. north ctrl. regional ctr. for rural devel. Iowa State U., Ames, 1994—, prof. agr., 2001—. Bd. dirs. Winfock Internat.; cons. USAID, 1981-91, Inter Am. Devel. Bank, 1992, UN, 1992. Author: Interactions between Agroecosystems and Rural Communities, Rural Communities: Legacy and Change; editor: Sustainable Agriculture, 1990, Rural Policy for the 1990s; contbr. articles to sociol. publs. Bd. dirs. N.W. Area Found., 1998—, Agrl. Nat. Rsch. Coun., 1996-98, Agrl. and Natural Resouces, NRC, NAS, Heartland Ctr. for Leadership Devel. Nat. Ctr. for Small Cmtys.; bd. dirs. Henry A. Wallace Inst. for Alt. Agr., 1994-99, pres., 1997-99. Recipient Outstanding Alumni award Coll. Agrl. and Life Scis., Cornell U., 1994; sr. fellow U. Minn. Sch. Agr. Endowed Chair in Agrl. Sys. Mem. Rural Sociol. Soc. (pres. 1988-89, Outstanding Rsch. award 1987), Latin Am. Studies Assn. (bd. dirs. 1982-84, pres. Midwest sect. 1989-90), Am. Sociol. Assn., Agr., Food and Human Values Soc. (pres. elect 2001—), Cmty. Devel. Soc. (v.p. 2001—). Mem. United Ch. of Christ. Office: Iowa State U N Ctrl Regional Ctr Rural Devels 107 N Curtiss Hl Ames IA 50011-0001 Office Phone: 515-294-1329. Business E-Mail: cflora@iastate.edu.

FLORA, KATHLEEN M., retired state representative; b. Dearborn, Mich., Nov. 10, 1952; m. James A. Flora; two children. BA, Mich. State U., 1975, MA, 1977. State rep. N.H. Ho. of Reps., 1996—2002. Mem. Bedford Rep. Com., 1996— Vol. adv. bd. VNA Hospice, 1996-97. Mem. ASTD. Office: NH State Legis State House Concord NH 03301 Office Phone: 941-907-6063. E-mail: kflora@tampabay.rr.com.

FLORA, LORETTA SUE, music educator; b. Washington Court House, Ohio, Jan. 25, 1964; d. Glen Mills and Christine Belle Jette. MusB, Milligan Coll., Johnson City, Tenn., 1986; MA in Tchg., East Tenn. State U., Johnson City, Tenn., 1991. Tchr. music Miami Troce Schs., Washington Court, Ohio, 1987—88; tchr. Johnson County Schs., Mountain City, Tenn., 1988—90, Fayette Christian Sch., Washington Court, 1990—91; tchr. music Washington Court City Schs., 1991—99, Greenfield Exempte4d Village Schs., 1999—2006. Recipient Acad. Excellence awards, Greenfield Exempted Village Schs., 2001, 2003, 2005, 2006. Mem.: Ohio Music Educators Assn., Little Theatre Off Broadway. Avocations: snorkeling, singing, acting. Home: 400Kimberly Dr Washington Court House OH 43160 Office: Greenfield Exempted Village Schs 200 N 5th St Greenfield OH 45123 Office Phone: 937-981-7731. E-mail: lflora@dragonbbs.com.

FLOREK, MICHAELINE, counselor; b. Gary, Ind., Sept. 12, 1953; d. William John and Josephine Smolinski; m. Fernando Florek, June 30, 1973; children: Joshua Lawrence, Jason Andrew, Bernadette Kathleen. BA, Purdue U., Hammond, Ind., 1995, MS in Edn., 1999. Coord. svcs. for students with disabilities Purdue U. Calumet, Hammond, 1997—. Avocations: reading, counted cross-stitch, gardening. Office: Purdue U Calumet Student Support Svcs 2200 169th St Hammond IN 46323-2094 Fax: 219-989-2736. E-mail: florekms@calumet.purdue.edu.

FLORENCE, JOYCE FRITZ, mathematics professor; b. Lexington, Ky., July 17, 1956; d. Joe and Elaine Humphrey Fritz; children: Donald Joe, Jillian Florence Anderson. Associates, Maysville C.C., 1997; Bachelors, U. Ky., 2000; Masters, Georgetown Coll., 2003, Ea. Ky. U., 2005. Travel agt. Wilco Travel Agy., Lexington, 1974—75; bookkeeper Fritz Distbg. Co. Inc., Cynthiana, Ky., 1977—90; travel agt. Going Places Travel, Georgetown, Ky., 1986—91, The Travel Shoppe, Winchester, Ky., 1991—2001; preschool tchr. United Preschool, Cynthiana, 1996—97; algebra, pre-algebra tchr. Harrison County HS, Cynthiana, 2000—03; algebra, problem solving tchr. Harrison County Mid. Sch., Cynthiana, 2003—. Life mem. Girl Scouts, N.Y.C., 1962—2006, troop leader Cynthiana, 1975—2006, day camp dir., 1975—2000; sec. Trials and Trowels Garden Club, Cynthiana, 1985—87; harrison county svc. unit chmn. Girl Scouts, 1987—90, 1996—99; Sunday sch. tchr. First United Meth. Ch., Cynthiana, 1986—90. Recipient Silver Cup award, Trials and Trowels Garden Club, 1985, Honor Pin, Wilderness Rd. Girl Scout Coun., 1990, Thanks Badge, 1999; Cmty. scholarship, Maysville C.C., 1998, Mason County Alumni scholarship, Mason County Alumni Assn., 1998. Mem.: Nat. Tchrs. Math. (assoc.), Ky. Edn. Assn. (assoc.), Ky. Tchrs. Math. (assoc.), Girl Scouts (life). Home: 207 Wilson Ave Cynthiana KY 41031 Office: Harrison County Mid Sch 269 Edn Dr Cynthiana KY 41031 Office Phone: 859-234-7123.

FLORENCE, MELANIE ANNE, biologist, writer; b. Grand Forks, ND, Nov. 27, 1953; d. W Lynn and Sylva Anne Smith; m. Scott Richard Florence, Aug. 19, 1978; children: Sylva Elaine, Kyle Allen. BS, Colo. State U., 1971—75; MA, Calif. State U., 1980—85. Cert. sec. sci. tchg. N. Mex., 1990. Range technician Bur. of Land Mgmt., Rawlins, Wyo., 1974—75; part time lab technician Colo. State U. Seed Lab, 1974—75; range technician Bur. of Land Mgmt., Ely, Nev., 1977, environ. edn. instr., 1978, range technician Folsom, Calif., 1979; botanist Forest Svc., Nevada City, Calif., 1980; plant breeder technician A.L. Castle Seed Co., Hollister, Calif., 1982—83; biol. cons. U. S. Pk. Svc., Pinnacles Nat. Monument, Paicines, Calif., 1985—86; biol. project aide N.Mex State U. Biology Dept., 1987—88; biol. cons. Nature Conservancy, Las Cruces, N.Mex., 1989; sub. tchr. Lake County Sch. Dist., Lakeview, Oreg., 1993—95; bus. edn. coord. Lake County, Lakeview, Oreg., 1995; owner, mgr. Bookworm Bookstore, Lakeview, Oreg., 1996—98; mktg. cons. Lake County Econ. Devel., Lakeview, Oreg., 1999—2000; botanist Bur. of Land Mgmt. (summer), Lakeview, Oreg., 2000; radiology clk. Lake County Dist. Hosp., Lakeview, Oreg., 2000—02; writer self-employed, Fairfax, Va., 2002—05; adj. prof. biology dept. Dixie State Coll., 2006—. Planning commn. mem. Town of Lakeview, Lakeview, Oreg., 1998—2002; chmn., revitalization com. Lake County C. of C., Lakeview, Oreg., 1999—2001; long range planning commn. mem. Lake Dist. Hosp., Lakeview, Oreg., 1999—2002; reporting-proof reading Greenbriar Flyer newspaper, Fairfax, Va., 2002—05; adj. prof. biology dept. Dixie State Coll., 2006—. Contbr.; author: (short stories) 2d and 3d Northwoods Anthologies, No Longer Dreams Horror Writers Anthology; contbr. articles to jours. Plant nursery vol. Zion Nat. Park, 2005—06. Mem.: Sisters in Crime. Democrat. Avocations: reading, gardening, hiking, cultural activities, travel. Personal E-mail: smskflor@yahoo.com.

FLORES, CANDACE, special events director; b. 1974; Owner The Stillwell House; special events dir. El Charro Cafe. Mem. Big Brothers/ Big Sisters, Humane Soc. Southern Ariz., Angel Charities, Jr. League, Tu Nidito. Named one of 40 Under 40, Tucson Bus. Edge, 2006. Office: The Still Well House PO Box 1203 134 S 5th Ave Tucson AZ 85702 Office Phone: 520-623-9123.*

FLORES, CHRISTINA ROSALIE, art educator; b. Tamuning, Guam, Nov. 17, 1947; d. George Pangelinan Franquez; m. Larry Blas Flores, June 20, 1970 (div. Nov. 1974); children: Tanisha, Briana. AA, Sacred Heart Coll., 1967; BA, San Diego State U., 1970; MA, Long Beach State U., 1979. Cert. art tchr. K-12, Guam. 5th grade tchr. Price Elem. Sch., Mangilao, Guam, 1970-80; 6th grade tchr. Harmon Loop Elem. Sch., Guam, 1980-82; 6th and 7th grade art tchr. Agueda Johnston Mid. Sch., Ordot, Guam, 1982—; art tchr. George Washington H.S., 1999—, Untalan Mid. Sch., 2003—04. Gifted and talented edn. art tchr. various elem. schs., Guam, summers, 1984-95; art instr. Fun in the Sun camp for handicapped children, summers 1975-82, Parks and Recreation Summer Camp, 1983-85; instr., tchr. workshops in art Simon Sanchez H.S., Yigo, Guam, 1988-92, art, reading summer sch. tchr. George Wash. HS, 1999-2003, part-time summer sch. tchr., 2004, 05; mem. adv. bd. Coun. Arts and Humanities, Maite, Guam, 1991-94, 2002, bd. dirs., 1995-99, 2002; chief advisor Crime Stoppers Agueda Mid. Sch., 1992—; advisor Nat. Jr. Honor Soc. Agueda Johnston Mid. Sch., 1987-99; part time art methods instr. Coll. Edn., U. Guam, 1994-2000; art dir. mural painting KGTF TV Sta., cmty walls Internat. Reading Assn., Guam, 2000—, bus stop painting project, 1993, 2000, 03, 05, Centennial mural Guam Internat. Airport, 1998; desinger coloring books Guam Meml. Hosp., 2001-06; designer valetine cards for Vets., 2001-06. Prin. works include George Washington H.S. Mural, Guam, 2006. Chief advisor Students Against Drunk Driving, Agueda Johnston Mid. Sch., 1987—; mem. Driver's Edn. Consortium, Guam, 1993-94; vol. Spl. Olympics, Guam, 1974—, ARC, Guam, 1992—, Festival of the Arts, Tahiti, 1985, Australia, 1988, Cook Islands, 1992, Western Samoa, 1996, New Caledonia, 2000, Koror, Palau, 2004, Am. Cancer Soc., Guam, 2001—, Relay for Life, 1999-2003, Blood Dr. Gift of Life, 2003, ARC Disaster Relief, 1997-2003, Am. Red Cross; instr. Pacific Region Ednl. Lab., 1993—; participant art auctions Am. Cancer Soc.,KPRG Radio Sta., Guam, 2000-06 Recipient Soil Conservation award, Coloring Book Design, 1987; Tchr. Inst. scholar Nat. Art Gallery, Washington, 1991. Mem. ASCD, Nat. Art Edn. Assn., Nat. Assn. Student Activity Advisers. Avocations: weaving, swimming, dance, paddling. Home: PO Box 1654 Hagatna GU 96932-1654

FLORES, KATHRYN LOUISE, mathematics educator; b. Midland, Mich., Sept. 28, 1963; d. George Homer and Mary Ruth Flores. BS in Chem. Engring., Tex. A&M U., Kingsville, 1985; MS in Chem. Engring., Tex. A&M U., College Station, 1989; PhD in Applied Math., U. Tex., Dallas, 2002. Asst. prof. math. McMurry U., Abilene, Tex., 2002—. With U.S. Army, 1992—97, PTO. Mem.: Am. Math. Soc., Math. Assn. America, Tau Beta Pi. Avocation: running. Office: McMurry U McMurry Sta Box 668 Abilene TX 79697

FLORES, ROBIN ANN, geriatric program and service consultant; b. Allentown, Pa., Oct. 6, 1949; d. Norman Henry and Ann May (Huff) F. BS in Edn., Kutztown U., 1971; MS in Adminstrn., U. Scranton, 1983. Exec. dir. Lehigh County Aging and Adult Svcs., Allentown, 1996—2004; pvt. cons. in geriatric and cmty. programs, 2004—. Lectr. cmty. svcs., family care giving and on aging process, utilization cmty. resources, Lehigh County; co-dir. The Ethics Inst., Inc., Allentown Mem. adv. bd. Cmty. Action Com. Lehigh Valley, 1979-82, Elder Well, 1987-90; Pa. del. White House Conf. on Aging, Hershey, Pa., 1981; bd. dirs. Vis. Nurse Assn. Lehigh County, 1982-98, Women Inc., 1983-87; mem. adv. bd. Homecare, Inc., 1982-91, Geriatric Edn. Modules, Allentown Osteo. Hosp., 1979; mem. profl. adv. com. Lehigh Valley Hospice, 1984-98; mem. utilization and rev. bd. Vis. Nurse Assn., 1979-98; consumer rep. Pa. Power and Light Co.; co-chmn. Human Svcs. Tng. Coop., 1975-81; bd. assocs. Lehigh Valley Hosp.; trustees Ethics Inst., Inc. Mem.: NAFE, United Way Alliance Aging, Nat. Assn. Area Agys. on Aging, Am. Soc. Aging, Allentown Art Mus., Quota Internat. Home: 2206 Overlook Ln Fogelsville PA 18051-1812 Office Phone: 610-248-5064. Personal E-mail: robina6@msn.com.

FLORES, ROBIN KAY, science educator; b. Fort Riley, Kans., Nov. 17, 1962; d. Anthony and June Brzezinski (Stepmother), Kay Bushnell; life ptnr. Ruben Flores, Aug. 30, 1986; children: Venesa Ann, Katy Renee. BS, Corpus Christi State U., Tex., 1985. Cert. sec. sch. tchr. Tex., 1991. Biology technician Nat. Marine Fisheries Svc. (NOAA), Aransas Pass, Tex., 1985—86; payroll clk. Herndon Marine Products, Inc., Aransas Pass, 1986—91; tchr. Cunningham Mid. Sch., Corpus Christi, 1991—97, A.C. Blunt Mid. Sch., Aransas Pass, Tex., 1997—. Cons. Edn. Svc. Ctr. Region 2, Corpus Christi, 2000—05, Tex. State Aquarium, Corpus Christi, 2001—06. Vol. City of Aransas Pass, 2002—06; faculty sponsor Sci. and Spanish Club Network (Gulf of Mex. Found.), Aransas Pass, 2002—06. Named Mid. Sch. Tchr. of the Yr., Coastal Bend Bays and Estuaries Found., 2004; recipient Campus Tchr. of the Yr., Aransas Pass ISD, 2003. Mem.: Am. Fedn. of Tchrs. (campus coord. 2004—06). Home: 2189 Timberleaf Cir Ingleside TX 78362 Office: AC Blunt Middle School 2103 Demory Ln Aransas Pass TX 78336 Personal E-mail: robinflores@hotmail.com.

FLORES, SYLVIA A., principal; BS in elem. edn., U. Houston, 1979; MS in sch. adminstrn., N. Mex. State U., 1995. Tchr. 1st grade Floresville (Tex.) Elem., 1980-82, tchr. 3d grade, 1982-85; tchr. 1st grade Ctrl. Elem., Artesia, N. Mex., 1985-87, Yucca Elem., Artesia, N. Mex., 1987-92; tchr. 4th grade, asst. prin. Hermosa Elem., Artesia, N.Mex., 1992—95; prin. Yucca Elem., Artesia, 1996—. Recipient N. Mex. Tchr. of the Year, 1995. Mem. Assn. Supr. and Curriculum Devel., Legis. and Salary Chairperson for Artesia Pub. Sch. Network. Home: 103 Marsha Dr Artesia NM 88210-9251 Office: 900 North 13th St Artesia NM 88210

FLORES, YOLANDA, speech pathology/audiology services professional, consultant; d. Samuel and Consuelo Flores; m. Manuel Moreno Jr., Nov. 17, 1985; children: Sasha Monik Moreno, Danielle Erika Moreno. BA in Speech, Hearing and Lang. Disability, U. Tex., El Paso, 1983, MS in Speech and Lang. Pathology, 1985. Cert. speech and lang. pathologist N.Mex., Tex., clin. competence in speech lang. pathology Am. Speech and Hearing Assn., 1990. Speech lang. pathologist Ysleta Ind. Sch. Dist., 1983—, Providence Meml. Hosp., 1995—98. Instr. ESL El Paso C.C., Tex.; off-campus grad. supr. U. Tex. El Paso, 1992—2004, Tex. Women's U., 2002—03; class sponsor Ysleta Ind. Sch. Dist., Tex., 2002—; technology and inclusion trainer Speak Up, Tex., Tex., 2005—. Mem.: N.Mex. Speech and Hearing Assn., El Paso Speech and Hearing Assn. (sec., pres. elect, pres.), Tex. Speech Lang. and Hearing Assn., Am. Speech and Hearing Assn. (continuing edn. award 1999, 2002, 2005). Roman Catholic. Avocations: travel, gardening, exercise, dance, sports. Home: 1363 Pony Trail Pl El Paso TX 79936

FLOREZ, DIANE O., county clerk; b. Pecos, Tex., Oct. 22, 1954; d. Leandro Tapia and Angelita Martinez (Carrasco) Orona; m. Margarito B. Florez, June 8, 1974 (div. June 1990); children: Bryan Gabriel, Jessica Ann. Student, Odessa (Tex.) Coll., 1972, 84-86. Adult probation officer 143d Jud. Dist. Probation Dept., Pecos, 1984-91; sec. Randall Reynolds, Atty., Pecos, 1992; dep. tax assessor Tax Office, Pecos, 1993; sec. Walter M. Holcombe, Atty., Pecos, 1994; pharmacist Reeves County Hosp., Pecos, 1994-95; county clk. Reeves County Clk.'s Office, Pecos, 1995—. Local registrar Reeves County, 1998—; spkr. in field. Bd. dis. X-Mas in April, 1995—; Cmty. Coun., 1997—, Lamar Elem. Sch. Improvement Campus Program, 1998—. Mem. Assn. County and Dist. Clks., Pecos C. of C. (bd. dirs. 1998—) Lions Club (bd. dirs. 1997—). Avocations: volleyball, swimming, dance, singing, coaching soccer. Home: 923 S Hickory St Pecos TX 79772-4910 Office: Reeves County Clk's Office PO Box 867 Pecos TX 79772-0867

FLOREZ, MARY A., artist; married; 5 children. Student, Boca Raton Art Mus., U. Cin., Thompson Art Studio. Exhibitions include Southeastern Ind. Art Guild, Aurora, Breast Cancer Awareness Brick Auction, Cin., 2002, Sharon Ctr. Hilltop Artists, 2003, 2004, Women in Visual Arts, Boca Raton, Fla., 2003, 2005, Fed. Credit Union Cin., 2003, Fitton Ctr. Creative Arts, Hamilton, Ohio, Cin. Acad. Medicine, Farbach Warner Nature Preserve, Cin., Town Club Cin, Ansonia High Sch., Conn., Evengale Recreation Ctr., Cin., 2004, Hamilton County Pub. Libr., 2004. Mem. Good Samaritan Hosp. Guild, Cin., St. Francis-St. George Hosp. Guild, Providence Hosp. Guild; fundraising chair Acad. Sacred Heart, St. Mary's Hosp. Mem.: Cin. Acad. Medicine Women's Aux., Hilltop Artists, Women Visual Arts, Cin. Town Club, Woman's Art Club, Cin. Woman's Club. Avocation: golf. Home: 797 Windings Ln Cincinnati OH 45220 E-mail: mflorez1@cinci.rr.com.

FLORI, ANNA MARIE DIBLASI, nurse anesthetist, educational administrator; b. Amsterdam, N.Y., Oct. 29, 1940; d. Tony and Maria (Macario) DiBlasi; children: Tammy, Tina, Toni; m. Gilberto Flori, May 24, 1986. Grad., Albany Med. Ctr. Sch. Nursing, 1962, Fairfax Hosp. Sch. Nurse Anesthetists, Va., 1972; BS in Anesthesia, George Washington U., 1979; M. in Bus. and Pub. Adminstrn., Southeastern U., Washington, 1982; PhD, Columbia Pacific U., 1983. Cert. registered nurse anesthetist. Staff nurse West Seattle Gen. Hosp., 1962-64; office nurse Filmore Buckner, M.D., Seattle, 1964-66; staff nurse anesthetist Fairfax Hosp., 1972-73; staff nurse anesthetist Potomac Hosp., Woodbridge, Va., 1973, chief nurse anesthetist, 1973—; dir. Potomac Hosp. Sch. for Nurse Anesthetists and Sch. for Nurse Anesthesia; faculty mem. Columbia Pacific U., 1973-90; chief nurse anesthetist No. Va. Anesthesia Assn., 1988—; guest lectr. No. Va. Community Coll., Inservice Potomac Hosp., George Washington U.; coord. Free Clinic Prince William County, Woodbridge, Va. Contbr. books on anesthesia. Mem. Am. Assn. Nurse Anesthetists, Va. Nurse Anesthesia Assn., Nat. Italian Am. Found. Home: 12954 Pintail Rd Woodbridge VA 22192-3831 Office Phone: 703-670-1357.

FLORIAN-LACY, DOROTHY, social worker, educator; b. Dearborn, Mich., Oct. 27, 1958; d. Raymond Joseph and Dorothy Mae Florian; m. Bill George Lacy, July 25, 1981; children: Jason M., Miles, Anderson. BS in Psychology and Edn., Eastern Mich. U., 1978, MA in Guidance and Counseling, 1979; EdD in Counselor Edn., Tex. Southeastern U., 1998. Lic. profl. counselor, Tex. Realtor Century 21, Ann Arbor, Mich., 1978—79; tchr. Adult Exception Ctr., Compton, Calif., 1979—81; owner, dir. Village Learning & Play Ctr., Houston, 1982—94; dept. chair spl. edn. Milby Sr. H.S., Houston, 1994—2000; therapist Houston Achievement Place, 1998—. Author: Fundamentals of Mathematics I, Fundamentals of Mathematics II, Consumer Math; co-author: Reference Manual for Special Education Department Chairpersons. Vol. Child Abuse Prevention, Houston, 1989-91, vol. coach YMCA, Houston, 1987-90. Recipient Adaptor grant Impact II, 1997, Study Group grant Impact II, 1998. Mem. ACA, Children's Mus Avocation: golf coach. Office: Houston Achievement Place 236 W 17th St Houston TX 77008-4002 Office Phone: 713-868-2909 272. Personal E-mail: dflorian@houstonisd.org. Business E-Mail: dlacy@h-a-p.org.

FLORIO, MARYANNE J., health and education research scientist; b. Queens, N.Y., Sept. 28, 1940; d. Edgar Vincent and Helen Louise (Schultze) Spaeth; m. James J. Florio, June 25, 1960 (div. 1985); children: Christopher, Gregory, Catherine. BS summa cum laude, Coll. N.J., 1979; MEd, Temple U., 1981, postgrad., 1982—. Cert. biofeedback therapist, tchr., N.J. Research and evaluation asst. Woodhaven Ctr., Phila., 1981-82; statis. and computer cons., program asst. Systems & Computer Tech. Corp., Phila., 1982-83; biofeedback therapist Ctr. for Creative Devel., Ardmore, Pa., 1984-85; evaluation coord. N.J. Dept. Edn., Trenton, 1987-88; computer scientist, stats. researcher N.J. Dept. Health, Trenton, 1987-88, research scientist for prenatal and neonatal care prog., 1988-97. Pvt. rsch. design and computing cons., 1983—; trainer computer and statis. software, N.J., Pa., 1984—, Camden County Commn. on Women, 1985—. Chmn. long-range planning, bd. dirs., 1st v.p. Camden County council Girl Scouts U.S., 1975—. Elks Club scholar, 1958, Systems and Computer Tech. Corp. scholar, 1982; Temple U. grad. fellow, 1984. Mem. Am. Edn. Research Assn., Biofeedback Soc. Am., Biofeedback and Behavioral Med. Soc. Pa. Avocations: reading, sports, tennis, volleyball, theater. Home: 290 Evergreen Rd Barrington NJ 08007-1432

FLORY, EVELYN LOUISE, educational administrator; b. N.Y.C., Mar. 23, 1935; d. George Louis and Evelyn Mathilda (Everson) Albert; m. Gaylord Gene Flory, June 10, 1961 (dec. Mar. 1982); 1 child, Charles Cameron. BA, Queens Coll., NY, 1956; MA, Northwestern U., 1957; PhD, NYU, 1969. Instr. Tex. Lutheran Coll., Sequin, 1959-60; tchr. Martin Luther H.S., Maspeth, N.Y., 1962-63; asst. prof. Queensborough C.C., Bayside, N.Y., 1970-76; tchr. Riverdale (N.Y.) Country Sch., 1976-83, head English dept., 1983-85, divsn. head grades 11-12, 1985-89; assoc. head Marin Acad., San Rafael, Calif., 1989-94; acting head, 1994-95; headmistress St. Paul's Sch. Girls, Brooklandville, Md., 1995—2002. Contbr. articles to profl. jours. and newspapers. Pres., sec., trustee Holy Trinity Luth. Ch., N.Y.C., 1970-72, 75-80, 85-89; bd. dir. BEST, 1995-2002, AIMS, 1999-2002. Fellow Woodrow Wilson Found., 1956-57, Northwestern U., 1958-59, N.Y. State Regents Coll., 1963. Mem. Phi Beta Kappa. Lutheran. Avocation: singing.

FLORY, JENNIFER MORGAN, conductor, educator; d. Charles Hermann and Ruth-Anne Hein Morgan; m. William Richard Flory, June 25, 2005. BA, B Music Edn., Otterbein Coll., Westerville, Ohio, 1995; MusM, U. Cin., Ohio, 2003, Dr. of Musical Arts, 2005. Gen./vocal music tchr. Cath. Diocese of Columbus, Ohio, 1995—98; vocal music tchr. Columbus Pub. Schs., Columbus, Ohio, 1998—2001; asst. prof. Ga. Coll. & State U., Milledgeville,

2005—. Choir dir. Faith Presbyn. Ch., Morehead, Ky., 1989—91; choir dir. for mid./high sch. choir Peace Luth. Ch., Gahanna, Ohio, 1995—97; interim dir. music ministries First United Meth. Ch., Milledgeville, 2005; dir. music First Presbyn. Ch., Glendale, Ohio, 2005; dir. Georgian Renaissance Singers, Macon, 2006—. Mem.: Chorus Am., Coll. Music Soc., Music Educators Nat. Conf., Am. Choral Dirs. Assn. Office: Georgia Coll & State Univ Cbx 066 Milledgeville GA 31061 Office Phone: 478-445-4839. Office Fax: 478-445-1633. Personal E-mail: jmflory@musician.org. Business E-Mail: jennifer.flory@gcsu.edu.

FLOTEN, BARBARA JEAN, educational dean; b. Mt. Clemens, Mich., Aug. 21, 1946; d. Joseph Michael and Dorothy Winston (Bowles) Sarto; m. Frederick Floten, Sept. 10, 1971. BA, Portlant State U., 1968; MA, Portland State U., 1970. Social worker Multnomah County, Portland, 1970—71; instr. Mt. Hood CC, Gresham, Oreg., 1971—74; dir. student programs Edmonds CC, Lynnwood, Wash., 1974—77, dean students, 1977—. Chair or mem. various profl. groups, 1971—; bd. dirs. Planned Parenthood, Snobomish County, 1978; mem. Joint Action Coun. Edn., Seattle, 1979. Named Honorary Triton, ASEdCC, 1975—78; recipient numerous profl. recognitions. Mem.: LWV, Am. Assn. of Univ. Women, Nat. Assn. Student Pers. Adminstrn., Wash. CC Adminstrs., Seattle Wash. Athletic Club. Office: Edmonds Community Coll 20000 68th Ave W Lynnwood WA 98036-5912 also: Bellevue Community Coll 3000 Landerholm Cir SE Bellevue WA 98007-6406

FLOURNOY, LINDA WESLEY, minister, educator; b. Minden, La., Aug. 29, 1957; d. John Henry and Lillie Anderson Wesley; m. Connell Flournoy, Feb. 14, 1975; children: Adrian Connell, Amber Nicole. AA, La. Tech. U., 1994, BA, 1996, postgrad., 1998. Ordained elder 1995. Prescription tutor Eckerd Drug Stores, Minden, 1982—84; accounts receivable clk. City of Minden, 1984—90; office mgr. Custom Windows and Glass, Shreveport, La., 1991; pastor, tchr. Christian Meth. Ch., Shreveport, 1991—, Hattiesburg, Miss., 1998—2002. Established youth and young adult outreach ministry, Bassfield, Miss., 1999. Recipient Devoted and Invaluable Svc. award, Webster Parish Penal Farm Ministry, Minden, 1992, 1994—95, Invaluable Svc. award, Town & Country Nursing Home Ministry, Minden, 1992. Democrat. Avocations: interior decorating, homebuilding, reading. Home: 137 Flournoy Dr Minden LA 71055 Office: Christian Meth Ch Holcomb Dr Shreveport LA 71103

FLOURNOY, NANCY, statistician, educator; b. Long Beach, Calif., May 4, 1947; d. Carr Irvine Flournoy and Elizabeth Flournoy-Rivera; m. Leonard B. Hearne, Aug. 28, 1978. BS, UCLA, 1969, MS, 1971; PhD, U. Wash., 1982. Dir. clin. stats. Fred Hutchinson Cancer Rsch. Ctr., Seattle, 1974-86; dir. stats. and probability NSF, Washington, 1986—; prof. stats. American U., Washington, 1988—2002; chmn., prof. stats. U. Mo., Columbia, Mo., 2002—. Mem. of corp. Nat. Inst. Statis. Scis., Research Triangle Park, N.C., 1990-97, coun. Inst. Math. Stats., 2004—. Editor Multiple Stats. Integration, 1991, Adaptive Designs, 1995, New Developments and Applications in Experimental Designs, 1998, Adaptive Designs in Clinical Trials, 2005; assoc. editor Jour. Statis. Planning and Inference, 1998-2004. Grant reviewer AAUW, NSF, NIH, Nat. Security Agy USPHS fellow, 1969-71; Nat. Cancer Inst. grantee, 1975-86, NSF grantee, 1989-90, 96-2001, Am. Math. Soc./Inst. of Math. Stats./Soc. of Indsl. Applied Math. grantee, 1989, 92, EPA grantee, 1994-2000; recipient Elizabeth Scott award Com. of Pres. of Statis. Socs., 2000. Fellow AAAS, Inst. Math. Stats., Am. Statis. Assn. (chair coun. sects. 1994), World Acad. Art and Sci., Washington Acad. Sci.; mem. Caucus for Women in Stats., Internat. Stats. Inst., Internat. Biometric Soc., Internat. Assn. for Statis. Computing. Democrat. Achievements include development of new statistical procedures for clinical trials and response-driven experimental designs; research on bone marrow transplantation, on graft versus leukemia, on infectious diseases in immuno-compromised hosts, on information management. Office: U Mo Dept Stats 146 Middlebush Columbia MO 65211-4100 Office Phone: 573-882-6376.

FLOWE, CAROL CONNOR, lawyer; b. Owensboro, Ky., Jan. 3, 1950; d. Marvin C. Connor and Ethel Marie (Thorn) Smith; children: Samantha Kathleen, Andrew Benjamin. BME magna cum laude, Murray State U., 1972; JD summa cum laude, Ind. U., 1976. Bar: Ohio 1977, U.S. Dist. Ct. (so. dist.) Ohio 1977, DC 1981, U.S. Dist. DC 1981, U.S. Dist. Ct. Md. 1983, U.S. Supreme Ct. 1987, U.S. Ct. Appeals (2d, 3d, 4th, 5th, 7th, and DC cirs.). Assoc. Baker & Hostetler, Columbus, Ohio, 1976—80, Arent Fox Kintner Plotkin & Kahn, Washington, 1980—87; dep. gen. counsel Pension Benefit Guaranty Corp., Washington, 1987—89, gen. counsel, 1989—95; ptnr. Arent Fox, PLLC, Washington, 1995—. Mem.: ABA, DC Bar Assn., Order of Coif, Phi Alpha Delta, Alpha Chi. Avocations: computers, reading. Home: 8608 Aqueduct Rd Potomac MD 20854-6249 Office: Arent Fox PLLC 1050 Connecticut Ave NW Ste 500 Washington DC 20036-5339 Office Phone: 202-857-6054. Business E-Mail: flowe.carol@arentfox.com.

FLOWER, JEAN FRANCES, art educator; b. Schenectady, N.Y., Apr. 12, 1936; d. Francis Tunis and Marjorie (Colcord) Fort; m. Wesley Allen Flower, Aug. 23, 1958; children: Kimberly Lynn, Kristina Kathleen. BA, Syracuse U., 1958; BFA cum laude, Western Mich. U., 1984, MFA magne cum laude, 1989. Free-lance artist, 1981-86; tech. grad. asst. Western Mich. U., Kalamazoo, 1988, grad. asst. early mgmt., 1989, instr. art, 1989-93, Kalamazoo Inst. Art, 1993—. One-woman shows include Peoples Ch., Kalamazoo, 1991; exhibited in group shows Kalamazoo Area Art Show, 1992, 94 95, 97, Nat. Art Show, Dallas, 1993, Libr., Parchment, Mich., 1993, EAA Aviation Internat. Art Show, 1992, 95; murals executed Kalamazoo Valley Pub. Mus., 1995, Kalamazoo Aviation History Mus., 1996. Pres., mem. Anna Cir. 1st United Meth. Ch., Kalamazoo, 1980—, mem. communications commn., 1994—; sec.-treas. Airward, Plainwell, Mich., 1986—. Mem. Am. Assn. Aviation Artists, Plainwell Pilots Assn., Kalamazoo Aviatrix Assn. (past v.p.). Avocations: flying, painting, golf, tennis, cross country skiing. Home: 8745 Marsh Rd Plainwell MI 49080-8818

FLOWER, RENÉE BEVILLE, artist; b. Chgo., Oct. 22, 1950; d. Milton Oliver and Doris Lea (Beville) F.; m. Victor Allan Spiegel, June 22, 1975 (div. June 1981); m. James Anderson MacKenzie, July 31, 1982. BA in Studio Art, U. Calif., Santa Cruz, 1979. Lectr. in field. Ilustrator: (books) The Complete Sylvie & Bruno, 1991, City Noise, 1994, School Supplies, 1996; one-woman shows include Eloise Pickard Smith Gallery, 1993; exhibited in group shows at Ste 311, Pacific Grove, 1985, Zaner Gallery, Rochester, N.Y., 1986, San Francisco Mus. Modern Art Rental Gallery, 1987, The Art Mus. Santa Cruz County, 1988, Christopher Grimes Gallery, Carmel, 1989, Susan Cummins Gallery, Mill Valley, Calif., 1990, One Market Plaza, San Francisco, 1991, Gallery 500, Elkins Park, Pa., 1992, Yummy! Eating Through A Day, 2000, and others.

FLOWERS, BETTY SUE, library director, educator; b. Waco, Tex., Feb. 2, 1947; d. Paul Davis and Betty Lou (Lewis) Marable; m. John G. Flowers III; 1 child, John Michael. BA with high honors, U. Tex., 1969, MA, 1970; PhD, U. London, 1973. With U. Tex., Austin, 1968—, dir. plan II honors program, 1987-91, assoc. dean Graduate Studies, 1979-82, 88-90, Kelleher prof. English, dir. creative writing English Dept.; dir. Lyndon Baines Johnson Libr. and Mus., Austin, Tex., 2002—. Cons. Exxon, IBM, Shell Internat., London. Author: Browning and The Modern Tradition, 1976, Four Shields of Power, 1987, Extending the Shade, 1990; editor: A World of Ideas, 1988, Joseph Campbell and the Power of Myth: Bill Moyers and Joseph Campbell in Conversation, 1988, (with Lynda E. Boose) Daughters and Fathers, 1988, Moyers: Healing and the Mind, 1992; contbr. chpts. to books, articles to profl. jours. Adv. bd. Salado Inst. for Humanities, 1980-84, bd. dirs., 1988; mem. exec. com. Tex. Com. for Humanities, 1987-90; bd. trustees Tex. Humanities Alliance, 1986-87. Recipient Amoco Teaching Excellence award 1979, Leadership Tex., 1985; Andrew W. Mellon fellow, 1976; faculty U. Rsch. Inst. grantee, 1983. Mem. MLA, Tex. Assn. Coll. Tchrs., Tex. Assn. Creative Writing Tchrs., AAUP, Nat. Poetry Therapy Assn. (bd. dirs. 1987—), NEH, Rotary, Phi Beta Kappa, Omicron Delta Kappa. Office: Lyndon Johnson Libr and Mus 2313 Red River St78705 Austin TX 78705-5702 Office Phone: 512-721-0200.*

FLOWERS, CYNTHIA, investment company executive; b. NYC, May 29, 1951; d. Bernard and Pearl (Davis) Heller; m. Robert Flowers, June 3, 1973; children: Perry, Lindsey. BS summa cum laude, Boston U., 1973; MBA with honors, NYU, 1976. Sr. mgr. portfolios Citibank NA, N.Y.C., 1973-82; v.p. Nat. Securities Corp., N.Y.C., 1982-87; pres. Stillrock Mgmt. Inc., N.Y.C., 1987-90; founder, pres. Flowers Capital Mgmt. Inc., N.Y.C., 1990—. Mem.: Westside Tennis Club, Beta Gamma Sigma. Avocations: tennis, antiques. Office: Flowers Capital Mgmt Inc 97 Groton St Forest Hills NY 11375-5956

FLOWERS, HELEN FOOTE, librarian, educator; b. Elizabethtown, Ky., Aug. 10, 1931; d. Arthur Alonzo and Mayme (Redmond) Foote; m. Elbert Conner Flowers Jr., June 19, 1954. BA, Peabody Coll., 1954; MSLS, Columbia U., 1962; EdD, Hofstra U., 1983. Cert. sch. dist. adminstr., libr. media specialist N.Y. Tchr. English St. Andrew's High Sch., Charleston, S.C., 1956-61; libr. Ashley Hall, Charleston, 1962-65; libr. media specialist Bay Shore (N.Y.) Pub. Schs., 1965-93. Adj. prof. Palmer Sch. Libr. and Info. Sci., L.I. U., Greenvale, N.Y., 1976-93, SUNY, Stony Brook, 1989-93; mem. task force White House Conf. on Librs., 1988—; mem. adv. com. on librs. N.Y. Regents, 1985-90; mem. NY Gov.'s Commn. on Librs., 1990; N.Y. del. to White House Conf. on Librs., 1991. Author: Sources for Teaching Long Island History, 1980, Public RElations for School Library Media Programs, 1998; editor: Sharing Showcase: A Book of Ideas that Work, 1985. Hofstra U. fellow, 1982-83; recipient N.Y. Libr. Assn. Outstanding Svc. to Librs. award, 1990. Mem. ALA (mem. best books for young adults com. 1991-92), N.Y. Libr. Assn. (pres. 1987). Avocations: opera, reading, singing. Home: 490 Fearrington Post Pittsboro NC 27312

FLOWERS, JUDITH ANN, marketing and public relations director; d. Woodrow Coleman and Ola Marie (Harding) Haynes; m. Sayles L. Brown Jr., Apr. 20, 1963 (div. Apr. 1974); children: Sayles L. III, Gregory A., Matthew C., Stephen W.; m. Taylor Graydon Flowers Jr., Apr. 27, 1979. Grad. high sch., Clarksdale, Miss. Office mgr. The KBH Corp., Clarksdale, 1964-69; office mgr., estimator Willis & Ellis Constrn., Clarksdale, 1969-75; with advt. prodn. Farm Press Pub., Clarksdale, 1975-79, advt. mgr., 1979-86, dir. advt. svcs., 1986-93; dir. mktg. and pub. rels. Cotton Club Casino, Greenville, Miss., 1992-95; dir. spl. projects C. of C., Clarksdale, Miss., 1996—; pres. JF Designs, Inc., 1999—. Adv. Moore Bayou Water Assoc., 2005. Counselor County Youth Ct., Clarksdale, 1985—; sec. Keep Clarksdale Beautiful, 1990-92; bd. dirs. Delta Arts Coun., 1994-95, Miss. Tourism Promotion Assn., 1996—; co-chair Tennessee Williams Festival, 1996, chair, 1999-2001; founding mem. Clarksdale Heritage Found., pres., 1997; advisor Moore Bayou Water Assn., 2005-06. Mem. NAFE, Bus. and Profl. Women (corr. sec. 1987-88, 1st v.p. 1989-90, pres. 1992-93), Agri-Women Am., Nat. Agri-Mktg. Assn. (v.p. Mid-south chpt. 1989-90, pres. 1990-91, nat. dir. 1991-93), Clarksdale C. of C. (chmn. agri-bus. commn. 1989-92, bd. dirs. 1989-92), So. Garden History Soc. (bd. dirs. 1992-95), The Garden Conservancy (city beautification 1996—), Miss. Tourism Promotion Assn. (bd. dirs. 1996—), Miss. Delta Arts Coun. (bd. dirs. 1996—), Clarksdale Women's Club (1st v.p. 2001-02) Republican. Baptist. Avocations: genealogy, gardening. Home: PO Box 26 Dublin MS 38739-0026 Office: JF Designs Inc PO Box 26 Dublin MS 38739-0026

FLOWERS, MARGUERITA DENISE, banker, educator; b. Memphis, June 24, 1951; d. Green William and Precious Loyal Flowers; m. Ira Demetrius Greene (div.); m. Calvin Lee Scorirons III (div.). BA Bus. Adminstrn., Fla. State Christian Coll., Ft. Lauderdale, 1977. Cert. loan agt. Br. mgr., exwc. v.p. prodn. All Cities Mortgage Co., Riverside, Calif., 1984—87; exec. v.p. DI Investments, Victorville, Calif., 1987—89; supr. Gold Card Harrah's Casino Resort, Reno, 1990—96; mgr. club svcs. Atlantis Casino Resort, Reno, 1996—98; coord. recruitment U. Nev. Reno, 1998—99, educator, 1999—; loan agt. we. divsn. mktg. HAVAS Leasing, Reno, 2004—. V.p. bd. dirs. New Project, Reno, 2003—05; mem. Racial Justice Com., Reno, 2004—05. Author: Poems. Mem. Sisters for Sisters adv. U. Nev. Reno, 2003—05; treas. Black Dem. Caucus, Reno, 2004—05; del., precinct capt. Washoe County Dem., Reno, 2004—05. Named to Wall of Tolerance, Montgomery, Ala., 2005; recipient Hand in Hand award, Nev. PEP, 2004. Islam. Avocations: reading, sports, gardening, politics. Home: 6139 Dawn View Ln North Las Vegas NV 89031 Office: HAVAS Leasing Mortgage Loan Divsn 3100 Mill St Ste 219 Reno NV 89502

FLOWERS, SANDRA JOAN, elementary school educator, educator; b. Newport, R.I., July 17, 1943; d. Joseph A. and Dolores A. (Martino) F. BA, Salve Regina Coll., 1965; MA in Teaching, R.I. Coll., 1968; postgrad., Salve Regina U., 1990—2006, cert. advanced grad. study, 1994, PhD, 2006. Cert. elem. tchr., R.I. Tchr. Newport Sch. Dept., 1965-95; ret., 1995; instr., edn. Salve Regina U., Newport, 1979—. Mem. adv. bd. Underwood Sch., Newport, 1986, mem. site-based mgmt. team, 1993—; mem. basic ednl. planning ream R.I. Dept. Edn., Barrington Pub. Schs., 1986; mem. planning team, reader Children's Reading Hour, Literacy Outreach, Newport. Mem. Funding and Expenditures Alternatives Strategic Planning, Newport, 1989—; mem. grad. student coun. Salve Regina U.; mem. Newport Dem. City Com., 2005—; religious edn. tchr. St. Joseph's Parish, Newport, 1995—, chair liturgy com., 2000—. sec. parish coun., 2001—; bd. dirs. Aquidneck Collaborative for Edn., 1993—, Vols. on Newport Edn., 2004, Friends of Newport Libr. Moore scholar Salve Regina Coll., 1961-65, R.I. State scholar, 1961-65; recipient Feinstein Enriching Am. award, 1999. Mem.: LWV, AAUW, ASCD, Newport County Ret. Tchrs. Assn., RI Ret. Tchrs. Assn., RI Assn. Tchr. Educators, US Naval War Coll. Found., Newport Irish Heritage Mus., Navy League US. Roman Catholic. Avocations: creative writing, reading, church work, drawing, painting. Home: PO Box # 114 16 Keeher Ave Newport RI 02840-2320 E-mail: sjf71743@hotmail.com, sjflowersphd@yahoo.com.

FLOWERS, V. ANNE, retired academic administrator; b. Dothan, Ala., Aug. 29, 1928; d. Kyrie Neal and Annie Laurie (Stewart) Flowers. BA, Fla. State U., 1949; MEd, Auburn U., 1958; EdD, Duke U., 1963. Teaching asst. Duke U., Durham, NC, 1963; elem. and secondary sch. tchr., adminstr. Dothan, Dalton, Ga., 1949-61; from assoc. prof. to prof. edn., head dept. Columbia (S.C.) Coll., 1963-68, from assoc. dean to dean, 1969-72; prof. edn. Va. Commonwealth U., 1968-69; tchg. asst. Duke U., 1963, assoc. dean, asst. provost, acting dean, vice provost Trinity Coll. Arts and Scis., 1972-74, prof. edn., chmn. dept., asst. provost ednl. program devel., 1974-80; dean Sch. Edn. Ga. So. Coll., Statesboro, 1980-85; asst. vice chancellor acad. affairs Univ. Sys. Ga., Atlanta, 1985-88, vice chancellor, 1988-90, ret., 1990, vice chancellor emerita, 1990—. Mem. coun. aging and human devel. Duke U., 1974—80; cons. in field. Co-author: Law and Pupil Control, 1964, Readings in Survival in Today's Society, 2 vols., 1978; mem. editl. bd. Ednl. Gerontology, 1979, Jour. Tchr. Edn., 1980—82; contbr. articles to profl. jours. Bd. dirs., mem. exec. com. Learning Inst. N.C., 1976—80; vice chmn. continuing commn. study black colls. related to United Meth. Ch., 1973—76; pres. univ. senate Bd. Higher Edn. and Ministry United Meth. Ch., 1977—80; adv. trustee Queens Coll., Charlotte, NC, 1976—78; mem. bd. visitors Charleston So. U., 1992—93. Delta Kappa Gamma scholar, Duke U., 1963, State of Fla. scholar, Fla. State U., 1949. Mem.: NEA, Nat. Orgn. Legal Problems Edn., Am. Assn. Colls. Tchr. Edn. (bd. dirs., mem. exec. com. 1979—84, pres. 1983—84), Kappa Delta Pi. Home and Office: 41 Williamsburg Pl Dothan AL 36305

FLOWERS-SCHOEN, MARYLU UTLEY, art educator; d. Lynwood Hugh and Mary Jane Utley Flowers. BA, Meredith Coll., Raleigh, N.C., 1974. Cert. art tchr. K-12 Dept. Pub. Instrn., N.C., 1974, Dept. Edn., NSW, Australia, 1975, art specialist Dept. Edn., Victoria, Australia, 1977, visual arts tchr. K-12 Dept. Pub. Instrn. N.C., 1985. Visual arts specialist Miller HS, New South Wales, Australia, 1974—76; contract creating art programs Dept. Edn., Carringbah and Corowa, New South Wales, Australia, 1976—80; visual arts specialist St. Anne's and Gippsland Grammar Sch., Sale, Victoria, Australia, 1980—81, Dept. Edn., Ballimore and Dubbo, New South Wales, 1981—85; graphic artist Fine Designs, Durham, 1985—90; visual arts specialist Durham City and Public Schs., 1987—; contract educator Ackland Art Mus., Chapel Hill, NC, 1990—; mixed media tchr. Durham Arts Coun., 1992—. Lead tchr., fellow Thomas Day Edn. Project, Durham, 1994—2004; A+ fellow Kenan Inst. for the Arts/ A+ Schs., Greensboro, NC, 1993—; presenter NCAEA Confs., 1993, 94, 98, 2005, PDS Conf., Louisville, 1995, Columbia, SC, 2000, Integrated Arts Conf., Tucson, 2003, Tucson, 05, N.C. Environ. Edn. Conf., 2005. Author (editor): (published history) Ballimore Public School, Centenary 1884-1984; mural, Our Ballimore; contbr. articles to profl. jours. Mem. Five Oaks Assn., Durham, 1994—99; cultural arts liaison PTA, Durham, 1996—. Recipient Miss NC Outstanding Arts Educators award, NC Dept. Pub. Instrn. and N.C. PTA, 1992, award for Excellence in Internat. Edn., Goldman Sachs Found., 2003; grantee Cultural Edn. Through the Arts, Bright Ideas/ Gen. Electric, 1988, Race Rels. through Arts, Z. Smith Reynolds Found., 1989, One World, Many Faces, Durham Pub. Edn. Network Tchr. Initiative Grants, 1995, Thomas Day Edn. Project, Nat. Endowment for the Humanities and N.C. Arts Coun., 1997, Mary Mac Mullen Fund for Art Edn., Nat. Art Edn. Found., 1999, History in a Green Box, Durham Pub. Edn. Network Tchr. Initiative Grants, 2003, New Hope Creek Project, 2005. Mem.: NEA, NC Art Edn. Assn. (treas., sec., mem. at large, and long range planning 1993—2006, N.C. Art Educator of Yr. 1996), Forest View Elem. PTA (membership chair 2003—06), Durham Assn. Educators (site rep. 1987—2006), Nat. Art Edn. Assn. (Art Educator of Yr. 1998), Phi Delta Kappa (Outstanding Educator of Yr. 2003). Achievements include students' artworks published in three Shakti for Children's books and Unicef 2000 Calendar. Avocations: cooking and catering, Japanese style gardening.

FLOYD, ANN R., elementary school educator; b. Mullins, S.C., June 29, 1951; d. Harry Theodore and Mary Elizabeth (Winburn) Richardson; m. Larry Dwight Floyd, Sr., Feb. 20, 1971; 1 child, Larry Dwight Jr. Student, Coastal Carolina, 1969-71; BA in Early Childhood Edn., Clemson U., 1981; MEd in Reading, Francis Marion U., 1990. Cert. early childhood edn., elem. edn. Fourth grade tchr. McKissick Elem., Easley, S.C., 1981-82; first grade tchr. Concrete Elem., Easley, 1983-84, third grade tchr., 1984-85; fourth grade self contained tchr. Royall Elem., Florence, S.C., 1985-91, sixth grade sci./health tchr., 1991-93, sci. specialist, 1993—99; 3rd grade tchr. Red Bank Elem., Lexington, SC, 1999—. Mem. Supts. Faculty Adv. Bd., 1993-99. Loyalty fund mem. Clemson U., 1981—, mem. Iptay, 1981—; active Friends of the Mus., S.C. State Mus., Columbia, 1988—, S.C. Wildlife Orgn., 1990—, Supt.'s Adv. Bd., Florence, 1993. Recipient Presdl. award for excellence in sci. tchg. NSF, 1995; grantee Pee Dee Edn. Found., 1995. Mem. NSTA, Internat. Reading Assn., S.C. Ednl. TV Endowment, S.C. Sci. Coun., S.C. Middle and Elem. Sch. Sci. Coun. (bd. dirs., charter mem.), S.C. Children's Sci. Coun. (exec. bd. 1995—), Nat. Wildlife Assn., Nat. Geographic Soc. Office: Red Bank Elem Sch 246 Community Dr Lexington SC 29073

FLOYD, CAROL ANN, musician, recording artist, pianist, educator; b. NYC; d. Frank Dallas and Marilyn Marcella Floyd; 2 children. B of Music, Boise State U., 1990; M of Music summa cum laude, Cin. Coll., 1993, D of Music, 1994; diploma in chamber music, Conservatoire de Musique, Fontainebleau, France, 1993. Pvt. instr. music, Idaho, 2000—; instr. Idaho Music Acad., 2005—. Concert pianist, chamber music coach and adviser Boise Tuesday Mus. Scholarships for Students, 1983—; writer, rschr., spkr., guest clinician music history NFMC, Idaho, 2005; spkr. in field. Musician (concert pianist): state, nat. and internat. performances, European piano premier, Am. woman composer (Amy Beach), (CD) Premiere, 2005. Fundraiser Cystic Fibrosis Found., Boise, 1994; mem. Am. Mothers, Inc. Recipient First Place award, Am. Mother's Inc., 2000. Mem.: Internat. Alliance Women Music, Music Tchrs. Nat. Assn., Nat. Fedn. Music Clubs (judge). Avocations: gardening, reading, writing. Business E-Mail: info@carolannfloyd.com.

FLOYD, DAISY HURST, dean, law educator; BA, MA in Polit. Sci., Emory U., 1977; JD cum laude, U. Ga., 1980. Bar: Ga., TEx. Dir. Legal Rsch. and Writing Prog. U. Ga. Sch. Law; atty. Alston, Miller & Gaines, Atlanta; prof. law Tex. Tech U. Sch. Law, assoc. dean academic affairs; dean Walter F. George Sch. Law, Mercer U., 2004—. Faculty mem. Nat. Inst. Trial Advocacy (NITA), Nat. Jud. Coll., Tex. Jud. Acad., Tex. Ctr. for Judiciary. Mem. bd. dirs. Lubbock Legal Aid Soc. Named Phi Alpha Delta Prof. of Yr., 2001, Carnegie Scholar, 2001; recipient New Prof. Excellence in Tchg. Award, 1995. Fellow: Am. Bar. Found.; mem.: Tex. Bar Found. Office: Mercer U Sch Law 1021 Georgia Ave Macon GA 31207-0001 Office Phone: 478-301-2602. E-mail: floyd_dh@mercer.edu.

FLOYD, HAZEL MCCONNELL, special education educator; b. Cumming, Ga., June 4, 1953; d. E.W. and Reatha Mae (Sosebee) McConnell; m. Nolan Trent Floyd, June 8, 1975; children: Jared Gordon, Nalanna Hope. BS in Elem. Edn., Ga. Southwestern Coll., 1974; MEd in Elem. Edn., North Ga. Coll., 1977; Specialist in Edn., U. Ga., 1991. Tchr. 2nd grade Midway Elem. Sch., Alpharetta, Ga., 1974-81; tchr. visually impaired Chestatee Elem. Sch./Forsyth County Schs., Gainesville, Ga., 1981—2002; ret.; tchr. visually impaired Dawson County Sch., Dawsonville, Ga., 2005—. Part-time Ga. Pines, 2005—. Composer songs: He Will Hear Me When I Pray, 1989, I Want to Work Till Jesus Comes Again, 1991. Panel mem. State Adv. Bd. for Spl. Edn., Atlanta, 1988-91, Local Edn. agy. for Vision tchrs., Macon, 1988-90; treas. Chestatee Elem. Sch. PTO, 1989-91; choir leader Children's Choir, Salem Bapt. Ch., Gainesville, 1986—. Named Tchr. of the Yr. Midway Elem. Sch., 1981. Mem. Ga. Assn. Educators (legis. chmn. 1987-92), Coun. for Exceptional Children, Assn. for edn. and Rehab. of Visually Impaired. Baptist. Avocations: singing, playing organ. Home: 6285 Keith Bridge Rd Gainesville GA 30506-3907 E-mail: canuchazel@juno.com.

FLOYD, KRISTI, counseling administrator; b. Omaha; d. Marie C. and Donald J. Floyd. BA, Dillard U., 1994; MA in Counseling (hon.), Prairie View A&M U., 1997; D in -Educational Leadership, Nova Southeastern U., 2005. Sch. counselor Tex., 2002. English tchr. Ft. Bend ISD, Houston, 1995—99; student svcs. coord. Lamar U., Beaumont, Tex., 1999—2000; h.s. counselor Port Arthur ISD, Port Arthur, Tex., 2000—03; elem. sch. counselor Alief ISD, Houston, 2003—. Safe & drug free coord. Alief ISD, Houston, 2003—, testing coord., 2003—, mentor coord., 2003—. Singer jazz singer, JOI (group name). Recipient Counseling Honor Soc., Chi Sigma Iota, 1997. Mem.: Alpha Kappa Alpha Sorority, Inc. (life). Home: 2255 Eldridge Pkwy #1616 Houston TX 77077

FLOYD, PAMELA KAY, elementary school educator, artist; d. Marie A. and Harold Raymond Floyd. M of Secondary Edn., U. No. Ariz., Flagstaff, 2004. Mgr. of AOK program Alhambra Sch. Dist., Phoenix, 1988—96; tchr., chmn. dept. Desert Sands Mid. Sch., Phoenix, 1996—. Handmaking teddy bears and dogs. Recipient Golden Bell award, Ariz. Sch. Bd. Assn., 2002. Mem.: NSTA. Home: 5520 W Onyx Ave Glendale AZ 85302 Office: Desert Sands Mid Sch 6803 W Campbell Phoenix AZ 85033 Office Phone: 623-691-2913. Business E-Mail: pfloyd@sand.cartwright.k12.az.us.

FLOYD, ROSALYN WRIGHT, pianist, accompanist, educator; b. Charleston, SC, Oct. 22, 1956; d. Reginald Abram and Dorothy (Brunson) Wright; m. Hernan Augustus Floyd, Nov. 27, 1987 (dec. Aug. 2004) BA, Talladega (Ala.) Coll., 1977; MusM in Piano Performance/Pedagogy, U S.C., 1981; D Musical Arts in Piano Performance, U. S.C., 1990. Music tchr. Charleston County Dist. 20, Charleston, 1977-78; grad. asst. U. S.C., Columbia, S.C., 1978-85; asst. prof. dept. music Benedict Coll., Columbia, SC, 1985—88; rehearsal accompanist Columbia Lyric Opera, 1983-86; prof. dept. fine arts Augusta (Ga.) State U., 1988—; rehearsal accompanist Augusta Choral Soc., 1994—. Bd. dirs. Augusta Choral Soc. Performer lectures and recitals; accompanist for Martina Arroyo and Myrtle Hall in their performances for Pope John Paul II, 1987. Evaluator, Arts Infusion program Greater Augusta Arts Coun., 1992, music panel Ga. Coun. for the Arts, 1997-98. Named Artist of Yr., Greater Augusta Arts Coun., 2005; Black Am. Music Symposium scholar, 1985; Ambrose Headen scholar Talladega Coll., 1973-77. Mem. Augusta Music Tchrs. Assn. (v.p. for membership 1998-2000), Ga. Music Tchrs. Assn., The Links Inc. (v.p. Augusta chpt. 1999-2001, pres. 2001-03), Ctr. for Black Music Rsch. (pres. 2001-03). Baptist. Avocations: crocheting, sewing, gardening, computing. Home: 2503 Larchmont Ct Augusta GA 30909-6567 Office: Augusta State U 2500 Walton Way Augusta GA 30904-4562 Office Phone: 706-667-4877. Personal E-mail: rosalynwf@cs.com. Business E-Mail: rfloyd@aug.edu.

FLOYD, RUTH CRUMMETT, elementary school educator; b. Staunton, Va., Apr. 9, 1947; d. Floyd E. and Marie (Redifer) Crummett; m. Ray Harold Floyd, Dec. 23, 1967; children: Kristal Marie, Kathy Rae. Diploma, Elizabeth Brant Bus. Sch., Staunton, 1967; BA cum laude, Mary Baldwin Coll., 1985. Tchr. Weyers Cave (Va.) Elem. Sch., 1985-95, Clymore Elem. Sch., Ft. Defiance, Va., 1995—. Avocation: bowling. Home: 287 Stokesville Rd Mount Solon VA 22843-9539 Office: Clymore Elem Sch 184 Fort Defiance Rd Fort Defiance VA 24437-9801 E-mail: riteach2@ntelos.net.

FLOYD, SUZANNE ELVIRA IZZO, music educator; b. Norristown, Pa., Sept. 27, 1950; d. Nicholas and Virginia Marsh Izzo; children: Jennie Rebecca, Andrea Roberta. MusB, U. Miami, Coral Gables, Fla., 1978; MusM, U. Miami, 1983. Music specialist Miami-Dade County Pub. Schs., Miami, Fla., 1978—; music tchr. L'Overture Elem. Sch., Miami. Supt.'s leadership cir. Miami-Dade County Pub. Schools/United Way, Miami, Fla., 2002—; dir. music First United Meth. Ch., Homestead, Fla., 1992—2001; adj. prof. Barry U., Miami Shores, Fla., 1997—; mem. U. Miami Pres. Cir., 2002—. Bd. trustees Greater Miami Youth Symphony. With WAC, 1970—72, Ft. McClellan, Alabama. Named Tchr. of the Yr., Miami Dade County Pub. Schs./Perrine Elem. Sch., 1989; recipient Outstanding Svc. award, U. of Miami, Frost Sch. of Music, 1988, 1990, 1992. Mem.: U. Miami Frost Sch. Music Alumni Assn. (pres. 1989—92), U. Miami Alumni Assn. (bd. dirs. 1992—95), Miami Dade County Music Educators Assn., Miami Dade County Music Tchrs.' Assn. (pres. 1990—2006), Sigma Alpha Iota (life; nat. v.p., alumnae chapters 2000—06, nat. dir. music edn. 1997—2000, Ring of Excellence 2005, Rose of Dedication 2003, Diamond Sword of Honor 1997, Rose of Honor 1991). Independent. Presbyterian. Avocations: gourmet cooking, counted cross stitch, travel, reading. Home: 10340 SW 120th St Miami FL 33176 Office Phone: 305-758-2600. E-mail: suefloyd@dadeschools.net.

FLUD, SHERRIE MAE, science educator; d. Samuel Woodson Nunn and Velma Cathryn Holmes; m. Jerry Duane Flud, Aug. 17, 1972; children: Starla Dawn, Melissa Renae. Assoc., Connors State Coll., Warner, Okla., 1972; BS, Cameron U., Lawton, Okla., 1973. Tchr. Hanna Pub. Sch., Okla., 1975—83, Eufaula Pub. Sch., Okla., 1983—. Site coord. BEACON, Eufaula, Okla., 1998—2002. Recipient Tchr. of Yr. award, Cooper McClain, 1999, Eufaula Pub. Sch., 2006, Eufaula Mid. Sch., 2006. Office: Eufaula Mid Sc 111 Forest Ave Eufaula OK 74432 Office Phone: 918-689-2711. E-mail: smflud@eufaula.k12.ok.us.

FLUKE, LYLA SCHRAM (MRS. JOHN M. (LYLA) FLUKE SR.), publisher; b. Maddock, ND; d. Olaf John and Anne Marie (Rodberg) Schram; m. John M. Fluke, June 5, 1937 (dec. 2002); children: Virginia Fluke Gabelein, John M. Jr., David Lynd. BS in Zoology and Physiology, U. Wash., Seattle, 1934, diploma tchg., 1935. H.S. tchr., 1935-37; tutor Seattle schs., 1980-84; pub. Portage Quar. mag. Hist. Soc. Seattle and King County, 1980-84. Hon. chmn. nanotech. rsch. U. Wash., 2000, hon. chmn. campaign, 2006—. Contbr. articles to profl. jours. Co-founder N.W. chpt. Myasthenia Gravis Found., 1953, Wash. Tech. Ctr., 1996, pres., 1960-66; obtained N.W. artifacts for Navy destroyer Tender Puget Sound., 1966; mem. Seattle Mayor's Com. for Seattle Beautiful, 1962; sponsor Seattle World's Fair, 1962; charter and founding mem. Seattle Youth Symphony Aux., 1974; benefactor U. Wash., 1982-01, sponsor first chair mfg., U Wash., 1982, nat. chmn. ann. giving campaign, 1983-84; benefactor Cascade Symphony, Salvation Army, Sterling Cir. Stanford U., MIT, 1984, Seattle Symphony, 1982-2002, Wash. State Hist. Soc., Pacific Arts Coun., Pacific Sci. Ctr., 2003-04, Twenty-Twelve Club, 1962-2002; mem. condr.'s club Seattle Symphony, 1978-; mem. U. Wash. Campaign Exec. Com., 2003-04, hon. mem. Campaign Com. NSF Grant to Nat. Nanotechnology Infrastructure Network, 1984; hon. exec. com. on nanotech. U. Wash. Coll. Engring., 2003-; benefactor Seattle Symphony, 2004, U. Wash., 2004; mem. Seattle Beautification Com., 1965-68. Recipient Crystal plaque Coll. Engring. U. Wash., 2002, Framed document Pres. U.S.; fellow Seattle Pacific U., 1972; named Father of Electronics in Wash. State, Gov. John Spellman, 1983. Mem. IEEE Aux. (chpt. charter mem., pres. 1970-73), Wash. Trust for Hist. Preservation, Nat. Trust for Hist. Preservation, N.W. Ornamental Hort. Soc. (benefactor, life, hon.), Nat. Assn. Parliamentarians (charter mem., pres. N.W. unit 1961-64), Wash. Parliamentarians Assn. (charter), Seattle C. of C. (women's divsn. 1965-66), Seattle Symphony Women's Assn. (life, charter, sec. 1982-84, pres. 1985-87), Hist. Soc. Seattle and King County (exec. com. 1975-78, pres. women's mus. league 1975-79, pres. Moritz Thomsen Guild of Hist. Soc., 1978-80, 84-87), Highlands Orthopedic Guild (life), Wash. State Hist. Soc., Antiquarian Soc. (v.p. 1986-88, pres. 1988-90, hon. mem. John Fluke Mfg. Co. 20 Year Club 1987—), Rainier Club, Seattle Golf Club, U. Wash. Pres.'s Club, Twenty-Twelve Club, Pacific Sci. Ctr, Seattle. Republican. Lutheran. Achievements include sponsorship of the Fluke Chair in Coll. of Engring. U Wash. Home: 1206 NW Culbertson Dr Seattle WA 98177-3942 Office Phone: 425-453-4590.

FLUMMER, SANDRA MOON, elementary school educator; b. York, Ala., Apr. 29, 1947; d. John James and Ruby Jeanette Moon; m. Jerone S. Flummer, June 1, 1968; children: William Jonathan, Matthew Todd. BS, U. So. Miss., Hattiesburg, 1969; EDS, U. Ala., Tuscloosa, 1995, MS, 1989. Tchr. Purvis Sch. Elem., Miss., 1969—70, WDRobbins, Mobile, Ala., 1972—73, Heritage, Montomery, Ala., 1973—74, Hooper Acad., Montgomery, Ala., 1974—76, Bethany Christian Sch., Mobile, Ala., 1978—79, Hooper Acad., Montgomery, Ala., 1980—83, Calhoun County Tng. Sch., Anniston, Ala., 1985—87, Oxford City Schs., Ala., 1987—. Coord. marathon St. Jude's Rsch. Hosp., Oxford, Ala., 1992—2006; mission trip team One Way Ministries, Sells, Ariz., 2000—06; vol. coord. World Changers Internat., Oxford/Anniston, Ala., 2000—06; tchr./celebration choir Grace Bapt. Ch., Oxford, Ala., 2000—06. Mem.: NEA, Assn. of Classroom Tchrs., Ala. Coun. of Tchr.'s of Math., Nat. Coun. of Tchrs.'s of Math., Oxford Edn. Assn. (pres., v.p., treas. 2000—06), Ala. Edn. Assn. (del. 2000—06). Independent. Baptist. Home: 410 Highland Lakes Blvd Anniston AL 36207 Office: Oxford City Schs 1401 Caffey Dr Oxford AL 36203 Office Phone: 256-241-3844. Home Fax: same; Office Fax: 256-831-3043. Personal E-mail: sjflummer@bellsouth.net. E-mail: sflummer.oe@oxford.k12.us.

FLURY, JANE MADAWG, artist, educator; b. Furstenfeldbruk, Germany, May 31, 1955; d. Richard Benjamin and Cara Mae (Vondrak) McKee; m. Speed Coseboom, Jan. 11, 1986 (div. Dec. 1989); m. John Flury, Sept. 2, 1990; 1 child, Ty. AA, Bakersfield Coll., 1981; BA, U. Calif. Santa Cruz, 1992. Cert. adult edn. Dir. Robertson's Art & Antiques, Carmel, Calif., 1989—94; mgr. Collectors Framing, Pacific Grove, Calif., 1986—90; instr. painting Pacific Grove Unified Sch. Dist., 1997—. Intern Monterey Mus. Art, 1990—; docent Monterey Art & History Assn., 1994-96, open studio, Artist Equity, 1998—; owner Noble Savage Fine Art and Antiques, 1997—; instr. painting Lyceum Monterey Mus. Art, Calif., 1997—, Monterey Bay Aquarium, 1997—; v.p., bd. dirs. Pacific Grove Art Ctr. Author: Jane Flury's Artists' Handbook, 2003. V.p. Pacific Grove Art Ctr., Neoists. Mem. Fluxus Home: PO Box 916 Pacific Grove CA 93950-0916 E-mail: artnants@aol.com.

FLYE, CAROLYN MARIE, minister; d. L.A. and Marjorie Janette Flye. Ordained min. Lighthouse Fellowship of Chs., Fla., 1995; cert. Mandt tng. Anthony Wayne Svcs., 2005, CPR and first aid for infants, children and adults YWCA, 2004. Follow-up min. Calvary Chapel, Fort Wayne, Ind., 1991—93, pastoral and ch. com. chairperson, 1992—, deaconness, 1992—94, singles and womens conf. event planner, spkr., 1993—, evangelism ministry head, instr., 1993—95; sr. elder, assoc. min. Lighthouse Deliverance Cathedral, Fort Wayne, Ind., 1995—, worship leader, 1998—2000, dir. faith based initiative program, 1999—2000; edn., employment adv. YWCA Domestic Violence Svcs., Fort Wayne, Ind., 2001—04, supr. shelter program, 2005; trainer Anthony Wayne Svcs., Fort Wayne, Ind., 2004—. Spkr. Youth Svcs., Fort Wayne, 1993—95, Wood Youth Svcs., Fort Wayne, 1993—95, Greater Mt. Ararat Bapt. Ch., Fort Wayne, 1999—2003, Kingdom Door Worship Ctr., Fort Wayne, 1999, Lion of Judah, Huntington, Ind., 2000, Taylor U., Chapel Svc., Fort Wayne, 2004; adv. YWCA Domestic Violence Svcs., Fort Wayne, 2001—04, supr., 2001—04; min. to youth Calvary Chapel, Wood Youth Ctr., Youth Svcs., Fort Wayne. Treas. Lighthouse Deliverance Cathedral, Fort Wayne, 1995—2005. Grantee, Taylor U., 2002—05; scholar, Grabill Bank, Ft. Wayne, 2002—05; Levi and Pearl Moser scholar, Ft. Wayne, 2005—. Avocations: travel, mentoring, singing, reading. Personal E-mail: carolflye7@yahoo.com.

FLYNN, GARY L., pharmaceutical executive; b. Columbus, Ohio, Oct. 8, 1949; BBA, Franklin U. Various fin. and mgmt. positions Abbott Labs., Abbott Park, Ill., 1971—, divisional v.p., contr. Ross Products divsn., 1993, v.p., contr., sr. v.p. Ross Products, 2001—. Mem. bd. dirs. Columbus Children's Hosp. Rsch. Inst.; bd. trustees Franklin U. Office: Abbott Labs 100 Abbott Park Rd Abbott Park IL 60064-6400

FLYNN, GINA PEREZ, lawyer; BA cum laude, Mary Baldwin Coll., 1995; MA, U. Melbourne, 1997; JD, Boston Coll., 2000. Bar: Mass. 2001. Assoc. Nixon Peabody, LLP, Boston, DLA Piper, Boston. Mem.: Women's Bar Assn., Boston Bar Assn. Office: DLA Piper Floor 26 33 Arch St Boston MA 02110 Office Phone: 617-406-6046. Office Fax: 617-406-6146. E-mail: gina.flynn@dlapiper.com.*

FLYNN, JOAN MAYHEW, librarian; b. Mpls., Sept. 13, 1927; d. Oscar Koehler and Mabel Victoria (Stein) Mayhew; m. Elliot Colter Dick, Jr., Aug. 19, 1950 (div. May 1966); children: Emily Diane Dick Tuttle, Elliot Mayhew Dick; m. Paul James Flynn, Nov. 4, 1967. BMus, U. Minn., 1950; MLS, U. Hawaii, 1972, cert. in advanced libr. and info. studies, 1986. Circulation clk., 1972-75; reference libr., 1975-85; dir. acad. support svcs., head Sullivan Libr. Chaminade U. of Honolulu, 1986—. Mem. Interlibr. Cooperation Coun., 1990, 91; supr. vocal music Forest Lake (Minn.) Pub. Schs. Asst. dir. races Norman Tamanaha Meml., 1982, dir. 1983; bd. dirs. Hawaii Kai Fun Runners. Mem. ALA, Hawaii Libr. Assn., MidPac Road Runners Assn. (bd. dirs.), Hawaii Masters Track Club, Beta Phi Mu, Pi Lambda Theta, Sigma Alpha Iota. Avocations: running, bicycling, swimming, weightlifting, reading. Office: Chaminade U 3140 Waialae Ave Honolulu HI 96816-1578 Home: 8927 N Fitzgerald Ln Tucson AZ 85742-4451

FLYNN, MARIE COSGROVE, portfolio manager, corporate financial executive; b. Honolulu, Jan. 1, 1945; d. John Aloysius and Emeline Frances Cosgrove; m. John Thomas Flynn, Jr., June 3, 1968; children: Jamie Marie, Jacqueline Elizabeth. BA, Trinity Coll., 1966. CFP, CFA. Analyst U.S. Govt., Washington, 1967-70; coord. nat. reading coun. F.X. Doherty Assocs., N.Y.C., 1970-71; security analyst Corinthian Capital Co., N.Y.C., 1971-73; portfolio mgr. Clark Mgmt. Co., Inc., N.Y.C., 1973-78; 1at v.p., sr. portfolio mgr. Lexington Mgmt. Corp., Saddle Brook, NJ, 1978-96; pres. Corinthian Capital Mgmt. Co., Inc., Morristown, NJ, 1996-99; 1st v.p., mng. dir., sr. portfolio mgr. Glenmede Trust Co., 1999—. Bd. dirs., v.p. First Call for Help, 1996—2000; bd. trustees N.J. Pension and Annuity Fund, 1996—, vice chair bd. trustees, 2006—; elected mem. Somerset County Rep. Com., 1994—98; treas. Bernardsville Rep. Com., 1996—98, Bernardsville Planning Bd., 1996—98; mem. Bernardsville Borough Coun., 1998—2004; mayor Bernardsville, 2002, 2004; commr. Bernardsville Police Commn., 2000—04; pres. Women's Polit. Caucus NJ, 2001—03; bd. dirs. Soc. Women's Health Rsch., 2004—. Recipient Tribute to Women award, Patriots' Path Coun., 2002, Somerset Commn. on Women, 2004. Mem. Fin. Analysts Fedn., Inst. Chartered Fin. Analysts, N.Y. Soc. Security Analysts. Home: 50 Pickle Brook Rd Bernardsville NJ 07924-1909 Office: 360 Mt Kemble Ave Morristown NJ 07960-6019 Office Phone: 973-451-3800.

FLYNN, PATRICIA M., director, special education educator, gifted and talented educator; b. East Cleveland, Ohio, Sept. 11, 1952; d. Harry L. and Eleanore (Mahon) Flynn. BS in Edn. magna cum laude, St. John Coll., Cleve., 1974, MS in Edn., 1975; cert., Notre Dame Coll., 1992, Ursuline Coll., 2001. Cert. elem. edn., prin., edn. handicapped Ohio Detp. Edn. Reading specialist East Cleveland City Schs., 1974—98, reading coord., 1998—2000, curriculum specialist, 2000—01; dir. pupil svcs. Fairview Park (Ohio) Schs., 2001—. Local coord. Reading Is Fundamental Project, East Cleveland, 1996—2000; coord. East Cleveland Elem. Acad., East Cleveland, 1999. Scholar, St. John Coll., 1974. Mem.: Nat. Assn. Fed. Edn. Program Adminstrs., Internat. Reading Assn., Ohio Assn. Adminstrs. State and Fed. Edn. Programs, Ohio Assn. Pupil Svcs. Adminstrs., Irish Am. Club, City Club Cleve., Kappa Gamma Pi. Roman Catholic. Office: Fairview Park City Schs 20770 Lorain Rd Fairview Park OH 44126 E-mail: pflynn@leeca.org.

FLYNN, PAULINE T., retired speech pathologist, educator; BA, Paterson State Coll., 1963; MA, Seton Hall U., 1966; PhD, U. Kans., 1970; cert. specialist in aging, U. Mich., 1982. Speech pathologist Bd. Edn., Parsippany-Troy Hills, NJ, 1963—67; prof., chmn. dept. audiology and speech scis. Ind. U. Purdue U., Ft. Wayne, 1970—2003, prof. emerita, 2003—. Ednl. cons. Retirement Ctr., Ft. Wayne, 1982-85. Contbr. articles to nat. and internat. jours. Recipient Outstanding Alumna award William Paterson Coll., 1973, Woman of Achievement award Ft. Wayne YWCA, 1992. Fellow Am. Speech, Lang. and Hearing Assn.; mem. Am. Speech, Lang., Hearing Assn., Ind. Speech, Lang. and Hearing Assn. (honors 2003).

FLYNN-BISSON, KATHLEEN MARY, school system administrator; b. Qunees, NY, Sept. 24, 1964; d. Arthur Henry Flynn and Teresa Agnes Hertz; m. Roderick Francis Bisson, Nov. 25, 1994; children: Elizabeth Ann Bisson, Alexander Roderick Bisson, Andrew Francis Bisson. MA in Cmty. Health, Adelphi U., 1994. Cert. health edn. specialist NY. Account exec. Wells, Rich, Greene Advt., NYC, 1986—88, Harriet Schoenthal Pub. Rels., NYC, 1988—90; acad. advisor, pub. rels. specialist Adelphi U., Garden City, NY, 1990—94; health edn. coord. student health svc. Stony Brook (NY) U., 1994—. Prevention through the arts cons., North Babylon, NY, 2000—. Co-author: Experiece Stony Brook Freshman Textbook. Recipient Creative Program of Yr. award, LI Coll. Pers. Assn., 1996, Outstanding Student Group award, Stony Brook U. Residential Programs, 1997, Outstanding Student Life Programs award, NY State Faculty Senate, 1997, Star Fish Flinger award, Stony Brook U. Student Health Svc., 2005. Mem.: LI Coll. Consortium on Alcohol and Substance Awareness (treas. 1998—2006), Am. Coll. Health Assn. (assoc.). Office: Stony Brook U Student Health Svc 1 Stadium Road Stony Brook NY 11794-3191 Office Phone: 631-632-6682. Office Fax: 631-632-6936. Business E-Mail: kflynnbisson@notes.cc.sunysb.edu.

FLYNN-CONNORS, ELIZABETH KATHRYN, reporter, editor; b. Chgo., Aug. 17, 1939; d. Timothy Carver Flynn and Elizabeth Eleanor (Tait) Scanlon; m. Gerald Martin Connors, Dec. 30, 1978; children: Andrew, Kathryn, Elizabeth. Student, Monmouth Coll., Ill., 1957-59; BA in Journalism, U. Wis., 1961, postgrad., 1965-66. Cityside reporter Mpls. Tribune, 1961-62, Chgo. Daily News, 1962-66, UN/N.Y. corr., 1966-75, Washington corr., 1968; writer, press officer UN, N.Y.C., 1975-82; sr. writer UN Chronicle, N.Y.C., 1982-85, editor-in-chief, 1985-96; chief editor Yearbook of UN, N.Y.C., 1996-99; chief UN pubs., N.Y.C., 1999—. Troop leader Girl Scouts U.S., Tarrytown, N.Y., 1993-95. Russell Sage fellow U. Wis., 1965-66; recipient Investigative Reporting award Sigma Delta Chi, 1962, 1st Pl. Spot News award AP, 1970. Mem. UN Corrs. Assn. (alumni), Sleepy Hollow Sr. Citizens Club (sec.), White Plains Garden Club, Phi Beta Kappa, Kappa Delta. Avocations: reading, watching old movies. Home: 238 Hunter Ave Sleepy Hollow NY 10591-1317 E-mail: betty1153@aol.com.

FLYNN-JAMES, STEPHANIE, biologist, educator; b. Richland, Wash., Nov. 1, 1974; d. George Frank and Terry Faye Flynn; m. Christopher Matthew James, June 29, 2002; 1 child, Sydney Faye James. BS in Biology, Gonzaga U., 1997; MS in Biology, Ea. Wash. U., 2000—00; MBA, City U., Bellevue, Wash., 2004. Mem. profl. staff U. Wash., Seattle, 2000—01; sr. rsch. technician NeoRx Corp., Seattle, 2001—02; rsch. assoc. Seattle Genetics, Bothell, Wash., 2002—05; assoc. faculty mem. biology Cascadia C.C., Bothell, 2004—. Presenter in field. Contbr. articles to profl. publs. Vol. City of Bothell North Creek Project, 2005—06. Recipient Outstanding Contbn. award, Vols. Am. Crosswalk, 1998; scholar Golf Scholarship, Ea. Wash. U., 1993-1995; acad. scholar, Gonzaga U., 1995—97, Swartz Biotechnology Grad. fellow, Ea. Wash. U., 1999—2000, Rsch. grantee, 1999. Mem.: Gonzaga U. Alumni Assn. (life), Phi Eta Sigma (assoc.), Phi Sigma (assoc.). Office: Cascadia CC 18345 Campus Way NE Bothell WA 98011

FLYNN-POPPEY, ELISSA, lawyer; BA, Bridgewater State Coll., 1994; JD cum laude, Suffolk U. Law Sch., 2000. Rsch. asst. (update Mass. Practice Series) to Hon. Joseph Nolan Supreme Judicial Ct., Mass.; law clk. Superior Ct. Mass.; dep. counsel to Gov. Romney Office Gov. Mass., dexec. dir. judicial nominating commn.; ptnr. Litig. Sect. Mintz, Levin, Cohn, Ferris, Glovsky and Popeo PC, Boston. Zoning bd. appeals Town of Norfolk, historical commn.; trustee Bridgewater State Coll. Office: Mintz Levin Cohn Ferris Glovsky and Popeo PC One Financial Center Boston MA 02111 Office Phone: 617-348-1868. Office Fax: 617-542-2241. E-mail: EFlynn-Poppey@mintz.com.*

FOARD, SUSAN LEE, editor; b. Asheville, NC, Aug. 1, 1938; d. Carson Cowan and Anne (Brown) F. AB, Salem Coll., 1960; MA, William and Mary Coll., 1966. Asst. editor Inst. Early Am. Hist. and Culture, Williamsburg, Va., 1961-66, assoc. editor, 1966; editor U. Va. Press, Charlottesville, 1966—2004.

FOCH, NINA, actress, creative consultant, film director, educator; b. Leyden, The Netherlands, Apr. 20, 1924; came to U.S., 1927; d. Dirk and Consuelo (Flowerton) F.; m. James Lipton, June 6, 1954; m. Dennis de Brito, Nov. 27, 1959; 1 child, Dirk de Brito; m. Michael Dewell, Oct. 31, 1967 (div.). Grad., Lincoln Sch., 1939; studies with Stella Adler. Adj. prof. drama U. So. Calif., Grad. Sch. Cinema & TV, L.A., 1966—68, 1978—80, adj. prof. film, 1987—; creative cons. to dirs., writers, prodrs. of all media. Artist-in-residence U. N.C., 1966, Ohio State U., 1967, Calif. Inst. Tech., 1969-70; mem. sr. faculty Am. Film Inst., 1974-77; founder, tchr. Nina Foch Studio, Hollywood, Calif., 1973—; founder, actress Los Angeles Theatre Group, 1960-65; bd. dirs. Nat. Repertory Theatre, 1967-75. Motion picture appearances include Nine Girls, 1944, Return of the Vampire, 1944, Shadows in the Night, 1944, Cry of the Werewolf, 1944, Escape in the Fog, 1945, A Song to Remember, 1945, My Name Is Julia Ross, 1945, I Love a Mystery, 1945, Johnny O'Clock, 1947, The Guilt of Janet Ames, 1947, The Dark Past, 1948, The Undercover Man, 1949, Johnny Allegro, 1949, An American in Paris, 1951, Scaramouche, 1952, Young Man with Ideas, 1952, Sombrero, 1953, Fast Company, 1953, Executive Suite, 1954 (Oscar award nominee), Four Guns to the Border, 1954, You're Never Too Young, 1955, Illegal, 1955, The Ten Commandments, 1956, Three Brave Men, 1957, Cash McCall, 1959, Spartacus, 1960, Such Good Friends, 1971, Salty, 1973, Mahogany, 1976, Jennifer, 1978, Rich and Famous, 1981, Skin Deep, 1988, Sliver, 1993, Morning Glory, 1993, 'Til There Was You, 1996, Hush, 1998, Shadow of Doubt, 1998, How to Deal, 2003; appeared in Broadway plays including John Loves Mary, 1947, Twelfth Night, 1949, A Phoenix Too Frequent, 1950, King Lear, 1950, Second String, 1960; appeared with Am. Shakespeare Festival in Taming of the Shrew, Measure for Measure, 1956, San Francisco Ballet and Opera in The Seven Deadly Sins, 1966; also many regional theater appearances including Seattle Repertory Theatre (All Over, 1972 and The Seagull, 1973); actress on TV, 1947—, including Playhouse 90, Studio One, Pulitzer Playhouse, Playwrights 56, Producers Showcase, Lou Grant (Emmy nominee 1980), Mike Hammer; series star: Shadow Chasers, 1985, War and Remembrance, 1988, LA Law, 1990, Hunter, 1990, Dear John, 1990, 91, Tales of the City, 1993, Dharma and Greg, 1999, Just Shoot Me, 2000, recurring role Bull, 2000-01, State of Grace, 2003, When We Were Grown-ups, 2004, NCIs, 2005, 06; many other series, network spls. and TV films; TV panelist and guest on The Dinah Shore Show, Merv Griffin Show, The Today Show, Dick Cavett, The Tonight Show; TV moderator: Let's Take Sides, 1957-59; assoc. dir. (film) The Diary of Anne Frank, 1959; dir. (nat. tour and on-Broadway) Tonight at 8:30, 1966-67, Family Blessings, 1997; assoc. producer re-opening of Ford's Theatre, Washington, 1968. Hon. chmn. Los Angeles chpt. Am. Cancer Soc., 1970. Recipient Film Daily award, 1949, 53. Mem. AAUP, Acad. Motion Picture Arts and Scis. (co-chair exec. com. fgn. film award, membership com., chair foreign lang. award com., 1998-99), Hollywood Acad. TV Arts and Scis. (bd. govs. 1976-77). Avocation: work. Office: PO Box 1884 Beverly Hills CA 90213-1884 Office Phone: 310-553-5805.

FOCHT, SANDRA JEAN, retired elementary school educator; b. Santa Monica, Calif., Aug. 1, 1944; d. George Allen and Pauline Estella De Bra; m. R. Duane Focht, Feb. 1, 1964; children: Jeremy D., Jennifer R. BS in Edn., Wright State Univ., 1969, MEd in Ednl. Media, 1981, cert. in Gifted Edn. 1-12, 1985. Cert. elem. tchr. Ohio, tchr. gifted Ohio. Tchr. Parkwood Elem., Beavercreek, Ohio, 1970—99, Ankeney Middle Sch., Beavercreek, 1999—2004; ret., 2004. Pres., dir. Beavercreek (Ohio) Cmty. Theatre, 1994—99; adv. Muse Machine, Dayton, Ohio, 1995—2004; founder Jr. Thespian Chpt. at Ankeney Middle Sch. Co-author: (textbook) Writing Step By Step, 1986. Recipient Golden Apple Achievement award, Ashland Oil, 1996; Jennings scholar, 1975. Mem.: NEA, Ednl. Theatre Assn., Ohio Edn. Assn., Nat. Coun. Tchrs. English, Phi Delta Kappa. Avocations: writing, directing plays and musicals, photography. Home: 224 Cleek Springs Ct Dayton OH 45440 Personal E-mail: sfocht@sbcglobal.net.

FODI, ALISON ELIZABETH, mathematics educator; b. Denville, N.J., Nov. 2, 1976; d. Michael Joseph and Sharon Ann Brown; m. Scot Edward Fodi, July 19, 2003; 1 child, Grant Edward. BS in Secondary Math Edn., U. Ill., Urbana-Champaign, 1999; MA in Secondary Math Edn., DePaul U., Chgo., 2002. Cert. tchg. Ill., 1999, Pa., 2001, ticket tech. Pa. State U., 2005. Math tchr. Wheaton (Ill.) North H.S., 1999—2001, Norwin H.S., Irwin, Pa., 2001—02, Seneca Valley Intermediate H.S., Harmony, Pa., 2002—. Editor: College Textbook. Instr. St. Thomas, Naperville, Ill., 1999—2001. Home: 212 Birch St Mars PA 16046 Office: Seneca Valley IHS 126 Seneca School Rd Harmony PA 16037 Personal E-mail: alisonfodi@zoominternet.net. E-mail: fodia@svsd.net.

FODOR, IRIS ELAINE, clinical psychologist, educator, psychotherapist; b. N.Y.C., May 26, 1935; d. Jack and Helen (Cantor) Goldstein; m. Harry Beilin, June 5, 1988; children: Anthony Fodor, Johanna Sperling. PhD, Boston U., 1965. Lic. psychologist, N.Y. Prof. NYU, 1970—. Office: NYU Dept Applied Psychology East 537-D New York NY 10003

FODOR, SUSANNA SERENA, lawyer; b. Tg-Mures, Romania, Apr. 24, 1950; came to U.S., 1963; d. Bela Akos and Rachel (Rafira) F.; 1 child, Brooke Alexandra Bodoki-Fodor. BS, U. Wis., Milw., 1969; JD, U. Wis., Madison, 1972. Bar: Wis. 1972, N.Y. 1974. In ho. counsel Wis. Dept. Devel. Natural Resources, Madison, 1972-73, U.S. EPA, N.Y.C., 1973-74, Urban Devel. Corp., N.Y.C., 1975-77; assoc. Schulte, Roth & Zabel, N.Y.C., 1977-79; ptnr. Weil, Gotshal & Manges, N.Y.C., 1979-85, Shea & Gould, N.Y.C., 1985-89, Jones Day, N.Y.C., 1989—. Editor chpt. to book; contbr. articles to profl. publs., chpt. to book. Mem. ABA (real property, probate and trust constrn. form com.), Am. Coll. Real Estate Lawyers, Profl. Women in Constrn., Real Estate Bd. N.Y. (owner labor coordinating com.), Am. Coll. Constrn. Lawyers, Am. Arbitration Assn. (large complex case panel), Comml. Real Estate Women N.Y. (editl. bd.), Urban Land Inst., CoreNet Global; CoreNet Learning Advisory Bd.; Wis. State Bar Assn., N.Y. State Bar Assn., Hungarian-Am. C. of C. of N.Y./N.J. Avocations: sports, art, languages. Home: 200 E End Ave Apt 14F New York NY 10128-7887 Business E-Mail: ssfodor@jonesday.com.

FODREA, CAROLYN WROBEL, adult education educator, researcher; b. Hammond, Ind., Feb. 1, 1943; d. Stanley Jacob and Margaret Caroline (Stupeck) Wrobel; m. Howard Frederick Fodrea, June 17, 1967 (div. Jan. 1987); children: Gregory Kirk, Lynn Renee. BA in Elem. Edn., Purdue U., 1966; MA in Reading and Lang. Devel., U. Chgo., 1973; postgrad., U. Colo.,

Denver, 1986—87. Cert. elem. tchr., Ind., Ill. Tchr. various schs., Ind., Colo., 1966-87; founder, supr., clinician Reading Clinic, Children's Hosp., Denver, 1969-73; pvt. practice Denver, 1973—87, Deerfield, Ill., 1973—; creator of pilot presch.-kindergarten lang. devel. program Gary, Ind. Diocese Schs., 1987—, therapist lang. and reading disabilities, 1987—; pres. Reading Rsch. Ctr., Arlington Heights, Ill., 2000—. Conducted Lang. Devel. Workshop, Gary, Ind. 1988; tchr. adult basic edn. Dawson Tech. Sch., 1990, Coll. Lake County, 1991, Prairie State Coll., 1991—, Chgo. City Colls., 1991, R.J. Daley Coll., 1991, Coll. DuPage, 1991—; condr. adult basic edn. workshops for Coll. of DuPage, R.J. Daley Coll., 1992, Ill. Lang. Devel. Literacy Program; tchr. Korean English Lang. Inst., Chgo., 1996, Lang. Devel. Program for Minorities, 2000; dir. pilot study Cabrini Green Tutoring Ctr., Chgo., 2000; presenter in field. Author: Language Development Program, 1985, Presch. Kindergarten Lang. Devel. Program, 1988, A Multi-Sensory Stimulation Program for the Premature Baby in Its Incubator to Reduce Medical Costs and Academic Failure, 1986, Predicting At-Risk Babies for First Grade Reading Failure Before Birth A 15 Year Study, A Language Development Program, Grades 1 to Adult, 1988, 92; editor, pub.: ESL For Native Spanish Speakers, 1996, ESL for Native Korean Speakers, 1996. Active Graland Country Day Sch., Denver, 1981-83, N.W. Ind. Children's Chorale, 1988—; Ill. state chair Babies and You com. March of Dimes, 1999—. Mem. NEA, Am. Ednl. Rsch. Assn., Internat. Reading Assn., Am. Coun. for Children with Learning Disabilities, Am. Acad. Environ. Medicine (chhmn. pub. rels., mktg. com., chmn. town meeting com. 2005), Assn. for Childhood Edn. Internat., Colo. Assn. for Edn. of Young Children, Infant Stimulation Edn. Assn., Art Inst. Chgo., U. Chgo. Alumni Club (Denver area ann. fund, Pres. fund com. 1988—, com. mem. Denver area chpt. 1974-87). Roman Catholic. Avocations: sports, cultural activities, sewing, literature. Office Phone: 847-632-0622, 888-748-0222, 888-748-0222. Business E-Mail: carolynfodreamille@sbcglobal.net.

FOERSTER, JANE A., music educator; d. Ronald A. and Mildred A. Youmans; m. John R. Foerster, July 2, 1994. MusB, U. Mo., Kansas City, 1981. Tchr. Brookfield Christian Sch., Wis., 1992—. Pvt. music tchr., Brookfield, 1992—. Deacon Elmbrook Ch., Brookfield, 1997—. Mem.: Music Educators Nat. Conf. Avocations: cooking, gardening, volleyball.

FOGARASSY, HELEN CATHERINE, writer; b. Gyula, Hungary, Oct. 30, 1949; arrived in U.S., 1957; d. Janos and Ilona (Skerl) Fogarassy; m. Karl Matlin, Aug. 23, 1972 (div. Aug. 1978). BA in Comparative Lit., Ind. U., 1972. Editor Scholastic Mag., N.Y.C., 1974—76, Sloan-Kettering Cancer Ctr., N.Y.C., 1976—79; owner, mgr. On Paper Office Svcs., N.Y.C., 1979—88. Author: Mix Bender, 1987, Mission Improbable: The World Community on a UN Compound in Somalia, 1999; contbr. Voices Unabridged.com. Mem.: Internat. Womens Writing Guild, Poets & Writers, Pen & Authors Guild. Democrat. Home and Office: PO Box 504 Lenox Hill Sta New York NY 10021 E-mail: helfog@aol.com.

FOGARTY, ELIZABETH RUMMANS, retired librarian, researcher; b. Portsmouth, Ohio, Nov. 1, 1916; d. George Rummans and Mattie Belle (Shaver) Jordan; m. Joseph Christopher Fogarty, Oct. 6, 1945 (dec. Jan. 1977); children: Patricia C., Michelle., Josephine S. BA magna cum laude, Ohio Wesleyan U., Delaware, 1938; MLS, U. Ill., 1939. Post libr. U.S. Army, Camp Atterbury, Ind., 1942-45; organizer of libr. Legis. Auditor's Calif. Capitol Office, Sacramento. 1952-53; med. rsch. libr. U.S. Army Med. Ctr., Ryukyu Islands, Japan, 1967-70, U.S. Army Hosp., Ft. Polk, La., 1970-72; libr. pub. svcs. McAllen Pub. Libr., Tex., 1974-76. Researcher for Calif. state legislators and physicians. Chmn. coun. on ministries, mem. adminstrv. bd. St. Mark United Meth. Ch., McAllen, 1975—; Germany country commr. North Atlantic Girl Scout Bd. Europe, 1961-63; pres. John Knox Village, 2003-05. Mem. AAUW (pres. McAllen br. 1977-81, bd. dir. internat. rels. Tex. state div. bd. 1981-84, cond. internat. rels. workshops at Tex. state and nat. convs. 1981—, Outstanding Woman of yr. award 1980), DAR (regent Sam Maverick chpt. 1983-85), Colonial Dames 17th Century (pres. Capt. Thomas Jefferson chpt. 1985—, Tex. state bd. 1985—, v.p. 1987—, Uni985—, v.p. 1987—), United Daus. Confederacy (treas. Palo Alto chpt. 1982-84, pres. 1990—, registarar 1987—), ALA, LWV, Mortar Board, U.S. Daus. 1812, The Jamestowne Soc., Nat. Soc. Daus. Am. Colonists, Nat. Soc. Colonial Dames (state pres. Tex. 1989—), Nat. Soc. Magna Charta Dames (pres. UDC Palo Alto chpt. 1990—), Nat. Soc. Colonial Dames XVII Century (Tex. state pres. 1989-91, libr. gen. 1991-93, 93-95, 95-97, v.p. gen., 1997-99, hon. v.p. life, 2001), UDC (chpt. pres. 1990—), New England Women, Dames of Ct. of Honor, Soc. of Ky. Pioneers, Colonial Order of the Crown, Ams. Royal Descent, Sons and Daughters of the Pilgrims, Phi Beta Kappa, Delta Delta Delta, Delta Sigma Rho. Home: John Knox Village Cottage 610 1204 S Border Ave Weslaco TX 78596-7447 Personal E-mail: bttyfogerty@aol.com.

FOGELMAN, ANN FLORENCE, nutrition consultant, educator, researcher; b. Reading, Pa., Oct. 12, 1924; d. George Franklin Fogelman and Ruth Amelia Swartley Fogelman. BS, U. Del., 1950; MPH, U. Calif., Berkeley, 1957. Registered dietitian Am. Dietetic Assn., lic. dietitian Tex. Cook Art Camp, Cragsmoor, NY, 1948; asst. dir. YWCA Camp Otonka, Dagsboro, Del., 1949; asst. dietitian Meml. Hosp., Wilmington, Del., 1950—51; dietetic intern Frances Stern Food Clinic, Boston, 1952; clinic and tchg. dietitian Vanderbilt U. Hosp., Nashville, 1953—56; nutritionist Charlotte (N.C.)-Mecklenburg Health Dept., 1957—60; nutrition cons. Md. State Dept. Health, Balt., 1960—63; nutritionist dept. ob-gyn. U. Tex. Med. Br., Galveston, 1963—91; ret. Dietary dir. Tex. Nutrition Survey, 1968—69; liaison Tex. Home Econs. Assn. Tex. Dietetic Assn. Exec. Bd., 1968—69; pres., various other offices and coms. Tex. State Nutrition Coun., 1976—78; Tex. del. Am. Home Econs. Assn. Nat. Conv., 1971, 73; rec. sec. Houston Area Home Econs. Assn., 1967—68; pres. South Tex. Dietetic Assn., 1969—70. Contbr. chapters to books, articles to profl. jours. Vol. Clear Lake Regional Med. Ctr., Webster, Tex., 1992—96, Meml. Hermann S.E. Hosp., Houston, 1994—, Vitas Healthcare, Friendswood, Tex., 1994—, Sr. Learning Ctr., Webster, 1997—; active Clear Lake Presbyn. Ch., 1992—, deacon, 1996, Stephen min., 2000. With WAVES, 1944—46. Named one of 10 Most Outstanding Students, Sch. Home Econs. U. Del., 1962. Mem.: Waves Nat. (life), Bay Area Writers League, U. Tex. Med. Br. Retirees, Sr. Friends (Clear Lake chpt.), The Women's Meml. (charter), Beta Sigma Phi (pres. Charlotte chpt. 1959—60, pres. Pasadena chpt. 1974—75, Dickinson chpt. Girl of Yr. 1966—67, Girl of Yr. 1974—75). Avocations: travel, dance, reading. E-mail: annbird@hotmail.com.

FOGER, FRANCES MURCHISON, minister; b. Alexandria, La., Dec. 31, 1941; d. Duncan Cameron and Marietta Mills Murchison; m. Carl Allen Foger, Dec. 18, 1982; m. Wallace Montgomery Driskell (dec.); 1 child, Stephen Driskell. Student, Rhodes Coll., Memphis, 1959—61; BA, La. Tech. U., Ruston, 1963; MS, Tex. Woman's U., Denton, 1984; MDiv, So. Meth. U., 2000. Adminstrv. mgr. The U. of Tex. Health Sci. Ctr. at Houston, 1970—84; adminstrv. asst. Baylor Coll. Medicine, 1989—93; min. United Meth. Ch., 1995—. Preschool bd. mem. First United Meth. Ch., LaPorte, Tex., 2000—02; ptnrs. in mission United Meth. Ch., Houston, 2001; spkr. Rotary Club Internat., Houston, 2001. Police chaplain LaPorte Police Dept., 2002; clinical mem. Assn. Clinical Pastoral Edn., 1995—96; mem. Coll. of Chaplains, 1995—96. Fellow: Am. Coll. Healthcare Execs.; mem.: Ministerial Alliance (sec. 2002—05). Democrat. Methodist. Avocations: piano, swimming, walking, crafts, organ. Home: 9825 Radio Rd Houston TX 77075 Office Phone: 713-649-1387.

FOGG, JANET, architectural firm executive; Prin. OZ Arch., Denver, mng. ptnr., CFO, dir. human resources Boulder (Colo.) Studio, bd. dirs. Chmn. Downtown Boulder (Colo.), Inc., bd. dirs. Office: OZ Architecture Inc 3012 Huron St Ste 100 Denver CO 80202

FOGGIN, BRENDA FRAZIER, retired state agency administrator, volunteer; b. Bogalusa, La., Jan. 24, 1942; d. Joseph Wiley Frazier and Virginia Mary Holmes; m. Joseph Jimes, Feb. 23, 1963 (div. May 1989); children: Jeffery, Joel, Christina; m. Howard Francis Foggin, Dec. 23, 1992. AA, La. Tech. U., 1998, BA, 1999. Cert. master gardener, La.; notary public. Supr. Dept. of Health, Bossier City, La., 1967-76; motor vehicle officer Dept. Pub. Safety, Bossier City, 1976-87; supr. State Employees Group Benefits, Shreveport, La., 1987-96. Author, editor: (short stories) Collage of Memories, 1998, poems. Mem. Citizens Leadership Acad. The Polit. Tng. Inst., Shreveport, 1998; mem. Highland Area Partnership, 1993-99, Nat. Trust Historic Preservation, 1997-99; sec. Profl. Rep. Women's Club, Shreveport, La., 2001-02. Mem. Highland Historic Preservation Assn., Golden Key, Krewe of Highland. Republican. Roman Catholic. Avocations: reading, writing, gardening, historic preservation. Home: 1122 Janther Pl Shreveport LA 71104-4126

FOGLE, JENNIFER FOX, elementary school educator; b. Pitts., Oct. 10, 1952; d. Cyrus Keener and Terrell Mae Fox; m. Alan Bruce Kalik, Aug. 5, 1995; children: Chip, Bradley Keener, Ellen Kalik, Annie Kalik. BA, Westminster Coll., 1974. Instructional Level II Pa., 1980, Nat. Bd. Profl. Tchg. Stds. Pa., 2001. Self employed piano, vocal instr., Pitts., 1980—2005; adminstrv. team mem. St. Agnes Sch., Diocese of Pitts., 2002—05, tchr., 1991—, asst. prin., 2005—. Assessor Nat. Bd. for Profl. Tchg. Stds., Pitts., 2001—. Dir.(director, quartet member): (barbershop singing) Sweet Adeline Director (Novice Dir. of the Yr., 1991). Deacon Presbyn. Ch., Pitts., 1996—98. Recipient Regional Medalist, Sweet Adelines Internat., 1995—2005, Championship Quartet, 1996, 2001. Mem.: Sweet Adeline (dir. 1991—96, Novice Dir. of the yr. 1991). Presbyterian. Avocations: singing, reading, creative arts. Home: 190 Jade Dr Verona PA 15147 Office: St Agnes Sch 120 Robinson St Pittsburgh PA 15213 Office Phone: 412-682-1129.

FOGLIA, MICHELLE LYNN, psychologist; b. Poughkeepsie, N.Y., Oct. 26, 1971; d. John Joseph and Diane Marie (Gunn) F. AA, Dutchess Cmty. Coll., Poughkeepsie, 1991; BA in psychology, Marist Coll., 1993; MA in counseling, Webster Univ., 1997. Hab tech./tchr. asst. Astor Home for Children, Rhinebeck, N.Y., 1992-93; sales assoc. Limited Express, Poughkeepsie, 1993-95, sales mgr. Charleston, S.C., 1995-96; support team mem. Cmty. Living of Wilmington, Wilmington, N.C., 1996-97; family & group therapist Oaks Pscyhiatric Hosp., Wilmington, N.C., 1996-97; CAP case mgr. Southeastern Ctr. for Mental Health, Wilmington, N.C., 1997—; child psychologist Beckman Mental Health Clinic, Greenwood, S.C., 1998. Mem. adv. com. Southeastern Mental Health, Wilmington, 1997—. Tutur, tchr. Cape Fear Literacy Coun., Wilmington, 1996; sponsor Christian Children's Fund, N.Y., 1991. Mem. Am. Counseling Assn., Young Men's Club of Am., Alzheimers Assn., Humane Soc. Avocations: exercise, jazz, ballet dance, yoga, gardening, spending time with my dogs. Office: Southeastern Mental Health Ctr 5041 New Centre Dr Ste 200 Wilmington NC 28403-1624 Home: 4115 Little River Rd Apt 24 Myrtle Beach SC 29577-0840

FOK, AGNES KWAN, retired cell biologist, educator; b. Hong Kong, China, Dec. 11, 1940; came to US, 1962; d. Sun and Yau (Ng) Kwan; m. Fok, June 8, 1965; children: Licie Chiu-Jane, Edna Chiu-Joan. BA in Chemistry, U. Great Falls, 1965; MS in Plant Nutrition and Biochemistry, Utah State U., 1966; PhD in Biochemistry, U. Tex., 1971. Asst. rsch. prof. pathology U. Hawaii, Honolulu, 1973-74, Ford Found. postdoctoral fellow, anatomy dept., 1975, asst. rsch. prof., 1975-82, assoc. rsch. prof., 1982—88, rsch. prof. Pacific Biomed. Rsch. Ctr., 1988-96, grad. faculty, dept. microbiology, 1977—2003, dir., 1994-96, dir., prof. biology program, 1996—2003, prof. emeritus, 2003—. Contbr. articles to profl. jours. Mem. Am. Soc. for Cell Biology, Soc. for Protozoologists, Sigma Xi (treas. Hawaii chpt. 1979-2002). Avocations: reading, gardening, hiking, sewing. Office: U Hawaii Biology Program Honolulu HI 96822 Business E-Mail: fok@hawaii.edu.

FOLAND, SARA, geologist, association executive; b. Anderson, Ind., May 6, 1956; d. James Phillip and June Irene (DeWood) F. BS in Chemistry, Ind. U., Ft. Wayne, 1978, BS in Geology, 1979; MS in Geology, U. Mont., 1982; Exec. MBA, Ind. U., Bloomington, 1994; postgrad., U. Calif., Santa Cruz, 1998—. Cert. petroleum geologist. Physician asst., Ft. Wayne, 1974-80; rschr. Los Alamos Nat. Lab., 1982; geologist, mgr. Amoco Prodn. Co., Denver, 1982-98; CEO, pres. Farallon Energy Group Ltd., Denver, 1998-99; CEO Geol. Soc. Am., Boulder, Colo., 1999—. Nat. corp. sec. Amoco Corp., Houston, 1996-98; chair Denver Outreach Com. for Elem. Edn., 1990-96; mem. adv. bd. Amoco Women's Employee Network, 1990-94. Contbr. more than 30 articles to profl. jours. Vice chair Colo. AIDS Inst. Found., Denver, 1998—; chair planning com. of bd. trustees U. Mont. Found., Missoula, 1996—. Assn. Western Univs. grantee, 1982. Mem. AAUW, Am. Geophys. Union (life), Am. Assn. Petroleum Geologists, Geol. Soc. Am., Sigma Xi. Avocations: skiing, golf, flying, fly fishing. Office: Geol Soc Am 3300 Penrose Pl Boulder CO 80301-1806

FOLAND-BUSH, TERRI, language educator, speech educator; d. James W. and Betty M. Foland; m. Roger R. Bush, Jan. 25, 1952; 1 child, Robeyn M. Bush. BS Edn., Ohio U., Athens, 1972; M Liberal Learning, Marietta Coll., Ohio, 1994. Cert. English Comprehensive; Comm. Ohio, 1972. Tchr. English and drama Morgan H.S., McConnelsville, Ohio, 1972—73; instr. lang. arts and speech Ft. Frye H.S., Beverly, Ohio, 1973—. Instr. tech. writing Wash. State C.C., Marietta, Ohio, 1993—95; instr. reading W.Va. U. Parkersburg, 2004—05. Nominee Ohio Tchr. of Yr., Ft. Frye Sch. Bd., 1997. Home: 2808 15th Avenue Vienna WV 26105 Office: Fort Frye HS Fifth St Beverly OH 45715

FOLCH-SERRANO, KAREN D., psychologist, consultant; b. Mayagüez, P.R., Feb. 20, 1969; d. José Folch and Digna J. Serrano. BA in Psychology, U. P.R., Mayaguez, 1991; MS in Clin. Psychology, Carlos Albizu U., San Juan, 1994, PhD in Clin. Psychology, 1998. Cert. forensic psychologist Carlos Albizu U., P.R., 1999, in gerontology U. P.R., San Juan, 2006. Asst. to dir. clin. tng. program Carlos Albizu U., San Juan, PR, 1997—98; dir. Centro Clinico Roig Lucy Lopez Roig and Assocs., San Juan, 1999; clin. psychologist Ramsay Youth Svcs. of P.R., San Juan, 1999—2000, Inst. Psychol. Treatment, San Juan, 2000—02, Clin. Support Group, Inc., San Juan, 2002—; pvt. practice San Juan, 2002—, Support Therapy Ctr., Inc., Caguas, PR, 2004—05. Cons. in field; lectr. in field; presenter in field. Named Outstanding Student Counselor of Yr., U. P.R., 1990. Mem.: APA. Roman Catholic. Avocations: reading, travel, collecting barbies. Office: Calle Manuel Pavia # 611 Ste 213 San Juan PR 00910-2239 also: Clin Support Group Inc 65th Infantry Plaza Iturregui Ste 217-A San Juan PR 00924 Office Phone: 787-722-3944. Personal E-mail: kdfolch@yahoo.com. E-mail: kdfolch@prdigital.com.

FOLEY, ANN, broadcast executive; BA, Mount Holyoke Coll., 1976. Exec. v.p. programming Showtime Networks, Inc., N.Y.C., 1988—96, exec. V.P. east coast programming, 1996—. Mem.: FCC Oversight Monitoring Bd., TV Parental Guidelines Monitoring Bd. Office: Showtime Networks Inc 1633 Broadway Fl 17 New York NY 10019-6708

FOLEY, APRIL H., ambassador; b. Avon Lake, Ohio, Aug. 9, 1947; Grad., Smith Coll.; MBA, Harvard U. With Pfizer Pharm. Co.; dir. strategy Reader's Digest Assn.; various positions in fin. mgmt., strategic planning, and mergers and acquisitions PepsiCo, Inc.; first v.p., vice chmn. Export-Import Bank U.S., 2003—05; U.S. amb. to Hungary, 2006—. Chmn. Alexis de Tocqueville Soc. Westchester and Putnam counties. Office: 5270 Budapest Pl Washington DC 20521*

FOLEY, BRIANA, music educator, consultant; b. Jersey City, N.J., Sept. 23, 1958; d. Daniel Joseph and Jane Catherine Moriarty; m. Gregory Howard Foley, Oct. 12, 1980; 1 child, Elizabeth Ann. Student, Fla. State U., 1978; B of Music Edn., Westminster Choir Coll., Princeton, N.J., 1981. Cert. music edn.K-12 Fla. Voice and piano instr. pvt. home studio, Clearwater, Fla., 1981—83; choral dir. N.W. Presbyn. Ch., St. Petersburg, Fla., 1981—94; music specialist Mildred Helms Elem. Sch., Largo, Fla., 1982—90, Garrison-Jones Elem. Sch., Dunedin, Fla., 1990—. Cons. profl. edn. music dept. Pinellas County Schs., Largo, 1986—2003; mem. Pinellas County Student Achievement Grant. Author: (study guide) The Florida Orchestra Youth Concert Series Guide, 1986—2003. Vol. Clearwater Jazz Holiday, 1984—87; coord. Adopt-a-Grandparent Program, Largo, 1985—89. Recipient grantee, Fla. Dept. Edn., 1989. Mem.: Music Educators Nat. Conf., Pinellas Classroom Tchrs. Assn. Achievements include development of first music inclusion program in Pinellas County School District. Avocations: yoga, walking, playwriting, reading, travel. Office: Garrison-Jones Elem Sch 3133 Garrison Rd Dunedin FL 34698 Office Phone: 727-469-5716.

FOLEY, ELLEN MADALINE, journalist; b. Chgo., Apr. 13, 1952; d. Thomas Jennings and Joan Ellen (Murphy) F.; m. Thomas Foley Mullaney, June 30, 1984; children: Kaitlin, Maura. BA in Polit. Sci., U. Wis., 1974, MA in Journalism, 1988. Mng. editor Menominee (Mich.) Herald Leader, 1976-78; copy editor The Milw.-Sentinel, 1978-79, The Detroit News, 1979-80; reporter, copy editor The Star-Tribune, Mpls., 1980-91, asst. features editor, food editor, 1991-93; features editor The Kansas City (Mo.) Star, 1993-96, asst. mng. editor/features, 1996—98; mng. editor The Phila. Daily News, Phila., 1998—2004; editor Wis. State Jour., Madison, 2004—. Mem. Jr. League of Mpls., 1980—, bd. dirs., 1989; founder Violence Against Women Coalition, Mpls., 1988-93. Recipient Minn. Page One award, 1987, Vol. of Distinction award Assn. Jr. Leagues Internat., 1996; named Pulitzer Prize juror, 2005, 06. Mem. Am. Assn. Sun. & Feature Editors (bd. dirs., conf. host. 1996-98, bd dirs. associated press mng. editors 2004—), Am. Soc. Newspaper Editors (bd. dirs. 2005) Avocations: reading, hiking. Office: Wis State Jour 1901 Fish Hatchery Rd PO Box 8058 Madison WI 53708 Office Phone: 608-252-6104. Business E-Mail: efoley@madison.com.

FOLEY, JANE DEBORAH, foundation executive; b. Chgo., May 30, 1952; d. Colin Gray Stevenson and Bette Jane (Cullenbine) Coleman; m. George Edward Foley, Jan. 29, 1972; children: Sy Curtis, Shelly. BA, Purdue U., 1973, MS, 1977, PhD, 1992. Cert. elem. adminstr., Ind., cert. elem. adminstrn. and supervision. Tchr. phys. edn. and health Lafayette (Ind.) Jefferson H.S., 1973-74; tchr. music and phys. edn. Valparaiso (Ind.) Cmty. Schs., 1974-79, tchr. elem. phys. edn., 1979-90; prin. South Ctrl. Elem. sch., Union Mills, Ind., 1990-93, Flint Lake Elem. Sch., Valparaiso, 1993-98; v.p. Milken Family Found., Santa Monica, Calif., 1998—2003, sr. v.p., 2003—. Mem. panel experts The Master Tchr., 1996—98, NEH; coord. Milken Nat. Educator Awards, Milken Scholars, Children of Willesden Ln, Milken Festival For Youth; spkr., presenter in field. Author: Technology Integration: A School Administrator's Guide, 1998, Success in Restructuring: A Road Map for Administrators, 1998, The Administrator's Technology Training Booklet, 1998; contbr. articles to profl. jours. and books. Mem. Valparaiso Sch. Sys. PTA, mem. exec. bd., 1993-98; co-chair Hold Onto Your Music Found.; bd. dirs. Wings Inc. Recipient Hoosier Sch. award, 1992, Ind. 2000 Designation award 1994, Outstanding Dissertation award Internat. Soc. Ednl. Planning, 1993, Nat. Educator award, Milken Family Found., 1994, Ind. Bell Ringer award Ind. Dept. Edn., 1994, Ind. 4 Star Sch. award, 1995, 96, 97, 98, Internat. Tech. Edn. Assn. award, 1995, Cmty. Improvement award Valparaiso C. of C., 1994, NCREL Pathways to Improvement Pilot Site, 1995, Ind. Sch. Improvement award, Ind. Dept. Edn., 1998, others; Ind. 2000 Planning grantee, 1993, Milken Educator Tech. Project leader, 1997, other grants. Mem.: ASCD (assoc.), Valparaiso Tchrs. Assn. (treas. 1989—90), Phi Kappa Phi. Avocations: running, reading, writing, computers. Office: Milken Family Found 1250 4th St Santa Monica CA 90401-1350 Office Phone: 310-570-4782. Business E-Mail: jfoley@mff.org.

FOLEY, LOUISE, medical educator, retired military officer; d. Archibald and Janet Cameron; m. John Foley, May 20, 1972. EdM, U. Ctrl. Okla., Edmond, 1981. Registered respiratory therapist AZ Bd. Respiratory Examiners, 1995. Officer USAF, 1971—92; respiratory care practitioner NW Med. Ctr., Tucson, 1995—2002; respiratory therapy instr. Pima Med. Inst., 2003—. Decorated Meritorous Svc. medal USAF. Mem.: Am. Assn. Respiratory Care, Air Force Assn. (life), Ret. Officers Assn. (life), Kappa Delta Pi, Lambda Beta (life). Office: Pima Medical Inst 3350 E Grant Tucson AZ 85716 Office Phone: 520-326-1600. E-mail: louise@wvcnet.com.

FOLEY, MARY E., medical association administrator, nursing administrator; Diploma in nursing, New Eng. Deaconess Hosp., 1973; BSN, Boston U., 1976; MS in Nursing Adminstrn. and Occupl. Health, U. Calif., San Francisco, 1994. RN. Asst. dir. ambulatory care rev. N.Y. County Health Svcs. Rev. Orgn.; med.-surg. nurse St. Francis Meml. Hosp., San Francisco, dir. nursing and chief nurse exec.; pres. ANA, Washington. Part-time clin. faculty San Francisco State U. Sch. Nursing; lectr. in field. Contbr. articles to profl. jours. Mem. Calif. Tuberculosis Elimination Task Force Dept. Health Svcs., 1993—94; mem. Mayor's HIV Task Force, San Francisco, 1989, Calif. RN Spl. Adv. Com. on Nursing Shortage, Dept. Consumer Affairs, 1989; project cons. tng. for devel. of innovative control tech. project Trauma Found. at San Francisco Gen. Hosp., 1990. Mem.: ANA (2d v.p. 1994—96, 1st v.p. 1996—2000, chair constituent assembly, ofcl. rep. to Internat. Coun. Nurses 1997, 1999, chair legis. com., mem. polit. action com. bd. dirs.), Calif. Nurses Assn. (pres., treas.). Office: American Academy Of Nursing 8515 Georgia Ave Ste 400 Silver Spring MD 20910-3492

FOLEY, PATRICIA JEAN, accountant; b. Bridgeport, Conn., Jan. 12, 1956; d. John Edward and Louise (Caselli) F AA, Housantonic C.C., 1978; BS, Ctrl. Conn. State Coll., 1980; MBA, U. Hartford, 1996. CPA, Conn. Staff acct. Spitz, Sullivan, Wachtel & Falcetta, Hartford, Conn., 1981—82, client acct., 1982—85, sr. acct., 1985—87, supr., mgr., 1987—97; mgr. Falcetta Wachtel & Knochenhauer LLC, Bloomfield, Conn., 1997—98; prin. Patricia J. Foley, CPA, Newington, Conn., 1998—. Mem. acctg. del. to Russia; Ukraine and Estonia citizens amb., 1993 Pres. Woodsedge Condominium Assn., Newington, 1989—92, treas., 1985—92; bd. dir. Friends Lucy Robbins Welles Libr., membership co-chair, 2000—, v.p., 2001, 2006, pres., 2002—04, immediate past pres., 2005—06. Mem. AICPA (mgmt. adv. svc. com. 1987—, info. tech. divsns., 1992—), Conn. Soc. CPA, Am. Women Soc. CPA, Cmty. Assn. Inst. (membership chair Conn. chpt. 1991-92), Nat. Assn. Women Bus. Owners (treas. 2001-03, 05-06, pub. policy com. 2000—) Home: 35 Woodsedge Dr Apt 1B Newington CT 06111-4271 Office: 35-1B Woodsedge Dr Newington CT 06111-4271 Office Phone: 860-667-1504. Personal E-mail: pattyjfoley@pattyjfoley.com.

FOLEY, REGINA M., lawyer; b. 1967; BA, Cath. U. of Am., 1989; JD, Widener U., 1992; grad., Nat. Inst. of Trial Advocacy. Bar: Pa., NJ, US Dist. Ct., NJ 1992. Mem. Raynes McCarty, Phila. Elected mem. Alumnae Bd., Mt. St. Joseph Acad. Mem.: ABA, Desmond J. McTighe Chap., Am. Inn of Cts., Montgomery County Bar Assn., Phila. Trial Lawyers Assn., Pa. Bar Assn., Pa. Trial Lawyers Assn. (bd. govs.), Phila. Bar Assn. Office: Raynes McCarty 1845 Walnut St, 20th Fl Philadelphia PA 19103 Office Phone: 212-568-6190. Office Fax: 212-998-0618. E-mail: rmfoley@raynesmccarty.com.*

FOLEY, RUTH IONA, music educator; d. John and Jolan Elizabeth Szakacs; m. Chris Charles Foley; children: Jonathan, Caralise. BA, BEd, U. Winnipeg, Man., Can., 1982; MMus, U. N.D., Grand Forks, 1989; DMA, U. Nebr., 2000. Assoc. prof. music Liberty U., Lynchburg, Va., 1992—; organist Luth. Ch., Lynchburg, Va., 2002—. Mem.: Choristers Guild, Am. Guild Organists, Nat. Assn. Tchrs. Singing. Home: 112 Westridge Circle Lynchburg VA 24502 Office: Liberty U Dept Fine Arts 1971 University Blvd Lynchburg VA 24502 Personal E-mail: rifoley@netscape.com. Business E-Mail: rifoley@liberty.edu.

FOLEY, TERESA A., psychologist; BA in Psychology, Antioch U., LA, 1995; MA in Clin. Psychology, Calif. Sch. Profl. Psychology, LA, 1998, PsychD in Clin. Psychology, 2000. Intern Cornerstone Day Care, Marina Del Rey, Calif., 1993, Windows Between Worlds, Marina Del Rey, 1994—96, Sojourn Battered Women's Shelter, Marina Del Rey, 1994—96; assessment intern Booth Meml., Lincoln Heights, 1997; intern therapist Pacific Ctr., LA, 1997, AIDS Svc. Ctr., Pasadena, Calif., 1998—99, Glendale Family Svc., Calif., 1998—99, LA Police. Dept., LA, 1999—2000, fellow behavioral scis. sect., 2000—01; self employed, 2000—05; rschr., liaison so. Ariz. area CFIDs Assn. Am. So., 2006—. Home: 2990 S Placinta Sam Javier Green Valley AZ 85614

FOLEY, VIRGINIA SUE LASHLEY, counselor, educational training consultant; b. Richmond, Ind., May 1, 1942; d. Robert E. and Flora Rose (Johnson) Lashley; m. Laurence Michael Foley Sr., Jan. 28, 1968 (dec. 2002); children: Megan Leigh, Jeremie Beth, L. Michael Jr. BA, Hanover Coll., 1964; MS, San Francisco State U., 1969. Cert. profl. counselor and internat. mental health tng. cons.; nat. bd. cert. hypnotherapist; Myers Briggs Type indicator cert. specialist. Vol. Peace Corps, Danao City, The Philippines, 1964-66; counselor, tng. cons. In Touch Found., U.S. Peace Corps., Asian Devel. Bank, Manila, Internat. Sch., 1981-85; counselor, tng. cons. to Overseas Briefing Ctr. U.S. Dept. of State, Washington, 1988-90; counselor, mental health cons. U.S. State Dept./U.S. Peace Corps, La Paz, Bolivia, 1990-92; mental health coord. U.S. Embassy, Lima, Peru, 1992—96; counselor, preferred provider Aetna/HAI, Lima, Peru, 1994-96, mental health cons., internat. tng. cons. Harare, Zimbabwe, 1996-2000, mental health cons., internat. tng. cons., archiving specialist Amman, 1996—2000; cons. USAID, U.S. State Dept., Washington, 2002—, field rep., life coach, population leadership program, 2002—. Archiving specialist USAID, Jordan, 2001—02. Author: Leisure Time Activities for Families in Manila, 1983; (manuals) Career Development Manual, 1984; writer mags. What's On in Manila, 1983-85, Off Duty Mag., 1985, USAID Frontlines, 1991—, Lima Times, 1994, Fgn. Svc. Jour., 1996; contbr. articles to mags. Mem. U.S. Embassy Mental Health Com.; chair Cmty. Morale Com. Recipient award of recognition Bukidnon State Coll., The Philippines, 1985. Mem.: ACA, Assn. Boliviana de Psicologia Humanista (founding), Internat. Assn. Marriage and Family Counselors, Royal Soc. for Conservation of Nature, Friends of Archeology, Am. Women's Assn. of Amman. Avocations: instrumental music, art, crafts, hiking, literature. Office Phone: 202-544-0558. Personal E-mail: virfoley@hotmail.com.

FOLGATE, CYNTHIA A., social services administrator; b. Chgo., Jan. 27, 1950; d. William C. and Cassie Edna (Sisemore) F. BA, No. Ill. U., 1974, MA, 1983. Cert. domestic violence profl. Ill. Sec. No. Ill. U., DeKalb, 1974—80, 1983—84, instr., 1984—92; outreach coord. Safe Passage, De-Kalb, 1992—96, crisis intervention/outreach coord., 1996—97, systems advocacy coord., 1997—2002, cmty. edn. and tng. coord., 2002—03, vol., cmty. coord., 2004—05, cmty. resources dir., 2005—. Instr. Waubonsee C.C., Sugar Grove, Ill., 1990—; mem. DeKalb County Domestic Violence Forum, 1990-91; family violence coord. coun. Ill. 16th Jud. Cir.; chmn. EMS tng. sub-com., 2005—; mem. adv. bd. Coop. Edn. Internship Office No. Ill. U. Speech cons. for various election campaigns DeKalb County, 1988—90; coord. DeKalb County Domestic Violence Initiative, 1998—2000; mem. bd. deacons 1st Congregational United Ch. of Christ, DeKalb, 1989—92. Mem.: Friends of Barb City Manor. Office: Safe Passage PO Box 621 Dekalb IL 60115-0621

FOLKERTS, JEAN, dean, journalism educator; b. Aug. 6, 1945; d. Leonard Folkerts and Betty Manahan; m. Leroy Towns, Aug. 11, 1984; children: Sean, Jenny. BA in Journalism cum laude, Kans. State U., 1967, MS in Journalism and Mass Comm., 1973; MPhil in Am. Studies, U. Kans., 1979, PhD in Am. Studies, 1981. Asst. prof. journalism U. Tex., Austin, 1982-85; assoc. prof., chmn. dept. comm. Mt. Vernon Coll., Washington, 1985-90; assoc. prof. journalism George Washington U., Washington, 1990-94, prof., chmn. dept. journalism, 1994—2006, from acting dir. to prof., dir. Sch. Media and Pub. Affairs, 1995—2001, interim dean Columbian Coll. Arts & Scis., 2001—02, assoc. v.p. special acad. initiatives, 2003—06; dean, disting. alumni prof. Sch. Journalism and Mass Comm., U. NC, Chapel Hill, 2006—. Cons. Food Lion Inc., 1997-98, Newseum, Freedom Forum Found., 1995, Nat. Bank Washington, 1988-89; writer Kans. State U. Counseling Ctr., 1967. Author: Media Voices: An Historical Perspective, 1992, Voices of A Nation: A History of Mass Media in the U.S., 1992, 4th edit., 2002, Media in Your Life: The Role of Mass Media In Society, 1998, 3d edit., 2003; editor Journalism and Mass Comm. Quar., 1992-2002. Grantee AT& T Corp, 1995, Ctr. for Washington Area Studies, 1992. Mem.: Orgn. of Am. Historians, Assn. for Schs. and Depts. of Journalism and Mass comm., Assn. for Edn. and Mass Comm., Phi Kappa Phi. Office: Sch Journalism and Mass Comm U NC at Chapel Hill Campus Box #3365 Chapel Hill NC 27599-1204 Office Phone: 919-962-1204. E-mail: jfolk@email.unc.edu.*

FOLKESTAD, RUTH L., mathematics professor; b. Tacoma, Wash., Nov. 6, 1951; d. Ray W. and Adeline Folkestad; 1 child, Amy. BS, U. N.D., Grand Forks, 1973. Cert. Math. Tchr. N.D., 1973. Tchr. math. Trenton H.S., ND, 1974—. Instr. Water Aerobics Williston Parks and Recreation, ND, 1995—. Named We. Math. Scholar; named to Who's Who in Edn., 1990, 2005, 2006. Mem.: Trenton Edn. Assn. (life; treas. 1974—2006). Avocations: swimming, pinochle. Home: 1722 West 27th St Williston ND 58801 Office: Trenton High School PO Box 239 Trenton ND 58853 Personal E-mail: ruth.folkestad@sendit.nodak.edu.

FOLLANSBEE, PATTI A., health educator, marriage and family therapist; d. Richard Moore and Stella Jenny Follansbee. BS in Edn., Bowling Green (Ohio) State U., 1974; MS in Edn., So. Ill. U., Carbondale, 1977; PhD, So. Ill. U., 1982; postgrad., U. Rochester, NY, 1992—96. Lic. marriage and family therapist NY, cert. family life educator Nat. Coun. on Family Rels. Asst. prof. health edn. SUNY, Brockport, 1982—; marriage and family therapist Rochester, 1997—. Adj. clin. psychologist U. Rochester Med. Ctr., 1997—. Bd. mem. Monroe County Bd. of Health, Rochester, 1986—89; vol. United Way Strengthening Families Impact Team, Rochester, 1998—2006. Mem.: NY Assn. Marriage and Family Therapists (sec., exec. bd. Genesee Valley chpt. 2004—), Am. Assn. Sex Educators, Counselors and Therapists, Nat. Coun. Family Rels., Am. Assn. Marriage and Family Therapists. Avocations: travel, sports. Office: SUNY Brockport Dept Health Sci 350 Campus Dr Rochester NY 14620 Office Phone: 585-395-5483. Business E-Mail: pfollans@brockport.edu.

FOLLETT, DEBORAH ELAINE, sales executive, director, radio director; b. Portsmouth, Va., Feb. 3, 1952; d. Robert Lee and Reba Deloris McCarty; m. Alan V Follett, Dec. 19, 1998; m. Llloyd Frederick Rahn, June 6, 1970 (div. Oct. 1, 1996); children: Shelby Lee Rahn, Jeffrey Scott Rahn. BA, Ea. Ill. U., Charleston, 1991. Media asst. Penta, Inc, Champaign, Ill., 1991—93; traffic dir. Illini Radio Group/Saga Comm., Champaign, Ill., 1993—. Pres./mem. Tuscola Schs. Bd. of Edn., Tuscola, Ill., 1983—96. Named Master Sch. Bd. Mem., Ill. State Bd. of Edn., 1993. Methodist. Home: 915 CR 900E Champaign IL 61822 Office: Illini Radio Group 2603 west Bradley Ave Champaign IL 61821 Office Phone: 217-355-2222. Office Fax: 217-352-1256. Personal E-mail: d.e.follett@sbcglobal.net. E-mail: deb@illiniradio.com.

FOLLINGSTAD, CAROL C., psychologist, consultant, educator; b. Rantoul, Ill., Jan. 21, 1956; d. James Harvey and Ella May Watson; m. Eugene M. Follingstad; children: Alisha, Angela, Anita, Alayna, Arlyn, Arick. BA, Moorhead State U., 1990, MS, 1992. Lic. sch. psychologist, Minn., clin. psychologist, Minn. Med. sec. Korda Clinic, Pelican Rapids, Minn., 1974-77; news reporter KBRF Radio, Fergus Falls, Minn., 1981-84; rschr. Moorhead State U., 1986-92; sch. psychologist Sheyenne Valley SPED, Valley City, N.D., 1992-93; ind. sch. psychologist Rothsay, Minn., 1993-94, Cass County Spl. Svc., Fargo, ND, 1994—99; prof. psychology Moorhead State U., 1997—. Dir. After Sch. Program, Moorhead, 1997-99; cons. 4-H Vols., Breckenridge, Minn., 1996-2001. Editor Children's Works mag., 1990-91. Vol. coord. Wilkin County Ext., Breckenridge, 1996-2001; Blandin Leadership coord. Rothsay Br., Minn., 1996—; adv. bd. Bapt. Ch., Rothsay, 1992-2001; pres. PTO, Rothsay, 1994; dist. rep. Head Start, Moorhead, 1980-86; Sunday sch. supt. Bapt. Ch., Rothsay, 1988-90. Mem. APA, Nat. Assn. Sch. Psychologists, N.D. Psychol. Assn., Minn. Sch. Psychol. Assn. Republican. E-mail: cfollingstad@hotmail.com.

FOLLIT, EVELYN V., former retail executive; b. Sept. 10, 1946; BA in Math., MBA in Fin. and Info. Sys.; degree in Exec. Planning and Tech., Cornell U., MIT. With Dunn & Bradstreet, 1984—96; v.p. ops. & engring. AC Nielson, 1996—97; sr. v.p., chief info. officer RadioShack Corp., 1997—2005, chief orgnl. enabling svcs., 2003—05. Bd. dirs. Catalina Mktg. Corp., 2000—, chmn. audit com., mem. fin. com.; chmn. CIO Coun. Nat. Retail Fedn., 2000—; mem. adv. bd. Ctr. Values Based Leadership, 2002—; bd. dirs. Winn-Dixie Stores Inc., 2006—. Bd. visitors Tex. Christian U., Fort Worth. Named one of Top 10 CIOs in Retailing, Retail Tech. Mag., 1999, Top 10 CIOs Across Am., Info. Week, 1999, 100 Premier IT Leaders in Country, Computerworld, 2001, 25 Most Influential People in Retail, Retail Info Sys. News, 2001, Pioneering Women in Tech., Am. Friends Jerusalem Coll. Tech., 2002; recipient Leadership and Innovation award, Exec. Tech. Mag./Compaq Computer, 2002.*

FOLSOM, ROSE, calligrapher, writer, artist; b. Madison, Wis., July 31, 1953; d. Ralph Dale and Sylvia Lynne Mitchell; m. Fred Gorham Folsom III, Apr. 24, 1982. Mem. adv. bd. Strathmore Arts Ctr., Rockville, Md., 1985; lectr. in field. Author: The Calligrapher's Dictionary, 1991; editor: Letter Arts Rev., 2000—. Resident Rehoboth (Del.) Art League, 1993. Grantee Hermann Zapf Fund, 1993. Mem. Washington Calligraphers Guild (v.p. 1987, pres. 1988), Third Order of St. Dominic. Home and Office: 212 Hillsboro Dr Wheaton MD 20902-3126

FOLSOM, VIRGINIA JEAN, music educator; b. Oakland, Calif., Mar. 26, 1944; d. John Dixon Vincent and Marjorie Estelle Toothaker; d. Virginia J. Hansen; m. Robert Bruce Folsom, Oct. 19, 1970; children: Paul Dixon, Colleen Marie, Katherine Anne. BFA cum laude, U. Utah, 1973. Piano recitalist, 1960—; tchr. music Salt Lake City, 1968—; lectr. music, 1972—; instr. piano U. Utah, Salt Lake City, 1982-83. Vol. Utah Pub. Schs., Salt Lake City, 1970-98. Mem. Music Tchrs. Nat. Assn. (chpt. v.p., Tchr.'s Enrichment grantee 2000), United Fedn. Music Clubs (chpt. treas., chpt. co-chair), Mu Phi Epsilon. Democrat. Mem. Lds Ch. Avocations: music, reading, cooking. Personal E-mail: gfols@yahoo.com.

FOLTZ, KATRINA MARIE, music educator; b. Dubois, Pa., Feb. 10, 1976; d. John Max and Mary Linda Foltz. MusB in Edn., Mercyhurst Coll., 1998; M in Ednl. Leadership, Gannon U., 2006. Pvt. music tchr., Erie, Pa., 1995—; music tchr. Our Lady of Peace Sch., Erie, 1998—2001, Jamestown (N.Y.) Pub. Schs., 2001; choral dir. Woodrow Wilson Mid. Sch., Erie, 2001—03, NW Pa. Collegiate Acad., 2003—04; music tchr. Wayne Sch., Erie, 2004—. Organist, pianist Sacred Heart Cath. Ch., Erie, 1998—2001; accompanist A Canterbury Feast Dinner Theatre, Erie, 2001—; organist, pianist St. Jude's Cath. Ch., Erie, 2002—; music dir. Our Lady of Peace Playhouse, Erie, 1998—, bd. dir.; music dir. Erie Playhouse, Pa., 2003; condr. Erie Playhouse, 2003, 05. Musician: St. Peter's Basilica, 2001, St. Patrick's Cathedral, 2002. Founding mem. Nat. Campaign for Tolerance, 2005. Mem.: Pa. State Educators Assn., Music Educators Nat. Conf. (v.p. 1996), Kappa Gamma Pi. Office: Wayne Mid Sch 650 East Ave Erie PA 16503

FONDA, BRIDGET, actress; b. Los Angeles, Jan. 27, 1964; SAG; d. Peter and Susan Fonda.; m. Danny Elfman, 2003; 1 child, Oliver Henry Milton. Films: Aria, 1987, You Can't Hurry Love, 1988, Shag, 1988, Scandal, 1989, Strapless, 1989, Frankenstein Unbound, 1990, The Godfather, Part III, 1990, Doc Hollywood, 1991, Out of the Rain, (also known as Remains), 1991, Single White Female, 1992, Singles, 1992, Bodies Rest and Motion, 1993, Point of No Return, 1993, Little Buddha, 1994, It Could Happen To You, 1994, Camilla, 1994, The Road to Wellville, 1994, Rough Magic, 1995, Balto (voice), 1995, Grace of My Heart, 1996, City Hall, 1996, South of Heaven, West of Hell, 2000, Delivering Milo, 2001, The Whole Shebang, 2001, Kiss the Dragon, 2001; TV appearances: (series) 21 Jump Street, 1989, Jacob Have I Loved, WonderWorks episode, 1989, (made for cable movie) Leather Jackets, 1991, Jackie Brown, 1997, A Simple Plan, 1998, Finding Graceland, 1998, The Break Up, 1998, South of Heaven West of Hell, 1999, South From Hell's Kitchen, 1999, Monkey Bone, 1999, Lake Placid, 1999; (TV movies) In the Gloaming, 1997, After Amy, 2001, The Snow Queen, 2002; (TV series) The Chris Isaak Show, 2001.

FONDA, JANE, actress; b. NYC, Dec. 21, 1937; d. Henry and Frances (Seymour) F.; m. Roger Vadim Aug. 14, 1965, (div. Jan. 16, 1973); 1 child, Vanessa; m. Tom Hayden, Jan. 20, 1973 (div. 1990); children, Troy Garity, Mary Luana Williams; m. Ted Turner, Dec. 21, 1991 (div. May 22, 2001). Student, Vassar Coll. Appeared on Broadway stage in There Was a Little Girl, 1960, The Fun Couple, 1962; appeared in Actor's Studio prodn. Strange Interlude, 1963; appeared in films Tall Story, 1960, A Walk on the Wild Side, 1962, The Chapman Resort, 1962, Period of Adjustment, 1962, Sunday in New York, 1963, In the Cool of the Day, 1963, The Love Cage, 1963, La Ronde, 1964, Cat Ballou, 1965, The Chase, 1966, Any Wednesday, 1966, The Game Is Over, 1967, Hurry Sundown, 1967, Barefoot in the Park, 1967, Barbarella, 1968, Spirits of the Dead, 1969, They Shoot Horses, Don't They?, 1969 (NY Film Critics Circle award for Best Actress), Klute, 1970 (NY Film Critics Circle award for Best Actress, Nat. Soc. Film Critics award, Golden Globe award for Best Actress, Acad. award for Best Actress), All's Well, 1972, Steelyard Blues, 1973, A Doll's House, 1973, The Blue Bird, 1976, Fun with Dick and Jane, 1977, Julia, 1977 (Golden Globe award for Best Actress), California Suite, 1978, Comes a Horseman, 1978, Electric Horseman, 1979, Nine to Five, 1980, On Golden Pond, 1981, Rollover, 1981, Agnes of God, 1985, The Morning After, 1986, Retour, 1987, Leonard Part 6, 1987, Old Gringo, 1988, Stanley and Iris, 1990, Monster-in-Law, 2005; actor, prodr., Coming Home, 1978 (LA Film Critic Assn. award for Best Actress, Golden Globe for Best Actress, Acad. award for Best Actress), The China Syndrome, 1979; (TV movies) A String of Beads, 1961, Lily: Sold Out, 1981, The Dollmaker(Emmy award for Best Actress), 1984; (TV miniseries) A Century of Women, 1994; author: Jane Fonda's Workout Book, 1981, Women Coming of Age, 1984, Jane Fonda's New Workout & Weight-Loss Program, 1986, Jane Fonda's New Pregnancy Workout & Total Birth Program, 1989, (autobiography) My Life So Far, 2005 (New York Times bestseller list); video: Jane Fonda Workout Video, 1982, 12 additional videos. Recipient Golden Globe award for Most Promising Newcomer, 1962, Golden Apple prize for Female Star of Year Hollywood Women's Press Club, 1977, People's Choice award for Favorite Motion Picture Actress, 1980-83, Career Achievement award Nat. Bd. Review, 2005. Office: Creative Artists Agy care Kim Hodgert 9830 Wilshire Blvd Beverly Hills CA 90212-1804

FONG, EDNA M., retired physician; b. Toi San County, Guang dong Province, China, Nov. 21, 1911; arrived in U.S., 1920; d. Wing Fong and Shee Yee; m. Arthur Wayson Chung, Oct. 15, 1977; m. Jehim Wong (dec.); children: Richard, Ronald, Rebecca. BS, MS, Pacific Union Coll., Angwin, Calif.; MD, Loma Linda Med. Sch., Calif., 1942. Cert. physician, surgeon Bd. of Med. Examiners of Calif. Asst. resident in pediat. The Children's Hosp., L.A., 1948—50; physician family practice Sacramento, 1950—76; physician personnel clinic City of L.A., 1976—80; physician Vet.'s Hosp., Yountville, Calif., 1980—85; ret., 1985. Home: 1265 Brockman Ln Sonoma CA 95476-7664

FONG, ELAINE SUSAN, middle school educator; d. David Y. and Connie M. Wong; m. Gary P. Fong; children: Angelina, Timothy, Steven, Jeffrey. BA, U. Calif., Berkeley, 1973; tchg. credential, Calif. State U., Hayward, 1996. Cert. clin. lab. scientist Dept. Health Svcs., Calif. Clin. lab. scientist Merritt Hosp., 1975—81; spl. edn. classroom aide Alvarado Mid. Sch., Union City, Calif., 1994—95, sci. tchr., 1996—. Head math./sci. dept. Alvarado Mid. Sch., 2000—03, head sci. dept., 2003—06; action rschr. on assessment Stanford U. Sch. Edn., Palo Alto, Calif., 2000—02. Contbg. author: Designing Everyday Assessment in the Science Classroom, 2005. Mem.: Calif. Sci. Tchrs. Assn., Calif. Tchrs. Assn. Office: Alvarado Mid Sch 31604 Alvarado Blvd Union City CA 94587 Office Phone: 510-489-0700. Fax: 510-475-3936. E-mail: elaine_fong@nhusd.k12.ca.us.

FONG, MARY, ethnic studies educator; BA, U. So. Calif., 1981; MA, Calif. State U., Lomg Beach, 1983; PhD, U. Wash., Seattle, 2004. Prof. Calif. State U., San Bernardino. Coord. Ethnic Studies Program, San Bernardino, 2004—. Contbg. author: (textbook) Communicating Ethnic and Cultural Identity. Named Advisor of Yr., Calif. State U., San Bernardino, 2005. Democrat. Office: Calif State U San Bernardino 5500 University Pky San Bernardino CA 92407 Office Phone: 909-537-5891. Office Fax: 909-537-7009. E-mail: mfong@csusb.edu.

FONG, PHYLLIS KAMOI, federal agency administrator, lawyer; b. Phila., Pa., Oct. 16, 1953; d. Bernard W.D. and Roberta (Wat) F.; m. Paul E. Tellier, Nov. 25, 1978. BA in Asian Studies, Pomona Coll., 1975; JD, Vanderbilt U., 1978. Bar: Tenn. 1978, DC 1982. Atty. U.S. Commn. on Civil Rights, Washington, 1978-81; asst. gen. counsel Legal Svcs. Corp., Washington, 1981-83; assoc. counsel to the insp. gen. U.S. Small Bus. Admin., Washington, 1983-88, asst. insp. gen. for mgmt. and policy, 1988-94, asst. insp. gen. for mgmt. and legal counsel, 1994-99, insp. gen., 1999—2002, USDA, Washington, 2002—. Mem. ABA, Tenn. Bar Assn., D.C. Bar Assn. Office: USDA Rm 117 W Jamie Whitten Bldg 1400 Independence Ave SW Washington DC 20250

FONTAINE, JENNIFER LYNNE, choreographer, educator; b. Lowell, Mass., Aug. 29, 1978; d. Jeffrey Victor and Donna Marie Fontaine. Student, Bradford Coll., Haverhill, Mass. Tchr. dance The Joan Izzo Acad. of Dance, Chantilly, Va., 2003—.

FONTAINE, JOAN, actress; b. Tokyo, Oct. 22, 1917; M. Brian Aherne 1939 (div. 1945), m. William Dozier 1946 (div. 1951) 1 daughter,m. Collier Young 1952 (div. 1961), m. Alfred Wright, Jr. 1964 (div. 1969) AlfredWright Jr. 1964 (div. 1969), student American School, Tokyo; film appearances include, No More Ladies, 1935, You Can't Beat Love, 1937, Quality Street, 1937, Rebecca, 1940 (Acad. Award nomination), Suspicion, 1941 (recip. Acad. Award), This Above All, 1942, The Constant Nymph, 1943, (Acad. Award nomination), The Emperor Waltz, 1948, September Affair, 1950, Born to Be Bad, 1950, Darling, How Could You!, 1951, The Devil's Own, 1966; actress: (Broadway) A Certain Smile, 1958, Tea and Sympothy, 1979, Lion in Winter, Vienna, Austria, 1982

FONTAINE, MARY C., lawyer; b. Chicopee, Mass., May 18, 1956; BA summa cum laude, Syracuse Univ., 1978; JD, Univ. Chgo., 1981. Bar: Ill. 1981, NY 1996. Assoc. Mayer Brown Rowe & Maw, Chgo., 1981—85, London, 1985—86, Tokyo, 1987; ptnr., fin. & securitization Mayer Brown Rowe & Maw LLP, Chgo., 1988—. Co-author: Illinois Commercial Financing Forms, 1993. Mem.: ABA, NY State Bar Assn. Office: Mayer Brown Rowe & Maw LLP 71 S Wacker Dr Chicago IL 60606-4637 Office Phone: 312-701-7106. Office Fax: 312-706-8132. Business E-Mail: mfontaine@mayerbrownrowe.com.

FONTAINE-WHITE, BARBARA FRANCES, art educator; b. Watervliet, NY, Aug. 31, 1955; d. Raymond Leo Fontaine and Caroline Elenor Harnish; m. William Daniel IV White, Jan. 9, 1981; children: Justin William White, Aaron Daniel White. BA, SUNY, Albany, 1978, MA, 1981; MFA, So. Meth. U., 1984. Cert. tchr. Tex. Adv. art instr. Eastfield Coll., Mesquite, Tex., 1984—96; continuing edn. art instr. So. Meth. U., Dallas, 1984—96, adj. art instr., 1985—87; art specialist, ESL tchr. Dallas Ind. Sch. Dist., 1993—96; asst. prof. art U. Mary-Hartin Baylor, Belton, Tex., 1997—. Exhibitions include Cultural Activities Ctr., 2000, Hermanas en Arte Exch. Show, 2001, Temple Coll. Downtown Ctr., 2003, Murray State Coll., 2004, Nat. Small Oil Painting Show, Wichita Ctr. for the Arts, 2004, 2006. Membership chmn. Dallas Area Educators of Art, 1993—96; col. Outback Steakhouse Cmty. Outreach, Killeen, Tex., 1997—. Recipient Meadows fellowship, So. Meth. U., 1982—84. Mem.: Tex. Interacholastic Press Assn. (award for yearbook 2001, 2002, 2003, 2004, 2005, 2006), Coll. Art Assn., Killeen C. of C., Harker Heights HS Booster Club (Sec. 2004—). Roman Catholic. Avocations: art history, exercise, reading. Home: 506 Impala Killeen TX 76548 Office: U Mary Hardin Baylor 900 College St Box 8012 Belton TX 76513 Personal E-mail: whitel@hot.rr.com. Business E-Mail: BFWhite@umhb.edu.

FONTANA, BARBARA, psychologist; b. N.Y.C., Oct. 9, 1946; d. Peter and Maria Leone Fontana; m. James Edward Durso, Aug. 7, 1971 (div. May 5, 1998); children: Gina Fontana Durso, David Fontana Durso. BS, St. John's U., N.Y.C., 1968; MS, Profl. Diploma, St John's U., N.Y.C., 1970; PhD, St. John's U., N.Y.C., 1975. Lic. psychologist N.Y., 1978, cert. Imago Relationship therapist Inst. of Imago Relationship Therapy, 2000. Sch. psychologist Bd. of Coop. Ednl. Svcs., Dix Hills, NY, 1970—71, Patchogue-Medford Pub. Schools, Patchogue, NY, 1971—79, Sachem Pub. Schools, Holbrook, NY, 1979—81; pvt. practice psychology Shoreham, NY, 1979—. Cons. Little Flower Children's Svcs., Wading River, NY, 1981—89, Mothers' Ctr. of Suffolk, Wading River, NY, 1987—90. Trustee and sec. Wading River Cemetery Assn., Wading River, NY, 2001—05; psychologist for pre-cana program St. John the Bapt. Roman Cath. Ch., Wading River, NY, 2001—05. Recipient Cert. of Appreciation, Mothers' Ctr. Of Suffolk, 1988, Woman of the Yr. in Health Care, Town of Brookhaven, Office of Women's Svcs., 2004. Mem.: Psychologists for Legislative Action in NY (bd. mem. 2001—03), Found. of the N.Y. State Psychol. Assn. (trustee 2001—02), Imago Relationship Theapists, Imago Relationships Internat. (N.Y. chpt. rep. to Imago global communities), Suffolk County Psychol. Assn. (bd. mem. 1993—2005, pres-elect 2003—05, pres. 2005—, Cert. of Appreciation 1987, 1993, Psychologist of the Yr. 1999), NY State Psychol. Assn. (coun. rep. 1997—2003, Disting. Svc. award 2001), APA, LI Paddlers (spl. events coord. 2001—05, President's award 2003). Roman Catholic. Avocations: kayaking, walking, travel, reading. Office: Barbara Fontana PhD Psychologist 45 Route 25A - Ste A2 Shoreham NY 11786 Office Phone: 631-821-1880. E-mail: drfontana@aol.com.

FONTANA, CAROL P., education educator; d. Paul J. and Irene Yurchak Palmitessa; 1 child, Sara A. AS, Keystone Coll., La Plume, Pa., 1973; BS in Elem. and Early Childhood Edn., Marywood Coll., Scranton, Pa., 1976, MS in Early Childhood Edn., 1978. Cert. trainer Pa. Pathways. From instr. to assoc. prof. Keystone Coll., La Plume, Pa., 1985—2005, prof., 2005—. Cons. Child Care Providers, Inc., Scranton, Pa., 1990—; cda trainer SLHDA Head Start, Scranton, 1990—. Office: Keystone Coll One College Green La Plume PA 18440 Office Phone: 570-945-8474. Business E-Mail: carol.fontana@keystone.edu.

FONTANA, SANDRA ELLEN FRANKEL, special education educator; b. N.Y.C., July 12, 1951; d. Robert Lowell and Mildred (Tropan) Sharoff; m. Jay Tommy Frankel, May 25, 1973 (div. 1993); children: Austin, Lauren; m. David Fontana, July 27, 2002; stepchildren: Troy, Tara. BS in Med. Tech., Rochester (N.Y.) Inst. Tech., 1973; MA in Linguistics, Galludet U., 1984. Cert. comprehensive permanent S.I.G.N. Nat. Assn. Deaf SIGN Instr. Guidance Network, 1985. Coord. bus. affairs/sign lang. program dept. bus. affairs Gallaudet U., 1980-83; head tchr. dept. sign communication faculty retreat N000, winter 1981; instr. dept. interpreter/translator instruction Gallaudet U., 1981-84, instr. in sign lang. dept. sign communication, spring 1982, ASL instr. dept. sign communication, 1982-84, coord. NDC sign lang. program dept. sign communication, 1984-88, instr. dept. sign communication, 1984-88, head instr./trainer, ASL instr. dept. sign communication, 1988-89, ASL instr. Coll. Continuing Edn. extension/summer programs, 1988; assoc. prof. interpreting preparation program CC Balt. County, 1990—2002; assoc. prof. interpreting preparation program/world langs. Riverside (Calif.) CC, 2002—. Evaluator Sign Instr. Guidance Network, Indpls., 1989-90; mem. Sign Instr. Guidance Network; bd. dir. State Md. Office Govr. Assistive Tech. Guaranteed Loan Program, 1999-2002. Mem. Am. Sign Lang. Tchr. Assn. (profl. cert. 1986—, nationwide evaluator 1990—, mem. L.A. chpt. 2002-), Nat. Assn. of the Deaf, Metro. Wash. Assn. of the Deaf, Md. Assn. of the Deaf. Home: 1540 Highridge Rd Riverside CA 92506 Office: Riverside CC 4800 Magnolia Ave Riverside CA 92506 Personal E-mail: sandrell@aol.com.

FONTANIVE, LYNN MARIE, special education administrator; b. Detroit, June 29; d. Edward and Violet Fontanive; m. Paul Adasek Jr., Nov. 8, 1985; 1 child, Paul Fontanive. BA, Marygrove Coll., Detroit; MA, Mich. State U.; EdS, EdD, Wayne State U. Audiologist Plymouth (Mich.) Ctr. for Human

Devel.; assoc. dir. Deaf Hearing & Speech Ctr.; from ednl. audiologist to dept. dir. ctr. programs Oakland Schs., Waterford, Mich., 1996—99; dir. presch. and assessment ctr. Macomb Intermed. Sch. Dist., Clinton Twp., Mich., 1999—. Lectr. in field. Adv. bd. Mich. Sch. for Deaf, Flint, 1986—91; pres. Suprs. for Programs for Hearing Impaired; bd. dirs. Career Leadership and Devel. Bd., 1987—90; bd. dirs., human svcs. coord. bd. HSCB, 1999—; pres. local coord. coun. LICC, 1999—; bd. dirs. State Spl. Edn. Adv. Com., 1994—98; adminstr. Macomb County Adminstrn. Spl. Edn., 1999—. Mem. Am. Speech and Hearing Assn., Mich. Speech, Lang., Hearing Assn. (v.p. 1986-90), Coun. for Exceptional Children Macomb County (membership chmn. 1988-90), Adminstrs. of Spl. Edn., Mich. Suprs. of Pub. Sch. Programs for Hearing Impaired (treas. 1996-97, pres. 1997-2000). Roman Catholic. Avocations: dance, aerobics, travel, biking, tennis. Office: Macomb ISD 44001 Garfield Rd Clinton Township MI 48038-1100 E-mail: lfontanive@misd.net.

FONTES, BIANCA MICHELLE, social studies educator; b. Nogales, Ariz., Mar. 23, 1968; d. Victor Manuel Fontes and Linda Carol Puchi; children: Lillian Christine Garcia-Fontes, Matthew Steven Garcia-Fontes. BS with hons. in Edn., No. Ariz. U., Flagstaff, Ariz., 2002; MEd with hons., Ariz. State U., Glendale, Ariz., 2005; grad., Scottsdale Culinary Inst. Tchr. social studies Phoenix (Ariz.) Union H.S. Dist., 2002—06; instr. Phoenix (Ariz.) Coll., 2006—. Mem.: NEA, Cert. Tchrs. Assn., Ariz. Edn. Assn. Independent. Home: 8352 North 5th Street Phoenix AZ 85020

FONTES, PATRICIA J., psychologist; b. Providence, Dec. 10, 1936; d. Manuel William and Sadie Elizabeth (Conceicao) Sousa F. BS in Edn., Boston U., 1957; MEd, Boston Coll., 1965, PhD, 1968. Tchr. Warwick (R.I.) pub. schs., 1957-59; religious sister/superior Sisters of Our Lady of Providence, 1959-65; asst. prof. U. R.I., Kingston, 1968-69; asst./assoc. prof. Salve Regina Coll., Newport, RI, 1969-72; cons. psychologist Girl Scouts of R.I., Inc., Providence, 1972-73; research fellow Ednl. Research Ctr., St. Patrick's Coll., Dublin, 1973-88; cons. psychologist Girl Scouts R.I., Providence, 1989-92; prof. CEFOPE/IEC U. Minho, Braga, Portugal, 1992—2003; ret. Lectr. in field. Author: Equality in Primary Teaching 1985, As Crianças como Agentes de Mudança Ambiental, 1998, Os Alunos com Necessidades Educativas Especiais, 1998; contbr. articles to profl. jours., chpts. to books. Boston U. scholar, 1953-57; Boston Coll. fellow, 1965-68; Inst. for Portuguese Lang. and Culture grantee, 1982. Mem. APA, Internat. Coun. Psychologists (sec.-gen. 1991-94). Roman Catholic. Avocations: biking, mountain walking, travel, gardening, reading, cooking. Personal E-mail: patfontes@netscape.com.

FOOSANER, JUDITH, artist, art educator; b. Sacramento, Aug. 10, 1940; d. Milton and Anna Yanker Foosaner. BA, U. Calif., Berkeley, 1964, MA, 1968. Prof. art U. Calif., Berkeley, 1975—77, Wimbledon Sch. Art, London, 1993, Calif. Coll. Arts, San Francisco, 1970—2004. One-woman shows include Wenger Gallery, San Francisco, 1971, 1973, 1979, 1980, William Sawyer Gallery, 1975, 1977, Meml. Union Art Gallery, Davis, Calif., 1978, John Bolles Gallery, Santa Rosa, Calif., 1981, Rolando Castellon Gallery, San Francisco, 1982, Space Gallery, LA, 1983, 1985, 1988, 1995, Jeremy Stone Gallery, San Francisco, 1983, 1985, 1987, 1988, Don Soker Gallery, 1992, 1994, R.B. Stevenson Gallery, La Jolla, Calif., 1993, 1995, 1997, 2001, 2006, Littlejohn Gallery, 1993, D.P. Fong Gallery, San Jose, Calif., 1995, Louis Stern Fine Arts, West Hollywood, Calif., 2000, 2001, 2004, Carl Cherry Ctr. Fine Arts, Carmel, Calif., 2003, Spheris Gallery, Bellows Falls, Conn., 2004, Pamela Skinner Gallery, Sacramento, 2005, Gallery 276, San Francisco, 2005, Busch Len-Mowatt Galleries, Palm Desert, Calif., 2006, exhibited in group shows at Crocker Art Mus., Sacramento, 1982, Walnut Creek Civic Arts Gallery, Calif., 1983, Newspace Gallery, San Francisco, 1984, Everson Mus. Art, Syracuse, Calif., 1985—86, Littlejohn-Sternau Gallery, NYC, 1987, 1992, 1993, Irvine Fine Arts Ctr., Calif., 1988, Helander Gallery, NYC, 1989, Ark. Arts Ctr., Little Rock, 1990, 1991, Morley Gallery, London, 1994, Gwenda Jay Gallery, Chgo., 1996, Pacific Heritage Mus., San Francisco, 1998, San Diego Mus. Art, 2000, Reeves Contemporary, NYC, 2003, Monterey Mus., Calif., 2005, Buschlen Mowatt Galleries, Palm Desert, Calif., 2005, Triangle Gallery, San Francisco, 2006, others, Represented in permanent collections Newport Harbor Art Mus., Calif., Albuquerque Art Mus., Bank of Am., San Francisco, Shalee Co., Oral-B, others, Crooker Art Mus., Sacramento, Everson Art Mus., Syracuse, NY, Mus. Haweaii, Honolulu. Fellow, Va. Ctr. Creative Arts, Sweet Briar, 1989; Yaddo fellow, Saratoga Springs, NY, 1983. Avocation: literature.

FOOTE, CHANDRA JEANET, education educator, writer, elementary school educator; b. Rochester, NY, Jan. 20, 1970; d. Theron A. and Patricia M. Foote; m. Christopher A. Robins, July 3, 1999; children Aidan M. Robins, Carson A. Robins. BS, Syracuse U., 1992, MA, 1994, PhD, 1996. Cert. in elem. edn., N.Y. Tchg. assoc. Syracuse U., NY, 1994-96; chair, prof. edn., dept. chair Niagara U., NY, 1996—. Project dir. Niagara Falls (N.Y.) Bd. Edn., 1998-99. Co-author: (book) Constructionist Teaching Practices; contbr. chpt. to books, articles to profl.jours. Leadership rep. The Higher Edn. Task Force for Quality Inclusion, N.Y. State, 1998—; cmty. rep. LaSalle Mid. Sch. Quality Coun., 2001—. Recipient Golden Apple award Niagara Falls City Sch. Dist., 1998-99, Dean's award Coll. Edn. at Niagara U., 1998; Goals 2000 grantee N.Y. State Dept. Edn., 1998-99; Office of Vocat. and Ednl. Svcs. for Individuals with Disabilities grantee, 2000, 02,03. Mem. Am. Ednl. Rsch. Assn., Assn. Tchr. Educators. Avocations: reading, travel. Office: Niagara U Dept Edn B 11 O'Shea Hall Niagara University NY 14109-2042 Fax: (716) 286-8561. E-mail: cjf@niagara.edu.

FOOTE, DOROTHY GARGIS, nursing educator; b. Sheffield, Ala., Jan. 27, 1942; d. Tracy E. and Mary Helen (Cox) Gargis; m. Avon Edward Foote, Mar. 15, 1960; children: Anthony E., Kevin A., Michele. Student, U. So. Miss., 1966-67; AS in Nursing, NW Coll., 1985; BS in Nursing, U. N. Ala., Florence, 1987; MS in Nursing, U. Ala., Huntsville, 1989; postgrad., U. North Ala., England and Scotland, 1990, 91; PhD in Higher Edn. Adminstrn., Miss. State U., 2003. RN Ala., cert. family nurse practitioner, gerontol. nurse practitioner. Real estate assoc. McWaters Realty & Appraisal Co., Athens, Ga., 1977-79; acctg. clk. U. Ga., Athens, 1979-81; nursing supr., nurse practitioner Mitchell Hollingworth Annex Eliza Coffee Meml. Hosp., Florence, 1985-92; v.p. Thornwood Books, Florence, 1982-93; instr. N.W. CC, Phil Campbell, Ala., 1992-93; asst. prof. U. Ala., Huntsville, 1993—; nurse practitioner N. Ala. Clinics, 2002—. Rsch. dir. Leadership Long Term Care, 1995—; co-donor Gulf War video collection U. Md., College Park, 2002; prin. investigator LTC Nursing Adminstr. Ednl. Needs, 2004; co-chair health fair U. Ala. Coll. Nursing Faculty Coun., Huntsville, 2001—, chair health fair, 2003—05; prof. studies abroad U. Ala., London, 2006. Editor: (newsletter) Dames Digest, 1970. Pres. Band Boosters, Athens, 1976. Mem.: ANA, Advanced Practice Council (chair 1999—2001), Ala. State Nurses Assn. (pres. dist. 1 1989—92, bd. dirs. 1989—92, chair gerontol. coun. 1992—93), Phi Theta Kappa, Beta Sigma Phi, Sigma Theta Tau (Beta Phi chpt. pres 2002—04). Home: 222 Shirley Dr Florence AL 35633-1434 Office Phone: 256-824-2439. Business E-Mail: footed@uah.edu.

FOOTE, EVELYN PATRICIA, retired military officer; b. Durham, N.C., May 19, 1930; d. Henry Alexander and Evelyn Sevena (Womack) Foote. BA summa cum laude, Wake Forest U., 1953, LLD (hon.), 1989; student, U.S. Army Command & Gen. Staff Coll., Leavenworth, Kans., 1971-72, U.S. Army War Coll., Carlisle, Pa., 1976-77; MS in Govt. and Pub. Affairs, Shippensburg State U., 1977; student, U. Va. Sch. Bus. Adminstrn., 1980. Commd. 1st lt. U.S. Army, 1960, advanced through grades to brig. gen., 1986, platoon officer WAC Ft. McClellan, Ala., 1960-61, selection officer 6th recruiting dist. Portland, Oreg., 1961-64; comdr. WAC Co. U.S. Army Engr. Brigade, Ft. Belvoir, Va., 1964-66; student Adj. Gen. Officer Advanced Course, Ft. Benjamin Harrison, Ind., 1966; exec. officer, chief adminstrv. div. pub. affairs office U.S. Army, Vietnam, 1967; exec. officer, office personnel ops. WAC, Washington, 1968-71, plans and programs officer OFC, dir., 1972-74; personnel mgmt. officer U.S. Army Forces Command, Ft. McPherson, Ga., 1974-76; comdr. 2d basic tng. bn. U.S. Army Tng. Brigade and Military Police Sch., Ft. McClellan, Ala., 1977-79; faculty mem. U.S. Army War Coll., 1979-82; student Fgn. Service Inst., Dept. of State, Washington, 1982-83; comdr. 42d Mil. Police Group, Mannheim, Fed. Republic of Germany, 1983-85; spl. asst. to comdg. gen. 32d Army Air Def. Command Hdqrs., Darmstadt, Fed. Republic of Germany, 1985-86; dep., insp. gen. for inspections Hdqrs. Dept. of the Army, Washington, 1986-88; dep. comdg. gen. Mil. Dist. Washington, comdr. Ft. Belvoir, Va., 1988-89; ret. U.S. Army, 1989, recalled to active duty Sr. Rev. Panel, 1996-97, ret., 1997. Lectr. various U.S. Army and civilian groups. Contbr. articles to mil. jours. and books. Mem. Am Battle Monuments Commn., 1994—2001; bd. visitors Wake Forest U., 1991—2003, chmn. bd. visitors, 2001—03; trustee Fund for Peace, 2002—; bd. dirs. U.S. Army Women's Mus. Found., 1995—2005. Decorated DSM, Legion of Merit with oak leaf clusters, German Cross of Svc. 1st class; named Spokesperson of the Yr., Dept. Army, 1997—98; named to Disting. Fellows Hall of Fame, U.S. Army War Coll., 1996, Regimental Hall of Fame, U.S. Army MP Corps, 1998; recipient Disting. Pub. Svc. award, Wake Forest U., 1987, DSM, Am. Battle Monuments Commn., 2001. Mem.: Vets. United For Truth (bd. dirs.). Democrat. Lutheran. Avocations: music, reading, hiking.

FOOTE, GWENDOLYN SUE, middle school educator, artist; b. Oklahoma City, Apr. 9, 1953; d. John Thurman and Dorothy Clow Foote; 1 child, Shawn Robert Scarbrough. BS in Biomed. Sci., Tex. A&M U., 1975; MA in Interdisciplinary Studies, U. Tex., 1985; BS in Elem. Edn. and Spl. Edn., Oglala Lakota Coll., 2004. Registered med. technologist Am. Med. Technology Soc.; cert. tchr., spl. edn. tchr. S.D., Fla. Owner Foote Fine Art Studio, 1983—97; supr. med. tech. St. Joseph's Hosp., Denver, 1988—90, St. Mary's Hosp., Tucson, 1990—91; tchr. Wounded Knee Sch., Pine Ridge Indian Reservation, SD, 2000—01; tchr. elem. sch. Little Wound Sch. Pine Ridge Indian Reservation, Kyle, SD, 2001—05; instr. Talented and Gifted Program Little Wound Sch., 2004—05; instr. dept. edn. Oglala Lakota Coll., Kyle, SD, 2003—05. Instr. Oglala Lakota Coll., 2004—06, Johns Hopkins U., 2004—06, U. S.D., 2004—06; spkr. on ecology and human rights. Exhibitions include, Palestine, Dallas, Las Vegas, Los Angeles, 1985—95, Australia, France, Ireland, US (Royal Rainer Family award, 1995), UNESCO, 1994, Universal Studios; mem. rev. bd.: Sci. Scope Mag. Rehabilitator Fed. Fish and Wildlife, Tex., 1983—87. Recipient award, Pediat. AIDS Soc., 1992, Recognition award, Oglala Lakota Tribe, 1994; grantee, Toshiba and NASA, 2005. Mem.: Am. Med. Tech. Soc., Tex. A&M U. Former Students, Internat. Sr. Citizens Assn. (v.p. 1994—97), Nat. Sci. Tchrs. Assn., Mus. Natural History, Earthwatch. Avocations: travel, hiking, reading, music, art. Office: Nautilus Middle Sch 4301 N Michigan Ave Miami Beach FL 33190 Personal E-mail: gwendolyn00@excite.com.

FOOTE, JILL, investment banker, educator; b. Covington, La., Nov. 1, 1964; d. Richard and Jo Lynn Foote; BA in Econ., Managerial Studies, Rice U., 1987; MA in Econ., NYU, 1992; PhD in Econ., Fordham U., 2002. Fixed income sales assoc. Goldman Sachs & Co., N.Y.C., 1987—93, v.p., 1993—99; lectr., dir. MA Rice U., Houston, 2002—. Bd. dirs. Rice U. Alumni, 1998—2002. Mem.: Houston Soc. Fin. Analysts, CFA Inst. Avocations: exercise, music, writing, reading. Office: Jones Grad Sch 6100 Main St Houston TX 77005 Home: 5011 Jackwood St Houston TX 77096-1506

FOOTE, SHERRILL LYNNE, retired manufacturing company technician; b. Marshalltown, Iowa, Apr. 19, 1940; d. Howard Raymond and Lois Ellen Ellis; m. Terry D. Downey, July 27, 1958 (div. 1978); children: Patrick L., Holly L. Harrelson; m. Frank H. Foote, Nov. 17, 1979 (div. 1989); stepchildren: Lauri K., Christopher R. Student, Marshalltown C.C., 1981. Receptionist Drs. Long & Clawson, Marshalltown, 1958—59; clk. Fisher Controls, Marshalltown, 1963—73, cost estimating analyst, 1974—82, sr. cost estimator, 1982—95; ret., 1995. Contbr. limericks Des Moines Register (Contest Winner), 1976, Marshalltown Times Rep., 1986. Mem. Mensa (contbr. Bull. Wordplay 1981—, limerick editor M-Pressions Ctrl. Iowa newsletter 1989-91, local sec. 1991-93). Democrat. Methodist. Avocations: games, reading, movies, plays. Home: 702 Ratcliffe Dr Marshalltown IA 50158-3453

FORBES, DORSEY CONNORS, commentator, journalist; b. Chgo. d. William J. and Sarah (MacLain) C.; m. John E. Forbes; 1 dau., Stephanie. BA cum laude, U. Ill. Fl. reporter WGN-TV Rep. Nat. Conv., Chgo., Dem. Nat. Conv., L.A., 1960. Conducted: Personality Profiles, WGN-TV, Chgo., 1948-49, Dorsey Connors Show, WMAQ-TV, Chgo., 1949-58, 61-63, Armchair Travels, WMAQ-TV, 1952-55, Homeshow, NBC,1954-57, NBC Today Show, Dorsey Connors program, WGN, 1958-61, Tempo Nine, WGN-TV, 1961, Society in Chgo, WMAQ-TV, 1964; writer: column Hi! I'm Dorsey Connors, Chgo. Sun Times, 1965—; Author: Gadgets Galore, 1953, Save Time, Save Money, Save Yourself, 1972, Helpful Hints for Hurried Homemakers, 1988. Founder Ill. Epilepsy League; mem. woman's bd. Children's Home and Aid Soc., mem. women's bd. USO. Named one of Am.'s Outstanding Irish Am. Women, World of Hibernia mag., 1995. Mem. AFTRA, NATAS (Silver Cir. award 1995), SAG, Mus. Broadcast Comm. (founding mem.), Soc. Midland Authors, Chgo. Hist. Soc. (guild com., costume com.), Chi Omega. Roman Catholic. Office: Chicago Sun Times 350 N Orleans St Ste 1270 Chicago IL 60654-2148

FORBES, JEANNE C., secondary school educator; b. Boston, Jan. 9, 1952; d. Paul Leonard and Mary Patricia (Hatch) Costello; m. Peter Ross Forbes, June 16, 1984; 1 child, Patrick John. BA in English, Mt. St. Mary Coll., Hooksett, NH, 1973; MEd, Northeastern U., Boston, 1981. Cert. tchr. Wash. Tchr. Milford (NH) HS, 1973—81, Lake Forest (Ill.) Acad., 1981—84, Yakima (Wash.) Valley C.C., 1984—85, Selah (Wash.) HS, 1985—. English dept. chair Selah HS, Selah, 1986—. Active Jeannine Hedwall Guild, Yakima, 2001—05. Independent. Roman Catholic. Avocations: swimming, bicycling, reading. Office: Selah High Sch 801 N First St Selah WA 98942

FORBES, KAREN KAY, science educator; d. Jerry and Sharon Dingus; m. Dave Forbes, Apr. 17, 1999; 1 child, Sean. BS in Edn. in Earth Sci. and Math., Cen. Mo. State U., Warrensburg, 1995; MA in Edn., Lindenwood U., St. Charles, 2000. Math tchr. Excelsior Springs H.S., Mo., 1995—96; tchr. earth sci. Mehlville H.S., St. Louis, 1996—. Class sponsor Mehlville H.S., St. Louis, 1998—, volleyball coach, 1996—. Mem.: NEA. Avocations: bowling, golf. Office: Mehlville HS 3200 Lemay Ferry Rd Saint Louis MO 63125 Office Phone: 314-467-6258.

FORBES, KRISTIN J., economics professor, former federal official; BA summa cum laude in Econ., Williams Coll., 1992; PhD in Econ., MIT, 1998. Fin. analyst, investment banking divsn., Fin. Institutions Group Morgan Stanley, NYC, 1992—93; project asst., policy rsch. dept. The World Bank, Washington, 1993—94; rsch. fellow Nat. Coun. of Applied Econ. Rsch, New Delhi, 1996; dep. asst. sec. quantitative policy analysis U.S. Dept. Treasury, Washington, 2001—02, dep. asst. sec of quantitative policu analysis, Latin Am. & Caribbean nations, 2002; asst. prof. mgmt. in Applied Econ. Group MIT Sloan Sch. Mgmt., Cambridge, Mass., 1998—2002, Mitsubishi devel. chair internat. mgmt., 2001—, assoc. prof. mgmt. applied econ. group, 2002—04, assoc. prof. mgmt., 2004—; mem. Coun. Econ. Advisers The White House, Washington, 2003—05; faculty rsch. fellow Nat. Bur. Econ. Rsch. Faculty rsch. fellow Nat. Bur. Econ. Rsch., 2000—05; vis. scholar Indian Coun. Rsch. on Internat. Econ. Rels. and Internat. Monetary Fund (ICRIER), 2000; vis. fellow U.S. Fed. Reserve Bd., 2001; vis. scholar IMF, 2002, Fed. Reserve Bank of Mpls., 2002; co-chair IMF rsch. program Project on Global Linkage, 2001—03; assoc. editl. bd. Emerging Markets Review, 2002—03; mem. editl. bd. Jour. Econ. Integration, 2002—03; mem. Coun. Fgn. Relations, 2004—; rsch. assoc. Nat. Bur. Econ. Rsch., 2005—. Contbr. articles to profl. jours. Named a Young Global Leader, World Econ. Forum, 2005; named 1 of 100 Global Leaders for Tomorrow, 2003; recipient David Wells prize in Econ., Williams Coll., 1992, Solow prize for Excellence in Rsch. & Teaching, 1998, Milken award Disting. Econ. Rsch., 2000, Teacher of the Year award, MIT Sloan Sch. Mgmt, 2001. Office: MIT Sloan Sch Mgmt 50 Memorial Dr Rm E52-455 Cambridge MA 02142 E-mail: kjforbes@mit.edu.

FORBES, MARY ALLISON, psychology educator, educator; b. Culpeper, Va., Jan. 29, 1978; d. Richard and Barbara Forbes. BS in Family and Child Devel., Va. Tech. U., 2000, BS in Psychology, 2000, MA in Counselor Edn., 2002. Rschr. dept. human devel. Va. Tech. U., Blacksburg, Va., 2000—01, rschr. dept. psychology, 2000—02; substitute tchr. Poe Mid. Sch., Annandale, Va., 2002—03; mem. faculty Gibbs Coll., Vienna, Va., 2002—. Nominee Tchr. of Yr. award, Gibbs Coll., 2004, Tchr. of Quarter award, 2004. Republican. Avocations: exercise, reading, scrapbooks. E-mail: maforbes02@hotmail.com.

FORBES, SALLY, researcher, editor, curator; d. William Shackleford Koontz and Mary Louise Kibler; m. Kenneth Frith Forbes, Oct. 15, 1944 (dec.); children: Philip Andrews, Melanie Kibler. BA in English and Speech, Ctrl. Meth. U., 1941. Libr., rschr., curator Standard Oil Co. NJ, NYC, 1945—57; freelance art rschr., curator NYC, 1957—. Exec. dir. The Beaux Arts Alliance, NYC, 1995—. Co-founder, prodr.: The Penny Bridge Players, 1976—97. Recipient Disting. Alumni award, Ctrl. Meth. U., 1980. Democrat. Episcopalian. Office: The Beaux Arts Alliance 119 East 74th St New York NY 10021

FORBES, SARAH ELIZABETH, gynecologist, real estate company officer; b. Currituck, N.C., May 4, 1928; d. Dexter and Mary (Brock) Forbes. BA, U. Rochester, 1949; MD, Med. Coll. of Va., 1954. Diplomate Am. Bd. Ob-Gyn. Intern Norfolk (Va.) Gen. Hosp., 1954-55; resident ob-gyn Johnston-Willis Hosp., 1955-56, Norfolk Gen. Hosp., 1956-57, chief resident, 1957-58; pvt. practice gynecologist Newport News, Va., 1958—; pres., real estate investor Mary B. Forbes Land Corp., Newport News, 1972—; pres. Sebrof Corp., Newport News, 1978—, Haras, Inc., Newport News, 1984—, S.S. U.S., Inc., Newport News, 1984—. Bd. dirs. Family Planning Coun.; mem. teaching staff ob-gyn dept. Riverside Hosp. Pres. Peninisula Soc. for Prevention Cruelty to Animals, 1966—; mem. adv. bd. Peninisula chpt. Parents without Ptnrs.; bd. dirs. Newport News chpt. Am. Cancer Soc., pres., 2d v.p., 1971-72, 1st v.p., 1972-73, pres., 1973-74, chmn. rsch., 1961-69; candidate for Newport News City Coun., 1986; bd. dirs. Va. Peninsula Boys and Girls Club, 1991-99, 1st v.p., pres. Va. Peninsula Boys and Girls Club, 2000—. Recipient AMA Physicians Recognition award for Continuing Edn., 1973-76, Twin award Va. Peninsula YWCA, 1987, Medallion award Peninsula Boys and Girls Club, 1993; named Woman of Yr. for Peninsula Area, 1975. Mem. Va. Peninsula Acad. Medicine (pres. 1973-74, v.p. 1972-73, sec., treas. 1971-72); fellow AMA, Va. Med. Soc., Newport News Med. Soc. Am. Coll. Ob-Gyn, Tidewater Ob-Gyn Soc. Office: 12420 Warwick Blvd Newport News VA 23606-3001

FORBES, SHARON ELIZABETH, software engineer; b. Lynn, Mass., Nov. 23, 1960; d. Leland James Brown and Vail (Wilkinson) Bartelson. BSChemE, U. Mass., 1983. Software engr. K&L Automation div. Daniel Industry, Tucson, 1983-86, asst. mgr. software systems, 1987; software mgr. Daniel Automation, Houston, 1987-91; sr. software engr. Praxis Instruments, Inc., Houston, 1991-93, Dresser Measurement, Houston, 1993-97, Dresser Roots Instruments Operation, Houston, 1997-98, Roots Meters and Instruments, Houston, 1999-2001, Dresser Inc., Houston, 2001; software engr. Omni Flow Computers, Inc., Sugar Land, Tex., 2002—. Republican. Avocations: church, contemporary jazz, computers. Home: 5735 Henniker Dr Houston TX 77041-6589 Office: Omni Flow Computers Inc 12620 W Airport Blvd Ste 100 Sugar Land TX 77478 Business E-Mail: sforbes@omniflow.com.

FORBES JOHNSON, MARY GLADYS, retired secondary school educator; b. Bend, Oreg., June 19, 1929; d. Percy Lloyd and Bertha May (Gettman) F.; married, 1996 BA in Edn. magna cum laude, Cascade Coll., 1951; BS in Edn., Western Oreg. State Coll., Monmouth, 1951, MS in Edn., 1968. Cert. tchr., Oreg. Tchr. Christian & Missionary Alliance, Mamou, Guinea, West Africa, 1952-54, Bend (Oreg.)-Redmond Christian Day Sch., 1954-56, Dalat Sch., Asia, 1956-76, Bend-LaPine Sch. Dist. 1, Bend, 1976-99, adminstr., tchr., 1981-87, tchr. kindergarten Thompson Sch., 1989-99. Cons. Chpt. I Program in Spl. Edn., 1976-88; supt. Sunday sch. Christian and Missionary Alliance, 1976-80, Faith Fellowship Four Sq., Madras, Oreg., 1981-88. Mem. Citizens for the Republic, Washington, 1989; mem. Rep. Nat. Com., 1990—. Recipient cert. of appreciation Hale Found., 1986, 87, Skyhook II Project, 1987, Concerned Women Am., 1987, Nat. Law Enforcement Officer Meml., 1991, Am. Indian Relief Coun., 1992. Mem. Am. Def. Inst., Nat. Right to Life Com., Coun. for Inter-Am. Security, Nat. Assn. for Uniformed Svcs., Concerned Women for Am., Capitol Hill Women's Club, Christian Coalition, Am. Ctr. for Law and Justice, Am. Life League, Oreg. Citizens Alliance, Heritage Found., Delta Kappa Gamma. Avocations: gardening, bicycling, hiking, farming. Home: PO Box 107 Bend OR 97709-0107 Office: Bend LaPine Sch Dist 1 520 NW Wall St Bend OR 97701-2608

FORBUSH, SANDRA M., artist, educator; b. Garden City, NY, Jan. 14, 1940; d. John Herbert Jr. and Mary Elizabeth (Keeler) Mears; m. Wade Hampton Massie III, Mar. 27 (div. Aug. 1980); 1 child, Nancy Massie Wiley; m. Lloyd Augustus Forbush, Sept. 6, 1982. Student, Md. Inst. Art, Balt., 1957-59. Fashion model Garfinckel & Co., Washington, 1960-65; fashion freelance model, commls. and TV Washington, Balt., N.Y.C; ballet tchr. Wakefield Country Day Sch., Huntly, Va., piano tchr.; profl. portrait artist, art tchr. self-employed, Flint Hill, Va. Ofcl. artist The Va. Gold Cup, Great Meadow, 2002, $100,000 Grand Prix Jumper Classic, Great Meadow, 2002. One-woman shows include Montpelier, Va., Middleburg Libr., Fifth St. Gallery; exhibited in shows at Am. Acad. Equine Art, 1999, The Dog Mus., St. Louis, Farmington Hunt Club, Beresford Gallery, Saratoga Springs, N.Y., Mus. of Hounds and Hunting, At the Dog Show, Wichita, Kans., Somoza Gallery, Houston, 2000, others; offl. artist Va. Gold Cup, 2002, Grand Prix, Gt. Meadow, 2002; works include sporting art in oil, numerous portraits in oil; contbr. articles to profl. jours. Mem.: Am. Acad. Equine Art (assoc.). Episcopalian. Home: Foxhall Farm Box 149 Flint Hill VA 22627 Office Phone: 540-636-1507. Personal E-mail: sforbush@lynxconnect.com.

FORCE, ELIZABETH ELMA, retired pharmaceutical executive; b. Phila., Sept. 6, 1930; d. Harry Elgin and Loretta G. (Werner) Force. BA, Temple U., 1952; postgrad., U. Pa., 1965-67; MPh, George Washington U., 1972, PhD, 1973. Cons. sr. scientist Booz-Allen Hamilton, Bethesda, Md., 1967-68; rsch. cons. scientist GEOMET, Inc., Rockville, Md., 1968-70; profl. assoc. div. med. scis. NAS-NRC, Washington, 1970-74; mgr. clin. adminstrn. dept. clin. rsch. and devel. Wyeth Labs., Radnor, Pa., 1974-77; exec. dir. regulatory affairs Merck Sharp and Dohme Rsch. Labs., West Point, Pa., 1977-88; cons. Clin. Regulatory Systems, Sarasota, Fla., 1988-91. Asst. prof. epidemiology and environ. health Sch. Medicine George Washington U., Washington, 1972—74; vis. assoc. prof. cmty. health and preventive medicine Med. Coll. Jefferson U., Phila., 1981—83. Editor: Clin. Rsch. Practice and Drug Regulatory Affairs, 1983—85, Drug Info. Jour., 1984—88; contbr. articles to profl. jours. Chmn. adv. coun. bd. trustees Ringling Mus. Art, 1992—95; pres. bd. dirs. Siesta Tower Condominium Assn., Sarasota, 1990—92; vice chmn. Com. Minority Contracts, Sarasota County, 1994; pres. Women's Resource Ctr., Sarasota, 1992—94; mem. adv. coun. Coun. Violence, Sarasota County, 1994; pres. Sterling Lakes Owners Assn., Boynton Beach, 1996—98; mem. steering com. Harid Conservatory Music, Lynn U., Boca Raton, 1999—2000; chmn. resident coun. Abbey Delray S., 2004—05. Pub. Health fellow, U. Pa. Sch. Medicine, 1965—67, Ruhland Pub. Health fellow, George Washington U. Sch. Medicine, 1971—73. Mem.: AAUW, Drug Info. Assn. (pres. 1986—87, Outstanding Dir. award 1985), Heritage Soc. George Washington U., Torch Club Boca Raton. Avocation: collecting oriental antiques. Home: 1717 Homewood Blvd Apt 247 Delray Beach FL 33445-6801

FORCHE, JENNIFER ROTH, clinical psychologist; b. Youngstown, Ohio, Feb. 27, 1960; d. Daniel Benjamin Roth and Merabeth (Meyer) Lurie; m. Jeffrey Paul Forche, Sept. 12, 1987; children: Daniel Robert, Rachel Marie, Kathryn Roth. BA, Miami U., Oxford, Ohio, 1981; MA, Bowling Green State U., 1984, PhD, 1987. Pvt. practice, Troy, Sterling Heights, Mich., 1987—.

Presenter at profl. confs. Mem. Am. Psychol. Assn., Mich. Psychol. Assn., Mortar Bd. Avocations: bicycling, photography, gardening. Home: 2477 Kingsbury Dr Troy MI 48098-4293 Office: 38800 Van Dyke Ste 700 Sterling Heights MI 48312

FORCIER, HELENE FRANCIS, secondary school educator; d. Jack Benny and Rose Epstein; m. Jay Stanley Forcier, Dec. 17, 1965; children: Jack William, AmyBeth Elise Smith, Jeremy Michael, Jeffery Howell. BA, Ariz. State U., Tempe, 1969, MA in English Edn., 1973. Cert. adminstr. Ariz., 1991. Tchr. Glendale (Ariz.) Union H.S. Dist., 1971—, prin. alternative programs, 1991—2001. Advisor Interact- Rotary, Phoenix, 2000—06. Democrat. Avocations: reading, travel, writing, cooking. Office: Washington High School 2217 W Glendale Ave Phoenix AZ 85021 Office Phone: 623-915-8400. Business E-Mail: hfforcie@guhsdaz.org.

FORD, ALMA REGINA, retired union official, educator; b. Owings, W.Va., Oct. 4, 1939; d. Charles Feathers and Pearl (Costello) Ford. AB, Fairmont State Coll., 1960; MA, W.Va. U., 1964, Ball State U., 1984; postgrad., Sorbonne. Cert. counselor. Tchr., Ohio, 1961—78, W.Va., 1961—78, Turkey, 1961—78, England, 1961—78, France, 1961—78, Italy, 1961—78, Germany, 1961—78; v.p., dep. rep. Dept. Def. Dependents Schs.-Europe; negotiator Overseas Fedn. Tchrs., 1978—80; tchr. Zweibrucken, Germany, 1980—, counselor, 1997; ret., 1999. Recipient Sustained Superior/Performance award, Dept. Army, 1972—76, Exceptional Performance award, 1984; NDEA fellow, 1968. Mem.: LWV, AARP, AAUW, Marion County Ret. Tchrs. Assn., W.Va. Sheriff's Assn., Overseas Fedn. Tchrs., Am. Fedn. Tchrs., Speech Assn. Am., Nat. Assn. Ret. People, Nat. Coun. Tchrs. English, Nat. Assn. Ret. Fed. Employees, Zweibrucken Alumnus Assn., Fairmont State Coll. Alumnus Assn., Ret. Eagles Club, W.Va. Travelers Club, Moose, Elks, Eagles Ladies Aux., Am. Legion Ladies Aux., VFW Ladies Aux., Alpha Psi Omega, Phi Delta Kappa. Home: RR 2 Box 365 Shinnston WV 26431-9616 Office Phone: 304-534-4091.

FORD, ANN K., lawyer; b. Cleve., July 12, 1954; BA, Georgetown Univ., 1976; JD, Duke Univ., 1980. Bar: DC 1981, NY 1987. Ptnr., nat. chair Trademark, Copyright and Media Practice Group DLA Piper US LLP. Contbr. articles to profl. jours. Mem.: ABA, Internat. Trademark Assn. Office: DLA Piper US LLP 1200 19th St NW Washington DC 20036-2412 Office Phone: 202-861-3920. Office Fax: 202-689-7540. Business E-Mail: ann.ford@dlapiper.com.

FORD, ANN SUTER, family practice nurse practitioner, consultant; b. Mineola, NY, Oct. 31, 1943; d. Robert M. and Jennette (Van Derzee) Suter; m. W. Scott Ford, 1964; children: Tracey, Karin, Stuart. RN White Plains Hosp., Sch. Nursing, NY, 1964; BS in Nursing with high distinction, U. Ky., 1967; MS in Health Planning, Fla. State U., 1971, PhD, 1975, MSN, 1992. Nurse U. Ky. Med. Ctr., 1964-65, Tallahassee Meml. Hosp., 1968-69; guest lectr. health planning dept. urban/regional planning Fla. State U., Tallahassee, 1973-76, health planner and research assoc., 1974-76, vis. asst. prof., 1976-77, asst. prof. and dir. health planning splty., 1977-83, assoc. prof., 1982-83, health care analyst and policy cons., 1983-86; med., health program analyst Aging and Adult Svcs. for State of Fla., 1986-90; coordinator Fla. Alzheimer's Disease Initiative, 1986-90; family nurse practitioner Capital Area Physicians' Svcs., 1993-94; assoc. prof. nursing Fla. A&M U., 1994—2002; clin. nurse Tallahassee Meml. Regional Ctr., 1990—. Bd. dirs. Regional Fla. Lung Assn., 1986-91; mem. exec. com. human services and social planning tech. dept. Am. Inst. Planners, 1977-83. Author: The Physician's Assistant: A National and Local Analysis, 1975; contbr. articles to profl. jours., chapters to books. USPHS grantee, 1965-67; HEW grantee, 1978; Univ. fellow Fla. State U., 1971-72; recipient Am. Inst. Planners' Student award, 1975. Mem. Am. Planning Assn. (charter mem. human services and social planning tech. dept. 1976-83, chmn. health planning session Oct. 1978, 79, health policy liaison 1979-83, author assn. health policy statement), Am. Health Planning Assn., Fla. Nurses Assn., Phi Kappa Phi, Sigma Theta Tau. Address: 2602 Cline St Tallahassee FL 32308-0810 Personal E-mail: annscott64@comcast.net.

FORD, ANNA MARIA, language educator; b. Starachowice, Poland, Aug. 17, 1940; arrived in U.S., 1954; d. Antoni Niedzwiedzki and Wanda Gluszkiewicz; married; 1 child, Alexandra Sky. BA, Wayne State U., 1963, MA, 1970. Cert. secondary edn. tchr. French, Spanish, English Mich., SC, advanced placement French tchr. SC, Adolescence Young Adulthood/English Lang. Arts Nat. Bd. Cert. Tchrs., 2001, nat. bd. cert. tchr. Tchr. French and Spanish Ford Mid. Sch., Highland Park, Mich., 1965-66; tchr. fgn. lang. dept. Highland Park Cmty. HS, 1966-97, head fgn. lang. dept., 1968-70, 73-78, lang. arts facilitator, 1991-94; owner, founder Horizons-Internat., Grosse Pointe Park, Mich., 1993-97; dist.-wide lang. cons./coord. Highland Park Pub. Schs., 1994-97; Spanish, French and English lang. tchr. Georgetown (S.C.) County Sch. Dist., 1997—. Ind. contractor, cons. Langs. and Svcs. Agy., 1993—; assessor, field study, tchr. performance lang. arts Nat. Bd. Profl. Tchg. Stds., Mich., 1994; scorer writing proficiency assessments Mich. Dept. Edn., 1994—97, trainer of tchrs., 1995, trainer of trainers, 1995—97, elem. and secondary content literacy com. mem., 1995—; instrnl./profl. devel. task force Mid. Cities Assn., Lansing, Mich., 1995—97; mem. North Ctrl. Accreditation Evaluation Teams, 1970—97; cons. Coastal Area Writing Project, SC, 1998—; ADEPT team evaluator, asst. tng. evaluator, SC, 1999—; advisor H.S. yearbook Polar Bear, 1985—86. Editor: (newsletter) Happenings, 1977—79, Mich. Writing Assessment News, 1994—97. Bd. dirs. Friends of Polish Art, Mich., 1995—97, French Inst. Mich., Southfield, 1985—97. Named Tchr. of Yr., Howard Adult Ctr., Georgetown, SC, 2005—06; recipient Big E award, Josten's Printing Divsn., 1986, cert. appreciation for participation in Classrooms of Tomorrow program, Mich. Gov., 1990. Mem.: AAUW, Alliance Francaise (Detroit/Grosse Pointe/Charleston), Alpha Mu Gamma. Roman Catholic. Avocations: travel, sailing, skiing, literature, music. Home: 38 Wexford Ln River Club Pawleys Island SC 29585-7614 Office: Horizons Internat 38 Wexford Ln Pawleys Island SC 29585-7614 Office Phone: 843-546-0219. Home Fax: 843-237-5352. Personal E-mail: anoushka@earthlink.net.

FORD, BARBARA G., secondary school educator; b. Houston, Aug. 17, 1952; d. Joe Marie Winters and Jesse Burton Ford. BFA, MA, Stephen F. Austin State U., Nacogdoches, Tex. Tchr. Winnsboro (Tex.) H.S., 1976—78; biology dept. purchasing agt. Rice U., Houston, 1978—80; credit mgr. Westin Hotels and Resorts, Seattle, 1980—90; tchr. Pearsall (Tex.) H.S., 1991—95, S. San Antonio H.S. West Campus, 1995—. Facilitator SureScore, Austin, Tex., 1998—2000; scorer Psychol. Corp., San Antonio, 1998—2001. Named Tchr. of Yr., S. San Antonio West Campus H.S.; recipient Thurston Dupar award, Westin Hotels and Resort Galleria, Dallas, 1980, Hon. Col. of the Rgt., S. San Antonio West Campus H.S., JROTC. Office: South San Antonio HS West Campus 5622 Ray Ellison San Antonio TX 78242 Office Phone: 210-623-1800. Home Fax: 210-623-1812; Office Fax: 210-623-1812.

FORD, BARBARA JEAN, librarian, educator; b. Dixon, Ill., Dec. 5, 1946; BA magna cum laude with honors, Ill. Wesleyan U., 1968; MA in Internat. Rels., Tufts U., 1969; MS in Libr. Sci., U. Ill., 1973. Dir. Soybean Insect Rsch. Info. Ctr. Ill. Natural History Survey, Urbana, 1973-75; from asst. to assoc. prof. U. Ill., Chgo., 1975-84, asst. documents libr., 1975-79, documents libr., dept. head, 1979-84, acting audiovisual libr., 1983-84; asst. dir. pub. svcs. Trinity U., San Antonio, 1984-86, assoc. prof., assoc. dir., 1986-91, acting dir. librs., 1989, 91; prof., dir. univ. libr. svcs. Va. Commonwealth U., Richmond, 1991-98; asst. commr. Chgo. Pub. Libr., 1998—2002; dir., disting. prof. Mortenson Ctr. Internat. Libr. Programs, U. Ill., Urbana, 2003—. Women's re-entry adv. bd. U. Ill., Chgo., 1980-82, student affairs com., 1978-80, student admissions, records, coll. rels. com., 1981-84, univ. senate, 1976-78, 82-84, chancellor's libr. coun. svcs. com. 1984, campus lectrs. com. 1982-83; admissions interviewer for prospective students Trinity U., 1987-91, reader for internat. affairs theses, 1985-91, libr. self-study com., 1985-86, internat. affairs com., 1986-91, inter-Am. studies com., 1986-91, faculty senate, 1987-90; libr. working group U.S./Mex. Commn. Cultural Coop., 1990; presenter in field Contbr. articles to profl. jours. Bd. dirs. Friends of San Antonio Pub. Libr., 1989-91; adv. com. chair Office for Libr. Pers. Resources, 1994-95; steering com. Virtual Libr. Va., 1994-98, chair user svcs. com., 1995-96. Celia M. Howard fellow Tufts U., 1969; sr. fellow UCLA Grad. Sch. Libr. and Info. Sci., 1993. Mem. ALA (conf. program com. 1985-91, libr. edn. assembly 1983-84, membership com. 1978-79, status of women in librarianship com. 1983-85, exec bd., 1996-99, Lippincott Award Jury 1979-80, Shirley Olofson Meml. award 1977), ALA Coun. (at-large councilor 1985-89, chpt. councilor Ill. Libr. Assn. 1980-84, com. on coms. 1987-88, spl. coun. orientation com. 1982-83, ALA exec. bd., 1996-99, pres.- elect 1996-97, pres. 1997-98), Assn. Coll. and Rsch. Librs. (bd. dirs. 1989-92, pres.-elect 1989-90, pres. 1990-91, publs. com. 1990-91, conf. program planning 1990-91), Nat. Assn. State Univs. and Land Grant Colls. (commn. info. tech. 1992-94), Internat. Fedn. Libr. Assns. and Instns. (sec. ofcl. pubs. sect., gen. info. com. 1985 conf., moderator Latin Am. seminar on ofcl. pubs. 1991, univ. and other rsch. librs. sect. standing com. 1999—, governing bd. 2005—), Spl. Librs. Assn. (program com. 1976-77, 80-82, publicity com. 1977-79, chair 1978-79, chair spl. projects com. 1981-82, sec./treas. divsn. social sci. internat. affairs sect. 1984-86), Assn. Libr. Info. Sci. Edn. (chair local arrangements conf. planning com. 1988, 92), Ill. Libr. Assn. (chair election com. 1976-77, exec. bd. 1978-79, 80-84, bd. govt. documents round table 1976-79, chair 1978-79, long range planning com. 1980-84), Tex. Libr. Assn. (pubs. com. 1985-87, legis. com. 1986-87, judge best of exhibits award 1987, task force Amigos Fellowship 1990, del. conf. on librs. and info. svcs., 1991), Va. Libr. Assn. (ad hoc. com. distance learning 1992), Va. State Libr. and Archives (Va. libr. and info. svcs. task force 1991-93, steering com. Arbuthnot lecture 1992-93, coop. continuing edn. adv. com. 1992-94), VIVA (steering com. 1994-98), Chgo. Libr. Club (2d v.p. 1983-84), Richmond Acad. Libr. Consortium (v.p. 1991-92, pres. 1992-93), Beta Phi Mu, Phi Kappa Phi, Phi Alpha Theta, Kappa Delta Pi. Office Phone: 217-244-1898. Business E-Mail: bjford@uiuc.edu.

FORD, BETTY ANN (ELIZABETH ANN FORD), former First Lady of the United States, health facility executive; b. Chicago, Apr. 8, 1918; d. William Stephenson and Hortence (Neahr) Bloomer; m. William G. Warren, 1942 (div. 1947); m. Gerald R. Ford (38th Pres. U.S.), Oct. 15, 1948; children: Michael Gerald, John Gardner, Steven Meigs, Susan Elizabeth. Studied, Bennington Sch. of Dance, 1936, 37; studied with Martha Graham, Graham Sch. of Dance, N.Y.C., 1937; LL.D. (hon.), U. Mich., 1976. Dancer Martha Graham Concert Group, N.Y.C., 1939-41; fashion dir. Herpolsheimer's Dept. Store, Grand Rapids, Mich., 1943-48; dance instr. Grand Rapids, 1932-48; First Lady of the United States, 1974—77. Co-founder Susan G. Komen Foundation, 1982; chmn., co-founder The Betty Ford Ctr., Rancho Mirage, Calif., 1982—. Author: (autobiography) The Times of My Life, 1978, Betty: A Glad Awakening, 1987. Bd. dirs. Nat. Arthritis Found. (hon.); trustee Martha Graham Dance Ctr., Eisenhower Med. Ctr., Rancho Mirage; hon. chmn. Palm Springs Desert Mus.; nat. trustee Nat. Symphony Orch.; bd. dirs. The Lambs, Libertyville, Ill.; co-founder (with Leonard Firestone) Betty Ford Ctr., Rancho Mirage, Calif., 1982. Named to Mich. Women's Hall of Fame, 1987; recipient Presidential Medal of Freedom, 1991, Living Legacy award, Women's Internat. Ctr., 1998, Congressional Gold Medal, 1999, C. Everett Koop Health award, Am. Hosp. Assn., 1999, Woodrow Wilson Pub. Svc. award, 2003. Republican. Episcopalian. Office: Gerald R Ford Library 1000 Beal Ave Ann Arbor MI 48109*

FORD, BURCH TRACY, headmaster; BA, Boston U.; MSW, Simmons Coll.; EdM, Harvard U. Former teacher and sch. counselor Groton Sch., 1978—88; former teacher & dean of students Milton Acad., 1988—93; head of sch. Miss Porter's Sch., Conn., 1993—. Former pres. Nat. Coalition of Girls Schools; former chair Commn. on Independent Schools, New England Assn. of Schools and Colleges; bd. mem. Nat. Assn. of Principals of Schools for Girls. Bd. mem. Chewonki Found., Nutmeg Big Brothers Big Sisters Found. Office: Miss Porter's Sch 60 Main St Farmington CT 06032

FORD, CAROL, science educator; m. Terry Ford, Aug. 8, 2004. BS in Edn., East Ctrl. U., Ada, Okla., 1995. Cert. tchr. NBPTS, 2004. Tchr. Noble H.S., Okla., 1997—. Office Phone: 405-872-3441. Personal E-mail: tcford@sbcglobal.net. E-mail: cford@nobleps.com.

FORD, CECILIA SPARKS, federal agency administrator; Grad., U. Va. Atty. Bus. and Adminstrv. Law Divsn. Health and Human Svcs. Office Gen. Counsel; bd. mem. U.S. Dept. Health and Human Svcs., Washington, 1980—99, chair departmental appeals bd., 1999—, also bd. dirs. Office: Dept Health & Human Svcs Departmental Appeals Bd MS 6127 DAB Chair & Appellate Division 330 Independence Ave Cohen Bldg Rm G-644 Washington DC 20201 Office Phone: 202-565-0200. Office Fax: 202-565-0238. Business E-Mail: cecilia.ford@hhs.gov.*

FORD, CHERYL ANISIA, elementary school educator; d. Reginald Annis and Joyce Elaine (Hall) Gale; m. Anthony Herbert Ford, Aug. 26, 1972. BA, Calif. State U., LA, 1973, MEd, 1978. Cert. tchr. Calif. Tchr. Montebello Unified Schs., Calif., 1974—, mentor, 1996—97. Avocations: reading, art, interior decorating. Home: 2009 N Palm Ave Upland CA 91784

FORD, CLARA S., retired secondary school educator; b. Oxford, N.C., Apr. 14, 1938; d. Nannie Laura (Bailey) Smith; m. Joseph J. Ford (dec. Apr. 2000); 15 foster children 1 child, Joseph III. Student, SUNY, 1978; A in Liberal Arts, Adelphi U., 1980, BS, 1983. Coord. Dept. Intergovt. Affairs Divsn. Employment and Tng., Massapequa, NY, 1984—88; tchr. Westbury (N.Y.) Sch. Dist., 1983—89, BOCES Spl. Edn., Dix Hills, NY, 1983—85, John Glenn HS, East Northport, NY, 1984—99, Elwood Sch. Dist., Huntington, NY, 1984—99; ret., 1999. Assembler Estee Lauder, Melville, NY, 1987—2005. Vol. Mentally Retarded Recreation Ctr., 1980—83; recruiter, trainer young adults for workforce; mem. Humane Soc., 2000—; cub den mother Boy Scouts Am.; vol. Am. Heart Assn., Suffolk Devel. Facility. Baptist. Avocations: reading, bicycling, writing, cooking, poetry. Home: 641 Commander Ave West Babylon NY 11704-2301

FORD, EILEEN OTTE (MRS. GERARD W. FORD), modeling agency executive; b. NYC, Mar. 25, 1922; d. Nathaniel and Loretta Marie (Laine) Otte; m. Gerard William Ford, Nov. 20, 1944; children: Margaret (Mrs. Robert Craft), Gerard William, M. Katie (Mrs. Andre Balazs), A. Lacey (Mrs. John Williams). BS, Barnard Coll., 1943. Stylist Elliot Clarke Studio, N.Y.C., 1943-44, William Becker Studio, 1945; copywriter Arnold Constable, N.Y.C., 1945-46; reporter Tobe Coburn, 1946; co-founder Ford Model Agy., N.Y.C., 1946—, now chmn. bd. Author: Eileen Ford's Model Beauty, Secrets of the Model's World, A More Beautiful You in 21 Days, Beauty Now and Forever, 1977. Bd. dirs. London Philharmonic, 1948—. Recipient Harpers Bazaar award for promotion internat. understanding., Woman of Yr. in Advt. award, 1983

FORD, FAITH, actress; b. Alexandria, La., Sept. 14, 1964; d. Charles and Pat F., m. Robert Nottingham, 1989 (div. 1996); m. Campion Murphy, June 27, 1998. Actress: (films) You Talkin' to Me, 1987, For Goodness Sake, 1993, North, 1994, Sometimes They Come Back.For More, 1999, The Pacifier, 2005; (TV series) One Life to Live, 1983, Another World, 1983-84, Popcorn Kid, 1987, Murphy Brown, 1988-97 (Emmy nominee Supporting Actress - Comedy Series, 1989, 90, 91, 94), Maggie Winters, 1998, The Norm Show, 1999, Hope and Faith, 2003-; (TV films) If It's Tuesday, It Still Must Be Belgium, 1987, Poisoned by Love: The Kern County Murders, 1993, A Weekend in the Country, 1996, Night Visitors, 1996, Her Desperate Choice, 1996, Moms on Strike, 2002; TV appearances include Hardcastle & McCormick, 1985, Webster, 1986, Scarecrow and Mrs. King, 1986, Cagney & Lacey, 1986, Thirtysomething, 1987, 88, Murder She Wrote, 1990, The Hidden Room, 1993, (voice) Family Guy, 2000.

FORD, GAIL, library administrator; b. Sacramento, Mar. 5, 1952; d. R. Eugene and Jeanne P. Ford; m. Clive Matson, Jan. 15, 1993; 1 child, Ezra John Matson-Ford. AB in Philosophy, Stanford U., 1973. Adminstrv. analyst U. Calif. Berkeley Libr., 1984—; pub. Broken Shadow Publs., Oakland, Calif., 1993—. Pub.: (book) Emptiness That Plays So Rough, 1995, Under a Gibbous Moon, 1996, Squish Boots, 2002. Home: 472 44th St Oakland CA 94609-2136

FORD, IRENE ELAINE, pastor; b. West Union, W.Va., Oct. 6, 1927; d. Clurel Cecil Powell and Lillian Violet Gaskins; m. Claudius Arnold Ford, Jan. 24, 1946 (dec. Oct. 20, 1997); children: Richard Freeman, Michael Leroy. Student, Northern C.C., Weirton, W.Va., W.Va. Wesleyan Coll., 1984—87, Duke Divinity, 1984—89. Ordained deacon United Meth. Ch., 1992. Pastor Bristol Charge United Meth. Ch., Bristol, W.Va., 1983—89, pastor Christ-Owings Charge Shinnston, W.Va., 1989—94, assoc., 1992; pastor Graysville-Washington Lands United Meth. Ch., Moundsville, W.Va., 1994—96, Nessly Chapel United Meth. Ch., New Cumberland, W.Va., 1997—. Parish coord. United Meth. Ch., Bristol, W.Va., 1986—89, Shinnston, W.Va., 1989—94; pres., v.p. WHG dist. United Meth. Women, 1980; coun. mem. Race Track Chaplaincy Am./Mountaineer Race Track, 2005—. Pres. W.Va. Congress Parent Tchr. Orgn., 1975—77; sch. bd. mem. Hancock County, 1979—84. Mem.: W.Va. Ann. Conf. (assoc.; deacon). Methodist.

FORD, JEAN ELIZABETH, retired language educator; b. Branson, Mo., Oct. 5, 1923; d. Mitchell Melton and Annie Estella (Wyer) F.; m. J.C. Wingo, 1942 (div. 1946); m. E. Syd Vineyard, 1952 (div. 1956); m. Vincent Michel Wessling, Feb. 14, 1983 (div. Dec. 1989). AA in English, L.A. City Coll., 1957; BA in English, Calif. State U., 1959; MA in Higher Edn., U. Mo., 1965; postgrad., UCLA, 1959-60, U. Wis., 1966, U. Mo. Law Sch., 1968-69. Cert. English tchr., real estate broker, Mo. Dance instr. Arthur Murray Studios, L.A., 1948-51; office mgr. Western Globe Products, L.A., 1951-55; pvt. dance tchr., various office jobs L.A., 1955-59; social dir. S.S. Matsonia, 1959; social worker L.A. County, 1959-61; 7th grade instr. Carmenita Sch. Dist., Norwalk, Calif., 1961-62; English instr. Leadwood (Mo.) High Sch., 1962-63; dance instr. U. Mo., 1963-66, SW Mo. State U., 1966-68, NW Mo. State U., 1970-76, Johnson County Community Coll., 1976-77; tax examiner IRS, Kansas City, Mo., 1978-80; tax acct. Baird, Kurtz & Dobson, Kansas City, Mo., 1981; dance tchr. Singles Program Village, Presbyn. Ch., Kans., 1981-96; pvt. practice, 1984—2002; ret., 2002. Substitute tchr. various sch. dists., 1976-85; dance chmn. Mo. Assn. Health, Phys. Edn. and Recreation, 1965-66, 68-69, dance chmn. ctrl. dist. AAHPER, 1972-73; vis. author Young Author's Conf., Ctrl. Mo. State U., 1987, 88, 89; speaker Am. Reading Assn., Grandview, Mo., 1990; real estate sales agt., Kansas City, 1980-84; real estate sales broker, Mo., 1990—, Kans., 1990-2000; spkr. in field Author: Fish Tails and Scales, 1982, 2d edit., 2000, The Other Side of the Coin, 2004 Mem. Am. Contract Bridge League, Kansas City Ski Club. Democrat. Presbyterian. Avocations: tennis, swimming, skiing, sailing, bridge. Home and Office: 142 Grandview Dr Bldg 4 #7 Branson MO 65616

FORD, JEANETTE WHITE, archivist, educator; b. Altus, Okla., Jan. 22, 1929; d. M. H. and Gladys Martin White; m. LeRoy Ford, June 3, 1950; children: Judy Rex, Daniel, Cindy Meyer. BA, Okla. Bapt U., Shawnee, 1949; MRE, Southwestern Bapt. Theol. Sem., Ft. Worth, Tex., 1966. Cert. archivist, tchr. Tex. Tchr. Tex. Wesleyan U., Ft. Worth, 1956—58, Ft. Worth Ind. Sch. Dist., 1968—72; archivist S.W. br. Nat. Archives, Ft. Worth, 1974—84. Author: Archival Principles and Practice, 1990, Archival Principles for Churches, 2001; co-author: Our Niche in History, 1994. Pres. Casa Hospice Group, Co., 1994—96; docent Amon Carter Mus. Am. Art, Ft. Worth, 2004—. Recipient Alumni Achievement award, Okla. Bapt. U., 2000, Outstanding Fed. Women award, Region 10 GSA, 1982. Democrat. Avocations: collecting Franksoma pottery, watercolor painting. Home: 5832 Sycamore Creek Rd Fort Worth TX 76134

FORD, JUDITH ANN TUDOR, retired natural gas distribution company executive; b. Martinsville, Ind., May 11, 1935; d. Glenn Leyburn and Dorotha Mae (Parks) Tudor; m. Walter L. Ford, July 25, 1954 (dec. 1962); children: John Corbin, Christi Sue. Student, Wichita State U., 1953-55; student, U. Nev.-Las Vegas. Legal sec. S.W. Gas Corp., Las Vegas, 1963-69, asst. corp. sec., 1969-72, corp. sec., 1972-82, v.p., 1977-82, sr. v.p., 1982-88, also bd. dirs., dir. 7 subs. Bd. dirs. NBA Svcs., Nev., residence for handicapped, 1989-97, treas., 1990-91, chmn., 1994-97; trustee Nev. Sch. Arts, Las Vegas, 1979-90, chmn. bd. dirs., 1985-86; trustee Disciples Sem. Found., Claremont Sch. Theology and Pacific Sch. Religion, San Francisco, 1985-91, 92-98, 99-2005, vice chmn., 1993-94, chmn., 1994-98; mem. Ariz. Acad., Ariz. Town Halls, 1986-92. Mem. Am. Soc. Corp. Secs., Greater Las Vegas C. of C. (bd. dirs. 1979-85), Pacific Coast Gas Assn. (bd. dirs. 1984-88), Ariz. Bus. Women Owners (exec. com. 1985-88). Democrat. Mem. Christian Ch. (Disciples Of Christ).

FORD, KARRIN ELIZABETH, music educator, musician; b. Waco, Tex., July 2, 1951; d. Joe Brown Ford and Lillian Pauline Phelps. B in Music Edn. magna cum laude, Baylor U., 1974; MusM, U. Kans., 1978; D in Musical Arts, Cin. Conservatory Music, 1984. With Burrus Fine Arts Acad., Houston Ind. Sch. Dist., 1975—76; asst. prof. music U. of the South, Sewanee, Tenn., 1985—86; assoc. prof. music, univ. organist Belmont U., Nashville, 1986—99. Faculty Tenn. Arts Acad., Nashville, 1987—94; recitalist annual meeting Music Tchrs. Nat. Assn., Mpls., 2000; lectr. in field. Contbr. articles to profl. jours. Mem.: Coll. Music Soc., Internat. Alliance Women in Music, Am. Guild Organists (assoc.; dean Nashville chpt. 1990—91), Pi Kappa Lambda, Mu Phi Epsilon. Achievements include research in historical keyboard music by women composers. Avocations: playing piano, playing organ, gardening, running. Home: 56 Dog Ln Storrs Mansfield CT 06268-2220

FORD, KATHERINE MICHELLE, special education educator; b. Gloversville, N.Y., Oct. 16, 1965; d. Michael Joseph Conte and Belle Mae Bruse; m. John Allen Ford, Aug. 16, 1997; 1 child, Garrett Michael. BS, U. Tenn., 1997, MEd, 2002; EdS in Ednl. Leadership, Lincoln Meml. U., 2004. Lic. spl. edn. tchr. Ga. Instr. Lexington Ctr., Gloversville, NY, 1987—95; mgr. group home Orange Group Ctr., Chattanooga, 1996—98; from tchr. spl. edn. Mid. Sch. to lead tchr. spl. edn. Elem. Sch. Whitfield County Pub. Schs., Dalton, Ga., 1997—2001, lead tchr. spl. edn. Elem. Sch., 2001—. Trainer new tchrs. Whitfield County Pub. Schs., 2003—; mem. leadership team New Hope Elem. Sch., Dalton, 2001—, Whitfield County Spl. Edn. Dept., Dalton, 2001—. Leader pioneer team Varnell (Ga.) United Meth. Ch., 2004—. Mem.: PTA (pres. 2004—05), Profl. Assn. Ga. Educators. Republican. Meth. Avocations: travel, camping, swimming, hiking. Office: New Hope Elem 1175 New Hope Rd Dalton GA 30720

FORD, LORETTA C., retired dean, educator, consultant, nurse; b. N.Y.C., Dec. 28, 1920; d. Joseph F. and Nellie A. (Williams) Pfingstel; m. William J. Ford, May 2, 1947; 1 child, Valerie. BSN, U. Colo., Boulder, 1949, MS, 1951, EdD, 1961; DSc (hon.), Ohio State Med. Coll., 1997; DSc (hon.), Simmons Coll., 1997, U. Colo., 1997; LLD (hon.), U. Md., 1990; DSc (hon.), U. Rochester, 2000; LHD (hon.), Binghamton U., 2001. RN N.J. Staff nurse New Brunswick Vis. Nurse Svc., 1941—42; supr., dir. Boulder County (Colo.) Health Dept., 1947—58; from asst. prof. to prof. U. Colo. Sch. Nursing, 1960—72; dean Sch. Nursing, DON, prof. U. Rochester, NY, 1972—86, acting dean Grad. Sch. Edn. and Human Devel. NY, 1988—89; vis. prof. U. Fla., 1968, U. Wash., Seattle, 1974, St. Lukes Coll. Nursing, Tokyo, 1987. Mem. educators adv. panel GAO; dir. Security Trust Co., Rochester, Rochester Telephone Co.; internat. cons. in field. Contbr. chapters to books, articles to profl. jours. Mem. adv. com. Commonwealth Fund Exec. Nurse Fellowship PRogram; bd. dirs. Threshold Alt. Youth Svcs., Easter Seal Soc., ARC, Monroe Cmty. Hosp. With Nurse Corps USAF, 1942—46. Named Colo. Nurse of Yr, Colo. Nurses Assn., Alumni of Century, U. Colo. Sch. Nursing Alumni Assn., 1998; recipient N.Y. State Gov.'s award for women in sci., medicine and nursing, Modern Healthcare Hall of Fame award, Modern Health Care Jour., 1994, Lillian D. Wald Spirit of Nursing award, N.Y. Vis. Nurse Svc., 1994, Lifetime Achievement award, Nat. Conf. Nurse Practitioners, 1999, Trailblazer award, Am. Coll. Nurse Practitioners, 2003, Elizabeth Blackwell award, Hobart and William Smith Colls., 2003, Amazing Exemplar award, Friends of Nat. Inst. Nursing, 2005, Second Century Excellence in

Health Care award, Columbia U., 2006. Fellow: Nat. League Nursing (Linda Richards award), Am. Acad. Nursing (Living Legend award 1999); mem.: NAS Inst. Medicine (Gustav O. Leinhard award 1990), ANA, APHA (Ruth B. Freeman award), Am. Coll. Nurse Practitioners (Crystal Trailblazers award 2003), Am. Coll. Health Assn. (Boynton award), Sigma Theta Tau, Alpha Omega Alpha (hon.). Personal E-mail: lorettaford@cfl.rr.com.

FORD, LUCILLE GARBER, economist, educator; b. Ashland, Ohio, Dec. 31, 1921; d. Ora Myers and Edna Lucille (Armstrong) Garber; m. Laurence Wesley Ford, Sept. 1, 1946; children: Karen Elizabeth, JoAnn Christine. AA, Stephens Coll., 1942; BS in Commerce, Northwestern U., 1944, MBA, 1945; PhD in Econs., Case Western Res. U., 1967; PhD (hon.), Tarkio Coll., 1991, Ashland U., 1995. Cert. fin. planner. Instr. Allegheny Coll., Meadville, Pa., 1945-46, U. Ala., Tuscaloosa, 1946-47; personnel dir., asst. sec. A.L. Garber Co., Ashland, Ohio, 1947-67; prof. econs. Ashland U., 1967-95, chmn. dept. econs., 1970-75; dir. Gill Ctr. for Econ. Edn. Ashland Coll., 1975-86, v.p., dean Sch. Bus., Adminstrn. and Econs., 1980-86, v.p. acad. affairs, 1986-90, provost, 1990-92; exec. asst. to pres., 1993-95; pres. Ashland Comm. Found., 1995—. Bd. dirs. Peco II, Inc., Western Res. Econ. Devel. Coun., Ohio Coun. Econ. Edn.; lectr. in field; mem. govs. adv. com. on econ. devel. Author: University Economics-Guide for Education Majors, 1979, Economics: Learning and Instruction, 1981, 91; contbr. articles to profl. jours. Mem. Ohio Gov.'s Commn. on Ednl. Choice, 1992; candidate for lt. gov. of Ohio, 1978; trustee Stephens Coll., 1977-80, Ashland U., 1995—, North Cen. State Coll., 1998-2005; elder Presbyn. Ch.; bd. dirs. Presbyn. Found., 1982-88; chair, trustee Synod-Presbyn. Ch., 1994-2000; active ARC. Named to Ohio Women's Hall of Fame, 2001; recipient Outstanding Alumnus award, Stephens Coll., 1977, Outstanding Profl. award, Ashland U., 1971, 1975, Roman F. Warmke award, 1981, Women of Achievement award, 1998, Outstanding Fundraiser award, Assn. Fund Raising Profls., 2001, Spirit of Chamber award, Ashland Area C. of C., 2001, Disting. Ashland H.S. award, Ashland City Sch. Acad. Found., 2002, Gleanch Clayton award, Ashland U., 2003. Mem. Am. Econs. Assn., Nat. Indsl. Rsch. Soc., Am. Arbitration Assn. (profl. arbitrator), Assn. Pvt. Enterprise Edn. (pres. 1983-84), North Ctrl. Assn. Colls. and Schs. (commr.), Omicron Delta Epsilon, Alpha Delta Kappa. Republican. Office: Ashland Co Comm Found 300 College Ave Ashland OH 44805-3803 Office Phone: 419-281-4733. Business E-Mail: accf@hmltd.net.

FORD, MARY PAT, art educator; d. Mary I. Ford; m. Hugh A. Weldon, July 25, 2004. BS in Art Edn., Pa. State U., 1983. Cert. instrnl. I Pa. State U., tchng. NJ. Related arts tchr. Pennsauken (NJ) HS, 1994—. Music dir. Queen Peace Ch., Ardsley, Pa., 2004—06. Home: 1322 Kirks Ln Dresher PA 19025 Office: Pennsauken Schs 800 Hylton Rd Pennsauken PA 19025 Office Phone: 854-662-8500 2048.

FORD, MARY (POLLY) WYLIE, retired physical education educator; b. Rock Hill, S.C., Oct. 20, 1927; d. William Calvin and Orene Poe Wylie; m. Jack Buening Ford, June 25, 1960 (dec. Aug. 25, 1992). BS cum laude, Winthrop U., 1948; MEd, U. Va., 1953; PhD, U. Iowa, Ames, 1957. Instr. Anderson (S.C.) Coll., 1948—50, Stratford Coll., Danville, Va., 1950—55; grad. asst. U. Iowa, Iowa City, 1955—57; asst. prof. Ea. Ill. U., Charleston, 1957—60; prof. dept. chair Winthrop U., Rock Hill, 1960—92; ret., 1992. Mem. phys. edn. textbook selection panel State Dept. Edn., Columbia, SC, 1995—95. Bd. dirs. Rock Hill YMCA, 1975—78; mem. adv. coun. home care Catawba Health Dist., Lancaster, SC, 1998—; adv. bd. Fewell Pk. Recreation Ctr., Rock Hill, 1998—2002; trustee Presbyn. Home S.C., Columbia, 2005—, Winthop U., Rock Hill, 2002—06; bd. dirs. Shepherd's Ctr. Rock Hill, 1993—95, pres., 1995; profl. adv. com. Home Health, Inc., Rock Hill, 1995—. Named to First Class of Disting. Phys. Edn. Alumni, Winthrop U., 2000. Mem.: AAHPERD (bd. govs., pres. So. dist. 1986—89, Honor award So. Dist. 1975, Profl. Svc. award So. Dist. 1991), S.C. Assn. for Health, Phys. Edn., Recreation and Dance (pres. 1970—71, President's Honor award 1970, Pres. Svc. award 1993), So. Assn. Phys. Edn. Coll. Women (pres. 1984—86), Perihelion Club (pres. 1994—96), Phi Kappa Phi. Democrat. Presbyterian. Avocations: bridge, tennis, travel. Home: 335 Shurley St Rock Hill SC 29732 Personal E-mail: pford@cetlink.net.

FORD, MARYESTELLE BEVERLY, piano educator, music researcher; b. St. Paul, Jan. 2, 1908; d. Harvey Louis Leander and Roberta Beverly (Finley) Glick; m. Ira Wilbur Ford, Mar. 23, 1928; 1 child, Mary Lou Ford Falkard. Student, L.A. Conservatory Music, 1957-58, U. So. Calif., 1961-63, UCLA, 1964, El Camino Jr. Coll., Redondo Beach, Calif., 1965-66, Calif. State U., Long Beach, 1966. Pvt. tchr. piano Alderman Studios, Fresno, Calif., 1926-28, El Segundo, Calif., 1928—. Adjudicator South Bay, El Segundo, 1966-71, El Camino Jr. Coll., 1971—. Mem., speech coord., liaison Am. Field Svc., El Segundo, 1950-60. Recipient hon. degrees in music child edn. specialist and pedagogy, Music. Tchrs. Assn. Calif. Plan. Mem. Music Tchrs. Nat. Assn., Piano Guild Internat., Music Tchrs. Assn. Calif. (charter, pres. 1956-58), South Bay Music Tchrs. Assn. (founding, cert. tchr., pres. 1956-58), Order Ea. Star, Bridge Club. Avocations: accompanying on piano for various organizations, gardening, reading, travel, collecting hummels.

FORD, MAUREEN MORRISSEY, civic worker; b. St. Joseph, Missouri, July 1, 1936; d. Albert Joseph and Rosemary Kathryne (FitzSimons) Morrissey; m. James Henry Lee Ford, Jr., Feb. 12, 1954; children: Kathryne Elizabeth, James Henry Lee III(dec.), William Charles, Maureen Lee. Student, U. N.Mex., 1953—54, U. Bridgeport, Conn., 1966—68; BS, Fairfield U., 1986, postgrad. in applied ethics, 1986—. Charity and sch. vol., 1959—; fundraiser for cmty. causes, mus., agy., 1964—; active presdl. campaign Barry Goldwater, 1963—64; congl. campaign Senator Lowell Weiker, 1968; pre-sch. tchr. Earth Place, 1966—68, trustee, v.p., bd. dir., 1968—75. Co-Author: (with Lisa H. Newton) Taking Sides: Controversial Issues in Business Ethics, 1990, 9th edit., 2005. V.p. Women's League, 1966-70; mem. exec. com. Rep. Women's Club, Westport, 1967-68; leader, trainer Troops on Fgn. Soil br. Girl Scouts US, Caracas, Venezuela, 1971-72; founding trustee, treas. Kara Mus., Norwalk, Conn.; mem. adv. coun. Fairfield County Conn. for spl. edn. Staples H.S.; bd. dir. CLASP; mem. exec. com. Group Home Search; pres. Ind. Assoc. Cons. Firm, 1991—; cons., facilitator life planning workshops Merideth Assocs., Westport; v.p., bd. dirs. Isaiah 61:1, Inc., 1989—; active grants com. Bridgeport Pub. Edn. Fund and Devel. Commn., 1984-2004; mem. first selectmen's com. on recycling, 1974-75; bd. dir. PTA, 1976-79; mem. YWCA of Bridgeport Com. of 100 and Task Force; v.p. bd. dir. YWCA, 1980-87, pres., 1984-85; v.p. Conf. Women's Orgns., Bridgeport; founding mem. Concerned Women Colleagues of Bridgeport; pres. Jr. League Ea. Fairfield County, Inc., 1977-78; v.p., sec. J.H.L.F., Inc. Westport; mem. grants com. Conn. Cares Hartford Fund, 1995-97. Mem. Jr. League Am. Assn., Westport Tennis Assn. Roman Catholic. Home: 204 Stillson Rd Fairfield CT 06825

FORD, NANCY LEONARD, retired special education educator; b. Marion, Va., July 15, 1955; d. Ray Wilburn and Thelma Lee (Bolt) Leonard; m. C. Phillip Ford III, Aug. 6, 1983; 1 child, Charles Patrick. BS in Spl. Edn., Radford Coll., Va., 1977; MS in Early Childhood Edn., Radford U., 1981. Cert. tchr. spl. edn., Va. Tchr. mentally handicapped Wythe County Sch. Bd., Wytheville, Va., 1977-83; program dir. Wythe County ARC, 1981-82; tchr. mentally handicapped Smyth County Sch. Bd., Marion, Va., 1983-95; reading tchr. Grace Presbyn. Day Sch., 1999—. Bd. dirs. Assn. for Retarded Citizens, Wytheville, 1981-82; leader Girl Scouts Am., Atkins and Wytheville, 1978-82, asst. cubmaster, dean leader Boy Scouts Am., 1992-95, also tiger organizer for tigers; mem. Family Life Bd., Marion, 1989-1995, PTA, PTO (sec. 1980-81), Child Devel. Coun.; organizer Spl. Olympics, Wythe and Smyth Counties, 1977-95. Mem. Parent Tchr. Assn. (sec., treas. 1981-82, Recognition award 1982), Assn. for Retarded Citizens, Parent Tchr. Orgn., AAUW, Jr. Women's Club. Avocations: computers, reading, coin and stamp collecting. Home: 6353 Eagle Valley Cv Bartlett TN 38135-7430

FORD, NANCY LOUISE, composer, scriptwriter; b. Kalamazoo, Oct. 1, 1935; d. Henry Ford III and Mildred Wotring; m. Robert D. Currie, June 7, 1957 (div. 1962); m. Keith W. Charles, May 23, 1964. BA, DePauw U., 1957; D of Arts (hon.), Eastern Mich. U., 1986; D of Fine Arts (hon.), DePauw U., 2002. Composer (with Gretchen Cryer): (off-Broadway musicals) Now is the Time for All Good Men, 1967, The Last Sweet Days of Isaac, 1970, I'm Getting My Act Together and Taking It On the Road, 1978, The American Girls Revue, 1998, Circle of Friends, 2001; composer: (Broadway musical) Shelter, 1972; scriptwriter (TV daytime serials Love of Life, 1971—74, Ryan's Hope, 1975; scriptwriter (TV daytime series) Ryan's Hope, 1983—84; scriptwriter: TV daytime serials Search for Tomorrow, 1981—82, Guiding Light, 1977—78, As the World Turns, 1978—80, 1987—95; performer: stage and cabaret. Trustee DePauw U., 1988-97. Recipient Emmy awards, 1983, 84. Mem.: AFTRA, League Profl. Theatre Women N.Y. (bd. dirs.), Am. Fedn. Musicians, Actors Equity, Writers Guild Am., Dramatists Guild (mem. coun.).

FORD, SHIRLEY GRIFFIN, science educator, pharmacist; b. Peoria, Ill., Dec. 21, 1946; d. Jesse Andrew Griffin and Dorothy Mae Lampert; m. William Herschel Ford, Dec. 19, 1970; children: Bret Andrew, Bryce Merritt, Heather Louise. BS, U. Ill., Urbana, 1968, MA in Tchg., 1970; PharmD, U. Pacific, Stockton, Calif., 1978. Registered pharmacist Calif., 1979. Tchr. East Lynn H.S., Ill., 1972—73, Wren H.S., Anderson, SC, 1973—74, Tri County Tech. Coll., Pendleton, SC, 1974—75, Stockton Unified Sch., Calif., 1976—87, Lodi Unified Sch., Stockton, 1987—, tchr. dept. sci., choir Bear Creek H.S., 2006—; pharmacist Dameron Hosp., Stockton, Calif., 1987—2006, Kaiser Permanente, Stockton, Calif., 2006—. Coach Sci. Olympiad team Lodi Unified Schs., 1987—; pharmacy intern Dameron Hosp., 1990—2006. Com. mem. Golden State Exams Com., Sacramento, 1985—2002, Supt's. Adv., Stockton, 2005—06; health acad. coord. Bear Creek H.S., Stockton, 1995—2002. State Tchr.'s scholar, State of Ill., 1964. Mem.: Minn. Bd. Pharmacy (licentiate), State of Calif. Pharmacists Assn. (licentiate; local officer 1987—91), NSTA (assoc.). Independent. Presbyterian. Avocations: singing, theater, scuba diving, travel. Office: Bear Creek High Sch 10555 N Thornton Rd Stockton CA 95204 Office Phone: 209-953-8060. E-mail: sford@lodiusd.k12.ca.us.

FORD, VICTORIA, retired public relations executive, writer, oral historian; b. Carroll, Iowa, Nov. 1, 1946; d. Victor Sargent and Gertrude Francis (Headlee) F.; m. John K. Frans, July 4, 1965 (div. Aug. 1975); m. David W. Keller, May 2, 1981 (div. Nov. 1985); m. Jerry W. Lambert, Mar. 30, 1991 (div. Aug. 2002). AA, Iowa Lakes C.C., 1972; BA summa cum laude, Buena Vista Coll., 1974; MA in Journalism, U. Nev., Reno, 1988. Parole officer juvenile Iowa Dept. Social Services, Sioux City, 1974—78; staff reporter Feather Pub. Co., Quincy, Calif., 1978—80; tng. counselor CETA, Quincy, 1980; officer libr. pub. info. U. Nev., Reno, 1982—84; exec. pub. rels. Brodeur/Martin Pub. Rels., Reno, 1984—87; dir. pub. rels. Internat. Winter Spl. Olympics, Lake Tahoe (Calif.) and Reno, 1987—89; owner Ford Factor Pub. Rels. cons. firm, Reno, 1989—2002. Staff writer Publs. and Pub. Info. Office Truckee Meadows C.C., 2001—05; comm. specialist U. Nev. Coop. Ext., Reno, 2005—. Author: Making Their Mark: Reno-Sparks YWCA History, 1997; author: (with R.T. King and Ken Adams) War Stories, 1997; author: Jean Ford: A Nevada Woman Leads the Way (oral history), 1998, Silver Peak Oral History Project, 2001, Charlotte Hunter Arley, 2001, Never a Ghost Town: Silver Peak, Nevada, 2002, Cliff Young, Chief Justice, Nevada Supreme Court, 2002, Arthur Bernard, Nevada Mine Inspector and Prison-Warden, 2003, Victor Kral (oral history), 2004, Through the Glass Ceilings, Sue Wagner, A Life in Nevada Politics, 2005; contbr. articles to profl. jours. Mem. adv. bd. Reno Philharm., 1985-87, Reno-Sparks Conv. and Visitors Authority, 1985-93; bd. dirs. Truckee Meadows Habitat for Humanity, 1992-93, half-time exec. dir., 1994; mem. Gov.'s Com. on Fire Prevention, 1991-92; mem. U. Nev. Reno Oral History Program, 1994; bd. dirs. Nev. Women's Archives, 1996; state sec. and roll of honor Nev. Women's History Project, 1998, 2001, com. Nev. Writers Hall of Fame, 1993-96; bd. dirs. Friends of the U. Nev. at Reno Libr., 1995-98. Mem.: NOW, Women Writing the West, Assn. Personal Historians, S.W. Oral History Assn. (bd. dirs. 2000—02, State Hist. Rec. adv. bd. 2002—), Pub. Rels. Soc. Am. (charter v.p. Sierra Nev. chpt. 1986—87, pres. 1987—88), Sigma Delta Chi. Democrat. Home and Office: PO Box 33993 Reno NV 89533-3993 Office Phone: 775-784-7070.

FORDEN, DIANE CLAIRE, magazine editor; b. NYC, Apr. 6, 1951; d. Joseph Anthony and Helen (Nash) F. BA in English Edn. summa cum laude, Montclair (N.J.) State U., 1973. Fashion editor Seventeen Mag., N.Y.C., 1975-81; fashion and beauty dir. YM Mag., N.Y.C., 1981-85; fashion dir. Avon Fashions, N.Y.C., 1985-87, Prima Mag., N.Y.C., 1987-88; from fashion and beauty editor to editor in chief and v.p. Bridal Guide Mag., N.Y.C., 1989—. Author: How to Have an Elegant Wedding-Without Going Broke, 2002, How to Find the Perfect Wedding Dress, 2003, New Etiquette for Today's Bride, 2004. Mem. Am. Soc. Mag. Editors, Fashion Group Internat., N.Y. Women in Comms. Avocations: piano, biking, skiing, photography. Home: 10 River Rd Apt F Nutley NJ 07110-3459 Office: Bridal Guide Mag 3 E 54th St New York NY 10022-3108 E-mail: dforden@ebridalguide.com.

FORDHAM, BEVERLY SURLES, middle school educator; d. Joseph E. and Peggy L. Surles; m. Kenneth E. Fordham, Sept. 14, 1997; children: Kelli M Fisher, Kevin, Joey Merchant, Ashley Merchant. BFA, Valdosta State U., Ga., 1977; MEd, Brenau U., Gainesville, Ga., 1988; EdS, Mercer U., Atlanta. Tchr. 6-8 Old Nat. Christian Acad., College Park, Ga., 1977—79; English tchr. 9-12 Darsey Pvt. Sch., Albany, Ga., 1981—83; tchr. reading 8, speech 9-12 Evang. Christian Schools, Inc., Cordova, Tenn., 1983—85; tchr. 6-8 Gwinnett County Pub. Schs., Lawrenceville, Ga., 1988—. Gift internship Sci.-Atlanta, Lawrenceville, 2001; gift facilitator Ga. Inst. of Tech., CEISMC, Atlanta, 1997; gift internship edn. dept. Zoo Atlanta, 1995—96, tchr. adv. coun., 2002—04. Curriculum guide, Against Extinction. Team mem., team capt. Relay for Life, Gwinnett County; mem. PTSA adv. coun. Lanier Mid. Sch., Buford, Ga.; small group facilitator divorce recovery for children Comeback Kids, Duluth, Ga. Finalist Local Sch. Tchr. of Yr.; grantee People's Bank of Gwinnett, Lanier Mid. PTSA. Avocations: audio/video production, gardening. Office Phone: 770-945-8419.

FORDICE, PATRICIA OWENS, civic leader, former state first lady; b. Jackson, Miss., Nov. 27, 1934; d. Lloyd Leon and Veo (McLelland) Owens; m. Daniel Kirkwood Fordice, Aug. 13, 1955 (div. Feb. 2000); children: Angela Leigh, Daniel Kirkwood III, Hunter Lloyd, James Owens. Student, Christian Coll., Columbia, Mo., 1952-53, Memphis State U., 1953-54. First lady State of Miss., Jackson, 1992-2000. Host radio talk show. Co-host TV show Woman to Woman. Responsible for art exhibit Palaces of St. Petersburg Russian Imperial Style, Jackson, 1996, Splendors of Versailles exhbn., Jackson, 1998, Majesty of Spain, 2001; creator Spendors of Miss. Project, Bucks for Books; host, hon. chmn. Internat. Ballet Competition, 1998, also mem. bd.; founder Miss. Gov.'s Initiative for Vol. Excellence Awards; creator SAFETY (Securing Brighter Future for Today's Youth); creator women's health initiative Heart of Miss. Women; hon. chmn., spokesperson for Friends of Children's Hosp.; spokesman Miss. Div. Tourism; hon. chmn. Spl. Olympics, Very Spl. Arts, Miss. Family for Kids; organizer fight against breast cancer Miss. Florist Assn., 1995, Miss. chpt. Am. Cancer Soc., also hosps. and clinics; founder, Power of One, Miss. Woman's Conf., from 1996; co-chmn. abstinence program Miss. Dept. Human Services; hon. pres. Gulf Pines coun. Girl Scouts U.S.A., 1994; past pres. Ofcl. Miss.'s Women's Club; hon. chmn., mem. founding bd. Miss. Commn. Volunteerism, 1993—; active Miss. Blood Svcs.; bd. dirs. Hospice Care Found., Vicksburg, Miss.; active Salvation Army; vol. Toys for Tots; participant Gateway Rescue Mission, 1998, Habitat for Humanity; keyperson key arts program Miss. Arts Commn.; spkr. to numerous chambers of commerce orgns., Rotary and Lions clubs, other civic and charitable groups; vol. Rankin County Human Resource Ctr.; promoter Good Neighbor Day; lobbyist for Medicare coverage of arthritis drugs; hon. chmn. emeritus of bd. Commn. for Internat. Cultural Exch.; bd. dirs. Miss. Symphony; Internat. Ballet Competition; amb. Ageless Heroes awards program Blue Cross & Blue Shield Miss.; spokesperson Arthritis Found; also others. Decorated knight Sovereign Order of Orthodox Knights Hospitaller of St. John of Jerusalem; named Miss.'s Outstanding Philanthropist, 1996; recipient Communicator award Soil and Water Conservation Soc., 1997, Need Knows No Svc. award Salvation Army, 1997, award as outstanding leader and vol. Miss. Blood Svcs., 1998, medal of honor DAR, 1999, medal of excellence Miss. U. for Women, 1999, Steward of Arts and Edn. award Phi Theta Kappa, 1999, Keep Ms Beautiful Louise Godwin award for excellence, 1999; inducted into Miss. Family for Kids' Hall of Fame, 1997. Mem. Nature Conservancy (life), Girl Scouts U.S.A. (life), United Meth. Women (life), Garden Club Soc. Miss. (life), Vicksburg Jr. Aux. (life, pres. 1970). Home: 207 Winter Teal Ct Madison MS 39110-9652

FORDIS, JEAN BURKE, lawyer; b. Ashiya AFB, Japan, Feb. 25, 1956; BA in Biology with distinction, Calif. State U., 1978; JD cum laude, Am. U., 1985. Bar: Md. 1985, US Ct. Appeals (Fed. Cir.) 1986, DC 1988, US Supreme Ct. 1993, Calif. 2005, registered: US Patent & Trademark Office. Law clk. to Hon. Philip Nichols Jr., Sr. Cir. Judge US Ct. Appeals (Fed. Cir.), 1985—86; biologist Nat. Inst. Health, Uniformed Services U. for Health Sci.; ptnr. Finnegan, Henderson, Farabow, Garret & Dunner LLP, Palo Alto, Calif., mng. ptnr. Pa. office. Mem. Am. U. Law Rev., 1983—85. Mem.: Md. Patent Law Assn. (sec. 1990—92, v.p. 1993—94, pres. 1995—97), Licensing Exec. Soc., Am. Intellectual Property Law Assn. (chmn. awards com. 1988—90), Phi Kappa Phi. Office: Finnegan Henderson Farabow Garrett & Dunner LLP 3300 Hillview Ave Palo Alto CA 94304-1203 Office Phone: 650-849-6600. Office Fax: 650-849-6666. Business E-Mail: jean.fordis@finnegan.com.

FORD-REED, LILLIE MAE, geriatrics services professional; b. Near Blackville, S.C., Oct. 9, 1939; d. William Henry and Joanne Coleman Reed; m. Phinnize Ford; children: Monica D. Ford, Marie C. Ford, William H. Ford, Maude L. Ford, Phinnize E. Ford, Lee A. Ford, Merlinda Ford, Christopher E. Ford. A in Paralegal, Orangeburg Calhoun Tech. Coll., 2000. Pres. usher bd. Thankful Bapt. Missionary, Bamberg, SC; program chairperson Bapt. Usher Bd. Union, Bamberg; therapeutic asst. Northhampton Assocs., Orangeburg, SC, S.C. Mentor Network, Columbia; insp. quality control Allied Signal Aerospace Electronics, Orangeburg; vol. solicitor's office, victim witness sect. Helpline, Aiken, SC; vol. VITA Tax Svc.; pvt. caregiver Aiken. Named to Wall of Tolerance So. Poverty Law Ctr., Mont.; recipient Honor award for Internship, Senator Strom Thurmon, 1984, Spl. Recognition award, Continental Challenge II Team, 2003, cert. of Appreciation, Girl Scouts U.S. Mem.: NAACP, Christian Burial Aid Assn. (pres. lodge #46), Smith-Hazel Phraise Modeling Team, Smith-Hazel Phraise Dance Group, Smith-Hazel Sr. Citizens Art and Crafts Club. Avocations: quilting, crafts, reading, sewing, dance.

FORE, HENRIETTA HOLSMAN, federal agency administrator; m. Richard L. Fore. AB, Wellesley Coll., 1970; MS, U. No. Colo., 1975. Pres. Stockton Wire Products, Burbank, Calif., 1977-89; chmn., pres. Pozacorp, Inc., 1981—89; asst. adminstr. for pvt. enterprise US Agy. for Internat. Devel., Washington, 1990-91, asst. adminstr. for Asia, 1991-93; dir. U.S. Mint US Dept Treasury, Washington, 2001—05; under sec. for mgmt. U.S. Dept. State, Washington, 2005—. Chmn. US Asia Environ. Partnership, 1991—93. Mem. Com. of 200. Mem. Young Pres. Orgn. Office: US Dept State 2201 C St NW Rm 7207 Washington DC 20520

FOREHAND, JENNIE MEADOR, state senator; b. Nashville; d. James T. and Estelle Meador; m. William E. Forehand, Jr.; children: Virginia, John. BS in Indsl. Rels., U. N.C., Chapel Hill. Reporter Charlotte (N.C.) News, 1954-56; probation counselor Juvenile Ct., Charlotte, 1958; tchr. Anne Arundel County, Md., 1958-60; statis. analyst NIH, Bethesda, Md., 1961-62; interior designer, owner Forehand Antiques and Interiors, Rockville, Md., 1970—; mem. Md. Ho. of Dels., Annapolis, 1978-94, Md. Senate, Annapolis, 1995—. Mem. appropriations com., joint capital budget com., health and environ. subcom., chair Montgomery County delegation transp. com., co-chair com. on mgmt. of pub. funds; mem. Senate jud. procs. com., exec. nominations Com., vice-chmn. Montgomery County Senate delegation; mem. children, youth and families com. Small Mus. Com., Regulatory Rev. Com.; co-chair Fed. Rels. com., co-chair Md./D.C./ Va Regional Transp. Commn., NIH Bio-Safety Com.; chair econ. devel., transp. and cultural affairs com. So. Legis. Conf., 1994—; mem. So. Tech. Coun.; chair Task Force on Genetic Techs. and Pub. Policy, vice chair transp. com. Nat. Conf. State Legislatures. Mem. planning bd. Montgomery County Health Sys.; consumer rep. Rockville Econ. Devel. Coun., Md. Cmty. Mental Health Adv. Bd.; pres. local civic assn., Girl Scout Adv. Coun.; bd. dirs. Montgomery County Hist. Soc., Md. Coll. Art and Design, Rockville Arts Place, Asbury Meth. Homes; mem. Peerless Rockville Hist. Preservation, Ltd. Recipient Bus. Leadership award Suburban Md. Tech. Coun.; named Outstanding Legislator Montgomery County Med. Soc., and Md. State's Attys. Assn., Biotechnology Leader of Yr., U. Md. Biotechnology Inst., 2006; named among Md.'s Top 100 Women. Mem. AAUW, Women's Caucus of Md. Gen. Assembly (pres.), Women's Polit. Caucus, Nat. Conf. State Legislatures (pres. Women's Legis. Network). Office: James Senate Ofc Bldg 110 College Ave Annapolis MD 21401-8012 Office Phone: 301-858-3134. E-mail: jennie_forehand@senate.state.md.us.

FOREMAN, BARBARA BLATT, healthcare facility administrator; b. Phila., Pa., Apr. 8, 1951; d. Raymond and Charlotte (Schiller) Blatt; m. Stewart Barry Foreman, May 15, 1981; children: Vicki Spitalnick Densen, Benjamin Blatt Spitalinick. BS, Pa. State U., 1971, MS, 1975. Secondary English instr. Abington (Pa.) Sch. Dist., 1972—81, faculty advisor, 1972—81; practice adminstr. Dr. S.B.F. Assoc., Inc., Pa., 1981—94; practice integrator multipractice program devel. U. Pa. Health Sys., Phila., 1994—97; healthcare cons. Health Power Assocs., Phila., 1998—2002; program dir. Cogent Healthcare, Boca Raton (Fla.) Cmty. Hosp., 2005—. Mem. exec. bd. Am. Heart Assn., Boca Raton, 2003—04. Mem.: Soc. Hospitalist Medicine, Rotary Club (mem. exec. bd. Boca Raton club 2003—04). Avocations: swimming, gardening, cooking. Office: Cogent Healthcare Boca Raton Cmty Hosp 800 Meadows Rd Boca Raton FL 33486 Office Phone: 561-955-3677. Business E-mail: foreman.barbara@cogenthealthcare.com.

FOREMAN, CAROL LEE TUCKER, consumer advocate; b. Little Rock, May 3, 1938; d. James Guy and Willie Maude (White) Tucker; m. Jay Howell Foreman, June 13, 1964; children: Guy Tucker, Rachel Marian. AA, William Woods Coll., 1958; AB, Washington U., 1960; postgrad., Am. U.; LLD (hon.), William Woods Coll., 1976. Rsch. asst. Com. Govt. Ops. U.S. Sen., 1961; assoc. Fed. Counsel Assocs., 1961-63; instr. Am. govt. William Woods Coll., Fulton, Mo., 1963-64; exec. asst. to Rep. James Roosevelt, 1964; dir. rsch. & publs. Dem. Nat. Com., 1965-66; Congl. liaison aide HUD, 1967-69; chief info. liaison Ctr. Family Planning Program Devel. Planned Parenthood-World Population, 1969-71; dir. policy coordination Commn. on Population and Am. Future, 1971-72; exec. dir. Citizens Com. on Population and Am. Future, 1972-73, Paul Douglas Consumer Rsch. Ctr., 1973-77, Consumer Fedn. Am., 1973-77; asst. sec. food and consumer svcs. Dept. Agriculture, Washington, 1977-81; dir. U.S. Commodity Credit Corp., 1977-81, U.S. Consumer Coop. Bank, 1977-81; pres. Foreman & Co., 1981-86, Foreman Heidepriem & Mager, 1986—99; disting. fellow, dir. The Food Policy Inst. Consumer Fedn. Am., 1999—. Mem. Pres.'s Commn. on White House Fellows, 1996—2001, Nat. Adv. Com. Meat and Poultry Inspection, 1997—2002, EU/US Consultative Forum Biotech., 2000, US Agriculture Policy Adv. Com. for Trade, 2002-; adv. com. Joint Inst. Food Safety and Applied Nutrition, 2000-05; mem. adv. com. on agrl. biotech. USDA, 2000—. Editor: Regulating for the Future, 1991. Exec. dir. Ctr. Women Policy Studies, 1983-84, mem. Interdeptl. Task Force on Women, 1973-74; bd. dirs. Consumer's Union, 1982-83, chmn., 1993—; bd. dirs. Food Rsch. & Action Ctr., 1983, Christianity and Crisis, 1990-92; vice chmn. Ctr. Nat. Policy, 1982-84, bd. dirs., 1981-99; trustee Washington U., St. Louis, 1987-95; bd. dirs. Bread for the World, 2000—. Recipient disting. alumni award Washington U., 1979, 2000. Mem. Women's Equity Action League (past pres. local chpt.), Nat. Policy Assn. (dir. 1985-97), Phi Beta Phi. Presbyterian. Home: 5600 Wisconsin Ave Ste 502 Chevy Chase MD 20815 Office: Consumer Federation Of America 1620 I St NW Ste 200 Washington DC 20006-4030 Office Phone: 202-797-8551. Personal E-mail: tuckfore@aol.com.

FOREMAN, GAIL LYNNE, secondary school educator; b. East Liverpool, Ohio, June 4, 1961; d. Frederick E. Burton and Virginia Lee Isett; life ptnr. Patricia Jane Cummins, Sept. 5, 1991. BS in Criminal Justice, Kent State U., Ohio, 1984; BS in Edn., Youngstown State U., Ohio, 1998, M of Spl. Edn.,

2001. Intervention specialist Leetonia Exempted Village H.S., Ohio, 1998—. Varsity softball coach Leetonia Exempted Village H.S., 2000—04, athletic dir., 2001—02; asst. varsity softball coach Crestview H.S., Columbiana, Ohio, 2004—. Nominee Disney Tchr. award nomination, 2004. Mem.: ASCD, NEA, Ohio Edn. Assn., Coun. for Exceptional Children (hon.), Phi Kappa Phi, Kappa Delta Pi, Golden Key Nat. Honor Soc. (hon.). Achievements include establishing a GO-GIRL-GO program to allow all young girls the opportunity to enjoy sports; Establishing and supervising various softball clinics for grades 3 to 12 acquiring university coaches and teams to share their knowledge and expertise. Avocations: outdoor activities, bicycling, hiking. Office: Leetonia Exempted Village HS 450 Walnut St Leetonia OH 44431

FOREMAN, GINI DIANE, English educator; d. Kennith Gerald and Monita Louise Sterling; m. Fred Samuel Foreman, Dec. 26, 1987; children: Freddie Samuel III, Christopher Adam, Aaron Michael. Bachelors, La. State U., Baton Rouge, 1983. Cert. English, social studies tchr. La., 1984, Tex., 1987. Tchr. sophomore English, Kingwood H.S., Tex., 2001—03, tchr. ap, pre-ap, level world history, 2003—. Acad. social studies coach Kingwood H.S., Tex., 2000—02, 2003—05, acad. spelling and vocabulary coach, 2005—. Baptist. Avocations: travel, shopping, reading. Home: 2019 Running Springs Kingwood TX 77339 Office: Kingwood HS 2701 Kingwood Dr Kingwood TX 77339 Office Phone: 281-641-8000.

FORERO, PAULA JULIANA, academic administrator, artist; b. Bogota, Colombia, Aug. 4, 1978; d. Orlando Prieto and Melba Rodriguez. BFA in Visual Arts, Los Andes U., Bogota, Colombia, 2001; MA in Art Adminstrn., Fla. State U., Tallahassee, 2005. Graphic designer & photographer Traz Digital Impresores, Bogota, 1996—2001; asst. to exec. dir. Rossier Prodns. Inc., Tallahassee, 2005; asst. to academic coord., museum studies program Fla. State U., Tallahassee, 2006—. Mem.: Profl. Colombians Living Abroad, Nat. Mus. Women in Arts, Am. Assn. Museums. Avocation: photography.

FORESE, LAURA LEE, hospital administrator, orthopedist; b. Suffern, NY, Aug. 17, 1961; m. Robert J. Downey; 3 children. BSE in civil engring. and ops. rsch. (summa cum laude), Princeton U., 1983; MD, Columbia U. Coll. Physicians and Surgeons, 1987; M in Health Svc. Mgmt., Columbia Sch. Pub. Health (now called Mailman Sch. Pub. Health), 1995. Intern, orthop. surgery NY Presbyterian Hosp., NYC, NJ, 1987—88, asst. attending orthop. physician, 1994, v.p. med. affairs, 2003—05; asst. attending physician Helen Hayes Hosp., West Haverstraw, NY, 1993—97, chief surgical and anesthesia services, 1994—97; resident, orthop. surgery Columbia U., 1988—93, vice chair, dept. orthopaedic surgery, 1998—2002; sr. v.p., chief med. officer NY Presbyterian Hosp./Weill Cornell Med. Ctr., NYC, 2005—, COO, 2006—. Faculty mem. specializing in pediatric orthopaedic surgery, assoc. clin. prof. Columbia U., 1993—; teaches physician-patient comm. to orthopaedic surgeons in the US; lectr. in field. Mem.: Am. Coll. Physician Executives, NY Acad. Medicine, Am. Acad. Orthopaedic Surgeons (editor-in-chief, Orthopedic Medical Legal Advisor, comm. skills mentor), Assn. Am. Med. Coll., Health Mgmt. Acad., Alpha Omega Alpha, Phi Beta Kappa. Office: NY Presbyterian Hosp/Weill Cornell Med Ctr M-106 525 E 68th St New York NY 10021*

FOREST, EVA BROWN, nursing home supervisor, composer; b. Ontario, Va., July 7, 1941; d. William Butler and Ruth Pauline (Simpson) Brown; m. Willie J. Forest Jr., Sept. 16, 1961; children: Gerald, Darryl, Angela. AA, Bismarck (N.D.) State Coll., 1981; BSN, U. Mary, Bismarck, 1984. RN Colo. Charge nurse St. Alexius Med. Ctr., Bismarck, 1984—85, Cedars Health Care Ctr., Lakewood, Colo., 1989—90; staff devel. coord. Pk. Ave. Bapt. Home, Denver, 1990—91; supr., charge nurse Cedars Health Care Ctr., Lakewood, Colo., 1991—; charge nurse Villa Manor Health Ctr., Lakewood, Colo., 1991—93, Stovall Care Ctr., Denver, 1995—96, supr., 1997—98, supr., charge nurse, 1999—2003; nursing supr. Rose Ter. Care Ctr., Commerce City, Colo., 2003—. Songwriter, prodr., 1999; recorded (CD) God Has Begun a Good Work in Me, 1999. Vol. for cultural exch. lang., culture and fashions YWCA, Kano, Nigeria; vocalist gospel music workshop, ND; pianist adult and children's choir, ND; mem. MADD, Habitat for Humanity Internat., HALT, Vols. of Am. Mem. Nat. Multiple Sclerosis Soc., DAV Commdrs. Club, Vols. of Am. Office Phone: 303-716-9346. Personal E-mail: Webmaster@foresteb.net.

FORESTER, JEAN MARTHA BROUILLETTE, retired librarian, educator, innkeeper; b. Port Barre, La., Sept. 7, 1934; d. Joseph Walter and Thelma (Brown) Brouillette; m. James Lawrence Forester, June 2, 1957; children: Jean Martha, James Lawrence. BS La. State U., 1955; MA, George Peabody Coll. Tchrs., 1956. Libr. Howell Elem. Sch., Springhill, La., 1956—58; asst. post libr. Fort Chaffee, Ark., 1958; command libr. Orleans Area Command, U.S. Army, Orleans, France, 1958—59; acquisitions libr. Northwestern State U., Natchitoches, La., 1960; serials libr. La. State U., New Orleans, 1960—66, mem. faculty Eunice, 1966—85, asst. libr., 1972—85, assoc. libr., 1985—87, acting libr., 1987—88, dir. libr., 1988—89, libr. emeritus, 1989—, asst. prof., 1972—85, faculty senator, 1978—80, 1985—86, 1987—89; innkeeper Crown'n'Anchor Inn, Saco, Maine, 1989—. Co-author: Robertsons's Bill of Fare; contbr. articles to profl. jours. Active Eunice Assn. Retarded Children. Fellow Carnegie, 1955—56. Mem.: UDC, La. Libr. Assn. (sect. sec. 1971—72, coord. serials interest group 1984—85), Delta Kappa Gamma (chpt. parliamentarian 1972—74, rec. sec. 1984—86), Order Ea. Star, Phi Mu, Phi Gamma Mu, Alpha Beta Alpha. Democrat. Baptist.

FORGASON, CHERYL L., secondary school educator; b. Peoria, Ill., Aug. 3, 1961; d. Robert Nelson and Linda Lee Forgason. BS, Bradley U., Peoria, 1983; MA, St. Xavier U., Chgo., 1998. Tchr. Bergan HS, Peoria, 1985—89, Peoria Notre Dame HS, 1989—91, Manual HS, Peoria, 1991—93, Tyng Primary Sch., Peoria, 1993—94, Richwoods HS, Peoria, 1994—. Named Tchr. of Yr., Richwoods HS faculty, 2004. Mem.: Ill. Assn. Phys. Edn., Recreation and Dance. Avocations: canoeing, hiking, reading. Home: 7720 W Hideaway Ct Mapleton IL 61547

FORKAN, EVELEEN, counselor, educator, researcher; b. Cloonmore, Mayo, Ireland, Jan. 8, 1927; arrived in U.S., 1970; d. Michael J. Forkan and Winnie Kate Sherlock. Studied Anthropology, Spirituality, Marist Inst., Eng., 1944—45; studied Philosophy, Psychology, Marist Inst., Paris, 1945—48; BA, Ottawa U., Canada, 1954, MEd, 1963; M in Counseling, St. Paul's U., Ottawa, 1980. Tchr. Primary Devel. Pub. Schs., New Brunswick, Canada, 1948—51, tchr. H.S., 1951—64; adminstr. Children's Home, Edmondston, Canada, 1964—70; tchr. St. Albert's Cath. Sch., Dearborn Heights, Mich., 1970—72, Wheeling Cath. Schs., W.Va., 1972—80; personal growth workshops PRH Internat., Detroit, 1982—, healing counselor personal growth, 1982—. Recipient Pepper award, 2004. Mem.: Marist Sisters. Avocations: reading, philosophy, anthropology, spirituality, psychology. Home: 16057 Hauss Eastpointe MI 48021 Office: St James Parish 241 Pearson Ferndale MI 48220

FORKAN, PATRICIA ANN, foundation executive; b. N.Y.C., June 13, 1944; d. Robert James and Elaine May F. BA in Polit. Sci., Pa. State U., 1966; postgrad., Am. U., 1968-69. Manpower analyst Dept. Labor, Washington, 1967-69; nat. coord. Fund for Animals, N.Y.C., 1970-76; v.p. program and comms. Humane Soc. of U.S., Washington, 1976-86, sr. v.p., 1987-91, exec. v.p., 1992—. Weekly web-active commentator Soap Box, 1999—2004; bd. dirs. Solar Elec. Light Fund, 1990-2000; mem. U.S. del. Internat. Whaling Commn., 1978, 93, 94 Re-negotiation of Conv. for Regulation of Whaling, 1978, U.S. del. North Pacific Fur Seal Commn., 1985; mem. U.S. Public Adv. Com. to Law of the Sea, 1978-83; bd. dirs. Coun. for Ocean Law; advisor, contbr. weekly TV show Living with Animals, 1985-91; advisor Animal Polit. Action Com.; sr. v.p. Humane Soc. Internat., 1991-2004; pres. Humane Soc. Internat., 2004—, Global Alliance Humane and Sustainable Devel., 2004—; coun. woman Friendship Heights (Md.) Village, 1993-2001; pres. Nat. Assn. Humane and Environ. Edn., 1994—; pres. Worldwide Network (Women in Devel. and Environ.), 1998-2004; presdl. appointed mem. trade and environment policy adv. com. U.S. Trade Rep., 2000—; bd. mem. Humane Farm Animal Care. Contbr. articles to environ. and animal welfare publs.; co-host weekly radio show, 1986-87. Office: Humane Soc of US 2100 L St NW Washington DC 20036

FORMAN, BETH ROSALYNE, specialty food trade executive; b. N.Y.C., Oct. 15, 1949; d. Philip and Dorothy Lea (Vilensky) F. BA in English with honors, NYU, 1971; MA with honors, Columbia U., 1972; MBA in Fin., Rutgers U., 1980. Asst. to contr. Colin Hochstin Co., N.Y.C., 1971-78; instr. Columbia U., N.Y.C., 1974-76; adj. faculty Bergen Community Coll., Paramus, N.J., 1985-87; communications cons. B.R. Forman & Co., Paramus, 1981-87; proposal mgr. Ogden Svcs.Corp., N.Y.C., 1988-89; dir. tech. svcs. Ogden Entertainment Svcs., Rosemont, Ill., 1990-92, dir. mktg. comms. N.Y.C., 1993-96; dir. mktg. Euro-Am. Brands, LLC, Paramus, N.J., 1999—. Bd. dirs. new leadership div. United Jewish Community Bergen County, River Edge, N.J., 1981-87, chmn. fundraiser, 1983, chmn. edn. com., 1983-86, treas., 1984-86; mem. steering com. Viewpoints div. Am. Jewish Com., 1991-93. Pres.'s fellow Columbia U., 1973; recipient Masters award Ogden Svcs. Corp., 1994. Mem. NAFE, Women in Comm. (v.p. spl. programs 1992-93 Chgo. chpt., mem. career devel. com. 1994-95, mem. pub. rels. com. and Matrix awards fundraising com. 1995-96), Columbia U. Club of N.Y., Mensa. Democrat. Avocation: acting. Home: 421 Yuhas Dr Paramus NJ 07652-4125 Office: Euro-Am Brands LLC 15 Prospect St Paramus NJ 07652-2712

FORMAN, MARY, dean; d. Major Neal Forman and Eugenia Therese Mis. PhD, Ctr. Medieval Studies, Toronto, Ont., Can., 1994. Assoc. dean St. John's U., Sch. Theology, Collegeville, Minn., 2005—06, asst. prof., 2000—06. Author: Praying with the Desert Mothers; contbr. articles to profl. jours. Bd. mem. Am. Benedictine Acad., Richardton, ND, 1994—2000, pres., 1996—98. Grantee, Coll. St. Benedict, St. John's U., 2006—; scholar, Benedictine Ctr., Sacred Heart Monastery, Richardton, ND, 1996—2000. Roman Catholic. Avocations: dance, tai chi, reading. Office: St Johns U Sch Theology PO Box 7288 Collegeville MN 56321-7288 Office Phone: 320-363-2618.

FORMAN, MICHELE, secondary school educator; b. Biloxi, Miss., Apr. 7, 1946; m. Dick Forman; children: Elissa, Laura, Tim. BA in hist., Brandeis U., 1967; MA in tchg., U. Vt. Cert. Profl. Tchg. Standards Nat. Bd. Tchr. Middleburg (Vt.) Union HS, 1986—. Alcohol drug edn curriculum spec. Vt. Dept. Edn. Mem. Vt. State Dept. Edn., Task Force HS Reform; vol. Peace Corp., Nepal, 1960. Named Nat. Tchr. of Yr., 2001, Vt. State Tchr. of Yr., 2001; recipient mary K. Bonsteel Tachau Pre-Collegiate Tchg. award, 1999. Mem.: Academic Coun. The Coll. Bd., Hist. Soc. Studies Academic Adv. Com., Nat. Bd Profl. Tchg. Standards. Office: Middlebury Union HS Hist Social Studies Dept 73 Charles Ave Middlebury VT 05753

FORMATO, JONELLE NANETTE, secondary school educator; d. James Robert and Sharon Olive Formato. BA in Comm., Radio, TV, Film, Marist Coll., Poughkeepsie, N.Y., 2002; student, Scuola Lorenzo de'Medici, Florence, Italy, 2001; MA in Social Sci. Edn., U. South Fla., Tampa, 2006; postgrad., Mt. St. Mary's Coll., Newburgh, N.Y., 2004. Cert. tchr. NY. Student asst. humanities and fgn. lang. Marist Coll., Poughkeepsie, NY, 1998—2001; summer sch. clk. Newburgh Enlarged City Sch. Dist., 1999—2001, substitute tchr. and head coach, 2002—04, social studies tchr., 2006—; intern, prodn. asst. FOX News Channel, N.Y.C., NY, 2002; internship Hillsborough County Sch. Dist., Plant City, Fla., 2006. Coach-jv and varsity volleyball Newburgh Enlarged City Sch. Dist., 2006—, head coach-modified, jv, varsity volleyball. modified basketball and softball., 2002—04; sports specialist-summer camp Gate Hill Day Camp, Stony Point, NY, 2003. Mem.: Nat. Coun. for the Social Studies, Kappa Delta Pi. Avocations: sports, travel.

FORMENTI, SILVIA C., radiation oncologist; b. Italy; MD, Universita degli Studi di Milano, 1980. Cert. Radiation Oncology 1991. Intern San Carlo Borromeo Hosp., Milan, 1980—83; fellow, hematology, oncology USC Med. Sch., Los Angeles, 1984—85; resident, radiation oncology Nat. Cancer Inst., Milan, 1984—88; resident, radiation oncology USC Sch. Medicine, Los Angeles, 1985—90; assoc. prof. radiation oncology and medicine USC, Keck Sch. Medicine, 1990—2000; assoc. dir. clin. rsch., leader of breast cancer rsch. program NYU Cancer Inst., 2000—; Sandra and Edward H. Meyer chmn. NYU Sch. Medicine, Radiation Oncology Dept., 2000—. Office: NYU Med Ctr Dept Radiation Oncology 566 First Ave New York NY 10016-6402

FORMICA, PALMA ELIZABETH, physician; b. Windber, Pa., June 14, 1928; d. Salvatore M. and Angela (Arrera) F.; m. John Rihacek, 1955 (dec. May 1977); children: Gregory, John, Alycia. BS, U. Pitts., 1948; MD, U. Rome, 1953. Intern Queens Hosp. Ctr., Jamaica, NY, 1954, resident in internal medicine, 1955-56; family practitioner pvt. practice, Old Bridge, NJ, 1959—; sch. physician Old Bridge Twp. Bd. Edn., 1959—; chmn. dept. family practice St. Peter's Univ. Hosp., New Brunswick, NJ, 1979—; co-founder, assoc. dir. Robert Wood Johnson Med. Sch., Dept. Family Medicine, New Brunswick, NJ, 1979—. Lay trustee St. Thomas the Apostle Ch., Old Bridge. Fellow Med. Soc. N.J., Am. Acad. Family Physicians; mem. AMA (bd. trustees 1990-99), Am. Acad. Family Practice, Am. Coll. Physician Execs., Am. Diebetic Assn., Acad. Medicine N.J. (pres., bd. dirs., exec. com., awards com.), N.J. Assn. Sch. Physicians, N.J. Acad. Family Practice, Middlesex County Med. Soc. (found. bd. trustees), Soc. Tchrs. Family Medicine, Orgn. State Med. Soc. Pres. Office: Saint Peter's Univ Hosp 254 Easton Ave New Brunswick NJ 08901-1766

FORNELLI, CYNTHIA M., bank executive; BA in Philosophy & Polit. Sci., Purdue U., 1985; JD magna cum laude, George Washington U. Nat. Law Ctr., 1990. Bar: DC. Assoc. Fried, Frank, Harris, Shriver & Jacobson, Washington, 1991—97; mem. of investment mgmt. practice group Dechert Price & Rhoads, Washington, 1997—99; sr. adviser to dir., div. of investment mgmt. SEC, Washington, 1999—2001, dep. dir., div. of investment mgmt., 2001—04; sr. v.p. & compliance exec. for securities regulation and conflict mgmt. Bank of Am., 2004—. Taught Russian Purdue U., 1985—86. Office: Bank of Am 100 N Tryon St Charlotte NC 28255

FORNERIS, JEANNE M., lawyer; b. Duluth, Minn., May 23, 1953; d. John Domenic and Elva Lorraine (McDonald) F.; m. Michael Scott Margulies, Feb. 6, 1982. AB, Macalester Coll., 1975; JD, U. Minn., 1978. Bar: Minn. 1978. Assoc. Halverson, Waters, Bye, Downs & Maki, Ltd., Duluth, 1978-81, Briggs & Morgan, P.A., Mpls., St. Paul, 1981-83; ptnr. Hart & Bruner, P.A., Mpls., 1983-86; assoc. gen. counsel M.A. Mortenson Co., Mpls., 1986-90, v.p., gen. counsel, 1990-96; with Gen. Counsel, Ltd., Mpls., 1997-98; v.p., sr. counsel Medtronic, Inc., Mpls., 1999—. Instr. women's studies dept. U. Minn., Mpls., 1977-79. Author profl. edn. seminars; contbr. articles to profl. jours. Bd. dirs. Good Will Indusries Vocat. Enterprises, Inc., 1979-81; chmn. bd. trustees Duluth Bar Libr., 1981; mem. United Way Family and Individual Svcs. Task Force, Duluth, 1981. Nat. Merit Assn. scholar, 1971. Fellow Am. Coll. Constrn. Lawyers (bd. dirs.); mem. AMA, Am. Arbitration Assn. (mem. large complex case panel), Minn. State Bar Assn., Minn. Women Lawyers (bd. dirs.), U.S. Dist. Ct. Hist. Soc. (pres.). Democrat. Roman Catholic. Office: Medtronic Inc 7000 Central Ave NE Minneapolis MN 55432-3576

FORNI, PATRICIA ROSE, nursing educator; b. St. Louis, Feb. 14, 1932; d. Harold and Glenda M. (Keay) Brown. BSN, Washington U., St. Louis, 1955, MS (USPHS trainee), 1957; PhD (USPHS fellow), St. Louis U., 1965; postgrad. (USPHS scholar), U. Minn., summers 1968, 70. Staff nurse McMillan EENT Hosp., St. Louis, summer 1955, Renard Psychiat. Hosp., St. Louis, part-time 1955-57; rsch. asst. Washington U. Sch. Nursing, St. Louis, 1957-59, rsch. assoc., 1959-61, asst. prof., 1964-66, assoc. dean in charge grad. edn., assoc. prof. gen. nursing sci., 1966-68; assoc. prof. pub. health nursing Wayne State U., Detroit, 1968-69; asst. dir. for manpower and edn. Ill. Regional Med. Program, Chgo., 1969-71; project dir. Midwest Continuing Profl. Edn. for Nurses, St. Louis U., 1971-75; dean, prof. nursing So. Ill. U., Edwardsville, 1975-88; dean Coll. Nursing U. Okla., Oklahoma City, 1988—2004, prof. Coll. Nursing, 1988—. Grant proposal reviewer Divsn. Nursing, USPHS, 1972-79, 88, 91, NSF, 1978, U.S. Dept. Edn., 1980; mem. Ill. Implementation Commn. on Nursing, 1975-77, Okla. State Health Plan Adv. Com., 1994—. Mem. peer rev. panel Nursing Outlook, 1987-91; mem. editl. bd. Health Care for Women Internat., 1984—, Jour. Profl. Nursing, 1988-90. Chairwoman articulation of nursing programs task force Okla. State Regents for Higher Edn., 1990-91; bd. dirs. Greater St. Louis Health Sys. Agy., 1976-81, Adult Edn. Coun. Greater St. Louis, 1973-76, Edwardsville unit Am. Cancer Soc., 1981-88. Fellow WHO, Sweden, Finland, 1985. Mem. Nat. League for Nursing (accreditation site visitor 1979—, nominating com. Coun. Baccalaureate and Higher Degree Programs 1979-82, pub. policy and legis. com. 1981-85, bd. dirs. 1991-93, treas. 1991-93, fin. com. 1991-95), Nat. League for Health Care (trustee 1991-93), Nat. League for Nursing Accrediting Commn. (peer review panel, baccalaureate and higher degree programs 1997-2000, 06, commr. 2000-06, chmn. 2001-06), Am. Nurses Assn. (chmn. continuing edn. publs. com. 1975-76), Mo. Nurses Assn. (chmn. edn. com. 1973-77), Greater St. Louis Soc. Health Manpower Edn. and Tng. (chmn. legis. com. 1974-75), Midwest Alliance in Nursing (1st governing bd. 1979-80, 93-96, chmn. nominations com. 1980-81, fin. com. 1993-94, chair fin. com. 1994-96, treas. 1994-96, pres. 1998-2000), Am. Assn. Colls. Nursing (hon., program com. 1978-82, mem.-at-large, bd. dirs. 1990-92, chair rsch. com. 1990-92), Ill. Coun. Deans/Dirs. Baccalaureate and Higher Degree Programs in Nursing (chmn. 1979-81), Am. Acad. Nursing (treas., chair fin. com., gov. coun. 1989-93, editor Newsletter 1982-87), Ill. Nurses Assn. (commn. on adminstrn. 1983-87, commn. on edn. 1987-89), Okla. Nurses Found. (pres. bd. trustees 1990-93), Sigma Theta Tau Internat. (charter mem. Epsilon Eta chpt. 1980). Office: U Okla Coll Nursing PO Box 26901 Oklahoma City OK 73190-0001

FORONDA, LISA, newscaster; b. Nashville; d. Judy Foronda. BS in Telecomm., U. Fla., 1991. Anchor Sta. KLST-TV, San Angelo, Tex., Sta. WEVU-TV, Ft. Meyers, Fla., WTSP-TV, Tampa, Fla., Sta. KHOU-TV, Houston, 1997—. Office: Sta KHOU-TV 1945 Allen Pkwy Houston TX 77019

FORONDA, MONICA F., graphics designer; b. Elmhurst, N.Y., Oct. 10, 1974; d. William and Teresa Foronda. BFA in Graphic Design and Psychology, St. John's U., Jamaica, N.Y., 1997; MS in Comm. Design, Pratt Inst., N.Y.C., 2000. Jr. prodn. designer NYSSCPA, N.Y.C., 1997—98, sr. graphic designer, 1998—2000; sr. designer Aspen Pubs. Inc., 2000—04, sr. designer, prodn. supr., 2004—. Mem.: Am. Inst. Graphic Artists. Avocation: skiing.

FORRER, NAN LOUISE, secondary school educator; b. Reading, Pa., May 3, 1954; d. Edward Charles and Leona Kathryn (Unger) Hilbert; m. Larry Lyn Forrer, Jan. 10, 1976; children: Katherine Carole, Benjamin Edward, Adam Jacob, Sallie Oleta. BS in Art Edn., Kutztown U., 1976, MEd in Art Edn., 1994. Cert. tchr., Pa. Elem. art tchr. Reading Sch. Dist., 1976-78, Muhlenberg Sch. Dist., Laureldale, Pa., 1987—; art dept. chair Muhlenberg Sch. Dist., 2003—. Adj. prof. Albright Coll., Reading, 1993—; freelance portrait and comml. artist for local bus. and customers, Reading, 1980—; dir., creator of cmty. creative arts camps for children, Reading, 1985—; spkr. for inclusion in the art classroom, Pa., 1993—. Author: Inclusion in the Art Room, 1994; portrait artist; contbr. articles to profl. jours. Sec. Muhlenberg Twp. Art Bd., Laureldale, 1985-88; prse. Muhlenberg PTO, Laureldale, 1986-89; sec., treas. ch. coun. Good Shepherd Luth. Ch., Muhlenberg Twp., 1984-89; organizer, v.p. cmty. group to create a local playground. Grantee Pa. Coun. of the Arts, 1990, 94, 2006. Mem. Pa. Art Edn. Assn., Nat. Art Edn. Assn. Democrat. Avocations: reading, drawing, cooking, gardening. Home: 1009 Hilldale Ct Reading PA 19605-3226 Business E-Mail: forrern@mail.mublsd.berksiu.k12.pa.us.

FORREST, KATHERINE B., lawyer; b. NYC, Feb. 13, 1964; BA with honors, Wesleyan Univ., 1986; MA, NYU, 1987, JD, 1990. Bar: NY 1991. Summer assoc. Cravath Swaine & Moore LLP, NYC, 1989, assoc., 1990—98, ptnr., litig., 1998—. Lectr. in field of antitrust, intellectual property law, gen. comml. litig. Contbr. chapters to books, articles to profl. jours. Named one of 40 Under 40, Global Competition Rev., 2006. Mem.: NY State Bar Assn., Assn. of Bar of City of NY. Office: Cravath Swaine & Moore LLP Worldwide Plz 825 Eighth Ave New York NY 10019-7475 Office Phone: 212-474-1155. Office Fax: 212-474-3700. Business E-Mail: kforrest@cravath.com.

FORREST, KELLY ALEXANDRA, psychology professor; BS in Engring., Duke U., 1983; JD, Seattle U., 1988; PhD, U. Wash., 1998. Bar: Wash. 1988; lic. mental health counselor Wash., 2001. Jud. law clk. Wash. State Supreme Ct., Olympia, 1988—89; assoc. atty. Riddell, Williams, Bullitt, and Walkinshaw, Seattle, 1989—91; jud. law clk. Wash. State Supreme Ct., Olympia, 1991—94; lectr. U. Wash., Bothell, 1999—2001; asst. prof., chair dept. psychology Franklin Coll., Ind., 2002—06; asst. prof. U. Wash., Tacoma, 2006—. Mental health law cons., mental health counselor, Seattle, 1999—2001. Individual Svc. Rsch. award, NIMH, 1997 - 1998. Mem.: APA, Internat. Soc. for Study of Dissociation (Pierre Janet Writing award 2002). Office: Univ Wash Tacoma Interdisciplinary Arts and Sci 1900 Commerce St Tacoma WA 98402 Office Phone: 253-692-4730. Business E-Mail: forrestk@u.washington.edu.

FORREST, LINDA DOTTS, elementary school educator, social studies educator; d. Edward and Phyllis Proctor Dotts; m. William M. Forrest, May 2, 1970; 1 child, Adam. BS in Edn., Gorham State Coll., Maine, 1970. Tchr. Havelock (N.C.) Jr. HS, 1970—72, Maddux Pvt. Sch., Brandon, Fla., 1980—87, Mann Mid Sch. (formerly Mann Jr. HS), Brandon, 1987—, Lockhart Elem., Tampa, Fla., 1988—90. Named Tchr. of the Yr., Mann Jr. HS, 1995—96. Mem.: Fla. Coun. Social Studies, Nat. Coun. Social Studies. Avocations: travel, reading, scrapbooks.

FORREST, PATRICIA ANNE, publishing executive, editor; b. Kingstree, S.C., July 16, 1935; d. John Symonds Hale and Clara Mae Smith; m. Richard Stockton Forrest, June 26, 1999; m. Dwight Ellsworth Whitton (div.); children: Laura Katherine, Robert Kennedy. BA, Agnes Scott Coll., 1955; MA, CUNY, 1969. Pub. New Plays Inc., Charlottesville, Va., 1962—, editor, 1962—. Lectr. in field. Author: Capture Them With Magic, 1982, Bringing the World Alive, 1996, (plays) The Little Mermaid, 1996, Puppet Heroes Around the World, 2006. Bd. dirs. Internat. Assn. of Theatre for Children and Youth, 1981—87. Recipient Oustanding Svc. award, East Ctrl. Theatre Coop., 1996, Sace Spencer Lifetime Achievement award, 1997, award, Children's Theatre Found., 2004, Woodrow Wilson Centennial Celebration Commn. Plays winner, Hall Mirr. Fellow: Coll. Fellows Am. Theatre; mem.: Am. Alliance Theatre and Edn. (chmn. exhibits 1991). Democrat. Avocations: camping, water aerobics, snorkeling, cats. Office: New Plays Inc PO Box 5074 Charlottesville VA 22905 Personal E-mail: patwhitton@aol.com.

FORRESTER, ALEXIS C.G., elementary school educator; d. Walter G. Jr. and Lorraine A. Golgart; m. Leonard Ray Forrester, Dec. 29, 1973; children: Christopher Leonard, Jill Marie. BA, Purdue U., 1973; MA, U. Va., 1990. Cert. reading specialist 1-12, gifted edn. tchr. 1-7, Va. Tchr. math. Lancaster (Va.) H.S., 1974; tchr. Lancaster Primary Sch., 1974—. Mem. NEA, Internat. Reading Assn., Va. Edn. Assn., Va. Reading Assn., Lancaster Edn. Assn., Delta Kappa Gamma (pres., sec.). Baptist. Avocations: sewing, crafts, nature protector, walking, singing. Office: Lancaster Primary Sch 36 Primary School Cir Lancaster VA 22503

FORRESTER, PATRICIA TOBACCO, artist; b. Northampton, Mass., 1940; Student, Yale Summer Sch. Music and Art, 1961; BA, Smith Coll., 1962; BFA, Yale U., 1963, MFA, 1965. Resident Yaddo Found., 1979, 81, The MacDowell Colony Residency, 1980, Hand Hollow Found., 1981, San Francisco Mus. Art, 1967. One woman shows include Trutton Gallery, San Francisco, 1968, Capper's Gallery, San Francisco, 1970, William Sawyer Gallery, San Francisco, 1974, 81, 83, Smith Coll. Fine Arts Bldg., Northampton, 1975, M. H. de Young Meml. Mus., San Francisco, 1977, Kornblee

Gallery, N.Y.C., 1978, 79, 81, 82, 83, Fendrick Gallery, Washington, 1978, 79, 81, 88, 90, Sebastian Moore Gallery, Denver, 1981, Contemporary Art Ctr., Honolulu, 1984, Frick Gallery, U. Pitts., 1984, 87, U. Conn., 1984, New Orleans Acad. Fine Arts, 1984, 91, Mattingly-Baker Gallery, Dallas, 1985, Fischbach Gallery, N.Y.C., 1987, 89, 90, 92, Reynolds/Minor Gallery, Richmond, Va., 1987, Braunstein/Quay Gallery, San Francisco, 1987, 89, 91, 94, 98, 2001, Gail Severn Gallery, Sun Valley, Idaho, 1988, Sierra Nevada Mus., Reno, 1988, N.Y. Stock Exch. Bldg., N.Y.C., 1989, Luria Gallery, Bay Harbor Island, Fla., 1990, Kalamazoo Inst. Arts, 1991, Stephen Scott Gallery, Balt., 1992, 97, Addison/Ripley Gallery, Washington, 1993, 96, 99, Gerald Peters Gallery, Santa Fe, 1994; exhibited in group shows Mattingly-Baker Gallery, Dallas, 1982, Springfield (Mo.) Art Mus., 1983, Pa. Acad. Fine Arts, Phila., 1983, Art Inst. Chgo., 1983, Corcoran Gallery, Washington, 1984, Bklyn. Mus., N.Y.C., 1985, William Sawyer Gallery, San Francisco, 1985, 88, Coll. of Mainland, Texas City, Tex., 1985, William's Coll. Art Ctr., Williamstown, Mass., 1985-86, Akron (Ohio) Art Mus., 1985-86, Madison (Wis.) Art Ctr., 1985-86, San Francisco Mus. Art, 1985-86, DeCordova and Dana Mus. Art, Lincoln, Mass., 1985-86, Archer M. Huntington Art Gallery U. Evanston, Ill., 1985-86, William's Coll. Art Ctr., Williamstown, Mass., 1985-86, Akron (Ohio) Art Mus., 1985-86, Madison (Wis.) Art Ctr., 1985-86, Metro. Mus., Miami, 1986, Springfield (Mo.) Art Mus., 1986, Art Mus. Santa Cruz County, 1987, The Sierra Nevada Mus. Art, Reno, Nev., 1988, William Sawyer Gallery, San Francisco, 1988, Kohler Arts Ctr., Sheboygan, Wis., 1988, Grand Ctrl. Art Galleries, N.Y.C., 1989, Fendrick Gallery, Washington, 1989, Gallery K., Washington, 1989, The Palmer Mus. Art, Pa., 1990, Steven Scott Gallery, Balt., 1990, Am. Acad. and Inst. Arts and Letters, N.Y.C., 1991, The Gallery at Bristol-Myers Squibb, Princeton, N.J., 1991, The Noves Mus., N.J., 1991, Ctr. Contemporary Arts, Miami, 1991, Nat. Mus. Women in the Arts, 1991-92, 2000, The Miyagi Mus. Art, Sendai, Japan, 1991-92, Sogo Mus. Art, Yokohama, Japan, 1991-92, Tokushima (Japan) Mod. Art Mus., 1991-92, Mus. Modern Art, Shiga, Japan, 1991-92, Kochi (Japan) Prefectural Mus. Folk Art, 1991-92; Kavesh Gallery, Ketchum, Idaho, 1993, Nat. Acad. Design, N.Y.C., 1993, Sewall Art Gallery Rice U., Houston, 1993, Gerald Peters Gallery, Santa Fe, N. Mex., 1993, Philbrook Mus., Davenport Mus., 2000, Meridian Internat. Ctr., Traveling to Vietnam, China, Singapore, Indonesia, 2000; represented in numerous pub. and pvt. permanent collections including The Achenbach Found., Art Inst. Chgo., Hawaii Arts Ctr., Indpls. Mus. Art., Meml. Art Gallery, Oakland Mus., N.Y. Pub. Lib., San Antonio Mus. Art, San Francisco Art Commn., Springfield Mus., The British Mus., The Brooklyn Mus., University Art Mus., Corcoran Gallery, Nat. Mus. Am. Art, Nat. Mus. for Women in the Arts; others. Guggenheim fellow in printmaking, 1967. Mem. Nat. Acad. Design, Phi Beta Kappa. Address: Addison Ripley Fine Art 1670 Wisconsin Ave NW Washington DC 20007

FORSBURG, SUSAN LOUISE, molecular geneticist; b. Berkeley, Calif., Oct. 9, 1962; d. Frank E. and Janet B. Forsburg. AB, U. Calif., Berkeley, 1984; PhD, MIT, 1989. Postdoctoral rsch. fellow Imperial Cancer Rsch. Fund, Oxford, U.K., 1989-93; jr. rsch. fellow Linacre Coll., Oxford U., 1990-92; asst. prof. The Salk Inst. for Biol. Studies, La Jolla, Calif., 1993—; adj. asst. prof. dept. biology U. Calif., San Diego, 1997—. Vis. prof. U. Copenhagen, 1995; mem. Am. Cancer Soc. Growth Control Rev. Panel, 1996—; ad hoc mem. NIH Molecular Cytology Study sect., 1996. Postdoctoral fellowship Helen Hay Whitney Found., 1989-92, NATO, 1992-93; scholar Leukemia Soc. Am., 1997—. Mem. Am. Soc. for Cell Biology (Women in Cell Biology jr. career recognition award 1996), Genetics Soc. Am., Am. Soc. for Microbiology. Office: Salk Inst for Biol Studies 10010 N Torrey Pines Rd La Jolla CA 92037-1099

FORSHEE, GLADYS MARIE, insurance agent, writer; b. Loveland, Colo., July 1, 1942; d. Henry William Hansen and Bird Marie Smith; m. Larry Bill Forshee, Aug. 27, 1960 (widowed Dec. 1992). Score grad., Small Bus. Adminstrn., 2003. Cert. ins. agt. Customer svc. rep., acct. mgr. various ins. agys., Denver, 1970—2000; property and casualty divsn. agy. mgr., 2004—05; owner Superior Janitorial Svc., Colo., 1975—2000, A Appletree Pub., Superior, 1991—. Author, pub.: (history book) Where Memories Linger, 1994, (cookbook) A Superior Centennial, Culinary Fest Cookbook, 1996, also 11 researched, published and continous updated family histories. Asst. organizer Superior Hist. Soc., 1998; town clk., recorder Town of Superior, 1970—73; cmty. svc. dir. Colo. State Grange, Aurora, 1992—99, Boulder county dep., 1999—2001; rsch. asst. Nat. Archives, Lakewood, Colo.; asst. organizer Superior Vol. Fire Dept., Colo., 1972—81; mem., vol. Adams County Hist. Soc., Henderson, Colo., 1991—2006; mem., vol. citizens adv. com. Boulder County Recycling and Composting Authority, 2000—05; mem. com. Boulder County Hist. Preservation, 2002—05; mem. Boulder County Resource Conservation Adv. Bd., 2002—04, chair, 2003—04; mem. Adams County Centennial Roundtable, 2002; mem. scholarship Colo. Preservation Conf., 2004, 2006; citizen shareholder Colo. Dept. Transp. Environ. Impact statements for US36 corridor and northwest parkway corridor projects, 2004—06; citizen adv. Town of Superior, Colo., 2003—05; event coord. Christian Clown Posse, 2003. Mem.: Nat. Womens History Mus., Green Valley Grange. Achievements include organized campaign for federal government legislation to create National Children's Day, 2006; organized placement of sign on Boulder County, Colo. open space property regarding the Denver and interurban railroad electric trolley line from Denver to Boulder, 2005 circa 1908-1926. Avocations: gardening, crocheting, reading, playing the stock market, photography. Home: 404 S 3d Ave Superior CO 80027

FORSLOFF, CAROL MARIE, rehabilitation services professional, consultant; b. La Grande, Oreg., Mar. 31, 1941; d. Ted Eugene and Faye Marie Matthews; m. Delbert Raymond Forsloff, Feb. 14, 1984; children from previous marriage: John Steven Czerniejewski, Eric Dale Czerniejewski. BA, U. Wash., Seattle; MA, SUNY, Albany, 1969. Cert. rehab. counselor, hypnotherapist. Evaluation coord., cons. Goodwill Industries, Honolulu, 1984—98; pres. Heritage Valley Pub., Honolulu, 1998—; owner, mgr., pres. Forsloff and Assoc., Honolulu, 1998—2005; owner, mgr. La Maison de Aloha, Natchitoches, La., 2005—. Supr. Crawford Healthcare Mgmt., Las Vegas, 1984—92; v.p., gen. mgr. Heritage Cons., Honolulu, 1993—2005; cons. in field. Author: Vocational Profiling: Workplace Solutions, 1987; contbr. articles to profl. jours. Pres. Orton Soc., Pitts., 1976—77, Rehab. Assn. Hawaii, 1996, Punahou Gardens, Honolulu, 1979—83; Katrina vol. counselor Red Cross, Natchitoches, 2005. Named Outstanding Spl. Edn. Tchr., Saddle River (NJ) Schs., 1969, Disting. Prof. in Rehab., Crawford Healthcare, Honolulu, 1985; recipient Elizabeth Ducey award, Portland State U., 1960. Mem.: Internat. Assn. Life Care Planners, Nat. Rehab. Assn., Am. Counseling Assn., Kiwanis. Avocations: writing, singing. Home: 220 Ragan St Natchitoches LA 71457 Office Phone: 318-354-1717. E-mail: carolforsloff@thehouseofaloha.com.

FORSSELL, LINDA LEE, secondary school educator, illustrator; d. Harrill Dean Johnson and Harriet Adelia Johns; children: Amy Maria Shane, Laila Katrina Lambrecht. BA in Art, Calif. State U., Sacramento, 1973. Educator Fairview Elem. Sch., Calif., 1988—2003, Fairfield H.S., 2003—. Mentor Fairfield Suisun Unified Sch. Dist., 1997—2000, educator adult sch., 2001—03, dist. devel. day presentor, 1995—96, dist. art shows coord. elem. schs., mid. schs. and high schs., 1996—; master tchr. Chapman U., 2002—03; dist. steering com. Local Edn. Arts Partnership, 2000—03. Illustrator, The Trouble With Secrets, raku sculpture, Symbolic Self Portrait (No. Calif. Juried Art Show Winner, 2001), Gentle (No. Calif. Juried Art Show Winner, 2002). Mem.: Calif. Tchrs. Assn. (assoc.). Office: Fairfield High School 205 EAtlantic Ave Fairfield CA 94533 Office Phone: 707-438-3000. Office Fax: 707-421-3977. Personal E-mail: lindafo@fsusdk12.ca.us.

FORST, CATHERINE PHILLIPS, library director; b. Plymouth, Mass., Dec. 11, 1956; d. Jim W and Joyce E Fisk; m. Michael James Forst, June 18, 1984; children: Garrett Fisk Phillips, Thomas Michael, Andrea Marie. M, U. of Mich., 1985—93. Librarian's Permanent Professional Certificate Libr. of Mich., 2000. Libr. dir. Springfield Twp. Libr., Davisburg, Mich., 1979—. Pres. Neighbor for Neighbor, Davisburg, Mich., 2002—05. Mem.: ALA, Am. Assn. of Univeristy Women, Mich. Libr. Assn. Catholic. Avocations: reading, cooking, antiques. Home: 9676 Susin Lane Clarkston MI 48348 Office: Springfield Township Library 12000 Davisburg Rd Davisburg MI 48350 Office Phone: 248-846-6550. Office Fax: 248-846-6555. E-mail: cforst@tln.lib.mi.us.

FORSYTH, BEVERLY K. (BEVERLY K. ROY DAVIDSON FORSYTH), language educator, writer; b. Memphis, June 05; d. Marian Davidson Roy and Oakley Eugene Stover, Johnny Roy. AA in Mass Comm., Odessa Coll., Tex.; BA in Mass Comm., U. Tex., Odessa, MA in English, 1995; PhD in English, Union Inst., Cin., 2001. Mem. faculty awards com. Odessa Coll. Co-author: The Texas Monthly Guidebook to Texas. 3rd edition, 1993, American Women Writers, 1900-1945, A Bio-Bibliographical Critical, 2000; author: (short stories) La Gringa Is My Name, 1999, Pontotoc Witch, 2000, One Last Secret, 2003, Amazon Heart, 2003, The Knock, 2002, Shadow's Edge, 2003; contbr. articles to profl. jours. Grantee Grace Mitchell/Learner Coun. Rsch. Travel, Union Inst., 2000; scholar, 2000, Agnes Rettig, 2000. Mem.: W. Tex. Writers, Tex. Assn. Creative Writing Tchrs., Tex. Coun. Tchrs. English (Pres.'s Classroom Rsch/Travel Study grantee 2001), Tex. C.C. Tchrs. Assn., Conf. Coll. Tchrs. English (exec. bd. councilors 2002—), S. Ctrl. MLA, Tex. Popular Culture Assn., S.W. Popular Culture Assn., Am. Culture Assn., Sigma Kappa Delta, Sigma Tau Delta (life). Office: Odessa Coll 201 W University Odessa TX 79764 Office Phone: 432-335-6661. Business E-Mail: bforsyth@odessa.edu.

FORSYTH, GARYFALLIA LILLIAN, nurse educator; b. Taunton, Mass., Sept. 22, 1920; d. Peter Halekas and Sophia Zakopoulos; m. Charles Clifford Forsyth, June 15, 1945 (dec.); 1 child, Charles Jr. BA in English, Fort Hayes State U., 1950; MS in Nursing, U.Colo., 1967; PhD in Nursing, Tex. Woman's U., 1977. U.S. Army nursing U.S. Hosp. Ship Okasa, 1943—46; op.rm. supr. Veteran's Hosp., Wichita, Kans., 1953—63; nursing faculty Wichita State U., 1963—70; v.p. nursing affairs Rush Presbyn., 1978—84; assoc. prof. nursing St. Luke's Med. Ctr., 1978—84. Contbr. articles to profl. jours. Mem. Am. Red Cross, 1942—80. Republican. Presbyn. Home: 1829 W Via Del Recodo Green Valley AZ 85614

FORSYTH, ILENE HAERING, art historian; b. Detroit, Aug. 21, 1928; d. Austin Frederick and Eleanor Marie (Middleton) H.; m. George H. Forsyth, Jr., June 4, 1960. AB, U. Mich., 1950; AM (univ. fellow), Columbia U., 1955, PhD (Fulbright, AAUW, Fels Found. fellow), 1960. Lectr. Barnard Coll., 1955-58; instr. Columbia U., 1959-61; mem. faculty U. Mich., Ann Arbor, 1961—, prof. history of art, 1974-97, prof. emerita, 1998—, Arthur F. Thurnau prof., 1984—; vis. prof. Harvard U., 1980; Mellon vis. prof. U. Pitts., 1981; vis. prof. U. Calif., Berkeley, 1996. Mem. Nat. Com. History Art, 1975-97; bd. dirs. Internat. Ctr. Medieval Art, 1970-95, 2005-, v.p., 1981-85; mem. supervisory com. Woodrow Wilson Found., 1985-88; Rome prize juror Am. Acad. in Rome, 1986-88; bd. advisors Ctr. Advanced Study in the Visual Arts, Nat. Gallery Art, 1985-88; mem. vis. com. medieval dept. Met. Mus. Art, N.Y.C., 1990-95; Samuel H. Kress prof. Ctr. Advanced Study in the Visual Arts, Nat. Gallery Art, 1998-99, bd. advisors, 1999-2000, U. Mich. Mus. of Art, 2005- Author: The Throne of Wisdom, 1972 (Charles Rufus Morey Book award 1974), The Uses of Art: Medieval Metaphor in The Michigan Law Quadrangle, 1993 (Annie award for non-fiction 1994); co-editor: Current Studies on Cluny, 1988; contbr. articles to profl. jours. Rackham research grantee and fellow, 1965-66, 75-76; grantee Am. Council Learned Socs., 1972-73; mem. Inst. Advanced Study Princeton, 1977 Mem. Coll. Art Assn. (dir. 1980-84), Archaeol. Inst. Am., Medieval Acad. Am. (fellow, 2006-, bd. advs. 1985-86, editorial bd. 1986-90), Medieval Club N.Y., Soc. francaise d'archéologie, Soc. Archtl. Historians, Acad. Arts, Scis. et Belles Lettres Dijon (France), Centre de recherches et d'études préromanes et romanes. Home: 5 Geddes Hts Ann Arbor MI 48104-1724 Office: U Mich Dept Art History Ann Arbor MI 48109

FORSYTH, LACEY LYNN, mathematics educator; b. Winterset, Iowa, Jan. 25, 1978; d. Gary Wayne and Suzanne Lynn Christensen; m. Jeffrey Ryan Forsyth, Sept. 16, 2000; children: Kade Ryan, Kael Wyatt, Haelynn Clare. BA, Simpson Coll., Indianola, Iowa, 2000; postgrad., Viterbo U. Tchr. h.s. math. Winterset Cmty. Sch. Dist., Iowa, 2000—. Mem.: Sch. Improvement Team (mem. 2001—06). Home: 1415 W Washington Winterset IA 50273

FORSYTH, ROSALYN MOYE, middle school educator; b. Pavo, Ga., Sept. 14, 1942; d. David Cody and Mary (Chapman) Moye; m. James Floyd Forsyth, Aug. 7, 1965. AB, Wesleyan Coll., Macon, Ga., 1964. Cert. paraprofl. Tchr. edn. Dougherty County Bd. of Edn., Albany, Ga., 1965-70, substitute tchr., 1972-88, paraprofl., 1988—. Editor: Membership Roll and Register of Ancestors, 1986. Mem. at large exec. com. South Ga. conf. United Meth. Women, 1972-74, dist. pres. Thomasville dist., 1977-78, rec. sec., 1979-83, sec. publicity and pub. rels., 1983-87, mem. com. on nominations Southeastern jurisdiction 1988-92). Mem. DAR (regent Chenaw chpt. 2005-), Profl. Assn. Ga. Educators, Bus. and Profl. Woman's Club (pres. 1973-75, dist. dir. Ga. Fedn., state chmn. Young Careerist 1977-79, state chmn. nat. found. 1979-81), DAR (regent Thronateeska chpt. 1986-88, state chmn. Am. Heritage 1986-88, dist. dir. Ga. soc. 1988-90, state officer, historian 1990-92, state chmn. textbook study nat. soc. 1992-94, state officer, registrar 1994-96, state officer, libr. 1996-98). Methodist. Avocations: reading, jogging, georgia bulldog activities, basketball, football. Home: 1706 Pineknoll Ln Albany GA 31707-3770 Office: Alice Coachman Elem 1425 Oakridge Dr Albany GA 31707

FORT, WANA ANN, retired pediatrician; b. Harrisonburg, La., June 21, 1924; d. David Wana Gibson and Olive Izetta Peters; m. Milton Giles Fort, Jr., June 14, 1946; children: Milton Giles III, David Gibson, Robert Gordon, Lewis Gregg, James Grady. BS, La. Tech U., Ruston, 1944; MD, Baylor Coll. Medicine, Houston, 1949. Lic. State Bd. Med. Examiners, Tex., 1949. Chem. lab. tech. Ammunitions Factory, Minden, La., 1944—45; med. lab. tech. Sentell Clinic and Minden Hosp., 1945; office sec. Chem. Diagnostic Lab., Houston, 1947; med. lab. tech. Pvt. Lab and Harris County TB Hosp., 1948; intern, resident Jefferson Davis Hosp. and Baylor Related Hosps., 1949—52; med. missionary Internat. Mission Bd., So. Bapt. Conv., USA, Sanyati Tribal Area and Harare, Zimbabwe, 1952—88; staff physician Bapt. Mission Zimbabwe, Sanyati Tribal Area, then Harare, 1952—88. Spkr. in field. Recipient Oustanding Women of Baylor U. award, Dallas Assn. Baylor U. Women Grads., 1990, Disting. Alumnus award, Baylor Coll. Medicine, 1990, Tower Medallion award Outstanding Alumni, La. Tech U., 1990; scholar, Harrisonburg H.S., La. Tech, 1941—44, So. Bapt. Fgn. Mission Bd., 1945—49. Mem.: AMA, Dallas Bapt. Missionary Fellowship (pres., prayer chmn.), Criswell Coll. Ladies Aux. (historian, writer for newsletter), Dallas Bapt. U. Women's Aux., Jr. Three Arts Club (pres., constn. chmn., parliamentarian). Conservative. Southern Baptist. Avocations: gardening, reading, writing, bible study, photography. Home: 4950 Ashbrook Road Dallas TX 75227-2913

FORTE, CHRISTINA KIRBY, financial analyst; b. McKinney, Tex., Sept. 1, 1973; d. Karen D. Whittington; m. Michael E. Forte, Feb. 27, 1993; children: Joshua Michael, Noah Nathaniel. AA in Acctg., Collin County C.C., 1996; BS in Acctg., U. Tex., 2005. Engring. clk. Fisher Regulators, Divsn. Emerson, McKinney, Tex., 1995—97, accts. payable, 1997—99, payroll, 1999—2000, gen. acctg., 2000—02, sr. credit & collections analyst, 2002—04. Mentor, tutor Cmtys. in Schools, McKinney, 1998—2003. Mem.: Golden Key Internat. Honour Soc. (life scholar 2003), Beta Gamma Sigma (life). Avocations: writing, reading, cub scouts. Office: Fisher Regulators Divisn Emerson 310 East Univ Dr Mc Kinney TX 75070 Office Phone: 972-542-5512.

FORTENBERRY, DELORES B., dean; b. McComb, MS, Jan. 31, 1933; d. Isaac and Maude Elma (Carmel) Brown; m. John Prowell, Jan. 22, 1956 (div. 1960); children: Dennis A. Prowell, Stevie G. Prowell; m. Fred D. Fortenberry, Dec. 3, 1971. BS, Jackson State U., 1963; MA, Ball State U., 1974, EdD, 1988. Sci. & math. tchr. McComb (Ms.) Pub. Schs., 1962-65; sci. tchr. Chgo. Pub. Schs., 1965-68; sci., art tchr. E. Chgo. Pub. Sch., Ind., 1968-80; sci. tchr. Ball State U. Lab Sch., Muncie, IL, 1980-81; sci., math. tchr., gen. edn. E. Chgo. Pub. Sch., Ind., 1981-89, dean, 1989—. Pres. Dist. Sci. Fair com., McComb, Miss., 1964-65; nat. chairperson Pike County Agrl. H.S. Alumni, Chgo., 1991-2000, Pike County Agrl. H.S. scholarship fund; chmn. sci. com. Nat. Alliance Black Sch. Educators, Washington, Chgo. Alliance Black Sch. Educators, 1984-86. Fellow NSF, 1963-64, Ball State U., 1980-81; sabbatical leave E. Chgo. Pub. Sch., 1980-81. Mem. AAUW, Nat. Alliance Black Sch. Educators, Chgo. Alliance Black Sch. Educators (certificate 1986), Afro-Am. History Club (chairperson 1999-2000), Pike County Agrl. H.S. Alumni (nat. chairperson 1991-2000, recipient plaques 1992-94, 96-98), Am. Fedn. Tchrs., Nat. Sci. Tchrs. Assn., Hoosier Assn. Sci. Tchrs., Assn. Supervision and Curriculum Devel., Kappa Delta Pi, Gamma Phi Delta (basileus, 1968-73), Phi Delta Kappa. Avocations: reading, travel, collecting recipes, collecting black history materials, sports. Home: 831 E 192nd St Glenwood IL 60425-2005 Office: Ctrl High Sch 1100 W Columbus Dr East Chicago IN 46312-2582

FORTENBERRY, NICHOLE AUDREY, paralegal, small business owner; d. Robert Donald Palmateer and Michelle Walker; m. Crinzel Frentez Fortenberry, June 22, 1996. BA in Justice, U. Alaska, Anchorage, 1995. Notary pub. Alaska. Legal sec. Holmes, Weddle and Barcott, Anchorage, 1997—98; legal asst. Keesal, Young and Logan, Anchorage, 1998—2001; owner, investigator alaskanparalegal.com, Anchorage, 1999—; litig. paralegal Law Offices Richard G. Haggart, PC, Anchorage, 2001—. Paralegal affiliate ATLA, 2005—. Mem.: ACLU, Alaska Assn. Paralegals, Nat. Fedn. Paralegals Assns., Alpha Phi Sigma. Office: Law Offices Richard G Haggart PC 1215 W 8th Ave Anchorage AK 99501 Office Phone: 907-278-2525. Office Fax: 907-278-3297. E-mail: nichole@haggart.com.

FORTI, LENORE STEIMLE, business consultant; b. Houghton, Mich., Sept. 9, 1924; d. Russell Nicholas and Agnes (McCloskey) Steimle; m. Frank Forti, May 29, 1950 (dec.). BBA summa cum laude, Northwood U., 1973, Dr.Laws, 1969. Asst. corp. sec., purchasing agt. Fed. Life & Casualty Co., Detroit, 1942-53; supr. sectl. J.L. Hudson Co., Detroit, 1953-57, adminstrv. asst. to exec. v.p., 1957-86; instr. Wayne State U. and U. Mich. Adult Edn., Detroit, 1958-71; creator, dir. Seminars for Profl. People, 1971—. Co-author: The Professional Secretary; contbr. articles to profl. jours. Asst. br. dir. planning City of Detroit for Civil Def.; chmn. bd. trustees PSI Rsch. and Ednl. Found.; trustee PSI Retirement Home Complex, Albuquerque; elected dir. Property Owners and Residents Assn., Sun City West Mcpl. Govt., 1994—97; past pres. Women's Bd. Northwood U., Midland, Mich.; past pres. parish coun. Our Lady of Lourdes Ch., Sun City West, Ariz., 1988, pres. ladies guild, 1990, 1995; 1st v.p. Vol. Bur. of Sun Cities, 1989; pres. Sun City West Found., 2002—03; bd. dirs. Sun City West Cmty. Fund, 1998—99. Elected One of Detroit's Top Ten Working Women, 1969; elected to Exec. and Profl. Hall of Fame. Mem. Internat. Assn. Adminstrv. Profls. (internat. pres. 1967-69), Future Secs. Assn. (nat. coord.), Lioness Club (pres. 1991-92), Sun City West Singles Club (pres. 1988). Republican. Roman Catholic. Avocations: bridge, Mah Jongg, dance. Home and Office: 12613 W Seneca Dr Sun City West AZ 85375-4635

FORTNER, NELL, professional athletics coach; b. Jackson, Miss. BS, U. Tex., 1982; MS, Stephen F. Austin U., 1987. Asst. coach women's basketball Stephen F. Austin U., Nacogdoches, Tex., 1986—90, Louisiana Tech U., 1991—95, USA Nat. Team, 1995—96; head coach women's basketball Purdue U., West Lafayette, Ind., 1996—97; head coach women's basketball, gen. mgr. Ind. Fever Women's Nat. Basketball Assn., Indpls., 1999—. Head coach women's basketball USA Basketball, 1997—2000, FIBA World Championship, 1998, R.William Jones Cup Tournament, Taiwan, 1998. Named Coach of Yr., Big Ten Conf., 1997, Nat. Coach of Yr., Basketball Times, 1997; recipient Gold medal, Olympic Games, 2000, FIBA World Championships, 1998, Olympic Games, 1996. Office: Indiana Fever 125 S Pennsylvania St Indianapolis IN 46204

FORTNEY, KIMBERLY BENSON, health and sports medicine educator; b. Morgantown, WV, Sept. 30, 1966; d. Stephen Theodore and Mary Rae (Spindler) Benson; m. Hugh Scott Fortney, June 30, 1990; children: Lane Benson, Atley Ray. BSc, W. Va. U., 1988; MA, Mich. State U., 1990. Tchr. Parkview H.S., Liesburg, Va., 1990—91, Walkersville Elem. Sch., Frederick, Md., 1991—93, athletic trainer, 1990—95; tchr. Thomas Johnson H.S., 1993—95; athletic trainer Urbana H.S., Ijamsville, Md., 1995—2000, tchr., 1995—. New tchr. mentor Frederick County Pub. Sch., 1998—, curriculum writer, 1995—. Mem.: NEA, Nat. Athletic Trainer Assn., Cure Action Now. Home: 15 Derby Pl Charles Town WV 25414

FORTUIN, DIANE HAY, historian, researcher; b. Portland, Maine, May 15, 1939; d. Wilfred A. Hay and Catherine T. Moore; m. Nicholas John Fortuin, Aug. 25, 1962; children: Elizabeth Steffensen, Julianne Savage, Karen Corsi. BA, Smith Coll., 1961. Field dir. Richardson-Merrell Internat., NYC, 1961—64; hist. rschr. Preservation Md., 1986—89, cons.; archeol./land rschr. Hist. & Environ. Clearance, Balt. City, 1988. With Mayor's Task Force Preservation, Balt. Mem. women's bd. Johns Hopkins Hosp., 1978—99, chmn. funding distbn., sustainer; bd. mem. Preservation Md.; bd. trustees Bryn Mawr Sch., Balt. Mem.: Green Spring Valley Garden Club, Green Spring Valley Hunt Club, Smith Coll. Club Balt. (pres. 1989—90). Avocations: writing, skiing, golf, bicycling. Home: 2929 Caves Rd Owings Mills MD 21117

FORTUNATO, JULIE MARIANNE, neurologist; b. Newark, Nov. 24, 1952; d. Antonio Gaetano and Julia Marianne Fortunato. AB magna cum laude, Drew U., 1974; MD, U. Medicine and Dentistry N.J., 1979. Diplomate Am. Bd. Psychiatry and Neurology, Am. Bd. Med. Examiners. Rsch. asst. dept. neuroscis. N.J. Med. Sch., 1974-75; intern dept. neurosci. Coll. Medicine and Dentistry of N.J.-Coll. Hosp., 1979-80; jr. resident neurosci. Coll. Hosp./East Orange VA Hosp., 1980-81, sr. resident, 1981-82, chief resident, 1982-83; rsch fellow demyelinating diseases U. Medicine and Dentistry of N.J., 1983-84; pvt. practice Westwood, N.J., 1984—; attending physician Holy Name Hosp., Teaneck, N.J., Pascack Valley Hosp., Westwood, Hackensack (N.J.) Univ. Med. Ctr. Contbr. articles to profl. jours. Recipient Dr. Miranti award, 1976, Ciba award, 1979, Lange Book award, 1979, Dr. Jesse McCall award Sussex County Med. Soc., 1979, others. Fellow ACP (assoc.), N.J. Acad. Medicine (assoc.); mem. Am. Acad. Neurology, N.J. Med. Women's Assn., Alpha Omega Alpha, Sigma Phi, Beta Beta Beta. Office: 10 Fairview Ave Westwood NJ 07675-2225

FORTUNATO, PAT DEAKIN, fine artist; b. Buffalo, Apr. 30, 1934; d. Edmund J. Deakin and Jane Wilson (Danahy) Ray; m. Thomas A. Fortunato, Apr. 7, 1956; children: Kathleen Yoder, Mark, Susan, Karen Voight, Steven, Thomas J. BS in Edn., State U., Buffalo, 1955. Elem. tchr. Buffalo Sch. System, 1955-57; substitute tchr. Williamsville (N.Y.) Schs., 1974-76; part-time workshop instr. Niagara C.C., Sanborn, N.Y., 1991-93. Workshop instr. 1990—, pvt. instr., Orchard Park, N.Y., 1992—. Exhibited at Albright-Knox Mems. Gallery, Buffalo, 1993, Burchfield-Penney Mus., Buffalo, 2004; travel exhibit Adirondacks Nat. Exhbn. of Am. Watercolors, 1999—, (award 2002); paintings included in several books. Liason Williamsville Sch. System, 1972-79. Recipient Award of Merit Nat. League of Am. Pen Women, 1988, Holbein award Batavia Internat. Exhibit, 1997. Mem. Midwest Watercolor Soc. (Award of Excellence 1987), Am. Watercolor Soc. (assoc.), Allied Artists of Am. (assoc.), Niagara Frontier Watercolor Soc. (editor 1983-87, chmn. 1988-94, Grumbacher Gold medal 1990, 2003), Buffalo Soc. of Artists (bd. dirs. 1994-95, 99—). Roman Catholic. Avocation: photography. Home and Office: 144 Lord Byron Ln Williamsville NY 14221-1998 E-mail: patfortunato@adelphia.net.

FORYS, LINDA R., science educator; b. Pensacola, Fla., Jan. 13, 1956; d. Robert J. and Jacquelyn D. Klarich; m. Michael H. Forys, Aug. 20, 1977; 1 child, Marianne. AAS in Dental Hygiene, Mich. C.C., Flint, 1977; BS in Elem. Edn., Reading Endorsement, U. Mich., Flint, 1991; MA in Gen. Tchg., MS Endorsement, Saginaw Valley State U., Saginaw, Mich., 1997. Cert.

adult, child, infant CPR, AED and First Aid instr.; lic. dental hygienist. Chairside dental asst. Kenneth E. Merckel, DDS, Mayville, Mich., 1972—74, Soll Gaynor, DDS, Flint, 1974—77; clin. dental hygienist Ralph Kretchmann, DDS, Yale, Mich., 1977—89, Lapeer (Mich.) Dental Assocs., 1988—89; tchr. 5th grade North Branch (Mich.) Area Schs., 1991—95, tchr. 8th grade sci., 1995—. Chair sci. dept. North Branch Schs., 1995—98, mem. sch. improvement team, 1992—; univ. supr. student tchrs. Cen. Mich. U., 1999, Saginaw Valley State U., 2005. CPR/AED/First Aid trainer ARC, Lapeer County, 1996—. Named Mich. Tchr. of Yr. finalist, Mich. Dept. Edn., 1998; recipient Excellence in Edn. award, Mich. Assn. Schs. Bds., 2002, Judy Stewart award for excellence, ARC, 2003. Mem.: NEA, North Branch Edn. Assn. (head negotiator 2002, pres. 2005—, bldg. rep. 2003—05, Disting. Svc. award 1997, 2005), Mich. Edn. Assn. Democrat. Roman Catholic. Avocations: swimming, snowmobiling, computers. Home: 2743 North Branch Rd North Branch MI 48461 Office: North Branch Area Schs PO Box 3620 6600 Brush St North Branch MI 48461 Office Phone: 810-688-4431.

FOSCARINIS, MARIA, lawyer; b. NYC, Aug. 8, 1956; d. Nicolas and Rosa F. BA, Barnard Coll., 1977; MA, Columbia U., 1978, JD, 1981. Bar: N.Y. 1982, U.S. Dist. Ct. (so. and ea. dists.) N.Y. 1983, D.C. 1986, U.S. Dist. Ct. D.C., U.S. Ct. Appeals (D.C. cir.). Law clk. to judge U.S. Ct. Appeals (2d cir.), N.Y.C., 1981-82; assoc. Sullivan & Cromwell, N.Y.C., 1982-85; counsel Nat. Coalition for Homeless, Washington, 1985-89; founder and dir. Nat. Law Ctr. on Homelessness and Poverty, Washington, 1989—. Notes editor Columbia U. Law Rev., 1980-81. Harlan Fiske Stone scholar, 1978-79; John Dewey fellow. Mem. ABA (commr. homelessness and poverty, 1989-95, 2004—). Office: Nat Law Ctr Homelessness and Poverty 1411 K St NW Ste 1400 Washington DC 20005-3404 Home: 1752 Swann St NW Washington DC 20009-5535 Office Phone: 202-638-2535. Business E-Mail: foscarinis@nlchp.org.

FOSDICK, CORA PRIFOLD (CORA PRIFOLD BEEBE), management consultant; b. San Francisco, Nov. 3, 1937; d. George and Beatrice (Ehni) Prifold; m. Ronald Beebe, Jan., 1959 (div.); m. Donald James Fosdick, Oct. 12, 1997. Student, Hollins Coll., Va., 1955-57, Am. U., DC, 1957-58; BA, U. Mich., Ann Arbor, 1959, MA, 1961; LHD (hon.), Southeastern U., Washington, D.C., 1993. Adminstrv. asst. Am. Polit. Sci. Assn., 1962-64; rsch. assoc. Inst. Comparative Studies of Polit. Systems, Washington, 1963-65; program planning and evaluation specialist U.S. Office Edn., Washington, 1965-68, planning coord., 1968-73, dir. planning and budget div., 1973-80; prin. dep. asst. sec. for elem. and sec. edn. Dept. Edn., Washington, 1980-81; asst. sec. adminstrn. U.S. Treasury Dept., Washington, 1981-84; dir. office of policy, budget and program mgmt. OSWER, EPA, Washington, 1984-86; dir. office of planning, budget and evaluation Dept. Commerce, Washington, 1986-87; commerce & justice br. chief Office of Mgmt. and Budget, 1987-94, advisor to assoc. dir. gen. govt. and fin., 1994; exec. dir. adminstrn., chief fin. officer Office of Thrift Supervision, Washington, 1994-99; v.p. Jefferson Consulting Group, Washington, 1999—2002; sr. assoc. Kelly, Amdersen & Assocs., Inc., Washington, 2002—. Mem. Washington Performing Arts Soc., 1983—, Coun. for Excellence in Govt.; bd. dirs. Treasury Hist. Assn., 2005—. Recipient HEW Superior Svc. award, Presdl. Rank award, 1989; Inst. World Affairs fellow, 1956, Am. Edn. Abroad former fellow, 1960. Fellow: Nat. Acad. Pub. Adminstrn. (vice chair 2002—03, bd. dirs.); mem.: Treasury Hist. Assn. (bd. dirs.), Hist. Assn. (bd. dirs. 2006, treas.), Nat. Press Club, Exec. Women in Govt. Program and Budget Analysis. Home: 1415 N Pegram St Alexandria VA 22304-1933 Personal E-mail: corabeebe@aol.com.

FOSLER, GAIL D., economist, government official; b. Los Angeles Dec. 7, 1947; d. Richard E. and Helen Elizabeth (O'Gorman) Deschner; m. R. Scott Fosler; 1 son, Michael. AB in Econs. U. So. Calif., 1969; MBA in Fin., NYU, 1972. Research analyst Chgo. Dept. Human Resources, 1970-72; research assoc. I.C.F., Inc., 1972-74; asst. v.p., economist Manufacturers Hanover, 1974-78; chief economist Senate Budget Com., Washington, 1981-89, dir. and chief economist, 1986-89; exec. v.p., chief economist The Conf. Bd., Inc., NYC, 1989-. Bd dirs. Unisys Corp., Baxter Internat., Caterpillar Inc., and DBS Holdings, Singapore. Office: The Conference Bd Inc 845 3rd Ave Fl 2 New York NY 10022-6600

FOSLER, NORMA LORRAINE, counselor; b. Chgo., Jan. 26, 1930; d. Walter Frederick and Josephine L. (Graft) Apel; m. Jay Vincent Woosley, June 8, 1954 (dec. Feb. 1958); m. Gail Marvin Fosler, Aug. 4, 1967; 1 child, Scott Edwin. BEd, Nat. Coll. Edn., Evanston, Ill., 1951; MA, Stanford U., 1963. Cert. in elem. edn. 5th grade tchr. Santa Cruz (Calif.) City Schs., 1951-53; 6th grade tchr. Redwood City (Calif.) Sch. Dist., 1954-55; substitute tchr. Palo Alto (Calif.) Elem. Schs., 1955-56; coll. admissions counselor Nat. Coll. Edn., Evanston, Ill., 1958-62; coll. counselor Ladue (Mo.) Sch. Dist., 1964-66, New Trier Sch. Dist., Winnetka, Ill., 1966-67; counselor Parkland Coll., Champaign, Ill., 1967-69, 78-94. Mem. H.S. Adv. Com. Champaign Sch. Dist., 1983-85; workshop dir. assertive tng. Champaign Sch. Dist., 1983-85. Mem. Carle Hosp. Aux., 1994—, scholastic chair, 2000—01; chmn. Carle Aus. Scholarship Com., 2005—; Election judge Champaign County Clks. Office, 1994—. Fellow Stanford U., 1963-64. Mem. ACA, Ill. Counseling Assn., U. Ill. Women's Club (v.p. Newcomers 1967-68). Presbyterian. Avocations: reading, swimming, golf. Home: 1011 W Healey St Champaign IL 61821-3926

FOSNAUGHT, PATRICIA S., art educator; b. Jersey City, Mar. 20, 1943; m. Robert A. Fosnaught, Nov. 26, 1964; 1 child, Nancy. BFA, U. Dayton, 1969; M. Art Edn., Wright State U., 1973. Art tchr. Dayton (Ohio) Pub. Schs., 1972-73; art tchr. Trotwood-Madison Schs., Trotwood, Ohio, 1973-78; instr. art Tenn. Tech. U., Cookeville, 1979-91; artist in residence Tenn. Tech. U./Tenn. Arts Commn., 1989-90; asst. curator edn. Tampa Mus. Art, 1992—2001; curator edn. Gulf Coast Mus., 2004—. Photographs of art included in Soft Jewelry, 1977, (Nancy Howell-Koehler, author) Photo Art Processes, 1980; exhibited in many shows. Recipient Purchase award Tenn. Arts Com., Cookeville, 1981, Gov.'s award/arts State of Tenn., 1982; named Profl. Woman of Yr. Cookeville Bus. and Profl. Women, 1991. Mem. Nat. Art Edn. Assn., Fla. Art Edn. Assn., Fla. Assn. Mus., Arts Complete Edn. Coalition. Avocations: travel, cultural activities. Home: 195 Corsica St Tampa FL 33606-3333 Office Phone: 727-518-6833. E-mail: pfosnaught@gulfcoastmuseum.org.

FOSS, LINDA JUDD, banker, lawyer; b. Cedar Rapids, Iowa, Mar. 18, 1949; d. Jesse Barid and Marian Louise (Roberts) Judd; m. Howard Wallace Foss, Mar. 21, 1973; children: Amy Judd, Christopher Judd. BS, Mid. Tenn. State U., 1970; JD, U. Calif. Berkeley, 1973. Bar: Calif. 1973. Law clk. L.A. Superior Ct., 1974—75; sr. v.p., corp. sec. Security Pacific Bank, L.A., 1975—. Mem.: State Bar Calif.

FOSS, MICHELLE MICHOT, think-tank executive, economist; BS, Univ. La., Lafayette, 1976; MS, Colo. Sch. Mines, 1985; PhD with honors, Univ. Houston, 1995; postgraduate, Tex. A&M Univ., Rice Univ. Coord. Energy & Minerals Field Inst., Colo. Sch. Mines, 1982—85; sr. assoc. & dir. rsch. Rice Ctr., 1985—88; dir. rsch. Simmons & Co. Internat., 1988—89; exec. dir. Inst. Energy Law & Enterprise, Univ. Houston, 1991—. Ptnr. Harvest Gas Mgmt. LLC, Tex. Mem. bd. editors Internat. Jour. Regulation & Governance. Mem. vis. com. div. Economics & Business, Colo. Sch. Mines. Mem.: Women's Energy Network, Houston Geol. Soc., Assn. Internat. Petroleum Negotiators, Council on Fgn. Rels., U.S. Assn. Energy Economics (pres. 2001), Internat. Assn. Energy Economics (pres. 2003). Office: Institute for Energy Law & Enterprise University of Houston 100 Law Ctr Houston TX 77204-6060

FOSS, VALERIE ANN, medical/surgical nurse; b. Rockville Center, N.Y., Aug. 30, 1931; d. Frank Blanchard and Faith Parsons (Smith) F. RN, Buffalo Gen. Hosp., 1952; BSN, U. Buffalo, 1963. Asst. dir. nursing Deaconess Hosp., Buffalo, 1971-85; dir. nursing Buffalo Gen. Hosp., 1985-86, nursing coord., 1986-87; dir. nursing Genesee Meml. Hosp., Batavia, N.Y., 1987-92; staff nurse ARC, 1992-96.

FOSTER, ANDREA SUSAN, science educator; b. N.Y.C., Mar. 4, 1960; d. Andre John and Margaret Alice (Haug) Ognibene; m. Robert George Foster, June 2, 1984; 1 child, Robert G. Foster III. BS, Tex. A&M U., 1982, MEd, 1984, PhD in Sci. Edn., 1998. Tchr. Wilchester Elem., Houston, 1982-83, St. Joseph Parochial Sch., Bryan, Tex., 1983-84; sci. tchr. Sul Ross MS, San Antonio, 1984-92, Katherine Stinson MS, San Antonio, 1992-95; rsch. asst., instr. Tex. A&M U., College Station, 1995-98; asst. prof. sci. edn. Sam Houston State U., Houston. Nat. team mem. AAAS Project 2061, Washington, 1989—; assessment writer Psychology Corp., San Antonio, 1987—; adv. bd. coord. math. Tex. Edn. Assn., 1993-94; adj. com. for essential elements, Tex. Edn. Agy., Austin, 1995. Contbr. articles to profl. jours. Com. mem. task for Youth Tobacco Am. Cancer Soc., 1993, pilot tchr. Sun Safety MD Anderson, Houston, 1994; tchr., trainer Keep Tex. Beautiful, Austin, 1992-94. Named Tchr. of Yr. Northside ISD, 1989, Excellence in Sci. Teaching award Sigm Xi, 1990, Excellence in Sci. Teaching award Tex. Medical Assn., 1993, Presdl. award for Excellence in Sci. Teaching NSF, 1994. Mem. Nat. Sci. Tchrs. Assn. (social functions mgr. 1989—), NEA, Am. Assn. Advancement Sci., Nat. Middle Sch. Assn., Phi Delta Kappa, Am. Assn. Univ. Women. Roman Catholic. Avocations: waterskiing, watercolors, travel, reading, dance. Office: Texas A&M U College Of Education College Station TX 77843-0001 Home: 20914 Manon Ln Spring TX 77388-5289 Office Phone: 281-772-0671. E-mail: asf004@shsu.edu.

FOSTER, BONNIE GAYLE, operating room nurse, real estate agent; b. Valentine, Nebr., Dec. 3, 1940; d. Isaac Robert and Helen Anita (Tucker) Bingham; m. Floyd E. Foster, July 4, 1973; m. Daniel A. Plummer, Aug. 8, 1963 (div. Oct. 1971). AA, RN, Oakland City Coll., 1963; BA in Sociology, U. Mo., Kansas City, 1975, M in Ednl. Adminstrn., 1978. RN Calif., Kans., Mo., cert. plastic surg. nursing. RN staff O.R. Herrick Hosp., Berkeley, Calif., 1963—64, Kaiser Hosp., Oakland, 1963—64; RN staff oper. room U. Kans. Med. Ctr., Kansas City, 1964—65; RN oper. room Rsch. Med. Ctr., Kansas City, Mo., 1965—78; RN, oper. room supr. Broadway Surg. Ctr., Kansas City, Mo., 1979—86; RN oper. room Menorah Med. Ctr., Kansas City, Mo., 1986—94, Sierra Surgi-Ctr., Walnut Creek, Calif., 1994—; realtor assoc. Pacific Real Estate Svcs., Pleasanton, Calif., 2003—; agt. Keller Williams Tri Valley. In svc. instr. Rsch. Hosp. and Med. Ctr., Kansas City, Mo., 1966—72, instr. CPR, 1976—88. Bus. assoc. Network Mktg.; chairperson fund raising program St. Paul's Episcopal Ch., Lee's Summit, Mo., 1976—94, chairperson bldg. expansion program, 1976—94, vestry mem., 1976—94; active St. Clare's Episcopal Ch., Pleasanton, 1994—. Mem.: Pleasanton North Rotary, Assn. Oper. Rm. Nurses (past pres. Greater Kansas City chpt., sec., chairperson Career Fair, co-chairperson Oper. Rm. Nurse of the Yr., panel moderator two-day inst., mem. several coms.). Republican. Episcopalian. Avocations: bicycling, hiking, golf, bridge, gardening. Home: 7567 Maywood Dr Pleasanton CA 94588 Office: Keller Williams Tri Valley Realty 5994 West Las Positas Blvd Ste 101 Pleasanton CA 94588 Office Phone: 925-462-3644. Business E-Mail: Bonnie@BonnieFoster.com.

FOSTER, ELAINE ELIZABETH, retired art educator; b. Lawrence, Mass., Jan. 13, 1934; d. Ernest Webster and Elizabeth Josephine (Dubuc) F. Cert., Sch. of the Worcester Art Mus., 1955; BA, Clark U., 1957, MA, 1961; profl. diploma, Columbia U., 1965, EdD, 1970. Supr. art Auburn (Mass.) Elem. Schs., 1957-59; tchr. art Auburn Pub. Jr. High Sch., 1959-61, Auburn Pub. High Sch., 1961-65; from asst. prof. to prof. art N.J. City Univ., 1966—99; ret., 1999. Author: Collage Film Guide, Crayon Film Guide, 1966, A Great School of Fine Arts in N.Y.C.: A Study of the Development of Art at Columbia University (1860-1914), 1970; lectr. The Brain and Art, 1975—; group shows include 25 exhbns. in N.E.; patentee for tie brooch design, 1988, 89. Mem. Nat. Art Edn. Assn., Univ. Council for Art Edn. (pres. 1980-82), Am. Assn. Univ. Profs. (pres. local chpt. 1978-80), Soc. N.Am. Goldsmiths, Am. Craft Council, N.Y., Tchrs.' Coll. Columbia U. Alumni Coun., Pen A Brush (bd.). Avc

FOSTER, EVALINE L., education educator, researcher; b. Natchez, Miss., Aug. 7, 1953; d. John and Augustine W. Lewis; m. James L. Foster, Apr. 16, 1972; children: Tanya Shontae Demby, Cedrick James, Laura Alisha Simmons, Jamie Ryan. Degree in elem. edn. and gen. studies, Alcorn State U., 1996, MEd, 2000; PhD, Nova Southeastern U., 2005. Cert. elem. tchr., guidence counselor La. Guidance counselor intern Natchez (Miss.) Adams Sch. Dist., 2000—01, guidance counselor, social worker, 2000—02, behavior enrichment instr., 2002—03, rschr., 2003—04, prin. investigator, rschr., 2003—04; adj. prof. Alcorn State U., Natchez, 2005—. Mem. disciplinary rev. com. mem. Natchez Adams Sch. Dist., 2000—02. Sec., Bible class tchr. Ch. of Christ, Natchez, 1973—2006. Named Bible Class Tchr. of Yr., Ch. of Christ, Natchez, 1986; recipient Trillium Staff Spl. Recognition award, Copiah-Lincoln C.C., Natchez, 1993, Spl. Recognition Student Support Svcs., 1994. Mem.: ASCD (assoc.). Achievements include research in implementation of a social skills curriculum to reduce behavior problems of African American boys in elementary classroom settings. Home: 376 Concordia Pk Vidalia LA 71373 Office: Alcorn State U 15 Campus Dr Natchez MS 39120 Office Phone: 601-392-9503(c). Home Fax: 1-318-336-5480; Office Fax: 1-318-336-5480. Personal E-mail: evalinefoster@yahoo.com.

FOSTER, HOPE S., lawyer; b. 1948; BA, Wellesley Coll., 1970; JD with honors, George Washington U., 1973. Bar: DC 1973. Mem. Mintz Levin Cohn Ferris Glovsky & Popeo PC, Washington, co-mgr., Health Care Sect. Contbr. articles to profl. jour.; spkr. in field. Mem.: Am. Health Lawyers Assn., ABA (white collar crime com., health care com., antitrust com., health care fraud & abuse subcom.), DC Bar. Office: Mintz Levin Cohn Ferris Glovsky & Popeo PC 701 Pennsylvania Ave NW Washington DC 20004 Office Phone: 202-661-8758. Office Fax: 202-434-7400. Business E-Mail: hsfoster@mintz.com.

FOSTER, JEANNE O'CAIN, poet, fine arts educator; b. Portsmouth, Va., Sept. 10, 1931; d. James and Julia Sutton (Taft) O'Cain; m. Lue Raymond Haywood, July 13, 1951; children: Joy, Lee, Bonnie, Gregory; m. Charles Wilton Foster (div. 1988). BFA with honors, Columbia Coll., 1994; MFA (hon.), Mellen U., 1995; postgrad., U. Wales, U. London, Old Dominion U. Cons., educator, 1985—; cons., min. White Swan Ministries, Lake Ozark, Mo., 1995—. Actress CBN-TV, Va., 1980—85; scriptwriter PBS-TV, SC, 1990. Author: Dance the Divine, 1989 (Nat. Endowment Arts award, 89), (plays) Colony at Santee; editor: Annie's Gazette, 1988; author: The Temple Beautiful, 2006. Sec. Citizens Coun., Richmond, Va., 1958; educator Omega Inst., Rhinebeck, NY, 1989; founder Gifted Children, Va., 1965—67; first arts chmn. Edgar Cayce Found., 1968; founder ADRA sacred dance, 1968, Theatre of Isis, 1996—; sec. Bill Story for Gov., Richmond, 1962. Named Internat. Poet, 1989, Hon. Heirophant, Fellowship of Isis, Ireland, 1996; recipient Golden Poet award, World of Poetry, 1988, Editor's Choice award, Nat. Libr. Poetry, 1993, hon. award, Writers Digest, 1996. Mem.: Internat. Women's Writing Guild. Republican. Unitarian Universalist. Avocation: cross cultural dance. Home: 4629 Shore Dr Apt 302 Virginia Beach VA 23455-2794

FOSTER, JODIE (ALICIA CHRISTIAN FOSTER), actress, film director, film producer; b. L.A., Nov. 19, 1962; d. Lucius and Evelyn (Almond) F.; children: Charles, Kit BA in Lit. cum laude, Yale U., 1985, DFA (hon.), 1997; DArts (hon.), U. Penn., 2006; degree (hon.), Smith Coll. Owner, chair Egg Pictures Prodn. Co., LA, 1990—2001. Acting debut in TV show Mayberry, R.F.D, 1969; numerous other TV appearances including My Three Sons, The Courtship of Eddie's Father, Gunsmoke, Bonanza, Paper Moon, 1974-75; TV spl. The Secret Life of T.K. Dearing, 1975; TV movies include Rookie of the Year, Smile, Jenny, You're Dead; motion picture appearances include Napoleon and Samantha, 1972, One Little Indian, 1973, Tom Sawyer, 1973, Alice Doesn't Live Here Anymore, 1974, Taxi Driver, 1976 (Acad. award nominee for Best Supporting Actress), Echoes of a Summer, 1976, Bugsy Malone, 1976, Freaky Friday, 1976, Moi, Fleur Bleue, 1977, Casotto, 1977, The Little Girl Who Lives Down the Lane, 1977, Candleshoe, 1977, Foxes, 1980, Carny, 1980, O'Hara's Wife, 1982, Hotel New Hampshire, 1984, The Blood of Others, 1984, Five Corners, 1987, Siesta, 1987, Stealing Home, 1988, The Accused, 1988 (Acad. award for Best Actress, 1989, Golden Globe award for Best Performance by an Actress, 1989), Backtrack, 1989, The Silence of the Lambs, 1991 (Golden Globe award for Best Actress in Drama, 1992, Acad. award for Best Actress, 1992, BAFTA award for best actress, 1992), Shadows and Fog, 1992, Sommersby, 1993, Maverick, 1994, Contact, 1997, Anna and The King, 1999, Panic Room, 2002, A Very Long Engagement, 2004, Flightplan, 2005, Inside Man, 2006; dir., actress: Little Man Tate, 1991; prodr., actress: Mesmerized, 1986, Nell, 1994 (Acad. award nominee for Best Actress 1995), The Dangerous Lives of Altar Boys, 2002; dir., prodr. Home For the Holidays, 1995; exec. prodr. (Showtime) Babydance, 1998, Waking the Dead, 2000.*

FOSTER, JOY VIA, retired library media specialist; b. Besoco, W.Va., Aug. 11, 1935; d. George Edward and Burgia Stafford (Earls) Via; m. Paul Harris Foster, Jr., Dec. 8, 1956 (dec. Dec. 20, 1962); children: Elizabeth Lee, Michael Paul. BS, Radford Coll., 1971; MS, Radford U., 1979. Cert. libr. Va. Clk. Va. Tech. and State U., Blacksburg, 1955—57, Christiansburg Primary Sch., Va., 1971—72, libr., 1972—85, Auburn Mid. and H.S., Riner, Va., 1985—2000; ret., 2000. Meml. chmn. Am. Cancer Soc., Christiansburg, 1965—66; block worker, 1985—91; area chmn. Am. Heart Fund, Christiansburg, 1990—93; pres. Montgomery County Ret. Tchrs. Assn., 2002—04; trustee Montgomery-Floyd Regional Libr. Bd, 2003—. Mem.: Va. Ednl. Media Assn. (Meritorious Svc. award 1999). Presbyterian. Avocations: reading, bowling, flea marketing, antiques.

FOSTER, JUDI, interior designer, artist; d. Harold Gordon and Edith Mae (Stevens) Miller; m. Peter H. Foster, Aug. 8, 1959 (dec. Nov. 20, 2004); children: Juliet Elise, Christel Elise. BSc cum laude, U. Conn., 1959; student in Art, U. N.Mex., 1960. Buyer Federated Dept. Stores, Albuquerque, 1960—65; tchr. home econs. So. Union Gas Co. Schs., Albuquerque, 1965—70; with inventory control Comml. Warehouse, Albuquerque, 1970—75; sales Amana/Quasar, Albuquerque, 1975—80; prin. owner Pinon Tree Gallery, Albuquerque, 1975—80; interior decorator pvt. practice, Albuquerque, 1980—; exec. asst. Dyncorp., Albuquerque, 1980—90. The Art of Layering, 2004, Making Connections, 2004, New Mexico Women in Business Directory, 25th Anniversary Edition, 2006. Mem.: Nat. Soc. Layerists Multimedia (mem. planning com.), Nat. Watercolor Soc., Am. Watercolor Soc., MasterWorks of N.Mex. (steering com. 2002—), Nat. Collage Soc., Soc. Layerists Multimedia, N.Mex. Watercolor Soc. (mem. exhbn. com.), Taos Nat. Watercolor Soc. (hon.; exhibitor). Avocations: jazzercise, travel, painting, historic restoration. Home and Office: 28 Juniper Hill Ct NE Albuquerque NM 87122 Office Phone: 505-249-7167. Personal E-mail: judistudio@aol.com.

FOSTER, KIM, art dealer, art gallery owner; b. Washington, Nov. 22, 1956; d. James R. and Clair Lynn (Block) Foster; m. Antonio Petracca, Oct. 30, 1994. BA, Sarah Lawrence Coll.; MA, Johns Hopkins U., Balt. Lic. stockbroker, N.Y. Asst. treas. Bankers Trust Co., N.Y.C., 1980-83; asst. v.p. Marine Midland, N.Y.C., 1984-85; commodities credit mgr. Shearson Lehman, N.Y.C., 1985-86; v.p. Bayerische Vereinsbank, N.Y.C., 1988-94; pres. Kim Foster Gallery, N.Y.C., 1993—. Bd. dirs. Foster Holdings, Inc., Pitts. Speech writer Gov. James R. Thompson, Chgo., 1975. Mem. Mus. Modern Art., Whitney Mus. Am. Art. Republican. Jewish. Avocations: swimming, travel. Office: Kim Foster Gallery 529 W 20th St New York NY 10011-2800 Office Phone: 212-229-0044. Personal E-mail: info@kimfostergallery.com.

FOSTER, LINDA LEE, artist; b. Portland, Oreg. Student, Bellevue C.C., Foothills Coll., Wash. State U., Pratt Inst.; pvt. instrn. with numerous artists, including Joseph Bohler, Jackie Brooks, Jane Burnham, Ernie Young, others. Instr. adult watercolor classes Bellevue (Wash.) Parks Dept., Kirkland (Wash.) Arts Ctr. Watercolorist snow and water and floral still lifes, portraits, and abstract work; represented in numerous pvt., local, nat., and internat. collections. Recipient award Bellevue Sch. Dist. Staff Art Fair, 1990, Pacific Northwest Arts & Crafts Fair, 1990, 3rd Pl. award Sky Valley Artist's Guild, 1993, Merit award Parkland Gallery, 1993, Ilwaco Heritage Mus., 1993, Grand award Donald L. Johnson Meml. Art Competition, 1995, Best of Show award Women Painters Wash., 1996, awards several internat., nat. and western juried shows, including 1st place Eastside Jour. Newspaper/1997 Photo Contest, 1997, 3d place Greater Marysville Artists Guild, Seafirst Bank, Marysville, Wa., 1996, Best of Show Women Painters of Wash., Moss Bay Gallery, Kirkland, 1996, Grand award 9th Ann. Donald L. Johnson Meml. Art Competition, Seattle Telco Fed. Credit Union, Seattle, 1995, Hon. Mention award Puget Sound Area Exhbn., Frye Art Mus., Seattle, 1994, others; selected juried exhbns. include Women Artists of the West, San Juan Capistrano, Calif., 1997, 98, 99, 4th Internat. Juried Competition, Biloxi, Miss., 1997, Northwest Watercolor Soc. Invitational Exhibit, Goldendale, Wash., 1997, ann. show Women Artists of the West, Taos, N.Mex., 1995-98, Women Painters of Wash., Juried Kuwait Exhbn. Millennium Images, 1999, Ireland and Am., Washington, 1999, Clymer Mus., Ellensburg, Wash., 1999, Ariz. Aqueous VII, Tubac, Ariz., 1993, Fla. 19th ann. Watercolor Soc., Panama City, Fla., 1993, Ga. Watercolor Soc. ann., Stone Mtn., Ga., 1992, Pacific Northwest arts and crafts fair, Bellevue Art Mus., 1990, 1991, Aqueous Open 1989, Pitts. Watercolor Soc. 52d, LaFond Galleries, Pitts., Pa., 1989, 91, Open Painting Exhbn., Kimball Art Ctr., Park City, Ut., 1998, Klamath Juried Open, Klamath Art Gallery, Klamath Falls, Oreg., 1993, NE Watercolor Soc. (Signature mem.), 17th ann. nat. exhbn., Trotting Ho. Mus., Goshen, N.Y., 1993, Western Washington Watercolor Soc. Juried Competition, Richland, Wash., 1993, 94. Mem. Women Artists of the West (signature mem.), Northwest Watercolor Soc. (signature mem.), Women Painters of Wash. Home and Office: Phantom Lake Studio 16424 SE 17th St Bellevue WA 98008-5122 Office Phone: 425-941-8233. E-mail: lindaleefoster@msn.com.

FOSTER, LINDA TIMBERLAKE, state legislator; b. Portland, Maine, Feb. 8, 1943; m. Bernard Scott; 3 children. BS, U. Maine, 1965. Rep. Hillsborough Dist. 4 N.H. State Ho. of Reps., 1992—; policy leader Dem. Party, NH. Bd. dirs. Family Strength. Mem. N.H. Assn. Residential Care Homes (adv. bd.), So. N.H. Svcs. (exec. bd.), Phi Kappa Phi. Office: NH Ho of Reps Com on Fin State Capitol Concord NH 03301

FOSTER, LUCILLE CASTER, retired school system administrator; b. Vallejo, Calif., Sept. 28, 1921; d. Lewis Caster and Mabel Estelle (Witt) Beidleman; m. Donald Foster, Nov. 21, 1942 (deceased). AB in History, U. Calif., Berkeley, 1943; MA in Elem. Edn., San Francisco State U., 1953; EdD, Stanford U., 1959. Cert. sch. adminstr., Calif. Elem. tchr. Alameda (Calif.) Unified Sch. Dist., 1948-55; curriculum cons. Laguna Salada Elem. Sch. Dist., Pacifica, Calif., 1955-60, asst. supt., 1960-81; ret., 1981. Fir br. Children's Med. Ctr. No. Calif. Co-author (handbooks) Selling Ventures, 2000, Grant Writing 4th edit., 2002, Fundraising, 2d edit., 2002, Resource Development, 2002; contbr. articles to Calif. Jour. Elem. Edn., 1957, 61. Mem. AAUW (Santa Rosa br.), Can. Fedn. Univ. Women (hon. life), Internat. Fedn. U. Women, Calif. Sch. Adminstrs. Assn. (life), Calif. Tchrs. Assn. (life), Calif. Sch. Personnel Commrs. Assn. (life), Nat. Assistance League, Assistance League Sonoma County (hon. life), LWV, Pi Lambda Theta, Delta Zeta. Avocations: community volunteer, bridge, travel. Home: 245 Mockingbird Cir Santa Rosa CA 95409-6245

FOSTER, LUCILLE STUART, music educator; b. Lexington, Ky., June 11, 1953; d. James Philip and Mabel (Stuart) Foster. AA, Edison C.C., Ft. Myers, Fla., 1973; MusB Edn., Fla. State U., Tallahasse, 1975. Tchr. music, chorus, band, and math. Immokalee Mid. Sch., Fla., 1975—2000; instr. music, dir. chorus Lake Trafford Elem. Sch., Immokalee, 2000—06, tchr. music, chorus, keyboards Ft. Myers, 2003—. Clarinetist Ft. Myers Symphony Orch., 1971—73; flutist Gulf Coast Symphony Orch., Ft. Myers, 2004—; pvt. music tchr., Ft. Myers, 1975—2000. Mem.: Delta Kappa Gamma. R-Consevative. Avocations: perfoming music, swimming, travel. Office: Lake Trafford Elementary School 3400 Lake Trafford Road Immokalee FL 34142 Office Fax: 239-377-7301. Personal E-mail: fluteluchristian@aol.com. E-mail: fosterlu@k12.fl.us.

FOSTER, MARY CHRISTINE, film producer, writer; b. LA, Mar. 19, 1943; d. Ernest Albert and Mary Ada (Quilici) Foster; m. Paul Hunter, July 24, 1982. BA, Immaculate Heart Coll., L.A., 1967; M in TV News Documentary, UCLA, 1968. Dir. R & D Metromedia Producers Corp., L.A., 1968-71; dir. devel. and prodn. svcs. Wolper Prodns., L.A., 1971-76; mgr. film programs NBC-TV, Burbank, Calif., 1976-77; v.p. movies and mini series Columbia Pictures TV, Burbank, 1977-81, v.p. series programs, 1981; v.p. program devel. Group W. Prodns., L.A., 1981-87; agt. The Agency, L.A., 1988-90, Shapiro-Lichtman Agy., L.A., 1990-99; ind. prodr., 1999—. Lectr. in field. Creator (TV series) Sullivan, 1985, Auntie Mom, 1986; author: Immaculate Heart High School: Memories of 100 Years 1906-2006, 2005. Trustee Immaculate Heart H.S., L.A., 1980—; exec. com. Humanitas awards Human Family Inst., 1985—; cmty. devel. com. Immaculate Heart Cmty., 2001—; exec. com. LA Roman Cath. Archdiocesan Comm. Commn., 1986—90; bd. dirs., treas. Catholics in Media, 1992—2004; vol. com., writer tour script, vis. book, newsletter and website Cathedral of Our Lady of Angels, 2002—; chmn. pastorial coun. St. Francis of Assisi, 2003—05, chmn. stewardship com. and renovation com. Democrat. Personal E-mail: fosterc@aol.com.

FOSTER, MERCEDES S., curator, research scientist; BA in Zoology, U. Calif., Berkeley, 1963, MA in Zoology, 1965; postgrad., Duke U., Durham, N.C., 1965, Orgn. Tropical Studies, Costa Rica, 1966, U. Chgo., 1968—69; PhD in Biology, U. South Fla., Tampa, 1974. 26th Paul L. Errington Meml. lectr. Iowa State U., 1990; curator of birds, rsch. zoologist biol. survey project USGS Patuxent Wildlife Rsch. Ctr. Nat. Mus. Natrual History, Washington. Contbr. articles. Master: Soc. Antioquena Ornitología (hon.); fellow: AAAS. Office: c/o Biol Survey Project USGS Patuxent Wildlife Rsch Ctr Nat Mus Natural History 10th and Constitution Ave NW Washington DC 20560-0111

FOSTER, NANCY HASTON, columnist, writer; b. Austin, Tex., June 07; d. Arch B. and Verlea Haston; m. Joe D. Foster Jr. (div.). BJ, U. Tex., BA in Sociology. Writer, pub. rels. dept. Trinity U., San Antonio, Tex.; social worker pub. welfare dept. State of La., Lafayette; instr. sociology U. Tex., Austin; columnist San Antonio Light, 1982-83, San Antonio Express-News, 1989-90; freelance writer, 1977—. Author: San Antonio, A Texas Monthly Guidebook, 1983, rev. edit., 1989, 94, 98, San Antonio, Lone Star Guide, 1999, 2000, The Alamo and Other Texas Missions to Remember, 1984, Texas Missions, A Texas Monthly Guidebook, 1995, Texas Missions, Lone Star Guide, 1999; contbg. editor, writer: Texas, Fodor's Travel Guides, 1985, rev. edit., 1991, Fodor's American Cities, 1986, rev. edit., 1988, Texas, A Texas Monthly Guidebook, 1993, 98; contbr. articles to popular mags. Mem. Women in Comm., Phi Beta Kappa. Avocations: conversation, photography, collectibles. Home and Office: 201 Prinz Dr San Antonio TX 78213-1921

FOSTER, ROSEMARY ALICE, lawyer, artist; b. Independence, Iowa, Oct. 2, 1944; d. James Charles Mooney and Hilda Marie Engelkes; m. Monty Foster, July 20, 1979 (dec. Jan. 17, 2000); 1 child, Daisy Ward. BA, Drake U., 1964; JD, George Washington U., 1967; MA in Psychology, U. Utah, 1973. Bar: D.C. 1968. Supr. neighborhood probation unit Second Dist. Juvenile Ct., Salt Lake City, 1968—73; legal cons. State of Idaho, Boise, Idaho, 1973—74; atty. Nat. Ctr. Law Handicapped, South Bend, Ind., 1974—75; adminstrv. law judge Wash. Office Adminstrv. Hearings, Olympia, Wash., 1976—2001; with STEPS Program Cmty. Mental Health, Homer, Alaska, 2001—02; hearing officer Workers Compensation Dept. Labor, Anchorage, 2002—. Exhibitions include Artist's Gallery, Olympia, Wash., 1995—97, Cuyamungue Stone Co., Homer, Alaska, 2003, Mystic Enterprises, 2003. Vol. Youth Ct., Olympia, 1998—2001; mem. Alaska Women's Polit. Caucus, Anchorage, 2003; bd. dir. South Peninsula Women's Svcs., Homer, Alaska, 2000—02. Recipient Svc. award, State of Wash., 2001. Mem.: LWV. Democrat. Roman Catholic. Office: 2440 E Tudor Rd Anchorage AK 99507

FOSTER, SALLY, interior designer; b. New Orleans, Nov. 6, 1927; d. Charles Shearer and Bessie Long Foster; m. Harold Barnett McSween, Dec. 21, 1948 (div. Mar. 1979); children: John Charles McSween, Robert Douglas McSween, Elizabeth McSween, Sally McSween Ward. BA, Tulane U., 1948. Interior designer, owner Sally Foster Designs, Alexandria, La., 1979—. Bd. dirs., past pres. Alexandria Mus. Art, 1988—92, 1999—, Kent Plantation House, Alexandria, 1964—67, 1998—; founding mem. bd. dirs. Rapides Symphony Orch., Alexandria, 1973; found. bd. Christus St. Frances Calstini Hosp., 2005—. Mem.: Alexandria Jr. League (pres. 1963—64), Nat. Soc. Colonial Dames Am., Alexandria Golf and Country Club, Alexandria Rotary Club, Chi Omega. Republican. Episcopalian. Avocations: antiques, travel, food, reading. Office: Sally Foster Designs 1307 Windsor Pl Alexandria LA 71303-2751

FOSTER, SERRIN MARIE, non-profit organization executive; b. Washington, Sept. 17; d. William A. and Donna R. (Hayden) F. BA in Pub. Rels., Old Dominion U., 1977. Freelance pub. rels. specialist, Springfield, Va., 1978-82; program mgr., regional rep. St. Jude Children's Rsch. Hosp., Arlington, Va., 1982-89; dir. devel. Nat. Alliance for Mentally Ill., Washington, 1989-94; exec. dir. Feminists for Life of Am., Washington, 1994-99, pres., 1999—. Mem. adv. bd. Ivy League Coalition for Life, Harvard U., 1997—, Am. Collegians for Life, Washington, 1998—. Author: (books) Pro-Women Answers to Pro-Choice Questions, 2003, Great Speeches in History, 2004—; contbr. Women's Rights, Boston Globe, Cost of Choice; editor-in-chief, contbr. The Am. Feminist mag., 1994—. Susan B. Anthony List, Alexandria, 1997—. Mem. Alpha Phi Women's Found. Avocations: gardening, travel, painting. Office: Feminists for Life of Am PO Box 206 Alexandria VA 22314

FOSTER, TERESA E., choral director, piano educator; b. Hardinsburg, Ky., Aug. 11, 1971; m. Michael S. Foster. B Music Edn., U. Louisville, 1993. Choral dir. Sacred Heart Acad., Louisville, Ky., 1997—, Louisville Youth Choir, Louisville, Ky., 2000—; pvt. voice tchr. Ursuline Sch. For The Performing Arts, Louisville, Ky., 1997—; chorus mem. Ky. Opera, Louisville, Ky., 1990—99; choral dir. Bullitt Ctrl. H.s., Shepherdsville, Ky., 1995—97, St. Patrick Sch., Louisville, Ky., 1993—95. Mem.: Nat. Cath. Educators Assn., Tri-M Internat. Music Honor Soc., Ky. Choral Dir.'s Assn., Am. Choral Dir.'s Assn., Ky. Music Educator's Assn., Music Educator's Nat. Conf., Delta Omicron (pres. 1994—95). Office: Sacred Heart Acad 3175 Lexington Rd Louisville KY 40206

FOSTER, VERNA LAVONNE, small business owner; b. Lubbock, Tex., Aug. 14, 1939; d. Robert Clyde and Murl Lucyle (Colwell) Camp; m. Wayne Henry Foster, June 14, 1958; 1 child, Jason Todd. BA, So. Mo. State U., 1960. Cert. secondary educator in English, Speech, French. Tchr. Reeds Spring (Mo.) Schs., 1960-61, Billings (Mo.) Sch., 1962-71, Morrisville (Mo.) Schs., 1971-72; bookkeeper Foster Farm, Morrisville, 1971—; bookkeeper, cashier Foster Auction Co., Morrisville, 1973-82, Lockwood (Mo.) Sales Barn, 1975-79; tchr. English Marion C. Early Schs., 1981-84; owner, mgr. Hooked on Books, Springfield, Mo., 1984—2005; ret. Class sponsor Reed Spring High Sch., 1960-61, Billings (Mo.) High Sch., 1962-71, Morrisville Schs., 1971-72, 81-84; play dir. in field. Contbr. articles to profl. jours. Pres. Climax Springs (Mo.) Alumni Assn., 1960; bd. dirs. S.W. Mo. English Assn., Springfield, 1983-84. Grantee S.W. Mo. State U., 1965. Mem. Nat. Fedn. Ind. Bus., Nat. C. of C. Avocations: reading, cooking, travel.

FOSTER, VICKI ANNE, secondary school educator; b. Sapulpa, Okla., Apr. 21, 1952; d. James Robert and Mary Louise Long; m. E. Bernard Foster, July 14, 1976; children: Seth Alden, Chelsea Marie Burgardt. BA, U. Wyo., Laramie, 1974, MS in Tchg., 1978, PhD, 2005. Tchr., grades 1-9 multiple sch. districts, Wyo., 1974—98; instrnl. assessment specialist Natrona County Sch. Dist., Casper, 1998—2001, mentoring program facilitator, 2001—03, coord. secondary curriculum, 2003—. Adj. faculty U. Wyo., Casper Ctr., 1999—2001. Dist. commr. US Pony Club branches, Casper, 1993—2000. Recipient Presdl. award Excellence Elem. Sci. Tchg., NSF, 1991. Mem.: ASCD, Nat. Staff Devel. Coun., Nat. Sci. Tchrs. Assn., Nat. Coun. Tchrs. Math., Phi Delta Kappa. Avocation: equestrian sports. Office: Natrona County School District 970 N Glenn Rd Casper WY 82601 Office Phone: 307-577-0200. Business E-Mail: vicki_foster@ncsd.k12.wy.us.

FOSTER, WILLETTA JEAN, music educator; b. Paris, Tex., Feb. 18, 1939; d. Eugene Curtis and Lyda Willetta (Murphy) Lawhorn; m. Paul Kenneth Foster, Mar. 4, 1961 (dec. Nov. 1986); 1 child, Paulette LaRee Foster Galbraith. AA, Tyler Jr. Coll., 1959; BS, Tex. Women's U., 1961, postgrad., 1961-63. Tchr. music pvt. practice, Ft. Worth, Houston, Tyler, Tex., 1959—; dir. music West. U. Meth. Ch., Houston, 1965-67; devel. specialist, tchr. music Palmer Sch., Houston, 1983-88; tchr. music Duchesne Acad., Houston, 1984-91, U. St. Thomas Sch. Little Children, Houston, 1989-90; co-owner, devel. specialist, program dir. Acad. Skills Svcs. Learning Ctr., Houston, 1983-88; instr. U. Tex., Tyler, 1993-95; developer, dir. Acad. Skills & Knowledge, Tyler, 1996-98; devel./cognitive cons. Bay Waveland Sch. Dist., Bay St. Louis, Miss., 1998—. Cons. and spkr. in field. Author, composer: (albums) These Are Me, I Can Be Any of These, Listen It's the Singing Me, Watch It's the Dancing Me, Bravo It's the Creative Me, I Can Go Left, Right, All About, My World and Me, Shh-It's the Listening Me; author: (video) I Can Run I Can Read. Big sister Convent of the Good Shepherd, Houston, 1965-66; vol. Rep. County Hdqrs., Houston, 1964. Recipient Book Golden Deeds, Exch. Club Houston, 1986. Mem. Nat. Music Tchrs. Assn., Am. Contract Bridge League, Tex. Music Tchrs. Assn., Tyler Music Tchrs. Assn. (treas. 1993-96). Presbyterian. Avocations: needlecrafts, bridge, gardening, reading. Office: Bay-Waveland Sch Dist Bay Saint Louis MS 39520 Home: 4806 Jefferson Ave Gulfport MS 39507-4405

FOSTER-CHEEK, KAYE I., health products executive; With Yellow Pages, Pfizer, Inc.; v.p. human resources North Am. Consumer Products Cos. Johnson & Johnson, New Brunswick, NJ, 2003—04, v.p. human resources Consumer and Personal Care Grp., mem. human resources leadership team, mem. consumer and personal care grp. operating com., 2004—05, v.p. human resources, mem. exec. com., 2005—. Office: Johnson & Johnson 1 Johnson & Johnson Plz New Brunswick NJ 08933*

FOSTER-HENNIGHAN, SHARI M., science educator; d. Sharon R. and Robert E. Foster; m. Doug J. Hennighan; children: Zaryn J. Hennighan, Becan S. Hennighan. M in Edn., U. Ctrl. Fla., 2005. National Board Certified Teacher-Biology Nat. Bd. for Profl. Tchg. Standards, 2004. Internat. baccalaureate and advanced placement biology tchr. Cypress Creek H.S., Orlando, Fla., 1995—, sci. dept. chairperson, 2005—. Lacrosse coach Cypress Creek H.S., 1997—, wrestling coach, 2004—; coach Orlando Hurricanes, US Power Soccer Assn., 2004—. Mem.: Fla. Assn. of Sci. Teachers, Assn. Ednl. Comms. and Tech., Nat. Assn. of Sci. Teachers. Home: 3857 Blackberry Circle Saint Cloud FL 34769 Office: Cypress Creek HS 1101 Bear Crossing Dr Orlando FL 32824 Office Phone: 407-852-3400. E-mail: fosters@ocps.net.

FOSTER-WELLS, KAREN MARGARET, artist; b. Pasadena, Calif., Oct. 26, 1942; d. Ray Russell Foster and Margaret Victoria Ray; m. David Roycroft Rory Wells, Sept. 17, 1988; children: John McCarthy, Sabisha Friedberg. AA, Orange Coast Coll., Costa Mesa, Calif., 1962; student, U. Calif., Irvine, 1967-68, Laguna Beach Sch. Art/Design, Calif., 1965-67. Illustrator, 1963—. One-woman shows include Santa Barbara (Calif.) of Natural History, 1979, Morro Bay (Calif.) Mus. of Natural History, 1988, Great Western Bank, San Luis Obispo, Calif., 1989, Cayucos (Calif.) Art Assn., 1993, Chelsea Bookshop, Paso Robles, Calif., 1993, Paso Robles Art Assn. Gallery, 1993, Wild Horse Found., Santa Barbara, Summerwood Winery, 2002; group exhbns. include Waterside Gallery, Morro Bay, Calif., 1997, 98, Johnson Gallery and Framing Studio, San Luis Obispo, 1999, 2000, Coll. of Creative Studies, Santa Barbara, 2000, Santa Barbara Mus. Natural History, 2000, Carnegie Western Art Gallery, Paso robles, 2000-2001, San Luis Obispo Art Ctr., 2001, Cayucos Art Assn., 2001, Biennale Internazionale Dell'arte Contemporanea, Florence, Italy, 2003, Mid-State Fair (Artist Achievement award 2003), Quick Draw Cowboy Festival, Santa Clarita, 2003, 2004, Cattlemen's Western Art Show, Paso Robles, 2004, (with pianist Hilary Anderson) Painting Concert, 2004; artist (cover) The Path of Return, 2001, Monterey Mus. Art, 2002. Recipient Bronze medal Art of Calif. Discovery awards, 1993, 1st Pl. Calif. Mid-State Fair Art Show, 1994, 98, 1st Pl. and Coord. award Calif. Mid-State Fair Art Show, 2000, Best of Show Paso Robles Art Assn., 2000, Color of Autumn award Paso Robles Art Assn., 2004. Mem. The Oak Group, Calif. Art Club, San Luis Outdoor Painters Enterprise (co-founder), Am. Soc. Portrait Artists, Women Artists of the West. Avocations: horses, natural history. Office: Karen Foster Artist dot com PO Box 1114 Templeton CA 93465 Office Phone: 805-239-8413. E-mail: horseart@tcsn.net.

FOTOPOULOS, SOPHIA STATHOPOULOS, medical research scientist, administrator; b. Kansas City, Mo., Nov. 6, 1936; d. Marinos G. and Stavroula (Fotopoulos) Stathopoulos; m. Chris K. Fotopoulos, Aug. 27, 1963 (div.) BA, U. Kans., 1958, MA, 1964, PhD, 1970. Diplomate Behavioral Scis. Regulatory Bd. State of Kans., Council for Nat. Register of Health Svc. Providers. Rsch. asst. U. Kans. Med. Ctr., Kansas City, 1958-61; rsch. assoc. Inst. Cmty. Studies, Kansas City, Mo., 1965-66; lectr. U. Kans., Lawrence, 1969-70; dir. Psychophysiology-pharmacology Lab. Greater Kansas City (Mo.) Mental Health Found., 1970-73; staff assoc. neuropsychophysiology, 1973, Midwest Rsch. Inst., Kansas City, Mo., 1974-75, sr. scientist, head Psychophysiology Lab., 1975-77, assoc. dir. chem. scis. div., 1977-79, dir. life scis. div., 1979-84; dir. rsch. Am. U., Washington, 1984-87; exec. v.p., CEO Immucomp, Inc., 1987-92; pres., CEO Bioactive Tech., 1992—. rsch. prof. dept. medicine Kansas U. Med. Ctr., 1987-97; spl. rev. com. Nat. Cancer Inst., 1978-98; mem. adv. com. Am. Cancer Soc., 1982-96; lectr. U. Mo.-Kansas City Sch. Medicine, 1970-84. NIH research fellow, 1962-64, HHS research fellow, 1965-69; recipient Creative Scientist award Am. Inst. Research, 1971. Mem. AAAS, Claude Bernard Soc., Internat. Soc. for Antiviral Rsch., N.Y. Acad. Scis., Biofeedback Soc. Am., Mo. Biofeedback Soc. (pres. 1979-80), Sigma Xi. Greek Orthodox. Clubs: Zonta Internat. (pres. KCII 1983-85), Philoptochos Soc. Contbr. articles to profl. jours. and books.

FOUAD, NADYA A., psychology professor; b. Ames, Iowa, Dec. 5, 1955; d. A. A. and Maria Elisabeth Fouad; m. Robert L. Leitheiser, Mar. 21, 1981; children: Nicholas Robert Leitheiser, Andrew James Leitheiser, Patrick Joseph Leitheiser. BS, Iowa State U., 1977; PhD, U. Minn., 1984. Lic. psychologist WI. Prof. U. Wis.-Milw., 1984—. Chair, bd. ednl. affairs APA, Washington, 2006—; chair Coun. Counseling Psychology Tng. Programs; editor-elect The Counseling Psychologist; pres. Soc. Counseling Psychology. Author: Career Theory and Practice, Becoming Culturally Oriented: Practical Advise for Psychologists; editor: Handbook of Social Justice in Counseling Psychology. Pres. Shorewood Excellence in Ednl. Devel., Wis., 2004—06. Recipient John Holland award. Fellow: APA. Office: U Wis Milw PO Box 413 Milwaukee WI 53201-0413 Office Phone: 414-229-6830. Business E-Mail: nadya@uwm.edu.

FOUCHA, LAURA THERESA, computer graphics designer, filmmaker, writer; b. New Orleans, Mar. 24, 1947; d. Frederick Lake and Lucille Mary (Normand) F. BA, U. New Orleans, 1973. Reg. radiologic technologist. Radiologic technologist Uptown Physicians Group, New Orleans, 1969-73; dept. mgr. D.H. Holmes, New Orleans, 1969-73; asst. mgr. Gen. Cinema Theatres, New Orleans, 1973-75; computer graphics designer New Orleans, 1975—; videographer Lens To Creation, New Orleans, 1993—. Camerawoman New Orleans Women in Video, 1982-89. Film maker: Gunchase to Nowhere, 1970 (1st prize 1970); author: (book) Tribunal of Anarchy, 1995. Vol. City of New Orleans, 1962-64; campaign worker Candidates Campaigns, 1964-74; activist NOW, New Orleans, 1979—. Recipient Certificate of Recognition award City of New Orleans, 1962, Key to the City, 1965, Cert. of Appreciation Vet's. Adminstrn., 1963, Best Actress award New Orleans Cmty. Theater, 1979. Mem. NOW (New Orleans chpt. pres. 1986-88), Agenda For Children, Timberwolf Preservation Soc., Soc. for Creative Anachronism, Ravenswood Archery Assn. (pres. 1995—). Avocations: archery, reading, movies, dance, video editing. Home: PO Box 113247 Metairie LA 70011-3247

FOUCHÉ, HELEN STROTHER, editorial design executive; b. Washington, Apr. 19, 1939; d. James Herschel and Elizabeth Ellen (Wright) Strother; m. Robert Michael Fouché, Oct. 20, 1962; children: James Michael, David Carroll, Stephen Charles. BA cum laude, Auburn U., 1960; student, Belles Artes, Managua, Nicaragua, 1964-65; student Intensive Lang. Tng., Fgn. Svc. Inst., 1961, 73; grad., Am. Transp. Inst., 1983. Asst. producer-dir. Internat. TV Svcs., U.S. Info. Agy., Washington, 1960-62; diplomatic svcs. with fgn. svc. husband U.S. Dept. of State, Europe, Africa, Cen./So. Am., 1963-81; art instr. for internat. children's classes La Paz, Bolivia, 1979; community liaison officer U.S. Embassy, La Paz, 1979-81; internat. group coord. Group Travel Unlimited, Alexandria, Va., 1983-84, mktg. creative/tech. writer, 1985-86; mng. editor Am. Leisure Industries, Lanham, Md., 1986-87; editor, cons. Washington Editl. Svcs., DC and Met. area, 1987-88, pres. Washington, Arlington, Va., 1988—2002. Founding bd. dirs. Fgn. Svc. Youth Found., Washington, 1989-91; cons. Overseas Briefing Ctr., Fgn. Svc. Inst., U.S. Dept. of State, Arlington, 1981-93; internat. tour mgr. Acad. Travel Abroad, Inc., 1990—; in mktg. sales Va. Divsn. of Tourism, 1994-97; media cons. designed slide shows, wrote scripts for non-profit causes. Contbg. editor, columnist: Diplomatic Digest, others; editor FS EYE for U.S. Dept. of State, 1991-94; mem. editorial bd. Fgn. Svc. Jour., 1989-92; executed murals, Crippled Children's Ward Managua (Nicaragua) Gen. Hosp., 1964, Montessori Sch., La. Paz, 1980; contbr. articles to profl. publs. Pres. Episcopal Ch. Women of St. Michael's, 1989-90, mem. vestry, 1990-94; mem. Altar Guild, 1982-99, lector, 1984-99; mem. Habitat for Humanity coms. St. Philip's Cathedral, Atlanta. Recipient Vol. of Yr. award, Tampa, Fla., 1970; named one of Outstanding Young Women of Am., 1973. Mem. AAUW, DAR, Assn. of Am. Fgn. Svc. Women (bd. mem., editl. com., newsletter editor), Nat. Press Club, Atlanta Press Club, Jamestown Soc. Democrat. Episcopalian. Avocations: art, theater, travel, hiking.

FOUCHT, JOAN LUCILLE, retired elementary school educator, retired counseling administrator; b. Glenford, Ohio, Feb. 26, 1931; d. Byron Ralph and Elsie Pauline (Tavenner) Foucht. BS in Elem. Edn., Ohio State U., 1953, MA in Guidance, 1967. Elem. sch. tchr. Southwood Elem. Sch., Columbus, Ohio, 1953—55, Suffern (N.Y.) Pub. Sch., 1955—56, N.E. Elem. Sch., Upper Montclair, NJ, 1956—60, Hubbard Elem. Sch., Columbus, 1960—67, Medary Elem. Sch., Columbus, 1986—93; counselor Medina Jr. H.S., Columbus, 1967—70; elem. sch. counselor various schs., Columbus, 1970—86; ret., 1993; sub. tchr. Columbus, 1996—. Elected delegate Ohio Edn. Assn. and Nat. Edn. Assn. Conv., 1966—77; treas. Columbus Assn. of Classroom tchr., 1964—66, pres. elect, 1966—67, pres., 1967—69; human rels. chairperson, coorndinated tchr. edn. study with Ohio State Univ., Sch. desegregation. Columbus Edn. Assn., 1973—77. Contbr. articles Career Education Interest Groups Ohio Sch. Coun., 1968. Counselor, advisor 4H Club, Columbus, 1971—73; pres. Women's Assn. Columbus Symphony Orch., 1991—92, Women's Assn. Symphony Columbus Orch., 2000—01; program chairperson bus. and prof. unit Women's Assn. Columbus Symphony Orch., 1990—2000, 2002—03; choir mem. Overbrook Presbyn. Ch., Columbus, 1945—. Recipient Rsena B. Willis Award, Nat. Edn. Assn. Convention, 1975, Coun. Award of the Yr. for Creative Multicultral Programs, Ohio Sch., 1982. Mem.: AAUW (choral group 1988—, membership treas. 1996—2001, co chairperson 2002—04), Clintonville Women's Club (chairperson bridge groups 1988—2001), Alpha Delta Kappa (chpt. pres. 1986—88). Democrat. Presbyterian. Avocations: gardening, music, travel, theater, reading. Home: 225 Webster Pk Columbus OH 43214

FOUDY, JULIE MAURINE, retired professional soccer player, Olympic athlete; b. San Diego, Jan. 23, 1971; m. Ian Sawyers, July 1995. BSW in Biology, Stanford U., 1993. Mem. U.S. Women's Nat. Soccer Team, 1987—2004, capt., 1992—2004; profl. soccer player San Diego Spirit, 2001—03. Color commentator Men's World Cup, ESPN, 1998. Mem. Tyresco Football Club, Sweden, 1994; pres. Women's Sports Found. Named World Cup Champion, 1991, 1999; recipient Gold medal, Centennial Olympic Games, 1996, Athens Olympic Games, 2004, FIFA Fair Play award, 1997, Silver medal, Sydney Olympic Games, 2000, Bronze medal, World Cup, 2003. Achievements include being a member of the Bronze medal winning team World Championships, Sweden, 1995; CONCACAF, Montreal, 1994; being voted number 1 most powerful in sports, Sports Business Journal, 2004. Office: c/o US Soccer Fedn 1801 S Prairie Ave # 1811 Chicago IL 60616-1319

FOUGERAT, KAREN KAY, mathematics educator; d. Ivan and Betty Nowotny; m. Kenneth John Fougerat, June 15, 1985; children: Kelsey Beth, Kendall Shea. BS in Edn., MS in Edn., SW Tex. State U., San Marcos. Lifetime tchg. cert. Tex. Edn. Assn., 1986. Tchr. Gonzales H.S., Tex., 1986—.

FOUGHT, LORIANNE, plant pathologist; b. Upper Darby, Pa., Oct. 5, 1962; d. Edwin Howard and Jeanette Marie Matthews; m. Daniel Lynn Fought, Jan. 22, 1990; children: Bethannie, Angelique, Daniel, Kaitlyn. BS, Pa. State U., 1985; MS, U. Ky., 1988, PhD, 1992; MBA, U. Kan., 1996. Rsch. aid Pa. State U., University Park, 1982-85; grad. rsch. asst. U. Ky., Lexington, 1985-91; chemist II Bayer Corp., Bayer Research Park, Kans., 1991-93; sci. and regulatory specialist Bayer Corp./Animal Health, Shawnee Mission, Kans., 1993-98; sr. field devel. rep. Bayer Corp. Crop Protection, Kansas City, Mo., 1998—2002; fungicide product devel. mgr. Bayer CropSci., Research Triangle Park, NC, 2002—. Contbr. articles to profl. jours. Tchr. So. Hills United Meth. Ch., Lexington, 1989-90; Bayer Corp. Cmty. amb. Sch.-to-Career Program. Dept. Plant Pathology fellow U. Ky., Lexington, 1985-91. Mem. Am. Phytopathol. Soc. (sec. grad. student com. 1990-91), Am. Chem. Soc., Gamma Sigma Delta. Republican. Achievements include research in metabolism of xenobiotics in plants and animals, compound isolated from cucumber tissues which induces systemic resistance to disease in cucumbers. Investigated metabolism of agricultural chemicals in plants and animals. Field research of crop protection products. Development of fungicides for argonomic crops. Office: PO Box 12014 Research Triangle Park NC 27709

FOUKE, JANIE M., academic administrator, educator; BS, St. Andrews Presbyn. Coll.; MS, PhD in Biomed. Math. and Engring., U. NC, Chapel Hill. Prof. Dept. Biomedical Engring. Case Western Reserve U., Cleve., 1981—99; div. dir. Div. of Bioengineering and Environ. Sys., NSF, Washington, DC; dean Coll. Engring. Mich. State U., 1999—2005; provost, sr. v.p. academic affairs U. Fla., Gainesville, 2005—. Adv. bd. mem. Engring. Directorate, NSF, Nat. Inst. of Bioimaging and Bioengineering, NIH. Author: Engineering Tomorrow, 2000 (Dexter Prize, Soc. for History of Tech.); contbr. articles to profl. jours. Fellow: AAAS, IEEE, Biomed. Engring. Soc., Am. Inst. Med. and Biol. Engring. Office: U Fla 235 Tigert Hall PO Box 113175 Gainesville FL 32611 Office Phone: 352-392-2404. Office Fax: 352-392-8735. E-mail: jfouke@aa.ufl.edu.

FOULKE, JUDITH DIANE, health physicist; b. Bucyrus, Ohio, Nov. 22, 1945; d. Lawrence Kern Foulke and Alberta Amelia (Foulke) Houpt; m. Mark Allen Elrod, July 17, 1981. BA, St. Mary of the Springs, 1967; MS, U. Mich., 1969; PhD, Purdue U., 1973. Health physicist NASA Goddard Space Flight Ctr., Greenbelt, Md., 1969-71, U.S. AEC, Washington, 1973-77; radiobiologist U.S. Nuc. Regulatory Commn., Washington, 1977-87; health physicist U.S. Dept. Energy, Washington, 1987—. Mem. Montgomery Village Cmty. Band, Gaithersburg. Mem. AAAS, Am. Nuc. Soc., Health Physics Soc. Democrat. Roman Catholic. Home: 10 Sunnyview Ct Germantown MD 20876-4025

FOULSTON, NOLA TEDESCO, lawyer; b. Mt. Vernon, N.Y., Dec. 14, 1940; d. Dominick J. and Theresa M. (Pellino) Tedesco; m. Steven L. Foulston, Jan. 2, 1983; 1 child, Andrew. BA, Ft. Hays State U., 1972; postgrad., U. Kans., 1972-73; JD, Washburn U., 1976. Bar: Kans. 1977, U.S. Dist. Ct. Kans., U.S. Ct. Appeals (10th cir.). Asst. dist. atty. 18th Jud. Dist., Dist. Atty.'s Office, Wichita, Kans., 1977-81; assoc. Foulston, Siefkin, Powers & Eberhardt, Wichita, 1981-86; ptnr. Foulston & Foulston, Wichita, 1986-89; dist. atty. Office of Dist. Atty. Eighteenth Jud. Dist. Sedgwick County Courthouse, Wichita, 1989—. Bd. dirs., legal counsel YWCA, Wichita, 1978-83, pres. 1980-81; active YWCA's Women's Crisis Ctr., Wichtia Area

Sexual Assault Ctr.; bd. dirs. Exploited and Missing Children's Unit, Project Freedom, Community Corrections, County-Wide Substance Abuse Task Force, State of Kans. Law Enforcement Coordinating Com., Community Rels. Task Force, Inter-Agy. Truancy Adv. Com., Women's Rsch. Inst., Crime Stoppers of Wichita Adv. Bd.; apptd. by Gov. Hayden of Kans. to the Weigand Commn. on State Expenditures. Named one of Outstanding Young Women of Am., Outstanding Young Wichitan, Wichita Jaycees, 1990; recipient Alumni Achievement award Ft. Hays State U., 1992, Law Enforcement Commendation medal SAR, 1992. Mem. ABA, Kans. Bar Assn., Wichita Bar Assn. (Outstanding Atty. of Achievement 1992), Nat. County and Dist. Attys. Assn., Kansas County and Dist. Attys. Assn., Golden Key (hon.). Democrat. Roman Catholic. Office: 535 N Main Wichita KS 67203-3702

FOUNDAS, ANNE LEIGH, psychiatrist; b. 1957; MD, La. State U., 1986. Bd. cert. neurology. Resident neurology U. Fla., Gainesville, fellow behavioral neurology-neuropsychology; assoc. prof. neurology Tulane U. Med. Sch., New Orleans; dir. neurology residency tng. program Tulane U. Health Scis. Ctr., New Orleans. Adj. asst. prof. psychology U. New Orleans, La. State U., Baton Rouge. Consulting editor: APA Jour. Neuropsychology. Recipient Norman Geschwind prize in behavioral neurology, Am. Acad. Neurology, 2003. Office: Tulane Univ Med Sch Dept Psychiatry 1430 Tulane Ave SL-2 New Orleans LA 70112

FOUNTAIN, KAREN SCHUELER, retired physician; b. Aberdeen, SD, Oct. 14, 1947; BA, No. State Coll., Aberdeen, S.D., 1968; MD, U. Md., Balt., 1972. Diplomate Nat. Bd. Med. Examiners, Am. Bd. Radiology in Therapeutic Radiology. Intern Md. Gen. Hosp., Balt., 1972-73, resident in radiation oncology, 1973-74; fellow in radiation oncology Mayo Clinic, Rochester, Minn., 1974-76, cons. in oncology, 1976-81; clin. asst. prof. Columbia U., N.Y.C., 1981-83, residency program dir. dept. radiation oncology, 1981—93, clin. assoc. prof., 1983—2001, ret., 2004. Mem. med. bd. Presbyn. Hosp., N.Y.C., 1983-86, Med. Res. Corps., 2004-; faculty coun. mem. Columbia U., 1982-89; del. N.Y. State Radiological Soc., N.Y.C., 1987-2004. Fellow Am. Coll. Radiology (councilor 1999-04), Am. Radium Soc. (exec. com. 2004-06), N.Y. Acad. Medicine; mem. Am. Soc. Therapeutic Radiology and Oncology, Radiol. Soc. N.Am., Am. Soc. Clin. Oncology, Am. Assn. for Women Radiologists (bd. dirs. 1995-96), So. Med. Assn., N.Y. Roentgen Soc. (sect. chmn. 1989-90), N.Y. State Radiol. Soc. (bd. dirs. 1996-02).

FOUNTAIN, LINDA KATHLEEN, health science association executive; b. Fowler, Kans., Apr. 30, 1954; d. Ralph Edward and Ruth Evelyn (Cornelson) Young; m. Andre Fountain. BS in Nursing, Cen. State U., Edmond, Okla., 1976. RN, Okla. Staff nurse med./surg. and coronary care unit Presbyn. Hosp., Oklahoma City, 1976-79; mgr. nursing Hillcrest Osteo. Hosp., Oklahoma City, 1979-80; staff nurse, mgr. Oklahoma U. Teaching Hosp., Oklahoma City, 1981-82; pres. New Life Programs, Oklahoma City, 1981-88, Nursing Entrepreneurs, Ltd., Oklahoma City, 1988—; mgr. Internat. Health Supply, Oklahoma City, 1988—. Coord. lactation cons. program State of Okla., 1981-98, new life car seat rental program at various hosps., 1983-92, also speaker Success Co., Oklahoma City, 1984—; owner Rainbows Overhead Graphic Media, Oklahoma City, 1984-91; speaker in field. Founder Praxis Coll., Oklahoma City, 1988. Named Mentor of Yr., Okla. Metroplex Childbirth Network, Oklahoma City, 1984; honored for vol. work with families and rescue after Oklahoma City bombing, U.S. Dept. Justice, 1995. Mem. Am. Nurses Assn., Internat. Lactation Cons. Assn., Internat. Platform Assn., Bodyworkers and Wellness Therapies Assn. Avocations: gemology, travel. Office Phone: 405-879-0224. Business E-Mail: Lfountain@praxiscollege.com.

FOUNTAIN, RUTH ANNE, elementary school educator; b. Arlington, Va., Aug. 9, 1956; d. Kenneth Scarborough and Gere Dell Karr; m. Lynn E. Fountain, Mar. 30, 1955; children: Jeffrey L., Brian L. BS in Elem. Edn., Iowa State U., Ames, 1978; MS in Elem. Edn., Creighton U., Omaha, Nebr., 1987. ESL Endorsement U. Omaha. Elem. tchr. Coun. Bluffs Cmty. Sch. Dist., Iowa, 1978—90, tchr. ESL grades K-9, 1990—2004, tchr. ESL grades K-12, 2004—. Coord. children and youth group First Bapt. Ch., Council Bluffs, 1994—2000, coord. youth camp, 1997—2006. Grantee, Iowa West Found., 2005. Mem.: Iowa State Edn. Assn., NEA. Office Phone: 712-328-6422.

FOUQUET, ANNE (JUDY FUQUA), musician, music educator; b. Wurtland, Ky., Oct. 2, 1938; d. John Paul and Garnet May (Gibson) Hillman; m. Warren Russell Fuqua, Dec. 21, 1961 (div. Dec., 1992); children: Bryan David, Faith Fuqua-Purvis, Paul Carroll. BMus., Am. Conservatory, Chgo., 1962; MMus., No. Ill. U., 1967; MFA, U. Iowa, 1971, D in Musical Arts, 1997. Organist various churches and denominations, Ill., 1960—; profl. accompanist Wis., Ill., 1970—; piano instr. Beloit (Wis.) Coll., 1972—; instr. Rockford (Ill.) Coll. Acad., 1991—; ind. instr. Keyboard Studio, Rockford, Ill., 1971—; clarinet player Rockford (Ill.) Park Band, 1995—. Composer: (song cycle soprano) Spinner of the Seasons, 1987, (suite for flute and hapsichord) Issar Suite, 1992; author: (play) Miracle of Love, 1982; (novel) If It Hadn't Been for Joel, 1980; (memoirs) Daddy Was a Farmer, Mother Was a City Girl, 1999; concert artist duo-piano with Robin Wooten, 1999, 2001; solo harpsichord recitals, 2001, 02. Mentor Helping One Student To Succeed, Structured Reading, Kishwaukee Sch., Rockford, Ill., 1997-98, adult lit. tutor READ Chatanooga, 1999—; interim organist, choirmaster Trinity Luth. Ch., 2000, Northminster Presbyn. Ch., Chattanooga, summer 2001; organist St Thaddeus Episcopal Ch., 2003—; Suzuki piano instr. Tenn. Valley area, 1998--; active concert artist, harpsichord, and piano. Nominee Best Classical Pianist Rockford Area Music Industry, 1996. Mem. Am. Guild of Organists, Music Tchrs. Nat. Assn., Ill. Music Tchrs. Assn. (adjudicator 1994-97), Kishwaukee Valley Concert Band, Szuki Assn. of the Americas, Midwest Hist. Keyboard Soc., Mendelsson Club (founder composer showcase concerts Rockford 1991-97, bd. dirs. 1993-97), Am. Fedn. of Musicians, Tenn. Music Tchrs. Assn. (adjudicator 1999-2000), Sierra Club. Avocations: hiking, languages, cooking, gardening, astronomy. Office: Cadek Conservatory Music U Tenn Chattanooga 724 Oak St Chattanooga TN 37403-2406

FOUREMAN, NANCY LEE, artist; b. Greenville, Ohio, June 24, 1944; d. LaVern Columbus and Adonia Pauline (Lane) Foreman; m. Richard Allen Foureman, June 29, 1963; children: Stacy Lee, Steven Allen. Student, Ind. State U., 1962; BFA, Miami U. Ohio, Oxford, Ohio, 1963; postgrad., Eldison State Coll., Art Instrn. Schs., Mpls., 1966. Owner, mgr. Studio Gallery, Greenville, 1970—. Bd. dirs. Darke County Fair, Greenville; condr., judge freelance workshops and seminars; mgr. Hatfield's Color Shop, Rockport, Mass., 1988-89; dir., chmn. over 50 exhibits in midwest region; chmn. Nat. Wildlife Exhbn., Greenville Guild Regional Exhbn. One-woman shows include Riverbend Art Ctr., Dayton, Ohio, Ind. U., Middletown Fine Arts Ctr., Parma Art Ctr., Cleve., Indlps. State Mus., Garst Mus., Ohio, Cincinnati Mus. Natural History, Cleve. Mus. Natural History, Ohio State Mus., Richmond Art Mus., Ind.; exhibited in group shows at Am. Painters in Paris, Dayton Painters and Sculptors Exhbn., Hoosier Salon, Indpls., others; represented in permanent collections Cleve. Mus. Natural History, corp. collections; editor Legacy News On-Line Mag.; regional editor Find Art Connoisseur Mag. Trustee Darke County Ctr. for Arts, Darke County Ctr. for Arts, 1988—; cons. Greenville Sch. Bd., 1990—; bd. dirs. Greenville Guild and Theater, 1970-83, Greenville City Art Sch., 1977; chmn. bd. Greenville Art Gallery. Recipient Best of Show award Art Instrn. Schs., 1970, Garst Mus., 1983, Burkner Nat. Exhibit, Troy, Ohio, 1990, David Humphrey Miller award Wassenburg Art Ctr., May Van Landingham merit award Winchester Court House, Agnes T. Lontz merit award for watercolor, pastel award Lima Art Assn., watercolor award Middletown Fine Arts Ctr., Judges Choice award, Oil Painters Am., Chgo., 1992; Susan K. Black grantee. Mem. North Shore Arts Assn., Tri Arts (Dayton, Ohio), Greenville Art Guild (pres. 1975-93), Darke County Agrl. Soc. (bd. dirs., sec. 1977-93), Preble County Art Assn., Art Assn. Richmond (Ind.) (hon.), Dayton Painters and Sculptors, Master Works for Nature Artists, Western Ohio Watercolor Soc., Hoosier Salon, Ind. Plein Air Painters Assn. Avocation: swimming. Home: 6441 Daly Rd Greenville OH 45331-8402 Personal E-mail: rfoureman@skyenet.net.

FOURKILLER, DIANA LYNN, elementary school educator; b. Clinton, Okla., Feb. 15, 1964; d. Nanny Sue Hummingbird; m. Jack A. Fourkiller, Apr. 10, 1982; children: Kristin Allison, Joshua Grant. BS in Edn., Northeastern State U., 1990, MEd in Reading, reading specialist, 1993. Tchr. Zion Elem. Sch., Stilwell, Okla., 1991—. Mem. NEA. Baptist. Avocations: reading, camping, swimming. Office: Zion Elem Sch RR 1 Box 347 Stilwell OK 74960-9710 Home: RR 3 Box 2455 Stilwell OK 74960-9540

FOURNARIS, CHRISTINA MESIRES, lawyer; b. Sept. 17, 1966; AB, Smith Coll., 1988; JD, Cornell Law U., 1991. Bar: Pa. 1991. Ptnr. Morgan, Lewis & Bockius LLP, Phila., asst. leader personal practice group. Mem.: Pa. Bar Inst.-estate law adv. com., Phila. Bar Assn.-probate & trust law sect., ABA-estate & gift tax com., ABA-taxation sect. Office: Morgan Lewis & Bockius LLP 1701 Market St Philadelphia PA 19103 Office Phone: 215-963-5649. Office Fax: 215-963-5001. Business E-Mail: cfournaris@morganlewis.com.

FOURNET, LISA CLARK, music educator; d. William Spiva and Patsy Dunigan Clark; m. Dickens Quin Fournet, May 13, 2000. MusB, U. Miss., 1983; MusM Edn., Miss. State U., 1986. Choral music tchr. Ridgeland H.S., Miss., 2002—, Holmes C.C., Goodman, Miss., 2001—02; music tchr. Neshoba Ctrl. H.S., Philadelphia, Miss., 1995—2000; pvt. piano studio Louisville, Miss., 1986—95; organist/youth choir dir. First Presbyn. Ch., Louisville, 1987—95. Musician teacher. Life mem. Louisville Jr. Aux., Louisville, 1987—2003; regional dir. Miss. Jr. Miss Assn., Meridian, Miss., 1993—95; mem. Lydian Music Club, Philadelphia, Miss., 1995—2000. Recipient Miss Miss. Farm Bur., Miss. Farm Bur. Fedn., 1981. Mem.: Miss. Profl. Educators, Music Educators Nat. Conf., Am. Choral Directors Assn. Avocations: Nascar fan, travel, judging pageants.

FOURNET, PATRICIA SIBLEY, retired secondary school educator; b. Beaumont, Tex., Aug. 21, 1936; d. George W. and Irma Turnbull Sibley; m. Kenneth Leon Fournet, June 26, 1990; 1 child, George Ray Jones. Med, U. Southwestern La., Lafayette, 1975. HS tchr. St. Martin Parish Sch. Bd., St. Martinville, La., 1963—93; missions dir. Evangeline Assn. Vacation Bible Sch., Lafayette, La., 2006. Cons. local bar assn. St. Martin Ville, La., 1972—74; singer Return to Bethlehem, 2005; organist, stage mgr. Our Town, 2006. Author: Experiments and Exercises; singer: (albums) Return to Bethlehem, 2005. Mem. Found. for the Blind, 1995—2005; missions dir. Evangeline Assn. Vacation Bible Sch., Lafayette, La., 2006—; treas. Little Theater, St. Martinville, La., 2002—06; bd. dirs. Evangeline Players, 2002—06. Recipient Outstanding Vol. award, 2004. Mem.: La. Ret. Tchrs. Assn., So. Med. Aux. Soc. Bapt. Achievements include development of a computer science course at the local high school. Avocations: travel, accompanist for community activites, church organist, bridge, walking. Home: 206 Allan St PO Box 224 Saint Martinville LA 70582 Home Fax: 337-394-4118.

FOURNIER, MAUREEN MARY, physical education educator; b. Chgo., Feb. 27, 1952; d. George Joseph and Lauretta Marie (Tangney) Lewis; m. Thomas Joseph Fournier, Sept. 21, 1979; children: Jennifer Lynn, Michele Marie. BS in Edn., No. Ill. U., 1973; MS in Edn., Chgo. State U., 1983. Recreation leader Alsip Park Dist., Ill., 1973-75; tchr. phys. edn. Sch. Dist. 126, Alsip, 1974—. Mem. Alsip Coun. Local 943 IFT, 1973—, pres., 1985—87, 1992—97, 2005—. Mgr. Oak Lawn (Ill.) Girls Softball, 1990—91, 1994—98, sec., 1998, Richard Area Swim Club, 1997—98; mem. internal rev. com. Sch. Dist. 126, Alsip, 1999—2006; NCA com. mem., sec. Richards HS Parent Boosters Club, 2000—. Mem.: AAHPERD, Ill. Assn. Health, Phys. Edn., Recreation and Dance (evaluator Blue Ribbon com.). Avocations: bowling, swimming, reading. Office: Sch Dist 126 Lane Sch 4600 W 123rd St Alsip IL 60803-2522 E-mail: mofournier@sd12.k12.il.us.

FOUSHEE-HIGGS, ROSA, elementary school educator, artist; b. Ramseur, N.C., Sept. 1, 1937; children: Gregory, Carl, Rosemarie, Jeffrey, Rachael. BS in Commerce, N.C. Ctrl. U., Durham, 1958; MA in Psychology, Columbia U., N.Y.C., 1985; postgrad., Coll. S.I., N.Y.C., U. N.C., Greensboro, NYU, Bklyn. Coll., Bank St. Coll., N.Y.C. Tchr. N.Y.C. Pub. Sch. Sys., 1959—99; owner, operator Foushee's Art Studio, Daytona Beach, Fla., 1999—. Author: This Woman's Life, 1985. Counselor ARC, Daytona Beach, 1989, contbr., 1996. Recipient Appreciation Cert., St. Timothy's Learning Ctr., 1991, Svc. Cert., N.Y.C. Bd. Edn., 1999, Svc. award, United Fedn. Tchrs., 1999. Mem.: APA (assoc.), Psi Chi. Democrat. Baptist. Avocations: reading, art, crafts, oil painting. Home: 1320 Redding Ave Daytona Beach FL 32114 Office: Foushees Art Studio 1320 Redding Ave Daytona Beach FL 32114 Office Phone: 386-383-7979.

FOUST, DONNA ELAINE MARSHALL, women's health nurse; b. Sacramento, May 11, 1959; d. Donald H. and Diana Janet (O'Day) Marshall; m. Jennings Franklin Foust, Mar. 29, 1980; children: Andrew Donald, Sheri Diane. LPN, Harriman Vocat. Sch., 1979; ADN, Walter State C.C., 1983. RN, Tenn.; cert. RN first asst., CNOR. Staff nurse labor and delivery Meth. Med. Ctr., Oak Ridge, Tenn., 1979-83, staff nurse oper. rm., 1983-90; 1st asst. ob/gyn office Women's Health Assocs., Oak Ridge, 1988—. Mem. Assn. Oper. Rm. Nurse, RN First Asst. Specialty Assembly. Democrat. Avocations: computers, photography, reading, cross stitch. Home: 2512 Clinton Hwy Powell TN 37849-7613 Office: Westmall Med Park 200 New York Ave Ste 150 Oak Ridge TN 37830-5227 also: 9330 Park West Blvd Ste 300 Knoxville TN 37923-4311 E-mail: whapc@icx.net.

FOUST, JULIE ANN, secondary school educator; d. Claude DeFoe and Jean Stolz Chamberlain; m. Anthony A. Foust, Aug. 15, 1970; children: Danielle Renee Derethik, Blair Allen. BA, Mich. State U., East Lansing, 1967, MA, 1972. Tchr. Warren (Mich.) Consol. Schs., 1967—77; tutorial coord. Children's Ctr., Detroit, 1982—83; tchr. Univ. Liggett Sch., Grosse Pointe, Mich., 1987—. Mem. Mayor's Task Force Prevention of Child Abuse, Detroit, 1980—85; chmn. children and youth com. United Cmty. Svcs., Detroit, 1985; established Emergency Child Care Assistance Fund, Detroit, 1985—; bd. dirs., mem. exec. com. Children's Ctr., Detroit, 1984—90; sec. Horton Bay (Mich.) Club. Mem.: AAUW, Jr. League Detroit, Detroit Inst. Arts. Home: 695 Lincoln Rd Grosse Pointe MI 48230 Office: Univ Liggett Sch 1045 Cook Rd Grosse Pointe MI 48236

FOUT, JEANINE MARIE, social studies educator; b. Lake Forest, Ill., July 10, 1964; d. Wesley Wallace Fout and Judith Marie Boysen. AS in Horticulture, Coll. of Lake County, Grayslake, Ill., 1987; BA in Elem. Edn., Nat. Louis U., Grayslake, 1995; MA in Tchg. and Leadership, St. Xavier U., Chgo., 2003. Elem. tchr. Ill. Floral designer Balmes Flowers Shop and Greenhouse, North Chicago, Ill., 1987—; tchr. 5th grade social studies St. Gilbert Sch., Grayslake, 1997—. Tchr. adviser Lake County Farm Bur., Grayslake, 2006; adviser scrapbook club St. Gilbert Sch., Grayslake, 2005—. Named Lake County Tchr. of Yr., Lake County Farm Bur., 2005, Ill. Tchr. of the Yr. Top 10, Ill. Farm Bur., 2005, 2006; recipient Colonial Williamsburg Fellowship, 2005. Mem.: Lake County Genealogy Soc., Foresters Brancho Lago (v.p. 2004—), Nat. Coun. Social Studies. Roman Catholic. Avocations: genealogy, coin collecting/numismatics, scrapbooks, travel, gardening. Office: St Gilbert Sch 231 E Belvidere Rd Grayslake IL 60030

FOUTS, ELIZABETH BROWNE, psychologist, metals company executive; b. New Orleans, July 5, 1927; d. Donovan Clarence and Mathilde Elizabeth (Hanna) B.; m. James Fremont Fouts, June 19, 1948; children: Elizabeth, Donovan, Alan, James. BA, Tulane U., 1948; MS, N.E. La. U., 1973, postgrad., 1984. Cert. sch. psychologist, La.; cert. reality therapist, La. Instr. spl. edn., psychol. cons. N.E. La. U., Monroe, 1971-73; sch. psychologist Ouachita Parish Schs., Monroe, 1973-87; sec.-treas. Fremont Corp., Monroe, 1967—, Auric Metals Corp., Salt Lake City, 1975-99. Dir. La Fonda Hotel, Santa Fe, N.Mex., 1993—; pres. Sunbelt Reality Therapist, 1989-90. Exec. bd. Episc. Diocese Western La., 1986-87, 99-2002, commn. ministry, 1987-94; res. family resource ctr. N.E. La. U., 1993-94; bd. dirs. Assn. for Retarded Citizens, Monroe, 1982-88, treas., 1984, pres., 1987. Named Outstanding Sch. Psychologist, State of La., 1987. Mem. Nat. Assn. Sch. Psychologists, La. Sch. Psychologists Assn. (pres. 1978-79, Outstanding Woman Sch. Psychologist 1984, newsletter editor 1988-93). Avocations: walking, swimming. Home: PO Box 7070 Monroe LA 71211-7070 Office: 4002 Bon Aire Dr Monroe LA 71203-3015

FOWLER, ALYCE MILTON, health facility administrator; BSBA, Almeda Coll.; MBA, Ea. Conn. State U. Cert. med. practice exec. Regional supr., acting adminstr. Kaiser Permanente, 1980—85; dir. vol. svcs. Windham Hosp., 1985—88; pvt. practice, 1988—92; regional mgr. HealthNet Corp., Oakland, NJ, 1992—94; practices mgr. St. Francis Hosp. and Med. Ctr., Hartford, Conn., 1994—96; dir. physician practice mgmt., dir. med. practice ops., physician recruiter Englewood (NJ) Hosp. and Med. Ctr., 1996—97; exec. adminstr. Fairfield County Allergy, Asthma and Immunology Assoc., 2000—04; dir. physician svcs. Ea. Conn. Cardiology, 2004—06; dir., health ctr. Champlain Valley Physicians Hosp., Plattsburgh, NY, 2006—. Com. mem. J. Paul Getty Trust Preservation. Named Mgr. of Yr., HealthNet Corp., 1993—94; recipient Caregiver award, Conn. Hosp., 1986, Conn. Connie Regional award, Am. Cancer Soc., 1986—87, Merit award, EastConn, 1986—87. Mem.: Conn. Women in Health Care Mgmt., Conn. Med. Group Mgmt. Assn., Am. Coll. Med. Practice Execs., Med. Group Mgmt. Assn. (cert.). Avocations: pottery, art. Home: 159 Prospect Cove Plattsburgh NY 12901 E-mail: ampersky@aol.com.

FOWLER, BETH, actress; b. Jersey City, Nov. 1, 1940; Actor: (Broadway plays) Gantry, 1970, A Little Night Music, 1974, 1600 Pennsylvania Avenue, 1976, Peter Pan, 1979—81, Baby, 1984, Take Me Along, 1985, Teddy & Alice, 1987—88, Sweeney Todd, 1989—90 (Tony nominee best actress musical, 1990), Beauty and the Beast, 1994 (LA Ovation award), Bells Are Ringing, 2001, The Boy From Oz, 2003 (Tony nominee best featured actress musical, 2004). Office: Imperial Theatre 249 W 45th St New York NY 10036

FOWLER, CAROL W., journalist, educator; b. Miw., Mar. 20, 1934; d. Alphonse John and Mildred Wilke (Mueller) Winter; m. T. Kenneth Fowler, Aug. 18, 1956; children: T. Kenneth Jr., John, Ellen Jones. BS, U. Wis., Madison, 1955. Feature writer, travel editor, arts writer, freelance journalist Contra Costa Times, Walnut Creek, Calif., 1976—99; instr. Emeritus Coll. of Diablo Valley Coll., Pleasant Hill, Calif., 1999—. Sec. Soc. Am. Travel Writers, Raleigh, NC, 2003—; bd. dirs. Soc. Am. Travel Writers Found. Author: Contributions of Women: Art, 1976, Daisy Hooee Nampeyo: The Story of an American Indian, 1978, Contributions of Women: Dance, 1979, Insiders' Guide to Berkeley and the East Bay, 2003; editor: 100 Best All-Inclusive Resorts of the World, 3d edit., 2004; co-editor: three cookbooks. Chair City of Walnut Creek Arts Commn., 2005—. Recipient Lowell Thomas award for Best Newspaper Travel Section in Circulation Category, gold, 1997, Lowell Thomas award for Best Newspaper Travel Section in Circulation Category, silver, 1999, Northern Lights award for Best Story on Can., 3d pl., 1999, multiple writing awards, Soc. Am. Travel Writers, We. chpt., 1996—2004, Frank Riley award, 1997, 1999. Mem.: San Fransisco Mus. Modern Art, Fine Arts Mus. San Fransisco, Diablo Regional Arts Assn. Avocations: reading, photography. Home: 221 Grover La Walnut Creek CA 94596 Personal E-mail: carolfow@aol.com.

FOWLER, FLORA DAUN, retired lawyer; b. Washington, Aug. 11, 1923; d. Herman Hartwell and Flora Elizabeth (Adams) Sanford; m. Kenneth Leo Fowler, Aug. 22, 1941; children: Kenneth Jr., Michael, Kathleen, Daun, Jonathan, Colin, Kevin, James, Shawn, Maureen, Wendelyn, Liam, Tobias, Melanie. Student, Wilson Tchrs. Coll., 1940-41; AA, U. Md., 1973; JD, U. Balt., 1976. Bar: Fla. 1977, U.S. Dist. Ct. (mid. dist.) Fla. 1979, U.S. Ct. Appeals (5th and 11th cirs.) 1981. Staff atty. Cen. Fla. Legal Services Inc., Daytona Beach, 1978-80, mng. atty., 1980-81; pvt. practice, Daytona Beach, 1981-93; ret., 2001. Past editor Seabrook Acres Citizens' League Newsletter; columnist Bowie Express & Community Times; contbr. poems to New Voices in American Poetry, 1974. V.p. Seabrook (Md.) Acres Citizens League, 1970; past v.p. Prince Georges County Civic Fedn., Md.; past unit chmn. League of Women Voters, Prince Georges County; past pres., v.p., publicity chmn. Lanham-Bowie Dem. Club, Seabrook. Recipient Evening Star Trophy award Prince Georges County Civic Fedn., 1969. Mem. Fla. S. Ct. Hist. Soc. Democrat. Roman Catholic. Avocations: swimming, creative writing, cursillo. Personal E-mail: daunfowler@msn.com.

FOWLER, JOANNA S., chemist; b. Aug. 9, 1942; BA, U. South Fla., 1964; PhD in Chem., U. Colo., 1967. Sr. rsch. assoc. U. East Anglia, Norwich, England, 1968; rsch. assoc., med. dept. Brookhaven Nat. Lab., 1969—71, assoc. chemist, med. dept., scientist, 1974—76, chemist, chem. dept., 1976—88, sr. chemist, 1988, dir., Ctr. Translational Neuroimaging. Adj. prof. chem. dept. and biomedical engrng. dept. Stony Brook U. Named Disting. Basic Scientist of Yr., Acad. Molecular Imaging, 2005; recipient Ernest Orlando Lawrence award, Dept. Energy, 1999, Alfred P. Wolf award, Soc. Nuclear Imaging in Drug Devel., 2000, Glen T. Seaborg award, nuclear and radiochemistry, Am. Chemical Soc., 2002. Mem. Soc. Nuclear Medicine, Am. Chem. Soc. (co-recipient Gustavus John Esselen Award for Chemistry in the Pub. Interest, northeastern sect., 1988, Francis P. Garvin & John M. Olin Medal, 1998), Nat. Acad. Sciences (mem. 2003). Office: Brookhaven Nat Lab Chem Dept Bldg 555A Upton NY 11973 Office Phone: 516-344-4365. E-mail: fowler@bnl.gov.

FOWLER, KAREN JOY, writer; b. Bloomington, Indiana; BA in Political Science, MA in Political Science, Berkeley U. Writer-in-residence Cleveland State U., 1990; instructor Clarion Writers Workshop, Mich. State U.; instructor & administrator Imagination Workshop, Cleveland State U.; instructor Stanford U., 1996—98. Published short stories & poetry in numerous magazines & journals including Asimov's, The Centennial Review, The California Quarterly, The Ohio Journal. Author: Peripheral Vision, 1990, Artificial Things, 1991, Letters from Home, 1991, Sarah Canary, 1998, The Sweetheart Season, 1998, Black Glass, 1999, Sister Noon, 2001, The Jane Austen Book Club, 2004, (short stories) Praxis, 1985, The Lake was Full of Artificial Things, 1985, War of the Roses, 1985, The Poplar Street Study, 1985, The Natives, 1985, Face Value, 1986, Wild Boys, 1986, The Dragon's Head, 1986, Contention, 1986, The Faithful Companion at Forty, 1987, Lily Red, 1988, Heartland, 1988, Duplicity, 1989, Game Night at the Fox and Goose, 1989, Faded Roses, 1989, Lieserl, 1990, The Dark, 1991, The Elizabeth Complex, 1996, Standing Room Only, 1997, Reefers, 1997. Recipient John W. Campbell award best new sci. fiction writer, 1987, Nebula nominee, 1987, 1990, 1991, 1992, 1997, 1998. Office: c/o Putnam Books 375 Hudson St New York NY 10014

FOWLER, LINDA MCKEEVER, health facility administrator, educator; b. Greensburg, Pa., Aug. 7, 1948; d. Clay and Florence Elizabeth (Smith) McKeever; m. Timothy L. Fowler, Sept. 13, 1969 (div. July 1985). Nursing diploma, Presbyn. U. Hosp., Pitts., 1969; BSN, U. Pitts., 1976, M in Nursing Adminstrn., 1980; D in Pub. Adminstrn., Nova U., 1985. Supr., head nurse Presbyn. Univ. Hosp., Pitts., 1969-76; mem. faculty Western Pa. Hosp. Sch. Nursing, Pitts., 1976-79; acute care coord. Mercy Hosp., Miami, 1980-81; asst. adminstr. nursing North Shore Med. Ctr., Miami, 1981-84, v.p. patient care, 1984-88, Golden Glades Regional Med. Ctr., Miami, 1988-89, Humana Hosp.-South Broward, Hollywood, Fla., 1989-91, assoc. exec. dir. nursing; v.p., chief nursing officer Columbia Regional Med. Ctr., Bayonet Point, 1991-96; COO, chief nursing officer Greenbrier Valley Med. Ctr., 1996-97; quality mgmt. coord. Greenbrier Valley Hospice, 1997-98; pvt. practice healthcare cons., 1998-99; chief nursing officer Marlboro Park Hosp., 1999—2002; pvt. practice healthcare cons., 2002—; chief clin. officer Intermedical Hosp. of S.C., 2003—. Mem. adj. faculty Barry U., Miami, 1984-97, Broward C.C., Ft. Lauderdale, 1984-85, Nova U., 1986-87; cons. Strategic Health Devel. Inc., Miami Shores, Fla., 1986-90, So. Coll., Cleveland, Tenn., 1995-96. Dept. HEW trainee, 1976, 79-80; bd. dirs. Pasco County Am. Cancer Soc., 1992-95. Mem. Am. Orgn. Nurse Execs. (legis. com. 1988-90), Fla. Orgn. Nurse Execs. (bd. dirs. 1986-88), S.C. Orgn. Nurse Execs., South Fla. Nurse Adminstrs. Assn. (sec. 1983-84, bd. dirs. 1984-86), U. Pitts. Alumni Assn., Presbyn. U. Alumni Assn., Portuguese Water Dog

Club Am. (bd. dirs. 1988-89), Ft. Lauderdale Dog Club (bd. dirs. 1981-82, 83-85, v.p. 1982-83), Am. Kennel Club (dog judge), Moore County Kennel Club, Sigma Theta Tau. Lutheran. Office: Taylor at Marion Sts Columbia SC 29220 E-mail: lfowler@intermedical.us.

FOWLER, SANDRA LYNN, poet; b. West Columbia, W.Va., Feb. 4, 1937; d. Okey Donly and Ramona Jean Fowler. Author: In the Shape of Sun, 1972—73, The Colors Cry in Rain, 1983, Ever Sunset, 1992; assoc. editor: Ocarina, 1978—89; contbr. poetry to jours. Founding mem. Holocaust Meml. Mus., Washington; hon. mem. steering com. Clinton-Gore Campaign, Washington, 1991, 1995, Gore-Lieberman Campaign, Washington, 1999. Nominee Pushcart prize, 1998; named to Internat. Poetry Hall Fame, 1997; recipient Wall of Tolerance honoree. Mem.: Nat. Women's History Mus. (charter mem., Internat. Poetry Hall of Fame 1997—). Democrat. Avocations: reading, music, collecting classical movies. Home: Rte 1 Box 50 West Columbia WV 25287 Personal E-mail: sandrafowler7@hotmail.com.

FOWLER, SUE ANN, elementary school educator; d. Dale H. and Judy A. Anderson; m. John B. Fowler, Sept. 27, 1997; children: Wyatt Jones, Jesse Dale. BS in Elem. Edn., U. Wis., Stevens Point, 1995, EdM, 2006. Cert. elem. edn. tchr. Dept. Pub. Instrn., 1995, math. edn. tchr. Dept. Pub. Instrn., 1995. Jr. high tchr. Sch. Dist. Auburndale, Wis., 1996—. Jr. high cheerleading advisor Auburndale Sch. Dist., 1997—2000, jr. high student coun. advisor, 1998—; jr. high yearbook advisor Sch. Dist. Auburndale, 2005—; organizer, chairperson area math. competition JH Math League Contest; presenter in field. Named Tchr. of Yr., Ctrl. Wis. Uniserve Coun., 2002. Mem.: Auburndale Edn. Assn. (bldg. rep. 2004—, chairperson sunshine com. 2004, chairperson pub. rels. 2005—), Nat. Coun. Tchrs. Math., Wis. Math. Coun. Office: Auburndale School District PO Box 190 Auburndale WI 54412 Office Phone: 715-652-2115. Office Fax: 715-652-6322. Business E-Mail: sfowler@aubschools.com.

FOWLKES, NANCY LANETTA PINKARD, social worker; d. Amos Malone and Nettie (Barnett) Pinkard; m. Vester Guy Fowlkes, June 4, 1955 (dec. 1965); 1 child, Wendy Denise. BA, Bennett Coll., 1946; MA, Syracuse U., 1952; MSW, Smith Coll., 1963; MPA, Pace U., 1982. Dir. publicity Bennett Coll., Greensboro, NC, 1946-47, 49-50; asst. editor Va. Edn. Bull. ofcl. organ Va. State Tchrs. Assn., Richmond, 1950-52; asst. office mgr. Cmty. Svc. Soc., NYC, 1952-55; social caseworker, asst. supr. Dept. Social Svcs. Westchester County, White Plains, NY, 1959-67, supr. adoption svcs., 1967-77, supr. adoption and foster care, 1977-89. Mem. adv. bd. White Plains Adult Edn. Sch. First v.p. Eastview Jr. HS, 1970-71; area chmn. White Plains Cmty. Chest, 1964; sec. Mt. Vernon Concert Group, 1952-54; fund raising co-chmn. Urban League Guild of Westchester, 1967; pres. White Plains Interfaith Coun., 1972-74; pres. northeastern jurisdiction United Meth. Ch., 1988-92; chmn. adminstrv. bd. Meth. Ch., 1970-72, 82-83, vice chmn., 1978-80, vice chmn. trustees, 1973-77, treas., 1978-83; lay spkr., v.p. Met. dist. United Meth. Women, 1977-79, exec. bd. NY conf.; NY conf. rep. Upper Atlantic Regional Sch., 1981-83, mem. nominating com., 1982-83, trustee NY conf., 1982-88, pres. NY conf., 1983-87; bd. dirs. Global Ministries United Meth. Ch., 1988-96, women's divsn., 1988-96, v.p., chair sect. finance women's divsn., 1992-96, supt., 1997—, chair program divsn. NY conf., 1989-93; v.p. superintendency commn. Met. North Dist., 1997—; chair Episcopal residence NY Conf. Episcopacy Com., 1997-2002; mem. NY Conf. Bd. Ordained Ministry, 2000—, Bishop's Ptnrs. in Mission Leadership Coun., 2005—, mem. nominating com. N.Y. conf., 2006—, mem. bd. laity N.Y. conf., 2006—; chmn. Dist. Coun. on Ministry, 2002-05, lay leader 2005; bd. dirs. Family Svc. Westchester, Bethel Meth. Home, Ossining, NY, White Plains YWCA, 1985-93, Scarritt Bennett Ctr., Nashville, 1990-2000, Gum Moon Women's Residence, San Francisco, 1992-96, White Plains-Greenburg NAACP, 1993-98. Mem. NASW, Acad. Cert. Social Workers, Jack and Jill of Am. Inc. (chpt. pres. 1954-56, regional sec.-treas. 1967-71), Nat. Bus. and Profl. Women's Club (chpt. sec. 1954-56), Internat. Platform Assn., Theta Sigma Phi (sec.-treas.), Zeta Nu Omega, Alpha Kappa Alpha (pres. 1960-64, treas. 1975-78), Regency Bridge Club (pres. 1963-65). Home: 107 Valley Rd White Plains NY 10604-2316 E-mail: npfvalley@aol.com.

FOX, BETH A., music educator; b. Quincy, Ill., June 15, 1966; d. Dean and Carolyn Dedert; m. Dennis Fox, Sept. 3, 1994; children: William, Abigail. MusB, So. Ill. U., Carbondale, 1988; MEd, CCNY, 2005. Music tchr. Indian River County Sch. Dist., Vero Beach, Fla., 1988—93, Indian Hills Exempted Village Sch. Dist., Cin., 1994—97. Organist Christ Episcopal Ch., Sparkill, NY, 2002—. Mem.: Autism Soc. Am. Office: South Orangetown Ctrl Sch Dist 160 Van Wyck Rd Blauvelt NY 10913 Office Phone: 845-680-1300. E-mail: bfox@socsd.org.

FOX, BETTY, financial services executive; b. Chgo., July 30, 1935; d. Abraham and Lucille (Manesewitz) Axelrod; children: Deborah Kravitz, Esther Fox, Adam Fox. Student, U. Ill., Chgo., 1953; CLU, The Am. Coll., 1989, ChFC, 1990. Art tchr. Suburban Fine Arts Ctr., Highland Park, Ill., 1963-75; commodities broker Rosenthal et al, Chgo., 1975-78; registered rep. AXA Advisors, LLC, Northbrook, Ill., 1978—2004; self employed, 2005—. Painter represented in nat. collection (blue ribbon award 1971). Bd. dirs., past pres., art tchr./painter Suburban Fine Arts Ctr., Highland Park, Ill., 1962—; vol Jewish Vocat. Svc., Chgo.; active Alliance for Mental Illness; mem. devel. com. Las Vegas Art Mus.; mem. Guggenheim Mu. Recipient Purchase prize Kemper Ins. Co., Nat. Wine Art Competition. Mem. Nat. Assn. Life Underwriters, Million Dollar Round Table, Chgo. Women Ins. Assn. (treas. 1989), Nat. Assn. Women Life Underwriters, Lake County Life Underwriters, 500 Club (pres. 1990, agy. CLU advisor 1989-92, chmn. Agts. Forum 1992-94), Axa Group.

FOX, CARMEN ALICE, retired medical/surgical nurse; b. St. Louis, Mo., July 18, 1944; d. Joseph and Alice Betker; children: Jacinta, Alicia. RN Calif. Nurse ICU, critical care unit various hosps., Calif., 1975—2000; ret., 2000. Author: (children's books) Hodgepodge the Hedgehog, 2004, Hodgepodge and Rose, 2004, The Return of Hodgepodge, 2004. Named to Jazz/Art Festival, 2006; recipient Hon. mention, West Colo. Art Ctr., 2005. Mem.: ART Ctr. (vol. 2004—06), Newcomers Club (v.p. 2006). Episcopalian. Avocations: writing, art, gardening, art collecting, hiking. Home: Condo 3 251 Beacon Ct Grand Junction CO 81503

FOX, DEBORAH LEE, elementary school educator; b. New Orleans, Nov. 24, 1957; d. Jerry Wallace and Joyce Lapouble Lee; m. Patrick Kevin Fox, June 8, 1979; 1 child, Rebecca Lee. BA, U. New Orleans, 1979, MEd, 1994. Nat. bd. cert. tchr. 2000. Tchr. Jefferson Parish Sch. Bd., Gretna, La., 1979—81, St. Mary Magdalen Sch., Metairie, La., 1987—93, Jefferson Parish Sch. Bd., Harvey, La., 1994—. Adj. instr. U. New Orleans, 2002—05; cons. State Dept. Edn., Baton Rouge, 2002—05. Sunday sch. tchr. St. Mary Magdalen, 1988—93. Republican. Catholic. Avocations: swimming, reading, bicycling.

FOX, DEBRA L., educational association administrator, business owner; m. Jules Rosen; children: Adam, Josh, Daniel, Rebecca. Reporter, anchor WTAE-TV, 1976—86; founder, owner, pres., CEO Fox Learning Systems Inc. (formerly Fox FarSight Prodn.), 1997—. Named One of Pa. Best 50 Women in Bus., 2004. Office: Fox Learning Systems Inc Manor Oak II 1910 Cochran Rd Ste 920 Pittsburgh PA 15220 Office Phone: 412-531-1889. Business E-Mail: debra@foxlearningsystems.com.

FOX, DIANE PORRETTA, nursing educator; d. Marvin and Mary Lou Porretta; m. Robert Curtis Fox, Nov. 7, 1975; children: Jesse Thomas Morgan, Patrick Robert. AS with honors, Washtenaw C.C., 1978; BA magna cum laude, Siena Heights Coll., 1989; BSN magna cum laude, U. Mich., 1997; MS in Nursing, Ea. Mich. U., 2003. Cert. tchg. healthcare sys., Ea. Mich. U., 2001; asthma educator Nat. Asthma Educator Certification Bd., 2003. Staff nurse, contingent ecmo nurse U. Mich. Hosp., Ann Arbor, 1990—; part-time faculty Monroe County C.C., 1990—2004; reg. respiratory therapist U. Mich., 1995—2000; staff nurse U. Mich.-Mich. Congenital Heart Ctr., 1997—99; asst. prof. nursing Sch. Nursing, Ea. Mich. U., Ypsilanti, 2004—. Dir. cardiopulmonary svcs. Saline Cmty. Hosp., Mich., 1988—95; adj. faculty Washtenaw C.C., Ann Arbor, 2000—04; presenter in field; ednl. leadership doctorate cohort Ea. Mich. U., 2005. Vol. Big Bros./Big Sisters, Adrian, Mich., 1997—2002. Named Outstanding Grad. Nursing Student, Ea. Mich. U., 2003; Joan Rodman Schrandt Nursing scholar, Saline Cmty. Hosp., 1995—97, Angell scholar, U. Mich., 1997. Mem.: AACN, Nat. Bd. Respiratory Care, Am. Assn. Respiratory Care, Transcultural Nursing Soc., Am. Assn. Adult and Continuing Edn., Stratford Shakespeare Soc., Golden Key Nat. Honor Soc., Sigma Theta Tau (assoc.; v.p. 2002—04, rsch. award 2003). Avocation: master gardener. Office: Ea Mich U 306 Marshall Ypsilanti MI 48197 Office Phone: 734-487-2154. Business E-Mail: dfox2@emich.edu.

FOX, DONNA BRINK, music educator; b. Pipestone, Minn., June 7, 1950; d. Carroll Marion and Nellie (De Groot) Brink; m. George Bernard Fox, Aug. 30, 1975; 1 child, Elizabeth Ann. BA, Calvin Coll., 1972; MMus, Ohio U., 1975; PhD, Ohio State U., 1982; postgrad. Mgmt. Devel. Program, Harvard U., 1996. Music tchr. Calvin Christian Schs., Grand Rapids, Mich., 1972-74; vis. instr. Ohio U., Athens, 1975-76; asst. prof. Ill. State U., Normal, 1980-84; from asst. prof. to prof. Eastman Sch. Music, Rochester, NY, 1984—98, Eisenhart Prof. Music Edn., 1998—, chair music edn. dept., 1992—2001, dir. summer session, 1998—2000, dean acad. affairs, 2004—05, 2006—. Bd. dirs. Aesthetic Edn. Inst., Rochester, NY, 1994—2000; cons. in field. Recipient Eisenhart award for disting. tchg., Eastman Sch. Music, 1996, Outstanding Alumni award, Ohio U., 1994, 2005, Parents Choice Approved award, 2004; grantee Young Audiences of Rochester, 1994, 1995. Mem.: ASCD, Music Tchrs. Nat. Assn. (early childhood chair NY chpt. 2004—06), NY State Sch. Music Assn. (chair early childhood group 1991—95), Am. Orff-Schulwerk Assn. (rsch. adv. rev. panelist 1992—96, devel. com. 2004—), Music Educators Nat. Conf. (early childhood spl. rsch. interest group 1986—90, interest group chair 1986—90, grantee 2002), Nat. Assn. Edn. Young Children, Am. Edn. Rsch. Assn. Office: Eastman Sch Music 26 Gibbs St Rochester NY 14604-2599 Home: 8 Cambridge Cir Victor NY 14564 Office Phone: 585-274-1020. E-mail: dbfox@esm.rochester.edu.

FOX, ELEANOR MAE COHEN, lawyer, educator, writer; b. Trenton, NJ, Jan. 18, 1936; d. Herman and Elizabeth (Stein) Cohen; children: Douglas Anthony, Margot Alison, Randall Matthew. BA, Vassar Coll., 1956; LLB, NYU, 1961. Bar: N.Y. 1961, U.S. Dist. Ct. N.Y. 1964, U.S. Supreme Ct. 1965. Ptnr. Simpson Thacher & Bartlett, 1970—76, of counsel, 1976—; prof. Law Sch. NYU, N.Y.C., 1976—, Walter J. Derenberg prof. trade regulation, 1999—. Mem. Pres. Carter's Nat. Commn. Rev. Antitrust Laws and Procedures, 1978-79; mem. adv. bd. Bur. Nat. Affairs Antitrust and Trade Regulation Reporter, 1977—; trustee NYU Law Ctr. Found., 1974-92; exec. com. Lawyers' Com. Civil Rights Under Law, 1988—, bd. dirs.; mem. Coun. Fgn. Rels., 1993—; mem. Pres. Clinton's internat. competition policy adv. com. to advise the U.S. Atty. Gen., 1997-2000; lectr. on antitrust law, European Union law, world competition, trade, and econ. devel. Author (with Byron E. Fox): Corporate Acquisitions and Mergers, 1968, 1970, 1973, 1981, 2005; author: (novel) W.L., Esquire, 1977; author: (with Lawrence A. Sullivan and Rudolph Peritz) Cases and Materials, U.S. Antitrust in Global Context, 2000; author: (with G. Bermann, R. Goebel, W. Davey) European Union Law, Cases and Materials, The Competition Law of the European Union--Cases and Materials, 2002; author: (with J. Fingleton, D. Neven, P. Seabright) Competition Policy and the Transformation of Central Europe, 1996; mem. editl. bd. NY Law Jour., 1976—99, Antitrust Bull., 1986—, Rev. Indsl. Orgn., 1990—2001, EEC Merger Control Reporter, 1992—, Gaceta Juridica de la CE y de la Competencia, 1992—2001, World Competition: Law and Economics Rev., 1999—, Inst. for Consumer Antitrust Studies, 2002—. Fellow Am. Bar Found., N.Y. Bar Found.; mem. ABA (chmn. merger com. antitrust sect. 1974-77, chmn. publs. com. 1977-78, chmn. Sherman Act com. 1978-79, coun. antitrust sect. 1979-83, 90-94, vice chmn. antitrust sect. 1992-94, chair NAFTA Task Force, 1993-99), N.Y. State Bar Assn. (chmn. antitrust sect. 1978-79, exec. com. antitrust sect. 1979-83), Fed. Bar Coun. (trustee 1974-76, v.p. 1976-78), Assn. of Bar of City of N.Y. (v.p. 1989-90, exec. com. 1977-81, chmn. trade regulation com. 1973-76, lawyer advt. com. 1976-77, chmn. com. on U.S. in global economy, 1991-94), Am. Law Inst., Assn. Am. Law Schs. (chmn. sect. antitrust and econ. regulation 1981-83), NYU Law Alumni Assn. (bd. dirs. 1974-79, 87-91), Am. Fgn. Law Assn. (v.p. 1979-82, 98-2001). Business E-Mail: eleanor.fox@nyu.edu.

FOX, INGRID, curator; b. Shoemaker, Calif., June 14, 1945; d. Mel V. and Margaret (Hubert) Allex; m. Frederick B. Fox Jr., Sept. 1, 1973; children: Vanessa Verena, Frederick Bain. AD in Design, Parsons Sch. Design, N.Y.C., 1968; BFA, The New Sch., N.Y.C., 1977. Graphic designer Pfizer, Inc., NYC, 1988-1992, curator, 1992—2004, Gallery at Nicholas F. Rizzo Fine Arts, Chatham, NJ, 2004—; ind. curator/art advisor, 2004—. Designer Montgomery Winecoff & Assocs., N.Y.C., 1969—75., 1976—87. Mem.: Art Table, Nat. Art Exhbns. by the Mentally Ill (bd. mem.). Episcopalian. Avocations: crafts, designing. Home and Office: 22 Pomander Walk Ridgewood NJ 07450-3711

FOX, JEANNE MARIE, lawyer; b. Phila., May 30, 1952; d. Samuel Cooper and Palmira Caroline (Ungerbuehler) F.; m. Stephan DeMicco, Sept. 29, 1979. BA, Rutgers U., New Brunswick, 1975; JD, Rutgers U., Camden, 1979; completed Program for State and Local Govt. Execs., Harvard U., 1990. Letter carrier U.S. Post Office, Wildwood, 1971, Delran, 1973, Willingboro, 1976; intern U.S. Dept. of Environ. Protection, Edison, Phila., 1974, 77; law clerk Bd. of Pub. Utilities, Newark, N.J., 1978, N.J. Supr. Court, Camden, N.J., 1978, 79; policy dir. N.J. Democrat. State Com., Trenton, N.J., 1979-80; atty. N.J. Office of the Sec. of State, 1980-81; regulatory officer N.J. Bd. Pub. Utilities, Newark, 1981-85, dep. dir., 1985-87; dir. N.J. Bd. of Pub. Utilities, Newark, 1987-90, sr. advisor for policy and mgmt., 1990-91; chief of staff N.J. Dept. of Environ. Protection and Energy, Trenton, 1991-92; dep. commr. N.J. Dept. Environ. Protection and Energy, Trenton, 1992-93, commr., 1993-94, commr. Delaware River Basin Commn., 1991-94; regional adminstr. Region II, EPA, N.Y.C., 1994-2001. Vis. lectr. in pub. and internat. affairs Woodrow Wilson Sch., Princeton U., 2001; vis. disting. lectr. Bloustein Sch. Planning & Pub. Policy Rutgers U., 2001; pres. N.J. Bd. Pub. Utilities, Newark, 2002—. Active Commn. on Status of Women, Middlesex, 1985—94, chmn., 1985—89; bd. dirs. Douglass Coll. Assoc. Alumnae, 1986—2001, 2003—; trustee Rutgers U., 1989—2001, trustee emerita, 2003—; mem. N.J. Commn. on Sex Discrimination in Statutes, 1989—94; bd. dirs. Girl Scouts Coun. at Del.-Raritan, 2004—; co-chair devel. com. Del.-Raritan coun. Girl Scouts USA, 2001—; del. Dem. Nat. Conf., 1992; pres. Middlesex County Women's Polit. Caucus, 1984—86; v.p. Nat. Women's Polit. Caucus, 1991—94, mem. steering and adminstrn. coms., 1989—94; chmn. Dem. Task Force Women's Polit. Caucus, NJ, 1991—94; co-chair edn. and tng. com. Women's Polit. Caucus of N.J., 2001—; pres. Women's Polit. Caucus N.J., 1988—91, bd. dirs., 2001—; del. Dem. Nat. Conf., 2004. Named Outstanding Young Woman NJ, NJ Woman of Achievement, NJ Women's Clubs and Douglass Coll., 1986, Jerseyan of Week, Star Ledger, 1986, Bus. and Profl. Woman of Yr., Bus. and Profl. Women, 1993, Environmentalist of the Yr., NJ Environ. Lobby, 2001; recipient Alumni Meritorious Svc. award Rutgers U. Alumni Fedn., 1991, award Douglass Soc., 1994, Waterfront Visionary award NY League Conservation Voters, 2000, Barbara Boggs Sigmund award Women's Polit. Caucus, NJ, 2000, Corwin award Douglass Coll., 2002; named to Rutger U. Hall of Disting. Alumni, 1997. Mem. NJ State Bar Assn., Rutgers Sch. of Law Alumni Assn. Democrat. Home: 227 New York Ave New Brunswick NJ 08901-1715 Office: NJ Bd Pub Utilities Two Gateway Ctr Newark NJ 07102

FOX, JENNIFER JOY, artist, educator; b. Lancaster, Pa. d. Max III and Linda Jane Fox. AA Visual Art and Photography, Harrisburg Area C.C., Pa., 1992; grad. cum laude, Towson U., Md., 2000. Asst. mgr. Md. Inst. Coll. Art, Balt., 1994—98; technician/photo lab. Balt., 1998; camp counselor Cmty. Arts Towson U., 1998—2000; substitute tchr. Balt. County Sch., 2000—; long-term substitute tchr. Parkville Mid. Sch., 2001; tchr. Perryville H.S., 2001—. Vol. Pets on Wheels, 1996—98, Lancaster County Hist. Soc., 1993—94; vol. student mentor, 2001—; camp counselor Nature Camp, 2001—02; mem. Cecil County Arts Coun. Charlette W. Newcombe scholar, 1998, 99, Hope Tchrs. scholar, 1999-2000, German Soc. Md. grantee, 1999-2000, Mac iBook technology grantee, 2002- Mem. AAUW, NEA, Md. SPCA (vol. 1996-2006), Md. Art Edn. Assn., Harrisburg Area C.C. Alumni, Nat. Art Edn. Assn Avocations: photography, dog walking, hiking, coaching tennis, interior decorating. Home: 834 Angel Valley CT Edgewood MD 21040-2181 Office Phone: 410-996-6000. Personal E-mail: jjoyfox@aol.com. Business E-Mail: JFox@ccps.org.

FOX, KELLY DIANE, financial advisor; b. Brockton, Mass., Sept. 9, 1959; d. James H. and Betty Jane (Calloway) F.; m. Alan David Goldberg, July 6, 1985; 1 child, Andrew Jason BA, Allegheny Coll., 1980; postgrad. Bus. Adminstrn., Suffolk U., 1983—84; student, Temple U., London, 1978, Syracuse U., 1979. Cert. fin. planner practitioner. Asst. mgr. Casual Male, Braintree, Mass., 1980, Hit or Miss, Braintree, 1981—82; merchandiser Foxmoor, West Bridgewater, Mass., 1982; distbr. Hill's Dept. Stores, Canton, Mass., 1982—85; asst. buyer BJ's Wholesale Club, Natick, Mass., 1985—92; advanced advisor team, personal fin. advisor Am. Express Fin. Advisors, 1993—. Mem. steering com. Am. Express Fin. Advisors Boston, diversity chair 1995-96; mem. spkrs. bur. Women's Union, 1997-2001; contbr. ADVICE + program State Atty. Gen's. Office for Elder Affairs; guest lectr. MBA in a Day program Wheaton Coll.; mem. Mass. Dept. Edn. Gifted and Talented Adv. Coun., 1999-2002; founder Women's Resource Room, 1995-97; cofounder The Women's Connection, 2001-2002; founding bd. dirs., treas. Women at Work Mus., 2003—; founding bd. dirs. Young Women's Fin. Network, 2004; mem. supervisory com. Nation's Heritage Fed. Credit Union, Attleboro, Mass. Contbr. columns in newspapers. Treas. Attleboro Area Coun. Children, 1993—2006, pres., 2006—, bd. dirs., 1993—2006, Attleboro Area Parents Anonymous, 1996, New Hope, 1996—98; cheerleading coach Avon H.S., Mass., 1982—83; co-chair enrichment program Falls Elem. Sch., 1994—95, 1997—98; mem. John Woodcock Sch. Coun., 1993—94; vol. Foxborough Regional Charter Sch. SABIS. Recipient Woman of Achievement award, Attleboro Area Bus. and Profl. Women, 2003, Athena award, 2004, Good Neighbor award, North Attleboro/Plainville C. of C., 2006. Methodist. Avocations: theater, travel, bell choir, art galleries. Office Phone: 508-695-2336. Business E-Mail: Kelly.D.Fox@AMPF.com.

FOX, LESLIE B., real estate company executive; MBA, JD, U. Denver. Exec. mgmt. positions NHP, Inc.; sr. mgmt. positions Asset, Investors Corp., Comml. Assets, Inc., 1993—96, pres., 1996—97; exec. v.p., COO, exec. v.p., investment mgmt. Lexford Residential Trust, 1997—99; pres., Lexford divsn. Equity Residential, Chgo., 1999—2001, exec. v.p., 0999—, chief info. officer, 2001—. Office: Equity Residential 2 N Riverside Plaza Chicago IL 60606

FOX, LORRAINE ESTHER, psychologist, human services consultant; b. S.I., N.Y., Aug. 27, 1941; d. Charles Frederick and Dorothy Elizabeth (Clohessy) F. BA, Northeastern Ill. U., 1973, MA, 1976; PhD in Clin. Psychology, Profl. Sch. Psychol. Studies, San Diego, 1989. Cert. in child care; cert. counselor and contract instr. U. Calif., Davis. Exec. dir. The Harbour, Des Plaines, Ill., 1975-81; asst. prof. Coll. St. Francis, Joliet, Ill., 1981-84; dir. clin. services Casa de Amparo, San Luis Rey, Calif., 1984-86; cons. San Clemente, Calif., 1986—; contract instr. San Diego State U., 2000—. Vis. lectr. U. Ill. Chgo., 1983-84; cons. Arthur D. Little, Washington, 1979-82; contract cons. U. Calif.-Davis; internat. cons. Author tng. tapes on child care info.; various media appearances; consulting editor Jour. Child Youth Care; pub. speaker; contbr. articles to profl. jours. Mem. ACLU, NOW, Psi Chi, Sierra Club. Avocations: outdoor activities, camping, reading. Home: 2838 Riachuelo San Clemente CA 92673-4045 Office: Profl Growth Facilitators PO Box 5981 San Clemente CA 92674-5981

FOX, MARY HAWKSHAW, early childhood special education educator, consultant; b. Washington, May 4, 1945; m. Paul L. Fox, 1972. BA in Sociology, U. Md., 1969; MA in Edn., George Washington U., 1973; PhD, Fla. State U., 1992. Cert. tchr. emotionally disburbed, Fla. Tchr. crisis resource D.C. Pub. Schs., Washington, 1969-71, 73, mem. mobile crisis team, dept. spl. edn., 1972-73; tchr. emotionally handicapped then tchr. presch. Fla. Pub. Schs., Volusia County, Daytona Beach, 1980-84; tchr. emotionally handicapped then ednl. specialist, tchr. Fla. Pub. Schs., Leon County, Tallahassee, 1984-85, 87; behavior specialist, parent trainer HRS, Youth and Family Svcs., Tallahassee, 1986-93; tchr. Varying Exceptionalities Presch., Lively Vocat./Tech. Sch., Leon County, 1988; instr. dept. spl. edn. Fla. State U., Tallahassee, 1988, grad. asst., 1988-90, asst. and adj. instr. dept. childhood edn., 1990-92; vis. prof. spl. edn. Univ. North Fla., Jacksonville, 1991-92; vis. rsch. assoc. sch. improvement support team Fla. State U., Tallahassee, 1992-93; instrnl. designer Fla. State U. Ctr. for Ednl. Tech., Schoolyear 2000, Tallahassee, 1992-93; asst. prof. Daemen Coll., Amherst, NY, 1994—2002, assoc. prof., 2002—, campus coord. Consortium for Innovative Environments in Learning. Staff asst. to early childhood edn. specialist Bur. Edn. Exceptional Students, Fla. Dept. Edn., Talahassee, spring 1987; instr. Ctr. Advancement Ednl., GEM Module, NOVA U., Ft. Lauderdale, Fla., 1988; coord. Consortium of Innovative Environments in Learning; cons., instr., presenter seminars, insvcs., confs. in field. Contbr. articles to profl. jours. Vol. Spl. Olympics, Daytona Beach, 1984-85; instr. Dick Howser Ctr., United Cerebral Palsy, Tallahassee, 1988-90; organizer Spl. Awards Program for Exceptional Children, Birney Elem., Washington, 1969-71. U.S. Dept. Edn./Office Spl. Edn. Rehabilitative Svcs. grantee, 1986; recipient federally funded fellowships George Washington U., 1971-72, Fla. State U., 1985-87. Mem. Coun. Exceptional Children (student vol. 1986, pres. N.Y. chpt. 402 1996-97, v.p. N.Y. divsn. for early childhood), Phi Delta Kappa. Home: 4253 Main St Buffalo NY 14226-3502 Office Phone: 716-839-8352. E-mail: mfox@daemen.edu.

FOX, MURIEL, retired public relations executive; b. Newark, Feb. 3, 1928; d. M. Morris and Anne L. (Rubenstein) F.; m. Shepard G. Aronson, July 1, 1955 (dec. Nov. 10, 2003); children: Eric R., Lisa S. Student, Rollins Coll., 1944-46; BA summa cum laude, Barnard Coll., 1948. Art critic, bridal editor Miami (Fla.) News, 1946; reporter U.P.I., 1946-48; polit. speechwriter, publicist, 1949-50; from TV-radio writer to exec. v.p. Carl Byoir & Assos., N.Y.C., 1950-85; pres. subs. MediaCom Comm. Tng., 1975-85, By/Media Inc., 1981-85; sr. cons. Hill & Knowlton, Inc., 1986-90. Dir. Harleysville Ins. Co., Rorer Group Inc.; Co-chmn. Vice Presdl. Task Force on Women, 1968; mem. steering com. Women's Forum, 1974-79, pres., 1976-78; mem. Women's Econ. Adv. Com., N.Y.C., 1974-78; mem. nat. adv. com. Nat. Women's Polit. Caucus; nat. adv. bd. Women Today, Ethnic Woman Bd. dirs. N.Y. Diabetes Assn., 1956-66, Holy Land Conservation Fund, United Way of Tri-State, Internat. Rescue Com., 1977-84; v.p. Rockland Ctr. for the Arts, 1985-2004, pres., 2004—; pres. Hickory Hill Coop., Inc., 1995-99; chair bd. dirs. Vet. Feminists of Am., 1997—. Named one of 100 Top Corp. Women Bus. Week mag., 1976; recipient Matrix award Women in Communications, 1977, Bus. Leader of Year award ADA, 1979; Disting. Alumna award Barnard Coll., 1985, Eleanor Roosevelt Leadership award, 1985 Mem.: NOW (v.p. 1967—70, chmn. bd. 1971—73, chair nat. adv. com. 1973—74, bd. dirs. legal def. and edn. fund 1974—, v.p. fund 1977—78, pres. 1978—81, chair bd. 1981—92, hon. chair bd. 1993—, founder, Muriel Fox Comm. Leadership award 1991, Our Hero award 1995, Caroline Lexow Babcock award 1997), Am. Arbitration Assn. (bd. dirs. 1983—87), Am. Women in Radio and TV (bd. dirs. 1950—51, chair nat. publicity com. 1955—57, chair nat. pub. rels. com. 1957—59, Achievement award 1983), Vet. Feminists of Am. (chair bd. dirs. 2000—). Home and Office: 66 Hickory Hill Rd Tappan NY 10983-1804 Office Phone: 845-359-6075. Personal E-mail: mfox66@optonline.net.

FOX, PATRICIA ANN, school librarian, media specialist; b. Peekskill, N.Y., Nov. 9, 1942; d. Martin Van Deusen and Martha M. Hunt; m. Charles James Fox, Aug. 14, 1966; children: Jeffrey Martin, Traci Lynn, Brandi Lynn. BA, SUNY, Albany, 1964. Cert. libr. media specialist. Tchr. social studies Gloversville (N.Y.) High Sch., 1964-66; elem. librarian Amsterdam (N.Y.) Sch. Dist., 1966-67; sch. libr. media specialist Greater Johnstown (N.Y.) Sch., 1967—, libr. media dept. chair, 1989—97; libr. and media cons., 1997—. Mem. adv. coun. Hamilton Fultom Montgomery Sch. Libr. System,. Johnston, 1986—, chmn. adv. coun., 1988-90; mem. steering com. Knox Jr. High Sch., Johnstown, 1992. Named Vol. of Yr., Charlotte Sun Newspaper, 2005. Mem.:

AAUW (v.p. membership 1984—85, pres. 1991—95), Eastern NY Libr. Assns., Eclectic Study Club. Home: PO Box 1093 Northville NY 12134-1093: 12981 SW Kingsway Cir Lake Suzy FL 34269 E-mail: brandi@klink.net.

FOX, PATRICIA SAIN, academic administrator; b. Indpls., Jan. 8, 1954; d. Thomas Troy and Faye Melba (Martinez) Sain; m. Donald Lee Fox, Aug. 26, 1978; children: Ashley Marie, Aimee Elizabeth. BS in Acctg., Ind. U., 1980; MBA, Butler U., 1985. Adminstrv. asst. Sch. Engring. and Tech. Ind. U.-Purdue U., Indpls., 1980-83, asst. to the dean Sch. Engring. and Tech., 1983-86, asst. dean Sch. Engring. and Tech., 1986—2002, assoc. dean, 2003—. Cons. Gene Glick Mgmt. Co., Indpls., 1986-87. Eucharistic min. St. Christopher Ch., Speedway, Ind., 1983. Mem. Am. So. for Engring. Edn. Roman Catholic. Avocation: walking. Office: Ind U-Purdue U Sch Engring & Tech 799 W Michigan St Indianapolis IN 46202-5195 Business E-Mail: psfox@iupu.edu.

FOX, PAULA (MRS. MARTIN GREENBERG), writer; b. NYC, Apr. 22, 1923; d. Paul Hervey and Elsie (de Sola) F.; m. Richard Sigerson (div. 1954); children: Adam, Linda, Gabriel; m. Martin Greenberg, June 9, 1962. Student, Columbia U. Condr. writing Seminars U. Pa. Author: 22 children's books and 6 novels, including How Many Miles to Babylon, 1966, Portrait of Ivan, 1968, Blowfish Live in the Sea, 1970; (novels) Poor George, 1967, Desperate Characters, 1970, The Western Coast, 1972, The Slave Dancer, 1974 (John Newbery medal), The Widow's Children, 1976, The Little Swineherd and Other Tales, 1978, A Place Apart, 1983 (Am. Book award), A Servant's Tale, 1984, One-Eyed Cat, 1985 (Newbery honor book 1985), Maurice's Room, 1985, The Moonlight Man, 1986, The Stone-Faced Boy, 1987, The Village by the Sea, 1988, Lily and the Lost Boy, 1989, The God of Nightmares, 1990, Monkey Island, 1991, Amzat and His Brothers, 1993, Western Wind, 1993, The Eagle Kite, 1995, Radiance Descending, 1997, Borrowed Finery: A Memoir, 2000 (PEN/Martha Albrand award), (memoir) The Coldest Winter, 2005. Recipient Arts and Letters award Nat. Inst. Arts and Letters, 1972, Hans Christian Andersen medal, 1978, fiction citation Brandeis U., 1984, Empire State award for children's lit., 1994; Guggenheim fellow, 1972. Mem. Authors League, Am. Acad. Arts and Letters (recipient medal and cash award). Office: care Robert Lescher 47 E 19th St New York NY 10003-1323

FOX, RENÉE CLAIRE, sociology educator; b. NYC, Feb. 15, 1928; d. Paul Fred and Henrietta (Gold) F. AB summa cum laude, Smith Coll., 1949, LHD, 1975; PhD, Harvard U., 1954; MA (hon.), U. Pa., 1971, U. Oxford, 1996; ScD (hon.), Med. Coll. Pa., 1974, St. Joseph's Coll., Phila., 1978; D (hon.), Katholieke U., Leuven, 1978; LHD (hon.), La Salle U., Phila., 1988; DSc (hon.), Hahnemann U., 1991, U. Nottingham, Eng., 2002. Rsch. asst. Bur. Applied Social Rsch., Columbia U., 1953-55, rsch. assoc., 1955-58; lectr. dept. sociology Barnard Coll., 1955-58, asst. prof., 1958-64, assoc. prof., 1964-66; lectr. sociology Harvard U., 1967-69; rsch. fellow Ctr. Internat. Affairs, 1967-68, rsch. assoc. program tech. and soc., 1968-71; prof. sociology, psychiatry and medicine U. Pa., Phila., 1969-98, Annenberg prof. social scis., 1978-98, chmn. dept. sociology, 1972-78, Annenberg prof. social scis. emerita, 1998—, sr. fellow Ctr. for Bioethics, 1999—2002, sr. fellow emeritus Ctr. for Bioethics, 2005—, affiliated faculty Solomon Asch Ctr. for the Study of Ethnopolit. Conflict, 2001—. Rsch. assoc. Refugee Studies Centre, Queen Elizabeth House, U. Oxford, 1998—; sci. advisor Centre de Recherches Sociologiques, Kinshasa, Zaïre, 1963-67; vis. prof. sociology U. Officielle du Congo, Lubumbashi, 1965; vis. prof. Sir George Williams U., Montreal, summer 1968; Phi Beta Kappa vis. scholar, 1973-75; dir. humanities seminar med. practitioners NEH, 1975-76; maitre de cours U. Liège, Belgium, 1976-77; vis. prof. Katholieke U., Leuven, Belgium, 1976-77; Wm. Allen Neilson prof. Smith Coll., Mass., 1980; dir. d'Etudes Associè, Ecole des Hautes Etudes en Sciences Sociales, Paris, summer 1989; George Eastman vis. prof. Oxford U., 1996-97; vis. scholar Tokyo Med. and Dental U., 2001; mem. bd. clin. scholars program Robert Wood Johnson Found., 1974-80; mem. Pres.'s Commn. on Study of Ethical Problems in Medicine, Biomed. and Behavioral Rsch., 1979-81; dir. human qualities of medicine program James Picker Found., 1980-83; Fae Golden Kass lectr. Harvard U. Sch. Medicine and Radcliffe Coll., 1983, Kate Hurd Mead lectr. Med. Coll. Pa./Coll. Physicians Phila., 1990, Lori Ann Roscetti Meml. lectr. Rush-Presbyn.-St. Luke's Med. Ctr., Chgo., 1990; vis. scholar Women's Ctr., U. Mo., Kansas City, 1990, vis. scholar Case Western Res. Sch. of Med., 1992; opening address 13th Internat. Conf. on Social Scis. and Medicine, Hungary, 1994, vis. prof. U. Calif., San Francisco Sch. of Medicine, 1994; lectr. founds. of medicine Faculty of Medicine McGill U., Montreal, 1995; Supernumerary fellow Balliol Coll. Oxford U., 1996-97; WHR Rivers disting. lectr. dept. social medicine Harvard Med. Sch., 1998; assembly series lectr. Washington U., St. Louis, 1998; William J. Rashkind Meml. lectr, Am. Heart Assn., 1998, Salinger-Forlang lectr. U. Tex. Health Scis. Ctr. at San Antonio, 1999, Frances H. Schlitz lectr. U. Kans., Wichita, 2002; Stambaugh lectr. U. Louisville Sch. Medicine, 2004. Author: Experiment Perilous, 1959; author: (with Willy De Craemer) The Emerging Physician, 1968; author: (with Judith P. Swazey) The Courage to Fall, 1974, rev. edit., 1978, 2002; author: Essays in Medical Sociology, 1979, 2d edit., 1988, L'Incertitude Medicale, 1988, The Sociology of Medicine: A Participant Observer's View, 1989; author: (with Judith P. Swazey) Spare Parts: Organ Replacement in American Society, 1992; author: In the Belgian Château: The Spirit and Culture of European Society in an Age of Change, 1994, French lang. edit., 1997, Organ Transplantation: Meanings and Realities (edited with Stuart Youngner and Laurence O'Connell), 1996; author: (in Japanese) Looking Intimately at Bioethics: Fifty Years as a Medical Sociologist, 2003; editor (with Victor N. Lidz and Harold J. Bershady): After Parsons: A Theory of Social Action for the Twenty-First Century, 2005; assoc. editor Am. Sociol. Rev., 1963—1196, Social Sci. and Medicine, Jour. Health and Social Behavior, 1985—87, Perspectives in Biology and Medicine, 1996—, mem. editl. com. Ann. Rev. Sociology, 1975—79, mem. editl. adv. bd. Tech. in Soc., Sci., 1982—83, mem. editl. bd. Bibliography of Bioethics, 1979—, Culture, Medicine and Psychiatry, 1980—86, Jour. of AMA, 1981—94, Am. Scholar, 1994—99, Current Revs. in Publs., 1994—, Am. Jour. Bioethics, 1999—, vice chair adv. bd. Am. Jour. Ethics and Medicine, A Festschrift published in her honor Society and Medicine: Essays in Honor of Renée Fox, 2003; contbr. articles to profl. jours. Bd. dir. Medicine in Pub. Interest, 1979-94; mem. tech. bd. Milbank Meml. Fund, 1979-85; mem. overseers com. to visit univ. health svcs. Harvard Coll., 1979-86; trustee Russell Sage Found., 1981-87; vice chmn. bd. dir. Acadia Inst., 1990-97; mem. adv. com. Sch. Nursing LaSalle U., 1998—; mem. advancement com. King Baudouin Found. US Inc., 1998—, mem., sec. bd. dir. Acadia Inst., 2002—; mem. info. sci. adv. coun. Innovia Found., Netherlands, 2002—; mem. external bd. Ctr. Bioethics, Columbia U., 2002—; mem. Internat. and Sci. Adv. Coun., 2002—. Recipient E. Harris Harbison Gifted Tchg. award Danforth Found., 1970, Radcliffe Grad. Soc. medal, 1977, Lindback Found. award for tchg. U. Pa., 1989, Centennial medal Grad. Sch. Arts and Scis. Harvard U., 1993, Chevalier de l'Ordre de Leopold II (Belgium), 1995, M. Powell Lawton Quality of Life award Phila. Corp. Aging, 2006; Wilson Ctr., Smithsonian Instn. fellow, 1987-88, Guggenheim fellow, 1962, Sr. fellow Ctr. Bioethics U. Pa., 1999—, Andrew W. Mellon Emeritus fellowship, 2004-05; Fulbright Short-Term Sr. scholar to Australia, 1994; 1st W.H.R. Rivers Disting. lectr. Harvard Med. Sch., 1998. Fellow African Studies Assn., AAAS (dir. 1977-80, chmn. sect. K 1986-87), Am. Sociol. Assn. (coun. 1970-73, 79-81, v.p. 1980-81), Am. Acad. Arts and Scis. (co-chair Class III section I membership com., 1994-96), Inst. Medicine of NAS (coun. 1979-82), Inst. Soc., Ethics and Life Scis. (founder, gov.); mem. AAUP, AAUW, Assn. Am. Med. Colls., Social Sci. Rsch. Coun. (v.p., dir.), Ea. Sociol. Soc. (pres. 1976-77, Merit award 1993), NY Acad. Scis., Soc. Sci. Study Religion, Inst. Intercultural Studies, 1969-93, (asst. sec. 1969-78, sec. 1978-81, 89-92, v.p. 1987-89), Am. Bd. Med. Specialists, Coll. of Physicians of Phila. (coun. 1993-98), Phi Beta Kappa (senate 1982-87, Ralph Waldo Emerson book award com. 1998-2001), Alpha Omega Alpha (hon.). Home and Office: The Wellington 135 S 19th St 1104 Philadelphia PA 19103-4912 Business E-Mail: rcfox@ssc.upenn.edu.

FOX, STACY L., lawyer; b. Ann Arbor, Mich., 1953; m. Michael Van Hemet; children: Kyle, Callan. BS with high distinction, U. Mich., 1974, JD, 1983. Assoc. Mintz, Levin, Cohn, Ferris, Glovskky & Popeo, P.C., Boston, 1983—88; gen. counsel Unisys Fin. Corp., 1988—89; group counsel automotive systems group and plastics tech. group Johnson Controls, Inc., 1989—93, group v.p., gen counsel automotive systems group, 1993—2000; sr. v.p. corp. transactions and legal affairs Visteon Corp., Dearborn, Mich., 2000—. Named one of 100 Leading Women in Automotive Industry, Automotive News, 2000. Office: Visteon Corp 1700 Rotunda Dr Dearborn MI 48120

FOX, TERRI JO, music educator; b. Milw., Oct. 17, 1976; d. Lee and Cheryl Songer; m. Tyson Stanley Fox, Dec. 27, 2003. MusB in Edn., U. Wis., Eau Claire, 2000. Choir tchr. Lake Jr. HS, Woodbury, Minn., 2001—03, Clermont Mid. Sch., Clermont, Fla., 2003—04, Windy Hill Mid. Sch., Clermont, Fla., 2004—. Profl. singer Walt Disney World, Lake Buena Vista, Fla., 2005. Mem.: Music Educators Nat. Conf. Office: Windy Hill Mid Sch 3575 Hancock Rd Clermont FL 34711 Office Phone: 352-394-2123.

FOX-CLARKSON, ANNE C., fundraising company executive; 1 child. BS in Edn., Bucknell U., 1967; MS in Reading, Syracuse U., 1973, PhD in Tchr. Edn., 1975. Cert. elem. tchr., adminstr., Idaho. Postdoctroal work in edn. adminstrn. U. Idaho; elem. sch. tchr.; prin., supt. pub. schs., 1978-84; assoc. prof. ednl. adminstrn. Gonzaga U., 1987-94; supt. pub. instrn. State of Idaho, 1995-98; v.p. ednl. markets Shop2gether.com, 2000; pres. Grant Writers, Inc., Boise, 2004—. Mem. State Bd. Edn., State Land Bd., State Libr. Bd., State Endowment Fund, State Investment Bd.; pres., co-founder Children's Village, Homes for Abused Children; grant writer, mgmt. cons.; spkr. in field. Former pres. Idaho State Elem. Prin. Assn., Wash. State Univ. Profl. Adminstr. Assn. E-mail: Raand29@aol.com.

FOXE, MARYE ANNE, academic administrator; b. Canton, Ohio, Dec. 9, 1947; m. James K. Whitesell, 1990; stepchildren: Christopher Whitesell, Robert Whitesell; children: Robert Fox, Michael Fox, Matthew Fox. BS, Notre Dame Coll. of Ohio, 1969; MS, Cleve. State U., 1970; PhD, Dartmouth Coll., 1974; postgrad., U. Md., 1974-76; DSc (hon.), Notre Dame Coll., 1994, Cleve. State U., 1998; JD (hon.), Sandhills Cmty. Coll., 2000; degree (hon.), Universite Pierre et Marie Curie, 2001; LHD (hon.), Texas A&M, 2002; degree (hon.), Universidad Nacional de Educacion a Distancia, Madrid, 2003. Prof. chemistry U. Tex., Austin, 1976-91, Rowland Pettit Centennial prof., 1986-92, M. June and J. Virgil Waggoner regents chair chemistry, 1992-98, v.p. rsch., 1994-98; chancellor N.C. State U., Raleigh, 1998—2004, U. Calif. San Diego, 2004—. Mem. Nat. Sci. Bd., 1991-96, vice-chair, 1994-96; bd. dirs. Kenan Inst. Engring., Tech., and Sci., 1998—, Microelectric Ctr., NC, 1998—, mem. sci. adv. bd. Robert A. Welch Found., 1998—, David and Lucile Packard Found., 1998—; mem. Coun. on Competitiveness, 1999—; bd. trustees Nat. Inst. Statistical Sciences, 2000—; bd. dirs. Nat. Inst. Environment, 2001—, Boston Sci. Inc., 2001—, mem. President's Adv. Coun. of Advisors on Sci. and Tech., 2001—; bd. dirs. NC Bd. Sci. and Tech., 2002—, PPD Inc., 2002—, Red Hat Inc., 2002, Nat. Assn. State Universities and Land Grant Coll., 2003— Assoc. editor Jour. Am. Chem. Soc., 1986-94; mem. adv. bd. Jour. Organic Chemistry, Chem. Engring. News, Chem. Rev. Bd. trustees U. Notre Dame, 2002—; bd. dirs. N.C. Citizens for Bus. and Industry, 2003—. Recipient Agnes Faye Morgan Rsch. award Iota Sigma Pi, 1984, Arthur C. Cope scholar award Am. Chem. Soc., 1988; Garvan medal Am. Chem. Soc., 1988, Havinga medal Leiden U., 1991, Monie A. Ferst award, 1996; named to Hall of Excellence, Ohio Found. Ind. Colls., 1987, The Best of the New Generation, Esquire Mag., 1984; Alfred P. Sloan Rsch. fellow, 1980-82, Camille and Henry Dreyfus tchr. scholar, 1981-85. Fellow AAAS, Assn. Women in Sci.; mem. NAS (co-chair, Govt.-Univ.-Industry Rsch. Roundtable, 1999-), Am. Acad. Arts and Sci., Am. Philos. Soc., Sigma Xi (pres. 2001-02). Office: U Calif San Diego Chancellors Office 9500 Gilman Sr La Jolla CA 92093-0005*

FOX-GENOVESE, ELIZABETH ANN TERESA, humanities educator; b. Boston, May 28, 1941; d. Edward Whiting and Elizabeth Mary (Simon) Fox; m. Eugene Dominick Genovese, 1969. BA, Bryn Mawr Coll., 1963; MA, Harvard U., 1966, PhD, 1974; LittD (hon.), Millsaps Coll., 1992. Teaching fellow Harvard U., Cambridge, Mass., 1965-66, 1967-69; asst. prof. U. Rochester, NY, 1973-76, assoc. prof. NY, 1976-80; prof. SUNY, Binghamton, 1980-86, Emory U., Atlanta, 1986—, Eleonore Raoul prof. of humanities, 1988—. Adj. prof. Auburn (Ala.) U., 1987; Eudora Welty prof. Millsaps Coll., 1990, Mem. Nat. Coun. Humanities, 2003-. Author: Origins of Physiocracy, 1976, (with others) Fruits of Merchant Capital, 1983, Within the Plantation Household, 1988, Feminism Without Illusions, 1991, Feminism Is Not the Story of My Life: How the Elite Women's Movement Has Lost Touch with the Real Concerns of Women, 1996, Women and the Future of the Family 2000; co-editor: Reconstructing History: The Emergence of a New Historical Society, 1999, (with Eugene D. Genovese) The Mind of the Master Class: History and Faith in the Southern Slaveholders' Worldview, 2005; mem. editl. adv. bd. First Things; mem. editl. bd. Books and Culture; editor Jour. Hist. Soc., 1999—; contbr. numerous articles to profl. jours. Mem. acad. adv. bd. Inst. for Am. Values, 1994—; adv. bd. Campaign for the Am. Family, 1995—, Ind. Women's Forum, 1993-2000, Women's Freedom Network, 1994-. Recipient Nat. Humanities Medal, 2003. Mem. MLA, Soc. Am. Historians, The Hist. Soc. (life, mem. bd. govs.), So. Hist. Assn. (life), So. Assn. for Women Historians (life), Am. Comparative Lit. Assn. (adv. bd. 1991-95), Orgn. Am. Historians (life, proglram com. 1991), Am. Studies Assn. (program com. 1987), Soc. for Study So. Lit. (exec. coun. 1990-93), South Atlantic MLA (chair women's studies network 1989-90), Social Sci. Hist. Assn. (exec. coun. 1986-88), Am. Polit. Sci. Assn., Am. Acad. Liberal Edn. (bd. dirs.), Nat. Coun. on Hist. Standards (steering commn.), Atlanta Hist. Assn. (acad. adv. com.), Am. Antiquarian Soc., Nat. Alumni Forum, Cosmos Club, Harvard Club of Boston, Harvard Club of NYC. Roman Catholic. Avocations: films, fashion, reading, major league baseball. Home: 1487 Sheridan Walk NE Atlanta GA 30324-3253 Office: Emory U Dept History Atlanta GA 30322-0001 Office Phone: 404-727-4063. Business E-Mail: efoxgen@emory.edu.

FOXWELL, ELIZABETH MARIE, editor, writer; b. Somerville, NJ, Aug. 30, 1963; d. James Adolph and Rita Ann (Drohan) F. BS in Journalism, U. Md., 1985; MA in Liberal Studies with distinction, Georgetown U., 1990. Coord. publs. internat. student exch. program Georgetown U., Washington, 1987-91; editor Am. Assn. Colls. for Tchr. Edn., Washington, 1992-97, dir. publs. and mktg., 1994-97; publs. mgr. Soc. for Am. Archaeology, 1998-2000; pubs. dir. sect. internat. law and practice ABA, 2000—02; mng. editor Heldref Pubs., 2001—, acquisitions editor, 2004—. Bd. dirs. Malice Domestic, Bethesda, Md., publicity liaison, 1988-94, vice-chair, 1993-95, chair, 1995-97; presenter Vera Brittain Centenary Conf., 1993, Popular Culture Assn. Conf., 1995-96. Co-author: The Robert B. Parker Companion, 2005; editor: The Usual Suspects, 1992—95, The 3rd Degree, 2003—04, The Sunken Sailor, 2004; cons. editor: MysteryScene, 2000—; co-editor: (anthologies) Malice Domestic 5, 1996, Malice Domestic 6, 1997; editor: Malice Domestic 7, 1998, Malice Domestic 8, 1999, Malice Domestic 9, 2000, Malice Domestic 10, 2001; co-editor: Murder, They Wrote I, 1997, Murder, They Wrote II, 1998, More Murder, They Wrote, 1999; editor (in-chief): The Armchair Detective, 1997—98; prodr., host It's a Mystery, WEBR, Fairfax, Va., 2005—, contbr. (short stories) Crime Through Time II, 1998, Cat Crimes Through Time, 1999, Crime Through Time III, Crafty Cat Crimes, 2000, Blood on Their Hands, 2003, Chesapeake Crimes, 2004; contbr.: short stories World's Finest Mystery and Crime Stories V, 2004; contbr. (short stories) Chesapeake Crimes II, 2005—; contbr.: short stories Death Dines In, 2004; mng. editor CLUES: A Jour. of Detection, 2004—; contbr. articles to profl. jours. Recipient 2d prize in play contest NJ Ctr. for the Performing Arts, 1981, honorable mention in writing contest Interlochen Arts Acad., 1981, 1st prize Cape Fear (NC) Crime Festival Short Story Contest, 2003, Agatha award for Best Short Story, 2004. Mem.: Authors Guild. Office: Heldref Publs 1319 18th St NW Washington DC 20036

FOXWORTH, JOHNNIE HUNTER, retired state agency administrator; b. Anderson, S.C., Feb. 13, 1921; d. John Ira and Bessie (Hatton) Hunter; m. Marvin Ardell, Sept. 21, 1941. Attended colls., univs., Atlanta, Bridgeport, Conn. Cashier examiner, office supr. Motor Vehicle Dept., State Conn., Bridgeport, 1957—72; br. office mgr. various locations in state, 1972—77; br. office dist. supr. Wethersfield, Conn., 1977—81; asst. dir., 1981—85; cons., tng. instr., 1985—88; ret. Writer: manual in field. Mem. Commrs. Affirmative Action Com., 1987. Recipient Profl. Achievement award, Bridgeport chpt. Nata. Bus. and Profl. Women, 1972, (2) Disting. Managerial Svc. award, State of Conn., Wethersfield, 1982, Woman of Yr. award, Nat. Coun. Negro Woman, Bridgeport, 1972. Mem.: The Links, Inc. (Waterbury) (pres. 1980—85), Les Treize (Bridgeport) (pres. 1966—68). Home: 496A Heritage Village Southbury CT 06488-1525

FOXX, VIRGINIA ANN, congresswoman, small business owner; b. NYC, June 29, 1943; m. Thomas A. Foxx; 1 child, 2 grandchildren. AB in English, U. NC, Chapel Hill, 1968, MACT, 1972; EdD Curriculum and Tchg./Higher Edn., U. NC, Greensboro, 1985. Sec., rsch. asst. U. NC, Chapel Hill; prof. Caldwell CC, Hudson, NC; prof. sociology Appalachian State U., Boone, NC, asst. dean gen. coll.; dept. sec. mgmt. NC Dept. Adminstrn.; pres., cons. Mayland CC, Spruce Pine, NC, 1987—94; owner, operator Grandfather Nursery, Banner Elk, NC; mem. NC State Senate, 1995—2004, US Congress from 5th NC dist., 2005—. Mem. agr. com. US Congress, mem. govt. reform com., mem. edn. and the workforce com. Mem. Watauga County Bd. Edn., 1976-88. Recipient Outstanding Pub. Official award, NC Christmas Tree Assn., Award for Outstanding Citizenship, Exceptional Pub. Svc., Watauga County League Women Voters, 1988, NC Disting. Women's award, 1990, Order of the Long Leaf Pine, NC Gov. Jim Martin, 1992, Disting. Fundraising award, YMCA, 1993, NC Carpathian award, 1994, Guardian of Small Bus. award, Nat. Fedn. Ind. Bus., 2000, Alan Keith-Lucas Friend of Children award, NC Child Care Assn., 2002, Contbns. to Sociology award, NC Sociol. Assn., 2002. Mem. Nat. Assn. Women Legislators, Am. Legis. Exch. Conf., NCCBI, NC Ctr. Pub. Policy Rsch., NC Women's Forum. Republican. Office: US House Reps 503 Cannon Ho Office Bldg Washington DC 20515-3305 Office Phone: 202-225-2071.*

FOY, PATRICIA SOLESBEE, music educator; b. Greenville, S.C., Apr. 28, 1955; d. Luke Julian and Betty (Sprouse) Solesbee; m. David Strickland Foy; children: Robert Strickland, David Christopher. MusB, Converse Coll., 1977; M of Music Edn., U. S.C., 1980, PhD, 1988. Pvt. practice, SC, 1976—84; tchr. music Sch. Dist. Greenville County, 1978—79; tchr. choral music St. John's H.S., Darlington, SC, 1980—84; tchr. music Darlington County Schs., 1985—86, Fair Oaks Elem. Sch., Marietta, Ga., 1986—90; assoc. prof. music edn. Converse Coll., Spartanburg, SC, 1990—. Steering com. Arts in Basic Curriculum Project, Rock Hill, SC, 1994—; chair performance-based stds. com. for music tchr. edn. S.C. Dept. Edn., Columbia, 2001—02, coord. com. for the revision of the S.C. visual and performing arts stds., 2001—03; choral adjudicator Music in the Parks/Festivals of Music, Douglassville, Pa., 1992—; bd. mem. S.C. Alliance for Arts Edn., 2004—. Music dir. Sharon United Meth. Ch., Greer, SC, 1997—; bd. dirs. Cmty. Concert Assn., Hartsville, SC, 1980—84. Grantee, S.C. Coun. Arts Edn. Pres., 2001—; Music Technology grant, S.C. Dept. Edn., 2001, Arts in Basic Curriculum grant, S.C. Arts Commn., 2001—06. Mem.: Music Educators Nat. Conf. (So. Divsn. bd. dirs. 2003—05), S.C. Music Educators Assn. (chair tchr. edn. 1997—2001, pres.-elect 2001—03, pres. 2003—05, v.p. 2005—), Soc. for Music Tchr. Edn., Nat. Assn. for Music Edn., Pi Kappa Lambda. Methodist. Office: Converse Coll 580 E Main St Spartanburg SC 29302 Business E-Mail: patti.foy@converse.edu.

FOYOUZI-YOUSSEFI, REYHANEH, pharmacologist; b. Tehran, Iran, Dec. 6, 1964; arrived in Switzerland, 1983. d. Amin and Seyedeh (Salimi-Eshkevari); m. Hamid R. Mostafavi, 2001; 1 child, Mahan Ali. Diploma of Asst. Pharmacist, Sch. Pharmacy, Geneva, Switzerland, 1988, Diploma of Pharmacy, 1991; PhD in Pharmacy, U. Geneva, Geneva, Switzerland, 1999. Pharmacist, Geneva, 1991—; sr. scientist Estee Lauder Cos., Inc., 2000—04. Contbr. articles to profl. jours.

FRACKMAN, NOEL, art critic; b. N.Y.C., May 27, 1930; d. Walter David and Celeste (Barman) Stern; m. Richard Benoit Frackman, July 2, 1950 (dec. Jan. 2, 2002); 1 child, Noel Dru Pyne. Student, Mt. Holyoke Coll., 1948—50; BA, Sarah Lawrence Coll., 1952, MA, 1953; postgrad., Columbia U., 1964—67; MA Inst. Fine Arts, NYU, 1976, PhD Inst. Fine Arts, 1987. Art critic Scarsdale (N.Y.) Inquirer, 1962—67, Patent Trader, Mt. Kiscoo, NY, 1962—71; assoc. Arts Mag., N.Y.C., 1968—92. Lectr. Aldrich Mus. Contemporary Art, Ridgefield, Conn., 1967—75, Gallery Passport Ltd., N.Y.C., 1968—96; curator edn. Storm King Art Ctr., Mountainville, NY, 1973—75; instr. continuing edn. divsn. SUNY, 1988—2002; contractual lectr. Met. Mus. Art, N.Y.C., 1994—95; adj. assoc. prof. humanities SUNY, 1997—. Contbr. articles and revs. to various mags., including Arts Mag., Harper's Bazaar, Feminist Art Jour., Art Voices. Bd. dirs. Friends of the Neuberger Mus. Art, 1994—; bd. trustees Purchase Coll. Found., 2006—. Scholar Sarah Williston scholar, 1948—50. Mem.: Coll. Art Assn., Art Table Inc., Internat. Assn. Art Critics.

FRADELLA, LAURA TONI, art educator, muralist; b. Bklyn., Oct. 13, 1949; d. Salvatore Esposito and Phyllis Giangrande; m. Charles John Fradella, Nov. 11, 1973; 1 child, Lauren Diana. BA in Studio Art, Queens Coll., Flushing, N.Y., 1999, MS in Art Edn. with grad. honors, 2003. Cert. tchr. art k-12 (permanent) N.Y. State. Page design comml. artist Alexander's Dept. Store, N.Y.C., 1970—72; art inst. Saturday enrichment and summer programs Manhasset Sch. Cmty, 1997—2004; intern Godwin-Ternbach Mus. Queens Coll., Flushing, 1999; tchr. art Pub. Sch. 87 Queens, Middle Village, 1999—. Adj. prof. elem. art Queens Coll., 2005—; chairperson Funnight publicity and yearbook Munsey Park Parent Coun., Manhasset, NY, 1989—93; dir. P.S. 87 Afterschool Art and Mural Club, Middle Village, 1999—2004; mem. partnership com. Ctr. Art Edn. Grant, N.Y.C., 2002—; layout designer and contr. Interdisciplinary Curriculum Book, 2001; supr. student stage designs, exhibitions. Contbr. articles to profl. jours.; exhibitions include Queens Mus. Art, 2001, Represented in permanent collections Rosenthal Libr., Queens Coll. Pre-cana marriage counselor St. Mary's Parish, 1998—2002; mem. exec. bd. Manhasset Sch. Cmty. Assn., Manhasset, NY, 1989—93, chair enrichment program, 1989—93; chairperson Funnight publicity and yearbook Munsey Park Parent Coun., 1989—93. Recipient Outstanding in Art Edn. Abilities award, Queens Youth Ctr. Arts, 1999, Doris Liebowitz Art Educator of Yr., NYCATA/UFT, 2003, Trash Masters Recycling Grant, 2003, Golden Apple award, Dept. Sanitation, 2003; grantee, P. Buckley Moss Found., 2002. Mem.: Assn. Help of Retarded Children (Manhasset chpt.) (membership chair 1992—94, chairperson evening fund raising events 1988—94, most recruitment mems. in 2 yr. period), Kappa Delta Pi. Avocations: painting, concerts, museums, Broadway theater. Office: PS 87 Queens 67-54 80th St Middle Village NY 11379 E-mail: Tweeti1013@aol.com.

FRADY, KISHA, professional sports team executive; Owner Oakland (Calif.) Banshees. Home: 5616 Broadway Oakland CA 94618-1551

FRADY, RITA R., music educator, information technology manager; d. Laurence Herbert and Evelyn T. Rice; m. Lamar K. Frady, Aug. 29, 1981; children: Leigha A., Keith B. MusB in Piano Performance, West Ga. Coll., 1980; M of Elem. Edn., Brenau U., 2005. Tchr. Cert. T-4 Ga., 1991. Music tchr. K-6 Cherokee County Bd. of Edn., Canton, Ga., 1991—. Intech redelivery Cherokee County Bd. of Edn., Canton, Ga., 2003—. Pres., v.p. Cherokee Basketball Boosters, Canton, Ga., 2000—02. Mem.: Music Educators Nat. Conf., Delta Kappa Gamma. Avocations: Tae Kwon Do, reading, travel. Home: PO Box 4925 Canton GA 30114-0246 Office: Hasty Elem Sch Canton GA 30114

FRAHM, SHEILA, association executive, academic administrator, former government official; b. Colby, Kans., Mar. 22, 1945; m. Kenneth Frahm; children: Amy, Pam, Chrissie. BS, Ft. Hays State U., 1967. Mem. bd. edn. State of Kans., 1985-88; mem. Kans. Senate, Topeka, 1988-94, senate majority leader, 1993-94; lt. gov. State of Kans., 1995-96; mem. from Kans., U.S. Senate, Washington, 1996; exec. dir. Kans. Assn. C.C. Trustees, Topeka, 1996—. Mem. AAUW (Outstanding Br. Mem. 1985), Thomas County Day Care Assn., Shakespeare Fedn. Women's Clubs, Farm Bur., Kans. Corn Growers, Kans. Livestock Assn., Rotary (Paul Harris fellow 1988). Republican. Home: 410 N Grant Colby KS 67701-2036 Office: 700 SW Jackson St Ste 1000 Topeka KS 66603-3757 Personal E-mail: sfrahm@st-tel.net.

FRAICHE, DONNA DIMARTINO, lawyer; b. New Orleans, Dec. 8, 1951; d. Anthony and Rose Mary (Batchelona) DiM.; m. John F. Fraiche, Dec. 27, 1974; children: Geoffrey Michael, Ariane Michele. Student, St. Mary's Dominican Coll., New Orleans, 1969, La. State U. and A & M Coll., 1972; JD, Loyola U., 1975. Bar: La. 1975, U.S. Dist. Ct. (ea., we., mid. dists.) La. 1975, U.S. Dist. Ct. (no. dist.) W.Va. 1984, U.S. Dist. Ct. D.C. 1984, U.S. Ct. Appeals (D.C. cir.) 1977, U.S. Ct. Appeals (3d, 4th, 5th, 10th, 11th cirs.) 1975, U.S. Supreme Ct. 1979, U.S. Ct. Claims 1979, U.S. Tax Ct. 1977; diplomate Am. Coll. Healthcare Execs. Shareholder Baker Donelson Bearma Caldwell & Berkowitz PC, New Orleans, Health Law and Pub. Policy Depts. Chair La. Health Care Commn.; with Joint Commn. on Accreditations Hosps., Leadership Accountabilities Taskforce, Sch. Pub. Health. Past chair bd. trustees Loyola U., New Orleans; past chair bd., past pres. New Orleans Regional Med. Ctr.; mem. City Bus. Publ. Roundtable, New Orleans, 1992, Healthcare Redesign Collaborative; past pres. and chair bd. dirs. World Trade Ctr.; chair long term com. planning taskforce La. Recovery Authority, 2005. Recipient Achiever's award Am. Coun. of Career Women, 1990, Role Model award Young Leadership Coun., 1991, Women of Distinction award S.E. La. Girl Scout Coun., 1992. Mem. ABA (health law sect. 1980—, chmn. New Orleans health law forum 1982, chair women rainmakers divsn. 1996—, co-chair 1999—), Am. Health Lawyers Assn. (bd. dirs. 1982, exec. com. 1984, pres. 1989, com. chair 1988-91), New Orleans Regional C. of C. (bd. dirs., com. on govtl. affairs, New Orleans polit. action com. chair 1998—, v.p. 2004-05, pres. 2005—, La. Bar Found. 2004-05). Office: Baker Donelson Bearman Caldwell & Berkowitz PC Ste 3600 201 St Charles Ave New Orleans LA 70170 Office Phone: 504-566-5201. Office Fax: 504-636-3901.

FRALEY, LINDA WILLIAMS DARNELL, music educator; b. Lamesa, Tex., Mar. 11, 1953; d. Floyd Holley and Helen Alice Williams; m. James Raymond Fraley, Mar. 12, 1982; children: Emily Anne, Sarah Elizabeth. MusB magna cum laude, U. Tex., Austin, 1971—75. Cert. tchr. all level music Tex. Edn. Agy., 1975, Orff level three Memphis State U., 1981. Tchr. music Austin Ind. Sch. Dist., Tex., 1975—82; tchr. kindergarten Grace Covenant Christian Sch., 1991—94; tchr. music Austin Ind. Sch. Dist., 1994—95, 1996—99, Leander Ind. Sch. Dist., 1999—. Pvt. piano instr., Austin, Tex., 1982—91. Fundraising Leander Band Boosters, Leander, Tex., 2000—06; charter mem. Blanton Mus. Art U. Tex., Austin, Tex., 2006—06. Mem.: Tex. Music Educators Assn., Tex. Exes U. Tex. (life), Leander Band Boosters, Alpha Lambda Delta, Phi Delta Kappa. Presbyterian. Avocations: West African drumming, travel, scrapbooks, reading, gardening. Office: Leander Ind Sch Dist 204 W South St Leander TX 78641 Office Phone: 512-434-5000. E-mail: linda.fraley@leanderisd.org.

FRALIX GOLD, CAROLYN M., medical/surgical nurse, educator, consultant; b. Pulaski, Tenn., Oct. 12, 1951; d. Gardner and Louetta (Miller) Fralix; children: Sean Adams, Amber Holcomb-Keene; m. Ronald David Gold, Jan. 1, 2000. ADN, San Antonio Coll., 1982; BSN, U. Tex. Health Sci. Ctr., San Antonio, 1988; MSN, U. Tex., San Antonio, 1995. RN; cert. EMT, BLS, CPR instr. Tchr., rsch. assoc. U. Tex. Health Sci. Ctr., San Antonio; staff devel. coord. St. Rose and Villa Rosa Hosp., San Antonio; neonatal ICU Santa Rosa Hosp., San Antonio, 1982; cons. for ednl. resources, med. surg. staff nurse Santa Rosa Health Care Corp., San Antonio, 1984-88; med.-surg. pool nurse Meth. Hosp., San Antonio, 1994-95; vocat. nursing instr. St. Philip's Coll., San Antonio, 1991-95; nursing instr. U. Tex. Health Sci. Ctr., San Antonio, 1995-98, rsch. nurse coord., 1999, asst. prof., 2006—; assoc. prof. Dept. Nursing San Antonio Coll., 1998-99; intake coord. SNU Methodist Hosp., 1999—2001. Adj. faculty dept. nursing U. Tex. Health Sci. Ctr., San Antonio, 2002, S.W. Tex. Meth. Women's Ctr., 2002-05; founder, owner Hearts Alive Inc., 2003—; cons. in field. Founder, first aid ministry Oak Hills Ch., San Antonio, 2004—, dir., first aid ministry, 2004—. Recipient various scholarships. Mem. ANA, Holistic Nurses Assn., Am. Urol. Assn. Allied, Tex. Nurses Assn., U. Tex. Nursing Alumni Assn. (past treas.), Tex. Jr. Coll. Tchrs. Assn., Rotary, Sigma Theta Tau.

FRAME, NANCY DAVIS, lawyer; b. Brookings, S.D., Dec. 13, 1944; m. J. Davidson Frame, Mar. 28, 1970 (div. Oct. 1994); 1 child, Katherine Adele; m. Kelly C. Kammerer, Oct. 2, 1999. BS, S.D. State U., 1966; MA, Georgetown U., 1968, JD, 1976. Bar: D.C. 1976. Atty., advisor AID, Washington, 1976-81, asst. gen. counsel, 1981-86; dep. dir. Trade and Devel. Agy., Washington, 1986-99. Bd. dirs. Daktronics, Inc. Recipient Superior Honor award AID, 1984, Presdl. Meritorious Rank award, 1993, Disting. Alumnus award S.D. State U., 1998, Presdl. Disting. Rank award, 1998; Fulbright fellow, 1966, NDEA fellow, 1967. Address: Chemin de la Bernarde Route de Lorgues 83300 Draguignan France Personal E-mail: ndframe@hotmail.com.

FRAME, SUSAN S., special education educator; b. Napoleon, Ohio, June 6, 1952; d. George Raymond and Virginia Sappington (Clabaugh) Schey; m. Thomas F. Baslaugh (div.); children: Thomas Adam Boslaugh, Benjamin Schey Boslaugh, Elizabeth V. Skinner; m. Dennis C. Frame, Jan. 2, 1999. BS in Edn. in Vocal Music, S.W. Mo. State U., Springfield, 1996, MS in Edn. in Spl. Edn., 2003. Lic. practical nurse, Mo.; cert. tchr. visual impairments Mo., tchr. learning disabilities Mo., tchr. vocal music Mo. Tax checker H&R Block, Springfield, 1981; nurse Vis. Nurses Assn., Springfield, 1990—92; tchr. visually impaired Marshfield (Mo.) Pub. Schs. Owner Fair Grove Plumbing. Co-author: (book) 50 Years of Flight with My Guardian Angel, 1990, composer songs. Choir mem. St. James Ch. Ozark Anglican Coun., 1979—; adviser Boy Scouts, Fair Grove, 1985—93, 4-H Club, Fair Grove, 1985—93. Mem.: DAR, Mo. State Tchrs. Assn., Assn. for Edn. and Rehab. of the Blind and Visually Impaired. Republican. Avocations: quilting, music. Office: Marshfield Pub Schs 650 N Locust Marshfield MO 65706

FRAMPTON, J. PAIGE, lawyer; b. Media, Pa., Dec. 3, 1970; BA, Temple U., 1993; JD, Widener U., 1999. Bar: Md. 2000, Pa. 2003. Asst. dep. atty. gen. Del. Dept. Justice, 1999; assoc. Martin, Banks, Pond, Lehocky & Wilson, Phila. Mem.: Phila. Bar Assn., Nat. Assn. of Disability Reps., Nat. Orgn. of Social Security Claimants Reps. Office: Martin, Banks, Pond, Lehocky & Wilson 1818 Market St, 35th Fl Philadelphia PA 19103 Office Phone: 215-587-8400. Office Fax: 215-587-8417. E-mail: jpframpton@paworkinjury.com.*

FRAN, GRANDMA See BROWN, FRANCES

FRANCES, MARIE CECILIA, theater producer, television producer; b. Bklyn., Jan. 18, 1937; d. Rocco Joseph Lucadamo and Yolanda Frances Romano; children: Arthur Robert, Elissa Marie, Marie Peggy. AA, George Washington U., 1962; BS, Md. U., 1966; MS, Northfield U., 2003. Pres., owner Marie Frances Prodns., Inc., Las Vegas, 1971—; nat. dir. Anti Drug Program, Exec. Office of Pres., Washington, 1972—75; field prodr. ABC's Ripley's Believe it or Not, 1980—85; exec. prodr. Mt. Kilimanjaro Marathon, Tanzania, 1991—, Miss Egypt Universe, Cairo, 1987—97, The Paramids Marathon, 1987—97. Pub. info. officer USAID, Cairo, 1981—85. Exec. prodr.: (video presentations projects) USAID, 1983—86 (Best Video Prodn. Food for Peace, 1983); exec. prodr.: (films) Acupuncture the Eastern Cure, 1971; prodr.: (radio show) The Marie Frances Hour, 1998, Miss Latin Star, 2005. Founder, pres. The Frances Found., Las Vegas, 2005—. Recipient Outstanding Achievement, Office of Pres., Washington, 1967. Mem.: Rotary. Roman Catholic. Avocations: music, piano, art. Home: 8120 Bay Harbor Dr Las Vegas NV 89128 Office: Marie Frances Prodns Inc 8370 W Cheyenne Ave Ste 109-365 Las Vegas NV 89129 Office Phone: 702-952-9940.

FRANCESCONI, LOUISE L., defense equipment manufacturing company executive; b. Calif., Mar. 1953; BA, Scripps Coll., 1975; MBA, UCLA, 1978. With Hughes Missile Systems Co., 1976—98, CFO, 1993, pres., 1996—98; sr. v.p. Raytheon Systems Co., 1998—99; v.p. Raytheon Co., 1999—; dep. gen. mgr. Raytheon Missile Systems, Tucson, 1998—99, gen. mgr., 1999—2002, pres., 2002—. Bd. dirs. Stryker Corp., 2006—; bd. trustees Tucson Med. Ctr. Healthcare, Tucson Airport Authority. Mem. Ariz. Gov.'s Coun. on Innovation and Tech., 2003—; nat. bd. advisors Eller Coll. Bus. and Pub. Adminstrn., U. Ariz.; bd. trustees Tucson Med. Ctr. Healthcare, Tucson Airport Authority. Named Tech. Exec. of the Yr., Eller Coll. & U. Ariz. Coll. Engring. & MInes, 2002; recipient Lifetime Achievement award, Women in Aerospace, 2005. Office: Raytheon Missile Systems 1151 E Hermans Rd Tucson AZ 85706*

FRANCHINI, ROXANNE, bank executive; b. NYC, Mar. 20, 1951; d. Tullio and Jean (Brady) Franchini. Student, Emerson Coll., Ricker Coll., New Sch. Social Rsch. With Princess Marcella Borghese divsn. Revlon, NYC, 1972-73, TWA Airlines, 1973-74; asst. to pres. NY Shipping Assn., NYC, 1974-79; benefits mgr. Kidde, Inc., NYC, 1979-83; 2d v.p. pension trust fin. svcs. Chase Manhattan Bank, N.A., NYC, 1983-85, v.p. mgr. global securities, 1985-89; v.p., sales dir. global custody worldwide securities svcs. Citibank, NYC, 1989-91; v.p. Mellon Bank, Pitts., 1991—2001; 1st v.p. Mellon Fin. Corp., Pitts., 2002—05, Phila., 2005—. Chair fin. local fund raising campaigns. Mem.: So. Assn. Coll. and Univ. Bus. Offices, Ea. Assn. Coll. and Univ. Bus. Offices, Nat. Assn. Coll. and Univ. Bus. Offices. Home: 1415 Ocean Shore Blvd Ormond Beach FL 32176-3673 Office Phone: 215-553-4398.

FRANCIOSI, L. PATT, psychologist, mental health services professional, consultant; b. Jersey City, Jan. 8, 1943; d. Arthur Francis and Leona (Quinn) Rodgers; m. Ralph Anthony Franciosi, Apr. 4, 1964; children: Michael, Patricia, James. PhD, Marquette U., 1996. Psychologist Marquette U., Milw., 1995—. Pres. for N.Am., World Fedn. for Mental Health, Va., 1996—; mem. adv. com. NIMH, Washington, 1990-94; chair Nat. Coalition for the Prevention of Mental and Emotional Disabilities, 1991-93; presenter in field. Contbr. numerous articles to profl. jours. Recipient Disting. Svc. awards for mental health promotion activities. Mem. World Fedn. for Mental Health (life), Jr. League of Milw. (pres. 1988-89), Nat. Mental Health Assn. (pres. 1990-91). Home: 932 W Shaker Cir Thiensville WI 53092-6032

FRANCIS, BARBARA JOAN, nurse, paralegal; b. Toledo, Ohio, Oct. 28, 1957; d. Robert Arthur and Patricia Louise (Hansen) Francis; children: Jessica Lynn, Zachary Alfred, Katherine Elizabeth. RN, Toledo Hosp. Sch. of Nursing, Toledo, Ohio, 1978; Nurse Paralegal, U. Toledo, Toledo, Ohio, 2001; BSN, Lourdes Coll., Sylvania, Ohio, 2002. RN Ohio, 1978, registered In Patient Ob., NCC, 1991, lic. Elec. Fetal Monitoring, NCC, 1998, cert. Advanced Life Support in Ob. Instr., The Am. Acad. of Family Physicians, 1998, Neonatal Resucitation Instr., Am. Acad. of Pediat./ Am. Heart Assn., 1989, Basic Life Support Instr., Am. Heart Assn., 1998. Staff nurse Toledo Hosp., Toledo, 1978—82, Flower Hosp., Sylvania, Ohio, 1982—97, Toledo Hosp., Toledo, 1986—97, 2004—; asst. nurse mgr. St. Vincent Hosp., Toledo, 1997—98, staff nurse, 1998—2004. Day care educator Day Cares, Toledo, 1997—2002. Mem.: NACC, ACNM, AWHONN (cert. prins. and practices fetal monitoring instr. 2005), Bus. and Profl. Women (assoc.), Sigma Theta Tau/Zeta Theta Chpt. (Clin. Practice Award 2002). Home: 3314 Stanhope Dr Toledo OH 43606 Office: Toledo Hosp 2142 N Cove Toledo OH 43607 Office Phone: 419-291-4325.

FRANCIS, ELIZABETH ROMINE, secondary school educator, theater director; b. Clarksburg, WVa., Sept. 10, 1920; d. John Ransel and Virginia Snider Romine; m. Jack Stanley Francis, Feb. 13, 1943; children: Michael Stanley, John Maurice. BM, WVa. U., 1942, MM, 1963, JD; grad. drama, Ohio U., 1980. Tchr. Elem. Sch., Clarksburg, W.Va., 1942—43, Jr. H.S., Clarksburg, W.Va., 1943—44, Sr. H.S., Clarksburg, W.Va., 1943—45, New Martinsville, W.Va., 1960—93; tchr. adult edn. WVa. U. Ext., New Martinsville, 1960—70; Fred Waring workshop staff mem. Waring Enterprises, Delaware Water Gap, 1988—90; dir. theater activities Park & Recreation, New Martinsville, W.Va., 1993—2001. Chmn. theater divsn. Parks and Recreation, New Martinsville, W.Va., 1993—2001. Prodr., dir.: (musical theater) Cmty. Theater, 1993—2001. Recipient Acad. Excellence award, State of WVa., 1985. Republican. Methodist. Avocations: golf, bridge. Office: New Martinsville Parks and Recreation 191 Main St New Martinsville WV 26155 Personal E-mail: eliza@ovis.net.

FRANCIS, JULIE, beverage company executive; d. Butch and Tonie. BBA, Alfred U., 1993. Dir. mktg. Rabun, Hatch & Assoc., Atlanta, 1993—95; key account category mgr. Coca-Cola Enterprises, Atlanta, 1995—96, key account mgr., 1996—97, market devel. mgr. NY divsn. NY, 1998—99, dir. sales NY divsn. NY, 1998—99, sales ctr. mgr. NY divsn. NY, 1999—2001, area v.p. Eastern Great Lakes divsn. Rochester, NY, 2001—02, area v.p. Lakeshore divsn., 2002—04, v.p., gen. mgr. Midwest Bus. Unit, 2005—. Named one of 40 Under 40, Crain's Chgo. Bus., 2005. Office: Coca-Cola Enterprises 2500 Windy Ridge Parkway Atlanta GA 30339*

FRANCIS, KERRI ANN, athletic trainer; b. Charleston, W.Va., Sept. 1, 1977; d. James Edwin Francis and Marsha Lee Booth. BA in Athletic Tng., Marshall U., Huntington, W.Va., 1999, MA in Phys. Edn., 2001. Cert. athletic trainer. Head athletic trainer Bluefield State Coll., W.Va., 2002—, sr. woman adminstr., 2002—. Co-adv. student athlete adv. com. Bluefield State Coll., 2003—, dir. sports info., 2004—05. Mem.: W.Va. Athletic Trainers Assn., Nat. Athletic Trainers Assn. Avocations: football, baseball, travel. Home: 137 Bratton Ave Apt 11B Princeton WV 24740 Office: Bluefield State Coll 219 Rock St Bluefield WV 24701

FRANCIS, LYNNE ANN, elementary school educator, music educator; b. Parkersburg, W.Va., May 18, 1961; d. Gale Meyer and Mabel Eileen Hains; m. Randal Craig Francis, June 17, 1989; 1 child, Brent. MusB, SUNY, Fredonia, 1982, MusM, 1984. Cert. Pathwise mentor, permanent cert. music tchr. Ohio, N.Y., W.Va., lic. supr. Ohio. Summer employee E.I. DuPont, Washington, W.Va., 1980—82; music specialist elem. sch. Marietta City Schs., Ohio, 1984—; tchr. adaptive music for spl. learners. Freelance harpist, Marietta, Ohio, 1982—2000; lectr. in field. Mem.: NEA, Ohio Music Edn. Assn., Music Educator's Nat. Conf., Ohio Edn. Assn., Sigma Alpha Iota. Avocations: crocheting, music, counted cross stitch, photography, computers. Home: 165 Edendale Ln Parkersburg WV 26101 Office: Marietta City Schs 701 3d St Marietta OH 45750 Office Phone: 740-374-6500. Personal E-mail: wvharpo2004@yahoo.com.

FRANCIS, TRINA MICHELE, elementary school educator; b. Palatka, Fla., Aug. 23, 1978; d. Charlie and Roberta Reed Francis. BS in Econs., U. Fla., Gainesville, 1996—2000. Cert. social scis. tchr. Fla. Dept. Edn., 2006. 8th grade history tchr. Crescent City Jr./Sr. HS, Fla., 2004—. Sunday sch. tchr. Zion Temple Ch. God Christ, Palatka, Fla., 2004—06. Grantee Fla. Gold Seal Scholarship, State Fla., 2000—01. D-Liberal. Pentecoastal. Avocation: reading.

FRANCISCO, ANA B., medical/surgical nurse, legal nurse consultant; b. Havana, Cuba, Oct. 19, 1955; arrived in U.S., 1959, naturalized; d. Jose M. and Rosario Aspillaga; children: Alex G., Ana Carolina. AA, Miami Dade C.C., Fla., 1975; BA in Psychology and Biol. Scis., Fla. Internat. Univ., Miami, 1976—78; MD, U. Central East, San Pedro, Dominican Rep., 1985; BSN, Fla. Internat. Univ., Miami, 2002. Legal nurse cons.: Legal Nurse Cons. Inst. 2004; RN Fla. Bd. Nursing, 2003, cert. ICD-9 coder specialist, Kendall Regional Medical Center, 2000, critical care nurse, Kendall Regional Medical Center, 2004, IV high-tech. nurse, NUS, Inc., 2003. EKG tech. Am. Hosp. Miami, Fla., 1978—79; telemetry and monitor tech. Coral Gables Hosp., 1979—80; utilization rev. coord. PAL-MED Health Svcs., Miami Lakes, 1989—91; Medicare and Medicaid quality improvement coord. Visiting Nurses Assn., Dade County, Miami, 1991—98; quality improvement officer, managed care and HMO's Preferred Med. Plans, Coral Gables, 1999—2000; quality assurance analyst and home health educator Medex Home Health Care, Miami, Fla., 2000—02; hosp. coord. Jackson Meml. Hosp., 2002—03; RN and case mgr. Am. Providers Home Health, 2002—03; RN ICU Kendall Regional Med. Ctr., 2003—04; weekend clin. nurse supr. and asst. adminstr. Hialeah Shores Nursing Home, 2003—04; adminstr. and dir. nursing Fla. Health Care Ctr., 2004—05; dir. nursing Total Home Health Care, Inc., 2005—; med. surg. nurse Larkin Hosp., 2005—. Bd. dirs. Home Health, Miami, Fla., 2004. Mem.: AACN (assoc.), Nursing Mgmt. Orgn. (assoc.), Nurses Services Orgn. (assoc.), Am. Diabetic Assn. (assoc.), Alzheimer's Assn. (assoc.), Am. Soc. Legal Nurse Consultants (assoc.), Am. Nurse Assn. (assoc.).

FRANCISCO, DEBORAH ANTOSH, educational administrative professional; b. Wilkes-Barre, Pa, Mar. 8, 1952; d. Albert and Marie Iris (Stuka) Antosh; m. John Thomas McCauley, Sept. 11, 1970 (div. Sept. 1983); 1 child, John-Austen; m. John Patrick Francisco, July 28, 1988; 1 child, Theresa. BA, Cedar Crest Coll., Allentown, Pa., 1984; EdM in Ednl. Adminstrn., Rutgers U., 2003. Cert. elem. tchr., Pa.; cert. elem. and nursery sch. tchr., N.J. Elem. tchr. Allentown Sch. Dist., 1984-88; tchr. basic skills Perth Amboy Sch. Dist., NJ, 1988-89, elem. tchr. NJ, 1989—90; tchr. St. Matthias, Somerset, NJ, 1993—96; order processor divsn. housing and confs. Rutgers U., 1997—99, asst. mgr. adminstrn. Coll. Ave. campus, 1999—. Democrat. Roman Catholic. Home: 14 Canadian Woods Rd Marlboro NJ 07746-1672

FRANCK, ARDATH AMOND, psychologist, educator; b. Wehrum, Pa., May 5, 1925; d. Arthur and Helen Lucille (Sharp) Amond; m. Frederick M. Franck, Mar. 18, 1945; children: Sheldon, Candace. BS in Edn., Kent State U., 1946, MA, 1947; PhD, Western Res. U., 1956. Cert. high sch. tchr., elem. supr., sch. psychologist, speech and hearing therapist. Instr. Western Res. U., Cleve., 1953, U. Akron, 1947—50; sch. psychologist Summit County Schs., Ohio, 1950—60; cons. psychologist Wadsworth Pub. Schs., Ohio, 1946—86; dir. Akron Edn. Ctr., Ohio, 1950—. Pres. Twirling Unlimited, 1982—; cons., dir. Hobbitts Pre-Sch., 1973—88. Author: Your Child Learns, 1976. Mem.: Ohio Psychol. Assn., Internat. Reading Assn., Am. Speech and Hearing Assn., Soroptimist (Akron), Mensa. Home: 631 Ghent Rd Akron OH 44333-2629 Office: Akron Edn Ctr 700 Ghent Rd Akron OH 44333-2698 Office Phone: 330-666-1161.

FRANCK CSJ, SUZANNE ELIZABETH, religious studies educator, minister; b. Bklyn., July 3, 1956; d. William Francis and Marie Salome Franck. BS in Sci. Edn., St. John's U., 1978; MS in Edn., Queen's Coll., 1985; MA in Theology, Seminary of Immaculate Conception, 1990; MPhil in Theology, Fordham U., 2004, PhD in Theology, 2006. Mem. Sisters St. Joseph of Brentwood. Jr. HS tchr. Blessed Sacrament Sch., Valley Stream, NY, 1980—82, St. Martha's Sch., Uniondale, NY, 1982—85, St. Philip Neri Sch., Northport, NY, 1985—87, youth mininstry rel. edn. dir., 1985—88; pastoral assoc. St. Elizabeth Ann Seton, 1988—95; campus min. and prof. St. Joseph's Coll., Patchogue, NY, 1995—. Founder, pres. Footsteps Toward Hope Ovarian Cancer Walkathon, LI, NY, 2003—; vol. Christa Ho., West Babylon, NY, 2000—; mem. Northport Regional Sch. Bd., 1985—95; diocesan dir. Rainbows Inc., Rockville Center, NY, 1989—97; retreat dir. various parishes, schs. and religious cmtys., 1985—. Mem.: Cath. Theology Soc., Cath. Theol. Soc. Am., Am. Acad. Religion. Avocations: tennis, sailing, reading, walking. Office: St Joseph's Coll 155 W Roe Blvd Patchogue NY 11772 Office Phone: 631-447-3372. Business E-Mail: sfranck.s@jcny.edu.

FRANCKE, GLORIA NIEMEYER, retired pharmacist, editor, writer; b. Dillsboro, Ind., Apr. 28, 1922; d. Albert B. and Fannie K. (Libbert) Niemeyer; m. Donald Eugene Francke, Apr. 15, 1956. BS in Pharmacy, Purdue U., 1942; PharmD (hon.), 1988—; PharmD, U. Cin., 1971; postgrad., U. Mich., 1945. Pharmacist Dillsboro Drug Store, 1943-44; instr. Sch. Pharmacy Purdue U., Lafayette, Ind., 1943; asst. to chief pharmacist U. Mich. Hosp., Ann Arbor, 1944-46; assoc. editor Am. Jour. Hosp. Pharmacy, Washington, 1944-64; asst. dir. divsn. hosp. pharmacy Am. Pharm. Assn., Washington, 1946-56; exec. sec. Am. Soc. Hosp. Pharmacists, Ann Arbor, 1949-60, acting dir. dept. comm. Washington, 1963-64; drug lit. specialist Nat. Libr. Medicine, Bethesda, Md., 1965-67; clin. pharmacy tchg. coord. VA Hosp., Cin., 1967-71; asst. clin. prof. clin. pharmacy Coll. Pharmacy U. Cin., 1967-71; chief program evaluation br. Alcohol & Drug Dependence Svc. VA Ctrl. Office, Washington, 1971-75; dir. Pharmacy Intelligence Ctr. Am. Pharm. Assn., Washington, 1975-85; ret., 1988. Mem. Roche Hosp. Pharmacy Adv. Bd., 1971-74; judge for ann. Lunsford Richardson Pharmacy awards, 1963, 64; mem. com. stds. for drug abuse treatment and rehab. programs Joint Commn. Accreditation of Hosps., 1974-75. Author: (with D.E. Francke, C.J. Latiolais and N.F.H. Ho) Mirror to Hospital Pharmacy, 1964; contbr. articles to profl. jours. Bd. dirs., mem. found., co-chair women's bd. Ingleside Presbyn. Retirement Cmty., Washington., 1999-2003. Recipient Harvey A.K. Whitney award Mich. Soc. Hosp. Pharmacists, 1953, Disting. Alumnus award Purdue U. Sch. Pharmacy, 1985, Remington Honor medal, 1987, Career Achievement award Profl. Frat. Assn., 1991, Fedn. Internat. Pharm. Lifetime Achievement in the Practice of Pharmacy award, 1996; also various commendations. Mem. Internat. Pharm. Fedn., Am. Inst. History of Pharmacy (exec. sec. 1966-78), Tex. Soc. Hosp. Pharmacists (hon.), Am. Pharm. Assn. (hon. chmn. 1986, Gloria Niemeyer Francke Leadership Mentor award named in her honor 1995), Am. Soc. Hosp. Pharmacists (Donald E. Francke medal 1995), Kappa Epsilon, Rho Chi. Presbyterian. Personal E-mail: glor238@aol.com.

FRANCKE, LINDA BIRD, journalist; b. NYC, Mar. 14, 1939; d. Samuel Curtis and Janet (King) Bird; m. G.D. Mackenzie, Jan. 12, 1961; 1 son, Andrew Mackenzie; m. Albert Francke III, Oct. 7, 1967; 2 daughters: Caitlin, Tapp. Student, Bradford Jr. Coll., 1958, New Sch. for Social Rsch., 1963—65. Copywriter Young & Rubicam, Inc., N.Y.C., 1960-63, Ogilvy & Mather, Inc., N.Y.C., 1965-67; contbg. editor N.Y. Mag., N.Y.C., 1968-72, 80—; gen. editor Newsweek Mag., N.Y.C., 1972-77; columnist N.Y. Times, 1977—; TV news commentator Spl. Edit., 1978-79. Dir. New Directions; juror Am. Book Awards, 1981; Co-chmn. Writer's Resource Center, Southampton, N.Y. Contbr. (works to anthologies including) The N.Y. Spy, 1967, The Power Game, 1970, Running Against the Machine, 1969, Women: A Book for Men, 1979, Hers: Through Women's Eyes, 1985, America Firsthand, Vol. II: From Reconstruction to the Present, 1994; author: The Ambivalence of Abortion, 1978, Growing Up Divorced, 1983, Ground Zero: The Gender Wars in the Military, 1997; collaborator: First Lady from Plains, 1984, Ferraro: My Story, 1985, A Woman of Egypt, 1987, Daughter of Destiny, 1989, Signature Life, 1998, Life So Far, 2000, On Faith, 2002, On The Road With Francis of Assisi: A Timeless Journey Through Umbria and Tuscany, and Beyond, 2005. Mem. Women's Commn. for Refugee Women and Children, Internat. Rescue Com. Inc.; chmn. East End Choice; candidate N.Y. State Assembly, 2d Dist., 1990; del. to Dem. Nat. Conv., 1992; bd. dirs. Bridgehampton Child Care & Recreational Ctr., Inc., The Retreat. Recipient award Cannes Film Festival, 1969, Nat. Clarion award, 1994; finalist Helen Bernstein Book award Excellence in Journalism, 1998. Mem. Authors Guild, Women's Media Group N.Y.C., Eastville Hist. Soc., Women Mil. Aviators, Inc. E-mail: linda@hamptons.com.

FRANCKE, REND RAHIM, former ambassador; b. Baghdad, Iraq, 1949; arrived in U.S., 1981, naturalized, 1987; d. Mahdi Rahim; m. Frederic B. Francke. MA in English, U. Cambridge; MA in French Lit., Sorbonne. Co-founder The Iraqi Found., Washington, 1991—2003, dir., 1991—2003; amb. Iraq Washington, 2003—06. Co-author: The Arab Shi'a: Forgotten Muslims, 2000. Office: The Iraq Found 1012 14th St NW Ste 1110 Washington DC 20005

FRANCKE, SUSAN, elementary school educator; b. Farmington, N.Mex., Sept. 11, 1959; d. Bob Dean and Angie Evelyn Fitt; m. Erich Lawrence Francke, June 6, 1981; children: Brittani Rae, Erich Lawrence. BS in Edn.,

N.Mex. State U., Las Cruces, 1981, MA in Edn., 1986. Coord. and tchr. phys. edn. Hobbs Mcpl. Schs., N.Mex., 1981—82, tchr. grade 2, 1982—88, tchr. grade 1, 1988—97, reading specialist, 1997—. Mem. writing com. social studies benchmarks and stds. N.Mex. State Dept. Edn., Hobbs, 1996—97; chair student assistance team Hobbs Mcpl. Schs., 1998—. Mem. Philanthropic Edn. Orgn., Hobbs, N.Mex., 2004—; deacon First Presbyn. Ch., 2006—. Mem.: Internat. Reading Assn., Phi Kappa Phi. Republican. Avocations: reading, gardening, walking. Home: 307 W Jason St Hobbs NM 88242-9732 Office: Hobbs Mcpl Schs 1515 E Sanger Hobbs NM 88240

FRANCKE, UTA, geneticist, educator; b. Wiesbaden, Germany, Sept. 9, 1942; arrived in U.S., 1969; d. Kurt and Gertrud Muller; m. Bertold Richard Francke, May 27, 1967 (div. 1982); m. Heinz Furthmayr, July 27, 1986. MD, U. Munich, Fed. Republic Germany, 1967; MS, Yale U., 1985. Diplomate Am. Bd. Pediatrics, Am. Bd. Med. Genetics (bd. dirs. 1981-84). Asst. prof. U. Calif., San Diego, 1973—78; assoc. prof. Yale U., New Haven, 1978—85, prof., 1985—88; prof. genetics Stanford (Calif.) U., 1989—. Investigator Howard Hughes Med. Inst., Stanford, 1989—2000, mem. sci. rev. bd., Bethesda, Md., 1986—88; mem. mammalian genetics study sect. NIH, Bethesda, 1990—94. Profl. advisor March of Dimes Birth Defects Found., White Plains, NY, 1990, Marfan Assn., Port Washington, NY, 1991. Mem.: Am. Soc. Human Genetics (pres. 1999, bd. dirs. Rockville, Md. chpt. 1981—84), Soc. for Inherited Metabolic Disorders, Soc. for Pediatric Rsch., Human Genome Orgn., Inst. Medicine of NAS (assoc.). Avocation: piloting. Office: Stanford U Med Sch Beckman Ctr Stanford CA 94305-5323 Office Phone: 650-725-8089. Business E-Mail: ufrancke@stanford.edu.

FRANCO, ANNEMARIE WOLETZ, editor; b. Somerville, N.J., Sept. 18, 1933; d. Frederick Franz and Bertha (Laugginger) Woletz; m. Frederick Nicholas Franco, June 11, 1977 (dec. Feb. 1998). Student, Wood Coll. of Bus. Editorial asst. Internat. Musician, then assoc. editor, 1965-88, ret., 1988. Republican. Presbyterian. Avocations: writing, music, cooking, travel. Home: 166 Wellstone Dr Palm Coast FL 32164-4111

FRANCO, BARBARA ALICE, museum director; b. NYC, Mar. 16, 1945; d. Alexander and Sarah E. (Johnson) F.; m. John A. Mayer, Apr. 8, 1973; children: Lee, Samantha. BA, Bryn Mawr Coll., 1965; MA, SUNY, Cooperstown, 1966. Curator of decorative arts Munson-Williams-Proctor Inst., Utica, NY, 1966-73; curator of collections Mus. of Our Nat. Heritage, Lexington, Mass., 1974-85, asst. dir., 1985-89; asst. dir. for museums Minn. Hist. Soc., St. Paul, 1990-95; exec. dir. Hist. Soc. Washington, 1995—2003, Penn. Hist. and Museum Com., Phila., 2003—. Author exhbn. catalogs; editor: Folk Roots, New Roots, 1988, Ideas and Images, 1992. Mem. Minn. Assn. Museums (chmn. 1992-93). Mem. Bryn Mawr Club (pres. 1982-84). Office: Penn Historical and Museum Com 300 N St Harrisburg PA 17120 E-mail: bfranco@state.pu.us.

FRANCO, ELAINE ADELE, librarian; b. N.Y.C., Jan. 24, 1948; d. Alexander and Sarah Eleanor (Johnson) Franco; m. James Paul Webster, Dec. 29, 1982 (dec. Sept. 1993). BA magna cum laude, Hope Coll., Holland, Mich., 1969; MLS, U. Mich., 1975, MA, 1976. Cataloger U. Nebr.-Lincoln Librs., 1977-81, prin. cataloger, 1981-90, Shields Libr., U. Calif., Davis, 1990—. Bibliographer: MLA International Bibliography, 1979—, First Printings of American Authors, 1977-79; editor conf. procs. Recipient Disting. Svc award Nebr. Libr. Assn. Coll. and Univ. Sect. 1984. Mem. MLA, ALA (councilor-at-large 1987-91), Assn. Libr. Collections and Tech. Svcs. (bd. dirs. 2005-06, chmn. coun. regional groups 2005-06), Calif. Libr. Assn. (pres. access, collections and tech. svcs. sect. 1998-99, assembly mem.-at-large 2006—), Calif. Acad. and Rsch. Librs., Beta Phi Mu. Office: U Calif Shields Libr 100 NW Quad Davis CA 95616-5292 Business E-Mail: eafranco@ucdavis.edu.

FRANCOEUR, CHRISTINA, special education educator; b. Springfield, Mass., Dec. 24, 1951; d. John Harry and Santa Martha (Pescetta) Malmborg; m. William John Weckerly; children: Lida Maria Powell, Danel Susan Eitel. BA, Westfield State Coll., 1998, MEd, 2000; cert. in Advanced Grad. Studies, Our Lady of the Elms, 2004. Spl. edn. tchr. Paper Mill Elem. Sch., Westfield, Mass., 1998—. With USAF. Mem.: Phi Kappa Phi. Roman Catholic. Avocations: snow shoeing, cross country skiing, reading, swimming, aerobics. E-mail: cwec@comcast.net.

FRANCOEUR, SHEILA T., state representative; b. Lowell, Mass., Feb. 18, 1938; m. Ronald Francoeur; two children. BA, Fla. State U., 1971. Banker, ret. 1993; ret., 1993; mem. dist. 15 N.H. Ho. of Reps., 1996—. Mem., chmn. econ. devel. com., City of Hampton; mem. vice-chmn. policy bldg. study com.; mem. mcpl. budget com.; spkr. Pro Tem, 2003-04. Bd. dirs. Leadership Seacoast; dir. Rockingham Econ. Development Corp.; chmn. Commerce Com., 2005. Mem. Rotary (v.p., bd. dirs.), AAUW (treas., bd. dirs.). Roman Catholic. Home: 88 Kings Hwy Hampton NH 03842-4317 Office: NH State Legis State House Concord NH 03301 E-mail: sheila.francouer@leg.state.nh.us.

FRANCOIS, LINDA JEAN, medical/surgical and psychiatric nurse; b. Cin., Nov. 4, 1938; d. Eugene Frederick and Hilda Barger (Patteson) Kaltenbrun; m. Leland E. Francois, Sept. 6, 1980; children: Christina, Robyne, Eric Striepeke Diploma, Christ Hosp. Sch. Nursing, Cin., 1960; student, Riverside City Coll., 1978—79. Staff nurse occupl. rehab. and psychiatry Cin. Gen., 1960—61; pvt. duty, 1962; float charge nurse San Francisco Gen., 1963—64; med. office relief nurse, 1966; med. office nurse, 1977; supr. Beverly Manor Psychiat. Hosp., Riverside, Calif., 1978—80. Former vol. Riverside Cmty. Players, Riverside Children's Theatre, Jr. League, Girl Scouts U.S., many geneal. orgns Mem. Nat. League Nursing

FRANEY, BILLIE NOLAN, political activist; b. Eveleth, Minn., Sept. 17, 1930; d. Mark and Ann Murray Nolan; m. Neil Joseph Franey; children: Kathleen, Timothy, Nora, Colin, Patrick. Student, Carleton Coll., 1948-49, U. Minn., 1949-50; BA, Coll. St. Scholastica, 1952. Social worker Cath. Welfare, Mpls., 1952-53. Contbr. articles to profl. jours. Chair Indian Affairs, Minn. Mrs. Jaycees, 1962; mem. Charter Commn., White Bear Lake, Minn., 1962-65; pres. White Bear Lake LWV, 1965-67; lobbyist Common Cause of Minn., 1979, Minn. LWV, 1980, AAUW, 1987-89; mem. met. futures task force Met. Coun., 1988-89; co-chair Women Come to The Capitol, Minn. Women's Consortium. Named Outstanding Young Women of Am., 1966; revipient Sister Ann Edward Scholar award The Coll. of St. Scholostica, 1992. Mem. AAUW (pres. 1992-94, St. Paul program v.p. 1990-92, legis. pub. policy chair 1987-89, Minn. chpt. legis. pub. policy v.p. 1987-89, scholarship named for as a gift from St. Paul AAUW 1989, Women as Agts. of Change award 1991, chair St. Paul scholarship trust 2001—), Coun. Met. Area LWV (chair 1981-83, program and study chair 1979-81, bd. mem. 1978-79). Avocations: reading, biking, cross country skiing, gardening. Home: 1323 Hedman Way Saint Paul MN 55110-3360

FRANEY, CATHERINE T., elementary school educator; b. Ashland, Pa., Nov. 6, 1943; d. George William and Elizabeth (McDonald) Dougherty; m. William George Franey, Nov. 18, 1966; children: William Sean, Molly Elizabeth Suplee, Ryan Patrick, Sarah Jeanne, Emily Therese. BS, U. Md., 1965; postgrad., Trinity Coll., Washington, 1992-96. Elem. sch. tchr., Prince Georges County, Md., 1965-71; life skills tchr. Severn Sch., Severna Park, Md., 1992—. Mem. Ward One Residents Assn., Annapolis, Md., 1995—. Mem. AAUW, ACA, Md. Assn. Counseling and Devel., Delta Gamma Sorority (Beta Sigma chpt. pres. 1964-65).

FRANGES, GAYLE LOUISE, elementary school educator; b. Bethlehem, Pa., July 17, 1947; d. Ellsworth Vance and Hildegarde Emma Wildoner; m. Charles Norman Franges, Oct. 26, 1968 (separated); children: Joel, Rori; 1 child, Fabricio Olsson. BSc in Edn., East Stroudsburg U., Pa., 1969. Cert. instrnl. I tchg. Pa., tchr. math. K-12 N.J. Tchr. kindergarten East Windsor Sch. Dist., Hightstown, NJ, 1969—76; office mgr. Burt Ins. Agy., Valapraiso, Ind., 1976—78; officer mgr./co-owner Bethlehem Woodworks Inc., Pa., 1987—96; substitute tchr. Saucon Valley Elem. Sch., Hellertown, Pa., 1986—97, learning support tchr., 1997—2001; tchr. 5th grade St. Thomas More Sch., Allentown, Pa., 2001—. Pvt. tutor, 1997—2006. Vol. ann. cancer boutique Am. Cancer Soc., Bethlehem, 1985—95; mem. Holy Child Missions Assn., 2004—, Grace Moravian Ch., Center Valley, Pa. Fellow, DaVinci Inst. Sci. and Tech., 2004—06. Mem.: Nat. Cath. Educators Assn., Kappa Delta Pi. Avocations: skiing, swimming, reading, music, gardening. Office: St Thomas More Sch 1040 Flexer Ave Allentown PA 18103 Personal E-mail: franggstm@yahoo.com.

FRANK, AMÉLIE LORRAINE, marketing professional; b. L.A., Feb. 5, 1960; d. Lawrence Bruce and Phébé Exilda (Brodeur) Frank. BA in English, Creative Writing, U. Calif., Irvine, 1981. Letters editor Petersen Pub., West Hollywood, Calif., 1983—85; owner, writer Mysterious Affairs, Hollywood, 1984—88; script svcs. supr. Universal City (Calif.) Studios, 1985—86; mkt. rschr. Universal Pictures Mktg., Universal City, 1986—94; owner, pub. Sacred Beverage Press, Venice, Calif., 1994—; rsch. coord. Buena Vista Pictures Mktg., Burbank, Calif., 1994—2004; events coord. Red Hen Press, 2005; copywriter Nat. Notary Assn., 2005—. Host poetry readings Hot House Cafe, North Hollywood, 1996—99, Exile Books & Music, 1999—2000; co-dir. Valley Contemporary Poets, 1999—2002; host Killer Poetry, 2000—01; co-webmaster Billybobapalooza Ofcl. Billy Bob Thornton website; mng. editor Gatsby Mag., 2006—. Author: (poems) A Resilient Heart and Other Visceral Comforts, 1992, Flame and Loss of Breath, 1996, Doing Time on Planet Billy Bob, 2000; co-author: Drink Me, 1997, Bird Interpretations, 1998; editor: (book) God the Motion Picture, 1994; co-editor: Blue Satellite Jour., 1994—2000; performer spoken word (albums) The Essential Girl, 2001, Retro Hell music reviewer Ind. Revs. Site; CD, Michael Shipp Xcursion "The Adventures of Roosterboy". Facilitator buddy program AIDS Project, L.A., Hollywood, 1988—92; trustee Beyond Baroque, 1999—, artist, cmty. advisor coun., 1998—99; mem. med. staff Disney Disaster Preparedness, Burbank, 1994—. Named L.A. Newer Poet, Beyond Baroque in conjunction with L.A. Poetry Festival, 1999; recipient award for favorite new poetry book, Readership, NEXT Mag., 1996, Spirit of Venice award, 2003. Mem.: NOW, Nat. Notary Assn., Poetry Soc. Am., Office Profl. Employees Internat. Union (newsletter editor 1991—94), PETA. Green Party. Avocations: reading, choral music, travel, films, working with animals. Office: The Sacred Beverage Press PO Box 10312 Burbank CA 91510-0312 Personal E-mail: poetamelie@aol.com.

FRANK, CHRISTINE MARIE, music educator; b. Akron, Ohio, Sept. 13, 1960; d. Alfred Maxwell Walker and Donna Jean Davis; children: Justin William, Kia Marie, Devin Michael. MusB, Bowling Green State U., Ohio, 1987; MA in Tchg., Marygrove Coll., Detroit, 2005. Cert. tchr. Ohio Dept. of Edn., 2003. Music tchr. Robinson Jr. H.S., Toledo, Ohio, 1989—; handbell choir dir. St. Peter's United Ch. of Christ, Millbury, Ohio, 1998—. Fine arts chairperson Robinson Jr. H.S., 1995—, dir. of the sch. musical, 1996—, dir. of the handbell choirs, 1995—; site coord. of making mid. grades work Making Mid. Grades Work/High Schools That Work/Robinson Jr. H.S., 2005—. Dir.(writer): (music video) Listen to the Cat (Toledo Winner of the Foot Locker School's Cool Video Contest, 1996). Active mem. St. Peter's United Ch. of Christ, Millbury, Ohio, 1988—2006. Recipient Gov.'s Ednl. Leadership award, Bob Taft, Gov. of the State of Ohio, 2004. Mem.: Toledo Fedn. Tchrs. (bldg. com. mem. 1993—, tchr. rep. 1993—2006), Music Educators Nat. Conf. D-Liberal. Protestant. Home: 16464 W Walbridge E Rd Graytown OH 43432 Office: Robinson Junior High School 1007 Grand Ave Toledo OH 43432 Office Phone: 419-244-3753. Personal E-mail: cfrank913@att.net. E-mail: christine.frank@tps.org.

FRANK, DEE, artist, educator; b. Greeley, Colo., July 5, 1931; d. Frank Albert Borton and Carolyn Frances Hayden; m. Leslie Arthur Frank, 1959 (div. 1978); children: Edward, David, Barbara. BFA, Idaho State U., 1953. Asst. med. illustrator Oreg. Health Scis. U., Portland, 1953-57, ophthalmic artist and technician, 1960-82; recreation leader U.S. Army, LaRochelle, France, 1957-59; pvt. practice graphic artist Portland, 1982-92; tour leader, 1992—. Elderhostel watercolor instr., 1992-2004; participant juried shows Watercolor Soc. Oreg., 1977—, N.W. Watercolor Soc., 1979, 82, 88, 89, 92, 96, 2002, 04Rocky Mountain Nat. Watermedia Exposition, 1987, 88, 97. One-person shows include The Main Gallery, Boise, 1990, The Dalles Art Ctr., 1987, Idaho State U., Transition Gallery, 1981, Galos Gallery, Boise, 1995, Artreach Gallery, Portland, 1998, Salem (Oreg.) Art Assn. Bush Barn Gallery, 2000, among others. Active Stanford Parents Club, Portland, 1980-83; vol. Ecumenical workcamp, P.R., 1951. Recipient numerous awards. Mem. Watercolor Soc. Oreg. (bd. mem. 1978-97, newsletter editor 1980-97, pres. 1995-96, Outstanding Svc. award 1992), N.W. Watercolor Soc., The Critique Group, Le Déjeuner Français. Avocations: reading, walking, crossword puzzles. Home and Office: Aquarelle Tours PO Box 10 Gladstone OR 97027-0010 Office Phone: 503-659-9443. E-mail: dbfrank1@yahoo.com.

FRANK, ELIZABETH, writer, educator; b. LA, Sept. 14, 1945; d. Melvin G. and Anne R. Frank; 1 child, Anne Louise Buchwald. Student, Bennington Coll.; BA, U. Calif., Berkeley, 1967, MA, 1969, PhD, 1973. Prof. modern langs. and lit. Bard Coll., Annandale-on-Hudson, NY, 1982—, faculty Ctr. Curatorial Studies, Joseph E. Harry prof. modern langs. and lit. Author: Jackson Pollock, 1983, Louise Bogan: A Portrait, 1985 (Pulitzer prize for biography, 86), Esteban Vicente, 1995, Cheat and Charmer, 2004; contbr. articles to profl. jours. Fellow, Ford Found., 1967—72, Temple U., 1977, The Newbery Libr., 1977, Am. Coun. Learned Socs., 1977, NEH, 1978. Office: Joy Harris Lit Agy 156 5th Ave Ste 617 New York NY 10010-7002 also: Bard Coll Dept Lang & Lit Annandale On Hudson NY 12504

FRANK, ELIZABETH AHLS (BETSY FRANK), retired art educator; b. Cin., Sept. 27, 1942; d. Edward Henry and Constance Patricia (Barnett) Ahls; m. James Russell Frank, Aug. 10, 1963; children: Richard Scott, Robert Edward. Student, Hiram Coll., Ohio, 1960—63; BA, U. Denver, 1964; MA, U. South Fla., 1988. Cert. profl. educator. Remedial reading tchr. Willoughby-Eastlake (Ohio) Schs., 1971-72; elem. tchr., grade level chmn. Lee County Pub. Schs., Ft. Myers, Fla., 1972-79, tchr. art, 1979—2002; ret., 2002. Mem. arts coun. Lee County Pub. Schs., mem. long range and model schs. planning coms., 1997—98. Contbr. chapters to books. Vol. Mann Performing Arts Hall, Ft. Myers, 1986-98, Harborside Conv. Ctr., 1991-95; sec. Colonial Acres Homeowners Assn., North Ft. Myers, Fla., 1994-99; chmn. nature com. McGregor Bay Assn., Ont., Can., 2001—. Named Golden Apple Tchr. of Distinction, Lee County Schs. Found., 1991—2002, Lee County Art Educator of Yr., 1982, 2002; recipient, Seminar Fla. Humanites Coun., 2000; Delta Kappa Gamma fellow, 1988. Mem.: DAR, NEA, Edison African Violet Soc. (1st v.p. 1997—2000), Tchrs. Assn. Lee County (rep. bd. 1972—99, mem. exec. bd. 1990—91, M.M. Bethune Humanities award 1992), Fla. Edn. Assn., Lee Art Edn. Assn. (pres. 1991—92, founder, Art Educator of Yr. 1991—92), Calusa Nature Ctr., Southwest Fla. Rose Soc., Fla. Art Edn. Assn. (workshop presenter), Nat. Art Edn. Assn., Greater Ft. Myers Rose Soc., Audubon of S.W. Fla. (rec. sec. 2002—03, Educator of Yr. 1998), Citrus County Audubon Soc. (rec. sec. 2004—), Riverhaven Garden Club, Crystal River Women's Club, Phi Kappa Phi, Delta Kappa Gamma (chpt. v.p. 1986—88, pres. 1988—90, sec. 1996—98, state chmn. arts and crafts com. 1997—99, sec. 2001—03, state mem. world fellowship com., Fla. scholar 1988), Phi Delta Kappa. Democrat. Avocations: gardening, camping, boating, arts and crafts, birdwatching. Home: 4583 S Sawgrass Cir Homosassa FL 34448 Home (Summer): Birch Island, Ontario Canada P0P1A0 Personal E-mail: jrfrank@mindspring.com.

FRANK, HILDA RHEA KAPLAN, dancer; b. Houston, Dec. 30, 1939; d. Sam and Bertha (Grevsky) Kaplan; m. Robert Stuart Frank, Feb. 28, 1960; children: Karen Denise Frank Hurwitz, Daniel Steven, Nancy Alyson. Student, Newcomb Coll., New Orleans, 1957-59, U. Houston, 1959-60, Butler U., 1960. Dance tchr. Joy Alexander Sch. Dance, Houston, 1955-57, Jane Browning Sch. Dance, Houston, 1965-69, Rudy Jenkins, Sch. Ballet, Houston, 1968-69, Xperience Gymnastic Team, Houston, 1972-75, Jewish Community Ctr., Houston, 1975-80, dance com. chmn., 1978—, bd. dirs., 1987-93. Mem., dance panelist Cultural Arts Coun. Houston, 1980-85, 1988, 93-95; creative artist panelist Cultural Arts Coun. Houston and Harris County, 1995-96; sec.-treas. Discovery Dance Group, Houston, 1981-84, pres., 1984-85; trustee Houston Dance Coalition, 1985-87, mem. 1985—. Choreographer: To Live Another Summer, 1980; Jewish Fairy Tale, 1974; My Son, The President, 1981; dir., choreographer Emanu El Israeli Dancers, Houston, 1973-89; co-chair The Jewish Festival, 1989. Bd. dirs. Jazz Dance World Congress, 1998; co-chair Patrons of the Arts for Jewish Cmty. Ctr., 1997-98; bd. dirs. Jewish Community Ctr., 1987-93, co-chmn. patrons of the arts, 1997-99; active Bus. Vols. for Arts, Tex. Arts Coun. Jacob's Pillow Dance Festival scholar, Lee, Mass., 1959; named Vol. of Yr., Jewish Community Ctr., Houston, 1985; recipient Pres. award, 1989; honored for chairing 25 years of dance by Jewish Cmty. Ctr., 2005. Mem. Internat. Tap Assn., Hadassah, Sisterhood of Emanu El (Israeli dance dir. 1973-89, Houston). Jewish. Home: 1 Woods Edge Ln Houston TX 77024-7525

FRANK, JEAN MARIE, educational association administrator, researcher; b. Sheboygan, Wis., July 22, 1954; d. Donald J. and Patricia Gudinas; children: Eric, Andrew, Jennifer. BS in Tech. and Mgmt., U. Md., 1988; MS in Bus., Johns Hopkins U., 1995. Rsch. asst. Howard C.C., Columbia, Md., 1988—90, rsch. analyst, 1992—99, policy specialist, 1996—98, sr. rsch. analyst, 1999—2005, asst. dir. instnl. rsch., 2005—; bd. examiners Program for Ednl. Excellence, 1999—; examiner U.S. Senate Productivity and Md. State Quality Award, 2001. Spl. rsch. projects for Howard County Office Human Rights, Columbia, 1990, Columbia Forum, 1991. Exec. bd. Bryant Woods PTA, Columbia, 1984-86. Merit scholar U. Md., 1985-86, Chancellor's scholar, 1986-87, Kelly Found. scholar, 1987-88. Mem. Am. Coun. on Edn. (instnl. rep. 1994—), Nat. Coun. Rsch. and Planning, Md. Assn. Instnl. Rsch. (exec. com., C.C. segmental rep. 1997-98), Md. Assn. for Higher Edn. (instnl. rep. 1998-99), Md. C.C. Rsch. Group (pres.-elect 1998-99, pres. 1999-2000), Phi Kappa Phi, Alpha Sigma Lambda.

FRANK, LILLIAN GORMAN, human resources executive, management consultant; b. N.Y.C., July 4, 1953; d. Helmuth H. and Ida (Malitsch) Degen; m. Stephen E. Frank, Feb. 10, 2001. BA in Psychology, Lehman Coll., CUNY, 1975; MA in Indsl. Psychology, Case Western Res. U., 1978, PhD in indsl. Psychology, 1979; MBA in Corp. Fin., U. So. Calif., 1986. Econ. benefits asst. Girl Scouts U.S.A., N.Y.C., 1971—75; psychologist Pers. Rsch. Svcs., Cleve., 1975—79; cons. psychologist Pers. Rsch. & Devel. Corp., Cleve., 1977—78; mgr. pers. rsch. 1st Interstate Bank, L.A., 1979—82, v.p., mgr. human resource planning and devel., 1982—85; v.p., mgr. human resource planning and exec. devel. 1st Interstate Bancorp, L.A., 1985—86; exec. v.p., human resources dir. First Interstate Bank of Calif., 1986—90; exec. v.p. human resources First Interstate Bancorp, 1990—96; sr. v.p. human resources Edison Internat., Rosemead, Calif., 1996—2000; prin. Frank Insights, L.A., 2000—05. Trustee Autry Mus. Western Heritage, 2001—05; bd. dirs. INROADS/So. Calif., 1986—2005, YMCA of Met. L.A., 2002—05, Nev. Women's Fund, 2005—. Mem. APA, Soc. for Psychologists in Mgmt. (bd. dirs. 1993-97), Orgn. for Women Execs., Soc. for Human Resources Mgmt., Nev. Womens Fund. Home and Office: 5865 Strasbourg Ct Reno NV 89511 Business E-Mail: lillian@avantwireless.com.

FRANK, LINDA MARIA, science educator; b. N.Y.C., Feb. 17, 1941; d. Felix G. and Angeline A. Frank; 1 child, Michael Santangelo, Jr. BS in Edn., St. John's U., N.Y.C., 1961; MS in Edn., St. John's U., 1964. Cert. tchr. sci., sch. adminstr. N.Y. Sci. tchr. Seaford Schs., Seaford, NY, 1965—96, sci. chair, 1991—96; adj. prof. Hofstra U., NY, 1996—; sci. edn. cons. BOCES, NY, 1997—2003. Vol. Fire Island Lighthouse, Fire Island, NY, 2004—, Ctrl. Park, N.Y.C., 2002—. Named Tchr. of the Yr., Seaford H.S., 1990; recipient award for encouraging women in sci. and tech. edn., AAUW, 1995. Mem.: Nat. Sci. Tchrs. Assn., L.I. Crosscountry Ski Club (pres. 2005—06). Avocations: cross country skiing, ice skating, kayaking.

FRANK, MARY LOU BRYANT, psychologist, educator; b. Denver, Nov. 27, 1952; d. W. D. and Blanche (Dean) Bryant; m. Kenneth Kerry Frank, Sept. 9, 1973; children: Kari Lou, Kendra Leah. BA, Colo. State U., 1974, MEd, 1983, MS, 1986, PhD, 1989. Tchr. Cherry Creek Schs., Littleton, Colo., 1974—80; grad. dir. career devel. Colo. State U., Ft. Collins, 1980—86; intern U. Del., Newark, 1987—88; psychologist Ariz. State U., Tempe, 1988—93; assoc., lead prof. psychology Clinch Valley Coll. U. Va., Wise, 1992—96, asst. acad. dean, 1993—95; head psychology dept., prof. North Ga. Coll. and State U., Dahlonega, 1996—2001; dean undergrad. and univ. studies, dean univ. coll., prof. psychology Kennesaw (Ga.) State U., 2001—06; assoc. v.p. for acad. affairs, prof. psychology Gainesville State Coll., Ga., 2006—. Chmn. bd. regents adv. com. Psychology, 2000—01; instr. Colo. State U., Ft. Collins, 1981—82, counselor, 1984—85, Ft. Collins, 1986—87; spkr. in field; cons. Nat. Resource Ctr. for 1st Coll. Yr. Author: (program manual) Career Development, 1986; contbr. book chpts. on eating disorders and existential psychotherapy, 1996, 1998, 1999, 2002; reviewer: Buros Mental Measurements Yearbook. Bd. dirs. Ct. Apptd. Spl. Advocates, 2000—, Enotah Legis. Dist., Helping Teens Succeed, 2003—, Possible Woman Found.; mem. Youth Adv. Coun. Lumpkin County, 2000—02; adv. bd. mem. Chatahoochee Tech. Coll., 2004—. Mem.: ACA, AAUP, APA, Atlanta Women's Network (adv. bd. 2004—), Atlanta Women's Alliance (mem. exec. com. 2004—), Ga. ACE Network (mem. exec. com. 2001—), Ga. Assn. Women Higher Edn. (pres. 2001—), Am. Assn. State Colls. and Univs., Southeastern Psychol. Assn. (chair undergrad. rsch. 1996—2000), Am. Assn. Higher Edn., Am. Counselor Edn. and Supv., Am. Assn. Counseling and Devel., Odeka, Phi Beta Kappa, Psi Chi (Ga. Woman of the Yr. com. 1999—2003, vice chair 2003—, documentary project), Pi Kappa Delta, Phi Kappa Phi (Internat. Woman's Day program com. 2003, planning com. so. women in pub. svc. conf. 2003—, pres. 2003—, Promotion of Excellence grantee 2002—03). Avocations: music, hiking, reading. Office: Gainesville State Coll Office Academic Affairs PO Box 1358 Gainesville GA 30503 Office Phone: 710-531-4555. Personal E-mail: maryloufrank@gmail.com. Business E-Mail: mlfrank@gsc.edu.

FRANK, NANCY, architecture educator; BS, U. Wis., 1977; MS, SUNY, Albany, 1978, PhD, 1982. Pres. pro tem faculty senate U. Wis., Milw., 1993—94; grad. faculty coun., vice-chair com. on revs., 1995—97; acting dean, assoc. prof. Sch. Arch. and Urban Planning U. Wis., Milw., dept. chair, 1997—, assoc. dean, 2001—. Author: Crimes Against Health and Safety, 1985, From Criminal Law to Regulation: A Historical Analysis of Health and Safety Law, 1880-1982, 1986; author: (with Michael J. Lynch) Corporate Crime, Corporate Violence, 1992; author: (with Ellen Hochstedler Steury) Criminal Court Process, 1996. Recipient Disting. Dissertation award, Rockefeller Coll. Pub. Affairs and Policy, SUNY, Albany, 1983. Mem.: Wis. Brownsfields Study Group, Stewardship Plan for Lincoln Creek (mem. planning team), Acad. Planning and Budget Com., Cmty. Open Space Partnership (mem. steering team 2001—), Urban Open Space Found. (pres. 2001—), Wis. Chpt. Am. Planning Assn. (editor WAPA News), Am. Planning Assn., Assn. Collegiate Schs. Planning (editor Update newsletter), Am. Inst. Cert. Planners, Phi Beta Kappa. Office: Univ Wis Milw Sch Arch and Urban Planning PO Box 413 Milwaukee WI 53201

FRANK, PAULA FELDMAN, business executive; b. Tulsa; d. Maurice M. and Sarah (Bergman) Feldman; m. Gordon D. Frank, Dec. 15, 1955; children: Cynthia Jan, Margaret Jill. B.S., Northwestern U., 1954. Directed, wrote and appeared in TV films for Nat. Safety Coun., Chgo., 1954-55; appeared in TV comnls., 1955-56; asst. prodn. mgr. Kling Films, Chgo., 1956; pres. Gaston Ave. Optical Inc., ret. 1990; Dallas. Social chmn. Baylor Hosp. Vol. Corp., Dallas, 1962—; asst. dir. Des Plaines (Ill.) Theater Guild, 1956-57, Pearl Chappell Playhouse, Dallas, 1962-63, Dallas Theater Center, 1964. Mem. Hockaday Alumni Assn., Tau Gamma Epsilon, Phi Beta, Sigma Delta Tau. Home: 7123 Currin Dr Dallas TX 75230-3645

FRANK, ROBERTA, literature educator; b. NYC, Nov. 9, 1941; d. Norman Berton and Doris F.; m. Walter André Goffart, Dec. 31, 1977. BA, NYU, 1962; MA, Harvard U., 1964, PhD, 1968. Asst. prof. U. Toronto, 1968-73, assoc. prof., 1973-78, prof. English, 1978-2000, Univ. prof., 1995-2000, dir. grad studies dept. English, 1980-85, dir. Ctr. for Medieval Studies, 1994-99;

Douglas Tracy Smith prof. English Yale U., 2000—. Mem. bus. bd. U. Toronto Press. Author: Old Norse Court Poetry, 1978, also articles; co-editor: Computers and Old English Concordances, 1970, A Plan for the Dictionary of Old English, 1973; gen. editor: Toronto Old English Series, 1976-2003; publs. of Dictionary of Old English, 1984-2003. Recipient Guggenheim award, 1985, Bowdoin prize in humanities Harvard U., 1968. Fellow Medieval Acad. Am. (councillor 1981-84, Elliott prize 1972), Royal Soc. Can.; mem. MLA (mem. Old English exec. com. 1974-78, 95-99), Internat. Soc. Anglo-Saxonists (pres. 1985-87). Home: 171 Lowther Ave Toronto ON Canada M5R 1E6 Office: Yale U Dept English New Haven CT 06520-8302 Office Phone: 203-432-2238. Business E-Mail: roberta.frank@yale.edu.

FRANK, ROBYN CLAIRE, librarian; b. Washington, July 28, 1945; d. Vincent Leonard and Ann Elizabeth (Richards) Gingerich; m. Luther Kyle Baugham, Dec. 16, 1966 (div. 1970); m. 2d, Stephen Earl Frank, Mar. 22, 1975; children: Evelyn, Ingrid. B.S., U. Md., 1967; M.L.S., 1972. Rsch. asst. Rsch. Info. Ctr., Pub. Schs. D.C., 1967-69; asst. project dir. U.S. Office Edn., Ednl. Reference Ctr., Am. Soc. Info. Sci., Washington, 1971-73; tech. info. specialist Food and Nutrition Ctr., U.S. Dept. Agr., Beltsville, Md., 1978-78, dir., acting dep. adminstr. food and nutrition info., 1978-83, chief food, nutrition and human ecology Nat. Agrl. Libr., 1983-87, head info. ctrs. br., 1987—; mem. young exec. com., 1976. Editor: Directory of Food and Nutrition Information Services and Resources, 1984, Directory of Food and Nutrition Information for Professionals and Consumers, 1992, Jour. of Agrl. & Food Info., 1992—. Recipient John Cotton Dana Libr. Pub. Rels. award, 1986. Mem. Spl. Librs. Assn. (pub. rels. com. 1992-94, sec. food agr. and nutrition div. 1984-85, chair food, agr. and nutrition div. 1987-88), Am. Libr. Assn., Libr. Adminstrn. and Mgt. Assn. (pub. rels. sect., John Cotton Dana Awards Com. 1991—, trends awareness com. 1990-93), Assocs. of Nat. Agrl. Libr., Alpha Chi Omega. Lutheran. Lodge: Vasa Order. Office: Nat Agrl Library Info Ctrs Br Info Ctrs Brg Rm 304 Beltsville MD 20705

FRANKE, KATHERINE M., law educator; BA magna cum laude, Barnard Coll., 1981; JD, Northeastern U., 1986; LLM, Yale U., 1993, JSD, 1998. Supervising atty. NYC Commn. on Human Rights, 1987—90; exec. dir. Nat. Lawyers Guild, 1990—91; assoc. prof. law U. Ariz. Coll. Law, 1995—97, Fordham Law Sch., 1997—2000; prof. law Columbia U. Sch. Law, 2000—, co-dir. Ctr. for Study of Law & Culture. Founder, dir. AIDS and Employment Project, San Francisco, 1986—87. Mem.: Am. Soc. for Legal Hist., Soc. Am. Law Tchrs., Law and Soc. Assn., Ctr. for Non-Violent Edn. (mem. adv. coun.), Ctr. for Lesbian and Gay Studies (mem. adv. bd.). Office: Columbia Law Sch 435 W 116 St New York NY 10027 Office Phone: 212-854-0061. Office Fax: 212-854-7946. E-mail: kfranke@law.columbia.edu.

FRANKEL, FRANCINE RUTH, political science professor; b. NYC, Aug. 31, 1935; d. William and Dora (Tuchschneider) Goldberg; m. Douglas Vernon Verney, Nov. 28, 1975. BA, CCNY, 1956; MA, Johns Hopkins U., 1958; PhD, U. Chgo., 1965. Asst. prof. U. Pa., Phila., 1965-70, assoc. prof., 1970-79, prof., 1979—, prof. South Asian studies, 1978—, Madan Lal Sobt prof. study contemporary India, 2004—06, dir. Ctr. Advanced Study of India, 1992—. Vis. fellow Ctr. of Internat. Studies, Princeton (N.J.) U., 1969-73; resident scholar Bellagio Study and Conf. Ctr., 1975; vis. mem. Inst. Advanced Study, 1976; mem.-at-large Commn. Internat. Rels., Nat. Acad. Scis., 1973-79; mem. del. South Asian specialists to China, 1986; founding mem., mem. governing coun. U. Pa. Inst. for Advanced Study of India, New Delhi, 1995—. Author: India's Political Economy, 1947-2004, 2d edit., 2005, The Gradual Revolution, 1978, Chinese edit., 1990, India's Green Revolution, 1971; editor, contbr. Dominance and State Power in Modern India, Decline of a Social Order, 2 vols., 1989-90, Bridging the Non-Proliferation Gap: India and the United States, 1995, Transforming India, Social and Political Dynamics of Democracy, 2000, The India-China Relationship: What the United States Needs to Know, 2004; contbr. articles on India's polit. economy, fgn. policy to profl. jours. Grantee Am. Inst. Indian Studies, 1979-80, Smithsonian Instn., 1983-86, Social Sci. Rsch. Coun., 1989-91; Woodrow Wilson fellow, 1997-98, Scholar in Residence Woodrow Wilson Internat. Ctr. for Scholars, 2006—. Mem. Am. Polit. Sci. Assn., Assn. Asian Studies, Coun. Fgn. Rels. Home: 104 Pine St Philadelphia PA 19106-4312 Office: Ctr Advanced Study of India 3600 Market St Philadelphia PA 19104 E-mail: ffrankel@sas.upenn.edu.

FRANKEL, JENNIE LOUISE, writer, composer, playwright; b. Chgo., Aug. 7, 1949; Student, Roosevelt U., 1968, U. Hawaii, 1969-71, Golden West Law Sch., 1976. Fashion model, singer/actor in TV commls., 1967—81; performer Comedy Store and the Improvisation, L.A., 1977—79. Co-author: You'll Never Make Love in this Town Again, 1996 (NY Times Bestseller), Unfinished Lives, 1996, Tales From the Casting Couch, 1996; composer network TV theme songs, 1998-99, Youth at the Greek, 1999, Heartwalk LA Theme; columnist. Active USO Vietnam Tour, 1968; bd. govs. Hollywood Scriptwriting Inst.; judge Cable Ace Awards, 1987—96. Mem. The Recording Acad. Grammys, Acad. TV Arts & Scis. (blue ribbon panel judge Emmys), Acad. Country Music, LA Women in Music (bd. dirs. 1991-92), Circumnavigators Club Avocation: comedy.

FRANKEL, JUDITH JENNIFER MARIASHA, clinical psychologist, consultant; b. Bklyn., May 25, 1947; m. Anthony R. D'Augelli, Sept. 1, 1968 (div. 1985); children: Jennifer Hadley Frankel, Rebekah Lindsey Frankel. BA, New Coll. at Hofstra U., 1968; MA, U. Conn., Storrs, 1971, PhD, 1972. Lic. psychologist, Pa. Rsch. psychologist Family Consultation Ctr., Roslyn, N.Y., 1968, Conn. State Dept. Mental Health, Hartford, 1969-71; staff intern VA Med. Ctr., West Haven, Conn., 1971—72; asst./assoc. prof., dir. program devel. and evaluation Pa. State U., University Park, 1972—81, spl. admissions asst. Schreyer Honors Coll. State Coll., 1998, pvt. practice psychology, clin. and consulting psychology, clin. health psychology, and exec. coaching State College, 1976—. Psychol. cons. PYRAMID Orgn., Walnut Creek, Calif., 1975-78, N.Y. Dept. Mental Health, 1976, Nat. Inst. Alcohol Abuse Prevention, Nat. Inst. Drug Abuse Prevention, Nat. Youth Alternatives Program, 1975-79, Meadows Psychiatric Ctr. Women's Program, 1993-95; v.p. Mental Health Profls., State College, 1978-80, pres., 1980-82; exec. bd. Ctrl. Pa. Psychol. Assn., 1989-90. Author: Decisions Are Possible, 1975, Communication and Parenting Skills, 1976, Helping Others, 1980; contbr. articles to profl. jours. Campaign cons. Stein for Rep., 1982, Wachob for Congress, 1984; chair cmty. action Congregation Brit Shalom, State College, 1985-87, coord. ednl. liaison, 1985-87; v.p. Jewish Cmty. Coun. Women, 1988-90, pres., 1990-93, bd. dirs. Congregation Brit. Shalom, 1985-87, 90-93; v.p. Hadassah, 1995-2001. USPHS fellow, U. Conn., 1969-71. Mem.: APA (clin. psychology, psychology of women, ind. practice, health psychology, internat. psychology and counseling psychology divsns.), Ctrl. Pa. Psychol. Assn. (exec. bd. 1989—90), Ea. Psychol. Assn., Pa. Psychol. Assn., Hadassah (v.p. programming 1995—98, v.p. fundraising 1998—2000, v.p. ednl. programming 2000—02), Jewish Cmty. Coun. Women (pres. 1985—87, bd. dirs. 1990—94, 1991—94), Jewish Cmty. Ctr. (cmty. action chair 1985—87), Phi Kappa Phi, Phi Beta Kappa. Democrat. Jewish. Avocations: art, music, films, literature, gardening.

FRANKEL, TERRIE MAXINE, writer, composer, playwright; b. Chgo., Aug. 7, 1949; Student, Roosevelt U., 1968, U. Hawaii, 1971, U. Hong Kong, 1979—80. Entertainer USO, Viet Nam, 1968; performer Comedy Store, Improvisation, others, 1969-79. Fashion model TV Commercials, 1967—81. Co-author: You'll Never Make Love in this Town Again, 1996 (N.Y. Times Best Seller List), Unfinished Lives, 1996; author, editor: Tales from the Casting Couch, 1996, theme song Youth at the Greek, 1998-99,Heartwlk L.A. Theme, 1999; columnist Fabulous Boomer Babes, 1999, sr. editor: The Industry Mag., 2000; model tv commercials, 1971-81 Judge, comedy Cable Ace Award, 1988—96. Mem. Producers Guild of Am. (bd. dirs., sr. editor POV mag. 1990-2001), Hollywood Script Writing Inst. (bd. govs.), Authors Guild, Circumnavigators Club. Avocation: speaking Cantonese and Mandarin Chinese.

FRANKENTHAL, DANIELLE, painter, sculptor; b. N.Y.C., Apr. 29, 1947; d. Leon and Eugenia (Tchudnovski) Frankenthal; m. David Joseph Ruzich, May 10, 1991. BA Philosophy, Brandeis U., 1969. (exhibitions) Gallery 23 Garden St., Cambridge, Mass., Galeria del Patronata de Bellas Artes, Guatemala City, Guatemala, Green County Coun. on the Arts, Catskill, N.Y., Retrospective Gallery, San Diego, Lawrence Price Gallery, N.Y.C., Reza Namazi Real Estate Corp., Full House Gallery, Hoboken, N.J., La Galeria Panajachel, Guatemala, 2002, Brodsky Gallery of Ets, Princeton, N.J., 2002, (group exhbns.) Novelle Gallery, Northampton, Mass., Bergen (N.J.) Mus. Art and Sci., Helo Gallery, N.Y.C., City Without Walls, Newark, Seton Hall U. Sch. Law, B. Beamsderfer Galley, Highland Park, N.J.; one-woman shows include Exhibit:A Gallery, N.Y.C., 2003, Mark Humphrey Gallery, South Hampton, N.Y., 2004, Wade Wilson Art, Houston, 2005, exhibited in group shows at Monmouth Mus., Lingraf, N.J., 2003, group exhbns., Sol del Rio Gallery, Guatemala City, exhibited in group shows at Palmer Mus., Springfield, N.J., 2003, Eugene Binder, Marfa, Tex., 2005, Charlotte Jackson, Santa Fe, 2005, Katharina Krohn, Basel, Switzerland, Installation, Reseve Natural Atitlon, Panagachel, Guatemala, 2003. Vol. Compassionate Care Hosp., Clifton, N.J., 1997-98; bd. dirs. Friendly Visitors Inc., Riker's Island, N.Y.C., 1999—. Office: 300 Observer Hwy 4th Flr Hoboken NJ 07030-2412

FRANKENTHALER, HELEN, artist; b. NYC, Dec. 12, 1928; d. Alfred and Martha (Lowenstein) F.; m. Robert Motherwell, Apr. 5, 1958 (div.); m. Stephen DuBrul, June 1994. BA, Bennington Coll., 1949; LHD (hon.), Skidmore Coll., 1969, Hofstra U., 1991; DFA (hon.), Smith Coll., 1973, Moore Coll. Art, 1974, Bard Coll., 1976, NYU, 1979; DFA, Phila. Coll. Art, 1980, Williams Coll., 1980; DFA (hon.), Marymount Manhattan Coll., 1989, Adelphi U., 1989, Washington U., St. Louis, 1989; DArt, Radcliffe Coll., 1978, Amherst Coll., 1979; DArt (hon.), Harvard U., 1980; DFA (hon.), Yale U., 1981, Brandeis U., 1982, U. Hartford, 1983, Syracuse U., 1985, Dartmouth Coll., 1994, Parsons Sch. Design, 1996, U. Pa., 1996, R.I. Sch. Design, 1996, Tufts U., 1998. Tchr., lectr. Yale U., 1966, 67, 70, Hunter Coll., 1970, Princeton U., 1971, Cooper Union, N.Y.C., 1972, Washington U. Sch. Fine Arts, 1972, Skidmore Coll., 1973, Swathmore Coll., 1974, Drew U., 1975, Harvard, 1976, Radcliffe Coll., 1976, Bard Coll., 1977, Detroit Inst. Arts, 1977, NYU, U. Pa., Sch. Visual Arts, Goucher Coll., Wash. U., Yale Grad. Sch., U. Ariz., 1978, Graphic Arts Council N.Y., 1979, Harvard U., 1980, Phila. Coll., 1980, Williams Coll., 1980, Yale U., 1981, Brandeis U., 1982, U. of Hartford, 1983, Syracuse U., 1985, Sante Fe Inst. Fine Arts, 1986, 90, 91; U.S. rep. Venice Biennale, 1966, lectr. in field. One-woman shows include, Tibor de Nagy Gallery, N.Y.C., 1951-58, Andre Emmerich Gallery, N.Y.C., 1959-73, 75, 77, 78, 79, 81, 82, 83, 84, 86, 87, 89, 90, 91, 92, 93, Jewish Mus., N.Y., 1960, Everett Ellin Gallery, Los Angeles, 1961, Galerie Lawrence, Paris, 1961, 63, Bennington Coll., 1962, 78, Galleria dell'Ariete, Milan, 1962, Kasmin Gallery, London, 1964, David Mirvish Gallery, Toronto, 1965, 71, 73, 75, Gertrude Kasle Gallery, Detroit, 1967, Nicholas Wilder Gallery, Los Angeles, 1967, Andre Emmerich Gallery, Zurich, 1974, 80, Swarthmore (Pa.) Coll., 1974, Solomon R. Guggenheim Mus., N.Y.C., 1975, Corcoran Gallery Art, Washington, 1975, Seattle Art Mus., 1975, Mus. Fine Arts, Houston, 1975, 85, 86, Ace Gallery, Vancouver, B.C., Can., 1975, Rosa Esman Gallery, N.Y.C., 1975, 83, 89, 3d Internat. Contemporary Art Fair, Paris, 1976, 81, retrospective Whitney Mus. Am. Art, 1969, Whitechapel Gallery, London, Eng., 1969, Kongress-Halle, Berlin, Kunstverein, Hannover, 1969, Heath Gallery, Atlanta, 1971, Galerie Godard Lefort, Montreal, 1971, Fendrick Gallery, Washington, 1972, 79, John Berggruen Gallery, San Francisco, 1972, 79, 82, Portland (Oreg.) Art Mus., 1972, Waddington Galleries II, London, 1973, 74, Janie C. Lee Gallery, Dallas, 1973, Houston, 1975, 76, 78, 80, 82, Met. Mus. Art, N.Y.C., 1973, Gallery Diane Gilson, Seattle, 1976, Greenberg Gallery, St. Louis, 1977, Galerie Wentzel, Hamburg, Germany, 1977, Jacksonville (Fla.) Art Mus., 1977-78, Knoedler Gallery, London, 1978, 81, 83, USIA exhbn., 1978-79, Atkins Mus. Fine Art, William Rockhill Nelson Gallery Art, Kansas City, Mo., 1978, 80, Saginaw Art Mus., Mich., 1980, Gimpel and Hanover and Andre Emerich Galleries, Zurich, 1980, Gallery Ulysses, Vienna, 1980, Knoedler Gallery, London, 1981, 83, Buschlen/Mowalt Fine Arts, Vancouver, 1989, Mus. Modern Art, N.Y.C., 1989, Douglas Drake Gallery, N.Y.C., 1989, Mizografia Gallery, L.A., 1989, Gerald Peters Gallery, Santa Fe, 1990, Kukje Gallery, Seoul, Korea, 1991, Assn. Am. Artists, N.Y.C., 1992, Knoedler & Co., N.Y.C., 1992, 94, 95, 96, 97, Nat. Gallery Art, Washington, 1993, San Diego Mus. Art, 1993, Mus. Fine Arts, Boston, 1994, Contemporary Arts Ctr., Cin., 1994, Meredith Long and Co., Houston, 1994, 95, 96, 97, Dennos Mus. Ctr. Northwestern Mich. Coll., Travers City, 1995, Tyler Graphics Ltd., Mt. Kisco, N.Y., 1995, Bobbie Greenfield Gallery, Santa Monica, Calif., 1995, Meyerovich Gallery, San Francisco, 1995, Greg Kucera Gallery, Seattle, 1995, Gallery One, Toronto, Canada, 1995, 97, Ace Contemporary Exhbns., L.A., 1996, Tasenda Gallery, L.A., 1997, Remba Gallery, West Hollywood, Calif., 1997, Thomas Segal Gallery, Balt., 1997, numerous others; exhibited in group shows including, Whitney Mus., 1958, 71, 75-79, 82, 89, Carnegie Internat., Pitts., 1955, 58, 61, 64, Columbus Gallery Fine Arts, 1960, Guggenheim Mus., 1961, 76, 80, 82, Seattle World's Fair, 1962, Art Inst. Chgo., 1963, 69, 72, 76, 77, 82, 83, San Francisco Mus. Art, 1963, 68, Krannert Mus., U. Ill., 1959, 63, 65, 67, 80, Washington Gallery Modern Art, 1963, Pa. Acad. Fine Arts, 1963, 68, 76, N.Y. World's Fair, 1964, Am. Fedn. Arts Circulating Exhbn., 1964, U. Austin Art Mus., 1964, Rose Art Mus. Circulating Exhbn., 1964, Detroit Inst. Arts, 1965, 67, 73, 77, U. Mich. Mus. Art, 1965, Md. Inst., 1966, Norfolk Mus. Arts and Scis., 1966, Venice Biennale, 1966, Smithsonian Instn., 1966, Expo '67, Montreal, 1967, Washington Gallery Modern Art, 1967, Ga. Mus. Art, Athens, 1967, U. Okla. Mus. Art, Norman, 1968, Philbrook Art Center, Tulsa, 1968, Cin. Mus., 1968, U. Calif. at San Diego, 1968, Mus. Modern Art, N.Y.C., 1969, 75, 76, 80, 82, Met. Mus., N.Y.C., 1969-70, 76, 79, 81, Va. Mus., Richmond, 1970, 74, 87, Balt. Mus. Art, 1970, 76, 89, Boston U., 1970, Boston Mus. Fine Arts, 1972, 82, 90, Des Moines Art Center, 1973, Mus. Fine Arts, Houston, 1974, 82, Smith Coll. Mus. Art, Northampton, Mass., 1974, El Instituto de Cultura Puertorriquena, San Juan, 1974, Basil (Switzerland) Art Fair, 1974, 76, Finch Coll. Mus. Art, N.Y.C., 1974, S.I. Mus., 1975, Denver Art Mus., 1975, Visual Arts Mus., N.Y.C., 1975, 76, Mus. Modern Art, Belgrade Yugoslavia, 1976, Chrysler Mus., Norfolk, Va., 1976, Everson Mus., Syaracuse, N.Y., Galleria d'Arts Moderna, Rome, 1976, Grey Art Gallery, N.Y.C., 1976-78, 81, Bklyn Mus., 1976-77, 82, Edmonton Art Gallery, Alta., Can., 1977, 78, Albright-Knox Mus., Buffalo, 1978, Fogg Art Mus., Harvard U., 1978, 83, Art Gallery Ont., 1979, Hirshorn Mus. and Sculpture Garden, Washington, 1980, Phoenix Art Mus., 1980, Nat. Gallery Art, Washington, 1981, Tate Gallery, London, 1981, Walker Art Ctr., Mpls., 1981, Milw. Art Mus., 1982, Mus. Fine Arts, Boston, 1982, Whitney Mus. Am. Art, N.Y., 1982, St. Louis Art Mus., 1982, High Mus. Art, Atlanta, 1989, Nelson-Atkins Mus. Art, Kansas City, Nat. Gallery Can., 1990, Williams Coll. Mus. Art, Williamstown, Mass., 1991, Aldrich Mus. Contemporary Art, Ridgefield, Conn., 1992, Mus. Modern Art, Mexico City, 1992, Yokohama Mus. Art, Japan, 1992, Marugame Inokuma-Genichiro Mus. Contemp. Art, 1992, Mus. Modern Art, Wakayama, 1992, Tokushima Modern Art Mus., Japan, 1992, Hokkaido Obihiro Mus. Art, 1993, Whitney Mus. Am. Art, Stamford, Conn., 1993, Gallery One, Toronto, Can., 1994; represented in permanent collections, Bklyn. Mus., Met. Mus. Art N.Y.,, Solomon R. Guggenheim Mus., NYU, Mus. Modern Art, Albright-Knox Art Gallery, Buffalo, Whitney Mus., N.Y.C., U. Mich., High Mus., Atlanta, Milw. Art Inst., Wadsworth Atheneum, Hartford, Newark Mus., Yale U. Art Gallery, U. Nebr. Art Gallery, Carnegie Inst., Pitts., Detroit Inst. Art, Balt. Mus. Art, Univ. Mus., Berkeley, Calif., Bennington (Vt.) Coll., Art Inst. Chgo., Cin. Art Mus., Cleve. Mus. Art, Columbus Gallery Fine Arts, Honolulu Acad. Arts, Contemporary Arts Assn., Houston, Pasadena Art Mus., William Rockhill Nelson Gallery Art, Kans. City, Kans., Kans. City Art Inst., Atkins Mus. Fine Arts, Kans. City, Kans., City Art Mus., St. Louis, Mus. Art, R.I. Sch. Design, Providence, San Francisco Mus. Art, Everson Mus., Syracuse, N.Y., Smithsonian Instn., Walker Art Inst., Mpls., Washington Gallery Modern Art, Wichita Art Mus., Brown Gallery Art, Nat. Gallery Victoria, Melbourne, Australia, Australian Nat. Gallery, Canberra, Victoria and Albert Mus., London, Eng., Tokyo Mus., Ulster Mus., Belfast, No. Ireland, Elvehjem Art Center, U. Wis., Israel Mus.-Instituto Nacional de Bellas Artes, Phila. Mus. Art, Phoenix Art Mus., Corcoran Gallery Art, Boston Mus. Fine Arts, Springfield (Mass.) Mus. Fine Arts, Witte Mus., San Antonio, Abbott Hall Art Gallery, Kendal, Eng., Mus. Contemporary Art, Nagaoka, Japan, Guggenheim Mus., N.Y.C., 1984, others; was subject of film Frankenthaler: Toward a New Climate, 1978. Trustee Bennington Coll., 1967—. Fellow Calhoun Coll., Yale U., 1968—; recipient 1st prize for painting Paris Biennale, 1959, Gold medal Pa. Acad. Fine Arts, 1968, Great Ladies award Fordham U., Thomas Moore Coll., 1969, Spirit of Achievement award Albert Einstein Coll. Medicine, 1970, Gold medal Commune of Catania, III Biennale della Grafica d'Arte, Florence, Italy, 1972, Garrett award 70th Am. Exhbn., Art Inst. Chgo., 1972, Creative Arts award Nat. Women's div. Am. Jewish Congress, 1974, Art and Humanities award Yale Women's Forum, 1976, Extraordinary Woman of Achievement award NCCJ, 1978, Alumni award Bennington Coll., 1979, N.Y.C. Mayor's award, 1986, Lifetime Achievement award Coll. Art Assn., 1994, Lotos medal of merit, 1994, Artist of Yr. award, 1995, Jerusalem prize, 1999, Lifetime Achievement award, 1999. Mem. NEA, Am. Acad. (vice-chancelor 1991), Am. Acad. Arts and Scis., Nat. Coun. Arts, Nat. Inst. Arts and Letters. Office: M Knoedler & Co Inc 19 E 70th St New York NY 10021-4907*

FRANKL, RAZELLE, management educator; BA in English, Temple U., 1955; MA in Polit. Sci., Bryn Mawr Coll., 1966, PhD, 1984; MBA in Orgnl. Devel., Drexel U., 1973. Chair codes and ordinance com. Exec Com. Neighborhood Improvement Program, Lower Merion Twp., 1967-68; pres. LWV Lower Merion Twp., 1967-68; v.p. for organizational affairs LWV, Springfield, Mass., 1968-70; chair environ. quality com. LWV Radnor Twp., 1970-71; instr. applied behavioral sci. Drexel U. Sch. Bus., 1972-73; planner office of mental health/mental retardation Dept. Pub. Health, City of Phila., 1971-73, planner office of health planning, 1971-73; coord. for health programs Phila. '76 Inc. (Official Bicentennial Corp.), 1972-74; adj. faculty dept. mgmt. adminstrv. studies divsn. Coll. Bus. Rowan U. (formerly Glassboro State Coll., Rowan Coll.), 1974-77, 81-82; asst. prof. Glassboro (NJ) State Coll., 1982-88, assoc. prof. dept. mgmt., 1988-95, prof., 1995—2002, prof. emerita, 2002—. Author: Televangelism: The Marketing of Popular Religion, 1987, Popular Religion and the Imperatives of Television: A Study of the Electric Church, 1984; author: (with others) Religious Television: Controversies and Conclusions, 1990, Teleministries as Family Businesses, 1990, New Christian Politics, 1984, Culture Media and Religious Right, 1997, The Encyclopedia of Religion and Society, 1997; contbr. (book chpt.) Transformation of Televangelism: Repackaging of Christian Family Values, 1997; contbr. articles to profl. jours. Dir. nat. bd. Allegheny U. Health Scis., chair spring program; chair, bd. dirs. Anti-Violence Partnership of Phila.; founder, chair Friends of Rowan U. Libr., 1995—. Rsch. grantee Rowan Coll. NJ (formerly Glassboro State Coll.), 1986-87, 90, 91, 93-94, 94-95, All-Coll. Rsch. grantee, 1987-88. Mem. Am. Acad. Mgmt. (chair membership com. divsn. mgmt. edn. and devel., chair media rels. com., divsn. women in mgmt.), Soc. for Human Resource Mgmt., Am. Sociol. Assn., Ea. Sociol. Soc., Assn. for Sociology Religion, Religious Rsch. Assn., Soc. for Sci. Study Religion (chair women's caucus), Internat. Sociol. Assn. Home: 536 Moreno Rd Wynnewood PA 19096-1121 Business E-Mail: frankl@rowan.edu.

FRANKLE, DIANE HOLT, lawyer; BA, Coll. of Wooster, 1975; JD magna cum laude, Georgetown Univ., 1979. Bar: DC 1979, Md. 1980, Calif. 1985. Law clk. Judge R. Dorsey Watkins, US Dist Ct. (Md. Dist.), 1979—81; assoc. Ginsburg, Feldman & Bress, Washington, 1981—84; ptnr., co-chmn. Mergers & Acquisitions practice group DLA Piper Rudnick Gray Cary, Palo Alto, Calif. Faculty mem. ABA Nat. Inst., 1997—, Practising Law Inst., 1995—. Editor (in chief): Guide to Calif. Securities Law Practice, 2004; contbr. articles to profl. jours. Mem. adv. bd. Corp. Counsel Inst., Georgetown Univ., 2003—04; mem. Cmty. Working group, Opportunity Ctr., Palo Alto, Calif. Named a No. Calif. Super Lawyer, San Francisco mag., 2004. Mem.: ABA (co-chmn. Task Force on Pub. Co. Acquisitions 1995—), State Bar Calif., Phi Beta Kappa. Office: DLA Piper Rudnick Gray Cary 2000 University Ave Palo Alto CA 94303 Office Phone: 650-833-2026. Office Fax: 650-833-2001. Business E-Mail: diane.frankle@dlapiper.com.

FRANKLIN, ARETHA LOUISE, singer; b. Memphis, Mar. 25, 1942; d. Clarence L. and Barbara (Siggers) Franklin; m. Ted White, 1961 (div. 1969); children: Clarence, Edward, Kecalf, Teddy; m. Glynn Turman, Apr. 11, 1978 (div. 1984); 3 stepchildren. First record at age 12, rec. artist with Columbia Records, N.Y.C., 1961, then with Atlantic records, now with Arista Records; singer: (albums) Aretha, 1961, Electrifying, Tender Moving and Swinging, 1962, Laughing on the Outside, 1963, Unforgettable, Songs of Faith, Running Out of Fools, 1964, Yeah, 1965, Soul Sister, 1966, Queen of Soul, Take It Like You Give It, Lee Cross, Greatest Hits, I Never Loved a Man, Once in a Lifetime, Aretha Arrives, 1967, Lady Soul, Greatest Hits, Vol. 2, Best of Aretha Franklin, Live at Paris Olympia, Aretha Now, 1968, Soul 69, Today I Sing the Blues, Soft and Beautiful, Aretha Gold's, Satisfaction, I Say a Little Prayer, 1969, This Girl's in Love with You, Spirit in the Dark, Don't Play that Song, 1970, Live at the Fillmore West, Young Gifted and Black, Aretha's Greatest Hits, 1971, Amazing Grace, 1972, Hey Hey Now, Firest 12 Sides, 1973, Let Me Into Your Life, 1974, With Every Thing I Feel in Me, You, 1975, Sparkle, Ten Years of Gold, 1976, Sweet Passion, 1977, Almighty Fire, Star Collection, 1978, La Diva, 1979, Aretha, 1980, Who's Zoomin' Who, 1985, One Lord, One Faith, One Baptism, 1987, Aretha Sings the Blues, 1965, 85, Lady Soul, 1988, Through the Storm, 1989, What You See is What You Sweat, 1991, Jazz to Soul, 1992, Aretha After Hours, Chain of Fools, 1993, Unforgettable: A Tribute to Dinah Washington, 1995, Love Songs, 1997, The Delta Meets Detroit, A Rose Is Still A Rose, 1998, Amazing Grace, 1999, The Queen in Waiting: The Columbia Years 1960-1965, 2002, So Damn Happy, 2003; actress (films) Blues Brothers, 1980, Shindig! Presents Soul, Shindig! Presents Groovy Gals, 1991, History of Rock 'N' Roll, 1995, Blues Brothers 2000, 1998, (TV films) Bob Hope on Campus, 1975, Aretha Franklin: The Queen of Soul, 1988, (TV miniseries) Motown 40: The Music Is Forever, 1998; performer (Showtime prodn.): Aretha, 1986; performer: (concert tours) in U.S. and Europe; performer: at Pres. Carter's Inauguration, 1977, at Pres. Clinton's Inauguration, 1992. Named Top Female Vocalist, 1967, Number One Female Singer 16th Internat., Jazz Critics Poll, 1968; named one of Greatest Rock 'n' Roll Artists of All Time, Rolling Stone mag.; named to Hollywood Walk of Fame, 1979, Rock and Roll Hall of Fame, 1987; recipient Grammy award for best female rhythm and blues vocal, 1967—74, 1981, 1985, 1987, for best rhythm and blues rec., 1988, for best soul gospel performance, 1972, for best rhythm and blues duo vocal (with George Michael), 1987, Am. Music award, 1984, Grammy Legend award, 1991, Kennedy Center Honor, 1994, 1994, Presdl. Medal of Freedom, The White House, 2005, Grammy Award for Best Traditional R&B Vocal Performance (A House is Not a Home), 2006. Achievements include first woman admitted in Rock & Roll Hall of Fame.*

FRANKLIN, BARBARA HACKMAN, former government official; b. Lancaster, Pa., Mar. 19, 1940; d. Arthur A. and Mayme M. (Haller) Hackman; m. Wallace Barnes, 1986. BA with distinction, Pa. State U., 1962; MBA, Harvard U., 1964. Mgr. environ. analysis Singer Co., N.Y.C., 1964—68; asst. v.p. Citibank, N.Y.C., 1969—71; White House staff asst. to the Pres. for recruiting women to govt. Washington, 1971—73; commr. U.S. Consumer Product Safety Commn., Washington, 1973—79, vice chair, 1973—74, 1977—78; sr. fellow, dir. govt. and bus. program Wharton Sch. U. Pa., Phila., 1980—88; pres., CEO Franklin Assocs., Washington, 1984—92; U.S. sec. commerce Dept. Commerce, Washington, 1992—93; pres., CEO Barbara Franklin Enterprises, Washington, 1995—; commentator Nightly Bus. Report, 1997—. Mem. Pres.'s Adv. Com. for Trade Policy and Negotiations, 1982—86, 1991—92, chair task force on tax reform, 1985—86, mem. NAFTA task force, 1991—92; alt. Rep. and public del. 44th session UN Gen. Assembly, 1989—90; mem. cons. panel U.S. Comptroller Gen., 1984—92, 1994—98; bd. dirs. Aetna, Inc., 1979—92, 1993—, GenVec, Inc., 2002—, Dow Chem. Co., 1980—92, 1993—, MedImmune, Inc., 1995—, Washington Mutual Investors Fund, 2005—. Trustee Pa. State U., 1976—82; bd. regents U. Hartford, 1986—88; bd. advisors Harvard Bus. Sch., 1998—2003, 2006—; co-chmn. nat. fin. com. George Bush for Pres., 1987—88, George W. Bush for Pres., 1999—2000. Named Dir. Yr., NACD, 2000, Outstanding Dir., Bd. Alert, 2003; named one of 50 Most Influential Corp. Dirs., Am. Mgmt. Assn., 1990; recipient Disting. Alumni award, Pa. State U., 1972, John J. McCloy award for audit excellence, 1992, Alumni Achievement award,

Harvard Bus. Sch., 2004. Mem.: U.S. China Bus. Coun. (vice-chair, dir.), Nat. Com. U.S.-China Rels. (dir.), Coun. Fgn. Rels. (dir.), Nat. Assn. Corp. Dir. (Blue Ribbon Commn., CEO evaluation 1994, Blue Ribbon Commn., audit effectiveness 1999, co-chair Blue Ribbon Commn., exec. compensation 2003), Atlantic Coun. (dir.), Internat. Women's Forum (founding mem.), Nat. Symphony Orch. (dir.), Heritage Found. (chair Asian studies adv. coun.), Econ. Club NY (chmn.). Avocations: exercise, hiking, reading, painting. Office: 2600 Virginia Ave NW Ste 506 Washington DC 20037-1905 Office Phone: 202-337-9100.

FRANKLIN, BONNIE GAIL, actress; b. Santa Monica, Calif., Jan. 6, 1944; d. Samuel Benjamin and Claire (Hersch) F. BA, UCLA, 1966. Mem. regional theatres in, N.Y., Mass., Ohio, Maine, N.H., Conn., Pa., 1972-99. Stage appearances include Your Own Thing, San Francisco, L.A., N.Y.C., 1968, Dames At Sea, 1969, Applause, N.Y.C., 1970-72 (Aegis Theatre Club award 1970, Theatre Club award 1970, Outer Critics Circle award 1960-70, Tony nomination), Happy Birthday and Other Humiliations, N.Y., 1987, Frankie & Johnny in the Clair de Lune, 1988, Grace & Glorie, 1996; tv appearances include One Day At A Time, 1975-84. Mem. AFTRA, SAG, Actors Equity Assn., Dirs. Guild Am. Democrat. Jewish.

FRANKLIN, BONNIE SELINKSY, retired federal agency administrator; b. Oakland, Calif., Mar. 17, 1944; d. Harold Joseph and Madge (Warden) Selinsky; m. Alfred Carl Franklin, Jan. 24, 1981; 1 child, Amy Beth. AB in Am. Studies, George Washington U., 1966, MBA in Acctg., 1977. Tax auditor IRS, Baileys Crossroads, Va., 1966-71, from program analyst to tax law specialist Washington, 1971-77, from program analyst appeals to chief procedures sect., 1979-82, tech. asst. to nat. chief appeals, 1985-2000, program mgr., 2000—01, regional analyst conf. Atlanta, 1977-79. Chair Arlingtonians for a Better County, Arlington, Va., 1994-97, archivist, 1999-2000; active Friends of the Libr., Arlington, 1996—. Recipient Albert Gallatin Devoted Svc. award, U.S. Treasury Dept. Mem. LWV (treas. Arlington Va. chpt. 1998-2001, pres. 2001-04, treas. National Capital area, 2004—, membership chair Va. 2005—), AAUW, Nat. Active and Ret. Fed. Employees Assn. (chpt. 7 1st v.p. 2005-06) Democrat. Lutheran. Avocations: reading, travel.

FRANKLIN, DARLENE KAY, elementary school educator; b. Klamath Falls, Oreg., Oct. 24, 1948; d. Elbert Lee Beck, Sr. and Nellie Jesse Harron; m. Donald Keith Knapp (div.); children: Scottie Vance, Monica Faye; m. Duane Dale Franklin, Feb. 12. Student in Hons. Colloquial Program, So. Oreg. State Coll., 1967—68, BSc, 1971, MSc, 1983. Tchr. elem. sch. Eagle Point (Oreg.) Sch. Dist., 1982—91, Scappoose (Oreg.) Sch. Dist., 1991—, dir. space sci. program, 2003. Mem. adv. bd. Oregonian Newspaper, Portland, Oreg., 1994—; unit team leader Scappoose (Oreg.) Sch. Dist., 2003—05; mem. coun. Regional Unusew, Gearhart, Oreg., 1994—99. Mem. com. Art Faire, 1992—. Named Regional Tchr. of Yr., Portland (Oreg.) C. of C., 2000, Outstanding Tchr. Field Study Rsch., Forestry Dept., Jacksonville, Fla., 2003. Mem.: NEA, Oreg. Reading Assn., Oreg. Edn. Assn. Avocations: theater, painting, music, dance. Home: 1470 Kings Hwy Medford OR 97501

FRANKLIN, IRIS, elementary school educator; b. Hartford, Conn., Nov. 16, 1952; children: Brent, Erin, Erica. BA, Rider Coll., 1974; MS, Fla. State U., 1977. Cert. reading specialist Pa., elem. tchr. Pa., reading tchr. NJ. Tng. specialist Ocean County Coll., Toms River, NJ, 1978—81; reading and math tchr. READS, Langhorne, Pa., 1997—99; curriculum coord., reading specialist Garfield Pk. Acad., Willingboro, NJ, 1999—2004, curriculum coord., 2005—; reading tchr. Levitt Mid. Sch., Willingboro, NJ, 2004—05. Mem.: ASCD, NJ. Reading Assn., Internat. Reading Assn. Avocations: travel, crafts, reading. Office: Garfield Park Acad 24 Glenolden Ln Willingboro NJ 08046 Office Phone: 609-877-4111 250. Office Fax: 609-877-5551.

FRANKLIN, LYNNE, corporate communications specialist, writer; b. St. Paul, Aug. 24, 1957; d. Lyle John Franklin and Lois Ann (Cain) Kindseth, Thomas John Kindseth (Stepfather); m. Lawrence Anton Pecorella, Sept. 12, 1989; 1 stepchild, Lauren Pecorella. BA in Psychology and English, Coll. St. Catherine, 1979; MA, Hamline U., 1989. Residential treatment counselor St. Joseph's Home, Mpls., 1979-80; staff writer Comml. West Mag., Mpls., 1980-81; acct. exec. Edwin Neuger & Assocs., Mpls., 1981-83, Hill and Knowlton, Mpls., 1983-84; mgr. pub. rels. Gelco Corp., Eden Prarie, Minn., 1984-86; dir. fin. rels. Dunstan & Assocs., Mpls., 1986; cons. MC Assocs., Chgo., 1986-87; v.p. Fin. Rels. Bd., Chgo., 1987—; prin. Wordsmith, Glenview, Ill., 1993—; trainer SkillPath Seminars, Mission, Kans., 2004—, 2004. Trustee Lawrence Hall Youth Svcs., chairperson pub. rels. com.; former pres., v.p., sec. Skokie Valley chpt. Bus. Networking Internat., 2003—05; judge achievement awards Internat. Assn. Bus. Comm., Mpls., 1986, Publicity Club Chgo., 1992—94; presenter in fin. rels., 1990; presenter ann. report seminar Nat. Investor Rels. Inst., Chgo., 1992; presenter investor rels. survey, 2003; mktg. presenter Nat. Assn. Profl. Organizers, Chgo., 2005, World WIT Nat. Conf., Lake Geneva, Wis., 2005. Author: (novels) Second Sight, 1989. Tchr. Great Books Program, St. Paul, 1976—79, Minn. Literacy Coun., 1985—87. Recipient Ann. Report Excellence award, Fin. World Mag., 1991—98, award, MerComm-ARC Competition, 1992—2003, Nat. Assn. Investors Corp., 1994—2003, Equities Mag., 1999—2002. Office: Wordsmith 2019 Glenview Rd Glenview IL 60025-2849 Business E-Mail: lynne@yourwordsmith.com.

FRANKLIN, MARGERY BODANSKY, psychology professor, researcher; b. N.Y.C., Mar. 18, 1933; d. Oscar and Barbara (Biber) Bodansky; m. Raymond S. Franklin, Aug. 22, 1962; children— Kenneth, David AB, Swarthmore Coll., 1954; MA, Clark U., 1956, PhD, 1961. Instr. psychology Vassar Coll., Poughkeepsie, NY, 1960-62, asst. prof., 1962-64; research assoc. Bank St. Coll. Edn., N.Y.C., 1967-72; prof. Sarah Lawrence Coll., Bronxville, NY, 1965—2002. Dir. Child Devel. Inst. Sarah Lawrence Coll., 2003—. Co-editor: Developmental Processes: Heinz Werner's Selected Writings, 1978, Symbolic Functioning in Childhood, 1979, Child Language: A Reader, 1988, Development and the Arts: Critical Perspectives, 1994; contbr. articles to profl. jours., chpts. to books. Fellow Am. Psychol. Assn. (pres. psychology and arts divsn. 1990-91); mem. Soc. for Rsch. in Child Devel. Avocation: photography. Office Phone: 914-395-2630. Business E-Mail: mbf@slc.edu.

FRANKLIN, NADINE KAREN, performing arts educator; d. Edward Charles Caliguir and Lucille Esther Caliguri; m. John Michael Franklin, May 18, 1990; children: Ethan, Emma. BS in Bus. and Mktg., No. Ill. U., Dekalb, 1978, MFA in Performing, 1988. Dir. theatre Kiskwaukee Coll., Malta, Ill., 1990—. Spkr. No. Ill. U., Dekalb, 2005. Co-founder Operation Bookbag, Dekalb, 2004—. Recipient Excellence in Tchg. award, Kiskwaukee Coll., 2000. Mem.: Black Grad. Student Assn., Assn. Theatre in Higher Edn. Democrat. Avocations: theater, movies, reading, running. Office: Kiskwaukee Coll 21193 Malta Rd Malta IL 60150 Office Phone: 815-825-2086. Office Fax: 815-825-2072. Business E-Mail: nadinefr@kiskwaukeecollege.edu.

FRANKLIN, PATRICIA LYNN POWELL, special education educator; b. East St. Louis, Ill., Nov. 28, 1953; d. William and Alice Alfreda (Sowers) Powell; 1 child, Ashley Lynn. BS in Edn., So. Ill. U., 1976, MS in Elem. Edn., 1992. Cert. elem. edn., early childhood spl.edn., learning disabilities, behavior disorder, and educable mentally handicapped tchr., Ill. Primary spl. edn. tchr. Highland Community Sch. Unit #5, Ill., 1976—; devel. therapist, early interventionist, evaluator Child and Family Connections, Ill. Dept. of Human Svc., 2002—. Mentor tchr., insvc. presenter Madison County Region II Svc. Ctr., Edwardsville, Ill., 1976, 89, 91, 92, coach, supr. Spl. Olympics, 1977-90; supervising tchr. So. Ill. U., Edwardsville, 1976, 91, 93, 96—, Greenville (Ill.) Coll., 1976-84; chmn. exec. orgnl. com. Very Spl. Arts Festival, Madison County Supr. Schs., Edwardsville, 1983; chmn. com. Very Spl. Arts Festival, Ill. Arts for Handicapped, 1983-855; participating tchr. Title IV-C learning disabilities program St. Clair County Supr. Schs., 1979-81; spl. edn. summer program tchr. Madison County Region II Svc. Ctr., 1998—. Vol. Angel choir St. Paul United Meth. Ch., Rosewood Heights, Ill., 1990-92; Sunday sch. tchr. St. John's United Meth. Ch., Edwardsville, brownie leader Girl Scouts U.S., 1991—; v.p., program chair Heritage Herb Assn., 1998-2000, pres. 2000—. Mem. Ill. Reading Assn., Tchrs. Applying Whole Lang., Zoo Tchrs., Coun. for Exceptional Children, Highland Profl. Educators, Lewis & Clark Reading Coun., Ill. Whole Lang., Early Childhood Spl. Interest Coun., Highland Edn. Assn., Ill. Edn. Assn.; clubs: Edwardsville Garden Club. Avocations: needlecrafts, crafts, gardening, fishing, travel. Office: 1800 Lindenthal St Highland IL 62249-2206

FRANKLIN, PAULA ANNE, artist, writer, psychologist; b. Wheaton, Ill., Feb. 2, 1928; d. Paul Spangler and Ella Creighton (Daniels) Fowler; m. Richard Clarence Franklin, Aug. 13, 1950; children: Jan Franklin BenDor, Timothy Vickery, Edward Lee. Student, Manchester (Eng.) U., 1946-47; BSc in History, Northwestern U., 1949, postgrad., 1975, So. Ill. U., 1959-61; MA, W.Va. U., 1970; PhD, Union Inst., 1980; BA with honors in Art, Towson U., Md., 2003. Lic. psychologist, Md. Dir. Franklinc Behavioral Sci. Consultants, Balt., 1969—; mem. human resource and orgnl. devel. faculty Johns Hopkins U., Balt., 1972-92; rsch. project dir. Social Security Adminstrn., Balt., 1973—99. Adj. faculty dept. psychology U. Balt., 1989-91. Author: (with R. Franklin) Tomorrow's Track, 1976, (with others) Disability in the U.S., 1990; editor: The Maryland Psychologist, 1994-98; contbr. articles to profl. jours. Mem. various coms. LWV, 1950-75; various positions Girl Scouts U.S., Boy Scouts Am., 1950-70. Mem. Am. Psychol. Assn., Am. Evaluation Assn., Assn. Am. Women in Sci. (v.p. Balt. chpt. 1987-89), Md. Psychol. Assn. (mem. various coms., Cert. of Recognition 1981). Unitarian Universalist. Avocations: music, theater, gardening, photography, travel. Home: 3946 Cloverhill Rd Baltimore MD 21218-1707 Office: Ste 3A 3946 Cloverhill Rd Baltimore MD 21218-1707 Office Phone: 410-235-8151. Personal E-mail: franklin@charm.net.

FRANKLIN, REBECCA, elementary school educator; d. Pearlene and Ronald Franklin; children: Lauren N., Mi'cah Z., Zacharius Z., Chandler G. Ross, Kiaja L. AS in Funeral Svc., Gupton-Jones Coll., Ga., 1990; BS in Math., Voorhees Coll., S.C., 1996; MEd, U. Cin., 1999. Cert. Mid. Grades Sci. and Math. tchr. Ga. Profl. Stds., 2005. Educator Ga. Dept. Def., Ft. Gordon, 2000—04, Burke County Mid. Sch., Waynesboro, Ga., 2004—. Vol. ARC, Augusta, Ga., 2005. Mem.: Alpha Kappa Alpha.

FRANKLIN, SHIRLEY CLARKE, mayor; b. Phila., May 10, 1945; d. Eugene Haywood Clarke and Ruth (Lyons) White; m. David McCoy Franklin, Feb. 5, 1972 (div. 1986); children: Kai Ayanna, Cabral Holsey, Kali Jamilla. BA, Howard U., 1968, LLD (hon.), 2002; MA, U. Pa., 1969. Contract compliance officer U.S. Dept. Labor, Washington, 1966-68; instr. social scis. Talledega Coll., 1969-71; from dir. to commr. Dept. Cultural Affairs, Atlanta, 1978-82; chief adminstrv. officer City of Atlanta, 1982-90, exec. officer for ops., 1990—2001, mayor, 2002—; pvt. practice, 1997—. Trustee Atlanta Symphony Orch., 1977-81, Atlanta Found., 1980—; mem. Ga. Council for the Arts, Atlanta, 1979-82, adv. bd. Ga. Women's Polit. Caucus, Atlanta, 1982-84; chmn. expansion arts panel Nat. Endowment for the Arts, Washington, 1980-82; bd. dirs. Nat. Urban Coalition, Washington, 1980-83; dep. campaign mgr. Young for Atlanta, 1981-82; sr. v.p. external rels. Atlanta Com. Olympic Games, 1991-97; majority ptnr. Urban Environ. Solutions, LLC, 1998-. Recipient Disting. Alumni award Nat. Assn. for Equal Opportunity Higher Edn., 1983, Leadership award Atlanta chpt. NAACP, 1987, John F. Kennedy Profile in Courage Award, John F. Kennedy Libr. Found., 2005; named to Acad. Women Achievers YWCA Greater Atlanta, 1986; named one of 100 Most Influential Black Americans, Ebony mag., 2006. Mem. Nat. Forum Black Pub. Adminstrs. Clubs: Chautauqua Circle. Democrat. Avocations: gardening, travel, politics, fine arts. Office: City Hall 55 Trinity Ave SW Atlanta GA 30303-3520*

FRANKLIN, SHIRLEY MARIE, marketing consultant; b. Kansas City, Mo., Apr. 13, 1930; d. Eric E. and Marie M. (Kilpatrick) Snodgrass; div. 1967; 1 child, Scot Wesley. BA, State U. Iowa, 1952; MS, Simmons Coll., 1954; MA, Kans. U., 1974. Cert. tchr., Kans., Mass., N.J., Ariz., Calif. Tchr., adminstr. various schs., 1952-76; gifted student program designer Leavenworth County (Kans.) Pub. Schs., 1976-77; sales cons., mgr. Sealight Co., Inc., Kansas City, Mo., 1978-82; dir. chain sales Haagen Dazs Ice Cream Co., Teaneck, N.J., 1982-87; program dir. case space mgmt. Ice Cream Industry, 1986-88; prin. Shirley Franklin Consulting, Basehor, Kans., 1987—; U.S. brands dir. Mövenpick Co., Zurich, Switzerland, 1990—94; mktg. cons. Franklin & Assocs., 1994—. Speaker at dairy industry meetings, seminars. Contbr. articles to profl. jours. and mags. Nat. com. steering com. U.S. Congress Arts Caucus, Washington, 1983—89; foster parent World Vision, Pasadena, Calif., 1986—99; vol. ct. appointed spl. advocate for children in trouble Kans., 1994—97; steering com. Fred Harvey Mus., 2000—03, grant writer, Fred Harvey home restoration, 2000—03; apptd. City Planning Commn., 1996—99; project dir. St. Paul Episc. Ch., 1995—2006, mem. vestry, 2003—; ESL com. Leavenworth City Schs.; bd. dirs. Preservation Alliance Leavenworth, 2004. Recipient Excellence in Sales Promotions award Dairy and Food Industries Supply Assn. Mem. Internat. Ice Cream Assn. (mktg. coun. 1979-2004), Internat. Platform Spkrs. Assn., Alpha Delta Kappa, Delta Delta Delta. Republican. Episcopalian. Avocations: writing, walking, reading, travel, bridge. Home and Office: 910 Columbia Ave Leavenworth KS 66048-3133

FRANKLIN, SUSAN DENISE, science educator; b. Topeka, Kans., Apr. 8, 1956; d. Andrew Wayne and Dora Lee Trinkle; m. Donald Eugene Weisz (dec.); children: Benjamin Andrew Weisz, Olivia Marie Weisz; m. Gerald C. Franklin, Apr. 19, 1986; children: Anna Kate, Kylee Renee. BS in Edn., Ctrl. Mo. State U., Warrensburg, 1981, BS, 1985. Tchr. sci., math Braymer C-4 Schs., Mo., 1985—87; tchr. sci. Norborne R-8 Schs., Mo., 1987—. Ch. organist Sacred Heart Cath. Ch., Norborne, Mo., 1981—. Recipient Conservation Tchr. of Yr. award, Carroll County Soil and Water Dist., 1999, 2002, Educator of Yr. award, Mo. Soil and Water Conservation Soc., 2002. Mem.: Sci. Tchrs. Mo., Mo. State Tchr.'s Assn. Achievements include coached state Science Olympiad teams 1999-2006; coached Envirothon teams to represent Missouri at 2001 and 2005 Canon N.Am. Envirothon. Home: 16162 CR 330 Norborne MO 64668 Office: Norborne R-8 Schs Sci Dept Norborne MO 64668 Office Phone: 600-593-3319. E-mail: franklin@greenhills.net.

FRANKLIN, TAMMY, performing arts educator; b. Blackfoot, Idaho, May 29, 1965; d. Harrison Paul and Rachel Elizabeth Gilbert; m. Eric Franklin, Mar. 5, 1995; children: Peter Gilbert, Nicholas Walt. BA, U. No. Colo., Greeley, 1990. Owner Rising Curtain Theatre and Dance Acad., 2006—. Troupe dir. Internat. Thespian Soc., Cin., 2004—; mem. Colo. Theatre Guild, Denver, 2004—; tchr. vocal music pvt. practice. Singer: (cd) Dedications; musician: (accompanist) Highlands United Methodist Church; dir.: (musical theatre) The Wizard of Oz, Brigadoon, Bye Bye Birdie, Disney's Beauty & The Beast, Rogers & Hammerstein's Cinderella, The Sound of Music, Musical Theatre Competitions of America (3rd Pl. Ensemble, 1st Pl. Costume Design, 1st Pl. Duet, 2nd Pl. Soloist, 2006), Damn Yankees, Shenandoah, Miracle on 34th Street. Worship com. Highlands United Meth. Ch., Denver, 2004—. Methodist. Avocations: scrapbooks, travel, cooking. Office: The Rising Curtain Theatre & Dance Acad PO Box 792 Arvada CO 80003 Office Phone: 720-308-2920. Personal E-mail: rising_curtain@yahoo.com.

FRANKLIN-GRIFFIN, CATHY LOU HINSON, nursing educator; b. Newton, NC, Nov. 8, 1950; d. Willie A. and Evelyn Irene (Thornton) Hinson; 1 child, John Eric; m. Harry Griffin. ADN, Western Piedmont Comm. Coll., 1971; BSN, East Carolina U.; postgrad., Med. U. SC; MA, Appalachian State U., 1990; PhD, U. NC, Greensboro, 2004. RN, N.C., S.C., Ga., Ala., N.D., Calif., Va. Patient educator Wayne County Meml. Hosp., Goldsboro, N.C., developer cardiac rehab. & permanent pacemaker implantation programs, 1980-81; infection control nurse Charleston (S.C.) Meml. Hosp., 1981-83; instr. nursing United Health Careers, Inc., San Bernardino, Calif., 1986-88, Caldwell C.C., CCC & TI, Hudson, NC, 1988—91; rsch. coord. weekend/evening nursing program CCC and TI, Boone, N.C., 1991-93; dean nursing & allied health Rockingham C.C., Wentworth, N.C., 1993-2000; freelance contract nurse edn. Rowan-Cabarrus C.C., 2000—04; dir. program svcs. NC C.C. Sys., 2004—05. Cons., contract grant writer, 2000—; spkrs. bur. Rockingham C.C.; bd. dirs. Rockingham Mental Health Ctr., Free Clinic Reidsville; legis. chair NC ADN Coun., 1997-99, pres. NC Conf. Dirs. ADN Programs, 1999-2000; nurse educator NC Bd. Nursing, 2000-02, bd. dirs.; spkr. in field. Author (with others): Fundamentals of Nursing, Nursing the Whole Person; author: Survival Guide for Directors of Nursing Programs in Community Colleges in North Carolina, 2002; pub.: CCC & TI Skillbook, editorial cons. and contbr.: Mosby Nursing Texts, ind. contractor: NCCCS manual. Capt. fundraising for Civic Ctr.; mem. faculty dept. Chairs Inst. Named one of Outstanding Young Women of Am., 1987. Mem. ADN (pres., bd. dirs., chmn. legis. adv. coun., liaison N.C. PN educators), Phi Theta Kappa, Phi Kappa Phi, Sigma Theta Tau. Office Phone: 919-807-7118. Business E-Mail: griffin@ncccs.cc.nc.us. E-mail: healthdean@aol.com.

FRANKLYN, AUDREY POZEN, talent promoter, television personality; b. Detroit, Dec. 8, 1930; d. Sidney Pozen and Rachel (Slobasky) Franklyn. AA, LA City Coll., 1952; BA, UCLA, 1955. Dir. pub. rels., radio disc jockey Gene Norman, LA, 1957-60; owner Franklyn Agy. Pub. Rels. Firm, LA, 1960—. Ptnr. A & E Prodns. Host (TV series) The Franklyn Interview, 1977—, promoter numerous celebrities, promoter Ella Fitzgerald, 1966—94, Pablo Records; prodr.: various commls. and talks shows for cable TV. Mem.: LA Press Club. Office: 1010 Hammond St Apt 312 West Hollywood CA 90069-3853 Office Phone: 323-272-6080.

FRANKS, AMY ANN, healthcare educator, medical educator; b. Killeen, Tex., June 29, 1977; d. Meg and Ron Rogers (Stepfather), Chuck and Marsha Barnes (Stepmother); m. Chad Franks, Feb. 1, 2003; children: Chloe Ann, Carson Jacob. BA in Psychology, U. Ill., Springfield, 2002. Resident advisor Mental Health Ctrs. Ctrl. Ill., Springfield, 1999—2000; substitute tchr., cheerleading coach Springfield Sch. Dist. #186, 2000—03; tchr. Meml. Med. Ctr., Springfield, 2004—. Head coach Jr. Novice Medium Team. Recipient Nat. Champions, AAU Jr. Olympics, 2004. Mem.: Am. Soc. Tng. & Devel. Avocation: cheerleading. Office: Meml Health Sys 701 N First St Springfield IL 62781-0001 Office Fax: 217-788-7056. Business E-Mail: franks.amy@mhsil.com.

FRANKS, BEVERLY MATTHEWS, retired psychotherapist, consultant; b. Denver, Mar. 13, 1936; d. William Harry and Helen Catherine Nissen; m. Dean Nolie Matthews, Dec. 12, 1954 (div. July 1974); m. Kenneth W. Franks Jr., May 14, 1988. BS, Colo. State U., 1977, MS, 1981; PhD, U. Wyo., 1988. Diplomate Am. Bd. Psychotherapy; cert. sch. psychologist, nat. bd. cert. sch. psychologist, counselor, lic. profl. counselor Wyo., sch. psychologist Wyo., psychol. technician Wyo. Instr. dept. psychology Colo. State U., Ft. Collins, 1979—80; staff psychologist Poudre R-1 Sch. Dist., Ft. Collins, 1980—83, Natrona County Sch. Dist., Casper, Wyo., 1983—85; counselor Univ. Lab Sch., Laramie, Wyo., 1985—86; clin. therapist Ctrl. Wyo. Counseling Ctr., Casper, 1986—88; staff psychologist Lake Wash. Sch. Dist. # 414, Kirkland, Wash., 1988—89, Fed. Way (Wash.) Pub. Schs., 1989—92, head psychologist, 1992—94; spl. edn. legal cons. B&K Tech., Seattle, 1994—95; psychotherapist Red Buttes Counseling, Laramie, 1996—, ret. Cons. Fed. Way Pub. Schs., 1995, Albany County Pub. Schs., 2002. Mental health therapist Downtown Clinic, Laramie, 1999—2002. Recipient Mature Woman's award, AAUW, 1975—76, Sr. Woman's award, 1976—77; Charles S. Hill Meml. scholar, Colo. State U., 1976—77. Mem.: Laramie Area Mental Health Profls. (treas. 2000—), Nat. Assn. Sch. Psychologists, Am. Psychotherapy Assn., Omicron Nu, Psi Chi, Phi Kappa Phi. Avocation: quilting. Office: Red Buttes Counseling 36 Arrowhead Dr--The Buttes Laramie WY 82070-6824

FRANKS, CANDACE ANN, bank executive; b. Memphis, Nov. 18, 1952; d. James William and Barbara Elizabeth Webb; m. Roger Allen Franks, July 23, 1977; 1 child, Ava Elizabeth. BA, Ark. State U., 1974, MA, 1976; JD, U. Ark., 1979. Bar: Ark. 1979. Gen. counsel Ark. State Bank Dept., Little Rock, 1980-95, dep. bank commr., 1995—. Mem. Gov.'s Task Force to Revise Banking Code, Legis. Task Force to Study NAFTA, 1995, Gov.'s Task Force on Interstate Banking, 1997—; mem. legis. com. Conf. State Bank Suprs., Washington, 1997—. Named one of Top 10 Women in Ark., Ark. Bus. Mag., 1996, 97, 98. Mem. Ark. Bar Assn., Pulaski County Bar Assn., Conf. State Bank Suprs. Office: Ark State Bank Dept Sedgwick Ctr 400 Hardin Rd Ste 100 Little Rock AR 72211-2613 Office Phone: 501-324-9019. E-mail: cfranks@banking.state.ar.us.

FRANKS, CINDI W., supervisor; b. Kosuiskco, Mo., Oct. 7, 1955; d. Cloys Paul and Amber Louise (Burney) Wylie; m. Jesse Robert Franks, Nov. 3, 1973; children: Jared Heath, Jonathan Luke. BA in Elem. Edn., McNeese State U., Lake Charles, La., 1984; MA in Adminstrn., McNeese State U., 1987. Cert. Reading Recovery Tchr. Leader Tex. Kindergarten tchr. Beauregard Parish Sch. Bd., De Ridder, La., 1984—85, 2nd. grade elem. tchr., 1985—96, adminstrv. asst. prin., 1992—96, instrnl. supr., 1997—. Adj.prof. McNeese State U., 1997—98. Avocation: reading. Office: Beauguard Parish sch Bd PO Drawer 938 Deridder LA 70634

FRANKS, JANE WOODALL, science educator; b. Atlanta, Dec. 26, 1965; d. Mary Wanda Woodall; children: Jennifer Kerbi, Zachary Robert. Bachelor, U. Ga., Athens, 1987; MEd, Clemson U., SC, 1999, edn. specialist, 2000. Cert. tchr. Nat. Bd. Profl. Tchg. Stds. Tchr. 8th grade sci. South Habersham Mid. Sch., Cornelia, Ga., 1987—. Office: S Habersham Mid Sch 237 Old Athens Hwy Cornelia GA 30531 Office Phone: 706-778-7121.

FRANKS, LUCINDA LAURA, journalist; b. Chgo., July 16, 1946; d. Thomas Edward and Lorraine Lois (Leavitt) F.; m. Robert M. Morgenthau, Nov. 1977; children: Joshua Franks Morgenthau, Amy Elinor Morgenthau. BA, Vassar Coll., 1968. Journalist specializing youth affairs, civil strife in No. Ireland UPI, London, 1968-73, NY Times, NYC, 1974-77; freelance writer NY Times Mag., NY Times Book Rev., Talk Mag., The Atlantic, The New Yorker, NY mag., The Nation. Vis. prof. Vassar Coll., 1977-82; Ferris prof. journalism Princeton U., 1983 Author: Waiting Out A War: The Exile of Private John Picciano, 1974, Wild Apples, 1991. Recipient Pulitizer prize for nat. reporting, 1971, NY Newspaper Writers Assn. award, 1971, Nat. Headliners award Soc. Silurians journalism award, 1976, EDI award for print journalism Easter Seals, 1999. Mem. Am. PEN Club (membership bd.), Author's League, Coun. on Fgn. Rels., Writers Rm. Inc. (past pres.). Address: 64 E 86th St New York NY 10028-1016

FRANKS, NATALIE ROSE, music educator; b. Huntingburg, Ind., Jan. 25, 1977; d. Kenneth Joseph and Justine Rose Schaefer, Barbara Marie Schaefer (Stepmother); m. Chad Alan Franks, Aug. 4, 2001. BS, Ball State U., 1995—2001. Choral dir. South Henry Cmty. Schools, Straughn, Ind., 2001—02, Zionsville Cmty. Schools, Zionsville, 2002—03; music specialist Portage Twp. Schools, Portage, 2003—; pvt. instr., owner Rose Music Studio, Portage, 2004—. Choral dir. Jones Elem. Sch. Choir, Portage, 2003—, drama co-dir., 2005—; choral dir. Myers Elem. Sch., Portage, 2005—. Music min. Our Lady of Sorrows Ch., Valparaiso, Ind., 2004—. Mem.: Am. Choral Director's Assn., Ind. Music Educator's Assn., Music Educator's Nat. Conf., Kappa Alpha Theta (life), Sigma Alpha Iota (life Ruby Sword of Honor, Coll. Leadership award 2000, 2001). Roman Catholic. Avocations: singing, reading. Office Phone: 219-763-2943. E-mail: rosemusicstudio@verizon.net.

FRANKSON-KENDRICK, SARAH JANE, publisher; b. Bradford, Pa., Sept. 24, 1949; d. Sophronus Athinus and Elizabeth Jane (Sears) McCutcheon; m. James Michael Kendrick, Jr., May 22, 1982. Customer svc. rep. Laros Printing/Osceola Graphics, Bethlehem, Pa., 1972-73; assoc. editor Babcox Publs., Akron, Ohio, 1973-74, Bill Comms., Akron, Ohio, 1974-75, sr. editor, 1975-77, editor-in-chief, 1977-81; assoc. pub. Chilton Co./ABC Pub., Chgo., 1981-83, pub., 1983-89, group pub. Radnor, Pa., 1989-93; group v.p. Cahners Bus. Info. (formerly Chilton Co.), Radnor, Pa., 1993-98; divsn. v.p. Primedia Intertec, Chgo., 1999—2001. Exec. MBA prof. Northwood U., mem. adv. coun. Mem. oper. com. Primedia Intertec. Recipient Automotive Replacement Edn. award Northwood Inst., 1983, award for young leadership and excellence Automotive Hall of Fame, 1984; bd. dirs. Automotive Hall of Fame.

Mem. Automotive Found. for Aftermarket (trustee), Automotive Parts and Accessories Assn. (bd. dirs., exec. com., sec., treas., strategic planning com., edn. com., Disting Svc. award 1993), Automotive Svc. Industry Assn. (bd. dirs. automotive divsn. com.), Automotive Svc. Banyan Golf Club (Wellington, Fla.), Palm Beach Polo and Country Club (Wellington, Fla.), Winged Foot Golf Club (Mamaroneck, N.Y.). Republican.

FRANTZ, BARBARA M., music educator; b. Princeton, NJ, July 2, 1953; d. Thomas O. and Elinor Klos Frantz; m. Patrick E. Hayden, May 29, 1982 (div. Nov. 2, 2005); children: Kat Hayden, Thomas E. Hayden, Andrew D. Hayden, Christopher M. Hayden. BA, Barry Coll., Miami Shores, Fla., 1975; MA, U. Notre Dame, Ind., 1981. Profl. tchg. lic. Tenn. Liturgy dir. St. Paul the Apostle Cath. Ch., Greensboro, NC, 1995—97; music specialist Shelby County Schs., Memphis, 2002—. Keyboard player Memphis Knights (formerly Mercedes Knights), 2002—; mgr. Memphis Knights Big Band, 2005—; tchr. Japan Fulbright Meml. Fund Tchr. Program, Tokyo, 2005. Music dir. U. Memphis Cath. Ctr., 2005—. Mem.: NEA, Am. Orff-Schulwerk Assn., Music Educators Nat. Conf. Roman Catholic. Avocations: big band music, travel, photography, gardening. Office Phone: 901-373-2600.

FRANTZVE, JERRI LYN, psychologist, educator, consultant; d. Rolland and Marjorie Weiland. Student, Purdue U., 1964-68; BA in Psychology and History, Marian Coll., 1969; MS in Organizational Psychology, George Williams Coll., 1976; PhD in Indsl. and Organizational Psychology, U. Ga., 1979. Sr. mktg. rsch. analyst Quaker Oats Co., Barrington, Ill., 1971-75; asst. prof. sch. of mgmt. SUNY, Binghamton, 1979-83; dir. employee rels. Conoco/DuPont, Ponca City, 1983-88; cons. psychologist Mass., 1988-89; assoc. prof. psychology Radford (Va.) U., 1989-94; mgmt. cons. J.L. Frantzve & Assocs., Placitas, N.Mex., 1994—; divsn. head human svcs. Coll. New Rochelle, 1994-99; affiliate prof. Milano Grad. Sch. of Mgmt. New Sch. U., N.Y.C., 1999—; sr. cons. Lead Life Inst., St. Charles, Ill., 2004—. Instrn. cons. USAF, Rome, N.Y., 1979-83; dir. Israel Overseas Rsch. Program, Ginozar, Israel, 1982, Japanese Overseas Rsch. Program, Tokyo, 1983; coord. rsch. Ctr. for Gender Studies, Radford U., 1989-94; adj. prof. dept. psychology Bklyn. Coll., 2000—. Author: Behaving in Organizations: Tales from the Trenches, 1983, Guide to Behavior in Organizations, 1983; contbr. articles to profl. jours. Bd. dirs. Broome County Alcoholism Clinic, Binghamton, N.Y., 1980-83, bd. dirs. Broome County Mental Health Clinic, Binghamton, 1981-83; del. Dem. Caucus, Okla., 1985. Mem. APA (com. on women in psychology 1986-88), AAUW, Acad. Mgmt., Internat. Pers. Mgmt. Assn., Assn. for Women in Psychology. Avocations: ceramics, jazz, murder mysteries. Home and Office: 2 Windmill Ct Placitas NM 87043 Office Phone: 505-771-8862. Personal E-mail: jfrantzve@aol.com.

FRANUIK, RANAE, psychology professor; BS, U. Ill., Urbana, 1996, MA in Psychology, 1998, PhD in Psychology, 2002. Asst. prof. U. Wis., Stevens Point, 2002—05, Aurora U., Ill., 2005—. Contbr. articles to profl. jours. Faculty Advisor Rsch. grant, Psi Chi, 2005. Mem.: Internat. Assn. Romantic Relationships, Assn. Women in Psychology, Soc. Personality and Social Psychologists. Office: Aurora Univ Dept Psychology 347 Gladstone Aurora IL 60506

FRANZ, ELIZABETH, actress; b. Akron, Ohio, June 18, 1941; Actress with Broadway credits in: Death of a Salesman, The Cripple of Inishmaan, Brighton Beach Memoirs (Tony and Drama Desk nominations), Broadway Bound, Uncle Vanya, Getting Married, The Cemetery Club, The Octette Bridge Club, The Cherry Orchard, Mornings at Seven, 2002; off-Broadway credits include: Sister Mary Ignatius (Obie award, Drama Desk nomination), Minutes from the Blue Route, The Comedy of Errors; regional credits include: Eleanor of Aquataine in The Lion in Winter (Cleve.), Amanda in The Glass Menagerie, Dividing the Estate (Great Lakes), A View From the Bridge, Woman in Mind (Berkshire Theatre Festival), Dolly in The Matchmaker, Agnes of God, Hamlet, Buried Child, The Wicked Witch in The Wizard of Oz, Miss Haversham in Great Expectations, The Bird Sanctuary, 2005; appeared in numerous TV series and movies including: Roseanne, Sister, A Town's Revenge (Emmy nomination), Notes for My Daughter, Nothing Personal, Shameful Secrets, Face of a Stranger, Dottie, The Rise and Rise of Daniel Rocket, Love and Other Sorrows, A Girl Thing, Death of a Salesman (Emmy nomination, 2000), Gilmore Girls, 2001, Judging Amy, 2001; film credits include: Sabrina, 1995, The Substance of Fire, 1996, The Pallbearer, 1996, Thinner, 1996, Twisted, 1997, Jacknife, 1989, Secret of My Success, 1987, School Ties, 1992 Winner 1999 Tony award for featured actress in Death of a Salesman, also Drama Desk award, Outer Critics Circle award.

FRANZ, IRIS VIVIAN (VIVIAN FRANZ), dean, director; b. Cin., Nov. 17, 1923; d. Edgar George Krueger and Vivian Agnes Mohn; m. Robert Vernon Franz (dec. 1981); children: Leslie Totis, Darryl Bayer(dec.), Linda(dec.), Kathleen Alexander. BS in Elem. Edn., Miami U., 1966, MEd in Diagnostic and Remedial Edn., 1968, PhD in Ednl. Adminstrn., Higher Edn., Pers., Curriculum, Psychology, 1972. Tchr. remedial reading Clermont Northeastern Dist., Batavia, Ohio, 1961—64, tchr. elem., 1964—66, tchr. adult basic edn., 1965—66, cons. reading, 1971—73; adminstrv. asst. reading ctr. Miami U., Oxford, Ohio, 1967—69, supr. student tchrs., 1969—70, instr., 1970—71; dir. coop. project State Dept. Edn., Miami U., 1973—75; dean program and instrn. So. State C.C., 1975—81; owner Lamplighter Ednl. Resource Ctr., Terrace Park, Ohio, 1983—2004, dir., 1983—. Recipient Adult Basic Edn. Panel of Experts Cert. of Appreciation, OH Dept. Edn., 1981. Home: PO Box 106 550 Ibold Rd Miamiville OH 45147

FRANZ, JUDY R., physics professor; BA in Physics, Cornell U., 1959; MS in Physics, U. Ill., 1961, PhD in Physics, 1965. Rsch. physicist IBM Rsch. Lab., Zurich, Switzerland, 1965-67; asst. prof. dept. physics Ind. U., 1968-74, assoc. prof., 1974-79, prof., 1979-87; prof. dept. physics W.Va. U., 1987-91, U. Ala., 1994—; exec. officer Am. Phys. Soc., 1994—. Vis. prof. Tech. U. Munich, 1978-79, Cornell U., 1985-86, 88, 90; assoc. dean coll. arts and scis. Ind. U., 1980-82; mem. coun. on materials sci. Dept. of Energy, 1997-2002; mem. rev. com. for materials sci and tech. divsn. Los Alamos Nat. Lab., 1999-2002; sec. gen. Internat. Union Pure & Applied Physics, 2002—, assoc. sec. gen., 1999-2002; mem. U.S. Commn. for UNESCO, 2005— Mem. editorial bd. Am. Jour. Physics, 1985-88; contbr. numerous articles to profl. jours. Mem. divsn. materials rsch. adv. com. NSF, 1986-89, mem. divsn. undergrad. edn. adv. com., 1991-93. Humboldt rsch. fellow Munich, 1978-79; recipient Distinguished Service Citation awd., Am. Assn. of Physics Teachers, 1993, Disting. Alumni award Coll. Eng., U. Ill., Urbana-Champaign, 1997. Fellow AAAS (coun. 1995-98), Am. Phys. Soc. (various coms. and offices, chair exec. com. divsn. condensed matter physics 1993-94), Assn. Women in Sci.; mem. Am. Assn. Physics Tchrs. (pres. 1990-91), Am. Inst. Physics (various coms., gov. bd. 1994—, exec. com. 1996-00), Coun. Sci. Soc. Pres. (exec. bd. 1990), Phi Beta Kappa, Sigma Xi (pres. local chpt. 1981-82). Avocations: hiking, reading. Business E-Mail: franz@aps.org.

FRANZE, LAURA MARIE, lawyer; b. Pitts., Apr. 20, 1956; d. Catherine Franze; m. Kenneth Charles Morton, Aug.13, 1977; 1 child, Irena Everly Morton. BA summa cum laude, Thiel Coll., 1976; JD, Duke U. Law Sch., 1979. Bar: Ohio 1979, Tex. 1982, Ohio 1990, N.Mex. 1990, US Ct. Appeals (no., so. and we. dists.) Tex.; cert. labor and employment law Tex. Bd. Legal Specialization 1984. Atty. Smith & Schnacke, Dayton, Ohio, 1979-81, Gardere & Wynne, Dallas, 1981-93, McKenna & Cuneo, Dallas, 1993-95, Akin, Strauss, Hauer & Feld, Dallas, 1995—, now ptnr., chair labor and employment practice group and mem. mgmt. com. Counsel Coalition of Responsible Employers; commentator (TV show) Ask a Lawyer. Sr. editor Texas Employment Law (2 vol.), 1998. Vice chair legal/ethical task force Dallas AIDS Commn., 1988. Recipient 40 under 40 award Dallas Bus. Jour., 1993, Top Practitioner, Texas Lawyer 2001, One of Best Lawyers in Dallas, D Mag. 1997, 2001, One of Best Labor & Employment Lawyers, Corporate Counsel Mag. 2002. Fellow Tex. Bar Found. Dallas Bar Found.; mem. Dallas Bar Assn., ABA, Dallas Employment Law Sect. (coun., officer 1993—), Dallas Area Labor and Employment Law Group (pres. 1986-87), State Bar Tex. (advanced labor law com. 1993—). Office: Akin Gump Strauss Hauer & Feld LLP 1700 Pacific Ave Ste 4100 Dallas TX 75201-4675 Office Phone: 214-969-2779. Business E-Mail: lfranze@akingump.com.

FRANZEN, JANICE MARGUERITE GOSNELL, magazine editor; b. LaCrosse, Wis. d. Wray Towson and Anna Gosnell; m. Ralph Oscar Franzen, 1964. BS cum laude, Wis. State U., LaCrosse; MRE, No. Bapt. Theol. Sem. Dir. Christian Writers Inst., 1950—63, dir. studies, 1964-86; fiction editor Christian Life Mag., Wheaton, Ill., 1950-63, woman's editor, 1964-72, exec. editor, 1972-86; mem. editorial bd. Creation House, Wheaton, 1972-86. Speaker writers confs. Author: Christian Writers Handbook, 1960, 61, The Adventure of Interviewing, 1989; editor: Christian Author, 1949-54, Christian Writer and Editor, 1955-63; compiler, contbr.: The Successful Writers and Editors Guidebook, 1977; contbr. articles to various mags. Sec., bd. dirs. Christian Life Missions, Lake Mary, Fla., 1971-95; bd. dirs. Ralph O. Franzen Charitable Found., 1990—, Wesley Luehring Found., 2000—. Home: 140 Windsor Park Dr Apt E201 Carol Stream IL 60188-5314

FRANZETTI, LILLIAN ANGELINA, former automobile dealership owner; b. N.Y.C., Nov. 24, 1925; d. Anthony and Jenny (De Santis) Spilotro; m. Louis Mario Franzetti, Apr. 27, 1946 (dec. Oct. 1986); 1 child, Paul. Clk. typist U.S. Guarantee Ins. Co., N.Y.C., 1943—44, asst. mgr. payroll, 1944—46; clk. typist N.J. Divsn. Motor Vehicles, Westwood, 1950—54; office mgr. Lakeview Motors, Inc., Woodcliff Lake, NJ, 1954—58, mgr., owner Westwood, 1958—93; ret., 1993. Sec. Tri-State Jeep, Eagle Adv. Assn., Tappan, N.Y., 1978-93. Recipient Bus. Mgmt. award, Am. Motors Corp., 1978. Republican. Roman Catholic.

FRANZONI, DELAINA DAY, special education educator, department chairman; b. Roswell, N.Mex., Jan. 4, 1961; d. Robert H. Day and Elaine French, Billy C. French (Stepfather); 1 child, Darin. BE, MEd, N.Mex State U. Cert. elem. edn. K-8, spl. edn. K-12, sch. adminstrn. Spl. edn. tchr. Valley View Elem., RISD, Roswell, N.Mex., 1983—92, Adolescent Day Treatment Ctr., RISD, Roswell, N.Mex., 1992—93, Roswell H.S., RISD, Roswell, N.Mex., 1993—99, spl. edn. dept. chair, 1999—. Instr. Positive Parenting, Roswell, 1990—90; tutor Roswell Assurance Home, Roswell, N.Mex., 1992—94; sponsor Conflict Mediation, Roswell H.S., Roswell, N.Mex., 1996—99. Mem.: Delta Kappa Gamma (Alpha Theta chpt.). Episcopalian. Avocations: choir, racquetball, needlepoint.

FRAPPIA, LINDA ANN, medical administrator; b. St. Paul, May 14, 1946; d. Orville Keith Ferguson and Marilyn Ardis (Morris) Bidwell; 1 child, Jennifer Frappia Barrett. Grad. high sch., Seattle. Cert. claims adminstr. Claims rep. Fireman's Fund Ins., L.A., 1965-68; adminstrv. asst. to v.p. Employee Benefits Ins., Santa Ana, Calif., 1969-72; claims specialist Indsl. Indemnity Ins., Orange, Calif., 1972-83; claims supr. CNA Ins., Brea, Calif., 1983-85; claims mgr. EBI Ins. Svcs., Tustin, Calif., 1985; v.p. United Med. Specialists, Santa Ana, Calif., 1985-91; chief exec. officer United Ind. Specialists, Santa Ana, 1990—; chief executive officer United Chiropractic Specialists, Santa Ana, 1987—. Instr. Ins. Edn. Assn., Brea, 1988—; speaker Western Ins. Info. Svc., Orange, 1976-83. Mem. Calif. Mfrs. Assn., Pub. Agencies Risk Mgmt. Assn., Calif. Self-Insured Assn., Toastmasters Internat. (v.p. Orange chpt. 1978). Republican. Avocations: sailing, reading, travel.

FRAPPIER, PEARL PETERS, retired bookkeeper; b. Woonsocket, RI, Mar. 27, 1928; d. Frank and Angele (VanMaldeghem) Peters; m. Dollard Zenon Frappier, Apr. 2, 1956 (dec. Dec. 20, 1972). Bookkeeper McCarthy Dry Goods Co., Woonsocket, 1945—56; ret., 1956. Mem. Rep. Nat. Com., 2004; gov. vol. during WWII; vol. JFK presdl. campaign, 1961; charter mem. Bush-Cheney presdl. campaign, 2004. Recipient Appreciation award, St. Francis Ho., 1996, 1997, Pearl Day award, 2004, Lifetime Opportunity award, RI Assn. Facilities & Svcs. for Aging, 1996. Mem.: The Smithsonian Inst. (assoc.), U.S. Holocaust Meml. Mus., Humane Soc. US, Father Paul Wattson, SA Heritage Soc., Soclumac Club, R.I. Hon. Soc. Republican. Roman Catholic. Avocations: philanthropy, travel, antiques, theater, reading. Home: 223 Burnside Ave Woonsocket RI 02895-2188

FRASER, ARVONNE SKELTON, retired diplomat; b. Lamberton, Minn., Sept. 1, 1925; d. Orland D. and Phyllis (Du Frene) Skelton; m. Donald M. Fraser, June 30, 1950; children: Thomas Skelton, Mary MacKay, John Du Frene, Lois MacKay (dec.), Anne Tallman (dec.), Jean Skelton Fraser. BA, U. Minn., 1948; LLD (hon.), Macalester Coll., 1979. Staff asst. Office Congressman Donald M. Fraser, 1963-70, adminstrv. asst., campaign mgr., 1970-76; regional coord. Carter-Mondale Com., 1976; counsellor office presdl. pers. The White House, 1977; coord. office women in devel. U.S. Agy. Internat. Devel., Washington, 1977-81; dir. Minn. and Chgo. coms. peace petition dr. Albert Einstein Peace Prize Found., Chgo., 1981-82; co-dir. ctr. on women and pub. policy Hubert H. Humphrey Inst. Pub. Affairs, U. Minn., Mpls., 1982-94; head U.S. del. Commn. On The Status of Women, UN, 1993-94, U.S. rep., amb., 1994; co-founder, dir. Internat. Women's Rights Action Watch, 1985-93. Bd. dirs. Minn. DFL Edn. Found.; U.S. del. Internat. Women's Yr. Conf., Mexico City, 1975, UN Commn. on Status of Women, 1974, 78, Internat. Bur. Edn. Conf., Geneva, 1977; cons. Kenya Women's Leadership Conf., 1984; organizer, chairperson Orgn. Econ. Coop. and Develp./Devel. Assistance com./Women in Devel. experts group for aid-donor nations, 1978-80; dir. Ford. Found. Women's Equity Action League Fund Intern Project and World Plan Project, treas. 1974-77, bd. dirs. 1970-77, 81-83, nat. pres. 1972-74, past legis. chair Washington office; pub. mem. Minn. Bd. Law Examiners, 1999-2005. Author: U.N. Decade for Women: Documents and Dialogue, 1987; (with others) Women in Washington: Advocates for Public Policy, 1983, Women, Politics and the United Nations, 1995; co-editor: Developing Power: How Women Transformed International Development, 2004. Trustee Macalester Coll., St. Paul, 1982-84; candidate Lt. Gov. Minn., 1986; pres. Friends of Mpls. Pub. Libr., 2002-04 Recipient Disting. Svc. award Women's Equity Action League, 1977, Superior Honor award U.S. Agy. Internat. Devel., 1981, Elizabeth Boyer award Women's Equity League, 1984, Leader of Leaders Outstanding Achievement award Mpls. YWCA, 1979, Resourceful Woman award Tides Found., 1992; sr. fellow Humphrey Inst. Pub. Affairs U. Minn., 1981-94, emeritus 1995; Prominent Women in Internat. Law award Am. Soc. of Internat. Law, 1995, Mpls. Internat. Citizen award, 1995. Home and Office: 821 7th St SE Minneapolis MN 55414-1331 Office Phone: 612-379-9451.

FRASER, CATRIONA TRAFFORD, art gallery director, photographer; b. Reading, Eng., Jan. 8, 1972; arrived in U.S., 1992; d. Nigel Trafford Fraser and Christine Ilsley; m. Florencio Lennox Campello, Jan. 7, 1995; 1 child, Callum Fraser-Sharp. Diploma, Plymouth Coll. Arts and Design, Devon, Eng., 1988—89; graduated, Wallingford Sch., Oxfordshire, England, 1988. Asst. photographer trainee Reading Evening Post, Reading, England, 1987; founder Cairn Photography, Fettercairn, Scotland, 1991; dir. Fraser Gallery, Washington, 1996—, Bethesda, Md., 2002—. Founder Secondsight, 2003—; dir. Bethesda Fine Arts Festival; chair Trawick Art Prize, Bethesda Painting Awards. Photographer Dunnottar Castle, 1992 (1st prize No. Va. Fine Arts Festival, 1995), Kinnaird Castle, 1992 (1st prize No. Va. Fine Arts Festival, 1994), Glamis Castle, 1992 (1st place 6th Ann. Roseville Photography Competition, Calif., 1993), Fleur No. II, 1992 (Best of Show 17th Ann. Internat. Photo Competition Ark., 1993); exhibitions include Nat. Art. Competition, 1996, Castlegait Gallery, Scotland, 1992, Sacramento Fine Arts Ctr., 1992, New Image Gallery, Va., 1992, Carnegie Mus., Pitts., 1992, St. Helena Art League, Calif., 1993, Brusque Mus., Santa Caterina Brazil, 1993, Art League Gallery, Va., 1994, 1995, Va. Commonwealth U., 1995, Eklektikos Gallery, Washington DC, 1996, Fraser Gallery, Washington DC, 1996, 1997, 1999, 2000, 2002, Infrared Gallery, Chgo., 1998, Bruce Gallery, Edinboro Coll., Pa., 2001, Am. Ctr. Physics, Md., 2004. Adv. panel Bethesda Art and Entertainment; adv. bd. Washington Sch. of Photography. Recipient Honor Award, 42d Ann. Boardwalk Internat. Arts Festival, 1998, Best of Show, Ann. Edzell Scottish Art Invitational, Paul Ostaseski Meml. Award, Roanoke Art Festival, 1998, Merit Award, Spring Stockley Gardens Art Festival, Va., 1995, 20th Ann. Princess Anne Art Show, Va., second place, 37th Ann. Northern Calif. Art Festival, 26th Ann. Otero Mus. Nat. Exhbn., Colo., Waynesboro Fall Arts Festival, Va., 1997, 1996, Bel Air Festival Arts, Md., 1994, Fall Stockley Gardens Art Festival, Va., 1995, Bellgrade Art Festival, Va., 1995, 1997, Judge's Award, 1994. Mem.: Art Dealers Assn. Greater Washington, Bethesda C. of C. Office: Fraser Gallery 7700 Wisconsin Ave Ste E Bethesda MD 20814 Office Phone: 301-718-9651. Office Fax: 301-718-9652. Business E-Mail: catriona@thefrasergallery.com.

FRASER, ELEANOR RUTH, radiologist, administrator; b. Woodlake, Calif., May 31, 1927; d. Morton William and Dorothy Jean (Harding) F. BA magna cum laude, Pomona Coll., Claremont, Calif., 1949; MD, Stanford U., Calif., 1954. Diplomate Am. Bd. Radiology. Resident in radiology Los Angeles County Hosp., 1957; radiologist St. Joseph Hosp., Orange, Calif., 1957—61; pvt. practice Anaheim, Calif., 1961—78; radiologist Radiology Nuc. Med. Group, Bakersfield, Calif., 1978—85; dir. radiology Kern Valley Hosp., Lake Isabella, Calif., 1985—, chief of staff, 1992—99. Mem. AMA, Calif. Med. Assn., Kern County Med. Assn., Kern Valley Exch. Club (sec. 1992-94), Phi Beta Kappa. Methodist. Avocations: music, writing. Home and Office: PO Box 1657 Lake Isabella CA 93240-1657 Office Phone: 760-379-2681 227. E-mail: elfray@myway.com.

FRASER, KATHLEEN JOY, poet, creative writing professor; b. Tulsa, Mar. 22, 1935; d. James Ian and Marjorie Joy (Axtell) F.; m. Jack Marshall, July 10, 1960 (div. 1970); 1 child, David Ian; m. Arthur Kalmer Bierman, June 30, 1984 BA in English Lit., Occidental Coll., 1958; doctoral equivalency, San Francisco State U., 1976. Vis. prof. writing, lectr. in poetry The Writer's Workshop, U. Iowa, Iowa City, 1969-71; writer in residence Reed Coll., Portland, Oreg., 1971-72; dir. Poetry Center San Francisco State U., 1972-75, prof. creative writing, 1972-92. Founder-dir. Am. Poetry Archives, San Francisco, 1973-75; founder-editor How(ever), Jour. for poets/scholars interested in modernism and women's innovative writing, 1983-91. Author: (children's book) Stilts, Somersaults and Headstands, 1967; (poetry) What I Want (New and Selected Poems), 1974, New Shoes, 1978, Something (even human voices in the foreground) A Lake, 1984, Notes Preceding Trust, 1988, When New Time Folds Up, 1993, Il Cuore: The Heart, Selected Poems 1970-95, 1997, Discrete Categories Forced Into Coupling, 2004, (essays) Translating the Unspeakable: Poetry and the Innovative Necessity, 2000. Recipient Frank O'Hara Poetry prize, 1964; Nat. Endowment for Arts fellow, 1978, Guggenheim fellow, 1981.

FRASER, MAIDA LYNN, director; d. Wilfred Eugene and Martha Mary Switzer; m. Craig Fraser, Oct. 29, 1983; children: Garrett James Thee, Allison Lynn Thee, Clayton Allan, Nicole Rene Knecht. BA, UCLA, 1968. Lic. Calif. Tchrs. Commn., 1968. Classroom educator, 1968—2004; dist. resource tchr. for new tchr. support Cupertino Union Sch. Dist., Calif., 2004—. Bd. dirs. Mammoth Lakes Unified Sch. Dist., Calif., 1981—83. Recipient Award for Acheivement, PTA, 2003. Mem.: Mammoth Lakes Edn. Assn. (assoc.; pres. 1975—78), Chi Omega (life; officer gamma beta chpt. 1966—68). Achievements include development of implemented the WEB program for all five middle schools in the district. Avocations: tennis, writing. Office: Cupertino Union Sch Dist 10301 Vista Dr Cupertino CA 05124 Office Phone: 408-252-3000 178.

FRASER, SHEILA, government agency administrator; 3 children. BS in Comm., McGill U., 1972; LLD, Simon Fraser U., 2004. Chartered acct., 1974, cert. FCA, 1994. Acct. Ernst & Young, prtnr.; deputy auditor gen., audit opers. Office of Auditor Gen. Canada, 1999—2001, auditor gen., 2001—. Chair Working Group Environ. Auditing, Sub-Com. Independence Supreme Audit Insts., Internat. Orgn. Supreme Audit Insts. Recipient Prix Emérite, 1993, Gov. Gen.'s medal. Fellow: Inst. Chartered Accts. Ont. and Quebec; mem.: Canadian Inst. Chartered Accts. Office: Office of the Auditor Gen of Canada 240 Sparks St Ottawa ON Canada K1A 0G6 E-mail: communications@oag-bvg.gc.ca.

FRASER-LIGGETT, CLAIRE M., research scientist, science administrator; BS in Biology, Rensselaer Poly. Inst., 1977, DSc (hon.), 2002; PhD in Pharmacology, SUNY, Buffalo, 1981; Doctorate (hon.), U. Bergen, Norway, 2000; DSc (hon.), Rensselaer Polytechnic U., 2002. Tchg. asst. dept. pharmacology and therapeutics SUNY, Buffalo, 1977—81, rsch. assoc. dept. pharmacology and therapeutics, 1981—82, rsch. instr. dept. biochemistry, 1982—83; cancer rsch. scientist III dept. molecular immunology Roswell Park Meml. Inst., Buffalo, 1983—84, cancer rsch. scientist IV dept. molecular immunology, 1984—85; sr. staff fellow Lab. Neurophysiology NINCDS, NIH, Bethesda, Md., 1985—87; sr. staff fellow, chief unit of receptor regulation, receptor biochemistry and molecular biology Lab. Molecular and Cellular Neurobiology, NINDS, NIH, Bethesda, Md., 1987—89; chief sect. on molecular neurobiology Lab. Physiologic and Pharmacologic Studies Nat. Inst. on Alcohol Abuse and Alcoholism, ADAMHA, Rockville, Md., 1989—92; v.p. for rsch., dir. dept. microbial genomics Inst. for Genomic Rsch., Rockville, 1992—98, pres., dir., investigator, 1998—. Mem. com. on countering bioterrorism and domestic animal genomics NRC; mem. rev. com. NSF, US Dept. Energy-NIH; lectr. Waksman Found. for Microbiology Lectures Program, 2000, 01; prof. pharmacology George Washington U., 2000, prof. microbiology & tropical medicine, 01; bd. dirs. Becton Dickinson & Co., 2006—. Mem. editl. bd.: Jour. Biol. Chemistry, reviewer sci. jours.:; contbr. articles to profl. jours. Named one of Leading Women and Minority Scientists, NY Acad. Sciences, 2005; named to, Md. Top 100 Women, 1997, 2000; recipient Computerworld Smithsonian award for innovation and info. tech., 1998, Inst. for Math. and Advanced Supercomputing award, 1999, Burroughs Wellcome Fund Visiting Scientist Professorship award, 1999, Fellows award, Rensselaer Alumni Assn., 2002, E.O. Lawrence award, US Dept. Energy, 2002, Md. Top 100 Women Circle of Excellence award, 2004, Charles Thom award, Soc. for Industrial Microbiology, 2005, Diversity in Sci. award for Leadership & Scientific Excellence, NY Acad. Sci., 2005; fellow, AAAS, 2004, Am. Acad. Microbiology, 2005. Office: Inst for Genomic Rsch 9712 Medical Center Dr Rockville MD 20850

FRATES, MEX (MRS. CLIFFORD LEROY FRATES), civic worker; b. Moweaqua, Ill., Jan. 15, 1908; d. William James and Gertrude (Gunderson) Rodman; m. Clifford L. Frates, Nov. 15, 1935; children: Rodman A., Kent F. Student, Pine Manor Jr. Coll., 1924; BA, U. Okla., 1929. Mem. bd. ARC, Oklahoma City; dir. Community Fund Bd.; trustee Jane Brooks Sch. Deaf, Okla. Art Center, Okla. Coll. for Women; chmn. adv. bd. Mercy Hosp., also trustee; bd. dirs. Okla. State Library, Library for Blind, dir. Jr. Leagues of Am.; mem. bd. Okla. Heritage Assn., Allied Arts of Oklahoma City, Oklahoma City Symphony, YWCA, Blood Inst., Better Bus. Bur.; mem. Children's Rehab. and Edn. Bd.; drive chmn. Central Vol. Bur.; chmn. women's div. United Fund; chmn. Art Center drive; chmn. Oklahoma City Savs. Bond Com.; chmn. Episcopal Women's Conf. Okla.; div. chmn. for Christian social relations; mem. Episcopal Bishop and Council; mem. vestry All Souls Ch. chmn. Re-act campaign for Oklahoma City Vol. Action Center, 1971. Recipient award NCCJ, Humanitarian award Oklahoma City Pub. Sch. Found., 1986, By-Liners award Women in Comm., 1979, Okla. Gov.'s Arts award, 1985, Mary Baker Rumsey award Jr. League Redlands, award for volunteerism Girl Scouts U.S., Richard Clements award United Appeal, Pathfinder award Oklahoma County Hist. Soc., Dean's award Coll. Medicine for Cmty. Svc.; named to Okla. Hall of Fame, 1969. Home: 2607 Warwick Dr Oklahoma City OK 73116-4208

FRATKIN, LESLIE, photographer; b. Schenectady, N.Y., 1960; BA in Comm., SUNY, Albany, 1983. Curator, coord., mgr. touring internat. photography exhbn., film series, web site and book project Sarajevo Self-Portrait: The View From Inside, 1995—. Exhibitions include Barney's, N.Y.C., 1995, Foster Goldstrom Gallery, 1995, Children in Crisis Benefit, Germany, 1997, Riverside Studios, London, 1998, Florence, Italy, 1999; contbg. photographer various publs., 1983—. The Trust for Mutual Understanding grantee, 1997, Individual Project fellow and grantee, Soros Found./Open Soc. Inst., 1997. E-mail: leslief@interport.net.

FRAUENHOFFER, ROSE MARIE, visual artist; b. Evanston, Ill., July 24, 1926; d. Edward John and Rose Louise (Pantle) Kossow; m. Harold Voight Frauenhoffer, Oct. 14, 1950. Lic. cosmetologist, Ill. Mgr., buyer Del-Mar, Evanston, 1948-52; asst. mgr., buyer House of Harold Salon, Evanston, 1952-2000; mgr. buyer House of Harold Gifts, Evanston, 1952—; mgr. House of Harold Gallery, Evanston, 1952-2000; asst. mgr., designer House of Harold Engraving, Evanston, 1952-2000; artist, designer House of Harold Studio, Evanston, 1999-2000; artist, dir. Peinture de la Monde Studio, Gallery divsn. House of Harold, Evanston, 2000—04; dir., visual artist Blue Door Art Gallery and Studio, 2004—. One-woman shows include Aurelia Gallery, Evanston, Garland Bldg. Gallery, Chgo., Bank of Lincolnwood, Levy Ctr. La-Petite Gallery, Loft Gallery, Skokie, Ill., Friends of the Wilmette Area Libr. Exhibit (Hon. Mention, 1992); group shows at Loft Gallery, John G. Blank Ctr. for Arts, Michigan City, Ind., Margaret Harwell Art Mus., Poplar Bluffs, Mo., Wilmette (Ill.) Pub. Libr.; Nappa valley Nat. Exhibit (Hon. Mention, 1992), Evanston Woman's Club Area Exhibit (Third Watercolor award, 1999), Margaret Marwell Art Mus. Nat. Small Painting Exhibit (Second Watercolor award, 2004); miniature paintings in juried nat. and internat. exhbns. Alumnus, vol. Evanston Citizens Police Acad., 1997—; co-chair Skokie Centennial Art and Craft Fair, 1988. Award winner Nat. Art Juried Show, 2004. Mem. Skokie Art Guild (v.p. 1980-81, pres. 1981-82), Transparent Watercolor Soc. Am., Nat. Mus. Women in the Arts, Ill. Arts Coun., Evanston Arts Coun., Chgo. Artists Coalition, Nat. Women's History Mus. Avocations: gardening, photography, sewing. Office Phone: 847-864-0791.

FRAWLEY BAGLEY, ELIZABETH, government advisor, ambassador; b. Elmira, NY, July 13, 1952; m. Smith Bagley; 2 children. BA in French and Spanish cum laude, Regis Coll., 1974; JD in Internat. Law, Georgetown U., 1987. Staff Office Congl. Rels. Dept. State, spl. asst. to Amb. Sol Linowitz, congl. liaison Conf. on Security and Cooperation in Europe, amb. to Portugal Washington, 1993-97, US adv. commn. pub. diplomacy, 2001—. Adj. prof. law Georgetown U. Washington, 1992-94. Home: 1539 29th St NW Washington DC 20007-3061

FRAWLEY-O'DEA, MARY GAIL, clinical psychologist, psychoanalyst, educator; b. Lowell, Mass. d. John Edward and Mary Gail (Quinn) Frawley; m. Dennis Michael O'Dea, Jan. 1, 1996; 1 stepson, Daniel Patrick; children: Igor Ibradzic, Mollie Gilmore Chun O'Dea. BA, St. Mary's Coll., Notre Dame, Ind., 1972; MBA, So. Meth. U., 1975; PhD, Adelphi U., 1988, postdoctoral diploma in psychoanalysis, 1996. Psychologist II Pomona (N.Y.) Mental Health Clinic, 1987-91; asst. clin. prof. Adelphi U., Derner Inst., Garden City, NY, 1989—91; pvt. practice clin. psychologist/psychoanalyst Nyack, NY, 1990—2000, New City, NY, 2000—. Faculty supr. Minn. Inst. Contemporary Psychoanalysis, Mpls.-St. Paul, 1996—; continuing edn. faculty N.Y. Psychol. Assn. for Psycholanalysis, 1998—; supr. and faculty Nat. Tng. Program for psychoanalysis, N.Y., 2000—; co-dir. Manhattan Inst. Psychoanalysis, 2001—; exec. dir. Manhattan Inst. Psychoanalysis Trauma Treatment Ctr., 2001—; mem. faculty supervisory tng. program Nat. Inst. for Psychotherapies, NY, 2002—; mem. adv. bd. Nat. Orgn. for Male Sexual Victims, 2002—, Psychoanalytic Perspectives; chair victims rights com. Archdiocese of Boston. Co-author: treating the Adult Survivor of Childhood Sexual Abuse, 1994, The Supervisory Relationship, 2000; mem. editl. bd. Studies in Gender and Sexuality; mem. adv. bd. Psychoanalytic Perspectives, 2003—; contbr. chpts. to books, articles to profl. jours. Mem.: APA (mem. pub. com. div. psychoanalysis 2001—), Manhattan Inst. Psychoanalytic Soc., N.Y. State Psychol. Assoc., Westchester Soc. Psychoanalysis and Psychotherapy. Avocations: hiking, cooking, theater, symphony, reading. E-mail: mgfod@aol.com.

FRAZEE, EVELYN, lawyer, educator; BA, SUNY, Oneonta, 1972; JD, Rutgers U., NJ, 1978. Bar: N.Y. 1979, N.Y. (U.S. Dist. Ct.) 1980, Justice Supreme Ct., Seventh Dist.: N.Y. 1993. Lectr. Office of Ct. Adminstrn. Judicial Seminars, 1994, U. Rochester, NY, 2002—. Lectr. U. Rochester, NY, 2002—. Editor-in-chief Rutgers-Camden Law Jour. (Corpus Juris Secundum award). Advisor YMCA Youth and Govt. Conf., 1989—91; adv. bd. Alzheimer's Family Outreach Program, 1989—94; bd. dirs. United Cerebral Palsy of Rochester, 1991—94, Rochester Gen. Hosp. Found., 1993—94; co-founder, advisory bd. co-chair Assisting Children through Transition Parent Edn., 1997—; panelist Nat. ADR Conf., 1998; co-chair N.Y. State Com. to Promote Public Trust and Confidence in the Judicial Sys., 1998—; chair N.Y. State Parent Edn. Adv. Bd., 2001—; mem. Fed./State Judicial Council, 2000—02. Recipient Catherine Booth award, Salvation Army, 1998, Distinguished Jurist award, N.Y. State Trial Lawyers Assn., 2005; fellow, Starkweather Inst., 2001. Mem.: N.Y. Assn. Supreme Ct. Justices (Ad Hoc com. for status of ct. reporters, chair 1993, pub. rels. com., mem. ann. convention com., co-chair 1997), Women's Bar Assn. of State of N.Y., Greater Rochester Assn. for Women Attys. (program com. 1992, nominating com., chair 2000—01, co-chair 2000—, Hanna S. Cohn Mentoring award 2004), AFCC (founding mem., 1st co-pres. 2003—). Office: 223 Hall of Justice Rochester NY 14614

FRAZEE, JANE, music educator; b. Cumberland, Wis., July 16, 1936; d. Herbert Clarence and Aleda Etta (Richardson) Christensen; m. James Lowell Frazee (div. Sept. 1978); m. Kent Kirby Kreuter, May 30, 1982. MusB, U. Wis., 1958; MA, U. Minn., 1961. Instr. music Northrop Collegiate Sch., Mpls., 1960-72; asst. prof. Hamline U., St. Paul, 1972—; Fulbright prof., 1981-82; dir. grad. music edn. program Hamline U., St. Paul, 1984—91; tchr. music St. Paul Acad., 1978—93. Instr. music Macalester Coll., St. Paul, 1968-73. Author: Discovering Orff, 1987; contbr. articles to profl. jours. Named Elem. Music Tchr. of the Yr., Minn. Music Educators Assn., 1986. Mem. Am. Orff-Schulwerk Assn. (pres. 1976-77), Alliance for Arts in Edn., Music Educators Nat. Conf. Democrat. Unitarian Universalist. Avocation: gardening. Home: 459 Mount Curve Blvd Saint Paul MN 55105-1325

FRAZELLE, RHONDA J., psychology professor, counselor; d. Robert E. and Karen J. Walker; children: Sarah J., Marie C. Frazelle-Bland, Robert D. AA, State Fair C.C., Sedalia, Mo., 1994; BS in Psychology, Ctrl. Mo. State U., Warrensburg, Mo., 1996, MS in Clin. and Counseling Psychology, 1998; EdD Ednl. Leadership and Policy Analysis, U. Mo., Columbia, Mo., 2005. Lic. profl. counselor Mo. Profl. Licensure Bd. Counselors, 2000. Supr. comprehensive psychiat. rehab. ctr. Pathways Cmty. Behavioral Healthcare, Clinton, Mo., 1999—2000, dir. children's svcs., 2000—01; counselor trio student support svcs. State Fair C.C., Sedalia, Mo., 2001—03, instr. psychology, 2004—. Dir. preschool Grover Pk. Bapt. Ch., Warrensburg, Mo., 1994—2006, tchr. Sunday sch., 1994—2006. Named Disting. Student of the Yr., State Fair C.C., 1994, Undergraduate Psychology Student of the Yr., Ctrl. Mo. State U., 1996; grantee, 1996—98; Warren & Waller Educatin Adminstrn. scholarship, 2006. Mem.: Mental Health Assn. Pettis County (pres. 2005—06). Avocations: gardening, interior decorating, travel. Office: State Fair Commuity College 3201 W 16th St Sedalia MO 65301 Office Phone: 660-530-5800 372. Business E-Mail: rfrazelle@sfccmo.edu.

FRAZER, JANET ELIZABETH, music educator; b. Tulsa, Okla., Oct. 21, 1965; d. Fred and Margaret Harrison; m. Christopher J. Frazer, Mar. 23, 1991; children: Rachel, Nathan. MusB Edn., U. Tulsa, Okla., 1987. Music instr. Jenks (Okla.) Pub. Schs., 1988—. Bldg. rep. Jenks Classroom Tchrs. Assn.; children's choir coord. First Bapt. Ch., Tulsa, 2001—. Grantee, Jenks Pub. Schs. Found. Office: Jenks Pub Schs 205 East B St Jenks OK 74037 Office Phone: 918-299-4415.

FRAZER, JENDAYI ELIZABETH, federal agency administrator, former ambassador; BA political sci., Stanford U., MA internat. policy/internat. devel., PhD political sci. Fellow Coun. Foreign Relations Internat. Affairs, 1998-99; asst. prof. pub. policy, John F. Kennedy Sch. Govt. Harvard U., 1999—2001; spl. asst. to the Pres. & sr. dir. for African Affairs NSC, Washington, 2001—04; US amb to South Africa US Dept. State, Pretoria, 2004—05, asst. sec. for African Affairs Washington, 2005—. Vis. fellow Ctr. Internat. Security and Arms Control, Stanford U.; rsch. assoc. Inst. Devel. Studies, U. Nairobi, Kenya; bd. dirs. African Devel. Found., 2005- Mem. Women in Internat. Soc. (exec. bd. 1998—). Office: US Dept State 2201 C St NW Rm 6234A Washington DC 20520*

FRAZER, JOY A., retired nurse; b. Louisa, Ky., Feb. 6, 1937; d. David Adams and Mary Delilah Shannon; m. Thomas Derifield Frazier, Sept. 17, 1959; children: Mark Thomas, Martha Joy. RN Louisville Gen. Hosp., 1957. Surg. nurse King's Dau.'s Hosp., Ashland, Ky., 1957—58; office nurse P.J. Winn, M.D., 1957—60; sch. nurse Owsley County Health Dept., Booneville, 1960—62; nurse ICU Meth. Hosp., Louisville, 1962—63; surg. nurse gynecol. fl. North Decatur Hosp., Ga., 1974—77; office nurse Michael Nash, M.D., 1977—91; dialysis nurse Rolling Meadows (Ill.) Dialysis Unit, Rolling Meadows, 1992—2002; ret., 1992. Mem. mission to Dominican Rep. First Presbyn. Ch., Arlington Heights, Ill., 2002; mem. mission to El Salvador Union Ch., Berea, Ky., 2004; mem. ch. choir. Mem.: Kentuckians Commonwealth. Avocations: hiking, quilting, reading. Home: 110 Castle Dr Berea KY 40403

FRAZER, SUSAN HUME, architectural firm executive; b. Hinton, W.Va., Jan. 3, 1949; d. Dennis Ray and Wanda Marrs Hume; m. John Walker Frazer Jr., Oct. 6, 1989; children: Andrew Reno Collier II., Amy Marie Wilson Collier. BA Psychology, Chapman U., 1972; MS Interior Environments, U. Wis., 1992; PhD Art History, Va. Commonwealth U., 2001. V.p., dir. mktg. Signature Cmtys., Alexandria, Va., 1984—88; v.p. mktg. Miller and Smith, McLean, 1988—90; ind. scholar/cons. Am. Architecture and Decorative Arts, Richmond, 1998—. Contbr. articles to profl. jours. Mem.: Soc. Archtl. Historians, Sigma Sigma Sigma (past pres.), Kappa Omicron Nu (hon.), Delta Omicron (hon.). Presbyterian. Avocations: piano, baking, antiques. Home and Office: 2023 Hanover Ave Richmond VA 23220 E-mail: hume-frazer@erols.com.

FRAZER, TERESA ELIZABETH, pediatrician, endocrinologist; b. Muncie, Ind., July 30, 1950; d. Lloyd Dudley Frazer and Althea Lewisa Thornburg; m. Juan Llado, June 13, 1980; children: Estebania Nicole Llado, Juan Andres Llado, Joaquin Alejandro Ronald Llado, Nicolas Esteban Llado, Lucas Eduardo Marshal Llado. MD, Purdue U., Ind., 1975. Prof. pharmacology and pediat. Ponce Sch. Medicine, PR, 1986—; pediatrician, pediatric endocrinologist Bluefield Regional Med. Ctr., W.Va., 2005—. Sec. Caribbean Sch., Ponce, 1991—96. Grantee, NIH, 1989—2001. Fellow: Am. Acad. Pediat. Society Of Friends. Achievements include research in Incidence and Genetic Type of Type 1 Diabetes in Puerto Rican Chidlren. Office: Bluefield Regional Medical Center 510 Cherry Street Bluefield WV 24701 Office Phone: 304-327-1630. Home Fax: 304-327-1660.

FRAZIER, AMY, professional tennis player; b. St. Louis, Mo., Sept. 19, 1972; Prof. tennis player WTA Tour, 1990—. Mem. 1995 U.S. Fed. Cup Team. Named World Team Tennis MVP, 1995. Achievements include winner 7 career Singles Titles and 5 career Doubles Titles, WTA Tour; appeared in 18 consecutive U.S. Open Tournaments. Avocations: ceramics, painting, bicycling. Office: USTA 70 W Red Oak Ln White Plains NY 10604-3602

FRAZIER, ELOISE M., minister; b. Gloversville, N.Y., Aug. 19, 1934; d. George T. and Sally M. Thompson; m. Robert G. Frazier, Oct. 19, 1963; children: Willie, Kevin, Charles. Lic. LPN, Bd. Certified Diploma, 1967. Dir. Christian edn. Mt. Olive Bapt. Ch., Schenectady, NY, 1988—2005; coord. payne satellite Payne Theol. Seminary, Albany, NY, 2000—05. Pres. Internat. Ministers Conf., Albany, NY, 1997—2000; coord. N.Y. Satellite Payne Seminary, ALbany, NY, 2000—05. Pres. Zonta Internat. Women's Club, Sxhenectady, NY, 1999—2001; chair and commr. Sxhenectady County Human Rights Commn., Sxhenectady. Recipient Woman of Achievment award, Young Women C Assn., Svc. award, Schenectady Family Health Ctr., 1996, cmty svc. award, Interfaith Cmty., 2001. Mem.: Dr. Martin L. King Commn. (chair 1995—2005), Internal. Min. (pres. 1997—2000).

FRAZIER, EMMA L., healthcare educator, researcher; 1 child, Emory. PhD, Med. U. S.C., Charleston, 1988. Math. statistician Centers Disease Control, Atlanta, 1989—97; rsch. assoc. prof. pub. health scis. Morehouse Coll., Atlanta, 2004—. Office: Morehouse Coll 830 Westview SW Atlanta GA 30310 Office Phone: 404-681-2800. E-mail: efrazier@morehouse.edu.

FRAZIER, JAN ELAINE, literature and language educator, writer; b. Macomb, Ill., June 2, 1947; d. James Christopher and Mabel Anna (Pollman) Hoyt; m. Carl Edward Frazier, Dec. 17, 1983; children: Dara Anne, Jenna Elaine. BA, Bradley U., Peoria, Ill., 1971; MA, Bradley U., 2004. Cert. sec. edn. Ill. Sec. Assn. of Commerce, Peoria, 1966—69, Time-Life, Amsterdam, Netherlands, 1972—74; tchr. English Lacaza Bus. Coll., Silver Springs, Md., 1974—75, Pekin Cmty. H.S., Ill., 1982—2002; prof. English Bradley U., Peoria, 2004—. Adv. bd. Ill. Edn. Assn., Pekin, 1998—2002. Author: (young adult books) Starlight Laser Express, 2003 (Tommy award, 2003), Ghost of Chance, 2004, Glimpse of Netherworld, 2005, Touched By a Ghost, 2006, (young adult books) Murder Times Three, 2005, Mission to Murder, 2006. Pub. spkr. civic orgn., Ill., 2002—; summer travel with students to Europe, 1990—; ednl. writing workshops pub./pvt. sch., Midwest, 2002—. Mem.: NEA, Ill. Edn. Assn., Ret. Tchrs. Assn., Tazewell County Hist. and Genel. Soc. Lutheran. Avocations: travel, creative writing, reading. Home: 1020 Washington Pekin IL 61554 Office: Bradley Univ 1501 W Bradley Ave Peoria IL 61625

FRAZIER, JO FRANCES, religious organization administrator, writer; b. Tulsa, Dec. 20, 1928; d. Joseph and Eva Mae Fulcher; m. Chester Jerome Frazier, July 19, 1950; children: David, Linda Frazier Parizo, Susan Frazier Kelly. Student, Duke U., 1946—49; BA, Tulsa U., 1950. Publicity chmn. Ventura (Calif.) County Mental Health Adv. Bd., 1978—81; adv. bd. mem. Charter Hosp. Bd. Trustees, Bakersfield, Calif., 1983—85, Desert Counseling Ctr., Bakersfield, 1983—85; founder, dir. Saints Alive Ministry, Bakersfield, 1995—. Lectr./spkr. in field. Prodr.: (films) Any One of Us, 1980, (video) Saints Alive Ministry, 1999; author: Second Chance, 1987, Saints for Today's Youth, Books 1, 2 and 3, 1995—2002, (children's books) Saints Thérèse of the Child Jesus, Joan of Arc, Francis of Assisi, Martin de Porres, Blessed Kateri Tekakwitha. Mem.: Audobon Soc., Nature Conservancy, World Wildlife Fund, Italian Cath. Fedn. (sec. 1984—86). Avocations: swimming, reading. Home: 300 Magnolia Ave Bakersfield CA 93305-1425 Office Phone: 661-326-1838.

FRAZIER, MARY ANN, artist; b. Tulsa, Okla., Sept. 11, 1937; d. Dolphus Leonard and Elouise (Reedy) Cagle; m. Robert E. Frazier, May 14, 1954 (div. Mar. 1971); children: Robert E. Frazier, Jr. (dec.), Robbyne Elisa. Student, Tulsa C.C., 1990—92; studied with numerous artists, including, David Leffel, Ben Konis, Doug Dawson, William Herring, Mary Russell, Del Gish, others. Oil portrait David Moss, David L. Moss Correctional Ctr., Tulsa; permanent collections of portrait and other paintings in pub. and pvt. collections throughout the U.S. Home: 3338 E 27th Pl Tulsa OK 74114-5910

FREAD, PHYLLIS JEAN, counselor, educator; b. Pahala, Hawaii, May 21, 1927; d. Logan Allen and Joyce (Barnes) Pruitt; m. John W. Fread (dec.); children: James R., John A. BA, Cornell Coll., 1948; MEd, U. Oreg., 1958. Cert. tchr., counselor, Oreg. Tchr. Seattle Pub. Schs., 1948-50, West Valley H.S., Millwood, Wash., 1950-52, Roseburg (Oreg.) Dist. 4, 1954-65, dean students, 1965-80; French instr. Umpqua C.C., Roseburg, Oreg., 1983—92; diagnostic counselor AFS, Portland, Oreg., 1988—, hosting dir., 1990—98. Mem. scholar interview team Ford Family Found., 1992—2003. Named Vol. of Month, Roseburg C. of C., Vol. of Yr., Hillside Retirement Cmty., 2005. Mem. AAUW (treas. 1958-63, co-pres. 2000-02), Yamhill County Oreg. Ret. Educators Assn. (pres. 2004-06), Zonta Club Roseburg (pres. 1976-78, 83-84, gov. dist. 8 1996-98), Zonta Club Portland. Republican. Methodist. Avocations: music, travel, reading. Home: 879 NW Meadowood Cir Mcminnville OR 97128-9530 Personal E-mail: phyllisf@onlinemac.com.

FREANEY, DIANE M., financial executive; b. Boston, Sept. 15, 1943; d. James A. and Dorothy (Biddle) Freaney; m. R. Michael Harter, Sept. 12, 1970 (div. 1978); 1 child, Allison E. Harter. BS in Acctg., Syracuse U., 1965. CPA N.Y., Pa. Auditor Ernst & Young, N.Y.C., 1965—70; asst. corp. contr. Kenton Corp., N.Y.C., 1970—72; planning officer Citibank, N.Y.C., 1972—74; mgr. fin. control ITT Corp., N.Y.C., 1974—77; dir. bus. analysis Cigna Corp., Phila., 1977—79; corp. contr. Safeguard Bus. Sys., Inc., Fort Washington, Pa., 1979—82, treas., 1982—87; v.p., CFO Windon Capital Mgmt., Bala Cynwyd, Pa., 1987—89; ptnr. Triage Inc., Lafayette Hill, Pa., 1989—. Founder Phila. Women's Network, 1978. Bd. dirs. Miquon Sch., Pa., 1980—87, Ambler YMCA, BBB SE Pa. Mem.: AICPA, Fin. Women's Assn. N.Y., Phila. Fin. Assn., Pa. Inst. CPA, N.Y. State Soc. CPA, Forum Exec. Women, Whissahickon Valley C. of C. (bd. dirs.). Office: Triage Inc 1232 Somers Rd # A Huntingdon Valley PA 19006-1918

FREAR, LORRIE, graphic designer, educator; b. Rochester, N.Y., July 23, 1955; d. Charles Richard and Muriel Jean F; m. John Paul Dodd, Feb. 29, 1992. BFA, Rochester Inst. Tech., 1978, MFA, 1981. Graphic designer Gannett (newspapers), Rochester, N.Y., 1981-82, Robert Meyer Design, Rochester, N.Y., 1981-82, Gregory Fossella Assocs., Boston, 1982-84, McKesson Corp., San Francisco, 1984-88, Landor Assocs., 1985, Great Ideas Advtsg., Buffalo, 1988-99, Lorrie Frear Design, Canandaigua, N.Y., 1990—; lectr. graphic design Rochester Inst. Tech., 1990—, asst. prof., 2005—. Art dir. Nat. Ctr. Missing & Exploited Children, Rochester, 1998; water safety instr., 1973-93; IDEA cert. fitness instr., 1987-93. Recipient winner, Graceful Envelope Contest, 2003—06. Mem. Lake County Garden Club (art dir. 1999—2004), Genesee Valley Calligraphy Guild, Phi Kappa Phi. Independent. Baptist. Avocations: calligraphy, exercise, movies, gardening, piano. Home: 5434 Lower Egypt Rd Canandaigua NY 14424-8850 Office: RIT Sch Design Coll Imaging Arts & Scis 73 Memorial Dr Rochester NY 14623 E-mail: lxfcad@rit.edu.

FREASIER, AILEEN W., special education educator; b. Edcouch, Tex., Nov. 12, 1924; d. James Ross and Ethel Inez (Riley) Wade; m. Ben F. Freasier (dec.), Mar. 9, 1944; children: Ben. C., Doretha J. Christoph, Barbara F. Protzman, Raymond E. (dec.), John F. BS HE, Tex. A and I Coll., 1944; MEd, La. Tech. U., 1966; postgrad. 90 hours, La. Tech. U. Tchr. Margaret Roane Day Care Ctr., Ruston, La., 1965-71; tchr. spl. edn. Lincoln Parish Schs., Ruston, 1971-81; individualized edn. program facilitator La. Tng. Inst. Monroe Spl. Sch. Dist. # 1, 1981-89; ednl. diagnostician LTI Monroe (La.) SSD # 1, 1985-95. Vol. tutor GED class, Lincoln Parish Detention Ctr., 1996-2006; citizen amb. People Conf. on Edn., Beijing, 1992, South Africa, 1995; presenter in field. Mem. editl. bd.: Jour. Correctional Edn., 1983—95, editor learning tech. sect.:, 1991—95; contbr. articles to ednl. publs. and profl. jours.; author: 5 comml. handwriting duplicating books. Treas. Ruston Mayor's Commn. on Women, 1996—; GED tutor Lincoln Parish Detention Class, 1995—. Named Spl. Sch. Dist. #1 Tchr. of Yr., 1988; recipient J.E. Wallace Wallin Educator of Handicapped award La. Fedn. CEC, 1994, Meritorious Svc. award La. Dept. Pub. Safety and Corrections, 1995, Pres.'s award La. CEC-Tech. and Media, 1997. Mem.: AAUW (state co-chair diversity task force 1993—94, state chmn. diversity com. 1994—2002, pres. North La. br. 1995—2005, state treas. 2001—03, La. Named Gift honoree AAUW Edn. Found. 1994), N.La. Am. Assn. U. Women (pres. 2004—06), Lincoln Parish Ret. Tchrs. Assn. (yearbook editor 1996—, pres. 1998—2000), Internat. Correctional Edn. Assn. (spl. edn. spl. interest group, newsletter editor 1991—94, chmn. 1994—96, editl. bd. CEA Yearbook of Correctional Edn. 1998—), CEC-Tech. and Media (treas. La. divsn. 1993—96, 2001—, Pres.'s award 1997), Nat. Soc. DAR (Long Leaf Pine chpt., regent 1997—99, constitution week chmn. 2000—), DAR (chmn. vets. patient com. 2000—), Kappa Kappa Iota (pres. Epsilon conclave 1985—87, state pres. 1991—92, nat. scholarship com. 1995—, nat. tech. com. 1997—99, chmn. nat. tech. com. 1999—2000, pres. Epsilon conclave 1999—2000, nat. profl. devel. com. 2001—03, v.p. 2003, chmn. bylaws com. 2003—04, chmn. Eta state scholarship com. 2003—05, Eta state scholarship com. 2003—, Loretta Doerr com. chmn. 2004—05, chmn. Loretta Doerr Achievement com. 2004—05, Epsilon Conclave pres. 2005—06, state scholar com. chair 2005—06, nat. scholar com. 2005—06, Eta State Loretta Doerr award 1995), Phi Delta Kappa (newsletter editor 1989—93, past pres. chpt. 1994—96, newsletter editor 1997—98, treas. 2002—). Home: PO Box 1595 Ruston LA 71273-1595 Personal E-mail: aileenwf@bayou.com.

FRECHETTE, BONNIE L., secondary school educator; b. Green Bay, Wis., Oct. 23, 1946; d. Frank martin and Grace Emilia (Yindra) Jirovetz; m. David H. Frechette, June 23, 1973. BS, U. Wis., Oshkosh, 1969; MA, Viterbo Coll., LaCrosse, Wis., 1992. English tchr. West DePere H.S., DePere, Wis., 1969—. Recipient Golden Apple Tchr. of Distinction award, 1996, Golden Apple award, 1998; named Dist. Tchr. of Yr., Wis. State Dept. Instrn., 1986-87; Kohl Found. scholar, 1997. Mem. Nat. Coun. Tchrs. English, Wis. Coun. Tchrs. English (dist. dir. 1987—). Avocations: reading, theater, films, walking. Office: West DePere HS 665 Grant St De Pere WI 54115-1367 E-mail: bfrechette@wdpsd.com.

FRÉCHETTE, LOUISE, international organization official; b. Montreal, Can., July 16, 1946; BA, Coll. Basile Moreau, 1966; licence es lettres degree in history, U. Montreal, 1970; postgrad. diploma in econ. studies, Coll. Europe, Bruges, Belgium, 1978; Doctorate (hon.), St. Mary's U., Halifax, 1993, Kyung Hee U., Seoul, U. Ottawa, U. Toronto, Laval U., Quebec. Mem. General Assembly, Canada, 1972; second sec. Canadian Embassy, Athens, 1972—75; with European Affairs Div., Dept. of External Affairs, Canada, 1975—77; first sec. Canadian Mission to the UN, Geneva, 1978—82; deputy dir. Trade Policy Div., Dept. of External Affairs, 1982—83; dir. European Summit Div., 1983—85; amb. to Argentina, Uruguay, Paraguay Govt of Can., 1985—88; asst. dep. min. for L.Am. and Caribbean Dept. External Affairs and internat. trade, 1988—91; asst. dep. min. for econ. policy and trade competitiveness Ministry of Fgn. Affairs, 1991-92; permanent rep. of Canada to UN, 1992—95; assoc. dep. min. Can. Dept. Fin., 1994-95; dep. minister def. Govt. of Can., 1995-98; dep. sec. gen. UN, 1998—2006; disting. fellow Ctr. Internat. Governance Innovation, Waterloo, Ontario, 2006—. Chmn., Steering Com. on Reform and Mgmt. Policy UN; chmn., advisory bd. UN Fund for Internat. Partnerships (UNFIP). Named Office of the Order of Can., 1998; named one of most powerful women, Forbes mag., 2005. Office: The Centre for International Governance Innovation 57 Erb St W Waterloo On N2L 6C2 Canada Office Phone: 519 885 2444. Office Fax: 519 885 5450.*

FRECKELTON, SONDRA, artist; b. Dearborn, Mich., June 23, 1936; d. William and Elizabeth (Zimmerman) F.; m. W.H. Jack Beal, Sept. 3, 1955. Student, Sch. Art Inst. Chgo., 1954—56, U. Chgo., 1954—56; LittD (hon.), Hollins Coll., 1994. Artist self-employed, 1958—, Tibor de Nagy Gallery, N.Y.C., 1953—64, B.C. Holland Gallery, Chgo., 1964—67, Lo Giudice Gallery, Chgo., 1968—71, Brooke Alexander Gallery, N.Y.C., 1975—85, 1991, Robert Schoelkopf Gallery, N.Y.C., 1986—91, Alice Simsar Gallery, Ann Arbor, Mich., 1987—, Maxwell Davidson Gallery, N.Y.C., 1991—98. Co-author: Dynamic Still-Lifes in Watercolor, 1983; one-person exhbns. include Robert Schoelkopf Gallery, 1986, 88, 90, John Berggruen Gallery, 1982, Brooke Alexander, Inc., 1976, 79, 80, 81, Fendrick Gallery, 1980, Allan Frumkin Gallery, Chgo., 1977, Lo Giudice Gallery, 1970, B.C. Holland Gallery, 1965, Tibor de Nagy Gallery, 1961, 63, Maxwell Davidson Gallery, 1994, Kalamazoo Inst. Arts, 1994, Huntington Mus., W.Va., 1998-99; group shows including Mt. Holyoke Coll., Yale U. Art Gallery, Art Mus. of Santa Barbara, Va. Mus. Fine Arts, 1987-88, Detroit Inst. Arts, 1991, Madison Art Ctr., Wis., 1998, Columbus Mus. Art, Ga., 1998, and others. Recipient Print award, Bradford Mus., 1979, Pollock-Krasner award, 2002; grantee, Grant Ingram-Merrill Found., 1960. Avocations: horticulture, gardening. Home and Office: 331 Epps Rd Oneonta NY 13820-6451 Office Phone: 607-433-2325. E-mail: freckbea@dmcom.net.

FREDERICK, AMY L., science administrator; b. Flint, Mich., Oct. 13, 1972; BA, Cumberland U., Lebanon, Tenn., 1994; MA, Howard U., 1996, PhD, 2000. Tech. commercialization fellow NASA, Greenbelt, Md., 1995—99; program adminstr. Global Sci. and Tech., Inc., Greenbelt,

1999—2000; sr. staff Sci. Applications Internat. Corp., Vienna, Va., 2000—; with IRS. Presenter in field. Author: The Election of Women and African-American to Congress; contbr. articles to profl. jours. Recipient NASA Goddard Space Flight Ctr. Group award, NASA, 1996; Hawthorne Dissertation fellow, Howard U., 1999, Cumberland U. scholar, 1992—94. Mem.: Phi Sigma Alpha. Office: Science Applicatios Internat Corp 8401 Corporate Dr Landover MD

FREDERICK, ELIZABETH ELEANOR TATUM, watercolor artist, retired educator; b. Clovis, N.Mex., Dec. 22, 1915; d. John Hardy Tatum and Bessie Elizabeth Weathers Tatum; m. George Achias Frederick, June 7, 1937 (dec. Apr. 1991); children: Ronald W., George Douglas, Barbara Elizabeth Frederick Ewing, John Lawrence. BS in Edn., U. N.Mex., 1937, MS, 1943; postgrad., Highland U., Las Vegas, N.Mex., 1944, Ea. N.Mex. U., 1944, 45. Tchr. Ctrl. H.S., Kirtland, N.Mex., 1936-37, Bellview HS, N.Mex., 1940-42, Hot Springs Jr. HS, N.Mex., 1943-45, N.Mex., 1951-53, N.Mex., 1954; ret., 1967. Exhibitions include Sierra Art Soc., Truth or Consequences, N.Mex., Willamette Oaks Retirement Ctr., Eugene, Oreg., 1991—, El Paso Mus. Art, N.Mex. Art League, N.Mex. Watercolor Soc., Albuquerque, Represented in permanent collections. Mem. Nat. League Am. Pen Women (pres. Rio Grande br. 1975-76), Sierra Art Soc. (pres. 1974-75, funding and program chmn. 1975-89), N.Mex. Watercolor Soc., Black Range Artists (sec.-treas. 1978-79). Republican. Avocations: sweepstakes, worldwide travel.

FREDERICK, JANET DENNIS, physical education educator; b. Toledo, Jan. 15, 1949; d. Jack William Dennis and C. Anna Wilson; 1 child, Margot Ann. BS, Bowling Green State U., Ohio, 1971, MEd, 1985. Cert. tchr. Ohio. Tchr. phys. edn. Liberty Ctr. Elem. Sch., Ohio, 1971—2001; instr. Bowling Green State U., 2001—. Workshop leader Educator's Profl. Devel. Inst., Muncie, Ind., 2001—02. Named Midwest Elem. Phys. Edn. Tchr. of Yr., Nat. Assn. Sports and Phys. Edn., 1992; recipient Accomplished Grad. award, Bowling Green State U., 1993. Mem.: Ohio Ret. Tchrs. Assn., Am. Alliance Health, Phys. Edn., Recreation and Dance. Democrat. Roman Catholic. Avocation: ballroom dancing. Office: Bowling Green State U 101 E North Eppler Bowling Green OH 43403 Office Phone: 419-372-6891.

FREDERICK, PAULA J., lawyer; b. Riverside, Calif., Apr. 11, 1958; d. Henry Lewis and Hattie Maude (McCollom) F. BA, Duke U., 1979; JD, Vanderbilt U., 1982. Bar: Ga. 1982, U.S. Dist. Ct. (no. dist.) Ga. 1982. Staff atty. Atlanta Legal Aid Soc., 1982-86, mng. atty., 1986-88; asst. gen. counsel State Bar of Ga., Atlanta, 1988-92, dep. gen. counsel, 1992—. Bd. dir. Ga. Legal Svcs. Found. Mem. ABA (chair standing com. on profl. discipline 2000-02, commr. Commn. on Opportunities for Minorities in the Profession 1994-96, mem. ho. of dels. 1993—, bd. gov. 2002-), Atlanta Bar Assn. (bd. dirs. 1994-96, pres. 1999-00), Ga. Assn. Black Women Attys. (pres. 1998), Ga. Assn. Women Lawyers (Kathleen Kessler award 2002). Office: State Bar of Georgia Suite 100 104 Marietta St NW Atlanta GA 30303-2702 Office Phone: 404-527-8720.

FREDERICK, VIRGINIA FIESTER, state legislator; b. Rock Island, Ill., Dec. 24, 1916; d. John Henry and Myrtle (Montgomery) Heise; m. C. Donnan Fiester (dec. 1975); children: Sheryl Fiester Ross, Alan R., James D.; m. Kenneth Jacob Frederick, 1978 (dec.). BA, U. Iowa, 1938; postgrad., Lake Forest Coll., 1942-43, LLD, 1994, MLS, 1999. Freelance fashion designer, Lake Forest, Ill., 1952-78; pres. Mid Am. China Exch., Kenilworth, Ill., 1978-81; mem. Ill. Ho. of Reps., Springfield, 1979-95, asst. minority leader, 1990-95. Alderman first ward, Lake Forest, 1974-78; del. World Food Conf., Rome, 1974; subcom. pensions and employment Ill. Commn. on Status of Women, 1976-79; co-chair Conf. Women Legislators, 1982-85; bd. dirs. Lake Forest Coll., 1995-98, Lake Forest Symphony Guild, 1998—; city supr. City of Lake Forest, 1995-98. Named Chgo. Area Women of Achievement, Internat. Orgn. Women Execs., 1978; recipient Lottie Holman O'Neal award, 1980, Jane Addams award, 1982, Outstanding Legislator award Ill. Hosp. Assn., 1986, VFW Svc. award, 1988, Joyce Fitzgerald Meml. award, 1988, Susan B. Anthony Legislator of Yr. award, 1989, Delta Kappa Gamma award, 1991, Outstanding Legislator award, 1995, Svcs. for Srs. award, Ill. Dept. Aging, 1991, Ethics in Politics award, Rep. Womens's Club, 1992, Woman of Achievement award YWCA North Eastern Ill., 1994, Ill. Women in Govt. award, 1994, Lifetime Achievement award Equip for Equality, 1999. Mem. LWV (local pres. 1958-60, state dir. 1969-75, nat. com. 1975-76), AAUW (local pres. 1968-70, state pres. 1975-77, state dir. 1963-69, nat. com. 1967-69, Legislator of Yr. 1993), UN Assn. (bd. dirs.), Chgo. Assn. Commerce and Industry (bd. dirs.). Home: 1290 N Western Ave Lake Forest IL 60045-1258 Personal E-mail: k13v16@aol.com.

FREDERICK-MAIRS, T(HYRA) JULIE, administrative health services official; b. Islip, N.Y., Jan. 4, 1941; d. Manuel and Thyra C. (Thorsen) Cajiao. BA, Adelphi U., 1961; MSW, U. So. Calif., 1972, MPA, 1991. Social worker L.A. County Dept. Social Svcs., 1966-67, social work supr., 1967-70, planning cons., 1972-76; dep. to supr. 4th dist. L.A. County, 1976-80; asst. dir. L.A. County Office Alcohol Programs, 1980-90; assoc. adminstr. ELACO Health Ctrs., 1990—2003; CEO East Country Health Ctrs.; health care process improvement and change mgmt. cons., 2003—. Fellow U. So. Calif., 1988-90. Author: (with others) Youth Program Planning, 1975. Trustee LEARNS, 1992; active L.A. Child Sexual Abuse Project, Commn. for Sexual Equality, L.A. Unified Sch. Dist., Harbor Policy Cmty. Adv. Coun., L.A.; mem. Perinatal Substance Abuse Coun. L.A.; mem. ops. com. Interagy. Coun. Child Abuse and Neglect; adv. com. UCLA Alcohol Rsch. Ctr. Mem. Los Amigos de la Humanidad, DHS Latino Mgrs., Alpha Epsilon Delta, Beta Beta Beta, Bus. and Profl. Women's Club, Soroptimists (pres. L.A. Club, dir. Found. of L.A. 1986-88). Office Phone: 818-512-0083.

FREDERICKS, BEVERLY MAGNUSON, artist; b. Colorado Springs, Colo., June 14, 1928; d. Oscar Frederick and India King (Glenn) Magnuson; m. Harvey Ray Fredericks (dec.); children: Annetta Louise(dec.), John Stafford, Jeffrey Robert. Student, Colorado Springs Fine Art Ctr., 1946—54, Antelope Valley Coll., Lancaster, Calif., 1960—61, Santa Monica City Coll., Calif., 1961—62. Receptionist Hughes Aircraft, LA, 1963—67; interior designer Gerald's Paint and Hardware, LA, 1967—69; owner, restorer, conservator Fine Art Beverly Fredericks, LA, 1980—. Lectr. in field. Editor: Art of Creating Monotypes, 1990; author: History & Heritage of Victoria County Texas, 2000; exhibitions include LA Co. Mus., Ringling Mus., Robiard Gallery, John Lane Galleries, Vega Fine Arts, Am. Inst. Fine Arts, Centennial Gallery, Warner Fine Art, one-woman shows include Riggs Galleries, Robertson Gallery, Armagost Fine Arts, Barton Galleries. Troop leader Girl Scouts Am., Colorado Springs, 1954—55; active Nat. Mus. Women in Arts, Washington, 1976. Named one of Ten Best Tchrs. on Tape, Arts Am., 1991; named to Alumni Hall of Fame, Colorado Springs HS, 1985. Fellow: Am. Inst. Fine Art (bd. dirs., treas. 1978—85); mem.: Am. Inst. for Conservation, Nat. League Am. Pen Women. Republican. Presbyterian. Avocations: genealogy, photography, dance, theater, travel. Home: 8227 Westlawn Ave Los Angeles CA 90045 Office: Fine Art Studio Beverly Fredericks 8227 Westlawn Ave Los Angeles CA 90045

FREDERICKS, SHARON KAY, nurse's aide; b. Grand Rapids, Mich., July 12, 1942; d. Leroy and Edith Luella (Crawford) Fredericks. Cert. in Interior Decorating, LaSalle U., 1975; AAS, Community Svc. Asst., Kalamazoo Valley Coll., 1982; A paralegal studies, Internat. Corr. Schs., Scranton, Pa., 1993; AAS in Bus. Mgmt., Davenport Coll., 1994, BBA in Bus. Adminstrn., 1997. Cashier Goodwill Industries, Battle Creek, Mich., 1963; dishwasher Woolworths, Kalamazoo, 1963; nurses aide Mary L. Bocher, Kalamazoo, 1964-69, Sisters St. Joseph, Nazareth, Mich., 1976-98; kitchen aide Saga Foods, Kalamazoo Valley C.C., 1981—82, Saga Foods, Nazareth Coll., 1983—84; ind. sales rep. Avon, 2000—01. Vol. Portage Ctrl. Jr. and Sr. HS, 1961—62, Bronson Meth. Hosp., Kalamazoo, 1961—62, nurse aide bloodmobiles, 1970—75; nurse aide ARC, 1964—69, Brogess Med. Ctr., 1977, CASA Kalamazoo Juvenile Ct., 1980—86; participant neighborhood watch Vine Neighborhood, Kalamazoo, 1985—88; vol., adminstrv. aide Cath. Family Svcs., Kalamazoo, 1991—; vol. monitor Kalamazoo Women's Festival, 1991, 1992; mem. grounds com. New Horizon Village, Kalamazoo, 1998, mem. neighborhood watch com., 1999, chair pet com.; active Mich. Campaign for Quality Care, 2002—; foster grandparent sr. svc. elem. sch., 2004—; sec.-treas. Order St. Francis Secular, 1976—79, pres. dir. pres. pub. rels. and bulls., 1979—81; vol. Cath. Family Svcs., 1991—. Named Vol. of the Month, Kalamazoo Regional Psychiat. Hosp., 1976, Vol. of the Week, Cath. Family Svcs., 1993, 1995; recipient John Edgar Hoover Gold medal, 1991; Thomas F. Reed Jr. scholar, Davenport Coll., 1993. Mem.: AARP (Mich. amb. vol. 2002—03, v.p., pub. rels. vol. A.A. chpt. 1020 Kalamazoo br. 2003—), Davenport U. Alumni Assn. Roman Catholic. Avocations: photography, textile painting, helping people, reading, learning wildlife, environnmental policies, pet policies, governmental policies. Home: 2310 Inverness Ln Apt 204 Kalamazoo MI 49048-1459

FREDERICKSON, CHRISTINE MAGNUSON, reporter, researcher, editor, writer; d. George Adolf and Pauline Hazen Magnuson; m. Arthur Robb Frederickson, June 6, 1970 (dec.); children: Timothy R., Nathan B., Julie H. Attended, Kalamazoo Coll., 1964—66; BA cum laude, U. NH, 1969; MEd, Boston Coll., 1974. Staff writer Computerworld Newsweekly, Newton, Mass., 1969—71; radio events editor Antique Radio Classified, Carlisle, Mass., 1986—97; ct. reporter, ind. contractor LA, 1999—2003. New script reader Fountain Theatre, LA, 1998—2003. Author: Doña Victoria-First Lady of San Gabriel, 1998; prodr.: Southwest Museum, 1999—2000. Docent San Gabriel Mission, Calif., 1997—2006, Homestead Mus., Industry, Calif., 1998—2004. Critic fellow, Nat. Critics Inst., Waterford, Conn., 2000. Mem.: Eugene O'Neill Soc., Internat. Bonhoffer Soc., Dramatists Guild (assoc.), Calif. Mission Studies Assn., Caltech Women's Club (bulletin editor 1998—2000). Avocations: ice skating, aerobics, reading. Personal E-mail: cmfrederickson1@comcast.net.

FREDERIKSEN, MARILYNN C., physician; b. Chgo., Sept. 12, 1949; d. Paul H. and Susanne (Ostergren) Conners; m. James W. Frederiksen, July 11, 1971; children: John K., Paul S., Britt L. BA, Cornell Coll., 1970; MD, Boston U., 1974; grad. Exec. Leadership in Acad. Medicine, Allegheny U. Health Scis., 1998. Diplomate Am. Bd. Ob-Gyn., Am. Bd. Maternal-Fetal Medicine, Am. Bd. Clin. Pharmacology. Pediat. intern U. Md. Hosp., 1974-75, resident in pediat., 1975-76; resident in ob-gyn. Boston Hosp. for women, 1976-79; fellow in maternal fetal medicine Northwestern U., 1979-81, fellow clin. pharmacology, 1981-83, instr. ob-gyn. Chgo., 1981-83, asst. prof. ob-gyn., assoc. clin. pharmacology, 1983-91, assoc. prof. ob-gyn., 1991—, sect. chief gen. ob-gyn., 1993—2001. Mem. gen. faculty com. Northwestern U., Chgo., 1994—97, mem. ob-gyn. adv. panel, 1985—2000, chair ob-gyn. adv. panel, 2000—05; mem. U.S. Pharm. Com. Revision, Rockville, Md., 1986—2005; del. U.S. Pharm. conv. Northwestern U. Med. Sch., 1990, 95, 2000; mem. gen. clinic rsch. ctr. com. NIH, 1989—93; chairperson, 1992—93; mem. Task Force Writing Group on Asthma in Pregnancy, Nat. Heart, Lung and Blood Inst., 1991—92; examiner Am. Bd. Ob-Gyn., 1997—; mem. Task Force Working Group, Nat. Bd. Med. Examiners, 1997—98, mem. acute care com., 1999—2001. Mem. editorial bd. Clin. Pharmacology & Therapeutics, 1993; contbr. numerous articles to profl. jours. Bd. dirs. Cornell Coll. Alumni Assn., Mt. Vernon, Iowa, 1986—90, PRCH, 1997—2005, Planned Parenthood of Chgo. Area, 1999—, Northwestern Med. Faculty Found., 1995—98. Recipient Pharm. Mfrs. Assn. Found. Faculty Devel. award, 1984-86, Civil Liberties award ACLU, 1991. Fellow Am. Coll. Ob-Gyn.; mem. Soc. Maternal Fetal Medicine, Ctrl. Assn. Obstetricians and Gynecologists (bd. dirs. 1997-99), Am. Soc. Clin. Pharmacology and Therapeutics (bd. dirs. 1994-97), Chgo. Gynecologic Soc. (treas. 1994-97); Phi Beta Kappa. Episcopalian. Avocations: gardening, needlecrafts. Office: Northwestern Perinatal Assocs 680 N Lake Shore Dr Ste 1230 Chicago IL 60611 Office Phone: 312-981-4350. Personal E-mail: npa@cypressmail.com. Business E-Mail: mcf810@northwestern.edu.

FREDERIKSEN, PATRICIA SULLIVAN, elementary school educator; b. Saint Louis, Mo., Jan. 23, 1952; d. Gregory and Dorothy Sullivan; m. Nicholas Frederiksen, Dec. 27, 1974; children: Seth, Ben. MA, Wash. U., 2004. Cert. Elem. Edn. Mo. Kindergarten tchr. Immacolata Sch., Saint Louis, Mo., 1985—. Home: 420 N Hanley Rd Saint Louis MO 63130 Office: Immacolata Sch 8910 Clayton Rd Saint Louis MO 63117 Office Phone: 314-991-5700.

FREDETTE, BARBARA WAGNER, art educator; b. Lima, Peru, Dec. 5, 1933; came to U.S., 1934; d. Lawrence A. and Anne A. (Sherwood) Wagner; m. John W. Fredette Jr., Dec. 28, 1953 (dec.); children: John W. III, Lawrence F. BA, Chatham Coll., 1955; MEd, U. Pitts., 1963, EdD, 1969. Supr. elem. art Hampton Sch., Allison Park, Pa., 1960-64; tchr. art edn. Carnegie Mellon U., Pitts., 1964; assoc. prof. U. Pitts., 1964—. Roundtable mem. Pitts. Fund for Arts Edn., 1988—. Mem. Nat. Art Edn. Assn., Pa. Art Edn. Assn. (Outstanding Art Educator award 1984), Am. Edn., Am. Edn. Rsch. Assn., Internat. Visual Litracry Assn., Phi Delta Kappa. Republican. Roman Catholic. Avocation: photography. Home: 939 Savannah Ave Pittsburgh PA 15221-3447 Office: U Pitts 4C31 Forbes Quad Pittsburgh PA 15260

FREDIANI, DIANE MARIE, graphics designer, interior designer, executive secretary; b. Bklyn., June 20, 1963; d. Albert Michael and Mary (Piantino) F. BFA in Graphic Design, Centenary Coll., 1985, teaching cert., 1991. Cert. graphic designer. Cashier, dept. supr. Reynolds, Hackettstown, N.J., 1982-85, window displays and promotions staff, 1985-86; clerical asst. AT&T, Basking Ridge, N.J., 1986-87, typesetter, bd. artist Parsippany, N.J., 1988-89, project mgr. interior design Basking Ridge, 1989-99, supplier diversity specialist supplier mgmt. divsn., 1999—. Graphic designer St. Mary's Sch., Hackettstown, 1985—; nominee for White House Fellowship Com., 1994. Mem. Centenary Alumni Assn. (forensic judge oral speaking competitions 1993—), N.J. Supplier Diversity Devel. Coun., N.Y./N.J. Minority Purchasing Coun. (sec. 1999—). Roman Catholic. Avocations: photography, painting, reading, going to sporting events. Home: 203 Hudson Ct Hackettstown NJ 07840-1690 Office: At T 900 US Highway 202 206 Bedminster NJ 07921-2662

FREDMAN, FAIYA RUBENSTEIN, artist; b. Columbus, Ohio, Sept. 8, 1925; d. David and Henrietta Baum (Hassel) Rubenstein; m. Milton Fredman, Feb. 14, 1947; children: Stephen Albert, Teri Lynn. BA in Visual Arts, UCLA, 1948. One-woman shows include La Jolla (Calif.) Mus. Contemporary Art, 1968, 74, 81, U. Calif.-Riverside, Irvine, 1984, U. Calif.-San Diego, 1984, Ruth Bachofner Gallery, L.A., 1985, 88, Santa Monica, 1990, Zach/Shuster Gallery, Boca Raton, Fla., 1989, Boehm Gallery, Palomar Coll., San Marcos, Calif., 1990, Southwestern Coll., Chula Vista, Calif., 1995, Porter Troupe Gallery, San Diego, 1996, Lipworth/Hartman Gallery, Boca Raton, Fla., 1998, Atheneum, La Jolla, 2003, Earl & Birdie Taylor Gallery, Pacific Beach, Calif., 2004; group shows include La Jolla Mus. Contemporary Arts, 1973, 78, 79, 81, 86, U. Sao Paulo (Brazil) Mus. Contemporary Art, 1980, Mus. Photog. Arts, San Deigo, 1987; represented in permanent collections Mus. Photog. Arts, Oakland (Calif.) Mus., La Jolla Mus. Contemporary Arts, Ariz. State U., Tempe; artist book collections: Getty Mus., San Francisco Mus. Contemporary Art, Mus. Modern Art N.Y.C., Chgo. Art Inst., UCLA, Nat. Mus. Women in the Arts, Washington. Recipient 1st prize juried show San Diego Pub. TV, 1978. Home: PO Box 2735 La Jolla CA 92038-2735

FREDRICK, SUSAN WALKER, tax company manager; b. Painesville, Ohio, Nov. 17, 1948; d. Floyd Clayton and Margaret (Merkel) Walker; m. Stephan Douglas Fredrick, Oct. 20, 1973. BS, Mt. Union Coll., Alliance, Ohio, 1970; MS, U. Conn., 1973. Rsch. asst. Boyce Thompson Inst., Yonkers, NY, 1971-74; dir. quality control Lawley, Matusky, Skelly, Tappan, NY, 1974-75; field supr. Ecological Analysts, Middletown, NY, 1975-76; scientist Pandullo Quirk Assocs., Wayne, NJ, 1976-78; editor Bioscis. Info. Service, Phila., 1978-80; tax preparer H&R Block, Inc., Malvern, Pa., 1978-80, dist. mgr. King of Prussia and West Chester, Pa., 1980—2002, franchise dist. mgr. Easton, Md., 2002—05, Mid-Atlantic franchise dist. mgr., 2005—. Guest lectr. Temple U., 1981-86. Mem. Nat. Assn. Enrolled Agts., Pa. Soc. Enrolled Agts., Nat. Assn. Underwater Instrs. (ret. instr.), Keystone Divers Club (West Chester, Pa.). Avocations: scuba diving, hiking, swimming. Office: 1510 Chester Pike Ste 150 Eddystone PA 17022

FREDRICKSON, KAREN LORAINE, librarian; b. Kansas City, Mo., Sept. 27, 1952; d. Kenneth Eugene Kruse and Loraine Lulu (Neugebauer) Morse; m. Timothy Dean Cox, Sept. 1, 1973 (dec. Sept. 1984); m. David Dean Fredrickson, June 10, 1989; children: Jennifer, Rachel. BS, Cen. Mo. State U., 1974, MS, 1979. Cert. tchr. Kans., Mo. Tchr./libr. Lone Jack (Mo.) Schs., 1974-76; tchr. Clarksville-Montgomery County Schs., Tenn., 1977; tchr./libr. St John's Luth. Sch., Indpls., 1978-82; libr. media specialist Lawrence (Kans.) Public Schs., 1985—. Mem. Lawrence In-Svc. Coun., 1986-88. Recipient Kans. Ednl. Excellence Program award Southwestern Bell, Lawrence, 1991, Lawrence Sch. Found. Tchr. Innovation grant, 2006. Mem. ALA, Am. Assn. Sch. Libr., Kans. Assn. Sch. Libr. Luth. Avocations: sewing, crocheting. Office: Langston Hughes Sch 1101 George Williams Way Lawrence KS 66049 Office Phone: 785-832-5890 106. E-mail: klfredri@usd497.org.

FREDRIK, BURRY, theater producer, director; b. NYC, Aug. 9, 1925; d. Fredric Kreuger and Erna Anita (Burry) Gerber; m. Gerard E. Meunier, Dec. 27, 1945 (div. 1949). Grad., Sarah Lawrence Coll., 1947. Ind. theatrical dir., producer U.S. and abroad, 1955—; lit. mgr., dir. Boston Post Road Stage Co., 1988—92; artistic dir. Fairfield County Stage Co. (formerly Boston Post Road Stage), 1992—93. Prodr.: (Broadway plays) Too Good to be True, 1964—65 (nominated Tony award, 1965), Travesties, 1976 (Tony award, 1976), An Almost Perfect Person, 1977, The Night of the Tribades, 1978, To Grandmother's House We Go, 1981, The Royal Family, 1975—76 (Drama Desk award, 1976), (off-Broadway plays) Thieves Carnival, 1955 (Spl. Tony award, 1955), Exiles, 1956 (OBIE award, 1956), Buried Child (Pulitzer prize, 1980); dir.: (nat. tours) Misalliance, 1953, Milk and Honey, 1963, Dark at the Top of the Stairs, 1958, Dear Love, 1971, To Grandmother's House We Go, 1982, (off-Broadway prodns.) The Decameron, 1961, Catholic School Girls, 1981, (Broadway prodn.) Wild and Wonderful, 1972; prodr.: (off-Broadway) Pretzels, 1974; dir.: (plays, Sad Hotel) White Barn Theatre, 2001—; (plays, Swansong), 2002—. Chmn. Weston Commn. Arts, 1997—2000; mem. fin. commn., trustee Long Wharf Theatre, New Haven, 1998—. Recipient Disting. Adv. Arts award, State of Conn. Commn. Arts, 2001. Home and Office: 51 Hillside Rd N Weston CT 06883-1513 Office Phone: 203-227-9349. Office Fax: 203-222-9478.

FREE, BARBARA A., psychotherapist, writer; b. Maryville, Mo., Dec. 20, 1942; d. Earl F. and Clara May Sexton; m. Ronald L. Drake, Jan. 21, 1967 (div. Apr. 1982); children: David R., Daniel P., John A., Kenneth L. Thomas; m. Jay J. Johnson Jr., Sept. 2, 1989. BA in English, U. Kans., 1965; MA in Counseling Psychology, Wash. State U., 1984. Lic. Alcohol and Drug Abuse Counselor, Profl. Clin. Counselor; cert. Master Addiction Counselor, Advanced Relapse Prevention Specialist. Therapist Cmty. Alcohol Svcs., Kennewick, Wash., 1983-84; therapist, Intensive Outpatient Program dir. Benton-Franklin Co. Alcohol and Drug Svcs., Pasco, Wash., 1984—89; therapist Ctr. Alcoholism, Substance Abuse and Addiction, U. N.Mex., Albuquerque, 1989-92, Meml. Hosp., Albuquerque, 1992-97; pvt. practice Relapse Prevention Svcs., Albuquerque, 1992—. Active Habitat for Humanity, Albuquerque, 1989-94, Am. Adoption Congress, 2000—; v.p., newsletter editor Operation Identity, Albuquerque, 1996—; active Disciples PEace Fellowship, 20/20 Club Visually Impaired; mem. Interfaith Alliance, Religious Coalition Reproductive Rights. Mem. AAUW, ACLU, Nat. Assn. Alcohol and Drug Counselors, N.Mex. Assn. Drug and Alcohol Counselors, Phillips U. Alumni & Friends Assn. Democrat. Mem. Christian Ch. (Disciples Of Christ). Avocations: hiking, camping, native american history, artifacts and arts. Home and Office: 1818 Somervell St NE Albuquerque NM 87112-2836 Office Phone: 505-275-9952.

FREE, HELEN MURRAY, chemist, consultant; b. Pitts., Feb. 20, 1923; d. James Summerville and Daisy (Piper) Murray; m. Alfred H. Free, Oct. 18, 1947 (dec. May 2000); children: Eric, Penny, Kurt, Jake, Bonnie, Nina. BA in Chemistry, Coll. of Wooster, Ohio, 1944, DSc (hon.), 1992; MA in Clin. Lab. Mgmt., Ctrl. Mich. U., 1978, DSc (hon.), 1993. Cert. clin. chemist Nat. Registry Cert. Chemists. Chemist Miles Labs., Elkhart, Ind., 1944—78, dir. mktg. svcs. rsch. products divsn., 1978-82; chemist, mgr., cons. Bayer HealthCare Diabetes Care, Elkhart, 1982—. Mem. adj. faculty Ind. U., South Bend, 1975—96. Author (with others): (books) Urodynamics and Urinalysis in Clinical Laboratory Practice, 1972, 1976; contbr. articles to encys. and profl. jours. Bd. dirs. Nat. Inventors Hall of Fame Found.; women's chmn. Centennial of Elkhart, 1958; mem. adv. bd. Intellectual Property Sch. Law, Akron U.; indsl. adv. bd. chemistry/chem. engring. Tri-State U., Angola, Ind. Named Woman of Yr., YWCA, 1993, Kilby Found. laureate, 1996; named to Hall of Excellence, Ohio Found. Ind. Colls., 1992, Nat. Inventors Hall of Fame, 2000, Engring. and Sci. Hall of Fame, 1996; recipient Disting. Alumni award, Coll. of Wooster, 1980, award, Medi Econ. Press, 1986, Nat. Leadership award, Lab. Pub. Svc., 1994. Fellow: AAAS, Royal Soc. Chemistry, Am. Inst. Chemists (co-recipient Chgo. award 1967); mem.: Nat. Com. Clin. Lab. Stds. (bd. dir.), Am. Soc. Clin. Lab. Sci. (chmn. assembly, Achievement award 1976), Soc. Chem. Industry (hon.), Assn. Clin. Scientists (diploma of honor 1992), Am. Assn. Clin. Chemistry (coun., bd. dir., nominating com. and pub. rels. com., coord. profl. affairs, nat. membership com., pres. 1990, Outstanding Contbn. award 2006), Am. Chem. Soc. (pres. 1993, bd. dir., chmn. Chemistry Week task force, bd. com. pub. affairs and pub. rels., chmn. women chemists com., internat. activities com., grants and awards com., prof. and mem. rels. com., nominating com., coun. policy pub. affairs and budget, councilor, chair Progress project, Garvan medal 1980, Svc. award local chpt. 1981, co-recipient Mosher award 1983, 1st recipient Helen M. Free Pub. Outreach award 1995, Helen M. Free award named in her honor 1995), Altrusa (pres. 1982—83, bd. dir.), Sigma Delta Epsilon (hon.), Iota Sigma Pi (hon.). Presbyterian. Achievements include patents in field. Home: 3752 E Jackson Blvd Elkhart IN 46516-5205 Office: Bayer HealthCare Diabetes Care Divsn 1884 Miles Ave Elkhart IN 46514-2291 E-mail: Hmfree23@aol.com, helen.free.b@bayer.com.

FREE, MARY MOORE, biological and medical anthropologist; b. Paris, Tex., Mar. 6, 1933; d. Dudley Crawford and Margie Lou (Moore) Hubbard; m. Dwight Allen Free Jr., June 26, 1954 (dec.); children: Hardy (dec.), Dudley (dec.), Margery, Caroline. Student, Ward-Belmont Coll., 1951; BS, So. Meth. U., 1954, MLA, 1981, MA, 1987, PhD, 1989. Instr. So. Meth. U., Dallas, 1982-89, prof. continuing edn., 1989-90; prof. So. Meth. U., Dedman Coll., Dallas, 1990—; adj. asst. prof. dept. anthropology So. Meth. U., Dallas, 1990—. Prof. Richland C.C., Dallas, 1986; house anthropologist Baylor U. Med. Ctr., mem. adv. bd. Inst. for Study of Earth and Man, 1995, preceptor clin. edn. affiliation, 1990—, chair Class 1954 sustentation drive, organ/tissue transplantation task force, 1997; cardiothoracic transplantation team Baylor U. Med. Ctr., S.W. transplantation team Baylor U. Med. Ctr./U. Tex. Southwestern Med. Sch., 1990— (cardiothoracic transplantation award for excellence in svc., 1998); adv. bd. geriatrics Vis. Nurse Assn., Dallas, 1984-91; presenter in field anthropology, medicine, women's issues; bd. Dedman Coll. SMU Excellence in Sci. Lecture Series, Dallas Soc. SMU, Collegium de Vinci, SMU; contbr. AMA/JAMA protocol on authorship; spokesperson, adv. bd. Lisa Landry Childress Found. for Organ Donation Awareness. Author: The Private World of the Hermitage: Lifestyles of the Rich and Old in an Elite Retirement Home, 1995; contbr. numerous chpts. in sci. books, ednl. TV, and articles to Anthropology Newsletter, Am. Anthropologist, Am. Jour. Cardiology, Cahiers de Sociologie Economique et Culturelle-Ethnopsycholie, Jour. Heart Failure, Jour. Internat. Soc. Dermatology, Jour. Leadership Ctr., Baylor Health Care System, Jour. Lisa Landry Childrens Found.,; mem. editl. bd. Baylor U. Med. Ctr. Procs.; editor/contbr. Jour. Kimberly H. Courtwright and Joseph W. Summers Inst. of Metabolic Disease, BUMC, 1998; contbr. numerous articles to profl. jours. Bd. dirs. New Hearts and Lungs, Baylor Med. Ctr., 1994—, Lisa Landry Childress Found. for Organ Donor Awareness, Victims Outreach, 1997—, Isis Soc. and internat. issues com. Baylor U. Med. Ctr.; active various svc. and social orgns. Named one of Notable Women of Tex., 1984; recipient Outstanding Svc. Cardiothoracic Transplantation award Baylor U. Med. Ctr., 1998; provide Dr. Mary Moore Free Endowment for grad. study fieldwork in anthropology So. Meth. U. Fellow Am. Anthrop. Assn., Inst. for Study of Earth and Man; mem. AAAS, Internat. Soc. Heart Failure (sci. adv. bd.), Internat. Acad. Cardiology

Inc. (internat. sci. adv. bd.), Internat. Congress Heart Disease (internat. sci. adv. bd.), Internat. Soc. Heart Disease (sci. adv. bd.), Soc. Heart Edn. (sci. adv. bd.), Dallas Women's Club, Dallas Petroleum Club, Brook Hollow Golf Club, Pi Beta Phi. Methodist. Achievements include development of position of house anthropologist in non-academic medical center, community medicine program; cross-cultural research on old age, women and cardiology. Home: 4356 Edmondson Ave Dallas TX 75205-2602 Office: Baylor U Med Ctr 3500 Gaston Ave Dallas TX 75246-2096

FREE, RHONA CAMPBELL, economics professor; BA, Sarah Lawrence Coll., 1978; MA in Econs., U. Notre Dame, 1980, PhD, 1983. Sr. tchg. fellow U. Notre Dame, 1981—83; asst. prof. Ea. Conn. State U., 1983—88, acting dept. chmn. Dept. Econs. and Mgmt. Sci., 1988, assoc. prof., 1988—93, prof., 1993—, dir. Ctr. Ednl. Excellence. Recipient Outstanding Master's Univ. and Coll. Prof. of Yr., Coun. for Advancement and Support of Edn. & Carnegie Found. for Advancement of Tchg., 2004. Office: Dept Econs Ea Conn State U Willimantic CT 06226 E-mail: free@easternct.edu.

FREED, JUDY GAYLE, literature and language educator; d. Vetus and Dolly Montgomery; children: Colby Lynn Edde, Erin Elizabeth Hale. BS in Edn., S.E. Mo. State, Cape Girardeau, 1967; MA in Counseling Psychology, Pepperdine U., Malibu, Calif., 1984. Lic. counseling intern Calif. Assn. Marriage and Family Therapists, 1984. English tchr. Overland (Mo.) Unified Sch. Dist., 1967—69, North Star Burroughs Sch. Dist., Fairbanks, Alaska, 1969—70, Saddleback Unified Sch. Dist., Mission Viejo, Calif., 1970—76, Irvine H.S., Calif., 1980—. Named Tchr. of Yr., Irvine H.S., 1990; recipient, 2006. Avocations: gardening, travel, golf. Office: Irvine High Sch 4321 Walnut Ave Irvine CA 92604 Office Phone: 949-936-7042. Personal E-mail: judyfreed1@cox.net. E-mail: jfreed@iusd.org.

FREED, KAREN SCHMIDT, elementary school educator; b. Elgin, Ill., Mar. 14, 1950; d. Delbert F. and Jeanette V. Schmidt; m. Ron W. Freed, June 24, 1972; children: Joshua A., Adam W. BS in Edn., No. Ill. U., DeKalb, Ill., 1972, MS in Edn., Curriculum and Instrn., 1988; postgrad., Drake U., Nat. Louis U., Xavier Coll., Aurora U., 1988—2004. Elem. tchr. Glenbrook Elem., Streamwood, Ill., 1972—98, Sycamore Trails Elem., Bartlett, Ill., 1998—2005. Staff devel., gifted contact com., report card devel. Sch. Dist. U-46, Elgin, Ill., 1972—2005. Contbr. articles pub. to profl. jour. Vol. YWCA, Elgin, Ill., 1981—85. Scholarship, Furnas Found., 1968—72. Mem.: NEA, Ill. Assn. for Gifted Children, Ill. Edn. Assn., Elgin Tchrs. Assn. Achievements include Golden Apple Award Nominee, Disney's American Teacher Award Nominee. Home: 36W624 River Grange Rd Saint Charles IL 60175

FREED, SHARON LOU, retired principal; b. LA, Feb. 23, 1944; d. Louis Robert Freed and Barbara Elizabeth Freed-Whitehead. BS Edn., U. So. Calif., 1965; MEd Curriculum Devel. and Instrn., Mich. State U., 1978. Cert. tchr. K-8 Calif., life credential K-8 Calif., credential tchr. K-8 Dept. Def. Dependent Schs., tchr. social studies and compensatory edn. grades 8-12 Dept. of Def. Dependent Schs., tchr. gifted and talented Dept. of Def. Dependent Schs., adminstr., Prin. elem. pre-K-8 Dept. of Def. Dependent Schs. Tchr. K-1 Amestoy Sch. L.A. Unified Sch. Dist., Gardena, 1965—68, tchr. grade 1 Amestoy Sch., 1969—70; tchr. grade 1 Chofu Elem. Sch. Dept. Def. Dependent Schs., Fuchu, Japan, 1968—69, tchr. grade 1 Darmstadt Am. Sch., 1970—73, tchr. K-2 Oberammergau Am. Sch., 1973—74, tchr. grade 3 RAF Lakenheath, England, 1974—82, tchr. compensatory edn., 1980—81, tchr. gifted and talented, 1981—82, prin. Uden Am. Sch. Netherlands, 1982—84, prin. W. F. Halsey Sch. Edzell, Scotland, 1984—90, prin. Woodbridge Elem. Sch. RAF Woodbridge, England, 1990—93, prin. Feltwell Elem. Sch. England, 1993—2000. Mem. early childhood progress report task force Dept. of Def. Dependent Schs. Europe, Weisbaden, Germany, 1994—95; mem. base closure/sch. closure task force USAF and Dept. of Def. Dependent Schs., RAF Woodbridge, RAF Upper Heyford, and UK dist., 1992—93; mem. accreditation team NCA, Upper Heyford, 1990. Sponsor Cub Scouts and Boy Scouts, RAF Edzell, 1984—90, RAF Woodbridge/RAF Bentwaters, 1990—93, RAF Feltwell, 1993—2000; voting mem. base scholarship com. and Angel Pin com. RAF Woodbridge/RAF Bentwaters, 1990—93, mem. Family Advocacy Bd., 1990—93, mem. Installation Adv. Coun., 1990—93, mem. Task Force on Base Closure, 1992—93; mem. exec. coun. Lakenheath Sch., 1998—2000; mem. Family Advocacy Coun., RAF Lakenheath, 1993—95, Installation Adv. Coun., RAF Lakenheath, Horringer Parish Coun. Assn., 1993—2006, Bredfield Village Assn., England; mem., spkr. Edzell Village Assn., 1984—90; participant Horringer Open Gardens for Charity, 2000—06; advisor Red Cross Vol. Bd., RAF Lakenheath, 1995—98; voting mem. Willie Johnson Scottish-American Sports Award Com., RAF Edzell/Edzell Village, 1984—90; mem. St. Andrew's Ch., Bredfield, 1990—93, Ch. of Scotland, Edzell, St. Leonard's Ch., Horringer, 1993—2006, mem. fete com., 1993—95; mem., spkr. Protestant Women of the Chapel, RAF Edzell, 1987—92. Named Student Tchr. of Yr., U. So. Calif., 1965, Tchr. of Yr., Atlantic Region, Dept. of Def. Dependent Schs., 1989, Prin. of Yr. UK East, Dept. of Def. Schs., 1989, 1990, 1992, 1999, Prin. of Yr. Atlantic Region, 1989—90, 1992—93, 1999—2000, Nat. Disting. Prin., Dept. Edn. and NAESP, 1989, 1999; recipient Sustained Superior Performance award, Dept. of Def. Schs., 1984—2000, cert. of appreciation, 1993, cert. of recognition, 1993, Rear Adm. William Thomas award letter of commendation, USN Security Group Comdr., Edzell, 1985, Travis Trophy award USN letter of commendation, Commdg. Officer, RAF Edzell, 1986, Guard award, Red Cross, 1997. Mem.: NAESP, U. So. Calif. Alumni Assn., Phi Delta Kappa (life). Presbyterian. Avocations: travel, reading, gardening, walking, attending the theatre. Home: 24525 Outlook Dr F21 Carmel CA 93923 also: Ashdown Cottage The Street Horringer Bury St Edmunds IP29 5SJ England Personal E-mail: slfcarmel@aol.com.

FREEDLENDER, SUSAN See HOMESTEAD, SUSAN

FREEDMAN, HELEN E., judge; b. NYC, Dec. 15, 1942; d. David Simeon and Frances (Fisher) Edelstein; m. Henry A. Freedman, June 7, 1964; children: Katherine Eleanor, Elizabeth Sarah. BA, Smith Coll., 1963; JD, NYU, 1967. Bar: N.Y. 1970, U.S. Dist. Ct. (so. and ea. dists.), U.S. Supreme Ct. 1979. Staff atty. office of gen. counsel Am. Arbitration Assn., N.Y.C., 1967-69; assoc. Hubbel, Cohen & Stiefel, N.Y.C., 1970-71, Shaw, Bernstein, Scheuer, Boyden & Sarnoff, N.Y.C., 1971-74; law sec. Civil Ct., N.Y.C., 1974-76; sr. atty. housing litigation bur. N.Y.C. Dept. Housing Preservation and Devel., 1976; supervising atty. Dist. Coun. 37 Legal Svcs. Plan, N.Y.C., 1976-78; judge Civil Ct., N.Y.C., 1979-88; acting justice Supreme Ct., N.Y.C., 1984-88, justice, 1989-95; apptd. to appellate term 1st dept. NY Supreme Ct., N.Y.C., 1995-99, apptd. to comml. divsn., 2000—, pres. judge mass tort litigation panel, 2002—. Co-chair State Judges Mass Tort Litigation Com.; mem. pattern jury instrns. com., Supreme Ct. Justices; adj. prof. N.Y. Law Sch., 1999, 2000, 03, 04; lectr. in field. Author: New York Objections, 1999, 6th revised edit., 2004; contbr. articles to profl. jours. Recipient Disting. Alumna award Smith Coll., 2000, Disting. Svc. award, Civil Ct. N.Y., 2004, Louis J. Capozzoli Gavel award N.Y. Ct. Lawyers Assn., 2005. Fellow Am. Bar Found., NY State Bar Found.; mem. ABA (chair small claims ct. com. 1986-89, bioethics com. nat. conf. spl. ct. judges, NY State Ct. del. to ann. meetings, nat. conf. spl. ct. judges, 1987-88, Spl. Cts. Conf. award 1987, 88, 93, Jud. Excellence award 1998), Nat. Assn. Women Judges, NY State Bar Assn. (del.), NY Fed. State Jud. Coun., NY Women's Bar Assn., NY State Assn. Women Judges (pres. 1995-97), Assn. of Bar of City of NY (com mem., chair com. med. malpractice, v.p. 1994-95), Judges and Lawyers Breast Cancer Alert (pres. 2001-03). Home: 150 W 96th St New York NY 10025-6469 Office: NY Supreme Ct 60 Centre New York NY 10007-1488 Office Phone: 646-386-3208.

FREEDMAN, JACQUELINE KAHANE, art educator; b. Bklyn., June 22, 1937; d. William and Yetta Kahane; m. Frederick Freedman (dec.), Oct. 16, 1960 (widowed July 1975); children: Stuart Morse Freedman, Rebecca Robin Freedman. BFA, Pratt Inst., 1958; MFA, Syracuse U., 1990. Layout artist A&S Dept. Store, Bklyn., 1957; textile designer M. Lowenstein & Sons, N.Y.C., 1958-60; graphic designer Ben Feder Inc., N.Y.C., 1960-61; textile designer M. Lowenstein & Sons, N.Y.C., 1961-63; freelance artist pvt. practice, Poughkeepsie, NY, 1968—73; designer Joan Luntz Studio, Cleve., 1973-75; art prof. Cuyahoga C.C., Highland Hills, Ohio, 1976—. Illustrator Today with Music, 1972, The Kitten in the Pumpkin Patch, 1973, The Big Sukkah, 1986, Jewish Stories One Generation Tells Another, 1986; commissioned works portraits, Jewish marriage contracts, landscapes and animals. Recipient First prize logo design, U.S. Navy, Bklyn., 1957. Mem.: No. Ohio Illustrator's Soc. Avocations: opera, classical music, electronic equipment. Home: 3317 Chadbourne Rd Shaker Heights OH 44120-3375 Office Phone: 216-987-2216. E-mail: jaqsart@wowway.com.

FREEDMAN, JOYCE BETH, academic administrator; b. Bklyn., Jan. 17, 1945; d. Nathan and Sarah (Minsky) Shlechter; m. Stuart Jay Freedman, Dec. 16, 1968; 1 child, Paul-Michael. BA in Psychology, UCLA, 1967. Various adminstrv. positions U. Calif., Berkeley, 1969-72; office coordinator Princeton (N.J.) U., 1972-75, dir. grad. admissions, 1975-76; various adminstrv. positions Stanford (Calif.) U., 1977-82; assoc. comptroller U. Chgo., 1982-86, asst. v.p. rsch., 1986—. Mem. Council on Govt. Relations, Nat. Council U. Research Adminstrs. Clubs: Quadrangle (Chgo.). Democrat. Jewish. Avocations: cross country skiing, handy-crafts, tennis. Office: U Chgo 970 E 58th St Chicago IL 60637-1432

FREEDMAN, JUDITH GREENBERG, retired elementary school educator, state legislator; b. Bridgeport, Conn., Mar. 11, 1939; d. Samuel Howard and Dorothy (Hoffman) G.; m. Samuel Sumner, Dec. 24, 1964; 1 child, Martha Ann. Student, Boston U., 1957—58, U. Mich., 1958—59; BS, So. Conn. State U., 1961, MS, 1972. Tchr. Hollywood (Fla.) Pub. Schs., 1961-62, White Plains (N.Y.) Pub. Schs., 1962-64, Wilton (Conn.) Pub. Schs., 1964-66, Weston (Conn.) Pub. Schs., 1966-72, 1982-84, tutor, 1977-80; owner Judith's Fancy, Westport, Conn., 1984—; mem. Dist. 26 Conn. Senate, Hartford, 1987—. Ranking mem. human svcs. com. Conn. Senate, 1987—88, ins. com., 1987—94, ranking mem. appropriations com., 1989—94, chmn. program rev. and investigation, 1992—94, chmn. commn. on innovation and productivity, 1994—95, ranking mem. edn. com., 1995—96, dep. pres. pro tem, 1995—97, 1995—2000, chair edn. com., 1998—2000, asst. minority leader, 1998—2002, co-chair edn. sub. com. appropriations, 1998—, mem. legis. mgmt. com., 1998—, mem. appropriation com., 1998—, ranking mem. higher edn. com., 2002—04; mem. exec. com. ea. region Coun. State Govts., chair program rev. and investigation, 2000—, dep. minority leader, 2000—02; edn. commn. of the states Conn. steering com., 2000—; mem. exec. com. ERCCSG, 2004—. Pres., v.p. 4th Congl. Rep. Women's Assn., 1976-80; pres. Rep. Women of Westport, 1976-79; mem. Bd. Edn., Westport, 1983-87, 89—; treas. Conn. Order Women Legislators. Mem. Order of Women Legislators (treas.), Weston Kiwanis, Fairfield County Navy Leagues. Jewish. Avocations: reading, art, golf. Home: 17 Crawford Rd Westport CT 06880-1823 Office Phone: 860-240-8826. Business E-Mail: judith.g.freedman@po.state.ct.us.

FREEDMAN, MARYANN SACCOMANDO, lawyer; b. Buffalo, Sept. 12, 1934; d. James Vincent Saccomando and Rosaria Rizzo; m. Robert P. Freedman, Apr. 9, 1961; children: Brenda M., Donald V. JD, U. Buffalo, 1958. Bar: N.Y., 1959; U.S. Dist. Ct. (we. dist.) N.Y., 1959; U.S. Bankruptcy Ct., 1959. U.S. Supreme Ct., 1963. Law clk. Saperston, McNaughton & Saperston, 1957-59, assoc., 1959-61; ptnr. Freedman & Freedman, 1961-75, 93-95; confidential legal rsch. asst. Buffalo City Ct., 1972-75; asst. atty. gen. N.Y. State Dept. of Law, 1975-77; law clk., matrimonial referee, hearing referee N.Y. State Supreme Ct., 1977-90, 80-90; spl. counsel Lavin & Kleiman, 1991-95; of counsel Cohen & Lombardo, P.C., 1995—. Hearing referee Jud. Conduct Commn., 1998—; founder and panel mem. Alliance for Dispute Resolution, 1997—; arbitrator, mediator U.S. Arbitration and Mediation of Upstate N.Y., 1992-94, arbitrator Am. Arbitration Assn., 1985—; lectr. Buffalo & Erie Co. Police Acad., 1975-86, Erie Co. Emergency Med. Tech. Tng. Program, 1975-83; asst. prof. paralegal studies Erie C.C., 1975-76; guest lectr. SUNY Buffalo, others. Contbr. articles to profl. jours. and publs. Mem. numerous civic orgns. including steering com. Women's Pavilion Pan Am 2001, 1999—, Italian-Am. Women of We. N.Y., 1994—, Temple Beth Zion Sisterhood, Buffalo Geol. Soc., others. Named Western N.Y. Women's Hall of Fame, 2001; recipient Outstanding Italian Am. Woman award, Ann. of Italian Am. Women, Western N.Y., 1989, Woman of Yr. award, Buffalo Philharmonic Orchestra, 1993. Mem.: ABA (ho. of dels. 1986—2002), Legal Svcs. for the Elderly (dir. 1978—85, others), Legal Aid Bur. (bd. dirs. 1980—81), Vol. Lawyers Project (adv. coun. 1982—86), Assn. Women Lawyers, Mid-Atlantic Conf. of State Bar Pres., N.Y. State Bar Jour. (bd. editors 1983—97), Pre-Trial Svcs., Inc. (pres. 1981), Erie County Aid to Indigent Prisoners Soc., Inc. (pres. 1981—82), Erie County Bar Found. (treas. 1962—63, bd. dirs. 1974—77, others), Erie County Bar Assn. (v.p. 1980—81, pres. 1981—82, others), N.Y. State Bar Found. (bd. dirs. 1982—, v.p. 1994—97, pres. 1997—2000, others), N.Y. State Bar Assn. (exec. com. 1982—89, sec. 1984—86, pres.-elect/chair ho. of dels. 1986—87, pres. 1987—88, Ruth G. Schapiro award 1994, others). Avocations: rocks, music, gardening, reading. Office: Cohen & Lombardo PC 343 Elmwood Ave Buffalo NY 14222-2203

FREEDMAN, SANDRA WARSHAW, former mayor; b. Newark, Sept. 21, 1943; m. Michael J. Freedman; 3 children. BA in Govt., U. Miami, 1965. Mem. Tampa (Fla.) City Coun., 1974—, chmn., 1983-86; mayor City of Tampa, 1986-95. Author: Specialties of the House (Recipes for People on the Go!), 2002. Bd. dirs. Jewish Cmty. Ctr., Boys and Girls Clubs Greater Tampa, Hillsborough Coalition for Health, Tampa Cmty. Concert Assn., Hillsborough Edn. Found., Judeo Christian Clinic, NCCJ, Human Rights Task Force; mem. sports adv. bd. Hillsborough Community Coll., 1975-76; sec. Downtown Devel. Authority, 1977-78; bd. dirs., v.p. Fla. Gulf Coast Symphony, 1979-80; vice chmn. Met. Planning Orgn., 1981-82; corp. mem. Neighborhood Housing Service; bd. fellows U. Tampa; mem. steering com. Hillsborough County Council of Govt.'s Constituency for Children; mem. exec. bd. Tampa/Hillsborough Young Adult Forum; chmn. bd. trustees Berkeley Prep. Sch.; trustee Tampa Bay Performing Arts Ctr., Inc., Tampa Mus.; mem. ethics com. Meml. Hosp.; mem. Tampa Preservation, Inc., Tampa/Hillsborough County Youth Council, Davis Islands Civic Assn., Tampa Hist. Soc., Met. Ministries Adv. Bd., Rodeph Sholom Synagogue, Sword of Hope Guild of Am. Cancer Soc., Friends of Arts. Recipient Spessar L. Holland Meml. award Tampa Bay Com. for Good Govt., 1975-76, Human Rights award City of Tampa, 1980, award Soroptimist Internat. Tampa, 1981, Status of Women award Zonta of Tampa II, 1986, Woman of Achievement award Bus. & Profl. Women, Jewish Nat. Fund Tree of Life award, Disting. Citizen award U. South Fla., 1995, Nat. Conf. of Christian and Jews Humanitarian award, 1995; named to Fla. Home Builders Hall of Fame. Mem. Hillsborough County Bar Aux., Greater Tampa C. of C., C. of C. Com. of 100 (exec. com.), Fla. League of Cities (bd. dirs.), Tampa Urban League, Nat. Council Jewish Women, U. Miami Alumni Assn., Athena Soc., Hadassah. Office: 3435 Bayshore Blvd Apt 700 Tampa FL 33629-8827

FREEDMAN, SARAH WARSHAUER, education educator; b. Wilimington, NC, Feb. 23, 1946; d. Samuel Edward and Miriam Warshauer; m. S. Robert Freedman, Aug. 20, 1967; 1 child, Rachel Karen. BA in English, U. Pa., 1967; MA in English, U. Chgo., 1970; MA in Linguistics, Stanford U., 1976, PhD in Edn., 1977. Tchr. English Phila. Sch. Dist., 1967-68, Lower Merion H.S., 1968-69; instr. English U. N.C., Wilmington, 1970-71; instr. English and linguistics Stanford U., 1972-76; asst. and assoc. prof. English San Francisco State U., 1977-81; asst. prof. edn. U. Calif., Berkeley, 1981-83, assoc. prof. edn., 1983-89, dir. Nat. Ctr for Study of Writing and Literacy, 1985-96, prof. edn., 1989—, sr. rschr. Human Rights Ctr., 2001—. Resident Bellagio Conf. and Study Ctr., Rockefeller Found., 1997; mem. nat. task force Nat. Writing Project, 1998—. Author: Response to Student Writing, 1987, Exchanging Writing, Exchanging Cultures, Lessons in School Reform from the United States and Great Britain, 1994, (with E.R. Simons, J.S. Kalnin, A. Casareno and M-Class teams) Inside City Schools, Investigating Literacy in Multi-cultural Classrooms, 1999; editor: The Acquisition of Written Language: Response and Revision, 1985, (with A. Ball) Bakhtinian Perspectives on Language, Literacy, and Learning, 2004; contbr. chpts. to books and articles to profl. jours. Recipient Richard Meade award for Pub. Rsch. in Tchr. Edn. Nat. Coun. Tchrs. English, 1989, 94, Ed Fry book award, 1996, 2000, Multicultural Book award, Nat. Assn. Multicultural Edn., 2000; fellow Nat. Conf. on Rsch. in English, 1986, Ctr. Advanced Studies in Behavioral Scis., 1999-2000, 06—; grantee Spencer Found. 1996-2003, Nat. Ctr. for Study of Writing and Literacy, Office Ednl. Rsch. and Improvement, 1985-95, Minority Undergrad. Rsch. Program U. Calif., 1988, 89, 92, 93, U.S. Inst. of Peace, 2003-06, numerous other grants. Mem. Nat. Coun. Tchrs. English (standing com. on rsch. 1981-87, ex-officio 1987-96, chair bd. trustees rsch. found. 1990-93, co-chair rsch. assembly 1999-2001, chmn. 2003-06), Am. Ednl. Rsch. Assn. (chair spl. interest group on rsch. in writing 1983-85, numerous other coms.) Office: U Calif Dept Edn Berkeley CA 94720-0001

FREEDMAN, WENDY LAUREL, astronomer, educator; b. Toronto, Ont., Can., July 17, 1957; arrived in U.S., 1984; d. Harvey Bernard and Sonya Lynn Freedman; m. Barry F. Madore, June 23, 1985, two children. BSc, U. Toronto, 1979, PhD in astronomy and astrophysics, 1984. Fellow Carnegie Observatories, Pasadena, Calif., 1984-87, faculty, 1987—, Crawford H. Greenewalt chair dir., 2003—. Bd. dirs. Assn. Univs. for Rsch. in Astronomy, Inc., Washington; co-chair com. on astronomy and astrophysics NRC, 2002—. Named a Fellow of Am. Acad. of Arts and Scis., 2000; recipient Marc Aaronson Lectureship and prize, 1994, John P. McGovern award, 2000, Helen Sawyer Hogg award, 2000. Mem. NASA (sci. oversight com. planning the Next Generation Space Telescope), Nat. Acad. Scis., Am. Astron. Soc., Can. Astron. Soc., Astron. Soc. Pacific, Am. Phys. Soc., Nat. Rsch. Coun. Bd. Physics and Astronomy, Ctr. Particle Astrophysics (mem. exec. bd.). Achievements include first to being first woman to join Carnegie's permanent scientific staff, 1987. Office: Carnegie Observatories 813 Santa Barbara St Pasadena CA 91101

FREEDSON, GRACE ELIZABETH, publishing executive; b. NYC, July 17, 1951; d. Oscar and Anna (Selzer) Chandler; m. Mark D. Freedson, June 6, 1971; 1 child, Brett Heather. BA, Boston U., 1972. Asst. dir. publicity Stein & Day Pubs., N.Y.C., 1973-75; freelance publicist L.I., N.Y., 1975-83; dir. pub. rels. and acquisitions Barron's Ednl. Series, Hauppauge, N.Y., 1983-90, managing editor, dir. acquisitions, 1990—2000; owner Grace Freedson's Pub. Network, Woodbury, NY, 2000—. Avocations: skiing, tennis. Office: Grace Freedsons Pub Network Ste 406 20 Crossways Park North Woodbury NY 11797

FREEHLING, BROOKE ANN, elementary school educator; b. Natrona Heights, Pa., May 31, 1976; d. Glenn Drane and Janet Eileen (Weber) Freehling. BSc, Pa. State U., 1999. Second grade tchr. Chatham County Schools, Pittsboro, NC, 2002—. Grand officer Internat. Order of the Rainbow for Girls, Pa., 1988—97. Mem.: NEA, Internat. Reading Assn., NC Assn. of Educators, Order of the Ea. Star. Democrat. Luth. Avocations: reading, walking. Home: 408 Harlon Dr B3 Cary NC 27511 Office: Chatham County Schools 369 W St P O Box 128 Pittsboro NC 27312 Office Phone: 919-542-3725. E-mail: rwf41298@yahoo.com.

FREELAND, CHRYSTIA, editor, director; b. Alta., Can., 1968; married; 2 children. BA history & lit., Harvard U., 1991; M in Slavonic studies, St. Anthony's Coll., Oxford U. Corr. FinancialTimes.com, Kiev, Ukraine, 1991—93, ea. Europe corr., 1994, Moscow bur. chief, 1995—98, UK nat. news editor, 1998—99, editor, 2001—02, editor Sat. ed., 2002—03, dep. editor, 2003—05, editor electronic svcs., 2005—06, US mng. editor, 2006—; dep. editor Globe & Mail, Toronto, 2002. Author: Sale of the Century: Russia's Wild Ride from Communism to Capitalism, 2000. Named a Young Leader of Tomorrow, World Econ. Forum, 2005; recipient Best Energy Submission, Bus. Journalist of the Yr. awards, 2004. Office: FinancialTimes.com 1330 Ave of the Americas New York NY 10019 Office Phone: 212-641-6503.

FREEMAN, ALLISON BROWNE, museum educator, researcher; b. Hartford, Conn., Oct. 18, 1975; d. Louis and Margaret A. Freeman; 1 child, Margaret Murdoch. BS in Langs., Georgetown U., Washington, D.C., 1998; student, U. Aix-Marseille, France, 1997; MA, Courtauld Inst. Art, London, 2001. Rsch. asst. Smithsonian Am. Art Mus., Washington, 2002, The Phillips Collection, Washington, 2002—05. Class agent The Hotchkiss Sch., Lakeville, Conn., 1994—. Mem.: The Norton Simon Mus., Caltech Women's Club (mem. bd.).

FREEMAN, ANGELA Y., assistant principal; d. Willie L. and Lillie M. Wright; m. Isaiah Freeman, III, Apr. 6, 1996; children: Isaiah IV, Christopher J., Stephen M., Jonathan D.; children: Chavonne R., Caitlin J., Joshua D., Alexa T. BS, SC State U., 1983; MA, The Ohio State U., 1986; postgrad., Wilmington Coll., 2005—. Cert. adminstrn. Band dir. Lantana Mid. Cmty. Sch., Fla., 1986—89; math tchr. Dover HS, Del., 1989—90; band dir. William Henry Mid. Sch., Dover, 1990—2002, Seaford Mid. Sch., Seaford, Del., 2002—03; asst. band dir. Seaford HS, 2002—03; asst. dean Cab Calloway Sch. Arts, Wilmington, Del., 2003—06; asst. prin. John Dickinson H.S. Red City Consolidated Sch. Dist., Wilmington, 2006—. Bd. mem. Cab Calloway Bd. Dirs., 2003—. Pres., founder Talitha Cumi, Inc., Wilmington, 2000; adminstrv. asst. United Ind. Christian Fellowship, Milford, Del., 2001; youth pastor New Galilee Missionary Bapt. Ch., Wilmington, 2003; mem. Cab Calloway Fund, 2003. Mem.: ASCD, Nat. Assn. Secondary Sch. Adminstrs., Del. Assn. Sch. Adminstrs., Phi Delta Kappa, Alpha Kappa Mu. Avocations: swimming, counseling. Office: Talitha Cumi Inc PO Box 5716 Wilmington DE 19808-0716 Office Phone: 302-651-2700, 302-992-5500. Home Fax: 302-994-3947; Office Fax: 302-425-4594. Business E-Mail: afreeman@talithacumi.org, angela.freeman@redclay.k12.de.us.

FREEMAN, ANNE HOBSON, writer, English language educator; b. Richmond, Va., Mar. 19, 1934; d. Joseph Reid Anderson and Mary Douthat (Marshall) Hobson; m. George Clemon Freeman, Jr., Dec. 6, 1958; children: Anne Colston McEvoy, George Clemon Freeman III, Joseph Reid Anderson Freeman. AB, Bryn Mawr Coll., 1956; postgrad. London U., 1956-57; MA, U. Va., 1973. Fiction writer, 1956—; reporter Internat. News Svc., Eastern Europe, 1957; editor Va. Mus. Fine Arts, Richmond, 1959-63; lectr. English, U. Va., Charlottesville, 1973-88; chmn. adv. com. Bryn Mawr Bull., Pa., 1978-81. Author: The Style of a Law Firm: Eight Gentlemen From Virginia, 1989, A Hand Well Played, the Life of Jim Wheat Jr., 1994; contbr. stories to various mags., anthologies, lit. jours. Bd. dirs. Va. Hist. Soc., 1984-90, Va. Commn. for Humanities and Pub. Policy, 1985-89, Nat. Coun. Friends of Kennedy Ctr., Washington, 1983-85, Mus. of Confederacy, Richmond., 1994-2001. Fulbright scholar, 1956-57; Va. Ctr. for Creative Arts fellow; MacDowell Colony fellow. Mem. Country of Va. Club, Woman's (Richmond) Club. Episcopalian. Home: Oyster Shell Point Farm 314 Oyster Shell Ln Callao VA 22435-0680 Personal E-mail: ahfreeman@aol.com.

FREEMAN, BABA FOSTER, editor; d. Festus Finley and Beatrice Michelson Foster; m. Monroe E. Freeman Jr, 1959; 3 children. BA in Polit. Economy, Bennington Coll., 1948. Mem. editl. staff The Blue Ridge Herald, Purcellville, Va., 1949—50; clk. Office Sci. Pers. Nat. Acad. Sci., Washington, 1950—52; head info. svcs. sect., Ops. Evaluation Group Office of Chief of Naval Ops., Washington, 1952—59. Rsch. dir. New Town Publs., Reston, Va., 1980—96. Dir., bull. editor LWV of Fairfax Area, 1967—71, v.p., 1999—; vol. Fairfax County Pub. Libr., 1976—; dir. governing bd. Reston Cmty. Ctr., 1976—80; commr., coach Reston Soccer Assn., 1978—82; bd. dirs. Reston Interfaith Housing Inc., 1980—93; Centreville (Va.) dist. rep. Adv. Social Svcs. Bd., Fairfax County, 1986—97; Hunter Mill dist. rep. Human Svcs. Coun., Fairfax County, 1997—; del. conv. LWV of the U.S., Washington, 2000; del. ann. coun. Diocese of Va., 1986—92. Achievements include development of machine literature search program for research and development program for USN. Office: LWV - Fairfax Area 4026 Hummer Rd Ste 214 Annandale VA 22003 Office Phone: 703-658-9150. Business E-Mail: lwvfa@ecoisp.com.

FREEMAN, CAROL LYN, business administrator; b. Loraine, Tex., May 3, 1949; d. James R. and Flora Lee (Tibbs) Turnbow; m. Donald Lee Freeman, July 2, 1987; children: Tracy Lyn, Warton Irvin, Rian, Makai Jenkins, Merritt Freeman. Student, Western Tex. Coll., Snyder. Pres. DC Sports, Roscoe, Tex.; purchasig agt. Bearings Inc., Sweetwater, Tex., Abilene, Tex.; in ops. Abilene Bearing Co.; br. mgr. Bearings Inc., Abilene, Tex.; computer programmer Freeman & Sons. Trucking, Roscoe, Tex. Co-owner DC Sports, Roscoe. Mem. NAFE. Address: 5249 Meadowick Ln Abilene TX 79606-4335

FREEMAN, CAROLYN RUTH, oncologist; b. Kettering, Eng., Jan. 2, 1950; emigrated to Can., 1974, naturalized, 78; d. Ivor Thomas and Winifred Mary (Scotney) F.; m. J.C. Negrete, July 25, 1981. Student, King's Coll. London U., 1967-69; MB, BS, Westminster Med. Sch. London U., 1972. Prof., chmn. dept. radiation oncology, faculty medicine McGill U., Montreal, 1979—; radiation oncologist-in-chief McGill U. Hosps., Montreal, 1979—. Contbr. articles to med. publs. Fellow Royal Coll. Physicians (Can.); mem. Can. Assn. Radiol. Oncologists (pres. 1991-93), Am. Soc. Therapeutic Radiology and Oncology. Home: 4270 deMaisonneuve W Montreal PQ Canada H3Z 1K6 Office: 1650 Cedar Ave Montreal PQ Canada H3G 1A4 Office Phone: 514-934-8040. Business E-Mail: carolyn.freeman@muhc.mcgill.ca.

FREEMAN, CATHERINE ELAINE, education educator; b. Independence, Kans., Oct. 18, 1956; d. John R. and Irma J. (Simmons) F. BA, Pitts. State U., 1978, MS, 1979, EdS, 1985; PhD, U. Tulsa, 1990; student, Oxford U., Eng., 1993. Residence hall dir. Pitts. State U., 1979-80; counselor, coord. orientation Mo. So. State U., Joplin, 1980-85, dir. coll. orientation and patron's scholarship coord., 1985-88, assoc. prof. of edn., dir. spl. projects, 1990—, asst. dir. honors program, 1992-93, prof. tchr. edn., 2002—; tchg. asst. U. Tulsa, 1988-90. Intern Okla. State Regents for Higher Edn., Oklahoma City, summer 1989, Pres.'s Office, U. Tulsa, 1988-89. Contbr. articles to profl. jours. First v.p. Mo. So. Women's Club, 1982-83; team capt., vol. Mo. So. State U. Fundraising Phon-a-Thon, 1982-88, 90—; team capt. United Way Mo. So. State U., 1991-94, 05-; mem. S.W. Mo. Cmty. Band. Mem. Am. Edn1. Rsch. Assn., Nat. Assn. Student Pers. Adminstrs., Internat. Alliance for Invitational Edn., S.W. Mo. Sch. Counselors Assn., Omicron Delta Kappa (faculty sec. 1987-88, 92—, Outstanding Faculty Sec. Province XI 1994, faculty province dir. 1995-00), Phi Delta Kappa. United Methodist. Avocations: travel, cultural events, spectator sports. Office: Missouri So State U 3950 Newman Rd Joplin MO 64801-1512

FREEMAN, CHANDA, executive secretary, elementary school educator; d. Charles and Cynthia (Walsh) Leggans; m. David Freeman, June 15, 1993 (div. June 26, 2003); children: Tyler, Breanna. AA in Law Enforcement, U. Ark.-Little Rock, 2002, BA in Sociology, 2002—02. Cert.: Ark. (Nat. Crime and Info. Ctr. Terminal Ops.) 1994. Asst. mgr. TCBY Yogurt, Little Rock, 1987—90, Domino's Pizza, Little Rock, 1990—92; exec. asst. to v.p. Greenfield Millworks, Maumelle, Ark., 1992—97; adminstrv. office supr. dept. math. and stats. U. Ark., Little Rock, 1997—2003; tchr. North Little Rock Sch. Dist., 2003—. V.p. staff senate U. Ark., Little Rock, 2001—03. Com. chairperson; mem. staff senate Helping Hands, Little Rock, 1999—2002; ambassador United Way, Little Rock, 1998—2002; peer mentor Adult Student Advocacy, Little Rock, 1998—2003; educator Ch. Rock Creek Care Ctr. Computer Lab., Little Rock, 2005—06. Recipient Staff Achievement award, U. Ark.-Little Rock, 1999, Svc. Pin, 2002. Mem.: Ctrl. Ark. Bicycle Youth Devel. Assn., Am. Mensa (life). Avocations: bmx racing, reading.

FREEMAN, CORINNE, financial analyst, retired mayor; b. NYC, Nov. 9, 1926; d. Bernard J. Hirschfeld and Sidonie (Daxe) Lichtenstein; m. Michael S. Freeman, Mar. 14, 1948; children: Michael L., Stephan J. Student, Adelphi Coll. Sch. Nursing, 1944—47. RN, N.Y., Mass. Nurse numerous hosps. in N.Y. and Mass., 1948-64; mayor St. Petersburg, Fla., 1977-85; mem. Pinellas County Sch. Bd., St. Petersburg, Fla., 1989-98, chmn., 1996-98; bd. trustees Palms of Pasadena Hosp., St. Petersburg, 1998—, dir., 1998—2004. Fin. advisor Prudential Securities, Wachovia Securities; bd. dirs. Creativity in Child Care. Chmn. Social Svc. Allocations Com., St. Petersburg, 1972-76, City Budget Rev. Com., 1973-76, Youth Svc. System, Pinellas County, 1975-76, West Coast Regional Water Supply Authority; past mem. community redevel. com. U.S. Conf. of Mayors; past pres. Fla. League Cities; past mem. Pinellas County Mayors Coun.; past mem. Nat. League of Cities Revenue and Fin. Task Force; pres. LWV, St. Petersburg, 1970-72, 75-76; trustee Fire Pension Bd., St. Petersburg, 1989-92, Bayfront Med. Ctr.; dir. Palms of Pasadena Hosp., 1999-2003; adv. com. Jr. League St. Petersburg, 1990-92. Recipient Disting. Alumni award Adelphi U. Mem. Fla. Nursing Assn. Mem.: Treasure Island Yacht and Tennis Club (bd. dirs. 2004—). Republican. Home: 2101 Pelham Rd N Saint Petersburg FL 33710-3659 Office: 100 Zndue South 400 N Saint Petersburg FL 33707-1728 Office Phone: 727-551-2303. Business E-Mail: corinne_freeman@wachoviasec.com.

FREEMAN, DEBRA, federal judge; b. 1957; BA, Yale Coll., 1979; JD, NYU, 1986. Bar: NY 1987. Assoc. Parker Auspitz Neesemann & Delehanty PC, 1986—87, Morrison & Foerster LLP, 1987—95, ptnr., litig., 1995—2001; magistrate judge US Dist. Ct. (So. Dist.) NY, 2001—. Bd. dir. Legal Aid Soc. NY, 1993—99. Office: US Courthouse Rm 631 40 Centre St New York NY 10007-1581

FREEMAN, DONNA COOK, small business owner; b. Waldron, Ark., Apr. 18, 1937; d. Oliver Raymond and Lura Edna (Doyel) Cook; m. Clarence Lee Freeman, Jan. 21, 1954; children: Scott, Kevin, Steven, Melissa, Melinda. Staff dept. aquaculture U. Calif. Bodega Marine Lab., 1976—77; real estate assoc., 1978—82; co-owner fishing vessel Noyo Belle, 1981—84; ptnr. Freeman's Union 76 Svc., Bodega Bay, 1983—93; designer Compass Rose Gardens, 1986—, owner, 1987—. Vice chmn. Shoreline Trust Ednl. Program Svcs., 1981—85; founding chmn. Bodega Bay Fisherman's Festival, 1973—74, 1983; chmn. Spud Point Adv. Bd., 1985—; grand juror Sonoma County, Calif., 1983—84; hon. dir. Sonoma County Fair, 1995—; dir. Bodega Bay Fire Protection Dist., 1987—; alt. mem. Dem. Ctrl. Com., 1982; mgr. polit. campaign, 1984; bd. dirs. Bodega Bay Area Rescue, 1973—74; mem. local bd. SSS, 1982—; bd. dirs. Sonoma County Fair, 1985—95, Coastal Fisheries Found., 1986—; mem. regional adv. bd. Sonoma County Libr. Commn., 2002—. Mem.: Bodega Bay Cmty. Assn., Bodega Bay C. of C. (pres. 1979—81, bd. dirs. 1982—86), Bodega Bay Fisherman's Auz., Bodega Bay Grange. Home: PO Box 1060 Bodega Bay CA 94923-1060 E-mail: donna@compassrosegardens.com.

FREEMAN, ELAINE LAVALLE, sculptor; b. Boston, May 22, 1929; d. John and Ellen (Tufts) Lavalle; m. Felix Joachim Freeman, Jr., June 16, 1951 (div. 1974); children: John Lavalle, William Baker, Ellen Candler. Student, NAD, 1973, Art Students League, N.Y.C., 1947-49, 70-73; BA, Fordham U., 1986. Profl. sculptor, N.Y.C. and Southampton, N.Y., 1973—; instr. Sculpture Ctr. Sch., N.Y.C., 1977-81; vol. gallery asst. Sculpture Ctr., N.Y.C., 1979-2000. Exec. com., sec., bd. trustees Sculpture Ctr., N.Y.C., 1985-2000. One-woman shows include Wheeler Gallery, Providence, 1979, Sculpture Ctr., N.Y.C., 1977, Southampton Gallery, N.Y.C., 1975; exhibited in group shows at Nat. Acad., Audubon Artists, Allied Artists, Parrish Mus., Nat. Arts Club, Am. Standard Corp. Gallery, Sculpture Ctr. Gallery, Huntington Twp. Art League, East Edn Arts Coun., others, 1973—; permanent collection include Martha Graham Sch. Contemporary Dance, Health Mgmt. Resources, N.Y., Southampton Hosp. Bd. dir. Southampton Fresh Air Home for Crippled Children, 1980-86, sec., 1981-83, treas. 1980. Recipient Judges award Parrish Art Mus., Southampton, 1974, Am. Carving Sch. award Allied Artists, N.Y.C., 1977. Mem. Portrait Soc. Am., Catharine Lorillard Wolfe Art Club (honored mem., bd. dir. 1997—, v.p. sculpture 1998-2001, Creative Hands award 2005, 1st v.p. 2001—2006, 1st prize sculpture 1994, Anna Hyatt Huntington award 1983), Southampton Bathing Corp., Colony Club, Meadow Club. Democrat. Episcopalian. Avocations: travel, watercolor painting. Home: 132 Post Ln Southampton NY 11968-4919

FREEMAN, JANET L., librarian; b. Winston-Salem, N.C., Nov. 5, 1946; d. Vernon Charles and Lula M. (McHan) F. BA, U. N.C., Greensboro, 1969; MLS, George Peabody Coll. Tchrs., 1971. Ref. libr. Ga. Southwestern Coll., Americus, 1971-73; tech. svcs. libr. Furman U., Greenville, S.C., 1973-75; dir. libr. svcs. Wingate (N.C.) Coll., 1975-84; coll. libr. Meredith Coll., Raleigh, N.C., 1984—. Mem. ALA, N.C. Libr. Assn. (bd. dirs. 1987-89, pres.-elect. 1989-91, pres. 1991-93), Southeastern Libr. Assn. Avocation: music. Home: 2800 Rue Sans Famille Raleigh NC 27607-3049 Office: Meredith Coll 3800 Hillsborough St Raleigh NC 27607-5237

FREEMAN, LESLIE JEAN, neuropsychologist, researcher; b. San Diego, Feb. 17, 1965; d. Richard Joseph and Jean Doris (Weber) Currier; m. Drue Scott Freeman, Sept. 6, 1986. BA, U. Calif., Irvine, 1989; MA in Clin. Psychology, Antioch U., L.A., 1992; postgrad., Calif. Sch. Profl. Psychology, Fresno, 1993-98. Marriage, family and child counselor intern So. Calif. Counseling Ctr., L.A., 1990-93; marriage, family, child counselor intern/psychology intern Bakersfield (Calif.) Med. Hosp., 1993-94; intern, resident in neuropsychology pvt. practice and Drs. Hosp., Modesto, Calif., 1994-97; resident in neuropsychology VA Med. Ctr., Cleve., 1997-98; resident, fellow in neuropsychology U. Rochester (N.Y.) Med. Ctr., 1998—. Guest lectr. in field. Contbr. articles to profl. jours. Mem. APA, Nat. Acad. Neuropsychology, Internat. Neuropsychol. Soc., Am. Neuropsychiat. Assn., Calif. Assn. Marriage and Family Therapy, Calif. Assn. Psychology Providers. Avocations: collecting first edition mystery novels, collecting original animation art and disneyana, cooking, skiing, photography. Office: U Rochester Rochester NY 14642-0001

FREEMAN, MYRNA FAYE, county schools official; b. Danville, Ill., Oct. 30, 1939; d. Thomas Gene and Dorothy Olive (Chodera) F.; m. Lonnie Lee Choate, Aug. 16, 1959 (div. 1987); children: Leslie Rene, Gregory Lonn. BA in Pub. Adminstrn., San Diego State U., 1977, MA in Edn. Adminstrn., 1987. Employee benefits mgr. City of San Diego, 1974-84; dir. San Diego County Office Edn., San Diego, 1984—. Instr. Sch. Bus. Mgrs. Acad., Assn. Calif. Sch. Adminstrs., 1985—, Ins. Edn. Assn., Cert. Employee Benefits Specialist courses, 1991—. Author: Adm. Impact of Implement Leg. 1987; Author: Article Risk Mgmt.-Emp. Benefits 1985, Risk Mgmt.-Workers' Comp. 1986, Risk Mgmt.-Loss Control 1986. Mem. Kaiser Consumer Coun., 1977-84, pres., 1979-80; bd. dirs. S.D. County Affirmative Action Adv. Bd., 1985; mem. adv. com. Vista Health Plan Pub. Policy, 1994—; adv. coun. Kaiser On-the-Job, 1994—. Recipient Appreciation award COMBO-Cultural Arts of San Diego 1977. Mem. Risk Ins. Mgmt. Soc. (pres. San Diego chpt. 1988), Calif. Assn. Sch. Bus. Ofcls. (chmn. risk mgmt. R&D comm. 1987-88), San Diego Group Ins. Claims Coun. (pres. 1987), S.D. Employers Health Cost Coalition (vice-chmn. 1987), Calif. Women in Govt. (bd. dirs. 1983-84), Calif. Assn. of Joint Powers Authority, Pub. Agys. Risk Mgmt. Assn., Pub. Risk Ins. Mgmt. Assn., Internat. Found. Employee Benefits Plans, San Diego Workers' Compensation Forum, Sigma Kappa, Phi Kappa Phi, Internat. Platform Assn Republican. Methodist. Home: 1545 Northrim Ct # 272 San Diego CA 92111-7341 Office: Mira Costa Coll One Bernard Dr Oceanside CA 92056 Office Phone: 760-795-6866. Business E-Mail: ffreeman@miracosta.edu.

FREEMAN, PATRICIA ELIZABETH, multi-media specialist, educational consultant; b. El Dorado, Ark., Nov. 30, 1924; d. Herbert A. and M. Elizabeth (Pryor) Harper; m. Jack Freeman, June 15, 1949; 3 children. BA, Centenary Coll., 1943; postgrad., Fine Arts Ctr., 1942—46, Art Students League, 1944—45; BSLS, La. State U., 1946; postgrad., Calif. State U., 1959—61, U. N.Mex., 1964—74; EdS, Vanderbilt U., 1975. Libr. U. Calif., Berkeley, 1946-47; libr. Albuquerque Pub. Schs., 1964-67, ind. sch. libr. media ctr. cons., 1967—. One-woman shows include La. State Exhibit Bldg., 1948; author: Pathfinder: An Operational Guide for the School Librarian, 1975, Southeast Heights Neighborhoods of Albuquerque, 1993; compiler, editor: Elizabeth Pryor Harper's Twenty-One Southern Families, 1985; editor: SEHNA Gazette, 1988—93. Mem. task force Goals for Dallas-Environ., 1977—82; pres. Friends Sch. Librs., Dallas, 1979—83; v.p., editor S.E. Heights Neighborhood Assn., 1988—93. With USAF, 1948—49. Named honoree, AAUW Ednl. Found., 1979, 1996; recipient Vol. award for Outstanding Svc., Dallas Ind. Sch. Dist., 1978; AAUW Pub. Svc. grantee, 1980. Mem.: LWV (sec. Dallas 1982—83, editor Albuquerque 1984—86, editor Albuquerque/Bernalillo County Voters' Guide 1986, 1988, editor N.Mex. 2004—, editor Albuquerque 2005—), AAUW (bd. dirs. Dallas 1976—82, bd. dirs. Albuquerque 1983—85, dir. N.Mex, editor 1999—2005, bd. dirs. Albuquerque 2003—, editor), ALA, N.Mex Symphony Guild, Nat. Trust Historic Preservation, Friends Pub. Libr., Colorado Springs Fine Arts Ctr., Alpha Xi Delta. Home: 612 Ridgecrest Dr SE Albuquerque NM 87108-3365

FREEMAN, PATSY L., director; b. West Columbia, Tex., Jan. 10, 1953; d. Herman Charles and Goldie Bertram; m. Jimmy R. Freeman, July 11, 1977; children: Shalene Rodgers, Michelle Caruth. A in Sociology, Coastal Bend Coll., Beeville, Tex., 1987; B in Sociology, Tex. A&M U., Corpus Christi, 1989, MS in Guidance and Counseling, 1993. Lic. profl. counselor Tex., 1998. Basic child care worker South Tex. Children's Home, Pettus, 1980—82, supr. Ind. Living Program, 1982—86, supr. Coll. Cottage Program, 1986—89, caseworker, 1989—91; case mgr. III Corpus Christi State Sch., Tex., 1991—93, case mgr. supr. Tex., 1993—95; spl. needs counselor Coastal Bend Coll., Beeville, 1995—2003, dir. fin. aid, 2003—. Named Outstanding Student of Am., 1989; named to Outstanding Women of Am., 1991. Mem.: Tex. Counseling Assn., ACA, Phi Theta Kappa Nat.Honor Alumni Assn. Republican. Baptist. Avocations: hunting, camping, ranching. Mailing: PO Box 4053 Beeville TX 78104 Office: Coastal Bend Coll 3800 Charco Rd Beeville TX 78102

FREEMAN, PAULA S., social worker; b. Cullman, Ala., Nov. 9, 1969; d. Leon Douglas and Mary Sue Freeman. Student, Wallace State Coll.; BSW, Jacksonville State U., 1992; MSW, Ala. A&M U., 1997. Lic. social worker, Ala. Svc. social worker Dept. Human Resources, Anniston, Ala., 1992-96; clin. social worker intern Family Svcs. Ctr., Huntsville, Ala., 1996-97; family svc. worker Three Springs, Inc., Trenton, Ala., 1997-99; project dir. Auburn (Ala.) U., 1999—2002; trainer State Dept. Human Resources, 2002—. Vol. Hospice Caring House, Hunstville, 2001-, Children's Hosp., Birmingham, 1993—, Mt. Olive Ch. Food Bank, 1999, Habitat for Humanity, Anniston, 1995-96, USA Weekend's Make a Difference Day, Anniston, 1995. Named Foster Care Worker of Yr., Dept. Human Resources, 1995, Hon. Recognition award USA Weekend, 1995. Mem. NASW. Avocations: exercise, travel, piano, running. Home: 110 Poplar Green Ln Harvest AL 35749 Office: Madison County DHR 2206 Oakwood Ave Huntsville AL 35801

FREEMAN, PHYLLIS RISË, psychology educator; b. Bklyn., July 3, 1948; d. Melvin Daniel and Helen (Yuder) F.; m. David Krikun, Oct. 9, 1977. AB cum laude, NYU, 1970; MA, Bryn Mawr Coll., 1973, PhD, 1975. Instr. NYU, Bronx, 1969-70; grad. asst. Bryn Mawr (Pa.) Coll., 1973-75; asst. prof. SUNY, New Paltz, N.Y., 1975-83, asst. dean, 1982-83, assoc. dean, 1984-85, assoc. prof. psychology, 1983—, dir. honors program, 1984-85, dir. psychology grad. program, 1986—, dean grad. sch., 1999—2004. Referee jours. Pharmacology, Biochemistry, Behavior; manuscript reviewer various textbook pubs. Co-author: (book) Wise Women: Reflections of Teachers at Midlife, 2000. Evaluation cons., clin. vol. Planned Parenthood Dutchess and Ulster Counties, 1976-83, chair, adv. bd. Inst. for Disaster Mental Health, SUNY, New Paltz, 2004—. Nat. Def. Edn. Act fellow Bryn Mawr Coll., 1970-73, Postdoctoral fellow U. Colo., Boulder, 1980; rsch. grantee SUNY Rsch. Found., 1979-80, 81-82, NEH, 1988, Sept. 11 Recovery Fund Grant ARC, 2005-06. Mem. APA, Phi Beta Kappa. Office: SUNY Dept Psychology Coll New Paltz New Paltz NY 12561 Office Phone: 845-257-3468. E-mail: freemanp@newpaltz.edu.

FREEMAN, SALLY ANN, writer, English language and literacy educator; b. Portland, Maine, June 20, 1937; d. Arthur Alfonso and Helen Dorothy (Goshen) Wilcox; m. Harry William Freeman, Jan. 2, 1959 (div.); children: Toby, Eben. Student, Antioch Coll., Yellow Spring, Ohio, 1957-58, New Sch., N.Y.C., 1960-62; BA, U. Maine, 1962. Editor Natural Lifestyles Mag., New Paltz, N.Y., Felton, Calif., 1970-74; project/module writer Boces Environ. Ednl. Project, New Paltz, 1978-79; editor Navigator, Hudson River Sloop Clearwater, Poughkeepsie, N.Y., 1982; ESL instr. CUNY, 1989-92; instr. ESL, grammar and writing divsn. continuing edn. N.Y.C. Coll. of Tech., Bklyn., 1983—. Literacy instr. N&CT divsn. Can., 2005—. Author: Drugs and Civilization, 1988, Herbs for All Seasons, 1991, Every Woman's Guide to Natural Home Remedies, 1996, Everywoman's Guide to Ageless Natural Beauty, 2000; co-author, editor: The Kitchen Almanac, 1975; co-author, editor-in-chief: The Green World, 1974; co-author: Cave of the Moon, 1974; contbr. articles to nat. mags. Helene Wurlitzer Found. residency, 1995. Mem. Internat. Women's Writing Guild (area rep. 1995-98). Democrat. Avocations: botany, travel, swimming, reading, cross country skiing. Home: 3300 Baker Hwy # 4 Mohegan Lake NY 10547-1765 Personal E-mail: sallyann16@juno.com.

FREEMAN, SHAREE M., federal agency administrator; b. N.Y. BA, St. Lawrence U., 1976; JD, Georgetown U., 1980. Law clk. to Hon. Norma Holloway Johnson U.S. Dist. Ct. D.C., Washington; asst. dist. atty. City of Phila., 1982—84; atty., Office Solicitor Gen. US Dept. Interior, 1984—97, acting asst. Solicitor Gen. Indian Legal Activities; counsel U.S. Ho. of Reps. Internat. Rels. Com., 1997—2001; dir. Cmty. Rels. Svc. US Dept. Justice, Washington, 2001—. Trustee St. Lawrence U., 2003—. Office: US Dept Justice Bicentennial Bldg 600 E St NW Ste 6000 Washington DC 20530*

FREEMAN, STACIE DRERUP, sociologist, educator; d. Walter Eugene Drerup and Judy Winstead Mathis; m. Michael Lynn Freeman, May 21, 1993; children: Erin Melton, Wil, Katie, Lillie. BS, U. Tenn., Martin, 1998; MS in Social Work, U. Tenn., Knoxville, 2005. Cert. master social worker Tenn. Residential technician West Tenn. Healthcare, Jackson, 1998—2001, intensive family preservation team leader, 2005, individual therapist; instr. of sociology Bethel Coll., McKenzie, Tenn., 2006—. V.p. Gleason Sch. Assn., Tenn., 2004; mem. Women's Missionary Union, Gleason, 2000. Recipient Chancellors award, Tenn. Bd. of Regents, 2005, 2006. Mem.: Psi Chi (life). Office: Bethel Coll 325 Cherry Ave Gleason TN 38229 Office Phone: 731-352-4000.

FREEMAN, SUSAN TAX, anthropologist, educator, culinary historian; b. Chgo., May 24, 1938; d. Sol and Gertrude Tax; m. Leslie G. Freeman, Jr., Mar. 20, 1964; 1 dau., Sarah Elisabeth. BA, U. Chgo., 1958; MA, Harvard U., 1959, PhD, 1965. Asst. prof. anthropology U. Ill., Chgo., 1965-70, assoc. prof., 1970-78, prof., 1978—, prof. emerita, 1999—, chmn., 1979-82. Rsch. assoc. dept. sociology and anthropology Mont. State U., Bozeman, 1992—; panelist NEH, Council for Internat. Exchange of Scholars; mem. anthropology screening com. Fulbright-Hays Research Awards, 1975-78; mem. ad hoc com. on research in Spain Spain-U.S.A. Friendship Agreement, various yrs., 1977-84; field researcher Mex., 1959, Spain, 1962—, Japan, 1983; instr. Radcliffe Coll. Seminars on Food in History and Culture, 1998. Author: Neighbors: The Social Contract in a Castilian Hamlet, 1970, The Pasiegos: Spaniards in No Man's Land, 1979; assoc. editor: Am. Anthropologist, 1971-73, Am. Ethnologist, 1974-76; editl. bd. Gastronomica, 2000—. Fellow Inst. for the Humanities, U. Ill. Chgo., 1987-88; Wenner-Gren Found. for Anthrop. Research grantee, 1966, 83; NIMH grantee, 1967, 68-71; NEH fellowships, 1978-79, 89-90. Fellow Am. Anthrop. Assn. (nominating com. 1981-82, Centennial Adv. Commn. 1999-2002), Royal Anthrop. Inst. Gt. Britain and Ireland; mem. Soc. for Anthropology of Europe (exec. com. 1987-88), Soc. Spanish and Portuguese Hist. Studies (exec. com. 1990-92), Coun. European Studies (steering com. 1980-83), Internat. Inst. Spain (corporator, bd. dirs. 1982-87, 2000-2003), Centro Estudios Sorianos (hon.), Assn. Anthropologia Castilla y Leon (hon.). Home: PO Box 369 Whitehall MT 59759 Office: U Ill Dept Anthro M/C 027 1007 W Harrison St Chicago IL 60607-7135 Office Phone: 312-413-3570.

FREEMAN-CLARK, J. P. LADYHAWK, vicar, underwater exploration, security and transportation executive, educator, model; b. Berkley, Calif., Feb. 21, 1951; d. Gilbert Richard Freeman (dec.) and P.M. (Ann) Raistrick; children: Jennifer Patricia (dec.), Schne F. (dec.), S. Lancelor (dec.), Simon L.G., Simone D. B., Simba Velvet, Scarlett; m. Joanne Marie Clark-Freeman. BA in English, Davis & Elkins Coll., W.Va., 1973; grad., USAF Air Weapons Controller Sch., Tyndall AFB, Fla., 1973, USAF Air Command and Staff Coll., 1982, U.S. Marine Corps Command and Staff Coll., 1982, Dept. Def. Computer Inst., 1984; M in Aviation Mgmt., Embry-Riddle Aeronautical U., Daytona Beach, Fla., 1986, postgrad., 1986; grad., USAF Air War Coll., Montgomery, Ala., 1988. Cert. EMT; ordained vicar Universal Ch., 2002. Mem. 56th spl. ops. rescue for Southeast Asia NKP Royal Thai Air Force Base, 1974, 75; chief wing radar standardization/evaluation RAF Alconbury, England, 1980-83; commdr. joint U.S. forces Operation Raleigh, 1986; support chief of staff Hdqs. NORAD, Colorado Springs, Colo., 1987-89; dep. base commdr. NATO Hdqs. Allied Forces No. Europe, Norway, 1989-91; chief airport mgmt. divsn. Whiteman AFB, Knob Noster, Mo., 1991-93; dir. spl. projects USAF Acad. Regional Hosp., Colorado Springs, 1993-94; systems performance specialist Colo. Sport & Spine Rehab., Colorado Springs, 1994-95; dir. FLEET Internat. Explorations and Svcs. Co., Colorado Springs, 1995-97; fashion model, 1996—2001; vicar, 2002—. Spl. adv. for anti and counter terrorist security design for 1994 Internat. Olympic Games, Oslo, Norway, 1989-91; designer Automated Provider Credentialing System USAF Acad. Regional Hosp., USAF Acad., Colo., 1993-94; spl. adv. comms. NATO German High Commd., 1977-80; paralyzed Vet. of Am., sr. legist. advocate. U.S. Congress for Colo., Mont. Ut. and Wyo., 2002-05; experience in 37 countries. Poet, poems included in numerous anthologies. Mem. bd. dirs. Johnson County (Mo.) United Way, 1991-93; surgery life support specialist ARC, USAF Acad. Regional Hosp., 1993-95; mem. nat. scholarship com. Red River Valley Fighter Pilots Assn., 1993-96; hosp. vol., med. technician, provider credentialing system designer, oral surgery life support system specialist. Recipient 53 awards and decorations including Defense Meritorious svc. medal with 1 oak leaf cluster, Meritorious Svc. medal with 2 oak leaf clusters, Joint Svc. Commendation medal with 1 oak leaf cluster, air force commendation medal, Armed Forces Expeditionary medal with 2 bronze stars, 2 Humanitarian Svc. medals, 2 Kuwait Liberation medals, 2 Southwest Asia medals; named Adminstrsn. Officer of Yr. USAF, 1986; named one of the six top Support Officers USAF, 1986-87; 1st woman named dir. Fleet Internat. Mem. VFW, DAV, Am. Legion, Air Force Assn., Soc. of Profl. Journalists, Assn. of Old Crows, Lambda Lambda Lambda, Alpha Phi Omega, Iota Beta Sigma. Mem. United Anglican Ch. Avocations: writing, skiing, horseback riding, painting, music. Home: 5913 Amber Station Ave Las Vegas NV 89131

FREEMAN-WILSON, KAREN, retired state attorney general, prosecutor, educational association administrator; m. Carmen Wilson; 1 child, Jordan; 3 stepchildren. BA cum laude, Harvard Coll., 1982, JD, 1985. Pub. defender Lake County; ptnr. Freeman-Wilson and Lewis; dir. Ind. Office Drug Control Policy; atty. gen., chief legal officer State of Ind., judge drug ct. Gary; pub. defender, exec. dir. Ind. Civil Rights Commn.; dep. prosecutor Lake County, 1985—88; exec. dir. Ind. Civil Rights commn., 1989—92; judge Gary City Ct., 1994—2000; atty. gen. State Ind., Indpls., 2000—01; exec. dir. Nat. Drug Ct. Inst., 2002—; CEO Nat. Assn. Drug Ct. Profls., 2002—. Instr. Valparaiso U. Law Sch., Ind. U. Sch. Law; bd. dirs. Conf. for Legal Edn. and Opportunity, Ind. Supreme Ct. Trainer rape awareness Gary Commn. for Women; active Harbor House; bd. dirs. Rainbow Shelter. Democrat. Address: 4900 Seminary Rd Ste 320 Alexandria VA 22311 Business E-Mail: kfwilson@nadcp.org.

FREEMONT, ANDRIA SHAMONA, lab administrator; b. Monroe, La., Mar. 10, 1971; d. Billy Joe Freemont and Barbara Jean Tillman. BS in Chemistry, Jackson State U., 1993. Lic. analyst, State of Ga. Rsch. scientist Upjohn Pharm. Co., Kalamazoo, Mich., 1993-94; chemistry tchr. Carroll H.S., Monroe, 1994-95; extraction chemist Analytical Svcs., Inc., Atlanta, Ga., 1997; sr. forensic toxicologist Ga. Bur. Investigation, Decatur, 1997-2000; adminstr. Biolab Inc., Decatur, 2001—. Lectr. Ga. Prosecution Attys. Coun., Atlanta, 1998-2000; with Howard Hughes Rsch. program, Jackson, Miss., 1989-93. Mem. Am. Chem. Soc., Alpha Kappa Alpha Sorority, Inc.,

Beta Kappa Chi Honor Soc., 1991. Democrat. Roman Catholic. Avocation: reading mystery novels. Office: 121 New St Decatur GA 30030 Home: 1295 Shelton Way Lawrenceville GA 30043-5814 E-mail: afreemont@usa.net.

FREENY, SARAH S., science educator; b. Memphis, Tenn., Mar. 13, 1957; d. John Payne and Joy Smythe Stone; m. Ted M. Freeny, Apr. 12, 1979; children: Emily Elizabeth, Leslie Freeny Houston. MEd., U. Miss., 2003. Lic. Educator Miss. Dept. Edn. Sci. tchr. North Delta Sch., Batesville, Miss., 1994—97, Water Valley (Miss.) H.S., 1997—2000, Oxford (Miss.) Mid. Sch., 2000—. Mem.: NSTA, Nat. Educators Assn., Miss. Sci. Tchrs. Assn. Presbyn. Office: Oxford Mid Sch 501 Martin Luther King Jr Dr Oxford MS 38655 Office Phone: 662-234-2288.

FREESE, CAROLYN LEE, art educator; b. Chgo., Ill., Apr. 4, 1947; d. Allen F and Ruth M McKee; children: Jewel, Philip. BSc in edn., No. Ill. U., 1965—69. Cert. Ill. Tchr. Cert. Art tchr. Simmons Jr. H.S., Auroroa, Ill., 1969—72; sub. tchr. Moose Heart Sch., 1986—87; art tchr. Yorkville Dist. H.S., 1988—; contractor edn. dept. Chgo. Field Mus., 2002—. Sponsor Art Club, Yorkville, Ill., 1988—. Future Educators Am., 1999—2002; visual art curriculum develop. Yorkville Dist. 115, 1990—. Pub. artwork, Nat. History Mag., Nature, Papers in Paleontology, exhibitions include Norris Gallery, St. Charles, Ill., 2004, Ariz. Sonora Desert Mus., Ironwood Gallery, Tucson, 2004, Orleans St. Gallery, St. Charles, 2004, Sprague Gallery, Joliet, Ill., 2005, Ill. Artisans Gallery, 1998—, Anti-Cruelty Soc., Chgo., 2003, 2005, 2006, James R. Thompson Ctr. Atrium, 2004, 2005, 2006, NY State Mus., Albany, 2006; art contbr. Life over Time exhibit, Chgo. Field Mus., 2001—04. Choir and Sunday sch. tchr. Congl. Ch., 1984—99. Named Tchr. of Yr., Yorkville H.S., 2006; recipient Educator of the Month, Coca-Cola Co., 1995, Most Influential Educator, Yorkville H.S. Students, 1996, 1997, 1998, 2001, 2002, 2005. Mem.: Ill. Artisian's Program, Guild of Natural Sci. Illustrators, Ill. Art Edn. Assn. Avocations: horseback riding, birdwatching, paleontology. Home: P O Box 259 400 Washington St Serena IL 60549 Office: Yorkville HS 797 Gamefarm Rd Yorkville IL 60560

FREESE, MELANIE LOUISE, librarian, educator; b. Mineola, N.Y., May 12, 1945; d. Walter Christian and Agnes Elizabeth (Jensen) F. BS in Elem. Edn., Hofstra U., 1967, MA in Elem. Edn., 1969; MLS, L.I. U., 1977. Cert. tchr., N.Y. Bibliographic searcher acquisitions dept. Adelphi U. Swirbul Libr., Garden City, NY, 1973—79, res. desk libr., 1979—83; catalog libr., assoc. prof. Hofstra U. Axinn Libr., Hempstead, NY, 1984—, asst. dean, chair libr. tech. svcs., 1998—2000, sr. cataloger, 2000—. Ch. librarian St. Peters Evang. Luth. Ch., Baldwin, N.Y., 1977—. Founder libr. Salvation Army Wayside Home and Sch. for Girls, Valley Stream, N.Y., 1993. Mem. ALA, Nassau County Libr. Assn. (corr. sec. acad. and spl. librs. divsn. 1986-88, v.p., pres.-elect 1989-90, pres. 1991), Bus. and Profl. Women's Club (pres. Nassau County chpt. 1990-92, 95-97, Woman of Yr. 1994). Republican. Avocations: needlecrafts, knitting, crocheting. Office: Hofstra U Axinn Library 1000 Fulton Ave Hempstead NY 11550-1030 Office Phone: 516-463-6423. Business E-Mail: melanie.l.freese@hofstra.edu.

FREESMEIER, RUTH ANN, music educator, director; b. Breese, Ill., June 21, 1955; d. Vincent Jerome and Marie Theresa Jansen; m. Daniel Paul Freesmeier, Sept. 17, 1977; children: Aaron, Jeris. Degree in Music Edn., SIU, Edwardsville, Ill., 1977. Dir. music/organist Diocese of Belleville St. Frances, Aviston, Ill., 1970—77; organist/choral dir. Trinity Episcopal, Lincoln, Ill., 1983—95; organist Diocese of Peoria-Holy Family, Lincoln, 1987—, dir. music, 1999—; tchr. gen. music Diocese of Peoria-Carroll Sch., Lincoln, 2001—. Grantee, Ctrl. Ill. Light Co., 2006. Mem.: Springfield Choral Soc. Office: Carroll Cath Sch 111 4th St Lincoln IL 62656 Business E-Mail: ruth.freesmeier@holy-familylincoln.com.

FREHM, LYNNE, painter; Exhibited in group shows at Yale U., 1968, Fed. Courthouse, NYC Orgn. Ind. Artists, 1977, Landmark, NYC, 1978, Attitude Art, 1987, Blondies Contemporary Art, 1991—94, Allan Stone, 1995, Beatrice Conde Gallery, 1997, The Fanelli Show, OK Harris Gallery, NYC, 1998, 181st Ann.: An Invitational Exhib. Contemporary Art, Nat. Acad. Mus., NYC, 2006, one-woman shows include Norwalk Mus., Conn., 1973, Bruce Mus., 1974, Ruth Siegel, NYC, 1991, Andre Zarre, 1996, 1997, 2002, Exhibit A, 2000, prin. works include Black Sails, 1975—78, Clown, 1976, King Bill, 1992, Wedding, 1993, Secret Places, 1995—96, Night Sail, 1997. Mailing: 108 Wooster St Apt 3G New York NY 10012-5232*

FREHNER, PATRICIA ANN, education educator, consultant; d. Arlen Joseph and Kenna Bowman Frehner. BA in Art History, U. Utah, Salt Lake City, 1981; MEd, Chapman U., Orange, Calif., 1992; MA in Edn. Adminstrn., Chapman U., 2001; PhD, Capella U., Mpls., 2004. Cert. Pub. Sch. Educator/Adminstr. State Ariz., 1992. Mid. sch. educator Cartwright Sch. Dist., Phoenix, 1992—2005; staff devel. specialist Cartwright Sch. Dist.-Estrella, Phoenix, 2005—. Ednl. cons. Frehner Consulting, Phoenix, 2004—; adj. prof. Ottawa U. Phoenix Ctr., 1995—. One-man shows include exhibition Exhibit 'A' Mask Images, The Faces of Illusion, Sumi-e and Ikebana, Masks, The University of Paper; author: (handbook) Training the Para-educator For the Classroom, Transitional Bilingual Guide for School Districts. Recipient Educator's Award, Wells Fargo Bank, 1997. Mem.: Nat. Assn. Bilingual Edn., Nat. Mid. Sch. Assn., Am. Fedn. Tchrs. (assoc.; Ariz. exec. v.p. 1996). Democrat-Npl. Achievements include research in Developing and implementing acitivities for connecting schools and families in the task of educating children; development of Educational series for educators working with Second Language Learners. Office: Cartwright Sch Dist- Estrella 3733 North 75th Ave Phoenix AZ 85033 E-mail: tfrehner@estr.cartwright.k12.az.us.

FREIBERGER, KATHERINE GUION, composer, retired piano educator; b. Mineral Wells, Tex., May 2, 1927; d. Waldo Burton and Kate Francis (Guion) Lasater; m. John Jacob Freiberger, July 22, 1950. AA, HocKaday Jr. Coll., Dallas, 1946; BA, U. Tex., 1949; MusB, So. Meth. U., 1966. Tchr. Dallas Ind. Schs., 1949-50; pvt. practice piano tchr. Dallas, 1961-85. Composer piano solos and duets, chamber, choral and incidental music. Mem. Dallas Civic Chorus, 1962-69, 72-76, chorus Dallas Civic Opera, 1959; alto soloist Preston Hollow Presbyn. Ch., Dallas, 1956-63; alto soloist, dir. youth choir Churchill Way Presbyn. Ch., Dallas, 1963-70; sole trustee David W. Guion Edn. and Religious Trusts I and II, Dallas, 1978-91; bd. dirs. Dallas Music Tchrs. Assn., 1979-91, Voices of Change, Dallas, 1980s, Dallas Civic Music, 1970s-80s, Durango/Purgatory Music in the Mts., Colo., 1990—, The Dallas Opera, 1989-97;artist in residence com. Ft. Lewis Coll., Durango, Co., 1998—.) Recipient; Elizabeth Mathias Award, Prof. Achievement, 2001. Mem. Musical Arts Club, Mu Phi Epsilon Alumni (First prize for composition 1989, Elizabeth Mathias award 2001). Home: 3825 Hawthorne Ave Dallas TX 75219-2212

FREIDHEIM, LADONNA, dance company director; b. Chgo., Nov. 15, 1967; d. J. Thomas and Janet Rae (Garr) F. BS, U. Ill., 1991. Corp. asst. dir. Advanced Quality Custom Graphics, Champaign, Ill., 1990-91; adminstrv. coord. Classical Symphony Orch., Chgo., 1991-92; adminstrv. asst. Chgo. Sinfonietta, 1992-93; bus. mgr. Organic Theater, Chgo., 1993-94, mng. dir., 1994-96, Hedwig Dances, Chgo., 1997—. Lighting designer, 1992-95; founding mem. Lucid Theatre Co. Bd. dirs. Ministry to the Disadvantaged, Champaign; vol. phys. assistance Rehab. Inst., Chgo., 1993-96; vol. dance instr. Pace Program, Evanston, 1993; vol. Children's Meml. Hosp., Chgo., 1996-99. Roman Catholic. Avocations: lighting design, exercise, bicycling. Office: Hedwig Dances Chgo Cultural Ctr 78 E Washington Chicago IL 60606

FREILICH, JOAN SHERMAN, utilities executive; b. Albany, NY, Nov. 3, 1941; d. Julius and Bess (Bergner) Sherman; m. Sanford J. Freilich, Jan. 24, 1965. AB in French magna cum laude, Barnard Coll., 1963; MA in French, Columbia U., 1964, PhD in French, 1971, MBA in Fin., 1980. Instr. CCNY, Columbia U., NYC, 1965-75; tchr. Walden Sch., NYC, 1970-74; asst. to dean Coll. of New Rochelle, NY, 1974-75, dir. admissions NY, 1975-78; sr. acct. Consol. Edison Co. NY, NYC, 1978-81, mgr. acctg. rsch., 1981-82, contr. power generation, 1982-86, gen. mgr. power generation, 1986-89, exec. asst. to pres., 1989, asst. v.p. corp. planning, 1989-90, v.p. corp. planning, 1990-92, v.p., contr., chief acctg. officer, 1992-96, sr. v.p., CFO, 1996-98, exec. v.p., CFO, 1998—2005, vice chmn., 2005—; also bd. dirs. Consol. Edison, Inc. and Consol. Edison of NY, Inc., NYC, 1997—2005. Author: Paul Claudel's "Le Soulier de satin": A Stylistic, Structuralist and Psychoanalytic Interpretation, 1973; assoc. editor Claudel Studies, 1973-78; contbr. articles to profl. jours. Vice chmn. bd. trustees Coll. New Rochelle; bd. dirs. Women's City Club, NY. Publ. grantee Humanities Rsch. Coun. Can., 1972; Pres.'s fellow Columbia U., 1964, Henry Todd fellow, 1967; recipient scholarship NY State Bd. Regents, 1959, Nat. Merit Found., 1959, Columbia U., 1965; Civic Spirit award Women's City Club of NY, 1999. Mem.: YWCA Acad. Women Achievers, Phi Beta Kappa, Beta Gamma Sigma. Office: Consolidated Edison Co NY 4 Irving Pl New York NY 10003-3598

FREILICHER, JANE, artist; b. NYC, Nov. 29, 1924; d. Martin and Bertha (Niederhoffer); m. Joseph Hazan, Feb. 17, 1957; 1 dau., Elizabeth. AB, Bklyn. Coll., 1947; postgrad., Hans Hoffman Sch. Fine Arts, 1947; MA, Columbia U., 1948. Vis. lectr., critic art schs., colls. One-woman shows include Tibor de Nagy, 1952-68, 98, 2000, 02, 04, 05, 06, John Bernard Myers Gallery, 1971, Fischbach Gallery, 1975, 77, 79-80, 83, 85, 88, 90, 92, 95, Utah Mus. Fine Arts, 1979, Lafayette Coll., 1981, Kansas City Art Inst., 1983, David Heath Gallery, Atlanta, 1990, Reynolds Gallery, Richmond, Va., 1993, Nat. Acad., 2002; group exhbns. include Met. Mus. Art, 1979-80, Denver Art Mus., 1979, Pa. Acad., 1981, Am. Acad. and Inst. of Arts and Letters, 1981, 84-85, Bklyn. Mus. 1984, Yale U., 1986, Tibor de Nagy Gallery, 1992, Whitney Mus., 1955, 72, 95, Whitney Mus., Stamford, Conn., 1999, Artists Eye NAD, 2002, Women of Acad. NAD, 2003; curator Nat. Acad., 2002; represented in permanent collections Met. Mus. Art, Hirschorn Mus., Bklyn. Mus., NYU, Rose Art Mus., Whitney Mus., Cleve. Mus. Art, San Francisco Mus. Art, others; travelling retrospective in Currier Gallery Art, Parrish Mus., Contemporary Arts Mus., McNay Mus., 1986-87; illustrator Turandot and Other Poems, 1953, Paris Review, 1965, Descriptions of a Masque, 1998. Recipient Eloise Spaeth award Guild Hall Mus., East Hampton, N.Y., 1991, Lifetime Achievement award Guild Hall Mus., 1996; AAUW fellow, 1974; Nat. Endowment Arts grantee, 1976; Benjamin West Clinedinst Meml. medal Artists' Fellowship, 1997. Mem. NAD (academician) (Saltus Gold medal 1987, Benjamin Altman landscape prize 1995, Edwin Palmer prize 2003), Am. Acad. Arts and Letters (Gold medal 2005).*

FREIS, KATHLEEN MARIE, educational association administrator; b. New Brunswick, N.J., Jan. 28, 1974; d. Maria Felicia and James Henry Freis. BA, Villanova U., 1996; MA, Columbia U., 2002. Program mgr. Nat. Puerto Rican Forum, Bronx, NY, 2002—03; program dir. Hague Appeal for Peace, N.Y.C., 2003—05; edn. dir. Internat. Ctr. Tolerance Edn., 2005—. Author: Speak English With Confidence and Assurance, 2000; co-editor: United Nations Global Atlas Human Rights Curriculum, 2001; editor: Peace Lessons from Around the World, 2006. Vol. FREE Arts, N.Y.C., 2004—05. Mem.: Hague Appeal for Peace (internat. adv. com. 2003—06), Kappa Delta Pi. Democrat. Avocations: yoga, writing, skiing, painting, tennis. Home: 421 Degraw St 4A Brooklyn NY 11217 Office: Internat Ctr Tolerance Edna 25 Washington St 4th Flr Brooklyn NY 11201 Office Phone: 718-237-6262 ext. 104. Office Fax: 718-237-6264. Personal E-mail: kayemf@gmail.com. Business E-Mail: kfreis@tmf-tolerance.org.

FREISCHLAG, JULIE ANN, surgeon; b. 1955; m. Phillip Roethle; 1 child, Taylor stepchildren: Paul, Matthew. BS, U. Ill., 1976; MD, Rush U., 1980. Asst. prof. in residence dept. surgery UCSD Med. Ctr., San Diego, 1987—89, UCLA Med. Ctr., L.A., 1989—92; chief vascular surgery sect. Wadsworth VA Med. Ctr., L.A., 1989—92, Zablocki VA Med. Ctr., Milw., 1992—96, chief surgery, 1996—98; assoc. prof. surgery, vice-chair sect. vascular surgery Med. Coll. Wis., Milw., 1997—98, prof. surgery, vice-chair sect. vascular surgery, 1997—98; prof. and chief vascular surgery UCLA Med. Ctr., 1998—2003; prof. and chief. divsn. vascular surgery David Geffen Sch. Medicine UCLA, L.A., 1998—2003, dir. Gonda (Goldchmied) Vascular Ctr., 1998—2003; head dept. surgery Johns Hopkins U.; surgeon in chief Hopkins Hosp., dir. surgery, 2003—. Named William Stewart Halsted Prof., 2003; recipient Outstanding Achievement award, Dept. Veterans, 1993. Fellow: ACS; mem.: Assn. Surg. Edn., Assn. VA Surgeons, Assn. Academic Surgery, Soc. Clin. Vascular Surgery, Peripheral Vascular Surgery Soc., Assn. Women Surgeons, Am. Assn. Vascular Surgery, Soc. Vascular Surgery, Soc. Univ. Surgeons, Ctrl. Surg. Assn. Achievements include first woman to be named surgeon in chief of The Johns Hopkins Hospital and Director of the Department of Surgery. Office: Dept Surgery Richard Staf Ross Rsch Bldg 720 Rutland Ave Rm 759 Baltimore MD 21205-2196

FREITAG, ANNA CAROL, endocrinologist, internist; b. Norwalk, Conn., Dec. 26, 1964; d. Arthur Richard and Sofia Boccanfuso Freitag. BA, Smith Coll., 1986; MD, U. Conn., 1994. Diplomate in internal medicine, endocrinology, diabetes and metabolism Am. Bd. Internal Medicine. Assoc. in rsch. Yale Sch. of Medicine, New Haven, Conn., 1986-90, U. Calif. San Diego Sch. of Medicine, 1990; resident in internal medicine N.Y. Hosp.-Cornell Med. Ctr., N.Y.C., 1995-97; fellowship in endocrinology and metabolism Albert Einstein Coll. of Medicine/Montefiore Med. Ctr., Bronx, 1997-99; endocrinologist, internist The Norwalk (Conn.) Med. Group, P.C., 1999—. Instr. endocrinology Albert Einstein Coll. of Medicine, 1998-99; attending physician in medicine and endocrinology Montefiore Med. Ctr., Bronx, 1997-99; instr. phys. diagnosis Cornell U. Med. Coll., N.Y.C., 1997, instr. medicine, G.I. physician asst. program, 1997. Editor-in-chief (newsletter) The Forum, 1997-98; contbr. articles to profl. jours. Fellow ACP; mem. AMA (resident del. 1995-99, reference com. mem. 1997, Physician's Recognition award 1999), Am. Med. Women's Assn. (bylaws com. 1997-99), Women's Med. Soc. of Fairfield County (bd. dirs. 2000--), N.Am. Menopause Soc., Am. Diabetes Assn. (governing coun. Fairfield County), Am. Thyroid Assn., The Endocrine Soc. Republican. Roman Catholic. Avocations: tennis, skiing, scuba, photography, writing. Home: 5 Butternut Ln Norwalk CT 06851-1009

FREITAG, CAROL WILMA, political scientist; Diploma in Dental Hygiene, Northwestern U., 1959; BA, Purdue U., Hammond, Ind., 1988. Registered dental hygienist, Ill. Pvt. practice dental hygiene Henry W. Freitag, D.D.S., Homewood, Ill., 1959-85; mem. group practice Chgo., 1970; faculty, interim dir. dental hygiene Prairie State Coll., Chgo. Heights, Ill., 1971-72; pvt. practice James J. Kreuz, D.D.S., Homewood, 1985-90. Contbr. articles to profl. jour. Chair US Constn. Bicentennial Commn., Village of Matteson, Ill., 1986-89; pres. Matteson Hist. Soc., 1987-89; panel spkr. South Suburban Heritage Assn., Homewood, 1990. Calumet rep. Bicentennial Com. Purdue U., 1988; vis. com. Northwestern Dental Sch., 1997-98; mem. centennial celebration com. Bloom Twp. HS, 2000; mem. Hist. Columbia Found. 2003—. Recipient Key to City, Village of Matteson, 1990, Svc. award Northwestern U., 1980, Good Neighbor award Village of Matteson, 1989, Outstanding Alumni 1950's Decade award Bloom Twp. H.S., 2000. Mem. Am. Dental Hygienists' Assn. (chair Ann. Session Program 1975), Ill. Dental Hygienists Assn. (pres. 1968-69, bd. dirs., Merit award 1979), G.V. Black Soc. (leader, pres. 1997-2001), Evelyn E. Maas Soc. (pres. 1989-90, bd. dirs., Merit award 1993), Northwestern Dental Sch. Alumni Assn. (bd. dirs. 1969-2001, pres. 1977-78, v.p. 1976-77, 90-93), Acad. Polit. Sci., Sigma Phi Alpha, Alpha Chi. Avocation: travel. Home: 117 Oak Trace Ct Chapin SC 29036

FREITAS, BEATRICE B(OTTY), musician, educator; b. Aug. 28, 1938; d. John and Pauline (Esterhay) Botty; m. Lewis P. Freitas, Nov. 30, 1963; children: Roslyn K., John B. BA, Oberlin Coll., 1958; MusM, Boston U., 1959; student, Julliard Sch. Music, 1959—62. Assoc. artistic dir. Hawaii Opera Theatre, Honolulu, pianist, organist, harpsichordist, tchr. Recipient Outstanding Achievement in Area of Arts award, YMCA, 1983.

FREMONT-SMITH, MARION R., lawyer; b. Boston, Oct. 29, 1926; d. Max and Frances (Davis) Ritvo; m. Joseph Miller, Sept. 12, 1948 (div.); children: Beth Miller Johnsey, Keith Lane Miller, E. Bradley Miller; m. Paul Fremont-Smith, July 6, 1961 (dec. July 2000). BA with high honors, Wellesley Coll., Mass., 1948; LLB cum laude, Boston U., 1951. Bar: Mass. 1951, U.S. Supreme Ct. 1979. Instr. dept. polit. sci. Wellesley Coll., 1958-59; asst. atty. gen. Commonwealth Mass., Boston, 1961-62; project dir. Russell Sage Found., Boston, 1963-65; assoc. Choate, Hall & Stewart, Boston, 1964-71, ptnr., 1971-96, sr. counsel, 1997—2004; ret., 2005. Sr. rsch. fellow Hauses Ctr. for Nonprofit Orgns., Harvard U., 1998—; dir. Fed. Tax Inst. New Eng., Aid to Artisans. Author: Foundations and Government: State and Federal Law and Supervision, 1965, Philanthropy and the Business Corporation, 1972, Governing Nonprofit Organizations: Federal and State Law and Regulation, 2004; contbr. articles to profl. jours. Past dir. Ind. Sector, Washington; hon. trustee Carnegie Endowment for Internat. Peace, Washington; trustee Mass. Environ. Trust. Fellow Am. Acad. Arts and Scis., Am. Bar Found., Am. Coll. Tax Counsel, Internat. Acad. Estate and Trust Law; mem. ABA (past chmn. com. on exempt orgns. tax sect.), Am. Law Inst. Office: 2 Internat Pl Boston MA 02110

FRENCH, CANDACE LEE, elementary school educator, music educator; b. Springfield, Mo., Aug. 17, 1956; d. Ronald Lee and Fern Elizabeth Affolter; m. Everett Earl French, Dec. 20, 1980; children: Gregory, Geoffrey. BS in Edn., So. Mo. State U., 1979, MEd in Music Edn., 1987. Tchr. piano, voice pvt. practice, Springfield, Mo., 1978—2003, Willard, 1978—2003; choral dir. Willard Jr. High Sch., 1979—; choir dir. Ctrl. Christian Ch., Springfield, 1995—. Mem.: Music Educators Nat. Conf., Mo. State Tchrs. Assn.

FRENCH, DOROTHY MARIE, music educator; b. Warrenton, Va., Mar. 5, 1964; d. Warren Douglass Thompson, Sr. and Iris Rebecca Thompson; m. Wayne James French; children: Megan, Samantha. BA in Music Edn., Marshall U., 1986. Music tchr. Prince William County Schs., Manassas, Va., 1986—. Pvt. music tchr., Manassas, Va., 1986—99, Gainsville, 2005—; ch. musician Haymarket Bapt. Ch., 1987—. Mem.: Am. Choral Dirs. Assn., Peadmont Music Fedn., Music Educators Nat. Conf. Bapt. Avocation: reading. Home: 7512 Melton Ct Gainesville VA 20155-1801 Office: Stage Presence Music Studio Gainesville VA 20155 Office Phone: 703-393-7608. Personal E-mail: wdfrench@verizon.net.

FRENCH, DORRIS TOWERS BRYAN, volunteer; b. Kissimmee, Fla., May 15, 1926; m. Lawrence Cornwell French, Sept. 7, 1947; children: Layne Bryan, Leyland Bradley. Student, Art Inst., Costa Rica, 1940-42; BFA, Tulane U., 1946; student, U. Mex., 1943-44. Fabric designer Wembley Co., 1945-46; designer silver and jewelry New Orleans, 1945-47; head art dept. pvt. sch., 1947. Columnist From the Mayor's Desk; editor pub. Paw Prints, 1981-93. Founder, v.p. Peoples Animal Welfare Soc., 1977-96; past art dir., coord. internat. gladiola show Garden Club, Binghamton. Mem. AAUW, Zeta Tau Alpha. Avocations: writing, art. Home: 3510 Aransas St Corpus Christi TX 78411-1302

FRENCH, ELIZABETH IRENE, biology professor, musician; b. Knoxville, Tenn., Sept. 20, 1938; d. Junius Butler and Irene Rankin (Johnston) F. MusB, U. Tenn., 1959, MS, 1962; PhD, U. Miss., 1973. Tchr. music Kingsport (Tenn.) Symphony Assn., 1962-64, Birmingham (Ala.) Schs., 1964-66; NASA trainee in biology U. Miss., Oxford, 1969-73; asst. prof. Mobile (Ala.) Coll. (name now U. Mobile), 1973-83, assoc. prof., 1983-94, prof., 1994—. Orch. contractor Am. Fedn. Musicians, 1983—; 1st violin Kingsport Symphony Orch., 1962-64, Birmingham Symphony Orch., 1964-66, Knoxville Symphony Orch., 1955-62, 66-68, Memphis Symphony Orch., 1970-73, Mobile Symphony Orch., 1974—. Pensacola Symphony Orch., Gulf Coast Symphony Orch., Mobile Symphony Players Com., 2001—; concertmaster Riviera Symphony Orch. and Chorus, Ala., 2005—. Violin recitalist Ala. Artists Series, 1978-81, Fairhope (Ala.) Concert Series, 1998. Mem. project Choctaw Nat. Wildlife Refuge, 1997-98. Named Career Woman of Yr., Gayfer's, Inc., 1985. Mem. Assn. Southeastern Biologists, Human Anatomy and Physiology Soc. (nat. com. to construct standardized test on anatomy and physiology), Wilderness Soc., Ala. Acad. Scis. (presenter 1996), Ala. Ornithol. Soc., Mobile Bay Audubon Soc. (bd. dirs. 1997—), Am. Fedn. Musicians, Ala. Fedn. Music Clubs (chmn. composition contest 1986-90, historian 1991-94), Schumann Music Club (pres. 1977-79, 85-87, 94-97, 2000-03, adv. bd. 2005—). Republican. Roman Catholic. Avocations: camping, photography, birdwatching. Home: 36 Ridgeview Dr Chickasaw AL 36611-1317 Office: U Mobile PO Box 13220 Mobile AL 36663-0220

FRENCH, JAE, theater producer, sculptor; b. Bklyn., Jan. 9, 1947; d. Benjamin Louis and Shirley Adel Shareff; m. John Herndon II French, May 30, 2001. BA, Pace U., N.Y.C. Assoc. prodr. Drama Desk Awards, N.Y.C., 2000—; dir. Times Square Group, N.Y.C., 2005—06, Dicapo Opera Group, N.Y.C., 2006. Home: PO Box 368 Newport RI 02840

FRENCH, JULIA MCALLISTER (JUDY MCALLISTER FRENCH), environmental consultant; b. NYC, Dec. 18, 1922; d. Addams Stratton and Home' Catharine McAllister; m. Judson Cull French, Aug. 1, 1951; 1 child, Judson Cull Jr. AA, George Washington U., 1943. Photographic libr. Nat. Geog. Soc., Washington, 1943—54; freelance lectr., cons. on environ., horticulture, L.Am. and Japanese history and culture Bethesda and Rockville, Md., 1955—81; pres. Judy French Assocs., Inc., Rockville, 1982—. Cons., spkr. in field; instigator, leader environ. tours. Contbr. to profl. publs., mags., books and radio and TV programs. Mem. steering com. Potomac Valley Conservation and Recreation Coun., 1962—71; vice chmn. Montgomery County Com., Md. Environ. Trust, 1968—76, chmn., 1977—; chmn. Md. state conservation com. Nat. Capital Area Fedn. Garden Clubs, 1970; mem. planning com., exec. planning coun., solid waste symposium Nat. Bur. Stds., Gaithersburg, Md., 1971; mem. citizen's adv. com. for waste-water treatment facility Montgomery County, 1972; mem. citizen's air pollution workshop com. Rockville Environ. Coalition, 1972; del., mem. water resources citizen adv. com. Met. Washington Coun. Govts. Water Resources Planning Bd., 1973—77; mem. citizen's adv. com. on storm water mgmt. in Watts Br. Basin Dept. Environ. Protection, Rockville, 1974; legis. chmn. steering com. Com. for a More Beautiful Montgomery County, 1977; mem. county line survey com. Md. Environ. Trust, 1978; mem. Solid Waste Energy Recovery Adv. Com., Montgomery County, 1981; mem. adv. coun. for Montgomery County U. Md. Coop. Extension Svcs., 1955—81; mem. adv. com. Green Park Farm, Montgomery County, 1955—81; mem. exec. com. Mt. Vernon Coll. Alumnae Assn., 1955—81; mem. del. Interstate Commn. on Potomac River Basin to Thames/Potomac Seminars, London, 1978; chmn. Vol. Guide Svc., U.S. Nat. Arboretum, 1974—84; v.p. State of Md. People to People, 1992—95, chmn. events and programs Nat. Capitol Area chpt., 1995—99. Recipient Sci. medal, Bausch and Lomb, 1941, award for exceptional achievement in pollution control activity, Md. Environ. Trust, 1972, Jean Ladson Legis. award, Nat. Capital Area Fedn. Garden Clubs, Inc., 1974, Conservation and Protection cert. of appreciation, Md. Environ. Trust, 1976, Environ. Action Leadership medal, Nat. Coun. State Garden Clubs and Sears Roebuck and Co., 1978.

FRENCH, LEURA PARKER, secondary school educator; b. Owensville, Ind., June 4, 1926; d. Arthur William and Mildred Ruth Parker; m. Alvin L. French, July 14, 1947 (dec. Sept. 1996); children: Bruce A., Dwight L. BA cum laude, God's Bible Sch. and Coll., 1950; BS in Edn., Wesleyan U., Marion, Ind., 1952; MS in Edn., Butler U., 1961; postgrad., U. Calif., Davis, 1970—73. Tchr. Moorhead Jr. H.S., Indpls., 1957-58, Washington H.S., Indpls., 1962-63, Bella Vista H.S., Fair Oaks, Calif., 1963-65, Casa Roble H.S., Orangevale, Calif., 1967-84, Valley Oak H.S., Oakdale, Calif., 1987—2004; ret., 2004. Study tours for WWII in Europe, China, Hong Kong, Bangkok, Singapore. Co-author booklet: Goals and Objectives for the San Juan Unified School District's Reading Program, 1972. Active Free Meth. Ch., Indpls., 1953-62, Orangevale, 1963-85, 89-96, Oakdale, 1985-89. Fellow Calif. Tchrs. Assn. Republican. Avocations: reading, research, writing, travel. Home: 209 Snowy Egret Ct Roseville CA 95611 E-mail: leurafrench@aol.com.

FRENCH, MARGARET DIANA, operating room nurse; b. Birmingham, Eng., Dec. 9, 1956; arrived in U.S., 1984; d. Almira Clarissa French; 1 child, Dwane. Diploma, Kingston Sch. Nursing, Jamaica, 1979; BSN, Pace U.,

NYC, 2004. RN, cert. nurse oper. rm., N.Y. Nurse Kingston Pub. Hosp., 1979-83, Jewish Meml. Hosp., Boston, 1984, Brookdale Hosp., Bklyn., 1985—, preceptor oper. room, 1990—; nurse Maimonides Hosp., Bklyn., 1993—. Mem. advance tech./laser/minimally invasive surgery splty. assembly, 1997. Appeared on cover Spectrum Mag., 1993. Mem. Assn. Oper. Rm. Nurses (local edn. com. 1992-93), N.Y. State Nurses Assn. Avocations: reading, travel, going to plays, decorating, cooking, music, tennis. Home: 547 Eagle Ave West Hempstead NY 11552-3725 Office: Brookdale Hosp Med Ctr 1 Brookdale Plz Brooklyn NY 11212-3139

FRENCH, MARGO ANN, financial planner; b. Morehead City, N.C., Jan. 9, 1948; d. Robert Arthur and Dolores (Holtman) F.; m. Edwin A. Vogt, May 29, 1971 (div. Sept. 1975). AS, St. Petersburg Coll., 1975; BA, U. South Fla., 1984; postgrad., U. Tampa, 1985-87; MS in Fin. Svcs., Coll. for Fin. Planning, Denver, 1997; postgrad., Calif. Coll. for Health Sci., 2003—. Cert. fin. planner; registered respiratory therapist. Rsch. technician Merrell Nat. Labs., Cin., 1966-73; respiratory therapist Tampa (Fla.) Gen. Hosp., 1975-86; fin. planner IDS/Am. Express, Tampa, 1986-89; pvt. practice Riverview, Fla., 1989—; corp. dir. of respiratory svcs. Mediplex Group, Wellesley, Mass., 1993—94; pvt. practice fin. planning, 1989—; respiratory cons. HCA South Bay Hosp., 1998—; med. cons., 1997—. Adj. clin. instr. St. Petersburg Jr. Coll., 1978-79, Erwin Tech. Ctr., 1989-91. Mem. Phi Theta Kappa.

FRENCH, MARILYN, writer, critic, historian; b. NYC, Nov. 21, 1929; d. E. Charles and Isabel (Hazz) Edwards; m. Robert M. French, Jr., June 4, 1950 (div. 1967); children: Jamie, Robert. BA, Hofstra Coll., 1951, MA, 1964; PhD, Harvard U., 1972. Secretarial, clerical worker, 1946-53; lectr. Hofstra Coll., 1964-68; asst. prof. Holy Cross Coll., Worcester, Mass., 1972-76; Mellon fellow Harvard U., 1976-77; writer, lectr., 1967—. Author: (criticism) The Book as World: James Joyce's Ulysses, 1976, Shakespeare's Division of Experience, 1981, The Women's Room, 1977, The Bleeding Heart, 1980, Beyond Power: On Women, Men and Morals, 1986, Her Mother's Daughter, 1987, The War Against Women, 1992, Our Father: A Novel, 1994, My Summer with George, 1996, A Season in Hell, 1998, From Eve To Dawn: A History of Women, Vol. I-III, 2002—03, (introductions) Summer and The House of Mirth, 1981, Her Mothers, 1985, A Weave of Women, 1985. Mem. Phi Beta Kappa. E-mail: mfrench187@aol.com.

FRENCH, PATSY, property manager, state representative; b. Randolph, Vt., Aug. 22, 1949; m. Patrick French; 2 children. BS in Edn., U. Vt., 1972. Owner, mgr. rental property; rep. Vt. State Ho. Reps., 2003—. Democrat. Home: 886 Harlow Hill Randolph VT 05060

FRENCH, STEPHANIE TAYLOR, cultural organization administrator; b. Newark; d. William Taylor and Connie V. French; m. Amory Houghton III, Sept. 8, 1979 (div.); children: Christina French Houghton, Amory Taylor Houghton. BA, Wellesley Coll., 1972; MBA, Harvard U., 1978. Freelance on-air performer, prodr. San Francisco and Oakland radio and cable TV stas., 1973-76; dir. European Gallery, San Francisco, 1974-75; acct. exec. Young & Rubican, NYC, 1978-79; acct. supr. Rives Smith Baldwin & Carlberg, Houston, 1980-81; mgr. cultural affairs and spl. programs Philip Morris Cos. Inc., NYC, 1981-86, dir. cultural and contbns. programs, 1986-90, v.p. corp. contbn. and cultural programs bds., 1990—2001; pvt. practice NYC, 2001—05; sr. v.p. US Trust Co., 2005—. Bd. dirs. New Mus. Contemporary Art, Mus. Arts and Design, Parsons Dance Co., Miller Theatre Columbia U., PERFORMA, Works and Process, Shen Wei Dance, Harkness Ctr. for Dance Injuries, Bus. Com. of the Met. Mus. Art, Arts and Edn. Adv. Coun. for Harvard Grad. Sch. Edn., Ballet Tech, Career Transitions for Dancers; bd. adv. com. Bill T. Jones/Arnie Zane Co.; dance com. Juillard Sch.; apptd. mem. Gov. of NY to Empire State Arts Commn., Mayor of NYC to the NYC Econ. Devel. Corp. Mem. Harvard Bus. Sch. Network of Women Alums, Wellesley Club.

FRENETTE, GERALDINE GLORIA, librarian; b. Dearborn, Mich., Dec. 27, 1928; d. Joseph and Victoria Frances Miklosky; div.; 1 child, Emily Frances Kliemann. BA, Wayne State U., 1950; MLS, U. Mich., 1953. Music libr. dept. music and performing arts Detroit Pub. Libr., 1956-72, chief dept. philosphy and edn., 1972—. Mem. Mich. Oriental Art Soc., Detroit Philos. Soc. (historian 1977-84), Philomusica (sec. 1992). Avocations: choral singing, gardening, birdwatching. Home: 6227 N Charlesworth St Dearborn Heights MI 48127-3921 Office: Detroit Pub Libr 5201 Woodward Ave Detroit MI 48202-4093

FRENIER, DIANE M., lawyer; b. Burlington, Vt., June 8, 1957; BS in mgmt. magna cum laude, Rutgers U., 1982, JD, 1986. Bar: NJ 1986. Assoc. Smith, Stratton, Wise, Heher & Brennan, Princeton, NJ, 1986—91, ptnr., 1993—2000; assoc. Hannoch Weisman, Roseland, NJ, 1991—93; ptnr. Reed Smith LLP, Princeton, NJ, 2000—, mem. exec. com. Mem.: NJ State Bar Assn., ABA (mem. bus. law sect.). Office: Reed Smith LLP Princeton Forrestal Village 136 Main St, Ste 250 Princeton NJ 08540 Office Phone: 609-514-5999. Office Fax: 609-951-0824. Business E-Mail: dfrenier@reedsmith.com.

FRENNNING, GINEEN F., elementary school educator; b. Buffalo, N.Y., May 9, 1959; d. Fay and Norma J. Skadan; m. John J. Frenning, July 27, 1985; children: Jillian Frenning, Jaclyn Frenning. AOS Paralegal, Bryant & Stratton, Buffalo, 1979; BA in Polit. Sci., Spanish, Canisius Coll., Buffalo, 1983; M in Multidisciplinary Studies, Buffalo State Coll., 1993. Cert. bus. edn., Spanish, elem. edn., social studies edn. N.Y. Tchr. social studies grade 7 Tonawanda City Schs., NY, 1992—. Mem. youth bd., sch. planning team, publicity coms. Tonawanda City Schs. Vol., Sunday sch. tchr. WNED, Buffalo, 1990; mem. Girl Scouts of Erie, Buffalo, 1994. Grantee, Best Buy, 2004. Mem.: Psi Sigma Alpha. Business E-Mail: gfrenning@tona.wnyric.org.

FRENTZ, YVONNE ELIZABETH, science educator, sports official; b. Balt., June 18, 1947; d. Charles Stanley and Virgie Grace Frentz; children: Sheila Ann Lambert, James Tyler Lambert, Donald Reginald Sanchez. BA in Chemistry, Towson State U., Md., 1970. Cert. advanced profl. Md. Sci. dept. head Balt. City Pub. Schs., 1969—; pres. Raebon Enterprises, Inc., Balt., 2006—. Mem. World Wildlife Fund, 1998—, Am. Indian - Smithsonian, Washington, 2003—, Olympics Supporter, 2000. Sci. grantee, U. Md., 2004. Mem.: Balt. Bd. Ofcls. Women's Sports (field hockey chair 1998—2000, treas. 1980—90), Md. Sci. Tchrs. Assn., Nat. Sci. Tchrs. Assn., Ladies Aux. Democrat. Roman Cath. Avocations: travel, camping, kayaking, sports, reading. Home: 16 Homberg Ave Essex MD 21221 Office: Raebon Enterprises Inc 450 Hillside Dr Mesquite NV 89027

FRERK, LORI ANN, mathematics educator; b. Green Bay, Wis., Dec. 31, 1968; d. John B. and Nancy J. Hansen; m. Brian D. Frerk, July 17, 1992; children: Autumn M., Joshua Lawrence. BS in Math., U. Wis., Green Bay, 1992; EdM, Marion Coll., Fondu Lac, Wis., 2005; M in Leadership, Cardinal Stritch U., Milw., 2006. Tchr. West DePere Schs., Wis., 1992—96, Green Bay Pub. Schs., 1996—. Recipient Farmington Tchr. of Yr., 2004. Business E-Mail: lfrerk@greenbay.k12.wi.us.

FRESCH, MARIE BETH, court reporting company executive; b. Norwalk, Ohio, Jan. 16, 1957; d. Ralph Roy and Vonda Mae (Brunkhorst) Spiegel; m. James R. Fresch, Aug. 5, 1978; 1 child, Alexandra Jane. AS in Bus., Tiffin U., 1977; cert. in ct. reporting, Acad. Ct. Reporting, 1979. Registered profl. reporter, Ohio. Ofcl. reporter Seneca County Common Pleas Ct., Tiffin, Ohio, 1979-80; owner, operator Marie B. Fresch & Assocs., Norwalk, 1980—. Coach indoor and outdoor Soccer teams, 1994-99, summer softball teams, 1994-2004, girls volleyball coach, 1999-2002; leader Girl Scouts Am., 1995-2002, sch. organizer, team leader, 1997-2002, parade organizer, 1998-2002. Recipient Cert. of Merit, Nat. Ct. Reporters Assn., 1990; named Outstanding Leader, Girl Scout Coun., 1998, Outstanding Vol., 2000. Mem. Nat. Ct. Reporters Assn., Ohio Ct. Reporters Assn. (student promotions and pub. rels. coms. 1986-90, dist. rep. 1994-95, fundraising com. 1993-96), NOW (sec. Port Clinton chpt. 1984-86, treas. 1986-87, 91), Am. Legion Aux., Kappa Delta Kappa. Lodges: Order of Eastern Star (esther 1979-81). Democrat. Methodist. Avocations: swimming, biking, gardening, hiking. Home and Office: 47 Warren Dr Norwalk OH 44857-2447 Office Phone: 419-668-7394. E-mail: mfresch@neo.rr.com.

FRESE, BRENDA, women's college basketball coach; b. Cedar Rapids, IA, Apr. 30, 1970; d. Bill and Donna Frese; m. Mark Thomas, Aug. 20, 2005. BS in Comm., U. Ariz., 1993; MS in Athletic Admin., Kent St. U., 1995. Asst. coach Kent St. U., 1994—95, Iowa St. U., 1996—99; head coach Ball St. U., 1999—2001, U. Minn., 2001—02, U. Md., 2003—. Named Coach Yr., MAC Conf., 2000, Big Ten Conf., 2002, Nat. Coach Yr., AP, 2002, NCAA, 2004. Achievements include coaching NCAA Women's Nat. Championship team, 2006. Office: U Md Athletic Dept 9658 Baltimore Ave College Park MD 20740*

FRESH, LINDA LOU, government official; b. Ashland, Pa., June 29, 1957; d. Harold Foster and Norma Jean (Thomas) Geist; m. Bruce Alan Fresh, June 18, 1977; 1 child, Niccole Patricia. AA in Bus. Mgmt., U. Md., Okinawa, Japan, 1981; BS in Psychology, U. Md., Heidelberg, Germany, 1987; EdM in Counseling, Boston U., Heidelberg, 1994. Clinic liaison specialist U.S. Army, Augsburg, Germany, 1985, fin. counselor New Cumberland, Pa., 1989-92, Hanau, Germany, 1992-94; family support program specialist U.S. Army Res., Ft. Belvoir, Va., 1994-95; family life specialist USAF, Washington, 1995-96; family advocacy prevention and edn. specialist USN, Washington, 1996-99; EEO mgr., fed. women's program mgr., mgr. Upward Mobility program, EAP counselor FBI, Washington, 1999—, sexual harassment coord., 2000—. Mem. interagy. com. Fed. Women's Program, Washington, 1999; cert. instr. FBI, 2003. Mem. Mus. for Women in Arts, Women's Meml. With U.S. Army, 1975-78. Mem. AAUW, Women in Mil. Svc. for Am., Women's Army Corps Vets. Assn., Federally Employed Women (regional rep. D.C. Metro region), Women in Fed. Law Enforcement Inc., Toastmasters (competent Toastmaster 2004). Avocations: travel, movies, writing, reading, teaching. Home: 12993 Queen Chapel Rd Woodbridge VA 22193 Office: FBI 935 Pennsylvania Ave NW Washington DC 20535-0001 E-mail: bfresh@comcast.net.

FRESHWATER, SHAWNA MARIE, neuropsychologist, clinical psychologist, cognitive neuroscientist; b. Roseau, Minn., Aug. 10, 1964; d. Robert D. and Andrea K. Porter; children: Michaël, David. BA (magna cum laude), U. Miami, 1995; MS in Clin. Psychology, Nova Southeastern U., Ft. Lauderdale, 1996, PhD, 2000, postdoc., 2002. Lic. Psychology Fla., 2001. Behavioral medicine/health psychology trainee Behavioral Medicine Clin. Rsch. Ctr., U. Miami, 1993—95; psychology intern Cmty. Mental Health Ctr., Nova Southeastern U., Ft. Lauderdale, 1995—96, psychology intern child and adolescent traumatic stress program, 1995—96, psychology intern program for seriously emotionally disturbed, 1995—96; intern Brain Injury Rehab. Program, Ft. Lauderdale, 1996—97, Brief Psychotherapy Program, Ft. Lauderdale, 1997—98, V.A. Hosp., Miami, 1997—99, resident East Orange, NJ, 2000, Cornell Med. Ctr., N.Y.C., 2000, N.Y. Presbyn. Hosp., N.Y.C., 2000; postdoc. fellow, faculty rschr. dept. Neurology U. Fla., Gainesville, 2000—02; dir., pres. Neuropsychological Inst., P.A., Miami, 2002—. Author: (jour. article) Nineteenth Ann. Procs. of Soc. for Behavioral Medicine, 1998, The Clin. Neuropsychologist, 1998, Archives of Clin. Neuropsychology, 1999—2000, Jour. of Clin. Geropsychology, 2001. Mem.: Fla. Soc. Neurology, Internat. Neuropsychological Soc., Nat. Acad. Neuropsychology, APA, Phi Theta Kappa, Phi Kappa Phi, Phi Beta Kappa. Office: Neuropsychological Inst PA 407 Lincoln Rd Ste 12-K Miami Beach FL 33139 Office Phone: 305-538-1585.

FRESTEDT, JOY LOUISE, research scientist, science administrator; b. Oak Park, Ill., Jan. 31, 1959; d. James Albert Machnicki and Wanda Louise (McConnaughhay) Katzman; m. Robert LeVance Frestedt, Aug. 8, 1987; 1 child, Megan Marie. BA Biology, Knox Coll., 1980; PhD Pathobiology, U. Minn., 1996. Rsch. asst. Knox Coll., 1978—80; cytogeneticist Ill. Masonic Med. Ctr., Chgo., 1980—81; med. tech., asst. scientist, rsch. scientist, lab. dir. U. Minn., Mpls., 1981—89, 1991—96; cancer rsch. scientist III, lab. dir. Roswell Park Cancer Inst., Buffalo, 1989—90; rsch. scientist, lab. dir. Mpls. Children's Med. Ctr., 1990—91; grad. fellow, safety expert, sr. scientist Sci. Mus. Minn., St. Paul, 1993—2001; rsch. scientist St. Jude Med. Inc., St. Paul, 1996—97. Adj. faculty Mpls. Cmty. Tech. Coll., 1996-99, North Hennepin CC, 1997-98, Anoka Ramsey CC, 1997-98, Rasmussen Bus. Coll., 1998-99, Medtronic/Mpls. Cmty. Tech. Coll., 1998, Normandale CC, 1999; mgr. Busulfex Clin. Devel. Orphan Med., Inc., 1999-2000; med. info. scientist AstraZeneca Pharm., 2000-01; ops. mgr. clin. trials svc. Mayo Clinic, 2001-03; contract compliance auditor, 3M, 2002; mgr. regional clin. affairs Ortho Biotech Products, LP, 2002-04; v.p. sci. affairs, v.p. clin. affairs, exec. dir. rsch. Humanetics Corp./Minn. Applied Rsch. Ctr., 2004—; adj. faculty Coll. St. Catherine, 2004-06. Co-author: Writing About Science, 1997, Considering Graduate School in the Sciences, 1999; reviewer Jour. Women and Minorities in Sci. and Engring.; contbr. articles to profl. jours. and books Mem.: Soc. Clin. Rsch. Profls., Am. Soc. Clin. Oncologists, Am. Assn. Pharm. Scientists (abstract reviewer for nat. meetings), Assn. Clin. Rsch. Profls. (co-chair programming com., editl. bd. jour. Monitor, coord. CEU), Grad. Women in Sci. (pres. 1996—97, bd. dirs. 1999—2003, chair bd. dirs. 2002—03), Assn. Women in Sci., Sigma Xi. Home: 2708 Vernon Ave S Saint Louis Park MN 55416-1838 Office Phone: 952-974-4370 ext. 232. Business E-Mail: frest001@umn.edu.

FRETWELL, DORRIE SHEARER, retired psychologist; b. Chgo., Jan. 2, 1927; d. Fred Wesley and Alice (Hassinger) Shearer; m. Elbert Kirtley Fretwell Jr., Aug. 25, 1951; children: Barbara, Margaret, James, Katharine. BMus, Drake U., 1948, MMus, 1949; MA in Community/Clin. Psychology, U. N.C., Charlotte, 1985. Lic. psychol. assoc., N.C. Psychologist Carolina Psychol. Resource Ctr., Charlotte, 1985—, Mercy Hosp. Rehab. Ctr., 1989—91, 2003—. Psychologist support group Metrolina Assn. for the Blind, Charlotte, 1991-93. Stress group tchr. Myers Park Presbyn. Ch., Charlotte, 1986-88, deacon, 1988-91; bd. dirs. Charlotte Symphony, 1980-89, Opera Carolina, Charlotte, 1979-89. Mem. AAUW, APA, Am. Acad. of Pain Mgmt., Assn. for Adult Devel. and Aging, Phi Kappa Phi, Pi Kappa Lambda. Avocations: music, reading, travel. Home: 3738 Cypress Club Dr Apt D411 Charlotte NC 28210-2492

FRETZ, DEBORAH MCDERMOTT, oil industry executive; m. Philip Fretz; two children. BS in Biology and Chemistry, Butler U., 1970; MBA, Temple U., 1977. Virologist Merck, Sharp & Dohme; fin. analyst Sun Co., Inc., 1977—, mgr. fin. analysis group, 1985-88, dir. wholesale fuels mktg., 1988-89, gen. mgr. fuels, 1989; pres. Sun Pipe Line Co. and Marine Terminals Sunoco, Inc., 1991—; sr. v.p. logistics Sunoco., Inc., 1994—2000; sr. v.p. lubricants Sunoco, Inc., 1997—2000, sr. v.p. MidContinent Refining, Mktg. and Logistics, 2000; pres., COO Sunoco Logistics Ptnrs., LP, 2001. Dir. GATX Corp., Cooper Tire and Rubber Co. Office: Sunoco Logistics Ptnrs LP Ten Penn Ctr 1801 Market St Ste Sl Philadelphia PA 19103-1699

FREUND, CAROL LOUISE, social services consultant; b. Mineola, N.Y., Feb. 21, 1933; d. Warren Edwin and Dorothy Geraldine (Gilbrech) Darnell; m. William O.H. Freund, Jr., Sept. 16, 1960; children: Carol Burnam, William O.H. III. BA, Allegheny Coll., 1954; MA, John Carroll U., 1982. Tchr. South Euclid Lyndhurst City Schs., Ohio, 1955—57; trainer Episc. Diocese of Ohio, Cleve., 1972—; exec. dir. Hitchcock Ho., Cleve., 1983—87. Mem., v.p. Children's Svcs., Cleve., 1965—75. Pres. Shaker Heights PTA, Cleve., 1975—76, Cleve. Internat. Program, 1980—83; 1st v.p. Coun. Internat. Program, Cleve., 1984—88, pres., 1988—91; mem. Roscoe Village Commn., 1990—, chair, 1992—; pres. Johnson-Humrickhouse Mus. Found., 1999—; trustee Roscoe Village Found., 1993—, pres., 1997—. Recipient cert. of recognition, Coun. Internat. Programs, 1981, Founding Trustee award, Edn. for Freedom of Choice in Ohio, 1982, Outstanding Vol. Svc. award, Cleve. Internat. Program, 1983, Vols. are the Heart of Hospice award, Ohio Hospice and Palliative Care, 2004, Blue Citation award, Allegheny Coll., 2005. Episcopalian. Avocation: flower arranging. Home: 699 High St PO Box 1240 Coshocton OH 43812-6240

FREUND, DEBORAH A., academic administrator; AB, Washington U., 1973; MPH, U. Mich., 1975, MA in Applied Econs., 1975, PhD in Econs., 1980. Rsch. asst. Washington U. Sch. Medicine, 1971—73; intern to dep. commr. for med. assistance N.Y. State Dept. Social Svcs., 1974; program asst. The Robert Wood Johnson Found., 1975—76; rsch. assoc. U. Mich., Mich., 1976—77; IPA Nat. Ctr. for Health Svcs. Rsch., Dept. Health and Human Svcs., 1977—79; core faculty mem. U. N.C., Chapel Hill, 1979—88, asst. prof., assoc. prof., 1979—88, dir. doctoral program, 1987—88; chair Sch. Pub. and Environ. Affairs Ind. U., 1987—88, dir. The Bowen Rsch. Ctr., 1989—99, assoc. dean for acad. affairs Bloomington, 1992—94, vice chancellor acad. affairs, 1994—99; prof. Syracuse (N.Y.) U., 1999—, vice chancellor, provost for acad. affairs, 1999—. Adj. asst. prof. Duke U., 1979—84; adj. prof. Ind. U., 1988—94, U. N.C., Chapel Hill, 1988—, SUNY, 2002—. Mem. editl. bd.: PharmacoEconomics, 1993—, Health Econs., 1994—2003, Med. Care Rsch. and Rev., 1994—2003; contbr. chapters to books, articles to profl. jours. Recipient Jay S. Drotman Meml. award, 1981, The Elvehjam Meml. medal, 1990, Kershaw Rsch. award, 1991; fellow, Kellogg Found. Nat. Leadership, 1986—89. Fellow: Nat. Acad. Social Ins.; mem.: N.Y. Acad. Medicine. Home: 5213 Silver Fox Dr Jamesville NY 13078 Office: Ctr for Policy Rsch 426 Eggers Hall Syracuse Univ Syracuse NY 13244-1020

FREUND, DEBORAH MIRIAM, transportation engineer; b. Bklyn., Apr. 9, 1957; d. Harry and Bertha (Fried) F.;m. Garey Douglas White, Feb. 22, 1981. BSCE, Washington U., 1979, MSc, 1982. Registered profl. engr., Tex. Grad. rsch. asst. Washington U., St. Louis, 1979-81; transp. planning engr. Mid-Am. Regional Coun., Kansas City, Mo., 1981-83; civil engr. Fed. Hwy. Adminstrn., Washington, 1983-85, rsch. hwy. engr., 1985-90, transp. specialist, 1990-92, sr. transp. specialist, 1992—99; sr. transportation specialist Fed. Motor Carrier Safety Admin., 2000—. Nat. tech. expert for vehicle rsch., 2001—; mem. com. operator and vehicle performance and simulation Transp. Rsch. Bd., Washington, 1993—96, mem. com. on vehicle user characteristics, 1997—2003, mem. com. on frt. econs. and regulation, 2000—, mem. com. on truck and bus safety, 2003—; presenter in field. Recipient award for meritorious achievement, Sec. of Transp., 1996, Forest R. McFarland Award, Soc. of Automotive Engrs., 2003; fellow, Coun. for Excellence in Govt., Washington, 1995—96. Mem. ASCE (sec. hwy. divsn. rsch. com. 1988-90), Soc. Automative Engrs. (co-chair total vehicle com. 1997-2003, vice chair comml. vehicle maintenance com. 2003-04, chair 2004—, mem. at-large comml. vehicle engring. activity exec. com. 2004—), Inst. Transp. Engrs., Sigma Xi (assoc.). Achievements include leadership in research on commercial motor vehicle driver safety; innovation in pavement infrastructure information systems. Office: Fed Motor Carrier Safety Adminstrn 400 7th St SW Washington DC 20590-0001 Office Phone: 202-366-4009. Business E-Mail: deborah.freund@dot.gov.

FREUND, ELAINE M., literature and language educator; b. Waterloo, Ind., Jan. 2, 1943; d. Joseph George and Vivian Marie Freund. BA in English, St. Louis U., Md., 1967; MA in Humanities, SUNY, Buffalo, 1980. Cert. tchr. Ill. and Mo. Tchr. St. Clare Parish, O'Fallon, Ill., 1967—69, St. Pius X H.S., Festus, Mo., 1969—74, St. Edmond H.S., Ft. Dodge, Iowa, 1974—75, Gibault H.S., Waterloo, Ind., 1975—78; sec. to provincial Red Bud, Ill., 1978—83; tchr. Gibault H.S., Waterloo, 1984—. Recipient M. Cathlin Casey award, St. Louis U., 1998. Mem.: Ill. Assn. Tchrs. of English, Nat. Coun. Tchrs. of English. Roman Catholic. Avocations: theater, travel, films, bowling. Home: 760 Marney Ln Waterloo IL 62298 Office Phone: 618-939-3883. Office Fax: 618-939-7215. E-mail: freund@adorers.org.

FREUND, EMMA FRANCES, technologist; b. 1922; d. Walter R. and Mabel W. (Loveland) Ervin; m. Frederic Reinert Freund, March 4, 1953; children: Frances, Daphne, Fern, Frederic. BS, Wilson Tchrs. Coll., Washington, 1944; MS in Biology, Cath. U., Washington, 1953; MEd in Adult Edn., Va. Commonwealth U., 1988. Tchr. math and sci. DC Sch. Sys., Washington, 1944-45; technician in parasitology lab. U.S. Dept. Agr., Beltsville, Md., 1945-48; histologic technician dept. pathology Georgetown U. Med. Sch., Washington, 1948-49; clin. lab. technician Kent and Queen Anne's County Gen. Hosp., Chestertown, Md., 1949-51; histotechnologist Med. Coll. Va. Hosp., Richmond, 1951—. Cons. profl. meetings and workshops; exam. coun. Nat. Credentialing. Agy. Med. Lab. Pers. Co-author: (mini-course) Instrumentation in Cytology and Histology, 1985; editor Histo-Scope Newsletter. Asst. den leader Robert E. Lee coun. Boy Scouts Am., 1967-68, den leader, 1968-70. Mem. AAAS, NAFE, AAUW, APS, Am. Mgmt. Assn., Am. Soc. Clin. Lab. Sci. (rep. to sci. assembly histology sect. 1977-78, chmn. 1983-85, 89-96), Va. Soc. Med. Tech. (Richmond chpt. corr. sec. 1977-78, bd. dirs. 1981-82, pres. 1984-85), Va. Soc. Histotech. (pres. 1994-96), Nat. Credentialing Agy. (clin. lab. specialist in histotech., clin. lab. supr. clin. lab. dir.), NY Acad. Scis., Am. Assn. Clin. Chemistry (assoc.), Am. Soc. Clin. Pathology (assoc., cert. histology technician), Nat. Geog. Soc., Va. Govtl. Employees Assn., Nat. Soc. Histotech. (by-laws com. 1981—, C.E.U. com. 1981—, program com. regional meeting 1984, 85, 87, 97, 2000, chmn. regional meeting 1987, program chmn. state meeting 1998-99, Conv. scholarship award 1997, Clin. Chemists' Recognition award 1995, 98, 2002, 04), Am. Mus. Natural History, Smithsonian Inst., Am. Mgmt. Assn., Am. Chem. Soc., Am. Soc. Quality, Clin. Lab. Mgmt. Assn., Van Slyke Soc., Soc. Human Resource Mgmt., Nat. Soc. Hist. Preservation, Math. Assn. Am., Sigma Xi, Phi Beta Rho, Kappa Delta Pi, Phi Lambda Theta. Home: 1315 Asbury Rd Richmond VA 23229-5305

FREUND, KRISTEN P., bank executive; 1 child. Student in Bus., Mich. State U.; MBA, Northwestern U. Kellogg Sch. Mgmt. With Exch. Nat. Bank; chief adminstrv. officer LaSalle Bank, grp. sr. v.p. Named one of Top 40 Under 40, Crain's Chgo. Bus., 2006. Office: LaSalle Bank Hdqs 135 S LaSalle St Chicago IL 60603*

FREUND, PEPSI, artist, art educator; b. NYC, Oct. 17, 1938; d. Patrick and Mary (Walsh) Gibbons; m. Frank Freund, Oct. 8, 1960; children: Gerard, Theresa. Tchr. Venice Art League, Sarasota Arts Coun. Workshop presenter, tchr., Sarasota, Fla., Venice (Fla.) Art Ctr., Smithtown Art Coun., East End Arts Coun., Riverhead, N.Y.; series demonstrator Art in the Park, Sarasota, Fla. Exhibitions include Goodard Ctr. for Visual Arts, Ardmore, Okla., U. Gallery, U. S.W., Sewanee, Tenn., Mus. of the S.W., Midland, Tex., Richmond Art Mus., Ind., Owatonna Arts Ctr., Minn., Kimball Art Ctr., Park City, Utah, Palm Ave. Gallery, Sarasota, Fla., Soundview Art Gallery, Port Jefferson, N.Y., Blue Door Gallery, NY; illustrator God's Tomatoes, Abuse, Offenses, Jezebel Spirit; prin. works include posters and art work in Ireland and England. Civil activist Elmont (N.Y.) Cmty., 1983. Mem. Nat. Art League (sec. 1986-87), Malverne Artists (newsletter editor), Floral Park Art League (newsletter editor), Nat. Assn. Women Artists (rev. com. 1993-94), Aquarelle, 30 Artists (pres.), East End Arts Assn. (Plein Air Leader). Avocations: reading, writing, swimming, evangelism. Home: 15 Penn Commons Yaphank NY 11980-2025 Personal E-mail: Pepsi2231@juno.com.

FREY, JOANNE ALICE TUPPER, art educator; b. Wakefield, Mass., Jan. 16, 1931; d. Arthur Andrew Tupper, Elva June Goddard, Joanne Alice Tupper; m. John Oscar Frey, June 14, 1953 (dec. Oct. 2000); children: David J., Donald A., Dale R., Alexandria Brennan. Grad. honors, Vesper George Sch. Art, Boston, 1951; student art history, NTL Art Gallery, London, 1979. Tchr. art Wishing Well Cards, Everett, Mass., 1951—54, Sarrin Studio, Wakefield, Mass., 1960—96; tchr. art oil, acrylic, and watercolor Wakefield H.S., Wakefield, 1997—. Antique and current doll authority; lectr. in field. Asst. resident dir. Bolt Home for Women, Wakefield, Mass., 1996—; bd. dirs. The Hartshorne House. Mem.: Collie Fancier League of N.E., The Kosmos Club (decorator 1997—). Republican. Congregationalist. Avocations: painting, reading, walking, gardening, art history. Home: 701 Haverhill St Reading MA 01867

FREY, JULIA BLOCH, language educator, art historian, educator; b. Louisville, July 25, 1943; d. Oscar Edgeworth and Jean Goldthwaite (Russell) Bloch; m. Roger G. Frey, Dec. 27, 1968 (div. Mar. 1976); m. Ronald Sukenick, Mar. 9, 1992 (dec. 2004); m. Guust Nolet, Mar. 8, 2006. BA,

Antioch Coll., 1966; MA, U. Tex., 1968; MPhil, Yale U., 1970, PhD, 1977. Instr. Brown U., Providence, 1972-73; chargée de cours U. Paris, 1974-75; lectr. Yale U., New Haven, 1975-76; prof. Inst. Internat. Comparative Law, U. San Diego, Paris, 1979-89, adminstrv. dir., 1989; prof. French, art history U. Colo., Boulder, 1976—2001, prof. emeritus, 2002—, dir. undergrad. studies, 1985-95, assoc. chmn. for grad. studies, 1996-97, 98-99, chmn., 1999. Guest prof. Sarah Lawrence Coll., Bronxville, N.Y., 1983; curator Toulouse-Lautrec Met. Mus. Art Denver Art Mus., 1999, Toulouse-Lautrec, Museo Vittoriano, Rome, 2003-04. Author: Toulouse-Lautrec, a life, 1994, Toulouse-Lautrec l'homme qui aimait les femmes, 1996; editor: Gustave Flaubert's La Lutte du Sacerdoce et de L'Empire (1837), 1981; contbr. articles and monographs to profl. publs., chpts. to books; translator: René. Recipient Conn. Grad. Study award, 1970-73; grantee NDEA, 1967, Brown U. Research and Travel, 1973, Boulder Arts Com., 1979, 80, Ctr. for Applied Humanities, 1985, S.W. Inst. for Research on Women, 1985-86, NEH, 1986; fellow NDEA, 1966-68, Yale U., 1968-72, Gilbert Chinard, Inst. Français de Washington, 1977, Big 12 2000, Humanities Rsch. Ctr., Australian Nat. U., 2000; Pen Ctr. USA West Lit. award for non-fiction, 1995; Finalist Nat. Book Critics Cir. award for Biography, 1994. Mem. MLA, PEN U.S.A., Coll. Art Assn., Yale Club. Unitarian Universalist. Home: 158 Herrontown Rd Princeton NJ 08540 E-mail: julia.frey@aya.yale.edu.

FREY, LUCILLE PAULINE, social studies educator, consultant; b. Huggins, Mo., Aug. 1, 1932; d. Albert Raymond and Gladys Pearl (Maxville) F. BS in Edn., Southwest Mo. State U., 1955; MA in English, Mo. U., 1963; MAT, Alaska Pacific U., 1975; PhD in Women's Studies, Union Grad. Inst., 1985. Tchr. Tex. County Rural Schs., Plato, Mo., 1949-53, Sullivan (Mo.) Pub. Schs., 1953-57, Anchorage Pub. Schs., 1957-70, social studies coord., 1970-75; ednl. cons. The Learning Tree, Alaska, 1975-85. Adj. prof. U. Alaska, 1970-77; owner Women's Bookstore, Anchorage, 1981-84; comml. fisherwoman Net Prophets, Bristol Bay, Alaska, 1980-85; real estate salesperson Dynamic Properties, Anchorage, 1989-94, Century 21 Peterson, Hermitage, Mo., 1995-2004. Author: (textbook) Eyes Toward Icebergia, 1963; editor: Women of Alaska Workbook, 1974, Alaska Studies Curriculum, 1975, Athabaskan Curriculum, 1980. Founding mem. Alaska Women's Edn. Caucus, Anchorage, 1970; mem. Alaska Women's Polit. Caucus, Anchorage, 1972; organizer various state edn. confs., 1976-83, women's conf., Alaska, 1982. Recipient Gov's. Vol. award, Alaska, 1984; named to Women's Hall of Fame, Alaska, 1991. Mem. AAUW, NOW, NEA (Women's Right award 1979, Renowned Alaskan award, 1986), Profl. Women's Assn. (sec.), Mo. Realtor's Assn., Mel Carnahan Club. Progressive. Avocations: historian, political activist, gardening, birdwatching, travel. Home: RR 1 Box 1965 Urbana MO 65767-9639

FREY, MARGO WALTHER, career counselor, columnist; b. Watertown, Wis., July 1, 1941; d. Lester John and Anabel Marie (Bergin) Walther; m. James Severin Frey, June 29, 1963; children: Michelle Marie Frey Loberg, David James. BA in French, Cardinal Stritch Coll., 1963; MS in Ednl. Psychology, U. Wis., Milw., 1971; EdD in Adult Edn., Nova U., 1985. Nat. bd. cert. career counselor; approved profl. counselor, Wis. Acad. counselor biology dept. Ind. U., Bloomington, 1975-76; dir. career planning and placement Cardinal Stritch Coll., Milw., 1977-89; pres. Career Devel. Svcs., Inc., Milw., 1989—. Weekly columnist Milw. Journ. Sentinel, 1994-95, 98—. Mem. Bloomington (Ind.) women's commn. com. on employment assessment Displaced Homemakers Task Force, 1975. Named to Practitioner's Hall of Fame, Nova U., 1985. Mem. ASTD (bd. dirs. 1992), Wis. Career Planning and Placement Assn. (bd. dirs. 1987), Wis. Assn. Adult and Continuing Edn. (bd. dirs. 1983-85), Milw. Coun. Adult Learning, Human Resource Mgmt. Assn., Tempo (bd. dirs. 1995-97). Avocations: reading, swimming. E-mail: margocds@execpc.com.

FREY, MARY ELIZABETH, artist; b. Yonkers, N.Y., Nov. 25, 1948; d. Harold and Matilda F.; m. William M. Bennett, Jan. 31, 1976; children: Jacob F. and Nicholas F. BA in Fine Arts, Coll. New Rochelle, 1970; postgrad., Pratt Inst., 1970-71; MFA in Photography, Yale U., 1979. Instr. photography Project Art Ctr., Cambridge, Mass., 1975-77, dir. photography, 1976-77; prof. photography Hartford Art Sch., West Hartford, Conn., 1989—. NEA, Washington, 1994; vis. artist Harvard U., Cambridge, 1984, Cooper Union, N.Y.C., 1985, Yale U., New Haven, 1986, NYU, N.Y.C., 1987, Cornell U., Ithaca, N.Y., 1988, Northfield Mt. Hermon, Northfield, Mass., 1989, Mills Coll., Oakland, Calif., 1989, Hampshire Coll., 1992; Harnish vis. artist Smith Coll., Northampton, Mass., 1994-95; guest lectr. Hudson River Mus., Yonkers, N.Y., 1984, Hartford Art Sch., 1988, Smith Coll. Mus. Art, Northampton, 1994. One-woman shows include Panopticon Gallery, Boston, 1974, Hollins College (Va.) Art Gallery, 1977, Project Art Ctr., Cambridge, Mass., 1979, Hudson River Mus., Yonkers, N.Y., 1984, Blue Sky Gallery, Portland, 1985, ZONE Art Ctr., Springfield, Mass., 1988, Ledel Gallery, N.Y.C., 1989, Arno Maris Gallery, Westfield, Mass., 1991, Springfield (Mass.) Mus. of Fine Arts, 1993, Ariz. State U., 1994, Laelia Mitchell Gallery, Boston, 1995, Marlboro (Vt.) Coll., 1998; group shows include Commonwealth Armory, Boston, 1974, Project Art Ctr., Cambridge, 1975, Boston City Hall, 1976, Yale U., New Haven, 1977, Webb & Parsons Gallery, New Bedford, Mass., 1978, Pleasant St. Gallery, Amherst, Mass., 1979, Hampshire Coll., Amherst, 1980, Light Gallery, N.Y.C., 1981, Memphis Acad. Art, 1982, Carpenter Ctr. for Visual Arts, Cambridge, 1984, Blue Sky Gallery, Portland, 1985, Mus. Modern Art, N.Y.C., 1986, Aperture Gallery, N.Y.C., 1986, 87, Real Art Ways, Hartford, Conn., 1988, MS Gallery, Hartford, 1990, Smith Coll. Mus. Art, Northampton, 1992, 100 Pearl St. Gallery, Hartford, 1993, Artspace, New Haven, 1994, ICP-Midtown Eye of the Beholder, 1997, Coll. of N.J., 2002, Smithsonian Instn., 2001, others; represented in permanent collections at Art Inst. Chgo., Mus. Fine Arts, Houston, Smith Coll. Mus. Art, Northampton, Internat. Polaroid Collection, Cambridge, Mus. Modern Art, N.Y.C., Coca-Cola Corp., Atlanta, Bank of Boston, Springfield Tech. C.C., Avon Corp., others. Home: 215 Crestview Cir Longmeadow MA 01106-2327

FREY, YVONNE AMAR, librarian; b. Chgo., Nov. 23, 1945; d. Wesley Francis and Yvonne Adele (Van Lent) Amar; m. Charles Jerry Frey, Sept. 20, 1975; 1 son, Benedict Francis Charles. A.B. with honors, Loyola U., Chgo., 1967; M.A., Johns Hopkins U., 1969; M.A. in Library Sci., Rosary Coll., 1981. Cert. tchr., Ill. Grad. asst. tchr. Johns Hopkins U., Balt., 1968-69; tchr. English, Montini High Sch., Lombard, Ill., 1970-73; instr. Western Ill. U., Macomb, 1973-78; antique dealer Frey's Tory Peddler, 1978—; instr. Bradley U. Peoria, Ill., 1981-82; supr. reference Ill. Valley Library System, Peoria, 1982-84; head children's room Peoria Pub. Library, 1985—89; dist. libr. Peoria Pub. Schs., 1989-2003; libr. Richwoods H.S., Peoria, 2003—; instr. children's lit. Ill. Cen. Coll., 1987—1997. Author: One-Person Puppetry: Streamlined and Simplified, 2005; contbr. articles and revs. to profl. jours. Woodrow Wilson scholar, 1967, Johns Hopkins U. scholar, 1968. Mem. ALA, Ill. Library Assn., Peoria Hist. Soc. (docent 1981—), Beta Phi Mu, Delta Kappa Gamma Soc. Roman Catholic. Home: 6523 N Imperial Dr Peoria IL 61614-2601

FREYD, JENNIFER JOY, psychology professor; b. Providence, Oct. 16, 1957; d. Peter John and Pamela (Parker) F.; m. John Q. Johnson, June 9, 1984; children: Theodore, Philip, Alexandra. BA in Anthropology magna cum laude, U. Pa., 1979; PhD in Psychology, Stanford U., 1983. Asst. prof. psychology Cornell U., 1983-87, mem. faculty coun. reps., 1986-87; assoc. prof. psychology U. Oreg., Eugene, 1987-92, mem. exec. com. Inst. Cognitive and Decision Scis., 1991—94, prof., 1992—, mem. dean's adv. com., 1990-91, 92-93, mem. exec. com. Ctr. for the Study of Women in Soc., 1991-93, mem. child care com., 1987-89, 90-91, mem. instnl. rev. bd., 2002—, dir. undergrad. studies dept. psychology, 2004—, mem. exec. com. dept. psychology, 2006—. Author: Betrayal Trauma: The Logic of Forgetting Childhood Abuse, 1996 (Disting. Publ. award Assn. of Women in Psychology 1997, Pierre Janet award Internat. Soc. for Study Dissociation 1997), Spanish edit., 2003; co-editor: (with A.P. De Prince) Trauma and Cognitive Science: A Meeting of Minds, Science, and Human Experience, 2001; mem. editl. bd. Jour. Exptl. Psychology: Learning, Memory, and Cognition, 1989-91, Gestalt Theory, 1985—, Jour. of Aggression, Maltreatment, and Trauma, 1997—, Jour. of Psychopathology and Behavioral Assessment, 2001-2003, Jour. Trauma Practice, 2003—, Jour. of Trauma and Dissociation, 1999-2005, assoc. editor, 2004, editor, 2005—; guest reviewer Am. Jour. Psychology, Am. Psychologist, others; contbr. articles to profl. jours. Grad. fellowship NSF, 1979-82, Univ. fellowship Stanford U., 1982-83, Presdl. Young Investigator award NSF, 1985-90, IBM Faculty Devel. award, 1985-87, fellowship Ctr. for Advanced Study in the Behavioral Scis., 1989-90, John Simon Meml. fellowship Guggenheim Found., 1989-90, Rsch. Scientist Devel. award NIMH, 1989-94, Pierre Janet award Internat. Soc. Study of Dissociation, 1997, 05, Psychologist-Scientist of Yr. award Lane County Psychologists Assn., 2006. Fellow AAAS, APA (liaison divsn. 35 to sci. directorate 1998—, chair sci. com. trauma psychology divsn. 2006—), Am. Psychol. Soc.; mem. Psychonomic Soc., Internat. Soc. Study of Traumatic Stress, Sigma Xi. Office: Dept Psychology 1227 U Oreg Eugene OR 97403-1227 Business E-Mail: jjf@dynamic.uoregon.edu.

FREYER, DANA HARTMAN, lawyer; b. Pitts., Apr. 17, 1944; m. Bruce M. Freyer, Dec. 21, 1969. Student, L' Institut De Hautes Etudes Internationales, Geneva, 1963-64; BA, Conn. Coll., 1965; postgrad., Columbia U., 1968, JD, 1971. Bar: NY 1972, Ill. 1974, US Dist. Ct. (no. dist.) Ill. 1974, US Ct. Appeals (7th cir.) 1976, US Supreme Ct. 1977, US Dist. Ct. (so. dist.) NY 1978, US Dist. Ct. (ea. dist.) NY 1981, US Ct. Appeals (2d cir.) 1982. Staff atty. Legal Aid Soc. Westchester County, Mt. Vernon, NY, 1971-72; assoc. Friedman & Koven, Chgo., 1973-77, Skadden, Arps, Slate, Meagher & Flom, LLP, NYC, 1977-88; spl. counsel Skadden, Arps, Slate, Meagher & Flom, NYC, 1988-93, ptnr., arbitration and alternative dispute resolution, 1994—, mem. internat. arbitration group, head corp. compliance practice. Pres. Westchester Legal Services, Inc., White Plains, NY, 1985-87, bd. dirs., 1978-98; US Coun. for Internat. Bus. Arbitration Com.; adv. bd. World Arbitration and Mediation Report; mem. Coun. on Fgn. Rels.; lectr. in the field; leader in dispute resolution, Practical Law Company's Global Counsel Dispute Resolution Handbook, 2003-04. Contbr. articles to profl. publs.; author and co-author (articles in profl. jours. and publs.), mem. adv. bd. Bur. of Nat. Affairs' Alternative Dispute Resolution Report, 1987—90, Am. Arbitration Assn. Dispute Resolution Jour., 1996—, World Arbitration and Mediation Report, 1990—. Bd. legal advisors Legal Momentum, 2002—. Named one of World's Leading Expert in Commercial Arbitration, Euromoney, 50 Top Women Litigators in Am., Nat. Law Jour. Fellow Chartered Inst. Arbitrators; mem. ABA, Bar Assn. of City of NY, Internat. Bar Assn., adv. and spl. coms. on Alternative Dispute Resolution, Internat. Bar Assn.; co-chair and co-founder, Global Partnership for Afghanistan, 2002-; arbitrator, mem. corp. coun. com. and law com., Am. Arbitration Assn. Office: Skadden Arps Slate Meagher & Flom LLP 4 Times Sq New York NY 10036 Office Phone: 212-735-2506. Office Fax: 917-777-2506. Business E-Mail: dfreyer@skadden.com.

FREYER, VICTORIA C., fashion and interior design executive; b. Asbury Park, N.J. d. Spiros Steven and Hope (Pappas) Pappaylion; m. Cyril Steven Arvanitis, Dec. 26, 1950 (div. 1975); children: Samuel James, Hope Alexandra. BA, Georgian Court Coll., 1950; student, N.Y. Sch. Interior Design, 1971-72. Mgr. Homestead Restaurant, Ocean Grove, N.J., 1946-58; art supr. Lakewood (N.J.) Pub. Schs., 1950-51; interior designer London, 1975-76, F. Korasic Assocs., Oakhurst, N.J., 1977-78; owner, operator Virginia Interiors, McLean, Va., 1974-90; interior designer Anita Perlut Interiors, McLean, 1986; owner, operator Victoria Freyer Interiors, McLean, 1986—; fashion cons. Nordstrom Splty. Store, McLean, 1988-92, fashion seminar coord. Tysons Corner, Va., 1992—. Lectr. Girl Scouts U.S., Rep. Women of Capitol Hill, Washington Hosp. Ctr., Women's Am. ORT, Nat. Assn. Cath. Women, Bethesda Naval Hosp., NIH, others. Pres. Monmouth County Med. Aux., 1964; originator 1st lecture series Monmouth Coll., Long Branch, N.J., 1965; guest moderator Alexandria (Va.) Hosp. Series, 1988; mem. Women's Symphony Com., Washington, 1988—; guest speaker Girl Scouts U.S. Coun. Nation's Capitol, 1988-90, Nuclear Energy Coun., 1989, pers. dept. CIA, 1989-90, Internat. Women's Group Washington, 1989-90. Recipient Recognition awards Girl Scout Coun. Nation's Capitol, 1990, No. Region Beta Pi, 1991, Beta Sigma Pi, 1991. Mem. AAUW (program chmn. 1968, guest speaker many orgns.). Greek Orthodox. Avocations: greek and roman archeology and antiquities, painting, gourmet cooking, travel. Home and Office: 44 N Sugar Rd Apt 315 New Hope PA 18938

FREYERMUTH, VIRGINIA KAREN, art educator; BFA cum laude, Boston U., 1973, MFA, 1975; edn. cert., Suffolk U., 1975; PhD in Interdisciplinary Studies, Art Edn., Union Inst. and U., 2003. Cert. art tchr., Mass. Grad. asst. Boston U., Mass., 1973-75; art tchr. Quincy Pub. Sch., Mass., 1975-76, Plymouth Pub. Sch., Mass., 1976-78, 83-85; painting tchr. Brockton Fuller Mus. Art, Mass., 1978-79; art coord. grades K-12 Duxbury Pub. Sch., Mass., 1985-99; vis. lectr. art edn. U. Mass., Dartmouth, Mass., 1999—2004; pres. Virginia K. Freyermuth, Inc., Carver, Mass., 2004—. Art reviewer Patriot Ledger, Quincy, 1975-85; dir. Freyermuth Fine Arts Ctr., Plymouth, 1990-94; mem. adv. coun. Mass. Field Ctr. Tchg. & Learning, 1993-96; tchr. in electronic residence MCET, Cambridge, 1993-95; instr. art Massasoit C.C., Brockton, 1991-92; dir. Helen Bumpus Gallery, Inc., Duxbury, 1992-94; forum tchr. Goals 2000 U.S. Dept. Edn., 1994—, internat. space camp, 1994; master tchr. Connecting Oceans Acad., ECHO Project, New Bedford, Mass, 2004— Columnist Learning for Life, 1994. Mem. commn. on common core of learning Mass. Dept. Edn., 1993-94; bd. dirs. Mass. Alliance for Arts Edn., 1994-95. Named Mass. Tchr. of Yr., Mass. Dept. Edn., 1994, Nat. Outstanding Visual Art Tchr., Walt Disney and McDonald's, 1995, 1995-96 Profiled in Disney Channel. Mem. Mass. Art Edn. Assn., Nat. Art Edn. Assn., Tchr. Leadership Acad. Mass. (bd. dirs., founding fellow), Lucretia Crocker Acad. of Tchg. Fellows (bd. dirs.). Personal E-mail: virginiafreyermuth@yahoo.com.

FREYRE, ANGELA MARIANA, lawyer; b. Havana, Cuba, Sept. 18, 1954; BA, Wellesley Coll., 1976; D.E.J.G. Mention Assez Bien, Univ. Paris, France, 1978; JD, LLM, Georgetown Univ., 1980. Bar: NY 1984. Ptnr. prin. Latin Am. practice Coudert Bros. LLP, NYC. Trustee NY Studio Sch. Drawing, Painting & Sculpture, 1984—, LongHouse Reserve Ltd., 2000—; mem. City of NY Conflicts of Interest Bd. Fulbright scholar. Mem.: Assn. Bar City of NY. Office: Coudert Bros LLP 1114 Ave of the Americas New York NY 10036 Office Phone: 212-626-4487. Office Fax: 212-626-4120. Business E-Mail: freyrea@coudert.com.

FREYTAG, SHARON NELSON, lawyer; b. May 11, 1943; d. John Seldon and Ruth Marie (Herbel) Nelson; children: Kurt David, Hillary Lee. BS with highest distinction, U. Kans., Lawrence, 1965; MA, U. Mich., 1966; JD cum laude, So. Meth. U., 1981. Bar: Tex. 1981, U.S. Dist. Ct. (no. dist.) Tex. 1981, U.S. Ct. Appeals (5th cir.) 1982, U.S. Supreme Ct. 1993, U.S. Dist. Ct. (so. dist.) Tex. 2001, U.S. Ct. Appeals (8th cir.) 2001, U.S. Ct. Appeals (fed. cir.) 2002. Tchr. English, Gaithersburg (Md.) H.S., 1966—70; instr. English, Eastfield Coll., 1974-78; law clk. U.S. Dist. Ct. (no. dist.) Tex., 1981-82, U.S. Ct. Appeals (5th cir.), 1982; ptnr., chmn. appellate practice sect. Haynes and Boone, Dallas, 1983—. Vis. prof. law So. Meth. U., 1985-86. Editor-in-chief Southwestern Law Jour., 1980-81; contbr. articles to profl. jours. Dir. devel. bd. U. Tex. at Dallas; bd. dir. Ctr. Brain Health. Named Tex. SuperLawyer, 2003, 2004, 2005; named one of 50 Women Tex. Super Lawyers, 2003, 2004, 2005, Best Lawyers in Am., 2005—, 2006; recipient John Marshall Constl. Law award, Baird Cmty. Spirit award, 1995; Woodrow Wilson fellow. Mem. ABA (mem. exec. com. and long range planning com., former chmn. program com., sec. coun. appellate lawyers, sec., chmn. task force appellate advocacy), Fed. Bar Assn. (co-chmn. appellate practice and adv. sect. 1990-91), State Bar Tex. (bd. dir., exec. com. 1997-2001, appellate coun. 1995-98), Dallas Bar Assn. (appellate section), Higginbotham Inn of Ct. (former barrister), Order of Coif, Phi Beta Kappa. Lutheran. Office: Haynes & Boone 901 Main Ste 3100 Dallas TX 75202 Office Phone: 214-651-5586. E-mail: sharon.freytag@haynesboone.com.

FREZZA, CHRISTINE ANNE, theater music composer; b. Rochdale, Eng., May 22, 1942; d. James Gaymond and Fanny (Leach) Chester; m. Daniel August Frezza, Sept. 29, 1973. MusB, U. Victoria, B.C., Can., 1967, MFA in Theatre, 1970; PhD in Theatre, U. Pitts., 1982. Guest artist U. Pitts. Theatre, 1981-85; resident composer Three Rivers Shakespeare Festival, Pitts., 1980—; lectr. U. Pitts. Theatre Arts, 1986—; planning adminstr. Three Rivers Shakespeare Festival, Pitts., 1986—; resident composer Utah Shakespearean Festival, Cedar City, Utah, 1985—. Composer in field. Composer: Two Gentlemen of Verona, 1987, Cloud Nine, 1985, Twelfth Night, 1985, Hearts and Diamonds, 1980. Grantee Pa. Coun. on Arts, 1983, 81. Avocations: cooking, dieting, sci. fiction. Home: 241 S Pacific Ave Pittsburgh PA 15224-1719 Office: U Pitts Theatre Arts # Cl1617 Pittsburgh PA 15260

FRIARS, EILEEN M., bank executive; b. Holden, Mass., June 3, 1950; d. Gordon Edward and Marjorie Ella Friars. BA, Simmons Coll., 1972; MBA, Harvard U., 1974. Mgmt. asst. U.S. Govt. Office Mgmt. and Budget, Washington, 1974-76; sr. v.p., dir. fin. svcs. practice The MAC Group, Chgo., 1976-90; sr. exec. v.p. C&S/Sovran, Virginia Beach, Va., 1990-92; pres. card svcs. Nations Bank, Charlotte, N.C., 1992-98; pres. consumer credit card svcs. Bank of Am., Charlotte, 1998-99. Mem. vis. com. Harvard Bus. Sch., 2000-; mem. adv. bd. McColl-Garella, 2003-. Editor: Financial Services Handbook; contbr. articles to profl. jours. Pres. Charlotte Repertory Theatre, 1997—98; bd. dirs. Com. of 200, Chgo., 1997—2003; trustee. Simmons U., Boston, 1997—, chair fin. com. Named Outstanding Bus. Leader, Northwood U., Palm Beach, Fla., 1998. Mem. Harvard Bus. Sch. Club Charlotte. Avocations: theater, hiking, writing, yoga.

FRIAS, SHIRLEE N., elementary school educator; b. Albuquerque, Jan. 27, 1969; d. Fred and Jackie Arellano; m. Don A. Frias, Nov. 5, 1994; children: Zacharie Ty, Alexis Sheree. B in bus., N.Mex State U., 1991; MBA, N.Mex Highland U., 2001. Cert. extra ordinary min. Queen of Heaven Parish; lic. elem. tchr. United Way liaison Intel Corp., Rio Rancho, N.Mex., 1995—2001; tchr. Queen of Heaven Sch., Albuquerque, 2002—, founder Summer Sch. Acad., 2003—. Cubmaster Cub Scouts, 2002—; vacation bible sch. instr. St. Thomas Aquinas Ch., 1998—; pastoral com. mem. Queen of Heaven Parish, 2003—, liturgy com. mem., 2004—, mem. Guadulupanas, 2005, vacation bible sch. coord., 2005, creator, coord. cheer squad, 2005—. Recipient Marian medal, Queen of Heaven Parish, 1980, Pope Puis VI Nat. award, Nat. Cath. Com. on Scouting, 2004—05. Mem.: DECA (sec. 1989, pres. 1990—91), Am. Mktg. Assn. (v.p. 1990—91), Veterans of Fgn. Wars Post 401 Ladies Aux. (nat. home chair 1998—2004, jr. v.p. 2001—02, cmty. svc. 2001—02, patriotic instr. 2001—03, Americanism chair 2001—03, dist. 2 nat. home chair 2002—03, sr. v.p. 2003—04, chair nat. home for children state 2003, dist. 2 cmty. svc. 2003—04, dist. 2 jr. v.p. 2003—04, dist. 2 sr. v.p. 2004—05, dist. 2 pres. 2005—, Nat. Recognition of Achievement for nat. home for children, Second Pl. Dept. N.Mex. Chairperson, First Pl. Dept. N.Mex. Chairperson), Delta Zeta Alumnae, Delta Mu Delta. Democrat. Roman Catholic. Office: Queen of Heaven Sch 5303 Phoenix Ave NE Albuquerque NM 87110 Personal E-mail: ztf@aol.com.

FRIAUF, KATHERINE ELIZABETH, metal company executive; b. Balt., Oct. 13, 1956; d. John Beecher Friauf and Elizabeth Withers (Wilson) Struever. Student, Columbia Coll., Chgo., 1979-81. Cert. sound engr. Owner, operator Midwest Emery Freight System, Chgo., 1978-80; driver BCB Dispatch, Inc., Rochester, N.Y., 1980-88, dispatcher, systems analyst LeRoy, N.Y., 1988-89; corp. controller Rochester Plating Works, Inc., 1988—; owner Rochester Vibratory Inc., 1991—. Dir. Rochester Plating Works, Inc., 1988-91. Mem. NAFE, Rochester Women's Network (patron mem.). Presbyterian. Avocations: classical piano, photography, gardening, gourmet cooking. Office: Rochester Vibratory Inc 4 Cairn St Rochester NY 14611-2416

FRICK, KELLY ADRIAN, editor; b. Standish, Mich., 1970; m. Christopher Frick; children: Emma, John. Reporter Bay City (Mich.) Times, 1993, enterprise editor, metro editor, 2006—. Office: Bay City Times 311 5th St Bay City MI 48708-5853 Office Phone: 989-894-9639.

FRICKE, JILL E., elementary school educator; b. New Bedford, Mass., Apr. 6, 1979; d. William and Wally Fricke. BS, Elon U., NC, 2001. Phys. edn. tchr. Alamance-Burlington (NC) Sch. Sys., 2001—. Office: E M Yoder Elementary School 301 N Charles St Mebane NC 27302 Office Phone: 919-563-3722. Business E-Mail: jill_fricke@abss.k12.nc.us.

FRICKER, BRENDA, actress; b. Dublin, Feb. 17, 1945; m. Barrie Davies (dec. 1990). Theatre work includes appearances with the Royal Shakespeare Co., London, Royal Court Theatre, London, Nat. Theatre, London; (stage) Cat on a Hot Tin Roof, 2005; other appearances include (films) Quatermas Conclusion, Bloody Kids, Our Exploits at West Poley, My Left Foot, 1989 (Acad. award for Best Supporting Actress 1989), The Field, 1990, Home Alone 2: Lost in New York, 1992, Utz, 1993, So I Married an Axe Murderer, 1993, Angels in the Outfield, 1994, A Man of No Importance, 1994, Deadly Advice, 1994, Moll Flanders, 1996, A Time to Kill, 1996, Swann, 1996, Masterminds, 1997, Painted Angels, 1998, Resurrection Man, 1998, Pete's Meteor, 1998, The War Bride, 2001, The Intended, 2002, Conspiracy of Silence, 2003, Veronica Guerin, 2003, Trauma, 2004, Inside I'm Dancing, 2004, Razor Fish, 2004, Milk, 2005, Tara Road, 2005; (TV series) Casualty; (TV Movies) Licking Hitler, 1978, The House of Bernarda Alba, The Ballroom Romance, 1982, The Sound and the Silence, 1992, Resurrection, 1999, Durango, 1999, Cupid & Cate, 2000, The American, 2001, Torso: The Evelyn Dick Story, 2002, Watermelon, 2003, Call Me: The Rise and Fall of Heidi Fleiss, 2004, Omagh, 2004; (miniseries) Brides of Christ, 1991, A Woman of Independent Means, 1995, Relative Strangers, 1999, I Was A Rat, 2001, No Tears, 2002.*

FRIDAY, ELEANOR SULLIVAN, federal official; Dep. assoc. dep. asst. sec. policy, portfolio oversight & execution U.S. Dept. Veterans Affairs, Washington. Named a Heroine in Tech., Women in Tech., March of Dimes, 2005. Office: Dept Veterans Affairs Rm 575F 810 Vermont Ave NW Washington DC 20420*

FRIDAY, LEAH REBECCA, portfolio manager; b. Houston, Nov. 12, 1968; d. Jerry Jefferson and Verena (Shuttlesworth) Bennett; m. Charles Kevin Friday, Aug. 26, 1995. BS, Tex. A&M U., 1991. CFA. Fixed income product specialist Am. Funds Group, L.A., 1992—95; portfolio mgr. King Investment Advisors, Houston, 1995—. Docent Houston (Tex.) Zoo. Mem.: Houston Soc. Fin. Analysts (edn. com. 1999—2001, edn. chmn. 2001—04, secr. 2002—03, treas. 2003—04, v.p. 2004—), Kappa Alpha Theta. Republican. Avocations: running, biking, tennis, reading, triathlons. Office: King Investment Advisors 1980 Post Oak Blvd #2400 Houston TX 77056 Office Phone: 713-961-0462.

FRIDLEY, SAUNDRA LYNN, private investigator; b. Columbus, Ohio, June 14, 1948; d. Jerry Dean and Esther Eliza (Bluhm) F. BS, Franklin U., 1976; MBA, Golden Gate U., 1980. Accounts receivable supr. Internat. Harvester, Columbus, Ohio, San Leandro, Calif., 1972—80; sr. internal auditor Western Union, San Francisco, 1980; internal auditor II County of Santa Clara, San Jose, Calif., 1980—82; sr. internal auditor Tymshare, Inc., Cupertino, Calif., 1982—84, divsn. contr., 1984; internal audit mgr. VWR Scientific, Brisbane, Calif., 1984—88, audit dir., 1988—89; internal audit mgr. Pacific IBM Employees Fed. Credit Union, San Jose, 1989—90, Westaff, Inc., Walnut Creek, Calif., 1990—2002; lic. pvt. investigator, owner Fridley & Assoc., 2000—. Dir. quality assurance, 1992-98, v.p. audit and investigations, 1998-2002; owner Dress Fore the 9's, Brentwood, Calif., 1994-2002; pres., founder Bay Area chpt. Cert. Fraud Examiners, 1990. Commr. Brentwood Art Commn., 2003—; mem. Brentwood Bus. Alliance. Mem. NAFE, Calif. Assn. of Lic. Investigators, No. Calif. Fraud Investigators Assn., Friends of the Vineyards, Internal Auditors Speakers Bur., Assn. Cert. Fraud Examiners (founder, pres. Bay area chpt., we. regional gov. 1996-97, Disting. Achievement award 1997, 98), Inst. Internal Auditors (pres., founder Tri-Valley chpt., internat. seminar com., internat conf. com.) Avocations: woodworking, gardening, golf, painting. Home: 19 Windmill Ct Brentwood CA 94513-2502 Office: Fridley & Assocs 601B 1st St # 19 Brentwood CA 94513 Office Phone: 925-634-3034. Personal E-mail: saunief@aol.com.

FRIE, DOROTHY GRACE, retired physical education educator; b. Toledo, Ohio, Apr. 4, 1923; d. George Ross and Helen Lichti Frie. BS, Miami U., Oxford, Ohio, 1945; MS, U. Wis., Madison, 1957. Lic. tchr. Colo. Tchr. phys. edn. Boulder (Colo.) Pub. Schs., 1945—50; instr. phys. edn. Westmar Coll., LeMars, Iowa, 1953—57; asst. prof. phys. edn. Northeastern State U., Tahlequah, Okla., 1957—83, ret., 1983. Recipient Pathfinder award, Nat. Assn. Girls, 2001. Mem.: Am. Assn. Health, Phys. Edn. and Dance (life). Avocations: golf, reading.

FRIED, BARBARA H., law educator; b. 1951; BA in English & Am. Lit., magna cum laude, Harvard U., 1977, MA in English & Am. Lit., 1980, JD cum laude, 1983. Bar: NY 1984. Law clk. to Hon. J. Edward Lumbard US Ct. Appeals 2nd Cir., 1983—84; assoc. tax dept. Paul Weiss Rifkind Wharton & Garrison, NYC, 1984—87; asst. prof. Stanford Law Sch., 1987—91, assoc. prof., 1991—93, prof. law, 1993—, Deanne Johnson faculty scholar, 1993—2003, William W. and Gertrude H. Saunders prof. law, 2003—. Vis. prof. NYU Law Sch., 1998—99, 2000. Author: The Progressive Assault on Laissez Faire: Robert Hale and the First Law and Economics Movement, 1998. Recipient John Bingham Hurlbut Award for Excellence in Teaching, Stanford Law Sch., 1991, 2000. Office: Stanford Law Sch Crown Quadrangle 559 Nathan Abbott Way Stanford CA 94305-8610 Office Phone: 650-723-2499. Business E-Mail: bfried@stanford.edu.

FRIED, LINDA P., medical educator; b. NYC, 1949; MD, Rush Med. Coll., 1979; MPH, Johns Hopkins U., Balt., 1985; BA in Polit. Sci., Colgate U. Diplomate Am. Bd. Internal Medicine. Intern Rush Presbyn. St. Luke's Med. Ctr., Chgo., 1979—80, resident in internal medicine, 1980—82; fellow in internal medicine Johns Hopkins Med. Inst., Balt., 1982—85, fellow in epidemiology, 1983—85, fellow in geriatrics, 1985—86, prof. medicine, epidemiology & health policy, dir. geriatric medicine & gerontology div., 2003—; legis. dir. Congresswoman Connie Morella, Washington, 1987—98; staff Johns Hopkins Hosp. Geriatrician and dir. Johns Hopkins Ctr. on Aging and Health; vice chair clin. epidemiology and health svcs. rsch. Johns Hopkins Dept. Medicine, mem. pres.'s coun.; advisor Paul Beeson Faculty Scholars in Aging Rsch., Health and Retirement Survey; staff liaison Congl. Caucus for Women's Issues, 104th Congress. Contbr. articles to profl. jours.; mem. editl. bd. Jour. Gerontology, Am. Jour. of Medicine. Pres. Women's Policy, Inc., 1999—; co-founder Experience Corps, Balt., 2002—. Named one of Md.'s Top 100 Women, (Md.) Daily Record, 2003; recipient Archstone award, APHA, 2000, Marion Spenser Fay award for the 2000 Disting. Woman Physician/Scientist, Herbert R. DeVries Disting. Rsch. award, Coun. on Aging and Adult Devel., 2000, Merit award, Nat. Inst. Aging; fellow Exec. Leadership in Acad. Medicine Program fellow; scholar Kaiser Found. scholar in gen. internal medicine. Fellow: Am. Heart Assn. (Coun. on Epidemiology and Prevention); mem.: ACP, SGIM, SER, AGS, Inst. of Medicine of NAS. Office: Ctr on Aging & Health Johns Hopkins Med Inst 2024 E Monument St Baltimore MD 21205*

FRIEDA-SIEPMANN, ELAINA M., psychology professor; d. Vincent M. and Adeline J. Frieda; m. Arndt Siepmann, Mar. 3, 2001; 1 child, Gabriel A Siepmann. BA, SUNY, Stony Brook, N.Y., 1992; MA, PhD, U. Ala., 1998. Adj. faculty U. Md., Schwaebisch Gmuend, Germany, 1999—2000; post-doctoral rsch. fellow The Ohio State U., Columbus, Ohio, 2000—02; asst. prof. Auburn (Ala.) U., 2002—. Named Tchr. of Yr., Psych Go Grad. Student Orgn. Auburn Univ, 2003—04, Psi Chi, 2004. Mem.: Acoustical Soc. Am., Am. Psychol. Soc. Achievements include research in study of language acquisition in children and adults. Office: Auburn University Department of Psychology 226 Thach Hall Auburn University AL 36849 Office Phone: 334-844-6498. Office Fax: 334-844-4447. Business E-Mail: friedem@auburn.edu.

FRIEDEN, FAITH JOY, obstetrician; b. N.Y.C., Sept. 15, 1960; MD, Mt. Sinai Sch. Medicine, 1984. Diplomate Am. Bd. Ob-Gyn., Am. Bd. Maternal and Fetal Medicine. Resident in ob-gyn. Beth Israel Med. Ctr., N.Y.C., 1984—88, attending physician, 1990—93; fellow in maternal fetal medicine Bellevue Hosp./NYU, N.Y.C., 1988—90; perinatology dir. maternal-fetal medicine Englewood (N.J.) Hosp. and Med. Ctr., 1993—, chief ob-gyn., 2001—. Mem. faculty Mt. Sinai Sch. Medicine, N.Y.C., 1991—. Named one of Top Drs. in N.Y. Metro Area, Castle Connolly, Top Drs. 2003, N.J. Monthly Mag. Office: Englewood Hosp and Med Ctr 350 Engle St Englewood NJ 07631 Office Phone: 201-894-3669.

FRIEDHABER-HARD, SUSAN MARGARET, library media educator; b. Holyoke, Mass., July 11, 1944; d. John Herbert and Anne Mary (Pruzinsky) Friedhaber; m. Robert Osvath, Feb. 17, 1973 (div. 1990); 1 child, Rebecca Jeanne Osvath. BA, Daemen Coll., 1967; MLS, State Univ. Coll., Geneseo, 1974; postgrad., Christ the King Sem., East Aurora, N.Y., 1999—. Tchr. English and French, DeSales H.S., Columbus, Ohio, 1967-68; housemother St. Vincent's Orphanage, Columbus, 1968; tchr. English and French Mater Dei H.S., New Monmouth, NJ, 1968-69; records libr. Children's Aid Soc., Buffalo, 1970; tchr. English, French and religion, libr. Archbishop Carroll H.S., Buffalo, 1970-74; libr. asst. Arcade (N.Y.) Free Libr., 1975-81; sch. libr. Pioneer H.S., Yorkshire, NY, 1981—, chmn. libr. dept., 1989-94, 2000—, co-chmn. libr. dept., 1998—99. Mem. coun. Cattaraugus-Allegany Sch. Libr. System, 1986-90, chmn. coun., 1989-90; lector, mem. liturgy com. St. Joseph's Ch., Bliss, N.Y., 1987-90. Mem. Citizens' Activist Group to fight zoning change, Arcade, 1982-83; tchr. St. Mary's Ch., East Arcade, N.Y., 1977-84, 97-2002, lectr., 1980-84, 97—, Eucharistic min., 2002—. Mem. ALA, AAUW, Am. WWII Orphans' Network, NY Libr. Assn., Sch. Libr. Assn. Western NY, Arcade Hist. Soc., Enchanted Mountains Sch. Libr. Assn. (treas. 1993-94, v.p. 1994-95, pres. 1995-96), Second Air Divsn. Assn., Eighth Air Force Hist. Soc. Western NY Roman Catholic. Office: Pioneer High Sch Libr PO Box 639 Yorkshire NY 14173-0639 Home: 146 Skyview Dr Arcade NY 14009-9521 Office Phone: 716-492-9324. Personal E-mail: barclaypenn@yahoo.com.

FRIEDLAND, BILLIE LOUISE, former human services administrator, educator; b. Los Alamos, N.Mex., Jan. 6, 1944; d. William Jerald and Harriet Virginia (Short) Van Buskirk; m. David Friedland. BS in Edn., California U. of Pa., 1972, MS in Psychology, 1986; EdD, W.Va. U., 1998. Sales mgr., buyer Friedland's Ladies Ready-To-Wear, Monessen, Pa., 1969-72; tchr. Belle Vernon (Pa.) Area Schs., 1973-74; head social scis. dept. Yeshiva Achei Tmimim, Pitts., 1974-75; caseworker, outreach to children and their families project Fayette County Mental Health and Mental Retardation Clinic, Uniontown, Pa., 1975, ctr. supr. outreach to children and their families project, 1976; case mgr., family support svcs. coord. Diversified Human Svcs. Inc., Monessen, 1978-89, supr. cmty. living arrangements, 1989-92; grad. asst. Affiliated Ctr. for Devel. Disabilities W.Va. U., Morgantown, 1992-93, grad. asst. dept. spl. edn., 1993-98, coord. inclusive schooling project, 1998-99; asst. prof. spl. edn. Ea. Ill. U., Charleston, 1999—2002, Del. State U., 2002—, assoc. prof. spl. edn., 2005—. Founder 1st Infant/Toddler Day Care Project, Fayette County, 1976-78. Mem. NAACP, CEC (sponsor student chpt.), Am. Assn. Mental Retardation, Assn. Supervision & Curriculum Devel., Am. Conf. Rural Spl. Edn. (reviewer RSEQ), W.Va. Fedn. Coun. for Exceptional Children (past pres. divsn. mental retardation/devel/ disabilites), Phi Delta Kappa, Sigma Rho Epsilon. Avocations: cross country skiing, canoeing, backpacking, hiking, bicycling. Office: Del State U EH 233 Edn & Human Performance 1200 N Dupont Hwy Dover DE 19901 Personal E-mail: bfriedladesu@comcast.net.

FRIEDLANDER, PATRICIA ANN, marketing professional, writer; b. Chgo., May 9, 1944; d. James Farrell and Therese Mary (Pfeiler) Crotty; m. Daniel B. Friedlander, July 3, 1971 (div. Apr. 1978); children: Michael Derek, David Colin. BA, Cardinal Stritch Coll., 1966; MA, U. Wis., Milw., 1968; postgrad., U. Chgo., Ill., 1968-69, U. London, 1968—. Instr. U. Wis., Milw., 1966-68, Chgo. State U., 1968-71, Argo Cmty. H.S., Summit, Ill., 1971-73, Park Dist., Park Forest South, Ill., 1973-77; counselor Will County Mental Health Clinic, Park Forest South, 1977-78; sales rep. Prentice-Hall, Inc., Englewood Cliffs, N.J., 1978-84; nat. sales mgr. Dow Jones-Irwin, Homewood, Ill., 1984-87; dir. mktg. Nat. Textbook Co., Lincolnwood, Ill., 1987-88; mgr. mktg. Scott Foresman & Co., Glenview, Ill., 1988-90; corp. advt. dir. Giltspur, Inc., Itasca, Ill., 1990-96; dir. Mktg. Comms. Exhibitgroup/Gitspur, Roselle, Ill., 1996-98; sales exec. Derse Exhibits, Chgo., 1998-99; dir. mktg. Exhibitor Mag. Group, 1999-2000; pres. Word-Up! Comms., 2000—. Dir. Printer's Row Bookfair, Chgo., 1985; cons.; spkr. and author in trade show. Den mother Cub Scouts Am., Park Forest South, 1981-84. Mem.: Bus. Mktg. Assn., Healthcare Conv. and Exhibitors Assn. Avocations: piano, reading, bicycling, swimming. Home and Office: Word-Up! 2320 W Farwell Ave Chicago IL 60645-4735 E-mail: pat@patfriedlander.com.

FRIEDLI, HELEN RUSSELL, lawyer; b. Indpls., July 8, 1956; d. William F. and Helen F. Russell; m. E. Kipp Friedli, May 19. BS, Purdue U., 1977; JD, Ind. U., 1980. Bar: Ill. 1980. Ptnr., mem. firm exec. mgmt. com. McDermott, Will & Emery, Chgo., 1980—. ABA. Office: McDermott Will & Emery LLP 227 W Monroe St Ste 4700 Chicago IL 60606-5096 Office Phone: 312-984-7563. Office Fax: 312-984-7700. Business E-Mail: hfriedli@mwe.com.

FRIEDMAN, ADENA T., finance company executive; b. 1967; d. Michael D. and Adena W. Testa; m. Michael Friedman, Aug. 21, 1993. BA in Polit. Sci., Williams Coll., Mass.; MBA with honors, Owen Grad. Sch. Mgmt. Vanderbilt Univ., Nashville. With NASDAQ Stock Market, Inc., 1993—; mktg. mgr. Nasdaq Trading and Market Svcs., dir., v.p.; exec. v.p. corp. strategy & data prods. NASDAQ Stock Market Inc., 2003—. Chmn. Econ. Adv. Bd.; bd. mem. Internat. Fin. Forum, Beijing. Office: The Nasdaq Stock Market One Liberty Plz 165 Broadway New York NY 10006*

FRIEDMAN, AMY LISA, social worker; b. N.Y.C., May 24, 1962; d. Victor E. Friedman and Kathleen Teltsch. BA, Haverford Coll., 1985; MSW, Simmons Coll., 1990. Lic. ind. clin. social worker, Mass. Crisis clinician, psychotherapist Tri-City Cmty. Mental Health and Retardation Ctr., Everett, Mass., 1990-98; pvt. practice clin. social work, Bedford and Carlisle, Mass., 1997—. Mem. NASW, Emdr Internat. Assoc. Home: 33 Pilgrim Path Carlisle MA 01741-1840

FRIEDMAN, CAITLIN, public relations executive; married; 2 children. Segment prodr. TV Food Network; account exec. Kratz & Co. Pub. Relations; publicity mgr. cookbook program Broadway Books; founder Caitlin Friedman Comm., 1999; cofounder (with Kimberly Yorio) YC Media. Co-author (with Kimberly Yorio): The Girl's Guide to Being the Boss (Without Being a Bitch): Valuable Lessons, Smart Suggestions and True Stories for Succeeding as the Chick-in-Charge, 2006 (Quills award business The Quills Literacy Found., 2006). Avocations: reading, tennis, dining out. Office: YC Media Ste 310 547 West 27th St New York NY 10001 Office Phone: 212-609-5009 ext. 1. Office Fax: 212-684-0059.*

FRIEDMAN, D. DINA, writer, educator; b. Takoma Pk., Md., June 13, 1957; d. Stanley David and Susan Loeserman Friedman; m. Shel Horowitz, Oct. 9, 1983; children: Alana Horowitz Friedman, Rafael Horowitz Friedman. BA in English, Cornell U., 1978; MSW, U. Conn., 1987. Co-dir. Accurate Writing & More, Northampton, Mass., 1987—; instr. Mt. Holyoke Coll., South Hadley, Mass., 1997—2002; instr. sch. mgmt. U. Mass., Amherst, 2000—. Writing workshop leader Amherst Writers and Artists, 1987—99; tchr. pub. speaking U. Mass., 1987—89. Author: Escaping Into the Night, 2006, Playing Dad's Song, 2006. Co-founder Save the Mountain, Hadley, Mass., 1999—. Recipient Pallas award, Athena Press, 1988, Reed Smith prize, Amelia Mag., 1989. Mailing: 16 Barstow Lane Hadley MA 01035 E-mail: dina@frugalfun.com.

FRIEDMAN, DEBBIE, singer, songwriter, religious studies educator; b. 1952; With New Reform Congregation, LA, 1984—87; former dir. Chalutzim Hebrew prog. Olin-Sang-Ruby Union Inst., Oconomowac, Wis., co-founder, co-leader Hava Nashira songleading & music workshop, 1992—. Singer: (albums) Sing Unto God, 1972, In the Beginning, 1994, Renewal of Spirit, 1997, You Shall Be a Blessing, 1997, The Journey Continues, 1997, Shirim al Galgalim: Songs on Wheels, 1998, Live at Carnegie Hall, 1999, It's You, 1999, The Alef Bet, 2001, The Water in the Well, 2001, Live at the Del, 2002, Worlds of Your Dreams, 2002, Shanah Tovah, 2002, Light These Lights, 2004, One People, 2006. Recipient Steven S. Wise Jewish Edn. award, Bennett H. Walzer Meml. Judaic Arts award, 1992, 1994, Covenant Found. award, Crown Family Found. & Jewish Edn. Svc. N.Am., 1996, Woman of Valor award, Jewish Fund for Justice, 1997, Myrtle Wreath award, Nassau region of Hadassah, 1997, US/Israel Women to Women award, 2000, Jewish Cultural Achievement in Performing Arts award, Nat. Found. Jewish Culture, 2002, Sherut L'Am award, Kalsman Inst. Hebrew Union Coll.-Jewish Inst. Religion, 2005, Heritage award, 1st Ann. Jewish Music Awards, 2005, Burning Bush award, University Women of U. Judaism, 2006. Mem.: Am. Conf. Cantors (hon.), Nat. Fedn. Temple Youth (hon. life). Jewish. Office: c/o Golden Land Concerts & Connections Ste 605 45 E 33rd St New York NY 10016 also: c/o Sounds Write Prodns Inc PO Box 601084 San Diego CA 92160-1084 Office Phone: 212-683-7816. Office Fax: 212-213-2033. E-mail: concerts@goldenland.com.*

FRIEDMAN, ELAINE FLORENCE, lawyer; b. N.Y.C., Aug. 22, 1924; d. Henry J. and Charlotte Leah (Youdelman) F.; m. Louis Schwartz, Apr. 10, 1949; 1 child, James Evan. BA, Hunter Coll., 1944; JD, Columbia U., 1946. Bar: N.Y. 1947, U.S. Dist. Ct. (so. and ea. dists.) N.Y., U.S. Ct. Appeals (2d cir.), U.S. Supreme Ct. 1954. Assoc. Oseas, Pepper & Siegel, N.Y.C., 1947-48, Bernstein & Benton, N.Y.C., 1948-51, Copeland & Elkins, N.Y.C., 1951-53; sole practice N.Y.C., 1953—. Bd. dirs. Health Ins. Plan of Greater N.Y. Mem. Fedn. Internat. des Femmes Juristes (v.p. U.S. chpt. 1993-95), N.Y. State Bar Assn., Hunter Coll. Alumni Assn., Columbia Law Sch. Assn. Jewish. Avocation: poetry. Home: 2 Agnes Cir Ardsley NY 10502-1709 Office: 60 E 42nd St New York NY 10165-0006 Office Phone: 212-687-6380.

FRIEDMAN, ELIZABETH ANN, educational administrator; b. N.Y.C., June 6, 1948; d. Aaron and Florence (Giatas) Zicherman; m. Paul Lawrence Friedman, May 25, 1975. BA cum laude, U. Pitts., 1970. Mgmt. analyst U.S. Dept. Commerce, 1970-73; tng. systems analyst Inst. Law and Social Research, Washington, 1973-78; dir. curriculum devel. and adminstrn. D.C. Bar (Unified), 1978-81; mgr. edn. programs Assn. Trial Lawyers Am., Washington, 1981-82; exec. dir. Inst. Profl. and Exec. Devel., Washington, 1982—2004; mem. community adv. council WETA Pub. TV/Radio, 1988-91; bd. dirs. Ctr. for dispute Resolution, 1995-2006, Fredrick B. Abramson Meml. Found., 1994-2005, v.p. for devel., 1997-2000; mem. bd. overseers Corcoran Mus. of Art, 1996-2002. Mem. WETA 2691 Club (leadership com. 1988-93, bd. dirs. Washington project arts, 1991-94). Home: 3218 Volta Pl NW Washington DC 20007-2731

FRIEDMAN, FRANCES, public relations executive; b. NYC, Apr. 8, 1928; d. Aaron and Bertha (Itzkowitz) Fallick; m. Clifford Jerome Friedman, June 17, 1950; children— Kenneth Lee, Jeffrey Bennett. BBA, CCNY, 1948. Dir. pub. rels. Melia Internat., Madrid, N.Y.C., 1971-73; sr. v.p. Lobsenz-Stevens, N.Y.C., 1973-75; exec. v.p. Howard Rubenstein Assocs., N.Y.C., 1975-83; pres., prin. Frances Friedman Assocs., N.Y.C., 1983-84; pres., chmn. bd. dirs. GCI Group Inc., N.Y.C., 1984-91, pub. rels. and editl. cons., 1991-93; mng. dir. L.V. Power & Assoc., Inc., 1993-97; pub. rels. cons. N.Y.C., 1997—. Media cons. White Ho. on Women's Issues, 1995; participant in Vital Voices Confs., Hillary Clinton's program for women in emerging democracies, 1996; feature writer Kenttribune.com, 2003—. Bd. dirs. United Nations Assn. (NW Ct. chpt.), 2003, Morris-Jumel Mansion, 1999-2001, Contemporary Guidance Svcs, 1999, 2001, City Coll. Fund, N.Y.C., 1970-79; mem. adv. bd. League for Parent Edn., N.Y.C., 1961-65; editor South Shore Democratic Newsletter, North Bellmore, N.Y., 1958-61, press sec. N.Y. State Assembly candidate, 1965, N.Y. State Congl. candidate, 1968; officer Manhasset Dem. Club, N.Y., 1965-69; mem. adv. com. N.Y.C. Coun. candidate, 1985. U. New Haven Bartels fellow, 1993. Mem. Pub. Rels. Soc. Am., Women in Comm. (Matrix award for pub. rels. 1989), The Counselors Acad., Pride and Alarm, City Club N.Y. Democrat. Jewish. Home: 30 Appalachian Rd Kent CT 06757-1009 Personal E-mail: ffried2078@aol.com.

FRIEDMAN, FRANCES WOLF, political fund raiser; b. Ft. Worth, June 14, 1940; d. Tobian Alexander and Ann (Katz) Wolf; m. Christopher I. Newman (div. 1984); children: Peter A., J. Hope; m. Frederick Friedman Sr., Jan. 3, 1986; stepchildren: Danielle F., David J. BA in Polit. Sci., Tulane U., 1961. Motion picture film prodn. office coord. Columbia Pictures Corp. Paramount Pictures, N.Y.C., 1965-72, Metro Goldwyn Mayer, N.Y.C., 1965-72; dir. vols. Congressman Bill Green, N.Y.C., 1984-86, fin. dir., 1988-92; nat. dir. Modrnpac, N.Y.C., 1993-2001. Bd. dirs. Family Connections, 1998-2004; domestic violence task force chair Adv. Bd. on the Status of Women-Essex County, Newark, 1997-2000; mem., co-founder Essex County Coalition on Domestic Violence Svc. Providers, Newark, 1997-2004. Mem. pub. rels. Concert Artists Guild, N.Y.C., 1982-84, LWV, Millburn-Short Hills, N.J., 1996-2004; v.p. Rep. Club, Millburn-Short Hills, 1996-2004; freeholder-at-large candidate Rep. Party, Essex County, N.J., 1996.

FRIEDMAN, FREDRICA SCHWAB, editor, publisher; b. N.Y.C., Aug. 29, 1939; d. Joseph H. and Ruth (Landis) Schwab; m. Stephen J. Friedman, June 25, 1961; children: Vanessa V., Alexander S. BA, Vassar Coll., 1961; MA, Columbia U., 1963. Assoc. articles editor Holiday Mag., N.Y.C., 1966-68; contbg. editor Travel & Leisure Mag., N.Y.C., 1969-70; editorial cons. Saturday Rev. Mag., N.Y.C., 1971-74; sr. editor Reader's Digest Press, N.Y.C., 1974-77; sr. staff editor Reader's Digest Condensed Books, N.Y.C., 1977-84; sr. editor Little, Brown & Co., N.Y.C., 1985-88, exec. editor, assoc. pub., v.p., editl. dir., assoc. pub., v.p., 1996; pres. Fredrica S. Friedman, Inc. Chair Matrix Awards, 1996. Recipient Matrix award Women in Comm., 1992. Mem. Women's Forum, Women's Media Group, The Peer Group, Leadership Circle of Woman's Campaign Fund.

FRIEDMAN, GLORIA LANDSMAN (MRS. DANIEL A. ROBLIN JR.), psychologist, educator; b. N.Y.C., Apr. 29, 1925; d. Benjamin F. Landsman and Helen (Siegler) Lehman; m. Daniel A. Roblin, Jr., May 22, 1949 (dec.); children: Diane Roblin Finlayson, Daniel Arthur III; m. Bennett Friedman. BA, Barnard Coll., 1945; MA, Columbia U., 1947; PhD, SUNY, Buffalo, 1963. Cert. sexologist clin. hypnotist. Instr. psychology dept. U. Richmond, Va., 1946-48, Columbia U., N.Y.C., 1948-49, Med. Coll. SUNY, Buffalo, 1963-65; research psychologist Research Found., SUNY, Buffalo, 1973—; professorial lectr. Coll. Arts and Scis., 1965—; clin. asso. prof. psychiatry Med. Coll., 1972, clin. prof., 1975—, coordinator, instr. programs on human sexuality, clin. hypnosis and psychopathology. Bd. dirs. Psychiat. Clinic, Buffalo, 1956-62, pres., 1961-63, spl. cons, 1962—; bd. dirs. Nat. Council Jewish Women, 1954-60, chmn. social legislation, v.p., 1956-57; mem. speakers bur. Erie County Republican Com., 1950—; bd. dirs. United Way, 1972—, Mental Hygiene Community Services of Erie County, 1979—; mem. council Religious Studies Center of Canisius Coll., 1970—. Fellow Soc. for Sci. Study of Sex (dir.); mem. Am. Psychol. Assn., N.Y. State Psychol. Assn., AAUP, Psychol. Assn. Western N.Y., Am. Soc. Clin. Hypnosis, Soc. Clin. and Exptl. Hypnosis, Am. Assn. Sex Educators, Counselors and Therapists, Sex Info. and Ednl. Council U.S., Sigma Xi. Clubs: Buffalo (Buffalo), Westwood Country (Buffalo); Barnard of Western N.Y. (past pres.); Met. (N.Y.C.). Home: 33 Gates Cir Apt 6G Buffalo NY 14209-1197 Office: Erie County Med Ctr 462 Grider St Buffalo NY 14215-3021

FRIEDMAN, JANE, publishing executive; BA in English, NYU, 1967. Joined Random House, 1968, with publicity dept., exec. v.p. Knopf Pub. Group, pub. Vintage Books, founder, pres. Random House Audio, exec. v.p. Random House Inc., mem. exec. com.; pres., CEO HarperCollins, NYC, 1997—. Co-chair pub. divsn., vice chair entertainment, media and comms. divsn. UJA; mem. Am. adv. com. Jerusalem Internat. Book Fair; chmn. bd. dirs., adv. com. Assn. Am. Pubs.; bd. dirs. Poets and Writers; adv. com. Literacy Ptnrs., Yale U. Press. Named Person of Yr., LMP, 1999; named one of 200 Women Legends, Leaders and Trailblazers, Vanity Fair, 1998, N.Y.'s 100 Most Influential Women in Bus., Crain's N.Y. Bus., 1999, Am.'s 100 Most Important Women, Ladies Home Jour., 1999, 101 Most Important People in Entertainment, Entertainment Weekly, 1999—2002; recipient Matrix award, Women Who Change the World, 2001. Office: HarperCollins 10 E 53rd St New York NY 10022-5299

FRIEDMAN, JOAN M., retired accountant, educator; b. NYC, Nov. 30, 1949; d. Alvin E. and Pesselle Gail (Rothenberg) F.; m. Charles E. Blair III, Sept. 20, 1992. AB magna cum laude, Harvard U., 1971; MA, Courtauld Inst., U. London, 1973; MS with honors, Columbia U., 1974; MAS, U. Ill., 1993. CPA, Ill. Asst. research librarian Beinecke Library, New Haven, 1974-75; asst. research librarian Yale Ctr. for Brit. Art, New Haven, 1975-76, curator of rare books, 1976-90; computer cons., teaching asst. dept. accountancy U. Ill., Champaign, 1990-95; vis. asst. prof. acctg. Ill. Wesleyan U., Bloomington, Ill., 1995-99, asst. prof. acctg., 1999—2006; ret., 2006. Cons. Johns Hopkins U., Balt., 1983; tchr. Sch. Library Service Columbia U., 1983-88, Sysop WordPerfect Users Forum on CompuServe, 1987-2000, Sysop, Tapcis Forum on CompuServe, 1988-95. Author: Color Printing in England, 1978; contbr. articles in field Recipient student achievement award Fedn. Schs. Accountancy, 1993; Nat. Merit scholar Harvard U., 1967; Moss Accountancy fellow U. Ill. 1990. Mem. ALA (chmn. rare books and manuscripts sect. 1982-83), Bibliog. Soc. Am. (coun. 1982-86, sec. 1986-88), Am. Printing History Assn., Phi Beta Kappa, Beta Phi Mu. Clubs: Grolier (N.Y.C.); Elizabethan (New Haven). Jewish. Avocations: microcomputers, bicycling, listening to the radio. E-mail: jfriedma@iwu.edu.

FRIEDMAN, KENNI, health facility administrator, councilman; BA, UCLA, 1963, MBA, 1964. Councilwoman City of Modesto, Calif., 1991-99, vice mayor, 2000—; mem. bd. Sutter-affiliated Meml. Hosps. Assn., Sacramento, chmn. bd., 1993-95; bd. dirs. Sutter Health Inc., Sacramento. Bd. dirs. Sutter Gould Med. Found., Modesto; active League Calif. Cities, United Way Sanislaus County, Modesto Symphony Assn.; former mem. state bd. dirs. and nat. bd. dirs. LWV; mem. policy bd. San Joaquin Valley Unified Air Pollution Control Dist. Mem. Modesto C. of C. (bd. dirs.).

FRIEDMAN, LINDA WEISER, operations researcher, educator; b. N.Y.C., July 4, 1953; d. Norman and Marion (Neiman) Weiser; m. Hershey Harry Friedman, June 8, 1972; children: Esther M., Pearl, Sarah, Rachel, Deborah A. BA in Statistics and Biology, Baruch Coll. (CUNY), 1976; MS in Applied Statistics, Poly. Inst. N.Y., 1980, PhD in Ops. Rsch., 1983. Adj. lectr. Poly. Inst. N.Y., Bklyn., 1978-80; asst. prof. Long Island U., 1980-81; instr. Baruch Coll., N.Y.C., 1981-83, asst. prof., 1983-86, assoc. prof., 1987-92, prof., 1993—; chairperson, 1993—98. Author: Comparative Programming Languages, 1991, (with others) Deadly Stakes, 1989, Simulation Metamodel, 1995; contbr. articles to profl. jours. Active Women's League for Community Svcs., Bklyn., 1978—. Mem. Assn. for Computing Machinery, Soc. for Computer Simulation, IEEE Computer Soc. Home: 1367 57th St Brooklyn NY 11219-4637 Office: Baruch Coll Dept Statistics/CIS Box B11 220 New York NY 10010

FRIEDMAN, LYNN JOSEPH, counselor; b. New Orleans, Jan. 12, 1949; d. Leonard Cerf and Paula Rose (Levy) Joseph; children: Rebecca, Naomi. BS, La. State U., 1970; MEd, U. Tex., 1971; PhD, U. New Orleans, 1995. Tchr. Orleans Parish Schs., New Orleans, 1971-73; rehab. counselor L.A. Div. Rehab. Svcs., Metairie, 1973-87, Intracorp, Metairie, 1987-91, GAB Robins/Med Insights, Metairie, 1991—. Counselor Metro Battered Women, Metairie, 1990-92; edn. dir. Congregation Gates of Prayer, New Orleans, 1971-75; nat. mgr. Crisis Intervention Program. Contbr. articles to profl. jours. Named Counselor of Yr. Goodall Rehab., 1980; recipient Cert. Appreciation Nat. Assn. Ret. Citizens, 1974, Magnolia Sch., 1976. Mem. ACA (La. Grad. Student of Yr. 1991), Nat. Rehab. Assn. (La. Counselor of Yr. 1979), Chi Sigma Iota (treas. 1990-91, v.p. 1991-92). Democrat. Jewish. Home: 4721 Loveland St Metairie LA 70006-4027 Office: GAB Robins/Med Insights 4721 Loveland St Metairie LA 70006-4027

FRIEDMAN, MARIA ANDRE, public relations executive; b. Jackson, Mich., June 12, 1950; m. Stanley N. Friedman; children: Alexandra, Adam. BA cum laude, U. Md., 1972, MA, 1979; DBA, Nova U., 1993. Writer U.S.

Bur. Mines, Washington, 1973-78; head writer Nat. Ctr. Health Svc. Rsch./Healthcare Tech. DHHS, Rockville, Md., 1978-85; chief publs. and info. br. Agy. for Healthcare Policy and Rsch., 1986-89; dir. office pub. affairs Healthcare Fin. Adminstrn., Washington, 1990—, acting assoc. adminstr. for comm., 1992-93, sr. rsch. advisor Balt., 1994-95, dir. disemination staff ORB, 1995-96, sr. advisor for ins. reform, 1997-99, Y2K outreach coord. for medicaid program, 1999—. Mem. Assn. Health Svcs. Rsch., Acad. of Mgmt. Office: Health Care Fin Adminstrn 7500 Security Blvd Baltimore MD 21244-1849 Home: 12535 Heurich Rd Silver Spring MD 20902-1441

FRIEDMAN, MARLA ILENE, director, educator; b. Miami, Fla., Sept. 19, 1972; d. Alice and Joseph Ostrower; m. Marc Richard Friedman, Feb. 27, 1999. BS, Emerson Coll., 1995, MA, 1996; postgrad., Nova Southea. U., 1998—. Regional dir. Bus. Network Internat., Albuquerque, 1992—94; intern, account asst. Ward Rovner Pub. Rels., Boston, 1994—95; mktg. project mgr. Nova Southea. U., Ft. Lauderdale, Fla., 1997—99, mktg. mgr., 1999—2000, adj. faculty mem., 1999—; assoc. dir. internat., online & grad. programs Nova Southea. U. Law Ctr., Ft. Lauderdale, 2000—. Co-facilitator Thyroid Cancer Survivors, Ft. Lauderdale; team capt. Multiple Sclerosis Soc. 150 Bike Ride, Fla. Mem.: Am. Mktg. Assn. (assoc.). Office: Nova Southea U Law Ctr 3305 College Ave Fort Lauderdale FL 33314 E-mail: friemar@nova.edu.

FRIEDMAN, MARY KATHLEEN, secondary school educator; d. John S. and Catherine M. Kelly; m. Matthew L. Friedman, July 13, 1997; 1 child, Talia Cealleigh. BA, U. Colo., Boulder, 1988. Cert. secondary social studies tchr. Colo., 2000, single subject tchr. Calif., 2005. Social studies tchr. Westlake Jr. H.S., Broomfield, Colo., 1990—94; history tchr. Horizon H.S., Brighton, Colo., 1994—97; substitute tchr. St. Joseph Sch. Dist., St. Joseph, Mo., 1998—99, Elwood Sch. Dist., Kans., 1999; history tchr., chmn. dept. SJ H.S., Carmichael, Calif., 2000—. Text book reviewer Jewish Fedn. Sacramento, 2005—; participant Holocaust Teachers Program, Israel, 1995, NSF Summer Inst., Boulder, 1994; presenter in field. Author: (poetry) The Kinetic Energy of Kosher Krishnas. Vol. Chevre Kadish Sacramento, 1999—2002; sec. bd. dirs. Twin Spires Inc., St. Joseph, 1998—99; bd. dirs. Samaritan Ctr., St. Joseph, 1998—99. Named Paul Harris fellow, Rotary Internat., 2006; recipient Innovative Classroom award, Adams County Five Star Sch. Dist., 1993. Avocation: travel. Office: Jesuit HS 1200 Jacob Lane Carmichael CA 95608 Office Phone: 916-482-6060. Personal E-mail: friedcat@yahoo.com. Business E-Mail: friedmanm@jhssac.org.

FRIEDMAN, MILDRED, architecture educator, design educator, curator; b. LA, July 25, 1929; d. Nathaniel and Hortense (Weinsveig) Shenberg; m. Martin Friedman; children: Lise, Ceil, Zoe. BA, UCLA, 1951, MA, 1952; DFA (hon.), Mpls. Coll. Art, 1984; DFA, Hamlin U., 1987. Instr. design L.A. City Coll., 1952-54; archtl. designer Cerny Assocs., Mpls., 1957-69; design curator Walker Art Ctr., Mpls., 1970-90; freelance cons. N.Y.C., 1990—. Mem. arch. and design panel Nat. Endowment Arts, 1975—78, mem. policy panel design arts, 1979—82, mem. presdl. design awards jury, 1991; mem. vis. com. Sch. Arch. and Planning MIT, 1985—88; mem. vis. com. Grad. Sch. Design Harvard U., 1994—; bd. dirs. Internat. Design Conf., Aspen, 1989—91, Chgo. Inst. Arch. and Urbanism, 1990—93, Nat. Inst. Archtl. Edn., 1993—; mem. deisgn jury Am. Acad. Rome, 1991; guest instr. UCLA, 1992; mem. jury to select architect for Whitehall Ferry Terminal, N.Y.C., 1992; vis. instr. Harvard U., 1993; cons. Battery Park City Authority, N.Y.C.; guest curator Bklyn. Mus., 1992—2002; guest curator for Frank Gehry retrospective exhbn. Solomon R. Guggenheim Mus., N.Y.C., 2001; guest curator for Vital Forms exhbn. Bklyn. Mus. Art, 2001—02. Author, editor: Gehry Talks, 1999; editor Design Quar., 1970-91, numerous catalogues; participating author for catalogue on the work of Jack Lenor Larson, Mus. Arts & Design, 2004. Recipient Outstanding Achievement award YWCA, 1984, Outstanding Svc. award U. Minn., 1991; fellow Intellectual Interchange program Japan Soc., 1982, Chrysler Design award, 2002; grantee Nat. Endowment Arts, 1992-93, Graham Found. for Advanced Studies in Fine Arts, 1997; recipient Graham Found grant for Design Quar. Anthology. Mem. AIA (hon., nat. awards jury 1981, 87, bd. dirs. Minn. chpt. 1984-86, Inst. Honors 1994). Office Phone: 212-647-1118.

FRIEDMAN, NICOLE, psychologist, consultant; d. Ira J. Friedman and Alice Davis. BA, Boston U., 1993; MA in Psychology, Yeshiva U., NYC, 1994; MS in Health Psychology, Calif. Sch. Profl. Psychology/Alliant U., San Diego, 1999; PhD in Health Psychology, Calif. Sch. Profl. Psychology/Alliant U., 2002. Lic. psychologist Calif. Rsch. asst. Harvard Med. Sch./McKinney Demonstration Project for the Homeless Mentally Ill, Boston, 1993, Columbia U. Coll. Physicians and Surgeons, NY Psychiat. Inst., NYC, 1995; health psychology clk. Scripps Clinic Wellness Program, La Jolla, Calif., 1996; health psychology intern AIDS Response Ctr., San Diego, 1997—98, Navy Med. Ctr., San Diego, 1998—2000; health psychology fellow Tripler Army Med. Ctr., Honolulu, 2001—02; psychologist Scripps Meml. Hosp. La Jolla, 2003—; psychologist dept. psychiatry, Sch. Medicine, U. Calif., San Diego, 2003—; clin. health psychologist, 2003—. Mem. exec. com. dept. psychology Scripps Meml. Hosp., 2004—; media cons., La Jolla, 2003—. Recipient Nursing Star of Excellence award, Tripler Army Med. Ctr., 2002. Mem.: APA. Achievements include research in Zen Breath Meditation improving heart rate variability in patients with coronary artery disease. Office Phone: 619-818-6777.

FRIEDMAN, PAULA KONOWITCH, dentist, academic administrator; b. Wildwood, N.J., June 22, 1948; d. Howard N. and Beatrice E. (Gibbs) Konowitch; m. Emanuel Friedman, Aug. 27, 1972; children: Daniel, Eric, Jeff. BS, U. Mass., 1970; DDS, Columbia U., 1974; MSD, Boston U., 1988, MPH, 1999. Attending dentist Beth Israel Med. Ctr., N.Y.C., 1975-78, Beth Israel Hosp., Boston, 1978-82; dir. DAU and TEAM program Boston U. Sch. of Dental Medicine, 1980-82, dir. divsn. of Oral Diagnosis and Radiology, 1982-87, asst. dean for adminstrn., 1987-91. Coord. GP residency Boston U. Sch. of Dental Medicine, 1980-82; assoc. dean adminstrn., 1991—; chair peer rev. panel HHS, BHPr, 1999-; acad. coord. Health Professions Edn. Program, 1998. Chair Coun. of Faculties Am. Assn., Dental Schs. Washington, 1997, adminstrv. bd. Cmty. and Preventative Dentistry, 1990-94. Recipient Disting. Alumni award Columbia U. Sch. of Dental and Oral Surgery, 1986. Fellow Am. Coll. Dentists, Internat. Coll. of Dentists; mem. ADA, Fisher Hill Assn. (bd. dirs. 1995—), Gerontol. Soc. of Am. (oral health v.p. 1994-97), Am. Assn. of Women Dentists, Am. Dental Edn. Assn. (pres. 2003-04, bd. dirs. 2002-), Phi Kappa Phi. Office: Boston U Sch of Dental Medicine 715 Albany St B308 Boston MA 02118-2308 Office Phone: 617-638-4741. Fax: 617-638-4729. E-mail: pkf@bu.edu.

FRIEDMAN, RACHELLE, music retail executive; b. Israel; m. Joseph Friedman; children: Jason, Daryn. Grad., Poly. Inst. of Brooklyn. Co-founder, co-CEO J & R Music World, N.Y.C., 1971—, J & R Computer World, N.Y.C., 1990—. Adv. bd. Dealerscope mag. Trustee Poly. U. N.Y. (bd. dirs. Y.E.S. Ctr. Promise Fund); bd. dirs. Heritage Trails., Alliance Downtown N.Y.; Grammy Awards host com. Mem. Nat. Assn. Record Merchandisers (mem. bd. dirs., chmn., 1998-99). Avocations: travel, boating, working out, reading. Office: J & R Music World 23 Park Row New York NY 10038-2397

FRIEDMAN, ROSELYN L., lawyer, mediator; b. Cleve., Dec. 9, 1942; d. Charles and Lillian Edith (Zalzneck) Friedman. BS, U. Pitts., 1964; MA, Case Western Res. U., 1967; JD cum laude, Loyola U., Chgo., 1977. Bar: Ill. 1977, U.S. Dist. Ct. (no. dist.) Ill. 1977. Mem. legal dept. No. Trust Co., Chgo., 1977-79; assoc. Rudnick & Wolfe, Chgo., 1979-84, ptnr., 1984-95, Sachnoff & Weaver, Ltd., Chgo., 1995—2006, ptnr., chmn. dept. estates and trusts, 2002—05; chief adminstrv. officer investment svcs. Joseph Freed and Assocs., Palatine, Ill., 2006—. Mem. Loyola U., Chgo. law rev.; mem. profl. adv. com. Chgo. Jewish Fedn., chmn., 1999-2001; mem. profl. adv. com. Chgo. Cmty. Trust, 2001-. Trustee Jewish Women's Found., 1997—2001; mediator Ctr. for Conflict Resolution, 2000—. Fellow Am. Coll. Trust and Estate Counsel; mem. ABA, Am. Jewish Congress (gov. coun. Midwest region 1995-97), Chgo. Bar Assn. (cert. appreciation continuing legal edn. program 1984, chmn. trust law com. 1989-90), Chgo. Estate Planning Coun. (program com. 1992-94, 98-2000, membership com. 1997-98, bd. dirs. 2001-2003), spkr. Ill. Inst. CLE, Chgo. Fin. Exch. (bd. dirs. 1995-97, sec. 1996-97). Office: Joseph Freed and Assoc 350 W Hubbard St Ste 620 Chicago IL 60610

FRIEDMAN, SALLY, artist, educator; b. NYC, Jan. 21, 1932; d. Isaac Mercado and Delicia (Elias) Hazan; children: Michael, Deborah. BA, Queens Coll., 1953, MA, 1959; postgrad., Ruskin Sch. Art, 1962-64, Art Students League, 1964-70. One-woman shows include Waverly Gallery, 1974, NYU, 1977, L.I. U., 1977, 92, Queens Coll., 1980, 90, Fairleigh Dickinson U., 1982, 93, Phoenix Gallery, 1978, 81-82, 84, Pratt Inst., 1985, Donnell Libr. Ctr., 1987, 97, Queens Coll., 1990, Coach Gallery, 2001, Clayton-Libertore Gallery, 2002, Kingsfoot Gallery, 2003; exhibited in group shows at Bklyn., Mus., 1975, Butler Inst. 1975, Phila. Mus., 1978, Sara Lawrence Coll., 1978, Marymount Coll., 1983, Adelphi U., 1987, Berkshire Mus., 1989, Art Expo, NYC, 2000, Guild Hall, East Hampton, NY, 2001, Ashawagh Hall, East Hampton, 2003, Donnell Libr., NY, 2006; represented in permanent collections Oklahoma City Art Mus., Mus. Arts & Scis., Daytona Beach, Fla., New England Ctr. Contemporary Art, Brooklyn, Conn. Mem. Nat. Assn. Women Artists (Paley prize 1975, Cotton prize 1978, Grumbacher award 1980, Winston Meml. prize 1982, Erlanger Meml. prize 1986), Art Students League (life). Avocations: skiing, golf, folk guitar. Home: 255 W 88th St Apt 4D New York NY 10024-1717 E-mail: sallylong@nyc.rr.com.

FRIEDMAN, SOFIA, social sciences educator, nutritionist, educator; b. San Carlos, Uruguay, Oct. 7, 1940; arrived in USA, 1988; d. Israel Iser and Szajndla Lea (Lebensohn) Friedman; m. Salomao Nejman, Dec. 26, 1959 (div. June 10, 1980); children: Helena (Nejman) Bardusco, Regina Nejman, Susana Nejman. BS nutrition, Univ. Rio De Janeiro, Rio de Janeiro, Brazil, 1979; MA social comm., Fed. Univ. of Rio de Janeiro, Rio de Janeiro, Brazil, 1987; MA polit. sci., City Univ. of Rio de Janeiro, New York, NY, 1995; PhD internat. studies, Fairfax Univ., London, Eng., 2000. Cert. Yoga Instr. Vayuananda Yoga Ctr./ Rio de Janeiro, Brazil, 1974, Internat. Sivananda Yoga Vedanta Ctr./Paradise Is., Bahamas, 1983. Asst. prof. Univ. of Rio de Janeiro, Rio de Janeiro, 1980—88; adj. instr. Hudson County Cmty. Coll., Jersey City, NJ, 1995—97, Stevens Inst. of Tech., Hoboken, NJ, 1997, La Guardia Cmty. Coll., NY, NY, 1995—2000. Founder, owner Redefining Life After Fifty ednl. seminars, Hoboken, 1997—. Author: (MA thesis dissertation) Food Scarcity and Abundance: Analysis of a Food Sys. in Natividade, Rio de Janeiro, 1987, The Emergence of a Condition of Food Insecurity in Brazil During the 1964-1985 Military Regime and the Rise of Civil Soc., 1995, (book) Brazil 1960-1990: Structures of Power and Processes of Change, 2003. Democrat. Jewish. Office Phone: 201-792-3815. E-mail: sfriedman@aol.com.

FRIEDMAN, SUE TYLER, technical publications executive; b. Nürnberg, Germany, Feb. 28, 1925; came to U.S., 1938; d. William and Ann (Federlein) Tyler (Theilheimer); m. Gerald Manfred Friedman, June 27, 1948; children: Judith Fay Friedman Rosen, Sharon Mira Friedman Azaria, Devora Paula Friedman Zweibach, Eva Jane Friedman Scholle, Wendy Tamar Friedman Spanier. Student, Beth Israel Sch. Nursing, 1941—43. Exec. dir. Ventures and Publs. Gerald M. Friedman, 1964—90; owner Tyler Publs., Watervliet and Troy, NY, 1979—86; treas., dir. Northeastern Sci. Found., Inc., Troy, 1979—; treas. Gerry Exploration, Inc., Troy, 1982—88; office mgr. Rensselaer Ctr. Applied Geology, Troy, 1983—. Pres. Pioneer Women/Na'amat, Tulsa, 1961-64, treas., Jerusalem, Israel, 1964, pres., Albany, N.Y., 1968-70; bd. dirs. Temple Beth-El, 1975-, dir. Hebrew Sch., 1965-80; mem. social program com. Internat. Sedimentological. Congress, 1979. Named Hon. Alumna Dept. Geology Bklyn. Coll. at CUNY, 1989; Sue Tyler Friedman medal for distinction in history of geology created in her honor Geol. Soc. London, 1988; recipient Disting. Svc. award Temple Beth-El, 1991, Scroll of Honor, State of Israel Bonds, 1981. Mem. Geology Alumni Assn. (hon.). Avocation: world travel. Office: Northeastern Sci Found Inc Rensselaer Ctr Applied Geology PO Box 746 Troy NY 12181-0746 Personal E-mail: gmfriedman@nycap.rr.com.

FRIEDMAN, SUSAN LYNN BELL, economist; b. May 23, 1953; d. Virgil Atwood and Jean Loree (Wiggins) B.; m. Frank H. Friedman, July 31, 1976; 1 child, Alex Charles. BA, Purdue U., 1975; MSc, Ind. State U., 1981. Asst. dir. pub. rels. Vincennes U. Jr. Coll., Ind., 1977-83; dir. Knox County C. of C., Vincennes, 1983-84; asst. to pres. Am. Assn. Cmty. and Jr. Colls., Washington, 1985-87; owner, pres. SBF Promotions, 1987—; mgr., program developer Family Resources, Inc., 1988-89; partnership coord. Beaufort (S.C.) County Sch. Dist., 1989-90; job tng. coord. Heart of Ga. Tech. Inst., 1990-92, v.p. econ. devel., 1992-96; exec. dir. Tex. Assn. Ptnrs. in Edn., 1996-98; dir. regional bus. assistance Thomas Jefferson Partnership for Econ. Devel., 1999—. Mem. Leadership Class, Charlottesville, Va., 2000; pres. Annandale BPW, Vincennes, Ind., BPW Dublin and Capital City; bd. dirs. United Way, Thomas Jefferson Area; mem. sch. bd., chair Albermarle Pub. Schs., Va., 2004—; bd. dirs. I Have A Dream Found., 2001—. Hoosier scholar, 1971, 1972. Mem. NAFE, LWV (v.p. chpt. 1982-84, pres. 2000-2002), ACLU, Nat. Assn. Ptnrs. in Edn., NOW, Rotary (v.p. 2000-01), Albemarle County Rotary (program chair 2006). Home: 2544 Brandermill Pl Charlottesville VA 22911-8253 Office: PO Box 1525 Charlottesville VA 22902 Office Phone: 434-979-5610. Personal E-mail: sue_friedman@hotmail.com.

FRIEDMAN, SUSAN O., retired academic administrator; b. Bklyn., Jan. 9, 1948; d. Frank and Rose (Epstein) F BS Genetics, Cornell U., 1968; MS Molecular Biology, Syracuse U., 1976; DEd Higher Edn., Pa. State U., 1985. Lab. technologist N.Y. Med. Coll., N.Y.C., 1968—69; rsch. technician U. N.C. Med. Sch., Chapel Hill, 1969—70; tchg. asst. Syracuse U., NY, 1971—75; instr. biology Allegheny Coll., Meadville, Pa., 1975—76; rsch. asst. Pa. State U., University Park, 1977—79; program advisor Thomas Edison State Coll., Trenton, NJ, 1979—82, degree coord. applied sci. techs., 1982—94, assoc. dean Applied Sci. and Tech., 1994—2004; ret., 2004; cons. Higher Edn. S.O. Friedman Consulting, East Windsor, NJ, 2004—. Contbr. articles to profl. jours Named Who's Who Edn., Who's Who Sci. and Engrng., Who's Who Am. Women, Who's Who East. Mem. Princeton Folk Music Soc. (pres. 1985-87, bd. dirs. 1980-89) Avocations: folk music, English history, computers, Arthurian legend.

FRIEDRICH, JENNIFER, lawyer; b. Summit, N.J., Aug. 22, 1972; m. Roman Friedrich, Sept. 19, 2004. BA in Sociology, St. Lawrence U., Canton, N.Y., 1995; JD, Hofstra U. Sch. Law, Hempstead, N.Y., 2002. Bar: N.Y. 2003, N.Y. Fed. Ea. Dist. 2003, N.Y. Fed. So. Dist. 2003. Assoc. atty. Kelly, Rode & Kelly, LLP, Mineola, NY, 2003—05, Lewis Johs Avallone Aviles, LLP, Melville, NY, 2005—. Office: Lewis Johs Avallone Aviles LLP 425 Broadhollow Road Ste 325 Melville NY 11747 Office Phone: 631-755-0101. Office Fax: 631-755-0117. Personal E-mail: jenniferfriedrich@hotmail.com. Business E-Mail: jcfriedrich@lewisjohs.com.

FRIEDRICH, MARGRET COHEN, guidance and student assistance counselor; b. Balt., June 4, 1947; d. Joseph Cohen and Judith (Kline) Cohen Roisman; m. Jay Joseph Friedrich, May 16, 1971; children: David Benjamin, Marc Adam, Samantha Lauren. BEd, U. Miami, Fla., 1969, MEd, 1970; PhD, Internat. U., 2003. Cert. alcoholism and addiction counselor, alcohol and drug counselor NJ. Grad. asst. U. Miami, Coral Gables, Fla., 1969-70; tchr. Balt. Bd. Edn., 1970; guidance counselor Ridgewood Bd. Edn., N.J., 1970—, student asst. coord. N.J., 1986—, chmn. student assistance com. NJ, 1986—98. Alcoholism counselor Bergen County Dept. Health, Paramus, N.J., 1981-82; in-service tchr. Ridgewood Bd. Edn., 1983, supr., coordinator peer counseling program H.S., 1978-93; with Assn. Mental Health and Counseling of No. N.J., 1985-89; pres. BFT, Maggie Assoc.; exec. officer BFPR; cons. N.J. Student Assistance Program, student asst. cons. N.J. Dept. Edn., chmn. student asst. com.; presenter Coll. Bd. Conf., 1992, CEEB Conf., Phila., 1992, Nat. Assn. Suicidology; working group partnership for Cmty. Health Addiction Prevention, Bergen City, 1997. Author tech. papers. Exec. bd. Hadassah, Ridgewood-Glen Rock, NJ, 1971-80; youth leadership com. United Jewish Appeal, Bergen County, 1974-75; sec. Bergen County Youth Com. Substance Abuse, Paramus, 1980-90, conf. coord. com., 1983; treas. Ridgewood Coalition Substance Use and Abuse, 1983-84, Ridgewood Substance Abuse Prevention Commn., 1989-91; active Pres.'s Drug-Free Am., Washington; facilitator Gov.'s NJ Drug-Free Teleconf.; co-chmn. fundraiser, treas. United Parents/Safe Homes, Ridgewood, 1984; core com. Ridgewood Against Drugs; lectr., educator Passaic County Juvenile Conf. Com., Paterson, NJ, 1984; steering com. Bergen County Addictions Prevention Working Group-Partnership Cmty. Health; mem. White House Adv. Conf. Commn. Reisman scholar, 1969; U. Miami teaching asst., 1970, recipient Recognition award, 1968, Disting. Leadership award N.J. Assn. St. Asst. Profls. Mem. NEA, N.J. Assn. Alcoholism and Drug Counselors, Nat. Assn. Suicidology, N.J. Edn. Assn., Ridgewood Edn. Assn., Bergen County Edn. Assn., N.J. Task Force on Women and Alcohol, Nat. Assn. Coll. Adminstr. Counselors, Bergen County Profl. Counselors Assn., N.J. Pers. and Guidance Assn., Women of Accomplishment, Sigma Delta Tau (exec. bd. 1965-69). Democrat. Jewish. Office: Ridgewood High Sch Ridgewood NJ 07451 Personal E-mail: peggy7502@hotmail.com.

FRIEND, CYNTHIA M., chemist, educator; b. Hastings, Nebr., Mar. 16, 1955; d. Matthew Charles and Elise Germaine Friend; children: Ayse K., Kurt Y. BS, U. Calif., Davis, 1977; PhD, U. Calif., Berkeley, 1981. Postdoctoral assoc. Stanford (Calif.) U., 1981-82; asst. prof. Harvard U., Cambridge, Mass., 1982-86, assoc. prof., 1986-89, prof., 1989—, and chair, dept. chemistry and chemical biology. Rsch. collaborator Nat. Synchrotron Light Source/Brookhaven Nat. Labs.; Lucy Pickett lectr. Mt. Holyoke Coll., 1991; Cargill lectr. U. South Fla., 1992; Robert Welch lectr., Bernhard vis. fellow Williams Coll., 1992; Procter & Gamble lectr. U. Cin., 1993. Recipient Presdl. Young Investigator award NSF, 1985, Am. Chem. Soc. Garvan medal, 1990, Iota Sigma Pi Agnes Fay Morgan award, 1991. Mem. Am. Phys. Soc., Am. Chem. Soc. (Francis P. Garvan-John M. Olin medal 1990), Am. Vacuum Soc., Phi Beta Kappa (hon., Iota chpt.). Avocations: golf, swimming, weightlifting. Office: Harvard U Dept Chemistry-Mallinckrodt 018 12 Oxford St Cambridge MA 02138-2902 Business E-Mail: friend@chemistry.harvard.edu.*

FRIEND, PATRICIA A., trade association administrator; b. Aug. 28, 1946; Student, Northeastern State Coll. Flight attendant United Airlines, 1966—. Mem. Dept. Transp. Rapid Response Team for Aircraft Security, 2001—. Mem.: Am. Fed. Labor Unions-Congress Indsl. Orgns., Assn. Flight Attendants (head United Coun. 8/ORD Chgo. local 1980—82, internat. pres. 1995—, v.p.). Mailing: 5th Fl 1275 K St NW Washington DC 20005

FRIES, HELEN SERGEANT HAYNES, civic leader; d. Harwood Syme and Alice (Hobson) Haynes; m. Stuart G. Fries, May 5, 1938. Student, Coll. William and Mary, 1935-38. Mem. nat. nurses aid com. ARC, 1958-59; dir. ARC Aero Club, Eng., 1943-44; supr. ARC Clubmobile, Europe, 1944-46; mem. women's com. Nat. Symphony Orch., Washington, 1959—, chmn. residential and fund dr. for apts., 1959; bd. dirs. Madison County Rep. Club, 1969-70; mem. nat. coun. Women's Nat. Rep. Club N.Y., 1963—, chmn. hospitality com., 1963-65; bd. dirs. League Rep. Women, 1952-61; patron mem., vol. docent Huntsville Mus. Art, Huntsville Lit. Assn.; vol. docent Weeden House, Twickenham Hist. Preservation Dist. Assn., Inc., Huntsville; mem. The Garden Guild, Huntsville, The Collectors Guild Constn. Hall Village, Huntsville, Hist. Huntsville Found., Huntsville Mus. Art., Corcoran Art Gallery. Recipient cert. of merit 84th Divsn., U.S. Army, 1945. Mem.: DAR, Assn. Preservation Va. Antiquities, Turkish-Am. Assn., English Speaking Union, Greensboro Soc. Preservation, Nat. Trust Hist. Preservation, Va., Nat., Valley Forge (Pa.), Eastern Shore Va., Nat. Soc. Colonial Dames Am., Daus. Am. Colonists, Huntsville-Madison County hist. socs., Friends of Ala. Archives, Nat. Soc. Lit. and Arts, Va. Hist. Soc., Cmty. Ballet Assn. Inc. (life bd. dirs.), Bot. Garden Club, Heritage Club, Redstone Yacht Club, Garden Club, Army-Navy Country Club, Capitol Hill Club, Washington Club, Army-Navy Club. Address: 6200 Oregon Ave NW Apt 480 Washington DC 20015-1549

FRIESEN, CYNTHIA DEANN, elementary school educator; b. Newton, Kans., Mar. 23, 1957; d. Joel Frank and Fern Pretty Friesen. BS in Secondary Phys. Edn. and Social Studies, Emporia State U., Kans., 1979, BS in Elem. Phys. Edn., 1987. Tchr. phys. edn. and social studies St. John-Hudson Unified Sch. Dist., St. John, Kans., 1979—. Presenter ctrl. dist. AAHPERD, Rapid City, SD, 2002. Co-author: (phys. edn. activity book) Beyond Activities, Susan P Kogut, editor, 2003. Mem. Martha Rebekah cir. First United Meth. Ch., St. John, Kans., 1998—. Mem.: Kans. AAHPERD (Model Elem. Phys. Edn. Program 1998, Secondary Tchr. of Yr. 1999), AAHPERD, Kans. Nat. Educators Assn. Avocations: yard work, collecting Coke memorabilia, pets, sports. Home: 209 W 4th St PO Box 96 Saint John KS 67576-0096 Office: St John Hudson Sch Dist 350 505 N Broadway Saint John KS 67576 Office Phone: 620-549-3518.

FRIESS, DONNA LEWIS, children's rights advocate; b. L.A., Jan. 16, 1943; d. Raymond W. Lewis, Jr. and Dorothy Gertrude (Borwick) McIntyre; m. Kenneth E. Friess, June 20, 1964; children: Erik, Julina, Daniel. BA in Comm., U. So. Calif., 1964; MA in Comm., Calif. State U., Long Beach, 1966; PhD in Psychology, U.S. Internat. U., San Diego, 1993. Cert. tchr., Calif. Prof. human comm. Cypress Coll., Calif., 1966—. Lectr. survivors of abuse, 1990—, mental health profls., 1990—; guest lectr. U. Tianjin, China, 2005; guest expert (TV) Sally Jessy Raphael, 1993, Leeza Gibbons Talk Show, 1994, Sonja: Live, 1994, Oprah Winfrey Show, 1991, others; presenter, spkr. in field. Author: Relationships, 1995, Just Between Us: A Guidebook for Survivors of Childhood Trauma, 1995, Cry the Darkness, 1993, European edit. 1995, Danish edit., 1999, Korean edit., 1995, Norwegian edit., 1998, Circle of Love: Secrets to Successful Relationships, 1996, 2d edit., 2002, Whispering Waters: The Story of Historic Weesha, 1998, Chronicle of Historic Weesha and the Upper Santa Ana River Valley, 2000; contbr. articles to mags. Del. to round table discussion on victims' issues U.S. Justice Dept., 2002—, apptd. consortium for victims affairs, 2003; nat. consortium of victim assistance experts U.S. Dept. Justice, 2003—05, adv. bd.; apptd. mem. adv. coun. victim sensitive issues Calif. Dept. Corrections and Rehab., 2006—. Recipient Author's award U. Calif. Friends of Libr., 1996, recognition from U.S. Justice Dept. for outstanding efforts to stop child abuse, 1995, Lee Steelmon award, Recognition cert. for work to prevent child abuse Calif. State Senate, 2000, Orange County (Calif.) Bd. Suprs.' Resolution for Outstanding Efforts for Children, 2000, Outstanding Speech Faculty award Calif. State U., 2001. Mem. Am. Coalition Against Child Abuse (founder), Task Force for ACCA to Educate American Judges on Issues of Sexual Abuse, One Voice, Calif. Psychol. Assn., Western Social Sci. Assn., Child Abuse Listening and Mediating (bd. dirs.), Am. Profl. Soc. on Abuse of Children, Mother Against Sexual Abuse (bd. dirs.), Laura's House for Battered Women (bd. dirs.), Calif. Tchrs. Assn., Faculty Assn. Calif. C.Cs., Speech Communication Assn. of Am., U.S. Internat. U. Alumni Assn. (bd. dirs.). Avocation: painting. Office: Cypress College Dept Human Communications Cypress CA 90630 Personal E-mail: donafriess@aol.com. Business E-Mail: dfriess@cypresscollege.edu.

FRIGARD, MONIQUE DENISE, journalist; d. Louis Theodore and Miriam Claudia Frigard. AA, Laney Coll., 1997; BA, San Francisco State U., 2001. Cmty. editor, author newsmakers and youth spotlight columns focusing on local citizens Las Vegas Rev.-Jour., 2003—. Guest reader to second graders Crestwood-Edison Elem. Sch. Editor: Laney Tower Newspaper; designer: newspaper layout (1st place on-the-spot layout for a tabloid newspaper, Journalism Assn. Cmty. Colls., 1995). Recipient Humanitarian award, Nev. Reading Week, cert. appreciation, 2004. Liberal. Avocations: reading, writing, gardening, movies, swimming. Office: Las Vegas Review Jour 1111 W Bonanza Rd Las Vegas NV 89125 Office Fax: 702-383-4676. Business E-Mail: mfrigard@reviewjournal.com.

FRINK, HELEN HILLER, language educator; b. Portsmouth, N.H., July 4, 1947; PhD, U. of Chgo., 1972. Asst. prof. modern langs. Keene State Coll., 1974—79; asst. prof. German & French, SUNY, Albany, 1979—81; prof. modern langs., women's studies, holocaust studies Keene State Coll., NH, 1981—. Author: (literary scholarship) Animal Symbols in the Works of Hugo von Hofmannsthal, (history) These Acworth Hills, Alstead Through the Years, (scholarly monograph) Women After Communism; the East German Experience, (scholarly monograph - translation) Lebenswege ostdeutscher Frauen. Grantee, Fulbright Commn., 1977; Travel And Rsch. grant, German Acad. Exch. Svc., 1972-1973, Rsch. And Travel grants, Marion and Jasper Whiting Found., 1985; 2000. Office: Keene State Coll Modern Langs 229 Main St Mailstop 1301 Keene NH 03435-1301 Office Phone: 603-358-2956. Personal E-mail: hfrink@keene.edu.

FRINK, JANE LOUISE, literature and language educator; b. Cincinnatus, NY, Mar. 22, 1938; d. Thomas Lowell and Cornelia Lenora Cass; m. Zane R. Frink, Feb. 8, 1999. AB, SUNY, Albany, 1959; MA, Middlebury Coll., 1964. English tchr. William Floyd Sch., Mastic-Shirley, NY, Valley Stream North H.S., Franklin Square, NY; trainer Baruch Ctr. Mgmt. CUNY, N.Y.C., NY, 1966—67; instr. English lit. Lebanese U., Beirut, 1966—67, Pinewood Coll., Beirut, 1966—67; English tchr. Gerard Inst. for Boys, Sidon, Lebanon, 1985—86; tchr. coll. writing and lit. Bd. do Cooperative Edn. Svcs., Cortland, NY, 2000—, Cincinnatus Ctrl. Sch., 2002—03. Trainer Baruch Ctr. Mgmt.; facilitator Great Neck (NY) Adult Ctr., Cultivating Change, Valley Stream (NY) Adult Programs, Bldg. Emotional Muscle Program; writer Models for Tchg. divsn. Prentice Hall; film dubber, salesperson TV svcs., Beirut; advt. salesperson Thomas Murphy Co., Red Oak, Iowa. Author: (poetry) Quill Books: Treasure the Moment. Coord. Freedom Support Act exch. program C.W. Post/L.I. U. E-mail: jenjoony@yahoo.com.

FRISCH, KATHERINE LEIGH, secondary school educator; b. St. Paul, Minn., Dec. 31, 1958; adopted d. John Dietrich and Katherine Cunliffe Boentje; m. Douglas Stuart Frisch, Sept. 19, 1981; children: Matthew Alexander, Katherine Cunliffe. BS, Midwestern State U., Wichita Falls, Tex., 1981; profl. developmental degree in sci. edn., U. Las Vegas, Nev., 1994. Employment interviewer I Tex. Employment Commn., Graham, 1983—88; math. tchr. Clark County Sch. Dist., Las Vegas, 1995—98, New Holstein (Wis.) Sch. Dist., 1998—. Home: 1404 Parkview Dr New Holstein WI 53061 Office: New Holstein Sch Dist 1715 Plymouth St New Holstein WI 53061 Office Phone: 920-898-4256. Business E-Mail: kfrisch@nhsd.k12.wi.us.

FRISCH, ROSE EPSTEIN, population sciences researcher; b. NYC, July 7, 1918; m. David H. Frisch; children: Henry J., Ruth Frisch Dealy. BA, Smith Coll., 1939; MA, Columbia U., 1940; PhD, U. Wis., 1943. Assoc. prof. population scis. Harvard U., Cambridge, Mass., 1984-92, assoc. prof. emerita, 1992—2006. Author: Female Fertility and the Body Fat Connection, 2002, paperback edit., 2004; contbr. articles to profl. jours. Recipient Disting. Prof. Emeritus Merit award, Harvard Sch. Pub. Health, 2005; John Simon Guggenheim Meml. fellow, 1975—76. Fellow: Am. Acad. Arts and Scis.; mem.: AAAS, Sigma Xi (nat. lectr. 1989—90). Office: Harvard U Ctr Population Studies 9 Bow St Cambridge MA 02138-5103 Office Phone: 617-495-3013. Business E-Mail: rfrisch@hsph.harvard.edu.

FRISWELL-JACOBS, TRACY, performing arts educator, dancer; b. Wilmington, Del., May 21, 1971; d. E. Charles and Donna Jean Friswell; m. Scott Adam Jacobs, Sept. 1, 2002; 1 child, Benjamin Charles Jacobs. BS in Edn., U. Del., Newark, 1993. Tchr. spl. edn., drama and musical theatre Cab Calloway Sch. of the Arts, Wilmington, 1994—2000; asst. to artistic dir. Del. Dance Co., Newark, 2005—; camp instr. The Tatnall Sch., Wilmington, 2000—; instr. Del. Dance Co., Newark, 2000—. Dir., choreographer Premier Centre Arts, Middletown, Del., 2004—; ednl. diagnostician Red Clay Consol. Sch. Dist., Wilmington, 1995—2000; dance instr., competition adjudicator StarQuest Talent Competition, NC, 2001—, Internat. Dance Challenge/Dance Olympus, LI, 2001—05. Dancer On Tap, Seussical the Musical; dir.(choreographer): (instructional theatre workshops) Annie, Oliver, The Wiz, Bugsy Malone Jr., Music Man Jr, Guys and Dolls Jr., (musical theatre performance) Annie; director of competition teams (dance and song/dance performance) Mulitple Titles. Vol. coord. Christina Edn. Enrichment Fund, Newark, 2003—06; vol. mentor Miss Del. Scholarship Pageant, 1995—2006. Recipient Outstanding Edn. Grad., Del. Assn. Sch. Adminstrs., 1993, Paul Harris award, Rotary Internat., 2005; grantee, Chase Manhattan Bank, 1998; scholar, Miss Del. Scholarship Orgn., 1994—95. Mem.: Nat. Dance Week (assoc.). Office: Delaware Dance Company 168 Elkton Road Suite 101 Newark DE 19711 Office Phone: 302-738-2023. Office Fax: 302-738-1820. Personal E-mail: tkfriz@aol.com.

FRITH, ANNA BARBARA, artist; b. Fort Collins, Colo., Jan. 3, 1925; d. Adam Christian and Rose Virginia (Ayers) Tepfer; m. Donald Eugene Frith, May 7, 1949; children: Eugenia, Martin, Johanna, Juliet. ABFA in Painting, Colo. Women's Coll., Denver, 1944; Cert. in Illustration, Cleve. Sch. of Art, 1946; BFA in Painting (Hon.), Cleve. Western Reserve U., 1947; MA in Painting, Denver U., 1950; attended, U. Ill., Champaign, 1975-89. Tchr. figure drawing Denver Art Mus.; tchr. figure drawing, summers Chappell House, Denver, 1942, 43, 44, 45; tchr. ceramic sculpture San Bernardino (Calif.) Jr. Coll., 1950, 51, 52; tchr. art H.S. San Bernardino, 1953; part-time tchr. women's classes U. Ill., Champaign, 1955-80. Tchr. Sat. and pvt. classes; conductor workshops in field. Exhbns. include Gilman/Gruen Gallery, Chgo., The Peoria (Ill.) Art Guild, Prairie House Gallery, Springfield, Ill., Mus. Modern Art, N.Y.C., 1950; one-woman shows include Julian McPhee Univ. Gallery, San Luis Obispo, Calif., Calif. Poly. U., 1996, Lompoc, Calif., 1999; participant Mural-in-a-Day, Lompoc, 1998, 99, 2001. Recipient Mary Agnes Page award Cleve. Inst. of Art, 1946, 5th Yr. Scholarship award, 1946, Excellence award for watercolor Picnic Calif. State Fair, 2002. Republican. Presbyterian. Avocations: tennis, swimming, dance, travel, music. Home: 310 Poppinga Way Santa Maria CA 93455-4204 Office Phone: 805-937-3719. E-mail: b.frith.dfrith@impulse.net.

FRITTS, ANNA NICOLE, psychologist; b. St. Paul, Minn., Feb. 10, 1971; d. Andre Jon and Kathleen Eleanor LaSalle; m. Daniel Ora Fritts, July 11, 2004; 1 child, Benjamin LaSalle. BS Magna Cum Laude, U. Wash., Seattle, Wash., 1993; MS, Syracuse U., Syracuse, N.Y., 1997, PhD, 1999. Cert. Ednl. Staff Assoc. - Sch. Psychology Wash. State, 1998, Supt. Credentials Gonzaga U., 2002. Instr. Syracuse U., Syracuse, NY, 1998; sch. psychologist Spokane Pub. Sch., Spokane, Wash., 1998—, spl. edn. facilitator, 2003—04; instr. Ea. Wash. U., Cheney, Wash., 2002. Victim adv. Luth. Social Svc., Spokane, Wash., 1991; exec. bd. officer Wash. State Assn. Sch. Psychologists, Seattle, 2001—05; guest lectr. Syracuse U., Syracuse, NY, 1997—98, Mukagowa U., Spokane, Wash., 2003—04, Ea. Wash. U., Cheney, Wash., 1999—2005; crisis interventionist Spokane Cmty. Mental Health, Spokane, Wash., 1992; therapist Syracuse U., Syracuse, NY, 1996—97; instr. Esd 101, Spokane, Wash., 1999—2000; spl. edn. tng. cadre Wash. Edn. Assn., Federal Way, Wash., 1999—; sch. psychology cert. work group Office of the Supt. of Pub. Instrn., Olympia, Wash., 2003—04, ell / spl. edn. joint cert. of mastery task force, 2003—04, spl. edn. assessment leadership team, 2003—, response intervention task force, 2005—; adv. bd. Ea. Wash. U., 2005—. Contbr. articles pub. to profl. jour. Bd. mem. and chairperson Jr. League, Spokane, Wash., 2000—; edn. work group One Spokane, 2002; mem. profl. edn. adv. bd Ea. Wash. U., 2005—. Recipient Order of Omega, U. Washington's Greek Sys., 1990 - 1993, Nat. Dean's List, U. Wash., 1990 - 1993, Bruce Hornung Award, Beta Lamda Delta, 1990 - 1993, McDonald Work Award, Gonzaga U., 2000, Ted Bernstein Award, Syracuse U., 1998; fellow Syracuse U. Summer Fellowship, 1995; scholar Henderson Scholarship, U. Tex., 1993. Mem.: Nat. Assn. Sch. Psychologists, Wash. State Assn. Sch. Psychologists (sec. 2002—05, Sch. Psychologist of Yr. 2004, finalist Nat. Sch. Psychologist of Yr. 2006), Spokane Mountaineers, Psi Chi, Phi Beta Kappa, Phi Kappa Phi, Golden Key Honor Soc., Phi Eta Sigma. Roman Cath. Avocations: hiking, cross country skiing, snow shoeing, golf, travel. Office: Spokane Pub Sch 3102 E Trent Ste 206 Spokane WA 99202 Office Phone: 509-354-7964.

FRITZ, BARBARA JEAN, occupational health nurse; b. Helena, Mont., Sept. 16, 1936; d. Marion Caldwell and Clara K. (Bernard) Heffern; m. Bernard John Fritz Sept. 2, 1961; children: Cathleen, Stephen, Elizabeth. Diploma in nursing, Sacred Heart Sch. Nursing, 1957; BS in Nursing, St. Louis U., 1959; postgrad., Oreg. State U., Portland State U., Oreg. Health Scis. U. Cert. occupl. health nurse. Occupl. health nurse Chloride Western Battery, Portland, Oreg., 1984-85; occupl. health nurse unit mgr. Pub. Health Dept. Fed. Occupl. Health, Portland, 1985-86; occupl. health relief nurse James River Corp., Portland, 1986-88; occupl. health nurse Harder Mech./James River Site, Camas, Wash., 1988; health and safety mgr. Armour Foods, Portland, 1988-90; occupl. health cons. Pacific Rim Occupl. Health & Safety Svcs., Portland, 1990—2005; occupl. health nurse mgr. Toyota Vehicle Processing, Inc., Portland, 1992-95; med. case mgr. Gates McDonald, Beaverton, Oreg., 1995-96; temp. occupl. health mgr. L.S.I. Logic, Gresham, Oreg., 1997; parish nurse St. Charles Cath. Ch., 2005—06; relief nurse Gen. Motors, 2000—06. Relief occupl. health cons. Atlas, Copco, Wagner Mining, Portland, 1986-99; instr. in field. Chmn. northeast citizen's adv. Portland Planning Commn., 1988, com. historic landmarks, 1988; mem. Urban Tour Group, Portland; leadership group Mid-County Sewer Project, 1991-92; vol. Portland Ctr. Performing Arts. Recipient Cert. of Appreciation, 25th Anniversary of Urban Tour Group, 1995. Mem. Am. Assn. Occupl. Health Nurses, Oreg. State Assn. Occupl. Health Nurses (registered lobbyist, historian 1992-96, govtl. affairs co-chair 1995-96, chair 1996-97, Nat. Govtl. Affairs award 1996, 98). Democrat. Roman Catholic. Avocation: floral arranging. Home and Office: 4705 NE Ainsworth St Portland OR 97218-1818 Office Phone: 503-288-1027. Personal E-mail: prohealthme@msn.com.

FRITZ, JEAN GUTTERY, writer; b. Hankow, People's Republic China, Nov. 16, 1915; d. Arthur Minton and Myrtle (Chaney) Guttery; m. Michael Fritz, Nov. 1, 1941; children: David, Andrea. BA, Wheaton Coll., Norton, Mass., 1937, LittD (hon.), 1987, Washington and Jefferson Coll., 1982. Rsch. asst. Dobbs Ferry (N.Y.) Libr., 1937—41, children's libr., 1955—57; founder, instr. Jean Fritz Writers' Workshops, Katonah, NY, 1962—70; tchr. Bd. Co-operative Ednl. Svc., Westchester County, NY, 1971—73; faculty mem. Appalachian State U., Boone, NC, 1980—82. Author: Fish Head, 1954, The Late Spring, 1957, The Animals of Doctor Schweitzer, 1958, The Cabin Faced West, 1958, How to Read a Rabbit, 1958, Brady, 1960, I, Adam, 1963, Magic to Burn, 1964, Early Thunder, 1967, George Washington's Breakfast, 1969, Cast for a Revolution, 1972, And Then What Happened, Paul Revere?, 1973, Why Don't You Get a Horse, Sam Adams?, 1974, Where Was Patrick Henry on the 29th of May?, 1975, Who's that Stepping on Plymouth Rock?, 1975, Will You Sign Here, John Hancock?, 1976, The Secret Diary of Jeb and Abigail, 1976, What's the Big Idea, Ben Franklin?, 1976, Can't You Make Them Behave, King George?, 1977, Brendon the Navigator, 1979, Stonewall, 1979, Where Do You Think You're Going, Christopher Columbus?, 1980, The Man Who Loved Books, 1981, Traitor: The Case of Benedict Arnold, 1981, The Good Giants and the Bad Pukwudgies, 1981, Homesick: My Own Story, 1982 (Am. Book award 1983, Child Study Book award 1983, Honor Book, Newberry Medal Book 1983), China Homecoming, 1985, The Double Life of Pocahontas, 1983 (Boston Globe/Horn Book award 1984), Make Way for Sam Houston, 1986 (Western Writers award 1987), Shh! We're Writing the Constitution, 1987, China's Long March, 1988, The Great Little Madison, 1989, Bully for You, Teddy Roosevelt!, 1991, Around the World in 100 Years, 1994, Harriet Beecher Stowe and the Beecher Preachers, 1994, You Want Women to Vote, Lizzie Stanton?, 1995, Why Not, Lafayette?, 1999, Leonardo's Horse, 2001, The Lost Colony of Roanoke, 2002. Recipient Christopher award Cath. Library Assn., 1982, Regina Medal Cath. Library Assn., 1985, Laura Ingalls Wilder award ALA, 1986, Nat. Humanities medal, 2003. Home: 50 Bellewood Ave Dobbs Ferry NY 10522-2302

FRITZ, JUDITH ANN, special education administrator, educator; b. Topeka, Kans., Feb. 9, 1938; d. John Conrad Meister and Ann Elizabeth (Meek) Jackson; m. Charles Vincent Ijams, Oct. 19, 1957 (div. 1966); children: Wendy Garrett, Roy Ijams; m. Walter Neil Fritz, July 1, 1967 (div. 1991); stepchildren: Howard, Russell, Laura Fritz Ogle; adopted child, Kenton. BEd, Washburn U., 1962; MEd, U. Kans., 1971; PhD, Kans. State U., 1982. Cert. adminstr. spl. edn. Elem. tchr. Rochester Sch., Shawnee County, Kans., 1962-63, Tecumseh (Kans.) Sch., 1963-65; spl. edn. tchr. USD #501, Topeka, 1965-68, Family Svc. Guidance Ctr., Topeka, 1968-71; jr. high sch. tchr. Wabaunsee East USD #330, Eskridge, Kans., 1972-74, spl. edn. tchr., 1974-81, program coord., 1981-88; asst. dir. spl. edn. Flint Hills Spel. Edn. Coop., Emporia, Kans., 1988-99; dir. spl. edn. Coffey County Edn. Coop., Burlington, Kans., 1999—2001; tech. asstance provider Three Lakes Ednl. Cooperative, 2001—. Spkr. in field. Editor Rural Spl. Edn. Quarterly, 1980-2000; contbr. Kans. Record, 1983. Pres. Kiwanis, Emporia, 1997; pres. bd. dirs. Mental Health Ctr. East Ctrl. Kans., Emporia, 1985—. Kans. Dept. Edn. grantee, 1981-97, Artist in Edn. grantee Kans Arts Commn., 1982-88. Mem. Am. Coun. Spl. Educators (editl. bd.), Kans. Assn. Spl. Edn. Adminstrs. (membership chair), Coun. Exceptional Children, Phi Delta Kappa. Democrat. Avocations: duplicate bridge, bowling, camping, reading, hiking. Home: 820 Weaver St Emporia KS 66801-3451 Office: Three Lakes Ednl Cooperative 1318 Topeka Ave Lyndon KS 66451 E-mail: jafritz@cadvantage.com.

FRITZ, KRISTINE RAE, retired secondary school educator; b. Monroe, Wis. BS in Phys. Edn., U. Wis., LaCrosse, 1970; MS in Phys. Edn., U. N.C., Greensboro, 1978. Softball and fencing program coord. Mequon (Wis.) Recreation Dept., 1970; phys. edn., health and English tchr. Horace Jr. H.S., 1970—81; phys. edn. and health tchr. Sheboygan (Wis.) South H.S., 1982—2004; emeritus tchr. Sheboygan Early Learning Ctr., 2004—05; basketball and volleyball coach, 1972—89; girls track coach, 1972—2004; active early childhood phys. activity pilot program SASD. Mem. dist. wide curriculum and evaluation coms., 1978—2004; mem. sch. effectiveness team, 1991—94; sch. evaluation consortium evaluator, 1988—93; inbound/outbound coach Sport for Understanding, 1991—96. Contbr. articles to profl. jours. Active Sheboygan (Wis.) Spkrs. Bur., 1987—95, Women Reaching Women. Recipient Nat. H.S. Coaches award for girls track, 1987, Womans Sports Advocates of Wis. Lifetime award, 2003. Mem.: AAHPERD (chair 2004, Midwest dist. Tchr. of Yr. 1995, Pathfinder award 1997, chair 2003—04), NEA, Sheboygan Edn. Assn., Wis. Assn. Health, Phys. Edn., Recreation and Dance (life; pres.-elect 1998—99, pres. 1999—2000, Phys. Edn. Tchr. Yr. 1993). Home: 1841 N 26th St Sheboygan WI 53081-2008

FRITZ, MARY ANN, music educator; b. Springfield, Mo. d. James Martin and Mary Lavon Fritz. BA, Drury Coll., 1982; MA in Ednl. Psychology, U. Nebr., 1984; MusM in Piano Performance, Southwestern Bapt. Theol. Sem., 1994, D in Musical Arts in Piano Pedagogy, 1998. Advanced cert. Creative Motion Alliance. Pvt. piano tchr., Ft. Worth, 1975—; piano tchr. Lake Arlington (Tex.) Acad., 1989—99. Adj. prof. piano Howard Payne U., Brownwood, Tex., 1993—94, Dallas Bapt. U., 1997—; tchg. fellow music edn. and piano Southwestern Bapt. Theol. Sem., Ft. Worth, 1994—98, adj. prof. music edn. and piano, 1999—2000; dir. children's choirs Overton Pk. Meth. Ch., Ft. Worth, 1996—2005; adjudicator piano festivals various music tchr. assns., 1995—; adjudicator piano auditions Am. Coll. Musicians, 1999—; clinician children's creativity camps various chs. and schs., Tex. and La., 1985—. Author: A Piano Pedagogy of Creative Motion, 1998; percussionist: mus. rec. Steal Away Home, 1995; editor: Jour. Creative Motion, 2000—. Pres.' Merit scholar Southwestern Bapt. Theol. Sem., Ft. Worth, 1994. Mem.: Creative Motion Alliance, Inc. (charter) (pres. 1994—98, clinician/workshop leader 1995—, 1st v.p. 1999—2001, pres. 2006—), Ft. Worth Music Tchrs. Assn., Ft. Worth Piano Tchrs. Forum (4th v.p. 1998—2002), Am. Coll. Musicians (adjudicator). Home: 5101 Mountain Spring Tr Fort Worth TX 76123 Office Phone: 214-333-5316.

FRITZSCHE, PEGGY J., medical association administrator, radiologist; b. Dayton, OH; m. Anton Hasso; children: Stephen, Martin. Undergrad., Andrews Univ., Berrien Springs, Mich.; MD, Loma Linda U. Intern Charles Kettering Mem. Hosp.; resident radiology White Memorial Medical Ctr., LA; med. dir. Riverside MRI Ctr., Riverside, Calif.; pres. Radiol. Soc. N.Am., Oakbrook, Ill., 2002—04; with San Bernardino MRI, Inland Empire Regional PET Ctr., Calif. Clin. prof. Loma Linda U. Sch. Medicine, 1970—, pres. med. staff; presenter scientific mtgs.; fellow U.C.L.A., 1973—74. Mem. editl. bd.: RadioGraphics, The Am. Jour. Roentgenology, Jour. Computer Assisted Tomography, scientific referee: Academic Radiology, Radiology; contbr. articles to numerous profl. jours., chapters to books; co-author: MRI of the Body, 1993. Recipient Charles J. Kettering Found. Scholarship. Fellow: ACR (councilor); mem.: AMA (gov. bd. women physician congress, deleg.), Am. Assn. Women Radiologists (pres.), Calif. Med. Assn. (deleg.), San Bernardino County Med. Soc. (pres., officer). Office: Radiological Soc North America Inc 820 Jorie Blvd Oak Brook IL 60523-2251

FROBOM, LEANN LARSON, lawyer; b. Ramona, S.D., May 31, 1953; d. Floyd Burdette and Janice Anne (Quist) L.; m. Richard Curtis Finke, May 19, 1973 (div. Jan. 1978); 1 child, Timothy; m. Dwayne Jeffery LaFave, May 31, 1981 (div. 1992); children: Jeffrey, Allison; m. Jerome B. Frobom, Aug. 21, 1999. BS, U. S.D., 1974, JD with honors, 1977. Bar: S.D. 1977, U.S. Dist. Ct. S.D. 1977, U.S. Ct. Appeals (8th cir.) 1977, N.D. 1978, U.S. Dist. Ct. N.D. 1978, Iowa 1998, Nebr. 2001. Asst. atty. gen. State of S.D., Pierre, 1977-78, 79-81; assoc. Bjella, Neff, Rathert & Wahl, Williston, ND, 1978-79, Tobin Law Offices, P.C., Winner, SD, 1981-83; assoc. dean, asst. prof. U. S.D. Sch. Law, Vermillion, 1983-86, dir. continuing legal edn., 1983-89, assoc. prof. law, 1986-89; ptnr. Aho & LaFave, Brookings, SD, 1990-91; pvt. practice Brookings, 1991-92; asst. U.S. atty. U.S. Dist. S.D., 1992-97; gen. counsel S.D. Auto Group, Inc., Sioux Falls, 1997-98; atty. Hughes Law Offices, Sioux Falls, 1998-99, Cline Williams Wright Johnson & Oldfather, Lincoln, Nebr., 1999—2003, Nebr. Legal Svcs., 2003—05; adjudicator N.E. Workforce Devel., Nebr., 2005—. Mem. S.D. Bd. Pardons and Paroles, 1987-90, chmn., 1989-90; comml. arbitrator Am. Arbitration Assn., 1985-92; prof. Kilian C.C.; tax preparer H&R Block Co., 1999— Contbr. articles to profl. jours. Mem. planning coun. Nat. Identification Program for Advancement Women in Higher Edn. Adminstrn., Am. Coun. on Edn., S.D., 1984-90; bd. dirs. Mo. Shores Women's Resource Ctr., Pierre, 1980, W.H. Over Mus., Vermillion, 1986-87, S.D. Vol. Lawyers for Arts, 1987-92, Brookings Interagy. Coun., 1990-91, Brookings Women's Ctr., 1990-94 Named S.D. Woman Atty. of Yr. Women in Law U. S.D., 1985. Mem. Epsilon Sigma Alpha (S.D. coun. sect. 1985-86). Episcopalian. Avocations: reading, quilting. Home: 4911 High St Lincoln NE 68506-3970

FROEDGE, SUSAN JANET, music educator; b. Taegu, Republic Of Korea, Sept. 25, 1976; d. Richard Lee and Kwon Si Baumgardner; m. Brian Paul Froedge, June 5, 2004; 1 child, Elizabeth Marie. B Music Edn., U. Ky., Lexington, 1998, M Music Performance-Instrumental Conducting, 2000. Cert. tchr. Ky., 2000. Tchr. instrumental music Radcliff Mid. Sch., Ky., 2000—. Pvt. flute instr., Elizabethtown, Ky., 2000—. Named Outstanding Young Band Dir. in Ky., Phi Beta Mu, 2005. Mem.: NEA, Flute Soc. of Ky., Ky. Leadership Acad., Flute Soc. of Ky. (bd. dirs. 2000—05), Ky. Educator's Assn., Ky. Music Educator's Assn. (bd. dirs. 2005—06), Music Educator's Nat. Conf., Fourth Dist. Band Director's Assn. (pres. 2002—05). Avocations: golf, scrapbooking, community band, landscaping. Home: 217 Emmaus Cir Elizabethtown KY 42701 Office: Radcliff Mid Sch 1145 S Dixie Blvd Radcliff KY 40160 Office Phone: 270-351-1171. Personal E-mail: bfroedge@comcast.net. Business E-Mail: susan.froedge@hardin.kyschools.us.

FROEMMING, BARBARA G., retired home economics educator; b. Peoria, Ill., June 5, 1933; d. Alva V. Gibson and H. Florence Johnson; m. Jack A. Froemming, Feb. 23, 1957 (dec.); children: John G., James A. BS in Home Econs. Edn., U. Wis., Madison, 1955; MS in Curriculum and Instrn., U. Wis., Milw., 1979. Tchr. home econs. Milw. Pub. Schs., 1955—59, Glendale-River Hills Sch., Wis., 1968—93. Dept. chmn. Glendale-River Hills Schs., 1975—93; Glen Hills sch. rep. Glendale Planning Coun., 1990—92. Coord. women's ministries Fox Point Luth. Ch., Wis., 1995—. Mem.: Dahlia Soc. Wis. (grower, exhibitor), Am. Assn. Family and Consumer Scis., Swedish-Am. Hist. Soc. (bd. dirs.), Phi Upsilon Omicron, Omicron Nu, Kappa Delta (nat. officer 1993—2002, Outstanding Alumni award 2004, Order of the Emerald 2005). Lutheran. Avocations: genealogy, travel, Dahlia growers exhibitor. Home: 151 W Blackhawk Rd Fox Point WI 53217 Fax: 414-352-4310. E-mail: bfroemm@aol.com.

FROETSCHER, JANET, social services administrator; m. Roy Froetscher; 2 children. Bachelor's Degree, U. Va., 1981; M in Mgmt., Northwestern U., 1983. Leveraged buyout specialist First Chgo. Corp.; v.p. corp. fin. Bankers Trust Co., N.Y.C.; founding mng. ptnr. Exec. Options; exec. dir. Fin. Rsch. and Adv. Com. Civic Com. of the Comml. Club Chgo., 1992—99; sr. v.p. seminars Aspen Inst., 1999—2000, exec. v.p., 2000—01, COO, 2001—02; pres., CEO United Way Chgo., 2003, United Way Met. Chgo., 2003—. Named mem. Coun. of 100, Northwestern U., mem., The Chgo. Network; named one of Chgo. Most Influential Women, Crain's Chgo. Bus., 1996, 40 under 40, 1997; Henry Crown fellow, Aspen Inst., 1998. Office: United Way Met Chgo 560 W Lake Chicago IL 60661

FROLICK, PATRICIA MARY, retired elementary school educator; b. Portland, Oreg., May 17, 1923; d. Fred Anthony and Clara Cecelia (Riverman) F. BS in Edn., Marylhurst Coll., 1960; MS in Edn., Portland State U., 1970; student, U. Oreg., 1975; MA in Theology, St. Mary's Coll., Moraga, Calif., 1977. Joined Roman Cath. Order Sisters of Holy Names of Jesus and Mary, 1943. Left order in 1974. Elem. sch. tchr. Catholic Sch. System, Oreg., 1943-69; tchr., libr. Hood River Pub. Schs., 1970-74, Bend-La Pine (Oreg.) Pub. Schs., 1981-93; ret., 1993. Part-time tchr.'s asst., Portland, 1993—2000. Mem. NEA, Oreg. Edn. Assn., Met. Mus. Art (assoc.), Nat. Mus. Women in Arts (charter). Democrat. Roman Catholic. Avocation: watercolor and oil painting. Home: 3465 SE 153rd Ave Portland OR 97236-2265

FROMAN, SANDRA SUE, lawyer; b. San Francisco, June 15, 1949; d. Jay and Beatrice Froman. AB with honors, Stanford U., 1971; JD, Harvard U., 1974. Bar: Calif. 1974, U.S. Dist. Ct. (cen. dist.) Calif. 1974, U.S. Dist. Ct. (so. dist.) Calif. 1976, U.S. Dist. Ct. (no. dist.) Calif., U.S. Ct. Claims 1979, U.S. Tax Ct. 1984, Ariz. 1985, U.S. Dist. Ct. Ariz. 1985, U.S. Ct. Appeals (9th cir.) 1986, U.S. Supreme Ct. 1986. Assoc. Loeb & Loeb, L.A., 1974-80, ptnr., 1981-84; assoc. Bilby & Schoenhair, P.C., Tucson, 1985, shareholder, 1986-89; ptnr. Snell & Wilmer, Tucson, 1989-99. Vis. asst. prof. law U. Santa Clara, Calif., 1983-85; mem. Pima County Commn. on Trial Ct. Appointments, 1996-98. Trustee NRA Civil Rights Def. Fund, 1992-98, NRA Found., pres. 1997-2000; bd. dirs. NRA, 1992-2005, pres. 2005-. Mem. Ariz. Bar Found. (pres. 1996—), Nat. 4-H Shooting Sports Found. (pres. 2002-04), Wildlife for Tomorrow Found. (pres. 1999-02). Office: Ste 140 200 W Magee Rd Tucson AZ 85704-6492 Address: NRA 11250 Waples Mill Rd Fairfax VA 22030

FRONTANI, HEIDI GLAESEL, geographer, educator; BS, Cornell U., 1987; MS, PhD, U. Wis., Madison, 1997. Vis. asst. prof. Mt. Holyoke Coll., 1997—98; asst. prof. geography Elon U., NC, 1998—2003, assoc. prof. geography, 2003—. Grant reviewer NSF, Fulbright-Hays Found.; presenter in field. Contbr. book reviews, chapters to books, articles to profl. jours. Fellow, U.S. Dept. Edn., 1992—94, Fulbright-Hays Found., 1995, 2001; scholar Marie Christine Kohler fellowship, Social Sci. Rsch. Coun., 1994;, U. Wis., Madison, 1996—97. Mem.: African Studies Assn., Assn. Am. Geographers.

FROSSARD, JANICE L., science educator; d. Wilfred and Jewel Frossard; m. Alvin V. Katz, Aug. 6, 1983; children: David Katz, Joseph Katz. BA in Edn., U. Fla., Gainesville, 1973; MS in Edn., Elmira Coll., NY, 1989. Cert. tchr. NY. Tchr. LaLuz Pvt. Sch., Miami, Fla., 1973—74, Dade County Pub. Schs., 1974—77; tchr. fgn. lang. Gulliver Acad., Coral Gables, 1977—81; tchr. sci., fgn. lang. St. Gertrude HS, Richmond, Va., 1981—; tchr. sci. South Seneca Ctrl. Schs., Ovid, NY, 1985—. Mentor new tchrs. South Seneca Ctrl. Schs., 1996—; advisor Environthon, 1994—. Com. mem. Ulysses Philomathic Libr., Trumansburg, NY; vol. State & Hangar Theatre. Fellow, Cornell Inst. Biology. Mem.: South Seneca Tchrs. Assn. (sec. 1985—), Delta Kappa Gamma. Avocations: gardening, reading, needlecrafts, travel.

FROST, AMY ROSALIE, choreographer, dancer, educator; b. Roanoke, Va., Apr. 29, 1978; d. Robert Frost and Celia McCormick; m. Jeffrey Michael Schultze, July 15, 2006. BA in Dance, Hollins U., Roanoke, 2004. Dancer So. Ballet Theater, Orlando, Fla., 1997—98; dancer, tchr. SW Va. Ballet, Salem, 1998—99; dancer Charleston Ballet Theater, SC, 1999—2001; dancer, tchr., choreographer Roanoke Ballet Theater, Roanoke, 2001—04; dancer, tchr.

Young Audiences Va., 2001—04; dance tchr. North Cross Mid. Sch., Roanoke, 2003—04, Am. Dance Festival, Durham, NC, 2001—; dancer, acad. dance tchr. NW Fla. Ballet, Fort Walton Beach, 2004—. Aerial dancer Roanoke Ballet Theater, 2001—04; guest artist Turks and Caicos Dance Festival, 2003, Dancenter South, Atlanta, 2005. Dancer (ballets) Tarantelle; dir.: (ballets) Pieta.

FROST, DEBORAH E., elementary school educator; b. Brookfield, Conn., Dec. 22, 1969; d. Ronald A. and Elizabeth H. Frost. MA in Tchg., Sacred Heart U., Fairfield, Conn., 1992. Profl. tchg. cert. Conn., 1992. Elem. sch. tchr. Salisbury Ctrl. Sch., Lakeville, Conn., 1992—97; pvt. tutor Sharon, Conn., 1999—2003; tchr. history and English Rochambeau Mid. Sch., Southbury, Conn., 2003—. Rsch. asst. Measurement Learning Cons., Cannon Beach, Oreg., 1997—98. Fellow, NSF/Edn. Connection, 1995—96. Mem.: NEA. Avocations: travel, auto racing. Office: Rochambeau Middle School Dist # 15 100 Peter Rd Southbury CT 06488 Office Phone: 203-264-2711. Business E-Mail: dfrost@region15.org.

FROST, ELIZABETH ANN MCARTHUR, physician; b. Glasgow, Scotland, Oct. 29, 1938; arrived in US, 1963; d. Robert Thomas and Annie M. (Ross) F.; m. Wallace Capobianco, Sept. 4, 1965 (dec. May 1988); children: Garrett, Ross, Christopher, Neil. MBChB, U. Glasgow, 1961. Diplomate Am. Bd. Anesthesiology, Royal Coll. Ob-Gyn., London. Intern in surgery Royal Infirmary, Glasgow, 1961-62; intern in medicine Victoria Infirmary, Glasgow, 1962; intern in obstetrics Royal Maternity Hosp., Glasgow, 1962-63; resident in internal medicine Englewood (N.J.) Hosp., 1963-64; resident in anesthesiology N.Y. Hosp., N.Y.C., 1964-66; instr. in anesthesiology Albert Einstein Coll. Medicine, Bronx, NY, 1966-68, asst. prof. to assoc. prof., 1968-81, prof. anesthesiology, 1981-91, mem. dept. history of medicine, 1973-91; prof. dept. anesthesiology N.Y. Med. Coll., Valhalla, 1992-99; clin. prof. dept. anesthesiology Mt. Sinai Med. Ctr., N.Y.C., 2000—; attending anesthesiology VA Bronx, 2000—04. Book reviewer New Eng. Jour. of Medicine, 1983—; editor Preanesthetic Assessment, Anesthesiology News, 1984—, Gen. Surgery News, 1991; author/contbr. books; contbr. articles to profl. jours. Mem. N.Y. State Soc. Anesthesiologists, Am. Soc. of Anesthesiologists, Assn. of Univ. Anesthesiologists, Soc. of Neurosurg. Anesthesia and Neurologic Supportive Care, Am. Assn. of Neurol. Surgeons, Anesthesia History Assn. Home: 2 Pondview West Purchase NY 10577 Office Phone: 212-241-7467. Personal E-mail: elzfrost@aol.com.

FROST, ELLEN ELIZABETH, psychologist; b. N.Y.C. d. John Joseph and Josephine Mary (Cornell) F.; m. Jerry Melnick, Jan. 8, 1982; children: Mariel Frost, Matt James. BA magna cum laude, St. John's U., 1969; MA, Fordham U., 1971, PhD, 1982; candidate NYU Postdoctoral Program for Psychotherapy and Psychoanalysis, 1982—84. Cert. Eye Movement Desensitization Reprocessing tng., 2000. Clin. psychology intern Columbia-Presbyn. Psychiat. Inst., N.Y.C., 1972-73; asst. team leader staff psychologist Bensonhurst inpatient unit South Beach Psychiat. Ctr., Bklyn., 1973-75, sr. psychologist, Bensonhurst outpatient dept., 1975-81, assoc. psychologist, supr., 1982-89; dir. Phobia Svc., 1982-89; pvt. practice, 1983—; clin. supr. New Hope Guild, Bklyn., 1983—2000. Faculty L.I. Inst. Mental Health, 1990-97, supr., 1993-97. N.Y. State regents fellow, 1969-72; USPHS fellow, 1969-72. Mem. Am. Psychol. Assn., EMDR Internat. Assoc., Sigma Xi. Office: 200 E 33rd St Apt 25J New York NY 10016-4831 Office Phone: 212-725-0543. Office Fax: 212-725-0543. Personal E-mail: efrostphd@aol.com.

FROST, ELLEN LOUISE, political economist; b. Boston, Apr. 26, 1945; d. Horace Wier and Mildred (Kip) F.; m. William F. Pedersen, Jr., Feb. 2, 1974; 1 son by previous marriage, Jai Kumar Ojha; children: Mark Francis Pedersen, Claire Ellen Pedersen. BA magna cum laude, Radcliffe Coll., 1966; MA, Fletcher Sch. Law and Diplomacy, 1967; PhD, Harvard U., 1972. Teaching fellow, instr. Harvard U., Wellesley Coll., 1969-71; legis. asst. Office of Senator Alan Cranston, Washington, 1972-74; fgn. affairs officer Dept. Treasury, Washington, 1974-77; dep. dir. Office of Internat. Trade Policy and Negotiations, 1977; dep. asst. sec. of def. for internat. econ. and tech. affairs Dept. Def., Washington, 1977-81; dir. govt. programs Westinghouse Electric Corp., Washington, 1981-88; corp. dir., internat. affairs United Techs. Corp., Washington, 1988-91; sr. fellow Inst. for Internat. Econs., Washington, 1992-93, 95-98, vis. fellow, 1998—; counselor to U.S. Trade Rep., Washington, 1993-95. Author: For Richer, For Poorer: The New U.S.-Japan Relationship, 1987, Transatlantic Trade: A Strategic Agenda, 1997; co-editor: The Global Century, 2001. Trustee Aspen Inst. Berlin, 1990—92. NSF trainee, 1967—69. Mem. Internat. Inst. Strategic Studies, Coun. Fgn. Rels., Phi Beta Kappa.

FROST, JUANITA CORBITT, retired hospital foundation coordinator; b. Rockford, Ill., Aug. 4, 1926; d. Mervin Charles and Eva Marie (Moberg) Corbitt; m. Thomas Tapenden Frost, Jan. 3, 1954; children: Annamarie, Thomas Tapenden. Student, Little Rock U., 1959—61. Med. sec. asst. clin. pathology lab. VA Hosp., Whipple, Ariz., 1951—54; exec. dir. Camp Fire Girls, Temple, Tex., 1967—72; exec. sec. Scott and White Meml. Hosp. Found., Temple, 1972—82; coord. hosp. found., exec. asst. to bd. Scott and White Meml. Hosp., Temple, 1982—98, Scott Sherwood and Brindley Found., Temple, 1982—98; ret., 1998. Vestrywoman Episcopal Ch., Temple, 1985-88, sr. warden, 1987, worship com., 1995-97, search com., 1996-97; active Com. on Bishops Address NW Region Diocese Episcopal Ch., Houston, 1988; mem. Bell County Choral Group, Belton, Tex., 1988-92, Temple Civic Theatre Guild, 1997; tchr. Lit. Coun., Temple, 1988-93; coord. capital campaign St. Francis Episcopal Ch., Temple, 2000, mem. Altar Guild, mem. Pastoral Care Com., 1986— Mem. Am. Hosp. Assn. Exec. Assts., Dau. of King (sec. St. Clare chpt. 1998-99, widows serving 2004—) Avocations: needlecrafts, reading. Home: 3902 W Adams Apt 122 Temple TX 76504 E-mail: jfrost6948@aol.com.

FROST, LAURA LYNN, microbiology educator; b. Charleroi, Pa., June 12, 1971; BS, California U. Pa., 1995; MS, Iowa State U., Ames, 1995; PhD, W.Va. U., Morgantown, 2003. Asst. prof. Gannon U., Erie, Pa., 2002—05; asst. prof. microbiology, genetics and biotech. Point Park U., Pitts., 2005—. Office: Point Pk U 201 Wood St Pittsburgh PA 15222 Office Phone: 412-392-3891. Business E-Mail: lfrost@pointpark.edu.

FROST, LINDA GAIL, clergyman, hospital chaplain; b. Louisville, Feb. 26, 1950; d. Halqua Mildon and Christena (Crisp) F. BA, Georgetown (Ky.) Coll., 1972; MDiv, So. Bapt. Sem., Louisville, 1978, DMin, 1982. Ordained to ministry Bapt. Ch., 1978; bd. cert. chaplain. Social worker Dept. Pub. Welfare, Corpus Christi, 1972-76; assoc. to pastor Walnut St. Bapt. Ch., Louisville, 1979-89; chaplain, clin. supr. Koala Hosp., Columbus, Ind., 1989-92; dir. chaplain svcs. St.'s Mary and Elizabeth Hosp., Louisville, 1993—. Advisor pastoral svcs. Hospice of S.E. Ind., Jeffersonville, 1993-98. Author: A Legacy in Missions and Ministry, 1993; contbg. author: Women at the Well, 2003. Bd. dirs., pres. Neighborhood Devel. Corp., Louisville, 1979-89; mem., sec. Old Louisville Neighborhood Coun., 1979-87; active ARC Disaster Svcs., 1999—. Mem.: Ky. Chaplain Assn. (pres. 1999—).

FROST, SUSAN BETH, theater producer; b. South Kingston, R.I., Nov. 1, 1955; d. Cyril E. and Martha (Smith) F.; m. Daniel Francis Renn III, Feb. 16, 1991; 1 child, Martha Hope Renn. B in Theater, Smith Coll., 1977. Freelance theatrical mgr., N.Y.C., 1977-84; assoc. prodr. Goodspeed Opera House, East Haddam, Conn., 1985—2005. Chair panel NEA/New Am. Works, Washington, 1991-93; awards panelist Loewe Award/New Dramatists, N.Y.C., 1994, 95; mem. com. Smith Coll./Theatre Alumni, N.Y.C., 1985—, Alliance Music Theatre, N.Y.C., 1991—. Office: Goodspeed Opera House PO Box A East Haddam CT 06423-0281

FROST-KNAPPMAN, (LINDA) ELIZABETH, publishing executive, editor, writer; b. Washington, Oct. 1, 1943; d. Edward Laurie and Lorena (Ameter) Frost; m. Edward William Knappman, Nov. 6, 1965; 1 child, Amanda. BA, George Washington U., 1965; postgrad., U. Wis., 1966, NYU, 1966. Editor Natural History Press, N.Y.C., 1967-69, William Collins and Sons, London, 1970-71; sr. editor Doubleday and Co., N.Y.C., 1972-80, William Morrow and Co., Inc., N.Y.C., 1980-82; founder, pres. New Eng. Pub. Assocs. Inc., Chester, Conn., 1982—. Lectr. New Eng. colls. and univs. Author: The World Almanac of Presidential Quotations, 1993, The ABC-CLIO Companion to Women's Progress in America, 1994 (Outstanding Acad. Book-Reference of Yr. award ALA), The Quotable Lawyer, 1986, 1998, Women Suffrage in America: An Eyewitness History, 1992, Courtroom Dramas, 3 vols., 1997; gen. editor: (CD-ROM) American Journey: Women in America, 1994, Women's Rights on Trial, 1998. Mem. Authors Guild. Avocations: knitting, tennis, travel, reading. Office: New Eng Pub Assocs Inc PO Box 361 Chester CT 06412-0005 Office Phone: 860-345-7323. E-mail: elizabeth@nepa.com.

FROT-COUTAZ, CECILE, television producer; b. Chambery, France, Apr. 18, 1966; m. M. Eliot Charles, Dec. 29, 2001; 1 child, Amelie. BA in Bus., ESSEC, 1988; MBA, INSEAD, 1994. Assoc. Mercer Mgmt. Consulting, London, 1988—93; exec. corp. strategy Pearson TV, London, 1994—98, dep. chief exec. officer So. Europe, mng. dir. France Paris, 1998—2000, head digital media, 2000—01; exec. v.p. comml. and ops. FremantleMedia N.Am., LA, 2001—02, COO, Santa Monica, Calif., 2002—, exec. prodr. Am. Idol, 2002—. Office: Fremantle Media Productions North America Inc 2700 Colorado Ave Ste 450 Santa Monica CA 90404

FRUEH, DEBORAH K.A. (DEBI FRUEH), artist, poet; b. St. Louis, Nov. 24, 1951; d. Louis J. and Dorothy M. Frueh. AA, St. Louis Coll., 1971; student, Fontbonne Coll. Art, St. Louis, 1971—72, St. Louis U., 1972. Profl. portraitist, Wickliffe, Ky., 1972—. Lectr. Paducah Art Guild, Ky., 1973; sculpture tchr. Paducah C.C., U. Ky., 1977—79. Author numerous poems; one-woman shows include Florissant Valley Art Gallery, St. Louis, 1970, Evansville Mus. Arts and Sci., Ind., 1973, Paducah Art Guild/Gallery, 1973, Paducah C.C., 1974, Peoples First Nat. Bank and Trust Co., Paducah, 1974, Spring Arts Show, 1975—76, Arts Coun., 1979, Represented in permanent collections Chester Meml. Hosp., Ill., Carmin Miranda Mus., Rio de Janeiro, Cairo Marine Svc., Ill., Huffman Towing Co., Clayton, Mo., Okie Moore Diving Co., St. Louis, Wis. Barge Lines, Cassville, Office of Congressman Ed Whitfield, Paducah, Paducah C.C., The White House, Washington. Fundraiser St. Mary's, Paducah, 2000—05, Yeiser Art Ctr., Paducah, 2001, 2005. Recipient Riverview Gardens Best in Art award, 1969, Duchess of Paducah award for excellence, 1976, Spl. award for creativity, Gamblin Artists Colors Co., 2003. Mem.: Am. Soc. Portrait Artists, Nat. Mus. Women in the Arts. Avocations: reading, gardening. Home: 1985 Deerfield Rd Wickliffe KY 42087 Office Phone: 270-335-3728.

FRUEHWALD, KRISTIN GAIL, lawyer; b. Sidney, Nebr., May 15, 1946; d. Chris U. and Mary E. (Boles) Bitner; m. Michael R. Fruehwald, Feb. 23, 1980; children: Laurel Elizabeth, Amy Marie. BS with highest distinction in History, U. Nebr., 1968; JD summa cum laude, Ind. U., 1975. Bar: Ind. 1975, U.S. Dist. Ct. (so. dist.) Ind. 1975. Assoc. Barnes & Thornburg, Indpls., 1975-81, ptnr., 1982—. Spkr. in field. Contbr. articles to profl. jours. Trustee The Orchard Sch., 1993—99, chmn., 1997—98, bd. govs., 2005—; bd. dirs. Indpls. Parks Found., 1995—2000, Arts Ind., 1994—98, Ind. Continuing Legal Edn. Forum, 1993—2001, pres., 2000—01; bd. dirs. James Whitcomb Riley Meml. Assn., 1995—, treas., 2000—; bd. dirs. Planned Giving Group Ind., Fedn. Cmty. Defenders, Inc., 1993—99, pres., 1999—2001; bd. dirs. Ind. affiliate Am. Heart Assn., 1977—81, vice chmn. Marion County chpt., 1981; bd. trustees Ctrl. Ind. Land Trust, 2005—. Fellow: ABA (chmn. distributable net income subcom 1985—91, mem. real property, probate and trust sect.), Ind. State Bar Assn. (chmn. probate, trust and real property sects. 1987—88, mem. ho. of dels. 1987—, bd. mgrs. 1989—90, treas. 1996—97, chair ho. of dels. 1998—99, pres. 2001—02, mem. sect. taxation), Ind. Bar Found. (bd. dirs. 2003—, bd. govs. 2004—), Am. Coll. Trust and Estate Counsel (chmn. Ind. state laws com. 1992—95); mem.: Indpls. (Ind.) Bar Found. (bd. dirs. 1992—, chmn. 1997—99), Ind. Code Study Commn., Internat. Assn. Fin. Planners, Indpls. Estate Planning Coun., Indpls. Bar Assn. (chmn. estate planning and adminstrn. sect. 1982—83, chmn. long range fin. planning com. 1988—89, pres. 1993). Office: Barnes & Thornburg 11 S Meridian St Indianapolis IN 46204-3535 Office Phone: 317-231-7245. Business E-Mail: kris.fruewald@btlaw.com.

FRUIA, CAROLYN CHRISTINE, hair designer, educator; b. Louisville, Ky., July 3, 1943; d. Cecil William Burruss and Virginia Elizabeth Wright; m. Frank John Fruia, June 19, 1976; children: Paul, Perry, Troy, Dwayne; m. Joseph Frederick Crutcher (div.); children: Simone Elise, Tanya Shantel. Student, Saint James, Louisville, 1961—62. Hair designer Nat. Cosmetologist, 1962—2006, Blue Grass Hair Fashion, Ky., 1966—76, Hair America, 1975—2006, Tex. Hair Fashion, 1976—99. Styles dir. Blue Grass Hairfashion, Ky., 1973—74; creative design com. Hair Am., 1978—79; styles dir. Lone Star Styles Com., Tex., 1980—81; educator, lectr., platform artist Clairol Platform Competition, 1975; cons. MaDona House, Houston, 1977—80; educator Look Good-Feel Better, Houston, 1996—2006; sub-tchr. Katy Ind. Schs., Tex., 1988—2000. Organizer, supporter Young Dem. Club, 1964—76. Recipient Woman of Yr., Xi Mu Eta, 2004. Mem.: Profl. Divers Assn., Nat. Assn. Self Employed, Am. Assn. Ret. People. Democrat. Roman Catholic. Avocations: art, fishing, swimming, scuba diving. Home: 21218 Park Bend Katy TX 77450 Office: CF Design Concepts/Carolines 5711 Fifth St Katy TX 77493 Personal E-mail: carolyn.fruia@sbcglobal.net.

FRUIHT, DOLORES GIUSTINA, artist, educator, poet; b. Portland, Oreg., Mar. 9, 1923; d. Erminio and Irene (Onorato) Giustina; m. Thos. Herman Fruiht, Dec. 20, 1947 (div. 1976); children: Justina, Bryce, Bradford, Erica, Renee. BS, RN, U. Portland, 1944; attended, U. San Francisco, 1971. Nurse, Nurse Corps U.S. Army, 1944-46; intravenous nurse St. Vincent's Hosp., Portland, 1946; staff nurse Dr. Shepard, Eugene, Oreg., 1947-49; surg. nurse Sacred Heart Hosp., Eugene, Oreg., 1949-52; tchr. Ursulina High Sch., Santa Rosa, Calif., 1976-78; artist Angela Ctr. for Adult Edn., Santa Rosa, Calif., 1978-88. Juror Bodega Bay Fisherman's Festival, Calif., 1992, Sebastopol Ctr. for the Arts, 1995. One woman shows include: "Expressions in Art", Abstract Photography, Paintings, and Images in Clay, Sonoma County Mus., Santa Rosa, 1992, Pottery Exhibit, Angela Ctr., 1980, Sonoma, 1976; exhibited in group shows at: Oreg. State U., 1999, Cultural Arts Coun. Sonoma County, 1998, Sebastopol Libr., 1992, Bodega Bay Allied Arts, 1991, 93-96, Nor Cal. State Art Exhibit, Nat. League of Am. Pen Women, Souverain Winery, 1985, "Tibetan Faces", Photography, Calif. Mus. of Art, Santa Rosa, 1985, Photography Exhibit, Angela Ctr., 1982, "The Healing Celebration of Art", Photography, San Francisco Civic Auditorium, 1981, Photography Show, Angela Ctr., 1980, Pottery Exhibit, 1975; contbr. articles to numerous profl. jours.; disting. lectr. Diplomat City of Sonoma, Russia, 1988. 1st Lt. U.S. Army Nurse Corps, 1944-46. Decorated Bronze Star for Luzon Campaign U.S. Army. Mem. Nat. League of Am. Pen Women (Biennial Selection award, 1986, Excellence award, 1985). Roman Catholic. Avocations: hiking, golf, reading. Home and Office: 1519 Parsons Dr Santa Rosa CA 95404

FRUMP, STEFANIE L., elementary school educator; b. Trenton, NJ, Sept. 11, 1979; d. Michael and Susan Janoski; m. Steven Frump, Apr. 24, 2004. BS in Marine Sci., Eckerd Coll., St. Petersburg, Fla., 2001. Edn. intern Mote Marine Lab., Sarasota, Fla., 1999—99; fisheries intern The Ocean Conservancy, St. Petersburg, 2000—02; instr. Fla. Aquarium, Tampa, 2002—03; marine sci. coord. Marine Sci. Ctr. Campbell Pk. Elem., St. Petersburg, 2003—. Dive vol. Fla. Aquarium, Tampa, 2003—. Scholar, St. Petersburg Audubon Soc., 2006. Mem.: Fla. Assn. Sci. Tchrs., Fla. Marine Sci. Educators Assn. Presbyterian. Avocations: scuba diving, travel, kayaking. Office: Campbell Park Elementary 1051 7th Ave South Saint Petersburg FL 33705 Office Phone: 727-893-2650. Personal E-mail: stefanie_frump@places.pcsb.org.

FRY, DONNA MARIE, military officer, educator; b. Altadena, Calif., Oct. 16, 1947; d. Hampton Scott and M. Genevieve (Wolff) F.; 1 child, Alicia Fay. BA, Rutgers U., 1981; MS, Air Force Inst. Tech., 1986. Enlisted USAF, 1968, advanced through grades to master sgt., 1981, commd. 2d lt., advanced through grades to capt., staff cost analyst Cost Rsch. Office Bergstrom AFB, Tex., 1986-88, instr. Air Force Inst. Tech. Wright-Patterson AFB, Ohio, 1989-91, chief divsn. exec. communications Maxwell AFB, Ala., 1991-92, chief divsn. analysis for resource mgrs., 1992-95, instr. Ctr. Profl. Devel., Profl. Mil. Comp. Sch., 1991-95, ret., 1995; sr. analyst, curriculum developer Budget Info. Sys. FIRST, MCR Fed., Inc., Maxwell AFB, Montgomery, Ala., 1999-2000; v.p. curriculum devel. Knowledge Mgmt. Solutions, Prattville, Ala., 2000—02; substitute tchr. Lighthouse Christian Acad., 2001—, Evangelical Christian Acad., 2001—03, Montgomery Cath. Prep. Sch., 2001—. Tchr. speech, pub. speaking andcomputers Covenant Acad., 1995—97; adj. faculty J. Patterson State Tech. Coll. (now H. Coun. Trenholm State Coll.), 1996; cons. in field. Mem. NAFE, Am. Soc. Mil. Comptrollers (v.p., project officer 1988-91, v.p. for Profl. Mil. Comptrollers' Sch. 1992), Air Force Assn. (life), Soc. Cost Estimating and Analysis, SALSAW (pres. Dayton chpt. 1990-91), Res. Officers Assn. (life), Non-Commd. Officers Assn. (life), Rutgers U. Alumni Assn. Republican. Roman Catholic. Avocations: travel, costume design, reading, swimming, knitting. Home: 7537 Halcyon Forest Trl Montgomery AL 36117-3493 E-mail: wafretiree@aol.com.

FRY, ELIZABETH H. W., lawyer; b. Willimantic, Conn., Mar. 31, 1951; AB, Yale U., 1973; JD cum laude, Fordham U., 1978. Bar: Conn. 1978, N.Y. 1979. Ptnr., co-leader Individual Client Svc. practice Pillsbury Winthrop Shaw Pittman, N.Y.C. Assoc. editor Fordham Law Review, 1977-78. Mem.: NY State Bar Assn., Assn. Bar City of NY. Office: Pillsbury Winthrop Shaw Pittman 1540 Broadway New York NY 10036 Office Phone: 212-858-1520. Office Fax: 212-858-1500. Business E-Mail: elizabeth.fry@pillsburylaw.com.

FRY, HEDY, Member of Parliament; 3 children. MD, Royal Coll. Surgeons, Dublin, Ireland, 1968. Pvt. practice; mem., sec. of state (multiculturalism) (status of women) Can. Parliament/Vancouver Ctr., Ottawa, 1996—2002; chair B.C. Caucus, 2002—; mem. spl. com. on non-med. use of drugs, mem. standing com. on health, standing com. on justice and human rights Can. Parliament, Ottawa, Canada, 2002. Dr. Hirsh Rosenfeld Disting. Lectr. in family medicine McGill U., 1994; featured on Doctor-Doctor, CBC TV series, 1985-89. Mem. editl. bd. Med. Post. Mem. com. Royal Commn. on Reproductive Technologies.dn. Learning for Living Adv. Bd.; mem. Mayor's Spl. Com. on Urban Natives; bd. dirs. St. George's sch., 1989-91; adv. bd. B.C. Physicians Against Nuclear War; co-chair Liberal Party Health and Social Issues sect., Aylmer Conf., 1992, mem. Leader's Nat. Task Force on Women, 1992-93; parliamentary sec. Min. of Health, 1993-96, mem. task force on reform of social security sys., 1994, standing com. on health, 1994, subcom. on AIDS, mem. caucus com. on social policy. Recipient Cmty. Svc. award Commonwealth Caribbean Club, 1991, Black Achievement award, 1994, Congress of Black Women award, 1994. Mem. B.C. Fedn. Med. Women (pres. 1977), Vancouver Women's Network, Vancouver Med. Assn. (pres. 1988-89), B.C. Med. Assn. (pres. 1990-91, chief negotiator 1991-93), Can. Med. Assn. (chair obstetrics task force 1986-87, chair multiculturalism com. 1992-93), Coun. of Healthcare and Promotion (B.C. rep. 1984-92). Avocations: travel, gardening, reading.

FRY, JANE MARIE, secondary school educator; b. Erie, Pa., Aug. 28, 1965; d. Charles Theodore and Olga (Maha) Fry. BA in Internat. Studies and Econ. Theory, Am. U., 1987, MA in Econs., 1992. Economist U.S. Dept. Commerce, Washington, 1987-98; social studies tchr. Montgomery County Schs., 1999—. Planning commr. City of Rockville, Md., 1994-98. Recipient Performance award U.S. Bur. Econs., Washington, 1991, 97. Mem.: Toastmaster (Dist.).

FRY, MILDRED COVEY, regional library executive director; b. Canton, Ohio, Mar. 31, 1940; d. Homer D. and Freda A. (Heldman) Covey; m. James W. Fry (div. 1985); 1 child, Christine Lee Fry Clarke. BA, Capital U., Columbus, Ohio, 1982; MLS, Kent (Ohio) State U., 1986. Libr. asst. Stark County Dist. Libr., Canton, Ohio, 1958—61; asst. dir. Mayne Williams Pub. Libr., Johnson City, Tenn., 1965—66; circulation desk supr. Ohio State U. Libr., Edn. and Psychology, 1966—82; training coord. Online Computer Libr. Ct., Columbus, 1982—84; asst. dir. Cleve. Area Met. Libr. Sys., 1986—97; owner Polaris Leadership Ctr., Marietta, 1996—; exec. dir. NOLA Regional Libr. Sys., 1997—99, SOLO Regional Libr. Sys., Caldwell, Ohio, 1999—2002. Mem. adv. coun. Ohio Libr. Svcs. and Tech. Act, 1998-99; mem. Ohio Statewide Resource Sharing Com., 1998-2001; mem. adv. coun. Sch. Info. and Libr. Scis., Kent State U., 1998—2001 v.p., pres.-elect alumni, 1997-98, pres.-alumni, 1999-2000. Developer Libr. Leadership 2000 Inst., Ohio, 1993-95. Recipient Leadership award for LL 2000, Assn. Specialized and Cooperative Library Agencies, 1996, Librarian of the Year, Ohio Library Coun., 1995; named Alumna of Yr. Kent State U. Sch. of Libr. and Info. Sci., 1998. Mem. ASTD, ALA, DAR, Continuing Libr. Edn. Network and Exch. Round Table (exec. bd., sec. 1990-92), mem. PLA (leadership devel. com. 1994-95), Libr. Adminstrn. and Mgmt. Assn., Am. Soc. Assn., Execs, Ohio Libr. Coun. (bd. dirs. 1990-93, govt. rels. com. 1998-2001), First Families of Ohio, First Families of Washington County (Ohio) Geneal. Soc. Democrat. Avocations: reading, writing, hiking, travel. Home: 105 Brittigan Cir Marietta OH 45750-1202 E-mail: milliecovey@charter.net.

FRY, THERESA EILEEN, therapeutic foster care aide; b. Bellefonte, Pa., July 20, 1968; d. James Allen Boob, Eileen Betty Boob; m. Shawn William Fry; children: Teri Shaffer, Melinda Shaffer. Student in social work, Lock Haven U., 1999—2003. Cert. nurse asst., 1991. Resident asst. Alterra, State College, Pa., 1998—99; technician mental health Meadows Psychiat. Ctr., Centre Hall, Pa., 2000—01; sec. Social Work Club, Lock Haven, 2000—; therapeutic foster care aide Hope For Kids, Inc., 2002—. Counselor Risk Reduction Test The Aids Project, State College, 2000—. Mem.: NASW (Pa. chpt., com. on nominations and leadership identification). Democrat. Methodist. Avocations: camping, hunting, fishing, travel. Home: 102 Front St Centre Hall PA 16828 Personal E-mail: theresa16828@yahoo.com.

FRYE, BRANDIE MARIE, personal trainer, educator; b. Wellsboro, Pa., Feb. 6, 1979; d. Kirk Robert MacClaren; m. William Joseph Frye, June 28, 2003. BS in Health Sci., Lock Haven U., Pa., 2001; MEd, Temple U., Phila., 2003. Cert. athletic trainer NATA Bd. Cert. Asst. athletic trainer, clin. instr. Stevens Inst. Tech., Hoboken, NJ, 2003—04; head athletic trainer, faculty Oak Knoll Sch., Summit, NJ, 2004—. Cert. athletic trainer USTA Jr. Internat. Grasscourt Championships, Phila., 2001—03. Mem.: Athletic Trainers Soc. NJ, Pa. Athletic Trainers Soc., Nat. Athletic Trainers Assn., Phi Sigma Pi. Achievements include research in glenohumeral joint stiffness and laxity are influenced by gender and athleticism.

FRYE, DELLA MAE, portrait artist; b. Roanoke, Va., Feb. 16, 1926; d. Henry Vetchel and Helen Lavinia Theradosia (Eardley) Pearcy; m. James Frederick Frye, Nov. 1, 1944 (dec.) May 5, 2004; children: Linda Jeanne Frye, James Marvin, David Scott. Student, Hope Coll., 1968, Grand Valley State Coll., 1969-71. Asst. med. records librarian Bapt. Hosp., Little Rock, 1944; receptionist, sec. Stephens Coll., Columbia, Mo., 1945-46; art tchr. Jenison (Mich.) Christian Sch., 1965-67, pvt. classes, 1964-74; realtor, 1978-80; with Diversified Fin., 1979-82; portrait artist, 1967—. Cons. World Traders, Grand Rapids, Mich., 1986—. Author various poems; exhbns. include Salon Des Nations (cert. honor), 1984, Ann Arbor (Mich.) Art Guild, Kalamazoo Artists, Internat. Art Gallery, Hawaii, La Mandragore Gallery Internationale D'Art Contemporain, songwriter: (album) I Love America, 2000-2002 Pres. mother's club Jenison Christian Sch., 1965-66; treas. Band Boosters, Jenison, 1966. Recipient awards for nat. contests in portrait painting. Republican. Baptist. Avocations: songwriting, swimming. Home: 7677 Steele Ave Jenison MI 49428 also: 8901 SE 120th Pl Belleview FL 34420

FRYE, HELEN JACKSON, federal judge; b. Klamath Falls, Oreg., Dec. 10, 1930; d. Earl and Elizabeth (Kirkpatrick) Jackson; m. William Frye, Sept. 7, 1952; children: Eric, Karen, Heidi; 1 adopted child, Hedy; m. Perry Holloman, July 10, 1980 (dec. Sept. 1991). BA in English with honors, U. Oreg., 1953, MA, 1960, JD, 1966. Bar: Oreg. 1966. Public sch. tchr., Oreg., 1956-63; with Riddlesberger, Pederson, Brownhill & Young, 1966-67, Husband & Johnson, Eugene, 1968-71; trial judge State of Oreg., 1971-80; U.S. dist judge Dist. Oreg. Portland, 1980-95; sr. judge U.S. Dist. Ct., Portland, 1995—. Coll. Arts and Sci. Alumni Fellow, Univ. Oreg., 1997—98. Mem. Phi Beta Kappa.

FRYE, LATOYA AISHA HORTENSE, newswriter; d. Lester Alton and Pansy Moraine (Williams) Frye. AS in Bus. Adminstrn., Piedmont Va. C.C., Charlottesville, Va., 1999; BS in Mktg., Va. Commonwealth U., 2000. Resident asst. Va. Commonwealth U., Richmond, 1998—2000; intern personal banker Bank of Am., Richmond, 1999; intern computer instr. Collis-Warner Found., Alexandria, 2000; mgmt. assoc. Wachovia Bank, Charlottesville, 2001—03, br. mgr., 2003—04; corresp. Charlottesville/Albernarle Tribune, 2004—. Vol. Salvation Army, Charlottesville, Va., 2002—. Mem.: Am. Mktg. Assn., Inroads/Richmond Inc. (Outstanding Acad. Achievement award 1999—2000), Golden Key, Phi Kappa Phi. Avocations: aerobics, rollerblading, tennis. Office: Charlottesville Albernarle Tribune 250 W Main St Ste 402 Charlottesville VA 22902

FRYE, LINDA BETH (LINDA BETH HISLE), elementary school educator, secondary school educator; b. Apr. 15, 1947; d. Roland Earl Jr. Hisle and Paralee M. Jones; m. Dennis Franklin Frye; children: Byron Franklin, Cody Earl, Matthew Cole. BA in Art and Elem. Edn., East Ctrl. State U., Ada, 1970; M.Ed. in Elem. Edn., East Tex. State U., Commerce, 1975. Tchr. Sherman (Tex.) Ind. Sch. Dist., 1969—2002. Specialist in lang., learning disabilities in spl. edn. Recipient Tex. Instrument Invention Conv. award, Tchr. award, Tex. Instrument Invention Convention; grantee Ada City Sch. Foundation, Ada City Sch. Foun. Mem.: Church of Christ. Home: 8380 CR 3510 Ada OK 74820-9619

FRYER, KAREN HELENE, geologist, educator; d. Donald M. and Elaine P. Fryer; m. Cameron Begg; 1 child, Gavin Fryer Begg. BA in Geology with honors, Wellesley (Mass.) Coll., 1979; PhD, U. Ill., Urbana-Champaign, 1986. Intern Lunar and Planetary Inst., Houston, 1979—79; geologist Consultants in the Geol. Scis., Urbana, Ill., 1980—86; from asst. to assoc. prof. geology Ohio Wesleyan U., Delaware, 1986—98, prof., chair dept. geology and geography, 1997—. Geoscis. councilor Coun. on Undergrad. Rsch., Washington, 1992—; chair geology rev. panel for course, curriculum and lab. improvement program NSF, Washington, 2001. Contbr. articles to profl. jours. Vol. Homeowners' Assn., Dublin, Ohio, 1993—. Grantee, NSF, 1989—91, 1994—96; Geologic Mapping grantee, NC Geol. Survey, 1990—2002, Eisenhower Program Tchg. grantee, Dept. of Edn., 1997—2001. Mem.: Mineral. Soc. Am., Am. Geophys. Union, Geol. Soc. Am., Nat. Assn. Geosci. Tchrs., Columbus Wellesley Club (treas. 2004—06), Sigma Xi (pres. local club 1988—89). Avocations: skiing, hiking, water activities, music. Office: Ohio Wesleyan U 61 S Sandusky St Delaware OH 43015 Office Phone: 740-368-3618. Office Fax: 740-368-3999. E-mail: khfryer@owu.edu.

FRYER, SHARA, newscaster; m. Barry Silverman. Grad., U. Tex., 1974. With Sta.KLRN-TV, Austin, Tex., KVUE-TV, Austin, KSAT-TV, San Antonio; anchor Sta. KTRK-TV, Houston, 1980—. Named Woman of Distinction, Crohn's and Colitis Found., 1998; recipient Humanitarian award, Jabboury Found. for Cancer Rsch., 2002. Office: KTRK-TV 3310 Bissonnet Houston TX 77005

FRYXELL, GRETA ALBRECHT, marine botany educator, oceanographer; b. Princeton, Ill., Nov. 21, 1926; d. Arthur Joseph and Esther (Andreen) Albrecht; m. Paul A. Fryxell, Aug. 23, 1947; children: Karl Joseph, Joan Esther, Glen Edward. BA, Augustana Coll., 1948; MEd, Tex. A&M U., 1969, PhD, 1975. Tchr. math and sci. jr. high schs., Iowa, 1948-52; research asst. Tex. A&M U., College Station, 1968-71, research scientist, 1971-80, asst. prof. oceanography, 1980-83, assoc. prof., 1983-86, prof., 1986-94, prof. emeritus, 1994—; adj. prof. botany U. Tex., Austin, 1993—. Vis. scientist U. Oslo, 1971; chmn. adv. commn. Provasoli-Guillard Ctr. for Culture Marine Phytoplankton, Bigelow Lab, Maine, 1985-87; hon. curator N.Y. Bot. Garden, 1992—; courtesy prof. U. Oreg., 1994-2000; sr. rsch. scientist U. Tex. Marine Sci. Inst., 1996-2003. Editor: Survival Strategies of the Algae, 1983; contbr. articles to profl. jours. Recipient Outstanding Woman award Brazos County, College Station, 1979, Outstanding Achievement award Augustana Coll., Rock Island, Ill., 1980; Faculty Disting. Achievement award in rsch. Tex. A&M U., 1991, Geoscis. and Earth Resources Adv. Coun. medal, 1993; grantee NSF. Fellow: AAAS; mem.: ACLU, Oceanographic Soc., Tex. Assn. Coll. Tchrs., Internat. Diatom Soc. (coun. 1986—92), Am. Soc. Plant Taxonomists, Internat. Phycol. Soc., Brit. Phycol. Soc., Phycol. Soc. Am. (editl. bd. 1976—79, 1982—85, chair Prescott award com. 1991, award of Excellence in Phycology 1996). Democrat. Unitarian-Universalist. Office: U Tex Sch Biol Scis Sect Integrative Biology Austin TX 78712 Mailing: 650 Harrison Ave Claremont CA 91711

FUCHS, ELAINE V., molecular biologist, educator; b. Hinsdale, Ill., May 5, 1950; m. David T. Hansen, Sept. 10, 1988. BS in Chemistry with highest distinction, U. Ill., Urbana, 1972; PhD in Biochemistry, Princeton U., 1977; PhD (hon.), Mt. Sinai U., 2003. Postdoctoral fellow dept. biology MIT, 1977-80; from asst. prof. to prof. U. Chgo., 1980—89, prof. Dept. Molecular Genetics and Cell Biology, 1989—2002; investigator Howard Hughes Med. Inst., 1988—; Rebecca C. Lancefield prof. mammalian cell biology and devel. Rockefeller U., NYC, 2002—. Assoc. editor Jour. Cell Biology, 1993—; contr. 225 articles to profl. jours. Recipient Bensely award Am. Assn. Anatomists, 1988, Searle Scholar award Chgo. Cmty. Trust, 1981-84, Presdl. Young Investigator award NSF, 1984-89, NIH Merit award, 1993, 98, Wm. Montagna award Soc. Investigative Dermatology, 1995, Keith Porter Lecture award Am. Soc. Cell Biology, 1996, Sr. Woman Achievement award, 1997, Cartwright award 2001, Richard Lounsbery award, 2001, Novartis award, 2003, Dickson prize, 2004. Fellow Am. Acad. Arts and Scis., Am. Assn. Microbiology, IOM, Am. Soc. Cell Biology (past pres.), Harvey Soc., Am. Philos. Soc., NY Acad. Sci., Phi Beta Kappa. Office: Rockefeller U Lab Mammalian Cell Biology and Devel 1230 York Ave Box 300 New York NY 10021*

FUCILLO, DAWN M., radiologic technologist; Dir. Samaritan Regional Cancer Ctr. and Mario Pastega Guest House, Corvallis, Oreg. Mem.: Am. Soc. Radiologic Technologists (chair 2005—06, past v.p., pres.-elect, pres. bd. dir.). Office: Samaritan Regional Cancer Ctr 501 NW Elks Dr Corvallis OR 97330 Office Phone: 541-768-5220.*

FUDA, SIRI NARAYAN K.K. (ELAINE T. BARBER), director; b. Albany, N.Y., June 13, 1941; d. Adam Henry and Anna Mae Farrell Barber; m. Michael G. Fuda, Nov. 23, 1962; children: Meredith-Anne Costello, Melanie Elsie Henderson, Michelle Germanne Fuda. BA in English with honors, SUNY, Albany, 1963, MA in English Lang. and Lit., 1965; postgrad., SUNY, Buffalo, 1967; MS in Exceptional Edn., Buffalo State Coll., 1982. Tchr. Albany Pub. Sch. Sys., 1964-67, curriculum developer, 1966-67; tchr. Buffalo Pub. Schs., 1981-99; dir. Ctr. for Healthy, Happy, Holistic Living, Buffalo, 1987—. Adj. prof. Buffalo State Coll., 1993—; edn. cons. just buffalo lit. ctr., 1990-99; yoga tchr. Women's Wellness Ctr. Western N.Y., 1999—, others; cons. SUNY, Buffalo, 1999; coord. Buffalo State Coll./Buffalo Pub. Schs. coop. program, 1993-99; writer-in-residence Khalsa Women's Tng. Camp, Espinola, N.Mex., 1993-94, just buffalo lit. ctr., 1994; developer, instr. Creative Writing Workshops, Buffalo, Santa Fe; reader Erie and Niagara County Writers Assn.; presenter workshops on yoga for personal stress reduction, expectant mothers and infants, and as metatherapy for emotionally disturbed students. Contbg. editor to lit. anthology Life Junkies: On Our Own, 1990; author: (poetry collections) Unconditional Love: The Sapphire Poems, 1992, Dancing with the Guru, 1994.; contbr. articles to profl. jours., poetry to Buffalo News, others. Founding mem. Lexington Real Foods Co-op, Buffalo, 1971; bd. dirs. Elmwood Ave. Bus. Assn., Buffalo, 1980-83; founder Children's Rm. Co-op Day Care Ctr., Buffalo, 1972-73. Recipient Labor in Lt. award AFL-CIO, Buffalo, 1995; grantee Arts Coun., Buffalo and Erie County, 1990. Mem. Buffalo Tchrs. Fedn. (coun. of dels. 1984-91), just buffalo lit. ctr., Internat. Kundalini Yoga Tchrs. Assn. Democrat. Sikh. Avocation: gardening. Home: 460 Ashland Ave Buffalo NY 14222-1502 Office: Ctr for Healthy Happy Holistic Living 460 Ashland Ave Buffalo NY 14222-1502 E-mail: SiriNarayan@aol.com.

FUDGE, ANN MARIE, advertising executive; b. Washington, Apr. 23, 1951; d. Malcolm R. and Bettye (Lewis) Brown; m. Richard E. Fudge, Feb. 27, 1971; children: Richard Jr., Kevin. BA, Simmons Coll., 1973; MBA, Harvard U., 1977; DHL (hon.), Adelphi U., 1995, Howard U., 1998, Simmons Coll., 1998, Marymount Coll., 1999. Manpower specialist GE, Bridgeport, Conn., 1973-75; mktg. asst. Gen. Mills, Mpls., 1977-78, asst. product mgr., 1978-80, product mgr., 1980-83, mktg. dir., 1983-86; assoc. dir., strategic planning Gen. Foods, White Plains, NY, 1986-87, mktg. dir., 1987-89, v.p. mktg. and devel., 1989-91, exec. v.p., gen. mgr., 1991-94; exec. v.p. Kraft Foods, 1994-97; pres. Maxwell House Coffee Co., White Plains, NY, 1994-97, Maxwell House Coffee and Post Cereal, Tarrytown, NY, 1997—2001; chmn., CEO Young & Rubicam, Inc., NYC, 2003—05, Y&R Brands, NYC, 2003—. Bd. dirs. GE, Marriott Internat.; trustee Am. Grad. Sch. Internat. Mgmt., Brookings Instn. Bd. dirs. Women's Econ. Devel. Corp., St. Paul, 1984-86; chair allocations panel United Way, Mpls., 1983-86; vol. Big Sisters/Big Bros., Fairfield County, Conn., 1988-90; bd. govs. Boys and Girls Clubs Am.; trustee Rockefeller Found., 2006-. Recipient Leadership award YWCA, Mpls., 1980, Black Achievers award Harlem YMCA, 1988, Candace award Nat. Coalition of 100 Black Women, 1991-92, Corp. Women's Network award, 1994, She Knows Where She's Going award Girls, Inc., 1994, Alumni Achievement award Harvard Bus. Sch., 1998; named Woman of Yr., Glamour Mag., 1995, Ad Woman of Yr., Advt. Women of N.Y., 1995, Sara Lee Frontrunner award, 1999, one of 50 Most Powerful Women in Am. Bus., Fortune mag.; one of 100 Most Influential Black Americans, Ebony mag., 2006. Mem. Exec. Leadership Coun. (pres. 1994-96, Achievement award 2000), Com. of 200, NY Women's Forum, Coun. on Fgn. Rels. Office: Y&R Advt 285 Madison Ave New York NY 10017-6486*

FUENTES, JUNE TORETTA, language educator; d. Anthony James and Fortuna Katherine (Bianco) Toretta; m. Antonio Fuentes, Dec. 20, 1974; 1 child, Noelle Marie. BA, Coll. of New Rochelle, N.Y., 1963; MA, Fordham U., Bronx, N.Y., 1969; PhD, U. Tex., Austin, 1988. Lic. tchr. Kans. Elem. tchr. Blessed Sacrament Sch., New Rochelle, NY, 1963—68; separate acct. cons. Equitable Life Assurance Soc., N.Y.C., 1969—74; Jr. H.S. tchr. St. Mary's Cathedral Sch., Austin, Tex., 1975—76; media cons. and ESL instr. U. Tex. and St. Edward's U., Austin, 1976—83; instr. English U. Tex. and Austin Cmty. Coll., 1980—88; prof. English and ESL Ind. U. and Purdue U., Ft. Wayne, 1988—91; prof. English Western State Coll., Gunnison, Colo., 1991—94; dir. ESL Bethany Coll., Lindsborg, Kans., 1994—96; instr. ESL Salina Unified Sch. Dist. 305, Salina, 1996—2004; prof. ESL Kans. Wesleyan U., Salina, 2005—. Editl. writer Ft. Wayne Cardiology, Ind., 1989; editl. adv. bd. Collegiate Press, Ft. Wayne, 1990; mem tactic team Gunnison (Colo.) Watershed Sch. Dist., 1993—94. Author: Maria's Secret, 1992; contbr. articles to profl. publs.;, author poetry. Pub. rels. chair AAUW Art in the Pk., Gunnison, Colo., 1992; pres. AAUW (Gunnison chpt.), 1992—94; bd. dir. Rotary Internat., Lindsborg, Kans., 1995—96; docent Raymer Soc., 1996—2002. Recipient Ursula Laurus citation, Coll. New Rochelle, 2005; grantee U. Tex. Intensive English Program Mini-Grant, 1979, IPFW Faculty Summer Grant, 1990, Western State Coll. Mini-Grant, 1993, Bethany Burmeister Grant, 1995, Salina Edn. Found., 2003. Mem.: TESOL (Kans. chpt), Phi Kappa Phi, Kappa Delta Pi, Pi Lambda Theta. Avocations: poetry, children's stories, water color, reading detective fiction.

FUENTES, MARTHA AYERS, playwright; b. Ashland, Ala., Dec. 21, 1923; d. William Herny and Elizabeth (Dye) Ayers; m. Manuel Solomon Fuentes, Apr. 11, 1943. BA in English, U. South Fla., 1969. Lectr., instr. workshops on drama, writing for TV. Author: The Rebel, 1970, Mama Don't Make Me Go To College, My Head Hurts, 1963, Two Characters in Search of An Agreement, 1970, A Cherry Blossom for Miss Chrysanthemum; contbr. articles to local, regional and nat. newspapers, feature artcles to nat. mags.; author TV plays and feature articles for children and young adults. Mem. Nat. Rep. Senatorial Com., Rep. Pres. Task Force, Rep. Nat. Com., Rep. Party, Fla. Recipient George Sergel drama award U. Chgo., 1969. Mem. AAUW, NAFE, S.E. Playwrights Project, The Alliance of Resident Theatres, Stageworks, Authors Guild, Dramatists Guild, Romance Writers Am., Southeastern Writers Assn., Fla. Studio Theatre, United Daus. Confederacy. Roman Catholic. Avocations: reading, theater, travel. Home and Office: 102 3rd St Belleair Beach FL 33786-3211 Office Phone: 727-596-5393. Personal E-mail: belfuentes@aol.com.

FUENTEZ, TANIA MICHELE, journalist; b. Manhattan, Nov. 21, 1966; d. C. Pedro Alvarez Carr and E. Kay (Samuels) Queally. BA in Comm. and Rhetorical Studies, Marquette U., 1991; MA in Mass Media Comm., U. Akron, 1996. Asst. rschr. V.I. Legislature, St. Thomas, 1991; reporter V.I. Daily News, St. Thomas, 1993-95; instr. news writing U. Akron, Ohio, 1995-96; copy editor The Akron Beacon Jour., 1997-2000; newswoman AP, Atlanta, 2000—03, nat. desk editor NYC, 2003—05, copy desk supr. graphics, 2006—. Adv. bd. diversity com. V.I. Daily News, 1993-95. Contbr. articles to profl. jours. Bd. dirs. U.S. V.I. League of Women Voters, 1994-95; mem. Am. Cancer Soc., 1993-95, mem. St. Thomas Arts Coun., 1992-95. Recipient Cmty. Svc. award Pan African Support Group, 1995; scholar John S. Knight Meml. Fund, 1996, U. Akron, 1995-96. Mem. Soc. Profl. Journalists, Nat. Assn. Hispanic Journalists, Nat. Assn. Black Journalists, Comm. Workers Am.-AFL-CIO, News Media Guild, Local 31222. Roman Catholic. Avocations: writing, travel, photography, hiking, cooking. Office: The AP 450 W 33d St New York NY 10001 Office Phone: 212-621-1500. E-mail: tfuentez@ap.org.

FUER-DAVIS, BEVERLY JEAN, retired elementary school educator; b. L.A., Jan. 3, 1940; d. George Harold Jr. and Lucille May (Jones) Davis; m. John Anthony Fuer, Oct. 21, 1972 (dec. 1996); m. Chester B. Davis, 2002. BA, UCLA, 1961; MEd, U. Ariz., 1981. Tchr. 5th grade L.A. City Schs., 1961-62; tchr. 6th grade San Luis Obispo (Calif.) City Schs., 1962-63, LaMesa-Spring Valley Sch. Dist., LaMesa, Calif., 1963-67, gifted edn. specialist, 1967-71; middle sch. tchr. Continental Sch. Dist., Green Valley, Ariz., 1971—2002, ret., 2002. Supt.'s designee; cons. No. Ariz. U. Ideanet Spanish program; dist. rep. Tucson-Pima Arts Coun. Named Dist. Tchr. of Yr., 1988; recipient youth activities recognition award Optimist Club, 1978, Delta Kappa Gamma Soc. State Achievment award, 1990, Am. History Tchr. award Madera chpt. DAR, 1992. Mem. ASCD, NEA, Ariz. Edn. Assn., AAUW, Continental Edn. Assn. (pres. 1986-87, 97-98, 2001-02), Delta Kappa Gamma (state pres. 1993-95), Continental Sch. Dist. Ednl. Found. (bd. dirs. 1993-), Greater Green Valley Arts Coun. (v.p. 2003-), The Animal League of Green Valley (pres. 2005-). Democrat. Home: 211 E Calle Herboso Green Valley AZ 85614-4114 Personal E-mail: bjeandf@aol.com.

FUERSTNER, FIONA MARGARET ANNE, ballet company executive, educator; b. Rio de Janeiro, Apr. 24, 1936; d. Paul G. and Agnes Ethel (Stothard) F.; m. Dane LaFontsee, June 7, 1969 (div. 1992); 1 child, Liana Marie. Studied with San Francisco Ballet, Royal Ballet (London), Ballet Rambert (London) Ballet Theatre Sch. (N.Y.C.), Sch. Am. Ballet (N.Y.C.). With corps de ballet San Francisco Ballet, 1952-55, soloist, 1955-58, prin. dancer, 1958-62; toured with Walter Terry's Am. Dances, 1962-63; prin. dancer Les Grands Ballets Can., Montreal, 1963-64, Am. Choreographer's Co. of N.Y., 1964, Pa. Ballet, 1965—74, ballet mistress, instr. co. class, apprentice class, 1974-77, ballet mistress, instr. co. class, 1977—86; ballet mistress Nashville Ballet, 1986-87, ballet mistress, asst. to artistic dir., 1987-91; ballet mistress Milw. Ballet, 1990-95, asst. to artistic dir. ballet mistress, 1995—2003. Guest dancer Ballet Concerto, Miami, 1967, 68, Erie Civic Ballet, 1969; guest instr. Marsha Woody Dance Acad., Beaumont, Tex., 1974, U. Louisville, 1977-78, co. class San Francisco Ballet, 1985, Tenn. Assn. Dance Nashville Conf., 1988, So. Regional Workshop Chgo., Nat. Assn. Dance Masters in Nashville, 1989, BalletMet, 1991, Memphis Classical Ballet, 1992, 97, 99, Nashville Ballet, 1992; guest ballet mistress BalletMet, 1993; faculty tchr. Sch. of Pa. Ballet, 1977-78, 78-86; organized concert group, ballet mistress, dancer Pa. Ballet, 1971; mem. dance panel Nat. Found. Advancement in the Arts, 1995-98; master tchr. South Eastern Regional Ballet Assn. Festival, 1998, Nat. Found. for Advancement in the Arts, 1999, 2001, 2005; guest tchr. Ind. U. Ballet Dept., 2000, Western Mich. U., 2002, DanceWorks Studio 1661, Milw., Wis., 2005, 06, Dancenter North, Libertyville, Ill., 2005, 06; master tchr. USDAN Ctr. for the Creative and Performing Arts, Wheatley Heights, NY, 2004—; vis. asst. prof. dance Wright State U., 2004; dance panelist Midwest Regional, Nat. Found. for Advancement in the Arts, 2001, 2002. Staged Allegro Brillante, Sch. Pa. Ballet Student Showcase, 1986, Nashville Ballet, 1988, Madrigalesco, Pacific NW Ballet, 1981, (parts) Nutcracker, Nashville Ballet, 1989, Carmina Burana (Butler), Milw. Ballet, 1989, Scotch Symphony, Pa. Ballet, 1993, Carmina Burana, Alberta Ballet, 1993, Concerto Barocco, Ballet Omaha, 1994, Ballet Met, 1995, Serenade, Milw. Ballet Sch., 1994, 95, 96, Serenade, Milw. Ballet, 1998-99, Serenade, Western Mich. U., 1999-2000, Concerto Barocco, The Four Temperaments for Milw. Ballet, 1999-2000, Allegro Brillante for Milw. Ballet, 2000-01, (excerpts) Who Cares?, Western Mich. U., 2003, Serenade, Wright State U., 2004. Office Phone: 414-254-4086. E-mail: fionafio@sbcglobal.net.

FUFUKA, NATIKA NJERI YAA, retail executive; b. Cleve., Feb. 21, 1952; d. Russell and Mindoro Reed. AA, AAB, Cuyahoga CC, Cleve., 1973; BA, Mich. State U., 1975; postgrad., Cleve. State U. Asst. pers. dir. May Co., Cleve., 1975—78; merchandiser J.C. Penney, Cleve., 1978—80; sports mgr. Joseph Hornes, Cleve., 1980—81; fashion buyer Higbee, Cleve., 1981—86; exec. v.p. Mindoro & Assocs., 1982—; merchandise exec. Fashion Bug, Euclid, Ohio, 1986—92; pres., CEO Mindy's Return to Fashion, Cleve., 1993—. Vice chmn. Joint Com. on Medicaid Provider Impact for State of Ohio, 1992; mem. Mayor's Census Task Force, Cuyahoga County Women Bus. Enterprise Adv. Coun., Cleve. Female Bus. Enterprise Adv. Coun.; pub. affairs com. Greater Cleve. Growth Assn.; active Displaced/Single Parent Homemakers Adv. Coun., Cuyahoga Cmty. Coun., Cuyahoga Hills Boys Adv. Coun., Black Aspiration Week Celebrationcom. Cleve. State U., 1990; cmty. rels. coun. Cleve. Job Corp., 1996; African Am. com. Cleve. Found., 1996; nat. nomination com. Outstanding Young Woman of Am., 1998, Outstanding Young Man of Am., 1998; chmn. Centralized Resource Referral Svc. Panel United Way, 1993l; mem. Gen. Assembly, 1993—, United Way Appeal Com., 1996, leadership devel. program; asst. dir. Project Vote, 1983-84; bd. dirs. Ohio Youth Adv. Coun., 1988-90; mem. Mayor Census Task Force, 1989-90; adv. coun. Displaced Single Parent Homemakers, Cuyahoga County Women Bus. Enterprises, Cleve. Female Bus. Enterprise; active Citizen League, Cleve. Mus. Art, Playhouse Square Found., Women in Apptd. Office Project, Planned Parenthood Greater Cleve., WCPN Radio.; bd. dirs. Ohio Youth Adv. Coun., Women Cmty. Found., 1993—, Career Beginning Program Bd., 1993—, Nat. Ctr. Non-Profit; mem. Nat. Coun. Christians and Jews, 1996 Recipient Jesse Jackson Voter Registration award, 1984, Leadership award, United Way, 1991, Cert. Appreciation award, 1998, 2001, Vol. Leadership recognition, City of Cleve., 1991, Cmty. Rels. Coun. Svc. award, Cleve. Job Corps., 1998; Ford Found. scholar, 1975. Mem. NAFE, Nat. Nominating Bd. Outstanding Ams., Assn. MBA Execs., Black Profl. Assn., Nat. Assn. Negro Bus./Profl. Women, Am. Profl. Exec. Women, Am. Women Bus. Assn., Nat. Assn. Black Female Entrepreneurs, Severance Merchant Mall Orgn., Op. Big Vote, Nat. Coun. Negro Women, Nat. Polit. Congress Black Women (nat. founder mem., founder mem. Ohio state chpt.), Nat. Hook-Up, 100 Black Women Coalition, Black Congl. Caucus Braintrust, Small Minority Bus. Braintrust, Corp. Braintrust, Nat. Non-Profit Bds., Black Women Agenda, Black Women Roundtable, Black Focus (pres. bd. trustees), 21st Congl. Dist. Caucus (exec. bd. mem., chair bus. women com., certs. of appreciation for outstanding svc. 1985, 86), Urban League Greater Cleve., Op. Push of Greater Cleve. (bd. dirs.), Project Vote (asst. dir., Voter Registration award 1984), Midwest Vote Project, Women Vote Project, WomenSpace, United Black Fund, Greater East Cleve. Dem. Club, Minority Women Polit. Action Com., LWV, Cuyahoga Women Polit. Caucus, Ohio Pub. Interest Campaign, Ohio Rainbow Coalition, Ohio Dem. Women Com., Network Together, Black Elected Dem. Ofcls. Ohio, Cleve. City Club, 16th Dist. Club, Project M.O.V.E, Kinsman Youth Devel. Program and Scholarship Cmty. Liasion Democrat. Pentecostal. Avocations: collecting African art, golf. Office: One Chagrin Highlands 2000 Auburn Drive Ste 200 Beachwood OH 44122 Personal E-mail: mindorohgcom@yahoo.com.

FUGATE, KELLY ANNE, nurse; b. Balt., Feb. 2, 1965; d. James D. and Anne D. (Kelly) F.; m. Jeffrey M. Sharpe, Aug. 16, 1987. BA, Case Western Res. U., 1987, D. of Nursing, 1989. Core mgr. Advocate Good Samaritan Hosp., Downer's Grove, Ill., 1994—. Fuld fellow. Mem. ANA, Ill. Nurses Assn., Chicagoland Nurses Assn., Assn. for Nurses in AIDS Care, Critical Care Nurses Assn., Am. Care Mgr. Assn., Sigma Theta Tau. Office: Dept Clin Excellence 3815 Highland Ave Downers Grove IL 60515

FUGATE, SHARON JEAN, biology professor; b. Hazard, Ky., Apr. 1, 1960; d. Harvey Edward and Gearldine (Slone) Whitaker; m. Archie Fugate, Jr., Dec. 12, 1981; 1 child, Samuel Archie. AS, Alice Lloyd Coll., Pippa Passes, Ky., 1980, BS in Biology Edn., 1982; MS in Biology, Morehead State U., Ky., 1990. Dir. biomonitoring McCoy & McCoy Environ. Labs., Madisonville, Ky., 1982—2003; instr., asst. prof. biology Madisonville C.C., Ky., 2003—. Adj. faculty biology KCTCS-Prestonburg C.C., 1991—2003; eye care chair, v.p. Madisonville Cmty. and Tech. Coll., 2003—; master advisor Madisonville C.C., 2005—06. Named salutatorian, Alice Lloyd Coll., 1982; recipient Biology award, 1980; Meml. scholar, 1978—82. Mem.: DAR (registrar, rec. sec. 2003—), Hon. Order Ky. Cols., Lions Club. Presbyterian. Avocations: travel, reading, piano. Office: Madisonville CC 2000 College Madisonville KY 42431

FUGETT, ROBERTA LYNN, special education educator; b. Dayton, Ohio, July 18, 1957; d. Ray Walton and Bertha Collinsworth; m. Jerry Winston Fugett, July 31, 1993; children: Sarah Elizabeth, Nathaniel Lee Whitt. BA in Edn., Morehead State U., Ky., 1995, MA in Edn., 2002. Cert. tchr. exceptional children, grades K-12 Ky., 1996, thcr. social studies grades 5-8 Ky., 1996. Spl. edn. resource classroom tchr. Powell County Schs., Clay City, Ky., 1996—97; tchr. spl. edn. Rowan County Schs., Morehead, 1997—2002; lectr. Morehead State U., 2002—; tchr. grade 5 Elliott County Schs., Sandy Hook, Ky., 2002—03; mid. sch. collaboration tchr. Clark County Schs., Winchester, Ky., 2003—05; online instr. Tchr. Edn. Inst., Winter Park, Fla., 2003—06; tchr. English Menifee County H.S., Frenchburg, Ky., 2005—06. Brownie troop leader Girl Scouts Wilderness Rd. Coun., Lexington, Ky., 2005—. Author: (poetry) Betrayal (Best Poets of Yr., 2006). Recipient Outstanding Undergrad. in Spl. Edn., Morehead State U., 1996. Mem.: Ky. Edn. Assn., Phi Kappa Phi. Christian. Avocations: reading, writing poetry.

FUGGI, GRETCHEN MILLER, education educator; b. Westerly, R.I., Aug. 26, 1938; d. John Louis and Harriet (Scheid) M.; m. William Joseph Fuggi, Aug. 15, 1960; children: Gretchen, Juliann, John, Kristen. BS, So. Conn. State U., New Haven, 1960, MS, 1969, 6th yr. diploma, 1991, 6th yr. Ednl. Leadership diploma, 1994. Reading cons. Washington Magnet Sch., West Haven, Conn., 1974—; adj. prof. So. Conn. State U., New Haven, 1988—. Pres. Cath. Charity League of Greater New Haven, 1989-90; bd. dirs. New Haven Symphony Aux., 1992—. Named Tchr. of Yr., West Haven Fedn. Tchrs., 1998-99. Mem. AAUP, Internat. Reading Assn., Conn. Reading Assn., Stonington Hist. Soc. of Conn., Delta Kappa Gamma Soc. Internat., Grad. Club New Haven. Roman Catholic. Home: 19 Westview Rd North Haven CT 06473-2013 E-mail: Fuggi@juno.com.

FUGO, DENISE MARIE, small business executive; b. Cleve., Apr. 4, 1953; d. William Anthony and Mary Magdelene (Madar) F.; m. Ralph Thomas Di Orio, Nov. 25, 1977; children: Dena J., Michael P. (dec.), Georgia N. BS in Communication, Ohio U., 1975; MBA, U. Chgo., 1977. Stockbroker Goldman, Sachs & Co., Chgo., 1977-79; fin. analyst Standard Oil Co., Cleve., 1979-81; dir. Charter One Bank, 1991—2004; pres. City Life Inc. (Sammy's), Cleve., 1980—. Bd. dir. Cleve. Coun. Smaller Enterprises, 1986-89; mem. mktg. com. Conv. and Visitors Bur., Cleve., 1984—, bd. dirs. 1986—; mem. Downtown Bus. Coun., Cleve., 1984—, United Way Investment Com., 1980-85, Cuyahoga C.C. Found., 2006—. Recipient Chivas Regal Young

Entrepreneur award 375 Spirits Co., N.Y., 1986; named one of Career Women of Achievement YWCA, 1989. Mem.: Nat. Restaurant Assn. Edn. Found. (trustee 2000—), Nat. Restaurant Assn. (bd. dirs. 1991—, chmn. 2000), One Fitness Ctr. Roman Catholic. Office: City Life Inc 1400 W 10th St Cleveland OH 44113-1215

FUHRER, LINDA LARSEN, social worker; b. Bayonne, N.J., Aug. 29, 1940; d. Joseph Martin and Metha Kirsten (Sorensen) Larsen; student U. Aix-Marseile (France), 1960-61; AB, Taylor U., 1962; MSW (VA fellow 1963-64, NIMH grantee 1964-65), U. Ill., 1965; m. Larry R. Fuhrer, Dec. 31, 1962; 1 son, Lance. Social worker children's div. Cook County (Ill.) Dept. Public Aid, 1962-63; dir. camp for delinquent girls under auspices Gov. Ind., 1964, social worker Wheaton (Ill.) Public Schs., 1965-68; family counselor La Grange (Ill.) Family Svcs., 1968; instr. social work Wheaton Coll., 1969-70; social worker spl. project for disadvantaged, elem. schs. Naperville (Ill.) Schs., 1971-72; social worker Regional Program of Hearing Impaired Students, Hinsdale Twp. (Ill.) HS, 1975—2004, adj. faculty Aurora U., 2004-; dir. Equity Realty Group, 1978-83; dir. Presdl. Svcs. Inc., 1978—; pvt. practice social work, 1985-; founding bd. dirs. DuPage Pastoral Counseling Ctr., Glen Ellyn, Ill., 1975-78. Deacon, 1st Presbyn. Ch., Glen Ellyn, 1973-76; co-chmn. Wheaton Swim Team Parents Group, 1977-80; Class IV swim ofcl. AAU (bd. mem.); bd. dirs. scholarship com. Longfellow Sch. PTA, Wheaton, 1976-77. Lic. clin. social worker, Ill. Mem. Nat. Assn. Social Workers, NEA, Acad. Cert. Social Workers, Taylor U. Alumni Assn., Alpha Chi. Office: 2808 Willow Ridge Dr Naperville IL 60564-8938 Office Phone: 630-355-6625. Business E-Mail: lindafuhrer@lindafuhrer.com.

FUHRMAN, SUSAN H., academic administrator, education educator, researcher; BA in history with highest honors, Northwestern U., 1965, MA in history, 1966; PhD in polit. sci. and edn., Columbia U., 1977. Prof. of edn. policy Eagleton Inst. of Polit. at Rutgers U., 1989—95; prof., dept. of pub. policy Edward J. Bloustein Sch. of Planning and Pub. Policy, Rutgers U., 1994—95; dean grad sch. edn. U. Penn, 1995—2006, George & Diane Weiss prof. edn.; pres. Tchrs. Coll., Columbia U., NYC, 2006—. Bd. mem. Carnegie Found. for the Advancement of Tchg.; founder and chmn. Consortium for Policy Rsch. in Edn. (CPRE), 1985—; former co-chair Nat. Adv. Panel for the Third Internat. Math and Sci. Study; bd. dirs. Nat. Coalition on Asia and Internat. Studies in the Schs. Editor: From the Capitol to the Classroom: Standards-Based Reform in the States, One Hundredth Yearbook of the National Society for the Study of Education, 2001, Designing Coherent Education Policy: Improving the System, 1993; co-editor (with Jennifer O'Day): Rewards and Reform: Creating Educational Incentives that Work, 1996; contbr. articles to profl. jours. Achievements include research in standards-based state education reform, state local relationships, state differential treatment of districts, federalism in education, incentives and systemic reform, legislatures and education policy. Office: Tchrs Coll Columbia U 525 W 120th St New York NY 10027 Office Phone: 212-678-3131. E-mail: susanf@itc.edu.

FUITEN, HELEN LORRAINE, small business owner; b. Grafton, ND, Nov. 13, 1923; d. Yat Wong and Anna Marie Schmitt; m. Robert Lester Fuiten, Mar. 15, 1947 (dec. Oct. 31, 2002); 1 child, Roderick L. Student, OReg. State Coll., Corvallis, 1943. Artist Photo Art Comml. Studios, Portland, Oreg., 1940—46; sec., bookkeeper Reo Oreg. Sales, Portland, 1942—43; draftsman engring. dept. Oreg. Ship Yard, Portland, 1943—46; pers. sec. St. Vincent Hosp., Portland, 1946—47; owner, ptnr. Forest Grove Plumbing, Oreg., 1948—50, Fuiten's Plumbing and Heating Co., Forest Grove, 1952—97, Fuiten Mech. Inc., Forest Grove, 1997—. Ptnr., owner R H & R Properties, Forest Grove, 1954—; owner, mgr. ladies' retail clothing store, Forest Grove, 1981—93. Office: Fuiten Mech Inc 1832 Pacific Ave Forest Grove OR 97116

FUKINO, CHIYOME LEINAALA, state agency administrator, public health service officer; B, Brandeis Univ.; MD, Burns Sch. Med., Univ. Hawaii, Manoa. Physician Fronk Clinic, 1982—85; private practice internal medicine, 1985—2002; staff mem. Leahi Hosp.; cons. Kahi Mohalu, 1988—92; med. dir. Queen's Physician Group, 1996—99; dir. Hawaii Health Dept., 2002—. Office: Hawaii Dept Health 1250 Punchbowl St Honolulu HI 96813 Mailing: Hawaii Dept Health PO Box 3378 Honolulu HI 96801*

FULBRIGHT, HARRIET MAYOR, educational association administrator; b. NYC, Dec. 13, 1933; d. Brantz and Evelyn (Griswold) M.; m. William Watts, Aug. 4, 1954 (div. 1975); children: Evelyn G. Ward, Shelby Funk, Heidi H. Mayor; m. J. William Fulbright, Mar. 10, 1990. BA, Radcliffe Coll., Cambridge, Mass., 1955; MFA, George Washington U., 1975; LLD (hon.), U. Scranton, 1986; LHD (hon.), L.I. U., Bank St. Coll., U. Devel. Studies, Tamale, Ghana, Pace U., 2006; D in Philosophy and Physics (hon.), Stevens Inst. Tech., 2006. Chair art dept. Maret Sch., Washington, 1975-80; asst. dir. Congl. Arts Caucus, Washington, 1980-82, Alliance of Ind. Coll. Art, Washington, 1982-84; exec. sec. Internat. Congress Art History, Washington, 1984-87; exec. dir. Fulbright Assn., Washington, 1987-91; pres. The Ctr. for Arts in the Basic Curriculum, Washington, 1991-96; exec. dir. Pres.'s Com. on the Arts and the Humanities, 1997-2000. Vice chair Reves Internat. Ctr., 1994-97, chmn. 1997-; mem. J.W. Fulbright Fgn. Scholarship Bd., 1992-98, Acad. for Ednl. Devel., 1995—; pres. Fulbright Ctr., 1996—; chmn. UNESCO leadership coun. U. Bahcesehir, Istanbul, Turkey, 2002-; unofficial amb. Fulbright Program's 50th Ann.; co-chair BTN Inst., 2005—. Author: How To Get Your Own Pre-School Play Group; editor: Fulbrighters Newsletter. Pres. Maret Sch. Bd., 1975; exec. dir. Pres.'s Com. for Arts and Humanities, 1997—2000; mem. U.S. Cuba Policy Project, Ctr. for Nat. Policy, 2001—. Honoree, Young Audiences, 1994; recipient El Order de Manuel Amador Querrero (Panama's highest civilian award), 1997, Arts in Edn. award Fillmore Arts Ctr., 2001, Medal Cross of the Order of Merit, Hungary, 2002, Hubert H. Humphrey Humanitarian award Assn. Tchrs. of Social Studies, 2003, Person of Yr. award Rotary Internat. 2005, Cassandra Pyle award Nat. Assn. Fgn. Student Advisors, 2005. Mem. Nat. Coun. Stds. in the Arts. Office Phone: 703-351-5717. Personal E-mail: hmful@aol.com.

FULKERSON, JODI LEE, secondary school educator; b. Evansville, Ind., Dec. 10, 1972; d. Truman Lee and Denita Jo Harding; m. Chad Edward Fulkerson, Nov. 27, 1993; children: Tyler, Ashlyn. BS in English Edn., U. So. Ind., Evansville, 2000; MS in Tchg. with Bldg. Adminstrn., Oakland City U., Ind., 2006. Lic. sch. prin., tchr. K-12 Ind. English tchr. Harrison H.S., Evansville, Ind., 2001—03, varsity head swim coach, 2001—03; English tchr. Tecumseh H.S., Lynnville, Ind., 2003—, varsity head swim coach, 2003—05. Bd. dirs., sec. Oakdale PTO, 2002—; bd. dirs. Boonville Jr. H.S. Panther Pak. Mem.: Am. Legion. Democrat. Presbyterian. Avocations: reading, travel, sports. Home: 177 S State Rd 161 Boonville IN 47601 Office: Tecumseh High School 5244 W State Rd 68 Lynnville IN 47619

FULLARD, HENRIETTA, minister; d. Henry Graham and Janie Lillie Scott; children: Adrienne Yolanda Small, John Harold. BS, SC State U., Orangeburg, 1964; MA, Columbia U., 1972; MDiv, New Brunswick Theol. Sem., NJ, 1992; EdD, DD, Faith Coll., Mobile, Ala., 1994. Cert. sch. adminstrn. St. John's U., 1982. Endocrinology rschr. Interfaith Hosp. (formerly Bklyn. Jewish Hosp.), Bklyn., 1964—65; tchr. Andrew Jackson H.S., Cambria Heights, NY, 1965—90, asst. prin. sci. Cambria Heights, NY, 1990—94; prin. Math., Sci. Rsch. And Tech. Magnet H.S., Cambria Heights, 1994—99; pastor Bethel AME Ch., Arverne, 1995—2004; presiding elder numerous chs. African Meth. Episcopal Ch., Phila., 2004—. CEO Bethel Arverne Cmty. Devel. Corp., Arverne, 1999—; founder, job-trainer, developer Bethel Home Health Aide Program. Advisor Arverne Civic Assn., 2000—; mem. Cmty. Planning Bd. 14, Arverne, 1998—; v.p. Rockaway/Inwood Ministerial Coalition, Far Rockaway, NY, 1999—; mem. AME Ch. Ministerial Alliance, N.Y.C., 1995—, Habitat For Humanity, Jamaica, NY, 2000—; pres. S.E. Queens Clergy For Cmty. Empowerment, Inc., Jamaica, NY, 1999—; sec. adv. bd. York Coll., Jamaica, 1998—; adv. bd. St. John's Episcopal Hosp., Far Rockaway, 1999—. Recipient Congl. Record Award Of The 107Th Session, U.S. Ho. of Reps., 2002, Women Of The Millennium award, Nat. Coun. Of Negro Women, 2000, citation, N.Y. State Assembly, 1998, Nassau County, N.Y., 2000, Svc. To Women award, Ladies Of Distinction, Inc., 2002. Democrat. Avocation: travel. Personal E-mail: hefullard@aol.com.

FULLENWIDER, NANCY VRANA, composer, dancer, musician, educator; b. Sheridan, Wyo., May 9, 1940; d. Jacob Allen and Edith Martha (Tripp) Fullenwider; m. Linsfred Leroy Vrana, Apr. 26, 1980. BA summa cum laude, U. Denver, 1962, MA, 1971, postgrad., 1974. Prin. dancer, instr. Colo. Ballet and Colo. Ballet Ctr., Denver, 1958-80; owner, instr. Idaho Springs (Colo.) Sch. Ballet, 1962-67, Sch. Ballet, Parker, Colo., 1974-79. Curriculum developer Career Edn. Ctr., Denver Pub. Schs., 1973; grad. asst. U. Denver, 1974; guest artist, choreographer, composer Young Audiences, Denver, 1975-80; instr. ballet Ballet Arts Ctr., Denver, 1992-98, Colo. Dance Ctr., Littleton, 1992—; music dir., accompanist for Western Chamber Ballet, Denver, 1994-98, Colo. Ballet, 1999, Arvada Ctr., 1998, Ballet Arts, 1998, Internat. Sch. Ballet, 2000. Composer (CD's) To the Pointe, 1997, Brava!, 1999, Curtain Call, 2000, Inner Dance, 2002, Prepare!, 2005; commissioned ballet works performed at Auditorium Theatre, Denver, 2000, Arvada Ctr. for Performing Arts, Colo., 1991, Aurora (Colo.) Fox Arts Ctr., 1989-92, Buell Theatre, Colo., 1993, Cleo Parker Robinson Dance Theatre, Colo., 1992, 2003, 04, Colo. Springs Fine Arts Ctr., 1991, Houston Fine Arts Ctr., Colo., 1971, San Luis Arts Festival, Colo., 1990, Bonfils Theatre, Colo., 1971, Denver Civic Theatre, 2000, Auditorium Theatre, Denver, 2000, 01, (TV series) Providence, 2000; pianist theatre restaurant Denver Ctr. Performing Arts, Denver, Colo., 2003-04. Grantee Douglas County Schs., Colo., 1998. Mem. ASCAP, Phi Beta Kappa, Alpha Lambda Delta. Avocations: hiking, fly fishing, theater, concerts.

FULLER, ANNE ELIZABETH HAVENS, English language and literature educator, consultant; b. Pomona, Calif., Jan. 20, 1932; d. Paul Swain and Lorraine Elizabeth (Hamilton) Havens; m. Martin Emil Fuller, II, June 17, 1961; children: Katharine Hamilton, Peter David Takashi. AB, Mount Holyoke Coll., 1953; BA (Fulbright scholar), Somerville Coll., Oxford U., 1955, MA, 1959; PhD (Univ. fellow), Yale U., 1958. Instr. English, Mount Holyoke Coll., 1957-59; instr. Pomona Coll., 1959-61; asst. prof. U. Fla., Gainesville, 1961-63; lectr. U. Denver, 1964-68, 71-73; assoc. prof., chmn. center for lang. and lit. Prescott (Ariz.) Coll., 1968-70; tchr. Colo. Rocky Mountain Sch., 1970-71; dean of faculty Scripps Coll., Claremont, Calif., 1973-80, prof. English, 1973-80; spl. asst. to pres., sec. to corp. Claremont U. Center, 1981-83; v.p. for acad. affairs Austin Coll., Sherman, Tex., 1982-84, faculty mem., 1984-96. Mem. SW dist. Rhodes Scholar Selection Com., 1975-83 Bd. dirs. Am. Council on Edn., 1979-81. Mem. Assn. Am. Colls. (dir. 1977-81, chmn. 1980-81), Am. Conf. Acad. Deans (dir. 1976-79), Commn. on Women in Higher Edn., Am. Assn. Higher Edn., Modern Lang. Assn. Am. Democrat. Episcopalian. Home: 11304 Pinos Altos Ave NE Albuquerque NM 87111-5701 E-mail: ahnefu@nmia.com.

FULLER, BETTY STAMPS, music educator; b. Prentiss, Miss., Feb. 19, 1938; d. Henry Buford and Genevieve (Bozeman) Stamps; m. Allan Riggs Fuller, Dec. 19, 1957 (dec. May 1987); children: Melodie, Valerie. Attended, Miss. Coll., 1958; BA, McNeese State U., 1983; post grad., Loyola U., 1985. Music tchr. Bearss Acad., Jackson, Miss., 1969—73, Episcopal Day Sch., Lake Charles, La., 1975—85, Our Lady's Sch., Sulpher, 1985—. Mentor tchr. Alliance for Cath. Edn., Notre Dame U., Notre Dame, Ind., 2000—01. Coord. youth orch. Miss. Coll., Clinton, Miss., 1967—72; bd. mem. Lake Charles (La.) Symphony Orch., 1975—77. Named Citizen of the Day, KLOU Radio Station, Lake Charles, 1975, Tchr. of Yr., KC Coun., 1994; Fine Arts grant, La. Divsn. of Arts, 1994—95, Arts and Humanities Coun. SW La., 1996. Mem.: Nat. Cath. Edn. Assn. Episcopalian. Avocations: production of musical plays, visual arts, historical preservation, environmental activities. Home: 2715 Roxton St Sulphur LA 70663

FULLER, BEVERLEY BOZEMAN, dancer, singer, actress, choreographer, director; b. Fresno, Calif., July 20, 1927; d. Ernest Edward Bozeman and Lola Lee Bills; m. Walter Dean Fuller Jr., Jan. 3, 1955 (div. July 1981); children: Liza Dean, John Whitney. Broadwy debut as dancer/singer Inside USA, 1948; appeared in Broadway prodns. Where's Charley?, 1949, Peer Gynt, 1951, Pal Joey, 1953, Anta Dance Series, As I Lay Dying, 1950's, Domino Furioso, 1950's; off-Broadway prodn. the Littlest Revue, 1956; Brit. touring co. prodn. Midsummer Night's Dream, 1931; national tours with The Desert Song, 1946, Pal Joey, 1954; choreographer, lead actress in regional tour of On The Town, 1950; co-prodr., choreographer with regional tour of A Connecticut Yankee, 1951; co-star in regional tour Three To One, 1952; choreographer stage and films Capriccio for Three, 1950's, the Mad Woman of Chaillot, 1950's, King of Hearts, 1950's, 1980s, regional theater prodns. of Pal Joey, No, No, Nanette, 1982, Panama Hattie, 1954, Wish You Were Here, 1952, Where's Charlie?, New Faces of 1952, Guys and Dolls (nominee Best Actress award The Sara Siddons Soc., 1955), The Golden Apple, 1955 (nominee Best Actress award The Sara Siddons Soc., 1955); appeared in TV programs Hallmark, Ed Sullivan Show; founder, moderator The Theatre Club, 1997-99; exhibits include China Inst., N.Y.C. and Chester (Conn.) Gallery; author Cooking On Your Knees, 1973; contbr. articles to profl. jours. Mem. Actors Equity Assn., Dramatists Guild. Democrat. Avocations: chinese brush painting, calligraphy, cooking, working out. Home: 205 W End Ave Apt 5M New York NY 10023-4818

FULLER, BONNIE, editor-in-chief; b. Toronto, Canada; m. Michael Fuller; 4 children. BA in History, U. of Toronto, 1977. Fashion reporter Toronto Star, 1978; sportswear editor Women's Wear Daily; editor-in-chief Flare mag., Canada, 1982, YM, NYC, 1989—94; founding editor Marie Claire, 1994—96; dep. editor Cosmopolitan, 1996—97; editor-in-chief Cosmopolitan Hearst Mags., N.Y.C., 1997—98; editor-in-chief Glamour, Conde Nast, 1998—2001; editor US Weekly, 2002—03; exec. v.p. Am. Media Inc., NYC, 2003—, chief editl. dir., 2003—. Author: From Geek to Oh My Goodness, 2003, The Joys of Much Too Much: Go for the Big Life--The Great Career, The Perfect Guy, and Everything Else You've Ever Wanted, 2006. Named Editor of Yr., Ad Age Mag. (twice); recipient Spotlight award, Amnesty Internat., 2000. Office: American Media Inc 1 Park Ave New York NY 10016

FULLER, CASSANDRA MILLER, applications specialist; b. Norwalk, Conn., Dec. 10, 1965; d. George Louis and Bernice (Simmons) Miller; m. David Norman Fuller, Dec. 24, 1988; 1 child, Jessica Ashley. BS, S.C. State Coll., 1987; MBA, U. Bridgeport, 1995. Interior decorator's apprentice Marty Rae Interiors, Orangeburg, S.C., 1984-85; asst. mgr. Dairy Queen, Orangeburg, S.C., 1986-87; day mgr. The Bedford, Stamford, Conn., 1987-88; dept. mgr. Burlington Coat Factory Warehouse, Danbury, Conn.; asst. mgr. Kidstuff, Inc., Orange, Conn., 1989-92; Postage By Phone customer assistance specialist Pitney Bowes, Stamford, Conn., 1992-95, programmer analyst, 1996-98; applications specialist GE Capital Vendor Fin. Svcs., Danbury, Conn., 1998—. Cons. Orangeburg Metro Transit 1987. Mem. Nat. Assn. Negro Bus. and Profl. Women's Clubs Inc., Nat. Black MBA Assn., NAFE, African Am. Forum, Kappa Omicron Phi. Democrat. Baptist.

FULLER, JANET MCCRAY, anthropologist, educator; b. Alma, Mich., June 24, 1962; d. Richard Milton and Judith McCray Fuller; m. David Marvin Johnson, Aug. 11, 2001; 1 child, Nicholas Matthew Johnson-Fuller; m. Lars Winfried Seiler, July 26, 1991 (div. Feb. 7, 1997); 1 child, Arlette McCray Seiler-Fuller. BA, Macalester Coll., St.Paul, 1984; MA, Freie Universitaet Berlin, 1992; PhD, U. S.C., Columbia, 1997. Asst. prof. Linguistics So. Ill. U., Carbondale, 1997—2003, assoc. prof. Linguistics, 2003—04, assoc. prof. Anthropology, 2004—. Editor: Readings in Contact Linguistics: Studies in Honor of Glenn G. Gilbert; contbr. articles to profl. jours. Mem.: Am. Dialect Soc., Am. Anthropology Assn., Linguistic Soc. Am. Office: Southern Illinois University Mailcode 4502 Carbondale IL 62901 Office Phone: 618-536-6651. E-mail: jmfuller@siu.edu.

FULLER, JEAN, school system administrator; AA, Bakersfield Cmty. Coll.; BA, Calif. State U., Fresno, 1972; MPA, Calif. State U., LA, 1982; PhD in Ednl. Policy and Orgnl. Studies, U. Calif., Santa Barbara, 1989. Cert. tchr. comm., English, Soc. Sci. Calif. State U., 1972. Elem. and secondary tchr., 1972—80; elem. and mid. sch. prin. Westside Union Sch. Dist, Calif., 1980—83, cons. 803 computer, 1987; elem. prin. and dir. of tech. svcs. Keppel Union Sch. Dist, 1983—88, dir. state and fed. projects, spl. edn. and pers., 1988, asst. supt., 1988—90, supt., 1990—99, Bakersfield City Sch. Dist, 1999—. Attendee U. So. Calif. Supt. Symposium, LA, 1991, Harvard Grad. Sch. of Edn. Supt. Seminars, Cambridge, Mass., 1998, Cambridge, 99; mem. Kern County Supt.'s Adv. Bd., 1999—. Mem. Jim Burke Ednl. Found., Vision 2020 Ednl. Com.; Mayor's Youth Devel. Coun.; mem. Kern County Network Children Bd.; bd. dir. Boys and Girls Club, 2002—, mem. mktg. com., 2002—. Recipient Calif. Supt. of Yr., Am. Assn. of Sch. Adminstrs., 1995, Nat. Leadership Learning award, 1998. Mem.: Am. Assn. of Sch. Adminstrs. Office: Bakersfield City Sch Dist 1300 Baker St Bakersfield CA 93305

FULLER, JENNIFER L., lawyer; b. Bellflower, Calif., Apr. 26, 1958; BA, Whittier Coll., 1982; JD, Loyola Law Sch., 1985; LLM in taxation, Georgetown Univ., 1988. Bar: Calif. 1987. Ptnr., tax group Fenwick & West LLP, Mountain View, Calif. Instr. Golden Gate Univ. Contbr. articles to profl. jours. Mem.: Calif. State Bar (no. Calif. chair internat. tax com.). Office: Fenwick & West LLP Silicon Valley Ctr 801 California St Mountain View CA 94041 Office Phone: 650-335-7284. Office Fax: 650-938-5200. Business E-Mail: jfuller@fenwick.com.

FULLER, KATHRYN SCOTT, former environmental services administrator; b. NYC, July 8, 1946; d. Delbert Orison and Carol Scott (Gilbert) F.; m. Stephen Paul Doyle, May 29, 1977; children: Sarah Elizabeth Taylor, Michael Stephen Doyle, Matthew Scott Doyle. BA English, Am. Lit., Brown U., 1968, LHD (hon.), 1992; JD with honors, U. Tex., 1976; postgrad., U. Md., 1980-82; DSci. (hon.), Wheaton Coll., 1990; LLD (hon.), Knox Coll., 1992. Bar: Tex. 1977, D.C. 1979. Rsch. asst. Yale U., New Haven, 1968-69, Am. Chem. Soc., 1970-71, Harvard U. Mus. Comparative Zoology, Cambridge, Mass., 1971-73; law clerk Dewey, Ballantine, Bushby, Palmer & Wood and Vinson & Elkins, N.Y.C., Houston, 1974-76, U.S. Dist. Ct. (so. dist.), Tex., 1976-77; atty., advisor Office Legal Counsel Dept. Justice, Washington, 1977-79, atty. Wildlife and Marine Resources sect., 1979-80, chief Wildlife and Marine Resources sect., 1981-82; exec. v.p., dir. Traffic USA, pub. policy, gen. counsel World Wildlife Fund, Washington, 1982-89, pres., CEO, 1989—2005. Contbr. articles to profl. jours.; bd. dirs. Alcoa Inc., 2002—, Student Conservation Assn., Fondo Mexicano para la Conservacion de la Naturaleza; mem. World Bank Adv. Com. on Sustainable Devel. Bd. trustees Ford Found., Brown U. Recipient William Rogers Outstanding Grad. award Brown U., 1990, UN Environment Programme Global 500 award, 1990; Named outstanding woman law student Tex. scholar, 1975. Mem. State Tex. Bar, D.C. Bar, Coun. Fgn. Rels., Zonta Internat. (hon.). Avocations: squash, trekking, scuba diving, gardening, fishing.

FULLER, KATHY J., special education educator, consultant, researcher; b. Lamar, Colo., Oct. 24, 1957; d. Alfred L. and Leona M. Fuller; 1 child, Samantha Devon Blake. MA, Calif. State U. Northridge, 1993; PhD in Psychol. Studies of Edn., UCLA, 2004. Prof. UCLA ext., 1999—, Pacific Oaks Coll., Pasadena, Calif., 2002—; cons. L.A. County of Edn., 2002—. Tchr. Pasadena Unified Sch. Dist., Calif., 1992—94; tchr., full inclusion specialist LA Unified Sch. Dist., 1994—2000; prof. Calif. State U., L.A., 1999—2002, adj. prof., 1997—; owner Teacher Talk, 2003—; presenter in field. Musician: (singer) New Life - Kora Music for the 21st Century (Prince Diabate CD); poet Helpless Hoping (Editor's Choice award); contbg. author: Rescued Tails, 2005; contbr. articles to profl. jours. Pet therapist Love on 4 Paws, L.A., 2002; edn. dir. Beagles & Buddies, Orange County Cavy Haven; vol. pet therapist Vitas Hospice, 2006—, Ronald McDonald Houses. Recipient 1st place Edn. award, 2001, 2d place Behavioral/Social Scis. award, 2002; grantee Nat. Rsch. grant, Nat. Assn. Alternative Cert., 1999—. Mem.: Nat. Assn. Alternative Edn., Am. Ednl. Rsch. Assn., Coun. for Exceptional Children (assoc.), Phi Lambda Theta. Achievements include design of Fuller-Blake Academic Inventory. Home: 790 Monterey Rd South Pasadena CA 91030 Office Phone: 626-685-2532. Personal E-mail: kfullerbla@aol.com.

FULLER, MARTHA M., poet; Author: Tattle Tales, 1997, Days Gone By, 1997 (Editor's Choice award Nat. Libr. Congress), Sounds of Poetry, 1998, After Thoughts, 2002, among others. Recipient numerous awards. Mem. Poetry Hall of Fame, Internat. Soc. Poets. Home: 34 Worthington Dr Apt 202 Westbrook CT 06498-1994 E-mail: quidfit@snet.net.

FULLER, MARY BAKER, chemistry educator; d. John Ambrose and Victoria Josephine Baker; m. William Fuller, Dec. 23, 1973; children: Kathleen Jeanne, Rebecca Jo. BS, Frostburg State U., Md., 1972; M in Liberal Arts, Johns Hopkins U., Balt., 1974. Advanced profl. tchg. cert. Md. State Dept. Edn., 2006. Biology/chemistry instr. Notre Dame Prep. Sch., Hampton, Md., 1972—73, Allegany County Career Ctr., Cresaptown, Md., 1973—82; owner/operator Eckhart Apts., Frostburg, 1979—; chemistry instr., sci. dept. chair Ft. Hill H.S., Cumberland, Md., 1982—. Mentor Allegany County Bd. Edn., Cumberland, Md., 1995—2006; owner, operator Fuller Earth Expdn., 1998—2006; presenter worshops on handheld computers. Grantee, Foundaton for Rural Md., 2005, 2006. Mem.: NEA. Roman Catholic. Avocations: travel, camping, canoeing, flying, reading. Office: Fort Hill High School 500 Greenway Ave Cumberland MD 21502 E-mail: mfuller@allconet.org.

FULLER, S(HERI) MARCE, energy executive; BSEE, U. Ala.; MS in Power System Engring., Union Coll. Student engr. Ala. Power (subs. The So. Co.), 1980-83; engr. power system engring. dept. GE, 1983-85; electric system planning engr. Ala. Power (subs. The So. Co.), 1985-87; sr. fin. analyst corp. finance So. Co. Svcs., 1987-89, prin. strategic planning, asst. to pres., 1989-91; bus. devel. mgr. So. Electric (subs. The So. Co.), 1991; v.p. domestic bus. devel. So. Electric, 1994-96, sr. v.p. domestic ops., 1996; pres., CEO Mirant Corp., Atlanta, 1999—. Bd. dirs. Curtiss-Wright Corp., Earthlink; chairperson electricity adv. bd. U.S. Dept. Energy; mem. bd. councilors The Carter Ctr.; mem. Pres. Internat. Bd. Advisors, Philippines. Trustee Atlanta Internat. Sch. Office: Mirant 1155 Perimeter Ctr W Atlanta GA 36338

FULLERTON, DAVINA, art historian, consultant, researcher; b. London, July 29, 1931; came to U.S., 1957; d. David George and Elsa Victoria Mandler; m. Kenneth James Fullerton, Aug. 16, 1952; children: Victoria. Honor. BS, London U., 1952, Boston U., 1972, MEd, 1974; Mus. Studies Cert., Tufts U., 1992. Jr. physiotherapist St. Mary's Hosp., London, 1953-54, sr. physiotherapist, 1954-57; physiotherapist Framingham (Mass.) Union Hosp., 1958-72; homecare physiotherapist Easter Seals, Boston, 1973-83; cons. physiotherapist Sudbury (Mass.) Pines, 1983-86; coord. pub. edn. Harvard U. Art Museums, Cambridge, Mass., 1990-98; lectr., art historian Humanities Internat., Boston, 1998—. Actor, appearing in numerous plays, 1959-90; voice-over for commls., 1970s—. Eucharistic lay min. St. Elizabeth's Ch., Sudbury, 1980-92, also thrift shop mgr.; lay reader Ch. of Messia, Woods Hole, Mass., 1992—. Mem. Doric Dames Inc. (bd. dirs. 1986—, exec. v.p. 1986-88). Episcopalian. Avocations: reading, gardening, swimming, exercise. Home: 44 Carey Ln Falmouth MA 02540-1604

FULLERTON, DENISE S.S., lawyer; married; 2 children. Grad. with honors, Gustavus Adolphus Coll., 1993, William Mitchell Coll. Law, 1998. Bar: Minn. 1998, US Dist. Ct. (dist. Minn.). Ptnr. Ramsay & DeVore, P.A., Roseville, Minn. Contbr. articles to profl. publs. Named a Rising Star, Minn. Super Lawyers mag., 2006. Mem.: Minn. State Bar Assn., Ramsey County Bar Assn., Hennepin County Bar Assn., Minn. Trial Lawyers Assn. (mem. no-fault com. 2001—, mem. bd. govs. 2003—, mem. exec. com. 2005, chair women lawyers sect.), Minn. Women Lawyers. Office: Ramsay & DeVore PA Rosedale Towers Ste 450 1700 W Hwy 36 Roseville MN 55113 Office Phone: 651-604-0000. E-mail: dfullerton@ramsaydevore.com.*

FULLERTON, GAIL JACKSON, retired academic administrator; m. Stanley James Fullerton, Mar. 27, 1967; children by previous marriage— Gregory Snell Putney, Cynde Putney Mitchell. BA, U. Nebr., 1949, MA, 1950; PhD, U. Oreg., 1954. Lectr. sociology Drake U., Des Moines, 1955-57; asst. prof. sociology Fla. State U., Tallahassee, 1957-60, San Jose (Calif.) State U., 1963-67, assoc. prof., 1968-71, prof., 1972-91, dean grad. studies and rsch., 1972-76, exec. v.p. univ., 1976-78, pres., 1978-91; ret., 1991. Bd. dirs. Assoc. Western Univs., Inc., 1980-91; mem. sr. accrediting commn. Western Assn. Schs. and Colls., 1982-88, chmn., 1985-86; mem. Pres.'s Commn. NCAA, 1986-91; bd. dirs. Am. Coll. Assn., 1991. Author: Survival in Marriage, 2d edit, 1977, (with Snell Putney) Normal Neurosis: The Adjusted American, 2d edit, 1966. Carnegie fellow, 1950-51, 52-53; Doherty Found. fellow, 1951-52. Mem. Phi Beta Kappa, Chi Omega.

FULLERTON, JEAN LEAH, retired language educator, researcher, census researcher; b. Johnstown, Pa., Aug. 5, 1929; d. Elmer M. and Elizabeth (Schultz) Daily; m. Bernell Houston Fullerton, Nov. 8, 1952; children: Kenneth Leon, Michele Marie Kelley, Brian Hugh, Madeline Elizabeth McMahon. BA, Seton Hill U., Greensburg, Pa., 1951; MS, Towson State U., 1980. Cert. English Tchr. Md., Master's Equivalency Cert. Tchr. English Balt. County Sch. Sys., Towson, Md., 1967—89; interviewer/rschr. Census Bur. US Dept. Commerce, Phila., 1990—. Author poetry. Vol. Rep. Party, Towson, 1960—82. Roman Catholic. Avocation: genealogy. Home: 185 Sandyhook Rd Ocean Pines MD 21811 Personal E-mail: b.fullerton@mchsl.com.

FULLERTON, JESSICA ANN, music educator; b. Newport News, Va., Dec. 31, 1980; d. William and JoEllen Fullerton. MusB Edn., Va. Commonwealth U., 2003. Cert. vocal/choral tchr. Va. Choral tchr. Binford Mid. Sch., Richmond, Va., 2003—; choral tchr., drama tchr. Albert Hill Mid. Sch., Richmond, 2003—. Chmn. music com. Tabernacle Bapt. Ch., Richmond, 2004—06. Mem.: Richmond Choral Dirs. Assn. (pres.), Am. Choral Directors Assn., Va. Music Educators Assn., Kappa Kappa Psi (founder local chpt. 2001—03, pres. 2002—03). Democrat. Baptist. Avocations: reading, travel. Office: Binford Middle Sch 1701 Floyd Ave Richmond VA 23220 Home: 3423 Parkwood Ave Richmond VA 23221 Office Phone: 804-780-6231. Office Fax: 804-780-6057. Business E-Mail: jfullert@richmond.k12.va.us.

FULLILOVE, MINDY THOMPSON, psychiatrist; b. Irvington, N.J., Oct. 15, 1950; d. Ernest Leroy and Margaret Aileen (Brown) Thompson; m. Michael J. Kaufman, Aug. 21, 1971 (div. Nov. 1983); children: Kenneth, Dina, Molly; m. Robert E. Fullilove, Dec. 23, 1983; 1 child, Robert E. AB, Bryn Mawr (Pa.) Coll., 1971; MS, Columbia U., 1974, MD, 1978; DHL (hon.), Chatham Coll., Pitts., 1999. Diplomate Am. Bd. Psychiatry and Neurology. Resident N.Y. Hosp., 1978-81, Montefiore Hosp., 1981-82, staff psychiatrist Bronx, 1982-83, Bayview-Hunter's Point Found., San Francisco, 1983-90; rsch. psychiatrist N.Y. State Psychiat. Inst., N.Y.C., 1990—; prof. clin. psychiatry and pub. health Columbia U. Author: House of Joshua, 1999. Avocations: photography, gardening. Office: New York State Psychiatric Inst 1051 Riverside Dr Unit 29 New York NY 10032-1013 E-mail: mf29@columbia.edu.

FULLWOOD, ALTBURG MARIE, women's health nurse; b. Scharbeutz, West Germany, May 6, 1933; d. Hans F. and Cacilie A. (Bliesmer) Burmann; m. Marvin Fullwood, Sept. 6, 1963; children: Randal O., Renée M. Diploma, St. Georg Hosp., Hamburg, West Germany, 1953, Kleemann Sch., Kiel, West Germany, 1954; ADN, U. N.C., Wilmington, 1984. RN, N.C.; cert. psychiat./mental health nurse. Nurse German Social Security System, Hamburg, 1954-57; exec. sec. to dir. Fla. State U., Eglin AFB, 1963-67; civil service pers. Dept. of Army, Southport, N.C., 1972-74; psychiat. nurse New Hanover Regional Med. Ctr., Wilmington, 1984—2005, Welcare Home Health, 2003—.

FULMER, AMY M., lawyer; d. M. and F. Fulmer; m. James S. Fulmer, May 21, 2000. BS in Agrl., Ohio State U., Columbus, 1992; JD, Capital U. Law Sch., Columbus, 1997. Bar: Ohio 1997. Atty., owner Thomas & Fulmer, Delaware, Ohio, 2003—05, Fulmer & Co., Dublin, 2005—. Photo journalist, numerous art shows and exhbns. Participant Tri Village Noon Lion's Club, Columbus, 2006. Mem.: Columbus Bar Assn. (assoc.). Rastafarian. Office Fax: 614-793-8483. E-mail: tigerinatrance@gmail.com.

FULMER, DEBORAH LEE, education educator, oncological nurse; b. Harrisburg, Pa., July 25, 1957; d. Donald Richard Petrovic and Nancy Lee Gruber. ADN, Harrisburg Area CC, Pa., 1991; B in nursing, Graceland U., Lamoni, Iowa, 1998; MS in Biology, Millersville U., Pa., 2001; PhD student, Touro U., San Francisco, 2003—. RN Am. Nursing Assn., Pa., 1991, cert. Oncology Nurse, Am. Nursing Assn., 1995. Oncology nurse Polyclinic Med. Ctr., Harrisburg, Pa., 1991—2000; pediatric nurse Pediatric Svc. of Am., Harrisburg, Pa., 1999—; instr. biology Harrisburg Area CC, 2004—. Vol. AIDS Cmty. Alliance, Harrisburg, 1999—2006. Prodr.: (pub. awareness presentation) Rebuilding Education: Afghanistan, (ednl. presentation) Landmines - A Day At The ICRC Rehabilitation Clinic In Afghanistan. Del. Global Exch./Afghans 4 Tomorrow, San Francisco, 2003; project coord. Cultural Embrace, Austin, 2006. Mem.: ARC (vol. 2004—06), Internat. Soc. Nursing (assoc.). Avocations: victorian gardening, travel. Home: 3024 Orchard Ln Middletown PA 17057 Office: Pediatric Svcs of America Prince St Harrisburg PA 17109 Office Phone: 717-540-1051. Personal E-mail: dfulm_2000@yahoo.com.

FULMORE, MARYANN, state agency administrator; b. Mar. 19, 1952; d. William Stewart and Etta Grace Anderson; m. Clifton Fulmore, Mar. 29, 1980. BA, N.C. Ctrl. U., Durham, 1974; MA, Kean U., Union, N.J., 1985. Cert. counselor dept. labor, N.J. Sr. vocat. counselor divsn. employment and tng. State of N.J., Plainfield; discretionary grants coord. Union County Dept. Human Svcs./Divsn. Employment and Tng., Elizabeth, N.J., 1992-98, dir. ops., 1998—. Editor-in-chief newsletter Shiloh Bapt. Sentinel, 1993-99. Recipient Women of Excellence award Union County Commn. on Status of Women, 1998, Freeholder Resolution award Bd. Chosen Freeholders, Union County, 1998. Mem. Nat. Assn. Univ. Women (past pres. Plainfield Brunswick br., Svc. award 1994-98), Garden State Employment and Tng. Assn., Shiloh Bapt. Ch. Women's Fellowship. Office: County Adminstrn Bldg Human Svcs Dept Elizabethtown Plz Elizabeth NJ 07207

FULTON, CHERYL L., customer service administrator; b. Chgo., Feb. 21, 1947; d. Theodore E. and Elsie A. Whiffen; m. Richard L. Gniadek, Nov. 15, 1969 (dec. Feb. 1979); m. Richard J. Fulton, Sept. 2, 1995. BSBA, Ill. State U., 1969. Prodn. sec. Universal Tng. Systems, Lincolnwood, Ill., 1969-71; exec. sec. Alliance Am. Insurers, Chgo., 1971-78; temp. sec. Kelly Svcs., Grand Rapids, Mich., 1978-79; sec. Honeywell, Internat., Grand Rapids, Mich., 1979—80, sales corr., 1980—81, adminstr. customer quality Ft. Washington, Pa., 1981—84, rep. customer svc. Valley Forge, Pa., 1984—88, fin. acct. Ft. Washington, 1987—91, br. support supr. Valley Forge, 1991—92, supr. Regional Customer Svc. Ctr. Ft. Washington, 1992—95, field svcs. mgr., 1995—. Mem. NAFE, Am. Bus. Women's Assn. (New Directions Charter chpt., pres. 1986, Woman of Yr. 1985), Instrument Soc. Am. (treas., edn. com. Phila. sect., sec., treas., 3d v.p., 2d v.p., 1st v.p., pres. 1994-95). Democrat. Roman Catholic. Avocations: needlecrafts, skiing, reading. Home: 857 Thoreau Ct Warminster PA 18974-2057 Office: Honeywell Internat 1100 Virginia Dr Fort Washington PA 19034-3264

FULTON, JUDITH P., management consultant; b. Princeton, N.J., Oct. 30, 1955; m. Mark P. Howard; children: David I. Fulton-Howard, Brian E. Fulton-Howard. BA in Computer Sci., Harvard U., 1978, MBA, 1983. Software devel. engr. Hewlett-Packard Co., 1978—81; dir. external sourcing, dir. strategic planning, bus. analysis mgr., mgr. mktg., MIS mgr. Bristol-Myers Squibb Co., 1983—90; mgr. flexible benefits bus. unit, mktg. mgr. Blue Cross & Blue Shield Md., 1990—94; dir. physician billing ops., dir. planning and bus. devel. HealthCare Automation Inc., 1995—97; CEO, treas. NovoVasc In., 1997—99; mgmt. cons. Eager St. Group, 1999—; CEO Cornerstone Mgmt., 2000—. Mentor Dingman Ctr. for Entrepreneurship, Smith Sch. Bus., U. Md., College Park, 1999—; mem. bd. trustees, sec., v.p. bd., mem. exec. com., chair com. on trustees, mem. mktg. and devel. coms., co-chair ann. fund raising Norbel Sch., 1995—; mem. bd. mgrs., chair program and membership com., chair ann. support campaign gen. teams Towson YMCA, 1993—96; adviser to pres., bd. Bright Vision Therapeutic Riding, 2000—. Recipient one of Md.'s Top 100 Women, Daily Record, 1998. Office: 1903 Indian Head Rd Baltimore MD 21204

FULTON ROSS, GALE, artist, actor; b. Medford, Mass., July 28, 1947; adopted d. Herman Fulton Jr. and d. Henrietta Kelly, d. Joseph, Barksdale, Jr.; m. Craig Ross Sr., Dec. 18, 1964 (div. Aug. 7, 1977); 1 child, Craig Jr. Ross. Studied with artist Melvin Johnson, Instr. Melvin George Sch. Art, Boston, 1965—76; studied with artist Cleveland Bellow, Oakland, Calif. of the DeYoung Mus., 1976—81; studied with artist Pierre Parsus, France, 1993; studied, Berlin, 1996, studied, 2005. Trustee Nat. Urban League, N.Y.C., 1976—78; local/state judge Miss Am. Pageant, 2000—. Paintings/traveling exhibition, Billie (Nat. Coalition of 100 Black Woman Artistic Achievement Award, 1995); actor(role of Hazel): (film) Blue Hill Avenue, (role of Tituba): The Crucible; exhibitions include Earth N' Arts Gallery, Oakland, 1971—76, Black Expo, San Francisco, 1972, Oakland Mus., 1971, The Gallery, LA, 1978, Brockman Gallery, 1984, Calif. African Mus., 1986, Cousen Rose Gallery, Boston, 1987—89, Phila. AA Hist. Cultural Mus., 1995, US Dept. Health and Human Svcs., Wash., 1996, Pa. State U., 1996, Chuck Levitan Gallery, NYC, 1996, Tampa City Ctr., Franceсsca Anderson Gallery, Lexington, Mass., Sarasota Ctr. for Visual Arts, 1997, SoBo Fine Art, Tulsa, 1999, Gallery Bershad, Boston, 1999, Artjaz Gallery, Phila., 1999, various others, one-woman shows include Nat. Coun. Chs. Hdqs., NYC, 1991, Castillion Fine Art, 1991, Zora Neal Hurston Mus., 1994, Monique Knowlton Gallery, NYC, 1994, Don Roll Gallery, Sarasota, 1995, African Am. Mus., Tampa, 1995, Represented in permanent collections Am. Mus. African Am. Artists, Ca. Mus. African Am. Art, Forbes Gallery, NYC, The Arthur Ashe Found., Thurgood Marshall Estate, NC U., Women's Mus Ar., Wash., commissioned works include, Archbishop Desmond Tutu, Nat. Orgn. Black Law Enforcement Officers, Congressman Ronald Dellums, Ambassador Bradlet Holmes, Gov. Michael Dukakis, Mayor Andrew Young, J. Bruce Llewellyn, Jackie Robinson for Mrs. Rachel Robinson, Dr. Arthur Logan for Marian Logan, Byard Rustin, Gov. L. Douglas Wilder, Pres. Coun. Chs. R. William David, Law office of Rosen & Shapiro, Sarasota, Law office of Shaffer Zapson, NYC, San Francisco Gen. Hosp., Singer Whitney Houston, 100 Black Women, Boston, Dr. Lorna Thomas, Former mayor of Detroit, Dennis Archer. Activie artistic development study program, Berlin; founder, pres. Fulton Ross Fund For Visual Artists, Inc., Sarasota, Fla., 1998. Recipient Atlanta Life Painters award, 1990, Artistic Achievement award, Nat. Coalition 100 Black Women, 1995, Humanitarian award, West Coast Ctr. Human Devel., 1996, Arts and Humanity award, Nat. Coalition of 100 Black Women; fellow, LaNapoule Found., 1990—92; grantee Merit Purpose award, Pollock-Krasner Found., 1993.

FUMAGALLI, BARBARA MERRILL, artist, printmaker; b. Kirkwood, Mo., Mar. 15, 1926; d. Harold C. and Mary Louise (Fitch) Ellison; m. Orazio Fumagalli, Aug. 15, 1948; children: Luisa, Piera, Elio. BFA, State U. Iowa, 1948, MFA, 1950; student, Mauricio Lasansky, Iowa City, 1945-50, Garo Antreasian, John Sommers, Jim Kraft, Albuquerque, 1980-81. Solo shows at Tweed Gallery, U. Minn., Duluth, 1955, 82, U. Minn., St. Paul, 1964, Mpls., 1965, Concordia Coll., Moorhead, Minn., 1965, Suzanne Kohn Gallery, St. Paul, 1967, Hamline U., St. Paul, 1969, 84, Paine Art Center and Arboretum, Oshkosh, Wis., 1973, St. Johns U., Collegeville, Minn., 1984, U. Louisville, 1993; group shows, Cork Gallery, Lincoln Ctr., N.Y.C., 1982, Baylor U., Waco, Tex., 1990, Abilene (Tex.) Christian U., 1991, Multnomah County Libr., Portland, Oreg., 1991, Hesston (Kans.) Coll., 1991, Henry Ford C.C., Dearborn, Mich., 1991, Grinnell (Iowa) Coll. Gallery, 1993, One West Contemporary Arts Ctr., Ft. Collins, Colo., 1994, Tarleton State U., Stephenville, Tex., 1994, Chadron (Nebr.) State Coll., 1994, Waldorf Coll., Forest City, Iowa, 1995, Ctrl. Coll., Pella, Iowa, 1996, Mo. Western State Coll., St. Joseph, 1996, Highland (Kans.) C.C., 1997, Indian Hills C.C., Ottumwa, Iowa, 1997, 98, Tex.-Dallas, Richardson, 1997, Truman State U., Kirksville, Mo., 1998, S.E. Mo. State U., Cape Girardeau, 1999, Albrecht-Kemper Mus. Art, St. Joseph, Mo., 2000, Butler C.C., El Dorado, Kans., 2000, Studio Channel Islands, Camarillo, Calif., 2000, 01, U. Ctrl. Ark., Conway, 2001, Focus On the Masters, Ventura, Calif., 2002, 03, Mo. Western State Coll., St. Joseph, 2003, Dickenson State U., N.D., 2004, Ventura County Arts Coun., 2004, Artist's Salon, Ventura, Calif., 2005, Ashford U., Clinton, Iowa, 2005, Art and Jazz Festival, Studio Channel Islands Art Ctr., Calif. State U., Channel Islands, Camarillo, Calif., 2006, others; represented in permanent collections Mus. Modern Art, N.Y.C., Nelson A. Rockefeller Collection, N.Y.C.; illustrator: Swing Around the Sun (Barbara J. Esbensen), 1965.

FUNDA, EVELYN, literature educator; b. Emmett, Idaho, Jan. 23, 1960; d. Lumir Earnest Funda and Antonia Kratochilova Funda. BA, Boise State U., Idaho, 1984, MA, 1986; PhD, U. Nebr., Lincoln, 1994. Asst. prof. Am. lit./Am. studies Utah State U., Logan, 1995—2001, assoc. prof. Am. lit./Am. studies, 2001—. Book rev. editor Western Am. Lit. (quar. jour.), Logan, 1997—2004. Contbr. articles, essays and poetry to publs. Recipient Hon. mention, Frederick Manfred Award for Creative Writing, 2004; Albert J Colton Rsch. fellow, Utah Humanities Coun., 2005—06, New Faculty Rsch. grantee, Utah State U., 1996. Mem.: Assn. for the Study Lit. and Environment, Western Lit. Assn. (J. Golden Taylor award for outstanding grad. student paper 1993). Office: Utah State University Dept English 3200 Old Main Hill Logan UT 84322-3200 Office Phone: 435-797-3653.

FUNDERBURG, JAN, telecommunications industry executive; Numerous positions including operator svcs., human resources, network ops., sales, mktg. Bellsouth Corp., v.p. customer svcs., 1997—2002, pres. interconnection svcs. Atlatna, 2002—. Active Am. Cancer Soc., Woodruff Arts, Jr. Acheivement, United Way; bd. dirs. ARC Disaster Svcs. Divsn. Recipient Oustanding Woman Achievement award, YWCA, 1997, Person Yr. award, Ga. Interconnection Assn., 1988.

FUNG, INEZ Y., science educator; SB in Applied Math., MIT, 1971, ScD in Meteorology, 1977. Prof. atmospheric sci. U. Calif., Berkeley Inst. Environ., co-dir. Featured in Women's Adventures in Sci. Recipient NASA Goddard Inst. for Space Studies Peer award, 1987, 1993, NASA Exceptional Scientific Achievement medal, 1989, NASA Goddard Inst. for Space Studies Most Valuable Paper award, 1990, 1996, Nat. Oceanic & Atmospheric Adminstrn. Disting. Authorship award, 1991; NASA Goddard Sr. Fellow, 1992—97. Fellow: Am. Meterological Soc., Am. Geophysical Union (Roger Revelle medal 2004); mem.: NAS. Office: U Calif Berkeley Inst Environ 399 McCone and 335 Hilgard Berkeley CA 94720-1250 Office Phone: 510-643-9367. Office Fax: 510-643-9980. Business E-Mail: inez@atmos.berkeley.edu.*

FUNG, MINA HSU, advertising executive; b. Kwangsi, China, Feb. 14, 1947; arrived in U.S., 1966, arrived in U.S., 1966; d. Man-Tak and Yu-Wen (Chew) Hsu; 1 child, Daniel. BA in Social Scis., U. Ill., Chgo., 1970; MBA in Mktg., Loyola U., Chgo., 1973. Project supr. Conway/Milliken Corp., Chgo., 1970—73; sr. assoc. rsch. dir. Grey Advt., N.Y.C., 1976—81, v.p., 1981—85, mgmt. planning dir., 1985—89, sr. v.p., 1989—. Mem.: Dir. Mktg. Assn., Am. Mktg. Assn., Advt. Rsch. Found. Office: Grey Advt 777 3rd Ave New York NY 10017-1401

FUNG, ROSALINE LEE, language educator; b. China, May 14, 1944; came to U.S., 1963; d. Frank Kwok-Wai and Teresa Wai-Hing (Cheung) Lee; m. Stephen Ying-Chung Fung, Aug. 23, 1968. BA, Briar Cliff Coll., 1966; MA, Idaho State U., 1968. Instr. Highland C.C., Freeport, Ill., 1968-69, Merced (Calif.) Coll., 1969-70; tchr. Linden (Calif.) High Sch., 1970-84; prof. San Joaquin Delta Coll., Stockton, Calif., 1984—. Cons. in field. Author: (textbooks) ESL Writing Manual, 1992, Patterns for Success, 4 vols., 1997, Basic Composition, 1997, Writing Essays, 1998, Writing Paragraphs, 1999. Coord. cultural exch. San Joaquin Delta Coll., 1995, 96, 98. Mem. NEA, Calif. Tchrs. Assn. Avocations: reading, writing, concerts, theater, surfing the net. Office: San Joaquin Delta Coll 5151 Pacific Ave Stockton CA 95207-6304 Office Phone: 209-954-5252. E-mail: rfung@deltacollege.edu.

FUNG-CHEN-PEN, EMMA TALAUNA SOLAITA, librarian, director; b. Pago Pago, Am. Samoa, Sept. 4, 1951; d. Talauna and Ema (Tauoa) S.; m. Su'a oelu T. Fung-Chen-Pen, Nov 1, 1971; children: John Kevin, Juliet Ruth, Jacqueline Josie, Jennifer Lorna, Jonathan Emosi. AA Gen. Edn., Am. Samoa C. C., 1973, AS Libr. Studies, 1974; BA, Brigham Young U., Honolulu, 1977; MS in Librarianship, U. Hawaii, 1979. Libr. clerk Libr. Svcs., Pago Pago, 1971-74, libr. technician, 1974-76, libr. II, 1976-79, program dir., 1980—. Sec. Seventh Day Adventist Leone (Am. Samoa) Ch., 1990-94; dir. Seventh Day Adventist Leone Pathfinder, 1993—; pres. Parent-Tchr. Assn.-Sch., 2000-; active SDA Sch. Bd., 1991-98, mem. exec. bd. Samoa Mission, 1999-; mem. libr. bd. Feleti Barstow Pub., 2000-; mem. Samoa bd. dirs., coun. Read to Me, 1998-; mem. TV ministry bd. Leone SDA Ch., 1999-. Avocations: volleyball, reading, walking. Home: PO Box 1952 Pago Pago AS 96799-1952 Office: Am Samoa-Office of Lib Svcs PO Box 1329 Pago Pago AS 96799-1329

FUNK, CARLA JEAN, library association director; b. Wheeling, W.Va., Sept. 21, 1946; d. David H. and Jean (Duffy) Belt. BA in Psychology, Northwestern U., 1968; MLS, Ind. U., 1973; MBA, U. Chgo., 1985. Libr. adult svcs. Northbrook (Ill.) Pub. Libr., 1973-77; dir. Warren-Newport Pub. Libr. Dist., Gurnee, Ill., 1977-80; cons. Suburban Libr. Sys., Burr Ridge, Ill., 1980-83; dir. automation and tech. svcs., med. student svcs. AMA, Chgo., 1983-92; exec. dir. Med. Libr. Assn., Chgo., 1992—. Adj. faculty Dominican U., 1986—2000. Contbr. articles to profl. jours. Mem. Internat. Fedn. Libr. Assns. and Insts. (treas., mgmt. libr. assn. sec.), Am. Soc. Assn. Execs. (cert. assn. exec.), Assn. Forum of Chicagoland, Beta Phi Mu, Delta Zeta. Office: 65 E Wacker Pl Ste 1900 Chicago IL 60601-7246 Business E-Mail: funk@mlahq.org.

FUNK, CHARLOTTE MARIE, art educator, artist; b. Milw., Sept. 27, 1934; d. Ernest Louis and Stacy Cecile (Radomski) Mueller; m. Verne James Funk, June 8, 1956; children: Tracy B., Kory V., Christopher J. BS, U. Wis., 1972; MS, Ill. State U., 1975, MFA, 1976. Instr. art dept. Tex. Tech. U., 1978-97. Instr. Arrowmont Sch. Arts & Crafts Summer program, 1981, spring 1988. One-person shows include McMurray U., Alilene, Tex., 1993, Hueser Art Ctr., Bradley U., 1990; exhibited in group shows at UT-PB, Odessa, Tex., 1993, Nat. Juried Exhbn., Iowa City, 1992, 93, Arrowmont Collection Eastern Shore Art Ctr., Fairhope, Ala, 1993, Nat. Women's Art Exhbn., Eastern New Mex. U., 1992, Textile Arts Ctr., Chgo., 1990, Waco Art Ctr., 1988, Downey Mus., Calif., 1987, Milw. Art Mus., 1987, Tenn. Fine Arts Ctr., Nashville, 1985, West Tex. Mus., 1985, Funk and Funk, Old Jail Art Ctr., Albany, Tex., 1996. Mem. Am. Craft Coun. Home: 15422 Kid Run San Antonio TX 78232-4043

FUNK, EDITH KAY, minister, consultant, social worker; b. Durham, Feb. 19, 1944; d. Clinton M. and M. Josephine Frick; m. Francis Lee Funk, Sept. 3, 1967; 1 child, Aaron Lee. B in Music Edn., Kans. State Tchrs. Coll., Emporia, 1966, MusM, 1968; MDiv, St. Paul Sch. Theology, Kansas City, Mo., 1984; MSW, Kans. U., Lawrence, 1997. Ordained minister Kans. E. Ann. Conf. United Meth. Clergy, 1983; LCSW State of Kans., 1995. Music tchr. Osage City Pub. Schs., Kans., 1969—72, Shawnee Mission Pub. Schs., Kans., 1972—74; pastor United Meth. Ch., various locations, Kans., 1984—90; chaplain Topeka State Hosp., 1990—93; preaching assoc. pastor 1st United Meth. Ch., Topeka, 1993—96; psychotherapist Woodridge Counseling Svc., Topeka, 1996—2003; chaplain The Menninger Clinic, Houston, 2002—05. Named Outstanding Young Educator, Osage City Jaycees, 1972; recipient Kimbrill award Excellence in Biblical Studies, St. Paul, 1983; grantee Ministry grant, St. Paul Sch. of Theology, 1984. Mem.: Kans. E. Conf. United Meth. Ch. (Elder 1983—). Democrat. Avocations: weaving, needlecrafts, gardening, cooking, woodcarving. Office: Menninger Clinic PO Box 809045 Houston TX 77280

FUNK-WERBLO, DOROTHY, elementary school educator; b. Chgo., Aug. 8, 1917; d. Adam and Emma G. Funk. BS, Ind. State Tchrs. Coll.; MA, U. Minn.; EdD, U. Ga. Cert. tchr. Tex. Tchr. Hammond Pub. Schs., Hammond, Ind. Spkr. in field. Contbr. articles to profl. jours. Grantee, U.S. State Dept., NSF. Home: 16315 Channing Way Cypress TX 77429-5013

FUQUA, JUDY See FOUQUET, ANNE

FURBEE, AMY H., social studies educator; b. Atlanta, May 25, 1971; d. Otis Merle and Joan Caldwell Hicks; m. Daniel Lee Furbee, Aug. 24, 1996; children: Katelyn Michelle, Joshua Hunter. BS in Edn. and Social Scis., West Ga. U., Carrollton, 1996. 6th social studies, sci., reading Whitewater Mid. Sch., Fayetteville, Ga., 1996—97; 7th social studies, reading tchr. Rising Starr Mid. Sch., Fayetteville, 1997—. Liturgical reader St. Gabriel's Cath. Ch., Fayetteville, 1991—2006. Mem.: PAGE (assoc.), Alpha Xi Delta (life; social chairperson 1992—93). Republican. Roman Catholic. Avocations: reading, travel, poetry, dance. Office: Rising Starr Middle School 183 Panther Path Fayetteville GA 30215 Office Phone: 770-486-2721.

FURDELL, ELIZABETH LANE, history professor; d. Lionel Kenneth Lane and Helen M. Jonas; m. Theophilus Christopher Prousis, Aug. 18, 1990; m. William J. Furdell, Dec. 14, 1968 (div. May 5, 1983); children: James Lionel, Andrew Lane. BA, U. Wash., Seattle, 1966; MA, Kent State U., Ohio, 1968, PhD, 1973. Assoc. prof. history U. Gt. Falls, Mont., 1971—83; prof. history U. North Fla., Jacksonville, 1983—. Author: (history) Medicine and Publishing in Early Modern England, The Royal Doctors, James Welwood, Great Falls, Textual Healing (Disting. Prof., 2002); editor. Grantee, Wellcome Trust, 2004, So. Conf. Brit. Studies, 2005; scholar, U. North Fla., 2006. Mem.: Leadership Jacksonville. Office: Department of History University of North Florida Jacksonville FL 32224 Office Phone: 904-620-1862.

FUREY, JENNIFER B., lawyer; b. Newton, Mass., Oct. 29, 1971; BA summa cum laude, Providence Coll., 1993; JD cum laude, Boston Coll., 1996. Bar: Mass. 1997, DC 1998. Assoc. Howrey & Simon, Washington, Hogan & Hartson, Washington, Cooley Manion Jones LLP, Boston. Mem.: Women's Bar Assn., Mass. Bar Assn. (labor and employment sect.). Office: Cooley Manion Jones LLP 21 Custom House St Boston MA 02110 Office Phone: 617-737-3100. Office Fax: 617-737-3113. E-mail: jfurey@cmjlaw.com.*

FURLANO, JOANNE ELIZABETH, science educator; d. John Frank and Joan Ann Furlano; m. Richard Michael Fink, July 27, 1980 (div. Aug. 2, 1993); children: Brandon John Fink, Tiffany Lynne Fink. BA in Biology, D'Youville Coll., 1973; MS, Buffalo State Coll., 1980. Cert. tchr. NY, 1978. Lab tech. Erie County Med. Ctr., Buffalo, 1973; tchr. sci. St. James Elem. Sch., St. Mary's Elem. Sch., Lancaster, 1980—86, Sch. # 81, Buffalo, 1986—90, Clarence Mid. Sch., 1990—. Fundraiser organizer Leukemia Soc., 2000—04; fundraising Save the Manatees, Homassasa, Fla., 1996—2000; fundraiser organizer Children's Hosp., Buffalo, 1974—86; holiday cards children Roswell Hosp., 1998—2004; vol. fundraiser Hospice, 2005; fundraising SPCA, 1990—95; vol. Mash Bash/ARC, 2006. Mem.: Roots and Shoots (assoc.). Avocations: dance, travel, crafts, aerobics, swimming. Home: 148 Redwood Terrace Williamsville NY 14221 Office: Clarence Middle School 10150 Greiner Road Clarence NY 14031 Office Phone: 716-407-9209. Home Fax: 716-407-9229. Personal E-mail: joanne3285@aol.com.

FURLONG, EBBA VON, science educator; d. Bobby Luther and Ebba Ann Barber; children: Matthew Escue, Joshua Escue. BS, Angelo State U., San Angelo, 1975. Tchr. sci. Lincoln Mid. Sch., San Angelo, 1978—, chair sci. dept., 1980—2000. Sponsor Peer-Meditation Group, San Angelo, 1990, Nat. Jr. Honor Soc., San Angelo, 2004—06. Named Tchr. of Yr., Lincoln Mid. Sch., 1983—84, Most Outstanding Sci. Tchr., Gt. Western Drilling Co., 2006; recipient Tchr. of Yr., Lincoln Mid. Sch., 1998—99, Andrew Wallace

Excellence in Edn. award, Dist. XI S.E.C., 2003. Mem.: Assn. Tex. Profl. Educators. Avocation: water sports. Home: Box 5973 San Angelo TX 76902 Office Phone: 325-659-3500. Business E-Mail: efurlong@saisd.org.

FURMAN, ELISE HILARY, middle school educator; d. David M. and Barbara M. Furman. BS in Secondary Edn., Ind. U, Bloomington; MA in Theater, Lindenwood U., St. Charles, Mo. Cert. tchr. Mo., Pilates instr. 7th grade tchr. Pky. South Mid. Sch., Manchester, Mo., 2001—. Cert. pilates instr. Pilates Unlimited, Dallas, 2004—. Project chair, vol. Back to Sch. Store, Nat. Coun. Jewish Women, St. Louis, 2001—. Office Phone: 314-415-5241.

FURNALD, LISA ANNE, lawyer; BA in English, Boston Coll., 1991; JD cum laude, Suffolk U., 1995. Bar: Mass. 1995, US Dist. Ct. (Dist. Mass.) 1999, US Ct. Appeals (1st Cir.) 1999. Assoc. Robins, Kaplan, Miller & Ciresi LLP, Boston. Mem.: Boston Bar Assn., Mass. Bar Assn., ABA. Office: Robins Kaplan Miller & Ciresi LLP Floor 25 800 Boylston St Boston MA 02199 Office Phone: 617-267-2300. Office Fax: 617-267-8288. E-mail: lafurnald@rkmc.com.*

FURNARI, ROSEMARIE ANN, secondary school educator, real estate agent; b. New Brunswick, N.J., Oct. 19, 1944; d. Anthony and Rose Nancy Furnari; children: Toni Lynn Carter, Neal Robert Pellis. BA, Carlow U., Pitts., 1962—66; MS in Edn., Shenandoah Coll., Winchester, Va., 1986—89. Cert. Tchr. Tex. Bd. Edn., 1978. Math. & computer sci. tchr., dept. chmn. St. Agnes Acad., Houston, 1982—96; math. & computer sci. tchr., former dept. chmn. Pearland Ind. Sch. Dist., Tex., 1997—. Curriculum writing com. Pearland Ind. Sch. Dist., 1997—, campus adv. com., 2001—04, taks curriculum devel., 2002—05, tchr. mentor, 2002—04, engring. dept. com. mem., 2004—05. Sec. Home Owner's Assn., Houston, 1996—99. Mem.: Tex. Classroom Tchr.'s Assn. (corr.). Republican. Roman Catholic. Avocations: career development, travel, teacher mentoring, student advocate, creative projects. Home: 3527 Teakwood Ln Pearland TX 77584 Office: Pearland HS 3775 S Main St Pearland TX 77581 Office Phone: 281-997-7445. Home Fax: 713-436-0544. Personal E-mail: rof45@hotmail.com. Business E-Mail: furnarir@pearlandisd.org.

FURNAS, VALERIE YVONNE, secondary school educator; b. Santa Barbra, Calif., Feb. 24, 1975; d. Stephen Kirk and Ann Nora Furnas. BS in History, U. North Tex., Denton, 1999. Cert. secondary edn. Tex., 1999. Tchr. Lewisville Ind. Sch. Dist., Tenn., 2000—03, Fowermound, Tex., 2004—. WILL mentor Lewisville Ind. Sch. Dist., Tex.; team leader. Home: 165 Forestbrook Dr 118 Lewisville TX 75067 Office: Lewisville ISD Old Settlers Rd Flowermound TX 75067 Office Phone: 214-284-5818.

FURNER, BONITA BAKER, retired banker, consultant; b. DesMoines, Aug. 22, 1942; d. Ralph Nicholson Baker and Dorothy Dale Miller; m. James William Furner, Aug. 5, 1967. BA, Miami U., Oxford, Ohio, 1964; M, Johns Hopkins U., Washington and Bologna, Italy, 1966. Platform asst. Germany, Austria, Netherlands dist., internat. divsn. Citicorp, NYC, 1966—67; loan officer export credits, guarantees and ins. divsn. Export-Import Bank of the US, Washington, 1968—70, sr. loan officer fin. analysis divsn., 1970—71, spl. asst. to the vice chmn., 1988—89; asst. cashier internat. divsn. Ctrl. Nat. Bank, Chgo., 1971—73; v.p., asst. mgr. Crocker Mid-Am. Internat. Bank, Chgo., 1973—76; v.p., mgr. corp. internat. unit Crocker Bank Internat., NYC, 1976—81, v.p., mgr. Asia Pacific unit, 1981—84; sr. v.p. trade fin. divsn. Nat. Westminster Bank USA, NYC, 1984—87; sr. assoc. First Wash. Assocs., Arlington, Va., 1990—2005. Mem. Dist. Export Coun. of NY, 1978—86, Export Awareness Com., NYC, 1984—87; spkr. in field. Bd. dirs. Pvt. Export Funding Corp., NYC, 1985—86. Mem.: Slaps Women's Interclub Golf Orgn. (v.p.), Delta Delta Delta, PEO Sisterhood (chpt. pres. 1998—2003, chmn. fin. com. Fla. chpt.). Episcopalian. Avocations: volunteer work, golf, tennis, hiking.

FURNESS, JANET ELISABETH, social work educator; b. Newark, Nov. 25, 1948; d. Charles Yardley and Margaret Sutherland F.; children: Philip Andrew Spressart, Jessie Marie Spressart. BS, Phila. Biblical U., 1970; MSW, Rutgers U., 1972; postgrad., U. Rochester, 1997—. Lic. master social worker NY. Dir. child welfare Goodwill Home and Rescue Mission, Newark, 1972-82; dir. child placement svcs. Christian Homes for Children, Hackensack, N.J., 1982-86; dir. statewide vol. programs Mental Health Assn. N.J., Montclair, 1987-94, dir. children's mental health legis. advocacy, 1987-94; assoc. dean, asst. prof. Carver Sch. Ch. Social Work, So. Bapt. Theol. Sem., Louisville, 1994-95; acting dean Carver Sch. Ch. Social Work So. Bapt. Theol. Sem., Louisville, 1995-96; assoc. prof. social work Roberts Wesleyan Coll., Rochester, N.Y., 1996—, dir. MSW program, 2005—. Chair parents and profls. in partnership statewide conf. Mental Health Assn. N.J., New Brunswick, 1990; chair legal issues task force Children's Svc. Coordinating Coun., N.J. Dept. Human Svcs., Trenton, 1990-94; cons. to pub. schs. regarding edn. reform Ky. Edn. Reform Act, Louisville, 1994-95; founding mem., leadership team mem. Christians Supporting Cmty. Orgn., Denver, 1997. Contbr. chapters to books. Mem., adv. Rochester Area Children's Collaborative, 1996—. Mem. NASW (cert.), Acad. Cert. Social Workers, N.Am. Assn. Christians in Social Work (sec./treas. 1987-89, pres. 1995-97, co-chair ann. conv. 2002), Coun. on Social Work Edn. Evangelical Covenant. Avocations: soprano vocalist, organist, pianist. Office: Roberts Wesleyan Coll 2301 Westside Dr Rochester NY 14624-1933 Business E-Mail: furnessj@roberts.edu.

FURNIVAL, PATRICIA ANNE, social worker; b. Poughkeepsie, N.Y., Feb. 3, 1938; d. Edwin A. and Esther L. Smith; BA, Maryville (Tenn.) Coll., 1960; MA, U. Chgo., 1970; m. George E. Furnival, Feb. 15, 1967. Cert. addiction profl.; lic. marriage and family therapist. Sr. caseworker Dutchess County Dept. Social Services, Poughkeepsie, 1961-67; rural resources dir. OEO, Freeport, Ill., 1967-68; program coordinator H. Douglas Singer Zone Ctr., Rockford, Ill., 1968-72; family therapist Bur. Alcohol Rehab., Avon Park, Fla., 1973-74; dir. Tri-County Alcoholism Rehab. Services, Inc., Avon Park, 1974-80; exec. dir. Tri-County Alcoholism Rehab. Services, Inc., Winter Haven, Fla., 1980—; exec. dir. adult and adolescent programs Tri-County Addictions Rehab. Services, 1986—; field instr. Fla. State U. Sch. Social Work, 1977—; instr. South Fla. Jr. Coll., 1979; pvt. practice psychotherapy, 1973—; bd. dirs. Pride of Polk County and Turnaround, Inc. drug rehab. ctr.; mem. alcohol and drug abuse task force Polk County Sch. Bd.; cons. in field. Mem. Nat. Assn. Social Workers, Acad. Cert. Social Workers, Fla. Alcohol and Drug Abuse Assn. (Bill Snyder meml. award 1986, bd. dirs.), Alcohol and Drug Problems Assn. N.Am., AAUW. Democrat. Mem. United Ch. Christ. Home (Summer): PO Box 245 Tenants Harbor ME 04860-0245 Office: PO Box 9306 Winter Haven FL 33883-9306 Home (Winter): 2233 Clifton St Sebring FL 33875

FURROW, VALERIE, mathematics educator, coach; d. David Haacke and Glenna Shank; m. Aaron Furrow, June 11, 2005. B in Elem. Edn. magna cum laude, Western Illinios U., Macomb, 2003. Math tchr. ROWVA Jr. High Dist. 208, Oneida, Ill., 2004—. Asst. coach boys track and field ROWVA H.S. Dist. 208, Oneida, 2003—. Office: ROWVA Jr HS Dist 208 PO Box 69 Oneida IL 61467

FURSE, ELIZABETH, retired congressman, small business owner; b. Nairobi, Kenya, 1936; came to U.S., 1958, naturalized, 1972; children: Amanda Briggs, John Briggs; m. John Platt. BA, Evergreen State Coll., 1974; postgrad., U. Wash., Northwestern U., Lewis and Clark Coll. Dir. Western Wash. Indian program Am. Friends Svc. Com, 1975-77; coord. Restoration program for Native Am. Tribes Oreg. Legal Svc., 1980-86; co-owner Helvetia Vineyards, Hillsboro, Oreg.; mem. 103rd-105th Congresses from 1st Oreg. dist., 1993-98, mem. commerce com. Exec. dir. Inst. for Tribal Govt., Portland State U. Co-founder Oreg. Peace Inst., 1985. also: Inst Tribal Govt PO Box 751 Portland OR 97207 Home: 7414 SW Miles Pl Portland OR 97219-3028

FURTADO, BEVERLY ANN, financial aid administrator; b. Bellville, Ill., Feb. 2, 1951; d. George C. and Bertha D. Carroll; m. James R. Furtado, July 18, 1970; children: Jeffrey, Cynthia. AS in Criminal Justice, Fisher Coll., Boston, 1994; BA in Liberal Studies, Western New Eng. Coll., 1998. Fin. aid counselor Fisher Coll., Boston, 1999; career cons. Job Tng. and Edn. Corp., Hyannis, Mass., 1998—2000; fin. aid assoc. Labouré Coll., Boston, 2000—01; fin. aid specialist Quincy Coll., Mass., 2001—; assoc. fin. aid dir. Quincy, Mass. Avocations: reading, quilting, sewing. Office: Quincy Coll 34 Coddington St Quincy MA 02169

FURTADO, NELLY KIM, vocalist; b. Victoria, BC, Can., Dec. 2, 1978; d. Maria Manuela and Antonio Jose Furtado; 1 child, Nevis. Signed to Dreamworks Records, 1999—2005, Geffen Records, 2005—. Singer: (albums) Whoa Nelly!, 2000, Folklore, 2003, Loose, 2006, (songs) I'm Like a Bird, 2000 (Juno award for Best Single, 2001, Grammy award for Best Female Pop Performance, 2002), Turn Off the Light, 2000, Promiscuous, 2006 (Choice Song of the Summer and Choice V Cast Music Artist, Teen Choice Awards, 2006); background vocals: albums Phrenology (The Roots), 2002, vocals: albums Bunkka (Oakenfold), 2002. Recipient 4 Juno awards: Best Single, Best New Solo Artist, Best Prodr., Best Songwriter, 2001. Office: c/o Chris Smith Mgmt Inc 5th Fl 21 Camden St Toronto ON M5V 1V2 Canada Office Phone: 416-362-7771. Office Fax: 416-362-6648. E-mail: info@ChrisSmithManagement.com.*

FURTADO-LAVOIE, JULIA, sales executive; b. Fall River, Mass., July 22, 1964; d. Manuel Lawrence and Mary Gloria (Mello) Furtado; m. Michael Lavoie. BA cum laude, U. Mass., 1987; postgrad., Emerson Coll., Boston, 1987—89. Dist. sales mgr. Paycex, Inc., Mansfield, Mass., 1996—. Recipient Freedom Torch award ABC6 and Providence Jour., 1996. Mem. C. of C. (amb.). Office: Paychex Inc 200 foxborough Blvd Unit 400 Foxboro MA 02035 Office Phone: 800-472-9019 2027. Personal E-mail: juliafurtado@msn.com.

FURTH, KAREN J., artist; BA in Am. History, U. Pa., 1983; MA in Photography, NYU, 1988. Photographer Smithsonian Instn., 1989—94; freelance photographer, 1994—; tchr., cons. Ctr. Urban Cmty. Svcs. The Times Sq., 1994—2002; tchr. Internat. Ctr. Photography at The Point, NYC, 1998—2005; adj. tchr. photography Eugene Lang Coll. New Sch. Social Rsch., 1999—2005. Artist-in-residence Creative Ctr. NYC Hosp., 2003—06; presenter in field. One-woman shows include 494 Gallery, NYC, 1991—92, 1994, Pulse Art Gallery, 1997, exhibited in group shows at 494 Gallery, 1991—92, Synchronicity Space, N.Y.C., 1995, Sullivan County Mus., 1995, Pulse Art Gallery, 1996, Golin/Harris, 1998, 2002, at A.I.R., 2004, others, curatorial projects include, The Times Sq. Photography Project, Met. Transp. Authority, 1999, Represented in permanent collections J.P. Morgan, Mt. Sinai Hosp., others; contbr. articles to profl. jours. Recipient Gilbert Graphic Paper award, 1993; fellow Open Soc. Inst. Individual Project fellow, Soros Found., 1997; Faculty scholar, U. Pa., 1979—83, Internat. Outreach grante, 1993—94. Personal E-mail: karen@karenfurth.com.

FURTH, YVONNE, advertising executive; BS in Mktg., Georgetown U., postgrad., DePaul U. Asst. account exec. Draft Worldwide, 1981—88, gen. mgr., 1988—92, pres. of Chicago office, 1992—96, pres. & COO US operations, 1996—2001, pres., COO Chgo., 2002—. Mem.: Chgo. Assn. Direct Mktg., Direct Mktg. Assn. Office: Draft Chicago 633 N St Clair St Chicago IL 60611

FURY, SARA JO, social studies educator, coach; d. Michael Rohn and Karen Marie Fury. BA, Hamline U., St. Paul, 2000. Tchr. Century H.S., Rochester, Minn., 2001—. Girl's basketball coach Century H.S., Rochester, Minn., 2003—. Dfl. Roman Catholic. Avocations: running, reading, golf, scrapbooks. Office Phone: 507-287-7997.

FUSCO, AURILLA MARIE, director; d. Delmar A. and Catherine F. (Bryan) Thibodeau; m. John A. Fusco (div.); 1 child, Craig L. Jr. BS in Paralegal/Govt. Bus., U. Md., 1986; MPA, Troy State U., 1990; postgrad., Concord Sch. Law. Staff asst. to Sen. George J. Mitchell U.S. Senate, Washington, 1981—85, staff asst. to Sen. Albert Gore, Jr. Nashville, 1985—86, staff asst, office mgr. subcom. on children, families, drugs and alcoholism, 1987; program analyst, adminstrv. officer Dept. of Army, Germany, 1987—91; dir. child care River Valley Child Devel., Huntington, W.Va., 1992—97; exec. dir. Child Advocates of Blair County, Altoona, Pa., 1998—2001; regional mr. capital gifts Bucknell U., Lewisburg, Pa., 2001—04; dir. devel. Main Campus Librs. Georgetown U., Washington, 2004—. Presenter Nat. Assn. for Edn. of Young Children; cons. W.Va. Welfare Reform Coalition, 1996—98; exec. dir. nonprofit R&D Gamday, LLC, Altoona, Pa., 2000—. Co-chair Children's Issues Advocates, W.Va., 1997—98; pres. Jr. League, Huntington, 1997—98; sustainer adviser Jr. League Williamsport, 2003—04; mem. devel. com. Heurich House Found.; mem. parents com. Bishop Ireton H.S. Hockey Team. Mem.: Sunrise Rotary. Office: Lavinger Libr Georgetown U 37th and O St NW Washington DC 20057-1174

FUSELIER, MARILYN MONIE, retired counselor; b. New Orleans, June 16, 1931; d. Maurice Roch and Margaret (Partlan) Monie; m. Edward F. Fuselier, Dec. 26, 1955; children: Rosemary, Edward, Stephen, Nancy, Linda. BA in Psychology, U. New Orleans, 1973, MEd in Counselor Edn., 1978, PhD in Counselor Edn., 1994. Tchr. Mt. Carmel High Sch., New Orleans, 1974-76, New Sarpy Middle Sch., La., 1976-77, Jefferson Parish Schs., Metairie, La., 1977-88, counselor, 1998—2003; ret., 2003. Mem.: ACA, La. Counseling Assn., Chi Sigma Iota, Delta Kappa Gamma. Roman Catholic.

FUSILLO, ALICE ELBERT, retired sociologist, sculptor; b. Balt., Dec. 13, 1922; d. Francis Wilson and Alice Margaret (Jones) Zeigler; m. Matthew Henry Fusillo, Sept. 13, 1947 (dec. Aug. 3, 1980); children: Lawrence Joseph, Lisa Ann, Jessica Jean, Susan Frances. BS, U. Md., 1948, MA, 1966. Pub. health analyst NIH, Bethesda, Md., 1968—74; statistician Bur. Census, SESA, Suitland, Md., 1974; consumer sci. specialist FDA, Washington, 1974—79; statistician Dept. Health and Human Svcs., Washington, 1979—88; sculptor Washington, 1988—. Contbr. articles to profl. jours.; exhibitions include Carego Foxley Leach Gallery, Washington, D.C., 1991, Whitehall Gallery, Corcoran, Washington, 1990, Washington Square Sculpture Show, 2003. Recipient Mary Lay Sculpture award, Corcoran Sch. Art, 1986, Visual Art award, Capitol Hill Art League, 2002. Mem.: AAUW, Goodwill Industries, Washington Sculptors Soc., Internat. Sculpture Ctr., The Art League (Best in Show 1988), Sierra Club. Achievements include patents for Dying Swan sculpture. Avocations: landscape and portrait painting, ballroom dancing. Home: Apt N604 560 N St SW Washington DC 20024-4617

FUSILLO, NANCY MARIE, medical/surgical, oncological, pediatric, community health and family nurse practitioner; b. Washington, Sept. 15, 1948; d. Leonard and Yolanda Rita (Tolatta) F. AA, Montgomery Jr. Coll., Takoma Park, Md., 1969; BA, U. Md., 1971; ADN, Daytona Beach C.C., 1986; BSN, U. South Fla., 1988; MS, Nat. Louis U., Tampa, Fla., 1992; MSN in Family Nurse Practitioner Program, U. Tampa, 2002. RN; cert. chemotherapy nurse 1991, med.-surg. nurse 1993, intravenous nurse 1993, oncology nurse, 1993,; diabetic educator, 1994, family nurse practitioner, 2003. Med.-surg. staff nurse Palms of Pasadena Hosp., St. Petersburg, Fla., 1986-87; home health nurse Paragon Nursing Fla., Inc., Clearwater, 1987-94; staff and home health nurse Upjohn Olsten Gentiva Intel Staff Healthcare Svcs., Clearwater, Fla., 1987—; intravenous nurse clinician New Eng. Critical Care, Tampa, 1989-91; oncology and med.-surg. nurse Suncoast Hosp., Largo, Fla., 1991-92; neonatal and pediat. clinician Pediat. Health Choice, Tampa, 1993-97; nurse clin. pediat., neonatal Pediat. Svcs. Am., St. Petersburg, Fla., 1994-96; nurse Hospice of Fla. Suncoast, 1990—2002; chemotherapy infusion nurse Fla. Cmty. Cancer Ctrs. Am., 2000—04; staff nurse med. oncology unit St. Anthony's Hosp., 2001—02. Pub. educator nurse, Triple Touch Health Instr. Am. Cancer Soc., 1987—, breast and cervical cancer sub-com., chair Tell-A-Friend mammogram project, 2001—02; item reviewer Nat. Coun. State Bds. Nursing, 1999; cmty. educator ARNP St. Petersburg Gen. Hosp., Fla., 2003—05. Manuscript reviewer: Jour. Hospice and Palliative Nursing, 2002, mem. editl. rev. bd.: Jour. Infusion Nursing; author: numerous poems, essays. Vol. nurse cmty. outreach program St. Anthony's Hosp., 1990—, distributor newspaper Voice of the Diabetic, Sojourn Bears for Cancer Patients, 2000—, Eucharistic min., Angels Passing By program Bon Secours Rehab. Ctr., St. Petersburg, 2005-. Recipient Masters scholar, Oncology Nursing Soc. Found., 2002. Mem.: Nat. Conf. Gerontol. Nurse Practitioners, Am. Acad. Nurse Practitioners, Am. Cancer Soc., Infusion Nurses Soc., Oncology Nurses Soc., Sigma Theta Tau.

FUTERKO, SUZANNE, art educator; d. John Peter and Nancy Lou F. BA, SUNY, Potsdam, 1989; MS in Art Edn., Syracuse U., 1991. Mus. tchr. Historic Cherry Hill, Albany, 1990; substitute tchr. Ray Middle Sch., Baldwinsville, N.Y., 1991; art tchr. Sharon Springs (N.Y.) Cen. Sch., 1992—. Mem. N.Y. State Art Tchrs. Assn., Nat. Art Edn. Assn. Avocations: skiing, ice skating, stamp collecting/philately. Office: Sharon Springs Ctrl Sch PO Box 218 Sharon Springs NY 13459-0218

FUTTER, ELLEN VICTORIA, museum administrator; b. NYC, Sept. 21, 1949; d. Victor and Joan Babette (Feinberg) F.; m. John A. Shutkin; children: Anne Victoria, Elizabeth Jane. Student, U. Wis., 1967-69; AB magna cum laude, Barnard Coll., 1971; JD, Columbia U., 1974, LLD (hon.), 1984, Hamilton Coll., 1985, NY Law Sch.; DHL (hon.), Amherst Coll., Hofstra U., 1994, CCNY, 1996, LI City Coll., 1995; DHL (hon.), Yale U., 2000; DL, Columbia U.; degree (hon.), Stadmore Coll., 2003, Williams Coll., 2004, Skidmore Coll., 2005. Bar: NY 1975. Assoc. Milbank, Tweed, Hadley & McCloy, NYC, 1974-80; acting pres. Barnard Coll., NYC, 1980-81, pres., 1981-93, Am. Mus. Natural History, NYC, 1993—. Bd. dirs. Am. Internat. Group, JP Morgan Chase, Consol. Edison of N.Y., Viacom Inc., Bristol-Myers Squibb Co.; overseer Meml. Sloan Kettering Cancer Ctr., NYC; trustee Am. Mus. Natural History Recipient L. Sachar award Brandeis U., Elizabeth Cutter Morrow, Distinction medal Barnard Coll., Excellence medal Columbia U., Gold medal award Nat. Inst. Social Scis., Legacy Conservation award Theodore Roosevelt Sanctuary, Visionary award New Vision in Pub. Sch., Alexander Hamilton award Manhattan Inst. Policy Rsch., 2002. Fellow Am. Acad. Arts and Scis.; mem. ABA, N.Y. State Bar Assn., Assn. Bar City N.Y., Nat. Inst. Social Scis., Coun. Fgn. Rels., Cosmopolitan Club, Century Club, Phi Beta Kappa. Office: Am Mus Natural History Central Park West at 79th New York NY 10024*

FYFE, DORIS MAE, elementary school educator; b. Shelby, Nebr., Sept. 5, 1930; d. Harold William Fyfe and Mae Emma Schmid. Assoc. in Elem. Edn., Scottsbluff Jr. Coll., Nebr., 1957; BS in Elem. Edn., Peru State Tchrs. Coll., Nebr., 1963; M in Urban Edn., U. Nebr., Omaha, 1980. Cert. K-12 tchr. Nebr. Tchr. K-8, Polk County Schs., Shelby, 1947—50, Banner County Schs., Harrisburg, Nebr., 1950—53; tchr. 2d grade Albin Consol. Schs., Albin, Wyo., 1953—57; prin., tchr. K-2, Union Pub. Schs., Nebr., 1957—61; tchr. 2d grade Nebraska City Pub. Schs., Nebr., 1961—63; intermediate tchr. Omaha Pub. Schs., 1963—90, substitute tchr., 1990—; adj. faculty Grace U., Omaha, 1984—. 4-H leader Agr. Coll. Ext. Svc. Polk County, 1947—50; vol. tutor Uta Halee Girls' Village, Omaha, 1995—; active Harvey Oaks Bapt. Ch., 1962—; dir. Midway Bible Camp, Thompson, Canada, 1970—90. Mem.: Omaha Area Ret. Tchrs. Assn., Olympian Club. Republican. Avocations: stamp collecting/philately, doll collecting, pencil collecting. Home: 6222 Ponderosa Dr Omaha NE 68137-4231

GAAR, MARILYN AUDREY WIEGRAFFE, political scientist, educator, property manager; b. St. Louis, Sept. 22, 1946; d. Arthur and Marjorie Estelle (Miller) W.; m. Norman E. Gaar, Apr. 12, 1986. AB, Ind. U., 1968, MA, 1970, MS, 1973. Mem. faculty Stephens Coll., Columbia, Mo., 1971—73, Johnson County CC, Overland Park, Kans., 1973—; vis. scholar Moscow (Russia) Symphony Orch., 2003. Interviewer fellowship candidates Fulbright Hayes Tchr. Exch., Kansas City, Mo., 1982—92; mem. state selection com. Congress Bundestag Youth Exch. Program, Kans., 1985; pres. faculty del. Kans. Assn. CCs, 1984—85; gov.'s appointee, admissions interviewer, mem. selection panel Sch. Medicine U. Kans., 1991—95, mem. admissions criteria and admissions process rev. com., 1992. Contbg. editor: (instr.'s manual) Am. Democracy (Thomas Patterson). Pres. LWV Johnson County, 1987—89, prodr. candidates forum, mem. governing bd., 1993—95; mem. Johnson County Elder Net Coalition, 1988; mem. governing bd. Johnson County Mental Health Ctr., 1981—86, chmn., 1985—86; vol., translator Russian Refugee Resettlement Program of Jewish Family and Children Svcs., Kansas City, 1979—81; treas. Heart of Am., Japan Am. Soc., 1979; hon. dir. Rockhurst Coll., Kansas City; sec. Ctrl. Slavic Conf., 2000—05; alt. mem. Rep. State Com., Kans., 1984—86; chmn. Rep. City Com., Shawnee, Kans., 1982—86; program chmn. Kans. Fedn. Rep. Women, 1984—87; bd. dirs. Substance Abuse Ctr., Johnson County, 1983—85, Huntington Farms Homes Assn., Leawood, Kans., 1984—87, Internat. Rels. Coun., Kansas City, 2001—04. Grantee, Europaische Akademie, West Berlin, 1984, 1992, 1997; Fulbright Hayes grantee, Japan, 1975, The Netherlands, 1982, NEH fellow, 1990, Johnson County C.C. scholar in residence, 1998, 1999, 2001, 2003, Johnson County C.C. sr. scholar awardee, 2003—05. Mem.: Ctrl. Assn. Russian Tchrs. Am. (bd. dirs. 2003—04), Assn. Russian and Am. Historians (sec. 1998—99), Internat. Rels. Coun. Kansas City (exec. com. 2001—03, governing bd. 2001—04), Kans. Polit. Sci. Assn., C.C. Humanities Assn., Russian and Am. Internat. Studies Assn. (sec. 1999—, 2000—), Nelson-Atkins Mus. Arts Soc. Fellows, People to People, Phi Beta Kappa, Dobro Slovo Nat. Slavic Honor Soc., Phi Sigma Alpha. Avocations: piano, gardening. Office: Johnson County C C 12345 College Blvd Shawnee Mission KS 66210-1283

GAARDER, MARIE, speech pathologist; b. New Britain, Conn., July 19, 1935; d. Nicholas and Clara (Sangeloty) Sarris; m. Kenneth R. Gaarder, Dec. 8, 1962; children: Jason, Galen. BS, U. Ill., 1957; postgrad., U. Md., 1962-63; postgrad. Our Lady of Lake U., Grad. Sch. Social Work, San Antonio, 1976-77. Founder speech therapy program Flossmoor (Ill.) Sch. Dist. 161, 1957-59; speech pathologist Prince George's County (Md.) Bd. Edn., 1959-65, Sidwell Friend's Sch., Washington, 1966-67, St. Maurice Sch. for Learning Disabilities, Potomac, Md., 1968-69; pvt. practice speech therapy Chevy Chase, Md., 1967—; adminstrv. officer Gaarder Med. Corp., Chevy Chase, 1977—. Pres., Prince George's chpt. Coun. for Exceptional Children, 1963-64; mem. Florence Crittenton Circle, 1966-69, Hospitality and Info. Svc. for Diplomats, 1967—; chmn. activities com. Jr. Teens, 1979-80; chmn. publicity YWCA Internat. Fair, 1977-79, chmn. entertainment, 1983, chmn., 1987-88; mem. internat. com. Woman's Nat. Dem. Club; co-chmn. Adv. Com. for Quality Integrated Edn. in Montgomery County, 1977-78; bd. dirs. D.C. br. YWCA, 1981-82, Washington Ctr.; chmn. oral history 65th Birthday Town of Chevy Chase; chmn. Mid-Atlantic regional adv. bd. Am. Found. for the Blind, 1984-85; founding mem. exec. bd. internat. adv. com. Very Spl. Arts, 1990-93; victim asst., ct. accompaniment, Divsn. Health & Human Svcs., Md., 2004-. Recipient Appreciation cert. Opera Guild San Antonio, 1977, Outstanding and Dedicated Svc. to 1987 Internat. Fair Plaque YWCA of the Nat. Capital Area, Nat. Svc. Registry award, 1990, Disting. Svc. in Profession citation, Appreciation cert. Internat. Tng. in Communication, 1994. Mem. Am. Speech, Lang. and Hearing Assn. (advanced cert.), Md. Speech, Lang. and Hearing Assn., Meridian Internat. Ctr., Salvation Army Women's Aux., World Affairs Coun. Washington, Soc. Internat. Devel., Asia Soc., Soc. Preservation Greek Heritage, Capitol Spkrs. Club (sec. chpt. III 1983-84), Zeta Phi Eta. Greek Orthodox. Home and Office: 4221 Oakridge Ln Bethesda MD 20815-6058 Personal E-mail: mariespeech@hotmail.com.

GABALDON, DIANA, writer; b. Williams, Ariz., Jan. 11, 1950; d. Jacqueline (Sykes) Gabaldon; m. Doug Watkins; children: Laura Juliet, Samuel Gordon, Jennifer Rose. BS in Zoology, Northern Ariz. Univ., 1973, PhD in Ecology, 1978; MS in Marine Biology, Univ. Calif., San Diego, 1975. Lab tech. Northern Ariz. Univ., 1972—73; post-doctoral appt. Univ. Pa., 1978—79; freelance writer UCLA, 1979—80; also writer Walt Disney Prodns., 1979—80; field ecologist Ariz. State Univ., 1980—92. Author:

Outlander, 1991 (Best First Novel award B. Dalton bookstores 1991, Best Book Yr. award Romance Writer's Am. 1991), Cross Stitch, 1992, Dragonfly in Amber, 1992, Voyager, 1994, Drums of Autumn, 1997, Fathers and Daughters: A Celebration in Memoirs, Stories, and Photographs, 1999, The Outlandish Companion, 1999, The Fiery Cross, 2001, Lord John and the Private Matter, 2003, A Breath of Snow and Ashes, 2005 (Quills award sci. fiction/fantasy/horror The Quills Literacy Found., 2006); software reviewer Byte mag.; contbr. articles to profl. jours.; author comic strips Disney. Mailing: #102-321 10810 N Tatum Blvd Phoenix AZ 85028 Business E-Mail: dgabaldon@aol.com.*

GABARRA, CARIN LESLIE, professional soccer player, professional soccer coach; b. East Orange, N.J., Jan. 9, 1965; m. Jim Gabarra. Degree in bus. mgmt., U. Calif., Santa Barbara, 1987. Mem. U.S. Nat. Women's Soccer Team, 1987—96; head coach, women's soccer Westmont Coll., 1987—88; assist. coach, women's Soccer Harvard U., Boston, 1988—93; head coach, women's soccer Navy, 1993—. Mem. U.S. Olympic World Festival team, 1986—89; mem. women's soccer U.S. Naval Acad., 1993. Named U.S. Soccer's Female Athlete of Yr., 1987, 1992; named to, U. Calif.-Santa Barbara Athletic Hall of Fame; recipient Golden Ball, FIFA Women's World Championship, China, 1991, gold medal, Atlanta Summer Olympic Games, 1996. Achievements include ranked as 3d-leading goal scorer in U.S. women's history; mem. CONCACAF Championship team, 1993, 94. Office: c/o US Soccer Fedn 1801 S Prairie Ave # 1811 Chicago IL 60616-1319

GABBARD, SUSAN J., art association administrator, educator; b. Ft. Worth, Tex., Oct. 7, 1949; d. Burton Edward Ellis and Mary Jane Denman; m. Jay McCray Gabbard, June 29, 1974. BA in Art Edn., U. North Tex., 1970, M in Art Edn., 1994. Cert. tchr. early adolescent and young adult art Nat. Bd. Profl. Tchg. Stds. Art tchr. San Antonio Ind. Sch. Dist., 1971—74, New World Sch., Oklahoma City, 1976—80; dir. Cmty. After Sch. Program, Norman, Okla., 1980—82; art tchr. George Lynn Cross Acad., Norman, 1982—87, Norman Pub. Schools, 1987—89, Carrollton (Tex.) Farmers Br. Ind. Sch. Dist., 1989—94, Oklahoma City Pub. Schs., 1994—2003, dir. of fine arts, 2004—; master tchr. in residence U. Ctrl. Okla., Edmond, 2003—04. Named Outstanding Visual Art Tchr., Walt Disney Am. Tchr. Awards, 1996, Disting. Alumna, U. North Tex., 2003; recipient Claire Flanagan Meml. Youth Art Month award, Art and Craft Materials Inst., 1987, Gov.'s Arts award, Okla. Art Coun., 2000, Okla. medal of excellence in tchr., Okla. Found. of Excellence, 2003. Mem.: Okla. Alliance for Arts Edn. (sec. 2001—04), Okla. Art Edn. Assn. (Okla. Art Educator of the Yr. 1995), Arts Edn. Partnership, Nat. Art Edn. Assn. (pres. 2005—, Marion Quin Dix award 2003). Office: Oklahoma City Pub Schs 900 N Klein Oklahoma City OK 73106 Office Phone: 405-587-0220. E-mail: sjgabbard@okcps.org.

GABBIN, JOANNE VEAL, education educator; b. Balt., Feb. 2, 1946; d. Joseph and Jessie Katie Veal; m. Alexander L. Gabbin, July 2, 1967; 1 child, Jessea Nayo. BA, Morgan State U., Balt., 1967; MA, U. Chgo., 1970, PhD, 1980. Asst. prof. Chgo. State U., 1972—74; assoc. prof. Lincoln U., 1977—85, James Madison U., Harrisonburg, Va., 1985—88, prof., dir., 1988—2006, dir., furrous flower, 2005—. Author: (books) Sterling A. Brown, 1985 (CLA award, 1986), I Bet She Called Me Sugar Plum, 2004, The Furious Flowering of African American Poetry. Office: James Madison Univ MSC 3802 Harrisonburg VA 22807

GABEL, CONNIE, chemist, educator; b. Green Bank, W.Va. d. William Ashby and Marie Lowry; m. Richard Gabel; children: Greg, Keith, Debbie. BS in Chemistry magna cum laude, James Madison U.; MA in Ednl. Adminstrn. summa cum laude, U. Colo., 1984, PhD in Ednl. Leadership and Innovation, 2001. Tchg. asst. U. Wis., Madison, 1969-70, specialist endocrinology, 1970-71; tchr. Dept. Def. Schs., Tokyo, 1972-74, Poudre R-1 Schs., Ft. Collins, Colo., 1975-78, Boulder (Colo.) Valley Schs., 1985-87, 96-98, intern asst. prin., 1984-85; intern supt. Jefferson County Schs., Golden, Colo., 1992; tchr. Mapleton Pub. Schs., Thornton, Colo., 1992-95; internat. studies Egyptian program Regis U., Denver, 1994; instr. chemistry Colo. Sch. Mines, 1995-98; dean students Horizon HS, Thornton, Colo., 1995-96; project 2061 coord. dept. chemistry/edn. U. Colo., Denver, 1998-2000; instr. St. Mary's Acad., Englewood, Colo., 2000—03, Met. State Coll. Tchr. Edn. and Chemistry, Denver, 2004—. Cons. sch. fin. Colo. Dept. Edn., Denver, 1984; rschr. AMC Cancer Rsch. Ctr., Denver, 1993, Colo. U. Med. Ctr., Denver, 1994; display tech. Boulder-Chemistry Rsch., 1995. Charter mem., pres. Friends Louisville (Colo.) Libr., 1985—; charter mem. Nat. Women's History Mus.; charter mem., pres., v.p. Coal Creek Rep. Women, Louisville, 1987—; sec., mem. Boulder County Reps., 1988—98, precinct chair; mem. Nat. Rep. Women, Washington, 1987—; sec. Dist. 17 Colo. Senate, Dist. 13 Colo. Ho., 1993—2002; mem. Colo. Fedn. Rep. Women, 1987—, Colo. Rep. Ctrl. Com. Mem.: AAUW, AAAS, ASCD, NY Acad. Sci., Math., Engring. and Sci. Achievement (dir., advisor 1992—97, mem. state level adv. bd. 1992—96), Colo. Chemistry Tchrs. Assn., Colo.-Wyo. Acad. Sci., Colo. Assn. Sci. Tchrs., Nat. Soc. Study Edn., Nat. Assn. Rsch. Sci. Tchg., Am. Chem. Soc., Nat. Assn. Sci. Tchrs., Am. Ednl. Rsch. Assn., Phi Delta Kappa. Avocations: reading, hiking, gardening. Business E-Mail: cgabel@mscd.edu.

GABEL, KATHERINE, retired academic administrator; b. Rochester, NY, Apr. 9, 1938; d. M. Wren and Esther (Conger) G.; m. Seth Devore Strickland, June 24, 1961 (div. 1965). AB, Smith Coll., Northampton, Mass., 1959; MSW, Simmons Coll., 1961; PhD, Syracuse U., 1967; JD, Union U., 1970; bus. program, Stanford U., 1984. Psychol. social worker Cen. Island Mental Health Ctr., Uniondale, NY, 1961-62; psychol. social worker, supt. Ga. State Tng. Sch. for Girls, Atlanta, 1962-64; cons. N.Y. State Crime Control Coun., Albany, 1968-70; faculty Ariz. State U., Tempe, 1972-76; supt. Ariz. Dept. of Corrections, Phoenix, 1970-76; dean, prof. Smith Coll., 1976-85; pres. Pacific Oaks Coll. and Children's Sch., Pasadena, Calif., 1985-98; western region v.p. Casey Family Program, Pasadena, 1998—2001; pvt. practice, 2001—. Advisor, del. UN, Geneva, 1977; mem. So. Calif. Youth Authority, 1986-91; west region dir. Lambda LegalDef. Fund, LA, 2003— Editor: Master Teacher and Supervisor in Clinical Social Work, 1982; author report Legal Issues of Female Inmates, 1981, model for rsch. Diversion program Female Inmates, 1984, Children of Incarcerated Parents, 1995. Vice chair United Way, Northampton, 1982-83; chair Mayor's Task Force, Northampton, 1981. Mem. Nat. Assn. Social Work, Acad. Cert. Social Workers, Nat. Assn. Edn. Young Children, Western Assn. Schs. and Colls., Pasadena C. of C., Athenaeum, Pasadena Rotary Club. Democrat. Presbyterian. Avocation: collecting south west Indian art, aviary. Personal E-mail: gabelk@prodigy.net.

GABEL, TERA CHRISTINE, secondary school educator; b. Guymon, Okla., Apr. 20, 1972; d. Terry Mack and Becky Moore; m. Sean Daniel Gabel, Nov. 19, 1994; children: Kambri Bret, Kyla Marie. BS in Secondary Edn., Okla. State U., Stillwater, 1996. Cert. secondary edn. Okla., 1996. Tchr. Guymon Pub. Schs., 1996—. Dance team coach Guymon Pub. Schs., 1997—, asst. volleyball coach, 2001—. Mem.: Zeta Psi chpt. Beta Sigma Phi (pres., v.p., rec. sec. 1999—2005, Pledge of Yr. 1999). Republican. Methodist. Avocations: reading, dance. Home: 6031 Sunset Dr Guymon OK 73942 Office: Guymon Public Schools 801 N Beaver Guymon OK 73942 Office Phone: 580-338-4350. Home Fax: 580-338-0994; Office Fax: 580-338-0994. Business E-Mail: tgabel@guymon.k12.ok.us.

GABELER, JO, artist; b. Baton Rouge, Feb. 14, 1931; d. Gustav Adolph Jr. and Ruth Hart Stein; m. Charles Pierce Gabeler Jr., Feb. 17, 1951 (div. Feb. 1973); children: Ann Speed, Charles Pierce III, T. Dolph, Caroline Hart. BA, Stephens Coll., 1950; studied with Edward Betts, Judi Betts, Al Brouillete, Jeanne Dobie, Ray Ellis, Dong Kingman, Fred Messersmith, Tony Van Hasselt, Millard Wells, Charles Reid. Illustrator: (with others) The Golf Courses at the Landings on Skidaway Island, 1993, The Galley Collection, 1998. One-woman shows include Elliott Mus., Stuart, Fla., 1986, Scarborough House, Savannah, 1988, John Tucker Fine Arts, 2000; exhibited in two-person show Al Stine Gallery, Anderson, S.C., 2002; exhibited in group shows at Fla. Watercolor Soc., Mus. Arts and Scis., Daytona, Fla., 1978, Brevard Art Ctr. and Mus., Melbourne, 1981, State Capitol, Tallahassee, 1982, Boca Raton Mus. Art, 1984, 86, Houston Pub. Libr., 1981, Galveston (Tex.) Art League, 1983; represented in permanent collections The Moody Found., Elliott Mus., The Rosenberg Libr., Transco Energy Co. Houston, Allied Bank of Seabrook, Hang with the Dolphin and the Mermaid Gallery, Thunderbolt, Ga., Gallery 209, Savannah,. Mem. Fla. Watercolor Soc. (Pres.'s award 1981, 82, Purchase award 1986, signature life mem.), Salmagundi Club, Galveston Art League (pres. 1981-82, Purchase award 1982), Profl. Artist Guild, Landings Art Assn. (pres. 1990). Home: 11 Mainsail Xing Savannah GA 31411-2723 Home Fax: 912-598-9817.

GABLER, ELIZABETH BRAND, film company executive; m. Lee Gabler. Agent motion picture literary dept. ICM; creative exec. Columbia Pictures; v.p. prodn. United Artists; with 20th Century Fox, Beverly Hills, Calif., 1988—, exec. v.p. prodn.; pres. Fox 2000 Pictures, 1999—. Mem. adv. bd. Ctr. Film, TV and New Media U. Calif., Santa Barbara. Named one of 100 Most Powerful Women in Entertainment, Hollywood Reporter, 2004, 2005. Office: 20th Century Fox PO Box 900 Beverly Hills CA 90213-0900

GABLIK, SUZI, art educator, writer; b. N.Y.C., Sept. 26, 1934; d. Anthony Julius and Geraldine (Schwartz) G. BA, Hunter Coll., 1955. Vis. prof. art Sydney Coll. Arts, 1980, U. of the South, Sewanee, Tenn., 1982, 84, U. Calif., Santa Barbara, 1985, 86, 88, Va. Commonwealth U., Richmond, 1987, Va. Tech., Blacksburg, 1990, U. Colo., Boulder, 1990. Endowed lectr. U. Victoria, B.C., 1983, Colo. Coll., 1983, U. Santa Barbara, 1985, Va. Tech., 1989. Author: Magritte, 1979, Has Modernism Failed?, 1984, The Reenchantment of Art, 1991, Conversations Before the End of Time, 1995, Living the Magical Life, 2002. Recipient Lifetime Achievement award, Women's Caucus for Art, 2003. Home: 3271 Deer Run Rd Blacksburg VA 24060-9075 E-mail: suzi@swva.net.

GABOR, ZSA ZSA (SARI GABOR), actress, cosmetics executive; b. Budapest, Hungary, Feb. 6, 1917; m. Conrad Hilton (div.); 1 child, Francesca Hilton; m. George Sanders (div.); m. Prince Frederick von Anholt, 1986. Student in, Budapest and Lausanne, Switzerland. Chmn. bd. Zsa Zsa Ltd. Stage debut, Europe; appeared in motion pictures Lovely to Look At, We're Not Married, The Story of Three Loves, Lili, Moulin Rouge, Three Ring Circus, Death of a Scoundrel, Girl in the Kremlin, For the First Time, Boys Night Out, 1962, Picture Mommy Dead, 1966, Jack of Diamonds, 1967, Won Ton Ton, The Dog Who Saved Hollywood, 1976, Hollywood, Here I Come, 1980, A Nightmare on Elm Street 3: Dream Warriors, 1987, Happily Ever After (voice), 1990, Naked Gun 2 1/2: The Smell of Fear, 1991, The Naked Truth, 1992, Est & Ouest: Les Paradis Perdus, 1993, The Beverly Hillbillies, 1993, A Very Brady Sequel, 1996; star stage prodn. Arsenic and Old Lace, 1975; author: Zsa Zsa's Complete Guide to Men, 1969, How to Get a Man, How to Keep a Man, How to Get Rid of a Man, 1971, one lifetime is not enough, 1991; exercise video: It's Simple, Darling, 1993.

GABOR-HOTCHKISS, MAGDA, research scientist, librarian; b. Paris, Mar. 21, 1934; arrived in U.S., 1967; adopted d. Andor and Olga (Halpern) Gabor; m. Rollin D. Hotchkiss, May 21, 1967 (dec. Dec. 2004). D of Natural Scis. summa cum laude, Eotvos Lorand Sci. U., 1963. Intern Plant Physiology Humboldt U., Berlin, 1957—58; rsch. asst., rsch. assoc. Inst. Genetics Hungarian Acad. Scis., Budapest, 1959—67; rsch. assoc. Rockefeller U., N.Y.C., 1967—82; asst., assoc. libr. Hancock Shaker Village Mus., Pittsfield, Mass., 1985—94, coord. libr. collections, 1995—99, vol. libr., archivist, 2000—. Postdoctoral Bacterial Genetics, Animal Viruses Cold Spring Harbor Lab. of Quantitative Biology, NY, 1965; guest investigator Rockefeller U., N.Y.C., 1964—66; mem. adv. bd. We. Mass. Libr. Assn., Hadley, 1996—97; adj. asst. prof. biology SUNY, Albany, NY, 1982—2002, multilingual contbg. indexer for film/lit. index, Film and TV Document Ctr., 1985—94. Author, compiler: Guide to Hancock Shaker Village Library Collections, 2001—03, annotator, editor: The Shaker Image, 1994; contbr. chpts. to sci. books, articles to sci. jours. Vol. libr. Berkshire Mus., Pittsfield, 1998—; tutor ESL Lit. Vols. Am., Pittsfield, 2001—. Mem.: N.Y. Acad. Scis., Genetics Soc. Am., Sigma Xi. Achievements include discovery of entry of various forms of purified DNAs into bacterial cells of pneumococcus progresses in a linear fashion; recombination patterns of induced bacterial diploids (via protoplast fusion in Bacillus subtilis) follow the classical mechanism found in eucaryotic cells. Avocations: reading, photography, yoga, languages.

GABOW, PATRICIA ANNE, internist, health facility executive; b. Starke, Fla., Jan. 8, 1944; m. Harold N. Gabow, June 21, 1971; children: Tenaya Louise, Aaron Patrick. BA in Biology, Seton Hill Coll., 1965; MD, U. Pa. Sch. Medicine, 1969. Diplomate Am. Bd. Internal Medicine, Am. Bd. Nephrology, Nat. Bd. Med. Examiners; lic. Colo. Internship in medicine Hosp. of U. of Pa., 1969-70; residency in internal medicine Harbor Gen. Hosp., 1970-71; renal fellowship San Francisco Gen. Hosp. and Hosp. of U. Pa., 1971-72, 72-73; instr. medicine divsn. renal diseases, asst. prof. U. Colo. Health Scis. Ctr., 1973-74, 74-79, assoc. prof. medicine divsn. renal diseases, prof., 1979-87; chief renal disease, clin. dir. dept. medicine Denver Gen. Hosp., 1973-81, 76-81, dir. med. svcs., 1981-91; CEO, med. dir. Denver Health and Hosps., 1992—. Intensive care com. Denver Gen. Hosp., 1976-81, med. records com., 1979-80, ind. rev. com., 1978-81, continuing med. edn. com., 1981-83, animal care com., 1979-83; student adv. com. U. Colo. Health Scis. Ctr., 1982-87, faculty senate, 1985, 86, internship adv. com., 1977-92; exec. com. Denver Gen. Hosp., 1981—, chmn. health resources com., 1988-90, chmn. pathology search com., 1989, chmn. faculty practice plan steering com., 1990-92. Mem. editorial bd. EMERGINDEX, 1983-93, Am. Jour. of Kidney Disease, 1984-96, Western Jour. of Medicine, 1987-98, Annals of Internal Medicine, 1988-91, Jour. of the Am. Soc. of Nephrology, 1990-97; contbr. numerous articles, revs. and editorials to profl. publs., chpts. to books. Mem. Mayor's Safe City Task Force, 1993; mem. sci. adv. bd. Polycystic Kidney Rsch. Found., 1984-96, chmn., 1991; mem. sci. adv. bd. Nat. Kidney Found., 1991-94; mem. Nat. Pub. Health and Hosps. Inst. Bd., 1993-2001, 03—. Recipient Sullivan award for Highest Acad. Average in Graduating Class, Seton Hill Coll., 1965, Pa. State Senatorial scholarship, 1961-65, Kaiser Permanente award for Excellence in Tchg., 1976, Ann. award to Outstanding Woman Physician, 1982, Kaiser Permanente Nominee for Excellence in Tchg. award, 1983, Seton Hill Coll. Disting. Alumna Leadership award, 1990, Florence Rena Sabin award U. Colo., 2000, Nathan Davis award AMA, 2000, Good Housekeeping Women in Govt. award, 2002; named one of The Best Doctors in Am., 1994-95, 2002; grantee Bonfils Found., 1985-86, NIH, 1985-90, 91-96, 96-00, W.K. Kellogg Found., 1997—, AHRQ, 2000-03; named to Colo. Women's Hall of Fame, 2004, One of the Top 25 Women in Healthcare, 2005, 100 Most Influential People in Healthcare in Modern Healthcare, Women Who Make a Difference International Women's Forum, 2005. Mem. Denver Med. Soc., Colo. Med. Soc., Am. Fedn. Clin. Rsch., Am. Physiol. Soc., Polycystic Kidney Disease Rsch. Found. (sci. advisor 1984-96), Western Assn. Physicians, Nat. Kidney Found. (sci. adv. bd. 1987-91), Women's Forum of Colo., Inc., Assn. Am. Physicians. Roman Catholic. Office: Denver Health 660 Bannock St Denver CO 80204-4506 Address: Denver Health 777 Bannock St Denver CO 80204

GABRIEL, DIANE AUGUSTA, artist, educator; b. N.Y.C., Sept. 12, 1947; d. Herbert N. and Jean L. (Wertheimer) Gabriel; m. Mark A. Stoler, Aug. 11, 1991; 1 child, Eben Gabriel Cahan. BA, Goddard Coll., Plainfield, Vt., 1976. Designer/owner Diane Gabriel Fiber Arts, Vt., 1977—93; instr. Firehouse Ctr. for the Arts, Vt., 1999; lectr. Helen Day Art Ctr., Stowe, Vt., 2000, Burlington City Arts, Vt., 2000; instr. Studio 250/Print Making Studio, Burlington, 2001, C.C. of Vt., 2003—. Founding mem. 215 Coll. Gallery, Burlington, 2005—; juried artist Vt. Arts Coun., Montepelier, 2005—. One and two person shows, The Doll Anstadt Gallery, Burlington, 1999, The Grannis Gallery, 2002, Lorraine B. Goode Gallery, 2002 (Barbara Smail award, 2003). Fellow, Vt. Studio Ctr., Johnson, 2006. Mem.: Mus. Women in the Arts. Home: 43 Prospect Hill Burlington VT 05401 Personal E-mail: dgabriel1@mac.com.

GABRIELE, MARGUERITE ANN (MARGIE ST. JOHN), artist, nursing educator; b. Glens Falls, N.Y., Jan. 27, 1930; d. Clifford Francis and Marguerite Cecilia St. John; children from previous marriage: Frederick, Michael, Marguerite, Peter. BA, Albertus Magnus Coll., New Haven, 1952; MSN, Yale U., New Haven, 1955, at art studies, 1994—96; at, Art Students League, N.Y.C., 1996. RN Conn. Instr. nursing Greenwich (Conn.) Sch. Nursing, 1955—56, Yale U., New Haven, 1956—58; asst. dir. pediat. clinic New Haven Hosp., 1958—59; assoc. dir. rsch. and open heart surgery Yale U., 1959—60; instr. nursing W. Va. Sch. Nursing, 1978—80; nursing home nurse Guilford, Conn., 1984—85; artist Margie St. John Paintings, White Plains, NY. Prin. works include Meditation of Hope, exhibitions include Ceres Gallery, N.Y.C., 1995, 1999, 2000, 2003, Prince St. Gallery, N.Y.C., 1996, Upper West Side Artists Coalition, 1997, White Plains (N.Y.) Women's Club, 1998, 1999, 2000, 2001, 2003, Artforum, N.Y.C., 2001, Yale Sch. Nursing, 2001, Palace Provisional Cultural Delegation Andalusia, Spain, 2002, Lincoln Ctr., N.Y.C., 2003, New Art Ctr., 2003, Westchester Arts Coun., 2004, Ezair Gallery, N.Y.C., 2004, one-woman shows include New Arts Ctr., 2005, Ezair Gallery, 2006. Treas. LWV, Morgantown, W.Va., 1990. Grantee, New Arts Ctr. N.Y.C., 2004. Fellow: Mus. Modern Art; mem.: Rockland Arts Coun., Upper West Side Arts Coalition, Nat. Mus. Women in Arts, Westchester Arts Coun., Women's Caucus Arts. Avocations: swimming, cross country skiing, yoga, fitness. Home: 41 Barker Ave White Plains NY 10601

GAC-ARTIGAS, PRISCILLA, foreign language educator; b. P.R. m. Gustavo Gac-Artigas; children: Melina, Alejandro. BA, U. P.R., Río Piedras, 1977; MA, Middlebury (Vt.) Coll., 1978; PhD, U. Franche-Comté, France, 1994. Assoc. prof. fgn. langs., chair dept. fgn. lang. studies Monmouth U., West Long Branch, NJ, 1995—. Author: Critical Study of Latin American Popular Theater in the Sixties, 1996, Melina, ConversacionesCon el Ser Que Seras, 2000; co-author: Directro al Grano, Spanish Grammar, 1998, Sans Detour, French Grammar, 1998, T the Point: English for Spanish Speakers, 1996; editor: (anthology) Reflexiones, Essays on Spanish Women Writers, 2 vols., Nos tomamos la palabra, (textbook) Hoja de Ruta, civilizacion y cultura de Latinoamerica. Office Phone: 732-571-3406. E-mail: pgacarti@monmouth.edu.

GAD, SIMONE, actress, performance artist, visual artist, writer; b. Brussels, Apr. 17, 1947; arrived in U.S., 1951; d. Rachmil and Bacia (Sztark) Gad. Student, Art Ctr. La. Instr. Art Ctr. Coll. Design, Pasadena, Calif., 1992-93, Westridge, Pasadena, 1992-93, Armory Ctr. for Arts, Pasadena, 1995-99. One-woman shows include Monique Knowlton Gallery, N.Y.C., 1984, Fun Gallery, N.Y.C., 1984, Molly Barnes Gallery, 1984, ID Galerie, Dusseldorf, Germany, 1990, Orlando Gallery, Van Nuys, Calif., 1995, No Name Exhbns., Mpls., 1995, Granados II Gallery, L.A., 1996, 2002-03, Musee D'Art Spontane, Brussels, 1998, MP and Pine Gallery, San Francisco, 1998, LZ Kontmeporary Gallery, Chinatown, LA, 2006; group shows include Leo Castelli Gallery, N.Y.C., 1980, ID Gallerie, Germany, 1990, Art in Gen., N.Y.C., 1992, Exit Art, N.Y.C., 1993, Stuart Katz Loft, 1997, Julie Rico Gallery, 1999, Dirt Gallery, 1999; represented in permanent collections Miss. Mus. Art, Tampa Mus. Art, Fresno Mus. Art, Calif. State U., Laguna Beach Mus. Art, Long Beach Mus. Art; performances include No Name Exhbns., Mpls., 1995, MaidenForms, 1996, Dark Night Memory, 1997, Geffen Contemporary at MOCA, 1998, Molested/Shoes, Glaxa Studios, 2000, Red Eye Theatre, 2002, Temple Mus., 2002, Cleve. State U. Factory Place Theatre, 2002. Grantee New Orleans Contemporary Art Ctr., 1984, Dolph & Esther Gottlieb Fedn., 2002, Cmty. Redevel. Agy., 1987, UCLA, 1992, Change Inc., 2002, Rauschenberg Fedn., 2002, Adolph and Esther Gottlieb Fedn., 2002. Mem.: AFTRA, SAG. Address: PO Box 39874 Los Angeles CA 90039-0874

GADBERRY, VICKI LYNN HIMES, librarian; b. Frederick, Md., Jan. 3, 1950; d. Guilford Swisher and Eloise Alberta (Twentey) Himes; m. Eric Brett Gadberry, Aug. 15, 1971. BS, U. Md., 1971; MLS, U. S.C., 1974; postgrad., Penland Sch. Crafts, 1989, 96, Sul Ross State U., 1997-98. Cert. media coord. N.C. Dept. Pub. Instrn. Media coord. N.C. Pub. Schs., Fayetteville, 1976-78, Hendersonville, 1980-85, Asheville, 1985-88; pub. svcs. coord. Mars Hill (N.C.) Coll., 1990-92, reference svcs. libr., 1992-97; asst. exec. dir., adminstrn. Fort Davis (Tex.) C. of C., 1998—; owner Off The Wall Photos & Art, 2001—. On-site dir. Children's Art in the Mountains Program, Marshall, N.C., summer 1992, tchr. fiber art, summer 1990; artist-in-residence Mountain Arts Program, Waynesville, N.C., 1990. Project designer book: Molas!, 1998; contbr. articles, revs., index to profl. publs. Mem. planning com. Beacon Handloom Weaving Show, Asheville, N.C., 1988, 90-92, chair, 1989; bd. dirs. Children's Art in the Mountains Program, Marshall, N.C., 1991-93. Mem. Handweavers Guild Am. (orgnl. C.O.E. Weaving com. co-chair 1992-94), S.W. Women's Fiber Art Collective, Mogollon Rim Fiber Guild (sec.). Avocations: weaving, photography. Home: 18 Gulch Ln Silver City NM 88061 E-mail: gadberry@gilanet.com.

GADDIS, BETTY H., retired elementary school educator; b. Carlisle, Ky. d. Walter Cornelius and Gertrue Mae (Earlywine) Hollar; m. Luther Herbert Goddis, Jr., Aug. 20, 1961. Ltd. Arts degree, Sue Bennett Coll., 1961; BS, Cumberland Coll., 1963; MA, Union Coll., Barbourville, Ky., 1976, postgrad., 1977—78. Elem. tchr. Knox County Bd. Edn., Gray, Corbin, Ky., 1964—96; ret., 1996. Cons. Knox Bd. Edn., Barbourville, 1994—2001; tchr. math. workshops, 1984—90. Vol. Food Pantry, Corbin, 1977—. Named Ky. col.; recipient Reading award, Reading in Primary, Ky.; Sci. grantee, Sci. in the Sch., Ky. Mem.: NEA, Ky. Edn. Ret. Tchrs., Presbyn. Women (pres., officer). Avocations: gardening, sewing, singing, writing, travel. Home: 164 Dr Jones Rd Gray KY 40734

GADDIS ROSE, MARILYN, literature educator, translator; b. Fayette, Mo., Apr. 2, 1930; d. Merrill Elmer and Florence Georgia (Lyon) Gaddis; m. James Leo Rose, Dec. 23, 1956 (div. 1966); m. Stephen David Ross, Nov. 16, 1968 (div. Sept. 2005); 1 child, David Gaddis Ross. BA, Central Meth. Coll., 1952; MA, U. S.C., Columbia, 1954-55; PhD, U. Mo., 1958; LHD, Ctrl. Meth. Coll., 1987. Instr. Stephens Coll., Columbia, Mo., 1958-68; assoc. prof. Ind. U., Bloomington, 1968; prof. comparative lit. SUNY, Binghamton, 1968—, disting. svc. prof., 1991—, dir. translation program, 1973—2002. Translator: (book) Axel, 1970, 1986, Eve of the Future Eden, 1981, Lui: A View of Him, 1986, Adrienne Mesurat, 1991, Volupté, The Sensual Man, 1995, Translation Horizon, 1996, Translation and Literary Criticism, 1998, Beyond the Western Tradition, 2000; editor, contbr.: book Translation Spectrum, 1981; editor: Translation Perspectives, (jour.) Women Writers in Translation, 1983—; contbr. articles to profl. jours. Fulbright fellow, U. Lyon, France, 1953—54, Humanities Rsch. Centre Sr. fellow, Australian Nat. U., 1977. Mem.: MLA (del. assembly 1974—78, pres. N.E. sect. 1975—76, del. assembly 1984—87, exec. coun. 2004—), Am. Translators Assn. (bd. dirs. 1986—88, mng. editor series 1986—96, endowed lectr. 1998—. Spl. Svc. award 1983, 1995, Alexander Gode award 1988), Am. Lit. Translators (sec.-treas. 1981—83), PEN N.Y. Home: Apt 508 5 Riverside Dr Binghamton NY 13905-4644 Office Phone: 607-777-6726. Personal E-mail: mgrose@binghamton.edu.

GADDY, SARAH ANN, elementary school educator; b. Powder Springs, Ga., Jan. 29, 1980; d. Freddy Lamar and Diane Streetman. BS in Mid. Sch. Edn., Kennesaw State U., Ga., 2002. Lead tchr. explorer's program Primrose Sch. at Macland Pointe, Marietta, Ga., 1998—2001; 6th grade math tchr. Cobb County Sch. Sys., Marietta, 2002—. Named Employee of Month, Primrose at Macland Pointe, 1999. Mem.: Cobb County Assn. Educators (assoc.). Office: Tapp Mid Sch 3900 Macedonia Rd Powder Springs GA 30127 Office Phone: 770-222-3758. Personal E-mail: sarah.gaddy@cobbk12.org.

GADDY, STEPHANIE ANN, director; b. Bloomington, Ill., Mar. 18, 1959; d. Eldon M. and Norma E. Rupp; m. David L. Gaddy Sr., Aug. 11, 1979; children: Amy, Lindsey, David Jr. BS, Ill. State U., 1989, MEd, 1995, EdD, 2004. Instr. Heartland Cmty. Coll., Normal, Ill., 1989—93; prof. Lincoln Coll., Normal, 1993—96, Lincoln, 1996—2006, dir. Office Disability Svc., 2006—. Contbr. articles to profl. jours. Mem.: Coun. Exceptional Children, Kappa Delta Pi. Office: Lincoln Coll 300 Keokuk Lincoln IL 62656 Office Phone: 217-732-3155. Business E-Mail: sgaddy@lincolncollege.edu.

GADIESH, ORIT, management consulting executive; b. Haifa, Israel, Jan. 31; BA in psychology summa cum laude, Hebrew U., Israel, 1973; MBA, Harvard Bus. Sch., 1977. Asst. to dep. chief of staff Israeli Army; asst. prof. Hebrew U., Israel; with Bain & Co., Boston, 1977—, head Boston office, 1991—93, chmn., 1993—. Bd. dir. Peres Inst. for Peace, Israel, WPP, World Econ. Forum; coun. mem. Harvard Bus. Sch., Kellogg Sch., Haute Ecole Commerciale, France; bd. mem. Fed. Reserve Bank of New Eng. Named one of 100 Most Powerful Women in World, Forbes mag., 2005—06; recipient Disting. Leadership award, IDC U., 2000, Alumni Achievement award, Harvard Bus. Sch., 2000. Mem.: Coun. Fgn. Rels.*

GADSBY, MONICA M., marketing executive; b. Brazil; m. Jon Gadsby; 3 children. BA in Liberal Arts, Univ. Tex., 1987, BS in Advt., 1987. Media asst., Procter & Gamble acct. Leo Burnett USA, Chgo., 1987, founding mem., Hispanic unit, 1987; now mng. dir., CEO, Tapestry Mktg. Agy. Starcom MediaVest Group, Chgo. Bd. dir. Pangea Ptnrs. Named Media Planning Exec. Yr., HispanicAd.com and Assn. Hispanic Advt. Agencies, 2002; named one of Top 42 US Hispanic Women, Vanidades Mag., 2003, 100 Most Influential Women, Crain's Chgo. Bus., 2004. Mem.: IAB Hispanic Com., Assn. Hispanic Advt. Agencies (co-chair, media com.). Fluent in Spanish, Portuguese, French, English. Office: Tapestry Mktg 35 W Wacker Dr Chicago IL 60601 Office Fax: 312-220-3381, 312-220-6561. Business E-Mail: monicam.gadsby@tapestrypartners.com.

GADSON, SANDRA L., nephrologist, medical association administrator; Grad., Hampton U.; MD, Meharry Med. Coll. Resident U. Ill. Med. Ctr., Chgo.; emergency room physician Meth. Hosp., Gary, Ind.; nephrologist, med. dir. N.W. Ind. Dialysis Ctr. Named one of 100 Most Influential Black Americans, Ebony mag., 2006. Mem.: Nat. Med. Assn. (mem. bd. trustees, pres. N.W. Ind. Chap., nat. pres. 2005—). Office: Nat Med Assn 1012 Tenth St, NW Washington DC 20001 Office Phone: 202-347-1895.*

GAETA, JANE, minister; b. Elizabeth, NJ, Dec. 7, 1942; d. Stanley Anthony Luboniecki and Stella Helen Misiur; m. Gerard Ralph Gaeta, Apr. 4, 1964; children: Gregory Mark, Susan Marie. AA, Thomas A. Edison Coll., 1978; MDiv, Trinity Sem., Columbus, Ohio, 1985; D Ministry, NY Theol. Sem., 1994; M Sacred Theology, Gen. Theol. Sem., 2002. RN NY; cert. chaplain Assn. Profl. Chaplains. Pastor St. Mark's Luth. Ch., Elmsford, NY, 1985—87; chaplain Amsterdam Nursing Home, N.Y.C., 1985—89; co-pastor ST. John's Luth. Ch., Lindenhurst, NY, 1989—93; chaplain Calvary Hosp., Bronx, NY, 1994—99; pastor Good Shepherd Luth. Ch., Bayside, NY, 1999—. Vacancy pastor Calvary Luth. Ch., Bronx, NY; instr. George Mercer Sch. Theology, Garden City, NY, 2000—; adj. prof. pastoral theology Gen. Theol. Sem., N.Y.C., 2005; spiritual dir. Mercer Sch. Theology, Garden City, 2002—; pastoral advisor Nassau Diakonia, Garden City, 2001—; book reviewer Trinity Sem. Rev., 2003—. Mem. exec. bd. Trinity Sem. Alumni, Columbus, Ohio, 2001—; active Bread for the World, Washington, 1970, Amnesty Internat., N.Y.C., 2004; mem. Lutherans Concerned, St. Paul, 2003—. Merit scholar, Maryknoll Sch. Theology, 1982, merit scholar, Trinity Luth. Sem., 1984. Mem.: Spiritual Dirs. Internat., Assn. Profl. Chaplains. Avocations: crocheting, cooking, swimming, singing, needlepoint. Home: 192 Garth Rd 3P Scarsdale NY 10583 E-mail: JSLGaeta@aol.com.

GAETA, MICHELLE, mathematics educator; b. Secaucus, NJ, July 3, 1979; d. Richie and Diane Gaeta. BA in Math., Sacred Heart U., Fairfield, Conn., 2001, MA in Tchg., 2002. Std. cert. tchg. math. NJ, 2004. Intern/student tchr. Trumbull H.S., Conn., 2001—02; math. tchr. Staples H.S., Westport, Conn., 2002—04, Pascack Hills H.S., Pascack Valley Regional H.S. Dist., Montvale, NJ, 2004—. Mem.: Nat. Coun. Tchrs. Math. Office: 225 West Grand Ave Montvale NJ 07645 Office Phone: 201-358-7020 3032.

GAETA, ROSEMARIE, social worker; b. Bklyn., Apr. 15, 1947; d. James and Rose (Scorcia) G. BS, Fordham U., 1968, MSW, 1970. Diplomate NASW; lic. clin. social worker, N.Y. Pvt. practice, S.I., 1973—. Bd. mem. Accreditation Council for Psychoanalytic Edn., 2004—. Recipient Disting. Practitioner, Nat. Acad. Practice in Social Work. Mem. N.Y. State Soc. Clin. Social Work Psychotherapists (diplomate, chair state com. on psychoanalysis 1987-91), Inst. Psychoanalytic Tng. and Rsch., Internat. Psychoanalytical Assn. Office: 416 Crown Ave Staten Island NY 10312-2828 Office Phone: 718-356-8881.

GAETH, ROXANNE, school psychologist; b. Defiance, Ohio, Feb. 4, 1949; d. Alvin Frederick and Emma Louise Warncke; m. William A. Gaeth (div.); children: Benjamin F., Joshua W. AA, Concordia Luth. Jr. Coll., Ann Arbor, 1968; BA, Concordia Tchrs. Coll., River Forest, Ill., 1970; EdM, Bowling Green State U., Ohio, 1974. Elem. tchr. Grace Luth. Sch., Queen Village, NY, 1970—71; tchr. spl. edn. Defiance Pub. Schs., Ohio, 1971—74; sch. psychologist Allen County, Lima, Ohio, 1974—79; sch. psychometrist Logansport Spl. Edn. Coop., Ind., 1979—81; cons. Berks County Head Start, Reading, Pa., 1981—83; sch. psychologist Woodridge Sch. Dist., Ill., 1984—86, Benjamin Sch. Dist. #25 Sch. Assn. Spl. Edn. in DuPage County, Carol Stream, 1987—97, Naperville Cmty. Unit Sch. Dist. #203, 1997—. Office: Naperville Cmty Unit Sch Dist 203 414 Orleans Ave Naperville IL 60565-2634

GAFFORD, MARY MAY GRIMES, retired humanities educator; b. Paris, Tex., Jan. 4, 1936; d. Benjamin Earl and Mary Elizabeth (Perfect) Grimes; m. Frank Hall Gafford, Dec. 31, 1958 (dec. May 2003); children: Michelle Marguerite, Georgette Marie. BA in English and Social Studies, North Tex. State U., Denton, 1957, MA in English, Spanish and History, 1958; postgrad., U. Nev., summer 1970. Tchr. English Alpine Pub. Schs., Tex., 1959-61; tchr. English and history Houston Sch. Dist., 1957-58; tchr. English and Spanish Grapevine Sch. Dist., Tex., 1958-59, Amarillo Sch. Dist., Tex., 1962-65; tchr. English, Spanish and Journalism Fabens Schs., Tex., 1965-67; tchr. English and Spanish Flagstaff Schs., Ariz., 1967-68, Mesa County Schs., Grand Junction, Colo., 1968-71; tchr. English Clark County Schs., Las Vegas, Nev., 1976—2004; ret., 2004. Editor: Ethnic Etchings, 1990-93 (award of Excellence 1991, 92); southern region project coord. Skirts That Swept the Desert Floor, vol. I. Vol. Am. Cancer Soc., Las Vegas, 1974—, So. Nev. Dems., Las Vegas, 1980, Very Spl. Arts Festival, 1990-92, youth health fair Nev. Bus. Svcs., Las Vegas, 1989; mem. Nev. Symphony Guild; chair Christopher Columbus Quincentinnial 1990—; bd. dirs., hospitality and publicity chair Summer Theatre, 2003-06; cultural arts bd. State Pks., 1990-2001; publicist Nev. Women's History Project, 1998-2002, 1st v.p., 2002—, state sec., 2003—; cultural chair Roy Martin Middle Sch., 2000-03; charter mem. Desert Arts Nev., Inc., publicist, 2005—; bd. dirs., publicist Super Summer Theatre, 2005-06, chair long range planning com.; project coord., Nevada Women's History Project. Recipient Nat. Defense Edn. Act. award U. Alaska, Fairbanks, 1966, Spanish Inst. Calif. Luth. Coll., Thousand Oaks, 1968, Las Vegas Centennial award Wall of Women, 2005, Pin recognition Super Summer Theatre Bd.; named Outstanding Woman of Las Vegas, Las Vegas (Nev.) Mus Mem. DAR (Francisco Garcés chpt., vice-regent 1983-90, regent 1990-92, chair Christopher Columbus Quincentennial 1990—, chair WWII 50th Anniversary Commemoration 1992—, chair U.S. Constn. week 1992—, Nev. state chair com. Am. Indians 2004—, Nev. state nominating com. 2006), Clark County Classroom Tchrs., Soc. Nev. Tchrs. of English, AAUW (life chair teen-age pregnancy study group chpt. 1983-92, pres. 1976-77, chair coupon clippers 1984-93, Sarah Winnemucca award for svc. 2003), Pilot Club (pres. 1989-90, hospitality chair 1993), Nev. Soc. Descs. Mayflower (lt. gov. 1997—, state sec. 2002—), Nev. State Women's History Project (state sec. 2004—, 1st v.p. so. region 2004—), Deserts Arts of Nev. (publicist 2005-06), Sons and Daughters of Pilgrims for Southern Nev. (charter mem., state sec. 2003—), Cameo Soc., Daughters of the Confederacy (Southern Nev. charter mem., v.p.), Paradise Dem. Club. Methodist. Avocations: numismatics, antiques, creative writing, collecting Native American artifacts. Home: 5713 Balzar Ave Las Vegas NV 89108-3184

GAGAN, SARAH K., lawyer; BA, McMaster U., 1991; JD, McGill U., 1994. Bar: Mass. 1998, Ontario, Canada 1996. Ptnr. Bingham McCutchen LLP, Boston, co-chairperson comml. tech. practice group. Contbr. articles to profl. jours. Mem.: Boston Bar Assn., Mass. Bar Assn., ABA. Office: Bingham McCutchen LLP 150 Federal St Boston MA 02110-1726 Office Fax: 617-951-8736, 617-951-8549. Business E-Mail: sarah.gagan@bingham.com.*

GAGE, BEAU, artist; b. Rye, N.Y., Dec. 3, 1945; d. John Alden and Frances (Johnston) G.; m. Glenn A. Ousterhout, May 24,1980. BA, St. John's Coll., Santa Fe and Annapolis, Md., 1971; student, Internat. Ctr. Photography, N.Y.C., 1981-82, 82-83, Art Students League N.Y., 1983-87, The Sculpture Ctr. Sch., N.Y.C., 1985-87, Nat. Acad. Design, 1988-89. Staff asst. to the pres. The White House, Washington, 1972-73; key accounts mgr. Sterling Drug, Inc., Montvale, NJ, 1975-79. Works exhibited at Internat. Ctr. Photography, 1981-83, Art Students League, 1984-87, The Sculpture Ctr., 1985-87, Westbeth Gallery, N.Y.C., 1984, 86, Sotheby's Auction House, 1990, others; permanent pub. sculpture Jacksonville (Fla.) Jaguars, Inc.; permanent exhbn. Jacksonville Mus. Sci. & History. Supporter, guild mem. Martha Graham Dance Co., N.Y.C., 1989—; canopy assoc. Rainforest Alliance, 2000—; mem. adv. bd. Buglisi/Foreman Dance Co., N.Y.C., 2001—; leader Perlman Music Program, N.Y.C., 2001—. Fellow Mus. Modern Art; mem. Met. Mus. Art, Internat. Ctr. Photography, Orgn. Ind. Artists, The Nature Conservancy, Mass. Soc. Mayflower Descendants, Poets House (N.Y.C.). Avocations: astronomy, sailing, yoga. Home: 320 E 46th St Apt 34E New York NY 10017-3039 Personal E-mail: beau7gage@aol.com.

GAGE, MIRIAM BETTS, retired nutritionist; b. Nelsonville, Ohio, Jan. 9, 1928; d. Charles Donald and Lillian Mary (Linscott) B.; m. Robert Averill Gowdy, Oct. 12, 1950 (div. 1977); children: Carol Jo, Robert Jr., Bruce; m. George Joel Gage, Aug. 16, 1997. BA in Home Econs., Ohio Wesleyan U., 1949; postgrad., Duke U., 1949-50, Calif. State U., L.A., 1975-76. Registered dietitian. Pvt. practice dietitian, L.A., 1977-91; cons. Nat.-in-Home Health, Van Nuys, Calif., 1984-87; clin. dietitian Lake Mead Hosp., 1991-94; pvt. practice Las Vegas, Nev., 1994-97; contract dietitian Pulse Health Svcs., Las Vegas, 1995-97; ret., 1997. Mem. Am. Diabetes Assn. (con. San Fernando Valley unit 1976-80, bd. dirs. N.W. chpt. 1977-82), Nev. Dietetic Assn. (nominating com. 1995-97), So. Nev. Dietetic Assn. (mem. chmn. 1991-92, pres. 1993-94), Cons. Nutritionists (chmn.-elect So. Calif. chpt. 1979-81), Calif. Dietetic Assn. (chmn. diabetes care practice 1979-81), Am. Heart Assn. (governing bd. N.W. chpt. 1988-89). Republican. Methodist. Home: 10813 Brinkwood Ave Las Vegas NV 89134-5248 Business E-Mail: miriamgage@cox.net.

GAGE, NANCY ELIZABETH, academic administrator, accountant, educator; b. Chgo., Aug. 22, 1947; d. Winfred Paul and Anne Ellen (Osbon) Rankhorn; m. Walter Howard Crane, June 14, 1969 (div. June 1977); 1 child, Patrick; m. James Lewis Gage, June 10, 1977 (div. Oct. 1981); 1 child, Laura Anne. BS, Ill. Inst. Tech., 1969; postgrad., Winona State U., 1978-80, U. Minn., 1981-82. Cert. Collegiate Mgmt. Inst.; cert. tchr. math., Wash., Mich., Ill.; Myers-Briggs Type Indicator qualified adminstr., interpreter. Tchr. math. St. Bede Acad., Eau Claire, Wis., 1977; accounts specialist U. Minn., Mpls., 1981, asst. adminstr., 1981-82, assoc. adminstr., 1982-83; grants acct. supr. Coll. of DuPage, Glen Ellyn, Ill., 1984, cash disbursements mgr., 1984-87, chief acct., 1987—. Founding mem. Ptnrs. in Edn. Coun., Coll. DuPage, 1997, chair bd/staff rels. com., 1990-92, mem. salary/benefits negotiating team, 1993-94, 98-99, pres. 1994-95, 2003-04; chmn. supervisory com. Fed. Credit Union, 1985-86, mem. project team payroll/pers. sys. implementation, 1985-87, mem. project team gen. ledger sys. implementation, 1987-88, 2003-05; project leader Y2K Conversion, gen. ledger sys., 1997-2000; mem. Baldrige Award Bd. Examiners, 2002—. Contbg. author math. curriculum, 1972; web developer, 1996—. Media contact coord. Common Cause, Manistique, Mich., 1975-76; bd. dirs., pres. Manistique Coop. Nursery Sch., 1974-75; mem. Bicentennial program com. Manistique Jr. Women's Group, Manistique, 1975-76, Chgo. Tchrs. Against the Vietnam War, 1969. Recipient Outstanding Svc. award Coll. of DuPage, 1987-88, 91-92, Spirit Svc. award, 2006; State of Ill. fellow, 1970; Ill. Inst. Tech. scholar, 1964. Mem. AAUW, Am. Soc. Profl. and Exec. Women, Am. Assn. Women in C.C.s (bd. sec. 1997-98), Classified Pers. Assn. (exec. bd. 1993-96), Cen. Assn. Coll. and Univ. Bus. Officers (2 yr. coll. com. 1990-93, drive in workshop com. 1993-97), Nat. Assn. Coll. and Univ. Bus. Officers, Manistique Ext. Homemakers Club (treas. 1974-76), Kappa Phi Delta (treas. 1967-68). Independent. Unitarian. Avocations: reading, writing, travel, social reform. Home: 2201 W Illinois Ave Aurora IL 60506-1530 Office: Coll of DuPage Fin Office 425 Fawell Blvd Glen Ellyn IL 60137-6599 Office Phone: 630-942-2404. Business E-Mail: gagena@cod.edu.

GAGGIANO, ANDREA JEAN, secondary school educator; b. Orange, Calif., Jan. 12, 1971; d. Thomas Edward Lareau and Joyce Loreen Molzahn Ours; m. Michael John Gaggiano, June 18, 1994; children: Joseph Dominic, Katherine Emalyne. BA in English, U. Calif., Irvine, 1993, BA in History, 1993; MS in Reading, Reading Specialist Credential, Calif. State U., Fullerton, 2005. Cert. English and history tchr., Calif. Thcr. English Trabuco Hills H.S., Mission Viejo, Calif., 1994—. Mem. Calif. Tchrs. Assn., Nat. Coun. Tchrs. English. Republican. Mem. Soc. Of Friends. Avocations: sewing, crafts, reading. E-mail: gaggianoa@svusd.org.

GAGLIARDI, CHARLOTTE MARIE, music educator, secondary school educator; b. Sayre, Okla., May 22, 1953; d. Charles Edward and Charlotte Thelma (Jean) Connally; m. Leonard F. Gagliardi, July 2, 1982; children: Colleen Marie, Marco Anthony. MusB in Edn., U. Okla., Norman, 1976. Dir. choral Noble Pub. Schs., Okla., 1976—80; tchr. music Carriage Hills Elem. Sch. Lawton Pub. Schs., Okla., 1981—84, dir. choral Ctrl. Jr. H.S., 1984—87, dir. choral Lawton H.S., 1987—2006. Pvt. music instr., Lawton, 1980—2006. Mem. com. women's choirs Okla. Music Hall Fame, 1990—97. Finalist ACE award, 1993; nominee Tchr. of Yr., NFL, 1997, 1998, 2000, Disney, 1997, 2002, others; named Tchr. of Yr., Lawton H.S., 1995, 2004, Tchr. of Today, Lawton Masonic Lodge, 1997, 2002. Mem.: NEA, Okla. Music Adjudicators Assn., Okla. Music Educators Assn. (chmn. chorus 1994), Profl. Educators Assn. Lawton, Okla. Educators Assn., Okla. Choral Dirs. Assn. (rep. S.W. chpt. 1996—2001, dir. honors choir, nominated Dir. Distinction award 1999), Kappa Kappa Iota (pres. 1990—91). Home: 3008 NE Heritage Ln Lawton OK 73507

GAGNE, MARY, academic administrator; Dir. Tex. Acad. Leadership in the Humanities Lamar U., Beaumont, 1998—. Recipient Blue Ribbon awards U.S. Dept. Edn., 1986-87, 90-91, Exec. Educator Best Prin. award, Nat. Tchg. award NCEA, Coca Cola Educator of Distinction award. 2000. Address: PO Box 10062 Beaumont TX 77710-0062 E-mail: gagneml@hal.lamar.edu.

GAGNON, NANCY SPEAR, secondary school educator, consultant; b. Portland, Me., July 14, 1958; d. Deon C. Spear, Jr. and Irene Johnson Spear; m. Edward F. Gagnon, June 17, 1981; children: Jessica, Amanda, Michael. BA, U. Me., Orono, 1980; MA, U. New Eng., Biddeford, Me., 1997. Tchr. Conual HS, Peterborough, NH, Mascenio HS, New Tosioch, NH; rehab. cons. Comprehensive Rehab., Bedford, NH. Bd. mem. N.H. Coun. Social Studies; steering mem. N.H. Geog. Alliance; tchr. cons. Nat. Geog. Fullbright Meml. fellow, Goethe Tops fellow, Korea Soc. Tchr. fellow. Mem.: NHCSS, NCSS. Office: 185 hancock Rd Peterborough NH

GAHAGEN, BONNIE KNEPP, elementary school educator; b. Pitts. d. James E. and Mary Ann Knepp; m. David Wayne Gahagen, June 16, 1984; children: Benjamin Andrew, Jonathan David. BS Elem. and Spl. Edn., California State U., Pa., 1983. Cert. elem.-mid. sch. tchr., tchr. spl. edn. endorsement in LD, emotionally disturbed, severe and profound mentally retarded K-12. Tchr. spl. edn. emotionally disturbed Sewell Sch. Handicapped Students, Barnwell, SC, 1983; tchr. spl. edn. learned disabled H.M. Pearson Elem. Sch., Warrenton, Va., 1984—87; tchr. spl. edn. emotionally disturbed Chancellor Elem. Sch., Spotsylvania, Va., 1987—88; tchr. 3d grade Farmington and Pearl Sample, Culpeper, Va., 1988—2006. Mem. Social Studies and Sci. Curriculum com., Culpeper, 1999—2004, Math. Curriculum Com., Culpeper, 2002—04. Leader Cub Scout Pack 198, Culpeper; missionary Jamaica and W.Va.; asst. youth leader Lake of Woods Ch., Locust Grove, Va.

GAHALA, ESTELLA MARIE, writer, consultant; b. Alva, Okla., Mar. 28, 1929; d. Ivan Grant Crouse and Margaret Estella Beck; m. Dale Lowell Lange, Apr. 18, 1998; m. John W. Gahala, Nov. 27, 1964 (dec. Aug. 1, 1989). BA magna cum laude, Wichita State U., Kans., 1953; MA, Middlebury Coll., Vt., 1963; PhD, Northwestern U., 1980. Tchr. Highland Pk. HS, Topeka, 1953—57, Amarillo (Tex.) HS, 1957—60, Glenbrook North HS, Northbrook, Ill., 1960—64; dept. chmn. Evanston (Ill.) Township HS, 1964—73; dir. curriculum Lyons Township HS, LaGrange, Ill., 1973—84; author, cons. Scott Foresman Pub., Glenview, Ill., 1984—94, McDougal Littell Pub., Boston, 1994—. Pres. Gahala Assocs., Pk. Ridge, Ill., 1980—96. Author: Son et Sens, 1984, Dis-moi, 1993, En Español, 2004, Avancemos, 2006; contbr. articles to profl. jours. Vol. Albuquerque (N.Mex.) Mus. Art, 1987—2003, Presbyn. Hospice Care, Albuquerque, 1991—2006; vol. working with homeless and abused women; mem. ch. counsel First United Meth. Ch. Named Chevalier Palmes Académiques, French Ministry Edn., 1975. Mem.: Am. Assn. Tchrs. French (chpt. pres. 1970—72, mem. exec. coun. 1976—81), Am. Coun. Fgn. Langs. Democrat. Avocations: art, genealogy. Home and Office: 2315 Madre Drive NE Albuquerque NM 87112 Personal E-mail: egahala@aol.com.

GAHRING, SANDRA ANN, secondary school educator, coach; b. Milw., Oct. 1, 1954; d. David Edward and Joan Mae Steward; m. Todd Russell Gahring, Nov. 3, 1990. BS in Phys. Edn., Calif. Poly., Pomona, 1976; MA in Edn., Azusa Pacific U., Calif., 1987. Cert. tchr. Calif., 1977, NATA, 1978. Tchr. Azusa Unified Sch. Dist., Calif., 1978—. Athletic dir. Azusa H.S., 1993—, athletic trainer, 1978—2006, softball coach, 1978—93. Named Tchr. of Yr., Azusa Unified Sch. Dist., 1990, Athletic Dir. of Yr., CSADA, 2003; recipient T.H.E. award, Azusa Unified Sch. Dist., 2004. Mem.: Calif. Assn. Health, Phys. Edn., Recreation and Dance, Foothill Citrus Athletic Assn., Calif. State Athletic Dirs. Assn. (at-large rep.). Avocations: exercise, water sports, reading, crafts, piano. Office: Azusa HS 240 N Cerritos Ave Azusa CA 91702 Personal E-mail: tsgahring@adelphia.net.

GAILIE, KRISTINA ANN, music educator; b. Newfane, NY, Apr. 3, 1979; d. James Richard Gailie and Denise Marie West. BM, Crane Sch. of Music at SUNY Potsdam, 1997—2001; EDM, U. at Buffalo, 2002—04. Instrumental music tchr. Niagara Mid. Sch., Niagara Falls, NY, 2001—. Edn./ performance intern Jazz at Lincoln Ctr., NY, 2001. Musician: (big band performance) Women of Jazz by Women of Jazz (Buffalo's Best Big Band, 2004). Mem.: NY State Mid. Sch. Assn., Music Educators Nat. Assn., Sigma Alpha Iota (treas. 1999—2000). R-Consevative. Roman Catholic. Avocations: scuba diving, skiing. Office: Niagara Middle Sch 6431 Girard Ave Niagara Falls NY 14304 Home: 6002 Stephenson Ave Niagara Falls NY 14304 Office Phone: 716-278-9120. Office Fax: 716-278-9122. Personal E-mail: gailie98@yahoo.com. E-mail: kgailie@nfschools.net.

GAILLARD, MARGARET, communications executive; m. Michael Gaillard, 1985. BA, Northeastern Mo. St. Univ., 1981; BS in Bus. Mgmt., Univ. Md., Coll. Park, 1996. Drafter, drafting supervisor, corp. design dept. ATC (now Time Warner Cable), 1981—83; owner, founder Butler Drafting Svc., 1983—85; designer, drafter United Cable, 1985—89; mgr., design and drafting Jones Intercable, 1989—96; project engr. TCI (now AT&T Broadband), 1996—. Mem.: Soc. Cable Telecom. Engrs. (Women in Tech. award 2000). Office: AT&T Broadband 1500 Market St Philadelphia PA 19102*

GAILLARD, MARY KATHARINE, physicist, educator; b. New Brunswick, NJ, Apr. 1, 1939; d. Philip Lee and Marion Catharine (Wiedemayer) Ralph; children: Alain, Dominique, Bruno. BA, Hollins Coll., Va., 1960; MA, Columbia U., 1961; Dr du Troiseme Cycle, U. Paris, Orsay, France, 1964, Dr-es-Sciences d'Etat, 1968. With Ctr. Nat. Rsch. Sci., Orsay and Annecy-le-Vieux, France, 1964-84, head rsch. Orsay, 1973-80, Annecy-le-Vieux, 1979-80, dir. rsch., 1980-84; prof. physics, sr. faculty staff Lawrence Berkeley lab. U. Calif., Berkeley, 1981—. Morris Loeb lectr. Harvard U., Cambridge, Mass., 1980; Chancellor's Disting. lectr., U. Calif., Berkeley, 1981; Warner-Lambert lectr. U. Mich., Ann Arbor, 1984; vis. scientist Fermi Nat. Accelerator Lab., Batavia, Ill., 1973-74, Inst. for Advanced Studies, Santa Barbara, Calif., 1984, U. Calif., Santa Barbara, 1985; group leader L.A.P.P., Theory Group, France, 1979-81, Theory Physics div. LBL, Berkeley, 1985-87; sci. dir. Les Houches (France) Summer Sch., 1981; cons., mem. adv. panels U.S. Dept. Energy, Washington; cons. Nat. Sci. Bd., 1996-97, 2002, bd. dirs., 1997-2002. Co-editor: Weak Interactions, 1977, Gauge Theories in High Energy Physics, 1983; contbr. articles to profl. jours. Recipient Thibaux prize U. Lyons (France) Acad. Art and Sci., 1977, E.O. Lawrence award, 1988, J.J. Sakurai prize for theoretical particle physics, APS, 1993; Guggenheim fellow, 1989-90. Fellow Am. Acad. Arts and Scis., Am. Phys. Soc. (mem. various coms., chair com. on women, J.J. Saburai prize 1993); mem. AAAS, NAS, Am. Philos. Soc. Office: U Calif Dept Physics Berkeley CA 94720-0001

GAINER, LEILA J., media relations executive, golf industry specialist; b. Balt., Dec. 4, 1948; d. Theodore and Leila Lee Dworkowski (dec.); stepmother: Madeline Dworkowski. BA, Frostburg (Md.) State Coll., 1970. Reporter, editor Labor Law Guide, Coll. and Univ. Report, Commerce Clearing House, Inc., Washington; dir. Ctr. for Regional Action Nat. Assn. Regional Coun. Local Govts., Washington; dir. nat. affairs Am. Soc. for Tng. and Devel., Alexandria, Va.; dir. pub. rels. Lesnik, Himmelsbach, Wilson, Hearl Advt., PR, Myrtle Beach, S.C. Freelance editor, writer. Co-author: Training in America: The Organization and Strategic Role of Training, Workplace Basics: The Essential Skills Employers Want, Workplace Basics: Training Manual, Training the Technical Workforce; author tng. monographs, articles on golf, golf course revs., personality profiles on golf course archs. and others, and equipment. Honored by Pres. Carter for Leadership on 1980 Rural Devel. Act. Office Phone: 843-448-1123. E-mail: lgainer@lhwh.com.

GAINES, BRENDA J., retired financial services company executive; b. Chgo., July 22, 1949; d. Clarence and DeLouise Gaines. BA, U. Ill., 1970; MA, Roosevelt U., 1976. Spl. asst. to regional adminstr then dep. regional adminstr. US Dept. Housing & Urban Devel., Chgo.; commr. Housing Authority City of Chgo., dep. chief staff to Mayor Harold Washington, 1985—87; advanced through co. in govt. and cmty. rels. to sr. v.p. residential lending Citigroup, Inc., Chgo., 1988—92; sr. v.p. Diners Club N.Am. (subsidiary of Citigroup), Chgo., 1992—99, pres., 1999—2004. Mem. Diners Club Internat. Global bd.; bd. dirs. CNA Financial, Nicor, Inc., Tenet Healthcare Corp., Office Depot, Inc, Fannie Mae, 2006—. Named Volunteer of the Yr., Boys & Girls Club Chgo., 1999; named one of 50 Most Powerful Black Executives in Am., Fortune, 2002, Chicago's 100 Most Influential Women, Crain's Chicago Business, 2004; recipient Black Achievers in Industry award, 1995, Pioneer award, Urban Bankers Forum, 1996, Woman of Achievement award, Anti-Defamation League, Otto Wirth award, Roosevelt U., 2000.*

GAINES, KENDRA HOLLY, language educator; b. Chgo., Dec. 6, 1946; d. Reuben B. and Frances P. Gaines; m. Kenneth C. Wolfgang, Feb. 18, 1989. BA with distinction, Mt. Holyoke Coll., 1968; MA with honor, Claremont Grad. Sch., 1971; MA, Northwestern U., 1974, PhD, 1982. Cert. life secondary and community coll. tchr., Calif., Ariz. Tchr. English, Claremont (Calif.) Collegiate Sch., 1969-72; teaching asst. Northwestern U., Evanston, Ill., 1975-78; instr. English, U. Mich., Ann Arbor, 1978-79; assoc. editor Scott, Foresman Co., Glenview, 1983-85; instr. English, sr. career tutor U. Ariz., Tucson, 1985—2002, mgr. Grad. Writing Resource website, 2002—; instr., faculty advisor Pima C.C., Davis-Monthan AFB, Ariz., 1987—. Head Grad. Writing Inst., U. Ariz., 1996—2002; editl. cons., freelance writer, 1969—; lectr. Suzhou U., Nanjing Normal U., China, 1999; mem. adv. bd. translation studies Pima C.C.; writing cons. U. Ariz. Coll. Law; trainer S.W. Gas Corp., Geico Ins.; writing cons. to Arizona Daily Star newspaper, Tucson,

2002—; online instr. Colo. Tech. U., 2005—. Contbr. articles to various publs.; writer radio scripts Holiday World of Travel, 1969—2000. Elected to The Imperial Russian Order of St. John of Jerusalem Ecumenical Found. (Knights of Malta), N.Y.; grantee State of Calif., 1970; Mills fellow, 1971; fellow Northwestern U., 1973-76. Mem. MLA, Nat. Coun. Tchrs. English, AAUW. Avocations: travel, photography, music, creative writing, aerobics. Home: 925 N Jerrie Ave Tucson AZ 85711-1153 Office: U Ariz Grad Coll Tucson AZ 85719 E-mail: kgaines@email.arizona.edu.

GAINES, LA DONNA ADRIAN See SUMMER, DONNA

GAINES, RUTH ANN, secondary school educator; BA in Drama and Speech, Clarke Coll.; MA in Dramatic Art, U. Calif., Santa Barbara. Tchr. drama East High Sch., Des Moines, 1971—. Host Classroom Connection Cable TV; former TV/radio prodr., talk show host TCI of Ctrl. Iowa, WHO; diversity facilitator Heartland Area Edn. Agy., Des Moines, 1979—; instr. speech and drama Des Moines Area C.C., 1971—. Bd. dirs. Very Spl. Arts, Hospice of Ctrl. Iowa, Westminster Ho.; former bd. dirs. YWCA of Greater Des Moines, Polk County Mental Health Assn., Drama Workshop, Des Moines Tutoring Ctr.; vice chair City Wide Strategic Plan, 1994-95; state senate candidate, 1994; racial justice coord. YWCA, 1992-93; chair Cross Cultural Rels., Des Moines Area Religious Coun., 1988-89; dir. religious edn. St. Ambrose Cathedral, 1981-83; grad. Leadership Iowa Class of 1997. Recipient Wal-Mart Tchr. of Yr., 1998, Iowa Tchr. of Yr., 1998, Angel in Adoption award, 1999, Friends of Iowa Civil Rights Commn. Tchr. of Yr. award, 2000, U. Iowa's Phyllis M. Yeager Commitment to Diversity award, 2001, I'll Make Me a World in Iowa Heritage Legacy, 2002, Des Moines Bus. Records' Woman of Influence, 2002, USA Today's All USA Tchr. Recognition 3d Team, 2002; grad. Greater Des Moines Leadership Inst., 2002; inducted into Nat. Tchr. Hall of Fame, 2003. Mem. Iowa Edn. Assn., Des Moines Edn. Assn., Delta Kappa Gamma, Phi Delta Kappa, Delta Sigma Theta, Delta Kappa Pi. Home: 3501 Oxford St Des Moines IA 50313-4562 Office: East High Sch 815 E 13th St Des Moines IA 50316-3499

GAINES-MASAK, ANNE FARLEY, artist, art educator; b. Grand Rapids, Mich., May 19, 1954; d. Ralph Clay and Nancy Bogue (Farley) G.; m. David Michael Masak, Nov. 26, 1999; stepchildren: Chad, Ryan. BA magna cum laude, Principia Coll., 1976; MA, MFA, Bowling Green State U., 1980. Instr. in color theory and fashion drawing Internat. Acad. Design and Tech., Chgo., 1987-92, 2000—; commd. muralist Sara Lee Bakery Headqtrs., Chgo., 1992-93; artist in residence Chgo. Jr. Sch., Elgin, Ill., 1993-94, art tchr. grades 1-8, 1994-95; vis. asst. prof. art Ripon (Wis.) Coll., 1995-97; adj. prof. of art and humanities Moraine Valley C.C., Palos Hills, Ill., 1997-99. Vis. scholar Principia Coll., Elsah, Ill., 1989; owner, artist Pilsen Screens, Chgo., 1990—; mem. adv. bd. Collegiate Press, 1998—; instr. at art workshops, Chgo., Mich., Fla. Illustrator: (book) From Greek to Graffiti, English Words that Survive and Thrive, 1981, (cover design) A Walking Tour of Wicker Park by Elaine Coorens, 2003; artist solo exhbns. include Lighthouse Gallery, Tequesta, Fla., 1983, South Haven (Mich.) Ctr. for Fine Arts, 1990, Wilderness at A.R.C. Gallery, Chgo., 1995, Strange Yards and Other Eulogies, Harper Coll., Palatine, Ill., Outer Depictions/Inward Questions, De Caprio Gallery, Moraine Valley C.C., Palos Hills, Ill., 1997, A.R.C. Galllery, Chgo., 2000; selected group exhbns.: Stockton State Coll., Pomona, N.J., 1985, Ill. State Mus., Springfield, 1985, Ukranian Inst. Art, Chgo., 1988, Alice and Arthur Baer Juried Competition, Beverly Art Ctr., Chgo., 1989, Quincy (Ill.) Art Ctr., 1989, Watercolor Alternatives -4 Chgo. artists- South Bend Art Ctr., Women's Art League Gallery, 1990, Botanics Gallery 10, Rockford, Ill. (1st place), 1991, Sacred Arts, Billy Graham Ctr. Mus., Wheaton (Ill.) Coll., 1992, Chgo. Botanic Gardens, Glencoe, Ill., 1992, Barrington (Ill.) Area Arts Coun. Gallery, 1993, Coll. Lake County, Grays Lake, Ill., 1993, Caestecker Gallery, Ripon (Wis.) Coll., 1995, P.E.A.C.E. Gallery, Chgo., 1996, Mus. Sci. and Industry, Chgo., 1996, Jacqueline Ross Gallery, Chgo., 1998, Landscapes, Portraits and a Touch of Fantasy, A.R.C. Gallery, Chgo., 2000, European Influence, 2003, Transformations, T2 Gallery, Chgo., 2003, numerous others; works in pub. collections: Am. Nat. Bank, Chgo., Borg Warner, Chgo., Bowling Green (Ohio) State U., Ernst & Young, Chgo., G.A.T.X. Corp., Chgo., Harper Elem. Sch., Wilmette, Ill., Nat. Soc. Am. Colls. and Univs., Washington, D.C., Rockford Art Mus., Sara Lee Bakery, Chgo.; major commns. include 21 x 8 mural, Conf. Rm., Bowling Green (Ohio) State U., 1979, 4 20 x 12 painted solar fabric murals, Sara Lee Bakery, Chgo., 1992-93, Palmer Ho., Chgo., mixed media installation and watercolors, office suite, Fox Valley Neurosurgery, McHenry Ill., 1995, 4 mixed-media panels Valley Hosp., Ridgewood, N.J., 1999, 5 x 8 painting mix media, 17th Church Christ, Chgo., 2001, 6 x 9 folding screen, Lockhart Nature Ctr., Lake Forest, Ill., 2001; chief designer, coord. set design PM&L Theater, Antioch, Ill. Lectr. com. chmn. 17th Ch. of Christ, Scientist, Chgo., 1996-98. Named Accomplished Grad. Honoree in Fine Arts, Bowling Green (Ohio) State U., 1992; grantee: Ill. Arts Coun., Chgo., 1986, Ripon (Wis.) Coll., 1995, 96, Chgo. Matters Mural Project, 2005-06. Mem. Nat. Assn. Women Bus. Owners, Coll. Art Assn., Women's Caucus for Arts, Chgo. Artists Coalition, A.R.C. Gallery (grant chmn., chair self-portrait show 1984-86), Pilsen Artists (chair open house 1981, 90, fund raising 1991-95). Avocations: playing classical piano, choral singing, gourmet cooking, renovating Victorian houses. Home: 713 W 19th St Chicago IL 60616-1023 Office: Pilsen Screens 713 W 19th St # 1 Chicago IL 60616-1023 Office Phone: 312-829-2746. E-mail: gainesart@yahoo.com.

GAINES-PAGE, RENA L., science educator; d. Llyod William Gaines and Jo-Dee Petre; m. David H. Page III, Apr. 19, 1987. BS in Phys. Anthropology, U. Calif., Davis, 1986. Cert. tchng. credential Calif. Secondary tchr. Wilson HS, LA, 1989—91; seconday tchr. Huntington Pk. (Calif.) HS, 1991—. Sci. dept. chairperson Huntington Pk. HS, 2003—05, sci. dept. coord., 2005—. Mem.: Calif. Tchg. Assn. Office: Huntington Park HS 6020 Miles Ave Huntington Park CA 90255 Office Phone: 323-583-3333.

GAIOTTI, REGINA, civil engineer, educator; b. Montreal, Que., Canada, Apr. 27, 1963; BEng, McGill U., Montreal, 1986; PhD in Civil Engring., McGill U., 1990. Registered profl. engr., Que., Can., 1987. Structural engr. Lavalin - Experts-Conseils Shawinigan Inc., Montreal, 1990—91; adj. prof. McGill U., 1991; structural engr. SNC-Lavalin Inc., Montreal, 1991—93; sr. static and dynamic engr., numerical analysis group Pratt & Whitney Can., Longueuil, Que., Canada, 1993—95; adj. assoc. prof. So. Meth. U., Dallas, 2001—06, lectr., 2006—. Faculty advisor Engrs. Without Borders - So. Meth. U. Student Chpt., 2006. Recipient Environ. and Civil Engring. Outstanding Faculty award, So. Meth. U., Sch. of Engring., 2005—06, Ernest Brown Gold medal, McGill U., 1986; scholar Postgrad. scholar, Natural Sci. and Engring. Rsch. Coun. (Can.), 1986—90. Mem.: Order of Engrs. of Que. Achievements include research in interactive effects of nonstructural elementson the behavior of tall building structures. Office: Southern Methodist University PO Box 750340 Dallas TX 75275-0340 Office Phone: 214-768-1721. E-mail: rgaiott@engr.smu.edu.

GAISSER, JULIA HAIG, classics educator; b. Cripple Creek, Colo., Jan. 12, 1941; d. Henry Wolseley and Gertrude Alice (Lent) Haig; m. Thomas Korff Gaisser, Dec. 29, 1964; 1 child, Thomas Wolseley. AB, Brown U., 1962; MA, Harvard U., 1966; PhD, U. Edinburgh, Scotland, 1966. Asst. prof. Newton (Mass.) Coll., 1966-69, Swarthmore (Pa.) Coll., 1970-72, Bklyn. Coll., 1973-75; assoc. prof. dept. Latin Bryn Mawr (Pa.) Coll., 1975-84, prof., 1984—. Martin Classical lectr. Oberlin Coll., 2000. Author: Catullus and his Renaissance Readers, 1993, Pierio Valeriano On the Ill Fortune of Learned Men, 1999, Catullus in English, 2001; editor Bryn Mawr Latin Commentaries, 1983—. Mem. Mid-East sel. com. Marshall Scholarships, Washington, 1975-89, chmn., 1984-89; mem. mng. com. Intercollegiate Ctr. for Classical Studies in Rome, Stanford, Calif., 1984-92, chmn., 1988-92. Decorated MBE; named Marshall scholar, U. Edinburgh, 1962—64, Phi Beta Kappa Vis. scholar, 1996—97, ACLS Travel grantee, 1985, fellow, ACLS, 1989—90, NEH sr. fellow, 1985—86, 1993—94, 1999; recipient NEH summer stipend, 1977, rsch. grantee, Am. Philos. Soc., 1980, 1993. Mem. Am. Philol. Assn. (dir. 1985-88, pres. 2000), Renaissance Soc. Am., Internat. Neo Latin Soc., Am. Philos. Soc. Office: Bryn Mawr Coll Dept Latin Bryn Mawr PA 19010

GAITHER, ANN HEAFNER, sales executive; b. Lincolnton, N.C., Feb. 12, 1932; d. James Harian and Evangeline (Houser) Heafner; m. Albert Cowles Gaither, July 25, 1953; children: William Harlan, Susan Gaither Jones, Lawson Heafner, Albert Comer. MusB, U. N.C., Greensboro, 1953; postgrad. in bus. adminstrn., Catawba Valley Tech. Coll., 1974-76. Music coord. city schs., Enterprise, Ala., 1953-54, Davidson, N.C., 1954-55; sales cons. Ridgeview Mills, Inc., Newton, N.C., 1973-74; from v.p. mktg. to sr. v.p. Heafner Tire Co., Inc., Lincolnton, 1974-84; pres. Heafner Data Svcs., Lincolnton, 1983—; exec. v.p., CEO J.H. Heafner Co., Lincolnton, 1984-86, pres., 1986-90, chairperson, 1988—, also bd. dirs. Bd. dirs. N.C. Nat. Bank, Lincolnton; mem. adv. bd. Bryan Sch. Bus. and Econs. U. N.C., Greensboro, 1989—. Bd. dirs. Catawba Valley Tech. Coll. Found., Hickory, N.C., 1985; mem. com. of 200, 1985—; bd. advisors Gardner-Webb Coll., Boiling Springs, N.C., 1982, chmn., 1983-85; bd. visitors Davidson Coll., N.C., 1985—, Wake Forest Univ. Babcock Sch. Mgmt., Winston-Salem, N.C., 1986; bd. dirs. Broyhill Acad. for Free Enterprise, 1980—, U.S. Small Bus. Adminstrn., 1987—, N.C. Citizens for Bus. and Industry, 1994—, N.C. Dept. Transportation, 1993—, Carolinas Partnership, 1993; trustee U. N.C., Greensboro, 1989, chmn., 1991; pres. svc. league Bas Blue Club, Newton, N.C., 1964-65; mem. Gov.'s Bus. Coun. on Arts and Humanities State of N.C., 1989—; mem. foresight com., econ. devel. com. Catawa County, N.C., 1986—. Recipient Bus. Leader of the Yr. award Bus. Coun. of Lenoir Rhyne Coll., 1995, Vocat. and Cmty. Svc. award Newton Conover Rotary Club, 1994; named to Savvy 60 List, Top Women Bus. Execs., 1990, one of Top 50 Women Bus. Owners, Working Woman Mag., 1993-95. Mem. Nat. Assn. Tire Dealers, Pvt. Brand Tire Dealers, Lincoln County C. of C. (bd. dirs.), Soc. Internat. Bus. Fellows, Hickory Choral Soc., Rotary (first woman mem.). Democrat. Presbyterian. Avocations: travel, arts, gardening.

GAITHER, SUSAN ANNE, business education educator; b. Madison, W.Va., June 21, 1952; d. Annie Sue and Charles Edward Harmon; children: Justin Alan, Kelly Suzanne, Joshua Aaron. ABD in Higher Edn., U. Ark., Little Rock, 2005. Bus. divsn. instr. Delight Pub. Schs., Ark., 1988—97, Nat. Pk. C.C., Hot Springs, Ark., 1997—. Recipient Outstanding Faculty award, Nat. Pk. C.C., 2005-2006. Mem.: Nat. Bus. Edn. Assn. Office: Nat Pk CC 101 College Dr Hot Springs AR 71913 Office Phone: 501-760-4257. Business E-Mail: sgaither@npcc.edu.

GAITSKILL, MARY LAWRENCE, writer, educator; b. Lexington, Ky., Nov. 11, 1954; d. Lawrence Russell and Dorothy Jane Gaitskill; m. Peter Jay Trachtenberg, Sept. 15, 2001. BA, U. Mich., Ann Arbor, 1981. Adj. prof. U. Calif., Berkeley, 1995; assoc. prof. U. Houston, 1996—97; vis. lectr. NYU, N.Y.C., 1999, New Sch., N.Y.C., 2000, Brown U., Providence, 2001; assoc. prof. Syracuse (N.Y.) U., 2002—. Author: (novel) Two Girls Fat and Thin, 1991, Veronica, 2005 (One of the 10 Best Books of the Yr. NY Times, 2005), (story collection) Bad Behavior, 1988, Because They Wanted To, 1997. Host mother Fresh Air Fund, N.Y.C., 2002—. Nominee Nat. Book Critics Cir. award, 2005; recipient Pen-Faulkner award nomination, 1998, Nat. Book award nomination, 2005; fellow, Guggenheim Found., 2002. Mem.: PEN. Avocation: acting in community theater. Office: 100 University 401 Hall Syracuse NY 13244

GAJDA, SHIRLI KUBIAK, literature and language educator; b. Ind., May 22, 1970; d. Ray and Nancy Kubiak; m. Paul Neil Gajda, June 10, 2006. BS in Mid. Sch. Edn., Ill. State U., Normal, 1993; M in Curriculum and Instrn., No. Ill. U., DeKalb, 2001. Title I reading tchr. Odell (Ill.) Grade Sch., 1994—98; tchr. lit. and lang. arts Lake Zurich Mid. Sch. North, Hawthorn Woods, Ill., 1998—. Volleyball coach Lake Zurich Mid. Sch. North, 2003—. Recipient Meritorious Svc. award, Dist. 95, 2004—05. Mem.: NEA (dist. union rep.), Lake Zurich Edn. Assn., Ill. Edn. Assn. Home: 2015 N Spruce Terr Arlington Heights IL 60004 Office: Lake Zurich Mid Sch N 95 Hubbard Ln Hawthorn Woods IL 60047 Office Phone: 847-719-3600. Business E-Mail: shirli.gajda@lz95.org.

GAJIC, RANKA PEJOVIC, secondary school educator; b. Mostar, Bosnia-Herzegovina, Apr. 30, 1928; came to U.S., 1953; d. Radovan Ilija and Darinka Ducic Pejovic; m. Sreten Gajic, Sept. 26, 1954 (dec. Apr. 1991). Student, Belgrade (Yugoslavia) U., 1947-52; B Art Edn., Northeastern Ill. U., 1973; M Slavic Langs. and Lit., U. Ill., Chgo., 1979, ABD, 1990; MLS, Chgo. State U., 1987; PhD in Edn., Century U., 1995. Acct. Field Enterprises Ednl. Corp., Chgo., 1955-59; ins. policy writer Alexander & Co. Ins., Chgo., 1959-64; fgn. ind. travel agt. Am. Express, Chgo., 1964-69; tchr. Chgo. Pub. Schs., 1974-84, 85—; tchg. asst. U. Ill., Chgo., 1984-85. Exhibited paintings in group shows at Northeastern Ill. U., Chgo., 1976 (3d prize) Mus. Sci. and Industry, Chgo., 1976 (Hon. Mention), North River Gallery, Chgo., 1977, 79 (2d prize 1977, Hon. Mention 1979). Chgo. State U. scholar, 1986; recipient Nat. Collegiate award U.S. Achievement Acad., 1987, Am. Medal of Honor ABI, 2000, Lifetime Achievement award IBC, Cambridge, Eng., 2002, Women of Yr. award ABI, 2002; named to Hall of Fame, ABI, 2003. Mem. Am. Assn. for Advancement of Slavic Studies, U. Ill. Alumni Assn. (life), Mus. Contemporary Art (comm. chair North Side Affiliates chpt. 1999—), Golden Key Nat. Honor Soc. Avocations: art, literature, languages, travel. Home: 5901 N Sheridan Rd Apt 12J Chicago IL 60660-3638

GAJL-PECZALSKA, KAZIMIERA J., retired surgeon, pathologist, educator; b. Warsaw, Nov. 15, 1925; came to U.S., 1970; d. Kazimierz Emil and Anna Janina (Gervais) Gajl; widowed; children: Kazimierz Peczalski, Andrew Peczalski. Student, Jagiellonian Univ., Cracov, Poland, 1945-47; MD, Warsaw U., Poland, 1951, PhD in Immunopathology, 1964. Diplomate Polish Bd. Pediatrics, Polish Bd. Anatomic Pathology, Am. Bd. Pathology. Attending pediatrician Children's Hosp. for Infectious Diseases, Warsaw, Poland, 1953-58, head, pathology lab., 1958-65; adj. prof. Postgrad. Med. Sch., Warsaw, Poland, 1965-70; fellow U. Minn., Mpls., 1970-72, asst. prof. dept. pathology, 1972-75, assoc. prof. dept. pathology, 1975-79, prof. dept. pathology, 1979-00, dir. immunophenotyping and flow lab., 1974-00, dir. cytology dept. pathology, 1976-95; ret., 2000. Author chpts. to book; contbr. of numerous papers to profl. jours. Fellow WHO, Paris, 1959, London, 1962, Paris, 1967, U.S. Pub. Health Svcs. fellow, 1968-69; recipient Scientific Com. award Polish Ministry of Health and Social Welfare, 1964. Mem. Am. Soc. Experimental Pathology, Am. Soc. Cytology, Internat. Acad. Pathology, British Soc. Pediatric Pathology, Polish Soc. Pathology, Polish Soc Pediatricians. Roman Catholic. Avocations: music, skiing.

GALA, DEBRA GAIL, elementary school educator; m. Edaward Gala, Aug. 28, 1983; children: Jordan, Jessica. BA, U. Calif., Santa Barbara. Tchr. Marshall HS, LA, 1990—2001, Irvine (Calif.) HS, 2001—. Home: 20612 Kelvin Ln Huntington Beach CA Office: Irvine High Sch 4321 Walnut Ave Irvine CA 92604 Business E-Mail: dgala@iusd.org.

GALAGAN, CAROL ANNE, special education educator; b. Vancouver, Wash., Dec. 26, 1963; d. John Michael and Madeline Galagan. AA, Bakersfield C.C., Bakersfieled, Calif., 1984; BA Liberal Studies, Calif. State U., Bakersfield, Calif., 1987. Calif. Asst. Tech. Project (CTAP) Levels I & II Kern County Supt. of Schools, 2003; Multiple Subject Tchg. Credential with Crosscultural Language & Academic Devel. Calif. Commn. on Tchr. Credentialing, 1999, Edn. Specialist Instruction Credential Calif. Commn. on Tchr. Credentialing, 2004, Crisis Prevention Inst. (CPI) Non-violent tng. Panama-Buena Vista Union Sch. Dist., 2005, cert. CPR Panama-Buena Vista Union Sch. Dist., 2005. Sub. tchr. Panama-Buena Vista Union Sch. Dist., Bakersfield, Calif., 1997—99; tchr., resource specialist Panama-Union Sch. Dist., Bakersfield, Calif., 1999—. Safety compliance coord. Freymiller Trucking, Bakersfield, Calif., Okla. City, 1991—97; english tchr. Ednl. Svcs. Exhchange with China, Tangshan City, China, 1991; student study team coord./facilitator Panama-Buena Vista Union Sch. Dist.: Panama Sch., Leo B. Hart Sch., Bakersfield, Calif., 2002—; sci. fair com. Panama-Buena Vista Union Sch. Dist., Leo B. Hart Sch., Bakersfield, Calif., 2005—06. Mem. talent show com. Leo B. Hart Sch., Bakersfield, Calif., 2004—06; team leader, coord. Mission to Mexico, All Saints Episcopal Ch., 1999, 2000, 2003; vol. Spl. Olympics, 2003, 2004; vestry, sr. warden, jr. warden, vestryman All Saints Episcopal Ch., Bakersfield, Calif., 1998—2002, vestryman, 2006—, youth dir./leader Bakersfield, Calif., 1997—2004, hearts and hands ministry leader, 2004—; vestry mem. Episcopal Ch. of the Resurrection, Oklahoma City, 1997; del. San Joaquin Diocesan Convention, All Saints Episc. Ch., Bakersfield, Calif., 1991—93, 1997—99, 2001—02, 2005—. Mem.: Coun. for Exceptional Children (membership chair, local u. chpt. 2002—03). R-Consevative. Episcopalian. Avocations: counted cross stitch, reading. Personal E-mail: cgalagan@bak.rr.com.

GALAMORE, SHANNON, mathematics educator; b. Birmingham, Ala., Mar. 24, 1971; children: Kelsey Nicole Price, William Allen Galamore Price. AA, U. Ala., Birmingham, 1999, EdM, 1995; BS, U. Montevallo, Ala., 1993. Cert. nat. bd. for profl. tchg. stds. Ala., 2004. Math. tchr. Hewitt-Trussville Mid. Sch., Ala., 1995—96, Clay-Chalkville Mid. Sch., Ala., 1996—2003, Shades Valley H.S., Irondale, Ala., 2003—, ITT Tech. Inst., Bessemer, Ala., 2005—. Math. tchr. Jefferson State C.C., Birmingham, 2000—. Mem.: Nat. Coun. Tchrs. Math. Office: Shades Valley High School 6100 Old Leeds Rd Irondale AL 35126 Office Phone: 205-379-5350.

GALANAKIS, PATRICIA SARIGIANIS, special education resource educator; b. Balt., Oct. 3, 1964; d. Jim and Diamando (Stamatopoulos) S.; m. Constantine J. Galanakis, July 18, 1998. BA in Elem. Edn., Loyola Coll., Balt., 1986; MS in Reading Specialist, Johns Hopkins U., 1990, CAGS in Early Childhood Spl. Edn., 2000. Spl. edn. tchr. Carroll County Bd. Edn., Westminster, Md., 1986—. Counselor Chesapeake Youth Coun. Camp, Glyndon, Md., 1985-98, St. Demetrios Ch. Young Adult League, Balt., 1988-98; Sunday sch. tchr. St. Demetrios Ch., 1977-2002, 2005—. Mem. Coun. for Exceptional Children (sec. 1990-94). Greek Orthodox. Home: 5969 Cecil Way Eldersburg MD 21784-8576 Office: Sandymount Sch 2222 Old Westminster Pike Finksburg MD 21048-1636

GALANG, MONICA LYNN, science educator, department chairman; b. Akron, Ohio, Sept. 4, 1970; d. Larry Eugene and Marilyn Anita VanCant; m. Nicholas Stith Galang, July 28, 2004; 1 child, Brianna Michele VanCant. BS cum laude, U. Akron, 1994; MA, Ashland U., 1999. Phys. sci. tchr. Copley-Fairlawn Mid. Sch., Ohio, 1994—. Vol. Julia de Burgos, Cleve., 2005—06. D-Conservative. Roman Cath. Avocations: reading, travel, cooking. Home: 55 Quaker Ridge Dr Akron OH 44313 Office: Copley-Fairlawn Mid Sch 1531 S Cleve Massillon Rd Copley OH 44321 Personal E-mail: mlvlatina@yahoo.com. Business E-Mail: mgalang@mail.neonet.k12.oh.us.

GALANTE, JANE HOHFELD, musician, music historian; b. San Francisco, Feb. 14, 1924; d. Edward and Lillian (Devendorf) Hohfeld; m. Clement Galante, Dec. 26, 1956; children: Edward Elio, John Clement. AB, Vassar Coll., 1944; MA, U. Calif., Berkeley, 1949. Instr. U. Calif. Ext., Berkeley, 1948—51, Mills Coll., Oakland, Calif., 1951—54. Founder, dir. Composers' Forum of San Francisco, 1946-56. Music editor Berkeley, A Jour. Modern Culture, 1944-52; concert pianist German tours for USIS, 1952-54; Young Audience Concerts, San Francisco, 1963-70; mem. Lyra Chamber Music Ensemble, 1980-90; transl.: Darius Milhaud (Paul Collaer) including revised and edited catalog Milhaud's Compositions, 1988, Darius Milhaud: Interviews with Claude Rostand, 2002. Trustee Morrison Chamber Music Ctr., San Francisco State U., 1956—; hon. trustee San Francisco Conservatory Music, 1970-99; co-founder San Francisco Friends of Chamber Music, 1999. Decorated chevalier de l'ordre des arts et des lettres; recipient Disting. Svc. award Chamber Music Am., 1992, Pres.'s medal San Francisco State U., 1998. Mem.: Am. Fedn. Musicians.

GALATAS, RUTH ANN, musician, publishing executive, educator; b. New Orleans, La., June 29, 1958; d. Robert I. and Shirley A. Galatas; m. Rick Sands. BFA, La. Tech., 1980; MFA, U. Fla., 1982; MusD, U. Miami, 1989. Tchr. Miami Dade C.C., Miami, 1994—98; prin., owner Rim Sky Pub., Miami, 1998—. US. liaison Lloyd's of London Music Found., 1990—94; chmn. Frank Angelo Music Fund, 1998—. Musician: (albums) Exhalation of The Soul, 1999, A More Gentle Time, 2001, My Fav Things, 2006; prodr.: (album) Juba Live, 1996, (edit prodr.) At Last, 2002 (Grammy award, 2002). Mem.: Nat. Music Tchrs. Assn. (v.p. 1996), Phi Mu, Sigma Alpha Iota. Methodist. Avocations: swimming, art collecting, miniatures. Office: Rim Sky Pub PO Box 558025 Miami FL 33255 Business E-Mail: rgalatas@bellsouth.net.

GALAZNIK, JUDITH ANN, elementary school educator; d. Thomas Elbert Gatbright and Mary Lucille Gotbright; m. Charlie Mack Galaznik, June 15, 1968; 1 child, Brian Charles. BS in Edn., U. Houston, 1968; MA in Edn., U. Colo., 1990. Tchr. Churchill Elem., Homewood, Ill., 1968—69, Braddock Elem., Alexandria, Va., 1970—72, North Elem., Colonial Hts., Va., 1972—74, Nashville Elem., Nash County, NC, 1974—75, Mission Viejo Elem., Aurora, Colo., 1978—84, Belleview Elem., Greenwood Vill, Colo., 1984—. Coord. elem. sci. Cherry Creek Sch. Dist., Greenwood Vill, 1999—2002, coop. tchr. student tchrs., 1983—2005, sci. rep. profl. learning cmtys., 2004—05. Pres. Homestead Youth Swim Club, Centennial, Colo., 1991; co-coord. deacon body Cherry Creek Presbyn., Greenwood Vill, 1991. Recipient Disting. Tchr. Cherry Creek Chpt. award, Colo. Awards Edn. and Civic Achievement, 1986. Mem.: Denver (Colo.) Mus. Nature and Sci., Nat. Sci. Tchrs. Assn., Denver (Colo.) Art Mus. Avocations: gardening, reading, birdwatching, cross country skiing, tennis. Office: Cherry Creek Schs Belleview Elem 4851 S Dayton St Centennial CO 80112

GALBRAITH, MARIAN, elementary school educator; Tchr. West Side Mid. Sch., Reading and Lang. Arts Dept., Groton, Conn., 1991—, various U., 1986—96; with Conn. State Dept. Edn., Fist Assessment Devel. Lab. Served various com. State Dept. Edn., 1986—93. Bd. dirs. Nat. Edn. Assn., 1993—99. Office: West Side Mid Sch Reading and Lang Arts Dept 250 Brandegee Ave Groton CT 06340

GALBRAITH, MARILYN ANN, secondary school educator; b. San Angelo, Tex., Feb. 1, 1956; d. Leander Victor and Elizabeth Katherine (Hoelscher) Braden; m. John Michael Galbraith, Aug. 20, 1977; children: Charlene, Charles, Kendall, Kimber, Curtis. BS, Tex. Tech. U., Lubbock, 1978, Elem. Endorsement, 1980. Tchr. Menard Elem., Tex., 1978—79; substitute tchr. Andrews Pub. Schs., Tex., 1979—80; tchr. St. John Neumann, Lubbock, 1980—82, Pearsall Elem., Tex., 1982—83; self-employed day care provider Havre, Mont., 1988—90, Ithaca, NY, 1990—98; elem. tchr. Country Day Sch., Gainesville, Fla., 1998—99; tchr. Blacksburg HS, Va., 1999—. Mem. site based com. Blacksburg HS, 2003—05. Adv. Family, Career and Cmty. Leaders Am., Blacksburg, 1999—2006, Future Educators of Am., 2004—06. Mem.: Nat. Tchrs. Assn., Montgomery County Tchrs. Assn.

GALBRAITH, RUTH LEGG, retired dean, home economist; b. Lecompte, La., Nov. 5, 1923; d. Byron S. and Dora Ruth (Lindley) Legg; m. Harry W. Galbraith, June 16, 1950; 1 son, Allan Legg. BS, Purdue U., 1945, PhD, 1950. Chemist E.I. duPont de Nemours, Waynesboro, Va., 1945-46; textile chemist Gen. Electric Co., Bridgeport, Conn., 1946-47; teaching asst. Purdue U., 1947-48, research fellow, 1948-50; prof. textiles and clothing U. Tenn., Knoxville, 1950-55; asso. prof. U. Ill., Urbana, 1956-64, prof., 1964-70, chmn. textiles and clothing div., 1962-70; prof., head consumer affairs dept. Auburn (Ala.) U., 1970-73; dean Sch. Home Econs., head home econs. research, 1973-85. Mem. task force on quality of living Dept. Agr., 1967-68; mem. nat. adv. com. Flammable Fabrics Act, 1971-73; mem. U.S. Dept. Agr. Com. of Nine, 1981-83, chmn., 1983 Mem. editorial bd.: Research Jour. Home Econs., 1973-77, chmn. policy bd., 1978-80; contbr. articles to profl. jours. Recipient Disting. Alumni award Purdue U., 1970 Fellow Am. Inst. Chemists; mem. Am. Home Econs. Assn. (chmn. agy. mem. unit 1975-76, chmn. research sect. 1978-80, Outstanding Home Economist award 1984), Ala. Home Econs. Assn. (pres. 1983-84), Am. Assn. Textile Chemists and Colorists, Am. Chem. Soc., ASTM (3d v.p. com. D-13 textiles 1975-79), Assn. Adminstrs. Home Econs., Nat. Council Adminstrs. Home Econs., AAUW, Sigma Xi, Omicron Nu, Phi Kappa Phi, Delta Kappa Gamma. Home: 368 Singleton St Auburn AL 36830-6317

GALBREATH, LESLIE M., academic administrator; BA in English and Criminal Justice, Northwest Mo. State U., Maryville, MSEd in Ednl. Leadership; EdD in Ednl. Leadership and Policy Analysis, U. Mo., Columbia. Dir., assist and student athlete success programs Northwest Mo. State U., Maryville, 1988—97, dir. talent devel. ctr., 1997—. Membership devel. rep. Midwest Plaines region Sweet Adelines Internat., Tulsa, Okla., 1995—98, internat. membership com., 1997—98; bd. dir. North Andrew H.S. Alumni Assn., Rosendale, Mo., 2005—06, St. Joseph Chorus of Sweet Adelines Internat., St. Joseph, Mo., 1996—99. Mem.: AAUW, Assn. of Higher Edn. and Disability, Nat. Coll. Learning Ctr. Assn., Internat. Coll. Reading and Learning Assn., Northwest Mo. State U. Band Alumni Orgn. Office: NW Mo State Univ 800 Univ Dr Maryville MO 64468 Office Phone: 660-562-1726.

GALE, MICHELLE SUE, retired clinical psychologist; b. Bklyn., Feb. 14, 1954; d. Aaron and Irene (Meizel) G. BA in Folklore, U. Pa., 1976; MA in Psychology, Ga. State U., 1985, PhD in Clin. Psychology, 1991. Lic. psychologist, Ga. Instr., grad. teaching asst. psychology Ga. State U., Atlanta, 1986-87; counselor Atlanta Women's Counseling Collective, 1984-88; psychology intern Counseling and Testing Ctr. U. Ga., Athens, 1990-91; postdoctoral fellow Hub Counseling and Edn. Ctr., Tucker, Ga., 1992-93; pvt. practice Stockbridge, Ga., 1993—; staff psychologist So. Regional Med. Ctr., Riverdale, Ga., 1995—2005; ret. Author: f-News, 1993. Mem. APA, Assn. for Women in Psychology, Ga. Psychol. Assn. Jewish. Home: 144 Grandiflora Dr Mcdonough GA 30253-4688

GALEF, SANDRA RISK, state legislator, educator; b. LaCrosse, Wis., May 7, 1940; d. William P. and Christine Risk; m. Steven Allen Galef, Mar. 30, 1963 (dec.); children: Gregory Todd, Gwendolyn. BS, Purdue U., 1962; MS in Edn., U. Va., 1965. Tchr. Albemarle Schs., Charlottesville, Va., 1962-65, Scarsdale (N.Y.) Schs., 1965-67; mem. Westchester County Bd. Legislators, 1980-93, minority leader, 1984-93; mem. N.Y. State Assembly, Dist. 90, 1993—, chair com. on librs. and ednl. tech. Bd. dirs. Children's Hosp. Found., 1998—, Bethel Nursing Home, 1999—2003; bd. dirs. United Way No. Westchester, 1973—, pres., 1979-80, v.p., 1975-79; trustee Ossining (N.Y.) Pub. Libr., 1975-80, Briarcliff (N.Y.) Nursery Sch., 1974-76; pres. chpt. LWV, 1973-75; chair Ossining Youth Employment Svc., 1977-80; bd. dirs Day Care Coun. Westchester, 1976-79; pub. affairs chair Jr. League Westchester-on-Hudson, Tarrytown, 1978-80, mem. tng. com., 1980-85; mem. adv. bd. Children's Village, Dobbs Ferry, N.Y., 1984—, Interfaith Coun. for Action, Ossining, 1983—; mem. Ossining Upward Bound Substance Abuse Coun., 1984—, Ossining Restoration Com., 1975-77; mem. nominating com. White Plains chpt. ARC, 1985-86; bd. dirs. Phelps Meml. Hosp. Ctr., Vis. Nurse Svcs. Westchester. Recipient Harold J. Marshall award United Way No. Westchester, 1981. Mem. N.Y. Assn. Counties (v.p. 1984-85, pres. 1985, mem. steering com. 1989-92, Legislator of Yr. 1993), Westchester Mcpl. Planning Fedn. (bd. dirs. 1982—), Westchester 2000 (mem. task force 1985), Ossining C. of C. Avocations: gardening, sewing, crafts, decorating. Office: 2 Church St Ossining NY 10562-4802 Office Phone: 914-941-1111. E-mail: galefs@assembly.state.ny.us.

GALESI, DEBORAH LEE, artist; b. Paterson, NJ, Oct. 08; d. John Michael Galesi and Ethel Marchitti; m. Samuel Peace Eagle Dolphin, Oct. 3, 1997. BFA, U. Colo.; studied with, Raymond Whyte and Gene Scarpentoni, NY, Benjamin Long, Florence; MA, Villa Schifanoia/Inst. Florence. One-woman shows include Lo Sprone, Florence, Italy, 1983, Spinetti Gallery, Florence, 1985, Benvenuti Gallery, Venice, 1986, Salaria Gallery, Spoleto, 1987, Lo Spirale, Prato, Italy, 1988, Traghetto Gallery, Venice, 1987; works exhibited at U. Colo., Boulder, 1980, NY Gallery, NYC, 1981, NJ Gallery, 1981, U. Avignon, France, 1981, Sieve Art Expo, Pontassieve, Italy, 1984, Cenacolo Gallery, Florence, 1985, Modigliani Gallery, Milan, 1990, Art Expo, Verona, 1990, Palazzo Congressi, Salsomaggiore, 1995, Palazzo, Florence, 1996, Montserrat Gallery NY, 1997; represented in permanent collections Montserrat Gallery Chelsey, NYC, Amsterdam Whitney Gallery, NYC; contbr. articles to profl. jours. Vol. Natural Resource Def. Coun., Washington, Pacific Whale Found., Hawaii, Ctr. for Marine Conservation, Washington, WWF, Greenpeace. Nat. Art Ctr. award, NY, 1978, others; recipient Stewardess of Ctr. of Light and Harmony award, Sierra Club. Mem. Ptnrs. of Destiny. Avocations: scuba diving, rollerblading, chinese painting, piano, ballet. Office: PMB 523 PO Box 959 Kihei HI 96753-0959

GALINDO, KARLA RAE, retired secondary school educator; b. Palestine, Tex., Nov. 28, 1945; d. C.E. and Doris Elizabeth (Gabourel) Holmes; m. Frank L. Galindo, June 30, 1969. BA, Lamar U., 1968. Cert. secondary tchr., Tex. Tchr., dept. chmn. S. San Antonio (Tex.) HS, 1968-72; curriculum cons. Harlandale Ind. Sch. Dist., San Antonio, 1972-73; tchr., dept. chmn. Harlandale HS, San Antonio, 1973—2002; ret., 2002. Mem. Am. Numismatic Assn., Tex. Numismatic Assn. (asst. medals officer), Soc. of Ration Token Collectors (librarian 1977-87), Daughters of the Rep. of Tex. (assoc. mem., Alamo Couriers Chpt.), DAR (James McHenry Chpt.), U.S. Mil. Vets. Parade Assn., San Antonio Fiesta Comm., Los Bexareños Geneaology Soc., Granaderos and Damas de Galvez, Tex. Connection to Am. Revolution, Gateway Coin Club, San Antonio. Methodist. Avocations: antiques, coin collecting/numismatics, collecting historical memorabilia, travel.

GALIPAULT, LORRAINE D., adult education educator; b. Waterbury, Conn., June 6, 1948; d. Vito John Decarolis and Josephine D'Ascenza; m. Robert Joseph Galipault, Apr. 28, 1973; children: Jennifer, Joanne. BS in Edn., St. John's U., Jamaica, NY, 1970; MS in Edn., Fla. Atlantic U., Boca Raton, 1977, postgrad. Educator Broward County Schs., Ft. Lauderdale, 1973—2006; adj. prof. Fla. Atlantic U., Boca Raton, 2006. Named Tchr. of Yr., Lloyd Estates, 1995. Mem.: Internat. Reading Assn. Home: 7931 NW 89th Ave Tamarac FL 33321

GALITELLO-WOLFE, JANE MARYANN, artist, writer; b. Torrington, Conn., Aug. 27, 1942; d. Morris D. and Rose A. (Abate) Galitello; children: Henry Berg III, Jason Sterling, Marissa Tracy. Student, Ward Sch. Elec., 1961, Porter-Chester Coll., 1982. Nurse aide, Palm Bay, Fla., 1989; decorator, designer Waterbury, Conn.; electronic engr. Torrington, Conn.; sales rep. Thomaston, Conn.; dance tchr. San Jose, Calif.; freelance artist, writer Torrington. Host radio show C.C. Fla., Ct. Teen St. Ministry. Author: Your Gift of Life, 1991 (award 1993), 2d edit., 2002, Snow Bird Melt, 1991, Tody, Heart Desire, Jumping for Jesus, World Wide Irrigation System, 2002; published 3 songs including Let Jesus Take Your Hand - Set You Free, You Answer All My Prayers, Unity Song; inventor hurricane, tornado and fire shelters. Faith healer; active Govt. for Abuse Through Nation and Unity of Nation; advocate for the homeless; active United We Stand in Love; min. Your Gift of Life, WBCC-CoCo Radio.

GALIZZI, MONICA, economics professor; b. Piacenza, Italy, Nov. 12, 1961; arrived in U.S., 1987; d. Giovanni and Giuliana (Vecchiotti) G.; m. Enrico Cagliero, June 25, 1994; children: Diana Anna, Erica B. BS, U. Cattolica, Milan, Italy, 1986; M in Polit. Economy, Boston U., 1990, PhD in Econs., 1994; D in Polit. Economy, U. Milan, Italy, 1990. Rsch. asst. dept. econs. Cath. U., Milan, 1986-87; instr. micro- and macro-economics, dept. econs. Boston U., 1989-92; postdoctorate rsch. fellow in econs. of labor markets U. Limburg, Maastricht, The Netherlands, 1993-94; economist Workers Compensation Rsch. Inst., Cambridge, Mass., 1994-98; adminstrv. dir. program on children Nat. Bur. Econ. Rsch., Cambridge, 1998-99; assoc. prof. dept. econs. U. Mass., Lowell, 1999—. Co-author (with L. Boden): What Are the Most Important Factors Shaping Return to Work? Evidence from Wisconsin, 1996; co-author: (with Boden and T. Liu) The Workers' Story: Results from a Survey of Workers injured in Wisconsin, 1998; co-author: (with G. Gotz and T. Lin) Predictors of Multiple Workers' Compensation Claims in Wisconsin, 2000; contbr. articles to profl. jours. Mem.: Soc. Labor Economists, Ea. Econ. Assn., Workers' Compensation Rsch. Group, European Econ. Assn., Am. Econ. Assn. Home: 76 Paul Revere Rd Lexington MA 02421-6638 Office: U Mass Lowell Dept Econs 1 University Ave Lowell MA 01854-2881 Office Phone: 978-934-2790. Business E-Mail: monica_galizzi@uml.edu.

GALL, LENORE ROSALIE, educational administrator; b. Bklyn., Aug. 9, 1943; d. George W. Gall and Olive Rosalie (Weekes) Gall Bryant. AAS, NYU, 1970, cert. tng. and devel., 1975, BS in Mgmt., 1973, MA in Counselor Edn., 1977; EdM, EdD, Columbia U., 1988. Various positions Ford Found., N.Y.C., 1967-75; dep. dir. career devel. Grad. Sch. Bus., NYU, N.Y.C., 1976-79; dir. career devel. Pace Lubin Sch. Bus., N.Y.C., 1979-82, Sch. Mgmt., Yale U., New Haven, 1982-85; asst. to assoc. provost Bklyn. Coll., 1985-88, asst. to provost, 1988-91; asst. to v.p. acad. affairs Fashion Inst. Tech., 1991-94; asst. provost curriculum and instrn. N.Y.C. Tech. Coll., 1994-2000, dean students and acad. svcs., 2000—. Adj. asst. prof. LaGuardia C.C., L.I. City, N.Y., 1981-90, Sch. Continuing Edn. NYU, 1983-84; dir., sec. devel. workshop Coll. Placement Svcs., Bethlehem, Pa., 1978-81. Bd. dirs. Langston Hughes Cmty. Libr., Corona, N.Y., 1975-83, 86-92, chair, 1975-79, 82-83, 89-92, 2d v.p., 1986, 1st v.p., 1987-88, chair awards com. Dollars for Scholars, Corona, 1976-99, pres., 1999-2003; active audience devel. task force Dance Theatre of Harlem, 1992-98, hon. co-chmn., 1994-95; active alumni coun. Tchrs. Coll., Columbia U., 2000—; bd. trustees Renaissance Charter Sch., 2002, Queens (N.Y.) Borough Pub. Libr., 2003. Recipient Concerned Women of Bklyn., Inc., 1994, Edn. award Stuyvesant Heights Lions Club, Bklyn., N.Y., 1997, Edn. award Girls HS Alumni Assn., Bklyn., N.Y., 2003, Edn. award Key Women Am., Concourse Village Beach, 2003; grantee Jewish Fedn. for the Edn. of Women, 1986-87. Mem. AAUW, Assn. Black Women in Higher Edn. (exec. bd., membership chair, pres.-elect 1988, pres. 1989-93), Am. Assn. Univ. Adminstrs., Nat. Assn. Univ. Women (chaplain 1987-88, 2d v.p. 1988, 1st v.p. 1988-92, dir. N.E. sect. 1993-96, nat. 2d v.p. 1996-98, nat. first v.p. 2000-2002, nat. pres. 2002), Tchr.'s Coll./Columbia U. Alumni Coun. (chmn. nominating com. 2001-), Nat. Assn. Women in Edn., Black Faculty and Staff Assn. Bklyn. Coll. (1st vice-chair 1986-87, chair 1987-88), New Haven C. of C. (chmn. women bus. and industry conf. 1984), Nat. Coun. Negro Women Inc. (life, 1st v.p. North Queens sect. 1986-89, pres. 1989-93), Nat. Assn. Negro Bus. & Profl. Women's Club (Sojourner Truth award 1991), Phi Delta Kappa, Kappa Delta Pi, Pi Lambda Theta, Delta Sigma Theta (chmn. nominating com. Queens Alumni chpt. 2001-03, chmn. tri-com.-arts and letters, project ch., May Week 1999-2002). Mem. A.M.E. Ch. Office: NYC Coll Tech 300 Jay St Jackson Heights NY 11201-1909

GALL, MARY SHEILA, former federal agency administrator; 2 children. BA, Rosary Hill Coll., 1971; MS in Edn., Old Dominion U., 1998. Staff mem. various mems. of Senate and Ho. of Reps., 1971-79; sr. legis. analyst study com. Ho. of Reps., 1980-81; dep. domestic policy adviser Office of V.P. of U.S., 1981-86; counselor to dir. U.S. Office Pers. Mgmt., 1986-89; asst. sec. human devel. svcs. HHS, Washington, 1989-91; commr. U.S. Consumer Product Safety Comm., Washington, 1991—2004. Chair Pres.'s Task Force on Adoption, 1987-89. Dir. rsch. George Bush for Pres. campaign, 1979-80; mem. Reagan-Bush Presdl. campaign and transition team, 1980-81; tchr. Sunday sch. Republican.

GALL, SIMONE ELLEN, music educator; b. Elyria, Ohio, Sept. 7, 1950; d. Rudy and Dorothy Maravich; m. Steven Joseph Gall, June 30, 1974; children: Julie Jeannine, Melanie Nicole. B of Music Edn., Bowling Green State U., 1972. Vocal music tchr. K-6 Elyria City Schs., 1972—78; vocal music tchr. K-8 Amherst (Ohio) Exempted Village Schs., 1985—; dir. Amherst Cmty. Chorus, 1996—. Dir. St. George Serbian Orthodox Ch. Choir, Lorain, Ohio, 1980—2000; dir. music Sandstone Summer Theater, Amherst, 1995—97. Named Lorain Internat. Queen, Lorain Internat. Festival, 1968. Mem.: Music Educators Nat. Conf., Ohio Edn. Assn. Democrat. Avocations: performing at retirement centers and nursing homes, singing and playing for weddings, organizing class reunions. Home: 764 Terra Ln Amherst OH 44001 Office: Amherst Jr H S 548 Milan Ave Amherst OH 44001 E-mail: simonegall51@aol.com.

GALLAGHER, ANNE PORTER, communications executive; b. Coral Gables, Fla., Mar. 16, 1950; d. William Moring and Anne (Jewett) Porter; m. Matthew Philip Gallagher, Jr., July 31, 1976 (div. July 1998); children: Jacqueline Anne, Kevin Sharkey. BA in Edn., Stetson U., 1972. Tchr. elem. schs., Atlanta, 1972-74; sales rep. Xerox Corp., Atlanta, 1974-76, Rosslyn, Va., 1976-81, No. Telecom Inc., Vienna, Va., 1981-84, account exec., 1984-85, sales dir., 1985-91, mktg. dir., 1995-96; v.p. Fed. Pub. Sector Timeplex Fed. Sys., Inc., Fairfax, Va., 1995-96; bus. devel. dir. Informix Software, Vienna, 1996-97; sr. v.p. Tricor Industries Inc., Alexandria, Va., 1997-98; sr. v.p. fed. sys. Metromedia Fiber Network, McLean, Va., 1999—2002; sr. v.p. bus. devel. Source1 Techs., Arlington, Va., 2002—04; pres. AG Consulting LLC, Alexandria, Va., 2004—. Mem. Info. Tech. Assn. Am., Pi Beta Phi. Episcopalian. Avocations: running, working out. Home: 4643 Kirkland Pl Alexandria VA 22311-4949 Office Phone: 703-626-9466. Business E-Mail: APGallaghe@aol.com.

GALLAGHER, CAROL JOY, bishop; b. San Diego, Calif., Dec. 24, 1955; d. Donald K. and Elizabeth Anne (WalkingStick) Theobald; m. Mark Paul Gallagher, 1975; children: Emily, Ariel, Phoebe. BA in Writing and Communication, Antioch Coll., Balt.; MDiv, Episcopal Div. Sch., Cambridge, Mass., 1989; ThM, Princeton Theol. Sem., 1998; PhD in Urban Affairs and Pub. Policy, U. Del., 2004. Ordained priest, 1990; asst. Cathedral of the Incarnation, Balt., St. Martin's Ch., Radnor, Pa.; priest-in-charge Trinity Ch., Collingdale, Pa.; rector St. Anne's Ch., Middletown, Del., 1996—2002; consecrated bishop, 2002; bishop suffragen Episcopal Diocese of So. Va., 2002—. Mem. editl. bd. First Peoples Theology Jour. Episcopalian. Office: Episcopal Diocese of So Va 600 Talbot Hall Rd Norfolk VA 23505 Office Phone: 757-423-8287. Office Fax: 757-440-5354.

GALLAGHER, CYNTHIA, artist, educator; b. N.Y. BFA in Painting, Phila. U. of Arts, 1972; MFA in Painting, Queens Coll., 1974. Instr. N.Y. Inst. Tech., N.Y.C., 1974-88; adj. prof. CUNY, Queens Coll., N.Y.C., 1974—90; instr. foundations dept. Parsons Sch. Design, 1994—2001. Critic Brown U., 1994, R.I. Sch. Design, 1994, Cooper Union for Advancement of Sci. and Art, 1994; selection com. vis. artists Fashion Inst. Tech., 1992-93; graphics cons. N.Y. State Found. Arts, 1978; vis. critic NYU, N.Y.C., N.Y., 1974-75; adj. asst. prof. Phila. (Pa.) Coll. Art, 1976—, Fashion Inst. Tech., N.Y.C., N.Y., 1976—; instr. summer sch. music and art Yale U., Norfolk, Conn., 1980—. One-woman shows include 55 Mercer St., N.Y.C., 1976, 1978, Grace Borgenicht Gallery, 1981, Luise Ross Gallery, 1988, Edward Thorden Gallery, Gothenborg, Sweden, 1989, Charles More Gallery, Phila., 1990, 1991, Mary Ryan Gallery, N.Y.C., 1992, Espace Crois, Barangnon, Toulouse, France, 1993, Johnson & Johnson, New Brunswick, N.J., 1998, exhibited in group shows at Weatherspoon Mus., Greensboro, N.Y.C., 1982, Castelli Graphics, N.Y.C., 1983, Bess Culter Gallery, 1984, Parrish Art Mus., Southampton, L.I., N.Y., 1991, Tiffany's, N.Y.C., 1993, Inst. for Art and Urban Resources, Inc., L.I. City, N.Y., 1982, Nat. Mus. Women in the Arts, Washington, 1996, Montclair (NJ) Mus. Art, 1997, Represented in permanent collections Met. Mus. Art, N.Y.C., Best Inc., Citibank, 1st Nat. Bank Chgo., Home Ins. Co., Owens Corning Corp., Salomon Bros., Shearson-Lehman Am. Express, N.Y.C., San Francisco, Skadden, Arts, Slate, Meagher and Flom, Johnson, Nat. Mus. of Women in the Arts, Whitney Mus. Am. Art, Met. Mus. Art, Nat. Women's Mus., Washington, D.C.; contbr. articles to profl. jours. Mem. adv. bd., bd. dirs. YWCA Elsa Mott Ives Gallery, 1992, curator, 1993. Grantee, Creative Artists Pub. Svc. Program, 1981—82, Nat. Endowment for Arts, 1983—84, 1989—90, N.Y. Found. for Arts, 1989—90.

GALLAGHER, ELLEN, artist; b. Providence, 1965; Student, Sch. Mus. Fine Arts, Boston, 1992, Skowhegan Sch. Art, 1993, Oberlin Coll. One-woman shows include Akin Gallery, Boston, 1992, Mario Diacono Gallery, 1994, Mary Boone Gallery, N.Y., 1996, Anthony d'Offay Gallery, London, 1996, Gagosian Gallery, 1998, Ikon Gallery, Birmingham, 1998, Galerie Max Hetzler, Berlin, 1999, Anthony d'Offay Gallery, London, 2000, Watery Ecstatic, ICA, Boston, 2001, Ellen Gallagher: Preserve, Drawing Ctr., NYC, 2002, Currents 88, St. Louis Art Mus., 2003, Murmur, Galerie Max Hetzler, Berlin, 2003, Orbus, Fruitmarker Galley, Edinburgh, 2004, deLuxe, Whitney Mus. Am. Art, NYC, 2005, Fluidity of Time, Mus. Contemporary Art, Chgo., 2005—06, exhibited in group shows at Brandeis U., Waltham, 1993, Mus. Fine Arts, Boston, 1993, Inst. Contemporary Art, 1994, 1996, Mus. Fine Arts, 1995, Whitney Mus. Am. Art, N.Y., 1995, Whitechapel Art Gallery, London, 1996, Mario Diacono Gallery, Boston, 1997, De Beyerd Ctr. Contemporary Art, Breda, The Netherlands, 1998, others, Represented in permanent collections Mus. Modern Art, N.Y., Whitney Mus. Art, Met Mus. Art, Guggenheim Mus., Mus. Fine Art, Boston, Mus. Contemporary Art, L.A., Denver Mus. Art, Moderna Museet, Stockholm; featured in numerous articles and revs. Recipient Am. Acad. award, Art; Ann. Gund fellow, 1993, Provincetown Fine Arts Work Ctr. fellow, 1995, Joan Mitchell fellow, 1997. Office: Gagosian Gallery 555 W 24th St New York NY 10011

GALLAGHER, LINDY ALLYN, banker, financial consultant; b. Kalamazoo, Sept. 27, 1954; d. Karl P. Joslow and Audrey S. Phillips; m. Thomas J. Gallagher, Nov. 29, 1975; children: James Allyn Buckley, Phillip Graham, Charles Bedloe. BS, U. Pa., 1975; MBA, Columbia U., 1982. Mem. faculty, rschr. U. Pa., Phila., 1976-80; corp. banking officer Bank of Montreal, N.Y.C., 1982-84; v.p. Citibank NA, N.Y.C., 1984-89; v.p., mgr. Chase Manhattan Bank, N.Y.C., 1989-90; pres. The Allyn Co., New Canaan, Conn., 1990-99; prin. State Street Global Advs., 1999; pvt. fin. cons., 2000—. Treas., dir. 957 Lexington Corp., 1981-87. Editor Columbia Jour. World Bus., 1980-82. Mem. Women's Nat. Rep. Club, 1986—; commr. Town of New Canaan, 1991-99; treas., sec. Young Women's League New Canaan, Inc., 1992-94; bd. dirs. Charlotte Latin Sch., 2000—. Mem. Stanwich Club, The Penn Club (N.Y.C.), The Breakers Club. Republican. Episcopalian. E-mail: lindy@carolina.rr.com.

GALLAGHER, M. CATHERINE, English literature educator; b. Denver, Feb. 16, 1945; d. John Martin and Mary Catherine Sullivan; m. Martin Evan Jay, July 6, 1974; children: Margaret Shana, Rebecca Erin. BA, U. Calif., Berkeley, 1972, MA, 1974, PhD, 1979. Asst. prof. U. Denver, 1979-80, U. Calif., Berkeley, 1980-84, assoc. prof., 1984-90, prof., 1990—. Author: The Industrial Reformation of English Fiction, 1985, Nobody's Story, 1994, The Body Economic, 2005; co-author: The Making of the Modern Body, 1987, Practicing New Historicism, 2000; editor Representation, 1983—. Guggenheim fellow Guggenheim Found., 1989; fellow NEH, 1990, ACLS, 1990, Mem. MLA (del. assembly mem. 1985-86, exec. com. lit. criticism divsn. 1991-94), Am. Acad. Arts and Scis., Acad. Lit. Studies, Brit. Studies Assn., The Dickens Soc. Office: U Calif Dept English Berkeley CA 94720-0001 Business E-Mail: cgall@berkeley.edu.

GALLAGHER, MAGGIE, columnist; B, Yale Univ., 1982. Articles editor Nat. Review; sr. editor City Jour., Manhattan Inst.; pres. Inst. for Marriage and Pub. Policy, Washington. Syndicated columnist; author: Enemies of Eros, 1989, The Abolition of Marriage, 1995. Sr. fellow, Ctr. for Social Thought. Mailing: Universal Press Syndicate 4520 Main St Kansas City MO 64111

GALLAGHER, PATRICIA CECILIA, author; b. Lockhart, Tex. d. Frank Joseph and Martha Leona (Rhody) Bienek; m. James D. Gallagher (dec.); 1 son, James Craig. Student, Trinity U., 1951. Novels include The Sons and the Daughters, 1961, Answer To Heaven, 1964, The Fires of Brimstone, 1966, Shannon, 1967, Shadows of Passion, 1971, Summer of Sighs, 1971, The Ticket, 1974, Castles in the Air, 1976, Mystic Rose, 1977, No Greater Love, 1979, All For Love, 1981, Echoes and Embers, 1983, On Wings of Dreams, 1985, A Perfect Love, 1987. Mem. Authors Guild, Romance Writers Am., Women in Communications, San Antonio Mag. Council.

GALLAGHER, PATRICIA E., government agency administrator; BA in Pub. Adminstrn. and Urban Studies, Elmhurst Coll., Ill.; MA in Pub. Policy Analysis, Northwestern U. Prin. P. Gallagher & Assocs., Chgo.; mgr. Chgo. River Devel. Plan; asst. commr. open space planning City of Chgo. Dept. Planning, dep. commr. strategic planning, 1999—2001; exec. dir. Nat. Capital Planning Commn., Washington, 2001—. Contbr. articles to profl. jours. Loeb fellow, Harvard U., 1999—2000. Office: Nat Capital Planning Commn 401 9th St NW Washington DC 20576 Office Phone: 202-482-7200.

GALLAGHER, PAULA MARIE, real estate appraiser; b. Omaha, Nov. 10, 1959; d. Kenneth Leroy and Phyllis Virginia (Stopak) G. Diploma, Nebr. Coll. Bus., 1979; student, Met. Tech. C.C., Omaha, 1979—81, U. Nebr., 1981—85, Coll. St. Mary, 1986—90; BS, Bellevue U., 1993. Lic. real estate appraiser and broker, Nebr. Legal sec. McCormick Cooney Mooney & Hillman P.C., Omaha, 1979; word processor Firstier Bank, Omaha, 1979-83, staff asst., 1983-84; sec. Morrissey Appraisal Svcs., Omaha, 1984—85; appraiser trainee Morrissay Appraisal Svcs., Omaha, 1985-88, real estate appraiser, 1988—. Residential mem. Am. Inst. Real Estate Appraisers. Boutique com. St. Stephen the Martyr Cath. Ch., 2000—, boutique co-chair, 2004—. Mem.: Am. Bus. Women's Assn. (rec. sec. 1984—85, treas. 1988—89, Woman of Yr. award 1989), Appraisal Inst. (sr. residential appraiser), Omaha Women's C. of C. (mem. edn. com. 1990—92, mem. fin. com. 1991—2003, dir. cmty. recognition 1992, dir. edn. 1993, chmn. fin. style show 1995, pres.-elect 1996, pres. 1997, immediate past pres. 1998). Roman Catholic. Avocations: counted cross stitch, sewing, reading, painting, stamp collecting/philately. Home: 16617 Monroe St Omaha NE 68135-2906 Office: Morrissey Appraisal Svcs 13825 P St Omaha NE 68137-2701

GALLAGHER-DALTON, TONYA MARIE, family support specialist; b. Great Falls, Mont., Aug. 2, 1971; d. Ronald A. and Sherry E. (Morris) G. BA in Psychology, U. Mont., 1994, BA in Comm. Studies, 1994, M in Interdisciplinary Studies, 1999. Cert. family support specialist II, Mont. Project asst./resource coord VVCAP, Missoula, Mont., 1993-96; grad. asst. dept. psychology U. Mont., Missoula, 1996-97; family support specialist Western Mont. Comprehensive Devel. Ctr., Missoula, 1997—. Mem. coun. Youth in Crisis Coalition, 1995—; bd. dirs. MCAT, 1999. Vol. coord. AmeriCorps, Missoula, 1996-2000; crisis vol. YWCA Domestic Violence Assistance Program, 1992-95. Recipient Children And Youth scholarship award Am. Legion, 1993, Heisey award Mont. Cascade Coun., 1992; Mountain West Regional scholar Golden Key Nat. Honor Soc., 1994-95; Early Intervention scholar, 1994-97. Mem. AAUW, Grad. Student Assn., Psi Chi, Alpha Phi (treas. 1989). Lutheran. Avocations: stamp collecting/philately, coin collecting/numismatics, poetry, skiing, hiking. Home: PO Box 2166 Kalispell MT 59903 Office: Child Devel Ctr 1725 Mont Hwy 35 Kalispell MT 59901

GALLAGHER-GRIFFITH, VICTORIA ALANA, secondary school educator; b. Queens, N.Y., Dec. 5, 1977; d. Daniel James Gallagher and Maryse Altagracia Moise-Gallagher; m. Christopher Griffith, Apr. 23, 2003. AA, Queensboro C.C., Queens, N.Y., 1998; BA in English and Secondary Edn., Queens Coll., Flushing, N.Y., 2001; MA in Guidance Counseling, St. John's U., Jamaica, N.Y., 2005. Cert. counselor CACREP, 2005. Tchr. English Queens (N.Y.) Gateway, 2001—03; summer tchr. English John Bowne H.S., Queens, 2002—03; tchr. English John Adams H.S., Queens, 2003—. Tchr. dance Mt. Sinai Coll., Queens, 2002—03, Queens (N.Y.) Coll., 2002—03; internship guidance counselor John Adams H.S., 2003—05; model mags., 2000—06. Mem.: United Fedn. Tchrs., Am. Counseling Assn. Avocations: dance, writing. Home: 121-18 Linden Blvd South Ozone Park NY 11420

GALLARDO, SISTER ARSENIA PULUMBARIT, elementary school educator; b. Bulacan, The Philippines, Nov. 16, 1931; came to U.S., 1979; d. Federico Santos and Juana (Cruz) Pulumbarit; m. Emmanuel Javate Gallardo, May 2, 1961; children: Emily Anne, Ellen Agnes, Effie Angeline Gallardo-Sanblom. BS in Edn., Far Ea. U., Manila, 1953. Cert. tchr., The Philippines. Tchr. E. Rodriquez Jr. H.S., Quezon City, The Philippines, 1954-79, Garapan Elem. Sch., Saipan, Mariana Islands, 1980—, sch. math. coord., art coord., 1985—. Mem. math. task force CNMI Pub. Sch. Sys., Saipan, 1985—, math. textbook selection com., 1992—, art task force, 1985—, person-in-charge Math. Olympiads for Elem. Sch., 1986—, mem. 5-yr. edn. plan, 1987-94, coach interscholastic math.-sci. bee competition, 1991—. Author (slide/cassette tape) Palauan Culture, 1985. Troop leader Girl Scouts Am., Saipan, 1992—; tchr. Cath. Christian Doctrine, Gualo Rai Parish, 1992—; mem. Artist of Rota, Tinian and Saipan, 1992—; organizer holiday fundraising projects, math. tutorial programs and others. Recipient Outstanding Secondary Tchr. award Divsn. Quezon City, 1968, Nat. Presdl. award for sci. and math. NSF, 1994. Mem. ASCD, Nat. Coun. Tchrs. Math. (State award 1989-90), Marianas Assn. Filipino Tchrs., Coun. for Presdl. Awardees in Math., Soc. for Elem. Presdl. Awardees. Avocations: doll making, embroidery, reading, gardening, creative crafts. Home: Garapan Village PO Box 1642 Saipan MP 96950-1642 Office: Garapan Elem Sch Beach Rd Saipan MP 96950

GALLARDO, HENRIETTA CASTELLANOS, writer; b. San Antonio, July 16, 1934; d. Francisco Garcia and Elisa Duarte (Moreno) Castellanos; m. Albert Joseph Gallardo, Aug. 19, 1965; children: Frank Cantu, Roger Cantu (dec.), Gloria Michelle. Cert., Draughn's Bus. Coll., San Antonio, 1952. Sec. Kelly Air Force Base, San Antonio, 1952-53; exec. sec. U. Tex., Dallas, 1974-82; interior decorator Plano, Tex., 1983-85; writer. Author: Tangled Web of Destiny, 1992, Marsh & Co., 1993, Everyday Heroes, 2002. Democrat. Roman Catholic. Avocations: photography, travel, reading, charity work. Home: 2212 Parkhaven Dr Plano TX 75075-2013 E-mail: hgallardo@comcast.net.

GALLARDO, SANDRA SILVANA, television producer, actress; b. Bronx, Jan. 13, 1947; d. Edward Francis and Grace (Mallory) G.; m. Gerald O'Connor, Jan. 21, 1968 (div. 1978); m. Billy Burrows, Sept. 21, 1985. Student, HB Studio, N.Y.C., 1964—72, CCNY, 1964—66. CEO Gallardo Studios, North Hollywood, Calif., 1980—; pres. Camellia Prodns., Studio City, Calif., 1987—. Guest spkr. IRS, Hollywood, Calif., 1990. Prodr., dir., writer The Acting Class, 1988; author: The Winning, 1998, Acting for Success, 1999, 2d edit., 2005 (Academic World Star); actress (film) Solar Crisis, The Windwalker, Death Wish II, Out of the Dark, The Tin Angel; (TV) Prison Stories: Women on the Inside, Calendar Girl Murders, The People vs. Inez Garcia, Days of Our Lives, NYPD Blue, Lou Grant, ER, Babylon 5, Providence, Strong Medicine, Golden Girls, Ressurection Blvd., Kingpin; appeared on stage in American Mosaic; writer, prodr. (films) The Anger, 2006, The Tin Angel, 2006 Recipient Bronze Star halo So. Calif. Motion Picture Coun., 1985, Golden Eagle award Nosotros, 1989. Mem. SAG (guest spkr. 1988-96), Am. Fedn. TV Arts Scis., Am. TV Arts & Scis., Equity. Avocations: writing, paddle tennis, hiking, museums. Studio: #641 11288 Ventura Blvd Studio City CA 91604 Office: Camellia Prodns #641 11288 Ventura Blvd Studio City CA 91604 Personal E-mail: sgalla2222@aol.com.

GALLARELLO, JOSEPHINE, performing arts educator, director; b. N.Y.C., June 2, 1942; d. Amedeo and Angelina Ammirata; m. John R. Gallarello, Aug. 1, 1965; children: Victoria Angela, Josephine M., John Amedeo. BS in music edn., NYU, 1964; MS in music edn., Queens Coll., 1966; profl. dip., Long Island U., 1994. Music tchr. So. Huntington Schs., Huntington Station, NY, 1964—68; soprano singer self employed, Long Island, NY, 1976—80; choral tchr. Sachem Schs., Holtsville, NY, 1980—86; choral dir. Kings Park (NY) Schs., 1986—96; dir. fine and performing arts Hauppauge (NY) Schs., 1996—. Past pres. NY Sch. Coun. of Admin. of Music Edn., Suffolk County, 1996—, Suffolk County Music Edn. Assoc., 1964—; fellow mem. PTA, So. Huntington, 1964—69, Kings Park, 1975—85, Hauppauge, 1996—. Mem.: NY State Coun. Admin. of Music Edn., Elem. Secondary PTA So. Huntington NY (life). Republican. Roman Catholic.

GALLATIN, JENNIFER, music educator; d. William and Joan Snodgress (Stepmother), Cynthia and Sergei Huffman (Stepfather); m. Charles Gallatin, July 30, 1994; children: Joseph, John. BS in Music Edn., Ball State U., Muncie, Ind., 1994. Band dir. Randolph Ea. H.S., Union City, 1994—95, Montpelier Sch., Ind., 1995—. Prodr.: various DVD prodns. Mem.: Ind. Bandmasters Assn. Office Phone: 765-728-2402.

GALLAWAY, MARILYN, performing arts educator, communications educator; b. Gunnison, Utah, Apr. 26, 1952; d. Standley and Verda Pickett; children: Kenneth, Andrea Smith, Mathew. AA, Snow Coll., Ephraim, Utah, 1972; BA in Speech and Theatre Arts, Brigham Young U., Provo, Utah, 1974, MA in Comm., 1977. Tchr. English, drama, speech, debate Manti H.S., Utah, 1974—78, Gunnison Valley H.S., Utah, 1984—92; tchr. theatre and concurrent enrollment comm. Murray H.S., Utah, 1992—. Tchr., svc. vol. LDS Ch., Salt Lake City, 1978—2006. Recipient Best Female Spkr. award, Snow Coll., 1972, U.S.O. Tour Germany, Brigham Young U., 1974, Best Grad. Tchr. in Comm. award, 1976, Best Dir., Best Show award, Salt Lake Valley Performing Arts, 2005, 2004, 1998. Achievements include 22 Years Of Overall Superior Ratings Of Drama Teams At The State Level, Numerous Acting And Directing Awards On A Regional, State, And Community Level.

GALLEGOS, DEBORAH E., pension fund administrator; BA in Polit. Econ., MBA in Polit. Econ., UC Berkeley, 1995. Pension fund cons. Callan Assoc.; with Morgan Stanley & Co.; v.p. JP Morgan Fleming Asset Mng., NYC; dep. investment officer State of N.M.; chief investment officer NYC, 2005—. Gov. bd. Robert Toigo Found., NYC. Office: Comptrollers Office Rm 736 One Center St New York NY 10007 Office Phone: 212-669-2020.

GALLEHER, GAY, psychologist; b. Delaware, Ohio, Nov. 3, 1946; d. Richard Adair Galleher and Ellen Jean Huntsberger; m. Charles Frost Gould III (div.). MS in Learning Disabilities, Med. Sci. Sch. U. Pacific, San Francisco, 1976; MA in Psychology, Pacific Grad. Sch. Profl. Psychology, Palo Alto, 1983, PhD, 1987. Bd. cert. diplomate in clin. psychology Am. Bd. Profl. Psychology, lic. psychologist Maine. Pvt. practice clin. psychologist Gay Galleher PhD, Kentfield, Calif., 1990—2000; clin. psychologist USAF, Lakenheath, England, 2001, Maine Gen. Med. Ctr., Waterville, 2002—04; pvt. practice clin. psychologist Gay Galleher PhD, ABPP, Bath, 2004—. Contbr. articles to profl. jours. Mem.: Am. Bd. Profl. Psychology, Nat. Register Health Svc. Providers, San Francisco Psychotherapy Rsch. Group. Democrat. Congregationalist. Avocations: painting, gardening, interior decorating, old house renovation. Home: 579 Berrys Mill West Bath ME 04530 Office: One Lincoln St Ste 4 Bath ME 04530 Office Phone: 207-443-4334.

GALL-IEMMA, JULIE JEANNINE, personal trainer; b. Oberlin, Ohio, Dec. 6, 1978; d. Steven Joseph and Simone Ellen Gall; m. Christopher Adam Iemma, July 16. BS, Mount Union Coll., Ohio; MEd, Cleve. State U. Cert. athletic trainer Cleve. Clinic Found., Lorain, Ohio, 2002, Vermilion HS, Ohio, 2002. Home: 4524 Fields Way Lorain OH 44053-4412

GALLIEN, SANDRA JEAN, social worker; b. Winchester, Mass., May 13, 1956; d. William Joseph and Shirley Ann (Ewing) Treacy. BA in Early Childhood Edn., U. Mass., 1979; Cert. Advance Study in Adminstrn., Mgmt., Harvard U., 1987; MBA in Mgmt., U. Conn., 1997; MSW, U. Conn., W. Hartford, 1998. Counselor Greater Newburyport Edn. Collaborative, Danvers, Mass., 1991-93; grad. student Inst. African Am. Studies U. Conn., Storrs, 1995-98, work study student Inst. Advancement Polit. Social Work Practice W. Hartford, 1996-98; intern Conn. Women's Edn. and Legal Fund, Hartford, 1996-97, United Way, Rocky Hill, Conn., 1997—. Contbr. papers to Credit Rsch. Found., 1989. Town precinct coord. congl. campaign, Reading, Mass., 1974; mem. Coventry Dem. Town Com., 1997-99, Unitarian Universalist Soc., East Manchester, Conn., 1999-2004. Mem. NASW, U. Mass. Alumni Assn., Emily's List. Avocations: leather and wreath crafting, bowling, woodworking. Home: 16 Vernon Ave Unit 50 Vernon Rockville CT 06066-6701 E-mail: Sandy.Gallien@ctunitedway.org.

GALLIGAN, CAITLIN MAUREEN, elementary school educator; d. Michael Gerard and Alice Cleary Galligan. Student, UMBC, Balt., 2000—04. Cert. secondary edn. Md., 2004. Social studies tchr. Calvert County Pub. Schs., Prince Frederick, Md., 2004—. Office: Calvert Middle School 435 Solomons Island Rd Prince Frederick MD 20678 Office Phone: 410-535-7355.

GALLIGAN, LYNDA T., lawyer; BA, Purdue U., 1991; JD cum laude, Boston Coll. Law Sch., 2000. Bar: Mass., NY. Assoc. ERISA/Employee Benefits Practice Goodwin Procter LLP, Boston, 2000—. Served to capt. USMC, aviation maintenance control officer USMC. Mem.: NY Bar Assn., Boston Bar Assn., ABA. Office: Goodwin Procter LLP Exchange Place 53 State St Boston MA 02109 Office Phone: 617-570-1090. E-mail: lgalligan@goodwinprocter.com.*

GALLO, JOAN ROSENBERG, lawyer; b. Newark, Apr. 28, 1940; BA in Psychology, Boston U., Mass., 1965; postgrad., We. Md. Coll., Westminster, 1966—67; postgrad, We. Grad. Sch. Psychology, 1966—67; JD magna cum laude, U. Santa Clara, 1975. Bar: Calif. 1975. Assoc. with Cynthia Mertens U, Santa Clara, Calif., 1975-76; sr. law clk. US Dist. Ct., Calif., 1976-78; assoc. Decker and Collins, San Jose, Calif., 1978-79; from dep. city atty. to city atty. City of San Jose, 1979-2000; ptnr. Terra Law LLP, San Jose, 2000—02, Realty Law, LLP, San Jose, 2002—03; of counsel Hopkins & Carley, 2004—. Mem.: Psi Chi. Office: Hopkins & Carley 70 S First St San Jose CA 95113 Office Phone: 408-286-9800. Business E-Mail: jgallo@hopkinscarley.com.

GALLO, MARTA IRENE, retired language educator; b. Córdoba, Argentina, Oct. 20, 1926; d. Gregorio and María Luisa (Teodoro) Gallo. Grad., U. Buenos Aires, 1951. Rschr. Inst. de Filologia, Univ. de Buenos Aires, 1960-61, asst. prof. Lit. Theory, 1961-66; vis. prof. U. Puerto Rico, 1967-68; prof. Spanish U. Calif., Santa Barbara, 1968-91, prof. emeritus, 1991—. Author: Novela Hispoamericana del siglo XIX, Relfexiones sobre espejos; contbr. articles to profl. jours. Mem.: MLA, Ling. Soc. Am., Internat. Assn. Semiotic Studies, Asociación Internat. de Hispanistas, Inst. Internat. de Literatura Iberoamericana, Asociación Española de Smiótica. Home: 2948 Kenmore Pl Santa Barbara CA 93105-2224 Personal E-mail: martagallo@earthlink.net.

GALLO, MARTHA J., diversified financial services company executive; married; 1 child. BS in Acctg., Cornell U., MBA. Tech. and ops. trainee J.P. Morgan Chase & Co., 1981, contr. tech. and ops., 1989, mng. dir., 1992—, co-head tech., 1993—96, CEO Credit Risk Bus., 1996, chief auditor, 1998. Co-pres. Battery Park City Neighbors and Parents' Assn., NYC. Office: JP Morgan Chase & Co 270 Park Ave New York NY 10017-2070 E-mail: gallo_m@jpmorgan.com.*

GALLOP, JANE (JANE ANNE GALLOP), women's studies educator, writer; b. Duluth, Minn., May 4, 1952; d. Melvin Gordon and Eudice Zelda (Titch) G.; children: Max Blau Gallop, Ruby Gallop Blau. BA, Cornell U., 1972, PhD, 1976. Lectr. French Gettysburg (Pa.) Coll., 1976; asst. prof. Miami U., Oxford, Ohio, 1977-81, assoc. prof., 1981-85; prof. women's studies Rice U., Houston, 1985-87, Autrey prof., 1987-90; prof. English U. Wis., Milw., 1990-92, Disting. prof., 1992—. NEH vis. prof. Emory U., Atlanta, 1984-85; Hill vis. prof. U. Minn., Mpls., 1987; dir. seminar for coll. tchrs. NEH, Milw., 1985, 88; instr. Sch. of Criticism and Theory, Dartmouth Coll., 1991; vis. disting. prof. Johns Hopkins U., Balt., 2006. Author: Intersections, 1981, The Daughter's Seduction, 1982, Reading Lacan, 1985, Thinking Through the Body, 1988, Around 1981, 1992, Feminist Accused of Sexual Harassment, 1997, Anecdotal Theory, 2002, Living with His Camera, 2003; editor: Pedagogy, 1995, Polemic, 2004. Guggenheim fellow, 1983-84. Mem. MLA. Office: Dept English Univ Wis - Milw PO Box 413 Milwaukee WI 53201-0413 Business E-Mail: jg@uwm.edu.

GALLOWAY, CATHERINE BLACK, writer, editor; b. Birmingham, Ala., Oct. 24, 1954; d. Robert Lee and Catherine Hicks Black; m. Michael Galloway, Aug. 25, 1984. Editl. prodn. coord. So. Med. Jour., Birmingham, Ala., 1975—2002, mng. editor, 2002—04; tech. writer, web editor NIH Viral Bioinformatics Resource Ctr., U. Ala., Birmingham, 2004—. Sec., treas. Vocat. Resources, Inc., Birmingham, 1997—2005. Mem.: Am. Med. Writers Assn. (cert. core curriculum program 1983). Office: Viral Bioinformatics Resource Ctr Bevill Biomed Rsch Bldg Rm 273-D U Ala Birmingham Birmingham AL 35294-2170 Business E-Mail: galloway@uab.edu.

GALLOWAY, EILENE MARIE, space and astronautics consultant; b. Kansas City, Mo., May 4, 1906; d. Joseph Locke and Lottie Rose (Harris) Slack; m. George Barnes Galloway, Dec. 23, 1924; children: David Barnes, Jonathan Fuller. Student, Washington U., St. Louis, 1923—25; AB, Swarthmore Coll., 1928, LLD (hon.), 1992; postgrad., Am. U., 1937—38, postgrad., 1943; LLD (hon.), Lake Forest Coll., 1990. Tchr. polit. sci. Swarthmore Coll., 1928-30; editor Student Svc., Washington, 1931; staff mem. edn. div. Fed. Emergency Relief Adminstrn., 1934-35; asst. chief info. sect. div. spl. info Library of Congress, 1941-43; editor abstracts Legis. Reference Svc., 1943-51, nat. def. analyst, 1951-57, specialist in nat. def., 1957-66; sr. specialist internat. rels. (nat. security) Congl. Rsch. Svc., 1966-75, cons. internat. space activities, 1975—. Staff mem. Senate Fgn. Rels. Com., 1947; profl. staff mem. U.S. group Interparliamentary Union, 1958-66; cons. Senate Armed Svcs. Com., 1953-74, Ford Found., 1958; spl. cons. Spl. Senate Com. on Space and Astronautics, 1958; spl. cons. to Senate Com. on Aero. and Space Sci., 1958-77; cons. to Senate Com. on Commerce, Sci. and Transp., 1977-82; chmn. com. edn. and recreation Washington, 1937-38; forum leader, 1976-79; guest Soviet Acad. Sci., 1982, adult edn. U.S. Office Edn., 1938; mem. Internat. Inst. Space Law of Internat. Astronautical Fedn., 1958—, U.S. bd. dirs., v.p., 1967-79, hon. dir., 1979—, Fedn. ofcl. observer at sessions UN Com. on Peaceful Uses Outer Space and legal sub-com., 1970-94, com. for rels. with internat. orgns., 1979—; space law and sociology com. Am. Rocket Soc., 1959-62; adv. panel Office Gen. Counsel, NASA, 1971; adviser outer space del. U.S. Mission to UN Working Group on Direct Broadcast Satellites, 1973-75; observer UN Conf. Exploration and Peaceful Uses of Outer Space, Vienna, 1982; lectr. NAS, 1972, U.S. CSC, Exec. Seminar Ctr., Oak Ridge, 1973-78; edn1. counselor Purdue U., 1974; lectr. Inst. Air and Space Law McGill U., 1975, Inter Am. Def. Coll., 1977-78, U. Akron, 1984, 91; mem. panel on solar power for satellites and U.S. space policy Office Tech. Assessment, 1979-80, 82-86, cons., 1982; cons. COMSAT, 1983, FCC Commn. on U.S. Telecomm. Policy, 1983-87; spkr. internat. space law UN, N.Y.C., 1995; mem. NASA Nat. Adv. Com. on Internat. Space Sta., 1996-99, NASA Spaceflight Adv. com., 2000-03, UN seminar Space Futures and Human Security, Alpbach, Austria, 1997, chmn. Session in Internat. Astronautical Fed. Congress Concepts of Space Law, 1997; active European Space Agy. Internat. Lunar Workshop, 1994, 97; chair UN Workshop UNISPACE III Space Treaties: Strengths and Needs, Vienna, Austria, 1999. Author: Atomic Power: Issues Before Congress, 1946; author: (with Bernard Brodie) The Atomic Bomb and the Armed Services, 1947; author: History of United States Military Policy on Reserve Forces, 1775-1957, 1957, The Community of Law and Science, 1958, United Nations Ad hoc Committee on Peaceful Uses of Outer Space, 1959, Space Policy Guidelines, 2003, Space Law for the Moon-Mars Program, 2004. Pres. Theodore Von Karman Meml. Found., 1973-84; mem. alumni council Swarthmore Coll., 1976-79; mem. organizing com., author symposium on Conditions Essential For Maintaining Outer Space for Peaceful Uses, Peace Palace, Netherlands, 1984; bd. advisers Student for Exploration and Devel. of Space, 1984—. Rockefeller Found. scholar-in-residence, Bellagio, Italy, 1976; elected to Coun. of Advanced Internat. Studies, Argentina, 1985, Uruguyan Centro de Investigacion y Difusion Aeronautica-Expacial, 1985; recipient Andrew G. Haley gold medal Internat. Inst. Space Law, 1968, Disting. Svc. award Libr. Congress, 1975, NASA Gold Medal for Pub. Svc., 1984, USAF Space Command plaque, 1984, Internat. Acad. Astronautics' Theodore Von. Karman award, 1986, Women in Aerospace Lifetime Achievment award Internat. Inst. Space Law, 1989, Leadership award NASA Johnson Space Ctr., 1997, NASA award for contbns. to internat. space sta., 1999, Cologne U. Inst. Air and Space Law and German Aerospace Ctr. award, 2003, Contbns. to Preserve Outer Space award UN Office Outer Space Affairs, NASA, Inst. Air and Space Law, Germany, Can. Space Agy., McGill U., 2006; Wilton Park fellow, Eng., 1968; Eilene M. Galloway award established by Internat. Inst. Space Law, 2000; honored Annals Vol. award Galloway NASA Adv. Com. on Internat. Space Sta., Internat. Inst. Space Laws, The Netherlands, 2006, UN Offices for Outer Space Affairs, NASA, Inst. Air and Space Law, U.S. Congress, Can. Space Agy., McGill U. Inst. Air and Space Law, 2006; dedication Informational Workshops on Policy and Law on Moon, Mars and Celestial Bodies, Montreal, 2006. Fellow: AIAA (hon.; tech. com. on legal aspects of aeros. and astronautics 1980—84, internat. activities com. 1985—, European space agy. internat. lunar workshop 1994, Pub. Policy award 2002, Pub. Svc. award and medal 2003), Internat. Acad. Astronautics (trustee emeritus, Social Scis. award 1999, Moot Ct. Best Brief award 2002), Am. Astronautical Soc. (John F. Kennedy Astronautics award 1999); mem.: Internat. Inst. Space Law, Nat. Aeronautic Assn. (Katharine Wright award 2003, 2003), Internat. Law Assn., LWV (chmn. study groups housing, welfare in D.C. 1937—38, mem. tech. com. on law and sociology task force on legal aspects 1979—), World Peace Through Law Ctr., Lamar Soc. Internat. Law, Am. Soc. Internat. Law, Kappa Alpha Theta, Phi Beta Kappa.

GALLOWAY, GLADYS, artist; b. Crane, Mo., May 25, 1918; d. Thomas Lloyd Kincaid and Mae Margaret Rickman; m. William Harold Galloway, May 21, 1939 (dec.); children: Bonnie Jean, William Thomas. Cert. in tchg., Tuscola County Normal Sch., Caro, Mich., 1937. Instr. porcelain painting, 1951—; organized and directed 6 reg. porcelain art shows, 1978-80; organizer, dir. Internat. Porcelan show, Detroit, 1980; participant Brazilian porcelain Art Conf., 1982; del. porcelain artists People to People Internat., Republic of China, 1983, Italy, 1991; leader effort to get porcelain painting recognized as a fine art, U.S., 1980; tchr. hundreds of seminars, workshops, lectures, 1960—; coord., dir. summer program for Porcelain art, Delta Coll., Midland, Mich., 1984-89; guest artist Porcelain Art Exposition, Lisbon, Portugal, 1996. Author: Sparkling Tables, 1984, 7th edit., 1999, Holidays and Special Moments, 1979, 10th edit., 1999, China Painting Fun and Basics, 1975, 16th edit., 1999, Step By Step Painting, 1970, and numerous bot. study booklets; fine art porcelain painter, 1949—. Trustee People to People Intrnat., 1981-96. Named Citizen of Yr. Caro C. of C., 1977. Mem. International Porcelain Art Tchrs. (pres. 1978-80, bd. dirs. 1978-94, dir. emeritus 1994—), Mich. China Painting Tchrs. Orgn. (charter), Caro Garden Club (pres. 1966). Avocations: watercolor, porcelain and oil painting, travel, gardening, cooking, the outdoors. Home: 670 Gibbs St Caro MI 48723-1447 Office Phone: 989-673-2447.

GALLOWAY, JANICE, writer, editor; b. Kilwinning, Scotland, Dec. 2, 1956; d. James and Janet (McBride) G.; 1 child, James Alexander Galloway McNaught. MA, Glasgow U., 1978. Tchr. Strathclyde Regional Coun., Ayrshire, Scotland, 1980-90. Music critic. Editor: The Scotsman and Orange Short Story Collection, 2005; editor: (with Hamish Whyte) New Writing Scotland, 1990, 1991, 1992; author: The Trick is to Keep Breathing, 1990, Foreign Parts, 1994, Where You Find It, 1996, Clara, 2002 (Saltire book of yr., 2002), Boy Book See, 2002; editor: The Scotsman & Orange Short Story Collection, 2005; author (with sculptor Anne Bevan): +Rosengarten, 2004; librettist (with sculptor Anne Bevan): Operas Pipelines, librettist (with composer Sally Beamish): Operas Monster. Recipient Mind/Allan Lane prize, 1990, CosmopolitanPerrier award, 1991, E.M. Forster award in lit. Am. Acad. Arts and Letters, 1994, McVitie's prize for Scottish Writer of the Yr., 1994, Saltire prize, 2002; Times Literary Supplement Rsch. fellow Brit. Libr., 1999. Office: care Jonathan Cape 20 Vauxhall Bridge Rd London SW1 6RB England also: care Derek Johns AP Watt Agy 20 John St London WCIN 2DR England E-mail: sarah@galloway.itol.org.

GALLOWAY, LILLIAN CARROLL, modeling agency executive, consultant; b. Hazard, Ky., Sept. 23, 1934; d. William Zion and Clemma (Lewis) Carroll; m. Thomas Roddy Galloway, Dec. 21, 1957; children: David Junkin, Scott Thomas, Donald Lewis. Student, Cumberland Coll., 1955, Ea. U., Richmond, Ky., 1956, U. Cin., 1958, John Robert Powers Sch., Cin., 1958. Tchr. Vandalia (Ohio) Elem. Sch., 1954-56, Kenwood Elem. Sch., Louisville, 1956-57, Cin. Pub. Schs., 1957-64; founder, pres. Fairfax Model Agy., Washington, 1964-67, Cin. Model Agy. Internat., 1967—, Lillian Galloway Modeling Acad., Cin., 1971—, Children Model Agy. Internat., Cin., 1985—, Lillian Galloway Fashion Show Prodn. Co., 1998—. Cons., co-owner John Robert Powers Modeling Sch., Cin., 1957-64; pres. Student Model Bds., Cin., 1984—; dir. Career Day, Cin., 1967—. Active Cin. Better Bus. Bur., 1967—; trustee Knox Presbyn. Ch. Named Cin.'s Outstanding Bus. Woman, Sta. WCPO-TV, 1985, Outstanding Alumni, Cumberland Coll., 1988, Cin. Bus. Woman of Yr., Leading Women Assn., 2004, Entrepreneurship award Reading Women Inc., 2004. Mem. DAR, Modeling Assn. Am. (chmn. convs. 1975-77), Am. Modeling Assn. Internat. (pres. 1976-77), Cin. Advertisers Club (membership and program coms., Outstanding Bus. Woman award 1985), Exec. Women Internat. (program com., chmn. bd. dirs. 1986, Woman of Achievement award 1986), Cin. C. of C., Cumberland Coll. Alumni Assn. (pres. 1982), English Speaking Union, Order Ky. Cols., Cin. Woman's Club (bd. dirs. 1992—, lecture/entertainment chmn. 1992-95), Town Club (bd. dirs. 1988—), Order Ea. Star (organist 1953—). Republican. Avocations: art, antiques, gardening, music, travel. Home: 6027 Stirrup Rd Cincinnati OH 45244-3917 Office: 6047 Montgomery Rd Cincinnati OH 45213-1611 Office Phone: 513-351-2700. Business E-Mail: cincinnatimodelagency@msu.com.

GALLOWAY, PATRICIA DENESE, civil engineer; b. Lexington, Ky., June 14, 1957; d. Howard John and Maudine Lou (Jones) Frisby; m. Kris Richard Nielsen, Mar. 16, 1987. BS in Civil Engring., Purdue U., 1978; MBA, NY Inst. Tech., 1984; PhD in Civil Engring., Kochi U. Tech., Japan, 2005. Registered profl. engr. Ky., NY, NJ, Ariz., Wis., Wyo., Fla., Wash., Colo., Pa., Man., Can., Australia. Project engr., insp. CH2M Hill, Milw., 1978-79, master program scheduler, 1979-81; sr. cons. Nielsen-Wurster Group, NYC, 1981-83, sr. engr., 1983-84, v.p., 1984-85, prin., exec. v.p., 1985-99, pres., 1999-2000, CEO, pres., 2001—04, CEO, 2004—. Lectr. Columbia U., U. Wis.-Madison; vis. prof. Kochi U. Tech.; presenter to numerous orgns; ptnr. Unionville Vineyards, Ringoes, NJ; pres. Unionville Ranch, L.L.C., Wash.; chief exec. Nielsen-Wurster Asia Pacific, Melbourne, Australia, 2001—, bd. dirs., mem. adv. bd. Contbr. articles to profl. jours. Named one of Top 10 Women in Constrn., Engring. New Record, 1986, one of Top 10 Women, Glamour Mag., 1987, 88, White House fellow regional finalist, 1990, Ky. Col., Gov. Patten, Sts. of Ky., 2002; named to Lafayette H.S. Hall of Fame, 2001; recipient Nat. Leadership Coun. Capital award, 1990, Engr. of Yr. award Mercer County Profl. Engrs., 1990, Nat. Leadership award Profl. Women in Constrn., 1995, Fed. Infrature Design award Whitehouse Commn., 1999, Upward Mobility award Soc. Women Engrs., 2003, Tribute to Women in Industry award, YWCA, 2004; named Disting. Engring. Alumnus, Purdue U., 1992, Celebration of Women, NAE, 2000. Fellow ASCE (instr. constrn. claims course, bd. chair task com. on women in civil engring. 1998—2000, internat. dir., bd. dirs. 1992-95, chmn. membership com. 2001—, pres.-elect 2003—, pres., bd. dirs. 2004 (1st woman); mem. NSF (dir. engring. 2004-), YWCA (Tribute to Women award), Am. Assn. Engring Socs., Nat. Soc. Professional Engrs., Am. Arbitration Assn., Professional Women in Construction, The Acad. Experts, UK, The Inst. Engrs., Australian Fellow, Soc. Women Engrs. (pres. Wis. chpt. 1980, pres. NY chpt. 1982, Disting. New Engr. 1980, Mobility award 2003-), Project Mgmt. Inst. (dir. pub. bd.), Am. Assn. Cost Engrs., Am. Nuclear Soc., Garden State Wine Growers Assn. (pres. 1990-92), Somerset County C. of C. (most outstanding woman in bus. and industry 1987), Purdue Engring. Alumni Assn. (bd. dirs., 1975-2001), Toastmasters, Sigma Kappa (fin. com. 1993-97), Tau Beta Pi. Republican. Methodist. Avocations: scuba diving, cross country skiing, hiking, horseback riding, wine making. Office: Nielsen-Wurster Group 719 Second Ave Ste 700 Cle Elum WA 98922 Fax: 609-497-3412. Office Phone: 509-857-2235. E-mail: patnwg@aol.com.

GALLOWAY, SHARON LYNNE, special education educator; b. Pensacola, Fla., Jan. 2, 1951; d. Richard Earl and Beatrice Kathlyn (Stone) G. AA, Pensacola Jr. Coll., 1995; BA, U. West Fla., 1998, MEd, 2000. Professionaly Recognized Spl. Educator, cert. Nat. Bd. Cert. Tchr. ENS-ECYA, 2005. Travel counselor, trainer Gulf Breeze Travel, Fla., 1985-95; sign lang. interpreter Pensacola Jr. Coll., 1995-97; tchg. intern Sherwood Elem., Pensacola, 1997-98; tchr. Sherwood Elementary, Pensacola, Fla., 1998—2006, Oriole Beach Elem., Gulf Breeze, Fla., 2006—. Coord. deaf ministries Gulf Breeze United Meth. Ch., 1995-2000, interpreter, 1995—, youth counselor anchor program, 1996-98; vol. Habitat for Humanity, Gulf Breeze, Pensacola, 1994-96, Gulf Coast Sports Ability Games, 1996, Special Olympics, 1999-02;

interpreter Ala.-West Fla. Annual Conf. United Meth. Ch., Montgomery, Ala., 1996-2004; server, cleanup com. Loaves and Fishes, Pensacola, 1996-97; reading camp tchr. U. West Fla., Pensacola, 1997, 99. Mem. NEA, Internat. Reading Assn., Student Coun. Exceptional Children (mem. chair 1996-98) Golden Key Internat. Honor Soc. (chpt. webmaster 1998-2002, chpt. treas. 1998), Coun. for Exceptional Children, Coun. for Children with Behavioral Disorders, Coun. for Children with Learning Disabilities, Alpha Sigma Lambda, Phi Delta Kappa (bd. dirs., chpt. webmaster, 2001—). Avocations: gardening, carpentry, interior design, webpage design. Home: 3367 Crestview Ln Gulf Breeze FL 32563 Office: Sherwood Elem Sch 501 Cherokee Trl Pensacola FL 32506-3519 Business E-Mail: sgalloway@escambiek12.fl.us.

GALLOZZI, MARIALUISA S., lawyer; b. Dec. 22, 1961; AB cum laude, Harvard U., 1982; JD, NYU, 1986. Bar: NY 1987, DC 1988. Law clk. for Judge Robert G. Doumar US Dist. Ct. (ea. dist.) Va., 1986—87; ptnr. Covington & Burling, Washington, co-chmn. recruitment com.; civil and child protection case mediator Superior Ct. DC. Office: Covington & Burling 1201 Pennsylvania Ave NW Washington DC 20004-2401 Office Phone: 202-662-5344. Office Fax: 202-778-5344. Business E-Mail: mgallozzi@cov.com.

GALLUCCI-BREITHAUPT, ADRIANNE, psychologist, social worker; b. Bridgeport, Conn., Nov. 17, 1959; d. Helen Mary and Alfred Joseph Gallucci; m. Mark Breithaupt, May 11, 2002. BA, Boston U., 1977—81, MSW, 1994—96; D of psychology, Mass. Sch. of Profl. Psychology, 1997—2002. Lic. psychologist Ariz., 2004, Md., 2004. Supr. Shawmut Bank, Boston, 1982—86; product mgr. Fidelity Investments, 1986—91; asst. v.p. Putnam Investments, 1991—94; crisis clinician Tri-City Mental Health, Lynn, Mass., 1996—97, Boston Emergency Services, 1997—99; psychotherapist Children's Charter, Inc., Waltham, Mass., 1998—99; rsch. cons. The Oak Group, Wellesley, Mass., 1999—2000; sr. psychologist No. Va. Mental Health Inst., Falls Church, Va., 2003—04. Mem.: Am. Psychology Assn. Liberal. Avocations: travel, amatuer aquarist, tennis, reading, music.

GALLUP, JANET LOUISE, management consultant; b. Rochester, N.Y., Aug. 11, 1951; d. John Joseph and Mildred Monica (O'Keefe) VerHulst; 1 son, Jason Hicks. BA, Hofstra U., 1973; MA, Calif. State U., 1979. Asst. trader E.F. Hutton, N.Y.C., 1975; instr. Calif. State U., Long Beach, 1978-79, grad. asst., 1979; fin. analyst Rockwell Internat., Seal Beach, Calif., 1979-85, coord. mgmt. and exec. devel. and succession planning, 1985-91; mgr. orgn. and employee devel. activities Hughes Aircraft, 1991-95; mgr. tng. ops. Smart & Final Co., L.A., 1995-98; mgr. human resources devel. Yons-A Safeway Co., Arcadia, Calif., 1998—2002; counselor Ctr. for Discovery, 2005; owner J. Gallup Cons., 2002—. Vol. Working Wardrobes of Orange County, Sr. Meals. Democrat. Office Phone: 562-708-7027. Personal E-mail: jlgallup@mindspring.com.

GALLUP, PATRICIA, computer company executive; Grad., U. Conn., 1979. Chmn. PC Connection, Inc., Milford, Mass., 1982—, CEO, 2002—, pres., 2003—. Named Entrepreneur of Yr., Ernst & Young, 1998, 2003, N.H. High Tech. Coun., 2003; named one of Top 50 Women Bus. Owners in U.S., Working Woman, 2000—03. Office: PC Connection Inc Rt 101A 730 Milford Rd Merrimack NH 03054-4631

GALOVICH, BEVERLY LUCILLE, psychologist; b. Detroit, Mich., Apr. 18, 1958; d. John Ralph and Barbara Phylis (Szalwinski) Horn; m. Michael Lewis Galovich (div.); children: Jennifer Silak, Stephanie, Michelle. AS, Oakland Cmty. Coll., Farmington Hills, Mich., 1990; BS, Madonna U., Livonia, Mich., 2002, MS, 2004. LLP Mich. Histologist Harper Hosp., Detroit, 1996—97, U. Mich. Dermatology Clinic, Ann Arbor, 1997—98, St. Mary's Hosp., Livonia, 1998—99; rsch. asst. Mich. State U., Lansing, 2001; therapist Positive Images, Detroit, 2002—. Vol. tutor computers Glengary Elem. Sch., Walled Lake, Mich., 1988; vol. tutor math Oakland Cmty. Coll., Farmington Hills, 1989, Walled Lake Ctrl. H.S., 1990. Mem.: Psi Chi (treas. 2002—04), Kappa Gamma Pi. Avocations: ice skating, singing, sewing, writing. Office: Positive Images 13336 E Warren Detroit MI 48215

GALTON, VALERIE ANNE, endocrinologist, educator; b. Louth, Eng., May 6, 1934; came to U.S., 1959; d. Wilfrid and Eileen (Watson) Hamilton; m. Michael Galton, Aug. 26, 1956 (dec. 1968); children: Ian Andrew, Kenneth Anthony. BSc with honors, U. London, 1955, PhD, 1958., 1967-75; Research assoc. Nat. Inst. Med. Research, Mill Hill, London, 1955-58; research assoc. Med. Sch., Harvard U., Boston, 1959-61; instr., then asst. prof. Dartmouth Med. Sch., Hanover, N.H., 1961-66, assoc. prof., 1968-75, prof., 1975—. Cons. NIH, Bethesda, Md., 1973-98. Mem. editl. bd. Endocrinology, 1982-85, Am. Jour. Physiology, 1982-85, 95—; contbr. articles to profl. jours. NIH grantee, 1962— Mem. Am. Thyroid Assn., Endocrine Soc. Home: 57 Jenkins Rd Lebanon NH 03766-2002 Office: Dartmouth Med Sch Lebanon NH 03756 Office Phone: 603-650-7735. Business E-Mail: val.galton@dartmouth.edu.

GALVAN, MARY THERESA, economics professor; b. Rockford, Ill., Dec. 19, 1957; d. Dino F. and Ida M. Dal Fratello; m. John D. Galvan, June 27, 1987; children: Marie K., John M., Kathleen T. BA, Rockford Coll., 1979; MA, No. Ill. U., 1981, PhD, 1988. Instr. No. Ill. U., DeKalb, 1979-81; asst. prof. Rockford Coll., 1981-87; assoc. prof. bus. and econs. St. Xavier Coll., Chgo., 1987-92; assoc. prof. mktg. North Ctrl. Coll., Naperville, Ill., 1992—, dir. Ctr. for Rsch., 1994—, chmn. bus. dept., 1998—, chair dept. bus., 1998. Chmn. grad. studies com. North Ctrl. Coll., 1996—; cons. Fed. Res. Bank Chgo., 1988—. Lector St. Elizabeth Seton Parish, Naperville, 1987—, mem. edn. commn. pastoral coun., 1998—, chmn. pastoral coun., 2001-2003, chmn. edn. commn., 2004, pres. Women's Network. Earhart Found. fellow, 1988; Hegelar Carus scholar, 1987. Mem. AAUW, Am. Econs. Assn., Am. Mktg. Assn., Am. Statis. Assn. (v.p. 1994—), Western Econs. Assn. Internat., Midwest Bus. Adminstrn. Assn., Midwest Econs. Assn., Acad. Mktg. Sci., Mktg. Educator's Assn., Phi Delta Kappa, Omicron Delta Epsilon, Mu Kappa Tau. Avocations: tennis, golf, sewing, hiking, reading. Office: North Ctrl Coll 30 N Brainard St Naperville IL 60540-4607 Office Phone: 630-637-5473. Business E-Mail: mtgalvan@noctrl.edu.

GALVIN, KATHLEEN MALONE, communications educator; b. N.Y.C., Feb. 9, 1943; d. James Robert and Helen M. (Sullivan) G.; m. Charles A. Wilkinson, June 19,1973; children: Matthew, Katherine, Kara. BS, Fordham U., 1964; MA, Northwestern U., 1965, 80, PhD, 1968. Tchr. Evanston (Ill.) Township High Sch., 1967-72; asst. prof. Northwestern U., Evanston, 1968-73, assoc. prof., 1973-78, prof., 1978—, assoc. dean, 1988-2001. Presenter workshops in field. Author: Listening by Doing, 1986, multiple articles and chpts. family communication; sr. author: Family Communication, 6th edit., 2004; co-author: Person to Person, 5th edit., 1996, Basics of Speech, 4th edit., 2004; co-editor: Making Connections, 4th edit., 2006, Communication Works!, 2000; developer, instr. 26-video series on Family Communication (PBS Adult Satellite Sys.). Office: Northwestern U Comm Studies Dept 2240 N Campus Dr Evanston IL 60208-3545 Office Phone: 847-491-2260. Business E-Mail: k-galvin@northwestern.edu.

GALVIN, KERRY A., lawyer; b. Greenville, SC, Jan. 27, 1961; BS in fgn. svc. cum laude, Georgetown U., 1983; JD cum laude, U. Mich., 1986. Bar: Tex. 1986. Assoc. Mayor Day & Caldwell, Houston; joined legal dept. as fin. counsel Lyondell Chem. Co., Houston, 1990, named assoc. gen. counsel, sec., 1998, assoc. gen. counsel internat. legal affairs Maidenhead, England, v.p., gen. counsel, sec. Houston, 2000—02, sr. v.p., gen. counsel, sec., 2002—. Office: Lyondell Chem Co 1221 McKinney St Ste 700 Houston TX 77010

GAMACHE, CLAUDETTE THERESA, artist, nurse; b. Fall River, Mass., Dec. 9, 1941; d. Raymond Alfred Cote and Yvette Marguerite Lavigne; m. Peter Paul Gamache, May 23, 1964; children: Daniel, Raymond, Christopher. Diploma, St. Anne's Nursing Sch., Fall River, Mass., 1962; BFA, U. Hartford, West Hartford, Conn., 1984; MA, Lesley U., Cambridge, Mass., 1985. RN Mass., N.Y., Calif., Conn., Me., N.H.; registered Am. Art Therapy Bd. RN Mt. Sinai Hosp., Hartford, Conn., 1984—86; expressive therapist Elmcrest Psychiat. Hosp., Portland, Conn., 1986—87; nurse clinician/expressive therapist, adolescent partial program New Britain Gen. Hosp., 1987—89; hospice nurse VNA Group, Hartford, 1989—93; hospice mgr. Portsmouth Visiting Nurses, NH, 1994—97; artist Claudette Gamache Gallery, Bath, Maine, 1997—. Pastel painting tchr. Heartwood Coll. Art, Kennebunk, Maine, 2000—02, Chocolate Ch. Art Ctr., Bath, 2003; vis. art tchr. Wells Mid. Sch., 2000; ind. pastel painting tchr., Bath, 2004—; spkr. in field of hospice nursing, 1990—97. Pastel painting, Reflection, 2001, Retreat, 2004, exhibitions include Internat. Pastel Soc., Raleigh, N.C., 2005, pub. in various profl. jours. Mem.: Am. Art Therapy Assn., Pastel Painters Me. (v.p. 2006), Pastel Soc. Am. Avocations: writing, astrology, piano, shaman drumming. Office Phone: 207-443-9978. Personal E-mail: claudettegamache@yahoo.com.

GAMBARO, RETHA WALDEN, artist; b. Lenna, Okla., Dec. 9, 1917; d. William Benson and Zella Athleen Walden; m. Stephen A. Gambaro, Sept. 24, 1945; children: Delia, Anna, Mario. Student, Corcoran Sch. Arts, Washington; apprentice with Berthold Schmutzhart, Washington. Curator various orgns., tech. adv.; lectr. in field; represented by Yah-Ta-Hey Gallery, New London, Conn., 1988—. One-woman shows include U.S. Dept. Health & Human Svcs., Washington, 1984, Children's Art Expo IV, Fredericksburg, Va., 1990, Buffalo Gallery, Alexandria, Va., 1992, Four Winds Gallery, Naples, Fla., 1995, exhibited in group shows at Fredericksburg Mus., 1993, Mcpl. Cultural Ctr., Frejus, France, 1993, Suffolk Mus., Suffolk, Va., 1995, exhibitions include Smithsonian Inst., Washington, 1982, 1983, Night of the First Americans, Kennedy Ctr., Washington, 1982, Nat. Cathedral, Washington, 1984, Art Inst. Phila., Fox-Chase Cancer Rsch. Ctr., Phila., 1985, State Botanical Garden of Ga., Athens, 1989, Peabody Mus., Hawack, Mass., George Washington U., Washington, 1982, Susquehanna Art Mus., Harrisburg, Pa., 1994, Represented in permanent collections Gallaudet Coll., Washington, Daybreak Star Art Ctr., Seattle, B'nai B'rith Mus., Washington, Howard U., Bacone Coll., Muskogee, Okla., Bust of Pres. John F. Kennedy, Internat. Franchise Found., Hawaii, Bust of Rev. Jesse Jackson, Convention Ctr., Washington, 1985, Bust of Martin Luther King, Jr., Howard U., Washington, Achievement award, Pfizer Rsch. Ctr., Groton, Conn. Founder, pres. Amerindian Circle. Mem.: Fredericksburg Ctr. for Creative Arts, Nat. Mus. Women in the Arts, Indian Arts & Crafts Assn., Artists Equity, Welcome to Wash. Internat. Club. Home and Studio: 74 Dishpan Ln Stafford VA 22554-5424

GAMBER, HEATHER ANNE, mathematics professor, statistician, consultant; b. Christchurch, New Zealand, Oct. 8, 1953; arrived in U.S., 1975; d. Leonard John and Sylvia Lorelei Lucas; m. James H. Gamber, Aug. 5, 1978; children: Jennifer, Carolyn, Catherine. BSc, U. Auckland, New Zealand, 1973, MSc with 1st class honors, 1975; PhD, U. Wis., 1978. Vis. asst. prof. Tulane U., New Orleans, 1978—79; assoc. prof. U. New Orleans, 1979—84; prof. math. Cy-Fair Coll., Cypress, Tex., 2003—. Owner Quality Decisions LLC, Houston, 2000—. Travel grantee, Fulbright Hayes Found., 1978, Project Access fellow, Math. Assn. Am./Am. Math. Assn. Two-Yr. Colls., 2004—05. Mem.: Am. Math. Assn. Two-Yr. Colls., Am. Soc. Quality, Am. Statis. Assn. Avocations: swimming, reading. Office: Cy-Fair Coll 9191 Barker-Cypress Cypress TX 77433 Office Phone: 281-290-5247. Business E-Mail: heather.a.gamber2@nhmccd.edu.

GAMBER, JAMIE SADDLER, athletic trainer; b. Metairie, La., Nov. 2, 1972; d. James David and Sonja Segura Saddler; m. James Carroll Gamber, III, June 3, 2000; 1 child, Christopher Britton. BS, U. La., Lafayette, 1995; MEd, Clemson U., SC, 1997; EdD, Auburn U., Ala., 2005. Cert. health fitness instr. Am. Coll. Sports Medicine, 2004. Grad. asst. athletic trainer Clemson U., 1995—98; asst. athletic trainer, instr. Mid. Tenn. State U., Murfreesboro, 1998—99; dir. Kenny Howard athletic tng. fellowship Auburn, 1999—2004; head athletic trainer Smiths Sta. H.S., Ala., 2004—05, Columbus Cottonmouths Hockey Club, Ga., 2005—. Lay eucharistic min. St. Dunstan's Episcopal Ch., Auburn, Ala., 2003—05. Scholar, SE Athletic Trainers' Assn., 2003; Jerry Rhea Sports Medicine scholar, Atlanta Falcons, 2002, Capt. Reginald E. and Geneva W. McKamie scholar, 2003. Mem.: Nat. Athletic Trainers' Assn. (cert.), SE Athletic Trainers' Assn., Ala. Athletic Trainers' Assn. (sec. 2005). Episcopalian. Avocations: travel, sailing, snorkeling, running, reading. Home: 420 Arnell Ln Auburn AL 36830 Office: Columbus Cottonmouths Hockey Club (SPHL) PO Box 1886 Columbus GA 31901 Personal E-mail: jsgamber@charter.net.

GAMBILL, CARA LEE, physician assistant; b. Waukesha, Wis., Nov. 30, 1968; d. Paul Alan and Joetta Lou (Powell) G. BA in Pub. Policy Studies, Duke U., 1991, M of Health Scis., physician asst. cert., 1997. Cert. physician asst. Nat. Commn. for Certification of Physician Assts. Rsch. assoc. Duke U. Med. Ctr., Durham, 1991-95; life skills trainer Carolina Learning Svcs., Durham, 1991-95; physician asst. Ctrl. Tex. Vets. Health Care Sys., Temple, 1998-2000, Kaiser Permanent, Sacramento, 2000—. Contbr. articles to profl. jours. Med. missionary Duke U. Med. Ctr., Haiti, 1996, Honduras, 1997; bd. dirs., cmty. devel. v.p. Round Rock (Tex.) Jaycees, 1998-99 Winner 3d pl. award Peter J. Nyquist Student Writing Competition, 1997, 2d pl. award Surg. Physician Asst. Writing Contest, 1998; health profl. scholar Dept. VA, 1995. Mem.: Calif. Acad. Physician Assts., Am. Acad. Physician Assts. Avocations: travel, sports. Office: Permanente Med Group Inc 1600 Eureka Rd Roseville CA 95661 Home: 201 W Tazewell St Apt 204 Norfolk VA 23510-1317 E-mail: clgambill@aol.com.

GAMBLE, CAHTINA ROBYNE, elementary school educator; b. Troy, NY, Jan. 26, 1973; d. John Robert and Sandra Dale Gamble. BA in Music Edn., Social Sci., U. Stonybrook, NY, 1997; M in Elem. Edn., Wilmington Coll., 2004. Cert. cosmetologist N.Y., Md., Del. Kindergarten tchr. PrimeTime Daycare and Develop. Ctr., Troy, NY, 1990—94; residential skills instr. Adults and Children with Learning Disabilities of Bethpage, NY, 1998; tchr. Delcastle Vocational Tech. H.S., Wilmington, Del., 1999—2001; mental health technician The Devereux Found., Malvern, Pa., 2002—03; 4th grade tchr. Highlands Elem. Sch., Wilmington, 2002—04; tchr. NY City Dept of Edn., Bklyn., 2006—. Mentor Jr. Achievement Inc., Newark, 2004—06; dance instr. Bethel Bapt. Ch. Youth Dept., 2005—. Youth mentor vol. Bethel Bapt. Ch., 2005—. Mem.: Wind and Fire Ministries. Avocations: singing, dance, music, writing poetry. Home: 200 8th St Troy NY 12180 Office: NYC Dept Edn PS 243 1580 Dean St Brooklyn NY 11213

GAMBLE, DESIRATA, artist, poet; b. Wilkesboro, NC; d. Robert Lee and Mary Etta Gamble; m. David Bullins, Feb. 14; 1 child, Zoe Bullins. AA with honors, Surry C.C., Dobson, N.C., 1983; BA in Psychology, U. N.C., Wilmington, 1985, BA in Studio Arts, 2001; postgrad., U. Ga., 1985—87. Ordained to ministry Apostolic Ch. Proofreader Joan S. Northrop, Wilmington, 1984—85; artist U. N.C., Wilmington, NC, 1996—2002; artist transp. MerleFest, Wilkesboro, NC, 1994—2005, 2006; prof. arts in art Buxton U., England, 2003; with Apollo Apostilic Svcs., 2005—. One-woman shows include The Morning Dew, Winston-Salem, NC, 1997—98, 2005, Claude Howell Gallery, Wilmington, 1998, 1999, The Deluxe, Wilmington, NC, 1998—99, 2006, The Beanstalk, Boone, NC, 1999—2001, Daughtry's Old Books, Wilmington, 2003, 2004, 2005, 2006. William Vance Nichols/Wilkes Art Gallery, Wilkesboro, NC, 2003, Nth Degree, Boone, 2006; artist, poet: Sights of the Wind, Her White Hair Peeps and We Heard the Music for Miles, 1985 (Book award for poetry U. N.C. Wilmington); Represented in permanent collections Daniel Hall, Wilkes C.C., Wilkesboro, NC, River Valley Animal Foods, Harmony, NC; author: numerous poems. Named State-wide Hon. Mention for the Lyricist, A Violet Letter from Frannie, 2005. Mem.: AAUW, Assn. Rsch. and Enlightenment, Smithsonian Inst., Acad. Am. Poets, Nature Conservancy, Southeastern Ctr. for Contemporary Art, Ala. State Poetry Soc. Personal E-mail: gambled1@excite.com.

GAMBLE, VANESSA NORTHINGTON, historian, healthcare educator, bioethicist; b. May 20, 1953; BA, Hampshire Coll., 1974; MD, U. Pa., 1983, PhD, 1987. Resident U. Mass. Med. Ctr.; visiting scholar Harvard U. Sch. Pub. Health; assoc. prof. family & cmty. medicine U. Mass.; asst. prof. history of medicine, science and family medicine U. Wis., Madison, 1989-93, assoc. prof., 1994—2000; dir. Ctr. for the Study of Race and Ethnicity in Medicine U. Wis. Sch. of Medicine, Madison, 1996—2000; v.p. Div. Comty. & Minority Programs Assn. Am. Med. Colleges, 2000—02; assoc. prof. health policy & mgmt. Johns Hopkins Bloomberg Sch. Pub. Health, 2002—04; dir. Nat. Ctr. Bioethics in Rsch. & Health Care Tuskegee U., 2004—, prof. bioethics & health care, 2004—. Adv. bd. Nat. Ctr. Primary Care Morehouse Sch. Medicine; adv. bd. Ctr. Study of Health Disparities Tex. A&M U.; adv. com. Soros Reproductive Health & Rights Fellowship; bd. trustees Ctr. for the Advancement of Health. Health commentator The Tavis Smiley Show, NPR; author: The Black Community Hospital: Contemporary Dilemmas in Historical Perspective, 1989, Germs Have No Color Line: Blacks & American Medicine 1900-1940, 1989, Making a Place for Ourselves: The Black Hospital Movement, 1920-1945, 1995 (Choice mag. Outstanding Academic Book). Chairwoman Tuskegee Syphilis Study Legacy Com., 1996—97. Mem.: Inst. Medicine. Office: Tuskegee University 1003 W Montgomery Rd Tuskegee Institute AL 36088*

GAMBLIN, CYNTHIA MACDONALD, mathematics educator, lobbyist; b. Chgo., Sept. 12, 1946; d. Robert Eugene and Janice (Billings) MacD.; m. James Bradford Gamblin, Sept. 6, 1969 (div. June 1980). BS, Washington U., St. Louis, 1969, MA in Teaching, 1971. Cert. tchr., Fla., Mo.; lic. basic ground instr. FAA. Tchr. maths. Mary Inst., St. Louis, 1969-70; exec. sec. Coalition for the Environment, St. Louis, 1971-72; office mgr. Around the World Food Corp., St. Louis, 1972-73; tchr. maths. Dunedin (Fla.) High Sch., 1973—. Mem. pub. policy com. Juvenile Welfare Bd., St. Petersburg, Fla., 1979-98, co-chmn. legis. subcom., 1989-90; advisor DHS Sailing Club, 2002—. Mem. Pinellas Classroom Tchrs. Assn. (lobbyist St. Petersburg chpt. 1979-92), Ctr. for Fla.'s Children, Jr. League of Clearwater, Phi Delta Kappa. Republican. Avocations: pilot, sailing, reading. Home: 1441 Fairway Dr Dunedin FL 34698-2270

GAMBRELL, LUCK FLANDERS, corporate financial executive; b. Jan. 17, 1930; d. William Henry and Mattie Moring (Mitchell) Flanders; m. David Henry Gambrell, Oct. 16, 1953; children: Luck G. Davidson, David Henry, Alice Kathleen, Mary G. Rolinson. Grad., St. Mary's Coll., Raleigh, N.C., 1948; AB, Duke U., Durham, N.C., 1950; diplome d'etudes françaises, L'Institut de Touraine, Tours, France, 1951. Chmn. bd. dirs. LFG Co., 1960—. Mem. State Bd. Pub. Safety, 1981—90, Chpt. Nat. Cathedral, Washington, 1981—85, World Svc. Coun. YWCA, 1965—; chmn. bd. dirs. Student Aid Found., Atlanta, 1992—99; life mem. bd. councilors Carter Ctr., Emory U.; mem. bd. advisors Emory U., Atlanta, 2001—04; coun. mem. Presbytery Greater Atlanta, 1988; elder First Presbyn. Ch., Atlanta; bd. dirs. Atlanta Symphony Orch., 1982—85. Recipient East Ga. Coll. Student Ctr. named in her honor, Swainsboro, Ga., 2002. Mem.: Atlanta Jr. League, Alpha Delta Pi.

GAMBRELL, SARAH BELK, retail executive; b. Charlotte, N.C., Apr. 12, 1918; d. William Henry and Mary (Irwin) Belk; m. Charles Glenn Gambrell (dec.); 1 child, Sarah Belk Gambrell Knight. BA, Sweet Briar Coll., 1939; D in Humanities (hon.), Erskine Coll., 1970, U. N.C., Asheville, 1986, Furman U., 1997, Johnson C. Smith U., 2003. Dir. Belk Inc., Charlotte, 1947—2005, dir. emeritus, 2005—. Bd. dirs. emeritus Belk Inc. Adv. bd. Erskine Coll. and Sem., Union PSCG, Opera Carolina; trustee Queens U., Charlotte; nat. bd. asset mgmt. and devel. com. YWCA; hon. trustee Cancer Rsch. Inst.; hon. trustee emeritus Princeton (N.J.) Theol. Sem.; trustee emeritus Furman U., Charlotte Mus. of History; bd. dirs. Parkinson's Disease Found., N.Y.C., N.C. Cmty. Found., Raleigh, Charlotte Philharmonic Orch., N.C. Transp. Mus., Spencer, NC; hon. bd. dirs. Hist. Rosedale, Charlotte, NC, YWCA, N.Y.C.; bd. dirs. YWCA of Ctrl. Carolinas; dir. Warren Wilson Coll., Asheville, NC. Recipient Algernon Sydney Sullivan award, Queens U., Charlotte, N.C., Univ. award, U. N.C. Chapel Hill, 1993, Woman of Achievement award, YWCA Charlotte, Mary Elizabeth Francis award, Florence Crittenton Svcs. Mem.: DAR, Fashion Group, Inc. (N.Y.C.), Jr. League Charlotte, Nat. Soc. Colonial Dames. Home: 300 Cherokee Rd Charlotte NC 28207-1908 Office: Belk Inc 2801 W Tyvola Rd Charlotte NC 28217-4500 also: 6100 Fairview Rd Ste 640 Charlotte NC 28210

GAMIN, JUDITH See GEMEINHARDT, JUDITH

GAMMEL, GLORIA L., secondary school educator; b. Aurora, Colo., June 19, 1979; d. Micheal Lanier and Linda Kay Gammel. B in Social Sci., U. Louisville, 2002; M in Secondary Edn., Drury U., Springfield, Mo., 2004. Tchr. Springfield Pub. Schs., Mo., 2004—. Office: Parkview High School 570 Meadowmere Springfield MO 65807 Office Phone: 417-523-9200.

GAMPEL, ELAINE SUSAN, investment company executive, consultant; b. New Haven, Apr. 12, 1950; d. Stanley Irwin and Marion (Levine) G.; m. Alan Joseph Tedeschi, Sept. 9, 1984; children: Zachary Joseph Gampel Tedeschi, Matthew Samuel Gampel Tedeschi. BS in Spl. Edn., Boston U., 1972; MS in Counseling, So. Conn. State U., New Haven, 1975; cert. investment mgmt. analyst, Wharton Sch. Bus., 1990. Spl. edn. tchr. Ansonia (Conn.) Pub. Schs., 1972-77; v.p., investment mgmt. cons. Paine Webber Inc., Denver, 1977-89; v.p. investments Dean Witter Reynolds, Denver, 1989-93, 1st v.p. investments, sr. cons., 1993-2000, sr. v.p. investments, sr. cons., 2000—, wealth advisor, 2002—. Bd. dirs. United Cerebral Palsy of Denver, 1984-93; outside editl. bd. Denver Post, 1991-94; chair investment com. Women's Found. Colo., Denver, 1995-97, treas. 1998, 99, chair bd. trustees, 2002; elected mem. Women's Forum of Colo., 2002; cmty. bd. Denver Nuggets, 1992-95; bd. dirs. Project PAVE, 2003—, Judith Ann Griese Found., 2004-05, Jewish Family Svc., 2006—; mem. investment com. Jewish Family Svc., 2005—. Recipient Women Leaders of Excellence award, Colo. Women's Leadership Coalition, 2003, Women of Distinction award, Miletti coun. Girl Scouts US, 2004. Mem. Investment Mgmt. Cons. Assn. (membership com., cert. com. 1990—), Denver Soc. Security Analysts. Avocations: tennis, running, biking. Office: Morgan Stanley 370 17th St Ste 5100 Denver CO 80202-5651 Office Phone: 303-595-2080. E-mail: elaine.gampel@morganstanley.com.

GAND, GALE, chef, restaurateur; b. Chgo. married; 1 child. Student, La Varenne, Paris. With Strathallen Hotel, Rochester, NY, Jam's, NYC, Carlos' Restaurant, Chgo., 1987; pastry chef Gotham Bar & Grill, NYC, Pump Room, Chgo., 1987, Stapleford Park, Leicestershire, England, Charlie Trotter's, Chgo., 1993; co-owner Trio, Chgo., 1993—95, Brasserie T, Northfield, 1995—2001, Vanilla Bean Bakery, Chgo., 1996—98; co-owner, exec. pastry chef Tru, Chgo., 1999—. Chef's coun. Chefs for Humanity. Host (TV series) Sweet Dreams, Food Network, 2000—; co-author (with Rick Tramonto, Julia Moskin): (cookbooks) American Brasserie, 1997 (finalist Julia Child Cookbook Awards); co-author: Butter Sugar Flour Eggs: Whimsical, Irresistible Desserts, 1999 (nominee James Beard award in baking and desserts category); co-author: (with Julia Moskin) Gale Gand's Just a Bite, 2001, Gale Gand's Short and Sweet, 2004; co-author: (with Rick Tramonto, Mary Goodbody) Tru: A Cookbook from the Legendary Chicago Restaurant, 2004. Named Top Pastry Chef of Yr., Best of Best Awards, Bon Appetit, 2001; named one of Top 10 Best New Chefs, Food & Wine, 1994, Chicago's 100 Most Influential Women, Crain's Chicago Bus., 2004; recipient Robert Mondavi award for culinary excellence, 1994, James Beard Found. award for outstanding pastry chef, 2001. Mem.: Culinary Coun., Marshall Field's. Mailing: Tru Restaurant 676 N St Clair St Chicago IL 60611 Office Phone: 312-202-0001.*

GANDEK, JEAN DAVIS, secondary school educator; b. Nashua, N.H., June 21, 1931; d. Townsend King and Helen Georgette (Butler) Davis; m. Andrew Gandek, Nov. 20, 1954 (dec. Aug. 1988); children: Barbara Lynne, Kathryn Lynne. BA, Mt. Holyoke Coll., 1952; MA, Columbia U., 1954. Rsch. technician Rockefeller Inst. for Med. Rsch., N.Y.C., 1952-53, 54-56, Alfred I. du Pont Inst., Wilmington, Del., 1956-57; substitute tchr. Seaford (Del.) Sch. Dist., 1977-93. Tutor Del. Tech. and C.C., Georgetown, 1993-02. Leader, cons., organizer Girl Scouts U.S.A., Seaford, 1970-81; v.p. Friends Seaford Dist. Libr., 1985-87; bd. commrs. Seaford Dist. Libr., 1987-96, v.p., 1988-90, treas., 1990-96; mem. Sussex County Libr. Adv. Coun., 1996-02, pres., 2001-02; mem. State Del. Coun. Librs., 2003—. Recipient Friend of Seaford

Edn., Seaford Bd. Edn., 1987. Mem. AAUW (edn. rep. Del. div. 1984-86, Seaford chpt. 1991-92, Ednl. Found. gift in her honor Del. div. 1986, Seaford 1989), Phi Beta Kappa. Unitarian Universalist. Avocations: reading, knitting, crossword puzzles, travel. Home: 745 Woodlawn Ave Seaford DE 19973-1237

GANDHI, PURVI B., psychologist; b. Navsari, Gurjarat, India, Aug. 15, 1970; arrived in U.S., 1975; d. Babu and Bharti Gandhi. BA, U. Ky., Lexington, 1994; MEd, U. Louisville, 1997; PsyD in Clin. Psychology, Spalding U., 2002. Lic. psychologist Bd. of Psychology, Calif. Crisis counselor Seven Counties Svc., Louisville, 1995—98, access counselor, 1997—98; adj. prof. Bellarmine Univ., Louisville, 1998—2000, acad. advisor, 1998—2000; psychologist Pacific Clin., Monrovia, Calif., 2001—. Cons./presenter in field. Participant for marathon Leukemia and Lymphoma Soc., 1999, 2005, 2006; bd. mem. Women's Indian Assn., 2004—05. Mem.: APA. Avocations: running, yoga. Office Phone: 626-357-3258.

GANDY, KIM ALLISON, feminist organization executive, lawyer; b. Bossier City, La., Jan. 25, 1954; d. Alfred K. and Roma Rae (Young) Gandy; m. Christopher Lornell; children: Elizabeth Cady, Katherine Eleanor. GBS, La. Tech. U., 1973; JD, Loyola U., 1978. Bar: La. 1978, U.S. Dist. Ct. (ea. and we. dists.) La. 1980, U.S. Supreme Ct. 1981, U.S. Ct. Appeals (5th cir.) 1982. Mgr. South Ctrl. Bell Tel. Co., New Orleans, 1973—77; asst. dist. atty. Orleans Parish, New Orleans, 1978—79; sole practice New Orleans, 1979—. Guest lectr. in field. Treas. ERA United Coalition La., 1977—78; chmn. New Orleans del. La. Dem. Conv., 1980, 1982; vice chmn. New Orleans del., 1984; dir. Women's Lobby Network, 1980—85; founder Greater New Orleans Assn. Dem. Women, 1984. Named New Orleans Outstanding Young Career Woman, New Orleans Bus. and Profl. Women, 1980; named one of New Orleans 100 Women in Forefront, 1986; recipient Law Alumni award, Loyola U., 1976, Milton Sheen award, 1978. Mem.: ABA, Assn. Women Attys., La. Trial Lawyers Assn., La. Bar Assn., NOW (nat. sec. 1987—91, exec. v.p. 1991—2001, pres. 2001—, Mid-South reg. dir. 1983—87, Woman of Yr.). Office: NOW 1700 Highland Dr Silver Spring MD 20910 Business E-Mail: president@now.org.

GANGLE, MELANIE JEAN, counselor; d. Eugene Martin and Sandra Smith Gangle; m. James Dewey. BS in Anthropology, Santa Clara U., 1993; MS in Edn., Western Oreg. U., 2000. Cert. rehab. counselor Commn. on Rehab. Counselor Certification, 2000. Human resources intern Stanford U. Hosp., Palo Alto, Calif., 1993, First Franklin Fin. Corp., San Jose, Calif., 1993—93; benefits coord. GAP, Inc., San Bruno, Calif., 1993—94; project rschr. Redbridge Disability Assn., London, 1995—97; disability svcs. grad. intern Portland State U., Oreg., 1999—2000; disability program grad. intern Pentagon, Dept. of Def., Washington, 2000; coord. office for students with disabilities, learning assistance counselor U. Portland, Oreg., 2000—. Facilitator speech therapy aphasia group Salem Hosp. Regional Rehab. Ctr., Salem, Oreg., 1997—98; group counselor Oreg. Youth Leadership Forum, Monmouth, 1999; adj. instr. rehab. counselor edn. Western Oreg. U., 2005—; presenter in field. Pub. rels. YWCA of Salem, Oreg., 1997; treas. Oreg. Parent Tng. Initiative, Inc., Salem, 1998—2000. Recipient Oreg. Scholar award, Gov. of Oreg., 1989, Witold Krassowski Anthropology/Sociology Rsch. award, Santa Clara U., 1993; scholar Honors scholarship, 1989-1993; scholarship, Salem Edn. Assn., 1989, Salem Hosp. Found., 1998-2000. Mem.: Assn. Higher Edn. and Disability (chair, vol. subcom. 2000—01), Oreg. Assn. Higher Edn. and Disability (pres. 2000—03). Achievements include Facilitated Governor's Award for College Student with a Disability, in partnership with Oregon Disabilities Commission Employment Committee, 2002; development of Electronic Text Guidelines and Presented to Oregon Association of Higher Education and Disability, 2003. Avocations: fiction author, poet, hiking, bicycling, travel. Office: U Portland 5000 N Willamette Blvd Portland OR 97203-5798 Office Phone: 503-943-7134. Office Fax: 503-943-7199. Business E-Mail: gangle@up.edu.

GANGLE, SANDRA SMITH, arbitrator, mediator; b. Brockton, Mass., Jan. 11, 1943; d. Milton and Irene M. (Powers) Smith; m. Eugene M. Gangle, Dec. 21, 1968; children: Melanie Jean, Jonathan Rocco. BA, Coll. New Rochelle, 1964; MA, U. Oreg.; JD, Willamette U., 1980. Bar: Oreg. 1980. Instr. French Oreg. State U., Corvallis, 1968-71, Willamette U., Salem, Oreg., 1971-74; instr. ESL Chemeketa C.C., Salem, 1975-79; labor arbitrator Salem, 1980—; pvt. practice, 1980-86, 96—; ptnr. Depenbrock, Gangle & Greer, 1986-96. Mem. Oreg., Idaho, Wash., Mont., Calif. and Alaska Arbitration Panels; mem. NASD securities arbitration and mediation panel, mediator employment bus. and disabilities disputes; clin. prof. Portland State U., 1981-84; cons. State Oreg., 1981; land use hearings officer City of Keizer, Oreg., 1985-91; mem. mediation panel for disabilities issues Key Bridge Found., 1995—; mem. USPS Redress mediation panel, 2000—. Contbr. articles to profl. jours. Land-use chmn. Faye Wright Neighborhood Assn., Salem, 1983-84; mem. Civil Svc. Commn., Marion County Fire Dist., Salem, 1983-89; mem. U.S. Postal Svc. Expedited Arbitration Panel, 1984-91; mem. Salem Neighbor-to-Neighbor Mediation Panel, 1986-91; mem. labor arbitrator panel Fed. Mediation & Conciliation Svc., 1986—; mem. panel Prudential APCOM reviewers, 1999-2000; ct. apptd. arbitrator, mediator Marion, Polk & Yamhill Counties, 1996—; mem. Marion County Cir. Ct. Dispute Resolution Commn., 1993-95; trustee Salem Peace Plaza, 1985-97; convenor Salem Peace Roundtable, 1995; bd. dirs. Salem YWCA, 1997-2002; bd. dirs. Salem City Club, 1998-2003, pres., 2001; chair planning com. joint conf. between Oreg. Women Lawyers and Assn. Women Solicitors, 1998; chair fgn. policy study group Marion-Polk LWV, 2001-05, pres., 2006-. NDEA fellow, 1967. Mem. Am. Arbitration Assn. (arbitrator/mediator), Assn. for Conflict Resolution (chpt. co-pres. 1993-94), Oreg. State Bar Assn. (ho. dels. 2005). Office: Sandra Smith Gangle PC PO Box 904 Salem OR 97308 Office Phone: 503-585-5070. Business E-Mail: gangle@open.org.

GANGLOFF, AMBER D., music educator; b. Charleston, Ill., July 4, 1980; d. Gary L. and Christine L. Gangloff. Student, Lincoln Trail Coll., Robinson, Ill., 1998—2001. Aide in computer dept. Marathon Ashland Petroleum, Robinson, 2000; libr. aide Lincoln Trail Coll., Robinson, 2001—04, guitar instr., 2004—. Accompanist Lincoln Trail Coll., Robinson. Recipient Svc. Recognition, Lincoln Trail Coll., 2005, 2006; scholar, ISAC/MAP LTC, 1998—2000. Office: Lincoln Trail College 11220 State Hwy 1 Robinson IL 62454 Office Phone: 618-544-8657. Business E-Mail: gangloffa@iecc.edu.

GANGOTENA, MARGARITA, educator, consultant; b. Quito, Ecuador, Dec. 6, 1948; d. Emilio and Carlota (Gonzalez) G.; m. Jorge F. Landivar, May 1982 (div. Apr. 1987); children: Emrys, Micaela. BA, U. Minn., 1971, MA, 1976, PhD, 1980. Cons., trainer, translator, S. Am., U.S.A., 1970—; mgr. U. Minn. - Citibank/Citicorps, Life/Dow Chems., San Juan, P.R., 1980-85; tchr. U. Minn., Mpls., 1988, U. Houston Downtown, 1988-92, Tex. A&M, College Station, 1992-96, Cen. Mich. U., Mt. Pleasant, 1994—. Coord. Fgn. Studies Degree program, Mpls., 1976-78; cons. various cos. including Powell Industries, Control Data, Ky. Fried Chicken, Quito, 1970—; head of adv. bd., sec. Ecuadorean Am. C. of C., Houston, 1989-92; co-founder U. San Francisco de Quito, Ecuador, 1983—; cons. trainer on supervisory mgmt. in cross-cultural work place; presenter in field. Contbr. articles to profl. jours.; contbg. author: Our Voices: Essays in Culture, Ethnicity, and Communication. An Intercultural Anthology, 1992, (recipient Disting. Scholarship Book Award, 1994). Speaker various civic orgns. Recipient McNamara fellowship World Bank's Rsch. Fellowship, 1983, Order of Ski-U-Mah, U. Minn., 1972, scholarship awards, 1967-72, others; grantee Tex. A&M U., 1995, U. Minn., 1976. Mem. Mortar Bd., Speech Comm. Assn. Am., Internat. Comm. assn., Soc. Intercultural Edn., Tng. and Rsch., Internat. Assn. Cross-Cultural Psychology, Latin Am. Psychol. Assn., Phi Kappa, others. Office: Speech Comm and Theater Arts Tex A&m Univ College Station TX 77843-0001 Office Phone: 979-209-7291. E-mail: eladev@verizon.net.

GANLEY, BETTY, artist; b. Rahway, N.J., Sept. 18, 1942; d. Walter George and Margaret Charlotte Kenney; m. John Charles Ganley, Feb. 6, 1965 (dec.); children: Scott Michael, Kyle Andrew, David Sean. Diploma in Nursing, Muhlenberg Sch. Nursing, Plainfield, N.J., 1965. RN Va., Md., N.J. Part-time nurse Holy Cross Hosp., Silver Spring, Md., 1979—2003. Artist-contbr., Fresh Flowers, The Best of Flower Painting, 1996, Splash 5 - The Glory of Color, 1998, The Artistic Touch 3, 1999, Splash 5, 2000, Splash 7, The Quality of Light, 2001, Splash 7, A Celebration of Light, one-woman shows include NIH, 1995, Glenview Mansion, Rockville, Md., 1997, The Manor House, Green Spring Gardens Pk., Alexandria, Va., 2002, exhibited in group shows at Quiet Waters Gallery, Annapolis, Md., 1996, Black Rock Art Ctr., Germantown, Md., 2003; cover artist, contbr. article Elan mag., 2000; Australian Artist mag., 2004; author: Secret Gardens in Watercolor, 2005, Artists Project You Can Paint 10 Secret Gardens No Watercolor, 2005. Named One of Nieman Marcus' Top 10 Artists of 2000; named one of Top 100, Arts for the Parks, 2001; recipient numerous awards for artwork, 1994—, Best of Show for watercolor, Rockville Art League 2001, McLean Art Club, Emerson Ramp Gallery Show, 2001, Potomac Valley Watercolor Soc., Bohrer Park Show, 2001, Best of Show, Vienna Art Soc., 1999, Best of Show and 1st Place for watercolor, Rockville Art League ann. spring show, 1997, Spl. award for watercolor, Va. Watercolor Soc. ann. Art Show, 2000, Top 10, Still Life Comp., Australian Artist Mag., 2004, numerous others. Mem.: Washington Watercolor Soc., Balt. Watercolor Soc., Va. Watercolor Soc. (Northlight award 2004), Potomac Valley Watercolor Soc., Internat. Soc. of Marine Painters, Reston Art League, Vienna Art Soc., So. Watercolor Soc., Rockville Art League. Home: 713 Forest Park Rd Great Falls VA 22066 Personal E-mail: bettyganley@hotmail.com.

GANN, ELIZABETH DIANNE, elementary school educator; b. Mena, Ark., Feb. 27, 1953; d. Royal D. Philpot and Lois Elizabeth Raines Philpot; m. Robert G. Gann, Aug. 15, 1987. BS in Edn., U. Ctrl. Ark., Conway, 1976; MS in Edn., Henderson State U., Arkadelphia, Ark., 1981. 6th grade math tchr. McNair Mid. Sch., Fayetteville, Ark., 2000—04; mid. sch. math coach Fayetteville Pub. Schs., 2004—. Recipient Entergy's Outstanding Tchrs. award, Enertgy Cooperation, 1997. Mem.: NW Ark. Coun. for Tchrs. Math., Ark. Coun. for Tchrs. Math. (Tchr. of Yr. 1997), Nat. Coun. Tchrs. Math. (assoc.), Delta Kappa Gamma (pres. elect 2006). Home: 277 Village Dr Fayetteville AR 72703 Office: McNair Middle School 3030 E Mission Blvd Fayetteville AR 72703 Office Phone: 479-527-3660. Office Fax: 479-527-3667. Personal E-mail: egann@fayar.net.

GANN, MELINDA DENISE, mathematics professor; b. Kosciusko, Miss., May 24, 1961; d. Gerrell Wayne and Annie Katherine Downs; m. Donald Ray Gann, June 4, 1983; children: Kelli Rhea, Michael Jeffrey. BS, Miss. State U., Starkville, 1983; M in Combined Scis., Miss. Coll., Clinton, 1990; PhD, U. So. Miss., Hattiesburg, 1999. Assoc. prof. math. Miss. Coll., 1990—. Cons. Miss. Pub. Schs., 1996—. Author: (mid. sch. tchg. manual) Algebric Thinking. Pres. PTA, Clinton, 1992—94. Named Outstanding Faculty Mem., Civitan Men's Club of Miss. Coll., 1995, Outstanding Alumnus of Yr., Miss. State U. Bapt. Student Union, 2002; recipient Outstanding Faculty award, Miss. Coll. Student Govt. Assn., 2001. Mem.: Miss. Tchrs. of Coll. Math., Miss. Coun. Tchrs. of Math., Nat. Coun. Tchrs. of Math., Mortar Bd. Baptist. Office: Miss Coll PO Box 4025 Clinton MS 39058 Office Phone: 601-925-3941. E-mail: gann@mc.edu.

GANN, PAMELA BROOKS, academic administrator; b. 1948; BA, U. N.C., 1970; JD, Duke U., 1973. Bar: Ga. 1973, N.C. 1974. Assoc. King & Spalding, Atlanta, 1973; 1975assoc. Robinson, Bradshaw & Hinson, P.A., Charlotte, 1974; asst. prof. Duke U. Sch. Law, Durham, 1975—78, assoc. prof., 1978—80, prof., 1980—99, dean, 1988—99; pres. Claremont McKenna Coll., Claremont, Calif., 1999—. Vis. asst. prof. U. Mich. Law Sch., 1977; vis. assoc. prof. U. Va., 1980 Author: (with D. Kahn) Corporate Taxation and Taxation of Partnerships and Partners, 1979, 83, 89; article editor Duke Law Jour. Mem. Am. Law Inst., Coun. Fgn. Rels., Order of Coif, Phi Beta Kappa Office: Claremont McKenna Coll Office Pres 500 E 9th St Claremont CA 91711-5903 Office Phone: 909-621-8111. Business E-Mail: pamela.gann@mckenna.edu.

GANNETT, DIANA RUTH, musician, educator; b. Davenport, Iowa, July 30, 1947; d. Wright Kent and Ruth Babette (Gebauer) Gannett; m. Dary John Mizelle, Dec. 17, 1974 (div. Oct. 1989); children: Adam Anthony Mizelle, Joseph Martin Mizelle, Agon Matthew Mizelle; m. Robert Cruden, 1996; stepchildren: Nathalie Cruden, Lyda Cruden. MusB with honors, U. Iowa, 1969; MusM, Yale U., 1972, DMA, 1977. Adj. lectr. double bass U. S. Fla., Tampa, Fla., 1973-75; instr. double bass Oberlin (Ohio) Conservatory, 1976-78; assoc. prof. double bass Lehman Coll., Bronx, NY, 1979-83, Yale U. Sch. Music, New Haven, 1984-92; tchr. double bass Hartt Sch. Music, Hartford, Conn., 1985-92; prof. double bass U. Iowa Sch. Music, Iowa City, 1992—2001; prof. double bass, doctoral advisor strings U. Mich. Sch. Music, Ann Arbor, 2002—. Prin. bass Black Hills Festival, SD, 1970—91, Gulf Coast Orch., Tampa, 1973—75, Eastern Music Festival, Greensboro, NC, 1975, Greensboro, 78, Greensboro, 1984—92, Quad City Symphony Orch., 1992—2001; numerous chamber & solo performances traditional, contemporary music. Mem.: Internat. Soc. Bassists (past pres.), Am. String Tchrs. Avocations: instrument building, drawing, calligraphy, Aikido. Home: 550 Woodhill Dr Saline MI 48176 Office Phone: 734-764-6515.

GANNON, SISTER ANN IDA, retired philosophy educator; b. Chgo., 1915; d. George and Hanna (Murphy) G. AB, Clarke Coll., 1941; A.M., Loyola U., Chgo., 1948, LL.D., 1970; PhD, St. Louis U., 1952; Litt.D., DePaul U., 1972; L.H.D., Lincoln Coll., 1965, Columbia Coll., 1969, Luther Coll., 1969; LHD, Augustana Coll., 1969; L.H.D., Marycrest Coll., 1972, Ursuline Coll., 1972, Spertus Coll. Judaica, 1974, Holy Cross Coll., 1974, Rosary Coll., 1975, St. Ambrose Coll., 1975, St. Leo Coll., 1976, Mt. St. Joseph Coll., 1976, Stritch Coll., 1976; LHD, Stonehill Coll., 1976, Elmhurst Coll., 1977, Manchester Coll., 1977, Marymount Coll., 1977; L.H.D., Governor's State U., 1979; LHD, Seattle U., 1981, St. Michael's Coll., 1984, Nazareth Coll., 1985, Holy Family Coll., 1986, Keller Grad. Sch. Mgmt., Our Lady of Holy Cross Coll., New Orleans, 1988. Mem. Sisters of Charity, B.V.M.; tchr. English St. Mary's High Sch., Chgo., 1941-47; residence, study abroad, 1951; chmn. philosophy dept. Mundelein Coll., 1951-57, pres., trustee, 1957—75, prof. philosophy, 1975-85, emeritus faculty, 1987—, archivist, 1986—. Contbr. articles philos. jours. Mem. adv. bd. Sec. Navy, 1975—80, Chgo. Police Bd., 1979—89; bd. dirs. Am. Coun. on Edn., 1971—75, chmn., 1974—75; nat. bd. dirs. Girl Scouts USA, 1966—74, nat. adv., 1976—85; trustee St. Louis U., 1974—87, Ursuline Coll., 1978—92, Cath. Theol. Union, 1983—89, DeVry, Inc., 1987—98, Duquesne U., 1989—91, Montay Coll., 1993—95, Mundelein Coll., 1957—75; bd. dirs. Newberry Libr., 1976—, WTTW Pub. TV, 1976—, Parkside Human Svcs. Corp., 1983—89. Recipient Laetare medal, 1975, LaSallian award, 1975, Aquinas award, 1976, Chgo. Assn. Commerce and Industry award, 1976, Hesburgh award, 1982, Woman of Distinction award Nat. Conf. Women Student Leaders, 1985, Outstanding Svc. award Coun. Ind. Colls., 1989, Woman of History award for edn. AAUW, 1989; named One of 100 Oustanding Chgo. Women, Culture in Action, 1994, Alpha Sigma Nu, 1996. Mem. Am. Cath. Philos. Assn. (exec. coun. 1953-56), Assn. Am. Colls. (bd. dirs. 1965-70, chmn. 1969-70), Religious Edn. Assn. Am. (pres. 1973, chmn. bd. 1975-78), North Cen. Assn. (commn. on colls. and univs. 1971-78, chmn. exec. bd. 1975-77, bd. dirs.), Assn. Governing Bds. Colls. and Univs. (bd. dirs. 1979-88, hon. bd. dirs. 1989-92). Home: Wright Hall 6364 N Sheridan Rd Chicago IL 60660-1726 Office: Gannon Ctr Piper Hall 6525 N Sheridan Rd Chicago IL 60626-5344 Office Phone: 773-508-8450. Business E-Mail: aganno2@luc.edu.

GANO, JANET ANNE, secondary school educator; b. Honolulu, May 23, 1948; d. Therman Lester and Caroline Marie Butts; children: Gregory Scott, Jeffery Michael. BA, U. Ctrl. Fla., Orlando, 1970. Tchr. mid. sch. Lake County Sch. Bd., Leesburg, Fla., 1972—73; tchr. migrant program Polk County Sch. Bd., Winter Haven, 1973—74, tchr. h.s. Auburndale, 1974, tchr. mid. sch. English, 1975—84, tchr. h.s. English, 1984—2005, Eagle Lake, 2005—. Co-chair recognition com. BARC Bloodhound Achievment Recognition Com., Auburndale, 1994—2000; co-chair dropout prevention program TAP, 2003—05; organizer and judge Sch. and Polk County Poetry Contest, 1986—2005. Mem.: Polk County Coun. Tchrs. English. Avocations: personal fitness trainer, reading, gourmet cooking, history. Office: Polk County Sch Bd 1915 S Floral Ave Bartow FL 33830 Office Phone: 863-534-0500. Personal E-mail: gddavis1031@hotmail.com.

GANOTE, ANGELA, newscaster; BA in Speech Comms., Ind. U. Intern WRTV-TV, Ind.; with Sta. WBC-TV, Columbus, Ind., Sta. WLFI-TV, Lafayette, Ind., Sta. WSBT-TV, South Bend, Ind.; anchor Sta. WCMH-TV, Columbus, Ohio, Sta. WXIN-TV, Indpls., 2001—. Office: WXIN Fox 59 6910 Network Pl Indianapolis IN 46278-1929

GANSLE, MARBRY L., physical education educator; d. Chester and Almeda Pulver; m. Stephen Gansle, Mar. 9; 1 child, Ashley. BS in Phys. Edn. and Health, Russell Sage U., Troy, N.Y., 1977, MS in Health Edn., 1983. Instr. phys. edn., instr. Shaker H.S., Latham, NY, 1977—. Office Phone: 518-785-5511 3347. Business E-Mail: mgansle@ncolonie.org.

GANTER, SUSAN LYNN, foundation administrator, retired mathematics professor; b. Waynesboro, Va., Jan. 29, 1964; d. Dorrance Lynn and Gertrude M. (Kirschner) G. B.Music Edn., BS in Math. Sci., So. Meth. U., Dallas, 1986; MA in Math., U. Calif., Santa Barbara, 1988; PhD in Math. Edn., U. Calif., 1990. Grad. math. instr. U. Calif., Santa Barbara, 1986-88; math. instr. Santa Barbara City Coll., 1988-90; asst. prof. math. Western Wash. U., Bellingham, 1990; dir. for program for promotion of inst. change Am. Assn. for Higher Edn.; math. sci. faculty Worcester Polytechnic Inst.; assoc. prof., math. sci. Clemson U., SC, 1999—2004; exec. dir. Assn. of Women in Sci., Washington, 2004—. Contbr. articles to profl. jours. Santa Barbara City Coll. faculty enrichment grantee, 1990, U. Calif.-Santa Barbara grantee, 1989. Mem. Nat. Coun. Tchrs. Math., Math. Assn. Am., Am. Math. Soc., Wash. Math. Coun., Soc. for Indsl. and Applied Math., Western Wash. U. Collegiate Chorale, Music Acad. of the West Opera, Kappa Mu Epsilon, Kappa Delta Pi, Mu Phi Epsilon. Roman Catholic. Avocations: singing, hiking, swimming. Office: Assn for Women in Sci Ste 650 1200 New York Av NW Washington DC 20005

GANTLEY, JUDY ANN, elementary school educator, retired music educator; b. Belleville, Ill., Aug. 24, 1941; d. Vernon Miller and Juanita Victoria Eckert. MusB, Stetson U., 1962; MusM, U. So. Calif., 1964. Tchr. L.A. (Calif.) Unified Sch. Dist., 1966—2003, ret., 2003. Chmn. Sch. Improvement Walter Reed Mid. Sch., L.A., 1993—2003. Singer: Roger Wagner Master Chorale, 1972—81. Vol. Doingsomething, 1991—2004, bd. dirs., 1991—2000. Grantee, U. So. Calif., 1991. Mem.: United Tchrs. L.A., Phi Beta. Avocations: photography, jewelry design, graphic design. Home: 1501 Pearl St 6 Santa Monica CA 90405 Personal E-mail: jgantley@verizon.net.

GANTZ, SUZI GRAHN, special education educator; b. Chgo., May 17, 1954; d. Robert Donald and Barbara Edna (Ascher) Grahn; m. Louis Estes Gantz, July 11, 1976; children: Christopher, Joshua. BS in Edn. of Deaf and Hard of Hearing, U. Ill., 1976. Tchr. A.G. Bell Sch., Chgo., 1976-80, 88—, facilitator Edn. Connection grant, 1999-2001; sales asst. Bob Grahn & Assocs., Chgo., 1982-84; with sales dept. Isis/My Sisters Circus, Chgo., 1984-86; interpreter Glenbrook North High Sch., Northbrook, Ill., 1986-87; interpreter, aide Lake Forest (Ill.) Dist. 67, 1987-88. Mem. Northbrook Citizens for Drug and Alcohol Alliance, 1988—; cubmaster Boy Scouts Am., Northbrook, 1990-93. Mem. Ill. Tchrs. of the Hearing Impaired, A.G. Bell Soc., Coun. on Exceptional Children. Avocations: dance, swimming. Home: 485 Laburnum Dr Northbrook IL 60062-2259 Office: O A Thorp Scholastic Acad 6024 W Warwick Chicago IL 60634 Office Phone: 773-534-3640. Personal E-mail: shopatnord@comcast.net.

GANTZER, MARY LOU, medical products executive; d. Richard John and Mary Jane (Capistrant) G. B in Chemistry, U. Minn., 1972, MS, 1976; PhD in Chemistry, U. Va., 1980. Instr., postdoctoral fellow dept. chemistry U. Va., Charlottesville, 1980—81; rsch. scientist diagnostics divsn. Miles, Inc., Elkhart, Ind., 1981—84, sr. rsch. scientist, 1984—86, staff scientist, 1986—87, supr. R&D, 1987—91, project mgr., 1991—98, coord. clin. and outcomes rsch., 1996—98; dir. clin. and sci. affairs Dade Behring, Inc., Newark, Del., 1998—2004, v.p., clin. and sci. affairs, 2004—. Mem. Women in Mgmt. del. to People's Republic of China, 1988; bd. dirs. Clin. and Lab. Stds. Inst. (formerly Nat. Commn. for Clin. Lab. Stds.), 2003-. Contbr. articles to chemistry jours.; patentee in field. Mem. Am. Assn. Clin. Chemistry (chmn. Chgo. sect. 1988, chair long range planning com. 1993-95, bd. editors Clin. Chem. News 1993-95, pres. 2002, Chmn.'s award 1988), Am. Heart Assn. (profl. mem.), Soc. Chest Pain Ctrs. Roman Catholic. Avocation: needlecrafts. Office: Dade Behring Inc (MS709) PO Box 6101 Newark DE 19714-6101

GANULIN, JUDY, public relations professional; b. Chgo., May 2, 1937; d. Alvin and Sadie (Reingold) Landis; m. James Ganulin, June 23, 1957; children: Stacy Ganulin Clark, Amy Ganulin Lowenstein. BA in Journalism, U. Calif., Berkeley, 1958. Copywriter-sec. Joe Connor Advt., Berkeley, 1958; exec. sec. Prescolite Mfg. Co., Berkeley, 1958-59; info. officer Office of Consumer Counsel, Sacramento, 1959-61; pub. rels. positions various polit. campaigns, Fresno, Calif., 1966; adminstrv. asst., editor, mktg. Valley Pubs., Fresno, 1971-80; staff asst. to county supr. Bd. Suprs., Fresno, 1980-82; field rep. Assemblyman Bruce Bronzan, Fresno, 1982-84; prin. Judy Ganulin Pub. Rels., Fresno, 1984—. Speaker new bus. workshop SBA/Svc. Corps Ret. Execs., Fresno, 1990—. Active Hadassah, Fresno, 1975—; pres. Temple Beth Israel Sisterhood, Fresno, 1976; panelist campaign workshop Nat. Women's Polit. Caucus, Fresno, 1994, 2001, publicity chmn. ctrl. Calif. chpt., 1999—2000; mem. C. of C. Art and Wine Festival Com., 1999—2000, Juvenile Justice Ctr. Task Force, 2001, Valley Women's Polit. Fund; bd. dirs. Temple Beth Israel, Fresno, 1972—75, Planned Parenthood Ctrl. Calif., Fresno, 1986—91, Empty Bowls, Sr. Companion Program. Mem. Pub. Rels. Soc. Am. (accredited pub. rels. practitioner, pres. Fresno/Ctrl. Valley chpt. 1994), Am. Mktg. Assn. (pres. ctrl. Calif. chpt. 1987-88), Calif. Press Women, Fresno Advt. Fedn., Fresno Comm. Network (v.p., pres. 1991-93), Fresno C. of C. (mem. mktg. com. 1988-), Fresno Comm. Network (formerly Pub. Rels. Roundtable). Democrat. Avocations: travel, reading, cooking. Office: Judy Ganulin Pub Rels 1117 W San Jose Ave Fresno CA 93711-3112 Office Phone: 559-222-7411. Personal E-mail: jganulin@comcast.net.

GANZEL, LINDA SUE, secondary school educator; b. Nebraska City, Nebr., Aug. 13, 1965; d. Robert and Ruby Ann Wrigg G. BA in Edn., Peru (Nebr.) State Coll., 1987; MA in Curriculum and Instrn., U. Nebr., 1998. Student tchr. Techumseh (Nebr.) Pub. Sch., 1987; tchr. English and art Macy (Nebr.) Pub. Schs., 1987-95; tchr. English and journalism Walthill (Nebr.) Pub. Sch., 1995—96; tchr., art, speech, drama and journalism Mead (Nebr.) Pub. Sch., 1996—98; ESL, dept. head Omaha Ctrl. H.S., 1998—2006. GED instr. Nebr. Indian C.C., Winnebago, Nebr., 1991-92; coord. Young Nebr. Animation project, Macy, Nebr., U. Nebr. at Kearny and Nebr. Arts Coun., 1992-94; instr. N.Am. Handicapped Riding Assn., 2006— Sponsor Fellowship of Christian Athletes, Macy, Nebr., 1991-2000; counselor, tchr. I Can Camps, Macy, 1991-95. Recipient Dorothea A. Kropp Art scholarship, Campbell Kropp Found., Nebr. City, 1983-87. Mem. NEA, Nat. Coun. Tchrs. of English, Nebr. Art Education Assn., Sigma Tau Delta, Kappa Delta Pi Republican. Avocations: art, piano, tennis, horseback riding, skiing. Office: Ctrl High Sch 124 N 20th St Omaha NE 68102

GAPEN, DELORES KAYE, librarian, educator; b. Mitchell, S.D., July 1, 1943; d. Lester S. and Lena F. G. BA, U. Wash., 1970, M.L.S., 1971. Gen. cataloger Coll. William and Mary, Williamsburg, Va., 1971-72; instr., asst. head Quick Editing Ohio State U., Columbus, 1972-74, head, 1974-77; asst. dir. tech. services Iowa State U., Ames, 1977-81; dean, prof. univ. libraries U. Ala., University, 1981-84; dean gen. library system U. Wis., Madison, 1984-91; exec. com. Council U. Wis. Libraries, 1985-87; cons. Northeast Mo. State U., 1980, Assn. Research Libraries task force on bibliog. control, 1981, Pa. State U., 1982, Conn. Coll., 1982; chmn. Coun. U. Wis. Librs., Madison, 1989-90; dir. libr. Case Western Res. U., 1991—. Vice chmn. exec. com. of bd. trustees U. Wis. Online Computer Library Ctr., Madison, 1984-86, also mem. research libraries adv. com. (chair task force on Future of Research Library Coop. in Changing Techs. Environment, 1986-89, chmn. com. short cataloging records, 1983-84), 1989; cons. Bryn Mawr Coll. Online System Planning, 1983, Council Library Resources Edn. Task Force on Future of Library Sch. Edn., 1983, Tex. A&I U. reaffirmation team cons. for So. Assn. Colls. and Schs., 1984, Dickinson Coll. Library Autocat System, 1987; chair Assn. of Research Libraries Task Force for Govt. Info. in Electronic Form, 1986-87; mem. Assn. of Research Libraries Task Force on Scholarly Communication, 1983-87; nat. cons. scholar librarian, IBM, 1989-90. Contbr. articles to profl. pubs. Mem. AAUP, ALA, Southeastern Libr. Assn., Ala. Libr. Assn., Assn. Rsch. Librs. (chmn. task force govt. info. in electronic form 1986-87, bd. dirs. 1987-90), Bus. and Profl. Women's Assn., Beta Phi Mu, Alpha Lamba Delta. Democrat. Roman Catholic. Office: Case Western Res U Libr 10900 Euclid Ave Cleveland OH 44106-1712

GAPPA, JUDITH M., academic administrator; Student, Wellesley Coll., 1957-60; BA in Music, George Washington U., 1968, MA in Musicology, 1970; EdD in Ednl. Adminstrn., Utah State U., 1973; cert. Inst. for Ednl. Mgmt., Harvard U., 1980. Lectr. George Washington U., Washington, 1968-69; dir. fine arts program The York Sch., Monterey, Calif., 1970; program cons. Western Interstate Commn. for Higher Edn., Boulder, Colo., 1973; coord. affirmative action program Utah State U., Logan, 1973-75, dir. affirmative action/equal opportunity programs, asst. prof., 1975-77, 78-80, project dir., 1979-81; sr. staff assoc. Nat. Ctr. for Higher Edn. Mgmt. Systems, Inc., Boulder, 1977-78; assoc. v.p. for faculty affairs, dean of faculty, prof. San Francisco State U., 1980-91; sr. assoc. Am. Assn. Higher Edn., 1995-97; prof. Purdue U., West Lafayette, Ind., 1991—, v.p. human rels., 1991-98. Served on numerous coms., couns. Utah State U., San Francisco State U.; cons. Assn. Governing Bds., 1994, U. Mich., Duluth, 1992, Calif. State U. Human Resources Mgmt. Office, 1992, Am. U., Washington, 1987, No. Rockies Consortium for Higher Edn. Conf., 1985, So. Utah State Coll., 1982, Nat. Ctr. for Rsch. in Vocat. Edn., 1980-81, Hood Coll., 1982-84, Am. Insts. for Rsch. in Behavioral Scis., 1980-81; condr. workshops on edn. Co-author: The Invisible Faculty, 1993; mem. editl. bd. Rev. of Higher Edn., 1994-97; contbr. numerous articles to profl. jours. Grantee Lilly Endowment, 1995, United Techs. Corp., 1992, TIAA-CREF/Lilly Endowment, 1990, Calif. State U., 1985, San Francisco State U., 1981, HEW, 1979-81, Nat. Inst. Edn., 1977, Utah State U., 1977, Fed. workshop grant, 1976, State of Utah, 1975, 76. Mem. Western Assn. Schs. and Colls. (accreditation team mem. Calif. State U.-L.A. 1990), Am. Assn. for Higher Edn. (sr. assoc. Washington chpt. 1995-97), Assn. for Study of Higher Edn. (nat. adv. bd. ASHE-ERIC Higher Edn. Report Series 1990-91, editl. bd. Rev. of Higher Edn. 1994-97, nominating com. 1986-87, program com. for 1986 nat. conf., membership com. 1982-84, conf. com. 1983, editl. bd. Rev. of Higher Edn. 1994-97), Am. Coun. on Edn. Nat. Identification Program (No. Calif. state coord. 1988-91). Office: Purdue Univ Coll Edn 1446 Liberal Arts Rd West Lafayette IN 47907-1075

GARABEDIAN-URBANOWSKI, MARTHA ANN, foreign language educator; b. Whitinsville, Mass., Dec. 8, 1953; d. Charles and Sadie (Madanjian) G.; m. William John Urbanowski, Jr., June 8, 1991. BA summa cum laude, Worcester State Coll., 1975; MA, U. Conn., 1978, PhD, 1984. Grad. tchg. asst. in Spanish U. Conn., Storrs, 1975-79; vis. asst. prof., lectr. Spanish Assumption Coll., Worcester, Mass., 1984-90; prof. Spanish Western New Eng. Coll., Springfield, Mass., 1990—. Adj. prof. Spanish, Worcester State Coll., fall 1985. Contbr. articles to profl. jours. The Josefina Romo-Arregui Meml. scholar U. Conn., Storrs, 1983. Mem. MLA, N.E. MLA, Am. Coun. on the Tchg. Fgn. Langs., Am. Assn. Tchrs. Spanish and Portuguese, Mass. Fgn. Lang. Assn., Worcester Art Mus., The Smithsonian, Libr. Congress, Phi Kappa Phi, Kappa Delta Pi. Armenian Evangelical. Avocations: golf, music, art, reading, travel. Home: 21 Pine Ridge Rd Southbridge MA 01550-2139 Office: Western New Eng Coll 1215 Wilbraham Rd Springfield MA 01119-2612

GARAS-YORK, KELI ANN, reading specialist; b. Buffalo, Aug. 4, 1973; d. Michael Edward and Tena Marie Garas; m. Richard David York, July 2, 2005. BS in Elem. Edn., SUNY, Oswego, 1994; MEd, St. Bonaventure U., 1999; PhD in Reading Edn., SUNY, Buffalo, 2005. Tchr. Buffalo Bd. Edn., NY, 1996—2002; rsch. asst. U. Buffalo, 2002—03; tchr. Buffalo Bd. Edn., 2004; reading specialist West Seneca Ctrl. Sch., NY, 2004—; grad. course instr. U. Buffalo, 2002, 2004, 2005. Author: (book) Tools for Teaching Literacy in the Third Grade, 2006. Pres. Niagra Frontier Reading Coun., 2006—. Mem.: NY State Reading Assn. (Charlotte award commn., children's choice award choir 2000—). Home: 50 Arlington Rd Buffalo NY 14221 Office: Winchester Elem 650 Harlem Rd Buffalo NY 14224

GARAVAGLIA, JAN C., forensic pathologist, chief medical examiner; m. Kevin Kowaleski, 1980; children: Alexander, Eric. AB magna cum laude, St. Louis U. Sch. Medicine, 1978, MD, 1982. Cert. Am. Bd. Pathology in combined anatomic and clin. pathology, Am. Bd. Pathology in forensic pathology. Tchg. Wis. Pub. Sch. Sys., 1979; fellowship, forensic pathology Dade County Med. Examiner's Office, Miami, Fla.; externship, psychiatric dept. Mass. Gen. Hosp., 1981; externship, Third World Crisis Medicine Cambodian Refugee Camp Hosp., Phanat Nikhom, Thailand, 1982; intern, internal medicine St. Louis U. Hosp., 1982, resident, anatomic/clin. pathology dept., 1983—87; assoc. med. examiner Duval County, Jacksonville, Fla., 1988—91, Ga., 1991—93; med. examiner Bexar County Forensic Sci. Ctr., San Antonio, 1993—2003; dep. chief med. officer Med. Examiner's Office, Orlando, Fla., 2003—04; chief med. examiner Orange-Osceola Med. Examiner's Office, Dist. 9, Orlando, Fla., 2004—. Clin. asst. prof., dept. pathology U. Tex. Health Sci. Ctr., San Antonio, 2000, mem. grad. faculty coun., grad. sch. biomedical sci.; given numerous presentations and lectures at various institutions. Published media Jour. of Forensic Sciences, Am. Jour. Forensic Medicine and Pathology, host Dr. G: Chief Medical Examiner (Discovery Channel), 2004—. Mentor Hispanic Ctr. of Excellence, U. Tex.; independent study mentor for HS students of gifted and talented program Tex. Recipient Hidalgo award, Bexar County Commissioners Ct., Tex., 2000. Mem.: Am. Acad. Forensic Sciences, Nat. Assn. Med. Examiners. Office: Dist Nine Medical Examiner's Office 1401 Lucerne Terr Orlando FL 32806

GARAY, DOLORES LOLLIE, science educator; m. Reynaldo Garay; children: Luz del Mar, Joaquin Alfredo. BA, U. Houston, 1972; MS in Tchg., Rice U., 2004. Lic. Am. Amateur Radio League. Sci. coord., sci. educator Redd Sch., Houston, 1987—. Tchr. liaison Space Found., 2005; tchr. Argonaut, Jason Found. for Edn., 2005—; Messenger Educator fellow Carl Sagan Ctr. for Earth and Space Sci. Edn., Univs. Space Rsch. Assn., 2004—. Contbr. articles to profl. jour. Finalist Presdl. award for Excellence in Math. and Sci., 2003; recipient Elem. Sci. Tchr. of Yr. award, Houston Mus. of Health/Med. Sci., 1999, Educator Achievement award, AIAA, 2005; grantee, Am. Inst. Aeronautics and Astronautics, 2005; Sci. Edn. Leadership fellow, Baylor Coll. Medicine, 2000-2001, Sci. Edn. Leadership Tng. fellow, HULINC-Baylor Coll. Medicine, 1999, Victor Clark Youth Incentive Program grantee, Am. Amateur Radio League, 2003. Mem.: Tex. Coun. Elem. Sci., Sci. Tchrs. Assn. Tex., NSTA, Bldg. a Presence for Sci. (assoc.; point of contact 2003—04), NW Amateur Radio Soc. Achievements include Science Program LABRATS: Learning About Research And Technology Through Science. Avocations: astronomy/space science, reading, travel, camping. Office: Redd School 4820 Strack Rd Houston TX 77069 Office Phone: 281-440-1106.

GARBACZ, PATRICIA FRANCES, school social worker, therapist; b. Hamtramck, Mich., Nov. 26, 1941; d. Stanley and Frances (Harubin) G. BS, Siena Heights Coll., 1969; M. Pastoral Counseling, St. Paul U., Ottawa, Can., 1972; ThM, St. John Provincial Sem., 1983; MSW, Wayne State U., 1989. Lic. social worker Acad. Cert. Social Workers; cert. sch. social worker; lic. marriage and family therapist; cert. addictions counselor level I; LMSW. Assoc. dir. vocations Archdiocese of Detroit, 1975-77; co-dir. of inst. for women Archdiocese of Lusaka (Zambia), 1977-78; pastoral minister Archdiocese of Detroit, 1979-80, assoc. dir. preformation, 1980-84; tchr., ministry coord. Bishop Borgess High Sch., Redford, Mich., 1984-86; tchr., dept. chair Aquinas High Sch., Southgate, Mich., 1986-88; therapist Community Coun. on Drug Abuse/Livonia (Mich.) Counseling, 1988-89; substance abuse therapist Oxford Inst., St. Clair Shores, Mich., 1989-91; sch. social worker Lakeshore Pub. Schs., St. Clair Shores, 1990—; therapist Macomb Child Guidance, 1989-96. Mem. NASW, Am. Assn. Marriage and Family Therapists, Mich. Assn. Sch. Social Workers. Avocations: reading, walking, piano, dulcimer, spinning and weaving. E-mail: pgarbacz1@comcast.net.

GARBECKI, ANN M., nurse; b. Springfield, Mass., Sept. 22, 1962; d. Robert H. and Diane (Donah) Branconnier; m. Brian E. Garbecki, Aug. 18, 1984; children: Marissa, Arianna, Faith, Matthew. BSN, Am. Internat. Coll., 1984. Cert. oncology nurse. Staff nurse Worcester (Mass.) Meml. Hosp., Arlington (Va.) Hosp.; asst. clin. nurse mgr. Roger Williams Hosp., Providence; staff nurse Baystate Med. Ctr., Springfield, nurse clinician. Mem.: Oncology Nursing Soc.

GARBE-MORILLO, PATRICIA ANN, preservationist; b. Paterson, NJ, Nov. 27, 1946; d. William Richard Garbe and Margaret Mary Quinn; m. Manuel Enrique Morillo, Sept. 9, 1985 (div.); 1 child, Christina Patricia Morillo (dec.). BA, U. Miami, Coral Gables, 1969; MA, U. Ariz., 1971; PhM, Columbia U., 1976. Truck driver N.Y. Daily News, N.Y.C., 1974—76; bus. mgr., contbr. Talking Wood environ. mag., Pompton Lakes, NJ, 1979—81; archtl. historian Divsn. Cultural and Hist. Affairs Bergen County Dept. Pks., Hackensack, NJ, 1981—83; archtl. historian Urban Rsch. & Design divsn., Jersey City Dept. Housing, 1983—85; preservation specialist N.Y.C. Landmarks Preservation Commn., 1985—95; preservation officer Bergen County Dept. Pks. divsn. Cultural and Hist. Affairs, Hackensack, NJ, 1996—2004; coll. archivist Miami Dade Coll., 2005—. Apprentice archaeologist archeol. excavations, Mexico, 1972—73; cons. N.J. State Hist. Preservation Consulting List, 1983—; chmn. Closter (N.J.) Hist. Preservation Commn., 1998—2005; prin. Preservation Planning & Heritage Devel., Closter, 1996—. Author (annotated bibliography): Kroeber Anthropological Society Papers, 1971; author: Closter and Alpine, 2001; project dir., tombstone restoration and mus. exhibit Closter: This is Your History, 1997 (Bergen County Historic Sites adv. bd. award); editor: Raid! The Tory Raid on Closter, May 9, 1779, 1999. Apptd. mcpl. historian Borough of Closter, 1996—; mem. environ. and hist. com. N.J. State Dem. Com., Rutgers U., 1981—83; mem. Closter Bus. & Industry Adv. Com., 1995—98; design advisor Downtown Renaissance Com., Closter, 1996—98. Recipient Women's Heritage Keeper award, Bergen County and N.J. State Assembly, 1999, Vol. of Yr. award, Bergen County, 1999, Hist. Preservation Leadership award, 2003; fellow Ford Found., 1972. Mem.: Soc. Fla. Archivists, Soc. Am. Archivists, Preservation New Jersey, Miami Design Preservation League, Nat. Trust for Historic Preservation, Closter Hist. Soc. (founder, pres. 1996—2005). Avocations: travel, gardening, Cuban culture and architecture, museums. Home: 2555 Collins Ave PH201 Miami Beach FL 33140 Office Phone: 305-237-3575. Personal E-mail: pmorillo@bellsouth.net.

GARBER, BETH CAROL, early childhood educator, music educator; b. Miami Beach, Fla., Oct. 1, 1952; d. Seymour Albert Bender and Marian Jane Ascher; m. Harold Garber, Feb. 19, 1984; 1 child, Mathew Eric. BS in Edn., U. Hartford, 1974; MA in Student Personnel Svcs., Kean Coll. N.J., 1981; MA in Rehab. counseling, Seton Hall U., South Orange, N.J., 1985. Cert. tchr. handicapped N.J., 1975, student personnel svc. instr. N.J., 1982, rehab. counselor N.J., 1985, elem. tchr. N.J., 1991. Resource rm. tchr. Lafayette Mid. Sch., Elizabeth, NJ, 1975—78, Battin Career Ctr., Elizabeth, NJ, 1978—81; learning resource ctr. tchr. Union County Regional High Schs., Springfield, NJ, 1981—83; rehab. specialist Ctrl. Rehab. Assocs., Freehold, NJ, 1985—87; music specialist tchr. Sundance Sch., North Plainfield, NJ, 1988—90; nursery dir., lead tchr. Bayonne Jewish Cmty. Ctr., NJ, 1990—91; music tchr. TMR program Jointure for Cmty. Adult Edn., Bound Brook, NJ, 1992—95; head tchr., music specialist Wee People, Bound Brook, NJ, 1991—96; music specialist Jewish Edn. Assn., Ctr. for Spl. Edn., Whippany, NJ, 1996—; head tchr., music dir. Mountain Top Presch. and Kindergarten, Warren, NJ, 1996—. Ednl. cons. Teen Parent Program, Elizabeth, NJ, 1978; Judaic programming cons. Mountain Top Presch. and Kindergarten, Warren, NJ, 1996—, mentor, 2000—01. Vol. Somerset County Food B ank, Bound Brook, NJ; mem. Somerset County Mental Health Players, Bridgewater, NJ; coord. Interfaith Hospitality Network, Temple Beth-El, Hillsborough, NJ, 2002—, founding mem. adult choir, mem., past pres. Sisterhood, 1996—98. Named Outstanding Child Care Profl., Somerset Alliance for the Future, 1993; fellowship, Seton Hall U., 1983. Mem.: Nat. Assn. Edn. of Young Children, N.J. Assn. for Edn. of Young Children, Rho Chi Sigma (pres. 1983—84). Avocations: guitar, family and friends, reading, travel, performing in community theater.

GARBRANDT, GAIL ELAINE, political science professor, consultant; b. Dover, Ohio, Oct. 10, 1955; d. Floyd Madison Grewell and Mary Catherine Sica; children: John Paul Marino, Vanessa Marie Marino. BA, Kent State U., Ohio, 1992; MA, U. Akron, Ohio, 1995. Pres. and CEO Citi-Energy Ops., Dover, Ohio, 1983—91; campaign coord. Senator Robert L. Burch, 1992—94; adj. prof. Stark State Coll., Canton, 1996—98, Malone Coll., 1998—2005, Mount Union Coll., Alliance, 1998—, Walsh U., N. Canton, 1998—; intern coord. and nat. campaign trainer Ray C. Bliss Inst. U. Akron, 2000—. Mem. adv. bd. Ctr. Women in Pub. Svc., Cleve., Canadian Studies U. Akron, North Am. Free Trade Agreement Program Ctr., Washington. Author: NWPC Campaign Training, 2005; contbr. articles to profl. jours. Vol. Main Street, New Philadelphia, Ohio, 2005—06, Tuscarawas County Hospice, 2005—06; mem. exec. com. Tuscarawas County Dem. Party, New Philadelphia, 2003—06; mem. think tank Ohio Dem. Party, Columbus, 2006. Named a Ky. Col., Gov. Ky., 2002, Woman of Worth, Worth Corp., Ltd., 2003; recipient Pioneer award, Mortar Bd., 2003. Mem.: Am. Acad. Polit. Cons. (bd. mem. 2005—, pres. midwest chpt. 2004—06), Nat. Women's Polit. Caucus (bd. mem. 2005—). Roman Catholic. Office: U Akron Olin Hall Rm 224A Akron OH 44325-0002 Office Phone: 330-972-5182.

GARCEAU, JO MILLS, writer; b. Portland, Oreg., Nov. 10, 1932; d. M. Pierre Mills and Mary Elizabeth Kies. BA in Polit. Sci., U. of Oreg., 1953; MA in Human Values, San Francisco Theol. Sem., 1982. Campaign dir. Dan Evans for Gov. Com., Spokane, Wash., 1968; asst. to the gov. Office of the Gov. State of Wash., Olympia, Wash., 1969—72, cabinet dir., 1972—76; campus min. The Evergreen Coll. Campus Ministry, Olympia, 1977—82; asst. min. Ananda Ch., Nevada City, Calif., 1982—89; writer Boring, Oreg., 1990—; customer svc. assoc. PacifiCorp, Portland, 1996—2006; owner, operator Manjusri Enterprises, 2006—. Chmn. affirmative action com. State of Wash., Olympia, 1973—77. Chmn. The Evergreen Coll. Campus Ministry, Olympia, 1976—78; bd. dir. Wash. Coun. of Ch., Seattle, 1977—82. Fellow Walden fellow, 1998; grantee, State of Oreg., 1949—51; scholar Hazel P. Schwering scholarship, U. of Oreg., 1952. Mem.: Nat. Assn. Securities Dealers (arbitrator 2003—), Willamette Writers (asst. treas. 2002), Oreg. Astrological Soc. Liberal. Buddhist. Avocations: astrology, psychology, spirituality.

GARCHIK, LEAH LIEBERMAN, journalist; b. Bklyn., May 2, 1945; d. Arthur Louis and Mildred (Steinberg) Lieberman; m. Jerome Marcus Garchik, Aug. 11, 1968; children— Samuel, Jacob BA, Bklyn. Coll., 1966. Editorial asst. San Francisco Chronicle, 1972-79, writer, editor, 1979-83, editor This World, 1983-84, columnist, 1984—; also author numerous book and movie reviews, features and profiles. Author: San Francisco; the City's Sights and Secrets, 1995; panelist (radio quiz show) Minds Over Matter; contbr. articles to mags. Vice pres. Golden Gate Kindergarten Assn., San Francisco, 1978; pres. Performing Arts Workshop, San Francisco, 1977-79; bd. dirs. Home Away From Homelessness, 1994-99. Recipient 1st prize Nat. Soc. Newspaper Columnists, 1992. Mem. Newspaper Guild. Democrat. Jewish. Home: 156 Baker St San Francisco CA 94117-2111 Office: San Francisco Chronicle 901 Mission St San Francisco CA 94103-2905 Business E-Mail: lgarchik@sfchronicle.com.

GARCIA, ANGELA G., lawyer; b. Manila, Philippines, 1960; BA cum laude, Mount Holyoke U., 1982; MPhil, U. Cambridge, 1984; JD cum laude, Georgetown U., 1989. Bar: N.Y. 1990, D.C. 1990, U.S. Dist. Ct. (so. and ea. dists.) N.Y. 1994, U.S. Ct. Appeals (2d cir.) 1996. Law clk. Hon. James Belson D.C. Ct. Appeals, 1989—90; atty. Skadden, Arps, Slate, Meagher & Flom LLP, N.Y., 1990—97, ptnr., 1997—. Office: Skadden Arps Slate Meagher & Flom LLP Four Times Sq New York NY 10036 Office Phone: 212-735-3000.

GARCIA, ANNETTE D'URSO, educational consultant; d. John Michael and Ann Ciccone D'Urso; m. Paul Charles Garcia, Aug. 16, 1980; children: Felicia C., Dominic P., Nicholas M. BA in Biology, Mercyhurst Coll., Erie, Pa., 1973; MA in Health Edn., U. No. Colo., Greeley, 1980. Tchr. Mercyhurst Prep. H.S., 1972—74, Adams County Sch. Dist., Commerce City, Colo., 1974—2006; asst. con. Coun. Real Edn., Englewood, 1977—78; tchr. health edn. U. No. Colo., Greeley, 1979—80; ednl. cons. Colo. Sch. Dists., 2006—. Textbook reviewer McGraw Hill, 2003—04. Named Tchr. Yr., Commerce City Wal-Mart, 2005; recipient Disting. Tchr. award, Colo., 1991. Mem.: VFW, NEA, Nat. Sci. Tchrs. Assn., Colo. Edn. Assn., Order Eagles.

GARCIA, BEATRICE MAUDE, social worker, director; b. Boston, Jan. 18, 1929; d. George Louis and Beatrice Lawrence (White) Joughin; m. Edward P. Black, June 4, 1950 (dec.); children: Victoria, Edward, Barbara; m. Marvin Victor Aquirre, May 10, 1956 (div.); children: Deborah (dec.), Michael; m. Peter Charles Garcia, Aug. 13, 1961. BA in Anthopology with honors and distinction, Sonoma State U., 1971; MA in Anthropology, San Francisco State U., 1979; postgrad., Sonoma State U., 1982—. Coord. Boyle Heights Coalition, L.A., 1953-55; dir. Truman Boyd Housing Assn., Long Beach, Calif., 1961-63; med. records supr. Crestview Hosp., Petaluma, Calif., 1979-81; investigator, ombudsman Sonoma County Ombudsman, Santa Rosa, Calif., 1984—88; dir. sr. svcs. Ctrl. YMCA, San Francisco, 1988-90; dir. case mgmt. East Valley Sr. Ctr., North Hollywood, Calif., 1994-98, regional mgr. Region VIII, long term care ombudsman LA, 2001—06; field coord. Health Ins. Counseling and Advocacy Program Lake and Mendocino Counties, 2006—. Sec. Red Banks Oaks Assn., 1998—, Dem. Club High Desert, 1999—; organizer campaigns Dem. Orgn., Santa Maria, Calif., 1964, Vallejo, Calif., 1968. Mem. AAUW (sec. Antelope Valley chpt. 1999—), No. Calif. Manx Assn. (adminstrv. 1999—). Democrat. Episcopalian. Avocations: reading, travel, antiques. Home: Box 221 9885 Lee Barr Rd Lower Lake CA 95457

GARCIA, CHRISTINE, academic administrator, educator, researcher; B Govt., U.Nex., 1961, M Polit. Sci. in Edn., 1964; PhD Polit. Sci., U. Calif., Davis, 1972. Prof. polit. sci. U. N.Mex., 1970—, asst. dir. divsn. govt. rsch., 1970—72, asst., assoc. dean Coll. Arts and Scis., 1975—80, dean coll. Arts and Scis., 1980—86, v.p. acad. affairs, 1987—90, interim provost, v.p. acad. affairs, 1993, 1998—2000, pres., 2002—. Tchr. various us.; rschr. in field. Author (editor): 10 books, 50 monographs; contbr. articles, chapters to books. Office: U NMex 115 Civic Plz Dr Taos NM 87571

GARCIA, DONNA M., science educator; d. Donald M. and Erma M. (Johnson) Amos; m. Jaime D. Garcia, Aug. 8, 1971; children: Christina Garcia Angelos, Laura A., Daniel I., David I. BS in Biology, No. Ill. U., Dekalb, 1971, MS in Edn., 1976, MS in Biol. Scis., 1992. Cert. secondary tchg. Ill. Tchr. adult basic edn.-ESL Elgin (Ill.) C.C., 1973—77, adj. instr. anatomy and physiology and microbiology, 1974—88, adj. instr. intermediate Spanish, 1978; grad. asst. anatomy and physiology No. Ill. U., 1989—90; adj. instr. anatomy and physiology Waubonsee C.C., Sugar Grove, Ill., 1993, Elgin C.C., 1994—99, instr. microbiology, 1999—. Transl. Comty. Crisis Ctr., Elgin. Mem.: Am. Soc. for Microbiology. Office: Elgin C C Elgin IL 60120

GARCIA, ELISA DOLORES, lawyer; b. Bklyn., Nov. 8, 1957; d. Vincent Garcia, Jr. and Dolores Elizabeth (Canedo) Marmo; m. John Jay Hasluck, Feb. 28, 1987; children: Brooke Elisabeth, John Neville. BA, MS, SUNY, Stony Brook, 1980; JD, St. John's U., 1985. Bar: N.Y. 1986. Cons. Energy Devel. Internat., Pt. Jefferson, N.Y., 1980-83; assoc. Willkie Farr & Gallagher, N.Y.C., 1985-89; sr. counsel GAF Corp./Internat. Specialty Products, Wayne, N.J., 1989-94; regional counsel for L.Am., Philip Morris Internat., Rye Brook, N.Y., 1994-2000; exec. v.p., gen. counsel Domino's Pizza, LLC, Ann Arbor, Mich., 2000—. Mem. Glen Rock (N.J.) Planning Bd., 1992-95, chmn., 1994-95. Mem. ABA, N.Y. State Bar Assn., Mich. Bar Assn., Assn. Corp. Counsel Assn. (pres. Mich. chpt.). Roman Catholic. Avocations: gardening, scuba diving. Office: Domino's Pizza LLC PO Box 997 30 Frank Lloyd Wright Dr Ann Arbor MI 48106-0997 E-mail: garciae@dominos.com.

GARCIA, EMMA YVETTE, music educator; d. Walter Larry and Berta Cecila Allen. B, U. Tex., San Antonio, 1996, M in Ednl. Counseling, 2004. Cert. music educator Tex. Dept. Edn., 1996. Band dir. McCollum H.S., San Antonio, 2000—05; band and choir dir. Burbank H.S., San Antonio, 2005—. Dir. concert band McCollum H.S., San Antonio, Burbank H.S. Co-recipient Sweepstakes award, Univ. Interscholastic League, 2004, Excellent choir rating, 2005; named to Nat. Dean's List, Coll. Bd., 2004; Marjorie Powell Music scholar, Music Dept. U. Tex. San Antonio, 1995. Mem.: Tex. Edn. Assn., Tex. Music Educators Assn. (life), Alpha Lambda Delta, Golden Key. Roman Catholic. Achievements include directed bands in Univ. Interscholastic League competition; band selected feature marching band at Disney World; directed first Burbank H.S. choir to attend Univ. Interscholastic League competition.

GARCIA, GRACE V. BACON, lawyer; b. 1972; BA cum laude, U. Rochester, 1994; JD cum laude, Boston U. Law Sch., 1998. Bar: Mass. 1998. Ptnr. Morrison Mahoney LLP, Boston. Legal writing and rsch. instr. Boston U. Sch. Law, 2003—06. Mem.: Boston Bar Assn. (co-chair new lawyer sect. 2002—04, task force pro bono and new lawyers 2002—03), Mass. Bar Assn. (new lawyer sect. coun. 2000—03, bus. law sect. coun. 2003—06, litig. sect. coun.). Office: Morrison Mahoney LLP 250 Summer St Boston MA 02210 Office Phone: 617-737-8822. Office Fax: 617-342-4914. E-mail: gbacon@morrisonmahoney.com.*

GARCIA, JULIA THERESA, secondary school educator; b. N.Y.C., Aug. 30, 1923; d. Ignatius Colletti-Riena and Julia Pendeleur; m. Frank Leonard Garcia, May 26, 1949 (dec. Aug. 1995); children: Julia, Frank, Annette. BA, Hunter Coll., 1951; MA, Columbia U., 1956. Cert. tchr. chemistry N.Y., asst. prin. supervision phys. scis. N.Y. Tchr. gen. sci. Alfred E. Smith Jr. H.S. Bd. Edn. N.Y.C., tchr. chemistry Alfred E. Smith H.S., asst. prin. supervision phys. scis. Alfred E. Smith H.S., prin. summer sch. Alfred E. Smith H.S. Bd. examiner sci. and math. Bd. Edn. N.Y.C., 1984—89. Active Diabetic Assn. Recipient award for dedicated svc. to children, N.Y.C. Sci. Chmn.'s Assn., 1989. Mem.: Am. Assn. Scientists, Phi Delta Kappa, N.Y.C. Acad. Sci.

GARCIA, JULIET VILLARREAL, academic administrator; m. Oscar E. Garcia; two children. BA in Speech, English, U. of Houston, 1970, MA in Speech, English, 1972; PhD in Communications & Linguistics, U. of Texas Austin, 1976. Teaching asst. U. of Houston, 1970—72; Instr. Pan American Univ. at Edinburg, 1972; teaching asst. U. of Texas Austin, 1974—76; adj. prof. Pan American U. Brownsville, 1977—79; instr. Tex. Southmost Coll., 1972—74, 1976—81, dir. TSC Self-Study, 1979—81, dean, arts and sciences, 1981—86, pres., 1986—92, U. Tex. at Brownsville, Tex. Southmost Coll., 1992—. Bd. dirs. Fed. Res. of Dallas/San Antonio br. of Tex. Commerce Bancshares Inc.; past bd. dirs. Am. Coun. Edn., chmn. bd. dirs. 1995. Bd. dirs. Carnegie Found. for Advancement of Teaching, Pub. Welfare Foun.; vice-chair adv. com. on Fin. Aid; appointed mem. White House Initiative on Ednl. Excellence for Hispanic-Ams. Named Woman of Distinction Nat. Conf. of Coll. Women Student Leaders, 1995, one of most influential Hispanics Hispanic Bus. Mag. Office: U Tex & Tex Southmost Coll Office of Pres 80 Fort Brown St Brownsville TX 78520-4956

GARCIA, JUNE MARIE, librarian; b. Bryn Mawr, Pa., Sept. 12, 1947; d. Roland Ernest and Marion Brill (Hummel) Traynor; m. Teodosio Garcia, July 17, 1928; children: Gretchen, Adrian. BA, Douglass Coll., 1969; MLS, Rutgers U., 1970. Reference libr. New Brunswick (N.J.) Pub. Libr., 1970-72, Plainfield (N.J.) Pub. Libr., 1972-75; br. mgr. Phoenix Pub. Libr., 1975-80, extension svcs. adminstr., 1980-93; dir. San Antonio Pub. Libr., 1993-99; CEO, CARL Corp., Denver, 1999-2001; v.p., chief amb. TLC/CARL, Denver, 2001—02; mng. ptnr. Dubberly Garcia Assocs., 2002—, E-Learn Librs., Inc., Nashville and Denver, 2004—. Recipient Productivity Innovator award, City of Phoenix, 1981. Mem. ALA (life, coun. 1986-90, 93-2001, pres. Pub. Libr. Assn. 1991-92, new stds. task force 1983-87, goals, guidelines and stds. com. 1986-90, chairperson 1987-90, resource allocation com. 1998-99), Freedom to Read Found. (bd. dirs.), Ariz. State Libr. Assn. (pres. 1984-85, Libr. of Yr. award 1986, Pres.'s award 1990), Pub. Libr. Internat. Network (exec. dir.), Beta Phi Mu. Office: 1195 S Harrison St Denver CO 80210 Office Phone: 303-757-7420. Business E-Mail: jgarcia@dubberlygarcia.com.

GARCIA, KATHERINE LEE, controller, accountant; b. Portland, Oreg., Nov. 4, 1950; d. Gerald Eugene and Dolores Lois (Erickson) Moe; m. Buddy Jesus Garcia; Nov. 19, 1977; children: Kevin, Brett, Rodd. BS cum laude, U. Nev., 1976. CPA Idaho, Nev.; cert. pub. fin. officer 2001. Retail clk. Raleys, Food King, Reno, 1968-76; sr. acct. Pieretti, Wilson and McNulty, Reno, 1976-78, Deloitte Haskins and Sells, Boise, Idaho, 1979-81, Washoe County, Reno, 1981-83, chief dep. comptr., 1983-94, comptroller, 1994—. Treas., bd. dirs. Friends of 4 (pub. TV), Boise, 1979-81; tutor RAD program, 1995-97; treas. Sierra Miners, 1998-99. Recipient Cert. of Excellence in Fin. Reporting, Govt. Fin. Officer's Assn., 1982-, Outstanding CPA in Govt., Nev, 2002-03. Mem. AICPA, Nev. Soc. CPAs (chmn. state and local govt. com. 1992-93, 98—), Govt. Fin. Officers Assn. (mem. spl. rev. com. 1989-97, 2004—, state rep.), Nev. Govt. Fin. Officers Assn. (treas. 1989-91), U. Nev. Reno Found. (trustee, audit com.). Republican. Avocations: jogging, sewing, biking, reading. Home: 655 Joy Lake Rd Reno NV 89511-5766 Office: Washoe County PO Box 11130 Reno NV 89520-0027 Office Phone: 702-328-2552. Business E-Mail: kgarcia@washoecounty.us.

GARCIA, LAURA CATHERINE, utilities executive; b. Hollywood, Fla., Mar. 11, 1957; d. Thomas Tubens and Felicia (Acebal) Garcia; children: Kristin Kaplan, Jonathan, Diana. BSEE, U. Miami, 1979. Utilities exec. Fla. Power and Light Co., Miami, 1980-93, ops. mgr. Dade County, 1991-93; pres. L.G.K. Assocs., Inc., Ft. Lauderdale, Fla., 1993—. Counselor Soc. Abused Children, Kendall, Fla., 1985-86; instr. Jr. Achievement, Miami, 1986-87, Adult Illiteracy Program, 1987; bd. dirs. YWCA, 1988-92, Convenant House, 1995-96; instr. Youth Ministry, 1999-2002, CHARLEE program, 2000-05. Early admission scholar U. Miami, 1975; recipient Hurricane Andrew Hero award Dade County Rebuilding Program, 1993. Mem. Leadership Miami Assn., Greater Miami C. of C. Clubs: Hurricane. Republican. Roman Catholic. Avocations: doll collecting, piano, scuba diving. Office: LGK Assocs Inc 6738 NW 110th Way Parkland FL 33076-3828 E-mail: lgkassoc@mindspring.com.

GARCIA, MARIA LUISA, biochemist, researcher; b. Valladolid, Spain, Oct. 9, 1953; came to U.S., 1979; d. Baldomero and Dolores (Garcia) G.; m. Gregory Kaczorowski, June 21, 1982. PhD, Autonoma U., Madrid, 1979. Sr. rsch. biochemist Merck & Co., Rahway, NJ, 1985—87, rsch. fellow, 1987—91, sr. rsch. fellow, 1991—97, sr. investigator, 1997—2003, disting. sr. investigator, 2003—. Invited speaker, presenter papers in field. Contbr. numerous articles and revs. to profl. jours.; patentee in field. Mem. AAAS, Am. Soc. Biol. Chemists, Biophys. Soc., N.Y. Acad. Sci. Home: 5 Ashbrook Dr Edison NJ 08820-4318 Office: Merck Rsch Labs PO Box 2000 Rahway NJ 07065-0900 Personal E-mail: maria_garcia@merck.com.

GARCIA, MARY FRANCES, science educator; b. Chgo., Ill., Sept. 30, 1962; d. Paul Charles and Mary Elizabeth Ragona; m. Bob Garcia, Apr. 25, 1962; children: Erika Kristine, Nicole Marie. MA in Edn., St Xavier U., Chgo., 2000. Tchr. Diamond Lake Sch. Dist 76, Mundelein, Ill., 1987—88, Northbrook Glenvier Sch. Dist. 30, Ill., 1998—. Recipient Leadership award, NEA/Ill. Edn. Assn. Mem.: NEA (v.p.), Ill. Edn. Assn. (v.p.). Home: 404 Normandy Ln Grayslake IL 60030 Office: Northbrook Sch Dist 30 2374 Shermer Rd Northbrook IL 60062 Office Phone: 847-400-8900. Personal E-mail: mgarcia@district30.k12.il.us. Business E-Mail: mgarcia@distrtict30.k12.il.us.

GARCIA, MELVA YBARRA, counseling administrator, educator; d. Estanislaso B and Ofelia M Ybarra; m. Frank Garcia, Dec. 28, 1974; children: Ruben Jesus, Luis Francisco, Ramon Estanislado. Student, San Francisco State U., 1969—72; B.A. in Sociology, Calif. State U., Hayward, 1974, MS in Counseling, 1983; PhD (hon.), U. Calif.-Berkeley, 1992. Cert. cmty. coll. counselor Calif., 1986, student pers. workers credential Calif., 1986. Dir. Chicano student counseling ctr. Wash. State U., Pullman, 1984—86; Chicano studies advisor U. of Calif., Berkeley, 1987—92; counselor/instr. Chabot Coll., Hayward, Calif., 1992—. Co-author (counseling manual) Counseling Chicanos: The Affects of Racial and Cultural Stereotype, 1985. Mem. Self-Help for the Hard of Hearing, 2001—; sponsor Children's Internat., Kansas City, Mo., 2002—; mem. La Alianza, Hayward, Calif., 1993; mentor Puente Program, Chabot Coll., 1992—; advisor Wash. State U.; ptnr. Spl. Olympics, 1995—; assoc. mem. Nat. Coun. of La Raza, Washington, 2000—. Mem.: Assn. Main United Farm Workers, So. Law Poverty Ctr., Chabot-Las Positas Faculty Assn., Faculty Assn of Calif. Cmty. Colls., Chicano/Latino Edn. Assn. (mem., 1992-present, co-chair 1998—99), NACADA. D-Liberal. Catholic. Avocations: travel, aerobics. Office: Chabot College 25555 Hesperian Blvd Hayward CA 94545 E-mail: mgarcia@chabotcollege.edu.

GARCIA, MINERVA A.F., microbiologist, research and clinical laboratory scientist; b. Santiago, Dominican Republic, Nov. 1, 1959; arrived in U.S., 1969; d. Seferino Frias and Lydia Hernandez; m. Jose N. Garcia, Aug. 25, 1985; 1 child, James. BS in Biology, St. Francis Coll., 1984; postgrad. Wagner Coll.; student, CUNY. Bacteriologist, S.I., NY. Poet Anthologies, 1994, Newspapers and Mags. Recipient award, Anaerobic Bacteriology, 1992, Mayor's scholarship, N.Y.C. Honor Citation award. Mem.: AAUW, Alliance for Prudent Use of Antibiotics, Am. Chem. Soc., N.Y. Acad. Scis., Am. Soc. Microbiology. Home: 29 Pontiac St Staten Island NY 10302-2213 Office: Beth Israel Med Ctr 1st Ave at 17th St New York NY 10003 Office Phone: 212-420-4040. E-mail: pferre@si.rr.com.

GARCÍA, NORMA GARZA, county treasurer; b. Donna, Tex., Oct. 5, 1950; d. Zacarias H. and Olivia (Cavazos) Garza; m. George A. García, Dec. 20, 1977 (div. Mar. 1993); children from previous marriage: Martha Ann, Lucas Aaron, Jorge Antonio II. Stenographer, San Antonio C.C., 1968; student, Pan Am. U., 1969-70, Southmost Coll., 1984. Cert. county treas. Tex. Assn. Counties; cert. investment officer Tex. Assn. Counties. Employment interviewer, supr. Tex. Employment Commn., Weslaco, 1969-80; real estate agt. M.F. Red Connor & Assocs., Weslaco, 1984-85; asst. dir. CBM Edn. Ctr., San Benito, Tex., 1985-87; legis. asst. State Rep. Juan Chuy Hinojosa, McAllen, Tex., 1987-88; income tax return preparer, co-owner H&R Block, Rio Grande City, Tex., 1988-95; county treas. Hidalgo County, Edinburg, Tex., 1995—. Child support investigator Tex. Atty. Gen., McAllen, 1993-94. Mayor City of Mercedes, Tex., 1986-93; dir. Amigos del Valle, McAllen, 1989-93; bd. mem. Planned Parenthood Hidalgo County, McAllen, 1990-92; pres., coun. of govts. Lower Rio Grande Valley Devel. Coun., McAllen, 1992-93; pres. Assn. Mayor, Coun. Mems. and Commrs., Austin, Tex., 1993; mem. County Treas.'s Polit. Action Com., Austin, 1995—. Named Outstanding Profl. Woman, Bus. and Profl. Women's Club, McAllen, 1988, Woman of the Yr., Mercedes C. of C., 1988, Outstanding Hispanic Mayor, Assn. Hispanic Mcpl. Ofcls., Austin, 1992. Democrat. Roman Catholic. Avocations: cake decorating, baking, piano, reading. Office: Hidalgo County Courthouse Annex Bldg Edinburg TX 78539

GARCIA, OFELIA, art educator, department chairman; b. Havana, Cuba, Feb. 12, 1941; d. Ramon Garcia-Castro and Nieves (Gomez de Molina) Garcia. Student, Escuela de Bellas Artes, Havana, 1958-60; BA, Manhattanville Coll., 1969; MFA, Tufts U., 1972; postgrad., Duke U., 1973-75; D. Fine Arts (hon.), Atlanta Coll. Art, 1991. Asst. prof., art dept. chair, div. dir. humanities and fine arts Newton (Mass.) Coll., 1969-75; dir. studio art Boston Coll., Chestnut Hill, Mass., 1975-76; exec. dir. The Print Club, Phila., 1978-86; critic Pa. Acad. Fine Arts, Phila., 1982-86; pres. Atlanta Coll. Art, 1986-91, Rosemont (Pa.) Coll., 1991—95; sr. fellow Am. Coun. on Edn., 1995—97; dean, coll. arts and comm., prof. William Paterson U., 1997—2006. Visual arts panelist State Coun. of the Arts, Pa. and N.J., 1985-86, Ga., 1990-91; mem. vis. com. dept. art and architecture Lehigh (Pa.) U., 1990-96; bd. mgrs. Haverford Coll., 1992—2004. Artist exhibitions of prints and drawings; curator, juror numerous nat. and internat. or regional art exhibitions. Nat. pres. Women's Caucus for Art, 1984-86; bd. dirs. Am. Coun. on Edn., 1993-96; co-chair Mayor's Commn. for Women, City Phila., 1992-97; Arts Adv. Com. Barnes Found. Bd., 1992-95; trustee Jersey City Mus., 2000—, chair, 2001—; bd. dirs. Caths. for Free Choice, 2000—, Artpride NJ, 2005—. Recipient Am. Bookbuilders prize Boston Mus. Sch., 1969, Park Found. award, 1974; Kent fellow Danforth Found., 1975-80. Fellow Soc. for Values Higher Edn.; mem. Coll. Art Assn. Am. (bd. dirs. 1986-90, bd. coms. 1986-92), Commn. on Women in Higher Edn., Am. Coun. on Edn. (chair 1990-91), So. Assn. Colls. and Schs. (accreditation evaluator 1990-91), ArtTable, Inc. Roman Catholic. Office: William Paterson U 300 Pompton Rd Wayne NJ 07470-2152 Business E-Mail: garciao@wpunj.edu.

GARCIA, PATRICIA A., lawyer; b. New Orleans, Feb. 18, 1956; d. Martin F. and Shirley (Polders) G. BA in History, U. New Orleans, 1976; JD, Loyola U., New Orleans, 1980. Bar: La. 1980, U.S. Tax Ct. 1982, U.S. Dist. Ct. (ea. dist.) La. 1984, U.S. Dist. Ct. (mid. dist.) La. 1986. Staff atty. office of chief counsel IRS, Washington, 1980-82; law clk. U.S. Ea. Dist. Ct. of La., New Orleans, 1983-86; assoc. Law Office of Eric A. Holden, New Orleans, 1986-89; ptnr. Holden & Garcia, New Orleans, 1990—2001; private practice, 2001—. Bd. dirs. La. Ctr. for Law and Civic Edn., 1992-96, pres., 1994-95, New Orleans Legal Assistance Corp., 1995-2000. Co-chair No/AIDS Task Force, 1997-01, sec./treas., 1994-97. Mem. ABA (comm. chair, exec. com. young lawyers divsn. 1990-91, gen. practice sect. gen. practice link conf. team 1994-99, vice chair sole practitioners and small firms com. 1990-92, vice chair law students com. 1991-96, vice chair law sch. curriculum com. 1991-94, La. dist. gov. 1979-80, project dir. model project for effective delivery of law-related edn. to low income families 1985-87, project dir. com. on substance abuse, chmn. delivery of legal svcs. com. young lawyers divsn. 1987, chmn. law student outreach com. 1988-91, asst. editor Affiliate mag. 1988-90, liaison to law student divsn. 1987-91, recipient Gold Key award 1980, regional coord. state and local bar liaison com. 1992-98, standing com. on Gavel awards 1994-97, project dir. com. on substance abuse 1994-97, ann. mtg. 1994 host com., ho. dels. 1994, 97-2000), La. Bar Assn. (chmn. law week 1986, mem. young lawyers sect. 1986-92, Achievement award 1985, 86, 87, mem. local and splty. bars com. 1992-98), New Orleans Bar Assn. (1st v.p. 1990-91, pres.-elect 1991-92, pres. 1992-93, chmn. TV com. 1992-98, com. on drugs and violence 1992-96, vice chmn. young lawyers sect. 1984-86, chmn. 1987-88, chmn. membership com. 1988-91, exec. com. 1988-94, vice chmn. increasing membership com. 1986-87, pub. rels. com. 1984-92, project grantee 1985-87), La. Ctr. for Law and Civic Edn. (pres. 1994-95, v.p. 1993-94, bd. dirs. 1992-96). Democrat. Roman Catholic. Office: PO Box 24098 New Orleans LA 70184-4098 Home: 1803 Edgemere Ct Se Huntsville AL 35803-3635 Office Phone: 504-288-3539. E-mail: pagarcia@pagarcialaw.com.

GARCIA, REBEKAH, elementary school educator; b. El Paso, Mar. 12, 1956; d. Rafael and Raquel Garcia. BS, Tex. Woman's U., Denton, 1978, MS, 1991. Tchr. Denton Ind. Sch. Dist., Tex., 1978—2006. Office: Ryan High School 5101 E McKinney Denton TX 76208 Office Phone: 940-369-3112.

GARCIA, SANDRA JOANNE ANDERSON, law and psychology educator; b. Buffalo, Aug. 10, 1939; d. James Edwards and Thelma Harriet (Crawford) Anderson; m. Gerard L. Garcia, Jr., June 11, 1960 (div. 1968); 1 child, Robert Vincent. BA, Tex. Western Coll., 1966; MA, U. Tex., El Paso, 1968; PhD, U. So. Calif., 1971; JD, Stetson U. Coll. Law, 1985. Rsch. assoc. Human Rsch. Office, George Washington U., El Paso, 1967-68; rsch. assoc. SW Regional Lab. for Ednl. Rsch. and Devel., Inglewood, Calif., 1968-69; asst. prof. English dept. UCLA, 1970-74; asst. prof. psychology U. South Fla., Tampa, 1974-80, assoc. prof., 1989-90, prof., 1990—, prof. interdisciplinary arts and scis., 1992—. Editor: Bionic Babies in High-Tech Families: New Issues in Child Psychology, 1988; co-editor: Current Perspectives in Legal, Psychological, and Ethical Issues, 1990. Recipient Equal Opportunity award U. South Fla., 1976; rsch. fellow Ford Found., Jerusalem, 1973-74, Am. Bar Found., 1989, 90, McKnight Found., 1989-90, Nat. Ctr. for State Cts., 1990—, Fla. Commn. on Human Rels., 1992—. Democrat. Avocations: running, race walking, travel. Home: 807 Lorena Rd Lutz FL 33548-4527

GARCIA, SARA KRUGER, lawyer; b. San Antonio, Dec. 12, 1975; d. Daniel Yahr and Chaddie Bruckman Kruger; m. Ryan Matthew Garcia. BA cum laude, Bryn Mawr Coll., 1997; JD, U. Tex., 2000. Rsch. atty. Supr. Ct. Calif., San Jose, 2001—03; briefing atty. U.S. Dist. Ct., San Antonio, 2003—05. Mediator, Tex., 1999—, Calif., 1999—. Recipient Peggy Guggenheim Internat. Studentship. Mem.: Nat. Order of Barristers. Home: 6600 Walebridge Ln Austin TX 78739-2025

GARCIA, SHARON D., elementary school educator; b. Morehead City, NC, May 25, 1960; m. Frank C. Garcia, May 28, 1988. BS, Music Edn., Old Dominion U., Norfolk, Va., 1984; MusM, Va. Commonwealth U., Richmond, 1989. Tchr. Portsmouth Pub. Schs., Va., 1986—92, Norfolk Pub. Schs., Va., 1992—2004, Virginia Beach City Pub. Schs., Va., 2004—. Flutist Va. Wind Symphony. Recipient Blue Ribbon award, Va. Music Educators Assn., 2001, 2005, 2006. Home: 115 North Shore Rd Norfolk VA 23505 Office: Brandon Middle Sch 1700 Pope St Virginia Beach VA 23464 Office Phone: 757-366-4545. Business E-Mail: sharon.garcia@vbschools.com.

GARCIA, SUSAN BREAUX, multi-media specialist, consultant; m. Gerard Garcia; children: Brandon, Caroline, Benjamin. BS in English Edn. magna cum laude, La. State U., 1973, MLS, 1977. Cert. secondary English, libr. sci. tchr. La. Elem. sch. libr. Iberia Parish Sch. Sys., Jeanerette, La., 1974—82, HS libr., 1982—93, dist. libr., media specialist supr. New Iberia, La., 1993—. Cons. storytelling Iberia Parish Sch. Sys., New Iberia, 1978—; cons. libr. sci. U. Southwestern La., Lafayette, 1995—2002, adj. instr. libr. sci.; storyteller. From pres. to sec. Entre Nous Club, Jeanerette, 1976—2005, chmn. Reading is Fundamental Project, 1979—2005; bd. dirs., sec. Friends of Iberia Parish Libr., New Iberia, La., 1998—2005; lector St. John the Evangelist Ch., Jeanerette, 1980—2005, mem. parish coun., 1999—2001. Named Outstanding Young Educator of La., La. Jaycees, 1980, Outstanding Young Educator, Jeanerette Jaycees, 1980, Outstanding Club Mem., Entre Nous Club, 1987, 1991, 2005; recipient Achievement award, Nat. Coun. Tchrs. English, 1970; scholar, La. State U. Alumni Fedn., 1970—73; Nat. Merit scholar, Texaco Merit scholar, Nat. Merit Scholarship Corp., 1970—73. Mem.: ALA, Title I Spl. Interest Coun., La. Reading Assn., Internat. Reading Assn., La. Libr. Assn., La. Assn. of Parish Textbook Adminstrs. (sec. 1999—2002), Alpha Beta Alpha, Alpha Lambda Delta, Beta Phi Mu, Phi Kappa Phi. Roman Catholic. Avocations: reading, storytelling, travel. Office: Iberia Parish Sch Sys 325 Provost St Jeanerette LA 70544 Office Phone: 337-364-7641.

GARCIA, VERONICA, school system administrator; BA, MA, U. N.Mex, EdD in Edn. Leadership. Exec. dir. N.Mex Coalition of Sch. Adminstrs.; supt. Santa Fe Pub. Schs.; regional supt. Albuquerque Pub. Schs.; sec. edn. N.Mex Pub. Edn. Dept., 2003—. Named one of Top Ten Hispanic Woman in N.Mex, N.Mex Legis., 2000; recipient Educator of Yr., N.Mex Rsch. and Study Coun., 2003, Lifetime Achievement award, Hispanic Mag., 2004. Office: NMex Pub Edn Dept 300 Don Gaspar Ave Santa Fe NM 87501-2752 Office Fax: 505-827-6696. E-mail: veronica.garcia@state.nm.us.

GARCIA, YVETTE, speech-language pathologist; b. Tampa, Fla. MS, U. South Fla., 1999. Cert. of clin. competence Am. Speech Lang. and Hearing Assn. Bilingual speech-lang. pathologist United Cerebral Palsy of Tampa Bay, Tampa, 1999—2000; speech-lang. pathologist Sch. Dist. of Hillsborough County, Tampa. Accent modification instr. U. South Fla.

GARCIA Y CARRILLO, MARTHA XOCHITL, pharmacist; b. Austin, Tex., Dec. 7, 1919; d. Alberto Gonzalo and Guadalupe Eva (Carrillo) Garcia; m. Jerjes Jose Rodriguez, Oct. 9, 1943 (dec. 1987); children: Marie Eugenia, Jerjes Alberto, Nicanor Francisco. BS in Pharmacy, U. Tex., 1944. RPh, Tex. Retail pharmacist Ward Drug Store, Austin, Tex., 1952-57, Sommer's Drug Store, San Antonio, 1957-62, Skillern's Drug Store, Dallas, 1962-66; hosp. pharmacist Brackenridge Hosp., Austin, 1968-75; retail pharmacist Thorp Lane Pharmacy, San Marcos, Tex., 1975-77, The Pharmacy, San Marcos, 1975-79, MHMR Pharmacy, Austin, 1975-78, Ace Drug Co., Austin, 1979-82; ret. Contbg. author: The New Handbook of Texas, 1996. Recipient Citation of Achievement Tex. State Bd. Pharmacy, 1996. Mem. Am. Pharm. Assn. (emeritus mem.), Tex. Pharmacy Assn., Capitol Area Pharmacy Assn., Tex. State Hist. Assn., Ex-Students Assn. U. Tex. (life, Golden Anniversary cert. 1994). Republican. Avocations: reading, playing piano, current events, pharmacy medicine.

GARD, JEAN, music educator; b. Huntsville, Mo., June 27, 1949; d. Jesse Edward and Dorothy Edna Bagby; m. Gregory Dennis Gard, Apr. 23, 1983; children: Candace Dawn Stone, Shauna Lea Jacks. MusB in Edn., NE Mo. State U., 1972; MusM in Edn., Mo. U., 1976. Jr high vocal music tchr. O'Fallon (Mo.) Schs., 1972—76; elem. vocal music tchr. Blue Springs (Mo.) RIV Schs., 1976—. Dir. music Parkview Cmty. Christ, Blue Springs, 1996—2005. Office: Blue Springs RIV Schs 1801 NW Vesper Blue Springs MO 64015 Office Phone: 816-478-9899.

GARDE, SUSAN REUTERSHAN, accountant; b. Southampton, N.Y., Sept. 5, 1953; d. Robert Gordon and Ann Patricia (Cronin) Reutershan; m. John Franklin Garde III, May 20, 1989 (div. 2000); children: John Franklin IV, Sean Robert. BS, Skidmore Coll., 1975; MBA, Fla. Inst. Tech., 1983, MS in Mgmt., 1991. Budget analyst Grumman Aerospace Corp., Bethpage, NY, 1975-76, program planner, 1976-79, sr. budget planner Stuart, Fla., 1979-81, program planner, 1981-82; adminstr. rsch. ctr. United Techs., Inc., West Palm Beach, Fla., 1982-86, sr. adminstr., 1986-87, 1988-94; cost acct. Harbor Br. Oceanog. Inst., Inc., Fr. Pierce, Fla., 1994-96, sr. cost acct., 1996—. Mem.: Am. Bus. Women's Assn. (pres. Orchid chpt. 1986—87, pres. Sailfish chpt. 1985, Woman of the Yr. Citrus chpt. 2000), Skidmore Alumni Assn., Skidmore Club S.E. Fla. Republican. Congregationalist. Avocations: reading, coin collecting/numismatics, needlepoint. Office: Harbor Br Oceanog Inst 5600 US Highway 1 N Fort Pierce FL 34946-7320 Home: 286 14th Ave Vero Beach FL 32962-2718 E-mail: SueGarde@excite.com, garde@hboi.edu.

GARDEBRING, SANDRA S., academic administrator; Grad., Luther Coll., Decorah, Iowa; JD, U. Minn. Dir. Region 5 U.S. EPA; commr. Minn. Pollution Control Agy., Minn. Dept. Human Svcs.; judge Minn. Ct. Appeals; assoc. justice Minn. Supreme Ct., 1991-98; v.p. univ. rels. U. Minn., 1998—2004; v.p. univ. advancement Calif. Polytech. State Univ., San Luis Obispo, 2004—. Bd. dirs. Nature Conservancy of Minn., Regions Hosp. Hearth Connection, Greater Mpls. Conv. and Visitors Assn. Mailing: 1055 Capistrano Ct San Luis Obispo CA 93405

GARDENIER, TURKAN KUMBARACI, statistician, researcher; b. Istanbul, Turkey, Nov. 10, 1941; arrived in U.S., 1958; d. Celal and Aysel (Triandafilidu) K.; m. John Stark Gardenier, June 18, 1977; children: Pamela Lee, George HalilBonneval, Jason Celal Stark. AB, Vassar Coll., 1961; MA, Columbia U., 1962, PhD, 1966. Ops. rsch. scientist IIT Rsch. Inst., Chgo., 1966-68; asst. prof., chmn. Middle East Tech. U., Ankara, Turkey, 1968-70; vis. scientist Brookhaven Nat. Labs., Upton, L.I., NY, 1970-71; assoc. dir. Pfizer Pharms., N.Y.C., 1971-73; asst. prof. N.Y. State Maritime Coll., Bronx, NY, 1973-78; health scientist U.S. EPA, Washington, 1978-81; assoc. prof. Am. U., Washington, 1982-84; pres. Pragmatica Corp., Vienna, Va., 1982—. Tech. cons. Analytic Services Corp., Arlington, Va., 1982-90; expert U.S. Energy Info. Adminstrn., Washington, 1982-84; statis. expert EEO, 1990—, statis. cons. Engring. Computer Optecnomics, Annapolis, Md., 1977—; cons. C.R. Cushing Co., Marine Engring., N.Y.C., 1974-77. Organizer, pub. Symposium on Data Efficiency Design; preprocessing pub. Garden-ear Math./Stat. Series for Quanititative Literacy. Corp. mem. Am. Friends of Turkey, McLean, Va., 1983-89; com. mem. World Mut. Service Com., N.Y.C., 1982—; bd. dirs., v.p. Friends of Am. BoardSchs. in Turkey, 1986-88, Am. Turkish Assn., Washington, 1988-90, Washington parents rep. Foxcroft Sch., Middleburg, Va., 1981-84. Grantee, NSF, 1980, CENTO, 1969, NIH/NCI, 1997-2000. Mem. Am. Statis. Assn. (audio-visual graphics com. 1979), Ops. Rsch. Soc. Am. (fin. com. 1980), Soc. Computer Simulation (assoc. editor jour. 1980-84), Soc. Risk Analysis (fin. com. 1980), AAAS (symposium organizer 1979-2003). Avocations: swimming, photography, music composition, multi-media training. Address: Pragmatica Corp 115 St Andrews Dr NE Vienna VA 22180-3660 Office Phone: 703-319-9009. E-mail: drgarden@verizon.net.

GARDINER, JILL KENNON, secondary school educator; b. Cary, N.C., Sept. 17, 1973; d. John S. and Diane S. Gardiner. B in Social Work, N.C. State U., Raleigh, 1995; MEd, U. NC, Charlotte, 1998. Social worker Pueblo Youth Svc. Bur., Colo., 1995—96; tchr., coach Charlotte-Mecklenburg Schs., NC, 1996—98; tchr. and coach Cabarrus County Schs., Concord, NC, 1998—. Contbr. conf. Field worker Salvation Army, Concord, NC, 1999, Dept. of Social Svcs., Concord, NC, 1999. Recipient Disney Worldwide Tchrs. award, Walt Disney World/Land Corp., 2005, 2006. Mem.: NCMTA, NCAE. Independent. Roman Catholic. Avocations: running, triathlons, sports, soccer, swimming. Office: Concord HS 481 Burrage Rd Concord NC 28025 Office Phone: 704-786-4161.

GARDINER, PAMELA NAN, performing company executive; m. David Edward Miller, 1974 (div. 1988); m. Anton Labuschagne, 1998 (div. 1999). BA, U. Wis.; MA, Columbia U.; JD, Case Western Res. U. Bar: Ohio 1975, Wis. 1982, Fla. 1999. Asst. trust officer Cleve. Trust Co., 1975-78; asst. dean acad. affairs Coll. Letters and Sci. U. Wis., 1978-84; exec. dir. Madison Festival of the Lakes, 1984-88, Miami City Ballet, Fla., 2000—, Gardiner & Fix LLC, Arts and Entertainment Atty., 2002—. Bd. dirs. Miami Performing Arts Ctr. Found.; mem. adv. bd. The Playground Theatre for Young Audiences. Office: Miami City Ballet 2200 Liberty Ave Miami Beach FL 33139-1641 Office Phone: 305-929-7000. Business E-Mail: pamela@miamicityballet.org.

GARDNER, BONNIE MILNE, theater educator, playwright; b. Cleve., Oct. 17, 1954; d. Alexander Robert and Lois Chase Milne; m. Bruce Andrew Gardner, July 9, 1977; children: Jesse Milne, Elizabeth Milne. BA in Theatre, Ohio Wesleyan U., 1977; MA in Theatre, U. Akron, 1980; PhD in Theatre, Kent State U., 1985. Intern Meri Mini Players, NYC, 1975; mng. dir. Theatre on the Square, Brecksville, Ohio, 1976—79; pub. rels. dir. Fairmount Theatre of the Deaf, Cleve., 1980—81; doctoral fellow Kent State U. Sch. of Theatre, 1981—84; dir. Kent State U., Youth Enrichment Program, 1982—83; instr. U. Akron, 1984—85; prof. theatre Ohio Wesleyan U., Delaware, 1985—. Author: The Emergence of the Playwright- Director in American Theatre, 2001; contbr. articles various profl. jours.; author: (plays) produced off Broadway and regional theatres. Adv. bd. mem. Arts Edn. Ohio Dept. of Edn., 1996—2002; mem. program rev. bd. Theatre Edn. Ohio Dept. of Edn., 1998—2000; program bd. mem. Del. County Cultural Arts Ctr., Ohio, 1990—92. Individual Artist grantee, Playwrights Ohio Arts Coun., 1994. Mem.: Ohio Theatre Alliance, Ohio Alliance for Arts Edn., Assn. for Theatre in Higher Edn., Dramatists Guild. Unitarian Universalist. Office: Ohio Wesleyan U Theatre 45 Rowland Ave Delaware OH 43015

GARDNER, DONNA RAE (DIEHL), education educator; b. Johnstown, Pa., Sept. 25, 1954; d. G. Edwin and Hilda M. (Batley) D.; m. William W. Gardner. BS in Edn., Geneva Coll., 1976; MEd, U. Pitts., 1984; EdD, U. Ga., 1997. Cert. tchr., Pa. Substitute 2d and 3d grade tchr. Portage (Pa.) Elem./Mid. Sch., 1976-77, 3d grade tchr., 1977-86, 2d grade tchr., 1986-87; from assoc. prof. to prof. Toccoa Falls Coll., Ga., 1987, prof. Ga., 1998—, asst chmn. Sch. Tchr. Edn., 2005—. Chair Curriculum Rev. Com. for Accelerated Christian Edn.; spkr. in field. Editor (newsletter) Chalk Talk, Pew Pal; contbr. revs., articles to profl. publs., and ch. newsletter. Mem. choir First Alliance Ch., Toccoa, 1989-92, 96—; storyteller Stephens County Schs., Toccoa. Named 1st Lady, Toccoa FAlls Coll., 2004; grantee U. Ga., 1991-92, Ga.'s Educators Profl. Devel. Mem. Internat. Reading Assn., Nat. Coun. Tchrs. English, Ga. Assn. Colls. Tchr. Edn., Ga. Assn. Ind. Colls. Tchr. Edn. Office: Toccoa Falls Coll PO Box 875 Toccoa Falls GA 30598 Office Phone: 706-886-6831. Business E-Mail: dgardner@tfc.edu.

GARDNER, ELIZABETH ANN HUNT, artist, poet, genealogist; b. Chgo., Aug. 8, 1916; d. William Luther and Elizabeth (Miller) Hunt; m. Vernon Everett Gardner, Mar. 25, 1950. Student, Wilson Tchrs. Coll., Washington, 1934-35. Art instr. Studio 6624, Falls Church, Va., 1968—. Vol. arts tchr. Anderson Orthopedic Hosp., Arlington, Va., 1958-66; flower judge, Alexandria, Va., 1965. Author: Nature-God's Realm Acknowledged, 2005; author and photographer: Accidental Surprises in Art, 2005, Spotlight on Little Mountain Garden Gems, Collection of Poetry on Current Themes Hand Illuminated, Gardens and Nurseries to Explore; photographer numerous color photographs Framed Restoration Worn Thin Keepsake Copy Salvadore Dali's Mystical Art, 2004; exhbn. Smithsonian Inst., Washington; one-woman show at Bowie Art Ctr., S.C., 1997; oil paintings, watercolors, brass rubbings included in area exhbns. including Brevard, NC, 2004; presenter recitation of original compositions including Winter Wonderland, Shut-In, Easter, Easter Haiku, 2004, Mother's Day, Father's Day, A Matter of Survival, 2005; author, compilor: Nature: God's Realm Acknowledged, 2004 Mem.: Nat. Wildlife Fedn., Cornell Lab. Ornithology, Nat. Audubon Soc., Nat. Home Gardening Club, Shillelaghs the Travel Club, Washington Figure Skating Club. Unitarian Universalist. Avocation: ornithology. Office Phone: 703-533-0999.

GARDNER, ELLA HAINES, artist; b. Montfort, Wis. d. Robert Daniel and Gena Helena (Helgeson) Haines; m. Russell Robert Gardner, June 1, 1937; children: Russell R., Wayne, Keith. One-woman shows include Bank of Granton, Wis., 1977—, Marshfield Living Ctr., 1985—, First Nat. Bank, Neillsville, Wis., 1982—84, Dept. Industry, Labor and Human Rels., Madison, Wis., 1987, Marshfield Libr., 1990, 1991, 2001, The Mabel Tainter Meml. Mus., Menomonie, Wis., 1996, McMillan Meml. Gallery, Wisconsin Rapids, Wis., 1997, Lucille Tack Ctr. for the Arts Mus., Spencer, Wis., 1998, Marshfield Pub. Libr., 2001, 2002, 2-woman shows, Jail Mus., Neillsville, 1985, exhibited in group shows at Rahr West Mus., Manitowoc, Wis., 1982, gov.'s Office, Madison, 1983, 1988—89, King Treatment Ctr., Wis., 1983, Tuffs Mus., Neillsville, 1983, Silverman Gallery, Spring Green, Wis., 1989, New Visions Gallery, Marshfield, 1989, 1990, 2002—04, Art for Faith, Janesville, 1990, Wis. Ctr., Madison, 1997, Porter Bulls Gallery, Meml. Union, 1998, Ctrl. Wis. Triennial, 2002—03, numerous pvt. collections; author: A Celebration of Life, 1998. Charter mem. Nat. Mus. Women in the Arts. Recipient K & M Kuemmerlin award, 1986, Grumbacher Bronze award, 1987, Northwood Art Assn. award, 1987, Traveling Show award, 1987, 97-98, Obermiller Edn. award, 1993, Ctrl. Wis. State Fair award, 1973-99, 2002, 03, 04, 05, State exhibit award 1998, 99, 2002, Kenneth Kummerlein Meml. award, 1998, Creative Souls Art Guild award, 1999. Mem.: Wis. Women in the Arts (Centerfold award for logo for Wis. Regional Artist Assn. 2001), Wis. Regional Artists Assn. (Contour award 1978, 1981, 1984, 1985, 1986, 1987, Meml. award 1988, Contour award 1988, 1991, 1993). Avocations: sewing, gardening. Home: 610 E 6th St Marshfield WI 54449

GARDNER, GRACE JOELY, writer, consultant, psychologist; b. Lynn, Mass., 1947; d. Joseph B. and Shirley E. (Phillips) Beatty; m. David C. Gardner, Mar. 24, 1984. BA, Simmons Coll., 1968; MEd, Boston U., 1972, EdD, 1979; PhD, Columbia Pacific U., 1984. Diplomate Am. Bd. Med. Psychotherapists (fellow), lic. psychologist Mass. Tchr. Braintree (Mass.) H.S., 1968—70; asst. prof. Quincy (Mass.) Jr. Coll., 1971—77; sr. rsch. assoc. Boston U., 1977—79; owner, mgr. Gardner Beatty Group, Rancho La Costa, Calif., 1979—; v.p. CyberHelp, Inc., Carlsbad, Calif., 1995—; pres. Self-Test Labs., Inc., 1999—; dir. human experience rsch. Rare Medium, Inc., 2001—; pres., CEO Human Factors Rsch., Inc., 2003—. Dir. human factors rsch. France Telecom R&D, 2001—03; pres., CEO Human Factors Rsch., Inc., 2003—; part-time faculty U. Calif., San Diego. Author (with David C. Gardner): Access for Windows 95, ACT 2.0 for Windows, Cruising American On-Line (2.0 and 2.5), Cruising CompuServe, Cruising Microsoft Network, Excel 5 for Mac: The Visual Learning Guide, Excel 5 for Windows: The Visual Learning Guide, Internet for Windows: The Visual Learning Guide (AOL 2.0 and 2.5 edits., Microsoft 95 edit.), Lotus 123 for Windows: The Visual Learning Guide (v4), Powerpoint for Windows 95: The Visual Learning Guide, Quicken 5 for Windows: The Visual Learning Guide, Windows 95: The Visual Learning Guide, WindFaxPro: The Visual Learning Guide (7.0), Word 7 for Windows 95: The Visual Learning Guide, WordPerfect 6 for DOS: The Visual Learning Guide, Words for Windows 95: The Visual Learning Guide, Dissertation Proposal Guidebook: How to Write a Research Proposal and Get It Accepted, 1979, Career and Vocational Education, 1984, Stop Stress and Aging Now, 1986, Never be Tired Again!, 1989 (Book-of-Month Club selection), Discover Internet Explorer, 1997, Discover Netscape Communicator, 1997, Windows NT 4.0 Workstation: Visual Desk Reference, 1997, Visual Guide to Installing Mandrae 7-1 on a Windows Machine, 2000, others. Home: 2844 Esturion Pl Carlsbad CA 92009-5819 Office: Human Factors Rsch Inc Ste 107-389B 3675 S Rainbow Blvd Las Vegas NV 89103 Personal E-mail: joelygardner@yahoo.com.

GARDNER, JANET PAXTON, journalist, film producer; b. Dayton, Ohio, Sept. 6, 1940; d. Edward Tytus and Mary Elizabeth (Paxton) G.; m. George Karl Debreczeny, Sept. 10, 1964 (div. Feb. 1970); 1 child, Karl Philip; m. George Edward Bradshaw Morren, Jr., Nov. 6, 1980. BFA in Art and Architecture, Cooper Union, NYC, 1965; MFA in Film Prodn., NYU, 1971; postgrad., Columbia U., NYC, 1976. Film editor, assoc. prodr. Sta. WRC-TV, NBC, Washington, 1972; asst. film editor NBC News, N.Y.C., 1973-74; newswriter, field prodr. NewsCenter4 NBC, N.Y.C., 1974-75; freelance film editor CBS News, N.Y.C., 1976-79; staff reporter, feature writer The Plain Dealer, Cleve., 1979-81; edn. columnist, editor Glamour mag., N.Y.C., 1981-82; staff writer Asbury Park Press, Neptune, N.J., 1985-86; press officer UN, 1989; owner, mgr. prodr. The Gardner Documentary Group, N.Y.C., 1991—. Adj. faculty journalism U. Coll., Rutgers U., Newark, 1988-92, Montclair State Coll., Upper Montclair, NJ, 1992; mem. LA Times pub.-prof. exch. program, 1989. Prodr., dir., writer documentary videos The United Nations: It's More Than You Think, 1991, Vietnam: Land of the Ascending Dragon, 1993, Children of the Night & Starting Over, 1994, A World Beneath The War, 1996, Dancing Through Death: The Monkey Magic & Madness of Cambodia, 1999, Precious Cargo: Vietnamese Adoptees Come of Age, 2001, Siberian Dream, 2004, The Last Ghost of War, 2006; editor CBS News documentary film The Black Robes, 1978; prodr. Preparing To Give Birth, 1977, Choices in Childbirth, 1977, (film) Inside Ladies Home Jour., 1970; contbr. to NY Times, Phila. Inquirer, Boston Globe, Newsday, The Nation, Glamour, Working Women, New Woman, Diversion, Health Week, Indochina Newsletter, NJ Monthly, others. Co-chair peace and social order com. Religious Soc. of Friends, Princeton, N.J., 1994; participant U.S.-Indochina Reconciliation Project Del. to Vietnam, 1987, to Cambodia, 1990. Nominee Emmy award Outstanding Hist. Programming, NATAS, 1997; recipient spl. citation, Edn. Writers Assn., 1983, 2d pl. for news reporting, N.J. Press Women, 1990, 1st pl. for newspaper feature writing, 1990, cert. of merit, Media & Methods mag., 1992, Lowell Thomas award for video on Vietnam, Soc. Am. Travel Writers Found., 1993, Bronze Apple award, Nat. Edn. Film and Video Festival, 1993, Golden Eagle award, CINE, 1994, 1999, 2001, 2004, Spl. Jury award, 2001, Silver Apple award, Nat. Edn. Film and Video Festival, 1997, Best Feature Reporting TV award, Soc. Profl. Journalists N.Y. chpt. Deadline Club, 1998, 2001, Bronze medal, Sigma Delta Chi, award, Chgo. Internat. Film Festival, 2002; Woolrich writing fellow, Columbia U. Sch. Gen. Studies, 1976. Mem. Soc. Profl. Journalists (juror nat. mag. awards 1985, scholastic press awards 1986, chief juror editl. writing awards 1988, recipient Best Feature Reporting TV award NY chpt. 2001), Investigative Reporters and Editors, Internat. Documentary Assn., North Jersey Press Club (2d pl. for bus. feature writing 1990, 1st pl. 1991, 1st pl. for best documentary 1992, 2d pl. for feature photography 1993), NY Women in Film and TV. Office: The Gardner Documentary Group 330 W 42d St Ste 2420 New York NY 10036-6902

GARDNER, JOAN, medical, surgical nurse; b. Ft. Worth, Oct. 5, 1950; d. Bert and Pearl (Sandgarten) G. BS in Edn., U. Tex., 1972, BS in Communication, 1976; diploma, Brackenridge Hosp., 1982. RN, Tex. Trust asst. Austin Nat. Bank, Tex.; tchr. English and reading Columbus Ind. Schs., Tex.; staff orthopedics nurse Seton Med. Ctr., Austin, 1982-83, staff nurse gyn. surgery and post partum, 1983-84, staff nurse post partum, 1984-85, staff nurse gyn. surgery and ear, nose, throat, and eye, 1986, charge nurse gen. surgery, 1988-92, staff nurse short-term surgery, 1992-99; radiology charge nurse South Austin Hosp., 1999—2003; CT/MCI nurse St. David's Med. Ctr., 2003—05; adult acute psychiat. svc. nurse Austin State Hosp., Tex., 2005—. Home: 6301 Niederwald Strasse Kyle TX 78640 Office: 901 W Ben White Blvd Austin TX 78704 E-mail: a1950jg@netzero.net.

GARDNER, JOAN ANDREWS, artist educator; b. Joliet, Ill., May 3, 1933; d. E. Willard and Elizabeth (Shaffner) Andrews; m. Frank T. Gardner, July 27. BFA, U. Ill., 1953, MFA, 1957. Instr. U. Utah, Salt Lake City, 1957-58, Lane Coll., Jackson, Tenn., 1964, So. Conn. State Coll., New Haven, 1965-67, U. New Haven, 1971-82, Kent (Ohio) State U., 1982—. Author: Rooms, 1980; co-author: If I Were A, 1979. Recipient Conn. Commn. on the Arts grant, 1980. Mem. Conn. Women Artists, Coll. Art Assn., Nat. Fulbright Hays Grant Com., Spaces. Avocations: photography, painting, art. Home and Office: 735 Silver Sands Rd East Haven CT 06512-4217 Office Phone: 203-468-2366. E-mail: gardner7@mac.com.

GARDNER, JULIE ISABEL, elementary school educator; b. Stamford, Conn., June 21, 1972; d. Thomas Mark and Linda Louise Hebert; m. Willis Gardner, June 24, 2006. BS, U. Maine, Farmington, 1994. Cert. tchr. Maine, 2002. Spl. edn. tchr. Waterville Pub. Schs., Maine, 1995—96; customer satisfaction specialist MBNA Am., Belfast, Maine, 1996—98; customer svc. specialist John Hancock Signature Svcs., Charlestown, Mass., 1999—2000; mut. fund acct. Forum Fin. Group, Portland, Maine, 2000—01; mid. sch. tchr. Maine Sch. Adminstrv. Dist., Presque Isle, Maine, 2001—. Mem. needs assessment com. Maine Migrant Program, Augusta, 2003—04; participant Maine Ednl. Assessment Standards Setting Com., Augusta, 2006, MBNA Leadership Devel. Program, Belfast, Maine, 1998. Fundraiser AIDS Rsch. Boston, 1999—2000; lector St. Bruno-St. Remi Cath. Ch., Van Buren, Maine, 2001—04. Recipient Golden Apple award, WAGM-TV, 2005. Mem.: NEA. Independent. Roman Catholic. Avocations: reading, travel, cooking, swimming. Office: Presque Isle Mid Sch 569 Skyway St Presque Isle ME 04769 Office Phone: 207-764-4474.

GARDNER, KAREN, mathematics educator, computer scientist, educator; BS in Math. and Computer Sci., Oakland U., Rochester, Mich., 1991; MA in Tchg. Math. and Computer Sci., Wayne State U., Detroit. Cert. Mich. Dept. Edn., 1998. Tchr. Detroit Pub. Sch., 1993—94, Romeo (Mich.) Cmty. Sch., 1994—. Advanced placement reading Coll. Bd. Office: Romeo Engring & Tech Ctr 62300 Jewell Washington MI 48094 Office Phone: 586-752-0245. Home Fax: 586-752-0452; Office Fax: 586-752-0452. Personal E-mail: karen.gardner@romeo.k12.mi.us.

GARDNER, KAREN HIGH, special education educator; b. Longview, Tex., Sept. 2, 1958; d. Lawrence Wayne and Mary Elizabeth; m. Flexton L. Gardner, Nov. 5, 1983; children: Flexton Lee, Alycia Yvonne. BS in Spl. Edn., Va. State U., 1981; MS in Secondary Edn., Old Dominion U., 2001. Cert. collegiate profl. cert. 1981. Spl. edn. tchr. Va. Beach Public Sch., 1981—, Princess Anne H.S., Va. Beach, 2001—. Dept. chair Windsor Oaks Elem., 1991—93, Corp. Landing Middle Sch., 1999—2001; mentor Va. Beach Public Sch., 1999—; coord. Ptnr. in Edn, Va. Beach, 2003—. Planning coun. Windsor Oaks Elem., 1992—93, Corp. Landing Middle Sch., 1997—99; child study team coord. Bayside Middle Sch., 1994—97; season for nonviolence sponsor Princess Anne H.S., 2003—. Recipient Human Rights award, Va. Beach Human Rights Commn., 2004. Fellow: Assn. Supervision and Curriculum Devel. Avocations: reading, bicycling, travel, chess. Home: 3545 Byrn Brae Dr Virginia Beach VA 23464 Office: Princess Anne HS 4400 Va Beach Blvd Virginia Beach VA 23462 Office Phone: 757-473-5000. Business E-Mail: khgardne@vbschools.com.

GARDNER, KERRY ANN, librarian; b. Honolulu, May 19, 1955; d. Byron Patton and Claire Gardner. BA in Polit. Sci. magna cum laude, Temple U., 1976; MA in L.Am. Studies, U. Ariz., 1983, MLS, 1990. Documents libr. FMC Corp., Chgo., 1977-78; grad. rsch. asst. U. Ariz., Tucson, 1983-86; rsch. cons., 1983-92; libr. asst. I Phoenix Pub. Libr., 1988-89; mgr. faculty resource libr., English 2d lang. U. Ariz. Ctr., 1989—90; project mgr. U. Ariz., 1990-92; mgr. faculty resource libr., English 2d lang. U. Ariz. Ctr., 1991—92; pub. svcs. libr. Bryan Wildenthal Meml. Libr., Sul Ross State U., Alpine, Tex., 1992-95; libr. dir. Am. U., Dubai, United Arab Emirates, 1995-96; literacy libr. Sterling Mcpl. Libr., Baytown, Tex., 1996-98; libr. Valle Verde campus, El Paso C.C., Tex., 1998—, co-head libr., 2001—02. Indexer Hispanic Am. Periodicals Index, 1995; maintain GPO Access Web site, 1998—. Contbr. articles to profl. publs. Tchr. English, Literacy Vols. Am., 1991-92, 96-98; mem. Friends of the El Paso Pub. Libr., 2004—, sec., 2006—. Named Libr. of Yr., Border Regional Libr. Assn., 2001; grad. scholar, U. Ariz., 1976—77, 1981—82. Mem.: NEA, ALA, Tex. C.C. Tex. Assn., Border Regional Libr. Assn. (chair publicity com. 1999—2002, chair. Libr. of the Yr. com. 2002—03), Assn. Coll. and Rsch. Librs., Tex. Libr. Assn. (legis. com. coll. and univ. librs. divsn. 1993—94), Beta Phi Mu. Avocations: travel, birding. Office: El Paso C C Valle Verde Campus PO Box 20500 El Paso TX 79998-0500

GARDNER, LIZ See WEDDINGTON, ELIZABETH

GARDNER, SANDI B., biology professor; b. Chicago Heights, Ill., June 24, 1959; d. Robert S. and Lenore M. (D'Arcy) Bushor; m. Daniel E. Gardner, Apr. 16, 1988 (div. 1997); m. Philliip K. Duncan, Feb., 2004; 1 child, C(atherine) J. BS in Phys. Edn./Recreation, U. Ill., Chgo., 1981; MS in Environ. Biology, Govs. State U., University Park, Ill., 1988; postgrad., Ill. Inst. Tech., Chgo., 1993-95; PhD, Walden U., Mpls., 1997. Profl. scout Wau Bon Girl Scout Coun., Fond Du Lac, Wis., 1981-82; pre-sch. tchr. Anita M. Stone Ctr., Flossmoor, Ill., 1982-84, Alsip (Ill.) Pre-Sch., 1984-85; tchg. asst. Govs. State U., 1986-89; park ranger Ind. Dunes Nat. Lakeshore, Porter, 1986-92; prof. biology South Suburban Coll., South Holland, Ill., 1990-96. Adj. prof. Ind. U.-N.W., Gary, 1990—92, Govs. State U., 1989—93; mem. spl. populations adv. bd. South Suburban Mental Health, South Holland, 1992—94; staff develop./curriculum specialist Purdue U., 1995—96, adj. faculty, 1996; prof. biology Triton Coll., River Grove, Ill., 1996—, chair sci. dept., 2001—, adv. pre-profl. orgn., 2002, faculty advisor, 2003—, grad. sch. advisor, 2003—; cons. Taylor U., Ft. Wayne, Ind., 1999—2001; grad. sch. adv. Excelsior U., NY, 2003—, Ellis Coll., 2004—, Western Internat. U., 2005—; scorer ACT and AP exams, 2004—05; grad. program faculty Aspen U., 2005—; workshop presenter, cons. in field. Author: Relationship Between Computer Anxiety and Computer Use, 1996, WebWeaver Environmental Science Online, 2001, Lab Manual Genetics, 2002, Student Study Guide, 2005; co-author: Case Studies for Anatomy and Physiology, 1992, Lab Manual for General Biology, 1994, 1999, 2001, Teachers/Student Guide to Virtual Biology Laboratory CD-ROM, 1997, WebWeaver Study Guide, 1998; editor: McGrawHill Pub., 2003, Pearson Pub., 2003. Leader, vol., trainer Calumet coun. Girl Scouts U.S., Highland, Ind., 1981-84, 93—; vol. Lincoln Park Zoo, 1986-88, Brookfield Zoo, 1996-2000; coach AYSO Soccer, River Forest, Ill., bd. dirs. 1999; adv. Phi Theta Kappa Triton Coll, River Grove, Ill., 1996-2000; vol. mentor West Lake Hosp., 2002; vol. Amb. Walden U., 2002; co-chair accreditation com. NCA, 2003. Recipient Spl. Achievement award Nat. Park Svc., 1988; Hand-On Sci. for Tchrs. award EPA, 1992; grantee R&D Triton, 1998—, On-line Biology, 1999, Plastination, 1999, HECA, 1999-2000, On-Line Tutoring Ctr., 2000-01. Mem. Nat. Sci. Tchrs. Assn., Nat. Assn. Biology Tchrs., Ill. Assn. C.C. Biology Tchrs. (pres. 1999-2001), Phi Delta Kappa (v.p. membership 1999-2003). Home: 1202 Havalina Rd Williamsburg NM 87942 Office: Triton Coll 2000 N 5th Ave River Grove IL 60171-1907 Personal E-mail: sbgardner@aol.com.

GARDNER, SHERYL PAIGE, gynecologist; b. Bremerton, Wash., Jan. 24, 1945; d. Edwin Gerald and Dorothy Elizabeth (Herman) G.; m. James Alva Beat, June 20, 1986. BA in Biology, U. Oreg., 1967, MD cum laude, 1971. Diplomate Am. Bd. Ob-Gyn. Intern L.A. County Harbor Gen. Hosp., Torrance, Calif., 1971-72, resident in ob-gyn., 1972-75; physician Group Health Assn., Washington, 1975-87; pvt. practice Mililani, Hawaii, 1987—; chmn. dept. ob-gyn. Wahiawa Gen. Hosp., 1994—. Med. staff sec. Wahiawa (Hawaii) Gen. Hosp., 1994-95. Mem. Am. Coll. Ob-Gyn., Am. Soc. Colposcopy and Cervical Pathology, Hawaii Med. Assn., N.Am. Menopause Soc., Sigma Kappa, Alpha Omega Alpha. Democrat. Office: 95-1249 Meheula Pkwy Ste B10A Mililani HI 96789-1763 Office Phone: 808-625-5277.

GARDNER, SONIA KAY, writer; b. Council, Idaho, Nov. 27, 1956; d. Kenneth A. and Vera E. (Jones) White; m. William D. Gardner, Aug. 7, 1982; 1 child, Shane. BA in edn., BSU, 1979. Elem. tchr. Cambridge Elem., Cambridge, Idaho, 1980-94; writer Homer, Ark., 2005—. Author: Eagle Feathers, 1997. Mem. Soc. Childrens Books Writers and Illustrators.

GARDNER, SUSAN KAY, elementary school educator; b. San Antonio, June 25, 1963; d. John Wayne and Jacklyn Pearl Gardner; life ptnr. Kevin Wayne Creamer; children: Tiffany Janice, Sunny Brianne. BS, Tex. A&M U., College Station, 1993. Tchr. Woodville Ind. Sch. Dist., Tex., 1994—99, Spurger Ind. Sch. Dist., 1999—2006. Chmn. dairy goat Tyler County Fair Bd., Woodville, 2000—06. Home: RR 3 Box 56 Woodville TX 75979 Office: Spurger Ind Sch Dist PO Box 38 Spurger TX 77660 Office Phone: 409-429-5152. Personal E-mail: gardners@spurger.k12.tx.us.

GARDNER, TRACY A., social studies educator; b. Pueblo, Colo., Dec. 17, 1966; d. Georgia Gardner. BS, U. So. Colo., Pueblo, 1996; MBA, Colo. State U., Pueblo, 2003. Lic. tchg. Colo. Dept. Edn., 1996. Social studies tchr. Pueblo East H.S., 1996—. Mem.: APA, NEA, Tchrs. Psychology in Secondary Schs., Colo. Edn. Assn. Office: Pueblo E HS 9 MacNeil Rd Pueblo CO 81001 Office Phone: 719-549-7724. Personal E-mail: gardnerteach@hotmail.com. Business E-Mail: tgardner@pueblo60.k12.co.us.

GARE, FRAN, nutritionist; b. Dec. 5, 1939; d. David and Henrietta Rhein; divorced; children: David, Marc. BA, Fairleigh Dickinson U., 1962; Naturopathic degree, Braintridge Forest Sch., U.K., 1978; MS in Clin Nutrition and Biology, U. Bridgeport, 1980. Corp. spokesperson Liggett & Meyers; pres. Nutriplan, Inc, 1980-96; dir. nutrition The Atkins Ctr. Complementary Nutrition, 1991-96, Dayton Med. Ctr.-Nutrition, North Miami Beach, Fla., 1996—; dir. natural medicine Columbia Miami Heart Ctr. for Alternative Medicine, 1998—; pres. and CEO The Sweet Life, Inc., 2002—. Lectr. in field. Co-author: Dr. Atkins Diet Revolution, 1972, The Diet Cookbook, 1974, Super Energy Diet Cookbook, 1978, The Mandell's Not Your Fault Your're Fat, 1983, The Allergy Cookbook, 1981, The New Diet Revolution Cookbook, 1994, The Sweet Miracle of Xylitol, 2002, Women's Health Book, 2003; radio host The Diet Revolution WEVD 1050 AM, WAXY 790, Miami; resident nutritionist CBS TV News, Miami; panelist Donahue, David Sussking, Geraldo. Office: 1111 Brictell Ave 11th flr Miami FL 33131

GAREY, PATRICIA MARTIN, artist; b. State College, Miss., Nov. 11, 1932; d. Verey G. Martin and Eva Myrtle Jones; m. Donald L. Garey, Aug. 1, 1953; children: Deborah Anne Garey Furst, Elizabeth Laird Garey Jones. BS in Costume Design, Tex. Women's U., 1953; MFA, Tex. Tech. U., 1973; postgrad. in art history, Two-Dimensional Studio Art, 1970-73. Prodn. mgr. Cox Advt. Agy., Roswell, N.Mex., 1958-63; art instr. Coll. of Southwest, Hobbs, N.Mex., 1967-69, 72-73, prof. art history, art appreciation, 1974-76; studio artist Hobbs, 1976—; prof. art/painting and drawing N.Mex. Jr. Coll., 1997-98. Instr. Cloudcroft Artists Sch., N.Mex., 1991; prof. drawing, painting N.Mex. Jr. Coll.; prof. art hist. Coll. of Southwest, 1999—2001; rep., drawing instr. Villa Maria Ctr. for the Arts, Perugia, Italy, 1996; apptd. commr. N.Mex. Arts Commn., 1999; artist-in-residence N.Mex. Art Commn., Santa Fe, 1975—76. Artist (one-woman shows) Sand Hills Mus., Kermit, Tex., 1968, N.Mex. Jr. Coll., Hobbs, 1969, 1985, Coll. of SW, 1974, 1979, Sangre de Cristo Arts Ctr., Puebl, 1979, U. Tex. of Permian Basin, Odessa, 1980, (exhibitions) Roswell Mus. Art, Four Women Artists of Hobbs, N.Mex., 1966, Lubbock Mcpl. Garden and Arts Ctr., 1966, Laguna Gloria Art Mus., 1968—, Southeastern N.Mex. Small Painting Exhibit, 1975 (2d pl., 1966, 2d pl. Graphics, 2d pl. Sculpture, 2d pl. Acrylics, 1st pl. Ceramics, 1st pl. Drawing, 2d pl. Painting), Americas Gallery, Taos, 1974, Blair Gallery, Santa Fe, 1976, Mus. Fine Arts, 1976, Tex. Tech. U. Grad. Show, 1977, Little Rock Art Ctr., Ark., 1978, Hills Gallery, Santa Fe, 1979, Dallas Mus. Fine Art, 1986, 1987, 1988, 1990, Beaux Arts Ball Art Auction, 1990, Okla. City Mus. Art nat. drawing competition, Little Rock Art Ctr., El Paso Sun Carnival, Tex., Govs. Gallery, State Capitol, Santa Fe, 1997, Llano Estacado Art Assn., Hobbs, N.Mex., 1999 (Best of Show, 1st pl. watercolor), (permanent collections) Home Scis. Dept., Tex. Tech. U., The Round House/State Capitol, Santa Fe, Villa Maria Ctr. for the Arts, Raimondi Collection, Perugia, Italy, State Capitol, Santa Fe, N.Mex. Jr. Coll., docent Meadows Mus. of Art So. Meth. U., Dallas, 1990, Govs. Invitiational, Govs. Gallery, 1996, 35 Clay Workers of N.Mex., artist (exhibitions) Southeastern N.Mex. Small Painting Exhibit, 1976, 1987, 1988, 1990, (represented by) Design Today, Lubbock, Tex., Sylvia Ullman Am. Crafts, Cleve.; represented by, DeLis Backdoor Gallery, N.Mex., Old Pecos Gallery, Carlsbad, N.Mex., Contemporary Arts Studio, Hobbs, N.Mex. Arts commr. State of N.Mex., 1999—2002, N.Mex. Arts Commn., 1999—2003; artistic bd. S.W. Symphony, Hobbs, 1987—99; Bd. dirs. The Bridge Breast Ctr., Dallas, 1992—93, Llano Estacado Art Assn. Recipient Best of Show award for mixed media Llano Estacado Art Assn. Regional Show, Hobbs, N.Mex., 1996, Best of Show award for ceramics, 1999, 1st pl. award for watercolor, 1999, Best of Show for oil painting, 2004, others. Mem. Delta Phi Delta, Chi Omega. Democrat. Methodist. Avocations: swimming, cooking, classical music, book collecting. Studio: 315 E Alto Dr Hobbs NM 88240-3905 also: Piney Woods Cloudcroft NM 88350 Office Phone: 505-393-8683.

GAREY, VELMA KAY, science foundation director, educator; d. Elizabeth Joann and James Lynn Thornton; m. Richard Griffith Garey, June 28, 1968; children: Richard James, Elisa Joanne. MS in Edn., BS in edn., New Paltz Coll., N.Y., 1990. Cert. Permanent Tchr. N.Y., 1986. Asst. planetarium dir. Newburgh Enlarged City Sch. Dist., NY, 2002—03; planetarium dir. Newburgh Enlarged City Sch. Dist., NY, 2003—. Fellow Empire State Challenger Fellowship for Tchrs., N.Y. State, 1987, 1989; scholar Bertha Herwig Connelly Meml. Scholarship, New Paltz Coll., 1986, Empire State Math and Sci. Tchrs. Scholarship, N.Y. State, 1985. Mem.: NSTA. Office: 201 Fullerton Ave Newburgh NY 12550 Office Phone: 845-563-5400. Business E-Mail: vgarey@newburgh.k12.ny.us.

GARFIELD-WOODBRIDGE, NANCY, writer; b. N.Y.C. d. Solomon and Betty Silbowitz; m. George Charles Woodbridge, Apr. 20, 1980; children from previous marriage: Maurice Garfield, Joshua Garfield. BA in Lit., Bennington Coll., 1955; MS in Edn., Hofstra U., 1972, postgrad., 1973. Cert. tchr. K-8, English 7-9 N.Y. Editl. asst. Wenner Gren Found. Anthropol. Rsch., N.Y.C., 1952—55; picture editor Forbes Mag., N.Y.C., 1955—56; editor-in-chief The Gifted Child Mag., N.Y.C., 1957—58; v.p. Info. Retrieval Systems, Great Neck, NY, 1958—72; rsch. assoc. to v.p. and editor N.Y. Inst. Tech., Westbury, 1972—73; dir. spl. projects Girl Scouts of USA, N.Y.C., 1973—2000; children's author, 2000—. Spkr. v.p.'s task force on youth employment, Little Rock, 1979, gov.'s conf. on juvenile justice, Baton Rouge;

presenter Edn. Commn. for the States, Denver, 1979. Author: The Tuesday Elephant, 1968, The Dancing Monkey, 1970, Juvenile Justice, 1981; contbr. articles to profl. jours. and mags. Vol. Kennedy Kenya Airlift Program, N.Y.C., 1962, Biafran Refugee Campaign, N.Y.-London, 1967; fundraiser Sara's Ctr. Very Spl. Arts Festival, L.I. to Washington. Scholar Breadloaf Writers Conf., Vt., 1967. Mem.: Acad. Am. Poets, The Author's Guild, Milford Fine Arts Coun., Soc. Children's Book Writers and Illustrators. Avocations: travel, reading, opera, painting, photography.

GARFINKEL, JANE E., lawyer; b. NYC, Dec. 2, 1952; d. Albert E. and Rita H. (Halpern) G.; m. Louis F. Solimine, May 20, 1979. BA, Wheaton Coll., 1974; MA, U. Mich., 1975, JD, 1979. Bar: Ohio 1980. Assoc. Smith & Schnacke, Cin., 1980-88, ptnr., 1988-89, Thompson Hine LLP, Cin., 1989—. Office: Thompson Hine LLP 312 Walnut St Ste 1400 Cincinnati OH 45202-4089 Office Phone: 513-352-6530. Business E-Mail: jane.garfinkel@thompsonhine.com.

GARFINKEL, RENÉE EFRA, psychologist; b. N.Y.C., May 26, 1950; d. Jacob Joseph and Miriam (Herc) Morgenstern; m. Jay Garfinkel, June 22, 1969; children: Elon J., Erica B. BA, Am. U., 1971; PhD, Lund U., 1975. Lic. psychology, Pa., Md., D.C., Va. Sr. clin. psychologist Phila. Geriat. Ctr., 1977-80; chief psychology dept. Grad. Hosp., Phila., 1980-85; dir. women's programs Am. Psychol. Assn., Washington, 1985-86; dir. Gerontology Svcs., Silver Spring, Md., 1986-97; founder, editor Adoption Quar., 1995-2000. Pres. Adoption Studies Inst., 1994-2000; bd. dirs. Hebrew Home of Greater Washington, Rockville, Md., Greater Washington Bd. of Jewish Edn., George Washngton U. Hillel, Red Cross Disaster Svcs.; vis. scholar Inst. for Crisis Disaster and Risk Mgmt. The George Washington U., 1998—; Coolidge Colloquium fellow, 2001. Author: A View from my Rooftop: Reflections of an Inner Life, 2000. Sec. Eldergames, Washington, 1986; bd. dirs. Sr. Citizen Judicare Project, Phila., 1983-85. Kellogg Found. scholar, 1983. Mem. Am. Psychol. Assn., Gerontol. Soc., N.Y. Acad. Scis., Nat. Coalition for Women's Mental Health, Women's Health Alliance Pa. (charter). Avocations: flying, writing, travel, photography, reading. Office: Ste 403 2515 K St NW Apt 403 Washington DC 20037-2013

GARFINKLE, ELAINE MYRA, writer; b. Canton, Ohio, July 24, 1936; d. Clifford and Dora Adelman Margolis; m. Jack George Garfinkle, Dec. 27, 1959; 1 child, Marcia Lizabeth. Gen. mgr., editor, pub. Stark Jewish News, Inc., Canton, 1970—83; owner, writer, rschr. Canton Writing Svc., 1978—90; pres., treas. Marce Pubs., Inc., Canton, 1979—83; owner, rschr. Leo Rsch. unlimited, Canton, 1979—83; cmty. rels. supr. Goodwill Rehab., Canton, 1984—87; advt. exec. Cmty. Newspapers, Massillon, Ohio, 1987—91. Historian, pub., compiler, author Through the Years, the Informal History of the Canton, Ohio, Area Jewish Community 1870-2005, 80 vols. Program presenter area nursing homes, 1970—2005; historian on local spl. PBS program on history of Canton, Ohio; adv. U.S. Holocaust Meml. Mus.; supporter Goodwill's Amb. of Goodwill; bd. mem., publicity chair Canton chpt. Hadassah; mem. Cleve. Jewish Genealogy Soc.; advocate for spl. edn., sr. adult and consumer product affairs; mem., supporter Stark County Hist. Soc., McKinley Mus.; vol. and program presenter Canton Jewish Cmty. Ctr. Mem.: Friends of Ctr. Jewish History, Ohio Libr., Am. Friends Hebrew U., Leo Baeck Inst., Friends North Canton, YIVO Inst. Jewish Rsch., Am. Jewish Hist. Soc., Canton Jewish Cmty. Fedn. (edn. com. mem., Outstanding Svc. award 1996—), Internat. Jewish Women (life; past pres., treas.), Am. Heart Assn. (cmty. rels. com. 1992—96, Outstanding Svc. award 1992—96), Am. Sephardi Fedn., Nat. Geographic Soc., Hadassah (program presenter 2003, former edn. com. mem., bd. mem., publicity chair Canton chpt.), Anti-Defamation League, Women's League Conservative Judaism, Shaaray Torah Sisterhood (former social action chmn.). Jewish. Avocations: photography, practical psychology, music, reading, studying Jewish history.

GARING, IONE DAVIS, civic worker; b. Huntsville, Ala., Jan. 8, 1930; d. Drury McNary and Ione (Thompson) Davis; m. John Seymour Garing, Apr. 26, 1952; children: John Davis, Susan Carolyn. BSc in Edn. cum laude, Ohio State U., 1951. Tchr. Columbus (Ohio) Pub. Schs., 1952-54, Upper Arlington Pub. Sch., Columbus, 1957-58; libr. Newton (Mass.) Libr., 1955; interviewer audits and surveys Elmo Roper, Boston, 1956. Adv. com. Sch. Com. on Spl. Edn., Lexington, Mass., 1979-80; adv. bd. Cary Meml. Libr., Lexington, 1989—. Elected Town Meeting mem., Lexington, 1980-2002, Lexington 2020 Vision Study, 2001; exec. bd. Lexington Dem. Com., 1987-89, mem., 1986—; del. Mass. Dem. Convs., 1986, 88, 90, 92, 94, 96, 98, 2000, 2002; exec. bd. Friends Coun. on Aging, 1986, PTA, 1965-79; vol. Meals on Wheels, 1985-89; pres. United Meth. Women, Lexington, 1973-75; bd. dir. Meth. Weekday Sch., 1971-80, chmn. bd. dir., 2004—; co-organizer 1st town-wide hazardous waste collection in U.S., Lexington, 1983; vol. Lexington Hist. Soc., 1978—; co-founder, chmn. Friends of Cary Meml. Libr. Orgn., 1990-97, bd. dir., 1990—; founding mem., treas., Precint 8 Residents Assn., 1996-2005. Mem. LWV (pres. Lexington 1983-85), AAUW (Mass. long range planning com.), DAR (vice regent 1977-80, Mass. chmn. scholarships and loan com. 1980-83), Florence Crittenton League, Outlook Club (pres. 1985-87, chmn. scholarships com. 1990-2002), Lexington Field and Garden Club (chmn. Wednesday Workshop 1998-2000, 2d v.p. 2000-02), North Shore Rock and Mineral Club (Peabody, Mass.), Brookline Bird Club, Minute Man Nat. Pk. Assn., Alpha Chi Omega. Avocations: conservation, gardening, birdwatching, genealogy, travel. Home: 157 Cedar St Lexington MA 02421-6507

GARITY, KATHLEEN MARY, nurse coordinator, director; m. Donald Garity, Oct. 22, 1988; children: Hannah C., Katherine M. BSN, Old Dominion U., 1980, BS in Psychology, 1980; MSN, Cath. U. Am., 1987. RN Va. Heart transplant coord. Fairfax Hosp., Falls Church, Va., 1986—88; cons. APACHE Med. Sys., Washington, 1988—89; cardiac clinical specialist GW Hosp., Washington, 1989—92; ICU nurse Inova Fairfax Hosp., 1992—97; dir. care coord. Compassionate Care Assoc., Burke, Va., 2002—, fed. occupl. health nurse coord. Washington, 2003—. Vol. Am. Heart Assn., 2005—, Fairfax Med. Reserves, 2005—. Wise fellow, George Wash. Med. Ctr., 1985, Nurse Traineeship fellow, HHS US Govt., 1986. Mem.: Omicron Delta Kappa (life), Sigma Theta Tau (life). Avocations: travel, snorkeling, scuba diving, exercise.

GARLAND, LARETTA MATTHEWS, psychologist, nursing educator; b. Jacksonville, Fla. d. Wilburn L. and Clyde-Marian (Chamberlin) Matthews; m. John B. Garland, Mar. 2, 1946; children: John Barnard, Brien Freeling, Amy-Gwin. Diploma, Fla. State Sch. Nursing, 1942; BSN, Emory U., 1950, MA, 1953; BA in Edn., U. Fla., 1951; cert. cardiovascular nurse specialty, Tex. Med. Ctr., 1965; EdD, U. Ga., 1975; postgrad. in counseling and guidance, Ga. State U., 1969; grad. cert. in gerontology, 1981. Cert. nat. counselor. Office and staff nurse, Lakeland, Fla., 1942, 45; nurse ARC, Buffalo, 1956; asst. prof. nursing Med. Coll. Ga., 1965-67; instr. Emory U., 1952-54, assoc. prof., 1967-71, prof., 1972-86, prof. emeritus, 1987—. Ednl. psychologist, dir. gerontol. nurse practitioner program, 1978-80, asst. to dean, 1983-86. Author: (with Carol Bush) Coping Behavior and Nursing, 1982; contbr. articles to profl. jours. With Nurse Corps, U.S. Army, 1942-45. Decorated 2 Bronze Stars; recipient Outstanding Tchg. award Emory U. Sch. Nursing Grad. Srs., 1977, Appreciation award So. Region Constituent Leagues, Nat. League for Nursing award, 1987, Mabel Korsell award of appreciation Ga. League Nursing, 1987, Spl. Recognition award Ga. Nurses Assn., 1988, 90, Nurse of Yr. award, 1992, Appreciation award Ga. Assn. Nursing Students, 1990, Van de Vrede award Ga. League Nursing, 1993; HEW fellow, 1967-68. Mem. APA, AACD, ANA, Ga. Assn. Nursing Students (hon.), Nat. League Nursing, Bs. and Profl. Women, China Burma India VA Assn. (mem. nat. bd. 1993—), 14th Air Force Asssn. (Flying Tigers), Hump Pilots Assn., Ormond Beach Womens Club, Ormond Beach Hist. Trust, Nat. Assn. Women Vet. (steering com.), Women in Mil. Svc. Meml. Found. (charter), ARC Nurses, Panhellenic Assn., Hist. Trust, Alpha Chi Omega, Sigma Theta Tau, Kappa Delta Pi, Alpha Kappa Delta, Omicron Delta Kappa. Office: Emory U Nell Hodgson Woodruff Sch Atlanta GA 30322-0001 Office Phone: 386-677-9466.

GARLAND, SYLVIA DILLOF, lawyer; b. NYC, June 4, 1919; d. Morris and Frieda (Gassner) Dillof; m. Albert Garland, May 4, 1942; children: Margaret Garland, Paul B. BA, Bklyn. Coll., 1939; JD cum laude, N.Y. Law Sch., 1960. Bar: N.Y. 1960, U.S. Ct. Appeals (2d cir.) 1965, U.S. Ct. Claims 1965, U.S. Supreme Ct. 1967, U.S. Customs Ct. 1972, U.S. Ct. Appeals (5th cir.), 1979. Assoc. Borden, Skidell, Fleck and Steindler, Jamaica, NY, 1960-61, Fields, Zimmerman, Skodnick & Segall, Jamaica, 1961-65, Marshall, Brater, Greene, Allison & Tucker, N.Y.C., 1965-68; law sec. to N.Y. Supreme Ct. justice Suffolk County, 1968-70; ptnr. Hofheimer, Gartlir & Gross, N.Y.C., 1970—. Asst. adj. prof. N.Y. Law Sch., 1974-79; mem. com. on character and fitness N.Y. State Supreme Ct., 1st Jud. Dept., 1985—, vice chmn., 1991—. Author: Workman's Compensation, 1957, Labor Law, 1959, Wills, 1962; contbg. author: Guardians and Custodians, 1970; editor-in-chief Law Rev. Jour., N.Y. Law Forum, 1959-60 (svc. award 1960); contbr. articles to mag. Trustee N.Y. Law Sch., 1979-90, trustee emeritus, 1991—; pres. Oakland chpt. B'nai Brith, Bayside, N.Y., 1955-57. Recipient Disting. Alumnus award N.Y. Law Sch., 1978, Judge Charles W. Froessel award N.Y. Law Sch., 1997. Mem. ABA (litigation sect., family law sect.), N.Y. State Bar Assn. (family law sect.), Queen's County Bar Assn. (sec. civil practice 1960-79), N.Y. Law Sch. Alumni Assn. (pres. 1976-77), N.Y. Law Forum Alumni Assn. (pres. 1963-65). Jewish. Home: 425 E 58th St New York NY 10022-2300

GARMAN, RITA B., state supreme court justice; b. Aurora, Ill., Nov. 19, 1943; children: Sara Ellen, Andrew Gil. BS in Econs., U. Ill., 1965; JD with distinction, U. Iowa, 1968. Asst. state atty. Vermilion County, 1969—73; pvt. practice Sebat, Swanson, Banks, Lessen & Garman, 1973; assoc. cir. judge, 1974—86; cir. judge Fifth Jud. Cir., 1986—95, presiding cir. judge, 1987—95; judge Fourth Dist. Appellate Ct., 1996—2001; justice Ill. Supreme Ct., 2001—. Mem.: Ill. Judge's Assn., Vermilion County Bar Assn., Iowa Bar Assn., Ill. State Bar Assn. Office: Ill Supreme Ct 160 N LaSalle St Chicago IL 60601*

GARMANY, CATHARINE DOREMUS, astronomer; b. NYC, Mar. 6, 1946; d. Edwin and Janet (MacMaster) Doremus; children: Richard, Jeffrey. BS, Ind. U., 1966; MS, U. Va., 1968, PhD, 1971. Rsch. assoc. U. Va., Charlottesville, 1971-73; rsch. assoc. Joint Inst. for Lab Astrophys. U. Colo., Boulder, 1977-84, sr. rsch. assoc. Joint Inst. for Lab Astrophys., 1984-2000; dir. Fiske Planetarium, 1991-2000; dir. astronomy Astronomy, Oracle, Ariz., 2000—03, NOAO, 2004—. Contbr. articles to profl. jours. Recipient Annie J. Cannon award AAUW, AAS, 1976; grantee NASA, NSF. E-mail: garmany@hnoao.edu.

GARMEL, MARION BESS SIMON, retired arts journalist; b. El Paso, Tex., Oct. 15, 1936; d. Marcus and Frieda (Alfman) Simon; m. Raymond Lewis Garmel, Nov. 28, 1965 (dec. Feb. 1986); 1 child, Cynthia Rogers; 1 stepchild, Christine Blum. Student, U. Tex., El Paso, 1954-55; BJ, U. Tex., Austin, 1958. Exec. sec. Nat. Student Assn., Phila., 1958-59, pub. rels. dir., 1960-61; sec. World Assembly Youth, Paris, Brussels, 1959-60; dictationist Wall Street Jour., Washington, 1961; libr., staff writer Nat. Observer, Silver Spring, Md., 1961-70; art critic Indpls. News, 1971-91, editor Free Time sect., 1975-91, critic radio and TV, 1991-95; theater critic Indpls. Star and News, 1995-99, Indpls. Star, 1999—2002, ret., 2002. Mem. Nat. Fedn. Press Women (1st Place Critics award 1974), Ind. Soc. Profl. Journalists (1st place criticism 2002), Hadassah Women's Zionist Orgn. Am. (life), Woman's Press Club Ind. (1st Place Critics award 1995, 2002). Jewish. Avocation: tennis. Home: 226 E 45th St Indianapolis IN 46205-1712 E-mail: mgarmel@earthlink.net.

GARNER, CARLENE ANN, not-for-profit fundraiser, consultant; b. Dec. 17, 1945; d. Carl A. and Ruth E. (Mathison) Timblin; m. Adelbert L. Garner, Feb. 17, 1964; children: Bruce A., Brent A. BA, U. Puget Sound, 1983. Adminstrv. dir. Balletacoma, 1984-87; exec. dir. Tacoma Symphony, 1987-95; prin. New Horizon Cons., Tacoma, 1995-98; co-owner Stewardship Devel., 1998—. Cons. Wash. PAVE, Tacoma, 1983-84. Treas. Coalition for the Devel. of the Arts, 1992-94; pres. Wilson High Sch. PTA, Tacoma, 1983-85; chmn. Tacoma Sch. Vol. Adv. Bd., 1985-87; pres. Emmanuel Luth. Ch., Tacoma, 1984-86, chmn. future steering com., 1987-93; sec.-treas. Tacoma-Narrows Conf., 1987-98; vice chmn. Tacoma Luth. Home, 1996-98; pub. mem. Wash. State Bd. Pharmacy, 1993-98. Mem. N.W. Devel. Officers Assn. (chair Tacoma/Pierce County com. 1994-96), Jr. Women's Club Tacoma (pres. 1975-76, pres. Peninsula dist. 1984-86), Gen. Fedn. Women's Club-Wash. State (treas. 1988-90, 3d v.p. 1990-92, 2d v.p. 1992-94, 1st v.p. 1994-96, pres. 1996-98, Clubwoman of Yr. 1977, Outstanding FREE chmn. Gen. Fedn. 1982), Commencement Bay Woman's Club (pres. 1990-92), Gen. Fedn. of Women's Club (bd. dirs., chair nat. conv. 1995, state pres. 1996-98, chair cmty. improvement program 1998-2000, treas. 2000—02, rec. sec. 2002-04, 2d v.p. 2004-06, 1st v.p. 2006—). Lutheran.

GARNER, JENNIFER ANNE, actress; b. Houston, Apr. 17, 1972; d. Bill and Pat Garner; m. Scott Foley, Oct. 19, 2000 (div. Mar. 30, 2004); m. Ben Affleck, June 29, 2005; 1 child, Violet. BFA, Dennison U., 1994. Actor: (TV miniseries) Danielle Steele's Zoya, 1995, Dead Man's Walk, 1996; (TV films) Harvest of Fire, 1996, The Player, 1997, Rose Hill, 1997, Aftershock: Earthquake in New York, 1999; (TV series) Swift Justice, 1996, Law & Order, 1996, Spin City, 1996, Fantasy Island, 1998, The Pretender, 1999, Significant Others, 1998, The Time of Your Life, 1999—2000, Alias, 2001—06 (Emmy nominee for outstanding lead actress in a drama, 2002, 2003, 2004, 2005, Golden Globe award for best actress in a television series, 2001, Saturn award for best actress in a television series, 2003, SAG award for outstanding performance in a drama series, 2005); (films) Deconstructing Harry, 1997, Washington Square, 1997, Mr. Magoo, 1997, In Harm's Way, 1997, Nineteen Ninety-Nine, 1998, Dude, Where's My Car, 2000, Pearl Harbor, 2001, Rennie's Landing, 2001, Catch Me if You Can, 2002, Daredevil, 2003, 13 Going On 30, 2004, Elektra, 2005. Recipient People's Choice award, favorite female TV star, 2006, People's Choice award, favorite female action star, 2006.*

GARNER, JOYCE CRAIG, artist; b. Covington, Ky., Dec. 4, 1947; d. William Fayette and Mildred Ollie (Hodge) Craig; m. Gordon Reed Garner, Aug. 19, 1967; children: Angie Reed, Craig Charles, Scott William, Will Michael. BS, U. Ky., 1968. One-woman shows include Ctrl. Bank Gallery, Lexington, 1988, 91, Yvonne Rapp Gallery, Louisville, 1989, 91, 93, 94, Bluegrass Airport Gallery, Lexington, 1991, Headley-Whitney Mus., Lexington, 1992, Malton Gallery, Cin., 1994, Jewish Cmty. Ctr., Louisville, 1995, Hot House Gallery, Indpls., 1996, 98, Carnegie Art Ctr., Covington, Ky., 1997; group exhibits include Three Rivers Art Festival, Pitts., 1995, Turman Gallery Ind. State U., Terre Haute, 1995, 96, Louisville Visual Art Assn., 1995, 96, Indiana (Pa.) U., 1995, 96, Indpls. Art Ctr., 1995, 96, Carnegie Art Ctr., Covington, Ky., 1995, 96, Midwest Mus. Am. Art, Elkhart, Ind., 1995, 96, many others; represented in permanent collections Grand Ctrl. Office Bldg., St. Louis, U. Hosp., Cin., St. Luke's Hosp., Newport, Ky., Assn. Met. Sewage Agys., Washington, C.P.I. Corp., St. Louis, KAISER, Atlanta, Ctrl. Bank, Lexington, Balke Properties, St. Louis, Brown & Williamson, Louisville, Riscorp., Sarasota, Fla., Peach Tree Ctr., Internat. Tower, Atlanta, others; art in embassies program U.S. Mission to European Cmtys., Brussels. Resident fellow Hambidge Ctr., 1994. Unitarian-Universalist. Home: 7300 Happy Hollow Rd Prospect KY 40059-9356

GARNER, MABLE TECOLA, health facility administrator; b. Sharon, Miss., June 11, 1931; d. Annie B. (Johnson) Garner; 1 child, Wendell Orson Siggers. BA, Fisk U., 1953; MD, Meharry Med. Coll., 1959; MTH, Springhill Coll., 1996. Diplomate Am. Bd. Clin. Pathology, 1967, Am. Bd. Anatomical Pathology, 1968. Intern Meharry Med. Coll., Nashville, asst. prof. pathology, 1968; resident in pathology Hubbard Hosp./Meharry Med. Coll., Nashville, 1963—66; sr. resident anataomny clin. and pathology VA Hosp., Nashville, 1966—67; USPHS spl. postdoctoral fellow dept. biochem. hypertension rsch. Case Western Res. U., Cleve., 1969—70; dir. health cons. Fayette St. Clinic Ltd., Shaw, Miss., 1979—. Mem.: Alpha Omega Alpha. Home and Office: PO Box 798 Shaw MS 38773-0798 Office Phone: 662-754-2314.

GARNER, SHIRLEY IMOGENE, retired music educator; b. Silverton, Oreg., June 8, 1932; d. Julius Edgar and Amelia Christine (Preszler) Herr; m. Steven Mead Garner, Feb. 24, 1952 (div. Dec. 15, 1987); children: Shelia Christine Garner-Ward, Mark Steven. MusB with honors, Univ. Oreg., Eugene, 1957. Elem. tchr. Springfield USD, Oreg., 1957—58; vocal music tchr. Berkeley USD, Calif., 1958—61, San Jose USD, Calif., 1961—66; lit. tchr. Napa USD, Calif., 1966—67; vocal music tchr. San Jose USD, Calif., 1968—99, ret., 1996, part-time tchr., 1996—99. Choir dir. various ch., Oreg., Calif., 1955—83, Pilgrim Haven Ret. Home, Los Altos, Calif., 1969—72, The Fun Time Singers, Campbell, Calif., 2000—02. Edn. adv. com. Restoration of the Statue of Liberty and The Bicentennial of the Constitution, Washington, 1986; vol. Castillero Music Performance. Recipient Hall of Fame award, Youth Focus., Inc., 1993, Appreciation cert., Calif. State Assembly, 1993, Cert. Recognition, Calif. State Senate, 1993, Svc. Pub. Edn., Masonic Lodge, Spl. Citation award, Hawaii-Calif. Elks Assn. Mem.: Music Educators Nat. Conf. Presbyterian. Avocations: gardening, flower arranging, reading. Home: 1085 Tasman Dr Space 805 Sunnyvale CA 94089 Personal E-mail: shigarner@aol.com.

GARNER, SHIRLEY NELSON, language educator; b. Waxahachie, Tex., Aug. 8, 1935; d. Cleo and Ruby D. Nelson; m. Frank L. Garner, Nov. 24, 1972; children: Hart Phillip, Celia Ann. AB magna cum laude, U. Tex., 1957; MA, Stanford U., 1966, PhD, 1972. Instr. Stanford (Calif.) U., 1964-65, instr., asst. to dir. fresh composition, 1967-70; asst. prof. U. Minn., Mpls., 1972-76, assoc. prof., 1976-86, assoc. mem. faculty Women's Studies, 1980—86, prof., 1986—, chair Women's Studies, 1989-90, dir. Ctr. Advanced Feminist Studies, 1990-94, chair English dept., 1994—2000, assoc. dean grad. sch., 2001—. Editor: (with Personal Narratives Collective) Interpreting Women's Lives: Feminist Theory and Personal Narratives, 1989, (with Madelon Sprengnether) Shakespearean Tragedy and Gender, 1995, Antifeminism in the Academy, 1996, (with VeVe Clark, Ketu Katrak, and Margaret Higonnet) Is Feminism Dead?, 2000; editor, contbg. author: (with Clare Kahane and Madelon Sprengnether) The (M)other Tongue: Essays in Feminist Psychoanalytic Interpretation, 1985; contbg. author: Bad Shakespeare: Revaluations of the the Shakespeare Canon, 1988, Seduction and Theory: Readings of Gender, Representation and Rhetoric, 1989, Shakespeare's Personality, 1989, Novel Mothering, 1991, Feminism and Psychoanalysis, Feminism and Philosophy: Essential Readings in Theory, Reinterpretation and Application, 1992, The Intimate Critique: Autobiographical Literary Criticism, 1993; founder, mem. editl. bd. Hurricane Alice, 1983-95; mem. editl. bd. Signs, 1992-95; contbr. articles, revs. to profl. jours. Recipient Horace T. Morse-Amoco award, 1982, Pres.'s award for outstanding svc., 1999; Phillips Petroleum Found. scholar, 1953-57; Woodrow Wilson fellow, 1959-60, Sorptimists' fellow, 1965-66, 66-67; grantee U. Minn. 1974-76, 81, 87-88, Bush Sabbatical, 1984-85, Office Internat. Edn., 1988, CLA, 1981, 84-90, UROP, 1991-92; named to U. Minn. Acad. Disting. Tchrs., 1999. Mem. MLA (co-chair Marriage and the Family in Shakespeare divsn., Shakespeare sect. 1979, chair 1980-82, chair/co-chair various seminars, symposia), Nat. Women's Studies Assn., Midwest Modern Lang. Assn. (sec. Shakespeare sect. 1972, chair 1973, nominations com. 1974-77, sec. Women and Lit. sect. 1978-79, chair 1980-81, nomination com. Women and Lit. sect. 1981-84), Shakespeare Assn. Office: U Minn English Dept 207 Church St SE Minneapolis MN 55455-0134 Office Phone: 612-625-3363. Business E-Mail: sngarner@umn.edu.

GARNER, TARALYN R., secondary school educator; BS, Kans. State U., Manhattan, 1976, MS, 1982. Instr. phys. edn. Manhattan Pub. Schs., Manhattan, 1984—88; instr. phys. edn. dept. Kans. State U., Manhattan, 1988—90; instr./ coach Park Hill Sch. Dist., Kansas City, Mo., 1990—. Recipient Spirit award, Park Hill Faculty, 1992; grantee, Park Hill Edn. Found. Adminstrn., 2006. Mem.: AAHPERD, Mo. AHPERD (adapted chairperson 1992—94). Office: Park Hill High School 7701 NW Barry Road Kansas City MO 64153

GARNET, EVA DESCA (EVA DESCA), dance educator, choreographer; b. Bronx, NY, Mar. 18, 1914; d. Louis and Berta Olugatch. AA in Sociology, LA City Coll., 1967; BA in Phys. Edn., LA State Coll., 1969; MS in Recreation Gerontology, Calif. State U., 1972. Apprentice performer Dennishawn Dance Co., 1932; Doris Humphrey asst. dir. Fed. Dance Theatre, 1939; mem. faculty Juillard Sch. Music, 1939; founder, geriatric calistenics Calif. Assn. Homes Aging, 1963; fitness instr. Irvine Valley Coll., 1991. Cons. Calif. Assn. Homes for Aging, 1963—66, lectr., 1963—66, fed. funded grant sponsor, 1965; workshop trainer US Labor Dept. Geriatric-Calisthics, 1965; cons. U. So. Calif. Gerontology Nursing Homes Tng. Project, 1973, lectr., 73. Author: (book) Movement is Life, 1982, (manual) Theory and Philosophy of Geriatric Calistenics. Named Tchr. of Yr., Part Time Emeritus Inst., Irvine Valley Coll., 2006; named to Wall of Tolerance, Montgomery, Ala., Nat. Mus. Dance Hall of Fame (as part of New Dance Group Co.), 2006; recipient Disting. Svc. award, Arthritis Found., 1993; grantee, UCI. Mem.: AAUW, Ams. For Arts, Calif. Ret. Tchrs. Assn., Am. Dance Therapy Assn. Democrat. Unitarian. Avocations: yoga, swimming, table tennis. Personal E-mail: egarnet@1world.net.

GARNETT, ADRIENNE WILMA, art educator; b. N.Y.C., Jan. 7, 1936; d. Maurice H. and Florence Schlang; m. T. G. Ritter (div.); children: Lianne A. Ritter (dec.), Louis A. Ritter; m. W. Gordon Garnett, July 19, 1966 (dec.); children: Daun E. Susan, Stephen G., Joan M. Falvey, Jeffrey G. BS in Art Edn., Regents Coll., 1980; MS in Studio Art, Coll. New Rochelle, 1984; profl. diploma in Dist. Level Adminstrn. and Supervision, Iona Coll., 1999. Tchr. art, cons., curator pre-K edn. and city art edn. programs, New Rochelle, N.Y., 1966-79; tchr. art Davis, Mayflower, Stephenson and Trinity Elem. Schs., New Rochelle, 1979-84, Daniel Webster Humanities/Arts Magnet Sch., New Rochelle, 1979-88, New Rochelle High Sch., 1988—2005; ret., 2005; freelance artist. Adj. prof. Iona Coll., Yonkers, N.Y., 1992; appointed mem. edn. com. Neuberger Mus., SUNY, 1988-89, tchrs. adv. com. Coll. New Rochelle, 1988-89; mem. core planning group tchrs. ctr. Tchrs. Coll., Columbia U., N.Y.C., 1989-90, art adminstrs. and suprs., 1989-90; guest lectr. Parsons Sch. Art and Design, 2001-03; N.Y.C. art critic Art of the Times: Mag. of Arts. Appointed mem. New Rochelle Coun. on Arts, 1989—; past bd. dirs. Castle Gallery Coll. New Rochelle. Recipient Tchr. Excellence award Marine Midland Bank, 1990; Honors Seminar fellow R.I. Sch. Design, 1989; Earth Day grantee Polaroid Corp., 1990, grantee E.A. Cohen Found., 1991. Mem. Nat. Art Edn. Assn., N.Y. State Tchr.'s Assn. (coun. adminstrs. of art edn., com. multicultural art edn., Art Educator of Yr. 1991), Phi Delta Kappa. Avocations: music, piano. E-mail: a@wholeart.net.

GARNO, JAYNE C., chemistry professor; d. Donald R. and Diana M. Garno. BS in Biology, U. Mich., Ann Arbor, 1981; BS in Chemistry, Saginaw Valley State U., 1992; PhD in Chemistry, Wayne State U., Detroit, 2002. Postdoctoral assoc. CUNY, NYC, 2002—03; NRC postdoctoral assoc. NIST, Gaithersburg, Md., 2003—04. Named Emerging Investigator in Analytical Chemistry, The Analyst, RSC publ., 2006; recipient David F. Boltz Grad. award in Analytical Chemistry, Wayne State U., 2000, Powe award, Oak Ridge Associated Univs., 2004; grantee, La. Bd. Regents Support Fund, 2006—; U. Mich. Alumni scholar, U. Mich., 1977, Hiatt Williams Meml. scholar, UAW Local 699, 1978—81, State of Mich. Competitive Scholarship grantee, State of Mich., 1977, Starter grantee, PRF G, ACS Petroleum Rsch. Fund, 2005—, Faculty rsch. grantee, L. State U. Coun. on Rsch., 2005—06, NSF-IGERT fellow, NSF, 1998—2002. Office: Louisiana State University 232 Choppin Hall Baton Rouge LA 70803 Office Phone: 225-578-8942.

GAROFALO, JANEANE, actress, comedienne; b. Newton, N.J., Sept. 28, 1964; d. Carmine Garofalo; m. Robert Cohen, Aug. 16, 1991 (separated). BA in History and Am. Studies, Providence Coll. Co-anchor Majority Report Air America Radio, 2004—. Actress (films) Late for Dinner, 1991, That's What Women Want, 1992, Armistead Maupin's Tales of the City, 1993, Suspicious, 1994, Reality Bites, 1994, Bye Bye Love, 1995, I Shot a Man in Vegas, 1995, Coldblooded, 1995, Now and Then, 1995, Sweethearts, 1996, The Truth About Cats & Dogs, 1996, The Cable Guy, 1996, Larger Than Life, 1996, HBO 1 Hour Special, 1997, Touch, 1997, Romy and Michele's High School

Reunion, 1997, Cop Land, 1997, The MatchMaker, 1997, The Thin Pink Line, 1998, Half Baked, 1998, Thick as Thieves, 1998, Permanent Midnight, 1998, Dog Park, 1998, Clay Pigeons, 1998, Can't Stop Dancing, 1999, The Minus Man, 1999, 200 Cigarettes, 1999, Dogma, 1999, Mystery Men, 1999, The Bumblebee Flies Anyway, 1999, The Cherry Picker, 2000, Steal This Movie, 2000, The Independent, 2000, The Adventures of Rocky & Bullwinkle, 2000, Titan A.E., 2000, Wet Hot American Summer, 2001, The Search for John Gissing, 2001, The Laramie Project, 2002, Martin & Orloff, 2002, Big Trouble, 2002, Manhood, 2003, Ash Tuesday, 2003, Wonderland, 2003, Nobody Knows Anything!, 2003, Junebug and Hurricane, 2004, Jiminy Glick in Lalawood, 2004, Duane Hopwood, 2005, Stay, 2005, The Wild, 2006, (TV films) Slice o' Life, 2003, Nadine in Date Land, 2005, (TV appearances) The Ben Stiller Show, 1992—93, The Larry Sanders Show, 1992—97, Saturday Night Live, 1994—95, Comedy Product, 1995, Mr. Show with Bob and David: Fantastic Newness, 1996, Ellen, 1996, Seinfeld, 1996, Home Improvement, 1997, Law & Order, 1997, The Simpsons, 1998, Felicity, 1999, Mad About You, 1999, Jimmy Kimmel Live, 2003, The King of Queens, 2004, The West Wing, 2006, King of the Hill, 2003; co-author (with Ben Stiller): Feel This Book, 2000. Office: UTA Inc 9560 Wilshire Blvd Fl 5 Beverly Hills CA 90212-2401 also: The Majority Report Air America Radio 641 Sixth Ave 4th Floor New York NY 10011

GARON, PHYLLIS S., retired elementary school educator; b. Mpls., Dec. 9, 1948; d. Harvey I. and Shirley Heiligman Ansel; m. Philip S. Garon, Mar. 22, 1970; children: Edward B., Sara Garon Berl. BS in Elem. Edn., U. Minn., 1970; MA, Alfred Adler Inst. of Minn., Hopkins, 1993. Tchr. 6th grade Robbinsdale (Minn.) Sch. Dist., 1970—72, lead tchr. sch. age child care, 1980—83; tchr. 6th grade Fairfax County (Va.) Pub. Schs., 1972—73; tchr. children and adults Computer Encounter, Plymouth, Minn., 1984—87; tchr. 3d and 4th grade St. Paul Talmud Torah Day Sch., 1988—89; tchr. gifted and talented K-6 Hopkins Sch. Dist., Minnetonka, Minn., 1994—2001. Facilitator groups for parents of gifted children, 2002—. Pres. Scopus Hadassah, Mpls., 1985—87; v.p. Beth El Synagogue, St. Louis Park, Minn., 1998—2001; vice chair edn. panel Mpls. Fedn. Jewish Svc., 2004—06. Avocations: physical fitness, reading, golf, bridge, educational classes.

GARONZIK, SARA ELLEN, stage producer; b. Phila., Jan. 12, 1951; d. Milton and Bernice (Kohn) Garonzik. BA in Spanish cum laude, Temple U., 1972. Producing artistic dir. Phila. Theatre Co., 1982—. Bd. dirs. Arts and Bus. Coun. Greater Phila., Phila. Theatre Co., Theatre Alliance Greater Phila., Phila. Cultural Fund. Recipient prize, Sigma Delta Pi, 1972, award of Honor, Alumnae Assn. Girls HS, 1997, Pres. award, Phila. Young Playwrights, 2006. Office: Phila Theatre Co 230 S 15th St Philadelphia PA 19102 Office Phone: 215-985-1400. Business E-Mail: sgaronzik@phillytheatreco.com.

GAROOGIAN, RHODA, librarian; b. Bronx, N.Y. d. David and Rose (Fried) Lillian; m. Andrew Garoogian, Feb. 19, 1954; children: David, Neill. BA, Bklyn. Coll., 1961, MA, 1970; MLS, Pratt Inst., 1971, postgrad., 1974. Reference librarian Medgar Evers Coll., Bklyn., 1976; asst. dean Grad. Sch. Library and Info. Sci. Pratt Inst., Bklyn., 1977-85; dir. Wilson Line Info. System, Bronx, 1985-88; asst. prof. Palmer Sch. Libr. & Info. Sci., Bronx, 1988-89; chairperson grad. libr. and info. sci. program Pratt Inst., Bklyn., 1989—. Author: Child Care Issues, 1977, Careers for Librarians, 1985; editor Software Rev., 1980-81; contbr. articles to profl. jours. Recipient Fannie L. Simone award Spl. Librarians Assn., 1988. Mem. ALA, Am. Soc. Info. Sci.

GARR, SALLY D., lawyer; b. Atlanta, June 10, 1952; BA magna cum laude, Ga. State U., 1977; JD cum laude, U. Ga., 1980. Bar: Ga. 1980, DC 1980, US Dist. Ct. (DC, Md., Colo., ea. Mich., no. Ill. dist), US Ct. Appeals (4th, 6th, DC cir.), US Supreme Ct. Former assoc. gen. counsel, labor & personnel Amtrak, Washington; ptnr., Employment Law, Litigation & Dispute Resolution practices, mem. mgmt. com. Patton Boggs LLP, Washington. Office: Patton Boggs LLP 2550 M St NW Washington DC 20037-1350 Office Phone: 202-457-6525. Office Fax: 202-457-6315. Business E-Mail: sgarr@pattonboggs.com.

GARR, TERI (ANN), actress; b. Lakewood, Ohio, Dec. 11, 1949; m. John O'Neil, Nov. 1993 (div. 1996); 1 adopted child, Molly. Began career as dancer performing with San Francisco Ballet at age 13; in original road show co. of West Side Story; stage appearences include One Crack Out, 1978, Broadway, 1978, Ladyhouse Blues, 1979, Night of 100 Stars II, 1985; appeared in films including Viva Las Vegas, Head, 1968, Maryjane, 1968, Moonshine War, 1970, The Conversation, 1974, Young Frankenstein, 1974, Won Ton Ton, The Dog Who Saved Hollywood, 1976, Oh God!, 1977, Close Encounters of the Third Kind, 1977, Mr. Mike's Mondo Video, 1979, The Black Stallion, 1979, Honky Tonk Freeway, 1981, The Escape Artist, 1982, Tootsie, 1982, One From the Heart, 1982, The Sting II, 1983, The Black Stallion Returns, 1983, Mr. Mom, 1983, Firstborn, 1984, After Hours, 1985, Miracles, 1987, Out Cold, 1988, Let It Ride, 1989, Short Time, 1990, Waiting for the Light, 1990, Mom and Dad Save the World, 1992, Ready to Wear, 1994, Dumb and Dumber, 1994, Michael, 1996, A Simple Wish, 1997, Changing Habits, The Definite Maybe, 1997, Kill the Man, 1999, Dick, 1999, The Sky is Falling, 2000, Life Without Dick, 2001; TV movies include Doctor Franken, 1980, Prime Suspect, 1982, The Winter of Our Discontent, 1983, To Catch a King, 1984, Intimate Strangers, 1986, Fresno, 1986, Pack of Lies, 1987, Teri Garr in Flapjack Floozie, 1988, Drive, She Said (Trying Times), 1987, Mother Goose Rock n Rhyme, Stranger in the Family, 1991, Deliver Them From Evil: The Taking of Alta View, 1992, Fugitive Nights: Danger in the Desert, 1993, Ronnie and Julie, 1996, Casper Meets Wendy, 1998, Half a Dozen Babies, 1999, A Colder Kind of Death, 2001; regular on TV series The Sonny and Cher Comedy Review, 1974, Good and Evil, 1991, Good Advice, 1994, Duckman, 1994, The Women of the House, 1995, Double Jeopardy, 1996, Nightscream, 1997, Murder Live!!, 1997; other TV appearances include Law and Order, 1976, Fresno, Late Night with David Letterman, the Frog Prince, Tales From the Crypt, Friends, 1997-98; guest appearances include Murphy Brown, 1993, Frasier, 1995, Sabrina, the Teenage Witch, 1997, ER, 1999, Felicity, 2001, Life with Bonnie, 2003; author (memoir): Speedbumps: Flooring it Through Hollywood, 2005. Office: William Morris Agy 151 S El Camino Dr Beverly Hills CA 90212-2775*

GARRAHAN-MASTERS, MARY PATRICIA, retired social worker, writer; b. Phila., June 6, 1951; d. Francis Edward and Mary Patricia McElduff Garrahan; m. Thomas Anthony Masters Mastrangelo, June 5, 1995 (div. Feb. 2000). Student, Georgetown U., 1971-72, Facultad Filosofia y Letras, Madrid; BA in Sociology with honors, Villanova (Pa.) U., 1973; M in Social Sci., M in Law and Social Policy, Bryn Mawr (Pa.) Coll., 1983. Geriat. case worker Schuylkill County Area Agy. on Aging, Pottsville, Pa., 1974-79; social svc. dir. Dowden Nursing Home, Newtown Sq., Pa., 1980-84; dir. admissions St. Francis County Ho., Darby, Pa., summer 1981; tchr. Delaware County Coll., Media, Pa., 1984; med. social worker VA Med. Ctr., Lebanon, Pa., 1985-88, Phila., Pa., 88-90. Part-time staff coord. Garrahan Equipment Inc., Havertown, Pa., 1973-92; part-time social worker Delta-T Home Health Agy., Bryn Mawr, 1992-97. Contbr. poetry to Lynx mag. Villanova U. Assoc. mem. Rep. Nat. Com., Washington, 1993-99; Eucharistic minister St. Richard's Roman Cath. Ch., Barnesville, Pa., 1974-79. Mem. Internat. Hypnosis Hall Fame Guild Inc., Nat. Assn. Ret. Fed. Employees, Soc. Friends of Touro Synagogue (assoc. mem.), Alpha Zeta Delta. Home: 501 Harriet Ln Havertown PA 19083-1817

GARRARD, PATRICIA RENICK, elementary school educator; b. Miami, Fla., Mar. 9, 1950; d. Ralph Apperson and Elizabeth (Henry) Renick; m. Walter Martin Garrard, Dec. 29, 1972; children: Elizabeth, Danielle. BA, Fla. State U., 1972. Tchr. St. Lawrence Sch., North Miami Beach, Fla., 1972—73, Citrus Grove Jr. H.S., Miami, Fla., 1973—76, Hialeah Jr. H.S., Fla., 1977—79; tchr. lang. arts Pioneer Mid. Sch., Cooper City, Fla., 1979—, chair dept. lang. arts, 1996—. Tchr. cons. South Fla. Writing Project, Ft. Lauderdale, 2001—. Mem.: Nat. Coun. Tchrs. English, Fla. Coun. Tchrs. English, Broward Coun. Tchrs. English, Alpha Chi Omega (province officer 1987—93), Kappa Delta Pi. Roman Catholic. Home: 10427 SW 53 St Fort Lauderdale FL 33328 Office: Pioneer Middle Sch 5350 SW 90th Ave Cooper City FL 33328 Business E-Mail: patricia.garrard@browardschools.com.

GARRELS, ANNE, news correspondent; b. July 2, 1951; m. Vint Lawrence Garrels. Grad., Harvard U., 1972. Various positions ABC News, 1975—85, Moscow bur. chief, Ctrl. Am. corr., 1984—85; State Dept. corr. NBC News, 1985—88; fgn. corr. Nat. Pub. Radio, Washington, 1988—. Recipient Alfred I. duPont-Columbia U. award, 1992, duPont-Columbia award, 1996, Whitman Bassow award, Overseas Press Club, 1999, Alumnae Recognition award, Radcliffe Assn., 2002, Courage award, Internat. Women's Media Found., 2003, George K. Polk award for radio reporting, 2004; Edward R. Murrow fellow, Coun. on Fgn. Rels., 1996. Mem.: Com. to Protect Journalists (bd. mem.). Office: NPR 635 Massachusetts Ave NW Washington DC 20001-3753

GARRELS, SHERRY ANN, lawyer; b. Chgo., Feb. 5, 1956; d. William Henry and Jacqueline Ann G.; m. Timothy Anthony Marion, Aug. 1, 1987 (div. June 1988); 1 child, William Garrels-Marion; 1 child, Georgianna Garrels-Rogers. BA, Barat Coll., 1980; certificate, Trinity Coll., 1989; JD, Western State U., 1990. Bar: Calif. 1992, U.S. Dist. Ct. (ctrl. dist.) Calif. 1992, U.S. Dist. Ct. (no. dist.) Calif. 1993, U.S. Dist. Ct. (so. dist.) Calif. 1996, U.S. Ct. Appeals (9th cir.) 1994, U.S. Tax Ct. 1996. Pvt. practice, Huntington Beach, Calif., 1992—; judge pro tem West Justice Ctr., Westminster, Calif., 1998—. Arbitrator Nat. Panel Consumer Arbitrators, Huntington Beach, 1996, State Panel Consumer Arbitrators, Huntington Beach, 1996, Better Bus. Bureau, 1996—, U.S. C. of C., 1996, Huntington Beach C. of C., 1996. Editor The Dictum, 1989. Active 4th of July Exec. Bd., Huntington Beach, 1996—. Mem. Assn. Trial Lawyers, L.A. Trial Assn., Orange County Bar Assn., St. Bonny Golf Classic (dir. 1991-97), Delta Theta Phi. Republican. Presbyterian. Avocations: swimming, golf, scuba diving. Office: 5942 Edinger Ave Ste 113-702 Huntington Beach CA 92649-1763 Home: 18377 Beach Blvd Apt# 102 Huntington Beach CA 92648 Fax: 714-374-0104.

GARRETT, AMY J., parks director, educational coordinator; b. Omaha, June 22, 1961; d. Robert E. Garrett. BS, Ctrl. Mich. U., Mt. Pleasant, 1995. Mgr. Waldenbooks, Waco, Tex., 1987—97; pk. ranger Yellowstone Nat. Pk., Wyo., 1997—99, Death Valley Nat. Pk., Calif., 1999—2001; pk. ranger, edn. coord. Homestead Nat. Monument Am., Beatrice, Nebr., 2001—. Contbr. articles to profl. jours. Mem. Nebr. Wildlife Fedn., 2001—03, Gage County Heritage Preservation, Beatrice, 2002—04. Sgt. U.S. Army, 1982—86, Ft. Hood, Tex. Recipient Nat. Freeman Tilden award, Nat. Pk. Svc., 2003. Mem.: Nat. Assn. Interpretation (life). Office: Homestead Nat Monument Am 8523 W State Hwy 4 Beatrice NE 68310 Office Phone: 402-223-3514. Office Fax: 402-228-4231. Business E-Mail: amy_garrett@nps.gov.

GARRETT, BETTY, actress; d. Curtis Garrett and Octavia Stone; m. Larry Parks, Sept. 8, 1944 (dec.); children: Garrett Parks, Andrew Parks. Grad., Annie Wright Sem., Tacoma, Wash., 1936; student, Neighborhood Playhouse, N.Y.C., 1936—38. Dancer Martha Graham Dance Group, N.Y.C., 1938—39; actress Orson Welles Mercury Theater, N.Y.C., 1938—39. Tchr., moderator musical comedy workshop Theatre West, L.A. Author book, writer/performer show: Betty Garrett & Other Songs; actor: (Broadway shows) Let Freedom Sing, 1941, Something for the Boys, 1942, Jackpot, 1943, Laffing Room Only, 1945, Call Me Mister, 1946, A Girl Could Get Lucky, 1950, Beg Borrow or Steal, 1958, Spoon River Anthology, 1963, Supporting Cast, 1982, Meet Me in St. Louis, 1989, Stephen Sondheim's "Follies", 2001, (L.A. shows) Spoon River Anthology, 1962, Who's Happy Now, Quilters, No Dogs or Actors Allowed, So There!, Mixed Couples, A Little Night Music, Nobody Safe Here, Tom Tom on a Roof Top, Tallulah & Tennessee, (nat. tours) Plaza Suite, Cactus Flower, Miss Reardon Drinks a Little, Variety Act with Larry Parks; (films) Big City, 1947, Words & Music, 1948, Take Me Out to the Ballgame, 1948, Neptune's Daughter, 1949, On the Town, 1950, My Sister Eileen, 1955, Shadow on the Window, 1956; (TV series) All in the Family, 1972—75, Laverne & Shirley, 1976—82, (guest appearances include) Golden Girls, Black's Magic, Townies, Union Square, Murder She Wrote, The Good Life, Harts of the West, The Love Boat, The Long Way Home, Boston Public, Becker (Emmy nominee, 2003). Chair, performer Southland Theatre Artist Goodwill Event, L.A., 1986—. Recipient Star on Hollywood Walk of Fame, L.A. C. of C., 2003. Mem.: AFTRA, SAG, Actors Equity. Avocations: songwriting, essay writing, tap dancing, exercise. Office: Theatre West 3333 Cahuenga Blvd W Los Angeles CA 90068 Office Phone: 323-851-4839.

GARRETT, CELIA ERICA, human services administrator, consultant; b. Asheville, N.C., Mar. 31, 1945; d. Willie Thomas and Barbara Anne (Roberts) Garrett. BA, N.C. Ctrl. U., 1967; MSSW, Columbia U., 1978. Caseworker Human Resource Adminstrn., N.Y.C., 1967-74, Adminstrn. for Children's Svcs., N.Y.C., 1974-85, supr. emergency children's svcs., 1985-88, dir. field office emergency children's svcs., 1988—; mental health profl. Trustees of Columbia U. CSS Program, 1979—; cons. Harlem Restoration Project Inc., 1998—. Cons. El Guapo, N.Y.C., 1998—; field instr. Columbia U., 1992—, Hunter Coll., N.Y.C., 1992—; adj. prof. NYU, 1991—. Mem. NASW, Delta Sigma Theta. Democrat. Roman Catholic. Avocations: reading, cooking. Home: 650 Lenox Ave Apt 3J New York NY 10037-1043

GARRETT, ELIZABETH, law educator, academic administrator; b. Oklahoma City, June 30, 1963; d. Robert D. and Jane (Thompson) G. BA in History with spl. distinction, U. Okla., 1985; JD, U. Va., 1988. Bar: Tex. 1988, D.C. 1989. Law clk. to Hon. Stephen Williams U.S. Ct. Appeals (D.C. cir.), 1988—89; law clk. to Hon. Thurgood Marshall U.S. Supreme Ct., 1989—90; legal adviser to Hon. Howard M. Holtzman Iran-U.S. Claims Tribunal, The Hague, Netherlands, 1990—91; legal counsel, legis. asst. Senator David L. Boren, 1991—93, legis. dir., tax counsel, 1993—94; vis. assoc. prof. U. Va., 1994—95; asst. prof. U. Chgo. Law Sch., 1995—99, prof., 1999—2003, dep. dean, 1999—2001; vis. asst. prof. Harvard U., 1998; vis. prof. Ctrl. European U., 1999—2003, Interdisciplinary Ctr. Law Sch., Tel Aviv, 2001, Calif. Inst. Tech., 2004, U. Va., 2001, U. So. Calif. Law Sch., 2002; dir. Caltech Ctr. Study Law & Politics U. So. Calif., 2003—, vice provost acad. affairs, 2005—; Sydney M. Irma prof. pub. interest law, legal ethics and polit. Sci. Calif. Inst. Tech., 2005—; vice provost acad. affairs U. So. Calif., 2005—. Bd. dir. Initiative & Referendum Inst. Articles editor U. Va. Law Rev.; contbr. articles to profl. jours.; mem edtl. bd. Election Law Journal Ewing fellow U. Okla. Fellow, Am. Bar Found.; mem. ABA, Am. Law & Econ. Assn., Fed. Bar Assn., Tex. Bar Assn., D.C. Bar Assn., Order of Coif, Mortar Bd., Phi Beta Kappa, Chi Omega. Office: Univ So Calif Rm 103 Bovard Adminstrn Bldg Los Angeles CA 90089-4019 Office Phone: 213-740-0064. Business E-Mail: vpaa@usc.edu.

GARRETT, FLORENCE ROME, poet; b. Bklyn., Sept. 10, 1912; d. George and Blanche Alice (Smith) Rome; m. Elmer Ellsworth Garrett, June 2, 1934 (dec. Oct. 1993); children: Susan Taylor, James Garrett. Profl. accompanist, N.Y., Conn., 1930-61; piano tchr. L.I., N.Y., 1930-55; editor Flume Press, Bridgewater and Hebron, Conn., 1975—. Poetry lectr., L.I., N.Y.; dir. poetry workshops, Conn. Author, editor: Looking for a View, 1997, Light Coming, 1995; author: A Sprig of Lilac, 1990, Japanese Sketches, 1980, Bridgewater Morning, 1986, The Mill and Us, 1978, On the Hill, 1977, More than the Quiet Pond, 1969, Edge of Day, 1954, More than All, 2001. Mem. Roxbury Dem. Town Com., 1972-73, Nat. Dem. Com., Hebron, Conn., 1992-98. Book inclusion in the collection The Ko MUs. of Haiku, Japan; works included in Walt Whitman Collection. Fellow Acad. of Poetry and Lit.; mem. Nat. League of Am. Pen Women (br. pres. L.I. br. 1954-56, poetry chair Conn. Pioneer br. 1959-61). Home: 52 Kellogg Rd Marlborough CT 06447-1238

GARRETT, KATHRYN ANN BYERS (KITTY GARRETT), legislative clerk; b. Antlers, Okla., July 10, 1930; d. Stansell Harper and Vena Clifford (Crawford) Byers; m. William Donald Garrett, Jan. 13, 1955 (dec. June 1992); children: William Mark, Amy Kathryn, Ann Elizabeth Garrett Jenni. Student, Okla. A&M U., 1948—50. Sec. Garform Industries, Wagoner, Okla., 1951—52; sec. to exec. sec. Okla. Edn. Assn., Oklahoma City, 1952—55; sec. revenue and taxation com. Ho. Reps., State of Okla., Oklahoma City, 1969—76, bill clk./ins. clk., 1976—84, asst. chief clk./jour. clk., 1985—93; ret., 1994. Mem. Okla. Heritage Assn., Gamma Book Club, Salvation Army Women's Aux Republican. Avocations: china painting, bridge, reading, travel. Home: 3432 NW 173d St Edmond OK 73003

GARRETT, LAURIE, journalist, global health scholar; b. LA, Sept. 8, 1951; d. Banning and Lou Ann (Pierose) G. BA in biology with honors, U. Calif., Santa Cruz, 1975; postgrad. work in dept. bacteriology and immunology, U. Calif., Berkeley; PhD (hon.), Wesleyan Ill. U., U. Mass., Lowell, 2002. Sci. reporter KPFA, Berkeley, Calif.; with Calif. Dept. Food and Agr.; freelance journalist So. Europe, E. Africa, 1979; freelance reporter, 1980-88; sci. corr. Nat. Public Radio, 1980—88; health and sci. writer Newsday, N.Y.C., 1988—2004; sr. fellow in global health Coun. Fgn. Relations, 2004—. Vis. fellow Harvard Sch. Pub. Health, 1992-93; Editor-at-large, SEED Mag., 2003-. Author: The Coming Plague: Newly Emerging Diseases in a World Out of Balance, 1994, Betrayal of Trust: The Collapse of Global Public Health, 2000 (George C. Polk Award for Best Book, 2000, Nat. Book Critics Award finalist, 2000, Madeline Dane Ross Award, Overseas Press Club of Am., 2001, First Prize Med. Book Competition, Brit. Med. Assn., 2002); contbr. articles to periodicals including Omni, Washington Post, L.A. Times, Foreign Affairs, Vanity Fair, others; frequent guest appearances on Dateline, Jim Lehrer Newshour, ABC Nightline, The Charlie Rose Show, BBC, NPR, CNN, others; contbr. reports including Science Story (George Foster Peabody Broadcasting Award, 1977), Hard Rain: Pests, Pesticides, and People (Edwin Howard Armstrong Award in Broadcast Journalism, 1978), The VDT Controversy (Best Consumer Journalism Award, Nat. Press Club, 1982), Why Children Die in Africa (Meritorious Achievement Award in Radio, San Francisco Media Alliance, 1983, First Prize in Radio, World Hunger Alliance, 1987), AIDS in Africa (J.C. Penney/Mo. Journalism Cert. Merit, Award of Excellence, Nat. Assn. Black Journalists, 1989), Breast Cancer (Best Beat Reporter, Deadline Club N.Y., 1993, First Place Award, Soc. Silurians, 1994), AIDS in India (Bob Considine Award, Overseas Press Club of Am. 1995), Ebola (Madeleine Dane Ross Award, Overseas Press Club of Am., 1996, Pulitzer Prize in Explanatory Journalism, 1996), Crumbled Empire, Shattered Health (George C. Polk Award for Internat. Reporting, 1998), Orphans of AIDS (First Place in Internat. Reporting, NY Assn. Black Journalists, 2000). Named Times Mirror Journalist of Yr., 1996, Alumna of Yr., U. Calif., Santa Cruz, 1996, Champion of Prevention, Centers for Disease Control and Prevention, 1997; recipient Award of Excellence, Nat. Assn. Black Journalists, 1989, Spl. Citation for Outstanding Journalism, AAAS, 1995, Disting. Achievement Award, Ednl. Press Assn. of Am., 1996, Presdl. Citation, APHA, 1996, Pub. Health Hero Award, NYC Dept. Health, 2000, Victor Cohn Prize for Excellence in Med. Sci. Reporting, Coun. for the Advancement of Sci. Writing, 2000, Rsch. in Action Award, Treatment Action Group, 2002. Mem.: Nat. Assn. Sci. Writers. Achievements include Only person ever to be awarded the George Polk Award for Journalism, the George Foster Peabody Award for Broadcasting, and the Pulitzer Prize. Office: Coun Fgn Rels Harold Pratt House 58 E 68th St New York NY 10021

GARRETT, MAGGIE M., retired literature educator; b. Goodman, Miss., Mar. 29, 1937; d. Edward Alvin and Annie Lee McCrory; children: Robert, Thomas, Todd, Jon Scott. BA, Delta State U., Cleveland, Miss., 1959; postgrad., U. So. Miss., Hattiesburg, 1978, U. Miss., Oxford, 1980, Miss. State U., Starkville, 1980, Sorbonne/U. Paris, 1989. English tchr. Biloxi Sch. Sys., Miss., 1959—60; French tchr. Cheyenne Sch. Sys., Wyo., 1960—62; English/French tchr. Ctrl. Holmes Acad., Lexington, Miss., 1978—88, Kosciusko Sch. Sys., Miss., 1988—98; tchr. Dept. Justice/Fed. Prison, Yazoo City, Miss., 2000—04; ret., 2004. Pres., mem. Nu chpt. Delta Kappa Gamma, Kosciusko, 1981—2000; owner Red Bud Inn, Kosciusko. Author: (cookbook) A Taste of the Redbud, 1996. Mem.: Carbon County Arts Guild (bd. mem. 2006—). Republican. Methodist. Avocations: painting, reading, golf, travel, crafts. Home: 1471 Kane Cir Red Lodge MT 59068

GARRETT, MARGO, pianist, music educator; b. Raleigh, N.C., July 25, 1949; d. Laurie William and Elizabeth (Snipes) G.; m. Charles D. Kavalovski, June 4, 1987. MusB, N.C. Sch. Arts, 1971; MusM, Manhattan Sch. Music, 1974. Faculty N.C. Sch. Arts, Winston-Salem, 1971-72, Sarah Lawrence Coll., Bronxville, N.Y., 1974-83, Manhattan Sch. Music, N.Y.C., 1974-83, Tanglewood Music Ctr., Lenox, Mass., 1979—97, The Juilliard Sch., N.Y.C., 1985—91, 2000—. Guest artist univs., 1974—; guest lectr. Westminster Choir Coll., Princeton, N.J., 1983-85; faculty, co-dir. accompanying dept. New Eng. Conservatory, Boston, 1986-92; chair accompanying and coaching, U. Minn., 1992-2004; faculty chair vocal programs Steans Inst. Young Artists, Ravinia Festival, 1999—. Pianist to instrumentalists, vocals in recitals and recs. Recipient Grammy award, 1992. Office: The Juilliard Sch 60 Lincoln Ctr Plz New York NY 10023 Personal E-mail: margogk@earthlink.net.

GARRETT, MARY JANE, director; b. Houston, Oct. 16, 1961; d. Neitha Mae Freeman. BS in Home Econs., Prairie View A&M U., 1985; child devel. assoc. cert., Houston C.C. Sys., 2000; MS in Human Svcs. and Consumer Sci., Tex. So. U., 2005. Cert. Child Devel. Assn. Owner, operator Ms. Mary's Day Home Care, Houston, 1991—96; dir. Kiddie Coll. Ctr., Houston, 1996—97; tchr. Young Scholar Acad., Houston, 1997—98; ctr. mgr. Village Green Head Start, Houston, 1998—99; asst. ctr. mgr. South Willow Head Start, Houston, 1999—2002, ctr. mgr., 2003—05; asst. ctr. mgr. Cook Rd. Head Start, Houston, 2003—, Braeburn Head Start, 2005—, Panda Path Early Head Start, 2005—. Active blood donor Buff Coast Regional Blood Ctr., 2000—; vol. worker Ada Edward Campaign, Houston, 2001; active Christmas Wish Tree Program Salvation Army, Houston, 2001—02; active Girls Scouts Am., 2001—02; mentor Cmtys. in Sch., Houston, 2002—03; active Dress for Success Orgn., 2004—05; vol. worker Texas Head Start Assn., 2004—05; mem. Southern Poverty Law Ctr., 2004—; social action health ministry com. The Shrine of the Black Madonna Ch., 2001—. Mem.: Houston Area Assn. for Edn. Young Children, Nat. Black Child Devel. Inst., Nat. Head Start Assn. Democrat. Avocations: bowling, painting, baking, speed walking, party planning. Home: 5500 Martin Luther King Blvd #3 Houston TX 77021 Office Phone: 713-922-6923. E-mail: marygarreth@aol.com.

GARRETT, PAULA KAY, special education educator; b. Oklahoma City, Okla., Oct. 6, 1955; d. Paul Donald and Elizabeth Blount Coffey; m. Jerry Franklin Garrett, Oct. 4, 1985; children: Christina Elizabeth Kinghorn, Amy Delynn Mogg. BS, Redlands Coll., Okla., 1975; BA, Ctrl. State U., Okla., 1978. Cert. Mid. Sch. English Okla. State Dept. Edn., 2004. Severe and profound tchr. Hilldale Elem., Oklahoma City, 1978—80, Lake Pk. DLC, Bethany, Okla., 1980—84; learning disabled tchr. Western Oaks Mid. Sch., Bethany, Okla., 1984—. Athletic sponsor Western Oaks Jr. High, Bethany, 1985—92, spl. edn. dept. head, 1993—99; 8th grade team leader Western Oaks Mid. Sch., 1999—2001, spl. edn. team leader, 2001—03, leadership/student coun. sponsor, 2001—. Avocations: reading, sewing, travel. Office: Western Oaks Mid Sch 7200 NW 23rd Bethany OK 73008 Office Phone: 405-789-4434. Personal E-mail: pkg55@cox.net.

GARRETT, ROBIN SCOTT, health facility administrator; b. Sparta, NC, Jan. 24, 1965; d. Milton William Scott, Peggie Adams Scott; m. William Earle Garrett; 1 child, Nicolas. BS in Mgmt. and Mktg. magna cum laude, U. S.C., 2004. Med. clk. WJBD VA Med. Ctr., Columbia, SC, 1986, sec., stenographer, 1986—91, civilian pay technician, 1991—95, lead civilian pay technician, 1995—97, fiscal adminstrn. supr., 1997—2000, adminstrv. officer, 2004—. Preparer strategic mgmt. plans Edward Jones Investments, Columbia, SC, 2002, Ashley Fetner Fine Art Photography, Columbia, 2002; notary pub. State of SC, Columbia, 1996—; adminstrv. mgmt. intern, VALUE, Atlanta, 2000. Named Fed. Woman of Yr., 1995; named to Nat. Dean's List, 2004; recipient CPCU Mem. Scholarship, Lanville Mengedoht, 2003, Honor Cord for Superior Academic Achievement, Darla Moore Sch. Bus., U. S.C., 2004. Mem.: Nat. Soc. Collegiate Scholars, Phi Beta Kappa, Golden Key, Beta Gamma Sigma. Baptist. Avocation: photography, travel, hiking, reading, music. Home: 101 Fox Run Dr Hopkins SC 29061-9231 Office Phone: 803-776-4000 ext. 6404. Personal E-mail: rgarrett@sc.rr.com.

GARRETT, SANDY LANGLEY, school system administrator; b. Muskogee, Okla., Feb. 8, 1943; 1 child, Charles Langley (Chuck). BS in Elem. Edn., Northeastern U., Tahlequah, Okla., 1968, MS in Counseling, 1980; grad. John F. Kennedy Sch. Govt., Harvard U., 1989. Lic. tchr., adminstr., supt. std., Okla. Tchr. Hilldale Schs., Muskogee, Okla., 1968-80; coord. gifted program Hillsdale Schs., Muskogee, Okla., 1980-82; coord. gifted and talented State Dept. Edn., Oklahoma City, 1982-85, dir. rural edn., 1985-87, exec. dir. ednl. svcs., 1987-88, state supt. pub. instrn., 1991-95; sec. edn. Gov.'s Office, Oklahoma City, 1988—; supt. pub. instrn. Okla. Dept. Edn., Oklahoma City, 1991—. Chair State Bd. Edn., Oklahoma City, 1991—, State Vo-Tech. Edn., Oklahoma City, 1991—; bd. dirs. So. Regional Edn. Bd.; regent Okla. Colls., 1991—; mem. Nat. Coll. Bd. Equality Project; chair. Okla. Lit. Initiatives Commn.; mem. So. Regional Ednl. Bd. Co-author: (curriculum guide) Gifted Galaxy; mem. editorial bd. Rural and Small Schs.; contbr. articles to profl. jours. Co-chair Dem. Party, Muskogee, 1978; del. Dem. Nat. Conv., N.Y.C., 1980, 82; mem. Leadership Okla., 1990. Recipient Cecil Yarbrough award, 1989, Claude Dyer Legis. award, 1989. Mem. Muskogee County Ednl. Assn., Delta Kappa Gamma, Phi Delta Kappa, Delta Kappa Gamma. Methodist. Avocations: tennis, swimming, computer programming, travel, politics. Office: State Dept Edn 2500 N Lincoln Blvd Oklahoma City OK 73105-4503

GARRETT, SHARON, health services company executive; B in Econs., MPH, PhD, UCLA. Formerly with Hyatt Med. Enterprises, VA, Am. Heart Assn., Cath. Hosp. Assn., Calif. Dept. Health Svcs.; former dep. dir. UCLA Med. Ctr.; chief info. officer The Walt Disney Co., 1989—2000; exec. v.p. enterprise svcs. PacifiCare Health Systems, Inc., Cypress, Calif., 2000—. Bd. dirs. Ross Stores, Corio. Office: PacifiCare Health Systems Inc 5995 Plaza Dr Cypress CA 90630

GARRETT, SHIRLEY GENE, nuclear medicine technologist; b. Evanston, Ill., Apr. 19, 1944; d. Nathan and Emma Louise (Uecker) G. AA, Oakton C.C., 1977; AS in Nuc. Medicine, Triton Coll., 1980; BA, Northea. Ill. U., 1983; MA, Govs. State U., University Park, Ill., 1985. Cert. nuclear medicine technologist. Nuc. medicine technologist Chgo. Osteo. Hosp., 1980-88, Little Co. of Mary Hosp., Evergreen Park, Ill., 1989; nuclear medicine technologist Lutheran Gen. Hosp., Lincoln Park, Ill., 1989; nuc. medicine technologist Mt. Sinai Hosp., Chgo., 1990-92; technologist nuc. medicine Swedish Covenant Hosp., Chgo., 1992-93; pres. Providence Hosp. of Cook County, Chgo., 1994—. Contbr. articles to profl. jours. Vol. Ravenswood Hosp., Chgo., 1986-2000, Mt. Sinai Hosp., 1990-92, Congl. Health Ministry, Ch. of St. Lukes. Mem. Soc. Nuc. Medicine (mem. bylaws com. technologist sect. Ctrl. chpt. 1982-83, 85-86, 92-2000, mem. continuing edn. com. 1986-87, chmn. nominating com. 1987-88, 92-93, mem. edn. com. 1988-89, pres.-elect 1989-90, mem. bd. govs. 1990-92, 97-2000, pres. 1991-92, chmn. bylaws com. 1992-93, bd. govs. ctrl. chpt. 1997-2000), Assoc. and Tech. Affiliates Chgo. Area (coord. edn. 1981-84, mem. adv. bd. 1983-84, 87-88, 96-97, pres. 1985-87, chmn. nominating com. 1987-89). Lutheran. Office Phone: 312-572-2127.

GARRETT, STEPHANIE KAY, history educator; b. Dallas, Dec. 18, 1957; d. Claude Edward and Doris Jean DeWees; children: Stephen Frank, Hunter Keller. BA, Dallas Bapt. U., 2000, MA in Tchg., 2003. Cert. tchr. Tex. State Bd. Edn., 2000. Tchr. K-6 Ashley's Pvt. Sch., Cedar Hill, Tex., 1991—96; spl. edn. aide Cedar Hill Ind. Sch. Dist., Tex., 1996—2000, U.S. history and geography tchr., 2000—03; U.S. history and govt. tchr. Mansfield Ind. Sch. Dist., Tex., 2003—. Mentoring advisor Mansfield Ind. Sch. Dist., Tex., 2004—; chairperson Faculty Adv. Coun., Mansfield, 2004—. Treas. Singing Women of Tex., Dallas, 1996—2006; pers. officer U.S. Naval Sea Cadet Corp, Ft. Worth, 1997—2006. Mem.: Assn. Tex. Profl. Educators (assoc.), Phi Delta Kappa (assoc.; sec. 2005—). Baptist. Avocations: reading, travel. Office: Mansfield Timberview High Sch 7700 S Watson Rd Arlington TX 76002 Office Phone: 817-299-2600. Office Fax: 817-472-2978. E-mail: garrst@mansfieldisd.org.

GARRINGER, BARBARA LOU, nurse; b. Jay County, Ind., Feb. 27, 1937; d. Grover C. and Mabel (Shaneyfelt) G. Diploma, Ball Meml. Hosp. Sch. Nursing, 1959; BA, Ball State Tchrs. Coll., 1959; MA, Ball State U., 1975. RN Ind. Charge nurse orthopedics Ball Meml. Hosp., Muncie, Ind., 1959, head nurse orthopedics, 1961-63; staff nurse Ctrl. Ind. Orthopedics, Muncie, 1963—2006. Leader workshops in field. Purdue Frederick fellow, 1983; recipient Outstanding Nursing award Ball State U. Nursing Alumni Assn., 1983, Sagamore of Walbash award Gov. of Ind., 2003. Mem. Assn. Oper. Rm. Nurses (cert. 1980-2005), Sigma Theta Tau. Home: 3613 W Peachtree Ln Muncie IN 47304-4243

GARRIS, ANNETTE D. FAILE, medical, surgical, and rehabilitation nurse; b. Homestead, Fla., July 3, 1963; d. Rex Pyron and Margie Ruth (Jordan) Faile; m. Larry Allen Garris, June 5, 1987; children: Lanette and Tiffany. LPN, Lancaster (S.C.) Vocat. Sch., 1987; ADN, U. S.C., Lancaster, 1990. RN, S.C.; cert. rehab. nurse. Nursing asst. Marion Sims Nursing Ctr., Lancaster; nurse Piedmont Med.Ctr., Rock Hill, S.C., Lancaster County Care Ctr., Lancaster, Rebound Inc., Lancaster, Elliot White Springs Meml. Hosp., Lancaster; RN, asst. dir. nursing Rebound, Inc., Lancaster. Asst. dir., Nursing at Meadow Haven Rehab. & Specialty Care Ctr., Rock Hill, SC, transitional care coord., Rehab. Care, Lancaster, SC, dir. case mgmt., Springs Hosp., Lancaster, SC. Recipient Francine Manion award, 1990. Home: 2468 Golf Course Rd Lancaster SC 29720-8416

GARRISON, ALTHEA, government official; b. Hahira, Ga., Oct. 7, 1940; d. Charles and Lenora Mae (Davis) G. AS, Newbury Jr. Coll., 1978; BS, Suffolk U., 1982; cert. in social studies, Harvard U., 1986; MS, Lesley Coll., 1984. Counselor, supr. Charlotte House Dorchester (Mass.), 1977-77; with EDP dept., sr. assessor Mass. Dept. Revenue, Boston, 1979-81; sr. examiner Office State Compt., Boston, 1982-90; human resource mgr. Office of State Comptr. Commonwealth of Mass., 1991—; state rep. gen. ct. 5th suffolk Rep. Dist., Mass., 1992-95. Bd. dirs. Uphams Corner Health Ctr., Dorchester, 1983—, v.p., 1987—, Disting. Svc. award, 1991. Charter mem. adv. bd. Christian Record Braille, Lincoln, Neb., 1983; alumna coun. Lesley Coll. Grad. Sch., Cambridge, Mass., 1986-88; active Nat. Rep. Congl. Com., 1988—, Rep. Presdl. Task Force, 1989—, Met. Area Planning Coun., 1994; charter founder Ronald Reagan Rep. Ctr., Washington, 1989; nominee City Coun. Dorchester, 1989, State Rep. Rep. Primary, 1990; town com. woman Ward 13, Boston, 1992, commn. vice-chair, treas. city com., 1994-96; exec. com. Met. Area Planning Coun., 1995-98; apptd. Notary Pub., 1994—, Justice of Peace, 1997; mem. Irish Immigration Ctr., 1996-98; coord. Toys for Tots, Office State Comptr., 1997; hon. mem. Profl. Women's Adv. Bd., 1999, Am. Biog. Inst., 1999. Recipient Senator's citation Commonwealth Mass., 1982, Merit medal Rep. Task force, 1989, Appreciation cert. Mass. Rep. Party, Outstanding Vol. award Suffolk U., 1991, Achievement cert. Conf. New Legislators, 1993, Rep. Leadership award, 1993-94, Book award Dearborn Middle Sch., 1994, Legis. Yr. award Gtr. Boston Labor Coun. AFL-CIO, 1994, Excellent Svc. award Holborn, Gannett, Gaston, Otisfield Betterment Assn., 1995, Cmty. Svc. Honor award Winthrop St. Crime Assn., 1996, Benefactor Cert. Mayo Found., 1998, Membership Achievement award WGBH, 1999, Cert. of Appreciation, Uphams Corner Health Ctr., 1999; hon. fellow John F. Kennedy Libr., 1987-90; named one of 100 Women Making History North Shore Women's Coalition, Rep. Presdl. Legion of Merit Honor Roll, 1993; cert. of appreciation USMC Res.; Cmty. Svc. Honor award Winthrop Street Crime Assn., 1996. Mem. Am. Mgmt. Assn., Nat. Assn. Govt. Employees (negotiator, organizer 1979-81), Suffolk U. Gen. Alumni Assn. (bd. dirs. 1986-89), Heritage Found., Nat. Found. Cancer Rsch. (hon., citation 1991), DAV Comdrs., World War II Soc. (charter mem. 2000). Roman Catholic. Avocations: walking, music, reading, research.

GARRISON, ARLENE ALLEN, academic administrator, engineering educator; BA in Liberal Arts, U. Tenn., 1975, PhD in Analytical Chemistry, 1981, BSEE, 1988. Instr. analytical chemistry, grad. rsch. asst. U. Tenn., Knoxville, 1975-81, rsch. assoc., 1981, sr. electonic design engr. dept. chemistry, 1985-89, rsch. asst. prof. dept. chemistry, 1989—; dir. measurement and control engrng. ctr. Coll. Engrng. U. Tenn., Knoxville; licensing exec. U. Tenn., Knoxville, 1998-99, dir. industry programs and tech. transfer, 1999-2000, asst. v.p., 2000—. Mem. NRC bd. assessment for Nat. Inst. Standards and Tech., Panel for Chem. Sci. and Tech., 1996-2001; mem. chemistry dept. alumni steering com. U. Tenn. Knoxville, 1994—; participant in NATO Advanced Study Inst. on Analytical Applications of Fourier transform infrared to Molecular and Biolog. Systems, Florence, Italy, 1980; organizer insl. spectroscopy symposium Internat. Conf. on Raman Spectroscopy, Hong Kong; co-chair Soc. Photo-Optical Instrumentation Engrs. conf. on optical methods for chem. process control, 1994; sci. bd. Iternat. Forum Process Analytical Chemistry, 1993-2002; presenter in field. Contbr. over 29 articles to profl. jours. Chair bd. trustees Fountain City United Meth. Ch., 1991-94; sec. Wesley Found. Bd., 1992-93; bd. dirs. Appalachian Sci. Fair, 1993-2003, WATTec, 1994-96, Discovery Ctr., 1995-98; mem. Pub. Bldg. Authority, 1995—, chair, 2000-02, Tenn. Econ. Coun. Women, 2002—. Recipient Chancellors Citation for extraordinay cmty. svc., 1993. Mem. Soc. for Applied Spectroscopy (Meggars award 1982), Soc. of Photo Instrumentation Engrs., Coblentz Soc. (bd. mgrs. 1989-92, pres. 1997-98), Am. Chem. Soc. (sec. East Tenn. sect. 1988-90, chair-elect 1991, chair 1992, steering com. divsns. chem. edn. and analytical chemistry, chair Williams Wright award com. 1991, 92). Phi Beta Kappa, Phi Kappa Phi, Alpha Lambda Delta, Tau Beta Pi. Office: U Tenn Office Rsch 1534 White Ave Knoxville TN 37996-1529 Office Phone: 865-974-6410. Business E-Mail: garrison@utk.edu.

GARRISON, BARBARA JANE, chemistry professor; b. Big Rapids, Mich., Mar. 7, 1949; BS, Ariz. State U., 1971; PhD in Chemistry, U. Calif., Berkeley, 1975. Rsch. fellow in chemistry Purdue U., Lafayette, Ind., 1975-77; lectr. U. Calif., Berkeley, 1977-78; from asst. prof. to assoc. prof. Pa. State U., University Park, 1979-86, prof. chemistry, 1986—, head dept. chemistry, 1989-94, Disting. prof. chemistry, 2000—02, Shapiro prof. chemistry, 2002—. Vis. asst. prof. Purdue U., 1978-79; vis. assoc. chemistry Calif. Inst. Tech., 1985-86. Alfred P. Sloan Found. rsch. fellow, 1980. Fellow Am. Phys. Soc., Am. Vacuum Soc.; mem. Am. Chem. Soc. (Francis P. Garvan - John M. Olin medal 1994). Office: Pa State U Dept Chemistry 104 Chemistry Bldg University Park PA 16802-4615

GARRISON, CAROL Z., academic administrator; b. Upper Montclair, N.J. BA, U. N.C., Chapel Hill, 1974; MS in nursing, U. Ala., Birmingham, 1976; PhD, U. N.C., Chapel Hill, 1982. Cert. nurse practitioner, U. Ala. Birmingham, 1978. Asst. prof. nursing U. Ala., Birmingham, 1976—78, U. N.C., 1978—82; faculty U. S.C., 1982—92, prof. and chair epidemiology and biostatistics, 1992—97, assoc. provost, 1994—97, dean grad. sch., 1994—97; provost U. Louisville, 1997—2002, acting pres., 2002; pres. U. Ala., Birmingham, 2002—. Office: AB 7070 1530 3rd Ave S Birmingham AL 35294-0110

GARRISON, ELIZABETH JANE, artist; b. Elmira, N.Y., Feb. 11, 1952; BFA, Ringling Sch. Art and Design, 1973; postgrad., Mansfield U., 1976—78; MS, Fla. State U., 1980. Exhibits include Mus. Contemporary Art, Netherlands, Mus. Fine Arts, St. Petersburg, Fla., Renwick Gallery, Smithsonian Inst., Washington, and others; represented in permanent collections Yale U. Art Gallery, New Haven, Conn., Kunstgewerbe Mus., Berlin, Honolulu Acad. Arts, Mus. Fine Arts, Houston Nat. Endowment Arts fellow, 1981, 88; Saltonstall Found. grantee, 1996 Home: 317 Elm St Ithaca NY 14850-3018

GARRISON, GENEVA, retired administrative assistant; b. Bowling Green, Ky., Feb. 14, 1933; d. Claude Harrison and Helen (Bohannon) Garrison; m. Marion Murphey Dare, Jr., Aug. 1955 (div. Mar. 1972); 1 child, Marcus Glenn. AAS, U. Louisville, 1975, BLS summa cum laude, 1977. Tchr. behavior disorders, learning disabilities, mentally handicapped Jefferson County Schs., Louisville, 1974—77; coord. parent edn. project U. Louisville, 1977—79; exec. sec. to dir. AHES Western Ky. U., Bowling Green, 1980, sec., asst. to dir. devel., 1980—84, exec. sec. to exec. v.p. adminstrv. affairs, 1984—87, sec. to pres., 1987—89; ret., 1989. Part-time crisis counselor LifeSkills Inc., Bowling Green, 1993—96. Author: (poetry) to profl. jours. Recipient Omicron Delta Kappa Outstanding Grad. Sr. award, U. Louisville, 1978. Mem.: AAUW, DAR, Warren County Ret. Tchrs. Assn., Ky. Ret. Tchrs. Assn., So. Appalachian Nature Photography Club, Internat. Soc. Poets, Phi Kappa Phi (scholar 1978). Avocations: photography, walking, reading, travel. Home: 733 Newman Way Bowling Green KY 42104-3810

GARRISON, GWEN E., educational researcher, consultant; d. Thomas B. and Peggy A. Garrison; life ptnr. Linda K. Hodson. BA in English cum laude, Seattle Pacific U., 1985; MA in Theology, Fuller Theol. Sem., 1992; PhD in Edn., Claremont Grad. U., 2003. Tchr. English Auburn Sch. Dist., Wash., 1986—89; mgr. Burns Espresso Co., Seattle, 1989—90; grad. academic advisor Fuller Theol. Sem., Pasadena, Calif., 1991—94, dir. academic advising, 1994—97; instl. rschr. Azusa Pacific U., Calif., 1997—98; rsch. assoc. Inst. at Indian Hill, Claremont, Calif., 1998—2001, dir. rsch. and ops., 2001—03; dir. student and applicant rsch. AAMC, Wash., 2003—. Prin. evaluator Inst. at Indian Hill, 2003—. Author: (rsch. report) The Impending Loss of Talent. Com. mem. Branford Pk. Home Owners Assn., Silver Spring, Md., 2005. Mem.: Assn. Study of Higher Edn. Independent. Christian. Avocations: dog training, hiking, music, bicycling. Home: 12006 Sawmill Ct Silver Spring MD 20902 Office: AAMC 2450 N St NW Washington DC 20037 Office Phone: 202-862-6186. Business E-Mail: ggarrison@aamc.org.

GARRISON, KATHRYN ANN, retired nutritionist; b. Prentiss, Miss., Dec. 30, 1929; d. Brooks Hilton and Irene Dale Polk; m. Rufus James Garrison, Dec. 30, 1953; children: Rufus James Jr., Karen D. Garrison Goff, David B. BS in Instnl. Mgmt., U. So. Miss., 1952. Dietetic intern Vanderbilt U. Hosp., Nashville, 1953; staff dietition Bapt. Hosp., Nashville, 1954, Children's Hosp., Louisville, Ky., 1954; cons. Murfreesboro (Tenn.) Med. Clinic, 1980-89; registered dietitian, 1989-96; ret., 1996. Pres., gen. mgr. Mid. Tenn. Choral Soc., 1983—; gen. mgr. Orpheus Vocal Competition, 1995—. Recipient Cmty. Svc. award, Daily News Jour. and Sun Trust Bank, 1999. Baptist. Avocations: music, travel, antiques, art. Home: 1941 Veranda Pl Murfreesboro TN 37130-3267

GARRISON, LATREASE E., association executive; b. Petersburg, Va., Aug. 8, 1972; d. Larry Boyd and Ruby (Williams) Evans; m. D'Vell Medley Garrison, Mar. 15, 1997; 1 child, Testimony Faith. BS in Chemistry, Howard U., 1995; postgrad., Strayer U., 1998—. Editl. sec. Am. Chem. Soc., Washington, 1992-95, program asst., 1995-96, staff asst., 1996-97, staff assoc., 1997-98, sr. staff assoc., student affiliates program, 1998-99, program mgr., 1999—2001, sr. edn. program mgr., 2001—. Editor Chemistry, 2003—; editor (newsletter) FANmail, 1998—. Active Antioch Bapt. Ch. Mem. Am. Chem. Soc., Alpha Kappa Alpha Sorority, Inc. Avocations: travel abroad, reading, poetry, cooking. Home: 5408 Quaint Dr Woodbridge VA 22192-5612 Office: Am Chem Soc 1155 16th St NW Washington DC 20036-4800

GARRISON, LINDA, retired foundation administrator; b. Lockport, NY, July 25, 1953; d. Robert Groves and Mary Jean Garrison. BS, Excelsior Coll., Albany, 1995; D (hon.), Pepperdine U., 1997; MA in Spiritual Psychology, U. Santa Monica, 2005. V.p. Headline Brokers, Secaucus, NJ, 1976-85; mgr. Forest Lawn Meml. Pks., Glendale, Calif., 1985-89; v.p. Forest Lawn Found., Glendale, Calif., 1993—98, pres., 1998—2003, ret., 2003. Dir., officer Goodwill Industries So. Calif., LA, 199-2001; dir., mem. exec. com. ARC, LA, 1993-2000; dir. Children's Bur. So. Calif., LA, 1998—, chmn. bd. 2002-05. Mem. So. Calif. Grantmakers (bd. dirs. 2000-03) Home: 8983 Whispering Pine Curve Sylvania OH 43560

GARRISON-FINDERUP, IVADELLE DALTON, writer, educator; b. San Pedro, Calif., Oct. 4, 1915; d. William Douglas and Olive May (Covington) Dalton; m. Fred Marion Garrison, Aug. 8, 1932 (dec. Nov. 1984); children: Douglas Lee, Vernon Russell, Nancy Jane; m. Elmer Pedersen Finderup, Apr. 8, 1994 (dec. Oct. 1997). BA, Calif. State U., Fresno, 1964; postgrad., U. Oreg., 1965, U. San Francisco, 1968. Cert. secondary tchr., Calif. Tchr. Tranquillity (Calif.) H.S., 1964-78, West Hills Coll., Coalinga, Calif., 1970-74. Lectr. in field. Author: Roots and Branches of Our Garrison Family Tree, 1988, Roots and Branches of Our Dalton Family Tree, 1989, The History of James' Fresno Ranch, 1990, 3d edit., 1993, There is a Peacock on the Roof, 1993; (with Vernon R. Garrison) William Douglas Dalton, a Biography, 1995, Sam (The Cat That Thought He Was a Boy), 1997, Amanda and Her Feathered Friends, 1997, Freddy Goes on a Trailer Outing, 1998, David Learns to Count, 1998, Laura and the Lizard: a fairy tale, 2001, A Mystery Story, 2005. Mem. Arne Nixon Ctr. Study Children's Lit., Henry Madden Libr. Mem. DAR (sec. 1987-89, regent 1989-91, regent Fresno chpt. 1999-2001, scholarship chmn. 2002, 05, nat. recognition for excellence in cmty. svc. Cert. of Award 1995), Nat. Trust for Hist. Preservation, Frazier Clan N.Am., Fresno City and County Hist. Soc. (life), Fresno Archaeology Soc. (sec. 1994), Children of the Am. Revolution (life patriot, sr. pres. 1991-97), Westerners Internat., Fresno Gem and Mineral Soc., Thora # 11 Dannebrog, Friends of the Libr. (Fresno), Chaffee Zool. Gardens of Fresno, Archaeol. Inst. Am. (San Joaquin Valley chpt., charter mem.), Fresno Met. Mus., Baker Hist. Mus. (life). Republican. Lutheran. Avocations: quilting, knitting. Office: Garrison Libr 3427 Circle Ct E Fresno CA 93703-2403

GARRISS, PHYLLIS WEYER, music educator, performer; b. Hastings, Nebr., Dec. 25, 1923; d. Frank Elmer and Mabelle Claire (Carey) Weyer; m. William Philip Garriss, Aug. 28, 1954; children: Daniel, Meredith, Margaret. AB, MusB, Hastings Coll., 1945; MusM, U. Rochester, 1948. Instr. DePauw U., Greencastle, Ind., 1948-51; assoc. prof. music Meredith Coll., Raleigh, N.C., 1951-94, assoc. prof. emerita, part-time prof., 1994—. Instr. Cannon Music Camp, Appalachian State U., Boone, N.C., 1973-98; vis. instr. Ball State U., Muncie, summers 1951, 53; dir. Lamar Stringfield Chamber Music Camp, Meredith Coll., 1980—; bd. dirs. Raleigh Symphony Orch., Raleigh Chamber Music Guild; mem. various symphonic groups as violinist, including Roanoke Symphony, Raleigh Civic Symphony, Duke U. Symphony, Tri-City Chamber Orch., Raleigh Symphony Orch., Capital Chamber Music Ensemble. Mem. Raleigh Civic Coun., 1958-60; bd. dirs. Raleigh Comty. Mus. Sch., 1993-97, N.C. Fedn. Music Clubs, 1988-96; mem. PEO. Recipient Medal of Arts, City of Raleigh Arts Commn., 1987. Mem. Am. String Tchrs. Assn. (corr. sec. 1950-54, Disting. Svc. award 1979), Music Tchrs. Nat. Assn., Music Educators Nat. Conf., Local 500 Musicians Assn. (bd. dirs. 1980—), Raleigh Music Club (pres. 1958-60, 93-95), Pi Kappa Lambda, Mu Phi Epsilon. Democrat. Presbyterian. Avocations: cooking, travel. Home: 3400 Merriman Ave Raleigh NC 27607-7004 Office: Meredith Coll 3800 Hillsborough St Raleigh NC 27607-5237 Office Phone: 919-760-2821. Business E-Mail: garrissp@meredith.edu.

GARRO-BISSETTE, SUSAN ANN, adult nurse practitioner; b. Lynchburg, Va., May 12, 1944; children: Lisa, Tony, Pilar. BSN, Cath. U. Am., 1984, MSN, 1995. RN, S.C.; cert. adult nurse practitioner. Adult nurse practitioner Dr. R.D. Gibbs, Moncks Corner, S.C., 1996-98, Ralph H. Johnson VA Med. Ctr., Charleston, S.C., 1998—; clin. faculty adult nurse practitioner program Med. U. S.C. Sch. Nursing, Charleston, 1997-2000. Guardian ad litem State of S.C. Office of Gov., Charleston, 1996—. Mem.: ANA, Am. Coll. Nurse Practitioners, S.C. Nurses Assn. and Advanced Practice Coun. (mem.-at-large 2001—03), Am. Acad. Nurse Practitioners, Low Country Advanced Practice Nurses (pres. 1998—2001), Sigma Theta Tau. Home: 22 Short St Charleston SC 29401-1908 Office: VA Med Ctr 109 Bee St Charleston SC 29401-5703 Office Phone: 843-789-6515. E-mail: susangarro@bellsouth.net.

GARROTT, FRANCES CAROLYN, architectural engineer; b. Bowling Green, Ky., Mar. 10, 1932; d. Irby Reid and Carrie Mae (Stahl) Cameron; m. Leslie Othello Garrott, Oct. 12, 1951 (dec. Feb. 1978); adopted children: Carolyn Maria(dec.), Karen Roxana children: Dennis Leslie, Alan Reid; m. Raymond William Scerbo, May 31, 1978 (div. Oct. 1990). Student, Fla. State U., 1951, St. Petersburg Jr. Coll., 1962—74; grad., Pinellas Vocat. Tech. Inst., 1975. With Sears, Roebuck and Co., Rapid City, S.D., 1951-52, St. Petersburg, Fla., 1961-62; bookkeeper Ohio Nat. Bank, Columbus, 1953-54, Sunbeam Bakery, Lakeland, Fla., 1955-56; with Christies Toy Sales, Pennsauken, N.J., 1958-60; exec. sec. Gulf Coast Automotive Warehouse, Inc., Tampa, Fla., 1970-73, office mgr., 1975-78; sec., treas., chief pilot, co-owner Tech. Devel. Corp., St. Petersburg, Fla., 1970-78. Freelance archtl. draftsman and designer, archtl. cons., constrn. materials estimator, Lakeland, Fla., 1995—, Seminole, Fla., 1975—95. Fla. judge Vocat. Indsl. Clubs Am. Skills Olympics, 1986. Nat. Assn. Women in Constrn. scholar, 1974. Mem. Nat. Assn. Women in Constrn. (scholar 1974), Alpha Chi Omega. Democrat. Home: 8156 Timberidge Loop W Lakeland FL 33809-2357

GARTON, JANETTE, music educator; b. Lawton, Okla., Sept. 26, 1965; d. Herbert F. and Jan P. Jacobs; m. Randy D. Garton, June 4, 1992; children: Ashley Diana, Melody Michelle. BS in Computer Sci., Cameron U., Lawton, 1987, B Music Edn., 1990. Band dir. Ctrl. HS, Marlow, Okla., 1990—2002, MacArthur Mid. Sch., Lawton, 2002—. Mem.: Okla. Adjudicators' Assn., Okla. Bandmasters Assn. Office: MacArthur Mid Sch 510 NE 45th St Lawton OK 73507

GARVEY, ARLENE P., media specialist, consultant; b. Butte, Mont., Aug. 6, 1946; d. Michael Joseph and Dorothy Louise G. BS in Edn., Ea. Mont. Coll., 1973; MA, Lesley Coll., 1993. Libr. Butte Silver Bow, 1965-71, Whitehall (Mont.) H.s., 1973-75, Sweetgrass County HS., Big Timber, Mont., 1975-78; libr., media specialist Sch. Dist. #1, Butte, 1979—. Mem. Am. Fedn. Tchrs., Mont. Fedn. Tchrs., AAUW. Democrat. Roman Catholic. Avocations: walking, reading, writing, travel.

GARVEY, DAWN ELAINE, elementary school educator; d. Dean Eugene and Emily Garvey; m. Bruce William Irish, July 28, 1990; children: Ian Justin Ginsberg, Deven Lynn Grimaldi, Kenneth Wayne Caudle. BS in Elem. Edn., Norfolk State U., Va., 1986—90. 6th grade English & social studies tchr. Va. Beach Pub. Schs., 1991—. With US Army, 1978—79. Recipient Tchr. of Yr., W.T. Cooke Elem., 1995, Disting. Tchr., Corp. Landing Mid. Sch., 2002—04, Tech. Tchr. of Yr., Sta. WHRO, 2004; grantee Tchr. Incentive grant, Va. Commn. for Arts, 2001—06, Bldg. Futures grant, Va. Beach Edn. Found., 2000—02, 2004. Mem.: Va. Social Studies Educators (corr.). Office: Corporate Landing Mid Sch 1597 Corporate Landing Pkwy Virginia Beach VA 23454 Office Phone: 757-437-6199. Office Fax: 757-437-6587. Business E-Mail: dawn.garvey@vbschools.com.

GARVEY, JANE, public relations executive; BA, Mount Saint Mary Coll.; MA, Mount Holyoke Coll.; fellowship program for pub. leaders, Harvard U. Assoc. commr. Mass. Dept. Pub. Works, Boston, commr., 1988-91; dir. Logan Internat. Airport, Boston, 1991-93; dep. adminstr. Fed. Hwy. Adminstrn. U.S. Dept. Transp., Washington, 1993-97, acting adminstr. Fed. Hwy. Adminstrn., 1997, apptd. 14th adminstr. FAA Washington, 1997—2003; exec. v.p., chmn. APCO Worldwide, 2003—. Lectr., rsch. scientist Ctr. for Transp. and Logistics, MIT, 2003—. Office: Apco Worldwide 700 12th St NW Ste 800 Washington DC 20005-3949

GARVEY, JOANNE MARIE, lawyer; b. Oakland, Calif., Apr. 23, 1935; d. James M. and Marian A. (Dean) Garvey. AB with honors, U. Calif., Berkeley, 1956, MA, 1957, JD, 1961. Bar: Calif. 1962. Assoc. Cavaletto, Webster, Mullen & McCaughey, Santa Barbara, Calif., 1961-63, Jordan, Keeler & Seligman, San Francisco, 1963-67, ptnr., 1968-88, Heller, Ehrman, White & McAuliffe, San Francisco, 1988—. Bd. dirs. Mex.-Am. Legal Def. and Ednl. Fund; chmn. Law in Free Soc., Continuing Edn. Bar; mem. bd. councillors U. So. Calif. Law Ctr. Recipient Paul Veazy award, YMCA, 1973, Internat. Women's Yr. award, Queen's Bench, 1975, honors, Advs. Women, 1978, CRLA award, Boalt Hall Citation award, 1998, Judge Lowell Jensen Cmty. Svc. award, 2001, Margaret Brent award, 2003, Latcham State and Local Disting. Svc. award, 2003, Lifetime Achievement award, Am. Lawyer mag., 2006. Fellow: Am. Bar Found.; mem.: ABA (gov., state del., chmn. SCLAID, chmn.delivery legal svcs., chmn. 10LTA), Calif. Women Lawyers (founder), Am. Law Inst., San Francisco Bar Assn. (pres., pres. Barristers), Calif. State Bar (v.p., gov., tax sect., del., Jud Klein award, Joanne Garvey award), Phi

Beta Kappa, Order of Coif. Democrat. Roman Catholic. Home: 16 Kensington Ct Kensington CA 94707-1010 Office: 333 Bush St San Francisco CA 94104-2806 Office Phone: 415-772-6729. Business E-Mail: joanne.garvey@hellerehrman.com.

GARVEY, SHEILA HICKEY, theater educator; b. Erie, Pa., Dec. 23, 1949; d. Robert Francis and Mary Virginia (Sullivan) H.; children: Sean Timothy, Darragh Burgess. BS, Emerson Coll., 1971; MA, Northwestern U., 1973; PhD, NYU, 1984; grad., The Circle in the Square, N.Y.C., 1975. Preceptor NYU, N.Y.C., 1978-80; sabbatical replacement Rutgers U., Camden, N.J., 1980-81; asst. prof. Dickinson Coll., Carlisle, Pa., 1981-88; full prof. So. Conn. State U., New Haven, 1988—. Editor: Jason Robards Remembered, 2002; contbr. articles to profl. jours.; actor: New Haven Gaelic Players, 1999, 2004, New Haven Internat. Festival Arts and Ideas, 2004, Long Wharf Theatre, 2006. Scholar JFK Ctr. Performing Arts, Am. Coll. Theatre Festival, 1993; Rsch. grantee Dickinson Coll., 1987-88, So. Conn. State U., 1988-90, 92, 94, 98, 2003, Faculty Devel. grant, 1988-90, 92, 94, 97; Dana fellow Dickinson Coll., 1987. Mem. New Eng. Theatre Conf. (bd. dirs., coll. divsn. 1992-95, chair coll. and univ. com. 1991-95, life mem. Coll. Fellows), Eugene O'Neill Soc. (bd. dirs. 1999—, pres. 2000-02, v.p. 2001—), Conn. Critics' Cir., Conn. Critics Cir. (bd. dirs.). Roman Catholic. Home: 273 Knob Hill Dr Hamden CT 06518-2737 Office: So Conn State U 501 Crescent St New Haven CT 06515-1330

GARVIN, MICHELE M., lawyer; b. Nov. 8, 1952; BA, Coll. William & Mary, 1974; MA, Boston Coll., 1977, PhD Sociology, 1981; JD, Suffolk Univ., 1987. Bar: Mass. 1988. Assoc. to ptnr. corp. dept. Ropes & Gray, Boston, 1988—, chmn. health care practice group. Contbr. articles to profl. jours., chapters to books. Mem.: ABA, Mass. Bar Assn., Boston Bar Assn., Jackson Hole Task Force on HCCPs. Office: Ropes & Gray 1 International Pl Boston MA 02110-2624 Office Phone: 617-951-7495. Office Fax: 617-951-7050. Business E-Mail: michele.garvin@ropesgray.com.

GARVIN, VAIL PRYOR, hospital administrator; b. Wilmington, N.C., Aug. 8, 1942; d. Henry Paul and Harriet Jane (Vail) Pryor; children: John P., Thomas P. BS in Nursing, Emory U., 1965; post grad. in Bus. Adminstrn., Temple U., 1978—79; DPA, Nova U., 1983. RN Emory U. Hosp. and Clinic, Atlanta, 1965—67; assoc. adminstr. Warminster (Pa.) Gen. Hosp., 1978—84, CEO, 1984—87; sr. v.p. corp. affairs Blue Cross Greater Phila., 1987—. Mem. govtl. services adv. coun. Atlanta Regional Commn., 1973—74, mem. emergency med. svcs. task force, 1973—74; mem. drug and alcohol abuse task force S.E. Pa. Health Systems Agy., 1979; cons. Med. Mgmt. Group, 1979—81; mem. drug adv. task force Pa. Gov.'s Council on Drug and Alcohol Abuse, 1980. Mem. comm. com. United Way, 1982—, mem. county coun. of execs., 1976—; mem. Warminster Twp. Drug and Alcohol Commn., 1981—; bd. dir. Women Organized Against Rape, 1981, ARC, 1981—82, Warminster Symphony Orch., 1980—, Bucks County Mental Health/Mental Retardation, 1981—, Bucks County Council on Alcoholism, 1981—, Warminster Cmty. Ctr., mem. fin. com., 1981—; bd. dir. Pa. Economy League, 1987—. Recipient Safety award, Ga. Safety Coun. and Sta. WSB, 1976, Heart of Yr. award, Am. Heart Assn., 1987, Ann. Freedom award, Freedom Valley Girl Scouts, 1987. Mem.: Hosp. Assn. Pa. (coun. psychiatric providers), Nat. League Nursing, Alcohol and Drug Problems Assn. N. Am., Am. Soc. Pub. Adminstrs., Health Care Fin. Mgmt. Assn., Am. Soc. Law and Medicine, Am. Soc. Mental Health Adminstrs., Am. Coll. Hosp. Adminstrs., Sigma Theta Tau. Episcopalian. Home: 1028 Cox Ave Washington Crossing PA 18977-1418 Office: Independence Blue Cross Ste 3 1901 Market St Philadelphia PA 19103-1475

GARWICK, CYNTHIA L., elementary school educator; b. Mpls., Minn., Nov. 2, 1952; m. Kenneth R. Garwick. Student, U. Minn., 1971—74; BS in edn., Kans. State U., 1976, MS in edn., 1982. Cert. Nat. Bd. Cert. Early Childhood Generalist 2002. First grade tchr. Morris Hill Elem., Ft. Riley, Kans., 1977—83, Bluemont Elem., Manhattan, Kans., 1983—84, 1985—2002, Eugene Field Elem., Manhattan, Kans., 1984—85, Northview Elem., Manhattan, Kans., 2002—. Tchr. Kans. State U., Manhattan, Kans., 1977—; trainer, cons. Foss/Delta Edn., 1999—; mentor USD 383, Manhattan, Kans., 1999—; scorer Kans. Performance Assessment, 2004—; vice chair State Kans. Profl. Stds. Bd., 2005—. Deacon elder, bell choir First Christian Ch., Manhattan, 1974—, group leader, tchr. Mem.: Nat. Coun. Tchrs. Math, Nat. Sci. Tchr. Assn., Nat. Edn. Assn. (local pres. 1999—2000). Office: Northview Elem 300 Griffith Dr Manhattan KS 66502 Business E-Mail: cindyg@manhattan.k12.ks.us.

GARWOOD, JULIE, writer; b. 1946; Author: (novels for young adults) A Girl Named Summer, 1985, (as Emily Chase) What's A Girl to Do, 1985, (historical romance novels) Gentle Warrior, 1985, Rebellious Desire, 1986, Honor's Splendor, 1987, The Lion's Lady, 1988, The Bride, 1989, Guardian Angel, 1990, The Gift, 1990, The Prize, 1991, The Secret, 1992, Castles, 1993, Saving Grace, 1993, Prince Charming, 1994, For the Roses, 1995, The Wedding, 1996, One Pink Rose, One White Rose, One Red Rose, Come the Spring, 1997, The Wedding, 1998, Ransom, 1999, Heartbreaker, 2000, Mercy, 2002, Killjoy, 2002, Killjoy, 2003, Murder List, 2004 (Publishers Weekly Bestseller), Slow Burn, 2005 (Publishers Weekly Bestseller). Office: PO Box 7574 Leawood KS 66207-0574 Address: Jane Rotrosen Agy 318 East 51st St New York NY 10022*

GARY, JULIA THOMAS, retired minister; b. Henderson, NC, May 31, 1929; d. Richard Collins and Julia Branch (Thomas) G. BA, Randolph-Macon Woman's Coll., 1951; MA, Mt. Holyoke Coll., 1953; PhD in Chemistry, Emory U., 1958; MDiv cum laude, Candler Sch. Theology, 1986. Ordained to Meth. Ch. as deacon, 1986, as elder 1989. Instr. Mt. Holyoke Coll., South Hadley, Mass., 1953-54, Randolph-Macon Woman's Coll., Lynchburg, Va., 1954-55; from asst. prof. to prof. chemistry Agnes Scott Coll., Decatur, Ga., 1957-84, dean, 1969-84; pastor-in-charge St. Matthew United Meth. Ch., East Point, Ga., 1987-92; ret., 1992. Bd. dirs. Global Health Action, Inc., Atlanta, treas., 1991-97, v.p., 1997—; chmn. coord. coun. Decatur Area Emergency Assistance Ministry, 1995-96. Contbr. articles to profl. jours. Recipient Alumnae Achievement award Randolph-Macon Woman's Coll., 1990. Mem.: Sigma Xi, Phi Beta Kappa. Avocation: music. Home: 4105 Springhouse Cir Stone Mountain GA 30087 Personal E-mail: revjtg@aol.com.

GARY, KATHLEEN NOLAND, public relations executive; b. Long Beach, Calif., July 3, 1945; d. Richard Lee and Grace Irene Noland; m. Richard N. Gary. BA U. Wash., 1967. Assoc. editor Kaiser News, Kaiser Aluminum & Chem. Corp., Oakland, Calif., 1968—73; dir. comm. Kaiser Engrs., Oakland, 1973—74; mgr. internal comm. Kaiser Industries Corp., Oakland, 1975—77; dir. pub. rels. and advt. Kaiser Steel Corp., Oakland, 1977—80, v.p. pub. affairs, 1979—80; former corp. v.p. pub. affairs and comm. Syntex Corp., Palo Alto, 1981. Co-author (with Don Fabun): (books) Children of Change, 1970, Dimensions of Change, 1971. Chmn. steering com. St. Mary's Coll. Exec. Seminar; mem. Bay area coun. steering com. Nat. Investor Rels. Inst.; bd. dirs. U. Wash. Devel. Fund. Mem.: Pharm. Mfrs. Assn. (pub. affairs. sect.), Calif. Mfrs. Assn., World Affairs Coun., Pub. Rels. Soc. Am., Forum West Club, Silverado Country Club.

GARZA, ANNABEL, elementary school educator; b. Alice, Tex., Sept. 27, 1956; d. Samuel Sr. and Maria Idolina (Najar) G. BS, Tex. A & I U., 1978. Cert. elem. tchr., biligual tchr. Tchr. Spanish Los Fresnos (Tex.) CISD, San Antonio Ind. Sch. Dist.; tchr. 3rd grade Los Fresnos CISD; tchr. 2nd grade San Diego Ind. Sch. Dist. Mem. TSTA, Sigma Delta Pi, Alpha Lambda Delta. Home: PO Box 516 Ben Bolt TX 78342-0516

GARZA, MELITA MARIE, journalist; b. Madrid, Oct. 19, 1959; came to U.S., 1961; d. Carlos Mario and Linda Rose (Caballero) G. BA, Harvard U., 1983; postgrad., Poynter Inst. Reporter, writer L.A. Times, 1984-85, Milw. Jour., 1986-89, Chgo. Tribune, 1989—. Discussion leader Am. Press Inst., Reston, Va., 1995; spkr., instr. Wildwind (Del.) Writers Workshop, 1995. Bd. dirs. SciTech mus., Aurora, Ill., 1991—; mem. com. on fgn. rels. Chgo. Coun. on Fgn. Rels., 1991—. Named one of top 20 young people in U.S. newspaper industry Newspaper Assn. Am., 1993, one of 100 Women Making a Difference Today's Chgo. Women, 1996; recipient Excellence in Journalism award Ill. Coalition for Immigrant and Refugee Protection, 1995, Cardinal's Comm. award for Profl. Excellence Archdiocese of Chgo., 1996. Mem. Nat. Assn. Hispanic Journalists (v.p. bd. dirs. 1989-94, Pres.' award 1994), Internat. Women's Media Found., Harvard Club of Chgo. (v.p. 1993-94), Radcliffe Club of Chgo. (pres. 1993-94). Roman Catholic. Avocations: tennis, aerobics, cooking, sewing, reading. Office: Chgo Tribune 435 N Michigan Ave Chicago IL 60611-4066

GARZARELLI, ELAINE MARIE, economist; b. Phila., Oct. 13, 1952; d. Ralph J. and Ida M. (Pierantozzi) G.; BS, Drexel U., 1973, MBA, 1977, Ph.D, 1992. With A.G. Becker, N.Y.C., 1973-84, v.p., economist, 1975-84, mgn. dir., 1984; ptnr., portfolio mgr. Lehman Bros. Inc., 1984-94; prin. Garzarelli Internat. Inc., Delray Beach, Fla., 1994—; lectr. in field. Named Businesswoman of Yr. Fortune Mag., 1987, # 1 in Quantitative Analysis, Instl. Investor Annual Contest. Mem. Nat. Assn. Bus. Economists, Women's Fin. Assn., Am. Statis. Assn., Women's Bond Assn. Developer Sector Analysis (econometric model for predicting industry profits and stock price movements, also predicted stock market crash of 1987).

GARZOLINI, JUDITH A., information technology manager; m. Michael Rusnack. BS in Textiles and Clothing, Ind. State U.; BSChemE, Wayne State U.; MBA, U. Calif., Davis. Staff Ford Motor Co., Detroit; rocket engine materials engr. AeroJet Strategic Propulsion Co.; prog. mgr. Hewlett-Packard, Boise, Idaho. Campus diversity coord. Hewlett-Packard-Purdue Tech. Recruiting Team. Co-chair logistics com. Ride Idaho Bicycle Tour, 2005. Mem.: Soc. Women Engrs. (sr.; pres. 2006—, Purdue indsl. adv. bd.). Achievements include patents in field; patents pending in field. Office: Soc Women Engrs 230 E Ohio St Ste 400 Chicago IL 60611 E-mail: president@swe.org.*

GASAWAY, LAURA NELL, law librarian, educator; b. Searcy, Ark., Feb. 24, 1945; d. Merel Roger and Carnell (Miller) Gasaway. BA, Tex. Woman's U., 1967, MLS, 1968; JD, U. Houston, 1973. Bar: Tex. 1973. Catalog libr. U. Houston, 1968—70, catalog-circulation libr., 1970—72, asst. law libr., 1972—73, asst. prof. law, 1973—75; dir. law libr. U. Okla., Norman, 1975—85, prof. law, 1975—85; dir. law libr. U. N.C., 1985—, prof. law, 1985—. Copyright cons. Author: Growing Pains: Adapting Copyright for Librs., Edn. and Soc., 1997; co-author (with Maureen Murphy): Legal Protection for Computer Programs, 1980; co-author: (with James Hoover and Dorothy Warden) Am. Indian Legal Materials, A Union List, 1981, 1981; co-author: (with Bruce S. Johnson and James M. Murray) Law Libr. Mgmt. during Fiscal Austerity, 1992; co-author: (with Sarah K. Wiant) Libraries and Copyright: A Guide to Copyright in the 1990s, 1994; co-author: (with Michael D. Chiorazzi) Law Librarianship: Hist. Perspectives, 1996. Recipient Calvert prize, U. Okla., 1973, 1981, Compton award, Ark. Librs. Assn., 1986. Fellow: Spl. Librs. Assn. (H.W. Wilson award 1983, John Cotton Dana award 1987, Fannie Simon award 1992, H.W. Wilson award 2005); mem.: ABA, Am. Assn. Law Librs. (pres. 1986—87), N.C. Bar Assn., State Bar Tex. Democrat. Office: U NC Law Libr CB 3385 Chapel Hill NC 27599-0001 Office Phone: 919-962-2295. Business E-Mail: laura_gasaway@unc.edu.

GASBARRO, DOTTIE FULLER, mathematics professor; d. Orlando Howard and Sarah Ellen (Schmidt) Dodson; m. Fred Gasbarro, Aug. 17, 2004; children: Amy Taylor, Alison True. BS in Edn., Athens State U., Ala., 1980; MA in Edn., U. N. Ala., Florence, 1985; EdS in Math., U. Ala., Tuscaloosa, 1999. Cert. AA Ala. State Dept. Edn. Instr. math. Decatur H.S., Ala., 1980—95, Huntsville H.S., 1996—2003; asst. prof. math. Athens State U., 2000—. Keyclub advisor Kiwanis, Huntsville, Ala., 1996; advisor and mem. So. Assn. Student Couns., 1997—2003; advisor and mem. math and computer sci. club Athens State U., 1998—; pres. N. Ala. Coun. Tchrs. Math., 1999—2003. Mem. and officer PTA, Huntsville, Ala., 1996—2003. Named Tchr. of Yr., Hutsville H.S. PTA, 2000—01. Mem.: Ala. Coun. Tchrs Math. (exec. bd. 2000—, dist. I dir. 2005—), Nat. Coun. Tchrs Math. (conf. chmn. 2005—), Kappa Mu Epsilon (advisor 1999—). Office: Athens State U 300 N Beaty St Athens AL 35611-1999 Office Phone: 256-233-8236.

GASCOINE-MOLINA, JILL VIOLA, actress, writer; b. London, Apr. 11, 1937; d. Francis Gascoine and Irene Ethel Greenwood; m. William Keith, Mar. 18, 1965 (div. June 1973); children: Sean William, Adam Francis; m. Alfred Molina, Mar. 1, 1985. Student, Theatre Sch., London. Actress theater, TV, films, London. Author: Addicted, 1994, Lilian, 1996, Just Like A Woman, 1997. Named Best Actress on TV, TV Times Mag. Viewers Vote, 1983, 1984. Avocation: designing gardens.

GASHAW-GANT, GEBAYNESH GELILA, psychologist, consultant; b. Addis Abeba, Ethiopia, Mar. 26, 1958; arrived in U.S., 1980; d. Gashaw Kebede and Mulunesh Million; m. James R. Gant, Oct. 10, 1980; 1 child, Gabriel Gashaw Gant. A, Irvine Valley Coll., Calif., 1987; B, Calif. State U., Fullerton, 1989; M, Nat. U., 1993; D, Alliant Internat. U., 2004. Mental health counselor intern County of Orange Perinatal Substance Abuse Program, Santa Ana, Calif.; mental health counselor Neighborhood House Head Start Program, San Diego; developer, dir. Project Essea, San Diego. Chair, developer African Health Collaborative, San Diego. Mem.: APA.

GASKELL, CAROLYN SUZANNE, librarian; b. Glen Cove, N.Y., Aug. 14, 1954; d. Duane Uson and Betty Jane G. BA, Pacific Union Coll., 1976; MA, U. Denver, 1977. Circulation libr. Walla Walla Coll., College Place, Wash., 1978-89, dr. librs., 1989—. Chmn. Adventist Library Information Cooperative (ALICE) Council, 2001-2002 Mem. ALA, Assn. Seventh-day Adventist Librs. (pres.-elect 1991-92, pres. 1992-93), ACRL (v.p., pres. elect Wash. state chpt. 1995-96). Avocations: hiking, flower arranging. Office: Walla Walla Coll Peterson Meml Libr 204 S College Ave College Place WA 99324-1139

GASKEY-SPEAR, NANCY JANE, nurse anesthetist; b. California, Pa. d. Frank and Rose Gaskey; m. Robert L. Spear (dec. Jan. 1998). RN, Mercy Hosp., Pitts., 1960, Nurse Anesthetist, 1963; BS in Nursing Edn., California (Pa.) U., 1970; MEd in Curriculum and Supervision, U. Pitts., 1975, PhD in Edn. Comm. and Tech., 1983. Cert. nurse anesthetist; RN, Pa. Staff nurse Mercy Hosp., Pitts., 1960-61, staff nurse anesthetist, 1963-70; dir. Sch. Nurse Anesthesia Western Pa. Hosp., Pitts., 1970-86; staff nurse anesthetist Western Pa. Anesthesia Assocs. Ltd., Western Pa. Hosp., Pitts., 1987—. On-site visitor Coun. on Accreditation Nurse Anesthesia Ednl. Programs, Schs., 1981-86; ednl. cons. Nursing Expo, Pitts., 1982; mem. Allegheny County Bd. Health, Pitts., 1976-85; instr. workshops, seminars, various orgns. Prodr. slide/cassette: Radial Artery Cannulation, Western Pa. Hosp. Sch. Anesthesia Recruitment, Instrns. for Assembling the Gould Transducer Pressure Monitoring Sys., Brachial Plexus Blocks: Interscalene Technique, Evolution of Inhalation Anesthesia; prodn. coord. videotapes Close-Ups in Anesthesia; contbr. articles to profl. jours.; mem. editl. bd. Current Revs. for Nurse Anesthetists; profl. corr. Antique Collector, Salem, Ohio, Bee Pub. Co., Newtowne, Conn. Recipient Cmty. Citation of Merit Allegheny County Bd. Commrs., 1985. Mem. Am. Assn. Nurse Anestetists (edn. com. 1973-74, rsch. in action recognition award 1985), Pitts. Bibliophiles, Mid-Atlantic Assn. Nurse Anesthetists (sec.-treas. 1970-71, chmn. elect 1971-72, chmn. 1972-73, chmn. program com. 1973-74), Southwestern Pa. Soc. Nurse Anesthetists (pres. 1972-73), Pa. Assn. Nurse Anesthetists (trustee 1972-74, pub. rels. com. 1972-74, safety com. 1974-75, pres.-elect 1975-76, pres. 1976-77, editor Pennsylvania Tidings 1976-77, founder, chmn. spl. com. Assembly Sch. Faculty), Hosp. Coun. Western Pa. (anesthesia circuits project com. 1982-83). Avocations: photography, antiques, art, gardening. Home: 552 N Neville St Pittsburgh PA 15213-2855 Office: Western Pa Hosp Liberty Ave Pittsburgh PA 15224

GASKILL, GAYLE, literature and language professor; b. Mapleton, Minn., Aug. 9, 1945; d. Courrier G. and Beryl Cornell Hubmer. BA, Mankato State U., Minn., 1966; MA, U. Nebr., Lincoln, 1970; PhD, U. Minn., Mpls., 1986. Lectr. English composition U. Minn., Mpls., 1973—93; lectr. English lit. Hamline U., St. Paul, 1979—80, Clarke Coll., Dubuque, Iowa, 1980—81; prof. English Coll. St. Catherine, St. Paul, 1987—. Contbg. author: Greenwood Companion to Shakespeare, Merchant of Venice: Critical Essays. Active mem. Cathedral of St. Mark, Mpls., 1973. Fellow, Amherst Ctr. Renaissance Studies, U. Mass., 2005, 2006. Mem.: Shakespeare Assn. Am. Dfl. Episcopalian. Avocation: travel. Office: College of Saint Catherine 2004 Randolph Ave Saint Paul MN 55105 Office Phone: 651-690-6857. Business E-Mail: ggaskill@stkate.edu.

GASKIN, FELICIA, biochemist, educator; b. Carlisle, Pa., Jan. 17, 1943; d. Joseph A. and Wanda J. (Rakowski) G.; m. Shu Man Fu, Nov. 29, 1969; children: Kai-Ming, Kai-Mei. AB in Chemistry, Dickinson Coll., 1965; MA in Organic Chemistry, Bryn Mawr Coll., 1967; PhD in Biochemistry, U. Calif., San Francisco, 1969. Postdoctoral fellow Stanford U., Palo Alto, Calif., 1969—71; rsch. assoc. Rockefeller U., N.Y.C., 1971—72, Columbia U., N.Y.C., 1972—74; asst. prof., then assoc. prof. Albert Einstein Coll. Medicine, N.Y.C., 1974—82; prof. Sch. Medicine U. Okla., Oklahoma City, 1982—88, U. Va., Charlottesville, 1988—. Mem. Okla. Med. Rsch. Found., 1982-88. Contbr. articles to profl. jours. Recipient rsch. career devel. award NIH, 1975-80; Nat. Inst. Neurol. Diseases and Stroke spl. fellow, 1972-74. Mem. AAAS, Am. Soc. Biochemistry and Molecular Biology, Soc. Neurosci. Office: U Va Sch Medicine Box 800203 Charlottesville VA 22908-0001

GASKIN-BUTLER, VIKKI TWYNETTE, clinical psychologist; b. St. Petersburg, Fla., Aug. 21, 1966; d. Don Ameche and Victoria Elizabeth (Martin) Gaskin; m. Malcolm Blaine Butler, June 20, 1992. BA, Spelman Coll., 1988; MSc, U. Fla., 1991, PhD, 1994; MDiv, Emory U., 2002. Lic. clin. psychologist, Tex., Ga. Clin. psychologist Coll. William and Mary, Williamsburg, Va., 1994-95; psychologist Tex. A&M U., Corpus Christi, 1995-99; min. edn. New Grove Bapt. Ch., 2004—. Contbr. articles to profl. jours. Sunday sch. tchr. St. Paul United Meth. Ch., Corpus Christi, 1997-99, chmn. Christian edn., 1997. Recipient O.C.T.A.A. award Prevention Rsch. Inst., 1996, United Meth. Seminary award, 2000; McKnight fellow Fla. Edn. Fund, 1988-94; Woodruff fellow, 1999-2002. Mem. Nueces County Psychol. Assn. (sec. 1997, pres. 1999), Theta Phi Theology Honor Soc., Nat. Coun. Negro Women, Ga. Psychological Assn. Avocations: writing, spiritual exploration/growth.

GASKINS, ANNE CARSON, retired human resources specialist; b. Nashville, Ga., Feb. 3, 1950; d. Joseph Ashmore and Edith Wilkes Carson; m. Walter Jeron Gaskins, Aug. 2, 1969; children: Jodi Hogan, Patrick R. B, Valdosta State U., Ga., 1976, M, 1980, Edn. Specialist, 1996. Tchr. Nashville Elem., 1976—93; resource specialist So. Pine Migrant Edn. Agy., Nasvhille, 1993—2005; ret., 2005. Spokesperson March of Dimes, Nashville; Sunday sch. tchr. 1st Bapt. Ch., Nashville, mem. fin. com., mem. long range planning com. Named Tchr. of the Yr., Nashville Elem. Sch. Mem.: Ga. Compensatory Ednl. Leaders, Ret. Tchrs. Berrien County. Avocations: swimming, travel, exercise. Home: 612 W Dennis St Nashville GA 31639

GASKINS, KAREN D., management consultant, research scientist; b. Ft. George Meade, Md., Mar. 23, 1953; d. Melvin Whittier Gaskins Sr. and Geneva K. Hill. AA in Nursing, Prince George's C.C., Largo, Md., 1978; BS in Psychology and Neurosci., U. Md., 2000. Substitute tchr. Prince George's Pub. Schs., Upper Marlboro, Md., 1998—2005. Freelance writer, orgnl. devel., social svc. worker, inventor, linguist Indo-European langs., cognitive psychology. Mem. Healing Waters, Inc., Ponderosa Project, KDG Assocs., Inc. Mem. Noetic Sci. (neuroscientist), Am. Psychol. Soc. E-mail: millicent71@yahoo.com.

GASNER, RENEE, music educator; b. Sioux Falls, SD, Jan. 5, 1958; d. Stanley and Ihlene Fillingsness; m. Donn Gasner, June 30, 1984; children: Jocelyn, Olivia. BA in Music, Augustana Coll., Sioux Falls, 1980; MA in Tchg., U. Wis., Whitewater, 1983. Instrumental music instr. Waupun Area Sch. Dist., Wis., 1983—. Flute instr. Marian Coll., Fond du Lac, Wis. Mem., participant Beaver Dam (Wis.) Area Cmty. Theater, 1992—2006. Mem.: NEA, Wis. Youth Band Dirs. Assn., Nat. Flute Assn., BIg Ten Investment Club (pres. 2001—02). Lutheran. Avocations: community theater, travel, music, sports mom, wine tasting. Home: 718 Neitzel St Horicon WI 53032 Office Phone: 920-324-9341.

GASPARRINI-ETHERIDGE, CLAUDIA, publishing executive, research scientist, writer; b. Genova, Italy, Apr. 25, 1941; arrived in US, 1984; d. Corrado and Tina (Pizzuti) G.; m. James K. Etheridge, Oct. 15, 1998. D in Earth Scis., U. Rome, 1965; cert. in English, U. Cambridge, Eng., 1965, Pitman Inst., London, 1965. Sr. tech. U. Toronto, Can., 1966-67, rsch. asst., 1967-70, rsch. assoc., 1970-72; phys. scientist II Geol. Survey Can., Ottawa, 1973; rsch. scientist Nat. Inst. for Metallurgy (now Mintek), Johannesburg, 1974-75; ind. cons. Toronto, 1976; pres., owner Minmet Sci. Limited, Toronto, 1977—, Jacksonville, Fla., 1982-86, Tucson, 1986—2000, The Space Eagle Pub. Co., Inc., Toronto, Tucson, 1986—, 1987—; writer, pub., 1989—. Adviser Chinese chpt. Internat. Precious Metals Inst., 1996—2000; guest lectr. U. Heidelberg, 1990, 91, Inst. Precious Metals, Kunming, China, 1984, U. Padua, U. Florence, 1995; presenter in field; assoc. Amazon.com, 2003—. Author: Gold and Other Precious Metals-The Lure and the Trap, 1989, How to Get the Most Out of the Legal System Without Spending a Fortune, 1990, Gold and Other Precious Metals-From Ore to Market, 1993, Murder of the Mind-The Practice of Subtle Discrimination, 1993, Murder of the Mind-The Practice of Subtle Discrimination, rev. 2d edit., 1996, When You Make the Two One, 1994, When You Make the Two One, rev. 2d edit., 1996; author: (as Gloria J. Duv) How to Run a Successful Mail Order Business by Defrauding the Public, 1995; author: Deceit-The Fad of the Nineties, 1997, Gold and Other Precious Metals-Occurrence, Extration, Applications, 2000, From Darkness to Light, 2001, Mechanics-Doctors, Does the Quality of Their Assistance Justify the Fees?, 2002, Subtle Discrimination, 2003, The Enemy Within, 2003, The Wrath of the Devil, 2004; mem. bd. editors: Chinese mag. Gold Sci. and Tech., 1996—2000; contbr. articles to profl. jours. and books. Scientist Sci. by Mail Program, Boston Mus. Sci., 1991-92; mem. rsch. bd. advisors Am. Biog. Inst., Raleigh, N.C., 1990—; hon. mem. Internat. Biog. Ctr. Adv. Coun., Cambridge, Eng., 1992—. Recipient Cert. Appreciation Outstanding Svc. Internat. Precious Metals Inst., 1994; named hon. mem. organizing com. Internat. Conf. on Precious Metals, Kosice, Slovakia, 1995. Avocations: classical music, computers, collecting books, crystals, precious and semi-precious stones. Home and Office: 9880 East Sterling View Tucson AZ 85749 Office: Minmet Sci Ltd/ The Space Eagle Pub Co Inc 1210 Sheppard Ave E # 200 North York ON Canada M2K 1E3 Office Phone: 520-760-0155. Personal E-mail: claudiaetheridge@thespaceagle.net, claudiaetheridge@comcast.net.

GASPARRO, MADELINE, retired banker; b. Jersey City, Oct. 5, 1928; d. Donato and Anna (D'Urso) D'Achille; m. Dominick J. Gasparro, Apr. 30, 1949; children: Dorothy, Joseph, Donato, Frank. Grad. high sch., Jersey City. Cert. St. Aloysius Eucharistic Min. 2003. Salesperson credit dept. and employee sales J.C. Penney, Parlin, N.J.; head teller Amboy Madison Nat. Bank, Old Bridge, N.J., bank mgr., br. mgr., 1983-97; ret., 1997. Chpt. chmn. South Amboy Hosp., mem. fin. com.; eucharist minister St. Bernadette Ch. of Parlin. Mem. NAFE, Nat. Assn. Bank Women (past hostess), Fin. Women Internat. (chmn. membership Raritan Bay group 1990-91, v.p. 1991-92, pres. 1992-93), Altar Rosary Soc. (past pres.). Address: 12 Baltusrol Dr Jackson NJ 08527-3991 E-mail: domgas@aol.com.

GASPER, JO ANN, social services administrator, consultant; b. Providence, Sept. 25, 1946; d. Joseph Siegleman and Jeanne Van Matre Shoaf; m. Louis Clement Gasper, Sept. 21, 1974; children: Stephen Gregory, Jeanne Marie, Monica Elizabeth, Michelle Bernadette (dec.), Phyllis Anastasia, Clare Genevieve. BA, U. Dallas, 1967, MBA, 1969. Adminstrv. asst. U. Dallas, 1964-68; asst. dir. adminstrn. Britian Convalescent Ctr., Irving, Tex., 1964-68; pres. Medicare Ctrs., Inc., Dallas, 1968-69; bus. mgr., treas. U. Plano, Tex., 1969-72; ins. agt. John Hancock Ins. Co., Dallas, 1972-73; systems analyst Tex. Instrument, Richardson, 1973-75; pvt. practice acctg., bus. cons. McLean, Va., 1976-81; editor, pub. Congl. News for Women and the Family, McLean, Va., 1978-81, Register Report, McLean, Va., 1980-81; dep. asst. sec. for social services policy HHS, Washington, 1981-85; exec. dir. White House Conf. on Agys., HHS, Washington, 1982-85; dep. asst. sec. for population affairs HHS, Washington, 1985-87; policy advisor to under sec. U.S. Dept. Edn., Washington, 1987-88, cons.; pres. Franklin Pk. Assocs., 1989—; exec. dir. Nat. Assn. for Abstinence Edn., 1989-94; mgr. TSR, 1995-98. Tchr. Grapevine-Colleyville Ind. Sch. Dist., 1998—. Co-chmn. St. John's Refugee Resettlement Commn., Va., 1977; bd. dirs., treas. Coun. Inter-Am. Security, Washington, 1978-80; active Fairfax County Citizens Coalition for Quality Child Care, Va., 1979-80; del. White House Conf. on Families, Va., 1979-80; mem. U.S. adv. Inter-Am. Commn. on Women, OAS, 1982-85; U.S. del. XVI Pan Am. Child Congress, Washington, 1984; mem. nat. family policy adv. bd. Reagan-Bush Campaign, 1980; mem. City of Colleyville Planning and Zoning Comm., 2000-02. Recipient Eagle Forum award, 1979, Wanderer Found. award, 1980, Bronze medal HHS, 1982; named Outstanding Conservative Woman, Conservative Digest, 1980, 81 Mem. Exec. Women in Gov. (treas. 1985, sec. 1986) Roman Catholic. Office Phone: 817-498-2671. Personal E-mail: joanngasper@yahoo.com.

GASPER, RUTH EILEEN, real estate executive; b. Valparaiso, Ind., July 16, 1934; d. Reuben John and Effie (Wesner) Tenpas; m. Ralph L. Gasper, May 25, 1957. Student, Purdue U., 1952—56; BA, Govs. State U., 1982. Analyst computer sys. Leo Burnett Advt., Chgo., 1958-69; nat. adminstr. registrars Sports Car Club Am., Denver, 1977-79; pres. Ainslie Inc., Port Orange, Fla., 1982—. Mem. North River Commn. Housing Com., Chgo., 1982-83, fin. com. Mayor's Task Force on Homelessness City of Chgo. Area coord. Concerned Action party, Lansing, Ill., 1977; chief race registrar Ind. N.W. Region Sports Car Club Am., 1969-80; co-founder, Single Rm. Operators Assn., 1987-98; treas. Sand Dollar Home Owners Assn. Inc. Mem. Dolphin Beach Club Condo Assn., Fantasy Island II Condo Assn. (sec.). Avocations: sports car racing, classical music. Personal E-mail: regasper@earthlink.net.

GASPERINI, ELIZABETH CARMELA (LISA GASPERINI), marketing professional; b. Newark, Sept. 26, 1961; d. Enrico Caesar and Wanda Claudia (Stanziale) G. BFA, Caldwell (NJ) Coll., 1983. Advt. specialist J.C. Penney Corp., Wayne, NJ, 1982-83; asst. prodn. mgr. Internat. Postal Mktg. Corp., Montville, NJ, 1983-84; art dir. Healy, Dixcy & Forbes, West Caldwell, NJ, 1984-86; sr. mktg. specialist Am. Varityper Corp., East Hanover, NJ, 1986-88; product promotion mgr. Brother Internat. Corp., Somerset, NJ, 1988-90; mktg. specialist Ishida USA Inc., Lincoln Park, NJ, 1990-92; mktg. promotions mgr. Nat. Electronic Info. Corp., Secaucus, NJ, 1992-95; pvt. practice Towaco, NJ, 1995—96; mgr. mktg. svcs. AmeriHealth Ins. Co. NJ, Iselin, 1996-98; mktg. cons. Towaco, 1998—2000; mgr. client segment mktg. Merck-Medco Managed Care LLC, Towaco, 2000—01; pvt. practice Mine Hill, NJ, 2001—. Telemarketing specialist Sears, Roebuck & Co., Fairfield, NJ, 1984-96; owner, cons. Gasperini Graphics, Towaco, 1984—; art cons. Italico Pubs., Livingston, NJ, 1982-92. Mem. NJ Art Assn., NJ Italian-Am. Assn. (cons. 1982-92). Republican. Roman Catholic. Avocations: photography, painting, piano, crafts, unique and antique jewelry collector. Home and Office: 7 Frank St Mine Hill NJ 07083 E-mail: lisa.gasperini@hotmail.com.

GASPERONI, ELLEN JEAN LIAS, interior designer; b. Rural Valley, Pa.; d. Dale S. and Ruth (Harris) Lias; student Youngstown U., 1952-54, John Carrol U., 1953-54, Westminster Coll., 1951-52; grad. Am. Inst. Banking; m. Emil Gasperoni, May 28, 1955; children: Sam, Emil, Jean Ellen. Mem. Coeurde Coeur Heart Assn., Orlando Opera Guild, Orlando Symphony Guild. Mem. Jr. Bus. Women's Club (dir. 1962-64), Sweetwater Country Club (Longwood, Fla.); Lake Toxaway Golf and Country Club (N.C.). Presbyterian. Home: 1126 Brownshire Ct Longwood FL 32779-2209 also: 963 Cold Mountain Rd Lake Toxaway NC 28747-9630

GASQUE, DIANE PHILLIPS, mortgage manager, marketing executive; b. Madison, Wis., Mar. 31, 1954; d. Codie Odel and Ruth Elaine (Oimoen) Phillips.; m. Wyndham Henry Burriss, Feb. 5, 1977 (div. 1989); m. Allard Harrison Gasque, Nov. 14, 1992; 1 child, Folline Elaine Gasque. BA, Midlands Tech., Columbia, S.C. Cert. Notary S.C. With inventory control Oxford Industries, Columbia, S.C.; processing agent NCR, Columbia, S.C.; comml. loan officer S.C. Nat., Columbia, S.C.; personnel dir. Witten Sales, Columbia, S.C.; funding agt. Resource Bankshares Mortgage Group, 1995—, sr. specialist; CEO Gasque's Internet Mktg. Co., Inc. Mem.: Order of Confederate Rose. Republican. Presbyterian. Avocations: bowling, coin collecting/numismatics. Home: 3728 Linbrook Dr Columbia SC 29204-4438 Fax: (803) 741-3595. Office Phone: 803-462-8147. E-mail: dgasque@sc.rr.com.

GASSMAN, STEPHANIE LYNNE, artist; b. Cin., Oct. 30, 1949; m. Norman David Gassman, Jan. 24, 1975. Grad., Art Acad Cin., 1971. Graphic artist, illustrator Ala. Farm Bur., Montgomery, 1970-72; graphic artist, illustrator, photgrapher Mktg. Comm., Inc., Cin., 1972-73; graphic artist, illustrator U. Cin. Publs., 1973-74; art dir., illustrator U.S. Shoe Corp., Cin., 1975; part owner, buyer, store design, display, advertising Foot-Lites Shoe Stores, Cin., 1975—. Artist: photography exhbn. Cin. Art Acad. 1972, entered in many alumni art shows, winner of numerous awards since. Commd. paintings, pastels and sculptures for private collections, number over 100; corp. commns. include the following: lobby wall sculptures Blue Ash (Ohio) Bank Tower, 1988, Mitchell's Inc., Cin. 1989, Holly Hills, Calif., Ky, 1990, Cellular One, Inc., Mason, Ohio, 1991, Cin. Zoo Ctr. for Reprodn. of Endangered Wildlife, 1991, Million Air Inc. Lunken Airport, Cin., 1992, Queen City Sports Medicine and Rehab., Cin., 1992; Evendale (Ohio) Recreation Ctr., 3 wall sculptures: lobby, mural in activity room, 1993, Fin. and Credit Svcs. Group Divsn. of Fed. Dept. Stores, Mason, Ohio, lobby wall sculpture, Drake Ctr., Cin. Tree of Life, W. Pavilion, 1995, U. Cin. Sch. of Nursing and Health, Cin., wall sculpture, multi-purpose area, 1996, St. Elizabeth Med. Ctr., Edgewood, Ky. Tree of Life, Family Birth Ctr., 1996, Children's Hosp. Med. Ctr., Cin. oncology dept. wall sculpture, 1997, Entek IRD Internat., Milford, Ohio, lobby painting, Spectrum (Christ Hosp.-Beechmont), Clermont County Courthouse, Ohio, 1998; wall sculpture with graphic, main area, 1997, J.&W. Seligman & Co. Inc., N.Y.C., 1999, Avaya Comm. Highlands Ranch, Colo., 2001, Marion County Publ. Lib., Fla., 2003. Recipient Art scholarship Art Acad Cin., 1967-71, Wilder Traveling scholarship, 1972; 3 percetn for art nat. competition comm., U. Ctrl. Fla., 1998, Mont. State U., 2000, Fla. A&M U., 2004. Home: 4219 Miriana Way Sarasota FL 34233-1466 Office Phone: 941-341-0721. Personal E-mail: slgassman@aol.com.

GASSON, JUDITH C., research scientist; m. David Kronemyer; children: Andrew, Lauren. BS in microbiology, Colo. State Coll., 1973; PhD in physiology, U. Colo., 1979; postdoctoral, Salk Inst., 1979—82. With UCLA Jonsson Comprehensive Cancer Ctr., 1983—, dir., 1995—; prof. medicine and biol. chemistry UCLA Sch. Medicine; and co-dir. UCLA Inst. Stem Cell Biology and Medicine, 2005—. Pres. Jonsson Cancer Ctr. Found., 1995—. Recipient Scholar award, Leukemia Soc. Am., 1988, Stohlman Scholar award, 1991, Women of Sci. award, UCLA, 1991, Am. Soc. Clin. Investigation award, 1994. Office: UCLA Jonsson Comprehensive Cancer Ctr 8-684 Factor Bldg 10833 Le Conte Ave Box 951781 Los Angeles CA 90095-1781*

GAST, ALICE PETRY, academic administrator, chemical engineering educator; b. 1958; BS, U. So. Calif., 1980; MA, Princeton U., 1981; PhD, Princeto U., 1984. Asst. prof. dept. chem. engring. Stanford U., Calif., 1985—90, assoc. prof., 1991—95, assoc. prof., chem. by courtesy, 1992—95, prof., 1995—2001; affiliated faculty Stanford Synchotron Radiation Lab., 1994—2001; prof. chem. engring., Robert T. Haslam Chair MIT, 2001—06, v.p. rsch., assoc. provost, 2001—06; pres. Lehigh U., Bethlehem, Pa., 2006—. Chair ACS Div. Colloid and Surface Chemistry. Recipient Allan P. Colburn award, 1992, Camille and Henry Dreyfus Tchr. award, Stanford Univ., Alexander von Humboldt award, 1998. Fellow: NSF (Pres. Young Investigator award), Am. Acad. Arts and Sci.; mem.: NAS (mem. bd. chemical sci., tech. 1999—2001), AAAS (bd. mem. 2005—), NAE, Am. Chemical Soc. (Langmuir Lectr. 1995). Achievements include discovery of scientific fidings having direct impact and applications in biotech., nanotech., advanced materials; research in field supported by NSF, NASA. Office: Lehigh U Office of Pres 618 Broadhead Ave Bethlehem PA 18015*

GASTON, BARBARA LOVELL, elementary school educator; b. Villa Rica, Ga., Nov. 15, 1950; d. Claude and Jessie Lovell; m. Ronald Gene Gaston, Apr. 19, 1969; 1 child, Rick Geoffrey. MEd, West Ga. Coll., Carrollton, 1974. Cert. tchr. West Ga. Coll., 1974. 5th grade tchr. Villa Rica Mid. Sch., Ga., 1972—96; tchr. Bay Springs Mid. Sch., Villa Rica, 1996—2001, Villa Rica Elem. Sch., 2001—. Team leader Bay Springs Mid. Sch., Villa Rica, 1996—2001. Recipient Tchr. of Yr., Villa Rice Mid.Sch., Bay Springs Mid. Sch. Mem.: Ga. Assn. Educators. D-Conservative. Baptist. Office: Villa Rica Elementary School 314 Peachtree St Villa Rica GA 30180 Office Phone: 770-459-5762.

GASTON, GINA, newscaster; m. Mario Elie Gaston, 2000; children: Gaston, Glenn, Lauren. Grad., U. So. Calif. Anchor, reporter Sta. KLTV-TV, Tyler, Tex., Sta. WHTM-TV, Harrisburg, Pa., Sta. WTSP-TV, Tampa, Fla.; anchor Sta. KTRK-TV, Houston, 1992—99, reporter, anchor, 2001—; with MSNBC, NYC, 1999—2001. Recipient News Reporting award, AP Broadcasters. Mem.: Nat. Assn. Black Journalists. Office: Sta KTRK-TV 3310 Bissonnet Houston TX 77005

GASTON, MARILYN HUGHES, health facility administrator; b. Cin. children: Amy Marie, Damon Allen. AB in Zoology, Miami U., Oxford, Ohio, 1960; MD, U. Cin., 1964. Diplomate Am. Bd. Pediats. Intern Phila. Gen. Hosp., 1964—65; resident in pediat. Childrens Hosp. Med. Ctr., Cin., 1965—67, asst. dir. out-patient dept., 1967—68, Convalescent Hosp. for Children, Cin., 1968—69; med. dir. Lincoln Heights (Ohio) Health Ctr., 1969—72; dir. Sickle Cell screening clinic Cin. Health Dept., 1972—76; med. expert Nat. Heart, Lung & Blood Inst./NIH, Bethesda, 1976—79; commd. 2d lt. USPHS, 1979—89; dir. divsn. medicine Bur. Health Professions, Rockville, Md., 1989—90; dir., asst. surgeon gen., assoc. adminstr. for bureau Bur. Primary Health Care, Rockville, Md., 1990—2002; chief medical officer National Minority Health Month, 2002; co-dir. Gaston Porter Health Improvement Ctr., Potomac, Md., 2002—. Instr. pediats. U. Cin. Coll. Medicine, 1967—68, asst. clin. prof. divsn. cmty. pediats., 1968—70, asst. prof. pediats., 1970—76, assoc. prof. pediats., 1976—77; asst. clin. prof. pediats. Cin. Tech. Coll., 1974—76, Howard U. Coll. Medicine, 1978—91, Uniformed Svcs. U. the Health Scis., 1987—; attending pediatrician Children's Hosp. Med. Ctr., 1969—76, attending pediatrician and clinician, 1969—76, dir. med. staff, 1969—76; attending pediatrician Bethesda Hosp., 1974—76; pediatrician Hosp. Albert Schweitzer Deschapelles, Haiti, 1967; presenter, lectr., spkr. in field. Author: AL Bibliography: Comprehensive Sickle Cell Centers, 1977; co-author (with C.L. Calhoun), 1981; author: Management and Therapy of Sickle Cell Disease, 1984, 1988, Prime Time: The African American Woman's Complete Guide to Midlife Health and Wellness, 2003; author: (with others) Newborn Screening for Sickle Cell Disease and Other Hemoglobinopathies, 1989; contbr. articles to profl. jours. Co-chair Nat. Sickle Cell Dirs., 1974; med. advisor Sickle Cell Awareness Group, 1971—77, State Crippled Children's Svcs., 1975—77; bd. trustees Child Health Assn., 1974—77; bd. dirs. U. Cin. Found., 1989—, George Washington U. Life Scis., 1993—, U. Md. Ctr. for Minority Rsch. External Adv. Bd., 1993—, Komen Found. for Breast Cancer, Wellesley Ctr. for Women, Nat. Black Woman's Health Project. Named Woman of the Yr. in Medicine, Harriet Tubman Black Women's Dem., 1976; named one of Outstanding Young Women in Am., 1973, Outstanding Black Women in Cin., 1974; named to Ohio Women's Hall of Fame, 1990; recipient Phyllis Wheatley award, State of Ohio, 1975, Hildrus A. Poindexter award, Pub. Health Svcs., 1990, State of Ohio Gov.'s award, 1987, Disting. Alumnae award, U. Cin., 1989, Pub. Health award, D.C. Health Care for the Homless Project, Inc., Nathan Davis award, AMA. Mem.: APHA, AAAS, Inst. of Medicine/NAS, N.Y. Acad. Scis., Am. Med. Women's Assn., Am. Pediat. Soc., Am. Soc. Hematology, Nat. Med. Assn. (Living Legend award), Nat. Assn. Med. Minority Educators, Am. Acad. Pediats., Alpha Kappa Alpha, Sigma Delta Epsilon. Office: Gaston Porter Health Improvement Ctr 8612 Timber Hill Ln Potomac MD 20854

GATERS, DOROTHY, basketball coach; b. Miss. 1 child. Student, Crane Jr. Coll.; grad., DePaul Univ. Dean of students John Marshall Met. High Sch., Chgo., and head girls' basketball coach, 1974—. Named Nat. Coach of Yr., Women's Basketball Coaches Assn., 1999, Coach of Yr., Ill. Baskeball Coaches Assn. (seven times), Dist. 1 Coach of Yr. (22 times); named one of 100 Most Influential Women, Crain's Chicago Business Mag., 2004; named to Women's Basketball Hall of Fame, 2000, Women's Basketball Coaches Assn. Hall of Fame, Chicagoland Sports Hall of Fame, Chgo. Public League Coaches Assn. Hall of Fame, Ill. Basketball Coaches Hall of Fame, Ill. Girls Assn. Hall of Fame; recipient Career Achievement award, Pres. Bill Clinton. Achievements include having a 90% winning average, 19 city titles, seven state titles; appeared in series of Nike commercials. Office: John Marshall Met High Sch 3250 W Adams St Chicago IL 60624

GATES, JANICE SUE, management consultant, educator; d. Claude Richard and Eleanor Lucille Pontifex; m. Thomas Patrick Gates, Sept. 21, 1974; children: Timothy Matthew, Sarah Elizabeth. Bachelors, Western Ill. U., Macomb, 1973, MBA, 1992. Clk. steno II, Western Ill. U., Macomb, 1974; acctg. asst./farm records coord. Farm Credit Svcs., Macomb, Ill., 1974—79, v.p. acctg., 1979—89; records admissions officer Western Ill. U., Macomb, 1990—96; tchr. bus. Dallas City H.S., Ill., 1996—97; instr. dept. mgmt. Western Ill. U., Macomb, 1997—. Vol. McDonough Dist. Hosp., Macomb, Ill., 1971—2006; treas., Sunday sch. tchr. Aldersgate Free Meth. Ch., Macomb, Ill., 1972—96; Sunday sch. tchr., coll. encouragement Maple Ave. Christian Ch., Macomb, Ill., 1996—2006. Mem.: Am. Soc. for Quality, Phi Kappa Phi. Avocations: collecting moose, walking, travel. Office: Western Ill Univ 1 University Cir Macomb IL 61455 Office Phone: 309-298-1018.

GATES, JOANNE FERRY, counselor; b. N.Y.C., Oct. 7, 1924; d. Joseph Rutherford and Constance (Riker) Ferry; m. Richard Judson Gates, Sept. 7, 1946; children: Pamela, Cynthia, Suzanne, Rebecca. BA, Conn. Coll., 1946; MA in Counseling, St. Josephs Coll., 1981; DHL (hon.), Centenary Coll., 1987. Mem. exec. bd. Jr. Leaghe Hartford, Conn., 1957-64; bd. dirs. Inst. of Living, 1968-69; counselor Counseling Ctr./Hartford Coll. for Women, 1981-92; bd. dirs. Hartford Symphony, 1973-76, aux. v.p. nominating chmn., 1977; with Greater Hartford Campus Ministry, 1981—, West Hartford Pastoral Counseling Ctr., 1985. Sec. Smith Gates Corp., Farmington, Conn. Trustee Children's Mus. Hartford, 1970-73, West Hartford Sch. Music, 1962-83, Hartford Coll. for Women, U. Hartford, 1997—; trustee Centenary Coll. for Women, N.J., 1968-86, trustee emeritus, 1986—, hon. chmn. capital campaign; pres. Jodik Found., 1977—; deacon 1st Ch. of Christ Congregational, 1977-79, tchr. religious edn., 1952-72, pres. women's guild, 1969-70; co-chmn. music and arts festival Trinity Coll., 1975; vol. Hartford Hosp., 1949-55, Meals on Wheels, 1977-80; v.p. women's bd., trustee, corporator Hartford Sem., 1978—; mem. alumnae exec. bd. Capital fund drives Northfield (Mass.) Mt. Herman Sch.; class agt. ann. fund Conn. Coll. Mem. Conn. Coll. Alumnae Assn., Northfield Mt. Herman Sch. Alumnae Assn., Seed and Weed Carden Cub, Stonington Country Club, Musical of Hartford Club, Watch Hill Yacht Club, Town and County Club of Hartford. Republican. Home: 5 Hunters Rd Granby CT 06035-2635

GATES, KATHERINE A., accountant, writer; b. Birmingham, Ala., May 8, 1955; d. Charles James Gates and Jacquie Katherine Kirk. Attended, Ohio State U., Columbus, 1974—77. Registered rep. NASD. Acctg. and quality rev. prof. Western So. Life, Cin., 1978—. Author: Reflective Meditation, 2002, The Power of Your Thoughts, 2002, Love, Relationships and Reflective Meditation, 2004. Vol. WCVO-Christian Radio Sta., Columbus, Ohio, 1978—85. Mem.: Mensa (sec. 1979—85, 2003—04). Avocations: hiking, swimming, cross country skiing, scuba diving. Home: 1642 Brandon Ave Cincinnati OH 45230

GATES, LAURA LOVE, physical education educator; d. Carlton B. and Nancy A. Love; m. Al Gates, June 11, 1994; children: Thomas Mitchell, Caroline Love. BA, Coastal Carolina U., Conway, S.C., 1988; Interdisciplinary MA, U. S.C., Columbia, 1993. Cert. elem. tchr. S.C., 1988. Tchr. Lexington H.S., SC, 1988—96, Lexington Mid. Sch., SC, 1996—2001, White Knoll Elem., West Columbia, SC, 2001—. Scholar, Japan Fulbright Meml. Fund. Mem.: SC. Phys. Edn., Recreation and Dance (assoc.). Office: White Knoll Elementary School 132 White Knoll Way West Columbia SC 29170 Office Phone: 803-957-7700.

GATES, MARTINA MARIE, food products company executive; b. Mpls., Mar. 19, 1957; d. John Thomas and Colette Clara Gates. BSBA in Mktg. Mgmt. cum laude, U. St. Thomas, 1984, MBA in Mktg., 1987. Tchrs. asst. Mpls. Area Vocat. Tech. Inst., Mpls., 1978-79; sec., regional sales mgr. Internat. Multifoods, Mpls., 1979, sec. bakery mix, mktg. mgr., 1979-80, sec., v.p. sales and new bus. devel., 1980, customer svc. rep. regional accounts, 1980-81, customer svc. rep. nat. accounts, 1981-82, credit coordinator indsl. foods divsn., 1982-85, asst. credit mgr. consumer foods divsn., 1985, advt./sales promotion mgr. indsl. foods divsn., 1985-86, asst. credit mgr. fast food and restaurant divsn., 1986-87, dir. devel. USA and Can. franchise area, 1987-89; dir. franchise devel. FIRSTAFF, Inc., Mpls., 1989-90; dir. adminstrn. Robert Half Internat., Inc., Mpls., 1990-94; dir. client svcs. The NPD Group, Inc., Chgo., 1994—. Vol. seamstress Guthrie Theater Costume Shop, Mpls., 1975—; alumni mem. New Coll. Student Adv. Council St. Thomas, St. Paul, 1984—; vol. Mpls. Aquatennial, 1987. Mem. Streeterville Orgn. of Active Residents, Omicron Delta Epsilon. Avocations: golf, fine arts, needlecrafts, tennis, skiing.

GATES, MELINDA FRENCH, foundation administrator; b. Dallas, Aug. 15, 1964; m. Bill Gates, Jan. 1, 1994; 3 children. BS in Computer Sci. and Economics, Duke U., 1986, MBA, 1987. Gen. mgr. info. products Microsoft Corp., Redmond, Wash., 1987—96; co-founder Bill & Melinda Gates Found., Seattle, 2000—. Bd. dir. drugstore.com, The Wash. Post Co., 2004—. Bd. trustee Duke U., 1996—2003; former co-chair Wash. State Gov. Commn. on Early Learning. Named one of Most Powerful Women, Forbes mag., 2005-2006; named one of three Persons of Yr., Time mag., 2005, 100 Most Influential People, 2006. Mem.: Bilderberg Group. Roman Catholic. Office: Bill & Melinda Gates Found PO Box 23350 Seattle WA 98102*

GATES, MIMI GARDNER, museum director; b. Dayton, Ohio, July 30, 1942; BA, Stanford U.; MA in Oriental and Chinese studies, U. Iowa; PhD in art hist., Yale U. Curator Asian art dept. Yale U. Art Gallery, New Haven, 1975—87, dir., 1987—94; Illsley Ball Nordstrom dir. Seattle Art Mus., Wash., 1994—. Instr. Chinese art hist. and mus. studies Yale U.; faculty mem. U. Wash.; chair Fed. Indemnity panel The Nat. Endowment, 1999—2002. Contbr. Bones of Jade, Soul of Ice: The Flowering Plum in Chinese Art, 1985, co-curator Stories of Porcelain, From China to Europe, 2000, Ancient Sichuan: Treasures from a Lost Civilization, 2001. Bd. mem. Downtown Seattle Assn., YWCA. Mem.: Assn. Art Mus. Dirs. (past pres.). Office: Seattle Art Mus 100 University St Seattle WA 98101

GATES, PENELOPE KANDIS, obstetrical nurse; b. Lapeer, Mich., June 1, 1957; d. Russell Leroy Firmingham and Mildred Ann Porritt; m. William James Gates, Feb. 15, 1997; children: Adrianna Dave, William James III, Krystal Ann children: Jeremy Russell Firmingham. Diploma in Nursing, Grace Hosp. Sch. of Nursing, Detroit, 1978. Perinatal nurse, ANA. Staff nurse Lapeer Regional Med. Ctr., 1982—. Mem.: Mich. Nursing Assn. (chap. rep. to bd. dirs. 2004). Avocations: quilting, travel, scrapbooks. Home: 727 S Saginaw St Lapeer MI 48446 Office: Lapeer Regional Med Ctr 1375 N Main Lapeer MI 48446

GATES, ROBERTA PECORARO, nursing educator; b. Elmira, N.Y., May 22, 1948; d. Patrick George and Verle Elizabeth (Warriner) Pecoraro; m. William Franklin Gates III, May 20, 1972; 1 child, William Franklin IV. BSN, U. Ariz., 1970; MSN in Family Nursing, U. Ala., Huntsville, 1981. Cert. clin. specialist in med.-surg. nursing; bd. cert. Advanced practice nurse; cert. lactation counselor. Charge nurse St. Mary's Hosp. and Mental Health Ctr., Tucson, 1970-72; asst. head nurse Torrance (Calif.) Meml. Hosp., 1973-74; dist. nurse Sierra Sands Sch. Dist., Ridgecrest, Calif., 1974-76; instr. Albany (Ga.) Jr. Coll., 1978-80, John C. Calhoun Coll., Decatur, Ala., 1981-83; learning resources coord. Albany State Coll., 1984-85; asst. prof. Sinclair C.C., Dayton, Ohio, 1990-91, Darton Coll., Albany, 1986-89, 92—. Bd. dirs. Network Trust, Albany; cons. Cmty. Health Inst., Albany, 1993, Early County Bd. Edn., Blakely, Ga., 1994, Ga. State U., 1996—, Ga. Interagy. Coordinating Coun., 1997—; mem. Dist. Health Perinatal Bd., 2002-05; mem. Breastfeeding Task Force, 2002; cons. Project SCEIs, Ga. State U., 1996—. Author: A Model for Adolescent Health Promotion in the Dougherty County Community, 1993. Mem. Ga. Coun. Prevention of Child Abuse, Albany, 1988, 93; mem. Albany Mus. Art, 1993—; mem. Cmty. Ptnrs. Health Care Initiative, Dayton, 1990-91; bd. dirs. March of Dimes, Albany, 1986-89; mem. Albany-Dougherty 2000, DOCO Alternative Adv. Bd., State Consortium Early Intervention, Babies Can't Wait, 1995. Recipient NISOD award tchg. excellence, 2002; Named to Outstanding Young Women of Am., 1983. Mem. Ga. Higher Edn. Consortium, Sigma Theta Tau, Phi Kappa Phi. Avocations: gardening, walking, boating, reading. Office: Darton Coll 2400 Gillionville Rd Albany GA 31707-3023 E-mail: roberta.gates@darton.edu.

GATES, SUSAN INEZ, magazine publisher; b. San Francisco, Jan. 14, 1956; d. Milo Sedgewick and Anne (Phelger) Gates. BA in English, French magna cum laude (hon.), U. Colo., 1978; MS in Journalism, Columbia U., 1983. With GEO Mag., N.Y.C., 1978—79, New York Mag., N.Y.C., 1981—82, Ladd Assoc., N.Y.C., 1983—85, Mc Namee Cons., N.Y.C., NY, 1986—88; founding pub. BUZZ Mag., L.A., 1989—97; co chmn. Mind Over Media, L.A., 1997—. Mem.: Phi Beta Kappa. Personal E-mail: sigates@adelphia.net.

GATH, JEAN MARIE, architectural firm executive; BS, SUNY, New Paltz; M in City and Regional Planning, Pratt Inst. Prin. Hardy, Holzman, Pfeiffer Assocs. LLP, N.Y.C., 2001—03, ptnr., dir. planning, 2003—. Fellow: Inst. for Urban Design; mem.: Soc. for Coll. and Univ. Planning, Am. Planning Assn. Office: HHPA 19th Fl 902 Broadway New York NY 10010

GATHERCOAL, KATHLEEN KLEINER, psychology educator; b. Phila., Nov. 12, 1958; d. William Anton and Marjorie Anne (Fine) Kleiner; m. Roy Owen Gathercoal, Aug. 9, 1988; children, Glen William, Owen Daniel. AB, Franklin & Marshall Coll., Lancaster, Pa., 1981; MA, PhD, Case Western Res. U., 1985. Teaching asst. Franklin & Marshall Coll., 1980-81; rsch. asst. Case Western Res. U., Cleve., 1981-85; researcher U. Calif., Berkeley, 1985-87; asst. prof. psychology Ind. U.-Purdue U., Indpls., 1987-93; assoc. prof. psychology, chair dept. psychology George Fox U., Newberg, Oreg., 1993—, prof., dir. rsch. grad. dept. clin. psychology. Summer faculty fellow Ind. U., Bloomington, 1988. Contbr. articles to profl. jours. Evaluation mem. Campaign for Healthy Babies, Indpls., 1990-92; active Yamhill County Commn. on Children and Families. Nat. Inst. Child Health and Human Devel. predoctoral fellow, 1981-85; Case Western Res. U. grad. alumni grantee, 1984, Project Devel. Program Interdisciplinary grantee Ind. U.-Purdue U., 1990, Intercampus Rsch. Funds, Ind. U., 1991. Mem. APA, Western Psychol. Assn., Soc. Rsch. in Child Devel., Internat. Soc. Infant Studies, Psi Chi. Mem. Soc. Of Friends. Avocations: painting, hiking. Home: 2504 Haworth Ave Newberg OR 97132-1951 Office: George Fox U 414 N Meridian St Newberg OR 97132-2697 Office Phone: 503-554-2754. E-mail: kgathercoal@georgefox.edu.

GATI, TOBY T., international advisor; b. Bklyn., July 27, 1946; m. Charles Gati; 2 children; 3 stepchildren. BA, Pa. State U., 1967; MA in Russian Lit., Columbia U., 1970, M in Internat. Affairs, 1972. Rsch. asst, project dir., dep. v.p., v.p., sr. v.p. UN Assn. of the U.S.A., 1972-93; spl. asst. to the pres. for nat. security affairs Nat. Security Coun., sr. dir. for Russia, Ukraine and Eurasian States, 1993; asst. sec. for intelligence and rsch. Dept. State,

Washington, 1993-97; sr. internat. advisor Akin Gump Strauss Hauer & Feld LLP, Washington, 1997—. Commentator CNN Headline News and CNN; cons. ABC World Tonight, 1986, Ford Found., 1987-89, BDM Internat., 1989; mem. Coun. on Fgn Rels., Internat. Inst. for Strategic Studies. Office: Akin Gump Strauss Hauer & Feld LLP Ste 400 1333 New Hampshire Ave NW Washington DC 20036-1564 Home: 2123 O St NW Washington DC 20037-1008 Office Phone: 202-887-4422. Business E-Mail: tgati@akingump.com.

GATIPON, BETTY BECKER, medical educator, consultant; b. New Orleans, Sept. 8, 1931; d. Elmore Paul and Theresa Caroline (Sendker) Becker; m. William B. Gatipon, Nov. 22, 1952 (dec. 1986); children: Suzanne, Ann Gatipon Sved, Lynn Gatipon Pashley. BS magna cum laude, Ursuline Coll., New Orleans, 1952; MEd, La. State U., 1975, PhD, 1983. Tchr. Diocese of Baton Rouge, 1960-74, edn. cons. to sch. bd., 1974-78; dir. Right to Read program Capital Area Consortium/Washington Parish Sch. Bd., Franklington, La., 1978-80; dir. basic skills edn. Capital Area Consortium/Ascension Parish Sch. Bd., Donaldsonville, La., 1980-82; instr. Coll. Edn. La. State U., Baton Rouge, 1982-84; evaluation cons. La. Dept. Edn., Baton Rouge, 1984-85; dir. basic skills edn. Capital Area Basic Skills/East Feliciana Parish Sch. Bd., Clinton, La., 1985-86; program coord. La. Bd. Elem. and Secondary Edn., New Orleans, 1987-89; dir. divsn. of med. edn., dept. family medicine Sch. Medicine La. State U. Med. Ctr., New Orleans, 1989—. Evaluator East Feliciana Parish Schs., 1982-86; presenter math. methods workshops Ascension Parish Schs., 1980-84. Author curriculum materials, conf. papers; contbr. articles to edn. jours. Curatorial asst. La. State Mus., New Orleans, 1987—; soprano St. Louis Cathedral Concert Choir, New Orleans, 1988—; chmn. Symphony Store, New Orleans Symphony, 1990—; lector St. Francis Xavier Ch. Mem. Am. Ednl. Rsch. Assn., Assn. Am. Med. Colls., Midsouth Ednl. Rsch. Assn., La. Ednl. Rsch. Assn., Soc. Tchrs. Family Medicine, New Orleans Film and Video Buffs, Phi Kappa Phi, Phi Delta Kappa. Roman Catholic. Avocations: music, aerobic walking, classic movies. Office: La State U Med Ctr Sch Medicine 1542 Tulane Ave New Orleans LA 70112-2825 Home: 3513 Lake Kristin Dr Gretna LA 70056 Business E-Mail: betty.gatipon@cox.net.

GATISON, KAREN ANN, private school educator; b. Bridgeport, Conn., Apr. 1, 1953; d. Harold George and Teresa Mary Russer; children: Jonathan Isaiah, Denise Nicole. AS in Office Tech. and Mgmt., Ctrl. Fla. C.C., Ocala, 1992, AA in Bus. Mgmt., 1994; BA in Bus. Mgmt., St. Leo Coll., 1996. Tchr. Cambridge Acad., Ocala, Fla., 1996—. Bd. dirs. Help Agy. Forest, Silver Springs, Md. Mem.: NAFE, Nat. Bus. Edn. Assn., Nat. Women's History Project, Nat. Coun. Tchrs. Math., Phi Beta Lambda (profl. divsn. 1995—, historian 1993—94, Most Valuable Mem. 1994).

GATONS, ANNA-MARIE KILMADE, government official; b. Albany, N.Y., Oct. 21, 1946; d. Daniel Joseph Jr. and Tomasina (Fallone) Kilmade; m. Robert A. McCarthy, Sept. 3, 1967 (div. Apr. 1990); children: Daniel Kilmade McCarthy, Kevin Michael McCarthy; m. Paul K. Gatons, July 28, 1991. BA, Coll. of St. Rose, 1970. Staff support positions HUD, Washington, 1976-79, mgmt. analyst, 1979-81, staff budget analyst, 1981-83, chief of the budget and legislation coord. br., 1983-91, dir. exec. secretariat, 1992-95; dir. exec. secretariat for atty. gen. Dept. of Justice, Washington, 1995—2001; corr. mgmt. officer Office of Asst. Atty. Gen. for Adminstrn., Washington, 2001—02; dir., exec. sec. Immigration and Naturalization Svc., Washington, 2002—03; dir., exec. secretariat U.S. Immigration and Customs Enforcement, Dept. Homeland Security, Washington, 2003—. Mem. St. Rose Alumni Assn. Roman Catholic. Avocations: reading, needlecrafts, decorating. Home: 7705 Huntsman Blvd Springfield VA 22153-3912 Office: US Immigration and Customs Enforcement Exec Secrt Rm 7045 Dept of Homeland Sec 425 I St NW Washington DC 20530 Office Phone: 202-514-2829. E-mail: akilmade@aol.com.

GATRIA, AMERICA I, retired writer; b. Havana, Cuba, Mar. 6, 1943; US, 1968; d. Jose F Gatria and Pilar T Varela. B, Havana's Inst., 1962. Clk. Citibank, NYC, 1969—70, asst. mgr., 1970—72, mgr., 1972—80, asst. v.p., 1980—90, v.p., 1990—95, sr. v.p., 1995—98; exec. dir. Dime Savings Bank, NYC, 1998—2002. Author: (book) Kristaluaght, 2004. Named Woman of the Yr., Hispanic Assn. Human Civil Rights, 1979, Hispanic Bus. Person of the Yr., State of NY, 1991. Republican. Avocations: writing, antiques, photography.

GATTING, CARLENE J., lawyer; b. Hartford, Conn., Apr. 12, 1955; d. Charles W. and Jean A. (Murkowicz) G. BS, U. Conn., 1977; JD, Rutgers U., 1983. Counsel Skadden, Arps, Slate, Meagher & Flom, N.Y.C., 1987—2001. Mem. ABA. Address: 26 Cow Bay Edgartown MA 02539 E-mail: cjgatting@msn.com.

GATWOOD, DIANNE N., music educator; b. Evansville, Ind., Aug. 25, 1946; d. Herve Joseph Normand and Clyta Mae Hart; m. Dwight Dean Gatwood, Jr., Dec. 26, 1971; children: David Alan. MusB, Brescia Coll., 1967; MusM, Peabody Coll., 1969, M in Music Edn., 1969. Cert. tchr., Ky., Tenn., Ohio. Instr. U. Tenn., Martin, 1973-74; assoc. prof. Dyersburg (Tenn.) State C.C., 1973-87; asst. prof. Lambuth Coll., Jackson, Tenn., 1977-81, Bethel Coll., McKenzie, Tenn., 1979-80; instr. Weakley County Schs., Dresden, Tenn., 1985-86; assoc. prof. Union U., Jackson, 1988—; dir. fine arts U. Sch. Jackson, 1990-91. Condr. Dyersburg (Tenn.) Choral Soc., 1981-87; soloist, clinician Tenn. Gov.'s Sch. Humanities, Martin, 1993-97; pres. West Tenn. Music Tchrs. Assn., Jackson, 1994-95; dir. 1st United Meth. Ch. Handbell Choir, Huntingdon, Tex. Author: Singing: A Manual for Singers, 1990. Faculty advisor Sigma Alpha Iota, Union U., 1992-99. NDEA grad. fellow Peabody Coll., Nashville, 1967. Mem. Internat. Soc. for Music Edn., Nat. Assn. Tchrs. Singing, Music Educators Nat. Conf. (clinician so. divsn. conf. 1997), Music Tchrs. Nat. Assn., Martin Area Music Tchrs. Assn. (pres. 1995-97), So. Bapt. Ch. Music Conf., Kappa Delta Pi, Pi Kappa Lamda (charter). Avocations: walking, biking, raising plants. Home: 109 S Dodd Dr Martin TN 38237-2302 Office: Union Univ 1050 Union University Dr Jackson TN 38305-3697

GAUCHER, JANE MONTGOMERY, retail executive; b. Houston, Feb. 11, 1936; d. Theodore Richard and Gertrude Paine (Daly) Heyck; m. Donald Holman Gaucher, June 15, 1957 (dec.); children: Susan Heyck Merrill, Beverly Jane. AB cum laude, Brown U., Providence, 1957. Mgr. Bride and Groom Registry Berings, Houston, 1990-99; asst. mgr. Pavillon Christofle, Houston, 1999—2002; mktg. rep. dinnerRings, 2002—. Pres. Antique Study Group, Houston, 1974—75. Mem. Kinkaid Sch. Alumni Bd., Houston, 1995—98, Mus. So. History Bd., 2000—; bd. dirs. Jr. League Houston, 1963, sustaining bd., 1990—93; rec. sec. Mus. So. History Bd., 2004—. Avocations: tennis, running, golf, mah jongg, bridge. Home: 4631 Ivanhoe St Houston TX 77027-4709

GAUDE, EMILY CAMP, elementary school educator; b. Knoxville, Tenn., July 19, 1945; d. William Mallory and Gladys (Isbell) Camp; m. William Conner Gaude, Mar. 29, 1969; children: Matthew McMaster, Nathan Burton, Katheryn Camp. BS, U. Tenn., 1966. Tchr. 5th grade Chattanooga City Schs., 1966-68; tchr. 6th grade Knoxville City Schs., 1968-70, tchr. 1st grade, 1978-80, tchr. 2d grade, 1980-81, tchr. 6th grade, 1981-88; tchr. 2d grade Nashville Metro, 1970-72; tchr. 6th, 7th grades Knox County Schs., Knoxville, 1988—. Faculty assoc. Coll. Edn., U. Tenn., 1987—2003; mem. tchg. staff Alternative Ctr. Learning, 1988—2003; cons. Tenn. Dept. Edn., 1998—; mem. validation panel Nat. Bd. Certification, 1999; mem. Tenn. Benchmarking Com. for Math. Objectives, 2001—02, Tenn. State Dept. Validation Com., 2003; panel mem. ACCLAIM, 2004—05. Recipient Golden Apple award, Knoxville News-Sentinel, 1986, Career Ladder III award, State of Tenn. Dept. Edn., 1986, Presdl. award, 1999, Excellence in Tchg. Math. Presdl. award, Princeton U., 2000—01, Tenn. State Tchr. Yr., Aerospace Edn. Found., 2001; grantee, Math. Dept. Title II Knox County, 1990—91, Jr. League Knoxville, 1990—91; Martin Marietta fellow, Acad. Tchrs. Sci. and Math. Mem.: AAUW, Smoky Mountain Math. Educators Assn. (instr. workshop 1988), Nat. Coun. Tchrs. Math. (spkr. regional conf. 1990), Tenn. Assn. Mid. Schs., Knoxville C. of C. (mem. leadership edn. class 1990—91, elected mem. Leadership Class of '92, BEST award 1989—90), U. Tenn. Faculty Women's Club, Old North Knoxville Assn. Presbyterian. Avocations: needlecrafts, reading, cooking, music, scrapbooks. Home: 517 E Oklahoma Ave Knoxville TN 37917-5623 Office: Gresham Middle Sch 500 Gresham Rd Knoxville TN 37918-3216

GAUDET, LAURA LATTA, psychologist, educator; b. Boston, Aug. 24, 1950; d. William Braden and Beatrice Lillian (Thompson) G. BS in Spl. Edn., U. Tex., 1973; MEd, Antioch Coll., 1976; PhD, U. No. Colo., 1995. Cert. in ednl. adminstrn., critical incidence traumatologist Fla. State U., bd. cert. expert in traumatic stress Am. Assn. Critical Incident Stress Mgmt., bd. cert. expert in forensic traumatology Am. Assn. Critical Incident Stress Mgmt. Instr. U. No. Colo., Greeley, 1991-95; asst. prof. U. Wis., Platteville, 1995-96; coord. emergency svcs., therapist Panhandle Mental Health Ctr., Scottsbluff, Nebr., 1996-98; assoc. prof. psychology Chadron (Nebr.) State Coll., 1998—2003, chair dept. counseling, psychology and social work, 2003—. Cons. on traumatic brain injury, domestic violence. Rsch. grantee. Mem. APA (rsch. award), Brain Injury Assn. Nebr. (bd. dirs. 1998—). Office: Chadron State Coll 1000 Main St Chadron NE 69337-2667 Home: 321 Chapin St Chadron NE 69337-2425 Office Phone: 309-432-6332. E-mail: lgaudet@csc.edu.

GAUDIO, MAXINE DIANE, biofeedback therapist, stress management consultant; b. Stamford, Conn., Oct. 7, 1939; d. Robert Fridolin and Doris (Altstadter) Goodman; m. Arthur Sebastian Gaudio, Oct. 7, 1962; 1 child, Dante Sebastian. Ordained minister, 2002. Relaxation therapist The Biofeedback Clinic, New Canaan, Conn., 1970-73; chief EEG technologist St. Barnabas, Bronx, N.Y., 1973-75; biofeedback therapist Biofeedback Clinic, Stamford, Conn. and Winston-Salem, N.C., 1973—; clin. dir. Biofeedback Unltd. N.C., 1979—; clin. dir. Creative Mind Systems, Stamford, Conn., 1980—; tech. advisor Creative Mind Systems N.C., 1980-83; indsl. cons. major corps. U.S.A., 1976—; writer, creator stress video Hartley Prodns., Old Greenwich, Conn., 1984—; writer, creator, narrator Robert Gross Assocs., Stamford, Conn., 1984; spkr. in field. Author, narrator video: Stress, 1984, Your Secret Energy Source, 1984; writer, dir. audio/visual package Captain Mind; creator, producer Stress and Relaxation, 1986-87; author, narrator book and tapes: Creative Union, 1980; author: Land Within the Shadow, 1980. Exec. dir. Friends of Children, Darien, Conn., 1985-87; dir. spl. projects Victim Svcs. Agy., N.Y.C., spl. events 1988-91; dir. pub. info. and devel. Louise Wise Svcs., N.Y.C., 1992-93; founder, chair bd. Kids with Kids, N.Y.C., 1991—; bd. dirs. cons. Childhope, N.Y.C., 1987-89. Mem. Am. Fed Press Women, Am. Soc. EEG Technologsts, Biofeedback Soc. Am., Biofeedback Soc. N.C., Internat. Platform Assn., Internat. Reiki Alliance. Avocations: swimming; fencing; flying; metaphysics; astrology; piano. Club: Conn. Press. Home: 19H Weaver Hill St Greenwich CT 06831-5118 Personal E-mail: emax3@earthlink.net.

GAUFF, LISA, broadcast journalist; b. Seattle; d. Joseph F. and Patricia A. (Lee) G. BA in Comm., U. Wash., 1987; MA in Journalism and Pub. Affairs, Am. U., 1988. Pub. info. asst. King County Coun., Seattle, 1985-86; reporter Sta. KUOW-FM, Seattle, 1985-86; news anchor Sta. KCMU-FM, Seattle, 1986-87; TV field prodr. Group W/Newsfeed Network, Washington, 1988-89; anchor, reporter Capitol TV, Washington, 1989-90, Newschannel 8, Washington, 1991-93; prodr., writer Sta. WJLA-TV, Washington, 1990-91; weekend anchor Sta. WHTM-TV, Harrisburg, Pa., 1993-94; morning anchor Sta. WJW-TV, Cleve., 1994-97; traffic anchor Sta. KNX-AM, L.A., 1998—2001, pub. rels. cons., 2001—. Freelance reporter KCBS-TV, KABC-TV, UPN-TV, Fox TV, Sunworld, Satellite News, Media Gen., NPR Radio, Shadow Broadcasting, 1988-89; ind. video prodr., 1989-91. Host, editor TV documentary Coming to Terms, 1993. Bd. dirs. NE Ohio AAU Baseball Com., 1995-96; moderator Ohio Acad. Decathalon, Cleve., 1995, 96; vol. United Way, Cleve., 1995, 96; honorary chair Women's Ctr. Greater Cleve., 1995; celebrity spokesperson Cleve. Christian Home for Children, 1995. Recipient John Merriman award Writer's Guild Am., 1988, Appreciation cert. United Negro Coll. Fund, 1995, 96; named One of 20 Top Women in Media, Washington D.C. Tchrs. Assn., 1993. Mem. NATAS, AFTRA. Avocations: art history, skiing, quiz shows. Office: Sta KNX-AM 6121 W Sunset Blvd Los Angeles CA 90028-6423

GAUGER, MICHELE ROBERTA, photographer; b. Elkhorn, Wis., Feb. 28, 1949; d. Robert F. and Christiane J. (Guiffaut) Marszalek; m. Richard C. Gauger, May 3, 1969 (div.). Student, U. Wis., Superior, 1967-69, U. Wis., Whitewater, 1978-80, Winona Sch. Profl. Photography, Chgo., 1984-91; MA in Photography, 1994. Wedding photographer Fossum Studio, Elkhorn, 1973-78; owner Photography by Michele, Whitewater, 1978-81; pres., photographer, mgr. Michele Inc. Wis., Delavan, 1981—, Foxes Reg., 1987. Founder, instr. Whitewater Experience Sch., 1997—2006, Yucatan Experience Sch., 1997—2006; spkr., lectr. in field; pres. Michele Inc. of Wis. Contbr. articles to profl. jours.; exhibitions include Chinese Nat. Gallery, Beijing, 1987, 1988 (2d pl. award, 1988), 1989 (Bronze medal, 1989), 1991, 1994, 1995, 1996 (Bill Stockwell Lifetime Achievement award, 1995). Mem. Nat. Arbor Found., Nebr., 1984—. Named to Wis. Ct. Honor, 1991, 1996; recipient 1st pl. Wedding Photography award, Internat. Wedding Photography, 1983—84, 1987—89, 1991, 1996, 2s pl. award, 1985, 1996, Grand award, 1988. Mem.: N.Am. Hunters Assn., Winona Sch. Profl. Photography Alumni Assn., Wedding & Portrait Photo Internat. Photographers Assn. (Lifetime Achievement award 2003), Profl. Photographers Am. (Nat. Loan Collectional 1984, Epcot Exhibit 1996), Whitewater C. of C., Turtle Lake Sportsman Club (chmn. bd. dirs. 2001—03). Republican. Roman Catholic. Avocations: world travel, big game hunting, horseback riding, cooking. Office: Michele Inc PO Box 856 Delavan WI 53115 Home: 833 Racine St Delavan WI 53115 Office Phone: 262-728-9707.

GAULKE, MARY FLORENCE, retired library administrator; b. Johnson City, Tenn., Sept. 24, 1923; d. Gustus Thomas and Mary Belle (Bennett) Erickson; m. James Wymond Crowley, Dec. 1, 1939; 1 son, Grady Gaulke (name legally changed); m. 22nd, Bud Gaulke, sept. 1, 1945 (dec. Jan. 1978); m. 3rd, Richard Lewis McNaughton, Mar. 21, 1983 (div. 1995). BS in Home Econs., Oreg. State U., Corvallis, 1963; MS in L.S., U. Oreg., Eugene, 1968; Phd in Spl. Edn., 1970. Cert. std. pers. supr., std. handicapped learner, Oreg. Head dep. home econs. Riddle Sch. Dist., Oreg., 1963-66; libr., cons. Douglas County Intermediate Edn. Dist., Roseburg, Oreg., 1966-67; head resident, head counselor Prometheus Project So. Oreg. coll.ect, Ashland, summers 1966-68; supr. librs. Medford Sch. Dist., Oreg., 1970-73; instr. psychology So.Oreg. Coll., Ashland, 1970-73; libr. supr. Roseburg Sch. Dist., 1974-91; resident psychologist Black Oaks Boys Sch., Medford, 1970-75. Mem. Oreg. Gov.'s Coun. Librs., 1979. Author: Vo-Ed Course for Junior High, 1965; Library Handbook, 9167, Instructions for Preparation of Cards for All materials Cataloged for Libraries, 1971, Handbook for Training Library aides, 1972. Coord. Laubach Lit. Workshops for High Sch. Tutors, Medford, 1972. Fellow Internat. Biog. Assn. (life); mem. ALA, So Oreg. Libr. Fedn. (sec. 1971-73), Oreg. Libr. Assn., Pacific N.W. Libr. Assn., Am. Biog. Inst. (lifetime dep. gov. 1987—), Internat. Biog. Ctr. (hon., adv. coun. 1990), Delta Kappa Gamma (pres. 1980-82), Delta Kappa Gamma (pres. 1980-82), Phi Delta Kappa (historian, rsch. rep.). Democrat. Methodist. Office Phone: 210-213-8833. Personal E-mail: ggmum1@earthlink.net.

GAULT, JUDITH, piano educator; b. Chgo., Jan. 11, 1934; d. Ray and Marguerite Louise Adkins; m. Richard J. Gault, Dec. 18, 1955; children: Laura, Sarah, Thom, David. BM, Western Mich. U., 1956. Cert. Nat. Music Tchrs. Assn. Pvt. piano tchr., 1960—; pianist Buchanan (Mich.) Pub. Schs., 1970—; dir. organist Ministry of Music, Buchanan, 1970—; dir. corp. choir Tyler BlueNotes, Niles, Mich., 1975—; orchestra dir. Brandywine Schs., Niles, 1964-70; choral dir. Area Choir, Buchanan, 1987-97. Actress various musicals and plays, 1970-90; dir. various choirs and cantatas, Buchanan and Niles, Mich., 1968—; Piano recitals and planner of Monster Concerts, South Bend, Ind., 1960—; singer chior tours of Europe and Canegie Hall, N.Y., 1982-99. Chmn. Buchanan Fine Arts Coun., 1980; pres. South Bend Area Piano Tchrs. Assn., 1990—; officer South Bend Symphony Guild, 1980-90; mem. South Bend Art League, Niles League of Women Voters, 1980-90. Mem. Nat. Piano Guild, Nat. Federation Music Clubs. Republican. Presbyterian. Avocations: travel, tennis, racquet ball. E-mail: JNRGault@aol.com.

GAULTIERE, KRISTI SOUTHARD, psychotherapist; b. Vancouver, Wash., May 24, 1965; d. Fred William and Lois Elizabeth Southard; m. William James Gaultiere, June 13, 1986; children: David, Jennifer Briana. BA, Oral Roberts U., 1986; MA in Marriage, Family and Child Counseling, Azusa Pacific U., 1988; D in Psychology, Newport U., 1990. Lic. marriage, family and child counselor, Calif. Exec. asst. Hour of Power, Syndey, Australia, 1985, computer programming asst. Orange, Calif., 1986-89; dir. coll. youth Crystal Cathedral, Garden Grove, Calif., 1986-88; marriage family trainee South Coast Psychol. Ctr., Irvine, Calif., 1987-89; marriage family intern City Psychol. Group, Garden Grove, 1988-90; psychotherapist New Hope, Tustin, Calif., 1990—; co-owner christian website. Spkr. in field. Co-author: Mistaken Identity, 1987. Mem. Calif. Assn. Marriage and Family Therapists, Am. Assn. Christian Counselors. Avocations: spirituality, exercise, travel. Office Phone: 949-262-3699.

GAUMOND, LYNN E., elementary school educator; b. Meriden, Conn., July 15, 1953; d. Richard Drake and Jean (Hall) Anderson; m. Gary Williams Gaumond, June 28, 1975; children: Jeffrey Ross, Kara Marie. BS in Edn. magna cum laude, Plymouth (N.H.) State Coll., 1975; MEd summa cum laude, U. Hartford, 1978. Tchr. grade 6 Squadron Line Sch., Simsbury, Conn., 1975-84, tchr. grade 3, 1984-86, tchr. kindergarten, 1986-89; tchr. grade 1 Tootin Hills Sch., West Simsbury, Conn., 1989—2000. Adj. prof. U. Hartford, 2002-; tchr. in residence bur. program and tchr. evaluation Conn. State Dept. Edn., 2000-2001, U. Hartford Magnet Sch., West Hartford, Grades 1, 2001-2003; logical math. essentialist, 2003-; cons. math program Primary Math. Series, Scholastic Book Pub., 1992-93; cons. math. manipulative project LEGO/DACTA, Enfield, Conn., 1990-91; tchr. PIMMS math recovery, 2002-. Contbg. writer/editor math program: Math Place, 1993-94; contbg. writer: CSDE Tchg. Handbook Portfolio. Mem. faculty, portfolio benchmarking, trainer, scorer, leader CSDE elem. edn., 1997-; trainer Ind. State Tchr.'s Portfolio, 2001, 2002; instr. CSDE Numeracy Acad., 1998-2000; com. mem. troop 177 Boy Scouts Am., Canton, Conn., 1992; coun. mem. Girl Scouts U.S., Canton, 1991—, leader troop 828, Canton, 1991—; mem. PTO, Canton Pub. Schs., 1985—; mem. Concerned Citizens for Canton, 1992—; bd. dirs. Canton Youth for Environ. Awareness, 1994—. Recipient Presdl. Award for Excellence in Sci. and Math. Teaching, NSF, 1993, state awardee, 1992, 93; Assoc. Tchrs. of Math. in Conn. grantee, 1993; semifinalist Conn. Tchr. of Yr., 2003, CREC Tchr. of Yr., 2003. Fellow Acad. for Edn. in Math., Sci. and Tech.; mem. NEA, ASCD, Conn. Edn. Assn., Simsbury Edn. Assn., Nat. Coun. Tchrs. Math., Assoc. Tchrs. of Math. in New Eng., Assoc. Tchrs. Math. in Conn., Coun. of Presdl. Awardees in Math., Soc. of Elem. Presdl. Awardees, Coun. for Elem. Sci. Internat., Nat. Sci. Tchrs. Assn. Democrat. Avocation: gardening. Home: 18 High Hill Rd Canton CT 06019-2225 Office: U Hartford Magnet Sch 196 Bloomfield Ave West Hartford CT 06117

GAUNT, KAREN KREIDER, lawyer; b. Cin., Aug. 14, 1971; BA, Denison U., 1993; JD, U. Cin. Coll. Law, 1997. Bar: Ohio 1997, US Ct. Internat. Trade 1999, US Dist. Ct. Southern Dist. Ohio 1999, US Ct. of Appeals Sixth Cir. 2003, US Dist. Ct. Eastern Dist. Mich. 2003. Ptnr. Keating Muething & Klekamp PLL, Cin. Named one of Ohio's Rising Stars, Super Lawyers, 2005, 2006; named to America's Leading Bus. Lawyers, Chambers USA, 2006. Mem.: Internat. Trademark Assn., Ohio State Bar Assn., Cin. Bar Assn. Office: Keating Muething & Klekamp PLL One E Fourth St Ste 1400 Cincinnati OH 45202 Office Phone: 513-579-6400. Office Fax: 513-579-6457.*

GAUNT, MARIANNE I., university librarian; BA, Montclair State U.; MLS, Drexel U. Rsch. libr. E. I. Dupont de Nemours Co., Wilmington, Del.; head Serials Dept. Brown U. Librs.; on-line reference coord. Rutgers U. Librs., NJ, circulation libr., dir. Humanities and Social Sci. Librs., assoc. univ. libr. rsch. and undergrad. svcs., acting univ. libr., univ. libr., 1997—. Contbr. articles to profl. jours. Mem.: NJ Libr. Assn. Office: Rutgers U Librs 169 College Ave New Brunswick NJ 08901-1163 Office Phone: 732-932-7505. E-mail: gaunt@rci.rutgers.edu.*

GAUNTNER, HEIDI LYNN, chemistry educator; b. Columbus, Ind., Aug. 23, 1963; d. Walter Phillip III and Marlene Sonia (Ames) Hallstein; m. Alan Thomas Gauntner, May 28, 1988; 1 child, Ethan Alan. BS in Geology, Kent State U., OH, 1987, BS in Edn., 1990, MS in Secondary Sci., 2000. Cert. tchr. Ohio, 2001. Tchr. Parma City Schs., Ohio, 1994—95, Hudson City Schs., Ohio, 1995—. Owner, chief instr. Isshinryu Karate Acad., Cuyahoga Falls, Ohio, 1990—. Avocation: Karate. Office: Hudson City Schs 2500 Hudson Aurora Rd Hudson OH 44236 Home: 60 Shawnee Dr Kent OH 44240-6000

GAUVEY, SUSAN KATHRYN, judge; b. Van Wert, Ohio, Mar. 1, 1948; d. Richard David and Asta Walburga (Frericks) G.; m. David E. Kern, May 10, 1975; children: Megan E. Gauvey-Kern, Kevin C. Gauvey-Kern, Elizabeth H. Gauvey-Kern. Student, Georgetown U., 1968-69; BA cum laude Polit. Sci., Rosary Coll, River Forest, Ill., 1970; JD, Northwestern U., 1973; postgrad. Mental Hygiene, Johns Hopkins U., 1976-77. Bar: Wash. 1974, Md. 1975. Law clerk to fed. dist. ct. judge We. Dist. Ct., Seattle, 1973-74; staff atty. Mental Health Law Project Legal Aid Bur., Balt., 1975-77, co-chief Mental Health Law Project, 1977-79; asst. atty. gen. Dept. Health and Mental Hygiene Office of Atty. Gen., Balt., 1979-81, asst. atty. gen. Civil Divsn., 1981-86, prin. counsel trial litigation, 1984-86; with litigation divsn. Venable, Baetjer and Howard L.L.P., Balt., 1986-96; magistrate judge U.S. Dist. Ct. for Md., Balt., 1996—. Contbr. articles to profl. jours. Chair bd. dirs. Marian House for Women. Mem. Nat. Assn. Women Judges, Wranglers Law Club, Lawyers' Roundtable, Sgt.'s Inn Network. Democrat. Office: US Courthouse 101 W Lombard St Baltimore MD 21201-2605 Office Phone: 410-962-4953. Business E-Mail: mdd_skgchambers@mdd.uscourts.gov.

GAVER, FRANCES ROUSE, lawyer; b. Lexington, Ky., Mar. 13, 1929; d. Colvin P. Rouse and Elizabeth Turner Sympson; m. Donald Paul Gaver, Jan. 24, 1953; children: Elizabeth, Donald, William. BA, Wellesley Coll., 1950; MA, U. Pitts., 1968; JD, Monterey (Calif.) Coll. of Law, 1986. Bar: Calif. 1986, U.S. Dist. Ct. (no. dist.) Calif. 1986; cert. specialist in probate, estate planing and trust law, Calif. Assoc. Hoge, Fenton, Jones & Appel, Monterey, 1986-93, Fenton & Keller, Monterey, 1993-97; ptnr. Johnson, Gaver & Leach, Monterey, 1997-99, of counsel, 2000—. Bd. dirs. Carmel (Calif.) Unified Sch. Dist., 1973-81, Monterey Coll. of Law, 1991-97, Legal Svcs. for Srs., Seaside, Calif., 1994-2000; bd. dirs. Monterey Peninsula Coll. Found., 2000-06. Mem. Monterey County Bar Assn. Avocations: playing recorder, swimming. Office: Johnson Gaver & Leach LLP 2801 Monterey Salinas Hwy Monterey CA 93940-6401 Business E-Mail: fgaver@jgllp.com.

GAVIN, MARY ELLEN, marketing professional, consultant; b. Chgo. d. Francis Edward and Agnes Mary (Rolder) Des Enfants; m. William Francis Gavin; children: Michael James, Terence Francis. MBA, U. Palmers Green, Eng., 1999. Lic. pvt. investigator. Analyst A.C. Nielsen, Chgo.; asst. br. mgr. Borg-Warner Fin. Svc., Chgo.; asst. leasing mgr. Borg-Warner Leasing, Chgo., midwest leasing mgr.; v.p. Gen. Equipment Leasing, Chgo.; leasing mgr. Pitney Bowes Credit Corp., Chgo.; ind. rep. Gen. Elec. Mobile Radio & Tele., Chgo.; pres. Gavin Communications, Annapolis, Md.; owner Gavin & Assocs., Chantilly, Va. Adult edn. tchr. Fairfax County, 1996—, Nova C.C., 2000—. Author: And Still We Celebrate, 2001, We Celebrate the Macabre, 2002, We Celebrate Food for the Soul, 2004; editor: Post War Letter Messages From the Heart, 1997. Mem.: Sisters in Crime, The Writers of Chantilly (founder), Nat. Assn. Writers, Women in Mgmt., Gulf Coast Writers, Internat. Women's Writing Guild, Associated Writing Program George Mason Univ., Nat. Writers Assn. Republican. Roman Catholic. Home: 8250 Vineyard Ave Apt 84 Rancho Cucamonga CA 91730-8707 E-mail: maryellengavin@yahoo.com.

GAVIN, MARY JANE, retired medical/surgical nurse; b. Prairie Du Chien, Wis., Sept. 1, 1941; d. Frank Grant and Mary Elizabeth Wolf; m. Alfred William Gavin, Nov. 9, 1963; children: Catherine Heidi Elizabeth, Carl Alfred Eric. Student, North Cen. Coll., Naperville, Ill., 1959-61; BS, RN, U. Wis., 1964; postgrad., Deepmuscle Tng. Ltd., 1980; postgrad. in deep muscle therapy. RN, Wis. Staff nurse U. Wis. Hosps., Madison; nurse home response VA, Milw.; ret., 2006. Unit chair Badger Girls State, 1991-2005; active Wis. Am. Legion Aux.; task force for handicapped Eastside Wis. Evang. Luth. Ch., Madison, 1993 U. Wis. scholar. Mem.: Monona Grove Am. Legion Aux. (pres. Unit 429 1990—2005). Achievements include writer material that made a federal law null and void.

GAVRIL, JEAN (JEAN VAN LEEUWEN), writer; b. Glen Ridge, NJ, Dec. 26, 1937; d. Cornelius Van Leeuwen and Dorothy Elizabeth Charlton; m. Bruce David Gavril, July 7, 1968; children: David, Elizabeth BA, Syracuse U., N.Y., 1959. Asst. editor TV Guide Mag., N.Y.C., 1959—60; libr. promotion asst. Abelard-Schuman, N.Y.C., 1960—63; from asst. editor to assoc. editor Random House, N.Y.C., 1963—68; assoc. editor Viking Press, N.Y.C., 1968—69; sr. editor Dial Press, N.Y.C., 1970—73; freelance writer, 1973—. Author: (children's books) Timothy's Flower, 1967, One Day in Summer, 1969, The Great Cheese Conspiracy, 1969, I Was a 98-Pound Duckling, 1972, Too Hot for Ice Cream, 1974, The Great Christmas Kidnapping Caper, 1975, Seems Like This Road Goes On Forever, 1979, Tales of Oliver Pig, 1979, More Tales of Oliver Pig, 1981, The Great Rescue Operation, 1982, Amanda Pig and her Big Brother Oliver, 1982, Benjy and the Power of Zingies, 1982, Benjy in Business, 1983, Tales of Amanda Pig, 1983, Benjy the Football Hero, 1985, More Tales of Amanda Pig, 1985, Oliver, Amanda, and Grandmother Pig, 1985, Dear Mom, You're Ruining My Life, 1989, Oliver and Amanda's Christmas, 1989, Oliver Pig at School, 1990, Amanda Pig on Her Own, 1991, Going West, 1991, The Great Summer Camp Catastrophe, 1992, Oliver and Amanda's Halloween, 1992, Emma Bean, 1993, Two Girls in Sister Dresses, 1994, Bound for Oregon, 1994, Across the Wild Dark Sea, 1995, Oliver and Amanda and the Big Snow, 1995, Blue Sky Butterfly, 1996, Touch the Sky Summer, 1997, Amanda Pig, 1997, A Fourth of July on the Plains, 1997, Amanda Pig and Her Best Friend Lollipop, 1998, The Tickle Stories, 1998, Growing Ideas, 1998, Nothing Here But Trees, 1998, The Srange Adventures of Blue Dog, 1999, Hannah of Fairfield, 1999, Hannah's Helping Hands, 1999, Hannah's Winter of Hope, 2000, Oliver and Albert: Friends Forever, 2000, Sorry, 2001, "Wait for me!" Said Maggie Mcgee, 2001, Lucy Was There, 2002, The Amazing Air Balloon, 2003, Amanda Pig and the Awful Scary Monster, 2003, The Great Googlestein Museum Mystery, 2003, Oliver the Mighty Pig, 2004, Cabin on Trouble Creek, 2004, Amanda Pig and the Really Hot Day, 2005 (Theodor Seuss Geisel Honor Book, 2006), Benny and Beautiful Baby Delilah, 2006, Oliver Pig and the Best Fort Ever, 2006 Avocations: gardening, antiques, music, tennis. Personal E-mail: jvgavril@att.net.

GAVRILOFF, KATRINA, writer; b. Erie, Pa., Aug. 5, 1978; d. Perry Richard and Susan Loraine Gavriloff. BA in English, Pa. State U., 2000. Asst. support technician Am. Online, Inc., Reston, Va., 2000—01; sr. tech. writer Am. Online, Inc. Systems Ops., Reston, Va., 2001—. Tool com., tool documentation, aided in tng. new writers Am. Online, Inc., Multi-departmental, Reston, Va., 2002—03; spkr. Pa. State U. Mem.: Soc. Tech. Communication. Avocations: travel, reading, theater. Personal E-mail: wutangaler@aol.com.

GAWKOWSKI, SPRING PAGE, social sciences educator, social worker; m. Harry Gawkowski; 1 child, Mary. MSW, Barry U., Miami Shores, Fla. LCSW Fla. Psychotherapist Banyan Group, West Palm Beach, Fla., 1995—; prof. Palm Beach C.C., Lake Worth, Fla., 2000—06. Pres. Advanced Psychoednl. Svcs., Wellington, Fla., 2005—. Author: (textbook) Introduction to Counseling and Interviewing. Bus. partnership com. PBCC Human Svcs., Lake Worth, Fla., 2004—06. Mem.: NASW, Phi Kappa Phi.

GAWRONSKI, ELIZABETH ANN, retired army officer, artist; b. Panama City, Fla., Oct. 11, 1943; d. Myron Harvey Belyeu Sr. and Irene (Sewell) Belyeu Coates; m. Kenneth E. Gawronski Sr., Sept. 16, 1972; 1 child, Kenneth Edward Jr. BS in Edn., Fla. State U., 1965; MA in Edn., U. Ala., 1974, EdS, 1975. Commd. 2d lt. USAR, 1965, advanced through grades to lt. col., 1986; comdr. Women's Army Corps, Aberdeen Proving Ground, Md.; asst. to chief-of-staff U.S. Army Missile Command, Redstone Arsenal, Ala.; officer-in-charge, instr. Women's Army Corps Sch., Ft. McClellan, Ala.; ops. officer 3392d USAR Sch., Huntsville, Ala.; occupl. splty. instr. 1163d USAR Sch., Bronx, NY; pers. mgmt. staff Adjutant Gen. Corps; staff officer LOGEX, Ft. Lee, Va., pers. staff officer Camp Pickett, Va.; postal staff officer Mil. Postal Svc. Agy., Alexandria, Va.; insp. gen. U.S. Army Missile Sch., Redstone Arsenal, sr. staff officer, various positions, 1988-94; comdg. officer 184th IMA Detachment, Redstone Arsenal, 1994-96; ret., 1996. Exhibitions include Signature 2000, Signature 2001, Limelight Series, 2002, Monte Sano Art Show, 2003, Carnegie Visual Arts Ctr., Decatur, Ala., 2004, Atrium Gallery, 2005, Huntsville-Madison County Pub. Libr., 2005, Artist Colony Internat. Online Exhbn., Gulf Breeze, Fla., 2006. Vol. Huntsville City Schs., 1988—96, Boy Scouts Am., Huntsville, 1993—95, Huntsville Art League, 1997. Decorated Meritorious Svc. medal; recipient Best in Acrylics, Fayetteville-Lincoln County Art Show, 2003. Mem.: Art League Madison, Watercolor Soc. Ala., Internat. Soc. Exptl. Artists, Res. Officers' Assn. (life), Phi Delta Kappa, Kappa Delta Pi. Methodist. Home: 8044 Lauderdale Rd SW Huntsville AL 35802-2916

GAY, AGNOLIA BEATRICE, actress, educator; d. Othel William Henry Gay and Georgia M. Hudson, Thomas Edward Hudson (Stepfather) and Betty Gay (Stepmother); 1 child, Chy'Na Beatrice Nellon. BFA, Ark. State U., Jonesboro, 1982. Actress, co-founder ACTS III: Drama Ensemble, Little Rock, 1993—; actress, founder An Intimate Exposure African Am. Artists, 2004—. Actor: (plays) An Evolution of Music. Mem.: Delta Sigma Theta. Office: Little Rock Central High School 1500 S Park Street Little Rock AR 72202 Office Phone: 501-447-1471. E-mail: agnolia.gay@lrsd.org.

GAY, FAITH E., lawyer, educator; BA with honors, Duke U., 1982; JD, Northwestern U., 1986. Bar: N.Y. 1987, U.S. Dist. Ct. (so. and ea. dists.) N.Y. 1987, U.S. Ct. Appeals (2d cir.) 1991, Tex. 1997, Ill. 1997, Fla. 1997, U.S. Ct. Appeals (8th cir.) 1999. Supervising atty., dep. chief civil rights divsn. U.S. Atty.'s Office for Ea. Dist. N.Y., N.Y.C., also dep. chief spl. prosecutions unit; ptnr. Sidley & Austin, N.Y.C. Instr. seminar complex criminal litigation Fordham U. Sch. Law, 1992. Angier B. Duke meml. scholar Duke U.

GAYDOS, MARY, writer, researcher, actress; b. Marblehead, Ohio, Feb. 13, 1936; d. George Joseph Gaydos and Dorothy Vargosick Gaydos Saunders. BFA, Ohio U., 1958; MLS, Queens Coll., 1972. Narrator various art programs, cable TV, 1992—; host Ballyhoo of Broadway exhbn. honoring the Broadway Musical, N.Y.C, 2004. Actress off-broadway, cinema, TV, 1958-70; writer, moderator (radio series) Fgn. Film Industry, 1970-71; prodr. Milliken Fabric's Fashion Show, 1978; book rev. critic MD Med. Newsmag., N.Y.C., 1973-76; stage mgr. Women in the Performing Arts Festival at Lincoln Ctr., 1977; narrator (film) The Art and Architecture of Belgrade and Kosovo (honoree World Lang. Inst., N.Y.C. 2001); narrator dedication of Nikola Tesla Meml. sponsored by Hons. R. Giuliani and G. Pataki, N.Y.C., 2001.; host of Broadway's 47th Ann. Drama Desk awards, 2002, 48th Ann. Drama Desk awards, 2003, 26th Ann. Medieval Festival, Cloisters Mus./Met. Mus. Art, 2003, Internat. POW-WOW welcoming media from 70 countries to N.Y.C., 2005. Fundraiser for non-profit orgns. including Skowhegan Sch. of Art and Design, The Spanish Inst., Legal Aid Soc., Nat. Energy Found., Archdiocese of N.Y.'s Inner-City Scholarship Fund, 1979-87. Named honoree, World Lang. Inst., 2001; recipient Mayor's Merit award, Hon. Ed T. Koch, N.Y.C., 1989. Mem. Actors Equity Assn., Screen Actors Guild, C.G. Jung Found., Am. Teilhard Assn. for the Future of Man, Am. Soc. of Psychical Rsch. Home: 101 W 85th St Apt 6-12 New York NY 10024-4487 E-mail: marygaydos@hotmail.com.

GAYLE, HELENE D., pediatrician, public health service officer; b. Buffalo; BS in Psychology cum laude, Columbia U., 1976; MD, U. Pa., 1981; MPH, John Hopkins U., 1981. Diplomate Am. Bd. Pediats. Intern then resident in pediats. Children's Hosp. Nat. Med. Ctr., Washington, 1981-84; epidemic intelligence svc. officer br. epidemiology divsn. nutrition Ctr. Health Promotion and Edn., 1984-86; preventive medicine resident divsn. evaluation and rsch. office internat. health program Ctrs. Disease Control Ga. State Dept. Health, 1986-87; med. epidemiologist pediats. and family studies sect., AIDS program Ctrs. Disease Control, 1987-89, acting spl. asst. minority HIV policy coordination office dep. dir. (HIV), 1988-89, asst. chief sci., 1989-90, chief internat. activity divsn. HIV/AIDS Atlanta, 1990-92, assoc. dir. Washington, 1994-96; agy. AIDS coord., chief divsn. HIV-AIDS Agy. Intl. Devel., Washington, 1992-94; dir. Nat. Ctr. HIV, Sexually Transmitted Diseases and Tb Prevention Ctrs. Disease Control, Atlanta, 1995—2001; dir. HIV, Tb, reproductive health Bill and Melinda Gates Found., 2001—06; pres., CEO Cooperative for Assistance and Relief Everywhere, Inc. (Care USA), Atlanta, 2006—. Lectr. Sch. Medicine Morehouse U., 1987—92; lectr. masters in pub. health program Emory U., Atlanta, 1989, 90, clin. asst. prof. cmty. medicine, 1996—; cons. WHO, others; bd. dir. Africa Am. inst. Global Health Coun., Internat. Ctr. Rsch. in Women, Inst. Medicine, Coun. Fgn. Rels.; adj. assoc. prof. Sch. Pub. Health U. Wash. Contbr. articles to profl. jours. Adm. USPHS. Merit scholar, 1981; recipient Henrietta and Jacob Lowenburg prize, 1981, Model Excellence award Colgate-Palmolive Co., 1992, Medal of Excellence Columbia U., 1996, Sec. Award Disting. Svc. US Dept. Health and Human Svcs., 1999, Disting. Svc. Award Nat. Med. Fellowships, 2003, Disting. Alumnus Award, John Hopkins U. Sch. Pub. Health; named Barnard Woman of Achievement Barnard Coll., 2001, Mem. AAS, AMA, APHA, Am. Coll. Epidemiology, Internat. AIDS Soc. (pres.), Soc. Against AIDS in Africa, Inst. Medicine, Coun. Fgn. Rels. Office: CARE USA 151 Ellis St NE Atlanta GA 30303

GAYNOR, ELLEN ROSE, hematologist; b. Chgo., 1948; MD, U. Wis., 1978. Cert. Am. Bd. Internal Medicine, 1982, in Med. Oncology 1985, in Hematology 1986. Intern Loyola U. Med. Ctr., Maywood, Ill., 1978—79, resident, 1979—82, fellow, oncology, 1980—81; fellow, hematology and oncology U. Chgo., 1982—84; assoc. prof. Loyola U., Stritch Sch. Medicine, Maywood, Ill. Office: Loyola Univ Health Sys 2160 S First Ave Maywood IL 60153

GAYNOR, LEAH, radio personality, commentator; b. Irvington, N.J., 1931; d. Jack and Sophia Kamish; m. Robert Merrill, Mar. 27, 1954 (dec.); children: Michael David (dec.), Lisa Heidi (dec.), Tracy Lynn (dec.). AA, Miami Dade C.C., 1970; BA, postgrad., Fla. Internat. U., 1975—. Owner, operator Lee Gaynor Assocs., pub. rels., Miami, Fla., 1970-72; exec. dir. Ft. Lauderdale (Fla.) Jaycees, 1970-71; host, interview program Sta. WGMA, Hollywood, Fla., 1971-73, stas. WWOK and WIGL-FM, Fla., 1973-79; occupational specialist Lindsey Hopkins Edn. Ctr. Dade County Pub. Schs., publicity-pub. rels., Miami, Fla., 1971-91; ednl. specialist Office Vocat., Adult, Career and Cmty. Edn. Dade County Pub. Schs., 1991-94; broadcaster talk show sta. WEDR-RM, 1983-93. Host, prodr. weekly half-hour pub. svc. talk program, The Leah Gaynor Show, 1985-94. Mem. Citizens Adv. Com. Career and Vocat. Edn., 1973; mem. adv. com. North Miami Beach High Sch., 1977-79; mem. publicity Com. Ctr. Fine Arts, Mus. Sci.; mem. Coalition Cmty. Edn.; bd. dirs. Alternative Programs, Inc. Mem. Women in Commn., Am. Women in Radio and TV (dir. publicity Goldcoast chpt. 1974-76), Alliance Career Edn. (publicity chmn.). Democrat. Personal E-mail: LKGaynor@bellsouth.net.

GAYOSKI, KATHLEEN MARY, counselor, minister; d. Thomas and Katherine Ida Gayoski. MA in Psychology and Religion, Andover Newton Theol. Sch., Mass., 2000; DEdn., Elfinstone Coll., 2004. Cert. holistic health counselor; RN Mass., cert. epidemiologist, CDC; ordained min. Universal Life Ch., 1997; cert. Reiki master tchr. Crystal Crossing Holistic Resource Ctr., Tapas accupressure technique Tapas Assn., Mass., Am. Soc. Alternative Therapists C.O.R.E. Counselor Inst. Transformational Studies, batter's treatment counselor EMERGE/Mass., Nat. Crisis Responder, Debriefer and Chaplain Nat. Office of Victims Assistance, traumatic bereavement specialist, 1999, and death notification specialist MADD, 1971, trainor Nat. Orgn. Victims Assistance, 2006, energy medicine specialist 2000, scientist and rsch. specialist in medicinal essential iol therapy. Psychiat. RN specialist Mass. Dept. Mental Health, Taunton, 1971—72; RN, health prevention specialist, alcohol rehab. counselor South Miami (Fla.) Hosp., 1972—73; state epidemiologist, RN Mass. Dept. Pub. Health, Boston, 1973—97; coord., traumatic bereavement specialist and trainer Project REACH, Ctr. for Health and Human Svcs., Inc, New Bedford, Mass., 1997—2002; ordained min., crisis chaplain Tender Spirit Ministries, Rochester, Mass., 1997—; cert. holistic health counselor, profl. lectr. and educator Eagle Feathers Healing Arts Garden, Wareham, Mass., 2002—; min. Old North Rochester Congl. Ch., 2005—. Poet, author, clay artist Eagle Feathers Healing Arts Garden, 2002—; poet, author, artist Tender Spirit Ministries, 1997—; author Mass. Med. Assn., Boston, 1995. Com. mem. Rochester Meml. Sch., 1982—88; commr. Rochester Pk. Dept., 1988—91; chair South Ea. Ednl. Collaborative, New Bedford; publicity dir. Emmaus Cmty., East Freetown, Mass., 1985—88; chaplain, counselor World AIDS Day; min. North Rochester Congregational Ch., 2004—. Named to Wall of Tolerance, 2003; recipient cert. appreciation, Bur. Family and Cmty. Health, Mass. Dept. Pub. Health, 1997, Silent No More cert. appreciation, U.S. Dept. Justice, 1999, Cert. of Achievement, MADD, 1999, cert. recognition for spiritual care for Egyptian Air Crash, ARC, 1999, letter appreciation for svc. response, Can. Consulate, 1999, cert. recognition for svc. to edn., ORPEA for crisis intervention and bereavement counseling, Old Rochester Regional Sch. Dist., 2000, cert. recognition, Sen. Edward M. Kennedy, U.S. Senate, Washington, 2001. Mem.: Nat. Office Victims Assistance Crisis Response Team, Greater New Bedford Trauma Response Team, Am. Soc. Alternative Therapists, Sisters of Mercy of the Ams. (assoc.; poet, author, nat. lectr.). Avocations: travel, writing, reading, expressive clay figures, hiking. Office: Eagle Feathers Healing Arts Garden 191 Main St Wareham MA 02571 Office Phone: 508-245-2860. E-mail: efhealingarts@aol.com.

GAYVORONSKY, LUDMILA, artist, educator; b. Kharkov, Ukraine, Dec. 4, 1939; arrived in U.S., 1980; d. Pavel Nikanorovich Nikitin and m. Eva Lazarevna Skibityanskaya; m. Alexander Vitalievich Eremenko, June 9, 1996; 1 child, Gleb. Diploma in Meteorology, Hydrometeorol. Inst., 1961; PhD in Geography, World Meteorol. Ctr., 1965; BFA, Acad. Fine Art Moscow, 1968. Engr.-climatologist Climatol. Obs., Samara, Russia, 1961—62; engr.-agrometeorologist World Meteorol. Ctr., Moscow, 1965—66; editor Inst. Tech. Info., Moscow, 1966—69, chief editor, 1969—79; instr. fine art Sts. Cosmas & Damian Human Svcs. Ctr., S.I., NY, 1983—93; prof. fine art Lebanon (NH) Coll., 1997—. Artist stage art constrn. for Childrens Week, Lincoln Ctr., N.Y.C., 1990, wall mural for Sinergia, Inc., N.Y.C., 1992-93, wall mural Town of Newport, N.H., 1998, backdrop panel Dicken's Fair, 1997. Named acad. knight Acad. Verbano, Italy, 1999; recipient Gold medal Festival of Art, Moscow, 1968, jurors prize distinction Spring Art Competition, Moscow, 1968, medal of honor, Ukrainian Inst. Am., N.Y.C., 1988, ABI, 2003, cert. of appreciation USCG, Govrs. Island, NY, 1989, Jurors prize distinction Sunapee Art Fair, N.H., 1999. Mem. World Phenomenological Inst. (artist-in-residence 1997—), N.H. Art Assn., Acad. Fine Arts, Acad. Verbano (Italy). Mem. Orthodox Ch. Of Am. Home: 26 Church St Newport NH 03773-1908 Personal E-mail: ludmila.gayvoronsky@verizon.net.

GAZAWAY, BARBARA ANN, music educator, art educator; b. Lebanon, Pa., Jan. 7, 1942; d. Ammon Mark Brubaker and Margaret (Lesher) Dierwechter; m. Hal Prentiss Gazaway; children: Farideh Dunford, Ramin Dunford, Ammon Dunford, Lavada Kahumoku, Rene Dunford. BS in Music Edn., West Chester State U., 1963; cert. in elem. edn., Brigham Young U., 1979. Cert. Multiple Subject Tchg. Credential 1984, type A tchg. cert. 1990. Elem. music tchr. Oxford (Pa.) Sch. Dist., 1963—65; elem. classroom tchr. Lebanon (Pa.) Sch. Dist., 1965—67; elem. music tchr. U.S. Dept. Edn., European Area, Bad Kreuznach, Germany, 1968—70, elem. classroom tchr. Darmstadt, Germany, 1972—74, elem. music tchr. Alconbury, England, 1974—75; instrumental music instr. Lebanon (Pa.) Cath. H.S., 1976—78, h.s. music tchr., 1976—77; music instr. Brigham Young U., Provo, Utah, 1978—79; elem. vocal music tchr. Bennett Valley Union, Santa Rosa, Calif., 1987—89; elem. vocal music instr. Anchorage Sch. Dist., 1990—2000; pvt. music studio practice, 2001—. Owner, dir. Millcreek Nursery Sch., Newmanstown, 1975—76; instr. Homestay Am. Japanese Exch. Program, Santa Rosa, Calif., 1987; show pianist Marquee Theater, Santa Rosa, Calif., 1985—85; governess, Stuttgart, Germany, 1967—68; opermädchen Internat. Student Info. Svc., Mautern, Austria, 1967; singer, waitress The Harbor View, Martha's Vineyard Is., Mass., 1964; singer, baker, pianist The Inn, Mt Gretna, Pa., 1963; active Experiment in Internat. Living Home Stay Program, Switzerland, 1962; gasthaus worker Am. Student Info. Svc., Feldkirch, Austria, 1965; pres. Internat. Reading Assn. Campus Chpt. Singer: Sister Quartet, 1956—64. Family Coun. sec. Anchorage Pioneer Home, 2001—02; sec. Alpine Condominium Assn., Anchorage, 2001—02; chair Beautification Com., Anchorage, 2001—02; co-tchr. Divorce Care for Kids, Anchorage, 2004—; co-chair County Rep. Com., Santa Rosa, 1984—84; co-chair mission com. Trinity Christian Reformed Ch., Anchorage, 2001—02, co-facilitator divorce recovery program, 1999—, co-facilitator adult divorce care program, 1999—. Mem.: NEA, Internat. Reading Assn. (pres.), Music Educators Nat. Conv. Avocations: travel, hiking, reading, gardening, cooking. Home and Studio: 8620 Boundary Ave Anchorage AK 99504 Office Phone: 907-338-8111. Personal E-mail: gazaway_barbara@hotmail.com.

GAZDAG, GAIL ELIZABETH, psychology associate; b. Rockville Center, N.Y., Mar. 4, 1950; d. Russell Carl and Claire Elizabeth (Robinson) G.; m. Jerry Michael Plummer, Apr. 14, 1990. BA in Psychology, L.I. U., 1972, MPS, 1979; PhD in Psychology, Vanderbilt U., 1994. Psychology asst. Manhattan Devel. Ctr., N.Y.C., 1972—78, Suffolk Devel. Ctr., Melville, 1978—82; psychology assoc. Rosewood Ctr., Balt., 1994—2002; assoc. psychologist Pilgrim Psychiat. Ctr., West Brentwood, NY, 2002—. Contbr. articles to profl. jours. Scholar, Comml. Travelers, 1979, Nat. Inst. Child Health and Human Devel., 1983—87. Home: 515 Devonshire Rd Hauppauge NY 11788-4528 Office: Pilgrim Psychiat Ctr B25 998 Crooked Hill Rd West Brentwood NY 11717

GEAR, KATHLEEN O'NEAL, archaeologist, writer; b. Tulare, Calif., Oct. 29, 1954; d. Harold Arthur and Wanda Lillie O'Neal; m. W. Michael Gear, Oct. 1, 1982. BA cum laude, Calif. State U., Bakersfield, 1976; MA summa cum laude, Calif. State U., Chico, 1979. Sr. mus. preparator Mus. Cultural Hist., L.A., 1980; city historian City of Cheyenne, Wyo., 1980-81; state historian U.S. Dept. Interior, Cheyenne, 1981-82, archeologist, 1982-86; buffalo ranch mgr. Red Canyon Ranch, Thermopolis, Wyo., 1992—; author TOR Books, DAW Books, Warner Books, N.Y.C., 1986—; prin. investigator Wind River Arch. Co., Thermopolis, 1990—. Bd. dirs. U. Press Colo., Boulder. Author: (historical) Sand in the Wind, 1990, This Widowed Land, 1993, Thin Moon and Cold Mist, 1995, (sci. fiction) An Abyss of Light, 1990, Treasure of Light, 1990, Redemption of Light, 1991, (booklet) Cheyenne and the Development of Wyoming, 1981; author (with W. Michael Gear): People of the Wolf, 1990, People of the Fire, 1991, People of the Earth, 1992, People of the River, 1992, People of the Sea, 1993, People of the Lakes, 1994, People of the Lightning, 1995, People of the Silence, 1996, People of the Mist, 1997, People of the Masks, 1998, The Visitant, 1999, The Summoning God, 2000, Dark Inheritance, 2001, Bone Walker, 2001, Raising Abel, 2002, People of the Owl, 2002, People of The Raven, 2003; contbr. articles to various mags. Scholar Am. Bible Study, 1975-76, Calif. State scholar Calif. State U., 1972-76. Mem. Nat. Bison Assn., Am. Assn. Physical Anthropologists, Am. Anthro. Assn., Soc. Hist. Archaeology, We. Writers Am., Sci. Fiction Writers of Am. Avocations: hunting, fishing, reading, camping, hiking. Home and Office: PO Box 1329 Thermopolis WY 82443-1329

GEARY, ALLYSON, secondary school educator; Tchr. secondary geography Ctrl. High Sch., Independence, Oreg. Recipient Disting. Tchr. K-12 award Nat. Coun. for Geog. Edn., 1992.

GEARY, HILARY R., society editor; d. J. Jeffrey Roche and Sidney B. Wood; m. John W. Geary II, Apr. 28, 1973 (dec. 1995); children: Alfred, John; m. Peter Green, 2000 (div. 2002); m. Wilbur Ross, Oct. 9, 2004. Student, Finch Coll. Society editor Quest Mag. Mem.: Southampton Rose Soc. Office: QUEST Media 920 Third Ave 6th Fl New York NY 10022 Office Phone: 646-840-3404 ext. 106. Office Fax: 646-840-3408.

GEARY, LAURA ALMA, mathematics professor; b. Rapid City, SD, Sept. 4, 1951; d. Richard James and Elda Pearl Mahoney; m. Patrick Michael Geary; children: Benjamin Richard, Deanna Kathleen Richardson, Lisa Michelle. MS in Math., SD Sch. Mines & Tech., Rapid City, 1982—84. Math. tchr. Stevens HS, Rapid City, 1975—78; math tchr. Nat. Coll. Bus., Rapid City, 1979—81; prof. math. SD Sch. Mines & Tech., 1984—. Mentor/advisor dept. math & computer sci. SD Sch. Mines & Tech., 1984—. Recipient Outstanding Mentor award, SD Sch. Mines & Tech., 2004, Outstanding Prof. Tchg. & Motivating Students award, 2006. Avocations: piano, gardening, reading. Office: SD Sch Mines & Tech 501 E St Joseph St Rapid City SD 57702 Business E-Mail: laura.geary@sdsmt.edu.

GEARY, MARIE JOSEPHINE, art association administrator; b. Boston, Dec. 1, 1933; d. Vincent and Maryanne (DeAngelo) Bianco; m. John Francis Geary, Oct. 11, 1959; 1 child, John Francis Jr. Grad., Medford H.S., 1951. Registrar grad./postgrad. div. Tufts U. Sch. Dental Medicine, Boston, 1951-60; reporter, arts editor Chelmsford (Mass.) Newsweekly, 1970-82; owner, mgr. Village Sq. Art Gallery, Chelmsford, 1976-80; founder, owner A Way With Words, Chelmsford, 1980—; founder, dir. Eastcoast Quilters Alliance, Westford, Mass., 1988—. Mktg. cons. Westford Regency Inn, 1991; cons. to arts orgns. for seminar planning, curator exhibits, 1999—. Contbr. articles to profl. mags. Pub. rels. dir. New England Quilt Mus., Lowell, 1986-88; founder, pres. Chelmsford Art Soc., 1970-75; founder, bd. dirs. Chelmsford Cultural Coun., 1980-84; founder, dir. pub. rels. Chelmsford Crafters, Inc., 1976-80; publicity dir. Chelmsford Town 4th of July Celebration, 1971-74; founder Women in Bus. Conf., 1994. Mem. Am. Quilting Soc., Chelmsford Quilters (pres. 1985-89, 99-2003), New Eng. Quilters Guild (Compass editor 1985-88), Chelmsford Book Discussion Soc., Quilters Connection (Quiltations editor 1992-93, v.p. 1994-95, pres. 1995-96), Middlesex Women's Network, Women in Bus. (formed 1993, coord. 1st conf. 1994), Enterprising Women. Republican. Roman Catholic. Avocations: art, antiques, reading, economics, marketing trends. Home: 38 Amble Rd Chelmsford MA 01824-1968 Office: Eastcoast Quilters Alliance PO Box 711 Westford MA 01886-0021 E-mail: eqaquilter@aol.com.

GEBBIE, KRISTINE MOORE, medical educator; b. Sioux City, Iowa, June 26, 1943; d. Thomas Carson and Gladys Irene (Stewart) Moore; m. Lester N. Wright; children: Anna, Sharon, Eric. BSN, St. Olaf Coll., 1965; MSN, UCLA, 1968; DPH, U. Mich., 1995. Project dir. USPHS Tng. Grant, St. Louis, 1972—77; coord. nursing St. Louis U., 1974—76, asst. dir. nursing, 1976—78, clin. prof., 1977—78; adminstr. Oreg. Health Div., Portland, 1978—89; sec. Wash. State Dept. Health, Olympia, 1989—93; coord. Nat. AIDS Policy, Washington, 1993—94; assoc. prof. Sch. Nursing Columbia U., 1994—; assoc. prof. Oreg. Health Scis. U. Portland, 1980—90. Chair secretarial panel on evaluation of epidemiologic rsch. activities U.S. Dept. Energy, 1989—90; mem. Presdl. Commn. on Human Imunodeficiency Virus Epidemic, 1987—88. Author (with Deloughery and Neuman): Consultation and Community Orgn., 1971; author: (with Deloughery) Political Dynamics: Impact on Nurses, 1975; author: (with Scheer) Creative Teaching in Clinical Nursing, 1976. Bd. dirs. Lusth. Family Svcs. Oreg. and S.W. Wash., 1979—84, Oreg. Psychoanalytic Found.1, 1983—87. Recipient Disting. Alumna award, St. Olaf Coll., 1979; scholar Disting. scholar, Am. Nurses Found., 1989. Fellow: Am. Acad. Nursing; mem.: Am. Soc. Pub. Adminstrn. (Adminstrn. award II 1983), N.Am. Nursing Diagnosis Assn. (treas. 1983—84), Inst. Medicine, Am. Pub. Health Assn. (exec. bd.), Assn. State and Territorial Health Ofcls. (pres. 1984—85, exec. com. 1980—87, McCormick award 1988). Office: Columbia U Sch Nursing 630 W 168th St New York NY 10032-3702 Business E-Mail: KMG24@columbia.edu.

GEBHARD, LAVERNE ELIZABETH, retired accounting educator; b. Milw., Aug. 30, 1936; d. Frank and Helen Gebhard. BS, Marquette U., 1958, MBA, 1964. CPA, cert. internal auditor, cert. cost analyst, cert. mgmt. acct. Internal auditor Fed. Res. Bank Chgo., 1958-60; gen. acct. City Products, 1960-61; tchr. bus. Milw. Pub. Schs., 1961-65; from instr. to lectr. to sr. lectr. U. Wis., Milw., 1966-93; cons. New Berlin, Wis., 1993—. CMA exam. adminstr. ICMA-Milw. site, Montvale, N.J., 1984-97. Contbr. articles to profl. jours. Vol. advisor Milw. Hist. Soc., La Farge Learning Ctr., others. Recipient Citizen Ambassador award People to People, Inc., 1991—. Mem. Inst. Internal Auditors, Wis. Inst. CPAs (ch. bd. dirs. 1984—, mem. numerous coms., cons. 1984-86), Inst. Mgmt. Accts., Beta Gamma Sigma, Delta Pi Epsilon, Beta Alpha Psi (faculty advisor, founder). Avocations: travel, reading, tennis, continuing education, volunteer work. Home: 12685 W Bobwood Rd New Berlin WI 53151-6975 E-mail: gebhard3@netzero.com.

GEBO, EMMA MARIE JOKI, education educator; b. Billings, Mont., Jan. 1, 1945; d. Waino August and Vera H. (Luoma) Joki; m. David Ray Gebo, Sept. 12, 1964; children: Lorri D., Paul A., Robyn J. BS in Home Econs., Mont. State U., 1966; MEd, U. Mont., 1971; PhD Vocat. Edn. Adminstrn., Colo. State U., 1988. Cert. secondary tchr., Idaho. Substitute tchr. various cities, Idaho, Mont., 1967-74; adult instr. Fashion Fabrics, Pocatello, Idaho, 1975-76; instr. clothing and tchr. edn. Idaho State U., Pocatello, 1975-80, chmn. dept. tchr. edn., 1980-92, prof., 1992-93, 94—. Pres., COO Crafts, Inc.; sec.-treas., COO Super Save Drug, Inc.; mem. Idaho Coun. on Vocat. Edn., 1992-1996, pres., 1995-1996; mem. Ben Franklin Retail Stores, Inc. Nat. Adv. Coun., 1995—, Southeast Idaho Pvt. Industry Coun., 1995-1996, chmn. sch. to work com.; chmn. Idaho State U. Coll. Bus. Entrepreneurship/Small Bus. Devel. Adv. Coun.; mem. Idaho Workforce Devel. Coun., 1996-2004, Idaho Econ. Advisors Coun., 2004—; bd. mem. Assn. Crafts and Creative Industries, 2001-2003, Idaho Dietetics Licensure, 2004—; bd. dirs. Crafts and Hobby Assn., 2004—, sec., 2005—. Editor: Idaho Adult Living/Teen Living, 1986, Idaho Cooperative Vocational Education, 1984, 86, Curriculum Guides for Home Economics, 1987. Named Outstanding Young Women of Am., 1978-81, Pocatello Disting. Young Woman, Jaycettes, 1981; Am. Vocat. Assn. fellow, Ellen S. Richards fellow, 1987; recipient: Person Yr., Idaho State Jour. Bus., 2002, Lifetime Svc. award, C. of C., 2002. Mem. Idaho Home Econs. Assn. (pres. 1983-85, Disting. Home Economist award 1985), Home Econs. Edn. Assn. (sec. 1989-91, publs. bd. 1986-87), Nat. Assn. Tchr. Educators Vocat. Home Econs. (newsletter editor 1986, sec. 1989-90, publs. bd. 1992—), Am. Assn. of Family and Consumes Scis. (nat. leader award 1995), Am. Home Econs. Assn. (by-laws com. 1983-85), Am. Vocat. Assn., Nat. Future Homemakers Am. (hon. Idaho chpt., tchr. task force 1984-88), Greater Pocatello C. of C. (pres. 1993-94), Pocatello Chiefs (Athena award 1995). Methodist. Avocations: whitewater rafting, skiing, backpacking, reading. Home: 2201 N Whitney Rd Pocatello ID 83204-7266

GEBO, SUSAN CLAIRE, consulting nutritionist; b. Bristol, Conn., June 22, 1954; d. Ernest Edward and Lena Clara (Julian) G.; m. Joseph Louis Vasile, Oct. 10, 1987. BS, Cornell U., 1976; MPH, U. Mich., 1980. Registered dietitian. Pub. health nutritionist Navajo & Apache County Health Dept., Holbrook and St. Johns, Ariz., 1976-77; coord., WIC nutritionist Miss. State Bd. Health, Tupelo, 1977-78; asst. state WIC nutrition coord. Conn. Dept. Health Svcs., Hartford, 1978-79; nutritionist Cmty. Health Svcs., Hartford, 1981-84; pvt. practice West Hartford, Conn., 1983—; faculty, nutritionist U. Conn. Family Medicine Residency Program, Hartford, 1985—; nutritionist Wesleyan U., Student Health Svcs., Middletown, Conn., 1988—. Adj. faculty U. Hartford, West Hartford, 1981-88, So. Conn. State U., New Haven, 1985-2002, Albertus Magnus Coll., 1991-2000, St. Joseph Coll., West Hartford, 1992—, Manchester C.C., 1994—; fellow Nat. Nutrition Consortium, Washington, 1980. Author: What's Left to Eat?, 1992; writer (video) The Diet Interview: A Guide for Paraprofessionals, 1980, featured in video Culinary Hearts Kitchen Course, Am. Heart Assn., 1988, panelist (PBS-TV spl.) Women's Hearts at Risk, 1996, featured nutrition expert (PBS-TV series) 3 episodes America's Walking, 2003; featured nutrition expert: Women's Health Series (Conn. Pub. TV), 2005. Bd. dirs. Am. Heart Assn., Hartford, chmn. program com. greater Hartford br., 1989-91; mem. com. State Communications, 1991-94, media spokesperson, 1991— (Outstanding program award 1990, Outstanding HeartGuide Spokeswoman 1990, Time, Feeling, and Focus award, 1992). Mem. AAUP, Am. Pub. Health Assn., Am. Dietetic Assn., Conn. Dietetic Assn. (co-chmn. pub. rels. com. 1991-93, mem. media spokesperson com. 1993-98, Registered Dietitian of Yr., 1994, del. 1996-99). Avocations: walking, photography, gardening. Office: 854 Farmington Ave West Hartford CT 06119-1587 Office Phone: 860-232-5415. E-mail: sgebo1@prodigy.net.

GECA, MONIQUE, psychologist; b. Lublin, Poland, Apr. 23, 1965; arrived in US, 1991; d. Henryk Geca and Zofia Geca-Wiraszka. Grad. in histopathology, Med. Acad., Lublin, 1987; BA in Theology and Bibl. Langs., Multnomah Bible Coll., 1994; Ma in Marriage and Family Therapy, George Fox U., 1996, MA in Clin. Psychology, 2001, PsyD in Clin. Psychology, 2003. Histopathology technician Jewish Hosp. Oncology, Lublin, 1987—89; mental health therapist Woodland Pk. Hosp., Portland, 1995; family therapist Pacific Gateway Hosp., Portland, 1995—96; mental health therapist Juvenile Det. Donald E. Long, Portland, 1996—98; mental health specialist Oreg. State Prison, Portland, 1998; mental health cons. Multnomah County Jail, Portland, 1998—2002; psychologist Patton (Calif). State Hosp., 2002—04, Napa (Calif.) State Hosp., 2004—. Recipient Minority award, George Fox U., 1997. Mem.: APA, Calif. Assn. Treatment Sex Offenders. Avocations: outdoor photography, hiking, jogging, reading, classical music. Office: Napa State Hosp 2600 Vallejo Hwy Napa CA Office Phone: 707-253-5071. Fax: 510-523-4137. Personal E-mail: mgeca@pacifier.com.

GECHTOFF, SONIA, artist; b. Phila., Sept. 25, 1926; d. Leonid and Etya (Freedman) G.; children: Susannah Kelly, Miles Kelly. BFA, Phila. Mus. Sch. Art, 1950. Instr. painting, drawing Calif. Sch. Fine Art, 1957-58; adj. asst. prof. art NYU, 1960—70; lectr. Queens Coll., N.Y.C., 1970-74; assoc. prof. U. N.Mex., 1974-75. Artist-in-residence Skidmore Coll., summers 1988, 89, 90, Adelphi U., N.Y., 1991, 93; vis. artist Chgo. Art Inst., 1989; instr. master classes Nat. Acad. Fine Art, NYC, 2000—. One-woman shows include DeYoung Mus., San Francisco, 1957, Ferus Gallery, L.A., 19l57, 59, Poindexter Gallery, N.Y.C., 1959, 60, Cortella Gallery, N.Y.C., 1976, 78, Gruenebaum Gallery, N.Y.C., 1979, 80, 82, 83, 85, 87, Witkin Gallery, N.Y.C., 1984, 89, Kraushaar Gallery, N.Y.C., 1990, 92, 95, Fine Arts Gallery, San Francisco, 1991, Adelphi U., 1993, Skidmore Coll., N.Y., 1995, Harrison Mus. Art, Utah, 1996, Kraushaar Gallery, NYC, 1998; group shows include Guggeneim Mus., N.Y.C., 1954, San Francisco Mus. Art, 1953-58, Brussels World's Fair, 1958, 1st Paris Biennale, 1959, Whitney Mus., N.Y.C., 1959, 60, Sao Paulo Biennale, 1961, Nat. Gallery Am. Art Smithsonian Instn., 1976, Mus. Modern Art, N.Y.C., 1977, Aldrich Mus. Contemporary Art, Ridgefield, Conn., 1981, Bennington Coll., Vt., 1985, Weatherspoon Gallery, Greensboro, 1987, Gruenebaum Gallery, 1987, The Butler Inst. of Am. Art: 56th Nat. Mid-Yr. Exhbn., Youngstown, Ohio, 1992, Santa Cruz (Calif.) Mus., 1993, Laguna Art Mus., Laguna Beach, Calif., 1996, San Francisco Mus. Modern Art, 1996, Worcester Mus. Art, Mass., 2001, San Jose Mus. Art, Calif., 2003, Whitney Mus., NYC, 2005, Pollock-Krasner House, East Hampton, NY, 2006, Menil Collection, Houston, 2006; represented in permanent collections, San Francisco Mus. Modern Art, Guggenheim Mus., Mus. Modern Art, Met. Mus., N.Y.C., Balt. Mus. Art, Harrison Mus. Art at Utah State U., Worcester (Mass.) Art Mus., Laguna (Calif.) Art Mus., Whitney Mus. Am. Art, NYC, San Jose Mus., Menil Collection, Houston; also pvt. and corp. collections. Ford Found. fellow Tamarind Inst., L.A., 1963; recipient Purchase awards San Francisco Mus. Art, 1955-59; grantee Esther and Adolph Gottlieb Found., 1987, Mid. Atlantic NEA, 1988, Pollock-Krasner Found., 1994, 2002, Richard Florsheim Art Fund, 1994. Mem. Nat. Acad. Design.

GEDDES, ANN, talent agency director; b. Evanston, Ill., Nov. 25, 1943; d. Robert Allen and Sara Elizabeth (Bonham) Geddes; 1 child, Peter Allen. Profl. model, Chgo., 1963—67; owner, dir. Geddes Agy., Chgo., 1968—83, co-owner Chgo., L.A., 1983—. Cons. Am. Nat. Bank, 1969, 1976—77, Walter Heller Corp., 1977, Worldbook Child Craft Internat., 1978. Office: 8430 Santa Monica Blvd # 200 West Hollywood CA 90069

GEDEON, LUCINDA HEYEL, museum director; b. Port Chester, NY, Oct. 13, 1947; d. Philip H. and Isabel (Oldham) H.; m. Francis A. Sprout, Feb. 8, 1987. BA, Calif. State U., Long Beach, 1978; MA, UCLA, 1981, PhD, 1990. Asst. curator Grunwald Ctr. UCLA, 1978-81, asst. dir. Grunwald Ctr., 1981-83, acting dir. Grunwald Ctr., 1983-85; chief curator Ariz. State U. Art Mus., Tempe, 1985-91; CEO, dir. Neuberger Mus. SUNY, Purchase, 1991—2004; dir. Vero Beach Mus. of Art, Fla., 2004—. Author: (exhbn. catalogues) Tamarind: Los Angeles to Albuquerque, 1985, Fiber Concepts, 1989 (book) The Art of Leonard Lehrer, 1986; gen. editor: Melvin Edwards Sculpture: A Thirty Year Retrospective, 1993, Shared Beginnings Separate Passages: A Retrospective of the Work of Carol Anthony and Elaine Anthony, 1996, June Wayne; A Retrospective, 1997, Elizabeth Catlett Sculpture: A Fifty-Year Retrospective, 1998, Marisol, 2001, Toshiko Takaezu, 2001, Grace Hartigan, 2001, Masters of Light: Selections of American Impressionism from the Manoogian Collection, 2006; contbr. articles to profl. jours. Chairperson Tempe Mcpl. Arts Commn., 1989-90; bd. dirs. Balboa Art Conservation Ctr., San Diego, 1986-91, ArtTable, N.Y., 1995-98, Westchester Arts Coun., 1998-2004. Recipient Individual Arts award Westchester Arts Coun., 2002, Chancellor's award Excellence, SUNY, 2002; Edward A. Dickson History of Art fellow UCLA, 1984, Afro-Am. Studies fellow, 1984. Mem. Am. Assn. Mus., Assn. Art Mus. Dirs. Office: Vero Beach Mus Art 3001 Riverside Pk Dr Vero Beach FL 32963 Office Phone: 772-231-0707 ext. 113. Business E-Mail: lgedeon@vbmuseum.org.

GEE, SHARON LYNN, funeral director, educator; b. Berea, Ohio, Jan. 11, 1963; d. Donald Edward Gee and Janet Lee Floyd. Cert. in mortuary sci., Wayne State U., 1986, BS Psychology, 1987. Mortuary sci. lic. Mich., Nat. Bd. Cert. Funeral Dir. Mgr., funeral dir. Pixley Funeral Home, Keego Harbor, Mich., 1996—; lectr. instr. dept. mortuary sci. Wayne State U., Detroit, 1996—2003, asst. prof. embalming, 2003—. Recipient Residential Beautification award, City of Royal Oak, Mich., 1993. Mem.: West Bloomfield C. of C., Tri City Bus. Assn., Mich. Embalmers Soc. (pres. 2000—), Mich. Funeral Dirs. Assn., Nat. Funeral Dirs. Assn. (pursuit of excellence achievement award 1997—), Optimist Internat., Keego Harbor Chpt. (Keego Harbor chpt.), A-Dock Sailing Club. Avocations: sailing, circa 1910 home renovation and restoration. Office: Pixley Funeral Home Godhardt-Tomlinson Chapel 2904 Orchard Lake Rd Keego Harbor MI 48320 Business E-Mail: ad7158@wayne.edu.

GEEHR, PATRICIA BRAY, education educator; b. Mechanicville, N.Y., Mar. 18, 1938; d. Frederick John and Jennie (DeMartino) De Casperis; m. Richard T. Bray, July 20, 1963 (dec. Aug. 1982); children: William, Jonathan; m. John E. Geehr, June 29, 1991. BA English, Coll. Mt. St. Vincent, Riverdale, N.Y., 1959; MPA, Suffolk U., 1982. Cert. tchr. social studies and English, Wis., Mass. Tchr. English North Babylon H.S., NY, 1959—63, Edgewood H.S., Madison, Wis., 1963—64, Natick H.S., Mass., 1980—90; tchr. ESL Kennedy Mid. Sch., Natick, 1990—91, County Coll. Morris, Randolph, NJ, 1992—; tchr. English Fairleigh Dickinson U., Madison, NJ, 1992—, dir. Acad. Support Ctr., 1998—. Active LWV Named Outstanding Adminstr. of Yr., Ednl. Opportunity Fund, 2005; recipient Pillar award, Fairleigh Dickinson U., 2005. Mem. NEA, Mass. Tchr. Assn., Natick Lit. Guild, Pi Alpha Alpha, Chi Alpha Epsilon (hon.) Home: 3 Alvord Rd Morristown NJ 07960-6301 Office: Fairleigh Dickinson U Acad Support Ctr 285 Madison Ave Madison NJ 07940 Office Phone: 973-443-8540, 973-443-8738.

GEER, LOIS MARGARET, music educator; b. Bethlehem, Pa., Mar. 16, 1957; d. Francis Levere Sterner and Doris Valeria Sterner-Young; m. Richard Charles Geer, July 21, 1994. MusB, U. Hartford, 1982. Cert. tchg. CT, 2001. Tchr. music Music, Movement and More, Hartford, Conn., 1982—91; tchr. elem. sch. music Old Saybrook Pub. Schs., Conn., 1992—. Dir. assoc. music Plainville Congl. Ch., Conn., 1991—96; dir. youth music Westbrook Congl. Ch., 1997—2003, dir. bell choir, 1997—2003. Singer weddings, funerals, events. Recipient Tchr. Yr., Kathleen E. Goodwin Sch. Faculty, 1993—94. Mem.: Old Saybrook Edn. Assn. (treas. 2002—03), Am. Guild English Handbell Ringers, Am. Orff Schulwerk Assn., Choristers' Guild (assoc.), Music Educators' Nat. Conf. (assoc.). Avocations: cooking, walking, travel. Office: Kathleen E Goodwin Elem Sch 80 Old Boston Post Rd Old Saybrook CT 06475 Business E-Mail: lgeer@oldsaybrook.k12.ct.us.

GEERLING, FALINDA SUE, language educator; d. Paul Doran and Barbara Elaine Hartsuff; m. Robert Rene Geerling, Mar. 9, 1973; children: Carolyn Ann, Benjamin Paul, Kevin Robert. BA, Albion Coll., 1971; MA in Mgmt., Aquinas Coll., 1991; PhD, Mich. State U., 2003. Adj. instr. Davenport U., Grand Rapids, Mich., 1991—98; writing specialist, asst. prof. Spring Arbor U., Kalamazoo, 1998—. Mem.: Assn. Continuing & Higher Edn., Mich. Assn. Adult & Continuing Edn., Am. Assn. Adult & Continuing Edn. Republican. Catholic. Avocations: reading, writing, bicycling, travel. Office: Spring Arbor U 3479 S 9th St Kalamazoo MI 49009

GEERTZ, HILDRED STOREY, anthropology educator; b. N.Y.C., Feb. 12, 1927; d. Walter Rendell and Helen (Anderson) Storey; m. Clifford Geertz, 1948 (div. 1979); children: Erika, Benjamin. BA, Antioch Coll., Yellow Springs, Ohio, 1948; PhD, Radcliffe Coll., 1956. Lectr. U. Chgo., 1963-68; assoc. prof. to prof. anthropology Princeton (N.J.) U., 1970-98, ret., 1998. Chmn. dept. anthropology Princeton U., 1972-77, 86, 88-89. Author: The Javanese Family, 1961, (with Clifford Geertz) Kinship in Bali, 1974, Images of Power: Balinese Paintings Made for Gregory Bateson and Margaret Mead, 1994, The Life of a Balinese Temple: Artistry, Imagination, and History in a Peasant Village, 2004, Tales from a Charmed Life: A Balinese Painter Reminisces, 2005, (with Geertz and Lawrence Rosen) Meaning and Order in Moroccan Society, 1979; editor: State and Society in Bali, 1992.

GEFFERS, BETTY J., secondary school educator; b. Cuba, NY, Jan. 24, 1957; d. Carlyle L. and Elizabeth A. Short; m. James P. Geffers, Mar. 1, 1975; children: Dominick R., Heather J. Fears, Bradley J. BS, U. Tex., Tyler, 1995. Cert. tchr. Tex., 1995. English tchr. Mt. Pleasant H.S., Tex., 1996—. Office: Mt Pleasant HS PO Box 1117 Mount Pleasant TX 75456 Office Phone: 903-575-2020.

GEFFKEN, CAROLYN D., special education educator; b. Ohio, 1952; m. John Geffken (dec.); 1 child. BS, U. Tulsa, 1975. Tchr. Tulsa Pub. Schs., 1978—79; forms control clk. St. Francis Hosp., Tulsa, 1979—80; printers helper, bindery Geneva Generics, Bloomfield, Colo., 1980—81; paste up artist The Paperwork Co., Tulsa, 1985—86; deaf edn. tchr. Mountain Home Pub. Schs., Ark., 1986—2002, ESL tchr., 1995—2002; spl. edn. tchr. Little Rock Sch. Dist., 2002—06. Mem.: NEA, Coun. on Exceptional Children, Ark. Edn. Assn., Phi Delta Kappa. Avocations: travel, camping, gardening, reading. Office: Little Rock Sch Dist Henderson Magnet Mid Sch 401 John Barrow Rd Little Rock AR 72205-4701 Business E-Mail: carolyn.geffken@lrsd.org.

GEFFNER, DONNA SUE, speech pathology/audiology services professional, audiologist, educator; d. Louis and Sally (Weiner) Geffner. BA magna cum laude, Bklyn. Coll., 1967; MA, NYU, 1968, PhD (NDEA fellow), 1970; postgrad., Advanced Inst. Analytic Psychology, 1973—75; EdD (hon.), Providence Coll., 2003. Asst. prof. Lehman Coll., 1971-76; assoc. prof. dept. speech St. John's U., 1976-81, prof., 1982—. Dir. Speech and Hearing Ctr., 1976—, chmn. dept. speech comm. scis. and theater, 1983—92, developer M.A. program in speech pathology and audiology, 1984, developer Au.D audiology and doctoral consortia, 2004, dir. grad. program in speech-lang. pathology and audiology, 1992—; pvt. practice, 1980—; cons. to corp. execs.; TV prodr. and hostess NBC, 1977—78, CBS, 1978—79; mem. N.Y. State Licensure Bd., 1993—97. Issue editor: Jour. Topics Lang. Disorders, 1980; editor: ASHA monograph, 1987; author: What Professionals Need to Know About Attention Deficit Hyperactivity Disorder, 2005, The Listening Inventory, 2005; contbr. articles to profl. jours., chapters to books. Recipient Emmy nomination for outstanding instrnl. program, 1978, award, Pres.'s Com. Employment Handicapped, Disting. Achievement award, N.Y.C. Speech-Lang.-Hearing Assn., 1994, Honors, L.I. Speech-Lang.-Hearing Assn., 1998; grantee, CUNY Rsch. Found., 1972, N.Y. State Dept. Edn., 1976—78. Fellow: Am. Speech, Lang. and Hearing Assn. (legis. councillor 1978—87, 1988—90, 1990—94, v.p. acad. affairs 1995—97, pres.-elect 1998, pres. 1999, past pres. 2000, ednl. standards bd. 1992—94); mem.: Coll. Bd. Com. on Literacy, Am. Guidance Svc. (mem. bd. advisors), Audiology Study Group N.Y., N.Y. State Speech and Hearing Assn. (pres. 1978—80, honors). Office: St John's U Speech and Hearing Ctr 8000 Utopia Pkwy Jamaica NY 11432-1343 Business E-Mail: geffnerd@Stjohns.edu.

GEGELMANN, SHARON FAY, piano teacher; b. Dickinson, N.D., Mar. 11, 1958; d. Jacob and Marjorie Jeanette (Hoff) G.; m. Mark D. Schields, Aug. 30, 1986; children: Rachel, Rebekah, Luke. BS, Moorhead State U., 1981; postgrad., U. of Mary, 1995. CPA, N.D. Dep. auditor Dunn County, Manning, ND, 1981-82; piano tchr., 1982—; sr. acct. ANG Coal Gasification Co., Dickinson, 1983-89; acct. Reichert Fisher & Co., Dickinson, 1990-91. Libr. Hope Christian Acad., Dickinson, 1997—; troop leader Girl Scouts, Dickinson, 1997-99. Mem. Music Tchrs. Nat. Assn. (sec.-treas. 1999-2001), Dakota Western Auto Club (treas. 1997-98, 2004—), St. Cecilia Music Club, Theodore Roosevelt Amateur Radio Club.

GEHLERT, SALLY OYLER, healing touch practictioner; b. Cin., Feb. 12, 1949; d. Ralph Thomas and Inez R. (Morgan) Oyler; m. Robert Gehlert; 1 child, Chloe. AS, U. Cin., 1971, M in Ednl. Adminstrn., 1976; BS in Allied Health Edn., U. Ky., 1974. Registered dental hygienist, Ohio; cert. healing touch practitioner. Dental hygienist, Cin., 1971—; dental cons. Proctor & Gamble Corp., Cin., 1985-95, John O. Butler Co., Chgo., 1990—; pvt. practice Cin., 1985—. Adv. bd. John O. Butler Co., Chgo.; cons. in field. Edit. adv. Journal of Dental Hygiene, 1993; author ednl. programs for dental profls. Mem. Am. Dental Hygienist Assn., Ohio Dental Hygienist Assn., Cin. Dental Hygienist Assn., Healing Touch Internat. (practitioner). Home: 2476 Walnutview Ct Cincinnati OH 45230-2455 Office Phone: 513-231-9783. Personal E-mail: sallygehlert@fuse.net.

GEHM, AMY K., lawyer; married; 2 children. JD cum laude, South Tex. Coll. Law, Houston, 1992. Cert.: Tex. Bd. Legal Specialization (family law) 2002. With Office of the Atty. Gen., Tex. Dept. Ins.; atty. Law Office of Jennifer Tull; prin. atty. Law Office of Amy K. Gehm, L.L.C., Austin, Tex. Named a Rising Star, Tex. Super Lawyers mag., 2006. Mem.: Collaborative Law Inst. Tex. Office: Law Office of Amy K Gehm LLC The Canyon at Wild Basin 115 Wild Basin Rd Ste 106 Austin TX 78746 Office Phone: 512-327-7272. E-mail: amy@amygehm.com.*

GEHRICH, LEONORA SUPPAN, artist, musician, German literature educator; arrived in US, 1963; d. Josef Cornelius and Josefine Maria Suppan; m. Heinz-Guenter Gehrich; children: Alan, Brian, Colleen. Diploma, Acad. Music, Vienna, 1958; MusM, Ind. U., 1965; PhD, Quincy U., 1988. Cert. performer Ind. U., 1965. Asst. prof. Western Ill. U., Macomb, 1965—68; artist-in residence Culver-Stockton Coll., Canton, Miss., 1968—75, Quincy U., 1977—2005. Musician, pianist (concerts), Austria, Germany, France, Italy, Poland, Hungary, Eng., Portugal, Can., Costa Rica, Mex., Holland, Czech Republic. Recipient City of Quincy Arts award, 1995. Mem.: Am. Coll. Musicians, Muddy River Opera (mem. bd. 2003), Hist. Soc. Avocations: sailing, tennis, swimming. Office: Quincy U 1800 College Ave Quincy IL 62301 Office Phone: 217-228-5460. Office Fax: 217-885-3024. Business E-Mail: ggehrich@msn.com.

GEHRING, ELIZABETH A., social studies educator; b. Camden, Ark., Aug. 11, 1951; d. James and Mary Sanders; m. Leonard Gehring; children: Rachel, Rebecca. BA Polit. Sci., Ouachita Bapt. U., Arkadelphia, 1972, MSE Social Studies, 1973. Tchr. Brinkley Pub. Schools, Ark., 1978—2004, literacy coach, 2004—. Leader GA's Mission Friends, Brinkley, 1987—92. Mem.: Internat. Reading Assn., Delta Kappa Gamma (pres. Gamma Theta chpt. 2004—06). Baptist. Avocation: reading. Home: 1923 Hwy 78 N Wheatley AR 72392

GEHRING, PATTI J., principal; d. Peter Edward Brunner and Sandra Ann Howdyshell; m. Jeffrey A. Gehring, July 3, 1992; children: Kyle, Lacey, Ryan. AA, Charles County C.C., LaPlata, Md.; BA with honors, St. Mary's Coll. Md., 1992; M in Ednl. Adminstrn. with honors, Trinity Coll., Washington, 2002. Cert. tchr. Md. State Dept. Edn. Tchr. St. Mary's Sch., Bryantown, Md., 1993—2002; prin. Little Flower Sch., Great Mills, Md., 2002—. Mem.: ASCD, Nat. Cath. Edn. Assn. Office: Little Flower Sch 20401 Point Lookout Rd Great Mills MD 20634 Office Phone: 301-994-0404. E-mail: gehringp@adwschool.org.

GEHRKE, KAREN MARIE, retired accountant; b. Gaylord, Minn., Apr. 12, 1940; d. Stanley Henry and Frieda Marie (Hammel) Ostermann; m. Orville Raymond Gehrke, Oct. 21, 1961 (div. Aug. 1994); children: Kimberly, Karla, Kent. Inspector Fingerhut Mfg., Gaylord, 1959-60; rewinder 3M, Hutchinson, Minn., 1960-61; sec. Boehmke Ins. Agy., Gaylord, 1961-63, Law Office of H.A. Knobel, Gaylord, 1964-68; teller First State Fed. Savs. and Loan, Hutchinson, 1969; sec. Wally's Tire Shop, Hutchinson, 1970, Lyle R. Jensen, CPA, Hutchinson, 1974-84; owner Karen M. Gehrke L.P.A., Hutchinson, 1984—2001; ret., 2001. Mem. Nat. Assn. Female Execs., Nat. Soc. Pub. Accts., Minn. Assn. Pub. Accts., Hutchinson Area C. of C.

GEHRMAN, JODY ELIZABETH, writer; b. Santa Rosa, Calif., Sept. 22, 1971; d. Sherry Garner and Ed Gehrman. M in Profl. Writing, U. So. Calif., L.A., 2001. Prof. Mendoccho Coll., 2001—. Author: (novel) Tart (Book Sense Notable, 2005, Best of its Genre Critics' award RT Bookclub Mag., 2005), Summer in the Land of Skin, 2004, (play) Tribal Life in America (New Women Playwrights award, 1995). Avocations: windsurfing, acting, songwriting. Business E-Mail: jgehrman@mendoccho.edu.

GEIBEL, SISTER GRACE ANN, university president; b. Sept. 17, 1937; BA in Piano and Music Edn., Carlow Coll., 1961; MA in Music Edn., U. Rochester, 1967, PhD in Music, 1975. Tchr. elem. and high schs., 1959-67; ch. musician, 1972-80; assoc. prof. and co-chmn. music dept. Carlow Coll., Pitts., 1981-82, acting acad. dean, 1982-83, dean, 1983-88, v.p. acad. affairs, 1984-88, pres., 1988—2005. Mem. adv. bd. Pitts. Symphony Soc.; bd. dir. Oakland Cath. H.S., Urban League Pitts., Penn. Econ. League. Office: Carlow Univ Office of the Pres 3333 5th Ave Pittsburgh PA 15213-3109 Business E-Mail: geibelga@carlow.edu.

GEIDE-STEVENSON, DORIS, adult education educator; b. Bad Homburg, Germany, Aug. 3, 1962; d. Kurt Oskar and Anna Elisabeth Geide; m. Mark Alan Stevenson, Aug. 19, 1989; children: Ella Elisabeth Stevenson, Sonja Rose Stevenson. PhD, SUNY, Buffalo, 1995. Prof. Weber State U., Ogden, Utah, 1996—. V.p. lifespan religious edn. Unitarian Universalist Ch. Ogden, Utah, 2006. Home: 1465 Mitchell Dr Ogden UT 84403 Office: Weber State University 3807 University Circle Ogden UT 84408-3807 Office Phone: 801-626-7634.

GEIER, KATHLEEN T., human resources specialist; b. Akron, Ohio, Aug. 7, 1956; BS, Heidelberg Coll., 1978. Indsl. engr., various human resources positions Goodyear Tire and Rubber Co., Akron, Ohio, 1978—86; ops. mgr. Cosmoflex (subsidiary of Goodyear Tire and Rubber Co.), 1986—90, plant mgr., pres. Mt. Pleasant, Iowa, 1992—94; bus. ctr. mgr. Goodyear Tire and Rubber Co., St. Marys, Ohio, 1990—92, dir. salaried human resources and employment practices Akron, Ohio, 1994—95, dir. human resources employment practices and systems, 1995—96, dir. human resources ctrl. svcs. N.Am. bus. unites and corp. staff, 1996—99, dir. human resources Europe, Africa,

Middle East region Brussels, sr. v.p. human resources Akron, 2002—. Office: Goodyear Tire and Rubber Co 1144 E Market St Akron OH 44316-0001 Office Phone: 330-796-2121. Office Fax: 330-796-2222.

GEIER, SHARON LEE, retired special education educator, realtor; b. Dayton, Ohio, Nov. 21, 1943; d. Robert Stanley Murphy and Mary Frances (Ross) Briggs; m. Arthur M. Geier, Jan 23, 1965; children: Arthur William, Bradford Robert. BA, Wilmington (Ohio) Coll., 1965; cert. spl. edn., Wright State U., 1976; MS in Edn., U. Dayton, 1995. Cert. elem. tchr., Ohio, edn. handicapped. Tchr. 1st grade Fairborn (Ohio) City Schs., 1965-66, Kettering (Ohio) City Schs., 1967-71, Xenia (Ohio) City Schs., 1975-81, tchr. 3rd grade, 1981-82, tchr. learning disabled, 1982—2004; ret., 2004; realtor Irongate Inc., Realtors, Beavercreek, Ohio, 2004—. Tchr. specifically learning disabled Camp Progress Centerville (Ohio) Schs., summers, 1977, 78; coord. MicroSoc. Program, 1995-2000, 2002-04. Founder, pres. Twig 6 Children's Med. Ctr. Aux., Dayton, 1971-73, chmn. Jr. Aux., 1972-74. Recipient Doer award Miami Valley Regional Ctr. and Dayton Area Citizens for Spl. Edn., 1988; Martha Holden Jennings scholar, 1980-81; named Spl. Educator of Yr., Spl. Edn. dept. Ctrl. State U., 1993. Mem. AAUW, ASCD, Coun. Exceptional Children (Outstanding Chpt. Pres. Ohio Fedn. 1989, pres. Greene County chpt. 1987-89, treas. Ohio divsn. learning disabilities 1989-91, pres. 1991-93, treas. Greene County chpt. 1999—), Ohio Fedn. Coun. for Exceptional Children (liaison S.W. region 1989-94, liaison chmn. 1992-93, 93-94, sec. 1994-97, v.p. 1997-98, pres. elect 1998-99, pres. 1999-2000, past pres. 2000-01, Tchr. of Yr., 2003), Green Key Honor Soc. Republican. Avocations: reading, music, plants, aerobics, golf. Home: 1134 Napa Rdg Centerville OH 45458-6017 Office Phone: 937-426-0800. E-mail: sharon@sharonGeier.com.

GEISELMAN, LUCYANN, college president; m. Robert L. Harrington; 1 child, Gabriella. BA in Religion, Tex. Christian U., MA in Theology; PhD in Edn., U. Chgo. Former v.p. Eisenhower Med. Ctr., Rancho Mirage, Calif.; v.p. for planning and Advancement Calif. Inst. of Arts, 1989-91; pres. Mt. Vernon Coll., Washington, 1991, Antioch Univ. So. Calif., LA, 2003—. Office: Antioch Univ 400 Corporate Pointe Culver City CA 90230

GEISELMAN, PAULA JEANNE, psychologist, educator; b. Ohio, June 30, 1944; d. Paul and Rosemary (Dawson) Parsley. AB in Psychology with honors, Ohio U., 1971, MS in Exptl. Psychology, 1976; PhD in Physiol. Psychology, UCLA, 1983. Adj. asst. prof. UCLA, 1986-91; dir. psychophysiol. rsch. UCLA Sch. Medicine, 1986-91; assoc. prof. dept. psychology La. State U., Baton Rouge, 1991—; adj. assoc. prof. Pennington Biomed. Rsch. Ctr. La State U., Baton Rouge, 1991—. Lectr. in field. Reviewer for Sci. Jour., Am. Jour. Physiology, Physiology and Behavior, Brain Research Bulletin, Appetite: Determinants and Consequences of Eating and Drinking; contbr. numerous articles to profl. jours. Mem. Soc. Neurosci., AAAS, N.Am. Assn. Study of Obesity, Women in Neurosci., Assn. Acad. Women, Am. Psychol. Assn., Am. Psychol. Assn., Eastern Psychol. Assn., Western Psychol. Assn. (head of physiol. psychol., chair. Animal Feeding and Behavior paper session 1981), Assn. Advancement Psychology, Internat. Brain Research Orgn., World Fedn. Neuroscientists, Brit. Brain Research Assn. (hon.), European Brain and Behavior Soc. (hon.), N.Y. Acad. Scis., Sigma Xi, Psi Chi. Achievements include research on the behavioral, nutritional and physiological mechanisms of energy, appetite and body weight regulation in humans and animal models; on the role of the liver, gut, vagus, sympathetic nervous system, enteric and pancreatic hormones in the control of food intake and body weight; on the role of macronutrients (especially carbohydrates and fats and their breakdown products) in the control of food intake and body weight; on the physiological and nutritional control of ingestive behavior in females across the estrous and menstrual cycles; on an animal model of anorexia nervosa; on meal-patterning analysis; on human taste psychophysiology, especially in smokers and in women across the menstrual cycle; on the relationship between smoking, food intake, and body weight control; and on patient compliance. Office: La State U Psychology Dept Pennington Biomed Rsch Ctr 6400 Perkins Rd Baton Rouge LA 70808-4124

GEISENDORFER, NANCY KAY, mathematics educator; b. Greeley, Colo., Apr. 9, 1970; d. Bernard and Lyn Stadler; m. Grant Geisendorfer; children: Garrett, Graham. AA, Northeastern Jr. Coll., Sterling, Colo., 1990; BA, U. No. Colo., 1992, MA, postgrad., U. No. Colo., 2006—. Tchr. math. Lester Arnold H.S., Commerce City, Colo., 1996—2001; tchr. John Mall High, Walsenburg, Colo., 2001—02, Conrad Ball Middle Sch., Loveland, Colo., 2003—04, U. No. Colo., Greeley, 2006—. Author: Beaver Creek Adventures. Mem. Colo. Tchr. Assn. (rep. 1994—), PTA (sec. 1998-2001). Avocations: writing, rock collecting, hiking. Home: 784 Lavastone Ave Loveland CO 80537

GEISER, ELIZABETH ABLE, publishing company executive; b. Phillipsburg, NJ, Apr. 28, 1925; d. George W. and Margaret I. (Ross) G. AB magna cum laude, Hood Coll., 1947. Promotion mgr. coll. dept. Macmillan Co., N.Y.C., 1947-54; promotion mgr. R.R. Bowker, N.Y.C., 1954-60, sales mgr., 1960-67, dir. mktg., 1967-70, v.p., 1970-73, sr. v.p., 1973-75, sr. v.p., pub. book divsn.; adj. prof., dir. U. Denver Pub. Inst., 1976—; sr. v.p. Gale Rsch. Co., 1976-91, cons., 1991—. Cons. Excerpta Medica, Elsevier, 1976-82; lectr. pub. procedures Radcliffe Coll., 1966-75; lectr. schs. libr. sci. U. Wash., U. So. Calif.; panel mem. TV series Living Library, 1970 Editor: The Business of Book Publishing, 1985; contbr. Manual of Bookselling, 1969. Trustee Hood Coll., 1993-99. Inducted into Pub. Hall of Fame, 1988; recipient PubWest Rittenhouse award for lifetime achievement contbn. to pub. in the west, Mem. Assn. Am. Pubs. (exec. coun. prof. and scholarly pub. divsn. 1989-91, adv. coun. Frankfurt book fair 1971, sch. and libr. promotion and mktg. com. 1972-76, bd. dirs. 1982-85), ALA (pres. exhibits roundtable 1968-70, bd. dirs. exhibits roundtable 1968). Presbyterian. Home: 3329 E Bayaud Ave Denver CO 80209 Office: Pub Inst 335 E 51st St Apt 5E New York NY 10022-6765 Office Phone: 212-752-8652. E-mail: egeiser@worldnet.att.net.

GEISINGER, JANICE ALLAIN, accountant; b. Iroquois County, Ill., June 21, 1927; d. Carl Oliver and Constance Kathryn (Risser) Irps Allain; m. Robert Bond Geisinger, Oct. 17, 1947 (div. 1976); children: Jacque K., Holly D., Terry Joe. AA, Blackburn U., Carlinville, Ill., 1947. Lab. technician Mich. Health Lab., East Lansing, 1947-48; with Southwestern Bell Telephone, Tulsa, 1948-49; bookkeeper Geisinger Ent., Dallas, 1951-69; salesman Earl Page Real Estate, Irving, Tex., 1969-71; food purchaser Town & Country vending, Dallas, 1971-75; bookkeeper/sec. Belco C & I Wiring Inc., Irving, 1976-85; leasing bookkeeper Copiers Etc., Inc., Dallas, 1985-89; bookkeeper Kennedy Elec. Inc., Mesquite, Tex., 1989; ret., 1990. Cons. Ross Mech., Irving, 1989—; bookkeeper Metroplex Dental Group (now Dr. Julian M. Chong), 1990—, Limpede, Inc., 1999—. Crew leader Census Bur., Dallas, 1990. Mem. Am. Contract Bridge Assn. Avocations: flying, gardening, knitting, rug making. Home: 1216 E Grauwyler Rd Irving TX 75061-5031

GEISLER, KAY, transportation executive; b. Indianapolis, May 24, 1951; d. Willis Manson and Virginia Mae (Altopp) Scobee; m. Donald Adam Geisler, June 26, 1971; 1 child, Melinda Kay Geisler. Co-owner/corp. sec. Geisler Trucking, Inc., Lebanon, Ind., 1980—; city council woman Lebanon, Ind., 1996—. Bd. dirs. Boone Co. Solid Waste, Lebanon, Ind., 1994—, Well Head Protection, Lebanon, 1998; mem. Teen Pregnancy Coun., 1998, Ind. Assn. Cities and Towns, Indianapolis, 1996, Boone Co. Republican Women, 1996, Boone Co. Symphony, 1997. Mem. Nat. League of Cities, Zonta Club of Lebanon (pres. 1994-96), Zonta Internat. (area 4 dir. 1996-98; dist. 6 sec. 1998-2000), Smile-A-While Homemakers Ext. Club (pres. 1992-94), Ulen Country Club, Kappa Kappa Kappa (Alpha Beta chpt.). Avocation: golf. Home: 2302 Golfside Dr Lebanon IN 46052-8175

GEISSLER, KRISTIANA ANDREA, secondary school educator; d. Harry Conrad and Joyce Ann Geissler. Degree cum laude, U. South Fla., 1987; MA, NYU, Manhattan, 1998. Cert. tchr. drama Fla., 1998, tchr. elem. edn. Fla., 1989. Tchr. elem. sch. Hillsborough County Schs., Tampa, Fla., 1989—95, St. Mary's Episcopal Day Sch., Tampa, 1995—96; tchr. drama Orange Grove Mid. Sch. Arts, Tampa, 1998—2000; tchr. N.E. H.S., Saint Petersburg, Fla., 2001—. Sponsor jr. thespian Orange Grove Mid. Sch. Arts, 1998—2000; sponsor thespian N.E. H.S., 2001—. Recipient Best Tech. Theatre Thespian Dist. IV award, 2004; scholar, NYU, 1996—97. Mem.: Golden Key. Home: 1333 51 Ave N Saint Petersburg FL 33703 Office: Northeast HS 5500 16th St N Saint Petersburg FL 33703 Personal E-mail: kgeissler@tampabay.rr.com. Business E-Mail: kristiana_geissler@places.pcsb.org.

GELB, JUDITH ANNE, lawyer; b. NYC, Apr. 5, 1935; d. Joseph and Sarah (Stein) G.; m. Howard S. Vogel, June 30, 1962; 1 child, Michael S. BA, Bklyn. Coll., 1955; JD, Columbia U., 1958. Bar: N.Y. 1959, U.S. Dist. Ct. (so. and ea. dists.) N.Y. 1960, U.S. Ct. Appeals (2d cir.) 1960, U.S. Ct. Mil. Appeals 1962. Asst. to editor N.Y. Law Jour., N.Y.C., 1958-59; confidential asst. to U.S. atty. ea dist. N.Y., Bklyn., 1959-61; assoc. Whitman & Ransom, N.Y.C., 1961-70, ptnr., 1971-93, Whitman Breed Abbott & Morgan LLP, N.Y.C., 1993-2000, Winston & Strawn LLP, NYC, 2000—. Mem.: ABA (individual rights sect., real property and trust law sect.), Assn. Bar City N.Y., N.Y. State Dist. Attys. Assn., N.Y. State Bar Assn. (trusts and estates com.), Fed. Bar Coun., Columbia Law Sch. Alumni Assn. (bd. dirs.), Princeton Club. Home: 169 E 69th St New York NY 10021-5163 Office: Winston & Strawn LLP 200 Park Ave New York NY 10166-0005 Business E-Mail: jgelb@winston.com.

GELB, LESA S., lawyer; b. Kinston, Pa., Jan. 20, 1961; d. Irwin H. and Judith Gelb; m. Barry H. Dyller, Aug. 1, 1993; children: Nathon Gelb-Dyller, Benjamin Gelb-Dyller. BA, Cornell U., Ithaca, NY, 1982; JD, Boston Coll., Boston, Mass., 1985. Atty. Deolo Assocs., W. Pittson, Pa., 1986—. Com. mem. Wilkes Barre Law Libr. Soc.; mem. Pa. Dem. State Com., 1990—; gov. apptd. Pa. Election Reform Task Force, Harrisburg, Pa., 2005; bd. mem. exec. com. Temple Israel, Wilkes-Barre, Pa., 2002—. Mem.: Am. Bus. Women's Assn., League Women Voter's. Democrat. Jewish. Avocations: gardening, swimming. Office: Cefalo Assoc 309 Wyoming Ave West Pittston PA 18643

GELBER, DANIELLE ARNA, broadcast executive; d. Morris and June Beverly Claman; m. Stephen Carl Gelber, Oct. 24, 1999; 1 stepchild, Joshua Austin 1 child, Alexandra Dylan; m. Stephen Carl Gelber (div.). BA, U. Calif., 1976—80; MA, Am. U., Washington, DC, 1980—82. Dir. of TV devel. Spelling TV, Inc., Los Angeles, Calif., 1983—92; sr. v.p. drama series programming Fox Broadcasting Co., Los Angeles, Calif., 1992—2000; v.p. original series programming Showtime Networks, Inc., Los Angeles, Calif., 2001—04, sr. v.p. original series programming, 2004—. Mem. Acad. TV Arts And Sciences, Los Angeles, Calif., 1987—; Am. U. nat. adv. bd. Am. U. Sch. Of Comm., Washington, 2002—. Recipient Wonder Woman of Yr., Multi-channel News, 2003. Mem.: Acad. of TV Arts And Sciences. Avocations: guitar, photography, travel. Office: Showtime Networks Inc 10880 Wilshire Blvd Los Angeles CA 90024 Office Phone: 310-234-5211.*

GELBERG, LILLIAN, family medicine physician, educator; b. LA, May 14, 1955; married; 3 children. BA, UCLA, 1977; MD, Harvard U., 1981; MSPH, UCLA, 1987. Diplomate Am. Bd. Family Practice. Robert Wood Johnson Found. clin. scholar UCLA/VA, 1984-86; asst. prof. UCLA, 1987-97, assoc. prof., 1997—, George F. Kneller prof. family medicine, 2001—. Contbr. chpts. to books, articles to profl. jours. Vol., com. chair various family clinics, Venice, Calif., 1984—. Recipient CAFP 1st Rsch. Excellence award, 2001; Robert Wood Johnson Found. scholar UCLA, 1984-86, Robert Wood Johnson faculty scholar, 1995-2001. Fellow Am. Acad. Family Physicians; mem. Soc. Gen. Internal Medicine, Assn. Health Svc. Rsch. (Young Investigator award 1995, Article of the Yr. award 1997), Soc. of Tchrs. of Family Medicine, Am. Pub. Health Assn., Inst. Medicine, 2004. E-mail: gelberg@ucla.edu.

GELFAND, JULIA MAUREEN, librarian; b. Cleve., Sept. 26, 1954; d. Lawrence Emerson and Miriam J. Ifland Gelfand; m. David Bruce Lang, Apr. 30, 1995. AB, Goucher Coll., 1975; MS in Libr. Sci., MA, Case Western Res. U., 1977. Reference libr. Penrose Libr. U. Denver, 1971-81; reference libr., bibiliographer U. Calif., Irvine, 1981-86, applied sci. and engring. libr., 1986—. Adj. faculty Sch. Info. Resources and Libr. Sci., U. Ariz., Tucson, 1998— Editor: (jour.) Grey Lit., 2000; co-editor: (jour.) Libr. Hi-Tech. News, 2001—. Bd. dirs. Orange County chpt. Am. Jewish Com., 1999—. Recipient U.S./UK Fulbright award Fulbright Commn., 1992-93, Literati award for excellence in Grey Lit., MCB Univ. Press, 1999, Literati award for leading editors MCB U. Press, 2003. Mem. ALA, AAAS, Am. Soc. Engring. Edn., Assn. Colls. and Rsch. Librs. (chmn. sci. tech. sect. 2005-06), Soc. Scholarly Pub., Internat. Fedn. Lib. Assns. (chmn. sci. tech. sect., 2001-05). Democrat. Jewish. Business E-Mail: jgelfand@uci.edu.

GELLAR, SARAH MICHELLE, actress; b. NYC, Apr. 14, 1977; d. Arthur and Roselen Gellar; m. Freddy Prinze Jr., Sept. 1, 2002. Appearances include (TV movie) Invasion of Privacy, 1983, (TV series) All My Children (Daytime Emmy award for outstanding younger leading actress in a daytime drama series 1995) 1993-96, Buffy The Vampire Slayer, 1997-2003 (Saturn Award Best Genre TV Actress, 1999), (films) I Know What You Did Last Summer, 1997 (Blockbuster Entertainment award for favorite best supporting actress-horror, MTV Movie award for best breakthrough performance), Scream 2, 1997, Beverly Hills Family Robinson, 1997, Cruel Intentions, 1999, Simply Irresistable, 1999, Scooby Doo, 2002, Harvard Man, 2002, Scooby-Doo 2: Monsters Unleashed, 2004, The Grudge, 2004, Southland Tales, 2006, The Grudge 2, 2006, others, also TV commls. Avocations: Tae Kwon Do, kickboxing, gymnastics.*

GELLER, BUNNY ZELDA, poet, writer, publisher, sculptor, artist; b. NYC, May 21, 1926; d. Herman and Shirley (Shoenfeld) Juster; m. Lester Roy Geller; children: Judy Lynn, Robert Douglas, Sheryl Sue, Wayne Mitchell. Student, UCLA, 1944-46, Fla. Internat. U., 1989-97. Invited artist Pegasus Internat. Corp., N.J., 1981-85, Internat. Art Expo., N.Y., 1982-83; invited guest artist Broward County Main Lib., Ft. Lauderdale, Fla., 1988; pres. BZG Enterprises. Author: Bunny Geller Original Poetry, 1995, Destiny, 1995, Choices (poetry), 1996, The Monkey and the Parakeet (A Poetic Tale for Children), 1997, Kaleidoscope (poetry), 1997, Impressions (poetry), 1999, Bunny Geller Original Sculpture, 1985; one woman sculpture shows include Bowery Savings Bank, N.Y.C., 1978, Lynn Kottler Galleries, N.Y.C, 1978, Hollywood (Fla.) Art Mus., 1978-79, Broward County Main Libr., Fla., Hallandale Cultural Ctr., 1996; group exhbns. include All Broward Exhibit 78, Ft. Lauderdale, Fla., 1978, Old Westbury Hebrew Congregation, Westbury, N.Y., 1978, De Ligny Galleries, Ft. Lauderdale, Fla., 1979, 1983-84, Internat. Treas. Fine Art, Plainview, N.Y., 1978, 79, 80, 81, Artists Equity Assn. Hollywood (Fla.) Art Mus., 1979, Limited Edition Galleries, Bal Harbour, Fla., 1979, Temple Beth-El, Boca Raton, Fla., 1979, Expo 79, Pompano, Fla., 1979, Hilda Rindom Galleries, Hallendale, Fla, 1980, Jockey Club Art Gallery, Miami, 1980, 81, 83, 84, Gallery SO-HO 7, Ltd., Great Neck, N.Y., 1979-80, Exhibition of Fine Art Nassau Mus. of Fine Art Assn., 1985, Gallery at Turnberry, Turnberry Isle, Fla., 1980-81, Galleria Martin, Palm Beach, Fla., 1981, Contextual Fine Arts, Ft. Lauderdale, Fla., 1980-81, Art and Culture Ctr. of Hollywood (Fla.), 1981, Miami Convention Ctr., 1981, Anita Gordon Gallery, Inc., North Miami Beach, 1981, Collier Art Internat., Ltd., Westbury, N.Y., 1981, Tavistock Country Club, Haddonfield, N.J., 1982, Internat. Art Expo, N.Y.C., 1982, 83, Ohio All Arabian Show and Buckeye Sweepstakes, Columbus, 1982, West Elec. Co., Hopewell, N.J., 1982, Devon (Pa.) Arabian Horse Show, 1982, Bondstreet Art Gallery, Pitts., 1982, Blumka II Gallery, N.Y.C., 1982, Korby Gallery, Cedar Grove, N.J., 1982, Washington Internat. Horse Show, Gaithersburg, Md., 1982, Pegasus Internat. Corp., Pennington, N.J., 1981, 82, 83, 84, 85, Patricia Judith Art Gallery, Boca Raton, Fla., 1983-84, Panache Gallery, Ft. Lauderdale, Fla., 1983, The Nelson Rockefeller Collection, Inc., N.Y.C., 1983, Shorr Goodwin Gallery, N.Y.C., 1983, Carrier Found. Auxiliary, Belle Meade, N.J., 1983, First Annual Internat. Wildlife Exposition, Atlantic City, N.J., 1983, Amann Gallery, Inc., Palm Beach, Fla., 1984-85, Robert's One-of-a-Kind, Bal Harbour, Fla., 1984, Hallandale (Fla.) Pub. Lib., 1984-85, Galleria Camhi, Bar Harbor Is., Fla., 1984-85, Tatem Galleries, Ft. Lauderdale, Fla., 1984-85, Westbury (N.Y.) Meml. Lib., 1984, Trenton Country Club, 1984, Designers' Showcase 1985 Cashelmara, Glen Cove, N.Y., 1985, UN Conf., Nairobi, 1985, Hallandale Cultural Ctr., Fla., 1998; sculptures on permanent exhibits; featured in (book) Artists/USA, 1979-80, The Am. Album, Nat. Mus. Women Arts permanent collection, Washington, 1985, Art Expo N.Y. catalogue, 1982, 83, 92, Limited Collectors Edition, 1982, Town and Country mag., 1982, Gold Coast Life mag., 1983, Art in America mag., 1983-84, Sunstorm Arts Mag., 1984; represented in permanent collection Kushi Found.; Wrote words, music to song One World, 1989. Pres. Sisterhood Westbury Hebrew Congregation, Westbury, N.Y., 1967-69; judge Fine Art and Craft Show, Ft. Lauderdale, Fla., 1979-81; art adv. coun. Westbury Meml. Libr., 1990-94. Recipient 1st prize Carrier Found. Aux. 2d Ann. Arts Festival, 1983; named to Internat. Poetry Hall Fame, 1996, Merit award, Hallandale Beach, Fla., 2004; inducted into Internat. Libr. Photography, 2002. Mem. Nat. Mus. Women in the Arts (assoc.), Nat. Libr. Poetry (Editor's Choice award 1995, published in Best Poems of the 90s 1996), Internat. Soc. Poets (disting. mem. 1995, Poet of Merit 1995, semi-finalist symposium 1995, inducted into Internat. Poetry Hall of Fame 1996), Nat. Trust for Historic Preservation. Avocations: tennis, all sports, cultural events, national events, art shows. Home: 400 Diplomat Pkwy Apt 711 Hallandale Beach FL 33009

GELLER, DEBRA F., academic administrator, educator; BA cum laude, U. So. Fla., 1986; MBA, Calif. Coast U., 1998; EdD, UCLA, 2004. Cert. salary adminstrn. ACA/World at Work, 1999. Asst. to dir. nursing systems UCLA Med. Ctr., 1992—94; bus. officer campus human resources UCLA, 1994—2006, chief adminstrv. officer student and campus life, acting dir., office internat. students and scholars, 2006—. Instr. L.A. City Coll. Chair, nominating com. Univ. Credit Union, 2001—02. Recipient Witness Program Wall of Fame, UCLA Sch. of Law. Mem.: Nat. Assn. Student Personnel Adminstr., Soc. Human Resource Mgmt., ACA/World at Work. Office: UCLA Box 951626 Los Angeles CA 90095-1626 Business E-Mail: dgeller@saonet.ucla.edu.

GELLER, EDITH HARRIET, elementary school educator; b. Bklyn., June 20, 1938; d. Rubin Stoller and Lillian Fine; m. Joseph Geller, Aug. 13, 1961; children: Mitchell Scott, Pamela Ann, Robin Mindy, Gregg Alan. BS, SUNY, New Paltz, 1960; MALS, SUNY, Stonybrook. Cert. K-8 tchr. and 8-12 lang. arts tchr. NY. 1st grade tchr. Washington St. Sch., Hempstead, NY, 1960—63; lang. arts tchr. South Ocean Mid. Sch., Patchogue, NY, 1975—2001. Author, editor: Youth Mag., 1980—96 (Tchr. of Yr. award, 95). Pres. Women's Am. Orgn. for Rehab. Thru Tng., Patchogue, Brookhaven Hosp. Women's Aux., Patchogue. Jewish. Avocations: travel, reading, gardening, hiking, swimming. Home: 282 S Country Rd East Patchogue NY 11772 E-mail: joenedyiegeller@pol.net.

GELLER, ESTHER (BAILEY GELLER), artist; b. Boston, Oct. 26, 1921; d. Harry and Fannie (Geller) G.; m. Harold Shapero, Sept. 21, 1945; 1 child, Hannah. Diploma, Sch. Boston Mus. Fine Arts, 1943. Tchr. Boston Mus. Sch., 1943, Boris Mirski Sch., 1945-49. Art cons. Leonard Morse Hosp., Natick, Mass. One-woman shows at Boris Mirski Art Gallery, Boston, 1945-46, 49, 52, 61, Addison Gallery Am. Art, Children's Art Centre, Andover, Mass., 1953-55, Mayo Gallery, Provincetown, Mass., 1958, Marion (Mass.) Art Centre, 1966, St. Mark's Sch., Southboro, Mass., 1969, Decenter Gallery, Copenhagen, 1969, Regis Coll., Weston, Mass., 1970, Am. Acad. Gallery, Rome, 1971, Newton (Mass.) Libr., 1973, Newton Art Centre, 1978, Artworks of Wayne, Providence, 1979, Stonehill Coll., Easton, Mass., 1986; 2-person show at The Ctr. for Arts in Natick, 2001; exhibited in group shows at San Francisco Mus., Va. Mus. Art, Chgo. Art Inst., Worcester Art Mus., U. Ill., Smith Coll., Inst. Contemporary Art, DeCordova Mus., USIA traveling show, USIS circulating exhbn., Far East, Boston Mus., Regis Coll., 1984, Danforth Mus. Art, 1995, Boston Ctr. for Arts, 1997, Firehouse Artists Show, Natiek, 1998, Univ. Place, Cambridge, 1999, Mass. State House, Boston, 2000, Boston U. Art Gallery, 2002, Visionary Decade Thorne-Sagendorph Art Gallery, Keene, N.H., 2003. Cabot fellow, 1949; Studios Am. Acad. fellow, 1949-50, 70-71, 75; MacDowell Colony-Yaddo fellow, 1945, 67, 69 Mem.: Arts Wayland Assn., Boston Visual Arts Union. Home: 9 Russell Cir Natick MA 01760-1223 Studio: 5 Summer St Natick MA 01760-4511

GELLER, ETHELL A., consulting clinical psychologist; b. Linz, Austria, Sept. 26, 1946; came to U.S., 1948; d. Abraham and Orinka (Brown) Avram; m. Ronald D. Geller, June 2, 1968. BA summa cum laude, Hunter Coll., 1970, MA, 1972; PhD, CUNY, 1977. Diplomate in Profl. Psychology Internat. Acad. Behavioral Medicine, Counseling and Psychotherapy. Prof. psychology Hunter Coll., N.Y.C., 1977-79; staff psychologist Albert Ellis Inst. for Psychotherapy, N.Y.C., 1979-89; pvt. practice clin. psychology, N.Y.C., 1980—. Rschr. in field. Contbr. articles to profl. jours. Mem. APA, N.Y. Acad. Scis., Am. Assn. Behavior Therapy, Soc. for Behavioral Medicine, Inst. for Rational Emotive Psychotherapy, Phi Beta Kappa. Avocations: cooking, martial arts, travel, languages, music. Office: 952 5th Ave New York NY 10021-1740 Office Phone: 212-861-7521.

GELLER, JANICE GRACE, nurse; b. Auburn, Ga., Feb. 25, 1938; d. Erby Ralph and Jewell Grace (Maughon) Clack; m. Joseph Jerome Geller, Dec. 23, 1973; 1 child, Elizabeth Joanne. Student, LaGrange Coll., 1955-57; BS in Nursing, Emory U., 1960; MS, Rutgers U., 1962. Nat. cert. group psychotherapist; cert. clin. nurse specialist. Psychiat. staff nurse dept. psychiatry Emory U., Atlanta, 1960; nurse educator Ill. State Psychiat. Inst., Chgo., 1961; clin. specialist in mental retardation nursing Northville, Mich., 1962; faculty Coll. Nursing Rutgers U., Newark, 1962-63, faculty Advanced Program in Psychiat. Nursing, 1964-66; faculty Coll. Nursing U. Mich., Ann Arbor, 1963-64; faculty, Teheran (Iran) Coll. for Women, 1967-69; clin. specialist psychiat. nursing Roosevelt Hosp., N.Y.C., 1969-70; faculty, guest lectr. Columbia U., N.Y.C., 1969-70; supr. Dept. Psychiat. Nursing Mt. Sinai Hosp., N.Y.C., 1970-72; pvt. practice psychotherapy N.Y.C., 1972-77, Ridgewood, N.J., 1977-96. Faculty, curriculum coord. in psychiat. nursing William Alanson White Inst. Psychiatry, Psychoanalysis and Psychology, N.Y.C., 1974-84; mem. U.S. del. of Community and Mental Health Nurses to People's Republic of China, 1983. Contbr. articles to profl. jours.; editorial bd. Perspectives in Psychiat. Care, 1971-74, 78-84; author: (with Anita Marie Werner) Instruments for Study of Nurse-Patient Interaction, 1964. Mem. Bergen County Rep. Com., 1989. Recipient 10th Anniversary award Outstanding Clin. Specialist in psychiat.-mental health nursing in N.J., Soc. Cert. Clin. Specialists, 1982; Fed. Govt. grantee as career tchr. in psychiat. nursing, Rutgers U., 1962-63; cert. psychiat. nurse and clin. specialist, N.J., N.Y. Mem. AAAS, ANA (various certs.), N.C. Nurses Assn., Soc. Cert. Clin. Specialists in Psychiat. Nursing (chmn.), Coun. Specialists in Psychiat./Mental Health Nursing, Am. Group Psychotherapy Assn. (cert. group psychotherapist), Am. Assn. Mental Deficiency, World Fedn. Mental Health, Sigma Theta Tau. Address: 307 Chatterson Dr Raleigh NC 27615-3137 Fax: (919) 518-0495.

GELLER, MARGARET JOAN, astrophysicist, educator; d. Seymour and Sarah Geller. AB, U. Calif., Bekeley, 1970; MA, Princeton U., 1972, PhD, 1975; DSc (hon.), Conn. Coll., 1995, Gustavus Adolphus Coll., 1997, U. Mass., Dartmouth, 2000. Rsch. assoc. Harvard Coll. Obs., Cambridge, Mass., 1978-80; asst. prof. Harvard U., Cambridge, 1980-83; astrophysicist Smithsonian Astrophys. Obs., Cambridge, 1983—. Goodspeed-Richardo lectr. U. Pa., 1992; Brickwedde disting. lectr. JHU, 1993; Hogg lectr. Royal Astro. Soc. Can., 1993; Bethe lectr. Cornell U., 1996; Hilldale lectr. U. Wis., 1999; disting. lectr. NSF, 2004; disting. fellow U. Calif., Irvine, Calif., 2006. Contbr. articles to profl. jours.; mem. editl. bd. Sci., 1991—94. Named Libr. Lion, N.Y. Pub. Libr., 1997; recipient Newcomb-Cleve. prize, 1989—90, Klopsteg award, Am. Assn. Physics Tchrs., 1996, ADION medal, 2003; fellow, MacArthur Found., 1990—95. Fellow: AAAS, APS; mem.: NAS (coun. mem. 2000—03), Assoc. Univs. Rsch. in Astronomy (dir.-at-large), Am. Astron Soc. (councillor), Am. Acad. Art and Scis. (coun. mem.), Internat. Astron Union, Phi Beta Kappa (senator 1998—99). Office: Smithsonian Astrophys Obs 60 Garden St Cambridge MA 02138-1516

GELLMAN, GLORIA GAE SEEBURGER SCHICK, marketing professional; b. La Grange, Ill., Oct. 5, 1947; d. Robert Fred and Gloria Virginia (McQuiston) Seeburger; m. Peter Slate Schick, Sept. 25, 1978 (dec. 1980); 2 children; m. Irwin Frederick Gellman, Sept. 9, 1989; 3 children BA magna cum laude, Purdue U., 1969; student, Lee Strasberg Actors Studio; postgrad., UCLA, U. Calif. Irvine. Lic. real estate Colwell Banker, Pa. Mem. mktg. staff Seemac, Inc. (formerly R.F. Seeburger Co.); v.p. V.I.P. Properties, Inc., Newport Beach, Calif.; pres. Glamglo Prodns.; realtor Coldwell Banker Preferred, West Chester, Pa. Host radio show Orange County Art Bytes, Sneak Previews from the Orange County Performing Arts Ctr.; prodr. corp. videos Profl. actress, singer, artist, writer; TV and radio talk show hostess, Indpls.; performer radio and TV commls.; feature writer arts and entertainment column H mag., The Grand Tour mag.; co-prodr. Fullerton: Then and Now (PBS); exec. prodr. (video) Paris Air Show, 2003, Tibet: Beyond Mystique (PBS, 2004 Emmy finalist); prodr. Art Bytes, The Destiny Report Devel. officer mission media Orange County Philharm. Soc., bd. dirs. women's com.; mem. Orange County Master Chorale, Orange County Performing Arts Ctr., v.p., treas. Crescendo chpt., Ctr. Stars, 1st v.p. membership; bd. dirs. Newport Harbor (Calif.) Art Mus., v.p. membership, mem. acquisition coun.; bd. dirs., mem. founders soc. Opera Pacific, mem. exec. com. bd. dirs.; patron Big Bros./Big Sisters Starlight Found.; mem. Visionaries Newport Harbor Mus., Designing Women of Art Inst. Soc. Calif.; past pres. Opera Pacific Guild Alliance; past pres. Spyglass Hill Philharm. Com.; v.p. Pacific Symphony Orch. League, chair endowment sect., spl. events chair; bd. dirs. Pacific Symphony Orch., v.p. cmty. affairs, vice chair vol. devel.; mem. U. Calif. Irvine Found. Bd., mem. devel. com., honors com., pub. affairs and advocacy com.; mem. social scis. dean's adv. coun. U. Calif. Irvine; chmn. adv. coun. Cold War Studies Ctr., Chapman U., Fashionables com.; chmn. numerous small and large fundraisers; mem. com. Red Cross; bd. dirs. Sta. KOCE PBS TV; bd. dirs., exec. com., nominating com., 25th anniversary com., devel. com., vice chmn. vol. devel. Pacific Symphony; fundraising cons. Mission Media Pa.; dir. devel. Mission Media Ministries, Pa., 2005 Recipient Lauds and Laurels award U. Calif., Irvine, 1994, Gellman Courtyard Sculpture honoring contbn. to Sch. of Humanities, U. Calif., Irvine, Most Outstanding Vol. award Pacific Symphony, 2002, Pacific Symphony Orch. League, 2002; finalist Emmy award, 2004 Mem. AAUW, AFTRA, SAG, NATAS, Am. Acad. Television Arts & Scis., Internat. Platform Assn., Actors Equity, U. Calif. Irvine Chancellor's Club, U. Calif. Irvine Humanities Assocs. (founder, pres., bd. dirs.), Mensa, Orange County Mental Health Assn., Seneca Network, Balboa Bay Club, U. Club, Club 39, Islanders, Covergirls, Pacific Symphony Supper Club (founder), Pacific Symphony "Symphony 100" (pres., founder), Sadsbury Village Home Owner's Assn. (pres.), Alpha Lambda Delta, Delta Rho Kappa Republican. Home: PO Box 189 Sadsburyville PA 19369 Personal E-mail: glamglo@comcast.net.

GELMAN, ROCHEL, psychology professor; b. Toronto, Ont., Can., Jan. 23, 1942; came to U.S., 1963; d. Isaac and Ida (Linver) G.; m. Charles R. Gallistel, Nov. 21, 1969; 1 child, Adam BA with first class honors, U. Toronto, 1963; MA, UCLA, 1965, PhD, 1967. Asst. prof. psych. Brown U., Providence, 1967—68, U. Pa., Phila., 1968-72, assoc. prof., 1972—77, prof., 1977—89; prof. psych. UCLA, 1989—2000; prof. psych. and cognitive sci. Rutgers U., New Brunswick, NJ, 2000—. Vis. asst. prof. U. Minn. Inst. Child Devel., Mpls., 1968; vis. scholar U. Calif. Sch. Social Scis.-, Irvine, 1973—74; dir. grad. studies psych. U. Pa., 1974—81; fellow Ctr. Advanced Study Behavioral Scis., 1977—78, 1984—85; assoc. dean grad. office U. Pa. Sch. Arts and Scis., 1981—82; vis. scholar Inst. Psych., Beijing, 1982, Penn Israel Exchange, Tel Avivi, Israel, 1987; chair devel. area UCLA, 1989—94; vis. scholar psych. NYU, 1995—96; dir. training grant in devel. cognitive sci. Nat. Inst. Mental Health, 1995—99; vis. prof. Rutgers U. Ctr. Cognitive Scis., 1999; emeritas prof. psychology UCLA, 2000—. Author: The Child's Understanding of Number, 1978; co-assoc. editor Internat. Ency. Psych Devel. secs.; editl. bd. Cognitive Psych., 1977-, Substratum, 1992-, Math. Cognition, 1994-, Applied Devel. Psych., 2000-; contbr. articles to profl. publs., chpts. to books Guggenheim fellow, 1973-74 Fellow Am. Psychol. Assn. (early career rsch. contbn. award 1976, pres. div. 7 1985-86, disting. sci. contbn. award 1995, mentor award div. 7 2003), Am. Psychol. Soc., Cognitive Sci Soc., Am. Acad. Arts Scis.; mem. Piaget Soc., Psychonomics Soc., Soc. Rsch. in Child Devel., Soc. Exptl. Psychologists, Phi Beta Kappa (foreign mem.), NAS. Office: Rutgers Ctr for Cognitive Sci Psych Bldg Addition Busch Campus 152 Frelinghuysen Rd Piscataway NJ 08854*

GELSKE, ANDREA JANNA, psychologist; b. Plantation, Fla., Dec. 13, 1979; d. Gary and Myra Zale; m. Thomas Edward Gelske, Sept. 5, 2004. BS Psychology, U. Fla., Gainesville, 1998—2002, Ednl. Specialist in Sch. Psychology, 2005. Human Participants Protection Edn. for Rsch. Teams NIH, 2003, cert. Health Ins. Protection and Portability Act U. Fla., 2003. Tchg. asst. exceptional student edn. Dept. Spl. Edn. U. Fla., Gainesville, 2001, grad. asst., autism inclusion project Dept. Spl. Edn., 2002, grad. asst., lit. initiative project Dept. Spl. Edn., 2003, grad. rsch. asst., aggression intervention study Dept. Spl. Edn., 2003—04; sch. psychologist Sch. Bd. Broward County, Fort Lauderdale, Fla., 2005—. Vol. Multidisciplinary Diagnostic and Tng. Program U. Fla., Gainesville, 2003; vol. Interface Youth Program divsn. Corner Drug Store, Inc, Gainesville, 2000—01; vol. Baby Gator Nursery Sch. Head Start Program U. Fla., Gainesville, 2000. Named to Pres.'s Honor Roll, U. Fla., 2001. Mem.: Broward Assn. Sch. Psychologists, Nat. Assn. Sch. Psychology (nat. cert. 2006), Fla. Assn. Sch. Psychologists, Sch. Psychology Grad. Student Assn., Nat. Acad. Honor Soc. for Freshman, Nat. Soc. Collegiate Scholars, Golden Key Honor Soc., Psi Chi. Office: 610 NE 13th Avenue Pompano Beach FL 33060 Personal E-mail: ufandi@aol.com. E-mail: andrea.gelske@browardschools.com.

GELSONE, AMY J., music educator; b. Statesville, NC, Oct. 30, 1955; d. Charles William Johnson and Norma Louise Compton; m. Gene Frank Gelsone, Jan. 18, 1991; 1 child, Melody Brooke; 1 child from previous marriage, David Charles Jackson. BA in Music Edn., Appalachian State U., Boone, NC, 1978; postgrad., U. Kans., Lawrence, 1985, Bowling Green State U., Ohio, 1990. Vocal music tchr. Graham HS, NC, 1979—83, Highland Park HS, Topeka, 1983—86, Anthony Wayne HS, Whitehouse, Ohio, 1986—. Recipient I Make a Difference award, Lucas County Ednl. Svcs., Toledo, Ohio. Mem.: Ohio Edn. Assn., Music Educators Nat. Conf., Am. Choral Dirs. Assn. Baptist. Avocations: scrapbooks, sewing, arranging jazz charts. Office: Anthony Wayne HS 59676 Finzel Rd Whitehouse OH 43571

GELTZER, SHEILA SIMON, public relations executive; b. N.Y.C. d. Sidney E. and Bertie (Rome) Simon; m. Howard E. Geltzer, Sept. 10, 1967; children: Jeremy Niles, Gabriel Lewis. BA, Queens Coll., 1961. With Philip Lesly Co., N.Y.C., 1962-63, Benjamin Co., N.Y.C., 1963-68; ptnr. Simon and Geltzer, Inc., N.Y.C., 1968-74, Ries and Geltzer, N.Y.C., 1974-79; pres. Geltzer and Co., Inc., N.Y.C., 1979—2000; mng. dir., exec. prin. Publicis Dialog, N.Y.C., 2000—. Mem. Pub. Rels. Soc. Am. (counselors acad.), Women in Comms., Women in Pub. Rels., Nat. Coun. of Women, Abingdon Theater. Business E-Mail: sgeltzer@geltzerco.com.

GELZER, LOIS AUGE, foundation administrator; b. Chgo., Oct. 9, 1942; d. William and Fern Bernice (Schwinkendorff) Auge; m. Lawrence Arthur Gelzer, Jr. (dec. Feb. 26, 1999); 1 child, Henry Lawrence. BA, No. Ill. U., 1964; MS in Edn., Shores Acad. Collegia, Miami Shores, Fla., 1982, M in Computer Sci., 1986. Ordained inter-faith min. 2005; cert. tchr. Ill., Mass., instr. USCG Aux., 1975, Usui Reiki master 2005, Qigong facilitator 2006. Tchr. Mc Henry Pub. Schs., Ill., 1964—65, No. Chicago Cmty. HS, 1965—69, Shores Acad., Miami Shores, Fla., 1980—82; tutor Gelzer Tutoring Svc., Oak Bluffs, Mass., 1983—94; tchr. Office for Job Partnerships, Edgartown, 1986—88, Fisher Jr. Coll., Hyannis, 1987; developer foundation not yet finalized, Oak Bluffs, 1995—2000, Cape Elizabeth, Maine, 2000—05, Standish, Maine, 2005—. Instr. USCG Aux., Martha's Vineyard, Mass., 1975—78. Contbr. to mags. and books. Communicator USCG Aux. Flotilla 1-1105, Martha's Vineyard, 1974—79; mgr. The Four PMers Net, 1992—95, Secretary-Treasurer, 1988—97; vol. 3 non-partisan polit. campaigns for selectman, Oak Bluffs, 1974—76; vol. tchrs.' aide Oak Bluffs Sch., 1977; Sunday sch. tchr. Trinity Unitd Meth. Ch., Oak Bluffs, 1977—79. Recipient award for five assists in one night, USCG, 1974. Mem.: AAUW, NAFE, No. Ill. U. Alumni Assn. (life). Meth. Avocations: stamp collecting/philately, genealogy, music, cooking, amateur radio. Home: 20 Libby Pines Rd Standish ME 04084

GEMEINHARDT, JUDITH M. (JUDITH GAMIN), writer, poet; b. Hillsborough, NJ, Oct. 30, 1939; 1 child, Ronald. BS in Psychology and Bus. Adminstrn., Ramapo Coll. of NJ. Columnist, reporter Collie Shetland Sheep Dog Rev., Calif., 1970—73; assoc. editor Off Lead Obedience Mag., NY, 1972—74. Reporter/columnist Collie-Shetland Sheepdog Rev.; reporter Collie Cues Mag.; assoc. editor feature articles on tng. dogs Off Lean Obedience Mag.; reporter Collie Club of Am. Bull.; reporter/columnist Chips Obedience Mag. Author: The Everly Brothers: A Celebration in Photos, Fantasy and Verse, 2006, Thanks for the Memories, 1998, Mental Menopause, 1998; author: (book) A Diary of a Woman in Anguish, 2006; poetry pub. in various mags., profl. pubs. Mem. Nat. Registery of Authors and Writers. Personal E-mail: jgamain@earthlink.net.

GEMMELL-AKALIS, BONNI JEAN, psychotherapist; b. Lansing, Mich., Mar. 11, 1950; d. James Stewart Gemmell and Alpha Alice (Hackenberg) Vanden Bosch; m. Gary Alfred Eddy, Jan. 1, 2001; 1 stepchild, Patrick Eddy; children: Scott Aaron, Ty Alexander, Zachary Alan. BS, Ctrl. Mich. U., 1972, MA, 1974. Ltd. lic. psychologist, Mich.; cert. social worker, Mich. Clin. psychologist, sr. mental health therapist Lincoln Ctr. for Emotionally Disturbed Children & Youth, Lansing, 1974-77; outpatient psychologist Grand Rapids (Mich.) Child Guidance Clinic, 1978-81; pvt. practice Grand Rapids Psychiat. Svcs., 1981-88, 96—, Associated Therapists, Inc., Grand Rapids, 1988-96, pres., 1989-90. Grad. fellow Ctrl. Mich. U., 1972-73. Mem. Mich. Psychoanalytic Coun., Mich. Women Psychologists, Mich. Assn. Profl. Psychologists, Am. Group Psychotherapy Assn. (founder nat. registry 1996), Grand Rapids Area Psychology Assn., Psi Chi. Home: 632 Duxbury Ct SE Ada MI 49301 Office: 1025 Spaulding Ave SE Ste B Grand Rapids MI 49546-3703 Office Phone: 616-285-9141.

GENDLER, ELLEN, dermatologist; b. Bklyn., Feb. 15, 1956; BA, Wesleyan Univ.; MD, Columbia U., 1981. Diplomate Am. Bd. Dermatology. Internal med. intern Lenox Hill Hospital, N.Y.C.; resident in dermatology NYU Med. Ctr., N.Y.C., 1982—85; pvt. practice dermatology N.Y.C., 1985—. Clin. assoc. prof. dept. dermatology NYU Sch. Medicine, N.Y.C., 1990—; trustee Dermatology Found.; consul., med. advisor to numerous cosmetics and health-care companies; spkr. in field. Contbr. articles to numerous profl. jours. Mem.: Am. Acad. Dermatology (assoc.; dir. cosmetics symposium). Office: 1035 Fifth Ave New York NY 10028*

GENDRON, MICHÈLE MARGUERITE MADELEINE, librarian; b. Paris, Mar. 15, 1947; came to U.S., 1950; d. Gerard Joachim and Denise Marie Louise (Le Moravan) G. BA, Orlinda Pierce Coll. for Women, Athens, Greece, 1969; MS, U. Ill., 1971. Libr. Free Libr. Phila., 1971-75, head, Kingsessing Br., 1975-76, head, Ramonita G. de Rodriguez Br., 1976-91, curator spl. collections ctrl. children's dept., 1991-92, head, lit. dept., 1992—. Cons. devel. Hist. Children's Lit. Collection Montgomery County-Norristown (Pa.) Pub. Libr., 1993-94; organizing mem. Pa. Libr. Assn.'s 1st Conf. Svcs. to Youth, Harrisburg, Pa., 1987-89, Women's Network's 1st Conf. on P.R. Woman in Phila., 1981. Author: (bibliographies) Booklist, 1983; contbr. bibliographies Destination World, 1979, Stories to Share, 1985. Trustee Legal Svcs. Fund Dist. Coun. 47 of Am. Fedn. State, County and Mcpl. Employees, 1985-95, mem. exec. bd. Local 2186, 1996—. Recipient Charles Scribner award Scribner Pub., 1976, Nat. Security Forum, Air War Coll., 1985. Mem. ALA (Assn. Libr. Svcs. Children, Mildred Batchelder award selection com. 1979-81, 85-87, internat. rels. com. 1981-85, chair 1984-85, libr. instrn. round table 1991-93), Pub. Libr. Assn. (mktg. to pub. librs. 1991—, svcs. to multicultural populations 1991, sec. exec. com. mktg. pub. libr. svcs. sect. 1995-96), Alliance Francaise de Phila., Franklin Inn Club, Beta Phi Mu. Roman Catholic. Office: Free Libr of Phila Lit Dept 1901 Vine St Philadelphia PA 19103-1116

GENDRON, SUSAN ANN, school system administrator; b. Tewksbury, Mass. m. Mark Gendron; children: Stacey, Matthew. BS in Elem. and Secondary Edn., U. So. Maine, Gorham, MS in Ednl. Adminstrn. From tchr. to supt. Scarborough Pub. Schs., Maine; supt. Windham Sch. Dist., 1997—2003; commr. of edn. State of Maine, Augusta, 2003—. Mem.: Maine Sch. Supts Assn. (Disting. Educator award 2001, Supt. of Yr. award 2002). Office: Commr of Edn State House Sta #23 Augusta ME 04333 E-mail: susan.gendron@maine.gov.

GENESI, SUSAN PETROVICH, school system administrator; b. Philipsburg, Pa., Mar. 24, 1957; d. Richard and Margaret (Ohs) Petrovich; 1 child, Lindsay Margaret. BS in Elem. Edn., Pa. State U., 1981, cert. ednl. adminstrn., 1998, MA in Edn. Adminstrn., 1999; PA Superintend Ency Letter of Eligibility, 2002. Cert. elem. tchr., Pa.; cert. kindergarten tchr., Pa.; cert. instrnl. tech. specialist; cert. grant specialist. Adminstr. Philipsburg-Osceola Area Sch. Dist., Pa., 1981—, prin., 1998. Commr. Pa. Profl. Stds. and Practices Commn., Harrisburg, Pa., 1995—; mem. content validation panel for early adolescence English Nat. Bd. for Profl. Tchg. Stds., Atlanta, 1997; workshop presenter on topics of coop. learning; presenter Keystone State Reading Assn., Hershey, Pa., 1995, 96; coop. tchr. Pa. State U., State College, 1994—; mem. various coms. throughout the sch. dist. Contbr. articles to profl. jours. Mem. Philipsburg Bicentennial Com., 1996-97; organizer Philipsburg Elem. Philipsburg Days, 1994. Mem. ASCD, NEA, Pa. State Edn. Assn., Philipsburg-Osceola Area Edn. Assn. (com. 1981—), Phi Delta Kappa. Republican. Presbyterian. Avocations: traveling and shopping with daughter, computer technology, exploring new trends in education and technology, relaxing at the beach. Office: North Lincoln Elem Sch/ Wallaceton Boggs Elem Sch 200 Short St Philipsburg PA 16866-2640 E-mail: sxg23@psu.edu.

GENESONI, JACQUELINE, mathematics educator; BA in Math., Columbia U., N.Y.C., 1999, MA, 2004. Cert. in tchg. NY, 2004, in sch. dist. adminstrn. NY, 2005. Math. tchr. Freeport HS, NY, 2001—, math. dept. chair, 2006—, prin. summer sch., 2006; asst. dir. Freeport Cmty Sch., 2006—. Mem.: Sch. Adminstrs. Assn. NY State, Am. Assn. Sch. Adminstrs., Kappa Delta Pi. Business E-Mail: jgenesoni@freeportschools.org.

GENEST, THERESA JOAN, lab technician; b. Detroit, May 29, 1950; d. Ted John and Dorothy Marie Bruske; m. Joseph William Genest, Apr. 23, 1971; 1 child, Joseph William Jr. Billing registration adminstrv. sec. St. John Hosp., Detroit, 1968—73; environ. lab tech. Shrader Lab., Detroit, 1990—. Panel mem. AIDS conf. Nat. Assn. Sch. Bd., Alexandria, Va. Pres., v.p., sec., treas. Macomb Intermediate Sch. Dist., Clinton Twp., Mich., 1994—; mem. Fed. Regulatio Com. Lobbying for Regulation in DC, 1995; legis. dinner chair Macomb County Sch. Bd. Legis. Com., 1995—; precinct del., 2003—; mem. bd. edn. Roseville Cmty. Sch., Roseville, Mich., 1988—, Macomb Intermediate Sch. Dist. Nominee Govs. Unsung Heroine award, Mich. Womens Commn., 2002; recipient award of merit, Mich. Assn. of Sch. Bd., 1996, cert. mem., 1991, Platinum Diamond award, Mich. Assn. Sch. Bds., 2005. Democrat. Roman Cath. Business E-Mail: tgenest@misd.net.

GENÉT, BARBARA ANN, accountant, travel company executive; b. N.Y.C., Oct. 14, 1935; d. Arthur Samuel and Louise Margaret (Scheider) G. Profl. cert. in acctg., U. Calif., La Jolla, 1995, student, 1996—; BS of Acctg., U. Phoenix, 2001; MBA, Keller Grad. Sch. Mgmt., 2003. Asst. to chmn. bd., asst. v.p. pub. rels. Brink's Inc., Chgo., 1976-78; co-owner, pres. Ask Mr. Foster, Chgo., 1982-90; with Profl. Cmty. Mgmt., Laguna Hills, Calif., 1990-92; travel counselor E.J. Brown & Assocs., San Diego, 1992-94; tchr.'s asst. U. Calif-San Diego, La Jolla, 1996—. Rep. Becker CPA-CMA Rev., San Diego, 1995—. Mem. campership cmty. coun. YMCA. Becker scholar, 1995, scholar Marks CPA Rev., 1996. Mem. Am. Soc. Woman Accts., Inst. Mgmt. Accts., Inst. Cert. Travel Agts., Order Ea. Star, Ladies of Shrine N.Am., Zonta Internat. of La Jolla (treas. 1998-2000, kids camp 2005). E-mail: barbaragenet@cox.net.

GENEWICK, TIFFANY BOQUARD, obstetrician, gynecologist; b. Buffalo, N.Y., July 5, 1970; d. Francis Joseph and Patricia Ann Boquard; m. Stephen Douglas Genewick, July 23, 1994; children: Paige Louise, Luke Stephen. MD, SUNY, Buffalo, N.Y., 1996. Diplomate Am. Bd. Ob-Gyn., 2003. Resident SUNY, Buffalo, 1996—2000; physician ob-gyn. Promedicus Health Group, West Seneca, NY, 2000—02, Aurora Med. Group, East Aurora, NY, 2002—04; pvt. practice Lancaster, NY, 2004—. Asst. clin. instr. SUNY, Buffalo, 2000—. Tyler Meml. scholarship, Alden H.S., 1988. Mem.: AMA (assoc.), Am. Coll. Of Obstetricians and Gynecologists (assoc.), Lancaster (Pa.) Schs. PTA. Independent. Office: Tiffany B Genewick MD PC 4731 Transit Road Lancaster NY 14043 Office Phone: 716-668-1902. Office Fax: 716-668-1919. Business E-Mail: tgenewick@verizon.net.

GENIA, VICKY, psychologist; b. N.Y.C., June 6, 1950; d. Vincent and Victoria (Bondzio) Auletta; m. Howard D. Genia Jr., Feb. 26, 1971 (div. Nov. 1984); 1 child, Howard D. III; m. Billy G. Witt, Jan. 11, 1985. BA in Math., Buffalo State Coll., 1971; MA in Psychology, U. No. Colo., 1981, D of Counseling Psychology, 1989. Lic. psychologist Md., Washington. Psychologist Ctr. Psychol. and Learning Svcs. Am. U., Washington, 1990—. Adj. prof. dept. psychology Am. U., 1995-96. Author: Counseling and Psychotherapy of Religious Clients, 1995; contbr. articles to profl. jours. With U.S. Army, 1974-76. Mem. Am. Psychol. Assn., Soc. Scientific Study Religion, Religious Rsch. Assn.

GENIESER, NANCY BRANOM, radiologist; MD, Med. Coll. Pa., 1962. Diplomate Am. Bd. Radiology, Am. Bd. Diagnostic Radiololgy, Am. Bd. Pediat. Radiology. Intern Phila. Gen. Hosp., 1962—63; resident radiology NYU Hosps., N.Y.C., 1963—65; prof. radiology NYU Med. Ctr.; staff Bellevue Hosp., N.Y.C.; cons. Manhattan VA; assoc. dean, admissions and fin. aid NYU Sch. Medicine, 2004—. Fellow Am. Coll. Radiology; mem. N.Y.C. Med. Soc., N.Y. Radiol. Soc., N.Y. State Radiol. Soc., Radiol. Soc. N.Am., Soc. Pediat. Rsch Fax: 212-263-7666.

GENIESER-DEROSA, ANYA, psychologist; m. Darren J. DeRosa, Apr. 23, 1994; 1 child, Emma S. DeRosa. BA in Econs., Gettysburg Coll., Pa., 1991; MS in Counseling Psychology, Chestnut Hill Coll., Pa., 1995; D Psychology, Phila. Coll. Osteo. Medicine, 2002. Lic. psychologist Pa. State Bd. Psychology, 2004. Psychologist Ctr. Mental Health Reading Hosp., West Reading, Pa., 2002—06, DGR Mgmt. Comprehensive Behavioral Health Svc., 2006—. Adj. prof. Phila. Coll. Osteo. Medicine, 2000—, Chestnut Hill Coll., 2005. Mem.: APA, Berks Area Psychol. Assn., Assn. Behavioral and Cognitive Therapies, Pa. Psychol. Assn. Office: 2201 Ridgewood Rd Ste 400 Wyomissing PA 19610 Office Phone: 610-378-9601. Personal E-mail: dranyaderosa@hotmail.com.

GENIS, ALICE SINGER, psychologist; b. Vilnius, Lithuania, June 8, 1926; d. Nahum Signer and Miriam Singer (Smith) Galerkin; widowed; children: naomi Genis-Mazin, Robert Genis. Esq., Ludwig Maximillian U., Munich, 1950; BA, Pace U., 1974; MA, Mercy Coll., Dobbs Ferry, N.Y., 1978, Coll. of New Rochelle, 1983. Cert. sch. psychologist. Lab. tech. Queens Gen. Hosp., N.Y.C., 1952-55; with Daycare Ctr. Presbyn. Ch., Peekskill, N.Y., 1972-73; psychologist Mental Health Clinic, Peekskill, 1978-80; asst. sch. psychology Pines Bridge Sch., Yorktown, N.Y., 1980-82; biofeedback therapist Med. Cmty. Ctr., Cortland, N.Y., 1985-94; sch. psychologist BOCES, Yorktown, N.Y., 1983-85. Presenter in field. Contbr. articles to profl. jours. Vol. Hosp. Aux., Peekskill, 1962-98; com. Heart Fund Ball, Westchester, 1970s, 80s; pres. Norchester Hadassam, Peekskill, 1983-85, 88-91; mem. The Field Libr., Peekskill. Named Woman of Merit, Westchester Hadassh, White Plaines, N.Y., 1996; recipient New Life award Israel Bonds, Peekskill, 1979, Presl. awards Norchester Hadassah, 1985, 91. Mem. Nat. Assn. Sch. Psychologists, Biofeedback and Psychophysiology Performing Ctr. for the Arts. Avocations: music, piano, swimming, gardening, travel.

GENN, NANCY, artist; b. San Francisco; d. Morley P. and Ruth W. Thompson; m. Vernon Chathburton Genn; children: Cynthia, Sarah, Peter. Student, San Francisco Art Inst., U. Calif., Berkeley. Lectr. on art and papermaking Am. Ctrs. in Osaka, Japan, Nagoya, Japan, Kyoto, Japan, 1979-80; guest lectr. various univs. and art mus. in U.S., 1975—; vis. artist Am. Acad. in Rome, 1989, 94, 2001. One-woman shows include, De Young Mus., San Francisco, 1955, 63, Gumps Gallery, San Francisco, 1955, 57, 59, San Francisco Mus. Art, 1961, U. Calif., Santa Cruz, 1966-68, Richmond (Calif.) Art Center, 1970, Oakland (Calif.) Mus., 1971, Linda/Farris Gallery, Seattle, 1974, 76, 78, 81, L.A. Inst. Contemporary Art, 1976, Susan Caldwell Gallery, NYC, 1976-77, 79, 81, Nina Freudenheim Gallery, Buffalo, 1977, 81, Annely Juda Fine Art, London, 1978, Inoue Gallery, Tokyo, 1980, Toni Birckhead Gallery, Cin., 1982, Kala Inst. Gallery, Berkeley, Calif., 1983, Ivory/Kimpton Gallery, San Francisco, 1984, 86, Eve Mannes Gallery, Atlanta, 1985, Richard Iri Gallery, L.A., 1990, Harcourts Modern and Contemporary Art, San Francisco, 1991, 93, 96, Am. Assn. Advancement of Sci., Washington, 1994, Anne Reed Gallery, Ketchum, Id., 1995, Michael Petronko Gallery, NY, 1997, Mills Coll. Art Mus., Oakland, Calif., 1999, Takada Gallery, San Francisco, 1999-00, 03, Ulivi Gallery, Prato, Italy, 2002, Fresno Art Mus., Calif., 2003, Bolinas Mus., Calif., 2003, Inst. Italiano di Cultura, Chgo., L.A., 2004, Inst. Italiano Di Cultura/Chgo. Art Inst., Flatfile Galleries, Chgo., 2005; group exhbns. include San Francisco Mus. Art, 1971, Aldrich Mus., Ridgefield, Conn., 1972-73, Santa Barbara (Calif.) Mus., 1974-75, Oakland Mus. Art, 1975, Susan Caldwell, Inc., NYC, 1974-75, Mus. Modern Art, NYC, 1976, traveling exhbn. Arts Coun. Gt. Britain, 1983-84, Inst. Contemporary Arts, Boston, 1977, J.J.Brookings Gallery, San Francisco, 1997, Portland (Oreg.) Art Mus., 1997—, Takada Gallery, San Francisco, 1999-00, Leighton Glalery, Blue Hill, Maine, 2005; represented in permanent collections Mus. Modern Art, NYC, NY Pub. Libr., Achenback Found., Palace of the Legion of Honour, San Francisco, Albright-Knox Art Gallery, Buffalo, Libr. of Congress, Washington, Nat. Mus. for Am. Art, Washington, LA County Mus. Art, Art Mus. U. Calif., Berkeley, McCrory Corp., NYC, Mus. Art, Auckland, N.Z., Aldrich Mus., Ridgefield, Conn., (collection) Bklyn. Mus., (collection) U. Tex., El Paso, Internat. Ctr. Aesthetic Rsch., Torino, Italy, Cin. Art Mus., San Francisco Mus. Modern Art, Oakland Art Mus., LA County Mus., City of San Francisco Hall of Justice, Harris Bank, Chgo., Chase Manhattan Bank, NYC, Modern Art Gallery of Ascoli Piceno, Italy, Mills Coll. Art Mus., Oakland, Calif., Mills Coll. Art, Oakland, Calif., various mfg. cos., also numerous pvt. collections; commd. works include, Bronze lectern and 5 bronze sculptures for chancel table, 1st Unitarian Ch., Berkeley, Calif., 1961, 64, bronze fountain, Cowell Coll., U. Calif., Santa Cruz, bronze menorah, Temple Beth Am, Los Altos Hills, Calif., 17, murals and 2 bronze fountain sculptures, Sterling Vineyards, Calistoga, Calif., fountain sculpture, Expo 1974, Spokane, Wash; vis. artist Am. Acad., Rome, 1989. U.S./Japan Creative Arts fellow, 1978-79; recipient Ellen Branston award, 1952; Phelan award De Young Mus., 1963; honor award HUD, 1968 Home: 1515 La Loma Ave Berkeley CA 94708-2033 Office Phone: 510-849-4366.

GENNINGS, KRISTEN ELLEN, music educator; d. Maurice and Catherine LeVine; m. David M Gennings, Nov. 1, 2003. BA in Music Edn., Wagner Coll., Staten Island, 1999; MS in Spl. Edn., CUNY, Staten Island, 2003. Band dir. NYC Bd. Edn., Staten Island, 1999—2001, South Plainfield Bd. Edn., NJ, 2001—. Musician numerous cmty. bands and recitals, Staten Island, 1995—. Mem.: NJ Edn. Assn., NJ Music Edn. Assn. Office Phone: 973-754-4620.

GENSHAFT, JUDY LYNN, psychologist, educator; b. Canton, Ohio, Jan. 7, 1948; d. Arthur I. and Leona (Caghan) G. BA, U. Wis., 1969; MA, Kent State U., 1973, PhD, 1975. Lic. psychologist, Ohio. Sch. psychologist Canton (Ohio) City Schs., 1972-75; asst. prof. Ohio State U., 1976-81, assoc. prof., asst. chmn., 1981-85, prof., 1985—92, asst. chair, 1985-86, chair, 1987—92, presdl. intern, acting assoc. provost, 1986-87; dean Sch. Edn. SUNY, Albany, 1992-95, interim v.p. for acad. affairs, 1995-97, provost, v.p. acad. affairs, 1997-2000; pres. U. So. Fla., Tampa, 2000—. Psychiat. social worker Canton Mental Health Clinic, 1970-72; vis. prof. U. British Columbia, Vancouver, Can., 1976-81. Contbr. numerous articles and book chpts. to profl. publ. Mem. Ballet Met., Columbus, 1986; cons. League Against Child Abuse, Columbus,

1978—, Bur. Vocat. Edn., Columbus, 1980—; mem. adv. bd. Support for Talented Students, Columbus, 1985—; bd dirs. H. Lee Moffitt Cancer Ctr. and Rsch. Inst., Fla. High-Tech Corridor, Greater Tampa Bay C. of C., Tampa Bay Partnership, Coun. of 100 (chair-designate). Nat. Rsch. grantee, 1984-85; recipient Kathryn Schoen Endowment award, 1986, Huelsman award, 1988, Hon. award Ohio Dept. Edn., 1984, Disting. Affirmative Action award, 1991, Leadership award Nat. Sch. Devel. Coun., Shirley A. Ryals award, Prevent Blindness, 2003. Mem. Am. Psychol. Assn., Nat. Assn. Sch. Psychologist, (sec. 1983-85, Presl. award 1982, 85, 87), Am. Assn. Counseling and Devel., Internat. Assn. Sch. Psychologists, Ohio Sch. Psychologist Assn. (ethics chmn. 1985-86), Sigma Xi. Avocations: sports, reading. Office: U So Fla Pres Office 4202 E Fowler Ave Tampa FL 33620-8000

GENTILCORE, EILEEN MARIE BELSITO, principal; b. Glen Cove, N.Y. d. Samuel Francis and Nellie Theresa (McKenna) Belsito; m. James Matthew Gentilcore, Aug. 4, 1951; children: Kevin, John, Scott BS Edn., SUNY, Potsdam; MS Edn., Hofstra U., 1968, profl. diploma, 1976, EdD, 1979. Tchr. first grade Sea Cliff Sch., NY, 1951—52; founder, pre-K Germany Officers Sch., Munich, 1952—53; tchr. first grade Peekskill Schs., NY, 1953—54; tchr. second grade Syosset Sch., NY, 1954—55, reading cons., 1970—84, head tchr., 1974—84, prin., 1985—96; ret., 1996. Bicentennial adv. bd. Syosset Cmty., 1976; adv. bd. Telicare, Uniondale, N.Y., 1978-80; mem. children immunized against polio, Med. Mission to India, 2004; mem. Gift of Life med. mission, Shanghai, Beijing and Hong Kong, 2003; cons. in field Author: Developmental Learning, 1979 Organizer med. team to Honduras, 1998; mem. Nassau County Graffiti Task Force, 1994—. N.Y. State PTA fellow, 1971-73, Hofstra fellow, 1971; recipient Jenkins award N.Y. State PTA, 1968, Hon. Life, 1976, Pius X award Rockville Ctr. Diocese, 1985, Disting. Svc. award, N.Y. State PTA Dist., 1996, Teddy Roosevelt Achievement award, 1999, Citation for meritorious svc., R.I. Internat. Found., 2002, Zone 32 Disting. Past Dist. Gov. award, Barcelona, Spain, 2002; named Woman of Distinction, N.Y. State Senate, 1998, 2003, Syosset-Woodbury Rep. Club and Senator Carl Marcellino Achievement award, 1999, Town Oyster Bay, 2004; grantee Karla Project, 1998; Queens Coun. Boy Scouts Am., 2003; scholarship named after N.Y. State Sen. Liberty award, 2006 Mem.: Profl. and Bus. Women (Rotary world literacy coord. 2005—), Syosset Prins. (pres. 1992), Rotary Internat. (pres. Syosset-Woodbury 1993—95, gov. aide 1995, launched Operation Mitch, Honduras 1996, Gift of Life pres., vocat. dir. dist. 7250 1996—97, med. mission to Honduras 1997, 1st woman dist. gov. dist. 7250 1998—99, children at risk task force 2000—, conf. chair Zone 32 2000—, coord. Internat. Avoidable Blindness task force 2002—, mem. internat. task force children at risk 2003—04, coord. literary task force zone 32 2003—04, coord. literacy task force zone 32 2003—, chair centennial com. dist 7250 2003—, coun. on legis. del. 2004, asst. gen. world coord. literacy task force 2004—, coord lit. gen. world 2005, strategic planning com. 2005—, coord. world health and hunger 2006—, med. mission to Russia dist. 7250 1995, coord. Internat. Children at Risk task force, v.p., presenter, Paul Harris fellow 1995, N.Y. State Senate Woman of Distinction 1998, Internat. Achievement award 1999, Outstanding Svc. award 1999, Abe Gordon V.P. Outstanding Svc. award 2000, Achievement award 2000, Meritorious Svc. citation 2002, Disting. Past Dist. Gov. Global award 2002, Internat. Global award 2002, Svc. Above Self award 2003, Lifetime Achievement award 2004—, Internat. Lit. award 2005, 4 Aves. Svc. citation 2006), Kappa Delta Pi, Alpha Sigma Omicron. Roman Catholic. Avocations: swimming, writing, reading, gardening. Fax: 516-921-0206. E-mail: genheart@optonline.net.

GENTILE, AMBER LEIGH, assistant principal; b. Reading, Pa., Oct. 17, 1974; d. Thomas W. and Margaret J. Scholvin; m. Marc A. Gentile, July 15, 2000. BA in Psychology summa cum laude, Dickinson Coll., Carlisle, Pa., 1997; MS in Counseling, West Chester U., Pa., 2002. Cert. tchr., spl. edn. tchr., counselor Pa. Emotional support instr. Chester County Intermediate Unit, Downingtown, Pa., 1998—2004, dean of students, 2003—04; juvenile edn. instr. Chester County Prison, West Chester, Pa., 1998—2003; program dir. alternative edn. program Phoenixville (Pa.) Area Sch. Dist., 2002—04, h.s. asst. prin., 2004—. Pvt. tutor, Phoenixville, Pa., 1994—2004. Team participant Nat. Multiple Sclerosis Soc., Phila., 1998—2006; com. chair relay for life Am. Cancer Soc., Phoenixville, 2004—05. Named Best SAP in Common Wealth, Pa. Assoc. Student Assistance Profls., 2003—04; recipient Fayette N. Talley award, Dickinson Coll., 1995, Wilbur Harrington and Helen Burns Norcross prize, 1996; scholar, 1997; Robert C. Byrd scholar, Pa. State, 1993. Mem.: ASCD (assoc.), Nat. Assoc. Secondary. Sch. Prins. (assoc.), Alpha Lambda Delta, Psi Chi, Phi Beta Kappa. Avocations: travel, reading. Office: Phoenixville Area High Sch 1200 Gay St Phoenixville PA 19460 Office Phone: 484-927-5100. Office Fax: 610-933-6009. Personal E-mail: amscholvin@hotmail.com. Business E-Mail: gentilea@pasd.com.

GENTILE, CAROLINE D., adult education educator; b. Presque Isle, Maine, Jan. 24, 1924; d. Gerado and Donata G. BS, Boston U., 1946; MA, NYU, 1952; postgrad., U. Wis., Columbia; LHD, U. Maine, Presque Isle, 1996. Instr. Aroostook State Normal Sch., Presque Isle, Maine, 1946-52; asst. prof. Aroostook State Tchrs. Coll., Presque Isle, 1952-58, assoc. prof., 1958-69, Aroostook State Coll. of the U. Maine, Presque Isle, 1969-71, U. Maine, Presque Isle, 1971—. Cons., editor: History of the Presque Isle Recreation Program. Organizer, founder Presque Isle Ice Skating Program; dir. ARC; mem. Presque Isle Parks and Recreation Bd.; bd. dirs. Opportunity Tng. Sch., chair bd. Mem. AAUP, AAUW, Maine Bus. and Profl. Women (pres. 1990-91), Delta Kappa Gamma (pres. 1986-88). Avocations: dance, sports, gardening, reading. Home: 13 Dudley St Presque Isle ME 04769-2423 Office: U Maine 181 Main St Presque Isle ME 04769-2844

GENTILE SACHS, VALERIE ANN, lawyer; b. Cleve., Aug. 4, 1955; d. John Charles and Doreen Phyllis (Neale) G. B.L.S., Bowling Green U., 1977; J.D., Case Western Res. U., 1981. Bar: Ohio 1981. Summer assoc. Arter & Hadden, Cleve., 1980, assoc., 1981-83; sec. Royal Petroleum Properties, Inc., Cleve., 1982-83; assoc. Baker & Hostetler, Cleve., M.A. Hanna Co., v.p., gen. counsel, sec. RELTEC Corp., 1997-2000; v.p., gen. counsel, Marconi Comm., Inc., 2000-01; exec. v.p., gen. counsel, 2001-02, gen. counsel, chief legal officer Marconi PLC, London, 2002-03; exec. v.p., gen. counsel, sec. Jo-Ann Stores, Inc., 2003-; Editor: Case Western Res. U. Law Rev., 1980-81, assoc. editor, 1979-80; assoc. editor Case Western Res. U. Jour. Internat. Law, 1978-79. Mem. Cleve. Citizens League, 1982-84; trustee Forest Hills Housing Corp., Cleve., 1982-84; mem. fgn. trade policy com. Cleve. World Trade Assn., 1982. Mem. ABA, Ohio State Bar Assn., Cleve. Bar Assn., Alpha Epsilon Delta, Beta Beta Beta, Alpha Lambda Delta. Office: Jo Ann Stores Inc 5555 Darrow Rd Hudson OH 44236-4011 Office Phone: 330-656-2600 2156. Office Fax: 330-463-6675.

GENTNER, DEDRE, psychology professor; PhD in psychology, U. Calif., San Diego, 1974. Sr. scientist Bolt Beranek and Newman; faculty mem. U. Wash., U. Ill., Urbana; prof. psychology, edn. and social policy Northwestern U., Evanston, Ill., 1990—. Fellow: Am. Acad. Arts and Scis. Office: Northwestern U 213 Swift Hall 2029 Sheridan Rd Evanston IL 60201 E-mail: gentner@northwestern.edu.

GENTRY, ALBERTA ELIZABETH, elementary school educator; b. Richter, Kans., Feb. 18, 1925; d. John Charles and Dessie Lorena (Duvall) Briles; m. Kenneth Neil Gentry, June 1, 1947; children: Michal Neil, Alan Dale, Elisa Ann. BE, Emporia (Kans.) Tchrs. Coll., 1975. Cert. tchr., Kans. Tchr. Chippewa Rural Sch., Ottawa, Kans., 1943-44; prin., tchr. Pomona (Kans.) Grade Sch., 1944-47, tchr., 1960-61, Silverlake Rural Sch., Pomona, 1947-48, Hawkins Rural Sch., Ottawa, 1948-49, Davy Rural Sch., Ottawa, 1950-53, Eugene Field Sch., Ottawa, 1953-54, Centropolis Grade Sch., Ottawa, 1964, Appanoose Elem. Sch., Pomona, 1964-90, ret., 1990. Trainer student tchr., 1985-86. Author: Proven Ideas for Classroom Teachers, 1988. Project leader, supporter 4-H, Franklin County, Kans., 1963-67; den mother Boy Scouts Am., Ottawa, 1955-66; dir. Bible sch., tchr. Trinity Meth. Ch., Ottawa, 1955-70, supt., 1955-66, mem. choir, 1947—. Named to Kans. Tchrs. Hall of Fame, 1991. Mem. NEA, Kans. Tchrs. Assn., Kans. Edn. Assn., Alpha Delta Kappa (sec. 1988-90). Republican. Methodist. Avocations: bird watching, arts and crafts, flower gardening, music, genealogy. Home: 1057 Hwy K68 Pomona KS 66076-9070

GENTRY, APRIL DAWN, liberal arts professor; b. Springfield, Ill., Sept. 7, 1974; d. James Paul Evers and Angela Ann Miller. BA, MacMurray Coll., Jacksonville, Ill., 1996; MA, Ohio U., Athens, 1998; PhD, So. Ill. U., Carbondale, 2003. ICI cert. grant writer 2005. Asst. prof. Savannah State U., Ga., 2003—. Reader Ga. Regents' Essay exam, 2004—, Advanced Placement Testing Program, 2005—, SAT essay, 2005—; grant editor Savannah State U., Office of Sponsored Rsch., 2006—; tutor Union Mission Family Literacy Project; presenter in field. Co-author: (reference book) A Critical Companion to Herman Melville, 2006; mem. editl. bd.: MP, An Internat. Feminist Online Jour., 2005—, guest editor: jour. issue Women Writers, 2005. Vol. Savannah's Step Up Poverty Initiative. Recipient Dean's award for faculty excellence, Coll. Liberal Arts and Social Scis., Savannah State U., 2004, Ann Moy Edn. award, United Way, 2006. Mem.: Popular Culture Assn., Postcolonial Studies Assn., Sigma Tau Delta (nat. com. mem. outstanding chpt./project grants 2005—, faculty sponsor SSU chpt.). Avocations: surfing, skating, soccer, writing. Office: Savannah State Univ Dept Liberal Arts PO Box 20029 Savannah GA 31404 Business E-Mail: gentrya@savstate.edu.

GENTRY, MARY JEAN ASHER, music educator; b. Outlook, Wash., Feb. 17, 1936; d. Robert arthur and Myrtle Gertrude (Ford) Asher; m. George Albert Gentry, Aug. 21, 1960; children: George Gregory, Michael Asher, Richard Wade, Brenda Renee. BA in Music, Wash. State U., 1959. Cert. in music edn. Substitute tchr. Katy (Tex.) Ind. Sch. Dist., 1979-94; piano tchr. Katy, 1979—. Mem. Houston Chorale Soc.; mem. St. Peter's Chancel Choir, Katy, 1980—, hand bell ringer, 1993—; mem. Women's Ensemble of St. Peters, Katy, 1990—. Mem. Katy Music Tchrs. Assn. (2d v.p. 1994-96), Mu Phi Epsilon. Home: 22715 Merrymount Dr Katy TX 77450-2319 Business E-Mail: gentryagentry@copper.net.

GENTRY, PENNY MICHELLE, elementary school educator; b. Bristol, Tenn., Mar. 23, 1972; d. Wayne William and Frances Katherine Duncan; m. Bud Gentry, July 20, 2002. BS, Va. Intermont Coll., Bristol, 1994. Phys. edn. tchr. Roan Creek Elem. Sch., Mountian City, Tenn., 1996—. Home: 939 Cold Springs Rd Mountain City TN 37683 Office: Roan Creek Elementary 2410 Roan Creek Rd Mountain City TN 37683 Office Phone: 423-727-4964. Home Fax: 423-727-2164; Office Fax: 423-727-2164. Personal E-mail: gentryp1@k12tn.net. Business E-Mail: gentryp1@tn.net.

GENTRY, SHIRLEY, music educator, writer; b. Trenton, N.J., Dec. 3, 1934; d. Howard E. and Wyvonne Robinson Gentry; m. David Lyman (div.). MusB in Edn., Ctrl. Meth. U., Fayette, Mo., 1957. Cert. tchr. Mo., 1960, Wash., 1965. Tchr. music Richland Schs., Wash., 1963—68; tchr. elem. sch. Hawaii Schs., Oahu, 1968—69; tchr. music Chariton Schs., Iowa, 1969—73, Tehran Am. Schs., Iran, 1973—76; with Chariton Phone Co., 1979—84; ret., 1984. Author: A Christmas In Rime, 2003, From the Pen of a Poetess, 2003, Posy Unsung, 2004. Sec. Dem. Party, Chariten, 1991—93. Scholar, Ctrl. Meth. U., 1953. Mem.: AARP, Mensa (contbr. mag. 1982—), Phi Kappa Theta. Democrat. Baptist. Avocations: piano, writing, poetry, crossword puzzles. Home: 511 Main 11 Trenton MO 64683

GENTRY, TINA, secondary school educator; b. Berwyn, Ill., June 19, 1967; d. Steve and Jean Serpico; m. James Gentry, Nov. 7, 1993; children: Joshua, Brittany. BA, Sam Houston State U., Huntsville, Tex., 1994. Cert. tchr. Tex. Tchr. Westfield H.S., Houston, Tex., 1997—. Pre-teen camp coord. WoodsEdge Cmty. Ch., The Woodlands, Tex. Named Distinguished Educator, 2006. Office: Westfield HS 16713 Ella Blvd Houston TX 77090 Office Phone: 281-586-1300. Business E-Mail: tinag@springisd.org.

GENYK, RUTH BEL, psychotherapist; b. Los Angeles, Apr. 5, 1955; d. John Douglas Bel and Ella Adiline (Lips) Medeiros; m. Edward A. Genyk, Aug. 8, 1983; children: Steven, Timothy, Devlon, Suzanne. Student, U. Copenhagen, 1975; BA, BSW, Whittier Coll., 1977; MA, U. Detroit, 1979; MSW, U. Mich., 1987. Lic. master social worker, Mich.; lic. marriage and family therapist, Mich. Social worker, community liaison Family Service, Whittier, Calif., 1976-77; social worker Children's Group Home, Detroit, 1977, Family Group Homes, Ann Arbor, Mich., 1977; probation officer Dept. Corrections, Detroit, 1978-86; cons. Cath. Social Svcs., Jackson, Mich., 1986-87; pvt. practice psychotherapy Jackson, Mich., 1987—, Chelsea, —, 1993—. Mem. Jr. League. Mem. AAUW, Am. Corrections Assn., Mich. Corrections Assn., Nat. Assn. Social Workers. Democrat. Unitarian Universalist. Avocations: classical music, jazz. Office: 2301 E Michigan Ave Ste 105 Jackson MI 49202-3765 Office Phone: 517-782-8313. Personal E-mail: egenyk@aol.com.

GEOGHEGAN, PATRICIA, lawyer; b. Bayonne, NJ, Sept. 9, 1947; d. Frank and Rita (Mihok) G. BA, Mich. State U., 1969; MA, Yale U., 1972, JD, 1974; LLM, NYU, 1982. Bar: N.Y. 1975. Assoc. Cravath, Swaine & Moore, N.Y.C., 1974-82, ptnr., 1982—. Mem. ABA, N.Y. State Bar Assn., Assn. of Bar of City of N.Y. Office: Cravath Swaine & Moore Worldwide Plz Fl 45 825 8th Ave New York NY 10019-7416 Office Phone: 212-474-1584. Office Fax: 212-474-3700. Business E-Mail: pgeoghegan@cravath.com.

GEORGE, BARBARA JEAN, literature and language educator, speech educator, communications educator; d. Ivan and Joan Hamel; m. Michael Edward George, June 5, 1981; children: Kelsie, Nikki, Jamie, Michelle. BS in Secondary English Edn., Kans. State U., Manhattan, 1985. Lic. Kans., 1985. English tchr. Unified Sch. Dist. 224, Clifton, Kans., 1991—; Cisco instr. Office Phone: 785-446-3444.

GEORGE, ELIZABETH (SUSAN ELIZABETH GEORGE), writer; b. Warren, Ohio, 1949; Student, Foothill Cmty. Coll.; graduate, Univ. Calif., Riverside; M in counseling, psychology, Univ. Calif., Fullerton; DHL (hon.), Calif. State U. English tchr. Mater Dei H.S., Santa Ana, Calif., 1974-75, El Toro (Calif.) H.S., 1975-87; creative writing tchr. Coastline Coll., Costa Mesa, Calif., 1988—92, Irvine (Calif.) Coll., 1989, U. Calif., Irvine, 1990. Author: A Great Deliverance, 1989 (Anthony award, Agatha award, 1989, Le Grand Prix de Litterature Policiere, 1990), Payment in Blood, 1989, Well Schooled in Murder, 1990 (MIMI award, Germany), A Suitable Vengeance, 1991, For the Sake of Elena, 1992, Missing Joseph, 1993, Playing for the Ashes, 1994, In the Presence of the Enemy, 1996, Deception on His Mind, 1997, In Pursuit of the Proper Sinner, 1999, A Traitor to Memory, 2001, Remember, I'll Always Love You, 2001, I, Richard, 2002, A Place of Hiding, 2003, Write Away, 2004, A Moment on the Edge, 2004, With No One as Witness, 2005 (Publishers Weekly bestseller list). Named Orange County Tchr. of Yr. Mailing: c/o Trident Media fl 36 41 Madison Ave New York NY 10010

GEORGE, GAY, lawyer; b. Hollywood, Calif., Mar. 3, 1955; d. Wallace Erby and Audrey Eva Elizabeth George. BS, Calif. Poly. U., 1977; MBA, U. Wyo., 1993, JD, 2001. Bar: Wyo. 2001. Peace Corps vol. U.S. Govt., Apia, Western Samoa, 1979—80; quality assurance mgr. Arnott's Biscuits, Auckland, New Zealand, 1981—88; R&D mgr. ETA Foods, Ltd., Auckland, 1988—99; tech. writer G&G Enterprises, Laramie, Wyo., 1991—98; law clk. to Hon. Barton R. Voigt Wyo. Supreme Ct., Cheyenne, 2001—03; corp. counsel Blue Cross Blue Shield Wyo., Cheyenne, 2003—. Contbr. chapters to books. Avocations: reading, films, theater, camping, backpacking. Office Phone: 307-432-2914. Business E-Mail: ggeorge77@earthlink.net.

GEORGE, JEAN CRAIGHEAD, author, illustrator; b. Washington, July 2, 1919; d. Frank Cooper and Carolyn (Johnson) Craighead; m. John L. George, Jan. 28, 1944 (div. Jan. 1964); children: Twig George Pittenger, John Craighead, Thomas Lothar. BA, Pa. State U., 1941. Reporter Washington Post, 1943-44; artist Pageant mag., 1945; reporter United Features, 1945-46; roving editor Reader's Digest, 1966-80; continuing edn. tchr. Chappaqua, NY, 1960-68. Author, illustrator: My Side of the Mountain, 1959, Summer of the Falcon, 1962, Gull Number 737, 1964, The Thirteen Moons, 1967-69, Coyote in Manhattan, 1968, River Rats, Inc., 1968, Who Really Killed Cock Robin, 1972, Julie of the Wolves, 1972, American Walk Book, 1978, Cry of the Crow, 1980, Journey Inward, 1982, The Talking Earth, 1983, One Day in the Alpine Tundra, 1984, How to Talk to Your Animals, 1985, One Day in the Prairie, 1986, Water Sky, 1987, (mus.) One Day in the Woods, 1988, The Shark Beneath the Reef, 1989, On the Far Side of the Mountain, 1990, One Day in the Tropical Rain Forest, 1990, The Missing 'Gator of Gumbo Limbo, 1992, The Fire Bug Connection, 1993, The First Thanksgiving, 1993, Dear Rebecca, Winter Is Here, 1993, Animals Who Have Won Our Hearts, 1994, Julie, 1994, To Climb a Waterfall, 1995, Acorn Pancakes & Dandelion Salad, 1995, There's an Owl in the Shower, 1995, Everglades, 1995, The Case of the Missing Cutthroat Trout, 1996, The Tarantula in My Purse, 1996, Look to the North, A Wolf Pup Diary, 1997, Julie's Wolf Pack, 1997, Arctic Son, 1997, Rhino Romp, 1998, Giraffe Trouble, 1998, Dear Katie, the Volcano Is a Girl, 1998, Survival Filmstrips, 1984, (film) My Side of the Mountain, 1965, Nature Filmstrips, 1978-80, One Day in the Woods Musical for Children (music by Chris Kubie), 1997, Elephant Walk, 1998, Gorilla Gang, 1999, Morning, Noon and Night, 1999, Frightful's Mountain, 1999, Snow Bear, 1999, How to Talk to Your Dog, 2000, How to Talk to Your Cat, 2000, Nutik, the Wolf Pup, 2001, Nutik & Amaoq Play Ball, 2001, Tree Castle Island, 2002, Cliff Hanger, 2002, Frightful's Daughter, 2002, Fire Storm, 2003, Charlie's Raven, 2004, Snowboard Twist, 2004, (musical) Julie of the Wolves, 2004, Luck, 2005, DVD Storyteller, 2005. Recipient Aurianne award, 1957, Newbery Honor Book award, 1961, medal, 1973, Hans Christian Andersen Honor List award, 1964, Pa. State Woman of Yr. award, 1968, World Book award, 1971, Kerlan award, 1982, U. So. Miss. award, 1986, Washington Irving award, 1991, 92, Knickerbocker award, 1991, Washington Post Children's Book Guild award, 1998, Empire State award, 1998, runner-up Lamplighter award, 2002, Regina medal Cath. Libr. Assn., Literary Lights award for children's lifetime work Boston Pub. Libr., 2003, Ludington award Am. Paperback Assn., 2004, Lamplighter Hon. Book, 2005. Address: 20 William Pl Chappaqua NY 10514-3114 E-mail: jeangeorgemail@aol.com.

GEORGE, JOYCE JACKSON, lawyer, writer, retired judge; b. Akron, Ohio, May 4, 1936; d. Ray and Verna (Popadich) Jackson; children: Michael Eliot, Michelle René. BA, U. Akron, 1962, JD, 1966; postgrad., Nat. Jud. Coll., Reno, 1976, NYU, 1983; LLM, U. Va., 1986. Bar: Ohio 1966, U.S. Dist. Ct. (no. dist.) Ohio 1966, U.S. Ct. Appeals (6th cir.) 1968, U.S. Supreme Ct. 1968. Tchr. Akron Bd. Edn., 1962-66; asst. dir. law City of Akron, 1966-69, pub. utilities advisor, 1969-70, asst. dir. law, 1970-73; pvt. practice Akron, 1973-76; referee Akron Mcpl. Ct., 1975, judge, 1976-83, 9th dist. Ct. Appeals, Akron, 1983-89, Peninsula, Ohio, 1989; U.S. atty. No. Dist., Ohio, 1989-93; v.p. adminstrn. Telxon Corp., Akron, 1993-96; pres. Ind. Bus. Info. Svcs., Inc., Akron, 1996—. Tchr., lectr. Ohio Jud. Coll., Nat. Jud. Coll.; cons. in field. Author: Judicial Opinion Writing Handbook, 1981, 3d edit., 1993, 4th edit., 1998, Referee's Report Writing Handbook, 1992; contbr. articles to profl. publs. Recipient Outstanding Woman of Yr. award Akron Bus. and Profl. Women's Club, 1982; Alumni Honor award U. Akron, 1983, Alumni award U. Akron Sch. Law, 1991; Dept. Treasury award, 1992; named Woman of Yr. in politics and govt. Summit County, Ohio, 1983. Mem.: ABA, Akron Bar Assn., Ohio Bar Assn. Fax: 330-668-2910.

GEORGE, JULIANNE MARY, music educator, conductor; b. Martinez, Calif., July 16, 1964; d. Robert Joseph and Marjorie C. George. BA, U. of the Pacific, Stockton, Calif., 1987. Tchr. instrumental music Sequoia Mid. Sch., Pleasant Hill, Calif., 1993—2006; tchr. choral and instrumental music Alhambra H.S. and Martinez Jr. H.S., Martinez, Calif., 2006—. Mem.: NEA, Am. Choir Dirs. Assn., Calif. Tchrs. Assn., Music Educators Nat. Conf., Am. String Tchrs. Assn., Nat. Assn. String Educators, Internat. Assn. Jazz Educators, Calif. Music Educators Assn. Avocations: gardening, birdwatching. Office: Alhambra HS 150 E St Martinez CA 94553 also: Martinez Jr HS 1600 Court St Martinez CA 94553 Office Phone: 925-934-8174, 925-313-0440 2099. Office Fax: (925) 946-9063.

GEORGE, KATIE, lawyer; b. Chillicothe, Ohio, Sept. 4, 1953; d. Harry Paul and Tina Lillian George; m. Nov. 25, 1972 (div. Nov. 1983); 1 child, Alison; m. Timothy John Nusser, June 30, 1985. BBA, U. Toledo, 1983, JD, 1986, MBA, 1989. Bar: Ohio 1987, U.S. Dist. Ct. (no. dist.) Ohio 1993, Fla. 1994. Law clk. Allotta, Singer & Farley, Co., LPA, Toledo, 1985-86; mgmt. specialist Dept. Pub. Utilities City of Toledo, 1987-91, acting commr. Dept. Health, 1992-93, acting mgr. Dept. Pub. Safety, 1991-94; pvt. practice Toledo, 1987-96, Pensacola, Fla., 1996—; asst. dist. legal counsel State of Fla., 1996-97, chief legal counsel, 1997—. Instr. U. Toledo, 1987-88, U. West Fla., 1997. Bd. dirs. Toledo BlockWatch, 1993, Ohio Pub. Employers Labor Rels. Assn., 1991-92; active Missing and Exploited Children Comprehensive Action Program, 1997-99. Mem. Fla. Bar Assn., Escambia Santa Rosa Bar Assn. Avocations: gardening, photography, scuba diving. Office Phone: 850-595-8057.

GEORGE, LILA GENE PLOWE KENNEDY, music educator; b. Sioux City, Iowa, Sept. 25, 1918; d. Eugene Preston Plowe and Lila Mazo Pickel; m. Richard Painter George; children: Eugenia, Richard Jr. BA in English and French, U. Okla., 1939, MusB in Theory, 1940; postgrad., Northwestern U., 1950, Columbia U., 1963—65; pvt. piano study with Egon Petri, Silvio Scionti & Edward Steuermann; pvt. composition study with Nadia Boulanger, Fontainebleau, France, 1971—78. Pvt. piano tchr., Oklahoma City, 1938—42, Talara, Peru, 1947—54, Houston, 1954—60, 1970—, Pelham Manor, NY, 1960—65. Soloist Oklahoma City Little Symphony, 1939, Houston Symphony, 1957; judge piano competitions Nat. Guild Piano Tchrs., Tex. State Music Tchrs. Recipient Houston Alumnae Music Leadership award, Sigma Alpha Iota, 2005. Mem.: Houston Tuesday Musical Club (pres. 1960), European Piano Tchrs. Assn., Am. Music Ctr. (composer), Sigma Alpha Iota (Music Leadership award Houston (Tex.) Alumnus chpt. 2005). Episcopalian. Avocation: genealogy. Home: 701 N Rusk Wharton TX 77488

GEORGE, LINDA SHUMAKER, freelance/self-employed writer; b. Lenoir, N.C., Sept. 24, 1949; d. Thomas Craig and Mary Poole Shumaker; m. Richard George, Feb. 14, 1986; 1 child, Alexander Thomas Oscar. BA, NYU, 1971; MA, Harvard U., 1975, PhD, 1980. V.p. internat. divsn. Mfrs. Hanover Trust Co., N.Y.C., 1981-87; adj. asst. prof. dept. history Drew U., Madison, N.J., 1989-91; vis. scholar Hagop Kevorkian Ctr. for Near Ea. Studies NYU, 1992-93; lectr. in Mid. Ea. langs. and civilizations Columbia U., N.Y.C., 1992-94; freelance writer, 1992—. Author: The Golden Age of Islam, 1998, Letters from the Homefront: World War I, 2001, Around the World in 800, 2002; editor: Far Brook Bull., 1995—2001. Charles McConn scholar NYU, 1967-68; fellow Ctr. for Arabic Study Abroad, Cairo, 1973-74; Radcliffe grantee for grad. women Harvard U., 1980, summer seminar for coll. tchrs. grantee NEH, 1991. Mem. The Authors Guild, Am. Rsch. Ctr. in Egypt (fellow 1977-78), Mid. East Studies Assn., Soc. Children's Book Writers and Illustrators. Avocations: opera, ice hockey.

GEORGE, MARY G., health scientist; d. C. and E. Gilbert; children: Brendon, Christian, Taryn. BS in Gen. Sci., U. Oreg., Eugene, BS in Chemistry, 1973; MD, Oreg. Health Scis. U., Portland, 1977; BS in Computer Sci., U. Tex. Permian Basin, Odessa, 2000; MSPH in Pub. Health Informatics, Emory U., Atlanta, GA, 2005. Diplomate Am. Bd. Plastic Surgery, 1986. Health scientist Northrop Grumman, Atlanta, Ga., 2006—. Marion Woodward Ottley scholar, Rollins Sch. Pub. Health Emory U., 2003—05. Fellow: ACS; mem.: N.Mex Bd. Med. Examiners (licentiate), Tex. Bd. Med. Examiners (licentiate), Am. Heart Assn. and Am. Stroke Assn. (assoc.), Tex. Soc. Plastic Surgeons (assoc.), Am. Soc. Plastic Surgeons (life), Phi Beta Kappa.

GEORGE, MERRILOU KAY, elementary school educator; b. Akron, Ohio, Jan. 2, 1947; d. Elmer Curtis and Rita Louise Shearer; children: Kristopher, Nicholas, Benjamin. BA, San Diego State U., 1969. Life tchg. credential. Tchr. Bassett Unified, La Puenta, Calif., 1970—74, Lincoln Unified, Stockton, Calif., 1984—85, Escondido (Calif.) Union, 1989—; dept. chair Grant Middle Sch., Escondido, 1998—99, grade-level leader, 2002—. Mem.: N County Doll Club, Delta Zeta. Republican. Methodist. Avocations: doll making, gardening, reading, crafts.

GEORGE, SONYA CAROL, customer service administrator, educator; b. Detroit, Aug. 7, 1958; d. Franklin Delano George and Ernestine Lee George (nee Nimmons); AA, Wayne Count C.C., 1990; B in bus. adminstrn., Detroit Coll. of Bus., 1990—94; MBA, Davenport U., 1999—2000. Document control clk. Detroit Edison Co, 1978—82, meter reader, 1982—88; field collector Detroit Edison, 1990—91; circuit analyst' Detroit Edison Co, 1993—96, consistency facilitator, 1996—99, field svc. rep., 1988—99, security investigator, 1999—2001; adj. instr. Rochester Coll., Mich., 2000—; adj. instuctor Cornerstone U., Grand Rapids, 2000—; adj. instr. Baker Coll., Auburn Hills, Mich., 2001—; supr., exception billing DTE Energy, Inc., Detroit, 2001—04, tech. trainer, 2005—; CFO Multiplicity Orgn. Devel. and Tng. Cons. Inc. Facilitator DTE Energy, Detroit, 1995—; supt. New Mt. Moriah Bapt. Ch., Pontiac, Mich., 1996—2001, leader deaf team, 1999—2003, leader leadership team, 2000—02; cons. Alma Bradley & Group, Pontiac, Mich., 2002—. Mem.: Nat. Assn. of Female Entrepreneurs (assoc.). Baptist. Avocation: roller skating. Personal E-mail: scwardlaw@msn.com. Business E-Mail: wardlaws@dteenergy.com.

GEORGES, MARA STACY, lawyer; b. Sept. 2, 1963; JD, Loyola U., 1988; BA, U. Notre Dame, 1985. Ptnr. Rock, Fusco, Reynolds, Crowe & Garvey, 1995-97; 1st asst. corporation counsel City of Chgo., 1997-99, corporation counsel, 1999—. Office Phone: 312-744-0220. E-mail: mgeorges@cityofchicago.org.

GEORGIEFF, ELLEN, nurse; b. N.Y.C., Apr. 3, 1948; d. Donald R. and Kathleen P. (Marren) Glynn; m. Gregory A. Georgieff (div.); 1 child, Ryan. Attended, U. Philippines, 1970—73; degree in nursing, U. State N.Y., Albany, 1975. RN Fla., Tex., N.Y., Utah. Oper. rm. tech. USAF, 1966—74, Bapt. Hosp., Miami, 1974—76; oper. rm. nurse Dr.'s Hosp., Coral Gables, Fla., 1976—78, Coral Gables Hosp., 1978—80, Primary Children's Hosp., Salt Lake City, 1980—83, Brownsville Med. Ctr., Tex., 1983—84, Dallas Children's Hosp., 1984—85, Parkland Regional Hosp., Dallas, 1985—90, Zale Lipsnit Hosp., Dallas, 1990—93, Northwest Med. Ctr., Margate, Fla., 2000—. Prodr. (dir.): (cable TV video) All That Jazz and Inner City Musical, 1992—96; photographer Garland Theater for Performing Arts, 1992—95. Recipient Crystal award, Dallas Cmty. TV, 1995. Avocation: photography. Personal E-mail: georgiee@bellsouth.net.

GEORGOPOULOS, MARIA, architect, artist; b. Moussata, Cefalonia, Greece, Apr. 2, 1949; came to U.S., 1973; d. Vassilios and Joulia Georgopoulos; 1 child, Demetrios. BArch, Nat. Poly. Sch. Greece, Athens, 1972; MS, Columbia U., 1976. Registered N.Y., Greece. Project mgr. Architects Design Group, N.Y.C., 1976—79, Griswold, Heckel & Kelly, N.Y.C., 1979—80; project dir. Lehman Bros., Kuhn Loeb Inc., N.Y.C., 1980—85; v.p. L.F. Rothschild Inc., N.Y.C., 1985—89; corp. art collection archivist, dir. facilities mgmt. The Dreyfus Corp., N.Y.C., 1989—. Mem. AIA, Greek Inst. Architects, Douglaston (N.Y.) Club. Home: 14 Melrose Ln Douglaston NY 11363-1221 Office: The Dreyfus Corp 200 Park Ave New York NY 10166-0099

GEPFORD, BARBARA BEEBE, retired nutrition educator; b. Buffalo, Sept. 2, 1930; d. Kenneth Hildreth and Martha Bell (Griswold) Beebe; m. William George Gepford, Dec. 28, 1952; children: David, Scott, Joanna, Andrea. BS in Home Econs. Edn., Iowa State U., 1952. Nutrition instr. Sidon Girl's Sch., Lebanon, 1953-56; instr. textiles and clothing Beirut Univ. Coll., Lebanon, 1955-56, 62-63; nutrition cons. Hong Kong Coun. of Social Svcs., 1967-71; commd. fraternal worker Presbyn. U.S.A., Lebanon, Hong Kong, 1953-71; mgr. Lila's Fabric Store, Cambridge, Ohio, 1973-74. Overseas missionary advisor to Assembly Coun. of Presbyn. Ch., U.S.A., 1971-72. Elder Presbyn. Ch., New Concord, Ohio, 1974-79, mem. com. on Ministry, Detroit, 1987-94; pres. Presbyn. Women of Littlefield Ch., 1987-89, mem. session, 2006-; vice-moderator Presbyn. Women of Presbytery of Detroit, 1985-87, moderator, 1997-99; synod of covenant women's rep. Churchwide Coordinating Team of Presbyn. Women, 1999-2002; chair Presbyn. Women Triann. Global Exch. to Africa, 2002-03; elder, session mem. Littlefield Presbyn. Ch., Dearborn, Mich., 2006—; advisor YWCA Head Start Program, Dearborn, Mich., 1988-91; bd. dirs. YWCA, 1985-96, pres., 1993-95. Named Ohio Mother of the Yr., Am. Mothers Com., New Concord, 1978. Mem., AAUW (bd. dirs. 1987-89, internat. rels. area rep.). Democrat. Avocations: reading, gardening, sewing, knitting. Home: 9421 Westwind Dr Livonia MI 48150-4530 E-mail: barbbgepford@msn.com, wiamfrd@msn.com.

GERAGHTY, DIANE C., law educator; BA, U. California; MA, U. Chgo., 1967; JD, Northwestern U. Faculty mem. Loyola U. Chgo., 1977—, prof. law, dir. Civitas ChildLaw Ctr., acting dean, 2004—05. Author: Juvenile Law Benchbook, Vols. I and II, 2001; co-author: Training the Lawyer to Represent the Whole Child: In re Pena, 2003; mem. editl. bd. Ill. Child Welfare; contbr. articles to law jours. Named Juvenile Justice Pioneer, 2000; recipient Livingston Hall Juvenile Justice Award, ABA, 2001, Leonard Jay Schrager Award, Chgo. Bar Found., 2003. Mem.: Ill. State Ct. Improvement Project (co-chair), Ill. Juvenile Justice Initiative (hon. bd. mem.), Citizens Com. on Juvenile Ct. (chair), Chgo. Children's Advocacy Ctr. (bd. mem., co-chair Strategic Planning Com.), Am. Civil Liberties Union (mem. Nat. Bd. Dirs.). Office: Loyola U Chgo Sch Law 1 E Pearson St Rm 506 Chicago IL 60611 E-mail: dgeragh@luc.edu.

GERAGHTY, ELIZABETH, food products executive; b. 1966; MBA, Northwestern Univ. Kellogg Sch. Mgmt., Chgo., 2000. With Sara Lee Corp., Chgo., 1990—, food sci., 1990, v.p. coffee and tea brand mgmt., 2005—. Named one of 40 Under Forty, Crain's Bus. Chgo., 2005. Office: Sara Lee Corp 3 First National Plz Chicago IL 60602-4260*

GERALD, CAROLYN AILEEN T., emergency physician; b. Hattiesburg, Miss., 1943; MD, U. Miss., 1980. Diplomate Am. Bd. Emergency Medicine. Intern USPHS, New Orleans, 1980-81; mem. staff Wesley Med. Ctr., Hattiesburg, Miss., Marion County Hosp., Columbia, Miss., Forrest Gen. Hosp., Hattiesburg, Miss., Gulf Coast Med. Ctr., Biloxi, Miss., Hancock Med. Ctr., Bay St. Louis; ind. contractor emergency medicine. Adj. faculty Ctr. for Cmty. Health, student health svc. physician U. So. Miss.; ind. contractor emergency medicine. Contbr. articles to profl. publs. Mem. AMA, Am. Bd. Quality Assurance and Utilization Rev. Physicians, Am. Coll. Emergency Physicians, Miss. State Med. Assn. Home: 9292 Janice Brooklyn Rd Brooklyn MS 39425-9689

GERARD, BARBARA, visual artist, educator; b. N.Y.C., Apr. 21, 1943; d. Arthur and Edith (Perrone) De Bernarda; m. Marvin Hartenstein, Sept. 18, 1976 (dec.); 1 son by aprevious marriage, David Gerard. BS, NYU, 1963; MA, 1966, postgrad., 1972—; profl. diploma, City Coll. CUNY, 1975; postgrad., Columbia U., 1977-79; EdD, Nova Southeastern U., 1994. Graphic designer C.A. Parshall Advt. Agy., N.Y.C., 1962; art tchr. Herman Ridder Jr. High Sch., N.Y.C., 1963-65; art chmn., 1967-70; freelance designer Sam Muggeo Advt. Inc., 1965-67; program counselor recruitment, tng. Spanish-speaking tchrs. N.Y.C. Bd. Edn., 1970-72; program coord. bilingual pupil svcs. Ctr. Bilingual Edn., 1972-75; dir. bilingual tchr.-intern program, 1975-79; dir. Ctr. Dissemination, 1979-81; dir. Project MASTER, 1983-87; spl. asst. to dep. chancellor, 1988-89; dir. staff devel., 1989-91; dir. staff and curriculum devel. office multi-cultural edn., 1991—95; owner, v.p. George Gerard Assocs., Inc., Port Washington, NY, 1995—98; with N.Y.C. Bd. Edn., 1998—. Adj. prof. Nova Southeastern U., 1995—, Hunter Coll., Queens Coll., L.I. U.; participant WNBC-TV, 1970, 75, 79; lectr. in field; cons. in field. Contbr. articles to profl. jours.; one woman ships inlcude Lincoln Inst. Gallery, N.Y.C., 1968, Henry Hicks Gallery, Bklyn., 1976, Second Story Spring St. Gallery, N.Y., 1976, Viridian Gallery, N.Y, 1977, 79; group shows include Loeb Student Ctr. Gallery, N.Y.C., 1962, 63, Riverdale Cmty. Gallery, N.Y., 1965, Environment Gallery, N.Y.C., 1969, Metamorphosis, N.Y., 1970, Concepts II, N.Y.C., 1971, Uion Carbide, N.Y., 1872, Lever House, 1973, Westchester Arts Soc., White Plains, N.Y., 1973, Gillary Gallery, Jericho, Long Island, 1974, Manhattan Savs. bank, 1976, Bklyn. Acad. Music, 1976, Pvt. Viewings/The Erlichs, The Colins, 1976, Gallery 91, Bklyn., 1976, Henry Hicks Gallery, Bklyn., 1975, 76, 77, Lincoln Ctr., Avery Fisher Hall, N.Y.C., 1976, second Story Spring St. Gallery, 1976, Bergdorf Goodman, White Plains, 1976, First Women's Bank, 1976, 80, Viridian Gallery, 1976, 77, 80, Womanart Gallery, 1976, Norman Kramer Gallery, Danbury, Conn., 1976, Mfrts. Hanover Bank, N.Y., 1977, 80, Union of Maine Artists, Portland, 1977, Northeastern U., Boston, 1978, Verd Internat. Gallery, East Hampton, 1978, Women in the Arts Gallery, 1979, Rensselaer Inst., Troy, 1979, Marie Pellicone Gallery, 1981, N.Y. Tech. Coll., 1982, guild Hall Mus., 1983, 84, Gov. of N.Y. - World Trade Ctr., 1985, Marte Previti Gallery, 1986, South Street Gallery, Guild Hall Mus., 1987, N.Y. Tech. Coll., 1988, CUNY, 1989; represented in permanent collections Mus. Contemporary Crafts, N.Y.C., BBD&O Advt., Inc., N.Y.C., Guild Hall, East Hampton; also pvt. collections. Chmn. Pres.'s Task Force on Bilingual edn., 1972; bd. dirs. Nat. Assn. Italian-Am. Dirs., 1982; v.p. Italian Bilingual Bicultural Educators Assn., 1982. HEW/Fed. govt. ESEA Title VII grantee, 1975-79; recipient Nat. Scene Award for Achievement in Arts and Culture, 1979. Mem. NEA, Nat. Assn. Bilingual Edn., Nat. Assn. Italian-Am. Women (bd.dirs. 1987—, pres. 1990-93), N.Y. State Assn. Bilingual Edn., coun. supervisory Adminstrs., NOW, Am. Coun. Arts, Coalition of Women Artists Orgn., Assn. Artist-Run Galleries, Women in the Arts, Advt. Women N.Y., Women Bus. Owners N.Y. Office: 30 Waterside Plz Apt 29F New York NY 10010-2626 E-mail: gerardba1@aol.com.

GERARD-SHARP, MONICA FLEUR, communications executive; b. London, Oct. 4, 1951; came to U.S., 1975; d. John Hugh Gerard-Sharp and Doreen May (Kearney) Dewhurst; m. Ali Edward Wambold, Nov. 21, 1981; children: Marina, Daniela, Dominica. BA in Philosophy and Lit. with honors, U. Warwick, Eng., 1973; MBA in Fin., Mktg. and Internat. Bus., Columbia U., 1980. Editor Inst. Chem. Engrs., London, 1973-74; sub-editor TV Times, London, 1974-75; press officer, editor UN, N.Y.C., 1975-78; bus. mgr. Time-Life Video, N.Y.C., 1980-81; mgr. fin. analysis Time-Life Films, N.Y.C., 1981; v.p. T.V.I.S., N.Y.C., 1982-83; dir. strategy and devel. HBO, ATC, N.Y.C., 1984-85; asst. treas., officer Time Inc., N.Y.C., 1985—87; pub. Travel Today and other mags. Fairchild Pubs. subs. Capital Cities/ABC, N.Y.C., 1987-88; dir. video programming Fairchild Pubs., Capital Cities/ABC, N.Y.C., 1988-89; pub. Entrée and Home Fashions Mags., N.Y.C., 1988-90; pres. Monali Inc., N.Y.C., 1991—. Cons. UN Bus. Council, N.Y.C., 1979; bd. rep. U.S.A. Network, N.Y.C., 1983-85. Editor: Everyone's United Nations, 1977; contbg. editor Asia Pacific Forum, 1976-77; contbr. articles to profl. jours. and mags., 1973-78. Treas. Help the Aged, Eng.; nat. devel. bd. Chances for Children, 1995-, pres. 2001-2003; adv. bd. Am. Mus. Natural History, 1998—; pres. bd. Am. Friends of Royal Ct. Theatre, 1998-2000. Bronfman fellow, 1979-80. Mem. Nat. Acad. Cable Programming, Am. Film Inst., Beta Gamma Sigma. Roman Catholic. Avocations: antiques, photography, wildlife. Home: Deer Park 128 Sunset Hill Rd Pleasant Valley NY 12569 Office: Monali Inc 26 E 80th St New York NY 10021-0110

GERBER, CECILIA ELENA, physics professor, researcher; m. Victor Daniel Elvira, Sept. 21, 1990; children: Pablo Daniel Elvira, Carina Cecilia Elvira. PhD, U. Buenos Aires, 1995. Rsch. assoc. Fermilab, Batavia, Ill., 1995—2000; assoc. prof. dept. physics U. Ill., Chgo., 2000—. Recipient Early Career Devel. Program CAREER award, NSF, 2003. Mem.: Am. Phys. Soc. Achievements include research in experimental high energy particle physics. Office: U Ill M/C273 845 W Taylor Chicago IL 60607 Office Phone: 312-996-2239.

GERBER, GWENDOLYN LORETTA, psychologist, educator; b. Calgary, Alta., Can. came to U.S., 1958; d. Ernest and Alma (Tesky) G. AB, UCLA, 1961, MA, 1964, PhD, 1967; cert. in psychoanalysis, NYU, 1970. Lic. psychologist, N.Y. Clin. psychologist Hillside Hosp., Glen Oaks, N.Y., 1970-73; asst. prof. psychology John Jay Coll. of Criminal Justice CUNY, N.Y.C., 1973-77, assoc. prof. psychology, 1977-90, prof., 1991—; pvt. practice in psychotherapy N.Y.C., 1970—. Contbr. chapters to books, articles to profl. jours. USPHS fellow, 1962-63, 66-67, NIMH fellow, 1967-69; CUNY grantee, 1989-92, 99-2000, 2002-05, 45 Found. grantee, 1991-96. Fellow: APA (bd. dirs. sect. III 1988—92, liaison divsn. 35 1989—, bd. dirs. sect. III 1994—95, bd. dirs. divsn. 39 1997—2005), N.Y. Acad. Scis. (chair psychology com. 1992—94, mem. steering com.); mem.: N.Y. State Psychol. Assn. (pres. acad. divsn. 1989—90, coun. rep. 1991—96, 2003—05, pres.-elect acad. divsn. 2006, William Wundt award 1993, Disting. svc. award 1996, Kurt Lewin award 1999), Phi Beta Kappa, Psi Chi, Chi Delta Pi. Office: John Jay Coll CUNY 445 W 59th St New York NY 10019-1104

GERBER, JANE SATLOW, history professor; d. I. David and Elsie Satlow; m. Roger Alan Gerber, Sept. 20, 1964; children: Dina Rakhel Huebner, Deborah Miriam Tor, Tamar Judith. BA, Wellesley Coll., Mass., 1959; MA, Radcliffe Coll., Cambridge, Mass., 1962; PhD, Columbia U., NYC, 1972. Asst. prof. CUNY Grad. Ctr., NYC, assoc. prof., 1981—93, prof. history dept., 1993—. Editor Jour. Jewish Social Studies, NYC, 1969—94; mem. academic coun. Ctr. Jewish History, NYC, 2002—; vis. prof. Hebrew U., Jerusalem, 1994, Harvard U., Cambridge, 1997, Yale U., New Haven, 1997, U. Pa., Phila., 1998. Author: Jewish Society in Fez:1450-1700, The Jews of Spain (Nat. Jewish Book Award, 1993), Sephardic Studies in the University. Pres. Assn. Jewish Studies, Cambridge, 1979—81; mem. academic coun. Ctr. Jewish History, NYC, 2002—; mem. editl. bd. Royal Inst. Interfaith Studies, Amman, Jordan, 2000—; bd. dirs. Westchester Jewish Conf., White Plains, NY, 1982—, Am. Sephardi Fedn., NYC, 2003—, Am. Jewish Hist. Soc., NYC, 1985. Wellesley scholar, Durant scholar. Mem.: Jewish Publ. Soc. (mem. publ. com. 2001—), Phi Beta Kappa. Office: CUNY Grad Ctr 365 Fifth Ave New York NY 10016 Office Phone: 212-817-1946.

GERBER, KIMBERLY ANN, music educator, singer; b. Columbus, Ohio, Aug. 23, 1972; d. E. Elliott and Barbara M. Gerber. MusB Edn., Bowling Green State U., 1994; MA in Edn., U. Phoenix, 2005. Soprano sect. leader USAF Singing Sgts., Washington, 1995—99; choir dir. Hill Country Mid. Sch., Austin, Tex., 1999—. Soprano: Conspirare: Craig Hella Johnson and Company of Voices. Sgt. USAF, 1995—99. Decorated Achievement medal USAF, Good Conduct medal, Commendation medal. Mem.: Tex. Music Educators Assn., Am. Choral Dirs. Assn. Home: 2882 Barton Skyway #245 Austin TX 78746 Office: Hill Country Mid Sch 1300 Walsh Tarlton Austin TX 78746 Office Phone: 512-732-9227 31806. Office Fax: 512-732-9229. Personal E-mail: kimberly823@ev1.net. Business E-Mail: kgerber@eanes.k12.tx.us.

GERBER, MARLENE, psychotherapist, health care administrator; b. Paterson, N.J., June 26, 1937; d. Nicholas and Evelyn (Zasa) D'Aurizio; m. Wilbur E. Smith, May 19, 1957 (div. Dec. 1977); children: Steven, Susan; m. Arthur Gerber, Apr. 20, 1986; children: Leslie, Pam, Denise. BA, Montclair State U., 1979, MA, 1983; EdS, Seton Hall U., 1996. Nat. bd. cert. counselor. Coord. crisis unit Alternatives to Domestic Violence, Hackensack, N.J., 1979-80; dir. social svc. Lincoln Pk. Intermediate Care Ctr., NJ, 1980-83; exec. dir. S.E. Sr. Ctr., Englewood, NJ, 1983—86, Whitehall Residence, Rochelle Pk., NJ, 1986—87; div. dir. Essex Assn. for Retarded Citizens, Livingston, N.J., 1988-89; pvt. practice Wayne, N.J., 1989—. Cons. 1st Reformed Ch., Pompton Plains, N.J., 1983—; creator, facilitor Women's Transition Group, 1977; creator, facilitator workshops, 1997-99. Sec. PTA, Rutherford, N.J., 1966; leader Girl Scouts U.S., Rutherford, 1966-67, organizer, 1967-73. Bergen County Community Devel. grantee, 1983-86. Mem. AACD. Democrat. Roman Catholic. Avocations: reading, history, interior decorating, cooking, opera. Home and Office: 116 Beechwood Dr Wayne NJ 07470-5612

GERBER, MELANIE K., lawyer; b. Jersey City, May 27, 1947; BA, Univ. Md., 1973; JD, Georgetown Univ., 1988. Bar: DC 1989, Pa. 1989, Supreme Ct. Pa., US Dist. Ct. (DC dist.), US Ct. Appeals (DC cir.), US Supreme Ct. Assoc. Morrison & Foerster, Washington; exec. dir. Legal Resource Ctr. for Housing & Cmty. Devel., Washington; pub. svc. counsel Patton Boggs LLP, Washington. Mem. oper. com. Whitman-Walker Legal Svc.; mem. adv. bd. DC Employment Justice Ctr.; mem. legal adv. bd. Capital Area Immigrants Rights Coalition; mem. editl. bd. Law Firm Pro Bono Project; vol. mentor Georgetown Univ. Law Ctr.; mem. regional leadership council Lawyers for Children Am.; mem. Legal Svc. Providers Consortium. Recipient Mayor's Arts award, DC Commn. on Arts & Humanities, 2003, Legal Assistance Disting. Svc. award, Sept. 11 Pro Bono Legal Relief Project, 2002, Servant of Justice award, Legal Aid Soc., 2001. Mem.: Washington Lawyers' Com. for Civil Rights (Vincent E. Reed award 2004, Outstanding Achievement award, Immigration & Refugee Rights 2003, Outstanding Achievement award, Equal Employment Opportunity 2000), Pa. Bar Assn., DC Bar (award for Pro Bono Work 2001). Office: Patton Boggs LLP 2550 M St NW Washington DC 20037-1350 Office Fax: 202-457-6315, 202-457-6312. Business E-Mail: mgerber@pattonboggs.com.

GERBERDING, JULIE LOUISE, federal agency administrator; b. SD, 1956; m. David Rose. BA in chemistry and biology, Case Western Reserve U., Cleve., MD; MPH, U. Calif., Berkeley, 1990. Intern and resident in internal medicine U. Calif., San Francisco, fellow in clin. pharmacology and infectious diseases; assoc. clin. prof. medicine Emory U.; assoc. prof. medicine, epidemiology and biostatistics U. Calif., San Francisco; founder, dir., Epidemiology Prevention and Interventions Ctr. San Francisco Gen. Hosp., 1987—98; dir., divsn. healthcare quality promotion CDC, Atlanta, 1998—2001, acting deputy dir. sci., 2001—02, dir., 2002—; adminstr. Agency for Toxic Substances and Disease Registry (ATSDR), 2002—. Dir., Prevention Epicenter U. Calif., San Francisco; mem., bd. scientific counselors CDC, mem., HIV adv. com., mem., scientific program com.; mem. Nat. Conf. Human Retroviruses; cons. NIH, AMA, Occupational Safety and Health Adminstrn., Nat. AIDS Commn., U.S. Congress, and WHO.; assoc. clin. prof. medicine (infectious diseases) Emory U. Edtl. bd. Annals of Internal Medicine, assoc. editor Am. Jour. Medicine, contbr. to profl. publs. and textbooks. Named one of 100 Most Powerful Women, Forbes mag., 2005—06. Fellow: Infectious Diseases Soc. Am. (chair and co-chair com. profl. devel. and diversity, mem. nominations com., co-chair. annual program com.); mem.: Inst. Medicine, Am. Epidemiology Soc., Am. Coll. Physicians, Soc. for Healthcare Epidemiology Am. (mem. AIDS/Tuberculosis com., bd. acad. counselor), Am. Soc. Clin. Investigation, Alpha Omega Alpha, Phi Beta Kappa. Achievements include first female director for the CDC. Avocations: scuba diving, reading, gardening. Office: CDC 1600 Clifton Rd NE 214 Atlanta GA 30333*

GERBERG, JUDITH LEVINE, management consultant; d. Murray Joseph and Pearl (Berens) Levine; m. Mort Gerberg; 1 child, Lilia Anya Berens. BS in Comparative Lit., Columbia U., 1963, postgrad. in organizational devel., 1989; MA in Psychology and Art, NYU. Registered art therapist; lic. clin. mental health counselor; cert. counselor, career mgmt. profl. Program dir. Women's Selling Game, N.Y.C., 1979-84; mem. faculty Parsons Sch. Design, N.Y.C., 1979-85; pres. gerberg & co., N.Y.C., 1984—. Orgnl. devel. mgmt., leadership devel., valuing diversity, team bldg., comm. skills, stress mgmt.; founder Powerhouse, 1st outplacement for creative profls.; mem. N.Y. steering com. Women's Study in Religion Program Harvard Div. Sch.; pres. Career Counselors Consortium, 2000-03. Co-author: The New York Women's Directory, 1973; contbr. articles and book revs. to profl. jours. Chmn. pub. rels. Profl. Women's Caucus, 1972; facilitator NYC Contr.'s Women's Econ. Task Force, 1994-95; mem. Harvard Divinity Sch.: Women in Religion Leadership Conf. NY State scholar. Mem.: Career Counselors Consortium (pres. 2000—03), Internat. Assn. Career Mgmt. Profl. (co-chair future focus com.), Women's Venture Fund, Fin. Women's Assn. (bd. dirs. 2003), The Forum at Stephen Wise (co-chmn. 1986—87), N.Y. Art Therapy Assn., Am. Art Therapy Assn. (life; bd. dirs. 1980—84). Office: 250 W 57th St Ste 2315 New York NY 10107-2315 Office Phone: 212-315-2322. Business E-Mail: gerberg@gerberg.com.

GERBI, SUSAN ALEXANDRA, biology professor; b. NYC, 1944; d. Claudio and Jeannette Lena (Klein) Gerbi; m. James Terrell McIlwain, Apr. 10, 1976. BA, Barnard Coll., 1965; MPhil, Yale U., 1968, PhD, 1970. NATO and Jane Coffin Childs Fund fellow Max-Planck Institut fur Biologie, Tubingen, Germany, 1970—72; asst. prof. biology Brown U., Providence, 1972—77, assoc. prof., 1977—82, prof., 1982—. Dir. grad. tng. program in molecular and cell biology, 1982-87, asst. dir. grad. program in molecular biology, cell biology and biochemistry, 1987-89, vice-chair sect. molecular, cellular and devel. biology, 1990-94, chair dept. molecular biology, cell biology and biochemistry, 1994-2004; vis. assoc. prof. Duke U., Durham, N.C., 1981-82; mem. genetics research grants rev. panel NSF, 1979-80; mem. genetic basis of disease com. NIH, 1980-84. Contbr. articles to profl. jours. Dist. commr. Palmer River Pony Club, 1973—75. N.Y. State Regents scholar, 1965; NIH fellow, 1966-70; NIH research grantee, 1974—, research career devel. award, 1975-80; recipient Gov.'s award for sci. achievement State of R.I., 1993. Mem. Fedn. Am. Socs. Exptl. Biology (pub. policy com. 1994-97, chair consensus conf. on grad. edn. 1996), Assn. Am. Med. Colls. (pub. policy com. 1994-98, chair grad. rsch. edn. and tng. group 1999), Am. Soc. for Cell Biology (program chair 1986, council mem. 1988-90, pub. policy com. 1991-97, pres. 1993), Soc. for Devel. Biology, Genetics Soc., RNA Soc., Sigma Xi (nat. lectr.). Office: Brown Univ Biomedical Divsn Providence RI 02912-0001 Office Phone: 401-863-2359. E-mail: susan_gerbi@brown.edu.

GERDNER, LINDA ANN, nursing researcher, educator; b. Burlington, Iowa, Sept. 17, 1955; d. Richard Paul and Edna Marie Gerdner. AA, Southeastern C.C., 1975, ADN, 1977; BSN, Iowa Wesleyan Coll., 1980; MA, U. Iowa, 1992, PhD, 1998. RN, Iowa, Ark., Minn. Staff devel. coord. Elm View Care Ctr., Burlington, Iowa, 1985—88, DON, 1988—89; tchg./rsch. asst. U. Iowa Coll. Nursing, Iowa City, 1989-92; nursing faculty Grand View Coll., Des Moines, 1992-93; project dir. Nat. Caregiver Tng. Project, U. Iowa Coll. Nursing, 1992-97, predoctoral fellow, 1996-98; postdoctoral fellow/faculty dept. psychiatry U. Ark. Med. Scis., VA Med. Ctr., Little Rock, 1998—2000; asst. prof. U. Minnesota Sch. Nursing, 2001—. Presenter in field; cons. Alverno Health Facility, Clinton, Iowa, 1997—2000. Mem. referee panel Clin. Nursing Rsch., 1997—, Western Jour. Nursing Rsch., 1998—, Jour. Gerontol. Nursing, 1999—, Internat. Jour. Geriatric Psychiatry, 2000—, Internat. Psychogeriatrics, 2002—, Alzheimer's Disease and Related Disorders, 2002—, Nursing Research, 2003—; contbr. chapters to books, articles to profl. jours. AARP Andrus Found. grad. fellow in gerontology Assn. Gerontology in Higher Edn., 1996-97, Rsch. award Am. Soc. Aging, 1999, mini-fellowship ethnogeriatrics, Stanford U., Palo Alto, Calif., 2004-. Mem.: ANA, Coun. Nursing and Anthropology, Am. Assn. Geriatric Psychiatry, Midwest Nursing Rsch. Soc. (Outstanding Poster award 1993), Mid-Am. Contress on Aging (Best Grad. Paper award 1994), Am. Geriatric Soc., Internat. Psychogeriatric Assn. (task force on behavioral and psychol. symptoms of dementia 1999—, scientific advisory com. 2001, IPA/Bayer Rsch. award 1999), Sigma Theta Tau (Best of Image award 1997). Avocations: reading, travel, walking, music, photography. Home: 1160 Cushing Cir Apt 318 Saint Paul MN 55108 Office: Weaver-Densford Hall 308 Harvard St SE Minneapolis MN 55455-0353 E-mail: gerdn001@umn.edu.

GEREIGHTY, ANDREA SAUNDERS, diversified financial services company executive, poet; b. New Orleans, July 20, 1938; d. Andrew Jackson and Jeanne Teresa (Martin) Saunders; m. Dennis Anthony Gereighty Jr., May 19, 1959 (wid.); children: Deni Ann, David Dennis, Peggy T. Cert., Exeter Coll., Oxford, Eng., 1972; BA, U. New Orleans, 1974, MA in English with distinction, 1978. Cotton analyst Anderson-Clayton, Metairie, La., 1956; records retrieval profl. Shell Oil Co., New Orleans, 1956-60; census coord. St. Vincent De Paul Ch., New Orleans, 1960-65; bldg. funds dir. St. Francis Xavier Ch., Metairie, 1965-70; tchr. spl. edn. Deckbar Elem. Sch., Jefferson, La., 1966-70; tchr. English Chalmette (La.) H.S., 1971-73; assoc. prof. English dept. U. New Orleans, 1973-75; tchr. secondary edn. Berlin-Am. H.S., 1980-81; owner, founder, CEO New Orleans Field Svcs. Assocs., 1974—. Guest speaker Delgado Coll., New Orleans, 1989; guest presenter Rabouin Vo-Tech., New Orleans, 1980; lectr., guest presenter poetry at New Sarpy Sch., 1994-95; guest presenter St. Mark's Episcopal Ch., Latter Libr.,

N.O. Pub. Libr., others. Author: (public opinon polls book) Asking Q's, 1980; (poetry) Illusions and Other Realities, 1974, Restless for Cool Weather, 1990, Season of the Crane, 1994; publ., editor Desire Street, 1997—; author numerous poems. Recipient Coda award Poets and Writers, 1983, Poetry award of honor Nat. League Am. Pen Women, 1973, Deep South Writers, 1984, 88, 90, 92, 94, 95, 96, 97, 98, 99, 2d place award Nuyarikin Poet's Cafe, N.Y.C., Ellipsis Poetry prize, 1983, 85, 87, 90, other poetry awards. Mem. Am. Mktg. Assn., Mktg. Rsch. Assn., Nat. Geneal. Soc., Jefferson Geneal. Soc., Geneaol. Soc. of New Orleans, New Orleans Poetry Forum (dir. 1990—), New Orleans Track Club. Democrat. Roman Catholic. Avocations: poetry, jogging, genealogy, camping. Office: New Orleans Field Svcs 257 Bonnabel Blvd Rear Office Metairie LA 70005-3738

GERGECEFF-COOPER, LORRAINE, artist, consultant; b. Ill. d. Harry Robert and Grace Johnson; m. George William Gergeceff (dec. 1984); m. John Cooper, Jr., May 30, 1992 (dec. 2002); children: Jill Gergeceff Lohnes, Jon Rice Gergeceff. Cert., Internat. Sommerakad., Salzburg, Austria, 1962, Sch. Landscape Painting, Dordogne, France, 1973; BS, So. Ill. U., 1953; MFA, U. Guanajuato, San Miguel Allende, Mex., 1970. Tchr., gallery dir. Ursuline Acad., Oakland, Mo., 1962-70; instr. McKendree Coll., Lebanon, Mo.; artist Forum Creative Dynamics, St. Louis, 1995, Unique Paintings, Webster Groves, Mo., 1997-98; owner LorPaint Gallery, Webster Groves, 1998—. Cons. JDR 3 Through Awareness Classroom Environment; founder, dir. Ursuline Art Gallery, Oakland, Mo. Author: Careers in Art, Self Designed Fabrics; one woman shows at Kinsella Gallery, Long Art Gallery, Ursuline Art Gallery, Notre Dame Coll., University City Libr., St. Louis U.; group shows include St. Louis Art Mus., Art Mus. St. Louis, Bellas Artes, Cuernavaca, Mex., Mus. Arts and Scis., Mo. Hist. Soc., Spete Kukla Gallery, Samos, Greece, Internat. Acad. Fine Arts, Salzburg, Austria, Highland Gallery, Atlanta, St. Louis Artists' Guild, 2002, Galeria Osman, Mex., Creative Art Gallery, St. Louis, 2001, 02, Centro Cultural El Nigromante, San Miguel de Allende, Mex., Art Expo '96, Webster Groves, Mo., Nat. Mus. Women in the Arts, Mo. Water Colo Assn., St. Peter's Cultural Art Ctr., 2001, 2002, 2003, Oil and Acrylic Nat. Exhbn., 2001, Collector's Choice, St. Louis, 2002, 2003, CJ Mggs Art Gallery, 2002, Oil and Acrylic Nat. Exhibit, 2002. Backer Repertory Theater, Webster Groves, Mo., 1996—. Best of Show Kinsella Gallery, Long Art Gallery, Ursuline Art Gallery; recipient prize St. Louis Artists' Guild, 1969, 71, 75; named Outstanding Secondary Educator, 1971. Mem. St. Louis Art Mus., Chgo. Art Inst., Guild of Opera Theater, Art St. Louis, St. Lousi Artists' Guild (spl. events, prize 1969, 71, 75), St. Louis Watercolor Soc. (signature), Soc. Multi Media Layerists. Avocations: travel, sailing, reading. Address: LorPaint Gallery 16 N Gore Ave Ste 201 Webster Groves MO 63119-2315 E-mail: lorpaint@aol.com.

GERHARDT, CAROL, artist; b. Wabash, Ind., Aug. 10, 1946; d. Dale Martin Ashby and Helen Irene Harper; 2 children from previous marriage. BS, U. Houston, 1986, postgrad., 1994—96. Exec. dir. Penguin Photography Studio, Houston, 1986—87, photographer, 1987—90; photojournalism faculty North Harris County Coll., Houston, 1990—92; art faculty Houston Ind. Sch. Dist., 1992—2006. Exhibitions include UN/UNIFEM, Marias do Mundo, Brazil, 2001, Diverse Works Art Space, Houston, 1996, Cultural Arts Coun. Houston, 2005, 125 Gallery, 2005, Commerce St. Artsts, Houston, 2005, Poissant Gallery, 2006.

GERHART, GLENNA LEE, pharmacist; b. Houston, June 11, 1954; d. Henry Edwin and Gloria Mae (Mrnustik) G. BS in Pharmacy, U. Houston, 1977. Registered pharmacist, Tex. Staff pharmacist Meml. City Med. Ctr., Houston, 1977—84; asst. dir. pharmacy Meml. Hosp.-Meml. City Med. Ctr., Houston, 1984-98; pharmacy supr. Meml. Hermann-Meml. City Hosp. Pharmacy, Houston, 1998—; investigational drug pharmacist Meml. City Med. Ctr., Houston, 2000—; staff pharmacist Christus St. Catherine Health and Wellness Ctr., 2000—02. Active Humane Soc. US. Mem.: Pharm. and Therapeutics Soc., Houston-Galveston Area Soc. Hosp. Pharmacists, Tex. Soc. Health-Sys. Pharmacists, Tex. Pharm. Assn., Am. Soc. Hosp. Pharmacists, Am. Pharm. Assn., Nat. Birman Fanciers, Humane Soc. U.S., U. Houston Alumni Orgn. (life), Houston SPCA, Plumeria Soc. Am., Nat. Cougar Club, Houston Cat Club, Slavonic Benevolent Order of Tex. SPJST Lodge #88, Kappa Epsilon. Republican. Methodist. Avocations: reading, gardening, running, raising cats. Home: 25527 Winston Hollow Katy TX 77494 Office: Memorial Hermann-Memorial City Hosp 921 Gessner Houston TX 77024-2312 Personal E-mail: glennacat@aol.com. Business E-Mail: glenna.gerhart@memorialhermann.org.

GERHART, LORRAINE PFEIFFER, elementary school educator; b. Porterfield, Wis., Mar. 13, 1939; d. Frank William and Michalena Mary (Kroll) Pfeiffer; m. Adolph Dietrich Gerhart, June 20, 1964; 1 child, Monika. BS, U. Wis., Oshkosh, 1961; cert. reading specialist, Carroll Coll., 1966; MA in Reading, Cardinal Stritch Coll., 1975. Tchr. Elmbrook Schs., Brookfield, Wis., 1961-67, reading specialist, 1967—, team leader and specialist, 1988—95; lectr., workshop coord. Cardinal Stritch Coll., 1975—95. Acad. staff U. Wis., Oshkosh, Madison. Co-author: Study Skills, 1977; cons. author for manuals with filmstrip set, 1979; cons. for reading strategies Scott Foresman Soc. St. text, 1988, 90; contbr. Middle School Content Reading, Middle School Thematic Series. Mem. fin. com. Village of Lac La Belle, 1983-84. Recipient Celebrate Literacy award Waukesha Reading Coun., 1986, 96. Mem. ASCD, Internat. Reading Assn. (mem. adv. bd. Jour. of Reading 1989-90, book reviewer Signal, 1975—90), N.E. Reading Coun., Wis. State Reading Assn. (pres. 1990-91, Friend of Literacy award 2000), Milw. Area Reading Coun., Nat. Coun. Tchrs. English., Delta Kappa Gamma. Republican. Roman Catholic. Avocations: reading, gardening, hiking, taking rubbings, making books. Home: 901 Fj St Crivitz WI 54114-1544 Office: 901 FJ St Crivitz WI 54114-1549

GERISH, DEBORAH ELAINE, history professor; b. Detroit, Sept. 14, 1965; BS, Northwestern U., Evanston, Ill., 1987; MA, PhD, U. Calif., Santa Barbara, 1999. Assoc. prof. Emporia State U., Kans., 2000—. Coord. Emporia State U., 2003—. Author: (scholarly book) Gender Theory in Palgrave Advances in the Crusades, edited by Helen J. Nicholson; contbr. articles to profl. jours. Recipient V.P. award Outstanding Tchg., Emporia State U., 2001, V.p. award Use Tech., 2002, Excellence in Tchg., Emporia State U., Coll. Liberal Arts & Scis., 2003. Office: Empoira State University Dept of Social Sciences box 32 Emporia KS 66801 Office Phone: 620-341-5579.

GERLACH, AMY LOUISE, physical education educator; d. Norbert E. and Carol Ann Gerlach. BA, Teikyo Westmar U., LeMars, Iowa, 1995. Cert. tchr. SD. Phys. edn. tchr. Lower Brule Sch., SD, 1998—, coach girls basketball, 1998, 2000, 2006, head coach girls track, 1999. Home: 1108 S Main St Chamberlain SD 57325

GERLACH, JEANNE ELAINE, English language educator; b. Charleston, W.Va., Oct. 20, 1946; d. Lafayette and Edith Lorraine (Robinson) Marcum; m. Roger Thomas Gerlach Sr., Dec. 30, 1966; children: Roger Thomas Jr., Kristen Elaine. BS, W.Va. State Coll., Institute, 1974; MA, W.Va. State Coll., 1979; EdD, W.Va. U., 1985, U. North Tex., 1992. Lang. arts tchr. Ohio County Schs., Wheeling, W.Va., 1974-79; English instr. West Liberty (W.Va.) State Coll., 1979-82; continuing edn. instr. Seattle Pacific U., 1982-85; asst. prof. English W.Va. U., Morgantown, 1985-86, Tarrant County Jr. Coll., Ft. Worth, 1986-88; dir. Communications Unlimited, Dallas, Pitts., 1986—; assoc. prof. English edn. W.Va. U., Morgantown, 1989-97, spl. asst. to the provost, 1994-97, dir. ctr. women's studies, 1993-94; dean coll. edn. U. Tex., Arlington, 1997—, assoc. v.p. K-16 initiatives, 2003—. Cons. to bus. and industry, 1986—; co-dir. advanced writing project W.Va. U., Morgantown, 1989, lang. arts camps, 1988, 89, 90, young writers inst. Editor: English Internat.; contbr. articles to profl. jours. Mem. LWV, W.Va., DAR, Young Republicans, W.Va.; participant Leadership Tex., 2005. Recipient 1st place Creative Writing award, W.Va. Women's Clubs, 1976, Great Tex. Woman award, Ft. Worth Bus. Press, 2002; Faculty Devel. grantee, W.Va. U., 1989. Mem. AAUW, AAUP, Nat. Coun. Tchrs. English (chair women's com. 1986—, chair nominating com. 1988-89, Outstanding Tchr. in Coll. of Human Resources and Edn. award W.Va. U. 1992, Rewey Belle Inglis award 1992), Am. Ednl. Rsch. Assn., W.Va. U. Alumni Assn. (sec. 1990, pres.), Nat. Women's Studies Assn., Nat. Soc. Daus. Am. Revolution. Republican. Methodist. Avocations: tennis, golf, poetry, photography, doll collecting. Business E-Mail: gerlach@uta.edu.

GERLITZKI, ANN L., music educator; BS of Vocal Pedagogy, Houghton Coll., N.Y., 1987; MusB in Edn., Millersville U., Pa., 1996; MusM in Edn., Duquesne U., Pitts., 2001. Cert. Kodaly tchr. West Chester U., 2004. Vocal and gen. music tchr. Lancaster Christian Sch., Pa., 1996—2000, Upper Adams Sch. Dist., Biglerville, Pa., 2000—. Ch. choir dir. Trinity U.C.C., Gettysburg, Pa., 2005—. Mem.: PA Music Educators.

GERLOVIN, SAMANTHA LEIGH, lawyer; BA, Dartmouth Coll., 1998; JD, Boston Coll., 2001. Bar: Mass., US Dist. Ct. (Dist. Mass.). Assoc. Brown Rudnick Berlack Israels LLP, Boston. Tchg. asst. Northeastern U. Sch. Law, 2002. Tchr. Citizen Schools Mock Trial Program; judge Grimes Moot Court Competition Boston Coll. Law Sch. Mem.: Women's Bar Assn., Boston Bar Assn., Mass. Bar Assn. (judge Mock Trial Competition). Office: Brown Rudnick Berlack Israels LLP One Financial Center Boston MA 02111 Office Phone: 617-856-8540. Office Fax: 617-289-0529. E-mail: SGerlovin@brownrudnick.com.*

GERMAIN, CLAIRE MADELEINE, law librarian, educator, lawyer; b. Chaumont, France, Sept. 22, 1951; d. Pierre and Jeanne (Despujols) G.; m. Stuart M. Basefsky, Aug. 16, 1976; 1 child, Nicolas. Licence-es. lettres, U. Paris, 1971, LLB, 1974; M in Comparative Law, La. State U., 1975; M in Law Librarianship, U. Denver, 1977. Reference librarian Duke U. Law Library, Durham, N.C., 1977-80, head reference librarian, 1982-84, asst. librarian, sr. lectr. comparative law, 1984-89, assoc. dir., sr. lectr. comparative law, 1989-93; Edward Cornell law libr., prof. law Cornell U., Ithaca, N.Y., 1993—. Research fellow Max Planck Inst., Hamburg, Federal Republic of Germany, 1980. Author: Germain's Transnational Law Research: A Guide to Attorneys, 1991, (with Szladits) Guide to Foreign Legal Materials, French, 2d edit., 1985; contbr. and editor articles to profl. jours. Mem. ABA, Am. Assn. Law Librs. (chair fgn. law sect. 1985-86, v.p., pres.-elect 2004—, chair-elect sect. librs. 2003-), Am. Assn. Law Schs. (chmn. libr. and tech. com., chmn. elect libr. sect. 2003—). Roman Catholic. Office: Cornell Law Libr Myron Taylor Hall Ithaca NY 14853 E-mail: cmg13@cornell.edu.

GERMAN, JENNIFER ELAM, elementary school educator, music educator; b. Memphis, Tenn., Aug. 3, 1973; d. Charles Marvin Glass and Teresa Jane Elam; m. Russell Wade German, Sept. 2, 2000. MusB in Music Edn., U. Tenn., Martin, Tenn., 1996; MA in Edn., Belmont U., Lebanon, Tenn., 2000. Tchr. music Drummonds (Tenn.) Elem. Sch., 2002—. Home: 2825 Hazel Grove Road Burlison TN 38015

GERMAN, JUNE RESNICK, lawyer; b. N.Y.C., Feb. 24, 1946; d. Irving and Stella (Weintraub) Resnick; m. Harold Jacob German, May 31, 1974; children: Beth Melissa, Heather Alice, Bret. BA, U. Pa., 1965; JD, NYU, 1968. Bar: N.Y. 1968, U.S. Dist. Ct. (ea. and so. dists.) N.Y. 1974, U.S. Ct. Appeals (2d cir.) 1973, U.S. Supreme Ct. 1973. Atty., sr. atty., supervising atty. Mental Health Info. Svc., N.Y.C., 1968-77; atty., advisor Course in Human Behavior Mems. of N.Y. State Judiciary, Nassau and Suffolk County, 1980; pvt. practice Huntington, NY, 1985—. Contbg. author: Bioethics and Human Rights, 1978, Mental Illness, Due Process and the Acquitted Defendant, 1979; contbr. chpts. to books, articles to profl. jours. Chmn. Citizen's Ad Hoc Com. Constrn. of the Dix Hills Water Adminstrn. Bldg., Huntington, N.Y., 1985-90; mem. Citizens Adv. Com. for Dix Hills Water Dist., Huntington, 1992—; dir. House Beautiful Assn. at Dix Hills, 1986—, Citizens for a Livable Environment and Recycling, Huntington, 1989-93; active Suffolk County (N.Y.) Dem. Com., 1986—, Deer Park Avenue Task Force, Town of Huntington, 1997-98, Dix Hills Revitalization Com., 1999-2000. Mem. Suffolk County Bar Assn. Jewish. Avocations: tennis, hiking, travel. Office: 150 Main St Huntington NY 11743-6908 Office Phone: 631-271-8711. Personal E-mail: junegerman@hotmail.com.

GERMANN, JOANN, mathematics educator; d. Patsy Restaino and Christina Spina; m. Albert Germann, July 26, 1970. BA, Coll. of NJ, Ewing, 1969. Cert. elem. tchr. Dept. Edn. N.J., 1969. Tchr. math. Lyndhurst Bd. Edn., NJ, 1969—. Office: Lyndhurst Bd Edn 281 Ridge Rd Lyndhurst NJ 07071 Business E-Mail: germann@lyndhurst.k12.nj.us.

GERRITSEN, MARY ELLEN, vascular and cell biologist; b. Calgary, Alta., Can., Sept. 20, 1953; arrived in US, 1978; d. Thomas Clayton and Alice Irene (Minton) Cooper; m. Paul William Gerritsen, May 24, 1975 (div. 1977); m. Thomas Patrick Parks, Oct. 11, 1980; children: Kristen, Madelene. BSc summa cum laude, U. Calgary, 1975, PhD, 1978. Postdoctoral fellow U. Calif., San Diego, 1978-80; asst. prof. N.Y. Med. Coll., Valhalla, 1981-86, assoc. prof., 1986-90; sr. staff scientist Pharm. divsn. Bayer Corp., West Haven, Conn., 1990-93, head inflammation exploratory rsch., 1990-96, prin. staff scientist, 1993-97; vis. scientist Harvard U., 1996; assoc. dir. cardiovasc. rsch. Genentech, South San Francisco, 1997—2001; sr. dir. Millennium Pharms., South San Francisco, 2003—04, Molecular and Cellular Pharm., Exelixis Inc., South San Francisco, 2004—. Cons. Insite Vision, Alameda, Calif., 1987-89, Boehringer Ingelheim Pharms., Ridgefield, Conn., 1985-88, Xoma, Berkeley, Calif, 2003-04, Frazier Health Care Ventures, Palo Alto, Calif, 2003—, Macusite, Union City, Calif., 2004—; adj. assoc. prof. N.Y. Med. Coll., 1990-99. Co-author: Masdevallias: Gems of the Orchid World, 2005; editor: N.Am. Vascular Biology Orgn. Newsletter, —; mem. editl. bd. Microvascular Rsch., 1988—96, Am. Jour. Physiology, 1983—90, Am. Jour. Cardiovasc. Pathology, 1996—98, Circulation Rsch., 1997—99, Endothelium, 1999—, editor-in-chief Microcirculation, 1993—98, cons. editor, 1998—; contbr. articles to profl. jours. I. W. Killam Found. fellow, 1976, Med. Rsch. Coun. Can. fellow, 1978. Mem. Am. Soc. for Pharmacology and Exptl. Therapeutics, Am. Physiol. Soc., Am. Soc. Investigational Pathology, Microcirculatory Soc. (mem. coun. 1989-92, chairperson publs. com. 1991-93, Mary Weideman award 1985, Young Investigator award 1984), N.Am. Vascular Biology Orgn. (mem. steering com. 1993, mem. coun. 1994-97, editor-in-chief newsletter 1994-97, sec.-treas. 1997-99, pres. 1999, chair devel. com., 2004-05), Peninsula Orchid Soc. (bd. dirs. 2001, v.p. 2005), Am. Orchid Soc., Pleurothallid Alliance. Avocations: orchids, horticulture. E-mail: meg570@comcast.net.

GERRY, DEBRA PRUE, psychotherapist, recording artist, writer; b. Oct. 9, 1951; d. C.O. and Sarah E. Rawl; m. Norman Bernard Gerry, Apr. 10, 1981 (div. 1998); 1 child, Gisele Psyche Victoria. BS, Ga. So. U., 1972; MEd, Armstrong State U., 1974; PhD, U. Ga., 1989. Cert. Ariz. Bd. Behavioral Health Examiners. Spl. edn. tchr. Chatham County Bd. Edn., Savannah, Ga., 1972-74; edn. and learning disabilities resource educator Duval County Bd. Edn., Jacksonville, Fla., 1974-77; ednl. resource counselor spl. programs adminstr. Broward County Bd. Edn., Ft. Lauderdale, Fla., 1977-81; pvt. practice Scottsdale, Ariz., 1990—. Contbr. author coll. textbooks; contbr. articles to profl. jours.; prodr. musical album Welcome to this World. Vol., fundraiser, psychol. cons., group leader Valley AIDS Orgns., Phoenix, 1990-96; fundraiser Hosp. Health Edn. Programs, Scottsdale, 1992-93; mem. com. for women's issues Plz. Club, Phoenix, 1992-93; pres. Laissez Les Bon Temps Rouler, Wrigley Club, Phoenix, 1993-96; mem. bd. Sojourner' Ctr., 1996, exec. bd., 1997-98, v.p., 1999; exec. bd. Breast Found., Inc., Phoenix, 1997-98; appointee Ariz. Supreme Ct., Foster Care Rev. Bd., Phoenix, 1996-2001. Recipient Rudy award Shanti Orgn., 1991. Mem. APA, NOW, ACA, Internat. Soc. Poets (disting., Poet of Merit award 1996), Nat. Assn. Women Bus. Owners, Assn. for Multicultural Coun., Assn. for Specialists in Group Work, Mensa, Phi Delta Kappa, Kappa Delta Epsilon, Sigma Omega Phi, Kappa Delta Pi. Avocations: ballroom dancing, playing musical instruments, singing, travel, air sports. E-mail: dgerryphd@aol.com.

GERSHENFELD, MATTI KIBRICK, psychologist; b. Phila. d. Hyman and Esther Kibrick; m. Marvin A. Gershenfeld, 1946 (dec. 1989); children: Robert, Howard, Richard, Kenneth. BA, U. Pa., 1947, M in Govt. Adminstrn., 1951; EdD, Temple U., 1967. Lic. psychologist, Pa.; cert. marriage and family therapist. Pres. MKG Assocs., Elkins Park, Pa., 1975—, Couples Learning Ctr., Jenkintown, Pa., 1975—. Adj. prof. Temple U., 1967—; grad. faculty mem. Pa. State U., Phila., dir. Inst. of Awareness; mem. organizing com., co-chair 1st Internat. Interdisciplinary Conf. on Women, Haifa, Israel, 1982. Author: Groups: Theory and Experience, 1973, 7th edit., 2004, Making Groups Work, 1983, How to Find Love, Sex and Intimacy after 50: A Woman's Guide, 1991; contbr. chpts. to Contemporary Marriage, 1986, Adult Development, 1984, conservation of Marriage and the Family Studies, 1986. Active Phila. City Planning Commn.; chair bd. dirs. Gratz Coll., Elkins Park, 2001-04; pres. Hillel Greater Phila., 1996-99; mem. pres.' coun. Gwynedd (Pa.) Mercy Coll., 1981—; past pres. Am. Diabetes Assn., Phila., 1987-90, chair. Fellow APA, Am. Assn. Marriage and Family Therapists; mem. Nat. Coun. on Family Rels., Pa. Coun. Family Rels. (past pres.), Assn. State Couns. Nat. Coun. Family Rels. (past pres.), Internat. Coun. Psychologists (sec.-gen.). Jewish. Avocations: travel, theater. Home: 8302 Old York Rd Philadelphia PA 19027-1522 Office Phone: 215-884-5964. E-mail: mattikg@comcast.net.

GERSHON, NINA, federal judge; b. Chgo., Oct. 16, 1940; d. David and Marie Gershon; m. Bernard J. Fried, May 15, 1983. BA, Cornell U., 1962; LLB, Yale U., 1965; postgrad., London Sch. Econs., 1965-66. Staff atty. NY Supreme Ct. (Appellate div.), 1966—68; asst. corp. counsel, Appeals div. State of NY, 1968—69; lectr. law and political sci. U. of Calif. San Diego, 1969—70; chief fed. appeals State of NY, 1972—75, chief consumer protection div., 1975—76; magistrate judge U.S. Dist. Ct. (so. dist.) N.Y., NYC, 1976—96; U.S. dist. judge Eastern Dist. N.Y., Bklyn., 1996—. Adj. prof. law Cardozo Sch. Law, 1986—88. Fulbright scholar. Office: US Courthouse 225 Cadman Plz E Brooklyn NY 11201-1818 Office Phone: 718-613-2650.

GERSKE, JANET FAY, lawyer; b. Nov. 14, 1950; d. Bernard G. Gerske and L. Fay (Knight) Capron. BS, Northwestern U., 1971; JD, U. Mich., 1978. Bar: Ill. 1978, U.S. Dist. Ct. (no. dist.) Ill. 1978. Pvt. practice, Chgo., 1978—80, 1984—2002; assoc. Jerome H. Torshen Ltd., Chgo., 1980—84. Chpt. chair Ind. Voters Ill./Ind. Precinct Orgn., Chgo., 1982—83; co-chmn. Ill. Women's Agenda Com., 1985—88, fin. officer, 1987—88; dir. Chgo. Abused Women Coalition, 1986—90, sec., treas., 1988—90; co-chair legal status of women com. Young Lawyers sect. Chgo. Bar Assn., 1984—85; co-chair rights of women com. Ill. Women's Bar Assn., 1985—86, dir., 1988—90. Democrat. Home: 850 W Oakdale Ave Chicago IL 60657-5122

GERSONI-EDELMAN, DIANE CLAIRE, author, editor; b. Apr. 16, 1947; d. James Arthur and Edna Bernice (Krinski) Gersoni; m. James Neil Edelman, Oct. 5, 1975; children: Michael Lawrence, Sara Anne. Asst. editor, then assoc. editor Sch. Libr. Jour. Book Rev., 1968—72; freelance writer, 1972—74, 1977—; writer, editor Scholastic Mags., Inc., N.Y.C., 1974—77. Cons., spkr. in field. Author: Sexism and Youth, 1974, Work-Wise: Learning About the World of Work from Books, 1980; contbr. articles and book revs. to anthologies, newspapers and mags.

GERSTEIN, ESTHER, sculptor; b. N.Y.C., May 20, 1924; d. Leon and Lillian (Peretz) Grizer; m. Leonard B. Gerstein, Mar. 31, 1946; children: Lee Steven, Laurie Susan. Student, Pratt Inst., 1941-42, NYU, 1942-43; pvt. study, various sculptors; student, Cooper Union, 1946-48. Asst. tchr. Art Students League, N.Y.C., 1944-46; painting tchr. pvt. sch. Great Neck, N.Y., 1961-63; founder, instr. sculpture and painting Studio 33, Westbury, N.Y., 1964-72; sculptor and painter pvt. studios, Boca Raton, Fla. Lectr. Norton Mus., Palm Beach, Fla., 1985. Exhibited in group shows at Hecksher Mus., Huntington, N.Y., Norton Mus., Palm Beach, Fla., Kellenberg Gallery, C.W. Post Coll., L.I., Firehouse Gallery, Nassau Cmty. Coll., L.I., Lever House, N.Y.C., Grace Bldg., N.Y.C., Hofstra U., Lighthouse Gallery, Tequesta, Fla., Montoya Art Gallery, Palm Beach, Del-Aire Country Club, Boca Raton, Fla., Bocaire Country Club, Boca Raton, Polo Country Club, Boca Raton, Nathan Rosen Gallery, Boca Raton, Lynn U., Boca Raton, Naza Gallery, Boca Raton; one man show includes TV spl.; represented in numerous pvt. and corp. collections throughout U.S. Art Students League scholar, 1944, Cooper Union scholar, 1946. Mem. Artists Guild Norton Mus., Nat. League Am. Pen Women. Avocations: reading, music.

GERSTEN, ELIZABETH WELLIVER, education educator, researcher; m. Lee Allan Gardner; children: Charlene Patricia McConnell, Connie Lee Brown. PhD, U. Ariz., Tucson, Ariz., 1994. RN Ariz. State Bd. Nursing, 1973; lic. hypnotherapist Nat. Hypnosis Soc., 2000, cert. FAA, 1988. Adj. faculty Pima Coll., Tucson, 1988—98, Victor Valley Coll., Victorville, Calif., 1999—. Developer, coord. supplemental instrn. and tutoring program Victor Valley Coll., Victorville, Calif., 2000—05; cons. rschr. in field. Bd. mem. Desert Communities United Way, Apple Valley, Calif., 2006—. Mem.: So. Calif. Balloon Assn. (safety com. mem. 2004—05). Avocations: flying hot air balloons, travel, gardening.

GERSTEN, SHIRLEY R., elementary school educator; b. Bklyn., 1931; d. Max and Zelda Rothstein; m. Jesse Jay Gersten, Dec. 25, 1951; children: Karen Ann(dec.), Michael Bruce. BA, Bklyn. Coll., 1952. Disability tchr. North Bellmore Sch. Dist., Bellmore, NY, 1964—74; convention planner Focus Rsch., West Hartford, Conn., 1986—96. Address: 38 E Nacoma Dr Sun Lakes AZ 85248

GERSTENBERGER, VALERIE, media specialist; b. Amherst, Ohio, Sept. 7, 1913; d. Frank Abraham Eppley and Ethel Elizabeth Dute; m. William Jacob Jenkins, Aug. 13, 1944 (div. May 1964); m. Henry Louis Gerstenberger, Nov. 8, 1984 (dec. Aug. 2001). BA, Baldwin-Wallace Coll., 1936; MA, Kent State U., 1963; postgrad., U. Iowa, 1938—39. Asst. drama dir. Baldwin-Wallace Coll., Berea, Ohio, 1936—38; English/speech tchr. St. Elmo (Ill.) H.S., 1940—42, Clearview H.S., Lorain, Ohio, 1942—57; speech tchr. Kent State U., Elyria, Ohio, 1963—66, Cleve. State U., Lakewood, Ohio, 1966—70; media coord. Amherst (Ohio) Pub. Schs., 1957—80; drama dir. Amherst (Ohio) Pub. H.S., 1957—60, 1975—78. Mem./pres. Amherst Pub. Libr. Bd., 1963—92; cons. for libr. expansion Am. Pub. Libr., 1972—73; costume designer various orgns. Founder Amherst Heritage House Mus., 2002; pres. Libr. Bd., 1984—86; founder Workshop Players, Inc., 1948, Cmty. Theater; vol. cataloging documents Amherst Hist. Soc. Named to Gallery of Success, Amherst (Ohio) HS, 1987, First Families of Lorain County, 1989, Hall of Fame, Ohio Cmty. Theatre Assn., 2003; recipient Merit award, Baldwin Wallace Coll., 1986; Paul Harris fellow, Rotary Internat., 1983. Mem.: Amherst Hist. Soc., Phi Mu. Republican. Congregationalist. Home: 439 Shupe Ave Amherst OH 44001

GERSTENLAUER, JOYCE ELAINE, elementary school educator; b. Ephrata, Pa., May 30, 1955; d. Richard N. and Alta S. Myer; m. David L. Gerstenlauer, June 4, 1977; 1 child, Joshua E. BS in Music Edn., Indiana U. Pa., 1977; M Music Edn., Pa. State U., University Park, 1986, postgrad., 1998—. Cert. music tchr. Pa., Tex. Tchr., Waynesboro, Tex., 1977—83; tchr. music, theater Westshore Sch. Dist., Etters, Pa., 1987, Susquenita Sch. Dist., Duncannon, Pa., 1998—2002; assoc. ministry musician Grace Luth. Ch., Camp Hill, Pa., 1987—97; fin. planner Mass. Mut./Wienken Assocs., Camp Hill, 1993—98; instr. fine arts Scotland Sch. for Vets.' Children, Pa., 2002—. Part-time music instr. Pa. State U., State College, 1983—87, Gettysburg Sem., Pa., 1987—95; part-time dir., artist Perry County Choral Soc., Duncannon, 1997—; pvt. voice coach, piano tchr., 1977—; choreographer various show choirs and theatrical prodns., 1977—. Mem. com. Mechanicsburg HS Ice Hockey Boosters, Pa., 2002—; bd. dirs., organist AGO, Harrisburg, Pa., 1985—2000; founding mem., treas. Assn. Luth. Ch. Musicians, Harrisburg, 1987—2000; nat. del. confs. Evang. Luth. Ch. Am., Chgo., 1990, Ind., 2001, mem. synod and ch. worship and music coms. Harrisburg, 1987—. Mem.: NEA (mem. Nat. Honor Roll 2006), Pa. Edn. Assn., Pa. Music Edn. Assn., Music Educators Nat. Conf., Am. Choral Dirs. Assn. Avocations: winetasting, travel, fitness, aerobics, sewing. Home: 824 Bonny Ln Mechanicsburg PA 17055

GERSTING, JUDITH LEE, computer scientist, educator, researcher; b. Springfield, Vt., Aug. 20, 1940; d. Harold H. and Dorothy V. (Kinney) MacKenzie; m. John M. Gersting, Jr., Aug. 17, 1962; children: Adam, Jason. BS, Stetson U., 1962; MA, Ariz. State U., 1964, PhD, 1969. Assoc. prof. computer sci. U. Ctrl. Fla., Orlando, 1980—81; asst. prof. Ind. U./Purdue U., Indpls., 1970—73, assoc. prof., 1974—79, prof., 1981—93, U. Hawaii, Hilo, 1994—. Staff scientist Indpls. Ctr. Advanced Rsch., 1982—84. Author: Mathematical Structures for Computer Science, 2006; contbr. articles to sci. jours. Mem.: Assn. Computing Machinery. Avocations: youth soccer, reading. Office: U Hawaii 200 W Kawili St Hilo HI 96720-4075 Business E-Mail: gersting@hawaii.edu.

GERTRUDE, KATY See WILHELM, KATE

GERTZ, SUZANNE C., artist; b. Chgo., Sept. 8, 1938; d. Henry A. Feldman and Helen Flanzer; m. Theodore G. Gertz, June 19, 1960; children: Craig M., Candace C., Scott W. Student, Art Inst. Chgo., 1960; BFA, Barat Coll., 1982. Exhibited in group shows at Art Inst. Chgo., San Jacinto Coll., Houston, 2001, New Horizons in Art, Chgo., Lake Forest Art Show, exhibitions include San Bernardino County Mus., Firehouse Gallery, N.Y., Evanston and Vicinity 12th Bienniel Exhbn., The Cmty. Gallery Art Coll. Lake County, Dittmar Gallery, Northwestern U., David Adler Cultural Ctr., Cindy Bordeau Gallery, others. Mem.: Cliff Dwellers Club. Democrat. Jewish. Home: 1894 Buckeridge Ct Gurnee IL 60031-6329

GERVAIS, CHERIE NADINE, small business owner; b. Marysville, Calif. d. Victor H. and Gladys A. (Poissant) Fehr; 1 child, Dublin M. Ryan. Student, Yuba Coll., Coll. of Marin, 1977, Sonoma State Coll., 1994, student, 2002. Owner, operator Grandma's Trunk Doll Hosp., San Francisco, 1969-72, San Rafael, Calif., 1972-92, Cherie's Doll Hosp., Petaluma, Calif., 1992-93. Model various local fashion shows, San Francisco and Marin County, Calif., 1973-87; docent Petaluma Mus. Editor: U.F.D.C. Doll Convention Book; contbr. numerous poems to profl. publs., articles in mags. on doll history; paintings and scultpures exhibited at show in Petaluma Mus. Recipient many 1st, 2d and 3d place ribbons at doll shows, ribbons for quilts at fairs in Sonoma and Marin County, 1st place ribbons for paintings and sculptures Sonoma Fair, 1993, Best of Show Sonoma-Marin Fair, 2004, 1st and 2d ribbons, 2005; named Poet of Month, San Rafael (Calif.) Pointer News, 1975. Mem. Dolls from the Attic (pres. 1988-02, 06, v.p.), 101 Doll Club (pres. 1975-76), San Francisco Doll Club (pres. 1976-77), Women of the Moose. Episcopalian. Avocations: painting, sculpting, writing, sewing. Home and Office: Cherie's Doll Hosp 45 La Cresta Dr Petaluma CA 94952-2460 Office Phone: 707-778-8534.

GERVAIS, SISTER GENEROSE, hospital consultant; b. Currie, Minn., Sept. 18, 1919; d. Philip Frederick and Elizabeth Eleanor (Sandgathe) Gervais. BS, Stout State U., Menomonie, Wis., 1945; M. Hosp. Adminstrn., U. Minn., 1954. Joined Sisters of St. Francis, Roman Catholic Ch., 1938; adminstrv. dietitian St. Marys Hosp., Rochester, Minn., 1948-50, adminstrv. asst., 1951-52, asst. adminstr., 1954-63, assoc. adminstr., 1963-71, hosp. adminstr., 1971-81, exec. dir., 1981-85, bd. trustees, 1968-86; hosp. cons., 1985-90. Cons. dietitian Mercy Hosp., Portsmouth, Ohio, 1950-51; bd. dirs. 1st Nat. Bank, Rochester, 1974-78, Fed. Res. Bank Mpls., 1978-86, St. Francis Med. Ctr., LaCrosse, Wis., 1979-87, S.E. Minn. Health Systems Agy., 1978-83, S.E. Minn. Health Coun., 1983-87, Unity Home Health Svcs., Inc., LaCrosse, 1994-95; v.p., sec. Family Health Ctr. LaCrosse, Inc., 1985-91, pres., 1991-93; mem. residency adv. bd. St. Francis-Mayo Family Practice, 1993-95; mem. v.p., bd. dirs. Caledonia Health Care Ctr., 1986-90; bd. dirs. Franciscan Health System, LaCrosse, 1987-94, mem., treas., bd. dirs. Franciscan Cmty. Programs 1985-94. Bd. dirs. United Way of Olmstead County, 1968-73, Sr. Citizens Svcs. Inc., Rochester, Minn., 1988-94, Diocese of Winona Found., 1991-2000; bd. dirs. Madonna Towers, Rochester, 1987—, chair, 1991-97, 2003-05; bd. dirs. Olmstead County Hist. Soc., 1994-97; bd. dirs. Regina Med. Ctr., Hastings, Minn., 1996-02, Madonna Meadows, 2002—; pres. Poverello Found., Rochester, 1983—; bd. adv. Winona State U. Rochester Ctr., 1985-93; mem. fin. coun. Diocese of Winona, 1986-91; mem. Franciscan Skemp Healthcare Cmty. Bd., LaCrosse, 1995—. Decorated Lady of Equestrian Order of Holy Sepulchre, 1989; recipient Alumni Disting. Service award U. Wis.-Stout, 1978, Teresa of Avila award Coll. of St. Teresa, 1980, Outstanding Achievement award Rochester chpt. U. Minn. Alumni Assn., 1981, Women of Achievement in Area of Bus. award YWCA, 1985, Pro Ecclesiae et Pontifice medal, 1985, Service to Mankind award Sertoma 700 Club, 1987, Mayor's Medal of Honor City of Rochester, 1990, The Athena award, 1994, Outstanding Alumni award Coll. Human Devel., U. Wis.-Stout, 2001; named Boss of Yr., Rochester Jaycees, 1980, named in her honor Sister Generose Gervais Bldg. St. Marys Hosp., 1991; Paul Harris fellow Nat. Rotary Club, 1998. Mem. Cath. Health Assn. U.S. (trustee 1979, vice chair 1981-82, chair 1982-83, speaker membership assembly 1983-84), Am. Coll. Hosp. Adminstrs., Am. Hosp. Assn., Minn. Hosp. Assn., Minn. Conf. Cath. Health Facilities (past dir.), Rochester Area C. of C. Republican. Address: 1216 2nd St SW Rochester MN 55902-1906 Office Phone: 507-255-5158. Business E-Mail: hanson.sandra@mayo.edu.

GERVAIS-GRUEN, ELIZABETH, lawyer; b. Papa, Hungary, Feb. 04; arrived in U.S., 1921; d. Samuel Friedmann and Vilma Kohn; m. Ralph Gervais, Feb. 7, 1970; m. Rudolph Gruen, Aug. 2, 1934 (div.); children: Richard Gruen, Robert Gruen, S. Daniel Gruen, David Gruen. Student, St. John's U., 1929—31, LLB, 1934. Bar: N.Y. 1936, N.Y. Supreme Ct. 1936, U.S. Supreme Ct. 1969. Law clk. Law Office of Samuel Newfield, 1934—36; ptnr. Rudolf Gruen and Elizabeth Gruen, 1936—38; asst. to town atty. James Dowsey, Jr. Nassau County, NY, 1938—40, asst. to county atty. James Dowsey, 1940—43; pvt. practice, 1943—58; pvt. practice Immigration and Naturalization Law, 1958—. Pres. Nassau County Women's Assn., 1968—70; bd. trustees Blumenthal Jewish Home, 1989—93; pres. Durham-Chapel Hill Jewish Fedn., 1988—90; chair Am. Affairs com. Hadassah, 1960—64, 1972—74; founder, mem. Women's Ctr., Chapel Hill, NC; chair, advisor youth activity com. Temple Beth El, Great Neck L.I., NY, chair, advisor Temple Teens, chair, advisor Coll. Youth com., pres. Sisterhood; mem. long-term planning com. Temple Beth Zion, Buffalo; chair women's group Judea Reform Congregation, Durham, NC, 1976—78, mem. long-term planning com., hon. chmn. Capitol Campaign. Recipient Sara Mutt Evans award, Jewish Fedn. and Cmty. Svc., 1992. Mem.: Commn.-Status of Women Attys. (Status of Women Attys. in N.C. com. mem.), N.C. Bar Assn. (chair Immigration and Nationality com. 1981—99), Am. Immigration Lawyers Assn. (chair N.C. chpt. 1980—84, bd. govs., founder N.C. chpt., hon. fellow 2002, Sam Williamson Mentor award 2000, Carolinas chpt. Mentor award in honor Elizabeth Gervais-Gruen established 1999, Elizabeth F. Gervais-Gruen Mentor award 1999, Pres.'s Commendation 1992). Avocations: reading, analyzing law, collecting Judaic artifacts, collecting ancient glass, collecting minerals and fossils, stamp collecting/philately. Office: 914 Crestwood Ln Chapel Hill NC 27517 Office Phone: 919-933-6810.

GESKE, JANINE PATRICIA, law educator; b. Port Washington, Wis., May 12, 1949; d. Richard Braem and Georgette (Paulissen) Geske; m. Michael Julian Hogan, Jan. 2, 1982; children: Mia Geske Berman, Sarah Geske Hogan, Kevin Geske Hogan. Student, U. Grenoble, U. Rennes; BA, MA in Tchg., Beloit Coll., 1971; JD, Marquette U., 1975, LLD, 1998, LLD (hon.), 1994; DHL (hon.), Mt. Mary Coll., 1999. Bar: Wis. 1975, U.S. Dist. Ct. (ea. & we. dists.) Wis. 1975, U.S. Supreme Ct. 1978. Tchr. elem. sch., Lake Zurich, Ill., 1970-72; staff atty., chief staff atty. Legal Aid Soc., Milw., 1975-78; asst. prof. law, clin. dir. Law Sch. Marquette U., Milw., 1978-81; hearing examiner Milw. County CETA, Milw., 1980-81; judge Milw. County Circuit Ct., Milw., 1981-93; justice Supreme Ct. Wis., 1993-98; disting. prof. law Marquette U. Law Sch., Milw., 1998—, interim Miles County exec., 2002, interim dean Sch. Law, 2002—03. Dean Wis. Jud. Coll.; mem. faculty Nat. Jud. Coll.; instr. various jud. tng. programs, continuing legal edn. Fellow ABA, mem. Am. Law Inst., Am. Arbitration Assn., Soc. Profls. in Dispute Resolution, Wis. Bar Assn., Wis. Assn. Mediators, Milw. Bar Assn., Nat. Women Judges Assn., 7th Cir. Bar Assn., Alpha Sigma Nu. Roman Catholic. Office: Marquette U Law Sch PO Box 1881 Milwaukee WI 53201-1881

GESKIN, LEAH, foreign language educator; b. Daugavpils, Latvia, Mar. 25, 1939; came to U.S., 1990; d. Isaac and Gitel (Shneyder) Kopman; m. Semen Geskin, Aug. 2, 1962 (dec. Aug. 1991); children: Gennady, Elina. MEd, Latvia State U., Riga, 1988. Translator Jewish Cmty. Coun., N.Y.C., 1990-91; site supr. Sara Shemrer Tchrs. Sem., N.Y.C., 1991-93; dir. Russian dept. YMHA and YWHA, N.Y.C., 1993—. ESL tchr. Bronx House, 1995—, Hebrew Home for Aged, 1996—. Republican. Jewish. Avocations: travel, classical music, books, theater. Office: YMHA and YWHA Washington Heights 54 Nagle Ave New York NY 10040-1406 Home: 4009 Monroe St Fair Lawn NJ 07410

GESLANI, GEMMA P., health studies educator; d. Justiniano P. Geslani and Paz Pareja. BS in Chemistry, Silliman U., Dumaguete City, Philippines, 1981; MS in Biochemistry, U. Philippines, Manila, 1988; MPH, U. SC, Columbia, 1998; PhD in Biochemistry, U. SC, 1996. Rsch. asst. U. of the Philippines, 1982—84, rsch. assoc., 1984—88; instr. RTR Sch. of Medicine, Tacloban City, Philippines, 1988—90; rsch. and tchg. asst. U. SC, 1990—98; health rschr. Survey Methods Group, San Francisco, 1999—99; asst. prof. Claflin U., Orangeburg, SC, 2000—05, assoc. prof., 2005—. Co-PI, co-dir. export grant Claflin U., 2005—, co-investigator, program coord. Kellogg grant, 2003—06, rsch. coord. Kellogg grant, 2005—. Co-author: Custom Made Laboratory Manual for Human Biology; contbr. articles to profl. jours. Active mem. Filipino-Am. Assn. of Greater Columbia, 1991—. Academic fellow, RTR Med. Sch., 1982—84, rsch. fellow, U. SC Sch. Pub. Health, 2006. Mem.: APHA, SC Pub. Health Assn. Roman Catholic. Avocations: reading, travel, gardening, cooking, dance. Home: 968 Freeland St Orangeburg SC 29115 Office Phone: 803-535-5775. Personal E-mail: ggeslani@claflin.edu.

GEST, KATHRYN WATERS, public relations executive; b. Boston, Mar. 20, 1947; d. Mendal and Anna Waters; m. Theodore O. Gest, May 28, 1972; 1 child, David Mendal. BS, Northwestern U., 1969; MS, Columbia U., 1970. Reporter The Patriot-Ledger, Quincy, Mass., 1968; writer Europe desk Voice of Am., Washington, 1969; reporter St. Louis Globe-Democrat, 1970-77, Congl. Quar., Washington, 1977-78, news editor, 1978-80, asst. mng. editor, 1980-83, mng. editor, 1983-87; St. Louis corr. Time Mag., 1975-77, The Christian Sci. Monitor, 1976-77; press sec. to Sen. William S. Cohen, Washington, 1987-96; chmn., U.S. del. Internat. Labor Orgn. Tripartite Meeting on Conditions of Employment and Work of Journalists, Geneva, 1990; exec. v.p., dir. internat. issues Powell Tate/Weber Shandwick, 1996—. Election observer Nat. Dem. Inst., Albania, 1996, Azerbaijan, 2003, Ukraine, 04, Palestinian Terrs., 2006—. Recipient award for investigative reporting Inland Daily Press Assn., 1975 Bd. dirs. Nat. Press Found. Soc. Profl. Journalists, Women's Fgn. Policy Group, Internat. Women's Media Fund, Nat. Press Club. Office: Powell Tate/Weber Shandwick 700 13th St NW Washington DC 20005-6618 Business E-Mail: kgest@aol.com.

GESUALDO, DEBORAH MARY, music educator; b. Downey, Calif., Nov. 3, 1981; d. Joseph and Deborah Louise Gesualdo. MusB in Edn., Gordon Coll., Mass., 2003. Lic. Tchr. The Commonwealth of Mass. Dept. of Edn., 2003. Mid. sch. chorale asst. dir. Hamilton-Wenham Regional Sch. Dist., Mass., 2003, tchg. asst., 2003—04, mid. sch. chorale dir., 2004; gen. music tchr. City of Malden Pub. Schs., Malden, Mass., 2004—. Spl. event music cons. Pvt., Danvers, Mass., 1999—. Decorated Commendation USMC, Cert. of Achievement U.S. Sec. of Def.; recipient Recognition award, U.S. HHS, 1999. Mem.: Malden Edn. Assn. (assoc.), Mass. Tchrs. Assn. (assoc.), Nat. Educators Assn. (assoc.), Mass. Music Educators Assn. (assoc.), Music Educators Nat. Conf. (assoc.). Conservative. Avocations: music, reading, exercise, sports, history. Office Phone: 781-397-7205.

GETER, JENNIFER L., psychologist; b. Washington, Mar. 12, 1970; d. Robert James and Delores Marie Geter. BA, Spelman Coll., 1992; PsyD, Nova Southeastern U., 1997. Lic. clin. psychologist Bd. Examiners in Psychology/Tenn., 2002. Lead children and youth therapist, case mgr. Midtown Mental Health Ctr., Memphis, 1998—2003; clin. psychologist NIA Therapy Svcs., Memphis, 1999—2003; sch. psychologist Memphis City Schs., 2003—; owner, clin. psychologist Imani Psychol. Svcs., Memphis, 2003—. Singer: (church choir) Greater Cmty. Temple Voices, (gospel choir) Marc Cooper and Friends and Miami Mass Choir. Pres. Greater Cmty. Temple Voices, Memphis, 2002—05; mem. Holy Nat. Ch. Memphis, 2006—. Post Doctoral fellow, U. Tenn., 1997—98. Mem.: APA (assoc.), Delta Sigma Theta. Mem. Church Of God In Christ. Avocations: music, basketball, swimming, travel. Office: Imani Psychol Svcs Ste 709 1407 Union Ave Memphis TN 38104 Office Phone: 901-726-5200. Personal E-mail: psyd4kids@aol.com.

GETTINGER, SUSAN BETH, literature and language educator; b. Columbus, Ohio, July 2, 1950; d. John Ralph and Norman Jean Fleming; m. Scott E. Gettinger, June 21, 1975; children: Nathan Douglas, Benjamin Scott, Jared Allen. Masters, Ohio State U., Columbus, 1975. Cert. tchr. Ohio, 1972, nat. bd. cert. tchr. Nat. Bd. for Tchg. Stds., 2003. Lang. arts tchr. Hilliard (Ohio) City Schs., 1985—. Lang. arts tchr. leader Hilliard City Schs., 1994—. Named Wal-Mart Tchr. of Yr., Wal-Mart, 1998. Office Phone: 614-529-7424. Business E-Mail: susie_gettinger@fclass.hilliard.k12.oh.us.

GETTY, AMY C., language educator, department chairman; b. Davenport, Iowa, Sept. 28, 1967; d. Sharon A. and Terence A. Getty; m. Edward R. Allen, July 10, 1991. PhD, Marquette U., Milw., 2000. English instr. Tillamook Bay CC, Oreg., 2000—02; assoc. prof. English Grand View Coll., Des Moines, 2002—. Literacy tutor Des Moines Area Cmty. Coll., 2003—06. Recipient Excellence and Innovation in Tchg. award, Grand View Coll., 2005. Office: Grand View Coll 1200 Grandview Ave Des Moines IA 50316 Business E-Mail: agetty@gvc.edu.

GETTY, ESTELLE (ESTELLE SCHER), actress; b. NYC, July 25, 1923; m. Arthur Gettleman, Dec. 21, 1946 (dec. 2004); children: Barry, Carl. Student, New Sch. for Social Rsch., Herbert Berghof Studios; studied with Gerald Russak. Actress: numerous stage prodns. on and off Broadway including Death of a Salesman, The Glass Menagerie, All My Sons, 6 Rms Rv Vu, Blithe Spirit, Arsenic and Old Lace, I Don't Know Why I'm Screaming, Widows and Children, Torch Song Trilogy, 1981-83; (films) Team-Mates, 1978, Tootsie, 1982, Deadly Force, 1983, Mask, 1985, Mannequin, 1987, Stop! Or My Mom Will Shoot, 1992, Stuart Little, 1999, The Million Dollar Kid, 2000; (TV movies) No Man's Land, 1984, Victims for Victims: The Teresa Saldana Story, 1984, Copacabana, 1985, A Match Made in Heaven, 1997, The Sissy Duckling, 1999; (TV series) The Golden Girls, 1985-92, (Emmy award for outstanding supporting actress in a comedy series, 1988, Golden Globe award for best performance by an actress in a TV series - comedy/musical, 1986, Am. Comedy award for funniest supporting female performer in a TV series, 1991, 92), Golden Palace, 1992-93, Empty Nest, 1994-95; author: If I Knew Then What I Know Now.So What?, 1988. ret. 2000. Spokesperson Alternative Living for the Aging.

GETZ, BETTINA, lawyer; b. Davenport, Iowa; BA with honors, Mich. State U., 1976; JD with honors, DePaul U., 1982. Judicial law clk. Ill. Appellate Ct., Chgo., 1982-84; assoc. atty. Isham Lincoln & Beale, Chgo., 1984-87, Mayer Brown & Platt, Chgo., 1987-90, ptnr., atty., 1990—. Mem. Chgo. Inn of Ct. Office: Mayer Brown & Platt 190 S La Salle St Ste 3100 Chicago IL 60603-3441

GETZENDANNER, SUSAN, lawyer; b. Chgo., July 24, 1939; d. William B. and Carole S. (Muehling) O'Meara; children— Alexandra, Paul. BBA, JD, Loyola U., 1966. Bar: Ill. bar 1966. Law clk. U.S. Dist. Ct., Chgo., 1966-68; assoc. Mayer, Brown & Platt, Chgo., 1968-74, ptnr., 1974-80; judge U.S. Dist. Ct., Chgo., 1980-87; ptnr. Skadden, Arps, Slate, Meagher & Flom, Chgo., 1987—2002. Recipient medal of excellence Loyola U. Law Alumni Assn., 1981 Mem. ABA, Chgo. Council Lawyers. Office Phone: 312-944-2629. E-mail: sgetzendanner@mindspring.com.

GEURDEN, TAMMY ANN, education educator, counselor; b. Washington, Oct. 3, 1967; d. David Lee and Sharon Mary Geurden. BS in Psychology, U. Wis., Oshkosh, 1993; MS in guidance and counseling, U. Wis., Whitewater, 1997. Sr. program coord. REM-Wis., Madison, 1998—2000; program mgr. REM-Nev., 2000—01; asst. dir. vocat. svcs. Easter Seals Nev., Reno, 2001—04; counselor pvt. practice, Reno, 2001—; tchg. asst. U. Nev., Reno, 2005—. Doctoral student U. Nev., Reno, 2004—. Author: (poem) Twilight Musings, 2005. Vol., grant writer U.S. Wallyball Assn., Reno, 2004—05; vol., coach Spl. Olympics, Reno, 2001—06; eucharistic min. St. Rose of Lima Cath. Ch., Reno, 2001—06; v.p. Reno Pops Orch., 2002—06; vol. Sierra Safari Zoo, Reno, 2001—03. Grantee Continuing Edn. Grant, U. Nev., 2005—06. Mem.: Women Execs. Accelerating Change Today, Nev. Assn. for Play Therapy, Internat. Assn. of Marriage and Family Counselors, Assn. for Spiritual, Ethical, and Religious Values in Counseling, ACA (conv. vol. 2005—06), Reno Ski & Recreation Club, Pi Lamda Theta. Independent. Roman Catholic. Avocations: piano, singing, reading, tennis, travel. Home: 4500 Mira Loma Dr #305 Reno NV 89502-5460 Office: Univ Nev Reno Coll of Edn Mailstop 281 Reno NV 89557-0213 Office Phone: 775-342-7803. Office Fax: 775-784-1990. Personal E-mail: dutchangel67@yahoo.com.

GEWIRTZ, MINDY L., organizational and leadership relations consultant; b. NYC, Mar. 19, 1951; d. Martin and Miriam (Altman) Lebovicz; m. Gershon C. Gewirtz, Sept. 7, 1971; children: Yussy, Henoch, Sora Leah, Adina, Doniel. MPS, N.Y. Inst. Tech., 1977; MSW, SUNY, Albany, 1981; PhD in Orgnl. Sociology, Boston U., 1995. Lic. ind. clin. social worker; diplomate Am. Bd. Clin. Social Workers. Project coord. Ringel Inst. Gerontology SUNY-Albany, 1980-82; coord. sr. adult dept. Jewish Family Svcs., Albany, 1983-84; dir. eldercare connection long distance caregiving svc. Jewish Family and Children's Svc., Boston, 1984-93; prin. GLS, Inc., Boston, 1988—; postgrad. fellow orgnl. devel. & human resources cons. Boston Inst. Psychotherapy, 1990; cons., 2005; pres. Collaborative Networks Internat., 2005—, GLS Consulting Ptnr., 1995—2005. Adj. asst. prof. Boston U. Sch. Social Work; cons. Ibis Cons. Group, Cambridge, 1990—; orgn. and mgmt. cons. Boston Digital Equipment Corp., Boston, 1988-92; orgnl. cons. Malden Mills, Lawrence, Mass., 1992-99; presdl. adviser Am. Type Culture Collection, 2002; co-founder Emerging Bus. Collaborative, 2006. Author (book chpt.) Peoak Power, UK Jour. IMIS, 2004; co-author: Sustaining Top Leadership: Promise and Pitfalls in Collaborative Work Systems, 2002; assoc. author: Human Dilemmas in Work Organizations, 1994; contbr. articles to profl. jours. and publs. Mem. Boston Work and Family Forum, New England Human Resources Assn., Greater Boston Orgnl. Devel. Network. Recipient Max Siporin Social Work fellow. Mem. NASW, ACSW (bd. cert. diplomate), Am. Assn. Bus. Women (career advancement fellow), Phi Beta Kappa. Home: 23 Browne St Brookline MA 02446-3804 Office Phone: 617-777-7360. Business E-Mail: mgewirtz@collaborativenetworks.net.

GEWIRTZ-FRIEDMAN, GERRY, editor; b. NYC, Dec. 22, 1920; d. Max and Minnie (Weiss) G.; m. Eugene W. Friedman, Nov. 11, 1945; children: John Henry, Robert James. BA, Vassar Coll., 1941. Editor Package Store Mgmt., 1942-44, Jewelry Mag., 1945-53; freelance editor promotion dept. McCall's Mag., Esquire, 1953-56; free-lance fashion and gifts editor Jewelers Circular Keystone, N.Y.C., 1955-71; editor, pub. The Fashionables, 1971-74, The Forecast, 1974—, Nat. Jeweler, Ann. Fashion Guide, 1976-80; editor, assoc. pub. Exec. Jeweler, 1980-83; editor The Fashion Source (formerly Internat. Fashion Index), N.Y.C., 1984—; freelance editor and mktg. specialist, 1995—. Ptnr. Gay Gewirtz-Editl. and Mktg.; free-lance editl. wrtier, 1995—. Corr. Internat. Mktg. News. Mem. exec. com. Inner City Council of Cardinal Cooke, N.Y.; chairperson women's task force United Jewish Appeal Fedn.; former bd. govs. Israel Bonds; former trustee Israel Cancer Research Fund, Central Synagogue; bd. dirs. Double Image Theater; former pres. women's aux. Brandeis U. Honored guest Am. Jewish Com., 1978; Israel Cancer Research Fund, 1978-81; recipient Disting. Community Service award Brandeis U., 1987; named to Jewelry Hall Fame, 1988. Mem. N.Y. Fashion Group, Nat. Home Fashions League (former pres.), Women's Jewelry Assn. (pres. 1983-87, named editor who has contbd. most to jewelry industry 1984, free lance editor). Home: 45 Sutton Pl S New York NY 10022-2444

GEWURZ, ANITA TARTELL, physician, medical educator; b. Buffalo, July 30, 1946; MD, Albany Med. Coll., 1970. Resident in pediat. U. Ill., Chgo., 1971—73; resident in allergy and immunology Rush-Presbyn.-St. Luke's Hosp., Chgo., 1974—76; fellow allergy and immunology Max Samter Inst., Grant Hosp., Chgo., 1976—77, Northwestern U. Med. Coll., Chgo., 1983—85; assoc. prof. immunology/microbiology, pediat. and internal med. Rush U. Med. Coll., Chgo., 1993—2003, prof. immunology/microbiology, pediat. and internal med., 2003—; physician Rush U. Med. Ctr., Chgo., 1974—. Chair, Tng. Program Dirs. Com. Am. Acad. Allergy, Asthma & Immunology, 2003—04; past chair Am. Bd. Allergy and Immunology; initial cert. task force Am. Bd. Medical Specialties, 2004—, chair, 2004—05, program dir., 2004—. Office: Rush Univ Med Ctr 1725 W Harrison St Ste 117 Chicago IL 60612 Office Phone: 312-942-6296. Business E-Mail: agewurz@rush.edu.

GEYER, GEORGIE ANNE, columnist, educator, commentator, writer; b. Chgo., Apr. 2, 1935; d. Robert George and Georgie Hazel (Gervens) G. BS, Northwestern U., 1956, LHD (hon.), 1993; postgrad., U. Vienna, Austria, 1956-57; LittD (hon.), Lake Forest Coll., 1980, Coll. Mt. St. Joseph, 1986, Notre Dame, 1986, Wilson Coll., 1987, Linfield Coll., 1987, St. Mary-of-the-Woods Coll., 1989, U. Indpls., 1991, Colby-Sawyer Coll., 1992, Franklin Coll., 1992, Cabrini Coll., 1994; LHD (hon.), Northwestern U., 1984, U. S.C., 1991, Rockhurst Coll., Kansas City, 1992, Spring Hill Coll., 1993, Lebanon Valley Coll., 1994, Hofstra U., 1995, Loyola U., Chgo., 1996, Westminster Coll., 1996, Govs. State U., 1997, Notre Dame Coll., 1999, Knox Coll., 1999. Reporter Southtown Economist, Chgo., 1958; soc. reporter Chgo. Daily News, 1959-60, gen. assignment reporter, 1960-64, corr. Lat. Am., Ctrl. Am., Soviet Union, Middle East, Europe, 1964-75, roving fgn. corr. and columnist, 1967-75; syndicated columnist Los Angeles Times Syndicate, 1975-80, Universal Press Syndicate, 1981—; Lyle M. Spencer prof. journalism Syracuse U., 1977. Regular news commentator PBS' Washington Week in Review; questioner on Presdl. debate, Oct., 1984; steering com. Aspen Inst. Latin Am. Governance Project, 1981-82; commentator on the BBC; regular panelist Voice of America; sent by Internat. Communication Agy. on 3 worldwide speaking tours on Am. journalism: Nigeria, Zambia, Tanzania and Somalia, 1979, Philippines and Indonesia, 1981, Iceland, Norway, Belgium and Portugal, 1982; rep. Fulbright scholar program 40th anniversary, New Zealand, 1987; commencement speaker various colls., univs. including U. S.Carolina, Rockhurst Coll., St. Mary's Notre Dame; sr. fellow Annenburg Washington, 1992-93; columnist on fgn. policy, internat. affairs The Chgo. Tribune, The Wash. Times, Universal de Caracas, The Dallas Morning News, Diario las Americas, The Denver Post, others; speaker, lectr. in field. Author: The New Latins, 1970, The New 100 Years War, 1972, The Young Russians, 1976; (autobiography) Buying the Night Flight, (Weintal prize citation Sch. Fgn. Svc. Georgetown U. 1984, Chgo. Found. for Lit. award 1984), 1983, reissued, 1996, Guerilla Prince, The Untold Story of Fidel Castro, 1991, Waiting for Winter to End, An Extraordinary Journey Through Soviet Central Asia, 1994, Americans No More: The Death of Citizenship, 1996, Tunisia: A Journey Through the Country that Works, 2003, When Cats Reigned Like Kings: On the Trail of the Sacred Cats, 2004; subjects of interviews include Prince Sihanouk of Cambodia, Yassar Arafat, Anwar Sadat, King Hussein of Jordan, Pres. Khaddafy of Libya, the Ayatollah Khomeini, Sultan Qaboos of Oman, Pres. Juan Peron of Argentina, Pres. Siad Barre of Somalia, Prime Minister Mauno Koivisto of Finland, Anastasio Somoza, Jerzy Urban, Janusz Onyszkiewicz, Prime Minister Edward Seaga of Jamaica, Pres. Ronald Reagan, Pres. George Bush, others; discovered and had first interview with second most-wanted Nazi, Walter Rauff in Tierra del Fuego, Chile, 1966; found Dominican pres. Juan Bosch in hiding in P.R. during Dominican revolution, 1965; held by Palestinians as Israeli spy, 1973; imprisoned in Angola for writing about revolutionary government, 1976; contbr. chpts. to books, articles numerous pubs. Active Orgn. for S.W. Community Chgo., 1960-64; trustee Am. U., Washington, 1981-86; Coun. Fgn. Rels. Recipient 1st prize Am. Newspaper Guild, 1962; 2d prize Ill. Press Editors Assn., 1962;

award for best writing on Latin Am. Overseas Press Club, 1967; Merit award Northwestern U., 1968; Nat. Headliner award Theta Sigma Phi, 1968; Maria Moors Cabot award Columbia U., 1970; Hannah Solomon award Nat. Council Jewish Women, 1973; Ill. Spl. Events Commn. Woman's award, 1975; Northwestern U. Alumni award, 1991; Fulbright scholar U. Vienna, 1956-57; Woodrow Wilson fellow Rollins Coll., Winter Park, Fla., 1982; Presdl. Citation award Am. Univ., 1985; Disting. fellow Mortar Bd. Nat. Sr. Honor Soc., Am. U., 1982, Sr. fellow Annenberg Washington Program, Washington, 1992-93; fellow Soc. Profl. Journalists, 1992; named Outstanding Illinoisian, Ill. State Assn., 2001; named to Hall of Fame of Soc. of Profl. Journalists, 2001, Stewart Alsop award Assn. Retired Intelligence Officers, 2001, Headliners Club Lifetime Achievement award, 2003, Woman Extraordiaire award Internat. Women Assn., 2004. Mem.: Coun. Fgn. Rels., Inst. Internat. Edn. (bd. dirs.), Soc. Profl. Journalists, Tavern Club (Chgo.), Cosmos Club (1st women mem.), Gridiron Club. Home and Office: The Plaza 800 25th St NW Washington DC 20037-2207 Personal E-mail: gigi_geyer@juno.com.

GEYER, KAREN LEA, writer; b. Pampa, Tex., June 6, 1952; d. W.D. "Dub" and Mardell (Mask) McKendree; m. David Wesley Geyer, Aug. 11, 1972; children: Nathan David, Neil John William, Kendra Lea. Student, West Tex. State U., 1970-71, Ctrl. Area Tech., Drumright, Okla., 1987. With Drumright News Jour., 1985—86; reporter Drumright Gusher, 1987—88; reporter, Lifestyles editor Cushing (Okla.) Daily Citizen, 1992—98; mng. editor Drumright Gusher, 1999, Cushing Daily Citizen, 2000—01. Author: The Scoop on Stacy, 2004; editor: Shoat: A Champion Roper, 2003; editor newspaper Cimarron Valley People in Cushing Oklahoma. Mem. promotion com. Downtown Main St. Recipient 1st Pl. award for feature writing Okla. Newspaper Found. Mem. Okla. Press Assn. (participant news clinics), Okla. Writers Fed., Inc., Cimarron Valley Writers (pres.). Republican. Baptist. Avocations: writing, photography. Home: 8439 S 465th West Ave Drumright OK 74030 Office: Cimarron Valley People 202 North Harrison Cushing OK 74023 Office Phone: 918-285-5555. E-mail: geyersglen@wmconnect.com.

GEYER, KATHY VAN NESS, retailer; b. Ft. Lee, Va., July 9, 1954; d. Joseph Clinton and Barbara Lee (Musser) Van N.; m. David Paul Geyer, Mar. 16, 1990 (div. 2002). BS, Purdue U., 1977. Sales mgr. Macy's, Atlanta, 1977-78, asst. buyer, 1978-79, buyer, 1979-80, group mgr., 1980-81, mdse. mgr., 1981-83, store mgr., 1983-84; dist. mgr. Eddie Bauer Inc., Seattle, 1984-85; asst. store mgr. Rich's Dept. Stores, Atlanta, 1985-88; store mgr. Upton's Dept. Stores, Atlanta, 1988-92; instr., dept. chair fashion merchandising div. Bauder Coll., Atlanta, 1992-94; owner, pres. Rings Around the Moon Llamas, Chelsea, Okla., 1994—; realtor Century 21 Group 1, Claremore, Okla., 1995—2003, OklaHomes Realty, Inc., Claremore, 2003—. Avocations: swimming, showing llamas, reading, travel. Home: 10071 S 4220 Rd Chelsea OK 74016-2140 Office Phone: 918-343-3158.

GEYSER, LYNNE M., lawyer, writer; b. Queens, N.Y., Mar. 28, 1938; d. Henry and Shirley Dannenberg; m. Lewis P. Geyser, 1956 (div. 1974); 1 child, Russell B. Geyser. BA, Queens Coll., 1960; JD, UCLA, 1968. Bar: Calif. 1969. Atty. Zagon, Schiff, Hirsch & Levine, Beverly Hills, Calif., 1969-70; atty., registered legis. advocate Beverly Hills, Malibu, Calif., 1973-75; atty. Freshman, Marantz, Comsky & Deutsch, Beverly Hills, Malibu, Calif., 1971-74; prof. law Glendale (Calif.) U. Law, 1974-76, U. Iowa Sch. Law, Iowa City, 1976-77, Pepperdine U., Malibu, 1977-78; pvt. practice Newport Beach, Calif., 1978-81, San Clemente, 1978—. Part-time prof. law Western State Law Sch., Fullerton, Calif., 1978; cons. atty. The Irvine Co., Newport Beach, 1981-86, Std. Mgmt. Co., L.A., 1987-88; instr. Saddleback Coll., Mission Viejo, Calif., early 1990's; lectr., instr. Calif. Assn. Realtors Grad. Realty Inst., 1972-78, U. So. Calif. brokers tng. courses, L.A., 1978-80, UCLA real estate and corp. courses for paralegals, 1973-76; creator and lectr. course on disclosure for licensees, L.A., San Diego and Orange Counties, Calif., 1978-81; faculty advisor, rev. advisor Glendale U. Coll. Law, 1975-76. Chief articles editor UCLA Law Rev., 1967; adv. bd. The Rsch. Jour., 1976; contbr. poetry and short stories to jours. Mem. exec. bd. L.A. County Art Mus. Contemporary Art Coun., L.A., 1971-73; bd. trustees Westwood (L.A.) Art Assn., 1974; bd. govs. La Costa Beach Homeowners Assn., Malibu, 1975; pres. Dana Point (Calif.) Coastal Arts Coun., 1989-90; teaching participant Jr. Achievement, Newport Beach, 1985. Recipient 6 Am. Jurisprudence awards, 1966-68, 2 West Hornbook awards, 1967; nom. Douglas Law Clk. UCLA Law Sch., 1967. Fellow The Legal Inst.; mem. AALS (chair-elect environ. law sect. 1977), San Clemente Sunrise Rotary, Order of Coif. Avocations: world travel, fine arts, writing, computers, performing arts, graphics. Office: PO Box 4715 San Clemente CA 92674-4715

GHAFFARI, AVIDEH BEHROUZ, interior designer; b. Tehran, Iran, Apr. 17, 1943; arrived in U.S., 1975, naturalized, 1984; d. Zabih and Homa Behrouz; m. Abbas Ghaffari, Feb. 2, 1976; children: Narsi Azima, Borzou Azima. Founder, pres. Polydecor Co., Tehran, Paris, 1962—68; pres. Pakab Co. Ltd., Tehran, 1963—75, Avidecor Co., Inc., N.Y.C., 1979—, Avida Internat. Ltd., N.Y.C., 1985—; v.p. William B. May Co., N.Y.C., 1985—2004; v.p., dir. Brown Harris Stevens, N.Y.C., 2004—. Recipient Merit award, Imperial Govt. Iran, 1969. Mem.: NAFE, Real Estate Bd. NY, Iran Inst. Interior Design, Internat,. Soc. Interior Designers, Am. Soc. Interior Designers. Home: 425 E 58th St New York NY 10022-2300 Office: 425 E 58th St # 3-h New York NY 10022-2300

GHARIB, SUSIE, newscaster; b. NYC, Nov. 27, 1950; d. Ali and Homa (Razzaghmanesh) Gharib; m. Fereydoun Nazem, Jan. 20, 1973; children: Alexander Nazem, Taraneh Nazem. BA magna cum laude, Case Western Res. U., 1972; M in Internat. Affairs, Columbia U., 1974. Reporter Cleve. Plain Dealer, 1972-73; assoc. editor Fortune Mag., N.Y.C., 1974-83; anchor, reporter Bus. Times/ESPN, N.Y.C., 1983-85; bus. reporter ABC News, N.Y.C., 1986-87; anchor Fin. News Network, N.Y.C., 1989-90, CNBC Network, Ft. Lee, NJ, 1993-98, Nightly Bus. Report, N.Y.C., 1998—. Moderator/host Xerox Corp., Stanford, Conn., 1989—95, KPMG Peat Marwick, N.Y.C., 1992—95; cons. Adam Smith's Money World/PBS, N.Y.C., 1987. Bd. dirs. First Fortis, Inc., 1991—2000, Ice Theatre N.Y., 1988—90; mem. SIPA adv. bd. Columbia U., 2006—; trustee Case Western Res. U., 2005—. Mem.: Econ. Club N.Y. (trustee 2003—), N.Y. Fin. Writers Assn., Fgn. Policy Assn., Phi Beta Kappa. Democrat. Avocations: ice skating, tennis, piano. Home: 44 E 73rd St New York NY 10021-4173

GHAZI, STEFANIE SARA, obstetrician, gynecologist; d. James Allen Gefroh and Marija Dianne Kemmer; m. Tarek S. Ghazi, Oct. 22, 2000. BA in Biology, Moorhead State U., Minn., 1996; J, U. ND, Grand Forks, 2000. Diplomate Am. Bd. Ob-Gyn. Staff physician Dakota Clinic/Innovis Health, Fargo, ND, 2004—. Home: 2809 38th Ave S Fargo ND 58104-7003

GHEBRHIWET, FREWEINY WENDY, real estate broker, consultant; d. Shashu Mana; children: Daniel Yafet Girmay, Abel Rafel Girmay. BBA, Coll. Alameda, Calif., 1990. Lic. real estate sales Calif., 1994. Sales/real estate broker Re/Max East Bay Hills, Oakland, Calif., 2000—02; assoc. sales Re/Max In Motion, Castro Valley, Calif., 2002—. Sales assoc. Better Homes, Oakland, Calif., 1998—2000; loan broker Am. Fin., Santa Rosa, Calif., 2006—. Author: (novel) The Magic Pill. Mem. exec. bd. Morris Cerullo World Evangelism, San Diego, 1995—2004. Mem.: Nat. Assn. Realtors (licentiate). Office Phone: 510-536-0596.

GHEZ, ANDREA MIA, astronomy educator, physics educator; b. NYC, June 16, 1965; d. Gilbert and Susanne; m. Tom La Tourette, May 1, 1993; 1 child, Evan LaTourette-Ghez. BS, MIT, 1987; MS, Calif. Inst. Tech., 1989, PhD in Physics, 1992. Hubble postdoctoral fellow U. Ariz., Tucson, 1992-93; vis. rsch. scholar Inst. Astronomy, Cambridge, England, 1994; asst. prof. physics and astronomy UCLA, 1994-97, assoc. prof., 1997—2000, prof., 2000—. Contbr. articles to profl. jours. Recipient Amelia Earhart award, 1987, Young Investigator award, NSF, 1994, Fullam/Dudley award, 1995, Maria Goeppert-Mayer award, Am. Phys. Soc., 1999, Sackler prize, U. Tel Aviv, 2004; grantee Pacific Telesis fellowship, 1991, Alfred P. Sloan Rsch. fellowship, 1996, David and Lucile Packard fellowship, 1996. Fellow: Am. Acad. Arts & Scis.; mem.: AAUW, Am. Astron. Soc. (Annie Jump Cannon award 1994, Newton Lacy Pierce prize 1998), NAS, Phi Beta Kappa. Achievements include discovery of formation of young low mass stars in multiple star systems; production of the first diffraction-limited image with the keck 10-m telescope (the largest telescope in the world); measurement of stellar motions which indicate the presence of a supermassive black hole at the center of our own galaxy. Office: UCLA Divsn Astronomy and Astrophysics Physics and Astronomy Bldg 430 Portola Plz Box 951547 Los Angeles CA 90095-1547 E-mail: ghez@astro.ucla.edu.*

GHINAUDO, PENNY ALICIA, science educator, department chairman; b. Temple, Tex., Aug. 2, 1963; d. Andrew D. and Paulette E. Ghinaudo. BA in Biology, St. Mary's U., San Antonio, 1995, MA in Ednl. Leadership, 1998. Cert. secondary sci. and math. tchr., adminstr. Tex. Sci. and math tchr. Judson HS, San Antonio, 2004—05; chmn. dept. Karen Wagner HS, San Antonio, 2005—. Lay min. St. Mark's Cmty. of Hope, San Antonio, 2003—06. Named Tchr. of Yr., East Ctrl. H.S., 2002—03; grantee, Ford Found., 2003. Mem.: NSTA (assoc.), NESLA (assoc.), Nat. Edn. Agy. (assoc.; grantee 2006), Nat. Coun. Tchrs. Math. (assoc.). Catholic. Avocations: travel, cooking, reading, chinchilla, meditation. Office: Karen Wagner HS 3000 North Foster Rd San Antonio TX 78209 Office Phone: 210-662-5000. Personal E-mail: paghinaudo@yahoo.com.

GHIU, SILVANA MELANIA STEFANIA, process and development engineer; b. Constanta, Romania, Dec. 27, 1971; d. Gheorghe and Camelia Ghiu. BSc, U. Bucharest, 1995, MSc, 1996, Ctrl. European U., Budapest, 1998; PhD, U. So. Fla., 2003. EIT 2000. Rsch. asst. Engring. and Environment Rsch. Inst., Bucharest, 1995—97; safeguards officer asst. Nat. Commn. of Nuc. Activities Control, Bucharest, 1996—97; rsch. asst. U. So. Fla., Tampa, 1999—2003; environ. engr. HSA, Tampa, 2004—06; sr. process and devel. engr. Doosan Hydro Tech., Tampa, 2006—. Contbr. articles to profl. jours. Fellow, U. So. Fla. Coll. Engring., 1998—2001, 2001; Govtl. fellow, U. Bucharest, 1995—96, George Soros Found. fellow, Ctrl. European U., 1997—98, Channabasappa Meml. scholar, IDA, 2001. Mem.: Internat. Desalination Assn., North Am. Membrane Soc., Am. Membrane Tech. Assn., Am. Water Works Assn. (v.p. Fla. sect. 2001—03), Nat. Soc. of Profl. Engr., Phi Kappa Phi. Achievements include patents pending for submersible pump; research in equations governing the process of direct osmosis. Office: Doosan Hydro Tech 9001 Brittany Way Tampa FL 33619 Office Phone: 813-549-0182. Personal E-mail: silvanaghiu@yahoo.com. Business E-Mail: sghiu@doosanhydro.com.

GHOLSON, MARTHA RACHEL, religious studies educator; d. Charles and Carol Gholson. BA, U. Mo., Columbia, Mo., 1989; MA, U. Southwestern La., Lafayette, La., 1991; PhD, Meml. U., St. John's, Nfld., Can., 2002. Assoc. prof. Mo. State U., Springfield, Mo., 2001—. Asst. dir. Ozarks Studies Inst., Springfield, Mo., 2005, dir., 2005—; folklorist Ark. Hist. Preservation Program, Little Rock, 1996—97. Cinematographer(co-dir., co-author): (films) Home, Community, Tradition: The Women of Temple Israel, 2004; prodr.: (TV series) Ozarks Craft Traditions and Self-Reliance: Rex Harral Profile, 2004; editor: OzarksWatch Mag., The Mag. of the Ozarks, 2006—; exhibitions include Mo. State, 2005. Grantee, Mo. Arts Coun., 2002—03, Cmty. Found. Ozarks, 2004—05. Mem.: DAR, Springfield (Mo.) Archives Com., MidWest Popular Culture Assn., Midwest Jewish Studies Assn., Am. Folklore Soc. (convener folklore and lit. sect. 2005—), Mo. Folklore Soc. (v.p. 2004, pres. 2005), Magna Carta Dames. Office: Missouri State University-English 901 South National Springfield MO 65897 Office Phone: 417-836-5180.

GHORAYEB, FAY ELIZABETH, nursing educator; b. Sydney, Australia, 1936; d. Claude Ernest and Doris Venezia (Shannon) Seabrook; m. Ibrahim Anis Ghorayeb, July 20; children: Anthony, Mark. RN, Royal Prince Alfred Hosp., Sydney, 1959; Postgrad. Diploma, St. Luke's Hosp., N.Y.C., 1961; BA, Rutgers U., 1992. Jr. sister and sr. sister Royal Prince Alfred Hosp., Sydney, 1959-60; vis. nurse Vis. Nurse Assn., N.Y.C., 1960-61; pub. health instr. Beirut Coll. for Women, Lebanon, 1967-71, instr. sport and pub. health, 1974-75; coord. Women's Wellness Ctr. U. Medicine and Dentistry N.J., New Brunswick, 1991-98. Mem. Theatre Guild, Naples Comty. Hosp. Aux.; vol. disaster relief Red Cross. Mem. Douglass Alumni Club, PEO, Naples Woman's Club (exec. bd. mem., pres. 2002-04), Internat. Club, Welcome to Fla., Episcopalian Women Trinity By the Cove. Mem. Ch. England. Avocations: travel, walking, swimming, reading, cooking, mah jongg. Personal E-mail: IGHORABYEB@aol.com.

GIACCHI, JUDITH ADAIR, elementary school educator; b. Rochester, N.Y., Dec. 8, 1947; d. William Robert Peters and L. Virginia (Coulter) Peters Sweet; m. Alphonse Robert Giacchi, Aug. 8, 1970; children: Christina Marie, Anthony Robert. BS, SUNY, Buffalo, 1969. Permanent cert. tchr., N.Y. Data processing control clk. Neisner Bros., Inc., Rochester, 1965—70; tchr. Syracuse City Sch. Dist., NY, 1970—. Tchr. insvcs. and workshops Syracuse sch. dists., 1972—; master tchr. Syracuse U., 1983—, chmn. bldg. level team, 1988—98, collaborative field team rep., 1988—2004, trainer, ednl. rsch. and dissemination thinking math I, II and III, 2001—; rep. N.Y. State Tchrs. Retirement Sys. convs. and N.Y. State United Tchrs. convs., 1987—89. Contbr. articles to profl. publs. Corr. sec., rec. sec., legis. chmn. Nate Perry Sch. PTA, Liverpool, N.Y., 1983-95; troop aide Girl Scouts U.S.A., Liverpool, 1982-86; rep., mem. strategy com. Syracuse Labor Coun., 1995-97; mem. Union Cities Planning Com., 1997. Recipient award N.Y. State Legislature, 1994, various minigrants. Mem. N.Y. State United Tchrs. Fedn. (rep. convs. 1990-92), Ctrl. N.Y. Romance Writers Group, Onondaga County Tchrs. Assn. (award 1989), Syracuse Tchrs. Assn. (various coms., chief bldg. rep. 1984-2005). Avocations: reading, writing, needlecrafts, music, computers. Office: Porter Magnet Sch Tech and Career Exploration 512 Emerson Ave Syracuse NY 13204

GIADONE, SUSAN, livestock office manager; b. Pueblo, Colo., Mar. 5, 1956; d. Eugene Joseph and Mary Josephine (Burnham) Ceasar; m. James Lenn, Sept. 13, 1975; children: James Lenn Jr., Eugena Anthonette. Clerk Clark Western Store, Pueblo, Colo., 1974-76; sec. Caprock Feedlots, Leoti, Ks., 1978-98; accounting office Loaf and Jug Stores, Pueblo, 1990-92; accts. payable Vidmar Motor, Pueblo, 1995-97; co-mgr. Gene Cesar Dairy, Pueblo, 1996—; office mgr. Fowler Livestock Exchange, Colo., 1997—. Mem. Pueblo County Stockman's Assn., sec.; mem. Fowler C. of C.; adv. Pueblo County FFA; pres. Pueblo County FFA Alumni, 1992—93; organizer Mo. Day Com., Ranch Rodeo, Fowler, 1999; cmty. rep. White Rock Cmty., 1988—. Mem.: Colo. Cattlemen's Assn. (conv. com., pub. rels. com.), U.S. Team Roping Corp., Fowler Roping Club (sec., treas.). Avocations: nature, music, family, cooking. Home: 67643 Hwy 10 Fowler CO 81039-9613

GIAIMO, KATHRYN ANN, performing arts company executive; b. Milw., Jan. 20, 1961; d. Samuel Patrick and Marilyn Eunice G. BA, U. Minn., 1983; MA, NYU, 1989. Adminstrv. dir. Thalia Spanish Theatre, Sunnyside, NY, 1989—. Mem. steering com. Coalition to Develop Young Theatre Audiences, N.Y.C., 1992; panelist Queens (N.Y.) Coun. Arts, 1992-93, Nancy Quinn Fund for Alliance of Resident Theatres, N.Y., 1994 and N.Y.C. Dept. Cultural Affairs, 1997, 2006. Mem. steering com. N.Y.C. Arts Coalition, 2002—. Recipient proclamation for women's history month N.Y.C. Coun., 2001. Office: Thalia Spanish Theatre PO Box 4368 41-17 Greenpoint Ave Long Island City NY 11104 E-mail: kgiaimo@thaliatheatre.org.

GIALLOMBARDO, LESLIE, publishing executive; Adv. dir. The Desert Sun, Palm Springs, Calif., The Idaho Statesman, Boise; v.p. adv. The Tennessean, 1995, sr. v.p. mktg., 1999, pres., pub., 2002—05; v.p. advertising, newspaper div. Gannett Co., 2006—. Mgmt. positions Reno (NE) Gazette-Jour., Statesman Jour., Salem, Oreg. Named seven time winner Pres.'s Ring. Office: Gannett Co Inc 7950 Jones Branch Dr Mc Lean VA 22107 E-mail: lgiallom@tennessean.com.*

GIAMPETRO, KATHLEEN A., school psychologist; b. Phila., Oct. 1943; d. Anthony N. and Theresa D. Giampetro. BA, Our Lady of Angels Coll., Ashton, Pa., 1973; MA, Immaculata Coll., Pa., 1989. Cert. sch. psychologist Rowan U., Glassboro, NJ, 1994, in supervision Rowan U., Glassboro, NJ, 1994, in social studies Rowan U., Glassboro, NJ, 1997, ednl. specialist Rowan U., Glassboro, NJ, 1999. Tchr. primary studies Sisters St. Francis, Phila. Found., Glen Riddle, Pa., 1964—70; interviewer, supr. Dept. Pub. Welfare, Phila., 1970—73; tchr. jr. HS Queen of Heaven Sch., Cherry Hill, NJ, 1974—86; prin. pre-kindergarten to grade 8 sch. Christ the King Sch., Haddonfield, NJ, 1986—92; sub. tchr. Audubon Jr.-Sr. HS, NJ, 1992—93; sch. psychologist Overbrook HS, Pine Hill, NJ, 1994—. Invited sch. psychologist Oxford Round Table Discussion, London, 2005. Mem.: NASP, Oxford Roundtable Sch. Psychologists (invited mem. 2005), NJ Edn. Assn., NJ Assn. Sch. Psychologists (co-chair com. children's svcs. 1994—97, newsletter editor 1995—97, editor newsletter 1995—97). Avocations: music, baking. Home: 6807 Normandy Dr Mount Laurel NJ 08054 Office Phone: 856-767-8000 ext. 3058. E-mail: k.giampietro@worldnet.att.net.

GIANINNO, SUSAN MCMANAMA, advertising executive; b. Boston, Dec. 25, 1948; d. John Carroll and Barbara (Frances) Magner; m. Lawrence John Gianinno, June 7, 1970; 1 child, Alexandra Christin. BA in English Lit. and Psychology cum laude, Boston Coll., 1970; MA in Ednl. Psychology, Northwestern U., 1973; postgrad. in behavioral scis., U. Chgo., 1974-78. Psychiat. asst. Quinn Psychiat., Pavilion St Elizabeth's Hosp., Brighton, Mass., 1967-70; research assoc. com. human devel., dept behavioral scis. U. Chgo., 1973-79; resident adv. U. Chgo. Housing Systems, from 1979; research assoc., then research supr. Needham, Harper and Steers Advt. Inc., Chgo., 1979-80, dir. life style rsch., from 1981; v.p., dir. creative rsch. Young & Rubicam NY, then sr. and exec. v.p., dir. rsch. svcs., 1982-86, exec. v.p., dir. mktg., 1986-90, exec. v.p., worldwide group dir., 1990-92, exec. v.p. worldwide acct. mng. dir., 1992-94; exec. v.p., sr. dir. BBDO, NYC, 1994; chief branding officer D'Arcy; chairwoman, CEO Publicis USA, 2003—. Bd. dirs. United Way of NYC. Contbr. papers, reports to profl. jours. Trustee Boston Coll., 1991—. Univ. scholar U. Chgo., 1975-77 Office: Publicis USA 4 Herald Sq 950 Sixth Ave New York NY 10001 Office Phone: 212-279-5550. Office Fax: 212-279-5560.*

GIANLORENZI, NONA ELENA, art dealer, painter; b. Virginia, Minn., July 20, 1939; d. Teto Nicholas and Lena Dora (Zini) Gianlorenzi; m. George Michael Devlin, July 20, 1966 (dec. Feb. 1990); children: Gian Loren Kjellesvig Waering, Helena Nicole Devlin Seidel. BA, Bklyn. Coll./CUNY. Painter self employed, N.Y.C., 1960—; asst. dir. Am. Art Gallery, N.Y.C., 1961-67; owner, dir. Asage Art Gallery, N.Y.C., 1977-88; pvt. art dealer Art Space Inc., Bklyn., 1989—. Tchr. art and aesthetics St. Francis Sch. Deaf, Bklyn., 1968-71, Mt. Carmel, Queens, N.Y., 1968-71, Charles Borromeo Sch., Bklyn., 1968-71. Ford fellow, 1992-94, Loy fellow, 1992-94; Art Studio scholar, 1961. Address: 415 Rugby Rd Brooklyn NY 11226-5611

GIANNINI, ANTOINETTE FRANCES, music educator, researcher; b. Worcester, Mass., Sept. 9, 1923; d. Domenic Giannini and Mary Margaret Amato-Giannini. MusB, Boston U., 1945, MA, 1948; postgrad., Juilliard Sch., N.Y.C., Columbia U. Dir. music pub. schs., Spencer, Mass., 1948—51; tchr. Worcester Pub. H.S., 1958—91, instr. music history, 1962—91; ret., 1991. Concert pianist, New Eng., 1932—41, on tour, 1941—48, NYC, 1948—88. Mem.: Nat. Guild Piano Tchrs. (adjudicator 1965—94), Mu Phi Epsilon. Independent. Roman Catholic. Home: 196 Pakachoag St Auburn MA 01501

GIANNINI, EVELYN LOUISE, retired library consultant; b. Evanston, Ill., June 19, 1924; d. Bernard Peter and Thelma Thy (Wescoat) Smith; m. Aldo Joseph Giannini, Mar. 23, 1946; children: Michael, John. Student, Northwestern U. Sch. Commerce, 1942-43. Library clk. Kemper Group, Chgo., 1959-64, acquisitions librarian, 1964-70, asst. librarian Long Grove, Ill., 1970-77, corp. librarian, 1977-87; exec. v.p. Arlington Group, Inc., Arlington Heights, Ill., 1987—2000. Mem. Am. Assn. Law Libraries, Chgo. Assn. Law Libraries, Spl. Libraries Assn., N.W. Suburban Spl. Libraries (co-founder). Independent. Episcopalian. Home: 1330 S Harvard Ave Arlington Heights IL 60005-3512 Personal E-mail: elg1330@comcast.net.

GIANNUZZI, JUDY L., psychologist; b. Lorain, Ohio, May 3, 1969; d. John Stephen Speckhart and Hilda Mae Gulett; m. Michael David Giannuzzi, Sept. 11; children: Cara, Michael. AA, Lorain City CC, Ohio, 1990; BA, Cleve. State U., 1992, MA in Clinical Counseling Psychology, 1996. Psychology specialist Cleve. State U., 1998. Intern sch. psychologist Maple Heights Schs., Ohio, 1996—97; sch. psychologist Elyria City Schs., 1997—. Office: Sch Psychologist 6409 Baldwin Blvd Lorain OH 44053-3809

GIANOS, DIANE, lawyer; BS, DePaul U., 1984; JD, Chgo-Kent Coll. Law, 1989. Bar: Ill. 1989, U.S. Dist. Ct. No. Ill. 1990, U.S. Ct. Appeals, 6th & 7th cir. 1990. Ptnr. Foley & Lardner, Chgo. Office: Foley & Lardner Suite 2800 321 N Clark St Chicago IL 60610

GIBB, ROBERTA LOUISE, lawyer, artist; b. Cambridge, Mass., Nov. 2, 1942; d. Thomas Robinson Pieri and Jean Knox Gibb. BS, U. Calif., La Jolla, 1969; JD, New Eng. Sch. Law, 1982. Bar: Mass. 1978. Legal aide Mass. State Legis., 1973; practice law Mass., 1980—. Assoc. MIT, 1972—85. Author: To Boston With Love, 1980, The Art of Inflation, 1981, The Art of Economics, 1982; co-prodr.: (documentaries) Lovins on the Soft Path; Exhibited in group shows at Geraci Galleries, Rockport, Mass., 1996—2005, Rockport Art Assn. Gallery, Rockport, 1996—2005, Represented in permanent collections, Nat. Art Mus. Art, Indpls.; prodr.: (documentaries) Where the Spirit Leads, 2001—; Albert Einstein, Pres. Carter, Pres. Johnson, Pres. Reagan, Mother Theresa, Eleanor Roosevelt, The Marathon, Fire Dancers, Birth, Olympia, The Family, The Left Handed Squash Player, Basketball, Germain Gliddin, others. Bd. dir. Essex County Environ. and Conservation, Rockport, Mass., 1980-85; adv. MGH Day Lab. Women winner Boston Marathon, 1966-68, 1st woman to run Boston Marathon, 1966; named to Road Runners of Am. Hall of Fame, 1982 Mem.: Inst. Study of Natural Sys. (founder, pres. 1976—), Rockport Art Assn., Mass. Bar, Nat. Sculpture Soc. (assoc.), Boston Athletic Assn.

GIBBON, MARY-LYNN, special education educator; b. La Jolla, Calif., Feb. 5, 1955; d. Leslie and Edith Gertrude Swaim; m. Mark Jeffrey Gibbon, Mar. 12, 1987; children: Shawna Odet Pedro, William Leslie Lower. BS, Excelsior Coll., 1995; MA in Edn., Chapman U., 1997; MA in Spl. Edn., Azusa Pacific U., 2004. Cert. mid. childhood generalist Nat. Bd. for Profl. Tchg. Standards, 2001. Substitute tchr. Dept. Def. Dependent Schs., Baumholder, Germany, 1993—94, Barstow Unified Sch. Dist., Calif., 1995—96; tchr. elem. Lenwood Sch., Barstow, 1996—97, Hinkley Sch., Barstow, 1997—2002, social studies tchr. mid. sch. spl. edn., 2002—04; tchr. sixth grade sci. and world history tchr. Barstow Intermediate Sch., 2004—. Bus. action plan com. mem. Barstow Unified Sch. Dist., Calif., 1996, report card revision adv. bd. mem., 1999—2000, schoolwide assessment rev. & revision adv. com. mem., 1999—2000, mem. sci., social studies standards adoption adv. com., 2000; tchr. participant Goldstone Apple Valley Radio Telescope, NASA, Barstow, Calif., 2002—04; mem. Excel tchr. tng. team Barstow Intermediate Sch., 2005—, provider Beginning Tchr. Support and Assessment, 2005—. Vol. Police Activities League, Barstow, Calif., 1997—2003; mem. delegation People to People, Beijing, 2005. Grantee, Barstow Rotary Club, 1996. Mem.: Delta Kappa Gamma (assoc.; chmn. spring fling fundraiser 2005—06, Continuing edn. grantee 2005), Pi Lambda Theta (hon.). Conservative. Roman Catholic. Avocations: reading, travel. Office: Barstow Unified Sch Dist 551 So Ave H Barstow CA 92311 Office Phone: 760-255-6304. Personal E-mail: mlg2555@cs.com.

GIBBONS, JULIA SMITH, federal judge; d. John Floyd and Julia Jackson (Abernathy) Smith; m. William Lockhart Gibbons, Aug. 11, 1973; children: Rebecca Carey, William Lockhart Jr. BA, Vanderbilt U., 1972; JD, U. Va., 1975. Bar: Tenn. 1975. Law clk. to judge U.S. Ct. Appeals, 1975-76; assoc.

Farris, Hancock, Gilman, Branan, Lanier & Hellen, Memphis, 1976-79; legal advisor Gov. Lamar Alexander, Nashville, 1979-81; judge 15th Jud. Cir., Memphis, 1981-83, U.S. Dist. Ct. (we. dist.) Tenn., Memphis, 1983—2002, chief judge, 1994-2000; judge U.S. Ct. Appeals (6th cir.), Memphis, 2002—. Recipient Outstanding Judge of Yr. award, Memphis Lawyers, 1985, She Knows Where She's Going award, Girls, Inc., 1992. Master: Leo Bearman, Sr. Am. Inn of Ct.; fellow: Memphis and Shelby County Bar Found., Tenn. Bar Found., Am. Bar Found.; mem.: Ctrl. Gardens Assn., Tenn. Women's Forum, Assn. for Women Attorneys (pres. 1993, Marion Griffin-Frances Loring award 1992), Fed. Judges Assn., Memphis Bar Assn. (Heroine for Women in Law award 2000, Outstanding Judge of Yr. award 2001), Memphis Rotary Club (Treasurer 1991—92, v.p. 1992—93, Paul Harris Fellow, president 1994—95), Phi Beta Kappa, Order of Coif. Presbyterian. Office: US Ct Appeals 1157 Federal Bldg 167 N Main St Memphis TN 38103-1816*

GIBBONS, KATHLEEN MARIE, lawyer; b. Evanston, Ill., Dec. 20, 1958; d. David Joseph and Marilyn Ann Gibbons. BEd magna cum laude, Ill. State U., 1981; JD, Loyola Law Sch., 1987; MA in Adminstrn., No. Ill. U., 2002. Bar: Ill. 1987; cert. spl. edn. Ill., 1981, adminstrn. Ill., 2002. Tchr. St. Eugene's, Chgo., 1981—83; atty. Tressler, Soderstrom, Maloney & Priess, Chgo., 1987—94; spl. edn. atty. Chgo. Bd. Edn., 1994—. Mem.: Chgo. Bar Assn., Coun. Exceptional Children. Avocations: antiques, travel. Home: 4044 N Paulina Chicago IL 60613 Office Phone: 773-553-1926. Business E-Mail: kgibbons@cps.k12.il.us.

GIBBONS, KAYE, writer; b. Nash County, N.C., 1960; Student, U. N.C., Chapel Hill. Author: Ellen Foster (Sue Kaufman award for 1st fiction, Acad. Arts and Letters), A Virtuous Woman, 1989, A Cure for Dreams, 1991 (PEN Revson award, 1990, Heartland prize for fiction, Chgo. Tribune, N.C. Sir Walter Raleigh award), Charms for the Easy Life, 1993, Sights Unseen, On the Occasion of My Last Afternoon, 1998; actor:. Recipient Chevalier de l'Ordre des Arts et des Lettres, Govt. France, 1996. Office: c/o GP Putnam & Sons Publicity 375 Hudson St New York NY 10014

GIBBONS, LEEZA, television and radio talk show host, entertainment reporter; b. Hartsville, SC, Mar. 26, 1957; m. John Hicks, 1980 (div. 1982); m. Chris Quinten, 1988 (div. 1990); 1 child, Lexi; m. Stephen Meadows, 1991; children: Troy, Nathan. Student, U. S.C. CEO Leeza Gibbons Enterprises; former co-host Entertainment Tonight, Hollywood, Calif.; co-host John and Leeza, Hollywood, 1993; host, exec. prodr. Leeza, 1994—99; host Lezza Live Westwood One, host Hollywood Confidential. Host Miss Universe Pageant, The Hollywood Christmas Parade; host, co-prodr. (series) Growing Up Together; film appearances include Robocop, 1987, Robocop 2, 1990, Soapdish, 1991, The Player, 1992, Last Action Hero, 1993. Office: c/o KBIG #800 330 N Brand Blvd Glendale CA 91203*

GIBBONS, MARY PEYSER, civic volunteer; b. N.Y.C., Dec. 15, 1936; d. Frederick Maurice and Catherine Mary (McKelvey) Peyser; m. John Martin Gibbons; children: Catherine Way, Mary Sloan, John, Fredericka Kerr, Myles. Trustee Wadsworth Atheneum, 1978-99, hon. trustee, 2000; trustee Hartford Art Sch., 1985-95; regent U. Hartford, 1988-2004; bd. dirs. Hartford Ballet, 1981-95, Conn. Valley Girl Scouts, 1994-95, U.S. Found. World Fedn., Friends of Museums, 1990—; vol. Com. Art Mus., U.S. and Can., 1982-91; pres. Am. Assn. Mus. Vols., 1983-91, adv. bd. mem., 1991—; corporator St. Francis Hosp., 1990—, Hartford Ballet, 1995-97, Conn. Inst. for the Blind; mem. alumnae bd. dirs. Convent of the Sacred Heart, 91th St., N.Y.C. Mem. Hartford Golf Club, Town and County Club.

GIBBONS, PAMELA R., professional athletic trainer; b. Orange, Calif., May 16, 1965; d. Donna L. and Greg S. Crandall (Stepfather), Richard P. Gibbons; 1 child, Savana R. AS in Sports Med./Athletic Tng., Rancho Santiago C.C., 1985; BS in Phys. Edn. and Athletic Tng., Calif. State U., 1989; MA in Ednl. Leadership and Adminstrn., Chapman U., 2001. Cert. athletic trainer 1989, cardiopulmonary resuscitation instr. ARC, 1985, lifeguard tng. instr. ARC, 1996, adv. first aid, basic first aid, basic lifesaving ARC, 1998, first aid for pub. safety personnel instr. ARC, 1998. Head athletic trainer Los Alamitos (Calif.) H.S., 1988—91; personal trainer, fitness instr. Los Caballeros Sports Village, 1990—91; legal asst., investigator Juvenile Law Ctr., Santa Ana, Calif., 1991—94; asst. athletic trainer Chapman U., Orange, 1991—98, head women's swimming coach, 1993—96, head athletic trainer, 1998—. Instr./instr.'s aid Rancho Santiago C.C., 1984—90; substitute tchr. Los Alamitos H.S., 1988—91; part time faculty Chapman U., 1994—; lifeguard tng. instr. City of Orange, 1996—2000; approved clin. instr. Chapman U., 2003—. Mem. ARC. Mem.: Far West Athletic Trainers' Assn., Coll. Athletic Trainers Soc., Nat. Athletic Trainers' Assn. Office: Chapman U One University Dr Orange CA 92866 Office Phone: 714-997-6640. Business E-Mail: gibbons@chapman.edu.

GIBBS, DOROTHY SCOTT, retired Latin educator; b. Chgo., May 8, 1927; d. Ewing Carruth and Dorothy Eleanor (Carnine) Scott; m. George Minnis Gibbs, Apr. 16, 1949; 1 child, Peter Carnine. Student, Colo. Coll., 1944-45; BA magna cum laude, Syracuse (N.Y.) U., 1948; MAT in French, U. Va., 1964. Cert. French, German and Latin tchr., Ohio. Tchr. English Aoyama Gakuin U., Tokyo, 1950-51; sec. Sch. of Nursing U. Va., Charlottesville, 1953-54; sec. Westminster Presbyn. Ch., Charlottesville, 1954-56; asst. dir. pub. rels. Internat. Christian U., Tokyo, 1957-59; tchr. Brookville (Ohio) High Sch., 1960-61, Fairmont High Sch., Kettering, Ohio, 1968-90. Sponsor Jr. Classical League, Kettering, 1972-90; state and nat. officers sponsor Ohio Jr. Classical League, 1978, 80, 84, 87, 88, 89; sponsor Ohio Sr. Classical League, 1990-92; team mem. North Cen. Accrediting Team, Bellbrook, Ohio, 1984; founder Arthur Rackham Soc., 1984, pres., 1984-97, 2001—, pres. emeritus, 1997—. Editor Jour. Arthur Rockham Soc., 1984-97, co-editor, 2002—. French coach Dayton Opera Fun-atics, 1979-86; host family for fgn. students, Kettering, 1968, 81-83, 85; tchr. in space candidate NASA, 1985; vol. trail worker Am. Hiking Assn., Mont., Alaska, 1986, 87, Calif., 1992; vol. in parks Rocky Mountain Nat. Park, 1995—; bd. dirs. Knoll-Willows Conservancy, 2002—. Jennings Found. scholar, 1986-87; recipient Tchr. Achievement award Ashland Oil, 1988, Ed Phinney Book award Nat. Jr. Classical League, 1990, 10-Yr. svc. award Elk Bugle Corps. Rocky Mt. Nat. Park, 2004, 2,000 Hour award Vols. in Parks Rocky Mt. Nat. Park, 2005; named to Chester A. Roush Ednl. Hall of Fame, 1992. Mem. NEA, Am. Classical League (McKinley scholar 1985), Ohio Classical Conf. (coun. mem. 1979-82, 85-88, Hildesheim Vase 1975, 82), Ohio Fgn. Lang. Assn. (Leona Glenn award 1984), Kettering Classroom Tchrs. Assn. (workshop organizer 1973, 78, 88), Delta Zeta (sec. Syracuse chpt. 1947-48), Delta Kappa Gamma (com. chmn., Ruth Grimes scholar 1985), Classical Assn. of Midwest and South. Republican. Presbyterian. Home: 1240 Devils Gulch Rd Estes Park CO 80517-9500 E-mail: dorothygibbs@arthurrackham.org.

GIBBS, ELSIE FRANCES, social worker; b. Perth Amboy, N.J., Sept. 16, 1919; d. John and Edith May (Henry) G. Social worker, exec. adminstr. Nat. Bd. YMCA, N.Y.C., 1949-80; vol. coord. Schumburg Ctr. for Rsch. in Black Culture N.Y. Pub. Libr., N.Y.C., 1986—. Mem. Perth Amboy Human Rels. Com., 1953-70, Perth Amboy Planning Bd., 1970-76; pres. Citizens Adv. Com. to Mayor, Perth Amboy, 1961-69; vice chmn., treas., mem. exec. coun. of vols. N.Y. Pub. Libr., 1992—. Mem. LWV (pres. 1970-72), NAACP, Nat. Black Child Devel. Inst., N.Y.C. Black Child Devel. Inst. (charter mem.). Democrat. Methodist. Home: 77 Fulton St # 18 J New York NY 10038

GIBBS, JEWELLE TAYLOR, retired clinical psychologist; b. Stratford, Conn., Nov. 4, 1933; d. Julian Augustus and Margaret Pauline (Morris) Taylor; A.B. cum laude, Radcliffe Coll., 1955; postgrad. Harvard-Radcliffe Program in Bus. Adminstrn., 1959; M.S.W., U. Calif., Berkeley, 1970, Ph.D., 1980; m. James Lowell Gibbs, Jr., Aug. 25, 1956; children— Geoffrey Taylor, Lowell Dabney. Jr. mgmt. asst. U.S. Dept. Labor, Washington, 1955-56; market research coord. Pillsbury Co., Mpls., 1959-61; clin. social worker Stanford (Calif.) U. Student Health Service, 1970-74, 78-79, research assoc. dept. psychiatry, 1971-73; asst. prof. Sch. Social Welfare U. Calif., Berkeley, 1979-83, acting assoc. prof., 1983-86, assoc. prof., 1986-92, Zellerbach prof. social policy, 1992—, chair of faculty Sch. Social Welfare, 1993-94; pvt. practice as clin. psychologist, 1983-91; fellow Bunting Inst., Radcliffe Coll., spring, 1985. Bd. regents U. Santa Clara (Calif.), 1980-84; mem. Minn. State Commn. on Status of Women, 1963-65; co-chairperson Minn. Women's Com. for Civil Rights, 1963-65; mem. adv. coun. Nat. Ctr. for Children in Poverty, 1987-95; bd. dirs. Ctr. for Populations Options, 1989-93; trustee Radcliffe Coll., 1991-95; disting. scholar Joint Ctr. Pol. & Econ. Studies, Washington D.C., 1991-92; vis. scholar U. London, 1993, U. Toronto, 1994. NIMH fellow, 1979; Soroptimist Internat. grantee, 1978-79. Fellow Am. Orthopsychiat. Assn. (bd. dirs. 1985-86); mem. Am. Psychol. Assn., Nat. Assn. Social Workers, Western Psychol. Assn., Am. Assn. Suicidology (McCormick award 1987). Democrat. Author: Children of Color: Psychological Interventions with Minority Youth, 1989, Race and Justice: Rodney King and O.J. Simpson in a House Divided, 1996; co-author Preserving Privilege: California Proposition Politics, and People of Color, 2001; editor, contbr. Young, Black and Male in America, 1988; mem. editorial bd. Am. Jour. Orthopsychiatry, 1980-84; bd. publs. Nat. Assn. Social Workers, 1980-82; contbr. chpts. to books and articles to profl. jours. Phi Beta Kappa (hon.). Office: U Calif Sch Social Welfare Haviland Hl Berkeley CA 94720-0001

GIBBS, JOHNIE ELIZABETH, information technology manager, educator, consultant; d. John J. and Ruth P. Gibbs. BS in Human Environ. Scis., cum laude, U. Ala., Tuscaloosa, 1984, MS in Consumer Scis., 1985, PhD in Instrnl. Leadership and Instrnl. Tech., 2003. Cert. online tchg. UCLA, 2001. Rsch. asst./assoc. Ctr. for Bus. and Econ. Rsch., U. Ala., Tuscaloosa, Ala., 1986—89; sr. rsch. assoc./computer lab asst. dir. Coll. of Human Environ. Scis., U. Ala., Tuscaloosa, Ala., 1989—94, computer coord., 1994—2001; instr. Dept. of Consumer Scis., U. Ala., 1989—2001; online course developer and online instr. Dept. of Distance Edn., U. Ala., 1999—2003; online program mgr. and cons. Tuscaloosa City Schs.; owner Gibbs Learning Techs., LLC, Northport, Ala., 2004. Editor (project coordinator): (book) Nothing but the Best: A Collection of Recipes from The University of Alabama Family; editor: (magazine/newsletter) Ala. Bus.; senior editor (book) Economic Abstract of Alabama 1989-90, Economic Abstract of Alabama 1987. Vol. webmaster Town of Brilliant, Ala. Mem.: Assn. for the Advancement of Computing in Edn., Internat. Soc. for Tech. in Edn., Am. Assn. for Family and Consumer Scis. (Ala. state sec. 1992—94, past state exec. com., state exec. bd. 1988—94, Ala. New Achiever's award 1993, cert. in family and consumer scis.), Kappa Delta Epsilon, Kappa Delta Pi, Gamma Beta Phi, Golden Key, Phi Upsilon Omicron. Church Of Christ. Personal E-mail: bgibbs@simplecom.net. Business E-Mail: bgibbs@gibbslearning.com.

GIBBS, JUNE NESBITT, state senator; b. Newton, Mass., June 13, 1922; d. Samuel Frederick and Lulu (Glazier) Nesbitt; m. Donald T. Gibbs, Dec. 8, 1945 (dec. 2001); 1 child, Elizabeth. BA in Math., Wellesley Coll., 1943; MA in Math., Boston U., 1947; postgrad. computer sci., U. R.I., 1981-84. Mem. from R.I. Rep. Nat. Com., 1969-80, sec., 1977-80; mem. R.I. Senate, Dist. 48, Providence, 1985—2003, R.I. Senate, Dist 12, Providence, 2003—, dep. minority leader. Mem. def. adv. com. Women in Svcs., 1970—72, vice chmn., 1972. Mem. Middletown (R.I.) Town Coun., 1974—80, 1982—84, pres., 1978—80. Lt. (j.g.) USNR, 1943—46. Avocation: windsurfing. Home: 163 Riverview Ave Middletown RI 02842-5324 Office: Senate Minority Office State House Providence RI 02903 Office Phone: 401-222-2708. Business E-Mail: sen-gibbs@rilin.state.ri.us.

GIBBS, LAURA ELIZABETH, lawyer; BA summa cum laude, Loyola U., 1997; JD cum laude, Boston Coll., 2000. Bar: Fla. 2001, Mass. 2001, US Dist. Ct. (Dist. Mass.). Assoc. Rackemann, Sawyer & Brewster PC, Boston; assoc. Gen. Comml. Litig. Practice Foley & Lardner LLP, Boston. Mem.: Mass. Bar Assn., Women's Bar Assn., Hispanic Nat. Bar Assn., Boston Bar Assn., Mass. Assn. Hispanic Attorneys (bd. dirs. 2004—). Office: Foley & Lardner LLP 111 Huntington Ave Boston MA 02199 Office Phone: 617-342-4041. Office Fax: 617-342-4000. E-mail: lgibbs@foley.com.*

GIBBS, PATRICIA LEIGH, social sciences educator, researcher; b. Vancouver, B.C., Canada, Dec. 4, 1961; d. Claude Leslie and Margaret Helen Rencher; m. Robert Owen Stayte, June 20, 1997; children: Angus A. Gibbs Stayte, Lachlan A. Gibbs Stayte, Emma Q. Gibbs Stayte. EdB, U. B.C., Can., 1981; MA in Leisure Studies, U. Alta., Can., 1989; MA in Sociology, U. Hawaii, 1995, PhD in Sociology, 1999. Instr. Coll. Rockies, Cranbrook, B.C., Canada, 1984—91; faculty human svcs. dept. and recreation and tourism studies depts. Malaspina U. Coll., Nanaimo, B.C., Canada, 1991—94; lectr. U. Hawaii, Honolulu, 1994—99; assoc. prof. sociology Foothill Coll., Los Altos Hills, Calif., 1999—, chair dept. sociology, 2000—. Freelance writer. Contbr. chapters to books, articles to profl. jours. Story evaluator Project Censored: A Media Democracy Orgn., Sonoma State U., Calif., 1997—. Recipient Appreciation award, Foothill Alpha Gamma Sigma Hon. Soc., 2003, Profl. Growth and Acheivement award, Foothill Coll., 2004, Sabbatical award, 2006; grantee, Malaspina U. Coll., 1992; scholar, Hawaii Cmty. Found., 1998; vis. scholar Asia Pacific scholar, U. Hawaii, 1994—96; Hawaii Vet.'s Meml. scholar, Hawaii Cmty. Found., 1998. Office: Foothill Coll 12345 El Monte Rd Los Altos Hills CA 94022 Personal E-mail: gibbspatricia@foothill.edu.

GIBBS, SARAH PREBLE, biologist, educator; b. Boston, May 25, 1930; d. Winthrop Harold and Edith Dorothea (Hill) Bowker; m. Robert H. Gibbs, June 9, 1951 (div. 1962); 1 dau., Elizabeth Dorothea; m. Ronald J. Poole, Feb. 2, 1963 (div. 1980); 1 son, Christopher Harold. AB, Cornell U., 1952, MS, 1954; PhD, Harvard U., 1962. Research assoc. Inst. Animal Genetics Edinburgh U., 1963-65; asst. prof. botany McGill U., Montreal, Que., Canada, 1966-69, assoc. prof. biology, 1969-74, prof., 1974-98, Macdonald prof. bot., 1998, Macdonald emeritus prof., 1999—. Recipient Darbaker prize, Bot. Soc. Am., 1975, Gilbert Morgan Smith medal, NAS, 2003; fellow, NSF, 1958—61, NIH, 1961—63. Fellow: AAAS, Royal Soc. Can.; mem.: Can. Assn. Univ. Tchrs., Phycol. Soc. Am. (award of excellence 1999), Am. Soc. Cell Biology, Phi Kappa Phi, Sigma Xi, Phi Beta Kappa. Home: 70 Henley Ave Montreal PQ Canada H3P 1V3 Office: McGill U Dept Biology 1205 Avenue Docteur Penfield Montreal PQ Canada H3A 1B1

GIBBS CRUZ, KATHERINE K., science educator; b. Santurce, P.R., Mar. 26, 1963; d. Charles A. Gibbs and Krimilda Cruz. BA in Edn., U. PR, Rio Piedras, 1986, MS in Adminstrn. and Sch. Supervision, 1996, postgrad., 2002. Cert. home econs., health and gen. sci. tchr. P.R. Health tchr. José Nevarez Landrin Sch., Toa Baja, PR; sci. tchr. Colegio San Antonio, Rio Piedras. Tech. cons. McGraw Hill, Rio Piedras, 2005; evaluation com. MSA Colegio San Antonio, Rio Piedras, 2000; reviewer Nat. Sci. Tchrs. Assn., 2001—02; condr. seminars, workshops in field; presenter in field. Named Tchr. of the Yr., Colegio San Antonio, 2000—01. Mem.: ASCD, Earth Sci. Tchrs. Assn., Nat. Sci. Tchrs. Assn. Avocations: sewing, writing short stories, reading. Office: Colegio San Antonio Apartado 21350 Rio Piedras PR 00928

GIBBY, DIANE LOUISE, physician, plastic surgeon; b. Miami, Feb. 5, 1957; d. John and Mabel (Kunce) G.; m. Rodney J. Rohrich, July 3, 1990; children: Taylor Rodney, Rachel Nicole. BS, Duke U., Durham, N.C., 1975; MD, U. Miami, 1980. Diplomate Am. Bd. Gen. Surgery, Bd. Plastic and Reconstructive Surgery. Clin. asst. prof. U. Tex. Southwestern, Dallas, 1987—; pvt. practice plastic surgery Med. City Dallas, 1987—. Founder Women's Ctr. for Plastic and Reconstructive Surgery, 1992. Fellow Am. Coll. Surgeons; mem. Am. Soc. Plastic and Reconstructive Surgeons, Am. Med. Soc., Tex. Soc. Plastic Surgeons, Dallas Soc. Plastic Surgeons, Aesthetic Soc. Office: 7777 Forest Ln Ste C820 Dallas TX 75230-2552 Office Phone: 972-566-6323. Business E-Mail: dgmdpa@aol.com.

GIBBY, MABEL ENID KUNCE, psychologist; b. St. Louis, Mar. 30, 1926; d. Ralph Waldo and Mabel Enid (Warren) Kunce; student Washington U., St. Louis, 1943-44, postgrad., 1955-56; B.A., Park Coll., 1945; M.A., McCormick Theol. Sem., 1947; postgrad. Columbia U., 1948, U. Kansas City, 1949, George Washington U., 1953; M.Ed., U. Mo., 1951, Ed.D., 1952; m. John Francis Gibby, Aug. 27, 1948; children— Janet Marie (Mrs. Kim Williams), Harold Steven, Helen Elizabeth, Diane Louise (Mrs. Roderick Rohrich), John Andrew, Keith Sheridan, Daniel Jay. Dir. religious edn. Westport Presbyn. Ch. Kansas City, Mo., 1947-49; tchr. elementary schs., Kansas City, 1949-50; high sch. counselor Arlington (Va.) Pub. Schs., 1952-54; counselor adult counseling services Washington U., 1955-56; counseling psychologist Coral Gables (Fla.) VA Hosp., 1956—; counseling psychologist Miami (Fla.) VA Hosp., 1956—, chief counseling psychology sect., 1982-86; sr. psychologist Office Disability Determination Fla. Hdqrs., 1987-94. Sec. bd. dirs. Fla. Vocat. Rehab. Found. Recipient Meritorious Service citation Fla. C. of C., 1965, President's Com. on Employment of Handicapped, 1965; commendation for meritorious service Com. on Employment of Physically Handicapped Dade County, 1965, named Outstanding Rehab. Profl., 1966, 81; named Profl. Fed. Employee of Year, Greater Miami Fed. Exec. Council, 1966; Outstanding Fed. Service award Greater Miami Fed. Exec. Council, 1966; Fed. Woman's award U.S. Civil Service Commn., 1968, Community Headliner award Theta Sigma Phi, 1968, Outstanding Alumni award Park Coll., 1968, Freedom award The Chosen Few, Korean War Vets. Assn., 1986; certificate of appreciation Bur. Customs, U.S. Treasury Dept., 1969, Fla. Dept. Health and Rehab. Svcs., 1970. Mem. Am., Dade County (past sec.) psychol. assns., Nat., Fla. (past dir. Dade County chpt.) rehab. assns., Nat. Rehab. Counseling Assn. (past sec.). Patentee in field. Home: 7107 Aberdeen Ave Dallas TX 75230-5406 Personal E-mail: jfgpc@aol.com.

GIBERSON, JOAN ALYNE, retired school nurse practitioner; b. Hammond, Ind., Jan. 10, 1947; d. John Harrison and Cleta Jean McFadden; m. Franklin Winston Giberson, Jan. 2, 1969; children: Patricia Melanie, Eric Louis. Diploma, James Ward Thorne Sch. Nursing, Northwestern U., Chgo., 1965—68. RN. Recovery rm. nurse Passayant Meml., Chgo., 1970—71; staff nurse Ingalls Meml., Harvey, Ill., 1972—74, Munster Cmty. Hosp., Ind., 1982—86; sch. nurse Hoover-Schrum Sch. Dist #157, Calumet City, 1986—2005; retired. Active South Side Christian Ch., choir mem., Sunday sch. tchr., past pres. Martha Group. Mem. Christian Ch. Avocations: music, drawing, sewing.

GIBLETT, ELOISE ROSALIE, retired hematologist; b. Tacoma, Wash., Jan. 17, 1921; d. William Richard and Rose (Godfrey) Giblett. BS, U. Wash., 1942, MS, 1947, MD with honors, 1951. Mem. faculty U. Wash. Sch. Medicine, 1957—, research prof., 1967—87, emeritus research prof., 1987—. Assoc. dir., head immunogenetics Puget Sound Blood Ctr., 1957—79, exec. dir., 1979—87, emeritus exec. dir., 1987—; former mem. several rsch. coms. NIH. Author: Genetic Markers in Human Blood, 1969; mem. editl. bd. numerous jours. including: Blood, Am. Jour. Human Genetics, Transfusion, Vox Sanguinis; contbr. over 200 articles to profl. jours. Recipient fellowships, grants Emily Cooley, Karl Landsteiner, Philip Levine and Alexander Wiener immunohematology awards, disting. alumna award, U. Wash. Sch. Medicine, 1987. Fellow: AAAS; mem.: NAS, Assn. Am. Physicians, Western Assn. Physicians, Am. Fedn. Clin. Rsch., Internat. Soc. Hematologists, Brit. Soc. Immunology, Am. Assn. Immunologists, Am. Soc. Hematology, Am. Soc. Human Genetics (pres. 1973), Alpha Omega Alpha, Sigma Xi. Home: 6533 53rd Ave NE Seattle WA 98115-7748 Office: Puget Sound Blood Ctr 921 Terry Ave Seattle WA 98104-1256

GIBLIN, PAMELA M., lawyer; b. N.Y.C., June 7, 1946; BA, U. Tex., 1967, JD, 1970. Bar: Tex. 1970. Mem. Jones, Day, Reavis & Pogue, Austin; ptnr. environ. dept. Baker Botts LLP, Austin, Tex. Gen. counsel Tex. Air Control Bd., 1970-76; chmn. Commn. on Electric Rates, Austin, 1975-76. Named a Texas Super Lawyer, Texas Monthly mag. & Law & Politics mag., 2003—04; named one of Top 50 Female Super Lawyers, 2003—04, Top 50 Regional & West Texas Region Super Lawyers, 2003—04; recipient Disting. Lawyer award, Travis County Bar Assn., 2003. Office: Baker & Botts LLP 98 San Jacinto Blvd Ste 1600 Austin TX 78701-4039 Office Phone: 512-322-2509. Office Fax: 512-322-8308. Business E-Mail: pam.giblin@bakerbotts.com.

GIBSON, ANN EDEN, art historian, educator; b. Hagerstown, Md., Apr. 30, 1944; d. James Orville and Mary Ellen (Ellis) G.; m. H. Thomas Simmons; 1 child, Jessica; m. Allan Federman, Jan. 10, 1982 (dec.); children: Elizabeth, Michele. BS, Kent State U., 1965, MA, 1970, U. Pitts., 1978; PhD, U. Del., 1984. Tchr. art pub. schs., Hinckley and Wooster, Ohio, 1966-69; studio adj. Kent (Ohio) State U., 1969-72, Akron (Ohio) State U., 1970-72; art history adj. U. Pitts., 1979; instr. art Art Inst. Pitts., 1972-75, Point Park Coll., Pitts., 1975-79; assoc. prof. history art Yale U., New Haven, 1981-91; assoc. prof. art history SUNY, Stony Brook, 1992-98, acting chair dept. art, 1993-94; chair dept. art history U. Del., 1998—. Author: Issues in Abstract Expressionism, 1990, Abstract Expressionism: Other Politics, 1997, Judith Godwin, Style and Grace, 1997, Norman Lewis, Black Paintings, 1946-1977, 1998; guest editor (with Stephen Polcari), Art Journal; also articles. Andrew W. Mellon fellow Met. Mus. Art, 1981-83; Morse fellow Yale U., 1987-88, sr. fellow, 1990-91; Ailsa Mellon Bruce fellow Ctr. for Advanced Study in Visual Arts, Washington, 1990, postdoctoral fellow Smithsonian Instn., 1990-91, Getty Rsch. Fellow, Guggenheim Meml. Found. Fellow, 2004; recipient Distinguished Alumna award, U. Pitts., 1995. Mem. Internat. Assn. Critics, Coll. Art Assn., Phi Kappa Phi. Office: U Del Dept Art History 206 Mechanical Hall Newark DE 19716 Business E-Mail: agibson@udel.edu.

GIBSON, ANNEMARIE, writer, editor; b. Linz, Austria, Oct. 6, 1947; d. Marion Alfred and Maria Anna (Ostermann) Green; m. Stephen Rawlings Gibson, Mar. 2, 1968; children: Stephanie Anne, Timothy Michael. AA, Cecil C.C., 1984; BA, Towson (Md.) State U., 1993. Editl. asst. US Army Environ. Hygiene Agy., Aberdeen Proving Ground, 1979-84, writer, editor, 1984-90; pub. affairs specialist US Army Ctr. for Health Promotion and Preventive Medicine, Aberdeen Proving Ground, 1990-95, supervisory tech. writer, editor, 1995-99, tech. writer, editor, mgr., 1999—, acting pub. affairs officer, 2003—, pub. affairs officer, co-lateral duty, 2003. Editl. adv. bd. US Army Ctr. for Health Promotion and Preventive Medicine, Aberdeen Proving Ground, 1990—, spkr. bur., 1993—, facilitator 1992—, mentor 1996—. Pres. Cecil County Ladies Aux. Md. State Firemen's Assn., Elkton, Md., 1995-98; sec. Ladies Aux. Water Witch Fire Co. Port Deposit, Md., 1985—. Mem. Federally Employed Women (life, sec. 1991—), US Army Environ. Hygiene Agy. (life). Office: US Army Ctr Health Promotion/ Preventive Medicine 5158 Black Hawk Rd Aberdeen Proving Ground MD 21010-5403 Office Fax: 410-436-1039. Personal E-mail: missanne1047@cs.com.

GIBSON, ARLENE JOY, headmaster; BA, Bryn Mawr Coll., 1965; MA, Georgetown U., 1969. Dir. middle school Bryn Mawr Sch., Balt., 1981-84; dir. lower sch. Holton Arms Sch., Bethesda, Md., 1984-87; headmistress Kent Place Sch., Summit, N.J., 1987-96; head of sch. Spence Sch., NYC, 1998—. Office: Spence Sch 22 E 91st St New York NY 10128-0657 E-mail: agibson@spenceschool.org.

GIBSON, DEANNA, actor; b. Greer, SC, Sept. 29, 1981; d. Edward Wakefield and Diane Anitra (Foster) Gibson. BA, Winthrop U., Rockhill, SC, 2002; MFA, Fla. State U., Sarasota, 2005. Apprentice Flatrock Playhouse, NC, 2002; tchr. asst. Asolo Conservatory, Fla. State U., 2002—05; actor Wooden Prodns., NYC, 2005; co. mem., actor Asolo Theatre Co., Sarasota, 2005—. Home: 32-86 34th St Apt 1D Astoria NY 11106

GIBSON, ELISABETH JANE, retired principal; b. Salina, Kans., Apr. 28, 1937; d. Cloyce Wesley and Margaret Mae (Yost) Kasson; m. William Douglas Miles, Jr., Aug. 20, 1959 (div.); m. Harry Benton Gibson Jr., July 1, 1970. AB, Colo. State Coll., 1954-57; MA, San Francisco State Coll., 1967-68; EdD, U. No. Colo., 1978; postgrad., U. Denver, 1982. Cert. tchr., prin., Colo. Tchr. elem. schs., Santa Paula, Calif., 1957—58, Salina, Kans., 1958—63, Goose Bay, Labrador, 1963—64, Jefferson County, Colo., 1965—66, Topeka, 1966—67; diagnostic tchr. Ctrl. Kans. Diagnostic Remedial Edn. Ctr., Salina, 1968—70; instr. Loretta Heights Coll., Denver, 1970—72; co-owner Ednl. Cons. Enterprises, Inc., Greeley, Colo., 1974—77; resource coord. region VIII Resource Access Project Head Star Mile High Consortium, Denver, 1976—77; exec. dir. Colo. Fedn. Coun. Exceptional Children, Denver, 1976—77; asst. prof. Met. State Coll., Denver, 1979; dir.

spl. edn. N.E. Colo. Bd. Coop. Edn. Svcs., Haxtun, Colo., 1979—82; prin. elem. jr. h.s. Elizabeth, Colo., 1982—84; prin., spl. projects coord. Summit County Schs., Frisco, Colo., 1985—92; prin. Frisco Elem. Sch., 1985—91; ret., 2002. Cons. Mont. Dept. Edn., 1978-79, Love Pub. Co., 1976-78, Colo. Dept. Inst., 1974-75, Colo. Dept. Edn., 1984-85, mem. proposal reading com., 1987—; pres. Found. Exceptional Children, 1980-81; pres. bd. dirs. N.E. Colo. Svcs. Handicapped, 1981-82; bd. dirs. Dept. Ednl. Specialists, Colo. Assn. Sch. Execs., 1982-84; mem. Colo. Title IV Adv. Coun., 1980-82; mem. Mellon Found. grant steering com. Dolo. Dept. Edn., 1984-85; mem. Colo. Dept. Edn. Data Acquisition Reporting and Utilization Com., 1983, Denver City County Commn. for Disabled, 1978-81; chmn. regional edn. com. 1970 White House Conf. Children and Youth; bd. dirs. Advs. for Victims of Assault, 1986-91; mem. adv. bd. Alpine Counseling Ctr., 1986-92; mem. placement alternatives commn. Dept. Social Svcs., 1986—; mem. adv. com. Colo. North Ctrl. Assn., 1988-91; sec. Child Care Resource and Referral Agy., 1992—; mem. Child Care Task Force Summit County, 1989-92; mem. tchr. cert. task force Colo. State Bd. Edn., 1990-91; chmn. Summit County Interagy. Coord. Coun., 1989-93. Co-author: (with H. Padzensky) Goal Guide: A minicourse in writing goals and behavioral objectives for special education, 1975, Assaying Student Behavior: A minicourse in student assessment techniques, 1974; contbr. articles to profl. jours. Recipient Vol. award Colo. Child Care Assn., 1992, Ann. Svc. award Colo. Fedn. Coun. Exceptional Children, 1981; San Francisco State Coll. fellow, 1967-68; named Vol. of Season, Hospice of Metro Denver, 2003. Mem. ASCD, Nat. Assn. Elem. Sch. Prins., Colo. Assn. Retarded Citizens, North Ctrl. Assn. (state adv. com. 1988-91), Order Ea. Star, Kappa Delta Pi, Pi Lambda Theta, Phi Delta Kappa. Republican. Methodist. Home: 4505 S Yosemite St Unit 114 Denver CO 80237-2520 E-mail: ejgibson@netzero.net.

GIBSON, FLORENCE ANDERSON, talking book company executive, narrator; b. San Francisco, Feb. 7, 1924; m. V.H. Carlos Gibson, Aug. 30, 1947; children: Nancy Derwent, Christopher Carlos, Katherine Wayne Bolland, Diana Corona. Student, Finch Jr. Coll., N.Y.C., 1941—42; BA in Dramatic Lit., U. Calif., Berkeley, 1944; student, Neighborhood Playhouse, N.Y.C., 1944—45. Radio actress, San Francisco, 1944, 46, 47; chmn. Washington com. Am. Field Svc., 1958-60, 62-65, founder, chmn. Peruvian Com. Lima, 1960-62; treas., distbn. mgr. Living Garden and Concern 1975 calendars, 1971-75; sec. exec. com Fgn. Student Svc. Coun., 1973-76; narrator Talking Books Libr. of Congress div. for Blind and Physically Handicapped, 1975-96; narrator Recorded Books, Inc., 1979; founder, pres. Audio Book Contractors, Inc., 1982—. Actress Blithe Spirit, the USO Camp Show, 1944, Ah, Wilderness, 1946, Equity Libr. Theater, NYC, (TV series) Traffic Ct., others, narrator more than 1,025 unabridged books on cassette; author: (children's book) Three Tales in Verse, 2006. Bd. dirs. Fgn. Student Svc. Coun., Concern, Inc., Rec. for the Blind, Children's Theater of Washington; vol. in occupational therapy Children's Hosp., Washington, 1949-50; vol. lobbyist student exch. program Am. Field Svc. Recipient Parents' Choice awards, 1983, 84, 86, Audiophile Earphone award, 1999; named Best Female Narrator, Book World, 1989; selected as A Notable Children's Recording, ALA, 1983, 87, 88, 89. Home: 4626 Garfield St NW Washington DC 20007-1025 Office: Audio Book Contractors Inc PO Box 40115 Washington DC 20016-0115 Office Phone: 202-363-3429. Personal E-mail: flogibsonabc@aol.com.

GIBSON, FRANCES ERNST, music educator; b. San Antonio, Dec. 7, 1925; d. Joseph Omer Ernst and Olga Catherine Ochs; m. Edwin Wray Gibson, Sr. MusB summa cum laude, Our Lady of the Lake U., 1947; MusM, U. Tex., 1970. Faculty piano dept. Our Lady of the Lake U., San Antonio, 1947—51; pvt. music tchr. Fredericksburg, Tex., 1951—. Piano accompanist Point Theater, Ingram, Tex., 1958; ch. organist St. Mary's Cath. Ch., Fredericksburg, 1965-70; participant Internat. Piano Workshops, 1979-91. Co-author: Music Lovers' Cookbook, 1992; performer Tex. Sch. of the Air, Austin, 1947, 125th Ann. Celebration, Fredericksburg, 1972. Free concert arranger Fredericksburg Music Club, Inc., 1987—; chmn. Concert Series, 1987—. Recipient Outstanding Alumni award Our Lady of the Lake U., San Antonio, 1997. Mem. Nat. Guild Piano Tchrs. (local chmn. 1952-93, adjudicator 1975-92), Music Tchrs. Nat. Assn., Fredericksburg Music Club, Inc. (bd. mem., program chair, pres. 1989-93), Frank van der Stucken Internat. Music Festival (bd. mem., program chmn. 1991-94, performer 1991, artistic dir.), Sigma Alpha Iota (Sword of Honor 1943), Sigma Alpha Iota Alumnae (pres. 1950-51), Alpha Chi, Delta Kappa Gamma Catholic Daughters. Roman Catholic. Avocations: reading, travel, gourmet cooking. Home: 809 W Travis St Fredericksburg TX 78624-2524

GIBSON, JANET MARIE, psychology educator; b. Phila., July 23, 1959; d. Howard Walter and Elinor Marie (Heil) G. BA, Temple U., 1981; MA, Rice U., 1987, PhD, 1990. Asst. prof. memory and cognition Grinnell Coll., Iowa, 1989—95, assoc. prof., 1995—2005, prof., 2005—. Ad hoc reviewer Memory & Cognition, 1990-94; co-exec. editor Jour. Gen. Psychology; contbr. articles to profl. jours. Am. Women in Sci. scholar, 1987-88; Rice U. fellow, 1984-85. Mem. APA, Am. Psychol. Soc., Midwest Psychol. Assn., Psychonomic Soc., Soc. for Judgment and Decision Making. Roman Catholic. Office: Grinnell Coll Dept Psychology Grinnell IA 50112

GIBSON, JANICE THORNE, developmental psychology educator, author, academic administrator; b. Hartford, Conn., Feb. 26, 1934; d. Peter Arnold and Marjorie Eleanor (Greenberg) Thorne; m. Robert Hahn Gibson, Feb. 13, 1957 (div. 1970); children: Robin Lynne, Mark Gregory. BA, U. Conn., 1955; MS, Brown U., 1957; Ed.D., U. Va., 1962. Asst. prof. psychology U. Pitts., 1962-70, assoc. prof., 1970-73; dir. Aegean Sch. Cultural Anthropology, Naxos, Greece, 1973; prof. devel. psychology U. Pitts., 1973—, chmn. dept. psychology in edn., 1986-87, assoc. dean Acad. Affairs and Research, Sch. Edn., 1987-92. U.S. Acad. Sci. rsch. scholar to USSR, 1978; vis. prof. U. London Inst. Edn., 1992-93; cons. on toy devel., mktg., children's videotapes, 1984—; psychol. cons. Mattel Toys, 1984, St. Martin's Press, 1987, Gund, Inc., 1989. Author: Psychology for the Classroom, 1976, Growing Up: A Study of Children, 1978, Living: A Study of Human Development, 1983, Discipline Is Not a Dirty Word, 1983, Educational Psychology: Mastering Learning, 1988; mem. editorial bd. Contemporary Ednl. Psychology, 1975-90, editor internat. issue, 1984; contbg. editor, monthly columnist One Year Olds, Parents mag., 1984-93; contbg. editor, columist Psychology Today, 1986; contbr. articles on edn. and child devel. to profl. jours. Fulbright research prof. Greece, 1972-73, Yugoslavia, Bulgaria, Cyprus, Israel, 1971-72, Philippines, 1990; research exchange scientist Nat. Acad. Scis., Moscow, 1977; vis. fellow Kennan Inst. Advanced Russian Studies Woodrow Wilson Internat. Ctr., 1978. Mem. Am. Psychol. Assn., Am. Ednl. Rsch. Assn., Internat. Round Table for Advancement of Counseling (bd. dirs. 1990), Internat. Ednl. Rsch. Assn., Northeastern Ednl. Rsch. Assn. (pres. 1981-82)

GIBSON, JANNETTE POE, educational consultant; b. Lubbock, Tex., Oct. 29, 1948; d. Hugh Miller and Norma Grace (Harrison) Poe; m. William Carroll Gibson, June 30, 1967; children: Darin L., Arminda L. Gibson Peery, Victoria L. Gibson Dixon. BS, East Tex. State U., 1971, MEd, 1981; postgrad., Tex. A&M U., Commerce, 1992—. Tchr. Como (Tex.)-Pickton Ind. Sch. Dist., 1971-77; tchr., cons. Diocese of Dallas, Diocese of Tyler, Tex., 1982-87; tchr., supr. Hyder Migrant Ctr., Dateland, Ariz., 1987-88; tchr., adult ESL edn. dir. Ariz. Western U., Hyder Campus, 1988-89; tchr. Sulphur Springs (Tex.) Ind. Sch. Dist., 1989-98; cons., presenter Multicultural/Migrant Edn., 1987—; edn. diagnostician Sulphur Springs ISD Spl. Edn. Dept., 1998—. Cons. ESL edn. and early childhood edn. and child devel. U.S. Dept. Edn., 1988-89; profl. adv. com. Sulphur Springs Ind. Sch. Dist., 1990, 92, 96; doctoral adv. bd. East Tex. State U., 1993-96; regional adv. com. migrant edn. Region V111 Svc., 1994-97, advisor Tex. Edn. Agy. assessments of ESL/LEP children, 1997-98; cons. for devel. of culture and lang. bias-free assessments to sch. dists. in Tex.; presenter in fields of migrant edn. and ESL; private cons. assessment in sch. dists., Tex. Mem. AAUW, NEA, Tex. State Tchrs. Assn., TAMU Doctoral Students Assn., TESOL, Classroom Tchrs. Assn. Tex., Tex. Ednl. Diagnosticians Assn., N.E. Tex. Assn. Ednl. Diagnosticians, Mensa, Alpha Chi, Phi Beta Kappa, Kappa Delta Pi. Democrat. Methodist. Avocations: reading, gardening. Office: 411 College St Sulphur Springs TX 75482-2809

GIBSON, JENNIFER ROSEANN, music educator; b. Kansas City, Mo., Dec. 14, 1978; d. Roger Durwood and Rosalie Eggers Gibson. B Instrumental Music Edn., Ctrl. Mo. State U., Warrensburg, 2001; M Music Edn., VanderCook Coll. Music, Chgo., 2005. Music tchr. Raymore-Peculiar Sch. Dist., Raymore, Mo., 2001—. Composer songs for choirs. Mem.: Am. Choral Dirs. Assn., Music Educators Nat. Conf. Avocations: composing, running, cooking.

GIBSON, JUDITH W., psychotherapist; b. Syracuse, NY, Apr. 27, 1942; d. Nathan Whitney and Helen-Alycia (Fancher) Watson; m. Robert Glenn Gibson, Aug. 1964 (dec. Oct. 1966); 1 child, Heidi. BA in English, Syracuse U., 1978, MA in Religion, 1985, MSW, 1987. LCSW Acad. Cert. Social Workers. Bookkeeper Stickley Furniture, Fayetteville, N.Y., 1965-67; adminstrv. asst. Agway Inc., Dewitt, N.Y., 1967-82; asst. dir. housing Syracuse U., 1983-87; dir. preventive svcs. The Salvation Army, Syracuse, 1990—2002; clinician Psychol. Health Care PLLC, Syracuse, 2002—. Mem. NASW. Roman Catholic. Avocations: reading, arts, travel. Home: 9 Carriage House E # A Manlius NY 13104-2355 Office Phone: 315-422-0300.

GIBSON, KAREN YVETTE, small business owner; b. Corpus Christi, Tex., July 16, 1964; d. Andrew Miles, Jr. and Leslie LaVerne Lockridge-Gibson. AAS, Del Mar Coll., Corpus Christi, 1985; BA, Tex. A&M, Corpus Christi, 1987; MA in Tech. Direction, U. Wash., Seattle, 1989; MPA, U. New Orleans, 1993; JD, Tex. Wesleyan U., Ft. Worth, 2004. Navy intern-pers. mgmt. U.S. Office Civilian Pers. Mgmt., Keyport, Wash., 1987—90; pers. mgmt. specialist U.S. Dept. Navy, New Orleans, 1990—92, dep. equal employment opportunity officer, 1992—94, equal employment specialist Washington, 1994—95; civil rights investigator U.S. Dept. Transp., Ft. Worth, 1995—2000; pres., CEO, owner KYG Assocs. LLC, Euless, Tex., 1998—. Active No Aids Task Force, Seattle, 1987—89, Bridge-Teenager Crisis Group, Washington, Seattle, 1987—88; v.p. Blacks in Govt., New Orleans, 1991—93; mem. adv. com. New Orleans Mayor's Office, New Orleans, 1990—92; active LG Polit. Action Caucus, New Orleans, 1989—91. Legal Assisting scholar, ABA, 1982, Comm./Theater scholar, Tex. A&M U., 1985—87. Mem.: ABA (assoc.), Assn. for Conflict Resolution (assoc.). Democrat. Avocations: tennis, racquetball, golf, bowling, singing. Office: KYG Assocs LLC Ste 200 1010 W Euless Blvd Euless TX 76040

GIBSON, KATHLEEN RITA, anatomy and anthropology educator; b. Phila., Oct. 9, 1942; d. Keath Pope and Rita Irene (Shewell) G. BA, U. Mich., 1963; MA, U. Calif., Berkeley, 1969, PhD, 1970. Teaching assoc. U. Calif., Berkeley, 1965-69; lectr., adj. assoc. prof., then adj. prof. Rice U., Houston, 1973-2000; asst. prof. U. Tex. Health Sci. Ctr., Houston, 1970-73, assoc. prof., 1973-80, prof., 1980—, chair dept. basic sci., 1998—2002. Mem. com. on parenting behavior Social Sci. Rsch. Coun., N.Y.C., 1980-89; mem. fellowship rev. panel NSF, 1992-95; vis. fellow Cambridge U., 1993; vis. scholar Oxford U., 1996. Editor: (with M. Thames and K. Molokon) Genealogy and Demography of the West Main Cree, 1989, (with S. Parker) Language and Intelligence in Monkeys and Apes, 1990, 94, (with A. Petersen) Brain Maturation and Cognitive Development, 1991, (with Tim Ingold) Tools, Language and Intelligence in Human Evolution, 1993, 94, 98, (with Paul Mellars) Modelling the Early Human Mind, 1996, (with Hilary Box) Social Learning in Mammals: Comparative and Ecological Perspectives, 1999 (with Dean Falk) Evolutionary Anatomy of the Primate Neocartin, 2001; contbg. editor Anthropology Newsletter, 1990-93; contbr. articles, commentaries and abstracts in profl. jours. Conf. grantee Wenner Gren Found., 1990, Sloan Found., 1985, travel grantee NSF, 1984, 86, Brit. Soc. Devel. Biology, 1982. Fellow AAAS, Am. Assn. Phys. Anthropologists, Am. Assn. Anthropologists; mem. Am. Assn. Anatomists, Internat. Primatol. Assn., Am. Assn. Dental Schs. (chmn. sect. anatomical scis. 1990), Am. Anthropol. Assn. (chmn.-elect biolog. anthropology sect. 1994-96, chair 1997-98, co-chmn. com. on ethics, 1994-95, chair 1996, chair com. scientific comm. 1997, mem. exec. bd. 1997, 99—2002, chmn. assn. oper. com. 2000—02, mem. nominations com., 2002—), Lang. Origins Soc., Am. Assn. Primatologists (publs. com. 1987-89). Office: Dept Nueorology and Anatomy U Tex Houston Houston TX 77225

GIBSON, KATHY, secondary school educator, art educator; BFA, U. Miss.; MEd, Miss. Coll. Tchr. art Warrenton Elem., Vicskburg, Miss., 1997—2002, Vicksburg H.S., 2002—. Mem.: Miss. Art Edn. Assn. (named Miss. Elem. Art Educator of Yr. 2002), Vicksburg Art Assn.

GIBSON, LISETTE L., elementary school educator, music educator; b. St. Louis, Dec. 14, 1945; d. Erwin L. and Anna Marie Lueker; children: Robert, Todd. BA, Concordia, River Forest, Ill., 1967; MA, U. Mich., 1989. Tchr. grades 3 and 4, music tchr. grades 5-8 St. Paul Luth. Ch. and Sch., Bay City, Mich., 1994—.

GIBSON, MARGARET FERGUSON, poet, educator; b. Phila., Feb. 17, 1944; d. John Spears and Mattie Leigh (Doyle) Ferguson; m. Ross Shackelford Gibson Jr., Aug. 27, 1966 (div. 1971); m. David W. McKain, Dec. 27, 1975; stepchildren: Joshua, Megan. BA, Hollins Coll., 1966; MA, U. Va., 1967. Instr. Madison Coll., Va., 1967-68, Va. Commonwealth U., 1968-70; asst. prof. George Mason U., Va., 1970-75; vis. prof. U. Conn., 1976-77, lectr., 1977-84; writer in residence Phillips Acad./Andover, Mass., 1984-87; vis. prof., MFA program Va. Commonwealth U., 1988-89, U. Mass., 1991-92; asst. prof. Ea. Conn. State U., 1989-91; vis. prof. U. Conn., 1992—. Author: Signs, 1979, Long Walks in the Afternoon, 1982 (Lamont Selection 1982), Memories of the Future, 1986 (co-winner Melville Cane award 1986-87), Out in the Open, 1989, The Vigil, 1993 (finalist Nat. Book award in poetry 1993), Earth Elegy, New and Selected Poems, 1997, Icon and Evidence, 2001, Autumn Grasses, 2003; contbr. poetry to anthologies including Ardis Anthology of New Am. Poetry, Contemporary New Eng. Poetry, Fifty Years of American Poets; contbr. to mags. including Ga. Rev., Prairie Schooner, Minn. Rev., Mich. Quar. Rev., Gettysburg Rev., Iowa Rev., Shenandoah. Woodrow Wilson grantee, 1966, Nat. Endowment for Arts grantee, 1985, Individual artist grantee Conn. Commn. on Arts, 1976, 88; Lila Wallace teaching fellow Woodrow Wilson Found., 1994—. Mem. Phi Beta Kappa. Democrat. Buddhist. Avocations: environment, hiking, gardening. Address: 154 Watson Rd Preston CT 06365-8837 E-mail: margibson@juno.com.

GIBSON, MARIENNE ANTOINETTE, retired special education educator; d. Ollie J. and Bessie (Marnez) Jackson; 1 child, Ingrid Marnez Gibson. BA, Tex. Coll., Tyler, 1960; MEd, St Louis U., 1969. Life Certifications K-12 Mo., 1963, cert. Tchr. Learning Disabilities K-12 Mo., 1963, Tchr. Behavior Disorders K-12 Mo., Tchr. Educable Mentally Disabled K-12 Mo., 1963, Tchr. Kinder Kind Mo., 1963, Tchr. Elem. Edn. K-8 Mo., 1963. Tchr. St. Louis Pub. Schs., 1963—2000; ret., 2000. Pres. NEA, St Louis, Mo., 1997—99; dept. head St Louis Pub. Schs., 1993—2000; supr., counselor Human Devel. Corp., St. Louis, 1970—73. Treas. Berean Seventh Day Adventist Ch., St. Louis, 1990—96, coord. cmty. svc., 2003—05. Home: 3829 Avondale Ave Saint Louis MO 63121

GIBSON, MELISSA UPCHURCH, elementary school educator; b. East Point, Ga., July 4, 1962; d. Harvell Marion and Vivian Hefner Upchurch; m. Michael Allen Gibson, July 29, 1989; children: Megan Erin, Abigail Elizabeth. Undergrad. in Mid. Sch. Edn., U. Ga., Athens, 1980—85, MEd in Computer Based Tech., 1985—87; BSED in Mid. Sch. Math., Ga. State U., Atlanta, 1987—92. Cert. T-6 Grades 4-8 Math, Science, Social Studies, Language Arts, Reading Ga. Dept. Edn., 2006, Gifted K-12 Math, Science, Social Studies, Language Arts, Reading Ga. Dept. Edn., 2006. Tchr. Fulton County Schools, Eastpoint, Ga., 1987—89, Clayton County Sch., Rex, Forest Park, 1989—96, Eagles Landing Mid. Sch., McDonough, 1996—. Team leader Eagles Landing Mid. Sch., 1996—98; sst team leader Eagles Landing Mid., 2005—; pub. rels. com. Eagles Landing Mid. Sch., 2005—, sacs com. for my sch., 2005—06. Dance team choreographer; musician (flute): (concert band, HS band) various musical orgns. (Governor's Honors, 1979); musician: (redcoat band, concert band, HS); georgette (dance team mem.) U. Ga. Bible sch. tchr. Hapeville Meth. Ch., 1985—87, pastor parish com., 1992—93, choir mem., musician(flute)soloists, 1989—2006; judge band auxilary groups Atlanta, 1985—90. Mem.: Atlanta Math Project, Kappa Kappa Gamma. Republican. Mem. Christian Ch. Avocations: learning, music, dance, travel. Office Phone: 770-914-8189.

GIBSON, SANDRA, painter, filmmaker; b. Portland, Oreg. BFA, RI Sch. Design, 1999; attended, Ecole des Beaux-Arts. Artist Whitney Biennial, Whitney Mus. Am. Art, 2004; dir.: (films) Cinematheque, ON, Pacific Film Archive, Anthology Film Archive, Rotterdam Film Festival, Ind. Exposure, Empire State Film Festival, Ann Arbor Film Festival, South Beach Animation Festival. Mailing: c/o Whitney Museum American Art 945 Madison Ave New York NY 10021 E-mail: sgibson31@hotmail.com.

GIBSON, SHERE CAPPARELLA, foreign language educator; b. Norristown, Pa. d. Anthony and Patsy (Robbins) Capparella. BA in Spanish and French, Rosemont Coll., Pa.; BA in Mktg., Ursinus Coll., 1991; student, Institut Internat. D'Enseignement de la Langue Française, France, 1992, Escuela de Idiomas, Spain, 1992; MEd in Multicultural Edn., Eastern Univ., 1993; studied ballet with, Novak and Kovalska; studied Spanish, flamenco, castanet with, José Greco; dance student, Harrisburg Dance Conservatory; PhD in Natural Health, Clayton Coll. Natural Health, 2005. Cert. tchr. Pa., 1992, Spanish and French Pa., 1992. Salesperson Spectrum Comm. Corp., Norristown, sales and mktg. mgr.; asst. sales and adminstrv. asst. Tettex Instruments, Inc., Fairview Village, Pa.; owner, instr. Shere's World of Dance and Fine Arts, Jeffersonville, Pa., 1982-88; multilingual adminstrv. asst. Syntex Dental Products, Inc., Valley Forge, Pa., 1984-86; v.p. Captrium Devel. Corp., Exton, Pa., 1987-89; cons. Mary Kay Cosmetics, 1988-96; sales mgr. Spectrum Comm., 1989-92; tchr. Spanish and French Middletown (Pa.) Area Sch. Dist., 1992-94; adj. prof. Spanish Messiah Coll., Grantham, Pa., 1996—; market rsch. analyst Capital Health Sys., Harrisburg, Pa., 1995; Spanish and French tchr. Elizabethtown (Pa.) Area Sch. Dist., 1996-97; tchr. Spanish, French, and German Milton Hershey Sch., 1997—98, tchr. Spanish, French and Italian, 2002—, world lang. chair, 2002—04. Tng. cons., 1999—; tech. recruiting specialist SHS Staffing Solutions, Harrisburg, 2000—01; trainer and curriculum developer Capital Region Health Sys., 2002—; mem. wellness com. Milton Hershey Sch., 2003—, site coord. year-round experience mid. divsn., 2005; v.p. La Bella Modeling Agy., Collegeville; choreographer and dance instr. La Bella Sch. Performance. Judge state and nat. pageants Miss Am. Scholarship, Jr. Miss. Nat. Teen and Pre-Teen, All-Am. Talent, Ofcl. Little Miss Am., Little Miss Diamond, Talent Olympics, Talent Unltd.; prodr., choreographer Miss Montgomery County Pageant, Plymouth Meeting, Pa., 1985; co-prodr., choreographer Miss Delaware Valley Pageant, Horsham, Pa., 1983-84; confraternity Christian Doctrine kindergarten tchr. Visitation Parish, 1987-88; adult leadership acad., Milton Hershey Sch., 2003. Recipient award Internat. Leaders in Achievement, 1989, Cmty. Leaders of Am., 1989; named Internat. Woman of Yr., 1999-2000. Mem. Am. Soc. Tng. and Devel., Am. Holistic Health Assn., Am. Naturopathic and Holistic Assn., Nat. Integrative Medicine Coun., Am. Coun. Tchrs. Fgn. Langs., Am. Assn. Tchrs. French, Pa. State MLA, Pa. State Edn. Assn., Christian Children's Fund, Am. Assn. Tchrs. Spanish, Kappa Delta Pi. Roman Catholic. Avocations: natural health, travel, dance, house restoration, canine adoption. Home: 4700 Cumberland St Harrisburg PA 17111-2725

GIBSON, STELLA EADES, art educator, photographer; b. Roanoke, Va., May 1, 1943; d. Leo Sanders and Alexandria Catherine Eades; children: Loring Leo, Mark Anthony. AA, Va. We. C.C., 1991; BA, Hollins U., 1993, MA, 1996; MEd, James Madison U., 1998. Cert. art tchr. Va., 1993, spl. edn. educator Va., 1998. Photographic artist Deyerle Studio, Roanoke, Va., 1964—, Lammies Color Lab., Roanoke, 1970—, Rudder Photo Lab., Roanoke, 1990—; tchr. spl. edn. Christiansburg Mid. Sch., 1999—2004, tchr. art., 2005—. Represented in permanent collections Gerald R. Ford Portrait, George Washington Masonic Inst., Alexandria, Va. Mem. Coun. Exceptional Children, 1997—2004. Home: 2755 Brandon Ave Apt 31 Roanoke VA 24015 E-mail: sgibson@rev.net.

GIBSON, TRACIE M., biology professor; d. Rudolph W. Gibson and Betty J. Brown. B, Cornell Coll., Mt. Vernon, Iowa, 1991; M, Purdue U., West Lafayette, Ind., 1996, PhD in Cell Biology, 2000. Postdoctoral rsch. scientist U. Wis., Madison, 2000—03; postdoctoral rsch. assoc. Salk Inst. Biol. Studies, La Jolla, Calif., 2003—05; vis. asst. prof. biology Purdue U., 2005—. Sci. reviewer NASA-Harriett G. Jenkins Predoctoral Fellowship Program, LA, 2004—; mem. adv. bd. Sci. on Wheels Lab., LA, 2005—06; cons. Multicultural Ctr. for Ednl. Excellence, Milw., 2001—03. Sci. HIV expert (Fox 6 news San Diego documentary) Life Lessons: Another Community at Risk. Vol. Lafayette Urban Ministry, Ind., 2006; spkr.on prevention and treatment of HIV chs., schs. and cmty. ctrs., San Diego. Recipient Tchg. honor, Purdue U., 1998, NIH-Ruth L. Kirschstein Nat. Rsch. Svc. award, Nat. Cancer Inst., 2002—05, Sci. Rsch. Travel award, Am. Soc. Virology, 2003; Purdue Grad. Opportunity fellow, 1993—94. Mem.: Am. Soc. Cell Biology (chair subcom. on postdoctoral tng. 2005—06, Sci. Rsch. Travel award 2000, 2002), Assn. Women in Sci. (co-chair stem cell workshop 2004—05). Roman Catholic. Achievements include development of a method to biochemically dissociate a motor protein, termed dynein; first African American post-doctorate research scientist at the McArdle Labortory for Cancer Research. Avocations: travel, Scrabble, science policy. Office Phone: 765-496-7095. Office Fax: 765-494-0876. E-mail: tgibson@purdue.edu.

GIBSON, VIRGINIA LEE, lawyer; b. Independence, Mo., Mar. 5, 1946; BA, U. Calif., Berkeley, 1972; JD, U. Calif., San Francisco, 1977. Bar: Calif. 1981. Assoc. Pillsbury, Madison & Sutro, San Francisco, 1980-83; ptnr. Chickering & Gregory, San Francisco, 1983-85, Baker & McKenzie, San Francisco, 1985—2001, White & Case, LLP, Palo Alto and San Francisco, 2001—. Mem. ABA (internat. law and practice sect., labor and employment law sect.), Nat. Assn. Stock Plan Profls., Nat. Ctr. for Employee Ownership, Calif. Bar Assn. (exec. com. tax sect. 1985-88), San Francisco Bar Assn. (internat. taxation sect.), Western Pension and Benefits Conf. (pres. San Francisco chpt. 1989-91, program com. 1984-88). Office: White & Case LLP 24th Fl 4 Embarcadero San Francisco CA 94111 also: White & Case LLP 5 Palo Alto Sq 3000 El Camino Real Palo Alto CA 94306 Business E-Mail: vgibson@whitecase.com.

GIDDENS, KATHLEEN COLETTE, artist, art educator; b. St. Petersburg, Fla., Apr. 20, 1949; d. Bernard Develira and Harriet Ann (Bruce) Cassidy; m. Marcus LaFayette Giddens Jr., Dec. 28, 1974. BFA, U. Fla., 1971, M Art Edn., 1979. Advt. specialist, Gainesville, Fla., 1978-80; coll. instr. Sampson Tech. Coll., Clinton, N.C., 1980-82, Rockingham C.C., Wentworth, N.C., 1983-85, Patrick Henry C.C., Martinsville, Va., 1983-85; homebound tchr. Pittsylvania County Schs., Chatham, Va., 1986-87; substitute tchr. Danville (Va.) Pub. Schs., 1988-89; art tchr. Cmty. Art Ctr., Waukesha, Wis., 1992. Vol. art tchr. Okeechobee (Fla.) Rehab. Ctr., 1997, Ctr. for Aging, WAukesha, 1990-92; docent Danville Mus. Natural History, 1985. One-person shows include Second Floor Gallery, Milw., 1991, Fla. State Capital, Tallahassee, 1998; exhibited in group shows at WARM Gallery, Mpls., 1960, Gallery Ten, Rockford, Ill., 1990, Cudahay Gallery, Milw. Mus. Art, 1992, Beaumont (Tex.) Art League, 1993, Breckenridge (Tex.) Fine Arts Ctr., 1993, J.R. Mooney Galleries Fine Art, San Antonio, 1994, Tex. Fine Arts Assn., Austin, 1994, Mus. N.W. Colo., Denver Colored Pencil Soc., 1996, Ridge Art Assn., Winter Haven, Fla., 1997, N.C. Zoo, Asheboro, 1997, Ctr. for Arts, Vero Beach, Fla., 1997,. Arts Ctr., St. Petersburg, 1997; commn. Danville Mus. Natural History, 1987. Recipient 1st pl. award art show Fayetteville (N.C.) Mus. Art, 1980, 1st pl. award Danville Art League, Danville Mus. Fine Arts and History, 1986, award Associated Artists of Southport (N.C.) Ann. Show, 1986, 2nd pl. award art show Accessible Parks Inc., Austin, Tex., 1994. Mem. Fla. Trail Assn., Sierra Club. Avocations: hiking, reading, sewing, gardening, environmental causes.

GIDEON, BRENDA K., mathematics educator; b. Clovis, N.Mex., Feb. 13, 1959; m. David Lee Gideon, July 16, 1977. BA, Coll. of S.W., Hobbs, N.Mex., 1993—95. Math tchr. Eunice Pub. Schs., N.Mex., 1995—. Youth worker Vista Point Bapt., Hobbs, 1995—97. Republican. Baptist. Avocations: swimming, reading, needlecrafts. Office: Eunice Pub Schs PO Box 129 Eunice NM 88231 Office Phone: 505-394-3338.

GIDEON-BRADLEY, ANISSA G., voice educator; d. Max G. and Diane Gideon; m. Charles R. Bradley, May 9, 1998. BA in Music Edn., Morehead State U., Ky., 1995; MA in Vocal Music Performance, Ind. State U., 2006. Music tchr. Perry Ctrl. Cmty. Schs., Leopold, Ind., 1995—99; flute tchr. Jasper Mid. Sch., Ind., 1995—2006; pvt. voice tchr. Ferdinand, Ind., 1999—; pvt. voice and flute tchr., 1999—. Area chair Ind. Choral Dirs. Assn., Indpls., 1996—. Awards chair Jasper Philharm. Club, 2005—06; actor/musician Ferdinand C. of C., 2002—06. Mem.: Nat. Assn. Tchrs. Singing, Ind. Choral Dirs. Assn., Jasper Philharmonic Club.

GIEBEL, MIRIAM CATHERINE, librarian, genealogist; b. Williamsburg, Iowa, Oct. 10, 1934; d. John Timothy and Helen Gertrude (Wright) Donahoe; m. William Herbert Giebel, Sept. 30, 1967; 1 child, Sara Ann Giebel Ward. BS, Marquette U., 1956; MLS, Rosary Coll., 1960; cert. in paralegal, Roosevelt U., 1992; cert. in family history rsch., Brigham Young U., 1992. Asst. acquisitions dept. Marquette U. Libr., Milw., 1956—58; tech. svcs. libr. Chicago Heights Pub. Libr., Ill., 1959—63, ext., reference libr., 1974—99, vol. coord./webmaster, 1999—2000, webmaster, 2000—01, geneal. rschr., 2002—; libr. Little Co. Mary Nursing, Evergreen Park, Ill., 1963—64; asst. libr. hdqrs. ALA, Chgo., 1964—67. Mem.: DAR (chpt. registrar 1994—2001), Fedn. Bus. Profl. Women (state libr. chair 1994—96), Daus. Union Vets. 1861-1865 (historian John Butler chpt. 2004—), Daus. Colonial Wars, Dames Ct. Honor (historian Ill. soc. 2003—), Ill. Cameo Soc. of DAR (state v.p. 1996—99, state pres. 1999—2001), U.S. Daus. of 1812 (chpt. pres. 1991—97, Ill. state registrar 1994—97, Ill. state pres. 1997—99, nat. chair lineage and geneal. records 1997—2000, chpt. registrar 1997—, hon. state pres. life), Soc. Ind. Pioneers (life). Roman Catholic. Avocations: reading, personal genealogical research, Web surfing. Personal E-mail: mirgiebel@aol.com.

GIELE, JANET ZOLLINGER, sociologist, educator; b. Medina, Ohio, Aug. 23, 1934; d. Albert Zollinger and Ellen Esther Nestor; m. David Lester Giele, Aug. 24, 1957; children: Elizabeth Ellen, Benjamin Zollinger. BA, Earlham Coll., Richmond, Va., 1956; MA, Harvard U., Cambridge, Mass., 1958; PhD, Harvard U., 1961. Instr. to asst. prof. Wellesley Coll., 1962—70; fellow Bunting Inst Radcliffe Coll, Cambridge, 1970—74; Ford faculty fellow Harvard U., 1974—75; assoc. prof. Heller Sch. Brandeis U., Waltham, 1976—2004; prof. emerita Brandeis U., 2004—. Contbr. chapters to books, scientific papers, articles to profl. jour. Warden and vestry mem. St. Andrew's Epsic. Ch. Grantee Lily Endowment, 1981—83; German Marshall Fund Fellowship, 1992—93. Mem.: Eastern Sociol. Soc., Internat. Sociol. Assn., Am. Sociol. Assn. Avocations: gardening, cooking, knitting.

GIELOW, KATHLEEN LOUISE, career planning administrator, consultant, special education educator; b. Buffalo, July 8, 1951; d. James Elbert and Billie Elaine Robinson; m. Arthur William Gielow, Sept. 1, 1973; 1 child, James Arthur. BS in Edn., SUCNY, Buffalo, 1973, MS in Edn., 1979. Spl. edn. tchr. Buffalo Pub. Schools, 1974—98, career devel. coord., 1998—; ednl. founds. faculty SUCNY, Buffalo, 2001—04, prin. investigator, 2002; entrepreneurship coord. Buffalo Employment and Tng. Ctr., 2002—; owner Queen Creations, 2005—. Profl. devel. provider various ednl. and cmty. orgns., NY, 1997—; profl. conf. workshop presenter, NY, 1998—; conf. workshop presenter Coun. of Gt. City Schs., San Francisco, 1999; careerzone trainer N.Y. State Dept. of Labor, 2000—; cons. Syracuse U., NY, 2001—; career plan trainer N.Y. State Edn. Dept., 2001—; edn. adv. bd. mem. N.Y. State Electric and Gas, Lancaster, 2001—. Editor: (career development best practices collec) Best Practices in Career Development; contbr. nysbest practices in career development Career Development in the Automotive Industry. Vol. Aids Cmty. Svcs., Aids Family Svcs., Buffalo, 1998—; eucharistic min. St. Joseph U. Cath. Ch., Buffalo, 2002—. Recipient Partnership Svc. award, Sch. to Work Family Resource Ctr., 1998, Career and Tech. Educator award, Buffalo Career and Tech. Educators Guild, 2002, Vol. of Yr. award, AIDS Cmty. Svcs., 2003, Pathfinders award for forging partnerships between bus. and edn. in western NY, 2004, Entrepreneur award, Nat. Consortium for Enterpreneurship, 2004, Nat. Leavy Entrepreneurship award, Freedom Found., 2006; grantee School-To-Work (for Buffalo Pub. Schools), NY State Edn. Dept., 1997-1999; Urban/Rural Opportunity grantee, US Dept. Labor, 1998-2003, Youth Entrepreneurship grantee, Kidsway, Inc., 2000, Workforce Devel. Entrepreneurship grantee, Workforce Investment Bd. of Erie County, 2002, Tech Prep Planning grantee, NY State Edn. Dept., 2002-2003, Cornell Workforce Devel. grantee, Cornell U., 2004. Mem.: Assn. for Career and Tech. Educators Adminstrs. (licentiate), Nat. Educators Assn. (licentiate), Buffalo Tchrs. Fedn. (licentiate). Roman Catholic. Avocations: scrapbooking, travel, reading, musical theater. Home: 300 Hamilton Blvd Kenmore NY 14217-1811 Office: Buffalo Pub Schs 2201 City Hall 65 Niagara Sq Buffalo NY 14202 Office Phone: 716-816-3656. E-mail: klg7851@aol.com, kgielow@buffalo.k12.ny.us.

GIER, AMY LOUISE, music educator; d. Keith LeRoy and Beverly Louise Ludwig; m. Douglas Guy Gier, May 26, 1973; children: Natalie Renee, Elisa Christine Taylor, Amanda Brooke, Philip Douglas Guy. MusB, SUNY, Fredonia, 1993, MusM, 1998. New York State Teachers Certification NY State Edn. Dept., 1993. Pvt. piano tchr. Pvt. Studio, South Dayton, NY, 1978—95; pub. sch. music specialist k-12 vocal/gen. Forestville Ctrl. Sch., NY, 1993—. Dir. SPEBSQSA Kings of Persia, Gowanda, NY, 1999—2003. Mem.: Music Educators Nat. Conf., Chautauqua County Music Teachers' Assn., NY State Music Teachers Assn. Avocation: music. Home: 8409 Rt 82 South Dayton NY 14138 Office: Forestville Central HS 4 Academy St Forestville NY 14062

GIERAS, ANGELA LEE, theater manager; d. Thomas and Linda Felts; m. John Gieras, Apr. 24; 1 child, Brett. BS in Fin., U. Fla., Gainesville, 1996; MBA, MA in Arts Adminstrn., So. Meth. U., Dallas, 2003. Asst. br. mgr. Am. South Bank, Jacksonville, 1996—98; comml. banking officer SunTrust Bank, Jacksonville, 1998—2000; devel. dir. Warehouse Theatre, Greenville, SC, 2000—03; fin. dir. Dallas Theater Ctr., gen. mgr., 2003—; assoc. mng. dir. Warehouse Theatre, 2000. Personal E-mail: angfuf1@hotmail.com.

GIESECKE, JOAN RUTH, librarian, dean; MS in Mgmt., Ctrl. Mich. U.; MLS, U. Md.; D in Pub. Adminstrn., George Mason U. Dean librs. U. Nebr., Lincoln. Author: Scenario Planning for Libraries, Practical Help for New Supervisors, Practical Strategies for Library Managers; former editor Library Administration and Management. Office: University of Nebr - Lincoln Librs 318 Love Library Lincoln NE 68588-4100 Office Phone: 402-472-2526. E-mail: jgiesecke1@unl.edu.*

GIESLER, KAREN HOFMANN, elementary school educator; b. St. Louis, Aug. 31, 1955; d. Earl Arthur and Deloris Marie Hofmann; m. Arthur Lewis Giesler, May 26, 1979; children: Lauren Elisabeth, Elizabeth Caroline. BA in Elem. Edn., Govs. State U., 1997. Cert. educator Tex., 1998, gifted and talented educator Tex., 2005. Sci. tchr. Grapevine (Tex.)-Colleyville Ind. Sch. Dist., 1998—. Coach Univ. Interscholastic League Sci., Colleyville, 1999—2005; sponsor Sci. Chicks, Colleyville, 2004—, Future City Competition, Colleyville, 2004—. Dir.: (sch. exhbn.) Texas Heritage Day. Grantee F is for Farad and Q is for Quark, Edn. Found. Grapevine-Colleyville, 2005. Mem.: Tex. Sci. Tchr. Assn., Nat. Sci. Tchr. Assn., Nat. Mid. Level Sci. Tchrs. Assn. Home: 2308 Woodmoor Ln Colleyville TX 76034 Office: Heritage Middle School 5300 Heritage Ave Colleyville TX 76034 Office Phone: 817-305-4790.

GIESSER, BARBARA SUSAN, neurologist, educator; b. Bronx, N.Y., Jan. 21, 1953; d. David and Evelyn (Cohen) G.; m. Philip D. Kanof, June 17, 1979; children: David, Marisa. BS, U. Miami, 1972; MS, U. Tex., Houston, 1974; MD, U. Tex., San Antonio, 1978. Diplomate Am. Bd. Psychiatry and Neurology. Intern Montefiore Hosp., Bronx, 1978-79; resident Bronx Mcpl. Hosp. Ctr. (Albert Einstein Coll. Medicine), 1979-82; asst. prof. neurology Albert Einstein Coll. Medicine, Bronx, 1983-91; med. dir. Gimbel MS Comprehensive Care Ctr., Teaneck, NJ, 1985-90, Rehab. Inst. of Tucson, 1991-95; assoc. prof. clin. neurology Ariz. Health Scis. Ctr., Tucson, 1993—2002; assoc. clin. prof. neurology UCLA, 2002—. Author: Neurology Specialty Board Review, 3d edit., 1986, 4th edit., 1996; contbr. articles to profl. publs. Dean's Tchr. scholar Ariz. Health Scis. Ctr., 1995; named to Best Drs. in Am., 2005-06. Fellow Am. Acad. Neurology (undergrad. edn. subcom. 1999—, Tchr. Recognition award 2002); mem. Nat. Multiple Sclerosis Soc. (rsch. grant 1989, 97, 2003, profl. adv. com. Desert S.W. chpt. 1994-2000, bd. dirs. 1994-2000, counselor Am. Acad. Neurology sect. on Multiple Sclerosis 1997-99, nat. chair client edn. com. 1999-2003, med. adv. bd. 1999-2003, Hall of Fame 2004). Office: UCLA Sch Medicine Neurology Reed Neurologic Rsch Ctr 710 Westwood Plz Los Angeles CA 90095 Office Phone: 310-825-7313. Business E-Mail: bgiesser@mednet.ucla.edu.

GIFFEN, LOIS KEY, artist, psychotherapist; b. Hollis, Okla., Dec. 18, 1932; d. Andrew Finley and Audra Agnes (Griffith) Key; m. Robert Edward Giffen, June 26, 1954; children: John Andrew, Mark Alexander. BA, U. Chgo., 1951; diploma, Inst. Psychosynthesis, London, 1988. Artist, 1945—; social group worker Neighbourhood Clubs, Oklahoma City, Okla., 1956-59; tchr. Unity of the Keys, Key West, Fla., 1994—. Workshop facilitator Fla. Coalition Peace and Justice, 1990; organizer tchg. student mediators in elem. schs. Peace Edn. and Awareness Ctr., Santa Barbara, 1992-93; mentor Take Stock in Children Program; tchr. art program children Fla. Keys Land and Sea Trust. Editor: The London Bridge Mag., 1981—84, The CCL Cookbook, 1986; one-woman shows include Gippsland Regional Art Ctr., Sale, Victoria, Australia, 1973, Anjuian Angkatan Pelakis Semalaysia, Kuala Lumpur, 1976, Am. Consulate-USIS, Benghazi, Libya, 1962, exhibitions include Sculpture Key West, 2001—06, Ft. Zachary Taylor State Parks Keys Women Arts, Key West Mus. Art and History, 2003—05, Gallery I, Artists in Paradise, Big Pine Key, Fla. V.p., mem. bd. dir. Internat. Women's Club, Benghazi, Libya, 1960-65; mem. bd. dirs. Gippsland Regional Art Ctr., Sale, Victoria, Australia, 1971-73; com. chmn., mem. bd. dirs. Am. Women's Club, London, 1981-88; mem. bd. dir. Commonwealth Countries League, London, 1982-88, Welcome to London Internat. Club, London, 1983-88; mem. Univ. Women's Club, London, 1985-88; bd. mem. Fla. Keys Coun. of the Arts, Inc.; vol. Practical Acad. Cultural Edn. program teenage girls at risk, mem. Voices Fla. Keys Children. Mem. Assn. Transpersonal Psychology, Assn. for the Advancement of Psychosynthesis, Bus. and Profl. Women's Club, Fla. Keys Art Guild, Fla. Keys Watercolor Soc., Lower Keys Artists Network, Marathon Sailing Club, Marathon Yacht Club. Democrat. Avocations: sailing, swimming, reading, astrology, gardening. Home: 2000 Manor Ln Marathon FL 33050

GIFFIN, MARGARET ETHEL (PEGGY GIFFIN), management consultant; b. Cleve., Aug. 27, 1949; d. Arch Kenneth and Jeanne (Eggleton) G.; m. Robert Alan Wyman, Aug. 20, 1988; 1 child, Samantha Jean. BA in Psychology, U. Pacific, Stockton, Calif., 1971; MA in Psychology, Calif. State U., Long Beach, 1973; PhD in Quantitative Psychology, U. So. Calif., 1984. Psychometrician Auto Club So. Calif., L.A., 1973-74; cons. Psychol. Svcs., Inc., Glendale, Calif., 1975-76, mgr., 1977-78, dir., 1979-94; rschr. Social Sci. Rsch. Inst., U. So. Calif., L.A., 1981; dir. Giffin Consulting Svcs., L.A., 1994—. Instr. Calif. State U., Long Beach, Long Beach, 1989—90; tech. adv. com. on testing Calif. Fair Employment and Housing Commn., 1974—80, steering com., 1978—80; pres. Pers. Testing Coun. So. Calif., 1980, exec. dir., 82, 88, bd. dirs., 1980—92. Mem. APA, Soc. Indsl. Organizational Psychology. Home and Office: 260 S Highland Ave Los Angeles CA 90036-3027 Office Phone: 323-939-0246. E-mail: peggygiffin@cs.com.

GIFFIN, MARJIE G., writer; b. Columbia City, Ind., Nov. 22, 1951; d. Robert Edwards and Harriett (Brown) Gates; m. Kenneth Neal Giffin, May 17, 1975; children: Christopher, Matthew, Elisabeth Anne. AB in Lit. magna cum laude, Ind. U., 1974; MA in Lit., Butler U., 1982. Cert. tchr., Ind., 1974, gifted and talented edn., 2000. Advt. writer Curtis Pub. Co., Indpls., 1974-75; pub. rels. dir. Dept. Parks and Recreation, Indpls., 1975-76; comms. dir. Acad. Pub. Svc., Indpls., 1976-78; editor Wayne Twp. Sch. Dist., Indpls., 1983-88; assoc. faculty Ind. U./Purdue U., Indpls., 1992-94; freelance writer Indpls., 1978—; rschr./ writer W.B. Brown historical Project, 2001. Mem. grad. sch. arts/scis. alumni bd. Ind. U., 1976-78; bd. dirs. Indpls. Pub. Libr., 1985-86; adv. bd. Ind. U. arts/scis. newsletter, 1977-78. Author: Water Runs Downhill, 1981, If Tables Could Talk, 1988, A Walk Through Time, 1989. Indpls. Zoo, Indpls. Children's Mus.; bd. dirs. Marion County Welfare Bd., 1981-82, Sycamore Sch. Assn., 1998-2001. Honoree Girls, Inc., Indpls. Forum Series, 1991. Honoree Ind. Authors Day, 1990. Mem. Ind. Hist. Soc., Hist. Landmarks found., Acad. Am. Poets, Kappa Alpha Theta. Republican. Roman Catholic. Avocations: water sports, poetry, reading, history, writing. E-mail: mggiffin@aol.com.

GIFFORD, FEREUZA, retired military officer; b. Keene, NH, May 24, 1917; d. John Amos and Leafie Mitchell Gifford; m. John Joseph Pydynkowski Jr., June 1936 (div. June 1941); 1 child, Patricia Mitchell Pydynkowski. Grad., Nat. Maritime Union, 1974; AS in Geology, City Coll. of San Francisco, 1981; AB, Maritime Acad., Piney Point, Md., 1992. Turbo-supercharger tester GE Lynn (Mass.) Riverworks, 1942—43; civilian recruit USN, Boston, Vallejo, Calif., 1943—45; stewardess for convoy SS Fermina, 1947, M.T. Ottawa, San Francisco, 1956, SS United States, N.Y.C., 1960—73, SS Santa Rosa, 1974; mil. petty officer; ret. Author: (poetry) The Falling Rain, 2000 (Editor's Choice award Internat. Libr. of Poetry). Mem.: VFW, Air Force Assn. Achievements include invention of safety handles, Gifford's Lizards, rescuing disabled submarines. Home: 330 Clementina St Apt 621 San Francisco CA 94103-4126

GIFFORD, HEIDI, writer, editor; b. New Haven, Jan. 28, 1961; d. Prosser and Dee Dee (O'Sullivan) Gifford; m. George Melas, July 15, 1995; children: Luke, Lily. BA in English Lit., Yale U., 1983; MPA in Internat. Econs., Columbia U., 1991. Editl. asst. Yale U. Press, New Haven, 1985; asst. to the dir. Gov.'s Office of Fed. Rels., Boston, 1987-89; asst. dir. internat. trade and econs. Coun. on Fgn. Rels., N.Y.C., 1991-94; elections analyst Nightly News with Tom Brokaw/NBC News, N.Y.C., 1995-96; writer and editor Comms. Devel., N.Y.C., 1997—. Assoc. USIA Fgn. Press Ctr., N.Y.C., 1990-91; bd. dirs. Beverly Hills Architecture Found. Mem. Inst. of World Affairs. Episcopalian. Avocations: crew, marathon running. E-mail: heidigiff@earthlink.net.

GIFFORD, KATHIE LEE, television personality, vocalist; b. Paris, Aug. 16, 1953; d. Aaron Leon and Joan Epstein; m. Paul Johnson, 1976 (div. 1983); m. Frank Gifford, Oct. 18, 1986; children: Cody Newton, Cassidy Erin. Student, Oral Roberts U., Tulsa. Gospel singer; singer $100,000 Name That Tune Quiz Show; co-host Morning Show, 1985-88, LIVE with Regis and Kathie Lee, 1988-2000, spl. corr. The Insider, 2005-; author: The Quiet Riot, 1976, I Can't Believe I Said That, 1992, (with Regis Philbin) Cooking With Regis and Kathie Lee, 1993, Entertaining With Regis and Kathie Lee, 1994, Christmas With Kathie Lee, 1997; marketer clothing collection Kathie Lee for Plaza South; singer (albums): Sentimental, 1993, It's Christmas Time, 1993, Born for You, 2000, A Gentle Grace, 2004; sang Nat. Anthem, Super Bowl, 1995; host, co-writer, co-producer, CBS television special, Kathie Lee.Looking for Christmas, 1994.; co-writer (with David Pomeranz), Under the Bridge (play), 2004, Hurricane Amy, 2005 Office: The Insider Paramount Pictures 5555 Melrose Ave Los Angeles CA 90038 also: William Morris Agy 1325 Ave of Americas New York NY 10019

GIFFORD, MARILYN JOYCE, emergency physician, consultant; b. Denver, Aug. 3, 1943; m. Leslie Arthur and Dorothy Marianne (Stevens) G.; m. Robert Bruce Caplan (div.); children: Eric Louis Caplan, Brian Matthew Caplan; m. Daniel Patrick McKenna, July 17, 1992. AA, Stephens Coll., Columbia, Mo., 1963; BS, Mich. State U., 1965; MD, Mt. Sinai Sch. Medicine, N.Y.C., 1971. Diplomate Am. Bd. Emergency Medicine. Emergency physician Longmont (Colo.) United Hosp., 1974-80, Boulder (Colo.) Cmty. Hosp., 1976-78; dir. emergency svcs. Meml. Hosp., Colorado Springs, Colo., 1980—. Physician advisor Colorado Springs Fire Dept., 1980—; bd. dirs. Nat. Registry Emergency Med. Technicians, Columbus, Ohio, 1983—. Co-author: Protocols for Prehospital Emergency Medical Care, 1984, Prehospital Emergency Care, 1996. Advisor E-911 Authority Bd., Colorado Springs, 1996—. Lt. USNR, 1971-72. Recipient Kim Langstaff Meml. award for excellence Region IV EMs Coun., 1986, Val. Wolhauer award for physician excellence Emergency Med. Technician Assn. Colo., 1982, Pres.'s Leadership award Nat. Assn. Emergency Med. Technicians, 1983, ACEP contbn. in EMS, 2001. Fellow Am. Coll. Emergency Physicians (chair EMS com. 1979-81, Colo. coun. 1978-85); mem. El Paso County Med. Soc. (pres. 1993-94). Avocation: skiing. Office: Meml Hosp 1400 E Boulder St Colorado Springs CO 80909-5599 Office Phone: 719-365-2000. Personal E-mail: marilyngifford@hotmail.com.

GIFFORD, MARJORIE FITTING, mathematician, educator, consultant; m. Frederick N. Fitting, Feb. 25, 1972 (dec. 1985); m. Forrest W. Gifford, May 28, 1988 (div. 1992). BS in Math., Mich. State U., PhD in Math. Edn., 1968; AM in Math., U. Mich., 1966; postgrad., U. Nev., Las Vegas, 1995—97. Cert. tchr., Mich. Grad. asst. Mich. State U., East Lansing, 1966-68; prof. emeritus math. and computer sci. San Jose State U., Calif., 1968-92; CEO Metier Cons., Kauai, 2004—. V.p. fin. Metra Instruments, San Jose, 1972—82; pres. Metier, San Jose, 1982—98; cons. San Jose Unified Sch., 1969—71; instr. U. Hawaii OutReach, 2006—. Author: (software) Math Test Generation, 1983; co-author: (book series) Computer Literacy Series, 1983-85, (book) Introduction to Geometry, 1996. Taxwise vol. AARP, 2006—. NSF fellow, 1965-66, Paul Harris fellow, Fulbright Sr. fellow, 1985-86. Mem. Am. Math. Soc., Calif. Math. Coun., Rotary, Zeta Tau Alpha. Roman Catholic. Avocations: gardening, bridge, photography, painting, kayaking.

GIFFORD, NANCY (MUMTAZ), artist, poet; b. Youngstown, Ohio, Feb. 24, 1948; d. John S. Baytos and Helen E. Yochman; m. Michael B. Gifford, Feb. 24, 1995; children: Harriet, Ben, Emma, Kristopher. Degree, Kent (Ohio) State U., 1970; student, Fashion Inst. of Am., 1970—71, The Film Sch., Half Moon Bay, Calif., 1975—76. One-woman shows include Argon Gallery, Venice, Calif., 1984, Merging One Gallery, Santa Monica, Calif., 1986, 1987, Carminel Gallery, N.Y.C., 1988, Schreiber/Cutler Gallery, 1988, L.A. County Mus. of Art, 1991, exhibited in group shows at Craft & Folk Art Mus., L.A., 1984, Bowers Mus., 1987, Carnegie Art Mus., 1987 (1st pl. award), Riverside (Calif.) Art Mus., 1988, Mus. of the Hudson Highlands, N.Y., 1989, Mus. of N.Mex., Santa Fe, 1990, Corcoran Gallery, 1990, Naples (Fla.) Art Mus., 2001, HW Gallery, Naples, Fla., 2002; author: (haiku poetry and drawings) The War Room, 2001, Modern Haiku, 2003. Patron, bd. dirs. Naples Art Assn., 1999—; patron Naples Art Mus., 1997—, Haiku Soc. of Am., 2002, Mus. of Contemporary Art, Miami, 2003. Recipient award of excellence, Scarsdale (N.Y.) Art Soc., 1987, Juror's award, Fine Arts of Burbank, Calif., 1987, award of excellence, Gallery 54, N.Y.C., 1988, award of merit, von Liebig Art Ctr., 2003. Avocations: swimming, hiking, yoga. Home: 568 9th St S Ste 354 Naples FL 34102 E-mail: nangifford@home.com.

GIFFORD, PAULA, elementary school educator; b. Oklahoma City, Feb. 1, 1962; d. Paul and Bonnie Gettle; m. Jeff Gifford, May 15, 1995; children: Kristen, Ryan Newman, Amber. BS in Edn., U. Ctrl. Okla., Edmond, 1997. Cert. tchr. State of Okla., Nat. Bd. Profl. Tchg. Stds., 2004. Third grade tchr. Santa Fe Elem. Sch., Moore, Okla., 1998—2000; fourth grade tchr. Kingsgate Elem. Sch., 2000—05; sixth grade tchr. Wayland Bonds Elem. Sch., 2005—. Webmaster Wayland Bonds Elem. Sch., Moore, Okla., 2005—, knowledge box coord., 2005—. Grantee, Moore Pub. Sch. Found., 2006. Office Phone: 405-735-4500.

GIGLI, IRMA, dermatologist, educator, academic administrator; b. Cordoba, Argentina, Dec. 22, 1931; d. Irineo and Esperanza Francisca (Pons de Gigli) Gigli; m. Hans J. Muller-Eberhard, June 29, 1985. BA, Liceo Nacional Manuel Belgrano, Cordoba, 1950; MD, Universidad Nacional de Cordoba, 1957. Intern Cook County Hosp., Chgo., 1957—58, resident in dermatology, 1958—60; fellow in dermatology NYU, 1960—61; mem. faculty Harvard Med. Sch., 1967—75, asso. prof. dermatology, 1972—75; chief dermatology service Peter Bent Brigham Hosp., Robert B. Brigham Hosp., 1971—75; prof. dermatology and exptl. medicine N.Y. U. Med. Center, N.Y.C., 1976—82, mem. Irvington House Inst., mem. faculty N.Y. Grad. Sch. Med. Scis., dir. Asthma and Allergic Disease Center for Immunodermatology Studies, 1980—91; prof. medicine, chief div. dermatology U. Calif.-San Diego, 1983—95; prof. medicine and dermatology, vice chair medicine for sci. U. Tex. Health Sci. Ctr., Houston, 1995—; assoc. dir. Inst. Molecular Medicine for Prevention Human Diseases U. Tex., Houston, 1998—2003, dep. dir., 2003—, Walter and Mary Mischer prof. molecular medicine Houston, 1998—; dir. Rsch. Ctr. Immunology and Autoimmune Diseases, 1995—. Mem. Nat. Inst. of Allergy and Infectious Diseases Coun., 1978—79, bd. sci. counselors, 1997—; chmn. study sect. Allergy and Immunology Inst., NIH, 1978—83; mem. Guggenheim Found. Western Hemisphere and Phillippines Com. of Selection; adv. bd. NIH Fogarty Internat. Ctr., 1984—97. Bd. dirs. U.S. Civilian R&D Found. for the Ind. States of the Former Soviet Union. Recipient Rsch. award, Am. Cancer Soc., 1970—72, NIH, 1972—76, Disting. Profl. Woman of Yr. award, U. Tex. Health Sci. Ctr. at Houston, 2003, David Martin Carter Mentor award, Am. Skin Assn., 2005; grantee, Guggenheim Found., 1974—75. Mem.: Acad. Medicine, Engring. & Sci. Tex. (bd. dirs.), Am. Acad. Arts and Scis., Henry Kunkel Soc. (councilor 1999—), PEW Latin Am. Fellows Program in Biomed. Scis. (nat. adv. com. 1998—2005), Inst. Medicine/NAS, Am. Dermatol. Assn., Assn. Am. Physicians, Am. Acad. Allergy, Am. Acad. Dermatology, Am. Assn. Immunologists, Am. Soc. Clin. Investigation, Soc. Investigative Dermatology (hon.; pres. 1990—91, Stephen Rothman Meml. award 1996). Office: U Tex Health Sci Ctr Inst Molecular Medicine 2121 W Holcombe Blvd Houston TX 77030-3303

GIGLIO, EMILY KRISTINE, athletic trainer, educator; b. Freeport, Ill., July 15, 1976; adopted d. Dominick Mario Giglio and Madelynn Irene Estwing, d. Curt Estwing (Stepfather). AS, Rock Valley Coll., Rockford, Ill., 1994—96; BS, Idaho State U., Pocatello, 1997—99; MS, Ill. State U., Normal, 1999—2001. ATC Nat. Athletic Trainer's Assn. Bd. Cert., Ill., 2002, cert. massage therapist Nat. Cert. Therapeutic Massage & Bodywork, N.Mex., 2003. Instr. Gymnastic Acad. Rockford, Ill., 1992—97, 2004—; trampoline coach Athletic Edge, Pleasant View, Utah, 2001—02; athletic trainer Hobbs Orthopaedic & Sports Therapy, N.Mex., 2002—04, USA Gymnastics Tumbling and Trampoline, Brownfield, Tex., 2003—, FHN, Freeport, Ill., 2004—. Mem.: USA Gymnastics, Nat. Athletic Trainer's Assn. Achievements include being part of the US National Women's Power Tumbling Team, world championships 1990, 92 & 94. Avocations: sports, photography, travel. Office: FHN 1045 W Stephenson St Freeport IL 61032 Personal E-mail: flip1976@yahoo.com.

GIGLIOTTI, AMY VERONICA, music educator; b. Phila., Nov. 7, 1976; d. Richard John and Frances Marie Gigliotti. MusB, Temple U., 2000; MA in Endl. Mgmt. Leadership and Policy, Seton Hall U., 2007. Cert. tchr. NJ. Gen. music tchr. Lake Tract Elem. Sch., Deptford, NJ, 2000—01; vocal music tchr., mus. dir., vocal coach Deptford HS, 2001—. Pvt. flute and piano tchr., Sewell, NJ, 1994—; vocal dir. Am. Music Abroad, Haddonfield, NJ. Mem.: South Jersey Choral Dirs. Assn., Music Educators Nat. Conf. (pres. collegiate level 1998—99), Deptford Edn. Assn. (bldg. rep. 2004—06), NJ Edn. Assn., Golden Key Nat. Honor Soc. (life; pres., collegiate advisor 1998—2000). Democrat. Roman Catholic. Avocations: singing, reading, flute, concerts. Home: 734 Sedgewick Ct Sewell NJ 08080 Office: Deptford HS 575 Fox Run Rd Deptford NJ 08096 Office Phone: 856-232-2713 7309. Office Fax: 856-374-9145. Personal E-mail: amy.gigliotti@comcast.net. Business E-Mail: gigliotti.a@deptford.k12.nj.us.

GIGNAC, JUDITH ANN, retired utilities executive, land developer; b. Detroit, Mich., Mar. 21, 1939; d. Durward Arthur and Gertrude Marian Du Pont; m. Oliver Otto Leininger, July 7, 1990; m. Paul Ross Gignac, Sept. 12, 1964 (div. Apr. 13, 1985); children: Beth Andrea Gignac-Hooper, Christopher Ross. Assoc., Broward Bus. Coll., 1958; student, U. Colo., 1967—69, Cochise Coll., 1975—76, U. Ariz.-South, 2002; LittD (hon.), U. Ariz., 2004. Data processor Kettelle, Colo. Springs, Colo., 1968—69; computer programmer RCA - Ballistic Missile Early Warning Sys., Colo. Springs, 1969—70; elected county supr. Cochise County Bd. of Supervisors, Bisbee, Ariz., 1977—88; vice pres., gen. mgr. Bella Vista Water/Ranches, Sierra Vista, Ariz., 1988—2004, ret., 2004; gen. mgr. Bella Vista Ranches, Sierra Vista, 2004—. Ptnr. Darby, Gignac & Associates, Inc, Sierra Vista, Ariz., 1982—88; mem. Ariz. Assn. of Counties, County Supervisors Assn., Phoenix; dir., sec. Orgn. of U.S. Border Cities & Counties, Ariz.; dir. Governing Bd. of Health Systems Agy. of SE Ariz.; chair San Pedro Water Resources Assn., Sierra Vista, Ariz.; mem. Governor's Workforce Devel. Policy Coun., Phoenix, State Task Force on Wastewater Treatment Facilities Constrn. Grants, Washington, D.C.; dir. Cochise County Water Mgmt. Coun., Bisbee, Ariz.; mem./chair Bur. of Land Mgmt. Pub. Lands Adv. Coun., Safford, Ariz.; dir. Water Utilities Assn. of Ariz., Phoenix, 1989—93, Ariz. Utilities Investor's Assn., 1995—; commr. Upper San Pedro Partnership Adv. Commn., Sierra Vista, Ariz., 2001—, chair exec. com.; mem./past pres. Ariz. Bd. of Regents, 1994—2002; dir. State C.C. Bd., Phoenix, 1994—2003, United Bank Bd., Phoenix, Bank of Cochise, Sierra Vista, Ariz.; dir./sec. Huachuca Fed. Credit Union, Sierra Vista, Ariz.; dir. letter U. Ariz., 2004. Dir. Wells Fargo Bank Adv. Bd., Sierra Vista, Ariz., 1999; mem./chair Cochise Coll. Presdl. Adv. Com., Sierra Vista, Ariz.; mem./dir. Sierra Vista C. of C., Ariz.; mem., chair Sierra Vista Bd. of Adjustment, Ariz.; co-chair platform subcommittee 1980 Rep. Nat. Conv., Detroit; keynote spkr. Ariz. Rep. Women; mem./chair Sierra Vista Charter Bd. of Freeholders, Ariz.; chmn. Cochise County Rep. Com., Bisbee, Ariz.; founder/mem./pres. Thunder Mountain Rep. Women, Sierra Vista; treas. Rep. State Party, Phoenix; dir./chmn. Ariz. Town Hall, Phoenix, 1978; dir. U. Found. Sierra Vista, Inc., Ariz. Recipient Woman of the Yr., Bus. & Profl. Women, 1974—75, Disting. Svc. award, U. of Ariz., Coll. of Edn., 2002, Lady of the Yr., Beta Sigma Phi, 1977, Leadership & Comm. award, Toastmasters Internat., 1982, Medal of Honor, DAR, 1988, Woman of the Yr., Cochise County Rep. Com., 1988, Citizen of the Yr., Sierra Vista C. of C., 1994, DeConcini award, Ft. Huachuca 50, 1995, Vision award, Commn. on the Status of Women, 2000, Outstanding Achievement award, U. of Ariz., Coll. of Edn., 2002. Mem.: U. Med. Ctr. (dir. 1997—), Upper San Pedro Partnership Adv. Commn. (commr. 2001), Ariz. Town Hall (chmn. bd. 2001—03). Avocations: reading, writing, gardening. Home: 1425 Via Viento Sierra Vista AZ 85635 Office: Bella Vista Ranches 5000 East Mediterranean Dr #C Sierra Vista AZ 85635 Office Phone: 520-459-3035. E-mail: jgignac@mindspring.com.

GIL, KAREN M., psychology professor; b. Bklyn., Aug. 8, 1956; BA in Psychology, SUNY, Stony Brook, 1974—78; MA in Clin. Psychology, West Va. U., 1980—82, PhD in Clin. Psychology, 1982—85. Internship Duke U. Med. Ctr., 1984—85, clin. assoc., 1985—86, asst. prof. med. psychology, 1986—92; asst. prof. psychology-social and health sciences Duke U., 1991—93, assoc. prof. psychology-social and health sciences, 1994—95, assoc. prof. med. psychology, 1992—95; assoc. prof. Dept. Psychology U. NC, Chapel Hill, 1995—2000, sr. assoc. dean undergrad. edn., 2001—04, prof. Dept. Psychology, 2000—, chair Dept. Psychology; prof. Dept. Psychiatry U. NC Sch. Medicine, Chapel Hill; adj. assoc. prof. Dept. Psychiatry and Behavioral Sciences Duke U. Med. Ctr. Office: Psychology Dept UNC-CH 254 Davie Hall Chapel Hill NC 27599-3270 Office Phone: 919-962-3991. E-mail: kgil@email.unc.edu.*

GILBERT, ANITA RAE, psychologist, educator; d. Marie Olivia Love; children: Ray Bernard, Lorin D'Andrew. PhD, Wright Inst., Berkeley, Calif., 1981. Lic. clin. psychologist Calif., 2001. Psychology instr. San Francisco City Coll., 1976—78; psychologist Bayview Mental Health Svc., San Francisco, 1980—82; lectr. U. of Calif., San Francisco, 1982—86; neuropsychologist San Francisco Gen. Hosp., 1982—84; forensic psychologist Calif. Dept. of Correction, San Francisco, 1985—; lectr. Calif. State U., Hayward, 1993—96, San Francisco State U., 2003—; clin. program dir. Westside Cmty. Mental Health, San Francisco, 1987—88; psychol. testing program dir. Calif. Med. Facility-Vacaville, Calif., 1984—86. Cons. psychologist Calif. Dept of Mental Health, San Francisco, 1987—88; cons. Asian Am. Residential Treatment Ctr., San Francisco. Mentor Cath. Charities, San Francisco, 1995—98. Fellow Doctoral fellow, APA, 1978—80. Mem.: Soc. for Personality Assessment, APA (assoc.). Achievements include research in depression, women's studies, issues in neuropsychology. Avocations: yoga, travel, exercise program, painting, dance. Personal E-mail: dragilbert@aol.com.

GILBERT, ANNA, mathematics professor; SB in Math. with honors, U. Chgo., 1993; PhD in Math., Princeton U., 1997. Summer intern AT&T Bell Lab., 1993—95; rsch. asst Princeton U., 1994—95; intern Lucent Technologies Bell Lab., 1996; postdoctoral rsch. assoc. Yale U. and AT&T Labs-Rsch., 1998—2002; sr. tech. staff mem., Information Sciences Rsch. Ctr. AT&T Labs-Rsch., 2002—04; asst. prof., dept. math. U. Mich., 2004—. Initiated AT&T Shannon postdoctoral fellowship, chaired search com., 2000—01; served AT&T Labs Fellowship program com., 2002—04; computing com. U. Mich., 2004—05, mem. applied and interdisciplinary math. grad. com., 2004—05, exec. com., 2005—06; invited spkr. in field. Contbr. articles to profl. jours.; assoc. editor Communications in Mathematical Sciences, referee IEEE Trans. on Information Theory, IEEE Trans. on Networking, IEEE Trans. on Signal on Processing, SIAM Jour. on Applied Mathematics, EURASIP Jour. Signal Processings. AT&T Found. Grad Rsch. Program for Women grant, 1993—97, AT&T Found. PhD fellowship, 1995—97, NSF University-Industry postdoctoral rsch. fellowship, 1997—99. Achievements include Patents filed. Office: Dept Math U Mich 4831 East Hall 530 Church St Ann Arbor MI 48109-1043 Office Phone: 734-763-5728. Office Fax: 734-763-0937. Business E-Mail: annacg@umich.edu.*

GILBERT, DEBBIE ROSE, entrepreneur; b. Indpls., Jan. 18, 1961; d. James Taylor and Rosemary (Robinson) Gilbert. BA, Ind. U., Bloomington, 1994; diploma computer literacy, St. Augustine Coll., Chgo., 1995. Student typing asst. Shortridge H.S. Indpls. Pub. Schs./Bd. Schs. Commrs., 1978—79; substitute tchr. Indpls. Pub. Schs./Bd. Sch. Commrs., 1985—89, Washington Twp. Schs., Indpls., 1992; CHA housewatcher, clothes distbr. Inner Voice, Inc., Chgo., 1994—95; vol. Lakefront Single Room Occupancy Employment Program, Chgo., 1997—. Dep. registrar O.N.E./Bd. Election Commrs., Chgo., 1996—; mem. People for Am. Way, Chgo., 1995-96; mem. Access Living, Chgo., 1996—, So. Poverty Law Ctr., Tchg. Tolerance, Militia Task Force, Klanwatch Orgn., Montgomery, 1998— Mem. ACLU, NOW, AAUW, NAACP, Nat. Mus. Women in Arts Orgn., Older Women's League, Voice of Midlife & Older Women, Mental Health Consumer Edn. Consortium, Inc Democrat. Baptist. Avocations: modeling, singing, race walking, Bingo, reading. Home: 5012 N Winthrop Ave Apt 224 Chicago IL 60640-3124 Office: 4753 N Broadway Ste 632/808 Chicago IL 60640-4986

GILBERT, ELLEN EFFMAN, music educator, conductor; b. New London, Conn., May 21, 1969; d. David Garth and Elaine Avery Effman; m. Steven Dale Gilbert, Dec. 25, 1995; 1 child, Eliza Avery. BS in Music Edn., U. Conn., 1991, MMus, 1995; Kodaly cert. in Music Edn., HARTT Sch. of Music, Hartford, Conn., 2001—. Music educator, bilingual Bridgeport (Conn.) Pub. Schs., 1992—93; choral condr. Hartford (Conn.) Camerata Conservatory, 1996—98; music educator Hartford Pub. Schools, 1996—98; choral condr. U. Conn. Treblemakers Cmty. Music Sch. of the Arts, Mansfield, Conn., 2003—; choir dir. Old Mystic (Conn.) Bapt. Ch., 2000—; music educator Mystic (Conn.) Mid. Sch., 1998—. Choral chairperson Ea. Region Music Festival, Waterford, Conn., 2002—; clinician/adjudicator R.I. Music Educators Conf., 2001—04; panel discussion rep. Providence Coll., Providence, 2000—00; presenter/condr. Gt. East Adjudication Festivals, Agawam, Mass., 1998—; presenter Conn. Music Educator's Conf., 2001, 03, 04, All State Elem. Gen. Mus. Conf., 2003, Franklin Pierce Coll., 2003; chmn. Children's Choir Repetoire and Stds. for Am. Choral Dir. Assn. Singer: Prov. Performing Arts Ctr.; contbr. articles to profl. jours. Member-at-large Stonington (Conn.) Players Thespian Assn., 2003; bd. of Christian edn. Old Mystic Bapt. Ch.; sec. Kodaly Educators of So. New Eng., Hartford, Conn. Grantee Celebration of Excellence, State of Conn., 2000, World Music Drumming in the Classroom, Stonington Edn. Fund, 2002, Recorder Consort, 2000, 100 Best Cmtys. Music Edn., 2002; scholar Young Artist Competition, Nat. Assn. of Teachers of Singing, 1990. Mem.: Am. Choral Directors Assn. (assoc.; presenter Mid. Sch. Festival, West Hartford, Conn. 1999—2003), Kodaly Educators of So. New Eng. (assoc.; sec. 1994—99), Orgn. Am. Kodaly Educators (assoc.), Conn. Music Educators Conf. (assoc.; presenter, Hartford 2001, choral chairperson 2002—03, presenter 2003—), Music Educators Nat. Conf. (assoc.). Democrat. American Baptist. Office: Mystic Mid Sch 204 Mistuxet Ave Mystic CT 06355 Office Phone: 860-536-9613. E-mail: egilbert@stoningtonschools.org.

GILBERT, HARRIETTE GURLEY, retired music educator; b. Cherryville, NC, Apr. 7, 1950; d. Robert Clifton and Ruth McDowell Gurley; m. Richard Lee Gilbert, June 16, 1973; children: Lindsay McDowell, Kerstin Blair. AA, Peace Coll., 1970; MusB, Appalacian State U., 1973, MA cum laude, 1974; postgrad., Duke U., 1976—77. Cert. music edn., supervisn., cmty. & jr. coll. curriculum Appalacian State U., NC. Instrumental music specialist Gaston County Sch. Sys., Gastonia, NC, 1976—2006; ret., 2006. Condr. N.C. Assn. Educators convention music groups, educator confs. & county edn. functions, 1976—. Chmn. Am. Cancer Soc., Cherryville, 2000, Am. Heart Assn., Cherryville, 2003; vol. Leukemia & Lymphoma Soc., Gaston County, 2004; organist First United Meth. Ch., Cherryville, 1981—84, St. Luke's Episcopal Ch., Lincolnton, NC, 1985—. Mem.: NEA, NC Assn. Classroom Tchrs., NC Assn. Educators, Music Educators NC, Cherryville Music Club (program chmn. 1980—97). Democrat. Episcopalian. Avocations: historic home restoration, gardening, genealogy, landscaping.

GILBERT, JENNIE, educator, consultant; b. Hagerstown, Md., Dec. 1, 1955; d. Tommy Bert and Edwige (Tokarz) G. BS, Pa. State U., 1977; MA, Western Mich. U., 1979; PhD, U. Ill., 1989. Head athletic trainer Pa. State U., Mont Alto, 1977-78; head women's trainer No. Ill. U., DeKalb, 1979-82; instr., athletic trainer George Williams Coll., Downers Grove, Ill., 1982-85; asst. prof. Calif. State U., San Bernardino, 1989—. Fitness cons. U. Redlands, Calif., 1990-91, youth sports, fitness camp fitness cons., instr., 1990—. Contbr. articles to profl. jours. Mem. Am. Coll. of Sports Medicine, Southwest Region Am. Coll. of Sports Medicine, Am. Alliance of Health, Phys. Edn., Recreation and Dance, Nat. Athletic Trainers Assn. (cert.). Avocations: stamp collecting/philately, running, hiking, bicycling. Office: Calif State U 5500 University Pkwy San Bernardino CA 92407-2318

GILBERT, JOAN STULMAN, retired public relations executive; b. NYC, May 10, 1934; m. Phil E. Gilbert Jr., Oct. 6, 1968; children: Linda Cooper, Dana McGrk, Patricia Novajosky. Student, Conn. Coll. Women, 1951-53. Br. coord. Vol. Svc. Bur., Westchester, NY, 1970-72; pub. rels. dir. Westchester Lighthouse, 1972-76; exec. dir. Westchester Heart Assn., 1976-77; mgr. cmty. rels. Texaco Inc., White Plains, NY, 1977-97. Vice chmn. ARC; chmn. The Street Theater, 1995—97; bd. dirs. Am. Heart Assn., Westchester Philharm., Jazz Forum Arts; former bd. dirs. Choate Rosemary Hall, United Way of Westchester; former bd. dirs., former trustee Westchester Coun. for the Arts; trustee, former bd. dirs. Teatown Lake Reservation. Recipient award, Youth Theater Interactions, Westchester Hispanic Coalition, Women in Comms., Am. Heart Assn., Am. Diabeters Assn., Westchester Putnam Affirmative Action Program, Arthritis Found., ARC, Urban League Westchester. Mem.: Sales and Mktg. Exec. Westchester (former dir.), Women in Comm. (award), Advt. Club (dir.), Pub. Rels. Soc. Am. (chpt. pres. 1977), Westchester County Assn. Home: Mystic Pointe 2 High Ridge Rd Ossining NY 10562 Personal E-mail: gilbertjs@aol.com.

GILBERT, JOANNE TOONE, director, educator; b. Chase City, Va., May 20, 1946; d. Walter and Emma Toone; m. Edward Cooper (div.); 1 child, Michael Cooper; m. Artist Gilbert, Aug. 4, 1990; children: Daren, Barbara, Robert. BSc, Hampton U., 1969; MEd, Va. State U., 1978; attended, San Diego State U., 1990—91, U. Calif., Riverside, 1998—2000. Tchr. Yonkers Bd. Edn., NY, 1969—70, Petersburg Pub. Schs., Petersburg, Va., 1973—83, Bd. Edn., Long Beach, Calif., 1983—90, Moreno Valley, Calif., 1990—96, dir. Calif. sch. age family edn. program, 1996—. Bd. dirs. Calif. Alliance Concerned Teen Age Pregnancy, Calif., 1998—2002; exec. bd. mem. Moreno Valley Educators Assn., Calif., 2000—01; bd. trustees Rialto Unified Sch. Dist., Calif., 2001, pres., 2003—04; dist. dir. area d San Bernadino County Sch. Bd., Calif., 2005—. Commr. City of Rialto, Calif., 1996—2004; pres. Rialto Dem. Club, 2003—04. Mem.: Nat. Sch. Bds. Assn., Calif. Sch. Bds. Assn., Nat. Coun. Negro Women (life; pres. 1996—98), East Rialto Kiwanis Club. Democrat. Avocations: gardening, pets. Home: 1490 N Marcella Ave Rialto CA 92376

GILBERT, KATHERINE E., literature and language professor; d. Joseph G. and Katherine Jennings Gilbert. BA, U. S.C., Columbia, 1990; MA, U. S.C., 1992, PhD, 1995. Grad. instr. of English U. S.C., Columbia, SC, 1990—95; prof. of English Midlands Tech. Coll., Columbia, SC, 1995—. Test writer ACT, Iowa City, 1997—. Contbr. articles and short stories to profl. jours. Co-founder U. S.C.Rape Awareness Coun., Columbia, 1989—90; pres. Free South Africa Alliance, Columbia, 1986—89, Alliance for Peace, Columbia, 1989—90. Recipient Excellence in Cmty. Action, Omega Psi, 1989. Mem.: Two-Yr. Coll. Assn., Philos. Assn. of the Carolinas, South Atlantic MLA, MLA. Office: English Dept Midlands Technical College PO Box 2408 Columbia SC 29202-9957 Office Phone: 803-738-7612, 803-822-3357. Personal E-mail: gilbertk@midlandstech.edu.

GILBERT, KATHIE SIMON, economist, educator; b. Akron, Ohio, Feb. 28, 1943; d. John Nicholas and Bernadine Mary (Ilg) Simon; m. John Randalph Gilbert, Jr., Jan. 28, 1964; children: Mark Ivan, Adam Stacy. BA, U. Ala., 1964; MA, La. State U., 1966, PhD, 1972; grad. mgmt. devel. program, Harvard U., 1989. Assoc. prof. econs. Miss. State U., 1968-78, prof. econs., 1978-93, prof. polit. sci., 1981-93, dept. head econs. and fin., 1985-93; prof. econs. Western N.Mex. U., Silver City, 1993—, v.p. acad. affairs, 1994—99, spl. asst. for quality initiatives, 1999—, amd., 2005—. Vis. sr. econ. analyst Miss. Rsch. and Devel. Ctr., 1985—; mem. adv. bd. Deposit Guaranty Nat. Bank, Starkville; bd. dirs. Quality N.Mex., 2003—. Contbr. articles to profl. jours. Vice chmn. Miss. Internat. Women's Yr. Com., 1977; chmn. Miss. State U. Faculty Coun., 1986-87; trustee Ednl. Found., 1993-96; bd. dirs. Oktibbeha County United Way, 1990-93, Starkville Area Habitat for Humanity; active Miss. Gov. Pvt. Sector Action Coun., Oktibbeha County Dem. Exec. Com., 1976-80, 84-88, N.Mex. First, 1994—, ACE nat. identification program, N.M. coord., 1997-99. Am. Council on Edn. fellow, 1979-80; Miss. Com. for Humanities grantee, 1975, 83 Mem. Am. Econ. Assn., So. Econ. Assn., Miss. Econ. Coun., Southwestern Econ. Assn. (pres.), Nat. Women's Studies Assn., Southeastern Women's Studies Assn. (pres.), AAUW (pres. Starkville br. 1977-79, v.p. Miss. div. 1980-82, pres. 1982-84, pres. Grant county br. 1986-87, nat. bd. dirs. 1987-89), LWV (treas. Starkville chpt. 1981-83), Southwestern Social Sci. Assn. (sec., pres. 1993-94), Silver City Grant County Econ. Devel. Assn. (pres. 1999-2003), Miss. State U. Faculty Women's Assn. (pres. 1981-82, 88-89), Mortar Bd., Phi Kappa Phi, Omicron Delta Epsilon, Beta Gamma Sigma. Democrat. Roman Catholic. Home: 3451 Ursa Minor Silver City NM 88061-6200 Office: Western New Mex U College Ave Silver City NM 88062-0610 Office Phone: 505-538-6348. E-mail: gilbertk@unmu.edu.

GILBERT, LINDA ARMS, education educator, educational association administrator; BS in Elem. Edn., Middle Tenn. State U., 1972, MA in Tchg., 1979, EdS in Adminstrn. and Supervision, 1991; EdD in Curriculum and Instrn., Tenn. State U., 1997. 8th grade tchr. Ctrl. Middle Sch., 1972-73; 5th-6th grade band tchr. Mitchell-Neilson Elem. Sch., 1987-90; 5th-6th grade band tchr., K-2 music tchr. Reeves-Rogers Elem. Sch., 1988-90; 5th-6th grade band tchr., K-6 music tchr., chorus tchr. Black Fox Elem. Sch., 1990-98; assoc. dir. instrn., staff devel. Murfreesboro City Schs., 1998—; asst. prof. Mid. Tenn. State U., 2000—. Pvt. music tchr., 1970—; presenter in field; guest conductor mass flute choirs Tenn. Flute Festivals; music adjudicator; adj. prof. Cumberland U., 2001—. Guest columnist for edn. Daily News Jour. Organist Bethel United Meth. Ch., various coms.; active Rutherford 2000, 1991-95; vol. VA Med. Ctr., guest spkr. civic orgns.; mem. Band of Blue Exec. Bd. Middle Tenn. State U.; chairperson edn. com. Am. Cmty. Summit of Rutherford County; bd. dirs. Arts and Humanities Coun.; mem. exec. bd. Murfreesboro Youth Orch., C. of C. Bus. Edn. Partnership. Named Tenn. State Tchr. of Yr., 1998, Radio Educator of Week, Sta. WGNS, Outstanding Tchr. Tenn. Gov.'s Sch. of the Arts, 1995; recipient Apple award WSMV TV's Tchr., 1998, Disting. Classroom Tchr. award, 1992, Spl. Recognition award Tenn. Environ. Edn. Assn.; inducted Band of Blue Hall of Fame, 1998. Mem. ASCD, Nat. Flute Assn., Middle Tenn. Flute Soc., Am. Orff-Schulwork Assn., Tenn. Educators Assn., Music Educators Nat. Conf., Tenn. Elem. Music Educators Assn., Tennesseans for the Arts, Tenn. Bandmasters Assn., Middle Tenn. Sch. Band and Orch. Assn., Middle Tenn. Vocal Assn. (accompanist mass choir 1992), Tenn. Edn. Assn. (human rels com. 1994-96, summer leadership sch. 1994-96, del. to rep. assembly 1992-96), Middle Tenn. Edn. Assn. (pres.), Murfreesboro Edn. Assn. (grievance com. chairperson, exec. bd., profl. adv. com. 1994-96, pres. 1994-96, pres.-elect, other coms.), Phi Kappa Phi, Kappa Delta Pi, Phi Delta Kappa, Delta Omicron, Delta Kappa Gamma. Office: Murfreesboro City Schs 2552 S Church St Murfreesboro TN 37127-6342 E-mail: lgilbert@cityschools.net.

GILBERT, LISA MARIE, social studies educator; b. Staten Island, NY, Nov. 19, 1963; m. Addison George Gilbert, Aug. 2, 1962. B in Edn., Fla. Atlantic U., Boca Raton, 1985, BS in Psychology, 1985; MS in Psychology, Nova U., Davie, Fla., 1990—90. Cert. tchr. Fla., 2006. Elem. sch. tchr. Sch. Bd. Palm Beach County, Boca Raton, Fla., 1985—93, social studies tchr., Olympic Heights H.S., 1993—2005, social studies tchr., Pk. Vista H.S. Lake Worth, Fla., 2005—. Cheerleader Miami Dolphins, Miami, 1991—92; fitness instr. Gold's Gym, Boca Raton, 1995—; choreographer drama dept. Olympic Heights H.S., Boca Raton, 1996—2004. Choreographer Into the Fire, 2002 (winner of group musical, state drama convention, 2002). Named Cheerleading Coach of Yr., Palm Beach County Athletic Assn., 1997, Social Studies Tchr. of Yr., Olympic Heights H.S., 2003—04; recipient nominated -Disney Tchr. of Yr., 2002. Mem.: NEA, Phi Kappa Phi, Nat. Thespian Soc. (hon.). Avocations: reading, exercise, dance, tennis, golf. Home: 7137 Michigan Isle Rd Lake Worth FL 33467 Office: Sch Bd Palm Beach County 7900 Jog Rd Lake Worth FL 33467 Office Phone: 561-491-8400. Business E-Mail: gilberl@palmbeach.k12.fl.us.

GILBERT, LUCIA ALBINO, psychology professor; b. Bklyn., July 27, 1941; d. William V. and Carmelina (Cutro) Albino; m. John Carl Gilbert, Dec. 18, 1965; 1 child, Melissa Carlotta. BA, Wells Coll., 1963; MS, Yale U., 1964; PhD, U. Tex., 1974. Lic. psychologist, Tex. Supr. research info. G.S. Gilmore Research Lab., New Haven, 1964-67; tchr. St. Stephen Sch., Austin, Tex., 1967-69; asst. prof. Iowa State U., Ames, 1974-76, U. Tex., Austin, 1976-81, assoc. prof., 1981-86, prof., 1986—, dir. women's studies, 1994—99, vice provost for undergrad. studies, 1999—2006; provost, prof. psychology Santa Clara U., 2006—. Author: Men in Dual Career Families, 1985, Sharing It All: The Rewards and Struggles of Two-Career Families, 1988, Two Careers/One Family: The Promise of Gender Equality, 1993, Gender and Sex in Counseling and Psychotherapy, 1999; editor spl. issue Parenting, Dual Career Families; assoc. editor Psychology of Women Quarterly, 1987—. Recipient Excellence in Teaching award U. Tex., 1981-86, Holland award, 1989, Carolyn Sherif award, 1998. Fellow AAUW, Am. Psychol. Soc., Am. Psychol. Assn. (rep. council 1980-83, 86-89, 93—); mem. Assn. Women in Psychology. Avocations: swimming, progressive country music, ecology, theater. Office: Santa Clara U 204 Walsh Hall 500 El Camino Real Santa Clara CA 95053 Office Phone: 408-554-4533. Office Fax: 408-551-6075. E-mail: lgilbert@scu.edu.

GILBERT, MARGARET P., philosophy professor, researcher; b. England; d. Peter and Miriam Gilbert. DPhil, Oxford U. Prof. philosophy U. Conn., Storrs, 1983—2006; prof., Abraham Melden chair moral philosophy U. Calif., Irvine, 2006—. Vis. prof. Princeton U., NJ, King's Coll., London; vis. fellow Wolfson Coll., Oxford; vis. mem., Herodotus fellow Inst. for Advanced Study, Princeton; rsch. fellow St. Hilda's Coll., Oxford, St. Anne's Coll., Oxford, England; vis. fellow Swedish Collegium for Advanced Study in The Social Scis., Uppsala, Sweden, 2004. Author: On Social Facts, 1989, Living Together: Rationality, Sociality, and Obligation, 1996, Sociality and Responsibility: New Essays in Plural Subject Theory, 2000, Marcher Ensemble: Essais sur les Fondements des Phenomenes Collectifs, 2003. Rsch. fellow, Am. Coun. Learned Socs., 1989—90, NEH fellow, 2003—. Office: U Calif Irvine 201 Humanities Office Bldg 2 Irvine CA 92697 Office Phone: 949-842-6520. E-mail: margaret.gilbert@uci.edu.*

GILBERT, MELISSA, former actors guild executive, actress; b. LA, May 8, 1964; d. Paul and Barbara (Crane) G.; m. Bo Brinkman, 1988 (div. 1994); 1 son, Dakota; m. Bruce Boxleitner, Jan. 1, 1995; 1 son, Michael; stepchildren: Lee, Sam. Student, U. So. Calif. Actress: (TV movies) Little House on the Prairie, 1974, Christmas Miracle in Caulfield, U.S.A., 1977, The Miracle Worker, 1979, The Diary of Anne Frank, 1980, Splendor in the Grass, 1981, Little House: Look Back to Yesterday, 1983, Choices of the Heart, 1983, Little House: Bless All the Dear Children, 1984, Family Secrets, 1984, Little House: The Last Farewell, 1984, Choices, 1986, Penalty Phase, 1986, Family Secrets, Killer Instincts, Without Her Consent, Forbidden Nights, 1990, Blood Vows: The Story of a Mafia Wife, Joshua's Heart, 1990, Donor, The Lookalike, 1990, Conspiracy of Silence: The Shari Karney Story, 1992, With Hostile Intent, 1993, Shattered Trust, 1993, House of Secrets, 1993, Dying to Remember, 1993, Cries From the Heart, 1994, Against Her Will: The Carrie Buck Story, 1994, The Babymaker: The Dr. Cecil Jacobson Story, 1994, Danielle Steel's 'Zoya', 1995, Christmas in My Hometown, 1996, Seduction in a Small Town, 1996, Childhood Sweetheart, 1997, Her Own Rules, 1998, Murder at 75 Birch, 1999, Switched at Birth, 1999, A Vision of Murder: The Story of Donielle, 2000, Sanctuary, 2001, Then Came Jones, 2003; (TV series) Little House on the Prairie, 1974-82, Little House: A New Beginning, 1983, Stand By Your Man, 1992, Sweet Justice, 1994-95 (TV spls.) Battle of the Network Stars, 1978, 79, 81, 82, Celebrity Challenge of the Sexes, 1980, Circus Lions, Tigers and Melissa, Too, 1977, Dean Martin Celebrity Roast, 1984, (stage prodns.) Night of 100 Stars, 1982, The Glass Menagerie, 1985, A Shayna Maidel, 1987 (Outer Critics Circle Award), (feature films) Nutcracker Fantasy, 1979, Sylvester, 1985, Ice House, 1989. Mem.: SAG (pres. 2001—05).

GILBERT, PAMELA, strategic services company executive; b. New Brunswick, NJ, Oct. 3, 1958; m. Charles R.E. Lewis, 1995; one child; one stepchild. BA, Tufts U., Medford, MA, 1980; JD, NYU, 1984. NY and DC bar assocs. Dir. consumer program U.S. Pub. Interest Rsch. Group, Washington; dir. Pub. Citizens Congress Watch, Washington; legis. counsel Malkin & Ross, Washington; exec. dir. Consumer Product Safety Commn., Bethesda, Md., 1996-2001; COO, M&R Strategic Svcs., Washington, 2001—. Office: M&R Strategic Svcs 2120 L St NW Ste 400 Washington DC 20037 E-mail: pgilbert@mrss.com.

GILBERT, RUTH ELIZABETH, inpatient obstetric nurse; b. Damariscotta, Maine, Aug. 25, 1950; d. Harry Elwood and Dorothy May (Richards) Percival; m. Raymond Scott Gilbert, Nov. 16, 1974. BS in Edn., Portland Gorham U. of Maine, 1973; A. in Nursing, U. Maine, Augusta, 1975. RNC inpatient obstetrics; cert. BLS, ACLS, neonatal resuscitation provider, nurses aide. Nurse aide Miles Hosp., Damariscotta, 1973-75, nurse, 1975-77, Parkview Meml. Hosp., Brunswick, Maine, 1977—. Health officer Town of Alna, 1975-79. Mem. AWHONN, Internat. Childbirth Educators Assn., Wiscasset Yacht Club (sec. 1992-93, membership com. chmn. 1993-94, rear comdr. 1994-96, vice comdr. 1996-98) Commodore (1998-99), Lamaze Internat. Avocations: sailing, knitting, sewing.

GILBERT, SANDEE R., art educator; d. Herbert Edward and Amanda Christine Sterling; m. Edward Raymond Gilbert, Apr. 3, 1971; children: Diane Christine, Sharon Corrine. BS in Art Edn., Kutztown U., 1971; profl.

cert. art tchr. K-12, West Chester U., 1987, profl. cert. mental and phys. handicapped, 2001. Art tchr. Devereux Kanner Learning Ctr., West Chester, Pa., 1972—75, 1986—, substitute tchr., 1984—86. Mem. adv. bd. 4H Chester County, West Chester, 1983—86, treas., 1985—. Named Outstanding Tchr., Friends of Seashore House Hosp. Avocations: flower arranging, jewelry design, children's murals. Office: Kanner Learning Ctr 390 E Boot Rd West Chester PA 19380 Office Phone: 610-431-8100.

GILBERT, SARA, actress; b. Jan. 29, 1975; d. Harold Abeles and Barbara Gilbert. Actor: (TV series) Roseanne 1988-97, Twins, 2005-, (TV movies) Sudie & Simpton, 1990, Calamity Jane, Broken Record, 1997, (TV spls.) ABC Weekend Spl., 1988, Valvolene Nat. Driving Test, 1989, 4th Ann. Am. Comedy Awards, 1990, Tom Arnold: The Naked Truth, 1991, In a New Light, 1992, 43 Ann. Foley's Thanksgiving Day Parade, 1992, CBS Schoolbreak Spls., 1992, (syndicated game show) Fun House, 1989, (talk show) At Rona's, 1989, (film) Poison Ivy, 1992, Outside Providence, 1998, Desert Blue, 1998, $30, 1999, Light It Up, 1999, The Big Tease, 1999, High Fidelity, 2000, Boys Life 3, 2000, Riding in Cars with Boys, 2001.

GILBERT-BARNESS, ENID F., pathologist, educator; b. Sydney, Australia, May 31, 1927; arrived in U.S., 1952, naturalized, 1975; d. Christian Henry and Mabel (Milne) Fischer; m. James Bryson Gilbert, Aug. 12, 1954; children: Mary M., Elizabeth A., James C. (dec.), Jennifer E., Rebecca D.; m. Lewis Barness, July 5, 1987. MBBS, U. Sydney, 1950, MD, 1983, MD (hon.), 1999; DSc (hon.), U. Wis., 1999; MD (hon.), U. Sydney, 2004. Diplomate Am. Bd. Pediat., Am. Bd. Clin. Pathology, Am. Bd. Anatomical Pathology, Am. Bd. Pediat. Pathology. Resident Children's Hosp., Boston, Phila., Washington, Brackenridge Hosp., Austin, Tex.; from asst. prof. to assoc. prof. U. W.Va., 1963-70; from assoc. prof. pathology and pediats. to prof. U. Wis., Madison, 1970-93, Disting. Med. Alumni prof., 1986-93, dir. pediat. pathology, 1970-93, prof. emeritus pathology and pediat., 1993—, Disting. Med. Alumni prof. emeritus, 1993—; prof. pathology, pediats. and ob-gyn. U. So. Fla., 1993—. Mem. editl. bds. Pediat. and Devel. Path. Med. jours., 1986—. Author: Introduction to Pathology, 1978, Genetic Aspects Developmental Pathology, 1987, Potters Pathology of the Fetus and Infant, 1997, Atlas Infant and Fetal Pathology, 1998, Metabolic Diseases, 2000, Atlas Embryo Fetal Pathology, 2004, Clinical Use of Pediatric Diagnostic Tests, 2003, Pediatric Autopsy Pathology, 2004; also numerous chpts., articles. Decorated Order of Australia; recipient Disting. Pathologist award, Royal Coll. Pathologists (Australia), 2002; grantee, NIH, 1972—92. Mem. Am. Soc. Clin. Pathology, Soc. Pediat. Pathology (pres. 1986-87), Internat. Acad. Pathology, Internat. Pediat. Pathology Assn. (pres. 1990-92), Teratology Soc., Cardiovasc. Soc. S.Am. (hon.), Am. Pediat. Soc., Am. Acad. Pediat., U.S. Can. Acad. Pathology, Arthur Purdy Stout Soc. Surg. Pathology, N.Y. Acad. Sci., Alpha Omega Alpha. Republican. Avocation: writing. Home: 3301 Bayshore Blvd #403 Tampa FL 33629 Office: Tampa Gen Hosp Dept Pathology Tampa FL 33601 Office Phone: 813-844-7565. Business E-Mail: egilbert@tgh.org.

GILBERTI, SHAUNA, music educator; b. Quincy, Calif., Mar. 30, 1980; d. Robert (Bob) Fausto and Susan Marie Gilberti. MusB in Edn., U. Nev., Reno, 2002. Dir. band & choir Sparks Mid. Sch., Nev.; dir. band Mendocino Unified Sch. Dist., Calif. Instr. clarinet Lake Tahoe Music Camp, Nev.; asst. dir. band Sugar Loaf Fine Arts Camp, Eldorado County, Calif.; prin. clarinetist Reno Pops Orch.; clarinetist Nev. Opera, Reno Philharm. Mem.: Nev. Music Educators Assn., Music Educators Nat. Conf.

GILBERT-STRAWBRIDGE, ANNE WIELAND, journalist; b. Chgo. d. David and Joy (Arnold) Wiel; m. George Gale Gilbert III (dec.); children: Douglas Gilbert, Christopher Gilbert; m. James Murry Strawbridge. BS, Northwestern U. Columnist Chgo. Daily News, 1971-78, United Features Syndicate, 1978-81; reporter NBC-TV Sunday in, Chgo., 1973; guest expert NBC-TV, N.Y.C. Today, 1974—. Mem. Newspapers Features Coun. Prodr.: WSNS-TV spl. Collectors World, 1971; performer: (TV series) KETC-TV, 1975, 1977; owner syndicated radio spot Antique Detective; author: Antique Hunters Guide: For Freaks and Fanciers, 1974, Collecting the New Antiques, 1975, How to be an Antiques Detective, 1978, Investing in the Antiques Market, 1980, Collectors Guide to American Illustrator Art, 1991, Design and Memorabilia 40s-50s, 1995, Design and Memorabilia 70s-80s, 1996, Collecting of Quilts; columnist: Antique Detective, 1983—2002. Mem.: Soc. Illustrators (assoc.), Alpha Gamma Delta. Presbyterian. Address: 854 Pruitt Cove Rd Laurel Springs NC 28644-8349 Office Phone: 336-359-2829. Personal E-mail: antique1@skybest.com.

GILBERT-TIEGS, MARION ANN, gifted and talented educator, consultant; b. Donora, Pa., Jan. 24, 1927; d. Walter C. and Madelyn Elaine Grantham; m. Albert D. Gilbert (div.); children: Eric Gilbert, Richard Gilbert; m. Frank Tiegs, May 5, 1996 (dec.). BS in Psychology, U. Pitts., 1950; MS in Edn., Ill. State U., Normal, 1970; EdD, Ill. State U., Normal, 1980. Tchr. We. Sch. Dist., Buda, Ill., 1968—78; adminstr. Ill. State Bd. Edn., Springfield, Ill., 1988—91, ret., 1991. Cons. Gifted Area Svc. Ctr., Bloomington, Ill.; gifted edn. del. to China Person to Person, gifted edn. del. to Russia, 2006. Gifted edn. del. Person to Person, China, 2005, Russia, 2006; mem. LWV. Mem.: Gifted Assn. for Gifted Children, Nat. Assn. Gifted Children. Independent. Protestant. Avocations: reading, travel, skiing. Home: 7367 Country Club Dr Pinetop AZ 85935

GILBREATH, SARAH BURKHART GELBACH, health facility administrator; b. Hagerstown, Md., Feb. 21, 1913; d. George and Carolyne Backer (Knode) Gelbach; m. Ylan Kailo Kealoha, Aug. 21, 1936 (dec. Nov. 9, 1944); 1 child, Ylan K. Kealoha; m. Junious Dewey Gilbreath, Apr. 13, 1946. BS in Edn., NYU, 1942. RN N.Y., lifetime Red Cross nurse. Newspaper reporter Herald Mail Publ. Co., Hagerstown, 1929—31; supr., instr. N.Y.C. Dept. Hosps., Seaview, S.I., 1934—36, supr. dept. Kings County, Bklyn., 1936—39, supr., ednl. dir. Goldwater Rsch. Hosp. Welfare Island, 1939—41; asst. dir. nurses Goldwater Rsch. Hosp., Welfare Island, 1941—46; supr. Kendall Hosp. Dade County Hosp. Sys., Fla., 1948—64; supr. Morris County Nursing Home, Morris Plains, NJ, 1964—74. Author (under pen name S. Burkhart Gilbreath): (book) Prayers of the Amwell Valley, 1987, Henry Stafford Little, Lawyer, 1993, Professor Benjamin B. Warfield, Princeton Clergy, 1996, Prayerful Praise-Sing Again in the Garden, 1999; contbr. poetry to various publs. Nurse Army Res. Hosp. Unit, N.Y. Harbor, Governor's Island, NY, 1939—45. Republican. Presbyterian. Home: PO Box 217 Quincy PA 17247

GILCHREST, BARBARA ANN, dermatologist; b. Port Chester, N.Y., 1945; MD, Harvard U., 1971. Diplomate Am. Bd. Dermatology, Am. Bd. Internal Medicine. Intern Boston City Hosp., 1971-72, resident internal medicine, 1972-73, resident dermatology, 1973-76; fellow photobiology Harvard U., Boston, 1974-75; chief dermatology U. Hosp., Boston, Boston City Hosp. (now Boston Med. Ctr.); prof., chmn. dermatology Boston U. Sch. Medicine, 1985—. Mem. AAAS, Am. Acad. Dermatology, Assn. Am. Physicians, Am. Soc. for Clin. Investigation, Inst. Medicine, Soc. for Investigative Dermatology. Office: Boston U Sch Medicine Dermatology 609 Albany St # J507 Boston MA 02118-2515

GILCHRIST, E. BRENDA, writer, freelance/self-employed editor; (parents Am. citizens); d. Huntington and Elizabeth (Brace) Gilchrist. BA, Smith Coll., 1951. Asst. Durlacher Bros. Art Gallery, NYC, 1954—57; art adminstrv. asst. Brussels World's Fair, Belgium, 1957—58; fundraiser Mus. Modern Art, NYC, 1959—62; reporter Show Mag., NYC, 1962—64; staff writer Am. Heritage Pub. Co., NYC, 1964; sr. editor Praeger Pubs., NYC, 1965—75; publs. editor Cooper-Hewitt Mus., NYC, 1976—81; freelance editor, writer, pub. Deer Isle, Maine, 1981—. Bd. dirs. Drawing Soc., mem. exec. com., 1960—. Author: (books) Yoga Mooseana Book, 2000, Flimflam for a Nephew: A Tale of Chairs, 2001, Paws for Peace, 2002, Gabi's Doggone Totally Awesome Guide to Maine, 2003; translator: Marc Chagall: The Ceiling of the Paris Opera (Jacques Lassaigne), 1966; editor: American Art & Artists Series, 1971—75; gen. editor Smithsonian Illustrated Library of Antiques, 1976—81, pub. (books) Braceypoint Press, 2000—; author: Eggemoggin Reach Review, 2004. Mem.: Victorian Soc. Am., Am. Assn. Mus., Coll. Art Assn., Soc. Archtl. Historians, Deer Isle Writers Group, Maine Writers and Pubs. Alliance, Deer Isle Yacht Club.

GILCRIST, TRACY ANN, science educator; b. Concord, Calif., Aug. 8, 1960; d. Albert and Janet Garcia; m. Robert Gilcrist, June 28, 1981; children: Seth, Leah, Heather. BS, Calif. Poly. State U., San Luis Obispo, 1982. Tchg. credential Calif. Sci. tchr. Vallejo Unified Sch. Dist., Calif., 1994—95, Lodi Unifed Sch. Dist., Calif., 1995—97; sci./agr. tchr. Tracy HS, Calif., 1997—99; sci. /computers/rsch. tchr. Delhi HS, Calif., 1999—2000; sci. tchr. Stella Brockman Sch., Manteca, Calif., 2000—01; acad. sci. tchr. Monte Vista HS, Danville, Calif., 2001—. Lead tchr. rsch. and tech. acad. Monte Vista HS, 2005—. Retail vendor chmn. Livermore (Calif.) Scottish Games, 2005—. Grantee San Ramon Valley Edn. Found., 2004, 2005, 2006, Toyota Tapestry, 2006, Partnership grantee, Chevron, 2006; scholar Outstanding scholar, Nat. U., 1997. Office: Monte Vista HS 3131 Stone Valley Rd Danville CA 94526 Office Phone: 925-552-5530.

GILES, AUDREY ELIZABETH, reference librarian; b. Menomonie, Wis., Oct. 31, 1931; d. Walter Fredrick and Gladys Merle (Drake) Stewart; m. Joe B. Giles, Nov. 18, 1950 (div. July 1979); children: Joe C., Fred A., Mark J., Laura E., John A. AS, North Ark. Cmty. Coll., 1977; BS in Edn., U. Ark., 1979; MLS, Tex. Womans U., 1987. Kindergarten tchr. Berryville Schs., Ark., 1979-84, KISD, Killeen, Tex., 1984-86; libr. Ark. Tech. U., Russellville, 1989-90; reference libr. U. of Mary Hardin Baylor, Belton, Tex., 1991—97; ret., 1997. Cons. libr. Fray Bartolme Libr., San Cristobal de las Casas, Chiapas, Mex., 1988; info. specialist Midwives Info. Libr. and Resource Ctr., London, 1987. Mem. ALA, AAUW, Tex. Libr. Assn., Am. Soc. Indexers, Assn. of Christian Librs., Kappa Delta Pi. Baptist. Avocations: swimming, walking.

GILES, DEBRA B., gifted and talented educator; b. Portsmouth, Va., Feb. 3, 1954; d. Harry Milton, Jr. and Janey (Wilman) Braudrick; m. Charle K. Giles, Oct. 23, 1975; children: Heather Giles Charlton, Justin Patrick Charlton. A in Elem. Edn., Tidewater CC, Virginia Beach, Va., 1973; BS in Elem. Edn., Old Dominion U., Norfolk, Va., 1975; MEd, Salisbury U., Md., 2005. Cert. early childhood tchr. Md. Tchr. Norfolk Pub. Sch., Worcester County Pub Sch.s, Newark, Md. Chair Gov's Green Schs., Balt. Named Tchr. of Yr., Pecomoke Elem., 1995, 1997, Md. State Tchr. of Yr., Johns Hopkins U., Balt., 2003; recipient Tech. cert., Worcester Pub. Sch., 2005. Mem.: Delta Kappa Gamma. Democrat. Methodist. Avocations: gardening, crafts, reading. Home: 1909 Kipling Dr Salisbury MD 21801 Office: Pocomoke Elem Sch 2119 Pocompke Beltway Pocomoke City MD 21851

GILES, JUDITH MARGARET, minister, educator, real estate broker; b. Sonora, Calif., Nov. 20, 1939; d. James Wilson and Phyllis Sue (Stafford) G. BA, Calif. State U., 1982; MA, Regent U., Virginia Beach, Va., 1986; A. Ministry, Christ for the Nations, Dallas, 1974; postgrad., Trinity Theol. Sem., 1996. Real estate broker Mason McDuffie, Berkeley, Calif., 1975-77, Taylor Realty, Sonora, Calif., 1978-82; pres., adminstr., instr. Christ for the People, Pleasant Hill, Calif., 1975-77; adminstr., pres. Mt. Zion Ministries, Dallas, 1977—98; instr. Calif. Assn. Realtors, Sacramento, 1980-82; adminstrv. asst., instr. Air Force Chaplaincy, Washington, 1983-84; asst. media/press coordinator Nat. Religious Broadcasters, Washington, 1983-86; grad. teaching asst. Regent U., Virginia Beach, Va., 1984-86; instr. Global Outreach Bible Inst., Modesto, Calif., 1987-92; real estate broker Weeks Real Estate, Modesto, Calif., 1987-94; assoc. prof. Southwestern Assemblies of God U., Waxahachie, Tex., 1994—2004; pres. Judith Giles Ministries, 1999—; assoc. prof. Speech Comms. Inst., Lansing C.C., Mich., 2005—. Lectr. in field; communications cons.; radio commentator; TV guest host. Author: A Historical Overview of the Women's Movement in America, 1986; producer, dir. TV documentary: The United Jewish Fedn., 1985, What's in a Name, 1985, Chiropractic, Lutheran Council, 1984. Mgr. pub. relations dir. South Lake Tahoe Community Choir, 1971. Mem. Calif. Assn. Realtors, Nat. Assn. Realtors, Women's Club, Pres.'s Club, Rainbow Girls. Republican. Avocations: golf, history, films, water sports, travel. Office Phone: 517-575-9380. E-mail: judigiles@aol.com.

GILES, KATHARINE EMILY (J. K. PIPER), retired administrative assistant, writer; b. Jackson Hole, Wyo., Jan. 9, 1938; d. William Lamar and Grace Hawley (Domrose) G.; children: Piper Lee Shanks, John Richard Hamlin. Diamond cert., Gemological Inst. Am., 1971. Adminstrv. asst. Matthiesen Equipment Co., San Antonio, 1993-96; driver USA Truck, Van Buren, Ark., 1996—. Top Gun, USA Truck, 148,900 accident free miles, 1997; 147,100, 1998. Author: The Marvelous Bean, 1989, The Lost Trident, 1991, The Missing Crystal, 1992, Jewel of Avalon, 1992, The Lost Kingdom, 1991, The Desert Sun, 1992, The Fire Sled, 1991, Knights of Glass, 1992, Black Pagoda, 1992, Memories from the Kitchen of Grace & Rich Williams, 1992, My Recipe Box, 2000. Home: 6700 Jefferson Paige Rd Lot 265 Shreveport LA 71119-4905 Personal E-mail: archer1@bellsouth.net.

GILES, KATHLEEN C., headmaster; m. Ralph Giles; children: Kait, Daniel, Eileen. AB in English and Am. Lit. magna cum laude, Radcliffe Coll.; JD cum laude, Harvard Law Sch. Teaching intern Groton Sch., coach; assoc. Gaston Snow, Boston; law clerk to Chief Justice Vincent McKusick Supreme Judicial Ct., Maine; coll. advisor Groton Sch., 1985—96, asst. dean of academic affairs, 1996—2002, dean of academic affairs, 2002—03; head of sch. Middlesex Sch., Concord, Mass., 2003—. Mem.: Phi Beta Kappa. Office: Middlesex Sch 1400 Lowell Rd Concord MA 01742-9122 Office Phone: 978-371-6537.

GILES, LYNDA FERN, clinical psychologist; b. Detroit, May 18, 1943; d. Samuel and Shirley (Finkelstein) S.; m. David Reuven Schenk, Sept. 5, 1965 (div. July 1975); children: Jared, Jamie; m. Conrad Leslie Giles, Nov. 26, 1978. BA, U. Mich., 1965, PhD, 1989; MSW, Wayne State U., 1977; PhD in Edn.-Psychology, U. Mich., 1989. Cert. social worker, clin. social worker. Clin. psychologist Counseling Assocs. Inc., Southfield, Mich., 1977—. Mem. com. on identity and affiliation Jewish Welfare Fedn., Detroit, 1985-88, com. on univ. rels., 1987—, com. on edn., 1987—, v.p. Agy. Jewish edn., 1995-97, pres. 1998-2000; v.p. Jewish Fedn. Metro Detroit, 2003—; mem. United Jewish Cmtys., 2005—, bd. trustees, 2005—. Mem. APA, Counseling Assocs. (chmn. Southfield gifted and talented program 1979-81), Mich. Soc. Clin. Social Workers. Clubs: Franklin Country. Democrat. Avocations: tennis, skiing. Home: 6300 Westmoor Rd Bloomfield Hills MI 48301-1359 Office: Counseling Assocs Inc 25835 Southfield Rd Southfield MI 48075-1827

GILES, PATRICIA CECELIA PARKER, retired art educator, graphic designer; b. Chgo., Mar. 8, 1925; d. Frederick Louis and Bernice Clara (Kennedy) Parker; m. Lewis Wentworth Giles, June 20, 1946 (div. 1960); children: Alan Julian, Kay Celeste. BS in Fine Arts, U. Ill., Urbana, 1946; postgrad., Howard U., Washington D.C., 1947, U. Mass., Amherst, 1974-75, Washington Sch. Psychology, 1962. Reg. sec. tchr. art Ill., 1972. Sec. tchr. art Randall Jr. High, Washington, D.C., 1947-48; art cons. Elem. Sch., Washington, 1952-53; tchr., chmn. art dept. Theodore Roosevelt H.S., Washington, 1959-60, Boys Sr. H.S., Washington, 1961-63, Carter G. Woodson Jr. H.S., Washington, 1963-72, Howard D. Woodson Sr. H.S., Washington, 1973-85; mgr. Foreverl Living Products, Washington, 1985—. V.p. D.C. Art Assn., 1964-65; cons. art-math. with humanities Upward Bounders U. Md., College Park, 1966-67; potential supr. of student tchg. in art therapy Planning Program Staff George Washington U., Washington, 1972; visual arts coord. D.C. Congress PTA Cultural Arts, Washington, 1972; artist-in-residence Washington Srs. Wellness Ctr., 1987-88, 97—, art therapist, 2002—; tennis instr. Tenn. Edn. Found.; calligraphy instr. D.C. Parks and Recreation, 1993, 34th Smithsonian Folklife Festival, 2000. Painter: (oil painting) Mud and Roots, 1971 (award), Mural: Infinite Joy, 1991 (Golden Dolphins Commendation award 1991), Kenkin, oils, 1992 (award); author: (poetry) Mud and Roots, 1976; illustrator: (children's book) Short Fuzzy Hair, 1999; exhibited at Benning Pub. Libr., Washington, 1962, two Washington pub. librs., 2002, M.L. King Pub. Libr., Washington, 2004, Brown Pub. Sch., 2005, Southeast, Georgetown, and Northwest Wash. DC Post Offices; designer schedule cover emblem, Washington Pub. Schs., 1976 (Flower Club award). Taught art workshop in cmty. Fort DuPont Civic Assn., Washington, 1960, defining creative art WOOK-TV, Washington, 1963, comparing and interacting with cultures and govts. Am. Forum for Internat. Study, Senegal, Ghana, Ethiopia, Kenya, Tanzania, 1970; peer leader in tennis and yoga Washington Seniors Wellness Ctr., Washington, 1995—; charter mem. Nat. Mus. Art Women. Recipient Commendation award, Ft. DuPont Civic Assn., Washington, 1960, 1st prize for watercolor, Arch.'s Wives Assn., 1962, Gold medal, D.C. Sr. Olympics in Tennis, 1993, 1995—97, Silver medal, 1998—99, Gold medal in Swimming, 1993, 2d Pl. trophy, NATA, 2001, 2 Gold medals, Sr. Olympics in Tennis, 2000, Am. Tennis Assn. Nat. Competition, 65 Doubles, Silver Plate (2d. Pl.), 2002, U.S. Tennis Assn./Mid-Atlantic Sectional Orgn. of the Yr. award, 2002, Dir. of Yr. award, Wash. Seniors Wellness Ctr., Tennis Set., U.S. Tennis Assn., Wash. Tennis Assn. Orgn., 2002, Gold medal in singles, D.C. Sr. Olympics, 2004, Silver medal in doubles, 2004. Mem.: Am. Art League Inc., Nat. Conf. of Artists, U.S. Tennis Assn. (pres.), U.S. Wash. Tennis Assn. (Outstanding and Dedicated Svc. award 2005, 80th Birthday Tennis award 2005), U.S. Nat. Tennis Assn., Deltakas Social Club, Swim Club Golden Dolphins (Outstanding Swimming Trophy 1993), Alpha Kappa Alpha. Democrat. Seventh Day Adventist. Avocations: tennis, swimming, yoga, gardening, painting. Home: 3942 Blaine St NE Washington DC 20019-3333

GILES, PATTY DAWN, school librarian; BS in Secondary Math Edn., Northeastern State U., 1994; MS in Instrnl. Tech., Ark. Tech U., 1999. Tchr. math. Arkoma (Okla.) H.S., 1994—98; libr. media specialist Poteau (Okla.) H.S., 1998—. Mem.: NEA, Okla. Edn. Assn. So. Bapt. Avocations: dance, reading. Office: Poteau High School 100 Pirate Lane Poteau OK 74953 Office Phone: 918-647-7716. Business E-Mail: gilesp@phs.poteau.k12.ok.us.

GILFILEN, TERI, artist; b. Columbia, S.C., Aug. 25, 1953; d. William Lee and Hilma Rehard Thomas; m. Dennis Jordan Gilfilen, June 30, 1973; children: Andrea Lee Hanson, Michael Jordan Gilfilen. Student, Ohio State U., 1971-73. Artist-in-sch. Dublin Mid. Sch., Ohio, 1988; mem. selection com. Dublin C. of C., 1987-88; presenter workshops in field. Artist: (book) Best of Watercolor, 1995; contbr. art to profl. jours. (Top 200 award 1994); one-woman shows include Zanesville Art Mus., Ohio, 1992, Middletown Arts Ctr., Ohio, 1994, The Ohio State U., Columbus, 1998. Mem. adv. bd. Dublin Cmty. Ctr., 1988. Mem. Nat. Acrylic Painters Assn. (Gold award 1999, CK award 1999), Salmagundi Nat. Assn. (Kanisky award 1995), Ohio Watercolor Soc. (trustee 1990, 94), Am. Artists Profl. League, Ky. Watercolor Soc. Avocations: fly fishing, archaeology, kayaking. Home: 1203 Sandoway Ln Delray Beach FL 33483-7133

GILFILLEN, REBECCA, soil scientist, educator; b. Ohio; BS in Biol. Scis., No. Ky. U., Highland Heights, 1989; MS in Agronomy, U. Ky., Lexington, 1994; PhD in Plant and Soil Scis., U. Tenn., Knoxville, 1999. Assoc. prof. soil sci. Western Ky. U., Bowling Green, 1998—. Contbr. articles to profl. jours. Named Outstanding Grad. Tchg. Asst., U. Tenn. Coll. Agrl. Scis. and Natural Resources, 1998, Outstanding Conservation Educator, Warren County Conservation Dist., 2002; Waste Mgmt. Rsch. grantee, USDA-ARS, 2001—06, Leaf Composting grantee, Bowling Green Mcpl. Utilities, 1998—2006. Mem.: Soil and Water Conservation Soc. (assoc.), Am. Soc. Agronomy (assoc.). Avocations: hiking, camping, needlecrafts, knitting, sewing. Office: Western Ky U 1906 College Heights Blvd # 41066 Bowling Green KY 42101-1066 Office Phone: 270-745-5970. Office Fax: 270-745-5972. Business E-Mail: becky.gilfillen@wku.edu.

GILFOYLE, NATHALIE FLOYD PRESTON, lawyer; b. Lynchburg, Va., May 4, 1949; d. Robert Edmund and Dorothea Henry (Ward) Gilfoyle; m. Christopher Y.W. Ma, Sept. 9, 1978; children: Olivia Otey. Rohan James. BA, Hollins Coll., 1971; JD, U. Va., 1974. Bar: Mass. 1974, D.C. 1977. Staff counsel Rate Setting Commn., Boston, 1974-76; ptnr. Peabody, Lambert & Meyers, Washington, 1976-84, McDermott, Will and Emery, 1984-96; gen. counsel Am. Psychol. Assn., 1996—. Bd. dirs. ACLU Nat. Capital Area, Washington, 1980-83, St. Columbia's Nursery Sch., 1992-99, D.C. Bar Atty. Client Arbitration bd., chmn., 1994-95. Mem.: ABA, Mass. Bar Assn., Women's Bar Assn., DC Bar Assn. (legal ethics com. 1999—2001, gen. counsel 2002—04, bd. govs. 2004—). Office: Am Psychol Assn 750 1st St NE Washington DC 20002-4241 Office Phone: 202-336-6186. Business E-Mail: ngilfoyle@apa.org.

GILHAM, HANNA KALTENBRUNNER, writer; b. Linz, Austria, July 1, 1943; arrived in U.S., 1977; d. Werner and Marianne Kaltenbrunner; m. Royce Edward Gilham, Sept. 13, 1971. BA, East Carolina U., Greenville, 1994. Office worker Teekanne, Salzburg, Austria, 1959—64; ground hostess Lufthansa, Frankfurt, Germany, 1965—66; distbr. Oefag Car Dealership, Salzburg, 1966—67; receptionist Europea Hotel Mirabell, Salzburg, 1968—71. Author: Sechsundsechzig Seiten, 1996, The Secret Rock, 1997, The King, Short Stories, 1998, Poetry, 1999, Elite, 2000, CET, Color Equals Time, 2000, Gravity, 2001, VS-VE=EA, 2002, Five Pieces, Five Narrative Renderings on Cloning, 2002, MS to VS-VE=EA, Mathematical Solution to Volume Sun Minus Volume Earth Equals Earth's Age, 2005, Die Fruehen, 2005. Roman Catholic. Avocation: painting. Home: 401 Summit St Greenville NC 27858 Office Phone: 252-758-7322.

GILHAM, JENNIFER ERIN, physical education educator, soccer coach; b. Buffalo, Dec. 17, 1976; d. Ronald S. and Judith A. Benson; m. Derek L. Gilham, July 29, 2000; 1 child, Mia. BS, Wingate U., N.C., 1999; MS, Canisius Coll., Buffalo, N.Y., 2002. Permanent tchg. cert. N.Y. State. Tchr. phys. edn. Kenmore Town of Tonawanda Union Free Sch. Dist., NY, 2002—. Coach girls varsity soccer Kenmore West H.S., 2003—. Mem.: AAHPERD, Nat. Athletic Tng. Assn. (cert. trainer). Avocations: travel, exercise. Office: Thomas Jefferson Elem Athens Blvd Kenmore NY 14223 Office Phone: 719-874-8418. E-mail: erin0576@aol.com.

GILKES, CHERYL LOUISE TOWNSEND, sociologist, educator, minister; b. Boston, Nov. 2, 1947; d. Murray Luke Jr. and Evelyn Annette (Reid) Townsend. BA, MA, PhD, Northeastern U.; postgrad., Boston U., 1988; DD (hon.), Ursinus Coll., Collegeville, Pa., 2006. Lectr. Univ. Coll. Northeastern U., Boston, 1973-78; instr. sociology Boston State Coll., 1974-78, U. Mass., 1976; asst. prof. sociology Boston U., 1978-87; MacArthur assoc. prof. African-Am. studies and sociology Colby Coll., Waterville, Maine, 1989-2000, MacArthur asst. prof., 1987-89, MacArthur prof. African Am. studies and sociology, 2000—. Vis. lectr. Tufts U., 1974, Ashland Theol. Sem., McCreary Inst., 2006; rsch. assoc., vis. lectr. sociology of religion Harvard U. Div. Sch., 1981-82, vis. lectr. African-Am. religious studies, 1992-93; vis. lectr. Afro-Am. studies Simmons Coll., Chgo. Theol. Sem., 1989, Iliff Sch. Theology, 1989, Temple U., 1989; faculty fellow Bunting Inst., Radcliff Coll., 1982-84; vis. scholar Episcopal Div. Sch., 1992-93; fellow W.E.B. DuBois Inst. for Afro-Am. Rsch., Harvard U., Inst. Advanced Study Religion, Yale U., 1999-2000; host gospel music radio sta. WMHB Waterville, 2002—. Author: If It Wasn't for the Women.: Black Women's Experience and Womanist Culture in Church and Community, 2000; contbr. articles and revs. to profl. jours., chpts. to books. Sec. Cambridge Civic Unity Com., 1978-87; mem. adv. com. Schlessinger Libr., Radcliffe Coll., 1984-86; pres. Cambridge Black Cultural and Hist. Assn., 1978-87; parliamentarian, asst. dean congress Christian Edn. United Bapt. Conv., Mass., R.I. and N.H., 1986—; assoc. min. Union Bapt. Ch., Cambridge, Mass., 1982-97, asst. pastor, 1998—. Nat. Fellowships fund dissertation fellow, 1977-78, Socialization Tng. fellow Northeastern U., 1970-73. Fellow: Inst. Advanced Study Religion; mem.: NAACP, Nat. Coun. Negro Women, Urban League Ea. Mass., Assn. for Sociology of Religion, Soc. Study Black Religion, Soc. Sci. Study of Religion (exec. coun. 1995—97), Sociologists Women in Soc. (lectr. 2002—), Assn. Black Sociologists, Soc. Study of Sybolic Interaction, Am. Acad. Religion, Assn. Humanist Sociology, Soc. Study of Social Problems (v.p. 1990—91), Mass. Sociol. Assn., Ea. Sociol. Soc. (v.p. 1995—96, Robin M. Williams lectr. 1998—99), Am. Sociol. Assn. (Spivak dissertation fellow 1977—78, mem. coun. 1995—98), Delta Sigma Theta, Phi Kappa Phi. Office: Colby Coll Dept Sociology Waterville ME 04901 Office Phone: 207-859-4715.

GILL, ANGELA SUE, clinical psychologist; b. Springfield, Mo., Mar. 8, 1972; d. Ronald Eugene and Connie Sue Gill. BS in Polit. Sci., S.W. Mo. State U., 1994, BS in Psychology, 1994; MA in Clin. Psychology, SW Mo. State U., 1999; PsyD in Psychology, Forest Inst. Profl. Psychology, 2002. Lic. clin. psychologist Mo., cert. pain mgmt. Intern Family Svc. and Guidance Ctr., Topeka, 2001—02, postdoctoral trainee, 2002—03, coord. ADHD program, 2002—04, supr., 2002—04; clin. psychologist St. John's Hosp., Springfield, Mo., 2004—. Mem.: APA. Office: St Johns Springfield MO 65804 Business E-Mail: agill@sprg.mercy.net.

GILL, BECKY LORETTE, retired psychiatrist; b. Phoenix, Mar. 16, 1947; d. David Franklin and Lorette (Cooper) Brinegar; m. Jim Shack Gill, Jr., Aug. 5, 1978. BA in Biology, Stanford U., 1968; MD, U. Ariz., 1973. Diplomate Am. Bd. Psychiatry and Neurology, cert. addiction counselor, substance abuse residential facility dir., addictions specialist, clin. supr. Clerk typist Ariz. Med. Ctr. Med. Libr., Tucson, 1970, asst. ref. libr., 1971; surg. extern Tucson Med. Ctr., summer 1970; med. extern Fed. Reformatory for Women, Alderson, W.Va., 1972-73; commd. lt. USN, 1974, advanced through grades to capt., 1992; intern in medicine USPHS Hosp., Balt., 1973-74; resident in psychiatry Nat. Naval Med. Ctr., Bethesda, Md., 1974-77; head alcohol rehab. svc./substance abuse dept., staff psychiatrist Naval Hosp., Camp Lejeune, N.C., 1977-85, head alcohol rehab. svc./substance abuse dept., head psych. Millington, Tenn., 1985-88, head alcohol rehab. dept. Long Beach, Calif., 1988-94; head Navy Addictions Rehab. and Edn. Dept., Camp Pendleton, Calif., 1994-2001; ret., 2001; owner, mgr. Curves of Chiefland, Fla., 2001—. Mem. tumor bd. Naval Hosp., Camp Lejeune, 1977—85, watch officer Acute Care Clinic, Millington, 1985—86; cons. Tri-Command Consol. Drug and Alcohol Adv. Coun., 1977—85, phys. fitness program com., 1980—85, med. liaison substance abuse, 1982—85, drug/alcohol program advisor, cons., 1983—85; cons. Counseling and Assistance Ctr., 1985—88, mem. bioethics com., chmn. med. records utilization rev. com., 1985—88, mem. exec. com. med. staff, chmn., 1986—87; psychiat. cons. NAS Brig, 1986—88, mem. quality assurance com., mem. pharmacy and therapeutics com., dir. surg. svcs., 1986, mem. credentials com., commd. duty watch officer, 1986—87, dir. med. svcs., 1986—88, watch officer Acute Care Clinic, 1987—88; mem., preceptor to social worker Navy Drug and Alcohol Adv. Coun., 1987—88, mem. pos. mgmt. com., mem. commd. retention coun., 1988; co-owner Curves, Chiefland, Fla., 2006—. Capt. USN. Decorated Legion of Merit. Mem.: Levy County Fla. Humane Soc., Nat. Assn. Alcoholism and Drug Abuse Counselors, Addiction Profls. N.C. (chmn. pub. info. com. 1979—80, eastern regional v.p. 1981—82, chmn. fall meeting planning com. 1983, sec. 1984—85), Am. Soc. Addiction Medicine, Am. Acad. Psychiatrists Alcoholism and Addictions (founding mem.), U.S. Lawn Tennis Assn. (life), U. Ariz. Alumni Assn., Stanford Alumni Assn., VFW Aux., Stanford Cardinal Club, Am. Legion, Stanford Cap and Gown. Democrat. Avocations: tennis, swimming, jogging. Home: PMB 8187 PO Box 2428 Pensacola FL 32513-2428 Office Phone: 352-490-6289.

GILL, DIANE LOUISE, psychology professor, dean; b. Watertown, N.Y., Nov. 7, 1948; d. George R. and Betty J. (Reynolds) G. BS in Edn., SUNY, Cortland, N.Y., 1970; MS, U. Ill., 1974, PhD, 1976. Tchr. Greece Athena High Sch., Rochester, N.Y., 1970-72; asst. prof. U. Waterloo, Ont., Can., 1976-78, U. Iowa, Iowa City, 1979-81, assoc. prof., 1981-86; assoc. prof. sport & exercise psychology U. N.C., Greensboro, 1987-89, prof. Greenboro, 1989—, assoc. dean Greensboro, 1992-97, head dept. exercise and sport sci., 1997-2000, dir. Ctr. for Women's Health and Wellness, 2002—04. Author: Psychological Dynamics of Sport and Exercise, 1986, 2000; editor Jour. of Sport and Exercise Psychology, 1985-90; contbr. articles to profl. jours. Fellow AAHPERD (rsch. consortium pres. 1987-89), APA (pres. divsn. 47 exercise and sport 1999-2001), Am. Psychol. Soc., Assn. for Advancement of Applied Sport Psychology, Am. Acad. Kinesiology and Phys. Edn.; mem. N.Am. Soc. for Psychology of Sport and Phys. Activity (pres. 1988-91). Democrat. Office: U NC Dept Exercise and Sport Sci Greensboro NC 27402-6170 Office Phone: 336-334-4683. Business E-Mail: dlgill@uncg.edu.

GILL, E. ANN, lawyer; b. Elyria, Ohio, Aug. 31, 1951; d. Richard Henry and Laura (Beeler) G.; m. Robert William Hempel, Aug. 4, 1973; children: Richard, Peter, Mary. AB, Barnard Coll., 1972; JD, Columbia U., 1976. Bar: N.Y. 1977, U.S. Supreme Ct. 1982. Assoc. Mudge, Rose, Guthrie & Alexander, NYC, 1976-77, Dewey Ballantine LLP, NYC, 1977-84, ptnr., 1985—2004, Thelen Reid & Priest LLP, NYC, 2004—. Mem. ABA, Nat. Assn. Bond Lawyers. Home: 255 W 90th St New York NY 10024-1109 Office: Thelen Reid & Priest LLP 875 Third Ave New York NY 10022 Office Phone: 212-603-2412. Personal E-mail: agill@thelenreid.com.

GILL, EVALYN PIERPOINT, editor, writer, publisher; b. Boulder, Colo. d. Walter Lawrence and Lou Octavia Pierpoint; m. John Glanville Gill; children: Susan Pierpoint, Mary Louise Glanville. Student, Lindenwood Coll.; BA, U. Colo.; postgrad., U. Nebr., U. Alaska; MA, Ctrl. Mich. U., 1968. Lectr. humanities Saginaw Valley State Coll., University Ctr., Mich., 1968-72; mem. English faculty U. N.C., Greensboro, 1973-74; editor Internat. Poetry Rev., Greensboro, 1975-92; pres. TransVerse Press, Greensboro, 1981—. Author: Poetry by French Women, 1930-1980, 1980, Dialogue, 1985, Southeast of Here: Northwest of Now, 1986, Entrances, 1996; editor: O. Henry Festival Stories, 1985, 87, Women of the Piedmont Triad: Poetry and Prose, 1989, Edge of Our World, 1990, A Turn in Time: Piedmont Writers at the Millennium, 1999. Bd. dirs. Eastern Music Festival, Greensboro, 1981-85, Greensboro Symphony, 1982-86, Greensboro Opera Co., 1982—, Weatherspoon Art Mus., 1980-; chmn. O Henry Festival, 1985, 95. Recipient numerous poetry prizes, Fortner award St. Andrews Coll., 1995, Altrusa Internat. Cmty. Arts award, Greensboro, 1998. Mem. MLA, Amn. Lit. Translators Assn., N.C. Poetry Soc., Phi Beta Kappa. Home: 2900 Turner Grove Dr N Greensboro NC 27455-1977

GILL, JANE ROBERTS, retired psychotherapist, clinical social worker; b. Boston, Dec. 6, 1923; d. Penfield Hitchcock and Cecilia (Washburn) Roberts. Student, Wellesley Coll., 1941-43; BA, Boston U., 1954, MSW, 1956; m. Peter Lawrence Gill, Dec. 24, 1943 (div. 1973); children: Jonathan Penfield, Dorcas Pearson, Nicholas Brinton, Timothy Roberts. Diplomate Clin. Social Work. Social worker Beth Israel Hosp., Boston, 1956-57, S. End Family Program, Boston, 1957-58, Margaret Gifford Sch., Cambridge, Mass., 1963-65; Adams House Psychiat. Clinic, Boston, 1967-76; supr. sr. clin. social work, coord. outpatient clinic, Faulkner Hosp., Boston, 1975-87, instr. family program NAMI, Springfield, Vt., staff mem. The Headache Rsch. Found., 1976-94; pvt. practice psychotherapy, Brookline, 1970-95; ret., 1995; With John R. Graham Headache Ctr., 1970-94; rsch. interviewer Stone Ctr. for Women's Studies, Wellesley Coll., 1989-90; clin. instr. Smith Coll. Sch. of Social Work, 1971-79; Contbr. chpt. to book, papers to profl. meetings; Mem. social svc. com. Am. Heart Assn., 1979-83; program chmn. Mass. Mental Health Ctr. Aux. Bd., 1969-71; bd. dirs. Rutland Corner House, 1982-96, Town of Putney Libr., 1996-2006; cons. to bd. dirs. Putney Cares, 1998-, invited spkr. Brazilian Headach Soc., 1996, poster Internat. Headache Soc., London, 1994, 2002, 04; mem. Dem. Town Com., Newton-Wellesley, 1959-64. Mem. NASW, Acad. Psychosomatic Medicine, Internat. Headache Soc., Internat. Stress and Tension Control Soc., Peacham (Vt.) Hist. Assn., Putney Sch. Alumni Assn. Home: 30 W Hill Rd Putney VT 05346 Personal E-mail: jrgill@sover.net.

GILL, JULIE FRANKS, education educator; b. Alexandria, La., Feb. 17, 1972; d. Sherman and Willie Franks; m. David Ralph Gill, Mar. 29; children: Jaycee, Zachary. BA in Fitness and Wellnes, La. Coll., Pineville, 1996; MEd in Exercise Sci., N.E. La. U., Monroe, 1997; postgrad., La. State U., Baton Rouge, 1999—. Exercise specialist II Rapides Regional Med. Ctr., Alexandria, La., 1997—98; asst. prof. La. State U., Alexandria, 1998—. Bd. dirs., sec. Boys and Girls Clubs Ctrl. La., Alexandria, 2002—. Recipient Cliff E. LaBorde Sr. Endowed Professorship award, La. State U., Alexandria, 2005—06. Mem.: AAHPERD, La. Assn. for Health, Phys. Edn., Recreation & Dance, Am. Coll. Sports Medicine. Republican. Baptist. Avocations: reading, walking. Office: La State Univ 8100 Hwy 71 S Alexandria LA 71302

GILL, KELLEY HENDERSON, elementary school educator; b. Gainesville, Ga., Sept. 28, 1964; d. Luke Knight and Doris Evelyn (Bray) G. BS in Early Childhood Edn., LaGrange Coll., 1986, MEd, 1993; degree in Ednl. Specialist, Troy State U., 2003. Cert. tchr., Ga. 3d grade tchr. Woodbury (Ga.) Elem. Sch., 1986-88; 4th grade and phys. edn. tchr. Manchester (Ga.) Elem. Sch., 1988-92; kindergarten tchr. Warm Springs (Ga.) Elem. Sch., 1992-94, pre-K tchr., 1994—, Mt. View Elem. Sch., Manchester, Ga., 1999—. Mem. Profl. Assn. Ga. Educators. Methodist. Avocations: crafts, music, reading. Office: Mountain View Elem Sch 2600 Judson Bulloch Rd Manchester GA 31816 Office Phone: 706-655-3969, 706-655-3969. Business E-Mail: khenderson@meriwether.12.ga.us.

GILL, LIBBY, television executive; BA in Theater magna cum laude, Calif. State U., Long Beach. Mgr., publicist Embassy Comm. and Columbia Pictures TV, Calif., 1986-89; dir. primetime publicity Columbia Pictures TV/TriStar TV, Calif., 1989-92; v.p. publicity and promotion Sony Pictures Entertainment TV Group, Calif., 1992-94; v.p. pub. rels. west coast Turner Entertainment Group, Calif., 1994-96; sr. v.p. media rels. Universal TV Group, Universal City, Calif., 1996—. Pub. rels. cons. for non-profit orgns., including Deaf Arts Coun. Mem. TV Publicity Execs. Com. (former chmn.).

GILL, LINDA A., advertising executive; b. Buffalo, May 8, 1942; d. Elvin R. Albee and Marian Elizabeth Beardsley; m. W. Richard Davy, Apr. 4, 1964 (div. Oct. 1973); children: Ashley, Jennifer, Kit; m. Edward W. Fallon, June 14, 1992. AS, Endicott Coll., 1962; student, Rutgers U., 1984—85. Sales rep., account mgr. Ciba-Geigy Pharm., Summit, NJ, 1980—87; account supr., v.p. Bozell, N.Y.C., 1987—90; sr. v.p., mgmt. supr. FCB, N.Y.C., 1990—94; exec. v.p., mng. dir. Healthworld, N.Y.C., 1994—. Tchr. music/piano, 1979—87. Recipient Clio award, 1986. Mem.: Healthcare Mktg. and Comm. Coun., Healthcare Bus. Woman's Assn., Jr. League. Avocations: piano, golf, reading, horseback riding. Office: Healthworld 100 6th Ave New York NY 10013 Business E-Mail: fallonle@yahoo.com.

GILL, MADELINE KAY, school and youth counselor; d. Joseph Paul and Earline Hart LeBlanc; m. H. Glenn Gill, Mar. 8, 1974; 1 child, Jason Glenn. Secretarial degree, Massey Bus. Coll., Nacogdoches, Tex., 1970; BEd, Stephen F. Austin U., Nacogdoches, 1979, MEd, 1982. LCSW Tex. Edn. Agy.; cert. mid-mgmt. Tex. Edn. Agy. Sec. Tom Senff, Atty., Nacogdoches, 1970—74; elem. tchr. Joaquin (Tex.) Ind. Sch. Dist., 1979—92; sch. counselor Garrison (Tex.) Ind. Sch. Dist., 1992—2004; youth counselor Joaquin Meth. Ch., 2002—; tutor for youth, dir. MK Leadership & Guidance, Joaquin, 2004—. Mem. Tex. Sch. Initiative, Austin, 2002—03; sec. Garrison Ind. Sch. Dist. Site Base Team, Garrison, 2003—04; cons. MK Leadership & Guidance, Joaquin, 2004—. Author: (guidelines) Seniors to College Freshman. Office mgr. vol. Shelby County Sheriff Office, Joaquin, 2005—; lobbier Tex. Counselor Assn., Austin, 2003—; program dir. Meth. Ch. Youth Program, Joaquin; vol. Tex. Counselor Assn. Growth Conf., El Paso, 2004—05. Named Counselor of Yr., Piney Woods Counseling Assn., 2002. Mem.: ACA (assoc.), Piney Woods Counseling Assn. (sen. 2001—), Tex. Assn. Adult Devel. and Aging (assoc.; sec.), Tex. Counseling Assn. (assoc. Award of Merit 2001—04), Delta Kappa Gamma, Chi Sigma Iota. Democrat. Methodist. Avocations: reading, dance, jet ski, church activities, scrapbooks. Home: 12113 FM 699 Joaquin TX 75954 Office: MK Leadership & Guidance 12113 FM 699 Joaquin TX 75954 Office Phone: 936-248-5307.

GILL, MILVI KOSENKRANIUS, artist, photographer; b. Geislingen, Germany, Sept. 25, 1948; d. Hans Edgar Kosenkranius and Georgine Marie Tomberg; m. Robert Earl Gill, Mar. 14, 1986; m. Robert Bruce Graham, Mar. 23, 1974 (div. Dec. 2, 1985); children: Dean James Graham, Alan Robert Graham. BA in Art History magna cum laude, U. Md. European Divsn., Brussels, 1992; cert. in Iconography, St. John of Damascus Sacred Art Acad., Ligonier, Pa., 1999. Cert. sys. adminstr. WANG Labs., Arlington, Va., 1987. Various office positions U.S. Army, Navy, Smithsonian Instn., NIH, Washington, 1973—83; office adminstrn. Smithsonian Instn., Washington, 1982—83, Office Sec. of Def., Arlington, 1983—84, Office Joint Chiefs of Staff, Arlington, 1984—88, NATO, Brussels, 1988—89; artist Old Towne Art Gallery, Fredericksburg, Va., 1993—98, Brush Strokes Gallery, Fredericksburg, 2004—, Edgy Studios, Fredericksburg, 2005—. Photographer (exhbn.) Corner Window, Fredericksburg (1st Pl., Bldg. and Arch. Category, 2005), Below Deck (Hon. Mention, Enhanced Photography, 2005), Old Vine (3d Pl., Buildings and Arch., 1995); exhibitions include Madonna and Child, The Plains, Va. (1st Pl., Mixed Media, 1994), Hanover Street Balcony, Fredericksburg (Hon. Mention, 2004), Bills (Hon. Mention, Drawing Category, 1994), Byzantine Angel (Hon. Mention, Mixed Media, 1995), Mary and Child, Old Towne Art Gallery (1st Pl., 1997), Father's Day (2nd Pl., 1997). Treas. Banner Plantation Homeowners Assn., Fredericksburg, 1998—2004; team leader Therapy Dogs Internat., Inc., Fredericksburg, 1996—2004; sponsor Christian Children's Fund, Richmond, Va., 1980—2006; treas. ASPCA, Fredericksburg, 1997—98, team leader, vis. pet program, 1994—98. Recipient Neighbors in Action - Adult Vol. of Yr., Rappahannock United Way, 1998, Best Essay, U. Md. European Divsn., 1991. Mem.: AAUW (assoc.), Nat. Mus. for Women in the Arts (assoc.), Fredericksburg Ctr. for Creative Arts (assoc.; ednl. com. 2005—06). Lutheran. Avocations: art workshops, computer graphics, travel, gardening. Home: 12720 Isle of Pines Blvd Fredericksburg VA 22407 Office: Brush Strokes Gallery 810 Caroline St Fredericksburg VA 22401 Office Phone: 540-368-0560. Personal E-mail: milvig@msn.com.

GILL, NIA H., state legislator; b. Mar. 15, 1948; BA in History and Polit. History, Upsala Coll.; JD, Rutgers Law Sch. Law clk. McTeer, Walls & Bailey, Greenville, Miss., 1973; legis. aide Sen. Wynona Lipman, NJ, 1973-74; trial atty. NJ Pub. Defenders Office, Essex & Passaic Counties, 1976-82; lawyer del. 3d Jud. Conf., 1987—; state legislator NJ Ho. of Reps., 1994—2001, mem., jud. law & pub. safety com., sr. citizen & social svc. com., task force on juvenile crime, criminal justice subcom., Dem. task force on crime & corrections, minority whip, 1996—2001; state legislator NJ State Senate, 2002—, chair, commerce com.; mem. judiciary com., legis. oversight com., legis. services commn.; ptnr. Gill & Cohen, PC, Montclair, NJ. Trustee Montclair Pub. Libr., 1978-83, Cmty. Nursing Svc., Montclair, 1986-87; bd. adjustment Montclair Twp., 1985; bd. dirs. Playwrights Theater NJ, 1993-94, Luna Theater, Montclair. Recipient legal profession award Nat. Coun. Negro Bus. Women, 1985, citizen award Montclair br. NAACP, 1988. Mem. ABA, Assn. Criminal Def. Lawyers NJ (trustee 1986-89), NJ State Bar Assn., Garden State Bar Assn., Essex County Bar Assn., Nat. Conf. Black Lawyers, Black Women Lawyers NJ, Assn. Trial Lawyers Am., Isis Literary Guild (pres.). Democrat. Office: NJ Senate Dist 34 425 Bloomfield Ave Ste 2 Montclair NJ 07042-3538 Office Phone: 973-509-0388, 609-292-5339.*

GILLAN, KAYLA J., lawyer; b. 1958; Grad., Calif. St. U.; JD, U. Calif., Davis, 1984. Gen. counsel Calif. Pub. Employees Ret. Sys., Sacramento, 1996—2002; v.p. Ind. Fiduciary Services, 2002—; mem. Pub. Co. Acctg. Oversight Bd., Washington, 2002—. Named one of Top 50 Women Lawyers Nat. Law Jour., 1998. Office: Pub Co Acctg Oversight Bd 1666 K St NW Washington DC 20006*

GILLAN, REBECCA JANE, music educator, composer; d. George Rozier and Hilda Marie Waller; m. Wynn William Gillan, June 18, 1953; children: Amy Leigh, Kelly Marie. B of Piano Performance, Hope Coll., 1977, B of Music Edn., 1977; M in Music Composition & Music Theory, Southeastern La. U., 1997. Cert. music edn. K-12 Mich., 1978, Okla., 1978, talented music tchr. La. State Bd. Edn., 1994, state music evaluator La. State Bd. Edn., 1996. Instr. piano., group. pvt. U. Redlands Cmty. Music, Calif., 1981—89; asst. dir. cmty. music programs U. Redlands, 1986—89; tchr. talented music St. Tammany Parish Sch. Bd., Covington, La., 1993—98, Livingston (La.) Parish Sch. Bd., 1999—; instr. group piano Crafton Hills Coll., Yucaipa, Calif., 1989; owner Rozier Press. Organist Luth. & Unitarian Chs., Hammond, La., 2000—05. Composer (pianist): (cd recording of 10 original piano solos) Impressions; composer, lyricist: musical Miracles: A Message of Hope; composer: (suite for strings and piano) American Landscapes, (vocal solo) Weeping Gently, Hear My Cry, (youth choir) The Mouse Poem, (instrumental solo) Time Will Tell. Mem. Nat. Multiple Sclerosis Soc., Washington, 1995—2005, walk chmn., 1996. Grantee, Office of Lt. Gov., State La., 2002—03. Mem.: ASCAP (writer, composer, pub.), New Orleans Musicians Union, Am. Fedn. Musicians, Music Educators Nat. Conf. (assoc.), Internat. Assn. Jazz Educators (assoc.; state sec. 2001—05). Democrat. Achievements include development of web page for MS clients of Biogen. Avocations: swimming, travel, Italian language & culture. Personal E-mail: rebeccagillan@charter.net.

GILLARD, BERYL L., mortgage company executive; d. James Howard and Doris Markland Gillard; life ptnr. Laura Ann Essick, July 23, 1997. BS in Agrl. Bus. Mgmt., U. Del., 1987. Foreclosure/REO sect. head USDA/Centralized Servicing Ctr., St. Louis, 2000—; co-owner, treas. Life Strategies, Inc., Clayton, Mo., 2001—. Bd. dirs., developer website Gateway Alliance, St. Louis, 1998—2001.

GILLEN, ADRIENNE KOSCIUSKO, librarian, researcher; b. Northampton, Mass., Jan. 7, 1947; d. Mitchell Fred and Gloria Theresa (Maynard) K.; m. William A. Gillen, May 24, 1986. BA, U. Mass., 1969. Library asst. Hotchkiss Sch., Lakeville, Conn., 1971-72; grants mgr. Conn. Planning Com. on Adminstrn., Hartford, 1972-73; researcher Dept. Youth Service, Bridgeport, Conn., 1974-75, White House, Washington, 1976; librarian Rep. Nat. Com., Washington, 1977-79; librarian U.S. Senate, Rep. Policy Com., Washington, 1979-82; library dir. White House, Washington, 1982—; exec. adv. com. mem. Fedlink Library of Congress. Republican. Roman Catholic. Office: Exec Office of Pres Library and Info Services Div Oeob Dv Rm 308 Washington DC 20503-0001

GILLEN, KATHERINE ELIZABETH, librarian; b. Washington, May 16, 1951; d. Hugh Chisholm and Norma Marie (Provost) G. BS, U. Md., 1973, MLS, 1976; MA, U. Phoenix, 1989; grad., Citizens Police Acad., Mesa, Ariz., 1993, Air Command and Staff Coll., 1996; student, Kino Inst., 2004—06. Mem. Order of Preachers Laiety, Dominical Laiety. Librarian Maricopa County Community Coll., Phoenix, 1982-84; librarian reference and serials Mesa (Ariz.) Pub. Library, 1981-92; libr. mgr. Denver Pub. Libr., 1992; libr. dir. USAF, Luke AFB, Ariz., 1993—. Book reviewer Libr. Jour., 1988—, KLIATT, 1991—; contbr. short stories to mags.; pub.: Felicia's First Christmas, 1994. Class mem. Mesa Leadership Tng. and Devel., 1991-92; chair Luke Officers' Wives Club scholarship program, 1998-2003; lector Luke Cath. Cmty., 1997—; vice-chair Avondale Libr. Bd., 2002-05, chair, 2005—. Mem. AAAS (reviewer 1982—), ALA (v.p. Armed Forces Librs. Roundtable 1997-98, pres. 1998-99), Ariz. State Libr. Assn. (exec. bd. 1991-92, serials roundtable chmn. 1991-92), Serials Specialists of Maricopa County, Mensa. Avocations: flying, ballet, reading. Home: 11301 W Orange Blossom Ln Avondale AZ 85323-3532

GILLENWATER-CATRON, TASHANNA SHANTAY, elementary school educator; b. Chgo., Dec. 25, 1973; d. Sheila Gillenwater and Paul Johnson; m. Devenchie Darrell Catron, July 4, 1999; children: DeVenchie Vincent Catron, Micah Parises Catron. BS in Exercise Sci., Iowa State U., Ames, 1998; MEd, Chgo. State U., 2001. Cert. Group Fitness Instr. Exercise Safety Assn., 2000, Personal Fitness Trainer Exercise Safety Assn., 2000, Yoga Instr. Exercise Safety Assn., 2005, Pilates Inst. Exercise Safety Assn., 2005, tchr. 2005. Phys. instr. Chgo. Pk. Dist., 1999—2005; tchr. phys. edn. Chgo. Pub. Schs., 2006—. Contracted fitness instr. Calumet Park Recreational Ctr., Ill., 2005—. Mem.: AAHPERD, Am. Coll. Sports Medicine, Personal Fitness Profl., Ill. AHPERD. Democrat-Npl. Office Phone: 708-799-3000 ext. 5333. Personal E-mail: deebomp@aol.com.

GILLEO, SANDRA V., elementary school educator; b. Somerville, N.J., May 8, 1944; d. Sam B. and Frances (Green) Hammer; m. Robert James Gilleo (div. Dec. 1981); children: Robert T.I., Felise V. BA, Trenton State Coll., NJ, 1967; MA, Newark State Coll., 1971. Cert. tchr., N.J., Pa. Tchr. elem. Franklin Twp. Sch. Dist., Quakertown, N.J., 1966-67, Bricktown (N.J.) Twp. Sch. Dist., 1967-69; reading specialist Lawrence Twp. Sch. Dist., Lawrenceville, N.J., 1969-72; elem. tchr. New Hope-Solebury (Pa.) Sch. Dist., 1972—. Libr. Village Libr. of Wrightstown, Pa., 1972—; vol. John B. Anderson presdl. campaing, Bucks County, Pa., 1980; mem. Second Monday adv. com. for women, Doylestown, Pa., 1982-894; tchr. Temple Judea of Bucks County, 1991; active James Michener Art Mus., Churchville Nature Ctr. With USNR, 1965-71. Mem. Franklin Twp. Edn. Assn., Brick Edn. Assn., Lawrenceville Edn. Assn., New Hope-Solebury Edn. Assn., Churchville Nature Ctr., Michener Art Mus. Jewish. Avocations: volunteering, tennis, hiking, tap and country western dance. Home: 2650 Windy Bush Rd Newtown PA 18940-3601 Office: New Hope-Solebury Elem Sch N Sugan Rd Solebury PA 18963-9998

GILLESPIE, DEIRDRE Y., pharmaceutical executive; BSc, MD, London U.; MBA, London Bus. Sch. Positions in bus. develop. 3 Dimensional Pharm.; positions in worldwide product planning and mktg. DuPont Merck Pharm. Co.; positions in clin. develo. Sandoz (now Novartis); sr. med. cons. Communications Strategy Group; COO, chief bus. officer Vical, Inc.; CEO, pres. Oxxon Therapeutics, Inc., 2001—06; CEO La Jolla Pharm. Co., San Diego, 2006—, also bd. dir., 2004—. Trustee Forsyth Inst. Office: La Jolla Pharm Co 6455 Nancy Ridge Dr San Diego CA 92121-2249*

GILLESPIE, DONNA FAY, novelist; b. Gainesville, Fla., July 21, 1948; d. Joe Gill and Orlene Fay (Cox) G. BA in Fine Art, U. Fla., 1970. Author: The Light Bearer (novel), 1994, Lady of the Light (novel), 2006, various freelance essays, 2004-06. Avocation: photography. Office: c/o Putnam Publicity 375 Hudson St New York NY 10014 Personal E-mail: donna.gillespie900@sbcglobal.net.

GILLESPIE, MARY KREMPA, psychologist, consultant; b. New Haven, Oct. 31, 1941; d. Albert Charles and Marye (Bemis) Krempa; m. J. Joseph Gillespie, Sept. 1, 1962 (div. 1979); children: Carolyn Gillespie Kottmeyer, James Joseph III (dec.). AA in Classical Music cum laude, Mount Aloysius Coll., 1961; BA in Psychology cum laude, Immaculata Coll., 1973; MA in Clin. Psychology, West Chester U., 1974; postgrad., Temple U., 1976-79; PhD in Psychology and Social Change, Walden U., 1988. Lic. psychologist, Pa. Dir. tng. Rape Crisis Coun., West Chester, Pa., 1974-77; exec. dir. Open Door Counseling Ctr., West Chester, 1975-77; therapist Temple U. Cmty. Counseling Clin., Phila., 1977-78; doctoral intern Coatesville (Pa.) Vets. Hosp., 1978-79; sr. psychologist Delaware Valley Pscyhol. Svcs., Phila., 1979-81; dir. substance abuse programs Resource Spectrum, Phila., 1980-81; psychologist 1810 Counseling Ctr., Phoenixville, Pa., 1983-85, Ambler (Pa.) Psychol. Svcs., 1980-83; clin. supr., profl. mentor Eaglesmere Psychology Assocs., Malvern, Pa., 1980—, dir., 1983—; mem. staff Eugenia Hosp., Lafayette Hills, Pa., 1988—. Dir. tng. Rape Crisis Coun., West Chester, Pa., 1974-77; vocat. counselor Haverford (Pa.) State Hosp., 1975; rsch. cons. Mind's Eye Ednl. Sys., Wayne, Pa., 1989-92; corp. cons. in field, 1975—; clin. cons. Chester County Hosp., Occupl. Health Ctr., 1988—, Children's Hosp. U. Pa., 1990—, The Reed Group, Rensselaer, N.Y., 1994—, Bus. Devel. and Tng. Ctr., Great Valley Ctr., Malvern, 1994—; occupl. health psychologist Sterling-Winthrop Drugs, Collegeville, Pa., 1992—; expert witness in field, 1979—; spkr. in field. Author: Outcome Study of an Innovative Paradoxical Treatment for Panic Attacks, 1988. Bd. dirs. Chester County Rape Crisis Coun., 1976-78; adminstr. U.S. Healthcare Managed Mental Health Care Capitation, 1979-90. Recipient Univ. fellowship Temple U., Phila., 1976-77. Fellow Pa. Psychol. Assn. (mem. legis. network 1980—), Coll. Physicians Phila. (devel. com.); mem. APA (cert., mem. legis. network 1980—), Am. Assn. Applied Psychophysiology and Biofeedback (cert. practitioner), Pa. Soc. Behavioral Medicine and Biofeedback, Am. Psychosomatic Soc., Prescribing Psychologists Register, Sierra Club (mem legis. network 1985—), Audubon Club (mem. legis. network 1985—), Phi Theta Kappa, Psi Chi. Avocations: classical music, photography, sailing, windsurfing, handicrafts. Office: Eaglesmere Psychology Assoc 2350 Pheasant Hill Ln Malvern PA 19355-9712 Office Phone: 800-673-9181.

GILLESPIE, PENNY HANNIG, business owner; b. Schenectady, N.Y., June 4, 1954; d. William Armand and Freda (Penney) H.; m. Kenneth Scofield Keyes, Jr., Sept. 2, 1984 (div. Aug. 1992) Student, U. Ariz., 1972—74. Cert. EMT, Ariz., N.Y.; completion in skills tng. for profls. in Hakomi psychotherapy, Oreg. Co-founder Ken Keyes Coll., Coos Bay, Oreg., 1982—91; pvt. practice counseling Eugene, Oreg., 1991—95; founder, pres. The Wellness Network, Eugene, 1994—. Co-author: Gathering Power Through Insight and Love, 1986, Handbook to Higher Consciousness: The Workbook, 1989; editor: How to Enjoy Your Life in Spite of It All, 1980, The Hundredth Monkey, 1982, Your Heart's Desire, 1983, Your Life Is a Gift, 1987, Discovering the Secrets of Happiness, 1988, PlanetHood, 1988, The Power of Unconditional Love, 1990 Bd. dirs. Living Love Ch., 1980-91, sec., v.p.; founding bd. dirs., sec., sec.-treas., v.p. The Vision Found., Inc., 1982-91; founding bd. dirs., sec., sec.-treas. Cornucopia, The Living Love Ch. Ky., 1982-91; vol. Victim Advocate Lane County Dist. Attys. Victim/Witness Svcs. Program, Oreg., 1993 Recipient Peace award Coalition for Justice and Peace, Ariz. State U. and the Inst. Peace Edn., 1989; Site Mgr. award for Anne Frank exhibit Jewish Fedn. Lane County, Oreg., 1993 Avocations: piano, bicycling. Home: PO Box 41532 Eugene OR 97404-0369

GILLET, PAMELA KIPPING, special education educator; EdB in Elem. Edn., Chgo. Tchrs. Coll., 1963; MA in Mental Retardation, Northeastern Ill. U., 1966; PhD in Gen. Spl. Edn./Adminstrn., Walden U., 1976. Cert. elem. edn., early childhood edn., learning disabled, mental retardation, behavior disorders, supt., supr. and dir. spl. edn. 4th grade tchr. Dist. # 83 Mannheim, Franklin Park, Ill., 1963—64; h.s. spl. edn. tchr. Dist. # 207 Maine Twp., Park Ridge, Ill., 1964—67, prevocational coord., 1967—69, dept. chmn. spl. edn. dept., 1969—70; dir. EPDA tchr. tng. program Chgo. Consortium Colls. and Univs., Northwest Ednl. Coop., Palatine, Ill., 1970—71; prin. West Suburban Spl. Edn. Ctr., Cicero, Ill., 1971—73; supr. West Suburban Assn. Spl. Edn., Cicero, 1973—75; asst. dir. Northwest Suburban Spl. Edn. Orgn., Palatine, 1975—78, supt. Mt. Prospect, Ill., 1978—96; spl. edn. cons., 1996—. Adj. instr. Northeastern Ill. U., Chgo. State U., Corcordia Coll., Barat Coll., Nat. Coll. Edn., Roosevelt U.; mem. task forces ISBE, 1975—2007, cons. career edn. project, 1977—78, spl. edn. demandate study group, 1983—85; cons. Ednl. Testing Svc.; tchr. edn. coun. Northeastern Ill. U., 1981—97, dean's grant program, 1982—97; workshop leader, 1974—; lectr., cons. in field. Author: Auditory Processes, 1974, rev., 1992, Career Education for Children, 1978, Of Work and Worth: Career Education Programming for Exceptional Children and Youths, 1981; contbr. articles to profl. jours., chapters to books. Bd. dirs. Found. Exceptional Children, 1996—, pres., 1999—2004. Recipient Cmty. Svc. award, Am. Legion, 1976, 1980, Alumnus of Yr. award, Northeastern Ill. U., 1984, Learning Disabilities of Am. Contributors award, Coun. Understanding Learning Disabilities, 1992, Those Who Excel award of excellence, Ill. State Bd. of Edn., 1994, Outstanding Svc. award, Divsn. Mental Retardation and Devel. Disabilities, 1994, Sleznick award, Coun. of Admin. of Spl. Edn., 1996, Outstanding Contbr. award, Coun. Exceptional Children, 1996, Burton Blatt award, Divsn. on Metal Retardation and Devel. Disabilities, 1997, Spl. Edn. Leadership award, Ill. Adminstrs. of Spl. Edn., 1995, Outstanding Spl. Edn. Adminstr. of Yr. award, 1997. Mem.: Found. for Exceptional Children (pres. 2000—04, v.p. CEC Pioneers divsn. 2006—), Ill. Adminstrs. Spl. Edn. (pres. 1994—95), Coun. Exceptional Children (pres. Ill. chpt. 1975—77, bd. govs. 1977—80, pres. mental retardation divsn. 1983—85, bd. govs. 1986, exec. com. 1989—92, v.p. internat. 1992—93, pres.-elect 1993—94, pres. 1994—95, bd. govs. 1996—2000, bd. dirs. 2000—04, pres.-elect 2005—06, Meritorious Svc. award Ill. 1983), Am. Assn. Sch. Adminstrs. Home and Office: 413 Courtlea Oaks Blvd Winter Garden FL 34787

GILLETT, MARY CAPERTON, military historian; b. Richmond, Va., Apr. 28, 1929; d. Lewis Hopkins and Mary Caperton (Horsley) Renshaw; m. Richard Clark Gillett, June 7, 1949; children: Richard Clark Jr., Glenn Douglas, Mary Caperton, Priscilla Elizabeth, Blakeney Diana. Student, Wellesley Coll., 1946-49; BA, Am. U., 1966, MA, 1971, PhD, 1978. Historian U.S. Navy Dept., Washington, 1966-69, U.S. Dept. Army, Washington, 1972-96. Author: The Army Medical Department, 1775-1818, 1981, The Army Medical Department, 1818-1865, 1988, The Army Medical Department, 1865-1917, 1995; contbr. articles to profl. jours. Mem. Am. Assn. for History of Medicine, Nat. Wildlife Fedn., We. Hist. Assn., The Nature Conservancy, The Wilderness Soc., The Sierra Club, Nat. Audubon Soc., Audubon Naturalist Soc. Avocations: backpacking, gardening. E-mail: mcgillett@mindspring.com.

GILLETT, PATRICIA, family and acute care nurse practitioner, clinical nurse; b. Mass., Jan. 2, 1948; d. Clyde and Estelle (Carter) Gleason; m. Warren Gillett, July 1968; children: Michael, James. ADN, Berkshire Community Coll.; BSN, U. N.Mex.; MSN, U. Tex., El Paso; FNP, Tex. Tech. Univ. Nursing instr. U. Albuquerque, Albuquerque T-VI; critical care edn. coord. St. Joseph Med. Ctr., Albuquerque VA Med. Ctr.; faculty U. N. Mex., Coll. of Nursing. Mem. ANA, AACN (Outstanding Cricital Care Educator 1989), Am. Acad. Nurse Practitioners, N.Mex. Nurses Assn. (award for clin. excellence 1994), Sigma Theta Tau.

GILLETTE, ESTELLA HERNANDEZ, government agency administrator; b. Mexico; BSBA, 1986, MS, 1994. Cert. English for Speakers of Other Langs. tutor. From cler-stenographer to dep. dir. NASA, Houston, chief Adminstrv. Support Office, dir. Equal Opportunity Programs Johnson Space Ctr. Mem.: Profl. Secretaries Internat. Office: NASA Johnson Space Ctr EOP Mailcode AJ Houston TX 77058

GILLETTE, ETHEL MORROW, columnist; b. Oelwein, Iowa, Nov. 27, 1921; d. Charles Henry and Myrne Sarah (Law) Morrow; student Coe Coll., 1939-41; BA, Upper Iowa U., 1959; MA, Western State Coll., 1969; m. Roman A. Gillette, May 6, 1944 (dec. 1992); children: Melody Ann, Richard Allan, William Robert (dec. 1993). Stenographer, Penick & Ford, Cedar Rapids, Iowa, 1941-43, FBI, Washington, 1943-44; tchr. Fayette (Iowa) H.S., 1959-60, Jordan Jr. H.S., Mpls., 1960-64, Montrose (Colo.) H.S., 1964-68; family living, religion editor The News-Record, Gillette, Wyo., 1977-79, columnist Distaff Side, 1979-84. Mem. Western Writers Am., WestWind Writers/NWC (founder, pres. 1992-96), Nat. Writers Club. Contbr. articles to popular mags.

GILLETTE, FRANKIE JACOBS, retired savings and loan association executive, federal agency administrator, social worker; b. Norfolk, Va., Apr. 1, 1925; d. Frank Walter and Natalie (Taylor) Jacobs; m. Maxwell Claude Gillette, June 19, 1976. BS, Hampton U., 1946; MSW, Howard U., 1948. Lic. clin. social worker; cert. jr. coll. tchr., life. Youth dir. YWCA, Passaic, N.J., 1948-50; dir. program Ada S. McKinley Community Ctr., Chgo., 1950-53; program dir. Sophie Wright Settlement, Detroit, 1953-64; dir. Concerted Services Project, Pittsburg, Calif., 1964-66, Job Corps Staff Devel., U. Calif., Berkeley, 1966-69; spl. program coordinator U.S. Community Services Adminstrn., San Francisco, 1969-83; pres. G & G Enterprises, San Francisco, 1985—. Chmn. bd. dirs. Time Savs. and Loan Assn., San Francisco, 1986-87. Commr. San Francisco Human Rights Commn., 1988-93; bd. dirs. Urban Econ. Devel. Corp., 1980-93, San Francisco Conv. and Visitors Bur.; trustee Fine Arts Mus. of San Francisco, 1993—; chmn. San Francisco-Abidjan Sister City Com., 1990—; founding bd. dirs. Mus. African Diaspora, 2002—. Mem. Nat. Assn. Negro Bus. and Profl. Women's Clubs (pres. 1983-87), The Links, Inc., Delta Sigma Theta, Inc. Office: G & G Enterprises 85 Cleary Ct Apt 4 San Francisco CA 94109-6518

GILLETTE, MURIEL DELPHINE, nurse; b. Pasadena, Calif., Nov. 10, 1945; d. Edwin and Jean Helen (Fremont) Gillette; m. Larry Houston Potter, Dec. 31, 1971 (dec. 1979); children: Melissa Darlene Genevieve Potter Stephens, Bryan Scott; m. Robert George Baumann Jr., Aug. 18, 1980; children: Robert George III, Michael Ray Alexander. Student, Western Coll. for Women, Oxford, Ohio, 1963-65; BSN, UCLA, 1968; M of Nursing, Oreg. Health Scis. U., 1991. Sch. nurse, health tchr. Hawthorne Intermediate Sch., Calif., 1969-70; nurse St. John's Hosp., Santa Monica, Calif., 1969-71; camp nurse L.A. Girl Scout Coun., 1969-71; nurse UCLA Med. Ctr., 1967-70; ICU/CCU/pediatrics nurse Mercy Med. Ctr., Roseburg, Oreg., 1971-79; nurse Umpqua Valley Community Hosp., Myrtle Creek, Oreg., 1981-91; camp nurse, health coord. Western Rivers Girl Scout Coun., Roseburg, 1984-90; health edn. dir. City of Myrtle Creek, 1986-91; nurse practitioner Umpgua Nat. Forest, Roseburg and Glide, Oreg., 1991-93; camp nurse, health coord. Oreg. Trail Boy Scout Coun., Roseburg, 1981-91, Western Rivers Girl Scout Coun., Roseburg, 1984-90; cmty. health cons. Roseburg, 1984-98; home health nurse, 1995-98; pub. health nurse State of Alaska Epidemiology, Anchorage, 1998—, Dept. Corrections, Alaska Psychiat. Hosp. Musician quartet, orch., soloist; artist in oils; poet. Bd. dirs. River 'N Dell Day Care Ctr., Myrtle Creek, 1983-85; trustee Augusta Bixler Farms, Inc., Stockton, Calif., 1976—; mem. Douglas County Cancer Screening Com.; vol. ARC, 1982-. Capt. USAF, 1970-89. Umpqua Valley Hosp. Aux. scholar, 1989; L.A. Watercolor Soc. traveling art collection award, 1963. Mem. DAR, UCLA Alumni Assn., Umpqua Valley Hosp. Aux., Oreg. Health Sci. U. Alumni Assn., OES, Delta Zeta. Republican. Presbyterian. Avocations: painting, tennis, music, skiing, raising arabian horses. Home: PO Box 521171 Big Lake AK 99652-1171 Office Phone: 907-269-7100. E-mail: alex7@gci.net.

GILLETTE, PATRICIA K., lawyer; b. LA, Aug. 7, 1951; AB, Occidental Coll., 1973; JD cum laude, U. San Francisco, 1976. Bar: Calif., Am. Bar Assoc. In-house counsel Bank of Am.; atty. private practice; ptnr. Heller Ehrman LLP, San Francisco, 1990—. Co-chmn. labor and employment practice group Heller Ehman LLP, co-chmn. gender diversity com., 2006—. Office: Heller Ehrman LLP 333 Bush St San Francisco CA 94104-2806 Office Phone: 415-772-6456. Business E-Mail: pgillette@hewm.com.

GILLETTE, SISTER JOSEPH ANN, education educator, educator; b. El Cayo de San Ignacio, Belize, Ctrl. Am., Jan. 1, 1929; came to U.S., 1947; d. Peter Edward Percival and Victoria Thomasina (Smith) G. BA, Cardinal Stritch Coll., Milw., 1965; MA, Tex. So. U., 1985. Joined Congregation of Sisters of Holy Family; cert. tchr., La., 1968. Tchr. 6th grade St. Paul Sch., New Orleans, 1949-50, tchr. grades 6 and 7, 1965-68; tchr. grades K-4 Holy Rosary Sch., Galveston, Tex., 1950-61; tchr. high sch. St. Mary's Acad., New Orleans, 1965-68; prin. St. Augustine Sch., New Orleans, 1968-69; vice prin., tchr. Austin High Sch., Belize, Calif., 1969-71; vice prin. St. Philip Neri Sch., Houston, 1972-78, 82-85; tchr. 1st grade St. Albert Sch., Compton, Calif., 1978-81, 87-93, vice prin., 1993—; tchr. 1st grade Regina Caeli High Sch., 1980-81; tchr. grades 6-8 St. Francis Xavier Sch., Baton Rogue, 1981-82; tchr grades 5-6 St. Joseph Sch., Marshall, Tex., 1985-87. Conductor workshops for tchrs. at convs., in-svc. meetings, adult evening classes, teaching techniques for pirmiary grades, music, arts and craft. Nat. leader San Jacinto coun. Girl Scouts U.S.A., Houston; vol. Peace Corps; active Project Score, Amnesty. Recipient awards for svc. to city, community, ch. and sch.; named Tchr. of Yr. Holy Redeemer Sch., 2004-. Mem. Houston/Galveston Art Edn. Assn., Art Students League, Artes del Centro Americano, Designers Guild, Nat. Cath. Edn. Assn., Sisters Coun. Houston. Roman Catholic. Avocations: designer, choreographer, director-producer children's plays, writing children's stories. Home: 801 E Redondo Beach Blvd Compton CA 90220-2528 Office: Sisters of the Holy Family 804 E Compton Blvd Compton CA 90220-1106

GILLI, LYNNE MARIE, academic administrator; b. Sidney, N.Y., May 4, 1954; d. Joseph Gerard and Marie Jane (Lese) Moore; m. Angelo Christopher Gilli, Sr., Dec. 22, 1983. BS, SUNY, Utica, 1978, MS, 1979; EdD, SUNY, Buffalo, 1983. Cert. ednl. adminstr. Tchr. Western Del. Bd. Coop. Ednl. Svcs., Sidney Center, N.Y., 1977-81; grad. asst. SUNY, Buffalo, 1981-82; specialist Div. Career and Tech. Edn. Md. State Dept. Edn., Balt., 1982-88, sect. chief, 1988-89, program mgr., 1989—. Contbr. articles to profl. jours. Mem.: Assn. for Career and Tech. Edn. (life). Office: Md State Dept Edn 200 W Baltimore St 3d Fl Baltimore MD 21201-2595 Home: 402 Idlebunny Rd Severna Park MD 21146-1661

GILLIAM, MARY, travel company executive; b. Pampa, Tex., Apr. 18, 1928; d. Roy and Hylda O. (Bertrand) Brown; divorced; 1 child, Terry K. AA, Amarillo Bus. Coll., Tex., 1949. Flight attendant Braniff Internat. Airways, Dallas, 1950-53; from reservation agt. to mgr. passenger sales Trans-World Airlines, various locations, 1953-81; exec. v.p. Lakewood (Colo.) Travel, 1981; mgmt. cons. Bank One Travel, Columbus, Ohio, 1981-82; pres. Icaria Travel, Inc., Green Valley, Ariz., 1986—, Intensive Trainers Inst., Tucson, 1983-92. Recipient Award of Excellence Trans-World Airlines, N.Y.C., 1972, Pres.' Hall of Fame award, 1973. Mem. Am. Soc. Travel Agts. (Industry Svc. award 1980), Inst. Cert. Travel Agts. Methodist. Avocations: reading, travel, music. Office: Icaria Travel Inc 1481 W Calle Mendoza Green Valley AZ 85614-1253 Office Phone: 520-625-4328. E-mail: mgill.418@aol.com.

GILLIG, PAULETTE MARIE, psychiatry educator, researcher; b. Boston, Mar. 24, 1949; d. Franklin Joseph and Marie Robichaud (Collins) G.; m. Douglas K. Fairobent, June 13, 1981. BA cum laude hons. psychology, SUNY, Buffalo; MA, PhD, Ohio State U., Columbus, 1973; MD, Med. Coll. Ohio, 1977. Diplomate Am. Bd. Psychiatry and Neurology, Am. Bd. Geriat. Psychiatry. Resident in neurology Med. Coll. Ohio, 1978-79, U. Mich., Ann Arbor, 1979-81; resident in psychiatry Ohio State U., Columbus, 1981-83; med. dir. North Ctrl. Mental Health Ctr., Columbus, 1985; clin. asst. prof. Ohio State U., Columbus, 1983-85; asst. prof. U. Cin., 1985-90; assoc. prof. Wright State U., Dayton, 1990-2000, prof. psychiatry, 2000—; chief clin. officer Mental Health Drug and Alcohol Svcs. Bd., Champaign and Logan Cos., 1995—2005. Prof. rural psychiatry Ohio Dept. Mental Health, 1997—; mem. strategic planning coun. Wright State U., Dayton, 1998-2001. Series editor Psychiatry, 2004—06; editor: (book) Clinical Guide to the Treatment of the Homeless Mentally Ill Person, 2006; contbr. chapters to books, articles various profl. jours. Founding Bd. Domestic Abuse and Violence Inst. of Dayton, 2000—; Patron Cin. Ballet Co., Xavier U., Humane Soc. U.S., Dayton Opera Co., Cin. Symphony Orch., Sorg Opera Co., Middletown, Ohio,Lebanon Police Children's Fund, Balletech Ohio, Warren County Animal Shelter, Nat, Wildlife Fedn.; chair Domestic Violence Rsch. Group, 1999-2002; examiner Am. Bd. Psychiatry and Neurology, 2006—. Recipient Clin. Neuroscis. award, Med. Coll. Ohio, Best Dr. in Am., Bestdoctors.com, 2005—06; grantee Pruitt Found., 1992, Ohio Dept. Mental Health, 1995—. Fellow Am. Psychiat. Assn. (disting.; com. on poverty, homelessness, and psychiatric disorders 1999-2006); mem. Am. Assn. Women Psychiatrists, Am. Assn. Cmty. Psychiatrists (Midwestern rep. 2002—, chair training com., Moffic award 1999), Ohio Psychiat. Assn. (chmn. com. on minorities 1999-2002, Pres.'s award 2001), World Health Orgn. (dir. internat. classification diseases), Nat. Wildlife Fedn. (cert.), Univ. Club, Nat. Bd. Psychiatry and Neurology (bd. examiner, 2005—), Alpha Omega Alpha. Avocations: classical piano, opera, companion animals, ballet, horticulture. Office: Wright State U Dept Psychiatry PO Box 927 Dayton OH 45401-0927 E-mail: paulette.gillig@wright.edu.

GILLIGAN, CAROL, psychologist, writer; b. NYC, Nov. 28, 1936; d. William Edward and Mabel (Caminez) Friedman; m. James Frederick Gilligan, June 12, 1960; children: Jonathan Mark, Timothy David, Christopher James. AB, Swarthmore Coll., 1958, degree (hon.), 1985; AM, Radcliffe Coll., 1961; PhD, Harvard U., 1964; degree (hon.), Regis Coll., 1983, Haverford Coll., 1987, Fitchburg State Coll., 1989, Wesleyan U., 1992, Smith Coll., 1999, John Jay Coll., 2006, U. Haifa, 2006. Instr. U. Chgo., 1965—66; lectr. Harvard U., Cambridge, Mass., 1967-69, rsch. asst., 1969-70, asst. prof., 1970-78, assoc. prof., 1978-86, prof., 1986—97, Patricia Alberg Graham prof. gender studies, 2001; Laurie chair in Women's Studies Rutgers U., New Brunswick, NJ, 1986-87; prof. NYU, N.Y.C., 2001—. Founding mem. Harvard Project on Women's Psychology and the Devel. of Girls, 1987—2001; co-dir., The Company of Women and Girls, 1991—96; mem. coun. scholars Erikson Inst. Ansten Riggs Ctr.; Pitt prof. U. Cambridge, 1992—93, vis. prof., 1993—94, fellow commoner Jesus Coll., 2004—. Author: In a Different Voice, 1982; author: (with Lyn M. Brown) Meeting at the Crossroads: Women's Psychology and Girls Development, 1992; author: (with J. Taylor and A. Sullivan) Between Voice and Silence: Women and Girls, Race and Relationship, 1995; author: The Birth of Pleasure: a new map of love, 2002; editor (with J. Ward and J. Taylor): Mapping the Moral Domain: A Contribution of Women's Thinking to Psychological Theory and Education, 1988; editor: (with N. Lyons and T. Hammer) Making Connections: Relational Worlds of Adolescent Girls at Emma Willard School, 1990; editor: (with A. Rogers and D. Tolman) Women, Girls, and Psychotherapy: Reframing Resistance, 1991, 2d edit., 2001. Bd. dir. Facing History and Ourselves. Sr. rsch. fellow Spencer Found., 1984—2001; Mellon Faculty fellow Bunting Inst.-Radcliffe Coll., 1982-83; recipient Grawemayer award U. Louisville, 1992, Heinz award, 1997, Medallion of the univ., SUNY, Albany, 2006. Fellow: Brit. Acad. Vis. Profs.; mem.: APA, Assn. Women in Psychology, Nat. Acad. Edn. Democrat. Jewish. Avocations: music, piano, modern dance, theater. Office: NYU Sch Law 511 Vanderbilt Hall New York NY 10012 Office Phone: 212-998-6048. Business E-Mail: carol.gilligan@nyu.edu.

GILLIGAN, COURTNEY, lawyer; b. 1977; BS, biology & philosophy, Univ. Scranton, 1999; JD highest honors, George Washington Univ., 2002. Bar: N.J., Pa., U.S. Ct. Appeals 8th cir. Law clk. U.S. Ct. Appeals (8th cir.), Fargo, ND, 2002—03; law clk. to Hon. William H. Rehnquist U.S. Supreme Ct., Washington, 2003—04; assoc. Baker Botts LLP, Washington, 2004—. Editor (articles): The George Washington Law Review. Mem.: Order of the Coif. Office: Baker Botts LLP The Warner 1299 Pennsylvania Ave Washington DC 20004-2400

GILLIGAN, SANDRA KAYE, private school director; b. Ft. Lewis, Wash., Mar. 22, 1946; d. Jack G. and O. Ruth (Mitchell) Wagoner; m. James J. Gilligan, June 3, 1972 (div. June 1998); 1 child, J. Shawn Gilligan. BS in Edn., Emporia State U., 1968, MS in Psychology, 1971; postgrad., Drake U., 1976, U. Mo., St. Louis, 1977-79. Tchr. Parklane Elem. Sch., Aurora, Colo., 1968-69, Bonner Springs (Kans.) Elem., 1970; stewardess Frontier Airlines, Denver, 1969; grad. teaching asst. Emporia (Kans.) State U., 1970-71; lead tchr. Western Valley Youth Ranch, Buckeye, Ariz., 1971-74; staff mem. program devel., lead tchr. The New Found., Phoenix, 1974; ednl. therapist Orchard Pl., Des Moines, 1974-76; ednl. cons. Spl. Sch. Dist. of St. Louis County, 1976-79; founding dir. The Churchill Ctr. and Sch. Learning Disabilities, St. Louis, 1978—. Instr. Webster Coll., Webster Groves, Mo., 1978-80; adj. prof. Maryville Coll., St. Louis, summer 1985; mem. exec. com. Ind. Schs. of St. Louis; keynote spkr. Miss. Learning Disabilities Assn. Conv., 1991; site visitor blue ribbon schs. program U.S. Dept. Edn., 1992; mem. evaluation rev. Com. Ind. Schs. of Ctrl. States; cert. trainer Human Potential Seminars; exec. com. Ind. Schs. St. Louis; presenter in field. Recipient Spirit Care & Counseling award, 2004. Mem. Learning Disabilities Assn., Internat. Dyslexia Assn. (chpt. bd. dirs.), St. Louis Jr. League. Avocations: gardening, painting. Office: The Churchill Ctr and Sch Learning Disabilities 1035 Price School Ln Saint Louis MO 63124-1596 Office Phone: 314-997-4343. Business E-Mail: sgilligan@churchillstl.org. E-mail: sgill@iganchurchillstl.org.

GILLIKIN, LYNN, retired psychologist; b. Camden, N.J., Dec. 10, 1945; d. Charles Leighton and Beulah (Eckard) Skerrett; m. Dennis O'Neil Gillikin, Apr. 30, 1983; children: David, Sarah, Robert. AB, Coll. William and Mary, Williamsburg, Va., 1967; MA, U. Va., Charlottesville, 1969, PhD, 1970. Lic. clin. psychologist Va., diplomate Am. Bd. Med. Psychotherapists. Asst. prof. U. Del., Newark, 1970—73; assoc. dean students and assoc. prof. Coll. William and Mary, Williamsburg, Va., 1973—98; pvt. practice, 1975—. Dir. psychology Rehab. Inst. Va., Newport News, Va. Contbr. scientific papers, articles to profl. jours. Grantee, NASA, 1995—98. Fellow: Am. Bd. Med. Psychotherapists; mem.: Psi Chi, Sigma Xi, Phi Beta Kappa. Achievements include research in psychological events and neurological EEG correlates. Home: PO Box 152 Mathews VA 23109-0152 Office Phone: 804-725-4884.

GILLILAND, LUCILLE MARY, artist, writer; b. N.Y. d. Lincoln Xaviar Waters and Irene Cecelia Stawarz; m. Charles Gilliland; children: Stephen, Brian, Kevin, Kathryn. BA magna cum laude, Lehman Coll., Bronx, N.Y., 1995. Cons., tchr. Bronx Coun. on the Arts, N.Y., YMCA, N.Y., JASA, N.Y., NBWNRA, N.Y., Neighborhood S.H.O.P.P., N.Y. Author: (column) Art of Craft and Needlework, (poetry); artist: (paintings). Roman Catholic.

GILLIOM, JUDITH CARR, federal official; b. Indpls., May 19, 1943; d. Elbert Raymond and Marjorie Lucille (Carr) G. BA, Northwestern U., 1964; MA, U. Pa., 1966. Feature writer, asst. women's editor Indpls. News, summers 1961-63; rsch. asst. cultural anthropology Northwestern U., 1963-64, asst. instr. freshman English, 1964; editorial asst. to dir. div. cardiology Phila. Gen. Hosp., 1965-67; asst. to ophthalmologist-in-chief Wills Eye Hosp., Phila., 1967-69; editor, writer Nat. Assn. Hearing and Speech Agencies, Washington, 1969-70; free-lance speech writer White House Conf. Children and Youth, 1969-70; free-lance editor, writer, abstractor, 1971-78; free-lance speechwriter President's Com. Mental Retardation, 1971-78; from dir. publs. to dir. comm. Nat. Assn. Hearing and Speech Action, Silver Spring, Md., 1972-77; editor Hearing & Speech Action mag., 1969-70, 72-77; program mgr. Interagy. Com. on Handicapped Employees, 1978, dep. exec. sec., 1979-83; mgr. disability program Dept. Def., 1983—. Cons. U.S. Archtl. and Transp. Barriers Compliance Bd., 1976-77, Office Ind. Living for Disabled, HUD, 1977-78, Office for Handicapped Individuals, HEW, 1978, Women's com. Pres.'s Com. Employment Handicapped, 1985-86. Mem. Nat. Spinal Cord Injury Assn., 1970-90, editor, pub. conv. jour., 1974-82, bd. dirs. D.C. chpt., 1975-81, 89-90, nat. trustee, 1975-81, nat. bd. dirs., 1978-79; bd. dirs. Nat. Ctr. for a Barrier-Free Environment, 1979-84, v.p., 1980-81, pres., 1981-82; nat. bd. dirs., treas. League Disabled Voters, 1980-85; local bd. dirs. Easter Seal Soc. Disabled Children and Adults, 1985-90; active Montgomery County Commn. on People with Disabilities, 1989-95; mem. Taxicab Svcs. Adv. Com., 1995-99. Recipient Smittkamp award Nat. Paraplegia Found., 1976, Outstanding Svc. award Fed. Asian Pacific Am. Coun., 1990, Geico Pub. Svc. award, 1996, Civilian Career Svc. award Office of Sec. of Def., 1997, Outstanding Leadership award Fed. Asian Pacific Am. Coun., 2002; Woodrow Wilson fellow, 1965. Mem. Phi Beta Kappa, Delta Delta Delta. Home: 901 Arcola Ave Silver Spring MD 20902-3401 Office: Dept Def The Pentagon Rm 5D641 Washington DC 20301-4000 Office Phone: 703-571-9330. Business E-Mail: judy.gilliom@osd.mil.

GILLIS, RHONDA RADFORD, elementary school educator; b. Louisburg, N.C., Feb. 5, 1963; d. W. Edward and Jessie Duke Radford; 1 child, Matthew. BS in Early Childhood Edn., Ga. So. Coll., Statesboro, 1987, MS in Early Childhood Edn., 1991; EdS in Elem. edn., Mercer U., Macon, Ga., 1994; EdD in Ednl. Leadership, Nova Southeastern U., Ft. Lauderdale, Fla., 2006. Nat. bd. cert. early childhood generalist. Tchr. Appling County Comprehensive HS, Baxley, Ga., 1987—88, Fouth Dist. Elem. Sch., 1988—91, Jeff Davis Primary Sch., Hazelhurst, 1991—98, Goodyear Elem. Sch., Brunswick, 1998—. Vol. The Gathering Place, Brunswick, Ga.; mem. St. Simons Cmty. Ch. Mem.: ASCD, Pi Lamda Theta. Avocations: reading, volunteering, travel, beach, skiing. Home: 106 Rosemont St Saint Simons Island GA 31522-1777 Office: Glynn County Bd Edn Egmont St Brunswick GA 31520

GILLIS, SUSAN FOX, judge; b. Cleve., Ohio, June 13, 1943; BA, DePaul U., Chgo., 1984; JD, Ill. Inst. Tech. Chgo. Kent, 1988. Bar: Ill. 1988. Atty. Querrey & Harrow, Chgo., 1987—92, Fischer & Kahn, Chgo., 1992—94, Schoer & Smith, Chgo., 1994—99, Fische & Kahn, Chgo., 1999; assoc. judge Cir. Ct. Cook County, Chgo., 1999—. Pres. Grateful House, Oak Park, Ill., 1998—2000. Named Outstanding Young Alumni, Ill. Inst. Tech. Chgo. Kent, 1996; recipient Golden Gavel award, Carpls, 2001. Mem.: Wayback Inn, Nat. Assn. Women Lawyers (pres. 1999—2000), Women's Bar Assn. Ill. (pres. 1994—95, 2004—05), Chgo. Bar Assn., Ill. Judges Assn. Avocations: travel, quilting, knitting, jewelry making. Office: Cir Ct Cook County 1708 R J Daley Ctr Chicago IL 60602

GILLISS, CATHERINE LYNCH, nursing educator; b. New Britain, Conn., Apr. 18, 1949; d. James A. and Lorraine Lynch; m. Thomas P. Gilliss, June 6, 1970. BS in Nursing, Duke U., 1971; MS in Nursing, Cath. U. Am., Washington, 1974; D of Nursing Sci., U. Calif., 1983; cert. adult nurse practitioner, U. Rochester, 1979. Staff and charge nurse Duke U. Med. Ctr., Durham, 1971, VA Hosp., Washington, 1971-72; asst. prof. U. Md., Balt.,

1974-76, The Cath. U. Am., 1976-79; assoc. prof. U. Portland, Oreg., 1979-83; lectr. in nursing Sonoma State U., Rohnert Park, Calif., 1983-84; prof., chmn. dept. family health care U. Calif., San Francisco, 1984-98, prof. emeritus, 1999—; prof. Sch. Nursing, Yale U., New Haven, 1998—2004, dean Sch. Nursing, 1998—2004, Duke U., Durham, NC, 2004—; vice chancellor nursing affairs Duke U. Health System, 2004—. Chair NIH, Nat. Inst. Nursing Rsch. Study Sect., 1997-99. Co-author: Toward a Science of Family Nursing, 1989, The Nursing of Families, 1993; mem. editl. bd. Families, Systems and Health, 1994-98, jour. Family Nursing; contbr. articles to profl. jours. Bd. dirs. Conn. Inst. for Child Health and Devel., Am. Acad. Nursing, U. Calif. San Francisco Ctr. for the Health Professions. Recipient Disting. Alumna award Duke U., 1991; Pres.'s fellow U. Calif., 1983; Se. fellow Ctr. for Health Professions, 1996-99, Primary Care Policy fellow USPHS, 1993; Regent U. Portland, Oreg., 1994-2000. Fellow Am. Acad. Nursing (bd. dirs. 1999-2004); mem. ANA, Nat. Coun. on Family Rels., Nat. Orgn. Nurse Practitioner Faculty (pres. 1995), Primary Care Fellowship Soc. (pres. 1996-97). Office: Duke Univ Sch of Nursing DUMC 3322 Durham NC 27710

GILLMAN, KAREN LEE, clinical psychologist; b. Wichita, Kans., Sept. 16, 1937; d. Raymond H. and Myra Ruth (Hudson) Hein; m. Louis Charles Thomason, Dec. 21, 1958 (div. 1980); children: Debra Lynn Roelke, Sandy River; m. Richard Earl Gillman, June 18, 1983. Student, Phillips U., 1955-58; BS, Okla. State U., 1959; MS, Va. Polytech. Inst., Blacksburg, 1974; PhD, SUNY, Albany, 1985. Lic. clin. psychologist, Maine, N.Y. Tchr. Washington Elem., Stillwater (Okla.) Jr. High Sch., Ponca City, 1959-64, West Hurley (N.Y.) Elem. Sch., 1971-72; therapist Family Svc. Ctr., Kingston, N.Y., 1974-77; sr. counselor Readiness Tng. Project, Ulster County C.C., Stone Ridge, NY, 1978—79; clin. dir. Greene County Mental Health Clinic, Cairo, N.Y., 1979-84; dir. student assistance program Rens. County Dept. Mental Health, Troy, N.Y., 1984-86; dir. intensive day treatment St. Lawrence Psychiat. Ctr., Ogdensburg, N.Y., 1986-89; pvt. practice Dover-Foxcroft, Skowhegan & Winslow, Maine, 1989—. Adj. prof. St. Lawrence U., Canton, N.Y., 1986; cons. Project Readiness Arbor Hill Dept. Labor, Albany, 1978, Overlook Pre-sch. Ctr., Woodstock, N.Y., 1974; vol. tchr. Ulster Acad., Kingston, 1974; music tchr. Headstart, Woodstock, 1970-71. Newspaper columnist The Apple Polisher, Ulster County Townsman; author: Whipped Cream on Rain, 2001, Mr. & Dr. Talking It Over, 2002, Ashes In the Wind, 2003; author of poems. Dir. Cmty. Vacation Ch. Sch., Woodstock, 1967-70; Head of Day Family of Woodstock, Inc., 1974-77. Fellow NSF, 1961. Mem. APA, LWV (bd. dirs., editor 1967-69) Am. Assn. Marriage & Family Therapists, Soc. Psychologists in Addictive Behaviors, Maine Psychol. Assn. (charter), Bd. Examiners Psychologists. Democrat. Avocations: music, tennis, swimming, bicycling, kayaking. Home: 959 Garland Rd Winslow ME 04901-0552 Office: 959 Garland Rd Winslow ME 04901-0552 Office Phone: 207-877-0718. Personal E-mail: drkaren@adelphia.net.

GILLMOR, HELEN, federal judge; BA, Queen's Coll. of CUNY, 1965; LLB magna cum laude, Boston U., 1968. With Ropes & Gray, Boston, 1968-69, Law Offices of Alexander R. Gillmor, Camden, Maine, 1970, Torkildson, Katz, Jossem, Fonseca, Jaffe, Moore & Hetherington, Honolulu, 1971-72; law clk. to Chief Justice William S. Richardson Hawaii State Supreme Ct., 1972; dep. pub. defender Office of Pub. Defender, Honolulu, 1972-74; dist. ct. judge per diem Family Ct. (1st cir.) Hawaii, 1977-83; per diem judge Dist. Ct., 1st circuit, 1983-85; pvt. practice Honolulu, 1985-94; district judge U.S. Dist. Ct. Hawaii, 9th circuit, 1994—2005, chief dist. judge, 2005—. Counsel El Paso Real Estate Investment Trust, 1969; lectr. U.S. Agy. Internat. Devel., Seoul, South Korea, 1969-70, Univ. Hawaii, 1975. Office: Prince J K Kuhio Fed Bldg 300 Ala Moana Blvd Rm C-400 Honolulu HI 96850-0400

GILLMOR, KAREN LAKO, state agency administrator; b. Cleve., Jan. 29, 1948; d. William M. and Charlotte (Sheldon) Lako; m. Paul E. Gillmor, Dec. 10, 1983; children: Linda D., Julie E., Paul Michael, Connor W., Adam S. BA cum laude, Mich. State U., 1969; MA, Ohio State U., 1970, PhD, 1981. Asst. to v.p. Ohio State U., Columbus, 1972-77, spl. asst. dean law, 1979-81, assoc. dir. Ctr. Healthcare Policy and Rsch., 1991-92; asst. to pres. Ind. Cen. U., Indpls., 1977-78; rsch. asst. Burke Mktg. Rsch., Indpls., 1978-79; v.p. pub. affairs Huntington Nat. Bank, Columbus, 1981-82; fin. cons. Ohio Rep. Fin. Com., Columbus, 1982-83; chief mgmt. planning and rsch. Indsl. Commn. Ohio, Columbus, 1983-86; mgr. physician rels. Ohio State U. Med. Ctr., Columbus, 1987-91; cons. U.S. Sec. Labor, Washington, 1990-91; mem. Regional Bd. Rev./Indls. Commn., Ohio, 1991-92; state senator Ohio Gen. Assembly, 1993-97; vice-chair State Employment Rels. Bd., 1997—. Legis. liaison Huntington Bancshares, Ohio, Ohio State U., Columbus; trustee Heidelberg Coll., 1999—, Rutherford B. Hayes Presd. Ctr., 2002—. Mem. adv. coun. The Childhood League Ctr., 2003—; nat. bd. dirs. Nat. First Ladies' Libr., 2004—; bd. dirs. Congl. Childcare Ctr., 2003—. Named Outstanding Freshman Ohio Legislator, 1994, Outstanding Nat. Freshman Legislator of the Yr., 1995, Watchdog of the Treasury, 1994, 1996, Hon. Alumna, Heidelberg Coll., 2006; named to Rocky River H.S. Hall of Fame, 1998; recipient Pres. award, Ohio State Chiropractic Assn., 1994, Pub. Svc. award, Am. Heart Assn., 1995, Ctr. Advancement and Study of Ethics award, Capitol U. and Trinity Luth. Sem., 1996, cert. of Achievement, U.S. Dept. of Army, 1997, Friend of Medicine award, Ohio State Med. Assn., 1997, Legis. Achievement award, Ohio chpt. Am. Acad. Pediat., 1997, Spirit of Women award, 1999; grantee, Andrew W. Mellon Found., 1978, Carnegie Corp., 1978. Mem.: DAR, Coun. Advancement and Support Edn., Am. Assn. Higher Edn., Ohio Fedn. Rep. Women, Women's Roundtable, Women in Mainstream, Phi Delta Kappa. Methodist. Office: 65 E State St Ste 1200 Columbus OH 43215-4209

GILLMORE, KATHLEEN CORY, lawyer; b. Louisville, July 10, 1947; d. Elmer Louis and Frances (Cory) Hoehn; m. David Newton Gillmore, Dec. 14, 1974. Student, U. Mich., 1965-66; B.A., Purdue U., 1969; J.D., Ind. U., 1972. Bar: Ind. 1972, D.C. 1973, Ky. 1979, Tex. 1986. Ptnr., firm E.L. Hoehn, Washington, 1972-78; staff atty. Ashland Oil, Inc., Ky., 1978-82, sr. atty., 1982-85; staff atty., Shell Oil Co., Houston, Tex., 1985-87, sr. environ. atty., 1987-96, sr. environ. counsel, 1996-98, 2002-; sr. environ. counsel Equiva Svcs. LLC, 1998-2002, sr. counsel Shell Oil Co., 2002—. Mem. ABA, D.C. Bar Assn., Ind. Bar Assn., Ky. Bar Assn., Tex. Bar Assn., Houston Bar Assn. (bd. dirs. environ. section 1994-98, 2002—), Am. Petroleum Inst. (vice chmn. subcomm. on environ. and health law 1995-95, chmn. 1996-98). Office: Shell Oil Co 910 Louisiana 1 Shell Plz Houston TX 77002-2463

GILLOM, JENNIFER, professional basketball player; b. Abbeville, Miss., June 13, 1964; Grad., U. Miss., 1986. Basketball player Italian League, Milan, 1987—91, Ancona, 1991—94, Messina, 1995—96, Athens, Greece, 1996—97, Phoenix Mercury, WNBA, 1997—2002, Los Angeles Sparks, WNBA, 2003—. Named an Sports Hall of Fame, U. Miss., 1999; named to All WNBA 2nd Team, 1997, All WNBA 1st Team, 1998, Inaugural WNBA All-Star Team, 2000; recipient Gold medal, Pan Am. Games, 1987, Olympic Games, 1988, Nat. Distinction award, U. Miss., 1998, Kim Perrot Sportsmanship award, 2002, USA Basketball World Championship Team, 2002. Office: Phoenix Mercury 201 E Jefferson St Phoenix AZ 85004-2412

GILLOOLY, EDNA RAE See BURSTYN, ELLEN

GILMAN, DOROTHY (DOROTHY GILMAN BUTTERS), author; b. New Brunswick, N.J., June 25, 1923; d. J. Bruce and Essa M. (Starkweather) G.; children: Christopher Butters, Jonathan Butters. Student, Pa. Acad. Fine Arts, 1940-45, Art Students League, 1963-64. Instr. creative writing Cherry Lawn Sch., Darien, Conn., 1969-70 Author young people's novels as Dorothy Gilman Butters, 1949-62, including Girl in Buckskin, 1956, Masquerade, 1961, Bells of Freedom, 1963; author fiction as Dorothy Gilman, 1966—, (including film starring Rosalind Russell The Unexpected Mrs. Pollifax, 1966) (Reader's Digest Book Club selection), Uncertain Voyage, 1967, The Amazing Mrs. Pollifax, 1970 (Reader's Digest Book Club selection), The Elusive Mrs. Pollifax, 1971, A Palm for Mrs. Pollifax, 1973 (Reader's Digest Book Club selection), Nun in the Closet, 1975 (Religious Book award), The Clairvoyant Countess, 1975, Mrs. Pollifax on Safari, 1976 (Reader's Digest Book Club selection), (non-fiction) A New Kind of Country, 1978; The Tightrope Walker, 1979 (Reader's Digest Book Club selection), The Maze in the Heart of the Castle, 1983, Mrs. Pollifax on the China Station (Readers Digest Book Club selection 1983), Mrs. Pollifax and the Hong Kong Buddha, 1985, Mrs. Pollifax and the Golden Triangle, 1988 (Reader's Digest Book Club selection), Incident at Badamyâ, 1989, Mrs. Pollifax and The Whirling Dervish, 1990 (Readers's Digest Book Club selection, Lit. Guild selection); contbr. short stories as Dorothy Gilman Butters to Redbook, Ladies Home Jour., McCalls, others. Mem. Authors Guild. Office: care Howard Morhaim Agy 175 5th Ave New York NY 10010-7703

GILMAN, SHARON LARIMER, biology professor; b. Abington, Pa., Aug. 10, 1963; d. Daniel McKenna and Vicki Lanning Larimer; m. Craig S. Gilman, Sept. 6, 1991; children: Jeff X., Nicole Skye. BA in Biology, McDaniel Coll., Westminster, Md., 1985; PhD in Oceanography, U. RI, Kingston, 1992. Oceanography lab instr. U. Victoria, BC, Canada, 1992—94; marine sci. lectr. Coastal Carolina U., Conway, SC, 1994—98, biology instr., 1998—2001, asst. prof. biology, 2001—. Mem. edn. and pub. awareness com. Ocean Rsch. Interactive Obs. Networks, Washington, 2005—. Contbr. articles to profl. jours. Mem. bd. Playcard Environ. Edn. Ctr., Loris, SC, 1998—2001. Hotel Environ. Edn. Pilot Program grantee, SC SeaGrant Consortium, 1998-1999, Cmty. Rivers Project Vol. Water Monitoring Program grantee, US EPA, 2000-2001, Peer-Led Team Learning Workshop Program Assoc. grantee, NSF, 2002-2003, Environ. Edn. Planning grantee, 2005—. Mem.: NSTA, Nat. Assn. Rsch. Sci. Tchg., Project Kaleidoscope, SC Acad. Sci. (councilor 2004—), Nat. Marine Educators Assn., Nat. Audubon Soc., Sierra Club. Avocations: reading, cooking, travel. Office: Coastal Carolina U 109 Chanticleer Dr Smith Sci Ctr Conway SC 29526 Office Fax: 843-349-2201. Business E-Mail: sgilman@coastal.edu.

GILMAN, SUSAN JANE, writer; b. NY; married. Grad, Brown Univ., 1986; MFA in Creative Writing, Univ. Mich. Reporter Jewish Week newspaper; tchr., writing, lit., poetry, drama Univ. Mich., Eastern Mich. Univ.; commentator World News Radio, Washington; columnist, editor-at-large Hues mag. Author: Kiss My Tiara, 2001, Hypocrite in a Pouffy White Dress, 2005. Recipient NY Press Assn. award for feature writing. Mailing: c/o Author Mail Warner Books 1271 Ave of Americas New York NY 10020

GILMAN-ANDERSON, SUSAN ELLEN, real estate company executive, consultant; b. Brockton, Mass., June 18, 1962; d. Alden Reed and Phoebe Ames Gilman. BA, Green Mountain Coll., 1985. Dir. relocation Relocation Resources Internat. Inc, Norwell, Mass., 1995—2002; dir. relocation and corp. svcs. ERA Stirling Properties, Covington, La., 2003—. Cons. relocation Rockport Co., Marlboro, Mass., 1995. Mem. Relocation Dirs. Coun. Mem.: Relocation Dirs. Coun., Profl. Employee Relocation Coun. (assoc. cert. relocation profl. 1998, PERC 2003), St. Tammany C. of C. Conservative-R. Protestant. Avocations: travel, swimming, camping, hiking. Office: ERA Stirling Properties 109 Northpark Blvd Ste 300 Covington LA 70433 Office Phone: 985-246-3400. Home Fax: 504-523-8577, 985-246-3420; Office Fax: 504-523-8577, 985-246-3420. Business E-Mail: sanderson@stirlingprop.com, sanderson@erastirling.com.

GILMARTIN, CLARA T., volunteer; b. East Stroudsburg, Pa., Jan. 23, 1922; d. Harry and Clarissa (Snearley) Treible; m. John Gilmartin, Jan. 18, 1945 (dec. Feb. 1956); children: Ronald, Donald; m. William Gilmartin, Sept. 8, 2002. BA, Rutgers U., 1961, MA, 1966. Elem. sch. tchr. Union Beach (N.J.) Pub. Sch., 1956-61; lang. arts tchr. Holmdel Village (N.J.) Intermediate Sch., 1961-82; Fulbright exch. tchr. New Zealand, 1973-74; mem. adv. bd. Juvenile Conf. Com., 1986—. Chair bd. trustees Grace Meth. Ch., Union Beach, 1997—. Mem. Monmouth County Ret. Educators Assn., Am. Legion (Post 321 Color Guard, scholarship com., trustee, chaplain), Triad. Democrat. Home: 122 Dock St Union Beach NJ 07735

GILMER, PENNY JANE, biochemist, educator; b. Hackensack, NJ, Aug. 19, 1943; d. Peter E. and Barbara D. (Joynt) Gilmer; m. Sanford A. Safron, Sept. 9, 1980; children: Helena M., Nathaniel S. BA in Chemistry, Douglass Coll., 1965; MA in Organic Chemistry, Bryn Mawr Coll., 1967; PhD in Biochemistry, U. Calif.-Berkeley, 1972; DSc in Sci. Edn., Curtin U. Tech., 2004. Bank Am.-Giannini postdoctoral fellow Stanford U. (Calif.), 1973—75, USPHS and NIH postdoctoral fellow, 1975—77, acting asst. prof. human biology, 1976—77; asst. prof. chemistry Fla. State U., Tallahassee, 1977—84, assoc. prof., 1984—96, interim assoc. dean coll. arts and scis., 1990—91, assoc. chair chemistry, 1991—93, prof., 1996—. Lectr. in field. Contbr. articles to profl. jour. Recipient Faculty Rsch. award, Fla. State U., 1978, 1984, 1986, 1990, Tchg. Incentive award, 1993—94, Outstanding Cmty. Women award, Am. Assn. U. Women, Tallahassee br., 2006; grantee NIH, 1979—81, Rsch. Corp., 1979—86, 1990—96, Am. Cancer Soc., 1981—83, Jessie Ball duPont Fund, 1987—89, Nat. Sci. Found., 1990—. Mem.: AAAS, Assn. Sci. Tchr. Edn. (Outstanding Sci. Tchr. Educator 2006), Nat. Assn. Rsch. Sci. Tchg. (bd. 2003—, pres.-elect 2006—), Assn. Women in Sci., Southeastern Immunology Conf. (dir. 1979—84, pres. 1982), Audubon Soc., Am. Chem. Soc., Fedn. Biol. Chemists, Zonta Internat. (pres. Tallahassee Club 1992—93), Sierra Club, Sigma Xi. Democrat. Office: Fla State U Dept Chemistry and Biochemistry Tallahassee FL 32306-4390 Office Phone: 850-644-4026. Business E-Mail: gilmer@chem.fsu.edu.

GILMER, STACI ROSE, special education educator; d. T. Carter and Marquita Denise Gilmer. BA, Hampton U., 1997; MEd, Bowling Green State U., 2002. Cert. tchr. Va., Ohio. Speech and lang. pathologist Richmond (Va.) Pub. Schs., 1997—2000; early childhood spl. edn. tchr. Prince William County Pub. Schs., Manassas, Va., 2003—. Tchr. rep. adv. coun. Ann Ludwig Sch., Woodbridge, 2004—05, preschool chmn., 2004—. Youth cmty. activist; children's choir dir., mem. women's ministry Mt. Olive Bapt. Ch.; participant/organizer Children's Miracle Network Dance -A- Thon, Bowling Green, Ohio, 2000—02. Fellow, Bowling Green State U., 2000—02; grantee, Lucas County Ednl. Svc. Ctr., 2001. Mem.: Coun. Exceptional Children (assoc.), Omicron Delta Kappa (assoc.). Avocation: travel. Office: Ann Ludwig Sch 2221 Opitz Blvd Woodbridge VA 22191 Office Phone: 703-491-6090. Office Fax: 703-491-7475. Business E-Mail: pooh1tchr@msn.com.

GILMORE, BRENDA RENÉ, literature and language educator, theater director; BA in English, Northern Ill. U., Dekalb, 1990; MA in speech, Northern Ill. U., Chgo., 2002. Theatre dir. Camp Kamaji, Benidji, Minn., 1990; speech coach Wanbondie Valley HS, Aurora, Ill., 1991—95; English tchr. Wanbondia Valley HS, Aurora, Ill., 1991—99, theatre dir., 1993—99, Neugua Valley HS, Naperville, Ill., 1999—2001, English and theatre tchr., 1999—; speech coach Nenqua Valley HS, Naperville, Ill., 1999—2000; theatre dir. Summer Place Theatre, Naperville, Ill., 2001, 2002. Prodr.: Boy the Musical, 2004; (plays) She Loves Me, 2005. Bd. mem. Summer Place Theatre, 2003—, sec., 2004—. Avocations: tennis, music, theater. Office: Neuqua HS 2360 95th St Naperville IL 60564

GILMORE, CONNIE SUE, director; b. Nashville, Sept. 3, 1951; d. Earl C. and L. Louise (Coleman) G. AA, Stephens Coll., 1971; BA, Vanderbilt U., 1973; MA, Cumberland U., 1992, postgrad., 1992—. Cert. tchr., Tenn. Tchr. Bellevue Presbyn. Ch., Nashville, 1980-83, dir., 1983-86; presch. tchr. St. Henry's Ch., Nashville, 1985-89, dir., 1986-90; comparative fin. analyst Vanderbilt U., 1998—. Tutor BellSouth Grant Reading Program, Lebanon, Tenn., 1990. Editor, author: Leadership, 1992. Mem. Nat. Assn. for Edn. Young Children, So. Assn. for Children Under Six, Tenn. Assn. for Young Children, Nashville Area Assn. for Young Children, So. Literacy Soc. (charter)., Kappa Delta Pi

GILMORE, DAWN S., music educator; b. Ontario, Calif., Oct. 6, 1956; d. Hubert and Sarah Lagasse; m. Glenn Gilmore, Nov. 27, 1982; children: Valerie Barnes, Marlena Vigeveno, Paul. BA, Azusa Pacific U., 1978, MusM, 1985. Cert. tchr. Calif. Music, drama tchr. Seattle Christian Sch., 1989—91; min. music North City Free Meth. Ch., Seattle, 1989—91, Antioch (Calif) Wesleyan Ch., 1992—93; min. of music Garden Grove (Calif.) Ch. of Nazarene, 1993—95; music tchr. Village Christian Schs., Sun Valley, Calif., 1995—; choir dir. Emmanuel Evang. Free Ch., Burbank, Calif., 2005—. Dir. Willing Heart, Seattle, 1988—90; singer Gary Bonner Singers, Orange, Calif., 1995—2006. Singer 18 CD recordings. Mem.: Choristers Guild, Am. Choral Dirs. Assn. (assoc.), Music Educators Nat. Conf. (assoc.). Office: Village Christian Schs 8930 Village Ave Sun Valley CA 91352 Office Phone: 818-767-8382. Office Fax: 818-768-2006. E-mail: dawng@villagechristian.org.

GILMORE, JENNIFER A.W., computer specialist, educator; b. San Fernando, Trinidad, Jan. 12, 1954; arrived in US, 1972, naturalized, 1993; d. Fitzroy Grant and Zelma (Williams) Oudkerk; m. Frederick R. Gilmore, June 17, 1983. BA, MA, Bklyn. Coll., NY, 1984; BBA, MS, Baruch Coll., NYC, 1993; MBA, LI U., NY, 1994; PhD, Kennedy-Western U., Cheyenne, Wyo., 2001, Walden U., Mpls., 2001. Cert. Microsoft Office Specialist (MOS) 2002, Internet Computing Core (IC3) Certiport, 2003, IC3 Instr. Certiport, 2003, Online Tchr. U. Md. Univ. Coll., 2003; coll. tchg. Kaplan U., 2005, blackboard tchg. Baker Coll., 2006. COBOL programmer MetLife, N.Y.C., 1972-86; project mgr., human resources adminstrn. mgmt. info. sys. City of N.Y., 1990—. Adj. prof. NYC Coll. Tech., 1997, Kingsborough C.C., 1998, St. Francis Coll., Bklyn., 1998, Medgar Evers Coll., 1998, Borough of Manhattan C.C., 1998, Touro Coll., 1999—, Baruch Coll., 1999—2000, Monroe Coll., 1999—, U. Md., 2003—, Kaplan U., 2005—, Baker Coll. Online, 2006—. Author: (books) A Case Study of Two System Development Projects and their Implementation, 2003, An Analysis of Computer and Telephone Usage in the New York City Metropolitan Area, 2003. Democrat. Adventist. Home: 47 Mckeever Pl Apt 16J Brooklyn NY 11225-2537 Office: NYC-HRA-MIS 15 Metrotech Brooklyn NY 11201 Personal E-mail: jgilmore102716560@yahoo.com.

GILMORE, JOAN ELIZABETH, small business owner, newspaper columnist; b. Waukegan, Ill., May 14, 1927; d. Joseph and Helen Ruth (Parks) G.; m. Alfred W. McLaughlin II, Mar. 25, 1974. BA, Drury Coll., 1951. Asst. soc. editor Springfield (Mo.) Newspapers, Inc., 1951; editor women's sect. Phoenix & Times-Dem., Muskogee, Okla., 1952; editor women's news sect. The Daily Oklahoman, Oklahoma City, 1952-80; met. news editor The Oklahoma and Oklahoma City Times, 1979-80; owner, pres. Joan Gilmore, Inc., Oklahoma City, 1980—; columnist The Jour. Record, Oklahoma City, 1982—. Bd. visitors U. Okla., Sch. Nursing, 2006—. V.p. Children's Miracle Network Telethon, 1986; charter bd. mem. Children's Med. Rsch. Inst., 1983; chair, adv. bd. U. Okla. Breast Health Inst., 2003—04; bd. dir. Okla. City Nat. Meml., 2003—. Named one of Outstanding Bd. Dirs., Okla. Soc. to Prevent Blindness, 1990, Outstanding Women in Comm., Red Lands coun. Girl Scouts Am., 1995; named to Okla. Journalism Hall of Fame, 1994; recipient Comm. award, Nat. Fedn. Colored Women's Clubs, 1970, Women in Comm., Inc., 1974, Gov.'s Arts award, Okla. Gov. Henry Bellmon, 1990, Drury U. Outstanding Alumnae, 2001, Oklahoma City U. Women of Distinction, 2002, Woman of the Yr. Lifetime Achievement award, Jour. Record, 2005. Mem.: Leadership Oklahoma City (charter, sec. bd. dirs. 1981, Founders award 1992). Avocations: volunteer, reading, travel. Home: 2415 NW 55th St Oklahoma City OK 73112-7720

GILMORE, JUDITH MARIE, physician; b. Houston, Dec. 28, 1942; d. Howard Ray and Mary Gardner (Currier) G.; m. Richard E. Kelley, July 21, 1974 (div. 1981); 1 child, Lisa Kelley. BA, U. Maine, 1965; MA, NYU, 1968; MD, Woman's Med. Coll., 1972. Diplomate Am. Bd. Internal Medicine, Am. Bd. Endocrinology. Resident St. Vincent's Hosp., N.Y.C., 1972-74; fellow in endocrinology St. Raphael's Hosp., New Haven, 1974-75, West Haven VA-Yale Hosp., New Haven, 1975-76; pvt. practice Bridgeport, Conn., 1976-80, Cranston, R.I., 1986—; mem. staff St. Joseph's Hosp., Providence, 1986—; mem. cons. staff Newport (R.I.) Hosp., 1986—; mem. courtesy staff Roger Williams Hosp., Providence, 1994—, R.I. Hosp., Providence, 1995, Kent County Hosp., Pawtucket Meml. Hosp. Lt. comdr. USNR, 1980-86. Mem. ACP, AMA, Am. Assn. Endocrine, Am. Diabetes Assn., R.I. Endocrine Assn. Avocations: hiking, music, art. Office: 725 Reservoir Ave Ste 2 Providence RI 02910-4450 Office Phone: 401-943-5120. E-mail: JP1994@msn.com.

GILMORE, JUNE ELLEN, psychologist; b. Middletown, Ohio, Oct. 22, 1927; d. Linley Lawrence and Elizabeth Kathleen (Barker) Wetzel; m. John Lester Gilmore, July 6, 1945; children: John Lester Jr., Michael Edward. BS, Miami U., Oxford, 1961; MS, Miami U., 1964. Lic. psychologist, Ohio. Intern in psychology Hamilton (Ohio) City Schs., 1963-64; psychologist Talawanda, Shiloh, Trenton Schs., Butler County, Ohio, 1964-66, Franklin (Ohio) City Schs., 1966-72, Wapakoneta (Ohio) City Schs., 1972-76, Cin. City Schs., 1978-86; pvt. practice psychology, 1975-95; planner, evaluator Warren/Clinton Counties Mental Health Bd., Ohio, 1986-88; adj. instr. Wright State U., Dayton, Ohio, 1989-90. Co-author: Summer Children-Ready or not for School, 1986, The Rape of Childhood--No Time to be a Kid, 1990. Sec. Tri County Drug Coun., Lima, Ohio, 1975; chmn. Auglaize County Social Svcs., Wapakoneta, 1973-75; bd. dirs. Butler County Alcohol and Drug Addiction Svcs. Bd., 1990-97, sec., 1992-94. Mem. Ohio Sch. Psychologists Assn. (exec. bd. 1982-86), Southwestern Ohio Sch. Psychologist Assn. (pres.), Southwest Council Exceptional Children (Pres.), Nat. Assn. Sch. Psychologists, Ohio Psychol. Assn., Butler County Retired Tchrs. Assn. (newsletter editor 2002-04, pres. 2004-), Butler County 648 Mental Health Bd. (bd. dirs. 1978-86, pres. 1983-84), Daughters of Am. Revolution Republican. United Methodist. Home and Office: 6120 Michael Rd Middletown OH 45042-9402

GILMORE, KATHI, former state treasurer; b. Dec. 23, 1944; m. Richard Gilmore; children: Suzi, Barb, Jeff, Amy. Mem. N.D. Ho. of Reps. from Dist. 6, 1989-92; treas. State of N.D., 1993—2004. Mem. Bd. Tax Equalization, State Hist. Bd., State Investment Bd., Tchrs. Fund for Retirement Bd., State Canvassing Bd., Bd. of Univ. and Sch. Lands Mem.: Assn. Securities Profls. (hon. co-chair pension fund conf. 1994, Task Forces Orgnl. Planning and Coordinating Com. 1993), Retirement and Investment Office Internal Audit Com., Nat. Assn. State Treas. (pension com.). Democrat. Presbyterian.

GILMORE, LOUISA RUTH, retired nurse; b. Pitts., Oct. 31, 1930; d. Albert Leonard and Bertha Christina (Birch) Huber; m. William Norman II Kemp (div. 1975); children: Janyce Louise Kemp Lipson, Barbra Lea Kemp Bilharz, Robert William, Paul Lee, Charles Albert; m. Robert James Gilmore, Sept. 1, 1989; stepchildren: Robi Lynn Lee, Donna Elizabeth Singleton. Diploma in nursing, San Bernardino C.C., Needles, Calif., 1983. Office nurse Santa Fe Clinic, Needles, 1953-57; spl. duty nurse Needles Cmtys. Hosp., 1957-62; nurse supr. Santa Fe Clinic, 1962-79; staff nurse in surgery Needles Desert Cmtys. Hosp., 1979-90; Cell Tech ind. distbr. Reliv Products, Temple, Tex., 1991-95; with Fine Host Corp., 1996—2001; food or product demonstrator Sam's Club #6336, 2000-2001, demonstrator jewelry dept., door greeter, 2001—. Instr. CPR Needles Desert Cmtys. Hosp., 1987-90; med. officer San Bernardino County Fire Dept., Needles, 1980-83, pub. info. officer, 1983-85, vol. fire fighter, 1983-90; ind. distbr. Reliv Products, 1991-95, Cell Tech., 1996. Mem. Calif. State Fireman Assn., Needles Firefighters Assn. (treas. 1987, 88), Beta Sigma Phi-Zeta Gamma (treas. 1966, sec. 1967, v.p. 1968, pres. 1969, named Sweetheart Queen 1969), Order of Rose (life). Avocations: travel, plastercraft and oil painting. Personal E-mail: fireangel5318@yahoo.com, rolukg2@yahoo.com. Business E-Mail: rgilmore@vvm.com.

GILMORE, MARJORIE HAVENS, retired civic worker, lawyer; b. NYC, Aug. 16, 1918; d. William Westerfield and Elsie (Medl) Havens; m. Hugh Redland Gilmore, May 8, 1942; children: Douglas Hugh, Anne Charlotte Gilmore Decker, Joan Louise. AB, Hunter Coll., 1938; JD, Columbia U., 1941. Bar: N.Y. 1941, Va. 1968. Rsch. asst. N.Y. Law Revision Commn., 1941—42; assoc. Spence, Windels, Walser, Hotchkiss & Angell, N.Y.C., 1942, Chadbourne, Wallace, Parke & Whiteside, N.Y.C., 1942-43; atty. U.S. Army, Washington, 1948-53. Sec., Thomas Jefferson Jr. High Sch. PTA, 1956-58; chmn. by-laws rev. com., Long Point Corp., Ferrisburg, Vt.,

1981-93; parliamentarian Wakefield High Sch. PTA, 1959-60, chmn. citizenship com., 1960-61; publicity chmn. Patrick Henry Sch. PTA, sec., 1964-65; parliamentarian Nottingham PTA, 1966-69; mem. extra-curricular activities com. Arlington County Sch. Bd.; area chmn. fund drive Cancer Soc., 1955-56; active Girl Scouts U.S.A., 1963-70; mem. '41 com. Columbia Law Sch. Fund. Recipient Constl. Law award Hunter Coll., 1938. Mem. Arlington Fedn. Women's Clubs (rec. sec. 1979-80), No. Dist. Va. Fedn. Women's Clubs (rec. sec. 1979-80), No. Dist. Va. Fedn. Women's Clubs (chmn. legis. com. 1986-88, chmn. pub. affairs no. dist. 1988-90), Williamsburg Woman's Club of Arlington (corr. sec. 1970-72, 97-98, 1st v.p. 1972-74, pres. 1974-76, 98-99, chmn. comms. 1981-82, chmn. legis. com. 1982-86, 90-98, pres. 1998-2000, pub. affairs chmn. 2000—), Columbia Law Sch. Alumni Assn., Alpha Sigma Rho. Presbyterian. Home: 12191 Clipper Dr Apt 304 Woodbridge VA 22192-2239

GILPATRICK, JANET, public relations executive, consultant; b. Seattle, Jan. 26, 1944; d. Donald Ernst Majer; children: Annie, Dawn. Dep. dir. Carter-Mondale Campaign, Wash., 1978—80; dist. dir. Spkr. of the House Thomas S. Foley, 1981—95; adminstr. asst. Office of Former U.S. Spkr. Thomas S. Foley, 1995—98; sr. cons. pub. affairs and pub. rels. Rockey-West Co., Spokane, 1998—2004; devel. dir. Inland N.W. Sci.-Tech., Spokane, 2004—. Owner JL Gilpatrick and Assocs., Spokane, 2004—. Bd. dirs. YWCA, Spokane, United Way, Women Helping Women, Mirabeau Point, Spokane Intercollegiate Rsch. Inst.; mem. Spokane Housing Commn.; mem. state bd. dirs. FEMA, Spokane. Office: JL Gilpatrick and Assoc So 922 Cowley Ave Spokane WA 99202 Personal E-mail: jlgilpatrick@aol.com.

GILPIN, JEANNY, elementary school educator; b. Fayette, Ala., July 27, 1962; d. Richard D and Jean McCracken; m. Eddy Dewayne Gilpin, Nov. 20, 1982; children: Kyle, Kirk. BS in Elem. Edn., Tenn. Tech. U., Cookeville, 1987; MA in Elem. Edn., U. Ala., Tuscaloosa, 1997. Cert. tchr. N-8 Va., 2002, tchr. Va., 2003. Headmistress Connally Christian Sch., Chimala, Tanzania; tchr. Coldwater Elem. Sch., Oxford, Ala., 1994—97, Glenvar Elem. Sch., Salem, Va., 1998—2001; math. tchr. Andrew Lewis Mid. Sch., Salem, 2001—. Author: (writing) Novel Guides. Named Tchr. of Yr., Roanoke County Sch. Sys., 2000; scholar, Va. Profl. Educators, 2005. Mem.: Va. Profl. Educators (Salem rep. 2005—06). Home: 1840 Tucker Ln Salem VA 24153 Office: Andrew Lewis Middle School 606 College Ave Salem VA 24153 Office Phone: 540-387-2513. Personal E-mail: gilpincrew@yahoo.com. Business E-Mail: jgilpin@salem.k12.va.us.

GILPIN, PERI, actress; b. Waco, Tex., May 27, 1961; m. Christian Vincent, 1999; children: Ava Vincent, Stella Vincent. Former student, Dallas Theatre Ctr., U. Tex., Brit.-Am. Acad., London. Owner prod. co. (with Jane Leeves) Bristol Cities. Actress (TV series) Frasier, 1993-2004 (SAG award outstanding performance ensemble, 2000), The Lionhearts (voice), 1998; (TV guest appearances) 21 Jump Street, 1988, Matlock, 1990, Wings, 1992, Designing Women, 1993, Cheers, 1993, Pride & Joy, 1995, The Outer Limits, 1996, Early Edition, 1996, Superman, 1998, Hercules (voice), 1998, Baby Blues, 2000, The Chris Isaak Show, 2001, King of the Hill (voice), 2003, Justice League (voice), 2003, I'm With Her, 2003; (TV movies) Fight for Justice: The Nancy Conn Story, 1995, The Secret She Carried, 1996, Laughter on the 23rd Floor, 2001, (films) Spring Forward, 1999, How to Kill Your Neighbor's Dog, 2000, Finaly Fantasty: The Spirits Within (voice), 2001; guest appearance Later with Greg Kinnear, 1994, Early Edition, 1996, The Outer Limits, 1995, Superman, 1996, Pride & Joy, 1995, Talk Soup, 1991, Matlock, 1986, 21 Jump Street, 1987. Office: William Morris Agy One William Morris Place Beverly Hills CA 90212-2775

GILSON, SUSAN LEE, performing arts educator; d. Izzy and Beatrice C. Westen; m. Robert Gilson, Sept. 6, 1970; 1 child, Tamara Shannon. AA, Santa Monica City Coll., 1964. Profl. dancer Dance Ctr. West, LA, 1964—69; dance instr., staff choreographer Palomar Coll., San Marcos, Calif., 1974—, dir. outreach program, 1997—; owner Georgia's Sch. Dance, 1997—. Bd. dirs. Jazz Dance World Congress, Chgo., Calif. Rhythm Tap Project, San Diego; musical theatre choreographer Palomar Coll., San Marcos, 1975—. Co-prodr., choreographer Gershwin in Revue, 1993, Ballads, Blues & Boogie Woogie, 1994, Stompin' at the Brubeck, 1996. Mem.: Escondido C. of C., Downtown Bus. Assn. Avocations: travel, shopping, dance, designing costumes. Office: Palomar Coll 1140 W Mission San Marcos CA 92069 Office Phone: 760-744-1150 ext. 5304, 760-745-6662.

GILSTRAP, LEAH ANN, media specialist; b. Seneca, S.C., Sept. 12, 1950; d. Raymond Chester and Eunice Hazel (Long) Gilstrap. AA, Anderson Coll., 1973; BA in History, Furman U., 1976, MEd, 1982; MLS, U. S.C., 1991. Cert. tchr., media specialist S.C. Tchr. Greenville (S.C.) County Sch. Dist., 1978-92, media specialist, 1992—. Mem.: ALA, NEA (del. 1991—95), Greenville County Coun. Media Specialists (bd. dirs. 1993—94), Greenville County Edn. Assn. (bd. dirs., governance chair 1988—98, v.p. 1996—97, pres. 1997—98), S.C. Edn. Assn. (bd. dirs. 1994—96), S.C. Assn. Sch. Librs. Democrat. Baptist. Avocations: travel, reading. Home: 19 Anson Ct Simpsonville SC 29681-5560 Office: Bryson Mid Sch 3657 S Industrial Dr Simpsonville SC 29681-3295 Office Phone: 864-355-2100. Business E-Mail: lgistra@greenville.k12.sc.us.

GIMBRÈRE, KATHREEN, psychiatrist, educator; b. Toledo, Ohio, Feb. 4, 1959; d. Rene Hubert Marie Gambrère and Suzanne Briley; m. Stanley Rill (div.). BA with Hons., Harvard U., Cambridge, Mass., 1981; MD with Hons., Cornell Med. Sch., N.Y.C., 1990. Lic. MD Wash. Adolescent fellowship U. Wash., Seattle, 1994; pvt. practice Port Townsend Pediatrics, Port Townsend, Wash., 1996—99; med. dir., juvenile rehab. adminstrn. DSHS, Olympia, 1999—2002; psychiat. residency U. Wash., 2002—05, asst. prof., psychiatry, 2005—. Pediatric cons. Gray Wolf Ranch, Port Townsend, 1996—99; admissions com. U. Wash., 2004—05. Contbr. articles articles to profl. jours. and pubs. Mem.: Am. Acad. Psychiatry, Noetic Scis., Seattle Jungian Soc., Amnesty Internat. Independent. Safi. Avocations: yoga, hiking, travel. Office: Univ Wash Harborview Med Ctr 401 Broadway Av Seattle WA 98112

GIMENES, SONIA REGINA ROSENDO, family therapist, psychologist; b. São Paulo, Brazil, Jan. 25, 1953; arrived in U.S., 1996; d. Joao Rosendo and Luzia Pragelis; m. Airton Jose Gimenes, May 7, 1976; children: Erika, Rodrigo. BS in Psychology, U. Mogi Cruzes, São Paulo, 1980; M in Sci. Psychology with honors, U. Americas, Mexico City, 1988; postgrad. in psychology; cert. in clin. psychology, U. Paulista, São Paulo, 1994. Registered family therapist intern Fla., lic. clin. psychologist Brazil. Family therapist intern Clinica Oira, Mexico City, 1987—88; psychologist intern Clinica Psicologia Objetivo, São Paulo, Brazil, 1994, Pontificia U. Cath., São Paulo, 1995; clin. psychologist Human Inst., São Paulo, 1995—96; family therapist Counseling and Hypnosis Inc., Miami, Fla., 1999—. Author: Domestic Violence, 2001; contbr. monography project Child Abuse, 1988, articles to profl. jours. Mem.: ACA, Am. Bd. Hypnotherapy, Am. Coll. Forensic Examiners, Am. Psychotherapy Assn., Rotary Internat. (Paul Harris medal of honor 1976). Avocations: music, dance, piano, arts and crafts. Office: Brickle Bayview Co Bus Ctr 80 SW 8th St Ste 2000 Miami FL 33130 Fax: 786-275-9514.

GIMON, ELEANOR HEWLETT, philanthropist; d. William and Flora Hewlett. Former mem. bd. dirs. Hewlett-Packard Co.; bd. dirs. William and Flora Hewlett Found., William R. Hewlett Revocable Trust. Former mem. library com. Brown U. Former trustee Brown U. Office: William and Flora Hewlett Found 2121 Sand Hill Rd Menlo Park CA 94025*

GIMON, JULIETTE, foundation administrator, volunteer; d. Eleanor Hewlett Gimon. BA in Anthropology, Columbia U. Mem. family council Flora Family Found.; fellow, trustee William and Flora Hewlett Found., 2000—; former instructor WorldTeach, Quito, Ecuador; former recycling prog. designer Fundación Natura; co-founder, outreach and develop. coordinator Global Philanthropy Forum (now project of World Affairs Council of No. Calif.). Bd. dirs. Synergos Inst., Global Fund for Children; adv. com. mem. Youth Philanthropy Worldwide, Global Philanthropy Forum. Office: Global Philanthropy Forum World Affairs Ctr 312 Sutter St Ste 200 San Francisco CA 94108*

GINER, A. SILVANA, lawyer; b. 1959; BA cum laude, Univ. Mass., Amherst, 1982; JD, Stanford Univ., 1985. Bar: Mass. 1985. Assoc. to ptnr. Wilmer Cutler Pickering Hale & Dorr, Boston, 1985—, vice chmn. Private Client dept. Contbr. chapters to books. Trustee Boston Social Law Libr., Brain Sci. Found., Medfield, Mass.; mem. adv. bd. Commonwealth Coll., Univ. Mass. Amherst; overseer Opera Boston. Fellow: Am. Coll. Trust & Estate Counsel; mem.: Boston Estate Planning Council, Phi Beta Kappa. Office: Wilmer Cutler Pickering Hale & Dorr 60 State St Boston MA 02109 Office Phone: 617-526-6327. Office Fax: 617-526-5000. Business E-Mail: nan.giner@wilmerhale.com.

GINGER, ANN FAGAN, lawyer; b. Nov. 25, 1925; Exec. dir. Meiklejohn Civil Liberties Inst., Berkeley. Vis. prof. law Univ. Calif. Hastings Coll., Univ. San Francisco, Univ. Santa Clara, New Coll. Calif., Univ. Puget Sound. Author: Calif. Criminal Law Practice (vol. I & II), The National Law Guide, Jury Selection in Civil & Criminal Trials, & other books and articles on civil liberties law. Office: Meiklejohn Civil Liberties Institute PO Box 673 Berkeley CA 94701-0673

GINGHER, MERLENE C., occupational therapist, educator; b. Buffalo, N.Y. d. Earl George and Merna Bethene Gingher. BS, SUNY, Buffalo, N.Y., 1970, MS, 1975, EdD, 1989. Physical therapist Erie Co. Home Infirmary, Buffalo, 1970—75; instr. SUNY, Buffalo, 1975—76; occupl. therapist, dir. Indendent. Living Project, Buffalo, 1976—80; asst. prof. SUNY, Buffalo, 1980—91, D'Youville Coll., Buffalo, 1991—. chairperson occupl. therapy, 1997—. Mem.: Program Dirs.Edn. Coun. (vice chmn. 2002—06), Am. Occupl. Therapy Assn. Avocations: singing, reading. Office: D'Youville Coll 320 Porter Ave Buffalo NY 14201 Office Phone: 716-829-7830. Business E-Mail: gingerm@dyc.edu.

GINGLES, MARJORIE STANKE, music educator; b. Bklyn., Jan. 30, 1938; d. E.C. and E.L. (Lewthwaite) Stromberg; m. Charles Frederick Stanke, Aug. 27, 1960 (div. Nov. 8, 1976); m. William Glen Gingles, Sept. 29, 1984. BS in Music Edn., W. Chester U., formerly W. Chester State Tchrs. Coll., 1959; MA in Edn., W. Chester U., formerly W. Chester State Tchrs. Coll., mem, 1969. Elem. music tchr. George Gray Elem. Sch., Wilmington, Del., 1959-60, Penn-Delco Pub. Schs., Aston, Pa., 1960-61; pvt. piano tchr. home studio Berwyn, Norwood, Devon, Malvern, Pa., 1963—; choral dir. Coterie Singers, Wayne, Pa., 1975-84; music dir. St. Francis-in-the-Fields Ch., Malvern, Pa., 1981-88; piano tchr. Acad. Cmty. Music, Fort Washington, Pa., 1997—. Mem. music com. Main Line Unitarian Ch, Devon, 1970—, chair music com., 1978-79; mem. music com. Dorothy Taubman Inst. Piano, Amherst Coll., 1988-97, adjudicator Pa. Govs. Sch. Arts, 1986; music dir. Pro-Arte Chorale, 1980-86, dir. world and area premieres of new works; instr. several vocal workshops in field; clinician PMTA Convention, 1999; presenter in field. Piano concert artist, Pa. and N.Y. State; duo pianist with William Gingles; performances (in Gingles Duo) Pa. Music Tchrs. Conv. Taubman Piano Study grantee Pa. Music Tchrs. Assn., 2000. Mem. Main Line Music Tchrs. Assn. (chair adult recitals, chair Prime Time Players). Unitarian-Universalist. Avocations: reading, swimming, decorating. Home and Office: 27 Cypress Ln Berwyn PA 19312-1004 Office Phone: 610-296-5908. Personal E-mail: wgingles@comcast.net.

GINN, SHARON PATRICK, mechanical engineer; BSME cum laude, La. Tech. U., 1976; MBA, Fla. Inst. Tech., 1990. Sr. specialist engr. Dyn McDermott, New Orleans, 1987-93; cons., 1993-97; lead facility engr. Miss. Space Svcs./Johnson Controls, Bay St. Louis, Miss., 1997-2000; dir. facilities mgmt. Pacific U., Forest Grove, Oreg., 2000—. Tutor for Cmty. Literacy program, 1995. Mem.: ASME, Assn. Higher Edn. Facility Officers, Internat. Faclty Mgmt. Assn., Soc. Coll. and Univ. Planners. Office: Pacific U 2043 College Way Forest Grove OR 97116-1797 Home: 13385 NW Westlawn Ter Portland OR 97229-5543

GINOSAR, D. ELAINE, elementary school educator; b. Red Lodge, Mont., June 14, 1937; d. Alvin Henry and Dorothy Mary (Roberson) Wedemeyer; children: Nathan B., Daniel M., David M. BA, Calif. State U., Northridge, 1964, MA, 1977. Cert. elem. tchr., reading and learning disabilities. Tchr. Sacramento City Unified Sch. Dist., 1997—, math. leader, 1992-95. Owner, operator rental properties. Pres. Davis (Calif.) Flower Arrangers, 1993-96, 2005—; host family for U. Calif. Davis to 15 fgn. students from Japan, Thailand, Mexico, South Korea, 1990-95. Named Woman of Yr. Am. Biog. Soc., 1996. Mem. AAUW (edn. equity chair 1993-95, edn. chair 1965-93, readers theater, women's history week 1990, 91, treas. 1993-98, pres. 1990-91, 98-2000), Calif. Tchrs. Assn., Delta Kappa Gamma (pres. 2000-02). Republican. Presbyterian. Home: 3726 Chiles Rd Davis CA 95616-4346

GINSBERG, NINA, lawyer; b. NYC, Nov. 12, 1951; BA with honors, U. Rochester, 1973; JD, Antioch Law Sch., 1978. Bar: DC 1978, Va. 1980, admitted to practice: US Supreme Ct. 1990. Ptnr. DiMuro Ginsberg PC, Alexandria, Va. Adj. faculty George Washington U. Law Ctr., Washington, 1994—; bd. editors Criminal Law Advocacy Reporter, 1993—; faculty mem. Va. State Bar Mandatory Course on Professionalism, 1990—92; practitioner's adv. com. US Sentencing Commn., 1990—2001. Named one of 75 Best Lawyers in Washington, Washingtonian mag., 2002. Mem.: Va. Coll. Criminal Def. Atty., Nat. Assn. Criminal Def. Atty. (chair, amicus com. 1988—90, bd. dir. 1989—95, chair, judicial liaison com. 1990—99, lawyers strike force com. 1997—, fed. sentencing guidelines com. 2000, vice chair, internat. law com. 2000—, UN Rep. 2003), Va. State Bar (8th dist. grievance com. 1986—89, advertising and solicitation com. 1990—93, vice chair, forfeiture com. 1992—2000, bar coun. 1997—2003, lawyers malpractice ins. com. 1998—, chair, lawyers malpractice ins. com. 2003—), Alexandria Bar Assn. (judicial screening com. 1989, fee arbitration com. 1989—90). Office: DiMuro Ginsberg PC 908 King St Ste 200 Alexandria VA 22314 Office Phone: 703-684-4333. Office Fax: 703-548-3181.

GINSBERG-FELLNER, FREDDA, retired pediatric endocrinologist, researcher; b. NYC, Apr. 21, 1937; d. Nathaniel and Bertha (Jagendorf) Ginsberg; m. Michael J. Fellner, Aug. 27, 1961; children: Jonathan R., Melinda F. Bramwit. AB, Cornell U., 1957; MD, NYU, 1961. Diplomate Am. Bd. Pediatrics, Am. Bd. Pediatric Endocrinology. Intern Albert Einstein Coll. Medicine, N.Y.C., 1961-62, fellow in pediatrics, 1962-63, 64-65, 66-67, resident in pediatrics, 1963-64, 65-66, clin. instr. pediatrics, 1967; assoc. in pediatrics Mt. Sinai Sch. Medicine, N.Y.C., 1967-69, asst. prof., 1969-75, assoc. prof., 1975-81, dir. div. pediatric endocrinology, 1987—96, prof. pediatrics, 1981-96; ret., 1996. Med. scis. rev. com. Juvenile Diabetes Found., 1985-88, scis. adv. bd., 1991-; mem. N.Y. State Coun. on Diabetes, Albany, 1988-89; chmn. Camp NYDA for Diabetic Children, Burlingham, 1977-1995. Recipient Humanitarian award Juvenile Diabetes Found., 1994; grantee NIH, 1977-93, Am. Diabetes Assn., 1978, March of Dimes, 1983-87, Juvenile Diabetes Found., 1982-88, 93-95, Wm. T. Grant Found., 1985-89. Fellow Am. Acad. Pediatrics; mem. Am. Diabetes Assn. (chmn. council diabetes in youth 1992-94, Outstanding Contbns. award 1991, Svc. award 1994), Soc. Pediatric Rsch., Am. Pediatric Soc., Endocrine Soc., Lawson Wilkins Pediatric Endocrine Soc., N.Y. Diabetes Assn. (pres.-elect 1985-87, pres. 1987-89, Svc. award Camp NYDA 1989, Max Ellenberg Profl. Svc. award 1993). Personal E-mail: freddagf@aol.com.

GINSBURG, IONA HOROWITZ, psychiatrist; b. N.Y.C., Dec. 2, 1931; d. A. Eugene and Gertrude (Seidman) Horowitz; m. Selig M. Ginsburg, Aug. 15, 1954 (div. 1984); children: Elizabeth, Jessica. AB, Vassar Coll., 1953; MD, Columbia U., 1957. Diplomate Am. Bd. Psychiatry and Neurology. Pvt. practice, N.Y.C., 1961—; instr. psychiatry Columbia U., N.Y.C., 1961-81, asst. clin. prof. psychiatry, 1981-95, assoc. clin. prof. psychiatry, 1995—; psychiatrist student health svc. NYU, N.Y.C., 1978—2000. Cons.-liaison psychiatrist N.Y. Presbyn. Med. Ctr., N.Y.C., 1982—. Contbr. articles to profl. jours. Med. adv. bd. Nat. Psoriasis Found. 1990-95. Recipient Josie Bradbury Travel award, Psoriasis Assn. Gt. Britain. Mem. Am. Soc. Adolescent Psychiatry, N.Y. Soc. Adolescent Psychiatry (pres. 1986, cert. of appreciation 1986), Am. Psychiat. Assn., Am. Psychosomatic Soc., Met. Coll. Mental Health Assn. (pres. 1980), Assn. Psychocutaneous Medicine N.Am. (sec.-treas. 1994-95, v.p. 1995-98, pres. 1998-2000). Office Phone: 212-289-5050.

GINSBURG, RUTH, state representative; b. Bklyn., July 18, 1931; m. George S.; two children. Grad., Bklyn. Coll., 1954. Mem. Mayor's Adv. Com. for Social Svc. Funding; mem. dist. 26 N.H. Ho. of Reps., 1996—. Mem. sci., tech. and energy com., children and family law com. N.H. Ho. Reps. Former mem. Nashua Sch. Bd.; bd. dirs. Nashua Children's Assn.; mem. Nashua Ethnic Awareness Com. Jewish. Office: NH State Legis State House Concord NH 03301

GINSBURG, RUTH BADER (JOAN RUTH BADER GINSBURG), United States Supreme Court Justice; b. Bklyn., June 23, 1933; d. Nathan and Celia (Amster) Bader; m. Martin David Ginsburg, June 23, 1954; children: Jane Carol, James Steven. AB, Cornell U., 1954; postgrad., Harvard Law Sch., 1956—58; LLB Kent scholar, Columbia Law Sch., 1959; LLD (hon.), Lund U., Sweden, 1969, Am. U., 1981, Vt. Law Sch., 1984, Georgetown U., 1985, DePaul U., 1985, Bklyn. Law Sch., 1987, Amherst Coll., 1991, Rutgers U., 1991, Lewis and Clark Coll., 1992, Radcliffe Coll., 1994, NYU, 1994, Columbia U., 1994, Smith Coll., 1994, L.I. U., 1994, U. Ill., 1995, Brandeis U., 1996, Wheaton Coll., 1997, Jewish Theol. Sem. of Am., 1997, George Washington U. Law Sch., 1997; DHL (hon.), Hebrew Union Coll., 1988. Bar: N.Y. 1959, D.C. 1975, U.S. Supreme Ct. 1967. Law sec. to Hon. Edmund L. Palmieri U.S. Dist. Ct. (so. dist.) N.Y., 1959—61; rsch. assoc. Columbia Law Sch., N.Y.C., 1961—62, assoc. dir. project internat. procedure, 1962—63; asst. prof. Rutgers U. Sch. Law, Newark, 1963—66, assoc. prof., 1966—69, prof., 1969—72, Columbia U. Sch. Law, N.Y.C., 1972—80; judge U.S. Ct. Appeals, (DC cir.), Washington, 1980—93; assoc. justice U.S. Supreme Ct., Washington, 1993—. Phi Beta Kappa vis. scholar, 1973—74; fellow Ctr. for Advanced Study in Behavioral Scis., Stanford, Calif., 1977—78; lectr. Aspen (Colo.) Inst., 1990, Salzburg (Austria) Seminar, 1984; gen. counsel ACLU, 1973—80, bd. dirs., 1974—80. Author (with Anders Bruzelius): Civil Procedure in Sweden, 1965, Swedish Code of Judicial Procedure, 1968; author: (with H.H. Kay & K. M. Davidson) Text, Cases and Materials on Sex-Based Discrimination, 1974; contbr. numerous articles to books and jours. Named one of World's 100 Most Powerful Women, Forbes mag., 2004, Most Powerful Women, 2005. Fellow: Am. Bar Found.; mem.: AAAS, Coun. Fgn. Rels., Am. Law Inst. (coun. mem. 1978—93). Office: US Supreme Ct One First St NE Washington DC 20543*

GINZBERG, ABIGAIL, video producer; b. NYC, June 6, 1950; d. Eli and Ruth (Szold) G.; 1 child, Sasha Sesser-Ginzberg. Student, London Sch. Econs., 1969-70; BA, Cornell U., 1971; JD, U. Calif., San Francisco, 1975. Bar: Calif. 1975, D.C. 1979, U.S. Supreme Ct. 1979. Instr. Boalt Hall Law Sch., Berkeley, Calif., 1975-76; atty. Zaks and Harris, San Francisco, 1976-79; litigation counselor U.S. Dept. Labor, Washington, 1979-80; staff counsel Cal/OSHA/Dept. Indsl. Rels., San Francisco, 1979-80; instr. New Coll. Sch. Law, San Francisco, 1980-84; video prodr. Ginzberg Video Prodns., Albany, Calif., 1983—. Pres. Nat. Lawyers Guild, San Francisco, 1988-91; cons. Dept. Labor, Washington, 1980-81, Dept. Health Svcs., Calif. and N.J., 1988-90, Bar Assn. of San Francisco, 1990-91. Prodr., dir.: (videos) Those Who Know Don't Tell, 1989 (Finalist award John Muir Med. Film Festival 1990, Silver Apple award Nat. Ednl. Film Festival 1990, Blue Ribbon award Am. Film and Video Festival 1990, Bronze award Houston Internat. Film Festival 1991, U.S. Environ. Film Festival award 1991), All Things Being Equal, 1989 (Golden Eagle award 1990, Finalist award Internat. Film and TV Festival N.Y. 1990), A Firm Commitment, 1990 (San Francisco AFTRA/SAG Am. Scene award 1991, silver plaque INTERCOM/Chgo. Film Festival 1991, Com. on Partnership award ABA 1992, Am. Scene award AFTRA/SAG 1992), All in A Day's Work, 1992 (E. Smythe Gambrell/ABA award 1993), Doing Justice: The Life and Trials of Arthur Kinoy, 1994 (Best of Festival award Vt. Internat. Film Festival 1994, CINE Golden Eagle award 1994, Silver Apple award Nat. Ednl. Film Festival, 1994), Inside/Out: A Portrait of Lesbian and Gay Lawyers, 1994, Breaking Down Barriers: Overcoming Discrimination Against Lawyers with Disabilities, 1994 (Silver plaque Intercom Film Festival 1995), Pulp Ethics, 1995 (Gold award World Fest Houston 1996, Gold plaque Intercom Film Festival 1996), The Unfinished Agenda: NIOSH's First 25 Years and Beyond, 1996 (Cert. of Merit, Intercom Film Festival 1996), Keeping the Door Open: Women and Affirmative Action, 1996 (Honorable mention Columbus Internat. Film Festival 1996), A Voice for Children, 1996, Movin' On Up, 1977, The Public's Health, 1997 (Gold award World Fest Houston 1998), Obstacle Courts, 1997 (Gold award Charleston World Fest 1997, others), Outlooks, 1998, Cracking the Habit: Drug Courts in Action, 2000 (CINE Golden Eagle 2001, Platinum award World Fest Houston 2001, Daughters of Justice 2001, Summary Judgments 2001, Silver award World Fest Houston 2002), others; co-prodr. Everyday Heroes, 2001, Recovering Lives, Uncovering Hope, 2002 (Gold award World Fest. Houston 2002), Growing Independence, 2002, If the Robe Fits, 2002, Changing Children's Lives, 2003, IFP, 2004, The Tale of Two Cities, 2005, Opportunity of a Lifetime, 2005, CINE Golden Eagle, 2005, Film Arts Festival, 2005, Soul of Justice: Thelton Henderson's American Journey, 2005, Mill Valley Film Festival, 2005, Pan African Film Festival, 2006, Ashland Film Festival, 2006. Bd. advisors KPFA, 1986-92; active Coalition for Civil Rights, San Francisco, 1988—; adv. bd. Ctr. Social Justice, U. Calif., Berkeley, 2002—; bd. dirs. Meiklejohn Civil Liberties Inst., 1991—; adv. bd. Impact Fund, 1993—. Recipient Cert. Recognition, Calif. Assembly, 1988, 2006, award Alice Toklas Dem. Club, 1988, Award of Merit from Bar Assn. San Francisco, 1994, 2005, Bronze Apple award Nat. Ednl. Media Network, 1997, Nat. Lawyers Guild Testimonial Dinner honoree, 2006. Mem. ABA (standing com. Gavel awards 1997-2000), APHA, State Bar Assn. Calif., D.C. Bar Assn., Bar Assn. San Francisco. Jewish. Avocations: swimming, photography. Home and Office: Ginzberg Video Prodns 1136 Evelyn Ave Albany CA 94706-2316 Personal E-mail: abbyginz@aol.com.

GIOMI, THELMA ANNE, clinical psychologist; b. Albuquerque, Feb. 26, 1947; d. James E. and Esma Anne (Snyder) G. BA cum laude, U. N.Mex., 1969, MA, 1972, PhD, 1974. Diplomate Am. Bd. Psychotherapy. Psychometrician Albuquerque Pub. Schs., 1969-70; intern Pitts. Child Guidance, 1974-75; clin. psychologist U. N.Mex., Albuquerque, 1975-81; pvt. practice clin. psychologist Albuquerque, 1981—. Dir. Psychology Internship Program, U. N.Mex., 1979-81; adj. asst. prof. psychiatry, U. N.Mex., 1980, clin. assoc. Author: (poetry) Jaleo, 1990, Winter's Inuitation, 1997. Nat. Sci. Found. grantee, 1968. Mem. Am. Psychol. Assn., N.Mex. Psychol. Assn., Nat. Register of Health Care Providers, S.W. Writers Workshop, Phi Beta Kappa, Phi Kappa Phi. Avocations: photography, gourmet cooking, writing poetry and fiction.

GIORDANO, MARIANNE, not-for-profit developer; d. Frank and Geraldine Giordano. BA, St. Joseph's Coll., Bklyn., 1984; MS in Spl. Edn., Coll. of S.I., N.Y., 1988; Profl. Diploma in Ednl. Supervision and Adminstrn., L.I. U., Bklyn., 1996. Cert. sch. adminstrn. and supervision adminstr. N.Y., tchr.spl. edn., nursery, K-6 N.Y. Spl. edn. tchr. N.Y.C. Bd. Edn., Bklyn., 1984—89; sr. spl. educator First Chance Program at Hosp. for Joint Diseases, N.Y.C., 1989—97; site dir., curriculum coord. Vols. of Am., Bronx, 1998—99, edn. dir., 1999—2002, divsn. dir., 2002—04; program dir. St. Vincent's Cath. Med. Ctr., Staten Island, 2004—05; dir. ops., edn. svcs. United Cerebral Palsy of N.Y.C., 2005—. Recipient Ednl. Leadership and Tech. award for excellence, L.I. U., Bklyn., 1996. Mem.: ASCD, Nat. Assn. for Edn. of Young Children. Avocations: gardening, cooking, baking. Office: United Cerebral Palsy of New York City 120 E 23d St 5th Flr New York NY 10010-5419

GIORGADZE, TAMAR ALFRED, pathologist, physician; b. Tbilisi, Georgia, Apr. 6, 1960; d. Alfred G. Giorgadze and Venera O. Iosava; m. Archil G. Tsuladze, May 26, 1991. MD, Tbilisi State Med. Inst., 1982, PhD, 1987.

Diplomate Am. Bd. of Pathology, 2002, in cytopathology Am. Bd. of Pathology, 2004, lic. physician Mich., 2002, Tenn., 2005. Resident in oncology Tbilisi State Med. Inst., Chair of Oncology, Tbilisi, Georgia, sr. lab. asst., 1985—94; staff oncologist Rep. Cancer Ctr., Dept. of Pediatric Oncology, Tbilisi, Georgia, 1984—85; rsch. fellow Patho Lab Ltd, Sci. Pk., Kiryat-Weizmann, Rechovot, Israel, 1995—96; pathology resident East Tenn. State U., Dept. Pathology, James H. Quillen Coll. Med., Johnson City, Tenn., 1998—2001, chief resident, 2001—02, asst. prof., 2004—; surg. pathology fellow Dept. Pathology and Lab. Medicine Hosp. U. Pa., Phila., 2002—03, cytopathology fellow Dept. Pathology and Lab. Medicine Hosp., 2003—04. Sr. lab. asst. editl. bd. chair of oncology Tbilisi State Med. Inst., Tbilisi, Georgia, 1987—89; manuscript reviewer Hosp. U. Pa., Phila., 2003—04, East Tenn. State U., 2006—. Contbr. chapters to books, articles to profl. jours. Grantee, ETSU. Fellow: Coll. Am. Pathologists; mem.: Internat. Acad. Cytology, Internat. Acad. Pathology, Am. Soc. Cytopathology, US and Can. Acad. Pathology. Orthodox Christian. Achievements include patents for Method of forming of the high oncoproctological risk groups; first to Innovative methodologies in cytopathology and endocrine pathology. Avocations: opera, art, reading, swimming, tennis. Office: East Tenn State Univ Dept Pathology PO Box 70568 Johnson City TN 37614 Office Phone: 423-439-6328. Business E-Mail: giorgadz@etsu.edu.

GIOSEFFI, DANIELA (DOROTHY DANIELA GIOSEFFI), poet, writer, playwright, critic; b. Orange, NJ, Feb. 12, 1941; d. Daniel Donato Gioseffi and Josephine Buzevska; m. Richard J. Kearney, Sept. 7, 1965 (div.); 1 child, Thea D. Kearney; m. Lionel B. Luttinger, June 6, 1986. BA, Montclair State U., 1963; MFA, Cath. U. Am., 1966. Cons., poet Poets-in-the-Schs., Inc., N.Y.C., 1972-85. Freelance writer, lectr. at numerous univs. throughout U.S. and Europe; appeared on Nat. Pub. Radio, CBC, BBC; spkr. on world peace and disarmament, 1979—; keynote spkr. Am. Forum for Global Edn. Nat. Conf., Miami, Fla., 1994, State Coun. Tchrs. English conf., Orlando, Fla., 1995, So. Edn. Found. Internat. Conf. of Tchrs. of English, Atlanta, 1997, IV Feminist Internat. Book Fair, Barcelona, 1989, Miami Internat. Book Fair, 1990. Author: The Great American Belly, 1977, The Great American Belly, 4th edit., 1979; author: (collections of poems) Eggs in the Lake, 1979, Word Wounds and Water Flowers, 1995, Going On, 2000, Symbiosis, 2002; author: Earth Dancing: Mother Nature's Oldest Rite, 1981, Women on War: International Voices for the Nuclear Age, 1988 (Am. Book award, 1990), rev. edit., 2003, On Prejudice: A Global Perspective, 1993—, Dust Disappears: Translations of Carilda Oliver Labra of Latin America, 1995—, (poems) In Bed With the Exotic Enemy, 1997—, (stories and novella) The Psychic Touch, 1996—; author: (play) The Golden Daffodil Dwarf, 1988—, Care of the Body, 1988—, The Sea Hag in the Cave of Sleep, 1988—; author: (radio play) Fathers and Children, 1988—, 1998—; author: Going On: Poems Via Folios, 2002, Symbiosis: Poems, 2003, Women on War: International Writings From Antiquity to the Present, 2003, Blood Autumn: New & Selected Poems, 2006; contbr. numerous periodicals and anthologies;, performer (stage presentations throughout U.S. and Europe), composer (and lyricist), singer (many concert series); editor-in-chief Wise Women's Web: Internet Mag. of Lit. and Art, — (Best of Web award, 1998), creator The First Bklyn. Bridge Poetry Walk, 1972; verses carved in marble: Penn Sta., 2002; mem. editl. bd. Voices in Italian Americana - Purdue U., 1990—; editor: poetry website www.PoetsUSA.com. Pres. Bklyn. Citizens for Sane Nuclear Policy, 1987—89; mem. exec. bd., chmn. media watch com. Writers and Pubs. Alliance for Nuclear Disarmament, 1978—91. Named Featured poet, The Peoples' Poetry Gathering: The Great Hall, Cooper Union, 2003; recipient World Peace award, Ploughshares Fund, 1989, 1999; grantee poetry and fiction, Creative Artists' Pub. Svc. Program - N.Y. State Coun. on Arts, 1971—77, Thanks Be to Grandmother Winifred Found., 1996. Mem.: Poet's House, Nat. Book Critics Cir., Actors Equity Assn., Acad. Am. Poets, PEN Am. Ctr. Office: Box 8G 57 Montague St Brooklyn NY 11201-3356 Office Phone: 718-643-3837. Personal E-mail: daniela@garden.net.

GIOVANNI, NIKKI (YOLANDA CORNELIA GIOVANNI), poet, educator; b. Knoxville, Tenn., June 7, 1943; d. Jones and Yolande Cornelia (Watson) G.; 1 son, Thomas Watson. BA in History with honors, Fisk U., 1967; postgrad. in social work, U. Pa., 1967; LHD (hon.), Wilberforce U., 1972, Worcester U., 1972; DLitt (hon.), Ripon U., 1974, Smith Coll., 1975, Coll. Mt. St. Joseph, 1983. Founder Nixtom Ltd., 1970; asst. prof. black studies Queens Coll., CUNY, 1968-69; assoc. prof. English Rutgers U., 1969-70; prof. creative writing Coll. Mt. St. Joseph, 1985-87; disting. prof. Va. Poly Inst. and State U., Blacksburg, 1987—. Vis. prof. English Ohio State U., 1984; Honors Week vis. prof. Humanities Tex. Christian U., 1991; co-chmn. Lit. Arts Festival, State of Tenn. Homecoming, 1986; Duncanson artist-in-residence Taft Mus., Cin., 1986; mem. Ohio Humanities Coun., 1987; dir. Warm Hearth Writer's Workshop, 1988—; bd. dirs. Va. Found. for Humanities and Pub. Policy, 1990-93; featured poet Internat. Poetry Festival, Utrecht, Holland, 1991. Poet, writer, lectr.; author: Black Feeling, Black Talk, 1968, Black Judgement, 1968, Re: Creation, 1970, Poem of Angela Yvonne Davis, 1970, Spin a Soft Black Song, 1971, Gemini, 1971 (Nat. Book award nomination 1973), My House, 1972, A Dialogue: James Baldwin and Nikki Giovanni, 1973, Ego Tripping and Other Poems for Young Readers, 1973, A Poetic Equation: Conversations Between Nikki Giovanni and Margaret Walker, 1974, The Women and the Men, 1975, Cotton Candy on a Rainy Day, 1978, Vacation Time, 1980, Those Who Ride the Night Winds, 1983, Sacred Cows.and other Edibles, 1988 (Ohioana Book award 1988), Conversations with Nikki Giovanni, 1992, Racism 101, 1994, Knoxville, Tennessee, 1994, Love Poems, 1997, Blues: For All the Changes, 1999, Quilting the Black-Eyed Pea: Poems and Not Quite Poems, 2002, The Collected Poetry of Nikki Giovanni: 1968-1998, 2003, Rosa, 2005 (Caldecott Honor Book, 2006); rec. artist: (albums) Truth Is on Its Way, 1971 (Nat. Assn. Radio and TV Announcers award best spoken word album 1972), Like A Ripple on a Pond, 1973, The Way I Feel, 1974, Legacies: The Poetry of Nikki Giovanni, 1976, The Reason I Like Chocolate, 1976, Cotton Candy on a Rainy Day, 1978, others; editor: Night Comes Softly, 1970, (with Jessie Carney Smith) Images of Blacks in American Culture, 1988, (with Cathee Dennison) Appalachian Elders: A Warm Heart Sampler, 1991, Grand Mothers: Poems, Reminiscences, and Short Stories About the Keepers of Our Traditions, 1994; TV appearances include Spirit to Spirit: The Poetry of Nikki Giovanni, PBS, 1986 (Silver Apple award Oakland Museum Film Festival 1988); participant Soul at the Center, Lincoln Center Performing Arts, NYC, 1972. Vol. worker Nat. Council Negro Women, now life mem. Recipient Omega Psi Phi Fraternity award for outstanding contbn. arts and letters, 1971, Prince Matchabelli Sun Shower award, 1971, Meritorious Plaque for Svc. Cook County Jail, 1971, Scroll, life mem. Nat. Coun. Negro Women, 1972, Woman of Yr.-Youth Leadership award Ladies Home Jour., 1972, Post-Corbett award, 1986, Disting. Recognition award Detroit City Coun., 1986, NAACP Image award, 1998, 2000, 2003, Va. Gov.'s award for the Arts, 2000, Rosa Parks Women of Courage award, 2001, 2002; elected Ohio Women's Hall of Fame, 1985; named Woman of Yr. Mademoiselle mag., 1971, Woman of Yr. Cin. Chpt. YWCA, 1983, Outstanding Woman Tenn., 1985, Woman of Yr. Lynchburg Chpt. NAACP, 1989; Ford Found. grantee, 1967; Nat. Endowment for Arts grantee, 1968; Harlem Cultural Coun. grantee, 1969.*

GIOVE, SUSAN NANCY, medical/surgical nurse, educator; b. Bklyn., Aug. 6, 1951; d. Salvatore T. and Theresa (Vitale) G. BSN, Hunter Coll., 1972; MA, NYU, 1975; EdD, Columbia U., 1992; cert. family nurse practitioner, Adelphi U., 1995. Asst. head nurse, med. svc. NYU Med. Ctr.-Univ. Hosp., N.Y.C., 1972-77; cardiovascular patient educator Heart Ctr.-St. Francis Hosp., Roslyn, N.Y., 1981-85; instr. Adelphi U., Garden City, N.Y., 1985, Queensborough C.C., Bayside, N.Y., 1984-85, Lehman Coll.-CUNY, Bronx, N.Y., 1986-87, Coll. of New Rochelle, 1989-95; Hunter Coll., Bellevue, 1993-95; Pace U., 1993-94; Lehman Coll., 1994; Adelphi U., 1995; per diem nurse neuroscil. svc. NYU Med. Ctr., 1989-95; nurse practitioner site coord., assoc. prof. Wilmington (Del.) Coll., 1995—98; cardiology assoc. nurse practitioner Dr. P. Monteleone, Roslyn, NY, 1995—. Co-dir. ann. health fair Coll. New Rochelle, 1989—92; ptnr., CFO Yokozuna Restaurant, Ocean City, Md., 2003—; mgr. Ristorante Zebra, Rehoboth Beach, Del., 1998—, A taste of Heaven, Lewes, Del., 1998. Contbr. articles to profl. jours. Mem. Mayor Koch's Anti-Drug Abuse Coun., 1988-89; mem. Bronx Borough Pres.'s Com. on Prevention of Drug Abuse, 1988-91. Mem. Acad. Nurse Practitioners, Internat. Assn. for Human Caring, N.Y. So. League for Nursing, Alumni Assn. Hunter Coll.-Bellevue, Alumni Assn. NYU, Mary Louis Acad. Alumnae Assn. (v.p., exec. bd.), Rotary (bd. dirs. Bronx chpt. 1988-95, pres. 1994-95), Lewes/Rehoboth Rotary Club, Wilmington Coll. Honor Soc., Sigma Theta Tau, Kappa Delta Pi. Home: PO Box 245 Rehoboth Beach DE 19971-0245

GIPSON, GLORIA LORRAINE, social worker; b. Jersey City, Aug. 8, 1947; d. Wilmon and Mary (Castelberry) F.; m. Gordon Gipson Jr., Mar. 30, 1968; children: Leshante, Anthony, Lareesa, Natalie. Assocs., St. Peter's Coll., Jersey City, 1986, BS, 1987; Social Svcs. Competency Tng. cert., Montclair State Coll., 1990. Tutor, trainer Lit. Vols. of Am. Inc., Jersey City, 1993—. Author: Poems of Purpose, 1993. Avocations: sewing, decorating, ping pong/table tennis, writing, singing. Home: 131 Bidwell Ave # 2 Jersey City NJ 07305-3326

GIPSON, ILENE KAY, ophthalmologist, educator; b. Hoberg, Mo., Oct. 13, 1944; d. Ferdinand Robert and Margaret Marie (Fritz) Quade; m. Philip Gipson, June 1967 (div. 1974); m. Henry T. Keutmann, June 23, 1984. BA in Biology, Drury Coll., Springfield, Mo., 1966; MS in Zoology, U. Ark., Fayetteville, 1968, PhD in Zoology, 1973; MA (hon.), Harvard Med. Sch., Boston, 1997; DSc (hon.), Drury U., Springfield, Mo., 1999. Rsch. assoc. dept. plant pathology U. Ark., Fayetteville, 1973-74; rsch. assoc., instr. dept. ophthalmology U. Oreg. Health Scis. Ctr., Portland, 1974-76, asst. prof., 1976-79; asst. prof. ophthalmology Harvard Med. Sch., Boston, 1979-85, assoc. prof., 1985—97, prof., 1997—; assoc. scientist Schepens Eye Rsch. Inst., Boston, 1979-83, sr. scientist, 1983—, ocular surface scholar, 1997—. Head morphology unit Schepens Eye Rsch. Inst., 1980—91, head cornea unit, 1985—94; mem. study sect. divsn. rsch. resources NIH, Bethesday, Md., 1983, 84, 88; mem. cornea diseases panel Nat. Eye Inst., 1990; Leverhulme vis. prof. dept. anatomy U. Bristol, England, 1997. Contbr. articles to profl. jours.; mem. editl. bd.: Ocular Surface, exec. editor cornea and ocular surface sect.: Exptl. Eye Rsch., 2001—, guest editor: Investigative Ophthalmology & Visual Sci. Bd. trustees Drury U., 1999—2003, 2004—. Recipient Rsch. Career Devel. award, Nat. Eye Inst., 1978—83, MERIT award, 1990—2000, Alcon Rsch. award, 1984, Rsch. to Prevent Blindness Sr. Sci. Investigator award, 2001. Mem.: Internat. Soc. Eye Rsch., Assn. Rsch. in Vision and Ophthalmology (2007 Friedenwald award), Am. Soc. Cell Biologists. Democrat. Achievements include patents in field. Avocations: birding, gardening, cooking, travel. Office: Schepens Eye Rsch Inst 20 Staniford St Boston MA 02114-2508 E-mail: gipson@vision.eri.harvard.edu.*

GIPSON, PAULINE, special education educator; b. Marionville, Mo., Jan. 13, 1937; d. Paul K. and Maud Ellen (Wolf) Kastendieck; m. Jerry E. Gipson, Feb. 19, 1956; children: Kent Edwin, Kevin STuart, Karen Annette. Student, U. Mo., 1955-56; BS, So. Mo. State U., 1971; MS, Drury Coll., Springfield, Mo., 1976, postgrad., 1980-82. Cert. elem. tchr., reading specialist, tchr. learning disabilities, Mo. Elem. tchr. Crane (Mo.) R-III Schs., 1971-80, tchr. reading, 1980-85, tchr. learning disabilities, 1985—2000; ret. Mem. Mo. Tchrs. Assn., Learning Disabilities Assn., Coun. for Learning Disabilities, Delta Kappa Gamma (sec. 1985-86, pres. 1990-92), Mo. Ret. Tchrs. Assn. Avocation: travel. Office: Crane R-III Sch PO Box E Crane MO 65633-0405

GIRA, CATHERINE RUSSELL, retired academic administrator; b. Fayette City, Pa., Oct. 30, 1932; d. John Anthony and Mary (Stephen) Russell; m. Joseph Andrew Gira, July 17, 1954 (dec.); children: Cheryl Ann, Thomas Russell. BS, Calif. State U., 1953; M.Ed., Johns Hopkins U., 1957, M.L.A., 1972; PhD, Am. U., 1975. Tchr. Balt. County, Balt., 1953-60, head dept., 1958-60; writing cons. Md. State Dept. Edn., 1960-68; instr. Johns Hopkins U., Balt., 1964-65; from asst. prof. to prof. U. Balt., 1965-81, acting dean, 1981-82, provost, 1982-91; pres. Frostburg State U., Md., 1991—2006. Contbr. articles to profl. jours. Bd. dirs. Western Md. Health Sys., 1996—; chair bd. dirs. Leadership Md., 2004—. Inductee Md. Women's Hall of Fame, 1999; Am. U. scholar, 1973-75. Mem. Am. Assn. Univ. Adminstrs. (bd. dirs. 1984-87, pres.-elect 1987, pres. 1988-90), Fedn. State Humanities Couns. (bd. dirs. 1990-94, vice-chair 1993-94), Md. Humanities Coun. (chmn. 1989-90), Md. Assn. Higher Edn. (bd. dirs. 1983-85, pres. 1986-87), Shakespeare Assn. Am., Edgar Allan Poe Soc. (bd. dirs. 1982—). Methodist. Home: 106 Jones Ct Frostburg MD 21532-1415*

GIRAL, ANGELA, librarian; b. Madrid, Aug. 11, 1935; came to U.S., 1956; d. Francisco Giral-Gonzalez and Petra (Barnés) Giral; m. James E. Irby, Aug. 4, 1956 (div. May 1972); children: Elizabeth Favaro, Francisco G. Student, Vassar Coll., 1953-54, Nat. U. Mexico, Mexico City, 1953-56; AB equivalent, U. Mich., 1957, AMLS, 1958, postgrad., 1958-59. Reference libr. Biblioteca Central Universidad Nacional Autónoma de México, 1955-56; upper sch. libr. Escola Americana, Rio de Janeiro, 1964-65; book scout Brazil Princeton U. Libr., 1964-65, descriptive cataloguer, subject analyst, 1962-64, sr. cataloguer, 1965-67; libr. Urban and Environ. Studies Libr. Sch. Architecture and Urban Planning Princeton U., 1967-75; chief libr. Frances Loeb Libr. Grad Sch. Design Harvard U., 1975-82; acting head sci. and engrng. divsn. Columbia U. Librs., 1990-91; dir. Avery Archtl. and Fine Arts Libr. Columbia U., 1982—. Mem. thesis review com. Boston Archtl. Ctr., 1978-79, mem. edn. com., 1979-80, mem. libr. com., 1981-82; chair libr. preservation com. Harvard U., 1980-82; cons. devel. Rensselaer Poly. Inst., Troy, 1982; panelist N.Y. State Libr. Assn. Meeting, Rochester, N.Y., 1986; panelist ARLIS/NA Conf., Washington, 1987, Am. Assn. Mus., San Francisco, 1987; cons. Archivos de Architectura de la Universidad de Puerto Rico, 1990-91; chair Edilia de Montequin Fellowship Soc. Archtl. Historians, 1992; chair archtl. archives session art librs. satellite meeting IFLA, Barcelona, 1993; mem. jury 1994 Internat. Book Awards Am. Inst. Architects, 1994; session moderator 7th Congress Internat. Confederation Archtl. Mus., 1994; bd. dirs. Internat. Coun. Archtl. Mus. Author: (with others) Equal Pay for Equal Work: Women in Special Libraries, 1976, The Architecture Library of the Future, 1989, Videotechnolgoy and Libraries, 1990, El Destierro Español en América, 1991; author: (preface) Mitchell's Choice: Highlights from 20 Years of Acquisitions for Avery Library, 1991, Contemporary Architectural Drawings: Donations to the Avery Library Centennial Drawings Archive, 1991; author: (introduction) Cataloging Architectural Drawings, 1992; editor: Harvard Research in Progress on Women, vol. 1, 1979; translator: Los Alquimistas: Fundadores de la Química Moderna (F. Sherwood Taylor) 1957. Grantee CLR, 1988-89. Mem. ALA (speaker 112th ann. conf. 1993), Am. Soc. Info. Sci. (speaker mid-yr. meeting 1992), N.J. Libr. Assn., Urban Info. Network N.Y., Art Librs. Soc. N.Am., Spl. Librs. Assn. (v.p. Princeton-Trenton chpt. 1969-70, pres. 1970-71, chairperson urban affairs sect. social scis. divsn. 1972-73, spl. com. pilot edn. project for equal opportunity for women 1974-76), Urban and Regional Info. Systems Assn., Social Responsibilities Roundtable, Coun. Planning Librs. (pres. 1974-75, organizer, moderator ann. conf. Vancouver, Can. 1975, panelist ann. conf. Miami 1979). Office: Columbia Univ Avery Archtl Fine Arts Libr New York NY 10027

GIRARD, ANDREA EATON, communications executive, consultant; b. N.Y.C., Oct. 16, 1946; d. Samuel Robert and Mimi (Eaton) Girard. Student, Syracuse U., 1964-66; BA cum laude, Finch Coll., 1968; MA, Columbia U., 1971. Talent coord./prodn. asst. Guber-Ford-Gross Prodns., NY, 1968-70; v.p. Charing Cross Press, N.Y.C., 1970-72; assoc. prodr., talent dir. TV shows "To Tell the Truth" and "Snap Judgement" Goodson Todman Prodns., N.Y.C., 1972-80; programming exec. David Letterman-NBC, N.Y.C., 1980; dir. of talent, prodr. Daytime/Arts and Entertainment Networks (Hearst/ABC Video Enterprises), N.Y.C., 1981-84; dir. current programming acquisition, sr. prodr. Lifetime Network (Hearst/ABC/Viacom Entertainment Svcs.), N.Y.C., 1984-86; pres. Girard Comm., N.Y.C., 1986—, dir. med. comm. advantage internat., 1990-91; v.p. PRNY, N.Y.C., 1990-92; CEO Panache Comm. Inc., N.Y.C., 1992—. Judge Emmy Awards Internat. Film and TV Festival; spkr. pub. rels. coun. Sch. Continuing Edn. NYU, N.Y.C.; media cons., 1987—. Prodr., writer: (documentaries) Cave Dwellers of Crete, 1974; Sponge Divers of Kalymnos, 1979; Gypsies of the Camargue, 1983. Active fund raising bd. Jersey Wildlife Preservation Trust, NY; active hospitality com. UN, N.Y.C.; active Big Apple Com. Benefit of Image of N.Y. Mem.: NAFE, NATAS, Internat. Assn. Cooking Profls., N.Y. Women Film and TV, Delta Soc. Avocations: goldsmith, horseback riding. Office: Panache Comms 201 E 77th St Ste 7F New York NY 10021-2082 Office Phone: 212-288-1348. E-mail: panacheinc@aol.com.

GIRARD, JUDY, broadcast executive; BS in Radio-TV-Film, Ithaca Coll. With WPVI-TV, Phila., 1968; program mgr. WBNG-TV, Binghamton, NY; sta. mgr. WOWK-TV, Huntington, W.Va.; dir. programming ops. and promotion WBAL-TV, Balt., WTAE-TV, Pitts.; dir. ops. and programming WTVJ-TV, Miami, 1987-89; dir. broadcasting WNBC-TV, 1989-91, v.p. broadcasting, 1991-93; sr. v.p. programming and prodn. Lifetime Television, NYC, 1993; pres. Food Network, 2001, Shop at Home, Nashville, HGTV, 2005—. Assoc. prof. NYU. Named Alumna of Yr., Ithaca Coll., 1992. Achievements include development of new movie franchise: Lifetime Original Movie. Office: Lifetime Tel 16th and 17th Fls 309 W 49th St New York NY 10019-7316*

GIRAUDO, SUZANNE MCDONNELL, psychologist; d. William and Theresa McDonnell; m. Louis John Giraudo, June 19, 1971; children: Bryan, Daniel, Denise, Izelle. BA, U. San Francisco, 1971, EdD, 1989; MA, San Francisco State U., 1981. Tchr. San Francisco Schs., 1978—79; learning specialist Archdiocese San Francisco, 1980—89; psychologist, dir. Calif. Pacific Med. Ctr., San Francisco, 1991—. Mem. adv. bd. Support for Families, San Francisco, 1998—; trustee U. San Francisco, 2002—; bd. dirs. Cmty. Alliance for Spl. Edn., San Francisco, 1999—. Contbr. chapters to books. Task force mem. 10 Yr. Homeless Plan, 2004; bd. dirs. Childrens Gardens Calif., San Rafael, 1990—96, Hamilton Family Ctr., San Francisco, 1993—99, Home Away From Homelessness, San Francisco, 1998—; com. chair 10 Yr. Homeless Plan, San Francsico, 2004, task force mem., 2004. Named Woman of the Yr., State Calif., 1998; recipient Knighthood of St. Gregory, Vatican Cath. Ch., 2000. Mem.: APA. Avocation: exercise. Office: Calif Pacific Med Ctr 3700 California St San Francisco CA 94118 Office Phone: 415-600-6200.

GIRDEN, ELLEN ROBINSON, retired psychology educator; b. Bklyn., May 14, 1936; d. Robert and Sarah (Bellinoff) Robinson; m. Edward Girden, Sept. 8, 1977. B.A., Bklyn. Coll., 1956, M.A., 1958; Ph.D., Northwestern U., 1962. Instr. psychology Northwestern U., Evanston, Ill., 1960-61; instr., asst. prof. Hobart and William Smith Coll., Geneva, N.Y., 1961-63; asst. prof., assoc. prof. Yeshiva U., N.Y.C., 1963-78; assoc. prof. Sch. of Profl. Psychology, Miami, Fla., 1978-81; assoc. prof. Nova U., Ft. Lauderdale, Fla., 1981-84, prof., 1984-93, supr. dissertations, 1981-93; ret., 1993; rsch. cons. Yeshiva U. Med. Sch., 1967-68. Author 2 books; contbr. articles to profl. jours. NIH grantee, 1963-64, 1966-67. Mem. Am. Statis. Assn. Democrat. Jewish. Avocations: cooking; tennis; swimming; theatre attendance; travel. Home: 2851 NE 183rd St Apt 1204 North Miami Beach FL 33160-2142 Personal E-mail: ellegirden@aol.com.

GIRGA, BARBARA, psychotherapist, college counselor; b. Rayland, Ohio, Oct. 11, 1937; d. Virgil and Marjorie Fisher; m. Andries Meuleman, 1997; children: Susan R., Robert E. BA, Bakersfield Coll., 1973; MA, Calif. State U., 1978; postgrad., Ky. Christian Coll., U. Calif., Santa Barbara, 1987. Lic. marriage, family, child counselor. With Water Assn. of Kern County, 1976-81; editor Bakersfield C. of C., 1977; diet counselor Nutra Systems, 1980; analyst Occidental Petroleum, 1981-86; mgr., 1986—; pvt. practice, clin. therapist Bakersfield Counseling Group, Calif., 1987-89; pvt. practice Bakersfield, 1989—96; dir. adolescent drug program Charter Hosp., 1989-91. Seminar leader, 1976—. Author numerous poems. Mem. AACD, Am. Assn. for Marriage and Family Therapy, Am. Businesswomen's Assn., Chi Sigma Iota. Home: 2401 San Ramon Ct Bakersfield CA 93304-6362

GIRGIS, MARY, counselor; b. Asyut, Egypt, Aug. 8, 1980; arrived in U.S., 1984; d. Khelela and Sameha Shafik Girgis. BA in psychology, Rutgers State U., N.J., 2002; MA in counseling, Montclair State U., N.J., 2006. Case mgr. Tri-City People's Corp., East Orange, NJ, 2002—04; counselor goals program Family Svc. Bur., Newark, 2004—05; MA intern Family Counseling Ctr., Verona, NJ, 2005; coll. support specialist Project GRAD, Newark, 2005—; group facilitator Strengthening Families Program, Jersey City, 2006—; in-home behavioral asst. Caring Family Solutions, Woodbridge, NJ, 2006—. Vol. BLESS USA, Cedar Grove, NJ, 1999—; Sunday sch. tchr. St. George & St. Shenanda Ch., Jersey City, 2000—; vol. for handicapped Abu Sefein Svc. for Handicapped, Jersey City, 1984—. Mem.: Am. Counseling Assn. Greek Christian Orthodox. Home: 38 Cliff St Jersey City NJ 07306 Personal E-mail: marmaora55@hotmail.com.

GIRGUS, JOAN STERN, psychologist, educator, director; b. Albany, N.Y., Mar. 21, 1942; d. William Barnet and Louise (Mayer) Stern; m. Alan Chimacoff, Jan. 2, 1981; 1 child, Katherine Louise Stern. BA, Sarah Lawrence Coll., 1963; MA, The Grad. Faculty New Sch. for Social Research, 1965, PhD, 1969. Asst. prof. dept. psychology CCNY, N.Y.C., 1969-72, assoc. prof., 1972-77, assoc. dean div. social sci., 1972-75, dean, 1975-77; prof. psychology Princeton U., 1977—, dir. Pew Sci. Program Undergrad. Edn., 1987—2002, chair dept. psychology, 1996—2002, spl. asst. to dean of faculty, 2003—. Contbr. articles and chpts. to profl. jours. and books. NSF fellow, NIH fellow; Research grantee CUNY, 1971-74; Nat. Inst. Child Health and Human Devel. research grantee, 1972-74; NSF grantee, 1975-79; NIMH grantee, 1985-91. Fellow APA, Am. Psychol. Soc.; mem. Eastern Psychol. Assn., Soc. Rsch. in Child Devel. Home: 306 Ridgeview Rd Princeton NJ 08540 Office: Princeton U Green Hall Princeton NJ 08544

GIRMAN, DEE-MARIE, artist, singer; b. Duquesne, Pa., Apr. 10, 1919; d. Michael Girman and Marie Schuster. Student, Pitts. Musical Inst., Fillion Ballet Sch.; studied dress design with Louise Salinger; student, Barry U. Singer, Pitts.; iconographer, artist Barry U., Miami Shores, Fla. Author: Sandtrap, The Mathematical Genius Dog, 2003; one-woman shows include Chase Showing, 1974, Barrry U., 1983, Miami Art Ctr. Entertainer specialist Spl. Svc., USAAC, 1942—45. Named to Hall of Fame, Barry U., 1995, Meml. Hist. Roll of Honor, Am. Meml. Found., 1997. Republican. Roman Catholic. Avocation: golf. Home: 1779 San Silvestro Dr Venice FL 34285 Personal E-mail: sansydee@msn.com.

GIRONE, JOAN CHRISTINE CRUSE, realtor, former county official; b. Kingston, Ont., Can., Aug. 30, 1927; d. Arthur William and Helen Wilson Cruse; m. Joseph MIchael Girone, June 26, 1954; children: Susan, Richard, William. Buyer Franklin Simon, Inc., N.Y.C., 1946-54; supr. Midlothian dist. Chesterfield County (Va.) Bd. Suprs., 1976-88, vice chmn., 1976-82; Founding mem. Capitol Area Agy. on Aging, 1973-89, Med. Coll. Va. Women's Health Adv. Coun., 1990-97, Chesterfield County Citizens for Responsible Govt., 1991—; comml. real estate agent Long and Foster Realtors, Richmond. Bd. dirs. Cen. Va. Ednl. TV Corp., 1989-94; commr., chmn. Richmond (Va.) Regional Planning Dist. Commn., 1976-88; Va. Power Consumer adv. bd.; chmn. cmty. edn. adv. com. Va. Bd. of Edn., 1972-79; mem. Va. Gov.'s Adv. Bd. on Aging, 1980-82; chmn. Richmond Met. Transp. Planning Orgn., 1981-88; bd. visitors Va. State U., 1980-84. Vice chmn., exec. com. Gateway Bus. Assn.; mem. Ctrl. Va. River Basin Com., 1985; mem. evaluation task force United Way of Greater Richmond, 1985; adv. bd. Chesapeake Bay Local Assistance Bd. Adv. Com. Midlothian YMCA, 2000; chmn. steering com. Bon Air Village Preservation, 1995—; mem. Coun. Advocates Va. Supportive Housing, 2001—; chmn. Chesterfield County Com. to elect John Warner and Paul Trible to U.S. Senate, 1979, 1982, 1984; Chesterfield chmn. Marshall Coleman for Gov., 1981—; chmn. Women for Reagen-Bush, 1984; vice chair Rt. 288 Freeway Comm., 1996, exec. com.; mem. candidate recruitment com. Va. Fedn. Rep. Women, 1995; bd. dirs. Maymount Found., 1982—89, YMCA Greater Richmond Metro, ARC Va. Capital chpt.; bd. mgrs. Chesapeake Bay Local Assistance Bd. Adv. Com. Midlothian YMCA, 1999, bd. dirs., 1994—, Caucus Future Ctrl. Va., 1994—, Coalition for Greater Richmond. Named Joan C. Girone Libr., Chesterfield Bus. County, 1995; recipient Good Govt. award, Richmond First Club, 1965. Mem. Va. Assn. Counties (exec. bd. 1982-87), Richmond Metro C. of C. (bd. dirs.

Chesterfield Bus. Coun. 1989—), Chesterfield County C. of C. (mem. gov. rels. com. 2004), Hugeunot Rep. Woman's Club (Rep. Woman of Yr. 1983), Virginians for High Speed Rail (bd. dirs. 2004). Home: 2609 Dovershire Rd Richmond VA 23235-2815 Office Phone: 804-560-7625, 804-327-1081. Business E-Mail: joan.girone@longandfoster.com.

GIROUARD, GAIL PATRICIA, family practice physician; b. Acushnet, Mass., Mar. 26, 1956; d. Ernest and Doris Elizabeth (Whalley) G. BS in Earth Sci. with honors, Bridgewater State Coll., 1978; MS in Molecular Biology with honors, Creighton U., 1989, MD, 1994. Cert. tchr., Mass., EMT, Mass. Sci. tchr. Keith Jr. H.S., New Bedford, Mass., 1978-89; resident Creighton Family Practice, St. Joseph's Hosp., Omaha, 1994—. Sci. tchr. Sea Lab, New Bedford, summer 1989; summer sch. tchr., New Bedford, 1980-89; personal fitness trainer, New Bedford, 1985-89; tchr., trainer weight training for women program Bright Nights, 1989; EMT, New Bedford, Mass. Physician at homeless clinics, Omaha, 1995. Mem. AMA, Am. Assn. Family Practice, Am. Med. Women's Assn. Roman Catholic. Avocations: sewing, embroidery, scuba diving, wind surfing, running. Office: 701 Grant St Atwood KS 67730

GIROUARD, PEGGY JO FULCHER, ballet educator; b. Corpus Christi, Tex., Oct. 25, 1933; d. J.B. and Zora Alice (Jackson) Fulcher; m. Richard Ernest Girouard, Apr. 16, 1954 (div. Mar. 1963); children: Jo Linne, Richard Ernest; m. James C. Boles, May 4, 1996. BS in Elem. Edn., U. Houston, 1970. Ballet instr. Emmamae Horn Studio, Houston, 1951-81; owner, dir. Allegro Acad. Dance, Houston, 1981—. Artistic dir. Allegro Ballet Houston, 1976—; asst. mgr. Sugar Creek Homes Assn., Sugar Land, Tex., 1979-90; coord. 1st Regional Dance Am. Nat. Festival, Houston, 1997. Choreographer (with Glenda W. Brown) Masquerade Suite, 1983, Sebelius Suite, 1983, Shannan, 1984, Papa Shamus, 1986, Silhouettes, 1987, Aspirations, 1989, Here Come the Clowns, 1990. Mem. Cultural Arts Coun. Houston; founding officer Regional Dance Am., 1988, bd. dirs., 1988—, sec., 1996-2001. Mem. Dance Masters Am. (dir. 1977-80), S.W. Regional Ballet Assn. (chmn. craft of choreography 1983-85, coord. to nat. assn. 1983-2003, Stream award 1986). Democrat. Home: 9945 Warwana Rd Houston TX 77080-7609 Office Phone: 281-496-4670. Personal E-mail: pgirouard77080@yahoo.com.

GIROUARD, SHIRLEY ANN, nurse, policy analyst; b. New London, Conn., Jan. 16, 1947; d. Maxime Albert Girouard and Irene Barbara (Arnold) Reid. BA in Sociology, Ea. Conn. State Coll., 1972; MA in Sociology, U. Conn., 1974; MSN, Yale U., 1977; PhD in Policy Analysis, Brandeis U., 1988. Nurse Woodstock (Conn.) Pub. Health Assn., 1968-70; staff nurse Clinton (Conn.) Convalescent Ctr., 1970-72; ins. edn. coord. Middlesex Meml. Hosp., Middletown, Conn., 1973-75; clin. nurse specialist Dartmouth Hitchcock Med. Ctr., Hanover, N.H., 1977-83, staff nurse, 1983-84; legis. cons., lobbyist N.H. Nurses Assn., Concord, 1985-87; program officer Robert Wood Johnson Found., Princeton, N.J., 1987-92; exec. dir. N.C. Ctr. Nursing, 1992-93, Am. Nurse's Assn., 1993-94; health policy and nursing cons. pvt. and pub. sector orgns., Washington, 1994-95; v.p. child health and financing Nat. Assn. Children's Hosps. and Related Instns., Alexandria, Va., 1995-99; cons., 1999—; assoc. prof. So. Conn. State U., 2001—. Pvt. practice cons., 1983-87; profl. devel. cons., Lebanon, N.H., 1983-87; health policy and nursing cons. Author: (chpt.) Health Policy and Nurse Services, 1989, 98, others; mem. editorial bd. Clin. Nurses Specialist Jour., 1986—, others; contbr. articles to profl. jours. State rep. N.H. Legislature, Concord, 1982-84; counselor City of Lebanon Coun., 1984-87. Fellow Am. Acad. Nursing; mem. ANA (project dir. 1986), Sigma Theta Tau. Democrat. Office Phone: 203-392-6479.

GIROUARD, TANDY DENISE, special education educator, psychology professor; b. Ft. Worth, Tex., Aug. 25, 1960; d. Nolan Ray and Barbara Gale (Miller) Rutledge; m. Jan. 22, 1980 (div. Dec. 1995); children: Michael, Christopher, Kaneissa. BS in Generic Spl. Edn., U. of Mary Hardin-Baylor; MEd in Spl. Edn., U. North Tex. Tchr. asst. spl. edn. Hurst-Euless-Bedford Ind. Sch. Dist., Bedford, Tex., 1988; tchr. asst. in spl. edn. McLennan County Dept. Edn., Waco, Tex., 1988-90; tchr. spl. edn. Moody Ind. Sch. Dist., 1991—94; tchr. resource reading LaVega Ind. Sch. Dist., 1994—95; tchr. life skills Waco Ind. Sch. Dist., 1996—98; tchr. 2d grade and spl. edn. Emma L. Harrison Charter Sch., 1998—99; tchr. resource Belton Ind. Sch. Dist., 1999—2000; tchr. spl. edn. Connally Ind. Sch. Dist., 2000—02; profl. scorer NCS Pearson Edn., 2003—04, NCS Pearson Ednl. Measurement, 2004—06. Mem. Internat. Assn. of Pers. in Employment Security, Ctrl. Tex. Coun. Tchrs. Math., Assn. Tex. Profl. Educators, PTA, Bedford-Euless Soccer Assn., Tex. State Edn. Assn., Pi Gamma Mu. Home: 500 Greenfield Dr Waco TX 76705-1705 E-mail: tdg0021@yahoo.com.

GIRTH, MARJORIE LOUISA, lawyer, educator; b. Trenton, NJ, Apr. 21, 1939; d. Harold Brookman and Marjorie Mathilda (Simonson) G. AB, Mt. Holyoke Coll., 1959; LLB, Harvard U., 1962. Bar: N.J. 1963, U.S. Supreme Ct. 1969, N.Y. 1976. Pvt. practice, Trenton, 1963-65; rsch. assoc. Brookings Instn., 1965-70; assoc. prof. law SUNY Law Sch., Buffalo, 1971-79, prof., 1979-91, assoc. dean, 1986-87; dean Ga. State U. Coll. Law, Atlanta, 1992-96, prof., 1992—. Vis. prof. U. Va. Law Sch., 1979-80, Southeastern Bankruptcy Law Inst., Emory Law Sch., spring 1991, vis. scholar 1996; vis. prof. Warsaw, Poland, 2003, Vytautus Magnus U., Lithuania, 2006; vis. legal educator W.Va. U. Coll. of Law Vis. Com., 1994-95; chancellor's search adv. com. Bd. of Regents, 1993-94; mem. com. on standards of the profession State Bar Ga., 1996-2005; mem. commn. on racial and ethnic bias in ct. sys. Ga. Supreme Ct, 1993-95, mem. commn. on equality, 1995-2004, sec., 1998-2000, mem. commn. on access and fairness in the cts., 2004-06. Author: Poor People's Lawyers, 1976, Bankruptcy Options for the Consumer Debtor, 1981, (co-author) Bankruptcy: Problem, Process, Reform, 1971. Bd. dirs. Buffalo and Erie County YWCA, 1972-76, Buffalo Unitarian-Universalist Ch., 1981-84, Feminist Women's Health Ctr., 1993-94, ACLU, Ga., 1995-2001, Unitarian-Universalist Congregation of Atlanta, 1999—2003; mem. commn. on peace, justice and human rights Internat. Assn. Religious Freedom, 1976-79; mem. Found. Freedom Commn., 2005-. Ga. ct. appeals Centennial Celebration, 2005-; chmn. Erie County Task Force on Status of Women, 1985-87 Recipient award for pioneering achievements N.Y. State 8th Jud. Dist. Splty. Bar Assn. and Com. on Women in the Cts., 2000. Fellow Lawyers Found. Ga.; mem. ABA (mem. coun. bus. law sect. 1985-89, chmn. consumer bankruptcy com. 1983-86), Am. Arbitration Assn. (comml. arbitration panel 1997—), Assn. Am. Law Schs. (profl. devel. com. 2002—06, nominations com. 1996), Am. Law Inst., N.Y. State Bar Assn. (mem. exec. com. bus. law sect. 1980-91, chmn. bankruptcy law com. 1980-82, chmn. banking corp. bus. law sect. 1986-87, mem. ho. of dels. 1990-91), Ga. Assn. Women Lawyers, Law Sch. Admissions Coun. (audit com. 1995-97, 1999—, fin. and legal affairs com., 1997-99), Mt. Holyoke Alumnae Assn. (Centennial award 1972). Unitarian Universalist. Office: Ga State U Coll Law PO Box 4037 Atlanta GA 30302-4037 Office Phone: 404-651-4916. E-mail: mgirth@gsu.edu.

GIRVIN, SHIRLEY EPPINETTE, retired elementary school educator, journalist; b. New Orleans, Apr. 16, 1947; d. Woodie Trevillion and Thelma Elizabeth (Axline) E.; m. Russell Robertson Girvin, Nov. 30, 1996. AA, East L.A. Coll., 1967; BA, Calif. State U., L.A., 1969, postgrad., 1969-70, U. So. Calif., 1982, Chapman Coll., 1983, Loyola Marymount U., L.A., 1986-87. Elem. tchr. Covina-Valley Unified Sch. Dist., 1970-74, San Gabriel (Calif.) Sch. Dist., 1974-75, Alhambra (Calif.) City Sch. Dist., 1976-78; elem. and program mentor tchr., faculty rep. L.A. City Unified Sch. Dist., 1978—2003; ret., 2003. Rewrite editor, staff writer San Gabriel Valley Newspaper Publs., 1975-76. Contbr. articles to profl. jours. Recipient TAP award Alhambra-San Gabriel dist. Soroptimist Club, 1975; Calif. State PTA scholar, 1981, Journalism Alumni Assn. scholar East L.A. Coll., 1967, Arthur J. Baum Journalism scholar Calif. State U., 1969. Mem. AAUW (com. internat. rels. 1977-78, chmn. ednl. com. 1978-79), NEA, Calif. Tchrs. Assn., LA City Tchrs. Math. Assn., United Tchrs. LA (chpt. chair 1994-95), Women in Comm., Nat. Press Women, Humane Soc. U.S., Soc. for the Prevention of Cruelty to Animals, Calif. Thoroughbred Breeders Assn., Thoroughbred Owners of Am., Sigma Delta Chi. Avocations: breeding, selling, and racing Thoroughbred race horses, gardening. Home: 8730 S East Ave Fresno CA 93725

GISH, AGNES BRIDGET, music educator; d. Phillip and Debra Gish. MusB, Ft. Hays State U., Kans., 2002, BA in French, 2002. Cert. tchr. music Kans. State Bd. Edn., 2002, tchr. French Kans. State Bd. Edn., 2002. Tchr. strings Unified Sch. Dist. 500 Kans. City Pub. Schs., Kans., 2002—. Asst. dir. hons. orch. Unified Sch. Dist. 500 Kans. City Pub. Schs., Kans., 2002—, asst. dir. harp ensemble, 2005—. Musician Theatre in the Park, Kansas City, Kans. Mem.: Am. String Tchrs. Assn.

GISOLFI, DIANA (DIANA GISOLFI PECHUKAS), art history educator; b. N.Y.C., Sept. 12, 1940; d. Anthony M. and Eleanor (Hayes) Gisolfi; m. Philip Pechukas, June 15, 1963 (div. Sept. 1991); children: Rolf, Maria, Sarah, Fiona (dec.), Amy. Student, Manhattanville Coll., 1958-60; BA magna cum laude, Radcliffe Coll., 1962; postgrad., Yale U., 1962-63; MA, U. Chgo., 1964, PhD, 1976. Instr. CUNY, 1967-68, Marymount Manhattan Coll., N.Y.C., 1977-79; asst. prof. art history Pratt Inst., Bklyn., 1979-84, assoc. prof., 1984-90, prof., 1990—, chmn. dept., 1981—99. Vis. asst. prof. Pratt Inst., 1976-79; dir. Pratt in Venice, Italy, 1984—; spkr. Conv. on Veronese, Venice, 1988, Conv. on Tintoretto, Venice, 1994, Symposium on Italian Art in Am., Fordham U., 1993, Mass. Coll. Art, 1998, AM Berger lecture, Manhattanville Coll., 2001; invited participant Veronese Reconsidered, CASVA, Washington, 1988; invited spkr. Coll. Art. Assn. 1990, 93, 95, 2002, discussant session Benedictine patronage, Medieval Conf., Kalamazoo, Mich., 2003; invited spkr. Medievel Conf. Kalamazoo, Mich., 2004; chmn. two Renaissance Art sessions, Renaissance Soc. Meeting, NYC, 2004; chair session Alterations in Italian Art, Italian Art Soc., Coll. Art Assn., 2006. Illustrator: On Classic Ground, 1982; designer: Caudine Country, 1987; author: (with S. Sinding-Larsen) The Rule, the Bible, and the Council: The Library of the Benedictine Abbey at Praglia, 1998; contbr. articles to profl. jours. Am. Philos. Soc. grantee, 1989, Delmas Found. grantee, 1995-96. Mem. Italian Art Soc., Renaissance Soc., Coll. Art Assn., Caucus for Design History, Phi Beta Kappa. Democrat. Roman Catholic. Home: 843 President St Brooklyn NY 11215-1405 Office: Pratt Inst Dept Art History East 250 Brooklyn NY 11205 Office Phone: 718-636-3598. Personal E-mail: dianagisolfi@aol.com. Business E-Mail: dgisolfi@pratt.edu.

GISOLO, MARGARET, dancer, educator; b. Blanford, Ind., Oct. 21, 1914; d. Nikolai and Matilde (Bellessa) Gisolo. BS, Ind. State Coll., 1935; MA, NYU, 1942; attended, U. Calif.-Berkeley, 1938, Pa. State U., 1947; doctorate (hon.), Ariz. State U., 1994, Ind. State U., 1996. Supr. Paris City Schs., Ill., 1937—42; asst. prof. Ind. State Coll., Indiana, Pa., 1947—52; asst. to full prof. Ariz. State U., Tempe, 1954—80, chairperson dance program, 1954—77. Mem. various local, regional and nat. coms. Am. Alliance for Health, Phys. Edn., Recreation and Dance, 1957—99; founding mem. Ariz. Dance Arts Alliance, 1973—2000; nat. mem. Coun. Dance Adminstrs., 1974—77. Choreographer (dance work) Women and Destiny, 1965, Carmina Burana, 1965, House of Malediction, 1963, 1966. Founding mem., donor Friends of Ariz. State U. Dance, Tempe, 1978—. Lt. comdr. USN, 1942—47. Named to Athletic Hall of Fame, Ind. State U., Terre Haute, 1998, Hall of Fame, Nat. Italian Am. Sports, 2004; recipient Disting. Achievement award, Coll. Fine Arts, Ariz. State U., 1985. Achievements include playing in boys' championship Am. Legion baseball team, 1928; written about in Her Story in Sport, Women At Play: The Story of Women in Baseball; Women in Baseball: The Forgotten History; nationally ranked sr. tennis player, singles and doubles, 1985-2000. Avocation: tennis.

GIST, REBECCA JANE, special education educator; BSE, Cen. Mo. State U., 1983; MEd, NW Mo. State U., 1988. Spl. svcs. tchr. Northwestern R-1 Sch. Dist., Mendon, Mo., 1983-85; behavior disorders tchr. Savannah (Mo.) R-III Sch. Dist., 1985-86; spl. svcs. tchr., guidance counselor Hardin (Mo.)-Cen. C-2 Sch. Dist., 1986-90; elem. counselor Lebanon (Mo.) R-III Schs., 1990-91; spl. edn. tchr. DoD Livorno Elem. Sch., Italy, 1991-92; spl. edn. tchr. Guam Dept. Edn., Agana, 1992—97, Dept. Def. Ednl. Activity Guam H.S., 1997—. Mem. Coun. Exceptional Children, Mo. State Tchrs. Assn., Nat. Assistance Project for Spl. Edn. Tech. (local chairperson 1984-85), Northwestern Community Tchrs. Assn. (v.p. 1984-85), Gentry County Assn. for Retarded Citizens (spl. Olympics coord. 1985-90, coach 1979-91). Home: RR 2 Box 29-a Mc Fall MO 64657-9709

GITENSTEIN, DONNA M., academic administrator; b. Florala, Fla. m. Donald Hart; children: Pauline, Samuel. BA in English, Duke U.; PhD in English and Am. Lit., U. N.C., Chapel Hill. Asst. prof. English Ctrl. Mo. State U.; prof. English SUNY, Oswego, chair English dept., assoc. provost; provost Drake U., 1992—98, exec. v.p., 1997—98; pres. Coll. of N.J., Ewing, 1998—. Commr. Mid. States Commn. on Higher Edn. Author: (book) Apocalyptic Messianism and Contemporary Jewish-Am. Poetry; contbr. articles and reviews on Jewish and Am. Lit. Named Salute to Policy Makers, Exec. Women of N.J., 2002, Tribute to Women, YWCA of Princeton, N.J., 2003; recipient Woman of Distinction award, Girl Scouts of Del.-Raritan Coun., 2002. Mem.: Am. Coun. on Edn. (mem. commn. on minorities in higher edn., pres. sponsor (N.J. chapt.) network of women leaders in higher edn.). Office: Office of the Pres Coll of NJ PO Box 7718 Ewing NJ 08628

GITTLER, JOSEPHINE, law educator; b. Richmond, Va., May 13, 1943; d. Joseph and Lamie Gittler. BA, Barnard Coll.; JD, Northwestern Coll., 1968. Bar: Conn. 1969. Law clk. US Dist. Ct., New Haven, 1969-70, Conn. Supreme Ct., Hartford, 1970-71, US Dist. Ct. Conn., 1971-72; assoc. prof. Coll. Law to prof. Coll. Pub. Health U. Iowa, Iowa City, 1973—2002, prof. Coll. Law, 2002—. Chief counsel subcommittee to investigate juvenile deliquency jud. com. US Senate, Washington, 1977-78; coord. US Surgeon Gen.'s Conf., Washington, 1988; mem. exec. com. Consortium Ctrs. on Children Families & Law, 1989-2000; legis. cons. Nat. Assn. State and Territorial Maternal and Child Health and Crippled Children's Progs., 1982-86, recipient Pub. Svc. award 1982, 84; counsel interim study com. juvenile justice Iowa Gen. Assembly, Des Moines, 1975-77; vis. scholar Justice Ctr. of Atlanta, 1999; cons. in field. Contbr. articles to profl. jours., chpts. to books. Chair Iowa Maternal and Child Health Adv. Coun., Des Moines, 1983-88; mem. Iowa Juvenile Justice Adv. Com., Des Moines, 1975—83, Iowa Crime Commn., Des Moines, 1974-75, interim com. Penal Reform and Correction, Des Moines, 1973-74. Office: Coll Law U Iowa 290 Boyd Law Bldg Iowa City IA 52242-1113 E-mail: josephine-gittler@uiowa.edu.

GITTLER, WENDY, artist, art historian, writer; b. Manhattan, N.Y. d. Lewis Frederic and Esther (Becker) G. Studied with George Grosz, Art Students League, N.Y., 1958-59; studied with Camillio Egas, N.Y.C., 1960; BS in Art History, Columbia U., 1963; MA in Art History, Hunter Coll., 1967; postgrad., NYU, 1968; MFA, Bklyn. Coll., 1973; postgrad., U. Paris, 1977-78. Lectr. art NYU, N.Y.C., 1966-68; lectr. art history Fairleigh Dickinson U., Teaneck, N.J., 1966-68; lectr., art history Hunter Coll., N.Y.C., 1968-80; lectr. art history Sch. Visual Arts, N.Y.C., 1979-86; lectr. Met. Mus., N.Y.C., 1988-89; lectr. art history Parsons Sch. of Design, N.Y.C., 1989-96; lectr. N.Y. Studio Sch., N.Y.C., 1991—. Instr. studio U. Haifa, Israel, 1971; curator First Street Gallery, N.Y.C., 1992; lectr. Brown U., R.I., 1993, South Fla. Art Ctr., 1990, Lowe Art Mus., U. Miami, Fla., 1984; moderator artists panels, bd. dir. Artists Equity, N.Y.C., v.p., 1995-2006, Liman Studio Gallery, Palm Beach, Fla., 2004-06. One-woman shows include 1st Street Gallery, N.Y.C., 1976, 82, 88, 95, 99, 2002, 2005, Artists Equity, 1999-2006; exhibited in group shows at Blue Mountain Gallery, Atlantic Gallery, N.Y.C., 1995-2005, N.Y. Studio Sch., 1996-2005, Savannah Coll. Art and Design, 1997,, S.E. Mo. State U. Mus., 1997, Fordham U., 1996, Ashawag Hall, East Hampton, N.Y., 1995, LeHigh U., Bethlehem, Pa., 1984, Gallery of Fine Arts, N.Y.C., 1976, N.Y. City C.C., 1975, McKee Gallery, N.Y.C., 1998, 1999-2003, 2006, N.Y. Studio Sch., 1999-2006; represented in permanent collections S.E. Mo. State U. Mus., Savannah (Ga.) Coll. Art and Design; contbg. author art jours., exhibit catalogues. Mem. Coll. Art Assn., Fedn. Modern Painters and Sculptors, Channel 13, Artist Equity (bd. dirs.), Internat. Assn. Art Critics. Avocations: archaeology, philosophy, travel. Home: 780 West End Ave Apt 11E New York NY 10025-5573

GITTMAN, ELIZABETH, educational consultant; b. NYC, Mar. 15, 1945; d. Kallman and Rebecca Gittman; 3 children. BS, NYU, 1966; MS, CUNY Queens Coll., 1969; PhD, Hofstra U., 1979, Cert. Advanced Study, 1987. Cert. elem. tchr., sch. dist. supr., N.Y. Tchr. NYC Bd. Edn., Kew Gardens, NY, 1966-68; instr. New Sch. for Social Rsch., NYC, 1980-81; ind. cons. for program evaluation, grant writing, data collection, 1981-84; coord. instl. rsch. and evaluation Bd. Coop. Ednl. Svc. of Nassau County, Westbury, NY, 1984-94; assoc. prof. NY Inst. Tech., Old Westbury, NY, 1994-97, adj. assoc. prof., 2003; cons., 1997-98; dir. instrnl. support svc. Commack Pub. Sch., NY, 1998-2000; ind. cons. for program evaluation, grant writing, data collection, 2002—. Adj. prof. L.I. U., Brookville, N.Y., 1987-93. Mem. high risk youth rev. com. Ctr. Substance Abuse Prevention, U.S. Dept. HHS, 1990-95; developer numerous ednl. programs. Recipient NYU Founders Day award, 1966; Hofstra U. Doctoral fellow, 1976. Mem.: ASCD, APA, Northeastern Ednl. Rsch. Assn. (membership com. 1989—90, program com. 1989—, nominating com. 1991—2003, program co-chair 1993, editor 1993—95, bd. dirs. 1993—98, treas. 1996—98, bd. dirs. 2003—06, mem. com. chair 2005—06), Nat. Coun. Measurement in Edn., Am. Evaluation Assn., Am. Ednl. Rsch. Assn., Phi Delta Kappa (rsch. rep. 1990—91, exec. bd. 1990—2006, sec. 1991—93, conf. co-chair 1992, v.p. 1993—94, pres. 1995—96, nominating com. 1996—2006, Svc. award 1998, 2005), Kappa Delta Pi. Democrat. Jewish. Avocations: computer applications, reading, writing. Business E-Mail: egittman@nyc.rr.com.

GIULIANI, JUDITH, not-for-profit executive; b. Hazelton, Pa.; d. Donald and Joan Stish; 1 child: Whitney; m. Rudy Giuliani, May 24, 2003. Since 2000, Mrs. Giuliani has been a Managing Director of Changing Our World, Inc., a national fundraising and philanthropic services company headquartered in New York. She is a registered nurse with an extensive medical and scientific background. She worked with U.S. Surgical Corporation and Bristol-Myers Squibb. Mrs. Giuliani coordinated the efforts at the Family Assistance Center on Pier 94 in the aftermath of the September 11, 2001 terrorist attacks. In 2001, she became a founding member of the Board of Trustees of the Twin Towers Fund, which raised and distributed all of the $216 million to over 600 families/individuals. Contributions to the fund helped to create the TTF Scholarship Fund, and America's Camp for victims' children. Mrs. Giuliani currently serves as the Executive Director of the Campaign for Saint Vincent Catholic Medical Centers in New York. This campaign includes the construction of a state-of-the-art Level 1 Trauma Center. As the only Level 1 Trauma Center below 14th Street, Saint Vincent's plays a key role in protecting the lives of hundreds of thousands of New Yorkers and visitors to New York City. The Trauma Center will also include a comprehensive educational and instructional component focusing on bio-terrorism. Mrs. Giuliani is the recipient of numerous awards, including the New York Junior League's "Community Award" for her commitment, support and love for New York City and its people. In November, 2005, she received the "Spirit of Cabrini Service Award" from the Cabrini Mission Foundation for her work with Cabrini High School for Girls in the Bronx. This award is presented to those who represent the finest in the tradition of public service to the community and who are involved in the facets of charity and philanthropy which are the hallmarks of the Cabrini Mission Foundation: healing, teaching and caring. In 2006, Mrs. Giuliani was awarded New York University's College of Nursing's "Humanitarian Award" in recognition of using her nursing identity for humanitarian work and charitable endeavors as well as for being a powerful voice that enhances the visibility of nursing and elevates the profession. Also in 2006, Mrs. Giuliani received the "St. Francis Xavier Cabrini Service Award" from Mother Cabrini High School an award honoring her commitment to young women and their education. She was further honored by the McCarton Foundation, who presented Mrs. Giuliani with their "Leadership Award" at the foundation's "Celebration of Learning 2006." The McCarton School is a full-time school in New York City dedicated to the treatment of children with autistic spectrum disorders. Mrs. Giuliani is a frequent speaker on medically related philanthropic issues. Office: Changing Our World Inc 420 Lexington Ave, Ste 2320 New York NY 10170*

GIULIANO, CONCETTA, physician; b. Vineland, N.J., June 27, 1969; d. Raffaele and Maria Giuliano. BS, Chestnut Hill Coll., Phila., 1991; DO, Phila. Osteo. Coll., 1995. Diplomate Am. Bd. Radiology. Resident in radiology Pa. Hosp., Phila., 1995—. Cotnbr. articles to profl. jours. Recipient George L. Harrison award Pa. Hosp., 1998; Internat. fellow AIFA, Milan, 1994; grantee St. George Med. Soc./Am. Cancer Soc., 1992. Mem. Am. Coll. Radiology, Radiol. Soc. N.Am. Avocation: travel. Home: 5732 Canton Cv Winter Springs FL 32708 E-mail: giulianomd@worldnet.att.net.

GIULIANTI, MARA SELENA, mayor; b. NYC, June 3, 1944; d. Leon and Bertha (Jablonky) Berman; m. Donald Giulianti, May 29, 1966; children: Stacey Alexander, Michael Alan. BA, Tulane U., 1966. Social worker L.A. County Social Svcs., 1966-68; adminstrv. asst. neurosurg. cons. D. Giulianti, MD, Hollywood, Fla., 1980-83; campaign mgr. City Commr. Suzanne Gunzburger, Hollywood, 1982; mayor City of Hollywood, 1986-90, 92—. Vice chmn. Broward Employment and Tng. Adminstrn., 1987-89, 92-94, 96-00, 01-02, chmn., 1989-90, 94-96, 00-01, Work Force One chmn., 2002-04, 06-, chmn. pro tem, 2004-05, vice chair 2005-06; exec. bd. Fla. League Cities, Tallahassee, 1986-90, 92—), bd. dirs.; econ. devel. pol. com. Nat. League Cities, Washington, 1987-90, human devel. policy com., 1992-94, fin., adminstrn. and intergovtl. rels. steering com., 1994-02; active Broward County Met. Planning Orgn., 1986-90. Columnist The Digest, Hallandale, Fla., 2001-02, South Fla. Sun-Times, 2002—, Beach Digest, 2002-03; contbr. articles to local newspapers. Pres. Women in Distress, Broward County, 1982-83, bd. dirs., 1983-90, 2006—, trustee, 1994-97, 05-; exec. bd. Nat. Jewish Cmty. Rels. Adv. Coun., 1985-87; v.p. CHARLEE Family Care Homes, Broward County, 1986-88, bd. dirs., 1988-92; mem. Broward County Commn. on Status Women, 1984-86, Fla. Commn. on Drug and Alcohol Concerns, Tallahassee, 1984-85, Broward County Dem. Exec. Com., 1984-88; pres. Hills Dem. Club, 1991-94; trustee Graves Mus. of Archeol. and Nat. History, Dania, Fla., 1993-97; bd. dirs. Hollywood Econ. Growth Corp., 1994-95, 98-99; chmn. Hollywood Comty. Redevel. Agy., 1992—; v.p. South Broward unit Am. Cancer Soc., 1992-93, bd. dirs., 1993-99. Recipient Hannah G. Solomon award, 1983, Giraffe Stick Your Neck Out award Women's Advocacy--the Majority/Minority, 1986, Leadership award Leadership Hollywood Alumni, 1987, City of Peace award Israel Bonds, Broward County, 1987, Menorah award Histadrut, 1990, Juliette Gordon Low award Girl Scouts Broward County, 1997, Govt. Leadership award, ArtServe, 2002, Gracias award Hispanic Unity, 2000, Cmty. Covenant award, Broward Outreach Ctr., 2001, Breaking the Glass Ceiling award, Ziff Jewish Mus. of Fla., 2002, Spirit of Excellence award Am Bus. Women's Assn., 2003, Woman of Valor award Broward County Jewish Cmty. Ctr., 2003, Founders award Chaminade-Madonna Coll. Prep., 2004; named Broward County Woman of Yr., Am. Jewish Congress, 1988, Woman of Yr. Women in Comms., Inc., 1990, Crystal Vision award Hollywood Art and Culture Ctr., 2000; Honoree Boys & Girls Clubs of Broward, 2001, honoree Holocaust Documentation and Edn. Ctr., 2005; inducted Broward County Women's Hall of Fame, 1996. Mem. Nat. Coun. Jewish Women (nat. bd. dir. 1985-89), Jewish Fedn. So. Broward (chair community rels. com. 1981-82, bd. dir. 1982-90), Broward County Med. Aux. (br. pres. 1977-78), Rotary. Democrat. Avocations: writing, volunteer work, travel. Office: PO Box 229045 Hollywood FL 33022-9045 Office Phone: 954-921-3321. Business E-Mail: mgiulianti@hollywoodfl.org.

GIULIVO, CYNTHIA ANN, secondary school educator; d. Robert Joseph and Anna Mary Mares; m. Michael Giulivo, Mar. 19, 1996. BS in Edn., Bowling Green State U., Ohio, 1981; MEd, Marygrove U., Mich., 1995. Dietetic tech. Cleve. (Ohio) Clinic, 1981—85; tchr. Parma (Ohio) City Schs., 1996—2002, tchr. sci. resource, 2002—. Office: Parma City Schs 3290 Forest Overlook Dr Seven Hills OH 44131

GIVEN, BARBARA (BARBARA KNIGHT), secondary school educator; b. Quenemo, Kans., July 17, 1935; d. Henry Taylor and Lucile Martha (Jolley) Knight; m. Bruce Willard Given, June 7, 1959 (div. 1983); children: Bryce Walton, Bethany Kay. AA, Colo. Women' Coll., 1955; BS in Elem. Edn., Kans. State U., 1958; MEd in Mental Retardation, U. Oreg., 1967; PhD in Edn. of the Exceptional, Catholic U. Am., 1974. Tchr. pub. schs., Kans., 1958—59, Oreg., 1959—63; dir. spl. edn., prin., instr. pediatrics John F. Kennedy Inst. Johns Hopkins Hosp. and U., Balt., 1969-70; tchr. children with learning disabilities Fairfax (Va.) Pub. Schs., 1972-73; mem. faculty dept. edn. George Mason U., 1974—2003, coord. learning disabilities tchr. preparation, 1979—95, co-dir. SE Regional Learning Styles Ctr., 1987—, dir. spl. edn. tchr. retraining inst., 1987-93, dir. ednl. study ctr., 1988—93, project dir. learning disabilities cert. program US Dept. Edn., 1989-93, co-dir. Adolescent and Adult Learning Rsch. Ctr., Krasnow Inst. Advanced Study, 2003—. Mem. edn. task force on identification of learning disabilities, Va. Commonwealth Dept. Edn., 1983-85, performance catalogue task force, 1983-86; cons. Fredrick County Pub. Schs., 1986-93; mem. adv. bd. No. Va. Literacy Coun.; presenter at seminars and profl. confs. Author: spl. edn. curriculum materials; contbr. articles to profl. publs., Learning Styles: A Guide for Teachers and Parents, 2000, Teaching to the Brain's Natuarl Learning Systems, 2002. Facilitator New Beginnings Support Group Separated and Divorced Persons, 1987-91. Grantee US Dept. Edn., 1975, 76-78, 80-83, 89-93, 1999— Mem. Internat. Assn. Children and Adults with Learning Disabilities, Coun. Exceptional Children, Coun. Learning Disabilities, International Alliance for Learning. Presbyn. Avocation: reading tutor. Office: George Mason U 4400 University Dr Fairfax VA 22030-4444 Home: 452 S Union St Alexandria VA 22314 Office Phone: 703-993-4406. Business E-Mail: bgiven@gmu.edu.

GIVEN, MELISSA ANN, elementary school educator, educational consultant; b. Charleston, West Virginia, June 5, 1961; d. Robert Carl and Janet (Barnette) Rehe; m. Bruce Owen Given. BS, West Va. State Coll., 1983; MA, West Va. U., 1989. Cert. elem. edn., mental retardation K-12, preschool handicapped, severe,profound handicapped. Tchr. Kanawha County Sch., Charleston, 1984—91, Monongalia County Sch., Morgantown, W.Va., 1991—94, Gwinnett County Sch., Buford, Ga., 1995—98, Kanawha County Sch., Dunbar, W.Va., 1998—. Course grader W.Va. U., Morgantown, 1991—94; cons., cadre tchr. Office Spl. Edn. W.Va. Dept. Edn., Charleston, 1999—; qualified mental retardation profl. Braley & Thompson, St. Albans, W.Va., 2000—01; qualified mental retardation prof. cons., 1999—2002; cadre tchr. Office Spl. Edn., W.va. Dept. Edn., 1999—2003; adv. com. mem. Office Assessment, W.Va. Dept. Edn., Charlston, 2003—. Named Tchr. of the Yr., West Va. Fedn. Coun. Exceptional Children, 2001. Mem.: Coun. Exceptional Children, La Belle Garden Club (co-v.p. 2001—, pres. 2003—). Episcopalian. Avocations: boating, swimming, photography. Home: 848 Alta Rd Charleston WV 25314 Office: Kanawha County Sch Dunbar Middle Sch 325 27th St Dunbar WV 25064 Business E-Mail: Wvcatlover39@aol.com.

GIVENS, CYNTHIA A., educator; d. James R. and LaVerne J. Givens. AA, Western Wyo. CC, Rock Springs, 1970; BA, U. Wo., Laramie, 1972; MA, Grand Canyon U., Phoenix, 2001, cert. in adminstrn. k-12, 2004. Tchr. Laramie County Sch. Dist., Cheyenne, 1972—81, 1990—, tchr. tchrs., paraprofls. and substitute tchrs., tchr., advocate at-risk students; tchr. Douglas County Sch. Dist., Glenrock, Wyo., 1982—83. Mem.: ASCD, Nat. Assn. Secondary Sch. Prins. Avocations: reading, travel. Office: Laramie County Sch Dist 2810 House Ave Cheyenne WY 82001 Business E-Mail: givensc@laramiel.k12.wy.us.

GIVENS, JANET EATON, writer; b. N.Y.C., July 5, 1932; d. Irving Daniel and Matilda (Schmelzle) E.; m. Richard Ayres Givens, Aug. 24, 1957; children: Susan Ruth, Jane Lucile. BA, Queens Coll., 1953; MA, Columbia U., 1955. Lic. tchr. NY. Tchr. pub. elem. schs., Silver Spring, Md., 1953—55, Mamaroneck, NY, 1955—59; supr. prospective tchrs., part-time ledctr. Queens Coll., N.Y.C., 1959—68. Author: The Migrating Birds, 1964, Something Wonderful Happened, 1982, Just Two Wings, 1984; contbg. author: Tensions Our Children Live With, 1959. V.p. PTA, Pub. Sch. 219, Queens, NY, 1972—73, del. to United Parents Assn., 1971—72, editor PS 219 News, 1971—73. Home: 600 E Cathedral Rd Ste D208 Philadelphia PA 19128-1928 E-mail: janet.givens@Owanputall.net.

GIVHAN, ROBIN DENEEN, journalist; b. Detroit, Sept. 11, 1964; d. Robert Earl and Stella Mae (Thompson) G. BA in English, Princeton U., 1986; MA in Journalism, U. Mich., 1988. Staff writer Detroit Free Press, 1988-92, San Francisco Chronicle, 1992-93; fashion editor Detroit Free Press, 1993-95, Washington Post, 1995—; assoc. editor Vogue, NYC, 2000. Recipient Outstanding Achievement in Media award Nat. Coalition of 100 Black Women, 1992, Pulitzer Prize for criticism, 2006. Methodist. Avocations: bicycling, aerobics, reading, photography. Office: Washington Post Style News Desk 1150 15th St NW Washington DC 20006 Office Phone: 212-445-4900. Office Fax: 202-334-5587. E-mail: givhanr@washpost.com.*

GLACEL, BARBARA PATE, management consultant; b. Balt., Sept. 15, 1948; d. Jason Thomas Pate and Sarah Virginia (Forwood Pate) Wetter; m. Robert Allan Glacel, Dec. 21, 1969; children: Jennifer Warren, Sarah Allane, Ashley Virginia. AB, Coll. William and Mary, 1970; MA, U. Okla., 1973, PhD, 1978. Tchr. Harford County Schs., Md., 1970—71, Dept. Def. Schs., Germany, 1971—73; ednl. counselor U.S. Army, Germany, 1973—74; mgmt. cons. Barbara Glacel & Assocs., Anchorage, 1980—86, Washington, 1986—88; ptnr. Pracel Prints, Williamsburg, Va., 1981—85; sr. mgmt. tng. specialist Arco Alaska, Inc., 1984—85; gen. mgr. mgmt. programs Hay Sys., Inc., Washington, 1986—88; CEO VIMA Internat., Burke, Va., 1988—99, chmn. emeritus, 2000; 2d v.p., bd. dirs. Chesapeake Broadcasting Corp. Md.; prin. The Glacel Group, 2000—. Adj. prof. U. Md., 1973—74, Suffolk U., Boston, 1975—77, C.W. Post Ctr., L.I. U., John Jay Coll. Criminal Justice, N.Y.C., 1979—80, St. Thomas Aquinas Coll., N.Y.C., 1981, St. Mary's Coll., Leavenworth, Kans., 1981, Anchorage C.C., 1982; acad. adviser Ctrl. Mich. U., 1981—82; asst. prof. U. Alaska, Anchorage, 1983—85; mem. adj. faculty Ctr. for Creative Leadership, 1986—; guest lectr. U.S. Mil. Acad.; mem. U.S. Army Sci. Bd., 1986—90, U.S. Dept. Def. Sci. Bd. Quality of Life Panel, 1994—95, Def. Adv. Com. on Women in the Svcs., 2000—02, Consumer Rev. Bd. DOD Breast Cancer Rsch. Program, 2001—02; mem. adv. coun. Reves Ctr. for Internat. Studies Coll. William and Mary, 2001—; bd. dirs. The Fund for William and Mary, 2001—. Author: Regional Transit Authorities, 1983; (with others) 1000 Army Families, 1983, The Army Community and Their Families, 1989, Light Bulbs for Leaders, 1994, Hitting the Wall: Memoir of a Cancer Journey, 2001. Chmn. 172d Inf. Brigade Family Coun. Recipient Comdr.'s award for pub. svc. U.S. Dept. Army, 1984, U.S. Army Patriotic Civilian Svc. award 1991, U.S. Army Forscom Svc. award 1993, Dept. of Army Outstanding Civilian Svc. medal, 1999, Yellow Rose of Tex. award, 1999, Helping Hand Cmty. Svc. award, 1999, Coll. William & Mary Alumna medallion, 2001; AAUW grantee, 1977-78. Mem. ASTD (bd. dirs. Anchorage chpt.), APA, Soc. for Indsl. and Orgnl. Psychology, Instrnl. Sys. Assn. (v.p. 1993-96), Soc. Alumni Coll. William and Mary (bd. dirs. 1992-98, v.p., 1997-98). Personal E-mail: bpglacel@aol.com.

GLAD, BETTY, political scientist, educator; b. Salt Lake City, Sept. 27, 1927; d. Harluf Anderson and Edna Janette (Geertsen) G.; m. Irving T. Diamond, Sept., 1954 (div. Jan. 1957). BS magna cum laude, U. Utah, 1949; PhD, U. Chgo., 1962. Instr. Mt. Holyoke Coll., 1958-59; lectr., instr. Bklyn. Coll., 1960-64; from asst. prof. to assoc. prof. U. Ill., Urbana, 1964-72, prof., 1973-89, dept. head, 1972-73; prof. U. S.C., Columbia, 1989-93, Caroline disting. prof., 1993-95, Olin D. Johnston prof., 1995—. Mem. hist. adv. com. U.S. Dept. State, Washington, 1990; rev. panelist NEH, Washington, 1980-83; chair Midwest Univs. Com. Seminar in U.S. Fgn. Policy, 1972. Mem. editl. bds., 1968-73; contbr. articles to profl. jours.; appeared on numerous TV and radio shows. Nat. Pub. Svc. fellow, 1952, Kappa Kappa Gamma nat. fellow, 1952. Mem. Internat. Soc. for Polit. Psychology (pres. 1993-94, Harold Lasswell award 1997), Am. Polit. Sci. Assn. (treas. 1978-79, v.p. 1994-95, pres. Presidency Rsch. Group 1989-90, women's caucus, Mentor of Distinction award 1989, Frank Goodnow award 2000), U. Utah Beehive Soc., Mortar Bd., Phi Beta Kappa. Democrat. Unitarian Universalist. Avocations: jazz, piano, dance, theater, travel. Home: 1317 Belmont Dr Columbia SC 29205-1507 Office: U SC Dept Polit Sci Columbia SC 29208-0001 Office Phone: 803-777-4544. Business E-Mail: glad@gwm.sc.edu.

GLADDEN, VIVIANNE CERVANTES, healthcare consultant, writer; b. Brookhaven, Miss., Oct. 8, 1927; d. Thomas James Guillory and Edna Beatrice Torry; m. Garnett Lee Gladden; children: Mark Lee, Jeanne Sue Wood. Grad., Edwin Lester Sch. Musical Theater, 1976; LittD (hon.), Union U., 1979; BA, Golden State U., 1980, PhD, DHL, Honolulu U., 1993. Ordained to ministry Cmty. Ch. of the Bay, 1985. Stage, film and TV actress, N.Y.C., Hollywood, 1950—64; model Harry Conover, N.Y.C., 1951; mannequin Jacques Heim, Paris, 1951; featured singer La Vien Rose, N.Y.C., 1951—52, Copa City, Fla., 1951—52; nutritional cons. Ctr. Holistic Health Cedars-Sinai Hosp., L.A., 1975—77; health and lifestyle counselor Beverly Hills and Newport, Calif., 1977—; lectr., cons. health sci. and products All Natural Products, Honolulu, Japan Life Inc., Tokyo. Radio ministry Sta. KIEV, Glendale, Calif., 1985—86; mem. adv. bd. Nat. Acad. Sports Medicine, Chgo., 1993—2002. Author (with Lee Gladden): (book) Heirs of the Gods, 1978 (Bronze Halo award So. Calif. Motion Picture Coun., 1982); author: (with Lee Gladden and Gary Couture) How to Win the Aging Game, 1979; author: Archeolinguistics, 1984. Chmn. Eco World, Hollywood, Calif., 1971; master of ceremonies Opening Ahmanson Theatre, L.A., 1976. Named to Hall of Fame, Oakwood Coll., Huntsville, Ala., 1956; recipient Gold award of merit, Martin Luther King Jr. Campaign Ctr., Port Arthur, Tex., 1988. Avocations: singing, piano, yoga, running. Office Phone: 888-991-2990 2733. Personal E-mail: gardant24@cs.com.

GLADSTEIN, MIMI REISEL, theater educator, literature educator; d. Emil and Regina Rosen Reisel; m. Jay Stephen Gladstein, Aug. 18, 1956; children: Clifford Eric, Denise Robin Halikman-Gladstein, Alfred Martin. BA in Speech and Drama, Tex. Western Coll., 1959; PhD, U. N.Mex, Albuquerque, 1973. Prof. English and Theatre U. Tex., El Paso, Tex., 1968—. Dir. Women's Studies Program U. Tex., 1981—83, chmn. Depts. English and Philosophy, 1985—88, chmn. Dept. English, 1985—88, exec. dir. Diamond Jubilee, 1988—90, dir. We. Cultural Heritage Program, 1995—97, assoc. dean, 1997—2002, chmn. Dept. Theatre, Dance, and Film, 2002—06. Author: 5 books; contbr. articles to profl. jours. Mem. edn. and content com. El Paso (Tex.) Holocaust Mus. and Study Ctr., 1995—2006. Named Woman of Yr., El Paso (Tex.) Women's Polit. Caucus, 1975; recipient Burlington No. award, 1988, Angeline Pruis award, 1987, Burkhardt award, 1996, Mentor Appreciation award, Ariz. State U., 2002, Disting. Achievement Svc. to Students award, UTEP, 2006; grantee, Fulbright Found., 1995, Outstanding Achievement award, Coll. Liberal Arts, 2003. Home: 5464 Cactus Hill Drive El Paso TX 79912 Office: University of Texas at El Paso El Paso TX 79968 Office Phone: 915-747-6259.

GLADUE, IRENE, elementary school educator; b. Belcourt, ND, Oct. 31, 1953; d. Alfred and Cecilia Belgrade; m. Patrick LaRocque; children: Jason LaRocque, Christie LaRocque, Laurie LaRocque; children: Lacey, Gaylen. BS, reading and math. cert., Minot State U., ND, 1993. Elem. tchr. Ojibwa Indian Sch., Belcourt, ND, 1993—97, Dunseith Elem., 1997—. Mem. crew Wildland Fire Fighter Camp, Turtle Mountain Forestry Svc., Belcourt, 2005—. Office: Dunseith Elem Sch PO Box 789 Dunseith ND 58329-0789

GLAESSMANN, DORIS ANN, former county official, consultant; b. Northampton, Pa., Feb. 18, 1940; d. Frank G. and Theresa (Fischl) Zwikl; m. Edward Glaessmann, Sept. 1, 1962; children: Edward Jr., Robert F. Grad. high sch., Northampton, 1958. Sec., bookkkeeper John F. Moore Agy., Inc., Allentown, Pa., 1958-64; ct. clk. Criminal div. Clk. of Cts. Office, Allentown, 1968-69, asst. dep. clk., 1969-76, chief dep. clk., 1976-82; clk. of cts., criminal and civil divsns. Lehigh County, Allentown, 1982-95; cons., 1995-2000; ret., 2001. Den leader, sec. Boy Scouts Am., Allentown, Pa., 1973-78; past bd. dirs.; mem. coun. St. Peter's Evang. Luth. Ch., Allentown, 1984-89. Mem. Pa. Prothonotaries and Clks. Assn. (past pres., treas. 1993-2006), Pa. Elected Women's Assn. (past. sec.-treas. and pres. Lehigh Valley chpt.), Quota Internat. of Allentown (pres. 1997-99, 2d dist. gov.). Democrat. Avocations: baking, reading, crocheting, walking. Home: 945 E Lynnwood St Allentown PA 18103-5250

GLANCY, DOROTHY JEAN, lawyer, educator; b. Glendale, Calif., Sept. 24, 1944; d. Walter Perry and Elva T. (Douglass) G.; m. Jon Tobias Anderson, June 8, 1979. BA, Wellesley Coll., 1967; JD, Harvard Law Sch., 1970. Bar: D.C. 1971, Calif. 1976, U.S. Dist. Ct. D.C. 1971, U.S. Ct. Appeals (D.C. cir.) 1972. Assoc. Hogan & Hartson, Wash., 1971-73; counsel U.S. Senate Judiciary Subcomm. on Constitutional Rights, Wash., 1973-74; fellow in Law & Humanities Harvard U., Cambridge, Mass., 1974-75; asst. to assoc. prof. law Santa Clara U., Calif., 1975-82, prof. law Calif., 1984—; vis. prof. law U. Arizona, Tucson, 1979; asst. gen. counsel U.S. Dept. of Agr., 1982-83. Cons. Commn. Fed. Paperwork, Wash., 1976; dir. summer Law Study Program in Hong Kong, 1985-90; advisor Restatement, Third Property: Servitudes, 1986-97; mem. ct. tech. adv. com. Calif. Jud. Coun. Dir. legal rsch. project regarding privacy and intelligent trnsp. systems Fed. Hwy. Adminstrn., 1993-95; bd. dirs. Presidio Hts. Assn. Neighbors, 1990—. Fellow Wellesley Coll., Harvard U. Mem. ABA (chair ethics com. of sect. on natural resources, energy and environ. law, 1993-95, coun. mem. 1995-98), State Bar Calif. (mem. environ. law sect., adv. exec. com. 1993-96, advisor 1996—), Am. Assn. Law Schs. (chair environ. law sect. 1992-93, chair property sect. 1996-97, chair defamation and privacy sec., 1997-98), Am. Law Inst., Calif. Women Lawers, Soc. Am. Law Tchrs., Phi Beta Kappa. Democrat. Avocations: gardening, travel. Office: Santa Clara U Sch Law Santa Clara CA 95053-0001 Business E-Mail: dglancy@scu.edu.

GLANTON, JERALINE CAIN, retired language educator; b. Wetumpka, Ala., Dec. 18, 1931; d. Allie and Alice Crosby Cain; m. Herbert Algenon Glanton Sr., Mar. 29, 1955; children: Venese Michelle, Virginia Glanton Gavin, Herbert Algenon Jr. BS, Ala. State U., 1954, MEd in English, 1964; postgrad., Troy U., 1960—61, Auburn U., 1980. Tchr. various secondary edn. sys., 1954—87. Chairperson English dept. Dothan (Ala.) H.S., 1956—67, chairperson summer sch. planning com., 1958—86, mem. curriculum adv. bd., 1977—87; chairperson English dept. Northview H.S., Dothan, Ala., 1977—87. Contbr. magazine. Bd. dirs. Am. Educators Ins. Co., Dothan, 1970—81; mem. Dothan City Constl. Bicentennial Com., Ala., 1987; contbr. Nat. Coun. Negro Women, Washington, 1984—2005; mem. Nat. Dem. Com., 1965—2005, Ala. Dem. Com., Dothan, 1985—2005. Grantee, Auburn U., 1981. Mem.: Ala. Edn. Assn., Delta Sigma Theta Inc. D-Liberal. Jehovah'S Witness. Achievements include first black person to chair English department in an integrated school in area; first black person to chair student government association in area. Avocations: cooking, canning, reading, gardening. Home: 2905 St Luke St Dothan AL 36303-5309

GLASBERG, LISA, radio personality; Disc jockey Sta. WQHT-FM, N.Y.C. Entertainment newscaster for various cable channels. Active in charity fundraisers. Avocation: jogging. Office: WQHT-FM/Emmis Broadcasting 395 Hudson St Fl 7 New York NY 10014-3600

GLASER, KANDACE KAYE, elementary school educator; m. Thomas L. Glaser, Jan. 17, 1970; children: John, Christine. BS in Edn., U. Tulsa, Okla., 1984; postgrad., U. N.Mex., Albuquerque, 2001, U. Tech. and Engring., Socorro, N.Mex., 2003. Lang. arts tchr. Immaculate Conception Sch., Tulsa, 1984—87, asst. prin., 1986—87; social studies tchr. Sts. Peter and Paul Sch., Tulsa, 1987—91; sci. tchr. Queen of Heaven Sch., Albuquerque, 1991—98, Lincoln Mid. Sch., Rio Rancho, N.Mex., 1998—. Dist. trainer Rio Rancho Schs., 2005—. Bd. dirs. Sci. Fair Regional Bd., Albuquerque, 1991—. Grantee Innovative Tchg. grantee, Dept. Edn., Santa Fe, N.Mex., 2001, Toyota Tapestry grantee, Nat. Sci. Tchrs. Assn., Washington, 2003. Mem.: Nat Sci. Tchrs. Assn., Kappa Delta Pi. Republican. Roman Catholic. Avocations: gardening, hiking, reading, stained glass. Office: Lincoln Middle School 2287 Lama Rd SE Rio Rancho NM 87124

GLASER, PATRICIA L., lawyer; b. Charleston, W.Va., Sept. 15, 1947; d. Richard Stanley and Tilda Jane (Rosen) G.; m. Samuel Hunter Mudie, May 19, 1978; stepchildren: Heather and Jason Mudie. BA, Am. U., 1969; JD, Rutgers U., 1973. Bar: Calif. 1973, U.S. Dist. Ct. (no. and cen. dists.) Calif. 1973, U.S. Dist. Ct. (so. dist.) 1976, U.S. Ct. Appeals (9th cir.), U.S. Supreme Ct. Law clk. to presiding justice U.S. Dist. Ct.; from assoc. to ptnr. Wyman, Bautzer, Rothman, Kuchel & Silbert, Los Angeles, 1973—. Judge pro tem West br. Los Angeles Mcpl. Ct., panelist legal continuing edn. programs. Mem. fund-raising com. Deukmejian for Gov. of Calif.; participant Parole-Aide program. Mem. Los Angeles County Bar Assn. (fed. cts. and practices com.). Avocations: travel, skiing, tennis, reading.

GLASER, VERA ROMANS, journalist; b. St. Louis, Apr. 21, 1916; d. Aaron L. and Mollie (Romans); m. Herbert R. Glaser, Apr. 16, 1939; 1 dau., Carol Jane Barriger. Student, Washington U., St. Louis, George Washington U., Am. U., 1937-40. Reporter-writer Nat. Aero. mag., 1943-44; reporter Washington Times Herald, 1944-46; pub. relations specialist Great Lakes-St. Lawrence Assn., 1950-51; promotion specialist, writer Congl. Quar. News Features, 1951-54; writer-commentator radio sta. WGMS, Washington, 1954-55; mem. Washington bur. N.Y. Herald Tribune, 1955-56; press officer U.S. Senator Charles E. Potter, 1956-59; dir. pub. relations, women's div. Rep. Nat. Com., 1959-62; press officer U.S. Senator Kenneth B. Keating, 1962-63; Washington corr. N.Am. Newspaper Alliance, 1963-69, bur. chief, 1965-69; columnist, nat. corr. Knight-Ridder Newspapers, Inc., 1969-81; assoc. editor Washingtonian Mag., 1981-88, contbg. editor, 1988—; columnist Maturity News Svc., 1988-94. Mem. Pres.'s Commn. on White House Fellows, 1969, Pres.'s Task Force on Women's Rights and Responsibilities, 1970; judge 1981 Robert Kennedy Journalism Awards. Free-lance writer nat publs., radio and TV appearances Stas. WTOP-TV, ABC, PBS, C-SPAN. Mem. nat. bd. Med. Coll. Pa., 1977-88; bd. dirs. Washington Press Club Found., 1986-88; bd. dirs. Internat. Women's Media Found., 1990-98. Mem. White House Corrs. Assn., Nat. Press Club (bd. govs. 1988, 89), Washington Press Club (pres. 1971-72), Cosmos Club. Unitarian Universalist. Home and Office: 5555 Friendship Blvd Apt 724 Chevy Chase MD 20815-7243

GLASGOW, CONSTANCE LENORE, pediatrician; b. N.Y.C., Jan. 31, 1934; d. Lester and Octavia Louisa Glasgow; m. Twitty Junius Styles, Aug. 11, 1962; children: Scott Peterson, Auria Octavia. BS, Hunter Coll., 1955; MD, SUNY Downstate, Bklyn., 1960. Intern Syracuse (N.Y.) Upstate Med. Ctr., 1960—61; resident Albert Einstein Bronx Mcpl. Hosp. Ctr., NY, 1961—63; rotating intern Upstate Med. Ctr., Syracuse, NY; pediat. resident Jacobi Hosp./Bronx Mcpl. Hosp. Ctr., Albert Einstein U., Bronx; pvt. practice physician Clifton Park, NY, 1966—. Mem. ethics com. Ellis Hosp., Schenectady, NY, 1993—. Fellow: Am. Acad. Pediat.; mem.: Capital Dist. Links (co-chair nat. trends com. 1999—). Meth. Avocations: travel, music, walking. Office: Capital Care Pediat Clifton Park 942A Route 146 Clifton Park NY 12065 Office Phone: 518-371-8000.

GLASGOW, DIANNE BRITT, education educator, writer, consultant; b. Shreveport, La., June 7, 1947; d. Carroll Kendrick and Mary Elmena Britt; m. James Michael Glasgow, June 3, 1968; children: Jamie Michele, Casey Rachelle. MS Human Ecology, La. Tech U., Ruston, La., 1992. Cert. Early Childhood Centenary Coll., 1985. Agcenter ext. educator La. State U., Shreveport, La., 2001—; writer LifeWay Pub. Co., Nashville, 1998—2005. Parent educator Providence Ho., Shreveport, La., 2002—; grant writer Children's Trust Fund, 2003—05; tchr. New Orleans (La.) Theol. Seminary; cons. in field. Composer: (songs) (preschool) lPrayer Is. and Who Teaches Me About Jesus?; co-author: Teaching in Christian Weekday Early Education; author: (column) City Lights Mag., (parenting edn. materials) Kids Under Contruction - Tools for Parenting; contbr. articles pub. to profl. jour. Mentor to single moms, Shreveport/Bossier, La., 1990—2005; parent educator Providence Ho., shelter for homeless families with children to prevent child abuse, Shreveport, La., 2002—05. Grantee Grant to Prevent Child Abuse, Chidlren's Trust Fund, 2003—05. Mem.: La. Bapt. Conv. (assoc.; chairperson 1992—2005), Nat. Assn. of Edn. of Young Children (assoc.), La. Bapt. Conv. Early Childhood Com. (assoc.; conf. chairperson 1998—2005), Nat. Assn. Edn. of Young Children (assoc.). Southern Bapt. Avocations: reading, travel. Office: La State Univ AgCtr 2408 East 70th St Shreveport LA 71105 Office Phone: 318-226-6805.

GLASGOW, ISTIHAROH, art administrator; b. Provo, Utah, Mar. 24, 1939; d. Lincoln Riter Le Vitre and Mildred Mae Young; m. Lukman Glasgow (dec.); children: Ra'uf, Hamidah, Istimah, Mutahar, Mutalib. Grad., Brigham Young U., 1960; BA in Arts Adminstrn., Union Inst., 1992; Ikebana cert., Sogetsu Sch., 92. Owner Eufloria, L.A., 1982—92; coord. folk and traditional art Harbor Art Ctrs. Cultural Affairs, L.A., 1996—97, dir., 1998—2000; dir. Barnsdall Art Ctr., Jr. Art Ctr. Cultural Affairs City of L.A., 2000—. Asst. to dir. Westwood Clay Nat., Fibre Structure Nat., Metal Nat., Ceramics Nat., L.A. and Sacramento. Floral designer (1st place award Winterfest, 85, 1st place award Nat. Florafax Design, 86), guest exhibitor L.A. County Fair, Pamona, 1982—92. Mem. Councilman Alatore's Blue Ribbon Com.; bd. dirs. Atalanta Crestone; trustee Lukman Glasgow Meml. Fund, Crestone; mem. com., councilman City of L.A., 1988—96; bd. dirs. Occidental Coll. Women's Club, L.A., 1983—, Eagle Rock C.C., L.A., 1988—94, My Neighborhood Internat., 2002—; dir. at large Subud USA, 2004—06. Recipient recognition for cmty. svc., L.A. City Coun., 1994, commendation, L.A. County Bd. Suprs., 1995, Calif. State Legislature, 1996. Mem.: Subud Cultural Assn. (bd. dirs. 2000—05), Subud Internat. Cultural Assn. (bd. dirs. 2000—05), L.A. C. of C. (chmn. street decorating 1987—95, chmn. pride in cmty. 1993—95), Alumni Assn. Union Inst. (pres. 1992—2005). Avocation: Japanese floral arranging. Office: Barndsall Art Ctr and Jr Arts Ctr 4800 Hollywood Blvd Los Angeles CA 90027 Office Phone: 323-644-6275.

GLASGOW, JORDANA BERKOWITZ, lawyer; b. Boston, 1967; BA magna cum laude, Brandeis U., 1989; JD cum laude, Boston Coll., 1992. Bar: Mass. 1992, US Dist. Ct. (Dist. Mass.), US Ct. Appeals (1st Cir.), US Supreme Ct. Ptnr. Edwards Angell Palmer & Dodge LLP, Boston. Mem.: Boston Bar Assn. (co-chair, fiduciary litig. com.), Phi Beta Kappa. Office: Edwards Angell Palmer & Dodge LLP 111 Huntington Ave Boston MA 02199 Office Phone: 617-239-0560. Office Fax: 617-227-4420. E-mail: jglasgow@eapdlaw.com.*

GLASGOW, KAREN, principal; b. N.Y.C., May 20, 1954; d. Douglas G. Glasgow. BS in Edn., U. Wis., 1976; MS in Spl. Edn., U. So. Calif., 1979; MA, Calif. State Univ., Los Angeles; PhD, Claremont Univ., 2001. Prin. Toluca Lake Elem. Sch., 2000—; adj. prof. Calif. State U. Northridge, Northridge, 2001—. Mem. Assoc. Adminstrs. L.A., Women in Ednl. Leadership, Assoc. of Calif. Sch. Adminstrn. of L.A.

GLASHAN, CONSTANCE ELAINE, retired nurse, volunteer; b. San Pedro, Calif., Oct. 15, 1932; d. Clyde Frizzell and Winifred Anne (Todd) Lapier; widow; children: Marilyn, Susan, Nanci, Linda. Dental and med. degrees, Lux Coll., San Francisco, 1953; student, Bryman Coll., San Jose, Calif., 1973; grad., Pacific Regional Staff Coll., 1998. With Family Practice Physician, 1974-80; pvt. home caregiver Carson City, Nev., 1980-91. Noon supr. Santee Sch., Franklin-McKinley Sch. Dist., San Jose, 1969-71; former leader Oak Hill 4-H Club; sec. Valley Glen Homeowner's Assn., 1967-70; exec. sec. Greater East San Jose Homeowners's Coun., 1969-82, del. to Calif. Met. Transp. Commn., 1972-82l exec. sec. UN Cultural Festival, Santa Clara County, Calif., 1969-75, exec. v.p., 1974-76; mem. Citizen's Cmty. Improvement Com., San Jose, 1969-82; former del. and mem. coordinating coun. on narcotics San Jose Police Dept., recorder for exec. bd. Anti-Crime Commn., from 1970; charter mem., exec. sec. Tchr.'s Day Com., 1970; citizen's coord. human rels. subcom. narcotics and cmty. rels. units San Jose Police Athletics League, 1971-72; former mem. bd. dirs. Pacific Neighbor's: San Jose's Sister Cities Program; formerly active Robert Smith Meml. Cultural Found.; charter mem. Performing Arts League, 1971—; charter mem. Coun. of Arts, City of San Jose; mem. Transp. Study Task Force, from 1972; former leader Brownies and Cadettes, Girl Scouts U.S.A.; formerly active San Jose C.C. Dist.; formerly active San Jose Mus. and Youth Sci. Inst., San Jose Hist. Mus.,

San Jose Zool. Soc.; formre mem. San Jose Mayor's Adv. Bd. Health.; vol. No. Nev. Healthfair, Carson City, 1982—, Make A Wish Found., 1984—; foster parent Spl. Olympics, 1984; nen, Advs. for Domestic Violence; lt., adminstrv. officer Carson Composite Squadron, CAP, Douglas County Composite Squadron, CAP; foster parent. Named Lady of Day, Sta. KARA, 1973. Mem. AAUW, Nat. Trust for Hist. Preservation, Beta Sigma Phi. Republican. Roman Catholic. Avocations: horseback riding, swimming, fly fishing, camping, fishing.

GLASHEEN, GLORIA D., secondary school educator; b. June 30, 1945; m. Michael J. Glasheen, Aug. 1, 1970; children: Catharine, Jeffrey, Gregory, Theresa. BA, Cedar Crest Coll., 1967. Tchr. English Bethlehem (Pa.) Area Schs., 1967-70, Prince George's County Schs., Upper Marlboro, Md., 1970-73; tchr., English, gifted program Pennsbury HS, Fairless Hills, Pa., 1997—. Educator advisor Edgar Allan Poe Nat. Hist. Site, Phila. Leader Boy Scouts Am., Holland, Pa., 1986-93. Recipient award, USA Today, 1999. Mem. NEA, NCTE, Pa. State Edn. Assn., Pa. Coun. Tchrs. English. Office: Pennsbury HS 705 Hood Blvd Fairless Hills PA 19030-3199 Office Phone: 215-949-6700.

GLASNER, CRISTIN ANNE, science educator; b. Cooperstown, N.Y., May 21, 1974; d. James and Doris Anne Quinn; m. James Andre Glasner, Apr. 19, 1999. A in Applied Sci., SUNY, Delhi, 1994; B in Biology Edn., SUNY Oneonta, 1998; Master's, Elmira Coll., N.Y., 2004. Lic. vet. technician N.Y., 1995; cert. tchr. biology secondary edn. N.Y., 2004. Vet. technician Westbrook Vet Clinic, Walton, NY, 1992—96, Millstone Vet Clinic, Dundee, NY, 2003—; sci. tchr. Horseheads H.S., NY, 1998—. Mem.: Horseheads Tchrs. Assn. Office Phone: 607-795-2500 ext. 1840.

GLASS, DOROTHEA DANIELS, physiatrist, educator; b. NYC; d. Maurice B. and Anna S. (Kleegman) Daniels; m. Robert E. Glass, June 23, 1940; children: Anne Glass Roth, Deborah, Catherine Glass Barrett, Eugene. BA, Cornell U., 1940; MD, Woman's Med. Coll. Pa., 1954; postgrad., U. Pa., 1960—61; DMS (hon.), Med. Coll. Pa., 1987. Diplomate Am. Bd. Phys. Medicine and Rehab. (guest bd. examiner 1978, 89). Intern Albert Einstein Med. Ctr., Phila., 1954-55, clin. asst. dept. medicine, 1956-59, attending phys. medicine and rehab., 1968-70, chmn. dept. phys. medicine and rehab., sr. attending, 1971-85; chief rehab. medicine VA Med. Ctr., Miami, Fla., 1985-95; clin. prof. dept. orthop. and rehab. U. Miami Sch. Medicine, 1985—. Lois Mattox Miller fellow preventive medicine Woman's Med. Coll. Pa., 1955-56, instr. preventive medicine, 1956-59, instr. medicine, 1960-62; resident phys. medicine and rehab. VA Hosp., Phila., 1959-62, chief phys. medicine and rehab., 1966-68, cons., 1968-82; asst. clin. dir. Jefferson Med. Coll. Hosp., Phila., 1963-66, Camden County Stroke Program, Cooper Hosp., Camden, N.J., 1963-66; gen. practice medicine, Phila., 1956-59; asst. med. dir., chief phys. medicine and rehab. Moss Rehab. Hosp., Phila., 1968-70, med. dir., 1971-82, sr. cons., 1982-; mem. active staff Temple U., Phila., 1968-, asso. prof. rehab. medicine, 1968-73, prof., 1973-, dir. residency tng. rehab. medicine, 1968-82; program dir. Rehab. Rsch. and Tng. Ctr., 1977-80, chmn. dept. rehab. medicine, 1977-82; staff physician Hosp. Med. Coll. Pa., Phila., 1955-59, vis. assoc. prof. neurology, 1973-79, clin. prof., 1977-82, vis. prof., 1982-96; mem. cons. staff Frankford Hosp., Phila., 1968-82, Phila. Geriatric Center, 1975-82; mem. active staff Willowcrest-Bamberger Hosp., Phila., 1980-82; asso. phys. medicine and rehab. U. Pa. Sch. Medicine, Phila., 1962-66; asst. prof. clin. phys. medicine and rehab., 1966-68; asst. clin. dir. dept. phys. medicine and rehab. Jefferson Med. Coll., Phila., 1963-66; cons. Vols. in Medicine Clinic, Stuart, Fla., 1996—. Contbr. articles to profl. jours. Mem. profl. adv. com. Easter Seal Soc. Crippled Children and Adults Pa., 1975-82; active Goodwill Industries Phila., 1973-82, Cmty. Home Health Svcs. Phila., 1974-82, Ea. Pa. chpt. Arthritis Found., 1968-82. Recipient Humanitarian Svc. cert. Gov.'s Com. on Employment Handicapped, 1974, Outstanding Alumnae award Commonwealth of Pa. Bd., Hosp. Med. Coll. Pa., 1975, Humanitarian award Pa. Easter Seal Soc., 1981, John Eiselie Davis award Am. Kinesiotherapy Assn., 1988, Carl Haven Young Svc. award, 1994, Disting. Career award Moss Rehab. Hosp., 1997, Outstanding Svc. and Accomplishments award Fla. Soc. Phys. Medicine and Rehab., 2001, Susan B. Anthony award LWV of Martin County, 2002. Fellow Am. Congress Rehab. Medicine; mem. AMA, Am. Acad. Med. Dirs., Am. Acad. Phys. Medicine and Rehab. (Disting. Clinician award 1995, Krusen award 2000), Am. Assn. Electromyography and Electrodiagnosis (assoc.), Am. Assn. Sex Educators, Counselors and Therapists, Am. Burn Assn., Am. Coll. Angiology, Am. Coll. Utilization Rev., Am. Congress Rehab. Medicine (bd. govs. 1979-85, pres. 1986-87, gold Key award 1989), Am. Heart Assn. (coun. on cerebrovascular disease), Am. Lung Assn. Phila. and Montgomery County (bd. dirs. 1977-79), Am. Med. Women's Assn., Assn. Acad. Physiatrists, Assn. Med. Rehab. Dirs. and Coords., Coll. Physicians Phila., Emergency Care Rsch. Inst., Gerontol. Soc., Internat. Assn. Rehab. Facilities, Internat. Rehab. Medicine Assn., Pan Am. Med. Assn., Fla. Med. Assn., Fla. Soc. Phys. Medicine and Rehab. (pres. 1975-77, Award for Outstanding Svc. in Rehab. Medicine 2001), Pa. Med. Soc. (phys. medicine and rehab. adv. com. 1975-82), Pa. Thoracic Soc., Delaware Valley Hosp. Coun. Forum, Phila. Med. Soc., Phila. PSRO (bd. dirs. 1975-82), Phila. Soc. Phys. Medicine and Rehab. (pres. 1968-69), Laennec Soc. Phila., Royal Soc. Health, Alpha Omega Alpha. E-mail: glassrd@earthlink.net.

GLASS, JULIA, writer; b. NY; d. John and Kerry G.; life ptnr. Dennis Cowley; children: Alec, Oliver. BA in Art summa cum laude, Yale Univ., 1978. Figurative painter; copy editor Cosmopolitan mag.; freelance editor JP MorganChase. Author: (novels) Three Junes, 2002 (Nat. Book award for fiction, 2002), The Whole World Over, 2006, (novella) Collies, 1999 (Faulkner Soc. medal for best novella, 1999). Recipient Nelson Algren award for a short story, Chgo. Tribune, 1993, two other Nelson Algren awards, Tobias Wolff award, Ames Meml. Essay award for nonfiction; grantee Nat. Endowment for the Arts fellowship, NY Found. for Arts fellowship, Radcliffe Inst. Fellow, 2004—05. Mailing: Author Mail - Pantheon Books Random House 1745 Broadway New York NY 10019*

GLASS, MARY JEAN, management executive; b. Urbana, Ill., Nov. 27, 1964; d. Sandra Kay and Bobby Dee Egner; 1 child, Jacob Steven. BS in Orgnl. Leadership, Mid-Continent U., 2001. Cert. quality auditor Am. Soc. Quality, 1995. Staff sgt. USAF, 1985, med. svc. specialist Belleville, Ill., 1985—89, med. svc. technician RAF Greenham Common, 1989—91; quality assurance technician North Star Steel Ky., Calvert City, Ky., 1991—99; quality assurance supr. Dura Automotive Sys., Inc., Fulton, Ky., 1999—2002; ISO coord. Jakel, Inc., Murray, Ky., 2002—04; with Newcomb Oil, Benton, Ky., 2004—. Internat. peace amb. Am. Biog. Soc.; capt. Dem. Nat. Party, Benton, Ky., 2003. Decorated Outstanding Unit with one oak leaf cluster USAF, Nat. Def. Svc. medal; named Woman of Yr., Am. Biog. Inst., 2002. Mem.: Am. Soc. Quality (publicity officer 1987—89). Democrat. Pentecostal. Avocations: reading, writing, internet. Home: 279 US Hwy 68E Benton KY 42025 Office: Newcomb Oil LLC 406 Main St Benton KY 42025 Office Phone: 270-527-3004. Personal E-mail: glaspane@bellsouth.net.

GLASS, SANDRA ANN, foundation administrator, consultant; b. Portland, Oreg., Feb. 14, 1936; d. Theodore Dunkin and Mary Ankelis; m. Stephen Lloyd Glass, June 16, 1957; children: Michael Stuart, Gregory Alan. BA, Pomona Coll., 1957; MA, U. Kans., 1964; PhD, Claremont Grad. U., 1970; LHD (hon.), Franklin & Marshall Coll. Instr. English Pitzer Coll., Claremont, Calif., 1965—67; dir. found. rels. Pomona Coll., Claremont, 1972—77, dir. devel., 1977—79; assoc. v.p. devel. Claremont U. Ctr., 1979; program officer W. M. Keck Found., LA, 1982—93, program v.p., 1993—98; cons. Philanthropy Advisors, Claremont, 1998—. Nat. steering com. Project Kaleidoscope, Washington, 1991—; nat. vis. com. Nat. Sci. Digital Libr., Washington, 1992—. Editor: (monograph) The Changing World of Foundation Fundraising, Approaching Foundations. Bd. dirs. Mt. San Antonio Gardens, Claremont, Calif., 2004—. Recipient Outstanding Contbn. to Pub. Understanding of Geology, Am. Geol. Inst., 1997, Disting. Alumna award, Claremont Grad. U., 1990; Merit scholar, Pomona Coll., 1953—57, Grad. fellow for Women, Danforth Found., 1967—69. Mem.: Mortar Bd., Phi Beta Kappa. Office: Philanthropy Advisors 157 W 7th St Claremont CA 91711 Office Phone: 909-621-3391. E-mail: saglass@gte.net.

GLASSER, LYNN SCHREIBER, publisher; b. Chgo., Sept. 19, 1943; d. Alexander Paul and Beatrice (Bollard) Schreiber; m. Stephen A. Glasser, Dec. 30, 1965; children: Susan, Laura, Jeffrey, Jennifer. BA, Chatham Coll., 1965. Publs. editor Inst. CLE U. Mich. Law Sch., Ann Arbor, 1966-68; asst. to dir. Practising Law Inst., N.Y.C., 1968-71; v.p., COO Law Jour. Press and Law Jour. Seminars, N.Y.C., 1971-78; exec. v.p., pub. Law & Bus./Harcourt Jovanovich, Inc., N.Y.C., 1978-86; co-pres. Prentice Hall Law & Bus., Englewood Cliffs, NJ, 1986-94; cons. Simon and Schuster, N.Y.C., 1994-95; pres. Glasser Publ. Inc., Little Falls, NJ, 1995—; co-pres. Glasser Legal Works, a Thomson Bus., 2003—04; pres. Sandpiper Ptnrs., LLC, Bloomfield, NJ, 2005—. Organizer, originator over 1000 CLE seminars, 1986—; organizer Woman Advt. Conf., N.Y.C., Chgo. and San Francisco, 1993-94; chmn. Woman Bus. Lawyer Conf., N.Y.C. and San Francisco, 1994; adj. assoc. prof. Stony Brook U., 2004-. Trustee N.J. Chamber Music Soc., Montclair, 1989—, Montclair Art Mus., 1998—; Cmty. Found. of N.J., Morristown, 1995—; co-donor Lynn & Stephen Glasser Scholarship Fund, Colgate U., 1988—, Bloomfield Coll., 1993—. Office: 1515 Broad St Bldg B Bloomfield NJ 07003

GLASSER, PAMELA JEAN, musician, music educator; b. Livonia, Mich., June 26, 1953; d. Walter and Margaret Julia (Geersens) Glasser; m. Richard Barth Turner, Sept. 7, 1996 (div. Mar. 2006). BEd in Music, Wayne State U., 1976; M of Music, Rice U., 1982. Prin. hornist Wyo. Symphony Orch., Casper, 1994—, Jackson Hole Symphony, 1999—2002; adj. prof. horn Casper Coll., 1998—2001; artistic dir. Casper Chamber Music Soc., 2001—; dir. music Fremont Sch. Dist. # 2, Dubois, Wyo., 2001—. Hornist music edn. programs Wyo. Arts Coun., 1993; hornist, solo performer Llangollen Eisteddfod North Wales, 1978. Mem.: SPLC, ACLU, NEA, Casper Chamber Music Soc. (edn. liaison 1997—2001), Wyo. Edn. Assn., Am. Fedn. Musicians. Democrat. Episcopalian. Avocations: field and space science, organic gardening, cross country skiing, science fiction, crystal and mineral collecting, world music, religion. Home: PO Box 1357 Dubois WY 82513-1357 E-mail: pjglasser@yahoo.com.

GLASSER, SUSAN BETH, journalist; b. Montclair, N.J., Jan. 14, 1969; d. Stephen A. and Lynn (Schreiber) G.; m. Peter Baker; 1 child, Theodore. AB, Harvard U., 1990. From staff writer to editor Roll Call Newspaper, Washington, 1990—98; joined Washington Post, 1998, dept. nat. editor, nat. polit. reporter, then co-bur. chief, Moscow, 2001—05, editor, Outlook sect., 2006—. Co-author (with Peter Baker): Kremlin Rising: Vladimir Putin's Russia and the End of Revolution, 2005. Office: Outlook Sect Washington Post 1150 15th St NW Washington DC 20071*

GLASSMAN, CAROLINE DUBY, state supreme court justice; b. Baker, Oreg., Sept. 13, 1922; d. Charles Ferdinand and Caroline Marie (Colton) Duby; m. Harry Paul Glassman, May 21, 1953; 1 son, Max Avon. LLB summa cum laude, Williamette U., 1944. Bar: Oreg. 1944, Calif. 1952, Maine 1969. Atty. Title Ins. & Trust Co., Salem, Oreg., 1944-46; assoc. Belli, Ashe, Pinney & Melvin Belli, San Francisco, 1952-58; ptnr. Glassman & Potter, Portland, Maine, 1973-78, Glassman, Beagle & Ridge, Portland, 1978-83; justice Maine Supreme Judicial Ct., Portland, 1983-97. Lectr. Sch. Law, U. Maine, 1967-68, 80 Author: Legal Status of Homemakers in State of Maine, 1977. Mem.: ATLA, Russian Am. Rule of Law Consortium, Maine Trial Law Assn., Maine Bar Assn., Calif. Bar Assn., Oreg. Bar Assn., Am. Law Inst., Supreme Ct. Hist. Soc. Roman Catholic. Home: 56 Thomas St Portland ME 04102-3639

GLASSMAN, CYNTHIA AARON, federal agency administrator, former commissioner; m. Len Glassman. BA, Wellesley Coll., 1967; MA in Econs., PhD in Econs., U. Pa., 1975. With Fed. Res. Bank, Phila, 1971—74; econ. supr. U. Cambridge, 1974—77; economist fin. structure sect., spl. asst. to Henry C. Wallich, economist capital markets sect., then chief fin. reports sect. Fed. Res. Sys., Washington, 1977—86; sr. economist Economists Inc., 1986—88; dir. rsch. then mng. dir. fin. services regulatory & pub. policy practices Furash & Co., 1988—97; dir. comml. bank risk mgmt. Ernst & Young, 1997—99, prin. nat. tax dept. quantitative economics & statistics divsn., 1999—2001; commr. SEC, NYC, 2002—06, acting chmn., 2005; under sec. for econ. affairs & statistics adminstrn. US Dept. Commerce, Washington, 2006—. Prof. econs. U. Cambridge, England, 1977—86; sr. mem. Lucy Cavendish Coll., England. Mem.: Commn on Savings and Investment in Am., Women in Housing and Finance, Fed. Res. Bd Credit Union, Nat Economists Club. Office: US Dept Commerce 1401 Constitution Ave NW Washington DC 20230*

GLASSMAN, DEBRA, dentist; m. Steven Glassman; 3 children. BA in dental hygiene, Columbia U.; DDS, NYU Col. Dentistry. Dentist Glassman Dental Care, NYC. Office: NYC Cosmetic Dentists Glassman Dental Care 160 West End Ave New York NY 10023 Office Phone: 212-787-4860. Office Fax: 212-787-9238.

GLASSMAN, JUDITH DALE, chocolate company owner, realtor; b. Newark, N.J., July 21, 1945; d. William Margo and Sonya (Janoff) Gale; m. Barnett Glassman, Nov. 24, 1967 (dec. Aug. 1976); children: Heather, Tara, Jolie. Student, U. Miami, 1967. Lic. realtor, Fla. Realtor, Miami, Fla., 1970—; owner chocolatier Tender Loving Chocolates, Hollywood, 1980—. Bd. dirs. Miami Chamber Symphony, 1991—. Democrat. Jewish. Avocations: arts, music. Office Phone: 305-653-5000. Business E-Mail: info@tenderlovingchocolates.com.

GLASSMAN, M. MELISSA, lawyer; b. Fort Rucker, Ala., 1955; BS summa cum laude, U. Tex., Austin, 1976; JD magna cum laude, George Mason U., Arlington, Va., 1987. Bar: Va. 1987, DC 1988, Md. 1995. Assoc. McGuire-Woods LLP, Tysons Corner, Va., 1987—96, ptnr., comml. litig. dept., 1996—, mng. ptnr. Tysons Corner office, 2004—. Mem.: Va. Bar Assn. (bd. mem. comml. litig. sect., chmn. constrn. & pub. contracts sect.). Office: McGuire-Woods LLP Ste 1800 1750 Tysons Blvd Mc Lean VA 22102-4215 Office Phone: 703-712-5351. Office Fax: 703-712-5228. Business E-Mail: mglassman@mcguirewoods.com.

GLAZEBROOK, RITA SUSAN, nursing educator; b. St. Paul, Apr. 26, 1948; d. David L. and Beverly Ruth (Penhiter) Beccue; m. Harold L. Glazebrook, Dec. 20, 1986; children: Julie, Robert J., Scott, Robert M., Katherine. Diploma, RN, Abbott Hosp. Sch. Nursing, Mpls., 1970; BS in Nursing, Augsburg Coll., Mpls., 1979; MS in Nursing, U. Minn., 1981, PhD in Edn. Adminstrn., 1987. Mem. staff, asst. head nurse United Hosps., Inc., St. Paul, 1970-78; mem. staff Med. Pers. Pool, St. Paul, 1978-81; prof. nursing, chmn. dept. St. Olaf Coll., Northfield, Minn., 1981—. Contbr. articles to profl. jours. Faculty devel. grant Evan. Luth. Ch. Am. Mem. ANA, Minn. Nurses Assn., Assn. of Women's Health Obstetric and Neonatal Nurses, Sigma Theta Tau. Home: 8941 Jasmine Ln S Cottage Grove MN 55016-3422 Office Phone: 507-646-3430. Business E-Mail: glazebro@stolaf.edu.

GLAZER, LEE MORRISON (LEE MORRISON), writer, choreographer; b. N.Y.C., Oct. 3, 1918; d. Henry and Ann (Rosan) Morrison; m. Donald Meyer, June 3, 1940 (div. Sept. 1948); m. Leland F. Cooley, Aug. 6, 1953 (div. June 1982); m. Bill Glazer, July 16, 2000. Student, N.Y. Sch. Applied Design for Women, 1937; student ballet arts, Carnegie Hall, N.Y.C., 1940-50; BA, U. Calif., Irvine, 1983. Ballet Met. Opera, N.Y.C., 1939—; tchr. ballet for srs. Oasis Sr. Ctr., Newport Beach, Calif., 1985. Tchr., author, lectr. Univ. De Catholique, Angers, France, 1979; Verano Internat. Irvine Sch. Dist., 1983; Leisure World, Laguna Hills, Calif., 1984. Dancer, Actress: Films with Warner Bros., Fox, and others, 1940-43, in Broadway Musicals, 1943-50; choreographer: CBS-Perry Como Show, Mel Torme-Peggy Lee Show, Vic Damone, and others; author: The Simple Truth About Land Investment, 1965, The Retirement Trap, 1966, Land Investment U.S.A., 1973, How to Avoid the Retirement Trap, 1974, Premedicated Murder, 1975, (with Miriam Spear) Redesigning Your Life, 1987. Dir. publicity U. Calif. Irvine Friends of the Library, 1966-70; bd. dirs. Peoples Clinic, Santa Ana, Calif., 1979-87; bd. dirs. United Way, Orange County, Calif., 1984-85. Mem. PEN, Emeritus Dancers Orange County, U. Calif.-Irvine Alumni Assn. Avocations: ballet, swimming, fishing, travel, ballroom dancing. Home: 2739 Fort Myer Ave Henderson NV 89052-7020

GLAZER, REA HELENE See KIRK, REA

GLAZIER, LINDA HATCH, mathematics educator; d. Burton Dilworth Hatch and Fern Lorea McGarry; m. John W. Glazier, Aug. 15, 1972; children: Ryan John, Aaron Burton, Matthew Claud, Scott Kyle, Spencer Mace. BS, Brigham Young U., Provo, Utah, 1974. Tchr. math. Kearns H.S., Utah, 1990—, Young Parents Ctr., West Valley City, Utah, 2002—04. Singer: (concerts, TV, radio, DVDs and CDs) Mormon Tabernacle Choir (Nat. Medal of Honor-Pres. of US, 2005), (10 CDs) Peace Like a River, etc. (Several Grammy awards). Pres. Women's Orgn., West Jordan, Utah, 1986—89. Office: Kearns HS 5525 S Cougar Ln Kearns UT 84118 Office Phone: 801-646-5380.

GLEASNER, DIANA COTTLE, author; b. New Brunswick, N.J., Apr. 26, 1936; d. Delmer Leroy and Elizabeth (Stanton) C.; m. G. William Gleasner, July 12, 1958; children— Stephen William, Suzanne Lynn. B.A., Ohio Wesleyan U., 1958; M.A., SUNY-Buffalo, 1965. Tchr. Kenmore (N.Y.) Sr. High Sch., 1958-64; instr. SUNY-Buffalo, 1970-76. Author: The Plaid Mouse, 1966; Pete Polar Bear's Trip Down the Erie Canal, 1970; Women in Swimming, 1975; Women in Track and Field, 1977; Hawaiian Gardens, 1978; Kauai Traveler's Guide, 1978; Oahu Traveler's Guide, 1978; Big Island Traveler's Guide, 1978; Breakthrough: Women in Writing, 1980; Illustrated Dictionary of Surfing, Swimming and Diving, 1980; Sea Islands of the South, 1980; Rock Climbing, 1980; Callaway Gardens, 1981; Inventions That Changed Our Lives: Dynamite, 1982; Charlotte: A Touch of Gold, 1983; Breakthrough: Women in Science, 1983; Inventions That Changed Our Lives: The Movies, 1983; Windsurfing, 1985; Lake Norman: Our Inland Sea, 1986, Governor's Island From the Beginning, 1988, RVing America's Backroads-Florida, 1989, Touring by Bus at Home and Abroad, 1989, Maui Traveler's Guide, 1996, Florida Off the Beaten Path, 2005, The Strange and Terrible Adventures of Popoki The Hawaiian Cat, 1996, Popoki's Incredible Adventures at the Volcano, 1999, Popoki The Hawaiian Cat, An Amazing Adventure With The Whale, 2004; contbr. numerous articles to mags., including Better Homes and Gardens, Home and Away, Travel America, Trail Blazer, numerous others; Mem. Soc. Am. Travel Writers, Travel Journalists Guild. Address: 7994 Holly Ct Denver NC 28037-9463 Office Phone: 704-483-9301. E-mail: dgleasner@aol.com.

GLEASON, BARBARA JO, literature and language educator; b. San Diego, Aug. 10, 1952; d. George Donald and Virginia Lee Gleason; m. Edward Gerard Quinn, Mar. 17, 2001. BS, U. Mo., Columbia, 1974; MA, Okla. State U., Stillwater, 1984; PhD, U. So. Calif., L.A., 1989. Vol. Peace Corps, Abong Mbang, Eastern Province, Cameroon, 1978—81; assoc. prof. english City Coll. N.Y., N.Y.C., 1990—, dir. composition, 1992—94, writing cons. supr. Ctr. Worker Edn., 1997—2006, dir. lang. and literacy, 2003—. Exec. bd. mem. Conf. Basic Writing, NY, 2005—. Co-editor: Composition in Four Keys; translator (contbg. author): Multiple Literacies for the 21st Century; Mainstreaming Basic Writers: Politics and Pedagogies of Access; author: College Composition and Communication; contbg. author: CityComp: Identities, Spaces, & Practices, Attending to the Margins: Writing, Researching, and Teaching on the Front Lines. Grantee, Fund for Improvement in Post-Secondary Edn., 1993—96. Mem.: Internat. Writing Ctr. Assn., Writing Program Adminstrn. Coun., Coll. Composition and Communication Conf., Nat. Coun. Tchrs. English. Office: City Coll NY 138th St at Convent Ave New York NY 10031 Office Phone: 212-650-6329. Personal E-mail: glsnbarb@aol.com. E-mail: bgleason@ccny.cuny.edu.

GLEASON, CAROL ANN, mental health nurse, educator; b. Fairfield, Iowa, Mar. 6, 1945; d. Maurice Alvin and Geraldine (Cook) Crist; m. Michael Gleason Jr., Nov. 26, 1966 (div. Nov. 1980); children: Daniel Lee, Raymond Joe, Christopher John, Crystal Dawn. ADN, Indian Hills Coll., 1977; AS in Adminstrn., Des Moines Area Coll., 1982; BSPA in Health Care, St. Joseph's, 1985; cert. nurses aides edn., U. Iowa, 1989; BSN, Drake U., 1997; grad., Nat. Inst. Paralegal Arts Sci., 2002. Lic. nursing home adminstr., Iowa; cert. psychiat. and mental health, gerontology ANA. Staff night charge nurse Mahaska Manor Nursing Home, Oskaloosa, Iowa, 1977; dir. nursing Tower Park Nursing Home, Oskaloosa, 1977—78, Pleasant Park Nursing Home, Oskaloosa, 1978—85, adminstr., 1985—86; staff nurse ICU-CCU Ottumwa Regional Hosp., Iowa, 1986; pellative care and chronic psychiat. nurse Knoxville Vets. Hosp., Iowa, 1986—. Coord., instr. Iowa Ednl. Inst., Oskaloosa, 1987—; cons. Tower Park Nursing Home, Oskaloosa, 1985-87, Siesta Park Nursing Home, 1985-87, Mahaska Manor, 1993-95; nurse New Sharon Care Ctr., Oskaloosa, 2004—, New Sharon Nursing and Rehab. Ctr., Iowa. Mem.: NAFE, Am. Fedn. Govt. Employers. Democrat. Roman Catholic. Avocations: football, walking, boating. Home: 220 Keomah Vlg Oskaloosa IA 52577-9671

GLEASON, CAROL ANN, rehabilitation nurse; b. Franklin, NH, June 17, 1950; d. Adam Victor and Rita T. (Robichaud) Novak; m. William J. Gleason, Aug. 24, 1974; 1 child, Stephen Bryan. Diploma, St. Elizabeth Hosp., Boston, 1971; M in Mgmt., Cambridge (Mass.) Coll., 1997. RN, Mass.; cert. rehab. RN; cert. case mgr.; lic. rehab. counselor. Surg. nurse St. Elizabeth Hosp., Boston, 1971-73; pvt. nurse for chief of otolaryngology Mass. Eye and Ear Infirmary, Boston, 1973-74; pvt. duty nurse Met. Nurses, Inc., Boston, 1975; liaison, mktg. RN Spaulding Rehab. Hosp., Boston, 1975-81; admissions nurse Shaughnessy-Kaplan Rehab. Hosp., Salem, Mass., 1982-86; mktg. assoc. New Medico Head Injury System, Lynn, Mass., 1986-88; asst. regional mgr. New Medico, Lynn, 1988-90; rehab. specialist Cost Containment Mgmt., Braintree, Mass., 1990-91; sr. rehab. cons. N.Am. Health and Rehab. Svcs., Nashua, N.H., 1991; sr. mktg. assoc. Greenery Rehab. Group, Newton, Mass., 1992-94; mgr. clin. bus. devel. Beverly Health & Rehab. Svcs., Inc., 1995-96; regional dir. mktg./census devel. Mariner Post Acute Network, 1997—99; dir. resource mgmt. Shaughnessy Kaplan Rehab. Hosp., Salem, Mass., 1999—2000, dir. admission, 2000—01; regional dir. admissions and mktg. Wingate Healthcare, Inc., Needham, Mass., 2001—04; dir. admissions and mktg. Jewish Meml. Hosp. and Rehab. Ctr., Boston, 2004—. Speaker Mass. Passenger Safety Bur., Boston, 1988-91; participant Nurse in Washington Internship, 1991; cons. in field Contbg. author: The Speciality Practice of Rehabilitation Nursing, A Core Curriculum, 3d edit., 1993, 4th edit., 2000, Rehabilitation Nursing Process and Application, 1996, Rehabilitation Nursing Process, Application, and Outcomes, 3d edit., 2002; contbr. articles to profl. jours. Vision/hearing tester Mass. Dept. Pub. Health, Boston, 1990-93; bd. dirs. Marblehead (Mass.) Festival of Arts, 1989-91, Jr. Aid Soc. Inc., Marblehead, 1979—; active MADD, Boston, 1990—. Recipient Occupant Safety award Mass. Nurses Assn., 1989, She Know's Where She's Going award Girls Inc., 1989. Mem. ANA, Mass. Nurses Assn., Nat. Head Injury Found., Nat. Assn. Rehab. Profls. in the Pvt. Sector (chpt. bd. dirs. 1987-90), Pro-Mass (chpt. bd. dirs. 1990-93), Mass. Coun. Nursing Orgns. (bd. dirs. 1986-96), Assn. Rehab. Nurses (chmn. mktg./pub. rels. 1990-91, health policy 1988-94, vice chmn. health policy 1991-92, chmn. health policy 1992-93, pres. bd. dirs. New Eng. chpt. 1988-89), Ins. Rehab. Nurses New Eng. (bd. dirs., co-pres. 1992-94, advisor 1994-99, legis. chair 1990-92, scholarship chmn. 1998--, conf. com. 2000--), Case Mgmt. Soc. New Eng. (bd. dirs. 1998-2004), Case Mgmt. Soc. Am. (bd. dirs. 2004—, nat. conf. chair 2005, vice-chair health policy 2005—) Democrat. Roman Catholic. Avocations: cooking, music, travel. Office Phone: 781-639-2797.

GLEASON, CINDY S., financial consultant, educator; b. Des Moines, Feb. 22, 1958; d. Claren E. and Dana Darlene Marsh; m. James F. Gleason, Nov. 1, 2002; 1 child, Dana D. Peralta. BS, Upper Iowa U., 1988. Cert. fin. planner, divorce fin. analyst. Fin. advisor Am. Express Fin. Adv., Indianola, Iowa, 1990—99, Diversified Fin. Group, Indianola, 1999—2000, Locust St. Securities, Bellevue, Iowa, 2000—02; fin. advisor, owner Gleason Fin. Group, Waterloo, Iowa, 2002—. Tchr., coach Hawkeye CC, Waterloo, 2005—, U. Book and Supply, Cedar Falls, Iowa, 2004—. Contbr. articles to Straight Talk e-zine newsletter. Pres., originator Milo Betterment Com., Milo Devel. Corp., Iowa, 1994—98; mentor, tutor Waterloo Expo Alternative H.S., 2005; charter bd. dirs. Warren County Leadership Inst., Indianola, 1994—96; bd. dirs. Warren County Econ. Devel. Corp., Indianola, 1994—97, pres., 1997. Named Citizen of Yr., Milo Lions Club, 1995. Mem.: Waterloo Bus. and Profl. Women (licentiate; pres. 2004—05). Avocations: riding a harley davidson, travel, fishing, writing, target shooting. Office: Gleason Fin Group 501 Sycamore St Ste 600 Waterloo IA 50703 Office Phone: 319-234-1213. Personal E-mail: cindy@gleasonfinancialgroup.com.

GLEASON, CYNTHIA S., public relations executive, educator; b. Portage, Wis., Mar. 2, 1949; d. Walter E. and Arleen (Slette) Gleason; m. William J. Kostka, Jr., Apr. 6, 1974; children: Jennifer Kostka, William J. Kostka III. BA in Journalism, U. Wis., 1972. Intern U. Wis.-Madison Med. Ctr. Office of Pub. Info., 1970, State of Wis. Dept. Natural Resources, Madison, 1971; writer-rschr., jr. account exec. William Kostka & Assoc., Denver, 1972—, sr. account exec., 1974—77, v.p., 1977—79, sr. v.p., 1979—81, exec. v.p., 1981—97; pres., CEO Kostka-Gleason Comms., Inc., Denver, 1997—. Instr. dept. journalism U. Colo. Active Guardians Ad Litem; bd. dirs. Juvenile Offenders in Need, Inc., Denver. Recipient Pub. Rels. Person of Yr. award, Southland Corp., 1976. Mem.: Pub. Relations Soc. Am. (accredited; counselors acad.), Denver Press Club. Office: Kostka-Gleason Comms Ste 250 820 16th St Denver CO 80202

GLEASON, JEAN BERKO, psychology professor; b. Cleve., Dec. 19, 1931; d. Arthur E. and Alice (Gelberger) Berko; m. Andrew Mattei Gleason, Jan. 26, 1959; children: Katherine, Pamela, Cynthia. AB, Radcliffe Coll., 1953, AM, 1955, PhD, 1958. USPHS fellow MIT, 1958—59; research assoc. VA Med. Ctr., Boston, 1961—2000; from vis. asst. prof. psychology to prof. emerita Boston (Mass.) U., 1972—2005, prof. emerita, 2005—, chairperson dept. psychology, 1985—89, acting chair dept. psychology, 1997, dir. grad program devel. psychology, 1975—78, 1982—85, dir. grad. program human devel., 1997—2002; research assoc. edn. Harvard U., Cambridge, Mass., 1968—70, prin. research assoc. psychiatry, 1970—72. Rsch. scholar in residence Inst. Linguistics, Hungarian Acad. Sci., 1981, 83; mem. mental retardation rsch. com. Nat. Inst. Child Health and Human Devel., 1981-85; trustee Ctr. for Applied Linguistics, Washington, 1989-94. Author: The Development of Language, 1983, 6th edit., 2005, You Can Take It with You, 1989, Psycholinguistics, 1993, 2nd edit., 1998; mem. editl. bd. Child Development, 1971—77, Discourse Processes, 1982—2002, assoc. editor Language, 1997—2000; contbr. articles. Recipient Editors award Jour. Speech and Hearing Research, 1970. Fellow: APA, AAAS (coun. del. 2002—05); mem.: ACLU, Internat. Assn. for Study of Child Lang. (pres. 1990—93), Soc. for Rsch. Child Devel., Linguistic Soc. Am. (chmn. program com. 1980—81, resolutions com. 2004), Radcliffe Alumni Assn. (bd. dirs. 1969—72), Radcliffe Grad. Soc. (past pres.), Gypsy Lore Soc. (exec. bd. 1983—87, 1992—2002, pres. 1996—99, exec. bd. 2003—06), Acad. Aphasia, Phi Beta Kappa (pres. Radcliffe chpt. 1965—68). Home: 110 Larchwood Dr Cambridge MA 02138-4639 Office: Boston U Dept Psychology 64 Cummington St Boston MA 02215-2407 Business E-Mail: gleason@bu.edu.

GLEASON, JOANNA, actress; b. Toronto, Ont., Can., June 2, 1950; d. Monty and Marilyn (Plotell) Hall. Grad., UCLA. Broadway debut I Love My Wife, Ethel Barrymore Theatre, 1977; Broadway appearances include Hey! Look Me Over, 1981, The Real Thing, 1984, A Hell of a Town, 1984, A Day in the Death of Joe Egg, 1985, It's Only a Play, 1985, Social Security, 1986, Into the Woods, Old Globe Theatre, San Diego and Martin Beck Theatre, N.Y.C., 1987 (Antoinette Perry award for leading actress in a mus., N.Y. Outer Critics Circle award, Drama Desk award), Nick and Nora, 1991, The Cartells, 2006; appeared in films Heartburn, 1986, Hannah and Her Sisters, 1986, Crimes and Misdemeanors, 1989, FX2: The Deadly Art of Illusion, 1991, Mr. Holland's Opus, 1995, Boogie Nights, 1997, American Perfekt, 1997, Dirty Rotten Scoundrels, 2005; TV appearances include Why Us?, 1981, Great Day, 1983, Still the Beaver, 1983, Life Under Water, 1989, The Boys, 1991, For Richer, For Poorer, 1992, Born Too Soon, 1993, For The Love of Aaron, 1994, series Hello, Larry, 1979-80, Chain Reaction, 1980, Love and War, 1992, Temporarily Yours, 1997, The West Wing, 2001-02. Mem. Actors' Equity Assn. Office: UTA 9560 Wilshire Blvd Fl 5 Beverly Hills CA 90212-2401*

GLEASON, JOYCE MARIE, educational consultant; b. Cambridge, Mass., Sept. 6, 1947; d. Antonino Jr. and Anne Margaret (Ianille) Laquidara; m. David Dickey Gleason, Oct. 11, 1969; 1 child, Andrew David. AB in Biol. Scis., Mt. Holyoke Coll., 1969; MLS, Wesleyan U., 1973; degree in Curriculum and Instrn., Boston (Mass.) Coll., 1995. Cert. tchr., Mass. Sci. tchr. Norwood (Mass.) Pub. Schs., 1969-95, chair K-12 curriculum project, 1990; sci. curriculum liaison Worcester (Mass.) Pub. Schs., 1995—2000; edn. specialist Harvard Smithsonian Ctr. Astrophysics, 2000—04; freelance ednl. cons. Punta Gorda, Fla., 2005—. Mem. vis. com. New Eng. Assn. Secondary Schs. and Colls., 1981; editor D.C. Heath, Lexington, Mass., 1983; supr. Boston Coll., Chestnut Hill, Mass., 1983-84; mem. program approval teams Mass. Dept. Edn., 1985, 86; chair pupil performance and evaluation ednl. results com., accreditation self-study Norwood High Sch., 1989-90; vis. clin. prof. Brown U., Providence, 1989-90; workshop presenter Mass. Assn. Sci. Tchrs., Mass. Assn. Sci. Suprs., NSTA, Nat. Assn. Biology Tchrs., N.J. Sci. Conv., New Eng. Biology Tchrs. Conf., Greater Boston Biology Tchrs., Providence Pub. Schs., Alpha Upsilon, Delta Kappa Gamma, Mass. Soc. for the Prevention of Cruelty to Animals, Boston Pub. Schs., Sci. Tchrs. Assn. N.Y. State; cons. Prime Sci., Ogunquit, Maine, 1993, 94, Nova Libr. Project, Sta. WGBH-TV, Boston, 1993; scorer Mass. Assessment Ednl. Progress. Co-editor (newsletter) Masthead, 1987-92; pre-publ. reviewer The Science Teacher; contbr. articles to profl. jours. Recipient Humane Educator of Yr. award Mass. Soc. for Prevention of Cruelty to Animals, 1991, award Am. Chem. Soc., 1993. Mem. NSTA (dist. I dir., 1999-2002, program coord. nat. convention, 1999, manuscript reviewer Sci. Tchr. 1992-95, mem. adv. panel Sci. Tchr. 1995-97, chmn. 1997-98), Mass. Assn. Sci. Tchrs. (v.p. 1992-94, pres.-elect 1994-96, pres. 1996-98, Norfolk County Sci. Educator of Yr. 1990, State Sci. Tchr. Yr., 2000), Mass. Tchrs. Assn. (mem. comm. com. 1984-90, 91-92, vice chair 1989-90, Affirmative Action award 1980-81), Delta Kappa Gamma (state 2d v.p. 1993-95, 1st v.p. 1995-97, pres. 1997-99) Avocation: folk dancing. Home: 3125 Guadalupe Dr Punta Gorda FL 33950

GLEASON, KATE, writer, educator, editor; b. Keene, N.H., Oct. 22, 1956; d. Allison Archie and Bertha Eleanor Sophie (Tonseth) Gleason. BA in Edn., U. Mass., 1981, postgrad., 1986; student, Amherst Writers and Artists, 1980-87. Editor, poetry editor Peregrine Lit. Jour., Amherst, Mass., 1985-91; proofreader Stratford Pub. Co., Brattleboro, Vt., 1994-95; poet-in-the-schs. Narragansett HS, Mass., 1994, Northfield Mt. Hermon, Mass.; creative writing workshop tchr. Writing From Your Inner Voice Workshops, Keene, 1992—; freelance editor Keene, 1994—. Author: (poems) Making As If to Sing, 1989, The Brighter the Deeper, 1995; contbr. poetry to anthologies and jours. Fellow, NEA/Ragdale, 1999. Mem.: N.H. Writers Project (Outstanding Emerging Writer award 1998).

GLEASON, KATHRYN L., lawyer; b. Nov. 20, 1959; BA, Johns Hopkins U., 1978; JD, Georgetown U. Law Ctr., 1981. Bar: D.C. 1981. Ptnr., mng. FDA/Healthcare Regulation Practice Group Morgan, Lewis & Bockius LLP, Washington. Contbr. articles to various profl. jour. Mem.: U.S. Food, Drug & Device Bar. Office: Morgan Lewis & Bockius LLP 1111 Pennsylvnia Ave Washington DC 20004 Office Phone: 202-739-5207. Office Fax: 202-739-3001. Business E-Mail: kgleason@morganlewis.com.

GLEIM, KATHY MARIE, music educator, performer, composer; b. Hammond, Ind., May 17, 1956; d. Erwin Albert and Elizabeth Ann (Raimey) Gleim; m. David Blake Hill, Dec. 17, 1983 (div. June 8, 1992); 1 child, Joshua Blake. B.Music in Piano Performance, Furman U., Greenville, S.C., 1978; M.Music in Piano Performance, U. Cin., 1981. Organist St. Michael's Luth. Ch., Doraville, Ga., 1972—74; grad. teaching asst. U. Cin., 1978—80; ind. piano instr., 1980—97; organist First Ch. of Christ Scientist, Vienna, 1982; piano instr. (Klavierlehrerin) Musikschule Neulengbach, Austria, 1982; sec. Internat. Atomic Energy Agy., Vienna, 1982—83; organist Prince of Peace Luth. Ch., Alpharetta, Ga., 1984—86; bilingual sec. ER-WE-PA USA, Ltd., Marietta, Ga., 1986—88; organist Eastminster Presbyn. Ch., Marietta, Ga., 1991—93; dir. Kindermusik by Sound Beginnings, 1995—97; admin. asst. WAGA TV, Atlanta, 1997—98, Nellon & Assoc., Atlanta, 1998—99; asst. to v.p. bus. fin. Agnes Scott Coll., Atlanta, 1999—2000; asst. bd. trustees Carter Ctr. Emory U., Atlanta, 2000—03; program asst. Task Force for Child Survival Devel., Atlanta, 2003—04; dir. membership Ctr. Academic Integrity, Duke U., Durham, NC, 2004—06; piano instr. Cary Sch. Music, NC, 2006—. Freelance pianist, 1989—; owner Spiral Soundcase Music, Raleigh, NC, 2001—. Composer; singer (under name Kathy Raimey): (cd) Flowers of Fire, 2001. U. Cin. scholar, 1978-80, Furman U. music scholar, 1974-78. Mem. Music Tchrs. Nat. Assn., ASPA. Avocations: composition, painting, writing, animals, healing arts.

GLENDON, MARY ANN, law educator; b. Pittsfield, Mass., Oct. 7, 1938; m. Edward R. Lev; 3 children. BA, U. Chgo., 1959, JD, 1961, M of Comparative Law, 1963, LLD (hon.), 1992; DHL (hon.), Brigham Young U., 1990. Bar: Ill. 1964, Mass. 1980. Legal intern EEC, Brussels, 1963; assoc. Mayer, Brown & Platt, Chgo., 1963-68; asst. prof. Boston Coll. Law Sch., 1968—71, assoc. prof., 1971—73, prof., 1973—86; prof. law Harvard Law Sch., Cambridge, Mass., 1986—, Learned Hand prof. law, 1993—. Vis. prof. Harvard Law Sch., 1974, U. Chgo. Law Sch., 1983, 84, 86, Gregorian U., Rome. Author: Abortion and Divorce in Western Law, 1987 (Scribes Book Award, Am. Soc. Writers on Legal Subjects, 1988), The Transformation of Family Law, 1989 (Order of the Coif Triennial Book Award, 1993), Rights Talk: The Impoverishment of Political Discourse, 1991, A Nation Under Lawyers, 1994, A World Made New: Eleanor Roosevelt and the Universal Declaration of Human Rights, 2001; co-author: Comparative Legal Traditions, 1994; editor: Intergenerational Solidarity, Welfare, and Human Ecology, 2004; author: Traditions in Turmoil, 2006; co-editor: Seedbeds of Virtue: Sources of Competence, Character, and Citizenship in Am. Soc., 1995. Foreign Law Fellow U. Libre de Bruxelles, 1962-63, Ford Found. Fellow, 1975-76, Fellow Radcliffe Inst., 1975-76; Nat. Humanities medal, 2005 Mem. Am. Acad. Arts & Sciences, Pres.'s Coun. Bioethics, Pontificial Acad. Social Sci. (pres. 2002-). Office: Harvard Law Sch 1563 Massachusetts Ave Cambridge MA 02138 Office Phone: 617-495-4769. Office Fax: 617-496-4913.

GLENN, CONSTANCE WHITE, art museum director, educator, consultant; b. Topeka, Oct. 4, 1933; d. Henry A. and Madeline (Stewart) White; m. Jack W. Glenn, June 19, 1955; children: Laurie Glenn Buckle, Caroline Glenn Galey, John Christopher. BFA, U. Kans., 1955; grad., U. Mo., 1969; MA, Calif. State U., 1974. Dir. U. Art Mus. & Mus. Studies program, from lectr. to prof. Calif. State U., Long Beach, 1973—2004, prof. and dir. emeritus, U. Art Mus. and Mus. Studies program, 2004—. Art cons. Archtl. Digest, L.A., 1980-89. Author: Jim Dine Drawings, 1984, Roy Lichtenstein: Landscape Sketches, 1986, Wayne Thiebaud: Private Drawings, 1988, Robert Motherwell: The Dedalus Sketches, 1988, James Rosenquist: Time Dust: The Complete Graphics 1962-92, 1993, The Great American Pop Art Store: Multiples of the Sixties, 1997, The Artist Observed: Photographs by Sidney B. Felsen, 2003, Candida Höfer: Architecture of Absence, 2004; contbg. author: Encyclopedia Americana, 1995-, The Grove Dictionary of Art, 1989-, Carrie Mae Weems: The Hampton Project, 2000, Double Vision: Photographs from the Strauss Collection, 2001, Tom Wesselmann, 2005. Vice-chair Adv. Com. for Pub. Art, Long Beach, 1990-95; chair So. Calif. adv. bd. Archives Am. Art, LA, 1980-90; mem. adv. bd. ART/LA, 1986-94, chair, 1992. Recipient Outstanding Contbn. to Profession award Calif. Mus. Photography, 1986, Women of Distinction award Soroptimist Internat., 1999. Mem. Am. Assn. Mus., Assn. Art Mus. Dirs. (trustee 2000-02, emeritus 2004—), Coll. Art Assn., Art Table, Long Beach Pub. Corp. for the Arts (Arts Adminstr. of Yr. 1989), Kappa Alpha Theta. Office: Calif State Univ Art Dept 1250 Bellflower Blvd Long Beach CA 90840-3501 Office Phone: 949-715-0933. Business E-Mail: cglenn@csulb.edu. E-mail: connieglenn@hotmail.com.

GLENN, DEBORAH ANN, economics educator, political science educator; BA in Polit. Sci., UCLA, 1986, MEd, 1987. Cert. single subject clear tchg. Calif. Commn. on Tchr. Credentialing, 1987. Tchr. govt. and econ. Upland H.S., Calif., 1987—. Trainer San Bernardino County Cmty. Coaltion, Calif., 1996—2001. Leader Girl Scouts of Am., Rancho Cucamonga, Calif., 2006—; pres. Upland Highland Rgt. Boosters, Calif., 2006—. Named Tchr. of Yr., Upland H.S., 2002. Mem.: Upland Tchrs. Assn. (past pres. 1990—, head negotiator 1990—), Baldy Vista Coun. for Social Studies (assoc.; v.p. 1995—2006), Calif. Coun. for Social Studies (assoc.), Nat. Coun. for Social Studies (assoc.), Gamma Phi Beta (life), Tau Beta Sigma (life). Avocations: reading, music. Office Phone: 909-949-7880.

GLENN, ETHEL CHAPPELL, educator; b. Dallas, Mar. 30, 1926; d. Frank Wilson and Nina Pearl (Wallace) Chappell; m. Robert J. Glenn, Mar. 30, 1950 (div. 1966); children: Christopher, Patricia, Phillip, Paul. BFA, U. Tex., 1946; MS, North Tex. State U., 1967; PhD, U. Tex., 1973. Tchr. Dallas Acad. Speech & Drama, 1946-67; instr. Bishop Coll., Dallas, 1967-71; from asst. to full prof. U. N.C., Greensboro, 1972—95, prof. emeritus, 1995—. Bus. mgr. Pearl Chappell Playhouse, Dallas, 1961-64; dir. oral communication program State Dept. Mental Health/Mental Retardation, Richmond, Va., 1972-75; cons. in field; numerous workshops. Author: Your Voice & Articulation, 1984, 4th edit., 1998, Public Speaking: Today & Tomorrow, 1989; contbr. articles to profl. jours. Vol. United Meth. Ch., English Spkg. Union, Broach Theatre, Greensboro Leadership Srs. Mem. Internat. Listening Assn. (1st v.p. 1989—, pres. 1990—, Outstanding Svc. award 1987), Carolinas Speech Comm. Assn. (v.p. to pres. 1975-78, Outstanding Svc. award 1992), So. Speech Comm. Assn., Speech Comm. Assn., Delta Kappa Gamma (v.p. 1987-89, pres. 1992-94). Avocations: reading, bridge, swimming, arts and crafts.

GLENN, SARA, religious studies educator, director; arrived in U.S., 1979, naturalized, 1986; d. Eli and Miriam Lahiani; m. John Glenn, Aug. 2, 1977; children: Eli, Dodi, Morgan. BS, BEd, Gordon Coll., Israel, 1975; MBA, Fla. Met. U., 1999. Cert. tchr. Dir. Hillel Sch., Tampa, Fla., 1993—99, Hebrew Acad. Tidewater, Virginia Beach, 2000—. Adj. prof. Old Dominion U., Norfolk, Va., 2005—. Office Phone: 757-424-4327.

GLENN, SHANNON LEA, music educator; b. Richardton, N.D., Apr. 5, 1968; d. Merwyn Andrew Wike and Doreen Anne (Nordin) Orf; m. Devin Clark Glenn; children: Alexandre Skye, Talyn Aeris. MusB in Edn. and Vocal Music, Concordia Coll., Morehead, Minn., 1999. Lic. profl. tchr. Colo. Performer Sheehan Aed. Medora Musical, Medora, ND, Plain People Entertainment, Fargo, ND; vocal and gen. music tchr. Sidney Cmty. Schs., Sidney, Iowa; choir dir. Prince of Peace Luth. Ch., Colorado Springs, Colo.; tchr. music Wildflower Elem. Sch., Colorado Springs, Colo. Asst. mgr. Long X Tr. Ranch, Grassy Battle, ND; program dir. and recreation asst. San Vito Air Sta. Cmty. Ctr., San Vito, Italy. Mailing: 4543 Desert Varnish Dr Colorado Springs CO 80922-2303

GLENN, VIOLETTA COLLEEN, retired secondary school educator; b. Houston, Sept. 11, 1949; d. Odis Everett Cooper and Ozamay Jacobs; m. Carl McKinney Glenn, Aug. 20, 1948. AA, San Jacinto Coll., Pasadena, Tex., 1970; BA, U. Houston, 1976; MA, U. Houston Clear Lake, Pasadena, Tex., 1983. Cert. secondary English and history tchr. Tex., 1976, K-12 reading specialist Tex., 1983. English tchr. Incarnate Word Acad., Houston, 1977—79; curriculum writer and history tchr. Houston Ind. Sch. Dist., 1979—81; tchr. reading, history, computer skills Pasadena Ind. Sch. Dist., Tex., 1981—2004; ret., 2004. Vol. asst. Alzheimer's patient, Houston, 2003—06. Named Pk. View Tchr. of Yr., Pasadena South Rotary, 1998—99. Republican. Avocations: computers, painting, travel.

GLESMANN, SYLVIA-MARIA, artist; b. Spardorf, Erlangen, Germany, June 8, 1923; arrived in the US, 1925; d. Rolf-Joseph and Auguste (Schultheiss) Hoffmann; m. John Brainerd Glesmann, Apr. 30, 1948; children: Glenn M., Eric B., Jonathan M. Degree, Acad. Fine Arts, Nurnberg, Germany, 1940, Acad. Fine Arts, Munich, 1944. Instr. Somerville Adult Edn. Exhibited in group shows at Carrier Clinic, 1993, Bergen Mus., 1993, Morris Mus., 1993, Nabisco Brands, 1993, Cultural and Heritage Gallery, Somerville, N.J., 1993-95, Salmagundi Club, 1994, Garden State Water Color Assn., Princeton, N.J., 1994, Barrons Art Ctr., 1993, Art on the Ave. Group Show of Flowers, 1991, Nat. Assn. Women Artists, N.Y.C., 1991, 94, SoHo, 1994, Bridgewater N.J. County Libr., 1996, 2001-02, Nat. Assn. Women Artists New World Art Ctr., Soho, N.Y., 1999, Children's Specialized Hosp., Westfield, N.J., 2002, Barrons Art Ctr, Woodbridge, 2002, Creative Arts Com. Show, Bridgewater, N.J., 2006, Trinity United Ch. Art Show, Warren, N.J., 2006; one-woman shows include Childrens Specialized Hosp., Mountainside, N.J., 2002, N.U.I. Corp., Bridgewater, 1987, Salmagundi Club, N.Y.C., 1995, 2000, Am. Artists Profl. League, 1995-97, Somerset County Libr., Bridgewater, 1996, 2001-02, Barrons Art Ctr., Woodbridge, 1997, Barrons Art Ctr., Bridgewater Mcpl. Bldg, 1999-2001, Nat. Assn. Women Artists, Balt. Conv. Ctr., 2000, Bridgewater Libr., 2001, Nat. Assn. Women Artists, UN Visitors Lobby, 2002, Georgio Zikos Gallery, New Hope, Pa., 2002-03, over 25 one woman shows; author numerous poems. Recipient over 50 awards in water color, Editor's Choice award, 1998, Poetry Editors Choice award, 2002, Poetry award, Intenat. Libr. Poetry, 2003. Mem. Am. Artists Profl. League (pres. N.J. chpt. 1988-91, 2001, Bridgewater NJ Artists shows, 2002-2003), Nat. Assn. Woman Artists, Raritan Valley Arts Assn. (pres. 1976-78), Somerset Art Assn. (chairwoman 10th outdoor art show), Salmagundi Club, Nat. Mus. for Women in Arts (charter). Lutheran. Avocations: sports, music, reading, poetry, traveling and sketching. Home and Office: 36 Twin Oaks Rd Bridgewater NJ 08807-2343

GLICK, ANNA H., lawyer; b. Salzburg, Austria, Apr. 25, 1947; BA, Bklyn. Coll., 1967; MA, Temple U., 1969; JD, NYU, 1982. Bar: N.Y. 1983. Ptnr., securitization, corp. fin. Cadwalader, Wickersham & Taft, N.Y.C. ABA (mem. bus. law sect.), Order of Coif. Office: Cadwalader Wickersham & Taft 1 World Financial Ctr New York NY 10281 Office Phone: 212-504-6309. Office Fax: 212-504-6666. Business E-Mail: anna.glick@cwt.com.

GLICK, ANNA MARGARET, real estate broker, consultant; d. John Dale and Lena Iris Thomas; m. Alfred Dean Glick, June 1, 1986; m. Lealon Maynard Stoy, Oct. 16, 1966 (div. July 8, 1983); children: Lee Matthew Stoy, John Dale Stoy. Student, Indiana-Purdue U., 1979—82, Okla. City C.C., 1985—86; cert., Coldwell Banker U., 1992, cert., 1999. Real estate broker State of Ind. Lic. Bd., 1989. Mathematician to sec. Lincoln Nat. Life Ins. Co., Fort Wayne, Ind., 1965—69; exec. sec. Magnavox Corp., Fort Wayne, 1969—71; tri-state dir. Tammey Jewels, Inc., Indpls., 1970—73; owner, operator LeAn's Family Footwear, Hamilton, Ind., 1973—78; dep. auditor DeKalb County Ct. Ho., Auburn, Ind., 1974—83; fin. contr. Price Comm., Inc, Oklahoma City, 1983—86; auditing State of Ind., State Bd. of Accounts, Idpls., 1987—90; trust, ira adminstr. Ft. Wayne Nat. Bank, Fort Wayne, 1987—90; real estate broker, realtor RE/MAX Results, Fort Wayne, 1989—. Presenter A & A Unlimited Budget Workshops, Fort Wayne, 2004—. Bd. dirs. Nat. Kidney Found. of Ind., Fort Wayne, 1986—95. Recipient Gift of Life award, Nat. Kidney Found. of Ind., 1987, President's Cir. award, Coldwell Banker, 1996, 1998, 2000—03, Diamond Cir. award, 1997, Multi-Million Dollar Club award, 1990—94, President's Elite Distinction, 1995, 100% Club, RE/MAX, 2004, 2005. Mem.: Ft. Wayne Area Assn. Realtors (forms and govtl. affairs com. mem. 2001—), Providence Seminars, Inc. (club net leader 2004—05). R-Conservative. Protestant. Avocations: genealogy, decorating, piano, computers, reading. Home: 11626 Sycamore Hills Dr Fort Wayne IN 46814 Office: RE/MAX Results 7806-A W Jefferson Fort Wayne IN 46804 Office Phone: 260-436-6363. Office Fax: 260-436-6364. E-mail: anna@annaglick.com.

GLICK, CYNTHIA SUSAN, lawyer; b. Sturgis, Mich., Aug. 6, 1950; d. Elmer Joseph and Ruth Edna (McCally) Glick; m. Paul Allen (dec. 2004). AB, Ind. U., 1972; JD, Ind. U.-Indpls., 1978. Bar: Ind. 1978, U.S. Dist. Ct. (so. dist.) Ind. 1978, U.S. Dist. Ct. (no. dist.) Ind. 1981, U.S. Supreme Ct. 2000. Adminstrv. asst. Gov. Otis R. Bowen of Ind., 1973-76; dep. pros. atty. 35th Jud. Cir., LaGrange County, Ind., 1980-82, pros. atty., 1983—90; pvt. practice LaGrange, Ind., 1979—. Campaign aide Ind. Rep. State Ctr. Com., Indpls., 1972-73; former chmn. La Grange County Rep. Ctrl. com. Named Hon. Spkr., Ind. Ho. of Reps., Sagamore of the Wabash. Fellow Ind. Bar Found.; mem. ABA, Ind. State Bar Assn., LaGrange County Bar Assn., DAR, Order Eastern Star, Phi Delta Phi, Delta Zeta. Methodist. Home and Office: 113 W Spring St Lagrange IN 46761-1843 Office Phone: 260-463-7414. Business E-Mail: sueglick@ligtel.com.

GLICK, GINA PHILLIPS MORAN, retired physician; b. Chgo., Dec. 6, 1931; d. Edward Langan Moran and Virginia Louise Phillips; m. L. Michael Glick, Feb. 9, 1957; children: Mark Michael, Celeste Michele, Felicia Michele, Matthew Michael. Student, Mundelein Coll., Chgo., 1949-52; MD, Loyola U., Chgo., 1956. Diplomate Am. Bd. Anesthesiology. Intern Mercy Hosp., Chgo., 1956-57; resident in anesthesia Chgo. Wesley Mem. Hosp., 1957-59; pvt. practice anesthesia Cumberland, Md., 1959-83; clin. instr. anesthesia U. Md., Balt.; chmn. dept. anesthesia Sacred Heart Hosp., Cumberland, 1967-83; asst. prof. anesthesia U. Tex. S.W. Med. Ctr., 1985—99; ret., 1999. Dir. Jenkins Anesthesiology Libr. Recipient gold, silver and bronze medals Md. chpt. Am. Heart Assn., Community Achievement award Sta. WCBC, 1981, St. Benedict medal St. Scholastica High Sch., Chgo., 1978. Mem. Am. Soc. Anesthesiologists, Tex. Soc. Anesthesiologists, Dallas County Soc. Anesthesiologists, Dallas County Med. Soc. Roman Catholic. Office: U Tex Sci Med Ctr Dept Anesthesiology 5323 Harry Hines Blvd Dallas TX 75390-7208

GLICK, JANE MILLS, biomedical researcher, educator; b. Memphis, Nov. 26, 1943; d. Albert Axtell Jr. and Mary Louise (Baynes) Mills; m. John Harrison Glick, May 25, 1968; children: Katherine Anne, Sarah Stewart. AB, Randolph-Macon Woman's Coll., 1965; PhD, Columbia U., 1971. Postdoctoral trainee NIH, Bethesda, Md., 1971-73; postdoctoral fellow Sch. of Medicine Stanford (Calif.) U., 1973-74; rsch. asst. prof. biochemistry Sch. Dental Medicine U. Pa., Phila., 1974-77; asst. prof. biochemistry Med. Coll. Pa., Phila., 1977-82, assoc. prof. biochemistry, 1982-90, prof. biochemistry, 1990-94; sr. rsch. investigator Inst. Human Gene Therapy Sch. Medicine U. Pa., 1994—2002, faculty adminstr. cell and molecular biology group. Mem. metabolism study sect. NIH, 1993—97; adj. assoc. prof. Sch. Medicine U. Pa., 1996—. Assoc. editor: Jour. Lipid Rsch., 1985-86, mem. editorial bd., 1987-99; contbr. articles to profl. jours. Trustee Episcopal Acad., Merion, Pa., 1989-95, Swarthmore Presbyn. Ch., 1995-97, pres. 1997. Recipient Rsch. Svc. award NIH, 1975-77, Young Investigator award, 1980-83, Teaching award Lindback Found., 1985. Mem. AAAS, AAUP (sec. 1990-92), Arteriosclerosis Coun. Am. Heart Assn. (program com. 1990-93), Am. Soc. for Biochemistry and Molecular Biology, Am. Soc. for Human Genetics, Phi Beta Kappa, Sigma Xi. Presbyterian. Office: U Pa Sch Medicine 652 BRB II/III 421 Curie Blvd Philadelphia PA 19104 Business E-Mail: glickj@mail.med.upenn.edu.

GLICK, MYRNA JOAN, psychologist; b. Newark, Aug. 7, 1936; d. Harry and Ida (Alter) Bergman; m. Carl Salamensky, Aug. 21, 1955 (dec. 1971); children: Shelley, David; m. Joseph M. Glick, Oct. 14, 1972 (div. Mar. 1993). BA, William Paterson U., 1966; MA, Columbia U., 1967, PhD, 1975. Lic. psychologist, N.J., Calif. Chmn. child study team Franklin Lakes (N.J.) Schs., 1969-85; psychotherapist Pascack Mental Health Clinic, Park Ridge, N.J., 1975-76; pvt. practice Pompton Plains, N.J., 1977—. Mem. NEA, Am. Psychol. Assn., N.J. Psychol. Assn., Calif. Psychol Assn., Monterey Bay Psychol. Assn. (forensic chair) Jewish. Avocations: theater, literature, travel, gardening, hiking, classical music. Office Phone: 831-646-9330. E-mail: mglickphd@aol.com.

GLICK, PAULA FLORENCE, art historian, author, lecturer; b. Balt. d. Emanuel and Hilda (Snyder) Erlich; m. Irving Isadore Glock; children: Stephen Paul, Judith Madeline Barringer. BA, George Washington U., 1976, MA, 1981; MPhil, Columbia U. Assoc. dir. Capricorn Galleries, Bethesda, Md., 1964-76, assoc. dir., mgr., 1976-85, co-dir., 1985—; instr. Cath. Univ. Am., Washington, 1985. Art cons., Silver Spring, Md., 1981—; lectr. in field. Co-author: Paul Sample, Painter of the American Scene, 1988, Sight and Insight, the Art and Work of Burton Silverman, 1998; contbr. articles to profl. jours. Mem. Coll. Art Assn., Am. Assn. Mus. (mem. registrars com.), Art Table, Am. Soc. Appraisers, Soc. Archtl. Historians, Assn. of Historians of Am. Art, Assn. Ind. Historians Art, Appraisers Assn. Am., Italian Art Soc. Jewish. Home and Office: 42842 Falling Leaf Ct Ashburn VA 20148-6928 Office Phone: 301-814-2406. Personal E-mail: paulaglickart@verizon.net.

GLICK, R. SARA, music educator and performer, composer, writer; b. Henderson, Nebr., Feb. 20, 1938; children: Ann Lorraine, Gregory Jon. Student, Bethel Coll., North Newton, Kans., 1956-59; BMusic, Kans. U., Lawrence, MMusic, 1965. Cert. tchr., Wash. Prof. organ and piano Park Coll., Parkville, Mo., 1967-68; prof. piano Olympic Coll., Bremerton, Wash., 1969-70; organist, choir master Silverdale (Wash.) Meth. Ch., 1969-71; instr. harpsichord Pacific Luth. U., Parkland, Wash., 1971-73; music tchr. Annie Wright Sch., Tacoma, 1974-78; organist, choir master St. Mary's Episcopal Ch., Tacoma, 1977-91, Mason Meth. Ch., Tacoma, 1991-95; music assoc. Trinity Luth. Ch., Parkland, 1995—98; music tchr. Charles Wright Acad., Tacoma, 1981—2003; ret. Soloist Bremerton (Wash.) Symphony, 1967; performer, recitalist Belvedere Consort, Tacoma Youth Symphony, various chamber groups, 1967-1998; accompianist Tacoma Youth Chorus, 1990-95. Author: (1-act play) Gingerbread Cake, 1981; composer: (song cycle) Greenwood Seasons, (piano teaching materials) Circle Zoo, Duets for Dinosaurs, Sea Modes, (songs for youth choruses) Twisters, Riddlers, Songs of the World, (organ pieces) Seasons; contbr. articles to profl. jours. Del., Dem. Caucus, Tacoma, 1970s; vol. Dem. Party, Gig Harbor, Wash., 1970s, Hillhaven Homes, Tacoma, Allenmore Hosp., Tacoma. Mem. Am. Guild Organists (dean 1974, bd. dirs. 1994-97), Wash. State Music Tchrs., Sigma Alpha Iota. Avocations: reading, hiking, family activities, woodworking, concerts. also: Trinity Luth Ch 12115 Park Ave S Tacoma WA 98444-3629

GLICK, RUTH BURTNICK, literature educator, writer; b. Lexington, Ky., Apr. 27, 1942; d. Lester Leon and Beverly (Miller) Burtnick; m. Norman Stanley Glick, June 30, 1963; children: Elissa, Ethan. BA, George Washington U., 1964; MA, U. Md., 1967. Lectr. S.W. Writers Conf., Houston, 1984, Nebr. Writers' Guild, Omaha, 1985, Bouchercon, Balt., 1986, Triangle Romance and Fiction Writers' Conf., Raleigh, 1988, Romantic Times Booklovers Conf., San Antonio, 1990, Orlando, 2001, Kansas City, 2003, St. Louis, 2005, Malice Domestic, Bethesda, 1993, Howard C.C., 1995—, World Fantasy Conv., 2003, Desert Dreams Conf., Phoenix, 2004, Writers Weekend, Seattle, 2004. Author: (with Nancy Baggett) Dollhouse Furniture You Can Make, 1977, Dollhouse Lamps and Chandeliers, 1979, Soup's On, 1985, Oat Bran Baking, 1989, Skinny Soups, 1992, 100 Percent Pleasure, 1994 (US Today list of 12 best cookbooks of 1994), Skinny Italian, 1996, One-Pot Meals for People with Diabetes, 2002; (with Eileen Buckholtz, Carolyn Males and Louise Titchener) Love Is Elected, 1982 (named one of best romances 1982), Southern Persuasion, 1983, (with Titchener) In the Arms of Love, 1983 (Romance best seller list), Brian's Captive, 1983 (Romance best seller list), Reluctant Merger, 1983 (Romance best seller list), Summer Wine, 1984, Beginner's Luck, 1984, Mistaken Image, 1985, Hopelessly Devoted, 1985, Summer Stars, 1985, Stolen Passion, 1986, Indiscreet, 1988, (with Baggett and Gloria Kaufer Greene) Don't Tell 'Em It's Good for 'Em, 1984, Eat Your Vegetables!, 1985, (with Buckholtz) End of Illusion, 1984, Space Attack, 1984, Mission of the Secret Spy Squad, 1984, Mindbenders, 1984, Doom Stalker, 1985, Captain Kid and the Pirates, 1985, The Cats of Castle Mountain, 1985, Logical Choice, 1986, Great Expectations, 1987, A Place in Your Heart, 1988, Saber Dance, 1988, Postmark, 1988, Roller Coaster, 1989 (Young Adult Best Seller List), Silver Creek Challenge, 1989, Needlepoint, 1989, Life Line, 1990, Shattered Vows, 1991, Whispers in the Night, 1991, Only Skin Deep, 1992, Trial By Fire, 1992, Hopscotch, 1993, Cradle and All, 1993, What Child is This, 1993, Midnight Kiss, 1994, Tangled Vows, 1994, Till Death Us Do Part, 1995, Prince of Time, 1995, Face to Face, 1996, For Your Eyes Only, 1997, Father and Child, 1997 (Peregrine Connection series) Talons of the Falcon, 1986, Flight of the Raven, 1986, In Search of the Dove, 1986 (Lifetime Achievement award for romantic suspense series 1987), (with Kathryn Jensen) The Big Score, 1989 (Young Adult Best Seller List), Night Stalker, 1989 (Young Adult Best Seller List), (sole author) Dollhouse Kitchen and Dining Room Accessories, 1979, Invasion of the Blue Lights, 1982, More Than Promises, 1985, The Closer We Get, 1989, Make Me a Miracle, 1992, Bayou Moon, 1992, Skinny One Pot Meals, 1994, The Diabetes Snack, Munch, Nibble, Nosh Book, 1998, Simply Italian, 1998, Nowhere Man, 1998, Shattered Lullaby, 1999, Midnight Caller, 1999, Never Too Late, 2000, Amanda's Child, 2000, Fabulous Lo-Carb Cuisine, 2001, The Man from Texas, 2001, Never Alone, 2001, Lassiter's Law, 2001, Body Contact, 2002 (Waldenbooks Series Best Seller List), From the Shadows, 2002, Phantom Lover, 2003, Killing Moon, 2003 (Berkley Sensation Launch Book), Intimate Strangers, 2003, Edge of the Moon, 2003, Witching Moon, 2003, Bedroom Therapy, 2004, Out of Nowhere, 2004, Undercover Encounter, 2004, Crimson Moon, 2005, Spellbound, 2005, Beyond Control, 2005, Riley's Retribution, 2005, others; contbr. articles to profl. jours. U. Md. Am. studies fellow, 1964-65; recipient Career Achievement award for series Romantic Mystery, 1994, Romantic Times Career Achievement award for series Romantic Suspense, 2000, Golden Leaf award for Best Long Contemporary novel and Best Novella, N.J. Romance Writers, 2001, Golden Leaf award for Best Paranormal novel N.J. Romance Writers, 2003, 04, Best Selling Author, NY Times, USA Today, 2003, Barclay Gold award for Best Futuristic, Fantasy and Paranormal novel Lake Country Romance Writers, 2004; nominee Best Series Romance Book of the Yr. 1993-94 Romantic Times, 1995, 99, 2001, nominee Series Storyteller of Yr., 1996, nominee Best Harlequin Intrigue of Yr., 1998, nominee Best Series Romantic Suspense Writer of Yr., 2000. Mem. Author's Guild, Romance Writers Am. (lectr. Detroit, 1984, Atlanta 1985, Dallas 1987, 96, 2004, Boston 1989, San Francisco 1990, New Orleans 1991, 2001, Denver 2002, N.Y.C. 2003, Reno, 2005), Washington Romance Writers (bd. dirs.), Sisters in Crime, Novelists Inc., Md. Romance Writers, Internat. Thriller Writers. E-mail: rglick@capaccess.org.

GLICKENHAUS, SARAH BRODY, speech therapist; b. Mpls., Mar. 8, 1919; d. Morris and Ethel (Silin) Brody; BS, U. Minn., 1940, MS, 1945; m. Seth Morton Glickenhaus, Oct. 23, 1944; children: James Morris, Nancy Pier. Speech therapist Davison Sch. Speech Correction, Atlanta, 1940-42; speech pathologist U. Minn., Mpls., 1945-46; speech therapist Queens Coll., N.Y.C., 1946-48; speech therapist VA, N.Y.C., 1949-50; pvt. practice, New Rochelle, N.Y., 1950-71; speech therapist Abbott Sch. United Free Sch. Dist. 13, Irvington, N.Y., 1971-79; pvt. practice, Scarsdale, N.Y., 1979—; tutor learning disabled children New Rochelle Public Schs., 1968-71. Mem. AAAS, Am. Speech Hearing & Lang. Assn., N.Y. State Speech &Hearing Assn., Westchester Speech & Hearing Assn. Club: Harvard (N.Y.C.). Jewish. Home and Office: 100 Dorchester Rd Scarsdale NY 10583-6051

GLICKMAN, BENITA, language educator, writer, poet; b. Bronx, N.Y., Oct. 21, 1952; d. Marcus and Esther Glickman. BA in Spanish magna cum laude, CCNY, 1973; MA in Spanish, Lehman Coll., 1976; postgrad., Manhattan Coll., 1980—84. Cert. tchr. Spanish 7-12 N.Y., tchr. ESL, tchr. jr. h.s. Spanish, bilingual common brs. grades 1-6. Tchr. Spanish and reading Gilbert Sch., Bklyn., 1973—74; adult edn tchr. Spanish and ESL William Howard Taft H.S., Bronx, 1974—75; bilingual tchr. P.S. 91, Bronx, 1975—78; tchr. ESL John F. Kennedy H.S., Bronx, 1978—91, Christopher Columbus H.S., Bronx, 1991—, Internat. House coord., 2003—; poet, writer, 2001—. Cons. Brown U.-The Edn. Alliance, N.Y.C., 2003. Contbr. short story Chicken Soup for the Sister's Soul, 2002 (Alice Minnie Hertz Heniger award for Children's Lit., 2001), poetry Wedding Blessings: Prayers and Poems Celebrating Love, Marriage and Anniversaries, 2003, poetry to 41 jours. Mem.: Tchrs. English to Students of Other Langs., Acad. Am. Poets, N.Y. State Writing Project, N.Y.C. Writing Project, Phi Beta Kappa. Avocations: reading, cooking, gardening, yoga, nature walking. Home: 55 Knolls Crescent Bronx NY 10463 Office: Christopher Columbus HS 925 Astor Ave Bronx NY 10469 E-mail: bgcchs@yahoo.com.

GLICKMAN, GLADYS, lawyer, writer; b. NYC, Feb. 28, 1920; d. Reuben and Sadie (Levy) Glickman. BA, Bklyn. Coll., 1939; JD, DePaul U., 1959. Bar: Ill. 1959, N.Y. 1961. Editor Bur. Nat. Affairs, Inc., Washington, 1942-44, Research Inst. Am., N.Y.C., 1944-48; asst. dir., labor rels. rsch. Continental Can Co., N.Y.C., 1948-51; supr. Wage Stabilization Bd., N.Y.C., 1951-53; writer, editor Matthew Bender and Co. a subsidiary of Lexis-Nexis, Inc., N.Y.C., 1959—; corp. counsel Parents Magazine Enterprises, Inc., N.Y.C., 1961-78; v.p. legal Gruner and Jahr, USA Pub., N.Y.C., 1978-93. Author: Franchising, 1969, (with others) and quadrennial supplements Warrens Forms of Agreement, 1964. Mem. ABA, N.Y. County Lawyers Assn. (com. mem.), Ill. State Bar Assn. Jewish.

GLICKMAN, MARLENE, non-profit organization administrator; b. Evansville, Ind., May 13, 1936; d. Morris Jack and Sarah (Krawll) Foreman; m. Marshall Levi Glickman, Jan. 9, 1956 (dec. 2002); children: Cynthia Anne, Joseph Leonard. Student, Ohio State U., 1954-56. Area dir. Am. Jewish Com., Buffalo, 1981-2000; v.p. adminstrn. and fin. Network of Religious Cmtys., 2000—05, co-pres., 2006—. Pres. Meals on Wheels of Buffalo and Erie County, 1981—83, N.E. Lakes Coun. and UAHC, Coun. Congl. Pres. Erie County, 1979—81; vice chair gen. campaign United Jewish Appeal, 1980, chair woman's divsn., 1979; pres. N.E. Lakes coun. Union Am. Hebrew Congregations, 1982—86; pres. Temple Beth Am, 1978—80, 2002—03, chair 50th anniversary, 2005; pres. Sisterhood Temple Beth Am, 1969—71, 1976—77; agy. allocations com. United Way, chair Towns and Villages divsn., 1981; pres. Human Rights Adv. Coun. Western N.Y., 1988—96; bd. dirs. YWCA, Buffalo and Erie County, 1990—96, Buffalo Fedn. Neighborhood Ctrs., Inc., 1994—98; exec. com., sec. Sheehan Meml. Hosp., Inc., 1994—98; pres., bd. dirs. Western N.Y. Martin Luther King Jr. Commn., 1991—97; active Western N.Y. Vision for Tomorrow 2000 C. of C./Buffalo Partnership. Recipient Abraham Pugash Cmty. Rels. award for establishing Kosher Meals on Wheels, Jewish Family Svc., Buffalo and Erie County, N.Y., 1975, NAACP Human Rels. award, 1997, Cmty. Rels. award Am. Jewish Com. Western N.Y., 2001; Marlene Glickman H.S. Human Rels. Award of Western N.Y. named in her honor for Am. Jewish Com., 2004; Am.-Pol Eagle Citizen of Yr., 1995. Mem. NAACP (life), Union Am. Hebrew Congregations (exec., bd. dirs. 1982-99, exec. com.), Commn. on Synagogue Music, Joint Cantorial Placement Commn., FRJ Admin. (budget and finance), New Congregations, Maintenance of Union Membership, Hadassah (life), Assn. Reform Zionists Am. (del. to Israel 1987), Brandeis Women's Com. (life), Nat. Coun. Jewish Women (life, Hannah G. Solomon award 1985), Assn. Jewish Comty. Rels. Workers, Jewish Communal Svc. Assn., Arza/World Union (bd. dirs. 1992-2000). Avocation: singing. Home: 94 Broadmoor Dr Tonawanda NY 14150-5532 Office: M&M Connections 94 Broadmoor Dr Tonawanda NY 14150-5532 also: PMB 361 425 Carr 693 Dorado PR 00646 Personal E-mail: mglickman5@cs.com.

GLICKMAN, SALLIE A., professional society administrator; BA, Temple U., 1988, EdM, 1991. With Crime Prevention Assn., Phila., 1989—94; sr. assoc. DTI Assocs., Arlington, Va., 1995—96; dir. membership svcs. Nat. Assn. Pvt. Industry Couns. (name changed to Nat. Assn. Workforce Bds.), Washington, 1996—98; v.p. instl. advancement Pvt. Industry Coun. Phila., 1998—99; founding exec. dir. & CEO Phila. Workforce Investment Bd., Inc., 1999—. Trustee US Conf. Mayors Workforce Devel. Coun., 2002—, pres., 2006—; co-founder, bd. mem. Life Sci. Career Alliance, 2003—; mem. Nat. Re-Entry Policy Coun., 2003—. Mem. econ. devel. cabinet City of Phila.; mem. Jewish Ednl. & Vocat. Svc. Coun., 2004—; co-founder, co-chair Graduate! Phila., 2005—; vol. United Way S.E. Pa., 2002—. Recipient 40 Under 40 award, Phila. Bus. Jour., 2006. Office: Philadelphia Workforce Investment Bd Ste 1500 1601 Market St Philadelphia PA 19103 Office Phone: 215-717-2010. Office Fax: 215-717-2020. E-mail: sglickman@pwib.org.*

GLICKSTEIN, EILEEN AGARD, librarian, consultant; b. Worcester, Mass., Aug. 26, 1948; d. Irving Howard and Mildred Maud (Dowling) Agard; m. Jonathan Andrew Glickstein, May 5, 1972; children: Ethan Agard, Samuel Agard. BA, Am. U., 1970; MLS, Columbia U., 1971; MA, NYU, 1975. Head instructional librs. Columbia U., 1985-88; dir. Barnard Coll. Libr., 1988—. Office: Barnard Coll Libr 3009 Broadway New York NY 10027-6501

GLICK-WEIL, KATHY, library director; b. Milw., Jan. 11, 1950; d. Irving Robert and Janice Esther (Rosner) Glick; m. Gordon Weil, June 20, 1971; children: Jeffrey, Aaron. BA, Tulane U., 1971; MLS, U. Calif., Berkeley, 1972. Children's libr. Thayer Pub. Libr., Braintree, Mass., 1972-73; reference libr. Stoughton (Mass.) Pub. Libr., 1973-77; br. libr. Brockton (Mass.) Pub. Libr., 1977-78; asst. dir. Medford (Mass.) Pub. Libr., 1978-84; dir. Lincoln (Mass.) Pub. Libr., 1984-93, Newton (Mass.) Free Libr., 1993—. Mem. ALA, Mass. Libr. Assn. (v.p. 2005, pres-elect 2005—). Home: 46 Acacia Ave Chestnut Hill MA 02467-1351 Office: Newton Free Library 330 Homer St Newton MA 02459-1429 Office Phone: 617-796-1400. Business E-Mail: kglickweil@mlnlib.net.

GLIER, INGEBORG JOHANNA, German language and literature educator; b. Dresden, Germany, June 22, 1934; came to U.S., 1972; d. Erich Oskar and Gertrud Johanne (Niese) G. Student, Mt. Holyoke Coll., 1955-56; Dr. phil. (Studienstiftung des deutschen Volkes), U. Munich, Germany, 1958; Dr. phil., Habilitation, 1969; MA (hon.), Yale U., 1973. Asst., lectr. U. Munich, 1958-69, universitätsdozentin, 1969-72; vis. prof. Yale U., 1972-73, prof. German, 1973—2004, chmn. dept., 1979-82, chmn. Medieval Studies New Haven, 1986-93, chmn. Women's Studies, 1995-96, sr. faculty fellow, 1974-75; vis. prof. U. Cologne, Germany, 1970-71, U. Colo., Boulder, spring 1983, U. Tubingen, summer 1984. Author: Struktur und Gestaltungsprinzipien in den Dramen John Websters, 1958, Deutsche Metrik, 1961, Artes amandi, Untersuchung zu Geschichte, Uberlieferung und Typologie der deutschen Minnereden, 1971; contbr. articles, book reviews to profl. jours. Mem.: Wolfram von Eschenbach Gesellschaft, Internat. Courtly Lit. Soc., Am. Assn. Tchrs. German, Medieval Acad. Am., MLA, Internat. Germanisten-Verband. Home: 111 Park St Apt 12T New Haven CT 06511-5421 Office: Yale Univ Dept Germanic Langs PO Box 208210 New Haven CT 06520-8210 Office Phone: 203-432-0788. E-mail: ingeborg.glier@yale.edu.

GLIMCHER, LAURIE H., immunology educator; MD, Harvard Coll., 1976. Irene Heinz Given prof. immunology Harvard Sch. Pub. Health; and prof. medicine dept. immunology and infectious diseases Harvard Med. Sch. Contbr. articles to profl. jours. E-mail: glimche@hsph.harvard.edu.

GLISMANN, CLEMENTINE, retired elementary school educator; b. Oakland, Nebr., Aug. 4, 1917; d. Louis Martin Larson, Edvinna Josephine Young; m. Leonard William Glismann, Feb. 24, 1940 (dec. Feb. 1997). BA, Midland Luth. Coll., Fremont, Nebr., 1939; postgrad., U. Nebr., 1942—43, Weber Coll., Ogden, Utah, 1945—47, U. Utah, 1963—78. Tchr. 1st grade Bd. Edn., Norfolk, Nebr., 1939—40, secondary tchr. Madrid, Nebr., 1941—42, 3d grade tchr. Ogden, Utah, 1945—56, 4th grade tchr., 1957—63, Salt Lake City, 1964—79; ret., 1979. Traveling dealer Lenswood, 1977—91. Author, prodr. (TV program) Wheels, KSL-TV Salt Lake City, Utah, 1951, Paper, 1952, Rubber, 1953, Clothes, 1954, Historical Masquerade (Great Americans), 1955, Mother Earth's Rock Family, Ogden City Schs. TV, 1962—63, There's More to Say to Your Story. State chmn. Luth. Ch. Women, Utah, 1963. Mem.: Golden Spike Gem and Mineral Soc., Delta Kappa Gamma. Republican. Lutheran. Achievements include having a 50-year collection of fossils, petrified wood, minerals and butterflies on permanent display at Midland Lutheran College in Fremont, Nebraska. Avocations: faceting gemstones, poetry.

GLOBUS, DOROTHY TWINING, museum director; b. Singapore, Aug. 31, 1947; d. Kinsley and Cynthia (Thébaud) T.; m. Stephen F. Globus, Sept. 9, 1973; children: Samuel Twining, Dorothy Schermerhorn. BA in Art History magna cum laude, Swarthmore Coll., 1969. Asst. to dir. Wilcox Gallery Swarthmore (Pa.) Coll., 1967-69; summer intern Smithsonian Instn., Washington, 1966-69, exhibits specialist Nat. Mus. Natural History, 1970-73, curator of exhbns. Cooper-Hewitt Nat. Mus. Design N.Y.C., 1973-92; mus. dir. Mus. at Fashion Inst. of Tech., N.Y.C., 1993—; curator of exhbns. Mus. Arts & Design, N.Y.C., 2004—. Mem. trustees coun. Preservation N.Y. State, 1989—. Mem. Fashion Group, Artable. Office: Fashion Inst of Tech Seventh Ave at 27th St New York NY 10001-5992

GLODOWSKI, SHELLEY JEAN, administrator, writer, musician; b. Stoughton, Wis., Jan. 27, 1950; d. Rodney Keller and Janet Maude (Nelson) Peterson; m. Randolph Raymond Glodowski, July 31, 1976. BA, Hamline U., St. Paul, Minn., 1972. Cert. secondary English tchr. Substitute tchr. Stoughton Schs., Wis., 1973-74; office worker Wis. Pharm. Assn., Madison, 1973-74; legal sec. Howard Hippman, Oregon, Wis., 1974-76; typist 3 dept. psychiatry U. Wis., Madison, 1976-78, supr., specialist fiscal affairs, 1978-79, grad. sec. dept. sociology, 1979-82, program asst. sch. music, 1982-84, dept. sec. sch. music, 1984-85, adminstrv. sec. phys. scis. lab., 1985-87, office mgr. instructional materials ctr., 1987-91, chairs' sec. dept. sociology, 1991-94, adminstr. dept. philosophy, 1994—. Sound engr. Midwest Book Rev. program, Madison, 1986-89; organizer Wis. State Employees Union 2412 Clerical Union, Madison, 1990-91. Profl. musician Z.B.M. Band, Oregon, Wis., 1986-2003, (CD) Pay the Price, 1991, Z.B.M., 2000; sr. book reviewer, Midwest Book Rev., 1975—; costume designer musical prodn. Godspell, Oregon Straw Hat Players, 1990; author: Murder on the Wrong Note, 2003, Murder on a Philosophical Note (Blood on the Lake Path), 2006. Canvasser Dem. Party, Stoughton, Wis., 1968; mem., organizer Wis. State Employees Union 2412 Clerical Union, Madison, 1990; vol. Wis. Libr. Assn., Madison, 1987-90; coord. fundraising cabaret Unitarian Ch., Madison, 1984-96; choir mem. Unitarian Universalist choir, Madison, 1979-96; mem. AFSME Union, to 1990. Mem. Letters and Sci. Adminstrs. Network (recording sec. 1996-97, pres. 2005—), Stoughton Fest. Choir, 2004. Avocations: reading, tennis, cross country skiing, gardening, dogs. Home: 137 Washington St Oregon WI 53575-1548 Office: Instrnl Materials Ctr 225 N Miller St Oregon WI 53575-1610 Personal E-mail: shelmyst@charter.net.

GLOGAU, LILLIAN FLATOW FLEISCHER, educational administrator; b. N.Y.C., Feb. 15, 1925; d. Henry and Diana (Heller) Flatow; m. Spencer Zeigen, Oct. 10, 1992; children: Jordan, Laurence, Alexander. BA cum laude, Bklyn. Coll., 1946; MA, Columbia U., 1949; EdD, NYU, 1969. Tchr. N.Y.C. Sch. System, 1946-49, Plainview (N.Y.) Schs., 1959-61, adminstr., 1961-66; prin. Spring Valley (N.Y.) Schs., 1966-87; edn. cons. Lillian Glogau Assocs., Ltd., Jamesburg, N.J., 1987—, Prins. Plus, Verona, N.J. Pres. Pragmatix Corp., South Orange, N.J., Travel-Wise Study Group Tours; lectr., cons. in field; pres. Prins. Pliest-Cons. Author: Nongraded Primary, 1967, You and N.Y. City, 1970, Let's See, 1971, The Elementary School Media Center, 1972; author children's book including Jerry and the Book of Tickets, TV scripts; contbr. articles to profl. jours. Recipient Founders Day award SUNY, 1970, award of excellence County of Rockland, 1986, cert. appreciation 22nd Congl. Dist. N.Y., 1986, cert. achievement Town of Ramapo, 1986, cert. merit N.Y. State Senate 38th Dist., 1986, cert. appreciation House of Reps. Congress, Washington. Mem. PTA (life), Am. Assn. Sch. Adminstrs. (recipient cert. merit 1986), Am. Soc. Curriculum Devel., N.Y. State Sch. Adminstrs. Assn., Kappa Delta Pi, Pi Lambda Theta. Home: 53 Nancy Blvd Merrick NY 11566-3122 Personal E-mail: lffgz@msn.com.

GLOVER, JANET BRIGGS, artist; b. Allahabad, India, June 22, 1919; came to U.S., 1924; d. George Weston and Mary Ames (Hart) Briggs; m. Alan Marsh Glover, Feb. 5, 1949; children: Keith Terrot, John Carroll, Beth Marsh Glover Wittig. BA, Bennington Coll., 1943; postgrad., New Sch. Social Rsch., 1969-70. Artist, draftsman Chartmakers, Inc., N.Y.C., 1943-45; apprentice to Oscar Ogg Book of Month Club, N.Y.C., 1946; 2d grade tchr. Hartridge Sch., Plainfield, N.J., 1947-48, Country Day Sch., Lancaster, Pa., 1948-49; chmn. art dept. Women's Club Chatham, N.J., 1964-65, lectr. art N.J., 1981-86; publicity chmn. N.J. Ctr. Visual Arts, Summit, 1980-81. One-man shows include Present Day Club, Princeton, N.J., 1967, Gallery 9 Upstairs, Chatham, 1978; group shows include Key Gallery, N.Y.C., 1980; contbg. editor N.J. Music and Arts Mag., 1970-71; art critic Madison Eagle, 1975-78. Recipient 1st prize Morris County Art Assn., 1966, Princeton Art Assn., 1969, Cmty. Art Assn., 1980. Mem. Chatham Twp. Art League (co-founder, 1st pres. 1988-90, editor Artist's Album 1993—, editor newsletter, 1996—), Drew U. Art Assn. (membership chmn. 1990-94, mem. directory illustrated 2000—). Democrat. Unitarian Universalist. Avocations: poetry, music.

GLOVER, KAREN ELAINE, lawyer; b. Nampa, Idaho, Apr. 14, 1950; d. Gordon Ellsworth and Cora (Frazier) G.; m. Thaddas L. Alston, Aug. 17, 1979; children: Samantha Glover Alston, Evan Glover Alston. AB magna cum laude, Whitman Coll., 1972; JD cum laude, Harvard U., 1975. Bar: Wash. 1975, U.S. Dist. Ct. (we. dist.) Wash. 1975. Assoc. Preston, Thorgrimson Ellis & Holman, Seattle, 1975-80; ptnr. Preston Gates & Ellis LLP, Seattle, 1981—2005, mng. ptnr., 2005—. Bd. dirs. Adaptis, Inc., 2001-, Attenex Corp., 2005-. Chmn. bd. dirs. United Way King County, Seattle, 1993-94; chmn. trustees Whitman Coll., Walla Walla, Wash., 2004-06; bd. trustees King County Libr. Sys., Seattle, 1992-01. Mem. Wash. State Bar Assn. (corp. and health sects.), Columbia Tower Club, Rainier Club. Episcopalian. Office: Preston Gates & Ellis 925 4th Ave Ste 2900 Seattle WA 98104-1158 Office Phone: 206-370-7624. Business E-Mail: karig@prestongates.com.

GLOVER, LISA MARIE, transportation executive, consultant; b. Detroit, Oct. 14, 1963; d. Ronald and Denise (Wellons) Glover. BS, Tuskegee U., 1986; MS, Morgan State U., 1988. Cert. Microsoft profl. Summer intern IBM, Charlotte, NC, 1982, GM, Pontiac, Mich., 1983-85, Turner Constrn., Detroit, 1986; grad. intern State of Md., Dept. Transp., Balt., 1987-88; planner Dept. Transp., Detroit, 1988-90, asst. to dir., 1990-91, mgr. Office of Contract Compliance, 1991-93; transp. engr., cons. M2 Internat., Detroit, 1993-94; transportation cons. Trans. Svcs., Inc., 1994-95; asst. venue transp. mgr. Atlanta Com. Olympic Games, 1996; ind. contractor, 1997-2000; staff asst., sta. svcs. Met. Atlanta Rapid Transit Authority, 1998, bus. analyst, info. tech., 1998, rsch. asst., strategic planning, 1999, rsch. analyst, project mgr. transit rsch., 1999-2000; sr. transp. planner Dekalb County Planning Dept., Decatur, Ga., 2000—04; transp. planning mgr. Henry County Bd. Commrs., Modonough, Ga., 2004—06; owner Sage Jewels, LLC, 2005, Ivy Vining Cons., LLC, 2006—. Dekalb County rep. Atlanta Regional Commn.-Transp. Coord. Com., 2000—04; mem. Transit Feasibility Study, 2000—03; mem. steering com. No. Sub-Area Study Ga. Regional Trans. Authority, 2001—04; mem. Atlanta Value Pricing Taskforce, 2001—03; mem. host com. RAIL-VOLUTION, Atlanta, 2001—03; mem. Regional Transit Action Plan, 2001—03, Marietta-Lawrenceville Transp. Study, 2001—05, Inner Core Transit Feasibility Study, 2003—04; mem. transp. coord. com. Henry County rep. Atlanta Regional Commn., 2004—06; access mgmt. com. Friend of Transp. Rsch. Bd., 2004; jewelry maker, owner Sage Jewels, LLC, 2005—; project mgr. Joint Henry Cities/County Transp. Plan, 2005—06. Corr. sec. Metro Atlanta chpt. Nat. Congress Black Women, 2001—; nat. nominating bd. Outstanding Young Ams., 1995—96; mem. Total Praise choir New Birth Missionary Bapt. Ch., Lithonia, Ga., 1997—2003, co-chair engring. ministry, 1999—2000, vol. registrar Lay Inst. Equipping, 1999—2000. Recipient cert. of Merit, Mayor Coleman A. Young City of Detroit, 1980. Mem.: NAACP (young adults com. 1989—91), Ga. Acad. for Econ. Devel., Am. Planning Assn., Urban Land Inst., Women Transp. Seminar (scholarship coord. 1988—2001, bd. dirs. 2003—05, nat. diversity com. 2004, nat. membership strategies taskforce 2004—), Assn. Gen. Contractors Am. (pres. 1985—86), Charleston Pointe Homeowners Assn. (pres. 2006—), Internat. Olympic Family, Atlanta Regional Leadership Inst., Tuskegee Nat. Alumni Assn., Sigma Lambda Chi (charter), Alpha Kappa Alpha (sponsor teen group 1989—95), Pi Alpha (corr. sec.). Baptist. Avocations: classical/jazz/gospel music, travel, remodeling projects, visual/theatrical arts. Address: Ivy Vining Cons LLC 1590 Charleston Walk SE Atlanta GA 30316 Office Phone: 404-272-1732, 678-610-6341. E-mail: gloveret@msn.com.

GLOYD, RITA A., retired social worker; b. Gaithersburg, Md., Sept. 10, 1918; d. Henry Dorsey Gloyd and Margaret Lavenia Arnold. RN, Georgetown U., 1939; BA in Art, Notre Dame Md., 1960; MSW, U. Md., 1970. Cert. Acad. Cert. Social Workers. Delivery rm. nurse Georgetown U. Hosp., Washington, 1939; obstet. nurse Washington, 1939; stewardess Am. Airline, Flushing, NY, 1940—43; from novice to superior Good Sherperd, Balt., 1943—68; social worker stroke unit Johns Hopkins Hosp., Balt., 1970—71; social worker Montgomery County Pub. Schs.-Mark Twain Spl. Sch., Rockville, Md., 1971—73; social worker, adminstr. Diagnosis and Profl. Support Team, Rockville, 1975—84; ret., 1984. Democrat. Roman Catholic. Home: Apt 315 403 Russell Ave Gaithersburg MD 20877 Personal E-mail: rgloydrag@aol.com.

GLUBE, CONSTANCE RACHELLE, retired judge; b. Ottawa, Ont., Can., Nov. 23, 1931; d. Samuel and Pearl (Slonemsky) Lepofsky; m. Richard Hillard Glube, July 6, 1952 (dec.); children: John B., Erica D. Glube Kolatch, Harry S., B. Joseph. BA, McGill U., Montreal, Can., 1952; LLB, Dalhousie U., Halifax, Can., 1955, LLD (hon.), 1983, Mount St. Vincent U., 1998, St. Mary's U., 2000. Bar: N.S. 1956, created queen's counsel, 1974. Assoc. Kitz, Matheson, Halifax, 1964-66; ptnr. Fitzgerald & Glube, Halifax, 1966-68; sr. solicitor City of Halifax, 1969-74, city mgr., 1974-77; puisne judge Supreme Ct. of N.S., Halifax, 1977-82, chief justice, 1982-98, N.S. Ct. Appeals, 1998—2004; ret., 2004. Vice chair Can. Judges Conf.; interim bd. dirs. Nat. Jud. Ctr., 1987; bd. dirs. Can. Inst. Adminstrs. Justice. Contbr. articles to profl. jours. Co-chair Can. Coun. Christians and Jews; bd. dirs. Halifax Heritage Found., 1984—95, Internat. Commn. Jurists, Can. br., 2003—, Queen Elizabeth II Found., 2005—, Can. Civil Liberties Assn., 2005—, Halifax Cmty. Learning Network, 2005; chmn. bd. N.S. Archives, 1998—2004; chmn. Lt. Govs. Arts Award Found.; chair (hon.) N.S. divsn. Can. Mental Health Assn., 1984—98; mem. adv. coun. Order N.S., 2001—04. Recipient award of merit City of Halifax, 1977, Frances Fish award, 1997, N.S. Women Lawyers Achievement award, Confedn. Can. medal (1867-1992), 1992, Commemorative medal Golden Jubilee of Her Majesty Queen Elizabeth II, 2002, Justice award Can. Inst. Adminstrn. Justice, 2003. Fellow: Law of the Future (hon.); mem.: Order of Can. (apptd. officer 2006), Order of N.S., Nat. Jud. Inst. (bd. dirs. 1998—2004), Can. Jud. Coun. (chmn. edn. com. 1986—88, adminstrn. of justice com. 1992—94, equality com. 1994—99, jud. benefits com. 1994—99, fin. com. 1999—2002, chmn. edn. com. 2000—04, exec. com. 2001—04, vice chair jud. conduct com. 2001—04), Assn. Women Judges (hon.), Internat. Assn. Women Judges (hon.), Can. Bar Assn. (hon.; fellow Law of the Future Fund), Golden Key Internat. Honor Soc. (hon.). Jewish. Avocations: swimming, gardening, bridge. Home: 5920 Inglewood Dr Halifax NS Canada B3H 1B1 Personal E-mail: cglube@judicom.ca.

GLUCK, ABBE R., lawyer; married. BA, Yale Univ., 1996, JD, 2000. Law clerk U.S. Ct. Appeals 2nd cir., 2001—02; assoc. Paul Weiss Rifkind Wharton & Garrison, N.Y., 2002—03; law clerk U.S. Supreme Ct. Just. Ruth Bader Ginsburg, Washington, 2003—04; atty. Legal Counsel Div., N.Y.C. Dept. Law, N.Y., 2004—. Vis. asst. prof. Brooklyn Law Sch., 2002—03, adj. prof., 2004—. Office: New York City Law Department 100 Church St New York NY 10007-2601

GLUCK, CAROL, history professor; b. Newark, Nov. 12, 1941; d. David E. and Doris S. Newman; m. Peter L. Gluck, May 1, 1966; children: Thomas Edward, William Francis. Student, U. Munich, 1960-61, U. Tokyo, 1972-74; BA, Wellesley Coll., 1962; MA, Columbia U., 1970, PhD, 1977. Asst. prof. Columbia U., N.Y.C., 1975-83, assoc. prof., 1983-86, prof., 1986-88, George Sansom prof. history, 1988—. Vis. rsch. assoc. faculty law Tokyo U., 1978-79, 85-86, 92; vis. prof. Harvard U., Cambridge, Mass., 1991, Inst. Social Sci. Tokyo U., 1993, Ecole des Hautes Etudes en Scis. Sociales, Paris, 1995, 98; fellow Inst. for Advanced Studies in the Behavioral Scis., 1999-2000; mem. Inst. for Advanced Study, Princeton, 2005-06; publs. bd. Columbia U. Press, N.Y.C., 1991-96; co-dir. project on Asia in the core Curriuculm NEH, N.Y.C., 1987—; Am. adv. com. Japan Found., 1986-96, chair, 1991-96; disting. lectr. N.E. Area Coun., 1988, Japan Soc. for Promotion of Sci., 1989. Author: Japan's Modern Myths, 1985 (Fairbank prize 1986, Trilling award 1987); co-editor: Showa: The Japan of Hirohito, 1992, Asia in Western and World History, 1997, Thinking with the Past, 2006; contbr. numerous articles to profl. publs. Mem. Coun. on Fgn. Rels., U.S.-Japan Friendship Commn., 1994—2001; mem. com. on rsch. librs. N.Y. Pub. Libr., 1987—, mem. humanities adv. coun., 1996—. Recipient Fulbright 50th Anniversary Disting. Fellow award, 2002, Order of Rising Sun, Japanese Govt., 2006; fellow, Woodrow Wilson Found.; grantee, Japan Found.; Fulbright grantee, 1985—86, Fgn. Area fellow. Fellow: Am. Acad. Arts and Scis.; mem.: Am. Philos. Soc., Asia Soc. (trustee 1992—98, 2002—), Japan Soc. (bd. dirs. 1990—), Assn. Asian Studies (coun. 1981—84, nominating com. 1985—86, pres. 1996—97, bd. dirs. 1995—99), Am. Hist. Assn. (coun. 1987—90), Phi Beta Kappa. Home: 440 Riverside Dr New York NY 10027-6828 Office: Columbia U East Asian Inst 420 W 118th St New York NY 10027-7213

GLÜCK, LOUISE ELISABETH, poet, educator; b. NYC, Apr. 22, 1943; d. Daniel and Beatrice (Grosby) G.; m. Charles Hertz (div.); 1 child, Noah Benjamin; m. John Dranow, 1977 (div.). Student, Sarah Lawrence Coll., 1962, Columbia U., 1963-65; LLD, Williams Coll., 1993, Skidmore Coll., 1995, Middlebury, 1996. Vis. poet Goddard Coll., U. N.C., U. Va., U. Iowa; Elliston prof. U. Cin., 1978; vis. faculty Columbia U., 1979; faculty M.F.A. program Goddard Coll., also Warren Wilson Coll., Swannanoa, NC; Holloway lectr. U. Calif., Berkeley, 1982; vis. prof. U. Calif.-Davis, 1983; Scott prof. poetry Williams Coll., 1983; Regents prof. poetry UCLA, 1985-88; faculty Williams Coll., 1984—, Preston Parrish 3d century prof., 1997—2003, Margaret Scott Bundy lectr., 2003—04; Rosenkranz writer-in-residence Yale U., New Haven, 2004—. Vis. prof. Harvard U., 1995; Hurst prof. poetry Brandeis U., 1996; delivered Phi Beta Kappa poem Harvard U. commencement, 1990; baccalaureate spkr. Williams Coll.; Hopwood lectr. U. Mich.; spl. cons. Libr. of Congress, 2000; judge younger poets competition Yale U. Press, 2003—. Author: Firstborn, 1968, The House on Marshland, 1975, Descending Figure, 1980, The Triumph of Achilles, 1985, Ararat, 1990, The Wild Iris, 1992 (Pulitzer Prize for poetry 1993), Proofs and Theories (collected essays), 1994, Meadowlands, 1996, Vita Nova, 1999, The Seven Ages, 2001, October (chapbook), 2004, Averno, 2006. Grantee Rockefeller Found., Nat. Endowment for Arts, 1969-70, 79-80, 88-89, Guggenheim Found., 1975-76, 87-88, NEA, 1988-89; recipient lit. award Am. Acad. and Inst. Arts and Letters, 1981, award in poetry Nat. Book Critics Cir., 1985, Melville Cane award Poetry Soc. Am., 1986, Sara Teasdale Meml. prize Wellesley Coll., 1986, Bobbitt Natil prize Libr. Congress, 1992, Pulitzer prize, 1993, William Carlos Williams award, 1993, PEN/Martha Albrand award Non-Fiction, 1995, Lannan Found. award in poetry, 1999, New Yorker mag. award, 1999, Ambs. award English Spkg. Union, 1999, 50th Anniversary medal MIT, 2000, Bollingen prize, 2001, Medal for lifetime distinction Barnard Coll., 2004; named Poet Laureate of Vt., 1994, U.S. Poet Laureate, 2003. Fellow Am. Acad. Arts and Scis.; mem. Am. Acad. Arts & Letters, Am. Acad. Poets (chancellor 1999—), Phi Beta Kappa (hon.).

GLUCK, MICHELLE H., lawyer; b. Apr. 1959; m. Robert J. Gluck. BA, JD, U. Mich. Bar: Va. 1983. Assoc. Hunton & Williams, 1983—89; legal cons. Am. Household Inc., 1996—99, Office Depot, 1996—99; v.p., assoc. gen. counsel, asst. sec. The Sports Authority Inc., Ft. Lauderdale, Fla., 1999—2001, Kmart Corp., Troy, Mich., 2001—03; exec. v.p., gen. counsel, corp. sec. LandAmerica Fin. Group Inc., Richmond, Va., 2004—. Mem.: Am. Corp. Counsel Assn. (sec., bd. mem. South Fla. Chpt. 2001). Office: LandAmerica Fin Group Inc PO Box 27567 Richmond VA 23261-7567 Office Phone: 804-267-8383. Business E-Mail: mgluck@landam.com.

GLUCKMANN, EMA, science educator; BS in Biological Sci., U. Calif., Davis, 1982; MPA, U. Southern Calif., 1992. Tchr. Sacramento (Calif.) City Unified Sch. Dist., 1985—. Office: Luther Burbank HS 3500 Florin Rd Sacramento CA 95823 Office Phone: 916-433-5100. E-mail: ema-gluckmann@sac-city.k12.ca.us.

GLUECK-RAMBALDI, MARY AUDREY, retired psychiatric and mental health nurse; b. Bridgetown, Barbados; arrived in U.S., 1952; d. Hubert and Christina Cumming; m. Stephen G. Glueck (dec.); m. Robert Rambaldi, May 15, 2005. Grad. sch. nursing, St. Joseph's Mercy Hosp., Georgetown, Guyana; paralegal diploma, Profl. Career Devel. Inst., 2000. RN, Calif. Asst. nursing educator in new employee orientation San Mateo County Gen. Hosp., San Mateo, Calif., also facilitator video insvcs. for nursing staff, tchr. safety and emergency response procedures to staff, ret., 1998. Vol. emergency room U. Physicians Health Care-Kino Campus, Tucson. Mem. Mid. Mgrs. Assn., Am. Psychiat. Nurses Assn. Home: 3692 S Desert Cache Rd Tucson AZ 85735-5078 Personal E-mail: mary-glueck@yahoo.com.

GLUSKER, JENNY PICKWORTH, chemist; b. Birmingham, Eng., June 28, 1931; came to U.S., 1955, naturalized, 1977; d. Frederick Alfred and Jane Wylie (Stocks) P.; m. Donald Leonard Glusker, Dec. 18, 1955; children: Ann, Mark John, Katharine. BA in Chemistry, Oxford U., Eng., 1953, MA, DPhil, Oxford U., Eng., 1957; DSc (hon.), Coll. of Wooster, Ohio, 1985. Postdoctoral rsch. fellow Calif. Inst. Tech., Pasadena, 1955-56; rsch. fellow Inst. Cancer Rsch., Phila., 1956, rsch. assoc., 1957-67, asst. mem., 1967, assoc. mem., 1967-79, sr. mem., 1979—. Adj. prof. U. Pa., 1969—; mem. U.S. Nat. Com. for Crystallography, 1974—90, sec.-treas., 1977—79, chmn., 1982—84; vis. fellow Oriel Coll., Oxford, England, 1994—95; vis. prof. Internat. Union Crystallography, Egypt, 1997, Nat. Inst. Health, Biophysics/Biochemistry A Study Sect., 1972—76; mem. Biotech. Rsch. Rev. Com., 1977—80, chmn., 1979—80; mem. Metallo Biochem. Study Sect., 1983—87, Divsn. Rsch. Grants Adv. Com., 1989—92, Rsch. Coun., 1995—99; mem. gov. bd. Cambridge Structural Database, England, 1988—2001, vice chmn., England, 1998—2001; mem. computer graphics lab. adv. com. U. Calif., San Francisco, 1985—, chmn., 1988—; cons., lectr. in field; dir.-at-large, mem. gov. bd. Am. Inst. Physics, 1980—83, exec. com., 1981—82; chmn. selection com. Rhodes Scholarship, Pa., 1984—89. Co-author (with K.N. Trueblood): (book) Crystal Structure Analysis: A Primer, 1972, Crystal Structure Analysis: A Primer, 2d edit., 1985; co-author: (with Dodson, Ramaseshan and Venkatesan) The Collected Works of Dorothy Crowfoot Hodgkin; editor: Structural Crystallography in Chemistry and Biology, Structures of Molecules of Biological Interest, 1981; co-editor (with McLachlan): Crystallography in North America, 1982; co-editor: (with S. Parthasarathy) Aspects of Crystallography in Molecular Biology, 1997; editor: Acta Crystallographica sect. D. Biological Crystallography; co-editor (with M. Lewis, M. Rossi): Crystal Structure Analysis for Chemists and Biologists, 1994; co-editor: (with Patterson and Rossi) Patterson and Pattersons, 1987; mem. adv. bd. Molecular Structures in Biology, 1991, mem. editl. bd. Biophys. Jour., 1981—86; contbr. articles to profl. jours. Hon. fellow Somerville Coll., Oxford U. (Eng.), 2001. Fellow AAAS; mem. Am. Assn. Cancer Rsch., The Chem. Soc., Am. Soc. Biol. Chemists, Biophys. Soc., Am. Crystallog. Assn. (pres. 1979, Pub. Svc. award 1991, Fankuchen Meml. award 1995), Am. Chem. Soc. (Phila. sect. award 1978, Garvan medal 1979), Am. Phys. Soc., Sigma Xi. Office: Inst Cancer Rsch Fox Chase Cancer Ctr Philadelphia PA 19111 Office Phone: 215-728-2220. Business E-Mail: jp-glusker@fccc.edu.

GLYNN, CARLIN (CARLIN MASTERSON), actress; b. Cleve., Feb. 19, 1940; d. Guilford Cresse and Lois Carlin (Wilks) G.; m. Peter Masterson, Dec. 29, 1960; children: Carlin Alexandra, Mary Stuart, Peter C.B. Student, Sophie Newcomb Coll., 1957-58. Prof. Columbia U. Grad. Film Sch., N.Y.C.; prof. MFA program Actors Studio at New Sch. U. Creative advisor Sundance Inst. Film Lab. Appeared in N.Y. as Miss Mona in: The Best Little Whorehouse in Tex., 1978-80; in London, 1981; starred in Pal Joey, Goodman Theatre, Chgo., 1988 (Joseph Jefferson award 1988), Cover of Life, Am. Place Theatre, N.Y., 1994, The Young Man from Atlanta, Signature Theatre Co., 1995 (Pulitzer prize for drama 1995), Amazing Grace, 1998, The Chemistry of Change, 1999, Frame 312, 2002, Safe, 2003, Spring Storm, 2004, The Oldest Profession, 2004, A Lovely Sunday for Creve Coeur, Hartford Stage, Conn., 2006; films include Three Days of the Condor, 1974, Resurrection, 1978, Continental Divide, 1981, Sixteen Candles, 1984, The Trip to Bountiful, 1985, Blood Red, Night Game, Convicts, 1989, Blessing, 1992, Judy Berlin, 1997, West of Here, 2001, Lost Junction, 2001, Intervention (now Whiskey Sch.), 2004; TV series Mr. President, 1987; dir. short film Love Divided By, 1993; dir. contemporary opera Cheri at Actors Studio, 2005. Recipient Theatre World award, 1978, Antoinette Perry award, 1979, best actress award in musical Soc. West End Theatres, Lawrence Olivier award, London, 1981 Mem. SAG, AFTRA, Actor's Studio (bd. dirs., co-artistic dir.), Actors' Equity Assn. Episcopalian.

GMACHL, CLAIRE, electrical engineer, educator; MS in Physics, U. Innsbruck, 1991; PhD in Electrical Engring., Tech. U., Vienna, 1995. Mem. tech. staff, Walter Schottky Inst. Tech. U., Munich, 1992—94, mem. tech. staff, Ctr. Microstructures Vienna, 1993—94, asst. prof., Dept. Solid State Electronics, 1995—96; post-doctoral mem. tech. staff Lucent Technologies-Bell Laboratories, NJ, 1996—98, mem. tech. staff NJ, 1998—2002, disting. mem. tech. staff NJ, 2002—03; assoc. prof. Dept. Electrical Engring. Princeton U., 2003—. Contbr. articles to profl. jour. Named a MacArthur Fellow, John D. and Catherine T. MacArthur Found., 2005; recipient Group Achievement award, NASA, 2000, Outstanding Performer award, US Dept. Def. (Def. Advanced Rsch. Projects Agy.), 2001, Commendation for Excellence in Tech. Comm., Laser Focus World mag., 2001, The Snell Premium award, IEE UK, 2003. Mem.: Laser and Electro-Optics Soc., Austrian Physical Soc. (Solid State Physics award 1996), AAAS, Optical Soc. Am., Am. Physical Soc., NY Acad. Sci., Internat. Soc. Optical Engring., Materials Rsch. Soc., IEEE (sr.). Achievements include granted 15 patents. Office: Princeton Univ Engineering Quadrangle B 326 Olden St Princeton NJ 08544 Office Phone: 609-258-4641. Office Fax: 609-258-3745. E-mail: cgmachl@princeton.edu.

GNEZDA, NICOLE M., art educator; b. Columbus, Ohio, Jan. 9, 1952; d. Walter F. Gnezda and Mary M. Winter; m. Gary A. Smith (dec.); children: Yvonne Smith, Anthony Smith, Katharine Smith; m. John I. Snouffer, June 21, 2001. BFA cum laude, Ohio Wesleyan U., 1973; MA, Ohio State U., 1981, PhD, 2001. Permanent tchg. cert. Ohio. Art tchr. Worthington (Ohio) Schs., 1973—80, 1993—; instr. Ohio State U., Columbus, 1980—86; presch. tchr. North Broadway Children's Ctr., Columbus, 1985—86; art tchr. Upper Arlington Schs., Columbus, 1987—89, Westerville (Ohio) City Schs., 1989—93. Founder, adminstr. Gary Smith Compassionate Tchg. Award, Worthington, 1998—; artist; spkr. in field. Author and illustrator: Teaching Difficult Students: Blue Jays in the Classroom, 2005. Mem. steering com. Gary Smith Worthington Classic, 1998—. Recipient cert. of merit, Ohio Domincan U., 2004. Mem.: NEA, Nat. Art Edn. Assn. Women's Caucus, Nat. Art Edn. Assn. Avocations: cooking, gardening.

GO, MARILYN DOLAN, federal judge; b. 1950; BA, Radcliffe Coll., 1973; JD, Harvard U., 1977. Bar: N.Y. 1978, Hawaii 1990. Law clk. to Hon. William M. Marutani, Pa. Ct. Common Pleas, Phila., 1977-78; asst. U.S. atty. for ea. dist. N.Y., U.S. Dept. Justice, Bklyn., 1978-82; ptnr. Baden Kramer Huffman Brodsky & Go, N.Y.C., 1982-92; magistrate judge U.S. Dist. Ct. (ea. dist.) N.Y., Bklyn., 1993—. Mem.: Fed. Bar Coun. (trustee 1993—2000). Office: US Dist Ct Eastern Dist New York 225 Cadman Plz E Brooklyn NY 11201-1818 Office Phone: 718-260-2550.

GOATS, DEBBIE, elementary school educator; b. Panorama City, Calif., July 11, 1964; d. Mandel and Joan Buchbinder; m. Michael Goats, May 26, 1991; children: Sarah, Mandy. EdB in Elem. Edn. summa cum laude, Temple U., Phila., 1990. Cert. elem. edn. Okla., sci. endorsement mid. sch./jr. HS Okla. 4th and 5th grade sci. tchr. Crutcho Pub. Schs., Oklahoma City, 1990—95, mid. sch. sci. tchr., 1995—2002; jr. high sci. tchr. Advanced Sci. and Tech. Edn. Ctr., Oklahoma City, 2003—05, sci. dept. chair, student health advisor, 2003—05; 6th grade tchr. McLoud (Okla.) Pub. Sch., 2005—. After sch. tutor Crutcho Pub. Schs., Oklahoma City, 1990—94, sci. club and field rsch. sponsor, 1996—97, sci. coord. lab. sci., sci. fair dir. local level, 1996—2002, asst. dir. bird and butterfly cmty. courtyard, 2002—03; sq. foot gardens facilitator, sci. fair dir. local level Advanced Sci. and Tech. Edn. Ctr., Oklahoma City, 2003—05. Recipient Dean Willard Zahn Tribute award, Temple U., 1990; Pres.'s scholar, 1990. Office: McLoud Schs 529 W Park Mcloud OK 74851 Office Phone: 405-964-3306.

GOBLER, BINA, assistant principal; d. Horace and Edith Dooley; m. Robert Gobler, June 24, 1978; children: Stephanie, Kyle. Edn. specialist, Valdosta State U., Ga. Tchr. Lanier County H.S., Lakeland, Ga., 1977—82, Lowndes Mid. Sch., Valdosta, 1982—86; sch. counselor Hahira (Ga.) Mid. Sch., 1986—91, Lake Pa. (Ga.) Elem. Sch., 1991—99; asst. prin. Lowndes Mid. Sch., Valdosta, 1999—. Vol. First United Meth. Ch., Valdosta, 1995. Mem.: PA Ga. Educators (bldg. rep. 2000). Office Phone: 229-245-2280.

GODBILLE, LARA, museum director; d. Donald and Shirley Tobias. BA, Pepperdine U., 1994, MA, 1997. Cert. archivist Acad. Cert. Archivists, instnl. protection mgr. Internat. Found. Cultural Property Protection. Mus. dir. Civil Engr. Corps/Seabee Mus., Port Hueneme, Calif., 2003—; adj. faculty Calif. State U., Northridge, 2001—02. Curator (exhibitions) A Patchwork History of the San Fernando Valley, assistant curator Expressions in the Gallery: Less Visible Material Culture in the Central Corridor; co-author: (book) The Human Tradition in the American West, (encyclopedia) Encyclopedia of Popular Culture. Office Phone: 805-982-5167.

GODDARD, LISA, meteorologist; b. Sacramento, Calif., Sept. 23, 1966; d. Glenn Kenneth Goddard and Marie Eleanor Betts; m. David Jeffrey Cooperberg, May 2, 1998; children: Matthew Hollis Cooperberg children: Samuel Jonathan Cooperberg. PhD, Princeton U., 1995. Project scientist, Internat. Rsch. Inst. Climate Prediction, Forecasting Group, climate rsch. divsn. Scripps Inst. Oceanography, La Jolla, Calif., 1995—99; rsch. scientist, Internat. Rsch. Inst. Climateand Soc., The Earth Inst. Columbia U., Palisades, NY, 2000—. Contbr. articles and revs. to profl. jours. Global Change fellow, NASA, 1993—95. Mem.: American Geophys. Union, Am. Meteorol. Soc. Office: IRI Earth Inst of Columbia U 61 Route 9W Palisades NY 10964 E-mail: goddard@iri.columbia.edu.

GODDARD, SANDRA KAY, retired elementary school educator; b. Steubenville, Ohio, Oct. 31, 1947; d. Albert Leonard and Mildred Irene (Hill) G. BS in Edn., Miami U., Oxford, Ohio, 1969; MEd, Miami U., 1973. Tchr. Gregg Elem. Sch., Bergholz, Ohio, 1969; media club advisor Springfield Mid. Sch., Bergholz, 2002—06; spelling bee coord., co-coord. Edison Local Spelling Bee, 2003; Praxis III assessor Ohio Dept. Edn., 2002—; tchr. elem. grades Springfield Mid. Sch., Bergholz, 1999—2006; ret. Curriculum and textbook com. Jefferson County Schs., Steubenville, 1994-95, textbook com., 2002; cooperating tchr. Franciscan U., 1972-77, 2002; presenter Ohio Regional Tchrs. Workshop, 1998, County Tchrs. Workshops for ARC/Jefferson County Tchrs., 1992-97, Jefferson County coord. Presch./Kindergarten Workshop for ARC first aid course, 2000, 2002. Publicity chmn., rec. sec., box office chmn., lead actress, asst. dir. Steubenville Players, 1981-83; mem. Edison Local Adv. Coun. on Drug Edn., 1987-99; mem. Edison Local Curriculum Instrn. Com., 1993-99; state judge Ashland Oil Tchr. Achievement awards, 1988-90; regional and state judge Odyssey of the Mind, 1992-97, bd. dirs. Region XI, 1993-97, regional dir., chair governing bd., bd. dirs. Ohio chpt., 1994-97; exec. com. Gregg Elem. PTO, 1990-92; instr. 1st aid, CPR, AED, ARC, 1990—, county disaster team, profl. rescuer status, 1997—, instr. trainer trainer, 2002; instr. CPR for Profl. Rescuer, 2002—. Martha Holden Jennings scholar, 1972-73; mini-grantee Jefferson County Schs., 1991, 94. Mem. NEA (del. to rep. assembly 1979, 85-88), Ohio Edn. Assn. (exec. com. 1983-89, pres.'s cabinet 1985-87, appeals bd. 1994-2002), Ea. Ohio Edn. Assn. (pres. 1978-79, exec. com. 1983-89), Edison Local Edn. Assn. (pres. 1974-75, v.p. 1986-91, exec. com. 1991-94, negotiation's team 1987, 90, 93), Ohio Valley UNISERV Coun. (treas. 1986-92), Delta Kappa Gamma (legis. chair 1990-92). Democrat. Methodist. Avocations: singing, reading, theater, collecting hummels and bells, photography. Home: 200 Fernwood Rd Apt 11 Wintersville OH 43953-9200 Office: Springfield Mid Sch 4569 County Hwy 75 Bergholz OH 43908-9801 Office Phone: 740-768-2420, 740-282-1124. E-mail: sgoddard@eohio.net.

GODDEN, JEAN W., columnist; b. Stamford, Conn., Oct. 1, 1933; d. Maurice Albert and Bernice Elizabeth (Warvel) Hecht; m. Robert W. Godden, Nov. 7, 1952 (dec. Dec. 1985); children: Glenn Scott, Jeffrey Wayne. BA, U. Wash., 1974. News editor Univ. Dist. Herald, Seattle, 1951-53; bookkeeper Omniarts Inc., Seattle, 1963-71; writer editorial page Seattle Post-Intelligencer, Seattle, 1974-80, editorial page editor, 1980-81, bus. editor, 1981-83, city columnist, 1983-91, Seattle Times, 1991—. Author: The Will to Win, 1980, Hasty Put Ins, 1981. Communicator of the Yr. U. Wash. Sch. of Comm., 1995. Mem. LWV (dir. 1969-71), Wash. Press Assn. (Superior Performance award 1979), Soc. Profl. Journalists, Mortarboard, City Club, Phi Beta Kappa. Office: The Seattle Times PO Box 70 Seattle WA 98111-0070

GODDESS, LYNN BARBARA, real estate investor; b. NYC, Mar. 3, 1942; d. Eugene David and Hazel Cecile (Kinzler) Goddess. BS, Columbia U., 1963, postgrad., 1964—66. Coord. John M. Burns Assembly Campaign, NYC, 1963; dir. spl. events, projects Kenneth B. Keating Senatorial Campaign, NYC, 1964; dist. dir. fund raising Muscular Dystrophy Assn. Am. Inc., NYC, 1965-66; exec. acct. fund raising, pub. relations Victor Weingarten Co., NYC, 1966-67, Oram Group (formerly Harold L. Oram Inc.), NYC, 1967-70; dir. devel. City Ctr. Music Drama Inc., NYC, 1970; sales person Whitbread-Nolan, NYC, 1971-73; from asst. v.p. to sr. v.p. Cross and Brown Co., NYC, 1973-1985; sr. dir., comml. real estate Cushman & Wakefield, Inc., NYC, 1985—2004; chmn./CEO LYNN LLC, 2004—. Trustee Young Adult Inst.; founder, chmn. The Hazel K. Goddess Fund for Stroke Rsch. in Women., 2000—; mem. external adv. bd. Ga. Brain and Spinal Injury Rsch. Ctr., 2004—. Mem. Nat. Soc. Fund Raisers, Assn. Fund Dirs., Real Estate Bd. NY (named Most Ingenious Broker Yr. 1975), Women's Forum (bd. dirs.). Personal E-mail: lbg22@earthlink.net.

GODENNE, GHISLAINE DUDLEY, physician, psychotherapist, educator; b. Brussels; came to U.S., 1951; d. Pierre and Olive Dudley (Short) G. BS, Universite Catholique de Louvain, Belgium, 1948, MD, 1952. Intern Providence Hosp., Washington, 1951-52; resident in pediatrics, 1952-54; fellow in pediatrics Mayo Clinic, Rochester, Minn., 1954-57; fellow in pediatric research Johns Hopkins U., 1957-58, assoc. prof. mental hygiene, 1966-82, assoc. prof. psychiatry and pediatrics, 1966-82, psychoanalyst, 1972—, prof. psychology, 1973-90, prof. psychiatry, pediatrics, and mental hygiene, 1982—; resident in psychiatry Johns Hopkins Hosp., Balt., 1958-62, chief adolescent psychiat. service, 1964-73, dir. counseling and psychiat. services, 1973-90, dir. health svcs., 1978-88, dir. emeritus, 1990—; mem. staff various hosps. Balt., 1978-88; clin. prof. psychiatry U. Md., Balt., 1986—. Cons. psychiatrist Cylburn Children's Home, Balt., 1960-81, Catonsville (Md.) C.C., 1968-75, Good Shepherd Ctr., Balt., 1970-74, Assoc. Cath. Charity, Balt., 1970-77, Jewish Family of Children's Svcs., Balt., 1972-77, Mt. Washington Pediat. Hosp., Balt., 1974-81, Sheppard and Enoch Pratt Hosp., Balt., 1973-80, Loyola Coll., Balt., 1990-92. Mem. editorial bd.: Adolescent Psychiatry, 1978-83, Clinical Update Adolescent Psychiatry, 1982-85; contbr. articles to profl. jours. Bd. dirs. Balt. Girl Scouts Assn., 1958-60, 81-82, Met. Balt. Assn. Mental Health, 1965-69, Florence Crittendon Home, 1966-68; trustee McDonough Sch., 1975-83; pres. bd. Trustees Richmond Fellowship Md., 1975-77. Decorated Knight and Officer Order of Leopold (Belgium); recipient Christophe Plantin prize, Belgium, 1989; awarded Nobility Concession with the title of Baroness (Belgium) 1991; recipient Career Teaching award NIMH, 1963-65, Schonfeld award Am. Soc. Adolescent Psychiatry, 1995; grantee Fulbright Found., 1951-52, Parke Davis Co., 1957-58, NIMH, 1961-63. Fellow ACP, Am. Psychiat. Assn. (life), APHA (life), Am. Orthopsychiat. Assn. (life), Am. Soc. Adolescent Psychiatry (life, pres. 1981-82);

mem. AAUP, Am. Psychoanalytic Soc., Md. Soc. Adolescent Psychiatry (pres. 1968-69), Md. Psychiat. Soc. (past chmn. program com., co-chmn. women's com. 1991-96), Md. State Conf. Social Welfare (past mem. child welfare com.), Am. Soc. Adolescent Medicine (charter), Am. U. and Coll. Counseling Ctr. Dirs., Internat. Soc. Adolescent Psychiatry (v.p. 1989-92, sec.-gen. 1992-95, v.p. 1995-99, co-editor monograph 2000-05), Women's Club of Johns Hopkins U. (pres. 1999-2000). Home: 15 Edgevale Rd Baltimore MD 21210-2215 Personal E-mail: g_godenne@comcast.net. Business E-Mail: gigodenn@jhmi.edu.

GODFREY, MARION ROSS, retired special education educator; b. Durham, N.C., Dec. 3, 1946; d. Norman Fletcher and Marjorie Glasson Ross; m. James Hendricks Godfrey; children: Jacob James, Anna Ross Godfrey Alig, Mary Elizabeth. BA in Psychology and Elem. Edn., Duke U., Durham, N.C., 1968; MA in Spl. Edn., George Peabody Coll. for Tchrs., Nashville, 1969. Cert. elem. edn. and spl. edn. N.C., Ga., Oreg., W.Va., Pa., Del. Tchr. learning disabled De Kalb County Schs., Decatur, Ga., 1969—70; coord. TMR program Corvallis Sch. Dist. 509J, Oreg., 1970—71, tchr. 2d grade, 1971—73, Red Clay Sch. dist., Wilmington, Del., 1991—92; tchr. spl. edn. Christina Sch. Dist., Wilmington, 1992—97. Mag. covers, Shanghai Expat. Assn., 1999—2000. Leader, area coord., program cons. Girl Scouts of Am., various locations, 1970—; crisis hotline vol. Contact Del., Wilmington, 2001—. Recipient Honor Pin, Girl Scouts of Am., 1999. Avocation: quilting. Home: 2401 W 17th St Wilmington DE 19806

GODINEZ, MARYE H., anesthesiologist; b. Louisville, Aug. 19, 1945; d. Jerome and Hilda Marye Durbin; m. Rodolfo I. Godinez, June 28, 1969; children: Lucas, Peter, Paul, Adela, Sarah, Ruth. BS, Gonzaga U., Spokane, Wash., 1967; MD, St. Louis U. Sch. Medicine, 1971. Diplomate Am. Coll. Anesthesiologists, 1974. Dir. ENT, neuro and opthalmology anesthesia Barnes Hosp., St. Louis, 1974—77; dir. Temple U. Hosp., Phila., 1978—79; rsch. assoc. Dept. Anesthesiology and Critical Care U. Pa., Phila., 1985—. Contbr. articles to profl. jours. Home: 1036 Speoul Rd Bryn Mawr PA 19010

GODLEY, JOANNE, city health department administrator; 2 children. BA in Human Biology, Stanford U., 1973; MPH, Yale U. Sch. Pub. Hlth., 1977; MD, Yale U. Sch. Medicine, 1977. Area med. officer Abidjan, Ivory Coast and Pretoria, South Africa Peace Corps; med. dir. Phila. Divsn. Social Services, Phila. Dept. Public Health, acting commr., 2005—. Mem.: Am. Bd. Quality Assurance and Utilization Review (diplomat), Am. Bd. Gastroenterology (diplomat), Am. Bd. Internal Medicine (diplomat). Office: Phila Dept Public Health 1101 Market St Ste 840 Philadelphia PA 19107 Office Phone: 215-685-5683. Office Fax: 215-685-5398.*

GODOFF, ANN, publishing executive; b. NYC, July 22, 1949; d. Boris and Marilyn (Rosenstock) G. BFA, NYU, 1972. Sr. editor Simon & Schuster, NYC, 1980-86; editor in chief Atlantic Monthly Press, NYC, 1986-91; exec. editor Random House Inc., NYC, 1991-96, pres., editor-in-chief, 1997—2003; pres., pub. Penguin Group USA, NYC, 2003—. Office: Penguin Group USA 375 Hudson St New York NY 10014*

GODONE-MARESCA, LILLIAN, lawyer; b. Buenos Aires, June 9, 1958; d. Armand C.E. Godone-Signanini and E. Nydia Soracco-Godone; m. Paul Alexander Maresca-Lowell (dec.); children: Catherine Victoria, Gerard Frank, Warren Paul. BA, Cath. U. Buenos Aires, 1975, MA, 1977, JD summa cum laude, 1979, advanced tchg. degree in jud. sci., 1981. Bar: Dist. Ct. Buenos Aires 1980, Calif. 1995, U.S. Dist. Ct. (ea. dist.) Calif. 1995, U.S. Dist. Ct. (so. dist.) Calif. 1998; lic. real estate broker, Calif. Advisor Sub-Sec. of State for Fgn. Trade, Buenos Aires, 1982; pvt. practice law Buenos Aires, 1982-86; therapist Ocean Pkwy. Developmental Ctr., N.Y., 1992; pvt. practice law Sacramento, 1995-96, San Diego, 1997—. Asst. instr. Cath. U., Buenos Aires, 1983-86; adj. instr. U.S. Internat. U., San Diego, spring 1998. Contbr. articles to profl. jours.; author of poetry. Vol. San Diego Vol. Lawyer Program, 1993-94, Legal Svcs. No. Calif., Sacramento, 1995-96; catechist St. Ignatius, Sacramento, 1995-96, St. Michael's, Poway, Calif., 1997-98. Mem. Internat. Soc. Poets (disting.), State Bar Calif., Mothers Twins Club. Republican. Roman Catholic. Avocations: spending time with her children, the right to life, writing. Home: 202 Calle Florecita Escondido CA 92029

GODRIDGE, LESLIE V., bank executive; married; 2 children. AB in History, Smith Coll., 1978; MBA, NYU, 1981. Head asset mgmt. and pvt. bank, head consumer bank and regional comml. lending Bank of NY, N.Y.C., 1981—, sr. exec. v.p., 2004—. Trustee Mus. City of NY; financial leadership forum NY Public Libr.; adv. coun. NY Botanical Gardens; bd. mem. Jr. Achievement of NY. Named one of 25 Women to Watch, US Banker Mag., 2003. Office: The Bank of NY One Wall Street New York NY 10286

GODSMAN, KATHERINE, retired psychologist, educator; b. West, Tex., June 21, 1922; d. William Ernest and Frances Chronie Gulos; m. Mitchell S. Godsman, Oct. 16, 1944; children: Frances Charlotte, Paul Bromley II, Cornelia Mitchell, Elizabeth Allen, William Pickett, Thomas Gregory. BA, Baylor U., 1942, MA with honors, 1943. Cert. sch. psychologist. Asst. to geophysicist Shell Oil Co., Houston, 1943-44; psychologist Juvenile Divsn., Berrien County, Mich., 1956-60; psychologist Title I, acting dir. ednl. measurement Grand Haven (Mich.) Pub. Schs., 1965-72; sch. psychologist Richmond (Va.) City Schs., 1972-84; psychologist Hilltop Rehab., Grand Junction, Colo., 1985-90; prof. Mesa State Coll., Grand Junction, 1985. Vol. psychologist Drug and Alcohol Rehab., Grand Junction, 1984-85; vol. tutor, Grand Junction, 1985-99; vol. sch. psychologist Pub. Schs. Dist. 51, Grand Junction, 1996-2000, vol. tutor, 1985—. Active Grand Junction Symphony Guild Children's Concert, 1995—; mem. Mesa County Rep. Women, 1985—; vol. Holy Family Sch., 2000-2003 Recipient cert. of recognition Sch. Dist. 51, Mesa County, 1997. Mem. APA (life), Friday Book Club (pres. 1987, historian 1996-99), Ea. Star. Episcopalian. Avocation: music. Home: PO Box 1825 Grand Junction CO 81502-1825

GODWIN, CAROL, mathematics educator; d. Miles Edward and Almeda Louise (Jones) Bone; 1 child, Marc. BS in Edn./Math. cum laude, SEMO U., Cape Girardeau, Mo., 1989. Cert. math. tchr. 7-12 Mo. DESE, 1989. Tchr. math. grades 9-12 Bloomfield R-14, Mo., 1989—91; tchr. math. grades 7-12 Lesterville R-4, Mo., 1991—. Recipient Pres. Honors, SEMO U., 1987—89. Mem.: Order Ea. Star, Kappa Delta Pi, Phi Theta Kappa, Alpha Chi. Independent. Avocations: camping, travel.

GODWIN, GAIL KATHLEEN, writer; b. Birmingham, Ala., June 18, 1937; d. Mose Winston and Kathleen (Krahenbuhl) G.; m. Douglas Kennedy, 1960 (div. 1961), m. Ian Marshall, 1965 (div. 1966). Student, Peace Jr. Coll., Raleigh, NC, 1955-57; BA in Journalism, U. NC, 1959, PhD (hon.), 1987; MA in English, U. Iowa, 1968, PhD, 1971; PhD (hon.), U. So.-Sewanee, 1994, SUNY, 1996. News reporter Miami Herald, 1959-60; rep., cons. US Travel Svc., London, 1961-65; editorial asst. Saturday Evening Post, 1966; instr. Univ. Iowa, Iowa City, 1967-71; lectr. Iowa Writer's Workshop, 1972-73, Vassar Coll., 1977, Columbia U. Writing Program, 1978, 81. Author: (novels) The Perfectionists, 1970, Glass People, 1972, The Odd Woman, 1974 (Nat. Book award nomination 1974), Violet Clay, 1978 (Am. Book award nomination 1980), A Mother and Two Daughters, 1982 (Nat. Book award nomination 1982), The Finishing School, 1985, A Southern Family, 1987, Father Melancholy's Daughter, 1991, The Good Husband, 1994, Evensong, 1999, Evenings at Five, 2003; (short stories) Dream Children, 1976, Mr. Bedford and The Muses, 1983; editor: (with Shannon Ravenel) The Best American Short Stories 1985, 1985, Evensong, 1999, Heart: A Personal Journey Through Its Myths & Meanings, 2001, Evenings at Five, 2003, Queen of the Underworld, 2006, The Making of a Writer: Journals, 1961-1963, 2006; librettist: (with Robert Starer) The Last Lover, 1975, Journals of a Songmaker, 1976, Apollonia, 1979, Anna Margarita's Will, 1981, Remembering Felix, 1987, Gregory The Great, 1996, The Other Voice: A Portrait of Hilda of Whitby in Words and Music, 1998, Magdalene At The Tomb, 1999, Abraham Remembers, 2000. Recipient Thomas Wolfe Meml. award Lipinsky Endowment of Western NC Hist. Assn., 1988, Janet Heidinger Kafka award U. Rochester, 1988; fellow Center for Advanced Study, U. Ill., Urbana, 1971-72; Am. specialist USIS, 1976; Nat. Endowment Arts grantee, 1974-75; Guggenheim fellow, 1975-76; recipient award in lit. Am. Acad. and Inst. of Arts and Letters, 1981 Mem. ASCAP, Authors Guild, Authors League. Mailing: PO Box 946 Woodstock NY 12498-0946

GODWIN, HILARY A., chemistry professor, research scientist; BS in chemistry with honors, Univ. Chgo., 1989; PhD in phys. chemistry, Stanford Univ., 1994; NIH post doctoral fellow, Johns Hopkins Univ. Sch. Medicine, 1994—96. Preceptor Interdepartmental Biol. Sci. Program Northwestern Univ., 1996—, asst. prof. Dept. Chemistry and Dept. Biochemistry, Molecular Biology & Cell Biology, 1996—2001, assoc. prof., 2001—. Mem. Lurie Cancer Ctr. Northwestern Univ., 1997—, Dow Chem. Co. Rsch. Prof. in Chemistry, 2002—; prof. Howard Hughes Med. Inst., 2002—. Recipient Stanford Centennial Tchg. Asst. Award, Stanford Univ., 1992, Toxicology New Investigator Award, Burroughs Wellcome Fund, 1998, CAREER Award, Nat. Sci. Found., 1999, Camille Dreyfus Tchr.-Scholar Award, 2000, Paul Saltman Award, 2001; grantee Grad. Rsch. Fellowship, Nat. Sci. Found., 1989—92, Postdoctoral Rsch. Fellowship, Nat. Inst. Health, 1994—96. Mem.: Am. Assoc. Women in Sci., Am. Assoc. for Advancement of Sci., Biophysical Soc., Soc. for Neuroscience, Am. Chem. Soc., Iota Sigma Pi, Phi Beta Kappa. Office: Dept Chemistry Northwestern Univ 2145 Sheridan Rd Evanston IL 60208-3113 Office Phone: 847-467-3543. Office Fax: 847-491-5937. E-mail: h-godwin@northwestern.edu.

GODWIN, MARY JO, editor, librarian, consultant; b. Tarboro, N.C., Jan. 31, 1949; d. Herman Esthol and Mamie Winifred (Felton) Pittman; m. Charles Benjamin Godwin, May 2, 1970. BA, N.C. Wesleyan Coll., 1971; MLS, East Carolina U., 1973. Cert. libr., N.C. From libr. asst. to asst. dir. Edgecombe County Meml. Library, Tarboro, 1970-76, dir., 1977-85; asst. editor Wilson Library Bull., Bronx, N.Y., 1985-89, editor, 1989-92; dir. govt. sales The Oryx Press, Phoenix, 1993-95, dir. mktg. svc., 1995-96, dir. mktg., sales and promotional svcs., 1996-2000; sr. mktg. mgr. Oryx, Greenwood Pub. Group, Westport, 2000—02; dir. mktg. Scarecrow Press and Scarecrow Edn., Rowman & Littlefield Pub. Group, Lanham, Md., 2002—. Mem. White House Conf. on Librs. and Info. Svcs. Task Force; bd. dirs. Libr. Pub. Rels. Coun., 1992-95. Bd. dirs. Friends of Calvert County Pub. Libr., 1994, Osborn Edn. Found., sec., 1997-98; mem. Ariz. Ctr. for the Book. Recipient Robert Downs award for intellectual freedom U. Ill. Grad. Sch. of Libr. Sci., 1992. Mem. ALA (bd. dirs. exhibitor roundtable 2004—, 3M/Jr. Mem. Roundtable Profl. Devel. award 1981), N.C. Libr. Assn. (sec. 1981-83), Info. Futures Inst., Ind. Librs. Exchange Roundtable (v.p., pres. elect 1994, pres. 1995-96). Democrat. Episcopalian. Office: Scarecrow Press 4501 Forbes Blvd Ste 200 Lanham MD 20706 Office Phone: 301-459-3366.

GODWIN, REBECCA THOMPSON, writer, educator, editor; b. Charleston, SC, July 9, 1950; d. Louis Bryan Thompson and Frances Carolyn Douglass; m. John K. Godwin, Oct. 28, 1968 (div. 1988); children: Melissa G. Buffington, Caroline K. Godwin; m. Deane O. Bogardus, Aug. 24, 1988. BA in English, Coastal Carolina Coll., Conway, S.C., 1977; MA in English, Middlebury Coll., 1988. Editor, writer Bennington (Vt.) Coll., 1992—2002; faculty mem. Bennington Coll., 2003—. Mem. faculty Bennington Writing Workshop, 1995, Wildacres Writing Workshops, Little Switzerland, NC, 1996, Bennington July Program, 1999, Bennington MFA in Writing Program, 2002. Author: (novels) Private Parts, 1992, Keeper of the House, 1994; contbr. fiction to Paris Rev., S.C. Rev. Epoch. Named winner, S.C. Fiction Project, 1988; fellow in lit., Nat. Endowment for Arts, 1994—95, MacDowell Colony, 2001. Mem Assoc. Writing Programs. Office: Bennington Coll 1 College Dr Bennington VT 05201 Business E-Mail: rgodwin@bennington.edu.

GODWIN, SARA, writer; b. St. Louis, Feb. 18, 1944; d. Robert Franklin, Jr. and Annabelle Godwin; m. Charles D. James, May 1, 1990; children: Jane, Josh. BA, Calif. State U., 1967; postgrad., UCLA, 1968-70, U. Calif., Berkeley, 1970-71, W.I. Inst. Fairleigh Dickinson U., St. Croix, V.I., 1971-72; MA, Dominican Coll., 1974. Writer, editor Ortho Books, Std. Oil Calif., San Francisco, 1975-77; writer, editor Gannett Corp., San Rafael, Calif., 1977-79; sr. writer Shaklee Corp., San Francisco, 1979-88; freelance writer Marin County, Calif., 1988—. Featured spkr. Ask the Gardener Sta. KSFO, San Francisco, 1980—81; contbr., prodr. Raw Radio Travel, 1998—. Author: (book) Seals, 1990, Gorillas, 1990, The Angler's Companion, 1992, Hummingbirds, 1991, The Gardener's Companion, 1992 (N.Y. Times Rev., Garden Book Club selection), Landscaping Decks and Patios, 1994, Scott's See and Do: Lawns and Groundcovers, 1995; contbr. book Last Puff, 1990 (Lit. Guild selection), book The Sea, 1993; author (with others): (book) Smith and Hawken Book of Outdoor Gardening, 1996; author: (screenplays) Discover Canada, Discovering The USA; manuscript editor: All About Perennials, 1992, prin. lexicographer: Nat. Gardening Assn. Dictionary of Horticulture, 1994; scriptwriter, prodr.: China: The Middle Kingdom; contbr. CD ROM Microsoft Complete Gardening, 1996, CD ROM Frommer's Boston, 1996, articles to numerous U.S. and fgn. mags. Recipient 1st prize for personal column, Calif. Press Women, 1984. Mem.: PEN, Garden Writers Assn., Am. Soc. Journalists and Authors, Authors Guild. Avocations: reading, travel, gardening, fly fishing. Home: PO Box 1503 Ross CA 94957-1503

GOEDKEN, ANN MARY, psychotherapist; b. Dubuque, Iowa, Feb. 28, 1949; d. Earl M. and Ruth A. (Evers) Wessels; m. Dennis D. Goedken, June 5, 1970; children: Eric, Jill. Diploma in nursing, Mercy Med. Ctr., Dubuque, 1970; BA, U. Wash., 1979; MS, Winona (Minn.) State U., 1989. RN, Wis.; approved psychotherapy provider, Wis.; cert. ind. clin. social worker, Wis., profl. counselor, Wis. Staff nurse, counselor to adolescents Mercy Med. Ctr., 1976-77; rsch. asst. U. Wash., Seattle, 1979; staff nurse, therapist St. Francis Med. Ctr., La Crosse, Wis., 1980, La Crosse Luth. Hosp., 1980-81, Trempealeau County Health Care Ctr., Whitehall, Wis., 1981-89, psychotherapist, educator, 1989—2003; clin. assessor No. Home Children & Family Svcs., Phila., 2003—04; psychotherapist Couseling Solutions, Madison, Wis., 2005. Mem. ACA, Nat. Honor Soc. Avocations: family activities, reading, theater, playing piano and guitar, singing.

GOEDKEN, JENNIFER LYNN, mathematics educator; b. Charlotte, NC; m. Eric Goedken; 1 child, Evan. BBA in Human Resource Mgmt., Tarleton State U., Stephenville, Tex., 1994. Tchr. Granbury Ind. Sch. Dist., Tex., 1998—99, Dublin Ind. Sch. Dist., 1999—2000, Cy-Fair Ind. Sch. Dist., Houston, 2000—. Presbyterian.

GOEHNER, DONNA MARIE, retired university dean; b. Chgo., Mar. 9, 1941; d. Robert and Elizabeth (Cseke) Barra; m. George Louis Goehner, Dec. 16, 1961; 1 child, Michelle Renee. BS in English, So. Ill. U., 1963; MSLS, U. Ill., 1966, CAS in L.S., 1974; PhD in Edn., So. Ill. U., 1983. Rsch. assoc. U. Ill., Urbana, 1966-67; high sch. librarian St. Joseph-Ogden Sch. System, St. Joseph, Ill., 1967-68; curriculum lab librarian Western Ill. U., Macomb, 1968-73, periodicals librarian, 1974-76, coordinator for tech. svcs., 1977-78, acquisitions and collection devel. librarian, 1979-86, acting dir. library, 1986, dean library svcs., 1988-97; assoc. Univ. librarian for tech. and adminstrv. svcs. Ill. State U., Normal, 1986-88; ret., 1998. Contbr. articles to profl. jours. Mem. ALA, Assn. Coll. and Rsch. Libraries (chmn. univ. libraries sect. 1988-89), Ill. Assn. Coll. and Rsch. Libraries (pres. 1985-86), Ill. Library Assn. (Acad.Librarian of Yr. 1989). Office: Univ Library Western Ill U Macomb IL 61455

GOEKE, LORISE ANN, principal, elementary school educator; b. Hoboken, N.J., July 22, 1961; d. MaryAnn and Walter George Carlson (Stepfather), Robert Ardito; m. Christopher John Goeke, Oct. 6, 2001; m. John Russo Mancuso, Sept. 24, 1981 (div. Feb. 15, 2001); children: Marc John Mancuso, Todd James Mancuso, Danielle Marie Mancuso. BA in Elem. Edn. and English Lit., William Paterson U.; MA in Ednl. Adminstrn. and Supervision, Seton Hall U.; EdD in Ednl. Leadership, Nova Southeastern U. English tchr. N.J., 2001, elem. edn. tchr. N.J., 2001, prin., supr. N.J., 2003. Tchr. St. Therese Sch., Paterson, NJ, 1994—2000; prin. Our Lady of Lourdes Sch., Paterson, 2000—03, Kingwood Twp. Sch., Frenchtown, NJ, 2003—. Adj. prof. William Paterson U., Wayne, NJ, 2003—05. Mem.: N.J. Prin.'s and Supervisors Assn., Garden State Prin.'s Assn., Nat. Coun. Tchrs. of English, Nat. Assn. Elem. Prins. Office Phone: 908-996-2941. Office Fax: 908-996-7268. Business E-Mail: lgoeke@kingwoodschool.org.

GOERNER, FREDA RUTH, secondary school educator; b. Gladewater, Tex., Apr. 21, 1953; m. Dennis Cornell Goerner, May 22, 1992; children: Brent, Ashley Lane Haden; children: Dustin Charles Bennett, Brittany Denese Bennett. BA, LeTourneau U., Longview, Tex., 1973—75. Cert. Tchr. Tex. Dept. Edn., 1988. Owner/operator Dance Studio, Longview, Tex., 1971—88; drill team dir. Bobcat Belles, Hallsville, 1988—. Drill team dir.: dance team. Recipient Nat. Grand Champion Drill Team, Showtime Internat., 1996, 1997, 1998, 1999, 2006. Mem.: Beta Sigma Phi (assoc. Pledge of Yr. 2002). Conservative. Baptist. Avocations: shopping, bowling, outdoor activities, travel. Home: 198 Simpson St Longview TX 75605 Office: Bobcat Belles PO Box 810 Hallsville TX 75650 Office Phone: 903-668-5990 ext 2035.

GOES, KATHLEEN ANN, secondary school educator; b. New Bedford, Mass., Jan. 13, 1951; d. Filento Andrade and Lillian (Cabral) G. BA in Psychology, U. Mass., North Dartmouth, 1976; postgrad., Ctrl. Conn. State U., 1987—98. Cert. K-8 elem. tchr., K-12 music tchr., Mass. Social worker Dept. Social Svcs., Cambridge, Mass., 1980-85; pvt. tchr. voice and piano, New Bedford, 1985-88; tchr. vocal music New Bedford Pub. Sch., 1985-90; tchr. music, choral dir. Fairhaven (Mass.) H.S., 1991—. Singer, actress, southeastern New Eng., 1974—; dir. music ministry St. Mary's Ch., South Dartmouth, Mass., 1988—; bd. dirs., sec. New Bedford Festival Theatre, 1990-97, v.p., 1997-99, mem. adv. bd., 1999—. Dir. musicals Guys and Dolls, State Fair, Me and My Girl, The Sound of Music, Cinderella, My Fair Lady, Bye, Bye Birdie, You're a Good Man Charlie Brown, How to Succeed in Business Without Really Trying, Little Shop of Horrors, The Boyfriend, Godspell, Jesus Christ Superstar; performed the mother in Amahl and the Night Visitors; actress, singer in musicals Fiddler on the Roof, Godspell, Phantom, The Sound of Music. Bd. dirs. New Bedford Symphony Orch., 1994-96. Named Promising Young Artist, Crescendo Club, Boston, 1981; recipient outstanding leadership award Fairhaven Assn. for Music Edn., 1995. Mem. NEA, Am. Choral Dirs. Assn., Nat. Pastoral Musicians Assn., New Eng. Theatre Conf., Drama League, Music Educators Nat. Conf., Mass. Tchrs. Assn., Mass. Music Educators Assn., Whale Hist. League. Roman Catholic. Avocations: cooking, crafts, computers, boating, scenic design. Home: 363 Maple St New Bedford MA 02740-1075 Office: Fairhaven HS 12 Huttleston Ave Fairhaven MA 02719-3122

GOESSL, CELINE, head of religious order; d. Irving Charles Goessl and Theresa Marie Decker. BS Edn., Alverno Coll., Milw., 1971; ThM, St. John U., Collegeville, Minn., 1973; D Ministry, St. Mary U. & Sem., Balt., 1988. Myers-Briggs Personality Profile MBTI, 1982, Enneagram Aspell Assocs., 1992. Dir. religious edn., musician Diocese of Superior Wis., Mercer, 1954—57; tchr., prin. St. Joseph Sch., Rhinelander, Wis., 1957—71; pastoral assoc. Diocese of Green Bay Wis, Appleton/Omro, 1976—85; pastoral adminstr. Diocese of Gaylord Mich., Bellaire, 1987—2004; provincial leader Holy Cross Sisters, Merrill, Wis., 2006—. Spiritual dir. Holy Cross Sisters, Merrill, 1990—. Dir.: (human development workshops) Titles are on web site www.crossbeams.org. Mem. Big Bros.-Big Sisters, Appleton, Wis., 1980—85, Bus. & Profl. Women, Mancelona, Mich., 1987—90, Midwest Pastoral Adminstrs., Racine, Wis., 1990—2005; treas. Women's Ordination Conf., Washington, 2004—06; bd. mem. Habitat for Humanity, Mancelona, 1988—91. Mem.: Leadership Conf. Women Religious (assoc.). Roman Catholic. Home: 700 East Riverside Avenue Merrill WI 54452 Office: Holy Cross Sisters 1400 O'Day Street Merrill WI 54452

GOESTENKORS, GAIL, basketball coach; b. Waterford, Mich., Feb. 26, 1963; m. Mark Simons. BA, Saginaw Valley State U., 1985. Grad. asst. Iowa State U., 1985-86; asst. coach basketball Purdue U., West Lafayette, Ind., 1986-92; head basketball coach Duke U., Durham, NC, 1992—. Coach U.S. Jones Cup Team, taiwan; head coach Festival Trials, 1991, 95; coach 1994 ACC All-Star Team, Latvia, Lithuania. Named ACC Coach of the Yr., 1995-96, 97-98, 98-99, Nat. Coach of Yr. 1999. Office: Duke University Cameron Indoor Stadium PO Box 90555 Durham NC 27708-0555

GOETHE, ELIZABETH HOGUE, music educator; b. Balt., May 4, 1943; d. Paul Robert and Charlotte H. (Rigney) H.; m. Frederick Martin Goethe, June 30, 1973; children: Elizabeth Anne, Jonathan David. BS, Towson U., 1965; MEd in Music, U. Md., 1972. Cert. tchr. piano. Accompanist Vera Hax Dance Studio, Balt., 1962-66; music tchr. Balt. County Pub. Schs., 1965-74; ch. choir dir. Glyndon, Ellicott City, Md., 1976-79; class piano tchr. Balt. County Pub. Schs., 1980—83; piano tchr. Reisterstown, Md., 1978—; pvt. piano tchr., 1978—; music tchr. St. John's Episcopal Pre-Sch., Glyndon, 1978—2000. Mem. Choristers Guild, 1976-79. Mem. Music Tchrs. Nat. Assn. (ea. divsn. sec. 1996-98), Md. State Music Tchrs. Assn. (convention chair 1991-93, v.p. student activities 1993-97, cert. com. 1991-97), Greater Columbia Music Tchrs. Assn. (sec. 1996-98), Greater Balt. Music Tchrs. Assn. (treas. 1997—), Nat. Guild of Piano Tchrs. (adjudicator), Am. Coll. Musicians. Republican. Episcopalian. Home and Office: 120 Nicodemus Rd Reisterstown MD 21136-3245

GOETSCH, LARA, marketing professional, director; d. Donald and Kathleen Goetsch. BS in Journalism, Northwestern U., Ill., 1993. Asst. theatre mgr. The Theatre Sch. at DePaul U., Chgo., 1993—95, pub. rels. dir., 1995—97, dir. mktg. and pub. rels., 1997—2006; dir. mktg. and comm. TimeLine Theatre Co., Chgo., 2006—. Prodr.: (theatre prodn.) Not About Nightingales (Joseph Jefferson Citation for Outstanding Prodn., 2001), The Crucible (Joseph Jefferson Citation for Outstanding Prodn., 2002), Awake and Sing! (Joseph Jefferson Citation for Outstanding Prodn., 2003). Mem. TimeLine Theatre Co., Chgo., 1997—2006. Mem.: League of Chgo. Theaters Mktg. Cmty (chair 2006—), Publicity Club of Chgo., Medill Alumni Club of Chgo. (co-chair 1998—2001).

GOETZ, BETTY BARRETT, physicist; b. Atlanta, Jan. 8, 1943; d. Vose Matthew and Fay (Howard) Barrett; m. Charles David Goetz, Mar. 25, 1972; children: Lisa Fay, Gayle Catherine. BA, Emory U., 1963, M in Med. Sci, 1972; BS, U. Ga., 1965. Tchr. jr. high sci. City of Decatur (Ga.) Bd. of Edn., 1965-66; tech. specialist, radiology Emory U. Sch. Medicine, Atlanta, 1967-72, sr. assoc. allied health professions, 1977-82, health physicist, 1973-92, sr. assoc. cmty. health, 1983-96, dep. radiation safety officer, 1993, radiation safety officer, 1994—. Adj. sr. assoc. Emory U. Sch. Pub. Health, 1991—; cons. in field. Contbr. articles to profl. jours. Mem. Decatur, Ga. Edn. Adv. Com., 1987, St. Thomas More Parents Club, Decatur, 1980-84, St. Thomas More Bd. Edn., 1981-85, Internat. Platform Assn., 1989-90, Ga. Conservancy, 1989—, Friends of Fernbank, 1989—. Mem. Health Physics Soc. (sec. Atlanta chpt. 1976-79, pres.-elect 1999), Am. Assn. of Physicists in Medicine (S.E. chpt.), Ga. Assn. Radio Physicists, S.E. U. Radiation Safety Officers. Republican. Methodist. Avocations: reading, gardening. Home: 1599 Rangewood Dr SW Lilburn GA 30047-4514 Office: Emory U Radiation Safety Ofc Atlanta GA 30322-0001 E-mail: bgoetz@ehso.emory.edu.

GOETZE, LYDIA B., biology educator; b. Bar Harbor, Maine, Feb. 4, 1941; d. E. Farnham and Gladys Whitmore Butler; m. Christopher Goetze, 1964 (dec. 1977); children: Elizabeth G. Record, Erica. AB cum laude, Harvard/Radcliffe U., Cambridge, Mass., 1963; MAT in Biology, Johns Hopkins U., Balt., 1964. Biology tchr. Southern HS, Balt., 1964, Newton (North) HS, Mass., 1964—69; editor, sci. texts D.C. Heath, Lexington, 1980; biology instr., dept. chair, coach, A. Wells Peck instructorship Phillips Acad., Andover, 1980—2005; photography workshop instr., 2005—. Cons., workshop instr. Internat. Acad. Partnership, Pakistan, 1995; steering com. Phillips Acad., 1995—96. Contbr. articles to magazines. Asst. editor Appalachian

Mountain Club, Boston, 1975—77; pres. LWV, Ipswich, Mass., 1975—77; bd. dirs. Randolph Mountain Club, NH, 2004—. Avocations: sailing, hiking, photography, choral singing, reading. Home: Box 429 Southwest Harbor ME 04679

GOETZINGER, ELEANOR, special education educator; BS, Northwestern Okla. State U., 1983; M in Edn., Southwestern Okla. State U., 1998; PhD (hon.), U. Okla., 2006. Cert. learning disability, mentally handicapped educator Okla., mild, moderate, severe, profound, multiple disabilities spl. edn.educator Okla., adminstrn., secondary level Okla., physical edn., health, safety, other health impairment educator Okla. Pastry chef apprentice Hyatt Hotel, Indian Wells, Calif., 1988—89; truman cottage mgr., sous chef Big Cedar Lodge, Branson, Mo., 1990—95; spl. edn. tchr. Albuquerque (N. Mex.) Pub. Schs., 1997; adj. prof. Southwestern Okla. State U., Weatherford, 1998—99; spl. edn. tchr. Putnam City HS, Oklahoma City, 2001—04, head spl. edn. dept., 2004—; spl. edn. tchr. Arapaho (Okla.) Pub. Schs. Sch. dist. cons. Self Employed, Oklahoma City, 2001—06. Commr. Planning & Zoning Commn., Village, Okla., 2003—06. Mem.: Coun. Children with Behavioral Disorders (assoc.), Kappa Delta Pi, Gamma Beta Phi, Phi Kappa Phi (assoc.). Achievements include research in response cards to enhance student participation and increase academics; study student participation and academic achieve. in a secondary spl. edn. classroom. Office Phone: 405-789-4350 2127.

GOFF, HEATHER ELIZABETH, psychiatrist; d. Christopher Wallick and Holly Lynn Goff. BA in Biochemistry, Swarthmore Coll., Pa., 1996; MD, NY Med. Coll., Valhalla, 2002. Resident in psychiatry Yale U. Sch. Medicine, New Haven, 2002—06; psychiatry fellow Yale Child Study Ctr., New Haven, 2006—. Coord. Conn. Residents Day, Farmington, 2003—05. Contbr. Vol. disaster mental health, post-Hurricane Katrina ARC, New Orleans, 2005. Grantee, Howard Hughes Med. Inst., 1995—96. Mem.: Yale Psychiatry Residency Assn. (sec. 2003—04), Am. Acad. Child and Adolescent Psychiatry, Am. Psychiat. Assn., Sigma Xi.

GOFF, MARILYN RUSSELL MCCLAIN, counselor; b. Laurelton, N.Y., Aug. 18, 1956; d. Russell H. and Lillian A. (Yarbrough) McClain; m. David W. Goff, Apr. 3, 2004; 1 child, Amy Lynne Roberts White. BS in Social Work, Harding U., 1977; MS in Adult Edn., Okla. State U., 1997. Career counselor Foothills Vo-Tech Sch., Searcy, Ark., 1977-78; social worker Dept. Social Svcs., Tulsa, 1978-79; owner, operator, instr. Spl. Deliveries Childbirth Preparation Ctr., Tulsa, 1980-85; mgr. One Hour Moto Photo, Tulsa, 1986-89; area mgr. Mervyn's, Tulsa, 1989-92; admissions counselor Rogers State U., Claremore, Okla., 1992-96, student counselor, 1996—2005, advisor specialist, 2000—05; asst. dir. Upward Bound, 2005—. Primary advisor Adult Students Aspiring Prosper, Claremore, 1993—2004; pres. Rogers U. Staff Assn., 1995—97, mem. staff senate, 1995—2003, CASA adv., 1997—; parent educator Parenting Ptnrs., Claremore, 1994—95. Mem. Oologah PTA, 1990—97; sec. Oologah-Talala Sch. Found., 1994—95, pres., 1995—99, trustee, 1994—2001; mem. statue and hotel com. Rogers County Hist. Soc., Claremore, 1994—2002. Mem.: Am. Assn. Adult and Continuing Edn., Okla. Acad. Advising Assn., Sertoma. Republican. Baptist. Avocations: needlepoint, reading, piano. Home: 18021 Oaklawn Dr Claremore OK 74017-3681 Office: Rogers State Univ 1701 W Will Rogers Blvd Claremore OK 74017-3259 Office Phone: 918-343-7572. Business E-Mail: mmcclain-goff@rsu.edu.

GOFFERJE, HADWIG, retired language educator; b. Frankfurt, Germany, Sept. 4, 1937; d. Karl and Edith Gofferje; m. Michael L. Dertouzos (dec.); children: Alexandra Rowe, Leonidas Dertouzos. Bachelors, U. Tubingen, Germany, 1959; PhD, MIT, Cambridge, 1967. Fulbright scholar, tchg. asst. Wellesley Coll., Mass., 1960—62; rsch. assoc. Boston (Mass.) U., 1967—70; German tchr. Brookline (Mass.) Pub. Schools, 1994—2004, Needham (Mass.) Pub. Schools, 1994—2004. Mem. Newton Music Sch., 1993—. Author: A Memoir in Letters, My Life on Both Sides of the Iron Curtain, 2005. Mem. corp. Newton Music Sch. Fulbright scholar, Wellesley Coll., 1960—61. Mem.: MIT Club Boston. Avocations: viola, chamber music.

GOFFNER, GWENDOLYN DENISE, elementary school educator; b. Lebanon, Ky., Nov. 19, 1963; d. James R. and Shirley A. Wright; m. Rory C. Goffner; children: Anthony, Branden. AA, U. Ky.; BA, MA, U. Louisville; postgrad., Western Ky. U. Mgr. Strategic Mortgage, Louisville; ops. sopr. Humana Corp., Louisville, human resources specialist; home sch. coord. Jefferson County Pub. Schs., Louisville, educator exceptional children, instnl. coach, elem. prin. intern. Appraisal coord. Strategic Mktg., Louisville. Author: Principals for Tomorrow, 2005, Women in School Administration, 2003—05. Mem. parent adv. coun. U. Louisville, 2005. Mem.: Delta Zeta, Phi Delta Kappa (co-v.p., membership officer 2002—04). Home: 5105 Dorose Ct Louisville KY 40291-1554

GOFORTH, CHERYL CLEWELL, medical/surgical nurse; b. Endicott, N.Y., Sept. 22, 1954; d. Robert G. and Althea (Keirle) Clewell; m. David L. Goforth, May 29, 1976; 1 child, Justin Tyler. BSN, Vanderbilt U., Nashville, 1976; MSN, Vanderbilt U., 1979; postgrad., U. Tenn., 1994. CEN; cert. trauma care nurse, BLS, ALS instr.; cert. family nurse practitioner. Asst. prof. Austin Peay State U., Clarksville, Tenn., 1979-81; clin. specialist, clin. nurse mgr. Vanderbilt U., 1981-84; asst. prof. U. Tenn., Knoxville, 1984-88; clin. mgr., clin. specialist emergency rm. Meth. Med. Ctr., Oak Ridge, 1988-94; family nurse practitioner, 1994—. Mem. Emergency Nurses Assn., Sigma Theta Tau. Home: 11425 Couch Mill Rd Knoxville TN 37931-2908

GOGGINS, COLLEEN A., health products executive; B in Mktg., U. of Wis.; grad., Northwestern U. Kellogg Sch. Mgmt., 1979. With Johnson & Johnson, New Brunswick, NJ, 1981—, dir. mktg. GmbH Germany, 1990—92, pres. Can., 1992—94, pres. consumer products, 1995—98, co. grp. chmn., 1998—2001, worldwide chmn. consumer and personal care grp., mem. exec. com. New Brunswick, NJ, 2001—. Exec. advisory bd. U. of Wis Madison Sch. of Bus. Named one of 50 Most Powerful Women in Business, Fortune mag., 2006. Office: Johnson & Johnson 1 Johnson & Johnson Plz New Brunswick NJ 08933*

GOGICK, KATHLEEN CHRISTINE, magazine editor, publisher; b. N.J., Aug. 3, 1945; d. Joseph John and Emeline (Radwin) Wadowski; m. Robert Joseph Gogick, Feb. 24, 1968; 1 son, Jonathan. BS, Fairleigh Dickinson U., Rutherford, N.J., 1967. Asst. beauty, fiction editor Cosmopolitan Mag., N.Y.C., 1967-68; mdsg. and publicity coordinator Co-ed Mag., N.Y.C., 1968-69, editor in chief, 1976-80; creative svcs. coord. Estee Lauder, Inc., N.Y.C., 1969-71; assoc. beauty, health editor Town and Country Mag., N.Y.C., 1971-75; editorial dir. home econs. div. Scholastic Inc., 1981-86; pres., pub. C.M.I. (formerly Corp. Mags. Inc.), 1986—98; v.p. Redwood Custom Comm., 1999—2002; pres. Danilo Black Custom Media Internat., 2002—05. Founder, editor: Student mag., 1989-96, College Counselor, 1993-96, Countdown to College Calendar, 1996. Trustee Fairleigh Dickinson U., 1980-89. Mem. Am. Student Assn., Inc. (founder, pres.). Clubs: University. Home and Office: 165 Lloyd Rd Montclair NJ 07042-1732 Business E-Mail: kathy@danitoblackusa.com.

GOGUE, SUSAN DIANE, elementary school educator; b. Baraboo, Wis., Aug. 7, 1948; d. William L. and Marian A. Schreiber; m. Buddy Gogue, July 16, 1977; children: Amy E. Frank, Marianne C. Steiner, Robyn L. MS in Ednl. Adminstrn., Winona State U., Minn., 1990. Tchr. grade 7 - 8 St. Joseph's Sch., Baraboo, Wis., 1971—74; tchr. social studies, dept. chair Jack Young Mid. Sch., 1974—; coord., tutor title VII Baraboo Sch. Dist., 1996—, coord. ACE program, 2005—. Cons. US Dept. Edn., Coun. Chief State Sch. Officers, Shepherdstown, W.Va., 1999; local coord. Japan-Wis. Edn. Connection, Baraboo, 2000—06; local coord. Japan sister sch. project Wis. Dept. Pub. Instrn., Madison, 1999—2002, cons. performance assessment project, 1996—2005. Recipient Tchr. Yr., Wis. Coun. Adminstrs. Spl. Edn., 1982, Severn Rinkob Secondary Tchr. Yr. award, Baraboo Sch. Dist., 1988, Senator Herb Kohl award, Herb Kohl Ednl. Found., 2004, Elgin Heinz Tchr. Yr. award, US - Japan Found., 2005, Little Red Pick-Up Truck award, Baraboo Sch. Dist., 2005; fellow, U.S. Japan Found., 1989, U. Colo., 1998, Fulbright Meml. Fund, 1999, Nat. Coun. Econ. Edn., 2003, Goethe Inst., 2004. Mem.: South Ctrl. Edn. Assn. (profl. devel. com. 1998—), Baraboo Edn. Assn. (sec. 1975—), Nat. Coun. Social Studies, Wis. Coun. Social Studies (v.p. 1998—2003). Presbyterian. Home: 209 Campus View Drive Baraboo WI 53913 Office: Jack Young Middle School 1531 Draper Street Baraboo WI 53913 Office Phone: 608-355-3930. Office Fax: 608-355-3998. E-mail: sgogue@baraboo.k12.wi.us.

GOH, CHAN HON, ballerina; b. Beijing, Feb. 1, 1969; arrived in Can, 1977; d. Choo Chiat and Lin Yee Goh. Attended Goh Ballet Academy, Vancouver. Corp de ballet dancer Nat. Ballet of Can., Toronto, 1988-90, second soloist, 1990-92, first soloist, 1992-93, prin. dancer, 1994—, The Suzanne Farrell Ballet, 1999—. Guest artist various ballet companies in Europe, Australia, N. Am., Asia; entrepreneur, owner Principal by Chan Hon Goh Inc., TM Dance Supplies and Dance Shoes, 1996—. Dancer (prin. roles) The Sleeping Beauty, La Fille Mal Gardée, Don Quixote, Romeo & Juliet, Tristan and Isolde, The Nutcracker, Taming of the Shrew, Swan Lake, Giselle, Cinderella, La Boutique Fantasque, La Sylphide, The Dream, Paquita, La Ronde, Desir, Mozartiana, La Bayadere, Apollo, Jewels, Afternoon of a Faun, Forgotten Land, others; author: Beyond the Dance: A Ballerina's Life, 2002; prodr., star and lead: The Stars of N.Am. Ballet, 2002; Dance at the Main Stage, 2003; An Evening with Dancers of the Nat. Ballet of Can, 2003. Recipient Prix de Lausanne, 1986, Solo Seal award, Royal Acad Dance, 1987, Silver Medal, Adelene Genee Comp, London, 1988, New Pioneers Arts award, 2005, ACCE Entrepreneurial award for the innovation of prin. shoes, 2005; Can. Coun. grantee, 1987. Office: Nat Ballet of Canada 470 Queens Quay W Toronto ON Canada M5E 3K4 Office Phone: 416-345-9686.

GOHEEN, DEBRA ELAINE, secondary school educator; b. Beaumont, Tex., Apr. 11, 1962; d. Kenneth Charles and Doris Elaine (Berry) Cloud; m. Norman Ray Goheen, June 3, 1994. BA, Tex. A&M U., Commerce, 1986. Cert. tchr. English and History, Tex. English tchr. South Garland H.S., Garland, Tex., 1986-94, history tchr., 1994—2005, freshman cheerleader coach, 1987—90, junior varsity/varsity cheerleader coach, 1990—94; lbr. Webb Middle Sch., Garland, 2005—. Active various coms. Heather Glen Elem. PTA, Garland, pres., 1997-99; dir. Pee Vee Drill Team, Garland Cheerleader Drill Team Assn., 1996-98, dir. Bison Pep Club; mem. Fisrt Christian Ch. (Disciples of Christ). Avocations: reading, archaeology, travel, dance. Office: Webb Middle Sch 1610 Spring Creek Garland TX 75040

GOIN, SUZANNE, chef; b. LA, Sept. 25, 1966; m. David Lentz. BA in History, Brown U.; apprenticeship, Ma Maison, L.A. Line cook Chez Panisse, Berkeley, Calif., 1990-92, Arpege Brigade, Paris, 1993; sous chef Olives, Boston, 1993; exec. chef Alloro, Boston, 1994-96, Campanile, LA, 1997-98; co-owner, exec. chef Lucques, West Hollywood, 1998—, A.O.C., 2002—, The Hungry Cat, 2005—. Author (with Teri Gelber): (cookbooks) Sunday Suppers at Lucques, 2005 (James Beard award, 2006). Named Best Creative Chef Boston mag., 1994, One of Best New Chefs, Food and Wine Mag., 1999, Best Chef award nominee, 2003, 2004, 2005, Best Chef: Calif. award of Excellence, James Beard Found., 2006. Office: Lucques 8474 Melrose Ave West Hollywood CA 90069-5313*

GOINS, JESSICA D., editor; d. James and Mildred L. Goins. BS in Bus. Adminstrn., Calif. State U. Dominguez Hills, Carson. Reporter Newsday, 1997; editl. asst. Entrepreneur Mag., 1997—98; copy editor Investor's Bus. Daily, L.A., 1998—99, LA Times Syndicate, 1999—2003, The Press-Enterprise, Riverside, Calif., 2003—05; editor Glencoe/McGraw-Hill, Woodland Hills, Calif., 2005—. Freelance editor and writer. Vol. Calif. African Am. Mus., L.A., 1993—97, L.A. County Mus. Art, 2003. Avocations: reading, writing, cooking, coin collecting/numismatics, travel. Office: Glencoe/McGraw-Hill Ste 500 21600 Oxnard St Woodland Hills CA 91367 Office Phone: 818-615-2720. Personal E-mail: jessica.goins@usa.net. Business E-Mail: jessica_goins@mcgraw-hill.com.

GOIZUETA, OLGA (OLGA CASTELEIRO DE GOIZUETA), foundation administrator, philanthropist; b. Havana, Cuba; arrived in US, 1960; m. Roberto Crispulo Goizueta, June 14, 1953 (dec.); children: Roberto Segundo, Olga M. Goizueta Rawls, Javier C., Carlos(dec.). Co-founder Goizueta Found., Atlanta, 1992—, chair exec. com.; bd. trustees Emory U., 1999—. Named a Dame of St. Gregory the Great, Pope John Paul II, 2003. Office: Goizueta Found Ste 520 4401 Northside Pkwy Atlanta GA 30327 Office Phone: 404-239-0390. Office Fax: 404-239-0018.

GOKTEPE, JANET ROSE, retired financial analyst; b. Anniston, Ala., Nov. 27, 1950; d. Clifton Frank and Bertha Ezel (Yates) Yeager; children: Katherine Emel, Joy Saadet. BS in Bus. & Mgmt. magna cum laude, U. Md., 1976, MBA with honors, 1979, PhD in Bus. & Mgmt. with honors, 1986. Sec. dept. of justice FBI, Washington, 1969-72, Dept. of Treasury, Washington, 1972-75; rsch. analyst Comptroller of Currency, Washington, 1975-77, fin. analyst, 1977, Interstate Commerce Commn., Washington, 1978-86, Farm Credit Adminstrn., McLean, Va., 1986—2005; ret., 2005. Lectr. bus. Montgomery Coll., Rockville, Md., 1979-80, U. Md., College Park, 1980-82, U. Md. Grad. Sch., College Park, 1988-89. Author: (with others) Small Groups and Social Interaction, 1983; contbr. articles to profl. jours. Co-chair fed. women's program Interstate Commerce Commn., Washington, 1980-81; vol. Seven Locks Elem. Sch., Bethesda, Md., 1986-94; chair child care task force Farm Credit Adminstrn., McLean, 1989-90. Recipient Outstanding Vol. Svc. certs. Seven Locks Elem. Sch., 1987, 91, 94, Commendation letter Pres. Gerald Ford, 1974. Mem. Nat. Assn. Female Execs., Nat. Capitol Women's Network, Exec. Women in Govt., Assn. Investment Mgmt. and Rsch., Wash. Assn. Money Mgrs., Beta Gamma Sigma, Phi Kappa Phi. Avocations: biking, walking, listening to music. Home: 1439 Mclean Mews Ct Mc Lean VA 22101-3800 Personal E-mail: janetgoktepe@yahoo.com.

GOLAN, YVETTE Y., consumer products company executive, lawyer; b. Netanya, Israel, July 9, 1978; arrived in U.S., 1981; d. Eddie Yehouda and Alisa Golan. BA summa cum laude, U. Tex., Austin, 1999; JD magna cum laude, Cornell U., Ithaca, N.Y., 2002. Clk. 9th Cir. Ct. Appeals, San Diego, 2002—03; assoc. Kirkland and Ellis, LLP, Chgo., 2003—05, Beck Redden and Secrest LLP, Houston, 2005; CEO World Innova Corp., Houston, 2005—. Contbr. articles to profl. jours. Mem. Child Adv. Inc., Houston, 2006. Mem.: ABA, Order of Coif. Office: World Innova Corp Two Allen Ctr 1200 Smith St Ste 1600 Houston TX 77002 Business E-Mail: ygolan@worldinnova.com.

GOLD, ALISON LESLIE, writer; b. N.Y.C. d. William I. and Shirley E. Greenwald; 1 child, Thor. BA, New Sch., N.Y.C., 1968. Author: (with Miep Gies) Anne Frank Remembered, 1987; author: Clairvoyant, 1991, Devil's Mistress, 1997, Remembering Anne Frank, 1997, A Special Fate, 2000, Fiet's Vose, 2003, Love in the Second Act, 2006. Recipient Merit of Ednl. Distinction award Anti-Defamation League, N.Y.C., 1987, Christopher award Christian Brothers, N.Y.C., 1988; named Best of Best Am. Libr. Assn., 1994.

GOLD, BETTY VIRGINIA, artist; b. Austin, Tex., Feb. 15, 1935; d. Julius Ulisses and Jeffie Mae (Meek) Lee; 1 child, Laura Lee Gold Bousquet. Student (hon.), U. Tex. Lectr. Gazi U., Ankara, Turkey, 1988, NAshida Gallery, Nara, Japan, 1989, Met. State Coll. Denver, 1992, Downey Mus., Calif., 1993, Foothills Art Ctr., Golden, Colo., 1994, Triskel Art Ctr., Cork, Ireland, 1994, ARmand Hammer Mus., L.A., 1994, Austin Art Mus., 1996. One-woman shows include Sol Del Rio Gallery, San Antonio, 1971, Parkcrest Gallery, Austin, 1972, Rubicon Gallery, L.A., 1973, Downtown Gallery, Honolulu, 1974, Esther Robles Gallery, L.A., 1975, Laguna Gloria Art Mus., Austin, 1976, Charles W. Bowers Meml. Mus., Santa Ana, Calif., 1977, Phoenix Art Mus., 1979, Baum-Silverman Gallery, L.A., 1988, Del. Art Mus., Wilmington, 1981, Univ. Art Mus., Austin, 1981, Decias Art, LaJolla, Calif., 1982, Patrick Gallery, Austin, 1983, Jan Baum Gallery, L.A., 1984, Boise State U., 1985, Purdue U., West Lafayette, Ind., 1986, Walker Hill Art Ctr., Seoul, Korea, 1987, Nishida Gallery, Nara, Japan, 1989, Armeson Fine Arts, Ltd., Vail, Colo., 1991, Downey Mus., Calif., 1993, ARt Mus. South Tex., Corpus Christi, 1995, Austin Art Mus., Austin, 1996, The Czech Mus. Fine Arts, Prague, 1998, Elite Gallery, Venice, 1998, retrospective, Palma-Mallorca, Spain, 2005—, Buschlen Mowatt Gallery, Palm Desert, Calif., 2006, others; group shows include Enhol Gallery, Dallas, 1971, Bestart Fallery, Houston, 1972, Gargoyle, Inc., Aspen, Colo., 1975, Aronson Gallery, Atlanta, 1976, Shidoni Gallery, Sante Fe, N.Mex., 1977, Elaine Horwich Gallery, Scottsdale, Ariz., 1981, Fordham U., Bronx, 1983, Nat. Mus. Contemporary Art, Seoul, 1987, John Thomas Gallery, Santa Monica, Calif., 1989, La Quinta Sculpture Park, Calif., 1994, Bova Gallery, L.A., 1995, Museo Nacional Centro de Arte Reina Sofia, Madrid, Spain, 1997, Threshold Gallery, Santa Monica, 1998, others; represented in permanent installations at RCA Bldg., Chgo., Cedars Sinai Hosp., L.A., Sinai Temple, L.A., Hawaii State Fond. Arts, Apollo Plastic Corp., Chgo., Houston First Savs., Pepperdine U., Malibu, Calif., No. Ill. U., Dekalb, Mus. Nacional-Centro de Arte Reina Sofia, Madrid, Texas U., Austin, City of Palma de Mallorca (1999), Spain, Duke U. Med. Ctr. (1999), Mary Baldwin Coll., Staunton, Va., 2001, Baylor U., Waco, Tex., 2002, Pres. Garden, Slovakia Republic (gift from U.S. Embassy), Pepperdine U., Malibu, Calif, 2003, Esbaulard Mus., Palma de Mallorca, Spain, 2004, Palm Springs Desert Mus., others. Fax: 310-399-3745. Office Phone: 310-399-5205. E-mail: bgold1324@earthlink.com.

GOLD, CALLA GISELLE, jewelry designer; b. L.A., Dec. 1, 1958; d. Robert Frederick Skeetz and Ruth Mary Connelly; m. Jeremy Peter Gold, July 15, 1979; 1 child, Daniel Jason. Grad. high sch., Berkeley, Calif. Sales rep. Fuller Brush, 1977-83; owner Cinderella Svcs., Santa Barbara, Calif., 1979-82, Ceiling Cleaning Co., Santa Barbara, Calif., 1982-83, Calla Gold Jewelry, Santa Barbara, Calif., 1983—. Spkr. Profl. Jeweler Show and Conf., Las Vegas, 2000. Contbg. author Profl. Jeweler mag., 1997, 98, 99. Orchard to Ocean run food dir. Carpinteria (Calif.) Edn. Found., 1999; fundraiser Kinderkirk Presch., Carpinteria, 1996; specific event fundraiser Villa Majella, Santa Barbara, 1997-2002, Holderman Endowment for La Patera, Lompoc Aquarium, 2000-02, Santa Barbara Women's Health Coalition, Santa Barbara County Med. Soc. Alliance; bd. dirs. Leads Club, 1995. Recipient Leadership award, Leads Club, 1996. Mem. Am. Jewelers Assn., Calif. Jewelers Assn., Santa Barbara Event Profls., Santa Barbara Jewelers Guild, South Coast Bus. Network, Toastmasters (competent Toastmaster 1991). Avocations: hiking, horseback riding, reading, scrapbooking. Office: Calla Gold Jewelry PO Box 40102 Santa Barbara CA 93140-0102 E-mail: gold2@cox.net.

GOLD, CAROL SAPIN, international management consultant, speaker, writer; b. NYC; d. Cerf Saul and Muriel Louise (Fudin) Rosenberg; children: Kevin Bart Sapin, Craig Paul Sapin, Courtney Byrens Sapin. BA, U. Calif., Berkeley, 1955. Asst. credit mgr. Union Oil Co., 1956; with U.S. Dept. State, 1964—66; mem. dept. pub. rels. Braun & Co., L.A., 1964—66; corp. dir. pers. tng. Gt. We. Fin. Corp., L.A., 1967—71; pres. Carol Sapin Gold & Assocs., L.A., 1971—. Bd. dirs. Marathon Nat. Bank, L.A.; host radio program The Competitive Edge; mem. expdn. to Syria and Jordan, 1994, to Morocco, 1995; mem. WORlD Bus. Acad.; instr. Learning Annex; instr. Asian program U. So. Calif., 1998; presenter, cons., spkr. in field. Author: Solid Gold Customer Relations and Success Secrets, Travel for Scholars, Paris, 1999; featured in tng. films Power of Words; author: Cassette Libraries, How to Present Seminars, Sound Selling. Bd. dirs. Ctr. Theatre Group, Town Hall, Music Ctr., Odyssey Theater; asst. dir. Burnhill Prodns., 1992—, asst. dir. Cabaret, Palisades Theatre; dir. Improv Corp.; vol. Exec. Svc. Corp., 1996—, CEO Leadership Forum. Mem. ASTD, Am. Film Inst. Assn., Sales and Mktg. Execs., Nat. Spkrs. Assn., Nat. Platform Assn., Women in Bus., KCET Women's Coun., Exec. Svc. Corps, World Affairs Coun., Blue Ribbon, Women in Arts, Women in Film, Manuscript Soc. Forum Scotland, Plato Soc., Brandeis U. Women, Sierra Club (Toure de Mt. Blanc), Supreme Ct. Hist. Soc., Dispute Resolution Svcs., Faces of History, Women of LA, Marina Del Rey C. of C., Internat. CEO Exec. Forum, Manuscript Soc., Brandeis Film Group. Avocations: collecting famous manuscripts, music, theater, writing. Office: PO Box 11447 Marina Del Rey CA 90295 Office Phone: 310-823-0202. Personal E-mail: cconsult@aol.com.

GOLD, CHRISTINA A., data processing company executive; b. Can. Grad., Carleton U., Ottawa; degree (hon.), U. Montreal, 1991. With human resources, sales, mktg., fin. and mgmt. depts. Avon Can., 1970-89, pres., CEO, 1989-93, head oper. bus. unit, 1993; sr. v.p., pres. Avon North Am., NYC, 1993-98; exec. v.p. Global Direct Selling Devel., NYC, 1997-98; co-CEO Teleglobe, Inc.; CEO Beaconsfield Group, 1998—99; chmn., pres., CEO Excel Comm., Inc., Dallas, 1999—2002; sr. exec. v.p. First Data Corp., 2002—, pres. Western Union, 2002—, CEO, bd. dir. Western Union, 2006—. Bd. dirs. Meredith Corp., 1999—2001, The Torstar Corp., The Conf. Bd., ITT Industries, NY Life Investment Mgmt. LLC. Named one of 50 Most Powerful Women in Business, Fortune mag., 2006. Mem.: Direct Selling Assn. (bd. dirs.), Conf. Bd. NY and Can. (bd. dirs). Office: First Data Corp 6200 S Quebec St Greenwood Village CO 80111*

GOLD, DEIDRA D., lawyer; b. Jan. 1955; m. Stephen A. Gold. BA, Wellesley Coll.; JD, Columbia U., 1979. Assoc. Jones Day Reavis & Pogue, Cleve., 1983—88, ptnr., 1988—91; v.p., gen. counsel Premier Industrial Corp., Cleve., 1991—97; ptnr. Goldberg Kohn Bell Black Rosenbloom & Mortiz, Chgo., 1998; counsel, corp. sec. Ameritech Corp., 1998—99; v.p., gen. counsel eLoyalty Corp., 2000—01; sr. v.p., gen. counsel, sec. United Stationers Inc., Des Plaines, Ill., 2001—. Office: United Stationers Inc 2200 E Golf Rd Des Plaines IL 60016-1267

GOLD, JANET NOWAKOWSKI, Spanish language educator; b. Torrington, Conn., Oct. 24, 1948; d. Peter S. and Virginia (Eseppi) Nowakowski; m. Hector Zamora, Dec. 1974 (div. Sept. 1978); m. Stephen Gold, June 28, 1981. BA, Albertus Magnus Coll., 1971; MEd, Worcester State Coll., 1981; PhD, U. Mass., 1990. Elem. sch. tchr., Tegucigalpa, Honduras, 1971-72; instr. English Centro Internat. de Idiomas, Cuernavaca, Mexico, instr. ESL, 1973; tchr. Spanish-English bilingual program Worcester (Mass.) Elem. Sch., 1974-82; tchg. asst. U. Mass., Amherst, 1984-88; instr. Spanish lang. and lit. Bates Coll., Lewiston, Mass., 1989-91; asst. prof. Spanish La. State U., Baton Rouge, 1991-95; assoc. prof. Spanish U. N.H., Durham, 1995—. Author: Clementina Suarez: Her Life and Poetry, 1995; contbr. books Reinterpreting the Spanish American Essay: Studies in Nineteenth and Twentieth Century Women's Essays, 1994, A Dream of Light and Shadow: Portraits of Latin American Women Writers, 1995; contbr. articles and revs. to Hispanic studies jours. Fulbright grantee, Honduras, 1988-89. Mem. MLA, Am. Assn. Tchrs. Spanish and Portuguese,Latin Am. Studies Assn., Millay Soc., Asociacion de Literatura Femenina Hispanica, Maine Writers and Publ. Alliance. Home: PO Box 357 Eliot ME 03903-0357 Office: U NH Dept Spanish Murkland 209 Durham NH 03824

GOLD, JUDITH HAMMERLING, psychiatrist; b. NYC, June 24, 1941; d. James S. and Anne (Linder) Hammerling; m. Edgar Gold, June 27, 1965. MD, Dalhousie U., 1965; DHumL (hon.), Mt. St. Vincent U., 2002. Intern Victoria Gen. Hosp., Halifax, N.S., Canada, 1964-65; resident Dalhousie U., Halifax, 1967-71; practice medicine specializing in psychiatry Halifax, 1971—2002; staff psychiatrist Dalhousie U. Student Health Clinic, 1971-73; vis. colleague U. Wales Med. Sch., 1973-75; asst. prof. dept. psychiatry Dalhousie U., Halifax, 1975-78, assoc. prof., 1978-80, part-time, 1980-87; pvt. practice Brisbane, 1998—. Vis. prof., reader in psychotherapy studies dept. psychiatry U. Queensland, Brisbane, 1998-99. Editor: Clinical Practice Series, 1987-2001, 6 books; contbr. articles to profl. jours. Bd. govs. Mt. St. Vincent U., 1981-87, chmn., 1986-87. Med. Research Council Can. fellow, 1973-75; Health and Welfare Bd. Can. grantee, 1976-78 Fellow Am. Psychiat. Assn., Am. Coll. Psychiatrists (1st v.p. 1990-91, pres.-elect 1991-92, pres. 1992-93); mem. Can. Psychiat. Assn. (pres. 1981-82), Royal Coll. Phys. Surgeons Can. (exec. mem. 1992-94, coun. 1991-98), Order Can., Alpha Omega Alpha. Office Phone: 61-7-3839-4788.

GOLD, LOIS MEYER, artist; b. NYC, June 2, 1945; d. Seymour Roy and Carol (Rubin) Meyer; m. Leonard Marshall Gold, Oct. 14, 1971 (dec. 1998); 1 child, Eric Marshall. BA, Boston U., 1967; MA, Columbia U., 1970. Tchr.

Lenox Sch., N.Y.C., 1972—84, Columbia Grammar Sch., N.Y.C., 1975—76; artist, freelance N.Y.C., 1976—; represented by Lizan-Tops Gallery, East-hampton, NY, Canyon Ranch, Lenox, Mass., Martha Keats Gallery, Santa Fe, Karin Zatt, L.A., Ruzetti and Gow, N.Y.C., Nutmeg Gallery, Kent, Conn., The Flinn Gallery, Greenwich, Conn., Cavalier Gallery, N.Y.C., 2005—06. Prin. works include Canyon Ranch, Bristol Myers Squibb, Imperial Oil, Bed, Bath and Beyond, Boston U., others, exhibitions include Florence Biennial, 2003, Represented in permanent collections Herbert F. Johnson Mus. Art, Ithaca, N.Y., Boston U. Libr., corp. collections, Bklyn. Union Gas Co., The Four Seasons, Dallas, Tex., NY Presbyn. Hosp., N.Y.C.; featured artist The Artists Mag., 1993, 2000 (Landscape award, 1993), Dan's Papers, 1999—2005, Pastel Artist Internat., 1999, Decor, 1999, Southwest Art, 2001, Pastel Jour., 2003, The Pastel Artist's Bible, Pure Color: The Best of Pastel, 2006, others, poster art represented in (films) My Big Fat Greek Wedding, Art International, 2003; various original posters; contbr. works to profl. jours.; work to books, including Pastel Painter's Solution Book, 1996, prints, Spiegel Catalog; contbr. Recipient Artists Mag. Landscape award, 1991, 1993, Best of Flower Painting award, North Light Books, Pastel Artist's Bible award, 2006, Pure Color the Best of Pastel, North Light Books; scholar Pastel Soc. Am. Juried, 1994—95. Mem.: Studio Ctr. Artist's Assn., Cassatt Pastel Soc., Nat. Assn. Women Artists (Pauline Law award 1988, Works on Paper award 1988), Pastel Soc. Am., Internat. Assn. Pastel Socs., Poetry Soc. Am. Avocations: bicycling, ballroom dancing, tennis, skiing, bicycling. Home: 45 E End Ave New York NY 10028-7953 Office Phone: 212-744-7503. Personal E-mail: lois.gold3@verizon.net.

GOLD, PHRADIE KLING See KLING, PHRADIE

GOLD, SARAE R., art educator; b. Mpls., Mar. 26, 1950; d. Samuel N. and Lillian Himmelfarb; m. Gary L. Nagel, Dec. 26, 1971 (div. Feb. 1991); children: Jill S. Nagel, Marcy B. Nagel; m. Herbert Arnold Gold, Feb. 18, 1996. BA in Art Edn., Northeastern Ill. U., 1970; MS in Art Edn., No. Ill. U., 1999; postgrad., Grand Valley State U., 2002, U. Nev. Las Vegas, 2003. Cert. tchr. Ill., Nev. Tchr. Chgo. Pub. Schs., 1970—74; sales rep. ARA Serve, Chgo., 1981—83; mgr. area ADIA Pers. Svcs., Chgo., 1983—84, NJ, 1984—86; pres. Photo Promotions Plus, NY and NJ, 1986—90; v.p. Olsten Profl. Acctg. Svcs., Chgo., 1990—93; pres. Photo Promotions Plus, Chgo., 1993—95; tchr. Chgo. Pub. Sch., 1995—99; dir. Fine Arts Grand Rapids Pub. Schs., Mich., 1999—2002; tchr. art Clark County Sch. Dist., Las Vegas, 2002—. Adj. art edn. prof. U. Nev., Las Vegas, 2004. Art Peoples Park, UNLV, 2003, Something Fishy in Grand Rapids, 2000, Santa Training School, N.J., 1987. Recipient Educator of Yr., Grand Rapids, 2002. Mem.: Nat. Art Edn. Assn., Art Educators So. Nev. (co-chair state conf. 2003, dir.-elect 2003—). Avocations: woodcarving, pastels.

GOLD, SHARON CECILE, artist, educator; b. N.Y.C., Feb. 28, 1949; d. Henry Joseph and Betty (Kopan) G.; m. William McKay Watson III, July 12, 1992; 1 child, Miranda Cecile. Student, CUNY, 1967-68, Columbia U., 1968-70; BFA, Pratt Inst., 1976. Adj. prof. Art NYU, 1983; vis. artist SUNY, Purchase, 1985; assoc. prof. painting and critical theory Syracuse (N.Y.) U., 1986—; vis. artist The Art Inst. Chgo., Chgo., 1990. Lectr. in field; guest critic Sch. Visual Arts, N.Y.C., 1987, N.Y. Studio Sch., 1988. Solo exhibits include Stephen Rosenberg Gallery, N.Y.C., 1987, 89, 91, 55 Mercer St., N.Y.C., 1986, John Davis Gallery, Akron, Ohio, 1986, Pam Adler Gallery, N.Y.C., 1986; group exhibits include IRIS House, N.Y.C., 1992, Everson Mus. of Art, Syracuse, 1991, ARTSTAR, L.A., 1991, Stephen Rosenberg Gallery, N.Y., 1991, Rose Art Mus. Brandeis U., 1990, Robert Pardo Gallery, N.Y.C., 2001; performance/video works include A Video Tape 1990-1991 Stephen Rosenberg Gallery, 1991, North South Consonance St. Stephen's Ch., N.Y.C., 1984. Pratt Inst. Acad. fellow, 1974-76, NEA grantee, 1981, Penny McCall Found. grantee, 1988. Home: 10 Leonard St New York NY 10013-2929 Office Phone: 212-925-6885. Business E-Mail: sharon@watsongold.com.

GOLD, SYLVIANE, editor, writer, film critic; b. Paris, Feb. 17, 1948; came to U.S., 1949; d. Jack and Annette (Movermann) G.; m. Lawrence Stanley Simonberg, June 30, 1972. Student, Queens Coll., 1964-68. Prodn. asst. Village Voice, NYC, 1968-70; editorial clerk, critic, reporter NY Post, NYC, 1970-77; arts editor Boston Phoenix, 1977-80; drama critic Wall St. Jour., NYC, 1983-89; entertainment editor Newsday, 1989-95, dance critic, 1996—2004; freelance writer, editor, 1995—; theater columnist Dance mag., 2000—. Adj. asst. prof. journalism dept. NYU, 1983-85. Contbr. stories and articles to numerous publs. including SoHo News, N.Y. Times, Elle, Boston Globe, USA Today, Vanity Fair, 1980—. Recipient George Jean Nathan award, 1982, Penney-Missouri awards, 1992, 93. Mem. NY Drama Critics Circle (emeritus), George Oppenheimer Playwriting Award Selection Com. (chmn.).

GOLDBACH, JENNIFER DEBERDINE, bank executive; b. Quarryville, Pa. married; 1 child. BA in Computer Scis., Dickinson Coll., 1984. Mgmt. trainee to v.p. residential mortgage mgr. Fulton Bank, Lancaster, Pa., 1984—95; from v.p. and mgr. mortgage lending to sr. v.p. retail lending Sterlin Fin. Corp., Lancaster, 1995—2000, sr. v.p. retail lending, 2000—02; pres., CEO First Nat. Bank North East, Md., 2002—. Past pres. Child Abuse Prevention Com. Ctrl. Pa.; mem. Union Hosp. Found., Elkton, Md., Cecil CC Found., North East, Md., North East C. of C., pres.; mem. mission outreach com. Salem United Ch. Christ; bd. dir. Am. Heart Assn. Named One of 25 Women to Watch, U.S. Banker Mag., 2003. Mem.: Mortgage Bankers Assn. Ctrl. Pa. (chmn. conf. 2000, 2001, past pres., past gov.). Avocation: golf. Office: First National Bank North East 14 South Main St North East MD 21901 Office Phone: 410-287-5000 ext. 114.

GOLDBARD, LAURA E., lawyer; b. NYC, June 14, 1956; BA, Emory Univ., Atlanta, 1978; JD, Univ. Miami, 1981. Bar: NY 1983. Adminstrv. ptnr., intellectual property practice area Stroock & Stroock & Lavan LLP, NYC. Contbr. articles to profl. journals. Mem.: ABA, Copyright Soc. USA, Internat. Trademark Assn. Office: Stroock & Stroock & Lavan LLP 180 Maiden Ln New York NY 10038-4982 Office Phone: 212-806-6675. Office Fax: 212-806-6006. Business E-Mail: lgoldbard@stroock.com.

GOLDBERG, ADELE J., computer scientist; b. July 1945; BS in Math., U. Mich.; MS in Info. Sci., U. Chgo., PhD in Info. Sci., 1973; PhD (hon.), Open U., 1998. Researcher, lab. mgr. Xerox Palo Alto Rsch. Ctr.; founder, chmn., CEO ParcPlace-Digitalk, Inc.; founder Neometron, Inc., Redwood City, Calif., 1996—; chief tech. officer AgileMind, Inc., San Francisco. Lectr. in field; cons. in field. Co-author, co-developer (books) Smalltalk-80 programming system; author: numerous papers on project mgmt., programming and analysis methodology using object-oriented tech., & on-line project communities; edited The History of Personal Workstations, 1988, co-editor Visual Object-Oriented Programming. Bd. dir. The San Francisco Exploratorium, chair, adv. coun.; bd. dir., trustee Internat. Computer Sci. Inst., Berkeley, Calif.; mem. vis. com., divsn. physical sciences U. Chgo. Recipient Lifetime Achievement award, PC Mag., 1990, Howard Vollum award, Reed Coll., 1995, Dr. Dobbs Mag. Excellence in Programming award, 2000. Fellow: Assn. Computing Machinery (pres. 1984—86, former nat. sect. and editor-in-chief, Computing Surveys, Software Systems award 1987). Office: Agile-Mind Inc 582 Market St Ste 1215 San Francisco CA 94104 E-mail: adele@neometron.com.*

GOLDBERG, ANNE CAROL, physician, educator; b. Balt., June 12, 1951; d. Stanley Barry and Selma Ray G.; m. Ronald M. Levin, July 29, 1989. AB, Harvard U., 1973; MD, U. Md., 1977. Diplomate Am. Bd. Internal Medicine, Am. Bd. Endocrinolgy and Metabolism. Intern in medicine Michael Reese Hosp., Chgo., 1977-78, resident in medicine, 1978-80; fellow in endocrinology Washington U., St. Louis, 1980-83, instr. medicine, 1983-85, asst. prof. medicine, 1985-94, assoc. prof. medicine, 1994—. Fellow ACP, Am. Heart Assn.; mem. AMA, Am. Diabetes Assn., Am. Med. Women's Assn., Endocrine Soc., Nat. Lipid Assn., Alpha Omega Alpha. Democrat. Jewish. Office: Washington U Med Sch Box 8127 660 S Euclid Ave Saint Louis MO 63110-1010

GOLDBERG, BETH SHEBA, artist, educator, art therapist; b. N.Y.C. d. Max and Hannah Segal; m. Benjamin Goldberg; children: Murray, Ilene, Gerald, Jeffrey. BA cum laude, Bklyn. Coll., 1955, MS in Guidance Sch. Counseling with honors, 1957; MA with distinction, Hofstra U., 1995. Tchr. Ohel Moshe Day Sch., Bklyn., 1954-55, N.Y. Bd. Edn., Bklyn., 1955-57, Amherst Sch. System, Snyder, N.Y., 1957-58, Farmingdale (N.Y.) Sch., 1959-60, Bd. of Edn. of Hebrew Acad. of Nassau, 1977-92; art therapy intern South Oaks, Amityville, 1994, South Nassau Hosp., Oceanside, 1995. Art therapy cons. L.I. State Vets. Home, 1998—2002, L.I. Breast Cancer Mem., 2004—05. Exhibited in various one-woman shows and group exhibits including Salmagundi, Firehouse Gallery, Island Artists Gallery, Chelsea, Heckscher Mus., Sumner Mus.; represented in pvt. collections including Dupont Corp., Cork Gallery, N.Y., NAssau County Mus., Roslyn Nat. Arts Club, Allied Artists Am. Hon. trustee Farmingdale Jewish Ctr., 1992—; v.p. Ea. L.I. Women's League, 1982-86; pres. Lionesses, Farmingdale, 1973-74; pres. Sisterhood Farmingdale Jewish Ctr., 1969-70. Recipient award of excellence Ind. Art League, award of merit Salmagundi Juried Show, Grumbacher medallion Ind. Art Soc., 1996, 98, 99, Julia Cohn award for creativity, 1994, 95, 96, 98, 99, Am. Artist award East Islip Juried Show, 2000, Award of Excellence, Town of Oyster Bay, 2003, Suprs. award Babylon Arts Coun., 2001, various awards for art; named Woman of Distinction in Art, Town of Oyster Bay, 2000, Woman of Distinction in Civic and Cmty. Affairs, 2003, George Estabrook Disting. Alumni, Hofstra U., 2004. Mem. Pequa Art Assn. (pres.), Nat. League Am. Pen Women (exec. v.p. 1995-2000, pres. 2000-02, 04—, N.Y. State treas. 2000-02, N.Y. state pres., award of excellence), Am. Art Therapy Assn., Clin. Art Therapy, Creative Art Therapist, Huntington Twp. Art League (L.I.), Allied Artist Am., Nat. Arts Club, Nassau County Mus., Visual Art Alliance League, Psi Chi (v.p.), Kappa Delta Pi (v.p.), Chi Sigma Iota. Avocations: painting, writing. Home: 23 Tanwood Dr Massapequa NY 11758-8548 Office Phone: 516-799-3990.

GOLDBERG, BONITA WILLIAMS, artist, consultant; b. Cin., June 30, 1947; d. Clifford James and Mary Margaret (Rolfsen) Williams; m. Michael Frederick, Nov. 16, 1968; children: Tracey, Scott, Jason. AA, Thomas More Coll., Crestview Hills, Ky., 1987, BES, 1988. Sr. sales rep. Cin. Bell, 1967-69; decorator sales Designs & Blinds, Fairfield, Ohio, 1980-84; art cons. Works of Art, West Chester, Ohio, 1987-90, Village Frame Schop, Cin., 1990-92; sales McAlpin, Cin., 1992-94; art cons. AB Closson Art Gallery, Cin., 1994—. Gallery docent Contemporary Art Ctr., Cin., 1988-90; sec.-treas. Base Art Gallery, Cin., 1990-97. Exhbns. include Middletown Fine Arts Ctr., 1988, 90, 91, 92 (1st place drawing award), Works of Art Gallery, 1989, Art Acad. of Cin., 1992, Mason Art Show, 1992 (hon. mention), Pendelton Art Ctr., 1993, Base Gallery, 1993-95, Women's Art Club, 1994, 95, Closson's Art Gallery, 1998, Embracing Color, Fitton Ctr. for the Arts, 2001, others. Art instr. YMCA, Florence, Ky., 1986. Mem. Fitton Art Ctr., Contemporary Art Ctr., Base Art (treas.-sec. 1993-95). Roman Catholic. Avocations: art, golf, bridge. Home: 15 Stablegate Ct Fairfield OH 45014-3980

GOLDBERG, CATHERINE T., lawyer; b. Devils Lake, ND, June 28, 1950; AB summa cum laude, U. ND, 1971; JD magna cum laude, U. N. Mex., 1975. Bar: N. Mex. 1975. Law clk. to Hon. Howard C. Bratton U.S. Dist. Ct., Dist. N. Mex., 1975—76; dir. Rodey, Dickason, Sloan, Akin & Robb PA, Albuquerque. Named to Best Lawyers in Am. in real estate and banking, 1995—, Chamber's America's Leading Lawyers for Bus., 2004, 2005. Mem.: Albuquerque Mus. Art, History & Sci. (found. bd. 1987—93, 1994—2000, art adv. com. 1996—, bd. trustees 2000—), Albuquerque Econ. Devel. Forum, Albuquerque Bar Assn. (former pres.), ABA (real property probate & trust law sect., bus. law sect.), Am. Coll. Mortgage Attys. (trustee, opinions com.), Am. Coll. Real Estate Lawyers (new mem.'s com.), Phi Beta Kappa, Order Coif. Office: Rodey Dickason Sloan Akin & Robb PA 201 Third St NW Ste 2200 PO Box 1888 Albuquerque NM 87103 Office Phone: 505-768-7318. Business E-Mail: ctgoldberg@rodey.com.

GOLDBERG, CHARLOTTE WYMAN, retired physical education educator, retired dean, retired counselor, retired travel company executive; b. Flint, Mich., July 3, 1914; d. Barney J. and Rose Wyman; m. Leo Goldberg, July 9, 1943 (dec.); children: Suzanne Goldberg Rosin, David, Edward. BS, Ea. Mich. U., 1936; MEd, Wayne State U., 1943. Cert. tchr., guidance counselor, Mass. Tchr. phys. edn. pub. schs., Muskegan Heights, Mich., 1936-37, Pontiac, Mich., 1937-44; asst. to dean Harvard Coll., Harvard U., Cambridge, Mass., 1967-68; guidance counselor Woburn (Mass.) H.S., 1968-72; travel agt. Travel Ctr., Tucson, 1978-97, ret. Pres. women's com. Brandeis U., Tucson, 1991. Mem. U. Ariz. Faculty Wives. Avocations: watercolor painting, lapidarist, golf, bowling. Home: 5700 E Rio Verde Vista Dr Tucson AZ 85750-1971

GOLDBERG, JOLANDE ELISABETH, law librarian, lawyer; b. Pforzheim, Germany, Aug. 11, 1931; came to U.S., 1967; d. Eugen and Luise Rosa (Thorwarth) Haas; m. Lawrence Spencer Goldberg, Sept. 7, 1969; children: Daniel Scott, Elisa Miriam, Clarissa Anna. Referendar, U. Heidelberg, 1957, PhD, 1963; postdoctoral, U. London, 1976-77. Bar: Germany 1961. Mem. rsch. staff Acad. Scis. and Humanities, Heidelberg, 1961-67; rsch. assoc. U. Heidelberg, 1964-67; cataloger, law specialist Libr. of Congress, Washington, 1967-72, asst. law classification specialist, 1972-80, law classification specialist, 1980—97, sr. cataloging policy specialist, 1997—. Sculptor, potter Torpedo Factory Art Ctr., Alexandria, Va., 1974—; lectr. Smithsonian Inst., Washington, 1988-90. Author: Probschlag & Meistersignatur, 1963, Library of Congress Law Library, and Illustrated Guide, 2005; contbr. articles to profl. jours. Exec. bd. dirs. Friends Torpedo Factory Art Ctr., Alexandria, 1987—2003. Volkswagenwerk Found. rsch. fellow, Fed. Republic of Germany, 1964-65, German Rsch. Assn. fellow, 1966, German Libr. Inst. grantee, 1981, Robbins Collection sr. rsch. fellow U. Calif. Berkeley, 1995; Hon. Mention award Best of Va. Artists and Artisans, 2005. Mem. ABA, ALA (Marta Lange award for disting. librarianship in law and polit. sci. 1999, Assn. Coll. and Rsch. Librs. divsn. Marta Lange Congl. Quarterly award 1999), Am. Soc. Internat. Law, Indigenous Rights Group (exec. bd. dir., 2005—), Internat. Assn. Law Librs., Am. Assn. Law Librs. (Tech. Svcs. Spl. Interest sect. exec. bd. dirs. 1987-91, 2003-05, ednl. com., 2006-, citation for exceptional contbn. 1992, Reneé Chapman Meml. award 1999, Joseph L. Andrews Bibliographie award 2002), Torpedo Factory Artist Assn., The Art League. Democrat. Jewish. Office: Libr Of Congress Washington DC 20540-4305 Office Phone: 202-707-4386. Office Fax: 202-707-6629. Business E-Mail: jgol@loc.gov.

GOLDBERG, LEE WINICKI, furniture company executive; b. Laredo, Tex., Nov. 20, 1932; d. Frank and Goldie (Ostrowiak) Winicki; m. Frank M. Goldberg, Aug. 17, 1952; children: Susan, Arlene, Edward Lewis, Anne Carri. Student, San Diego State U., 1951—52. With United Furniture Co., Inc., San Diego, 1953—83, corp. sec., dir., 1963—83, dir. environ. interiors, 1970—83; founder Drexel-Heritage store Edwards Interiors subs. United Furniture, 1975; founding ptnr., v.p. FLJB Corp., 1976—86; 1980founding ptnr., sec., treas. Sea Fin., Inc., 1980; founding ptnr. First Nat. Bank San Diego, 1982. Den mother Boy Scouts Am., San Diego, 1965; vol. Am. Cancer Soc., San Diego, 1964-69; chmn. jr. matrons United Jewish Fedn., San Diego, 1958; del. So. Pacific Coast region Hadassah Conv., 1960, pres. Galilee group San Diego chpt., 1960-61; supporter Marc Chagall Nat. Mus., Nice France, U. Calif. at San Diego Cancer Ctr. Foun., Smithsonian Instn., L.A. (Calif.) County Mus., San Diego (Calif.) Mus. Contemporary Art, San Diego (Calif.) Mus. Art; pres. San Diego (Calif.) Opera, 1992-94; bd. dirs. The Old Globe, 2002-05 Recipient Hadassah Svc. award San Diego chpt., 1958-59; named Woman of Dedication by Salvation Army Women's Aux., 1992, Patron of Arts by Rancho Santa Fe Country Friends, 1993. Republican. Jewish.

GOLDBERG, LENA G., lawyer, investment company executive; b. 1949; BA, Chatham Coll.; JD, Harvard Univ., 1978. Bar: Mass. 1978. Sr. v.p., gen. counsel FMR Corp. (Fidelity Investments), Boston. Dir. New Eng. Legal Found.; mem. exec. com. Boston Lawyers Group; mem. bd. overseers Mass. Supreme Judicial Ct. Hist. Soc. Mem.: Boston Bar Found. (pres. bd. trustees 2003—04), Boston Bar Assn. Office: FMR Corp 82 Devonshire St Boston MA 02109

GOLDBERG, LINDA, utilities executive, professional society administrator; b. Balt., Feb. 17, 1954; m. Stephen M. Goldberg; 1 child, Sarah. BS, U. Md., 1975; M in Health Sci., Johns Hopkins U., 1980; MA, U. Balt., 1992. Rsch. technician NIH, 1975—78; indsl. hygienist U.S. EPA, 1980; sr. indsl. hygienist Balt. Gas & Electric, 1980—82, supr. accident prevention and indsl. hygiene, 1982—89, supr. employee programs, interim supr. nuc. employment, 1989—91, supr. employment planning and support, 1991—94, sr. human resources analyst, 1992—94, dir. human resource devel., 1994—97, dir. employment, 1997—98; dir. human resource svcs. Constellation Enterprises, Inc., Balt., 1998—; pres. bd. Women's Indsl. Exch. Balt. City, Inc., Balt. Mem. diversity-affirmative action com. Edison Electric Inst., 1993—97; mem. conf. bd. Coun. on Workplace Diversity, 1995—97. Treas. Balt. Choral Arts Soc., 1997—99, v.p., 1999—; v.p. pres. adv. bd. on bus. outreach U. Md. Balt. County, 1997—; bd. mem. Woman's Indsl. Exch. Balt. City, Inc., 1997—98, pres. bd. dirs., 1998—; mem. Merrick adv. bd. U. Balt. Merrick Sch. Bus., 1996—99; bd. mem., chairwoman pers./adminstrn. com. The Family Tree, 1995—98; bd. mem. Balt. Choral Arts Soc., 1995—97; bd. mem. pres. adv. coun. on bus. outreach U. Md. Balt. County, 1995—98. Recipient H. Mebane Turner Svc. award, U. Balt. Alumni Assn., 1999. Mem.: Chesapeake Human Resources Assn., Am. Compensation Assn., Soc. for Human Resources gmt., Beta Gamma Sigma. Office: 333 N Charles St Baltimore MD 21201 also: Constellation Enterprises Ste 530 111 Market Pl Baltimore MD 21202-4035

GOLDBERG, LOIS D., health facility administrator, disability analyst; b. Mar. 30, 1940; m. Gerald Allen Goldberg, Dec. 18, 1960; children: Sheri, Nancy, Karen. BS, U. Wis., Milw., 1961, MS, 1977. Cert. Am. Inst. Hypnotherapy and Psychotherapy, disability analyst. Health svcs. adminstr. Eastside Clinic, Milw., 1985—; acupuncture detox specialist, 1992-98. Pres. Fox Point PTA, Milw., 1980; bd. dirs. Close Encounters Chamber Music. Recipient Fighting Back Initiative cert. of recognition, Milw. County for Reduction of Substance Abuse and Improvement of Life of Milw. County Residents, 1995. Mem.: Pi Lambda Theta (assoc. v.p. 1982). Avocations: music, swimming, tennis. Personal E-mail: LG507@comcast.net.

GOLDBERG, LUELLA GROSS, diversified financial services company executive; b. Mpls., Feb. 26, 1937; d. Louis and Beatrice (Rosenthal) Gross; m. Stanley M. Goldberg, June 23, 1958; children: Ellen Goldberg Luger, Fredric, Martha Goldberg Aronson. BA, Wellesley Coll., 1958; postgrad. in philosophy, U. Minn., 1958-59. Dir. Reliastar Fin. Corp., 1976—2000, NRG Energy, Inc., Mpls., 2001—04. Bd. dirs. Northwestern Nat. Life Ins. Co., Mpls. TCF Fin. Corp., Mpls., Hormel Foods Corp., Austin, Minn., Personnel Decisions Internatl., 1997-2004, dir. Communications System, Inc., 1997—, ING Group, Amsterdam, 2001—. Pres. Minn. Orch. Women's Assn., Mpls., 1972-74; bd. dirs. Minn. Orch. Assn., 1972—, chmn., 1980-83, Mpls. chpt. United Way, 1978-88, Ind. Sector, Washington, 1984-90; regent St. John's U., Collegeville, Minn., 1974-83; trustee U. Minn. Found., Mpls., 1978—, chmn. bd. trustees, 1996-98; mem. bd. overseers Sch. Mgmt., U. Minn., Mpls., 1980—; chmn. bd. trustees Wellesley (Mass.) Coll., 1985-93, acting pres., 1993; trustee Wellesley Coll., 1978-96, emerita, 1996—, Northwest Area Found., 1994—. Recipient Disting. Svc. award, Minn. Orch. Assn., 1983, Community Svc. Leadership award, Mpls. YWCA, 1986, Disting. Svc. to Higher Edn. award, Minn. Pvt. Coll. Coun., 1992, Humanitarian award, NCCJ, 1992, Regents award, U. Minn., 2000, Alumnae Achievement award, Wellesley Coll., 2002, Disting. Women's award, Northwoods U., 2001, Lifetime Achievement award as Outstanding Dir., Twin Cities Bus. Monthly, 2001, Minn. Bus. Hall Fame, Jr. Achievement Upper Midwest, 2005. Mem. Minn. Women's Econ. Round Table, Mpls. Club, Phi Beta Kappa. Avocations: water-skiing, wind surfing, travel. Home: 7019 Tupa Dr Minneapolis MN 55439-1643

GOLDBERG, MAUREEN MCKENNA, state supreme court justice; b. Pawtucket, RI, Feb. 11, 1951; m. Robert D. Goldberg. Grad., St. Mary's Acad., 1969; AB cum laude, Providence Coll., 1973; JD cum laude, Suffolk U., 1978, LLD (hon), 1999. Bar: R.I. 1978, Mass. 1978, U.S. Ct. of Appeals (1st cir.) 1979. Asst. atty. gen. Adminstr. of the Criminal Divsn., 1978-84; town solicitor South Kingstown, 1985-87, Town of Westerly, 1987-90, acting town mgr., 1990; spl. legal counsel RI State Police; apptd. assoc. justice Superior Ct., 1990-96; assoc. justice RI Supreme Ct., 1997—. Mem. Com. to Study Proposed Amendments to R.I. Rules of Evidence, 1998—99; co-chair R.I. Supreme Ct. Law Day Com., 2001—, Advisory Com. on Code of Jud. Conduct, 2002; chair Indigent Defense Task Force, 2003, Jud. Performance Evaluation Com., 2003. Mem. ABA, R.I. Bar Assn., R.I. Trial Judges Assn., Pawtucket Bar Assn., R.I. Bar Found., Nat. Assn. of Women Judges, Mass. Bar Assn. Office: Rhode Island Supreme Ct 250 Benefit St 7th Fl Providence RI 02903-2719*

GOLDBERG, NANCY G., business owner, community volunteer; b. Pitts., 1942; d. Henry and Rose Gross; m. Gerald Sanford Goldberg, 1966; children: Brian Michael (dec.), Sheri Goldberg Glickman. Student, U. Laval, Que., Can., 1962; BA, U. Pitts., 1963; MAT, Johns Hopkins U., Balt., 1965. French tchr. secondary schs., Balt., 1965, Arlington, Va., 1965-68; travel agt. with various agys., Plantation, Fla., 1984-94; interior decorator Nancy G. Goldberg, Interiors, Plantation, 1983-92; pres., owner Creative Inspirations, Inc., Rockville, Md., 1992—. Owner, dir. Creative Inspirations Gallery, Fort Lauderdale, Fla., 1994—96; bd. dirs. Child Advocacy, 1978—81, Jewish Family Svcs., 1982; owner, dir. Creative Inspirations Gallery, Plantation, Fla., 1996—98, Delray Beach, Fla., 2001—02; owner ArtisticJewelry.com, Ci-Gallery.com. Chair for internat. health Broward County Med. Assn. Aux., 1982—83, mem., 1974—85; women's com. Brandeis U., 1975—; bd. dirs., chair for Broward County Mosaic, Jewish Life in Fla., Ft. Lauderdale, 1977—81; bd. dirs. Greater Ft. Lauderdale Sister Cities Internat., 1996—2004. Recipient awards for cmty. svc. Mem.: NOW, Women's Am. ORT, Nat. Coun. Jewish Women (various offices), Sigma Kappa Phi, Phi Beta Kappa. Democrat. Jewish. Avocations: art, gourmet cooking, gardening, world travel.

GOLDBERG, NIECA, cardiologist, educator; b. Bkyln., Oct. 21, 1957; BA, Barnard Coll., 1979; MD, SUNY, Bklyn., 1984. Diplomate Am. Bd. Internal Medicine. Resident in internal medicine St. Lukes-Roosevelt Hosp., N.Y.C., 1985-87; fellow in cardiology SUNY Health Sci. Ctr., Bklyn.; chief women's cardiac care Lenox Hill Hosp., N.Y.C.; asst. clin. prof. of medicine NYU Sch. Medicine. Nat. spokesperson Am. Heart Assn, adv. bd. Women's Day mag. Author: Women Are Not Small Men: Life-Saving Strategies for Preventing and Healing Heart Disease in Women, 2003, The Women's Health Heart Program: Life-saving Strategies for Preventing and Healing Heart Disease in Women, 2006. Named to New York mag. Best Doctors issue, 1999, 2000, 2001, 2004, 2005. Mem. ACP, Am. Coll. Cardiology, Am. Heart Assn., Am. Soc. Echocardiography, Am. Coll. Physicians. Office: Total Heart Care PC 177 E 87th St #503 New York NY 10128 Office Phone: 212-289-2045.

GOLDBERG, PAMELA WINER, entrepreneur, educator; b. Boston, Oct. 14, 1955; d. Arthur Leonard and Marilyn (Miller) Winer; children from previous marriage: Frederick Warren, Alyssa Rachel, Meredith Hayley. BA, Tufts U., 1977; MBA, Stanford U., 1981. Day care dir. Cmty. Action Inc., Haverhill, Mass., 1977-79; lending assoc. Bankers Trust Co., N.Y.C., 1980-81; mgr., bank officer, corp. fin. dept. Citicorp, N.Y.C., 1981-82; assoc. dir., mergers and acquisitions group State St. Bank, Boston, 1983-85; ind. strategic cons. Wellesley, Mass., 1986-97; dir. bus. rels. Babson Coll., Wellesley, 1998—2002; prof., dir. Ctr. for Entrepreneurial Leadership Tufts U., 2002—. Exec. bd. friends Beth Israel Hosp., Boston, 1987—96; trustee Recuperative Ctr., Boston, 1988—95; exec. bd. trustees Temple Beth Elohim, Wellesley, 1992—2000, treas., 1997—2000, Synagogue 2000 nat. com., 2000—04; bd. dirs. Hunnewell Sch. PTO, 1991—96, Wellesley LWV, 1995—98. Avocations: swimming, tennis, singing. Home: 34 Ivy Rd Wellesley MA 02482-4554 Office: Tufts University 4 Colby St Medford MA 02155 Office Phone: 617-627-2153. Personal E-mail: pwg14@aol.com. Business E-Mail: pamela.goldberg@tufts.edu.

GOLDBERG, RITA MARIA, foreign language educator; b. NYC, Oct. 1, 1933; d. Abraham Morris and Hilda (Weinman) G. BA, Queens Coll., 1954; MA, Middlebury Coll., 1955; PhD, Brown U., 1968. Mem. faculty Queens Coll., N.Y.C., 1956, Oberlin (Ohio) Coll., 1957; mem. faculty St. Lawrence U., Canton, NY, 1957—2001, Dana prof. modern langs., 1975—2000, emerita, 2001—, chmn. dept., 1972—75, 1983—91, 2000—01. Chmn. Regional Conf. Am. Programs in Spain, 1979-81; mem. Nat. Fulbright Selection Com., 1990-92; mem. advanced placement devel. com. for Spanish, Ednl. Testing Svc., 1993-2000, chair, 1996-99, chief reader AP Spanish 2000-04. Spanish Ministry of Fgn. Affairs scholar, 1954-56; Danforth grantee, 1960-62, 63-64; N.Y. State Regents scholar, 1950-54, Brown U. scholar, 1960-62. Mem. Am. Assn. Tchrs. Spanish and Portuguese, AAUP, MLA, Am. Council Teaching of Fgn. Langs., N.Y. State Assn. Fgn. Lang. Tchrs., Phi Beta Kappa, Sigma Delta Pi. Roman Catholic. Office: St Lawrence U Dept Modern Langs Lits Canton NY 13617 Business E-Mail: ritagoldberg@stlawu.edu.

GOLDBERG, SUSAN, editor; b. 1959; m. Gary Blonston (dec. Apr. 1999). Reporter Seattle Post-Intelligencer; asst. city editor Detroit Free Press, San Jose Mercury News, 1987—89, acting city editor, mng. editor, 1999—2003, v.p., 2001—, exec. editor, 2003—; dep. mng. editor USA Today, 1989—99. Chair mng. editors leadership and mgmt. com. AP. Mem. bd. visitors Northwestern U. Medill Sch. Journalism; bd. mem. Silicon Valley chpt. Am. Cancer Soc., 2003—. Mem.: Downtown San Jose Rotary Club. Office: San Jose Mercury News 750 Ridder Park Dr San Jose CA 95190-0001

GOLDBERG, WHOOPI (CARYN ELAINE JOHNSON), actress, comedienne; b. N.Y.C., Nov. 13, 1955; d. Robert and Emma (Harris) Johnson; m. Alvin Martin, 1973 (div. 1979); 1 child, Alexandrea Martin; m. David Claessen, 1986 (div. 1988); m. Lyle Trachtenberg, 1994 (div. 1995). Mem. San Diego Repertory Theatre, 1975—80, Blake St. Hawkeyes, Berkeley, Calif., 1980—84. Actor: (plays) Living on the Edge of Chaos, 1988 (Calif. theatre award outstanding achievement, 1988); prodr.: (Broadway plays) Thoroughly Modern Millie (Tony award for best musical, 2002); actor: A Funny Thing Happened on the Way to the Forum, 1996—98, Funny Girl, 2002; actor, prodr. (Broadway plays) Ma Rainey's Black Bottom, 2003, actor, writer (one-person show Broadway plays) Whoopi Goldberg on Broadway, 1984—85; actor: (films) Citizen, 1982, The Color Purple, 1985 (Golden Globe for best actress motion picture drama, 1986), Jumpin' Jack Flash, 1986, Burglar, 1986, Fatal Beauty, 1987, The Telephone, 1987, Clara's Heart, 1988, Homer and Eddie, 1989, Beverly Hills Brats, 1989, Comicitis, 1989, The Long Walk Home, 1990, Ghost, 1990 (Acad. award for best supporting actress, 1991, Golden Globe for best supporting actress motion picture, 1991), Soapdish, 1991, Blackbird Fly, 1991, The Player, 1992, Sister Act, 1992, House Party 2, 1992, Sarafina!, 1992, Made in America, 1993, National Lampoon's Loaded Weapon 1, 1993, Sister Act 2: Back in the Habit, 1993, Naked in New York, 1993, (voice) The Lion King, 1994, Naked in New York, 1994, The Little Rascals, 1994, Corrina, Corrina, 1994, Star Trek: Generations, 1994, (voice) The Pagemaster, 1994, Boys on the Side, 1995, Moonlight and Valentino, 1995, Theodore Rex, 1995, Bogus, 1996, The Ghost of Mississippi, 1996, Eddie, 1996, Tales from the Crypt Presents: Bordello of Blood, 1996, The Associate, 1996, (voice) A Christmas Carol, 1997, How Stella Got Her Groove Back, 1998, (voice) The Rugrats Movie, 1998, Alegria, 1998, Deep End of the Ocean, 1999, Jackie's Back!, 1999, Girl, Interrupted, 1999, (narrator) A Second Chance at Life, 2000, More Dogs Than Bones, 2000, Kingdom Come, 2001, Monkeybone, 2001, Rat Race, 2001, (narrator) Golden Dreams, 2001, Star Trek: Nemesis, 2002, Blizzard, 2003, Jiminy Glick in La La Wood, 2004, (voice) Pinocchio 3000, 2004, (voice) Racing Stripes, 2005, (voice) Doogal, 2006, (voice) Everyone's Hero, 2006; (TV films) My Past Is My Own, 1989, Kiss Shot, 1989, Defenders of Dynatron City, 1992, (voice) Yuletide in the 'hood, 1993, In the Gloaming, 1997, (voice) Mother Goose: A Rappin' and Rhymin' Special, 1997, Cinderella, 1997, A Knight in Camelot, 1998, Jackie's Back!, 1999, The Magical Land of the Leprechauns, 1999, Alice in Wonderland, 1999, (voice) Madeline: My Fair Madeline, 2002, It's a Very Muppet Christmas Movie, 2002; actor, exec. prodr. (TV films) Call Me Claus, 2001, What Makes a Family, 2001, actor, prodr. Good Fences, 2003; actor: (TV series) Star Trek: The Next Generation, 1988—94, (voice) Captain Planet and the Planeteers, 1990, Baghdad Cafe, 1990, (voice) Happily Ever After: Fairy Tales for Every Child, 1997, (voice) Foxbusters, 1999, (voice) Liberty's Kids, 2002, Littleburg, 2004; host: (TV series, talk show) The Whoopie Goldberg Show, 1992—93; actor, exec. prodr. (TV series) Whoopi, 2003; actor: (TV specials) Circus of the Stars #15, 1990, Tales from the Whoop: Hot Rod Brown, Class Clown, 1990; dir., writer, performer (TV specials) Comic Relief, 1986; co-prodr.: (films) The Mao Game, 1999; exec. prodr.: (TV films) Ruby's Bucket of Blood, 2001; prodr.: (TV series) Hollywood Squares, 1998—2002; exec. prodr.: Strong Medicine, 2000; prodr.: (TV miniseries) Oh What A Time It Was, 1999; author: Alice, 1992, Whoopi Goldberg Book, 1997, Whoopi's Big Book of Manners, 2006. Named Entertainer of the Yr., NAACP, 1990; recipient Grammy award for album of Broadway show, 1985, Hans Christian Andersen award for outstanding achievement by a dyslexic, 1987, Humanitarian of Yr. award, Starlight Found., 1989, Star on Hollywood Walk of Fame, 2001, Mark Twain Prize for Am. Humor, Kennedy Center, 2001.*

GOLDBERGER, BLANCHE RUBIN, sculptor, jeweler; b. N.Y.C., Feb. 2, 1914; d. David and Sarah (Israel) Rubin; m. Emanuel Goldberger, June 28, 1942 (dec. 1994); children— Richard N., Ary Louis. B.A., Hunter Coll., N.Y.C., 1934; M.A., Columbia U., 1936; Certificat d'Etudes, Sorbonne, Paris, 1936; postgrad. Westchester Arts Workshop Sculpture and Jewelry, White Plains, 1961-70, Silvermine Coll. Arts, 1962, Nat. Acad. Arts, N.Y.C., 1968. Tchr. French and Hebrew, N.Y.C. High Sch. System, Scarsdale Jr. and Sr. High Schs. One-woman shows include: Bloomingdale's, Eastchester, N.Y., 1975, Scarsdale Pub. Library, N.Y., 1976, Temple Israel, White Plains, N.Y., 1975, Greenwich Art Barn, Conn., 1972 Westlake Gallery, White Plains, N.Y., 1981; exhibited in group shows at Hudson River Mus., Yonkers, N.Y., 1978, Silvermine-New Eng. Ann., Silvermine, Conn., 1979; represented in permanent collection at Scarsdale High Sch. Library, N.Y.; sculpture commn. Jewish Community Ctr. White Plains, N.Y., 1988; commn. Manchester, Vt.; also pvt. collections. Recipient Beaux Arts of Westchester, White Plains, N.Y., 1967, First Prize, White Plains Art Show, Holocaust Meml. Bronze Plaque for Synagogue Congregation Israel, Manchester, Vt.; various commns. for calli collis calligraphic collages. Mem. Nat. Assn. Women Artists, Nat. Assn. Tchrs. French, Scarsdale Art Assn. (bd. dirs.; first prizes for sculpture). Jewish. Avocations: lecturing on sculpture, reading contemporary lit. in Hebrew, the violin, classical music concerts, callicollies. Home: Sterling Glen of Rye Brook 1200 Rye King Box #316 Rye Brook NY 10573

GOLD-BIKIN, LYNNE Z., lawyer; b. N.Y.C., Apr. 23, 1938; d. Herbert Benjamin Zapoleon and Muriel Claire (Wimpfheimer) Sarnoff; m. Roy E. Gold, Aug. 20, 1956 (div. July 1976); children: Russell, Sheryl, Lisa, Michael; m. Martin H. Feldman, June 28, 1987. BA summa cum laude, Albright Coll., 1973; JD, Villanova Law Sch., 1976; degree (hon.), 1996. Bar: Pa. 1976, U.S. Dist. Ct. (ea. dist.) Pa. 1976, U.S. Supreme Ct. 1979. Assoc. Pechner, Dorfman, Wolffe, Rounick & Cabot, Norristown, Pa., 1976-81; ptnr. Olin, Neil, Frock & Gold-Bikin, Norristown, 1981-82; pres. Gold-Bikin, Welsh & Assocs., Norristown, 1982-96, Wolf, Block, Schorr & Solis-Cohen, Norristown, 1996—. Course planner for 12 manuals on continuing legal edn., 1978—; pres. coun. Albright Coll., Reading, Pa., 1982-87. Author: Pennsylvania Marital Agreements, 1984, Divorce Practice Handbook, 1994, The Divorce Trial Manual, 2003; contbg. editor, Fairshare Mag., 1987—. Bd. trustees Albright Coll., 2000—. Named Pa. Honor Roll of Women, 1996, Pa. Super Lawyers, 2004. Fellow Am. Acad. Matrimonial Lawyers, Internat. Acad. Matrimonial Lawyers, Am. Coll. Matrimonial Trial Lawyers, Am. Bar Found., Am. Law Inst., Pa. Bar Found.; mem. ABA (family law sect. chair 1994-95, ho. of dels. 1995-2001, 2002—, bd. govs. 1998-2001), Pa. Bar Assn. (family law sect. coun. mem. 1980-89), Montgomery County Bar Assn. (chmn. family law com. 1984-86), Pa. Trial Lawyers Assn. (chmn. family law sect. 1988-90). Office: Wolf Block Schorr & Solis-Cohen One West Main St Norristown PA 19401-0869 Office Phone: 610-278-1511. Business E-Mail: lgold-bikin@wolfblock.com.

GOLDBLATT, BARBARA JANET, sex therapist, educator; b. Denver, June 22, 1937; d. Robert and Esther Mae Gamzey; m. Arnold L. Goldblatt; children: Sheri, Neil. BA, U. Denver, 1958; MA, Goddard Coll., 1978. Tchr. Denver Pub. Schs., 1958—59; sex educator, therapist Denver, 1978—85; prin., owner Cultural Expeditions, Denver, 1985—90; CEO, founder Magnets for Health, Denver, 1997—2002. Founder Old Myths and New Realities workshop, 1977; spkr. Jewish Fedn., 1983; spkr. in field. Fundraiser various cultural orgns.; planning com. Am. Jewish Com., 1977; bd. dirs., tchr., program developer Learning for Living, Met. State Coll., Denver, 1972—78; bd. dirs. Colo. Sex Therapists, Denver, 1978—85. Mem.: NARAL, Jewish Allied Fedn., Hadassah, Emily's List. Democrat. Jewish. Avocations: golf, bridge, concerts, opera, book club. Home: 3042 S Fillmore Way Denver CO 80210

GOLDEN, AMY PATRICE, actress, performing company executive; b. Livingston, NJ, Jan. 21, 1977; d. William Francis Golden and Margaret Ann Vivino; m. Eric Olaf Stiner, May 29, 2004. BA, Rutgers U., 1999; Profl. Cert., Atlantic Theater Conservatory, NY, 2003. Exec. dir. The Mgmt.: Black and Blue Theater, N.Y.C., 2004—. Actor(lead actress): (theater prodn.) When Santo Domingo Isn't Enough (Best Play award, 2006), (prodr.) The Long Christmas Dinner, 2005, Look Back in Anger, 2005, Aloha Say the Pretty Girls, 2005 (Grant from PNC Bank for Artistic Contbn. to the Cmty., 2005). Mem. Big Bros. Big Sisters of Hudson County, Jersey City, 2003—06. Mem.: Off Off-Broadway Cmty. Dish (assoc.). Achievements include development of accessible theater for the tri-state area. Office: The Management: Black and Blue Theater 50 Bright St Ste 3R Jersey City NJ 07302 Office Phone: 646-320-1318. Personal E-mail: cataluna77@yahoo.com.

GOLDEN, CHRISTIE M., mathematics educator; b. Jackson, Tenn., Feb. 23, 1972; d. Raybon and Hope B. Moore; m. Scott M. Golden, Mar. 23, 2003; 1 child, Ela B. BS in Math., Union U., Jackson, Tenn., 1994; BS in Physical Therapy, U. Tenn., Memphis, 1996; MEd, Union U., 1999. Math. tchr. U. Sch. of Jackson, Jackson, Tenn., 1999—. Home: 11 Silverdale Lane Jackson TN 38305

GOLDEN, JUDITH GREENE, artist, educator; b. Chgo., Nov. 29, 1934; d. Walter Cornell and Dorothie (Cissell) Greene; m. David T. Golden, Oct. 10, 1955 (div.); children: David T. Golden III, Lucinda Golden Rizzo. BFA, Art Inst. Chgo., 1973; MFA, U. Calif., Davis, 1975; PhD Art (hon.), Moore Coll. Art, Phila., 1990. Assoc. prof. art U. Ariz., Tucson, 1981-88, prof. art, 1989-96, prof. emerita, 1996—. NEA forum pub. grants panelist, 1987; project dir. U. Calif. L.A. NEA Lecture series, 1979, 84; founder Ctr. Creative Photography, Tucson, 1996. One woman shows include Women's Bldg., LA, 1977, G. Ray Hawkins Gallery, LA, 1977, Quay Gallery, San Francisco, 1979, 81, A. Nagel Galerie, Berlin, 1981, Ctr. Creative Photography, U. Ariz., 1983, Colburg Gallery, Vancouver, Can., 1985, Etherton Gallery, Tucson, 1985, 89, 91, 95, Mus. Photog. Arts, San Diego, 1986, Friends of Photography, Carmel, Calif., 1987, Tucson Mus. Art, 1987, Mus. Contemporary Photography, Chgo., 1988, Visual Arts Ctr., Anchorage, Alaska, 1990, Temple Music and Art, Tucson, 1992, 97, 05, Scottsdale (Ariz.) Ctr. Arts, 1993, Arte de Oaxaca, Mex., 1995, Etherton Gallery, Tucson, 1995, Columbia Art Ctr., Dallas, 1997, U. Arts, Phila., 2002, Temple Music & Art, Tucson, 2005; exhibited in group shows at Centre Georges Pompidou, Paris, 1981, Security Pacific Bank, LA, 1985, Phoenix Mus. Art, 1985, LA County Mus. Art, 1987, 03, Tokyo Met. Mus. Photography, 1991, Laguna Art Mus., 1992, U. N.Mex. Mus. Art, Albuquerque, 1993, LA County Mus., 1994, Hara contemporary Mus., Tokyo, 1995, Mus. Women in Arts, Washington, 1997, Santa Barbara Mus. Art, Calif., 1997, 05, Mus. Cont. Photography, 1998, Tucson Mus. Art, 1999, Calif. Mus. Photography, 1999, Ctr. for Creative Photography, 1999, 04, Santa Barbara Mus. Art, 1999, 05, Mus. Fine Arts, Santa Fe, N.Mex., 2002, U. Ariz. Mus. Art, 2003, Akron (Ohio) Mus. Art, others; represented in permanent collections at Art Inst. Chgo., Calif. Mus. Photography, Ctr. Creative Photography U. Ariz., Denver Art Mus., Fed. Res. Bank San Francisco, Fogg Mus. Art, Grunwald Ctr. Graphic Arts, UCLA Mus. Continued Art, Internat. Mus. Photography George Eastman House, LA County Mus. Art, Mpls. Inst. Arts, Mus. Photographic Arts, San Diego, Calif., Mus. Fine Arts, Santa Fe, N.Mex., Newport Harbor Mus. Art, Oakland Mus. Art, Photography Mus. Osaka, Polaroid Corp., San Francisco Mus. Modern Art, Security Pacific Bank, Tokyo Met. Mus. Photography, Tucson Mus. Art, Weisman Found., LA, Mus. Cont. Photography, Chgo., Seattle Art Mus., Wash., Akron (Ohio) Art Mus., Avon Collection, N.Y.C.; resident Harvard Mus. Art, Taos, N.Mex., 2006. Individual artist grantee Tucson Pima Arts Coun., 1987; faculty rsch. grantee U. Ariz., 1986-87, 93-94; Ariz. Found. grantee U. Ariz., 1984; fellow Ariz. Commn. Arts, 1984; individual photography fellow NEA, 1979; Regent's faculty fellow Creative Rsch. U.Calif. L.A., 1977. Personal E-mail: judithgolden@earthlink.net.

GOLDEN, LIBBY, artist; b. N.Y.C. d. Simon and Anna (Guskoff) Siegel; m. Alfred Golden. Diploma in Arts, Cooper Union Art Sch., 1932; postgrad., Hunter Coll., 1934-36, NYU, 1937. One-woman shows include Seligmann Galleries, N.Y.C., Arwin Galleries, Detroit, De Boicourt Gallery, Birmingham, Mich., Chapman Gallery, Toledo, Gallery Three, Boston, Scottsdale (Ariz.) Ctr. for the Arts, 1982, Phila. Mus. Art, Preston Burke Galleries, Detroit, 1988; exhibited in group shows at Met. Mus. Art, N.Y.C., Associated Am. Artists, N.Y.C., Boston Mus. Art, Nat. Acad. Art (Prize award), Seattle Art Mus., Phila. Mus. Art (Purchase award 1962), Colorprint, U.S.A. (Prize award 1964), Mich. Painters and Printmakers (Prize award 1960), Butler Inst. Art, Bklyn. Mus.; represented in permanent collections Detroit Inst. Arts, Grand Rapids (Mich.) Art Mus., Flint (Mich.) Inst. Art, Colby Coll. Art Mus., Art Mus. Richmond, Matthews Ctr., Scottsdale Ctr. for the Arts, U.S. State Dept., AMA, Mich. Blue Shield, Owens-Ill. Print Collection, Nat. Bank Detroit, Chrysler Corp., Fed. Mogul Corp., The Clarke Collection, London, Temple Beth El, Denver and Birmingham, The Temple, Sylvania, Ohio, St. Vincents Med. Ctr., Toledo, Blain Clinic, numerous others; represented in numerous pvt. collections; commd. oil painting Ctr. for Beethoven Studies, San Jose (Calif.) U., 1986. Home and Office: 1209 E Loma Vista Dr Tempe AZ 85282-2515

GOLDEN, MARITA, English language educator, foundation executive; b. Washington, Apr. 28, 1950; d. Francis Sherman and Beatrice Lee Golden; m. Joseph Butlar Murray, Aug. 23, 1991; 1 child, Akintunde Michael Kayode. BA, Am. U., 1972; MSc, Columbia U., 1973; LittD (hon.), U. Richmond, 1998. Lectr. U. Lagos, Nigeria, 1975-79; asst. prof. Roxbury C.C., Boston, 1979-81, Emerson Coll., Boston, 1981-83; assoc. prof. George Mason U., Fairfax, Va., 1989-94; prof. English, Va. Commonwealth U., Richmond, 1994—2001. Author: Migrations of the Heart, 1983, A Woman's Place, 1986, Long Distance Life, 1989, And Do Remember Me, 1992, Wild Women Don't Wear No Blues, 1993, Saving Our Sons, 1995, Skin Deep, 1997, The Edge of Heaven, 1998, A Miracle Everyday, 1999, Gumbo, An Anthology of African American Writing, 2003, Don't Play in the Sun: One Woman's Journey Through the Color Complex, 2004. Pres. Hurston Wright Found., Hyattsville, Md., 1990—. Recipient Disting. Alumni award Am. U., 1994, Woman of Yr. award Zeta Phi Beta, 1997, Writers for Writers award Poets and Writers mag., 2001, Authors Guild Disting. Svc. award, 2002; named to Literary Hall of Fame, Chgo. State U., 2000. Mem. African Am. Writers Guild (pres. Washington 1986-90). Office: Hurston Wright Found Ste 531 6525 Belcrest Rd Hyattsville MD 20782

GOLDEN, OLIVIA ANN, human services administrator; b. NYC, May 23, 1955; BA in Philosophy and Govt., Harvard U., MPP, PhD. Budget dir. office human svcs. State of Mass., 1983-85; lectr. in pub. policy J.F. Kennedy Sch. Govt. Harvard U., Cambridge, Mass., 1987-91; dir. programs and policy Children's Def. Fund, Washington, 1991-93; commr. on children, youth and families HHS, Washington, 1993-97, prin. dep. asst. sec. for children and families, 1997, asst. sec. for children and families, 1997—2001; dir. D.C. Child and Family Svcs. Agy., 2001—04; sr. fellow Urban Inst., Washington, 2004—. Mem. adv. com. children and youth City of Cambridge. Author: Poor Children and Welfare Reform, 1992. Candidate for state senator, Mass. Office: Urban Inst 2100 M St NW Washington DC 20037 Business E-Mail: ogolden@ui.urban.org.

GOLDEN, PAULA ENGLANDER, social work educator, consultant, addiction educator, consultant; d. Josef Aaron and Erna (Lezer) Englander; m. David E. Golden, July 18, 1962; children: Jeff Bertram, Leila Justine. BS in Physics, Bklyn. Coll., 1956; MS in Physics, NYU, NYC, 1961; MA in Psychology, U. Nebr., Lincoln, 1974, PhD in Psychology, 1977. Cert. therapist and rschr. Level 2 Internat. Bd. Regression Therapy. Sr. scientist Lockheed Missiles and Space Co., Palo Alto, Calif., 1962—67; asst. project dir. U. Okla., Okla., 1975—76, prof., 1976—89; dir. grad. program chem. dependency studies Okla. Alcohol/Drugs Info. Clearinghouse, 1979—89, dir. chem. dependency tng. cert. program, 1979—89, dir., 1980—83, prof. women's studies, 1982—89. Dir. tng., founder Say It Straight Found., Carlsbad, Calif., 1982—; prof. dept. rehab., social work and addictions U. North Tex., Denton, 1989—2004; founder Inst. Studies in Addiction. Author (with Virginia Satir): Say It Straight: From Compulsions to Choices, 1990. V.p. Internat. Coalition Addiction Studies Educators, 1995—97; mem. adv. team Gov.'s Com. Aging, Oklahoma City, 1970, 1980; mem. adv. com. Tex. Commn. Alcohol and Drug Abuse, Austin, 1990. Recipient Citation Classic, Sci. Citation Index, 1981, Safe, Disciplined and Drug Free Schs. award, US Dept. Edn., Wash., 2001, award, Ctr. Substance Abuse Prevention, Wash., 2003, Dept. Juvenile Justice, Wash., 2005. Mem.: APA, AVANTA, Satir Internat. Network (mem. internat. com. 1984—, 1990). Achievements include development of three videotapes for the US Department of Education: Say It Straight: In the Classroom; Say It Straight: Student Support Group; Say It Straight: Family-Community Series. Avocations: yoga, travel, water aerobics. Office: Say It Straight Found 6254 Paseo Elegancia Carlsbad CA 92009 Office Fax: 509-278-7009. Business E-Mail: sayitstraight-info@sayitstraight.org, golden@pacs.unt.edu.

GOLDEN, SHAWNA, biomedical researcher; b. Brooklyn, Dec. 2, 1973; d. Stephen and Heather Rubenstein; m. Thomas Klever, 1997 (div. 1999); 1 child, Amanda Erin Klever; m. Daniel Golden, 2003; children: Amy Ruby, Adam Robert. BS in Molecular Bio., Johns Hopkins U., Balt., 1995. Staff scientist Vian Labs, Rye, NY, 1995—2000; rsch. Meriks Rsch. Ctr., Dix Hills, NY, 2000—05, assoc. rschr., 2005—. Contbr. articles to profl. jours., scientific papers. Mem.: Am. Soc. Law Medicine Ethics, Assn. Advancement Med. Instrumentation, Kappa Alpha Theta. Jewish. Avocations: gardening, crafts. Office: Meriks Rsch Ctr 8 Jordan Ct Dix Hills NY 11746-8319 Business E-Mail: goldensha@meriks.net.

GOLDEN, SHEILA S., retired special education educator; d. Harley Wade and Ruby Richards Golden. Student, Salem Coll., 1966—68; BS in Speech Pathology and Audiology, W.Va. U., 1970. Advanced Profl. Cert.in Spl. Edn.Grades K-12 Md. State Dept. Edn., 1980. Speech, lang. pathologist Bd. of Edn. of Mineral County, Keyser, W.Va., 1971—74; spl. edn. inclusion support tchr. Bd. of Edn. of Allegany County, Cumberland, Md., 1974—2004. Speech, lang. pathologist for summer head start program Bd. of Edn. of Mineral County, Keyser, 1971; ednl. coord. for summer programs for disabled students Clary St. Learning Ctr., Keyser, 1972—77. Contbr. articles to profl. jours. Vol. crisis counselor Family Crisis Ctr., Inc., Keyser, 1982—87, bd. dirs., 1982—87, sec., 1982—87, pres., 1982—87; vol. during 1985 flood disaster ARC; vol. Fire Escape Youth Ctr., Keyser, W.Va., 2005—; mem. Keyser-Mineral County C. of C., 1984—86, Mineral County Hist. Soc., Keyser, 2003—, Keyser Mineral County Friends of Libr. Assn., 2003—, vol., 2005—; mem. relay for life team Am. Cancer Soc., 2003—04; sec. exec. com. McNeill's Rangers Apple Alley Players, Inc., 1983—87, mem. funding com., 1983—87, chairperson box office, 1983—87, pub. rels. and media coord., 1983—87; bd. dirs. Potomac Kinship, 1983—86, pres., 1983—86, mem. spl. events com., 1983—86, chairperson, 1983—86, chairperson pub. rels. com., 1983—86; steering com. mem. Mineral County Substance Abuse Task Force, 1984—87, chairperson intervention com., 1984—87; bd. dirs. Mineral County Chpt., Am. Cancer Soc., 1984—87, fundraising chairperson, 1984—87, media chairperson, 1984—87; mem. programming com. Highland Arts Unlimited, Inc., 1982—89, 2003—05, mem. publicity com., 2003—, mem. accountability com., 2003—; mem. AAUW, 1985—87; life mem. Westernport Elem. Sch. PTA, Md., 2005—, Md. PTA, 2005—; vol. fundraiser Warm the Children Project, 2005—, shopper, 2005—; vol. Keyser After-Sch. Program, 2005—; mem. RCIA program Ch. of the Assumption, 1990—98; nursing home vol. Heartland of Keyser, 1999—, Clarksburg Continuous Care Ctr., Clarksburg, W.Va., 1987—, Moran Manor Care & Rehab. Ctr., Westernport, Md., 2000—. Named Vol. of Yr., Mineral County Mental Health Assn., 1985, Clarksburg Continuous Care Ctr., 2000; recipient Cert. of Appreciation for Outstanding Svc. to Cmty. and to Victims of Domestic Violence, Family Crisis Ctr., Inc., 1987, Plaque of Appreciation, Recognition as Exec. Com. Sec. and Publicity Coord., McNeill's Rangers, Apple Alley Players, Inc., 1987, Rose Dunlap award for Outstanding Vol., Heartland of Keyser, 2004, Cert. of Recognition for Vol. Svcs., 2005, Cert. of Recognition for Vol. Svc., Clarkesburg Continuous Care Ctr., W.Va., 2005, Heartland of Keyser Nursing Ctr., W.Va., 2005; scholar, scholar, 1968. Mem.: NEA (life), Nat. Ret. Tchrs. Assn. (life), Allegany County Tchrs. Assn. (life), Md. State Tchrs. Assn. (life). Roman Catholic. Achievements include research in Co-authored a research study on receptive language assessment scales; 1973-74. Avocations: volunteering-particularly with the geriatric population, attending concerts and stage shows, walking, crafts, reading. Personal E-mail: sgolden@pennswoods.net.

GOLDEN, THELMA, curator; BA in Art History & African Am. Studies, Smith College. Visual arts dir. Jamaica Arts Ctr., Jamaica, NY, 1989—91; dir., exhbn. coord. Whitney Mus. Am. Art at Philip Morris, 1991—93; assoc. curator, dir. br. museums Whitney Mus. Am. Art, 1993—96, curator, 1996—98; spl. projects curator Peter Norton Family Found., 1998—99; dep. dir. exhbns. and programs Studio Mus., Harlem, NY, 2000—05, chief curator, 2000—, exec. dir., 2005—. Lectr. in field. Curator (exhibitions) Black Male: Representations of Masculinity in Contemporary American Art, 1994, Bob Thompson: A Retrospective, 1998, Isaac Julien: Vagabondia, 2000, Martin Puryear: The Cane Project, 2000, Freestyle, 2001, Black and Green, 2001, Yinka Shonibare, 2002, Black Romantic: The Figurative Impulse in Contemporary American Art, 2002, Aaron Siskind: Harlem Document, 2003, Harlemworld: Metropolis as Metaphor, 2004, others. Office: The Studio Mus in Harlem 144 W 125th St New York NY 10027 Office Phone: 212-864-4500. Office Fax: 212-864-4800.*

GOLDEN, VIRGINIA ANN, principal; b. Cleve. d. James Alexander and Georgia Mae Cargile; m. George Phillip Golden Jr., July 27, 1985. BA, W. Henbert U., Springfield, Ohio, 1978; MA, Cleve. State U., 1994. Sales Kellogg's, Indpls., 1978—82; tchr. Cleve. Pub. Schs., 1982—94, Bedford City Schs., 1994—98, adminstrv. intern, 1998—99, prin. elem. sch., 1999—2001, dir. secondary edn., 2001—06, prin. mid. sch., 2006—. Foster mother, group home mother Bellefaire Jewish Children's Home, Cleve., 1985—2001. Mem.: Eta Phi Beta, Phi Delta Kappa. Avocations: bowling, cooking, reading. Office: Heskett Mid Sch 5771 Perkins Rd Bedford Heights OH 44146

GOLDENBERG, ELIZABETH LEIGH, finance company executive; b. Dayton, Ohio, Oct. 29, 1963; d. Neal and Myrna (Gallant) G. AB in Philosophy and Politics, Mount Holyoke Coll., 1985. Intern, spokeswoman The White House, Washington, 1984; trainee Nat. Westminister Bank USA, N.Y.C., 1985-86, asst. to v.p. fin. and strategic planning ops. div., 1986-87; asst. dealer Toronto-Dominion Bank, N.Y.C., 1987-88, dealer money markets, 1988-90, sr. dealer money markets, 1990-91, sr. dealer, sr. mgr. short term asset trading, 1991-93; sr. dealer, sr. mgr. short term loan participations TD Securities, Inc., N.Y.C., 1993-97, v.p., dir. short term money-market trading and origination, 1997-99; freelance journalist, author, 2000; reporter Bloomberg News, 2000—01, editor, team leader, 2001—02, mng. editor debt, currencies and derivatives, 2002—06; bus. mgr. fixed income Bloomberg LP, 2006—. Econ. commentator, 1993-2000. Contbr. articles and photographs to mags. Bd. dirs. USA Rugby Met. N.Y., 1987-89, N.Y. Rugby Club, 1995-98; publicist, spokesperson, com. on image and mktg. USA Rugby, 1993; U.S.A. Eagles publicist USA Rugby, Colorado Springs, Colo., 1989-94; chair Youth Rugby for Harlem Devel. Com., 1994-95. Mem. Pub. Securities Assn. (chmn. money market com. 1990-92, bd. dirs. 1990-92, mem. polit. action com.

1990-92, program com. 1990-92, awards com. 1991-93, chmn. money market com. 1997-99, bd. dirs. 1997-99). Avocations: photography, rugby, cooking, baking, ballet. Home: 355 S End Ave Apt 20J New York NY 10280-1007 Business E-Mail: egoldenberg2@bloomberg.net.

GOLDENBERG ABLER, MATHILDA MASLOW, artist; b. Brooklyn, N.Y., Mar. 7, 1920; d. Arthur and Harriet (Herrmann) Loebel; m. Ralph Maslow, Aug. 24, 1941 (dec. June 1976); children: Arthur, James, Elizabeth; m. Ely Goldenberg, July 1, 1984. Student, Cooper Union, 1942; BS, SUNY, 1965. Head dept. art Han. Poster Art, N.Y.C., 1937-43; designer furniture ads A.J. Kirven, Dayton, Ohio, 1944-45. Represented in permanent collections. Mem. Westchester (N.Y.) Art Assn., Scarsdale (N.Y.) Art Assn. Avocation: cooking. Home: 230 Garth Rd Apt 701 Scarsdale NY 10583-3960

GOLDFARB, MURIEL BERNICE, marketing consultant, advertising consultant; b. Bklyn., Mar. 29, 1920; d. Barnett and May (Steinberg) Goldfarb. BA, U. Miami, Coral Gables, Fla., 1942; postgrad., CCNY, 1950. Pub. info. asst. UNESCO, Paris, 1946—47; advt. mgr. Majestic Specialties Co., NYC, 1947—50; retail promotion mgr. Glamour Mag., 1955—61; advt. dir. Country Tweeds Co., NYC, 1961—65, S. Augstein & Co., NYC, 1966—72, Feature Ring Co., Inc., Gotham Ring Co., Inc., Fidco Inc., NYC, 1972—77; dir. advt. promotion Wasko Gold Products Corp., NYC, 1977—81; advt. mktg. cons. specializing promotions sale vintage jewelry Bric-a-Brac, 1982—. Lt. WAVES, 1943—46. Mem.: Women's Jewelry Assn. (corr. sec. 1983—85). Jewish.

GOLDFARB, RUTH, poet, educator; b. Bklyn., Aug. 13, 1936; d. Nathan Alter and Florence Goldfarb. BA in Psychology, L.I. Univ., 1980; MA in Edn., NYU, 1984. Tchr. kindergarten N.Y.C. Bd. Edn., 1963-64, early childhood tchr., 1993-94, N.Y.C., Bklyn., 1970-84; tchr. common br. Bklyn. Bd. Edn., 1986-93; clk. Primary Health Care Ctr. North Broward Med. Ctr., Pompano Beach, Fla., 1998—. Author (poetry) Whispers and Chants, 1997, Poems That Elevate the Soul, 2006; CD recs. include Christmas Memories, 1999, The Miracle of Christmas, 2000, Songs of Praise, 2000. Mem.: AARP, Gold Coast Poetry Group, Acad. Am. Poets, Internat. Soc. Poets. Avocations: poetry, music, sculpture, writing stories.

GOLDFINE, BEATRICE, artist; b. Phila., Aug. 17, 1923; d. Samuel and Esther (Sacks) Rubin; m. Leonard Goldfine, May 22, 1955; children: Carole Goldfine Ben-Maimon, Neil. Cert. in art history, Barnes Found., 1967; cert. in art, Pa. Acad. Fine Arts, Phila., 1980; student, Cheltenham Sch. Fine Arts, Phila., 1970; studied with Morris Blackburn, Phila., 1980-94. Studio, Phila., 1980—. Art works include bronze bust of Golda Meir (Jewish Cmty. Rels. Com. award 1984), Winston Churchill (Technion-Israel Inst. tech. award 1982). Bd. dirs. Bezelel Sch. Art and Design, Israel, 1990. Recipient Bok award Harrisburg Mus. Art, 1984, Selected Artist award Lind Creed Breast Cancer Found., 1994. Fellow Pa. Acad. Fine Arts (Mary Butler Meml. award 1992); mem. Pastel Soc. Am., North Light Book Club (Cover Competition award 1994), Artist's Cultural Exch. (Outstanding Achievement award 1988), Phila. Sketch Club (1st prize 1985), Woodmere Mus. Art (1st prize 1979), Friends of Barnes Found., Pastel Soc. Am., Phila. Art Alliance, Phila. Watercolor Club. Avocations: golf, tennis, walking. Studio: 1913 Guernsey Ave Abington PA 19001 Office Phone: 215-376-0128.

GOLDIE, DOROTHY ROBERTA, retired counselor; b. Phila., Apr. 7, 1922; d. Abe and Esther (Zupnick) Zafman; m. Ray Robert Goldie, Dec. 2, 1941 (dec. July 7, 2002); children: Deanne, Dale, Ron. MA in Humans Svcs., U. Calif., Riverside, 1976; postgrad., U. So. Calif. Bd. dirs. Family Svcs., San Bernardino, Calif.; counselor, instr. Suicide Crisis Hotline Inland Empire, San Bernardino; founder, counselor, instr., bd. dirs. Suicide Crisis Hotline Mountain Cmtys., Calif.; pres. Counsel of Mirage Inn, Rancho Mirage, Calif., 2004—05; ret. Mem. Amnesty Internat., Animal Samaritans SPCA, Inc.; charter mem. Women's Action Counsel Arthritis Found.; scholarship sponsor U. So. Calif. Law Sch., L.A., U. So. Calif. Keck Sch. Medicine, L.A., amb. to pres.; founder McCallum Theatre Bob Hope Cultural Ctr., Rancho Mirage, Eisenhower Hosp., Rancho Mirage; mem. Ctr. Sci. Pub. Interest, Jewish Family Svcs., Riverside Sheriff's Assn.; officer Sisterhood Temple Emanuel, San Bernardino, Sisterhood Temple Sinai. Mem.: AAUW, San Bernardino Lawyers Wives, B'nai B'rith (bd. dirs., pres.), U. So. Calif. Assocs. (life), U. So. Calif. Alumni Assn. (life), Rancho Mirage Calif. (life), Lake Arrowhead Country Club Women's Assn. (officer, bd. dirs.).

GOLDIE, SUE J., health service researcher; b. Washington, Dec. 14, 1961; m. Aaron Bradley Waxman, Apr. 17. 1986; children: Jacob Benjamin Waxman, Matthew Ariel Waxman. BS, Union Coll., 1984; MD, Albany Med. Coll., 1988; MPH, Harvard U., 1997. Bd. cert. Nat. Bd. Med. Examiners; diplomate, bd. cert. Am. Bd. Internal Medicine; lic. physician, Conn., Mass. Intern in internal medicine Yale New Haven Hosp., Yale U. Sch. Medicine, 1988-89, resident in internal medicine, 1989-91; fellow AHCPR policy award Harvard Sch. Pub. Health, Boston, 1996-98; attending physician Yale New Haven Hosp., 1990, Brigham and Women's Hosp., 1998; clin. asst. prof. medicine Yale U. Sch. Medicine, 1994-98; instr. medicine Harvard Med. Sch., Boston, 1998; asst. prof. health policy and health decision sci. Harvard Sch. Pub. Health, Boston, 1998, 1998—. Presenter in field. Contbr. articles to med. jour. Dana scholar Charles A. Dana Found., 1981, Dana fellow, 1982-84; Charles P. Drumm and Harold C. Wiggers merit scholar, 1984-88; MacArthur Fellow, John T. and Catherine MacArthur Found., 2005. Mem.: Soc. Med. Decision Making (editl. bd.), Am. Program Dirs. Internal Medicine (Original Investigation Competition award for innovative programs in med. edn. 1995), Soc. Gen. Internal Medicine (Larry Lynn award 1998), ACP, Alpha Omega Alpha. Office: Harvard Sch Pub Health 718 Huntington Ave Fl 2D Boston MA 02115-5924 Office Phone: 617-432-2010. Office Fax: 617-432-0190. E-mail: sgoldie@hsph.harvard.edu.

GOLDING, CAROLYN MAY, former government senior executive, consultant; b. Essex County, N.J., July 1, 1941; d. Wesley Irwin and Florence Grace (Smith) G.; m. Gary Anthony Derosa, Oct. 18, 1975 (div. Sept. 1982). BA, Duke U., 1963, postgrad., 1965—66. English tchr. Parkersburg (W.Va.) H.S., 1963; asst. to registrar Duke U., Durham, NC, 1963-65; mgmt. intern Dept. Labor, Washington, 1966-67, various other positions, 1967-72; dep. assoc. regional adminstr. Employment and Tng. Adminstrn., San Francisco, 1972-77, comptroller Washington, 1977-78, regional adminstr. San Francisco, 1979-82, dir. Unemployment Ins. Svc. Washington, 1982-87, adminstr. employment security, 1987-88, dep. asst. sec. employment and tng., 1988-96. Cons. on mgmt., labor force, long-range planning, workforce edn. issues and exec. coaching, 1996—; judge Arthur S. Flemming Award for Excellence in Fed. Svc. Recipient Disting. Career Svc. award Dept. Labor, 1979, Fed. Women's Career award Sec. Labor, 1983, Presdl. Meritorious rank, 1987, 95, Philip Arnow award Dept. Labor, 1988. Mem. Internat. Women's Forum, Women's Forum of Washington, Coun. for Excellence in Govt. (prin.), Women Mean Business (co-chair, Judge Arthur S. Flemming award Excellence Pub. Svc.) Episcopalian.

GOLDING, SUSAN G., former mayor; b. Muskogee, Okla., Aug. 18, 1945; d. Brage and Hinda Fay (Wolf) G.; children: Samuel, Vanessa. Cert. Pratique de Langue Francaise, U. Paris, 1965; BA in Govt. and Internat. Rels., Carleton Coll., 1966; MA in Romance Philology, Columbia U., 1974. Assoc. editor Columbia U. Jour. of Internat. Affairs, N.Y.C., 1968-69; teaching fellow Emory U., Atlanta, 1973-74; instr. San Diego Community Coll. Dist., 1978; assoc. pub., gen. mgr. The News Press Group, San Diego, 1978-80; city council mem. City of San Diego, 1981-83; dep. sec. bus., transp., housing State of Calif., Sacramento, 1983-84; county supr. dist. 3 County of San Diego, 1984-92; mayor City of San Diego, 1992—2000; pres. & CEO The Golding Group, Inc., San Diego, 2000—; head Homeland Security Office, Titan Corp., San Diego, 2000—. Chmn. San Diego Drug Strike Force, 1987-88, Calif. Housing Fin. Agy., Calif. Coastal Commn.; bd. dirs. San Diego County Water Authority; trustee So. Calif. Water Com., Inc.; founder Mid City Comml. Revitalization Task Force, Strategic Trade Alliance, 1993, Calif. Big 10 City Mayors, 1993; mem. Gov. Calif. Mil. Base Reuse Task Force, 1994; established San Diego World Trade Ctr., 1993, San Diego City/State/County Regional Permit Assistance Ctr., 1994; mem. adv. bd. U.S. Conf. of Mayors, 1994; chair Gov. Wilson's Commn. on Local Governance for 21st Century. Bd. dirs. Child Abuse Prevention Found., San Diego Conv. and Vis. Bur., Crime Victims Fund, United Cerebral Palsy, San Diego Air Quality Bd., San Diego March of Dimes, Rep. Assocs.; adv. bd. Girl Scouts U.S.; trustee So. Calif. Water Comm.; mem. Rep. State Cen. Com.; co-chair com. Presidency George Bush Media Fund, Calif.; chair San Diego County Regional Criminal Justice Coun., race rels. com. Citizens Adv. Com. on Racial Intergration, San Diego Unified Sch. Dist.; hon. chair Am. Cancer Soc.'s. Residential Crusade, 1988. Recipient Alice Paul award Nat. Women's Polit. Caucus, 1987, Calif. Women in Govt. Achievement award, 1988, Willie Velasquez Polit. award Mex. Am. Bus. and Profl. Assn., 1988, Catalyst of Chance award Greater San Diego C. of C., 1994, Woman Who Means Bus. award San Diego Bus. Jour., 1994, Internat. Citizen award World Affairs Coun., 1994; named One of San Diego's Ten Outstanding Young Citizens, 1981, One of Ten Outstanding Rep. County Ofcls. in U.S.A., Rep. Nat. Com., 1987, San Diego Woman of Achievement Soroptimists Internat., 1988. Mem. Nat. Assn. of Counties (chair Op. Fair Share, mem. taxation and fin. com.), Nat. Women's Forum. Republican. Jewish. Office: The Golding Group Inc 9276 Scranton Rd Ste 600 San Diego CA 92121 E-mail: commerce@golding.org.

GOLDMAN, BARBARA BAY, physical therapist; b. Chgo., July 30, 1935; d. Anthony and Janice Livingstone Bay; m. Ronald Leslie Goldman (div.); 1 child, Allison Kittay. BA, U. Calif., Berkeley, 1957; cert. in Phys. Therapy, U. Calif., San Francisco, 1958. Phys. therapist Peralta Hosp., Oakland, Calif., 1959—60, St. Mary's Hosp., San Francisco, 1962—63; chief phys. therapist Unity Hosp., San Francisco, 1965—74; pvt. phys. therapist Parnassus Heights Phys. Therapy, San Francisco, 1974—86; phys. therapist ReadiCare Health South U.S. Healthworks, Inc., South San Francisco, 1986—. Mem.: Friends of Earth, San Francisco Opera Guild, Sierra Club. Democrat. Avocations: drawing, fly fishing, photography, gardening. Office: 192 Beacon St South San Francisco CA 94080

GOLDMAN, JANICE GOLDIN, psychologist, educator; b. Phila., Feb. 15, 1938; d. Samuel and Dorothea (Berenson) Goldin; m. Arthur S. Goldman, Aug. 31, 1958; children: Jill Ann Goldman-Callahan, Joshua N., Jennifer S. BA, U. Pa., 1960, MA, 1962; MS, Hahnemann Med. Coll., 1972, D in Psychology, 1975. Lic. psychologist, Pa. Chief psychologist Charles Peberdy Child Psychiatry Ctr. Hahnemann U., Phila., 1975-87, from clin. asst. to assoc. prof., 1985-87; pvt. practice Jenkintown, Pa., 1977—. Cons. Haverford (Pa.) State Hosp., 1982, Assn. for Mental Health Affiliates with Israel, 1984, 86; mem. profl. adv. bd. Pub. Radio Sta WHYY, Phila., 1984-86; workshop leader Women's Ctr. of Montgomery County, Jenkintown, 1982—. Contbr. articles to profl. jours. Board dirs. Assn. for Mental Health Affiliate with Israel, nationwide, 1984-88, Or Hadash Synogogue, Wyncote, Pa., 1989, 96-2000. Mem. APA, Am. Family Therapy Acad., Nat. Register Health Svc. Providers, Phila. Soc. Clin. Psychology (sec. 1977-79), Am. Amnesty Internat., Internat. Soc. for Study Dissociation, Greater Phila. Soc. Clin. Hypnosis, Phi Beta Kappa. Democrat. Avocations: tennis, bicycling, cooking, reading, writing. Office: The Plaza 1250 Greenwood Ave Jenkintown PA 19046-2901 Office Phone: 215-572-1355. Personal E-mail: jgold1332@aol.com.

GOLDMAN, LYNN ROSE, medical educator; b. Galveston, Tex., Apr. 24, 1951; d. Armond Samuel and Barbara Jean (Bangert) G.; m. Douglas George Hayward. BS, U. Calif., 1976; MPH, Johns Hopkins U., 1981; MS, U. Calif., Berkeley, 1979; MD, U. Calif., San Francisco, 1981. Diplomate Am. Bd. Pediatrics; lic. physician, Calif. Resident in pediatrics Children's Hosp. Med. Ctr., Oakland, Calif., 1985; resident in preventive medicine U. Calif., Berkeley, 1985; pub. health med. officer Calif. Dept. Health Svcs., Berkeley, 1985-91, pub. health med. adminstr., 1991-93; asst. adminstr. Office of Prevention, Pesticides and Toxic Substances, EPA, Washington, 1993-98; prof. Sch. Hygiene and Pub. Health, Johns Hopkins U., Balt., 1999—. Democrat. Office: Johns Hopkins U Bloomberg Sch Pub Health 615 N Wolfe St Rm W8511 Baltimore MD 21205-1900 E-mail: lgoldman@jhsph.edu.

GOLDMAN, PHYLLIS E., psychology educator; BA, Rutgers U., 1966; MA, Seton Hall U., 1969; MS, Stevens Inst. Tech., 1978; EdD, Seton Hall U., 1983. Rsch. asst. Rutgers Univ., Newark, 1965-66; counselor N.J. Dept. of Labor and Industry, Newark, 1967-69; prof., psychology County Coll. of Morris, Randolph, N.J., 1969—; pvt. practice cons., 1978—. Author: Academic Self-Concept, 1992; editor: Dimensions of Work and Human Behavior, 1980, 85, (jour.) Morris Manager, 1988, 89, 90; contbr. articles to profl. jours. Mem. speakers bur. County Coll. Morris, Randolph, 1976—; bd. advisors Cath. Cmty. Svcs., Newark; mem. U.S. Postal Svc. Adv. Coun., 2003—04. Mem. Am. Psychological Assn., Psi Chi, Kappa Delta Pi, Phi Delta Kappa. Avocation: reading. Office: County Coll of Morris Rt 10 & Center Grove Rd Randolph NJ 07869 Office Phone: 201-328-5622.

GOLDMAN, RENITTA LIBRACH, special education educator, consultant; b. St. Louis, Aug. 15, 1938; d. Frank and Sally (Krantz) Librach; m. Jay Goldman, Dec. 20, 1959. BA, Washington U., St. Louis, 1960; MS, N.C. State U., 1967; PhD, U. Mo., 1978. Cert. tchr. Mo., sch. psychometrist Mo. Tchr. English and social sci. University City (Mo.) Pub. Schs., 1960-61; substitute tchr. St. Louis County Schs., St.Louis, 1961-64; rsch. asst. N.C. State U., Raleigh, 1967-68; counselor Columbia (Mo.) Pub. Schs., 1968-85; adj. asst. prof. U. Mo., Columbia, 1978-85; prof. spl. edn. U. Ala., Birmingham, 1985—. Cons., Birmingham, 1985—; sr. scientist Injury Prevention Rsch. Ctr. U. Ala., Birmingham, 1990—; spkr. in field. Author: Silent Shame: The Sexual Abuse of Children, 1986; sr. editor: Children at Risk, 1990; co-author: Issues and Trends in Education, 2002, 2nd edit., 2006; contbr. articles to profl. jours. Bd. dirs. Jefferson County Prevention Child Abuse, 1986—, Healthcare for Homeless, Birmingham, 1990—; bd. dirs., officer Jewish Family Svc., Birmingham, 1988—. Grantee UAB Injury Prevention Ctr., 1987, 1990, U.S. Dept. Edn., 1987, 1990, 1999, 2002. Mem.: Am. Assn. Counseling Devel., Assn. Children Learning Disabilities, Coun. Exceptional Children, Ala. Coun. Children Behavior Disorders (pres. 1988—89), U. Ala. Birmingham Faculty Women's Club, Phi Beta Kappa, Phi Delta Kappa, Phi Kappa Phi. Avocation: reading. Home: 6068 Brookhill Cir Birmingham AL 35243 Office: U Ala 210A Edn Bldg University Station Birmingham AL 35294 Office Phone: 205-934-3440. Business E-Mail: rgoldman@uab.edu.

GOLDMAN, TERI B., lawyer; b. Oklahoma City, Jan. 28, 1952; d. Howard L. and Betty J. Raskin; m. Gary S. Goldman, May 19, 1974; children: Geofffrey M., Eric R. BA, Stephens Coll., Mo., 1973; MA in Libr. Sci., U. Mo., 1985; JD, St. Louis U., 1990. Atty. Bryan Cave, 1990—92; prof. Washington U. Sch. Law, St. Louis, 1992—94; atty. Pepper Martin, LLC, 1993—98; atty., ptnr. Blackwell, Sanders, LLC, 1998—2000, Mickes, Tueth, LLC, 2000—02, Teri B. Goldman, LLC, 2002—. Office: 36 Four Seasons Ctr #337 Chesterfield MO 63017

GOLDSCHEIDER, FRANCES K., sociologist, educator; b. Balt., June 12, 1942; d. George Hyde and Ida Thomas (Sledge) Engeman; m. David R. Kobrin, Sept. 23, 1961 (div. 1978); children: Sarah, Janet; m. Calvin Goldscheider, Aug. 18, 1983. BA, U. Pa., 1965, MA, 1967, PhD, 1971. Asst. prof. sociology Skidmore Coll., 1969-74, Brown U., Providence, 1974-86, prof., 1986—, chair dept. sociology, 1984-87, dir. Social Sci. Data Ctr., 1984-85, dir. Population Studies and Tng. Ctr., 1989-92, 94-95, 2003—04; rsch. assoc. RAND Corp., 1980—, Inst. Social Rsch., U. Mich., Ann Arbor, 1989—. Vis. assoc. prof. demography The Hebrew U., 1983—84; vis. prof. sociology Stockholm U. Author: (with C. Goldscheider) The Ethnic Factor in Family Structure and Mobility, 1978, Ethnicity and the New Family Economy, 1989, (with Linda Waite) New Families, No Families: The Transformation of the American Home, 1991, (with C. Goldscheider) Leaving Home Before Marriage, 1993, (with C. Goldscheider) The Changing Transition to Adulthood: Leaving and Returning Home, 1999; editor: Demography, 1994-95; assoc. editor: Jours. of Gerontology, 1992-94, Am. Sociol. Rev., 1990-92, 2005—, Jour. Marriage and Family, 1987—, Demographic Research, 2002-; contbr. articles to profl. jours. NEH grantee, 1973-74; Fulbright fellow, 1983-84, 2001-02. Mem. Am. Sociol. Assn. (chair population sect. 1988-89), Internat. Union for Sci. Study of Population, Population Assn. Am. (bd. dirs. 1987-90, 2nd v.p. 1991-92, chair Dorothy Swaine Thomas Award com. 1985-86, chmn. pubs. com. 2002-03). Office: Brown U Dept Sociology Providence RI 02912-0001 Home: 2737 Devonshire Pl NW Apt 423 Washington DC 20008 Office Phone: 401-863-2535. Business E-Mail: frances_goldscheider@brown.edu.

GOLDSCHMIDT, AMANDA (AMY) O'CONNELL, food service executive; d. Edward Joseph O'Connell and Kay Grace Timmerman; m. Richard Steven Goldschmidt, Nov. 6, 1981; children: Edward O'Connell, Timothy O'Connell, William O'Connell, Rose Catherine. BA in English, U. Mo., St. Louis, 1981. Cert. tchr. English Mo., 1981. Tchr. All Souls Sch., Overland, Mo., 1982—92, St. Dismas Sch., Florissant, Mo., 1993—2004; asst. mgr. McDonald's, St. Louis, 2005—. Eucharistic min. St. Ferdinand Ch., Florissant, Mo., 1998. Personal E-mail: amyog@hotmail.com.

GOLDSCHMIDT, EVA, librarian; arrived in U.S., 1938; d. Phillipp Loewenfeld and Charlotte Winkler; m. Aron Goldschmidt (div.); children: Judith Anne, Leah Ruth. BA, Manchester Coll., Ind., 1943; MA, U. Chgo., 1944; MLS, Columbia U., N.Y.C., 1969. Rsch. analyst Office Strategic Svcs., Washington, 1944—45; rsch. writer UN Dept. Pub. Info., N.Y.C., 1946—49; sec., mgr. import, v.p. Textile Imports C. Hoedke Co., N.Y.C., 1951—67; adminstrv. asst. Walter E. Mayer Rsch. Inst. Law Columbia U., N.Y.C., 1967—69; reference libr. Rsch. Libr. N.Y. Pub. Libr., 1969—73; assoc. editor Fgn. Lang. Index Pub. Affairs Info. Svc., N.Y.C., 1973—86; libr. French Inst. Alliance Francais U., N.Y.C., 1986—94; libr. Lan Baeck Inst., N.Y.C., 1995—. Mem.: ACLU, Nature Conservancy, Sierra Club, Adirondack Mountain Club, Appalachian Mountain Club. Democrat. Avocations: reading, knitting, hiking, theater, concerts.

GOLDSCHMIDT, LYNN HARVEY, lawyer; b. Chgo., June 14, 1951; d. Arthur and Ida (Shirman) H.; m. Robert Allen Goldschmidt, Aug. 27, 1972; children: Elizabeth Anne, Carolyn Helene. BS with honors, U. Ill., 1973; JD magna cum laude, Northwestern U., 1976. Bar: Ill. 1976. Ptnr. Hopkins & Sutter, Chgo., 1976-2001, Foley & Lardner, Chgo., 2001—02; prin. D and G Cons. Group, 2002—. Articles editor Northwestern U. Law Rev. Mem. Airport Coun. Internat., N. Am., Order of Coif. Personal E-mail: lhg@dg-cg.com.

GOLDSCHMIDT, MYRA MARGARET, literature and language professor; d. Sidney and Ruth Straus; m. Michael Goldschmidt, Aug. 6, 1978; children: Kyle, Claire. BS, Towson State Coll., Md., 1970; MS, U. Pa., Phila., 1986, PhD, 1993. Tchr. English Montgomery Village Jr. H.S., Gaithersburg, Md., 1970—74, Seneca Valley HS, Germantown, 1974—78; prof. ESL Villanova U., Pa., 1986—97; asst. prof. linguistics Pa. State U., Media, 1997—. Concert violinist, Md., 1968—72; prof. dancer, Washington, 1970—78; dir. ESL program Villanova U. - Pa. State U., 1986—; cons. and rsch. evaluator, South Africa, 2003—04; cons. and grant evaluator State of N.J., 2005; founder Civic Engagement Minor Pa. State U., 2005—06; plenary spkr. U. Botswana, 2005; invited lectr. Oxford U. Round Table, England, 2006. Contbr. chapters to books, articles to profl. jours. Named Tchr. of Yr., Peace and Justice Dept. Villanova U., 1997. Mem.: Tchrs English to Students Other Langs., Am. Assn. Applied Linguistics, Internat. Assn. Applied Linguistics. Avocations: dance, travel. Office: Pa State U 25 Yearsley Mill Rd Media PA 19063-5522 Office Phone: 610-892-1465. Business E-Mail: mmg5@psu.edu.

GOLDSLEGER, CHERYL, artist, educator; b. Phila., Dec. 16, 1951; d. Abraham and Ruth Edith (Richman) G.; m. Larry Wayne Millard; 1 child, David Richman. Student, Tyler Sch. Art, Temple U., Rome, Italy, 1971; BFA, Phila. Coll. Art, Pa., 1973; MFA, Washington U., St. Louis, Mo., 1975. Asst. prof. Western Carolina U., Cullowhee, NC, 1975-77, Piedmont Coll., Demorest, Ga., 1988—2001, Ga. State U., Atlanta, 2001—. Vis. lectr. Ga. Southern Coll., Statesboro, Ga., 1981; artist in residence East Carolina U., Greenville, N.C., 1986. One woman shows include Miss. Mus. Art, Jackson, 1983, Southeastern Ctr. for Contemporary Art, Winston-Salem, N.C., 1985, High Mus. Art, Atlanta, 1985, Heath Gallery, Atlanta, 1980, 83, 89, Arden Gallery, Boston, 1988, 90, 92, Jessica Berwind Gallery, Phila., 1992, Bertha Urdang Gallery, N.Y.C., 1982, 84, 87, 89, 91, 93, Rosenberg & Kaufman Fine Art, N.Y.C., 1996, 98, 99, 2001, 02, 05, Halsey Gallery, Coll. Charleston, S.C., 2002, Greenville (S.C.) County Mus. Art, 2002, Macon (Ga.) Mus., 2002, Kidder Smith Gallery, Boston, 2003, Mus. Contemporary Art Ga., 2003; exhibited in group shows at The Inst. Contemporary Art, Phila., 1983, Islip (NY) Art Mus., 1984, Va. Mus. Fine Arts, 1985, Alternative Mus., N.Y.C., 1985, Greenville Mus., S.C., 1985, Mint Mus. Charlotte, 1986, New Orleans Mus., 1986, 87, Ivan Dougherty Gallery/City Art Inst., Australia, 1986, Bklyn. Mus., 1986, Am. Acad. and Inst. of Arts and Letters, N.Y.C., 1987, Ga. Mus. Art, Athens, Ga., 1987, Norton Gallery, Palm Beach, Fla., 1987, Corcoran Gallery, Washington, D.C., 1989, Israel Mus., Jerusalem, 1989, Perugia, Italy, 1991, Stephen Rosenberg Gallery, N.Y.C., 1994, U. Tenn., Knoxville, 1999, Montclair (N.J.) Mus., 2000, N.C. Mus. Art, Raleigh, 2000, Krannert Mus., Champaign, Ill., 2002, Cin. Art Mus., 2002, Bowdoin (Maine) Coll. Mus. Art, 2002; permanent collections include Albright Knox Art Gallery, Buffalo, Bklyn. Mus., High Mus., Atlanta, Israel Mus., Jerusalem, Mus. Modern Art, N.Y.C., Tel Aviv Mus., Israel, R.I. Sch. Design Mus. Artist fellow Pa. Coun. on the Arts, 1981, Sr. Artists fellow Ohio Arts Coun., 1982, Sr. Artist's fellow Nat. Endowment for the Arts, 1982, 91, RJR fellow Southeastern Ctr. for Contempory Art, 1986, Artist's fellow Ga. Coun. for the Art's, 1991, U.S./France fellow Nat. Endowment for the Arts, 1993, La Napoule Found. fellow, France, 1994; 5th Fl. Found. grantee, 1999. Mem. Coll. Art Assn. Home: 170 Greenwood Dr Athens GA 30606-4704 Office: Ga State U Sch Art & Design Atlanta GA 30303 E-mail: cgold@gsu.edu.

GOLDSMITH, BARBARA, writer, historian; d. Joseph I. and Evelyn (Cronson) Lubin; children: Andrew Goldsmith, Alice Elgart, John Goldsmith. BA, Wellesley Coll., Mass., 1958; DLitt (hon.), Syracuse U., N.Y., 1980; LHD (hon.), Pace U., N.Y.C., 1982; DLitt (hon.), Lake Forest Coll., Ill., 1996. Contbr. N.Y. Herald Tribune, Esquire Mag., 1958—64; founder, contbg. editor N.Y. Mag., 1968—; sr. editor Harpers Bazaar Mag., N.Y.C., 1970-74. Lectr. NYU, 1969, 75. Spl. writer TV documentaries and entertainments; author: (novel) The Straw Man, 1975; (non-fiction) Little Gloria.Happy at Last, 1980, Johnson v. Johnson, 1987, Other Powers: The Age of Suffrage, Spiritualism and the Scandalous Victoria Woodhull, 1998, Obsessive Genius: The Inner World of Marie Curie, 2005. Pres. Com. for Preservation and Access, 1990—95; mem. Pres.'s Commn. on Celebration of Women in Am. History, 1998—2001; mem. jr. coun. Mus. Modern Art, N.Y.C., 1951—73, mem. internat. coun., 2004—; mem. acquisitions com. Friends of Whitney Mus. Art, 1964—; mem. exec. bd. PEN Am. Ctr., 1984—2006; chmn. permanent paper com. PEN Freedom to Write Com., 1989—; founder Ctr. for Learning Disabilities, Albert Einstein Coll. Medicine; trustee N.Y. Pub. Libr., 1985—, mem. exec. com., 2003—, mem. nominating com., 2004—; gubernatorial appointee N.Y. State Coun. on Arts, 1990; founder Barbara Goldsmith/PEN Freedom to Write awards, Barbara Goldsmith/N.Y. Pub. Libr. Conservation and Preservation Divsns., Barbara Goldsmith/NYU Preservation and Conservation Dept.; founder, trustee Am. Acad. in Rome Barbara Goldsmith Rare Book Rm., 1988—; bd. dirs. permanent paper task force Nat. Libr. Medicine, 1989—97; bd. dirs. Parks Coun. N.Y.C., 1965—82, Nat. Dance Inst., 1979—, Goldsmith Found., 1981—. Recipient Brandeis U. Library Trust award, 1980, Albert Einstein Spirit of Achievement award, 1988, Permanent Paper citation N.Y. Pub. Libr., Lit. Lions award N.Y. Pub. Libr., 1988, Pubs. 1st Ann. award Lit. Market Place, 1990, Rome medal Am. Acad. in Rome, Nat. Libr. Medicine Lit. award, 1991, Nat. Archives award, 1991, NYU Presdl. Citation award, 1993, Lifetime Achievement award Guild Hall Acad. Arts, 1999, Poets and Writers Lit. award, 1999, Presdl. citation for pub. svc., 2000, (4) Notable Book awards NY Times, (5) Editor's Choice NY

Times, Lit. award, 2006. Mem. Authors Guild, Century Assn., Am. Acad. Arts and Scis., Guild Hall Acad. Arts (Lit. Achievement award 1999). Office: Janklow & Nesbit Attn Ms Lynn Nesbit 598 Madison Ave New York NY 10022-1614

GOLDSMITH, BETTY F., counselor; BS, East Tex. State Univ., Commerce, Tex., 1994; MS, Tex. A & M, Commerce, Tex., 2002. Cert. Nat. Counselor, lic. profl. counselor. Counselor Glen Oaks Hosp., Greenville, Tex. Mem.: ACA, Tex. Counseling Assn., Chi Sigma Iota.

GOLDSMITH, CATHY ELLEN, retired special education educator; b. NYC, Feb. 18, 1947; d. Eli D. and Gertrude A. G. BS, NYU, 1968, MA in Elem. Edn., 1971, MA in Ednl. Psychology, 1974. Cert. phys. handicapped, K-6 elem. edn. tchr., N.Y. 2d grade tchr. N.Y.C. Bd. Edn., 1968-69, tchr. learning disabled students (spl. edn.), 1969-86, tchr. emotionally disturbed learning disabled students, 1986-87, tchr. learning disabled students, 1987-88, tchr. trainable retarded students, 1988-2000, tchr. mixed disabilities class, 2000-01; ret., 2001. Represented in permanent collections Bobst Libr. NYU. Recipient Charles Oscar Maas Essay Am. History award NYU, 1968, Disting. Alumni Svc. award NYU, 1987. Mem. AAUW, Nat. Mus. Women in Arts, Nat. Women's History Mus., Nat. Trust for Historic Preservation, Hadassah (life, Youth Aliyah honoree 2006), NYU Alumni Assn. (past rec. sec., v.p.), NYU Alumni Assn., Peninsula Hosp. Ctr. Aux. (life, sec.), NYU Alumnae Club (past v.p.), Pi Lambda Theta (past pres., past historian, past mem. chair), Kappa Delta Epsilon. Home: 418 Beach 133d St Belle Harbor NY 11694-1416

GOLDSMITH, DONNA, sports association executive; b. Long Island; Degree in comm., SUNY, Oswego. Worked at Swatch Watch USA, Revlon Inc.; v.p. licensing NBA; sr. v.p. consumer products World Wrestling Fedn. Entertainment Inc., Stamford, Conn., 2000—. Mem.: NY Women in Comm. Office: World Wrestling Fedn Entertainment Inc 1241 E Main St Stamford CT 06902 Office Phone: 203-328-2561. E-mail: donna.goldsmith@wwecorp.com.

GOLDSMITH, ELEANOR JEAN, retired hospital administrator; b. Mount Vernon, N.Y., Aug. 16, 1929; d. Elias Benjamin Jacobson and Rose Millicent Liebowitz; m. Myles Robert Goldsmith, Mar. 8, 1981 (dec.); m. Marshall H. Numark (div.); children: Deborah Lynn Numark, Laura Ellen Madere, Neil Joseph Numark. BS in commerce, Coll. of New Rochelle, N.Y., 1949; MA in Edn., NYU, 1950, EdD, 1979. Cert. tchr. N.Y., 1950, lic. nursing home adminstr. Tex., 1983. Tchr. Mount Vernon Sch. Bus., Mount Vernon, 1949—50, Northport HS, NY, 1950—51; supr. recreation Greystone Park Psychiatric Hosp., Morris Plains, NY, 1969—80; dir. activities therapy Bellevue Psychiatric Hosp., N.Y.C., 1980—82; adminstr. Mesquite Tree Nursing Home, Tex., 1983—84; edn. coord. dept. ophthalmology U. Tex. Southwestern Med. Ctr., Dallas, 1984—92; ret., 1992. Author several mag. articles. Elected mem. Bd. Edn., Fair Lawn, NJ, 1957—59. Mem.: Women's Am. ORT, Bridgeport Upper Merion Lions Club (v.p.). Avocations: travel, reading, bridge, skiing, ice skating. Home: 3000 W Valley Forge Cir #941 King Of Prussia PA 19406 Personal E-mail: elgoldsmith@comcast.net.

GOLDSMITH, ETHEL FRANK, medical social worker; b. Chgo., May 31, 1919; d. Theodore and Rose (Falk) Frank; m. Julian Royce Goldsmith, Sept. 4, 1940; children: Richard, Susan, John. BA, U. Chgo., 1940. Lic. social worker, Ill. Liaison worker psychiat. consultation svc. U. Chgo. Hosp., 1964—68; med. social worker Wyler Children's Hosp., Chgo., 1968—98. Treas. U. Chgo. Svc. League, 1958-62, bd. dirs.; chmn. camp Brueckner Farr Aux., 1966-72; pres. Bobs Roberts Hosp. Svc. Commn., 1962; bd. dirs. Richardson Wildlife Sanctuary, 1988-2000; mem. Field Mus. Women's Bd., 1966—; bd. dirs. Hyde Park Art Ctr., 1964-82, Chgo. Commons Assn., 1967-77, Alumni Assn. Sch. Social Svc. Adminstrn., 1976-80, Self Help Home for Aged, 1985-2000; vol. Chgo. Found. for Edn.; mem. womens bd. U. Chgo., 1999—. Recipient Alumni Citation Pub. Service, U. Chgo., 1972. Mem. Phi Beta Kappa. Home: 5550 S Shore Dr Apt 1313 Chicago IL 60637

GOLDSMITH, JANET JANE, pediatric nurse practitioner; b. Creston, Iowa, Mar. 3, 1942; d. Paul William and Mary Lucille (Crow) Schafroth; m. Olin Russel Goldsmith, Aug. 31, 1963; children: Rodney, Scott, Kristen. Diploma, Iowa Meth. Hosp. Sch. Nursing, Des Moines, 1963; PNP, U. Iowa, 1982; BSN, Graceland U., Lamoni, Iowa, 1984. Cert. pediatric nurse practitioner. Staff nurse Rosary Hosp., Corning, Iowa, 1963-66, 71-72; sch. nurse Corning Commun. Schs., 1966-67; area adminstr., occupant protection program adminstr. Iowa Gov.'s Traffic Safety Bur., Des Moines, 1985—2002; ret., 2002; sch. nurse West Des Moines Sch. Sys., 2004—; clin. study coord. Heartland Med. Rsch., 2004—. Clin. instr. Southwestern C.C., Creston, Iowa, 1970, adj. faculty, 1985—86; health/handicap coord. Matura-Head Start, Creston, 1973—81; pediat. devel. nurse Child Diagnostic and Planning Svc., Creston, 1975—81; pediat. nurse practitioner physician's office, Lenox, Iowa, 1982—84, Otologic Med. Svcs., Iowa City, 1982—87, Taylor County Pub. Health, Bedford, Iowa, 1982—87, Heart and Hands, Des Moines, 2003—04; cons. Hwy. Safety Area, adv. bd. Iowa Ctr. for Agrl. Safety and Health; sexual assault nurse investigator, 2002; presenter, cons. in field. Author booklets, tng. video, articles, tng. curricula. Recipient Recognition of Accomplishment award Gov. of Iowa, 1989. Mem. Internat. Assn. Forensic Nurses, Iowa Pub. Health Assn. (exec. bd., legis. com.) Nat. Assn. Pediatric Nurse Assocs. and Practitioners (pub. rels. com.), Iowa Nurses Assn. (local treas., state policy com.), Iowa Assn. Nurse Practitioners (constn. and by-laws chmn., pres.), Iowa Traffic Control and Safety Assn. (bd. dirs., treas., sec., v.p., pres.). Methodist. Home: 1675 Walnut Woods Dr West Des Moines IA 50265-8511 Office Phone: 515-669-0641.

GOLDSTEIN, BARBARA BLOCK, education educator, director; b. Newport News, Va., Dec. 25, 1942; d. Irving Block and Rita Shirley (Sarfan) Spirn; m. Ralph Martin Goldstein, June 23, 1963; children: Irving Block, Beth Conn, Jay Alan. BA, Duke U., 1963; MA, Coll. William and Mary, 1984, postgrad., 1984—. Tchr. Newport News Sch. System, 1963-87, reading tchr., 1977-87, instrnl. specialist, 1987-89; prin., 1989—98; coord. sch. of edn. Coll. of William and Mary, Williamsburg, Va., 1999—. Bd. dirs. Newport News Reading Coun., 1977—. Mem. Tidewaters Assn. Early Childhood Devel. (bd. dirs.), Newport News Coun. Jewish Women (past treas.), Hadassah (officer), Delta Kappa Gamma (bd. dirs.). Home: 240 W Tazewells Way Williamsburg VA 23185-6524 Office: Coll of William and Mary Sch Leadership Inst 208 S Boundary St Williamsburg VA 23187

GOLDSTEIN, DEBRA HOLLY, judge; b. Newark, Mar. 11, 1953; d. Aaron and Erica (Schreier) Green; m. Joel Ray Goldstein, Aug. 14, 1983; children: Stephen Michael, Jennifer Ann. BA, U. Mich., 1973; JD, Emory U., 1977. Bar: Ga. 1977, Mich. 1978, D.C. 1978, Ala. 1984. Tax analyst atty. Gen. Motors Corp., Detroit, 1977-78; trial atty. U.S. Dept. Labor, Birmingham, Ala., 1978-90; U.S. adminstrv. law judge office disability and justice review Social Security Adminstrn., Birmingham, 1990—. New judge faculty U.S. adminstrv. law judges Social Security Adminstrn., 1991,93-, mem. Gov.'s Commn. Quality Tchg., 2006-. Troop leader Girl Scouts, 1992—2004, bd. dirs. Cahaba coun., 1996—2002; active Momentum, 2002—03; chmn. Success By 6 Blue Ribbon adv. com., 2003—05; active Leadership Ala., 2004—05; bd. dirs. Temple Emanu-El, 2000—03, Leadership Birmingham Assn., 2004—, United Way, Birmingham, 2004—, exec. com., 2005—; bd. dirs. YWCA, 2002—. Mem. ABA, Ga. Bar Assn., D.C. Bar Assn., Birmingham Bar Assn. (bd. dir. women's sect. 1999-2003), Ala. Bar Assn. Forum (pres. 2004—), Zonta, B'nai B'rith Women, Hadassah, Women's Network. Jewish. E-mail: debra.goldstein@ssa.gov.

GOLDSTEIN, DORA BENEDICT, pharmacologist, educator; b. Milton, Mass., Apr. 25, 1922; d. George Wheeler and Marjory (Pierce) Benedict; m. Avram Goldstein, Aug. 29, 1947; children: Margaret E. Wallace, Daniel P., Joshua S., Michael B. Student, Bryn Mawr Coll., 1940-42, Stanford U., 1945. Rsch. assoc. Stanford U., 1955-70, sr. rsch. assoc., 1970-74, adj. prof., 1974-78, prof. pharmacology, 1978-92, prof. pharmacology emerita, 1992—, co-dir. faculty mentoring program sch. medicine, 1994—2001. Author: Pharmacology of Alcohol, 1983; contbr. articles to sci. jours. Bd. dirs. Parents, Families and Friends of Lesbians and Gays, 2000-06. Mem.: Intersex Soc. N.Am. (med. adv. bd. 2003—05). E-mail: dody@stanford.edu.

GOLDSTEIN, DORIS MUELLER, librarian, researcher; b. Somerville, N.J., Mar. 11, 1942; d. Henry Frederick and Sophie Mueller; m. Steven Morris Goldstein, July 4, 1971. BA, U. Nebr., 1964, MA, 1966; cert., Goethe U., Frankfurt, Fed. Republic Germany, 1966; MLS, U. Md., 1973. Vol., instr. Peace Corps, Addis Abeba, Ethiopia, 1966-68; cataloger Libr. of Congress, Washington, 1968-69; instr. Bowie (Md.) State Coll., 1969-72; libr. Kennedy Inst. of Ethics Georgetown U., Washington, 1973-81, dir. libr. and info. svcs., 1981—, dir. Nat. Reference Ctr. for Bioethics Lit., 1984—. Cons. dept. nursing George Mason U., Fairfax, Va., 1984-89; adj. faculty mem. in libr. sci. U. Md., 1990. Author: Bioethics: A Guide to Information Sources, 1982; editor Scope Note Series, 1985—; co-editor Bibliography of Bioethics, 2002-; contbr. articles to profl. jours. Mem. Phi Beta Kappa, Alpha Lambda Delta, Delta Phi Alpha, Beta Phi Mu. Office: Georgetown U Kennedy Inst Ethics Washington DC 20057-1212

GOLDSTEIN, JANE D., lawyer; b. Oct. 21, 1960; BA magna cum laude, Boston Univ., 1982, JD magna cum laude, 1989. Bar: Mass. 1989. Assoc. Ropes & Gray, Boston, 1989—98, ptnr. corp. dept., 1998—, head, retail & consumer branded products practice group. Mem.: Mad River Ski Club (bd. dir.). Office: Ropes & Gray 1 International Pl Boston MA 02110-2624 Office Phone: 617-951-7431. Office Fax: 617-951-7050. Business E-Mail: jane.goldstein@ropesgray.com.

GOLDSTEIN, JOYCE, special education educator; b. Bklyn., July 7, 1949; d. George and Eleanor (Mittleman) Kluback; m. Charles Irwin Goldstein, May 31, 1975; children: Andrew, Roger. BA, CUNY., Queens, 1971; MS, C W Post, 1975, MS, 1990. Sci. tchr. IS 151, Bronx, 1972-76; spl. edn. tchr. of emotionally handicapped Bd. Coop. Ednl. Svcs. 2, Sayville, NY, 1989-91; spl. edn. tchr. emotionally handicapped Bd. Coop. Ednl. Svcs., West Islip, NY, 1991—2004; global studies tchr., spl. edn. Bellport Acad. Ctr., NY, 2004—. Contbr. articles to profl. jours. V.p. Young Republicans, Queens, 1969-71. Mem. Coun. for Exceptional Children. Avocations: reading, fishing, travel. Home: 49 Empress Pines Dr Nesconset NY 11767-3128 E-mail: cgoldi@optonline.net.

GOLDSTEIN, JOYCE ESERSKY, restaurant owner; b. Bklyn., July 17, 1935; d. Gerry Lewis and Jeanne (Salata) Esersky; m. Marc Evan Goldstein, Sept. 15, 1957 (div. Aug. 1972); children: Evan Matthew, Karen Anne, Rachel Laura. BA, Smith Coll., 1956; MFA, Yale U., 1959. Painter, San Francisco, 1961-65; cooking tchr., 1965-71; tchr., dir. Calif. St. Cooking Sch., San Francisco, 1971-76; tchr. U. Calif., Berkeley, 1976-83; chef, mgr. Chez Panisse Cafe, Berkeley, 1981-83; chef, owner Sq. One Restaurant, San Francisco, 1984—. Author: Feedback, 1977, The Mediterranean Kitchen, 1989, Back to Square One, 1992, Festive Occasion, 1993, Mediterranean The Beautiful, 1994; columnist Bon Appetit mag., 1982—, San Francisco Chronicle, 1986—, James Beard Perrier Jour., Best Chef in Calif., 1993. Named one of Top 25 Am. Cooks, Cooks mag., 1985. Mem. San Francisco Food Soc., Am. Inst. Food and Wine (bd. dirs. No. Calif. chpt. 1985-87). Jewish.

GOLDSTEIN, JUDITH SHELLEY, director; b. Bklyn., Mar. 5, 1935; d. Maurice and Mary (Goldstein) G. BA, Adelphi U., 1956; MA, Columbia U., 1957; EdD, Hofstra U., 1984. Cert. permanent tchr. in reading, spl. and elem. edn., N.Y. Early childhood tchr. N.Y.C. Sch. System, Bklyn., 1957-80; reading specialist Southampton Unified Sch. Dist., NY, 1981-87; spl. edn. tchr. Amagansett Sch., NY, 1987-88; mem. adj. faculty C.W. Post Campus, L.I. U., Brookville, NY, 1984-88, supr. clin. practice Southampton Campus, 1988-95. Exec. dir. nursery sch. Jewish Ctr. of Hamptons, East Hampton, N.Y., 1988-89; adj. assoc. prof. Southampton Campus L.I. U., 1989-94, Dowling Coll., 1990-92; chmn. edn. Hadassau, 2003-; adj. asst. prof. Suffolk County C.C., 1989-95, adj. assoc. prof. 1995-2005, adj. prof., 2005—. Mem. Guild Hall, East Hampton, 1980—; v.p. edn. Hadassah, East Hampton, 1989-92, chmn. edn., 2003; chair Am. Affairs, 1993-96, Hadassah edn. chair 2002-03; tchr. religious ch. Jewish Ctr. of the Hamptons, 1990-98; vol. Bay St. Theatre, Sag Harbor, N.Y., Long House Res., East Hampton; mem., vol. Friends of Guild Hall, East Hampton; mem. Jewish Ctr. Hamptons, 1974-98. Mem. AAUW (v.p. programming 1987-89, sec. 1993-99, 2003). Democrat. Avocations: gardening, museums, theater. Home: 138 Windward Rd East Hampton NY 11937-3189

GOLDSTEIN, LISA JOY, writer; b. LA, Nov. 21, 1953; d. Harry George and Miriam (Roth) G.; m. Douglas Andrew Asherman, Jan. 12, 1986. BA, UCLA, 1975. Author: The Red Magician, 1982 (Am. Book award for best paperback 1983), The Dream Years, 1985, paperback edit., 1986, A Mask for the General, 1987, paperback edit., 1988, Tourists, 1989, paperback edit., 1994, Author's Choice Monthly: Daily Voices, 1989, Strange Devices of the Sun and Moon, 1993, paperback edit., 1994 (Sci. Fiction Book Club selection), Summer King, Winter Fool, 1994, paperback edit., 1995, Travellers in Magic, 1994, paperback edit., 1997, Walking the Labyrinth, 1996, paperback edit., 1998, Dark Cities Underground, 1999 (Sci. Fiction Book Club selection), paperback edit., 2000, The Alchemist's Door, 2002, paperback edit., 2003. Office: care Tor Books 175 5th Ave New York NY 10010-7703

GOLDSTEIN, MARCIA LANDWEBER, lawyer; b. Bklyn., Aug. 7, 1952; d. Jacob and Sarah Ann (Danovitz) Landweber; m. Mark Lewis Goldstein, June 3, 1973. AB magna cum laude, Cornell U., 1973, JD cum laude, 1975. Bar: NY 1976, US Dist. Ct. (So. and Ea. dists.) NY, US Ct. Appeals (2nd, 3rd, 5th, 7th and 9th cirs.); cert. mediator, So. Dist. NY. Assoc. Weil, Gotshal & Manges LLP, NYC, 1975-83, ptnr. to mng. ptnr., 1983—, co-chair, bus. fin. & restructuring devel. Adv. bd. Colliers on Bankruptcy, 15th edit., editor (15th edit. revised); vis. lectr. Yale Law Sch., 1986-88; lectr. Columbia Law Sch., Practicing Law Inst. ALI-ABA, Southeastern Bankruptcy Law Inst., NYU bankruptcy workshop; served as mediator for several Chapter 11 cases; trustee Chapter 11; serves on the Law Sch. Adv. Coun.; mem. Cornell Law Sch. Dean's Spl. Leadership Com. Articles editor Cornell Law Review, 1974—75. Mem. ABA (com. on creditors' rights, corp. counse. com.), Assn. of Bar of City of NY (chair bankruptcy and reorgn. com.), Nat. Bankruptcy Conf. (chair misc. com.), Am. Coll. Bankruptcy, Internat. Insolvency Inst. Office: Weil Gotshal & Manges LLP 767 5th Ave New York NY 10153 Office Phone: 212-310-8214. Office Fax: 212-310-8007. Business E-Mail: marcia.goldstein@weil.com.

GOLDSTEIN, MARGARET FRANKS, special education educator; b. Toledo, July 3, 1940; d. Ray E. and Esther R. (Drewicz) Franks; m. William D. Goldstein, July 30, 1961; children: Sheldon, Benjamin, Marshall, Rochelle. BS in Edn., Bowling Green (Ohio) State U., 1975; MEd, U. Toledo, 1984. Cert. spl. edn. and indsl. arts educator. Tchr. indsl. arts Toledo Pub. Schs., 1970-77, tchr. devel. handicapped/behavior disordered, 1980-86, tchr. devel. handicapped/transitional tchr., 1986—99, severe behavior disability career ladder tchr., 1987—2000, mem. state supt.'s spl. edn. adv. coun., 1988—, chair, 1999—. Mem. state supt.'s task force for preparing spl. educators Toledo Pub. Schs., 1986—. Mem. Am. Fedn. Tchrs. (conv. del.), Ohio Fedn. Tchrs. (exec. coun., publicity and svcs. com., elections com., chmn., conv. del.), Toledo Fedn. Tchrs. (bd. dirs.), NW Ohio Spl. Edn. Assn. Office: McTigue Jr HS 5537 Hill Ave Toledo OH 43615-4699

GOLDSTEIN, MARJORIE TUNICK, special education educator; b. Port Chester, NY, Oct. 20, 1940; d. Abraham and Gertrude (Gluckman) Tunick; m. Herbert Goldstein, May 27, 1973. BA, Syracuse U., 1961; MA, George Washington U., 1968; PhD, Yeshiva U., N.Y.C., 1979. Spl. edn. tchr. Lancaster (Pa.) City Pub. Schs., 1962-63, Hempfield Union Schs., Landisville, Pa., 1963-64, Montgomery County (Md.) Pub. Schs., 1964-65; edn. specialist U.S. Office Edn., Washington, 1965-69; coord. field ops. Curriculum R&D Ctr., Yeshiva U., N.Y.C., 1969-78; supr. spl. edn. E. Ramapo Cen. Sch. Dist., Spring Valley, N.Y., 1978-79; adj. asst. prof. Herbert Lehman Coll., Bronx, 1980-83; spl. edn. coord. Ednl. Improvement Ctr./NE, W. Orange, N.J., 1981-83; prof. William Paterson U. of N.J., Wayne, N.J., 1983—. Spl. needs book reviewer Instr. mag., N.Y.C., 1984-90; co-developer entry level cert. tests Pa. Ednl. Testing Svc., Princeton, 1985-88; prin. investigator Project Link, a Transition Program, 1987-90. Cons. editor Career Devel. for Exceptional Individuals, 1988-97, 2004—; contbr. articles to profl. jours. Office Spl. Edn. and Rehab. Svc./Dept. Edn. grantee, 1987-90; named Educator of Yr., Morris County ARC, 1991, N.J. Assn. Retarded Citizens, 1991. Mem. ASCD, Coun. Exceptional Children (sec. N.J. div. on career devel. 1988, pres. 1992-93, 2001-04), Am. Ednl. Rsch. Assn., N.J. Assn. Supervision and Curriculum Devel. (assoc. exec. dir. 1984-85, 86-87, 89-91, pres. 2006—). Office: William Paterson Univ NJ Dept SPED & CSL 300 Pompton Rd Wayne NJ 07470-2103 Office Phone: 973-720-3092. Business E-Mail: goldsteinm@wpunj.edu.

GOLDSTEIN, MARSHA FEDER, tour company executive; b. Chgo., July 7, 1945; d. Charles S. and Geraldine (Shulman) Feder; m. Michael Warren Goldstein, Dec. 26, 1966; 1 child, Paul Goldstein. BA, Roosevelt U., 1967. Tchr. art Chgo. Pub. Schs., 1967-68; freelance artist Chgo., 1968-71; tchr. arch. Brandeis U., Northfield, Ill., 1974-80; tour guide My Kind of Town Tours, Highland Park, Ill., 1975-79, owner, 1979—. Owner Tours at the Mart, 1992-95; art cons. Randall Pub. Co., Inc., 1984—. Editor: Highland Park by Foot or Frame, 1980; contbr. to book in field. Charter mem. Nat. Mus. Women in the Arts; commr. and chmn. Highland Park Hist. Preservation Comm.; mayoral appt. Sister Cities Com., 1998; chmn. Paris Sister Cities, 2000—05; bd. dir. Roosevelt U., Chgo., Art Encounter, Parisian Salon Concerts; mem. adv. bd. and benefit chmn. Gene Siskel Film Ctr.; mem. devel. bd. Feltre Sch., 1999—2004. Recipient Cert. of Completion, Chgo. Arch. Found., 1975; named Disting. Alumni of Yr. Roosevelt U., 1997. Mem.: Chgo. Conv. and Tourism Bd. (devel. com.), Women's Exec. Network, Nat. Assn. Women Bus. Owners (bd. dir. Chgo. chpt., pres.), Assn. Destination Mgmt. Execs. (founder), The Auditorium Bldg. Soc. (chmn. 1994, founder), Brandeis U. Nat. Women (v.p. 1977—, bd. dir.), Union League Club (standing com., art com.). Jewish. Office: My Kind of Town 1585 Tara Ln Lake Forest IL 60045-1221 Office Phone: 847-295-8221. E-mail: info@mykindoftown.net.

GOLDSTEIN, MARY KANE, physician; b. NYC, Oct. 24, 1950; d. Edwin Patrick and Mary Kane; m. Yonkel Noah Goldstein, June 24, 1979; children: Keira, Gavi. Degree in Philosophy, Barnard Coll., 1973; MD, Columbia U., 1977; MS in Health Svcs. Rsch., Stanford (Calif.) U., 1994. Resident Duke U. Med. Ctr., Durham, NC, 1977-80; asst. prof. medicine U. Calif., San Francisco, 1980-84; clin. instr. dept. family and cmty. preventive medicine Stanford U., 1984-85, dir. grad. med. edn. divsn. gerontology, 1986-93, Agy. for Health Care Policy Rsch. fellow Sch. Medicine, 1991-94, asst. prof. medicine Med. Ctr. Line, 1996—99, with Ctr. Primary Care and Outcomes Rsch., 1998—, assoc. prof. medicine Med. Ctr. Line, 1999—2005, faculty fellow Inst. for Rsch. on Women and Gender, 2000—01, prof. medicine Med. Ctr. Line, 2005—; staff physician Mid-Peninsula Health Svc., Palo Alto, Calif., 1986-88; sect. chief for gen. internal medicine Palo Alto VA Med. Ctr., 1994-96, rsch. assoc. health svcs. R & D, 1996—2002; assoc. dir. clin. svcs. VA Geriatric Rsch. Edn. and Clinical Ctr., Palo Alto, 1999—. Editor Computer Ctr. Pubs., N.Y.C., 1971-72; computer programmer Columbia U., N.Y.C., 1972-73; governing coun. evidence-based practice ctr. U. Calif., Stanford, 1998—; automated decision support VA Health Svc. Rsch. & Devel., 2004, VISN collaborative for hypertension, 2005. Author chpt. to book; contbr. articles to profl. jours. Recipient Clin. Practice Guildelines for Hypertension award, VA Health Svc. R & D, 1997, Automated Decision Support Hypertension award, 2004, Practice Guidelines Multisite Study award, 2000, Dissemination Supplement to Drug Therapy Hypertension Multisite Study award, 2004, VA Intelligent Critiquing of Med. Records award, NIH/NLM, 2001, Disutility of Functional Limitations award NIH/NIA, 2001, VA Hosp., VISN Collaborative Improving Hypertension Mgmt. with ATHENA-HTN award, 2006-. Fellow: Am. Geriat. Soc. (bd. dirs. 1997—2002); mem.: Coll. Physicians and Surgeons. Office: VA Palo Alto Health Care Sys GRECC 182B 3801 Miranda Ave Palo Alto CA 94304-1290 Office Phone: 650-858-3933. Business E-Mail: goldstein@stanford.edu.

GOLDSTEIN, MARY WISEMAN, education educator; d. Leo J. and Helen Crooks Bittner; m. Harvey Goldstein; m. Charles Wiseman (div.); m. John O'Connor (div.); 1 child, Emily. BA, St. John's Coll., Annapolis, 1959; MA, Harvard U., Cambridge, Mass., 1969; PhD, Columbia U., N.Y., 1974. Philosophy prof. Bklyn. Coll., Bklyn., 1972—99, CUNY, N.Y.C., 1983—99. Home: 4936 Curly Hill Rd Doylestown PA 18901-9727

GOLDSTEIN, PHYLLIS ANN, art historian, educator; b. Chgo., Apr. 27, 1926; d. Frederick and Belle Florence (Hirsch) Jacoby; m. Seymour Goldstein, Nov. 19, 1947 (dec. 1980); children: Arthur Bruce, Kathy Susan Goldstein Maultasch. BA, Hunter Coll., 1948; MA, Hofstra U., 1985. Tchr. home econs. Cin. Pub. Schs., 1948-50; nutrition instr. Brandeis U. Nat. Women's Com., Westbury, N.Y., 1975-78, instr. art history, 1984-91; lectr. art history Brandeis U./Nat. Women's Com., Westbury, N.Y., 1985-92; instr. art history Herricks Adult Cmty. Edn. Program, 1990-91. Camp counselor, troop leader Girl Scouts U.S., N.Y.C., Cin., 1942-51; cub leader Boy Scouts Am., Westbury, 1963-64; active Sisterhood of Temple Beth Avodah, Westbury, 1958-80, pres. 1964-65; active Sisterhood of Temple of Beth Am., Merrick, N.Y., 1980-91; life mem. Brandeis U. Nat. Women's Com., lectr. art history, 1992—; Meadowbrook chpt. pres., 1985-87, South Dade chpt., 1996-98, mem. Fla. regional bd., 1998-99; vol. Fairchild Tropical Botanic Gardens, 1994—. Mem. Williamsburg Mus., Mus. Art Ft. Lauderdale, Met. Mus. Art N.Y., Hadassah (life). Democrat. Avocations: sewing, swimming, needlecrafts, quilting, travel. Home: 90 Edge Water Dr Apt 1001 Coral Gables FL 33133

GOLDSTEIN, SANDRA CARA, lawyer; b. Bklyn., May 12, 1964; BA, Barnard Coll., 1984; JD, NYU, 1987. Bar: N.Y. 1988. Assoc. Cravath Swaine and Moore LLP, NYC, 1987—94, ptnr., 1994—, mng. ptnr. litig., 2005—. Office: Cravath Swaine & Moore LLP Worldwide Plz 825 8th Ave Fl 38 New York NY 10019-7475 Office Phone: 212-474-1000. Office Fax: 212-474-3700. Business E-Mail: sgoldstein@cravath.com.

GOLDSTEIN, SHARI, healthcare educator; b. Syosett, NY, July 10, 1976; MS, Fla. Atlantic U. Asst. dir. pre-health professions advising Fla. Atlantic U., Boca Raton, 2000—. Recipient Excellence in Undergrad. Advising, Fla. Atlantic U., 2001. Mem.: NAAHP. Office: Florida Atlantic U 777 Glades Rd Boca Raton FL 33431 Office Phone: 561-297-0064.

GOLDSTEIN, SYDNEY RACHEL, photographer, writer, radio producer; b. San Francisco, Oct. 13, 1944; d. Edward William and Dorian Claire G.; m. Charles R. Breyer, Jan. 18, 1976; children: Katherine, Joseph. Grad. h.s., San Francisco. Photographer, writer, 1970—; prodr., founding exec. dir. City Arts & Lectures, Inc., San Francisco, 1981—; exec. prodr. City Arts & Lecturs, Radio Broadcasts, 1997—. Author: Earned Income, 2001. Adv. bd. Grants for the Arts, San Francisco Hotel Tax Fund, 1979-82. Recipient Koret Israel prize Koret Found., 1990. Democrat. Office: City Arts & Lectures Inc 1955 Sutter St San Francisco CA 94115

GOLDWASSER, SHAFRIRA, computer scientist; b. NYC, 1958; BS in math., Carnegie Mellon U., 1979; MS in computer sci., PhD in computer sci., U. Calif., Berkeley. RSA prof. elec. engring. and computer sci.; co-leader cryptology and info. security group Lab. Computer Sci. Prof. math. scis. Weitzmann Inst. Sci., Israel. Recipient Göbel prize, Theoretical Computer Sci., 1993, 2001, ACM Gracy Murray Hopper award, 1996, RSA award in math., 1998. Mem.: NAE, Am. Acad. Arts and Scis., NAS. Office: MIT Dept Elec Engring and Computer Sci 77 Massachusetts Ave Cambridge MA 02139 Business E-Mail: shafi@csail.mit.edu.*

GOLDWASSER, SHIRLEY WHITEMAN, educational psychologist; b. Atlanta, June 25, 1935; d. Ben W. and Sarah R. (Abelman) Whiteman; m. M. Robert Goldwasser, June 24, 1956; children: Elise S., Kenneth L. BA, Ga. State U., 1976, MEd, 1978, PhD, 1988. Grad. rsch. asst. Ga. State U., Atlanta, 1978-79, assoc. grant dir., 1981-82, instr., tcg. fellow, 1979-83, program devel. specialist, 1984-86; edn. cons. Galloway Sch., Atlanta, 1986-88; prof. Piedmont Coll., Demorest, Ga., 1990-93; ednl. psychologist Raleigh, N.C., 1993—. Presenter in field. Co-editor: Minimum Competency Education: Issues, Methodology and Policy for Local Sch. Systems, 1982. Docent N.C. Mus. Art, Raleigh, 1993—; mem. speaker's bureau Prevent Child Abuse N.C., Raleigh, 1993—. Teaching fellow Ga. State U., 1979-83. Mem. APA, Nat. Women's Studies Assn., Southeastern Psychol. Assn., Psy Chi. Avocations: travel, classical music, opera. Home and Office: 33 Renwick Ct Raleigh NC 27615-2990 Business E-Mail: gapeach24@bellsouth.net.

GOLDWATER, EDNA M., retired public relations executive; d. Herman Goldwater and Lillie Rothstein. BA, Columbia U., 1971, MA, 1973. Assoc. editor Film News, N.Y.C., 1946—47; staff writer World Video, Inc., N.Y.C., 1947—48; writer, film prodn. asst. Victor Weingarten Pub. Rels., N.Y.C., 1953—56; pub. rels. dir. Am. Phys. Therapy Assn., N.Y.C., 1957—58; asst. dir. pub. rels. NASW, 1958—60; dir. pub. info. Cancer Care, N.Y.C., 1960—64; pub. rels. dir. United Negro Coll. Fund, N.Y.C., 1964—65. Lectr. contemporary films Inst. Ret. Profls., NY, 1987—95, City Coll., N.Y.C., 1995—2000. Prodr., writer: (documentaries) The Return, 1958. Lectr., writer Soc. for Advancement of Judaism, N.Y.C., 1980—; reporter Nation Assocs., N.Y.C., 2000—. With WAC, 1944—45. Mem.: Tchrs. Coll. Alumni Assn., Columbia Alumni Fedn. Democrat. Jewish. Avocations: reading, gardening, films. Home: 110 West End Ave New York NY 10023 E-mail: emgold94@verizon.net.

GOLDWATER, MARILYN R(UBIN), medical/surgical nurse, state legislator; b. Boston, Jan. 29, 1927; d. Frederick and Rebecca (Geller) Rubin; m. William H. Goldwater, Aug. 8, 1948; children: Charles Alan, Diane Louise. Diploma, Mt. Sinai Hosp. Sch. Nursing, N.Y.C., 1948. RN, Md. Legislator State of Md., Annapolis, 1975-86; dir. Office Fed. Rels. Md. Dept. Health and Mental Hygiene, 1987-90; exec. asst. for health issue Gov.' Office, 1990—; mem. Md. Ho. of Dels., 1995—. Speaker on econs. and politics of health care; faculty assoc. U. Md., George Mason U. and Johns Hopkins U. schs. nursing. Author: (with Mary Jane Lloyd Zusy) Prescription for Nurses: Effective Political Action, 1990; mem. editl. adv. bd. Policy, Politics, and Nursing Practice, 2000; contbr. articles to profl. jours. Recipient Ann London Scott Legis. Excellence award, 1979, Legislator of Yr. award Md. Pub. Health Assn., 1982, Legis. Contbns. to Home Health Care award Upjohn Co., 1982, Disting. Alumna award Mt. Sinai Hosp. Sch. of Nursing, 1993; honored MedStar Health Vis. Nurse Assn., 2000. Fellow: Am. Acad. Nursing (hon.); mem.: ANA (bd. dirs. Hon. Recognition award 1980), Nat. Assn. Jewish Legislators, Order Women Legislators, Sigma Theta Tau. Office: Md Gen Assembly Lowe House Office Bldg Rm 221 Annapolis MD 21401-1691 Home: Apt 1927 5801 Nicholson Ln Rockville MD 20852-5738

GOLDWAY, RUTH Y., federal agency administrator; b. N.Y., Sept. 17, 1945; d. David and Mahilda G.; chldren: Casey, Anthony, Julie. BA, U. Mich., 1965; MA, Wayne State U., 1968; postgrad., UCLA, 1970-71. Asst. dir. Dept. Consumer Affairs, L.A., 1975-78; mayor City Santa Monica, Calif., 1979-83; dir. pub. affairs Calif. State U., L.A., 1984-91; mgr. pub. affairs Getty Trust, L.A., 1991-94; commr. postal rate commn., Washington, 1998—. Chair and founder Santa Monica Pier Restoration Corp., 1981-94; founding mem. Consumer Adv. Panel, GTE, San Francisco, 1974-76. Author: Letters From Finland, 1998; contbr. articles to profl. jours., 1994-97; actress in film Dave, 1992. Bd. dirs. So. Calif. Consumer Affairs Profls., 1986-92. Recipient Best Diplomatic Role Model, Helsinik City Mag., 1996. Avocations: biking, cooking, travel. Office: Postal Rate Commn 1333 H St NW Ste 300 Washington DC 20268-0002 Office Phone: 202-789-6810. Business E-Mail: goldwayr@prc.gov.

GOLEMBESKI, BEVERLY LONG, artist, art educator; d. Charles Wesley and Evelyn Mae (Hinchman) Long; m. Francis Gerald Golembeski, Feb. 24, 1962; children: Scott Fitzgerald, Cortlyn Elizabeth, Deidre Aleece, Tyler Gerard. BA in Fine Arts, Montclair State, NJ, 1962; studies watercolor with profl. artists, 1997—2003. Cert. art tchr. K-12. Art tchr. Ctrl. Regional High Sch., Bayville, NJ, 1962—66; recreation dir. Borough of Seaside Park (N.J.), 1963—67; art coord. Athletic Booster Club, Bayville, NJ, 1973—78. Adj. instr. Georgian Ct. Coll., Lakewood, NJ; profl. artist, instr., demonstrator, lectr., judge, 1980—2005; ofcl. artist USCG; cons. in field. Illustrator summer program booklets Borough of Seaside Heights, 1972—73, Toms River Soccer and Lavallette Little League, NJ, 1976—78; office designs, GTECH Corp., Mexico and Argentina, 1992—94, mural, Shore Cmty. Bank, Toms River, N.J., 1994, Brass Beds Antique Shoppe, Beachwood, N.J., 1995; illustrator various covers Jersey Shore Mag., Bayhead, N.J., 2000—03; exhibitions include N.J. Mus., Montclair, Monmouth Mus., Shrewsbury, N.J., Noyse Mus., Barnegat, N.J., John Hopkins U., Washington, Robertson Ctr., Delaware County, N.Y., Cooperstown Mus., NY, exhibited in group shows at Arts for the Parks, Jackson Hole, Wyo., 2005—06. Activities coor; activities coord. Seaside Park Fire Co., 1970—76; asst. Girl Scouts U.S.A., Ocean County, NJ, 1977—82; pres., chair various activities Seaside Park Sch. PTA, 1975—85. Recipient award, Trenton Mus., NJ, 2001, Jane Law's Art Gallery, Long Beach Island, Surf City, N.J., 2001, NJAAPL, 2000—03, Nat. Watercolor Soc. and Phila. Watercolor Soc. Pine Shores Art Assn. Manahawkin, N.J., 2002, Pine Shores Art Assn., 2002—03, Audubon Artists-Dick Blick award, Salmagundi Club, Merit award, R.I. Watercolor Soc., 2004, 3rd Pl., Ocean County's Artist show, 2005, Ida Wills and Clara Stroud award, NJ Am. Artists Profl. League, 2005, hon. mention, RI Watercolor Soc. Nat. Watermedia Competition. Fellow: Nat. Am. Watercolor Soc.; mem.: Audubon Artists Inc., N.J. Watercolor Soc. (bd. dirs., A.G. Edwards award), Pa. Watercolor Soc., Am. Artists Profl. League (award Salmagundi Club 2002, Pauline Wick award 2005), Ocean County Artists' Guild (past pres.), Garden State Watercolor Soc., Phila. Watercolor Soc. (signature). Avocations: gardening, bicycling, cooking, snowmobiling, swimming. Home: 16 I St Seaside Park NJ 08752-1525 Office Phone: 732-793-8224. E-mail: Beviemae@aol.com.

GOLIAN-LUI, LINDA MARIE, librarian; b. Woodbridge, NJ, Mar. 27, 1962; d. Joseph John Golian and Mary Grace (Juba) Rodriguez; m. Gary S. Lui, Oct. 6, 1988; 1 child, Katherine Jana Lui-Golian. BA, U. Miami, 1986; MLIS, Fla. State, 1988; EdS, Fla. Atlantic U., 1995, EdD, 1998; postgrad., Fla. Gulf Coast U., 1999—2002. Libr. tech. asst. U. Miami, 1981-86; serials control libr. U. Miami Law Sch., 1986-89; serials dept. head Fla. Atlantic U., Boca Raton, 1990-97; univ. libr. Fla. Gulf Coast U., Ft. Myers, 1997—2002, adj. instr. Coll. Arts and Scis., 1999—2002; libr. dir. U. Hawaii, Hilo, 2002—. Adj. instr. Fla. Atlantic U. Coll. Continuing & Distance Edn., 1993-97, U. So. Fla. Coll. Libr. Sci., 1995-2002; program specialist Marriott Statford Ctr. Sr. Living Cmty., Boca Raton, 1994-96. Vol. storyteller Aid to Victims of Domestic Assault, Delray Beach, Fla., 1994—96. Named Hawaii County Woman of Yr., 2005; recipient Mover and Shaker award, Libr. Jour. Mem. NOW, AAUW (by laws chair Hawaii and Pacific chpt. 2005—), NAFE, ALA, Hawaii Libr. Assn. (state chpt. councilor 2003-), Spl. Libr. Assn., N.Am. Serials Interest Group (co-chair mentoring com. 1996-97), ASCD, Southeastern Libr. Assn., Assn. Libr. and Info. Sci. Educators, Am. Libr. Assn., Am. Assn. Higher Edn., Assn. Libr. Collection & Tech. Svcs., Libr., Adminstrn. & Mgmt. Assn., Reference & User Svcs. Assn. (continuing libr. edn. network & exch. round table, intellectual freedom round table, libr. instruction round table, new members round table, staff orgn. round table, women's studies sect. comm. com. 1994—, serials nomination com. 1993, Miami local arrangements com. 1994, chair libr. sch. outreach 1994—, pres. 1998-99, 3M profl. devel. grantee 1995), Assn. Coll. Rsch. Libr. (Lazerow rsch. fellow 1997), Laubach Literary Vols. of Am., Am. Assn. Adult and Continuing Edn., Fla. Libr. Assn. (serials libr. or yr. 1994, grantee 1987, Libr. Jour. Mover and Shaker 2005), Am. Coun. Edn. Hilo Chpt. Women in Edn., Zonta (fellowship com. 2002—). Roman Catholic. Avocations: reading, fishing, ceramics, tennis. Office: U HI Hilo Edwin H Mookini Lib & Graphic Ser 200 W Kawili St Hilo HI 96720-4091 Office Phone: 808-933-3132. Business E-Mail: golianlu@hawaii.edu.

GOLICI, ANA, artist; b. Romania, 1955; arrived in US, 1987; With Podul Printmaking Workshop, Romania; mem. faculty continuing edn. Hunter Coll., NYC. Exhibitions include NY Hall of Sci., Hunter Coll. Times Sq. Gallery, East-West Gallery, NY, Internat. Print Ctr. NY, Holiday Show, Gallery 49, NYC, 2003—04, exhibited in group shows at 181st Ann.: An Invitational Exhib. Contemporary Art, Nat. Acad. Mus., NYC, 2006. Office: Hunter Coll Continuing Edn 695 Park Ave East Bldg 10th Fl New York NY 10021*

GOLKE-BAHNSEN, MORNA RAELYNNE ELSIE, secondary school educator; d. Arnold Wilhelm Karl Golke and Elsie Pauline Kwiram-Golke; m. Gill Stanford Bahnsen, July 3, 1988; children: Kyle Drew Arnold Bahnsen, Raena Elyse Bahnsen. MEd, U. Wash., 2002. Cert. tchr. Gen. Conf. Seventh-day Adventists, Wash. English tchr. Highland View Acad., Hagerstown, Md., 1986—91, asst. dean of women, 1986—88; English tchr. Auburn (Wash.) Adventist Acad., 1991—2001, Emerald Ridge H.S., Puyallup, Wash., 2001—02; online educator Adventist Edn. for 21st Century, Apopka, Fla., 2002—. Mem.: ASCD, ISTE, NCSS, Nat. Coun. Tchrs. English. Avocations: reading, cooking, travel. Office: Adventist Education for the 21st Century 3909 E Semoran Blvd Apopka FL 32703 Office Phone: 407-772-3789. Business E-Mail: mbahnsen@ae21.org.

GOLLIN, SUSANNE MERLE, cell biologist, researcher; b. Chgo., Sept. 22, 1953; d. Harvey A. and Pearl (Reiffel) G.; m. Lazar M. Palnick; 1 child, Jacob Hillel. BA in Biology, Northwestern U., 1974, MS, 1975, PhD, 1980. Diplomate Am. Bd. Med. Genetics with cert. in clin. cytogenetics; cert. food protection specialist. Postdoctoral fellow U. Rochester (N.Y.) Med. Ctr., 1979-81; rsch. assoc. in cell biology Baylor Coll. Medicine, Houston, 1981-83, rsch. assoc. in genetics, 1983-84; asst. prof. dept. pathology and pediat. U. Ark. for Med. Sci., Little Rock, 1984-87; dir. cytogenetics lab. Ark. Children's Hosp., Little Rock, 1984-87; assoc. mem. Pitts. Cancer Inst., 1987-95, mem., 1995—; dir. U. Pitts. Cancer Inst. Cytogenetics Facility, 1989—; asst. prof. human genetics U. Pitts., Grad. Sch. Pub. Health, 1987-95, dir. clin. cytogenetics lab., 1988-99, assoc. prof., 1995—2003, prof., 2003—, prof. human genetics, otolaryngology, pathology, 2003—; dir. rsch., clin. cons. Pitts. Cytogenetics Lab., 1999—. Pediat. oncology group, exec. com. Ark. Genetics Program, 1984-87; organizing com. Am. Cytogenetics Conf., 1990-2002; mem. Allegheny County Bd. Health, 1992-2004, vice chmn., 1997, 2000-04; bd. dirs. Tobacco-Free Allegheny; clin. lab. improvement adv. com. Ctrs. Disease Control and Prevention, HHS, 1994-2000, mem. genetic testing subcom., 1997-2000; vis. sci. German Cancer Rsch. Ctr., Heidelberg, 1995; cons. med. devices adv. com. FDA, 1996—; mem. oral biol. med. I study sect. NIH, 1997; master gardener, 2000; spl. emphasis panel Nat. Cancer Inst., 2000; genetics spl. emphasis panel ZRG1-GEN-01S, NIH Ctr. for Sci. Rev., 2000, spl. emphasis panel Nat. Cancer Inst., Minority Instn./Cancer Ctr. Partnerships, 2000, 05, mammalian genetics study sect., 2002; lectr. U.S.-Japanese Cancer Rsch. Collaborative Conf., Tokyo, 2001; lectr. 1st Dhirubhai Ambani Life Scis. Symposium, Mumbai, 2006; immunol. devices panel FDA, 2004—; lectr. in field. Contbr. articles to profl. jours., chpts. to books; mem. editl. bd. Cytogenetics and Genome Rsch., 2005— Mem. deans' adv. com. Pa. Sch. Excellence for Healthcare Profls., 1991-95; v.p. faculty senate U. Pitts. Grad. Sch. Pub. Health, 1994-95, senate anti-discriminatory policies com., 1999-2002, faculty senate athletics com., 2004—, search com. dean Grad. Sch. Pub. Health and chair human genetics, 2004-06., faculty adv. promotion tenure com., 2005—; vol. Lighthouse for Blind, Houston, 1983; vol. hort. dept. Pitts. Zoo, 2000-2001; chmn. med. ethics and civil liberties com. ACLU, Pitts., 1989-91; alt. del. Dem. Nat. Conv., 1992, 96, 2000, mem. rules com., 2004. Fellow Am. Coll. Med. Genetics (founder); mem AAAS, Am. Assn. Cancer Rsch., Am. Soc. Human Genetics (info. and edn. com. 2004-2005, mem. program com. 2005—), Am. Soc. Cell Biology, Soc. Analytical Cytology, Pitts. Cancer Inst., Pitts. Cytogenetics Club (founder, coord. 1989-95), Phipps/Pitts. Garden Place, Western Pa. Conservancy, Rivers Club, Carnegie Museums, Pitts. Zoo, Sigma Xi. Avocations: mountain dulcimer, gardening, photography, pulled thread embroidery. Office: U Pitts Dept Human Genetics Grad Sch Pub Health 130 Desoto St Pittsburgh PA 15213-2535 Office Phone: 412-624-5390. Business E-Mail: sgollin@hgen.pitt.edu.

GÖLLNER, MARIE LOUISE, musicologist, retired educator; b. Ft. Collins, Colo., June 27, 1932; d. Francis Gilbert and Gertrude Valentine (Steele) Martinez; m. Theodor W. Göllner, Sept. 30, 1959; children: Katharina, Philipp. BA, Vassar Coll., 1953; postgrad., Eastman Sch. Music, 1953-54, U. Heidelberg, Germany, 1954-56; PhD summa cum laude, U. Munich, 1962, Dr. phil. habil., 1975. Research asst. Bavarian State Library, Munich, 1964-67; lectr. Coll. Creative Studies, U. Calif., Santa Barbara, 1968; asst. prof. UCLA, 1970-74, assoc. prof., 1974-78, prof. musicology, 1978-2000, chmn. dept. music, 1976-80, chmn. dept. musicology, 1985-89; ret., 2000. Author: Die Musik des frühen Trecento, 1963, Katalog der Musikhandschriften der Bayerischen Staatsbibliothek München, vol. 2, 1979, vol. 1, 1989, Joseph Haydn, Symphonie 94, 1979, Orlando di Lasso: Sämtliche Werke, Neue Reihe, Das Hymnarium, (1580-82), 1980, Eine neue Quelle zur italienischen Orgelmusik des Cinquecento, 1982, The Manuscript Cod. lat. 5539 of the Bavarian State Library (Musicological Studies & Documents 43), 1993, Essays on Music and Poetry in the Late Middle Ages, 2003, The Early Symphony: 18th-Century Views on Composition and Analysis, 2004, The Echo of Music: Essays in Honor of Marie Louise Göllner, 2004; contbr. articles to profl. jours. NEH grantee, 1983, Fulbright grantee, 1954-56; Gordon Anderson Meml. lectr. U. New Eng., Armidale, Australia, 1984 Mem. Internat. Assn. Music Libraries, Am. Musicol. Soc., Internat. Musicol. Soc., Medieval Acad. Am. Episcopalian. Home: 817 Knapp Dr Santa Barbara CA 93108-1941 Business E-Mail: gollner@ucla.edu.

GOLOMB, CLAIRE, psychology educator; b. Frankfurt am Main, Germany, Jan. 30, 1928; came to U.S., 1958; d. Chaskel and Fanny (Monderer) Schimmel; m. Dan S. Golomb, Feb. 24, 1954; children: Mayana, Anath. BA, Hebrew U., Jerusalem, 1954; MA, New Sch. for Social Rsch., 1959; PhD, Brandeis U., 1969. Instr. psychology Wellesley (Mass.) Coll., 1969-70; asst. prof. Brandeis U., Waltham, Mass., 1971-74; assoc. prof. psychology U. Mass., Boston, 1974-77, prof., 1977—. Author: Young Children's Sculpture and Drawing, 1974, The Child's Creation of a Pictorial World, 1992, 2nd. edit., 2004, Child Art in Context: A Cultural and Comparative Prespective, 2002; editor: The Development of Artistically Gifted Children: Selected Case Studies, 1995. Fellow APA; mem. Jean Piaget Soc.

GOLSTON, JOAN CAROL, psychotherapist; b. Vancouver, B.C., Can., Aug. 10, 1947; came to U.S., 1958; d. Stefan and Lydia Barbara Golston. Student, Reed Coll., Portland, Oreg.; BA, U. Wash., Seattle, 1977, MSW, 1979. Lic. ind. clin. social worker; bd. cert. diplomate in clin. social work Am. Bd. Examiners in Clin. Social Work. Clin. supr. Crisis Clinic, Seattle, 1975-77; psychiatric social worker Valley Gen. Hosp., Renton, Wash., 1979-82; psychotherapist pvt. practice, Seattle, 1981—. Sch. counselor Northwest Sch., Seattle, Seattle Acad.; clin. cons. outpatient dept. Valley Cities Cmty. Mental Health, Renton, 1991, Seattle Counseling Svcs., 1991-96, emergency svcs., 1975-89; mem. faculty Internat. Soc. Study Dissociation Psychotherapy of the Dissociative Disorders, 2004-; cons., trainer and presenter in field. Contbr. articles to profl. jours. Bd. dirs. Open Door Clinic, Seattle, 1975-76, Northwest Family Tng. Inst., Seattle, v.p., 1990, pres., 1991, mem. exec. com., 1988-91; mem. adv. bd. Ctr. Prevention of Sexual and Domestic Violence, 1993—95, AIDS Risk Reduction Project Sch. Social Work U. Wash., 1988-93. Nat. Merit scholar, 1964. Fellow Internat. Soc. Study of Dissociation; mem. NASW (diplomate, Social Worker of Yr. 2006), Wash. State chpt. NASW (chmn. com. on inquiry ethics 1996—, mem. com. 1992—), Internat. Soc. Trauma Stress Studies, Acad. Cert. Social Workers. Avocation: antiques. Office: 726 Broadway Ste 303 Seattle WA 98122-4337 Office Phone: 206-328-1366.

GOLUB, SHARON BRAMSON, retired psychologist, educator; b. N.Y.C., Mar. 25, 1937; m. Leon M. Golub, June 1, 1958; children: Lawrence E., David B. Diploma, Mt. Sinai Hosp. Sch. Nursing, 1957; BS, Columbia U., 1959, MA, 1966; PhD, Fordham U., 1974. Head nurse Mt. Sinai Hosp., N.Y.C., 1957—59; contbg. editor RN Mag., Oradell, NJ, 1967—74; asst. prof. psychology Coll. New Rochelle, NY, 1974—79, assoc. prof., 1979—86, prof., 1986—98, prof. emeritus, 1998—; ret. Pvt. practice individual and group psychotherapy, 1976—2005; dir. women's studies Coll. New Rochelle, 1978—79, chmn. dept. psychology, 1979—82; adj. prof. psychiatry N.Y. Med. Coll., Valhalla, 1980—94. Editor: Menarche, 1983 (Assn. Women in Psychology Disting. Pub. award 1984, Book of Yr. award Am. Jour. Nursing 1984), Lifting the Curse of Menstruation, 1983, Health Care of the Female Adolescent, 1984, Health Needs of Women as They Age, 1984, PERIODS from Menarche to Menopause, 1992; (with Rita Jackaway Freedman) Psychology of Women: Resources for a Core Curriculum, 1987; editor Women and Health, 1982-86, mem. editorial bd., 1986—; mem. editorial bd. Psychology of Women Quar., 1989-2000. Grantee Nat. Libr. Medicine, 1983-84; NIH rsch. fellow, 1971-74. Fellow Am. Psychol. Assn. (chmn. task force on teaching psychology of women 1980-83), Am. Psychol. Soc.; mem. Soc. for Menstrual Cycle Rsch. (pres. 1981-83, bd. dirs. 1981-93), Assn. Women in Psychology, Westchester County Psychol. Assn. (pres. acad. divsn., Disting. Svc. award 2003), Phi Beta Kappa, Sigma Xi, Psi Chi. E-mail: sgolubny@aol.com.

GOMBER, MARY (DEE), real estate broker; b. Roseville, Mich., June 12, 1937; d. Edward Thomas and Doris Gertrude (Misener) Calomeni; m. Richard E. McGuire (div. 1974); children: Richard K., Victor S., Kevin M., René E., Robin E., Alice K., Marty T. and Christopher A. McGuire; m. Timothy James Gomber, Dec. 20, 1975. Student, Manatee Jr. Coll., Venice, Fla. Sec. Gen. Motors, Warren, Mich., 1955-57; owner, tchr. Dee's Decoupage Studio, Venice, 1972-74; real estate sales J. Booth & Co., Venice, 1975-81; real estate sales and mgr. Jacaranda County Club Villas, Venice, 1981-83; real estate sales Sorrento Realty Inc., Osprey, Fla., 1983-89; owner, mgr. Gulf Wind Adult Congregate Living Facility, 1988-89; real estate sales Michael Saunders & Co., Venice, 1989-91, Calusa Lakes Realty Inc., Nokomis, Fla., 1991-97, real estate sales and broker, 1998—. Pres. Women's Coun. of Realtors, Venice. Mem Venice Area Bd. Realtors (chair grievance com., Realtor Assoc. of Yr.), Sarasota Area Bd. Realtors, Nat. Assn. Realtors, Sarasota Home Builders Assn., Nat. Home Builders Assn. Avocations: decoupage, watercolor, garden club, stock club, book club. Home: 1957 White Feather Ln Nokomis FL 34275-5316

GÓMEZ, ANGELA GONZÁLEZ, art educator; b. Laredo, Tex., Oct. 29, 1953; d. Alberto and Aurora Benavides González; m. Albérico Michael Gómez, Aug. 7, 1982 (div. Feb. 1998); 1 child, Albérico Michael Gómez III. AA, Laredo Jr. Coll., Tex., 1973; BS in Art Edn., S.W. Tex. State U., 1975; M of Edn. in Art, Sul Ross State U., 1985. Cert. tchr. Tex. Art tchr. M.B. Lamar Jr. High, Laredo, 1975—83, United Mid. Sch., Laredo, 1989—. One-woman shows include Sal Ross State U., Alpine, Tex., Grad. Level Art Exhbn., 1984, Laredo Ctr. for the Arts., 1997—2002, United Mid. Sch., Laredo, 1989—2005. Adv., com. mem. Fine Arts Fiesta, Laredo, 1998—2005; com. mem. Youth Art Month, Laredo, 1976—83. Mem.: NEA, Tex. State Tchrs. Assn., Kappa Pi, Phi Theta Kappa. Avocations: art, travel, museums, movies, dance. Home: 1323 Kimberly Dr Laredo TX 78045 Office: United Mid Sch 700 E Del Mar Blvd Laredo TX 78045

GOMEZ, MARGARITA, language educator, researcher; b. Barranquilla, Atlantico, Colombia, Feb. 11, 1970; adopted d. Nestor Garcia and Carmen Barros de Garcia; m. Laureano Lavis Visbal, June 19, 1998; children: Miguel Angel Visbal, David Visbal. B in Modern Langs., Universidad del Atlantico, Barranquilla, Colombia, 1993; MEd, Universidad del Norte, Barranquilla, Colombia, 2002. Cert. internat. educator Dept. Edn. S.C., 2006. Tchr. Spanish Colegio Eucaristico de la Merced, Barranquilla, 1996—97; tchr. English Colegio de San Jose, Barranquilla, 1998—2004; prof. Universidad del Atlantico, Barranquilla, 2003—04; tchr. ESOL Lancaster Sch. Dist., SC, 2004—. Coord. Colegio de San Jose, 2004. Dir.: (school news) Eucanoticias. Singer Coro Juvenil Franciscano, Barranquilla, 1987—2002; vol. MCIC, Lancaster, 2004—06. Mem.: VIF. Achievements include research in helping children with selective mutism; developing mathematical critical thinking in kindergarteners. Avocation: singing.

GOMEZ, MELISSA MORDELL, trial consultant; b. Phila., Oct. 28, 1973; d. Leonard E. and Virginia M. Mordell; m. Nicolas Luis Gomez, May 4, 2002. Vis. student, Cath. U., Leuven, Belgium, 1993—94; BA, Loyola Coll., Balt., 1995; MS in Edn., U. Pa., Phila., 1997, PhD, 2001. Cert. sch. psychologist Pa. Sr. assoc. cons. Hay Group, Jersey City, 2000—02; trial cons. TrialGraphix, Inc., N.Y.C., 2003—05, Phila., 2005—. Child and family therapist Cmty. Counsel Phila., 1999—2001, clin. supr., 1999—2001; cons. Kenwood Psychol. Assocs., N.Y.C., 2000—01; group therapist for sexually abused children and their non-offending parents U. of Medicine and Dentistry N.J., Stratford, 1998—99; prof. psychology of personality U. Pa., 1999—2000, seminar leader grad. student practicum in psychol. svcs., 1998—2000; presenter in field. Illustration for coll. publ., The Forum; contbr. articles to profl. jours. Recipient dissertation rsch. grant, Applied Psychol. Measurement Inc., 2000. Mem.: APA, Am. Soc. of Trial Consultants (mem. rsch. and membership com. 2004—05), Psi Chi. Achievements include research in Parent Ratings of Behavior: Contextually Based Assessment for Children and Adolescents. Independently developed behavior-rating scale, designed research methodology, collected and analyzed data. Avocations: travel, running, studio arts, writing. Office Phone: 215-988-8200. Business E-Mail: mgomez@trialgraphix.com.

GOMEZ, PASTORA, medical/surgical nurse; b. Medellin, Colombia, Apr. 10, 1948; came to U.S., 1981; d. German and Lourdes (Escobar) G. Gen. nurse cert., U. Antioquia, Medellin, 1971, BSN, 1979. Cert. chemotherapist; RN N.Y., ACLS, cert. oncology nurse. Staff nurse, head nurse Inst. de Seguros Sociales, Medellin, 1972-81; LPN Parkway Hosp., N.Y.C., 1983-85, Elmhurst City Hosp., N.Y.C., 1985-87, staff nurse, 1987-90, asst. head nurse, 1990—. Bd. dirs. Queen Mary Anne Corp. Mem.: Oncology Nursing Soc., Am. Nephrology Nurses Assn. Roman Catholic. Avocations: music, art, travel, reading. Home: 88-02 35th Ave Flushing NY 11372-5710

GONDEK, MARY JANE (MARY JANE SUCHORSKI), property manager; b. Milw, May 19, 1958; d. Zigmund Alexander and Felicia Theodore (Staszewski) Suchorski; children from previous marriage: Amy Lynn Seamars, Joseph Alexander, Christine Ann. Student, S.W. Tech. Coll., 1989, 94, Internat. Correspondence Sch., 1995. Cert. nursing asst., CPR. Nursing asst. Lancaster Living Ctr., 1988-89, 95-96, Franciscan Villa Nursing Home, South Mil., Wis., 1990-92; home care provider Homeward Bound, Inc., Lancaster, 1994-95; dietary aide St. Joseph's Convent, Milw., 1995-96; on-site mgr. Meridian Group, Inc., Middleton, Wis., 1997-98; home care provider Supported Home Care Options, Inc., Wauwatosa, Wis., 1999, Anew Home Care Options, Wauwatosa, Wis., 1999—; nursing asst. Allis Care Ctr., West Allis, Wis., 1998, 99-2000, VA Med. Ctr., Milw., 2000—; rep. and beauty cons. Avon, 2002—; owner Mary's Treasured Gifts, 2002—05. Democrat. Roman Catholic. Avocations: gardening, canning, genealogy. Address: 1232 S 46th St Milwaukee WI 53214 Personal E-mail: mjgcna@yahoo.com.

GONG, GLORIA MARGARET, lawyer, pharmacist; b. Yreka, Calif., Oct. 12, 1953; d. Kenneth Wayne and Patricia Ann (Farley) McCain; m. Peter-Poon Ming Gong, Apr. 3, 1976; children: George-Wayne, Cynthia-May, Miranda-Lin. Pharmacist Degree, U. of the Pacific, Stockton, Calif., 1976; JD, Calif. Pacific Law Sch., Bakersfield, 1992. BAr: Calif. 1992, U.S. Dist. Ct. (ea., ctr. and so. dists.) Calif. 1992. Pharmacist Gong's Pharmacy, Tehachapi, Calif., 1978-93; atty. Gong & Hirsch, Bakersfield, 1994-97; pvt. practice, 1997—. Mem.: ATLA, ABA, Kern County Bar Assn., L.A. County Bar Assn., Lambda Kappa Sigma. Office: 6840 District Blvd Bakersfield CA 93313 E-mail: ggong@legalemail.com.

GONG, NANCY Y., artist, small business owner; b. Rochester, N.Y., 1957; d. Don S. and Sue Gong; m. Peter W. Fisk, 1983. Student Sch. for Am. Craftsmen, Rochester Inst. Tech., 1973—78; student, Champlain Coll., 1975—76, Empire State Coll., 1976—77, Naples Mills Sch. Arts & Craft, 1976. Propr., artist Gong Glass Works, Rochester, NY, 1979—; presenter glass art tech. workshops and confs. Rochester Mus. & Sci Ctr., 1979—83; coord. spl. projects Pyramid Art Gallery, Allofus Art Workshop, Inc., Rochester, 1979—86. Educator ALLOFUS Art Workshop, Inc., Rochester, 1976-80, PORTCON "82 Art Glass Conf., San Diego, 1982, Environ. Art Glass Conf., Oklahoma City, 1989, Profl. Art Glass Sem., San Antonio, 1990, Pub. Art Politics and Processes Symposium, Arts for Greater Rochester, 1990, Glass Art Soc. Conf., Monterey, Calif., Corning, N.Y., 1993, Huntington, W.Va., Toronto, Ont., Can., 1978—; instr. Rochester Mus. and Sci. Ctr., 1979-86, ALLOFUS Art Workshop, 1979-86, Jewish Community Ctr., 1979-86, Norman Howard Sch., 1979-86, cons. Edge Pub. Group, 1989-93, Profl. Stained Glass Guild, Brewster, N.Y., 1989-93, Arts for Gtr. Rochester, 1990; presenter numerous seminars; speaker numerous orgns. Exhibited at Lincoln First Plaza Gallery, Rochester, Meml. Art Gallery U. Rochester (Excellence award 1981), Glassmasters Guild Finalist N.Y.C., 1981, First Place, San Francisco, 1982, Oakland County Cultural Offices, Southfield, Mich., 1987 (Best Stained Glass), Glass Growers Gallery, Erie, Pa., Kunst Art & Form Internat., Vienna, Austria, Galerie, NY, 1988-89, Greater Rochester Internat. Airport, 1991, Crafts Nat. 27, 1993, Women's Art Works 4, 1994, 6, 1996, Kraft Lieberman Gallery, 2002, Glass Gallery, 2002, Kane Marie Gallery, 2002, Galleria of Sculpture, 2002, Lockhart Gallery, 2002, Swanson Reed Gallery, Glass Now, 2003, 04, Maitlins, 2003, Artform Internat., 2003, The Glass Gallery, 2003, 04, Kraft Lieborman Gallery, 2003, Mattlins, 2003, Collectors Fine Art, 2004, Pritam and Eames, 2004, Crafts Nat. 38 Zoller Gallery, 2004, 05, Sofa Chgo., 2004, Port of Rochester Pub. Art Competition, 2004; represented in permanent collections Blue Cross & Blue Shield, Meml. Art Gallery Rochester, Women's Coun. Room, Cornell U. Ithaca Faculty Club, Paychex, Inc., LiDestri Foods Inc., GM, Genesee Region Home Care Assn. Hospice Unit, Eastman Kodak Co., Lodge at Woodcliff, Monroe C.C., Duke U. Fuqua Sch. Bus. Conf. Ctr., Genesee Hosp., Rochester Gen. Hosp., Kemper, Virgin Vacations, Virgin Atlantic, Time Warner, Corning Tropel Corp., Graham Mfg., Strong Meml. Hosp., St. John Fisher Coll., U. Rochester, N.Y. State Appellate Ct. House, Rochester Yacht Club, Oak Hill Country Club, Key Bank, Port of Rochester, Rochester Inst. Tech., Lidestri Foods, Inc., St. Ann's Cmty., Constellation, Key Bank; appeared in numerous mags.; contbr. articles to profl. jours. Past bd. dirs. Arts for Greater Rochester, 1991; trustee Sta. WXXI Pub. Broadcasting Svc.; mem. Meml. Art Gallery Univ. Rochester, hon. adv. Arts for Greater Rochester Mem. Glass Art Soc., Am. Crafts Coun., Toastmasters Internat., Rochester Women's Network, Women and Minority Bus. Enterprise. Studio: Gong Glass Works 42 Parkview Dr Rochester NY 14625-1034 Office Phone: 585-288-5520.

GONGLEWSKI, GRACE, actress; b. Johnstown, Pa., Oct. 31, 1963; d. Zygmund Anthony John and Sylvia Blanche (MacFadyen) G. BFA, N.C. Sch. Arts, 1987. Outreach mem. The Walnut St. Theatre, Phila., 1987-88, The Drama Guild, Phila., 1993-94; tchr. teen acting Arden Theatre Co., Phila., 1990—; tchr. adult improvisation Wilma Theatre, Phila., 1995—; tchr. styles class U. Arts, 1997—. Appeared in performances at Arden Theatre Co., Walnut St. Theatre, Derby (England) Playhouse, The Wilma Theatre, others; voiceover clients include Acme, Campbells, Peco Energy, McDonald's, Trump Marina, others; plays include Hedda Gabler, A Little Night Music (Barrymore award best supporting actress, 1995), A Midsummer Night's Dream, The Beard of Avon, 2006. Recipinet F. Otto Haas award Performing Arts League Phila., 1995. Mem. NOW, AFTRA, SAG, Actors Equity Assn. Democrat. Brethren. Avocation: gardening. Home: 2825 Poplar St Philadelphia PA 19130-1222*

GONNERMAN, JENNIFER, writer, journalist; b. Jan. 24, 1971; Attended, Cambridge U.; BA, Columbia U., 1994. Staff writer The Village Voice, 1997—2006. Author: Life on the Outside: The Prison Odyssey of Elaine Bartlett, 2004 (Nat. Book Award finalist, 2004). Finalist Nat. Mag. Award; recipient Livingston award, Gold Typewriter Award, N.Y. Press Club, Meyer Berger Award, Columbia U. Sch. Journalism, Front Page Award, Newswomen's Club N.Y. Office: Village Voice 36 Cooper Square New York NY 10003

GONSALVES, MARGARET LEBOY, elementary school educator; b. Paia, Maui, Hawaii, Feb. 10, 1935; d. John Algarin and Antonia (Leboy) G. BS in Edn., Marylhurst U., 1959; elem. tchr. cert., U. Hawaii, 1971. Cert. elem. tchr., Hawaii. Nurses' aide St. Vincent Hosp., Portland, Oreg., 1956; office clk. Bur. Med. Econs., Honolulu, 1959; tchr. State of Hawaii Dept. Edn., Honolulu, 1959—, Benjamin Park Sch., Kaneohe, Hawaii, 1966-92. Tchr. ESEA-Title I Chpt. I reading and math. fed. program, 1979-92, coord. Parker Sch. Chpt. 1 reading and math. program. Vol. Am. Cancer Soc., Honolulu, 1979, Am. Diabetes Assn., Honolulu, 1992; reporter Nat. Data Corp.-Price Waterhouse, Springfield, Va., 1991-2002. Mem. NEA, Internat. Reading Assn., Hawaii State Tchrs. Assn. (faculty rep. 1960-62, 87-89, Golden Heart cert., 2003), Sigma Delta Pi. Roman Catholic. Avocations: reading, sweepstakes, fishing, gardening, travel. Home: 1328 Maalahi St Honolulu HI 96819-1727

GONSALVES, PATRICIA E., surgical nurse; b. N.Y.C., Oct. 28, 1943; d. John A. Gonsalves and Julia Rivera Brosa. Diploma in practical nursing, Caledonian Hosp., Bklyn., 1963; student, Cornell Med. Ctr., 1965-66, L.I. U., 1971, SUNY, L.I., 1988. Lic. practical nurse; cert. surg. technologist, preceptor, oper. rm., med. photographer. Lic. practical nurse Luth. Med. Ctr., Bklyn.; assoc. primary nurse, lic. practical nurse Maimonides Med. Ctr., Bklyn., LPN, surg. technologist, oper. rm. vascular surg. specialist, sr. tech. and neuro., 1980—. Contbr. articles to profl. jours. Guild del. Local 1199, Freedom of Health Choice; polit. Dem. endorser; lay min. Bay Ridge Christian Ctr., Bklyn. Mem.: NAACOG (Outstanding Leadership Recognition award), Found. for Advancement of Innovative Medicine, Nat. Ctr. Homeopathy, Assn. Surg. Technologists (pres. chpt. Metro 47 1994—96, nat. bd. dirs. 1993—94, apptd. mem. exam. rev. com. various awards 1992), Soc. Peripheral Vascular Nursing, Nat. Surg. Asst. Assn., Nat. Assn. Practical Nurse Edn. and Svc. Home: 814 57th St Apt 2A Brooklyn NY 11220-3631

GONYO, MARILYN E., education educator; b. Perth Amboy, N.J., Oct. 29, 1943; d. John M. and Catherine (Kozak) G. BA, Glassboro (N.J.) State Coll., 1965; MA, Kean Coll., Union, N.J., 1968; EdD, Rutgers U., 1976. Cert. elem. tchr., reading tchr., cons., learning disabilities tchr., tchr. of handicapped, supr., prin., sch. adminstr., N.J. Asst. prof., coord. learning disabilities programs Montclair (N.J.) State Coll., 1974-81; cons. Child Diagnostic Ctr., Woodbridge, N.J.; ednl. specialist N.J. Dept. Edn., Trenton, 1981-85; prof. edn., dir. Learning Ctr., Georgian Court Coll., Lakewood, N.J., 1985—. Mem. rsch. bd. advisors Am. Biog. Inst., adv. bd. Learning Disabilities Assn. Am. Mem. N.J. Gov.'s Conf. Com. Libr. and Info. Svc., juvenile conf. com. Twp. of Woodbridge; judge oratorical contest. Recipient Disting. Svc. award Rutgers U., 1986. Mem. N.J. Assn. Learning Cons. (past pres., Anita McKean Svc. award 1985), N.J. Coun. for Learning Disabilities (pres.), Internat. Reading Assn. (past pres. Middlesex coun.), N.J. Reading Tchrs. Assn. (bd. dir.), Nat. Assn. Parliamentarians, N.J. Schoolwomen's Club (past pres.), Phi Delta Kappa, Delta Kappa Gamma (past pres. N.J. state), Kappa Delta Pi, Alpha Delta Kappa. Home: 4 Fawn Way Clarksburg NJ 08510-1511

GONZALES, ELIZABETH BETSY BARNES, elementary school educator, consultant; d. Edward Francis Barnes and Carol Ann Funel; m. Stephen Louis Gonzales, July 27, 1973; 1 child, Nicole Renee. BS, La. State U., Baton Rouge, 1979; MEd, SW Tex. State U., San Marcos, 1988. Tchr. East Baton Rouge Parish Schs., 1983—85, Leander Ind. Schs., Tex., 1985—95, Leander Ind. Sch. Dist., Cedar Park, 1995—; chair social studies dept. Cedar Pk. Mid. Sch., 2001—. Cons. Law Related Edn. State Bar of Tex., Austin, 2004—; we the people dist. coord., tex. 31 Ctr. Civic Edn., We The People, 2002—; v.p. Capital Area Coun. Social Studies, Austin, 2004—, membership chair, 2002—04. Named Tchr. Yr., Capital Area Coun. Social Studies, 2005, Tex. Coun. Social Studies, 2005; recipient award, Jewish Fedn. Austin, 1998—99. Mem.: Tex. Social Studies Supervisors Assn., Nat. Coun. Social Studies, Tex. Coun. Social Studies, Capital Area Coun. Social Studies (v.p. 2004—06, pres. 2006—). Avocations: travel, gourmet cooking. Office: Cedar Park Middle School 2100 Sun Chase Blvd Cedar Park TX 78613 Office Phone: 512-434-5025. Office Fax: 512-434-7539. Personal E-mail: ebgonzales@austin.rr.com. E-mail: betsy_gonzales@leanderisd.org.

GONZALES, LOUISE MICHAUX, lawyer; b. Baltimore, Dec. 28, 1949; BA, Univ. Md., 1971, JD, 1976. Bar: Md. 1976. Atty. Blades & Rosenfield, Baltimore, Md., 1976—80; ptnr. Hylton & Gonzales, Baltimore, Md., 1980—. Bd. dir. Legal Mutual Insurance. Bd. regents Univ. Sys. Md., 1997—2002; bd. visitors Univ. Md. Law Sch., 2003. Recipient Md. Leadership in Law, 2001. Fellow: Md. Bar Found.; mem.: Am. Bar Found., Bar Assn. Balt. City, Md. State Bar Assn. (pres. 1991—92), ABA (bd. gov. 2004—). Office: Hylton & Gonzales Suite 2200 201 N Charles St Baltimore MD 21201

GONZALES, MARTHA, elementary school educator; b. San Jose, Calif., Apr. 23, 1967; d. Paul H. and Magdalena Gonzales. Student, Biola U., 1985; BA, Calif. State-San Bernardino, 1990. Preliminary credential-multiple subject Calif. Bd. Edn., preschool tchr. cert. Calif. Bd. Edn. Tchr. asst. Athena Learning Ctr., Palm Desert, 1993, Fernangeles Elem., Sun Valley, Calif., 1993—94, Coachella Valley Recreation Pk. Dist., Indio, 1994; preschool tchr. asst. YMCA Daycare Pre-K, LaQuinta, 1994—95; substitute tchr., Mecca Sch. Coachella Valley Unified Sch. Dist., Mecca, 1995—97, substitute tchr., Saul Martinez Elem., 1997—2000; preschool tchr. Eagle Mountain Child Devel. Ctr., Desert Center, 2000—01; substitute tchr. Desert Sands Unified Sch. Dist., LaQuinta, 2002; music tchr. Tools for Tomorrow, Coachella Valley, 2004. Author: (books) Cindy Lou Gets Lost, 1978 (Young Author award, 1978), Hermit and The Flying Machine, 1979 (Young Author award, 1979). Long term missionary Spearhead, Mexico, 1987; tutor Biola Cmty. Svc., S. Ctrl. LA Ch., 1985—86; short term missions YUGO, Mexico, 1988; child sponsor Compassion Internat., Bolivia, 2000. Mem.: Calif. Tchrs. Assn., Am. Fedn. Tchrs. Protestant. Avocations: writing, music, sports, travel, doll collecting. Home: 49938 Ave DePlatina Coachella CA 92236

GONZALES, SARAH, women's organization director; b. 1976; Dir., Racial Justice Prog. YWCA. Mem. Ariz. Collegiate Leadership Conf. Mem. Jewish Cmty. Rels. Coun., Tunnel of Oppression, U. Ariz., Tucson Save Darfur Coalition. Named one of 40 Under 40, Tucson Bus. Edge, 2006. Office: YWCA 738 N 5th Ave Tucson AZ 85705 Office Phone: 520-884-7810. Office Fax: 520-884-5205.*

GONZALEZ, ANGELA E., obstetrician, gynecologist; b. NYC, Nov. 18, 1969; d. Francisco Gonzalez and Leyda Velez-Gonzalez; m. Fernando Figueras, May 20, 2001; 1 child, Ethan. BSc, Sophie Davis Sch., NY, 1992; MD, NY Med. Coll., Valhalla, 1994. Ob-gyn resident Our Lady of Mercy, Bronx, 1994—98, attending physician, 1998—, dir. urogynecology, 2000—, outpatient svcs.; attending physician Soundshore Med. Ctr., New Rochelle, NY, 2005—. Mem. hosp. adv. com. Our Lady of Mercy, Bronx, 2004—. Recipient Excellence in Laparoscopy, Soc. Gyn. Laparascopy, 1998, Physician Recognition award, AMA, 2000—. Mem.: ACOG. Avocations: art, baking, running, writing. Home: 78 Central Pkwy Mount Vernon NY 10552 Office: Our Lady of Mercy Med Ctr 600 E 233d St Bronx NY 10466

GONZALEZ, CECELIA, lawyer; BA, McGill U., Can., 1976; JD, Georgetown U., 1979. Bar: DC Bar 1980, registered: US Ct. Appeals, Fed. Cir., US Dist. Ct., DC, US Ct. Internat. Trade, US Internat. Trade Commn., US Dept. Commerce, US Customs Svc., Office of US Trade Rep. Ptnr. Intellectual Property Practice Group Mgmt. Team, mem. exec. bd., co-chmn. bus. affairs com., Howrey Simon Arnold & White LLP, Washington, 1986—. Author: (chpt.) ABA Sect. on Intellectual Prop. Law in "Patent Litig. Strategies Handbook", 2000. Mem.: US Internat. Trade Commn. Trial Lawyer Assn., Minority Corp. Counsel Assn. (top minority IP ptnr.), Hispanic Bar Assn., Am. Intellectual Property Law Assn. (Intellectual Property Law Sect.), ABA, DC Bar Assn. Office: Howrey Simon Arnold & White LLP 1299 Pennsylvania Ave NW Washington DC 20004-2402 Office Phone: 202-383-6595. Office Fax: 202-383-6610. Business E-Mail: GonzalezC@howrey.com.

GONZALEZ, IRMA ELSA, federal judge; b. Palo Alto, Calif., 1948; BA, Stanford U., 1970; JD, U. Ariz., 1973. Law clk. to Hon. William C. Frey US Dist. Ct. (Ariz. dist.), 1973-75; asst. U.S. atty. US Attys. Office Ariz., 1975-79, US Attys. Office (ctrl. dist.) Calif., 1979-81; trial atty. antitrust divsn. US Dept. Justice, 1979; assoc. Seltzer Caplan Wilkins & McMahon, San Diego, 1981-84; judge US Magistrate Ct. (so. dist.) Calif., 1984-91; ct. judge San Diego County Superior Ct., 1991-92; judge US Dist. Ct. (so. dist.) Calif., San Diego, 1992—, chief judge, 2005—. Adj. prof. U. San Diego, 1992; trustee Calif. Western Sch. Law; bd. visitors Sch. Law U. Ariz. Mem. Girl Scout Women's Adv. Cabinet. Mem. Lawyers' Club San Diego, Inns of Ct. Office: Edward J Schwartz US Courthouse 940 Front St Ste 5135 San Diego CA 92101-8911

GONZALEZ, IVETTE, biomedical engineer; b. N.Y.C., Dec. 25, 1964; d. Jesus and Isabelle Gonzalez. B, N.Y. Inst. Tech., Westbury, 1988. Master: GE Elfuns. Achievements include invention of hand-key glove. Avocations: hiking, photography, biking, travel, volunteering. Home: 7450 NW 18th St Apt 206 Margate FL 33068-6879 Office: Cedars Med Ctr 1400 NW 12th Ave Miami FL Office Phone: 305-325-5929.

GONZALEZ, MANDY, actress; b. LA; Actress (regional plays) Warm, When You Wish, Go-Go Beach, Drive All Night, The Color Purple, Wicked, Beehive on Broadway, In the Heights, The Best Little Whorehouse in Texas, (Off-Broadway plays) Eli's Comin' (Obie award for performance, Village Voice), (Broadway plays) Aida, 2001, 2003—04, Dance of the Vampires, 2004, Lennon, 2005.

GONZALEZ, NANCY BERGER, healthcare professional, educator; b. N.Y., Aug. 14, 1942; d. Jack and Ruth (Blierer) Berger; m. Rafael González; 1 child, Adam Matthew. BA in Edn., U. Toledo, 1964; Montessori degree, Fairleigh Dickinson U., 1966; MS in Anthropology and Education, Queens Coll., 1968. Prin. Escuelas Las Nereidas, San Juan, P.R., 1966-71, Montessori Sch., Brooklyn, N.Y., 1971-73; sch. dir. Associated YM-YWHAs of Greater N.Y., Brooklyn, 1972-78; mktg. and recruitment dir. Cmty. Blood Ctrs. South Fla., Ft. Lauderdale, 1991; dir., recruitment Am. Red Cross Blood Svc., 1992-94; patient svc. administrator Nat. Parkinson Found., 1995-98; dir. Rehab. Facility Nova SE Univ., Fort Lauderdale, Fla., 1999—. Mem. Am. Parkinson Disease Assn. Democrat. Avocations: travel, painting, attending interest classes, cultural anthropology. Office: Nova SE Univ Health Profl Divsn 3200 S University Dr Fort Lauderdale FL 33328-2018

GONZÁLEZ ECHEVARRIA, AMELIA L., librarian, counseling administrator; b. Santurce, P.R., June 22, 1950; d. Raul A. and Arminda (Echevarria) Gonzalez; m. Angel Sepulveda, Sept. 11, 1980 (div. 1982). BA, U. P.R., Rio Piedras, 1967, MLS, 1975, MA, 1989; EdD, Interam. U., San Juan, 1992—. Tchr. spl. edn. Colegio Bautista Carolina (P.R.), 1972-73; dist. supr. Youth Program of P.R., Carolina, 1973-75; libr. dir. New Hampshire Coll., San Juan, P.R., 1985-89, Municipality of San Juan, 1975—. Counselor Fundacion Sida P.R., San Juan, 1987—; mem. Asegrab, San Juan, 1984—, Pracde, San Juan, 1985—. Mem. coun. Mcpl. Assembly, Municipality of Carolina, 1972-75; sec. Democrat. Com. of Carolina, 1969-72; mem. Consejo Vecinal Seguridad, Isla Verde, Carolina, 1989—; asst. treas. Salon de la Fama Deporte, Carolina, 1984-86; bd. dirs. Condominium St. Tropez, pres. 1989—, sec. 1987-88; sec. Asociación Condominios de Isla Verde, P.R., 1989-92; mem. Vecinal Coun. for Security, 1989—; vol. AIDS Found. of P.R., 1987—, counselor, 1987—. Mem. ALA, Sociedad de Bibliotecarios, Federación Nacional Puertorriqueña de Análisis Transaccional Inc., Assn. de Ex-Alumnos de la Escuela Graduada de Bibliotecología (sec. 1984-86), P.R. Assn. for Counselling and Devel. Baptist. Avocations: reading, theater and arts, travel, sewing. Home: PO Box 29700 San Juan PR 00929-0700

GONZALEZ-FALLA, SONDRA GILMAN, art collector; Trustee Whitney Mus. Am. Art, NYC; chmn. bd. Am. Theatre Wing. Avocation: collector of Am. photography. Mailing: c/o Whitney Mus Am Art 945 Madison Ave New York NY 10021 also: c/o American Theatre Wing 570 Seventh Ave Ste 501 New York NY 10018

GONZALEZ-HERMOSILLO, BRENDA, economist, researcher; b. Mexico City, Oct. 28, 1955; d. Jesus and Emilia (Gonzalez Watkins) G. BA in Econs., Inst. Tech. Autonomo de Mexico, Mexico City, 1979; MA in Econs., U. Western Ont., London, 1980, PhD in Econs., 1983. Rsch. asst. Bank of Mex., Mexico City, 1977; economist Banco Nacional de Mex., Mexico City, 1978, Min. of Fin., Mexico City, 1979, Bank of Montreal, Toronto, Ont., 1983-84, Bank of N.S., Toronto, 1985-89; sr. economist Bank of Can., Ottawa, Ont., 1989-94, Internat. Monetary Fund, Washington, 1994—. Contbr. articles to profl. jours. Recipient Govt. of Can. award to fgn. nationals, 1980-83; Inst. of Tech. scholar, 1976-78, U. Western Ont. scholar, 1979-80. Mem. Can. and Am. Econ. Assn. Achievements include research on financial crises, financial markets, monetary policy, medicare. Home: 4332 Leland St Chevy Chase MD 20815-6064 Office: Internat Monetary Fund 700 19th St NW Washington DC 20431-0001

GOOCH, AUDREY SMITH, retired education educator; b. St. Louis, July 7, 1925; d. James Irving and Mabel Dorthea (Higgins) Smith; m. Robert Thomas Gooch; children: Keith Ewing, Robert Kenneth. BA, Stowe Tchrs. Coll., 1947; MA in Tchg., Webster U., 1971. Cert. elem. tchr., reading specialist, coll. instr., child care. Elem. tchr. St. Louis Pub. Schs., 1947-66; edn. dir. Project Head Start, St. Louis, 1966-69, project dir., 1969-72; dir. Right to Read, St. Louis, 1972-74, Forest Park C.C., St. Louis, 1974-79; coord. Family Support Svcs., St. Louis, 1979-84; dir. Early Childhood Edn. Unit, St. Louis, 1984-90. Adj. faculty Harris Tchrs. Coll., St. Louis, 1972, Forest Park C.C., 1973; adv. bd. Learning Tree Day Care Ctr., St. Louis, 1991-97; cons. St. Louis Urban League, Right to Read Nat. Office, Washington, 1974, Mo. Vol. Accredition EOC, Jefferson City, 1989-90. Author: (booklet) A Guideline For Head Start Curriculum, 1967, Read On, 1973, Handbook for Reading Tutors, 1974. Mem. collections com. Mo. History Mus., St. Louis; mem. scholarship com. U. Mo., St. Louis; vice chmn. Kirkwood (Mo.) Human Rights Commn.; v.p. Kirkwood Hist. Soc., 2000; Oasis tutor Kirkwood Pub. Schs. Recipient Gateway medal City of St. Louis, 1972, Outstanding Vol. Svc. award at Mo. Hist. Soc., Union Electric and City of St. Louis, 1996, Woman of Achievement award St. Louis Globe Dem., 1985, Disting. Alumni award Harris-Stowe State Coll., 1992. Mem. Mo. Assn. for Edn. of Young Children (sec.), Gideon Internat. Aux. (v.p. 1993), Links Inc. (fin. sec. 1994), Delta Sigma Theta. Lutheran. Avocations: reading, volunteering. Home: 302 W Rose Hill Ave Saint Louis MO 63122-5942

GOOCH, CAROL ANN, psychotherapist, consultant; b. Meridian, Miss., Apr. 17, 1950; d. James Tackett and Chris M. Page; (div.); 1 child, Aaron Patrick Gooch. BS, Fla. State U., 1972, DS, 1975; MS, Troy State U., 1974. Lic. profl. counselor Tex., chem. dependency counselor Tex., marriage and family therapist Tex., cert. chem. dependency specialist Tex., compulsive gambling counselor Tex., tobacco addiction counselor ACP Tex., bereavement counselor. Tchr. Okaloosa Sch. Dist., Fort Walton, Fla., 1972-77; counselor USAF, Osan AFB, Korea, 1977-79; sch. counselor Tomball (Tex.) Sch. Dist., 1983-90; cons. Montgomery (Tex.) Sch. Dist., 1992—; pvt. practice Houston, 1990—; dir. cmty. rels. Cypress Creek Hosp., 1998—. Dir. bus. devel. Kingwood Pines Hosp., 2006; coord. sr. program Forest Springs Hosp., Houston, 1993—, Cypress Creek Hosp., 1994—; cons. in field. Vol. cons. PTO, Woodlands, Tex., 1990; bd. dirs. Leadership Montgomery County. Named Outstanding H.S. Counselor, Tomball Ind. Sch. Dist., 1989, Diplomat of Yr., Woodlands C. of C., 2001, 2002, 2004, Coun. Lake Conroe C. of C., 2004, Conroe County C. of C., 2005; named to Leadership Montgomery County; recipient Nat. Disting. Svc. award, Ex Coun. U.S. Pubs., N.J., 1989; fellow, Fla. State U., Tallahassee, 1973. Mem.: NAFE, ASCD, ACA, AAUW, Montgomery County Assn. Bus. Women (founder, exec. dir.), Am. Bus. Women's Assn., Tex. Mental Health Counselors Assn., Am. Mental Health Counselors Assn., Tex. Sch. Counselors Assn., Fla. State U. Alumni Assn., Woodlands C. of C. (life), Kappa Delta Pi. Avocations: travel, dance, boating. Home and Office: Carol A Gooch MS LPC PO Box 1308 Montgomery TX 77356-1308 Office Phone: 713-256-8002. E-mail: psychstages@aol.com.

GOOCH, DEBORAH ANN GRIMME, medical, surgical nurse, administrator; b. Covington, Ky., Aug. 30, 1951; d. Homer and Betty Jean (Conley) Grimme; m. James Gooch, May 10, 1975 (div. 1988); 1 child, Joshua James. AS, No. Ky. State Coll., Park Hills, 1971; BSN, No. Ky. U., Highland Hts., 1987. Cert. operating room nurse. Head nurse St. Luke Hosp. East, Ft. Thomas, Ky., 1987, asst. oper. rm. mgr., 1989, perioperative nurse mgr., 1989—. Mem. Assn. Operating Rm. Nurses, Soc. Gastroenterology Nurses. Home: 4 Upland Ct Cold Spring KY 41076-2186

GOOCH, NANCY EUGENIA SOUTH, retired secondary school educator, librarian; b. Big Spring, Tex., Sept. 21, 1945; d. James Lawton and Eugenia (Routh) South; m. James B. Gooch, Dec. 23, 1968; children: James Eric, Kim Hyo Eugenia. BA in Chemistry, Hardin-Simmons U., 1968; MLS, U. Tex., Austin, 1972. Cert. secondary tchr., Tex., nat. cert. chemistry/gen. sci. Tchr. Del Valle (Tex.) High Sch., 1979-82, Santa Anna (Tex.) High Sch., 1982-85, Mineral Wells (Tex.) High Sch., 1986-90; libr. Glen Rose (Tex.) Intermediate Sch., 1992-93; tchr. math. and phys. sci. Paradise (Tex.), Austin, 1993—99; libr. cons. Fairfield (Tex.) HS, 1998—2006, tchr. math and drama, 1999—2006; ret., 2006. Mem. Am. Geneal. Soc., Assn. Tex. Profl. Educators (pres. 2003—), Tex. Tchrs. Assn. (pres. chpt. 1978-79), Tex. Libr. Assn., Amen Libr. Assn., Fairfield (Tex.) History Club, Ednl. Theatre Assn., Delta Kappa Gamma (corr. sec. 1990-92). Democrat. Presbyterian. Avocations: reading, quilting. Home: 410 Meadowbrook Ln Fairfield TX 75840-1829 E-mail: negooch@hotmail.com.

GOOD, AMY, educational association administrator; Exec. dir. Alternatives for Girls, Detriot. Recipient Use Your Life award, Oprah's Angel Network. Office: Alternatives for Girls 903 W Grand Blvd Detroit MI 48208-2365 E-mail: afg.dev.spec@att.net.

GOOD, BILLIE B., sales executive, athletic trainer; b. Junction City, Oreg., Oct. 5, 1977; d. Richard Lee Wunderlich and Pamela Jo Godd. BS, Pacific U., Forest Grove, Oreg., 1999; MS in Sports Medicine, Ga. State U., Atlanta, 2004. Athletic trainer, prof. Anges Scott Coll., Decatur, Ga., 2001—03; athletic trainer Pace Acad., Atlanta, 2003—04; orthoped. surgeon asst. Peachtree Orthopedic, Atlanta, 2004—05; med. sales cons. Landmark Med., Atlanta, 2005—. Home: 172 Elysian Way NW Atlanta GA 30327

GOOD, EDITH ELISSA (PEARL WILLIAMS), writer, lexicographer; b. Hollywood, Calif., Jan. 10, 1945; d. Jack Brian and Rose Marie (Miller) Good; m. Michael Lawrence Black, Dec. 18, 1986 (dec.). Student, UCLA and U. Calif., Berkeley, 1962—92, Ballet Folklorico, Mex., 1963; BA in English summa cum laude, Calif. State U., Northridge, 1974. Explorer Mayan ruins, Mex., 1963; author, pub. Gull Press, L.A., 1990—. Participant numerous dance, art, music, lit., math. and sci. classes; dancer Hajde Dance Troop, Berkeley, Calif., 1962-66. Artist one-woman shows, L.A., 1962-95; singer in various langs. at various venues, L.A., 1986—; author: (pseudonym Pearl Williams) The Trickster of Tarzana, 1992, Short Stories, 1995, Mad in Craft, 1995, Missives, 1995, others; contbr. numerous poems to lit. publs., CDs, radio, ipods and internet broadcasts. Fundraiser, del. to local convs. Dem. clubs, Calif. and Mex., 1962—; supporter mental health orgns., sensitivity tng. encounter groups, 1962—; participant consciousness raising groups, del. encounter groups, sensitivity tng., local convs., fundraiser, canvasser, office worker, driver, participant W.E.B. DuBois Club, Congress Racial Equality, San Francisco, Berkeley, L.A., and Oakland, 1965, Peace in Alliance for Survival, Berkeley, Oakland, L.A., 1964-80, women's rights Westside Women's Ctr., Woman's Bldg., L.A., 1974-80, Environment in Earth Day, L.A., 1977, phys. and mental health VA, cons. book reviewer, tutor, Mental Health Assn., L.A., 1962—; supporter residential collectives, 1985—; mem. adv. bd.

American Biog. Inst. Mem. Mensa, Am. Soc. Composers, Authors, and Pubs., Plummer Park Writers, Westside Writers. Achievements include writing chosen by a jury of experts for inclusion in the permanent collecton of the Library of Congress. Home: 1470 S Robertson Blvd Apt B Los Angeles CA 90035-3402 Office Phone: 310-276-8933.

GOOD, ESTELLE M., minister; b. Charleston, S.C., Oct. 5, 1927; d. John Wesley and Minnie Estelle Hilton; divorced; children: Raymond L., Lee Good Sanders. BTh, Clarksville Sch. Theology, 1972, ThM, 1975, ThD, 1976, ThD, 1978, B in Sacred Music, 1980; PhD of Christian Psychology, Cornerstone U., 1992. Ordained to preach 1955; cert. hypnotherapist Internat. Assn. Counselors and Therapists, 1994. Organizer, pastor Covenant Life Cathedral, Macon, Ga., 1962—. Pres. Lighthouse Bible Tng. Ctr., 1976—88. Fellow: Nat. Christian Counselors Assn. (diplomate 1993, lic. temperament therapist 1991, Christian counselor and therapist 1992); mem.: Women Preachers Coun. Am., Full Gospel Fellowship of Churches and Ministers Internat. Office: Covenant Life Cathedral 4543 Bloomfield Rd Macon GA 31203

GOOD, JENNIFER L., pharmaceutical executive; BBA, Pacific Lutheran U. Various positions including audit mgr. Ernst & Young LLP, 1987—93; corp. contr., corp. dir. fin. Penford Corp., 1993—97; CFO Penwest Pharmaceuticals Co., 1997—2005, COO, 2005—06, pres., 2005—, CEO, 2006—. Office: Penwest 39 Old Ridgebury Rd Ste 11 Danbury CT 06810*

GOOD, JOAN DUFFEY, artist; b. Irvington, N.J., Apr. 8, 1939; d. Joseph Edmund and Mary Kathleen Duffey; m. Robert Whitney Meyers, Feb. 19, 1960; children: Robert Whitney Jr., Mary Kathleen; step-children: Alison H., Forrester H.; m. Allen Hovey Good, June 12, 1976. Student, Rosemont Coll., 1958-59, Summit Art Ctr., 1973-78; BA in Psychology and Studio Art, Drew U., 1987. Represented by Jain Marunouchi Gallery Soho, N.Y.C., 1991-92, Abney Gallery Soho, N.Y.C., 1992; exec. dir. New Jersey Ctr. Visual Arts, Summit, N.J. Interior designer Maytime Festival of Homes, 1985; freelance interior design cons., 1987-89; v.p. Atlantic Nat. Acquisition and Mergers, Inc., Short Hills, N.J.; bd. dirs. N.J. Ctr. for Visual Arts, Summit, curatorial assoc. gallery com., 1989-90, co-curator exhbns., 1990-94, asst. gallery curator, 1991-92, gallery curator, 1992-94, pres. 1994-95, exec. dir., 1995—; archivist Oak Knoll Sch., 1988-95. One-woman show World Trade Ctr., N.Y.C., 1988; exhibited in group shows at Madison (N.J.) Pub. Libr., 1986, Chatham (N.J.) Pub. Libr., 1987, Korn Gallery, Drew U., 1986-87, 89-90, N.J. Ctr. for Visual Arts, 1987-90, Oak Knoll Sch. Alumnae Art Exhibit, 1989-90; represented in numerous private collections, Mass., Fla., Tex., N.J., N.Y., Calif. V.p., pres., membership chmn. PTO, 1966-69; homecoming com. mem. Oak Knoll Sch. Alumnae Bd., Summit, 1989-90, historian, 1988-94, archivist, 1988-95. Mem. N.J. Ctr. for Visual Arts, The Drew Art Assn., Chatham Fish & Game Assn., Mantoloking Yacht Club, Summit Tennis Club. Republican. Roman Catholic. Avocations: psychology, floriculture, photography, tennis, sculpting. Address: NJ Ctr Visual Arts 68 Elm St Summit NJ 07901

GOOD, LINDA LEE, music educator, musician; b. Seattle, Jan. 24, 1940; d. Roy S. Grannis and Florence Virginia (Sprague Grannis) Shropshire; m. Leonard J. Good, Apr. 22, 1962; children: Nancye. BA, U. Wash., 1964; MA, U. Hawaii, 1970. Tchr. Pacific Prep. Acad., Honolulu, 1965; tchr., co-founder Island Strings, Langley, Wash., 1974—; tchr. Evergreen Sch., Seattle, 1976-78, Skagit Valley Coll., Langley, 1981-85. Performer (string band) Indigo, 1986—, (tape) Gather 'Round, 1992, (CD) Clara's Fiddle, 1996. Pres. Island Arts Coun., Whidbey Island, Wash., 1986-88, bd. dirs., 1980-93; bd. dirs. Cmty. Concerts Assn., Whidbey Island, 1984-87; music dir. Unitarian Universalist Congregation, Whidbey Island, 1994—. Recipient grant Hawaii Found., 1966. Mem. Suzuki Assn. of Americas, Internat. Suzuki Assn., Wash. State Suzuki Assn., Nat. Music Tchrs. Assn., Citizens for Sensible Devel., Whidbey Environ. Action Network. Avocations: sailing, gardening, yoga, learning japanese language, travel. Home and Office: PO Box 131 Langley WA 98260-0131

GOOD, MARY LOWE (MRS. BILLY JEWEL GOOD), investment company executive, educator; b. Grapevine, Tex., June 20, 1931; d. John W. and Winnie (Mercer) Lowe; m. Billy Jewel Good, May 17, 1952 (dec. 2005); children: Billy, James. BS, Ark. State Tchrs. Coll., 1950; MS, U. Ark., 1953, PhD, 1955, LLD (hon.), 1979; DSc (hon.), U. Ill., Chgo., 1983, Clarkson U., 1984, Ea. Mich. U., 1986, Duke U., 1987, St. Mary's Coll., 1987, Kenyon Coll., 1988; degree (hon.), Stevens Inst. Tech., 1989, Lehigh U., 1989, Northeastern Ill. U., 1989, U. SC, 1989, NJ Inst. Tech., 1989; degree in law (hon.), Newcomb Coll. Tulane U., 1991; LLD (hon.), Coll. William Mary, 1992; DSc (hon.), Manhattan Coll., 1992, Ind. U., 1992, SUNY, Binghamton, 1994, Rensselaer Polytechnic Inst., 1994, Monmouth U., 1995, La. State U., 1995, Ill. Inst. Tech., 1997, Mich. State U., 1997, U. Mich., 1998; DEng (hon.), Colo. Sch. Mines, 2000. Instr. Ark. State Tchrs. Coll., Conway, summer 1949; from instr. to asst. prof. La. State U., Baton Rouge, 1954—58, Boyd prof., 1978—80; assoc. prof. to Boyd prof. U. New Orleans, 1958—78; pres. Signal Rsch. Ctr. Inc., 1983—85; pres. engineered materials rsch. divsn Allied-Signal Inc., Des Plaines, Ill., 1986—87, sr. v.p.-tech. Morristown, NJ, 1987—93; under sec. of commerce for technology Dept. of Commerce, Washington, 1993-97; mng. mem. Venture Capital Investors LLC, Little Rock, 1997—2005, Fund for Ark., 2005—; Donaghey Univ. prof., dean Coll. Info. Sci. & Systems Engr U. Ark., Little Rock, 1998—. Chmn. Pres.'s Com. for Nat. Medal Sci., 1979-82; adv. bd. NSF Chemistry Sect., 1972-76; com. medicinal chemistry NIH, 1972-76, Office of USAF Rsch., 1974-78, chemist divsn. Brookhaven and Oak Ridge Nat. Labs., 1973-83, chem. tech. divsn. Oak Ridge Nat. Lab., catalysis program Lawrence-Berkeley Lab.; bd. dirs. BiogenIdec, Inc., Delta Bank and Trust, Acxiom Inc.; bd. chem. sci. and tech., Nat. Rsch. Coun., 2003-04, Govt. U., industry roundtable, NRC, 2000-05, Ark. Sci and Tech. Authority, 1998-03, Dialoge Com, Am. Chem. Coun., 2002-05. Contbr. articles to profl. jours. Mem. Nat. Sci. Bd., 1980-91, vice chair, 1984-88, chair, 1988-91; mem. Pres.' Coun. Advisors for Sci. and Tech., 1991-93. Recipient Agnes Faye Morgan rsch. award, 1969, Disting. Alumni citation U. Ark., 1973, Scientist of Yr. award Indsl. R&D mag., 1983, Delmer S. Fahrney medal Franklin Inst., 1988, N.J. Women of Achievement award Douglass Coll., Rutgers U., 1990, Indsl. Rsch. Inst. medal, 1991, Disting. Svc. award NSF, 1992, Roe award ASME, 1993, Gold medal SME, 1995, Earle Barnes award ACS, 1996, Priestley medal, 1997, UCLA Glenn T. Seaborg medal, 1996, Nat. Materials Advancement award Fedn. Materials Socs., 1996, Othmer medal award Chem. Heritage Found., 1998, Henry Michel award, Civil Engring. Rsch. Found., 1998, Heinz award for tech. The Economy and Employment, 2000, Vannevar Bush award NSF, 2004; AEC tng. grantee, 1967, NSF Internat. travel grantee, 1968, NSF rsch. grantee, 1969-80, Albert Fox Demers award, 1992. Fellow AAAS (Abelson award 1999, pres. 2000, chmn. bd. dirs. 2001), Am. Inst. Chemistry (Gold medal 1983), Chem. Soc. London, Royal Soc. Chemistry (hon.); mem. NAE, Acad. Arts and Scis, Am. Philos. Soc., Swedish Acad. Engring., Am. Chem. Soc. (1st woman dir. 1972-74, regional dir. 1972-80, chmn. bd. 1978, 80, bd. publs., pres. 1987, mem. bd. pub. 2002-, Garvan medal 1973, Herty medal 1975, award Fla. sect. 1979, Charles Lathrop Parsons award 1991), Internat. Union Pure and Applied Chmistry (pres. inorganic div. 1980-85),Alliance for Sci. and Tech. Rsch. in Am. (chmn. bd. dirs. 2000-), Zonta (past pres. New Orleans club, chmn. dist. status of women com. and nominating com., chmn. internat. Amelia Earhart scholarship com. 1978-88, pres. internat. Found. 1988-93, mem. internat. bd. 1988-90), Rotary Internat., Phi Beta Kappa, Sigma Xi, Iota Sigma Pi (regional dir. 1967-93, hon. mem. 1983), Ark. Women's Forum. Home: 13824 Rivercrest Dr Little Rock AR 72212-1521 Office: U Ark at Little Rock Coll Info Sci/Sys Engring 2801 S University Ave Little Rock AR 72204-1000 Office Phone: 501-569-8189. Personal E-mail: thegoods@aristotle.net. Business E-Mail: mlgood@ualr.edu.

GOODACRE, GLENNA, sculptor; b. 1939; m. CL Mike Schmidt. Vietnam Women's Meml., 1993, statue of Ronald Reagan, Reagan Library, Calif., 1998, Crossing the Prairie, 2002, Sacagawea (appears on dollar coin issued by US Mint), 2000, Irish Meml., 2002, statue of West Point Coach Col. Earl 'Red' Blaik, 2003, & many others. Named to Cowgirl Hall of Fame, 2003; recipient Tex. Medal Arts, 2003. Fellow: Nat. Sculpture Soc.; mem.: Nat. Acad. Design (academician 1994—). Mailing: c/o Galleria Silecchia 12 S Palm Ave Sarasota FL 34236 E-mail: goodacre@glennagoodacre.com.

GOODACRE, JILL, model; b. Lubbock, Texas, Mar. 29, 1965; m. Harry Connick, Jr., Apr. 16, 1994, 3 children. Model Elite Model Mgmt. Corp. Appearances include Victoria's Secret catalogues; (TV Series) Friends, 1994, Duckman, 1997, (films) Odd Jobs, 1984, Ladybird Ladybird, 1994, The Uninvited, 1997.

GOODALE, TONI KRISSEL, research and development company executive; b. NYC, May 26, 1941; d. Walter DuPont and Ricka Krissel; m. James Campbell Goodale, May 3, 1964; children: Timothy Fuller, Ashley Krissel, Clayton A. (Ward). AB cum laude, Smith Coll., 1963; student, U. Geneva, 1962-63; postgrad., Hunter Coll., 1964-65. Congl. intern Senator Keating U.S. Senate, Washington, 1963; broadcast analyst FCC, Washington, 1963-64; adminstrv. asst., dir. grant rsch. dept. Ford Found., NYC, 1964-67, cons. pub. edn. dept., 1968-69; N.Y. rep. Smith Coll., NYC, 1975-78, asst. dir. devel., 1978-79; pres. Goodale Assocs., NYC, 1979-92, chmn., CEO, 1992—; vice-chmn. Metropolitan Mus. Bus. Com., NYC. Mem. NYC 2000 Millennium Coun.; vis. com. continuing edn. New Sch. Social; mem. bd. advs. First Women's Bank; bd. dirs. N.Y. Outward Bound., mem. exec. com., chmn. alumni com.; lectr., writer in field. Columnist Fund Raising Mgmt., NY Social Diary. Bd. dirs. N.Y. Pub. Libr.; bd. dirs., mem. exec. com. Pen Am. Ctr., chmn.; mem. Women's Fgn. Policy Group; mem. UNA Chmn. Coun.; lectr. U.S. Naval Acad.; mem. alumnae fund com. Smith Coll., v.p. class, chmn. 25th reunion, Women's Forum; univ. chmn.'s coun., trustee, alumnae fund chmn., mem. alumnae coun.; bd. dirs. Brearley Sch.; mem. exec. com. Parents' Assn., St. Bernard's Sch.; mem. benefit com. N.Y. Philharmonic; trustee, bd. govs. Churchill Sch.; co-chmn. spl. events com. Carnegie Hall, The Joffrey Ballet Opening Gala; chmn. Coro Benefit Dinners; trustee N.Y. Inst. Child Devel.; mem. women's divsn. Legal Aid Soc.; mem. N.Y. com. Joffrey Ballet; mem. benefit com. Grosvenor House; vice chmn. N.Y.C. Opera Benefit, Peir Ctr. Benefit; mem. com. Sch. Am. Ballet; active Women's Forum, mem. bus. com. Met. Mus. Mem. Am. Coun. Arts (vice-chmn. bd., exec. com., chmn. nat. patrons commn., chair long range planning com.), Nat. Cultural Alliance (bd. dirs.), Am. Assn. Fund-Raising Counsel (bd. dirs. trust for philanthropy), Nat. Assn. Fund Raising Execs., Assn. Healthcare Philanthropy, Brearley Sch. Alumnae Assn., Smith Coll. Alumnae Assn., Cosmopolitan Club, Smith Club, Washington Club, Seventh Regiment Armory Club, Doubles Internat. Club, Women's Forum (Women's Leadership Forum select cir., transition team, NYC pub. adv.). Office: 52 E 66 St New York NY 10021 Office Phone: 212-759-2999, 212-472-0300. Office Fax: 212-472-0311. Personal E-mail: riowoman@aol.com.

GOODALL, JANE, zoologist; b. London, Eng., Apr. 3, 1934; d. Mortimer Herbert and Vanne (Joseph) Morris-Goodall; m. Hugo Van Lawick, 1964 (div. 1974); one child, Hugo Eric Louis; m. Derek Bryceson, 1975 (dec. 1980). PhD in Ethology, Cambridge U., 1965; degree (hon.), Wesleyan Coll., Macon, Ga., 2000, U. Minn., 2001, U. Buffalo, N.Y., 2001, Ryerson U., Toronto, Ont., Can., 2001, Providence U., Taiwan, 2001, Elon U., N.C., 2002, Sweet Briar Coll., Va., 2002, U.Ctrl. Lancashire, U.K., 2003, Pecs U., Hungary, 2005, Syracuse U., N.Y., 2005, Rutgers State U., N.J., 2005, numerous other univs., 1975—99. Asst., sec. to Dr. Louis S. B. Leakey Coryndon Meml. Mus. Nat. History, Olduvai Gorge, Tanzania; rschr. in animal behavior, sci. dir. Gombe Stream Rsch. Ctr., Tanzania, 1960—2003. Vis. prof. psychiatry, human biology Stanford U., 1971-75; hon. vis. prof. zoology U. Dar Es Salaam, Tanzania, 1973—; lectr. Yale U., 1973; adj. prof. dept., environ. studies Tufts U. Sch. Vet. Medicine, 1987-88; assoc. Cleve. Natural History Mus., 1990; disting. adj. prof. occupl. therapy and anthropology U. So. Calif., 1990; Andrew D. White prof.-at-large Cornell U., 1996-2002; messenger of peace UN, 2002—;; spkr. 20/20, Nightline, Good Morning America. Author: My Friends the Wild Chimpanzees, 1967, In the Shadow of Man, 1971, The Chimpanzees of Gombe, 1986 (R.R. Hawkins award for outstanding tech., sci. or med. book, 1986, Award for Outstanding Pub. in Wildlife Ecology and Mgmt., Wildlife Soc. U.S.A., 1986), The Chimpanzee Family Book, 1989, Through a Window, 1990, Visions of Caliban, 1993 (N.Y. Times "Notable Book", 1993, Libr. Jour. "Best Sci-Tech.Book, 1993), Jane Goodall: With Love, 1994; author: (with Philip Berman) Reason for Hope, 1999; author: Dr. White, 1999, 40 Years at Gombe, 1999, Brutal Kinship, 1999, The Eagle and the Wren, 2000, Africa in My Blood: An Autobiography in Letters, 2000, Chimpanzees I Love: Saving Their World and Ours, 2001, Beyond Innocence: An Autobiography in Letters, 2001; author: (with Marc Bekoff) The Ten Trusts: What We Must Do To Care for the Animals We Love, 2002; contbr. Primate Behavior, 1965, Primate Ethology, 1967, Am. Handbook of Psychiatry, 1976, Understanding Chimpanzees, 1990; author (with H. van Lawick): (children's book) Grub: The Bush Baby, 1972; author: My Life With the Chimpanzees, 1988 (Parenting's Reading-Magic award for outstanding book for children, 1989), The Chimpanzee Family Book, 1989, Jane Goodall's Animal World: Chimps, 1989, Animal Family Series, 1989, With Love, 1994, Dr. White, 1999, The Eagle and the Wren, 2000, Chimpanzees I Love: Saving Their World and Ours, 2001; author: (with Alan Marks) Rickie and Henri: ATrue Story, 2004; author: (films) Miss Goodall and the Wild Chimpanzees, 1963, Among the Wild Chimpanzees, 1984; author: (with Hugo van Lawick) People of the Forest, 1988; author: Chimpanzee Alert, in the Nature Watch Series, 1990, The Life and Legend of Jane Goodall, 1990, The Gombe Chimpanees, 1990, Jane Goodall: Reason for Hope, 1999, Chimps R Us, 2001, Jane Goodall's Wild Chimpanzees, 2002; contbr. numerous articles to profl. jours.; author: Harvest for Hope: A Guide to Mindful Eating, 2005. Founder Jane Goodall Inst. Wildlife Rsch., 1977—; sci. gov. Chgo. Acad. Scis., 1981—; internat. dir. ChimpanZoo, 1984—; trustee Jane Goodall Inst. U.K., 1988—, Jane Goodall Inst. Can., 1993—; adv. bd. Advocates for Animals, Scotland, 1990—, Albert Schweitzer Inst. for Humanities, 1991—, Trees for Life, 1994—, Dolphin Project Internat. and Dolphin Project Europe, 1995—, Fred Found., Netherlands, 1996—, Lab. Primate Advocacy Group, 2001—, Initiative for Animals and Ethics, Harvard U., 2004—, Friends of Africa Internat., 2005—; mem. internat. adv. bd. Tchrs. Without Borders, 2001—; adv. coun. Cin. Zoo, 2005—. Decorated Dame of Brit. Empire, Legion of Honor (France); named Internat. Patron, Immortal Chaplains Found., 2006; recipient Franklin Burr award, Nat. Geographic Soc., 1963, 1964, Centennial award, 1988, Hubbard medal, 1995, Conservation award, Women's Br. N.Y. Zool. Soc., 1974, Albert Schweitzer award, Internat. Women's Inst., 1987, Kyoto prize, Inamori Found., 1990, Tanzanian Kilimanjaro medal for Contbn. to Wildlife Conservation, Pres. Mwinyi, 1996, Mt. Kilimanjaro award, 1996, Pub. Svc. award, Nat. Sci. Bd., 1998, John Hay award, Orion Soc., 1998, Huxley Meml. medal, Royal Anthrop. Inst. Gt. Britain and Ireland, 2001, 2002, Gandhi/King award for Non-Violence, 2001, Benjamin Franklin medal in Life Sci., 2003, Prince of Asturias award, 2003, Gandhi/King award, Nierenberg Prize for Sci. in the Pub. Interest, 2004, European Heroes award, Time Mag., 2004, President's Medal for Exemplary Achievement, Westminster Coll., 2005, Natura award, Pax, 2005, Gold medal award, UNESCO, 2006, numerous others. Fellow: Royal Anthropol. Inst. Gt. Britain and Ireland (hon.); mem.: Academia Scientiarium et Artium Europaea Austria, Deutsche Akademie der Naturforscher Leopoldina (Germany), Soc. Women Geographers, Am. Philos. Soc., Rsch. Ctr. for Human Ethology (fgn.), Am. Acad. Arts and Sci. (hon. fgn.) (hon.), Explorer's Club (N.Y.). Achievements include research in in behavior of free-living chimpanzees in the Gombe National Park, Tanzania; social behavior of the spotted hyena, crocutta crocutta Ngorongoro Conservation Area; on behavior of the olive baboon, Papio anub is, Gombe National Park. Business E-Mail: jginformation@janegoodall.org.

GOODE, CONSTANCE LOPER, elementary school principal; b. Camden, N.J., Dec. 8, 1950; d. Joseph R. and Cora F. (Loper) Stallings; m. Thomas L. Goode, Mar. 24, 1973; children: Bryan Thomas, James Robert. BS, Duquesne U., 1973; MEd, Coll. William and Mary, 1989; advanced degree in Adminstrn. and Supervision, George Washington U., 1996. Cert. elem. tchr., Va. Tchr. spl. edn. Las Cruces (N.Mex.) Pub. schs., 1973-74; elem. tchr. Va., 1974-89; elem. counselor Newport News (Va.) Pub. Schs., 1989-91, staff devel. coord., 1991-95; asst. prin. Carver Elem. Sch., Newport News, 1995-97; prin. Briarfield Elem. Sch., Newport News, 1997—2002, Palmer Elem. Sch., 2002—06; ret. Recipient oustanding svc. award; scholar Mennon Co. Mem. Newport News Edn. Assn. (past pres.), Newport News Reading Coun., Sigma Lambda Delta, Delta Kappa Gamma. Home: 112 Hilda Cir Hampton VA 23666-4723

GOODE, CORALYN, lawyer; b. New Brunswick, NJ, 1956; AB, Georgetown U., 1978; JD, Coll. William & Mary U., 1981. Bar: DC 1981, US Dist. Ct., DC 1993. Ptnr., energy, project finance Squire, Sanders & Dempsey, LLP, Houston, mem. mgmt. com., mng. ptnr.-Houston Office. Fluent in Spanish. Office: Squire Sanders & Dempsey LLP 6250 Chase Tower 600 Travis St Houston TX 77002-3000 Office Phone: 713-546-3355. Office Fax: 713-546-5830. Business E-Mail: cgoode@ssd.com.

GOODE, CYNTHIA A., social studies educator, secondary school educator; BA in History, St. Anselm Coll., Manchester, NH, 1998; MEd, U. Mass., Boston, 2002. Tchr. social studies Marshfield H.S., Mass., 1999—. Advisor Book Club, Marshfield, 2005—. Office: Marshfield Public Schools 167 Forest Street Marshfield MA 02050 Office Phone: 781-834-5050. E-mail: cgoode@mpsd.org.

GOODE, ELIZABETH ANN, music educator; b. Cliffside, N.C., Jan. 9, 1932; d. Broadus B. Goode and Mary Elizabeth Hames. BA Duke U., Durham, N.C., 1954; MA Adelphi U., Garden City, N.Y., 1961; PhD U. Cin., 1978. Tchr. piano Kings Mountain Schs., NC, 1954—55; tchr. vocal music Plainview Schs., NY, 1956—61, Raleigh Schs., NC, 1961—63; dir. choral, tchr. music theory E. Meadow Schs., NY, 1963—92; ret., 1992. Adjudicator NY State Sch. Music Assn., 1966—92. Poll asst. and judge Rutherford Co. Bd. of Electors, Ellenboro, NC, 1994—2003. Mem.: DAR, United Daus. of Confederacy, Nassau Music Educators Assn., N.Y. State Sch. Music Assn. (Piano Com. 1957—92), Manual Com. 1976—92), Music Educators Nat. Conf., Am. Choral Dir. Assn. (life), Soc. Dames and Barons of Magna Charta, Jamestowne Soc. (life), Old Tryon County Geneal. Soc. (life), Iron Dukes, Guilford County Geneal. Soc. (life), Pi Kappa Lambda, Delta Phi Alpha, Sigma Kappa (life). Republican. Methodist. Avocations: genealogy, reading, sports. Home: 390 NC 120 Hwy Mooresboro NC 28114

GOODE, ERICA TUCKER, internist; b. Berkeley, Calif., Mar. 25, 1940; d. Howard Edwin and Mary Louise (Tucker) Sweeting; m. Bruce Tucker (div. 1971); m. Barry Paul Goode, Sept. 1, 1974; children: Adam Nathaniel, Aaron Benjamin. BS summa cum laude, U. Calif., Berkeley, 1962, MPH, 1967; MD, U. Calif., San Francisco, 1977. Diplomate Am. Bd. Internal Medicine. Chief dietitian Washington Hosp. Ctr., Washington, 1968; pub. health nutritionist Dept. Human Resources, Washington, 1969—73; intern Children's Hosp. (now Calif. Pacific Med. Ctr.), San Francisco, 1977—78, resident, 1978—80, chief med. resident internal medicine, 1979—80; pvt. practice internal medicine San Francisco, 1980—. Expert witness med.-legal issues, Calif., 1990—; lectr., tchr. med. house staff Calif. Pacific Med. Ctr. Hosp., 1982—; assoc. prof. medicine U. Calif., San Francisco, 1984—; apptd. mem. Calif. Commn. on Aging, 2003—. Contbr. articles to profl. publs. Co-chair Physicians for Clinton, No. Calif., 1992, 96 Mem. AMA, ACP, Calif. Med. Assn., Calif. Soc. Internal Medicine, San Francisco Med. Soc. (mem. editl. bd.), U. Calif. Alumni Assn. (del.), Alpha Omega Alpha (named Best Doctor's list 1998-2005) Office: CPMC Inst for Health & Healing Clinic 2300 California St Ste 200 San Francisco CA 94115-2754 Office Phone: 415-600-3503.

GOODE, REBEKAH EVELYN, literature and language educator; b. Princeton, NJ, Dec. 14, 1978; d. Charles Genther and Belva Marie Luther; m. Pete Michael Goode, June 23, 2001. BA in Hispanic Studies, East Carolina U., Greenville, NC, 2000; MEd in Tchg. ESL, U. NC, Charlotte, 2006. Spanish tchr. Pitt County Schs., Greenville, 2001; ESL tchr. Rowan-Salisbury Schs., Salisbury, NC, 2002—. Presenter in field. Sec. Cedarcraft Homeowners Assn., Mooresville, NC, 2001—03; Sunday sch. tchr. Grace Covenant Ch., Cornelius, NC, 2005—06. Mem.: Fgn. Lang. Honor Soc., Golden Key Honor Soc., Nat. Honor Soc. Avocation: community outreach. Home: 5901 Redding Rd Charlotte NC 28216

GOODELL, KATHY SUSAN, artist, educator; d. Herbert Sumner and Celestine Goodell; m. Ralph James Rogers, June 30, 1996. BFA, San Francisco Art Inst., 1969—71, MFA, 1972. Instr. Calif. Coll. of Arts and Crafts, San Francisco, 1974—77, San Francisco (Calif.) State U, 1978—81, The San Francisco Art Inst., 1978—80; lectr. U Calif., Davis, 1981—82; assoc. prof. Moore Coll. of Art and Design, Philadelphia, 1984—91; instr. sculpture The Sch. of Visual Arts, N.Y.C., 1986—; prof. painting, drawing SUNY, New Paltz, 1993—. Juror sculpture fellowship N.Y. Found. For The Arts, N.Y.C., 1995; juror Nat. Scholastic Award Nat. Scholastic Soc., N.Y.C., 1999; lectr.,workshops at various colls.,univs., film festivals. lectr. in field. Contbr. video Unterbrochene Karrieren Hannah Wilke Berlin,Germany, 2000, video Crumb Sony Classics, 1994, book Art in the San Francisco Bay Area 1945-1980, 1985, book New Bay Area Painting and Sculpture, 1982, articles and reviews numerous mentions 1976-2003; one-woman shows include Queens Art Ctr., Queens,N.Y., 2000, Willoughby Sharp Gallery, N.Y.C., 2000, Calkins Gallery, Hofstra U, 1982, Gallery Paule Anglim, San Francisco,Calif., 1982, Atholl McBean Gallery, 1981, Axel Raben Gallery, N.Y.C., 2003, mid-Manhattan br. N.Y. Pub. Libr., 2004, Chappell Gallery, Boston, 2004, exhibited in group shows at The Chandler Gallery-Faculty Exhbn. SUNY, New Paltz,N.Y., 2002, Paul Morris Gallery, N.Y.C., 2001, Wake Forest U., Winston-Salem, N.C., 2000, Nicolai Fine Art, N.Y.C., 1999, The Islip Mus., East Islip, N.Y., 1998, Satellite, AT, Long Island,N.Y., 1997, URBANGLASS, N.Y.C., 1996, The Boise Mus., Boise,Id., 1994, numerous group shows at galleries and univs., 1977—, Represented in permanent collections DeSaisset Mus., Santa Clara,Calif., The Samuel Dorsky Mus., New Paltz,N.Y., Fortroyal Found., Fultonville,N.Y., Calif. Pacific Corp., San Francisco,Calif., The Oakland Mus., Oakland, Calif., The Albuquerque Mus., Albuquerque,N.M., The Inst. of Plastic Arts, Bucharest, Romania, The Ctr. for Visual Arts, Anchorage, AK. Recipient James D. Phelan Award, Internat. award to a Calif. born artist., James D. Phelan, 1983; grantee Fellowship, N.Y. Found. for the Arts, 1997, 1993, Pollock-Krasne Found. Grant In Sculpture, 1991, Artist In Residence, N.Y. Council for the Arts, 1985, Fellowship in Sculpture, Nat. Endowment for the Arts, 1983, 1979, Fulbright-Hays Fellowship - Romania, Fulbright-Hayes Foun. Mem.: Tribera Organ. of Artists, United Fed. of Tchrs. Home: 401 Washington St New York NY 10013 Office: SUNY 75 South Manheim Blvd New Paltz NY 12561 Business E-Mail: ksg454@aol.com.

GOODFELLOW, ROBIN IRENE, surgeon; b. Xenia, Ohio, Apr. 14, 1945; d. Willis Douglas and Irene Linna (Kirkland) G. BA summa cum laude, Western Res. U., Cleve., 1967; MD cum laude, Harvard U., 1971. Diplomate Am. Bd. Surgery. Intern, resident Peter Bent Brigham Hosp., Boston, 1971-76; staff surgeon Boston U., 1976-80, asst. prof. surgery, 1977-80; pvt. practice medicine specializing in surgery Jonesboro, La., 1980-81; practice medicine specializing in surgery Albion, Mich., 1984-87, Coldwater, Mich., 1987—. Bd. Overseers Case Western Res. U., 1977-82. AAUW fellow, 1970. Fellow ACS; mem. AMA, Phi Beta Kappa. Republican. Methodist.

GOODIN, JULIA C., forensic specialist, state official; b. Columbia, Ky., Mar. 10, 1957; d. Vitus Jack and Geneva Goodin. BS, Western Ky. U., 1979; MD, U. Ky., 1983. Diplomate Am. Bd. Clin. and Anatomic Pathology, Am. Bd. Forensic Pathology. Intern Vanderbilt U. Med. Ctr., Nashville, 1983, resident in anatomic and clin. pathology, 1984-87; fellow in forensic pathology Med. Examiner's Office, Balt., 1987-88; asst. med. examiner Office of Chief Med. Examiner, Balt., 1988-90; dep. chief med. examiner State of Tenn., 1990-94; asst. med. examiner Nashville, 1990-93; chief med. examiner, 1993-94; asst. med. investigator State of N.Mex., Albuquerque, 1994-96; asst. prof. U. N.Mex., Albuquerque, 1994-96; clin. assoc. prof. U. of South Ala. Sch. Medicine, 1996-99; state med. examiner Ala. Dept. Forensic Scis., Mobile, 1996-99; chief state med. examiner State of Iowa, Des Moines, 1999—. Clin. prof. U. Md. Med. Sch., Balt., 1988-90, Vanderbilt U. Med. Ctr., 1990-94. Capt. USNR, 1985—. Mem. Am. Acad. Forensic Sci., Assn.

Mil. Surgeons of U.S., AMA. Avocations: long-distance running, weightlifting, photography, studying French. Home: 100 Market St Unit 414 Des Moines IA 50309-4765 Office: 2250 S Ankeny Blvd Ankeny IA 50023-9023 Office Phone: 515-725-1400.

GOODING, GRETCHEN ANN WAGNER, physician, educator; b. Columbus, Ohio, July 2, 1935; d. Edward Frederick and Margaret (List) Wagner; m. Charles A. Gooding, June 19, 1961; children: Gunnar Blaise, Justin Mathias, Britta Meghan. BA magna cum laude, Ohio Dominican U., 1957; MD cum laude, Ohio State U., 1961. Diplomate Am. Bd. Diagnostic Radiology. Intern Univ. Hosps., Columbus, 1961-62; rsch. fellow Boston City Hosp., 1962-63, Boston U., 1963-65; with dept. radiology U. Calif., San Francisco, 1975—, assoc. prof. in radiology, 1981-85, prof., vice chmn., 1986—2003; asst. chief radiology VA Med. Ctr., San Francisco, 1978-87, chief radiology, 1987—2003, chief ultrasonography, 1975—. Chair com. acad. pers. U. Calif., San Francisco, 1993-94, bd. dirs. commn. accreditation vascular labs., 1993-96. Co-editor Radiologic Clinics of N.Am., 1993—; mem. editl. bd. San Francisco Medicine, 1986—, Applied Radiology, 1987-89, Current Opinion in Radiology, 1992-93, The Radiologist, 1993—, Emergency Radiology, 1993-2003, Jour. Clin. Ultrasound, 1997—; guest editor Emergency Radiology, 1999; contbr. articles to profl. jours. Recipient Recognition award Inter Societal Commn. for Accreditation of Vascular Labs., 1997, Disting. Alumna award, Ohio State U. Coll. Medicine and Pub. Health, 2001. Fellow Am. Coll. Radiology (mem. commn. on ultrasound 1984-2000, chair stds. com. commn. on ultrasound 2004-05, chmn. com. practice guidelines and tech. standards 2004-06), Am. Inst. Ultrasound in Medicine (bd. govs. 1981-84, chair conv. program 1986-88, Presdl. Recognition award 1984), Am. Soc. Emergency Radiology, Soc. Radiologists U.S.; mem. AMA, San Francisco Med. Soc. (chmn. membership com. 1992-94, bd. dirs. 1996—), RSNA (course com. 1984-88, tech. exhibit com. 1992-96, mem. site med. advisor 2005-06), Bay Area Ultrasound Soc. (pres. 1979-80), Soc. Radiologists Ultrasound (chair membership com. 1991-93, chair corp. com. 1996-97), ARRS, AUR, CRS, Calif. Med. Assn., Am. Assn. Women Radiologists (pres. 1984-85, trustee 1991-94, Alice Ettinger Disting. Achievement award 2003), VA Chiefs of Radiology Assn. (pres.-elect, pres. 1994-95), San Francisco Radiol. Soc. (pres. 1990-91), Hungarian Radiol. Soc. (hon.), Pakistan Radiol. Soc. (hon.), Cuba Radiol. Soc. (hon.). Office: VA Med Ctr Radiology Svc 4150 Clement St San Francisco CA 94121-1545 E-mail: gretchen.gooding@radiology.ucsf.edu.

GOODKIN, DEBORAH GAY, corporate financial executive; b. Oceanside, N.Y., Dec. 8, 1951; d. Harold and Rose (Mostkoff) G.; m. Glenn Richard; children: Samuel Goodkin Richard, Sarah Goodkin Richard. BA, Syracuse U., 1972; M in Urban Planning, NYU, 1977. Planner Nassau-Suffolk Planning, Hauppauge, N.Y., 1972; asst. to treas. Nat. Assn. Savs. Banks, N.Y.C., 1973; planning aide Dept. City Planning, N.Y.C., 1973-79; planner, real property mgr. N.Y.C. Bd. Edn., 1979-81; dir. Capital Budget Bur., 1981-85; supervising mgmt. engr. Port Authority N.Y. & N.J., 1985-90, mgr. fin. sys., 1989-96; mutual funds ops. mgr. Tchrs. Ins. Annuity Assn., N.Y.C., 1997-99, tuition savs. program ops. mgr., 1999—2002; v.p. Citigroup Coll. Savs., 1999—2005; dir. Legg Mason, 2005—. Cons. C Corp., L.A., 1983—88. Author: (zoning law) Bay Ridge Zoning Dist., 1978; artist Show of Selected Works, Sireuil, France, 1983. Security cons. Dem. Nat. Com., N.Y.C., 1980; founder, pres. Allendale Opportunity and Enrichment Program. Recipient CEO Award of Excellence, 1987, 92. Mem. Women in Govt. (guest lectr. 1983), Syracuse U. Alumni Assn., NYU Alumni Assn. Office: Legg Mason 300 1st Stamford Pl Stamford CT 06902

GOODKIND, JOAN CAROL, librarian; b. Los Angeles, Oct. 27, 1938; d. William Casper and Edna Viola (Johnson) Jagy; m. Charles R. Troutman, Aug. 1, 1963 (div. 1966); m. Stephen J. Seligman, Aug. 8, 1968 (div. 1973); m. Richard I. Goodkind, July 6, 1980; 1 child, Rebecca Louise Troutman BA, UCLA, 1963, M.L.S., 1964. Cert. profl. librarian, N.Y. Research librarian Inst. for Library Research, Los Angeles, 1966-68; library systems analyst Columbia U., N.Y.C., 1969-72; mgr. Book and Game Land, N.Y.C., 1974-75; chief acquisition div. N.Y. Pub. Library, N.Y.C., 1975—. Mem. Book Industry Systems Adv. Com. Mem. ALA Clubs: Town Tennis, Appalachian Mountain (N.Y.C.). Democrat. Avocations: playing chamber music (viola); hiking; tennis; opera. Home: 500 E 77th St New York NY 10162-0025 Office: NY Pub Libr Fifth Ave at 42nd St New York NY 10018 also: Simon's Rock Bard Coll Great Barrington MA 01230

GOODMAN, ALLEGRA, writer; b. Bklyn., 1967; married. BA magna cum laude, Harvard Univ., 1989; PhD in English, Stanford Univ., 1996. Author: (short stories) (collection) Total Immersion, 1989, The Family Markowitz, 1996 (NY Times Notable Book Yr., fiction winner First Annual Salon Book awards), (novels) Kaaterskill Falls, 1998, Paradise Park, 2001, Intuition, 2006; contbr. articles New Yorker, Good Housekeeping, Slate, Am. Scholar. Named one of 20 Best Writers under 40, New Yorker Mag.; recipient Whiting award. Mailing: Author Mail Bantam Dell Publ 1745 Broadway New York NY 10019*

GOODMAN, CAROL HOCKENBURY, retired elementary school educator, consultant; b. Chgo., Nov. 12, 1943; d. Norman J. and Margaret Griffith Hockenbury; children: Kellie S., Krista L., Kirk A. BS, Lock Haven U., Pa., 1965; MEd, Shippensburg U., 1968. Cert. permanent tchg. cert. Pa. Elem. tchr. Wyalusing (Pa.) Area Sch. Dist., 1965—69, N.E. Bradford Sch. Dist., Rome, Pa., 1988—2004; adj. prof. Pa. State U., State College, 2001—, ret., 2004. Dir. Goodwriting Assocs., Wyalusing, 2002—; adj. prof. Keystone Coll., La Plume, Pa., 2005—. Dir., author, choreographer: elem. sch. musicals Broadway Dreams, American Pride, The Great American Vacation, others. Mem.: NEA (assoc.), Delta Kappa Gamma (state com. chair 2001—). Avocations: writing, reading, travel, grandchildren. Home: PO Box 254 Wyalusing PA 18853 Personal E-mail: cgoodman@epix.net.

GOODMAN, ELIZABETH ANN, retired lawyer; b. Marquette, Mich., Aug. 11, 1950; d. Paul William and Pearl Marie Goodman; m. Herbert Charles Gardner, Sept. 24, 1977. Student, U. Munich, 1970-71; BA cum laude, Alma Coll., Mich., 1972; JD cum laude, U. Mich., 1977. Bar: Minn. 1978, Mich. 1978, U.S. Dist. Ct. Minn. 1979. Cert. real property law specialist, real property sect. Minn. Bar Assn. High sch. tchr. Onaway (Mich.) High Sch., 1973-74; assoc. Dorsey & Whitney LLP, Mpls., 1978-82; ptnr. Dorsey & Whitney, Mpls., 1983-99; v.p., chief gen. counsel Ryan Cos., 2000—03; ret., 2003.

GOODMAN, ELLEN HOLTZ, journalist; b. Newton, Mass., Apr. 11, 1941; d. Jackson Jacob and Edith (Weinstein) Holtz; m. Robert Levey; 1 dau., Katherine Anne. BA cum laude, Radcliffe Coll., 1963; degree (hon.), Mt. Holyoke Coll., Amherst Coll., U. Pa., U. NH. Researcher, reporter Newsweek Mag., 1963-65; feature writer Detroit Free Press, 1965-67; feature writer columnist Boston Globe, 1967-74, assoc. editor, 1986—2001; syndicated columnist Washington Post Writers Group, 1976—; radio commentator Spectrum, CBS, 1978-80, NBC, 1979-80; commentator NBC Today Show, 1979-81. Vis. prof. Stanford U., 1995. Author: Close to Home, 1979, Turning Points, 1979, At Large, 1981, Keeping in Touch, 1985, Making Sense, 1989, Value Judgments, 1993, (with Patricia O'Brien) I Know Just What You Mean, 2000, Paper Trail, 2004. Trustee Radcliffe Coll.; judge Livingston Awards for Young Journalists, 1986—. Nieman fellow Harvard U., 1974, Lyndhurst fellow, 2000; named New Eng. Newspaper Woman of Year New Eng. Press Assn., 1968; recipient Catherine O'Brien award Stanley Home Products, 1971, Media award Mass. Commn. Status Women, 1974, Columnist of Year award New Eng. Women's Press Assn., 1975, Pulitzer Prize for Commentary, 1980, prize for column writing Am. Soc. Newspaper Editors, 1980, Hubert H. Humphrey Civil Rights award, 1988, William Allen White award 1995. Office: 5 JFK St Cambridge MA 02138 E-mail: ellengoodman@globe.com.

GOODMAN, ERIKA, dancer, actress; b. Phila. d. A. Allan and Laura (Baylin) G. Student, Sch. of Am. Ballet, 1961-63; BA in Theatre and Dance, Empire State Coll., 1993; master classes, Princeton Ballet, 1994, Hartford Ballet Co., 1995, Va. Intermont Coll., 1995—. Mem. faculty Actors and Dirs. Lab., N.Y.C., 1979—; founding mem. ensemble theater co. The Barrow Group, N.Y.C., 1986—; mem. dance faculty CCNY, 1990. Mem. dance faculty CCNY, 1990; guest tchr. ballet Balettakademein, Stockholm, 1986, 89; instr. master classes Rutgers U., East Carolina U., 1989, Hofstra U., U. Kans., 1990, Harvard U., summer 1993, Cornell U., Skidmore Coll., Vassar Coll., 1992—. Conn. Coll.; vis. prof. ballet, head ballet dept. CCNY, 1992—, lectr. world arts, 1993—. Dancer N.Y.C. Ballet Co., 1964-65, prin. dancer Joffrey Ballet, N.Y.C., 1966-75; performer (with Barrow Group) Seymour in the Heart of Winter, Perry St. Theatre, N.Y.C., 1986, When You Comin' Back Red Rider, 1987, Feather Hat, Three Sisters, 1989; casting dir. (films) Hazing in Hell, Neon Red; dir. ballet rehearsal Ballet Hispanico. Richard Porter Leach fellow, 1992-93.

GOODMAN, GAIL BUSMAN, small business owner; b. NYC, Feb. 8, 1953; d. Irving Laurence and Harriet (Topol) Busman; m. Laurence Goodman, June 17, 1979 (div. 1987). Student, Northwestern U., Evanston, Ill., 1970—72; BS magna cum laude, Tufts U., Medford, Mass., 1975. Staff occupational therapist St. Joseph's Hosp., Yonkers, N.Y., 1975-77; sr. occupational therapist N.Y. Hosp., White Plains, 1977-79; chief occupational therapist Phelps Hosp., Tarrytown, N.Y., 1979-80; occupational therapy cons. Elmwood Manor Nursing Home, Nanuet, N.Y., 1982-83; from v.p. tng. to pres. Facelifters, Bklyn., 1981-86; pres. Visual Impact, Rye, N.Y., 1987—; owner, pres. ConsulTel, Inc., White Plains, N.Y., 1988—. Guest speaker Columbia U., N.Y.C., 1977, 78, 79, 82. Mem. Women in Sales (pres. Westchester chpt. 1989-91). Democrat. Jewish. Avocations: reading, movies, needlepoint, antique refinishing, horseback riding. Office Phone: 914-242-1108. Personal E-mail: phoneteach@aol.com.

GOODMAN, GERTRUDE AMELIA, civic worker; b. El Paso, Tex., Oct. 24, 1924; d. Karl Perry and Helen Sylvia (Pinkiert) G. BA, Mills Coll., 1945. Pres. El Paso chpt. Tex. Social Welfare Assn., 1963-65, bd. dirs. 1965-70, state bd. dirs., 1965-70; state bd. dirs. Pan-Am. Round Table, El Paso, 1966—, bd. dirs. 1970-71, sec., 1973-74, life mem.; founder, 1st chmn. El Paso Mus. Art Mem. Guild, 1962-68; bd. dirs. Mus. Art Assn., 1962-69, also v.p.; chmn. dir. El Paso C. of C. women's Dept., 1976-77; bd. dirs. Rio Grande Food Bank, 1988-94; bd. dirs. El Paso Pub. Libr., 1972-80, pres. bd. dirs., 1978-80; pres. El Paso County Hist. Soc., 1981-82, bd. dirs., 1986-92; mem. planning com. El Paso United Way, 1953—; mem. El Paso Mus. Art Bd. Coun.; pres. Las Comadres, 2000-01. Recipient Hall of Honor award El Paso County Hist. Soc., Nat. Human Rels. award NCCJ, 1981, numerous awards for civic vol. work. Avocations: tennis, travel, art, books. Home: 905 Cincinnati Ave El Paso TX 79902-2435

GOODMAN, JESSICA MUI KWAI, secondary school educator; d. Bob and Robin Haycock; m. Michael Edward Goodman. BA in Biology, U. Colo., Boulder, 2000. Lic. tchr. secondary edn. Colo., 2001. Tchr. biology Pomona H.S. Jefferson County Pub. Sch., Arvada, Colo., 2001—.

GOODMAN, JOAN FRANCES, avionics manufacturing executive; b. N.Y.C., Oct. 25, 1941; d. Jack and Evelyn (Fine) G.; m. Stephen Gordon Glatzer, Oct. 2, 1982 (dec. Dec. 1987). BS, Alfred U., 1963; MA, NYU, 1967. RN, N.Y. Psychiat. liaison nurse Hosp. Albert Einstein Coll. Medicine, N.Y.C., 1968-73; nursing care coord. United Hosp., Port Chester, NY, 1974-80; asst. to pres. Emergency Beacon Corp., New Rochelle, NY, 1980—87, pres., CEO, 1988—. Mem. MBA adv. group Westchester Grad. campus L.I. U. Mem. ANA, Nat. League Nursing, Westchester Assn. Women Bus. Owners (pres. 2004-06), Nat. Bus. Aviation Assn., Women in Aviation Internat. Office: Emergency Beacon Corp 15 River St New Rochelle NY 10801-4351

GOODMAN, JUDITH ROSS, psychotherapist; b. St. Louis, June 12, 1950; d. Bernard Alan and Elizabeth (Schnitzer) Ross; m. Mark E. Goodman; children: Lauren, William, Evan. BA with Psi Chi Honors in Psychology, Tulane U., 1972; postgrad., U. Colo., 1973; MSW, Washington U., St. Louis, 1974. Cert. St. Louis Psychoanalytic Inst., 1983, ACSW, 1976, AASECT, 1980, Diplomate, 1989. Health educator St. Louis County Health Dept., St. Louis, 1972-73; after sch. coord. St. Louis County Juvenile Ctr., St. Louis, 1973-74; med. social worker Dept. Community Health and Med. Care, St. Louis, 1974-80; project dir. Springboards, Inc., St. Louis, 1982-83; psychotherapist Women's Care Group, St. Louis, 1980-84; health reporter Sta. KSDK-TV (NBC affiliate), St. Louis, 1986-89; pvt. practice St. Louis, 1984-91; dir. pub. rels. Lents and Assocs., St. Louis, 1990—. Lectr. Jr. League early childhood ctrs., 1980—; cons. Family Planning Coun.; adj. prof. Washington U. Cons. for ednl. entertainment video, 1983; contbr. articles to profl. jours. and newspapers. Founder Kids at Home NCJW, Super Sibling Classes; pres. Friends of Ctr. of Contemporary Arts; bd. dirs. St. Louis Nursery Found. Gifted Resources Coun., GWB Sch. Social Work, Washington u.; adv. bd. St. Louis County Dept. Cmty. Health and Med. Care; bd. dirs. St. Louis Regional Child Care Ptnrship., St. Louis Psychoanalytic Inst., Clayton Sch. Dist. Vol.; bd. of Aldermen City of Clayton, 2003-06. Recipient Orgn. award St. Louis Bus. and Profl. Women, 1989. Avocations: dance, tennis. Home: 17 Wydown Ter Saint Louis MO 63105-2218 Office: 1750 S Brentwood Blvd Ste 552 Saint Louis MO 63144-1302

GOODMAN, KAREN LACERTE, financial services executive; b. Mesa, Ariz., Nov. 9, 1946; d. Howard Lee and Margaret (Duncan) G.; m. Grant A. Lacerte, Feb. 1, 1964; children: Arthur Grant Jr., Arcel Leon Rene. Student, George Washington U., 1974-76. Prodn. mgr. Data Corp. of Am., Reston, Va., 1967-73; pres. Transco Leasing Co., Washington, 1974-78; sec., treas. to v.p. Certa Data Corp., Orlando, Fla., 1989—; pres. Fin. Rsch. Assocs., Inc., Orlando, 1979—. Cons. in field, 1979—; dir. statis. seminars in field. Editor, pub.: Financial Studies of the Small Business (annual publ.), 1976—. Mem. Am. Heart Assn., Winter Haven, Fla., MADD, 1985—. Mem. Greater Orlando C. of C. Republican. Home: 6759 Winterset Gardens Rd Winter Haven FL 33884-3154 Office: 203 Ave A NW Ste 202 Winter Haven FL 33881-4503 Office Phone: 863-299-2400. E-mail: kgoodman@certipay.com.

GOODMAN, KIM, marketing professional, computer company executive; B in Polit. Sci., Stanford U., M in Indsl. Engring.; MBA, Harvard U., 1992. V.p. Bain & Co., Inc.; v.p. bus. devel., exec. asst. to the CEO Dell Inc., 2000, v.p., gen. mgr. for networking product group; v.p. mktg. Dell Americas Public Sector, Round Rock, Tex., 2003—. Office: Dell Inc One Dell Way Round Rock TX 78682

GOODMAN, N. JANE, law librarian; b. Monett, Mo., May 9, 1946; d. William F. and Audie L. (Stolle; m. Douglas L. Goodman, May 9, 1969; children: Kelly, Gregory, Kristi, Anthony, Richard. Student, Drury Coll., Springfield, Mo., 1969-70; AA summa cum laude, Crowder Coll., Neosho, Mo., 1997; BS summa cum laude, S.W. Mo. State U., 1999; JD, U. Tulsa, 2003; MLS, U. Mo., 2005. Lic. real estate salesperson, Mo. Supr. Family Svcs., Aurora, Mo., 1972-87; exec. sec. Little Tikes Toy Co., Aurora, 1987-90, buyer, 1990-97; owner DJ's Catering, Aurora, 1997—2000; real estate salesperson Monett Realty, 1997—2005, ref. libr., 2005—. Author: South American Travel, 1985. Area rep. Am. Intercultural Student Exch., Aurora, 1989—; treas. for state rep. polit. campaign. Mem. NAFE, Am. Purchasing Soc., Optimist Club (charter pres., lt. gov. Western Mo. dist. 1996—), Phi Theta Kappa, Lambda Pi Eta, Phi Alpha Delta, Golden Key Honor Soc., Tex. Libr. Assn. Avocations: travel, music, foreign languages, studying south american cultures, reading. Home: 7614 Laguna Del Mar Ct #311 Laredo TX 78041

GOODMAN, PAULINE ROSE, retired secondary school educator; b. Marlow, Okla., Nov. 13, 1915; d. Edwin Lankford Kirtley and Olina Talle; m. Ben Lester Goodman, Jan. 10, 1942; children: Diane E. Lepawsky, Ben L. Jr., Lynn B., Cynthia H. Mumma. BA, Phillips U., Enid, Okla., 1938; BS in Medicine, U. Okla., Okla. City, 1940; MS in Chemistry Methods, U. Okla., 1976. Cert. secondary educator Okla., 1938. Tchr. sci. H.S. Garber (Okla.) Pub. Schs., 1942—44, Enid (Okla.) Pub. Schs., 1960—82, ret., 1982. Editor: Crest Chronicle, 2006. Vol. Contact Suicide Prevention, Enid, 1983—86. Named Outstanding Biology Tchr. of Yr., Nat. Assn. Biology Tchrs., 1982. Mem.: Okla. Ret. Tchrs. Assn. Democrat. Unitarian. Avocations: reading, walking, writing, opera. Home: 800 Hausman Rd Allentown PA 18104

GOODMAN, PHYLLIS L., public relations executive; b. N.Y.C., Sept. 7, 1946; d. Bernard Jacob and Claire (Rosenberg) Goodman. BS, Cornell U., 1967. Ext. home economist Nassau County Ext. Svc., Mineola, N.Y., 1967-68; editl. asst. Funk & Wagnalls, N.Y.C., 1968-69; sr. v.p. Glick & Lorwin, Inc., N.Y.C., 1969-80, Sci. and Medicine, N.Y.C., 1980-82; v.p. Hill and Knowlton, Inc., N.Y.C., 1982-85; assoc. v.p. comm. and pub. affairs St. Luke's-Roosevelt Hosp. Ctr., N.Y.C., 1985-92; owner Goodman Pub. Rels., Albuquerque, 1993-95; v.p. corp. comm. Sun Healthcare Group, Inc., Albuquerque, 1995-2000; v.p. mktg. and comms. St. Vincent Hosp., Santa Fe, 2000-01; v.p. mktg. and comm. Cin. Children's Hosp. Med. Ctr., 2001—. Mem. com. pub. affairs Greater N.Y. Hosp. Assn., 1988-92. Bd. dirs. Chamber Music Albuquerque, 1998-2001. Mem. Am. Soc. Health Care Mktg. and Pub. Rels. (treas. N.Mex. chpt. 1993-94), Pub. Rels. Soc. Am. (accredited, pres. N.Mex. chpt. 1996), Healthcare Pub. Rels. and Mktg. Soc. Greater N.Y. (pres. 1990-91), Westside C. of C. N.Y.C. (bd. dirs. 1986-92), Pi Lambda Theta. Office: Cin Childrens Hosp MLC 9102 3333 Burnet Ave Cincinnati OH 45229

GOODMAN, SHERRI WASSERMAN, lawyer; b. NYC, Apr. 9, 1959; m. John B. Goodman, Aug. 8, 1987. BA, Amherst (Mass.) Coll., 1981; JD, MPP, Harvard U., 1987. Bar: Mass. 1988, D.C. 1990. Analyst Sci. Applications, Inc., McLean, Va., 1981-83; counsel Senate Armed Svcs. Com., Washington, 1987-90; assoc. Goodwin, Procter & Hoar, Boston, 1990-93; dep. under sec. for env. security Dept. Def., Washington, 1993-2000; sr. fellow Ctr. for Naval Analyses, Alexandria, Va., 2001—. Cons. Def. Nuclear Facilities Safety Bd., Washington, 1990-92; signatory, Energy Future Coalition, 2005. Author: The Neutron Bomb Controversy, 1983, Weapons Acquisition, 1988; contbr. articles to profl. jours. Mem. Coun. on Fgn. Rels. Office: The CNA Corp 4825 Mark Center Dr Alexandria VA 22311

GOODMAN, SUSAN, curator; b. Phila. d. Maurice and Carolyn Kunst Tumarkin; m. Jerry Goodman, Oct., 1968; children: Micah, Nina. BA in Art History, U. Pa., 1956; MA in Art History, Columbia U., 1961. Editl., rsch. asst. The Solomon R. Guggenheim Mus., 1965-67; asst. curator The Jewish Mus., 1967-72, chief curator exhibns., 1972-98, sr. curator-at-large, 1999—. Fellow Meml. Found. Jewish Culture; grantee NEA, Trust for Mutual Understanding The Rockefeller Found. Mem. Am. Assn. Mus., N.E. Mus. Assn., N.Y. Assn. New Ams. (visual arts com.), Coll. Art Assn., Arttable. Address: 1140 5th Ave New York NY 10128-0806 Office: The Jewish Mus 1109 5th Ave New York NY 10128-0118 E-mail: sgoodman@thejm.org.

GOODMAN, SYLVIA KLUMOK, film center executive; b. Moorhead, Miss., June 19, 1940; d. Sol Harry and Fannie Ida (Davidson) Klumok; m. Carl Gerald Goodman, June 5, 1960; children: Lisa Wynne Goodman Stone, Gary Steven, Jeffrey David. BS in Zoology with honors, Newcomb Coll., 1962; M in Zoology, Tulane U., 1963; postgrad., Harvard U., summer 1990. Tchr. Midway Jr. H.S., Shreveport, La., 1963-68; instr. biology La. State U., Shreveport, 1967-68; instr. physiology, asst. coord. plans La. State U. Med. Ctr., Shreveport, 1970-74; chmn. bd. dir. Goldring Woldenberg Inst. So. Jewish Life, 2000—03; pres., CEO Robinson Film Ctr., Shreveport, La., 2004—. Pres. Shreveport Jewish Fedn., 1982—83; mem. C. of C. 100 Women of the Century; chmn. Food Project, Shreveport, 1990—92; chair beautification com. Shreveport Regional Airport, 1990—94, So. Jewish Inst., 2000—; pres. Sci-Port Discovery Ctr., 1993—95; trustee Shreveport-Bossier Cmty. Fedn., chmn., 1993—; vice chmn. Meadows Art Mus., 1995; mem. Shreveport Mayor's Women's Commn., 1986—90; vice-chair La. State Mineral Bd., Baton Rouge, 1988—92; bd. dir. Sci-Port Discovery Ctr., Shreveport, 1990—, Meadows Art Mus., 1991—97, La. Endowment Humanities, 1996—99, La. Film Theater, 2003—, chair capital campaign, 2003, pres., 2005—; mem. chancellor's adv. com. LSU-S, 1996—; chmn. bd. dir. Goldring/Woldenberg Inst. So. Jewish Life, 2000—. Recipient Humanitarian award NCCJ, Humanitarian award Caddo Commn., 1991, Vol. Fundraiser award Nat. Fedn. Fundraising Execs., 1996, Angel award Blue Cross Blue Shield, 1998, award Point of Light Found., 1999, Friend of Edn. award Caddo Assn. Educators, 2001, Heroines award La., 2006, La. Legend award, 2006; named Women Who Made a Difference Shreveport Celebration of Women Week, 1996, Best-Dressed Woman of No. La. Shreveport Times, 1998, Women of Century, Shreveport C.of C. Mem. Jr. League Shreveport (Sustainer of Yr. award 1995, Daily Point of Light 1999), Mensa, Phi Beta Kappa, Alpha Epsilon Phi. Jewish. Avocations: theater, piano, dance, taking courses, movies. Home: 409 Southfield Rd Shreveport LA 71106-2213 E-mail: gigigood@aol.com.

GOODMAN, VALERIE DAWSON, psychiatric social worker; b. Bluefield, W.Va., Feb. 2, 1948; d. Francis Carl and Lesly (Collett) Dawson; m. David William Goodman, June 9, 1985; 1 child, Amanda Lynn. BS, W.Va. U., 1970, MS, 1972; MSW, U. Md., 1980. Lic. clin. social worker, Md. Social worker Md. Children's Aide Family Svcs. Soc., Balt., 1972-78; social worker III Montgomery County Dept. Social Svcs., Rockville, Md., 1980-81; clin. social worker Johns Hopkins Hosp., Balt., 1981-83; pvt. practice Suburban Psychiat. Assoc. Hopkins at Greenspring Station, Balt., 1986—. Supr. Johns Hopkins Hosp., 1983-86, chair Brogden com., 1984-85, spl. events com. depression and related affective disorders dept. psychiatry, 1994; spkr. in field. Parent vol. Park Sch. Mem. Kappa Delta. Avocations: reading, piano, gourmet cooking, weightlifting. Home: 54 Bellchase Ct Pikesville MD 21208-1300 Office: Suburban Psychiat Svc Md Adult Ctr ADD Johns Hopkins at Greenspring Sta Falls Concourse Falls Rd Ste 306 Lutherville MD 21093 Office Phone: 410-583-2723.

GOODMAN-MILONE, CONSTANCE B. (CONNIE GOODMAN-MILONE), writer; b. Phila., Sept. 3, 1963; d. Marvin Joshua and Linda S. Goodman; m. David C. Milone, May 5, 2002. BA in Psychology, George Washington U., 1985; MSW, Barry U., Miami Shores, Fla., 1999. Freelance writer, Phila., 1987—88, N.Y.C., 1989—96; social work intern Vets. Adminstrn. Med. Ctr., Miami, 1999; case mgr. Health South Drs. Hosp., Skilled Nursing, Coral Gables, Fla., 2000; freelance writer Miami, 2001—. Author: (poetry, photo) Medicinal Purposes Lit. Rev., 1995—2003, (poem, article, photos) Vitas Vital Signs, 2001—03, (poem) Today's Caregiver, 2002, The Grief Observer, 2006; contbr. poetry and articles to newspapers and jours. Mem. Dem. Nat. Com., Washington, 1996—; hospice vol. Vitas Healthcare, Miami, 2000—; leadership coun. So. Poverty Law Ctr., Montgomery, Ala., 2002—; charter mem. women's action coun. Amnesty Internat., N.Y.C., 2004—; chair creative writing contest Jr. Orange Bowl Com., Coral Gables, Fla., 2003—; supporter Am. Jewish World Svc., NYC, 2005—; mem. Dem. Congl. Campaign Com., Washington, 2003—; bd. dirs. Jr. Orange Bowl Com., 2006. Mem.: Acad. Am. Poets, Amnesty Internat., Assn. for Death Edn. and Counseling South Fla. chpt. (outreach chair 2002—), Nat. Writers Union, South Fla. Writers Assn. (v.p. mktg. 2003—05, dir. cmty. rels. 2005—06, sec. 2006—, Bill Katzker Mem. of Yr. award 2003, Bereavement Vol. of Yr. Vitas Dade Program 2001), Soc. Social Work Leaders in Health Care (Fla. Chpt.), Nat. Assn. Social Workers, Nat. Assn. Poetry Therapy, Phi Eta Sigma, Psi Chi, Delta Epsilon Sigma. Democrat. Jewish. Avocations: volunteering, photography, tennis, walking, books. Home and Office: 12920 SW 95 Ave Miami FL 33176-5792 Personal E-mail: cgmilone@bellsouth.net.

GOODRICH HARWOOD, GAIL LEE, management consultant; b. Nashville, Tenn., June 17, 1947; d. Jack Beverly and Mildred Redmon Goodrich; m. Everett Walter Harwood, Nov. 19, 1994. BS in Edn., U. Tenn., 1969; MBA, U. Chgo., 1979; cert. in orgn. design, U. So. Calif., 2004. Regional mgr. human resources United Airlines, San Francisco, 1989—92, mgr. orgn. devel. Chgo., 1992—2005. Bd. mem. Orgn. Design Forum, 2000—03. Exhibitions include Ind. State Fair, 1996—2004, Harrison Ctr. Arts, 2001—04, Safeco Art Competition, Indpls., 2001. Bd. dirs., pres. N.W. Indsl. Coun., Chgo., 1985—87; bd. dirs. Jr. Achievement, Chgo., 1985—89, Orgn. Indsl. Coun. West, San Francisco, 1989—92, Chinese for Affirmative Action,

San Francisco, 1989—92, PALCARE Child Care Consortium, San Francisco, 1989—92; com. mem. Greater Indpls. Progress Com., 1994—96; bd. of directors Habitat for Humanity of Greater Indpls., 1996—2003; del. to Russia People to People Amb. Program, Indpls., 1999; co-founder, bd. dirs., pres. Old Centrum Found., Inc., Indpls., 1999—2004; lay leader, cert. lay spkr. Ctrl. Ave United Meth. Ch., Indpls., 1996—2004. Mem.: Orgn. Design Forum (assoc.; bd. mem. 2000—03), Chi Omega Alumnae Assn. (life). Non-Partisan. United Methodist. Avocations: travel, art, golf, reading, writing.

GOODRUM, SHANDA S., science educator; b. Danville, Ill., Mar. 18, 1966; d. Emmet O. and Joyce E. Hussar; m. John P. Goodrum, June 1991; children: Garrett R., Raina S. Masters, Ea. Ill. U., Charleston, 1994. Cert. zoology tchr. Ill., 1988. Tchr. sci. Potomac H.S., Ill., 1990—92, Urbana Sch. Dist. 116, Ill., 1992—. Office: Urbana HS Dist 116 1002 S Race St Urbana IL 61081 Office Phone: 217-384-3505. E-mail: sgoodrum@usd116.org.

GOODSPEED, BARBARA, artist; b. Sept. 1, 1919; d. George Daniel and Bernice (Lucas) G. Diploma, Stoneleigh Coll., 1939, Famous Artist Schs., Westport, Conn., 1955. Freelance photographer, N.Y.C., 1941-52; Christmas card designer Sherman, Conn., 1952-69; oil and watercolor, fine arts artist, 1969—. Forever Flowers, 1979; contbr. Best of Oil Painting, Best of Watercolor-Light and Shadow, Landscape Inspirations, Best of Watercolor, Vol. 3, The Complete Best of Watercolor. Recipient Merit award Sheffield Arts League, 1979, 81, 83, others; named Artist of Yr., Art League of Harlem Valley, 1981. Fellow Am. Artists Profl. League (John Dole Meml. award, Parsons award 1991); mem. Salmagundi Club (Jane Peterson Meml. award, Samuel Shaw Meml. award 1997, Arthur Hill award 1998), Hudson Valley Art Assn. (bd. mem.), Acad. Artists, Nat. League Am. Pen Women, Allied Artist Am. (N.Y.C.), Butler Mus., Kent Art Assn. (trustee), Inc. (pres. 1970-72, 80-83, 85-88, 91-93, 97, 98, medal of Merit 1979, Grumbacher Gold medal 1989, 91, K.A.A. award 1995, 96, 97, 2006), Housatonic Art League (v.p., bd. dirs. 1977-83), Catharine Lorillard Wolfe Art Club (bd. dirs. 1990-93, 98-01, travel show 1996, Corp. award), Candlewood Art League (award 2006). Avocations: camping, crafts. Home: 11 Holiday Point Rd Sherman CT 06784-1624 Office Phone: 860-354-3384. Personal E-mail: bgoodspeedb@aol.com.

GOODSPEED, KATHRYN ANN, pre-school educator; b. Elgin, Ill., Oct. 2, 1939; d. Earle Muller and Ruby Vera Curtiss; m. Robert Harrison Goodspeed, Feb. 4, 1961; children: Julie, Jill, Jerry, Jeff, Jennifer. BS, No. Ill. U., 1961. Tchr. spl. edn. Sch. of Hope, Rockford, Ill., 1962—65; home day care provider, 1971—78; tchr. presch., dir. Melrose DayCare Ctr., Iowa City, 1978—89; tchr. Blind Children's Learning Ctr., Santa Ana, Calif., 1989—92, dir. early childhood ctr., 1992—2001, asst. exec. dir., 2001—, interim exec. dir., 2004—05. Bd. pres. So. Calif. Network Serving Infants and Preschool Children with Visual Impairments, 1998—; cons. Supporting Early Edn. Delivery Sys. Co-treas. Joint Action Com. Visually Impaired, Calif., 1997—; co-chair Infant Vendor Com., Santa Ana, 2000; mem. adv. bd. Calif. Deaf-Blind Svcs.; edn. commn. head Yorba Linda United Meth. Ch., 1998—2002. Named Laywoman of Yr., Yorba Linda United Meth. Ch., 2000. Mem.: Family Support Network Bd., Assn. Edn. and Rehab. Blind and Visually Impaired, Coun. Exceptional Children, Calif. Transcribers & Educators Multihandicapped Specialist, Calif. First Chance Consortium (co-chair, bd. dir., family support network com., mem. camp TLC). Avocations: reading, cooking, travel. Home: 856 Amber Ln Anaheim CA 92807 Office Phone: 714-573-8888.

GOODSPEED, LINDA A., manufacturing executive; BSME, Mich. State U., 1984, MA in Bus. Adminstrn., 1989. Engr. Ford Motor Co., 1984—89; with R&D dept. Nissan, 1989—96; with GE, 1996—2001, range product devel. mgr., 1997, gen. mgr. Six Sigma divsn., 1999, product gen. mgr. GE Appliances, 1999—2001; pres., COO Partminer, Inc., 2001; chief tech. officer Lennox Internat., Richardson, Tex., 2001—. Bd. dir. Am. Electric Power, Columbus McKinnon Corp. Office: Lennox Internat 2140 Lake Park Blvd Richardson TX 75080*

GOODSTEIN-SHAPIRO, FLORENCE (FLORENCE GOODSTEIN WALTON), artist, art historian; b. N.Y.C., July 22, 1931; d. Philip and Cecelia (Pletchnow) Goodstein; m. Ivan Shapiro, June 24, 1951 (div. Jan. 1957); 1 child, Lisa Jean Shapiro; m. John A. Walton, Sept. 30, 1968. BS, CCNY, 1952; student, Cooper Union Inst., N.Y.C., 1950-52, Hans Hofmann Sch. Fine Arts, 1956-58, U. Calif., Long Beach, 1970-71; MA in Art History, U. Minn., 1973. Asst. prof. art history Lakewood Coll., White Bear Lake, Minn., 1971-72; lectr. art history Mpls. Inst. Art, 1973-74. Bd. dirs. Banfill-Locke Cmty. Art Ctr., Fridley, Minn., 1981. Exhibited in shows at Roko Gallery, N.Y.C., 1962, Smithsonian Inst., Washington, 1963, Aspects Gallery, N.Y.C., 1964, Loeb Gallery/NYU, 1966, Los Angeles County Art Mus., 1969, Bonython Gallery, Sydney, Australia, 1969, Peter M. David Gallery, Mpls., 1985, 91, Artbanque, Mpls., 1986, Coll. St. Catherine, St. Paul, 1988, McGallery, Mpls., 1994, Groveland Gallery, Mpls., 1998, Klevit Fine Arts Gallery, Silver Springs, MD, 1999, Johnson Heritage Post Art Gallery, Grand Marais, 1999, Mifa Artists Gallery, 2000; represented in collections at 3M Co., St. Paul, U. Minn. Mus., Martin Luther King Jr. Mus., Atlanta, Fairview Southdale Hosp., Mpls., Ctrl. Lakes C.C., Brainerd, Minn., Boyadjian Collection, Zurich, Ethan Coen, NYC, others. Mem. Cooper Union Alumni Assn. Democrat. Jewish. Avocations: camping, gardening, travel, sewing, reading. Office: Goodstein-Shapiro Studio 9983 Egret Blvd NW Coon Rapids MN 55433-6402 Office Phone: 763-767-2535. Personal E-mail: goodsteinshapiro@aol.com. Business E-Mail: fgwalton@aol.com.

GOODWIN, BEATRICE, nursing educator, consultant; d. David and Myrtle Goodwin. BS in Nursing, Vanderbilt U., 1955; MA, NYU, 1960, PhD, 1970; PhD (hon.), Valparaiso U., 2003. RN NY, 1958. Prof. nursing CUNY, NYC, 1970—98; vis. prof. Catholic U. Chile, Santiago, 1972—73, U. Conception, Chile, 1984—88, U. Los Andes, Santiago, 1999—2000, U. Chile, Santiago, 2006—, U. Andres Bello, Santiago, Chile, 2006—; adj. prof. nursing NYU, NYC, 1998—. External reviewer U. Ottawa, Canada, 1978; cons. clin. nursing Surgeon Gen., US Air Force, DC, 1980—82; cons. curriculum in baccalaureate nursing World Health Orgn., DC, 1986—88; dir. Latin Am. projects NYU Coll. Nursing, NYC, 1998—; keynote spkr. Nat. Colloquium Nursing Rsch., Bogota, Colombia, 2001, Internat. Nursing Conf., Chile, 2002, Colombia, 04; curriculum cons. programs in nursing Colombian Assn. Faculties Nursing, Chile, 2006—; vis. prof. U. Andrés Bello, Santiago, Chile, 2006—, U. Chile, Santiago, 2006—. Founding editor (profl. jour.) Image. Mem. Career Devel. Bd., US Air Force Nurse Corps, DC, 1979—81, NYU Nurse Alumni Assn., NYC, 2002—. Decorated Meritorious Svc. Medal US Air Force. Mem.: Internat. Ctr. Nursing Rsch., Chilean Assn. Nursing Edn. (hon.), Chilean Assn. Edn. in Nursing (hon.), Sigma Theta Tau (life), Kappa Delta Pi (life). Home: 220 E 65th St Apt 21K New York NY 10021 Personal E-mail: beagoodwin@aol.com.

GOODWIN, BECKY K., educational technology resource educator; Sci. tchr. USD 233 Sch. Dist., Olathe, Kans. Christa McAuliffe fellowship grantee State of Kans., 1992, 94, 97; named Kans. Tchr. of Yr., 1995; recipient Presdl. award for Excellence in Sci. and Math. Secondary Sci. for Kans., 1992, Outstanding Biology Tchr. award Nat. Assn. Biology Tchrs., 1992, Sci. Teaching Achievement Recognition Star award NSTA, 1993, Milken Nat. Educator award, 1995, Tandy Tech. Tchr. award, 1998. Office: USD 233 14090 Black Bob Rd Olathe KS 66063

GOODWIN, BEVERLY ANN, elementary school educator; b. Worcester, Mass., May 12, 1952; d. Richard Harvey Bejune; m. Jeffrey Scott Goodwin, June 29, 1974. BS in Edn., Westfield State Coll., Mass., 1974. Cert. elem. tchr. Mass., 1974. Tchg. asst. grades k-5 Agawam Pub. Schs., Mass., 1974—75, second grade tchr., 1975—2005; ELL, ESL tchr. Agawam Mid. Sch., 2005—. Vol. Westfield Soup Kitchen, Mass., 2002—05; tchr. rep., coord. parent/tchr./student activities PTO, 1995. ESL Profl. Devel. Leadership grantee, Agawam Pub. Schs., 2006. Mem.: Mass. Teacher's Assn. (licentiate). Republican. Avocations: languages, youth art and academic sponsor, future teacher mentoring, travel. Home: 46 Neptune Ave West Springfield MA 01089 Office: Agawam Mid Sch Main St Agawam MA 01001

GOODWIN, DANIELLE MARIE, mathematician; b. Havre de Grace, Md., 1977; m. Danny Goodwin, Dec. 22, 2004. BS in Math., U. Md. Ea. Shore, Princesse Anne, 1998; MS, Rensselaer Poly. Inst., Troy, NY, 2000. Tutor U. Md. Ea. Shore, 1994—98; tchg. asst., instr. dept. math. Rensselaer Poly. Inst., 1998—2001; lectr. SUNY, Utica and Rome, 2000—01; instr. math. Hudson Valley CC, Troy, 2001, NH Cmty. Tech. Coll., Manchester, 2001—03; mem. faculty dept. math. U. Mass., Lowell, 2001—04, No. Essex CC, Haverhill, Mass., 2003—04; math. content specialist Enablemath, Cambridge, Mass., 2004—05; math. edn. specialist Ctr. for Advancement Math. and Sci. Edn., Black Hills State U., Spearfish, SD, 2005; lead math. instnl. designer CompasLearning, Austin, Tex., 2006—. Author: (workbook) Why Do I Need Calculus? An Architecture, Humanities and Social Sciences Approach, 2000; pub.: Teaching Integrals That Involve Natural Logarithms, 2002; co-author: A Passion for Pi, 2003, Positivism and Post-Positivism: A Qualitative Mathematics Perspective, 2004. Recipient Ralph Ernest Huston award for excellence in tchg. Mem.: NCSM, Am. Math. Soc., Nat. Coun. Tchrs. Math., Math. Assn. Am. Avocations: music, reading, mathematical art, history, philosophy.

GOODWIN, DORIS HELEN KEARNS, historian, writer; b. Bklyn., Jan. 4, 1943; d. Michael Alouisius and Helen Witt (Miller) Kearns; m. Richard N. Goodwin, 1975; children: Richard, Michael, Joseph. BA magna cum laude, Colby Coll., 1964; PhD, Harvard U., 1968. Intern US Dept. State, Washington, 1963, Ho. of Reps., 1965; rsch. assoc. U.S. Dept. Health, Edn., & Welfare, 1966; spl. asst. to Willard Wirtz U.S. Dept. Labor, 1967; staff asst. to President Lyndon B. Johnson The White House, 1968; prof. govt. Harvard U., Cambridge, Mass., 1969—79. Spl. cons. to Pres. Lyndon Johnson, 1969-73; hostess "What's the Big Idea", WGBH-TV, Boston, 1972; polit. analyst news desk, WBZ-TV, Boston, 1972; mem. Women's Polit. Caucus, Mass., 1972, Dem. Party Platform Com., 1972; reg. panelist News Hour with Jim Lehrer; commentator NBC, MSNBC. Author: Lyndon Johnson and the American Dream, 1976, The Fitzgeralds and the Kennedys: An American Saga, 1987, No Ordinary Time: Franklin and Eleanor Roosevelt: The Homefront in World War II, 1994 (Harold Washington Lit. award, New England Bookseller Assn. award, Ambassador Book award, Wash. Monthly Book award, Pulitzer Prize for History, 1995), Wait Till Next Year: A Memoir, 1997, Team of Rivals: The Political Genius of Abraham Lincoln, 2005; numerous articles on politics and baseball; contbr.: Telling Lives: The Biographer's Art, 1979; forward: Mortal Friends: A Novel, 1992, Kennedy Weddings: A Family Album, 1999. Trustee Wesleyan U., Colby Coll., Robert F. Kennedy Found. Named Fulbright fellow, 1966, White House fellow, 1967, recipient: Charles Frankel prize from Nat. Endowment for Humanities, Sara Josepha Hale medal, Lincoln prize, Gettysburg Coll., 2006. Mem. Am. Polit. Sci. Assn., Coun. Fgn. Relations, Women Involved, Group for Applied Psychoanalysis, Signet Soc., Soc. Am. Historians, Am. Acad. Arts & Scis., Harvard U. Bd. Overseers, Phi Beta Kappa (outstanding young women of yr. award 1966), Phi Sigma Iota. Roman Catholic. Office: c/o Dori Lawson Soldier Creek Assoc PO Box 477 Rockport ME 04856*

GOODWIN, HEATHER MARIE, educational consultant; b. Houston, May 19, 1968; d. Ron and Cynthia Coffman. BA in Humanities, Trinity U., San Antonio, 1990, MA in Tchg., 1991. Cert. tchr. spl. edn. pre-sch.-12, elem. self-contained 1-6, elem. English 1-6, elem. history 1-6, English as 2d lang. pre-K-12. Life skills tchr. for students with mild-moderate disabilities Alief Ind. Sch. Dist., Houston, 1991—94, tchr. spl. edn. and literacy, 1994—96, dist.-wide behavior/inclusion specialist, 1996—99; ednl. cons. Stetson & Assocs., Houston, 1999—2001; dir. behavior programs Sopris West Ednl. Svcs., Longmont, Tex., 2001—04; owner HMG Ednl. Svcs., Inc., 2004—. Mentor gifted/talented students Saturday Morning Experience, San Antonio, 1989—90; mentor, tutor h.s. students Upward Bound, San Antonio, 1990—94; adult literacy instr. Neuhaus Ctr., Houston, 1994—96; presenter in field. Author, cons.: sci. textbook McGraw-Hill Science 2000, 1998. Recipient Tchr.-Rschr. grant, NICHD. Mem.: CEC, Coun. for Children with Behavior Disorders, Assn. for Curriculum and Devel. Avocations: travel, running, hiking, water-skiing, bicycling. Home: 1423 Ashland St Houston TX 77708 E-mail: heathermarie0519@yahoo.com.

GOODWIN, JEAN MCCLUNG, psychiatrist; b. Pueblo, Colo., Mar. 28, 1946; d. Paul Stanley and Geraldine (Smart) McClung; m. James Simeon Goodwin, Aug. 8, 1970; children: Laura (dec.), Amanda Harding Goodwin, Robert Caleb, Paul Joshua, Elizabeth Cronin Goodwin. BA in Anthropology summa cum laude, Radcliffe Coll., 1967; MD, Harvard U., 1971; MPH, UCLA, 1972. Diplomate Am. Bd. Psychiatry and Neurology, Am. Bd. Forensic Psychiatry, added qualifications in forensic psychiatry Am. Bd. Psychiatry and Neurology, cert. adult psychoanalysis Am. Psychoanalytic Assn. Resident in psychiatry Georgetown U. Hosp., Washington, 1972-74, U. N.Mex. Sch. Medicine, 1974-76, asst. dir., dir. psychiat. residents tng., 1979-85; prof. Med. Coll. Wis., 1985-92, U. Tex. Med. Br., Galveston, 1992-98, prof. clin. psychiatry, 1998—; pvt. practice in gen. psychiatry, psychoanalysis. From instr. to assoc. prof. dept. psychiatry U. N.Mex. Sch. Medicine, 1976-85; cons. protective services Dept. Human Services, N.Mex., 1976-84; faculty Houston-Galveston Psychoanalytic Inst., 1999—; founding bd. dirs. Houston-Galveston Trauma Inst.; lectr. in field Author: Effects of High Altitude on Human Birth, 1969, Sexual Abuse: Incest Victims and Their Families, 1982, 2d edit., 1989, Rediscovering Childhood Trauma: Historical Casebook and Clinical Applications, 1993, Mischief and Mercy, 1993; co-author (with Reina Attias) Splintered Reflections: Images of the Body in Trauma, 1999; mem. editl. bd. Jour. Traumatic Stress, 1985-93, Dissociation, 1988-98, Psychotherapy Rev., 1998-2000, Trauma and Dissociation, 2000—; contbr. articles to profl. jours. Chmn. work group on child sexual abuse Surgeon Gen.'s Conf. on Violence and Pub. Health, Leesburg, Va., 1985; mem. adv. bd. Nat. Resource Ctr. on Child Sexual Abuse, 1989-96. Recipient Esther Haar award Am. Acad. Psychoanalysis, 1990, Cornelia Wilbur award Internat. Soc. for Study of Dissociation, 1994; Nat. Cen. Child Abuse and Neglect grantee, 1979-82, Nat. Inst. Aging grantee, 1980-85. Fellow Internat. Soc. Study Dissociation (exec. com. 1991-96), Am. Psychiat. Assn. (dist. br. treas., sec. N.Mex. br. 1980-82, exhibits and programs subcoms. 1985-91) Democrat. Roman Catholic. Office: 4925 Fort Crockett Blvd Apt 510 Galveston TX 77551-5949 Office Phone: 409-762-1101. Personal E-mail: jmgoodwin@aol.com.

GOODWIN, NANCY LEE, computer company executive; b. Peoria, Ill., Aug. 11, 1940; d. Raymond Darrell and Mildred Louise (Brown) G. BA (Nat. Meth. scholar, Nat. Merit scholar), MacMurray Coll., 1961; MA, U. Colo., 1963; PhD, U. Ill., 1971. Tchr. Roosevelt Jr. High Sch., Peoria, 1961-62; counselor U. Ill., Urbana, 1963-66, staff assoc., asst. prof. edn. measurement Chgo., 1967-71; asst. v.p., assoc. prof. stats. Fla. Internat. U., Miami, 1971-78; pres. Greenfield (Mass.) Community Coll., 1978-82, Arapahoe Community Coll., Colo., from 1982; corp. owner MTF Enterprises; prof. Nat. U.; owner C.A.T.S. Inc., 1987—; corp. mgr. DRM Enterprises. Dir. Cons. Mid-Am. Computer Corp., First Chance Network U.S. Office Edn., 1972-78 Mem. Com. on Ill. Govt., Higher Edn. Task Force; mem. Vol. Action Center, Miami, 1972-78; active Girl Scouts U.S.A.; mem. Franklin/Hampshire Area Service Planning Team, 1978; incorporator Franklin County (Mass.) United Way, Farren Meml. Hosp.; adv. Franklin County Public Hosp.; bd. dirs. Women's Inst. Fla., Franklin County Arts Council, Franklin County Devel. Corp., Western Welcome Week, Inc.; bd. dirs., mem. fin. monitoring com. New Eng. Soy Dairy, 1980. Recipient Merit award Chgo. Tchrs. Assn., 1969; citation Girl Scouts U.S.A., 1973 Mem. NEA, Am. Assn. Higher Edn., Am. Ednl. Research Assn., Assn. Instl. Research, Centennial C. of C. (dir. 1983) Home: 5228 Del Rey Ave Las Vegas NV 89146-1414

GOODWIN, REBECCA, literature and language educator; MEd, U. Del., 2002. Cert. Reading Specialist Del. Reading specialist Christina Sch. Dist., Newark, Del., 2000—. Ind. literacy workshop cons. Del. Reading Project, Newark. Mem.: Internat. Reading Assn., Golden Key Nat. Honor Socitey, Kappa Delta Pi.

GOODWIN, RHODA SHERMAN, psychologist; b. Boston, Feb. 6, 1938; d. Harry and Edith (Nathanson) Sherman; m. Herbert Naradof Goodwin, Mar. 31, 1962; children: Joanne, Lauren, Carolyn. BA, Boston U., 1959, AM, 1960, PhD, 1979; diploma, Mass. Inst. Psychoanalysis, 2001. Lic. psychologist. Rsch. asst. Med. Coll. Cornell U., N.Y.C., 1960-62; rsch. psychologist Walter Reed Army Inst. Rsch., Washington, 1962-66; infant observer Group Health Assn., Washington, 1963-66; rsch. psychologist Tufts New Eng. Med. Ctr., Boston, 1967-69; sr. rsch. asst. Grad. Sch. Edn. Harvard U., Cambridge, 1969-70; rsch. psychologist MIT, Cambridge, 1970-74; postdoctoral rsch. fellow Children's Hosp. Med. Ctr., Boston, 1979-81; psychol. cons. Harvard U., Cambridge, 1981-83; psychologist Mass. Mental Health Ctr., Boston, 1982-90; staff psychologist Fresh Pond Mental Health Ctr., Cambridge, 1990—2000. Pvt. practice psychotherapy and psychoanalysis, Brookline, Mass., 1988—. Mem. Am. Psychol. Assn., Boston Psychoanalytic Soc. and Inst., Inc., Mass. Inst. for Psychoanalysis. Home: 47 Manchester Rd Brookline MA 02446-6061 Office: 1330 Beacon St Brookline MA 02446-3282

GOODWIN, SHARON ANN, academic administrator; b. Little Rock, May 19, 1949; d. Jimmy Lee and Eddie DeLois (Cluck) G.; m. Mitchell Shayne Mick, May 4, 1968 (div. Mar. 1973); 1 child, Heather Michelle; m. Raymond Eugene Vaclavik, June 24, 1974 (div. Aug. 1982); 1 child, Tasha Rae Vaclavik. BA in Psychology, U. Houston-Clear Lake, 1980; MEd in Higher Edn. Adminstrn., U. Houston, 1990. Various clerical positions Gen. Telephone Co., Dickinson, Tex., 1969-80; state dir. Challenge, Inc., Oklahoma City, 1980-82; gen. mgr. Mr. Fix It, Houston, 1982-85; assoc. dir. admissions U. Houston, Tex., 1985-92; adminstr. Inst. for the Med. Humanities U. Tex. Med. Br., Galveston, 1992—. Contbr. poetry to World of Poetry Anthology, 1986, 87, 90, 91, Nat. Libr. of Poetry Anthology, 1997, 99, 2001, SOL Mag., 1997-2000, Lucidity Jour., 1997, New Winds Jour., 1997, Galveston Writers Anthology, 1998-99, Nat. Poetry Guild Anthology, 1998; author (poetry exhibited) Moody Med. Libr., UTMB, 2003. Mem. legis. com. Comm. Workers, Dickinson and Austin, 1975; mem. centennial choir U. Tex. Med. Br., Galveston, 1992-2000; vol. Dickens on the Strand, Galveston, 1993-2000. Recipient award of merit World of Poetry Anthology, 1986, 91, Golden Poet award, 1987, Silver Poet award, 1990, rd 1990, Golden Poet award, 1991, hon. mention SOL Mag., 1997, 98, 1st pl., 1998, 2d pl., 1998; named to Internat. Poetry Hall of Fame, 1997. Avocations: travel, music, sports, books, movies. Office: Univ Tex Med Br Inst for the Med Humanities 301 University Blvd Galveston TX 77555-1311 Home: PO Box 1346 League City TX 77574 Office Phone: 409-772-5838. Business E-Mail: sgoodwin@utmb.edu.

GOODWIN, TONJA TRISTA, secondary school educator; b. Gibson City, Ill., Dec. 26, 1972; d. Helen Marie and Richard Dale Manuel; m. Dana Andrew Goodwin, June 14, 2003; 1 child, Kendra Heleen. B of Arts in English Edn., Drake U., Des Moines, Iowa, 1995, MS in Edn., 2001. English tchr. Ames (Iowa) HS, 1996—. Sponsor InterVaristy Christian Fellowship, Des Moines, 2005—06. Lutheran. Avocations: creative writing, scrapbooks. Home: 1330 Woodstock Ave Ames IA 50014 Office: Ames High Sch 1921 Ames High Dr Ames IA 50010 Personal E-mail: tonja.goodwin@ames.k12.ia.us.

GOODWIN CLARK, ANN ELIZABETH, music educator; b. Cameron, Mo., Aug. 16, 1961; d. David Laverne and Kathryn Annabelle Goodwin; m. Dennis Michael Clark, July 8, 2005; 1 child, David Michael Clark. B in Music Edn., U. Kans., Lawrence, 1983; M in Music, Bowling Green (Ohio) State U., 1989. Cert. tchr. Mo. Dir. of bands Gallatin Sch. Dist., Mo., 1984—87, Nevada Sch. Dist., Mo., 1989—97, Oak Pk. HS, Kansas City, Mo., 1997—98, Park Hill Sch. Dist., Kansas City, 1998—. Pres. SW Mo. Music Educators Assn., Mo., 1996—97. Contbr. articles to profl. jours. Mem. Northland Symphony Orch., Kansas City, 1998—2000, bd. dirs., 1999—2003; tchr. 1st Bapt. Ch., Nevada, 1991—97. Named Outstanding Tchr., Joplin (Mo.) Globe, 1994, Band Dirs. Who Make a Difference Mo. honoree, Sch. Band and Orch. Mag., 2003; named one of Outstanding Young Women of Am., 1984; recipient Bell Ringer award, Supt. of Schs. Park Hill Sch. Dist., 2002, 2003, Legion of Honor, John Philip Sousa Found., 2004. Mem.: Mo. Women Band Dirs. Nat. Assn. (pres. 1998—2000), Mo. Bandmasters Assn. (pres. 2004—06), Mo. Music Educators Assn. (band v.p. 1998—2000), Music Educators Nat. Conf., Tau Beta Sigma (hon. life 2003). Methodist. Avocations: travel, tennis. Home: 122 E Evergreen Cameron MO 64429 Office Phone: 816-359-4000.

GOODWYN, BETTY RUTH, librarian; b. Jasper, Ala., Oct. 7, 1930; d. Elzie Ervin and Nellie Virginia (Blackwell) O'Rear; m. Edward T. Goodwyn, Dec. 22, 1951. BA in English, Mt. Union Coll., 1962; MA in Edn., U. No. Ala., 1969; MLS, Geo. Peabody Coll., 1972; EdS, U. Ala., Birmingham, 1979; PhD, U. Ala., Tuscaloosa, 1984. Acting dir. publicity dept. Mt. Union Coll., Alliance, Ohio, 1958-60; tchr. English, dept. head Alliance (Ohio) City Schs., 1962-68; libr. Knoxville (Tenn.) City Schs., 1969-72; libr., dir. Mountain Brook High Sch. Libr., Birmingham, 1972-94. Bd. dirs. Friends of Ala. Librs., Birmingham. Author: (with others) Alabama St. Dept. of Education, 1978, 83, 84; town historian, editor The Village Voice. City mother for inc. of home area Village of Indian Springs, 1990. Mountain Brook City Schs. grantee, 1990, 93. Mem. ALA, NEA, Ala. Libr. Assn., Ala. Edn. Assn., Mountain Brook Edn. Assn., Beta Phi Mu, Phi Delta Kappa. Lutheran. Avocations: reading, photography, interior decorating, hiking.

GOODY, JOAN EDELMAN, architect; d. Beril and Sylvia (Feldman) Edelman; m. Marvin E. Goody, Dec. 18, 1960 (dec. 1980); m. Peter H. Davison, Aug. 11, 1984 (dec. 2004). BA, Cornell U., 1956; MArch, Harvard U., 1960. Prin. Goody, Clancy & Assocs., Inc., Boston. Asst. prof., design critic Harvard U., Cambridge, Mass., 1973-80, Eliot Noyes vis. critic, 1985; faculty Mayors Inst. for Design, 1989—; lectr. in field. Mem. Boston Landmarks Commn., 1976-87; chair Boston Civic Design Commn., 1994-2005; bd. dirs. Historic Boston. Fellow AIA (design awards, 1980), Boston Soc. Architects (award of honor 2005), Boston Archtl. Ctr. (hon.), Saturday Club, Tavern Club. Office: Goody Clancy & Assocs Inc 420 Boylston St Boston MA 02116-3866

GOOGINS, SONYA FORBES, state legislator, retired banker; b. New Haven, Nov. 9, 1936; d. Edward and Madeline Forbes; m. Robert Reville Googins, June 21, 1958; children: Shawn W. and Glen. R. BE, U. Conn., 1958. Tchr. Manchester (Conn.) High Sch., 1958-61; pres. Colonial Printing Co., Glastonbury, 1971-76; bank officer Conn. Nat. Bank, Hartford, 1982-89; mem. Conn. Ho. of Reps., 1994—. Mem. Conn. employment and tng. commn. Greater Hartford United Way, 1995; vice-chair commerce Nat. Conf. State Legislatures; mayor Town of Glastonbury, 1983—85, 1987—91, 1993—95; mem. Town Coun., 1979—94, Rep. Town Com., Capitol Region Coun. Govts., 1983—94, chmn., 1989—94; chair Conn. Adv. Commn. Intergovtl. Rels., 1992—; chair fin. svc. com. Nat. Conf. of State Legislators, 2002—; advocacy com. Am. Diabetes Assn.; bd. dirs. Conn. Capitol Region Growth Coun., 1994—96, Conn. Audubon Soc., 1997—99, Hartford Symphony Orch., 1997—. Recipient Outstanding Svc. award Friends of Glastonbury Youth, 1990, Disting. Svc. award Conn. Capitol Region Coun. Govts., 1994, Svc. award Women's Campaign Sch. at Yale, 2004; named Glastonbury Rep. of Yr., 1992. Mem. Auto Assn. Am. Allied Group Inc. (bd. dirs. 1994—), Glastonbury Bus. and Profl. Women (past pres. and founder, Woman of Yr. 1988), Glastonbury C. of C. (bd. dirs. 1994—), Glastonbury Jr. Woman's Club (past pres.). Roman Catholic. Avocations: golf, tennis, sailing. Home: 74 Forest Ln Glastonbury CT 06033-3918 Personal E-mail: sonya.googins@cga.ct.gov.

GOOLDY, PATRICIA ALICE, retired elementary school educator; b. Indpls., Nov. 23, 1937; d. Harold Emanuel and Emma Irene (Wade) VanTreese; m. Walter Raymond Gooldy, May 4, 1968. BS, U. Indpls., 1959; MS, Butler U., 1963. Tchr. Franklin Twp. Cmty. Schs., Indpls., 1959-68, 72-99, USA Dep. Schs., Bad Kreuznach, Germany, 1969-72; ret., 1999. Owner Ye Olde Genealogie Shoppe, Indpls., 1972—; lectr. in field. Author: 21 Things I Wish I'd Found, 1984; editor: Indiana Wills to 1880: Index to

Indiana Wills, 1987; co-editor: Indiana Manual For Gen, 1991, Illinois Manual For Gen, 1994. Named Ky. Col., 1995; named one of Outstanding Elem. Tchrs. of Am., 1974. Mem. Franklin Twp. Hist. Soc. (founder), Ind. Geneal. Soc. (chartered). Office: Ye Olde Genealogie Shoppe PO Box 39128 Indianapolis IN 46239-0128 Office Phone: 317-862-3330, 800-419-0200. Personal E-mail: yogs@iquest.net.

GOOLKASIAN, PAULA A., psychologist, educator; b. Methuen, Mass., Aug. 9, 1948; d. Paul K. and Sadie T. (Touma) G.; m. Francis C. Martin, July 29, 1978; 1 child, Christopher. BA, Emmanuel Coll., 1970; MS, Iowa State U., 1972, PhD, 1974. Asst. prof. U. N.C., Charlotte, 1974-79, assoc. prof., 1979-85, prof. psychology, 1985—, pres. faculty, 1989—. Cons. in field. Exec. editor: Jour. Gen. Psychology. NDEA fellow, 1971-74; grantee NSF, NIH, numerous others. Fellow APA, Am. Psychol. Soc.; mem. Psychonomics Soc., Soc. for Computers in Psychology (sec.-treas. 1989-91, pres. 1994), Sigma Xi, Phi Kappa Phi. Office: U NC Dept Psychology 9201 University City Blvd Charlotte NC 28223 Office Phone: 704-687-4749. Business E-Mail: pagoolka@uncc.edu.

GOOREY, NANCY JANE, dentist; b. Davenport, Iowa, May 8, 1922; d. Edgar Ray and Glenna Mae (Williams) Miller; m. Douglas B. Miller, Sept. 12, 1939 (div. 1951); children: Victoria Lee, Nickola Ellen, Douglas George, Melahna Marie; m. Louis Joseph Roseberry Goorey, Feb. 22, 1980. Student, Wooster (Ohio) Coll., 1939-40; DDS, Ohio State U., 1955. Cert. in gen. anesthesiology. Mem. faculty coll. dentistry Ohio State U., Columbus, 1955-86, dir., chmn. div. dental hygiene coll. dentistry, 1969-86, asst. dean coll. dentistry, 1975-86, mem. grad. faculty colls. dentistry and medicine, 1980-86, asst. dean, prof. emeritus colls. dentistry, 1986—. Moderator, prodn. chmn. Lifesavers 40 Prodns., 1981—; mem. task force on sch. based-linked oral health project Ohio Dept. Health, 1999—. Producer, video program Giving Your Mouth a Sporting Chance, 1990, video Operation TACTIC. Chmn. State Planning Com. for Health Edn. in Ohio, Columbus, 1976-77, 87-88, 95-97; founder Coun. on Health Info., Columbus, 1980, del., 1981-85, chmn., pres., 1985-86, chmn. prodn. com., 1986-2003, chmn. mktg. com., 2003—, chmn. Capital Campaign; trustee Caring Dentists Found., Mayor's Drug Edn. and Prevention Program, Columbus, 1980-90; mem. exec. com. Franklin County Rep. com., exec. com., 1993—; mem. human svcs. com. The Columbus Found.; pres. Worthington Arts Coun., 1998-2000, chmn. Capital Campaign, 2000-. Recipient Vol. of Yr. award Columbus Health Dept., 1988-89, Dental Hygiene Nancy J. Goorey award Ohio State U., 1988, Drug Free Sch. Consortium award, 1996, Champion of Children's Oral Health award Ohio Dept. of Health Dental Divsn., 1997, Disting. Alumnus award Ohio State U. Coll. Dentistry, YWCA Women of Achievement award, 2000; named Nancy J. Goorey Ednl. Suite in her honor Ohio State U. Coll. Dentistry, 2004. Fellow: Internat. Coll. Dentists, Am. Soc. Dental Anesthesiology, Am. Coll. Dentists (chmn.-elect 1989—90, chmn. Columbus sect.); mem.: ADA (nat. consumer advisor 1975—78, coun. edn. and licensure 1997—), Cols. Med. Assoc. Mem. Sports Med. Comm., Ohio Dept. Health (sch. linked oral health project 1999), Ohio State Med. Assn. Alliance (chmn. state com. legis. affairs 1993—94, chmn. state health promotions com. 1994—95, v.p. 1995—97, pres.-elect 1997, pres. 1998), The Found. of the Acad. of Medicine (v.p. 1993—94), Columbus Dental Soc. (pres. bd. dirs. 1986—87, 1989—91, chmn. coun. on constn. and bilaws on jud. affairs 1989—2003, chmn. sports dentistry com. 1995—), Ohio Dental Assn. (cons. 1979—, mem. subcoun. on dentists concerned for dentists 1994—96, chmn. subcoun. chem. dependency, prin. investigator, chair smokeless tobacco rsch., Ohio Disting. Dentist 1983, Disting. Svc. award 2002—03), Am. Assn. Dental Schs. (pres. 1972—77, v.p.), Caring Dentists Found. (trustee), The Columbus Found. (human svcs. com.), Acad. of Medicine Aux. (pres. 1992—93, 1996—97, chair mouthguard project), Ohio State U. Faculty and Profl. Womens Club (pres. 1971—72), Ohio State U. Starling Womens Club (pres. 1982—83), Omicron Kappa Upsilon. Republican. Episcopalian. Avocations: camping, travel, bridge, cooking, wine. Office: Ohio State U Coll Dentistry 305 W 12th Ave Columbus OH 43210-1267

GOOTEE, CHRISTY BECK, minister, educator; b. New Orleans, Oct. 5, 1951; d. John Warren and Conchita Curnault Beck; m. Jim Edward Gootee, July 8, 1984; children: Jan, Joe, Joyce, Jeff, Jill, Jason, J.J. BA in French, English with honors, U. New Orleans, La., 1973; MA in Comparative Lit., Ind. U., Bloomington, 1976, PhD in Comparative Lit., 1982. Tchr. comparative arts Ind. U., Bloomington, 1977—79; tchr. ESL Delgado Coll., New Orleans, 1982—83; tchr. freshman composition Tulane U., New Orleans, 1983—84; tchr. world lit. and conversational English Loyola U., New Orleans, 1983—84; co-founder Two Hearts Gospel Ministry, New Orleans, 1984; co-dir. Christos Ho. of Prayer, Gautier, Miss., 1986—98; minister, bd. dirs. Two Hearts Gospel Ministry, Inc., Alexandria, La., 1998—. Retreat dir. Mary Hill Renewal Ctr., Pineville, La., 2002—; spkr. various religious confs. Prodr.: (radio program) Moments of Light, 1985—88; prodr.: (radio program) Moments of Light, 2001—; author: (poetry collection) Winter Arches with Goldenrod, 1972; editor: The Gist of Life, 1974; author: (book on inner healing) Peace Is My Gift, 1992; assoc. editor: Vision mag., 1984. Recipient poem Calvary chosen for The Sound of Poetry collection, Internat. Libr. Poetry, Md., 2001. Mem.: Mensa. Roman Catholic. Achievements include 8th ranked woman chess player in the U.S., 1970. Avocations: art, music, reading, dogs. Office: Two Hearts Gospel Minstry Inc PO Box 7206 Alexandria LA 71306

GOOTNICK, MARGERY FISCHBEIN, lawyer; b. Rochester, N.Y., Oct. 24, 1927; d. Morris R. and Regina (Kroll) Fischbein; m. Lester T. Gootnick, Mar. 1, 1952; children— Jonathon, David, Amy. B.A., Harvard U., 1949; J.D., Cornell U., 1952. Bar: N.Y. 1952. Assoc. Stone & Hoffenberg, Rochester, N.Y., 1952-55; sole practice, Rochester, 1968—; permanent arbitrator Am. Airlines and Assn. Profl. Flight Attendants, NW Airlines and Teamsters Local 2000, Presbyn. Hosp.-N.Y. State Nurses Assn., U. Rochester and U. Rochester Security Guards Union, numerous others; chmn. Fgn. Service Impasse Disputes Panel, Washington, 1983-97; apptd. fgn. svc. grievance bd. U.S. State Dept., 1997; mem. exec. com. N.Y. State Bar, 1998. Mem. Rep. Jud. Screening Com., Rochester, 1976—. Mem. ABA, Fed. Bar Assn., Nat. Acad. Arbitrators (v.p. 1992-94, chair membership com. 1988-91, exec. com. 1987, bd. govs. 1983-86), N.Y. State Bar Assn. (labor and employment sect. chair elect 1994—, exec. com. 1982—), Soc. Fed. Labor Rels. Profls. (1st v.p. 1993—), Am. Arbitration Assn. (upstate N.Y. labor adv. panel). Office e-mail: mornings@ix.netcom.com. Home and Office: 46 Knollwood Dr Rochester NY 14618-3513 E-mail: mgootnich@ix.netcom.com.

GOPMAN, BETH ALSWANGER, retired elementary school educator; d. Abraham Harry and Frieda (Lelowsky) Alswanger; m. Herbert Leon Gopman, Mar. 5, 1955; children: Paulette, Judith, Jonathan. BEd, U. Miami, Coral Gables, Fla., 1955; MS in Elem. Edn., Nova U., 1980. Cert. state cert. pre-sch., elem. edn. Fla. Tchr. kindergarten, 1st and 2d grades Dade County Pub. Sch., Miami; ret. Bd. dirs. Commn. on Status of Women, Miami Beach, Hearing and Speech Ctr., Miami. Author: (book) Siblings, 2002. Bd. dirs. Comty. Devel. Ch., Miami Beach. Mem.: United Tchrs. of Dade Retirees (bd. dirs. union), Dem. Women's Club (v.p.), Lions Club (bd. dirs.), Alpha Omicron, Alpha Delta Kappa. Avocation: musician. Home: 709 E DiLido Dr Miami Beach FL 33139-1239

GORA, JOANN M., academic administrator; BA, Vassar Coll.; M in Sociology, D in Sociology, Rutgers U. Dean Coll. Arts and Scis., sr. dean Madison campus Fairleigh Dickinson U., 1985—92; provost, v.p. for acad. affairs, prof. sociology Old Dominion U., Norfolk, Va., 1992-01; chancellor U. Mass., Boston, 2001—04; pres. Ball State U., Muncie, Ind., 2004—. Author: The New Female Criminal: Empirical Reality or Social Myth?; co-author: Emergency Squad Volunteers: Professionalism in Unpaid Work; contbr. numerous articles to profl. jours. Office: Ball State U Office Pres AD Bldg 101 Muncie IN 47306 Office Phone: 765-285-5555. Business E-Mail: president@bsu.edu.

GORA, SUSANNAH PORTER MARTIN, journalist, poet; b. NYC, Sept. 4, 1977; d. Joel Mark and Ann Ray Martin Gora; m. Zachary Abella, July 22, 2006. BA in English cum laude with high distinction, Duke U., Durham, N.C., 1999. Intern NY1 News, NYC, 1994, CBS News, NYC, 1996, Brillstein-Grey Entertainment, Beverly Hills, Calif., 1998; prodn. asst. ABC TV, NYC, 1999—2000; asst. to the editor Premiere Mag., NYC, 2000—01, assoc. editor, 2001—04; entertainment journalist publs. including Elle, Variety and Woman's Day, 2004—; host, writer Classics on Film, 2005—. Contbr. of entertainment coverage AP Radio, NYC, 2002—05. Author: (poetry) Where Home Is, 1999, numerous poems. E. Blake Byrne scholar, Duke U., 1997. Mem.: The Authors Guild, NY Women in Comm., Inc., Phi Eta Sigma, Kappa Kappa Gamma (life; dir. of pub. rels. 1998—99). Personal E-mail: susannahgora1@aol.com.

GORAL, JUDITH ANN, language educator; b. Cleve., July 12, 1947; d. Chester and Elenore (Majka) C. BA, Cleve. State U., 1969; postgrad., Inst. Am., Guadalajara, Jalisco, Mex.; MAT, Marygrove Coll., 1998. Cert. Spanish and English tchr., Ohio. Tchr. Spanish Wiley Mid. Schs., Cleveland Heights, Ohio; advanced courses coord. Inst. Cultural Mexicano Norteamericano de Jai, Guadalajara, tchr. bus.; tchr. Colegio Victoria, Guadalajara; tchr. Spanish Brecksville Sr. H.S., Ohio; tchr. English Cleveland Heights H.S., 2003—. Mem. ASCD, Nat. Coun. Tchrs. English, Internat. Reading Assn., Am. Assn. Tchrs. Spanish and Portuguese, MEs. Assn. Tchrs. Eng. to Speakers of Other Langs. (2d v.p. acad. programs and events 1985-86, pres. 1986-87), Ohio Fgn. Lang. Assn., Phi Beta Omicron. Office: Cleve Heights HS 13263 Cedar Rd Cleveland OH 44118 Office Phone: 216-371-7101. Personal E-mail: judygoral@earthlink.net. E-mail: j_goral@chuh.org.

GORBY-SCHMIDT, MARTHA LOUISE, pharmacologist, researcher; d. Charles and Louise Gorby. BS in Nursing, Villanova U., 1983. RN Pa., 1983; cert. paralegal. Clin. rsch. asst. Scirex, Blue Bell, Pa., 1996—97; mgr. data quality compliance Aventis Pharma/Rhone Poulenc Rorer, Bridgewater, NJ, 1998—2001; mgr. clin. data rev. Premier Rsch. Worldwide, Phila., 1997—98; assoc. dir. Yamanouchi Pharma Am., Paramus, NJ, 2001—04; global project data mgr. Merck Rsch. Labs., Blue Bell, 2004—. Meddra blue ribbon panel Northrup Grumman, Alexandria, Va., 2003; spkr. in field. Editor: Pen and Ink Mag. (Svc. Award, 1979). Office vol. adminstr. Ch. Good Samaritan, Paoli, Pa., 1990—94, 12 step group facilitator, 1990—94, music dir. sch. com., advt. chmn., 1990—94. Mem.: NAFE, Am. Assn. Critical Care Nurses, ANA, N.Y. Acad. Scis., Oncology Nurse Soc., Am. Chem. Soc., Am. Heart Assn., Assn. Clin. Rsch. Profls., Soc. Clin. Data Mgmt., Regulatory Affairs Profl. Soc., Am. Soc. Clin. Oncology (assoc.), Drug Info. Assn. (assoc.; spl. interest action com. 2003—). Episcopalian. Achievements include research in oncology-early to late stage development. Avocations: music, travel, reading, comedy, hiking. Office: Merck Rsch Labs 785 Jolly Rd UNC-221 Blue Bell PA 19422 Office Phone: 484-344-2148. Personal E-mail: mlgs2327@aol.com. Business E-Mail: martha_schmidt@merck.com.

GORDLY, AVEL LOUISE, state legislator, political organization worker; b. Portland, Oreg., Feb. 13, 1947; d. Fay Lee and Beatrice Bernice (Coleman) G.; 1 child, Tyrone Wayne Waters. BS in Adminstrn. of Justice, Portland State U., 1974; Grad. John F. Kennedy Sch. Govt., Harvard U., 1995; grad., U. Oreg. Pacific Program, 1998. Phone co. clk. Pacific West Bell, Portland, 1966-70, mgmt. trainee, 1969-70; work release counselor Oreg. Corrections Divsn., Portland, 1974-78, parole and probation officer, 1974-78; dir. youth svcs. Urban League of Portland, 1979-83; dir. So. Africa program Am. Friends Svc. Com., Portland, 1983-89, assoc. exec. sec., dir. Pacific N.W. region, 1987-90; freelance writer Portland Observer, Portland, 1988-90; program dir. Portland House of Umoja, 1991; mem. Oreg. Ho. of Reps., Portland, 1991-96, mem. joint ways and means com., adv. mem. appropriations com., rules and reorgn. com., low income housing com., energy policy rev. com., others; mem. Oreg. Senate from 10th dist., Salem, 1997—; mem. crime and corrections com., trades econ. devel. com. Oreg. Senate, 1997, mem. joint ways and means com. on pub. safety, 1997, mem. joint ways and means com. on edn., 1999, mem. joint ways and means pub. safety com., 2005—, mem. joint ways and means edn. com., 2005—, chair, joint ways and means, full com., 2005, emergency bd., co-chair, interim task force on parental and family abductions, 2003—04. Mem. joint ways and means com. on edn., mem. gov. drug and violent crime policy bd., mem. Oreg. liquor control commn. task force, mem. sexual harrassement task force, mem. Hanford waste bd., mem. Gov.'s Commn. for Women, Gov.'s Drug and Violent Crime Policy Bd.; originator, producer, host Black Women's Forum, 1983-88; co-producer, rotating host N.E. Spectrum, 1983-88. Mem. corrections adv. com. Multnomah Cmty.; mem. adv. com. Oregonians Against Gun Violence; mem. Black Leadership Conf.; treas., bd. dirs. Black United Fund; co-founder, facilitator Unity Breakfast Com.; co-founder Sisterhood Luncheon; past project adv. bd. dirs. Nat. Orgn. Victims Assistance; past citizen chmn. Portland Police Bur.; past mem. coordinating com. Portland Future Focus Policy Com.; past coord. Cmty. Rescue Plan; past vice chmn. internat. affairs Black United Front; past sec. Urban League Portland, past vice chmn. and exec. com.; past adv. com. Black Ednl. Ctr.; past vice chmn. Desegregation Monitoring; also past adv. com., past chmn. curriculum com., founder African Am. Leg. Issues Roundtable; founder Black Women Gathering; other past orgn. coms.; elected state senate First African Am. Woman, 1996. Recipient Outstanding Cmty. Svc. award NAACP, 1986, Outstanding Women in Govt. award YWCA, 1991, Girl Scout-Cmty. Svc. award, 1991, N.W. Conf. of Black Studies-Outstanding Progressive Leadership in the African-Am. Cmty. award, 1986, Cmty. Svc. award Delta Sigma Theta, 1981, Joint Action in Cmty. Svc.-Vol. and Cmty. Svc. award, 1981, Quality of Life Photography award Pacific Power & Light Co., 1986, Am. Leadership Forum Sr. fellow, 1988, Equal Opportunity award, Urban League, 1996, Outstanding Alumni, 1996, PSU, Causa '98 En Defensa de la Comunidad award, 1997, Matrix award Assn. for Women in Comm., 1999, Pres.'s award Portland Oreg. Visitors Assn., 1999, Legacy award Black United Fund, 2000, Leadership award Albina Ministerial Alliance, 2000 Mem. NAACP. Avocations: reading, photography, walking. Home: 6805 NE Bradway St Portland OR 97213-5304

GORDON, ALICE JEANNETTE IRWIN, retired secondary school educator, retired elementary school educator; b. Detroit, Mar. 18, 1934; d. Manley Elwood and Jeannette (Coffron) Irwin; m. Edgar George Gordon, Feb. 4, 1967; children: David Alexander, John Scott. BA in Elem. Edn., Mich. State U., East Lansing, 1956; MA in Child Devel., U. Mich., 1959, EdS in Ednl. Psychology, 1967, MA in Reading, 1990; postgrad., Western Mich. U., Kalamazoo, 1990-97. Cert. K-12 tchr., Mich.; cert. K-12 reading specialist. Elem. tchr. Detroit Pub. Schs., 1956-67, reading tchr., 1967-68; secondary tchr. English and reading Parchment Pub. Schs., 1989-94; secondary reading specialist Kalamazoo Pub. Schs., 1994-96; jr. high reading specialist South Middle Sch., Kalamazoo, 1996-99; tchr. Milwood Elem. Sch., Mich., 1999-2001; ret. Reading therapist Western Mich. U., Kalamazoo, 1992-97; participant Ednl. Leadership Acad., 1998-99; bd. dir. U. Mich. Coll. Edn. Mem. alumni bd. Mich. State U. Coll. Edn., 1992-96; chmn. Century Ball, Nazareth Coll., Kalamazoo, 1987; co-chmn. Evening of Nte, Kalamazoo Symphony, 1989; precinct del. Kalamazoo Rep. Com., 1989, 92, 96, 99-2004; mem. Mich. Adult Edn. Practitioner Inquiry Project, 1994, 95, 96; docent Kalamazoo Inst. Art, 2002-2004; bd. mem. Ready to Read, 2002-2004, Literacy Coun., 2002-2004; bd. dirs. U. Mich. Coll. Edn., 2003—, alumni bd. Coll. Edn. Western Mich. U., 2003—; bd. dirs. Ready to Read, 1998-, Kalamazoo Literacy Coun., 2002—; mentor, tutor Cmty. in Schs. Americorps, 2002-05, vista mem. 2003-05; docent Kalamazoo Inst. Arts, 2003-06. Recipient Crystal Apple award Mich. a., 1990, 2002, Excellence in Edn. grantee, 1997, Kalamazoo Pub. Edn. Found. grantee, 1997, 98, Arts Coun. Greater Kalamazoo mini-grantee, 1997, 2000, State Dept. Arts grantee, 1997, Kalamazoo Pub. Edn. Found., 1998; Third Coast Writing fellow, 1998; MLPP grantee, 2001. Mem. Internat. Reading Assn., Mich. Reading Assn., Homer Carter Reading Assn., P.E.O. (pres. 2003-05), Jr. League, Lawyers Wives Aux. (bd. dirs. 2002—, pres. 2003-06), Phi Delta Kappa (pres. 1998-01, bd. dirs. 2002—), Alpha Omega Pi, Delta Kappa Gamma (bd. dirs. 2002-2005). Presbyterian. Avocations: miniatures, antiques, reading, genealogy, public education. Home: 4339 Lakeside Dr Kalamazoo MI 49008-2802 Office Phone: 269-337-0530.

GORDON, ANNE KATHLEEN, editor; m. Phillip L. Berman; 1 child, Aaron. BA speech pathology and audiology, U. Denver, 1979; postgrad., Columbia Grad. Sch. Journalism, 1983. Fin. writer Rocky Mountain Bus. Jour., Denver, 1981, Sun-Tattler, Hollywood, Fla., 1982-83, fin. editor, 1983; asst. bus. editor Ft. Lauderdale (Fla.) News, 1983-85; bus. editor The Denver Post, 1985-88, asst. mng. editor, 1988; news cons. Sta. KCNC-TV, Denver, 1988-89, assignment mgr., 1989-90; editor Jackson Hole News, 1990-92; editor Sunday Mag. The Plain Dealer, Cleve., 1993-99; arts and entertainment editor The Phila. Inquirer, 1999—2000, from assoc. mng. editor to dep. mng. editor arts and features, 2000—02, mng. editor, 2002—. Comm. dir. Colo. Dem. Party, Clinton presdl. campaign, 1992. Author: A Book of Saints, 1994. Recipient Best of Show award Colo. Press Assn., 1981, 86, Woman of Yr. award Broward County Bus. and Profl. Women's Assn., 1983, 1st Pl. Spot News award Colo. Associated Press, 1986, 1st Pl. Breaking News award Colo. Press Assn., 1986, Gen. Excellence award Wyo. Press Assn., 1991, Gen. Excellence award Nat. Newspaper Assn., 1992; Eisenhower fellow, 2000. Home: 149 Fairview Rd Narberth PA 19072-1330 Office: The Philadelphia Inquirer 400 N Broad St Philadelphia PA 19130-4015 E-mail: agordon@phillynews.com.

GORDON, AUDREY KRAMEN, healthcare educator; b. Chgo., Nov. 18, 1935; d. Edward J. and Anne (Levin) Kramen; children: Bradley, Dale, Holly. BS with highest distinction, Northwestern U., 1965, MA, 1967, postgrad., 1971; MA, U. Chgo., 1970; PhD, U. Ill., Chgo., 1991. Cert. in clin. pastoral edn. Lectr. Northwestern U., Evanston, Ill., 1966-74; vis. asst. prof. Beloit (Wis.) Coll., 1974-75; research specialist U. Ill., Chgo., 1983-86, dir. continuing edn. Sch. Pub. Health, 1986-91, lectr. cmty. health scis., 1988-91, dir. coll. advancement Sch. Pub. Health, 1991-92, asst. prof., 1992—, sr. rsch. specialist Inst. for Health Rsch. and Policy, 1992—, dir. instnl. rev. bd., 1998—2004, dir. human subjects rsch. Inst. Health Rsch. and Policy, 2001—, exec. dir. Ill. Ombudsman Study, Ctr. for Rsch. on Health and Aging, 2005—06; coord., counselor Jewish Hospice, Chgo., 1984-89. Lectr. Loyola U. Stritch Sch. Medicine, Maywood, Ill., 1982—90; pres. Rainbow Hospice Orgn., 1984—88, cons., 1988—92, rsch. cons., 2001—; exec. dir. S.E. Lake County Faith in Action Vols., Highland Pk., 2003—. Co-author: (book) They Need to Know: How to Teach Children About Death, 1979; co-editor: Hospice and Cultural Diversity, 1995. Bd. dirs. AIDS Pastoral Care Network, 1999—2001. Recipient Merit award, Northwestern U. Alumni, 1993, Heart of Hospice award, Nat. Coun. Hospice Profls., 1997. Mem.: APHA (Betty Clerkley award for minority rsch. 2004), Nat. Hospice Orgn. (mem. ethics com. 1997—2000), Ill. Hospice Orgn. (pres. 1989—90, v.p. 1997—98), Ill. Pub. Health Assn., Delta Omega, Alpha Kappa Lambda, Alpha Sigma Lambda.

GORDON, CECELIA T., lawyer; b. 1975; BA magna cum laude, Harvard U., 1997; JD, NYU, 2000. Bar: Mass. 2001. Assoc. Hospitality and Recreation Group, Real Estate Group Goulston & Storrs PC, Boston. Office: Goulston & Storrs PC 400 Atlantic Ave Boston MA 02110-3333 Office Phone: 617-574-3656. Office Fax: 617-574-7524. E-mail: cgordon@goulstonstorrs.com.*

GORDON, DOROTHY K., silversmith, goldsmith; b. Boston, May 7, 1919; d. Barney and Sarah M. Kazer; m. Benjamin Gordon, Mar. 27, 1949; children: Judith, Ellis, William. Student, Mus. Sch. Art, Boston, Cath. U., Montgomery Coll. Tchr. metalsmithing D.C. Dept. Recreation, USDA Grad. Sch.; lectr. in field. Exhibited in group shows at YWCA, Washington, Smithsonian Instn. and Nat. Housing Ctr., St. John's Episcopal Ch., McLean, Va., Jewish Cmty. Ctr., Rockville, Md., Temple Micah, Washington, Crafts of the Synagogue touring exhbn, Plum Gallery, Kensington, Md., 1987, Nat. Mus. Am. Jewish History, Phila., 1990, Target Gallery, Alexandria, Va., 1993, B'nai B'rith Klutznick Nat. Jewish Mus., Washington, 1997, Washington Hebrew Congregation, 1998, 2000, Goldman Gallery, Jewish Cmty. Ctr., Rockville, 1999, television series, HGTV Modern Masters, 2003. Mem.: Soc. Am. Silversmiths (artisan mem.), Am. Art League, Washington Guild Goldsmiths. Avocation: painting. Home: 2856 Davenport St NW Washington DC 20008

GORDON, ELLA DEAN, nursing educator, women's health nurse; b. Chgo., Jan. 19, 1947; d. Ed and Mozelle (Jordan) Hall; m. Starling Alexander Gordon, Aug. 2, 1969; children: Gerald Alexander, Dana Rolean. Diploma, Grady Meml. Hosp., 1968; student, Ga. State U., 1969-75; BSN, Med. Coll. Ga., 1976; M in Health Sci., Armstrong State Coll., 1983. RN, Ga., Tex. Charge nurse pediatrics evenings Grady Meml. Hosp., Atlanta, 1968-71; staff nurse pediatrics Dr.'s Meml. Hosp., Atlanta, 1971; charge nurse Pediatricians Office, Decatur, Ga., 1971-72; staff nurse VA Hosp., Atlanta, 1972-76, nurse primary care med. ICU San Antonio, 1983; charge nurse, army nurse corps Eisenhower Army Med. Ctr., Ft. Gordon, Ga., 1976-79; staff nurse obstet. Noble Army Hosp., Ft. McClellan, Ala., 1984; instr. clin. nursing Jacksonville (Ala.) State Coll. Nursing, 1984-85; clin. nurse obstet. Gorgas Army Hosp., Republic of Panama, 1987-89; charge nurse oncology days Eisenhower Army Med. Ctr., Ft. Gordon, Ga., 1989-90; charge nurse obstet. Brooke Army Med. Ctr., Ft. Sam Houston, Tex., 1990-96; mem. labor & delivery Wilford Hall Air Force Med. Ctr., Lackland AFB, Tex., 1996; charge nurse orthopedics Brooke Army Med. Ctr., Ft. Sam Houston, Tex., 1996-99, health/nurse educator Health Promotion Ctr., 2000—, head nurse allergy/immunology svc., 2005—. Cons. health edn. ETOWAH County Clinics, Gadsden, Ala, 1985; health educator Cardiovascular Coun. of Savannah, Ga., 1983, Parent/Child Devel. Svcs., Savannah, 1982. Contbr. articles to profl. jours. Instr. ARC, Ft. McClellan, 1985-86, chmn., vols., 1986-87. Capt. U.S. Army, 1976-79; col. USAR, 1991, ret., 1998. Named One of Outstanding Young Women in Am., 1979, 83. Mem. Ret. Army Nurse Corps Assn., Orthopaedic Nurses Assn., Officers Wives Club (publicity chmn. 1982-83), Sigma Theta Tau. Democrat. Avocations: cross-stitching, bowling, reading, ceramics. Home: 12810 El Marro St San Antonio TX 78233-5832 Office: Brooke Army Med Ctr Fort Sam Houston TX 78234 Office Phone: 210-916-4139. Personal E-mail: satxella33@hotmail.com.

GORDON, ELLEN RUBIN, candy company executive; d. William B. and Cele H. (Travis) Rubin; m. Melvin J. Gordon, June 25, 1950; children: Virginia, Karen, Wendy, Lisa. Student, Vassar Coll., 1948—50; BA, Brandeis U., 1965; postgrad., Harvard U., 1968. With Tootsie Roll Industries, Inc., Chgo., 1968—, corp. sec., 1970-74, v.p. product devel., 1974-76, sr. v.p., 1976-78, pres., COO, 1978—; v.p., dir. HDI Investment Corp. Mem. coun. on divsn. biol. scis. and Pritzker Sch. Medicine U. Chgo.; mem. med. sch. adv. coun. for cell biology and pathology Harvard U.; mem. bd. fellows Faculty of Medicine, Harvard Med. Sch. Mem. adv. coun. J.L. Kellogg Grad. Sch. Mgmt. at Northwestern U.; mem. univ. resources and overseers com. Harvard U.; mem. bd. advisors Women Inc. Recipient Kettle award, 1985. Mem. Nat. Confectioners Assn. (bd. dirs.). Office: Tootsie Roll Industries Inc 7401 S Cicero Ave Chicago IL 60629-5885

GORDON, EMMAJEAN ELIZABETH, farmer, entrepreneur, consultant; b. Fresno, Calif., Dec. 10, 1920; d. John Peter and Emilie (Kromberg) Wagenleitner; div. 1976; children: Marilyn Gordon Johnson, Glenda Rouzaud Farrer. Bus. cert., 4 C's Bus. Sch., 1941; provision teaching credential, Fresno State U., 1942; BA, Chico State U., 1955, MA, 1963. Lic. tchr., supervision, adminstr. edn., life credentials. Tchr. Fresno (Calif.) County Schs., 1945-47, Shasta County Schs., Redding, Calif., 1947-49, Enterprise Elem. Sch., Redding, 1949-58; tchr. team sports Redding Recreation Dept., 1945—47; tchr. Redding Elem. Sch., Bonneyview, 1958-59, Enterprise High Sch., Redding, 1959-60, counselor, 1960-83; beauty cons. Mary Kay Cosmetics, Fresno, 1988—; farmer Fresno, 1978—95; investor E.J. Gordon Enterprises, Fresno, 1976—2003. Mem. salary com. Shasta-Union High Dist., Redding, 1973-75. Ch. choir leader Redding Ch., 1948-52; bd. mem., chmn. Redding Jr. Acad., 1973-76; chmn. county sr. adv. Shasta Coll., Redding, 1983-84, mem. med. adv. bd., 1979-82; mem. adv. bd. Shasta County Woman's Refuge, Redding, 1980-83. Named Gold Star Foster Parent, Shasta County Foster Parent Assn., 1968, 86; recipient Golden Nike award Bus. and Profl. Women, Reading, 1983. Mem. NEA (life), AAUW (life), NAFE, Women in Agr. and Raisen Wives, Shasta Retired Tchrs. Assn. (life), Fresno Bus. and Profl. Women (v.p. 1980, pres. 1981, scholarship chmn. 1989—, sec. 1990, No.

Dist. I.D. Speech winner 1985), Profl. Women's Bowling Club, Palm Lakes Women's Golf Assn., Fresno Fig Garden Woman's Fedn., Edison Social Club Women's Aux., Woodard Exec. Estates Condo Assn. (beautification chmn. 1989-91). Republican. Avocations: arts and crafts, bowling, creative writing, golf, travel. Office Phone: 559-328-7485.

GORDON, FRAN, writer; b. Bklyn., 1965; BSChemE, U. Va., 1986; MFA in Creative Writing, Vt. Coll., 1996. Tchr. English dept. Rutgers U.; tchr. writing program New Sch. U. Vis. writer Am. Acad. Rome. Author: (novel) Paisley Girl, 1999; contbr. (nonfiction) The Practical Writer, 2004, The Future Dictionary of America, 2004. Bd. govs. Nat. Arts Club. Recipient Award for Precocious Youth, Johns Hopkins, Gold medal Nat. Art Club, Nat. and Cmty. Svc. Edn. award; Yaddo fellow; fiction scholar Wesleyan U. Writers Conf. Mem. SAG, Writers Room (N.Y.C.).

GORDON, HELEN TATE, program assistant; b. Washington, Ga., Dec. 17, 1948; d. Geraldine Tate; m. Marvin Gordon (div. 1968); children: Stedric, Itanza. Grad. high sch., Atlanta; cert. acad. excellence, Atlanta Met. Coll., 1990. Cert. nurse asst. Data transcriber IRS, Chamblee, Ga., 1966-67, sec.-steno Atlanta, 1967-70, U.S. Dept. Labor, Atlanta, 1970-77, U.S. Dept. Transp., Atlanta, 1977-80, equal opportunity specialist, 1980-83, adminstrv. officer, safety officer, 1984-85; adminstrv. sec. Atlanta Job Corps/MTC, Atlanta, 1986-90; adminstrv. asst. Spelman Coll., Atlanta, 1990-93; cert. nurse asst. Imperial Health Care Ctr., Atlanta, 1995-97, Sun Rise Care & Rehab., Atlanta, 1997-98, IHS of Atlanta Buckhead, 1999-2001; nurse asst. Universal Health Care, Atlanta, 2001—02, Personal Care Inc., Decatur, Ga., 2002—; program asst., receptionist DHR/Divsn. Family and Children Svcs., Atlanta, 2004—. Recipient Adminstr. Safety award Fed. Hwy. Adminstrn., 1985. Baptist. Avocation: sewing. Office: DHR/Divsn Family and Children Svcs 18th Fl 2 Peachtree St Atlanta GA 30303 Home: 2125 Simpson Rd #48C Atlanta GA 30314 Office Phone: 404-657-3400. E-mail: htgordon@dhr.state.ga.us, helentgordon@yahoo.com.

GORDON, JASMINE ROSETTA, elementary school educator; b. Fort William, Westmoreland, Jamaica, Feb. 21, 1948; came to U.S., 1991; d. Terrence Gordon and Mavis Collins; children: Nigel Jordan, Marcia Muir. BSc in Middle Grade Edn., We. Carolina U., 1985; MA in Counseling and Psych. Svcs., Clark Atlanta U., 1993; EdD in Ednl. Leadership and Adminstrn., U. Sarasota, 1999; student, Atlanta Tech. Inst., 1999—. Cert. counselor, tchr. Ga. Tchr. Mt. Alvernia H.S., Montego Bay, Jamaica, 1980-87; tchr. lang. arts, social studies, religious edn. Anchovy H.S., St. James, Jamaica, 1987-88; instr., lectr. Bethlehem Tchr.'s Coll., St. Elizabeth, Jamaica, 1988-91; intern Inman Middle Sch., Atlanta, 1992-93; counselor Morris Brown Coll., Atlanta, 1994; sch. counselor Oakhurst Elem. Sch., Decatur, Ga., 1994-95; grad. asst. Sch. Edn. counseling and human devel. dept. Clark Atlanta U., 1994-96; tchr. 4th grade math. and lang. arts Cook Elem. Sch., 1995—; skill tchr. Atlanta Pub. Sch., Emory U., 1998—. Workshop facilitator Elem. Sci. Edn. Ptnrs. program Emory U., Atlanta, 1998—, mem., steering com. 1998—; facilitate staff devel. workshops Emory U., Atlanta Pub. Schs., 1999, tchr. in-service workshop Cook Elem. Sch., 1998-99, City Sch. Decatur, 1994-95, workshop ednl. profls. Savannah, Ga, 1994; substitute tchr. Atlanta Pub. Sch., 1992-94; spkr. Emory U., Atlanta Pub. Schs. ESEP Program, Assn. Village Pride, Fayetteville, Ga., U. Sarasota, 1999. Author rsch. papers. Vol. counselor Ga. Baptist Hosp., Atlanta, 1998—; contbr. various civic orgns. DeWitt Wallace-Reader's Digest scholar 1993-94; recipient Stanley Motor award Mico Tchrs. Coll., Jamaica, 1979-80. Mem. NEA, ABA (assoc.), Am. counseling Assn., Ga. Assn. Educators, Ga. Sch. Counselors Assn., Atlanta Assn. Educators, Atlanta Jamaican Assn. (edn. com. 1998—), Jamaica Tchrs. Assn., Jamaica Tchrs. Credit Union, Jamaica Assn. Tertiary Educators (profl. devel. com.). Methodist. Avocations: sewing, reading, crochet, travel, sports. Office: Atlanta Bd Edn 210 Pryor St SW Atlanta GA 30303-3624 E-mail: jrgordon@acninc.net.

GORDON, JULIE PEYTON, foundation administrator; b. Jacksonville, Fla., June 21, 1940; d. Robert Benoist Shields and Bessie (Cavanaugh) Peyton; m. Robert James Gordon, June 22, 1963. BA, Boston U., 1963; MA, Harvard U., 1965, PhD, 1969. Asst. prof. English Ill. Inst. Tech., Chgo., 1968-75, assoc. prof., 1975-77, asst. dean students, 1975-78; asst. dean acad. affairs Northwestern U., Evanston, Ill., 1978-80, lectr. English, Univ. Coll., 1978—2001, assoc. dean Univ. Coll., 1980-85, sec. Econometric Soc., 1975—, exec. dir. Econometric Soc., 1985—. Mem. nat. adv. com. ALA, Chgo., 1983—86; lectr. English Northwestern U., Evanston, 2003—. Author: Seasons in the Contemporary American Family, 1984. Grantee NEH, 1971-73; project scholar NEH, 1983-86. Mem.: Phi Beta Kappa. Avocation: writing. Home: 202 Greenwood Evanston IL 60201-4714 Office: Northwestern U Dept Econs Econometric Soc Evanston IL 60208-2600 Office Phone: 847-491-3615. Business E-Mail: jpg@northwestern.edu.

GORDON, LANA G., state representative; b. Kansas City, Mo., Aug. 20, 1950; m. Arnold Gordon; children: Jennifer, Stacey, Jamie. BS in Edn., U. Kans., 1971. Subst. tchr., Mo., 1971—72; tchr. Lee's Summit (Mo.) Pub. Sch., 1972—73; test adminstr. State of Kans., 1978—80; sec., treas. Cardinal Bldg. Svcs., 1997—2001; office gen. Cardinal DBA/BG Svc. Solution, 2002—; mem. Kans. Ho. of Reps., 2001—. Bd. dirs. Kansas, Inc. Sec. citizens adv. coun. USD 501 Dist., 1982—85; bd. dirs. USD 501 Sch. Found., 1994—97, Vol. Ctr. Topeka, 1998—, Jr. League Topeka, 2002—04, Topeka Conv. and Visitors Bur., Topeka C. of C., 2006—. Republican. Jewish. Office: 181-W State Capitol 281 W 10th Ave Topeka KS 66612 Address: 5820 SW 27th St Topeka KS 66614

GORDON, LEE DIANE, school librarian, educator; b. Lafayette, Ind., Oct. 30, 1948; d. Henry Charles and Leonora (Brower) G.; m. James J. Thomas, Aug. 27, 1977 (div. Feb. 1994); m. Daniel L. Weber, July 10, 1999. BA, Calif. State U., Long Beach, 1970; MEd, U. Nev., Las Vegas, 1980. Cert. tchr., Nev., Calif.; cert. libr., Nev. Tchr. Carmenita Jr. High Sch., Cerritos, Calif., 1971-77, Jim Bridger Jr. High Sch., North Las Vegas, Nev., 1977-79, libr., 1979-84, Eldorado High Sch., Las Vegas, 1984—2001, Sierra Vista H.S., Las Vegas, 2001—. Adj. faculty U. Nev.-Las Vegas, 1997—. Co-author: The Overworked Teacher's Bulletin Board Book, 1981; filmstrips, 1983; author: World Historical Fiction Guide for Young Adults, 1996; contbr. articles to profl. jours. Mem. Am. Assn. Sch. Librs. (affiliate del., various coms. 1987—; dir. Region VII 1999-2001), Nev. Assn. Sch. Librs. (chair 1987), Clark County Sch. Librs. Assn. (pres. 1987-88), Delta Kappa Gamma (Iota chpt. pres. 1990-92). Office: Sierra Vista High Sch 8100 W Robindale Rd Las Vegas NV 89113

GORDON, LISA M., music educator; b. Kingston, Pa., Dec. 5, 1970; MusB, Wilkes U., Wilkes-Barre, Pa., 1992. Cert. music tchr. N.J., 2000. Music tchr. Freehold Twp. Schs., Freehold, NJ, 1999—. Freelance musician, Freehold, NJ, 1988—. Mem.: NEA, Music Educators Nat. Conf., N.J. Edn. Assn. (assoc.; rep. 2002—06, head rep. 2003—04), Am. Fedn. Musicians (assoc.). Democrat-Npl.

GORDON, LORI HEYMAN, psychotherapist, author, educator; b. S.I., NY, Jan. 31, 1929; d. Julius and Bertha (Hahn) Heyman; m. Morris Gordon, Sept. 5, 1982 (dec.); children: Beth, Jonathan, David, Seth. BS, Cornell U., 1950; MSW, Cath. U. Am., 1963; PhD, Summit U. La., 1993. Lic. clin. social worker, accredited supr., Va. Founder/dir. Family Rels. Inst., Falls Church, Va., 1969; condr. psychoednl. tng. seminars nat. and internat. PAIRS (Practical Application Intimate Relationship Skills), Falls Church. Instr. family therapy Am. U. Grad. Sch. Counseling Edn., Washington; field supr. Cath. U. Am. Sch. Social Work, Washington; presenter profls. cons. Am. Assn. Marriage and Family Therapy Conf., 1988-91, Va. Assn. Marriage and Family Therapy Conf., 1989, ABA Family Law divsn. ptnrs. program, 1994; founder Ctr. for Separation and Divorce Mediation, 1980; founder, dir. PAIRS Ltd., 1984, PAIRS Inst., 1990; founder, exec. dir. PAIRS Found., Inc., 1991, dir. tng., 1995 Author: Love Knots--How To Untangle Daily Frustrations, 1990, Passage to Intimacy, 1993, rev. edit., 2001, If You Really Loved Me, 1996, Pairs Participant Handbook, Paris Curriculum Guide and Training Manual vol. I, II, revised, 1999, The Peers Experience, 1999, Breaking the Code of Jealousy: Seven Steps to Healing, 2004; co-author: Prepairs, A Guide for Catholic Couples, 1999, Preventive Approaches to Couples Therapy, 1999, Prepairs, A Guide for Jewish Couples, 2001, Prepairs: A Guide for Christian Couples, 2001, Christian Pairs, 2002, Dare to be: The Autobiography of Rabbi Morris Gordon, 2006; contbr. articles to profl. jours. and mags., chpts. to books. Mem. Internat. Human Lng. Resource Network, Avanta-The Va. Satir Tng. Orgn., Inst. Noetic Scis., Coalition Marriage, Family and Couples Edn. (bd. dirs.). Office: PAIRS Found Ltd 1056 Creekford Dr Weston FL 33326-2836 Office Phone: 954-385-1775. Personal E-mail: pairsline@aol.com.

GORDON, LYNDA L., art educator; b. Lynwood, Calif., Apr. 9, 1949; BS, Long Beach State U., 1967, MA, 1973; ArtsD, Idaho State U., 1975. Prof. San Diego (Calif.) City Coll., 1975—89, Long Beach (Calif.) City Coll., 1989—. Vol. tutor Calif. State U., Long Beach, Calif., 2005—06. D-Liberal. Office: Long Beach City Coll 4901 E Carson St Long Beach CA 90808 Office Phone: 562-938-4630. Business E-Mail: lgordon@lbcc.edu.

GORDON, MARJORIE, lyric-coloratura soprano, music educator, opera producer; b. N.Y.C. d. Theodore and Minnie (Glantz) Fishberg; m. Nathan Gordon; children: Maxine, Peter Jon. BA cum laude, Hunter Coll. Nat. cert. voice tchr. Prof. voice Duquesne U., 1957-59, Wayne State U., 1961-91, Nat. Music Camp, Interlochen, 1963-65, Meadowbrook Sch. Music, 1966-71, U. Mich., 1970, Mich. State U., 1971; soloist, tchr. Am. U.-Wolf Trap Program, Washington, 1973. Spl. edn. cons. Detroit Grand Opera Assn.; adj. prof. Oakland (Mich.) U.; pres., gen. dir. Piccolo Opera Co., Inc. Solo debut N.Y. Philharm. Symphony, 1950, soprano soloist, N.Y.C. Opera, 1955-57, Chautauqua Opera Co., 1949-61, Pitts. Opera, 1956; dir. Detroit Opera Theatre, 1960-72, Piccolo Opera Co., 1961—; soloist with Chgo. Symphony, Phila. Symphony, Pitts. Symphony, other orchs., opera cos., summer stock, on radio and TV; recitals U.S., Greece, Europe, Can., Israel; editor: Opera Study Guide, 1968—. Mem. music adv. panel Mich. Arts Coun., 1980-90; mem. Palm Beach County Cultural Commn., 1992—; opera producer Blue Lake Fine Arts Camp, 1993—. Recipient resolution honoring 25th Anniversary Piccolo Opera Co., Mich. Senate; established voice scholarship in perpetuity Nat. Opera Assn. Mem.: AFTRA, Nat. Assn. Tchrs. Singing, Met. Opera Guild, Ctrl. Opera Svc., Nat. Opera Assn., Music Tchrs. Nat. Assn., Am. Guild Mus. Artists, Mich. Music Tchrs. Assn. (voice chmn. 1970—76), Fla. Music Tchrs. Assn., Boca Delray Music Soc., Broward County Music Club, Mu Phi Epsilon. Avocations: handcrafts, swimming, reading, sketching. Office Phone: 800-282-3161. Office Fax: 561-394-0520. Personal E-mail: leejon51@msn.com.

GORDON, MARSHA L., dermatologist; b. Annapolis, Md., 1958; BA, Rutgers U., 1980; MD, U. Pa., 1984. Diplomate Am. Bd. Dermatology. Intern Cooper Med. Ctr., Camden, 1984—85; resident in dermatology Mt. Sinai Med. Ctr., N.Y.C., 1985—88, chief cons., 1988—, vice chair dermatology, 1996—. Asst. prof. Mt. Sinai Sch. Medicine, N.Y.C., 1988—97, assoc. clin. prof., 1997—. Office: Mount Sinai Med Ctr Box 1048 5 E 98th St New York NY 10029-6501 Office Phone: 212-241-9773.

GORDON, MARY CATHERINE, writer; b. L.I., N.Y., Dec. 8, 1949; d. David and Anna (Gagliano) G.; m. James Brain, 1974 (div.); m. Arthur Cash, 1979; children: Anna Gordon, David Dess Gordon. BA, Barnard Coll., 1971; MA, Syracuse U., 1973. Tchr. English Dutchess Community Coll., Poughkeepsie, N.Y., 1974-78, Amherst (Mass.) Coll., 1979-80, Barnard Coll., 1988—. Author: (novels) Final Payments, 1978, The Company of Women, 1981, Men and Angels,1985, The Other Side, 1989, The Rest of Life, 1993, Spending, 1998, (short stories) Temporary Shelter, 1987, Good Boys and Dead Girls and Other Essays, 1991, The Rest of Life: Three Novellas, 1993, The Shadow Man, 1996, Seeing Through Places, 2000, Joan of Arc, 2000. Guggenheim fellow; recipient Kafka prize for Fiction, 1979, 82, Lila Acheson Wallace Reader's digest award. Roman Catholic. Office: Barnard Coll Dept English 3009 Broadway New York NY 10027-6501 Agent: Sterling Lord Literistic 65 Bleecker St Fl 12 New York NY 10012-2420

GORDON, MILDRED HARRIET GROSS, hospital executive; b. Phila., Mar. 13, 1934; d. Nathan and Kate (Segal) Gross; m. Ivan H. Gordon, June 13, 1954; 1 child, Radene Lara. BS, Kutztown State U., Pa., 1960; MS, Med. Coll. Pa., 1970, PhD in Psychiatry, 1972. Tchr. sci. pub. schs., 1961—66; with Family Guidance Ctr., 1960—70; dir. dept. psychiatry Mental Health Treatment Ctr., Reading Hosp., West Reading, 1972—. Cons. Ctr. Mental Health-Reading Hosp. and Med. Ctr.; clin. instr. dept. psychiatry Med. Coll. Pa., Phila., 1972—78; clin. asst. prof. dept. psychiatry Temple U. Med. Sch.; pvt. practice DGR Mgmt., Inc., Wyomissing, Pa.; mem. Pa. Gov.'s Counl. on Drug and Alcohol Abuse, 1972—78. Bd. dirs. Confront, 1971—73, Coun. on Chem. Abuse, 1971—73. Named to Ct. Hon. Disting. Daus., Phila. H.S. Girls, 2002; recipient Svc. award, Reading Hosp. and Med. Ctr., 2003, Jasper G. Chen See M.D. Healthcare Profl. award, Caron Found., 2003; fellow, Falk Found. Mem.: APA, Am. Coll. Forensic Examiners. Home: 1850 Oak Ln Reading PA 19604-1641 also: 560 Van Reed Rd Wyomissing PA 19610-1799 Office Phone: 610-988-4943.

GORDON, PAMELA ANN WENCE, pianist; b. Dayton, Ohio, Apr. 28, 1943; d. Arthur Elbert and Melva C. (Coleman) Wence (dec.); m. Clifford Elwood Gordon, Oct. 23, 1971. BS, Ind. State U., Terre Haute, 1966. Pvt. practice, 1957—; round dance leader, 1973—98. Organist Ctrl. Seventh Day Bapt. Ch., 1989-2005, choir dir. 2000-04; Christmas carol pianist Williamsburg, Va., 2001-04, sunshine chmn., outreach chmn., 2003— Recipient Appreciation award Rock Eights, 1985. Mem. ROUNDALAB (charter mem., chair survey com. 1985-86, Maestro trophy 1998), Round Dance Tchrs. Assn. Greater D.C. Area (v.p.), Nat. Capital Area Sq. Dance Leaders Assn. (treas.), Washington Music Tchrs. Assn. (treas.), Greenbelt Astronomy Club Avocations: travel, reading, box turtles, piano, doll collecting. Mailing: 219 Rainbow Dr # 11963 Livingston TX 77399-2019 E-mail: pcgordon@escapees.com.

GORDON, RITA SIMON, civic leader, former nurse, educator; b. Frederick, Md., Feb. 1, 1929; d. Jacob and Anna (Stein) Simon; m. Paul Perry Gordon, July 2, 1948; children: Stuart Yael, Hugh Ellis, Myla. RN, Frederick Meml. Hosp., 1949. RN, md surg. staff nurse Prince Georges Gen. Hosp., 1949-50; ped. staff nurse (part time) Frederick Meml. Hosp., 1950-54; surg. office nurse, 1960-62; nurse blood prog. ARC, 1954-83. Author: (with Paul P. Gordon) Textbook History of Frederick County, 1975, Playground of the Civil War, 1994, Never the Like Again, 1995. Mem. Frederick County Bd. Edn., 1975-85, pres., 1979-80, 83-84; mem. exec. com. Md. Assn. Bd. Edn., Annapolis, 1978-85, pres., 1983-84; trustee Jewish Mus. of Md. 1998—2004; bd. assocs. Hood Coll., Frederick 1985-94; mem. Md. Task Force on Ednl. Funding, Annapolis, 1983-84, Md. Values Edn. Com., Annapolis, 1979-83, Fed. Relations Network, Nat. Sch. Bd. Assn., 1978-82; bd. dirs. Community Commons, Frederick, 1983-85; area field rep. Am. Field Svc., Frederick, 1970-75; assoc. mem. adv. com. Vocat. Tech. Edn., publicity com. 1973 Snow Ball, Frederick Meml. Hosp. Aux.; past bd. dirs., vice pres. Beth Sholom Sisterhood; pres. Beth Sholom Congregation, 1988-90; past bd. dirs. Nat. Counc. Jewish Women, Frederick; vol. aide frederick Waverly Elem. Sch.; ofcr., chmn. fund raising North Market St. Sch.; active Girl Scouts U.S.A.; past pres., v.p. Frederick Improvement Found., editor: Town Crier; trustee Community Found., Frederick County, 1991-1995. Named Woman of the Yr., Bus. and Profl. Woman's Club, 1975; Frederick's Outstanding Woman, Internat. Woman's Yr., 1975. Mem. Frederick Sect. Nat. Counc. Jewish Women (pres. 1986-88), C. of C. (Planned Growth-2000 com.), Md. Hist. Soc., Internat. Graphoanalysis Soc., Md. Jewish Hist. Soc., Frederick County Hist. Soc. Clubs: Rotary Inner Wheel (Frederick, Md.). Avocation: history. Home: 202 Meadowdale Ln Frederick MD 21702-4036 Personal E-mail: prg202@adelphia.net.

GORDON, ROBBIE, television producer; Investigative prodr. Primetime, ABC-TV, NYC, 1989—. Lectr. Duke Univ., Univ. Syracuse, Univ. Tenn., Univ. Mass. Author: We Interrupt This Program: A Citizen's Guide to Using the Media for Social Change, 1978. Co-recipient CINE Golden Eagle award, 2004, Clarion award for TV Investigative Feature or Series - Nat., 2005; recipient RFK Journalism awards (hon. mention), 1991, IRE award (large mkts.), 1991, Headliner award (2nd place), news mag. program, 1999, George Polk award for TV reporting, 2005. Office: ABC Primetime 7 W 66th St New York NY 10023

GORDON, SARAH BARRINGER, law educator; BA, Vassar Coll., 1982; JD, Yale U., 1986, MAR (Ethics) magna cum ladue, 1987; PhD in History, Princeton U., 1995. Law clk. to Hon. Arlin M. Adams US Third Cir. Ct. Appeals, 1986—87; assoc. Fine, Kaplan & Black, Phila., 1987—89; asst. prof. law U. Pa. Law Sch., Phila., 1994—98, prof. law and history, 1998—, assoc. dean, 2000—02. Author: The Mormon Question: Polygamy and Constitutional Conflict in Nineteenth-Century America, 2002; contbr. articles to law jours. Mem.: ABA, Utah State Hist. Soc., Libr. Co. of Pa., Hist. Soc. of Pa., Am. Assn. Univ. Profs., Mormon History Assn., Soc. Am. Law Tchrs., Law & Soc. Assn., Western History Assn., Am. Acad. of Religion, Am. Soc. for Legal History, Orgn. Am. Hist., Am. Hist. Assn. Office: U Pa Law Sch 3400 Chestnut St Philadelphia PA 19104 Office Phone: 215-898-3069. Office Fax: 215-573-2025. E-mail: sgordon@law.upenn.edu.

GORDON, SHARON ANN, mathematics educator, pre-school educator; b. Newton, NJ, Aug. 8, 1945; d. Kenneth William Gordon and Hazel Emma Pascoe. Attended, Centenary Coll., 1963—64; BA in Math., Chemistry, and History, Drew U., 1967; MEd, Montclair U., 1970. Cert. Secondary Sch. Math. Tchr. (seventh through twelfth grades) NJ Bd. Examiners, 1969. Math. tchr. Sparta HS, NJ, 1968—2000; pre-sch. tchr. aide Cir. Friends Pre-Sch., Sparta, 2000—. Mem. Sparta United Meth. Ch., 1956—. Recipient Creative Writing award, Centenary Coll., 1963. Mem.: NEA, Sussex County Retired Educators Assn., NJ Retired Educators Assn., Jack Russell Terrier Club Am., Phi Theta Kappa. Methodist. Avocations: poetry writing, baking, cooking, counted cross stitch, reading.

GORDON, SHARON J., special education educator; b. Calif., 1972; m. Ted H. Gordon, 1972; 1 child, Matthew. BA, San Jose State U., 1969, MA, 1973. Cert. tchr., Calif. Speech lang. pathologist Walnut Creek (Calif.) Elem. Sch. Dist., 1969, San Ramon Unified Sch. Dist., Danville, Calif., 1969-75, Cotati-Rohnert Park (Calif.) Sch. Dist., 1975-80, spl. edn. educator lang. handicapped students, 1980-92, spl. edn. educator, 1992—2002; spl. edn. dept., adj. instr. Dominican U. of Calif., 2002—. Mem. leadership team Waldo Rohnert Sch., 1993—2002. Pres. Congregation Rodef Sholom, San Rafael, Calif., 1989-91; social action chair no. Calif. Union Am. Hebrew Congregations, San Francisco, 1985-88; chair Jewish Cmty. Rels. Coun., San Rafael, 1992-94. Named Woman of Yr. ORT, 1991. Mem. Am. Speech Lang. Hearing Assn., Calif. Speech Lang. Hearing Assn., Calif. Tchrs. Assn. Avocation: community service projects. Office: Dominican U Calif 50 Acacia Ave San Rafael CA 94901

GORDON, SHIRLEY BLOM, college president; b. Bremerton, Wash., Feb. 26, 1922; d. Waldemer and Edith Mary (Sterns) Blom; m. Thomas I. Gordon, Aug. 18, 1944. BS, Wash. State U., 1944, MA, 1947, PhD, 1957; postgrad., U. Calif., 1959, Seattle U., 1960, Reed Coll., 1961. Instr. in chemistry Wash. State U., 1946-49; instr. in chemistry and math. Grays Harbor Coll., 1950-57; tchr., math./sci. coordinator Highline Sch. Dist., Seattle, 1957-61; dean instrn. Highline Community Coll., 1961-72, v.p., 1972-76, pres., 1976—. Mem. Nat. Commn. on Excellence in Edn.; co-chmn. Wash. Commn. on Ednl. Excellence Mem. various community coms. and adv. groups.; Active United Way of King County. Mem. Am. Assn. Community and Jr. Colls. (dir.), N.W. Assn. Schs. and Colls. (dir., mem. Commn. on Colls.), Wash. Assn. Community Coll. Pres. (pres.), Delta Delta Delta, Iota Sigma Pi, Pi Lambda Theta. Episcopalian. Home: PO Box 98318 Seattle WA 98198-0318

GORDON, STORROW MOSS, information technology executive, lawyer; b. 1952; married; 2 children. BA, U. Tex.; JD, So. Meth. U. Bar: 1978. Ptnr. Johnson & Wortley, P.C.; sr. atty. Electronic Data Sys. Corp., Plano, Tex., 1991, legal mgr., corp. acquisitions and fin., 1992—96, sec. governance com. bd. dirs., 1996—99, dir. bd. ops., 1999—2000, dep. gen. counsel, 2002—05, exec. v.p., gen. counsel, 2005—. Named Super Lawyer, Tex. Monthly mag., 2004, 2005. Office: Electronic Data Sys Inc 5400 Legacy Dr Plano TX 75024 Office Phone: 972-605-6000.*

GORDON, SUZANNE, information technology executive; BS, MS, NC State Univ. Positions through v.p. SAS Info. Sys. Div. SAS Inst. Inc., Cary, NC, 1980—2003; v.p. info. tech. & chief info. officer SAS Inst., Inc., Cary, NC, 2003—. Trustee NC State Univ.; mem. adv. bd. NC State Univ. Coll. mgmt. Office: SAS Institute Inc 100 SAS Campus Dr Cary NC 27513-2414*

GORDON-HARRIS, CASSANDRA I., curator, educator; b. New Orleans, Jan. 23, 1948; d. Kevin Michael Gordon and Mary Frances Roberts; m. Eugene L. Harris, June 6, 1977. A in Drawing, Casa de La Cultura, Guayaquil, Ecuador, 1964; BA in Art History, U. Fribourg, Switzerland, 1968. Mem. faculty The Arts Ctr., St. Petersburg, Fla., 1998—; curator Galleries at Salt Creek, St. Petersburg, 2000—03. Co-founder Santa Fe Multi-Cultural Artist Group, 1980—83; west coast mem. chair Fla. chpt. Womens Caucus for Art, 2001—03; co-designer, artist State N.Mex., Santa Fe, 1982; cons., designer, artist City St. Petersburg, 2000—01; designer, sponsor Ctr. Against Spousal Abuse, 2001; bd. dirs. Fla. Artist Group, 2002—, area chair, 2003—, v.p., 2004—. One-woman shows include Gallery One, Coconut Grove, Fla., Anna Sklar Gallery, Bal Harbour, Fla., 1986, DeMayo Gallery, Guayaquil, Ecuador, 1989—91, Synthesis Fine Arts, Tampa, 1999, Mahaffey Theatre, St. Petersburg, Fla., 2000, Avalon Island Gallery, Orlando, 2002, Confident Gallery, St. Petersburg, 2003, Garden Gallery, Palm Beach Gardens, Fla., 2005, exhibited in group shows at Hilderbrand Gallery, New Orleans, La., 1995, 1996, Soho South Gallery, St. Petersburg, Fla., 1998, Fusion Gallery, 1998, Salt Creek Artworks, 1999, 2000, 2001, Rosemary Court Galleries, Sarasota, Fla., 2000, The Venice Arts Ctr., Fla., 2001, 2002, 2003, Big Arts Gallery, Sanibel Island, Fla., 2002, St. Augustine Art Assn., 2003, Confident Gallery, 2004, Galler in Cork St., London, Eng., 2004, Greenwich St. Gallery, N.Y.C., 2004, Boca Raton (Fla.) Mus. Art, 2005, Cornell Mus. Art, Delray Beach, Fla., 2005. Mem. steering com. Pinellas County Arts for Complete Edn., co-chair adminstrv. com., 2005—06, chair, 2006—. Named Artist in Residence, Pinellas Arts Coun., 2001—06, Best of Bay 2001 Promoter of Women Artists, Weekly Planet Newspaper, 2001; recipient Cert. Spl. Recognition, Sociedad Amazonica, 1984. Mem.: AAUW, Nat. Assn. Women Artists, Artist Equity, Art Beyond Borders, Nat. Mus. Women in Art. Studio: 719 Central Ave Saint Petersburg FL 33701 Home: 2000 28th Ave North Saint Petersburg FL 33713 Business E-Mail: casgohart@att.net.

GORDON-LARSEN, PENNY, nutritionist, educator, researcher; m. Robert A. Larsen; children: Isabella, Frederick. PhD, U. Pa., 1997. Instr. U. Pa., 1995—98; Dannon postdoctoral fellow U. N.C. Chapel Hill, 1998—2000, asst. prof. nutrition, 2000—. Rev. panels, obesity rsch. NIH, Bethesda, Md., 2003—; sci. meeting planning com. N.Am. Assn. for Study of Obesity, Silver Spring, Md., 2004—, mem. pediat. obesity sect., 2004—; cluster head macro & built environment U. N.C. Chapel Hill, 2004—. Mem. editl. bd. obesity rsch.: Boston Med. Ctr., 2004—, Obesity Rsch., —. Chair pers. com. Chapel Hill Day Care Ctr., 2002—03. Recipient Young Investigator Awards, N.Am. Assn. for Study of Obesity; Ind. Rsch. Grants, NIH, 2002—, Dannon Nutrition Inst. Postdoctoral Fellowship Interdiscplinary Rsch., Dannon, 1998—2000. Fellow: Ctr. for Regional and Urban Studies (assoc.), Carolina Population Ctr. (assoc. Fellow 2001-present); mem.: N.Am. Assn. Study Obesity (gov. coun.), Obesity Soc. (pediat. obesity coun.). Achievements include research in obesity, pediatric and adolescent medicine, interdisplinary studies, health disparities; development of population-based GIS methods for epidemiologic research. Avocations: running, swimming, cooking. Office: Univ NC-Chapel Hill Univ Sq CPC 123 W Franklin St Chapel Hill NC 27516 Office Phone: 919-843-9966. Office Fax: 919-966-1959. E-mail: pglarsen@unc.edu.

GORE, REBECCA ESTES, science educator; b. Charlottesville, Va., Mar. 6, 1948; d. James Smith and Margaret Sprinkel Estes; m. Thomas B. Gore, June 21, 1969 (dec.); children: Thomas William, Margaret-Anne Gore Hawley. BSc in Secondary Sci. Edn., U. Va., 1972. Sci. tchr. Madison County HS, Va., 1972—91, head softball coach, 1972—91, asst. basketball coach, 1973—78; sci. tchr. Orange County HS, Va., 1991—, lead tchr., sci. dept., 2001—, softball coach, 1992—94. Exec. bd. mem. Va. HS Coaches Assn., 1986—91. Leader Va. 4-H Clubs, Madison County, Orange County, 1972—; adult advisor BASS, Orange County, 1999—, 4-H Club, Orange County, 1999—; treas. Madison County Womens Club, 1972—91. Recipient Tchr. of Yr., Va. Jaycees, 1983, Softball Coach of Yr., Va. HS League Coaches Assn., 1988, Nat. HS Coaches Assn., 1988, Nat. Outstanding Jr. BASS Fedn. Chpt. of Yr. award, ESPN, 2004, Youth Adv. award, Orange County, 2004. Mem.: DAR, NEA, Bass Anglers Sportsman's Soc. of Am. Inc., Madison County Rescue Squad, Va. Sci. Tchrs. Assn., Orange County Edn. Assn., Va. Edn. Assn., Descendants Colonial Clergy Assn., U. Va. Alumnae Assn. Independent. Avocations: hiking, travel, kayaking, fishing. Home: 5274 Shelby Rd Rochelle VA 22738 Office: Orange County Public Schs 428 Waugh Blvd Orange VA 22960

GORE, TIPPER (MARY ELIZABETH GORE), wife of the former vice president of the United States; b. Washington, Aug. 19, 1948; m. Albert Gore Jr., May 19, 1970; children: Karenna, Kristin, Sarah, Albert III. BA in Psychology, Boston U., 1970; MA in Psychology, Vanderbilt U., 1975. Freelance photographer; photographer Nashville Tennessean. Mental health policy advisor to pres. Author: Raising PG Kids in an X-Rated Society, 1987, Picture This: A Visual Diary, 1996; co-author The Spirit of Family, 2002, Joined at the Heart: The Transformation of the American Family, 2002; co-prodr. (with Nat. Mental Health Assn.) Homeless in America: A Photographic Project. Co-founder Parents Music Resource Ctr., Arlington, Va., 1985; founder Tenn. Voices for Children, 1990; co-chair Am. Goes Back to Sch. Initiative, 1996—; chair Congl. Wives Task Force, 1978-79' co-founder The Climate Project, 2006-. Democrat. Office: 2100 West End Ave Nashville TN 37203

GOREAU, ANGELINE WILSON, writer; b. Sept. 12, 1951; d. Theodore Nelson and Eloise (Keaton) G.; m. Stephen Jones McGruder, Mar. 19, 1983; 1 child, Keaton Angeline BA, Barnard Coll., 1973. Hodder fellow Princeton U., NJ, 1982—83; lectr. Vassar Coll., Poughkeepsie, NY, 1984—90. Judge for various prizes Author: Reconstructing Aphra, 1980, The Whole Duty of a Woman, 1984; contbr. articles to mags., newspapers, essays to books Fellow NEH, 1976, Nat. Endowment Arts, 1981, Belgian Ministry Culture Mem. PEN, Book Critics' Cir., Authors' Guild Office: c/o Georges Borchardt 136 E 57th St New York NY 10022-2707 Personal E-mail: agoreau@aol.com.

GORELICK, JAMIE SHONA, lawyer; b. NYC, May 6, 1950; d. Leonard and Shirley (Fishman) Gorelick; m. Richard E. Waldhorn, Sept. 28, 1975; children: Daniel H. Waldhorn, Dana E. Waldhorn. BA magna cum laude, Harvard U., 1972, JD cum laude, 1975. Bar: DC 1975, US Dist. Ct. DC 1976, US Tax Ct. 1976, US Ct. Claims 1976, US Ct. Appeals (DC cir.) 1976, US Ct. Appeals (5th cir.) 1977, US Supreme Ct. 1979, US Ct. Apepals (Fed. cir.) 1982, US Ct. Internat. Trade 1984, US Dist. Ct. Md. 1985, US Ct. Appeals (4th cir.) 1986, US Ct. Appeals (3d cir.) 1988. With Miller, Cassidy, Larroca & Lewin, Washington, 1975-79, 80-93; asst. to sec., counselor to dep. sec. US Dept. Energy, 1979—80; gen. counsel Dept. Def., 1993—94; dep. atty. gen. Dept. Justice, Washington, 1994-97; vice chair Fannie Mae, Washington, 1997—2003; ptnr. litigation, co-chmn. Nat. Security & Govt. Contracts dept., co-chmn., Public Policy & Strategy group WilmerHale, Washington, 2003—. Mem. chmn.'s adv. coun. US Senate Jud. Com., 1988—93; tchr. Trial Advocacy Workshop Harvard Law Sch., Cambridge, Mass., 1982, Cambridge, 84; vice chair task force evaluation audit investigative inspection components Dept. Def., 1979—80; mem. sec.'s transition team Dept. Energy, 1979; bd. dirs. United Techs. Corp., Schlumberger Ltd., Lucent Govt. Adv. Bd., Best Editors Adv. Bd. Mem. editl. bd. Corp. Criminal Liability Reporter, 1986—93; contbr. articles to profl. jours. Mem. nat. security adv. panel CIA, 1997—2005; mem. Pres.'s Intelligence Rev. Panel, 2001—02; mem. threat reduction adv. com. Dept. Def.; co-chair adv. com. Presdl. Commn. Critical Infrastructure Protection, 1997—99; mem. Nat. Commn. Support Law Enforcement, Washington, 1995—97; commr. Nat. Commn. Terrorist Attacks Upon US (9-11 Commn.), 2002—04; bd. dirs. John D. & Catherine T. MacArthur Found., Fannie Mae Found., 1997—2005, Urban Inst., 1999—2003, Am.'s Promise-Alliance Youth, 1997—2004, Nat. Pk. Found., 1997—2004, Carnegie Endowment, 1989—93, Nat. Women's Law Ctr., 1991—93, Washington Legal Clinic Homeless; bd. overseers Harvard Coll., 1998—2004; mem. coun. Am. Law Inst., 1997—2000, DC Bar Found.; mem. selection com. Supreme Ct. Jud. Fellow, 2003—06; bd. dirs. Legal Affairs, 2004—06. Named one of Top 30 Lawyers in Washington, Washingtonian mag., 100 Most Powerful Women, 50 Most Powerful Women in Bus., Fortune mag., America's Top Businesswomen, forbes.com, 50 Smartest Women in Money Bus., Money Mag.; recipient Corp. Leadership award, DC C. of C., 2003, Aiming High award, NOW Legal Def. & Edn. Fund, 2002, Judge Learned Hand award, Am. Jewish Com., 1999, Wickersham award for exceptional pub. svc., 1998, Outstanding Advocate of the Year, Equal Justice Works, 1997. Fellow: Am. Bar Found. (Star of the Bar award 2003); mem.: ABA (vice-chair complex crimes litig. com. 1983—84, chair complex crimes litig. com. litig. sect. 1984—87, sec. litig. sect. 1988—90, coun. mem. 1990—93, mem. com. profl. discipline, ho. dels. 1991—93, 1997—, Margaret Brent award 1997), Coun. Fgn. Rels., Am. Law Inst. (couns.), Women's Bar Assn. (Lawyer of the Yr. award 1993), DC Bar (pres. 1992—93, bd. govs. 1982—88, sec. bd. govs. 1981—92, bar found. advisors 1985—93, mem. legal ethics com.). Office: WilmerHale 1875 Pennsylvania Ave NW Washington DC 20006 Office Phone: 202-663-6500. Office Fax: 202-663-6363. Business E-Mail: jamie.gorelick@wilmerhale.com.

GORELOVA, LINDA M., elementary school educator; b. East St. Louis, Ill., Sept. 29, 1957; d. Winford and Mary Ellen Morris; 1 child, Nikolai. BA, Ind. U., Bloomington, 1983; MEd, Ohio U., Athens, 1995. Cert. tchr. Ohio, 1998. Tchr. Adina Local Schs., Frankfort, Ohio, 1998—2002, Circleville City Schs., Ohio, 2002—. Interpreter Russian-English State Dept., Washington; also New Eng. newspaper assn., Boston. Recipient Hon. mention, GlimmerFrain Literary Contest. Mem.: Delta Kappa Gamma.

GOREN, JUDITH ANN, retired psychologist; b. Detroit, Apr. 5, 1933; d. Herman and Evelyn (Apple) Wise; m. Robert Goren, Dec. 20, 1953; children: Gary, Steven, Nancy. BA, Wayne State U., 1954, MEd, 1972; PhD, Union Grad. Sch., 1983. Lic. psychologist, Mich. Tchr., Detroit, 1954—57; pvt. practice Oakland County, Mich., 1971—96; tchr. Birmingham, Mich., 1970—80; ret., 1995. Author: (poetry) Coming Alive, 1975, Traveling Toward the Heart, 1994, Sharing the Journey: A Psychotherapist Reflects on her work, 2004; contbr. poetry to jours., anthologies. Personal E-mail: judithg@comcast.net.

GORENCE, PATRICIA JOSETTA, judge; b. Sheboygan, Wis., Mar. 6, 1943; d. Joseph and Antonia (Marinsheck) G.; m. John Michael Bach, July 11, 1969; children: Amy Jane, Mara Jo, J. Christopher Bach. BA, Marquette U., 1965, JD, 1977; MA, U. Wis., 1969. Bar: Wis. 1977, U.S. Dist. Ct. (ea. and we. dists.) Wis. 1977, U.S. Ct. Appeals (7th cir.) 1979, U.S. Supreme Ct. 1980. Asst. U.S. atty. U.S. Atty.'s Office, Milw., 1979-84, 1st asst. U.S. Atty., 1984-87, 89-91, U.S. Atty., 1987-88; dep. atty. gen. State of Wis. Dept. Justice, Madison, 1991-93; assoc. Ginbel, Reilly, Guerin & Brown, Milw., 1993-94; U.S. magistrate judge U.S. Dist. Ct. Wis., Milw., 1994—. Mem. judge adv. com. U.S. Magistrate, 2006—. Bd. dirs. U. Wis.-Milw. Slovenian Arts Coun., 1989—, treas., 1989—, Milw. Dance Theatre, 1993-98; bd. chair Bottomless Closet, 1999-2006. Recipient Spl. Commendation, U.S. Dept. Justice, 1986, IRS, 1988. Mem. ABA, Am. Law Inst., Nat. Assn. Women Judges, US Magistrate Judges (mem. adv. group 2006-), Fed. Magistrate Judges Assn. (cir. dir. 1997-2000), Milw. Bar Assn. (chair cmty. rels. com. 2000-03, Prosecutor of Yr. 1990, Disting. Svc. award 2003, Wis. Law Jour. Innovator of Yr. award 2003), State Bar Wis. (chair lawyer dispute resolution com. 1986—, chair professionalism com. 1988-00, vice chair legal edn. commn. 1994-96, Pres. award 1995), 7th Cir. Bar Assn. (chair rules and practices com. 1991-95), Wis. Bar Assn. (bd. dirs. ea. dist. 2004—), Assn. Women Lawyers, Profl. Dimensions (sec. 1998-00, v.p. adminstrn. 2000-02).

GORIN, SUSAN, medical association administrator; Asst. exec. dir. Coun. for Exceptional Children, 1981—93; exec. dir. Nat. Assn. Sch. Psychologists, Bethesda, Md., 1993—. Adv. bd. Ctr. on Personnel Studies in Spl. Edn. Office: Nat Assn Sch Psychologists Ste 402 4340 East West Hwy Bethesda MD 20814 Office Phone: 301-657-0270 ext. 221. Business E-Mail: sgorin@naspweb.org.

GORMAN, ANGELA SUE, dental assistant; b. Rolla, Mo., July 22, 1967; d. Gary Paul and Barbara Sue (Mooney) Hogan; m. Alan RAy Gorman, July 27, 1991; 1 child, Aaron Alan. Grad. high sch., Salem, Mo. Cert. CPR, IV, nitrous cert. Office mgr., dental asst., denture therapist Salem Dental Clinic, 1985-90; office mgr., dental asst. Dr. Ted Ziske, Salem, 1990-92; pharmacy technician Wal-Mart Pharmacy, Salem, 1993-94; lab technician Crosby Dental Lab., Springfield, Mo., 1995-96; dental asst. Cherokee Family Dentistry, Springfield, 1996—, Dr. Michael P. Glouse DDS, 1997—. Mem. Sing in Praise Team, KingsWay Christian Ch. Baptist. Avocations: roller skating, woodworking, going to gym. Home: 1505 Mary Ln Aurora MO 65605

GORMAN, GAYLA MARLENE OSBORNE, consumer affairs executive; b. Owenton, Ky., Aug. 9, 1956; d. Frederick Clay and Helen Beatrice (Mason) O. AAS, No. Ky. U., 1982, BS, 1986; cert. in Chinese Mandarin, Def. Lang. Inst., 1975. Pers. clk. Dept. Edn. State Ky., Frankfort, 1974; sec. Dept. Health, Edn., Welfare Nat. Inst. Occupational Safety Health, Cin., 1977-79; specialist sales promotion U.S. Postal Svc., Cin., 1980, coord. customer liaison, task force pub. image, account rep., 1986-87, with stamp distbn. task force, 1993—; reservation sale agt. Delta Airlines, 1987-89. Councilmember Florence City Coun., Ky. 1984-87; vol. Children's Home, Covington, 1982, 87. With USAF, 1974-76. Named to Hon. Order Ky. Cols. Mem. Disabled Am. Veterans, No. Ky. U. Alumni Assn., Nat. Assn. Postmasters U.S., Boone County Fraternal Order Police, Ky. Assn. Realtors, Nat. Bd. Realtors, Women in Mil. Svc. for Am. (charter). Clubs: Fraternal Order Police. Democrat. Baptist. Avocations: horseback riding, travel, organizing seminars. Home: 8395 Juniper Ln Florence KY 41042-9279

GORMAN, JOYCE J(OHANNA), lawyer; b. NYC, Aug. 23, 1952; d. Peter J. and Jane M. (Kelly) G. Student, Williams Coll., 1972-73; BA, Smith Coll., 1974; JD with honors, U. Md., 1977. Bar: Md. 1977, D.C. 1988. Assoc. Miles & Stockbridge, Balt., 1977-84, ptnr., 1984-87, Washington, 1987-88, Ballard, Spahr, Andrews & Ingersoll, Washington, 1988-94, Piper & Marbury, Washington, 1994-98; spl. counsel Cadwalader, Wickersham & Taft LLP, Washington, 1998—. Bd. dirs. Va. Opera, 1994-98. Mem. Md. Bar Assn. (sec. corp. banking and bus. sect. 1983-84, vice chmn. 1984-85, chmn. 1985-86), Merchants Club (Balt. bd. dirs. 1980-87). Roman Catholic. Avocations: swimming, gourmet cooking, travel. Home: 9492 Lynnhall Pl Alexandria VA 22309-3064 Office: Cadwalader Wickersham & Taft LLP Ste 1100 1201 F St NW Washington DC 20004

GORMAN, KAREN MACHMER, optometric physician; b. Poughkeepsie, N.Y., June 4, 1955; d. James Andrew and Joan (Benton) Machmer; m. D.L. McCartney III, Aug. l6, l976 (div. June l982); m. N. David Gorman, Oct. l6, l985; 1 stepchild, Danette Y. Gorman. BS in Optometry, U. Houston, 1976, OD, 1978; therapeutic pharm. lic., U. Mo., St. Louis, 1993. Diplomate Nat. Bd. Examiners Optometry; lic. optometrist, Colo., Mo., Tex. Pvt. practice, Dallas, 1978-83, 1984-85, Hurst, Tex., 1984-85, St. Joseph, Mo., 1986-2000; councilwoman, chmn. pub. safety com. City Coun., City of St. Joseph, 1997—2006, chmn. parks exec. com., 2005—06; pvt. practice Maryville, Mo., 1999—. Charter mem. optometric adv. panel Pearle, Inc., 1991-93; lectr. on eyecare to community groups; free-lance journalist St. Joseph News-Press, Benson (N.C.) Rev., jazzreview.com, Jazz Amb. mag.; with Fly-In, Washington, 2001-2005. Contbr. poetry to lit. jours. including Nat. Libr. of Poetry, Typo mag., Edge mag., articles to profl. jours. including St. Joseph News Press and Benson (N.C.) Review; lead actress (play) None Come Back Innocent, Robidoux Resident Theatre, St. Joseph, 1990, Hay Fever, 1991, The Best Man, 1992, Wedded But No Wife, 1993, Mousetrap, 1993, Diary of Anne Frank, 1994, Death and the Maiden, 1995, Veronica's Room, 1996, Plaza Suite, 1997, Dial M for Murder, 2000, The Laramie Project, 2002, The Atonement, Grace Evangelical Church, 2005, On Golden Pond, 2006 Vol. Dallas Humane Soc., 1981, YWCA Women's Abuse Shelter; patron Robidoux Resident Theatre, St. Joseph, 1988-92, Ice House Theatre, St. Joseph, Kemper Albrecht Art Mus., St. Joseph, St. Joseph Animal Shelter; patron Second Harvest Food Bank, 1998-2003; sponsor, coach, cheerleader and drill team Mo. Western State Coll., St. Joseph, 1985-86; legis. corr. Humane Soc. U.S., 1990-92; mem. Nat. Soc. Newspaper Columnists; mem. St. Joseph (Mo.) City Coun., 1997—, chmn. landfill and water pollution com., 1998-2005, parks and rec. com., 2005-, pub. safety com.; bd. dirs. Robidoux Resident Theater, 2006—. Recipient Optometric Recognition awards Pearle, Inc., 1986-90; U. Houston scholar, 1972-76 Mem.: DAR (Pony Express chpt.), Nat. Assn. Newspaper Columnists, U. Houston Alumni Assn., St. Joseph Lit. Guild, Tau Sigma. Avocations: jazz concerts, reading, writing, poetry, piano. Office: 1712 S Main Maryville MO 64468 Office Phone: 660-582-8911. E-mail: eyeDrKim@aol.com.

GORMAN, KATHLEEN JEAN, performing arts educator, choreographer; b. Mpls., Apr. 9, 1956; d. John William and Ruth Mary Gorman; m. Robert Chetwyn Glise, June 1, 1996; children: Zoe Mei Glise, Annie Li Glise. BA in Dance, Coll. of St. Teresa, Winona, Minn., 1980; MA in Dance Pedagogy, Brigham Young U., Provo, Utah, 1997. Dancer, choreographer Pasticcio Dance Ensemble, Mpls., 1981—83; dance faculty dept. theatre arts Viterbo U., LaCrosse, Wis., 1984—2000; artistic dir., tchr. dance The LaCrosse Dance Ctr., Wis., 1985—2001; artistic dir., choreographer, dancer The LaCrosse Dance Co., Wis., 1985—2001; dance faculty dept. exercise and sports sci. U. Wis., LaCrosse, 1997—, choreographer dept. theatre arts, 1998—. Choreographer numerous musicals and plays, artistic dir., choreographer Nutcracker Ballet, 1990—2000. Home: 959 Oak Timber Dr Onalaska WI 54650 Office: Univ Wis 1725 State St La Crosse WI 54601 Office Phone: 608-785-8180. E-mail: gorman.kath@uwlax.edu.

GORMAN, MARCIE SOTHERN, personal care industry executive; b. Feb. 25, 1949; d. Jerry R. and Carole Edith (Frendel) Sothern; m. N. Scott Gorman, June 14, 1969 (div.); children: Michael Stephen, Mark Jason; m. Stanley E. Althof, Jan. 24, 2004. AA, U. Fla., 1968; BS, Memphis State U., 1970. Tchr. Memphis City Sch. Sys., 1970-73; tng. dir. Weight Watchers Palm Beach County, Weight Watchers So. Ala., West Palm Beach, Fla., 1973-97; pres. Weight Watchers Franchise Assn., 1999—. Pres. Markel Enterprises, LLC (formerly Markel Ads, Inc.). Cubmaster Boy Scouts Am.; hon. lt. col. a.d.c. Ala. Militia; bd. dirs. Crossroads Program, Palm Beach C.C., 2001—, Cmtys. in Schs., West Palm Beach, 2003—. Named Woman of Distinction, March of Dimes, 2004; recipient Athena award, Nat. C. of C., 2004. Mem. NAFE, NOW, Women Am. ORT (program chmn. 1975), Weight Watchers Franchise Assn. (chair mktg. com., advt./mktg. coun., chairperson region IV bd. dirs., treas., 2d v.p. 1991, 1st v.p., region IV co-chair 1998-99, bd. dirs., nat. pres. 1999—), Exec. Women of Palm Beaches, Am. Bus. Women's Assn., Women's C. of C. (Giraffe award West Palm Beach chpt. 2004), Zonta. Office: Weight Watchers 1111 Hypoluto Rd Ste 106 Lantana FL 33462 Office Phone: 561-964-8100.

GORMAN, MARGARET NORINE, probation officer, chemical dependency counselor; b. St. Louis, Aug. 28, 1945; d. Joseph Tarkington and Mary Jo (Steil) Whitman; m. Thomas Edwin Gorman, Oct. 24, 1970; children: Mary Gorman Ray, Suzanne. BA, Ctrl. Meth. Coll., Fayette, Mo., 1967; student, Pan Am. U., Brownsville, Tex., 1985-90. Cert. alcohol and drug counselor; lic. chem. dependency counselor; cert. probation officer. Supr. Mo. Dept. Pub. Welfare, St. Louis County, 1968-71; child abuse investigator Tex. Dept. Child Welfare, Cameron County, 1974-84; adult probation officer, supr. substance abuse program Cameron County Cmty. Supervision and Corrections Dept., Brownsville, 1985—; instr. dept. continuing edn. U. Tex., Brownsville, 1999—2001. Bd. dirs. Palmer Drug Abuse Program, Brownsville, 1995-96. Mem. com. Brownsville Ind. Sch. Dist., 1994—; bd. dirs. Tip o' Tex. coun. Girl Scouts USA, Weslaco, 1980-82. Mem. AAUW. Avocation: tai chi. Office: Cameron County CSCD 854 E Harrison St Brownsville TX 78520-7121

GORMAN, MAUREEN J., lawyer; b. Rockford, Ill., Dec. 17, 1955; d. John William and Joanne Mary (Ollman) G.; m. Alan O. Sykes, 1980. BA, Coll. William and Mary, 1978; JD, Yale U., 1981. Bar: D.C. 1983, Ill. 1987. Law clk. to Hon. Warren W. Eginton U.S. Dist. Ct. Conn., 1981-82; assoc. Caplin & Drysdale, Washington, 1982-85; legis. atty. joint com. on taxation U.S. Congress, Washington, 1985-86; assoc. Mayer, Brown & Platt, Chgo., 1986-88, ptnr., 1988—. Mem. ABA (chairperson subcom. tech. corrections, employee benefits com., tax sect. 1987-91). Home: 343 E 1st St Hinsdale IL 60521-4241 Office: Mayer Brown & Platt 190 S La Salle St Ste 3100 Chicago IL 60603-3441

GORMAN, PATRICIA JANE, editor; b. Oak Ridge, Tenn., Feb. 28, 1950; d. Joseph Francis and Ruth (Kommedahl) G.; m. Adrian Thomas Higgins, Apr. 22, 1978; children: Mary Catherine, Patrick Edward. BJ, U. Mo., 1972. Feature writer, copy editor Northamptonshire Evening Telegraph, Eng., 1972-76; asst. editor Am. Tchr. newspaper Am. Fedn. Tchrs., AFL-CIO, Washington, 1976-82, editor, 1982-2000; exec. editor editl. dept. Am. Fedn. Tchrs., Washington, 2000—. Mem. delegation of labor editors to Israel, AFL-CIO, Washington, 1983 Author TV study guides for tchrs., 1979-83 Mem. Internat. Labor Communications Assn. Democrat. Roman Catholic. Office: Am Fedn Tchrs 555 New Jersey Ave NW Washington DC 20001-2029

GORMLEY, PAMELA D., controller; BBA, So. Methodist U., Dallas. With U.S. Bancorp, Portland, Oreg., 1980—93; CFO, Society Nat. Bank Keycorp, Cleveland, Ohio, 1994, CFO, Great Lakes Regional Bank; dir. fin. BankBoston, 1998—99; corp. contr. FleetBoston Fin. Corp. (BankBoston and Fleet Fin. Group merged), 1999—. Mem. Fleet's Leadership Adv. Group. Office: FleetBoston Fin Corp 100 Federal St Boston MA 02110

GORN, JANET MARIE, government official; b. Fond du Lac, Wis., Sept. 29, 1938; d. A. Reinhold Walter and Glady Lucille (Schulze) G.; m. Ronald Lee Braun, June 20, 1959 (div. Mar. 1980); children: Suzette Karen Braun Batchelder-Mitchell-Fulton, Gregory Reinhold William. BA, Drew U., 1973; MA, San Jose State U., 1982; postgrad., George Washington U., 1984-86. Policy analyst City of San Jose, Calif., 1975-76; rsch. asst. Brookings Instn., Washington, 1978; rsch. analyst Congl. Rsch. Svc., Washington, 1978-79; program analyst Nuclear Regulatory Commn., Washington, 1980-82, congl. affairs officer, 1982-87, sr. internat. rels. officer, 1988-99; sr. fgn. affairs officer U.S. Dept. of State, 1999—. Staff alt. Presdl. Task Force-State Planning Coun. Radioactive Waste Mgmt., Washington, 1980-82; mem. Internat. Atomic Energy Agy. Com. Devel. Code of Practice Internat. Transfers of Radioactive Waste, 1989-90, U.S. del. Internat. Atomic Energy Agy. Com. Control Radiation Sources and Devices, 1988-96, dep. head del., head of del., 1997—, steering com. Nuclear Energy Agy. Internat. Orgn. Econ. Cooperation and Devel., 1991—, commd. mem. solid waste mgmt. adv. com., 1992-2000, head U.S. delegation spent fuel and radioactive waste convention, 2003, 2006; councilman Quantico Civilian-Mil. Cmty. Rels. Coun., 1995—; mem. adv. coun. Internat. Policy Inst., 1993—; secretariate Internat. Nuc. Regulators Assn., 1997-99; com. mem. Sanitary Landfill Oversight Com. Prince William County, Va., 1990-92; commr. Prince William County Commn. on Future, 1989-90; sub-com. chmn. Prince William County Commn. and Libr. Planning Commn., Va., 1987-88 Author: Analysis of Low-Level Radioactive Waste Burial Site Capacity, 1981. Co-organizer, den mother, coach Pack 124 Cub Scouts Morris-Sussex Area coun. Boy Scouts Am., 1969-73; chairperson State Ad Hoc Com. to Establish Bus. Women and Adv. Bd., N.J., 1971-72; mem. Peralta Adobe Restoration Commn., San Jose, Calif., 1974-76, San Jose Bicentennial Commn., 1974-76, Mayor's Adv. Commn., Vienna, Va., 1978-79; bd. dirs. Prince William Libr. Found., 2004—, pres., 2005— Recipient commendation U.S. Nuclear Regulatory Commn. Chmn., 1990, Superior Honor award U.S. Dept. State, 2003; named Outstanding County Leader, Monmouth County, N.J., 1968, Woman of Yr., Morristown Jr. Woman's Club, N.J., 1969, West Valley Federated Woman's Club, San Jose, 1973; named to State Honor Role, N.J. Federated Woman's Clubs, 1973; acad. scholar Drew U., Madison, N.J., 1969, 70, 71, 72. Mem. AAUW (v.p. chpt. 1978-79), LWV (v.p. chpt. 1966-67, pres. 1968-69), Am. Nuclear Soc., Nuclear Women in Energy, European Nuclear Soc., Women in Energy (nat. v.p. 1984-86), Masons (Demolay club pres. 1978-79), Montclair Property Owners Assn. (bd. dirs. 2000—, pres. 2003-04) Republican. Episcopalian. Office: Nuclear Energy Safety and Security US Dept State Washington DC 20520 Business E-Mail: gornjm@state.gov.

GORNIK, KATHY, electronics executive; Co-founder & pres. THIEL Audio, 1975—. Bd. dirs. Lexington Partnership for Workforce Devel., Econs. Am.-Ky. Named Top 40 Women in Bus., The Lane Report; recipient Ky. / So. Ind. Entrepreneur of Yr., Ernst and Young, Inc. Mag. and Merrill Lynch. Mem.: Electronics Industries Alliance (bd. govs.), Consumer Electronics Assn (co-vice chair, chair 2003, bd. dirs & exec. com., former chair, Audio Div. & Specialty Audio Sub-div.), Electronic Industries Found. Achievements include being the first women, the first executive of a small manufacturing company, and the first representative of the high-end audio cmty. to serve as Chair for the Consumer Electronics Assn. bd. dirs. Avocations: reading, skiing. Office: THEIL Audio 1026 Nandino Blvd Lexington KY 40511-1207

GORON, MARA J., social studies educator, assistant principal; b. Jackson Heights, N.Y., Apr. 9, 1968; d. Stuart Platt and Joan (Arkin) Scolnick. BA, The George Washington U., 1990, MA, 1992; MEd, U. Md., 1995. Cert. secondary social studies and spl. edn. adminstrn. Resident asst., adminstr., supr. The George Washington U., Washington, 1989-92; tchr. religion Temple Sinai, Washington, 1990-96; peer tutoring coord. The George Washington U., 1991-92; adult edn. tchr. Montgomery County Pub., Rockville, Md., 1992; spl. edn. tchr. Alexandria (Va.) Pub. Schs., 1992, Prince Georges Pub. Schs., Upper Marlboro, Md., 1992-93; tutor Lab Sch. Washington, 1992—2002; spl. edn. tchr. Howard County Pub. Schs., Ellicott City, Md., 1993-96, social studies tchr., 1996-99; asst. prin. Centennial H.S., Ellicott City, 1999—2001; inaugural asst. prin. Reservoir H.S., 2001—02; asst. prin. Spanish River Cmty. H.S., Boca Raton, Fla., 2002—. Adviser Howard County Assn. Student Couns., 1997—99; pres. Howard County Coun. for Social Studies, 1997—99; adj. prof. Towson U., 1998, 99, Palm Beach C.C. Troop leader Girl Scouts of Am., 1994-95. Mem. ASCD, Nat. Assn. Secondary Sch. Prins., Pi Kappa Phi, Omicron Delta Kappa. Avocations: walking, hiking, knitting, reading, scrapbooks. E-mail: goronm@palmbeach.k12.fl.us.

GORRELL, NANCY S., English language educator; b. NYC, Mar. 6, 1946; d. Robert Morris Schwartz and Lillian Moskowitz; m. Joseph Gorrell, June 18, 1967; children: Sara Kate, Elizabeth Marie. BA summa cum laude, SUNY, Stony Brook, 1968, MA, 1970. Tchr. Harbor Country Day Sch., St. James, N.Y., 1970-72; English tchr. Morristown (N.J.) High Sch., 1972—. Tchr. summer training inst. Lincoln Ctr. Inst. for Arts in Edn. at Julliard, N.Y.C., 1983—; dir. Seeking Edn. Equity and Diversity, 1993—; project dir. Poem Pals Project, 1989—; active Geraldine R. Dodge Found. Poetry Coun., 1991. Contbr. articles to profl. jours. V.p. Temple Sholom, Bridgewater, N.J. A+ for Kids Tchr. Network grantee Sta. WWOR-TV, 1989, Dodge Found. Summer Opportunity grantee, 1991; recipient Innovative Teaching award Bus. Week Mag., 1990; named N.J. State Tchr. Yr., 1992, Educator of Yr. award NJ Coun. of Tchr. of Eng., 2001; named one of Tchr. Tribute Honorees Morris Ednl. Found., 2005. Mem. Nat. Coun. Tchrs. English (mem. English tchrs.

and sch. pub. com., state judge English lit. mag. ranking competition), Internat. Women's Writers Guild, Nat. Coun. Jewish Women. Office: Morristown High Sch 50 Early St Morristown NJ 07960-3898

GORTON-HORAN, ANN HILBERT, vice principal; b. N.Y.C., Mar. 30, 1937; d. Clarence Webb and Irene Madden Hilbert; children: Gwynne Gorton Zisko, Melissa Gorton Sadin, Lara Leigh Groton. BS in Elem. Edn., SUNY, 1959; MA in devel. reading, Coll. NJ, 1986. Cert. K-8 elem. sch. tchr., NJ tchr. of reading, reading specialist. Tchr. Mamaroneck Sch. Dist., NY, 1959—61, Bridgewater-Raritan Sch. Dist., NJ, 1961—63, Hillsborough Township Sch. Dist., NJ, 1965—76, Branchburg Twp. Sch. Dist., NJ, 1977—98; asst. prin. Whiton Sch., 1998—. Contbr. articles various profl. jours. Mem., v.p. BOE, Hillsborough Twp., NJ, 1972—89. Named Citizen of Yr., Rotary Club, 1974, Media Ctr. named after Ann Hilbert Gorton-Horan, Hillsboroughť BOE, 1990, Tchr. of Yr., Branchburg Twp. Sch. Dist., 1985, Reading Tchr. of Yr., NJRA Mary Filosa award, 1990. Mem.: Reading Recovery Coun. of N. Am., NJ Prin./Suprv. Assn., Assn. for Suprv. of Curriculum Devel., Nat. Coun. of Tchrs. of English, Ctrl. NJ Reading Coun., NJ Reading Assn., Internat. Reading Assn., Delta Kappa Gamma, Kappa Delta Phi. Avocations: knitting, crewel, reading, travel. Home: 10 Fairmont Ave Somerville NJ 08876 Office Phone: 908-371-0842. Office Fax: 908-369-1582. E-mail: aghoran@aol.com.

GORZKA, MARGARET ROSE, retired elementary school educator; b. Akron, Ohio, Sept. 2, 1945; d. Alfonso Sebastian and Hannah Jean (Morris) Brown; m. Joseph Frank Gorzka Sr., Nov. 24, 1966; children: Joseph Frank Jr., Julie-Anne. BS in Elem. Edn., Akron U., 1968; MS in Elem. Edn., Nazareth Coll., 1986. Permanent cert. N-6. Tchr. 1st grade # 3 Sch. Rochester (N.Y.) City Schs., 1967-68, St. John the Evangelist, Rochester, 1968-70, Mother of Sorrows, Rochester, 1971-72; tchr. kindergarten St. John's Sch., Spencerport, N.Y., spring 1978; tchr. 1st, 2d, 3d grades St. Rita's, West Webster, N.Y., 1978-79; tchr. 1st grade St. Anne's, Rochester, 1979-81, St. Jerome's, East Rochester, N.Y., 1981-86; tchr. kindergarten, 1st grade East Rochester Union Free Schs., East Rochester, 1986-91; tchr. 1st grade Fairport (N.Y.) Ctrl. Schs., 1991—2001, kindergarten tchr., 2001—04; ret., 2004. Geselle trainer East Rochester Union Free Schs., 1987—, essential elements of effective instrn. trainer, 1987-91, clin. supervision trainer, 1987-91; cons. and presenter in field. Mem. fundraising com. Advent House, Fairport, 1993—; PTA chair for Parent Edn., 1995-96; mem. staff devel. Fairport Cen. Sch. Dist., 1996-2002; mem. policy bd. Fairport Tch. Ctr., 1999—; chair Daffodil Day, 1994—; vol. Prince William Hosp., Glenkirk Elem. Sch.; mem. fund raising com. Noesville Vol. Fire Dept. Grantee Sci. Wizards at Work, 1994; recipient Disting. Svc. award East Rochester PTA, 1986, Crystal Apple award, 1995, PASE award, 1995, 98, Team Performance Recognition award for Fairport Cen. Sch. dist., 1993-94, Phoebe Apperson Hearst Outstanding Edn. Excellence award 1996. Mem. AAUW, N.Y. State United Tchrs., Fairport Edn. Assn., Prince William Hosp. Auxilliary, Phi Mu Alumnae (v.p. 1970s). Republican. Roman Catholic. Home: 6801 Tred Avon Pl Gainesville VA 20155 Personal E-mail: jgorzkasr@comcast.net.

GOSCHKE, LINDA FRY, artist; b. Ridley Park, Pa., July 17, 1957; d. Dale Eugene Fry and Annie Josephine Rhoades; m. John Phillip Goschke, Apr. 7, 1990. BFA in Painting with Distinction, Pa. State U., 1979; MA, Phila. Coll. Art, 1985; tchg. cert., Temple U., 1988; MFA, Pa. Acad. Fine Arts, 2002. Art instr. Camden County Coll., Blackwood, NJ, Holy Family Coll., Phila., Cabrini Coll., Radnor, Pa., Berkeley Edn. and Tng. Ctr., Bala Cynwyd, Pa., Del. County CC, Media, Pa., 1985—2000; comml. printing instr. Eastern Montgomery County Vocat.-Tech. Sch., Willow Grove, Pa., 1986—91; asst. curator Pa. Acad. of Fine Arts Studio Sch. Gallery, Phila., 2001; internship Greater Phila. Cultural Alliance, 2001. Artist, designer Barbara Kates Designs, Bala Cynwyd, 1980—90, 1993—94, NDI Engrng. Co., Pennsauken, NJ, 1981—86, Cornerstone Media, Ambler, Pa., 1998, Enterprise Mktg. & Comm., Cherry Hill, NJ, 1999—; set designer, prodn. designer Hatboro-Horsham HS, Pa., 1989—; rostered artist Pa. Coun. on the Arts, Arts-in-Edn. Artist-in-Residence Program, Harrisburg, 1991—. One-woman shows include Springfield Pub. Libr., Pa., 1979, Benjamin Rush Gallery at Unitarian Universalist House, Phila., 1996, touring exhbn., People's Republic of China, 1986—87, exhibitions include Ctrl. Pa. Festival Arts, HUB Gallery, 1979, University Park, 2001, CAC, Wallingford, Pa., 1980, 1981 (First prize Pastel, 1980, 1981), Terrance Gallery, Palenville, NY, 1981, Rittenhouse Sq. Fine Arts Ann., Phila., 1981, The Print Club, 1981, 1982, Provident Nat. bank, 1982, Glassboro State Coll., 1991, Allied Artists Winston-Salem, NC, 1992, Woodmere Art Mus., Phila., 1994, Main Line Arts Ctr., Haverford, Pa., 1994, Printmaking Coun. NJ, Somerville, 1996, 1997, 1998 (Johnson & Johnson Purchase prize), Camden County Coll. Art Gallery, 1998, 1999, Pa. Acad. Fine Arts, 2000—02, Mus. Am. Art, Pa. Acad. Fine Arts, Phila., 2002, West Chester Arts Walk, 2004, Jenkins Arboretum Greenhouse Gallery, Devon, Pa., 2005, numerous others. Recipient Images '97 Hon. Mention, Ctrl. Pa. Festival of Arts, 1997, Second prize, Photography, Best of Pa. Artists & Artisans, 2005, First prize, ArtAbility, 2006. Mem.: Nat. Assn. Photoshop Profls. Avocations: travel, sewing, nature. Home: 169 W Abbottsford Ave Philadelphia PA 19144 Office Phone: 215-848-2014. Personal E-mail: lafrites@aol.com.

GOSFIELD, MARGARET, secondary school educator, school system administrator, consultant, editor; b. Marshall County, Minn., Mar. 9, 1942; d. William Jay and Evelyn Pearl (Anderson) Wayne; m. Amor Gosfield, Aug. 21, 1964. BA in History, U. Calif., Santa Barbara, 1966, secondary tchrs. credential, 1968, MA in Edn., 1976. Cert. tchr. Calif. Tchr. Ventura (Calif.) Unified Sch. Dist., 1969-89, coord. gifted and talented edn. program, 1982-97; cons. gifted edn. Author: (book) History of the Anderson Family, 1981, History of the Wayne Family, 1983; editor: Meeting the Challenge: A Guidebook for Teaching Gifted Students, 1996, Gifted Edn. Communicator, 1998—. Named Calif. Outstanding Educator, Johns Hopkins U., 1994; recipient Ednl. Achievement award, Phi Delta Kappa, 1997. Mem.: Calif. Assn. for the Gifted (regional rep. 1990—94, v.p. 1994—96, pres. 1996—98, Tchr. of the Yr. 1985), Santa Barbara Mus. Art. Avocations: travel, writing, gardening. Home: 3136 Calle Mariposa Santa Barbara CA 93105-2775 Office: 1215 K St Ste 940 Sacramento CA 95814 Office Phone: 916-441-3999. Personal E-mail: gosfield@cox.net.

GOSNELL, NANCI LITTLE, information technology executive, nurse; BS in Nursing, Old Dominion Univ., Norfolk, Va., 1978; MBA, Marymount Univ., Arlington, Va. Staff nurse, emergency dept. and operating room Sibley Mem. Hosp., Washington; mgr., clin. applications Inova Health Sys., Falls Church, Va., 1990—99, asst. v.p., info. svc., 1999—2002, and interim chief info. officer, 2000—02, v.p., info. svc. & chief info. officer, 2002—. Adj. prof. George mason Univ. Mem.: Coll. of Healthcare Info. Mgmt. Executives. Office: VP & CIO Inova Health Sys Ste 200 2990 Telestar Ct Falls Church VA 22042

GOSPODAREK, ANGELA M, science educator; b. Oshkosh, Wis., May 14, 1974; d. Michael and Luanne Gospodarek; m. J. Nathan Henderson, June 26, 1999; children: Reed Henderson, Graham Henderson. BS in Marine Biology, U. NC, Wilmington, 1996; MS in Ecology and Evolutionary Biology, U. Conn., Storrs, 1998. Mem. field team Environ. Monitoring and Assessment Program, Wilmington, NC, 1995; mem. rsch. team U. Conn. Harbor Br. Oceanog. Inst., Barbados, 1997; grad. rsch. asst. U. Conn., Storrs, 1996—98; 8th grade sci. tchr. Greenfield Mid. Sch., Greenfield, Mass., 1998—99; marine biologist Fla. Fish and Wildlife Rsch. Inst., St. Petersburg, 1999—2000, biol. scientist ii, 2000—02; 7th grade sci. tchr. Iber Holmes Gove Mid. Sch., Raymond, NH, 2003—. Grade level leader Iber Holmes Gove Mid. Sch., Raymond, NH, 2004—, computer workshop instr., 2005—, soccer coach, 2004—. Recipient Mem., Pi Kappa Phi Nat. Honor Soc., 1994—96, Phi Sigma Pi Coll. Honor Soc., 1993—96, Chancellor's Achievement award, U. NC at Wilmington, 1993, 1994; grant, Hudson River National Estuarine Research Reserve and National Oceanographic and Atmospheric Assn. Mem.: NSTA. Office: Iber Holmes Gove Mid Sch 1 Stephen Batchelder Parkway Raymond NH 03077 Office Phone: 603-895-3394. Business E-Mail: agospodarek@raymond.k12.nh.us.

GOSS, GEORGIA BULMAN, freelance/self-employed translator; b. NYC, Dec. 1, 1939; d. James Cornelius and Marian Bright (McLaughlin) Bulman; m. Douglas Keith Goss, Dec. 21, 1957; children: Kristin Anne, David. BA, U. Mich., 1961. Libr. High Altitude Obs., Boulder, Colo., 1963-64, U.S. Bur. Stds., Boulder, Colo., 1964-65, cons. editor Spanish lang. pilot's tng. manual, 1981-82; freelance translator, 1982—. Mem. U. Mich. Alumni Assn., Phi Sigma Iota. Republican. Episcopalian. Home: 9 Dayton Cir Fredericksburg VA 22406-7486

GOSS, MARTHA CLARK, consulting company executive; b. Glen Ridge, NJ, May 31, 1949; d. David Ormiston and Marion Jane (Drury) Clark; m. Richard Keith Dentel, Dec. 29, 1972 (dec. Feb. 1974); m. Joseph Coyle Briley, Mar. 25, 1978 (div. May 1993); children: Christopher Briley, Alexis Briley; m. David Charles Goss, June 18, 1994. AB, Brown U., 1971; MBA, Harvard U., 1978. CLU, ChFC. Trainee, credit analyst Chase Manhattan Bank, NYC, 1972-74, asst. treas., 1974-76, 2d v.p., 1976, v.p., team leader, 1978-81; v.p. corp. fin. Prudential Ins. Co. Am., Newark, 1981-83, v.p., treas., 1983-88; pres., CEO Prudential Power Funding Assn., Newark, 1989-92; pres. Prudential Asset Mgmt. Co., Newark, 1992-94; sr. v.p., enterprise integrated control officer Prudential Ins. Co. Am., Newark, 1994-95; v.p., CFO Booz Allen and Hamilton Inc., Parsippany, NJ, 1995-99; ptnr., CFO, The Capital Market Co., NYC, 1999-2001, Blaqwell, Inc., NYC, 2001—; COO, CFO Amwell Holdings/Hopewell Holdings LLC. Bd. dirs. Foster Wheeler Corp., Clinton, NJ, Am. Water; mem. met. regional bd. Chase Manhattan Bank, NYC, 1997-2002. Active Women's Campaign Fund, Washington, 1989—; trustee Ind. Coll. Fund NJ, 1984-96; trustee, treas. Brown U., 1987-98; trustee Stuart Country Day Sch. of Sacred Heart, 1989-95; bd. dir. Fin. Women's Assn. Co-recipient (with Lady Margaret Thatcher) Independent Man award, Brown U., 1996. Mem. Fin. Women's Assn. (pres.-elect 2005), Com. of 200. Republican. Presbyterian. Avocations: skiing, travel, gardening, wine collection.*

GOSS, MARY E. WEBER, sociology educator; b. Chgo., May 8, 1926; m. Albert E. Goss, 1945; 1 son, Charles. BA in Sociology with distinction (Univ. Merit scholar 1946-47, Chi Omega Sociology prize 1947), U. Iowa, 1947, MA, 1948; PhD (Gilder fellow 1951-52), Columbia U., 1959. Rsch. asst. U. Iowa, 1947-48, Amherst Coll., 1949; instr. Smith Coll., 1949-50, U. Mass., 1950-51, 55-56, adj. mem. grad. faculty, 1961-66; rsch. assoc. Bur. Applied Social Rsch., Columbia U., 1952-53; cons. sociology, mem. rsch. staff, rsch. coord. N.Y. Hosp.-Cornell U. Med. Center, N.Y.C., 1957-66; mem. faculty dept. medicine Cornell U. Med. Coll., 1959-72, prof. sociology in pub. health, 1973-92, prof. emerita, 1992—. Author: Physicians in Bureaucracy, 1980; also numerous articles; editor: Jour. Health and Social Behavior, 1976-78; co-editor: Comprehensive Medical Care and Teaching: A Report on the N.Y. Hospital-Cornell Medical Center Program, 1967; mem. editorial bd. profl. jours. Fellow APHA, N.Y. Acad. Medicine; mem. AAAS, AAUP, Am. Sociol. Assn., Assn. Tchrs. Preventive Medicine, Acad. Health, Internat. Sociol. Assn., Ea. Sociol. Soc., Phi Beta Kappa, Sigma Xi. Home: 25 Hillcrest Drive Piscataway NJ 08854

GOSSETT, BARBARA JEAN, voice educator; b. Chgo., Jan. 28, 1955; d. Vernon Arthur and Lois Virginia Haggenjos; m. George Robson Gossett, Dec. 28, 1974. BFA, Monmouth Coll., Ill., 1979. Cert. K-12 music Ill., 1979, elem. edn. Ill., 1984. K-12 vocal music instr. Yorkwood Cmty. Unit Sch. Dist. #225, Monmouth, 1979—. Pvt. piano tchr., Roseville, Ill., 1980—. Dir. children's music Faith United Presbyn. Ch., Monmouth, Ill., 1988—, clk. session, 2000—03, organist, 2001—. Mem.: Am. Guild Organists (sec. 2005—06), Am. Legion Aux. R-Liberal. Presbyterian. Avocations: synthesizer, arranging music, singing, gardening, piano, organ. Office: Yorkwood CUSD #225 2140 State Hwy 135 Monmouth IL 61462 Office Phone: 309-734-8511. Business E-Mail: bgossett@roe27.k12.il.us.

GOSSETT, JANINE LEE, middle school educator; b. Carlsbad, N.Mex., Jan. 22, 1950; d. William Adair and Anita Jeanne (Hilty) G. BS, N.Mex. State U., 1974, MA, 1992. Tchr., dir. Sunshine Sch., Parker, Ariz.; tchr. spl. edn. Lubbock (Tex.) State Sch.; tchr. regular and accelerated lang. arts Carlsbad Mcpl. Schs.; tchr. 7th & 8th gr. advanced ednl. placement Carlsbad Mcp. Schs.; ret., 2005. Mem. Nat. Coun. Tchrs. English, Nat. Mid. Sch. Assn., N.Mex. Coun. Tchrs. English (past treas., directory/membership chair). Personal E-mail: ninigo98@hotmail.com.

GOSSETT, LINDA KELLEY, retired secondary school educator; b. Maysville, Ky. d. Harvey Early and Nancy Kelley; m. Robert Lebus Gossett, June 3, 1968; children: Robert Kelley, Richard Lebus. BS, Morehead State U., 1966, MA, 1969. Bus. tchr. Harrison County H.S., Cynthiana, Ky., 1966—67, Ripley-Union-Lewis H.S., Ripley, Ky., 1967—75, Fleming County H.S., Flemingsburg, Ky., 1975—2004, dept. head, 1987—2003; founder Panther Bank, Flemingsburg, 1996; ret., 2004. Dept. head Fleming County H.S., 1987—, adv., 2000—; tax prep. Kelley Tax Svc., Flemingsburg, 1998—. Adv. FBLA, 1999—2004. Mem.: NEA, Fleming County Retired Tchrs. Assn. (sec.), Ky. Retired Tchrs. Assn., Ky. Edn. Assn. Retired. Avocations: reading, travel, golf tournaments. Office: Kelley Tax Service 113 W Water Flemingsburg KY 41041

GOTBAUM, BETSY, municipal official; b. NYC; m. Victor Gotbaum; 1 child. Student, Barnard Coll.; BA, George Washington U., 1961; MEd, Columbia U., 1968. English instr. Brazil; asst. edn. City NY; exec. dir. NYC Police Found., 1977-82, Nat. Alliance Against Violence, 1982-86; assoc. Prospect Group, 1986-90; commr. NYC Parks & Recreation, 1990-94; pres. NY Hist. Soc., 1994—2001; public advocate NYC, 2001—. Office: 1 Centre St 15th Fl New York NY 10007*

GOTHART, PAMELA CAMPBELL, history educator; b. Huntsville, Ala., June 10, 1960; d. William Hence and Joyce Mary Ann Campbell; m. Ronald Wayne Gothart, Jan. 9, 1982; children: Christopher, Christa. BS in Social Sci., Athens State U., Ala., 1995. Tchr. Madison County Schs., Huntsville, Ala., 1995—2002; staff devel. coord. Tchg. Am. History Madison County Schs., 2002—05, project dir., 2005—. Prin.'s adv. bd. Early Works Mus., Huntsville, Ala., 2003—; edn. cons. Veteran's Meml. Mus. Founding mem. Hellfighters Motor Cycle Ministry, Huntsville, Ala., 2005. Grantee, U.S. Dept. Edn., 2002, 2005, Gilder Lehrman Inst. of Am. History, 2003. Mem.: Ala. Coun. Social Studies (bd. mem. 2004—). Avocation: motorcycling. Home: 124 Naugher Rd Huntsville AL 35811 Office: Madison County Schs 1275 E Jordan Rd Huntsville AL 35811 Office Phone: 256-837-0331.

GOTLIEB, DOROTHY A., deputy commissioner of education; b. Cambridge, Eng., July 31, 1944; arrived in U.S., 1949; d. Walter and Esther Calire (Genauer) Felsenburg; m. Jerome Mark Felsenburg Gotlieb, June 19, 1965; children: Adam B., Rachel B., Joshua J. BA, U. Calif.-Berkeley, 1965. Ombudsman, sch. improvement, accountability liaison Denver Pub. Schs., Colo., 1983—; dir., Office of Profl. Svcs. and Educator Licensing Colo. Dept. Edn., Denver, dep. commr., 2005—. Contbr. articles to profl. jours. Chmn. com. decelerating resources Rocky Mountain Sch. Study Coun., Denver, 1979—81; trustee Colo. Honor Band Assn., Denver, 1979—; v.p. Ctrl. Agy. Jewish Edn., Denver, 1980—84; vice chmn. Coloradans in Action for Drug Free Youth, Denver, 1982; dir. at large Nat. Assn. State Bds. Edn., Alexandria, Va., 1983—85; mem., chmn. Colo. State Bd. Edn., Denver, 1979—85; western area dir. Nat. Assn. State Bds. Edn. Recipient Legis. award, Colo. Assn. Guidance Counseling, 1983, In Appreciation of Svc. award, Colo. State Bd. Edn., 1983, 1985. Mem.: Colo. Commn. Higher Edn., First Cong. Dist. Rep. Adv. Com., Sigma Tau Sigma, Delta Kappa Gamma. Jewish. Office: CDE 201 East Colfax Ave Denver CO 80203

GOTLIEB, JAQUELIN SMITH, pediatrician; b. Washington, Oct. 20, 1946; d. Turner Taliaferro and Lois Barbara (Fisk) Smith; m. Edward Marvin Gotlieb, June 25, 1970; children: Sarah Ruth, Aaron Franklin, David Jacob. BS in Zoology, Duke U., 1968; MD, Med. Coll. Va., 1972. Diplomate Am. Bd. Pediat. Rotating intern Med. Coll. Va. Hosps.-Va. Commonwealth U., Richmond, 1972—73, resident in pediat., 1973—74; pvt. practice Richmond, 1974—75, Stone Mountain, Ga., 1976—86, 1987—; resident in pediat. U. Colo., Denver, 1975—76; med. dir., cons. CIGNA Healthplan Ga., Atlanta, 1986—87. Sch. physician Richmond City Schs., 1974-75. Bd. dirs. Ga. Health Found., Atlanta, 1985-95, 2005-, vice chmn., 1995-99, chmn., 1999-2005.2005 Recipient Tee Rae Dismukes award, 2003. Fellow Am. Acad. Pediat. (Ga. chpt. bd. dirs. 1996-99, coord. state chpt. pediat. rsch. in office settings, 1996—, mem. steering com., 2005—); mem. Med. Assn. Ga., Ga. Perinatal Assn. (bd. dirs. 1994-2002, pres. 1999-2000), DeKalb Med. Soc. (chmn. com. 1976). Office: Pediatric Ctr 5405 Memorial Dr Ste D Stone Mountain GA 30083-3236 Office Phone: 404-296-3800. Personal E-mail: jackiegotlieb@earthlink.net.

GOTO, MIDORI, classical violinist; b. Osaka, Japan, Oct. 25, 1971; Attended, Juilliard Sch. Music; grad., Profl. Childrens Sch., 1990; BA in Psychology and Gender Studies, NYU, 2000. Performer worldwide, 1982—; founder Midori and Friends, 1992; faculty Manhattan Sch. Music, 2001—. Recordings on Philips, Sony Classical, Columbia Masterworks; performed with N.Y. Philharmonic Orch., Boston Symphony Orch.; worldwide performances include Berlin, Chgo., Cleve., Phila., Montreal, London; recordings include Encore, Live at Carnegie Hall; recordings (albums) Paganini: 24 Caprices, 1989, Encore!, 1992, Midori's 20th Anniversary CD, 2001. Named Best Artist of Yr. by Japanese Govt., 1988; recipient Dorothy B. Chandler Performing Arts award, L.A. Music Ctr., 1989, Crystal award Ashani Shimbun Newspaper contbn. arts, Suntory award, 1994. Office: Midori And Friends 352 7th Ave Rm 201 New York NY 10001-5012

GOTO, TOSHIKO, retired art educator; b. San Pedro, Calif., Aug. 19, 1929; d. Kimitaro and Tora Yasui Goto. AA, L.A. Harbor Jr. Coll., Wilmington, Calif., 1952; BA, Calif. State U., Long Beach, 1954; MA, Calif. State Coll., Long Beach, 1956; postgrad., Sch. Pond Farm Pottery, Guerneville, Calif., 1959, postgrad., 1960, postgrad., 1961. Tchr. Long Beach Unified Jefferson, 1961—64; art tchr. Long Beach Unified Jordan HS, 1964—79, Long Beach Unified Milliken HS, 1979—89; part-time art edn. tchr. Long Beach State Coll., 1960—64; part-time pottery tchr. Chapman Coll., Orange, Calif., 1964—73, Long Beach C.C., 1976—2005; ret., 2005. Pres. Art Tchrs. Assn. Long Beach, 1964—76; mem., corr. sec. Calif. Art Educators Assn., L.A., 1964—76. Exhibitions include Chapman Coll., Long Beach C.C., Fullerton Art Mus., 2002, Calif. State U., San Bernardino, 2002. Active Higashi Hongan Buddhist Ch., L.A. Scholar, Ebell Club, 1953—54, Space Workshop, 1966. Mem.: NEA, Calif. Ret. Tchrs. Assn., Calif. Tchrs. Assn. Avocations: woodblock printing, writing Haiku, jewelry making. Home: 1431 Fifth Ave Redlands CA 92374

GOTSHALL, JAN DOYLE, financial planner; d. Edward Albert and Rose M. (Leahy) Doyle; m. Ralph M. Gotshall Jr.; children: Rosemarie, Annmarie, Elizabeth Marie. AA, Neuman Coll., 1979; MSM, Am. Coll., Bryn Mawr, 1997. CFP; registered investment advisor. Co-founder Radnor Planning Assocs., Devon, Pa., 1979-82; fin. cons. Exeter Fin. Svcs. Co., Devon, 1982-85; owner, pres. GM Fin. Planners, Inc., Devon, 1985—. Minority-majority insp. Del. County Electorate, Broomall, Pa., 1973-83; mem. fin. bd. St. Pius X Ch., Broomall, 1988, 2002—; Archbishop Prendergast H. Sch., Drexel Hill, 2003-. Mem. Inst. CFP (CFP, pres. 1986-87, chmn. 1987-89), Internat. Assn. Fin. Planners (v.p. 1980-88, pres. 1991-92, chmn. 1992-93), Nat. Assn. Ins. Women (cert. profl. ins. woman 1985, bd. dirs. local chpt. 1980-82), Del County Estate Planning Coun. (exec. com. 1989-90, 96—, v.p. 1991-94, pres. 1994-96, dir. 1996-98). Republican. Avocations: reading, golf, tennis. Office: GM Fin Planners Inc 49 Chestnut Rd Paoli PA 19301-1502 Office Phone: 610-644-0101.

GOTT, PATRICIA A., literature educator; b. Superior, Wis., Dec. 10, 1966; d. George and Dorothy M. Gott. BA, U. Minn., Mpls., 1989; MA, U. Mo., Columbia, 1992; PhD, So. Ill. U., Carbondale, 2000. Asst. prof. English Dakota Wesleyan U., Mitchell, SD, 2001—02, U. Wis., Stevens Point, 2002—. Contbr. articles to profl. jours. Advisor Women's Resource Ctr., Stevens Point, 2004—06. Mem.: Phi Kappa Phi, Sigma Tau Delta. Office: Univ Wis-Stevens Point 426 Collins Classroom Center Stevens Point WI 00481 Office Phone: 715-346-4347. Business E-Mail: pgott@uwsp.edu.

GOTTESMAN, SUSAN, federal agency administrator; BA magna cum laude, Radcliffe Coll., 1967; PhD, Harvard U., 1972. Postdoctoral fellow, lab. molecular biology Nat. Cancer Inst., NIH, Bethesda, Md., 1971—74, rsch. chemist, sr. investigator, lab. molecular biology, 1976—85, acting chief, biochemical genetics sect., lab. molecular biology, 1985—86, chief, biochemical genetics sect., lab. molecular biology, 1987—; rsch. assoc., dept. biology MIT, 1974—76. Mem., Risk Assessment Subcommittee, Phage Working Group, Human Gene Therapy Working Group, chmn., RAC Working on major revisions of the guildlines NIH Recombinant DNA Molecular Program Advisory Committee (RAC), 1978—87; chair Gordon conf. on biol. regulatory mechanisms, 1986; mem. EPA Biotechnology Sci. Adv. Com., 1987—89, chair, subcommittee on premanufacture notification, 1995; mem. NIH ORS adv. com., 1986—89; bd. scientific advisors Jane Coffin Childs Meml. Fund for Med. Rsch., 1988—96; NSF adv. panel for Prokaryotic Genetics, 1988—89; co-organizer Cold Spring Harbor Mtg. on Molecular Genetics of Bacteria and Phage, 1991—95; AdHoc mem. NIH Microbial Physiology and Genetics Study Sect., 1994; mem. rsch. scholars adv. program panel com. Howard Hughes Med. Inst., 1989—92, mem., rsch. tng. fellowships med. students review com., 1995—97; chair, Found. Advanced Edn. Sciences John Hopkins U. Cooperative PhD program com., 1994—; mem. Fogarty Internat. Ctr. Scholars Adv. Panel, 1990—94, chair, 1992—94. Contbr. articles to profl. jours.; mem. editl. bd. Jour. Bacteriology, 1987—89, assoc. editor, 1989—99, mem. editl. bd. Genes & Develop., 1992—. Nat. Merit Scholar, 1963, NSF postdoctoral fellow, 1969, Jane Coffin Childs Meml. fund for med. postdoctoral fellow, 1971. Mem.: Am. Soc. for Biochemistry and Molecular Biology (coun. mem. 1992—95), AAAS (coun. mem. 1992—95), Am. Soc. Microbiology (chmn. divsn. genetics and molecular biology 1985—86, divsn. group rep. 1988—90, chair ethical practices com. 1991—97), Genetics Soc. Am., Am. Acad. Microbiology, NAS (councilor 2006—). Office: Lab Molecular Biology Nat Cancer Inst NIH Bldg 37 Rm 2E18 37 Convent Dr MSC 4255 Bethesda MD 20892-4255 Office Phone: 301-496-3524. Office Fax: 301-496-3875. Business E-Mail: susang@helix.nih.gov.*

GOTTFRIED, ROSALIND B., humanities educator; children: Rachel J., Kara A. PhD, Brandeis U., Waltham, Mass., 1981. Faculty Albuquerque TVI, 1988—96; instr. Delta Coll., Stockton, Calif. Office: Delta College 5151 Pacific Ave Stockton CA 95207 Office Phone: 209-954-5735. Personal E-mail: rosalindgottfried@sbcglobal.net. Business E-Mail: rgottfried@deltacollege.edu.

GOTTHARDT, MARY JANE, religious studies educator; b. Davenport, Iowa, Sept. 22, 1940; d. Harry Claus and Roseanne (Beulah May) Stoltenberg; m. Lawrence John Gotthardt, July 8, 1967; children: Michael John, Paula Formold. BA, DeLourdes Coll., 1987; MAT, Nat. Louis U., 1999. RN Ill. Nurse Resurrection Hosp., Chgo., 1960—70; chmn. pub. rels. Mark Hopkins Sch., Elk Grove, Ill., 1975—78, Transfiguration Night Train, Wauconda, Ill., 1980; tchr. religious edn. Transfiguration Sch., Wauconda, 1979—2002, tchr. and libr. aid, 1979—2000, tchr., 2000—; tchr. religious edn. St. Peter Ch., Volo, Ill., 1998—2002, dir. religious edn., 2000—. Co-owner Mannheim Rental Equipment, Franklin Pk., Ill., 1968—. Sec. Homeowner's Assn., Wauconda. Mem.: AAAS, Nat. Mid. Sch. Assn., Pope John Paul II Cultural Ctr., Smithsonian Inst., Gallop Poll, Hist. Ill. Preservation Soc., Phi Delta Kappa. Roman Catholic. Avocation: travel. Office: Transfiguration Sch 316 W Mill St Wauconda IL 60084

GOTTI, VICTORIA, columnist, writer, actress; b. Bklyn., Nov. 27, 1962; d. John J. and Victoria (DiGiorgio) Gotti; m. Carmine Agnello, 1984 (div. Feb. 2002); children: John Gotti Agnello, Carmine Gotti Agnello, Frank Gotti Agnello. BA, St. John's U. Weekly features columnist NY Post; entertainment corr. EXTRA!, 2002; columnist Star mag., exec. editor-at-large; editor-in-chief Red Carpet mag. Actress & exec. prodr. (reality TV series) Growing Up Gotti, A & E, 2004—05; author: Women & Mitral Valve Prolapse: A Comprehensive Guide to Living & Coping With MVP & Its Symptoms, 1995, The Senator's Daughter, 1997 (Mystery of Yr., Mystery Writers Assn.), I'll Be Watching You, 1998, Superstar, 2000, The Fifth Avenue Club, The Loyal Son, Hot Italian Dish: The Victoria Gotti Cookbook, 2006; actor: (plays) We're Still Hot, 2005. Named Woman of Yr., Nat. Chpt. Am. Heart Assn., Writer of Yr., Women's Writer's Guild, Woman of Yr., Women's Coalition for Equal Rights; recipient Outstanding Humanitarian, St. Frances Guild Inc. Mailing: c/o Theatre at St Luke's 308 West 46 St New York NY 10019

GOTTLIEB, ALICE B., dermatologist; PhD in Immunology, Rockefeller U., 1979; MD, Cornell U., 1980. Diplomate Am. Bd. Dermatology, bd. cert. rheumatology and internal medicine. Fellow in rheumatology Cornell U. Hosp. for Spl. Surgery, N.Y.C., 1982—84; resident in internal medicine N.Y. Hosp., N.Y.C., 1980—82, resident in dermatology, 1990—93; chair dermatology, dermatologist-in-chief Tufts-New Eng. Med. Ctr., Boston, 2005—. Office: Tufts-New Eng Med Ctr 750 Washington St Box 114 Boston MA 02111 Office Phone: 617-636-5370.

GOTTLIEB, KATHERINE, health facility administrator; BA, Alaska Pacific U., 1990, MBA, 1995. Cmty. health aide, Seldovia, Alaska, 1987; pres., CEO Southcentral Found., Anchorage, 1987—. Named MacArthur Fellow, John D. and Catherine T. MacArthur Found., 2004. Achievements include development of over 75 medical, behavioral health and community programs that service Native Alaskans. Office: Southcentral Found 4501 Diplomacy Dr Anchorage AK 99508 Office Phone: 907-729-4955. Office Fax: 907-729-5000.

GOTTLIEB, MARISE SUSS, epidemiologist, physician; b. N.Y.C., July 16, 1938; d. Lester J. and Fannie (Freeman) Suss; m. A. Arthur Gottlieb, June 8, 1958 (dec.); children: Mindy Cheryl Davidson, Joanne Meredith. AB, Barnard Coll., 1958; MD, NYU, 1962; MPH, Harvard U., 1966. Intern, Mass. Meml. Hosp., 1962-63; resident preventative medicine dept. epidemiology Harvard U. Med. Sch., 1965-68, instr. dept. medicine, H.M., Boston, 1969-70, also fellow, asst. in Medicine Peter Bent Brigham Hosp.; dir. chronic disease control N.J. Dept. Health, Trenton, 1970-75; asst. prof. dept. community medicine Rutgers Med. Sch., Piscataway N.J., 1972-75; assoc. prof. dept. medicine Tulane U. Sch. Medicine, New Orleans, 1975-91; assoc. prof. dept. epidemiology Sch. Pub. Health, 1975-80; chief chronic disease control, La. Dept. Health and Human Resources, New Orleans, 1975-85; dir. clin. and regulatory affairs, v.p. med. affairs Imreg Inc., New Orleans, 1985-98; sec. treas. Pres. Endeavor Corp., 1998—; mem. bd. alumni coun. Harvard U. Sch. Pub. Health, 2005—; mem. epidemiology and disease control study sect. NIH, Bethesda, Md., 1982-85. NIH traineeship, 1965-66, spl research fellow Nat. Inst. Arthritis, Metabolism and Digestive Diseases, 1966-68. Diplomate Am. Bd. Preventive Medicine. Fellow Am. Coll. Preventive Medicine, Am. Coll. Epidemiology; mem. Am. Diabetes Assn., Soc. Epidemiol. Rsch., Am. Fedn. Med. Rsch., Am. Pub. Health Assn. Contbr. articles to profl jours. Home: 215 Chestnut Hill Rd Chestnut Hill MA 02467-1313 Business E-Mail: marsgott@massmed.org.

GOTTLIEB, SHERRY GERSHON, writer, editor; b. L.A., Apr. 6, 1948; d. Harry L. and Evelyn Jellen) Gershon; m. David Neil Gottlieb, Aug. 12, 1971 (div. 1973). BA in Dramatic Arts, U. Calif., Berkeley, 1969. Exec. sec. Budget Films, L.A., 1970-72; script reader United Artists, L.A., 1971-74; owner A Change of Hobbit bookstore, L.A. and Santa Monica, Calif., 1972-91, Career Boost Résumés, Ventura, Calif., 1999—. Class coord. UCLA Extension, 1982. Author: Hell No, We Won't Go! Resisting the Draft During the Vietnam War, 1991, Love Bite, 1994, Worse Than Death, 2000, Pup Fiction, 2005. Named Spl. Guest of Honor, Westercon, 1979. Democrat. Avocations: reading, cooking, Scrabble, trivial pursuit, travel. Office Phone: 805-658-1612. E-mail: writer@wordservices.com.

GOTTSCHALK, DEBBRA J., lawyer; b. Nov. 4, 1952; d. Mark A. and Armella B. Gottschalk; m. Mark A. Williams; children: Amanda Katherine Williams, Alexandra Samantha Williams. BA English, Pittsburg U., Kans., 1973; JD, U. Tulsa, 1976. Bar: Okla. Pvt. practice, Tulsa, 1976—. Vol. Domestic Violence Intervention Svc., Tulsa, 1976—84, bd. dirs., pres. Mem.: ATLA, Creek Nation Bar Assn., Tulsa County Bar Assn. (AIDS vol. 1997—, Pro Bono award 1997), Okla. Trial Lawyers Assn. (adv. bd.), Okla. Bar Assn. Office: 2518 E 71st St Tulsa OK 74136

GOTTSCHALK, SISTER MARY THERESE, nun, hospital administrator; b. Doellwang, Germany, June 21, 1931; arrived in U.S., 1953, naturalized, 1959; d. John and Sabina (Dietz) G. BS in Pharmacy, Creighton U., 1960; M.H.A., St. Louis U., 1970; DHL (hon.), U. Okla., 2001. Joined Sisters of the Sorrowful Mother, Roman Cath. Religious Order, 1952. Dir. pharmacy St. Mary's Hosp., Roswell, N.Mex., 1960-68, CEO, 1972-74; asst. adminstr. St. John Med. Ctr., Tulsa, 1970-72, pres., CEO, 1974-99, St. John Health Sys., Tulsa, 1982—; pres. Marian Health Sys., Tulsa, 1980—. Recipient Alumni Merit award, Creighton U., 2003. Fellow: Am. Coll. Healthcare Exec.; mem.: Cath. Health Assn. (bd. dirs. 1995—2001), Tulsa C. of C., Okla. Cath. Health Conf. (past pres.), Tulsa Hosp. Coun. (past pres.), Okla. Hosp. Assn. (pres. 1984), Am. Hosp. Assn. (ho. of dels., regional policy bd., governing coun., Disting. Svc. award 1999). Office: St John Health System 1923 S Utica Ave Tulsa OK 74104-6502

GOTTSCHALL, JOAN B., judge; b. Oak Ridge, Tenn., Apr. 23, 1947; d. Herbert A. and Elaine (Reichbaum) G. BA cum laude, Smith Coll., Mass., 1969; JD, Stanford Univ., Calif., 1973. Bar: Ill. 1973. Assoc. Jenner & Block, 1973-76, 78-81, ptnr., 1981-82; staff atty. Fed. Defender Program, 1976-78, Univ. of Chgo., Office of Legal Counsel, 1983-84; magistrate judge U.S. Dist. Ct. (no. dist.) Ill., Chgo., 1984—96, judge, 1996—. Mem. vis. com., past chair Divinity Sch., U. Chgo., 1984—97. Bd. dirs. Martin Marty Ctr., U. Chgo. Div. Sch., Ill. Humanities Coun. Mem.: ABA, Divinity Sch. (vis. com.), Chgo. Bar Assn. Office: US Dist Ct no dist Ill Everett McKinley Dirksen Bldg 219 S Dearborn St Ste 2356 Chicago IL 60604-1877

GOTTSEGEN, GLORIA, psychologist, educator; b. N.Y.C., Nov. 15, 1930; d. Marco and Flora (Salti) Behar; m. Paul D. Park, Jan. 10, 1981; children: Abby Jean, Paul Richard. BA, N.Y. U., 1950; MA, CCNY, 1951; PhD, N.Y. U., 1967. Lic. psychologist, N.Y. Postgrad. fellow N.Y. Med. Coll., N.Y.C., 1957-58; remedial psychologist Jewish Child Care Assn., N.Y.C., 1958-61; psychologist Bronx (N.Y.) Consultation Center, 1961-64, supervising psychologist, 1964-68; asst. prof. Hebert H. Lehman Coll., City U. N.Y., Bronx, 1968-75; asso. prof. Herbert H. Lehman Coll., CUNY, 1975-79; prof. Hebert H. Lehman Coll., CUNY, 1979-91; chmn. dept. specialized services edn. Hebert H. Lehman Coll., City U. N.Y., 1976-81; prof. emeritus, 1991—; pres. Sch. Psychology Educators Council N.Y. State, 1977-78. Editor: Professional School Psychology, Vols. I-III, 1960, 63, 69, Confrontation: Encounters in Self and Interpersonal Awareness, 1971, Group Behavior: A Guide to Information Sources, 1979, Humanistic Psychology: A Guide to Information Sources, 1980; assoc. editor: Psychotherapy: Theory, Research and Practice, 1976-82. Fellow APA (pres. divsn. humanistic psychology 1976-77, sec. divsn. psychotherapy 1975-78, rep. to coun. 1978-85, 93—, chmn. bd. conv. affairs 1983-84, mem. membership com. 1986-88, 91-93, chair membership com. 1993, mem. task force on centennial celebration 1989-92, pres. divsn. family psychology 1986-87, pres. divsn. clin. psychology sect. clin. psychology of women 1994, mem. policy and planning bd. 1994-96); mem. N.Y. Psychol. Assn. (pres. divsn. sch. psychology 1975-76), Fla. Psychol. Assn., S.E. Psychol. Assn.

GOUCKENOUR, SHARON CRAFT, elementary school educator; b. Columbus, Ohio, Feb. 7, 1944; d. Woodrow Albert and Mary Anna (Belcher) Craft; m. William Gouckenour, Dec. 27, 1965. BS, U. Charleston, 1967; Masters in Reading, Marshall U. Tchr. Littlepage Elem. Sch., Charleston, W.Va., 1967-69, Ravenswood (W.Va.) Grade Sch., 1969-70, Henry J. Kaiser Elem. Sch., Ravenswood, 1970—. Mem. Sch. Improvement Coun., Ripley, W.Va., 1990—, Jackson County Sick Leave Bank Bd., Ripley, 1990—. Mem. Jackson County Arts Coun., Ripley, 1980—. Grantee W.Va. Tchrs. Acad., 1989, W.Va. Edn. Found., 1990, Jackson County Schs., 1992. Mem. W.Va. Profl. Educators (v.p. 1990—), W.Va. Reading Coun. (pres. 1987-90), AAAUW (pres. Ravenswood), Alpha Delta Kappa (pres. 1989-92). Democrat. Roman Catholic. Avocations: tennis, skiing, bridge. Home: 605 Hillcrest Ave Ravenswood WV 26164-1456 Office: Henry J Kaiser Elem Sch Kaiser Ave Ravenswood WV 26164 Business E-Mail: sgoucken@access.k12.wu.us.

GOUDELOCK, CAROL V., library consultant; b. Milw., Dec. 25, 1938; d. Leo Michael and Regina Mary (Gasper) Schueller; m. Donald Ray Goudelock, July 2, 1971. BA, Marquette U., 1960, MA, 1962; MLS, U. Wis., Milw., 1977. Libr. asst. Milw. Pub. Libr., 1962-65, 74-76; instr. English U. Wis., Oshkosh, 1965-68; asst. prof. Milw. Sch. Engring., 1969-72; libr. Inglewood Pub. Libr., Calif., 1977-83, Hughes Aircraft Co., El Segundo, Calif., 1984-88; ret., 2005. Libr. cons. Teradata Corp., El Segundo, 1989-90, Kaiser Permanente, Pasadena, Calif., 1991, Getty Conservation Inst., Marina Del Ray, Calif., 1992, First Interstate Bank Legal Svcs., L.A., 1992-96, Nissan N. Am. Calif., 1997-2006; cataloging cons. Iolab Corp., Claremont, Calif., 1991-95. Mem. So. Calif. Assn. of Law Librs. Office: PO Box 459 Joshua Tree CA 92252-0459

GOUDY, JOSEPHINE GRAY, social worker; b. Des Moines, Nov. 30, 1925; d. Gerald William and Myrtle Maria (Brooks) Gray; m. John Winston Goudy, June 5, 1948; children: Tracy Jean, Paula Rae. BA, State U. Iowa, 1954, MSW, 1966; cert. in gerontology, U. Ill. LCSW, lic. ind. social worker Iowa, cert. social worker Iowa, Ill. Child welfare supr. Iowa Dept. Social Svcs., 1960-68; psychiat. social worker Cmty. Mental Health Ctr., Scott County, Iowa, 1966-71; social work instr. Palmer Jr. Coll., Davenport, Iowa, 1967-70; psychiat. social worker, chief social svcs. Jacksonville (Ill.) State Mental Hosp., 1971-74; coord. cmty. mental health outpatient svcs. McFarland Mental Health Ctr., Springfield, Ill., 1974; exec. dir. Macoupin County Mental Health Ctr., Carlinville, Ill., 1974-98, Youth Attention Ctr., Jacksonville, Ill., 1998-99; pvt. practice, 1999—. Chmn. Human Svcs. Edn. Coun., Springfield, 1979—81; bd. mem. Alzheimer's Disease and Related Disorders Assn., Springfield; past exec. Davenport Cmty. Welfare Coun.; adj. prof. dept. psychiatry So. Ill. U., Springfield. Mem.: AAUW (br. pres. 1964—66, state bar 1966—68, br. grantee 1975, br. pres. 2006—), NASW (del. to China 2000—06, Social Worker of Yr. Ctrl. Ill. area 1983), APA, Internat. Fedn. Univ. Women, Am. Psychotherapy Assn., Acad. Cert. Social Workers, Bus. and Profl. Women (Woman of Yr. 1983), U. Iowa Alumni Assn., Carlinville Women's Club (pres. 1975—77, 1996—98), Delta Kappa Gamma. Republican. Methodist. Home: 5347 Chapel Hill Rd Davenport IA 52802-9502

GOUGH, GEORGIA BELLE, art educator; b. Oklahoma City, Dec. 21, 1920; d. George John and Lillie Belle (Massongill) Leach; m. Clarence Ray Gough, Feb. 7, 1975. BS, Ctrl. State Coll., 1941; MS, North Tex. State U., 1946; PhD, U. Okla., 1962. Tchr. elementary Dist. 16/Noble County Okla., Lucien, 1941-42; tchr. elementary, art Denison (Tex.) Sch. Dist., 1942-43; tchr. elementary art Oklahoma City Sch. Dist., 1943-47; instr., asst. prof., assoc. prof., prof., prof. emerita U. North Tex., Denton, 1947—. Sec. Nat. Coun. on Edn. Ceramic Arts, 1970-73; craftsman/trustee Am. Crafts Coun., 1976-80; U.S. Del. World Crafts Coun., 1978, 80; sec., pres., hon. mem. Tex. Designer/Craftsmen. Artist one-woman shows Earth, Water, Fire, Air, 1996, Family Reunion, 2000; contbr. articles to profl. jours.; designer of wall hanging Greater Denton Arts Coun., 1985. Bd. dirs. Greater Denton Arts Coun. Recipient Cmty. Arts Recognition award Denton Arts Coun., 1995. Democrat. Home: 1813 Willowwood St Denton TX 76205-6992

GOUKER, JANE ANN, music educator; b. York, PA, Sept. 6, 1953; d. Ray Calvin and Freida Louise Gouker. B Music Edn., Ind. U., 1976, M in Music Edn., 1990. Elem. strings tchr. Fairfax County Pub. Schs., Va., 1976—77; elem./mid. sch. strings tchr. Manassas City Pub. Schs., Va., 1977—80; elem./mid. sch./h.s. orchestra dir., dept. chair Monroe County Cmty. Sch. Corp., Bloomington, Ind., 1980—; double bass tchr., ensemble dir. Ind. U. Summer Music Clinic, Bloomington, 1996—. Office Phone: 812-330-7714. Business E-Mail: jgouker@mccsc.edu.

GOULD, ANNE AUSTIN, special education educator; b. Detroit, Mich., Jan. 5, 1961; d. John David and Jane Brown (Austin) G. BS in Edn. magna cum laude, Lesley Coll., Cambridge, Mass., 1983; MA summa cum laude, Appalachian State U., 1988. Cert. spl. edn. tchr., elem. tchr. Spl. edn. tchr. Northwest Ministries Devel. Day Sch., Winston-Salem, N.C., 1983-84, Winston-Salem/Forsyth County Schs., 1984—. Tutor, Winston-Salem, 1988-94; respite provider, 1986-90; cons., 1988-94; habilitation, technician/respite provider Substitute Horizons Residential Care Rural Hall, N.C., 1991-92; caretaker Tanglewood Farm, Clemmons, N.C., 1999-. Treas. Winston-Triad chpt. Lupus Assn., 1983-84; Rites of Christian Initiation of Adults sponsor Holy Family Cath. Ch., Clemmons, N.C., 1989-90; vol. Cath. Hispanic Ctr., East Bend, N.C., 1989. Mem. NEA. Democrat. Avocations: crafts, reading, computers, quilting, horseback riding. Home: 105 Bradford Lake Ct Lewisville NC 27023-8662

GOULD, CHERYL, broadcast executive; BA, Princeton U., 1974. On-air reporter WOKR-TV, Rochester, NY; with NBC News, 1977—, field prodr., radio reporter Paris Bur., prodr. London Bur., prodr. NBC Nightly News weekend edit. NYC, 1981, sr. prodr. NBC Nightly News with Tom Brokaw, 1985—96, acting exec. prodr., v.p., 1993—2005, v.p. CNBC, 2001—05, sr. v.p. NYC, 2005—. Prodr.: D-Day Plus 40; co-creator, sr. prodr. NBC News Overnight (Alfred I. duPont-Columbia U. Award), contr. NY Times, Newsweek. Recipient Emmy Award for Nightly News, 1989. Mem.: Internat. Women's Media Found. Office: NBC News 30 Rockefeller Plz # 280 New York NY 10012

GOULD, CLAUDIA, museum director; BA in Art History, Boston Coll.; M in Mus. Studies, NYU. Curator, project dir., curator exhbns. Wexner Ctr. Arts, Ohio State U., 1989-91; ind. curator N.Y.C., 1992-94; exec. dir. Artists Space, N.Y.C., 1994-99, Inst. Contemporary Art, Phila., 1999—. Office: Inst Contemporary Art 118 S 36th St Philadelphia PA 19104-3289 Office Phone: 215-573-9973. E-mail: clgould@pobox.upenn.edu.

GOULD, DOROTHY MAE, executive secretary, soprano; b. Bridgeport, Conn., Sept. 9, 1927; d. Clifford Alexander and Mary Irene Hedin; m. John Colquitt Gould, Nov. 26, 1958; children: Natalie Mary, Clifford Gardner, Andrew Woodhouse. BA in English Lit. and Creative Writing, U. Mont., 1997; studied voice with Estelle Liebling, Julliard, 1959—63, studied voice with Bernard Taylor, 1943; studied voice with Alexander Kipnis, Met. Opera, 1968—72; scholar, New Eng. Conservatory. Legal sec. Thompson Knight, Dallas, White, McElroy, Dallas, Gibbons, Tucker, Smith, McEwen, Coxer and Taub, Tampa, Fla., Curtis, Trevethan & Gerety, Bridgeport, Conn., Music Corp. Am., N.Y.C., NY; sec. GE Co., Bridgeport, Columbia Artists Mgmt., N.Y.C., AMF, Greenwich, Conn.; soprano USO, Conn., 1944—45, Tampa Opera, 2002—; oratorio singer, soloist soprano N.Y., Conn., Fla. Sec. Music Corp. Am., N.Y.C. Finalist Barnum Festival Jenny Lind contest, 1948, Stamford Advocate, Greenwich Times contest, 1985—86. Home: 13871 N 91st Ln Peoria AZ 85381 Personal E-mail: colquitt3@msn.com.

GOULD, EMILY, editor; b. 1982; BA, New Sch., NYC, 2004. Editl. asst. Hyperion Books, NYC, 2004—05, asst. editor, 2005—06; co-editor-in-chief Gawker.com, NYC, 2006—. Co-author: Hex Education; author: (blogs) www.EmilyMagazine.com, 2005—. Office: Gawker Media 76 Crosby New York NY 10012 Office Phone: 212-655-9524.*

GOULD, LILIAN, writer; b. Phila., Apr. 19, 1920; d. Reuben Barr and Lilian Valentine (Scott) Seidel; m. Irving Gould, Nov. 16, 1944; children: Mark, Scott, Paul, John. Student, U. Pa., Charles Morris Price Sch. of Advt. and Journalism, Phila. Copywriter, mgr. advt. agys., Phila. Author: Our Living Past, 1969, Jeremy and the Gorillas, 1977 (award 1977); freelance journalist mags. and newspapers. Mem. Authors Guild, Phila. Children's Reading Roundtable, Phila. Writers Orgn., Soc. of Children's Book Writers and Illustrators. Home: 772 Newtown Rd Villanova PA 19085-1121

GOULD, MARTHA BERNICE, retired librarian; b. Claremont, N.H., Oct. 8, 1931; d. Sigmund and Gertrude Heller; m. Arthur Gould, July 29, 1960; children: Leslie, Stephen. BA in Edn., U. Mich., 1953; MS in Libr. Sci., Simmons Coll., 1956; cert., U. Denver Libr. Sch., 1978. Childrens libr. N.Y. Pub. Libr., 1956-58; adminstr. libr. svcs. act demonstration regional libr. project Pawhuska, Okla., 1958-59; cons. N.Mex. State Libr., 1959-60; children's libr. then sr. children's libr. L.A. Pub. Libr., 1960-72; acctg. dir. pub. svcs., reference libr. Nev. State Libr., 1972-74; pub. svcs. libr. Washoe County (Nev.) Libr., 1974-79, asst. county libr., 1979-84, county libr., 1984-94; ret., 1994. Cons. Nev. State Libr. and Archives, 1996—2003; part-time lectr. libr. adminstrn. U. Nev.; acting dir. Nev. Ctr. for the Book; vice-chair Nat. Commn. in Librs. and Info. Sci., 1993—2000, chair, 2000—03; mem. adv. coun. Nev. Coun. on Librs. and Literacy, 2001—05; mem. adv. bd. Fleischmann Planetarium, 1999—2003. Co-editor: Nevada Women's History Project Annotated Bibliography, 1999; contbr. articles to jours. Exec. dir. Kids Voting/USA, Nev., 1996; treas. United Jewish Appeal, 1981; bd. dirs. Temple Sinai, Planned Parenthood, 1996-97, Truckee Meadows Habitat for Humanity, 1995-98; trustee RSVP, North Nevadans for ERA; No. Nev. chmn. Gov.'s Conf. on Libr., 1990; bd. dir. Campaign for Choice, No. Nev. Food Bank, Nev. Women's Fund (Hall of Fame award 1989); mem. No. Nev. NCCJ, Washoe County Quality Life Task Force, 1992—, Washoe County Elections Taskforce, 1999—; bd. dirs. KUNR Pub. Radio, 1999-00, chair bd. dirs., 2000-04; chair Sierra Nevada Cmty. Access TV; adv. bd. Partnership Librs. Washoe County; co-chair social studies curriculum adv. task force Washoe County Sch. Dist.; mem. Nev. Women's History Project Bd.; chair Downtown River Corridor Com., 1995-97; vice chair Dem. Party Washoe County, 1998-00; v.p. Nev. Diabetes Assn. for Children and Adults, 1998-02, pres., 2002-04, mem. adv. bd., 2004-06; chair devel. com. Planned Parenthood, 2002-; bd. dir. Washoe Libr. Found., 2003-05; mem. adv. Adv. Coun. on Edn./to the Holocaust, 2000-; chair Washoe County Dem. Women's Club, 2003-05; coord. Diabetes Edn. Prevention Program, Nev., 2005—; chair 2nd Century Endowment for Friends of Washoe County Libr., 2005—. Recipient Nev. State Libr. Letter of Commendation, 1973, Washoe County Bd. Commrs. Resolution of Appreciation, 1978, ACLU of Nev. Civil Libertarian of Yr. 1988, Freedom's Sake award AAUW, 1989, Leadership in Literacy award Sierra chpt. Internat. Reading Assn., 1992, Woman of Distinction award 1992, Cornerstone award Sierra chpt. Assn. Fundraising Profls., 2003, Women Helping Women award Soroptimist Internat., 2005, Alumni Achievement award Simmmons Coll. Grad. Sch. Libr. and Info. Sci., 2006. Mem. ALA (bd. dirs., intellectual freedom roundtable 1977-79, intellectual freedom com. 1979-83, coun. 1983-86), ACLU (bd. dir. Civil Libertarian of Yr. Nev. chpt. 1988, chair gov.'s conf. for women 1989), Nev. Libr. Assn. (chmn. pub. info. com. 1972-73, intellectual freedom com. 1975-78, govt. rels. com. 1978-79, v.p., pres.-elect 1980, pres. 1981, Spl. Citation 1978, 87, Libr. of Yr. 1993). E-mail: mgould@unr.edu.

GOULD, MARY ANN CARPENTER, nephrology nurse consultant; b. Phila. d. Jonas and Mary (Minke) Carpenter; m. Scott Robert Gould, Apr. 23, 1988; children: Samuel Jonas, Joanna Miriam. BA in Sociology and Anthropology, Marquette U., 1972; BSN, Widener U., 1975; MSN, U. Pa., 1984. RN, Pa.; cert. BCLS, ACLS, nephrology nurse, hemodialysis practitioner. Staff nurse Kidney Ctr. Delaware County, Chester, Upland, Pa., 1975-78, team leader, 1978-80, ednl. coord., 1980-84, dir. clin. ops., 1987-89; dir. nursing BMA, Abington, Pa., 1984-86; pvt. cons. Broomall, Pa., 1989—2002, 2004—. Presenter in field. Ctr. dir. Phila. Area Physician's Dialysis, 2002. Mem. Am. Nephrology Nurses Assn. (life)(Judy Sloan Meml. fellow 1985, 88, Keystone chpt. pres. 1988-89, 2001-02, nat. program chair 1989-90, bylaws com. Keystone chpt. 1990-91, 91—, chairperson clin. practice com. 1991-93, nephrology nurse educator, 1992, N.E. region chpt. coord.-elect 1994-95, chpt. coord. 1995—, pres. elect 2000-01, Keystone chpt. Outstanding Contbn. award 1994, Nat. award 1995), Nat. Kidney Found. (Delaware Valley affiliate bd. dirs., Disting. Svc. award 1989, 91, 93, 95, chairperson patient svcs. commn. 1988-91, regional devel. prog. 1991-93, Nat. Vol. Svc. award 1992, ann. recognition dinner), BMA of Abington Pa. (dir. of nursing 1984-86), Phila. Nurses Council of Hadassa (bd. dirs. 2005—), Sigma Theta Tau Internat.

GOULD, TAFFY, Internet company executive, real estate executive; b. Miami, Fla., Apr. 14, 1942; d. Emil J. and Estelle F. Gould; m. Bernard Arthur Beber, Apr. 5, 1964 (div. Jan. 1975); children: Karen B. Futernick, J. Gregory Beber. BA, Smith Coll., 1963. Cert. real estate broker, Fla. Pres. Housing Engrs. Fla., Inc., Miami, 1977—; chmn. e-Med. Edn., LLC, Fla., 1999—; chmn. coun. Oceania U. Medicine, Samoa; vice chmn. Non-Invasive Monitoring Sys., Inc. Lectr. Potomac Spkrs. Bur., Washington, 1993-98. Author: South Africa: Land of Hope, 1989, White Woman Witchdoctor, 1993 (Best Seller 1994); co-author: Create Your Own Future, 1996; newspaper columnist Miami Today, 1983-88, Miami Today, Miami Herald; radio talk host WINZ, Miami, 1986-88. Mem. nat. com. Zionist Orgn. Am., N.Y., 1995—; bd. dirs. Alexander Muss H.S. in Israel, Miami, 1995—, Cen. Agy. for Jewish Edn.; dir. U. Miami, Miami Hot Glass, Coral Gables, Fla., 1998—; governing coun. Fla. Philharmonic Orch., 1998—; bd. trustees Miami Mus. Sci., 2003. Recipient Humanitarian and Arts award Internat. Bolivarian Soc., Miami, 1994, City of the Future award City of Ariel, Israel, 1999, Louis Brandeis award Zionist Orgn. Am., N.Y., 2000. Avocations: classical music, reading. Home: 10 Edgewater Dr Apt 14F Coral Gables FL 33133-6968 Home Fax: 305-668-3298. Personal E-mail: taffyg@bellsouth.net. E-mail: taffygould@taffygould.com.

GOULDER, CAROLJEAN HEMPSTEAD, retired psychologist, consultant; b. Houston, Minn., Apr. 9, 1933; d. Orson George and Jean Helen (Lischer) Hempstead; m. L. Lynton Goulder, Jr., May 26, 1953 (div. 1978); children: Jean Virginia, David Thomas, Ann Rachel; m. John T. Blake, Apr. 12, 1986. BS, Hamline U., 1956; MA Sch. Psychology, R.I. Coll., 1972, CAGS, 1975; postgrad., Nova U., 1977—78. Cert. sch. psychologist, R.I. Dept. head, instr. Highsmith Hosp., Fayetteville, NC, 1956—57; instr. nursing New Eng. Deaconess Hosp., Boston, 1957—58; dir. psychol. svcs. Burrillville Sch. Dept., Harrisville, RI, 1972—79, sch. psychologist, 1972—2000; cons. Norton Schs., Mass., 2001—01; retired psychologist; embroidery quilting educator and fiber artist, 1992—. Coord. presch. handicapped, 1985-86; lectr. pediatric problems Sturdy Meml. Hosp., Attleboro, Mass., 1970-72; cons. Wheeler Sch., Providence, 1970-73. Chmn. 2d Congl. Ch. Sch., Attleboro, Mass., 1962-65, mem. religious edn. com., kindergarten com. and choir, 1965; active 1st Unitarian Ch., Providence, 1982-86; mem. Providence Presbyn., 2005-. Mem.: APA (assoc.). Avocations: creative cooking, crewel embroidery, nature study, concerts, quilting. Office: 6 Dail Drive Providence RI 02911

GOULDIN, JUDITH ANN, nuclear medicine physician; b. Binghamton, NY, Nov. 20, 1947; d. Paul C. and Virginia E. (Millen) G.; m. Anthony M. Parente, May 15, 1982. AB, U. Mich., 1968; MD, Hahnemann U., 1972. Resident in internal medicine Mayo Grad. Sch. Medicine, Rochester, Minn., 1972—75; resident in nuclear medicine Stanford (Calif.) U. Hosps., 1975—77; med. dir. nuclear medicine Williamsport (Pa.) Hosp. and Med.

Ctr., 1977—. Mem.: AMA, Lycoming County Med. Soc. (pres. 1994), Pa. Med. Soc., Soc. Nuclear Medicine. Office: Williamsport Hosp & Med Ctr 777 Rural Ave Williamsport PA 17701-3198

GOULDING, NORA See CLARK, SUSAN

GOULEKAS, KAREN, special effects supervisor; b. Conn., Aug. 2, 1962; Digital artist: Last Action Hero, 1993; missiles and smoke animation: True Lies, 1994; digital effects supr.: Apollo 13, 1995; Strange Days, 1995; T2 3-D: Battle Across Time, 1996; The Fifth Element, 1997; digital compositor: Titanic, 1997; assoc. visual effects supr.: Godzilla, 1998; Spider-Man, 2002; visual effects supv.: Eight Legged Freaks, 2002; The Day After Tomorrow, 2004; visual effects plate photog. supr.: Venom, 2005. Nominee Best Spl. Effects, Saturn Awards, 2003; recipient Best Single Visual Effect of the Yr., Visual Effects Society, 2005. Office: Twentieth Century Fox 31/32 Soho Sq London W1D 3AP England

GOULET, CHRISTINE SWEENEY, elementary school educator; b. Hornell, NY, Feb. 27, 1977; d. Daniel Edward Sweeney; m. Jeremy Michael Goulet, July 12, 2003. A in Natuaral Resource Conservation, Finger Lakes C.C., Canandiagua, NY, 1998; degree in environ. sci., So. Vt. Coll., Bennington, 2000. Tchr. 6th grade Scarborough Mid. Sch., Maine, 2003—, coach 7th grade girls basketball, 2006—. Avocations: Boston terriers, walking, bicycling. Office: Scarborough Middle School 44 Gorham Road Scarborough ME 04074

GOULET, LORRIE, sculptor; b. Riverdale, N.Y., Aug. 17, 1925; Student, Inwood Potteries Studios, N.Y.C., 1932-36, Black Mountain Coll., N.C., 1943-44. Tchr. Mus. Modern Art, 1957, 64, Scarsdale Studio Workshop, 1959, 61, New Sch., 1961—75, Art Students League, 1981—2006. One-woman shows include Clay Club Sculpture Ctr., N.Y.C., 1948, 1955, Cheney Libr., Hoosick Falls, N.Y., 1951, Contemporaries Gallery, N.Y.C., 1959, 1962, 1966, 1968, Rye (N.Y.) Art Ctr., 1966, New Sch. Assocs., N.Y.C., 1968, Temple Emeth, Teaneck, N.J., 1969, Kennedy Galleries, N.Y.C., 1971, 1973, 1975, 1978, 1980, 1982, 1986, Carolyn Hill Gallery, 1988, 1991, Caldwell (N.J.) Coll., 1989, Nat. Mus. Women in the Arts, Washington, 1998, Harmon-Meek Galleries, Naples, Fla., 2000, David Findlay Jr. Gallery, 2001, 2002, 2004, 2005, exhibited in group shows at Mus. Natural History, 1936, Whitney Mus. Am. Art, N.Y.C., 1948—50, 1953, 1955, Met. Mus. Art, 1951, Detroit Inst. Art, 1960, Pa. Acad., 1950—52, 1954, 1959, 1964, AD, N.Y.C., 1966, 1975, 1977, Corcoran Gallery, Washington, 1966, Hofstra Mus., N.Y.C., 1990, The McNey Mus., 1990, The Copley Soc., Boston, 1991, The Spanish Inst., 1992, Lehigh U. Art Gallery, 1992, Iowa State U. Brunne Gallery, 1992, Paine Art Ctr., Oshkosh, Wis., 1992, Mitchell Art Gallery, St. John's Coll., Annapolis, Md., 1992, Erie (Pa.) Art Mus., 1995, Nat. Sculpture Soc., 2001, Art Students League, N.Y.C., 2003, David Findlay Jr. Gallery, 2005, Represented in permanent collections Hunter Mus., Chattanooga, N.J. State Mus., Wichita Mus. Art, Hirschhorn Sculpture Mus., Washington, The Philharm. Ctr., Naples, Fla., Art Students League, N.Y.C., Savannah Coll. Arts. Recipient Malvina Hoffman award Nat. Acad. Design, 2001, others; grantee Fhorsheim Art Fund, 1997. Mem.: NAD (academician 1989, mem. coun. 1994), Fine Arts Fedn. (pres. 1998—2002, hon. v.p. 2003), N.Y. Artists Equity Inc. (pres. 1998—2002), Visual Artists and Galleries Assocs., Sculptors Guild.

GOULETAS, EVANGELINE, investment executive; m. Hugh L. Carey, 1981. MA in Math, Northeastern Ill. State Coll. Formerly mem. faculty dept. Chgo. Bd. Edn.; prin. Am. Invsco Corp., Chgo., 1969—; ptnr. Electronic Realty Assn., IMB (Internat. Mcht. Banking), N.Y.C., 1969—. Formerly trustee DePaul U.; trustee Chgo. City Library, Com. for Thalassemia Concern; chairperson Combined Cardiac Research Women's Found., U. Chgo., N.Y. State Watch Com.; mem. exec. bd. Chgo. City Ballet, N.Y.C. Meals-On-Wheels, LaGuardia Community Coll. Recipient Great Am. award B'nai B'rith, 1977, Businesswoman of Yr. award Soc. of the Little Flower, 1979, Exec. Businesswoman of the Yr. Internat. Orgn. of Women Execs., 1980, Tree of Life Honor, Jewish Nat. Fund, 1981, Myrtle Wreath award, Nassau County Hadassah, 1981, Paedia award DePaul U., 1982, Eleanor Roosevelt Humanities award, State of Israel Bonds, 1983, humanitarian award Assn. for Children with Retarded Mental Devel., 1985, Woman of Distinction Pan Euboean Soc. of Am., 1985; two residences named in her honor Fedn. of P.R. Orgns., Bronx, United Cerebral Palsy, Staten Island; Evangeline Gouletas-Carey Leadership award presented annually in her name by LaGuardia Community Coll. of CUNY. Mem. Nat. Assn. Realtors, Inst. Real Estate Mgmt., Pres.'s Assn. of Am. Mgmt. Assn. Greek Orthodox.

GOUMNEROVA, LILIANA CHRISTOVA, physician, neurosurgeon, educator; b. Jakarta, Indonesia, Sept. 27, 1956; arrived in U.S., 1988; d. Christo Todorov and Jeanne Dimitrova (Petkova) G. BSc, Faculty of Medicine, Sofia, Bulgaria, 1977; MD, U. Toronto, Can., 1980. Intern U. Toronto, 1980-81; resident in neurosurgery U. Ottawa, Canada, 1981-86; fellow in pediatric neurosurgery Hosp. Sick Children, Toronto, 1987-88, assoc. staff neurosurgeon, 1987-88; assoc. staff surgeon Ottawa Civic Hosp., 1986-87; Dana fellow in neurosurgery U. Pa., Phila., 1988-90; assoc. in neurosurgery Children's Hosp., Boston, 1990—, dir. clin. pediat. neurosurg. oncology, 1999—; assoc. in neurosurgery Brigham & Women's Hosp., Boston, 1990—; cons. neurosurgeon Dana Farber Cancer Inst., Boston, 1990—, dir. clin. pediat. neurosurg. oncology, 1998; asst. prof. surgery Sch. Medicine Harvard U., Boston, 1990—2005; assoc. prof. surgery Harvard U. Sch. Medicine, Boston, 2005—. Mem. Am. Assn. Neurol. Surgeons (Young Investigator award 1996). Office: Childrens Hosp 300 Longwood Ave Boston MA 02115-5737 Office Phone: 617-355-6364. Business E-Mail: liliana.goumnerova@childrens.harvard.edu.

GOURDINE-TYSON, NATACHIA, investment company executive, writer; BSc, Morgan State U.; degree in Justice Adminstrn., Ctrl. Mich. U. Officer spl. projects Nations Bank Corp., Silver Spring, Md., 1992—93; adminstr. Dept. Vets. Affairs, Washington, 1993—96; transp. officer U.S. Army Res., Port Eustis, Va., 1988—98; prin., owner Gourdine Investment Co., Brandywine, Md., 2000—. Adv. Celia & Sons Restaurant, St. Stephen, SC, 2000—03. Author: Legacy of Love, 2001, Legacy of Love, II, 2005. Sec. Am. Assn. Disabled Vets., Washington, 1994—96; vol. Isaac Gourdine County Coun. Campaign, Oxon Hill, Md., 1994—98. Mem.: Internat. Assn. Adminstrv. Profls., Sigma Gamma Rho (sec. 1993—94). Home: 13501 Brandywine Rd Brandywine MD 20613 Office: Gourdine Investment Co PO Box 654 Bowie MD 20718 Personal E-mail: gourdineinvestments@verizon.net.

GOUREVITCH, JACQUELINE, artist; b. Paris, Oct. 28, 1933; came to US, 1940; d. Henry and Sophie (Eliasberg) Herrmann; m. Victor Gourevitch, June 18, 1954; children: Marc, Philip. Student, Black Mountain Coll., NC, 1950; BA, U. Chgo., 1954; student, Art Inst. Chgo., 1955-57. Vis. artist Wesleyan U., Middletown, Conn., 1967-71, Hartford Art Sch., 1973-78; vis. artist, lectr. U. Calif., Berkeley, 1974, Vassar Coll., Poughkeepsie, NY, 1977; prof. painting and drawing Wesleyan U., 1978-89; adj. faculty Cooper Union, NYC, 1989-92; vis. prof. Mt. Holyoke Coll., South Hadley, Mass., 1995. Represented by Mary Ryan Gallery, NYC. Solo exhbns. at Eleanor Rigelhaupt Gallery, Boston, 1967, 69, Tibor de Nagy, NYC, 1971, 72, 73, Wadsworth Atheneum, Matrix Gallery, Hartford, 1975, Gallery Marina Dinkler, Berlin, 1988, New Britain Mus. Am. Art, New Britain, Conn., 1994, Paesaggio Gallery, West Hartford, Conn., 1993, 96, 99, DFN Gallery, NYC, 2000, 02, Mary Ryan Gallery, NYC, 2005; group exhbns. including Invitational, Nat. Acad. Design, NYC, 2002, Watercolor, NY Studio Sch., 2002, Sky/Ground, Paessaggio Gallery, West Hartford, 2003, Modern Shadows, The Painting Ctr., NYC, 2003, Skies and Scapes, DFN Gallery, NYC, 2004, Invitational, Am. Acad. Arts and Letters, NYC, 2004, 181st Ann.: An Invitational Exbhn. Contemporary Art, Nat. Acad. Mus., NYC, 2006; represented in pub. collections at Wadsworth Atheneum, Menil Collection, Houston, De Cordova Mus., Lincoln., Mass., U.Calif., Berkeley, Yale U. Art Gallery, Conn. NEA grantee, 1976; Conn. Commn. Arts grantee, 1983; Tamarind Inst. fellow, 1973; recipient Obrig prize, Nat. Acad. Design, NY, 2002, Academy award, Am. Acad. of Arts and letters, 2004. Home: 120 Duane St Apt 6 New York NY 10007-1113

GOURLEY, JACQUELYN ELISE, information technology manager, researcher; b. Westminster, Md., Sept. 5, 1969; d. Frank Rittenhouse Gourley and Carolyn P. Boyd; m. Scott James Dietrich, Oct. 12, 2001; children: Sunny Lyn Dietrich, Violet Carver Dietrich. BA in Art History, U. Calif., Santa Barbara, 1991; MA in Art History, George Washington U., Washington, 2000. Program asst. artists' programs & panel ops. Mid Atlantic Arts Found., Balt., 1997—99; asst. dir. commns. and gov. rels. Am. Assn. Collegiate Registrars and Admissions Officers, 1999—2001; project mgr. Md. Artsource, Libr. Digital Programs, Johns Hopkins U., 2001—. Office: The Johns Hopkins University 3400 N Charles St Baltimore MD 21218 Personal E-mail: jacque_gourley@yahoo.com.

GOURLEY, PAULA MARIE, art educator, artist, writer, publishing executive; b. Carmel, Calif., Apr. 29, 1948; d. Raymond Serge Voronkoff and Frances Eliseyvna Gourley; m. David Clark Willard, Feb. 10, 1972 (div. Oct. 1973). AA, Monterey (Calif.) Peninsula Coll., 1971; BA, Goddard Coll., 1978; MFA, U. Ala., 1987; pvt. bookbinding study with, Donald Glaister, Roger Arnoult, Paule Ameline, Michelene de Bellefroid, Francoise Bausart, Sun Evrard, James Brockman. Radiologic technologist Cen. Med. Clinic, Pacific Grove, Calif., 1970-71, Community Hosp. of Monterey, 1972-75, Duke U. Med. Ctr., Durham, N.C., 1975-77; dept. head, ultrasound technologist Middlesex Meml. Hosp., Middletown, Conn., 1977-79; asst. prof. U. Ala., Tuscaloosa, 1985-93, assoc. prof., 1993-98. Established Pelegaya Press and Paperworks, 1978, Lilyhouse Studio Editions, 1999; asst. dir. Inst. for Book Arts U. Ala., 1985—88, coord., 1988—94, co-dir. MFA program in the book arts, 1994—97; U.S. rep. Les Amis de la Reliure d'Art, Toulouse, France, 1989—; founding dir. Southeastern chpt. Guild of BookWorkers, 1995—99; guest artist Marriott Libr. Book Arts Program U. Utah, 1999—2003; guest artist Ariz. State U., 2004, Jaffe Book Arts Collection, Fla. Atlantic U., 2002—04; contbr. journalist for U.S. to Art et Metiers du Livre Revue Internat., Paris; adj. faculty Lane Micro Bus./Lane C.C., resource and edn. coord., 2002—04; Saturday Market resource coord., Eugene, Oreg., 2001—; instr. Downtown Initiative for Visual Arts, 2004—; tchr. coord. Cultural Homestay Internat., 2004—; bd. dirs. Eugene (Oreg.) Saturday Mkt., Oreg. Micro Enterprise Network, Oreg. Coun. Bus. Edn.; small bus. counselor, lectr. Bus. Devel. Ctr., Lane CC; coord. Life-Enhancing Activity Programs Pearl Buck Ctr., Eugene, Oreg., 2005—. Editor First Impressions (newsletter), 1988-97; contbr. articles to profl. jours.; numerous nat. and internat. bookbinding exhbns., 1978—; contbr. editor Resource Corner, Saturday Market Newletter. Vol. PLUS Literacy Program, Tuscaloosa, 1991-96. U. Ala. grantee, 1988, 89, 90, 92; recipient Diplôme d'Honneur Atelier d'Arts Appliques, France, 1986, Craft fellowship Ala. State Coun. on Arts, 1993-94. Mem. Guild of Bookworkers (founder and bd. dirs. Southeastern regional chpt., editor, pub. newsletter True Grits, mem. exec. com.), Hand Bookbinders Calif., Bookbinders Internat. (v.p. U.S. 1989-92), Pacific Ctr. for the Book Arts, Am. Craft Coun., Ala. Craft Coun., Can. Bookbinders and Book Artists Guild, Nat. Mus. Women in Arts, Willamette Jazz Soc. (founding mem.), Artists Equity of the Ctrl. Coast, Downtown Initiative for the Visual Arts, Handcrafted Soapmakers Guild. Avocations: photography, reading, cuisine, travel, knitting. Studio: 1936 W 34th Ave Eugene OR 97405-1709 Office Phone: 541-686-0947. E-mail: lilyhousestudio@aol.com.

GOURLEY, SARA J., lawyer; b. 1955; AB cum laude with honors, Ripon Coll., 1977; JD, Univ. Ill., 1980. Bar: Ill. 1980, US Dist. Courts (no. dist. Ill. and dist. of Ariz.), US Ct. of Appeals (4th, 7th, 8th. and 11th circuits). Ptnr. product liability litig. Sidley Austin LLP (formerly Sidley Austin Brown & Wood LLP), Chgo., mem. exec. com. Mem. Univ. Ill. Law Rev., 1978—80. Mem.: ABA, Def. Rsch. Inst. Office Phone: 312-853-7694. Office Fax: 312-853-7036. Business E-Mail: sgourley@sidley.com.

GOUSKOS, LISA MARIE, elementary school educator, music educator; b. Chgo., Jan. 14, 1966; d. Clarence Edward and Peternella Jean Zieman; m. Bill John Zieman, July 29, 1990; children: Carissa Loren, Joshua Peter. MusM in Edn., No. Ill. U., DeKalb, Ill., 2005. Tchr. music and drama Carol Stream (Ill.) Sch. Dist., 1998—, dir. choral Roy DeShane Sch., 1998—. Grantee, PEP Grant Com. DuPage County, 2000. Office Phone: 630-462-8925. Business E-Mail: lgouskos@ccsd93.com.

GOUVELLIS, MARY C., utilities executive; b. Chester, Pa., Sept. 1, 1950; d. Nicholas Demitruis and Olga Gouvellis; m. Robert E. Zacconi, Dec. 25, 1976 (div. Sept. 30, 1999); 1 child, Kara. BA, U. Del., 1974; MBA, Ctrl. Mich. U., 1977. Mgr. PPG Industries, Inc., Pitts., 1975-90; mgr. pub. edn. and tng. Orange County Utilities, Orlando, Fla., 1990—. Co-chair Quality Clearing House, Orlando, 1997—. Contbr. articles to profl. jours. Mem. Assn. for Quality and Participation, Am. Water Works Assn., Water Environment Fedn. Home: 710 Terrace Blvd Orlando FL 32803-3241

GOUW, JULIA SURYAPRANATA, bank executive; b. Surabaya, Indonesia, Aug. 22, 1959; came to U.S., 1978; d. Moertopo Suryapranata and Indira (Koelani) Suryapranata; m. Ken Keng-Hok Gouw, June 1, 1981. B.S. with highest honors, U. Ill., 1981. CPA, Ill. Acct., Texaco, Inc., Los Angeles, 1981-83; from asst. acct. to sr. audit mgr. KPMG Peat Marwick, LA, 1983-89; joined East West Bank as v.p., contr., San Marino, CA, 1989, exec. v.p., CFO, East West Bancorp Inc., 1994-, dir., 1997- Bd. dirs. Huntington Meml. Hosp.; bd. visitors UCLA; bd. overseers LA Philharmonic; mem. Alexis de Tocqueville Soc. United Way. Named Philanthropist of Yr., United Way's Women Leaders for Giving and Nat. Assn. Bus. Owners, 2003, LA Bus. Jour. Women Making a Difference Awards, 2003; Named one of The Top 25 Most Powerful Women in Banking, US Banker mag., 2003, 2005. Mem. Chinese Am. CPA's, Nat. Assn. Female Execs., Beta Alpha Psi, Fin. Execs. Inst., Calif. Soc. CPA's. Office: East West Bank 415 Huntington Dr San Marino CA 91108 Office Phone: 626-583-3512, 626-583-3512. Office Fax: 626-799-2799. E-mail: jgouw@eastwestbank.com.

GOWING, PATRICIA M., retired elementary school educator; b. Hillsdale, Kans., Mar. 16, 1933; d. Carl Burton and Elsie Ida (Craven) White; m. Thomas Lee Gowing, June 10, 1956; children: Darrell Lee, Gerald Dean, Gregory Eugene. BS in Edn., Kans. State Tchrs. Coll., Pittsburg, 1955; MS in Edn., Kans. State Tchrs. Coll., Emporia, 1960; postgrad., Kans. State Tchrs. Coll., 1961-86. Cert. elem. tchr., jr. high subjects, counselor K-9. Tchr. grades 1-8 Dist. #11 Star Valley Rural Sch., LaCygne, Kans., 1951-54; tchr. McKinley Jr. High, Clay Center, Kans., 1955-56, Old Mission Jr. High, Shawnee Mission, Kans., 1956-61; tchr. grade 2 Prairie View Unified Sch. Dist. #362, Fontana, Kans., 1970-72, elem. counselor LaCygne, Parker, Fontana, 1972-74, Centerville, 1972-74, tchr., title I reading grades K-6 La Cygne, Fontana, Parker; ret., 1998. Kansas-China Exch. in Edn., 1986; People-to-People Amb. Reading Del. to Russia, Czech Republic, 1998. Mem. NEA (life), NEA Ret. (life), Kans. NEA Ret. (life), AAUW (life, sec., v.p., pres. 1970—), Kans. Ret. Tchrs. Assn., Miami County Area Kans. Ret. Tchrs. Assn., Pi Lambda Theta (study tours Australia, New Zealand, 1992, Scandinavian Countries, 1996, Orient, Manila, 1998, South AFrica 2000), Alpha Delta Kappa (rec. sec., v.p., pres. 1976—, South Ctrl. Regional scholar 1986, pres., corr. sec. Kans. Mu chpt.). Avocations: card ministry for church, travel, reading, word finds, bird watching. Home: 23573 Brown Rd Parker KS 66072-9612

GOWLER, VICKI SUE, newspaper editor, journalist; b. Decatur, Ill., Apr. 16, 1951; d. Carroll Eugene and Audra Janet (Briggs) G. BS in Journalism, U. Ill., 1973. Reporter Iroquois County Daily Times, Watseka, Ill., 1973-75, Quincy (Ill.) Herald-Whig, 1975-78; from reporter to mng. editor Miami (Fla.) Herald, Stuart, Delray Beach, West Palm Beach, 1089-88; asst. news editor Knight-Ridder Washington Bur., 1988-93; exec. editor Duluth (Minn.) News-Tribune, Knight-Ridder newspaper, 1978—2001, editor and v.p., 1993—97, editor, 2001—; mng. editor Pioneer Press, Knight-Ridder newspaper, 1997—2001, editor, 2001—; sr. v.p. and editor St. Paul Pioneer Press, Knight-Ridder newspaper, 2001—. Recipient numerous awards for journalistic works, including RFK award, state AP awards in all categories. Mem. Am. Soc. Newspaper Editors. Methodist. Avocations: reading, tennis, playing clarinet, travel, visiting with her family.

GOYAK, ELIZABETH FAIRBAIRN, retired public relations executive; b. Chgo., Oct. 7, 1922; d. Lewis Howard and Berenice Marie (Bowers) Fairbairn; m. Edward Anthony Goyak, May 20, 1951. BEd, So. Ill. U., 1943; MA, No. Ill. U., 1979. Reporter Internat. News Svc., Chgo., 1945-49, Chgo. Tribune, 1949-52; writer Gardner & Jones, Chgo., 1954-59, Aaron Cushman & Assocs., Chgo., 1959-60; v.p. Daniel J. Edelman, Chgo., 1960-76; mgr. pub. rels. Stone Container Corp., Chgo., 1976-82; pres. pub. rels. Firm Chgo. Connection, Matteson, Ill., 1982-98. Dir. pub. rels. Ill. Dem. Women for Adlai Stevenson, 1952; founder, pres. bd. dirs. Matteson Pub. Libr., 1958-87; chmn. Matteson Bicentennial Commn., 1973-76. Mem. Pub. Rels. Soc. Am. (accredited, Silver anvil award 1975), Publicity Club Chgo. (sec., bd. dirs. 1964-76, Golden Trumpet award 1965, 66, 75), Chgo. Jour. Assn. Mem. United Ch. Christ. Home: 9200 Lalique Ln Apt 1503 Fort Myers FL 33919-7408

GOYER, VIRGINIA L., accountant; b. Troy, N.Y., July 19, 1942; d. Clarence Archie and Edna Alice (Toussaint) G.; m. James Cobb Stewart, May 17, 1986. BS, Rochester Inst. Tech., 1975, MBA, 1976. Tax mgr. Deloitte Haskins & Sells, Rochester, N.Y., 1976-82; pres. Lamanna & Goyer, PC, CPAs, Rochester, 1982-89; owner Goyer & Assocs., CPAs, Rochester, 1989-93; pres. Virginia L. Goyer, CPA, P.C., Rochester, 1993—. Mem. adv. bd. Salvation Army, Rochester, 1985-88, Rochester Inst. Tech. Deferred Giving, 1988-89; mem. bd. Nat. Women's Hall of Fame, 1993-98; bd. dirs., treas. Friends of Women's Rights Nat. Park Inc., 2000-05, pres., 2005—. Mem. AICPA (nat. coun. 1995-98), Fla. Inst. CPAs, N.Y. State Inst. CPAs (bd. dirs. 1990-93, v.p. 1994-95, 1st woman pres. Rochester chpt. 1988-89), Rochester Women's Network, Nat. Assn. Women Bus. Owners (bd. dirs. 1992-93), Estate Planning Coun. (bd. dirs. 1987-89), NOW, Century Club Rochester (bd. dirs., fin. chair 2001-05) Office: 354 Westminster Rd Rochester NY 14607-3233

GOZEMBA, PATRICA ANDREA, women's studies and English language educator, writer; b. Medford, Mass., Nov. 30, 1940; d. John Charles and Mary Margaret (Sampey) Curran; m. Gary M. Gozemba, Sept. 4, 1967 (div. Feb. 1975). BA, Emmanuel Coll., Boston, 1962; MA, U. Iowa, 1963; EdD, Boston U., 1975. Tchr. Waltham (Mass.) H.S., 1963-64; prof. Salem (Mass.) State Coll., 1964—. Vis. fellow East-West Ctr., 1995; vis. prof. U. Hawaii, 1997-98; co-chair The History Project, Boston, 2000—; bd. dirs. Healthlink, Salem Alliance for the Environment, 2001—. Editor: New England Women's Studies, 1977—87; mem. editl. bd.: Thought and Action, 1990—93; contbr. articles to profl. jours.; author: Pockets of Hope: How Students and Teachers Change the World, 2002. Bd. dirs. Salem Alliance for the Environment, 2003—. Mem. NEA (standing com. 1982-93), NOW, NAACP, Nat. Women's Studies Assn. (gov. bd. 1977-89), Nat. Coun. Tchrs. English, Nat. Gay and Lesbian Task Force, Mass. State Coll. Assn. (editor 1982-90, 92-97), Herb Soc. Am. Democrat. Avocations: walking, tennis, gardening, photography. Home and Office: 17 Sutton Ave Salem MA 01970-5728

GRABER, DORIS APPEL, political scientist, writer, editor; b. St. Louis, Nov. 11, 1923; d. Ernest and Martha (Insel) Appel; m. Thomas M. Graber, June 15, 1941; children: Lee Winston, Thomas Woodrow, Jack Douglas, Jim Murray, Susan Doris AB, Washington U., St. Louis, 1941, MA, 1942; PhD, Columbia U., 1947. Feature writer St. Louis County Observer, Univ. City Tribune, 1939—41; civilian dir. U.S. Army Ednl. Reconditioning Program, Camp Maxey, Tex., 1943—45; editor legal mags. Commerce Clearing House, Chgo., 1945—46; lectr. polit. sci. Northwestern U., 1948—49, U. Chgo., 1950—51, rsch. assoc. Ctr. for Study Am. Fgn. and Mil. Policy, 1952—71; lectr. polit. sci. North Park Coll., 1952; mem. faculty U. Ill., Chgo., 1964—, assoc. prof. polit. sci., 1964—69, prof., 1970—; editor textbooks Harper & Row, Evanston, 1956—63. Vis. prof. Harvard U., 1996 Author: The Development of the Law of Belligerent Occupation, 1949, 68, Crisis Diplomacy: A History of U.S. Intervention Policies and Practices, 1959, Public Opinion, The President and Foreign Policy, 1968, Verbal Behavior and Politics, 1976, Mass Media and American Politics, 1980, 84, 89, 93, 96, 2001, 2005, Crime News and the Public, 1980, (with others) Media Agenda Setting in a Presidential Election, 1981, Processing the News: How People Tame the Information Tide, 1984, 88, 94, Public Sector Communication: How Organizations Manage Information, 1992; editor, contbr. The President and the Public, 1982; editor, contbr.: Media Power in Politics, 1984, 90, 94, 2000, 2006; editor: Political Comm., 1992-98, founding editor emeritus, 1998—, mem. editl. bd., 2001—; editor: (with others) The Politics of News: The News of Politics, 1998, Processing Politics: Learning from Television in the Internet Age, 2001 (Goldsmith Book prize 2003), The Power of Communication, 2003; book rev. editor Polit. Psychology, 1998—; mem. editl. bd. Polit. Sci. Quarterly, 1978—, Human Comm. Rsch., 1979-80, Pub. Opinion Quarterly, 1980-84, 93-98, Jour. Comm., 1985-91, 99—, Social Sci. Quarterly, 1989-2003, P.S.: Polit. Sci. and Politics, 1990-93, Discourse and Soc., 1990—, Discourse and Comm., 2006, Orgnl. Comm: Emerging Perspectives, 1994—, Jour. Health Comm., 1995-98, Harvard Internat. Jour. Press/Politics, 1995—, Acta Politica: Internat. Jour. Polit. Sci., 1997—, Comm., Soc. and Politics Series, Cambridge U. Press, 1999—, Polit. Comm., 2001—, Media and Am. Politics Ency., 2003—; contbr. articles to profl. jours Recipient Disting. Alumna award, Washington U., 2001, Univ. Scholar award, U. Ill., Chgo., 2003—. Mem. LWV, Am. Assn. Pub. Opinion Rsch., Midwest Assn. Pub. Opinion Rsch. (coun. 1978-83, program chmn. 1978-79, pres. 1980-81, Career award 1988), Midwest Polit. Sci. Assn. (past pres. 1972-73, coun. 1973-74, program sect. chair 1979, Career award 1994), Am. Polit. Sci. Assn. (coun. 1978-79, v.p. 1980-81, program chmn. 1984, chmn. polit. comm. sect. 1989-91, chmn. editl. bd. Polit. Sci. 1992-94), Internat. Polit. Sci. Assn., Internat. Comm. Assn. (divsn. program chmn. 1978-80, divsn. chmn. 1980-82, chmn. program 1990, chmn. pre-program 2004, Career award 1996), Assn. Edn. for Journalism, Acad. Polit. Sci., Am. Acad. Polit. and Social Sci., Internat. Soc. Polit. Psychology (coun. 1992-93, 95-98, co-program chmn. 1993-94, pres. 1995-96), Phi Beta Kappa (pres. Iota of Ill. chpt. 1991-92), Pi Sigma Alpha, Pi Alpha Alpha Home: 2895 Sheridan Pl Evanston IL 60201-1725 Office: U Ill 1007 W Harrison St Chicago IL 60607-7135 Office Phone: 312-996-3108. E-mail: dgraber@uic.edu.

GRABER, SUSAN P., federal judge; b. Oklahoma City, Okla., July 5, 1949; d. Julius A. and Bertha (Fenyves) Graber; m. William June, May 3, 1981; 1 child, Rachel June-Graber. BA, Wellesley Coll., 1969; JD, Yale U., 1972. Bar: N.Mex. 1972, Ohio 1977, Oreg. 1978. Asst. atty. gen. Bur. of Revenue, Santa Fe, 1972—74; assoc. Jones Gallegos Snead & Wertheim, Santa Fe, 1974—75, Taft Stettinius & Hollister, Cin., 1975—78; assoc., then ptnr. Stoel Rives Boley Jones & Grey, Portland, Oreg., 1978—88; judge pro tem Multonomah County Dist. Ct., 1983—88; arbitrator Oreg. Circuit Ct., 4th Jud. Dist., 1985—88; mediator US Dist. Ct., Dist. Oreg., 1986—88; judge, then presiding judge Oreg. Ct. Appeals, Salem, 1988—90; assoc. justice Oreg. Supreme Ct., Salem, 1990—98; judge US Ct. Appeals (9th cir.), Portland, 1998—. Mem. Gov.'s Adv. Coun. on Legal Svcs., 1979—88; mem. bd. visitors Sch. Law, U. Oreg., 1986—93; bd. dirs. U.S. Dist. Ct. of Oreg. Hist. Soc., 1985—, Oreg. Law Found., 1990—91. Mem.: Am. Law Inst., ABA, Am. Inns of Ct. (master), Oreg. Appellate Judges Assn. (sec.-treas. 1990—91, vice chair 1991—92, chair 1992—93), Oreg. Jud. Conf. (edn. com. 1988—91, program chair 1990), Ninth Cir. Jud. Conf. (chair exec. com. 1987—88), Oreg. State Bar (jud. adminstrn. com. 1985—87, pro bono com. 1988—90), Phi Beta Kappa. Mailing: US Ct Appeals 9th Cir Pioneer Courthouse 555 SW Yamhill St Portland OR 97204*

GRABLE, KRISTEN HEATHER, psychiatrist; b. Dallas, July 6, 1967; d. Nick and Frances Grable. BA, U. Tex., Austin, 1990; MD, U. Tex., Houston, 1994. Lic. Am. Bd. Psychiatry and Neurology. Resident in psychiatry U. Tex. Southwestern Med. Ctr. Dallas, 1994—98; staff psychiatrist Dallas Metrocare

Svcs., 1998—2003, med. dir., 2003—. Vol. Youth 2000, Dallas, 1998—99. Mem.: North Tex. Soc. Psychiat. Physicians, Am. Psychiat. Assn. Avocations: hiking, cooking. Office: Dallas Metrocare Svcs 1380 River Bend Dallas TX 75247 Office Phone: 214-275-7393.

GRABOWSKY, GAIL LEANNE, education educator, consultant; b. L.A., Jan. 12, 1963; d. Wallis Richard and Margaret Theresa (Cowley) Grabowsky. BS, Duke U., Durham, N.C., 1986, Dr. in Zoology, 1993. Rsch. technician Duke U., Durham, 1985—87; postdoctoral rschr. U. Hawaii, Honolulu, 1993—95; prof. Chaminade U., Honolulu, 1997—. Project coord. Nat. Audubon Soc., Honolulu, 1995—99; rsch. cons. Western Pacific Regional Fisheries Mgmt. Coun., Honolulu, 1997—2000. Author: (jour. articles) Evolution. Mem. adv. bd. Circles of Light, 2000—06; appointee Northwestern Hawaiian Islands Coral Reef Ecosystem Res. Adv. Coun., Hawaii, 2000—06; appointee environ. coun. Hawaii State Dept. Health, 2002—06; elected counselor Hawaii Acad. Sci., 2001—03. Recipient athletic scholarship, Duke U., 1982—86, Rookie Faculty of Yr. award, Chaminade U., 1997, Everyday Hero award, ARC Hawaii Chpt., 2000; fellow, U. Hawaii, 1993—95, rsch., Calif. Acad. Scis., 1995; grantee, Sigma Xi, 1992, CoCos Found., 1992—93; E. Baynard Halsted fellowship, Duke U., 1987—91. Mem.: Am. Soc. Naturalists, Soc. for the Study of Evolution, Soc. Conservation Biology. Democrat-Npl. Avocations: Polynesian outrigger canoe racing, swimming, running, movies. Office: Chaminade Univ 3140 Waialae Ave Honolulu HI 96816 Office Phone: 808-735-4834. Business E-Mail: ggrabows@chaminade.edu.

GRACE, BETTE FRANCES, certified public accountant; b. Hanford, Calif., Apr. 16, 1957; d. Boyd Lowell Sharp and Janet Praria; m. Clyde Jon Nold, May 4, 1974 (div. 1987); children: Mandolin P., Christopher J.; m. Michael E. Grace, Feb. 14, 1996. AA in Bus., Gavilan Coll., Gilroy, Calif., 1992; BS in Bus./Acctg., San Jose State U., 1994, postgrad., 1994—. CPA, Calif. Fin. controller Hollister (Calif.) Disposal, Inc., 1984-92; owner, operator Hollister Bookkeeping and Tax Svc., 1985-98; acct. mgr. Ridgemark Golf & Country Club, Hollister, 1992-98; CPA, owner Grace & Assocs CPAs, Hollister, 1998—. Fin. controller John Smith Landfill, Inc., Hollister, 1986-92, Ajax Portable Svc., Hollister, 1987-92. Supporter Monterey County (Calif.) Symphony Guild, 1991—; parent mem. Calif. High Sch. Rodeo Assn., Hollister, 1991—; dir. 33rd Dist. Agrl. Assn., San Benito County Fair Bd., 1992-96; fin. chmn. AT&T Pebble Beach Nat. Pro-Am. Mem. AICPA, El Gabilan Young Ladies Inst. Republican. Roman Catholic. Avocation: water and snow skiing. Office: Grace & Assocs CPAs PO Box 1352 Hollister CA 95024-1352

GRACE, JULIANNE ALICE, retired biotechnologist; b. Riverdale, NY, Oct. 29, 1937; d. Arthur Edward and Julia May (McCarthy) Thompson; m. Daniel Vincent Grace, July 2, 1960; children: Daniel Vincent III, Deirdre Elizabeth Beck. BA, Marymount Manhattan Coll., 1959; MA, Fordham U., 1960. Dir. admissions Marymount Manhattan Coll., N.Y.C., 1966-72; mgr. human resources The Perkin-Elmer Corp., Norwalk, Conn., 1972-78, dir. human resources, 1978-81, asst. sr. v.p. semiconductor equipment, 1981-83, asst. pres., 1983-85, v.p., asst. to CEO, 1985-86, v.p. adminstrn., 1986-90, v.p. corp. rels., 1990-95; pres. The Jagcom Group, New Canaan, Conn., 1995—2004; ret., 2004. Bd. dirs. Norwalk and Wilton chpts. ARC, 1975—85, Metropool, 1991—98; pres., bd. dirs. Waveny (Conn.) Care Ctr., 1998—99; bd. dirs. Waveny Network, 1988—; trustee Norwalk YMCA, 1986—94; active Norwalk C.C. Found., 1986—90, Fairfield 2000; mem. corp. cabinet U. Conn. Downstate Initiative, 1995—98, mem. adv. com., lectr. exec. edn. program U. Conn., 1996—2001; bd. dirs. New Canaan Cmty. Found., Conn., 2004—. Fellow Woodrow Wilson Nat. Found., 1959—60. Mem.: Fairfield Pub. Rels. Assn., Nat. Investor Rels. Inst. (sr. exec. roundtable), Econ. Soc. Conn., Saugatuck Harbor Yacht Club (bd. govs., flag officer fleet capt.), Wolfpit Running Club, Sports Car Club Am. Home and Office: 54 Louises Ln New Canaan CT 06840-2120

GRACE, L.A., fine artist, designer; b. N.Y.C., 1952; BFA Dean's list honors, Coll. New Rochelle, N.Y., 1986; attended, Cornell U., Ithaca, N.Y., 1985; student inviational Study Abroad Pilot Program, Les Ateler, Paris; attended Computer Applications, Westchester C.C., 1982, attended Auto. Cad., 2000—02; attended, Iona Coll., New Rochelle, N.Y., 1984. Cert. residential drafting & 30 CAD interior design. Interior designer Interscenes, Inc., New Rochelle, 1979-95; graphic designer Grace Designs & Panel Art, Ltd., New Rochelle, 1986—99; pvt. studio tutor, art workshop instr. Thornton Donovan Sch., New Rochelle, N.Y., 1998—2005, New Fairfield H.S., Conn., 1998—2005. Solo shows: Laurence Galleries, N.Y.C., 1987-92, Coll. New Rochelle, 1990 (blue ribbon award 1st Annual Juried Alumni Art Exhbn.), U.S. Libr. Congress fine artwork patent registry; represented in permanent corp. and pvt. collections in U.S. and Europe; group exhibits: Les Atalers, Paris, 1985, Coll. New Rochelle 1985, 88, 90, 91, 92; participant numerous soc. exhibits, arts & crafts shows. Lutheran. Avocations: photography, swimming, ice skating, flower arranging, reading.

GRACE, MARCIA BELL, advertising executive; b. Pitts., July 29, 1937; d. Daniel Henry and Gertrude Margaret (Loew) Bell; m. Roy Grace, May 16, 1966; children: Jessica Bell, Nicholas Bell. AB, Harvard U., 1959. V.p., assoc. creative dir. Doyle Dane Bernbach, N.Y.C., 1964-77; sr. v.p., creative dir. Wells, Rich, Greene, Inc., N.Y.C., 1977-85, exec. v.p., creative dir., 1986-90; cons. Marcia Grace & Co., N.Y.C., 1990—. Represented in permanent collections Mus. Modern Art. Recipient 1st Pl. ANDY award Advt. Club N.Y., 1968, 70, 72, 75, 1st Pl. Gold award The One Show, 1973, 78, Hall of Fame award The Clio Show, N.Y.C., 1982, 86. Avocations: horseback riding, gardening.

GRACE, NANCY A., news correspondent, former prosecutor; b. Macon, Ga., Oct. 23, 1958; d. Mac and Elizabeth Grace. BA, Mercer U., 1981; JD, Walter F. George Sch. Law, 1984; LLM, NYU. Bar: 1984. Law clk. to fed. ct. judge; practiced law with Fed. Trade Commn.; asst. dist. atty., Fulton County Atlanta, 1987—96; host Closing Arguments, Court TV, 2001—; sub. host Larry King Live, CNN, 2003—05; radio show host Rapid Fire with Nancy A. Grace, Clear Channel's KNEW-AM, 2004—; host CNN Headline News, 2005—. Lit. instr. Sch. Law, Ga. State U.; bus. law instr. Sch. Bus., Ga. State U.; appeared as legal commentator on ABC's The View, The Oprah Winfrey Show and numerous other cable and network programs. Contbr. articles to ABA Jour., various law reviews, and op-eds; author: Objection!: How High-Priced Defense Attorneys, Celebrity Defendants, and a 24/7 Media Have Hijacked Our Criminal Justice System, 2005 (Publishers Weekly Harcover bestseller list, 2005). Staff Atlanta Battered Women's Ctr. Hotline. Mem.: State Bar Ga. Achievements include while at Atlanta Fulton County Dist. Atty. Office, compiled a perfect record of nearly 100 felony convictions at trial and no losses. Office: Court TV 600 Third Ave 3rd Fl New York NY 10016 Office Phone: 212-973-7933.*

GRACE-CRUM, PHYLLIS VENETIA, military officer; b. Phila., Jan. 16, 1957; d. Philip Dean, Doris Eleanor Dean-Hagood; m. H. Ellis, Apr. 14, 2001. BS, Lincoln U., Oxford, Pa., 1979. Lic. ministry, 2003. Petroleum platoon leader 590th Combat Support and Combat Svcs. Support Co., Zebra Base, Saudi Arabia, 1991—91; chief billeting and housing Hdqrs. and Hdqrs. Co., 1st Area Support Group, Damman, Saudi Arabia, 1991—91; exec. officer Hdqrs. and Hdqrs. Co., 22nd Support Ctr., Dammam, Saudi Arabia, 1991—92; supply and svcs. platoon leader 226th Supply and Svcs. Co., Fort Stewart, Ga., 1992—93, platoon leader Ft. Stewart, Ga., 1992—93; with 632nd Maintenance Co. 87th Corps Support Bn., Ft. Stewart, Ga., 1993—94, asst. supply and svcs. officer, 1995—96; U.S. Army Recruiting Co. comdr. Pitts. Recruiting Bn., 1st Recruiting Brigade, 1996—99; co. comdr. 183rd Maintenance Co., 68th Corps Support Battalion, 43rd Area Support Group, Ft. Carson, Colo., 1999; logistics ops. officer 3/345th Regiment, 4th Brigade, 87th DIV (Tng. Support Divsn.), Forest Park, Ga., 2000—; promoted 2d lt., IMAR02 to major, 1991—. Environ. health specialist Ft. Devens, 1986—88. Contbr. The Logistician, 1996. Supt. ch. edn. Manna Missionary Baptist Ch., Chesapeake, Va., 2003; dir. tng. Word of Life Sch. Gifts, 2004. Decorated Army Achievement medal U.S. Army, Army Commendation medal, Nat. Def. medal, Joint Meritorious Unit award, Meritorious Svc. medal. Mem.: Am. Legion, Alpha Kappa Delta, Delta Sigma Theta. Avocations: horseback riding, ballroom dancing, reading, weightlifting. Office: 3/345th CS/CSS TS Bn Bldg 207B 4653 N First St Forest Park GA 30297-5000 Home: PO Box 61937 Virginia Beach VA 23466-1937 Office Phone: 757-788-2757. Personal E-mail: phylliscrum@hotmail.com.

GRACHEK, MARIANNA KERN, healthcare administrator; b. Amsterdam, The Netherlands, Oct. 6, 1949; d. Johannus J. and Paulina G. (DeHaas) Kern; m. Kenneth A. Grachek, June 12, 1971; children: Ellen, Brett. Grad., St. Vincent Med. Ctr., Toledo, 1971; BSN, U. Toledo, 1978; MSN, Med. Coll. of Ohio, 1987. Lic. nursing home adminstr.; cert. gerontol. nurse; cert. DON Nat. Assn. Dirs. of Nursing Adminstrn; cert. nursing home adminstr. and assisted living adminstr., ACHCA. Clinician gerontol. nursing, staff devel. educator St. Vincent Med. Ctr., Toledo, 1982-87; instr. St. Vincent Sch. Nursing, Toledo, 1985; dir. nursing svcs. Lake Park Nursing Care Ctr., Sylvania, Ohio, 1987-90; nursing home adminstr. St. Luke's Transitional Care Ctr., Maumee, Ohio; long term care surveyor Joint Commn. on Accreditation of Health Care Orgns., 1993—97; exec. dir., Long Term Care Accreditation Program Joint Commn. on Accreditation of Healthcare Orgn., Oakbrook Terrace, 1997—2006; pres., CEO Am. Coll. Health Care Administrators, Alexandria, Va., 2006—. Recipient Sigma Theta Tau (Zeta Theta Chpt.) Rsch. award, 1987; MCO Satellite scholar, 1986. Mem. Nat. Gerontol. Nursing Assn. (regional bd. dirs. 1988-93), N.W. Ohio Gerontol. Assn. (chair budget com. 1987-91), Alzheimer's Assn. (pres. N.W. Ohio chpt. 1991-93), ALHCA (bd. dirs. 1999-2003), Sigma Theta Tau. Office: Am Coll Health Care Administrators 300 N Lee St Ste 301 Alexandria VA 22314

GRADDICK-WEIR, MIRIAN, human resources specialist; d. Sam Massenberg. BA, Hampton U.; MS, PhD, Penn State U. With AT&T, Bedminster, NJ, 1981—, various positions in human resources and customer svc., 1981—94, v.p. multimedia products group, exec. v.p. human resources. Bd. dirs. Harleysville Ins. Cos., Joint Ctr. Polit. and Econ. Studies, Human Resources Policy Assn. Named Human Resources Exec. of Yr., Human Resources Exec. mag., 2000; recipient Disting. Psychologist in Mgmt. award, Soc. Psychologists in Mgmt., 2003. Fellow: Nat. Acad. Human Resources. Office: AT&T Corp One AT&T Way Bedminster NJ 07921 Office Phone: 908-221-2000. Office Fax: 908-532-1673.

GRADO-WOLYNIES, EVELYN (EVELYN WOLYNIES), nursing educator; b. N.Y.C., Apr. 2, 1944; d. Joseph Frederick and Evelyn Marie (Ronning) Grado; m. Jon Gordon Wolynies, July 12, 1964; children: Jon Andrew, Kristine Elisabeth; m. Brian Bereika, 1999. AAS, Burlington County Coll., 1990; AS, Camden C.C., 1990; BSN cum laude, Thomas Jefferson U., 1991, MSN summa cum laude, 1992; postgrad., Johns Hopkins U., 1993-95. RN N.J., Pa. Charge nurse Hampton Hosp., Westampton, N.J., 1990-92; adjunct clin. instr. psychiat. nursing Burlington County Coll., Pemberton, N.J., 1992-93; project leader Alzheimer's disease clin. drug study Olsten Health Care, Cherry Hill, N.J., 1992-95, psychiat. case mgr., 1992-94; CNS neuropsych in Huntingtons Disease Dr. Allen Rubin, Camden, N.J., 1992; psychiat. case mgr. Moorestown (N.J.) Vis. Nurses Assn., 1992; charge nurse, group therapist, rschr. Friends Hosp., Phila., 1994-99; clin. mgr. The Caring Link partial geriatric outpatient program Frankford Hosp., Phila., 1996-99; psychotherapist Penn Friends, Marlton, NJ, 2000—02. Pvt. practice hypnotherapy/psychotherapy; cons. psychiat. care, Alzheimer's Disease, RN/home health aide instr. Olsten-Kimberly Home Care; clin. preceptor U. Pa. Sch. NSG, MSN, GNP and Adult Mental CS Programs. Contbr. articles to nursing jours. Mem. Burlington County Coll. Alumni Bd.; founder, dir. Support Group for Adult Children with Aging Parents; Developed music therapy/exercise program for Geriatric Psych patients. Recipient Juanita Wilson award, 1991, Farber fellowship, 1991-92.; Nurse in Washington intern, 1992; named to Burlington County Coll. Hall of Fame, 1994 Mem. Am. Assn. of Neuroscience Nurses, Am. Psychiat. Nurses Assn., N.J. State Nurses Assn., Sigma Theta Tau (Delta Rho chpt.), Phi Theta Kappa. Home: PO Box 3604 Cherry Hill NJ 08034-0550

GRADY, JOYCE (MARIAN JOYCE GRADY), psychotherapist, consultant; b. Riverside, N.J., Sept. 27, 1930; d. David and Agnes Marian (Conroy) Lawber; children: Andrea, Christine; m. James F. Moller, June 11, 1983. BA in Clin. Psychology, U. Penna, 1951; M in Social Work, certificate in alcohol studies, Rutgers U., New Brunswick, N.J., 1968; certificate in psychotherapy, Inst. Psychoanalytic Psychotherapy, 1973. Lic. clin. social worker, N.J. Caseworker Upward Bound Program, Rutgers U., New Brunswick, summer 1966; psychiat. social work supr., chief psychiat. social worker Roosevelt Hosp., Edison, N.J., 1968-92, in-svc. educator in nursing and social work, 1972-92, support group caregiver, 1970-92; nursing home cons. Abbot Manor Nursing Home, Plainfield, N.J., 1984-92; pvt. practice psychotherapy, Highland Park, N.J., 1975—. Adj. prof., field instr. grad. sch. social work Rutgers U., New Brunswick, 1970-92; guest lectr. depression and geriatrics Rutgers Sch. Social Work, New Brunswick, 1975-92; cmty. lectr. dying, aging, loss, and depression in long term care; outreach cons. personal assistance and homebound elderly, Middlesex County, N.J., 1975-78; mem. adv. bd., chmn. Middlesex County Adv. Coun. Aging, North Brunswick, N.J., 1973-95. Contbr. papers, panelist in field. Advocate, Middlesex County Adv. Coun. on Aging, North Brunswick, 1970-92; mem. Cmty. Outreach Adv. Coun.; participant seminars svc. providers, Middlesex County, N.J., 1995. Mem.: NASW (guest panel mem., guest spkr. psychotherapy confs.), Rutgers Club, Penn Club N.Y.C. Avocations: writing, decorating, music, computers, gardening. Office: 12 N 4th Ave Highland Park NJ 08904-2736

GRADY, PATRICIA A., federal agency administrator; Diploma in nursing, St. Francis Hosp. Sch. Nursing, 1964; BSN, Georgetown U., 1967; MS in nursing, U. Md., 1968, PhD in physiology, 1977, D (hon.) in Pub. Svc., 1996; cert. in sr. mgrs. in govt., John F. Kennedy Sch. Govt., Cambridge, 1994. Instr. Sch. Nursing Washington Hosp. Ctr., 1966-67; from instr. to rsch. asst. prof. Sch. Nursing U. Md., Bethesda, 1968-88, rsch. assoc., 1976-77; health sci. administrator Nat. Inst. Neurol. Disorders and Stroke, NIH, Bethesda, 1988-92, asst. dir., 1992-93, dep. dir., 1993—95, acting dir., 1993-94; dir. Nat. Inst. Nursing Rsch., NIH, Bethesda, 1995—. NIH fellow, 1973-76; NIN(C)DS grantee, 1976-88; recipient Sol Greenberg Award for leadership ability and clin. excellence St. Francis Hosp., 1964, Rozella M. Schlottfeld Disting. Lecture Award Case Western Reserve U., 1996, Centennial Achievement Medal, Georgetown U. Fellow Am. Heart Assn. Stroke Coun. (Excellence in Nursing Lectr. Award 1995); Mem. AAAS, ANA, Am. Acad. Nursing, Am. Lung Assn., Am. Soc. Profl. and Exec. Women, Am. Acad. Neurology (lectr. 1993-95), Am. Neurol. Assn., Soc. Neuroci., NY Acad. Sciences, Neurotrauma Soc., Sigma Theta Tau (award 1966), Inst. Medicine. Office: Nat Inst Nursing Rsch NIH Bldg 31 Rm 5B05 31 Center Dr Bethesda MD 20892-2178 Office Phone: 301-496-8230. Office Fax: 301-594-3405. E-mail: gradyp@mail.nih.gov.*

GRADY, SANDRA C., minister, counselor; b. Kinston, N.C., July 8, 1941; d. William Devereaux Cobb and Nora Cathleen Davenport; m. Sanders W. Grady; children: Daniel, Dean. BS in Bus. and Eng. Edn., East Carolina u., Greenville, N.C., 1963, MS in Counseling and Edn., 1971; ThD, Wagner Leadership Inst., Colo. Springs, Colo., 2000. School tchr. and counselor, Calif., Conn., and Ark., 1965—94; owner and instr. Grady Studies, Fairfax, Va., 1975—; founder and dir. Va. Prayer Network, Fairfax, Va., 1990—, Master's Keys, Fairfax, Va., 2002—. Prayer coord. Well Builders, Aledo, Tex., 1991—; mid-Atlantic dir. and coord. U.S. Strategic Prayer Network, Washington, 1998—, intercessional counselor Eagles team, 1998—, mem. nat. adv. bd., 2003—; mem. adv. bd. Nat. Coun. Govt. Intercessions, 2005—, Internat. Leadership Embassy, Washington, 2005—; instr. The Citadel, Washington, 2000—, Colombia; internat. spkr. and Biblical counselor 1990—. Mem.: Nat. Fedn. Music Tchrs., Internat. Coalition of Apostles. Republican. Avocations: writing, composition.

GRAEBE, ANNETTE MULVANY, professor emeritus, retired university administrator; b. Benton, Ill., Feb. 11, 1943; d. Augusta (Magnabosco) Mulvany; m. William Fredrick Graebe, Jr., Feb. 23, 1974; 1 child, Justin William. BS, So. Ill. U.-Carbondale, 1962, MA, 1964. Rsch. asst., speech instr. So. Ill. U.-Carbondale, 1962-64; chmn. speech and theater dept. McKendree Coll., Lebanon, Ill., 1964-68; dir. info. center, So. Ill. U., Edwardsville, 1968-90, assoc. prof. speech communication, 1968-88, mem. faculty bd. govs.; cons. communications, pub. speaker. Contbr. articles to profl. jours.; book reviewer. Coord. Edwardsville Autumn Festival Children, Bicentennial Celebrations South Ill. U. Recipient Ill. and U.S. Bicentennial Commn. citations, 1976, Coun. for Advancement and Support of Edn. exceptional achievement community rels. and publ. rels. awards, Washington, 1976, 77, 81, Toronto, Can., 1982, Silver Medal for Pub. Rels. Projects, Coun. Advancement and Support of Edn., 1986, Bronze Quill award Internat. Assn. Bus. Communicators, 1986; named Woman of Year, Bus. and Profl. Women's Club, Edwardsville, 1983, Outstanding Faculty Advisor of Midwest Pub. Rels. Student Soc. Am., 1988. Mem. Pub. Rels. Soc. Am. (edn. chmn., treas., bd. dirs. St. Louis chpt. 1986-90, Outstanding Faculty Adviser 1982), Univ. Ambassadors (hon.), Pi Kappa Delta, Kappa Delta Pi, Zeta Phi Eta, Alpha Phi Omega, Alpha Phi. Office: PO Box 561 Collinsville IL 62234-0561

GRAF, DOROTHY ANN, human resources specialist; b. Nashville, Mar. 21, 1935; d. Henry George and Martha Dunlap (Hill) Meek; m. Peter Louis Graf, Oct. 28, 1971; children: Sidney E. Pollard, Deborah Lynn Pollard, Robert George Pollard, Michelle Joy Graf. Student, Montgomery Coll., 1979—. Office mgr. Pa. Life Ins. Co., Miami and Dallas, 1957-72; exec. sec. to med. dir. Pitts. Children's Hosp., 1974; sec. GE/TEMPO, Washington, 1974-76; adminstrv. asst. to sr. v.p. Logistics Mgmt. Inst., Washington, 1976-81, dir. adminstrv. svc., 1981-97, dir. recruiting and tng., 1995-97, dir. human resources, 1997-99; cons. human resources specialist, 1999—2000. Dir. KHI Svcs., Inc. Mem. Washington Tech. Pers. Forum. Democrat. Baptist. Home: 1400 Newry Circle Ormond Beach FL 32174 Personal E-mail: dotsie123@earthlink.net.

GRAF, STEFFI, retired professional tennis player; b. Bruhl, Germany, June 14, 1969; d. Peter and Heidi Graf; m. Andre Agassi, 2001; 2 children. Founder Steffi Graf Marketing, 1996—; designer Steffi Graf Handbags, 2002—. Amb. World Wildlife Fund (WWF); founder Children of Tomorrow, 1998—. Winner numerous profl. women's tennis tournaments including The Golden Grand Slam (Australian Open, French Open, Wimbledon, U.S. Open, Olympics), 1988, Berlin Open, 1988, Wimbledon, 1989, 91, 92, 93, 95, 96, U.S. Open, 1989, 93, 95, 96, Australian Open, 1989, 1990, 94, French Open, 1993, 95, 96, 99, Olympic Gold Medal, 1988; ret. from competition, 1999; named WTA Player of Yr., 1987-90, 1993-96; recipient Olympic Medal of Honor, IOC, 1999, Female Sports Award of the Last Decade, Espy, 1999. Achievements include 107 Career Titles; finished WTA season ranked no. 1, 1987-90, 1993-96; ranked no. 1 in world for more consecutive weeks than any other player in tennis history; ranks 1st all-time in career proze money ($21 million); only person to win a Grand Slam on four different surfaces; only person to win a Golden Grand Slam. Office: Steffi Graf Sport GmBH Mallaustrasse 75 68219 Mannheim Germany

GRAFF, CHERYL L., medical facility program administrator; b. Vancouver, Wash., Sept. 30, 1958; d. Russell C. and M. Gayle Obbink; 1 child, Jason G. Waugaman. Diploma in nursing, Citizens Gen. Sch. Nursing, New Kensington, Pa., 1979; BSN, U. Wyo., 1995. RN; cert. inpatient obstetrics. Obstetrical nurse Citizens Gen. Hosp., New Kensington, 1979-81, Wyo. Med. Ctr., Casper, 1982-95, nursing coord. women's svcs., 1995—. Mem. Natrona County Health Adv. Bd., Casper, 1995—; vice chair program svc. com. Wyo. chpt. March of Dimes. Mem. Soroptimist Internat. (chair membership Ctrl. Wyo. chpt. 1996—). Republican. Home: 3410 Saratoga Rd Casper WY 82604-4808 Office: Wyo Med Ctr 1255 E C St Casper WY 82601-2100

GRAFF, CYNTHIA STAMPER, health facility administrator; b. Fairbanks, Alaska, May 22, 1953; d. Marshall Bernard and Nell (Buntyn) Stamper; m. Grant H. Van de Walker, July 13, 1974 (div. 1980); m. Dennis Alan Graff, July 10, 1990 (div. 1996). BS in Fin., Calif. State U., Long Beach, 1975; LLB, York U., Toronto, 1985. Pres. MC Fin., Inc., Salt Lake City, 1976-82; founder, pres. The Road Butler, Toronto, 1985-86; house counsel Polyvoltec Inc., Toronto, 1986-87; v.p. Lindora Med. Clinics, Costa Mesa, Calif., 1988-91; pres. Lindora, Inc., Costa Mesa, 1992—. Mem. Am. Soc. Bariatric Physicians, Young Pres.'s Orgn. Republican. Avocations: golf, skiing, reading. Office: Lindora Med Clinics 3505 Cadillac Ave Ste N-2 Costa Mesa CA 92626-1466

GRAFF, PAT STUEVER, secondary school educator; b. Tulsa, Mar. 24, 1955; d. Joseph H., Sr. and Joann (Schneider) Stuever; m. Mark A. Rumsey; children: Earl, Jr., Jeremy. BS in Secondary Edn., Okla. State U., 1976; postgrad., U. N.M., 1976-87. Cert. tchr. lang. arts, social studies, journalism, French, N.Mex. Substitute tchr. Albuquerque Pub. Schs., 1976-78; tchr. Cleveland Mid. Sch., Albuquerque, 1978-86, La Cueva H.S., Albuquerque, 1986—, co-chair English dept., 1996—, chair sch. restructuring coun., 1999-2001. Adviser award winning lit. mag. El Tesoro, sch. newspapers The Edition, Huellas del Oso; instr. journalism workshops, N.Mex. Press Assn., Ind. U., Bloomington, Nat. Scholastic Press, Mpls., Kans. State U., Manhattan, Interscholastic Press League, Austin, Tex., St. Mary's U., San Antonio, Ala. Scholastic Press Assn., Wash.; keynote spkr. at numerous confs. in Ohio, Ind., Kans., S.C., Utah, La., Okla., Ala., N.Mex., Tex., Wash., Idaho, and N.Y.; reviewer of lang. and textbooks for several cos.; instr. Dial-A-Tchr., N.Mex., 1991-05; texbook evaluator Holt Pub., Inc., 1991; nat. bd. cert. tchr. adolescent/young adult English lang. arts, 2001—; mem. N.Mex. Network of Nat. Bd. Cert. Tchrs., 2002—, 2d v.p., 2003-; state bd. dirs. N.Mex. Coun. for the Social Studies, 1998-, chair state conf., 2001, state pres., 2002-03, state treas., 2003-; comm. officer, sec. ABQ Tchrs. Fedn. 2003-05. Author: Journalism Text, 1983; contbg. author: Communication Skills Resource Text, 1987, Classroom Publishing/Literacy, 1992; contbr. articles to profl. jours. Troop leader Girl Scouts U.S., 1979—90, coord. various programs, asst. program com. chmn. Chaparral Coun., 1988—89, chmn. adult recognition task force, 1991—96, bd. dirs., 1991—98; active PTA Gov. Bent Elem. Sch., 1983—86, v.p., 1985—86, Osuna Elem. Sch., 1986—92, N.Mex. PTA, 1994—2000; pub. various children's lit. mags., 1987—; pub. parent's newsletter, 1986—; newsletter layout editor Albuquerque Youth Soccer Orgn., 1985—88; active YMCA youth and govt. model legis.; faculty advisor La Cueva del., 1986—2002, press corps advisor, 1987—2001, asst. state dir., 2001—; asst. den. leader Boy Scouts Am., 1987—88, den leader, 1988—91. Recipient Innovative Tchg. award Bus. Week mag., 1990, Svc. commendation Coll. Edn. Alumni Assn., Okla. State U., 1990, Alumni Recognition award, 1993, Mem. Yr. Svc. award Bernalillo County Coun. Internat. Reading Assn., Thanks to Tchrs. award Apple Computers, 1990, Spl. Recognition Albuquerque C. of C., 1992, Disting. Svc. award NCTE, 2002; Gov.'s Outstanding Women in N.Mex. honoree, 2004; named Spotlighted Mem. Phi Delta Kappa, 1990, Spl. Recognition Advisor Dow Jones Newspaper Fund, 1990, Nat. H.S. Journalism Tchr. of Yr., 1995, Disting. Advisor, 1991, U.S. West Tchr. Yr. finalist, 1991, N.Mex. Pubs. Adviser of Yr., 1991, N.Mex. State Tchr. of Yr., 1993, finalist Nat. Tchr. Yr., 1993, finalist Am. Tchr. Awards, Disney, 1998; named USA Today All-Am. Tchr., 1999; grantee Phi Delta Kappa 1989, 91, Geraldine R. Dodge Found., 1990, 92, 95-97, Learn and Serve Am., 1999. Mem.: AAUW (chpt. newsletter editor 1995—2001, local v.p. 1997—99, state program v.p. 1997—99, state media chair 2000—03), ASCD (editor newsletter 1991—92, focus on excellence awards com. 1992—94, state bd. dirs. 2002—, Focus on Excellence award 1990), Albuquerque (N.Mex.) Tchrs. Fedn. (PR and comms. officer 2003—, sec. 2003—), N Mex. Coun. for Social Studies (mem. bd. 1999—2002, state v.p. 2001—02, pres. 2002—03), N. Mex. World Class Tchr. Network (state vice-pres. 2002—), N.Mex. Goals 2000 (panel mem. 1994—97), Quill & Scroll (adv. La Cueva chpt. 1986—, judge nat. newspaper rating contest 1988—97), Albuquerque Press Women (v.p. 1994, pres. 1995, Communicator of Achievement award 1993), N.Mex. Press Women (state scholarship chair 1994, publicity chair 1995—96, state treas. 1996—98, state v.p. 1998—99), N.Mex. Scholastic Press Assn. (state v.p. 1985—89, coord. workshop 1986, editor newsletter 1986—89, asst. chair state conf. 1988, 1989, state bd. dirs. 1991—2000, state v.p. 1992—95), N.Mex. Coun. Tchrs. English (regional coord. Albuquerque 1983—86, chair state confs. 1985—87, editl. bd. N.Mex. English Jour. 1986—88, state pres.

1987—88, chair facilities for Fall conf. 1988—93, chair English Humanities expo com. 1988—99, adv. mgr. 1989—90, editor N.Mex. English Jour. 1999—2003, Svc. award 1989, Outstanding H.S. English Tchr. N.Mex. 1991), Journalism Edn. Assn. (judge nat. contests 1988—, mem. nat. cert. bd. 1989—99, presenter nat. convs. 1989—, cert. journalism educator 1990, nat. bd. 1991—2002, master 1991—), Nat. Fedn. Press Women, Nat. Sch. Pub. Rels. Assn. (issues seminar planning com. 1990, chair 1991, master journalism educator 1991—, nat. conf. chmn. 1997—99, Zia chpt., contest winner 1991—94, Pres.'s award 1993), Nat. Coun. Tchrs. English (nat. chair com. English Tchrs. and Pubs. 1988—91, chair English Humanities Expo com. 1990—99, standing com. affiliates 1991—94, nat. chair 1995—98, chair English Humanities Expo com. 2001—03, nat. exec. com. 2001—03, nat. chair assembly for advisors of student pubs., regional rep. Tex., La., N.Mex., chair English Humanities Expo com. 2005—, Disting. Svc. award 2002), Nat. Alliance High Schs. (tchr. rep. 1997—2000), Nat. Assn. Secondary Sch. Prins. (Breaking Ranks tchr. rep.), Phi Delta Kappa (pres. U. N.Mex. br. 2002—), Delta Kappa Gamma (state profl. affairs com. chair 2003—), Pi Lambda Theta (Ethel Mary Moore award Outstanding Educator 1993, Gov.'s Outstanding Women in N.Mex. 2004). Roman Catholic. Avocations: soccer, running, hiking, travel, skiing. Home: 8101 Krim Dr NE Albuquerque NM 87109-5223 Office: La Cueva H S 7801 Wilshire Ave NE Albuquerque NM 87122-2807 Fax: 505-797-2250. Office Phone: 505-823-2327. Personal E-mail: pgraff@aol.com.

GRAFF, RANDY, actress; b. Bklyn., May 23, 1955; Grad., Wagner Coll. Profl. theater debut in Gypsy, Village Dinner Theater, Raleigh, N.C.; appeared in Godspell, Raleigh; other appearances include Pins and Needles, Roundabout Theatre, N.Y.C., 1978, Something Wonderful, Westchester Regional Theatre, Harrison, N.Y., 1979, Sarava, Mark Hellinger Theatre, N.Y.C., 1979, Coming Attractions, Playwrights Horizons, Mainstage Theatre, N.Y.C., 1980, Keystone, McCarter Theatre, Princeton, N.J., 1981, A My Name is Alice, Village Gate Theatre, N.Y.C., 1984, Amateurs, Playhouse in the Park, Cin., 1985, Fiorello!, Goodspell Opera House, East Haddam, Conn., 1985, Absurd Person Singular, Phila. Drama Guild, Phila., 1986, Les Miserables, Broadway Theatre, N.Y.C., 1987, City of Angels, Va. Theatre, N.Y.C., 1989 (Drama Desk award Featured Actress in Musical 1989, Tony award Supporting of Featured Actress in Musical 1990), Falsettos, 1993, Laughter on the 23rd Floor, 1993, Moon Over Buffalo, Martin Beck Theatre, 1995-96, High Society, St. James Theatre, N.Y.C., 1998, A Class Act, Ambassador Theatre, N.Y.C., 2001, Fiddler on the Roof, Minskoff Theatre, 2004, The Lady with All the Answers, 2005; (TV shows) include Mad About You, Law & Order, Love & War, Pros & Cons; (films) Key's to Tulsa, 1995. Office: TRI Richard Stable 321 W 44th St Ste 805 New York NY 10035-5404

GRAFF, SHERRY, adult nurse practitioner; b. Providence, Aug. 3, 1947; d. Morris and Sylvia Saslaw; m. Frederick Robert Graff, Aug. 24, 1969; children: David, Michele. BSN, San Jose State U., 1969; MSN, U. Phoenix, San Jose, Calif., 1999. RN, registered nurse practitioner, cert. diabetes educator, registered diagnostic med. sonographer, cert. advanced diagnostic mgr. Staff nurse San Leandro (Calif.) Dr.'s Hosp., 1969—71; staff nurse, labor and delivery Santa Clara Valley Med. Ctr., San Jose, Calif., 1971—78, fetal testing RN, 1978—83, clin. coord. fetal testing lab., 1978—2004, nurse practitioner, 1983—, CNS-DM in pregnancy, 1984. Clin. preceptor San Jose State Nursing Program, 1985; instr. EPA Nurse Practitioner Program, Campbell, Calif., 1980—88. Vol. Diabetes Mellitus Soc., San Jose, 1981—99. Mem.: Assn. Ultrasound in Medicine, Assn. Women's Health, Am. Assn. Diabetes Mellitus Educators (chair ob-gyn./neonatal com., pres.). Achievements include development and running of a nurse-run maternal-fetal testing unit; development and running of a diabetes in pregnancy program, with nurse practitioner as primary prenatal provider and diabetes mellitus manager. Home: 2516 SW 45th St Cape Coral FL 33914-6104

GRAFFEO, MARY THÉRÈSE, music educator, performer; b. Mineola, N.Y., Jan. 20, 1949; d. Michael Joseph and Florence Marie (Lonette) G. BA in Music Edn., Adelphi U., 1972; MusM in Vocal Performance, Kent State U., 1982. Cert. music tchr. NY. Tchr., therapist Nassau County Bd. Coop. Ednl. Svcs., Westbury, NY, 1972-85; tchr. music, developer curricula Great Neck (N.Y.) Pub. Schs., 1985-87; tchr. music Syosset (N.Y.) Pub. Schs., 1987-88, 89-90, Jericho (N.Y.) Pub. Schs., 1988-89; tchr. music, developer creative programs Lawrence (N.Y.) Pub. Schs., 1990-92; tchr. music Herricks Pub. Schs., New Hyde Park, NY, 1992-93, Hempstead (N.Y.) Pub. Schs., 1993—. Music dir. summer programs Friends Acad., Locust Valley, N.Y., 1989-95. Author: Creative Enrichment Programs/America: The First 300 Years in Song, 1990, (curriculum) Music for the Trainable Mentally Retarded, 1973, Music for the Early Childhood Center of Hempstead Public Schools, 2002, (book) Composing with Kindergarten, 2006; co-author: The Remediation of Learning Discrepancies Through Music, 1980; composer: (plays) Red Riding Hood's Day, 1993, The Bell of Atri, The Children's Song, 1995. Cultural adv. bd. Lawrence Pub. Schs., 1990-92, Hempstead Pub. Schs., 1993—; founding mem. United We Stand Am., Dallas, 1992-93. Scholar Adelphi U., 1968-72, Blossom Festival Sch., Kent, Ohio, 1978-79. Mem. NEA, Am. Fedn. Tchrs., Music Educators Nat. Conf., N.Y. State United Tchrs., N.Y. State Sch. Music Assn., Nassau Music Educators Assn. Democrat. Roman Catholic. Avocations: aviculture, needlecrafts, travel, photography, concerts. Home: 18 Osborne Ln Greenvale NY 11548-1140 Office: Early Childhood Ctr 436 Front St Hempstead NY 11550-4212 Office Phone: 516-489-2424. E-mail: mgraffeo@optonline.net.

GRAFSTEIN, BERNICE, physiology and neuroscience educator, researcher; BA, U. Toronto, Ont., Can., 1951; PhD, McGill U., Montreal, Que., Can., 1954. Prof. physiology and biophysics Cornell U. Med. Coll., NYC, 1973—, disting. prof. neurosci., 1984—. Office: Cornell U Weill Med Coll Dept Physiology New York NY 10021 Office Phone: 212-746-6364. E-mail: bgraf@med.cornell.edu.

GRAFTON, BETH P., music educator; b. Altoona, Pa., Dec. 16, 1957; d. Robert R. Reifsteck, Sally A. Reifsteck; m. Dirk S. Grafton; children: Christopher, Diana. MA in Music Edn., Indiana U. of Pa., 1994. Cert. Instrnl. II Pa., 1979. Tchr. music Indiana Area Sch. Dist., Indiana, Pa., 1979—; violist Altoona Symphony Orch., Altoona, Pa., 1975—94. Violist Johnstown Symphony Orch., Johnstown, Pa., 1979—99. Musician (condr., dir.): Indiana Area H.S. Pit Orch. V.p. Zion Luth. Ch. Coun., Indiana, 1998—2000. Mem.: Pa. State Edn. Assn., Pa. Music Educators Assn., Kappa Delta Pi (life), Delta Omicron (life). Lutheran.

GRAFTON, SUE, novelist; b. Louisville, Apr. 24, 1940; d. Cornelius Warren and Vivian Boisseau (Harnsberger) G.; children: Leslie, Jay, Jamie; m. Steven Humphrey, Oct. 1, 1978. BA, U. Louisville, 1961. Lectr. L.A. City Coll., Long Beach (Calif.) City Coll., U. Dayton (Ohio) Writers Conf., Midwest Writers Conf., Canton, Ohio, Calif. Luth. Coll., Thousand Oaks, Santa Barbara (Calif.) Writers Conf., L.A. Valley Coll., Antioch Writers Conf., Yellow Springs, Ohio, S.W. Writers Conf., Albuquerque, Smithsonian Campus on the Mall, Washington, and others. Author: (novels) Keziah Dane, 1967, The Lolly-Madonna War, 1969, "A" is for Alibi, 1982 (Mysterious Stranger award 1982-83), "B" is for Burglar, 1985 (Shamus award 1986, Anthony award 1987), "C" is For Corpse, 1986, "D" is for Deadbeat, 1987, "E" is for Evidence, 1988 (Doubleday Mystery Guild award 1989), "F" is for Fugitive, 1989 (Doubleday Mystery Guild award 1990, The Falcon award 1990), "G" is for Gumshoe, 1990 (Doubleday Mystery Guild award 1991, Anthony award 1991, Shamus award 1991), "H" is for Homicide, 1991 (Doubleday Mystery Guild award 1992), "I" is for Innocent, 1992 (Doubleday Mystery Guild award 1992, Mystery Scene Am. Mystery award 1993), Kinsey and Me, 1992, "J" is for Judgement, 1994, "K" is for Killer, 1994 (Shamus award 1994), "L" is For Lawless, 1995, "M" is For Malice, 1996, "N" is for Noose, 1998, "O" is for Outlaw, 1999, "P" is for Peril, 2001, "Q" is for Quarry, 2002, "R" is for Ricochet, 2004, "S" is for Silence, 2005; editor: Writing Mysteries, 1992; author short fiction, short stories, screenplay, teleplay TV episodes. Named to, Am. Acad. Achievement, 2000. Mem. Writers Guild Am. West, Mystery Writers Am. Inc. (pres. 1994), Private Eye Writers Assn. (pres. 1989-90, Life Achievement award 2003), Crime Writers Assn. Address: Penguin/Putnam 375 Hudson St New York NY 10014-3672

GRAGG, JULIE ANN, music educator; b. Kalamazoo, Mich., Dec. 21, 1965; d. James Alton and JoAnn Porter; m. Donald Ray Gragg. MusB in Edn., We. Mich. U., Kalamazoo, 1984—88; MusM in Instrumental Music Edn. with honors, VanderCook Coll. Music, Chgo., 1995—98. Cert. tchr. Ariz., 1990. Music tchr. Kazoo Sch., Kalamazoo, 1989—90, Montessori Sch., Kalamazoo, 1989—90, Kingman Unified Sch. Dist. #20, Ariz., 1990—, dist. music coord., 2001—. Bd. mem. Kingman Cultural Arts Commn., 1996—99; band chairperson NW Ariz. Mid. Sch. Music Festivals, Flagstaff, 2002—04; state standards revision com. mem. Ariz. Dept. Edn., Phoenix, 2005—06. Guest condr., prin. clarinetist Kingman Concert Band, clarinetist Lake Havasu Symphonic Winds, substitute condr., clarinetist Mohave Community Orchestra. Pres. Kingman Jr. C. of C., 1998—99; v.p. Ariz. Jr. C. of C., Phoenix, 1999—2001; local pres. & state v.p. US Jr. C. of C., 1998—2001. Recipient Jaycee of Yr. award, Kingman Jr. C. of C., 1998, Top State V.P. of Yr. award, US C. of C., 2000, Teacher of Yr. award, Kingman Jr. HS. Mem.: Music Educators Nat. Conf. (assoc.). Home: PO Box 6414 Kingman AZ 86402 Office: Kingman Unified Sch Dist #20 1969 Detroit Ave Kingman AZ 86401 Personal E-mail: bandldr@npgcable.com. Business E-Mail: jgragg@kusd.org.

GRAHAM, ALMA ELEANOR, editor, writer, educational consultant; b. Raleigh, N.C., Nov. 13, 1936; d. David Robert and Irene G. (Knott) G. BA in English with honors, U. N.C., 1958; MA in Contemporary Lit., Columbia U., 1970. Exec. editor Am. Heritage Dictionary, 1970—75; editl. mgr., exec. editor McGraw-Hill, 1976—87; free-lance author, corp. cons., 1987—90; editor New World Outlook mag. United Meth. Ch., N.Y.C., 1991—2001; ret., cons. N.Y.C., 2001—. Cons. in bias-free lang. and images; cons. USIA, 1978-80. Author: Our Nation, Our World, 1983, 86, 88, McGraw-Hill Educational Software, 1988, North Carolina: The Land and Its People, 1988, Basic Map Skills, 1991; co-author: Success With Words, 1983, Bridging Worlds Through General Semantics, 1984. Pres. Laymen's Club, trustee Cath. Ch. St. John the Divine, N.Y.C., 1994-99. Named one of 50 Extraordinary Women of Achievement, N.Y. region NCCJ, 1978; Woodrow Wilson fellow, 1958-59. Mem. NOW, Associated Ch. Press, Nat. Coun. for Social Studies, Org. for Equal Edn. the Sexes, Phi Beta Kappa. Achievements include first lexicographer to put courtesy title Ms. into dictionary, 1972. Home: 380 Riverside Dr New York NY 10025-1819 E-mail: montsea@aol.com.

GRAHAM, ANNA REGINA, pathologist, educator; b. Phila., Nov. 1, 1947; d. Edward Nelson and Anna Beatrice (McGovern) Chadwick; m. Larry L. Graham, June 29, 1973; 1 child, Jason. BS in Chemistry, Ariz. State U., 1969, BS in Zoology, 1970; MD, U. Ariz., 1974. Diplomate Am. Bd. Pathology. With Coll. Medicine U. Ariz., Tucson, 1974—, asst. prof. pathology, 1978-84, assoc. prof. pathology, 1984-90, prof. pathology, 1990—. Fellow Am. Soc. Clin. Pathologists (bd. dirs. Chgo. chpt. 1993-2003, sec. 1995-99, v.p. 1999-2000, pres.-elect 2000-01, pres. 2001-02), Internat. Acad. Pathology, Am. Telemedicine Assn., Coll. Am. Pathologists; mem. AMA (alt. del. Chgo. chpt. 1992-99, del. Chgo. chpt. 1999-2004), Ariz. Soc. Pathologists (pres. Phoenix chpt. 1989-91), Ariz. Med. Assn. (treas. Phoenix chpt. 1995-97). Republican. Baptist. Avocations: motorcycles, piano, choir. Office: Ariz Health Scis Ctr Dept Pathology 1501 N Campbell Ave Tucson AZ 85724-5108 Office Phone: 520-626-6828. Business E-Mail: agraham@umcaz.edu.

GRAHAM, BARBARA ANNE, secondary school educator; b. Bussfield, Miss., Dec. 29, 1947; d. Hollie E. and Mona M. Hudson; m. Stephen Norris Graham, June 1, 1968; children: John Stephen, Jeffrey Todd. BS, U. So. Miss., Hattiesburg, 1969; MA, Nichols State U., Thibodeaux, La., 1978; degree, William Carey Coll., Hattiesburg, 1984. Sr. instr. English Collins H.S., Collins, Miss., 1969—75; mgr. Plantation Tree Apts. Delta Properties and Mgmt., Thibodeaux, La., 1977—78; instr. English Prentiss H.S., Prentiss, Miss., 1981—82, Bassfield H.S., Bassfield, Miss., 1982—84; instr. Advanced Placement English Sumrell H.S., Miss., 1984—. Mem. adv. bd. U. So. Miss., Hattiesburg, Miss., 2005; chmn. Onward Toward Excellence Sumrall H.S., 1995—, chmn. quality bearying com., 1999—. Mem. literacy com. Gov. Hattiesburg, 2000—02; sec. bd. dirs. Lucille Parker Mus. Art, Sumrall, 2000—. Named Tchr. of Yr., Sumrall H.S., 2004, Miss. Star Tchr. eight times. Mem.: Am. Cancer Soc. (chmn. 1999—). Avocations: travel, shopping, skiing, reading. Home: 51 Graham Rd Sumrall MS 39482 Office: Sumrall High Sch PO Box 187 Sumrall MS 39482

GRAHAM, BARBARA J., special education educator; b. Sioux City, Iowa, Oct. 7, 1948; d. James H. and Mary A. (Ostmeyer) G.; m. Richard L. Hollinger, Dec. 27, 1986; stepchildren: Greg, Mark. BS in Edn., U. S.D., 1970; MS in Edn., U. Wis.-Stout, Menomonie, 1988; postgrad., Kearney (Nebr.) State Coll. Cert. elem. tchr., spl. edn. tchr., Nebr. Spl. needs tchr. Owatonna (Minn.) Pub. Schs., Dist. 916 Pub. Schs., White Bear Lake, Minn.; spl. needs tchr. and facilitator St. Paul Schs.; spl. needs tchr. Lexington (Nebr.) Pub. Schs. Bd. dir. So. Ctrl. chpt. ARC; regional bd. dir. Mem. Coun. Exceptional Children (bd. dir. south ctr. region II adv. bd., 1991—), Regional Devel. Disabilities Coun., CED-DCD, Alpha Delta Kappa.

GRAHAM, CYNTHIA ARMSTRONG, banker; b. Charlotte, N.C., Jan. 3, 1950; d. Beverly Weller and Katherine (Anderson) Armstrong; m. Walter Raleigh Graham Jr., May 23, 1970. AB in Chemistry, Bryn Mawr Coll., 1971; MBA in Fin. with distinction, U. Pa., 1976. Computer programmer Philco-Ford, Ft. Washington, Pa., 1973-74; asst. dir. admissions Wharton Sch., U. Pa., Phila., 1974-76; asst. v.p. N.C. Nat. Bank, Charlotte, 1976-80; v.p. Barclays Am. Corp., Charlotte, 1980-86; sr. v.p. Barclays Bank Del., N.A., Wilmington, 1986-87, Barnett Banks, Inc., Jacksonville, Fla., 1987-97; chmn., pres. Barnett Mcht. Svcs., Inc., Jacksonville, 1987-89, TeleCheck Southcoast, 1987-89, Barnett Card Svcs. Corp., Jacksonville, 1989-97; exec. v.p. customer info. and segment mgmt. Nat. City Corp., Cleve., 1998-2000; sr. v.p. customer info. & programs J.P. Morgan Chase & Co., N.Y.C., 2000—. Bd. advisors Nat. DAta Corp., Atlanta, 1987-88; delivery sys. advisor VISA U.S.A., Inc., San Mateo, Calif., 1987-91; mcht. svcs. advisor MasterCard, Internat., N.Y.C., 1989-92; mem. U.S. regional bus. com. MasterCard, 1992-97, strategic adv. Bank Adminstr. Inst., 1999—, adv. com. Direct Mktg. Assn., 2000—; card products advisor VISA U.S.A., Inc., San Mateo, 1991-94, VISA Internat., 1994, mem. mktg. com., 1994-97; bd. dirs. Inst. for Servant Leadership. Mem. Jacksonville Women's Network, 1988-92, bd. dirs., 1991-92, treas., 1992; mem. bd. suprs. Spaceport Fla., 1990-92. Mem. Am. Bankers Assn. (exec. com. card divsn. 1991-94, vice chmn. 1993, chmn. 1994), Jacksonville C. of C.

GRAHAM, DEBORAH DENISE, minister, educator; b. Akron, Ohio, Dec. 15, 1961; d. Douglas Eugene Ward and Ruby Lucille (Head) Lockett; m. Curnell Graham, May 21, 1988; children: Shakira Denaé, Victoria Patrice. BA, U. Akron, 1984, PhD, 1998; MDiv, Duke U., 1987. Ordained elder East Ohio Conf. English tchr. Upward Bound Program, Akron, 1982—87, dormitory counselor, 1982—87; tchg. asst. Duke U., Durham, NC, 1984—87; rschr., tchr. U. Akron, 1987—94, adminstrv. asst. women's studies, 1987—94; sr. pastor Holy Trinity United Meth. Ch., Akron, 1987—. Bus. adminstr. Holy Trinity United Meth. Ch., Akron, 1987—; profl. counselor Juvenile Ct., Akron, 1987—; leadership trainer Akron Dist./Shirley Caesar, 1996—. Spkr. M. King Fed. Ctr., Battle Creek, 1999; expert in residence Kellog Found., Battle Creek, Mich., 1998; bd. mem. InterFaith Caregivers, Akron, 1999—2000. Named Most Loved Pastor, Gospel Today Mag., 2001; recipient Cmty. Leadership award, God First Ministries, 2002. Mem.: East Ohio Bd. Ordained Mins., Delta Sigma Theta. Democrat. Avocations: organ, reading, journaling, running, dining. Home: 1291 Morse St Akron OH 44320 Office: Holy Trinity UMC 1127 Copley Rd Akron OH 44320

GRAHAM, DOROTHY E., elementary school educator; b. Orangeburg County, S.C., Jan. 13, 1941; d. Benjamin Howard Easterlin and Charlie Belle Murray; m. Thomas Wayne Graham, Sept. 3, 1959; children: Janet Elizabeth, Katherine Elaine. BA with hon., McNeese State U., 1967; diploma in religious edn., New Orleans Bapt. Theol. Sem., 1963; diploma in Japanese lang. and culture, Kansai Gakuin U., 1971. Cert. tchr. State of Fla., 1996. Elem. sch. tchr. Lake Charles Sch. Dist., La., 1967—68; missionary, tchr. Japan Bapt. Conv., Kobe, 1968—94; min. children First Bapt. Ch., Ft. Myers, Fla., 1994—96; tchr. elem. sch. Lee Dist. Sch., 1996—. Dir., organizer 100 Voice Children's Chorus, Cape Coral, 2000—06, After Sch. Arts Programs Children, Cape Coral, Fla., 2000—04, Japanese Children's Chorus, Kobe, 1986—93; choral dir., organizer City Wide Cmty. Chorus, Kobe, 1980—94; dir., organizer. sr. chorus First Bapt. Ch., Ft. Myers, 1994—96. Recipient Mayor's award for Outstanding Cmty. Svc., City Kobe, Japan Mayor Miyazaki, 1992, Outstanding Tchr. award, C. of C., 2000—01, 2001—02, Sam's Club Outstanding Tchr. Yr., Sam's Club Stores, Ft. Myers, Fl, 2003. Mem.: Fla. Music Educator's Assn. Avocations: travel, reading, classical music. Home: 1230 Braman Avenue Fort Myers FL 33901 Office: Cape Elementary School 4519 Vincennes Blvd Cape Coral FL 33904 Personal E-mail: grahamprs@aol.com.

GRAHAM, ELEANORE DAVIS, elementary school educator; b. Seville, Fla., Feb. 3, 1954; d. Nathaniel Williams and Virginia Hildajean Hightower; m. LaGoge Wick Graham, May 8, 1976; children: Jeneen Alicia, Janelle Nichole, Kayla Janae, LaGoge Donovan. BS, NC A&T U., Greensboro, 1976; MA, SC State U., Orangeburg, 1980; postgrad., Union Inst. & U., Cin., 2000—. Cert. tchr. Tex., Fla. Pub. health nutritionist Sumter County (SC) Health Dept., 1976—80; pediat. dietitian St. Joseph Hosp., Omaha, 1981—84; tchr. secondary math. and sci. Dept. Def. Dependent Schs., Kaiserslautern, Germany, 1985—90; elem. tchr. San Antonio Ind. Sch. Dist., 1991—96, Orange County Pub. Schs., Orlando, Fla., 1996—. Cons. Gordon Learning Ctr., Orlando, 2005—. Contbr. articles to jours. Mem. bus. adv. coun. Women of Renewing Minds, Sanford, Fla., 2002—03; internet voting poll attendant Orange County, Orlando, 2003—04; mem. bus. adv. coun. Nat. Rep. Congressional Com., Washington, 2005—; liaison United Meth. Ch., Casselberry, Fla., 2003—; bus. dir. Cmty. Options of Ctrl. Fla., Orlando, 2004—. Named Silver Medal Universal Literacy Tchr., 2002—03, Gold Medal Universal Literacy Tchr., 2004—05, Outstanding Bus. Woman, Nat. Rep. Congressional Com., 2005—06. Mem.: NAFE, AAUW, Nat. Alliance Black Educators. Avocations: reading, arts and crafts, travel, dance, music. Home: 1361 Cree Trl Casselberry FL 32707 Office: Cmty Options of Ctrl Fla Inc 1310 W Colonial Ste 8 Orlando FL 32804 Office Phone: 407-999-9039. Office Fax: 407-999-5608. Personal E-mail: onegram50@aol.com.

GRAHAM, FRANCES KEESLER (MRS. DAVID TREDWAY GRAHAM), psychologist, educator; b. Canastota, N.Y., Aug. 1, 1918; d. Clyde C. and Norma (Van Surdam) Keesler; m. David Tredway Graham, June 14, 1941; children: Norma, Andrew, Mary. BA, Pa. State U., 1938; PhD, Yale U., 1942; DSc (hon.), U. Wis., 1996. Acting dir. St. Louis Psychiat. Clinic, 1942-44; instr. Barnard Coll., 1948-51; research assoc. Sch. Medicine, Washington U., St. Louis, 1942-48, 53-57, U. Wis., Madison, 1957-64, asso. prof. pediatrics and psychology, 1964-68, prof., 1968-86, Hilldale research prof., 1980-86; prof. U. Del., Newark, 1986-89, prof. emerita, 1989—. Disting. faculty lectr., U. Del., Newark, 1989; cons. Nat. Inst. Neurol. Diseases and Blindness perinatal research br.; mem. exptl. psychology research review com. NIMH, 1970-74, NRC, 1971-74; mem. bd. sci. counselors NIMH, 1977-81, chmn., 1979-81; mem. Pres.'s Commn. for Study of Ethical Problems in Medicine and Biomed. and Behavioral Research, 1980-82 Mem. editorial bd. Jour. Exptl. Child Psychology, 1964-67, Child Devel., 1966-68, Jour. Exptl. Psychology, 1968-73, Psychophysiology, 1968-73; contbr. articles to profl. jours. Recipient Rsch. Scientist award NIMH, 1964-89, Disting. Alumna award Pa. State U., 1983, Wilbur L. Cross medal Yale U., 1992, Gold medal Am. Psychol. Found., 1995. Fellow AAAS (chmn. sect. psychology 1979, mem. nominations com. 1992-95), APA (coun. 1975-77, pres. div. physiol. and comparative psychology 1978-79, G. Stanley Hall award 1982, Disting. Scientist award 1990); mem. NAS, Am. Psychol. Soc. (William James fellow 1990), Soc. Rsch. Child Devel. (council 1965-71, pres. 1975-77, Disting. Sci. Contbns. award 1991), Soc. Psychophysiol. Rsch. (dir. 1968-71, 72-75, pres. 1973-74, Disting. Contbns. award 1981), Soc. Exptl. Psychologists, Soc. Neurosci., Fedn. Behavioral Psychol. and Cognitive Scis. (exec. com. 1991-94), Psychonomic Soc., Acoustical Soc. Am., Internat. Soc. Devel. Psychobiology, Phi Beta Kappa, Sigma Xi. Home: PO Box 1347 Wilmington DE 19899-1347 E-mail: fkgraham@udel.edu.

GRAHAM, GINGER L., pharmaceutical executive; b. Springdale, Ark., Nov. 18, 1955; m. John Graham; 3 stepchildren. BS in Agrl. Economics, U. Ark., 1979; MBA, Harvard U., 1986. With Elanco Eli Lilly and Co., 1979—92, pres., CEO Advanced Cardiovascular Systems, 1993—2000; group chmn., Office of Pres. Guidant Corp., 2000—03; CEO Amylin Pharmaceuticals Inc., 2003—, pres., 2003—, mem. fin. com. Bd. dirs. Amylin Pharmaceuticals Inc., 1995—, Pharmaceutical Rsch. and Manufacturers of Am., Calif. Coun. on Sci. and Tech.; adv. bd. Kellogg Ctr. for Exec. Women; bd. dean's adv. Harvard Bus. Sch., health industry alumni bd.; health sciences adv. bd. U. Calif. San Diego; spkr. in field. Recipient Emerging Co. Exec. of Yr. award, Pharm. Achievement Awards, 2005. Office: Amylin Pharmaceuticals Inc Ste 110 9360 Towne Centre Dr San Diego CA 92121*

GRAHAM, GLORIA FLIPPIN, dermatologist; b. Durham, N.C., Mar. 3, 1935; d. James Meigs and Ida Mae (Boyd) F.; m. Douglas Graham (div.); 1 child, Wayne Meigs Graham; m. James Herbert Graham, July 29, 1989. BS, Wake Forest U., 1957; MD, Bowman-Gray Sch. Medicine, 1961. Diplomate Am. Bd. Dermatology. Intern Sch. Medicine Vanderbilt U., Nashville, 1961—62; resident dermatology U. Va. Med. Ctr., Charlottesville, 1962—65; pvt. practice Columbia, SC, 1965—66; physician, owner Wilson Dermatology Clinic, NC, 1966—94; physician, dermatologist Grahams' Dermatology Svcs., Morehead City, 1992—2005; attending physician Crystal Coast Dermatology Svcs., P.A., Morehead City, 2000—01; physician, dermatologist Down East Med. Assocs., Morehead City, 2005—. Cons. Carteret Gen. Hosp., Morehead City, 1986-2000; clin. attending prof. Bowman Gray Sch. Medicine, Winston-Salem, N.C., 1991-2000; adj. clin. prof. U. N.C. Sch. Medicine, Chapel Hill, 1995-2001; assoc. prof. dermatology Wake Forest U. Med. Sch., 2001-20, bd. visitors, 2003—. Co-exhibitor: Two Hereditary Osseocutaneous Syndromes, Acad. Dermatology, 1965 (Silver award), So. Med. Assn. Exhibit Hereditary Acrokeratotic Poikiloderma, 1970 (Third Place award). Named Woman of Yr., Women's Residence Coun. Wake Forest U., 1982, Practitioner of Yr., Dermatology Found., 1998. Mem.: Internat. Soc. Cryosurgery (v.p. 2001—05, honorary mem. 2005), Women's Dermatologic Soc. (pres. 1997—98, Rose Hirschler award 2001), Am. Dermatologic Assn. (elect), Am. Acad. Dermatology (bd. dirs. 1991—96, audit com. 1996—2000, ethics com. 1996—2001, nominating com. 2002—, chair nominating com. 2003, honorary mem. 2005, Fox award 2003), N.Am. Clin. Dermatologic Soc. (bd. dirs. 1995—2001), World Congress Dermatology (co-chmn. cryosurgical symposium 1997, 2001), Wake Forest U. Sch. Medicine Alumni Assn. (bd. dirs. 2003—06). Avocations: travel, fishing. Home: 106 Cypress Dr Pine Knoll Shores NC 28513-6706 Personal E-mail: ggfgraham@aol.com.

GRAHAM, HEATHER, actress; b. Milw., Jan. 29, 1970; Film appearances include License to Drive, 1988, Drugstore Cowboy, 1989, I Love You to Death, 1990, Guilty as Charged, 1991, Diggstown, 1992, 6 Degrees of Separation, 1993, Don't Do It, 1994, Swingers, 1996, Boogie Nights, 1997 (MTV movie award 1998), Scream 2, 1997, Austin Powers: The Spy Who Shagged Me, 1999, Bowfinger, 1999, Kiss & Tell, 2000, Sidewalks of New York, 2001, From Hell, 2001, Killing Me Softly, 2002, The Guru, 2002, Aliene Love Triange, 2002, Anger Management, 2003, Hope Springs, 2003, Blessed, 2004, Gray Matters, 2005, Mary, 2005, Cake, 2005; (TV series) Emily's Reasons Why Not, 2006; (TV appearances) Growing Pains, 1987, Twin Peaks, 1991, Fallen Angels, 1995, The Outer Limits, 1996, Fantasy Island, 1998, Sex in the City, 2002, Arrested Development, 2004, Scrubs, 2004, 2005. Recipient ShoWest award for Female Star of Tomorrow, 1999. Office: Creative Artists Agency 9830 Wilshire Blvd Beverly Hills CA 90211

GRAHAM, HILDA RENAE, mathematics educator; b. Hampton, Tenn., May 17, 1952; d. Ronda B. and Mina Street; m. Lynn Edward Graham, June 2, 1973 (dec. Aug. 17, 1977). MA, Tusculum Coll., Greeneville, Tenn., 1998; BA, East Tenn.State U. Cert. tchr. Tenn., 1973. Math dept. chair, tchr. Hampton H.S., Tenn., 1993—. Named Carter County Tchr. of the Yr. Mem.: Carter County Edn. Assn. (treas.), Alpha Delta Kappa (life; pres.). Home: 106 Old 19E Hwy Hampton TN 37658-3618 Office: Hampton High School 766 First Ave Hampton TN 37658 Office Phone: 423-725-5200. Personal E-mail: hnae03@hotmail.com.

GRAHAM, JANET LORRAINE, music educator; b. Halifax, NC, Jan. 15, 1947; d. Lloyd Cartez and Waline Wilkins; m. Aaron Richard Graham, June 21, 1969; children: Andrea Yvonne, Aaron Richard II. BA, NC Ctrl. U., 1969. Cert. music tchr. N.C., Ohio, N.J. 4th grade tchr., H.S. chorus dir. Scotland Neck (NC) Schs., 1969; elem./jr. high music tchr. Akron (Ohio) schs., 1969—71; gen. music tchr. grades K-6 Bergenfield (NJ) schs., 1971—. Composer: (songs) Lessons for Kindergarten, 2005. Bd. dirs. Bergen Philharm., Englewood, NJ, 1997—. Named Tchr. of Yr., State of NJ Dept. Edn., 1994. Mem.: NEA, No. NJ Orff Schulwerk Assn. (pres. 1999—2002), Bergenfield Edn. Assn., Tri-M Music Honor Soc. (life). Achievements include featured in music textbooks on music methods. Avocations: travel, reading, dance. Home: 86 Church St Teaneck NJ 07666 Personal E-mail: Janyvo25@yahoo.com.

GRAHAM, JEWEL FREEMAN, social worker, lawyer, educator; b. Springfield, Ohio, May 3, 1925; d. Robert Lee and Lula Belle Freeman; m. Paul N. Graham, Aug. 8, 1953; children: Robert, Nathan. BA, Fisk U., 1946; student, Howard U., 1946-47; MS in Social Svc. Adminstrn., Case Western Res. U., 1953; JD, U. Dayton, 1979; LHD (hon.), Meadville-Lombard Theol. Sch., 1991. Bar: Ohio; cert. social worker. Assoc. dir. teenage program dept. YWCA, Grand Rapids, Mich., 1947-50, coord. met. teenage program Detroit, 1953-56; dir. program for interracial edn. Antioch Coll., Yellow Springs, Ohio, 1964-69, from asst. prof. to prof., 1969-92, prof. emeritus, 1992—. Mem. Ohio Commn. on Dispute Resolution and Conflict Mgmt., 1990-92. Mem. exec. com. World YWCA, Geneva, 1975-83, 87—, pres., 1983; bd. dirs. YWCA of the U.S.A., 1970-89, pres., 1979-85; bd. dirs. Antioch U., 1994-96. Named to Greene County Women's Hall of Fame, 1982, Ohio Women's Hall of Fame, 1988; named 1 of 10 Outstanding Women of Miami Valley, 1987; recipient Ambassador award YWCA of the U.S.A., 1993. Mem. ABA, Nat. Assn. of Social Workers (charter), Nat. Coun. of Negro Women (life), Alpha Kappa Alpha. Democrat. Unitarian Universalist. Avocations: bicycling, swimming, walking, needlecrafts. Office: Antioch Coll Livermore 51 Yellow Springs OH 45387 Business E-Mail: jgraham@antioch-college.edu. E-mail: jewelg@aol.com.

GRAHAM, JORIE, writer, educator; b. NYC, May 9, 1951; d. Curtis Bell and Beverly (Stoll) Pepper; m. James Galvin. BFA, NYU, 1973; MFA, U. Iowa, 1978. Asst. prof. Murray (Ky.) State U., 1978-79, Humboldt State U., Arcata, Calif., 1979-81; instr. Columbia U., N.Y.C., 1981-83; mem. staff U. Iowa, Iowa City, 1983—99, prof. English, dir. Writer's Workshop, 1999; Boylston Prof. of Oratory and Rhetoric Harvard U., 1999—. Poetry editor Crazy Horse, 1978-81; chancellor Acad. Am. Poets, 1997-2003. Author: Hybrids of Plants and of Ghosts, 1980 (Great Lakes Colls. Assn. award 1981), Erosion, 1983, The End of Beauty, 1987, Region of Unlikeness, 1991, Materialism, 1993, The Dream of the Unified Field: Selected Poems 1974-94, 1995, The Errancy, 1997, Swarm, 1999, Never, 2002, Overlord, 2005; editor: Earth Took of Earth: 100 Great Poems of the English Language, 1996; co-editor: The Best American Poetry 1990. Recipient Am. Acad. Poets award, 1977, Young Poet prize Poetry Northwest, 1980, Pushcart prize, 1980, 82, American Poetry Review prize, 1982, Pulitzer prize in poetry, 1996, Lavan award Acad. Am. Poets, 1991, Martin Zaubel award Acad. and Inst. of Arts and Letters, 1992; Bunting fellow Radcliff Inst., 1982, Guggenheim fellow, 1983, John D. and Catherine T. MacArthur Found. fellow, 1990; grantee Ingram-Merrill Found., 1981. Office: Harvard U English Dept Barker Cntr 12 Quincey St Cambridge MA 02138

GRAHAM, K(ATHLEEN) M. (K. M. GRAHAM), artist; b. Hamilton, Ont., Can., Sept. 13, 1913; d. Charles and G. Blanche (Leitch) Howitt; m. J. Wallace Graham, Dec. 17, 1938; children: John Wallace, Janet Howitt. BA, U. Toronto, Ont., 1936. (one-woman shows) Carmen Lamanna Gallery, Toronto, 1967, Trinity Coll., U. Toronto, 1968, Founders Coll., York U., Toronto, 1970, Pollock Gallery, Toronto, 1971,73,75, Art Gallery Coburg, Ont., 1973, City Hall, Toronto, 1974, David Mirvish Gallery Gallery, Toronto, 1976, Klonaridis, Inc., Toronto, 1978, Watson-Willour Gallery, Houston, 1980, Downstairs Gallery, Edmonton, Alta., 1980, 82, Lillian Heidenberg Gallery, N.Y.C., 1981,86, Klonaridis, Inc., Toronto, 1981-85, 87, 88, 90, ELCA London Gallery, Montreal, Que., Can., 1983, MacDonald-Stewart Art Centre, Guelph, Ont., 1984, Glenbow Mus., Calgary, 1984, Concordia Gallery, Montreal, 1984, Hart House Gallery, Toronto, 1985, Lillian Heidenberg Gallery, N.Y.C., 1986, Klondaridis Inc., Toronto, 1985, 87, 88, 90, 91, Feheley Fine Arts, Toronto, 1989, Douglas Udell Gallery, Vancouver, 1993, Meml. Art Gallery, St. Johns, N.F., 1994, Beaverbrook Gallery, Fredericton, N.B., 1994, Costin and Klintworth, Toronto, Ont., 1994, 95, The Art Gallery of Ont., 1997, The Moore Gallery, Toronto, 2000, 2001, (group shows) Montreal Mus. Fine Arts, 1976, Hirshhorn Mus., Washington, 1977, Edmonton (Alta., Can.) Art Gallery, 1977, Norman MacKenzie Art Gallery, Regina, Sask., Can., 1977, David Mirvish Gallery, Toronto, Watson De Nagy Gallery, Houston, Galerie Wentzel, Hamburg, Fed. Republic Germany, Beaverbrook Gallery, Fredericton, N.B., Associated Am. Artists, N.Y.C., 1986, 88, Elca London, Montreal, 1987, Klondaris Inc., Toronto, 1987, 91, Douglas Udell Gallery, Vancouver, 1987, Associated Am. Artists, N.Y.C., 1988, Feheley Fine Art, Toronto, 1989, (other) (traveling shows) CanadaxTen, 1974, The Can. Canvas, 1975-76, Changing Visions, 1976-77, The Shell Canada Collection, 1977, The Fauve Heritage, 1997, 14 Canadians Hirschhorn Mus., Washington, 1977, Certain Traditions, 1978, 79, (travelling shows), (permanent collections) Nat. Gallery Can., Ottawa, Edmonton Art Gallery, Art Gallery Ont., Art Gallery Hamilton, Ont., MacDonald-Stewart Art Gallery, Guelph, Ont., Toronto City Hall, The Brit. Mus., London, Art Gallery Vancouver, Agnes Etherington Art Centre, Kingston, Ont., Can., Musee d'Art Contemporarin Montreal, Beaverbrook Art Gallery, Frederickton, N.B., Art Gallery Nfld.and Labrador, Art Gallery, Peterborough, Ont., Robert McLaughlin Gallery, Oshawa, Ont., Kitchener Waterloo Art Gallery, McMichael Can. Art Gallery, Hart House Art Gallery, Toronto, also numerous corp. collections. Hon. fellow Trinity Coll., U. Toronto, 1988. Mem. Royal Can. Acad.

GRAHAM, LAUREL SUSAN, elementary school educator; b. Columbus, Ohio, June 15, 1556; d. Encil Glen and Nancy Louise Keyser; m. Donald Wayne Graham (div. Mar. 1990); 1 child, Douglas Edward. BA in Elem. Edn., Bowling Green State U., Ohio, 1978. Tchr. educable mentally retarded South-Western City Schs., Grove City, Ohio, 1978—81; kindergarten tchr. Kinder Care, Grove City, 1981—83; kindergarten-3rd grade tchr. NE Storyland Elem. Sch., Columbus, 1984—87; substitute tchr. Columbus Pub. Schs., 1987—90, elem. tchr., 1991—. Cons. in field. Troop advancement chair Boy Scouts Am., Dublin, Ohio, 2004—. Named Worthy Matron, Ea. Star, 1996. Mem.: Columbus Edn. Assn. Republican. Lutheran. Avocations: history, camping, horseback riding, reading. Home: 6261 White Sulphur Ct Grove City OH 43123 Office: Columbus Pub Schs West Broad Elem West Broad St Columbus OH 43204

GRAHAM, LAUREN, actress; b. Honolulu, Mar. 16, 1967; d. Lawrence Graham and Donna Grant. BA in English, Barnard Coll., Columbia U.; MFA in acting, So. Meth. U., 1992. Founder Good Game prodn. co. Actor: (TV series) Good Company, 1996, Townies, 1996, Conrad Bloom, 1998, M.Y.O.B., 2000, Gilmore Girls, 2000—; (films) Nightwatch, 1997, Confessions of a Sexist Pig, 1998, One True Thing, 1998, Dill Scallion, 1999, Sweet November, 2001, Chasing Destiny, 2001, Bad Santa, 2003, Lucky 13, 2004, Seeing Other People, 2004, The Moguls, 2005, The Pacifier, 2005; prodr.: Something More, 2003; actor(guest appearance): (TV series) Caroline in the City, 1995—96, 3rd Rock from the Sun, 1996, Law & Order, 1997, Seinfield, 1997, NewsRadio, 1997. Office: ICM 8943 Wilshire Blvd Beverly Hills CA 90211-1934

GRAHAM, LAURIE, editor, writer; b. Evanston, Ill., Nov. 22, 1941; d. Thomas Harlin and Mary Elisabeth (Stoner) Graham; m. George McKay Schieffelin, Dec. 12, 1980 (dec. Jan. 1988); m. Robert Dale Shearer, Apr. 6, 1994 (dec. Nov. 2002). Student, Mt. Holyoke Coll., 1959-61; BA, U. Colo., 1963. Editor Charles Scribner's Sons, NYC, 1969-87. Originator, co-project dir. The Greater Pitts. Poem Chase, 2001; bd. dirs. Pitts. Arts and Lectures. Author: Rebuilding the House, 1990, Singing the City, 1998; mem. editl. bd. Creative Nonfiction, 1994—, (press series) Emerging Writers in Creative Nonfiction, Duquesne U., 1994—; contbg. author: Pittsburgh Sports, 2000, Creative Nonfiction, 2003, 05. Mem.: PEN, NY Jr. League, Colony Club. Personal E-mail: lauriegraham@comcast.net.

GRAHAM, LINDA OHLSON, artist; b. Worcester, Mass., Dec. 16, 1947; d. Henry William Russell and Rose Marie (Magnan) Ohlson; m. Douglas John Merton Graham, Feb. 14, 1984; 1 child, Isis Marina. Cert. nurse's aide. Freelance photographer, 1969—; co-dir. The Turner Mus., Denver, 1981-96, trustee, 1983-96; nurse's aide Pleasant Bay Nursing & Rehab., Brewster, Mass., 1996—. One woman shows include Boatslip Restaurant, 1997, Cape Cod 5 Bank, Wellfleet, 1997, Compass Rose Bookstore, Orleans, 1998, 99, 2000, Wellfleet Libr., 1999, Truro Libr., 2000, Snow Libr. Orleans, 2000, Republic Bank, Fla., 2003, Cape Mus. Arts, in Polhermus and Savery Gallery, Mass., 2002, Visions Bookstore, 1997; exhibited in group shows, New East End Gallery, Provincetown, Mass., 1989, Foothills Art Ctr., Golden, Colo., 1990, Photo Mirage Gallery, Denver, 1990, Alternative Arts Alliance, Denver, 1990, Wellfleet Libr., 1998, ArtCenter Manatee, 2006; guest on Surreal News, Radio Sta. Wslr, Sarasota, 2006. Chair music performance Jr. Symphony Guild, Denver, 1992-93. Mem. Unity Ch. Avocations: sailing, bicycling. Mailing: PO Box 17523 Sarasota FL 34276-0523

GRAHAM, LOUVENIA DORSEY, science educator; d. Mary Della Williamson; m. Charles Graham, Sr. (dec.); children: Kevin, William, Marisara. BS, Ala. State U., Montgomery, 1968, EdM; AA, Auburn U., Montgomery, Ala. Cert. tchr. sci. Ala. Dept. Edn. Tchr. Talbat County Bd. Edn., Talbatton, Ga.; proofreader Herf Jones Yearbook Co., Montgomery, Ala.; tchr. Montgomery County Bd. Edn.; program coord. Montgomery br. NAACP. Office: Floyd Magnet Sch Math Sci Tech 3444 Le Bron Rd Montgomery AL 36111-1395

GRAHAM, MARGARET KATHERINE, retired secondary school educator; b. Grass Valley, Calif., Dec. 21, 1941; d. Carroll Joseph and Mary Barbara (Clark) Coughlan; m. Denis David Graham, Aug. 31, 1968; 1 child, Kathleen Ann. BA, U. Nev., 1963. Cert. secondary tchr., Nev. Case aide Catholic Social Svcs., San Francisco, 1963-64; tchr. Sparks (Nev.) HS, 1965-67; history tchr. Carson City (Nev.) HS, 1968-71; tchr. 7th/8th grades St. Teresa's Catholic Sch., Carson City, 1983-87; sex edn. tchr. Washoe County Sch. Dist., Reno, 1988—2002; ret., 2002; sales assoc. Cavanaugh's Furniture Store, 2005—. Sex edn. adv. bd. Carson City Sch. Dist., 1984-85; counselor marriage preparation and annulments Our Lady Snows Cath. Ch., 2005—. Mem. NEA, Washoe County Tchr.'s Assn., PEO, Serra Club (treas. 1992). Democrat. Roman Catholic. Avocations: travel, reading, walking. Home: 3056 Bramble Dr Reno NV 89509-6901 Personal E-mail: margaretgraham@charters.net.

GRAHAM, NANCY G., elementary school educator; d. Samuel Blair and Betty Browning Griffin; m. Charles A. Graham, June 29, 2002; children: Amanda M. Bouchillon, Elizabeth B. Bouchillon. BS, Winthrop U., Rock Hill, S.C., 1982; MEd, Furman U., Greenville, S.C., 1986. Lic. tchr. SC., 1982. Tchr. Berea Mid. Sch., Greenville, SC, 1982—. Math rep. Neufeld Learning Systems Inc., London, 2005—06. Mem.: GCCTM. Office Phone: 864-355-1734. Personal E-mail: ngraham234@aol.com. E-mail: ngraham@greenville.k12.sc.us.

GRAHAM, NANCY LOVE, music educator; arrived in U.S., 1954; d. George D. and Margaret W. Graham; children: Scott Richardson, Whitney Richardson. BA, Capital U., Columbus, Ohio, 1973; MusM, Westminster Choir Coll., Princeton, N.J., 1992; Doctorate in Sacred Music, Grad. Theological Found., South Bend, Ind. Cert. tchr. Ohio. Music dir. Montgomery Acad., Ala., 1992—2001, Immanuel Presbyn. Ch., Stuart Country Day Sch., Princeton, NJ, 2001—, St. Cecilia's Ch., Monmouth Junction, NJ, 2002—. Evaluator So. Assn. of Ind. Schs., Ala., 1996—97; chorus master Montgomery Symphony, Montgomery, Ala., 1994—2001; newspaper article critic. Recipient Disting. Tchr. award, U. Chgo., 2000; fellow, U. St. Andrews, Scotland, 2000. Mem.: Presbyn. Assn. of Musicians, Music Educators Nat. Conf., Am. Choral Dir. Assn., Hymn Soc. Avocation: organist. Office: Stuart Country Day Sch 1200 Stuart Princeton NJ 08540

GRAHAM, OLIVE JANE, retired medical/surgical nurse; b. Waterford, Wis., Mar. 23, 1932; d. Theodore Joseph Auterman and Edna Wilhelmina Sophia Boldt-Auterman; m. Charles E. Briggs (div.); children: Charles E. Briggs Jr., Joette A. O'Neill, Michael W. Briggs; m. Albert Frank Graham, Sept. 1, 1986. Diploma, St. John's Sch. Nursing, 1952. Cert. oper. room nurse, in oper. room tech., Johns Hopkins Hosp., 1953. Staff nurse Gibson Cmty. Hosp., Gibson City, Ill., 1952—53, Wesley Mem. Hosp., Chgo., 1953—54, Mercy Hosp., Champaign, 1954—55, Ho. Good Samaritan Hosp., Watertown, 1955; oper. rm./emergency rm. supr. Gibson Comty., Gibson City, 1956—58; staff nurse Cole Hosp., Champaign, 1958—59; office nurse Dr. Paul Sunderland, Gibson City, 1960—61; staff nurse Jefferson County Hosp., Ft. Atkinson, Wis., 1962—63, Charleston Meml. Hosp., Ill., 1964—68; tchr. Lamaze Dr. Pearman, Dr. Ferneau, Columbia, Mo., 1968—69; staff nurse Boone Hosp. Ctr., 1969—72, Harry S. Truman Meml. VA, 1972—92; ret. Co-dir.: (video) Pre-Operative Visit, 1982. Asst. leader Green Meadows Coun. Girl Scouts Am., Gibson City, 1958—59, neighborhood chmn., 1959—60; mem. Federated Jr. Womans Club, 1955—61, v.p. 17th dist., 1961—62; vol. blood drives ARC, 1993—2000; mem. bd. Rainbow Ho., Temporary Home for Children in Crisis, Columbia, 1996—2005, pres., 1998—99; mem. Lois Mikeut Century Cir. Internat. ORder King's Daus. and Sons., Inc., 1997—; mem. bd. King's Daus. Home, Mexico, 2001—03; docent Boone County Hist. Mus., 1995—2006; mem. U. Mo. Ext. Wives, 1993—2006; candidate Columbia City Coun., 1977; mem. choir, prayer chain, care givers Trinity Luth. Ch., Columbia, 1968—; mem. United Meth. Women, 1993—2001. Mem.: Nat. Assn. Fed. Retirees, U. Mo. Alumni Assn., U. Mo. Quarterback Club, Beta Kappa (master), Beta Sigma Phi (charter pres. Xi Epsilon Theta, coun. pres., Girl of Yr. 1984). Lutheran. Avocations: walking, reading, bridge.

GRAHAM, PATRICIA, information technology executive; With Prudential; dir. info. sys. Prudential Fin., Roseland, NJ. Past officer Data Mgmt. Assn. N.J.; presenter in field. Named one of Premier 100 Info. Tech. Leaders, ComputerWorld, 2003. Office: Prudential Group and Fin Svcs 55 Livingston Ave Roseland NJ 07068

GRAHAM, PATRICIA ALBJERG, education educator; b. Lafayette, Ind., Feb. 9, 1935; d. Victor L. and Marguerite (Hall) Albjerg; m. Loren R. Graham, Sept. 6, 1955; 1 child, Marguerite Elizabeth. BS, Purdue U., 1955, MS, 1957, DLett (hon.), 1980; PhD, Columbia U., 1964; MA (hon.), Harvard U., 1974; DHL (hon.), Manhattanville Coll., 1976; LLD (hon.), Beloit Coll., 1977, Clark U., 1978; DPA (hon.), Suffolk U., 1978, Ind. U., 1980; DLitt (hon.), St. Norbert Coll., 1980; DH (hon.), Emmanuel Coll., 1983; DHL (hon.), No. Mich. U., 1987, York Coll. of Pa., 1989, Kenyon Coll., 1991, Bank St. Coll. Edn., 1993; LLD (hon.), Radcliffe Coll., 1994, Salem State Coll., 1998; LLD (hon.), DePaul U., 2006. Tchr. high sch., Norfolk, Va., 1955-56, 57-58, N.Y.C., 1958-60; lectr., asst. prof. Ind. U., 1964-66; asst. prof. history of edn. Barnard Coll. and Columbia Tchrs. Coll., N.Y.C., 1965-68, assoc. prof., 1968-72, prof., 1972-74; dean Radcliffe Inst., 1974-77; also v.p. Radcliffe Coll., Cambridge, Mass., 1976-77; prof. Harvard U., Cambridge, Mass., 1974-79, Warren prof., 1979—2001, Warren Rsch. prof., 2001—06, dean Grad. Sch. Edn., 1982—91, emerita, 2006—; pres. Spencer Found., Chgo., 1991-2000. Author: Progressive Education: From Arcady to Academe, 1967, Community and Class in American Education: 1865-1918, 1974, S.O.S. Sustain Our Schools, 1992, Schooling America, 2005. Bd. dirs. Dalton Sch., 1973-76, Josiah Macy, Jr. Found., 1976-77, 79—; trustee Beloit Coll., 1976-77, 79-82, Northwestern Mut. Life, 1980-2005, Found. for Teaching Econs., 1980-87; bd. dirs. Spencer Found., 1983-2000, Johnson Found., 1983-2001, Hitachi Found., 1985-2004, Carnegie Found. for Advancement of Tchg., 1984-92, Ctrl. European U., Budapest, 2002—, Apache, 2002—. Mem.: AAAS (coun. 1993—96, v.p. 1998—2001), Ctr. for Advanced Study in the Behavioral Scis. (bd. dirs. 2001—), Am. Philos. Soc., Am. Hist. Assn. (v.p. 1985—89), Nat. Acad. Edn. (pres. 1984—89), Sci. Rsch. Assocs. (dir. 1980—89), Phi Beta Kappa. Episcopalian. Office: Harvard U Grad Sch Edn Cambridge MA 02138

GRAHAM, PAULA LEE, nurse; AS in Nursing, Maria Coll., 1977; BS in Bus. Adminstrn., U. Phoenix, 1983, MS, Pace U., 1993, postgrad. cert., 1993, cert. program in Holistic Nursing Seeds and Brdiges, Inc., Shutesbury, Mass., 1999-2000, cert.program in Parish Nursing, The Blenton Peale Inst., Bronxville, N.Y., 2001. RN charge nurse Valley Children's Hosp., Fresno, Calif., 1977-79, charge nurse pediatric ICU, 1979-81; staff nurse pediatric ICU Moffitt Hosp.-U. Calif., San Francisco, 1981-82; pediatric supr. Kaiser Found. Hosp., Hayward, Calif., 1982-84; Head Start nurse Westchester Community Opportunity Program, Port Chester, N.Y., 1990-91; per diem nurse in pediatrics unit Putnam Hosp. Ctr., Carmel, N.Y., 1992-93; grad. asst. in nursing lab. Pace U., Pleasantville, N.Y., 1992-93, also adj. prof., lectr. continuing edn., 1993—; nurse-pediatric endocrinology metabolism and nutrition N.Y. Med. Coll., Valhalla, 1994-95, clin. specialist and intravenous nurse A&T Healthcare, 1995-96; clin. specialist and pediat. case mgr. Olsten Kimberly Quality Care, 1995-96; maternal child nurse in home care N.Y. United Hosp., Port Chester, N.Y., 1999; pediatric case mgr. PTS Westchester, White Plains, N.Y., 1996-; acting dir. nursing edn. St. Mary's Rehab. Hosp. Children, Ossiming, N.Y., 2001-2002; clin. coord. Phelps Hosp., Sleepy Hollow, N.Y., 2002-. Author, editor newsletter Child and Parent Edn. Soc., 1984-86. Den leader Cub Scouts, Pleasantville, 1992-99, awards coord., 1994-95; mem. evangelical com., 1996-; tchr. Pleasantville Ecumenical Vacation Bible Sch., 1989-94, mem. curriculum com., 1995; tchr. Sunday Sch. Presbyn. Ch., Pleasantville, 1989-95, parish nurse, 2001—. Mem. ANA, Nat. Assn. Clin. Nurse Specialists, Intravenous Nurses Study, N.Y. State Nurses Assn. (author newsletter dist. 16 1993), Nat. Assn. Pediat. Nurse Assocs. and Practitioners, Soc. Pediat. Nurses, Alpha Xi Delta, Sigma Theta Tau (spkr., com. mem. holistic conf.), Parish Nurse Task Force (co-chair), Presbyn. Women's League (moderator). Home: 49 Brentwood Dr Pleasantville NY 10570-1220

GRAHAM, PRISCILLA MANN, librarian; b. Highland Park, Ill., Jan. 3, 1915; d. William David and Isabel (Browning) Mann; m. Myron J. Graham, Oct. 14, 1939; children: Wendy Stevens, Peter Mann, Robert Allen Student, Northwestern U., 1936; BS, Calif. Poly. State U., 1970; MLS, San Jose State U., 1972. Ref. libr. Calif. Poly State U. Libr., San Luis Obispo, 1970—80; substitute libr. Cuesta C.C., San Luis Obispo, 1988—91. Staff Historic Preservation Survey, City of San Luis Obispo, 1980-85 Trustee City Libr., San Luis Obispo, 1968-69, mem. cultural heritage com., 1981-91 Am. Beautiful grantee, 1972 Mem. AAUW, LWV, Libr. Assn. Calif. Poly., Alpha Phi, Beta Phi Mu Home: 61 Los Palos Dr San Luis Obispo CA 93401-7725

GRAHAM, SUSAN LOIS, computer scientist, consultant; b. Cleve., Nov. 16, 1942; m., 1971 AB in Math., Harvard U., 1964; MS, Stanford U., 1966, PhD in Computer Sci., 1971. Assoc. rsch. scientist, adj. asst. prof. computer sci. Courant Inst. Math. Sci., NYU, 1969-71; asst. prof. computer sci. U. Calif., Berkeley, 1971-76, assoc. prof., 1976-81, prof. computer sci., 1981—, Chancellor's prof., 1997—2000, Pehong Chen disting. prof., 2001—; chief computer scientist NSF Nat. Partnership for Advanced Computational Infrastructure, 1997—2005; sr. scientist Lawrence Berkeley Nat. Lab., Calif., 1999—. Vis. scientist Stanford U., 1981; mem. adv. com. div. computer and computation rsch. NSF, 1987-92, mem. program sci. and tech. ctrs., 1987-91, Alan T. Waterman award com., 2001-04; mem. vis. com. elec. engring. and computer sci. MIT, 1989—; mem. vis. com. for engring. and applied sci. Calif. Inst. Tech., 1994-99; mem. vis. com. applied scis. Harvard U., 1995—; mem. commn. on phys. sci., math. and applications NRC, 1992-95; mem. Pres.'s Com. on Nat. Medal Sci., 1994-00; mem. Pres.'s Info. Tech. Adv. Com., 1997-03; bd. dirs. Harvard Alumni Assn., 1997-2000; mem. bd. overseers Harvard U., 2001-; co-chair Nat. Rsch. Coun. Study Future Supercomputing, 2002-04. Co-editor: Comms. ACM, 1975—79; editor: ACM transactions on Programming Langs. and Systems, 1978—92. Mem. bd. trustees Calif. Performances, 2005-. NSF grantee. Fellow AAAS, Assn. for Computing Machinery, Am. Acad. Arts and Sci.; mem. IEEE, NAE. Office: U Calif-Berkeley Computer Sci Div EECS 771 Soda Hall 1776 Berkeley CA 94720-1776 Office Phone: 510-642-2059. Business E-Mail: graham@CS.Berkeley.edu.

GRAHAM, SUSAN LOUISE, religious studies educator, consultant; d. Howard Lee and Mary Margaret Graham. BA with Distinction, U. Calif., Berkeley, 1976; MA in Theology, Dominican Sch. of Philosophy and Theology, 1987, U. Notre Dame, 1996; MDiv, Dominican Sch. of Philosophy and Theology, 1999; PhD, U. Notre Dame, Ind., 2002. Vis. lectr. Mt. Holyoke Coll., South Hadley, Mass., 2000—01, vis. asst. prof., 2001—02; asst. prof. St. Peter's Coll., Jersey City, 2002—. Ministry cons., 1989—; mem. steering com. Byzantine Cool. N.Y.C. Mem.: Soc. Bibl. Lit., Am. Soc. Ch. History (membership com. 1995—), N.Am. Patristics Soc. Avocation: travel. Office: St Peters Coll Dept Theology 2641 Kennedy Blvd Jersey City NJ 07306 Office Phone: 201-918-9231. Office Fax: 201-451-6278 call first. E-mail: sgraham@spc.edu.

GRAHAM, SYLVIA ANGELENIA, wholesale distribution executive, retail buyer; b. Charlotte, NC, Mar. 27, 1950; d. John Wesley and Willie Myrl (Ray) White; m. James Peter Cleveland Fisher, Apr. 23, 1967 (div. Sept. 1972); 1 child, Wesley James Fisher; m. Harold Walker Graham, Sept. 14, 1972 (dec. June 1994); 1 child, Angelique Jane Graham. Cert., Naval Res. Force Detachment Mgmt. Sch., 1985; air cargo specialist cert., Air U., 1987; grad., U.S. Naval Acad./Global Material Transp. Sch., 2003. Store owner Naval Air Terminal/Naval Transp. Support Unit, Norfolk, Va., 1985—; fleet liaison technician Naval Material Transport Orgn., Norfolk, 1988-93, passenger svc. rep. Naval Transp. Support Unit, 1996—; distbr. Blair Divsn. of Mchts., Lynchburg, Va., 1988—, Mason Shoe Co., Chippewa Falls, Wis., 1988—, mem. dealer adv. bd., 1997—; driver Greater Charlotte Transp. Co., 1988—, Watkins Products, Winona, Minn., 1992—, Citizens Def. Products, St. Joseph, Mo., 1993—; dealer Creative Card Co. Products, Chgo., 1995—, Home Showcase Products, Lynchburg, 1995—; driver Carolina Transp., Charlotte, 2000—; distbr. Navy Leager Tng. Unit, Little Creek, Va., 2002; security officer Vance Uniformed Protective Svcs., Oakton, Va., 2005. Mem. Nat. Safety Coun., Charlotte, 1988-, "C" team Watkins Products, Lincoln, Nebr., 1992—, RBC Ministries, Grand Rapids, Mich., 1998-, ARC United Response Citizen Corps, 2003, Employer Support of the Guard and Res., 2003; sec. Popular Club Plan, Dayton, NJ, 1990—; pub. Citizens Def. Products, 1993—; jewelry dealer Merlite Industries, NYC, 1994; sponsor The Paralyzed Vets. Am., Wilton, NH, 1994—; dealer Creative Cards, Chgo., 1995—. Crusader Cancer Ctr. for Detection and Preventin Drive, Seattle, 1991—; block chmn. Easter Seal Soc., 1988—; census taker Census 2000, Charlotte, 2000—; active ARC; With USN, 1991, Persian Gulf; USNR, 1992-2005, Somalian Relief Effort; USN, 1993-94. Named Top Dealer, Home Showcase Products, Lynchburg. Mem. NAFE, Am. Assn. Ret. Persons, Nat. Enlisted Res. Assn., Naval Enlisted Res. Assn., First Class Petty Office Assn., Nat. Assn. Uniformed Svcs., Nat. Pk. and Conservation Assn., Nat. Trust Hist. Preservation, Direct Selling Assn., Navy League of the U.S., Libr. of Congress Assocs., Nature Conservancy, Nat. Audubon Soc., N.C. Sheriffs Assn. (hon. citizen mem. 2000-03), Handyman Club Am. (ofcl.), Nat. Health and Wellness CLub. Democrat. Pentecostal. Avocations: stamp collecting/philately, reading, bicycling, dance, painting. Home: PO Box 16066 Charlotte NC 28297-6066 Personal E-mail: esgr27@yahoo.com.

GRAHAM, SYLVIA SWORDS, retired secondary school educator; b. Atlanta, Nov. 15, 1935; d. Metz Jona and Christine (Gurley) Swords; m. Thomas A. Graham, Nov. 29, 1958 (div. 1970). BA, Mary Washington Coll., Fredericksburg, Va., 1957; MEd, W. Ga. Coll., Carrollton, 1980; SEd, W. Ga. Coll., 1981; postgrad., Coll. William and Mary, 1964-67. Tchr. Atlanta pub. schs., 1957-58, Newark County pub. schs., Newark, Calif., 1960-61; tchr. history Virginia Beach (Va.) pub. schs., 1964-75, Paulding County pub. schs., Dallas, Ga., 1976-97, ret., 1997. Tour dir. Paulding High Sch. trips, Far East, 1985, USSR, 1989, Australia, 1988-89. County chmn. Rep. Party, 1987-89, county chmn. for re-election of Newt Gingrich, 1982; mem. Gingrich edn. com., 1983, 88; 1st vice chmn. 6th Congl. Dist., 1989-90, chmn. 1989-90; chmn. 7th Congl. Dist., 1992-95; del. Nat. Rep. Conv., 1992. Named Star Tchr., Paulding County C. of C., Dallas, Ga., 1989, 97. Mem. Dallas Woman's Club (pres. 1982-84, 1st v.p. 1986-88, pub. affairs chmn. 1986—, treas. for Civic Ctr. fund 1984—), Phi Kappa Phi. Republican. Baptist. Avocations: travel, reading, piano, bridge. Personal E-mail: grahams35@earthlink.net.

GRAHAM, VIOLET JOYCE, writer; b. Brilliant, Ala., Apr. 29, 1931; d. William Middleton Collins and Phyllis Beryl Reynolds; m. Arlee John Graham, Aug. 2, 1953; children: John, James, Guy, Daniel, David, Julie. BA in sociology, Quincy Coll., 1973. Author: (book) Ain't No Chicken in my Dumplins!, 2000, Swamp Castle, 2003; contbr. columns in newspapers Buffalo, Wyo. Newspaper. Avocation: writing. Home: 103 Herbert St Thomaston GA 30286 Office Phone: 307-684-0993. Personal E-mail: vcross@vcn.com, missjoyce@altel.net.

GRAHAME, HEATHER H., lawyer; b. 1955; BA in Human Biol., Stanford Univ., 1978; JD, Univ. Oreg., 1984. Bar: Alaska 1984. Atty. Bogle & Gates PLLC, Anchorage; ptnr., co-chair, telecom. practice group Dorsey & Whitney LLP, Anchorage. Editor-in-chief Oreg. Law Rev., 1983—84. Pres. Alaska Dance Theatre, 2002—. Named Assoc. Mem. Yr., Alaska Telephone Assn., 1993. Mem.: ABA, Alaska Bar Assn., Federal Comm. Bar Assn. (Pacific NW chapt.). Achievements include Sixth place, US Cycling Team Time Trial Championships, 1988; Seventh place, Women's World Championship Sled Dog Race, 2002. Avocation: dog sledding. Office: Dorsey & Whitney LLP Ste 600 1031 W Fourth Ave Anchorage AK 99501-5907 Office Phone: 907-257-7822. Office Fax: 907-276-4152. Business E-Mail: grahame.heather@dorsey.com.

GRAHN, ANN WAGONER, retired science administrator; b. Phila., Feb. 28, 1932; d. George and Marjorie Sharps (Jefferies) W.; m. Douglas Grahn, May 19, 1973. BA magna cum laude with honors, Bryn Mawr Coll., Pa., 1953; MA, Middlebury Coll., Vt., 1954; MBA with distinction, Keller Grad. Sch., Chgo., 1986; DHL (hon.), Hanover Coll., Ind., 2004. Asst. to dir. overseas programs Am. Coun. Edn., Washington, 1955-56; asst. to dir. mat. dist. div. Dem. Nat. Com., Washington, 1956; with geophysics and space sci. NAS, Washington, 1956-70, staff dir. coms. of space sci. bd., 1970-74; coord. Ctr. Policy Studies, assoc. dir. devel. U. Chgo., 1974-79; exec. officer Argonne Univs. Assn., Argonne Nat. Lab., 1979-82, U. Chgo. Office at Argonne Nat. Lab., Argonne, 1982-83. Spl. editor jour. Perspectives in Biology and Medicine, 1980; editor numerous books and reports. Bd. dirs., founding exec. dir. Community Found. of Madison and Jefferson County, 1992-96; mem. City of Madison Port Authority; adminstr. Christ Episcopal Ch., 1996-98, coord., Collaborative Mktg. Project of Jefferson Cty., 1999-03, bd. dirs., Madison-Jefferson Cty. Econ. Devel. Corp. 1997-, chair, Info. Tech. Infrastructure Task Group, 2003-. Fulbright scholar, 1953-54; recipient NASA Pub. Svc. award Nat. Acad. Scis. Space Medicine Com., 1974, Cmty. Svc. award, C. of C., 2000. Mem. Jefferson County Hist. Soc. (bd. dirs. 1989-92). Republican. Episcopalian. Home: 218 Walnut St Madison IN 47250-3556

GRAINGER, AMANDA R., lawyer; b. Little Rock, Sept. 2, 1973; BS, Cornell U., 1995; MBA, JD, Emory U., 1999. Bar: Tex. 1999. Assoc. Winstead, Sechrest & Minick, Dallas, 1999—2004; assoc., pub. law & policy strategies group Sonnenschein Nath & Rosenthal LLP, Washington, 2004—. Office: Sonnenschein Nath & Rosenthal LLP Ste 600, E Tower 1301 K St NW Washington DC 20005 Office Phone: 202-408-3223. Office Fax: 202-408-6399. Business E-Mail: agrainger@sonnenschein.com.

GRAINGER, MARY MAXON, civic volunteer; b. Arlington, Va., Apr. 14, 1957; d. Fred J. and Grace A. (Ziel) Maxon; m. Bradley R. Grainger, Aug. 18, 1979; children: Aileen, Maura, Erin. BS, Cornell U., 1979, MPS, 1987. Dir. pub. rels. Cazenovia (N.Y.) Coll., 1979-80; assoc. dir. admissions Cornell U., Ithaca, N.Y., 1980-85. V.p. Cornell Class of 1979, 1984-99, 2004—, reunion chair, 1999—. Mem. devel. and mktg./pub. rels. com. Sciencenter, 1993-2003, mem. Gala com., 1996-2001; mem. comms. com. 1st Congl. Ch., 1985-2003 (mem. adv. bd.); pres. Cayuga Heights PTA, 2001-02; newsletter editor Ithaca H.S. PTA, 2001—; leader Girl Scouts, 1991—; chair equity com. Boynton Mid. Sch. PTA, 1997-2001, chmn. comms. com., 2003—; adv. Cayuga Heights Sch., literary mag., 1996-2002; bd. dirs. Cornell Alumni Fedn., Ithaca Pub. Edn. Initiative; coun. rep. 1997-2005, devel. com. chair, 2004—, Ithaca PTA, 1996-; mem. Cornell Coun., 2003—. Named Girl Scouts Seven Lakes Coun. Woman of Excellence, 2005, Vol. Fundraiser of Yr., 2003; recipient Agda Osborn award, 2002. Mem. AAUW (chair ednl. equity Ithaca br., event coord. Sister to Sister, 2000—), Cornell Alumni Fedn. (comms. chair), Tompkins Girls Hockey Assn. (v.p. 2002-05, sec. 2005—). Home: 421 Highland Rd Ithaca NY 14850-2215 Fax: 607-257-0483. E-mail: mmgithaca@aol.com.

GRAIS, ALEXANDRA, art appraiser, director; d. Dragan Lukic and Yelitsa Gligorijevic; m. Wafik Grais, Jan. 25, 1973; children: Menelik, Yelitsa, Alexandre. French baccalaureat, Présentation de Marie, St. Julien-en-Genevois, France, 1968; post grad., Davis Sch., Cambridge, England, 1969; post grad. in Linguistics, Santander U., Spain, 1968; BA in Translation French, English and Spanish, Geneva U., 1973. Instr. Cycle d'Orientation, Geneva; dir. Soimca, Montreal, Canada, 1978; tchr. Georgetown Prep, Rockville, Md., 1985—88; dir. C. G. Sloan's Auction Galleries, Washington, 1988—96, v.p. European, Asian and Am. decorative arts, antiquities, 1996—99, cons., 2000—02; dir. Asian and ethnographic dept. antiquities, Pre-Columbian, Islamic art Sloans and Kenyon, Bethesda, Md., 2003—. Condr. seminar appraisal study program George Washington U., Washington; appraisal cons. Pres. Clinton, U.S. Treasury; estate appraiser Elisabeth du Pont, Bayard Weedon; lectr. in field. Mem.: Washington Oriental Ceramic Soc., Asia Soc. Home: 5615 Grove St Chevy Chase MD 20815 Office: Sloans and Kenyon 7034 Wis Ave Bethesda MD 20815 Office Phone: 240-505-1441.

GRALIK, NANCY ELLEN, healthcare consultant; b. Niagara Falls, NY, May 4, 1946; d. Marvin William and Muriel Alice (Dean) S.; m. Edwin Anthony Kowal, May 4, 1968 (div. Jan. 1988); children: Lisa Michelle Herman, Bryan Richard Kowal, Denise Karen Kowal; m. Daniel Joseph Gralik, Apr. 22, 1995. Diploma in nursing, SUNY Buffalo, 1966. RN, N.Y. Supervisor plasmorphoresis ctr. Somerset Labs., Williamsville, NY, 1978-86; br. mgr. Niagara Homemakers H.C., Williamsville, NY, 1986-87; mgr. quality mgmt. HMO/BC/BS Western N.Y., Buffalo, 1987-94; dir. quality mgmt. FHP/Great Lakes Health, Oakbrook Terrace, Ill., 1994-95, HIP Health Plan Fla., Hollywood, Fla., 1996-97; cons. Coopers and Lybrand, LLP, Phila., 1997—. Mem. Nat. Assn. Healthcare Quality, N.Y. State Assn. Healthcare Quality Profls. (publ. team 1992-95), Fla. Assn. Healthcare Quality, Broward Assn. Healthcare Quality. Avocation: cooking. Office: Coopers & Lybrand 2400 Eleven Penns Ctr Philadelphia PA 19144 Home: 91 Parkview Dr Grand Island NY 14072-2958

GRALNEK, MINDA, retail executive; Exec. art dir. Dayton Hudson Dept. Stores; creative dir. US Comm., Target Corp., 1990—2002, v.p., creative dir., 2002—. Spkr. in field. Mem. bd. Frederick R. Weisman Art Mus., Minneapolis, Minn. Office: Target Corp 1000 Nicollet Mall Minneapolis MN 55403*

GRAMER, DOROTHY ANNE, secondary school educator; b. Chgo., Mar. 21, 1933; d. Valentine and Delia (McDonagh) G. BA, Rosary Coll., River Forest, Ill., 1955; MS, U. Ill., 1959. Tchr. math Lane Tech High Sch., Chgo., 1955-93. Mem. Nat. Coun. Tchrs. Math., Grad. Women in Sci. Roman Catholic. Avocation: travel. Home: 130 Ingalton Ave West Chicago IL 60185-2208 Office: Lane Tech High Sch 2501 W Addison St Chicago IL 60618-5945

GRAMES-LYRA, JUDITH ELLEN, artist, educator, municipal official; b. Inglewood, Calif., Feb. 7, 1938; d. Glover Victor and Dorothy Margaret (Burton-Bellingham) Hendrickson and Carolyne Marie Carrick Hendrickson (stepmother); children: Nanséa Ellen Ryan, Amber Jeanne Shelley-Harris, Carolyn Jane Angel Longmire, Susan Elaine Gomez, Robert Derek Shallenberger; m. Jon Robert Lyra, Feb. 14, 1997. Cert in journalism, Newspaper Inst. Am., N.Y.C., 1960; AA, Santa Barbara City Coll., 1971; BA, U. Calif., Santa Barbara, 1978. Cert. tchr. Calif., 1979, tchr. K-12 adult 1983, bldg. insp., plumbing insp. Calif. Editor, reporter, photographer Goleta Valley Sun Newspaper, Santa Barbara, 1968-71; editor, team asst. Bur. of Ednl. Rsch. Devel., Santa Barbara, 1971; bus. writer, graphics cons. Santa Barbara, 1971-77; art and prodn. dir. Bedell Advt. Selling Improvement Corp., Santa Barbara, 1979-81; secondary sch. tchr. Coalinga Unified Sch. Dist., Calif., 1981-83; bldg. insp. aide Santa Barbara County, Lompoc, 1983-88, from bldg. engring. inspector I to III, 1988-99, asst. plans examiner, 1999—2003. Exhibited in group shows at Foley's Frameworks and Interiors, 1984, Grossman Gallery, 1984, 98, Lompoc Valley Art Assn., 1984— (Best of Show 1985, 1st pl. 1984, 94, 2002, 04, 05, 2d pl. 1984, 86, 88, 96-97, 99, 3d pl. 1987, 89, 97, 2003-05, Judge's Choice award 2004, others), Brushes and Blues Invitational, 1998; featured artist Harvest Arts Festival, 1989, Cypress Gallery, 1994, 2004; author numerous poems Mem. disaster response team Calif. Bldg. Ofcl., 1992-2003, cmty. emergency response team; exec. bd. dir. Lompoc Mural Soc., 1991-2003; planning commr. City of Lompoc. Recipient scholarship, Delta Kappa Gamma. Mem. NOW, Nat. Abortion Rights Action League, Nat. Mus. of Women in the Arts (charter), Nat. Womens History Mus. (charter), Lompoc Valley Art Assn. (bd. dirs.), Toastmasters Internat. (Outstanding Spkr. award 1991-93). Avocations: painting, stained glass, illustrating note cards, creative writing, home improvement.

GRAMLING, AUDREY, library media specialist, educator; d. J.D. and Glenda Van Winkle; m. Mike Gramling; children: Laura, Jeff children: Jay. BS in Elem. Edn., Okla. Christian U., Okla. City, 1975; M in Libr. and Info. Studies, U. Okla., Norman, 1996. Cert. libr. media specialist Okla., elem edn. tchr. Okla., nat. bd. cert. tchr. 2005. Classroom tchr. Crowley's Ridge Acad., Paragould, Ark., 1975—77, Living Word Acad., Oklahoma City, 1977—81; libr. media specialist Windsor Hills Elem., Putnam City Schs., Oklahoma City, 1996—97, Monroe Elem., Norman Pub. Schs., Okla., 1997—. Fellow Okla. A+ Schs., Edmond, 2004—. Named Tchr. of Yr., Monroe Elem., 2002; recipient Polly Clarke award, Okla. Assn. Sch. Libr. Media Specialists, 2003. Mem.: ALA, NEA, Okla. Edn. Assn., Am. Assn. Sch. Librs., Okla. Libr. Assn., Okla. Assn. Sch. Libr. Media Specialists (awards chair 2004—06).

GRAMM, WENDY LEE, economics professor, retired government agency administrator; b. Waialua, HI, Jan. 9, 1945; d. Joshua and Angeline (AnChin) Lee; m. Phil Gramm, Nov. 2, 1970; children: Marshall Kenneth, Jefferson Philip. BA in Econs., Wellesley Coll., 1966; PhD in Econs., Northwestern U., 1971. Staff dept. quantitive methods U. Ill., 1969; asst. prof. Tex. A&M U., 1970-74, assoc. prof. dept. econs., 1975-79; research staff Inst. Def. Analyses, 1979-82; asst. dir. Bur. Econs. FTC, 1982-83, dir., 1983-85; adminstr. Office Info. and Regulatory Affairs, OMB, 1985-87; chmn. Commodity Futures Trading Commn., 1988-93; prof. econs. and pub. adminstrn. U. Tex., Arlington, 1993; chmn., regulatory studies prog. & disting. sr. fellow, Mercatus Ctr. George Mason U. Bd. dirs. Enron Corp., 1993—2002, Tex. Pub. Policy Found.; legal adv. bd. Nat. Fedn. Ind. Bus. Contbr. articles to profl. jours. Mem.: Ind. Women's Forum (bd. dirs.). Office: GMU Mercatus Ctr 3301 N Fairfax Dr, Ste 450 Arlington VA 22201

GRAMMER, LESLIE CARROLL, allergist; b. St. Louis, Mo., 1952; MD, Northwestern U., 1976. Cert. internal medicine 1979, allergy and immunology 1981, diag. lab. immunology 1986, occupational medicine 1989. Intern Northwestern U., Chgo., 1976—77, resident, medicine, 1977—79, fellowship, allergy and immunology, 1979—81; allergist Northwestern Meml. Hosp., Chgo., 1981—; prof. medicine Northwestern U. Med. Sch., 1990—. Office: Northwestern U Feinberg Sch Medicine 676 N St Clair Ste 14018 Chicago IL 60611-3093 Office Phone: 312-695-4000.

GRAMSTORFF, JEANNE B., retired farmer; b. Floydada, Tex., June 23, 1930; d. David Stephen Battey and Ruth Asbury Pitts; m. John C. Gramstorff, Feb. 14, 1951 (dec. Feb. 1993); children: Susan G. Gramstorff Fetzer, John C. BA, Tex. Tech U., 1951. Cert. tchr. Tex. Tchr. Perryton (Tex.) Mid. and HS's, 1951-66; farmer Gramstorff & Son, Farnsworth, Tex., 1951-2000; ret., 2000. Bd. dirs. Perryton Nat. Bank. Trustee, officer Perry Meml. Libr., Perryton, 1956—, pres., 2000—03; officer Tex. Panhandle Libr. Sys. Coun., Amarillo, 1978—, chmn., 2001—02; bd. dirs. Lydia Patterson Inst., 1993—2000; sec. Accord Agr., Inc., Farnsworth, 1995—; historian, v.p., pres. N.W. Tex. United Meth. Women; chmn. religion and race com., chmn. dist. mission N.W. Tex. Conf. United Meth. Ch., 2004—06, chmn. comm. religion and race, 2004—05, mem. ann. conf., 1976—2004, mem. conf. ministry team, 2004—06. Avocations: reading, needlepoint. Home: PO Box 250 Farnsworth TX 79033-0250 Personal E-mail: jgram@starband.net.

GRANADE, CALLIE VIRGINIA SMITH, federal judge; b. Lexington, Va., Mar. 7, 1950; d. Milton Hannibal and Callie Dougherty (Rivers) Smith; m. Fred King Granade, Oct. 9, 1976; children: Taylor Rives, Milton Smith, Joseph Kee. BA, Hollins Coll., 1972; JD, U. Tex., 1975. Bar: Tex. 1975, Ala. 1976, U.S. Ct. Appeals (5th cir.) 1976, U.S. Dist. Ct. (so. dist.) Ala. 1977, U.S. Supreme Ct. 1980, U.S. Ct. Appeals (11th cir.) 1981. Law clk. to chief judge John Godbold US Ct. Appeals (5th cir.), Montgomery, Ala., 1975-76; asst. US atty. US Dept. Justice, Mobile, 1977, sr. litigation counsel, 1987-90; chief criminal sect. US Atty.'s Office, Mobile, 1990-97; 1st asst. US Atty. Southern Dist. of Ala., 1997—2001, interim US Atty., 2001—02, judge, 2002—, chief judge, 2003—. Mem. ABA, Fed. Bar Assn., Ala. State Bar Assn., Tex. State Bar Assn., Mobile Bar Assn., Am. Coll. Trial Lawyers. Presbyterian. Office: US Courthouse 113 St Joseph St Mobile AL 36602

GRANATI, DIANE ALANE, retired ophthalmic nurse; b. Bethlehem, Pa., Sept. 23, 1952; d. William Edward and Martha Lou (Bradford) Reichard; m. Joseph P. Granati, June 15, 2000. Diploma, Abington (Pa.) Meml. Hosp., 1973. Cert. RN in ophthalmology, Nat. Certifying Bd. Ophthalmic Registered Nurses, ophthalmic exec., Nat. Bd. Certification Ophthalmic Execs. Med.-surg. nurse St. Luke's Hosp., Bethlehem, 1973-76; ophthalmic nurse physician's office, Pitts., 1976-77, Everett & Hurite Ophthalmic Assocs., Pitts., 1977-80; exec. dir. Assocs. in Ophthalmology, Inc., Pitts., 1980—2005. Speaker in field. Contbr. articles to profl. jours. Mem. NAFE, Founders Soc., Am. Soc. Ophthalmic Registered Nurses, Abington Nurses Alumnae, Am. Soc. Ophthalmic Adminstrs. Home: 109 BEnt Birch Ln Beaver Falls PA 15010 Office: 500 Lewis Run Rd Ste 218 Pittsburgh PA 15122-3057 also: 125 Daugherty Dr Ste 320 Monroeville PA 15146-2749 also: 2 W Main St Ste 508 Uniontown PA 15401-3403 Address: Ste 230 300 Belmar Dr Pittsburgh PA 15205 also: 2000 Tower Way Ste 2037 Greensburg PA 15601 Personal E-mail: spacesongs@aol.com.

GRANATO, CATHERINE (CAMMI GRANATO), Olympic athlete; b. Downers Grove, Ill., Mar. 25, 1971; d. Natalie and Don Granato. Student, Providence Coll., R.I., 1989-93, Concordia U., 1994-97. Hockey player U.S. Nat. Team, 1992—. Recipient Gold Medal, Women's Ice Hockey, Nagano Olympic Games, 1998, Silver Medal, Salt Lake City Olympic Games, 2002. Office: USA Hockey Inc 1775 Bob Johnson Dr Colorado Springs CO 80906-4090

GRANDCHAMP, JEANNE P., literature educator; b. Warwick, RI, Mar. 21, 1952; d. Louis E. and Estelle C. Grandchamp. AA, RI Jr. Coll., Providence, 1972; BA, RI Coll., Providence, 1974; MA, U. Conn., Storrs, 1977. Cert. adult devel. edn. Appalacian State U. Instr. U. Conn., Storrs, 1976; prof. English Bristol C.C., Fall River, Mass., 1978—. Editor (with F. Hahb Colloquia): Journal of Teaching and Learning, 2005; contbr. articles various profl. jours. Recipient Sceptre and Scroll award, Bristol C.C., 1985, Pride in Performance award, Commonwealth Mass., 1985. Mem.: Nat. Assn. Tchrs. English, Cranston Historical Soc. Avocations: walking, travel, reading, writing. Office: Bristol CC 777 Elsbree St Fall River MA 02720 Office Phone: 508-678-2811.

GRANDI, LOIS A., theater director, choreographer, actor; b. Phila., June 9, 1941; d. John R. and Rosina H.R. Grandinetti; m. Robert Leonard Sieben (div.); children: Laurey Dawn Heinrich, Paul Leonard Sieben. Student, Keith Davis Voice Studio, NYC, 1963—70, Neighborhood Playhouse, 1964—70, Met. Opera Ballet. Actress PBS, San Francisco, 1983; acting tchr. Performing Arts Acad., Walnut Creek, Calif., 1984—; dir. Willows Theatre Co., Concord, Calif., 1990—91, Calif. Conservatory Theatre, San Leandro, Calif., 1992—94; artistic dir. Playhouse West, Walnut Creek, 1995—. Music Man, Merry Widow, Little Me, The Rainmaker, The World Goes 'Round; dir., dir.: The Boy Friend, (Best Entire Prodn., Best Dir. awards), Betrayal, After the Fall, New Wrinkles (3 Critic's Cir. awards), Force of Nature, Taking Sides, Proof (Best Dir., 03), Whispers on the Wind (Best Dir., Critic's Cir.); actor: Light Sensitive (Best Actress Critic's Cir., 00), Lovers and Other Strangers, Two For the Seesaw, Smile, Oklahoma!, Carousel, The Sound of Music; actor, actor: The Boy Friend, (Best Entire Prodn., Best Dir. awards), He Who Gest Slapped, Very Good Eddie, Finian's Rainbow, West Side Story, (PBS TV series) Up and Coming, numerous training and indsl. films, commls.; guest dancer The White House. Recipient recognition, Arts and Culture Commn. Contra Costa County, 1998, 10 Drama-Logue awards, 1997; honored by State Sen. Tom Torlakson and Assemblywoman Lynne Leache for contbn. to arts, 2002. Mem.: SAG, AFTRA, Actors Equity Assn. (mem. adv. bd. 1975). Democrat. Avocations: classical music, piano. Home: 2245 Gladwin Dr Walnut Creek CA 94596

GRANDIN, TEMPLE, industrial designer, science educator; b. Boston, Aug. 29, 1947; d. Richard McCurdy and Eustacia (Cutler) Grandin. BA in Psychology, Franklin Pierce Coll., 1970; MS in Animal Sci., Arizona State U., 1975; PhD in Animal Sci., U. Ill., Urbana, 1989; D (hon.), McGill U., 1999. Livestock editor Ariz. Farmer Ranchman, Phoenix, 1973-78; equipment designer Corral Industries, Phoenix, 1974-75; ind. cons. Grandin Livestock Systems, Urbana, 1975-90, Fort Collins, Colo., 1990—; lectr., prof. animal sci. dept. Colo. State U., Fort Collins, 1990—. Chmn. handing com. Livestock Conservation Inst., Madison, Wis., 1976—; surveyor USDA. Author: Emergence Labelled Autistic, 1986, Recommended Animal Handling Guidelines for Meat Packers, 1991, Livestock Handling and Transport, 1993, 2d edit., 2000, Thinking in Pictures, 1995, Genetics and the Behavior of Domestic Animals, 1998, Beef Cattle Behavior Handling and Facilities Design, 2000, Animals in Translation, 2005 (One of Top Sci. Books of Yr., 2005), Developing Talents, 2005; contbr. articles to profl. jours. Named Woman of Yr. in Svc. to Agr. Progressive Farmer, 1999; named one of Processing Stars of 1990, Nat. Provisioner, 1990; recipient Meritorious Svcs. award Livestock Conservation, Madison, Wis., 1986, Disting. Alumni award Franklin Pierce Coll., 1989, Industry Innovators award Meat Mktg. and Tech. Mag., 1994, Brownlee award for internat. leadership in sci. publ. promoting respect for animals Animal Welfare Found. of Canada, 1995, Harry Roswell award Scientists Ctr. for Animal Welfare, 1995, Humane Ethics in Action award Geraldine R. Dodge Found., 1998, Forbes award Nat. Meat Assn., 1998, Founders award Am. Soc. Prevention Cruelty Animals, 1999, Humane award Am. Vet. Med. Assn., 1999, Joseph Wood Krutch award, Humane Soc. of U.S., 2001, Knowlton Innovation award in Meat Mktg. and Tech. Mag., 2001, 2002, Animal Welfare award, Brit. Soc. Animal Sci. and Royal Soc. Prevention Cruelty to Animals, 2002, Pres.'s award, Nat. Inst. Animal Agr., 2004. Mem.: Am. Soc. Agrl. Cons. (bd. dirs. 1981—83), Am. Registry Profl. Animal Scis., Am. Meat Inst. (supplier mem., Industry Advancement award 1995), Am. Soc. Agrl. Engrs., Am. Soc. Animal Sci. (Animal Mgmt. award 1995, Disting. Svc. award We. sect. 2003), Autism Soc. Am. (bd. dirs. 1988—, Trammel Crow award 1989). Republican. Episcopalian. Achievements include patents in field; design of stockyards and humane restraint equipment for major meat packing companies in the U.S., Canada and Australia; development of objective scoring system used for monitoring animal welfare in slaughter plants. Office: Colo State U Animal Sci Dept Fort Collins CO 80523-0001 Office Phone: 970-229-0703.

GRANDIZIO, LENORE, social worker; b. N.Y.C., Apr. 20, 1952; d. Louis and Angelina (Pre de Garcia) G.; m. Lenny Mars Rothbart; 1 child, Angelica M. BA, SUNY, Geneseo, 1973; MSSW, Columbia U., 1978. Cert. social worker, N.Y.; cert. child psychiatry and child guidance; diplomate clin. social work. Assoc. staff mem. Child, Adolescent and Family Clinic Postgrad. Ctr. for Mental Health, N.Y.C., 1981-83, assoc. staff mem. Adult Clinic, 1984-87; social worker East Harlem Consultation Svc., N.Y.C., 1983-84; sr. worker Jewish Bd. Family and Children's Svcs., Bklyn., 1984-85; sch. social worker N.Y.C. Bd. Edn., 1985—. Co-chair regional staff devel. com. N.Y.C. Bd. Edn., 1996-98; presenter in field, N.Y.C., 1995-97. Mem. NAFE, NASW. Home: 229 W 105th St Apt 53 New York NY 10025-3918

GRANESE, JUDITH ANN, secondary school educator; b. Corona, NY, Sept. 23, 1947; d. Edward Charles Granese and Ginevra Palazzo. BA, St. John's U., Jamaica, NY, 1969, MA, 1973. Instr. English Sewanhaka Ctrl. H.S. Dist., Floral Park, NY, 1969—77; instr. English and Latin Valley H.S., Las Vegas, 1977—2001; instr. English C.C. So. Nev., 1983—95; educator English and Latin Centennial H.S., 2001—; instr. Latin U. Nev., 2005—06. Owner Learning Designs by Judith, Las Vegas, 1998—. Author: (monograph) How to be a Great Club Advisor, 1992, Teaching the Short Story, 1996. Recipient Elizabeth Watkins Latin Tchr. award, Am. Classical League, 2005, Am. Hero Edn., Reader's Digest, 1993. Mem.: Am. Classical League, Kiwanis (bd. dirs. 1993—2006, Judith A. Granese scholar 2004, G. Harold Martin fellow, Hixson fellow, Tablet of Honor). Avocations: travel, researching vampire folklore, reading. Office: Centennial High School 10200 Centennial Parkway Las Vegas NV 89149

GRANET, EILEEN, secondary school educator; AA, Palomar Coll., 1974; BA, San Diego State U., 1977, MA, 1983. Cert. social sci., math, history, spl. edn. tchr. Calif. and Wash., lang. devel. specialist, c.c. instr., tchr. handicapped. Circulation clk. San Diego Union-Tribune, Escondido, Calif., 1974-82; exec. sec. State Mutual Life, San Diego, 1978-79; basic skills & social skills tchr. Mira Costa Coll., Oceanside, Calif., 1984-86; spl. edn. tchr. Escondido Union Sch., 1979-85, tchr. 6th grade history and math, 1985-88, tchr. 7th grade math., 1988-91; tchr. 6th grad history, math., computers and drama cre, 1991-95; tchr. 7th and 8th grade history Escondido Union Sch. Dist., 1995—. Master tchr. student tchrs. Nat. U., Vista, Calif., San Diego State U., 1984—; dist. cons., tchr. coach Escondido Union Schs., 1987—, dist. mentor tchr./trainer, 1988-92, mem. dist. ednl. tech. planning com., 1996—; dept. chairperson Grant Mid. Sch., Escondido, 1988-93, 95—; presenter in field. Internat. conf. presenter Nat. Assn. Vocat. Edn. Spl. Needs Pers., Am. Vocat. Assn., Nat. Rehab. Assn., Chgo., 1983; conf. copresenter Northwest Regional Ednl. Lab., Oregon State U., 1991; conf. presenter San Diego County Partnership Symposium, Oceanside, Calif., 1998, Calif. Coun. Social Sci., Santa Clara, 1999. Fellow NEH, 1997, Calif. History/Social Sci. Project, Schs. Calif. Online Resources for Edn., 1997; named Tchr. of Yr., Escondido Elem. Educators Assn., 1984, 88. Mem. AAUW, NAFE, Nat. Tchr.'s Assn., Calif. Coun. Social Studies, Computer Using Educators, Phi Delta Kappa. Avocations: reading, travel, photography, craft sewing, internet research. Home: PO Box 670 Escondido CA 92033-0670

GRANGE, JANET LENORE, lawyer, accountant, consultant; b. Chgo., Sept. 5, 1958; d. Albert Edward and Marie Loretta (Hart) G. BS in Acctg., U. Ill., Chgo., 1980; JD, U. Ill., 1983. Bar: Ill. 1983; CPA, Ill. Sr. tax cons. Grant Thornton, Chgo., 1983-85, Deloitte, Haskins & Sells, Chgo., 1985-86, Kraft, Inc., Glenview, Ill., 1986-88; assoc. prof. acctg. Chgo. State U., 1989—; sole practitioner of law. Nissan HBCU fellow, 1992; mem. hearing bd. Ill. Atty. Registration and Disciplinary Com., 1994-2003. Mem.: Ill. State Bar Assn., Beta Gamma Sigma. Avocation: golf. Office: Fed and State Tax Office 11070 S Western Ave Chicago IL 60643-3928 Fax: 708-481-5364. Office Phone: 773-995-3967. E-mail: j-grange@csu.edu.

GRANGER, KAY, congresswoman; b. Greenville, Tex., Jan. 18, 1943; children: John Dean, Chelsea, Brandon. BS magna cum laude, Tex. Wesleyan U., 1965, DHL (hon.); D in Pub. Svc. (hon.), Tenn. Wesleyan Coll. Prin., owner G&R Ins. Agy., Ft. Worth, Kay Granger & Assocs.; mem. zoning com. City of Ft. Worth, 1981—89; mem. pvt. industry coun., 1988-89; mem. City Coun., Ft. Worth, 1989-91; mayor Ft. Worth, 1991-95; mem. US Congress from 12th Tex. dist., 1997—, dep. majority whip, mem. appropriations com. Bd. visitors USAF Acad.; bd. trustees Southwestern U. Author: What's Right About America?, 2006. Recipient Woman of Yr. award, 1987, Bus. and Profl. Woman award, 1987, YMCA Congl. award, 2004, Nat. Assn. Mfrs. award, PE4LIFE Legislator of Yr. award, 2004, Cmty. Health Defender award Nat. Assn. Cmty. Health Ctrs., 2006; named Exec. of Yr., Ft. Worth Bus. Hall of Fame, 1999; inductee Tex. Women's Hall of Fame, 1999. Mem. Am. Planning Assn., Internat. Sister Cities Assn., Women's Policy Forum (bd. dirs.), East Ft. Worth Bus. and Profl. Assn. (bd. dirs.), Ft. Worth Bus. and Estate Planning Coun., Meadowbrook Bus. and Profl. Womens Assn., East Ft. Worth C. of C. (vice chmn.). Republican. Methodist. Office: US Ho Reps 440 Cannon Ho Office Bldg Washington DC 20515 Office Phone: 202-225-5071.*

GRANHOLM, JENNIFER MULHERN, governor; b. Vancouver, B.C., Can., Feb. 5, 1959; arrived in U.S., 1962; d. Civtor Ivar and Shirley Alfreda (Dowden) Granholm; m. Daniel Granholm Mulhern, May 23, 1986; children: Kathryn, Cecelia, Jack. BA, U. Calif., Berkeley, 1984; JD, Harvard U., 1987. Bar: Mich. 1987, U.S. Dist. Ct. (ea. dist.) Mich. 1987, U.S. Ct. Appeals (6th cir.) 1987. Jud. law clk. 6th Cir Ct. Appeals, Detroit, 1987—88; exec. asst. Wayne County Exec., Detroit, 1988—89; asst. U.S. atty. Dept. Justice, Detroit, 1990—94; corp. counsel Wayne County, Detroit, 1994—98; atty. gen. State of Mich., Lansing, 1999—2002, gov., 2003—. Gen. counsel Detroit/Wayne County Stadium Authority, 1996—98. Contbr. articles to profl. jours. Commr. Great Lakes Commn.; mem. bd. Cyberstate.org YWCA. Mem.: Inc. Soc. Irish Lawyers, Women's Law Assn., Detroit Bar Assn. Democrat. Roman Catholic. Avocation: running. Office: Gov Office PO Box 30013 Lansing MI 48909 Office Phone: 517-335-3400. Office Fax: 517-335-6949.*

GRANN, PHYLLIS E., editor, former publisher executive; b. London, Sept. 2, 1937; d. Solomon and Louisa (Bois-Smith) Eitingon; m. Victor Grann, Sept. 28, 1962; children: Allison, David, Edward. BA cum laude, Barnard Coll., 1958. Sec. Doubleday Pubs., N.Y.C., 1958-60; editor William Morrow Inc., N.Y.C., 1960-62, David McKay Co., N.Y.C., 1962-70; sr. editor Simon & Schuster Inc., N.Y.C., 1970—74, editor-in-chief, Pocket Books paperbacks divsn., 1974—76; editor-in-chief G.P. Putnam's & Sons, N.Y.C., 1976—79, editor-in-chief, pub., 1979—84, pub., pres., 1984—86; pres. Putnam Berkley Group, N.Y.C., 1986—87, pres., CEO, 1987—91, chmn., CEO, 1991—96; pres., CEO Penguin Putnam, Inc., 1996—2001; vice chmn. Random House, 2002, sr. editor, Doubleday Broadway Publishing Co., 2003—. Adj. asst. prof. fin. and economics Columbia Bus. Sch., N.Y.C., 2003—; bd. dirs. Warner Music Group Corp., 2006—. Co-founder Victor & Phyllis Grann Family Found.*

GRANNAN, KATY, photographer; b. Arlington, Mass., 1969; BA, U. Pa., 1991; MA, Harvard U., 1993; MFA, Yale U., 1999. One-woman shows include Dream Am., Kohn Turner Gallery, LA, 2000, 51 Fine Art, Antewerp Belgium, 2001, Morning Call, Salon 94, NYC, 2003, Sugar Camp Rd., Artemis Greenberg Van Doren Gallery, NYC, 2003, Arles Photography Festival, Arles, France, 2004, Emily Tsingou Gallery, London, 2005, Jackson Fine Art, Atlanta, Ga., 2005, exhibited in group shows, ArtSpace, New Haven, Conn., 1998, Another Girl, Another Planet, Lawrence Rubin Greenberg Van Doren Fine Art, NY, 1999, Reflections Through A Glass Eye, Internat. Ctr. Photography, NY, 2000, Smile, Here, NY, 2001, Boomerang: Collector's Choice II, Exit Art, NY, 2001, Women by Women, Cook Fine Art, NY, 2002, True Blue, Jackson Fine Art, Atlanta, 2002, Girls Night Out, Orange County Mus. Art, LA, 2003, Moving Pictures, Guggenheim Mus., Bilbao, Spain, 2003, Open House: Working in Bklyn., Bklyn. Mus. Art, 2004, Whitney Biennial, Whitney Mus. Am. Art, 2004, From NY with Love, Covivant Gallery, Tampa, Fla., 2004, Land of the Free, Jack Hanley Gallery, San Francisco, 2004. Recipient Bucksbaum Award, 2004; Rema Hort Mann Found. Grant, 1999. Mailing: c/o Artemis Greenberg Van Doran Gallery 730 Fifth Ave 7th Floor New York NY 10019

GRANNE, REGINA, artist, educator; b. NYC, Jan. 16, 1939; d. Meyer and Mildred Biernoff; m. Martin Granne, Oct. 27, 1963; 1 child, Michael. Cert., Cooper Union, 1956—59; student, Hunter Coll., 1959—60; BFA, Yale U., 1961, MFA, 1963. Instr. painting and drawing Ridgewood Sch. Art, 1967—73; asst. prof. art Bard Coll., Annandale-on-Hudson, NY, 1973—74; lectr. art CUNY Queens Coll., Flushing, NY, 1973—84; instr. painting and drawing Parsons Sch. Design, NYC, 1979—93, coord. MFA program, 1993—2002, mem. faculty, 2001—05, Bard Coll. Milton Avery Sch. of the Fine Arts, Annandale, 1983—2005. Vis. artist Lakehead U., Ont., Canada, 1989; vis. instr. Moore Coll Art, Phila., 1990—92; vis. artist Art Acad. Cin., 1994. One-woman shows include Tatistcheff Gallery, NYC, 1989, Genovese Sullivan Gallery, Boston, 1991, 1996, 1997, 1999, 2003, A.I.R. Gallery, NYC, 1995, 1997, 1999, 2002, Lehman Wing Sch. Internat. Studies, Columbia U., 2000, Univ. Art Gallery, Sewanee, Tenn., 2001, exhibited in group shows at 181st Ann.: An Invitational Exhbn. Contemporary Art, Nat. Acad. Mus., NYC, 2006. Home: 237 Bleecker St New York NY 10014 Personal E-mail: rgranne@verizon.net.

GRANSDEN, CHARISSA SHARRON, music educator; d. Charles Paul and Bertha Brown (Stepmother); m. Joseph Gransden, June 8, 2002. MusB Edn., Ga. State U., 1997. Cert. music tchr. Ga. Profl. Stds. Commn., 1997. Assoc. dir. band Mt. Zion H.S., Jonesboro, Ga., 1997—2001; dir. band Kittredge Magnet Sch., Atlanta, 2001—. Mentor Dekalb County Schs., Atlanta, 2001—; chair person Cultural Diversity Com., Atlanta, 2004—. Recipient Rising Star Tchr. award, Ga. Perimeter Coll., 1998. Mem.: Music Educators Nat. Conf., Ga. Music Educators Assn. Roman Catholic.

GRANSKOG, JANE ELLEN, anthropologist, educator; b. Mich., June 10, 1946; d. E. Walfred and Dorothy Granskog. BS, Mich. State U., East Lansing, 1968; PhD, U. of Tex., Austin, 1974. Mediation skills for resolving conflicts Ariz. Prof. of anthropology Calif. State U., Bakersfield, 1974—. Chair women's studies program com. Calif. State U., Bakersfield, 1988—2003; v.p. Bakersfield chpt. Calif. Faculty Assn., Bakersfield, 2001—03. Co-editor (with Anne Bolin): Athletic Intruders: Ethnographic Research on Women, Culture and Exercise; contbr. poetry to anthologies. Bd. dirs., pres. Ctr. for Prosperous Living, Laguna Beach, Calif., 2005—06; vice chair governing coun. PeaceWeb Inc, Tucson, 2003—06. Mem.: Southwestern Anthrop. Assn. (pres.-elect, pres. 2001—03), Am. Anthrop. Assn. New Thought. Avocation: triathlete. Office: Calif State U 9001 Stockdale Hwy Bakersfield CA 93311-1022 Office Phone: 661-654-3117. Business E-Mail: jgranskog@csub.edu.

GRANT, AMY, singer, songwriter; b. Augusta, Ga., Nov. 25, 1960; d. Burton and Gloria Grant; m. Gary Chapman, 1983 (div. 1999); children: Matthew Chapman, Millie Chapman, Sarah Chapman; m. Vince Gill, 2000; 1 child, Corrina Grant Gill. Student, Furman U., Vanderbilt U., Coll. Arts & Sci., 1982. Albums include Amy Grant, 1977, My Father's Eyes, 1979, Never Alone, 1980, Amy Grant in Concert, 1981, Amy Grant in Concert II, 1981, Age to Age (Grammy award), 1982, A Christmas Album, 1983, Straight Ahead, 1984, Unguarded (Grammy award), 1985, The Collection, 1986, Lead Me On (Grammy award), 1988, Heart in Motion, 1991, Home for Christmas, 1992, House of Love, 1994, Behind the Eyes, 1997, A Christmas to Remember, 1999, Legacy Hymns & Faith, 2002, Simple Things, 2003, Greatest Hits 1986-2004, 2004, Rock Of Ages.Hymns & Faith, 2005; host (TV series), Three Wishes, 2005. Recipient 24 Dove awards Gospel Music Assn., Grammy award contemporary album, 1983, Grammy award best gospel performance, 1984-86, Grammy award best contemporary album, 1988; honored Walk of Fame, 2001; named to Music Hall of Fame, 2005. Office: c/o Blanton Harrell Cooke & Corzine Ste 100 5300 Virgina Way Brentwood TN 37027 Office Phone: 615-627-0450.

GRANT, BARBARA, venture capitalist; PhD in Organic Chemistry, Stanford U., 1974. Rsch. scientist rsch. divsn. IBM, 1975-86; product mgr. IBM Sys. Printer Products, 1986-91; dir. IBM Storage Divsn. Magnetic Recording Head Bus. Unit, 1991-94; v.p. bus. devel. IBM Storage Sys. Divsn., 1994-95, v.p., gen. mgr. Removable Media Storage Solutions Bus. Unit, 1995—96; pres., CEO Siros Technologies, 1996—2004; exec.-in-residence Amer. River Ventures, 2004—. NSF fellow. Office: Amer River Ventures 2270 Douglas Blvd Ste 212 Roseville CA 95661

GRANT, BARBARA ROSEMARY, science educator, researcher; b. Arnside, Eng., Oct. 8, 1936; d. Alexander and Hilda Gwendoline (Peace) Matchett; m. Peter R. Grant, Jan. 4, 1962; children: Nicola, K. Thalia. BSc with honors, U. Edinburgh, Scotland, 1960; PhD, Uppsala U., Sweden, 1985; DSc (hon.), McGill U., Montreal, Can., 2000, U. San Francisco, Quito, Ecuador, 2005. Rsch. assoc., lectr. U. BC, Vancouver, Canada, 1960—64; rsch. assoc. Yale U., New Haven, 1964—65, McGill U., 1973—77, U. Mich., Ann Arbor, 1977—85; sr. rsch. scholar Princeton U., 1987—. Vis. prof. U. Zurich, Switzerland, 2002. Author: Evolutionary Dynamics of a Natural Population, 1991 (Wildlife Publ. award, 1991); contbr. articles to profl. jours. Recipient Leidy medal, Acad. Natural Scis., Phila., 1994, E.O. Winslow prize, Am. Soc. Naturalists, 1998, Darwin medal, Royal Soc., London, 2002, Miller award, 2003, Grinnell medal, 2003, Balzan prize, 2005. Fellow: Royal Soc. Can. (fgn.), German Ornithology Assn. (hon.); mem.: Am. Acad. Arts and Scis. Office: Dept Ecology and Evolutionary Biology Princeton U Princeton NJ 08544 Office Phone: 609-258-6290.

GRANT, BEATRICE, underwriter, consultant; b. Evanston, Ill., July 26, 1954; d. Roosevelt Lee and Mollie (Webb) Lee; m. David Grant, Oct. 6, 1973; children: Anton Lavon, Anita Leona Grant-Leigh. Student, Northeastern Ill. U., Chgo., 1972-74. Rating clk. Warner Ins. Group, Chgo., 1975-78, underwriter, 1981-85; underwriting technician CNA, Chgo., 1978-81, sr. underwriter, 1985-89; underwriting cons., br. bus. unit CNA Comml. Ins., Chgo., 1989—. Underwriting cons. Election judge Cook County, Country Club Hills, Ill., 1997—. Mem. Nat. Assn. Ins. Women, Chgo. Assn. Ins. Women (1st v.p. 1993-94, pres. 1995-96, 2000-01, Profl. Ins. Woman of Yr. 1996, state dir.-elect Ill. State Coun. 1999-2000, state dir. 2000-01, 04—, regional v.p. 2001-02). Office: CNA CNA Plz 37S Chicago IL 60685-0001 E-mail: beatrice.grant@cna.com.

GRANT, BETTY RUTH, retired elementary school educator; b. Alexandria, La., Apr. 14, 1937; d. Delila and Vonnie (Rogers) Nugent; m. Donald Eugene Grant, Mar. 28, 1958; children: David Nugent, Kenneth Don. BA, La. Coll., 1958; MA in Edn., Northwestern State U., Natchitoches, La., 1965; postgrad., East Tex. State U., 1975. Cert. elem. tchr., La., Tex. Classroom tchr. Woodland Elem. Sch., Pineville, La., 1958-66; 4th grade tchr. C.A. Tosch Elem. Sch., Mesquite, Tex., 1970—2003, ret., 2003. Active Homeowners Assn., Mesquite, 1969—, Polit. Action Com., Mesquite, 1970-85. Mem. AAUW (pres. 1982), Mesquite Edn. Assn. (pres. 1977-78), Assn. Tex. Profl. Educators, PTA (treas. 1970, life), Mesquite Assn. Ret. Sch. Employees (sec.), United Meth. Women (pres.), Alpha Delta Kappa (pres. 1984). Methodist. Home: 2537 Belhaven Dr Mesquite TX 75150-5201

GRANT, CARMEN HILL, psychologist, psychotherapist; b. Denver, Feb. 10, 1935; d. Floyd Vernon Hill and Ena Celeste Turner; m. Donald Roger Grant, Aug. 4, 1964; stepchildren: Roger W., David M. BA, U. Colo., 1957; PhD, U. Nebr., 1967. Diplomate in clin. psychology Am. Bd. Profl. Psychology, 1977, cert. Nebr. State Bd. Examiners Psychologists, Colo. State Bd. Examiners Psychologists. Clin. psychology intern Southwestern Med. Sch., Dallas, 1960—61; psychology trainee VA Hosp., Omaha, 1962—64; asst. clin. psychologist Nat. Jewish Hosp., Denver, 1962; clinic asst. U. Nebr., Lincoln, 1963—64; staff psychologist U. Health Ctr., U. Nebr., Lincoln, 1964—67, clin. psychologist and clinic coord., 1967—70, clin. psychologist/outreach staff coord., 1970—78; pvt. practice Lincoln, 1978—. Mem. U. Nebr. Task Force on Drug Edn., 1972—75; commr. and health com. chair Lincoln-Lancaster Commn. on Status of Women, 1976—80; sports psychology cons. U. Nebr., 1980—86; pres., sec., bd. dirs. Nebr. Soc. Profl. Psychologists, Lincoln, 1985—88; vice chair, mem. State Bd. Psychologists, 1997—2004; co-developer program on wellness lifestyles U. Health Ctr., Lincoln; presenter in field. Contbr. articles to jour.; co-author: (NETV videotape) Nonverbal Comm. in Counseling, 1974. Co-founder Lincoln Personal Crisis Svc., Inc., 1970—74, v.p., 1970—74, sec., 1970—74, bd. dirs., 1970—74; pres. Lancaster Co. Assn. Mental Health, Lincoln, 1972—75, bd. dirs., 1972—75, profl. adv. bd., 1972—75; com. mem. Mayor's Task Force: Domestic Violence, Lincoln, 1980. Recipient A Peer Group Approach to a Smoking Edn. Program in U. Setting award, Nat. Clearinghouse on Smoking and Health, USPHS Contract, U. Health Ctr., Lincoln, Nebr., 1966—69. Fellow: Acad. Clin. Psychology; mem.: APA, Nebr. Psychol. Assn. (pres./officer/bd. dirs. 1991—96, liaison to State Bd. Examiners of Psychologists 1995—97), Sigma Xi. Avocations: books, travel, tennis, golf, landscape gardening.

GRANT, COLLEEN, information systems specialist; b. Sunnyvale, Calif., Nov. 16, 1963; d. James Thomas and Hypatia May (Brierly) Walsh; m. Richard Michael Grant, May 30, 1999. Customs liaison Miami Valley Transportations Cons., Dayton, Ohio, 1984-8; sys. intergration coord. NCR Corp., Dayton, 1990-93; rsch. analyst Coding Svcs., Centerville, Ohio, 1993-94; office mgr. LaForsch Orthopedic, Dayton, 1994-95; office adminstr. CH2M Hill, Inc., Dayton, 1995-98; sr. adminstr. The Iams Co, Dayton, 1998-99, human resource info. specialist, 1999—. Mem. Phi Theta Kappa Internat. Republican. Avocations: boating, music, arts, travel. Office: The Iams Co 7250 Poe Ave Dayton OH 45414-5801

GRANT, CYNTHIA D., writer; b. Brockton, Mass., Nov. 23, 1950; d. Robert Cheyne and Jacqueline Ann (Ford) G.; m. Daniel Heatley; 1 child: Morgan; m. Erik Neel; 1 child, Forest. Author: Joshua Fortune, 1980 (Woodward Park Sch. annual book award 1981), Summer Home, 1981, Big Time, 1982, Hard Love, 1983, Kumquat May, I'll Always Love You, 1986, Phoenix Rising, 1989 (Mich. Libr. Assn. Young Adult Caucus best book of yr. 1990, PEN/Norma Klein award 1991, Detroit Pub. Libr. Author Day award 1992), Keep Laughing, 1991, Shadow Man, 1992, Uncle Vampire, 1993 (ALA best books for young adults list 1994), Mary Wolf, 1995, The White Horse, 1998, The Cannibals, Starring Tiffany Spratt, 2002. Recipient Book of Distinction award Hungry Mind Review, 1993, 94. Mem.: PEN (Norma Klein award 1991). Avocations: reading, volunteer work, Cloverstock. Home: PO Box 95 Cloverdale CA 95425-0095 Office: Writers House LLC 21 W 26th St New York NY 10010

GRANT, ELAINE MARION, music educator, voice educator; b. Buffalo, N.Y., Mar. 20, 1967; d. Richard George Becker, Sr. and Donna Lea Becker; m. Gary Edward Grant, Apr. 3, 1993; children: Dylan Jameson, Jakob Alexander, Samuel Caleb. BS in Music Edn., Nazareth Coll., Pittsford, N.Y., 1989; MusM in Voice Performance, Ithaca Coll., N.Y., 1992. Tchr. music West Seneca East Elem. Sch., NY, 1992—93, Kenmore Mid. Sch., NY, 1993—. Bd. dirs. Freudig Singers of Western N.Y., Buffalo, 2005—06. Mem.: Erie County Music Educators Assn., Am. Choral Dirs. Assn., Music Educators Nat. Conf. Democrat. Lutheran. Avocations: singing, reading, yoga, reiki, jewelry-making. Office: Kenmore Mid Sch 155 Delaware Rd Kenmore NY 14217

GRANT, FRANCES BETHEA, editor; b. Sumter, S.C., Jan. 25, 1932; d. Edward Samuel and Mildred (Ladson) Bethea; m. Victor Rastafari Grant, July 2, 1960 (div.); children: Christine Sharon, Pamela Ellen. BA, SUNY, Albany, 1954; postgrad., Temple U., summers 1955-59; MS, Coll. St. Rose, Albany, 1984. Cert. social studies tchr., N.Y. Tech. editor GE Knolls Atomic Power Lab., Schenectady, NY, 1976-89; tech. editor, writer Westinghouse Machinery Apparatus Operation, Schenectady, 1989-96. 1st black effective listening instr. GE Knolls Atomic Power Lab., Schenectady, 1988-89, Westinghouse Machinery Apparatus Operation, Schenectady, 1992; effective listening trainer Grant Enterprises, Albany, N.Y., 1988. Author, editor: Something to Believe In, 1973; author: (poetry) There's More to Tell, 1976, Waiting to Blossom, 2002; puppeteer, ventriloquist Puppet People, 1978-95; editor newsletter Jayncee, 1967-68. Founder, dir. Minority Women's Breast Cancer Network, Albany, 1992—; v.p. Empire State Black Arts and Cultural Festival Com., Albany, 1984-86; YWCA of Albany, 1986-92, YWCA of Schenectady, 1992-95; founder, 1st chairperson Diversity in Schenectady, AAUW Study Group, 1993-95; mem. nat. nominating com. YWCA/USA, Eastern states region, 1994-96; com. mem. Troy Conf. Ethnic Minority Scholarship Com., Latham, N.Y., 1990-96; vol. Reach to Recovery, Raleigh, 1997—, N.C. Assn. for Edn. of Young Children, 1998; bd. mem. Make a Joyful Noise, Raleigh, 1997-2002, Loaves and Fishes, Raleigh, 1998-2002, Nat. Coalition Bldg. Inst., Durham, N.C. Recipient Centennial award GE Knolls Atomic Power Lab., Schenectady, 1978, Scholar award First Reformed Ch., Albany, 1980, award of excellence Westinghouse Machinery Apparatus Operation Facility, Schenectady, 1994, Women of Note award, African Am. Cultural Complex, Raleigh, N.C., 2000, Disting. Alumni award, Coll St. Rose, Albany, NY, 2003. Mem. AAUW (life, chairperson internat. rels. 1973-74, chairperson vol. interpreters directory com. 2002, scholar award 1981, 83, cmty. action grant 1992, Edn. Found. grant honoree 1995), NAACP (life), Nat. Orgn. Black Chemists and Chem. Engrs. (copy editor newsletter 1995-97), Nat. Assn. Black Storytellers, Internat. Listening Assn. (life), Assn. Black Psychologists (life), Nat. Coun. Negro Women (life, co-founder Capital area sect. NC 1997), Nat. Story Telling Assn., N.Am. Assn. Ventriloquists, Puppeteers of Am., Fellowship of Christian Puppeteers, Nat. Women's History Mus. (charter mem.). Avocations: blues guitar, ventriloquist, poet, freelance writer, puppeteer.

GRANT, FRANCES ELIZABETH, retired educator; b. West Chester, Pa., Dec. 2, 1921; d. Howard Morris and Mary (Dunnigan) G.; B.S. in Mus. Edn., Wilberforce U., 1944; Ed.M. in Psychology of Reading, Temple U., 1969, Ed.D. in English Edn., 1974. Tchr., Christiansburg Ind. Inst., Cambria, Va., 1944-45; P.S. Jones High Sch., Washington, 1945, Coatesville and Twin Oaks, Pa., 1946; faculty Harbison Jr. Coll., Irmo, S.C., 1949, Wayne County Tng. Sch., Jessup, Ga., 1950; tchr. Downingtown, Pa., 1953-57, Sch. Dist. Phila., 1957-70; assoc. prof. Temple U., Phila., 1978-83, resident prof. Temple U. staff devel. program, Abraka, Bendel State, Nigeria; recruiter, counselor Gwynedd-Mercy Coll., Gwynedd Valley, Pa., 1986—; asst. prof. West Chester (Pa.) State Coll., summer 1973; vis. prof. LaSalle Coll., Phila; cons. in field. Bd. dirs. NW Br. ARC, 1980-82; bd. mem. Presbyn. Children's Village, Carson Valley Sch., 1983-1995. Recipient Chapel of Four Chaplains award, 1965; Leadership award United Negro Coll. Fund, 1976; Service award, Wilberforce U., 1976. Mem. Internat. Reading Assn., Nat. Council Tchrs. English, Assn. Supervision and Curriculum Devel., Wilberforce Alumni Assn. (dir., sec. nat. assn. 1976-79), Phi Lambda Theta, Phi Delta Kappa. Presbyterian.

GRANT, IRENE H., epidemiologist; b. NYC, Nov. 7, 1953; d. Benton Hanchett and Irene Allen Grant; m. Anton Bluman (div.); children: Cedric Bluman, Sergei Bluman. BA cum laude, U. Pa., Phila., 1975; postgrad., Columbia U., NYC, 1975—78; MD, Albert Einstein Coll. Medicine, Bronx, NY, 1982; cert. in accupuncture, NY Med. Coll., Valhalla, 1997. Diplomate Am. Bd. Internal Medicine, Am. Bd. Infectious Diseases. Fellow infectious disease Meml. Sloan Kettering Cancer Ctr., NYC, 1985—88; infectious disease specialist Bronx Lebanon Hosp. Ctr., 1985—96, assoc. dir. AIDS program, 1992—98; exec. Integrative Medicine Group, Tarrytown, NY, 1996—; pres. Grant Mfg., Vanderbilt, Mich., 2004—, Grant Airmac Corp., Stamford, Conn., 1994—. Author: IBS for Dummies, 2005; contbr. articles to profl. jours., chpt. to book. Named Outstanding Med. Resident, Montefiore Hosp., 1985; nutrition fellow, NY Acad. Medicine, 1992. Mem.: Am. Assn. Oriental Medicine, Am. Coll. Nutrition, Infectious Disease Soc. Am., NY State Bd. Acupuncture. Office: Integrative Med Group 200 S Broadway Ste 205 Tarrytown NY 10591

GRANT, ISABELLA HORTON, retired judge; b. L.A., Sept. 24, 1924; d. John Daniel and Hannabelle (Horton) Grant. BA, Swarthmore Coll., 1944; MA, UCLA, 1946; JD, Columbia U., 1950; LLD (hon.), Molloy Coll., 1976. Jr. profl. asst. OSS, Washington, 1944-45; economist Inst. Indsl. Rels., UCLA, 1946-47, Office Price Stblzn., L.A., 1951-52; ptnr. Livingston, Grant, Stone & Kay, San Francisco, 1953-79; judge Mcpl. Ct., San Francisco, 1979-82, Superior Ct., San Francisco, 1982-97; ret., 1997. Bd. dirs. Kid's Turn, Pocket Opera; mem. San Francisco Ethics Commn., 1997-2002, chair, 2001. Fellow ABA; mem. Am. Arbitration Assn. (action dispute resolution, resolution remedies), San Francisco Bar Assn. (bd. dirs. 1978-79), Acad. Matrimonial Lawyers (pres. No. Calif. chpt. 1976), Assn. Family and Conciliation Cts. (pres. Calif. chpt. 1987-89), Nat. Coll. Probate Judges (William W. Treat award 2000), Queen's Bench (pres. 1964), Calif. Tennis Club, Phi Beta Kappa. E-mail: ihortongrant@cs.com.

GRANT, JANETT ULRICA, medical/surgical nurse; b. Mavis Bank, St. Andrew, Jamaica, Jan. 15, 1956; came to U.S., 1990; d. John Edgerton and Daisy Ann (Sterling) Welsh; m. Aurnandy Alfanso Grant, Nov. 25, 1978; children: Avril, Adrian, Christophe. Grad., Kingston (Jamaica) Sch. Nursing, 1978, diploma in midwifery, 1988; BSN, N.J. City U., 1998. RN, N.J.; cert. med.-surg. nurse. Mem. staff med. surg. nursing Isaac Barrant Hosp., St. Thomas, Jamaica, 1978-79, Kingston Pub. Hosp., 1979-87, acting sister supr., 1988-90; mem. staff med. surg. nursing Newark Beth Israel Med. Ctr., 1990—, team leader Med.-Surg. Unit, 1995—97. Alt. unit rep. Coun. Nursing Practice, Newark Beth Israel Med. Ctr., 1994; pain resource nurse, 1996—. Mem. planning com. Salvation Army Basic Sch., Kingston, 1988-90. Mem. N.J. State Nurses Assn., Jamaica Nurses Assn. (N.J. chpt.). Methodist. Avocations: reading, sewing, cooking, gardening, craft work.

GRANT, JEAN TERRY, educational consultant; b. Apr. 27, 1930; d. Herbert Lewis and Flossie Mae (Stokes) Terry; m. Joseph Simeon Grant Jr., Oct. 22, 1955; children: Terry Von-Eric, Ericka Jeannine. BS, Howard U., 1953. Libr. asst. Howard U., Washington, 1953-59, Martin Luther King Libr., Columbus, Ohio, 1970-72; head of libr. Shepard Branch Libr., Columbus, Ohio, 1972; edn. cons. Ohio Dept. Edn., Columbus, 1972—. Creator performing exhibiting art shows Afroganza, Columbus Gallery of Fine Arts, 1972, 73, A Night to Remember, 1982-92. Creator performing/exhibiting art show: Afroganza, Columbus Gallery of Fine Art, 1972, 73. Bd dirs. YWCA, 1972-75, asst. treas. 1973-75; bd. dirs. Speech/Hearing Bd., 1989; mem. Govs. Coun. Genetic Diseases, 1975. Avocations: painting, reading, gardening, interior decorating. Office: Dept Edn 65 S Front St Rm 810 Columbus OH 43215-4183

GRANT, JOAN JULIEN, artist; b. Cornwall, Ont., Can., Apr. 15, 1934; d. John Duncan Julien and Winnifred Josephine McCormick; m. Douglas MacDougal Grant, Sept. 24, 1955; children: Stephen John, Ann Elizabeth, Abigail Jennifer, David King. AA, West L.A. C.C., 1975; BFA, Otis Art Inst., 1977, MFA, 1979. Instr. Plymouth (N.H.) State Coll., 1998; pvt. art instr. Represented in permanent collections; author, editor: Terrestis, 1995, Flight of the Muse, 2002. Active Citizens for a Livable Culver City, 1998—2000. Avocations: reading, book discussion groups, walking, hiking. Home: 4274 LeBourget Ave Culver City CA 90232 Office Phone: 310-839-6638. Personal E-mail: joan.grant@earthlink.net.

GRANT, KAY LALLIER, early childhood education educator; b. Leavenworth, Kans., Oct. 22, 1951; d. Leon Ernest and Retha Pearl (Poos) Lallier; m. Cary Benson Grant, Aug. 12, 1972; children: Shannon, Ryan. BA in Psychology, Human Devel. & Family Life, U. Kans., 1973; MA in Spl. Edn., U. Tulsa, 1982; EdD in Curriculum & Instrn., Okla. State U., 1990. Cert. early childhood and spl. edn.-mental retardation tchr. Kindergarten tchr. Muskogee (Okla.) Day Nursery, 1973; presch. tchr. Children's House Montessori Sch., Muskogee, 1974; kindergarten tchr. Haskell (Okla.) Pub. Schs., 1974-75; dir., tchr. presch. for handicapped Muskogee Pub. Schs., 1975-78; dir. child care ctr. Muskogee Gen. Hosp., 1982-84; instr. early childhood edn., field svc. coord. Northeastern State U., Tahlequah, Okla., 1985-88, program chair early childhood edn., 1988—92, asst. prof. early childhood Coll. of Edn. Tahlequah, Okla., 1990—92; dir. early childhood edn. Muskogee Pub. Schs., 1992—99; asst. dean coll. edn. Northeastern State U., 1999—2001, interim dean, 2001—03, dean, 2003—. Reviewer Music and Child Devel., 1988, Total Learning: Curriculum for Young Child, 1987, The Boy Who Would Be a Helicopter, 1990; contbr. articles to profl. jours. Elder Bethany Presbyn. Ch., Muskogee, 1991—99. Recipient scholarship award Okla. Assn. on Children Under Six, 1988, Faculty Rsch. grant Northeastern State U., 1989. Mem. Okla. Assn. Childhood Edn. Internat. (pres. 1991-1999), Nat. Assn. Edn. Young Children, Okla. Assn. Early Childhood Tchr. Educators, So. Early Childhood Assn., Okla. Inst. Child Advocacy (bd. dirs. 1999-2001), Internat. Reading Assn., Phi Delta Kappa, Delta Kappa Gamma, Kappa Delta Phi, Okla. Assoc. Colls. Edn. Office: Northeastern State U Coll Edn Tahlequah OK 74464 E-mail: grantk1@nsuok.edu.

GRANT, LEE (LYOVA HASKELL ROSENTHAL), actress, television and film director; b. N.Y.C., Oct. 31, 1931; d. A.W. and Witia (Haskell) Rosenthal; m. Arnold Manoff (dec.); 1 dau., Dinah; m. Joseph Feury; 1 dau., Belinda. Student, Julliard Sch. Music, Neighborhood Playhouse Sch. Theatre, Met. Opera Ballet Sch. Stage debut as child in L'arocolo, Met. Opera House, N.Y.C., 1934; Broadway appearances include Detective Story (Critics Circle award 1949), Lo and Behold, A Hole in the Head, Wedding Breakfast; toured with The Maids (Obie award), Electra, Silk Stockings, St. Joan, Arms and the Man, Prisoner of Second Avenue; with road co. Two for the Seesaw, The Captains and the Kings, N.Y. Shakespeare Festival; motion pictures include Detective Story, 1952 (best actress Cannes Film Festival), Storm Fear, 1956, Middle of the Night, 1959, Affair of the Skin, The Balcony, 1963, Divorce American Style, 1967, Valley of the Dolls, In the Heat of the Night, 1968, Marooned, 1970, There Was a Crooked Man, 1970, The Landlord, 1970, Plaza Suite, 1971, Shampoo, 1975 (Acad. award for best supporting actress), Voyage of the Damned, 1976, Airport '77, 1977, The Swarm, 1978, The Mafu Cage, 1978, Damien-Omen II, 1978, When You Comin' Back, Red Ryder, 1979, Little Miss Marker, 1980, Charles Chan and the Curse of the Dragon Queen, 1981, Visiting Hours, 1982, Teachers, 1984, The Big Town, 1987, Defending Your Life, 1991, Under Heat, 1994, The Substance of Fire, 1996, It's My Party, 1996, The Amati Girls, 2000, Dr. T and the Women, 2000; TV series include Search for Tomorrow, 1953-54, Fay, 1975, Peyton Place (Emmy award for best supporting actres 1966), White Fang, 1993, Mulholland Drive, 1999; TV movies include Night Slaves, 1970, The respectfull Prostitute (BBC), Neon Ceiling (Emmy award), Ransom for a Dead Man, Lieutenant Shuster's Wife, 1972, Partners in Crime, 1973, What Are Best Friends For?, 1973, Perilous Voyage, 1976, The Spell, 1977, The Million Dollar Face, 1981, For Ladies Only, 1981, Thou Shalt Not Kill, 1982, Bare Essence, 1982, Will There Really Be A Morning?, 1983, The Highjacking of the Achille Lauro, 1989, She Said No, 1990, Something to Live For: The Allison Gertz Story, 1992, In My Daughter's Name, 1992, Citizen Cohn, 1992 (Emmy nomination, Supporting Actress - miniseries, 1993); dir. TV spl. Shape of Things, 1973; dir. play Private View, 1983; dir, (feature film) Tell Me A Riddle, 1980, Women of Willmar, 1982, Feature A Matter of Sex, 1983, Nobody's Child, 1986 (Dirs. Guild Am. award), Down and Out in America, 1987 (Acad. award), No Place Like Home, 1989, (feature comedy) Staying Together, 1989; dir. documentary Women on Trial, 1992, Breast Cancer Say it! Fight it! Cure it!, 1997; dir. TV film Season's of the Heart, 1994, Reunion, 1994, Sing Me The Blues, Lena, 1994. Recipient Congl. Arts Caucus award U.S. Govt., 1983, Lifetime Achievement award Women in Film, 1989.

GRANT, LESLIE EDWINA, dentist, dental association administrator; b. Charlotte, N.C., June 24, 1954; d. Charles G. and Gwendolyn M. James. BS summa cum laude, Boston U., 1976; MSPA, U. Wash., 1978; DDS, U. Md., 1986. Lic. dentist, Md.; cert. ASHA, Md. Speech lang. pathologist North Jersey Devel Ctr., Totowa, NJ; resident St. Joseph's Hosp., Paterson, NJ; dental contractor Dental Power, Towson, Md.; dentist Balt. Named one of Most Influential Black Americans, Ebony mag., 2006; recipient Freeman King scholarship, 1985. Mem. Nat. Dental Assoc.(pres.), Am. Soc. of Dentistry for Children, Am. Soc. of Dental Anesthiology (Achievement award, 1986), Am. Speech-Lang. Hearing Assoc., Acad. of Gen. Dentistry. Office: 5800 Loch Raven Blvd Baltimore MD 21239 also: Nat Dental Assn 3517 16th St, NW Washington DC 20010 Office Phone: 410-532-1024. Office Fax: 410-592-7416.*

GRANT, LINDA KAY (LINDA KAY SCOTT), small business owner, sales executive; b. Galesburg, Ill., Oct. 15, 1949; d. Claire Arline Tabb and Addie Mae (Smith) Stedman; m. James G. Scott, Feb. 20, 1968 (div. Dec. 1977); children: Angela Christine, Aaron Christopher; m. Daryl Quinn Grant, Sept. 20, 1986; 1 child, Rachael Jane. Student, Balckhawk East Coll., 1984-86. Sec. Flynn Beverage, Inc., Rock Island, Ill., 1972-76, Lee's Place, Inc., Rock Island, 1976-81; merchandising rep. Polaroid Corp., Boston, 1981-84; sales rep. Drawing Bd. Greeting Cards, Dallas, 1984-86; owner Card Creations, Galva, Ill., 1986-90; mktg. rep. Q.C. Metall. Labs., Davenport, Iowa, 1989-94; contract pharmacy rep. PDI Corp./Johnson & Johnson, Mahwah, N.J., 1994-96; sales rep. Innoves Inc./Novartis Corp., Parsippany, NJ, 1996-2000; contract pharmacy rep. Ventiv Health, Inc., Somerset, NJ, 2000—04, Helfter Enterprises, Inc., 2004—; owner Spiritwood Farms, Kewanee, Ill., 2001—. Mem. Henry County Rural Revolving Loan Bd., 1994—. Mem. Dem. Women for Henry County, Cambridge, Ill., 1985—; pres. Galva/UA C. of C., 1988; advisor Galva/UA Econ. Devel. Com., 1989. Mem. NOW, NAFE. Methodist. Achievements include patent for Wound Flush. Home: RR 1 Kewanee IL 61443-9801 Address: 10128 E 2300 St Kewanee IL 61443

GRANT, LUCILLE, hospital administrator, social worker; b. N.Y.C., Aug. 29, 1942; d. Thomas Charles and Julia Mae Oliver; m. James Allen Grant Jr. (div.); children: Lucille Grant-Werts, James Allen Grant III. BSW, Adelphi U., 1976, MSW, 1977. LCSW, cert. Sr. addiction counselor Scant. Bd. of Edn., N.Y.C., 1971. Coord. social svcs. Julia Richmond H.S., N.Y.C., 1977—80; supr. social work, coord. Cmty. Mental Health Ctr., Queens Hosp. Ctr., Jamaica, NY, 1980—82, program dir. Teenage Pregnancy Program, 1982—99, program dir. Aspire program, 1999—2002. V.p. Laurelton Civic Assn., NY, 2001—, Family Life and Marriage Enrichment Inc; pres. Thankful Missionary Bapt. Ch. of Thankful Cmty. Devel. Corp., Thankful Women's Ministry. Named Social Worker of Yr., N.Y.C. Health and Hosp. Corp., 1998, Mgr. of Yr., N.Y.C. Managerial Employee Assn., 2002, Lucille Grant Day proclaimed in her honor, Queens, N.Y.; recipient Outstanding Svc. award, NASW, 1993. Mem.: NAACP (life). Baptist. Avocations: reading, travel. Home: 4342 Cedar Lake Cove Conley GA 30288

GRANT, MARILYNN PATTERSON, secondary school educator; b. Washington, Oct. 26, 1952; d. Rossie Lee and Mattie (Pringle) Patterson; m. David Michael Grant, Oct. 11, 1980; children: Karissa Joy, Jared David Michael. BA in History, U. Rochester, 1975, MS in Edn., 1982, postgrad; Cert. advanced studies, SUNY, Brockport, 1987. Cert. tchr., sch. adminstr., supr., N.Y. Jr. high coord. Rochester (N.Y.) City Sch. Dist., 1980-81, team tchr., 1981-83, skills cluster tchr., 1983-85, jr. high tchr., 1985-86, alternative to suspension, 1986-87, 89-90, dean of students, 1987-88, curriculum coord., 1988-89, acting house adminstr., 1990-91, social studies tchr., 1991—96, dir. of social Studies & multicultural edn., 1996—2002; prin. Joseph C. Wilson HS, Rochester, 2002—. Bd. dirs., allocations com. Rochester Monroe County Youth Bd., 1990-92; active Mt. Olivet Bapt. Ch., 1990—. Named one of Outstanding Young Women Am., 1984; recipient Volunteerism award Mayor of Rochester, 1991, Jack & Jill of Rochester Disting. Mother, 2000-01, RCSD Staff excellance award, 2001. Mem. Christian Visitor's Com. (chmn. 1990—), Rochester Urban League Guild (v.p. 1982-83), Jack & Jill of Am. (corr. sec. 1991-92, group leader 1992-93), Zeta Phi Beta (pres. 1985-87, parliamentarian 1985-87), Kappa Delta Pi. Democrat. Avocations: event planning, singing, drama, reading, writing. Home: 227 Genesee Park Blvd Rochester NY 14619-2459

GRANT, MARY ALVERSON, music educator; b. Lexington, Ky., Nov. 23, 1958; d. Welch and Geneva Elizabeth Alverson; m. Robert Cecil Grant, July 12, 1980; 1 child, Robert Clarke. MEd, Ga. Southwestern U., Americus, 2004; MusB in Edn., U. Ky., Lexington, 1976—80. Cert. tchr. level T-5 Ga. Profl. Standards Commn., 1982. Music educator Griffin-Spalding County Schs., Griffin, Ga., 1982—. Christian edn. First Christian Ch., Griffin, Ga., 1982—. Recipient Tchr. of Yr., Orrs Elem. Sch., 1996. Mem.: Profl. Assn. Ga. Educators, Nat. Assn. Music Edn. Mem. Christian Ch.(Disciples Of Christ). Avocations: music, reading. Home: 1113 Maple Dr Griffin GA 30224 Office: Moreland Rd Elem Sch 455 Moreland Rd Griffin GA 30224 Office Phone: 770-229-3755. E-mail: aravismag@aol.com.

GRANT, MARY LYNN JOHNSON, academic administrator, literary scholar; b. Corpus Christi, Tex., Sept. 28, 1937; d. William Linnaeus and Sarah Lewis (Stevenson) Johnson; m. Dale E. Woolley, Aug. 13, 1963 (div. 1965); m. John E. Grant, Mar. 9, 1974; children, William Josiah, Michael E., Kenneth M. BA, U. So. Miss., 1956, MA, Tulane U., 1958, PhD, 1962. Instr. Delta State Coll., Cleveland, Miss., 1960, La. State U., Baton Rouge, 1960-62; asst. prof. U. Ill., Champaign, 1962-69; assoc. prof. Ga. State U., Atlanta, 1969-78; vis. prof. Cornell Coll., Mt. Vernon, Iowa, 1979, 80, 81; vis. assoc. prof. Coe Coll., Cedar Rapids, Iowa, 1980-81, 82; spl. asst. to pres. U. Iowa, Iowa City, 1983—2000. Co-author: Blake's Four Zoas: The Design of a Dream, 1978; co-editor: Blake's Poetry and Designs, 1979, rev. edit., 2006, Reconciliations, 1983. Am. Philos. Soc. grantee, 1977, NEH grantee, 1981, Beinecke Libr. grantee, 1993, Newberry Libr. grantee, 1993. Mem. MLA, Wordsworth-Coleridge Assn., Am. Soc. for Eighteenth Century Studies. Home: 407 Magowan Ave Iowa City IA 52246-3726

GRANT, MICHELE BYRD, educator; b. Kansas City, Mo., Oct. 30, 1926; d. Ernest Louis and Violetta (Wallace) Byrd. B.S., Lincoln U., 1952; M.S. in Sci. Edn., U. Ill., 1955, advanced cert., 1964. Tchr., Unit 4, Champaign, Ill., 1956-66; tchr. sci. St. Louis Pub. Schs., 1966—, dept. head, 1978—, Mo. Outstanding Biology Tchrs. program dir., 1974—; participant NSF Summer Inst., CCNY, 1968-69; instr. Webster Coll. Upward Bound Program, 1969-70; judge Monsanto-St. Louis Post Dispatch Sci. Fair, 1970. Developer, edn. dir. Adventures in Medicine and Sci., 1992; coord., co-develpper Vashon Interdisciplinary Project for Edn. Reform, 1999-2000. Mem. Cath. Sch. Bd., St. Louis, 1982-83; mem. life aux. Barnes Hosp., 1968—; trustee Meml. and Planned Funeral Soc., 1980. Recipient Mo. Outstanding Biology Tchr. award, Nat. Biology Tchrs. Assn., 1974, One of 50 Nationwide Unsung Heroes award Newsweek, 1987, Excellence in Leadership award Lincoln U., 1987, Newsweek Mag. Unsung Hero Satte Mo., 1987, Monsanto Sci. Tchg. award, 2001; named STARS Tchr., Solutia-NSF, 1999. Mem. ASCD, Nat. Sci. Tchrs. Assn., Nat. Assn. Biology Tchrs., Biology Tchrs. Assn., Mo. Sci. Tchrs. Assn., Mo. Acad. Sci., Alpha Kappa Alpha, Kappa Delta Pi. Roman Catholic. Office: 3405 Bell Ave Saint Louis MO 63106-1604

GRANT, NANCY MARIE, marketing professional, journalist; b. Tilden, Nebr., Jan. 2, 1941; d. William Gerald and Evelyn Marie (Baughman) Whitford; m. Marvin Ostberg, 1961 (div. 1969); children: Jill Marie Ostberg Bennett, Carrie Ostberg Chun; m. Richard Grant, 1973 (div. 1975). BA in Journalism, U. Nebr., 1963; postgrad., U. Oreg., 1968; MBA, Portland State U., 1978; postgrad., U. Wash., 1979-83; diploma, Bailie Sch. Broadcasting, Seattle, 1984; postgrad., Seattle Cen. C.C., 1992, Computer & Bus. Tng. Inst., Bellevue, Wash., 1993. Internship gen. assignment reporter Lincoln (Nebr.) Jour., 1962-63; asst. state editor Lexington (Ky.) Leader, 1963; freelance writer Shreveport Times, AP, Natchatoches, La., 1964; info. rep. 1 & 2 Univ. Oreg. News Bur., Old Oreg. Alumni Mag., Faculty Staff Newsletter, Eugene, 1965-70; dir. pub. rels. U. Portland, Oreg., 1971; info. rep. 3 Oreg. Hwy. Div. and Motor Vehicles, 1972-77; founder, bus. mgr. Grant Mktg., Seattle, 1979; exec. dir., founder Wash. Neurol. Alliance, Seattle, 1985—. Editor U. Oreg. Faculty-Staff Newsletter, 1969; editor, writer U. Portland Alumni Mag., 1970, Hwy Newsletter and film, 1971-77. Lobbyist, newsletter editor Wash. Neurol. Alliance; mem. Gov.'s Com. on Disabaility Issues and Employment, 1983-86; bd. dirs. Wash. Assembly, 1983-86, Highland Community Ctr., Bellevue, Wash., 1984-86. Recipient Hearst award, 1963, No. 1 in country for hwy. pub. affairs event, 1973. Mem. NAFE, LWV (Seattle and Princeton, N.J.), Am. Assn. Women Bus. Owners (Seattle and Princeton), Internat. Platform Assn. Democrat. Unitarian Universalist. Avocations: hiking, climbing, bicycling, swimming.

GRANT, PAULA DIMEO, lawyer, nursing educator, mediator; b. Bridgeport, Conn., Aug. 3, 1943; d. Samuel Peter and Emilie Alyce (DiChiera) DiMeo; m. James Mullett Grant, Nov. 26, 1975. AS in Nursing, U. Bridgeport, 1973; BSN cum laude, Boston Coll., 1975; JD, No. Va. U., 1982; MA in Nursing, NYU, 1994. Bar: D.C. 1985, U.S. Ct. Appeals (D.C.) 1985, U.S. Dist. Ct. D.C. 1985, U.S. Supreme Ct. 1989, U.S. Dist. Ct. Md. 1995. RN, Conn. Coronary care nurse Cornell Med. Ctr., N.Y.C., 1969-70; with Trans World Airlines, Chgo. and N.Y.C., 1980—84; pvt. practice Washington, 1986-98; of counsel Ross & Hardies, Washington, 1998—2004; pvt. practice Washington, 2004—06; pntr. DiMeo and Grant Law Firm, 2006—. Mediator Superior Ct. D.C., 1991—2003; clin. asst. prof. cmty. and preventive medicine N.Y. Med. Coll., 1992—96; adj. prof. dept. nursing Columbia U. Tchrs. Coll., N.Y.C., 1993, 94; adj. asst. prof. nursing Sacred Heart U., Fairfield, Conn., 1998—99, mem. adv. coun., 1998—2000; co-chair Annual TAANA Conf., Washington, 2003; adj. faculty Mercy Coll., White Plains, NY, 2001—. Mem. task force for women Boston Coll., 2003. Mem. ABA, D.C. Bar Assn., Am. Assn. Nurse Attys., Inc. (co-chmn. legis. affairs com. 1987-91, bd. dirs. N.Y. Met. chpt. 1986-88, 2005-, sec. 1986-87, nat. bd. dirs. 1996-2000, 04, 05), Conn. Nurses Assn. (chmn. cabinet on econ. and gen. welfare 1985-88), Assn. Bar City N.Y., N.Y.U. Alumni Assn., The Am. Assn. Nurse Atty. Found. (pres., 1998-2001), Sigma Theta Tau (Cynthia Ellen Northrop award 2001). Roman Catholic. Avocations: reading, theater, music. Office Phone: 202-638-6956. Personal E-mail: pdmgrant@aol.com.

GRANT, PEGGY (MARGARET MARY GRANT), art gallery administrator, artist, consultant; b. Balt., Sept. 19, 1929; d. Edward J. and Estelle T. (Smith) Brennan; m. Adam M. Grochowski Grant (dec. June 1992); children: Thomas Gregory, Adam Mark. BFA, Md. Inst. Coll. Art, 1952. Designer Palmer Paint, Detroit, 1953-55, Craftmaster Corp., Toledo, 1956-80; art curator Owens-Ill. Corp., Toledo and N.Y.C., 1981-84; art cons., Toledo, 1985—; dir. 20 North Gallery, T, 1995—. Writer art exhibit catalogs, 1981—. Bd. dirs. Arts Commn. Greater Toledo, 1991—, Blair Mus. Lithophanes, Toledo, 1993—, Friends of the Libr. U. Toledo, 1996—; mem. Poznan (Poland)-Toledo Sister City Alliance, 1994—; mem. com. for cultural diversity Toledo Mus., 1991—; mem. docent bd. Toledo Mus. Art, 1988—. Recipient Disting. Svc. in Art Edn. award Ohio Art Edn. Assn., 1984. Mem. Glass Art Soc., Athena Art Soc. (bd. dirs., chmn. jury), Glass Collectors Club Toledo (bd. dirs. 1985—, pres. 1992-93). Roman Catholic. Home: 2821 Latonia Blvd Toledo OH 43606-3625 Office: 20 North Gallery 20 N Saint Clair St Toledo OH 43604-1028

GRANT, SUSAN, television executive; b. Boston, Dec. 23, 1954; d. Robert Nathan and Barbara (Weil) G.; m. Steven W. Korn, June 17, 1976 (div. Apr. 1982). AB, Vassar Coll., 1976. Rsch. asst. corp. devel. Cornell U., Ithaca, N.Y., 1976-78; asst. to v.p. fin. dept. Turner Broadcasting System, Atlanta, 1978-79; dir. pub. rels., regional sales mgr. Turner Cable News Network, 1979-81, dir regional sales and mktg., nat. sales mgr., 1982-85; v.p. sales Magnicom Systems, Inc., Stamford, Conn., 1985; dir. nat. accounts Intec Systems, West Palm Beach, Fla., 1985; account exec. Columbia Pictures TV, Atlanta, 1986-88, v.p. syndication S.E. region, 1989—94; pres. Turner Program Services, 1994, CNN Newsource Sales and Turner Living; exec. v.p. CNN News Services. Bd. dirs. Zoo Atlanta; bd. dirs. mng. com. Literacy Action, Inc. Named Woman of Yr. Tech. (enterprise bus.), (WIT) Women in Tech., 2006. Mem.: Women in Cable (pres. 1980). Office: CNN News Services One CNN Ctr Atlanta GA 30303*

GRANT, SUSAN J., federal agency administrator; Grad., Professional Military Comptroller Sch., Maxwell Air Force Base, 1982, Sr. Exec. Fellows Program, John F. Kennedy Sch. of Govt., Harvard U., Cambridge, 1992, Fed. Exec. Inst., Charlottesville, Va., 1994. Various positions including budget officer, manpower mgr., program analyst, logistics mgmt. specialist US Dept. Def., Washington, 1972—99, former dep. dir. for budget, resource mgmt. directorate, defense fin. acctng. svc., 1999—2001, CFO, dir. corp. resources, defense fin. acctng. svc., 2001—04; CFO, dir. office of mgmt., budget and evaluation US Dept. Energy, Washington, 2004—. Office: US Dept Energy Rm 4A-253 Washington DC 20585-0701

GRANT GOLDMAN, PAMELA, journalist, writer; b. N.Y.C., Sept. 2, 1961; d. Daniel B. and Shirley (Dworsh) G.; m. Joel S. Telpner, Oct. 29, 1995. BA in Polit. Sci., SUNY, Binghamton, 1984; MA in Journalism, Columbia U., 1990. With Sportset Inc., Syosset, N.Y., 1984-87; page NBC TV, Manhattan, N.Y., 1988; researcher NBC News, 1989, David W. Jayne meml. fellow, 1989-90, fgn. desk editor, field producer, 1990-91; freelance journalist Barcelona, 1991-92; assoc. prodr. The Brokaw Report, 1992-93; writer NBC Nightly News, 1993-95; freelance writer and prodr., 1996—. Writer/prodr. Who's Going to Care For These Kids, 1991 (Emmy award for News & Pub. Info. Programming). Recipient Emmy award for news and pub. info. category, 1991. Mem. Soc. Profl. Journalists, N.Y. Deadline Club. Avocations: exercise, travel, reading. Home: 111 E 30th St Apt 15a New York NY 10016-7368

GRANTHAM, JOYCE CAROL, small business owner, music educator; b. Alameda, Calif., Jan. 4, 1940; d. John Charles and Shirley Anne (Maze) G. AB in Music Composition, Mills Coll., 1961; student, LaSalle Extension U., 1965-69; MBA in Gen. Mgmt., Golden Gate U., 1980. Various secretarial and supervisory positions UNIVAC div. Sperry Rand Corp., San Francisco, 1962-68; various mgmt. positions Decimus Corp., San Francisco, 1969-77, sec. policy rev. com., 1976-81, v.p. personnel, 1977-81; product mgr. Bank of Am., San Francisco, 1981-83, asst. v.p., mgr. ops., mktg. and product mgmt., 1984-85; owner Grantham Assocs./White Rabbit Bus. Graphics, Walnut Creek, Calif., 1985—99. Tchr. piano Joyce Grantham Piano Studio, Walnut Creek, 1985—. Composer (piano piece) Sarabande, 1959, (song cycle) Sing the Forsaken, 1960, String Trio, 1961 (Elizabeth Mills Crothers prizes, 1961). Bd. dirs. San Leandro Symphony Assn., 1965-66. Francis J. Hellman scholar, 1957, Calif. State scholar, 1957. Mem. Nat. Guild of Piano Tchrs. (scholar 1957), Am. Coll. of Musicians, Calif. Assn. Profl. Music Tchrs. (bd. dirs. 1998—, v.p. membership 2000-02, v.p. dists. and chpts. 2004—, president elect 2004—), Music Tchrs. Nat. Assn., Music Tchrs. Assn. Calif. Democrat. Episcopalian. Avocations: gardening, collecting art and antiques. Office Phone: 925-938-5284.

GRANVILLE, LAURA, professional tennis player; b. Chgo., May 12, 1981; d. Charles and Elizabeth. Student, Stanford U., 1999—2001. Profl. tennis player, 2001—. Named Coll. Player of the Yr., Tennis Mag./ITA, 2000, 2001, NCAA Singles Champion, 2000, 2001; recipient 2 Women's Circuit Singles Title, ITF. Office: WTA Tour Corporate Headquarters One Progress Plz Ste 1500 Saint Petersburg FL 33701

GRANVILLE, PAULINA, independent music scholar, educator; b. Palmerton, Pa., Jan. 5, 1928; d. Paul Edward and Ethel (Hallock) Delp; m. Joseph Ensign Granville, July 11, 1950 (div. June 1980); children: Leslie, Blanchard, Leona, Sara (dec.), Paul (dec.), Mary, Johanna, John. BS, The Juilliard Sch., 1949; MA, Columbia U., 1950; PhD, Fla. State U., 1987. Cert. tchr., Fla. Theatrical organist, Lehighton, Pa., 1941-44; ch. organist, pianist, choir dir., 1938-88; voice accompanist Greenwich Village, N.Y.C., 1945-50; dir. pvt. piano studio for individual and group lessons, 1944-89; dir. gen. music studies, organist, choir leader St. James Episcopal Sch., Ormond Beach, Fla., 1967-72; elem. pub. sch. music specialist Volusia County, Fla., 1972-78; music specialist Bonner Elem. Sch., Daytona Beach, Fla., 1988-90; lectr./recitalist in Fla. and on cruise ships in the Caribbean, 1991-94; pvt. studio Ormond Beach, 1995—. Piano performances at internat. piano workshops in Salzburg, Austria, and Lausanne, Switzerland, 1979-80. Mem. Habitat for Humanity, Daytona Beach, 1993—, Symphony Soc., Daytona Beach, 1989—, Christian Med. Found. Internat., 1980—, Am. Fedn. Police and Concerned Citizens, Assn. Handicapped Artists, others; chairperson Social Ministry, Ormond Beach, Fla., 1999— Mem. NEA, AAUW, Fla. Music Edn. Assn., Music Educators Nat. Conf., Nat. Music Tchrs. Assn., Fla. Music Tchrs. Assn., Volusia County Music Tchrs. Assn. (co-founder 1973), Pres.'s Club Fla. State U., Juilliard Alumni Assn., Am. Orff-Schulwerk Assn., Phi Kappa Phi, Pi Kappa Lambda. Republican. Lutheran. Avocations: reading, gardening, walking, swimming, travel. Home: 40 Juniper Dr Ormond Beach FL 32176-2406

GRAPIN, JACQUELINE G., economist; b. Paris, Dec. 15, 1942; came to U.S., 1985; d. Jean and Raymonde (Ledru) G.; m. Michel Le Goc, June 4, 1971; children: Claire, Julien. Degree, Institut d'Etudes Politiques, Paris, 1966; Degree in Law, U. Paris, 1967; Auditeur, Inst. des Hautes Etudes de Def. Nat., Paris, 1980. Staff writer LeMonde, Paris, 1967-81; dir.-gen. Interavia Pub. Group, Geneva, 1982-86; pres. The European Inst., Washington, 1989—; assoc. prof. Am. U. Econ. corr. Le Figaro, Washington, 1987—; prof. Inst. d'Etudes Politiques, Paris, 1974-77. Author: Guerre Civile Mondiale, 1977, Radioscopie des Etats-Unis, 1980, Fortress America, 1984, Pacific America, 1987, Transatlantic Interoperability in Defense Industries, 2002; pub. European Affairs; contbr. articles to profl. jours. Trustee Aspen Inst. for Humanistic Studies, N.Y.C., 1981—96; bd. dirs. French Am. C. of C., Washington, Internat. Action Against Hunger. Recipient Prix Vauban Inst. des Hautes-Etudes, Paris, 1977, Officer in Order of Legion of Honor, 2001. Mem.: Internat. Inst. Strategic Studies, Cosmos Club, Nat. Press Club, Pen Club. Office: The European Inst 5225 Wisconsin Ave NW Ste 200 Washington DC 20015-2014 Home: 4201 Cathedral Ave NW Washington DC 20016

GRASER, SUSAN VINCENT, physical education educator; b. Panorama City, Calif., Oct. 4, 1967; d. William J. and Diana L. Vincent; m. Bart L. Graser, Dec. 21, 2005. BS, Brigham Young U., Provo, Utah, 1992, MS, 1997; PhD, Ariz. State U., Tempe, 2001. Phys. edn. tchr. Orangedale Elem. Sch., Phoenix, 1992—94, Kyrene de los Ninos Elem. Sch., Tempe, Ariz., 1994—95; elem. phys. edn. tchr. Horizon Cmty. Learning Ctr., Chandler, Ariz., 1997—98; asst. prof. Brigham Young U., Provo, 2001—. Mem.: AAHPERD (sec. 2001—, sw dist., Presdl. citation 2002, Presdl. Citation 2004), Ariz. Alliance for Health, Phys. Edn., Recreation, and Dance, Nat. Assn. Sport and Phys. Edn., Utah Alliance for Health, Phys. Edn., Recreation, and Dance (sec. 2005—), Phi Kappa Phi. Conservative. Mem. Lds Ch.

GRASHAM, CLARA LANGAN, reading specialist; b. Mobile, Ala., Nov. 3, 1946; d. John C. and Lucile K. Langan; m. Michael W. Grasham, Aug. 27, 1974 (div. Mar. 2, 2000); children: Michael W., Katie M., Dan D., Matthew T. BS, Miss. State U., Starkville, 1968, MEd, 1974, Oklahoma City U., Okla., 1989. Cert. reading specialist Okla. Elem. tchr. Meridian Pub. Schs., Miss., 1968—69, Escambia County Pub. Schs., Pensacola, Fla., 1969—73, Meridian Pub. Schs., Miss., 1974—75; tchr. presch. Pali Presch., Honolulu, 1976—77; tchr. learning disabled Chesapeake Individualized Learning Ctr., Va., 1979—80; reading specialist Choctaw Pub. Schs., Okla., 1981—83; tchr. gifted and talented Elmhurst Sch. for Gifted, Oklahoma City, 1987—88; tchr. H.S., Millwood Pub. Schs., Oklahoma City, 1988—89; reading specialist

Midwest City-Del City Pubs. Schs., Okla., 1990—. Recipient Tchr. of Yr. award, Choctaw-Nicoma Pk. Pub. Schs., 1982-83, MIdwest City-Del City Pub. Schs., 2005-2006. Mem.: Mid-Del Reading Coun. (pres. 1993—94).

GRASMICK, NANCY S., school system administrator; b. Balt. m. Louis J. Grasmick. BS in Elem. Edn., Towson State U., 1961; MS in Deaf Edn., Gallaudet U., 1965; PhD in Communicative Scis. with distinction, Johns Hopkins U., 1979; LHD (hon.), Towson State U., 1992, Goucher Coll., 1992, U. Balt., 1996, Villa Julie Coll., 1998. Tchr. deaf William S. Baer Sch., Balt., 1961-64; tchr. hearing and lang. impaired children Woodvale Sch., Balt., 1964-68; supr. Office Spl. Edn. Balt. County Pub. Schs., 1968-74; prin. Chatsworth Sch., Balt., 1974-78; asst. supt. Balt. County Pub. Schs., 1978-85, assoc. supt., 1985-89; sec. juvenile svcs. Dept. Juvenile Svc., Balt., 1991; spl. sec. children, youth and families Gov.'s Exec. Office, Balt., 1989-94; supt. schs. Md. Dept. Edn., Balt., 1991—. Mem., chmn. interagy. com. on sch. constrn. Gov.'s Subcabinet for Children, Youth and Families; mem. Gov.'s Workforce Investment Bd.; mem. profl. stds. and tchr. edn. bd. Md. Assocs. for Dyslexic Adults and Youth; mem. State Bd. Edn. profl. adv. bd. Met. Balt. Assn. Learning Disabled Children. Trustee Md. Retirement and Pension Sys.; active Women Execs. in State Govt.; mem. adv. coun. Scholastic, Inc. Recipient Medallion award Jimmy Swartz Found., 1989, Louise B. Makofsky Meml. award Md. Conf. Social Concern, 1990, Child Advocacy award Am. Acad. Pediat., 1990, Humanitarian award March of Dimes, 1990, Disting. Citizen's award Md. Assn. Non-pub. Spl. Edn. Facilities, 1991, Women of Excellence award Nat. Assn. Women Bus. Owners, 1991, Andrew White medal Loyola Coll., 1992, Nat. Edn. Adminstr. of Yr. award Nat. Assn. Ednl. Office Profls., 1992, Nat. award computing to asst. persons with disabilities Johns Hopkins U., 1992, Vernon E. Anderson Disting. Lecture award for outstanding leadership in edn. Coll. Edn., U. Md., 1992, DuBois Circle Award of Honor, 1992, Disting. Alumna of Yr. award Johns Hopkins U., 1992, Pub. Affairs award Md. C. of C., 1994, Educator of the Yr. award Am. Coun. on Rural Spl. Edn., Profl. Legal Excellence-Advancement of Pub. Understanding of Law award Md. Bar Found., Inc., Pressley Ridge award, Victorine Q. Adams Humanitarian award; named Communicator of Yr. by Speech and Hearing Agy., 1990, Marylander of Yr. by Advt. and Profl. Club of Balt., 1990, Marylander of Yr. by The Balt. Sun, 1997, Most Disting. Woman Girl Scouts Ctrl. Md., 1994, Cmty. Honoree 9th Ann. Heartfest Johns Hopkins Hosp., 1999; selected as one of Md.'s Top 100 Women, Warfields Bus. Record, 1996, 98. Fellow Nat. Assn. Pub. Adminstrs.; mem. Phi Delta Kappa (Excellence in Edn. award), Pi Lambda Theta. Office: Md Dept Edn 200 W Baltimore St Baltimore MD 21201-2595

GRASSELLI, MARGARET MORGAN, curator; b. Worcester, Mass., Mar. 1, 1951; d. Paul Shepard and Anne Piersol (Murray) Morgan; m. Nicholas Eugene Grasselli, May 24, 1981; children: James, Juliana, Anne Regina. AB magna cum laude, Radcliffe Coll., 1973; AM in Fine Arts, Harvard U., 1977, PhD, 1987. Curatorial asst. drawing dept. Fogg Art Mus., Cambridge, Mass., 1974-75, curatorial asst. print dept., 1977-78; asst. curator prints and drawings Nat. Gallery of Art, Washington, 1984-89, curator of Old Master Drawings, 1989—. Tutor fine arts dept. Harvard U., Cambridge, Mass., 1977; guest curator exhbn. Nat. Gallery of Art, Washington, 1980-84; professorial lectr. Georgetown U., Washington, 1988. Author: (exhbn. catalogs) Eighteenth-Century Drawings from the Collection of Mrs. Gertrude Laughlin Chanler, 1982, Colorful Impressions: The Printmaking Revolution in Eighteenth-Century France, 2003; co-author: (exhbn. catalogs) Renaissance and Baroque Drawings from the Collection of John and Alice Steiner, 1977, Old Master Drawings and Bronzes from the Cottonian Collection, 1979, Watteau 1684-1721, 1984-85, Master Drawings from the Armand Hammer Collection, An Inaugural Celebration, 1989, Art for the Nation, Gifts in Honor of the 50th Anniversary of the National Gallery of Art, 1991, Dürer to Diebenkorn: Recent Acquisitions of Art on Paper, 1992, Drawings from the O'Neal Collection, 1993, The Touch of the Artist: Master Drawings from the Woodner Collections, 1995, Mastery and Elegance: Two Centuries of French Drawings from the Collection of Jeffrey E. Horvitz, 1998, The Drawings of Annibale Carracci, 1999; mem. editl. bd. Master Drawings, 1994—; contbr. articles to profl. jours. Agnes Mongan Travelling fellow Harvard U., 1978-79, Samuel H. Kress Pre-doctoral fellow Samuel H. Kress Found., 1979-80, Ailsa Mellon Bruce Curatorial fellow Ctr. for Advanced Study in Visual Arts, 1989-90. Mem. Print Coun. Am. (bd. dirs. 1993-96). Office: Nat Gallery of Art 2000B S Club Dr Landover MD 20785-0001

GRASSERBAUER, DORIS, computer scientist, mathematician, educator; Diplom-Ingenieurin, Vienna U. Tech., 2003. Hardware and software engr. Andronic Gmbh, Vienna, 1991—95; dir. of the multimedia ctr. CCNY, 2001—. Office Phone: 212-650-5795. Personal E-mail: doris@dograba.com. Business E-Mail: dgrasserbauer@ccny.cuny.edu.

GRATZ, CINDY CARPENTER, dance educator, choreographer; b. Corpus Christi, Tex., Nov. 20, 1958; d. Regan and Sara (Medellín) Carpenter; m. Robert David Gratz, Dec. 30, 1995. BA, UCLA, 1980, MA, 1982; PhD, NYU, 1990. Adj. instr. dance NYU, N.Y.C., 1987-90, adj. asst. prof., 1990-91; asst. prof. dance Sam Houston State U., Huntsville, Tex., 1991-97, assoc. prof. dance, 1997—2003, prof. dance, 2003—. Artist-in-residence Dan-Ching Acad., Taiwan City, Taiwan, 1986, Brenau Coll., Gainesville, Ga., 1988, U. Nebr., Lincoln, 1989; dir. Washington Square Repertory Dance Co., N.Y.C., 1990-91; founder, dir. Janus Dance Projects, N.Y.C., 1986-91, Prime Time: Srs. in Motion Dance Co., Huntsville, 1992—, The Cindy Carpenter Dance Co., Huntsville, 1995-99, Tex. World Dance Co., Huntsville, 2001—. Choreographer, performer Afterimages, 1992, Gigglefeet Dance Festival, Ketchikan, Alaska, 2002; choreographer, dir. Post Post Dances: Another Artist Slips Away, 1995; dir., choreographer, performer (play) Stepping Out, 1995; choreographer Cheval, 1995, Prelude: Gathering of the Misfits, 1996, Starving, 1997, Excerpts from the Point, 1998, Requiem, 1999, Madwoman of Chaillot, 2001, Go, 2002, Bus Stop, 2003, Equus, 2003, Meatless Variations, 2004, Classical Coconuts, 2004; performer Hula Halau Ohana Elikapeka, 1999-2000; elephant rider, showgirl Ringling Bros. and Barnum and Bailey Circus, 1977-78; guest artist, choreographer Stephen F. Austin State U., Nacogdoches, Tex., 2002; costume design and constrn. Cinderella, 2003; choreographer, presenter A Night to Heal Through the Performing Arts, French Alliance Theatre, N.Y.C., 2004; dancer Halau Ho'ola Ka Mana O Hawaii, 2004. Founding mem. exec bd. World dance inst.; mem. exec. bd. Huntsville Cmty. Theatre, 1994-97, 98—. Grantee Chi Tau Epsilon, 1994, Huntsville Arts Commn., 1994-97. Mem. AAUP (pres. local chpt. 1994-97), AAUW (officer 1994-96), Sam Houston State U. Women (officer 1991-96), ACDFA (nat. bd. 2002—). Avocations: swimming, horses, Spurs fan. Home: 2223 Mustang Ln San Marcos TX 78666-1120 Office: Sam Houston State U PO Box 2269 Huntsville TX 77341-2269 Office Phone: 936-294-1311.

GRATZ, KIM L., psychologist, researcher; b. Syracuse, NY, July 1, 1974; d. David Kenneth and Linda Lee Gratz; m. Matthew Thomas Tull, June 13, 2004. BA, Tulane U., New Orleans, 1996; MA, U. Mass., Boston, 2000, PhD, 2003. Asst. rsch. psychologist McLean Hosp./Harvard Med. Sch., Boston, 2004—05; rsch. asst. prof. U. Md., College Park, 2005—. Dir. personality disorders divsn. Ctr. for Addictions, Personality, and Emotion Rsch., U. Md., College Park, 2005—. Contbr. articles to profl. jours., chapters to books. Recipient Shelley W. Coverman Meml. award, Tulane U., 1996, Student Rschr. award, Disaster and Trauma Spl. Interest Group, Assn. for Advancement of Behavior Therapy, 2000, Clin. Psychology Book award, U. Mass., Boston, 2001, Young Investigator's award, Nat. Edn. Alliance for Borderline Personality Disorder, 2005; grantee, Office of Rsch. and Sponsored Programs, U. Mass. Boston, 2001; Psychosocial fellow, McLean Hosp./Harvard Med. Sch., 2003—05, Rsch. grant, 2004—05. Mem.: Assn. Behavioral and Cognitive Therapies (program com. 2006), Phi Beta Kappa. Democrat. Office: Univ Md Dept Psychology College Park MD 20742 Office Phone: 301-405-3551. Office Fax: 301-405-3223. Personal E-mail: klgratz@aol.com.

GRAU, MARCY BEINISH, real estate broker, former investment banker; b. Bklyn., Aug. 7, 1950; d. Joseph Beinish and Gloria (Rosenbaum) Bennett; m. Bennett Grau, Nov. 19, 1978; 3 children. AB with high honors, U. Mich., 1971; postgrad., Columbia U., 1972, N.Y. Inst. Fin., 1973. Asst. to chmn. Bancroft Convertible Fund, N.Y.C., 1973-75; precious metals trader J. Aron & Co., N.Y.C., 1975-81, mgr. metals mktg., 1981-83; v.p. Goldman, Sachs & Co/J. Aron, N.Y.C., 1983-88; investment banking cons. N.Y.C., 1988-90; real estate broker Fox Residential Group, 1998-99, Stribling & Assoc., N.Y.C., 1999—2004, v.p., 2004—05, sr. v.p., 2005—. Editor Precious Metals Rev. and Outlook, 1980—; contbr. article to profl. jours. Vol. worker pediatrics dept. Lenox Hill Hosp., N.Y.C., 1978-79; asst. The Holiday Project, The Hunger Project, N.Y.C., 1978-83; vol. Yorkville Common Pantry, N.Y.C., 1984; tutor Yorkville Neighborhodd Assn., N.Y.C., 1984; assoc. Child Devel. Ctr., N.Y.C.; trustee Congregation B'nai Jeshurun, 1989—, pres., 1991-94, chair, 1994-97; trustee Ethical Fieldston Fund, 1994-2000. Mem. Phi Beta Kappa. Avocations: interior design, fashion, cooking, piano. Home: 300 West End Ave New York NY 10023-8156 Office: 924 Madison Ave New York NY 10021-3577 Office Phone: 212-452-4361. Personal E-mail: marcyg300@aol.com.

GRAU, SHIRLEY ANN (MRS. JAMES KERN FEIBLEMAN), writer; b. New Orleans, July 8, 1929; d. Adolph and Katherine (Onion) G.; m. James Kern Feibleman, Aug. 4, 1955; children: Ian, James, Nora Miranda, William, Katherine. BA, Tulane U., 1950. Author: (short stories) The Black Prince and Other Stories, 1955, The Hard Blue Sky, 1958, The House on Coliseum Street, 1961, The Keepers of the House, 1964 (Pulitzer prize for fiction 1965), The Condor Passes, 1971, The Wind Shifting West and Other Stories, 1973, Evidence of Love, 1977, Nine Women, 1986, Roadwalkers, 1994, Selected Short Stories, 2004; writer publs. including Holiday, New Yorker, New World Writing, Mademoiselle, Saturday Evening Post, Atlantic, The Reporter, 1954—. Mem. Phi Beta Kappa. Office: PO Box 9058 Metairie LA 70055-9058 Personal E-mail: shirleygrau@bellsouth.net.

GRAVELY, MARY JEANE, volunteer; b. East Orange, N.J., July 15, 1920; d. William Chauncey and Marguerite (Guilbert) Ripley; m. Herbert Carlyle Gragely Sr., Sept. 18, 1943; children: Cynthia, David, Carlyle, Marshall, Peter. Student, Wells Coll., 1941. Bd. dirs. York Pl. Children's Home, 1980-85; vol. Grand Stand Humane Soc., Myrtle Beach, S.C., 1985-95; mem. diocesan coun. Episcopal. Ch., Charleston, S.C., 1985-86; pres. ch. women Trinity Ch., Myrtle Beach, 1983-84, vestry, 1986-89. Republican. Home: 5004 Pine Lake Dr Myrtle Beach SC 29577-2437

GRAVER, MARY KATHRYN, medical/surgical nurse; b. Rehrersburg, Pa., Nov. 8, 1934; d. Levi B. and Emma A. (Sensenig) Gibbel; m. C. W. Graver, June 27, 1959; children: Elizabeth Ann, Craig Warren, Timothy John, Kathryn Renate. RN, Coatesville (Pa.) Sch. Nursing, 1956; BA, Eastern Coll., St. Davids, Pa., 1994. Staff nurse pediatrics unit Phila. Gen. Hosp., 1956; staff nurse med./surg. unit Coatesville Hosp., 1957; staff nurse maternal and med./surg. units Ephrata (Pa.) Hosp., 1958-59; staff/clinic nurse Bryn Mawr (Pa.) Hosp., 1976-93, vol., 2001—.

GRAVER, SUZANNE LEVY, English literature educator; b. NYC, Aug. 17, 1936; BA summa cum laude, CUNY, 1958; MA, U. Calif., Berkeley, 1960; PhD, U. Mass., 1976. Tchr. English Berkeley HS, 1960-61, Culver City HS, 1961-62; asst. prof. Berkshire CC, 1966-72; vis. asst. prof. Tufts U., 1976-78; assoc. ind. study Empire State Coll., SUNY, 1978; lectr. Williams Coll., Williamstown, Mass., 1976, 78-82, coord. writing workshop, 1981-85, asst. prof., 1983-87, chair dept. women's studies, 1988-89, assoc. prof. English, 1988-91, assoc. dean faculty, 1990-91, dean of faculty, 1991-94, prof., 1991—2002, John Hawley Roberts prof. English prof. emerita, 2002—, vis. prof. English, 2003—05. Manuscript reader Ind. U. Press, Victorian Studies, Victorian Periodicals Review, PMLA; fellowship and grants application reader NEH, Nat. Humanities Ctr., The Grad. Ctr., CUNY; Andrew W. Mellon emeritus fellow, 2005-06. Author: George Eliot and Community: A Study in Social Theory and Fictional Form, 1984, and numerous essays and revs. in Victorian lit. and culture. U. fellow U. Mass., Amherst, 1974-76, Am. Coun. Learned Socs. fellow, 1985-86, 89-90, Nat. Humanities Ctr. fellow, 1989-90, NEH fellow, 1995-96, Andrew W. Mellon Emeritus fellow, 2005-06. Mem. AAUP, ACLU, NOW, MLA (rep. to del. assembly 1988-91), Amnesty Internat., Wilderness Soc., N.E. MLA (chair English novel sect. 1980). Office: Williams Coll Stetson Hall Williamstown MA 01267-0141 Office Phone: 413-597-2559. Business E-Mail: sgraver@williams.edu.

GRAVES, ANNA MARIE, lawyer; b. Arlington, Va., Sept. 26, 1959; d. George W. and Anna (Czikora) G. AB cum laude, Cornell U., 1981; JD, U. Va., 1985. Bar: Calif. 1985, U.S. Dist. Ct. (cen. dist.) Calif. 1986. Corp. assoc. Memel, Jacobs, Pierno, Gersh & Ellsworth, L.A., 1985-87, Stroock & Stroock & Lavan, L.A.; ptnr., co-chmn. Restaurant Food & Beverage industry group Pillsbury Winthrop Shaw Pittman, LA. Chmn. UCLA Extension Calif. Restaurant Industry Conf. Named a So. Calif. Super Lawyer, LA Mag., 2004. Mem. ABA, Beverly Hills Bar Assn., Calif. Women Lawyers. Democrat. Office: Pillsbury Winthrop Shaw Pittman 725 S Figueroa St Los Angeles CA 90017 Office Phone: 213-488-7164. Office Fax: 213-226-4017. Business E-Mail: anna.graves@pillsburylaw.com.

GRAVES, KATHRYN LOUISE, dermatologist; b. Kansas City, Kans., Mar. 9, 1949; d. Jack Clair and Ruth Marjory (Prentice) Schroll; m. Jeffery Jackson Graves, Mar. 31, 1973; children: Jeffery Justin, Jonathon Tyler, Kathryn Camille. BA, U. Kans., 1971; MD, U. Kans., Kansas City, 1974. Diplomate Am. Bd. Dermatology. Intern St. Lukes Hosp., Kansas City, 1975-76, resident in internal medicine, 1976; resident dermatology Sch. Medicine U. Kans., Kansas City, 1976-79; dermatologist Hutchinson (Kans.) Clinic P.A., 1979—; mem. med. staff Hutchinson Hosp., 1979—. Fellow Am. Acad. Dermatology; mem. AMA, Kans. Dermatology Soc., Kans. Med. Assn., Hutchinson C. of C., Gamma Phi Beta (standards chair 1973—). Republican. Methodist. Avocations: reading, walking, golf, jetskiing. Home: 130 Hyde Park Dr Hutchinson KS 67502-2840 Office: Hutchinson Clinic 2101 N Waldron St Hutchinson KS 67502-1197 Office Phone: 620-669-2570.

GRAVES, LESLIE HILL, secondary school educator; b. Knoxville, Tenn., Nov. 26, 1971; d. Roy Lynn and Doris Ellison (Richardson) Hill; m. Jeffrey Todd Graves, June 27, 1998; children: Todd Franklin, Claire Elise. BS in Music Edn. magna cum laude, U. Tenn., Knoxville, 1995, MS, 1998; EdS in Adminstrn. and Supervision, Lincoln Meml. U., Harrogate, Tenn., 2004. Choral music tchr. Gibbs HS, Corryton, Tenn., 1996—. Pianist and choir dir. St. Luke's United Meth. Ch., 1990—2000; painist Fountain City United Meth. Ch., 2000—. Mem.: Am. Choral Dirs. Assn., Music Educators Nat. Conf. Methodist. Avocations: singing, piano. Home: 5900 Zachary Rd Corryton TN 37721 Office: Gibbs High Sch 7628 Tazewell Pike Corryton TN 37721 Personal E-mail: lesliesing1@yahoo.com.

GRAVES, LORRAINE ELIZABETH, dancer, educator, coach; b. Norfolk, Va., Oct. 5, 1957; d. Thomas Edward and Mildred Fayette (Odom) G. BS, Ind. U., 1978. Dancer, Regisseuse Dance Theatre of Harlem, N.Y.C., 1978—, ballet mistress, 1980—, prin. dancer, 1980, artistic asst., 1998—. Artistic advisor Va. Ballet Theatre, 1997—; tchr./coach Dance Theatre of Harlem, 1998-99, 2001, guest ballet mistress, 2001—; guest tchr. N.C. Sch. of Arts, Winston-Salem, 1987, 93, Gov.'s Sch. for Arts, U. Richmond, 1990—, Carlton Johnson Acad. of Dance, 1991-95, Okla. Summer Arts Inst., 1993-94, The Flint Sch. Performing Arts, Flint Youth Ballet, 2001—, Dance Theatre of Harlem, Kennedy Ctr. Residency Program, 1993-95, 98—, Worcester Sch. Performing Arts, 1997, Greenville Ballet, 2001; resident guest tchr. Gov.'s Sch. for Arts, Norfolk, Va., 1988-91, mem. faculty, 1996—; guest tchr. Worcester Sch. Performing Arts, 1997; resident guest tchr. S.C. Gov.'s Sch. for Arts, 1995-97; guest tchr. Va. Ballet Theatre, 1996—, artistic advisor, 1998—; guest tchr. Va. Sch. for the Arts, 1997—, resident guest tchr., 2003—; educator, judge Dance Olympus, 1997—; judge Internat. Dance Challenge, 1998—; guest faculty Mid-States Regional Dance Festival, 1999; mem. faculty SERBA Festival, Roanoke, Va., 2003. Dancer Dance Theatre of Harlem as Princess of Unreal Beauty in live TV prodn. of Firebird, 1982, as Myrta, Queen of the Willis in NBC prodn. of Creole Giselle, 1987, performed at White House, 1981, also at the closing ceremonies of the 1984 Olympics, toured with Dance Theatre of Harlem, USSR, 1988, South Africa, 1992, guest artist Young People's Concert series, N.Y. Philharm., 1988, Detroit Symphony, 1989, River City Ballet, Memphis, 1991, 1992, N.W. Fla. Ballet, 1994, prin. dancer Va. Ballet Theatre, Norfolk, 1996—, Dance Theatre of Harlem, 1999, guest ballet mistress, 1999—, regisseuse Dance Theatre of Harlem, 1989—96. Mem. artistic com. Young Audiences of Va.; sec. Norfolk Commn. on the Arts and Humanities, 2002—; mem. program com. Young Audiences Va.; sec., treas. Graves Funeral Home, Inc. Fellow Am. Guild Mus. Artists. Episcopalian. Avocations: modeling, teaching younger dancers.

GRAVES, MARGERY A., elementary school educator; b. Champaign, Ill., Dec. 16, 1931; d. Herbert L. and Margery E. (Fish) White; m. John E. Graves, June 23, 1956; children: Beth Graves Lenz, Cheryl Graves Mehta. BA, Drury Coll., 1953; MS Edn., Drake U., 1991. Tchr. Des Moines Pub. Schs., 1953-56, Ames (Iowa) Pub. Schs., 1956-59, Newton (Iowa) Comm. Schs., 1967-95. Mem. coms. lang., social studies, whole lang., early childhood, report card, Newton Schs., 1977-94; founder pub. ctr. for student books, Emerson Hough Sch., Newton, 1988. Pres. LWV, Newton, Willowbrook Adult Day Care Bd., Newton. Mem. Delta Kappa Gamma. Democrat. Unitarian Universalist. Home: 7006 S 28th Ave E Newton IA 50208-8129

GRAVES, MAUREEN ANN, self esteem and spirituality consultant; b. Sioux City, Iowa, July 10, 1946; d. Jack Milford and Elizabeth Mildred (St. George) Dryden; m. Thomas Darrel Graves, Oct. 9, 1965; children: Michael James, Lorrie Michelle. Grad. 1-yr. program, Gestalt Inst. Iowa, 1980. Cert. profl. asst., U. SD; cert. success in motivational coaching; cert. hypnotherapist, Wellness Inst., Seattle. Counselor Siouxland Coun. on Alcoholism and Drug Abuse, Sioux City, 1979-81; counselor, co-founder New Hope Alcohol and Addiction Ctr., South Sioux City, Nebr., 1981-98; Reiki practitioner, 1997—. Cons. St. Luke Hosp. Addiction Ctr., Sioux City, 1987—; trainer Va. Satir-Internat. Tng. Inst., Crested Butte, Colo., 1988-89. Vol. co-facilitator Siouxland Coun. on Alcoholism and Drug Abuse, Sioux City, 1976—79; exec. team couple Worldwide Marriage Encounter, N.E., Nebr., 1979—82; trainer Va. Satir-Internat. Tng. Inst., Crested Butte, Colo., 1992; co-leader Satir Family Camp, 1992—2006; active Avanta Faculty Governing Coun., 1994—2006. Mem. Avanta Network, Moscow Inst. for Profl. Devel. of Psychologists and Social Workers (founding). Roman Catholic. Avocation: reiki master. Home and Office: 1814 N 155th Ave Omaha NE 68154-4123 Office Phone: 402-932-3584.

GRAVES, MAXINE, medical and surgical nurse; b. Mobile, Ala., July 16, 1941; d. Leon Sr. and Mary E. (McDaniel-Lane) Grove; m. Perry R. Graves, Oct. 29, 1966; children: Dennis, Anita Graves Ricks. AD, Delaware County Community Coll., Media, Pa., 1972; BSN, Gwynedd Mercy Coll., Gwynedd Valley, Pa., 1983. Tchrs. aide Chester (Pa.)-Upland Sch. Dist.; simulation lab. instr. Delaware County Community Coll.; ambulatory care staff nurse Crozer-Chester Med. Ctr.; nurse mgr. Crozer Internal Medicine Assocs., Upland, Pa.; staff nurse transitional care ctr. Crozer Chester Med. Ctr., Upland, case mgr. nurse, 1998—. Editor newsletter Sleuth, 1989. Mem. ANA, Pa. Nurses Assn. (past. chmn. membership com.). Office: Croze Home Care 1 Medical Center Blvd Chester PA 19013-3902

GRAVES, NADA PROCTOR, retired elementary school educator; b. Kewaunee, Wis., Oct. 9, 1933; d. John and Martha Proctor; m. Harmon Sheldon Graves III, Dec. 28, 1958; children: Jessica, Gemont. BS, U. Wis., 1956. With TWA, Chgo., 1956-58; tchr. Denver Pub. Schs., 1959-61, Cherry Creek Schs., Englewood, Colo., 1980—99. Membership chmn. Denver Art Mus., 1966-68; treas. Glenmoor Homeowners, 1991-92; mem./vol. D.A.M., Mus. Nat. History, Ctrl. City Guild, The Guild Diabetes, Denver Lyric Opera Guild, Gathering Place., P.E.O., D. of the King Home: 17 Glenmoor Cir Englewood CO 80110-7121

GRAVES, PAMELA KAY, music educator; b. Cleve., Ohio, Oct. 29, 1953; d. Frank Michael and Harriet Gertude Duncan; m. Garry Thomas Graves, Aug. 17, 1979; 1 child, Tyler Logan. MusB, BE, Capital U., 1976. Bookkeeper McDonald Restaurants, Mayfield, Ohio, 1970—80; music tchr., instrumental dir. St. Joseph & John Sch., Strongsville, Ohio, 1985—2000; adj. music Ohio Music Educator Assn., Ohio, 1993—. Instrumental dir., tchr. Wickliffe Mid. Sch., Ohio, 1993—; freelance musician, Ohio, 1985—; guest conductor Ohio State Fair Band, Ohio, 1980—; piano tchr. Piano Turner Sch., Ohio, 1986. Contbr. articles to profl. jour., 2002. Mem.: Nat. Assn. of Music Edn., Levy Com., Wickliffe Parent and Tchr. Together (sec. 2001—03). Avocations: photography, crafts, gardening. Home: 1717 Robindale St Wickliffe OH 44092 Office: Wickliffe Mid Sch 29240 Eudid Ave Wickliffe OH 44092

GRAVES, PIRKKO MAIJA-LEENA, clinical psychologist, psychoanalyst; b. Tampere, Finland, Jan. 20, 1930; came to U.S., 1957; d. Frans Vilho and Bertta Katariina (Katajisto) Lahtinen; Mag.Phil. (Finnish State scholar 1949-52), 1954; French Govt. scholar, U. Paris, 1954-55; Ph.D. (Fulbright scholar 1957-58, Lucy E. Elliott scholar 1958-59), U. Mich., 1964; postgrad. Washington Psychoanalytic Inst.; m. Irving Lawrence Graves, Dec. 31, 1969. Psychologist, U. Mich. Psychol. Clinic, 1960-63, asst. study dir. Survey Rsch. Ctr., 1961-63, instr. psychology, 1964-70; asst. prof. Johns Hopkins U., 1970-76, prin. investigator under-nutrition and infant devel. Internat. Ctr. for Rsch., Calcutta, India and Kathmandu, Nepal, 1970-73, asst. prof., lectr., sr. rsch. psychologist Precursors Study Med. Sch., 1979—; assoc. clin. prof. U. Md. Med. Sch.; dir. rsch. Mental Health Study Center, NIMH, 1976-79, supervising and training analyst Washington Psychoanalytic Inst., 1990—; cons. in field. Fellow Md. Psychol. Assn.; mem. Am. Psychol. Assn., Am. Psychoanalytic Assn., Internat. Psychoanalytic Assn. Author articles in field, chpts. in books. Home: 1017 Cherry Point Dr White Stone VA 22578-2607

GRAVES, RUTH ELAINE, minister, educator; b. West Point, Miss., May 9, 1953; d. Charlie Mattice and Ruth Jones Graves. BS, Miss. State U., 1974; MS, Nova U., Las Vegas, 1983; MDiv, Interdenominational Theol. Ctr., Atlanta, 1987; PhD, Jackson State U., Miss., 2004. English instr. Las Vegas Pub. Schs., 1976—78, 1980—85; ordained minister United Meth. Ch., Full Gospel Min., Winona & Canton, Miss., 1987—92, City of Light Ch., Inc., Canton, Miss., 1993—2003; English instr. Miss. Pub. Schs., Carthage, McGee, Jackson, 1993—98, Mary Holmes Coll., West Point, 1992—94; psychology rsch. fellow Howard Univ., Washington, 2003—, faculty, 2004—. Recipient The Craig Brandenburg award, United Meth. Ch., Nashville, 1998. Mem.: Assn. Black Psychologists, Christian Counselors Assn., APA, Clark County Tchrs. Assn., Am. Fedn. Tchrs., Canton Ministerial Assn. Avocations: piano, reading, poetry, writing. Home: 4409 Clermont Dr NE 254 Washington DC 20011 Office: Howard Univ Hosp 530 Coll St Washington DC 20059 Office Phone: 202-806-7707. Personal E-mail: revelainegraves@att.net.

GRAVES, VICKI LLOYD, retired mechanical engineer; b. Phoenix, Ariz., Aug. 5, 1935; d. Margarite Marie Hogue and Lonnie Hershal Lloyd, adopted d. Ivan Burton and Dorothy Carol Lloyd; m. William S. Graves, June 24, 1966; stepchildren: Kay Levy, Lynn Neilson, Diane Graves-Dolk children: Darlene Ann Clow, Diane Jeanette Clow, Anthony Thomas Clow. Mech. Engrng. Design, Marietta Cobb Tech., 1969. Cons. Engrng. Cons. Designer, St. Petersburg, Fla., 1968—82; art designer Vicki Quail Run Art Studio, Mesa, Ariz., 1992—. Membership chmn. Scottsdale Artist League, Ariz., 1998—2000. Mem.: Scottsdale Artist League, Mesa Artist League. Address: 234 E Bakerview Rd Apt # 106 Bellingham WA 98226

GRAY, AMY CASTLE, lawyer; b. Austin, Tex., July 14, 1967; BA in Spanish, Vanderbilt U., 1989; JD, So. Meth. U., 1993. Bar: Tex. 1993. Assoc. Godwin, Pappas, Langley & Ronquillo, L.L.P., Dallas. Named a Rising Star, Tex. Super Lawyers mag., 2006. Office: Godwin Pappas Langley Ronquillo LLP Renaissance Tower Ste 1700 1201 Elm St Dallas TX 75270 Office Phone: 214-939-4691. E-mail: agray@godwinpappas.com.*

GRAY, ANN MAYNARD, broadcasting company executive; b. Boston, Aug. 22, 1945; d. Paul Maynard and Pauline Elizabeth MacFadyen; children: Richard R. Gray III, Dana Maynard Gray. BA, U. Mich., 1967; MBA, NYU,

1971. With Chase Manhattan Bank, N.Y.C., 1967-68, Chem. Bank, N.Y.C., 1968-73, asst. sec., 1971-73; asst. to treas., then asst. treas. ABC, Inc., 1974-76, treas., 1976-81, v.p. planning, 1979-86; v.p. Capital Cities/ABC, Inc. (merged 1986), 1986—; sr. v.p. fin. ABC TV Network Group, 1988-91; pres. Diversified Pub. Group Capital Cities/ABC, Inc., 1991—; bd. dirs. Cyprus Empire Corp. Bd. dirs. Cyprus AMAX Minerals Co., Duke Energy Corp. Trustee Martha Graham Ctr. of Contemporary Dance, N.Y.C., 1989-92, Cancer Care, Inc., 1991—.

GRAY, ARLENE, music educator, musician; b. The Dalles, Oreg., Dec. 15, 1948; d. Irving Bernard and Sarah Grace (Adamson) Elle; m. David Leroy Gray, Oct. 20, 1972; children: Mark, Stephanie, Brian, Timothy. BS in Elem. Edn., Oreg. State U., 1970; BA in Music Performance, U. Mary, 1994. Nat. cert. tchr. of music Music Tchrs. Nat. Assn., 1996. Tchr. kindergarten, Fairview, Mont., 1972; pvt. piano tchr. Mandan, ND, 1973—, Bismarck, ND. Coll. choir accompanist Bismarck State Coll., ND, 1994—, tchr. piano and organ, 1998—. Organist Presby. Ch., Mandan, 1982—98, First Presbyn. Ch., Bismarck, 2005—. Grantee, N.D. Coun. on Arts, 2004, 2005; P.E.O. grantee, 1992. Mem.: Jr. Fed. Music Club (chmn. The Playing Keys 1980—), Nat. Fed. Music Clubs, N.D. Music Tchrs. Assn. (sec. 1996—98, co-chmn. state conv. 2003, state newsletter editor 2004—), Am. Coll. Musicians (chmn. 1987—, judge 1997—), Am. Guild Organists, Nat. Music Tchrs. Assn. (state bd. dirs.). Avocations: reading, gardening, swimming, sewing, baking. Home: 4525 Camden Loop Bismarck ND 58503 Office: Bismarck State Coll 1500 Edwards Ave Bismarck ND 58501 Office Phone: 701-224-5510. Business E-Mail: arlene.gray@bsc.nodak.edu.

GRAY, BARBARA L., assistant principal, tax specialist; b. Memphis, Aug. 3, 1947; d. Willie Odum Register and Virginia Adline Garcia; children: Bryant, Yolanda, LoMay. BS in Chemistry, LeMoyne Owen Coll., Memphis, 1972; MEd, Memphis State U., 1989. Tchr. math and sci. Shelby County Schs., 1972—97, asst. prin., 1987—; tax specialist H & R Block, Millington, Tenn., 1998—. Pres. Shelby County Edn. Assoc., 2005—. Mem. City of Millington Appeal and Grievance Bd., 2001—, City of Millington Mcpl. Airport Auth., 2002—04, Pulvair Site Citizens Advisory Group, 2004—. Mem.: ASCD, Nat. Coun. of Tchrs. of Math., Nat. Sci. Tchrs. Assn. Church Of Christ. Avocations: reading, exercise, walking. Home: 7709 Tecumseh Millington TN 38053 Office: Shelby County Schs 5885 Woodstock Millington TN 38053 Office Phone: 901-386-8771. Personal E-mail: bgray901@aol.com, sceapres@bellsouth.net.

GRAY, BARBARA MAY, artist; b. N.Y.C., Apr. 29, 1934; d. Samuel David and Sadie Blum Ampolsey; m. Edward Gray, Aug. 29, 1954; children: Karen, Douglas. BA, CUNY, 1955; postgrad., Art Student League, 1965; MA, NYU, 1996. Graphics design Fred Kessler Collectors, N.Y.C., 1955; draftsman J. Rowland AIA, Kinston, N.C., 1955-57; art instr. Strathmore Sch., Matawan, N.J., 1963; instr. Guild of Creative Art, New Shrewsbury, N.J., 1965-66; art tchr. St. Mary's Town and Country Sch., London, 1967-68; lectr. Ctrl. Sch. of Art, London, 1975; art instr. Norwalk (Conn.) C.C., 1985-86, 95. Bd. dirs. Westport (Conn.) Ctr. for Arts, 1984-86 Creator Haiga-Haiku, 1982; collaborator (catalog) Five, 1979, Inner Eye, 1975; exhibns. in three cities in Europe; invited artist-in-residence Atelier A, Apricale, Italy, 1998. Mem. Conn. Women Artists, Westport, 1997-99. Recipient Best in Graphics Fairfield U. Gallery, 1988. Mem. AAUW, Soc. Am. Graphic Artists, Ulla Surland Gallery Eleven. Avocations: theater, dining out, bicycling, poetry, travel. E-mail: bgray1@optonline.net.

GRAY, CARI LAIRD, economics educator; b. Rockdale, Tex., Aug. 17, 1960; d. Lloyd Edward and Margaret Frankie Laird; m. Randal C. Gray, July 9, 1981; children: Chase Alan, Haley Anne. BA, U. Tex., San Antonio, 1988. Cert. Tchr. Tex., 1996. Tchr. econs. New Braunfels H.S., Tex., 1996—. Faculty adviser New Braunfels H.S. Nat. Honor Soc., 2003—; co-sponsor New Braunfels H.S. Model UN, 2000—. Leadership New Braunfels C. of C., 2005—06; mem. Mid-Tex. Symphony Guild, New Braunfels, 2000—06, Sophienburg Mus. & Archives, New Braunfels, 1992—2006, New Braunfels Rep. Women, 2003—06; mem. and hospitality chairperson Bulverde Area Rep. Women, Tex., 2003—06; mem. Canyon Lake Rep. Women, Tex., 2003—06, First United Meth. Ch., New Braunfels, 1989—2006. Named Tchr. Hero, New Braunfels H.S. Students, 2000, 2005, Tex. Econs. Tchr. of Yr., Tex. Coun. Econ. Edn., 1999—2000; named to Who's Who Among Am. H.S. Tchrs., New Braunfels H.S. Students, 2003—04, 2004—05; recipient Nasdaq Ednl. Found. Tchg. Award, Tex. Coun. Econ. Edn., 1999. Achievements include Selected presenter, College Board National Conference, July 2006; Selected contributor to Apple computer teaching website regarding the use of technology in the classroom 2005-06; Selected contributor to teacher's edition of Glencoe-McGraw-Hill's textbook Economics: Principles and Practices, 2000. Avocations: travel, gardening, reading. Office: New Braunfels High School 2551 Loop 337 North New Braunfels TX 78130 Office Fax: 830-627-6001. E-mail: cgray@newbraunfels.txed.net.

GRAY, CAROLYN DOPPELT, lawyer; b. Elmira, NY, Apr. 10, 1940; d. Frederic Amster and Lucille (Greenebaum) D.; m. Thomas Allen Gray, 1982; 1 child, Emilie Sara Gray. AA, Stephens Coll., 1959; BA in Journalism, U. Mo., 1961; JD, Ind. U., 1979. Dir. pub. rels. Ft. Wayne (Ind.) Fine Arts Found., 1962-65; pres., treas. The Toidey Co., Ft. Wayne, Ind., 1965-81; pvt. practice Ft. Wayne, Ind., 1979-81; dir. Office Women's Bus. Ownership, SBA, Washington, 1981-85; pres. Appalachian Found., Washington, 1985-86; dep. asst. sec. Office Human Devel. Svcs., HHS, Washington, 1986-88, commr. Adminstrn. Devel. Disabilities, 1988-89; spl. counsel Saul, Ewing, Remick & Saul, Washington, 1990-92; ptnr. Epstein Becker & Green, P.C., Washington, 1992—2003, Barnes & Thornburg, LLP, Washington, 2003—; adv. com. White House Conf. on Aging, 2005. Gen. counsel, sec., treas. Inst. Disability Resources, Washington, 1994-1997; pres. Gray Devel. Group, Inc., Rockville, Md., 1989—; participant White House Conf. on Aging, 2005. Author: (handbook) What You Absolutely Must Know About The Americans with Disabilities Act, 1992, (handbook) The ADA: Next Steps for Employers: How to Successfully Fit the ADA Into Your Workforce Picture, 1993; editl. adv. bd. Disability Law Reporter Svc., 1993; editl. bd. Nat. Disability Law Reporter, 1991—; contributing editor: Disability Compliance Bulletin, 1991—. Mem. task force on pediatric AIDS and HIV, HHS, 1988-89; exec. dir. Pres.'s Adv. Com. on Women's Bus. Ownership, 1983-84; mem. Pres.'s Task Force for Legal Equity for Women, 1983-86; participant White House Conf. on Aging, 2005. Recipient Disting. Svc. award Ft. Wayne (Ind.) Jaycees, 1975. Mem. ABA, Ind. Bar Assn., D.C. Bar Assn., Jr. League of Washington, Univ. Club; bd. overseers Hebrew Union Coll. Jewish Inst. Religion, N.Y., 1990-. Republican. Jewish. Avocation: residential and commercial design. Office: Barnes & Thornburg Ste 900 750 17th St NW Washington DC 20006-4607 Office Phone: 202-371-6364.

GRAY, DEBORAH DOLIA, business writing consultant; b. Elmo, Mo., Jan. 25, 1952; d. Gerald Lee and Rosalie (Thompson) G. BS in Music and Journalism cum laude, U. Nebr., 1976; MFA, Columbia U., 1988. Reporter Lincoln (Nebr.) Star, 1975-78; spl. writer, feature projects Ft. Lauderdale (Fla.) News, 1978-79; reporter Miami (Fla.) News, 1979-80; curriculum specialist John Jay Coll. Criminal Justice, CUNY, N.Y.C., 1980-84; tng. specialist Mgmt. Devel. Systems Inc., N.Y.C., 1985—. Writing cons. various non-profit agys. and corps. Contbr. articles to profl. jours. Hollingsworth fellow Columbia U., 1985. Avocations: songwriter, keyboard player, poet. Home: 900 W 190th St Apt 9R New York NY 10040 Office Phone: 212-326-3665. Business E-Mail: ddgray@jonesday.com.

GRAY, DEBORAH MARY, wine importer; b. Sydney, NSW, Australia, Feb. 4, 1952; came to U.S., 1973; d. Anthony Eric and Mary Patricia (O'Mullane) Gray. Student, Eckerd Coll., 1988—90. Fin. counselor Wuesthoff Meml. Hosp., Rockledge, Fla., 1973-75; admintrv. dir. Dresden & Ticktin, MDs, P.A., St. Petersburg, Fla., 1976-80; exec. dir., v.p. Am. Med. Mgmt., Inc., Clearwater, Fla., 1980-90; pres., dir. All Women's Health Ctr., Inc., various locations, Fla., 1980-90, Lakeland Women's Health Ctr., Fla., 1980-90, Ft. Myers Women's Health Ctr., Fla., 1980-90, Nat. Women's Health Svcs., Inc., Clearwater, Fla., 1983-90, Women's Ob-Gyn. Ctr. Countryside, Inc., 1984-90, D.M.S. of Ft. Myers, Inc., 1985-90; treas., v.p., dir. Birthing Mgmt. Inc., 1985-90; healthcare cons., 1990-92; N.Am. mgr. Cowra Wines, Australia, 1991-95; owner Australian Wine Connection, Inc., Carlsbad, Calif., 1992—2004, CEO, shareholder, 2004—. Mem. bd. agy. that facilitates hard to place children adoptions One Ch. One Child, 1990-94.

GRAY, DONNA LEA, small business owner; b. Snyder, Tex., Sept. 5, 1937; d. Dee Roy Chapman and Esther Weaver; m. C. D. Gray, Jr., Dec. 27, 1953; children: Donna Faye Gray Rosson, Cassandra L. Gray-Ratliff. Asst. postmaster USPS, Dunn, Tex., 1955—58; clk. J.C. Penney, Snyder, 1958—59, Fabric Mart, Snyder, 1959—60; owner, operator Donna's Beauty Shop, Snyder, 1963—65; owner, mgr. La Charme' Health Spa, Snyder, 1968—75, Snyder Bookstore and Gift Shop, 1978—90; part-owner, sec. Ice Melt Products LLC, Snyder, 1992. Active United Way, Heart Assn., Am. Cancer Soc., Snyder; dist. chmn. March of Dimes, Snyder, 1984; bd. dirs. Scurry County Fair Assn., Scurry County Hist. Commn.; bd. dirs., treas. Scurry County Child Welfare Bd. Recipient Soze,pre award, 1994, 1997, 1999. Mem.: Am. Bus. Women's Assn., Am. Booksellers Assn., Christian Booksellers Assn., Goldcoat Orgn., Snyder C. of C. Office: 8860 Road Runner Path Snyder TX 79549-1110 Office Phone: 325-573-6373.

GRAY, ELIZABETH VAN DOREN, lawyer; b. Columbia, S.C., Jan. 3, 1949; d. Robert Lawson and Elizabeth Dacus (Gaines) Van Doren; m. James Cranston Gray, Jr., Apr. 30, 1982; children: James Cranston III, Elizabeth Gaines. BA in Internat. Studies, U. S.C., 1970, JD cum laude, 1976; student, St. Mary's Coll., Raleigh, N.C., 1966-67. Bar: S.C. 1977, U.S. Dist. Ct. S.C. 1977, U.S. Ct. Appeals (4th cir.) 1980, U.S. Ct. Appeals (6th cir.) 1989, U.S. Supreme Ct. 1998. Assoc. McNair Law Firm, PA, Columbia, 1977-82, shareholder, 1982-87; ptnr. Glenn Irvin Murphy Gray & Stepp, Columbia, 1987—2000; now ptnr. Sowell Gray Stepp & Lafitte, LLC, Columbia. Contbr. articles to profl. jours. Mem. ABA, Am. Coll. Trial Lawyers, John Belton O'Neal Inn of Ct., S.C. Bar (pres. 2001-02), S.C. Women Lawyers Assn. (bd. dirs. 1995-99, sec. 1997-98), Richland County Bar Assn. Episcopalian. Office: Sowell Gray Stepp & Lafitte LLC PO Box 11449 Columbia SC 29211 Home: 8 Mahalo Ln Columbia SC 29204-3380

GRAY, FRANCES BOONE, minister; b. Miami, Fla., Aug. 23, 1939; d. Roy and Willie Artis Boone; m. Joel A. Gray, Apr. 17, 1959 (dec. Nov. 2002); children: Linda Lamarsh, Joel A., Frances S. AA, Miami Dade Jr. Coll., Miami, 1959; BS, U. Miami, 1965; MDiv, Jacksonville Theol. Sem., Jacksonville, Fla., 1995; PhD, Jacksonville Theol. Sem., 1999. RN 1965. Nurse Jackson Meml. Hosp., Miami, 1954—65, Mt. Sinai Hosp., Miami, 1965—70, Miami Heart Hosp., 1970—77; minister Temple Missionary Bapt. Ch., Miami, 1988—95; pastor Jesus Christ Unltd. Ministry, Miami, 1995—. Tchr. Lindsey Hopkins Sch., Miami, 1966—67. Bd. dirs. United Way, Miami; asst. sec. SCIC, Miami, 1984—90; mem. NAACP. With USPHS, 1970—75. Mem.: Order Eastern Star (worthy matron 1981—88). Democrat. Avocations: reading, sewing, swimming, singing. Home: 1510 NW 114th St Miami FL 33167

GRAY, FRANCINE DU PLESSIX, writer; b. Warsaw; came to U.S., 1941, naturalized, 1952; d. Bertrand Jochaud and Tatiana (Iacovleff) du Plessix; m. Cleve Gray, Apr. 23, 1957; children: Thaddeus Ives, Luke Alexander. BA, Barnard Coll., 1952; Litt.D. (hon.), CUNY, Oberlin Coll., U. Santa Clara, St. Mary's Coll., U. Hartford. Annenberg fellow Brown U., 1997. Disting. vis. prof. CCNY, 1975; vis. lectr. Yale U., New Haven, 1981-82; Ferris prof. Princeton U., 1986; Disting. vis. prof. Vassar Coll., 1999. Author: Divine Disobedience: Profiles in Catholic Radicalism, 1970 (Nat. Cath. Book award), Hawaii: The Sugar-Coated Fortress, 1972, Lovers and Tyrants, 1976, World Without End, 1981, October Blood, 1985, Adam & Eve and the City, 1987, Soviet Women: Walking the Tightrope, 1989, Rage and Fire: A Life of Louise Colet, 1994, At Home with the Marquis de Sade: A Life, 1998, Simone Weil, 2001, Them: A Memoir of Parents, 2005 (Nat. Book Critics Cir. award for autobiography, 2005). Guggenheim Found. fellow, 1991-92. Fellow, Am. Acad. Arts & Sci.;mem. Am. P.E.N., Am. Acad. Arts and Letters. Democrat. Roman Catholic.

GRAY, GLORIA MEADOR, librarian; b. Marshall, Tex., Aug. 24, 1935; d. Alfred E. and Julia (Whitfield) Meador; m. Philip R. Gray, Mar. 23, 1955; children: Brian, David, Gordon. BA, U. North Tex., 1970, MLS, 1974. Libr. Richardson (Tex.) Ind. Sch. Dist., 1971-91. Mem.: ALA, Tex. Libr. Assn. Democrat. Methodist. Avocations: reading, skiing, community volunteering.

GRAY, HANNA HOLBORN, historian, educator; b. Heidelberg, Germany, Oct. 25, 1930; d. Hajo and Annemarie (Bettmann) Holborn; m. Charles Montgomery Gray, June 19, 1954. AB, Bryn Mawr Coll., 1950; PhD, Harvard U., 1957; MA, Yale U., 1971, LLD, 1978; LittD (hon.), St. Lawrence U., 1974, Oxford U., Eng., 1979; LLD (hon.), Dickinson Coll., 1979, U. Notre Dame, 1980, Marquette U., 1984; LittD (hon.), Washington U., 1974; HHD (hon.), St. Mary's Coll., 1974; LHD (hon.), Grinnell Coll., Iowa, 1974, Lawrence U., 1974, Denison U., 1974, Wheaton Coll., 1976, Marlboro Coll., 1979, Rikkyo U., Japan, 1979, Roosevelt U., 1980, Knox Coll., 1980, Coe Coll., 1981, Thomas Jefferson U., 1981, Duke U., 1982, New Sch. for Social Research, 1982, Clark U., 1982, Brandeis U., 1983, Colgate U., 1983, Wayne State U., 1984, Miami U., Oxford, Ohio, 1984, So. Meth. U., 1984, CUNY, 1985, U. Denver, 1985, Am. Coll. Greece, 1986, Muskingum Coll., 1987, Rush Presbyn. St. Lukes Med. Ctr., 1987, NYU, 1988, Rosemont Coll., 1988, Claremont U. Ctr. Grad Sch., 1989, Moravian Coll., 1991, Rensselaer Poly. Inst., 1991, Coll. William and Mary, 1991, Centre Coll., 1991, Macalester Coll., 1993, McGill U., 1993, Ind. U., 1994, Med. U. of S.C., 1994; LLD (hon.), Union Coll., 1975, Regis Coll., 1976, Dartmouth Coll., 1978, Trinity Coll., 1978, U. Bridgeport, 1978, Dickinson Coll., 1979, Brown U., 1979, Wittenburg U., 1979, Dickinson Coll., 1979, U. Rochester, 1980, U. Notre Dame, 1980, U. So. Calif., 1980, U. Mich., 1981, Princeton U., 1982, Georgetown U., 1983, Marquette U., 1984, W.Va. Wesleyan U., 1985, Hamilton Coll., 1985, Smith Coll., 1986, U. Miami, 1986, Columbia U., 1987, NYU, 1988, Rosemont Coll., 1988, U. Toronto, Can., 1991; LDH, LHD, Haverford Coll., 1995; LDH (hon.), Tulane U., 1995; LLD (hon.), Harvard U., 1995; LHD (hon.), McGill U., 1993, Macalester Coll., 1993, Ind. U., 1994, Med. U. S.C., 1994, Haverford Coll., 1995, Tulane U., 1995; LLD (hon.), Harvard U., 1995, U. Chgo., 1996; DL (hon.), Pontifical Inst. Mediaeval Studies, Toronto, 2005. Instr. Bryn Mawr Coll., 1953—54; tchg. fellow Harvard, 1955—57, instr., 1957—59, asst. prof., 1959—60, vis. lectr., 1963—64; asst. prof. U. Chgo., 1961—64, assoc. prof., 1964—72; dean, prof. Northwestern U., Evanston, Ill., 1972—74; provost, prof. history Yale U., 1974—78, acting pres., 1977—78; pres. U. Chgo., 1978—93, prof. dept. history, 1978—, Harry Pratt Judson disting. svc. prof. history, 1994—. Fellow Ctr. for Advanced Study in Behavioral Scis., 1966—67, vis. scholar, 1970—71; vis. prof. U. Calif., Berkeley, Calif., 1970—71. Co-editor (with Charles Gray): Jour. Modern History, 1965—70; contbr. articles to profl. jours. Active Nat. Coun. on Humanities, 1972—78; trustee Yale Corp., 1971—74; past bd. regents Smithsonian Instn.; past chmn. bd. Andrew W. Mellon Found.; chmn. bd. Howard Hughes Med. Inst., Marlboro Sch. Music. Decorated Grosse Verdienstkreuz Germany; named Pontifical Justice Medieval Studies, Toronto, Can., 2005; recipient Grad. medal, Radcliffe Coll., 1976, Yale medal, 1978, Medal of Liberty award, 1986, Laureate Lincoln Acad. Ill., 1988, Medal of Freedom, 1991, Frontrunner award, Sara Lee, 1991, Charles Frankel prize, 1993, Centennial medal, Harvard U., 1994, Disting. Svc. award in edn., Inst. Internat. Edn., 1994, Medal of Distinction, Barnard Coll., 2000, Fritz Redlich Disting. Alumni award, Internat. Inst. Edn., 2004, The Newberry Libr. award, 2006; fellow Newberry Libr., 1960—61, St. Anne's Coll., Oxford U., 1978—; Fulbright scholar, 1950—51. Fellow: Am. Acad. Arts and Scis.; mem.: Coun. Fgn. Rels. N.Y., Coun. Fgn. Rels. Chgo., Nat. Acad. Edn., Am. Philos. Soc. (Jefferson medal 1993), Renaissance Soc. Am., Phi Beta Kappa (vis. scholar 1971—72). Office: U Chgo Dept History 1126 E 59th St Chicago IL 60637-1580 Business E-Mail: h-gray@uchicago.edu.

GRAY, HAZEL IRENE, retired special education educator, counselor, consultant; b. Van Nuys, Calif., July 2, 1921; d. Charles Clayton Cramer and Ida Mae (Leffler); m. Reed A. Gray; children: Mildred Lorene(dec.), Paul Charles; m. Neil Chapin Smith (dec.). BA, San Jose State Coll., Calif., 1964, MA, 1968; EdD, U. So. Calif., LA, 1977. Itinerant tchr. hearing impaired Santa Cruz County Office of Edn., 1964—66; resource specialist Santa Cruz Pub. Schools, 1966—68; psychologist Santa Cruz County Office of Edn., 1968—71; psychologist, cons. and parent counselor Project Idea, San Jose, 1971—72; dir. spl. edn. Live Oaks schs. Santa Cruz County Office of Edn., 1972—74; cons. Calif. State Dept. of Edn., Sacramento, 1975—76; adminstr. San Jose City Coll., 1976—78; dir. pupil pers. Campbell Union Sch. Dist., Calif., 1978; pvt. practice marriage counseling, 1971—. Cons. Catholic Pre-Sch., LA; lectr. Calif. State U, San Jose, U. Calif., Santa Clara, Santa Cruz; with Med. Info. Svcs. Co-author: (book) Behavior Modification, 1971. Mem. rescue team Calif. Coast Guard, 1971—76; team mem. marriage family and child counseling license rev. Calif. State Dept. of Licensing, Sacramento. Mem.: San Jose Movie and Video Club, Camera Club. Republican. Mem. Lds Ch. Avocations: travel, photography.

GRAY, HELEN THERESA GOTT, editor; b. Jersey City, July 2, 1942; d. William E. and Cynthia B. Gott; m. David L. Gray, Aug. 15, 1976; 1 child, David Lee Jr. BA, Syracuse U., 1963; M in Internat. Affairs, Columbia U., 1965. Editor religion sect. The Kansas City (Mo.) Star, 1971—. Tchr. Bible sch. Pleasant Green Bapt. Ch., Kansas City, Kans., 1975—, counselor, 1978—; former owner of a Christian book store. Co-author, editor several books; contbr. articles to profl. jours. Recipient writing award Valley Forge Freedom Found., 1967; John Hay Whitney Found. grantee, 1963-64; named 100 Most Influential African Ams. in Greater Kansas City. Mem. Religion Newswriters Assn., Kansas City Assn. Black Journalists (Life Achievement award 1998). Baptist. Office: The Kansas City Star 1729 Grand Blvd Kansas City MO 64108-1458 Office Phone: 816-234-4446. E-mail: hgray@kcstar.com.

GRAY, INA TURNER, fraternal organization administrator; b. Eagleville, Mo., July 25, 1926; d. Farris T. and Teloir (Anderson) Turner; m. Wallace G. Gray Jr., Dec. 18, 1948; children: Toni Jo, Tara Joy BS with high honors, Cen. Meth. Coll., 1948; MA, Scarritt Coll., 1952; postgrad., U. Hawaii, 1969. Tchr. Rutherford-Met. Sch. Bus., Dallas, 1948-49; dir. Christian edn. 1st Meth. Ch., Lawton, Okla., 1953-54, Winfield, Kans., 1957-58; dir. religious life Southwestern Coll., Winfield, 1958-59; dir. commn. on archives and history Kans. West Conf., Winfield, 1960-78; exec. dir. Pi Gamma Mu, Winfield, 1976-96. English tchr. JoGakuin Jr. High, Hiroshima, Japan, 1971-72, Kitakyushu U., Japan, 1997-98 Mem. editorial bd. Fire on the Prairie, 1961-69; mem. editorial and pub. coms. The Lure of Kansas, 1990 Bd. dirs. Cowley County Hist. Soc., 2004—. Named to Hall Fame, Pi Gamma Mu, 2005. Mem. Assn. Coll. Honor Socs. (del. 1986-96), Commn. Archives and History (local Ch. History award 1982—), Kans. State Assn. Parliamentarians (v.p. Walnut Valley unit 1991-92, 99-2000), Faculty Dames (pres. 1981-82). Republican. Avocations: travel, historical research, Japanese flower arranging. Home: 1701 Winfield Ave Winfield KS 67156-1919 Personal E-mail: gray@sckans.edu.

GRAY, JANET ETHEL, elementary school educator; b. Snyder, Tex., Dec. 15, 1942; d. James Lavern and Irene McClain (Brown) Cotton; m. Richard Lee Gray, June 24, 1960; children: Melinda, Eric, Heidi, Keith. BS in Edn., Abilene Christian U., 1964; degree in kindergarten-early childhood, Tex. Christian U., 1972. Tchr. Abilene Pub. Schs., Tex., 1964—67, Castleberry Ind. Sch., Fort Worth, 1967—84, Conroe Ind. Sch., Tex., 1984—2002. Tech Elem. Coord. Conroe ISD, 2002—03. Recipient Presdl. award for excellence in sci. and math. teaching NSF, 1994, Presdl. award for excellence in sci., Tex., 1994. Mem. Sci. Tchrs. Assn. Tex., Nat. Sci. Tchrs. Assn., Soc. Elem. Presdl. Awardees, Coun. for Elem. Sci. Internat., Tex. State Tchrs. Assn. (bldg. rep. 1992-95), ASCD. Office: Anderson Elem Sch 1414 E Dallas St Conroe TX 77301-2100 Business E-Mail: jgray@conroeisd.net.

GRAY, JOAN S., head of religious order; Grad., Columbia Theological Seminary, 1976. Rev. College Park Church, Smyrna Presbyterian Church, Good Shepherd Church, Hemphill Church, Columbia Presbyterian Church, Oglethorpe Presbyterian Church, Fellowship Presbyterian Church, Word of Sacrament Church; titular leader Presbyterian Church USA, 2006—. Moderator of the Permanent Judicial Commission Presbyterian Church USA, mem., GA Advisory Com. on the Constitution, Advocate for International Mission, Presbytery Council, Christian Edn. Div., mem. exec. com., mem. Calvin Center Div, mem. Task Force to Combat Racism; adjunct faculty mem. Columbia Theological Seminary, Johnson C Smith Seminary. Contbr. articles to numerous profl. jours. Mem.: Presbyterian Women (hon.). Office: Presbyterian Church USA 100 Witherspoon St Louisville KY 40202-1396 Fax: 502-569-8005.*

GRAY, JOHANNA JILL, music educator; b. Two Rivers, Wis., Apr. 30, 1956; d. George Albert and Nancy Jane Hansen; m. Viron Leo Gray, Dec. 21, 1991. BA in Instrumental Music K-12, U. Wis., Green Bay, 1979; MA in Secondary Edn., Adams State Coll., Alamosa, Colo., 1991; Kodaly cert., Silver Lake Coll., Manitowoc, Wis., 2001. Guild cert. Feldenkrais practitioner Feldenkrais Guild of N.Am., lic. tchr. Colo. Dept. Edn. Pvt. studio tchr. Rio Grande Studio, Creede, Colo., 1979—; instr. band and gen. music South Conejos Sch. Dist., Antonito, Colo., 1981—83; instr. gen. music MacKntosh Acad., Denver, 1985—86; band tchr. Sanford Schs., Colo., 1987—88; flute instr. Adams State Coll., Alamosa, Colo., 1987—2005; band tchr., instr. gen. music Lamb Elem., Creede, 2002—. Mem.: OAKE, Nat. Flute Assn., Music Educators Nat. Conf. Avocations: silk ribbon embroidery, sewing, hiking, cross country skiing, reading. Home: PO Box 242 Creede CO 81130 Office: Lamb Elem Sch Box 429 Creede CO 81130

GRAY, KARLA MARIE, state supreme court justice; b. Escanaba, Mich., May 10, 1947; BA, Western Mich. U., MA in African History; JD, Hastings Coll. of Law, San Francisco, 1976. Bar: Mont. 1976, Calif. 1977. Law clk. to Hon. W. D. Murray U.S. Dist. Ct., 1976-77; staff atty. Atlantic Richfield Co., 1977-81; pvt. practice law Butte, Mont., 1981-84; staff atty., legis. lobbyist Mont. Power Co., Butte, 1984-91; justice Mont. Supreme Ct., Helena, 1991-2000, chief justice, 2000—. Mem. Mont. Supreme Ct. Gender Fairness Task Force. Fellow Am. Bar Found., Am. Judicature Soc., Internat. Women's Forum; mem. State Bar Mont., Silver Bow County Bar Assn. (past pres.), Nat. Assn. Women Judges. Avocations: travel, reading, piano, genealogy, cross country skiing. Office: Supreme Ct Mont PO Box 203001 Helena MT 59620-3001*

GRAY, LAURA B., psychology professor, counselor; d. Harold Herman and Deborah Bowman; m. Philip Lempert, Feb. 24, 1991; 1 child, Jermey. BS, Cornell U., Ithaca, NY, 1966, MA, 1967; post grad., Phillips Inst., Encino, Calif. Lic. perm. tchr. NY State, tchr. Calif., cert. child devel. dirs. Calif., career devel. NJ. Cons., 1982—92; dir. training and devel. Age Wave Inc., Emertville, Calif., 1992—94; v.p. edn. Hosp. Coun., Pleasanton, Calif., 1992—94; v.p. career svcs. Right Mgmt. Cons., LA, 1996—99; dir. career devel. Pepperdine U., Mailbu, Calif., 1999—2001; assoc. prof., counselor Harbor Coll., Wilimington, Calif., 2001—. Bd. dirs. Nat. Employment Counseling Assn., 2002—04; presenter annual symposium Am. Coll. Personnel Assn., 2002. Adv. bd. Powerhouse Theater, Venice, Calif., 2001—04; recruitment bd. mem. Cornell U. Alumni Amb., LA, 2003—; trustee Cornell U., Ithaca, NY, 2006—. Named Outstanding Performer in Training Mgmt., Training Dirs. Forum, 1993. Mem.: Nat. Assn. Edn. of Young Children, Nat. Career Devel. Assn., Am. Counseling Assn. Avocations: ballet, photography, hiking, swimming. Office: 3015 Main St Ste 320 Santa Monica CA 90405

GRAY, LEANN MARIE, special education educator; b. Bryan, Tex., Aug. 30, 1968; d. Albert Ernest and June Catherine (Channing) Smith; m. Gregory James Gray, Dec. 28, 1991; children: Katelyn, Lauren. BS, Ga. So. U., 1991. Inter-related tchr. Jackson Road Sch., Griffin, Ga., 1991; mild intellectual disabilities tchr. Leslie J. Steele Sch., Decatur, Ga., 1991—98; presch., kindergarten tchr. Berkmar United Meth. Ch., 2001—06. Vol. Am. Cancer Soc., Griffin, 1990. Fellow Profl. Assn. Ga. Educators, Coun. for exceptional Children. Personal E-mail: llgk@bellsouth.net.

GRAY, LINDA ALYN, artist, educator; b. Sacramento, Oct. 18, 1948; d. Jack Erwin Evans and Mary Louise Conner; adopted by Feorge Fiene, 1960; m. Gary Grover Gray, June 1, 1968; children: Nathan McMillen, Thaddeus Conner. Student, Am. Internat. Acad., Europe, 1968, 69, Fla. State U., Tallahassee, 1969-71; BA, Albertus Magnus Coll., New Haven, 1986. Cert. instr. art K-12, Fla. Designer, freelance artist, owner design bus., Fla., N.J., Okla., 1968-82; owner/mgr. retail operation, Wellington, Fla., 1981-83; adminstr. non-profit orgns., 1982-97; edn. coord. Old Sch. Sq. Cultural Arts Ctr., Delray Beach, Fla., 1990-93; dir. Glade Youth Discovery Ctr., Belle Glade, Fla., 1993-95; project adminstr. L.E.A.P., Palm Beach County, Fla., 1996-97; instr. Palm Beach County Schs., 1996—. Mem. ednl. panel Norton Mus. Art, West Palm Beach, 1996-97. Executed mural Palm Beach County Pub. Libr., 1994-95, H.L. Brumbach Health Clinic Pediatrics Wing, 1996, Migrant Edn. Bldg. Exterior, 1998. Supporter Nat. Arbor Day Found., Defenders of Wildlife, Nature Conservancy, Nat. Parks and Conservation. MacArthur Found. grantee, 1995-96, others. Mem. NEA, Palm Beach County Art Tchrs. Assn., Fla. Art Tchrs. Assn., Classrm. Tchrs. Assn. Palm Beach County, Fla. Tchg. Profls.

GRAY, LISA HART, secondary school educator; b. Evansville, Ind., Mar. 8, 1962; d. Carl Levi and Bernice Hazel Hart; m. Dennis Patrick Gray, Apr. 5, 2002. BA in English, Ind. State U., 1986; BA in Journalism, U. So. Ind., 1993; MEd, Ind. Wesleyan U., 2004; EdD in Instnl. Leadership, Argosy U., 2005. Legislative asst. Ind. Ho. of Reps., Indpls., 1993—96; exec. asst. Rexam Metallising, Greenfield, Ind., 1996—98; tchr. Indpls. Pub. Schs., 1999—2001, Patrick Henry H.S., Stockbridge, Ga., 2002—. Mem.: ASCD. Avocations: reading, travel. Office Phone: 770-507-6414.

GRAY, LISA MARIE, language educator; b. Sheridan, Wyo., Jan. 31, 1963; d. Walter E and Mollie E Gray; 1 child, Zoe Madison. BA, U. of Wyo., Laramie, 1987. Cert. tchr. Wyo., 1987. English tchr. Eads H.S., Eads, Colo., 1988—91, Riverside H.S., Basin, Wyo., 1991—. Treas. Basin City Arts Ctr. and Theater, Basin, Wyo., 2005—06. Mem.: NEA (local pres. 2000—). Office: Riverside High School 919 West B St Basin WY 82410 Office Phone: 307-568-2416. Office Fax: 307-568-2415.

GRAY, LOIS MITTINO, biologist, educator; b. Detroit, July 18, 1951; d. Louis and Lina Casteller Mittino; m. James Alexander Gray, Apr. 9, 1976; children: Michael, Martyn. BS summa cum laude, Mich. State U., East Lansing, 1973; MS summa cum laude, U. So. Ind., Evansville, 1993. Ranger/naturalist Nat. Pk. Svc., Bedford, Va., 1973—74; career naturalist Ind. Divsn. State Pks., Mitchell, 1974—82; cons. naturalist Force of Nature, New Harmony, Ind., 1982—; tchr. biology New Harmony Sch., Ind., 1987—; prof. biology U. So. Ind., Evansville, 2005—. Sec. New Harmony Pks. Bd., Ind., 2002—. Recipient Creative Tchr. award, Lilly Found., 1998, Tchr. of Yr. award, Pasey County Farm Bur., 1994. Mem.: NEA (New Harmony br. sec. 2004—). Roman Catholic. Avocations: botany, birding, hiking, reading, travel. Home: 1500 Harmonie State Pk New Harmony IN 47631 Office: New Harmony Sch 1000 East St New Harmony IN 47631 Office Phone: 812-682-4401.

GRAY, LUCY, secondary school educator; d. George Richard and Jean Crawford (Gallery) Borich; m. Peter Brandon Gray, Nov. 19, 1994; children: Julia Katheryn, Henry Crawford. BA, Beloit Coll., 1989; MEd, Nat. Louis U., 2002. Tchr. Chgo. Pub. Schs., 1990—98, U. Chgo. Lab. Schs., 2000—. Disting. educator Apple Computer, Cupertino, Calif., 2005—. Local sch. coun. cmty. rep. John B. Murphy Sch. - Chgo. Pub. Schs., 2004—06. Grantee, The Rochelle Lee Fund, 1994. Mem.: Assn. for Supervision and Curriculum Devel., Internat. Soc. for Tech. in Edn. Avocations: photography, travel, digital media, tennis. Office: Univ Chicago Lab Schs 1362 E 59th St Chicago IL 60637 Office Phone: 773-702-5418. Business E-Mail: lgray@ucls.uchicago.edu.

GRAY, MARGARET EDNA, nursing educator, department chairman, dean; b. Norfolk, Va., June 11, 1931; d. William E. and Margaret E. (Smith) G. Diploma Norfolk Gen. Hosp., Sch. Nursing, 1952; BSN, Columbia U., 1956; MS, U. Md., 1966; EdD, Va. Poly. Inst. and State U., 1980. Staff nurse Norfolk Gen. Hosp., 1952-55, asst. night supr., 1953-54, instr. med.-surg. nursing, 1956-58, Riverside Hosp. Sch. Nursing, Newport News, Va., 1958-64; ednl. dir. Va. Bd. Nursing, Richmond, 1965-69; coord. health technology Va. Dept. C.C., Richmond, 1969-72; assoc. prof. nursing, dir. nursing program Va. Appalachian Tricoll., Abingdon, 1972-78; grad. rsch. asst. Va. Poly. Inst. and State U., Blacksburg, 1979; mem. adj. faculty outreach grad. program U. Va. Sch. Nursing, Charlottesville, 1977-79, asst. prof. nursing grad. program, 1980-82; chmn. dept. nursing Va. State U., Petersburg, 1982-87; prof., dean sch. nursing Ga. Southwestern Coll., Americus, 1988-96; ret., 1996. Cons. nursing programs various c.cs. in Va., 1969—; mem. adv. com. ARC Health Systems Agy., Va. and Tenn., 1977—78; mem. Rosalyn Carter Inst. tng. com. Contbr. articles on health care edn. to profl. publ. Mem. human rights com. Southside Tng. Ctr. and mem. adv. com. allied health programs John Tyler C.C., Chester, Va. Recipient Woman of Achievement award Americus/Sumter County Bus. and Profl. Women, 1989-90; pres. Americus/Sumter County BPW, 1993-94. Mem. ANA, Nat. League Nursing, Ga. League Nursing, Ga. Nurses Assn. (cabinet on continuing edn.), Ga. Southwestern Coll. Honor Soc., Sigma Theta Tau Internat. (charter mem. Mu Pi chpt., Lifetime Achievement award 1996). Presbyterian. Home: 933 Cedar Rd Apt 336 Chesapeake VA 23322

GRAY, MARILYN F. GRINWIS, elementary school educator, music educator; b. Paterson, N.J., July 3, 1927; d. John and Florence Abert Grinwis; m. Donald M. Gray. BS in Edn., Coll. NJ, 1948; MA in Music Edn., NYU, 1968; postgrad., Syracuse U., Fairfield U., Conn., William Paterson U., U. Conn., Caldwell Coll., NJ. Lic. tchr. N.Y., N.J., cert. N.J., music tchr. N.Y. Pianist: Wilmington Hilton, Lower Cape Fear Hospice, Festival of Trees, Old Wilmington Candlelight Ho. Tour, 1997—2004, Landfall Chapel, 1999—2004, N.C. Sirosis, 2005—. Pianist New Hanover Health Network, Wilmington, NC, 2005—; rep. Salvation Army, Wilmington, 2002—04; pianist Christmas Cape Fear Hosp., Wilmington, 1997—2003. Recipient Blue Ribbon award, Fed. Women's Clubs, 2005. Mem.: Delta Kappa Gamma (chmn. music), Sigma Alpha Iota. Presbyn. Avocations: baking, photography, swimming, music. Home: 1808 Mews Dr Wilmington NC 28405 Personal E-mail: mfgrgr@bellsouth.net.

GRAY, MARY JANE, retired obstetrician, gynecologist; b. Columbus, Ohio, June 13, 1924; BA, Swarthmore Coll., 1945; MD, Wash. U., 1949; DS, Columbia U., 1954. Diplomate Am. Bd. Ob-Gyn. Intern Barnes Hosp., St. Louis, 1949-50; resident in ob-gyn. Presbyn. Hosp., N.Y.C., 1950-56; fellow Columbia U., 1953—54, instr., 1956-60; asst. prof. ob-gyn. Coll. Medicine U. Vermont, 1960-63, assoc. prof., 1963-69, prof., 1969-76; adj. prof. U. N.C., 1976-85, prof., asst. dean Coll. Medicine, 1985-90, prof. emeritus ob-gyn., 1990—; ret., 1996. Mem. AMA, Am. Coll. Ob-Gyn., Soc. Gynecol. Investigation.

GRAY, MARY MARGARET, nephrology and dialysis nurse; b. Kansas City, Kans., Nov. 5, 1963; d. Darwin Douglas and Marjorie Mary (McGrath) Minnis; children: Michael, Mary, Jane, Joseph. ADN, Mo. Western State Coll., St. Joseph, Mo., 1986. RN, Mo. Dialysis nurse Heartland Health System, St. Joseph, Renal Mgmt. Inc., St. Joseph. Business E-Mail: mary.gray@davita.com.

GRAY, MARY WHEAT, statistician, lawyer; b. Hastings, Nebr., 1939; d. Neil C. and Lillie W. (Alves) Wheat; m. Alfred Gray, Aug. 20, 1964. AB summa cum laude, Hastings Coll., 1959; postgrad., J.W. Goethe U., Frankfurt, Fed. Republic Germany, 1959-60; MA, U. Kans., 1962, PhD, 1964; JD summa cum laude, Am. U., 1979; LLD (hon.), U. Nebr., 1993; LHD (hon.), Hastings Coll., 1996. Bar: D.C. 1979, U.S. Supreme Ct. 1983, U.S. Dist. Ct., D.C. 1980. Physicist Nat. Bur. Standards, Washington, summers 1959-63; asst. instr. U. Kans., Lawrence, 1963-64; instr. dept. math. U. Calif., Berkeley, 1965; asst. prof. Calif. State U., Hayward, 1965-67, assoc. prof., 1967-68; assoc. prof. dept. math., stats. and computer sci. Am. U., 1968-71, prof., 1971—, chmn. dept., 1977-79, 80-81, 83—; statis. cons. for govt. agys., univs. and pvt. firms, 1976—. Vis. prof. King's Coll., London, 2004. Author: A Radical Approach to Algebra, 1970; Calculus with Finite Mathematics for Social Sciences, 1972; contbr. numerous articles to profl. jours. Nat. treas., dir. Women's Equity Action League, from 1981, pres., from 1982; bd. dirs. treas. ACLU, Montgomery County, Md.; mem. adv. com. D.C. Dept. Employment Services, 1983—; dir. Amnesty Internat. USA, 1985—, treas., 1988-93, chair, 1993-95; mem. Commn. on Coll. Retirement, 1984-86; bd. dirs. Am.-Middle East Edn. Found., 1983—, chair, 1998--. Recipient U.S. Presdl. award for excellence in sci., engrng. and math. mentoring, 2001; Fulbright grantee, 1959-60; NSF fellow, 1963-64, NDEA fellow, 1960-63 Fellow AAAS (chmn. com. on women, com. on investments, com. on sci. freedom and responsibility, Lifetime Mentoring award 1995); mem. AAUP (regional counsel 1984—, com. on acad. freedom 1978—, dir. Legal Def. Fund 1974-78, bd. dirs. Exxon Project on Salary Discrimination 1974-76, com. on status of women 1972-78, Georgina Smith award), Am. Math. Soc. (v.p. 1976-78, coun. 1973-78), Amnesty Internat. (internat. treas. 1995-2001, chair USA 1993-95), Conf. Bd. Math. Scis. (chmn. com. on affirmative action 1977-78), Math. Assn. Am. (chmn. com. on sch. lectrs. 1973-75, vis. lectr. 1974—), Assn. for Women in Math (founding pres. 1971-74, exec. com. 1974-80, gen. counsel 1980—), D.C. Bar Assn., ABA, Am. Soc. Internat. Law, London Math. Soc., Societe de Mathematique de France, Brit. Soc. History of Math., Can. Soc. History of Math., Assn. Computing Machinery, N.Y. Acad. Scis., Am. Statis. Assn., Phi Beta Kappa, Sigma Xi, Phi Kappa Phi, Alpha Chi, Pi Mu Epsilon. Home: 6807 Connecticut Ave Chevy Chase MD 20815-4937 Office: Am U Math & Stats Dept Washington DC 20016 Office Phone: 202-885-3171. Business E-Mail: mgray@american.edu.

GRAY, NANCY ANN OLIVER, academic administrator; b. Dallas, Apr. 23, 1951; d. Howard Ross and Joan (Dawkins) Oliver; m. David Nelson Maxson, Oct. 5, 1985; children by previous marriage: Paul, Jeff, Scott. BA, Vanderbilt U., 1973; MEd, North Tex. State U., 1975; postgrad., Vanderbilt U., 1976-79; PhD (hon.), Presbyterian Coll., 2002. Cert. fund raising exec. Tchr. Highland Park High Sch., Dallas, 1973-75; chmn. drama dept. Harpeth Hall Sch., Nashville, 1975-77; assoc. dir. devel. Vanderbilt U., Nashville, 1977-78, assist. dean students, 1978-80; dir. spl. gifts U. Louisville, 1982-86; dir. major gifts Oberlin (Ohio) Coll., 1986-90; dir. capital programs The Lawrenceville (N.J.) Sch., 1990-91; v.p. devel. and univ. rels. Rider U., Lawrenceville, 1991-98; v.p. sem. rels. Princeton (N.J.) Theol. Sem., 1998-99; pres. Converse Coll., Spartanburg, SC, 1999—2004, Hollins U., Roanoke, Va., 2005—. Trustee Princeton Theol. Sem., 2000—, Spartanburg Day Sch., 2000-2002, Vanderbilt U., Nashville, 1973-77, Found. Ind. Higher Edn., 2006-; bd. dirs. Brevard Music Ctr., 1999—2005, Wye Faculty Seminar, 2000-04. Home: Hollins U PO Box 9630 Roanoke VA 24020 Office: Hollins U PO Box 9625 Roanoke VA 24020 Office Phone: 540-362-6321. Business E-Mail: ngray@hollins.edu.

GRAY, PAMELA, gifted and talented educator; b. Newark, Nov. 11, 1940; d. Irving William and Helen (Gail) G.; m. Robert Emil Kohn, Feb. 19, 1962 (div. 1978); children: Randall Evan Kohn, Andrew Robert Kohn, Cynthia Lee Kohn; m. John Goodman, Mar. 27, 1997. BA, Upsala Coll., 1970; MA in Teaching, Seton Hall U., 1972, EdS, 1980, EdD, 1986. Cert. prin., supr., tchr., N.J. Tchr. 2nd through 5th grade South Orange-Maplewood Bd. Edn., NJ, 1972-81, adminstv. and supervisory intern N.J., 1980-81, tchr. of gifted N.J., 1981; enrichment coordinator Mountainside (N.J.) Bd. Edn., 1982-85; coordinator, tchr. of gifted Livingston (N.J.) Bd. Edn., 1985-89. Mem. adminstrv. com. N.E. Olympics of Mind, N.J., 1984-85; supv. edn. program, Springfield, N.J.; creator Gifted and Talented Assn., Union County, N.J.; instr. Kean Coll. Grad. Sch.; ednl. cons. in field. Author: Happy Birthday U.S.A., 1975, America Is Having A Birthday, 1976. Bd. dirs., treas., jour. chmn. Ruth Kohn Community Service, 1972-78. Boston U. scholar, 1979-80; State Dept. Gifted Edn. grantee, 1988-89. Mem. ASCD, Kappa Delta Pi. Avocations: opera, tennis. Home: 2 Frederick Pl Chester NJ 07930-2913

GRAY, PAMELA, screenwriter, educator; b. Bklyn., Feb. 28, 1956; d. Lawrence Maurice and Arlene Gloria G.; 1 child, Andrew Lowe, Feb. 19, 1983. BA in English, SUNY, 1978; MA in Creative Writing, Boston U., 1980; MFA in Screenwriting, UCLA, 1993. Prof. San Francisco State U., 1982-86, U. Calif. Berkeley Extension, Berkeley, 1988-89; screenwriter Miramax Films, N.Y.C., 1997-99, Paramount Pictures, L.A., 1998-99, Disney Studios, L.A., 1998-99, Universal Pictures, L.A., 1998—, Bedford Falls, L.A., 1999—. Guest spkr. Writers Guild Found., L.A., 1999, NOW Ann. Conf., L.A., 1999; keynote spkr. Catskills Inst. Conf., N.Y., 1999. Screenwriter: (feature films) A Walk on the Moon, 1999, Music of the Heart, 1999, (teleplays) Star Trek: The Next Generation, 1992, Calm at Sunset, 1996, The Love Letter, 1998, Once and Again, 1999. Vol. zookeeper for Exotic Feline Breeding Compound for endangered big cats. Recipient First Place Samuel Goldwyn Writing award Samuel Goldwyn Found., 1992, Scriptwriting Internship award Acad. TV Arts and Scis., 1991; chosen One of Ten Screenwriters to Watch Variety mag., 1999. Mem. Writers Guild Am. West, Dramatists Guild. Democrat. Jewish. Avocation: rare book collecting.

GRAY, PATRICIA B., retired librarian, information specialist; b. Lumberton, N.C., Feb. 10, 1938; d. Carl Webster and Gladys (Newman) Barbee; m. James William Gray, Jr., Sept. 2, 1961 (dec. Apr. 1987); children: Susanna Gray Lund, James William III. BA magna cum laude, U. N.C., 1960, MS in Libr. Sci., 1965. Cert. libr. N.C., Va. Bookmobile libr. Sheppard Meml. Libr., Greenville, N.C., 1958, 59; libr. asst. U. Miami Libr., Coral Gables, Fla., 1960; French tutor U. N.C., Chapel Hill, 1960-62; libr. Sch. Libr. Sci., Chapel Hill, 1960-62; govt. documents libr. Pub. Libr. Charlotte (N.C.), 1962-63; ref. libr. Norfolk (Va.) Pub. Libr., 1966-77, asst. dept. head ref. and adult svcs., 1990—; dir. Barron F. Black Libr., Norfolk, 1977-88, Larchmont Libr., Norfolk, 1988-90. Libr. dir. search com. Va. Wesleyan U., Norfolk, 1967-68. Contbr. articles to profl. jours., book revs. to newspaper. Mem. Friends of the Libr., Chesapeake, Va., 1977-81; chmn. United Way Campaign, Libr. Dept., Norfolk, 1984; vol. Tidewater coun. Boy Scouts Am., 1987-93; vol. driver ARC, DAV, 2003—. Mem. ALA, AAUW (bd. dirs. 1965, 66, 80, rsch. analyst 1966-70), Southeastern Libr. Assn., Va. Libr. Assn., Va. Assn. Law Librs., Tidewater Assn. Law Librs., Phi Beta Kappa, Beta Phi Mu, Phi Alpha Theta. Methodist. Avocations: travel, translating french, bowling, swimming, gardening.

GRAY, PAULETTE STYLES, federal agency administrator, biologist; b. Chattanooga, Feb. 21, 1944; d. Paul Styles and Louise (Hill) Dennis; m. Walter Leonard, May 10, 1964; children: Walter Leonard Jr., Daniel Allen. BS in biology, Tuskegee Inst., 1966; MS in mycology, Atlanta U., 1976, PhD in cellular and devel. biology, 1978. Asst. prof., dir. electron microscopy lab. Atlanta U., 1978-79; research assoc. U. Kaiserslautern, Germany, 1979-81; instr. U. Maryland, Kaiserslautern, 1980-82; supr. clin. microbiology sect. Landstuhl Army Regional Med. Ctr., Germany, 1981-82; exec. sec. Divsn. Extramural Activities, Nat. Cancer Inst., Bethesda, Md., 1983-84, spl. review officer, 1984, chief rev. logistics br., 1988, assoc. dir. extramural applications, dep. dir., 1997—2005, acting dir., 2003—05, dir., 2005—. Tchr. Sun. Sch. Alfred St. Bapt. Ch., Alexandria, Va., 1982-89, supt., 1988-89; judge sci. and engrng. fair Fairfax County pub. schs., 1984-89; speaker Med. Coll. Ga., Augusta, 1985. Recipient Lederle Labs. award, 1977, H.E. Finley Meml. award Atlanta U., 1978, Outstanding Performance award Nat. Cancer Inst., 1983; Josiah Macy Jr. fellow, 1979, Hon. Fulbright Hays fellow, 1979-81, Spl. Act. of Achievement award, 1992, 93, EEO Spl. Recognition award, 1991, NIH Dir.'s award, 1990, Cert. Recognition and Spl. Achievement award, HHS, 1988-93. Mem. Am. Soc. Zoology, Nat. Inst. Sci., Atlanta U. Ctr. Honor Soc. (biology), Am. Assn. Cancer Rsch., Inc., Am. Assn. Cell Biology, Internat. Platform Assn., Women in Cancer Rsch., Assn. Women in Govt., Nat. Assn. Exec. Women. Avocations: cooking, reading, jogging, writing. Office: Nat Cancer Inst Divsn Extramural Activities 6116 Executive Blvd Rockville MD 20852 Office Phone: 301-496-5147. E-mail: pg36f@nih.gov.*

GRAY, PHYLLIS ANNE, librarian; b. Boston, Jan. 2, 1926; d. George Joseph and Eleanor (Morrison) G. PhB, Barry Coll., 1947, MBA, 1979; MS in LS, Cath. U. Am., 1950. Librarian U.S. Air Force Base, Miami, Fla., 1952-53; asst. librarian Brockway Meml. Library, Miami Shores, Fla., 1953-55; head librarian North Miami Pub. Library, 1955-59; supervising librarian Santa Clara County Library, San Jose, Calif., 1959-61; library dir. City of Commerce (Calif.) Pub. Library, 1961-68; adminstrv. librarian Miami Dade Pub. Library, 1969-76; library dir. Miami Beach (Fla.) Pub. Library, 1978-86; dir. Surf-Bal Bay Pub. Library, Surfside, Fla., 1987-91. Democrat. Roman Catholic. Councilwoman Bal Harbour Village, 1979-83; treas. Women in Govt. Service, 1981-86, pres., 1988-89. Mem. ALA, Barry U. Alumni Assn., Fla. Pub. Library Assn. Clubs: Pilot (rec. sec. 1981-82, pres. 1982-83). Democrat. Roman Catholic. Home: 618 Oakmont Ave Unit 2307 Las Vegas NV 89109-0205

GRAY, SHEILA HAFTER, psychiatrist, researcher; b. N.Y.C., Oct. 19, 1930; MD, Harvard U., 1958. cert. Washington Psychoanalytic Inst., 1969. Intern St. Elizabeths Hosp., Washington, 1958-59; resident McLean Hosp., Belmont, Mass., 1959-61; clin. and rsch. fellow Mass. Gen. Hosp., Boston, 1961-62; staff psychiatrist Chestnut Lodge, Inc., Rockville, Md., 1962-64; practice medicine, specializing in psychiatry and psychoanalysis Washington, 1964—; clin. asst. prof. psychiatry U. Md. Sch. Medicine, Balt., 1968-75, clin. assoc. prof., 1975-83, clin. prof., 1983-96; instr. Washington Psychoanalytic Inst., 1971-75, tchg. analyst, 1975-96, Balt.-Washington Inst. for Psychoanalysis, 1996—; clin. prof. psychiatry Uniformed Svcs. U. Health Scis., 1997-99, adj. prof. psychiatry, 1999—. Staff U. Md. Hosp., Balt., 1970-96; physician mem. Commn. on Mental Health, Superior Ct. of D.C., 1972-98; bd. govs. Nat. Capital Reciprocal Ins. Co., 1981-98; treas. NCRIC Physicians Orgn., 1994-97; cons. Walter Reed Army Med. Ctr., Washington, 1983—. Active Mayor's Adv. Com. on Mental Health Svcs. Reorgn., Washington, 1984; adv. panel Mayor's Environ. Design Awards Program, 1988-89; exec. com. D.C. Fedn. Civic Assns., 1984—, asst. rec. sec., 1985, rec. sec., 1986-88, 2d v.p., 1989-90, pres., 1991-92, del.-at-large, 1993—; v.p. programs Women's Equity Action League Met. D.C., 1986; commr. D.C. Adv. Neighborhood Commn., 1986-88; mem. Met. Washington Coun. of Govt.'s Partnership for Regional Excellence, 1992; trustee Accreditation Coun. for Psychoanalytic Edn., Inc., 2002—, sec., 2004—. Fellow: Am. Psychiat. Assn. (chair com. quality assurance and improvement, Coun. on Econ. Affairs, 1996—97, disting. life fellow); mem.: Washington Psychoanalytic Soc. (chmn. bd. dirs. psychoanalytic clinic and councillor ex officio 1987—90), Med. Soc. D.C. (exec. bd. 1982, ho. dels. 1992—97), Washington Psychiatric Soc. (councillor 1981—83), Am. Acad. Psychoanalysis (trustee 1996—99, pres.-elect 1999—2000, pres. 2000—01, editl. bd. jour. 2002—), Am. Psychoanalytic Assn. (parliamentarian 2006—, diplomate Bd. Profl. Stds.), Palisades Citizens Assn. (bd. dirs. 1980—, treas. 1983—84, pres. 1984—86). Office: PO Box 40612 Palisades Sta Washington DC 20016 Office Phone: 202-338-1955.

GRAY, TONJA LOUISE, literature and language educator; b. Moultrie, Ga., May 2, 1970; d. Richard Monroe and Reba Marilyn Seagroves; m. Paul Victor Gray, Nov. 13, 1969; children: Kristen Marie, Shannon Victoria. AA, Abraham Baldwin U., Tifton, Ga., 1991; BA, U. Ga., Athens, 1993. Tchr. Athens Tutorial Ctr., 1991—93, Berkshire Sch., Homestead, Fla., 1993—95, Colonial Christian Sch., Homestead, 2000—. Head English dept. Colonial Christian Sch., Homestead, 2004—06, coach varsity cheerleading, 2002—05, coach varsity basketball, 2005—06. Editor: (book) Not Quite Aesop, 2004, Our Favorite Things, 2005. Named Tchr. of Yr., Colonial Christian Sch., 2004. Mem.: Xi Kappa Kappa (v.p. 2000). Avocation: reading. Home: 20241 SW 317th St Homestead FL 33030 Office: Colonial Christian Sch 17105 SW 296th St Homestead FL 33030

GRAY, VIRGINIA HICKMAN, political science professor; b. Camden, Ark., June 10, 1945; d. George Leonard and Ethel Massengale (Bell) Hickman; 1 child, Brian Charles. BA with honors, Hendrix Coll., 1967; MA, Washington U., St. Louis, 1969, PhD, 1972. Asst. prof. polit. sci. U. Ky., Lexington, 1971-73; from asst. prof. to assoc. prof. U. Minn., Mpls., 1973-83, prof., 1983-2000, chairperson dept. polit. sci., 1985-88; Winston Disting. prof. polit. sci. U. N.C., Chapel Hill, 2001—. Guest scholar Brookings Inst., Washington, 1977-78; vis. prof. U. Oslo, 1985, Nankai U., 1988, U. B.C., 1992, U. N.C., 1993-94; NSF vis. prof. for women, 1993-94. Co-author: The Organizational Politics of Criminal Justice, 1980, Feminism and the New Right, 1983, Politics in the American States, 1983, 8th edit., 2004, American States and Cities, 1991, 2d edit., 1997, The Population Ecology of Interest Representation, 1996, Minnesota Politics and Government, 1999. Bd. dirs. Health Ptnrs. Inc., 1992-2001, chair, 1999-2001. Fellow Woodrow Wilson Found., 1970, NDEA, 1969-70; grantee Swedish Bicentennial Found., 1985; recipient rsch. assistantship NSF, 1968-69, rsch. grant NSF, 1997-2001; scholar in residence Rockefeller Ctr., Bellagio, Italy; Investigator award Robert Wood Johnson Found., 2003-05; named Disting. Alumnus Hendrix Coll., 2005. Mem. Am. Polit. Sci. Assn. (coun. 1990-92), Midwest Polit. Sci. Assn. (coun. 1984-86, v.p. 1997-99, pres. 2003-2004), Policy Studies Orgn. (coun. 1977-79), So. Polit. Sci. Assn., Western Polit. Sci. Assn. Democrat. Unitarian Universalist. Home: 2 Heather Ct Chapel Hill NC 27517 Office: U NC Dept Polit Sci CB 3265 Hamilton Hall Chapel Hill NC 27599-3265 Office Phone: 919-843-5602. E-mail: vagray@email.unc.edu.

GRAYBEAL, TRACY LYNN, secondary school educator; b. Kingsport, Tenn., Aug. 3, 1969; d. Oscar and Priscilla Irvin; m. Christopher Graybeal, Jan. 26, 2002. BA, King Coll., Bristol, Tenn., 1991. Cert. tchr. Tenn., 1992. Student asst. provider Frontier Health, Kingsport, 1992—97; English tchr. Sullivan Ctrl. H.S., Blountville, Tenn., 1997—. Varsity volleyball coach Sullivan Ctrl. H.S., Blountville, 1997—. Active Poplar Grove Primitive Bapt. Ch., Kingsport, 1977. Named Volleyball Coach of Yr., NE Tenn. Sports Writers, 2001, 2004; recipient Dist. Coach of Yr., Tenn. Athletic Coaches' Assn., 2002. Mem.: NEA (assoc.), Sullivan County Edn. Assn. (assoc.), Tenn. Edn. Assn. (assoc.). Baptist. Avocations: volleyball, reading. Home: 929 Old Elizabethton Hwy Bluff City TN 37618 Office: Sullivan Central High School 131 Shipley Ferry Rd Blountville TN 37617 Office Phone: 423-354-1200. Personal E-mail: ladycougarsvbcoach@yahoo.com.

GRAYBIEL, ANN M., medical educator; AB magna cum laude, Harvard U., 1964; PhD, MIT, 1971. Woodrow Wilson fellow Tufts U., New Haven, 1965—66; Walter A. Rosenblith prof. neuroanatomy dept. brain and cognitive sci. MIT, Cambridge, Mass. Chair sect. neurobiology NAS; bd. neurosci. and behavioral health Inst. of Medicine; mem. nat. adv. mental health coun. NIMH. Recipient Williams and Wilkins award, Charles Judson Herrick award, McKnight award. Mem.: Am. Acad. Arts and Sci., Inst. of Medicine of NAS, Royal Acad. Medicine (Spain) (hon.). Achievements include research in on cortico basal ganglia circuits and the role of these circuits in learning and the adaptive control of complex behaviors; on the structure of the brain has advanced the understanding of brain regions involved in neurological and neuropsychiatric disorders. Office: MIT Dept Brain/Cognitive Sci 45 Carleton St Bldg E25-618B Cambridge MA 02139-4307

GRAY-BUSSARD, DOLLY H., energy company executive; b. Wilmington, Del., July 29, 1943; d. Henry Odell and Dorothy (Knotts) Gray; m. Robert William Bussard, Mar. 17, 1981. BA in History and English Lit., U. Calif., San Diego, 1984; MA in History, Georgetown U., 1990. Cert. Orgn. Human Devel., San Diego, 1977-78; owner, prin. Hello Dolly, La Jolla, Calif., 1978-80; ptnr. Linda Chester Lit. Agy., La Jolla, 1978-80; owner, pres. Unicorn Literary Agy., La Jolla, 1980-85; pres., chmn. bd. Energy/Matter Conversion Corp., San Diego and Santa Fe, 1988—. Vis. lectr. writers' confs. U. Calif., San Diego, 1979-81. Co-author: The Best of San Diego, 1981. Mem. adv. bd. Women's Voices; mem. majority coun. Emily's List; mem. nat. coun. Aspen Santa Fe Ballet. Mem. NAFE, Am. Hist. Assn., The 1782 Soc.

Wash. Coll., Phi Alpha Theta. Episcopalian. Avocations: book collecting, skiing, mountain climbing. Office: EMC2 2658 Del Mar Heights Rd Ste 360 Del Mar CA 92014-3100 Business E-Mail: emc2qed@comcast.net.

GRAYER, ELIZABETH L., lawyer; b. Boston, June 19, 1964; BA magna cum laude, Amherst Coll., 1986; JD cum laude, Harvard Univ., 1989. Bar: NY 1990. Law clk., Hon. Miriam Goldman Cedarbaum US Dist. Ct., So. Dist. NY; assoc. Cravath Swaine & Moore LLPq, NYC, 1990—97, ptnr., litig., 1997—. Mem.: ABA, Assn. of Bar of City of NY, NY State Bar Assn., Phi Beta Kappa. Office: Cravath Swaine & Moore LLP Worldwide Plz 825 Eighth Ave New York NY 10019-7475 Office Phone: 212-474-1604. Office Fax: 212-474-3700. Business E-Mail: egrayer@cravath.com.

GRAY-LITTLE, BERNADETTE, psychologist, educator; b. Washington, N.C., Oct. 21, 1944; d. James and Rosalie (Lanier) Gray; m. Shade Keys Little, Nov. 21, 1971; children: Maura, Mark. Asst. prof. psychology U. N.C., Chapel Hill, 1971-76, assoc. prof., 1976-82, prof., 1982—, chair dept., 1993-98, assoc. dean, 1999—. NIMH fellow, 1967-68, Fulbright fellow, 1970-71, NRC fellow, 1982-83. Fellow Am. Psychol. Assn.; mem. Phi Beta Kappa. Office: U NC Psychology Dept Cb # 3270 Chapel Hill NC 27599-0001

GRAY MCCRAY, ROSALIND, assistant principal; b. Fort Lauderdale, Fla., Mar. 26, 1965; d. Samuel Gray and Willie Austin; m. Charles McCray, May 5, 2004; children: Selena Gray, Elizabeth Gray, Bethany Gray. BA, City Coll., N.Y.C., 1988; MEd, Lynn U., Boca Raton, Fla., 2005; student, Nova Southeastern U., Ft. Lauderdale, Fla. Speech/lang. pathologist Westward Elem., West Palm Beach, Fla., 1995—99; 1st grade tchr. Pilgrim Christian Acad., Bklyn., 2000; 4th grade tchr. Our Lady of Sorrows, N.Y.C., 2000—01; HS ESE tchr. Roosevelt Full Svc. Ctr., West Palm Beach, 2001—04; asst. prin. Palm Beach Lakes HS, West Palm Beach, 2004—. Avocation: singing.

GRAY-NIX, ELIZABETH WHITWELL, occupational therapist; b. Milton, Mass., Apr. 9, 1956; d. Roland and Susan (Brooks) Gray; m. Ronald Harding Nix; 1 child, Roger Harrison Nix. BS, Syracuse U., N.Y., 1978. Registered occupl. therapist. From occupl. therapist to clin. supr. Walter E. Fernald State Sch., Waltham, Mass., 1978-97; dir. occupl. therapy The Fernald Ctr., 1997—. Trustee Mass. Jaycees Charitable Trust, Mansfield, 1983-91; dir.-at-large South End Hist. Soc., Boston, 1983-85, fundraising dir., 1985-87; alumni rep. Beaver country Day Sch., Brookline, 1974-99, alumni sec., 1988-94. Recipient Baystater award #060, Mass. Jaycees, 1984, Armbruster Keyman award, 1981, Merit award, Maddak, Inc., 1991, 96, Jaycee Internat. Senatorship award, 1992, Mass. State Employee Svc. award, 1998, Paul Duhamel Svc. award, 2000. Mem. Mass. Occupl. Therapists Assn., State Employed Occupl. Therapists Assn. (union rep.), Am. Occupl. Therapists Assn., World Fedn. Occupl. Therapists, Mass. Nurses Assn.(occupl. therapy rep. 1981—, bd. dirs. 2002, bd. dirs. labor seat 2003—), Jaycees Internat. (Mass. sec., pres. Riverside chpt. 1983, mem. coun. Newton chpt. 1979-82, state sec. 1994-95), Boston Ctr. for Arts (mem. coun. 1979-84). Home: 90 Pelham Island Rd Sudbury MA 01776-3132 Office: The Fernald Ctr 200 Trapelo Rd Ste 1 Waltham MA 02452-6302

GRAYSON-JORDAN, CARRIE See JORDAN, CARRIE

GRAZIANI, LINDA ANN, secondary school educator; b. Erie, Pa., Aug. 16, 1951; d. Edward and Christine (Karsznia) Grzelak; m. Richard Martin Graziani, Aug. 4, 1973; 1 child, Kristen Lynn. BS, Pa. State U., 1973; MBA, Gannon U., 1978. Asst. twsp. sec. Lawrence Park Twsp., Erie, Pa., 1968-73; bus. edn. tchr. Millcreek Sch. Dist., Erie, 1973-74, Fairview (Pa.) Sch. Dist., 1983—, Girard (Pa.) Sch. Dist., 1976; adult edn. instr. Erie (Pa.) County Tech. Sch., 1978-85. Active Bus. Adv. Coun., Millcreek, Pa., 1994-2002. Bd. dirs. Lake Erie Jr. Women's Club, Erie, 1977-83, St. Stephen's Preschool, Fairview, 1982-83; mem. adv. com. Erie Bus. Adventure, 2002—; eucharistic min. Holy Cross Ch., Fairview, 1982—, steering com., 2002-03. Mem.: Inst. Mgmt. Accts., Erie County Bus. Edn. Assn., Nat. Bus. Edn. Assn., Pa. State Alumni Assn., Beginners Luck Investment Club, Phi Chi Theta. Democrat. Roman Catholic. Avocations: aerobics, tennis, golf, cross country skiing, reading, cooking. Home: 680 Hawthorne Trce Fairview PA 16415-1723 Office: Fairview HS 7460 Mccray Rd Fairview PA 16415-2401 Office Phone: 814-474-2600.

GRAZIANO, CATHERINE ELIZABETH, state legislator, retired nursing educator; b. Providence, Dec. 2, 1931; d. William J. and Catherine E. (Keegan) Hawkins; m. Louis W. Graziano, Oct. 9, 1954; children: Mary Lou, William F., Catherine E., Paul, Carol. BS, Salve Regina Coll., Newport, R.I., 1953, MS, 1984, Boston Coll., 1965; PhD, Pacific Western U., 1988. Instr. nursing Salve Regina U., 1953-66, asst. prof., 1966-74, assoc. prof., 1974-82, prof., 1982-97, chair dept. nursing, 1974-93, ret., 1997; staff-charge nurse St. Joseph's Hosp., Providence, 1953-93, part-time faculty, 1960, 65; mem. R.I. Senate, Dist. 5, Providence, 1992—2002. Mem. R.I. Bd. Nurse Registration and Edn., 1970-79, pres., 1977-79; charter mem., sec. R.I. Health, Sci. and Edn. Council, 1972-78; adj. asst. prof. Coll. Nursing U. R.I., 1986-2000; mem. R.I. Senate, Providence, 1992-2002, chairperson health, edn. and welfare com., 2001-02. Mem. adv. coun. John E. Fogarty Ctr./ARC, Fruit Hill Day Care Elderly Ctr., Ret. Sr. Vol. Program; mem. R.I. Commn. on Women, 1993—; active local and nat. senatorial campaigns. Named Outstanding RI Pro-Life Legislator, 2001; recipient Regina medal, Salve Regina U., 1997, Bishop's award, 2001. Mem. ANA, AARP (legis. chair, exec. coun., nat. legis. coun. 2004, mem. health and long term care com. 2004), R.I. Nurses Assn. (pres. 1969-71, 73-75), R.I. State Nurses Assn. (treas. 2004—), Women Educators (charter), Nursing Leadership Coun. R.I. (charter, chair 1981-82, sec. 1982—), Nat. League Nursing (accreditation site visitor 1990-96), R.I. Cancer Coun., R.I. Health Policy Coun., Shape Health Care Study, Silver Haired Legislature, Ret. Sr. Vols. (co-chair adv. coun.), Sigma Theta Tau. Roman Catholic. Home: 42 Rowley St Providence RI 02909-5521 Personal E-mail: sengraz@yahoo.com.

GRAZIANO, MARGARET A., chaplain, recreational therapist, educational consultant, volunteer; b. Portland, Ore., Nov. 25, 1916; d. Agostino Graziano and Madeline Rinella; children: Vincent, Margaret, Salvatore, Anne, Agatha, Prudence, Rosemary, Joseph. BA, Holy Names Coll., 1946; BM, Maryhurst Coll., 1951; MEd, U. Portland, 1961. Cert. correctional chaplain Am. Correctional Cath. Chaplains Assn., Am. Correctional Chaplains Assn., 2000, alcohol counselor Oreg., in adminstrn. and supervision U. Portland. Tchr. Sister of the Holy Names, Ore., 1937—75; music tchr. Montessori, Eugene, Oreg., 1974—76; young musicians artist camp Maryhurst Coll., 1972—73; specialized counselor Triple H. Ranch, Jasper, Oreg., 1972—74; chem. dependancy counselor Treatment Ctr. Youth, Eugene, Oreg., 1975—79; asst. vol. coord. Lane County Adult Corrections, Eugene, Oreg., 1976—2006, chaplain, 1995—2006; recreational therapist Johnson Unit, 2004—05. Chem. dependency facilitator Internal Treatment Program, Eugene, Oreg., 1997—2006; pres. Internat. Correctional Arts Network, 2000—06. Co-editor (with Susan Clayton): Best in the Business-Corrections Today, 1999. Vol. Ptnrs. for youth, 2000—06, St. Vincent de Paul Soc. Lane County, 2006; bd. dirs. Cath. Worker John Bosce Ho., 2000—06; rep. Lane County Human Potential Workshop, Eugene, Oreg., 1970; chmn. Governors Task force on Vol., 1965; cmty. svc. Inner City Burnside Area, Portland, Oreg., 1972; mem. planning com. Seattle Diocese against Death Penalty, 1968. Named one of four honorees, Newman Ctr./ U. Ore., 2005; recipient Alumni award, St. Mary's Acad., 2005, E.R. Cass award, ACA, 2003, Murname Soc. Justice award, Cath. Cmty. Svc., 2004. Mem.: Willamette Bus. Leaders, Sisters of the Holy Names (superior 1958), Sons of Italy (trustee/chaplain 1998—2006, bd. dirs. 2006). Roman Catholic. Avocations: travel, art, music, drama, films. Home: 100 E 11th Ave Apt 208 Eugene OR 97401 Office: Lane County Adult Corrections 101 W 5th Ave Eugene OR 97401 Office Phone: 541-682-2174.

GRAZIOLI, MARGARET, librarian; b. Weehawken, N.J., Aug. 28, 1917; d. Russell A. and Mary (Wilson) Keenan; B.A., Rutgers U. 1938; m. Roger Grazioli, Aug. 28, 1937; children— Kathleen (Mrs. Paul Freitag), Roger. Children's librarian Weehawken Public Library, 1956-61, dir., 1966—, also trustee; dir. Secaucus (N.J.) Pub. Library, 1961. A founder Sr. Citizens Secaucus, 1962, now gold card holder; v.p. publicity Secaucus Child Guidance; chmn. Secaucus Girl Scout drive, 1968-69, Weehawken ARC, 1956-57; 8th dist. chmn. Garden's Conservation, Women's Clubs, 1969-72; v.p. Secaucus Child Guidance, 1969-71; chmn. UN Observance for Secaucus, 1967—; sec. Secaucus Citizens Against Narcotics, 1969-71; Secaucus rep. on drugs Mayor's Council Hudson County, 1971-72; mem. Secaucus Bd. Edn. 1975—, v.p., 1978—; Bicentennial chmn. Town of Secaucus. Named Woman of Achievement for outstanding library work Jersey Jour., 1967; recipient Disting. Service award Town of Secaucus, 1978. Mem. Am., N.J., Hudson County (pres. 1968-72) library assns., Woodrow Wilson P.T.A. Weehawken (pres. 1957-61), Weehawken Hist. Soc. (charter), Secaucus Bus. and Profl. Women, Deborah. Clubs: Elks; Weehawken Garden (chmn. flower show 1966, 70, pres. 1967-69); Secaucus Women's (garden chmn. 1969-70). Home: 4 Millridge Rd Secaucus NJ 07094-4304

GREALY, MARY R., medical association administrator; b. Ft. Lauderdale, Fla. B, Mich. State U.; JD, Duquesne U. Speech and hearing pathologist; COO & exec. counsel Fedn. Am. Hospitals; sr. Washington counsel Am. Hosp. Assn., 1996—99; pres. Healthcare Leadership Coun., Washington, 1999—. Office: Healthcare Leadership Coun 1001 Pennsylvania Ave NW Ste 550 S Washington DC 20004 Business E-Mail: mgrealy@hlc.org.*

GREANEY, JENNIFER ELLEN, lawyer; b. Holyoke, Mass., May 24, 1970; BA, Coll. Holy Cross, 1992; JD magna cum laude, Boston U. Sch. Law, 1999. Bar: Mass. 1999. Reporter Worcester, Massachusetts Telegram & Gazette, 1993—96; assoc. Goulston & Storrs, PC, Boston, 1999—2001, Sally & Fitch LLP, Boston, 2001—. Office: Sally & Fitch LLP One Beacon Street Boston MA 02108 Office Phone: 617-542-5542. Office Fax: 617-542-1542. E-mail: jeg@sally-fitch.com.*

GREASER, CONSTANCE UDEAN, retired automotive executive; b. Jan. 18, 1938; d. Lloyd Edward and Udean Greaser. BA, San Diego State Coll., 1959; postgrad., U. Copenhagen Grad. Sch. Fgn., 1963, Georgetown U. Sch. Fgn. Svc., 1967; MA, U. So. Calif., 1968; exec. MBA, UCLA, 1981. Advt., publicity mgr. Crofton Co., San Diego, 1959-62; supr. Mercury Publs., Fullerton, Calif., 1962-64; supr. engring. support svcs. divsn. Arcata Data Mgmt., Hawthorne, Calif., 1964-67; mgr. computerized typesetting dept. Continental Graphics, LA, 1967-70; v.p., editl. dir. Sage Publs., Inc., Beverly Hills, Calif., 1970-74; head publs. RAND Corp., Santa Monica, Calif., 1974-90; mgr. svc. comms. Am. Honda Motors Co., Torrance, Calif., 1990—2002; ret., 2002. Co-author: Quick Writer-Build Your Own Word Procesing Users Guide, 1983, Quick Writer-Word Processing Center Operations Manual, 1984; editor: Urban Research News, 1971-74; mng. editor: Comparative Polit. Studies, 1971-74; contbr. articles to profl. jours. Nat. com. Million Minutes of Peace Appeal, 1986, Nat. Info. Stds. Orgn., 1987-93, Global Cooperation for Better World, 1988. Recipient Berber award Graphic Arts Tech. Found., 1989. Mem.: Soc. Tech. Comm., Women in Comm., Soc. for Scholarly Pubs. (nat. bd. dirs.), Graphic Comm. Assn. (bd. dirs. 1994—99), Women in Bus. (pres. 1977—78), So. Calif. Women for Understanding (chair LA/Valley chpt. 2004—06).

GREAUX, CHERYL PREJEAN, federal agency administrator; b. Houston, July 30, 1949; m. Robert Bruce Greaux. BA, Tex. So. U., 1967; MA, U. Tex., 1973. Mgr. compliance programs Dept. Labor, N.Y.C., 1973-80; corp. human resources mgr. Allied Signal Inc., Morristown, NJ, 1980-85; account exec., sourcing specialist Dean Witter Reynolds, N.Y.C., 1986-88; dir. civil rights staff USDA Rural Devel., Washington, 1994—. Cons. Seagrams, N.Y.C., 1984, Gen. Foods, White Plains, NY, 1985. Author: Struggling Within or Success from Within?, 1973. Lectr. Nat. Urban League, 1980—; cons. Nat. Urban Affairs Coun., NY, 1981—86; bd. dirs. Ednl. Opportunity Fund, NJ, 1985—87. Mem.: Edges Group, Delta Sigma Theta. Office: Dept Agr 14th And Independence SW Washington DC 20250-0001 Office Phone: 202-692-0204. Business E-Mail: cheryl.greaux@usda.gov.

GREAVER, JOANNE HUTCHINS, mathematics educator, writer; b. Louisville, Aug. 9, 1939; d. Alphonso Victor and Mary Louise (Sage) Hutchins; 1 child, Mary Elizabeth. BS in Chemistry, U. Louisville, 1961, MEd, 1971; MAT in Math., Purdue U., 1973. Cert. tchr. Pres. Math Mentors Inc., 1962—. Part-time faculty Bellarmine Coll., Louisville, 1982-2002, U. Louisville, 1985—; project reviewer NSF, 1983—; advisor Council on Higher Edn., Frankfort, Ky., 1983-86; active regional and nat. summit on assessment in math., 1991, state task force on math., assessment adv. com., Nat. Assessment Ednl. Progress standards com.; charter mem. Commonwealth Tchrs. Inst., 1984—; mem. Nat. Forum for Excellence in Edn., Indpls., 1983; metric edn. leader Fed. Metric Project, Louisville, 1979-82; mem. Ky. Ednl. Reform Task Force, Assessment Com., Nat. Framework, Nat. Assessment Ednl. Progress Rev. Com.; lectr. in field. Author: (workbook) Down Algebra Alley, 1984; co-author curriculum guides. Named Outstanding Citizen, SAR, 1984; named to Hon. Order Ky. Cols.; recipient Presdl. award for excellence in math. tchg., 1983; grantee, NSF, 1983, Louisville Cmty. Found., 1984—86. Mem. Greater Louisville Coun. Tchrs. of Math. (pres. 1977-78, 94-95, Outstanding Educator award 1987), Nat. Coun. Tchrs. of Math. (reviewer 1981—), Ky. Coun. Tchrs. of Math. (pres. 1990-91, Jefferson County Tchr. of Yr. award 1985), Math. Assn. Am., Phi Delta Kappa Internat., Kappa Delta Pi, Delta Kappa Gamma, Zeta Tau Alpha. Republican. Presbyterian. Avocations: tropical fish, gardening, handicrafts, travel. Home: 11513 Tazwell Dr Louisville KY 40241 E-mail: jogreaver@aol.com.

GREBNER, BERNICE PRILL, author, astrological counselor; b. Peoria, Ill. d. John Elmer and Emma (Duhs) Prill; m. Arthur Conrad Grebner (div. 1974); children: David Arthur, Marjorie Welsch. Astrological counsellor. Pres. Grebner Books Pub. Author: Lunar Nodes, 1980, The Decannates, 1980, Everything Has a Phase, 1982, Mercury, The Open Door I, 1988, Mercury, The Open Door II, 1990, Day of Your Birth, 1990, Bee's Flight, 1991, ABCs of Astrology and Astronomy, 1993; author of poetry. Chmn. Woodford County (Ill.) Citizens for John Kennedy. Mem. Am. Fedn. Astrologers (accredited profl.). Avocation: music: composing and performing for audiences. Home and Office: 5137 N Montclair Ave Peoria IL 61616-5221

GRECO, JANICE TERESA, psychology educator; b. N.Y.C., May 14, 1948; d. Joseph Ralph and Harriett May (McArdle) G.; m. Forlano, July 29, 1969 (div. Feb. 1993); children: Christopher, Jason, Jennifer. BS, MEd, U. Houston, 1975; PhD, U. Tex., 1992. Ins. clk. John Hancock Life Ins. Co., West Islip, N.Y., 1965-69; instr. San Jacinto Jr. Coll., Houston, 1976-77; with assessment & referral divsn. Employee Assistance Program, U. Tex., Houston, 1987-88; instr. psychology Houston C.C., 1977—, head behavioral stats.; adj. prof. HFH SCh. Social Work and Coll Pharmacy. Guest lectr. in stats. and rsch. design U. Houston. Vol. Huppotherapy Group, Galveston, Tex., 1990-91, fellowshp., Automated Lectr., Instrl. Computing, 1998, web access to statistics course, 1998. Fellow Instructional Computing, 1998, Coll. Computer Program. Mem. ACA, Tex. Assn. Counseling and Devel., Tex. Jr. Coll. Tchr. Assn., Stats. for Behavioral Scis. (rsch. com.). Avocations: horse-back riding, travel, reading, billiards, lionel collector. Home: 5322 Dana Leigh Dr Houston TX 77066-1604 Office Phone: 713-718-5537.

GRECO, MARY CEBULSKI, elementary school educator; b. Gainesville, Ga., Sept. 16, 1952; d. Henry Joseph and Angela Marie (Beltran) Cebulski; m. Joel Randy Blake, Nov. 1971 (div. Feb. 1975); 1 child, Jason; m. Steve Frank Greco, June 6, 1980. Student, DeKalb Community Coll., Ga. STate U., 1987. Cert. tchr., Ga. Day care worker Kiddie Kapers, Conyers, Ga.; tchr. aide J.H. House Elem. Sch., Conyers; youth worker UGA Cooperative Extension Service, Conyers; tchr. Flat Shoals Elem. Sch., Conyers, 1987-90, Hightower Trail Elem. Sch., Conyers, Ga., 1990—. Mem. long range planning curriculum com. and sci. com. Rockdale County Bd. Edn.; v.p. RCAE/GAE. Named Tchr. of Yr., Hightower Trail Elem. Sch., 1990, Pine St. Elem. Sch., 1996, 2006. Mem. NEA (Student Tchr. of Yr. S.E. region 1987), Internat. Reading Assn., Ga. Edn. Assn., Ga. Presch. Assn. (presenter at S.E. region conf.), Sci. Tchrs. Assn. Rockdale, Norris Lake Homeowners Assn. (sec.). Roman Catholic. Avocations: reading, writing, camping, swimming, river rafting. Home: 2371 Fairhaven Cv NE Conyers GA 30012-2664

GREEN, AIMEE MELISSA, physical education educator; b. Mission Viejo, Calif., June 29, 1976; d. Stephen Dallas and Catherine McCreery Green. BA in Theatre and Dance, Chapman U., Orange, Calif., 1998, single subject credential in phys. edn., 2001; MS in Phys. Edn., Azusa (Calif.) Pacific U., 2006. Phys. edn. tchr. Murrieta Valley HS, Calif., 2001—. Office Phone: 951-696-1408 ext 5270. E-mail: amgreen@mvusd.org.

GREEN, ANDREA M., college administrator; b. Newark, June 12, 1939; d. Robert and Pearl (Tauder) Freund; m. Alan Charles Green, Dec. 20, 1958 (div. June 1981); children: Keith, Adam BA English, Theater, U. N.Mex., 1962; MA English, Seton Hall U., 1972, EdD Coll. Adminstrn., 1986. Lic. tchr. English, theater, speech, psychology; lic. coll. adminstr. Faculty Union Coll., Cranford, NJ, 1972—85, chmn. humanities divsn., 1986—. Cons. Bellcore, Piscataway, N.J., 1991, ETS, Princeton, N.J., 1989, Johnson & Johnson, New Brunswick, N.J., 1990, AT&T, Murray Hill, N.J., 1989 Playwright: (one-act play) With No Apologies, 1993, For Tiger Lilies Out of Season, 1995 (Critics Choice award), (3-act play) Joel and Julia, Like Bees to Honey, 2001 Named Woman of Excellence, Student Govt. Assn., Union Coll., 1996; recipient Excellence in Higher Edn. award Union County Commn. on Status of Women, 1997 Mem. AAUP, Am. Coun. Educators Nat. Identification Program, Phi Kappa Phi, Pi Lambda Theta

GREEN, ANGELA MARIE, biology educator; b. Plainfield, N.J., Apr. 14, 1976; d. William A. and Phyllis E. Gallagher; m. Cameron J. Green. BS in Biology, Coll. St. Elizabeth, Morristown, N.J., 1998. Lic. biology secondary edn N.J. Bd. Edn., 1999. Tchr. South Plainfield H.S., NJ, 1998—. Advisor SADD, South Plainfield, 2000. Office: South Plainfield High Sch 200 Lake St South Plainfield NJ 07080 Personal E-mail: angea22@aol.com.

GREEN, BARBARA MARIE, publisher, journalist, poet, writer; b. N.Y.C., Mar. 21, 1928; d. James Matthew and Mae (McCarter) G. BA, CCNY, 1951, MA, 1955; ABD, NYU, 1978. Adminstr., tchr. English, 1952-82; tchr. English Newtown High Sch., Elmhurst, Queens, N.Y., 1961; asst. prin. Jr. High Sch. 142, Queens, N.Y., 1963; founder, pub. The "Creative" Record, Virginia Beach, Va., 1988-92. Keynote speaker; pres. Bar 'JaMae Comm. Inc. Founder, publisher The Good News, East Elmhurst, N.Y., 1985-88; author: (book of poetry) Love Pain Hope, 1990, More Poetic Thoughts, 1993, Dreams and Memories, 1996, Spirit, 1997; contbr. poetry to publs. Ch. and cmty. reporter N.Y. Voice; mem. libr. action com. Corona (N.Y.)-East Elmhurst, Inc.; mem. Langston Hughes Cmty. Libr. and Cultural Ctr., Corona, Harpers Ferry Hist. Assn., Va. Symphony League; mem. Crispus Attucks Theater Restoration Com., Norfolk. Recipient Profl. award Nat. Assn. Negro Bus. and Profl. Women's Club Inc., 1964, Trophy "Career Woman of Yr.", County Line Guild of Career Women, 1967, Cert. of Appreciation Women's Equality Action League, 1978, First Lynnhaven Bapt. Ch., Virginia Beach, Va., 1982, Cert. of merit City of N.Y., 1982, Community Svc. award Arlene of N.Y., 1990, N.Y. State Resolution commemorating the "Good" News, 1985, participation award Coalition of 100 Black Women, Valuable Service citation Phi Delta Kappa, cert. of appreciation Houston C.C., 1998, plaque U.S. Army and USAF N.G. Bur., Ageless Hero for Creativity award Blue Cross/Blue Shield, 1998; named Star Among Stars, 1991, Keeper of the Flame, 1997, Hampton Roads Poet Laureate, 2002; named to African-Am. Biographies Hall of Fame, Atlanta, 1994; elected to Hunter Coll. Alumni Hall of Fame, 1997; named poet laureate-in-residence First Lynnhaven Bapt. Ch., Virginia Beach, Va., 1996—, Hampton Roads Poet Laureate, New Jour.-Guide Newspaper, 2002. Mem. Am. Bus. Women's Assn. (Elizabeth River Charter chpt.), Nat. Assn. Negro Musicians (life; bd. dirs. Chgo. 1984-91, ea. region dir. 1990-91), Harpers Ferry Hist. Assn., Poetry Soc. Va., Nat. Assn. Black Journalists, Zonta Internat., Va. Fedn. Bus. and Profl. Women's Clubs (corr. sec. 1992, 1st v.p. 1993, pres. 1993, chair coastal region pub. rels. com. state level 1994-95), N.Y.C. Ret. Suprs. Assn., Phi Delta Kappa, Alpha Kappa Alpha. Baptist. Office Phone: 757-547-7440.

GREEN, BETTY NIELSEN, education educator, consultant; b. Copenhagen, Apr. 30, 1937; came to U.S., 1979; d. Alfred Christian Josef and Lilly Nielsen; m. Philip Irving Green, Apr. 16, 1962; children: Ruth, Erik, Nils. AA in Fgn. Lang., Daytona Beach C.C., 1981; BA in Liberal Arts, U. Ctrl. Fla., 1986; MS in TESOL, Nova Southeastern U., 1988; EdD in Curriculum and Instrn., U. Ctrl. Fla., 1994. Cert. tchr., Fla.; cert. TESOL trainer, Fla. Tchr. TESOL, program mgr. English Lang. Inst. Daytona Beach C.C., Fla., 1986—91; tchr. TESOL, fgn. lang. specialist Volusia County Schs., Daytona Beach, 1991—; tchr. trainer, facilitator Nova Southeastern U., Ft. Lauderdale, Fla., 1991—. Cons. TESOL, Ormond Beach, Fla., 1991; adj. faculty, Daytona Beach, 1997—; chair Fla. Consortium Multilingual-Multicultural Edn., 2001— Author, editor Teaching Assistant Manual, 1987; editor Unitarian Universalist Soc. newsletter, 1987—, religious editl. dir., 1996—; editor Fla. Fgn. Lang. Assn. Newsletter, UN Local Chptr. News Letter, 2006—. Pres. Unitarian Universalists, Ormond Beach, 1982-84, N.E. Cluster Unitarian Universalists, Volusia, 1982-86; pres., v.p. S.E. Unitarian Universalists Sem. Inst., Blacksburg, Va., 1985-89. Mem. TESOL, ASCD, Sunshine State TESOL (mem.-at-large 1999—, 2d v.p., 1st v.p., pres. 2003-04, editor messanger newsletter), N.E. Fla. TESOL (pres. 1995—, editor newsletter 1998—), Nat. Coun. Tchrs. English, Fla. Fgn. Lang. Assn. (membership bd., editor 2002—), Fgn. Lang. Adminstrn. and Mgmt. Edn. (sec. 1995-97, pres. 1998), Fla. Assn. Bilingual Edn. Suprs. (sec. 1995), Fla. Consortium on Multicultural Edn. (chair), Phi Kappa Phi, Kappa Delta Pi, Pi Delta Kappa, Phi Delta Kappa Democrat. Avocations: foreign languages, research on second language and multi-cultural educations, music, travel. Home: 771 W River Oak Dr Ormond Beach FL 32174-4641 Office: Volusia County Schs 729 Loomis Ave Daytona Beach FL 32114-4723 Office Phone: 386-255-6475 ext 60147. Personal E-mail: bngreen@fastmail.us. Business E-Mail: bngreen@volusia.k12.fl.us.

GREEN, CARLA RAE, music educator; b. Platte, S.D., July 13, 1971; d. Allen Henry and Sharon Elaine Timmermans; m. Damon E. Green, Dec. 17, 2005 (div.); 1 child, Isaiah. BA in Music Edn., Nebr. Wesleyan, Lincoln, 1995. Tchr. Omaha Pub. Schs., 1995—97, Orange County Pub. Schs., Orlando, Fla., 1997—2001, Akron Westfield Cen. Sch. Dist., Iowa, 2001—. Mem.: ACDA, AOSA (v.p.). Office: Akron Westfield 850 Kent Dr Akron IA 51001

GREEN, CARMEN R., anesthesiologist, pain medicine physician; b. Lockbourne AFB, Ohio; BS in Biology, U. Mich.-Flint; MD, Mich. State U. Coll. Human Medicine, 1988. Cert. Anesthesiology, Pain Mgmt. Resident, anesthesiology with subspecialty tng. in ambulatory and obstetrical anesthesiology U. Mich. Health Sys., 1993; fellow, pain mgmt. U. Mich. Health Sys., Multidisciplinary Pain Ctr.; fellow, health services rsch. Assn. Am. Med. Colleges Health Sciences Rsch. Inst.; assoc. prof. anesthesiology U. Mich. Med. Sch., med. dir., Pain Rsch. Divsn., dept. anesthesiology, dept. anesthesiology edn. and rsch. com. mem.; attending physician, Multidisciplinary Pain Ctr. U. Mich. Health Systems. Prin. investigator M-POST; assoc. dir. for the investigator core Mich. Ctr. for Urban African Am. Aging Rsch.; founding chair, pain mgmt. steering com. U. Mich. Health Sys.; U. Mich. Health Sys. institutional lead Joint Commn. on Accreditation of Healthcare Organizations Pain Initiative; assoc. dir. Med. Student Edn. Anesthesiology Clerkship; departmental coord. Midwest Anesthesia Residents' Conf.; mem. Violence Against Women Task Force U. Mich., developed and directed, Med. Student Anesthesiology Summer Rsch. Preceptorship; invited spkr. in field. Guest editor Pain Medicine, spl. issue on unequal burden of pain, mem. editl. bd. Pain Medicine, Journal of Pain, serves on editl. bd. for several jours.; contbr. articles to profl. jours. Bd. dir. Nat. Pain Found., Cmty. Dental Ctr., Mich. Visiting Nurses. Recipient Robert Wood Johnson Health Policy Fellow, IOM, 2006, Several awards for cmty. svc. and rsch.; fellow Am. Assn. Med. Coll. Health Services Rsch. Inst., Hedwig van Ameringen Exec. Leadership in Academic Medicine; Mayday Pain and Soc. Fellow, 2004. Mem.: Gerontological Soc. Am., Am. Acad. Pain Medicine, Am. Soc. Anesthesiologists (mem. com. on pain mgmt., mem. com. on profl. diversity, mem. com. on practice parameters), Am. Pain Soc. (founding chair spl. interest group for pain and disparities, mem. ann. mtg. com.), Alpha Omega Alpha. Office: U Mich Med Ctr Dept Anesthesiology 1H247 UH Box 0048 1500 E Medical Ctr Dr Ann Arbor MI 48109-0048 Office Phone: 734-936-4240. Office Fax: 734-936-9091. Business E-Mail: carmeng@umich.edu.*

GREEN, CAROL H., lawyer, educator; b. Seattle, Feb. 18, 1944; BA in History/Journalism summa cum laude, La. Tech. U., 1965; MSL, Yale U., 1977; JD, U. Denver, 1979. Reporter Shreveport (La.) Times, 1965-66, Guam Daily News, 1966-67; city editor Pacific Jour., Agana, Guam, 1967-68, reporter, editl. writer, 1968-76, legal affairs reporter, 1977-79; asst. editor editl. page Denver Post, 1979-81, house counsel, 1980-83, labor rels. mgr., 1981-83; assoc. Holme Roberts & Owen, 1983-85; v.p. human resources and legal affairs Denver Post, 1985-87, mgr. circulation, 1988-90; gen. mgr. Distbn. Systems Am., Inc., 1990-92; dir. labor rels. Newsday, 1992-95, dir. comm. and labor rels., 1995—96; v.p. Weber Mgmt. Cons., 1996—98; v.p. human resources and labor rels. Denver Post, 1998—2000; v.p. human resources, labor rels. Denver Newspaper Agy., 2001—06, sr. v.p., labor rels. and legal affairs, 2006—. 1985 speaker for USIA, India, Egypt; mem. Mailers Tech. Adv. Com. to Postmaster Gen., 1991-92. Recipient McWilliams award for juvenile justice, Denver, 1971, award for interpretive reporting Denver Newspaper Guild, 1979. Mem.: ABA, Soc. Human Resources Mgmt., Colo. and Internat. Women's Forum, Denver Bar Assn. (co-chair jud. selection and benefits com. 1982—85, 2nd v.p. 1986), Newspaper Assn. Am. (mem. human resources and labor rels. com.), Colo. Bar Assn. (bd. govs. 1985—87, chair BAR-press com. 1980), Leadership Denver. Episcopalian.

GREEN, CAROLE L., lawyer; b. Queens, NY, Mar. 17, 1959; d. Gerald Harry and Mary (Clark) Green. AB cum laude with distinction, Dartmouth Coll., 1980; JD, Harvard Law Sch., 1983. Bar: NY. Congl. aide to rep. John Conyers U.S. House of Reps., Washington, 1980; assoc. real estate Kaye Scholer LLP, NY, 1983—85, Richards & O'Neil, N.Y.C., 1985—87; gen. counsel Petrie Stores Corp., Secaucus, N.J., 1987-88; assoc. counsel Mfrs. Hanover Trust Co. (now JP Morgan Chase Bank), N.Y.C., 1988-91; v.p., asst. gen. counsel Chem. Bank (now JP Morgan Chase Bank), N.Y., 1991-96; contract atty. N.Y.C., 1996—; pub. arbitrator NASD Dispute Resolution, 1996—. Mem.: ABA, Practicing Attys. for Law Students, Inc. (founding mem. 1986—95, bd. dirs. 2004—), Assn. Bar City N.Y., N.Y. State Bar Assn., Black Alumni of Dartmouth Assn. Avocations: travel, jazz, reading. Office Phone: 212-613-0099.

GREEN, CHERYL FAYE, counseling administrator, educator; d. Walter Larry Green and Sarah Dean McCain; children: Lamont Elon, Jasmine Adelaja. BS in Psychology, Manchester Coll., Ind., 1982; PhD in Counseling Psychology, So. Ill. U., 1996. Cert. crisis intervention specialist World Crisis Intervention Network. Dir. career devel. U. Mich., Flint, 1987—89; chair dept. counseling Chgo. State U., 2005—. Rsch. chair Am. Black Women In Higher Edn., Chgo., 2003—; grievance chair Univ. Profls. Ill., Chgo., 2003—, co-chair women, human and civil rights task force, 2004—; internat. pub. health profl. People to People Amb. Program, Washington, 2004—. Contbr. articles to profl. jours. Bd. dirs. Cmty. Mental Health Coun., Chgo., 1996—2003. Recipient resolution, Flint, Mich. City Coun., 1989, Genessee County Bd. Commrs., 1989. Mem.: APA. Democrat. Baptist. Avocations: reading, African art collecting, jazz, antiques. Office Phone: 773-995-2383. Personal E-mail: cgreen21@csu.edu.

GREEN, CHRISTINA MARIE, literature and language professor; b. St. Louis, Mo., Nov. 1, 1952; d. Edward Walter and Mary Ann Czebrinski; m. James Leo Green, July 11, 1953; children: Erin Elizabeth, Ryan Daniel. M, Webster U., St. Louis, Mo., 1978; M in English, U. of Mo., 1998. Life Certification 7-12 Education Mo. Dept. of Edn., 1974. Secondary english tchr. Pattonville H.S., St. Louis, 1974—79, Villa Duchesne, St. Louis, 1980—81, Marian H.S., Omaha, 1982—83; english instr. St. Louis C.C., 1991—97; secondary english tchr. Christian Bros. Coll. High, St. Louis, 1997—98; assoc. prof. of english Lindenwood U., St. Charles, Mo., 1998—. Avocations: reading, hot air ballooning. Office: Lindenwood Univ 209 S Kings Hwy Saint Charles MO 63301 Office Phone: 636-949-4560. E-mail: cgreen@lindenwood.edu.

GREEN, DANA I., lawyer, human resources specialist; b. 1949; BA, Ind. Univ., 1971, JD, 1974; LLM in taxation, DePaul Univ., 1990. Bar: Ill. 1974. Atty. through dept. dir., employee rels. Walgreen Co., 1974—98, div. v.p., employee rels., 1998—2000, corp. v.p., human resources, 2000—04, sr. v.p., 2004—05, sr. v.p., gen. counsel, corp. sec., 2005—. Office: Walgreen Co 200 Wilmot Rd Deerfield IL 60015 Office Phone: 847-914-2500. Office Fax: 847-914-2804. E-mail: dana.green@walgreens.com.*

GREEN, ELEANOR MYERS, veterinarian, educator; b. Phila., Feb. 10, 1948; d. Wade Cooper and Eleanor Ruth (McWherter) Myers; children: George Ashby Jr., Stacy Elizabeth, William Wade. Student, U. South Fla., 1965-67, U. Fla., 1967-69; DVM, Auburn U., 1973. Diplomate Am. Coll. Vet. Internal Medicine, Am. Bd. Vet. Practitioners (pres. 1993-95, past pres. 1995-96). Ptnrship, owner Guntown (Miss.) Vet. Clinic, 1973-76; asst. prof. Miss. State U., Starkville, 1976-84; assoc. prof. U. Mo., Columbia, 1984-91; prof. U. Tenn., Knoxville, 1991-96; prof., chair dept. U. Fla., Gainesville, 1996—. Named Disting. Practitioner Nat. Acads. of Practice, Coll. Agrl. and Life Scis. award of distinction, 2004. Mem. Am. Assn. Equine Practitioners (bd. dirs. 1997-99), Fla. Vet. Med. Assn., Am. Vet. Med. Assn., Internat. Soc. Vet. Perinatology, Am. Assn. Vet. Clinicians (Faculty Achievement award 1999, pres. 1995-96, past pres. 1996-97), Nat. Acad.'s Practice (Disting. Practitioner 1998—), Fla. Thoroughbred Owners and Breeders Assn., Fla. Quarter Horse Assn. (bd. dirs.), Rotary Internat. Presbyterian. Avocations: horseback riding, tennis, painting. Office: U Fla Coll Vet Medicine Dept Large Animal Clin Scis Gainesville FL 32610-0136 E-mail: greene@mail.vetmed.ufl.edu.

GREEN, G. DORSEY, psychologist, author; b. Balt., Aug. 18, 1949; d. John Summerfield Green III and Gertrude Dixon (Dorsey) Wilson. AB, Dickinson Coll., 1971; MA, Bowling Green State U., 1972; PhD, U. Wash., 1981. Psychologist pvt. practice, Seattle, 1982—; clin. instr. U. Wash., 1992—. Cons. Hearing, Speech, Deafness Ctr., Seattle, 1987-88. Co-author: Lesbian Couples, 1988, 2000, The Lesbian Parenting Book, 1995, 2003; mem. edit. bd. Women and Therapy, 1995-98; contbr. articles to profl. jours. Vol. Am. Friends Svc. Com., Seattle, 1981-96; bd. dirs. Seattle Counseling Svc. for Sexual Minorities, 1981-84; exec. com. mem. Friends Com. For Nat. Legis., 2005—. Mem. APA (divsn. 44 Edn. and Tng. award 1996), Feminist Therapy Inst. Mem. Soc. Of Friends. Avocations: sailing, playing bridge, reading mysteries. Home: 1118 37th Ave Seattle WA 98122-5231

GREEN, JEAN HESS, psychotherapist; b. Flushing, Mich., Aug. 10, 1930; d. Ozro Kline and Thelma Lucille (Cook) Hess; m. Warren Dale Sarley, Mar. 21, 1952 (div. 1971); children: Gaie Lee, Patton Garret, Erin Jessie; m. Peter B. Green, Jan. 4, 1972 (div. 1998). BA, Mich. State U., 1955; MS, Columbia Pacific U., San Rafael, Calif., 1988, PhD, 1994. Cert. Rubenfeld synergist, 1995; diplomate Am. Psychol. Assn., 2000. Tchr. secondary English, Norwich (N.Y.) Pub. Schs., 1960-61; claims rep. Social Security Adminstrn., Rochester, N.Y., 1961-63; mgr. Maplewood Apts., Syracuse, N.Y., 1972-76; dir. overseas scholarships Episcopal Ch., USA, N.Y.C., 1979-81; dir. audio books N.Y. Pub. Libr., N.Y.C., 1987-89; pvt. practice psychotherapy, N.Y.C. and Mt. Vernon, N.Y., 1985—. Workshop presenter Mariandale Ctr., Ossining, NY., 1986—. Trustee Kristine Mann Libr., N.Y.C., 2000—01. Mem. Assn. for Humanistic Psychology, C.G. Jung Found., Analytical Psychology Club N.Y. (rec. sec. 1988-94, pres. 1994-96, v.p., 1998-2002). Democrat. Roman Catholic. Avocation: poetry. Home and Office: 210 Ridge Rd Roxbury NY 12474 Office Phone: 607-326-2967.

GREEN, JILL I., dance educator, researcher; b. Bklyn., June 19, 1954; d. Charles M. and Selma Z. (Stein) Green. BS summa cum laude, Bklyn. Coll., 1976; MA, NYU, 1981; PhD, Ohio State U., 1993. Lic. tchr. dance K-12, N.C., tchr. Kinetic Awareness. Dance instr. NYU, N.Y.C., 1981; dance tchr. Pub. Sch. 46, Bronx, N.Y., 1981-83; dance and movement instr. Lee Strasberg Theatre Inst., N.Y.C., 1983-86; dance tchr. Sheepshead Bay H.S., Bklyn., 1985-89; movement and relaxation specialist Columbus (Ohio) Psychol. Ctr., 1989-92; tchg. assoc. Ohio State U., Columbus, 1989-92, lectr., 1992-93; movement and body awareness educator Columbus Somatics Ctr., 1992-93; asst. prof. dance U. N.C., Greensboro, 1993—, coord. dance edn. program, 1993—. Cons. for dance curriculum N.C. State Dept. Instrn., Raleigh, 1995-96; editl. cons. Ind. U. Press, 1995-96. Contbr. chpt. to book, articles to profl. jours.; co-editor Dance Rsch. Jour., 2003—. Vol. tchr. Very Spl. Arts Festival, Greensboro, 1994—, N.C. 4-H Coun., Greensboro, 1993—; demonstration classes N.C. Pub. Schs., 1993—; ednl. facilitator for homeless women WINGS Ctr. for SelfDiscovery, Columbus, 1992-93. New Faculty grantee, 1993-95; Dance Connections grantee Cmty. Found. Greater Greensboro, 1997; Ctr. for Study of Social Issues grantee, 1997—; Fulbright scholar Theatre Acad. Finland, Helsinki, 2004; recipient U. N.C. Tchg. Excellence award Sch. of Health and Human Performance, 1998. Mem. Nat. Dance Edn. Org., N.C. Dance Alliance (bd. dirs. 1996-98), Congress on Rsch. in Dance (bd. dirs. 1998—), The Somatics Soc., Natl. Dance Edn. Assn., Am. Ednl. Rsch. Assn. Office: U NC at Greensboro Dept Dance PO Box 26169 Greensboro NC 27402-6169 Office Phone: 336-334-4064. E-mail: jillgreen@uncg.edu.

GREEN, JOYCE, book publishing company executive; b. Taylorville, Ill., Oct. 22, 1928; d. Lynn and Vivian Coke (Richardson) Reinerd; m. Warren H. Green, Oct. 8, 1960. AA, Christian Coll., 1946; BS, MacMurray Coll., 1948. Pres. Warren H. Green, Inc., St. Louis, 1992—, Affirmative Action Register, 1977—, InterContinental Industries, Inc., 1980—; chief exec. officer Pubs. Svc. Ctr.; pres. Epoch Press, 2004—. Mem. St. Louis C. of C., Jr. League Club, Media Club, Mo. Athletic Club. Office: 8356 Olive Blvd Saint Louis MO 63132-2814 Home (Summer): 12120 Hibler Dr Saint Louis MO 63141 E-mail: JRG1036@aol.com.

GREEN, JOYCE HENS, federal judge; b. NYC, Nov. 13, 1928; d. James S. and Hedy (Bucher) Hens; m. Samuel Green, Sept. 25, 1965 (dec.); children: Michael Timothy, June Heather, James Harry. BA, U. Md., 1949; JD, George Washington U., 1951, LLD, 1994. Practice law, Washington, 1951-68, Arlington, Va., 1956-68; ptnr. Green & Green, 1966-68; assoc. judge Superior Ct., D.C., 1968-79; judge U.S. Dist. Ct. for D.C., 1979—; judge presiding U.S. Fgn. Intelligence Surveillance Ct., 1988-95. Bd. advisors George Washington U. Law Sch., 1991-2001; jud. br. com. Jud. Conf. U.S., 1995-2001. Co-author: Dissolution of Marriage, 1986, supplements, 1987-89, Marriage and Family Law Agreements, 1985, supplements, 1986-89. Chair Task Force on Gender, Race and Ethnic Bias for the D.C. Cir. Recipient Alumni Achievement award George Washington U., 1975, Profl. Achievement award, 1978, Outstanding Contbn. to Equal Rights award Women's Legal Def. Fund, 1976, hon. doctor of Laws George Washington U., 1994, U.S. Dept. Justice Edmund J. Randolph award, 1995, Professionalism award D.C. Cir., Am. Inns Ct., 2004. Fellow Am. Bar Found.; ABA (jud. adminstrn. divsn., chair nat. conf. fed. trial judges 1997-98), Fed. Judges Assn., Nat. Assn. Women Judges, Va. Bar, Bar Assn. D.C. (jud. honoree of Yr. 1994), D.C. Bar, D.C. Women's Bar Assn. (pres. 1960-62, woman lawyer of yr. 1979), Exec. Women in Govt. (chmn. 1977), Woman's Forum of Washington D.C. Office: US Dist Ct E Barrett Prettyman US Courthouse 333 Constitution Ave NW Washington DC 20001-2802

GREEN, KAREN F., lawyer; b. 1956; AB magna cum laude, Radcliffe Coll., 1978; JD cum laude, Harvard Univ., 1981. Bar: Mass. 1981. Law clk. Judge W. Arthur Garrity, US Dist. Ct. (Mass. dist.), 1981—82; assoc. Hale & Dorr, Boston, 1982—84; asst. U.S. atty. civil div., U.S. Dept. of Justice, Boston, 1984—86; assoc. Hale & Dorr, Boston, 1987—88, jr. ptnr., 1988—90, sr. ptnr., 1990—93; chief of staff Mass. Gov. William F. Weld, 1993; dep. U.S. atty. U.S. Dept. of Justice, Boston, 1994—96; sr. ptnr. Hale & Dorr, Boston, 1996—2004; ptnr., co-chmn. Litigation dept., mem. exec. com. Wilmer Cutler Pickering Hale & Dorr, Boston, 2004—. Co-chmn., transition team for exec. office of health & human svc. Mass. Gov.-elect William F. Weld, 1990—91; bd. dir. Fiduciary Trust Co.; mem. spl. commn. on Suffolk County Sheriff's Dept. for Mass. acting Gov. Jane Swift; vice chmn. com. on pro bono legal svc. Mass. Supreme Judicial Ct.; mem. gender bias com. US Ct. Appeals (1st cir.); mem. com. to revise local criminal rules & com. on alternative dispute resolution US Dist Ct. (Mass. dist.); instr. Harvard Law Sch. Trial Advocacy Workshop, U.S. Atty. Gen. Advocacy Inst. Mem. exec. com. Mass. Judicial Nominating Council; dir. Children's Trust Fund. Named one of Boston's Top Women Lawyers, Boston Globe, 1996, Top 100 Mass. Super Lawyers & Top 50 Female Mass. Super Lawyers, Boston Mag., 2004; recipient award for Outstanding Svc. to City of Boston, Park St. Forum, 1997, Leading Women award, Patriot's Trail Girl Scout Council, 2000, Women's Bus. Hall of Fame award, 2001, honoree for pro bono legal work, Granada House, 2002. Mem.: Boston Bar Found. (trustee), Boston Bar Assn. (council mem. & chmn. Fed. Practice & Procedure com.), Boston Club (dir.), Phi Beta Kappa. Office: Wilmer Cutler Pickering Hale & Dorr 60 State St Boston MA 02109 Office Phone: 617-526-6207. Office Fax: 617-526-5000. Business E-Mail: karen.green@wilmerhale.com.

GREEN, KAREN INA MARGULIES, psychologist; b. N.Y.C., Jan. 27, 1939; d. Irwin Margulies and Roberta Rose (Goodbinder) Margulies-Varon; m. L.R. Green, Dec. 22, 1961 (div. June 1981); children: Garth Lorin, Allison Dawne. BA in Psychology with distinction, Duke U., 1959; MA, Boston U., 1960, postgrad., 1960-63; MA in Lit., Am. U., 1973. Lic. psychologist, D.C. Pvt. practice psychotherapy Green Assocs., Washington, 1968—; English tchr. Md. Sch. of Art & Design, Wheaton, 1980; cons. psychologist Providence Hosp., Washington, 1981-82, New Ventures, Inc., Bowie, Md., 1984, Hood Coll., Frederick, Md., 1985; psychologist cons. Associated Health Practitioners, Washington, 1987-90, Behavioral Factors, Inc., Washington, 1986-89; prof. lit. U. D.C., Washington, 1991—. Adj. prof. lit. U. D.C., Washington; sch. psychologist Pub. Schs. D.C., Washington, 1967-68; rsch. psychologist President's Commn. on Obscenity and Pornography, Washington, 1968-70; cons. psychologist Pub. Defender Svc., Washington, 1968-70. Playwright: These Dead Ladies Are My Friends, 1983 (winner of playwriting contest, 1983); dir. plays: Songs We've Never Sung, 1984, Where Has Love Gone, 1985; author (short story) Repetition, 1990, Late Night Blossoms, 2001; contbr. articles to profl. jours. Mem. Am. Psychol. Assn. (assoc.), Internat. Coun. Psychologists, D.C. Psychol. Assn., Nat. Register Health Svc. Providers, Phi Beta Kappa. Avocations: flamenco dancing, writing, acting, swimming, jazz. Home and Office: 1632 44th St NW Washington DC 20007-2051

GREEN, KAREN MARIE, science educator, gifted and talented educator; b. Littlefield, Tex., Aug. 12, 1954; d. Franklin Bernard Green and Lydia Maria Jungman; m. Jeffrey Michael Hilgart, Sept. 23, 1986; children: Amelia Hilgart, Alice Hilgart, Amber Hilgart;children from previous marriage: Jeremiah Bennack, Aaron Bennack. AS, South Plains Coll., Levelland, Tex., 1974; BS, Sul Ross State U., Alpine, Tex., 1976, MSc, 1980. Sci. educator Lago Vista Ind. Sch. Dist., Tex., 1989—.

GREEN, KELLI CHARNELL, psychiatrist; d. Charles Cleveland and Eleanor Faith Green; m. Glenn Turner Gholston, Mar. 1; children: Sofia Brooks Gholston-Green, William Carlo Gholston-Green; m. John Peter Flynn (div.). BA, Yale U., New Haven, Conn., 1982; MD, Vanderbilt U., Nashville, Tenn., 1986. Diplomate Am. Bd. Psychiatry and Neurology, 1999. Intern in surgery U. Ariz., Tucson, 1986—88; physician Indian Health Svc., Sells, Ariz., 1988, El Pueblo Clinic, Tucson, 1989, Flag Pond Med. Clinic, Ariz., 1989—92; resident in psychiatry U. Wash., Seattle, 1994—97; pub. health officer State of Tenn., 1994; pvt. practice psychiatrist NC, 1997—2000; psychiatrist Vets. Adminstrn., Knoxville, Tenn., 2000—02, Broadlawns Med. Ctr., Des Moines, 2002—; pvt. practice Innovate Psychiat. Care, Des Moines, 2004—. Physician Emergency Room various locations, 1997—2000. Home: 639 40th St Des Moines IA 50312-3319

GREEN, KELLY ALLYSON, gifted and talented educator, entrepreneur; d. William Ray and Lois Janet Martin; m. Stephen Anthony Green, Mar. 29, 2003. BS, U. North Tex., Denton, 1997. Cert. edn. with specialization in reading Tex. Edn. Agy. 8th grade lit. tchr. Lakeview Mid. Sch., Lewisville Ind. Sch. Dist., The Colony, Tex., 1998—, EPIC tchr. (at-risk), 2000—02. Reading dept. chairperson Lakeview Mid. Sch., Lewisville Ind. Sch. Dist., 1999—. Alumnae advisor Chi Omega, Denton, 2004—06. Grantee, Lewisville Ind. Sch. Dist., 2006. Mem.: Tex. Fedn. Tchrs. Roman Catholic. Office Phone: 469-713-5974.

GREEN, LENNIS HARRIS, psychologist; b. Indpls., July 14, 1940; d. William James and Anna Jane (McLane) Harris. BS, Ohio State U., 1962, MA, 1966, PhD, 1971. Lic. psychologist, Ohio. Program dir. Lattie Lazarus Counseling Ctr., Columbus, 1971-72; pvt. practice psychology Columbus, Ohio, 1968—. Bd. dirs. North Area Mental Health, Inc., Columbus, 1980-85, clin. cons., 1985—; clin. cons. Midwest Career Ctr., Columbus, 1985-90, Worthington Counseling Ctr., Columbus, 1986-87; prin. rsch. investigator Proctor Fund, Honolulu, 1984. Contbr. articles to mags. Del. Nigerian Consultation, Episc. Ch., Geneva, Switzerland, 1983; bd. dirs. Transcultural Family Inst., Columbus, 1983-84. Behavioral and Sci. Inst. fellow, U. Hawaii, Honolulu, 1985. Mem. Internat. Council Psychologists, Internat. Assn. Crosscultural Psychology, Am. Psychol. Assn., Am. Anthropology Assn. Avocations: music, art. Home and Office: 85 Forest Ridge Dr Columbus OH 43235-1410

GREEN, LINDA GAIL, retired international healthcare and management consultant, nursing educator; b. Kalamazoo, Nov. 29, 1951; d. Jesse Floyd and Mattie Dean (Fulcher) G. BS in Nursing, Fla. State U., Tallahassee, 1974; postgrad., Nova U., Ft. Lauderdale, Fla. Staff nurse med./surg. unit St. Mary's Hosp., West Palm Beach, Fla., 1974, staff nurse coronary care, 1974-75, relief charge nurse ICU, 1975-76, asst. nursing care coord. post anesthesia recovery rm., 1976-78, insvc. instr., 1978-81, asst. dir. staff devel. and edn., 1981-83; dir. insvc. H.H. Raulerson Hosp., Okeechobee, Fla., 1983-84; adminstr. Med. Personnel Pool, Palm Beach, Fla., 1984-90; regional exec. healthcare divsn. Interim Svcs., Inc. (formerly Pers. Pool of Am., an H&R Block Co.), Ft. Lauderdale, 1990-93; pres. L.G.I. Consulting/Cmty. Health Educator, West Palm Beach, 1993—2000. Dir. ednl. svcs., nurse educator Intracoastal Health Svcs., Inc., Good Samaritan Med. Ctr., St. Mary's Med. Ctr., West Palm Beach, Fla., 1998—2000; bd. dirs. at large Earthworkers Unltd., Inc., 2005—; spkr. in field. Author: Sexual Harassment in Home Healthcare, 1993. Past bd. dirs. Vinceremos Therapeutic Riding Ctr., Inc. for Physically and Mentally Challenged, 1990-95; chair Helen K. Persson Endowment Scholarship, 1999-2000; mem. Palm Beach County Workshop Devel. Bus. Partnership Coun., 1999. Mem. ANA, AHA (heart walk industry leader 1994, 95), Palm Beach County Health Educators (past sec.), Palm Beach County Patient Educators (pres. 1989, Leadership and Spirit awards 1989), Royal Palm Beach Bus. Assn., Palms West C. of C. (v.p. 1987-88, Dedicated and Outstanding Svc. award 1989, Cert. of Appreciation 1986, 87), Zonta Internat. (pres. 1994-95, past v.p. Palms West chpt., del. to internat. conf., Hong Kong, 1992).

GREEN, LINDA KAY, retired dermatologist; b. Knoxville, Tenn., May 28, 1958; d. Charles Kenneth Green; m. Steve G. Ferguson, May 21, 1988; children: Mary Alice Ferguson, Karen Ferguson. BA, Tex. A&M U., College Sta., 1980; MD, U. Tex. Med. Br., Galveston, 1984. Diplomate Am. Acad. Dermatology, 1988. Resident internal medicine Med. Coll. Va., Richmond, Va., 1985; resident dermatology U. Ala., Birmingham, Ala., 1988; dermatologist Dermatology Assoc. East Tenn., Knoxville, Tenn., 1988—2003; ret., 2003. Founder and fundraiser tumor fund Bapt. Hosp., Knoxville, Tenn., 2003—; sponsor summer swimathon for tumor fund Wellness Cmty., 2006, fundraiser; bd. mem. Girl Scouts USA, Knoxville, Tenn., 2006. Recipient Joy Dirksen Baker award, Bapt. Hosp. Found., 2006. Fellow: Am. Acad. Dermatology (life); mem.: East Tenn. Dermatol. Soc., Exec. Women's Assn. Avocations: swimming, reading, stained glass. Home: 1935 Lyons Bend Rd Knoxville TN 37919-8972

GREEN, LISA CANNON, online editor; b. Marshall, Ky., May 7, 1962; d. Walter L. and Phyllis (Jones) Cannon; m. Bob Dale Green, May 31, 1980; children: Emily, Ethan. BA in Journalism and English, Murray State U., 1983. With The Post-Intelligencer, Paris, Tenn., 1983-84, The Jackson (Tenn.) Sun, 1984-90, The Tennessean, Nashville, 1990—. Office: The Tennessean 1100 Broadway Nashville TN 37203-3134 Office Phone: 615-259-8275. Business E-Mail: lgreen@tennessean.com.

GREEN, LYNN TESSON, science educator, secondary school educator; m. Gordon B. Green; 1 child, Alex. BS, La. State U., Baton Rouge, 1982, EdM, 1998. Cert. tchr. Colo. H.s. sci. tchr. Heritage Christian Schs., Fort Collins, Colo., 1999—2000, Dayspring Christian Schs., Greeley, Colo., 2001—. Office: Dayspring Christian Schools 3734 W 20th St Greeley CO 80634 Office Phone: 970-330-1151.

GREEN, MARY JEAN MATTHEWS, foreign language educator; b. Honesdale, Pa., July 27, 1944; d. Joseph Robert and Garnet Barbara (Bayly) Matthews; m. Ronald Michael Green, June 25, 1965; children— Julie Elisabeth, Matthew Daniel. A.B., Brown U., 1965; A.M., Harvard U., 1966, Ph.D., 1974. Teaching fellow Harvard U., 1966-68; instr. Colby Sawyer Coll., New London, N.H., 1969-72; instr. Franconia Coll. (N.H.), 1972-73; asst. prof. French, Dartmouth Coll., 1973-81, assoc. prof., 1981-87, prof., 1987—, co-chmn. Women's Studies Program, chmn. dept. French and Italian, 1991-93, assoc. dean for Humanities, 1993—. Author: Louis Guilloux: An Artisan of Language, 1980; Fiction in the Historical Present: French Writers and the Thirties, 1986, Marie-Claire Blais, 1995; editor: Quebec Studies, 1983-89, Postcolonial Subjects: Francophone Women Writers, 1996, Ecritures de femmes, 1996; assoc. editor Internat. Jour. Canadian Studies, 1991. Vis. scholar U. Calif.-Berkeley, 1984—; Can. Govt. Faculty Enrichment grantee, 1984; recipient Donner medal in Can. Studies. Mem. Am. Council for Que. Studies (pres. 1981-82), Assn. Can. Studies in U.S. (exec. councillor 1983-87), MLA, Am. Assn. Tchrs. French, Northeast Modern Lang. Assn. Office: Dartmouth Coll Dept French And Italia Hanover NH 03755

GREEN, MAY CLAYMAN, elementary school educator, education administrator; b. Bklyn., Apr. 8, 1923; d. Joseph and Anna (Steinger) Clayman; m. Jerome E. Bloom, Oct. 14, 1945 (div. May 1963); children: Jeffrey Clayman Bloom, Claudia J. Segal; m. Milton Green, May 10, 1963; stepchildren: Carol R. Green, Peter A. Green. BA, Adelphi U., 1944; MA, NYU, 1956; postgrad., C.W. Post Coll./Long Island U., 1978. Rsch. asst. Winston Pub. Co., Phila., 1953-55; various positions Roslyn (N.Y.) Jr. H.S., 1956-80; adminstrv. asst. to dir. Afro-Am. affairs NYU, 1971-72; owner, exec. adminstr. New Horizons Country Day Sch., Palm Harbor, Fla., 1984-96; pres. New Horizons Edn. Cons. Firm, Palm Harbor, 1996—; bus. mgr. Curves For Women, Chantilly, Va., 2000—, Middleburg, Va., 2002. Adv. bd. St. Petersburg Jr. Coll., Tarpon Springs, Fla., 1992; pres. New Horizons Edn. Found., Palm Harbor, 1992, New Horizons in Learning-Child Care Mgmt., Tarpon Springs, 1983-88, New Horizons Rsch. Cons., New Horizons Rsch. Divsn., 2003—; validator Nat. Acad. for Early Childhood Programs; adv. bd. Cmty. Sch., Tarpon Springs, 1982-85; bd. dirs. Rexall Showcase Internat., Prentice Health Care; mgr. Curves for Women, Middleburg, Va., 2002; rsch. dir. to author, 2003—. Pres. L.I. Riding for the Handicapped, Brookville, NY, 1978-80; audience devel. Fla. Orch., Tampa, 1995; adv. com. Heritage Hall, Leesburg, Va., 1998—; adv. bd. Fla. Symphony, 1995—; bd. dirs. North Suncoast Fla. Symphony, 1995-96, Middleburg Riding for the Handicap, 2005; active Christmas in April, 1999-2000; chair Middleburg Point to Point Race Com., 2003 Recipient Svc. Appreciation award Nassau County Children's Mus., 1960, Nassau County Girl Scouts, 1961, Inst. Afro-Am. Affaris, NYU, 1979, Jenkins Meml. award NY State PTA, 1980, Pres.'s award Hempstead Child

Care Ctr., 1962 Mem. ASCD, Nat. Tchrs. Assn., Roslyn Tchrs. (Ret.) Assn., Nat. Assn. for Edn. of Young Children, Middleburg Hunt Club. Avocations: travel, reading, knitting, water aerobics, theatre and music. Office: New Horizons Edn Consulting Firm # 1122 19385 Cypress Ridge Ter Leesburg VA 20176-5171 Office Phone: 703-858-5466. Personal E-mail: mayc45@aol.com.

GREEN, MEYRA JEANNE, banker; b. Cleve., Oct. 17, 1946; d. Meyrick Evans Green and Jeanne Bynon (Griffiths) Strauss; m. Frank W. Horn, Dec. 10, 1977 (dec. 1983); 1 stepchild, Donna; m. John Joseph Fleming, Aug. 29, 1987; 1 stepchild, Kerry. BA, Lake Erie Coll., 1968; MBA, NYU, 1973. Corp. planner Chem. Bank, N.Y.C., 1968-72, CitiBank, N.Y.C., 1972; security analyst Bank of N.Y., 1972-74; asst. treas. Credit Lyonnais, 1974-84; v.p. Wachovia Bank, Summit, 1985—. V.p. Kent Pl. Sch. Alumnae Bd.; vol. Atlantic Health Systems Hospice, Summit, NJ, 1985—. Mem. AAUW, NYU Stern Grad. Sch. Bus. Alumni, Madison Fitness Coalition (chmn.) Republican. Home: 111 Woodland Rd Madison NJ 07940-2827 Office: Wachovia Bank 190 River Rd Summit NJ 07901-1412 Office Phone: 908-598-3728. Business E-Mail: meyra.green@wachovia.com.

GREEN, MILLIE ANN, mathematician, educator; d. James Richard Caudle and Martha Grace Lewis; m. Charles Earl Irvin, June 14, 1964 (div. Aug. 1981); children: Karl Anne Irvin, Jan Richard Irvin; m. Kenneth M. Green, June 12, 1992. BSc, Calif. Polytech., 1979; tchr.'s credential, U. Redlands, 1988; postgrad., U. Calif., 1989—90; M in Adminstrn., Internat. U., 1999. Cert. in adminstrn., home econs., math., sci., and phys. sci. Tchr. math. Ladera Vista Jr. H.S., Fullerton, Calif.; tchr. 6th grade Fontana, Calif., 1988—90. Mem. San Gorgonio Girl Scout Coun., Colton, Calif., 1984—88. Home: 25041 Acacia Ln Laguna Hills CA 92653-4961

GREEN, MIMI THERESA, social services administrator; b. Phila., June 7, 1954; d. Frank Ralph and Anne Ellen (Toroni) Murdock; m. Joseph S.U. Bodoff, Mar. 28, 1981 (div. Mar. 1986); m. Thomas Anthony Green, Oct. 18, 1987; 1 child, Heather Anne. BA in Edn., Rosemont (Pa.) Coll., 1976; MS in Counseling and Human Rels., Villanova (Pa.) U., 1983. Cert. tchr., Pa.; cert. cognitive behavioral therapist; cert. forensic counselor. Art educator Tredyffin/Eastham Schs., Berwyn, Pa., 1976-92, varsity boy's track coach, 1984-86; CEO Wayne (Pa.) Art Ctr., 1992-97, program dir. edn., 1997-98; CEO, founder Latch Key Concepts, Inc. and Oasis Home Edn., LLC, Wayne, 1993—. Admissions counsel Rosemont Coll., 1976-77; CEO, Wayne Art Ctr., 1998—2001. One-woman show at Berwyn Libr., 1986, two-woman show Rosemont Coll., 1976. Charity fashion announcer Wayne Art Ctr., 1989—; woman's group leader St. Isaac Joques Parish, Valley Force, Pa., 1991-92; committeeperson Rep. Party, East Whiteland, Pa., 1991-93; com. mem. Wayne Art Ctr. Craft Forms, 1995—. Mem. ACA, NEA, Nat. Curriculum Assn., Lions (pres. Charity Ball 1995—), Malvern Bus. Assn. Roman Catholic. Avocations: equestrian, canoeing, outdoor activities, swimming, watercolor painting. Home: PO Box 540 Sadsburyville PA 19360 Office: Oasis Home Edn LLC 17 W Central Ave Paoli PA 19301-1315 Office Phone: 610-296-9432. E-mail: WisteriaMi@aol.com.

GREEN, NANCY LOUGHRIDGE, publishing executive; b. Lexington, Ky., Jan. 19, 1942; d. William S. and Nancy O. (Green) Loughridge. BA in Journalism, U. Ky., 1964, postgrad., 1968; MA in Journalism, Ball State U., 1971; postgrad., U. Minn., 1968; EdD, Nova Southeastern U., 2003. Tchr. English, publs. adv. Clark County H.S., Winchester, Ky., 1965-66, Pleasure Ridge Park H.S., Louisville, 1966-67, Clarksville (Ind.) H.S., 1967-68, Charleston (W.Va.) H.S., 1968-69; asst. publs., pub. info. specialist W.Va. Dept. Edn., Charleston, 1969-70; tchr. journalism, publs. dir. Elmhurst H.S., Ft. Wayne, Ind., 1970-71; adviser student publs. U. Ky., Lexington, 1971-82; gen. mgr. student publs. U. Tex., Austin, 1982-85; pres., pub. Palladium-Item, Richmond, Ind., 1985-89, News-Leader, Springfield, Mo., 1989-92; asst. to pres. newspaper divsn. Gannett Co., Inc., Washington, 1992-94; exec. dir. advancement Clayton State Coll., Morrow, Ga., 1994-96; v.p. advancement Clayton Coll. & State U., Morrow, Ga., 1996-99; v.p. comm. Ga. GLOBE U. Sys., 1999-2000; dir. circulation/distbn., sales & mktg. Lee Enterprises, Davenport, Iowa, 2000—02; v.p. circulation LEE Enterprises, Davenport, 2002—; pub. The Courier, 2004—. Dir. Dow Jonesurban journalism program Harte-Hanks, 1984, Louisville Courier-Jour. and Lexington Herald-Leader, 1976-82; pres. Media Cons., Inc., Lexington, 1980; sec. Kernel Press, Inc., 1971-82. Contbr. articles to profl. jours. Bd. dirs. Studen Press Law Ctr., 1975-2005, Richmond Cmty. Devel. Corp., 1987-89, United Way of the Ozarks, 1990-92, ARC, 1990-92, Springfield Arts Coun., 1990-91, Bus. Devel. Corp., 1991-92, Bus. Edn. Alliance, 1991-92, Caring Found., 1991-92, Cox Hosp. Bd., 1990-92, Springfield Schs. Found., 1964-82, Jr. League, Lexington, 1971-82, Manchester Ctr., 1978-82, pres., 1979-82; chmn. Greater Richmond Progress Com., 1986-87, bd. dirs., 1986-89; pres. Leadership Wayne County, 1986-87, bd. dirs. 1985-89; adv. bd. Ind. U. East, 1985-89, Richmond C. of C., 1987-89, Ind. Humanities Coun., 1988-89, Youth Comm. Bd., 1988-92, Opera Theatre No. Va., 1992-94, Atlanta chpt. AIWF, 1995-2000. Recipient Coll. Media Advisers First Amendment award, 1987, Disting. Svc. award Assn. Edn. Journalism and Mass Comm., 1989; named to Ball State Journalism Hall of Fame, 1988, Coll. Media Advisers Hall of Fame, 1994. Mem. Student Press Law Ctr. (bd. dirs. 1975-05, pres. 1985-87, 94-96, v.p. 1992-94), Assoc. Collegiate Press, Journalism Edn. Assn. (Carl Towley award 1988), Nat. Coun. Coll. Publs. Advs./Coll. Media Advisers (pres. 1979-83, Disting. Newspaper Adv. 1976, Disting. Bus. Adviser 1984), Columbia Scholastic Press Assn. (Gold Key 1980), So. Interscholastic Press Assn. (Disting. Svc. award 1983), Nat. Scholastic Press Assn. (Pioneer award 1982), Soc. Profl. Journalists, Internat. Newspaper Mktg. Assn. N.Am. (bd. dirs. 2002—), Newspaper Assn. Am. (postal com. 2001—, readership adv. group 2002—, diversity subcom. 1991-05, circulation fed. bd. 2002—, 2d v.p. 2006), Clayton County C. of C. (adv. bd. 1995-99, chmn. internat. com. 1996-98), Cedar Falls C. of C. (bd. dirs. 2005—) Office: The Courier 501 Commercial St Waterloo IA 50701 Office Phone: 563-383-2126, 319-291-1500. Business E-Mail: nancy.green@lee.net.

GREEN, PATRICIA PATAKY, school system administrator, consultant; b. NYC, June 18, 1949; d. William J. and Theresa M. (DiGianni) P.; m. Stephen I. Green, Dec. 7, 1975. BS, U. Md., 1971, MEd, 1977, PhD, 1994. Tchr. Prince George's County Pub. Sch., Md., 1971-83; elem. instrnl. adminstrv. specialist Thomas Stone Sch., Mt. Ranier, Md., 1984-85, Glenridge Sch., Lanham, Md., 1984, Greenbelt Ctr. Sch., Md., 1983-84, Prince George's County Pub. Schs., 1985-91; prin. Columbia Pk. Sch., Landover, Md., 1985-91; asst. supt. Prince George's County Pub. Sch., 1991-95, assoc. supt., chief divsn. adminstr., 1995-99, assoc. supt. for pupil svc., 1999—2001, acting dep. supt. for instrn., 2000—02, fellow Broad Ctr. Supt., Bd. Found., 2002; supt. sch. North Allegheny Sch. Dist., Pitts., 2002—. Exec. dir. North Allegheny Found.; cons. nationwide sch. systems; presenter in field. Featured in numerous mag. and on TV shows; contbr. articles to profl. jour. Apptd. commr. Prince George's Commn. for Children, Youth and Families; mem. Prince George's County Cmty. in Sch., 1998—2002; trustee North Allegheny Found., 2002, exec. dir., 2002—. Recipient Nat. Sch. Recognition award US Dept. Edn., 1988, Outstanding Adminstr. award Prince George's County C. of C., 1990, Outstanding Rsch. award Md. Assn. Supervision and Curriculum Devel., 1995, Outstanding Educator award Prince George's County, 1983, Spotlight on Prevention award Md. State Atty. Gen., 1998, Disting. Achievement award North Allegheny Sch. Dist., 2002, Outstanding Profl. award U. Md. Coll. Edn., 2003. Mem. NAESP (Excellence of Achievement award 1988), ASCD, Am. Assn. Sch. Adminstrs., Pa. Assn. Sch. Adminstrs., Pa. Assn. Supr. and Curriculum Devel., Pa. Sch. Bds. Assn., Phi Kappa Phi. Kappa Delta Pi. Avocations: landscape gardening, photography, reading, writing, bicycling. Business E-Mail: pgreen@northallegheny.org.

GREEN, RHONDA BEVERLY, management consultant; b. Bklyn., June 18, 1958; d. Lawrence and Miriam (Hodosh) Stern; m. Jeremy Eric Green BA summa cum laude, Bklyn. Coll., 1979, postgrad., 1983. Instr., dept. chairperson, adminstr. Adelphi Inst., Bklyn., 1980—84; dir. edn. Crown Bus. Inst., N.Y.C., 1984—85; dir. N.Y. schs. Robert Fiance and Am. Hi-Tech Bus. Schs., N.Y.C., 1985—87; v.p. Elle Internat., N.Y.C., 1987—. Mem. NAFE, ASCD, Am. Mgmt. Assn., Am. Soc. Quality, Bus. Edn. Assn., Phi Beta Kappa, Pi Delta Phi

GREEN, RICKI KUTCHER, television producer; b. Sioux City, Iowa, Sept. 20, 1943; d. Louis Jacob Kutcher and Annabelle (Emlein) Shapiro; m. Thomas C. Green, Nov. 1976 (div.); children: Joshua, Marisa; m. Jeffrey Graham Spragens, May 18, 1984 (div. Oct 1996). Student, Newcomb Coll., 1961-63; BA in Polit. Sci., U. Calif., Berkeley, 1965; postgrad., Stanford U., 1990-91. Sec. U.S. Mission to UN, N.Y.C., 1965-67; publs. coord. Nat. Urban Coalition, Washington, 1968-70; press officer Presdl. Commn. on Population Growth, Washington, 1970-72; mng. editor legis. newsletter Women's Equity Action League, Washington, 1972-74; writer, film producer Md. Pub. TV, Owings Mills, 1975-78; assoc. producer WETA TV, Washington, 1978-79, producer, 1979-83, exec. producer, 1983-92, v.p. news and pub. affairs, 1984-92; pres. Ever Green Communications Co., 1992—; prod. Religion and Ethics NewsWeekly on PBS, 1995—99. Producer TV specials The Power and the Glory, 1982 (Emmy 1983), Summer of Judgment: Watergate Hearings, 1983 (ABA award 1984); exec. producer TV series Making Sense of the 60's, 1991; producer, exec. producer TV series Washington Week in Review, 1980-90 (several awards); series producer Religion and Ethics News Weekly, PBS, 1997-99. Bd. dirs. Women in Film and Video, Washington, 1979-; mem. exec. bd. Women's Equity Action League, Washington, 1973-76. John S. Knight Prof. Journalism fellow, 1990-91. Mem. Soc. Profl. Journalists, Radio-TV Corrs. Assn., Women in Film & Video. Avocations: hiking, photography. Office: 2947 Macomb St NW Washington DC 20008 Fax: (202) 244-1673. E-mail: rickigr@aol.com.

GREEN, RUTHANN, marketing and management consultant; b. Streator, Ill., July 14, 1935; d. John Joseph and Edna Marie (Peters) G. BS in Edn., U. Ill., l957. Elem. tchr. Jefferson Sch., Davenport, Iowa, 1957-59; tchr. Hinsdale (Ill.) Jr. High Sch., 1959-62; edn1. cons. Harcourt Brace & World, Chgo., 1962-63; exec. sec. Everpure, Inc., Oakbrook, Ill., 1963-68; ednl. cons. Houghton Mifflin Co., Europe, 1968-69, Palo Alto, Calif., 1969-77, sr. mktg. mgr. Boston, 1977-87; v.p., nat. sales mgr. Riverside Pub. Co., Chgo., 1987-89; v.p., dir. mktg. McDougal, Littell & Co., Evanston, Ill., 1990-92; v.p., gen. mgr. Open Court Pub. Co., Chgo., 1992-94; pres. Peters & Green, Inc. Mktg. Svcs. and Bus. Devel., Chgo., 1994—. Author: WSIL: Why Should I Listen, 1987, 1993, 2004, A Garfield Memoir, 1995. Recipient Svc. award Am. Arbitration Assn., 1987, Golden Reel of Excellence Internat. TV Assn., 1983. Mem. ASCD, Am. Mktg. Assn., Nat. Assn. Women Bus. Owners, Internat. Reading Assn., People for Am. Way, Am. Arbitration Assn., Urban Gateways (v.p. bd. dirs., v.p.), Ritchie Tower Condo Assn. (bd. dirs., sec.). Avocations: reading, fitness activities, travel, art. Home and Office: 1310 N Ritchie Ct Apt 21A Chicago IL 60610-8405 Office Phone: 312-787-2767. E-mail: petersgreen@att.net.

GREEN, SHARON JORDAN, interior decorator; b. Mansfield, Ohio, Dec. 14, 1948; d. Garnet and L. Wynell (Baxley) Fraley; m. Trice Leroy Jordan Jr., Mar. 30, 1968 (dec. 1973); children: Trice Leroy III, Caerin Danielle, Christopher Robin; m. Joe Leonard Green, Mar. 13, 1978. Student, Ohio State U., 1966-67, 75-76, U. St. Thomas, 2001, Rice U., 1998—. Typist FBI, Washington, 1968; ward clk. Means Hall, Ohio State U. Hosp., Columbus, 1970; x-ray clk. Riverside Hosp., Columbus, 1971; contr., owner T&D Mold & Die, Houston, 1988—; interior decorator, franchise owner Decorating Den, Houston, 1989-91; owner T&D Interior Decorator, Houston, 1992—; custom window designer The Great Indoors, 2001—. Tchr. aide Bedford Sch., Mansfield, Ohio, 1976-77, Yeager Sch., 1981-82; pres. N.W. Welcome Wagon, Houston, 1980-81, Welcome Club, El Paso, 1986-87; active North Houston Symphony, 1992—, North Houston Performing Arts, 1993—, Mus. Fine Arts, Houston, 1993—, Edn. and Design Resource Network, 1993—, The Wellington Soc. for Arts, 1994, Jr. Forum, 1995, Rep. Nat. Com., 1995—, The Heritage Soc., 1999—; vol. Harris County Juvenile Probation Dept., 1996; chmn. N.W. Houston Symphony Student Competition, 1998-99, founding mem. The Centrum Arts League, 1998-99, mem. Ptnrs. of the Woodlands Arts Ctr., 1998-99, mem. The Shepard Sch. Music, Rice U., 1998—, Heritage Soc., Houston. Mem. United Daus. of Confederacy. Home: 15107 Parkview Dr Houston TX 77068

GREEN, SHARON VINCENTINE, counselor, consultant; b. Omaha, June 19, 1943; d. Clifford Dominic and Esther Jane (Copp) Szarkowski; m. Jasper E. Green Jr., July 12, 1986; children: Charity J. Green Keierleber, M. Robin Green Denke, Jasper E. III, Henry L., Rose Green Zaschlag. BS, Black Hills State U., 1981; MEd, S.D. State U., 1985. Lic. profl. counselor; cert. counselor, chem. dependency counselor level III. Social worker S.D. Dept. Social Svc., Deadwood, 1980-84; psychol. asst. Intercept, Custer, S.D., 1984-86; counselor River Park, Rapid City, S.D., 1987-89; program coord. Parkside River Park, Rapid City, S.D., 1989-90; clin. dir. Pennington Program, Rapid City, S.D., 1991-93, Project Acorn, Rapid City, S.D., 1992—; pvt. practice, 1990—; state senator State of S.D., 1992—. Pres. S.D. Chem. Dependency Assn., Rapid City, 1989-93, West River Counseling Assn., Rapid City, 1991; mem. appropriations com. S.D. Senate, 1992—. Bd. dirs. Big Bros./Big Sisters, 1991—, Minneluzehan Sr. Ctr., 1991—; mem. Women's Network, 1992—, Health and Human Resources Bd., 1993—. Democrat. Avocation: reading. Office: Sharon Green Counseling 430 E Waterloo St Rapid City SD 57701-1076

GREEN, SHIA TOBY RINER, therapist; b. N.Y.C.; d. Murray A. and Frances Riner; student CCNY; BA, Antioch Coll., MA, 1976; m. Gary S. Green, Sept. 4, 1957; children: Margot Laura, Vanessa Daryl, Garson Todd. Pres. and legis. sec. U.S. Ho. of Reps., Washington, 1960-71; cons. Rehab. Services Adminstrn., Social and Rehab. Services, HEW, 1972-73; asst. dir. State of Md. Foster Care Impact Demonstration Project, 1977-78; therapist Alexandria (Va.) Narcotics Treatment Program, 1979-84, Assocs. Psychotherapy Ctrs., Gaithersburg, Md., 1984—; mem. treatment com. Alexandria Case Mgmt. and Treatment of Child Sexual Abuse. Mem. exec. bd. Children's Adoption Resource Exchange, Washington; vol. worker Girl Scouts U.S.A., also Boy Scouts Am., 1970-74. Diplomate Am. Coll. Forensic Examiners; mem. APA, Md. Psychol. Assn., Am. Assn. Marriage and Family Therapy. Co-author: Permanent Planning in Maryland— A Manual for the Foster Care Worker. Office: 8915 Shady Grove Ct Gaithersburg MD 20877-1308 Home: 21150 NE 38th Ave Apt 2804 Aventura FL 33180-4043

GREEN, SHIRLEY MOORE, retired communications executive, public information officer; b. Graham, Tex., Dec. 21, 1933; d. N. Edgar and Cora Day (Morrow) Moore; m. Paul M. Green, Aug. 26, 1967 (div. 1981); children: Ruth Lynn, Tracy Moore Anderson. Student, Midwestern U., Wichita Falls, Tex., 1952; BBA, U. Tex., 1956. Staff asst. Rep. Party, Austin, Tex., 1965-67; press asst. Bob Price U.S. Rep., Washington, 1967; coordinator Tex. and Ark. Bush for Pres. Campaign, Houston, 1979-80; dep. press sec. V.p. Bush, Washington, 1984, acting press sec., 1983; dir. pub. affairs NASA, Washington, 1985-86, dep. assoc. adminstr. communications, 1987-89; spl. asst. to the Pres. White House, Washington, 1989-92, dep. asst. to Pres., 1992; dir. Pres. Bush Transition Office, Washington, 1993; dir. program support Internat. Rep. Inst., Washington, 1993-96; dir. corr. and constituent svcs. Gov. George W. Bush, Austin, 1996-2001; dir. comm. svcs. Atty Gen. John Cornyn, 2001—03. Local chmn. Jim Baker for Atty. Gen., 1978, Pres. Ford Com., San Antonio, 1976; trustee S.W. Found. Forum, San Antonio, 1974-78; bd. dirs. Child Welfare Bd. Bexar County, 1975-79; presdl. apptd. mem. J. William Fulbright Scholarship Bd. Recipient Exceptional Svc. medal NASA, 1989. Mem.: Tex. Fedn. Rep. Women (editor Partyline mag. 1969—72, one of 10 Outstanding Rep. Women Tex. 1979). Presbyterian. Avocations: reading, travel. Home: 1513 W 30th St Austin TX 78703-1403

GREEN, SONIA MARIA, automotive executive; Dir. U.S. Hispanic mktg. div. Avon Co.; dir. Hispanic diversity mktg. and sales GM, 2001—: Past pres. Nat. Hispanic Corp. Coun.; mem. bd. Las Madrinas Mentoring Program, Nat. Task Force on Early Edn. for Hispanics, Nat. Hispanic Leadership Inst.; spkr. in field. Named to Elite Women, Hispanic Bus. Mag., 2005.

GREEN, TAMMIE, professional golfer; b. Somerset, Ohio, Dec. 17, 1959; Degree in recreation, Marshall U. Prol. golfer, 1986—. Mem. exec. com LPGA, 1992-94. Named Rookie of Yr. LPGA, 1987; 6 career wins including 1989 du Maurier Ltd. Classic, Healthsouth Palm Beach Classic, Rochester Internat., 1993, Youngstown-Warren LPGA Classic, 1994, Sprint Titleholder Champion, Gaintt Eagle LPGA Classic, 1997, LPGA Corning Classic, 1998. Avocations: fishing, gardening, horseback riding, sports. Office: 3990 Twp Rd 147 Somerset OH 43783

GREEN, THERESA DIANE, social worker; b. Port Angelas, Wash., Oct. 10, 1939; d. Walter Arnold and Edna Katherine (Lanich) Vickery; m. Norman Edward Green, Sept. 5, 1964 (div. June 1983); children: Darrin Scott, Brian Allen. BS in Psychology, Wash. State U., 1961; MSW, U. Denver, 1969. Child welfare worker Spokane (Wash.) County State Dept Pub Assistance, 1962-64, State Dept Pub Assistance, Colfax, Wash., 1970-72; asst. prof. social work Wash. State U., Pullman, 1970-76; diagnostic intake worker Whitman County Mental Health, Pullman, 1974-76; child abuse psychiat. social worker Humboldt Child Care Council, Eureka, Calif., 1978-84; pvt. practice in social work Arcata, Calif., 1983—. Cons. Hoffman Inst., San Francisco, 1984—, Humboldt and Del Norte Counties, Eureka, 1985—, Rural Human Services Domestic Violence Program Services to Children, 1986, Humboldt Women for Shelter-Therapist to Child Victims of Domestic Violence; spkr. Carl Rogers 100th Anniversary Internat. Conf., Rio de Janeiro, 2006. Recipient Redwood Broadcasting Heroism award, 1982; named Outstanding Faculty Mem. of Yr. Wash. State U., 1974. Mem. Nat. Assn. Social Workers (cert.), Inst. for Advancement Human Behavior (presenter on child abuse 1988), Women Against Pornography, Serious Legis. Against Molesters, Psi Chi. Democrat. Avocations: art, music, creative visualization. Home and Office: 1179 Stromberg Ave Arcata CA 95521-5121 Office Phone: 707-822-4056.

GREEN, VICKIE, music educator; b. Shawnee, Okla., Jan. 2, 1952; m. Richard David Green, June 22, 1990; children: Angela Dawn Copeland, Richard David II. B. in Music Edn., Okla. Bapt. U., 1974. Music tchr. Krouch Elem. Sch., Tecumseh, Okla., 1975—78; clk. Okla. Gas & Electric, Oklahoma City, 1985—90; computer clk. SW Med. Ctr., Moore, Okla., 1990—93; music tchr. Apple Creek Elem. Sch., Moore, Okla., 1993—2005, Wayland Bonds Elem. Sch., Moore, 2005—. Dir. Moore Elem. Honor Choir, Okla., 1993—. Mem.: Music Educators Nat. Conf., Orgn. Nat. Kodaly Educators, Orgn. Okla. Kodaly Educators, Nat. Educators Assn., Okla. Educators Assn. Home: 213 North Wyndemere Lakes Dr Moore OK 73160 Office: Wayland Bonds Elem Sch 14025 S May Ave Oklahoma City OK 73170 Office Phone: 405-735-4500. Personal E-mail: muslcmom@aol.com.

GREENAWALT, PEGGY FREED TOMARKIN, advertising executive; b. Cleve., Apr. 27, 1942; d. Bernard H. and Gyta Elinor (Arsham) Freed; m. Gary Tomarkin, Aug. 7, 1966 (div. 1981); children: Craig William, Eric Lawrence; m. William Sloan Greenawalt, Oct. 31, 1987. BS, Simmons Coll., 1964. Asst. account exec. Howard Marks/Norman, Craig & Kummel, Inc., N.Y.C., 1964-66; account exec. Shaw Bros. Advt. Co., N.Y.C., 1966-67; copywriter Claire Advt. Co., N.Y.C., 1967; ptnr. Copywriters Coop., Hartsdale, N.Y., 1970-73; copy chief Howard Marks Advt., N.Y.C., 1973-80; sr. copywriter Wunderman, Ricotta & Kline, N.Y.C., 1980-82; v.p., assoc. creative dir. Ayer-Direct (N.W. Ayer), N.Y.C., 1982-84; sr. v.p. creative dir. D'Arcy Direct (D'Arcy MacManus & Masius), N.Y.C., 1984-86; pres. Tomarkin/Greenawalt, Inc., N.Y.C., 1986—. Judge Echo Awards, Caples Awards, Fin. Comm. Soc. Awards. Author: Kiss, The Real Story, 1980. Dem. dist. leader. Mem. Direct Mktg. Assn., Women in Comms., Direct Mktg. Club N.Y., Westchester Assn. Women Bus. Owners (past pres.). Office: 24 Lewis Ave Hartsdale NY 10530 Office Phone: 914-683-8833. E-mail: pegdirect@aol.com.

GREENBERG, ANGELA BARMBY, lawyer; b. Kansas City, Mo., 1969; m. Andrew Greenberg; 1 child. BA, U. Kans., Lawrence, 1992; JD, U. Tulsa Coll. Law, 1996. Bar: Tex. 1997. Assoc. Lanier Law Firm, Houston, 2000—. Mem. editl. bd.: Energy Law Jour., 1996. Named a Rising Star, Tex. Super Lawyers mag., 2006. Mem.: Trial Lawyers for Pub. Justice, Assn. Trial Lawyers of Am., Houston Young Lawyers Assn., ABA, Houston Bar Assn. Office: Lanier Law Firm PC 6810 FM 1960 West Houston TX 77069 Office Phone: 713-659-5200.*

GREENBERG, ARLINE FRANCINE, artist; b. NYC; m. Sidney Greenberg. BA, Hunter Coll.; postgrad., NYU; AS, Parson Sch. Design, Pratt Inst. Ind. practice cons. firm in jewelry and design; v.p. Reliable Textile Co., NYC; fashion dir. Burlington Klopman Fabrics, NYC, 1988—92. Guest lectr. AWED, Fashion Inst. Tech. Contbr. articles to newspapers. Mem. Citizens Union, Opera Guild, Smithsonian, Met. Mus. Art, Preservation Soc. Recipient medal in Fine Arts; scholar, NYU. Mem.: Victorian Soc. NYC. Avocations: travel, art, architecture, opera, music. Home: 555 Kappock St Apt 15D Riverdale NY 10463-6458

GREENBERG, BONNIE LYNN, music industry executive; b. Roslyn Heights, NY, May 22, 1956; d. Morris U. Greenberg and Rozlyn (Wilner) Sadkin. BA, U. Denver, 1975; JD, Southwestern U., 1978. Bar: Calif. 1979, NY 1980. Lawyer ABC Records, Inc., LA, 1977-79; dir. bus. affairs MCA Records, Inc., Universal City, Calif., 1980-83, Paramount Pictures, 1984; co-chmn. Media MusiCons., LA, 1988-93; CEO Ocean Cities Entertainment, Inc., Santa Monica, Calif., 1993—. Judge anti-drug video contest NY Dept. Edn., 1988; prof., music supr. UCLA. Author: Negotiating Contracts in the Entertainment Industry, 1987, Music Volume; theatre prodr.: Getting Through the Night, 1985; music. supr. motion pictures include Hairspray, Book of Love, Menace II Society, The Mask, Corrina, Corrina, The Santa Clause, Flirting with Disaster, Dead Presidents, The Truth about Cats and Dogs, The Long Kiss Goodnight, My Best Friend's Wedding, Pleasantville, Parent Trap, The Muse, EdTV, How The Grinch Stole Christmas, What Women Want, Unconditional Love, Undercover Brother, Stuart Little 2, Peter Pan, Something's Gotta Give, Son of the Mask. Atty. Bet Tzedek, LA, 1987. Recipient Gov's. plaque NY, 1988. Democrat. Avocations: photography, sports, writing, languages, music.

GREENBERG, CAROLYN PHYLLIS, retired anesthesiologist; b. San Francisco, July 7, 1941; AB, Stanford U., 1962; MD, U. Calif., San Francisco, 1966. Diplomate Am. Bd. Anesthesiology. Rotating intern L.A. County Hosp., 1966-67; resident in anesthesiology Presbyn. Hosp., NYC, 1967-69, vis. fellow in anesthesiology, 1969-70, asst. attending anesthesiologist, 1971-90, assoc. attending anesthesiologist, 1990-99, med. dir. ambulatory surgery, 1986-96, attending anesthesiologist, 1999; asst. attending anesthesiologist NY Hosp., 1970-71; attending anesthesiologist NY Presbyn. Hosp., 1999—2006; ret., 2006. Instr. anesthesiology Cornell Med. Sch., 1970—71; assoc. anesthesiology Columbia U., NYC, 1971—74, asst. prof. clin. anesthesiology, 1974—90, assoc. prof. clin. anesthesiology, 1990—99, prof. clin. anesthesiology, 1999, prof. emerita anesthesiology, 1999—; clin. prof. anesthesiology Cornell Med. Sch., 1999—2006. Contbr. book chpts., articles to profl. jours. Mem. Am. Soc. Anesthesiologists, NY State Soc. Anesthesiologists (Media award 1992), Med. Soc. NY, Soc. Ambulatory Anesthesia (treas. 1994-98, 2nd v.p. 1998-99, 1st v.p. 1999, Ambulatory Anesthesia Rsch. Found. award 1992), Malignant Hyperthermia Assn. of US (hotline cons. 1983-99, partnership award 1996). Jewish. Avocations: swimming, reading, piano, travel. Personal E-mail: cgfcalvin@yahoo.com.

GREENBERG, CORINNE HUNT, psychotherapist; b. Little Rock, Dec. 12, 1941; d. O.T. and Virginia Elizabeth Hunt; m. David H. Greenberg, June 1, 1964; children: Tracy Elizabeth Wolff, Ashley Corinne Petzold. BS in Edn., Henderson State U., 1963; MS, Nova U., 1994, EdD, 1998. Cert. tchr., Fla., Mo.; lic. mental health counselor, Fla. Tchr. Post (Tex.) Elem. Sch., 1963-64, Margate (Fla.) Elem. Sch., 1981-85; psychotherapist Meridian Behavioral Healthcare, Dixie/Gilchrist Counties, Fla., 1994—. Pvt. practice counseling, Gainesville, Fla., 1998—. Author: Parent Idea Book: Enjoy Your Children and Maintain Control at the Same Time, 1998. Leader Girl Scouts U.S., Del Mar, Calif., 1970's, Memphis, 1970's, Coral Springs, Fla., 1980's. Mem.

ACA, Nat. Bd. Cert. Counselors, Assn. for Play Therapy, Inc., DAR, Rep. Women's Club, Altrusa Internat. Methodist. Avocations: running marathons, painting, reading. Home: 8107 SW 43d Pl Gainesville FL 32608

GREENBERG, ELINOR MILLER, director, consultant; b. Bklyn., Nov. 13, 1932; d. Ray and Susan (Weiss) Miller; m. Manuel Greenberg, Dec. 26, 1955; children: Andrea, Julie, Michael. BA, Mt. Holyoke Coll., 1953; MA, U. Wis.-Madison, 1954; EdD, U. No. Colo., 1981; LittD (hon.), St. Mary-of-the-Woods, Ind., 1983; LHD (hon.), Profl. Sch. Psychology, Calif., 1987. Speech pathologist U. Colo., Denver, 1954—69, mem. faculty, 1967—69, exec. dir., Arapahoe Inst. for Cmty. Devel., 1969—71; founding dir., nat. coord. Univ. without Walls, Loretto Heights Coll., Denver, 1971—79, asst. acad. dean, 1982—84, asst. to pres., 1984—85; regional exec. officer Coun. for Adult and Experiential Learning, Chgo., 1979—91; founding exec. dir. US West Comm.-CWA, Pathways to the Future, 1986—91; rsch. assoc. Inst. Rsch. on Adults in Higher Edn., U. Md., U. Coll., 1991; exec. dir. Project Leadership, 1986—. Project dir. Healthcare Seminars, Colo. Rural New Economy Initiative, 2000-02; pres., CEO EMG and Assocs., 1991—; cons. US West Found., No. Telecom, Rose Found., U. Colo. at Denver, Cogeoinfo., 1992-96, NEON Project, State Scholars Initiative, Western Interstate Commn. Higher Edn., 2003—06, NEAT Project, U. Wis., 2003—2006, Colo. Dept. Labor and Employment, 2004-05, Colo. AHEC Sys., U. Colo. Health Scis. Ctr.; founding regional coord. Mountain and Plains Partnership, 1996-02; adminstr. Visible Human Project-Undergrad., 2002-04. Co-editor, contbr.: Educating Learners of All Ages, 1980; co-author: Designing Undergraduate Education, 1981, Widening Ripples, 1986, Leading Effectively, 1987, In Our Fifties: Voices of Men and Women Reinventing Their Lives, 1993, MAPP Online Voices, 2000; editor, contbr.: New Partnerships: Higher Education and the Nonprofit Sector, 1982, Enhancing Leadership, 1989; author: Weaving: The Fabric of a Woman's Life, 1991, Journey for Justice, 1993; guest editor Liberal Edn. Jour.; gen. editor Seven MAPP Studies, 2002; feature writer Colo. Woman News, 1993-96, Women's Bus. News, 1995-96; contbr. Sculpting The Learning Organization, 1993; contbr. articles to profl. jours. Bd. dirs., exec. com. Anti Defamation League of B'nai B'rith, Denver, 1981-99, chair women's leadership com., 1991-93, bd. dirs., 1985-95; mem. Colo. State Bd. C.C. and Occupl. Edn., 1981-86, vice-chair, 1984-85; bd. dirs. Internat. Women's Forum, 1986-88, Internat. Women's Forum Leadership Found., 1991-95, Griffith Ctr., Golden, Colo., 1982-86, Colo. Bd. CLE and Jud. Edn., 1984-96; bd. dirs. Colo. Jud. Inst., 2004—, vice chair, 2005-; mem. Women's Forum Colo., 1981-, pres. 1986; v.p. Women's Forum Colo. Found., 1987; adv. bd. Anchor Ctr. Blind Child, Colo. Coalition Prevention Nuclear War, Mile Hi Girl Scouts, Nat. Conf. on Edn. Women's Devel.; cmty. adv. bd. Colo. Woman News; adv. com. Colo. Pvt. Occupl. Sch., 1990-98, Colo. Cmty. Incentive Fund; co-chair Gov.'s Women's Econ. Devel. Taskforce, Women's Econ. Devel. Coun., 1988-96; bd. visitors U. Hosp., U. Colo., 1990-91, gov. apptd. Colo. Math., Sci. and Tech. Commn., chair, 1991-93, co-telecom. adv. commn. TAC 14, chair, 1993-95; founding steering com. Colo. Women's Leadership Coalition, 1988-96; mem. interdisciplinary telecomm. program, exec. bd. U. Colo., 1992-03; U.S. Dept. Edn., mem. Tech. Panels, 1991—, mem. Expert Panel on Lifelong Learning, 1999-02, Western AHEC Reg. Learning System, chair, coursework com., 1998; bd. dirs. Colo. Rural Tech. Program, 1996-00, Housing for All/Metro Denver Fair Housing Ctr., 1999-03, chair, 2002-03; chair Colo. Coalition for the Advancement of Telehealth, 2002-03; co-chair Colo. Coun. on Telehealth, 2003; mem. U. Physicians Inc. Task Force on Telehealth, 2003; mem. industry adv bd. MESA, 2002-05, bd. dirs., 2005-; mem. planning com. Colo. Women's Health Rsch. Symposium, 2004-05. Named Citizen of Yr., Omega Psi Phi, Denver, 1966, Woman of Decade Littleton Ind. Newspapers, 1970; recipient Sesquicentennial award Mt. Holyoke Coll. Alumni Assn., 1987, Minoru Yasui Cmty. Vol. award, 1991, Women of Excellence award Colo. Women's Leadership Coalition, 1996, Founding Mothers award, 1997, Woman of Dist., Mile High Girl Scouts, 1997, Martin Luther King Disting. Svc. award to Littleton Coun. for Human Rels., Arapahoe C.C., 2003, 06, Arthur and Bea Branscombe Meml. award Housing for All: The Metro Denver Fair Housing Ctr., 2003, Martin Luther Kind Disting. Svc. award, Araphoe C.C., 2006, MESA Disting. Svc. award, 2006; grantee W. K. Kellogg Found., 1982, Weyerhaeuser Found., 1986, Fund for Improvement of Post Secondary Edn., 1977, 80, Robert Wood Johnson Found., 1997-2002. Mem. Kappa Delta Pi. Democrat. Jewish. Home: 6725 S Adams Way Littleton CO 80122-1801 Office Phone: 303-771-3560. Business E-Mail: ellie.greenberg@uchsc.edu.

GREENBERG, HINDA FEIGE, library director; b. Bayreuth, Germany, Feb. 26, 1947; arrived in U.S., 1951; d. Samuel Leon and Sima (Schampagnere) F.; m. Joseph Lawrence, July 6, 1968; children: David Micah, Jacob Alexander. BA, Temple U., 1969; MLS, Rutgers U., 1981; PhD, Drexel U., 1999. Assoc. librarian Ednl. Testing Svc., Princeton, NJ, 1981-86; dir. info. ctr. Carnegie Found., Princeton, 1986-97, Robert Wood Johnson Found., Princeton, 1997—. Former pres. Consortium of Found. Librs. Avocation: travel.

GREENBERG, JOANNE, author, anthropologist; b. Bklyn., Sept. 24, 1932; m. Albert Greenberg, 1955; children: David, Alan. BS in Anthropology and English Lt., Am. U., Washington; postgrad., U. London, U. Colo.; DHL, Gallaudet Coll., 1979; DL, Western Md. Coll., 1977; DHL, U. Colo., 1987. Assoc. prof. anthropology Colo. Sch. of Mines. Speaker in field; condr. seminars and workshops in field; tutor in Latin and Hebrew. Author: The King's Persons, 1963, I Never Promised You a Rose Garden, 1964, The Monday Voices, 1965, Summering: A Book of Short Stories, 1966, In This Sign, 1970, Rites of Passage, 1972, Founder's Praise, 1976, High Crimes and Misdemeanors, 1979, A Season of Delight, 1981, The Far Side of Victory, 1983, Simple Gifts, 1986, Age of Consent, 1987, Of Such Small Differences, 1988, With The Snow Queen, 1991, No Reck'ning Made, 1993. Condr. Bar Mitzveh preparation Beth Evergreen Congregation. Recipient H. and E. Daroff Meml. award, 1963, William and Janice Eppstein Fiction award, 1964, Cmty. Grange Award for Citizenship, Fromm Reichmann award, 1967, Kenner award, 1971, Christopher award, 1971, Rocky Mountain Women's Inst. award, 1983, Cmty. Grange award, Denver Pub. Libr. Bookplate award, 1990, Colo. Author of Yr. award, 1991. Home: 29175 Summit Ranch Dr Golden CO 80401-9765

GREENBERG, JUDITH HOROVITZ, geneticist; b. Phila., Apr. 2, 1947; d. Monty B. and Evelyn (Cohen) Horovitz; m. Warren Greenberg, June 8, 1969; 1 child, Elyssa H. BS in Biology, U. Pitts., 1967; MA in Biology, Boston U., 1970; PhD in Biology, Bryn Mawr Coll., 1972. Rsch. assoc. ARC, Bethesda, Md., 1971—74; postdoctoral fellow NIH, Bethesda, 1974—75, sr. staff fellow, 1975—81, health scientist adminstr., 1981—88; dir. divsn. genetics and devel. biology NIH, Nat. Inst. Gen. Med. Scis., Bethesda, 1988—; acting dir. Nat. Inst. Gen. Med. Scis. NIH, Bethesda, 2002—03. Recipient Pub. Health Svc. Spl. Recognition award, 1991, Presdl. Meritorious Exec. award, 1999, NIH Dirs. award, 2004, 06. Mem. Soc. Devel. Biology, Am. Soc. Cell Biology, Am. Soc. Human Genetics, AAAS, Sigma Xi. Office: NIGMS NIH 45 Center Dr Bldg 45 Bethesda MD 20892-6200 E-mail: greenbej@nigms.nih.gov.

GREENBERG, LENORE, public relations professional; b. Flushing; d. Jack and Frances Orenstein. BA, Hofstra U.; MS, SUNY. Dir. pub. rels. Bloomingdale's, Short Hills, N.J., 1977-78; dir. comms. N.J. Sch. Bds. Assn., Trenton, 1978-82; dir pub. info. N.J. State Dept. Edn., Trenton, 1982-90; assoc. exec. dir. Nat. Sch. Pub. Rels. Assn., Arlington, Va., 1990-91; pres. Lenore Greenberg & Assocs., Inc., 1991—. Adj. prof. pub. rels. Rutgers U. Freelance feature writer N.Y. Times. Mem. bd. assocs. McCarter Theatre, Princeton, N.J.; mem. Franklin Twp. Zoning Bd. Adjustment; mem. Franklin Twp. Human Rels. Commn.; chair Somerset County LWV; instr. Bus. Vols. for the Arts. Recipient award Am. Soc. Assn. Execs., award Women in Comms., award Internat. Assn. Bus. Communicators; Gold Medallion awrd Nat. Sch. Pub. Rels. Assn. Mem. Pub. Rels. Soc. Am. (accredited; pres. N.J. State chpt., nat. nominating and accreditation coms., Silver Anvil award), Nat. Health/Edn. Consortium. Home and Office: 30971 Carrara Rd Laguna Niguel CA 92677-2757

GREENBERG, LINDA GARRETT, education educator, volunteer, singer; b. Hanover, Pa., June 8, 1941; d. Richard Barnhart and Lillian (Shaffer) Garrett; m. Frederic Greenberg, Apr. 2, 1966; children: Timothy, Richard, Joshua. BA, Bucknell Univ., Lewisburg, Pa., 1963; MA, Columbia Univ., NY, NY, 1964. Asst. prof., speech and theatre Montclair State Coll., Montclair, NJ, 1964—70; actor, children's theatre Pushcart Players, Caldwell, NJ, 1972—73; tchr. John Robert Power Sch., NYC, 1964—67, NY Bus. Sch., NYC, 1967—68; adj. prof. Fairleigh Dickinson Univ., Rutherford, NJ, 1991—93, Montclair State Univ., Montclair, NJ, 1993—99, ret., 1999. Singer: (oratorio) NY Oratorio Soc., 1964—69; performer: (plays) Caldwell Players, 1970—74; singer: (oratorio) NJ Oratorio Soc., 1970—74; performer: (plays) Caldwell Players, 1980, Glen Ridge Cmty. Players, 1991; soloist: Keys Chorale (Key West). Trustee Bucknell Univ., Lewisburg, Pa., 1995—, alumni bd. dir., 1991—95; mem. mktg. com. Cmty. Found., Key West; bd. mem. The Actors Co. Theatre, NYC, 2005—; bd. dirs. Founders Soc., Key West, 2005—. Mem.: ednl. organizations (v.p.), Key West Arts and Hist. Soc. (soloist), Assn. of Gov. Bd. (AGB), Assn. of Univ. Women (AAUW), Turnip Theatre (bd. mem. 1990—2000), Arts Coun. of the Essex Area (v.p. 1973—80), Jr. League of Montclair (pres. 1976—78), art organizations (v.p.). Jewish. Avocations: singing, travel, reading, attending concerts and theatre, museums. Home (Winter): 17027 Flying Fish Lane Sugarloaf FL 33042 Home (Summer): 45 E 89th St Apt 31E New York NY 10128 E-mail: lgreenb@msn.com.

GREENBERG, ROSALIE, child psychiatrist; b. Bklyn., Dec. 21, 1950; d. Sam and Molly G.; BA, NYU, 1972; student Upstate Med. Ctr., Syracuse, 1972-73; MD, Columbia U., 1976. Intern Overlook Hosp., Summit, N.J., 1976-77; resident in gen. psychiatry Columbia Presbyn. Med. Ctr., N.Y. State Psychiatric Inst., N.Y.C., 1977-80, fellow in child and adolescent psychiatry, 1979-81, dep. dir. pediatric psychiatry outpatient clinic, 1981-82; dir. child and adolescent outpatient services Fair Oaks Hosp., Summit, N.J., 1982—; instr. Columbia U., 1981—. Mem. Am. Psychiat. Assn., Am. Acad. Child and Adolescent Psychiatry, AMA. Office: Fair Oaks Hosp 19 Prospect St Summit NJ 07901-2531

GREENBERGER, ELLEN, psychologist, educator; b. NYC, Nov. 19, 1935; d. Edward Michael and Vera (Brisk) Silver; m. Michael Burton, Aug. 26, 1979; children by previous marriage: Kari Edwards, David Silver. BA, Vassar Coll., 1956; MA, Harvard U., 1959, PhD, 1961. Instr. Wellesley (Mass.) Coll., 1961—67; sr. rsch. scientist Johns Hopkins U., Balt., 1967-76; prof. psychology and social behavior U. Calif., Irvine, 1976—. Author: (with others) When Teenagers Work, 1986; contbr. articles to profl. jours. USPHS fellow, 1956-59; Margaret Floy Washburn fellow, 1956-58; Ford Found. grantee, 1979-81; Spencer Found. grantee, 1979-81, 87, 88-91. Fellow Am. Psychol. Assn., Am. Psychol. Soc.; mem. Soc. Rsch. in Child Devel., Soc. Rsch. on Adolescent Devel. Office: U Calif 3340 Social Ecology II Irvine CA 92697-7085 Business E-Mail: egreenbe@uci.edu.

GREENBERGER, MARCIA DEVINS, lawyer; b. Apr. 24, 1946; AB, U. Pa., 1967, JD, 1970; LLD (hon.), Lafayette U., 2000. Bar: D.C. 1970. Co-pres. Nat. Women's Law Ctr., Washington; atty. Caplin & Drysdale, Wash., 1970—72; dir. Women's Rights Project Ctr. Law and Social Policy (now Nat. Women's Law Ctr.), 1972—81, co-pres. Named Woman Lawyer of Yr., D.C. Women's Bar Assn., 1996; named one of 25 Heroines, Working Women Mag.; recipient Woman of Distinction award, Soroptimist Internat., 2000, William J. Brennan award, D.C. Bar, 1994. Fellow: Am. Bar Found.; mem.: ABA (coun. individual rights and responsibilities sect.), Am. Law Inst. Office: Nat Womens Law Ctr Ste 800 11 Dupont Circ NW Washington DC 20036 Office Phone: 202-588-5180.

GREENBERGER, MARSHA MOSES, sales executive; b. Lakewood, N.J., Mar. 15, 1943; d. Bernard David and Ethel (Gordon) Moses; m. Paul Edward Greenberger (div. 1969); 1 child, Nathan Scott. Student, Kent (Ohio) State U., 1961-62. Mgr. gen. sales Ellison Products, Fairfield, N.J., 1972-79; gen. mgr. Indsl. Maintenance Corp., Cherry Hill, N.J., 1979-83; co-owner corp. sect. Ven-Mar Sales, Inc., Blairstown, N.J., 1983-89; pres. MGM Sales, Inc., 1989—. Avocations: skiing, world travel, egyptology. Office: MGM Sales 29 High Ridge Rd Randolph NJ 07869-4567

GREENBLATT, HELLEN CHAYA, immunologist, microbiologist; b. Frankfurt au Main, Germany; came to U.S., 1948; d. Gedaljie and Sara (Glass) Greenblatt. BA, CCNY, 1968; MS, U. Okla., 1971; PhD, SUNY Downstate Med. Ctr., Bklyn., 1977. Microbiologist Walter Reed Army Inst., Washington, 1978-80; sr. rsch. immunoparasitologist Merck Sharp & Dohme, Rahway, NJ, 1980-81; assoc. Albert Einstein Coll. Medicine, Bronx, NY, 1981-84; dir. rsch. and devel. Clin. Scis. Inc., Whippany, NJ, 1984-86, dir. new bus. and sci. devel., 1986-88; sr. devel. virology E.I. DuPont, Wilmington, Del., 1988-90; mng. dir. M-CAP Techs. Internat./DCV, Wilmington, 1990-93; tech. rep. BTR Separations, Wilmington, 1993-94; v.p. R & D, DCV Biol. Scis., Wilmington, 1994-97; v.p. devel. Life Scis. divsn. DCV BioNutrition, Wilmington, 1997-2000; v.p. Legacy USA, Melbourne, Fla., 1999—2002; exec. v.p. Legacy for Life, 2002—04, chief sci. officer, 2004—. Numerous internat. and domestic tech. presentations in field. Contbr. chpt. to book, numerous articles to peer-review profl. jours. Tutor Lit. Vols. Am., 1992—97; bd. dirs. Interfaith Housing of Del., 1993—97. Recipient Outstanding Young Woman award Competitive Resident Rsch. Coun., Washington, 1978; grantee NRC, 1978-80; fellow NRC. Mem.: NY Acad. Scis., Am. Acad. Anti-Aging Medicine, Del. Acad. Medicine. Achievements include patents for gastroprotective, anti-inflammatory and anti-diarrheal properties of immune egg; among the foremost authorities on polyvalent hyperimmune egg (PHIE) for human and pet applications. Office: Legacy for Life 2725 Ctr Pl Melbourne FL 32940 Office Phone: 800-825-9601. Business E-Mail: hgreenblatt@legacyforlife.net.

GREENBLATT, MIRIAM, writer, editor, educator; b. Berlin; d. Gregory and Shifra (Zemach) Baraks; m. Howard Greenblatt (div.). BA magna cum laude, Hunter Coll.; postgrad., U. Chgo. Editor Am. People's Ency., Chgo., 1957-58, Scott Foresman & Co., Chgo., 1958-62; pres. Creative Textbooks, Chgo., 1972—. Tchr. New Trier (Ill.) HS, 1978—81. Author (with Chu): The Story of China, 1968; author: (with Cuban) Japan, 1971; author: The History of Itasca, 1976; author: (with others) The American People, 1986; author: James Knox Polk, 1988, Franklin Delano Roosevelt, 1989, John Quincy Adams, 1990; author: (with Welty) The Human Expression, 1992; author: Cambodia, 1995; author: (with Jordan and Bowes) The Americans, 1996; author: Hatshepsut and Ancient Egypt, 2000, Alexander the Great and Ancient Greece, 2000, Augustus and Imperial Rome, 2000, Peter the Great and Tsarist Russia, 2000, Genghis Khan and the Mongol Empire, 2002, Elizabeth I and Tudor England, 2002, The War of 1812, 2003, Iran, 2003, Charlemagne and the Early Middle Ages, 2003, Suleyman the Magnificent and the Ottoman Empire, 2003, Lorenzo de Medici and Renaissance Italy, 2003, Afghanistan, 2003, Julius Caesar and the Roman Republic, 2005, Han Wu Di and Ancient China, 2005, Napoleon Bonaparte and Imperial France, 2005; author: (with Lemmo) Human Heritage, 2006; editl. cons. Peoples and Cultures Series, 1976—78, subject area cons. World Geography and Cultures, 1994; contbg. editor: A World History, 1979. Mem. nat. exec. coun. Am. Jewish Com., 1980—84, v.p. Chgo chpt., 1977—79; treas. Glencoe Youth Svcs., 1981—83. Mem.: Cliff Dwellers, Nat. Assn. Scholars. Jewish. Address: 2754 Roslyn Ln Highland Park IL 60035-1408

GREENBURG, SHARON LOUISE, psychologist; b. Chgo., Aug. 29, 1941; d. Irving and Ethel (Vinitzky) Rosenholtz; m. Joel H. Greenburg, Apr. 11, 1963; children: Douglas Neil, Jayne Ellen. BS, Northwestern U., 1963; MEd, Loyola U. Chgo., 1978, PhD, 1981. Pvt. practice psychologist, Chgo., 1981—, Arlington Heights, Ill., 1987—. Adj. prof. Loyola U., Chgo., 1981-86; cons. Cyborg Corp., Chgo., 1986—, Premark Corp., Deerfield, Ill., 1986—. Author: (with others) Casebook of Multimodal Therapy; contbr. articles to profl. jours. Bd. dirs. Chgo. chpt. Am. Jewish Com. Mem. Am. Psychol. Assn. (div. 42 psychologists in ind. practice), Ill. Psychol. Assn. Office: 1655 N Arlington Heights Ste 205E Arlington Heights IL 60004

GREENE, ADELE S., management consultant; b. Newark; d. Adolph and Sara (Schubert) Shuminer; m. Alan Greene (div.); 1 child, Joshua. Student, Juilliard Sch. Music, 1942-44, NYU, 1942-44, New Sch. Social Research, 1944-47; diploma in mgmt., Harvard Bus. Sch., 1978. Account exec. Ruder and Finn Inc., N.Y.C., 1964-66, sr. assoc., 1966-68, v.p., 1968-72, sr. v.p., 1972-76; v.p. pub. affairs Corp. Pub. Broadcasting, Washington, 1976-78; pres., CEO TV Program Group, Washington, 1978-80; pres. Greene and Assocs., N.Y.C., 1981—. Exec. dir. Am. Friends of Brit. Mus., 1994—; instr. pub. relations and community affairs, NYU 1974-76; bd. dirs. Sci. Program Group, Washington 1976-81; treas., bd. dirs. Coliseum Park Apts. Author Sara's Legacy, 2005; co-author: Teen-Age Leadership, 1971. Advisor The Acting Co., Understudies, N.Y.C., 1987—; pres., CEO Am. Craft Coun., 1980-81, trustee, 1976-81; bd. dirs. Union Settlement, N.Y.C., 1987-90; trustee Duke Ellington Sch. Arts, Washington, 1977-81, Inst. for Cancer Prevention, 2002—. Mem. Pub. Relations Soc. Am. (silver anvil award 1971), Nat. Assn. Edn. Broadcasters, Am. Women Radio and TV. Home and Office: 30 W 60th St New York NY 10023-7902

GREENE, ANNIE LUCILLE, artist, retired art educator; b. Waycross, Ga. d. Henry William and Ella Mae (Hall) Tarver; m. Oliver Nathaniel Greene; children: Zinta LaRecia Greene Perkins, Oliver N. Greene, Jr. BS, Albany State Coll., 1954; MA, NYU, 1961. Art tchr. Thomasville (Ga.) Sch. Sys., 1954—55, Troup County Sch. Sys., LaGrange, Ga., 1955—89; ret., 1989. Apptd. mem. Ga. Humanities Coun., 2002—; artist in residence Matthew Elem. Sch., Columbus, Ga., Thomasville Elem. Sch., Thomason Mid. Sch., Ga., West Side Magnet Sch., LaGrange, Ga. 46 one-woman art shows, 1976—, 163 group exhbns., 1962— (numerous awards). Past mem. Neighborhood Housing Svcs. Pub. Rels. com.; Grand Marshall Sweet Land of Liberty July 4th Parade, LaGrange, 2001; pianist St. Paul African Meth. Episcopal Ch. and McGhee Chapel African Meth. Episcopal Ch., Hogansville, Ga., trustee, chmn. stewardship and fin. commn.; bd. dirs. March of Dimes, 1991—; bd. mem. Keep Troup Beautiful, 1997—2001; past bd. dirs. LaGrange Meml. Libr. Named one of Gracious Ladies of Ga., 1998; recipient Outstanding Svc., St. Paul A.M.C. Ch., 2000, Citizen of Yr. award, McGhee Chapel A.M.E. Ch., 1999. Mem.: LaGrange Symphony Guild, LaGrange Artist Guild, Troup Ret. Tchrs. Assn. (past sect.), Chattahoochee Valley Art Mus. (past bd. mem.), The Links, Inc. (pres. 1985—87, Outstanding Svc. award 1987, sec. 1995—99, parliamentarian 1999—2001, pres. 1999—2001, Presdl. award 2001, sec. 2003—05, LaGrange chpt., Outstanding Svc. award 1987, Presdl. award 2001), Alpha Phi Alpha, Delta Sigma Theta (pres. 1991—93, LaGrange Alumnae chpt. Presdl. awards 1993—97, pres. 1995—97, fund raiser chair 2001—05, LaGrange Alumnae chpt. Presdl. awards 1993—97, Annie B. Singleton award 2000, numerous other awards). Avocations: music, crafts, reading, photography, travel. Home: 712 Pyracantha Dr Lagrange GA 30241

GREENE, CHRISTINE ELIZABETH, artist; b. Chelm, Poland, Mar. 29, 1945; came to the U.S., 1949; d. Stanley and Irene (Gering) Lipert; m. Stephen M. Greene, Aug. 25, 1974; 1 child, Valerie I. Diploma, Newark Sch. Fine Indsl. Arts, 1965; BFA, Moore Coll. Art, 1968. Textile designer Lowenstein & Sons, N.Y.C., 1968-71, Schwartz & Leibman Textiles, N.Y.C., 1971-77; party caricaturist Syosset, NY, 1981—; owner Caricatures by Chris Greene, 1984—. Recipient Art award Grumbacker Art Supplies, 1981, Award of Excellence Channel 21 Art Show, 1982, Huntington Twp. Art League, 1983. Mem. Nat. Caricaturist Network. Avocations: tropical fish breeding, gardening. Home and Office: 17 Edward Ln Syosset NY 11791-3502 Office Phone: 516-921-6892. E-mail: chris@artistchrisgreene.com.

GREENE, CLAUDIA, education associate; b. Orangeburg, S.C., Aug. 16, 1947; d. Joseph Elijah Randolph and Mazie Stephens; m. Kaponden McKinley, June 13, 1972; children: Karen Denise, Kory McKinley. BA in Elem. Edn., S.C. State U., Orangeburg, 1969, MA in Spl. Edn., 1973, EdD in Ednl. Adminstrn., 1990. Notary pub., S.C. Tchr. Colleton County Schs., Walterboro, S.C., 1969-70, Dillon County Schs., Dillon, S.C., 1970-71, Orangeburg Dist. I, Branchville, S.C., 1971-73; tchr., supr. Calhoun County Schs., St. Matthews, S.C., 1973-83; tchr. Orangeburg Dist. 5, 1983-92; edn. assoc. S.C. State Dept. Edn., Columbia, 1992—. Vis. prof. S.C. State U., Orangeburg, summers 1984-86. Adminstr. TEAM program St. Paul Bapt. Ch., Orangeburg, 1993—. Mem. NAACP, Coun. for Exceptional Children (Spl. Educator award 1999), Am. Bus. Women;s Assn., Protection an Advocacy. Avocations: reading, gardening, fishing, tutoring, teaching. Home: 544 Rosemont Dr Orangeburg SC 29115-2137 Office: State Dept Edn 1429 Senate St Columbia SC 29201-3730 E-mail: csgreene@sde.state.sc.us.

GREENE, DIANE, information technology executive; m. Mendel Rosenblum. BS in mech. engring., U. Calif., Berkeley; M in computer sci. and naval architecture, MIT. Joined Sybase, 1986; various tech. leadership positions Tandem, Silicon Graphics Inc.; co-founder, CEO Vxtreme (sold to Microsoft Corp.), Palo Alto, Calif., 1995—98; founder, pres. VMware (sub. of EMC), 1998—. Named one of 50 Most Powerful People in Networking, Network World mag., 2003. Office: VMware Inc 3145 Porter Dr Palo Alto CA 94304 Office Phone: 650-475-5000, 877-486-9273. Office Fax: 650-475-5005.

GREENE, ELAINE D. G., environmental science educator; b. Hartford, Conn., Aug. 3, 1937; d. George A. and Helene (Meyen) Gianopoulos; m. Jeremiah Evarts Greene Jr., June 5, 1971; children: Anne (dec.), Anthony, Meredith, Edward. BS in Biology, U. Hartford, Conn., 1970; MEd, Fitchburg State Coll., Mass., 1987. Staff technologist Hartford Hosp., 1957-61; asst. chief technologist Office Dr. Gilbert Heublein, Hartford, 1961-67; faculty, adminstr. Middlesex Community Coll., Middletown, Conn., 1969-71; staff technologist Mass. Gen. Hosp., Boston, 1971-72; supply tchr. William Penn High Sch., New Castle, Del., 1973-76, Catholic Sch., Leominster, Mass., 1980-87, Commonwealth of Mass., 1987-89; radiation therapist Worcester City Hosp., 1989-91, Holy Family Hosp., Methuen, Mass., 1992; instr. Fisher Coll., Marlborough, Mass., 1993—98, Commonwealth of Mass. Mt. Wachuset C.C., 1998—. Mem. Appalachian Mountain Club (naturalist). Avocations: mountain climbing, reading, sewing, knitting.

GREENE, ELLIN, library service educator; b. Elizabeth, NJ, Sept. 18, 1927; d. Charles M. and Dorothea (Hooton) Peterson. A.B., Rutgers U., 1953, M.L.S., 1957, Ed.D., 1979. Children's librarian Free Pub. Library, Elizabeth, 1953-57, specialist in group work with children, 1957-59; asst. group work specialist NY Pub. Libr., NYC, 1959-64, supervising children's librarian, Bronx, 1964, asst. coord. children's services, 1965-67, dir. Early Childhood Project, NY Pub. Libr., 1986-89; adj. faculty Rutgers U. Grad. Sch. Libr. and Info. Studies, New Brunswick, NJ, 1968-97; vis. prof. Nat. Coll. Edn.-McGaw Grad. Sch., Chgo., 1976-77; dean students U. Chgo. Grad. Libr. Sch., 1980-82, assoc. prof., 1980-85; cons. libr. svcs. to children, 1985—; vis. prof. U. Ill. Grad. Sch. Libr. and Info. Sci., 1979; adv. com. NY Pub. Libr. Early Childhood Resource & Info. Ctr., 1982—89; adv. bd. Nat. Clearing House for Info. on Storytelling, 1986-88. Author: Recordings for Children, 1964; A List of Stories to Tell and to Read Aloud, 1965; Films for Children, 1966; (with Augusta Baker) Storytelling: Art and Technique, 1977, 3d edit., 1996; (with Madalynne Schoenfeld) A Multimedia Approach to Children's Literature, 1972, 2d edit., 1977; (with George Shannon) Storytelling: A Selected Annotated Bibliography, 1986, Books, Babies, and Libraries: Serving Infants, Toddlers, Their Parents and Caregivers, 1991; Roger Duvoisin: The Art of Children's Books, 1989, Read Me a Story: Books & Techniques for Reading Aloud and Storytelling, 1992; (with others) Best-Loved Stories Told at the National Storytelling Festival, 1992; co-author, contbr. to numerous ednl. books and profl. jours.; mem. nat. editorial bd. Arrow Book Club, 1975-85; adv. com. Bull. of Ctr. for Children's Books, 1980-85; mem. editl. bd. Library Quar., 1980-85; editl. coun. Nat. Storytelling Jour., 1983—85. Books for children include: The Pumpkin Giant, 1970; Princess Rosetta and the Popcorn Man, 1971; The Rat-Catcher's Daughter: A Collection of Stories by Laurence Housman, 1974; Clever Cooks, 1973, 1977; Midsummer Magic, 1977, The Legend of the Christmas Rose, 1990, The Legend of the Cranberry, 1993, Billy Beg and His Bull, 1994, Li-Ling and the Phoenix Fairy, 1996, The Little Golden Lamb, 2000. Acad. specialist grantee U.S. Info. Agy. Bur. Ednl. and Cultural Affairs, 1989. Recipient Lifetime Achievement award Nat. Storytelling Network Oracle, 2002. Mem. ALA, Assn. Libr. Svc. to Children, Authors Guild Inc., Nat. Storytelling Network, Soc. Children's Book Writers and Illustrators, Douglass Soc., Psi Chi Office: 113 Chatham Ln Point Pleasant NJ 08742-2005

GREENE, GAIL PURCHASE, medical/surgical nurse; b. Northampton, Mass., Dec. 17, 1951; d. Albion Francis and Helen Loretta (Golash) Purchase; m. Paul Franklin Greene, Sept. 2, 1972; children: Stephanie Lynn, Paul Franklin Jr. BSN cum laude, U. South Fla., 1982; AA, Greenfield C.C., 1971. Lic. LPN 1972, Internat. Bd. Lactation Cons. Staff nurse East Pasco Med. Ctr., Zephyr Hills, Fla., 1982—88, Humana Hosp. Pasco, Dade City, Fla., 1988, Hosp. Corp. Am. Raulerson Hosp., Okeechobee, Fla., 1988-89, Tucson Med. Ctr., 1989—2000, Meml. Med. Ctr., Savannah, Ga., 2000—. Office: Meml Hosp Univ Med Ctr Inc Mother Baby Unit 4700 Waters Ave Savannah GA 31403

GREENE, GERALDINE MARIE, family therapist, consultant; b. N.Y.C., Aug. 5, 1944; d. Daniel Joseph and Helen (Skelly) Callahan; m. Robert Jack Kisslinger, Feb. 14, 1981; 1 child, Sean. BA, Mercy Coll., Dobbs Ferry, N.Y., 1966; MSW, Fordham U., 1969; cert. advanced clin. social work, Hunters Coll., 1983; postgrad., Adelphi U., 1982-85. Cert. social worker, N.Y.; diplomate Am. Bd. Examiners in Clin. Social Work. Psychotherapist Cath. Charities Guidance Inst., Yonkers, N.Y.; clin. supr. St. Germaine's Homes, Peekskill, N.Y.; assoc. exec. dir. St. Mary's-in-the-field, Valhalla, N.Y.; dir. family svcs. Cath. Family & Cmty. Svcs., Paterson, N.J., 1976-79; exec. dir., CEO, Scarsdale (N.Y.) Family Counseling Svc., 1980—. Adj. prof. psychology Mercy Coll.; peer reviewer Coun. Accreditation of Svcs. to Families and Children. Contbr. articles to mags. and newspapers. Mem. NASW. Avocations: skiing, dance. Office: 25 Hill St Mahopac NY 10541 Office Phone: 845-628-7629.

GREENE, JANE, health educator; b. L.A., Apr. 14, 1954; d. Ben Louis and Julie Eisen Cohen; m. Russell Edward Greene, Jan. 3, 1981; children: Rachael, Lisa, Joshua. Student, UCLA, 1971-75, MSN, 1981-83; BSN, Calif. State U., Long Beach, 1978. Cert. pediat. nurse practitioner. Dietitian's asst. Century City Hosp., L.A., 1972-76; nurses aide Long Beach (Calif.) Cmty. Hosp., 1976-78; charge nurse oncology dept. Children's Hosp. Orange County, Orange, Calif., 1978-80; staff nurse Children's Hosp. Boston, 1980-81, Cedars Sinai Med. Ctr., L.A., 1981-83; pediat. instr. Washburn U. Sch. Nursing, Topeka, 1983-85; mem. fitness staff Popeyes Cardiofitness, Topeka, 1988-90; phys. edn. instr., tchr. Topeka Collegiate Sch., 1991—94; tchr. Pediatrics PA, 1990—96, nurse practitioner Topeka, 1990-96; teen health instr. Topeka Collegiate Sch., 1996—2001; tchr. Nat. Conf. Cmty. and Justice, 2001—. Girls varsity basketball coach Bellflower (Calif.) H.S., 1975, 76; basketball boach Topeka Collegiate Sch., 1995-97, volleyball coach, 1996-98. Candidate for Kans. Legislature, 1994; asst. coach Woman's Jr. Nat. AAU, 1997; v.p. Temple Beth Sholom, 1997-99, pres., 1999; asst. varsity basketball and softball Tarbut V'Topah Sch., 2001. Named to U.S. Olympic Festival Team, Amateur Racquetball Assn., 1993; Allstate Ins. scholar, 1977-78, Auxilary of Garfield Hosp. nursing scholar, 1977-78. Mem. Nat. Assn. Pediat. Nurse Practitioners, Kans. Nurses Assn., Am. Amateur Racquetball Assn. (Kans. Women's Open State Champion 11 yrs.). Democrat. Jewish. Avocations: racquetball, tennis, jogging, bicycling, skiing. Home: 6800 SW Aylesbury Rd Topeka KS 66610-1442

GREENE, JANETTE ZAHER, elementary school educator; arrived in US, 1984; d. Elias and Salma Zaher; children: Elias, Nur, Fadi. BA, Tchrs. Coll., 1970, MA, 1973. Cert. math. Math. tchr. UN Schs., Jordan, Saudi Arabia. Bd. mem. Tchrs. Union, Jordan. Contbr. articles to newspapers. Bd. mem. Lego Maria Ch., Jordan. Recipient PTA award, Brandy Wine Sch. Dist. Mem.: Women League, Jordan, Parents Without Ptnrs. Avocations: art, antiques, politics.

GREENE, JANICE SCHNAKE, biology professor; d. J.B. and Imogean Schnake; m. Brian David Greene; children: Amy, Stephanie. PhD, Tex. A&M U., College Station, 1992. Conservation edn. coord. Rob & Bessie Welder Wildlife Found., Sinton, Tex., 1992—93; prof. biology Mo. State U., Springfield, 1993—, dir. Bull shoals field sta., 2002—. Commr. Mo. Clean Water Commn., Jefferson City, 1999—2004. Recipient Educator of Yr., Leopold Edn. Project, 1999, Environ. Educator of Yr., Mo. Forestkeepers Network, 2002, 2003. Mem.: Nat. Assn. of Biology Teachers (chmn. role and status of women in biology edn. 2005—06, Excellence in Encouraging Equity 1998). Avocations: reading, music. Office: Missouri State U 901 S National Ave Springfield MO 65897 Office Phone: 417-836-5306. Office Fax: 417-836-8886. Business E-Mail: janicegreene@missouristate.edu.

GREENE, JO, school system administrator; d. Thomas Elmo McKee and Elizabeth Louise McKee-Puckett; m. Allan Robert Greene, Aug. 10, 1976; 1 child, Jennifer Lynn. BS in Elem. Edn., Northwestern Okla. State U., Alva, 1977; M in Elem. Admin., Ctrl. Mo. State U., Warrensburg, 1995; cert. edn. Specialist in elem. adminstrn., Ctrl. Mo. State U., 1997. Lifetime cert. elem. edn. K-8 Mo., cert. admin. II, prin. K-8 Mo., admin. II, prin. 4-8 Mo. Reading tchr., basketball/track coach Prog. Sch., Fairmount, Okla., 1977—78; 3d grade tchr. Yuma Pub. Schs.-Roosevelt, Ariz., 1978—82; 6th grade sci./math tchr. Ft. Osage Schs.- Mid. Sch., Independence, Mo., 1982—89; 3d grade tchr. Ft. Osage Schs.-Blue Hills, Independence, 1989—95; vice prin. Ft. Osage Schs.-Cler-Mont, Independence, 1995; prin. Grain Valley Schs.-Matthews, Mo., 1997—2000; instrnl. coach Kansas City Schs.-Pinkerton, Mo., 2000—. CARE team mem. Ft. Osage Schools/Kansas City Mo. Sch. Dist., 1978; mem. profl. devel. com. Ft. Osage Schs., 1983—94; computer curriculum cons. Pearson Edn., Inc., Chgo., 2000; assessment coord. Kans. City Mo. Schs., 2000—. Mem. Jackson County Crisis Team, Mo., 1997—2000. Named Ft. Osage Mid. Sch. Educator of Yr., Independence Mentor of Yr.; recipient Very Influential Person award. Mem.: Phi Delta Kappa. Avocations: travel, sports, writing, music, hunting. Office Phone: 816-418-1604.

GREENE, JUDITH ORINDA, theater educator, theater director; d. Jerry G. Eldridge and Floyd E. Jones, John R. Morris (Stepfather); children: Stacia Y. Leach, Sarah M., Samantha C., J. Alex. AA, St. Charles C.C., St. Peters, Mo., 1997; BA in Edn., Theatre, and Art, Lindenwood U., St. Charles, Mo., 1999, M, 1999. Tchr., dir. Marquette H.S., Chesterfield, Mo., 1999—. Chair St. Louis CAPPIES, 2005—. Mem.: Mo. State Thespian Soc. (bd. dirs. 2004—, conf. site coord. 2004—), Internat. Thespian Soc. (assoc.). Office: Marquette High Sch 2351 Clarkson Rd Chesterfield MO 63017 Office Phone: 636-537-4300.

GREENE, JUDY, secondary school educator; b. Pikeville, Ky., June 9, 1945; d. Patton and Ella Syck; m. David Keith Greene, Jan. 23, 1965; 1 child, Byron Keith. BS, Pikeville Coll., 1968; MA Morehead State U., 1978. Tchr. Pike County Schs., Pikeville, Ky., 1966—67, Zane Trace Schs., Chillicothe, Ohio, 1968—69, Huntington Schs., 1969—. Exec. com. Ohio Edn. Assn., Columbus, 1988—2002; bd. dirs. NEA, Washington, 1994—2002. Lobbyist NEA, Washington, 1994—2002. Mem.: Nat. Coun. Accreditation Tchr. Edn. (bd.examiners 2001—04). Democrat. Avocations: reading, gardening, travel, scrapbooks, writing. Home: 1256 Mingo Rd Chillicothe OH 45601 E-mail: jmg4nea@bright.net.

GREENE, LILIANE, literature and language educator, editor; b. Salonica, Greece, Oct. 10, 1928; came to U.S., 1941; d. Maurice and Daisy (Kohn) Massarano; m. Thomas McLernon Greene, May 20, 1950; children: Philip James, Christopher George, Francis Richard BA, Hunter Coll., 1948; MA, Columbia U., 1949; PhD, Yale U., 1969. Asst. in instrn. French Yale U., New Haven, 1964-65, instr., 1967-68, lectr., mng. editor Yale French Studies, 1980-94 (ret.); instr. Conn. Coll., New London, 1968-69, asst. prof., 1970-75. Contbr. articles to profl. jours. Fullbright fellow, 1949-50. Mem. MLA, Am. Assn. Tchrs. French, Ctr. Ind. Study (founding mem., pres. 1978-79, bd. dirs. 1977-89), Conn. Acad. of Arts and Scis. Democrat. Avocations: travel, theater. Home: 125 Livingston St New Haven CT 06511-2428

GREENE, LYNNE JEANNETTE, wellness consultant, artist; b. Albany, N.Y., Aug. 27, 1938; d. Zebulon Stevens and Helen Matilde (Maier) Robbins; m. Stanley E. Greene, Jan. 31, 1962 (dec. June 27, 1987); 1 child, Stuart Nathaniel; m. Michael Alan Karlan, Sept. 29, 1991. Student, Goucher Coll., 1956-57; BA with honors, Parsons Sch. Design, 1960. Asst. designer Haymaker Sportswear (David Crystal), N.Y.C., 1959-61; designer Craig Craely Sportswear and Dresses, N.Y.C., 1961-63, Flair Lingerie, N.Y.C., 1964-66; designer, owner Kaleidoscope Lingerie, N.Y.C., 1966-67; head designer Contessa/Monique/Fisher Lingerie, N.Y.C., 1967-71; creative dir. Eye of the Peacock Sportswear, N.J., 1968-72; head designer, owner Lynne Greene Designs Retail, Montclair, N.J., 1972-74; designer, pres. Little Greene Apples Inc., Montville, NJ, 1971—2005; designer, dir. mktg. Lady Lynne Lingerie, Guy Laroche Lingerie, N.Y.C. and Paris, 1973-93, Paris, 1973—93, Val Mode by Lynne Greene, N.Y.C., 1993-97; v.p. design and merchandising The Intapp Group/Go Figure, N.Y.C., 1997-99; pres. Vital Advantage LLC, 1999—, owner, 1999—. Lingerie critic Pratt Inst., 1984-2001. Patentee in field; illustrator books, pamphlets in fashion and packaging fields; comml. artist and illustrator Home & Office Design. Active participant Montville Soccer Assn, 1972-88, fund drives for Am. Heart Assn., Cancer Inc., March of Dimes, Spl. Olympics. Recipient Humanitarian award, Polar Bear Project, Nikken Inc., 2003, honors in field. Mem.: The Fashion Group, 200 Club N.J., Kiwanis (pres. 2004—05, Kiwanian of Yr. 2002—03). Republican. Avocations: sketching, portraiture, cooking, sewing, painting. E-mail: maklynne@optonline.net.

GREENE, MARCIA SLACUM, editor; With Phila. Inquirer, St. Petersburg (Fla.) Times, Washington Post, Washington, 1983—, city desk editor, 2004, asst. dist. editor for politics & govt., city editor, 2006—. Office: Washington Post 1150 15th St Washington DC 20071*

GREENE, MARGARET H., telecommunications industry executive; b. Nebr. JD, U. Nebr., 1972; LLD (hon.), Georgetown Coll., 1975. Assoc. solicitor Dept. Energy, Washington; atty. pvt. practice; with legal dept. South Ctrl. Bell, 1983; pres. Bellsouth Corp., Ky., 1991—95; cabinet sec. Gov. Commonwealth Ky., 1996; v.p., gen. counsel Bellsouth Telecomm., 1996—98; pres. regulatory and external affairs Bellsouth Corp., Atlanta, 1998—. Mem. adv. com. rsch., devel. and tech. So. Govs. Assn.; bd. dors. High Mus. Art, Atlanta; mem. nat. bd. vis. U. Louisville Bus. Sch. Mem.: ABA, Nebr. Bar Assn., Ky. Bar Assn., D.C. Bar Assn., Ala. Bar Assn., U.S. Telecom Assn. (chair).

GREENE, MELINDA JEAN, retail maintenance analyst; b. Warren, Pa., Jan. 15, 1963; d. Nancy Louise Stanko, Gerald Paul Stanko (Stepfather). BA, Malone Coll., 1999. Customer svc. Blair Corp., Warren, Pa., 1980—92; retail clerk BP Products N.Am. Inc., Wexford, Pa., 1992—95, asst. maintenance and constrn., 1995—96, maintenance asst. Warrensville, Ohio, 1996—98, account svc. rep. Cuyahoga Heights, Ohio, 1998—2000, retail maintenance analyst Alpharetta, Ga., 2000—. Protestant. Office: BP Products NAm Inc 2475 Northwinds Pkwy Ste 400 Alpharetta GA 30004 Home: 566 Declaration Ln Aurora IL 60504-7341 Personal E-mail: greenemj@bp.com.

GREENE, MICHELLE RENEE, mathematics educator; d. Larry Edwin Greene and Mary Lyon Green. BS, Francis Marion U., Florence, SC, 1990; MS, U. Ga., Athens, 1996. Cert. tchr. SC, nat. bd. cert. tchr. Math. tchr. Lamar HS, SC, 1996—; math. instr. Francis Marion U., 2005—. Vol. McLeod Regional Med. Ctr., Florence, 2005. Named Dist. Tchr. of Yr., Darlington County Sch. Dist., 2004—05, Tchr. of Yr., Lamar HS, 1997—98, 2004—05; recipient Mark W. Buyck Polit. Sci. award, Francis Marion U., 1990—91. Mem.: NEA, Palmetto State Tchrs. Assn., Am. Statis. Assn., Nat. Coun. Tchrs. of Math. (assoc.), Am. Polit. Sci. Assn (assoc.). Home: 110 Gann Dr Darlington SC 29532 Office: Lamar HS 216 N Darlington Ave Lamar SC 29069 Office Phone: 843-326-7544. Office Fax: 843-326-7507. E-mail: mgreene@darlington.k12.sc.us.

GREENE, MONICA LYNN BANKS, psychologist; b. Washington, Sept. 24, 1969; d. John Thomas and Priscilla (Sneed) Banks. BS in Microbiology, Howard U., Washington, 1986; MBA/MGA, U. Md., College Park, 2000, PhD, 2005. Cert. therapeutic recreation specialist, activity cons. Therapeutic recreation specialist Dept. Human Svcs., Washington, 1986-91; dir. activities, vols., transp. Independence Ct. Hyattsville, Md., 1991-93; dir. therapeutic activity svcs. Asbury Meth. Village, Gaithersburg, Md., 1993—; dir. therapeutic activities and vol. svcs. Presdl. Woods Health Care Ctr., Adelphi, Md.; owner, pres. Excell Eldercare Mgmt., Inc.; asst. adminstr. St. Thomas More Nursing & Rehab. Ctr., Hyattsville, Md.; exec. dir. Morningside HOuse of St. Charles, Waldorf, Ind., 2003—; pvt. practice psychology Largo, Md., 2005—; clin. psychologist, therapist Laurel Regional Hosp.; owner It's All About Us! LLC, Excell ElderCare Mgmt., Inc. Mem.: Alpha Kappa Alpha. Democrat. Baptist. Avocations: swimming, jet skiing, horseback riding, snorkeling. Home: 1210 Blue Wing Ter Upper Marlboro MD 20774 E-mail: monicagreene01@comcast.net.

GREENE, SHEREE' JEANE, elementary school educator, consultant; d. Floyde Eugene and Betty Etheridge Greene. B in Early Childhood Edn., Wesleyan Coll., 1984; M in Early Childhood Edn., Piedmont Coll., 1996. In-Tech Certification Ga. State Bd. Edn., 2005; PBT-5 tchg. cert. in early childhood edn. Ga. State Bd. Edn., 2005, cert. tchr. support specialist Ga. State Bd. Edn., 1997. Elem. educator Northside Elem. Sch., Griffin, Ga., 1984—86; receptionist/sec. Athens (Ga.) Regional Youth Devel. Ctr., 1986—87; elem. educator Ila (Ga.) Elem. Sch., 1987—. Motivational spkr./cons. Nat. and State Inclusion Confs., Athens, 1992—; ednl. rsch. cons. U. Ga. Sch. Edn., Athens, 1993—94, vol. mentor (open door classroom observations), 1994—96; ednl. rsch. cons. U. Ga., Athens, 1994—95; portfolio evaluator Madison County Tchr. of the Yr. Evaluation Com., Danielsville, Ga., 1996—97; so. accreditation of colleges and schools steering com. co-chairperson Ila Elem. Sch., 1999—2004; motivational spkr. Emmanuel Coll., Franklin Springs, Ga., 2003—. Composer: (written lyrics and melody) Single Married Man (Ga. Songwriters Association's Top Ten Songwriters, 1992). Exec. com. co-chairperson/social events coord. Friends of the Madison County Libr., Danielsville, Ga., 1994—96; motivational spkr./singer various chs., Ga., 2004—. Recipient Leadership/Future Tchr. award, Alpha Delta Kappa, 1980, Tchr. of Yr. Cmty. award, Madison County Optimist Club, 1996, Tchr. of the Yr., Ila Elem., 1995, Madison County Sch. Sys., 1996; Future Tchr. scholar, Kappa Delta Epsilon, 1980. Avocations: songwriting, singing, gardening, creative writing, event planning. Office: Ila Elementary School 150 Sewell Mill Rd Ila GA 30647 Office Phone: 706-789-3445. Business E-Mail: sgreene@madison.k12.ga.us.

GREENE, TENA LORRAINE, singer, educator, actor; d. Roy and Kathryn Correen (Case) Greene. MusM in Voice Performance, Converse Coll., Spartanburg, S.C., 2001. Voice tchr. Limestone Coll. Acad., Gaffrey, SC, 1995—97, Converse Pre-Coll., Spartanburg, 1999—2002, U. S.C., Spartanburg, 1999—2003, Mars Hill (N.C.) Coll., 2003—. Singer: various local cmty. theater and opera cos. Sec. bd. dirs. Tryon Little Theater, 1993—, fund raising performer, ARC, Tryon, Columbus, NC, 2000—05. Named Dist. winner, Nat. Assn. Tchrs. Singing, 2001; A. J. Fletcher Found. scholar, Gardner-Webb U., 1987. Mem.: Foothills Music Club. Home: 49 Locust St Columbus NC 28722 Office: Mars Hill Coll Music Dept PO Box 370 Mars Hill NC 28754-0370

GREENE, WENDY SEGAL, retired special education educator; b. New Rochelle, N.Y., Jan. 9, 1929; d. Louis Peter and Anna Henrietta (Kahan) Segal; m. Charles Edward Smith (div. 1952); m. Richard M. Greene Jr. (div. 1967); children: Christopher S., Kerry William, Karen Beth Greene Olson; m. Richard M. Greene Sr., Aug. 29, 1985 (dec. 1986). Student, Olivet Coll., 1946-48, Santa Monica Coll., 1967-70; BA in Child Devel., Calif. State U., Los Angeles, 1973, MA in Elem. Edn., 1975. Cert. tchr. Calif., Specially Designed Acad. Instrn. in English 1999. Counselor Camp Watitoh, Becket, Mass., 1946-49; asst. tchr. Outdoor Play Group, New Rochelle, 1946-58; edn. sec. pediatrics Syracuse (N.Y.) Meml. Hosp., 1952-53; with St. John's Hosp., Santa Monica, Calif., 1962-63; head tchr. Head Start, L.A., 1966-77; tchr. spl. edn. L.A. Unified Sch. Dist., 1977—2005, Salvin Spl. Edn. Ctr., L.A., 1976—85, Alfonso B. Perez Sch., L.A., 1986—2005. Instr. mktg. rsch. for motivational rsch. Anderson-McConnell Agy., 1966; mentor tchr. L.A. Unified Sch. Dist., 1992-99; mem. adv. com. for spl. edn. Tustin Unified Sch. Dist. Comty., 1994-2004. Contbr. to house organ of St. John's Hosp.; co-editor of newspaper for Salvin Sch., L.A.; contbg. reporter El Aquilar (The Eagle), Perez. Mem. coun. LEARN, Perez, 1996—2005; bd. dirs. Tustin Area Coun. for Fine Arts, 2002—, Richland Ave Youth House, L.A., 1960—63, Emotional Health Assn., L.A., 1961—66, Richland Ave. Sch. PTA, L.A., 1959—63. Mem.: AAUW, Cmty. Advisory Advocacy Assistance (com. mem. 2000—), Tustin Area Woman's Club, United Tchrs. L.A., Tustin Hist. Soc., Olivet Coll. Alumni Assn., Tustin Cmty. Chorus, Celebration of Life Singers, Westside Singers (L.A.), Kappa Delta Pi. Jewish. Avocations: music, writing, theater, travel. Home: 14291 Prospect Ave Tustin CA 92780-2316 E-mail: wendygeewhiz@yahoo.com.

GREENE OSTER, SELMAREE, medical anthropologist, researcher; b. Phila., Feb. 17, 1949; d. Boisey and Elizabeth (Lewis) Greene; m. Gerald Oster, Apr. 11, 1973 (dec. Oct. 1995); 1 child, Alexander S. BS in Anthropology and Biology, U. Pa., 1969, CUNY, 1973, MSc, 1979, PhD, 1980. Cert. clin. lab. specialist N.Y. Dept. Health. Tchr. U.S. Peace Corps, Washington, 1975-77; med. rschr. Mt. Sinai Sch. Medicine, N.Y.C., 1978-88; pres., exec. officer Oster Children's Fund, N.Y.C., 1996—. Contbr. articles to sci. jours. Founder Gerald Oster Sch. for Peace Edn., Haiti. Tropical medicine grantee Friends of Children of Haiti, 1984-90. Mem. Am. Soc. Clin. Pathologists (lic. lab. pathologist and clinician). Democrat. Roman Catholic. Avocations: horseback riding, swimming. Home: PO Box 988 Village Sta New York NY 10014 Office: Peace Action Edn Rm 4050 866 United Nations Plz New York NY 10017 Fax: 609-871-5999.

GREENFIELD, LINDA SUE, nursing educator; b. Dover, Del., Aug. 5, 1950; d. Norman Raymond and Eleanor Henrietta (Harmon) Connell; m. Douglas Herman Greenfield, Dec. 27, 1976; children: Leah, Paige. BSN, Cath. U., 1972; MSN cum laude, Boston U., 1977; postgrad., Coll. New Rochelle, 1986-88; PhD, Adelphi U., 1998. RN, N.Y. Staff nurse emergency rm. and ICU Washington Hosp. Ctr., 1974-75; operating rm. nurse Mass. Eye & Ear, Boston, 1975; ICU nurse Peter Bent Brigham Hosp., Boston, 1975-76; surg. nurse practitioner Kingsbrook Jewish Hosp., Bklyn., 1976-79; nurse anesthetist student Metropolitan Hosp., 1979—81; cert. registered nurse anesthetist Brookdale Hosp., Bklyn., 1981-92, Winthrop U. Hosp., Mineola, N.Y., 1992-94; adj. prof. Adelphi U., Garden City, N.Y., 1995-99; adj. prof. nursing N.Y. Inst. Tech., Old Westbury, 1998-99; clin. supr. Midtown Ctr. Complementary Care, N.Y.C., 1999-2000; clin specialist St. Francis Hosp., Roslyn, N.Y., 2000-01; asst. prof. nursing Adelphi U., 2001—. Bd. officer Manhasset Newcomers, N.Y., 1988-90; bd. dirs. Friends of Manhasset Libr., N.Y., 1990-94; mem. Make a Wish Found., Port Washington, N.Y., 1990—. Lt. U.S. Army, 1970-74. Mem.: ANA, Nat. Assn. U. Women, Nat. Assn. for Holistic Nurses, Nat. Assn. Homeopathy, Noetic Soc., Sch. Cmty. Assn., Am. Assn. Nurse Anesthetists, Sigma Theta Tau. Avocations: skiing, sailing, dance. Office Phone: 516-877-4515. Personal E-mail: doclsg@aol.com. Business E-Mail: greenfi2@adelphi.edu.

GREENFIELD, PATRICIA ANN MARKS, psychology educator; b. Newark, July 18, 1940; d. David and Doris Jeannette (Pollard) Marks; m. Sheldon Greenfield, Mar. 13, 1965 (div.); children: Lauren, Matthew Michael. AB summa cum laude, Radcliffe Coll., 1962; PhD in Social Psychology, Harvard U., 1966. Research fellow in psychology Ctr. for Cognitive Studies Harvard U., Cambridge, Mass., 1968-72; vis. asst. prof. psychology Stanford (Calif.) U., 1972-73; asst. prof. U. Calif., Santa Cruz, 1973-74; assoc. prof. UCLA, 1974-78, prof., 1978—. Bd. dirs. Harvard-Radcliffe Club So. Calif.; external examiner U. Lagos, 1977-79; collaborating scientist Yerkes Regional Primate Ctr., Emory U., 1979—. Contbr. articles to profl. jours. Recipient 1st award Am. Insts. Rsch., 1967, award for disting. teaching in psychology Am. Psychol. Found., 1992; named Sci. scholar Bunting Inst. Radcliffe Coll., 1986-87. Fellow AAAS (Behavioral Sci. Rsch. prize 1992), APA (award divsn. 2 1986), Am. Psychol. Soc.; mem. Soc. Rsch. in Child Devel. Home: 42 Park Ave Venice CA 90291-3222

GREENFIELD, SUSAN L., lawyer; m. Lawrence Abramson; children: Rebecca, Kate. BA, Wayne State U., 1970, JD, 1975. In house atty. Fruehoff Trailer Corp., Valeron Corp., 1977—87; staff atty. Guardian Industries Corp., 1987—94; with Palace Sports and Entertainment Inc., 1994—, v.p. & gen. counsel; v.p. - legal Detroit Pistons. Office: Palace Sports & Entertainment Inc 4 Championship Dr Auburn Hills MI 48326

GREENHILL, LISA MICHELLE, professional society administrator; b. Richmond, Va., Feb. 2, 1973; d. Edward Wingfield and Angela Elaine Daniels Greenhill. BA, George Mason U., 1995, MPA, 2000. Legis. mgr. Assn. Women's Health, Ob.-Neonatal Nursing, Washington, 2001; assoc. exec. dir. for diversity Assn. Am. Vet. Med. Colls., Washington, 2004—. Mem. Nat. Adv. Environ. Health Scis. Coun., Washington, 2005—. Contbr. articles to profl. jours. Treas. Hunting Creek Condominium Assn., Alexandria, Va., 2003—05; troop leader Girl Scouts USA, Arlington, Va., 2004—05. Mem.: Women in Govt. Rels. Baptist. Office: Assn Am Vet Med Colls 1101 Vermont Ave NW Ste 301 Washington DC 20005 Office Phone: 202-371-9195 47. Office Fax: 202-842-0773. Business E-Mail: lgreenhill@aavmc.org.

GREENHOUSE, LINDA JOYCE, journalist; b. NYC, Jan. 9, 1947; d. Herman Robert and Dorothy Eleanor (Greenlick) Greenhouse; m. Eugene R. Fidell, Jan. 1, 1981; 1 child, Hannah Margalit Fidell. BA, Radcliffe Coll., 1968; M of Studies in Law, Yale U., 1978; DHL (hon.), Brown U., 1991, Binghamton U., 2006; LLD (hon.) (hon.), Colgate U., 1993, Northeastern U., 1997, CUNY, 1997; LLD (hon.), U. Miami, 2004, Georgetown U., 2004. Asst. to James Reston The N.Y. Times, N.Y.C., 1968—69, met. reporter, 1970—74, state polit. reporter, 1974—77, supreme ct. corr. Washington, 1978—85, 1988—, congl. corr., 1986—88. Author: Becoming Justice Blackmun: Harry Blackmun's Supreme Court Journey, 2005. Adv. com. Schlesinger Libr. on the History of Women in Am., Radcliffe Coll., 1995—2002; mem. Schlesinger Libr. Coun., 2003—; bd. dirs. Yale Law Sch. Fund, New Haven, 1984—91. Recipient Pulitzer prize in journalism for beat reporting, 1998, Carey McWilliams award, Am. Polit. Sci. Assn., 2002, Henry J. Friendly medal, Am. Law Inst., 2002, Golden Pen award, Legal Writing Inst., 2002, Goldsmith Career award, John F. Kennedy Sch. Govt., Harvard U., 2004, Pres.'s Spl. award, N.Y. Women's Bar Assn., 2004, John Chancellor award for excellence in journalism, 2004, Anvil of Freedom award, Estlow Internat. Ctr. for Journalism and New Media, U. Denver, 2005, William Green award Profl. Excellence, U. Richmond Law Sch., 2005, medal of distinction, Barnard Coll., 2006, medal, Radcliffe Inst., 2006. Fellow: Am. Acad. Arts and Scis. (mem. coun. 2004—); mem.: Women's Forum of Washington (v.p. 2003—05), Yale Law Assn. (exec. com. 1993—97), Am. Law Inst. (hon.), Am. Philos. Soc., Harvard Club of Washington (bd. dirs. 1989—92), Phi Beta Kappa (vis. scholar 2004—06). Office: The NY Times 1627 I St NW Washington DC 20006-4007 Office Phone: 202-862-0371. Business E-Mail: ligree@nytimes.com.

GREENLAW, MARILYN JEAN, retired adult education educator; b. St. Petersburg, Fla., Apr. 1, 1941; d. Hinckley and Dorothy Rebecca (Ball) G. BA, Stetson U., 1962, MA, 1965; PhD, Mich. State U., 1970. Elem. tchr. Broward County schs., Ft. Lauderdale, Fla., 1962-64; ele. cons. Harper and Row Publs., Evanston, Ill., 1965-69; from asst. to assoc. prof. U. Ga., Athens, 1970-78; from assoc. to full prof. U. North Tex., Denton, 1978-87, regents prof., 1987—2005, ret., 2005. Cons. Scholastic Publs., N.Y.C., 1978-87, Houghton Mifflin Co., Boston, 1984-94, Tex. Instruments, Dallas, 1981-85, Coordinating Bd., Austin, Tex., 1987-91. Author: Ranch Dressing: The Story of Western Wear, 1993, Welcome to the Stock Show, 1997; co-author: Storybook Classrooms, 1985, Educating the Gifted, 1988; editor book rev. column Jour. Reading, 1981-84, The New Adv., 1987-94. Mem. Friends of the Denton Pub.Libr., 1984—, pres., 1995-97, 2001-, Keep Denton Beautiful, pres., 2003; bd. dirs. Denton Libr., 1992-97, chair, 1995-96. Recipient

Arbuthnot award, 1992, Disting. Svc. award Tex. State Reading Assn., 1996, Pres.'s Coun. Disting. Svc. award U. North Tex., 1996. Mem.: ALA (com. chairperson 1984—85), Internat. Reading Assn. (com. chairperson 1980—90, Arbuthnot award 1992), Nat. Coun. Tchrs. of English (com. chairperson 1980—, Outstanding Leadership in Edn. award 1976), Kiwanis (pres. 2002—), Phi Kappa Phi (v.p. 1986—87), Phi Delta Kappa (pres. 1982—83, Outstanding Young Educator award 1981). Republican. Avocations: reading, gardening, photography. Home: 2600 Sheraton Rd Denton TX 76209-8620

GREENLEAF, VIRGINIA M. See KOCH, VIRGINIA

GREENLEE, MICHELLE JAYNE ORY, science educator; b. Jasper, Ala., June 20, 1979; d. Robert W. and Betty Bobo Ory; m. Todd Christian Greenlee, Dec. 18, 2004. BS in Gen. Sci. and Secondary Edn., U. North Ala., Florence, 2001. Mem. briefing staff, counselor U. S. Space and Rocket Ctr., Huntsville, Ala., 2002; sci. tchr. Lexington (Ala.) H.S., 2002—03; tchr. chemistry and physics Ctrl. H.S., Florence, Ala., 2003—. Office: Ctrl HS 3000 County Rd 200 Florence AL 35633 Office Phone: 256-764-2903.

GREENMAN, JANE FRIEDLIEB, lawyer, human resources executive; b. NYC, Sept. 9, 1950; d. Morton Jerome and Isabelle Irene (Bisgyer) F.; m. Charles P. Greenman, Nov. 23, 1975; children: Margot, Jaclyn, Danielle. BS, Cornell U., 1972; JD, NYU, 1975, LLM in Labor Law, 1981. Bar: NY 1976, NY 1986. Assoc. Wolf Haldenstein, N.Y.C., 1975-79; faculty NYU Law Sch., 1979-81, Bklyn. Law Sch., 1981—82; assoc., counsel Hughes Hubbard & Reed, N.Y.C., 1982-91, ptnr., chair employee benefits dept., 1991-96; v.p., dep. gen. coun. human resources Honeywell Internat., Inc., Morristown, NJ, 1996—2003; v.p. compensation, benefits and labor rels. Tyco Internat., N.Y.C., 2003—. Adj. prof. Bklyn. Law Sch., 1982-92, 95, Hofstra U.; bd. dirs. Women's Fund of N.J., NYC Bound Outward. Mem. Temple Sinai of Summit, Religious Action Ctr. Commn. for Social Action. Mem. ABA, N.Y.C. Bar Assn., N.Y. State Bar Assn. Jewish. Office: Tyco International PO Box 5260 Princeton NJ 08543-5260

GREENMAN, PAULA S., lawyer; b. Putnam, N.Y., 1951; BA cum laude, Yale U., 1972; JD, Boston Coll., 1976. Bar: Conn. 1976, N.Y. 1995. Atty. Skadden, Arps, Slate, Meagher & Flom LLP, N.Y., ptnr., 2001—. Office: Skadden Arps Slate Meagher & Flom LLP Four Times Sq New York NY 10036

GREENSLADE, CINDY LOUISE, psychologist; b. Balt., Nov. 9, 1959; d. John Robert and Doris Ann Weeks; m. Ivor David Greenslade, Sept. 11, 1982. AA in Nursing, Catonsville CC, Md., 1980; BS in Psychology cum laude, Liberty U., 1993; MA in Clin. Psychology, Biola U., 1997, PhD in Clin. Psychology, 2001. Lic. psychologist Calif.; RN Calif. Psychotherapist Deaf Journey Counseling Program, Orange, Calif., 1997—99; instr. West Coast Deaf Bible Coll., Long Beach, Calif., 1998—99; intern and staff psychotherapist St. John's Child and Family Devel. Ctr. and Deaf Program, Santa Monica, Calif., 1999—2001; staff psychologist deaf program Patton State Hosp., Calif., 2001—02; ednl. psychologist Calif. Sch. for the Deaf, Riverside, 2000; psychotherapist Meier Clinics, Long Beach, 2002—06; pvt. practice Garden Grove, 2006—. Cons. forensic deaf mental health Patton State Hosp., 2001—; cons. deaf and hearing mental health Meier Clinics, 2002—06; cons. in field. Mem.: APA, Adv. Coun. Abused Deaf Children, Nat. Assn. of the Deaf, Am. Deafness and Rehab. Assn. Achievements include co-establishment of the first deaf community counseling center in California. Avocations: backpacking, music, bicycling, stain glass. Office: 12792 Valley View St Ste 209 Garden Grove CA 92845 Office Phone: 714-403-7356.

GREENSPAN, DEBORAH, dental educator; 2nd BDS, U. London, 1960, BDS, 1964, DSc, 1991; fellow in Dental Surgery (hon.), Royal Coll. Surgeons, Edinburgh, 1994; LDS, Royal Coll. Surgeons, Eng., 1964; ScD (hon.), Georgetown U., 1990. Registered dental practioner, U.K.; diplomate Am. Bd. Oral Medicine. Vis. lectr. oral medicine U. Calif., San Francisco, 1976-83, asst. clin. prof., 1983-85, assoc. clin. prof., 1985-89, clin. prof., 1989-96, prof. clin. oral medicine, 1996—, interim chair dept. orofacial scis. Sch. Dentistry, 2004—, interim chair dept. orofacial scis., 2004—. Lectr. in oral biology, U. Calif., San Francisco, 1972, clin. dir. Oral AIDS Ctr., 1987—, active Sch. Dentistry coms. including admissions com., 1985—, chair task force on infection control, 1987—; cons. Joint FDI/WHO Working Group on AIDS, 1989—, EEC, 1990, WHO, 1990, 91, Dept. Health State Calif., 1991, others; ad hoc reviews Epidemiology and Disease Control Sect. Div. Rsch. Grants NIH, 1987—; mem. programs adv. com. Nat. Inst. Dental Rsch., 1989—, mem. spl. ad hoc tech. rev. panel, 1991, mem. panel Fed. Drug Adminstrn., 1991-94; other svc. to govtl. agys.; participant numerous sci. and profl. workshops, meetings, and continuing edn. courses, numerous radio, TV, and press interviews concerning AIDS and infection control in dentistry. Author: (with J.S. Greenspan, Pindborg, and Schiødt), AIDS and the Dental Team, 1986 (transl. German, French, Italian, Spanish, Japanese), AIDS and the Mouth, 1990, (with others) San Francisco General Hospital AIDS Knowledge Base, 1986, Dermatologic Clinics, 5th edit., 1987, Infectious Disease Clinics of North America, 2nd. edit., 1988, Oral Manifestations of AIDS, 1988, Contemporary Periodontics, 1989, Opportunistic Infections in AIDS Patients, 1990, AIDS Clinical Review, 1990, Oral Manifestations of Systemic Disease, 1990, others; mem. editl. bd. rev. Jour. Am. Coll. Dentists, 1991; mem. editl. bd. Oral Diseases, 1999; ad hoc referee Jour. Oral Pathology, 1983—, Cancer, 1985—, Jour. Acad. Gen. Dentistry, 1986—, European Jour. Cancer & Clin. Oncology, 1986, Archives of Dermatology, 1988—, Jour. AMA, 1988—, AIDS, 1991; contbr. numerous articles to profl. jours. Mem. dental subcom. of profl. edn. com. Calif. div. Am. Cancer Soc., 1982-90, profl. health care providers task force, 1991. Nat. Cancer Inst. fellow, 1978-79, Am. Coll. Dentists fellow, 1988; recipient Woman of Distinction award, London, 1986, Commendation cert. Asst. Sec. for Health, 1989; named Seymour J. Kreshover lectr. Nat. Inst. Dental Rsch., 1989, Hon. Lectr. United Med. and Dental Schs. of Guys and St. Thomas Hosps., U. London, 1991. Fellow AAAS, Royal Soc. Medicine, Royal Coll. Surgeons; mem. ADA (vis. lectr. speaker's bur. 1988—, cons. coun. on dental therapeutics 1988—, mem. coun. sci. affairs 1999—), Am. Assn. Dental Rsch. (session chair 1986-87, constitution com. 1988-91, chair 1990-91, pres. San Francisco sect. 1990—, treas. 1992—), Am. Acad. Oral Pathology, Am. Soc. Microbiology, Am. Assn. Women Dentists, Am. Acad. Oral Medicine, Am. Assn. Dental Schs., Internat. Assn. Dental Rsch. (pres. exptl. pathology group 1989-90, v.p. 2004-05, other coms. and offices), Internat. Assn. Oral Pathologists, Internat. Assn. for Dental Rsch. (v.p. 2005—), Calif. Dental Assn., San Francisco Dental Soc., Internat. AIDS Soc., Inst. of Medicine. Achievements include rsch. on oral candidiasis in HIV infection, on HIV-associated salivary gland disease, on oral hairy leukoplakia, and on the prevalence of HIV-associated gingivitis and periodontitis in HIV-infected patients. Office: U Calif Sch Dentistry Dept Orofacial Scis S 612 513 Parnassus Ave Box 0422 San Francisco CA 94143-0422

GREENSPAN, VALEDA CLAREEN, nursing educator, consultant; b. Ellsworth, Kans., Sept. 10, 1940; d. Theodore Frederick and Clara Lydia (Weinhardt) Steinle; m. Edward Phil Fabricius, June 10, 1962 (div. 1973); children: Craig Philip, Sheri Kay; m. Barney Greenspan, June 7, 1999. BS, Ft. Hays State U., 1962; M Nursing, Ind. U., 1966; cert. in gerontology, North Tex. State U., 1980, PhD, 1982. Instr. Bartholomew County Hosp., Columbus, Ind., 1971-72; asst. prof. Ft. Hays State U., Hays, Kans., 1973-74, Tex. Woman's U., Denton, 1974-80, Minot (N.D.) State U., 1980-82, dean, 1982—99; mem. clin. faculty George Mason U., Fairfax, Va., 2003; curriculum cons. Boise (Idaho) State U., 2004—. Cons., expert witness Zuger & Bucklin, Bismarck, N.D., 1982-83; mem. N.D. adv. bd. No. States Power Co., 1989-92; treas. health bd. 1st Dist., 1994-97. Matthews fellow North Tex. State U., 1979; grantee Bush Found., 1983-84; recipient Excellence in Writing award Am. Jour Nursing, 1987. Mem. ANA (del. 1986-87), Nat. League Nurses (bd. rev. 1992-95, baccalaureate higher degree programs site visitor 1983-1998), Nat. Gerontol Assn., N.D. Nurses Assn. (treas. dist. 2 1982-84, nominating com. 1984-85, 93-94, v.p. 1989-92, Phi Delta Kappa, Sigma Theta Tau. Avocations: reading, sewing, cooking, crafts, hiking. Home: 2250 E Mozart Ct Meridian ID 83642-1124 Business E-Mail: vgreenspan@boisestate.edu.

GREENSPAN-MARGOLIS, JUNE E., psychiatrist; b. NYC, June 28, 1934; d. Benjamin Robert and Theresa (Cooperstein) Edelman; divorced; 1 child, Alisa Greenspan; m. Gerald J. Margolis. AB, Bryn Mawr Coll., 1955; MD, Med. Coll. Pa., 1959; grad., Inst Phila Assn Psychoanalysis, Bala Cynwyd, 1975. Intern Albert Einstein Med. Ctr., Phila., 1959-60; pvt. practice medicine specializing in pediatrics Cinnaminson, N.J., 1961-67; psychiat. resident Hahnemann Med. Coll., Phila., 1967-71; practice medicine specializing in adult and child psychiatry, psychoanalysis Jenkintown, Pa., 1971—. Instr. U. Pa. Sch. Medicine, Phila., 1975—77, clin. assoc., 1977—81, clin. asst. prof., 1981—86, clin. assoc. prof., 1986—; tng. and supervisory analyst Psychoanalytic Ctr. Phila., 1986—. Fellow Am. Coll. Psychoanalysts, Am. Psychiat. Assn.; mem. AMA, Am. Psychoanalytic Assn. (cert. adult and child psychoanalysis), Am. Acad. Child Psychiatry, Ctr. for Advanced Psychoanalytic Studies (Princeton). Office: The Pavilion Ste 434 261 Old York Rd Jenkintown PA 19046 Office Phone: 215-887-5355.

GREENSPOON, IRMA NAIMAN, travel company executive; b. Washington, Oct. 18, 1920; d. Harry H. and Ada Marie (Himmelfarb) Naiman; m. Benjamin Greenspoon, July 10, 1960; children: Laurence, Julie. AB, George Washington U., 1942. Lic. tour guide, Washington, 1970—84; pres., CEO Guide Svc. of Washington, 1984—89. Bd. dirs. Washington Conv. and Visitors Assn., 1984-89, Am. Diabetes Assn., Washington, 1966-80; pres. Park View Citizens Assn., Chevy Chase, Md., 1986; Juvenile Justice Com. Montgomery County, Md., 1999—2003 Democrat. Jewish. Home: 3223 Park View Rd Chevy Chase MD 20815-5643 E-mail: birma01@comcast.net.

GREENSTEIN, LAURA M., education educator, department chairman; b. New York, NY, Sept. 8, 1950; d. Abraham and Gertrude Kass; m. Eric R. Greenstein, Sept. 1, 1973; children: Andrew, Casey. BS, U. Conn., 1973; MS, State U. of NY Coll. at Oneonta, 1978; EdD, Johnson and Wales U., 2004. Dir. edn. PPADOC, Oneonta, NY, 1975—78; coord., instr. Mohegan Cmty. Coll., Norwich, Conn., 1978—81; program dir. Nary Family Svc. Ctr., Groton, Conn., 1981—84; dir. Hospice of Southeast Conn., 1984—87; tchr., dept. chair Montville Bd. Edn., Oakdale, Conn., 1987—. Pres. NCC Children's Ctr., Niantic, Conn., 2004—; sec. U. Conn. Parent's Assn., 1998—2002. Mem.: Nat. Assn. Family Consumer Sci., ASCD. Home: PO Box 337 East Lyme CT 06333 Office: Montville Schools Old Colchester Rd Oakdale CT 06370

GREENSTEIN, RUTH LOUISE, think-tank executive, lawyer; b. N.Y.C., Mar. 28, 1946; d. Milton and Beatrice (Zutty) G.; m. David Seidman, May 19, 1972. BA, Harvard U., 1966; MA, Yale U., 1968; JD, George Washington U., 1980. Bar: D.C. 1980. Fgn. service info. officer USIA, Washington and Tehran, Iran, 1968-70; adminstrv. asst. Export-Import Bank U.S., Washington, 1971-72; asst. dean Woodrow Wilson Sch. Pub. and Internat. Affairs, Princeton U., 1972-75; budget examiner U.S. Office Mgmt. and Budget, Washington, 1975-79; budget coordinator U.S. Internat. Devel. Coop. Agy., 1979-81; dep. gen. counsel NSF, 1981-84; treas., then v.p. and gen. counsel Genex Corp., Gaithersburg, Md., 1984-90; v.p. fin. and adminstrn., gen. counsel Inst. for Def. Analyses, Alexandria, Va., 1990—. Mem. acad. adv. panel to tech. transfer intelligence com. CIA, 1983-90; mem. def. trade adv. group U.S. Dept. State, 1994-96; mem. com. for protection of human subjects ARC, 1996—; dir. VSA Arts, 1998—2005, PLATO Learning Inc., 2002--. Mem. NAS (panel on future design and implementation of nat. security export controls 1989-91), AAAS (com. on sci. freedom and responsibility 1987-93), D.C. Bar Assn. Home: 2737 Devonshire Pl NW Apt 511 Washington DC 20008-3458 Office: Inst for Def Analyses 4850 Mark Center Dr Alexandria VA 22311-1882 Business E-Mail: rgreenst@ida.org.

GREENTHAL, JILL A., investment banker; b. Milw. m. Tom Eisenmann; 2 children. Grad. mem. The Academy, Simmons Coll., 1978; MBA, Harvard Bus. Sch., 1983. Joined Salomon Smith Barney; assoc. Shearson Lehman Hutton (now Lehman Brothers), 1985; head media group Lehman Brothers, 1990—94; mng. dir. Media and Communications Investment Banking Group Donaldson, Lufkin and Jenrette, Boston, 1996; co-head Boston office, mem. exec. bd. investment banking Credit Suisse First Boston; sr. mng. dir. corp. advisory services Blackstone Group, 2003—. Bd. dirs. Martha Stewart Living Omnimedia Inc., NYC, 2006—. Mem. investment com. Noble and Greenough Sch. Office: Blackstone Group 345 Park Ave New York NY 10154*

GREENWALD, ALICE MARIAN, museum director; b. Oceanside, NY, Jan. 2, 1952; d. Edmund M. G. and Emily Leona (Liebman) Greenwald Meyer; m. David Pearce Ward, Oct. 10, 1976; children: Nathaniel, Leda Ward. BA, Sarah Lawrence Coll., 1973; MA in History of Religions, U. Chgo., 1975. Curatorial asst. Maurice Spertus Mus. of Judaica, Chgo.; asst. curator Hebrew Union Coll. Skirball Mus., LA, 1975—78, curator, 1978—81, acting dir., 1980; exec. dir. Nat. Mus. Am. Jewish History, Phila., 1981-86; prin. Alice M. Greenwald/Mus. Svcs., Washington, 1986—2001; assoc. mus. dir. mus. programs US Holocaust Meml. Mus., Washington, 2001—06; dir. World Trade Ctr. Meml. Mus., 2006—. Cons., tech. advisor Pew Charitable Trusts, Phila., 1987-90; chair, Coun. Am. Jewish Museums, 1984-86. Contbr. articles to profl. jours. Mem., advisor Local Assistance Bd., West Windsor, NJ, 1992. NEA fellow, 1981, Danforth Found. fellow, 1973-75. Democrat. Jewish. Avocations: cooking, travel, poetry.*

GREENWALD, CAROL SCHIRO, professional services marketing research executive; b. Phila., Mar. 2, 1939; d. Sidney L. and Adele R. (Rosenheim) Schiro; children: David Bruce, William Michael. BA cum laude, Smith Coll., 1961; MA, Hunter Coll., 1965; PhD in Polit. Sci., CUNY, 1972. Instr. polit. sci. Queen's Coll., CUNY, 1970-73; asst. dir. Evaluation N.Y.C. Adminstrv. Decentralization Project, 1971-73; asst. prof. Richmond Coll., CUNY, 1973-76, Bklyn. Coll., CUNY, 1976-77; research assoc. Bunting Inst., Radcliffe Coll., 1977-79; project dir. Jobs in the 1980s Pub. Agenda Found., N.Y.C., 1979-81; assoc. dir. Grant Thornton acctg. firm, 1984-86; sr. mgr. Seidman and Seidman, 1986-87; market research mgr. KPMG Peat Marwick, 1988-90; cons., 1990-91, 2002—; mktg. dir. Haight, Gardner, Poor & Havens, 1991-92; dir. comm. Richard A. Eisner & Co., LLP, 1993-97; dir. mktg. Hamilton, HMC divsn. Kurt Salmon Assoc., 1997—, Whitman Breed Abbott & Morgan LLP, 1998-2000; cons. MarketForce, a divsn. of Hildebrandt, Internat., 2002; pvt. practice, 2002—. Author: Group Power: Lobbying and Public Policy, 1977; mem. editl. bd. Mktg. Rev., 1997—; contbr. articles on polit. sci. to profl. jours. Lilly Found. fellow Mem. Am. Mktg. Assn. (chair profl. devel. leadership coun. 1995—, mem. editl. bd. 1996—), Common Cause (chmn. N.Y. 1981-83, nat. dir. 1978-84), Westchester Women in Comm. (treas. 1993-95). Home: 688 Forest Ave Larchmont NY 10538-1535 E-mail: greenwaldcarol@hotmail.com.

GREENWALD, JULIE, recording industry executive; b. 1970; 1 child, Tallulah Rose G. BA in polit. sci., Tulane Univ. Personal asst. to pres. Def Jam Records, 1992, head of mktg.; pres. Island Records; exec. v.p. Island Def Jam Records, 2002; pres. Atlantic Records Group, 2004—. Office: Atlantic Records 1290 Ave of the Americas New York NY 10104 Office Phone: 212-707-2000. Office Fax: 212-405-5475.*

GREENWALD, SHEILA ELLEN, writer, illustrator; b. N.Y.C., May 26, 1934; d. Julius and Florence (Friedman) Greenwald; m. George E. Green, Feb. 18, 1960; children: Samuel Green, Benjamin Green. BA, Sarah Lawrence Coll., 1956. Author over 24 children's books, including Give Us a Great Big Smile Rosy Cole, 1980, Valentine Rosy, 1984, Rosy Cole's Great American Guilt Club, 1987, Write on Rosy, 1988, Rosy's Romance, 1989, Here's Hermione, 1991, The Mariah Delany Author of the Month Club, 1990, Rosy Cole Discovers America, 1992, My Fabulous NewLife, 1993, Rosy Cole, She Walks in Beauty, 1994, Rosy Cole: She Grows and Graduates, 1997, Stucksville, 2000, Mariah Delany Lending Library Disaster (The Mariah Delany Author of The Month Club 1999), Stucksville, 2001, The Hot Day reissued by Silver Mountain, 2002, Rosy Cole's Worst Ever, Best Yet Tour of New York City, 2003, Rosy Cole's Memoir EXPLOSION, 2006. Mem.: PEN, Authors League. Jewish. Office: Melanie Kroupa Books Ferrar Straus & Geroux 19 Union Sq W New York NY 10003 E-mail: sheilagreenwald@usa.net.

GREENWALD, THERESA MCGOWAN, health services administrator, rehabilitation nurse; b. Scranton, Pa., Feb. 8, 1950; d. Robert Bell and Agnes (Butler) McGowan; m. David Jeffrey Greenwald, Oct. 26, 1996; 1 child, Jennifer Emilie Nicole Drescher. Diploma nursing, Hosp. U. Pa., 1970. RN, Ohio; cert. rehab. nurse, case mgr. Staff nurse, asst. head nurse Riddle Meml. Hosp., Media, Pa., 1971-80; rehab. nurse, mgr. Upjohn Rehab. Scvs., Phila. and Cin., 1980-85; cons., life care planner Occupl. Health Resources, Cin., 1985-87, Springfield, Va., 1987-88; dir. life care planning Rehab. Experts, Vienna, Va., 1988-89; program mgr., account exec. Comprehensive Rehab. Assocs., Cin., 1989-93; dir. managed care case mgmt. Sheakley Med. Mgmt. Sys., Cin., 1993-95; clin. program coord. Mayfield Clinic and Spine Inst., Cin., 1996—2005; sr. mgr. health svcs. Cin. Bell, 2005—; dir. Nat. Bd. Certification Continuity of Care, 1998-99. Mem. cmty. adv. bd. Drake Ctr., Inc., 1998-2000. Mem. Nurse Case Mgrs. of S.W. Ohio (membership chair 1994-99), Case Mgmt. Resource Network (v.p., pres. elect, 2005). Office: Cincinatti Bell 221 E 4th St Cincinnati OH 45202 Office Phone: 513-397-1008. Personal E-mail: theresa.greenwald@cinbell.com.

GREENWAY-AUGUST, KRISTIN LEE, dancer, educator; b. Phoenix, Ariz., Aug. 30, 1972; d. James Edward Greenway and Laurie Jo Lamson; m. Clint Joseph August, Sept. 29, 2001; children: Dylan Michael August, Gavin Reid August. BFA in Dance, U. Ariz., Tucson, 1994; MAT, Nat. U., San Diego, 2004. Tchg. credential Nat. U., 1997. Dist. sales mgr. ADP, San Diego, 1995—97; tchr. dance Sweetwater Union H.S. Dist., Chula Vista, Calif., 1997. Dancer Castle Park Dance Company. Liberal. Presbyterian. Avocations: travel, reading, dance, art. Home: 445 Whispering Willow Unit D Santee CA 92071 Office: Sweetwater Union HS 1130 Fifth Ave Chula Vista CA 91911 Office Phone: 619-691-5500.

GREENWELL, MARY JANE, middle school educator; b. New Haven, Ky., Aug. 12, 1945; d. Ned Bell and Edna (Ballard) Johnson; m. Roger Greenwell, July 3, 1975; children: Charles, Michael, Veronica. AB, Brescia Coll., 1968; MA, Morehead U., 1974. Cert. tchr., Ky. Tchr. St. Francis Elem. Sch., Loretto, Ky., 1968-70, St. Charles High Sch., Marion County Schs., St. Mary's, Ky., 1970-74, Bardstown (Ky.) Ind. Schs., 1974—. Part-time tchr. St. Catharine (Ky.) Coll., 1993. Mem. community coun. Prichard Com., Lexington; mem. site based coun. Bardswotn Mid. Sch., 1992-94; active Dem. Women's Club Ky., Nelson County. Recipient 1st Class award Bardstown Nelson County Leadership, 1989, plaque, Nelson County State Bicentennial Com., 1992, Concerned Parents award for Non-Minority Person, 1991. Mem. NOW, ACLU, Nat. Coun. for Social Studies, Ky. Coun. for Social Studies, Bardstown Edn. Assn. (exec. bd., pres. 1983-84, 94-99), Bardstown Woman's Club (pres. 1985-86), Amnesty Internat., Fourth Dist. Edn. Assn. (v.p. 2000-05, pres. 2005-06), Nelson County Dem. Party (sec. 2000-06). Roman Catholic. Home: 113 Edgewood Dr Bardstown KY 40004-1104 Office: Bardstown Mid Sch 410 N 5th St Bardstown KY 40004-1616

GREENWOOD, ANNA STARBUCK, librarian; b. Glendale, Calif., May 13, 1923; d. David Arnold and Margaret Lucinda (McVey) Starbuck; m. David Charles Greenwood, June 15, 1962 (dec. 1984). BA, U. So. Calif., 1953; MLS, Cath. U. Am., 1966. Tchr. Torrance (Calif.) Sch. Dist., 1953-56, Wiseburn Sch. Dist., Torrance, 1956-61; libr. Montgomery County Pub. Schs., Rockville, Md., 1961-83, Rock Creek Parish, Washington, 1980—. Reviewer Sch. Libr. Jour., 1968-71. Mem. Ch. and Synagogue Libr. Assn. (pres. 1988-89), Montgomery County Sch. Libr. Assn. (pres. 1973-74). Democrat. Episcopalian. Avocations: genealogy, local history.

GREENWOOD, JANE, costume designer, educator; b. Liverpool, England, Apr. 30, 1934; d. Harold Ralph Pate and Florence Sarah Mary (Humphrey) G.; m. Ben Edwards, children: Sarah, Kate. Attended, Central Sch. of Arts & Crafts, London, England. Teacher Lester Polakov Design Studio, New York, NY, Julliard Sch., New York, NY; assoc. prof. of design Yale U., New Haven, 1977—. Stage work includes: The Ballad of the Sad Cafe, 1963, Hamlet, 1964, Incident at Vichy, 1964-65, Tartuffe, 1965, Half a Sixpence, 1965-66, A Race of Hairy Men!, 1965, Nathan Weinstein, 1966, Where's Daddy?, 1966, How's the World Treating You?, 1966, More Stately Mansions, 1967-68, The Prime of Miss Jean Brodie, 1968, Seven Descents of Myrtle, 1968, I'm Solomon, 1968, The Wrong Way Light Bulb, 1969, The Penny Wars, 1969, Angela, 1969, Sheep on the Runway, 1970, Othello, 1970, Gandhi, 1970, Hay Fever, 1970, Les Blancs, 1970, Antigone, 1971, Wise Child, 1972, Look Away, 1973, Finishing Touches, 1973, A Moon for the Misbegotten, 1973-74, Cat on a Hot Tin Roof, 1974, 2003-04, Same Time Next Year, 1975-78, A Matter of Gravity, 1976, California Suite, 1976, A Texas Trilogy, 1976, Otherwise Engaged, 1977, Anna Christie, 1977, Vieux Carre, 1977, The Night of the Tribades, 1977, An Almost Perfect Person, 1977, A Touch of the Poet, 1977, Cheaters, 1978, The Kingfisher, 1978, Faith Healer, 1979, Knockout, 1979, Romantic Comedy, 1979, To Grandmother's House We Go, 1981, The Supporting Cast, 1981, The West Side Waltz, 1981-82, Duet for One, 1981, Medea, 1982, The Queen and the Rebels, 1982, Plenty, 1983, Heartbreak House, 1983-84, The Golden Age, 1984, Alone Together, 1984, The Iceman Cometh, 1985, Lillian, 1986, So Long on Lonely Street, 1986, Ah, Wilderness, 1988, Long Day's Journey into Night, 1988, Our Town, 1988, The Secret Rapture, 1989, Lisbon Traviatta, The Circle, 1989, The Tenth Man, 1990, The Big Love, 1991, I Hate Hamlet, 1991, Park Your Car in Harvard Yard, 1991, A Streetcar Named Desire, 1992, The Price, 1992, Lips Together, Teeth Apart, The Sisters Rosensweig, 1993-94, Abe Lincoln in Illinois, 1993, She Loves Me, 1993, Passion, 1994, The Heiress, 1995, A Month in the Country, 1995, Sylvia, Death Defying Acts, Master Class, 1995, A Delicate Balance, 1996, Once Upon a Mattress, 1996, The Last Night of Ballyhoo, 1997, An American Daughter, 1997, The Little Foxes, 1997, Proposals, 1997, The Scarlet Pimpernel, 1997, The Deep Blue Sea, 1998, Honour, 1998, High Society, 1998, James Joyce's The Dead, 2000, A Moon for the Misbegotten, 2000, The Dinner Party, 2000-01, Major Barbara, 2001, Bea Arthur on Broadway, 2002, Fortune's Fool, 2002, The Retreat from Moscow, 2003-04, The Violet Hour, 2003, The Caretaker, 2003-04, Oldest Living Confederate Widow Tells All, 2003, Who's Afraid of Virginia Woolf?, 2005, On Golden Pond, 2005, Lennon, 2005, Absurb Person Singular, 2005, Heartbreak House, 2006; TV work includes: The House Without a Christmas Tree, 1972, The Easter Promise, 1975, Beyond the Horizon, 1976, Addie and the King of Hearts, 1976, The Royal Romance of Charles and Diana, 1982, The Shady Hill Kidnapping, 1982, The File on Jill Hatch, 1983, Kennedy, 1983, Johnny Bull, 1986, Ike, 1986, Heartbreak House, 1986, Lyndon Johnson, 1987, Dialogue of the Carmelites, 1987, Liberace: Behind the Music, 1988, Our Town, 1989, The Ivory Hunters, 1990, Sensibility and Sense, 1990, Three Hotels, 1991, The End of a Sentence, 1991, A Life in the Theatre, 1993, The Mother, 1994; film work includes: Last Embrace, 1979, Can't Stop the Music, 1980, The Four Seasons, 1981, Arthur, 1981, Wetherby, 1985, Sweet Liberty, 1986, The Squeeze, 1987, Jacknife, Mr. Destiny, 1990, Glengarry Glen Ross, 1992, Oleanna, 1994, Other Voices, Other Rooms, 1995. 14 Tony nominations.*

GREENWOOD, JANET KAE DALY, psychologist, academic administrator, marketing professional; b. Goldsboro, N.C., Dec. 9, 1943; d. Fulton Benton and Kelminy Ethel Esther (Ball) Daly; 1 child, Gerald Thompson. AA, Peace Coll., 1963; BS in English and Psychology, East Carolina U., 1965, MEd in Counseling, 1967; postgrad., N.C. State U., 1967-69, U. London, 1969; PhD in Counseling and Higher Ednl. Adminstrn., Fla. State U., 1972. Tchr. English Kinston (N.C.) City Schs., 1965-66, Goldsboro City Schs., 1966-67; counselor and psychometrist primary and secondary schs. County of Wake, NC, 1967-69; coord. Am. Inst. for Fgn. Study, 1969; supr. student tours in Eng., France, Switzerland, Italy, and Capri, 1969; counselor Fla. State U., Tallahassee, 1969-72; asst. dir. counseling Rutgers U., New

Brunswick, NJ, 1972-73, cons. to v.p. for student svcs., 1973-74, lectr. in counseling psychology, 1972-74; coord. and assoc. prof. counselor edn. U. Cin., 1974-77, adviser to grad. students, 1974-77, vice provost student affairs, 1977-81; pres. Longwood Coll., Farmville, Va., 1981-87, U. Bridgeport, Conn., 1987-92; cons., ptnr., dir. Heidrick & Struggles, Washington, 1992-2000; v.p. A.T. Kearney, Inc., 2000—04; owner, ptnr. Greenwood & Assocs., Inc., 2004—. Guidance cons. South Plainfield Pub. Schs., 1973-76; adviser Parents without Ptnrs., 1976; bd. dirs. Hydraulic Co.; mem. Gov.'s Partnership To Prevent Substance Abuse in the Workforce, mem. audit com. and cmty. and govt. rels. com. Contbr. articles to profl. jours. Mem. Gov.'s Ad Hoc Edn. Com. on Tchr. Edn. and Counselor Edn., State of Ohio, 1975; mem. state planning commn. Nat. Identification of Women Project; chair Twin Rivers Tenants Rights Assn., 1972-74; bd. dirs. Bridgeport Hosp., Bridgeport Bus. Coun.; mem. adv. com. Bridgeport Pub. Edn. Fund; bd. dirs. Conn. Ballet Theatre, chair South End streeting com; mem. mgmt. adv. com. City of Bridgeport; mem. adv. com. United Way Tri-State; chair South End Partnership Com; mem. The Schiavone Steering Com./Downtown Bridgeport Project, YWCA Bd., Champion/United Way, United Way Community Human Svcs. Planning Coun., Bridgeport Symphony Bd., Bridgeport Opera Bd., Bridgeport Area Coll./Univ. Consortium, Conn. Conf. Ind. Colls., The Newcomen Soc. of U.S., The United Way Ea. Fairfield County; mem. adv. bd. Sacred Heart/St. Anthony Sch.; Roosevelt Sch; mem. ct. com. Regional Plan Assn. Fairfield 2000; bd. dirs. Conn. Ballet Theatre; chair The Bridgeport Regional Bus. Coun. Brass Ring Task Force on Leadership; bd. govs. Fairfield County Study; mem. hon. bd. dirs. Conn. Earth Day 20, Inc.; chair L.I. Sound Western Regional Coun.; founding mem. L.I. Sound Assembly; mem. membership com., campus partnership subcom. Drugs Don't Work program, 1989-91. Recipient Spl. award Black Arts Festival, Meritorious Svc. award Am. Assn. State Colls. and Univs. Mem. AAUP, Am. Coll. Pers. Assn. (editor and chair media bd. 1975—), Am. Pers. and Guidance Assn., Cin. Pers. and Guidance Assn., Ohio Psychol. Assn., Cin. Psychol. Assn., Organizational Behavior Assn., Am. Sch. Counselors Assn., Ohio Sch. Counselors Assn., Assn. for Women Faculty, Ohio Counselor Edn. and Supervision Assn., Kappa Delta Pi.

GREENWOOD, MONIQUE, innkeeper, writer, restaurant owner; b. Wash., DC; m. Glenn Pogue. Grad. magna cum laude, Howard U. Lifestyle dir., style editor Essence mag., 1996—98, exec. editor, 1998—2000, editor-in-chief, 2000—01; owner, innkeeper Akwaaba Mansion Bed & Breakfast, Bklyn., 1995—, Akwaaba by the Sea, Cape May, NJ, 2001—; owner Akwaaba Cafe, Bklyn. Co-founder, pres. Go On Girl! Book Club. Author: Having What Matters: The Black Woman's Guide to Creating the Life You Really Want, 2001. Bd. mem. Bklyn. Urban League, Central Bklyn. Partnership, Bridge St. Devel. Corp. Recipient Points of Light award, Pres. Bush. Avocations: reading, antiques, travel, interior decorating. Mailing: Akwaaba Mansion Bed & Breakfast 347 MacDonough St Brooklyn NY 11233 Office Phone: 718-455-5958. Office Fax: 718-774-1744.

GREENWOOD, PILAR FERNÁNDEZ-CAÑADAS, language and literature educator; b. Herencia, La Mancha, Spain, Feb. 26, 1940; came to U.S., 1965. d. Isidro Fernández-Cañadas and Maria Rosario González-Ortega; m. Davydd James Greenwood, June 19, 1965; 1 child, Alex David Greenwood. MA, U. Pitts., 1967, Cornell U., Ithaca, 1979, PhD, 1981. Head resident Grinnell (Iowa) Coll., 1963-64; lectr. Cornell U., Ithaca, N.Y., 1972-75, Wells Coll., Aurora, N.Y., 1987, vis. asst. prof., 1988-90, asst. prof., 1990-94, prof. Spanish, 1995, assoc. prof., 1994—, Sara Niles Georges prof. fgn. lang. and lit., 2001. Author: Pastoral Poetics, 1983, also children's plays; contbr. numerous articles to profl. jours. Vol. CIVITAS, Ithaca, N.Y., 1983. Grantee Program Cultural Cooper, U. Minn., 1987. Mem. MLA, Assn. Cervantists, Feministas Unidas, Am. Assn. Tchrs. Spanish and Portuguese, Assn. Licenciados y Doctores Españoles en Estados Unidos, Phi Kappa Phi. Roman Catholic. Avocations: travel, music, performing arts, visual arts, gardening. Office: Wells Coll Rt 90 Aurora NY 13026 Office Phone: 315-364-3306. E-mail: pgreenwood@wells.edu.

GREENWOOD, SARAH ELIZABETH, lawyer; d. David Franklin Greenwood, Jr. and Janet Lee Greenwood. BA in English, Lynn Coll., Batesville, Ark., 2000; JD, U. Little Rock, 2003. Assoc. Huckabay, Munson, Paulett and Moore, Little Rock, 2001—. Mem.: AAWL, Inn of Cts., Lynn Pres.'s Coun. Avocations: reading, exercise, running. Office: Huckabay Munson Paulett & Moore Ste 1900 400 W Capitol Little Rock AR 72201

GREENZANG, KATHERINE, lawyer, insurance company executive; b. 1964; BA, Johns Hopkins Univ.; JD, NYU. Bar: NY 1990. Assoc. Dewey Ballantine, NYC, 1990—94; corp. counsel Assurant Inc., NYC, 1994—95, asst. v.p., corp. counsel, 1995—96, v.p., corp. counsel, 1996—2001, sr. v.p., gen. counsel, sec., 2001—. Mem.: ABA, Assn. Corp. Counsel, NY State Bar Assn. Office: Assurant Inc 41st Fl 1 Chase Manhattan Plz New York NY 10005

GREER, BONNIE BETH, educator; b. Toledo, Sept. 13, 1946; d. Therron Otto and Betty Mae Kleckner; m. John Garland Greer, July 9, 1977; children: Christopher John, Tiffany Maye. AB, Ind. U., 1968; MEd, Okla. U., 1969, PhD, 1971. Instrnl. tchr. No. Ind. Children's Hosp., South Bend, 1968; tchr. 6th grade Blanchard Pub. Schs., Okla., 1968—69; grad. asst., spl. instr., lectr. Okla. U., 1969—72; program dir. Stone Belt Ctr. for Retarded, Bloomington, Ind., 1972—73; asst. prof. Bridgewater State Coll., Mass., 1973—74; prof. spl. edn. and rehab. U. Memphis, 1974—2004, prof. emeritus, 2004—. Lectr. in field. Co-author: Practical Strategies in Working with the Trainable Mentally Retarded, 1975; contbr. chapters to books, articles to profl. jours. Mem.: Assn. for Retarded Citizens, Coun. Exceptional Children, Delta Kappa Gamma.

GREER, CAROLYN A., guidance counselor; b. Dallas, Oct. 27, 1943; d. Billy Bryan and Estelle Catherine (Haney) Harris; m. Charles David Melton, Nov. 25, 1965 (div. Aug. 1991); 1 child, Melissa Gayle Melton Brydson; m. Robert S. Greer, Aug. 16, 1991. BA in English, U. North Tex., 1965, MEd in Counseling, 1971, mid-mgmt. cert., 1987, supt. cert., 1992, EdD, 1997; spl. edn. endorsement, Tex. Christian U., 1973. Lic. profl. counselor, Tex; approved supr. for lic. profl. counselors; cert. supt., Tex.; cert. mid-mgmt. adminstr., Tex.; cert. provisional secondary English, Tex.; cert. provisional secondary history, Tex. Tchr. English Carrollton-Farmers br. Ind. Sch. Dist., 1970-71, Onslow County Schs., NC, 1967, Dallas Ind. Sch. Dist., 1965-66, 68, 69; counselor Hurst-Euless-Bedford Ind. Sch. Dist., 1973-90; program dir. guidance and counseling Ft. Worth Ind. Sch. Dist., 1990-96; asst. prof. ednl. leadership and counseling dept. Sam Houston State U., 1996-98; instrnl. officer guidance and counseling Katy Ind. Sch. Dist., Tex., 1998—2001; cons. secondary assessment ACT, Inc., Austin, 2001—03; dir. enrollment Big Bros. Big Sisters Ctrl. Tex., 2003—. Adj. prof. U. H-Victoria, 1999-2000; part-time instr. psychology Tarrant County Jr. Coll., 1974-85; mem. Tex. Atty. Gen. Task Force on Sch. Violence Prevention, 1999-00; adv. mem. Tex. State Bd. for Educator Certification, 1998-2000; presenter workshops in field. Author: (books) Comprehensive Guidance Program—Ft. Worth, 1991, Administrv. Guide to Bias Free Classrooms, 1993; editl. adv. bd. Student Assistance Jour., 1989-91. Mem. women's issues com. Sam Houston State U., Huntsville, Tex., 1997-98; mem. zoning Commn., Bedford, Tex., 1990-92; mem. adv. for counselors Tex. Edn. Agy., Austin, Tex., 1998-99. Recipient Pub. Awareness award Tarrant County Mental Health Assn., 1995. Mem. ASCD, ACA (govt. rels. com. 1991-92, 99-2000), Am. Sch. Counselors Assn. (chair pub. rels. com. 1996-98), Assn. Counselor Educators and Supr. (chair sch. issues 1995-97), Nat. Career Devel. Assn. (chair sch. and bus. partnerships spl. interest group com. 1995-98), Tex. Counseling Assn. (senator 1985-88, sec. 1990-91, dir. region IV 1994-96, 1996 local conf. coord., pres.-elect 1997-98, pres. 1998-99, Rhosine Fleming Outstanding Sch. Counselor award 1989, Molly Gerold Human Rights award 1995), Tex. Sch. Counselor's Assn. (pres. 1989-90), Tex. Assn. for Counselor Educators and Supr. (pres. 1995-96), Tex. Career Guidance Assn. (bd. dirs. 1993-96, pres. 1996-97), Tex. Assn. for Supervision and Curriculum Devel., Tex. Coun. Women Sch. Exec., North Cen. Tex. Counseling Assn. (pres. 1980-81, Outstanding Counselor award 1988, Caring Counselor award 1993). Avocations: walking, gourmet cooking, gardening. Office: Big Brothers Big Sisters of Ctrl Texas 1400 Tillery Austin TX 78721 Home: 20421 Haystack Cv Spicewood TX 78669-6441 E-mail: greerc@act.org.

GREER, CAROLYN ARLENE, music educator, elementary school educator; b. Aberdeen, Wash., Apr. 29, 1961; d. Kenneth Junior and Alice Lorraine Linder; m. Ronald Keith Greer, Aug. 20, 1983; children: Tiffany Joy, Crystal Lynn, Brianna Nicole. AA in Gen. Studies, Grays Harbor Coll., 1982, N.W. Nazarene U., 1987; BA in Elem. Edn., St. Martin's Coll., 1999; student, Seattle Pacific U., 2002—. Cert. tchr. K-8; Music K-12 Wash., 1999. Med. records clk. Dr.s Morgan, Morgan & Worth Family Practice Ctr. of GH, Aberdeen, Wash., 1980—83; med. receptionist, bookkeeper Dr.s Magsalay, Caratao & Hutton (Pediat.), Aberdeen, 1988—96; elem. music tchr. Hoquiam (Wash.) Sch. Dist., 1999—, elem. band tchr., 1999—. Musician, worship leader, children's music ministries Immanuel Bapt. Ch., Hoquiam, 1994—; h.s. choir accompanist Hoquiam (Wash.) HS, 1996—97; accompanist all-state competition Hoquiam (Wash.) Sch. Dist., 1996—97, asst. elem. girls track coach, 2001—04; judicator Ann. River Festival City Hoquiam, 2000—03. Author: (plays) Christmas With Grandma, 1977; editor: (plays) Christmas With Grandma; dir., prodr.: (plays) Christmas With Grandma. Mem.: NEA (assoc.), Wash. State Music Tchrs. Assn., Grays Harbor Chpt., Ret. Tchrs. Assn. (assoc.), Music Educators Nat. Conf. (assoc.). Republican. Avocations: kite festivals, camping, canoeing, singing, gardening, crafts.

GREER, CHERYL L., middle school educator; b. Hammond, Ind., Oct. 27, 1954; d. Roger R. and Margaret L. Potts; m. David E. Greer, June 8, 1974 (div. May 17, 2001); children: Kristen M., Jessica L. Student, Butler U., 1972—74; MusB, Wayne State U., 1976; MA in Edn., We. Ky. U., 1995; Rank I in Edn., U. Louisville, 2004. Asst. mgr., treas. Royal Oak Cmty. Credit Union, Mich., 1977—82; note teller Farmer's Bank & Trust, Bardstown, Ky., 1982—85; owner, mgr. Sweets 'n Things, Bardstown, 1985—90; substitute tchr. Hardin County Pub. Schs., Elizabethtown, Ky., 1990—93; dir. band, tchr. music Bullitt Lick Mid. Sch., Shepherdsville, Ky., 1993—2005, Eastside Mid. Sch., Bullitt County, Ky., 2005—. Musician: River Cities Concert Band, 2004. Musician 1st Christian Ch., Elizabethtown, 1992—95, Sunday Sch. tchr., 1992—95, Rineyville Bapt. Ch., Rineyville, Ky., 1996—97; musician Bardstown Meth. Ch., Bardstown, Ky., 2001—; mem. I.U.S. Concert Band, 2002—. Mem.: Ky. Educators Assn., Ky. Music Educators Assn. (sec., treas. 5th dist. 2001—), Music Educators Nat. Conf. Business E-Mail: cheri.greer@bullitt.k12.ky.schools.us.

GREER, FRANCES ELLEN DUBOIS, JR., (NANCY GREER JR., NANCY GREER HAMILTON), retired statistician, volunteer; b. Fort McPherson, Ga., June 11, 1947; d. Robert William (Alonzo Jr.) and Frances Ellen (DuBois) Greer; m. Richard Alonzo Hart, Jan. 1, 2001. AB in Psychology, Wesleyan Coll., Macon, Ga., 1969; MA in Spl. Studies, George Washington U., Washington, 1975; MA in Indsl. Psychology, George Mason U., Fairfax, Va., 1992. Cert. Myers Briggs Type Indicator, 1987. Adj. instr. No. Va. Cmty. Coll., Alexandria and Annandale, 1975—76; owner and liturgical designer Divine Designs, Inc., Atlanta, 1976—79; adj. instr. Auburn U., Montgomery, Ala., 1979—81; program mgr. USAF, Bolling AFB, DC, 1981—89, U.S. Marine Corps, Arlington, Va., 1981—89; human resource adminstr. SRA Technologies, Merrifield, 1991—96; sr. rsch. analyst L-3 Corp., Chantilly, 1996—2004; ret., 2004. Contbr. articles to profl. jours. Charity quilter Quarterly Quilters, Alexandria, Va., 2003—; feline rescue vol. 4 Paws, Inc., Fairfax County, 2002—, King St. Cats, Inc., Alexandria, 2003—; costumed vol. Mt. Vernon Estate, Mt. Vernon, 2004—; head pastoral care St. Adrian's Ch., Alexandria, 2003—, head Octoberfest festival, 2004—. Named Outstanding Young Woman of Am., 1979, Personel Program Mgr. of Yr., 1982, Plankholder, U.S. Navy, 1988; recipient Sustained Superior Performance award, U.S. Marine Corps, 1983, 1988, EEO cert. merit, 1983. Mem.: PEO Internat., Mount Vernon Country Club, Phi Delta Epsilon. Democrat. Episcopalian. Avocation: genealogy. Home: 3300 Wessynton Way Alexandria VA 22309-2229

GREER, JULIANNA PATTERSON, not-for-profit administrator; b. Greenville, Tex., Dec. 5, 1953; d. Malcolm Boyd and Mary Helena Patterson; m. William Nathaniel Greer, Apr. 8, 1978. Student, Inst. Am., Aix-en-Provence, France, 1974—75; BA, Trinity U., San Antonio, 1976; MA, U. North Tex., 1981. V.p. of events Ill. St. Andrew Soc., North Riverside, Ill., 1996—2001; v.p. ops. Frank Lloyd Wright Preservation Trust, Oak Park, Ill., 2001—. Author: (monograph) Beyond the Regulations: Building Superior Facilities for the Aged. Mem.: Phi Beta Kappa. Unitarian Universalist. Avocations: travel, dance. Home: 667 Glen Haven Ln Glen Ellyn IL 60137 Office: Frank Lloyd Wright Preservation Trust 931 Chicago Ave Oak Park IL 60302 Office Phone: 708-848-1976. Office Fax: 708-848-1248. Personal E-mail: jpgreer@wowway.com. Business E-Mail: greer@wrightplus.org.

GREER, RENEE MICHELLE, elementary school educator; b. Peoria, Ill., Nov. 29, 1964; d. James and Ede Stickelmaier; m. Steven Paul Greer, June 28, 1990; children: Gillian, Cullen, Makinzie, Madalyn. BS, Bradley U., Peoria, 1999. Cert. elem. tchr. Ill., 1999. Sci. tchr. grades 7 and 8 St. Thomas Sch., Peoria Heights, Ill., 2000—01; sci. tchr. grade 7 Germantown Hills Mid. Sch., Metamora, Ill., 2001—. Office: Germantown Hills Middle School 103 Warrior Way Metamora IL 61548 Office Phone: 309-383-2121. Business E-Mail: greerr@schools.mtco.com.

GREER, SARAH ROLSTON DOXEY, retired elementary school educator; b. Holly Springs, Miss., Mar. 13, 1933; d. Hindman and Mary Amis (Bitzer) Doxey; m. Lloyd O'Neil Tate, Dec. 25, 1960 (div. July 16, 1986); children: Katherine Bitzer Tate, William Hindman Tate, Marisa O. Tate Stone, Frances Tate Johnson; m. Curtis Aquilla Greer, Jan. 22, 2006. AS, Belhaven Coll., 1951; BA in Art Edn., U. Miss., 1954, postgrad., 1981—83, Miss. So. U., 1986—89. Tchr. 2d and 4th grades Canton Pub. Schs., Miss., 1954—59; tchr. 3d grade Holly Springs Schs., 1959—60; art supr. 5 schs. Clarksdale Pub. Elem. Schs., Miss., 1961—62; art supr. 5 elem. schs. Tupelo Pub. Schs. ETV Art, Miss., 1962—69; tchr. kindergarten and pvt. sch. Playhouse, Tupelo, 1970—73; tchr. h.s. art and journalism Tupelo Pub. Schs., 1974—75, tchr. jr. high gifted edn., 1977—80; tchr., libr./media ctr. Lee County Schs., Tupelo, 1985—96. Pianist receptions, rehearsal dinners Tupelo Country Club, 1985—. Grand marshal Tupelo Christmas Parade, 2002; pres. bd. Friends of Lee County Libr., 2001—04; elder 1st Presbyn. Ch.; past pres., moderator Presbyn. Women, Tupelo; bd. dirs., past pres. Faith Haven, Inc. Home for Children, 1976—; head counselor Camp DeSoto Camp for Girls, Mentone, Ala., 1972—95; founder Ch. After Sch. Assn., Lee County, 1982—, civic chmn. Fortnightly Musicale, 1963—, pres., 1965; pianist Salvation Army Ch. Svcs., Tupelo. Named one of Mississippians Who Have Made a Difference, Miss. Mag., 1985, Outstanding Women of Am., 1967; recipient Freedom Found. Valley Forge Tchr.'s medal, 1969, Outstanding Citizen award, Tupelo Jr. Aux., Inc., 1999. Mem.: DAR (regent 1970), N.E. Miss. Ret. Tchrs. Assn. (dist. pres. 1997—99), Tupelo-Lee County Miss. Assn. Educators. Meth. Avocation: playing piano. Home: 620 Woodland Heights Holly Springs MS 38635

GREGERSON, LINDA KAREN, poet, language educator, critic; b. Elgin, Ill., Aug. 5, 1950; d. Olaf Thorbjorn and Karen Mildred Gregerson; m. Steven Mullaney, 1980; children: Emma Mullaney, Megan Mullaney. BA, Oberlin Coll., 1971; MA, Northwestern U., 1972; MFA, U. Iowa, 1977; PhD, Stanford U., 1987. Actress Kraken Theater Co., 1972—75; asst. poetry editor The Atlantic Monthly Press, 1982—86; staff editor Atlantic Monthly, Boston, 1982—87; asst. prof. Dept. English U. Mich., 1987—91, William Wilhartz asst. prof. English, 1991—94, assoc. prof. Dept. English, 1994—2001, prof. Dept. English, 2001—03, Frederick G. L. Huetwell prof., prof. English, 2003—, dir. MFA program in creative writing, 1997—2000. Mem. usage panel Am. Heritage Dictionary, 1987—; vis. asst. prof. creative writing program Dept. English Boston U., 1985—86; instr. lit. MIT, 1985—87; asst. editor Mich. Quarterly Rev., 1987—; editl. cons. Cambridge Univ. Press, 1989—, Harvard Univ. Press, 1989—, Oxford Univ. Press, 1989—, Wesleyan Univ. Press, 1989—, Ind. Univ. Press, 1989—, Bedford Books, 1989—, Univ. Mich. Press, 1989—, Wayne State Univ. Press, 1989—. Author: Fire in the Conservatory, 1982, The Reformation of the Subject: Spenser, Milton, and the English Protestant Epic, 1995, The Woman Who Died in Her Sleep, 1996, Negative Capability: Contemporary American Poetry, 2001, Waterborne, 2002, (poems) Illinois Again, 1975, Alone, 1977, Man Sitting in the Sun, 1979, To Albert Speer, 1980, (poetry) Ex Machina, 1982, Halfe a Yard of Rede Sea, 1983, Mother Ruin, 1984, Blazon, 1984, An Arbor, 1990, For the Taking, 1993, Fish Dying on the Third Floor at Barney's, 1996, Eyes Like Leeks, 2000, Pass Over, 2001, A History Play, 2002, Maculate, 2002. Recipient Levinson Prize award Poetry, 1991, Consuelo Ford award, Poetry Soc. Am., 1992, Isabel MacCaffrey award, Spenser Soc. Am., 1992, Pushcart prize, 1994, 2004, Acad. award in Lit., Am. Acad. Arts and Letters, 2002; fellow, Nat. Endowment Arts, 1985, 1992, Mellon, Nat. Humanities Ctr., 1991—92, Guggenheim, 2000; grantee Arts Found., Mich., 1994; Ingram Merrill grant, 1982—84. Mem.: MLA, Inst. Advanced Study (vis. mem. 1993—94), Milton Soc., Internat. Spenser Soc. (Isabel MacCaffrey award 1992), Renaissance Soc.Am., Shakespeare Assn. Am. Office: U Mich Dept English Lang and Lit 3147 Angell Hall Ann Arbor MI 48109-1045

GREGG, CYNTHIA LOUISE, music educator; b. Charleroi, Pa., May 7, 1952; d. Michael Richard and Helen Marie Bucci; m. Thomas Lee Gregg, May 27, 1978; children: Ashley Marie, Tommy Lee. MusB, W.Va. U., 1974, MusM, 1976; postgrad., Duquesne U., 1993, Ind. U. Pa., 1994. Cert. tchr. Pa, Orff cert. level 1 Nat. Am. Orff Schulwerk, Orff cert. level 2 Nat. Am. Orff Schulwerk. Piano tchr. Trombino's Music, Belle Vernon, Pa., 1972—75; piano instr. W.Va. U. Prep. Dept., Morgantown, 1972—74; music tchr. Barbour County Schs., Phillippi, W.Va., 1974—75, Washington (Pa.) Sch. Dist., 1975—. Organist, choir dir. St. Anne, 1972—99. Nominee Am. Tchr. award, Disney, 2001; named one of Outstanding Am. Tchrs., Nat. Honor Roll, 2006; recipient Tchr. Excellence award, Tchr. Excellence Ctr., 2006; Melvin Jones fellow, 2004. Fellow: Lions (dir. music necrology svc. 1998—99, pres. Rostraver Twp. 2002—04, zone chmn. 2003, v.p. care-a-van 2005, fellow 2005). Roman Catholic. Avocations: travel, music, crafts, reading. Home: 1130 Willowbrook Rd Belle Vernon PA 15012 Office: Washington Park Sch 801 E Wheeling St Washington PA 15301 Office Phone: 724-223-5000. Personal E-mail: tomgregg1@earthlink.net.

GREGG, ELLA MAE, writer; b. Appalachia, Va., Sept. 29, 1949; d. James Andrew Weatherly and Jewel Audrey Ramey; div.; children: Jeanie Barnett, Marcella Grooms, Jimmie Blazer. Offset pressman, Morritown, 1983; beautician, Knoxville Sch. Beauty, 1985; ins. Liberty Nat., Knoxville Sch. Ins., 1990. Tax cons. Exact Tax, Newport, Tenn.; owner, operator Hair Unltd., Tootie Fruitie's Beauty Shop, Newport. Mem. Mystery Writers Am., Women Guild Am., Police Writers Am. Avocations: walking, dance, reading. Home: PO Box 1214 Newport TN 37822-1214 Office: 543 Freeman Ave Newport TN 37821-3840

GREGG, ELLEN M., lawyer; b. Elkton, Md., July 9, 1961; BA summa cum laude, Campbell U., 1983; JD cum laude, Campbell U. Sch. Law, 1986. Bar: NC 1986, admitted to practice: All NC Fed. Dist. Cts., Ct. Appeals (4th Cir.). Intern Md. State Atty. Office, Cecil County, 1982; clerk to Hon. Gerald Arnold NC Ct. Appeals, 1984, jud. clerk to Hon. John C. Martin, 1986—87; mem. Womble Carlyle Sandridge & Rice, PLLC, Winston-Salem, NC. Membership editor Campbell Law Review; contbr. articles to profl. jours. Mem. jail manual adv. bd. Inst. Govt., Univ. NC. Named Region Champion, Nat. Trial Competition, 1986; recipient Lewis F. Powell Medallion for Excellence in Advocacy, Book Awards in Civil Procedure, Trial Advocacy, Criminal Procedure & Jurisprudence. Mem.: ABA (mem. litig. sect.), Forsyth County Young Lawyers Assn. (mem. litig. sect., mem. career develop. com., mem. trial practice general curriculum com.), NC Bar Assn. (mem. young lawyers divsn., mem. litig. sect.), Forsyth County Bar Assn. (mem. young lawyers sect.), Omicron Delta Kappa, Phi Kappa Phi. Office: Womble Carlyle Sandridge & Rice PLLC One W 4th St Winston Salem NC 27101 Mailing: Womble Carlyle Sandridge & Rice PLLC PO Box 84 Winston Salem NC 27102 Office Phone: 336-721-3729. Office Fax: 336-733-8384. Business E-Mail: egregg@wcsr.com.

GREGG, KATHY KAY, school system administrator; b. Washington, N.C., Aug. 26, 1956; d. Merwin Jack and Mary Elizabeth Gregg. BS, East Carolina U., 1978; MA, Appalachian State U., 1980; MEd, U. South Fla., 1993; PhD, Union Inst., Cin., 1998. Cert. educator Fla. Dept. Edn. Guidance counselor Waycross (Ga.) H.S., 1981—82; family life educator Family Svc. Ctrs., Clearwater, Fla., 1982—84; guildance counselor Pinellas County Schs., Largo, Fla., 1984—92, full svc. sch. coord., 1992—96, sch. adminstr., 1996—. Prof. Eckerd Coll., St. Petersburg, Fla., 1994—. Grantee Challenge Ropes Course, Jr. League St. Petersburg, 1997. Mem.: Assn. Experiential Edn. Avocations: reading, writing, sports, nature photography. Office: Northeast Cmty Sch 1717 54th Ave N Saint Petersburg FL 33714

GREGG, MARIE BYRD, retired farmer; b. Mount Olive, NC, Jan. 12, 1930; d. Arnold Wesley and Martha (Reaves) Byrd; m. Robert Allen Gregg, July 11, 1953 (dec.); children: Martha Susan, Kathryn Elizabeth, Kenneth Allen. BA in Elem. Edn., Furman U., Greenville, S.C., 1951. Tchr. 3rd grade Greenville City Sch., SC, 1951-53; med. social worker Ctrl. Carolina Rehab. Hosp., Greensboro, NC, 1959-61; window display designer Kerr Rexall Drugs, Durham, NC, 1960's; shop owner Something Else Antiques, Lima, Ohio, 1979-81; farm owner Mt. Olive, 1978-92. Democrat. Methodist. Avocations: collecting antiques, travel, reading, interior decorating. Home and Office: 212 Baucom Park Dr Greer SC 29650-2972

GREGOIRE, CHRISTINE O., governor, former state attorney general; b. Auburn, Wash., Mar. 24, 1947; m. Michael Gregoire; children: Courtney, Michelle. BA in Speech & Sociology, U. Wash., 1969; JD cum laude, Gonzaga U., 1977, LLD (hon.), 1995. Clerk, typist Wash. State Adult Probation/ Parole Office, Seattle, 1969; caseworker Wash. Dept. Social and Health Scis., Everett, 1974; asst. atty. gen. State of Wash., Spokane, 1977—81, sr. asst. atty. gen., 1981—82, dep. atty. gen., 1982—88, atty. gen., 1992—2005, gov. Olympia, 2005—; dir. Wash. State Dept. Ecology, 1988—92. Chair States/B.C. Oil Spill Task Force, 1989—92, Puget Sound Water Quality Authority, 1990—92, Nat. Com. State Environ. Dirs., 1991—92. Bd. dirs. Wash. State Dept. Ecology, 1988—92. Named Woman of Yr., Am. Legion Aux., 1999; named one of 25 Most Influential Working Mothers, Working Mother mag., 2000; recipient Conservationist of Yr. award, Trout Unlimited/N.W. Steelhead & Salmon Coun., 1994, Gov.'s Child Abuse Prevention award, 1996, Myra Bradwell award, 1997, Wyman award, 1997—98, Bd. of Gov.'s award for professionalism, WSBA, 1997, Kick Butt award, The Tobacco Free Coalition of Pierce County, 1997, Wash. State Hosp. Assn. award, 1997, Citizen Activist award, Gleitsman Found., 1998, Woman of Achievement award, Assn. for Women in Comm. Matrix Table, 1999, Pub. Justice award, WSTLA, 1999, Excellence in Pub. Health award, Wash. State Assn. Local Pub. Health Ofcls., 1999, Women in Govt. award, Good Housekeeping, 1999, Spl. Recognition award, Wash. State Nurses Assn., 2000. Mem.: Nat. Assn. Attys. Gen. (consumer protection and environment com., energy com., children and the law subcom., pres. 1999—2000). Democrat. Office: Office of Gov PO Box 40002 Olympia WA 98504 Office Phone: 360-753-6780. Office Fax: 360-753-4110.*

GRÉGOIRE, IDA, nursing administrator; d. Theodore George and Marie Cecile Grégoire. A in Applied Arts, Maria Coll., 1968; BSN, Coll. Tech., 1981; MSc in Nursing, Clin. Care Specialist, Syracuse U., 1985, MSW, 1990. RN NY, 1974, cert. in Pub. Health, ANCC, 1987, in Gerontology, Maria Coll., Albany, NY, 2003; Lic. Masters Social Worker NY, 1990. LPN St. Peter's Hosp., Albany, NY, 1969—74, RN, 1974—79; RN health educator Arthritis Found., Syracuse, 1981—82; pub. health nurse staff, clinic mgr. Onondaga County Health Dept., Syracuse, 1982—2002; RN case mgr. SUNY Upstate Med. Ctr., Syracuse, 2002—03; RN supr. Menorah Pk., Syracuse, 2003—; RN assessment coord. Francis House, Syracuse, 2004—. Congl. citizens com. mem. Medicare, 1995; adv. bd. mem. Peace Inc., Syracuse, 2000, advocacy bd. mem., 2002—; cons. Brady Faith Ctr., Syracuse, 1990—. Mem. Religious Sisters Mercy of Americas, 1965—. Nominee NY State Nurse Distinction in

Onondaga County, Syracuse, 1992; recipient Legis. recognition during Ice and Summer Storms, ARC, 1998. Mem.: ANA Coun. Nurses in Advanced Practice, Assn. Women's Health Obstetric and Neonatal Nurses, NY State Nurses Assn., Sigma Theta Tau Internat. Nursing Honor Soc. Roman Catholic. Avocations: cross country skiing, reading. Office: 4101 E Genesee St Syracuse NY 13203

GREGOR, DOROTHY DEBORAH, retired librarian; b. Dobbs Ferry, NY, Aug. 15, 1939; d. Richard Garrett Heckman and Marion Allen (Richmond) Stewart; m. A. James Gregor, June 22, 1963 (div. 1974). BA, Occidental Coll., 1961; MA, U. Hawaii, 1963; MLS, U. Tex., 1968; cert. in Library Mgmt., U. Calif., Berkeley, 1976. Reference libr. U. Calif., San Francisco, 1968-69; dept. libr. Pub. Health Libr. U. Calif., Berkeley, 1969-71, tech. services libr., 1973-76; reference libr. Hamilton Libr., Honolulu, 1971-72; head serials dept. U. Calif., Berkeley, 1976-80, assoc. univ. libr. tech. svcs. dept., 1980-84, univ. libr., 1992-94; chief Shared Cataloging div. Libr. of Congress, Washington, 1984-85; univ. libr. U. Calif.-San Diego, La Jolla, 1985-92, OCLC asst. to pres. for acad. and rsch. libr. rels., 1995—98; docent Asian Art Mus., San Francisco, 1997—, ret. Instr. sch. libr. and info. studies U. Calif., Berkeley, 1975, 76, 83; cons. Nat. Libr. of Medicine, Bethesda, Md., 1985, Ohio Bd. Regents, Columbus, 1987; trustee Online Computer Libr. Ctr., 1988-96; dir. Nat. Coordinating Com. on Japanese Libr. Resources, 1995-98; docent Asian Art Mus., San Francisco, 1997-. Mem.: ALA, Libr. Info. Tech. Assn., Program Com. Ctr. for Rsch. Librs. (bd. chair 1992—93, Hugh Atkinson award 1994). E-mail: dgregor@mcn.org.

GREGORIE, CORAZON ARZALEM, operations research specialist; b. Bethesda, Md., Aug. 6, 1947; d. Faustino and Rosalina Arzalem. AA in Bus. Adminstrn., Palm Beach Coll., 1967; postgrad., Fla. Atlantic U., 1967; BA in Bus. Adminstrn., U. Fla., 1969. Mgmt. trainee Burdines Dept. Store, West Palm Beach, Fla., 1969; adminstrv. asst. divsn. econs. Nat. Food Processors Assn., Washington, 1970-71, statis. analyst divsn. econs. and stats., 1972-77, acting dir. divsn. econs. and stats., 1978; asst. editor Airfare Pub. Co., Washington, 1979-81; product specialist Arbitron Co., Beltsville, Md., 1982-83, tng. supr. Laurel, Md., 1984-87, night shift ops. supr. Columbia, Md., 1988—95, survey supr., 1996—. Collective mem., bd. dirs. Glut Food, Mt. Rainier, Md., 1973-78. Force vol. Nat. Park Svc., Washington, 1973-76; coord. College Park Food Coop., Md., 1970-72. Mem. Lotus Ltd. (bd. dirs. 1974—, treas., parts and tech. chmn., membership dir., corr. sec.). Avocations: photography, sports cars. Office: Arbitron Co 9705 Patuxent Woods Dr Columbia MD 21046-1572

GREGORIUS, BEVERLY JUNE, retired obstetrician-gynecologist; b. Ottawa, Ill., June 21, 1915; d. Henry Godfrey and Arline (Barry) Pruette; m. Hans Harvey Gregorius, Apr. 6, 1939 (dec.); 1 child, Joan Gregorius Jones. BS, Madison (Tenn.) Coll., 1935; MD, Loma Linda (Calif.) U., 1946, postgrad, 1947-48, MS, 1953. Intern, Los Angeles County Gen. Hosp., 1946-47; resident in ob-gyn, White Meml. Hosp., Los Angeles, 1949-52; practice medicine specializing in ob-gyn, Burbank, Calif., 1953-77; assoc. clin. prof. Loma Linda U. Med. Sch., also U. So. Calif. Med. Sch., 1956-94; clin. prof. ob-gyn U. So. Calif. Med. Sch., 1985-94, emeritus clin. prof., 1994—; program dir. ob-gyn residency program Glendale (Calif.) Adventist Med. Ctr., 1976-82, chmn. dept. ob-gyn, 1981-83, cons., 1983—. Bd. dirs. Arroyo Vista Family Health Ctr.; adminstrv. bd. dirs. Glendale Adventist Ch., 1985—; mem. bd. councilors Loma Linda U., 1991— (Honored Alumnus 1991). Diplomate Am. Bd. Ob-Gyn. Fellow Am. Coll. Ob-Gyn, ACS, Internat. Coll. Surgeons; mem. AMA, CMA, Assn. Profs. Ob-Gyn., Los County Med. Assn., Los Angeles Ob-Gyn Soc. (coun. 1979-86, pres. 1984-85).

GREGORY, BETTINA LOUISE, retired journalist; b. NYC, June 4, 1946; d. George Alexander and V. Elizabeth Friedman; m. John P. Flannery, II, 1981 (div. 2001); 1 child, Diana Elizabeth. Student, Smith Coll., 1964-65; diploma in acting, Webber-Douglas Sch. Dramatic Art, London, 1968; BA in Psychology, Pierce Coll., Athens, Greece, 1972; PsyD, George Washington U., 2002; LittD (hon.), Susquehanna U., 1988, St. Thomas Aquinas U., 1992; LLD (hon.), Wilmington Coll., 1989; D in Journalism (hon.), U. Findlay, 1990; LittD (hon.), Bethany Coll., 2000. Reporter Sta. WVBR-FM, Ithaca, 1972-73, Sta. WCIC-TV, Ithaca, 1972; reporter, anchorwoman Sta. WGBB, Freeport, NY, 1973, Sta. WCBS, N.Y.; freelance reporter, writer AP, N.Y.C., 1973-74; freelance reporter N.Y. Times, 1973-74; with ABC News, 1974—2001, corr. Washington, 1977-79, White House corr., 1979, sr. gen. assignment corr., 1980, host The American Family, Goodlife TV Network, 2002—; pres. Sunshine State Telephone Co., Miami, Fla., 2004—05, Hollywood Internet Protocols, Inc., 2004—. Elected rep. for corrs. ABC News Women's Adv. Bd.; adj. prof. Robert H. Smith Sch. Bus.; adj. prof. exec. masters in bus. adminstrn. U. Md. Reporter TV spl. Flaws in the Shield, 1989 (1st pl. Headliner award), A&E's Biography of Hillary Rodham Clinton, 1994 (Best Documentary ACE award 1994), Murder Trial O.J. Simpson (Edward R. Murrow award Best News Series 1996), Hannibal Lecter: the Honey in the Lion's Mouth, Am.Journal Psychotherapy, 2002. Recipient 1st Place award Nat. Feature News, Odyssey Inst., NY, 1978, Clarion award Women in Communications, Inc., 1979, hon. mention Nat. Commn. on Working Women, 1979, Media award for Am. Agenda segment on homeless World Hunger Found., 1990, Cable Ace Best Documentary award, 1995, Edward R. Murrow award for coverage of O.J. Simpson Murder trial, 1996, Telly award for Bipolar Teens, 2004; named one of top 10 investigative reporters, TV Guide, 1983. Mem. Radio TV Corrs. Assn., White House Corrs. Assn. Clubs: Newswomen's NY (recipient Front Page award 1976); Nat. Press; Washington Press. Office Phone: 703-283-9088. Personal E-mail: bettinagre@aol.com.

GREGORY, CHERI B., biology educator; d. Mary Sue and William Thomas Buchanan; m. Thomas Scott Gregory, June 16, 1984; children: Thomas Brett, William Taylor. AS, Motlow State C.C., 1982; BS, Mid. Tenn. State U., 1984, MS, 1984—87. Sch. tchr. State of Tenn., Tullahoma, 1984—88; assoc. prof. Motlow State C.C., Tullahoma, 1988—. Recipient Faculty Excellence award, Motlow State C.C., 2004—05. Mem.: AAUP (assoc.). Office: Motlow State Cmty Coll PO Box 8500 Lynchburg TN 37352-8500 Office Phone: 931-393-1721. Business E-Mail: cgregory@mscc.edu.

GREGORY, DOLA BELL, bishop, customer service administrator; d. Earl James Barnett and Wilda May Claspell-Barnett; 1 child, James DeWayne Gregory. Student, Frontier C.C., 1982—83, Kishwaukee C.C., 1987—88, Inst. Theology, 1995—97; min. lic., Full Gospel Chs. Internat., 1997. Supr. DDT Career Devel. Ctr., Fairfield, Ill., 1981—86; asst. tchr. DeKalb County Spl. Edn., Cortland, Ill., 1986—88; leadership Assembly of God/Full Gospel, Rochelle, Ill., 1988—99; sr. pastor, founder Rock House Ministries I, Rockford, Ill., 1999—, Rock House Ministries II, Demonte, Ind., 2002, Rock House Ministries III, Forest Lake, Minn., 2003; sr., pastor, founder Rock House Ministries IV, Lakeland, Minn., 2005—; customer rels. Credit Union, Rockford, 2001—. Coach Spl. Olympics, Bloomington, Ill., 1981—86; spiritual leader Tres-Dias, Rockford, 1997—98; fundraising chmn. PTA, Fairfield, 1984—86. Author: (audiotape) Spiritual Education, Spiritual Welfare, 2000. Referral sponsor Hope for Women, Rochelle, Ill., 1997—; vol. Rockford Rescue Mission, 1999—. Recipient Eunice Kennedy Spl. Olympics award, 1984. Mem.: Rockhouse Outreach Children Klub (founder, dir. 2005), Women's Aglow Internat. (educator 1993—95), Women in Ministry of Rockford (facilitator 2002—03, 2006). Avocations: reading, motorcycling, singing, sewing, remodeling. Office: Rock House Ministries 1325 7th St Rockford IL 61104 Office Phone: 815-962-5067.

GREGORY, J. L., secondary school educator; Cert. tchr. Conn. Tchr. Ctrl. HS, Bridgeport, Conn., 1999—. Officer Dem. Town Com., Milford, Conn., 2005—06. Recipient numerous rsch. grants.

GREGORY, JEAN WINFREY, ecologist, educator; b. Richmond, Va., Feb. 13, 1947; d. Thomas Edloe and Kathryn (McFarlane) Winfrey; m. Ronald Alfred Gregory, Dec. 13, 1973. BS in Biology, U. Mary Washington, 1969; MS in Biology, Va. Commonwealth U., 1975, postgrad., 1982—90; MA in Environ. Sci., U. Va., 1983. Cert. fisheries sci. Lab. specialist A Cardiovascular Divsn. Med. Coll. Va., Richmond, 1969-70; pollution specialist State Water Control Bd. (now Dept. Environ. Quality), Richmond, 1970-77, pollution control specialist B, 1977-81, ecologist, 1981-85, ecology programs supr., 1985-88, environ. program mgr., 1988-2000, environ. mgr. II, 2000—. Adj. faculty Va. Commonwealth U., Richmond, 1978-93. Contbr. articles to profl. jours. Named One of Outstanding Young Women of Am., 1974; EPA fellow, Va., 1974-76. Mem. Am. Soc. Limnology and Oceanography, N.Am. Lake Mgmt. Soc., N.Am. Benthological Soc., Ecol. Soc. Am., Am. Inst. Biol. Scis., Assn. Trad. Hooking Artists, Sisters in Crime. Democrat. Methodist. Avocations: herb gardening, walking, rug hooking, dalmation rescue. Office: Office Water Quality Programs PO Box 10009 Richmond VA 23240-0009 Office Phone: 804-698-4113. E-mail: jwgregory@deq.virginia.gov.

GREGORY, JENNIFER DARYL, mathematics educator, small business owner; d. Clinton Wrenny Gregory Jr. and Myrtle R. Gregory; children: Christopher Todd Gunter, Samuel Gray Gunter, Rebekah Wrenn Gunter, Tiffany Renee Gunter, Adam Haynes Gunter. BS, Averett Coll., Danvill,e Va., 1988. Lic. tchr. Va. Math tchr. Stokes County Schs., Danbury, NC, 1988—2000; tchr. Accomack County Schs., Accomac, Va., 2000—01; math tchr. Patrick County Schs, Stuart, 2003—. Poll ofcl. Patrick County, Stuart, 2005. Named Female Student of Yr., Patrick Henry C.C., 1984. Mem.: NEA, Va. Edn. Assn. Mem. Lds Ch. Avocations: singing, dance, reading, needle work. Office: Patrick HS Stuart VA 24171 Office Phone: 276-694-7137. Personal E-mail: hs-math4@patrickcounty.org.

GREGORY, LYNNE WATSON, oncology clinical nurse specialist, health facility administrator; b. Atlanta, Dec. 4, 1946; d. Stephen Lawton and Louise (Baxter) Watson; m. Gerardo A. Gregory, July 10, 1976; children: Max, Alex, Sara. BSN with honors, Fla. State U., 1968; MN, Emory U., 1973; postgrad., U. Ga., 1983-88. RN, Tex.; cert. clin. nurse specialist, oncology cert. nurse. Evening charge nurse, emergency room Lakeland (Fla.) Gen. Hosp., 1968; staff nurse U.S. Army Hosp., various assignments, 1969-72, Emory U. Hosp., Atlanta, 1971-73; oncology nurse clinician Walter Reed Army Med. Ctr., Washington, 1974-77; instr. to asst. prof., Sch. of Nursing U. Tex. Health Sci. Center, San Antonio, 1977-80; asst. prof. dept. nursing Avila Coll., Kansas City, Mo., 1980-81; res. nurse USA Hosp., Ft. Ord, Calif., 1981-83; staff nurse to adminstrv. asst., staff dir. Hospice of the Monterey Peninsula, Carmel, Calif., 1981-83; res. nurse 382d. Field Hosp., Augusta, Ga., 1983-85; dir. St. Joseph Hospice St. Joseph Hosp., Augusta, Ga., 1985-88; nurse cons. N.Am. Health and Rehab. Svcs., Dallas, 1989-90; staff nurse, oncology Providence Meml. Hosp., El Paso, Tex., 1990-92, clin. nurse specialist, oncology svcs., 1992-94, clin. nurse specialist, continuing care divsn., 1994—, asst. v.p., interim chief nursing officer, patient care svcs., 2003—. Presenter in field. Maj. Army Nurse Corps, 1969-76. Decorated Army Commendation medal with oak leaf cluster; recipient cert. of appreciation Bexar County unit Am. Cancer Soc. Mem. Am. Cancer Soc. (patient edn. com., screening com.), Oncology Nursing Soc. (cert. chemotherapy instr., treas. Rio Grande chpt.). Presbyterian. Home: 909 La Cabana Pl El Paso TX 79912-1852 Office: Providence Memorial Hosp 2001 N Oregon St El Paso TX 79902-3368

GREGORY, M. CHRISTINE, science educator; d. Dana M. and John R. Phillips, Marcia L. Phillips (Stepmother); m. Tom Gregory; children: Jakaelin, Jasmine, Deondre, Donald. BS in Secondary Edn., Miami U., Oxford, Ohio, 1992—96; MS in Space Studies, U. N.D., Grand Forks, 1999—2003. Cert. Tchr. Ill. Dept. Edn., 1996, Tchr., Gifted Edn. Ill. Dept. Edn., 2000. Sci. tchr. Heyworth HS, Ill., 1998—, Bethany HS. Solar sys. amb. NASA-JPL; intern mentor NAS-JPL Mars Exploration Rover Athena Sci. mission; reviewer NASA Robotics Curriculum Clearinghouse. Tchr. Christian Life Club. Recipient Earth Sci. Educator of Yr., Earth Sci. Enterprise, 2004; grantee Math Sci. & Tech., State of Ill., 1998, Tech Prep in the Heartland, 1998—2002, ETC mini-grant, Edn. to Careers, 2002. Mem.: NEA (memb. chair), NSTA, Ill. Edn. Assn., NESTA. Independent. Office: Heyworth HS 308 W Cleveland Heyworth IL 61745 Office Phone: 309-473-2322. Office Fax: 309-473-2323. Business E-Mail: gregoryc@husd4.k12.il.us.

GREGORY, MARIAN FRANCES, retired elementary school educator, retired principal; b. Gary, Ind., Apr. 24, 1919; d. August Robert and Agnes Mae (Sturgess) Kuhn; m. Robert Wayne Gregory. BS in Edn., Ind. U., 1941; MA in Counseling, Columbia U., 1960. Elem. tchr. Bremen (Ind.) Schs., 1941-46, Gary Pub. Schs., 1947-56, tchr. remedial reading, 1956-68; elem. prin. Spaulding and Lincoln schs., Gary, 1968-74; student tchr. cons. Ind. U., Bloomington, 1974-91; sec. Heritage Motors, Hammond, Ind., 1974; ret. Contbr. articles to profl. jours. Mem., poll watcher LWV, Hammond, 1980-95, 98; mem. Master Gardners Purdue U., Crown Point, Ind., 1977—; elder Presbyn. Ch. Mem. AAUW (pres. 1956-57), DAR, Bus. and Profl. Women's Club (pres. 1957-58), N.W. Ind. Women's Club (1st v.p. 1994-96), Delta Kappa Gamma, Kappa Kappa Kappa. Avocations: genealogy, gardening, stock market, history, swimming. Home: 2238 Ridge Rd Highland IN 46322-1562

GREGORY, PATRICE D., retired nurse, small business owner; d. Urcel B. and Gale Murray Holloway; m. G. W. Gregory, Sept. 11, 1976. RN with honors, BS with honors, U. Calif., San Francisco, 1974. Rn, CA, 1974; grad. gemologist Gemological Inst. Am., 2002. Staff nurse ICU Nat. Naval Med. Ctr., Bethesda, Md., 1974—76, head nurse ICU, 1976—78; nursing coordinator ICU Wash. Hosp. Ctr., 1978—79; nursing supr. Kaiser Hosp., San Diego, 1979—80; office adminstr. Ashworth & Gregory Cardiac Surgery, Reading, Pa., 1980—95; ret., 1995. Gemologist GWG Enterprises, Kerrville, Tex., 1995—. Lt. USN, 1974—78. Independent. Home: 2105 Crown Ridge Dr Kerrville TX 78028 Home Fax: 830-515-5776. E-mail: sweetp@stx.rr.com.

GREGORY, PAULA ELAINE, gifted and talented educator; d. Howard Willard and Alma Louise (LaMasters-McClellan) Rasor; m. Harold W. Gregory, June 2, 1963; children: Carla Louise Perna, Cherissa Dawn, Regina Craig, Renae Johnson, Adam. BA in Family Scis., Miss. U. Women, 1996, MEd, 1997. Instr. Mich. U. Women, Columbus, 1995—97; tchr. Tuscaloosa City Schs., Ala., 1997—. Grader level chair Tuscaloosa City Schs., team leader gifted edn., 2003. Recipient Geography award, Tuscaloosa City Schs., 2003, GEM award, Pella, Tuscaloosa, 1999—2005. Mem.: Tuscaloosa Ballroom Dancing, Ballroom Dance Club (regent), Phi Upsilon Omicron (v.p. 1996—97), Mu Ro Sigma (pres. 1996—97). Office: Tuscaloosa City Schs 2000 Rock Quarry Dr Tuscaloosa AL 35406 Home: # 20 3004 Edward Hoffman Dr Champaign IL 61822

GREGORY, PEGGY J., music educator; b. Dallas, Sept. 15, 1935; d. Garnald Morris and Thelma Christean (Turner) Gregory; m. John Curtis Jones, Aug. 24, 1957 (div. June 1980); children: Lewis Gregory, Michael Wayne, Scott Carlton, Cynthia Luanne. BS in Home Econs., Baylor U., 1956; MS in Housing and Interior Design, Okla. State U., 1957; student, Rykyu Classical Acad., 1964—68, Hampton Inst., 1968—70. Nat. cert. tchr. music; cert. profl. master. Pvt. practice piano tchr., 1964—2002; founder, dir., tchr. piano, thcr. music theory Music Arts Conservatory, Albuquerque, 1984—2002; ret., 2002. Mem. piano faculty Summer Piano Camp at Mary Hardin-Baylor U., Belton, Tex., summers 1980, 86. Performed two-piano and duet music, 1980-85; performed with ptnr. in master classes for well-known duettists. Choir dir., pianist and organist various chs., Okinawa, 1964-68, Hampton, Va., 1969-72, Las Vegas, Nev., 1972-74; talent judge Miss Teen Pageant, Albuquerque, 1993-96. Mem. Profl. Music Tchrs. N.Mex. (state membership chair 1982-83, pres. 1986-88, adjudicator 1975—, Tchr. of Yr. 1998), Music Tchrs. Nat. Assn., Nat. Guild Piano Tchrs., Tex. Music Tchrs. Assn. Avocations: downhill skiing, hiking, gardening.

GREGORY, ROBIN N., lawyer; b. Syracuse, NY, Feb. 16, 1956; BS magna cum laude, Syracuse U., 1978; JD, Villanova U., 1981. Bar: NY 1982, US Dist. Ct. So. Dist. NY, US Dist. Ct. Ea. Dist. NY. Asst. dist. atty., Kings County, NY, 1981—85; ptnr. Wilson, Elser, Moskowitz, Edelman & Dicker LLP, NYC. Mem.: Am. Bd. Trial Advocates, Assn. of the Bar of the City of NY. Office: Wilson Elser Moskowitz Edleman & Dicker LLP 23rd Fl 150 E 42nd St New York NY 10017-5639 Office Phone: 212-490-3000 ext. 2650. Office Fax: 212-490-3038. Business E-Mail: gregoryr@wemed.com.

GREGORY, SARA SUSAN (SUDIE), musician, singer, lyricist, poet, recording industry executive, sound recording engineer, archivist; b. DeQueen, Ark., June 24, 1952; d. Eugene Cluran Gregory and Maxine Louise Fulton; m. Steven Eugene Thomas, Nov. 18, 1977 (div. Dec. 1, 1995). Student, East Tex. State U., 1964—66, So. Meth. U., 1967—69, U. Okla., 1971, Southeastern Okla. State U., 1972—75, U. Denver, 1974, Oklahoma City U., 1981, San Francisco State U., 1996, U. North Tex.; Master classes in trumpet, Nat. Trumpet Symposium, North Tex. State U. Auditor, payroll, ins. agt. Okla. Employment Svc., Oklahoma City, 1975—80; acct. Steven E. Thomas, CPA, Oklahoma City, 1980—82; musician, audio engr., record prodr. World Evangelism Svcs., Oklahoma City, 1983—94; owner Times Two Records and Pub., Oklahoma City and San Francisco, 1986—94, North Beach Rec., San Francisco, 1990—94; receptionist San Francisco Planning and Urban Rsch., 1996—; audio/video engr. Bill Graham Presents, San Francisco, 1996, archivist, 1996; event staff San Francisco Performing Arts Found., 1996—98, Bay Area Music Awards, 1996—98, Black and White Ball, 1996; publicist Daniel Castro Blues Band, 1996—98; prodr. Kimpton Prodns. Live from the Starlight Room TV show, 1998; hostess Little City & Tavolino Restaurants, 1998; enumerator U.S. Dept. Commerce-Census 2000, 2000; archivist George Tsongas, 2001. Judge No. Calif. Songwriters Assn., San Francisco, 1997; prodr./engr. performance and program com. Upper Grant Ave Fall Art Fair, 2003—. Prodr.: (rec.) Sheer Joy, 1983; prodr., engr., writer, musician: rec. Steve & Sara, 1986, prodr., engr., writer, performer, distbr.: Frontlines, 1988; prodr., engr., writer, performer, distbr.: Songs of the Street, 1992; prodr., engr., writer, performer, distbr.: Streetsinger, 1992, Christmas by the Sea, 1992; author: Collected Lyrics and Poetry, 1999; mem. prodn. crew 150th Anniversary Statehood Celebration, Sacramento, Calif., 1999, audio engr. Trieste Music, North Beach, San Francisco, 2003—, City Lights 50th Anniversary and Landmarking Celebration, 2002, 2003, Tele-Hi Neighborhood Ctr., 2002—, Indonesian Consultate and Telegraph Hill Dwellers Tsunami Relief Benefit, 2005; co-editor: Trieste Music News. Mem. Common Cause, Telegraph Hill Dwellers Assn., San Francisco, 1994—; mem. comm. com. Pioneer Park Project at Coit Tower, San Francisco, 1996—2001, 400 Trees Project Telegraph Hill Dwellers and Friends of the Urban Forest, San Francisco, 1996—98; mem. jazz band S.E. Okla. State U., 1972—75; concert band trumpet soloist Madrigal Singers and Opera Workshop; founder Nat. Campaign for Tolerance, 2005; poll worker presdl. election, 1996, 2000, 2004. Named to, Okla. All Dist. Band, 1965—70, Okla. All-State Band, 1969, 1970; recipient John Philip Sousa award, Broken Bow H.S., 1970, pvt. endowment, Elizabeth Styll Smith, 1983—94. Mem.: LWV, NARAS (staff 1997), Audio Engring. Soc., Music Educators Nat. Conf., Brass Quintet (outstanding brass ensemble 1969—70), Dixieland Combo-SE Okla. Dist. Tchrs., Okla. Music Educator's Conv., Four States Band Masters Conv., 4H Club, Dist. 3 Dem. Club. Democrat. Roman Catholic. Avocations: cooking, sewing, ceramics. Home: PO Box 330522 San Francisco CA 94133 E-mail: sarasgregory@yahoo.com.

GREGORY, STEPHANIE ANN, hematologist, educator; b. Vineland, NJ, June 23, 1940; d. Andonetta Gregory; m. Sheldon Chertow; children: Elizabeth Chertow, Jennifer Chertow, Daniel Chertow, Erica Chertow. BS cum laude, Boston Coll., 1961; MD cum laude, Med. Coll. Pa., 1965. Diplomate in internal medicine and hematology Am. Bd. Internal Medicine. Internal medicine intern Presbyn.-St. Luke's Hosp., Chgo., 1965-66, resident in internal medicine, 1966-68, fellow in hematology, 1969—72; chief resident in internal medicine Presbyn.-St. Lukes Hosp., Chgo., 1968-69; chief spl. morphology lab. sect. hematology Rush-Presbyn.-St. Luke's Med. Ctr., Chgo., 1972-76, dir. sect. hematology divsn. hematology/oncology, 1994—, Elodia Kehm prof. medicine, dir. hematology and stem cell transplantation, 1995—; from asst. prof. medicine to assoc. prof. medicine Rush Med. Coll., Chgo., 1972-86, prof. medicine, 1986—; adminstr., dir. Consultants in Hematology Rush U. Med. Ctr., Chgo., 1985—, sr. attending physician, 1982—, dir. sect. hematology and stem cell transplant divsn. hematology, 2004—06. Coord. continuing edn. sect. hematology Rush-Presbyn.-St. Luke's Med. Ctr., Chgo., 1970-76, dir. transfusion therapy svc. sect. hematology, 1972-76, asst. chmn. dept. medicine, 1972-77, clin. dir. Sheridan Rd. Pavilion, 1976-77, acting dir. sect. clin. hematology, 1980-81, assoc. dir. sect. hematology, 1993-94, asst. chair dept. medicine, 1993-94; co-dir. Lymphoma Ctr., Rush Univ Medical Ctr., Chgo., 1992—; mem. UN Security Coun. Commn. Experts, 1994; mem. med. adv. bd. Leukemia Rsch. Found., 1996—, Leukemia/Lymphoma Soc. Am., Lymphoma Rsch. Found.; chair B-cell Edn. Malignancies program, 2005-. Mentor Lean on Me support group for young adults with cancer Rush Univ. Medical Ctr., Chgo., 1992—. Recipient award Am. Women's Med. Assn., 1965, William B. Peck Sci. award for rsch. in hematopoietic stem cell studies Sci. Assembly of Interstate Postgrad. Med. Assn., 1973, Outstanding Alumni award MCP-Hahneman Med. Sch., 1998, Excellence in Medicine award Rush U. Med. Ctr., 2006; grantee Schweppe Found. Rsch., 1969-72, NIH tng. grantee Nat. Heart, Lung and Blood Inst., 1974-79; Schweppe fellow, 1969-72. Fellow ACP (mem. Ill. coun. 1994—, mentor physician mems. for advancement to fellowship designation ann. meeting 1996, Ill. Laureate award 1996); mem. AMA, Internat. Soc. Hematology (Inter-Am. divsn.), Internat. Soc. Exptl. Hematology (charter), Leukemia Soc. Am. (bd. trustees Ill. chpt. 1987—, chmn. patient aid com. Ill. chpt. 1988-90, treas. Ill. chpt. 1992-93, chairperson patient fin. aid com. Ill. chpt. 1992—, v.p. Ill. chpt. 1991-94, mem. med. adv. bd. Ill. chpt. 1996—), Am. Soc. Clin. Oncology, Am. Soc. Hematology (co-editor, 2005-), Cell Proliferation Soc., Ea. Coop. Oncology Group, Inst. Medicine Chgo., Chgo. Soc. Internal Medicine (exec. com. 1992—, sec.-treas. 1992-93, v.p. 1993-94, pres. 1994-95), Aplastic Anemia Found. Am. (hon. bd. trustees 1988—), Mark H. Lepper M.D. Soc. Tchrs. (elected), Alpha Omega Alpha, Sigma Xi. Office: Rush Univ Medical Ctr 1725 W Harrison St Ste 834 Chicago IL 60612-3861 Office Phone: 312-942-5982. Business E-Mail: stephanie_gregory@rush.edu.

GREGORY, VALISKA, writer; b. Chgo., Nov. 3, 1940; d. Andrej and Stephania (Lascik) Valiska; m. Marshall W. Gregory, Aug. 18, 1962; children: Melissa, Holly. BA cum laude, Ind. Ctrl. Coll., 1962; MA, Univ. Chgo., 1966; postgrad., Vassar Inst. Pub. Writing, 1984, Simmons Coll., 1986. Music and drama tchr. White Oak Elem. Sch., Whiting, Ind., 1962-64; tchr. Oak Lawn (Ill.) Meml. H.S., 1965-68; lectr. English U. Wis., Milw., 1968-74; adj. prof. English U. Indpls., 1974-83, Butler U., Indpls., 1983-85, writer-in-residence, 1993—; fellow Butler Writer's Studio, 1989-92. Founding dir. Butler U. Midwinter Children's Litf. Conf., 1989—; spkr., workshop leader schs., libr., confs., 1993—. Author: Sunny Side Up, 1986 (Chickadee Mag. Book of Month award 1986), Terribly Wonderful, 1986 (Grandparent's Mag. Best Book award 1986), The Oatmeal Cookie, 1987 (Best of Best Book list Chgo. Sun-Times), Riddle Soup, 1987 (Best of Best Book list Chgo. Sun-Times), Through the Mickle Woods (named Pick of List Am. Booksellers Assn. 1992, Parent's Choice award, 1992; State Ind. Read Aloud-List 1993), Happy Burpday, Maggie McDougal!, 1992 (State Ind. Read-aloud List 1993), Babysitting for Benjamin (Parent's Choice Honor award 1993), Kate's Giants, 1995, Loooking for Angels, 1996, (named Picked of the List Am. Book Sellers Assn., 1996), When Stories Fell Like Shooting Stars, 1996, (Family Circle Mag. Critics Choice, 1996), A Valentine for Norman Noggs, 1999, Shirley's Wonderful Baby, 2002. Recipient Ill. Wesleyan U. Poetry award, 1982, hon. mention Billee Murray Denny Nat. Poetry Award Bilee Murray Denny Poetry Found., 1982, Hudelson award Children's Fiction Work-In-Progress, 1982, Artistic Excellence and Achievement award State Art Treasure Arts Ind., 1989; Individual Artist Master fellow Ind. Arts Commn. and Nat. Endowment for Arts, 1986. Mem. AAUW (Creative Writer's pres. 1984-86), Author's Guild, Authors League Am., Soc. Children's Book Writers and Illustrators, Nat. Book Critic's Circle, Children's Reading Round Table, Soc. Midland Authors. Democrat. Office: Butler U 4600 Sunset Ave Indianapolis IN 46208-3487

GREGORY, YVONNE ELIZABETH HEYNING, interior designer; b. The Hague, The Netherlands, Apr. 2, 1952; arrived in U.S., 1953, naturalized, 1966; d. Joan Marinus Heyning and Johanna Alving; m. Hugh Martin Smith, Apr. 24, 1976 (div. Jan. 1990); 1 child, Erica Renee Smith; m. Walker Shelton Gregory, Aug. 8, 1992. AA, El Camino Coll., 1974; student, Harbor Coll., San Pedro, Calif., 1974-76, Torrance (Calif.) Art Ctr., 1976-79. Owner, designer HM Smith Constrn., San Pedro, Calif., 1974—90, San Pedro Renaissance Gallery, 1983—88, Nuhome Designs, Mt. Pleasant, SC, 1989—, Comml. Designs, Mt. Pleasant, 1997—2003. Bd. dirs. Wild Dunes (S.C.) Cmty. Archtl. Rev. Bd., 1998-2001; v.p. Leads for Women, San Pedro, 1985-88. Recipient Best Model Home Merchandising award Charleston (S.C.) Homebuilders, Best Lobby Remodel award Clear Channel Comm., Charleston, 1999. Mem. Charleston Trident Homebuilders Assn., Am. Soc. Interior Designers, Internat. Furnishings and Design Assn., BBB, S.C. Real Estate Commn., The Gibbes Art Mus. Democrat. Avocations: painting, reading, craft work, art work, jewelry making. Office: 3036 Intracoastal View Dr Mount Pleasant SC 29466-9022 Office Phone: 843-881-1597.

GREGUS, LINDA ANNA, government official; b. Hartford, Conn., Mar. 24, 1956; d. Steven and Sylvia Christine (Ramunno) G. AB, Bowdoin Coll., 1978; MA in Law and Diplomacy, Tufts U., 1985. Vol. VISTA, Phoenix, 1978-79; research asst. Econ. Research Assocs., Boston, 1979; ops adminstr. CRT Inc., Hartford, Conn., 1980-82; program officer U.S. Dept. of State, Washington, 1986-90; intelligence officer CIA, Washington, 1990—2004, U.S. Dept. State, 2004—. Recipient Milo Peck Scholarship Town of Windsor, Conn., 1984. Home: 9950 Unvie Pl Dulles VA 20189 Personal E-mail: gregusl@aol.com.

GREHER, GENA R., music production company executive; b. N.Y.C., Dec. 7, 1951; d. Henry and Pearl (Berman) G.; m. Lawrence Berger, Dec. 22, 1973; 1 child, Carla Tracey. MusB, Queens Coll., 1974; MS in Broadcasting and Film, Boston U., 1976; MA, Columbia U., 1998, EdD, 2002. Music/radio producer Young & Rubicam, N.Y.C., 1981-83; music producer Ogilvy & Mather, N.Y.C., 1983-85, Hea Prodns., N.Y.C., 1985-88; dir. music prodn. Lintas: N.Y., N.Y.C., 1988-91, Michael Whalen Music, N.Y.C., 1991—99; project dir. Columbia U., 1999—2002; asst. prof. U. Mass., Lowell, 2002—. Creator, producer radio series They Called it Jazz, WBUR-FM, 1975; creator, dir. audio cassettes, Russian Legends, 1986, Fairytales, 1986; music producer Atari comml., Dig Dug, 1983 (Clio award); contbr. articles to profl. jour. Mem. Internat. Congress of Strings, Am. Fedn. Musicians, 1973. Mem. SAG. Avocations: tennis, skiing, gourmet cooking. Office: Univ Mass 35 Wilder St Lowell MA 01854 Office Phone: 978-934-3893. Business E-Mail: gena_greher@uml.edu.

GREIDER, CAROL WIDNEY, molecular biology professor; b. San Diego, Apr. 15, 1961; BA in Biology, U. Calif., Santa Barbara, 1983; PhD in Molecular Biology, U. Calif., Berkeley, 1987. Fellow Cold Spring Harbor Lab., NY, 1988-90, asst. investigator NY, 1990-92, assoc. staff investigator NY, 1992-94, investigator NY, 1994-97; assoc. prof. dept. molecular biology and genetics, Johns Hopkins U. Sch. Medicine, Balt., 1997—99, prof., 1999—2002, acting dir., 2002—03, Daniel Nathans prof. and dir., 2003—; prof., dept. oncology Johns Hopkins U. Sch. Medicine, Balt., 1999—. Organizer Gordon Rsch. Conf. on Nucleic Acids, Providence, 1998, Cold Spring Harbor Lab. Seminar on Telemeres and Telemerase, 1999; mem., site visit com. NIH, 1992, mem. RFA study sect., 98, 93, mem., Ad hoc reviewer, Molecular Cytology Study Sect., 94; mem. Nat. Bioethics Adv. Commn., 1996—2001. Mem. editl. bd. Cancer Cell, 2001-, Molecular Cance Rsch., 2003-;contbr. numerous articles, revs., book chpts. Regents scholar U. Calif., 1981, Pew Biomed. Scis. scholar, 1990-94; recipient Allied Signal Outstanding Project award, 1992, Glenn Found. award Am. Assn. Cell Biology, 1995, Schering-Plough Sci. Achievement award, Am. Soc. for Biochemistry and Molecular Biology, 1997, Ellison Medical Found. Sr. Scholar award, 1998, Gairdner Found. award 1998, Passano Found. award 1999, Rosenstiel award in basic med. rsch. 1999, Harvey Soc. Lecture, 2000; co-recipient Albert Lasker award for Basic Med. Rsch., Lasker Found., 2006 Fellow Am. Acad. Arts and Sciences; mem. NAS (Richard Lounsbery award, 2003), Am. Soc. for Cell Biology (coun. mem., 1998-2001, Glenn Found. award, 1995), RNA Soc., Am. Assn. for Cancer Rsch. (Pezcoller award com. mem., 1999, organizer, program com. mem. ann. mtg., Phila., Pa., 1999, Gertrude Elion Cancer Rsch. award, 1994, Cornelius Rhoads award, 1996), Am. Soc. for Microbiology, AAAS, Phi Beta Kappa. Office: Johns Hopkins U Sch Med 601 PCTB 725 N Wolfe St Baltimore MD 21205 Office Phone: 410-614-6506. Office Fax: 410-955-0831. Business E-Mail: cgreider@jhmi.edu.*

GREILICH, AUDREY, administrative assistant; b. Wayne, N.J., July 23, 1933; d. Kenneth J. Holmes and Majorie I. Paige; m. Gerald D. Thompson, June 23, 1956 (dec. 1980); children: Gerald D. Jr., Kerry O., Christopher K., Linda G., Jeffrey L., Bonnie J. Thompson; m. William H. Greilich, June 21, 1986. Cert. profl. sec., Office Profls. Internat., 1993. Statis. typist various CPAs, Paterson, N.J., 1951-52; svc. rep. Bell Telephone, Newark, N.J., 1952-57; compensatory aide Vernon (N.J.) Twp. Schs., 1979-83; sec. Jansen Real Estate, Vernon, 1977-79; adminstrv. asst. U.S. Army TACOM-ARDEC, Picatinny Arsenal, N.J., 1983—. Mem. Bus. Profl. Women Internat. (chmn. scholarship fund 1985—). Baptist. Avocation: church organist. Home: PO Box 113 Glenwood NJ 07418-0113

GREINER, HELEN, mechanical engineer; b. London, Dec. 6, 1967; BS in Mech. Engring., MIT, 1989, MS in Computer Sci., 1990. Worked with NASA Jet Propulsion Lab., MIT, Artificial Intelligence Lab.; co-founder IS Robotics (now iRobot Corp.), Burlington, Mass., 1990—, pres., head of rsch.; also chmn. bd. iRobot Corp., Burlington, Mass. Lectr. in field; invited to the World Econ. Forums as a Global Leader of Tomorrow. Named Innovator for the Next Century, Technology Review Mag., (with Colin Angle) Ernst and Young New England Entrepreneurs of Yr., 2003; named one of Top 10 Innovators in the US, Fortune Mag.; recipient DEMO God award, DEMO conf. Achievements include inventor of the ROOMBA robotic vacuum. Avocations: reading, gardening, kayaking, mountain climbing, snowboarding. Office: iRobot Corp 63 South Ave Burlington MA 01803 Office Phone: 781-345-0200. Office Fax: 781-345-0201.

GREINER, NICOLE K. HUDAK, physical education educator; b. Erie, Pa., May 24, 1976; d. Francis Joseph and Sharon Ann Hudak; m. Nathan Reid Greiner, July 14, 2006. BS, Ohio No. U., Ada, 1998; tchg. cert., Edinboro U., Pa., 1999; MEd, U. Va., Charlottesville, 2004. Cert. Nat. Athletic Trainer. Tchr. elem phys. edn. Fairfax County Pub. Schs., Va., 2006—. Mem. Health and Phys. Edn. Adv. Com., Va.; co-chair after-sch. 6th grade girls program Girl Power!. Mem.: NEA, Fairfax Edn. Assn. Avocations: exercise, reading, dance, travel.

GREJDA, GAIL FULTON, dean; b. Clarion, Pa., Aug. 31, 1937; d. Ralph Jay and Virginia Agnew Fulton; m. Edward Stanley Grejda, Aug. 31, 1958; children: Richard Edward, Steven Douglas. BS, Clarion U., 1966, MEd, 1968; PhD in Instrnl. Sys. Design, Pa. State U., 1988. Cert. level 2 in elem. edn. and spl. edn., Pa. Tchr. Brookville (Pa.) Area Sch. Dist., 1966-69, Clarion (Pa.) Area Sch. Dist., 1969-87, dir. gifted programs, 1977-82; tchr. Beijing Internat. Embassy Sch., 1980-81; computer instr. Sch. of Am. Embassy, Bridgetown, Barbados, 1987-88; asst. prof. Clarion U., 1988-93, assoc. prof., 1993-97, prof., 1997-98, dean Coll. Edn. and Human Svcs., 1998—. Author: (book chpt.) Guidelines for Interpreting Educational Research, 1994; contbr. articles to profl. jours. Grantee U.S. Dept. Edn., 1999, Bell Atlantic Found., 1998, NSF, 1999-2003, 2003—. Mem. Am. Assn. Colls. for Tchr. Edn., Assn. Tchr. Educators (commn. on utilizing tech. for ednl. reform 1988—), Tchr. Edn. Coun. State Colls. and Univs., Assn. for Ednl. Comms. and Tech., Pa. Assn. Coll. Tchr. Educators (bd. dirs. 1988—), Phi Delta Kappa (v.p. 1982—), Pi Lambda Theta. Avocations: travel, reading, golf. Office: Clarion U 101 Stevens Hall Clarion PA 16214 E-mail: grejda@mail.clarion.edu.

GREMMLER, MARGO ROWDER, art director; b. Plano, Tex., Sept. 23, 1977; d. Richard Edward and Cheryl Bauer Rowder; m. Jed Randolph Gremmler, Aug. 31, 2003. BFA, U. North Tex., 1999. Creative intern McConnaughy Stein Schmidt Brown, Chgo., 1999—99, McCann-Erickson, Dallas, 1999—2000; asst. art dir. Ogilvy & Mather, Chgo., 2000—02; art dir. Point B Comm., Chgo., 2003—04, Ryan Partnership, Chgo., 2004—. Set dresser: (short film) Soap & Roses, 2002 (Best Student Film, Kodak product grant- Reel Women Internat. Film Festival, 2005); contbr. I Was a Mathlete Until I Met Margo Marris, 2003 (appeared in Chgo. Internat. Film Festival (2003), Tribeca Film Festival, Newport Beach Film Festival, Sidewalk Moving Picture Festival (2003), 2004). Recipient Gold Adrian award, Hospitality Sales and Mktg. Assn. Internat., 2004, Silver Adrian award, 2004. Mem.: Am. Mensa. Avocations: fiction-writing for teens, martial arts, drums, fitness. Office Phone: 312-321-7414. Personal E-mail: margocole@hotmail.com. Business E-Mail: mgremmler@ryanchicago.com.

GRENEN, JUDIE SANN, librarian; b. Jersey City, Mar. 21, 1937; d. Albert A. and Miriam Resnick Sann; m. Carl Mark Grenen; children: James F., Amy Grenen Levantin. BS, Arcadia U., Glenside, Pa.; MLS, Villanova U., Pa. Logistician, librarian M&T Co., King of Prussia, Pa. Home: 346 E Lancaster Ave Apg 607 Wynnewood PA 19096-2234

GRENZ, M. KAY, manufacturing executive; b. Minn., Dec. 1946; m. Rod Grenz; 1 child, Jenni. BA in Sociology, U. SD. Cord. 3M Co., 1969—71, salary adminstr., 1971—76, mgr., 1976—84, dir. human resources, 1984—96, v.p. human resources, 1996—98, sr. v.p. human resources, 1998—. Bd. dirs. Gillette Children's Specialty Healthcare. Mem.: Human Resource Planning Soc.

GRENZIG, GAIL A., school system administrator, consultant; d. Daniel Tkatch and Virginia Mary Cosgrave; m. Edward W. Grenzig, June 23, 1990; children: Christopher Edward, Brittany Marie. Post Grad. Profl. Diploma, L.I. U., 1989; MS, Adelphi U., 1985, BS, 1983. Cert. SDA Ednl. Adminstrn. NY State Bd. of Regents, 1994. Tchr. spl. edn. Glen Cove City Sch. Dist., NY, 1985—94; ednl. cons. Grenzig Consulting, Nesconset, NY, 1993—; adj. prof. Dowling Coll., Oakdale, NY, 1994; coord. of pupil pers. svcs. Mid. Country Ctrl. Sch. Dist., Centereach, NY, 1999—2002; asst. prin. Harry B. Thompson Mid. Sch. Syosset (NY) Ctrl. Sch. Dist., 2002—04; asst. supt. personnel Sachem Cen. Sch. Dist., Holbrook, NY, 2004—. Varsity coach Glen Cove City Sch. Dist., 1985—94. Vol. soccer coach Smithtown Kickers, NY, 1997—2003; editor - newsletter Nesconset Elem. PTA, 1996—2003; religion tchr. Parish of Holy Cross, Nesconset, 1999—2004. Mem.: ASCD, NASSP, L.I. Assn. Sch. Pers. Adminstrs., Nat. Mid. Sch. Assn., Coun. of Exceptional Children (spkr., presenter N.Y. State Conf. 2002), L.I. Assn. of Spl. Edn. Adminstrs. Avocations: reading, travel, gardening, sports. Office: Sachem Cen Sch Dist Office Pers 245 Union Ave Holbrook NY 11741 Personal E-mail: ggrenzig@sachem.edu.

GRESHAM, KAREN RENEE, music educator, singer; b. Dallas, Jan. 3, 1969; d. Robert James and Beverly Bailey Vinklarek; m. Mark Keith Gresham, Sept. 18, 1993; 1 child, Rachel Bailey. BS in Speech Comm., U.Tex., Austin, 1991. Cert. tchr. Tex., 2001. Music tchr. grades pre-K through 6th, Encore choir dir. Brazosport Ind. Sch. Dist., Lake Jackson, Tex., 1999—; profl. singer The Nailers Band, Lake Jackson, Tex., 1998—. Sales/advt. cons. KGNB/KNBT Radio Sta., New Braunfels, Tex., 1991—92; bodily injury claim's adjuster State Farm Ins. Co., Houston, 1992—96. Singer: The Nailers Band. Mem.: Delta Kappa Gamma (licentiate), Alpha Xi Delta (life; songleader 1989—90). Roman Catholic. Avocations: singing, acting. Home: 209 Tearose Ln Lake Jackson TX 77566 Office: Brazosport Independent School District PO Drawer Z Freeport TX 77541 Office Phone: 979-730-7160 11220. Home Fax: 979-285-2082. Personal E-mail: mgresham@houston.rr.com. Business E-Mail: kgresham@brazosport.isd.net.

GREVILLE, FLORENCE NUSIM, secondary school educator, mathematician; b. Lynn, Mass., Nov. 19, 1913; d. Melach Joseph Nusim and Lillian Montrose; m. Thomas N.E. Greville (dec. Feb. 18, 1998). AB, Cornell U., 1935; MA, Columbia U., 1947. Sub. tchr Wis. Pub. Schs., Madison, 1975—80; tchr. math. Madison Area Tech. Coll., 1980—81; lectr. math. Piedmont C.C., Charlottesville, Va., 1982—84; sub. tchr. Charlottesville Pub. Schs., 1987—99. Instr. in math Oswego State Coll., 1947—48; tchr. Am. sch., Rio de Janeiro, 1953—54; program dir. AAUW, Monona, Wis., 1966—68, Charlottesville, Va., 2001—02. Author: Computer Oriented Basic Math, 1970, Breakfast Gems, 2002, By The Numbers, 2005. Fellow: AAAS; mem.: Math. Assn. Am. Avocation: playing classical piano. Home: 2600 Barracks Rd Apt 207 Charlottesville VA 22901-2100 Personal E-mail: flogrev@cstone.net.

GREW, PRISCILLA CROSWELL, academic administrator, geologist, educator; b. Glens Falls, NY, Oct. 26, 1940; d. James Croswell and Evangeline Pearl (Beougher) Perkins; m. Edward Sturgis Grew, June 14, 1975. BA magna cum laude, Bryn Mawr Coll., 1962; PhD, U. Calif., Berkeley, 1967. Instr. dept. geology Boston Coll., 1967-68, asst. prof., 1968-72; asst. rsch. geologist UCLA, 1972-77, adj. asst. prof. environ. sci. and engring., 1975-76; dir. Calif. Dept. Conservation, 1977-81; commr. Calif. Pub. Utilities Comm., San Francisco, 1981-86; dir. Minn. Geol. Survey, St. Paul, 1986-93; prof. dept. geology U. Minn., Mpls., 1986-93; vice chancellor for rsch. U. Nebr., Lincoln, 1993-99, prof. dept. geoscis., 1993—, prof. conservation/survey divsn. Inst. Agr., 1993—, dir. U. Nebr. State Mus., 2003—, fellow Ctr. for Great Plains Studies, 2003—; coord. Native Am. Graves Protection and Repatriation Act, 1998—. Vis. asst. prof. geology U. Calif., Davis, 1973-74; chmn. Calif. State Mining and Geology Bd., Sacramento, 1976-77; exec. sec., editor Lake Powell Rsch. Project, 1971-77; cons., vis. staff Los Alamos (N.Mex.) Nat. Lab., 1972-77; com. on minority participation in earth sci. and mineral engring. Dept. Interior, 1972-75; chmn. Calif. Geothermal Resource Task Force, 1977, Calif. Geothermal Resources Bd., 1977-81; earthquake studies adv. panel US Geol. Survey, 1979-83, adv. com., 1982-86; adv. coun. Gas Rsch. Inst., 1982-86, rsch. coord. coun., 1987-98, vice-chmn., 1994-96, chmn., 1996-98, sci. and tech. coun., 1998-2001; bd. on global change rsch. NAS, 1995-99, subcom. on earthquake rsch., 1985-88, bd. on earth scis. and resources, 1986-91, bd. on mineral and energy resources, 1982-88, bd. on internat. sci. orgns., 2006—; mem. Minn. Minerals Coord. Com., 1986-93, US nat. com. for internat. union of geol. scis. (IUGS), 1985-93, US nat. com. for the internat. union of geodesy and geophysics 2001—, chmn., 2003—; mem. US Nat. Com. on Diversitas, 2000—, vice chmn., 2004—; adv. bd. Stanford U. Sch. Earth Scis., 1989—, Sec. of Energy Adv. Bd., 1995-97; com. on equal opportunities in sci. and tech. NSF, 1985-86, adv. com. on earth scis., 1987-91, adv. com. on sci. and tech. ctrs. devel., 1987-91, adv. com. on sci. and tech. ctrs., 1996, adv. com. on geoscis., 1994-97; mem. State-Fed. Tech. Partnership Task Force, 1995-99, Fed. Coun. for Continental Sci. Drilling, 1992-98, Gt. Plains Partnership Coun., 1995-99; trustee Am. Geol. Inst. Found., 1988— (Ian Campbell medalist 1999). Contbr. articles to profl. jours. Trustee 1st Plymouth Congl. Ch., Lincoln, 1997—2000; mem. edn. and outreach steering com. Earth Scope, 2005—; bd. dirs. Abendmusik:Lincoln, 1995—97. Fellow, NSF, 1962—66. Fellow AAAS (chmn. electorate nominating com. sect. E 1980-84, mem.-at-large 1987-91, chmn.-elect 1994, chmn. 1995, coun. del. 1997-98), Geol. Soc. Am. (nominations com. 1974, chmn. com. on geology and pub. policy 1981-84, audit com. 1988-90, chair 1990, com. on coms. 1986-87, 91-92, chmn. com. on coms. 1995, chair Day medal com. 1990, councilor 1987-91), Mineral. Soc. Am. (mem. Roebling medal com. 1999-2003), Geol. Assn. Can., Ctr. Great Plains Studies; mem. Am. Geophys. Union (chmn. com. pub. affairs 1984-89), Soc. Mayflower Descs., Nat. Parks and Conservation Assn. (trustee 1982-86), Nat. Assn. Regulatory Utility Commrs. (com. on gas 1982-86, exec. com. 1984-86, com. on energy conservation 1983-84), Nat. Sci. Collections Alliance (bd. dirs. 2006—), Interstate Oil and Gas Compact Commn. (mem. Petroleum Profls. Task Force, 2001-03), Cosmos Club, Rotary, Country Club of Lincoln, Sigma Xi (pres. U. Minn. chpt. 1990-91). Congregationalist. Office: U Nebr State Mus 307 Morrill Hall Lincoln NE 68588-0338 Office Phone: 402-472-3779. Business E-Mail: pgrew1@unl.edu.

GREWE, MARJORIE JANE, retired protective services official; b. Baltimore County, Md., Nov. 10, 1931; d. Wilbur Guy and Mary Alice (Stover) Gregory; m. Harold Henry, Oct. 31, 1954 (dec.); children: Dorothy Lee Gorkey, Eva-Maria Marjorie Shaeffer. Student, Essex County Coll., 1979-80, U. Md. Law Enforcement Inst., 1967—68. Demonstrator Tupperware, Balt., 1951—58; dep. area coord. civil def. City of Balt., 1956—59; matron Balt. City Jail, 1957—58; compiling stats., map making various orgns., Phila., 1959; profl. interviewer med. studies Johns Hopkins U., Balt., 1959; profl. interviewer U.S. Dept. Commerce, Phila., 1959—65; dep. sheriff Balt. County Sheriff's Dept., Towson, Md., 1966—87; ret., 1987. Freelance interviewer, 1959—65. Gossip columnist: local newspapers, 1959—65. Founder Md. Sheriff's Youth Ranch; sec. Dem. Clubs, Baltimore County, 1959—66; mem. Adv. for Wildlife; activist EPA, Am. with Disabilities, Animal Rights, Rights of Virginians with Disabilities; mem. polit. action com., 1965. Mem.: Baltimore County Sheriff's Dept., Nat. Sheriffs Assn. (state dir. 1986—87), Md. State Sheriffs Assn. (life; sec. 1967—86), Fraternal Order Police (life), VFW Aux., Moose Aux. Presbyterian. Avocations: doll collecting, travel, gardening, cooking, genealogy. Home: Baldwin Hills Estates Der Palast at 115 Baldwin Ln Staunton VA 24401-8950

GREY, MARGARET, nursing educator; b. Easton, Pa., Sept. 25, 1949; m. Michael Lauterbach. BSN, U. Pitts., 1970; MS in Nursing, Yale U., 1976; PhD, Columbia U., 1985. Nurse clinician Yale-New Haven Hosp.; asst. clin. prof. Columbia U., N.Y.C.; assoc. prof. U. Pa., Phila., dir. primary care grad. program; with Yale U. Sch. Nursing, New Haven, 1993—, founder, doctoral program, 1994, Independence Found. prof. nursing, dir. Ctr. for Self & Family Mgmt., Annie Goodrich prof. nursing, 2005—, assoc. dean, dean, 2005—. Rudin Clin. Nursing Rsch. scholar, Disting. Fellow, NAPNAP, 1990, Robert Wood Johnson Exec. Nurse Fellowship, 1999-2001; Sch. Nursing Teaching award, UPenn., 1990, Virginia Herderson award for Outstanding Contributions to Nursing Rsch., 1997, Applied Nursing Rsch. award, Coun. Nurse Researchers, ANA, 1998, Disting. Alumni award, U. Pitts. Sch. Nursing, 1999, Achievement in Rsch. award, Natl. Org. Nurse Practitioner Faculties, 2000, Excellence in Nursing Rsch. award, Assn. Faculties of PNP Programs, 2000, Fellow Soc. Behavioral Medicine, Am. Acad. Nursing; mem. ANA (mem. coun. nurse researchers, primary care providers), NAPNAP (membership com.), APHA, Am. Diabetes Assn., Am. Sociol. Assn., Nat. Assn. Pediatric Nurse Assocs. and Practitioners (pres. 1992-93), Inst. Medicine; Sigma Theta Tau. Office: Yale U Sch Nursing PO Box 9740 100 Church St S New Haven CT 06536 Office Phone: 203-785-2393. Office Fax: 203-785-3554. E-mail: margaret.grey@yale.edu.

GREY, RUTHANN E., corporate communications specialist, director; b. Buffalo, May 13, 1945; d. Wilson Campbell and Rosalie (Briggs) Evege; m. Daine A. Grey, Aug. 25, 1990; children: Daine, Jr., Keenan, Nichole. BS, SUNY, Buffalo, 1966, MS, 1970, PhD, 1980; postgrad., Harvard U., 1988. Tchr. Bennett H.S., Buffalo, 1966-69; prof. Erie C.C., Buffalo, 1970-73; adminstr. No. Va. C.C., Annandale, 1975-76, Wayne State U., Detroit, 1978-80; dir. pub. affairs Burroughs Corp., Detroit, 1981-86; exec. asst. to chmn. bd. dirs. The Equitable, N.Y.C., 1986-89; mgr. pub. affairs N.Y. Times, N.Y.C., 1989-90; mgr. divsn. corp. rels. Pub. Svc. Corp. Colo., Denver, 1990-93; v.p. comm. and pub. affairs Hoechst Celanese, Bridgewater, NJ, 1993—; v.p. global media and external rels. Hoechst Marion Roussel, Bridgewater, NJ, 1996—; comm. chief Ednl. Testing Svc., Princeton, NJ; with The Caunos Group, Watchung, NJ, 1998—; dir. global comm. Ethicon, Somerville, NJ. Cons. A+ For Kids, Newark, 1989-90, Rockefeller Found., N.Y.C., 1989-90. Bd. dirs. Citizens Scholarship Found., Minn., 1990-94. Mem. Pub. Rels. Seminar, Arthur Page Soc., The Wisemen, Pub. Rels. Rsch. Found. Avocations: gardening, walking. Home and Office: Ethicon Route 22W PO Box 151 Somerville NJ 08876 Office Phone: 908-377-0180, 908-218-3538. Personal E-mail: regrey1@earthlink.net. E-mail: rgrey1@ethus.jnj.com.

GREY-BETHIEL, SHARI, artist, sculptor, apparel designer; b. N.Y.C., July 27, 1959; d. Charles and Jean S. Grey; m. David Howard Bethiel, June 24, 1990; 1 child, Jonathan Blair. BFA with high honors, Pratt Inst., 1982; MA with high honors, NYU, 1993. Pres. Grey Originals, Inc., N.Y.C., 1999—. Sculptures in numerous corp. and pvt. collections including The Castle at Tarrytown, N.Y., Solid Ideas, Inc., Grand Prarie, Tex., N.W. Cmty. Hosp., Chgo. Avocations: skiing, music, writing, reading. Home: 12 Everett Pl Halesite NY 11743-2211

GREYSON D'OTAZZO, MEAGHAN REGINA, literary critic; b. Havana, Cuba, Sept. 7, 1942; arrived in US, 1962; d. Miguel Blanco and Virginia Mary de Barzaga-De Herrera; m. Neil Alfred D'Otazzo, Sept. 8, 1958; children: Jesse, Vivian, Patrick, Ann Shirley. B in psychology, U. Ga., 1972, M in hist. and lit., 1973, M in edn., 1976, PhD in hist. and lit., 1984. Tchr. Clark County Dist., Athens, Ga., 1971—75; rschr. Emory U., Psychology Dept., Atlanta, 1975—85; journalist freelance, N.Y.C., 1986—94, Orlando, Fla., 1995; literary critic various newspapers and mags., Los Angeles, Calif., 1995—97, London, 1997—; rschr. US Capitol Hist. Soc., Wash., DC, 2000—02, Smithsonian Inst., Wash., DC, 2003—04, Libr. of Congress, Wash., DC, 2004—. Author: La Musica de Haiti & Others, 1960, Literary Criticism: Conceptual Approach to Theatrical Reviews, 2004; contbr. articles various profl. jours. Poll judge Rep. Party, N.Y.C., NY, 1980—2004; tchr., autistic and deaf children. Mem.: Assn. Am. Writers, Assn. Reviewers and Editors. Republican. Roman Catholic. Avocation: piano. Home: 6150 Forland Garth 204 Columbia MD 21045 Office Phone: 443-319-5871. E-mail: meaghan7@aol.com.

GRIDER, RHONDA PATRIECE, elementary school educator, writer; b. Grider, Dec. 4, 1968; d. George William and Ida Jane Grider; children from previous marriage: Samuel Henry Scott, David Joseph Henry. BS cum laude, Harris Stow State Coll., Mo., 1988—91; M, U. Mo., 1996. Tchr. Ferguson Florissant Schs., St. Louis, 1989—96; tchr., playwright Hazelwood Schs., 1992—93; tchr. Chgo. Pub. Schs., 1997—2000, Broward County Schs., Ft. Lauderdale, Fla., 2000, DeKalb County Schs., Decatur, Ga., 1996—97, 2000—; asst. prin., educator Archdiocese Atlanta, 2003—04; founder, dir., adminstr. R.S.H Learning Programs, Covington, Ga., 2000—. Instr. Upward Bound Program, St. Louis, 1984—87; life scis. instr. Girls Club of St. Louis, 2005, 06. Author of poems, (handbook) R.S.H. Handbook: Mother and Son, 2004. Foster parent, St. Louis, Atlanta, 1995, 2004; vol. Nat. Jr. Beta, Atlanta, 1996—97, ARC, 2004—; donation collector Diabetes and MS Walkathon. Recipient Forum Honoree, John Ashcroft Leadership Forum, Fitness USA Merit award, All Around Athlete award, Drama Festival award Excellence, Archdiocese Tex., 1982, Class Favorite award, 1983, award, Am. Legion; Gus T. Ridgel fellow, U. Mo., 1991. Mem.: ASCD, Soc. Indsl. and Applied Math., St. Pius ProLife Vols., Internat. Soc. Poets, Kappa Delta Pi (pres. 1990—91). Avocations: swimming, aerobics, track, football, golf. Office: R S H Learning Programs PO Box 82605 Conyers GA 30013

GRIDER WATSON, MARY ELIZABETH, small business owner; b. Stevenson, Ala., July 22, 1941; d. James William and Villie Louise Grider; m. Frank Lee Watson Jr. June 28, 1960 (div. July 1971); children: Celena, Jeff, Kim. Student, Auburn U., U. Ala. Substitute tchr. Mobile County Schs., Mobile, Ala., 1974-75; exec. sec. Corrugated Paper Mills, Stevenson, Ala., 1975-78; br. mgr. Dept. Indsl. Rels., Stevenson, 1978—; owner ReSell, Stevenson. Rep. Ala. Reunion, Stevenson, 1988; mem. adv. bd. The Daily Sentinel, Scottsboro, Ala., 1996—. Recipient award Legion of Leaders, 1985-87, Cert. of Recognition, Ala. Rehab. Assn., 1981. Mem. Jackson County C. of C., Stevenson C. of C. (vice chmn. 1986-87, bd. dirs. 1991-92). Avocations: fishing, gardening, softball, quilting, cooking. Mailing: POB 952 Stevenson AL 35772

GRIEB, ELIZABETH, lawyer; b. Chestertown, Md., Nov. 14, 1950; d. Henry Norman and Lillian (Ballard) Grieb; m. George Stewart Webb, Aug. 18, 1979 (div. 1990); children: Timothy Stewart, Margaret Elizabeth; m. Walter George Lohr, Jr., Feb. 15, 2003. BA English, Wells Coll., 1972; JD cum laude, U. Balt., 1977. Bar: Md. 1977. Assoc. Piper & Marbury, Balt., 1977-84; ptnr. Piper & Marbury (now Piper Marberry Rudnigh & Wolfe LLP), Balt., 1984—2002; pres., CEO The Md. Zoo (formerly Balt. Zoo), 2002—. Adv. bd. U. Md. Sys. Downtown Ctr., Balt., 1990-92; bd. dirs., sec. Choice Jobs, Inc., Balt., 1991-93; pres. U. Balt. Alumni Assn., 1994-95; bd. dirs. Balt. Zoo, 1995-2002, pres. bd. dirs., 1999-2002. Mem. Md. State Bar Assn. (chair securities laws com. 1990-92), Ho. of Ruth (bd. dirs. 1994-97), Ctr. Club. Episcopal. Office Phone: 410-396-7102. E-mail: bgrieb@marylandzoo.org.

GRIEBEL, KAREN ANN, music educator; b. Chgo., Ill., Aug. 28, 1978; Bachelor's in Music Edn., Master's in Music Edn., DePaul U., Chgo. Band dir. Sch. Dist. # 143, Midlothian, Ill., 2000—. Composer: (concert band lit.) Anjin's Journey Beyond, Duke William's Kaer; musician: (compact disc) Shades of Autumn. Lector St. Daniel the Prophet Ch., Chgo., 1992—2006, Eucharistic min., 1995—2006. Mem.: S.W. Cmty. Concert Band (sec. 2004—06), IJEA, Music Educator's Nat. Conf. Roman Catholic. Office: School Dist # 143 14959 S Pulaski Midlothian IL 60445 Office Phone: 708-385-0045. Personal E-mail: thebandnerd@gmail.com.

GRIEBENAUW, LIZA-MARIE, secondary school educator; b. Cape Town, South Africa, Oct. 10, 1963; d. Hubert Oswald Beuster and Martha Maria Wilson; 1 child, Liebe. BS, U. Stellenbosch, South Africa, 1984; BA in Recreation and Sports Mgmt. with honors, U. Pretoria, South Africa, 1987; MS, Katholieke Universiteit Leuven, Belgium, 1998; postgrad., U. Va., Charlottesville, 2000—. Instr. phys. tng. South African Police Tng. Coll., Pretoria, 1985—87; tchr. h.s. Pub. Edn., 1987—90; lectr. U. Limpopo, Sovenga, 1990—2000; tchr. Albemarle County Schs., Charlottesville, Va., 2003—05. Cons. in field, Charlottesville, Va., 2000—. Contbr. chapters to books. Vol. firefighter and EMT Monticello Fire and Rescue, Charlottesville, 2001; rep. African continent Internat. Fedn. Adapted Phys. Activity, 1995—2000; instr. various disability activity orgns., Charlottesville, 2000; dir. Camp Holiday Trails, 2003—03. Mem.: Am. Coll. Sports Medicine, Am. Assn. Health, Phys. Edn., Recreation and Dance, Internat. Fedn. Adapted Phys. Activity (bd. mem. 1995—2000), Charlottesville Obesity Task Force. Avocations: travel, piano, guitar, gardening, reading. Home: 4030 Rolling Rd Scottsville VA 24590 Personal E-mail: lg8x@virginia.edu.

GRIEGO, ANGELIC, marketing professional; b. N.Mex., Aug. 8, 1974; m. Paul Sandoval, Sept. 17, 2005. BBA, N.Mex. State U., Las Cruces. Program mgr. U. N.Mex, Albuquerque, 2002—04; mktg. mgr. Comml. Data Systems, 2004—. Wish granting vol., com. mem. Make Wish Found., Albuquerque, 2003—06. Mem.: Am. Mktg. Assn.

GRIEGO, LINDA, entrepreneur; b. Tucumcari, N.Mex., 1949; m. Ronald C. Peterson. BA in history, UCLA, 1975. Pres., CEO Griego Enterprises, Inc., 1985—; restaurant founder, mng. ptnr. Engine Co. No. 28, 1988—; dep. mayor for econ. devel. City of LA, 1991—93, candidate for mayor, 1993; pres., CEO Rebuild LA Inc., 1994—97; pres. Zapgo Entertainment Group LLC, 1997—99; interim pres. & CEO LA Cmty. Devel. Bank, 1999—2000. Mem. Am. Devel. Bank Cmty. Adjustment Com., 1995—2000; sr. fellow UCLA Sch. Pub. Policy, 1998—2000; bd. dirs. Fed. Res. Bank San Francisco, 1998—2003, Granite Construction Inc., 1999—, Southwest Water Co., 2001—, City Nat. Corp., 2006—. Bd. trustees Robert Wood Johnson Found., 1995—2003, 2005—, Cedars Sinai Med. Ctr., 2004—, David & Lucile Packard Found., 2006—.*

GRIER WALLEN, MARY ELIZABETH, retired psychologist; b. Waukesha, Wis., June 27, 1912; d. James Harold and Edith Rosetta (Jacobson) Grier; m. Lawrence Jacques, Sept. 10, 1938 (div. 1953); m. Richard Wallen, Nov. 10, 1956 (div. 1966); stepchildren: Karen W. Bauman, Drew R.E. Wallen. AB in Philosophy, U. Chgo., 1936, MS in Psychology, 1938, PhD in Human Devel., 1947. Diplomate Am. Psychol. Assn. Rsch. assoc. U. Chgo., 1947-54, Northwestern U., Chgo., 1954-56; supervisory psychologist U.S. VA Hosps. and Clinics, Maywood, Chgo., Cleve., Ill., Ohio, 1956-66, D.C. Health and Human Svcs., 1967-77. Avocations: poetry, gardening, photography, recorder, handbells. Home: 10450 Lottsford Rd Cottage 1014 Mitchellville MD 20721-2745

GRIES, ROBBIE RICE, geologist, gas and petroleum company executive; Student, Del Mar Junior Coll., Corpus Christi, Tex.; BS in Geology, Colo. State U.; MS in Geology, U. Tex., Austin, 1970. Cert. petroleum geologist 1985. Geology tchr. Wichita State U.; with Texaco, Inc., Denver, 1973—76; staff geologist Reserve Oil Inc., 1976—80; ind. geologist, cons., 1980—92; founder Priority Oil & Gas, LLC, Denver, 1992—, pres., CEO, 1995—. Dir. Colo. Oil and Gas Assn. Mem. adv. coun. Geology Found., U. Tex., Austin. Named Leadership Honoree, Key Women in Energy awards, RaderEnergy, 2004; recipient Disting. Svc. award, Rocky Mountain Assn. Geologists. Mem.: Soc. Sedimentary Geology, Geol. Soc. Am., Am. Assn. Petroleum Geologists (hon.; sec. 1995—97, pres. 2001—02, A.I. Leverson award 1985, Disting. Svc. award 1991, named hon. mem. 1998). Achievements include First woman to serve as president of the Ammerican Association of Petroleum Geologists. Office: Priority Oil & Gas PO Box 27798 Denver CO 80227-0798

GRIESBAUM, KAMELA LEE, music educator; d. Raymond Edgar and Judy Lee Davenport; m. Douglas Frederick Griesbaum, Oct. 9, 1999; children: Mallory Lee, Connor Frederick. BS in Music Edn., Quincy U., Ill., 2003. Dir. sch. music Griggsville (Ill.) Sch. Dist., 1993—95; dir. vocal music Liberty (Ill.) Sch. Dist., 1995—96, Ill. Valley Ctrl. Sch. #321, Chillicothe, 1996—. Mem.: NEA, Ill. Edn. Assn., Music Educators Nat. Conf., Ill. Music Educator Assn. Office: Illinois Valley Central School #321 914 West Truitt Chillicothe IL 61523 Office Phone: 309-274-6266. Office Fax: 309-274-2010. Business E-Mail: kgriesba@roe48.k12.il.us.

GRIESEMER, CAROL J(OSEPH), counselor; b. Billings, Mo., Feb. 26, 1936; d. Joseph John and Margaret Catherine (Arend) G. BS in Edn., Mo. State U., 1957; MRE, St. Meinrad Sch. Theology, 1974; MA in Counseling, U. Mo., 1984. Lic. profl. counselor. Dir. Koinonia House, Columbia, Mo., 1984-88; case mgr. Sexual Assault-Family Violence, Joplin, Mo., 1988-90; dir. Midpoint Counseling Ctr., Joplin, 1991—2004. Chair Four-State Behavioral Health Network, 2003. Author numerous poems. Mem. AAUW, Am. Counseling Assn., Am. Counseling Assn.-Mo. (trustee 2006—), Am. Assn. Adult Devel. and Aging, Assn. Spirituality, Ethics, Religion and Values in Counseling, Internat. Assn. Marriage and Family Counselors, Amnesty Internat. Personal E-mail: carolgriesemer@cableone.net.

GRIESINGER, EMILY ANN, literature and language professor; b. Fort Worth, Tex., Feb. 7, 1954; d. John Graves and Elizabeth Jane Killebrew; m. Donald William Griesinger, July 30, 1988. BA, Baylor U., Waco, Tex., 1976, MA, 1979; PhD, Vanderbilt U., Nashville, 1989. Lifetime tchg. credential Tex., 1976, Ill., 1977. Tchr. English and Spanish Jane Addams Jr. H.S., Schaumburg, Ill., 1976—77; grad. tchg. fellow Baylor U., Waco, Tex., 1977—79, Vanderbilt U., Nashville, 1980—83; asst. to exec. dir. Grad. Mgmt. Ctr. Claremont Grad. Sch., Calif., 1983—89; prof. English Azusa Pacific U., 1990—. Author and editor: essay collection The Gift of Story: Narrating Hope in a Postmodern World, 2006; contbr. articles to literary jours. Recipient Charles J. Miller Best Essay award, Christian Scholar's Rev., 1999, Lionel Basney Best Essay award, Christianity and Lit., 2001. Mem.: MLA, Conf. on Christianity and Lit. (bd. mem. rep. western region 2003—), Kappa Delta Pi, Sigma Delta Pi, Sigma Tau Delta (faculty sponsor 1999—2006). Avocations: reading, piano, guitar, gardening, singing, jogging. Office: Azusa Pacific Univ English Dept 901 E Alosta Ave Azusa CA 91702 Office Phone: 626-815-6000.

GRIFALCONI, ANN, author, illustrator, producer; b. N.Y.C., Sept. 22; d. Joseph and Mary Hays (Weik) G. BS, NYU, 1954; cert. in design, Cooper Union, N.Y.C., 1950. Artist, N.Y.C.; designer Cin.; tchr. fine arts N.Y.C. Pub. Libr.; illustrator N.Y. Pubs., N.Y.C., 1960—; pres. Media Plus, Inc., N.Y.C., 1968-75, Greyfalcon House, N.Y.C., 1975—. Founder N.Y. Feminist Credit Union, 1973-80. Author: Not Home; author: (illustrator) numerous books, and plays, 1965—. Mem. Mus. TV & Radio. Recipient Caldecott Honor Jane Addams award, 2003. Mem. Author's Guild. Democrat. Avocation: travel. Office: Greyfalcon House 332 Bleecker St Ste 443 New York NY 10014-2980 Office Phone: 212-777-9042. Personal E-mail: anngrifalconi@verizon.net. Business E-Mail: greyfalconhouse@verizon.net.

GRIFFEN, AGNES MARTHE, retired library administrator; b. Ft. Dauphin, Madagascar, Aug. 25, 1935; d. Frederick Stang and Alvilde Margrethe (Torvik) Hallanger; m. Thomas Michael Griffen (div. Nov. 1969); children: Shaun Helen Griffen D'Antoni, Christopher Patrick, Adam Andrew; m. John H.P. Hall, Aug. 26, 1980. BA cum laude in English, Pacific Luth. U., 1957; MLS, U. Wash., 1965; Urban Exec. cert., MIT, 1976; postgrad., Harvard U., 1993. Cert. librarian, Wash., Md., Ariz. Area children's libr. King County Libr. Sys., Seattle, 1965-68, coord. instl. librs., 1968-71, dep. libr. for staff and program devel., 1971-74; dep. libr. dir. Tucson Pub. Libr., 1974-80; dir. Montgomery County Dept. Pub. Librs., Rockville, Md., 1980-96; libr. dir. Tucson-Pima Pub. Libr., 1997—2003; ret., 2003. Lectr. Grad. Libr. Sch., U. Ariz., Tucson, 1976-77, 79; vis. lectr. Sch. Librarianship, U. Wash., Seattle, 1983. Contbr. articles to library periodicals and profl. jours. Active Md. Humanities Coun., Balt., 1986-92, Ariz. Humanities Coun., Phoenix, 1977-80; charter mem. Exec. Women's Coun. of So. Ariz., Tucson, 1979-80; mem. coun. Nat. Capital Area Pub. Access Network, 1992-94, pres. bd., 1993-94, Ariz. Statewide Libr. Devel. Commn., 2000-02' mem. adv. coun. to Ariz. State Libr., 1998--. Recipient Helping Hand award Md. Assn. of the Deaf, 1985, Cert. Recognition Montgomery County Hispanic Employees Assn., 1985; Henry scholar U. Washington Sch. Librarianship, 1965. Mem. ALA (exec. bd. 1989-93, divsn. pres. pub. libr. assn. bd. 1981-82, councilor-at-large 1972-76, 86-93, chmn. com. on program evaluation and support 1987-88, legis. com. 1998-2002), Ariz. State Libr. Assn. (legis. com. 1997--), Md. Libr. Assn. Democrat. Home: 1951 N El Moraga Dr Tucson AZ 85745-9070

GRIFFIN, BETTY JO, elementary school educator; b. Monroe, La., Jan. 12, 1947; d. Julia Odell (Foster) Calhoun; divorced; 1 child, James Odell Griffin, Jr. BA, So. U., 1969; MA, San Francisco State U., 1975; PhD, LaSalle U., 2000. Cert. elem. tchr., Calif. Tchr. lang. arts Oakland (Calif.) Unified Sch. Dist., 1970-73, Garfield Elem. Sch., 1973-77, Stonehurst Elem. Schs., 1977-96; splty. prep. libr. and lang. arts tchr. Webster Acad., 1996—. Trustee Allen Temple Bapt. Ch., Oakland, Calif., 1987—; lit. tutor Delta Sigma Theta, Oakland, 1990—; chairperson African Am. Chain Read In, 1995—. Recipient Libr. Protection Fund award State Dept. Edn., 1997, Leadership award Dem. Nat. Com., 1997. Mem. NAACP, NEA, Oakland Edn. Assn. (bd. dirs.), Calif. Tchrs. Assn. (coun. of edn. 1996), Nat. Alliance Black Sch. Educators, Delta Sigma Theta, Phi Delta Kappa. Democrat. Avocations: reading, helping others, public speaking. Home: 2559 Oliver Ave Oakland CA 94605-4820 E-mail: BettyJGri@aol.com.

GRIFFIN, BETTY LOU, not-for-profit developer, educator; d. Julius Craven and Rachel Idell Best; m. Jack Wayne Griffin, May 28, 1960; children: Cheryle Louann, Melanie Lynn Young, Penelope. BS in Elem. Edn. magna cum laude, Campbell U., 1967; ME in Adult and Cmty. Coll. Edn., N.C. State U., 1974; ME in Adminstn. and Supervision, Fayetteville State U., 1995. Tchr. Sampson County Schs., Clinton, NC, 1965-67, Clinton City Schs., 1967-87; founder, exec. dir. U Care Inc., Sampson County Domestic Violence and Sexual Assault Program, Clinton, 1996—2005; CEO, bd. dirs., exec. dir. On Track Youth Svcs., Clinton, 2000—02. Evening bus. math. instr. Sampson CC, 1973—75, instr., 1975—77; notary pub. State of NC, 1995—2005. Contbr. articles tp Transformation Times, Triunity Dimensions, poetry to anthologies. Founder, dir. Sampson County Women's Assembly, 1994, 1996, 1998; legis. chmn., monitor chmn. Youth Adv. Coun., Sampson, 1994—98; founder, pres., exec. dir. Sampson County Coun. Women, 1995—. Named N.C. Dem. Women Poet Laureate, 1997, Sampson County Disting. Woman of the Yr., Sampson County Coun. Women, 1998; recipient Carpathian award, N.C. Equity, 1996. Mem.: DAR U. D.C., N.C. Dem. Women (mem. exec. bd. 1995—99, 1st poet laureate 1997—), Sampson County Dem. Women (v.p. 1993, pres. 1994—95, 2d v.p. 1996—97, pres. 1998—99, 2d v.p. 2000—03, v.p. 2006, 1st v.p. 2006—), Order of Eastern Star, Delta Kappa Gamma. Democrat. Methodist. Avocations: reading, creative writing, arts and crafts, hunting, fishing. Home and Office: 2535 Rosebory Hwy Clinton NC 28328

GRIFFIN, CHRISTINE M., commissioner; b. Boston; Grad., Mass. Maritime Acad., Boston Coll. With U.S. Atty.'s Office, Boston, FDA; atty. advisor US Equal Employment Opportunity Commn., 1995—96, commr., 2006—; exec. dir. Disability Law Ctr., Boston, 1996—2005. Interim pres. Mass. Maritime Acad., 1993—94. Former mem. nat. Social Security Adminstrn. Ticket to Work Advisory Panel, Mass. Devel. Disabilities Coun., Mass. Bd. Higher Edn. Served with U.S. Army. Named one of Lawyers of Yr., Lawyers Weekly USA. Office: EEOC 1801 L St NW Washington DC 20507 Office Phone: 202-663-4900.*

GRIFFIN, JEAN LATZ, political strategist, writer, publisher; b. Joliet, Ill., Mar. 6, 1943; d. Carl Joseph and Helene Monica (Bradshaw) Latz; m. Dennis Joseph Griffin, Sept. 16, 1967; children: Joseph, Timothy, Peter. BS in Chemistry, Coll. St. Francis, Joliet, 1965; MS in Journalism, U. Wis., 1967. Clin. investigation coord. Baxter Labs., 1967-68; reporter Joliet Herald News, 1968-70, Raleigh (N.C.) Times, 1974-75, Suburban Trib, Hinsdale, Ill., 1976-78, regional edn. reporter, 1978-82; gen. assignment reporter Chgo. Tribune, 1982-84, edn. writer, 1984-88, pub. health writer, 1988-94, govt., politics, and pub. policy reporter, 1994-97, econ. devel. reporter, 1997; strategist The Strategy Group, Chgo., 1998—; owner CyberINK, 1998—. Adj. journalism instr. Roosevelt U., Chgo., 2001—; facilitator U. Phoenix, 2004—. Author: One Spirit, 2006, In The Same Breath, 2006. Bd. dirs. Residents for Emergency Shelter, Chgo., 1978-82, Genesis House, Chgo., 1995-98, vol. cook, 1994-98; devel. com. mem. Hope Now, Inc., 1998-00; membership chair Arlington Hts. C. of C., 2001-02; vol. Taoist Tai Chi instr., 2001-; pres. Taoist Tai Chi Soc.-Midwest, 2005-. Recipient Writing award Am. Dental Assn., 1969, Alumna Profl. Achievement award Coll. St. Francis, Joliet, 1985, First Prize in ednl. writing Edn. Writers Am., 1986, Grand prize, 1988, Benjamin Fine award Nat. Assn. Secondary Sch. Prins., 1988, Edward Scott Beck award for reporting Chgo. Tribune, 1988, Peter Lisagor award for pub. svc. Soc. Profl. Journalists, Chgo. chpt., 1988, Mark of Excellence Chgo. Assn. Black Journalists, 1992, Cushing award for Journalistic Excellence, Chgo. Dental Soc., 1992, Human First award Horizon Cmty. Svcs., Chgo., 1993, Robert F. Kennedy Grand Prize in Journalism, 1994, Editl. Excellence award Ill. Merchandising Coun., 1994; finalist Pulitzer Prize, 1994. Mem. Taoist Tai Chi Soc. USA-Ill. (pres. 2003-05). Office: CyberINK 621 N Belmont Ave Arlington Heights IL 60004 Office Phone: 847-506-4214. Personal E-mail: jlgrif@earthlink.net.

GRIFFIN, JULIA WALLACE, real estate broker; b. Medford, Mass., Mar. 1, 1961; d. Peter Russel and Katherine Daab Clapp; m. Payton Townsend Griffin, Oct. 24, 1992; children: Lucian Wallace, Greer Van der Veer. Student, Hawaii Loa Coll., Kaneohe, U. Hawaii, Honolulu. Lic. real estate broker N.Y. State. Real estate salesperson James Marsden, Warwick, NY, 2002—04; assoc. broker D. L. Hawkins & Assocs., Warwick, 2004—. Mem. citizens' adv. bd. to Mayor Newhard Village of Warwick; auction chair Warwick Theraeutic Rehab. Ctr., 2005—06; invitation chair St. Anthony Cmty. Hosp., Warwick, 2005—06. Mem.: Orange County Citizens Found., Orange County Assn. Realtors. Avocations: yoga, water sports. Home: 66 West St Warwick NY 10990 Office: D L Hawkins & Assocs 100 Main St Warwick NY 10990

GRIFFIN, KATHY, comedienne, actress; b. Oak Park, Ill., Nov. 4, 1966; d. John and Maggie Griffin; m. Matthew Moline, Feb. 18, 2001 Studied acting, Lee Strasberg Inst. Actress playing Vicki Groener on Suddenly Susan NBC-TV, 1996—. Actor (films) The Unborn, 1991, Shakes the Clown, 1992, It's Pat, 1994, Pulp Fiction, 1994, Courting Courtney, 1995, Four Rooms, 1995, The Cable Guy, 1996, Trojan War, 1997, Can't Stop Dancing, 1999, Dill Scallion, 1999, Muppets From Space, 1999, (voice only) Lion of Oz, 2000, The Intern, 2000, On Edge, 2001, (voice) Dinotopia: Quest for the Ruby Sunstone, 2005, Her Minor Thing, 2005, Bachelor Party Vegas, 2006; (TV movies) The Barefoot Executive, 1995, A Diva's Christmas Carol, 2000; (TV series) Saturday Night Special, 1996, Suddenly Susan, 1996-2000, (voice) Dilbert, 1999-2000; (TV appearances) ER, 1994, Caroline in the City, 1995, Comedy Central, 1995, Mad About You, 1995, Seinfeld, 1996, Partners, 1996, (TV spls.) HBO Comedy Half-Hour: Kathy Griffin, 1996, The VH1 Fashion Awards, 1996; actor, exec. prodr. (TV series) My Life on the D-List, 2005-. Office: United Talent Agy 9560 Wilshire Blvd Ste 500 Beverly Hills CA 90212*

GRIFFIN, KELLY ANN, public relations executive, consultant; b. Buffalo, May 20, 1964; d. Michael Gerald and Patricia Frances (Lippert) G.; m. Thomas Richard Kleinberger, Oct. 11, 1992. B in Polit. Sci., SUNY, Geneseo, 1986; postgrad., CUNY, Bklyn., 1994—96. Legis. asst. to N.Y. State Assembly Spkrs. Stanley Fink and Mel Miller, Buffalo, 1986-87; acct. exec. Griffin Media Group, N.Y.C., 1987-88, acct. supr., v.p., 1988-90, pres., CEO, 1990-94; pub. rels. cons. N.Y.C., 1994—. Assoc. dir. N.Y. State Funeral Dirs. Assn., N.Y.C., 1992-94, Met. Funeral Dirs. Assn., N.Y.C., 1992-94, County Execs. of Am., N.Y.C. and Washington, 1993-2000; dep. exec. dir. County Execs. Am., 2000—; instr. remedial reading Cornell U. Sch. Industry/Lab. Rels., Buffalo, 1987; v.p. Fairfield Owners Cooperative, Riverdale, 1996-2000. Editor N.Y. State AFL-CIO Unity, 1988-90, County Execs. News, 1993—, N.Y. State Funeral Dirs. Assn./Met. Funeral Dirs. Assn. News, 1992-94, Amalgamated Transit Union News, 1988-90. Cons. Interfaith Assembly on Homelessness, N.Y.C., 1994-97, Voter Assistance Commn., N.Y.C., 1990-92; participant, cons. Erie County Dem. Party, Buffalo, 1985-87; mem. assocs. steering com. Children's Health Fund, N.Y.C., 1991-97; bd. dirs. Kingsbridge Hts. Cmty. Ctr., Bronx, 1999-2005, sec., 2000-01, chair, 2001-04; mem. Parents' Assn., Frances Schervier Home and Hosp. Childcare Ctr., Bronx, 1997-2000, Support Our Schs. Com., Bronx, 1999-2000; class parent Prospect Hill Sch. PTA, Pelham Manor, 2001-05, rec. sec., 2003-04, pres.-elect, 2004-05, pres., 2005-06, v.p. fundraising, 2006—; mem. fundraising com. Transition Learning Ctr., New Rochelle, N.Y.; mem. citizens nominating com. Pelham, N.Y., 2006—. Recipient Acad. award DAR, 1978. Mem. PTA (rep. Pelham coun. 2006—), Pub. Rels. Soc. N.Y.C., The Manor Club (Pelham Manor, N.Y.), N.Y. Athletic Club. Roman Catholic. Avocations: reading, running, yoga, ice skating, tennis. Home: 1061 Hunter Ave Pelham NY 10803-3409 Office: Griffin Media Group Ste 910 1100 H St Washington DC 20005 Office Phone: 800-296-8438. E-mail: kgrif@optonline.net.

GRIFFIN, LAURA MAE, retired elementary and secondary school educator; b. Woodland, Calif., Aug. 14, 1925; d. George Everette Ramsey and Bertha (Storz) Ramsey Lowe; m. Roy J. Griffin, Nov. 19, 1944; children: Robert Eugene, Dennis Charles, Kathleen Ann. AA in Social Sci., Sacramento City Coll., 1969; BA in Geography, Calif. State U., Sacramento, 1972. Cert. elem. and secondary tchr., Calif.; Master Gardener. Sec. Alameda Naval Air, Alameda, Calif., 1944-45, Cal-Western Life Ins., Sacramento, 1945-47, Pacific Sch. Dist., Sacramento, 1956-57; substitute tchr. Sacramento Unified Sch. Dist., 1974-75; tchr. Mt. Diablo Unified Sch. Dist., Concord, Calif., 1976-91, tchr. shorthand, adult edn., 1981—91; ret., 1991. Dir. Heather Farm Garden Ctr., Walnut Creek, Calif., 1985-86, edn. chmn., 1986-87, pres., 1987-88, fin. sec., 1993-94; sec. investment group AAUW, Walnut Creek, 1978-79. Guardian Jobs Daus.-Bethel 325, Walnut Creek, 1978-79; leader Girl Scouts Am., Sacramento, 1971-72; den mother Boy Scouts Am., Sacramento, 1957-60; publicity chmn. membership Northgate Music Boosters, Walnut Creek, 1976-77; tchr. women's Bible study group Christ's Greenfield Luth. Ch., 2003-04. Recipient Bert A. Bertolero Gardening award, 1996. Mem. Calif. Garden Clubs (hon. life), Heather Farm Garden Club (pres. 1987-88, Outstanding Svc. award 1995), Walnut Creek Garden Club (pres. 1983-84, civic project chmn. 1994-95, 95-96), Order Ea. Star. Republican. Avocations: reading, travel, bowling, golf, music, gardening.

GRIFFIN, MARY FRANCES, retired media consultant; b. Cross Hill, S.C., Aug. 24, 1925; d. James and Rosa Lee (Carter) G. BA, Benedict Coll., 1947; postgrad., S.C. State Coll., 1948—51, Atlanta U., 1953, Va. State Coll., 1961; MLS, Ind. U., 1957. Tchr., libr. Johnston Tng. Sch., Edgefield County Sch. Dist., SC, 1947—51; libr. Lee County Sch. Dist., Dennis H.S., Bishopville, SC, 1951—52, Greenville County Sch. Dist., SC, 1952—66; libr. cons. S.C. Dept. Edn., Columbia, 1966—87; ret., 1987. Vis. tchr. U. S.C., 1977. Bd. dirs. Greater Columbia Lit. Coun.; mem. Richland County unit Assault on Illiteracy. Recipient Cert. of Living the Legacy award Nat. Coun. Negro Women, 1980. Mem. ALA, Assn. Ednl. Comms. and Tech., S.C. Assn. Curriculum Devel., AAUW (pres. Columbia br. 1978-80), Southeastern Libr. Assn. (sec. 1979-80), S.C. Libr. Assn. (sec. 1979), S.C. Assn. Sch. Librarians, Nat. Assn. State Ednl. and Media Pers. Baptist. Home: 108 Jennings St Laurens SC 29360

GRIFFIN, PENNI ONCKEN, social worker, educator; b. Cedar Rapids, Iowa, Nov. 11, 1945; d. Edward Charles and Rita Margaret Oncken; m. Walt Griffin, Dec. 6, 1980; children: Rebecca, Kathleen, Shawn, Megan. BA, Coe Coll., 1970; MSW, U. Cin., 1992. LMSW S.C. Lead social worker Iowa Dept. Social Svcs., Cedar Rapids, 1975—79; dir. homemaker svcs. Family Svc. Agy., Cedar Rapids, 1979—80; investigator protective svcs. Iowa Dept. Social Svcs., Waterloo, 1982—89; med. social worker S.C. Dept. Health and Environ. Control, 1992—95; asst. prof. Limestone Coll., Gaffney, SC, 1995—, dir. social work program, 1995—2002, asst. dean, dir. Social Work Program, 2002—06. Founding bd. dir. LinnHaven Home Retarded Adults, Cedar Rapids, 1976—78; mem. adv. bd. Make Today Count, Cedar Rapids, 1976—79, Cherokee County Alcohol and Drug Abuse Commn., Gaffney, SC, 2001—05. Chmn. fin. Linn County Dems., Cedar Rapids, 1979—80, Steve Sovern U.S. Congress, Cedar Rapids, 1980; bd. dirs. Gaffney (S.C.) Little Theatre, 1994—2001. Mem.: NASW, Internat. Assn. Social Workers, Social Work Baccalaureate Program Dirs., Coun. Social Work Edn. Democrat. Avocations: reading, travel. Home: 1008 College Drive Gaffney SC 29340 Office: Limestone College 1115 College Drive Gaffney SC 29340 Office Phone: 864-488-4526. Business E-Mail: pgriffin@limestone.edu.

GRIFFIN, SALLIE T., artist, photographer, retired technologist; b. Whiteville, NC, Sept. 2, 1940; d. Benjamin Oliver and Virginia Alma (Ponton) Thompson; m. C.H. Griffin, Dec. 26, 1964; children: A.F. Griffin, M.A. Griffin. Grad., St. Mary's High Sch. and Jr. Coll., Duke U. Med. Ctr., Sch. Radiological Tech. and Nuclear Medicine; student, Anson Tech. Coll., Ctrl. Piedmont C.C., 1976-80, Wingate U., 1976-91, 97; studied with Sally B. Miller. With Stanley Meml. Hosp., Albermark, N.C.; technician, tchr. Moses Cine Hosp. Founding mem. Union Co. Art Coun., Monroe, N.C., 1980-84., found. first libr. gallery Union Co. Libr., Marshville, N.C., 1998. One woman shows include: Union County Pub. Libr., Monroe, N.C., 1980, 82, Wingate Coll., 1980, United Carolina Bank, 1981, Ivey's Southpark, Charlotte, 1985, Dove Pottery and Gallery, Monroe, 1990, Stanley County Libr., Albemarle, 1992, Artisan Ctr., Kannapolis, 1992, St. Mary's Coll., 1992, Union County Arts Coun., 1995, 50 piece show, 2000; Group shows include: Blooming Arts Festival (named Union County's Finest, 1981, 1st place winner, 1994), N.C. State U. Show, 1988, Dove Pottery and Gallery, 1991, Watercolor Soc. N.C., 1995, U. N.C. 1996, Myrtle Beach Convention Ctr., 1996, 22nd Nat. Show, Shelby, 1996, Greensboro Cultural Ctr., 1997, Mus. of York County, 1997, Shelby Nat. Show #23, 1997, Greenhill Gallery of N.C. Art, 1998, Taladega Mus., Ala., 1998, Wingate U., 1998, Union County Libr., 1998, Weatherspoon Gallery, 1999, Fayetteville Mus. Art, 1999, 25th Ann. Art Show of N.W., Fla., 1999, Burroughs and Chapin Art Mus., Myrtle Beach, S.C., 1999, MOMA, N.Y.C., 2000; Fe-Mail E-Mail 2000. Bd. dirs. Wingate Coll. Libr., Wingate, NC, 1985-89, Union County Arts Coun., Monroe; founder Union County Arts Coun. NE N.C. Mem. The Marshville Rsch. Club, The Union Co. Art League (pres. 1986-87, 2000-01), The Watercolor Soc. N.C., Ariz., Ala., Conn., The Guild of Charlotte Artists, The Charlotte Art League, The Jaycettes (founder, bd. mem. 1965-75, pres. 1965-67). Democrat. Baptist. E-mail: salliegriffin@altel.com.

GRIFFIN, SHARON GRASS, elementary school educator; b. Geary, Okla., Dec. 1, 1940; d. Donald and Fern La Vera (Coleman) Grass; m. Dorman Griffin, Nov. 19, 1960 (dec. May 2, 2002); children: Jeffrey Mark, Valerie Ann, Robert Scott. BS in Elem. Edn., Cen. State U., Edmond, Okla., 1962. Tchr. math. Piedmont Pub. Schs., Okla.; elem. tchr. Yukon Pub. Schs., Okla., Piedmont Pub. Schs.; owner D&S Pool Svc. and Supplies, Yukon, Okla., 1985—. Mem. NEA, Okla. Edn. Assn., Cen. Okla. Tchrs. Math. Office: D&S Pool Svc 702 Kouba Yukon OK 73099 Office Phone: 405-354-6164.

GRIFFIN, SHEILA MB, strategic marketing excutive; b. June 17, 1951; d. George Michael and Frances Josephine (Sheehan) Spielman; m. Woodson Jack Griffin, Dec. 30, 1972; children: Woodson Jack II, Kelly Sheehan. BS, U. Ill., 1975, MBA, 1979. Personal banking rep. Am. Express Banking, Boeblingen, Germany, 1973-74; market rsch. analyst Market Facts, Chgo., 1975-77; mgr. strategic rsch. Motorola, Inc., Schaumburg, Ill., 1977-83, mgr. mktg. resource, 1985-88, mgr. spl. projects corp. strategy office, 1988-89, dir. corp. advt. worldwide, 1989-93, dir. bus. assessment corp. strategy office, 1993-94, dir. multimedia strategy office, 1994-96, dir. global applied market rsch., 1996-98, v.p., dir. strategic mktg. office, 1999—2001; pres. Griffin Holdings, Inc., 2001—. Gen. mgr. mktg. rsch. and info. Ameritech Mobile Comm., Inc., Schaumburg, 1983-85. Founding trustee, chmn. Ill. Math. and Sci. Acad., 1985—; Lincoln Series for Excellence in the Pub. Sector fellow, 2002. Mem. U. Ill. Chgo. MBA Alumni Assn. (founder, pres. 1984-86), U. Ill. Alumni Assn. (bd. dirs. 1984-86), Disting. Alumni 1985, Constituent Leadership award 1989). Home: 3017 Glen Eagles Ct Saint Charles IL 60174-8832 Office: Griffin Holdings Inc PO Box 3702 Saint Charles IL 60174 Office Phone: 630-721-3017. E-mail: griffinholdings@gmail.com.

GRIFFIN, SUSAN, secondary school educator; BS, Clemson U., SC, 1973; MS, U. Md., College Park, 1980. Cert. tchr. La., Nat. Bd. Profl. Tchg. Stds. Tchr. Ruston (La.) HS, 1994—. Office: Ruston HS 900 Bearcat Dr Ruston LA 71270 Office Phone: 318-255-0807.

GRIFFIN, SYLVIA GAIL, reading specialist; b. Portland, Oreg., Dec. 13, 1935; d. Archie and Marguerite (Johnson) G. AA, Boise Jr. Coll., 1955; BS, Brigham Young U., 1957, MEd, 1967. Cert. advanced teaching, Idaho. Classroom tchr. Boise Pub. Sch., Idaho, 1957-59, 61-66, 67-69, reading specialist Idaho, 1969-90, 91-95, 98-2001, inclusion specialist Idaho, 1995-98, early childhood specialist Idaho, 1990-91. Tchr. evening Spanish classes for adults, 1987-88; lectr. in field; mem. cons. pool US Office Juvenile Justice and Delinquency Prevention, 1991—. Author: Procedures Used by First Grade Teachers for Teaching Experience Readiness for Reading Comprehension, The Short Story of Vowels, A Note Worthy Way to Teach Reading, The Little Black Schoolhouse, Hellside Elementary School, Reading, Righting, and Revenge, Memorandum: Murder, Once Upon a Trial; composer: The Second Coming, Progression. Advisor in developing a program for dyslexics Scottish Rite Masons of Idaho, Boise. Mem.: NEA, Actor's Guild, Idaho Edn. Assn. (pub. rels. dir. 1970—72), Boise Edn. Assn. (pub. rels. dir. 1969—72, bd. dirs. ednl. polit. involvement com. 1983—89), Alpha Delta Kappa. Avocations: music, creative writing. Home: 9948 W Sleepy Hollow Ln Boise ID 83714-3665 Personal E-mail: readwell2@yahoo.com.

GRIFFIN, TAMMY LYNN, industrial engineer; b. Atlanta, Jan. 15, 1961; married July 30, 1999. BS in Indsl. Engring., Ga. Inst. Tech., 1982; MBA, Ga. State U. Registered profl. engr., Ga. Imagery scientist CIA, Washington, 1983-84; indsl. engr. N.Am. Philips, Little Rock, 1984-86; sr. quality assurance engr. Emerson Electric Co., Sanford, Fla., 1986-88; mgr. quality assurance J&J, Inc., Hampton, Ga., 1988-93; quality assurance mgr. Goody Products, Manchester, Ga., 1993-95. Asst. treas. Starr's Mill Bapt. Ch., Fayetteville, Ga., 1993—, mem. fin. com., 1994-95. Mem. Ga. Soc. Profl. Engrs. (treas. C-H-F chpt. 1992-93, v.p. 1993-94, pres. 1994-95, Young Engr. of Yr. award 1994). Avocations: golf, jazzercise. Home: 195 Grindstone Way Senoia GA 30276-1602

GRIFFIS, THERESA A., secondary school educator; d. George Earl and Frances Inez Griffis. BS in Edn., U. Ark., Little Rock, 1976; MS in Edn., La. Tech. U., 1984. Tchr., coach Bearden Pub. Schs., Ark., 1976—79, Lewisville Sch., 1979—81, Webster Parish Sch., Minden, La., 1981—2001; tchr. Texarkana Ind. Sch. Dist., Tex., 2001—. Vol. Artex Animal Welfare, treas., 2000—; coach, vol. Callenger, 1999—. Mem.: Ted. Fedn. Tchrs. Avocations: golf, woodworking, photography. Office: Tex Mid Sch 2100 College Dr Texarkana TX 75503

GRIFFITH, CATHLEEN ANN, principal; b. Kalamazoo, Mich., Dec. 27, 1955; d. Edward and Janet Dawn Sweet; m. Paul Charles Griffith, Oct. 11, 1980. BS, Western Mich. U., 1978; M Guidance and Counseling, U. Toledo, 1984. HS tchr. Ida (Mich.) Pub. Schs., 1978—85, HS counselor, 1985—2004, HS prin., 2004—. Co-chmn. Relay for Life local divsn. Am. Cancer Assn., Ida, 2004—05; founder Christmas fundraiser for local families. Named Counselor of Yr., Monroe County Counselors, 2002, Tchr. of Yr., Toledo Blade, 2003; recipient award for student coun. work, Ida Pub. Schs. Mem.: Nat. Assn. Secondary Sch. Prins., Nat. Assn. Secondary Sch. Prins., Mich. Edn. Assn., Monroe County Prins. (pres. 2005—06), Ida Edn. Assn. (pres. 2002—04). Avocations: reading, antiques, travel. Home: 9261 Pixley Rd Palmyra MI 49268 Office: Ida HS 3145 Prairie St Ida MI 48140

GRIFFITH, GLORIA JEANETTE, finance educator; b. Jasonville, Ind., Aug. 16, 1926; d. Gilbert Owen Thomas and Artie Leora Harris-Thomas; m. Charles Herschel Holmes Griffith, June 3, 1949; children: Janet Susan, Diane Kay Barnett. BS, Ind. U., Bloomington, 1948, MS, 1950. Tchr. Westport High Sch., Ind., 1949—50, Trenton High Sch., Ohio, 1962—64, Warwick High Sch., RI, 1964—65, Fugazzi Bus. Coll., Lexington, Ky., 1967—68; tchr. bus. Bluegrass C.C., 1968—91. Actor: (TV comml. with George Clooney at Fugazzi Coll.). Mem. Planned Parenthood Bd., Stonewall Neighborhood Assn., treas., 2001; pres. bd. Donavan program U. Ky. Mem.: Bluegrass Ret. Tchrs. Assn. Independent. Avocations: bridge, exercise, music box collecting, piano, travel. Home: 3340 Grasmere Dr Lexington KY 40503

GRIFFITH, JEANNETTE TERESA, elementary school educator, education educator; b. Albany, Ga., Jan. 14, 1963; d. Ileana Rivera Alderman; m. Eric Michael Griffith, June 2000; children: Alexander Michael Barba, Lane Elizabeth. M in Liberal Arts, Rollins Coll., Winter Park, Fla., 2004. Cert. tchr. Fla. Tchr. Chain of Lakes Mid. Sch., Orlando, Fla., 1999—; prof. Valencia CC, Orlando, 2004—. Capt. Am. Cancer Soc., Orlando, 2006, WalkAmerica, Orlando, 1998. Recipient Teacherrific award, Walt Disney World, 1993. Home: 9300 Daney St Gotha FL 34734 Office: Chain of Lakes Mid Sch 8700 Conroy Windermere Rd Orlando FL 32835 Office Phone: 407-909-5400. Office Fax: 407-909-5410. Personal E-mail: jgriffith7@cfl.rr.com. Business E-Mail: griffij@ocps.net.

GRIFFITH, LINDA G. (LINDA GRIFFITH-CIMA), biomedical engineer, chemical engineer, educator; BSChemE, Ga. Inst. Tech., 1982; PhD in Chem. Engring., U. Calif., Berkeley, 1988. Postdoctoral assoc. chem. engring. MIT, 1988—90, asst. prof. chem. engring., 1991—96, assoc. prof. chem. engring., 1996—2002, assoc. prof. chem. and biol. engring., 1998—2002, prof., 2002—03, dir. Biotechnology Process Engring. Ctr., 2003—, prof. mech. and biol. engring., 2003—. Asst. prof. Harvard U.-MIT Divsn. Health Sci. and Tech., 1991—93; H.L. Doherty chair, 1991—93; Karl van Tassel chair, 1993—98; editorial bd. mem. Jour. of Biomaterials Sci. Contbr. articles to profl. jours.; mem. editl. bd.: Jour. Biomaterials Scis. Named one of Brilliant 10, Popular Sci. mag., 2002; recipient Presdl. Young Investigator award, NSF, 1991; fellow Am. Inst. Med. & Biol. Engrs., 1998, Biomaterials Sci. & Engring., Internat. Union of Soc. for Biomaterials Sci. & Engring., 2000; MacArthur fellow, John D. MacArthur and Catherine T. MacArthur Found., 2006. Renowned for human tissue engineering research and development. Office: MIT 77 Mass Ave Room 16-429 Cambridge MA 02139 E-mail: griff@mit.edu.*

GRIFFITH, MELANIE, actress; b. NYC, Aug. 9, 1957; d. Tippi Hedren; m. Don Johnson, Jan. 1972 (div. July 1976); m. Steven Bauer May 1982 (div. 1987); 1 child, Alexander; m. Don Johnson, June 26, 1989 (div. Feb. 1996); 1 child, Dakota; m. Antonio Banderas, 1996; 1 child, Stella. Student, Hollywood Profl. Sch., 1981; studied acting with, Stella Adler. Acting debut in Night Moves, 1975, other films include The Drowning Pool, 1975, Smile, 1975, One on One, 1977, Roar, Joyride, 1977, Underground Aces, Body Double, 1984, Fear City, Something Wild, 1986, Cherry 2000, 1988, The Milagro Beanfield War, 1988, Stormy Monday, 1987, Working Girl, 1988 (Acad. Award nominee), In the Spirit, The Grifters, Pacific Heights, 1990, Bonfire of the Vanities, Shining Through, Paradise, 1991, A Stranger Among Us, 1992, Born Yesterday, 1993, Milk Money, 1994, Nobody's Fool, 1994, Two Much, 1996, Mulholland Falls, 1996, Now and Then, 1996, Shadow of Doubt, Another Day in Paradise, Lolita, 1996, Celebrity, 1998, Crazy in Alabama, 1999, Cecil B. DeMented, 2000, Forever Lulu, 2000, Tart, 2001, Stuart Little 2 (voice), 2002, The Night We Called It a Day, 2003, Tempo, 2003, Shade, 2003; TV appearances include (series) Carter Country, (mini-series) Once an Eagle, Buffalo Girls, 1995, (TV movies) She's in the Army Now, 1981, Golden Gate, 1981, Alfred Hitchcock Presents, 1985, Women and Men: Stories of Seduction, 1990, Buffalo Girls, 1995, RKO 281, 1999, Heartless, 2005, (pilots) Golden Gate; (TV series) Twins, 2005-; (Broadway plays) Chicago, 2003. Recipient Golden Globe award, 1989.

GRIFFITH, NICOLA, writer; b. Leeds, Yorkshire, Eng., Sept. 30, 1960; life ptnr. Kelly Eskridge. Formerly ins. clk., waitress, singer, songwriter, tchr. self defense. Author: Ammonite, 1993 (Ga. and Atlanta Lit. prizes, Lambda Lit. award 1993, Tiptree Meml. award 1994), Slow River, 1995 (Lambda award, Nebula award), The Blue Place, 1999, Stay, 2002; co-editor: (short fiction series) Bending the Landscape. Office: care Shawna McCarthy Scovil Chichak Galen 381 Park Ave S Ste 1020 New York NY 10016

GRIFFITH, PATRICIA BROWNING, writer, educator; b. Ft. Worth; d. Robert Browning and Alonza Lee Johnston; m. William Byron Griffith; 1 child, Ellen Flannery. BA, Baylor U. Assoc. prof. creative writing and playwriting George Washington U., 1991—. Pres. PEN/Faulkner Found. Award for fiction, Folger Libr., Washington. Author: The Future is Not What it Used to Be, Tennessee Blue, The World Around Midnight, 1992, (One of Notable Books of 1992, ALA), Supporting the Sky, 1996; contbr.: Skin Deep, Black Women and White Women Write About Race, 1995, paperback edit., 1996; playwright Outside Waco, 1984, Safety, 1987, Risky Games, 1992; screenwriter. Mem. PEN, Author's Guild, Dramatist's Guild, Tex. Inst. Letters.

GRIFFITH, PATRICIA KING, journalist; b. San Francisco, Jan. 20, 1934; d. Earl Beardsley and Frankie Mae (Kelly) King; m. Winthrop Gold Griffith, Oct. 4, 1958 (div. Jan. 1986); children: Kevin Winthrop, Christina Suzanne. BA, Stanford U., 1955. Copy asst., reporter Washington Post, 1956-57, 60-64; reporter San Francisco Examiner, 1957-59; Washington bureau chief Monterey Herald and Toledo Blade, Washington, 1979-81; investigative reporter Monterey (Calif.) Peninsula Herald, 1973-79, city editor, 1981-83, mng. editor, 1983-88; Washington bureau chief, White House corr. Toledo Blade and Pitts. Post-Gazette, Washington, 1988-99. Bd. dirs. Lyceum of Monterey Peninsula, 1977-79, All Sts. Episcopal Day Sch., Carmel, Calif., 1977-79, Monterey Coll. Law, 1978-79; sr. warden St. Dunstan's Episcopal Ch., Carmel Valley, Calif., 1983-84; warden St. Margaret's Episcopal Ch., Belfast, Maine, 2004-05. Recipient Silver Gavel award ABA, 1978. Mem.: Stanford Alumni Assn., Nat. Press Club, Gridiron Club, Stanford Cap and Gown Soc. Home: 103 Dockside Ln Belfast ME 04915

GRIFFITH, ROBERTA, art educator; b. Hillsdale, Mich., May 14, 1937; d. Robert Charles Griffith and Jane Marie (Randolph) Griffith Elliott; m. Ray Schillmoeller, Mar. 26, 1966 (div. Oct. 6, 1995); children: David Robert, Raymond Mark. BFA, Chouinard Art Inst., 1960; MFA, So. Ill. U., 1962. Cert. tchr., N.Y. Tchr. art Am. Sch., Barcelona, Spain, spring, 1964; ceramic designer Design Technics, N.Y.C., 1965-66; Arkell Hall prof. art Hartwick Coll., Oneonta, N.Y., 1966—, chairperson art dept., 1974-91. Lectr. in field. Contbr. articles to profl. jours.; one-woman shows include Munson Williams Proctor Inst. Sch. Art Gallery, Utica, N.Y., 1988, Foreman Gallery, Hartwick Coll., Oneonta, N.Y., 1989, Winfisky Gallery, Salem (Mass.) State Coll., 1992, Warren Gallery, Yager Mus., Hartwick Coll., Oneonta, N.Y., 1994, 50 Yr. Retrospective Hartwick Coun., Yager Mus., 2003; exhibited in numerous group shows, including Wichita Falls (Tex.) Mus. and Art Ctr., 1991; revs. and photographs of work rep. in books, newspapers, mags. and exhbn. catalogues in U.S., Spain, France, Mex., and Japan. Sec., Upper Catskill Community coun. on Arts, 1974-78, v.p. 1978-79, pres. 1979-80; del.-at-large Nat. coun. Edn. for Nat. Ceramic Arts, 1984-86, dir. publs., 1986; cons. in field. Recipient award Young Am., 1962, Mus. Contemporary Crafts, Craftsmen USA, 1966; grantee NEH, 1991, rsch. grantee Hartwick Coll., 1992-2005, 93. Mem. AAUP (v.p. 1983-87, pres. Hartwick Coll. chpt. 1986-89), Humanities Div. Hartwick Coll. (chairperson 1988-89), Nat. Coun. Edn. Ceramic Arts (bd. dirs.), Upper Catskill Com. Coun. Arts (bd. dirs.), Nat. Coun. Art Adminstrs., Am. Assn. Univ. Women., Coll. Art Assn. Am., Am. Crafts Coun., Cooperstown Art Assn., MOMA, Whitney Mus. of Art, Met. Mus. Art. Republican. Episcopalian. Avocations: swimming, tennis, travel. Home: PO Box 112 Otego NY 13825-0112 E-mail: griffithr138@yahoo.com.

GRIFFITH, SIMA LYNN, investment banker, consultant; b. N.Y.C., Sept. 7, 1960; d. Morris Benjamin and Mary (Buberoglü) Nahum; m. Clark Calvin Griffith, Sept. 13, 1987. BA in English, Amherst Coll., 1982. Account exec. D.F. King & Co., Inc., N.Y.C., 1982-84, asst. v.p., 1984-86, v.p., 1986-88, Wells & Miller, Mpls., 1988; with Griffith, Levi Capital, Inc, Mpls., 1988-96; prin. Aethlon, Capital LLC, Mpls., 1996—, mng. prin. Co-chmn. PRSA, IR seminars, 1987; bd. adv. Pacer, Inc. Bd. dirs. Children's Hosps. and Clinics, 2004—; bd. govs. Children's Theater Co., 1999—2005; bd. adv. PACER; co-chair Women-to-Women. Named one of Top Women in Fin., Fin. and Commerce newspaper, 2003, Twin Cities Women to Watch, The Bus. Jour., 2002; recipient Vision award, Nat. Assn. Women Bus. Owners, 2003. Mem.: Pub. Rels. Soc. Am. (bod. govs., investor rels. sec. 1987—89), Assn. Bus. Communicators (bd. govs. 1987—88). Office: Aethlon Capital LLC 4920 IDS Ctr 80 South 8th St Minneapolis MN 55402-2100 Office Phone: 612-338-0934, 612-338-6065. E-mail: sgriffith@aethlon.com.

GRIFFITH, YOLANDA EVETTE, professional basketball player; b. Chgo., Mar. 1, 1970; d. Harvey G.; 1 child, Candace Michelle. Student, Palm Beach Jr. Coll., Fla. Atlantic U. Basketball player Palm Beach Jr. Coll., Fla. Atlantic U., 1992—93; profl. basketball player Germany, 1993—97, Long Beach StingRays, ABL, 1997—98, Sacramento Monarchs, WNBA, 1999—. Mem. USA Basketball Women's Sr. Nat. Team, 1998, 99, 2000, 04. Named ABL Defensive Player of Yr., 1997-98; recipient MVP award, 1999. Achievements include mem. US Women's Basketball Gold Medal Team, Sydney Olympics, 2000; mem. US Women's Basketball Team, Athens Olympics, 2004. Avocations: softball, music. Office: Sacramento Monarchs One Sports Pkwy Sacramento CA 95834

GRIFFITHS, BARBARA LORRAINE, psychologist, writer, marriage and family therapist; b. Glendale, Calif., July 15, 1927; d. David William and Mabel Augusta (Gaarder) G.; m. Dale Elmo Rumbaugh, Mar. 28, 1948; 1 child, David Wynn. AA in Journalism, Valley C.C., 1958; BA in Psychology, U. Calif. Riverside, 1972; MS in Rehab. Counseling, Calif. State U., 1976; PhD in Clin. Psychology, Calif. Grad. Inst., 1984. Cert. Diplomate Am. Psychotherapy Assn., 1998, cert. addicition specialist, Marriage and Family Therapist 1979. Alcoholism counselor Kaiser Permanente, L.A., 1976-82; pvt. practice Hollywood, L.A., 1979-89, Glendale, Burbank, Calif., 1989-97, L.A., 1997—2005. Mem. State of Calif. Med. Diversion Evaluation Com., 1998—2003; screener 6th and 7th Prism awards Entertainment Industry Coun. Film, 2001—02; sci. expert reviewer 6th annual Prism Awards Entertainment Industry Coun., 2002—03; reviewer 6th and 7th Ann. PRISM awards Entertainment Industry Coun. Film, 2002; clinical psychologist Calif. Youth Authority, 2002—03. Editor (child abuse newsletter): Directions, 1976—86; writer, prodr.: (short film) Silver Bullet Kid, 2003; contbr. short stories, feature articles, columns to various mags., newspapers and profl. mags. Mem. Glendale Rotary, 1990-95, Verdugo BPW, 1988-91; Nat. Ski Patrolwoman #122, 1952-56. Recipient Editor's Choice award for poetry, 1997. Mem. APA (assoc.), Los Angeles County Psychol. Assn. Avocations: script writing, tennis, skiing, swimming and water sports, reading. Home and Office: 5159 Lakewood Dr San Bernardino CA 92407-3529 Office Phone: 909-887-8793.

GRIFFITHS, JEM, singer; b. Cardiff, Wales, 1975; JD, Sussex U. Singer: (albums) Finally Woken, 2004; composer (films) The Prince & Me, 2004, guest appearance (TV series) The O.C., 2004, Kelly, 2005, T4, 2005, composer (TV series) Desperate Housewives, The O.C., 24. Office: ATO Records Sam Shah 157 Chambers St 12th Fl New York NY 10007

GRIFFITHS, RACHEL, actress; b. Melbourne, Australia, June 4, 1968; d. Anna Griffiths; m. Andrew Taylor, Dec. 31, 2002; children: Banjo Patrick, Adelaide Rose. BEd in Drama and Dance, Victoria Coll. Actor: (films) Muriel's Wedding, 1994 (Best Supporting Actress Australian Film Critics award, Best Supporting Actress Australian Film Inst. award, 1995), Jude, 1996, To Have and To Hold, 1997, My Best Friend's Wedding, 1997, Hilary and Jackie, 1998 (nominee Best Supporting Actress Oscar, 1999), My Son, the Fanatic, 1998, Among Giants, 1998, Amy, 1998, Me Myself I, 1999, Blow, 2001, The Rookie, 2002, The Hard Word, 2002, Ned Kelly, 2003, Angel, 2005, Step Up, 2006; (TV series) Secrets, 1993, Jimeoin, 1994, Six Feet Under, 2001—05 (Best Suppporting Actress Golden Globe award, 2001), Brothers & Sisters, 2006; (TV films) The Feds, 1993, Since You've Been Gone, 1998, Plainsong, 2004.*

GRIFFITHS, SYLVIA PRESTON, physician, educator; b. London, Dec. 25, 1924; d. Wheeler Bate and Dorothy (Hartley) Preston; m. Raymond B. Griffiths; 1 dau., Wendy Elizabeth. BA, Hunter Coll., 1944; MD, Yale U., 1948. Intern Grace-New Haven Community Hosp., 1948-49, resident, 1949-52; fellow in pediatric cardiology Yale U., 1952-54; asst. to prof. clin. pediatrics Columbia U., N.Y.C., 1955, prof. clin. pediatrics, 1977-90, prof. emerita, 1990—. Recipient career scientist award Health Research Council, City of N.Y., 1963-69 Mem. N.Y. Heart Assn. (dir. 1977-83), Am. Acad. Pediatrics, Am. Pediatric Soc., Am. Heart Assn., Am. Coll. Cardiology, Babies Hosp. Alumni Assn. (pres. 1991-92). Office: Columbia Presbyterian Med Ctr 622 W 168th St New York NY 10032-3720

GRIGGS, BOBBIE JUNE, civic worker; b. Oklahoma City, Feb. 14, 1938; d. Robert Jefferson and Nora May (Green) Fish; m. Peter Harvey Griggs, Apr. 16, 1955; children: Diana (dec.), Terry, James. Grad. high sch., Salina, Kans. Commissary rep. Family Mag., Charleston AFB, S.C., 1976—; rep. Avon Corp., Charleston, S.C., 1976—; freelance demonstrator to USAF and USN orgns. Charleston, 1976—; rep. Salute Mag., Charleston AFB, 1986—; consumer edn. counselor Air Force-Navy exchs. Oster Kitchen Appliances, Charleston, 1987-90. Contbr. World's Largest Poem for Peace, 1991, Selected Works of our Best Poets, 1992, In A Different Light, 1992. Youth advisor, Charleston AFB, 1966-78; vol. doll distbn. program Salvation Army; clinic vol. ARC, Charleston AFB, 1967-75, chmn. family svcs. publicity and spl. projects, 1989; clinic vol. Clara Barton award, 1972; vol. Spoleto Festival, 1989—, Twin Oaks Retirement Ctr., 1992—, Chapel SUMMOM program, 1991—; asst. coord., publicity chmn. Family Svcs., 1967-83, named vol. of quarter, 1970, 72, 74, 76, named vol. of yr., 1970; active various scouting orgns., 1967—; asst. kindergarten Sunday sch. supt. Chapel I, 1966-68; active North Charleston (S.C.) Christian Women's Club, 1988—, hosp. chmn., mem. Charleston AFB Protestant Women's Club., 1965—; tchr. Bible sch., 1984-89; vol. tutor Lambs Elem., 1992, Trident Literacy Assn. (Laubach Literacy Action cert. 1992); coun. rep. Charleston AFB parish coun., 1988—; mem. Rocketeers Actors Group, Goals 2000 com. 1993—, Barnabas Outreach program, 1991—, Clown Ministry Charleston AFB, 1993—; chairperson Helping Hands Charleston AFB, 1991—, Voyagers Sunday Sch. Class Project, Summerville Homeless Shelter Charleston AFB, 1993—, Publicity Protestant Women, 1993—; vol. Lambs Elem., 1992—, Twin Oaks Retirement Ctr., 1992—, Barnabas Outreach Com., 1991—, Military Retirees, 1994—; counselor Jr. Achievement Program, 1994; mem. Charleston Raptor Ctr., 1996, S.C. Homeless Shelter Planning com., 1995-96, Am. Indian Heritage Coun., 1996; vol. tutor Lambs Elem., Charleston County, S.C., 1990—, jr. achievement counselor, 1992—, career day spkr., 1998 Recipient 1,000 Hours award Air Force Times, 1971, 1st Pl. award Designer Craftsman show, 1967-71, Dedicated Svc. award Charleston AFB, 1981, Hurricane Hugo Hero award, 1989, 1st Pl. award Bake-Off Contest YMCA, 1981, Hist. Charleston Trail Hike award Cub Scouts, 1988, Family Svcs. Vol. of Quar. award, 1990, Family Svcs. 6,000 Hour award, 1990, Golden Poet award, 1991, 1992, In a Different Light award Libr. Congress, 1991; named Enlisted Wife of Yr., Charleston AFB, 1974, Family Svcs. Vol. of Quarter Charleston AFB, 1990, Family Svcs. 6000 Hour award, 1991, Outstanding Vol. Svc. award Operation Desert Shield/Storm, 1991, Family Svcs. Spl. Recognition award, 1991, Appreciation acknowledgement Pres. of U.S., 1991, 98-99, First Lady Barbara Bush, 1992, Pres. of U.S., 1994, First Lady Hillary Clinton, 1994, Disting. Vol. award Charleston County Sch. Dist., 1995, Retiree Volunteer of the Quarter Charleston AFB, 1995, Vol. of Month Lambs Elem. Sch., 1995, Voting Slogan award Sec. Def., 1995, Family Svcs. Vol. of Quarter, 1996, Disting. Vol. award Lambs Elem., 1995-98, Family Mag. Poster/Display award Charleston Air Force Base, 1998, Disting. Vol. award Charleston County Sch. Bd., 1995-99, Vol. of Month Lambs Elem., 1998. Mem. Nat. Trust Hist. Preservation, Smithsonian Inst., Charleston AFB Non-Commd. Officers' Wives Club (pres. 1971-73, publicity chmn. 1969-70, wife of month 1967, wife of quarter 1973), Rocketeers Actors Group, Friends of Dock St.-Ushers. Avocations: cooking, sewing, collecting antiques, writing, decorating.

GRIGGS, CELIA JOSEPHINE, music educator; d. John Joseph and Dee Pickens Bryan; m. William Mace Griggs; children: Amy Katherine Cliett, Christy Lee Sheives, Paul Stephen Stanford. BME, Tex. Christian U., Ft. Worth, 1972. Cert. All Level Music Grades K-12 Tex., 1972, Provisional Life/Elementary 1-8 TX Dept of Educ, 1972. Music tchr. Everman ISD, Tex., 1973—76, Port Arthur ISD, Tex., 1976—77; jr. high math tchr., elem. music admin. asst. Cathedral Christian Sch., Beaumont, Tex., 1983—2000; math. tchr. Dayton ISD, Tex., 2000—01; music tchr. Nederland ISD, Tex., 2001—. Ch. organist First United Meth. Ch., Port Neches, Tex., 1992—2004. Mem. Hillcrest Bapt. Ch., Nederland, Tex., 2000—06. Mem.: Tex. Music Educators, Alpha Delta Kappa (treas. 2006—), Delta Kappa Gamma. Avocations: reading, piano, camping. Office Phone: 409-722-4324.

GRIGGS, LINDA L., lawyer; b. May 20, 1949; BA, Smith Coll., 1971; JD, U. Cin. Coll. Law, 1974. Bar: OH 1974, DC 1980. Spl. counsel SEC Division Corp. Fin.; chief counsel to chief acct. SEC; ptnr., bus. & fin. practice group Morgan, Lewis & Bockius LLP, Washington. Office: Morgan, Lewis & Bockius LLP 1111 Pennsylvania Ave NW Washington DC 20004 Office Phone: 202-739-5245. Office Fax: 202-739-3001. Business E-Mail: lgriggs@morganlewis.com.

GRIGGS, NINA M., realtor; b. NYC, Sept. 21, 1932; d. John Malcolm Miller and Kathryn Ruth Wilenzick; m. Charles Guy Moseley, Aug. 28, 1954 (dec. Feb. 1970); children: Charles Edward Keeble Moseley, Kathryn Drew Moseley Kristofik; m. Bancroft Gerardi Davis, Dec. 31, 1971 (dec. Dec. 1980); m. Richard Curtis Miles, Feb. 5, 1983 (dec. Sept. 1987); m. Northam Lee Griggs, Feb. 13, 1993 (dec. Mar. 2002). BA, Vassar Coll., 1954; MA, U. Va., 1956; postgrad., Columbia U. Exec. assoc., part-time rsch. assoc., 1961-63; founder, pres. Adventures Abroad, Ltd., 1964-71; also asst. to dir. profl. exams. divn. Psychol. Corp., N.Y.C., 1968-71; program officer Internat. Inst. Ednl. Planning/UNESCO, Paris, 1971-72; program adminstr. French and

German lang. tchg. asst. prog. Inst. Internat. Edn., N.Y.C., 1973-85; dir. women's program Internat. Exec. Svc. Corps, 1988-91; real estate associate New England Land Co, Greenwich. Founder, dir. Women's Talent Corps, 1965-67; mem. N.Y. Jr. League; dir. Masters Nursery and Children's Ctr., 1972-81. Author: U.S. Citizenship Today, 1963; editor: (with Kertis, O'Driscoll) English Language and Orientation Programs in the United States, 1978, 80; contbr. articles to profl. jours. Trustee, chmn. nominating com. Dobbs Sch., 1968-71. Mem. Hyannisport Club, N.Y. Jr. League, Harvard Club of N.Y., Delta Delta Delta. Home: 9 Country Rd Westport CT 06880-2524 Office: New England Land Co 783 North St Greenwich CT 06831-3105 Personal E-mail: ninagriggs@aol.com.

GRIGGS, ROZELLEN, elementary school educator; b. Union City, Ky., July 21, 1919; d. Samuel Ogg Griggs and Nannie Ellen Minor. BS in Edn., Ea. Ky. State U., 1943; M, U. Ky., 1950. Tchr. to prin. Madison County Elem. Sch., Ky., 1940—43; tchr. to supr. Erlanger (Ky.) Elem. Sch., 1943—48, Ft. Thomas (Ky.) Elem. Sch., 1948—85; supr. student tchrs. No. Ky. U., Highland Heights, 1985—2002. Mem.: No. Ky. Tchrs. Assn. (pres.), Ft. Thomas Woman's Club (pres. 1990—92), Delta Kappa Gamma (state pres.). Democrat. Home: 822 N Ft Thomas Ave Fort Thomas KY 41075 Personal E-mail: rozeller@yahoo.com.

GRIGSBY, SHARLYN ANN, human resources specialist; b. Greevsville, SC, Nov. 6, 1949; d. Defoy and Nannie Ruth Palmer; 1 child, Kenan Dion. BA cum laude, Knoxville Coll., 1971; MA, Trinity Coll., 1975. Personnel mgmt. specialist Dept. of Navy, Wash., DC, 1974—75, US Dept of Treas, Wash., 1975—79; supr. personnel mgmt. specialist US Dept. of Treas., Wash., 1979—80; sr. personnel mgmt. specialist US Dept. of Treas. Office of Sec., Wash., 1981—87, equal employment opportunity comm. dir., 1987—92; dir. of personnel Nat. Labor Relations Bd., Wash., 1992—99; dir. civil svcs. personnel mgmt. US Dept of State, Bur. of Human Resources, Wash., 1999—. Mem.: Internat. Personnel Mgmt. Assn., Alpha Kappa Alpha Sorority, Inc (v.p. Theta Omega Omega Chpt. 1999—2000, pres. Theta Omega Omega Chp. 2001—02, Pres. of Yr. Large Chpt. North Atlantic Region 2002). Democrat. Bapt. Office: US Dept of State 2401 E St NW Washington DC 20522 Office Fax: 202-663-2261. E-mail: sagkdg@aol.com.

GRILLO, JANET, film producer; m. David O. Russell. Assoc. prodr.: (films) Pump Up the Volume, 1990; Love Crimes, 1992; Who's the Man?, 1993; exec. prodr.: House Party 2, 1991, Hangin' With the Homeboys, 1991, House Party 3, 1994, Spanking the Monkey, 1994, Joe the King, 1999; prodr.: Searching for Paradise, 2002. Office: New Line 888 7th Ave Fl 19 New York NY 10106-1997 Fax: 212-649-4966.

GRIM, ELLEN TOWNSEND, retired art educator; b. Boone County, Ind., Nov. 1, 1921; d. Horace Wright and Sibyl Conklin (Lindley) Townsend; m. Robert Little Grim, Apr. 5, 1952; children: Nancy Ellen Grim Garcia, Howard Robert. Student, Our Lady of the Lake U., San Antonio, Tex., 1939-41, U. Tex., Austin, 1941-42; BA in Art, U. Wash., Seattle, 1946; MA in Art, UCLA, 1950; postgrad., Otis Art Inst., L.A., 1970-71. Cert. secondary tchr., Calif. Art tchr., chairperson secondary Calif. and L.A. Unified Sch. Dist., 1947—82; retired, 1982; artist L.A., 1975—. Guest speaker on art TV and cable, L.A., 1993. One-woman shows include Ventura County Mus. Art, 1982, Riverside Mcpl. Mus., 1984, Craft and Folk Art Mus., L.A., 1986, S.W. Mus., L.A., 1987, Calif. Heritage Mus., 1991, Brand Art Ctr., Glendale, 1996, Wurdermann Gallery, L.A., 1997, Kraft Gallery, L.A., 2005, 06, Village Square Gallery, Montrose, Calif., 2005, 06, others. 1st lt. USMC, 1943-45. Recipient Purchase prize Gardena Fine Arts Collection, 1982, Watercolor West award San Diego Watercolor Soc. Internat., 1983, N.Mex. Watercolor Soc. award, 1989, 1st pl. award Fine Arts Fedn., 1987, 1st pl. award Art Educators L.A., 1988, 89, 1st pl. award Collage Artists Am., 1995, 2002, Brand Art Ctr. Watercolor West award, 1999, Painting award Valley Inst. of Visual Art, San Fernando Valley, 1999, 2001, Long Beach Arts painting award, 1999, 2000. Mem.: Alliance of Women Vets., Women Marines Assn., Collage Artists Am. (1st Place award 1995, 2002), Pasadena Soc. Artists (Painting award 1986, 1988, 1990, 1992—93, 1999, 2001—02), L.A. Art Assn. (bd. dirs. 1993—95), Women Painters West (membership chair, mem.-at-large 1983—89, Painting award 1985—86, 1989, 1992—93, 1995, 1999—2001, Best of Show award 2000), Nat. Watercolor Soc. (historian 1989—90, Painting award 1984, 1999—2000), Women in Mil Svc. for Am., Pi Lambda Theta, Alpha Phi. Avocations: Native American and Latin American culture, travel, Southwestern history.

GRIMALDI, KATHLEEN GALVIN, literature and language educator, poet; b. Waterbury, Conn., Mar. 19, 1942; d. Francis Xavier Galvin and Margaret Cecelia Brett; m. Philip Vito Grimaldi, Apr. 4, 1970; children: Lynnette Marie, Joseph Christopher. BA in English, Fordham U., 1968; MA in Liberal Studies, Stony Brook U., 1972, Immaculate Conception Sem., 1983. Cert. Secondary Edn. English Tchr. NY, 1968. English tchr. Cardinal Spellman HS, Bronx, NY, 1968—70, Mid. Country Sch. Dist., Centereach, NY, 1975—97; asst. to dean St. Joseph's Coll., Patchoque, NY, 1998—2003, English lectr., 1985—. Co-founder HS Performing Arts, Centereach, 1985—89, tchr., 1985—89; participant Frost Festival Poetry, 2003, 04, 05. Poet: poem Dungarvan Water Dance, 1996, Angels' Wings, 1997—98, Question Asked by Granddaughter, 2004. Tchrs.' rep. Am. Fedn. Tchrs., Centereach, 1976—78; pres. Infant Jesus Sch. Bd., Port Jefferson, NY, 1983—84. Mem.: Acad. Am. Poets, Internat. Soc. Poets (Editor's Choice award 1998). Avocations: hiking, travel, sewing, reading.

GRIMES, DAPHNE BUCHANAN, priest, artist; b. Tulsa, Apr. 12, 1929; d. George Sidney and Dorothy Elnora (Dodds) Buchanan; m. Thomas Edward Grimes, Nov. 6, 1964 (dec. Oct., 1986). BFA, U. Houston, 1952; MA, Columbia U., 1954; MA in Religion, Episcopal Seminary of the Southwest, 1985. Ordained deacon Episcopalian Ch., 1982, priest, 1986. Tchr. history Rockland County Day Sch., Nyack, N.Y., 1959-61; dir. Am. Sch., Tunis, Tunisia, 1962-64; priest vicar St. Andrew's Ch., Meeteetse, Wyo., 1987-90; bd. dirs., pres. Thomas the Apostle Ctr., Cody, Wyo., 1990—; assoc. priest Christ Ch., Cody, 1994—. Stewardship chmn. Diocese Wyo., 1979-85, mem. bd. diocesan coun., 1987-90, chmn. social svcs., 1987-91. Author poems, Journeys of the Spirit, 2005, Journeys in Time and Space, 2006. Chaplain West Park County Hosp., Cody, Wyo., 1981-84, West Park County Long Term Care Ctr., Cody, 1982-99; bd. dirs. Park County Arts Coun., 1995-98. Mem. Cody Country Arts League, Cmty. of Celebration (spiritual adv. 1990—), Cmty. of the Holy Spirit (assoc.), Compass Rose Soc. (bd. dirs.), N.Am. Regional Coun., St. George Coll. Jerusalem (bd. dirs.) Avocations: reading, science, theology, travel, journaling. Office: Thomas The Apostle Ctr 16 Thomas The Apostle Rd Cody WY 82414-9601 Personal E-mail: daphneg@tritel.net.

GRIMES, HEILAN YVETTE, publishing executive; b. Hamilton, Ohio, Sept. 16, 1949; d. J and Claudette (Hinkle) G. Grad., New Eng. Sch. Photography, 1987. Founder, pres. Dot & Line Graphics, 1975—, Color Computer Weekly, 1982—, Hollow Earth Pub., 1983—. Adj. prof. U. Mass., Lowell. Author: Norse Mythology, 1984, Legend of Niebelungenlied, 1984, Using QuarkXPress 3.3, 1994, Beginning Internet, 1994, Filemaker Pro Developer's Guide, 1997, Netiquette and E-Commerce Marketing, 2004, Runes, 2005; founder Byte Mag., 1974, Macpower Mag., 1993 Democrat. Avocations: magic, juggling, hiking, travel. Office: PO Box 51480 Boston MA 02205-1480 Office Phone: 617-249-0161. E-mail: yvettegr@hotmail.com.

GRIMES, KRISTEN, public health service officer; b. Milwaukee, Wis., 1976; d. Brophy; m. Matthew Grimes, 2003. BSc in Cmty. Health Edn., U. Wis., La Crosse, Wis., 1999; MA in Orgnl. Mgmt., U. Phoenix, Online, 2004. Cert. Health Edn. Specialist Nat. Commn. for Health Edn. Credentialing, 1999. Hiv/sexual assault prevention outreach worker Sixteenth St. Cmty. Health Ctr., Milw., 1999; youth at risk prevention specialist AIDS Resource Ctr. of Wis., Appleton, Wis., 1999—2000; pub. health educator ii City Milw. Health Dept., Milw. Adolescent Pregnancy Prevention Consortium, Milw., 2000—01; project mgr. Children's Health Alliance of Wis., Milw., 2001—; cons. Creative Memories, West Allis, 2005—. Mem.: Am. AAHPERD, Wis. Pub. Health Assn. Office: Children s Health Alliance Wis 1533 N River Ctr Dr Milwaukee WI 53212 Office Phone: 414-390-2189. Business E-Mail: kgrimes@chw.org.

GRIMES, MARGARET KATHERINE, English educator; b. Thomasville, N.C., May 20, 1955; d. Van Dolan and Edith Catherine (Bevan) G. BA, Catawba Coll., 1977; MA, U. N.C., 1978; PhD, U. N.C., Greensboro, 1993. Instr. Western Piedmont C.C., Morganton, N.C., 1979-83; teaching fellow U. N.C., Greensboro, 1983-88; instr. English Louisburg (N.C.) Coll., 1988-90; asst. prof. English, Ferrum (Va.) Coll., 1991-92, adj. instr., 1992—95, acad. advisor, 1995—97, pub. rels. feature writer, 1994, dir. First Yr. Experience, 1997—2003, assoc. prof. English, 2003—. Home: 730 Thompson Ridge Rd Ferrum VA 24088-2732 Office: Ferrum Coll Ferrum VA 24088 Office Phone: 540-365-4264. E-mail: kgrimes@ferrum.edu.

GRIMES, MARTHA, author; b. Pittsburgh, Pa. d. D.W. and June (Dunnington) G.; div.; 1 s.: Kent Van Holland BA, MA, U. Md. Formerly instr. English U. Iowa, Iowa City; asst. prof. Frostburg State Coll., Frostburg, Md.; prof. Montgomery Coll., Takoma Park, Md., 1970—; instr., writing seminars program Johns Hopkins Univ. Author: mystery novels The Man With a Load of Mischief, 1981, The Old Fox Deceiv'd, 1982, The Anodyne Necklace, 1983 (Nero Wolfe Award for best mystery of yr.1983), The Dirty Duck, 1984, The Jerusalem Inn, 1984, Help the Poor Struggler, 1985, The Deer Leap, 1985, I Am the Only Running Footman, 1986, The Five Bells and Bladebone, 1987 (NY Times Bestseller), The Old Silent, 1989 (NY Times Bestseller), Send Bygraves, 1989, The Old Contemptibles, 1991 (NY Times Bestseller), End of the Pier, 1992, The Horse You Came In On, 1993, Rainbow's End, 1994, Hotel Paradise, 1996, The Case Has Altered, 1997, The Stargazey, 1998, Biting the Moon, 1999, Lamorna Wink, 2000, Hotel Paradise, 1994, Cold Flat Junction, 2001, The Blue Last, 2001 (NY Times Bestseller), The Grave Maurice, 2002, Foul Matter, 2003, The Winds of Change, 2004 (Publishers Weekly Bestseller). Mailing: c/o Viking Pub Author Mail Penguin Putnam 375 Hudson New York NY 10014

GRIMES, NANCY GUERARD, secondary school educator; b. Nashville, Mar. 13, 1953; d. Franz Engels and Mary Ann Rylander Guerard; m. Robert Dale Grimes, May 26, 1975; children: Robert D., Franz E.G., Amelia Rose. BA, U. South, Sewanee, Tenn., 1975; MS, U. Tenn., Knoxville, 1978. Tchr. Sacred Heart Sch., Knoxville, 1976—78; tchr., dept. chair St. Bernard Acad., Nashville, 1978—85; tchr. U. Sch. Nashville, 1985—92, Harpeth Hall Sch., Nashville, 1992—, dept. chair, acad. dean, dir. curriculum. Mem. Jr. League, Nashville, 1992—. Recipient Excellence in Tchg. award, Harpeth Hall Sch., 2003. Democrat. Avocations: writing, reading, hiking, swimming. Office Phone: 615-298-8184.

GRIMES, PAMELA RAE, retired elementary school educator; b. Cumberland, Md., Dec. 30, 1943; d. Robert Elmer and Mary Evelyn (Hill) McFarland; m. George Edward Grimes, Feb. 9, 1962; children: George Edward Jr., Robert Eric, Jonathon William, David James, Richard Allen. AA, American River Coll., 1965; BA, MA, Calif. State U., Sacramento, 1975, adminstrv. credential, 1999; cert. in computer literacy, Sacramento Unified Sch. Dist., 1981. Cert. elem. tchr., Calif.; cert. adminstrv. credential. Tchr. aide O.W. Erlewine Elem. Sch., Sacramento, 1965-67, elem. gate tchr., 1969-71; tchr. aide Cohen Elem. Sch., Sacramento, 1967-69; libr., tchr. 1st through 6th grades Golden Empire Elem. Sch., Sacramento, 1979-89; tchr. Hubert Bancroft Elem. Sch., Sacramento, 1989-95; staff tng. specialist Literacy Curriculum & Instrn. Dept., 1995-97; reading coach Sacramento Unified Sch. Dist., 1998—2002; ret., 2002. Mentor tchr. Sacramento City Unified Sch. Dist., 1985-95; fellow, mem. Calif. History/Social Sci. course of study, 1991; mem. libr./lit. course of study, 1975, mem. CORE lit. com., 1979, mem. lang. arts assessment com., 1990—, mem. CLAS adv. com., 1993-94, mem. literacy task force, 1995-97, mem. adv. com. on assessment testing, 1995, co-chairperson 20-1 class size reduction program, mem. Young Authors program, mem. curriculum alignment project; literacy leader, facilitator CSIN, 1995—; No. Calif. coord. Ottawa U., 1991—; mem. lang. arts/literacy/ELD Task Force, 1996-97. Ednl. cons. Children's Mus. Com., 1985—, Sacramento History Ctr., 1985. Fellow Calif. Lit. Project, 1989, Area III Writing Project, 1988, Calif. Social Studies Inst., 1990. Fellow Calif. Geog. Inst., East Asian Humanities Inst.; mem. NEA, ASCD, SARA, CRA, IRA, Nat. Coun. Tchrs. English, Geography Inst. (mem. social studies project. stds. com. 1991), Calif. Alliance Elem. Edn., Calif. English Tchrs. Assn., Calif. Tchrs. Assn. Democrat. Methodist. Avocations: reading, writing, gardening. Home: 9005 Harvest Way Sacramento CA 95826-2203 Personal E-mail: grampam43@aol.com.

GRIMES, RUTH ELAINE, city planner; b. Palo Alto, Calif., Mar. 4, 1949; d. Herbert George and Irene (Williams) Baker; m. Charles A. Grimes, July 19, 1969 (div. 1981); 1 child, Michael; m. Roger L. Sharpe, Mar. 20, 1984; 1 child, Teresa AB summa cum laude, U. Calif., Berkeley, 1970, M City Planning, 1972. Coord. rsch. and evaluation Ctr. Ind. Living, Berkeley, 1972—74; planner City of Berkeley, 1974—76, analyst, 1976—83, sr. planner, 1983—2004, cons., 2004—. Bd. dirs. Vets. Asssistance Ctr., Berkeley, pres., 1978-93; bd. dirs. Berkeley Design Advocates, treas., 1987-94 Author: Berkeley Downtown Plan, 1988; contbr. numerous articles to profl. jours. and other publs Bd. dirs. Berkeley-Sakai Sister City Assn., pres., 1995-97; bd. dirs. Ctr. Ind. Living; mem. energy commn. City of Berkeley, 2005—, vice chair, 2006; bd. dirs. Cmty. Energy Svcs. Corp., pres. bd. dirs., 2006— Honored by Calif. State Assembly Resolution, 1988; Edwin Frank Kraft scholar, 1966 Mem. Am. Inst. Cert. Planners, Am. Planning Assn., Mensa, Lake Merrit Joggers and Striders (sec. 1986-89, pres. 1991-93, bd. dirs.), Lions Internat. (bd. dirs. Berkeley club 1992-94, 2000-02, v.p. 1997-98, pres. 1998-99, chair membership com. 1999-2000), U. Calif. Coll. Environ. Design Alumni Assn. (bd. dirs. 1992-98, treas. 1994-96, disting. alumnus com. 1997-2003) Avocation: long distance running. Home: 1330 Bonita Ave Berkeley CA 94709-1925

GRIMES, SALLY, marketing professional; m. Steve Grimes; 2 children. Grad., U. Chgo. Grad. Sch. Bus., 1997. With Kraft Foods, Inc., 1997—, brand mgr. e-commerce, dir. integrated mktg. North Am. grocery sector, 2005—. Named one of Top 40 Under 40, Crain's Chgo. Bus., 2006. Office: Kraft Foods Inc Three Lakes Dr Northfield IL 60093*

GRIMES, SUZANNE, publishing executive; married; 2 children. BA in Internat. Mgmt., Georgetown U. With NY Times; advt. dir. Success; with TV Guide, 1990—94, nat. advt. dir., 1994—95, sr. v.p., pub., 1995—97; pub. Women's Sports & Fitness, 1997—2000, Allure, 2000—01; pub., v.p. Glamour Mag., 2001—04; v.p. media group Conde Nast, 2004—. Office: Conde Nast 4 Times Sq New York NY 10036-6522

GRIMES, TERRIE LYNN, elementary school educator; b. Dallas, July 29, 1955; d. Robert Alexander and Ruth O. (Roberts) Heatherly; m. Boyd H. Grimes, Dec. 28, 1995. BS, U. North Tex., 1977, MEd, 1979. Cert. reading specialist. From title I tchr. to instrl. specialist Carrollton (Tex.) Farmers Br. Tex. Ind. Sch. Dist., 1977—2004, instrl. specialist Carrollton (Tex.) Farmers Br., 2004—. Named Outstanding Young Women of Am., 1981. Mem. AAUW (sec. 1991-92), NEA, Tex. State Tchrs. Assn., Carrollton-Farmers Branch Edn. Assn. (v.p., Friend of Edn. award 1982, scholarship 1985), U. North Tex. Alumni Assn., Phi Delta Kappa, Am. Mensa (cert. testing proctor). Baptist. Avocations: reading, travel, walking. Office: McLaughlin Elem Sch 1500 Webbs Chapel Rd Carrollton TX 75006-7741

GRIMES, TRESMAINE JUDITH RUBAIN, psychology educator; b. NYC, Aug. 3, 1959; d. Judith May (McIntosh) Rubain; m. Clarence Grimes, Jr., Dec. 22, 1984; children: Elena Joanna, Elijah Jeremy. BA, Yale U., 1980; MA, New Sch. for Social Rsch., 1982; MPhil, PhD, Columbia U., 1990. Advanced tchg. fellow Jewish Bd. Family and Childrens Svcs., N.Y.C., 1980-82; tchg./rsch. asst. Columbia U. Tchrs. Coll., N.Y.C., 1983—84; rschr., historian Youth Action Program, N.Y.C., 1984-86; psychologist Hale House for Infants, N.Y.C., 1986-89; asst. rschr. Bank St. Coll., N.Y.C., 1988; addiction program adminstr. Harlem Hosp. Ctr., N.Y.C., 1989-91; asst. prof. psychology S.C. State U., Orangeburg, 1991-96, assoc. prof., 1996—2000, chmn. psychology & sociology, 1998-2000; asst. prof. psychology Iona Coll., 2001—02, assoc. prof., 2002—. Adj. prof. psychology Tchrs. Coll., Columbia U., N.Y.C., 1990-91; adj. prof. Iona Coll., New Rochelle, N.Y., 2000-01. Named one of Outstanding Young Women of Am., 1981. Mem.: APA, Soc. for Psychol. Study of Social Issues, Soc. for Tchg. of Psychology, Ea. Psychol. Assn., Psi Chi, Kappa Delta Pi, Delta Sigma Theta. Democrat. Avocations: singing, drama. Office: Iona Coll 715 North Ave New Rochelle NY 10801 Home: 9 Woodbine Ave New Rochelle NY 10801-3207 Personal E-mail: newgrimes@yahoo.com. Business E-Mail: tgrimes@iona.edu.

GRIMES-DAVIS, DANNA ELIZABETH, elementary school educator, consultant; b. Tampa, Fla., Aug. 21, 1969; d. Virgil John Grimes and Jan Strickland; m. James Gordon Davis Jr.; children: Chance Reed, Carson Joel. BA, U. Ala., Tuscaloosa, 1991; M in Ednl. Leadership, U. Ctrl. Fla., Orlando, 2004. Art tchr. Orange County Pub. Schs., Orlando, Fla., tchr., instrnl. coach. Profl. developer Reading First Fla. Dept. Edn, Tallahassee. Mailing: 32302 Fish Hook Loop Wesley Chapel FL 33544-1635

GRIMLEY, JANET ELIZABETH, newspaper editor; b. Oelwein, Iowa, Dec. 3, 1946; d. Harold E. and Ida Mae Teague; m. Terry L. Grimley, June 15, 1968; 1 child, Brynn Sara Mae Grimley. BA, U. Iowa, Iowa City, 1969; attended, U. Wash., Seattle, 1979-82. Asst. mng. editor Seattle Post-Intelligencer; publs. dir. Marycrest Coll., Davenport, Iowa, 1969-70; reporter Quad-Cities Times, Davenport, Iowa, 1970-74, Seattle Post-Intelligence, Seattle, feature reporter and editor, 1976-95, asst. mng. editor, 1995—. Past pres. Am. Assn. Sunday and Feature Editors; mem. Newspaper Features Coun. Mem. Shoreline Strategic Planning Com., Seattle, 1993, Shorewood Site Coun., 1997-99, Shorewood Boosters; co-chair Shoreline Capitol/Bond Com., Seattle, 1994, Einstein Site Coun., Seattle, 1994-96; bd. dirs. Ctr. for Human Svcs. Mem. Junior League of Seattle (bd. dirs. 1989-90, exec. bd. 1991-92), Washington Athletic Club, City Club Seattle. Avocations: sailing, skiing, gardening. Office: Seattle Post Intelligencer 101 Elliott Ave W Ste 200 Seattle WA 98119-4295

GRIMM, MELISSA, sports association executive; Port dir. Phila. and Camden; sr. cons. Phila. Sports Congress Phila. Convention & Visitors Bur.; exec. dir. Phila. 2016 Working Group, 2006—. Named one of 40 Under 40, Phila. Bus. Jour., 2006. Office: Phila Sports Congress 1700 Market St, Ste 3000 Philadelphia PA 19103 Office Phone: 215-636-3417.*

GRIMM, NANCY JO See MCCLAIN, SYLVIA

GRIMME, A. JEANNETTE, retired elementary school educator, retired small business owner, volunteer; b. Eaton, Ohio, Jan. 13, 1921; d. Charles H. and Nelle L. (Scott) G. BA, Ohio Wesleyan U., 1943; MA, Oberlin Sch. Theology, 1953. Tchr. Eaton Pub. Sch., 1943-47, Zanesville (Ohio) Religious Edn. Coun., 1947-49; dir., tchr. Findlay (Ohio) Religious Edn. Coun., 1949-64; tchr. Findlay Pub. Schs., 1964-65, Consol. Dist. 2, Mo., 1965-83; dir. Christian edn. Unity of Independence, 1983-85. Co-owner Bess's Tea Room, Independence, 1996-98. Author: What is the Church, 1953; editor: Mutant Message Downunder (by Marlo Morgan), 1991; contbr. chpt. to books and articles to profl. jours. Program coord. Shepherd's Ctr. of Independence, 1987—, pres., 2000—. Mem. AAUW, Mission Work Area, Edn. Work Area, Raytown Ret. Tchrs. (pres. 1989-90), Delta Kappa Gamma. Meth. Avocations: travel, clown ministry.

GRIMMER, BEVERLEY SUE, consumer products company executive; b. Olathe, Kans., June 9, 1950; d. Edward Mathines Rice and Jessie LaVaun (Cade) Waymire; m. Danny Joe San Romani, June 4, 1977 (div. May 1991); 1 child, Justin (dec.); m. Gary G. Grimmer, June 21, 1992. Student, Kans. State Tchrs. Coll., 1968-71, U. Kans., 1975-77. Employee trainer, dept. mgr. T.G.&Y. Stores, Emporia, Kans., 1968-70; office mgr. Office of Staff Judge Adv. 3d Armored Div., Frankfurt, Fed. Republic of Germany, 1971-75, Don W. Lill, Atty. at Law, Emporia, 1976-77; instr., sub. tchr. Kodiak (Ala.) C.C. and Kodiak Pub. Sch. System, 1979-81; legal sec. Kaito & Ishida, Honolulu, 1983-84; adminstr. Alcantara & Frame, Honolulu, 1984-86; ind. contractor Hughes Hubbard & Reed, N.Y., Honolulu, 1986-88; paralegal Carlsmith, Ball, Wichman, Murray, Case, Mukai & Ichiki, Honolulu, 1988-91; spl. agt. Vanuatu (Hawaii) Maritime Agy., 1989—; ch. adminstr. Ctrl. Union Ch., Honolulu, 1991-94; owner Gentle Memories, Kailua, Hawaii, 1995—. Gubernatorial coun. appointee Juvenile Justice State Adv. Coun., 1993-94; mem. women's health work com. State of Hawaii, Commn. on Status of Women, 1994. 1st v.p. Christmas in April Oahu, 1995, bd. dirs., 1995-97; auction pub. chair Acad. Arts Guild, 1993; mem. Contemporary Arts Mus.; cmty. rels. and arrangements chairs for Tuxes 'n Tails Black and White Ball, Hawaiian Humane Soc., 1993, 94, silent auction Walkin in the Country, Boys & Girls Club; mem. Hawaii Lupus Found.; bd. dirs. Armed Forces YMCA, 1995-97; mem. vestry St. Christopher's Ch., 1995-98; chair silent auction Contemp '98, 100th Ann. Gala Honolulu Symphony, 1999. Recipient Order of Golden Swivel Shot award Comdt. USCG, 1981, 89, 1st Runner-up Maritime Week Maritime Employee award Propeller Club U.S., 1986, Letter of Appreciation, Dept. Navy, 1983, Cert. of Commendation, U.S. Army, 1975. Mem. Am. Heart Assn. (chair Celebrity Celebration 1994, silent auction co-chair 1996 Heart Ball, co-chair 1997 Heart Ball, Mary Lou Brogan award 1997), Coast Guard Officers' Spouses Club (nominating chair 1989, pres. 1982, 87, 88), Awa Lau Wahine (Coast Guard rep. 1988, 87, corr. sec. 1983, Boutiki chair 1982), Rotary (vice chair Friends of Foster Kids Picnic 1994, chair 1995), Jr. League (cmty. v.p. 1993, rec. sec. 1990, sustainer chair Honolulu 1999, sustainer chair 75th Gala 1999), Navy League, Propeller Club Port of Honolulu (bd. govs. alt. 1990), Hawaii Legal Aux. (v.p. 1994, pub./publs. chair 1994). Republican. Episcopalian. Avocations: golf, tennis, needlepoint, reading, community voluntarism. Home and Office: 159 Kakahiaka St Kailua HI 96734-3474

GRIMMER, MARGOT, dancer, choreographer, director; b. Chgo., Apr. 5, 1944; d. Vernon and Ann (Radville) G.; m. Weymouth Kirkland; 1 child, Ashley Samantha Grimmer Kirkland. Student, Northwestern U., 1964-68. Dancer N.Y. City Ballet prodn. of Nutcracker, Chgo., 1956-57, Kansas City Starlight Theatre, 1958, St. Louis Mcpl. Theatre, 1959, Chgo. TentHouse-Music Theater, 1960-61, Lyric Opera Ballet, Chgo., 1961, 63-66, 68, Ballet Russe de Monte Carlo, N.Y.C., 1962, Ruth Page Internat. Ballet, Chgo., 1965-70; dancer-choreographer, artistic dir. Am. Dance Co., Chgo., 1972—. Dancer, choreographer Bob Hope Show, Milw., 1975, Washington Bicentennial Performance, Kennedy Ctr., 1976, Woody Guthrie Benefit Concerts, 1976-77, Assyrian Cultural Found., Chgo., 1977-78, Iranian Consulate Performance, Chgo., 1978, Israeli Consulate Concert, Chgo., 1980, Chgo. Coun. Fine Arts Programs, 1978-87, U.S. Boating Indsl. Show, 1981-2001; dir.-tchr. Am. Dance Sch., 1971—; tchr. master classes U. Ill., 1975, 83, Anderson Hall, Occidental and Sebastopol Cmty. Ctr., Calif., 1988-90, Park Point Club, Santa Rosa, Calif., 1988-89, Oakland (Calif.) Dance Collective, 1989—, U. Calif., Berkeley, 1995, Mills Coll., 1996; soloist Showcase to Benefit Sebastopol Ctr. for Arts, Calif., 1990, benefit performances Chgo. Area Settlement Houses, Lake Forest, Ill., 1991-94, Milw. Charities, 1992; choreographer Oakland (Calif.) Dance Collective performances at Zellerbach Theatre, U. Calif., Berkeley, 1995, Mills Coll. Theatre, Oakland, Calif., 1996, Oakland Arts in the Schs. performance Series and Nutcracker Highlights, 1997, 98, 99, 00, 01, 02; choreographer Reno and Las Vegas performances of My Way (Sinatra tribute), 1998, For George & the Duke (Gershwin-Ellington tribute), 1999, Decades In Song & Dance, 2000, Fred & Ginger, 2001 Best of Broadway, 2002, Thanks for the Memories (Bob Hope Tribute), 2003, Chicago Musical, 2004; appeared in TV commls. and indsl. films for Libbys Foods, Sears, GM, others, 1963—, also in feature film Risky Business, 1982; soloist in ballet Repertory Workshop, CBS-TV, 1964, dance film Statics (Internat. Film award), 1967; soloist in concern Ravinia, 1973; important works includ ballets In-A-Gadda-Da-Vida, 1972, The Waste Land, 1973, Rachmanioff: Theme and Variations, 1973, Le Baiser de la Fee and Sonata,

1974, Four Quartets, 1974, Am. Export, 1975, Earth, Wind and Fire, 1976, Blood, Sand & Empire, 1977, Disco Fever, 1978, Pax Romana, Xanadu, 1979, Ishmael, 1980, Vertigo, 1982, Eye in the Sky, 1984, Frankie Goes to Hollywood, 1986, Power House Africano, 1987, Cole Porter Tribute, 1994, In the Mood, 1995, The Cranberry Pieces, 1996, Ozymandias, 1998, Ray of Light, 1999, All That, 2000, Santanatural, 2001, So Addictive, 2002, Return of No Point, 2003, Cold Play, 2004. Ill. Arts Coun. grantee, 1972-75, 78; Nat. Endowments of the Arts grantee, 1973-74. Mem. Actors Equity Assn., SAG, Am. Guild Mus. Artists. Home: PO Box 2495 Sebastopol CA 95473-2495 Office Phone: 707-823-8544. E-mail: wk@dejavuvideography.com.

GRIMSLEY, BESSIE BELLE GATES, retired special education educator; b. Iola, Kans., Feb. 22, 1938; d. Dwight Leonard and Ruth Bebee (Colwell) Gates; m. Dale Dee Grimsley, Feb. 14, 1959; 1 child, Lendi Lea Grimsley Bland. BS in Edn., Emporia State U., 1962, MS in Edn., 1970. Music tchr., Hamilton, Kans., 1957-58; music tchr. Belle Plaine, Kans., 1958-59; 3rd grade tchr. Johnson, Kans., 1959-61; mid. sch. tchr. Kendall, Kans., 1961-63-68; kindergarten tchr. Alma, Kans., 1968-69; music, reading, phys. edn., math. tchr. Council Grove, Kans., 1969-94; Title I reading and math tchr., 1994-2000. Polit. chmn. USD #417 Tchr.'s Orgn., Council Grove, 1992-94, pres., 1987-89, uniserve rep., 1987-93, sec., 1997-2000; adv. prof. Emporia State U., 2003. Vice chmn. Lyon County Dem. com., 1988-94; mem. planning bd. Americus, Kans. zoning commn., 1985-97; mem. Americus Fall Festival com., parade chmn., 1992-94, 97; pres. WKDC, 1997-98; chmn. Americus Days, 1997-2000. Mem. Americus C. of C. (pres. 1993-95, 97-99), Ret. Tchrs. Assn. (pres.-elect), Emporia Antique Auto Club (sec.-treas. 1993-94, pres. 2001-2003), 4-H Alumni, VFW Aux., Am. Legion Aux., Woman's Kans. Day Club (2d v.p. 1994, state pres. 1997-98), Lyon County Hist. Soc. (pres. 2004-05), Antique Tractors Club (sec.), Flint Hills Antique Power Assn. (sec., hist. 2004—), Emporia Area Ret. Sch. Pers. (pres. elect 2005, pres., 2006—), Delta Kappa Gamma (pres. 2000-2002) Presbyterian. Avocations: tennis, tap dancing, running, softball, bowling. Home: PO Box 147 Americus KS 66835-0147

GRIMWOOD, HELEN PERRY, lawyer; b. Phoenix, Aug. 9, 1953; BSBA magna cum laude, Univ. Ariz., 1973; JD magna cum laude, Ariz. State Univ., 1980. CPA Ariz., 1979. Law clerk Judge L. Ray Haire, Ariz. Ct. of Appeals, 1980—81, Judge William C. Canby Jr., U.S. Ct. of Appeals, Ninth Cir., 1981—82; judge pro tempore Ariz. Superior, Maricopa County, 1993—, Ariz Ct. of Appeals, 1998; ptnr. Grimwald Law Firm plc, Phoenix. Named a Fellow, Am. Bar Found., 2000; named one of the Valley's Most Influential in Law, Bus. Journal, 2000; recipient Friedman award for excellence in legal edn., Maricopa County Bar Assn., 1995, Justice Gordon award for pro bono svc., 1996, Solin award for outstanding leadership, Ariz. Women Lawyer's Assn. Mem.: Ariz. Women Lawyer's Assn. (pres. 1996—97), Nat. Conf. of Women's Bar Assn. (dir. 1977—), Maricopa County Bar Assn. (dir. 1992—96, chair, comml. litig. CLE Com. 1993—96), Ariz. State Bar Assn. (mem., bd. gov. 1997—, pres.-elect 2004). Office: Grimwood Law Firm plc Ste 940 3101 N Central Ave Phoenix AZ 85012-2666

GRINDAL, MARY ANN, former sales professional; b. Michigan City, Ind., Sept. 9, 1942; d. James Paxton and Helen Evelyn (Koivisto) Gleason; m. Bruce Theodore Grindal, June 12, 1965 (div. Sept. 1974); 1 child, Matthew Bruce. BSBA, Ind. U., 1965. Sec. African studies program Ind. U., Bloomington, 1965-66; rsch. aide Ghana, West Africa, 1966-68; exec. sec. divsn. biol. scis. Ind. U., Bloomington, 1968-69; office asst. Dean of Students office Middlebury (Vt.) Coll., 1969-70; exec. sec. Remo, Inc., North Hollywood, Calif., 1974-76; sec., asst. to product mgrs. in cosmetic and skin care Redken Labs., Canoga Park, Calif., 1976-79; various sec. and exec. sec. positions L.A., 1979-81, 85-89; exec. sec. Sargent Industries, Burbank, Calif., 1981-85; sales asst. Chyron Graphics, Burbank, Calif., 1989-97; adminstrv. sec. divsn. instructional svcs. Burbank Unified Sch. Dist., 1998—. Author of poems and essays. Mem. U.S. Navy Meml. Found. Mem. DAR (chpt. registrar 1988-91, chpt. regent 1991-94, chpt. chmn. pub. rels. and pub. 1994-2001, chpt. chaplain 1994-2001, mem. spkrs. staff 1995-2001, state chmn. Am. Heritage 1994-96, state chmn. Calif. DAR scholarship com. 1996-98), Daus. of Union Vets. of Civil War, 1861-65, Inc., Ladies of the Grand Army of the Republic, Nat. Soc. Dames of the Ct. of Honor (state chaplain 1997-2001). Episcopalian. Avocations: travel, writing, genealogy.

GRINNAN, KATIE, artist; b. Richmond, Va., 1970; Attended, Studio Arts Ctr. Internat., Florence, Italy, 1991; BFA in Painting, Carnegie Mellon U., 1992; attended, Skowhega Sch. Painting & Sculpture, Skowhegan Maine, 1992; MFA in Sculpture, UCLA, 1999. One-woman shows include Rock Bottom, ACME, L.A., 2001, 2003, Whitney Mus. Am. Art at Altria, 2003, exhibited in group shows at UCLA MFA Thesis Exhbn., New Wight Gallery, LA, 1998, As I love you you become more pretty, 937 Hudson Ave., LA, 2000, Legal Paper Work, Beyond Baroque, LA, 2000, katie grinnan alice konitz christie frields, Guggenheim Gallery, Chapman U., Calif., 2000, Snapshot, UCLA Hammer Mus., 2001, Sharing Sunsets, Mus. Contemporary Art, Tucson, 2001, Bommerang: Collector's Choice, Exit Art, NYC, 2001, Anti-Form, Soc. Contemporary Photog., Kans. City, Mo., 2002, Officina Am., Galeria D'Arte Monderna, Bologna, Italy, 2002, Drive-By, Reynolds Gallery, Richmond, Va., 2002, Strolling Through an Ancient Shrine & Garden, ACME, LA, 2002, Out of the Ground Into the Sky Out of the Sky Into the Ground, Pond, San Francisco, 2002, Wit Form Rainbow (Part I), The Project, LA, 2003, Whitney Biennial, Whitney Mus. Am. Art, NYC, 2004, Material Faith, Kontainer Gallery, LA, 2004, Real World: Dissolving Space of Experience, Modern Art Oxford, England, 2004, Art on Paper, Weatherspoon Art Mus., U. NC, 2004. Mailing: c/o ACME 6150 Wilshire Blvd #1 Los Angeles CA 90048

GRINSTEIN RICHMAN, LOUISE SONIA, mathematics professor; b. Buffalo, Sept. 28, 1929; d. Mark and Esther (Alpert) G.; m. Jack Richman, Aug. 4, 1985. BA, U. Buffalo, 1950, MA, 1952; postgrad., U. Mich., 1953—56; PhD, Columbia U., 1965. Lectr. Hunter Coll. CUNY, 1956—58; systems analyst Rep. Aviation, Farmingdale, NY, 1958—61; ops. rsch. analyst System Devel. Corp., Paramus, NJ, 1961—63; programmer N.Y. Naval Shipyard, Bklyn., 1963—65; ops. rsch. analyst Naval Supply R & D Facility, Bayonne, NJ, 1965—66; prof. Kingsborough C.C. CUNY, Bklyn., 1966—92; prof. emerita Kingsborough C.C. CUNY, Bklyn., 1992—. Referee Historia Math., 1979; mem. adv. bd. Community Rev., 1979; referee Maths. and Computer Edn., 1985—. Co-editor: Calculus: Readings From Mathematics Teacher, 1977, Women of Mathematics, 1987 (Best Ref. Book award 1987), Mathematics Education in Secondary Schools and Two Year Colleges, 1988, Women in Chemistry and Physics, 1993, Women in the Biological Sciences, 1997, Encyclopedia of Math Education, 2001; author: Mathematical Book Review Index, 1800-1940, 1992; mem. editl. bd. UMAP Jour., 1983-86; contbr. articles to profl. jours U. Mich. fellow, 1953-56. Mem. Am. Math. Soc., Math. Assn. Am., Nat. Coun. Tchr.'s Maths., Sch. Sci. and Maths. Assn., Kappa Delta Pi, Sigma Xi, Pi Mu Epsilon. Office: Kingsborough Community Coll Oriental Blvd Brooklyn NY 11235

GRISHAM, MICHELLE LUJAN, state agency administrator; 2 children. JD, Univ. N.Mex. Dir. lawyer referral for the elderly prog. N.Mex State Bar; dir. N.Mex Agy. on Aging, 1992—2004; sec. N.Mex. Dept. Health, Santa Fe, 2004—. Office: Dept Health 1190 S St Francis Dr Santa Fe NM 87502*

GRISKEY, PAULINE BECKER, education educator, researcher; b. Pitts., Oct. 30, 1933; d. William and Dorothy (Dzienis) Becker; m. Richard G. Griskey, June 11, 1955; children: Paula Louise, David Richard. B.S., Duquesne U., 1955; M.S., Radford U., 1966; ED.D., Nova U., 1985; postgrad. U. Denver, U. Del., Carnegie-Mellon U. Tchr. Pitts. Pub. Schs., 1955-58; concertmistress Eastern Shore Symphony, Salisbury, Md., 1958-60; tchr. Blacksburg High Sch., Va., 1962-66; lectr. Arapahoe Jr. Coll., Littleton, Colo., 1966-68; head English dept. Mt. Pleasant High Sch., Livingston, N.J., 1968-71; acting dir., coord., lectr., researcher dept. learning skills U. Wis.-Milw., 1971-85; tchr. advanced placement program Livingston (N.J.) High Sch., 1985—; reviewer Houghton, Mifflin, Boston, 1983—, Holt, Rhinehart Winston, N.Y.C., 1982—; adj. prof. Milw. Area Tech. Coll., 1981—. Author: Critical Reading, 1978; Speed Reading, 1982; editor Effective Study Strategies, 1978. Solicitor, Pub. TV Fund Raising, Milw., 1981, March of Dime, Milw., 1980, Univ. Sch. Milw., 1978-79. Recipient Outstanding Achievement award U. Wis.-Milw., 1975, Disting. Service award, 1980, Outstanding Tchr. Gov. N.J., 1995; U. Wis. System Minority Disadvantaged grantee, 1977; HEW fellow, 1964-66. Mem. MLA, Coll. Reading Assn., Western Reading Assn., Internat. Reading Assn., Adult Edn. Assn. E-mail: rgriskey@verizon.net.

GRISWOLD, ELAINE C., nurse, consultant; b. Quincy, Mass., Sept. 22, 1946; d. Clayton A. and Joan E. (McCausland) Sheppard; m. Gordon D. Griswold, June 15, 1968; children: Eric, Donald. BSN, Boston U., 1968. RN Calif. Dir. nursing svcs. Albany (Oreg.) Care Ctr., 1993-96; quality cons. pvt practice Best Practices in Long Term Care, 1993—. !n cons. Pharmacy Corp. Am., 1987-92; past chair adv. bd. Sch. Nursing Linn Benton C.C., 1987-93. Author: What has Happened to Me. Adv. bd. Benton Cmty. Coll. Mem.: Calif. Receiver Team. Home: 36295 Hillside Ln Lebanon OR 97355-9224 Office Phone: 541-990-5775.

GRITSCH, RUTH CHRISTINE LISA, editor; b. Duisburg, Germany, July 18, 1931; came to the U.S., 1941; d. Carl and Maria Augusta (von Schuman-Janssen) Sandman; m. Eric Walter Gritsch, June 4, 1955 (div. 1993); children: Deborah, Erika. BA, NYU, 1953. Assoc. Inst. for Internat. Edn., N.Y.C., 1953-55; sec. Zeigler Bros., Inc., Gardners, Pa., 1993—2003. Translator: (books) Liberty, Equality, Sisterhood, 1978, Office of the Ministry, 1981, Huldrich Zwingli, 1983, Unity of the Churches, 1984, I Am a Palestinian Christian, 1995, Violence, 1996; co-translator: Luther's Works, Vols. 39, 41, 1966, 67; editor: Roly, 1988; translator, editor: Justification of the Ungodly, 1968; editor, co-translator: Thomas Müntzer, A Tragedy of Errors, 1989. Active So. Poverty Law Ctr., Adams Co. Arts Coun. Mem.: LWV (bd. dirs., v.p. 1969—90, 1999—2001), Internat. Platform Assn. Democrat. Lutheran. Avocations: reading, collecting art. Home: 1 West St Gettysburg PA 17325-2130

GRIZZARD-BARHAM, BARBARA LEE, artist; b. Roanoke, Va., Apr. 4, 1935; d. Alton Lee and Mable (Jewell) Grizzard; m. Charles Thomas Barham, Sr., June 25, 1955; children: Charles Thomas, Christopher. BS in Edn., Va. Commonwealth U., 1971, postgrad. Educator Colonial Heights (Va.) Sch. Sys., 1971—88; represented by Agora Gallery, NYC, 1999—2001, 2002, Amsterdam Whitney Gallery, NYC, 2003—05. One-woman shows include Wakefield (Va.) Ctr. for Arts, 1992, 1993, 1994, Petersburg (Va.) Area Art League, 1993, 1995, 2000, Rappahannock Westminster-Canterberry Gallery, Va., 1995, Assn. for Visual Artists Gallery, Chattanooga, Tenn., 1999, Rappahanock Westminster Canterberry Gallery, Va., 1999, Williamsburg Regional Libr./Gallery/Theater Complex, 1999, exhibited in group shows at Richmond (Va.) Jewish Cmty. Ctr., 1991, 1993, Rappahannoc Art League Show, Va., 1995, Assoc. Artists Winston-Salem, N.C., 1991, 1992, 1996, Hoyt Inst. Fine Arts, Pa., 1998, Fredericksburg (Va.) Creative Ctr. Art, 1999, Richmond Shockoe Creative Ctr. Art, 1999, Richmond Women's Caucus for Art, 1999—2000, Shockoe Bottom (Va.) Art Ctr., 1999—2000, Agora Gallery, 1999, 2000, N.Y.C., 2001, 2002, Amsterdam Whitney Gallery, 2003, 2004, Limner Gallery, 2001. Recipient awards for art. Mem. Petersburg Area Art League, Va. Mus. Art, Whitney Mus. Art, Mus. Modern Art. Republican. Episcopal. Avocations: judging and breeding American Cocker Spaniels, piano. Home: 701 Forestview Dr Colonial Heights VA 23834-1116

GRIZZEL, PATSY (PAT) PAULINE, human services administrator; b. Clintwood, Va., Aug. 13, 1955; d. James Joshua and Eliza Elton Grizzel. BA, Ea. Ky. U., 1977; MPA, James Madison U., 1991. Lic. prevention profl. alcohol, tobacco and other drugs Substance Abuse Certification Alliance of Va.; cert. playground insp., Nat. Playground Safety Inst. Adv. social worker Valley Program for Aging Svcs., Inc., Waynesboro, Va., 1978; social worker Staunton (Va.)-Augusta County Dept. Social Svcs., 1978-86; coord. Staunton (Va.)-Augusta County D.S.S., 1986-88; exec. dir. Waynesboro Office of Youth, 1988-91; substance abuse prevention specialist, student assistance coord. Harrisonburg (Va.) High Sch., 1991—99; prog. admin. specialist Va. Dept. of Soc. Svcs., 1999. Adj. trainer Va. Dept. Youth and Family Svcs. Mem. Collegial Assn. for Devel. and Renewal of Educators, Va. Delinquency Prevention and Youth Devel. Assn., Assn. Va. Student Assistance Profls., Va. Edn. Assn. Avocations: photography, hiking, reading. Home: PO Box 1070 Verona VA 24482-1070

GRMEK, DOROTHY ANTONIA, accountant; b. Cleve., July 7, 1930; d. Louis and Antonia (Korosec) Lipanye; m. Charles Stelmach, June 13, 1953 (div. May 1977); children: Monica Doran Meade, Dwayne Alan Stelmach, Dale Richard Stelmach; m. William Edward Grmek, Aug. 18, 1978 (dec. Nov. 2003). BBA in Acctg., Fenn Coll., 1953. Chief acct. Pyromatics, Inc., Willoughby, Ohio, 1975-87; acct., exec. sec. Auctor Assocs., Inc., Cleveland Heights, Ohio, 1972-96; tax cons. Avon, Ohio, 1980—2005; contr., human rels. specialist Telefast Industries, Inc., Berea, Ohio, 1988-94; treas., buyer River Toy Box, Inc., Rocky River, 1990-2001. Mem.: Slovene Nat. Benefit Soc. (ins. agt. 1982—, charter mem., fin. sec. lodge 781 1982—, Cleve. Fedn. Lodges rec. sec. 1968—72, fin. sec. 1972—82). Home: 1925 Pembrooke Ln Avon OH 44011-1659

GROAH, LINDA KAY, nursing administrator, educator; b. Cedar Rapids, Iowa, Oct. 5, 1942; d. Joseph David and Irma Josephine (Zitek) Rozek; m. Patrick Andrew Groah, Mar. 20, 1975; 1 child, Kimberly stepchildren: Nadine, Maureen, Marcus. Diploma, St. Luke's Sch. Nursing, Cedar Rapids, 1963; student, San Francisco City Coll., 1976-77; BA, St. Mary's Coll., Moraga, Calif., 1978; BSN, Calif. State U., 1986; MSN, U. Calif., 1989. Staff nurse to head nurse U. Iowa, 1963-67; clin. supr., dir. oper. and recovery rm. Michael Reese Hosp., Chgo., 1967-73; dir. oper. rms. Med. Ctr. Ctrl. Ga., Macon, 1973-74; dir. oper. and recovery rms. U. Calif. Hosps. and Clinics, San Francisco, 1974-90, asst. dir. hosps. and clinics, 1982-86; v.p. patient care svcs., COO Kaiser Found. Hosp., San Francisco, 1990—2004, COO, nurse exec., 2004—. Asst. clin. prof. U. Calif. Sch. Nursing, San Francisco, 1975—; cons. to oper. rm. suprs. and divsn. ednl. resources and programs Assn. Am. Med. Colls., 1976—; condr. seminars. Author: Perioperative Nursing Practice, 1983, 3d edit., 1996; contbr. articles to profl. jours., chapters to books; author, prodr. audio-visual presentations; author: computer software. Named Most Influential Women in Bus., San Francisco Bus. Times, 2006; recipient Calif. Excellence in Nursing Leadership award, Nursing Spectrum, 2005, award for Nursing Leadership, Calif. Nurse Week, 2005, Nurse Leader of the Yr., 2005. Fellow: Am. Acad. Nursing; mem.: ANA (vice chmn. oper. rm. conf. group 1974—76), Nat. League Nurses, Assn. Oper. Rm. Nurses (mem. com. nominations 1979—84, treas. 1985—87, 1993—95, bd. dirs. 1991—93, pres.-elect 1995—96, pres. 1996—97, pres. found. 1992—95, trustee found. 1995—97, Excellence award in Preoperative Nursing 1989), San Francisco C. of C. Home: 5 Mateo Dr Belvedere Tiburon CA 94920-1071 Office: 3020 Bridgeway Ste 399 Sausalito CA 94965-2839 Office Phone: 415-833-3317. Personal E-mail: lindag1005@aol.com. Business E-Mail: linda.groah@kp.org.

GROBLEWSKI, JANE (JANE CAMPBELL), secondary school educator; b. Eau Claire, Wis., Apr. 16, 1953; d. Norman O. and Bethe M. Campbell; m. Russ S. Groblewski, Aug. 20, 1977; children: Meg, Bethe. Student, U. de Los Andes, Bogota, Colombia, 1974; BA in L.Am. Studies, U. Wis., Eau Claire, 1975; MA in Ibero-Am. Rels., U. Wis., 1977. Spanish tchr. Plymouth HS, Wis., 1975—81, 1988—; instr. Spanish, Latin Am. culture Lakeland Coll., Sheboygan, 1986-88. Pres. cmty. chpt. Am. Field Svc., Plymouth, 1985-87. Meth. Sunday sch. tchr., Sheboygan, 1981-1997; bd. mem. Children's Svc. Soc., Sheboygan, 1982-83. Recipient Tchr. of Yr., Plymouth Joint Sch. Dist., 1994—95, Woman of the Yr., Plymouth Professional Women, 2003. Mem. Am. Assn. Tchrs. Fgn. Lang., Wis. Assn. Tchrs. Spanish and Portuguese, Plymouth Profl. Women (Woman of Yr. 2003), Plymouth (Wis.) Club. Home: 814 Oak Ridge Dr Plymouth WI 53073-4026

GROBMAN, HULDA GROSS (MRS. ARNOLD B. GROBMAN), health science educator; b. Phila., Aug. 2, 1920; d. Joseph and Dora (Abrahams) Gross; m. Arnold B. Grobman, Feb. 20, 1944; children— Marc Ross, Beth Alison Burruss. AB, U. Pa., 1940; MPA, U. Mich., 1941; EdD, U. Fla., 1958. Rsch. asso. Western Interstate Commn. on Higher Edn., Boulder, Colo., 1959-60; staff cons. Biol. Scis. Curriculum Study, Boulder, 1960-65, Joint Council on Econ. Edn., NY, 1965-66; prof. edn. N.Y. U., 1966-72, Bklyn. Coll., City U. N.Y., 1972-73; sr. rsch. assoc. ADA, Chgo., 1973-74; dir. edn./career mobility, area health edn. system, prof. med. edn. U. Ill. Med. Center, 1973-75; prof. health scis. edn. St. Louis U. Med. Ctr., 1975-88; prof. emeritus St. Louis U. Med. Center, 1988—. Cons. Sci. Edn. Center, U. Sao Paulo, Brazil; vis. prof. Asian Assn. Biol. Edn., Hebrew U. Jerusalem Inst. on Test Writing, 1972; cons. Fundacao Carlos Chagos, Sao Paulo, Brazil. Author: Developmental Curriculum Projects, 1970, Evaluation Activities of curriculum Projects, 1968, also articles; cons. editor Jour. Ednl. Rsch., 1973-80, Am. Ednl. Rsch. Jour.; mng. editor Serin Press. Bd. dirs. LWV Fla., 1950-55; candidate for City Commn., Gainesville, Fla., 1955; mem. Bd. State Dept. Children and Families, Dist. 15, 1997-2000. Recipient A-Individual Achievement award 3d Army Res. Command, 1956. Fellow AAAS (council 1967-73); mem. Asian Assn. Biology Edn. (charter hon. mem.), Am. Ednl. Research Assn. (sec. div. I 1979-81). Home: 5000 SW 25th Blvd Unit 1115 Gainesville FL 32608 E-mail: agrobman@aol.com.

GROBSTEIN, RUTH H., health facility administrator; 3 children. BA, NYU, 1945; PhD in Biology, Yale U., 1957; MD, UCLA, 1976. Post-doctoral fellow Yale Med. Sch., Calif., mem. staff microbiology Calif.; prin. investigator U. Calif., San Diego, asst. prof. radiation oncology San Francisco, 1980—83; divsn. head radiation oncology Scripps Clin., La Jolla, Calif. Dir. The Ida M. and Cecil H. Green Cancer Ctr. Grantee Atomic Energy Commn., 1966, Nadonal Inst. Health, 1966.

GRODE, SUSAN A., lawyer; BFA, Cornell U., 1964; JD, U. So. Calif., 1977. Bar: Calif. 1977. V.p. Harry N. Abrams, Inc.; ptnr. Kaye, Scholer, Fierman, Hays & Handler, LLP; ptnr., co-chair Entertainment and Media Dept. Katten Muchin Zavis Rosenman, LA. Author: Visual Artist Manual, 1985. Mem.: ABA, Calif. Women's Law Ctr., State Bar Calif., LA County Bar Assn., Beverly Hills Bar Assn., Alpha Alpha Gamma, Phi Kappa Phi. Office: Katten Muchin Zavis Rosenman Ste 2600 2029 Century Park E Los Angeles CA 90067 Office Phone: 310-788-4410. Office Fax: 310-712-8422. E-mail: susan.grode@kmzr.com.

GRODECKI, MERRILYN, private school educator; b. Malden, Mass., Oct. 27, 1947; d. Daniel Gordon and Alice Louise MacLeod; m. James Frances Grodecki; children: Gary Steven, Carly Erin. BA, Boston U., 1969; MS in Child Devel. and Early Childhood Edn., Wheelock Coll., Boston, 1995. Infant-toddler coord. Mulberry Child Care, Acton, Mass.; 4th grade tchr. Agape Christian Acad., Winchester, Mass., 1995—99; grades 7-11 English tchr. Trinity Christian Acad., Hyannis, Mass., 1999—. Office: Trinity Christian Acad 979 Mary Dunn Rd Barnstable MA 02630-1807 Office Phone: 508-790-0114. Personal E-mail: balnamoon@comcast.net.

GRODSKY, JAMIE ANNE, law educator; b. San Francisco; d. Gerold Morton and Kayla Deane (Wolfe) G. BA in Human Biology/Natural Scis. and History with distinction, Stanford U., 1977; MA, U. Calif., Berkeley, 1986; JD, Stanford Law Sch., 1992. Ednl. dir. Oceanic Soc., San Francisco, 1979-81; rsch. asst. Woods Hole (Mass.) Oceanographic Inst., 1983; analyst Office Tech. Assessment U.S. Congress, Washington, 1984-89; counsel Com. Natural Resources, U.S. Ho. of Reps., Washington, 1993—95; counsel to Com. on Judiciary U.S. Senate, Washington, 1995-97; jud. clk. with chief judge U.S. Ct. Appeals (9th cir.), 1997-98; sr. advisor to the gen. counsel U.S. EPA, Washington, 1999—2001; assoc. prof. law U. Minn. Law Sch., Mpls., 2001—05; assoc. prof. Law Sch. George Washington U., Washington, 2005—. Articles editor Stanford Law Rev.; contbr. articles to profl. jours. Trustee Desert Rsch. Inst. Found. Mem.: D.C. Bar Assn., Calif. Bar Assn., Supreme Ct. Bar Assn.

GRODSKY, SHEILA TAYLOR, art educator, artist; b. Newark, May 7, 1933; d. Joseph and Rebecca Gerber Taylor; m. Leonard H. Grodsky, June 19, 1955 (dec.); children: David Mark, Robert Steven, Daniel Howard. BA in Fine Arts, Douglass Coll., New Brusnwick, NJ, 1954; postgrad., Md. Inst. Art, Balt., 1968—69. Tchr. art history Dover High Sch., NJ, 1955—56; substitute tchr. US Mil. Schs. Dependents, Ft. Bragg, NC, 1959—61, Ft. Lewis, Wash., 1962—65, Ft. Meade, Md., 1968—70, Chitose, Japan, 1965—68, Stillwater Township Sch., Stillwater, NJ, 1970—75. Pres. Gallery 23, Inc., Blairstown, NJ, 2002—. Exhibitions include Garden State Watercolor Soc. (Best in Show, 2004), Skylands Juried Exhbn., Newton (Best in Show, 2004), Internat. Soc. Cornell Mus. (Best in Show, 2005). Fellow: Internat. Soc. Experimental Artists; mem.: Nat. Assn. Women Artists, NJ Watercolor Soc. Jewish. Avocations: reading, politics, theater, gardening. Home: 940 W End Dr Newton NJ 07860

GRODY, DEBORAH, psychologist, director; b. Munich, Mar. 10, 1949; d. Sol and Jenny Chinitz; m. Allan David Grody, June 6, 1970; 1 child, Michael Brandon. BS in Psychology, Queens Coll., 1970, MS and Advanced Cert. in Sch. Psychology, 1972; PhD, Hofstra U., 1982. Lic. psychologist N.Y., cert. sch. psychologist N.Y. Clin. dir., founder Personal Resources, Inc., Employee Assistance Programs, N.Y.C., 1986—; clin. psychologist in pvt. practice N.Y.C., 1983—. Mem.: APA, Am. Psychological Assn., N.Y. State Psychol. Assn. Avocations: gardening, bicycling, writing. Home: 169 E 69th St New York NY 10021 Office: 11 E 68th St New York NY 10021 Office Phone: 212-288-1980. E-mail: grodyd@optonline.net.

GROGAN, VIRGINIA S., lawyer; b. Pasadena, Calif., Nov. 19, 1951; d. Bruce Mason and Helen Maude Gorsuch; m. Aug. 17, 1973 (div. June 1975); m. Allen R. Grogan, Jan. 10, 1982; children: Travis, Tess. BS, Occidental Coll., Eagle Rock, Calif., 1973; JD, U. So. Calif. Bar: Calif. 1979. Assoc. Latham & Watkins, LA, 1979-86, ptnr., 1987-97, chmn. assocs. com., 1995-97, mng. ptnr. Orange County Office Costa Mesa, Calif., 1997—. Mem. exec. roundtable U. Calif., Irvine, 1998—; mem. adv. com. Orange County Performing Arts, Costa Mesa, 1998—, Mem. ABA, Los Angeles County Bar Assn., Orange County Bar Assn. (judiciary com. 1998—), Legion Lex. Avocations: tennis, classical music. Office: Latham & Watkins 650 Town Center Dr Costa Mesa CA 92626-1989

GROHSKOPF, BERNICE, writer; b. Troy, N.Y. m. Herbert Grohskopf (div.); 1 child, Margaret Ellen. MA, Columbia U., 1954. Writer-in-residence Sweet Briar Coll., Va., 1978—82; rsch. assoc. Work and Correspondence of William James, Charlottesville, Va., 1984—95; freelance writer, book reviewer. Author: The Treasure of Sutton Hoo, 1970, 1973, 2000. Mem.: PEN, Nat. Book Critics Cir., Authors Guild.

GRONER, BEVERLY ANNE, retired lawyer; b. Des Moines; d. Benjamin L. and Annabelle (Miller) Zavat; m. Jack Davis; children: Morrilou Davis Morell, Lewis A. Davis, Andrew G. Davis; m. Samuel Brian Groner, Dec. 17, 1962. Student, Drake U., 1939-40, Cath. U., 1954-56; JD, Am. U., 1959. Bar: Md. 1959, U.S. Supreme Ct. 1963, D.C. 1965. Pvt. practice, Bethesda Md., Washington, 1959-99; ret., 1999. Chmn. Md. Gov.'s Commn. on Domestic Relations Laws 1977-87; exec. com. trustee Montgomery-Prince George's Continuing Legal Edn. Inst., 1983-99, pres., 1992-98; lectr. to lay, profl. groups; speaker to Bar Assns. and numerous seminars; participant continuing legal edn. programs, seminar leader, participant, faculty mem. trial demonstration films Am. Law Inst.-ABA Legal Consortium; participant numerous TV, radio programs; seminar leader, expert-in-residence Harvard Law Sch., 1987, Family Law, Georgetown U. Law Ctr., 1988, 89; mem. gov.'s com. ERA, 1978-80; faculty mem. Montgomery County Bar Assn. Law Sch. for the Pub., 1991, Inst. on Professionalism, 1992. Cons. editor Family Law Reporter, 1986-90, MD Family Law Monthly, 1993-99; mem. bd. editors Fairshare 1992-97; contbr. numerous articles to profl. jours. Pres. Am. Acad. Matrimonial Lawyers Found., 1994-98. Named One of Leading Matrimonial

Practitioners in U.S., Nat. Law Jour., 1979, 87, Best Divorce Lawyer in Md., Washingtonian Mag., 1981, One of Best Matrimonial Lawyers in U.S., Town and Country mag., 1985, Best Lawyers in Am., 1987—; recipient Disting. Svc. award Va. State Bar Assn., 1982, Okla. Bar Assn., 1987, Md. Gubernatorial citation, 1987. Fellow Am. Acad. Matrimonial Lawyers (pres. Md. chpt. 1992-98, pres.-elect found. 1993-94); mem. Bar Assn. Montgomery County (exec. com. chmn. family law sect. 1976, chmn. fee arbitration panel 1974-77, legal ethics com.), Md. State Bar Assn. bd. of govs., (gov., chmn. family law sect. 1975-77, vice chmn. com. continuing legal edn., ethics com. 1991-99, mem. inquiry panel and grievance com., 1991-99, faculty mem. on Professionalism 1992), ABA (chmn. family law sect. 1986-87, rep. to White House conf. on Yr. of Child 1984, sec. family law sect. 1983-84, vice chmn. 1984-85, chmn. sect. marital property com., assn. adv. to nat. conf. commrs. on uniform marital property act, mem. faculty family law advocacy inst. 1988, 90), Am. Acad. of Matrimonial Lawyers, Md. State Bar Assn. (mem. inquiry panel and grievance com. 1991—), Phi Alpha Delta. Home: 5600 Wisconsin Ave Apt 1602 Chevy Chase MD 20815-4413

GROOM, MITZI D, music educator, department chairman; b. Cullman, Ala. d. Arnold Hugo Danker and Louise Barbara Sperber; m. Joe Groom, July 2, 1978; 1 child, Joseph Jr. BA, Florence State U., 1972; MA, U. North Ala., 1975; PhD, Fla. State U. Choral dir. Davis Hills Mid. Sch., Huntsville, Ala., 1972—74, Deshler Jr./Sr. H.S., Tuscumbia, Ala., 1974—77; instr. U. Ala., 1980—83; choral dir. Athens City Sch., Ala., 1982—89; prof. music Tenn. Tech. U., 1989—2001; dept. head Western Ky. U., 2001—. Music dept. chmn. Tenn. Tech. U., 1999—2001; guest clinician, 1978—. Editor: (newsletter) Ala. ACDA Reprise; mem. editl. bd. The Choral Jour., 1976—77. Ch. musician various Ala. churches, 1964—94; bd. mem. Bowling Green Western Symphony Orch., Ky., 2001—. Recipient Alumni of the Yr., U. North Ala., 2004, Award of Musical Excellence, Baxter Elem. Sch., 1997—2001. Mem.: Nat. Assn. Schs. of Music (vis. evaluator 2003—), Am. Choral Dir. Assn. (nat. offier 2001—), Pi Kappa Lambda, Phi Kappa Phi, Delta Omicron. Office: Western Ky U 1906 College Heights Blvd #41029 Bowling Green KY 42101-1029 Office Phone: 270-745-3751.

GROOS, APRIL COX, secondary school educator; d. Charles G. and Jessie L. Cox; m. Edward L. Groos, June 5, 1976. AA, San Antonio Coll., 1967; BA, Our Lady of the Lake Coll., San Antonio, 1969, MA in English, 1970. English tchr. St. Mary's Hall, San Antonio, 1970—2006. English instr. San Antonio Coll., 1971—76; dir. of humanities St. Mary's Hall, San Antonio, 1983—93. Recipient Disting. Tchr. award, White Ho. Commn. on Presdl. Scholars, 1995. Mem.: Nat. Coun. Tchrs. English. Office: Saint Mary's Hall Box 33430 San Antonio TX 78265-3430 Office Phone: 210-483-9100.

GROOVER, LORI MOBLEY, athletic trainer; b. Savannah, Ga., May 26, 1967; d. Bobby Lee and Sandy Kaye Mobley; m. Gary Michael Groover, May 17, 2003. BS, Valdosta State U., Ga., 1992; MS, Ga. So. U., Statesboro, 1998. Lic. Ga. Bd. Athletic Trainers, 1992, cert. Nat. Assn. Orthop. Technologists, 2006. Athletic trainer Candler Sports Medicine, Savannah, 1994—97, Meml. Sports Medicine, Savannah, 1997—98; head athletic trainer Woodward Acad., College Park, Ga., 1998—2006; physician extender fellow U. Orthopaedics, Decatur, Ga., 2006—. Mem.: Ga. Athletic Trainers Assn. (assoc.; vice-president 2003—05, pres. 2005—), SE Athletic Trainers Assn. (assoc.; sec. 2006), Nat. Athletic Trainers Assn. (assoc.; cert.). Home: 1503 Macedonia Rd Newnan GA 30263 Office: University Orthopaedics 1014 Sycamore Drive St B Decatur GA 30030 Office Phone: 404-299-1700.

GROPPE, ELIZABETH T., education educator; d. John Daniel and Rose Marie (Nigro) Groppe; m. John Henry Sniegocki; 1 child, John David Groppe Sniegocki. PhD, U. Notre Dame, Ind., 1999; BA, Earlham Coll., 1985. Asst. prof. theology Xavier U., Cin., 2001—. Author: (book) Yves Congar's Theology of the Holy Spirit, 2004. Delores Zohrab Liebmann Fellowship, U. Notre Dame, 1996—99. Mem.: Cath. Theol. Soc. Am. Office: Xavier Univ 3800 Victory Pkwy Cincinnati OH 45207-4442 Office Phone: 513-745-3734. Business E-Mail: groppe@xavier.edu.

GROSCH, LAURA DUDLEY, artist, educator; b. Worcester, Mass., Apr. 1, 1945; d. Daniel Swartwood and Edith Dudley (Taft) G. BA in Art History, Wellesley Coll., 1967; BFA in Painting, U. Pa., 1968. Solo exhbns. include Mint Mus. Art, Charlotte, N.C., 1974, Jerald Melberg Gallery, Charlotte, 1984, 87, Greenville (N.C.) Mus. Art, 1987, Greenville County Mus. Art, 1987, Christa Faut Gallery, Davidson, N.C., 1990, 93, 96, Rock Sch. Arts Found., Valdese, N.C., 2000, Millennium exhbn., Valdese, 2000, others; group exhbns. include Impressions Gallery, Boston, 1973, Rose Mus. Glenbow-Alberta Gallery, Can., 1974, New Orleans Mus. Art, 1975, Bklyn. Mus., 1976, Visual Arts Ctr. Alaska, 1978, Print Club, Phila., 1980, Palazzo Venezia, Rome, 1984, Syracuse U., N.Y., 1987, Wellesley (Mass.) Coll., 1997, Mint Mus. Art, Charlotte, N.C., 2002, Christa Faut Gallery, Cornelius, N.C., 2003, 04, 05, 06, Charlotte Wine and Food, 2004, 250 Years of Art, Winston-Salem, N.C., 2004; represented in pub. collections Boston Pub. Libr., Bowdoin Coll., Brunswick, Maine, Brit. Mus., London, Bklyn. Mus., Fla. State U., Manhattan Coll., Mus. Fine Arts, Boston, N.Y. Pub. Libr., Ringling Mus., Sarasota, Fla., Smithsonian Inst., Washington, UCLA, Newark Pub. Libr., Minn. Inst. Arts, Honolulu Acad. Arts, Dayton (Ohio) Art Inst., Carnegie Mellon U., Pitts., Free Libr. Phila., Victoria and Albert Mus., London, many others. Office: PO Box 10 Davidson NC 28036-8006 Office Phone: 704-892-1723.

GROSECLOSE, JOANNE STOWERS, special education educator; b. Bland, Va., Dec. 15, 1956; d. Claude Swanson and Josephine (Mustard) Stowers; m. John Vincent Groseclose, June 24, 1979; children: Jouette Nicole, Nicholas Vincent. BS, Radford Coll., 1979; MS, Radford U., 1983. Cert. tchr., Va, exceptional needs specialist, Nat. Bd. Profl. Tchg., 2001. Tchr. kindergarten Bland (Va.) Combined Sch., Bland County Sch. Bd., 1979; tchr. 4th grade Marion (Va.) Intermediate Sch., Smyth County Sch. Bd., 1979-80, tchr. learning disabled 4th, 5th, 6th grades, 1980—. Instr. adult basic edn. Smyth County Schs., Marion, 1989-90. Technician Bland County Rescue Squad, 1975-78; bd. dirs. Am. Cancer Soc., 1985-88, Marion United Way, 1989-91, Smyth County Assn. for Retarded Citizens, 1982-85, Smyth County Cmty. Hosp., 1993-98; sec., vice chair Smith County Cmty. Found., 1998—; vol. Mt. Rogers Smyth House Group Home for Retarded Adults, 1983-85; mem. Hospice of Smyth County; mem. S.W. Va. Reading Coun., 1989-91, 94—, Smyth County Humane Soc.; mem. area Luth. ch. coun., 1996-99. Named Outstanding Young Careerist Marion Bus. and Profl. Women, 1983, Outstand Young Woman of Am., Marion Bus. and Profl. Women, 1981, Radford U. Outstanding Alumi, 1990, Va. Tchr. of Yr. Ency. Britannica/Good Housekeeping/Coun. of Chief State Sch. Officers, 1991. Mem. NEA (del. conv.), Smyth County Edn. Assn. (rep. 1979, 82, 93—, treas. 1981-83, pres. 1985), Smyth County C. of C., Va. Edn. Assn. (del. conv.), Marion Book and Study Club, Phi Kappa Phi, Kappa Delta Pi. Avocations: reading, travel, camping, playing bridge, tennis. Home: 241 Magnolia St Marion VA 24354-4413 Office: Marion Intermediate Sch 820 Stage St Marion VA 24354-4000 Office Phone: 276-783-2609.

GROSECLOSE, WANDA WESTMAN, retired elementary school educator; b. Clarks, Nebr., Oct. 5, 1933; m. B. Clark Groseclose; children: D. Kim, Byron C. Jr., Eric P., A. Glenn. B degree, Brigham Young U., 1976; M in Tchg., St. Mary's Coll., Moraga, Calif., 1981. Cert. tchr., Calif. 5th grade tchr. Brentwood (Calif.) Union Sch. Dist., 1977-97; ret. Art tchr., mentor tchr. Contra Costa County Program of Excellence. Author: American Music in Time, 1992, In the Shadow of Our Ancestors, vol. I, vol. II, 2004, The Lees of Southwest Virginia, 2004. Human rels. bd. dirs. City of Livermore, 1968—70. Republican. Mem. Lds Ch. Avocations: painting, sewing, gardening, genealogy. Home: 2763 St Andrews Dr Brentwood CA 94513 Personal E-mail: grosclos@ecis.com.

GROSHOLZ, EMILY ROLFE, philosopher, educator, poet; b. Phila., Oct. 17, 1950; d. Edwin DeHaven and Frances Skerrett Grosholz; m. Robert Roy Edwards, Jan. 2, 1987; children: Benjamin, Robert, William, Mary-Frances. BA, U. Chgo., 1972; PhD in Philosophy, Yale U., 1978. Fellow Nat. Humanities Ctr., Research Triangle Park, NC, 1985-86; sr. rsch. fellow Inst. History & Philosophy of Sci. & Tech. U. Toronto, Canada, 1988-89; assoc. Ctr. for Philosophy of Sci. U. Pitts., 1992—. Adj. assoc. prof. dept. philosophy U. Pa., Phila., 1992; prof. philosophy Pa. State U., University Park, 1993—, affiliate African and African-Am. studies, 1997—, fellow Inst. for the Arts and Humanities, 1995—; mem. poets' prize com. Nicholas Rsch. Mus., N.Y.C., 1993—. Author: Cartesian Method and the Problem of Reduction, 1991, Eden, 1992, The Abacus of Years, 2002; co-author: Leibniz's Science of the Rational, 1998; adv. editor: The Hudson Rev., 1984—, mem. editl. bd.: Jour. History of Ideas, 1998—, Studia Leibnitiana, 2001—. Fellow Nat. Humanities Ctr., 1985-86, Guggenheim Found., 1988-89, Am. Coun. Learned Socs., 1997, NEH, 2004—; Transatlantic Cooperation Rsch. grantee Alexander von Humboldt Found., 1994-97. Mem. Am. Philos. Assn., Leibniz Soc. N.Am., Leibniz Assn., Clare Hall U. Cambridge Club (life), Philosophy Sci. Assn. Democrat. Episcopalian. Office: Pa State Univ Dept Philosophy 240 Sparks Bldg University Park PA 16802 Home: 116 Kennedy St State College PA 16801-7805 E-mail: erg2@psu.edu.

GROSHONG, LAURA WOLF, psychotherapist, researcher; b. Chgo., Oct. 24, 1947; d. Henry Peter and Janyce Faye (Gluck) Wolf; m. Geoffrey Groshong, June 8, 1969; children: Joseph, Jacob. AM, U. Rochester, 1969; MusB, U. Chgo., 1974. Registered lobbyist Wash. State, 1996. Psychiat. social worker Harborview Med. Ctr., Seattle, 1974-77; pvt. practice in psychotherapy Seattle, 1977—. Master's mental health adv. com chair, Wash., 2001—04. Mem. NASW, Wash. State Soc. Clin. Social Workers (bd. dirs. 1993—), Wash. State Coalition Mental Health Profls. and Consumers (legis. chmn. 1994—), Psychoanalytic Assn. Seattle (pres. 1983-85), Nat. Com. Psychoanalysis (bd. dirs., area chmn. 1992—, nat. legis. chmn. 1995—, nat. membership com. on psychoanalysis in clin. social work), Nat. Acads. Practice Social Work Acad., Clin. Social Work Fedn. (gov. rels. chair, 2000—). Democrat. Jewish. Avocations: music, hiking. Home: 3413 NE 193rd St Seattle WA 98155-2533 Office: 4026 NE 55th St Seattle WA 98105-2262

GROSKLOS, HOLLIE JO, music educator; d. Jack Louis and Carol Ann Grosklos. MusB, Tex. Christian U., 1986—91, BA in hist., 1991—93, MusM in flute performance, 1991—93; D of musical arts, U. of North Tex., 1994—2001. Grad. fellowship in flute U. of North Tex., Denton, Tex., 1994—96; pvt. flute instr. Coppell Ind. Sch. Dist., Coppell, Tex., 1995—97; instrumental music buyer Pender's Music Co., Denton, Tex., 1996—98; asst. h.s. band dir. Putnam City Schools, Okla. City, Okla., 1998—99; h.s. asst. band dir. Duncan H.S., Okla., 1999—2001; mid. sch. band dir. Southlake Carroll Ind. Sch. Dist., Tex., 2001—. Music dir. Smithfield UMC, North Richland Hills, Tex., 2002—03, handbell dir., 2001—. Robert B. Toulouse Scholarship in Grad. Study, U. of North Tex., 1994—96, Tchg. Assistantship in Musicology, Tex. Christian U., 1992—93, Performance Scholarship, 1986—91, Academic scholarship, 1986—91. Mem.: Tex. Music Educator's Assn. (assoc.), Nat. Flute Assn. (assoc.), Pi Kappa Lambda (assoc.), Mu Phi Epsilon (v.p. 1989—90), Tau Beta Sigma (assoc.; parliamentarian 1989—90). Protestant. Avocations: travel, crafts, golf, reading, gardening. Office: Dawson Middle School 400 S Kimball Ave Southlake TX 76092

GROSS, AMBER SAVAGE, social sciences educator; b. Upland, Calif., Feb. 1, 1981; d. Kent and Barbara Savage. BA in Social Sci., Biola U., La Mirada, Calif., 2002. CLEAR credential Calif., 2003. Tchr. social studies Downey (Calif.) H.S., 2003—. Girls' volleyball coach Downey H.S., 2000—; curriculum com. mem. Donwey Unified Sch. Dist., 2005—; avid coord. Advancement Via Individual Determination, Los Angeles County, 2005—. Mem.: Am. Hist. Soc., Phi Alpha Theta.

GROSS, AMY, editor-in-chief; Features editor and spl. projects editor Vogue, 1978—88; founding editor Mirabella, 1988—93, editor-in-chief, 1995—97; edtl. dir. Elle, NYC, 1993—96; editor-in-chief O, The Oprah Mag., 2000—. Co-author: (books) Women Talk About Breast Surgery: From Diagnosis to Recovery, 1991, Women Talk About Gynecological Surgery: From Diagnosis to Recovery, 1992. Office: O The Oprah Mag 1700 Broadway New York NY 10019-6708*

GROSS, CAROL ANN, lawyer; b. St. Louis, Mo., May 25, 1951; m. William H. Gross. B in journalism, U. Mo., 1973; JD cum laude, Seton Hall U. Sch. Law, 1985. Bar N.J., 1985, Pa., 1985, N.Y., 1995, U.S. Dist. Ct., 1985. Law clerk N.J. office atty. gen., Trenton, 1983-85; assoc. Lowenstein, Sandler, Kohl, Fischer & Boylan, Roseland, NJ, 1985-90, Jones, Day, Reavis & Pogue, N.Y., 1990-96; ptnr. pvt. practice, Somerville, NJ, 1996—. Co-Author: (book) N.J. Environmental Law Handbook, 1989; contbr. Environmental Reporter's Handbook, 1988; co-editor (newsletter) Enviro-Notes, 1989-90; contbr. author: Legal Guide to Working with Environmental Consultants. Recipient Responsible Journalism award, N.J. Press Assn., 1982, Interpretive Writing award, N.J. Press Assn., 1980, Journalistic Excellence Under Deadline Pressure award, Soc. Profl. Journalists, 1979, Good Citizen award, Gannett Co., Inc., 1979, Merit award, Union Co. Civil Defense/Disaster Control, 1978. Mem. ABA, N.J. Bar Assn., Pa. Bar Assn. Avocations: gardening, guitar, cooking. Office: 79 Davenport St Somerville NJ 08876-1921

GROSS, DOROTHY-ELLEN, library director, educator; b. Buffalo, June 13, 1949; d. William Paul and Elizabeth Grace (Hough) Gross. BA, Westminster Coll., 1971; MLS, Benedictine U., 1975; MDiv, McCormick Theol. Sem., 1975. Jr. cataloger McCormick Theol. Sem., Chgo., 1972-75; head tech. svcs. Barat Coll., Lake Forest, Ill., 1975-79, head libr., 1980-82; dir. coll. libr. North Park Coll. and Theol. Sem., Chgo., 1982-87, dir. coll. and sem. librs., 1987-96, assoc. dean, 1990-96, prof., 1991—. Cons. acad. librs.; spkr. various profl. meetings and confs. Author (with Karsten): From Real Life to Reel Life, 1993; editor: LIBRAS Handbook and Directory, 1982—96; co-editor: North Park Faculty Publs. and Creative Works, 1992; contbr. chpt. in book, articles, book reviews to profl. jours. Dir. rsch. United Way, Chgo., 1996—99; bd. dirs. Eldredge Libr., 2000—, pres. bd. dirs., 2004—. Recipient Melvin R. George award, 1996. Mem.: LIBRAS (pres. 1983—85), ALA, Pvt. Acad. Librs. Ill. (pres. 1981—83, 1994—95, newsletter editor, contbr.), Assn. Coll. and Rsch. Librs. Presbyterian. E-mail: dottie@c4.net.

GROSS, HARRIET P. MARCUS, religious studies and writing educator; b. Pitts., July 15, 1934; d. Joseph William and Rose (Roth) Pincus; children: Sol Benjamin, Devra Lynn AB magna cum laude, U. Pitts., 1954; cert. religious tchg., Spertus Coll. Judaica, Chgo., 1962; MA, U. Tex., Dallas, 1990, postgrad., 1998. Assoc. editor Jewish Criterion Pitts., 1955—58; publs. writer B'nai B'rith Vocat. Svc., 1956—57; group leader Jewish Cmty. Ctrs. Met. Chgo., 1958—63; columnist Star Publs., Chicago Heights, Ill., 1964—80; pub. info. specialist Operation ABLE, Chgo., 1980—81; dir. religious sch. Temple Emanu-El, Dallas, 1983—86; freelance writer, 1986—; columnist Dallas Jewish Life Monthly, 1992—96, Dallas Jewish Week, 2000—04, Tex. Jewish Post, Dallas, 2004—. Lectr. U. Tex., Dallas, 1994-98; tchr. writing Homewood-Flossmoor (Ill.) Park Dist., Brookhaven Jr. Coll., Dallas; advisor journalism program Prairie State Coll., Chicago Heights, 1978-80; mem. adv. bd. The Creative Woman Quar. Publ., Gov.'s State U., Governors Park, Ill., The Mercury U. Tex., Dallas bd. dirs., sec. Family Svc. and Mental Health Ctr. South Cook County, Ill., 1965-71; active Park Forest (Ill.) Commn. on Human Rels., 1969-80, chmn., 1974-76; bd. dirs. Ill. Theatre Ctr., 1977-80, Jewish Family Svc. Dallas, 1982-95, Dallas Jewish Hist. Soc., 1995—; mem. Dallas Jewish Edn. Com., 1992-95 Recipient Humanitarian Achievement award Fellowship for Action, 1974, Honor award Anti-Defamation League B'nai B'rith, 1978, Cmty. Svc. award Dr. Charles E. Gavin Found., 1978, 1st Ann. Leadership award Jewish Family Svc., 1990, Katie award Dallas Press Club, 1995; inducted into Park Forest Hall of Fame, 2000, Tex. Press Women State Writing award, 2003 Mem. Nat. Fedn. Press Women, Press Women Tex., Ill. Woman's Press Assn. (named Woman of Yr. 1978), Intertel (pres. Gateway Forum Dallas 1984-85), Nat. Assn. Temple Educators, Mensa, Soc. Profl. Journalists, Dallas Press Club, Nat. Soc. Newspaper Columnists, Am. Jewish Press Assn. (Simon Rockower Personal Commentary award 2006), Phi Sigma Sigma Jewish. Achievements include development of 1st community newspaper action line column. Office: 8560 Park Ln Apt 23 Dallas TX 75231-6312 Office Phone: 214-691-8840. E-mail: harrietgross@sbcblogal.net.

GROSS, JUDY E., publishing executive; B in Math. cum laude, Vassar Coll., 1984; MBA, U. Chgo., 1988. Asst. mgr. Chem. Banking Corp.; planning analyst prodn. dept. N.Y. Times, N.Y.C., 1990—92, planning mgr. in prodn. dept., 1992—95, mgr. in strategic planning dept., 1995—97, mng. dir. gen. classified advt., 1997—99, mng. dir. customer order fulfillment, 1999—2001, group dir. customer order fulfillment, 2001—04, v.p. pub. ops., 2004—. Office: NY Times 229 W 43rd St New York NY 10036-3959

GROSS, KAREN CHARAL, lawyer; b. NYC, Nov. 25, 1940; d. Harry B. and Adele (Hook) Charal; m. Meyer A. Gross, Aug. 16, 1964; children: Dana Leslie, Jennifer P., Pamela A. AB, Barnard Coll., 1962; JD, NYU, 1965. Bar: N.Y. 1965. Atty. Wolder & Gross, NYC, 1965-78, Wolder, Gross & Yavner, NYC, 1978-86; sr. v.p. legal and bus. affairs GoodTimes Entertainment LLC, NYC, 1986—2004; of counsel Schweitzer Cornman Gross & Bondell LLP, NYC, 2005—. Editor NYU Law Rev., 1963-65. Parent liaison Ramaz Sch., N.Y.C., 1980-86; del. Dem. County Com., N.Y.C., 1988—; legal mentor to students Barnard Coll., N.Y.C. John Norton Pomeroy scholar NYU, 1963-65. Mem. Internat. Trademark Assn., Copyright Soc. USA. Avocation: travel. Office: Schweitzer Cornman Gross & Bondell LLP 292 Madison Ave New York NY 10017 Office Phone: 646-424-0770.

GROSS, KATHY ALDRICH, mathematics professor; d. Richard Harold and Barbara Ann (Masters) Aldrich; m. Gordon Burnell Gross, II, Aug. 28, 1993; children: Eric Masters, Jon Philip. AA in Liberal Arts, Cayuga C.C., Auburn, 1986; BA in Math., Le Moyne Coll., Syracuse, N.Y., 1988; MS in Maths. Edn., SUNY, Cortland, 1993; devel. edn. specialist, Appalachian State U., Boone, N.C., 1994. Maths. specialist Cayuga C.C., Auburn, 1988—96; learning specialist LeMoyne Coll., Syracuse, 1996—2000; instr., asst. prof. maths. Cayuga C.C., Auburn, 2000—. Treas. Finger Lakes Minor Soccer League, Auburn, 2002—04; cubmaster pack 52 Boy Scouts Am., Elbridge, NY, 2004—, unit commr. pack 52, 2006—. Mem.: N.Y. State Math. Assn. of 2-Yr. Colls., Phi Theta Kappa (adviser 2000—). Avocations: scrapbooks, visiting national parks.

GROSS, LAURA ANN, marketing and communications professional, herbalist, acupuncturist; b. Kew Gardens, N.Y., July 11, 1948; d. Melvin Fredericks and Harriette (Levy) G. BA, Boston U., 1970; MA, Columbia U., 1974; MS, Pacific Coll. Oriental Medicine, 1996. Staff writer Am. Banker, N.Y.C., 1974-82, assoc. editor, 1982-88; dir. fin. svcs., instns., communications Am. Express Travel/Related Svcs. Co., N.Y.C., 1988-89; dir. sales promotion and pub. rels. Am. Express Travelers Cheque Group/Am. Express Travel Svcs., N.Y.C., 1989-92; dir. strategic bus. comm. Am. Express Travel Related Svcs., N.Y.C., 1992-93; pres. Strategic Comm. Cons., N.Y.C., 1993-2000; founder Alternative Ctr. for Natural Healing, 1997—; exec. v.p. mktg. Letsgotrade, Inc., 2000-01; sr. v.p. mktg./ebusiness Muriel Siebert & Co., Inc., 2001—. Spkr. fin. svcs. and Chinese medicine. Author, editor consumer surveys and articles. Recipient editorial awards Pannell Kerr Forster, 1984, N.E. Bus. Press Editors, 1986, N.Y. Bus. Press. Editors, 1987, first Boston U. Coll. of Liberal Arts Young Alumni award, 1985. Avocations: fiction writing, travel, snorkeling.

GROSS, LESLIE PAMELA, sales executive, consultant; b. NY, Aug. 23, 1952; d. Gerald Jay and Pearl (Meltzer) G.; m. Ned T. Ashby (div. Mar. 1997); 1 child, James Warren Taylor Ashby; m. Russell A. Brown, Nov. 2003. AB, Cornell U., 1976. Ins. agt. Equitable Life, San Francisco, 1976-79; sales assoc. Digital Equipment Corp., San Francisco, 1979-81, from sales rep. to sales exec. Santa Clara, Calif., 1981-87, corp. acct. mgr. San Francisco, 1987-92; area mgr. WordPerfect Corp., Orem, Utah, 1992-94; sr. account mgr. Novell, Inc., Santa Clara, Calif., 1994-97; sr. client rep. IBM, Menlo Park, Calif., 1997—2001, client exec., 2001—. Missionary, LDS Ch., Boston, 1973-75; jr. Sunday sch. tchr., Menlo Park, Calif., 1993-95, 1996-98, 2002-04; pres. Women's Relief Soc., Stanford, Calif., 1986, counselor, Palo Alto, Calif., 1987-88, counselor, stake pres., Menlo Park, 1991-92, edn. com. 1999-2001, vis. tchg. supr., 2006—; sec. Channing Pl. Homeowners Assn., Palo Alto, 1987-88, 90-91, pres., 1988-90 Avocations: travel, cinema, exercise. Personal E-mail: lpgross@pacbell.net. Business E-Mail: lpgross@us.ibm.com.

GROSS, LINDA ARMANI, social studies educator; b. Andrews AFB, Md., May 11, 1973; d. Thomas Anthony and Donna Lee Armani; m. Michael Frank Gross, July 10, 2003. B, George Mason U., Fairfax, Virginia, 1996; M, George Mason U., 2001. Lic. Tchr. State Va., 1999. Tchr. spl. edn. Broad Run H.S., Ashburn, Va., 1999—2003; tchr. social studies Potomac Falls H.S., Va., 2001—02, Dominion H.S., Sterling, Va., 2002—04, Briar Woods H.S., Ashburn, 2005—. Cons. Lououn County Pub. Schs., Ashburn, 2004—. Mem. Cross Current Ministeries, Ashburn, 1999—2006. Office: Briar Woods High School 22525 Belmont Ridge Drive Ashburn VA 20148 E-mail: lgross@loudoun.k12.va.us.

GROSS, MARJORIE K., education educator, educator, small business owner; b. Detroit, Feb. 20, 1942; d. Paulus John and Marjorie Elizabeth (Towler) Keppel; m. Gene Herbert Gregg, June 8, 1963 (div. Jan. 1973); children: Kurtis Lowell, Marjorie Elizabeth, Andrea Lynn; m. James William Gross, Dec. 19, 1976 (dec. July 2004). BA magna cum laude, Western Coll., Oxford, Ohio, 1963; MA, Miami U., Oxford, Ohio, 1965; postgrad., U. Cin., 1971-73. Grad. teaching asst. Miami U., Oxford, 1963-65; instr. Western Coll., Oxford, 1965-68, asst. prof., acting dept. chair, 1969-71; instr. Dowling Coll., Oakdale, N.Y., 1968-69, Suffolk County C.C., Selden, N.Y., 1968-69; grad. teaching asst. U. Cin., 1971-73; instr. Northern Ky. State Coll., Erlanger, 1971-73, Carteret C.C., Morehead City, NC, 1985—. Adv. bd. Dept. Agr. Ext. Office Homemakers divsn., Cadiz, Ohio, 1975—79; owner Beacon of Opportunity, Morehead City, NC, 1997—. Mem.: N.C. Math. Assn. Two-Yr. Colls., N.C. Coun. Tchrs. Math. Presbyterian. Avocations: ceramics, computers. Home: 126 Caswell Dr Newport NC 28570-4502 Office: Carteret Community College 3505 Arendell St Morehead City NC 28557-2905 Office Phone: 252-222-6234. E-mail: mkg@carteret.edu.

GROSS, MICHELLE BAYARD, dancer, educator; b. N.Y.C., Apr. 13, 1954; d. Leo and Elizabeth (Teichman) Bayard; children: Melanie Bayard, Rebecca Bayard. BA, CUNY, 1975; MA, NYU, 1979; postgrad., Temple U., Phila., 1987—, Rowan U., 1992. Dance instr. Bayards Dance and Drama Sch.; freelance dancer, actress; prof. dance U. Nev., Reno, dir. dance program; prof. dance Atlantic Cape C.C., Mays Landing, NJ. Spkr. in field. Choreographer (concerts) U. Nev., Reno, Nev., 1981—85; author: Let's Learn About Dance, 2000; contbr. articles to profl. jours. Grant panelist Nev. State Coun. Arts; active causes N.J. Legis. Recipient Mentoring award, Atlantic Cape C.C., 2003, 2004. Mem.: Nat. Dance Educators Orgn., Nat. Dance Assn. Avocations: walking, films, reading, dance. Office: Atlantic Cape Cmty Coll Dance Program 5100 Black Horse Pike Mays Landing NJ 08330 Office Phone: 609-343-4900.

GROSS, PATRICIA LOUISE, neuropsychologist; b. Lisbon, Portugal, Feb. 29, 1952; came to U.S., 1955; d. Martin Arthur and Eva Delle (Stregevsky) G. BA magna cum laude, U. Calif., Irvine, 1974; MA, U. So. Calif., 1982, PhD, 1985. Lic. psychologist, Calif., N.C.; diplomate Am. Bd. PP, 1997. Psychology intern Sepulveda (Calif.) VA Med. Ctr., 1983-84, L.A. Child Guidance Clinic, 1984-85; rsch. assoc. Del Amo (Calif.) Psychiat. Hosp., 1984-85; postdoctoral fellow Neuropsychiat. Inst., UCLA, 1985-86; neuropsychologist West Los Angeles VA Med. Ctr., 1986; chief neuropsychology assessment lab., geropsychologist Sepulveda (Calif.) VA Med. Ctr., 1986-89; assoc. chief neuropsychiatry clinic, 1988-89; dir. brain injury program, neuropsychologist Charlotte (N.C.) Inst. of Rehab., 1989-91; dir. med. psychology, neuropsychologist Carolinas Med. Ctr., Charlotte, 1991—; dir. neuropsychology assessment lab., 1994—. Contbr. articles to profl. jours.

Mem. disaster mental health com. ARC, Charlotte, 1995—; pres. Western Carolina Alzheimer's Assn., 1999-2002. Oakley fellow, 1980-83; Sigma Xi grantee, 1984. Mem. APA, Internat. Neuropsychol. Soc., Nat. Acad. Neuropsychology, Mecklenburg Psychol. Assn. (pres. 1994), Nat. Head Injury Found., N.C. Head Injury Found., Alzheimer's Assn. (spkr.'s bur. Charlotte 1990—, bd. dirs. 1996—, v.p. 1998), Phi Beta Kappa. Democrat. Avocations: travel, movies, reading. Office: Charlotte Inst Rehab 1100 Blythe Blvd Charlotte NC 28203-5814

GROSS, SHARON RUTH, forensic psychologist, researcher; b. LA, Mar. 21, 1940; d. Louis and Sylvia Marion (Freedman) Lackman; m. Zoltan Gross, Mar. 1969 (div.); 1 child, Andrew Ryan; m. Ira Chroman, June 1994. BA, UCLA, 1983; MA, U. So. Calif., L.A., 1985, PhD, 1991. Diplomate Am. Bd. Psychol. Spltys. Tech. Rytron, Van Nuys, Calif., 1958-60; computress on tetrahedral satellite Space Tech. Labs., Redondo Beach, Calif., 1960-62; owner Wayfarer Yacht Corp., Costa Mesa, Calif., 1962-64; electronics draftsperson, designer stroke-writer characters Tasker Industries, Van Nuys, 1964-65; pvt. practice cons. Sherman Oaks, Calif., 1965-75, 77-80; printed circuit bd. designer Systron-Donner, Van Nuys, Calif., 1975-76; design checker, tech. writer Vector Gen., Woodland Hills, Calif., 1976-77; undergrad. adv. U. So. Calif., L.A., 1987-89, rsch. asst. prof., rsch. assoc. social psychology, 1991—. Owner Attitude Rsch. Litigation and Orgn. Cons.; prof. Pierce Coll., Woodland Hills, Calif., 2000—. Contbr. chapters to books, articles to profl. jours. Recipient Haynes Found. Dissertation fellowship U. So. Calif., 1990. Fellow Am. Coll. Forensic Examiners, mem. APA, AAAS, Computer Graphics Pioneers, Am. Psychol. Soc., Western Psychol. Assn. Democrat. Jewish. Office: 4570 Van Nuys Blvd #357 Sherman Oaks CA 91403 Office Phone: 818-905-1770. E-mail: sharonrgross@cs.com.

GROSS-BREIN, EVELYN, counseling administrator, real estate broker; b. Greenwood, SC, Sept. 30, 1926; d. Ernest Royal and Alyce Dreyfus (Kahn) Rosenberg; m. Leonard Gross, 1950 (dec.); children: Gayle Gross de Nunez, Sally Alyce Gross, Ernest Kent Gross; m. Irving Brein (dec.). BA, Tulane U., New Orleans, La., 1947; MS, Fla. Religious Studies Inst., 1994, PhD, 2002. Exec. dir. MCK Real Estate Edn. Ctr., Ft. Lauderdale, Fla., 1977—78; co-owner Real Estate Salesmanship Ctr., Ft. Lauderdale, 1974—77, Real Estate Edn. Ctr., Ft. Lauderdale, 1975—80. Chaplain Hospice, 1994—2001. Co-author: (textbook) Real Estate for New Practitioner, 1976. Vol. HIV/AIDS sr. prevention program Broward County Health Dept., 2003—; trustee Ft. Lauderdale Coll., 1971—75; life-long vol. Charities, 1970—2000. Jewish. Avocations: dance, exercise. Home: 555 Oaks Lane #101 Pompano Beach FL 33069

GROSSET, JESSICA ARIANE, computer executive; b. Paris, Aug. 31, 1952; came to U.S., 1970; d. Raymond Louis and Barbara Ann (Byrne) G.; m. Bruce Edward Kaskubar, May 23, 1986. AA, Berkshire Community Coll., Pittsfield, Mass., 1972; BS, SUNY, Potsdam, 1979; postgrad., Ariz. State U., 1980, U. Minn., 1980-81. Computer programmer Kay-Bee Toy and Hobby Shops, Lee, Mass., 1974-78; adminstr. Mayo Clinic, Rochester, Minn., 1981—. Voting staff Mayo Clinic, Rochester, 1996. Mem. Nat. Assn. Female Execs. Avocations: reading, sailing, travel, horseback riding, skiing. Office: Mayo Clinic 200 1st St SW Rochester MN 55905-0002

GROSSETETE, GINGER LEE, retired gerontology administrator, consultant; b. Riverside, Calif., Feb. 9, 1936; d. Lee Roy Taylor and Bonita (Beryl) Williams; m. Alec Paul Grossetete, June 8, 1954 (div.); children: Elizabeth Gay Blech, Teri Lee Maclennan. BA in Recreation cum laude, U. N.Mex., 1974, M in Pub. Adminstrn., 1978. Sr. ctr. supr., Office of Sr. Affairs, City of Albuquerque, 1974-77, asst. dir. Office of Sr. Affairs, 1977-96. Conf. coord. Nat. Consumers Assn., Albuqeruque, 1978-79; region 6 del. Nat. Coun. on Aging, Washington, 1977-84; conf. chmn. Western Gerontol. Soc., Albuquerque, 1983; N.Mex. del. White House Conf. on Aging, 1995; mem. adv. coun. N.Mex. Agy. on Aging, 1996-2002; mem. City of Albuquerque Affordable Housing Com., 2002—. Contbr. articles to mags. Campaign dir. March of Dimes N.Mex., 1966-67; pres. Albuquerque Symphony Women's Assn., 1972; exec. com. Jr. League Albuquerque, 1976; mem. Gov.'s Coun. on Phys. Fitness, 1987-91, chmn. 1990-91; bd. dirs. N.Mex. Sr. Olympics, 1995-2001; chmn. YWCA Alumnae Assn. for Women on the Move, 1999-2001; mem. Mayor's Affordable Housing Com., 2002—. Recipient N.Mex. Disting. Pub. Service award N.Mex. Gov.'s Office, 1983, Disting. Woman on the Move award YWCA, 1986, Outstanding Profl. award N.Mex. State Conf. on Aging, 1995, Presdl. citation S.W. Soc. on Aging, 1995, Gov.'s award for Outstanding N.Mex. Women, 2001; inductee Albuquerque Sr. Citizens Hall of Fame, 1998. Fellow Nat. Recreation and Pk. Assn. (bd. dirs. S.W. regional coun. rep., bd. dirs. leisure and aging sect., pres. N.Mex. chpt. 1983-84, 97-98, bd. dirs. N.Mex. Sr. Olympics, 1994-2001, pres. leisure and aging sect. 1997-98, Outstanding profl. award 1982); mem. ASPA (pres. N.Mex. coun. 1987-88), S.W. Soc. on Aging (pres. 1984-85, bd. dirs., Outstanding Profl. award 1991, Presdl. citation 1996), U. N.Mex. Alumni Assn. (bd. dirs. 1978-80, Disting. Alumni award 1985), Las Amapolas Garden Club (pres. 1964), Phi Alpha Alpha, Chi Omega (pres. alumni 1959-60). Avocations: tennis, water-skiing, skiing, racewalking, arts and crafts. Home: 805 Suzanne Ln SE Albuquerque NM 87123-4502 Personal E-mail: gingergro@gmail.com.

GROSSETT, DEBORAH LOU, psychologist, consultant; b. Alma, Mich., Feb. 16, 1957; d. Charles M. and Margaret A. (Roethlisberger) G. BS, Alma Coll., 1979; MA, Western Mich. U., Kalamazoo, 1981; PhD, Western Mich. U., 1984. Lic. psychologist, Tex.; cert. in diagnostic evaluation, Tex.; bd. cert. behavior analyst, Tex. Grad. rsch. and tchg. asst. Western Mich. U., 1979-84; asst. group home supr., cmty. outreach Residential Opportunities, Kalamazoo, 1982-84; psychologist Richmond State Sch., Tex., 1984-87, Shapiro Devel. Ctr., Kankakee, Ill., 1987-88; clin. coord. Monroe Devel. Ctr., Rochester, NY, 1988; chief psychologist Denton State Sch., Tex., 1989-90; dir. psychol./behavioral svcs. Ctr. for the Retarded, Houston, 1990—2002; psychologist Mental Health and Mental Retardation Authority of Harris County, Houston, 2002—, Behavior Treatment and Tng. Ctr., 2005—06; pvt. practice, 2004—. Behavioral cons. Ctr. for Developmentally Disabled Adults, Kalamazoo, 1984, Goodman-Wade Enterprises, Houston, 1987; instr. psychology Houston C.C., 1985-86, U. Houston-Clear Lake, 1987, 92, 95—. Contbr. chpt. to book, articles to profl. jours. Western Mich. U. fellow, 1984. Mem. Am. Psychol. Assn., Am. Assn. on Mental Retardation, Assn. for Behavior Analysis (chair Outreach Bd. 1989-91), Tex. Assn. for Behavior Analysis (bd. dirs. 1989-91, program chair 1996, pres. 1997). Democrat. Presbyterian. Avocations: golf, camping, gardening. Home: 9750 Ravensworth Dr Houston TX 77031-3130 Office: MHMRA Harris County 7011 SW Freeway Houston TX 77074 Office Phone: 713-970-7129. Business E-Mail: deborah.grossett@mhmraharris.org.

GROSSI, LINDA MARIE, elementary school educator; b. Providence, Jan. 27, 1955; d. Francesco and Helen Marie Grossi; children: Anna Lee Cogean, Karena Lyn Cogean, Joseph William Cogean Jr. BS in Health Sci. and Phys. Edn., RI Coll., Providence, 1995, MEd, 2004. Cert. adapted phys. edn. RI Dept. Edn., nonviolent crisis prevention Crisis Prevention Inst., Inc., teach to change Americorps. Camp dir. Girl Scouts RI, Inc., Providence, 1990—93; health and phys. ed. tchr. Cranston Sch. Dept., RI, 1995—97, Providence Sch. Dept., 1998—; instr. Bristol C.C., Fall River, Mass., 2000—. Leader trainer Girl Scouts RI, Inc., 1994—2002; grad., active mem. Warwick Citizen's Police Acad., RI, 2005—06. Recipient Sr. Departmental award, RI Coll., 1996, Project Sch. Spirit award, Mayor David Cicciline, City of Providence, 2004, 25 Yrs. Svc. award, Girl Scouts RI, Inc., 1997; grantee Go Girls award, Nat. Assn. for Girls and Women in Sports, 2006. Mem.: AAHPERD, Am. Assn. Health Edn., Nat. Assn. Sports and Phys. Edn., RI Assn. Health, Phys. Edn., Recreation and Dance (treas. 2004—, grantee 2005—06), Warwick Citizen's Police Acad. (v.p. 2005—06), Kappa Delta Pi. Office: Gilbert Stuart Mid Sch 188 Princeton Ave Providence RI 02888 Office Phone: 401-456-9340. Office Fax: 401-453-8659. Personal E-mail: physedtchrri@aol.com. Business E-Mail: linda.grossi@ppsd.org.

GROSSI, ROSE B., director; b. Rochester, NY, May 16, 1913; Secretarial grad. course, Rochester Bus. Inst., Rochester, NY, 1934. Med. sec. PF Metaldi, Rochester, NY; dir. Mt. Carmel House Inc., Rochester, NY. Author: Poetry Collection, Look up to Love, 1975; editor, Lay Carmelites of Rochester Sec., 1960-75. Recipient, Unsung Hero, City of Rochester, 1998, Charitable Svc. Awd., Roch. COmmty. of Churches, 1996. Roman Catholic. Avocation: writing. Home: 1550 Portland Ave # 1307 Rochester NY 14621-3005

GROSSMAN, BARBARA ANNE, nurse; d. Cornell and Anna Pazderski; m. Charles Marx (dec.); children: Michael Ralston, Elizabeth Ralston; m. Michael Grossman, Oct. 1, 1998. A of Nursing, Elgin C.C., Ill., 1978; BSc, U. St. Francis, Ill., 1992. Cert. orthop. nurse 1992. Staff nurse Northwest Cmty. Hosp., Arlington Heights, Ill., 1978—97; case mgr. Provina Health Care, Elgin, Ill., 1997—2005; unit mgr. Manor Care, Arlington Heights, 2005—06, Luth. Home, Arlington Heights, 2005—06; nurse cons. MetLife, Mt. Prospect, Ill., 2006—. Mem.: Nat. Assn. Orthop. Nurses (pres. Metro. chpt. Chgo. 2002—05). Avocations: horses, dogs, gardening. Office: MetLife 1660 Feenhand Dr Mount Prospect IL E-mail: barbaragrossman@comcast.net.

GROSSMAN, BONNIE, art gallery director; m. Sy Grossman. Former kindergarten teacher; founder The Ames Gallery, Berkeley, Calif., 1970—. Lectr. on Am. folk art and outsider art. Exec. prod., co-dir., prod. nine TV programs on Calif. artists; contbr. articles to profl. publs. Avocations: cake sculpture, knitting. Office: The Ames Gallery 2661 Cedar St Berkeley CA 94708 Office Phone: 510-845-4949. Office Fax: 510-845-6219. E-mail: amesgal@comcast.net.

GROSSMAN, CAROLYN SYLVIA CORT, retired elementary school educator; b. Cleve., Apr. 26, 1928; d. Louis J. and Esther (Matyas) Cort; m. Melvin J. Grossman, Aug. 7, 1949; children: Richard, Susan, Elaine. BS in Edn., Flora Stone Mather Coll., 1949; MS in Edn., Kent State U., 1974. Tchr. Columbus City Schs., Ohio, 1949—52; tchr. presch. Jewish Cmty. Ctr., Cleve., 1965—68, Carol Nursery, University Heights, Ohio, 1968—70; tchr. Cleveland Heights Schs., Ohio, 1970—93; ret., 1993. Bd. dirs., officer, pres. S. Euclid Lyndhurst (Ohio) LWV, 1957-74; coord. John W. Raper Open Sch., Cleve., 1965-73; bd. dirs. Greater Cleve. Tchr. Ctr., 1974-80; founder, pres., bd. dirs. Heights Parent Ctr., Cleveland Heights, 1975-80, hon. life trustee, 1985; co-chair Hello Israel program Nat. Coun. Jewish Women, Cleve., 1995-00, chair, 2000—. Martha Holden Jennings Found. scholar, 1975; recipient Achievement award City of University Heights, 1992, Arline B. Pritcher award Nat. Coun. Jewish Women-Cleve. Sect., 1998; named Carolyn Grossman award in her honor Heights Parent Ctr., 2003. Mem. Cleve. Heights Tchrs. Union (v.p. 1985-90, Ellen Krebs award 1983), Heights Ret. Tchrs. (founder, officer, bd. dirs. 1993-96). Jewish.

GROSSMAN, EDITH MARIAN, translator; b. Phila., Mar. 22, 1936; d. Alexander and Sally (Stern) Dorph; children: Matthew, Kory. BA, U. Pa., 1957, MA, 1959; postgrad., U. Calif., Berkeley, 1960-62; PhD, NYU, 1972. Translator: Love in Time of Cholera (Garcia Márquez), 1988, General in his Labyrinth (Márquez), Maqroll (Alvaro Mutis), 1992, Strange Pilgrims (Márquez), 1993, Of Love and Other Demons (Márquez), 1995, The Adventures of Maqroll (Mutis), 1995, Death in the Andes (Vargas Llosa), 1996, In The Palm of Darkess (Mayra Montero), 1997, The Feast of the Goat (Vargas Llosa), 2001, The Red of His Shadow (Mayra Montero), 2001, Monstruary (Julian Rios), 2001, Don Quixote (Miguel de Cervantes), 2003; also others. Avocations: reading, music.

GROSSMAN, ELIZABETH, lawyer; BA, JD, U. Mich. Atty. EEOC, 1993—, regional atty. NYC, 2004—. Office: EEOC 33 Whitehall St New York NY 10004 Office Phone: 212-336-3696. Office Fax: 212-336-3623.

GROSSMAN, FRANCES KAPLAN, psychologist; b. Newport News, Va., May 28, 1939; d. Rubin H. and Beatrice (Fischlowitz) Kaplan; m. Henry Grossman, July 26, 1970; children: Jennifer, Benjamin. BA, Oberlin (Ohio) Coll., 1961; MS, PhD, Yale U., 1965. Diplomate Am. Bd. Profl. Psychology. Asst. prof. Yale U., New Haven, 1965-69, Boston U., 1969-71, assoc. prof. psychology, 1971-82, prof. psychology, 1982—2002, prof. emeritus, 2002—. Author: Brothers and Sisters of Retarded Children, 1971, Pregnancy, Birth and Parenthood, 1980, With the Phoenix Rising, 1999. Trustee Oberlin Coll., 1990-92, pres. Alumni Assn., 1979-80. Recipient Cert. of Appreciation Oberlin Coll. Alumni Assn., 1983. Fellow APA (mem. ethics com. 1994-97); mem. New Eng. Soc. Study Treatment Trauma and Dissociation (bd. dirs. 1995-99), Mass. Psychol. Assn. (chair ethics com. 1989-91, Career Contbn. award 1991), Sigma Xi, Phi Beta Kappa. Jewish. Office: Boston Univ Dept Psychology 64 Cummington St Boston MA 02215-2407 Office Phone: 617-332-6505. E-mail: frang@bu.edu.

GROSSMAN, GINGER SCHEFLIN, advocate; b. Bklyn., June 24, 1919; d. Louis Scheflin and Rose Taggert; m. Arthur I. Grossman, Apr. 6, 1941; children: Lynn Grossman Balaban, Boni Grossman Smith. Del. UN Conf. Global Environment, Rio de Janeiro, 1985; mem. adv. bd. South Fla. Food Recovery, 1985—; charter mem. Dade County Women's Coalition for Healthy Planet, 1985; mem. Dade County Commn. on Status of Women, 1983—95, mem. older women's task force, 1990—95; co-founder, v.p. Kids in Dade Soc., 1987—; exec. v.p. Rood Alzheimer's Found., 1989—92; chmn. long-term and managed care task force Alliance for Aging, 1989—93, chmn. advocacy and edn. com., 1990—, bd. dirs., 1999—2002; mem. adv. bd. South Fla. Theater of Deaf, 1991—2004; founder, pres. Aventura-Turnberry chpt. Women's Am. ORT, 1991—95; co-founder, v.p. Youth Cadets of Dade County, 1991—2003; Dem. exec. committeewoman Nassau County, NY, 1971—75, Dade County, Fla., 1981—; founder, pres. William Lehman NE Dade Involved Democrats, 1990—; bd. dirs. Aventure-Turnberry Jewish Ctr., 1991—, Dade County Transit Coalition, 1987—. Named Best Friend, City of North Miami, Fla., 1995, Super Vol., Alliance for Aging, Dade County, Fla., 1999, Woman of Valor, Aventura-Turnberry Jewish Ctr., Fla., 2000; recipient Dr. Jean Jones Purdue award for spl. achievement, Alliance for Aging, 2001. Mem.: Profl. Bus. Women's Assn. Democrat.

GROSSMAN, JOAN DELANEY, literature and language professor; b. Dubuque, Iowa, Dec. 12, 1928; d. Francis Joseph and Opal (Desmond) Delaney; m. Gregory Grossman, June 16, 1972. BA, Clarke Coll., Dubuque, 1952; MA, Columbia U., 1962; PhD, Harvard U., 1967. Asst. prof. Russian Mundelein Coll., Chgo., 1967-68; asst. prof., assoc. prof. then prof. Slavic langs. and lit. U. Calif.-Berkeley, 1968-93, prof. emeritus, 1993—, prof. grad. sch., 1995—. Author: Edgar Allen Poe in Russia: A Study of Legend and Literary Influence, 1973, Valery Bryusov and the Riddle of Russian Decadence, 1985; co-editor: Creating Life: The Aesthetic Utopia of Russian Modernism, 1994. Guggenheim fellow, 1978; Soviet Acad. Scis. fellow, Am. Acad. Learned Socs., 1978, 86, NEH fellow, 1992. Mem. Am. Assn. Advancement of Slavic Studies (v.p. 1988, pres. 1989), Am. Assn. Tchrs. Slavic and Eastern European Langs., Western Slavic Assn. (pres. 1984-86). Office: Univ Calif Dept Slavic Langs And Lits Berkeley CA 94720-2979

GROSSMAN, JOANNE BARBARA, lawyer; b. Brookline, Mass., Oct. 23, 1949; d. Bernard R. and Beatrice G. (Quint) G.; m. John H. Seesel, Dec. 30, 1973; children: Benjamin P., Rebecca A. AB, Radcliffe Coll., 1971; JD, U. Calif., Berkeley, 1975. Bar: Calif. 1975, D.C. 1976, U.S. Dist. Ct. D.C. 1976, U.S. Ct. Appeals (D.C. cir.) 1976, U.S. Supreme Ct. 1979. Assoc. Covington & Burling, Washington, 1975-83, ptnr., 1983—. Office: Covington & Burling PO Box 7566 1201 Pennsylvania Ave NW Washington DC 20044

GROSSMAN, JOYCE RENEE, pediatrician, internist; b. Bklyn., Nov. 15, 1951; d. Norman and Sydell (Rashbaum) Katz; m. Arthur Robert Grossman (div.); 1 child, Justin BS, Bklyn. Coll., 1973; MS, Cornell Med. Coll., Ithaca, N.Y., 1980; MD, Downstate Med. Coll., 1986. Adj. prof. Downstate Med. Ctr., Bklyn., 1994—; attending physician N.Y. Hosp. Network, Bklyn., 1996—97, Beth Israel Med. Ctr., Bklyn., 1997; assoc. med. dir. Cigna of N.Y., N.Y.C., 1998—. Author: (with others) Pediatric Aspects of Tuberculosis & Clinical Handbook, 1995 Fellow: Am. Acad. Physicians, Am. Acad. Pediat. Achievements include patents in field of gene therapy, antibiotics and chemotherapeutic agents.

GROSSMAN, MARY MARGARET, elementary school educator; b. East Cleveland, Ohio, Sept. 26, 1946; d. Frank Anthony and Margaret Mary (Buda) G. Student, Kent State U., 1965—67; BS in Elem. Edn. cum laude, Cleveland State U., 1971; postgrad, Lake Erie Coll., 1974—77, Cleveland State U., 1985, John Carroll U., 1978, postgrad, 1981—83, postgrad, 1985. Cert. elem. sch. tchr. grades 1 to 8 Ohio, cert. data processing Ohio. Tchr. Cleve. Catholic Diocese, Cleve., Ohio, 1971-72, Willoughby-Eastlake Sch. Dist., Willoughby, Ohio, 1972—. Participant Nat. Econ. Edn. Conf., Richmond, Va., 1995. Eucharistic min. St. Christine's Ch., Euclid, 1988—, mem. parish pastoral coun., 1995—2000. Recipient Samuel H. Elliott Econ. Leadership award, 1986-87, Consumer Educator award NE Ohio Region, 1986, 1st pl. award for excellence in tchg. Tchrs. in Am. Enterprise, 1984-85, 89-90; Martha Holden Jennings scholar, 1984-85. Mem. NEA, Ohio Edn. Assn. (human rels. award 1986-87, cert. merit 1987-88), NE Ohio Edn. Assn. (Positive Tchr. Image award 1988). Roman Catholic. Avocations: racquetball, softball, walking, tennis, bicycling. Home: 944 E 225th St Cleveland OH 44123-3308 Office: McKinley Elem Sch 1200 Lost Nation Rd Willoughby OH 44094-7324

GROSSMAN, MELANIE, dermatologist; AB in Biology, Princeton U., N.J., 1984; MD, NYU, 1988. Diplomate Am. Bd. Dermatology. Intern Yale U. Med. Ctr., New Haven, 1988—89; resident in dermatology Presbyn. Hosp./Columbia U., N.Y.C., 1989—92; fellow in laser dermatology and photodynamic therapy Mass. Gen. Hosp. and Wellman Labs., Boston, 1993—95; asst. attending dermatologist NY Hospital, N.Y.C., 1998, Cornell Univ., 1998; pvt. practice dermatology N.Y.C., 1992—. Asst. attending dermatology Presbyn. Hosp., N.Y.C., 1992—, Cornell U., N.Y.C., 1998—, N.Y. Hosp., N.Y.C., 1998—, St. Luke's Roosevelt Hosp. Ctr., N.Y.C., 1995—; attending physician dept. plastic surgery N.Y. Eye and Ear Infirmary, N.Y.C., 1996—; assoc. clin. in dermatology Columbia U., N.Y.C., 1992—; dir. clin. and laser rsch. studies Laser and Skin Surgery Ctr. of N.Y., N.Y.C., 1995; clin. affiliate dermatology N.Y. Hosp., N.Y.C., 1996—97; clin. instr. dermatology Cornell U. Med. Ctr., N.Y.C., 1996—97; clin. fellow dermatology Mass. Gen. Hosp.-Harvard Med. Sch., Boston, 1993—95. Contbr. articles to profl. jours. Fellow: Am. Soc. for Dermatologic Surgery, Am. Soc. for Laser Medicine and Surgery (socioecon. affairs com. 1997—2000, nominating com. 2000); mem.: Women's Dermatologic Soc., Women's Med. Soc. N.Y., Dermatologic Soc. Greater N.Y. (comm. com., exec. com.), Med. Soc. State of N.Y., Am. Acad. Dermatology (chair photobiology task force 1998—99, melanoma task force, comm. com. 1998—2000, comm. study group for 21st century, sports ad hoc com., chair socioecon. affairs com. 1999—2000). Office: 161 Madison Ave Ste 4 NW New York NY 10016 Office Phone: 212-725-8600. Office Fax: 212-725-8620.

GROSSMAN, PATRICIA, writer; b. Cleve., June 2, 1951; d. Carol Klein and James Grossman; life ptnr. Helene Kendler. BFA, Pratt Inst., Bklyn., 1971; MFA, Sarah Lawrence Coll., Bronxville, NY, 1976. Author: (novel) Inventions in a Grieving House, Four Figures in Time, Unexpected Child, Brian in Three Seasons, Looking for Heroes (forthcoming), (children's book) The Night Ones, Saturday Market. Vol. Gay Men's Health Crisis, N.Y.C., 1986—93, Learning Leaders, N.Y.C., 2001—04. Recipient Parent's Choice and ABA Pick of the Lists citations for children's books, Parent's Choice Mag. and Am. Book Assn., 1991, 1995. Mem.: PEN Am. Progressive. Office Phone: 212-653-8146. Personal E-mail: pattygrossman@earthlink.net.

GROSSO, CAMILLE M., nurse; b. Geneva, N.Y., Sept. 28, 1938; d. Frank and Gaetana (Luongo) Balistreri; m. Gerard Michael Grosso, Apr. 8, 1961; children: Gerard II, Gina M. BS, George Mason U., 1976; MSN, Catholic U. Am., 1978; PhD, Case Western Res. U., 1995. RN. Staff nurse Project Hope, Saigon, Vietnam, 1961-62; head nurse Fairfax Hosp., Falls Church, Va., 1972-76; clin. specialist Arlington (Va.) Hosp., 1978-82; faculty Catholic U., Washington, 1982-89, U. Md., Balt., 1990-92; pvt. practice psychotherapist Annandale, Va., 1980—. Roman Catholic.

GROSSO, DOREEN ELLIOTT, management consultant; d. John and Hilda Elliott; m. Joseph Anthony Grosso, May 30, 1971; children: John Cesar, Michael Steven, Joseph Armando. BS, Fordham U., 1971; MBA, Pace U., 1979. V.p. Chem. Bank, NYC, 1981—91; pres. Change Creates Opportunity, Inc., Flushing, NY, 1991—. Dir. ARIL/CrossCurrents, NYC, 1995—2003. Participant, alum Coro-Leadership NY, NYC, 1990—90. Named Woman of Future, NY Women's Agenda, 2001. Mem.: Orgn. and Devel. Network Greater NY, World Future Soc. Roman Catholic. Business E-Mail: ccoi@nyc.rr.com.

GROTA, BARBARA LYNN, academic administrator, educator; d. Jerome A. and Laura B. Grota; m. James William Murphy, Apr. 30, 1988 (dec. Sept. 30, 1991). BA, Southeastern Mass. U., North Dartmouth, MA, 1976—79; MS, Syracuse U., Syracuse, NY, 1980—82; PhD, Walden U., 2005. Orgnl. devel. cons. Carrier Corp., Syracuse, NY, 1980—81; social sci. - adj. faculty New Eng. Inst. of Tech., Warwick, RI, 1982—85, coop. edn. founder/coord., 1983—85; coop. edn. asst. dir. Roger Williams U., Bristol, RI, 1985—2000, social sci. adj. faculty, 1988—2000, asst. prof. of mgmt., 2000—, asst. dean, asst. prof., 2000—. Pres. New Eng. Assn. for Coop. Edn. and Field Experience, Boston, 1990—90; supervising editor NEACEFE newsletter, New Eng. Assn. for Coop. Edn. and Field Experience, Boston, 1991—92; mem. bd. of directors Riverwood Rehab. Services Inc., Bristol, RI, 1995—2000, co-president bd. of directors, 1997—99; strategic planning cons./facilitator Bristol Econ. Devel. Commn., Warren, RI, 2000—00; facilitator/trainer RI Probate Ct., West Greenwich, RI, 2002—02. Author (co-author): (rsch. article) Procs. of the 2002 Symposium for the Mktg. of Higher Edn. of the Am. Mktg. Assn., (pub. rsrch.) Procs. of the 1987 Nat. Coop. Edn. Assn. Conf. Canvas com. mem. Fairhaven Unitarian Universalist Ch., Fairhaven, Mass., 1999—99; exec. dir. evaluation com. mem. Riverwood Rehab. Services, Inc., Bristol, RI, 1995—2000; mem. Child and Family Services of Newport County, Newport, RI, 1999—99. Recipient The Excellence in Tchg. Award, Alpha Chi - Nat. Honor Soc., 1997, Psi Chi - Psychology Nat. Honor Soc., 2000, Honor Soc. Induction, Sigma Beta Delta - Internat. Honor Soc. in Bus., Mgmt., and Adminstrn., 2000, Outstanding Women On Campus award, Roger Williams U. Women's Ctr., 1998, 2002. Mem.: Am. Mktg. Assn., Am. Psychol. Assn. (APA), Roger Williams U. Dean's Diversity Coun., Nat. Academic Advising Assn. Avocations: hiking, gourmet cooking, reading. Office: Roger Williams University One Old Ferry Rd Bristol RI 02809 Office Phone: 401-254-3092.

GROTENRATH, MARY JO, lawyer, writer; d. Joseph Albert and Mary Della (Castrigano) Grotenrath. BA in History cum laude, Dunbarton Coll. Holy Cross, 1955; JD, Georgetown U., 1959. Bar: Ohio 1959, DC 1959, US Ct. Appeals (DC cir.) 1959, US Ct. Mil. Appeals 1959, US Supreme Ct. 1962. Pvt. practice, Columbus, Ohio, 1962—67; atty. US Dept. Justice, Washington, 1967—2002; chief atty. Bd. Immigration Appeals, 1976; gen. counsel Interpol-U.S. Nat. Ctrl. Bur., 1984—88, assoc. dir. criminal divsn., office of internat. affairs, 1988—2000, chief fugitive unit, 1994—2002. Author: The Interpol Imbroglio, 2004. Named Hon. Deputy, US Marshall, 1997, Hon. Detective, Metro Toronto Fugitive Squad, 1997; recipient Honor plaque, FBI, Dept. of State counter-Terrorism Unit, US Secret Svc., US Postal Inspection Svc., Elvyn Holt award, Nat. Assn. Extradition Ofcls., 1999, St. Gabriel Possenti Honor medal, 2001. Mem.: Pi Gamma Mu, Kappa Gamma Pi. Home: 1000 Urlin Ave Summit Chase Unit 209 Columbus OH 43212

GROTH-MARNAT, GABRIELLE, counselor; b. LA, Sept. 17, 1947; d. Rudolph Sibo and Barbara Banks Groth-Marnat, Carolyn Groth-Marnat (Stepmother); children: Kimberly Laura Andrews, Kip(dec.), Banks(dec.). BS in Med. Tech., Colo. Women's Coll., 1968; BS in Interdisciplinary Studies & Human Svcs., Lewis Clark State Coll., 1994; MEd, U. Idaho, 1997. Cert. Am.

Soc. Clin. Pathology, Idaho Licensure Bd., 1976; LSW Idaho Licensure Bd., 1994; coach Hudson Inst., Calif., 1994, pupil personnel Bd. Edn., Idaho, 1999, Bd. Edn., Idaho, 2004. Social worker Kootenai Med. Ctr., Coeur d'Alene, Idaho, 1993—99; sch. counselor St. Marie's Joint Sch. Dist. #41, Idaho, 1999—2002, Lake Pend Oreille Sch. Dist. #84, Sandpoint, Idaho, 2003—; PSR worker Panhandle Horizons, Sandpoint, 2004—. Counselor, youth group domestic violence program Post Falls Police Dept./OASIS, Idaho, 2002—03; summer youth coord. Idaho Dept. Labor, Coeur d'Alene, 1999. Sec., bd. mem. Camp Fire Girls & Boys Am., Coeur d'Alene, 1982—85. Mem.: Idaho Sch. Counselors Assn. (assoc.), Am. Psychology Assn. (assoc.), Am. Sch. Counselors Assn. (assoc.), Peace Corps (assoc.; RPCV - Ivory Coast, West Africa 1972—74), C.A.R.E. (assoc.). Home: Smoke Rising Ranch PO Box 226 Bayview ID 83803-0226 Office: Lake Pend Oreille Sch Dist #84 Southside Elem PO Box 159 Cocolalla ID 83813 Office Phone: 208-263-3020. Office Fax: 208-265-4836. Personal E-mail: gabigm@imbris.com. Business E-Mail: gabrielle.grothmarnat@sci84.k12.id.us.

GROTZINGER, LAUREL ANN, librarian, educator; b. Truman, Minn., Apr. 15, 1935; d. Edward F. and Marian Gertrude (Greeley) G. BA, Carleton Coll., 1957; MS, U. Ill., 1958, PhD, 1964. Instr., asst. libr. Ill. State U., 1958-62; asst. prof. Western Mich. U., Kalamazoo, 1964-66, assoc. prof., 1966-68, prof., 1968—, asst. dir. Sch. Librarianship, 1965-72, chief rsch. officer, 1979-86, interim dir. Sch. Libr. and Info. Sci., 1982-86, dean grad. coll., 1979-92, prof. univ. libr., 1993—. Author: The Power and the Dignity, 1966; mem. editl. bd. Jour. Edn. for Librarianship, 1973-77, Dictionary Am. Libr. Biography, 1975-77, Mich. Academician, 1990—; contbr. articles to profl. jours., books. Trustee Kalamazoo Pub. Libr., 1991-93, v.p., 1991-92, pres., 1992-93; pres. Kalamazoo Bach Festival, 1996-97, bd. dirs. 1992-98, exec. com. 1996-98. Mem. ALA (sec.-treas. Libr. History Round Table 1973-74, vice chmn., chmn-elect 1983-84, chmn. 1984-85, mem.-at-large 1991-93), Spl. Librs. Assn., Assn. Libr. Info. Sci. Edn., Mich. acad. Sci., Arts and Letters (mem.-at-large, exec. com. 1980-86, pres. 1983-85, exec. com. 1990-94, pres. 1991-93, vice chmn. libr./info. scis. 1996-97, chair 1997-98), Internat. Assn. Torch Clubs (v.p. Kalamazoo chpt. 1992-93, pres. 1993-94, exec. com. 1989-95), Soc. Collegiate Journalists, Phi Beta Kappa (pres. S.W. Mich. chpt. 1977-78, sec. 1994-97, pres. 1997-99), Beta Phi Mu, Alpha Beta Alpha, Delta Kappa Gamma (pres. Alpha Psi chpt. 1988-92), Phi Kappa Phi. Home: 2729 Mockingbird Dr Kalamazoo MI 49008-1626 Office Phone: 269-387-5418. Business E-Mail: laurel.grotzinger@wmich.edu.

GROVE, CHERYLEE VEGA, special education educator; b. L.A., Oct. 23, 1980; d. Elizalde and Rosario Abad Vega; m. Kevin Grove, Aug. 7, 2005. BA, U. So. Calif., L.A., 2002. Cert. CLAD-ELA U. La Verne, 2002. Eld/ela tchr. Lorbeer Mid. Sch., Diamond Bar, CA, Calif., 2002—06; intervention tchr. specialist Pomona (Calif.) Unified Sch. Dist., 2006—. Advisor Calif. Jr. Scholarship Fedn., Lorbeer MS Chpt., Diamond Bar, 2004—06. Mem. Leukemia and Lymphoma Soc., L.A., 2005—06. Avocations: marathons, travel, baking, card making, scrapbooks. E-mail: cherylee.grove@pusd.org.

GROVE, MYRNA JEAN, elementary school educator; b. Bryan, Ohio, Oct. 24, 1949; d. Kedric Durward and N. Florence (Stombaugh) G. Student, Bowling Green State U., 1970-71; BA in Edn., Manchester Coll., 1971; postgrad., U. No. Colo., 1974-76, Purdue U., 1977, St. Francis Coll., Ft. Wayne, Ind., 1986, Coll. Mount St. Joseph, Ohio, 1986; MLS, Kent State U., 1999. Cert. elem. tchr., Ohio, 1971, permanent cert., 1999. Tchr. elem. sch. Bryan City Schs., 1972—. Author: Asbestos Cancer: One Man's Experience, 1995, Legacy of One-Room Schools, 1999; editor newspaper column Education Today, 1975-82, newsletter N.W. Ohio Emphasis, 1981-83 (award 1981). Dir., violinist Bryan String Ensemble, 1981—; organist Trinity Episc. Ch., Bryan, 1979-89; active Lancaster Mennonite Hist. Soc., Hans Herr Found.; trustee Bryan Area Cultural Assn., 1984-89; bd. dirs. Williams County Cmty. Concerts; sec. Black Swamp Arts Coun., 2001-2004. Jennings scholar Martha Holden Jennings Found., Bowling Green State U., 1982-83. Mem. ALA, NEA (Ohio del., state contact 1986-87), Ohio Edn. Assn. (presenter 1984, del. global issues 1986, sec. N.W. Ohio Tchrs. Uniserv. 1975-78), Bus. and Profl. Women Ohio (individual devel. com. 1986-90, speaking skills cert. 1987), N.W. Ohio Manchester Coll. Alumni Assn. (past pres.), Bryan Edn. Assn. (exec. com., pres. 1985-86), Williams County Geneal. Soc., Williams County Hist. Assn., P. Buckley Moss Soc., Trees of Life (v.p. 1994-2001, regional Moss docent), Alpha Delta Kappa (pres. 1996-98), Alpha Mu. Avocations: collecting dolls, playing piano, organ and violin, reading, travel. Business E-Mail: graf24@cityofbryan.net.

GROVE, NANCY CAROL, academic administrator; b. Johnstown, Pa. d. Henry and Marie (Boerstler) Frambach; m. William M. Grove; children: Eric William, Carol Ann. BS in Nursing, U. Pitts., 1968, MEd, 1972, PhD, 1988; MS in Nursing, Duquesne U., 1980. Staff nurse Conemaugh Valley Meml. Hosp., Johnstown, 1963-66, head nurse, 1967, 70, nursing care supr., 1968-71, instr., course dir. Sch. Nursing, 1971-79, dir. Sch. Nursing, 1979-91; assoc. prof. RN-BSN program, dir. Sch. Nursing U. Pitts., Johnstown, 1990—. Instr. refresher course Votech. Sch., Johnstown, 1973-76; adj. assoc. prof. U. Pitts., 1979-91; site visitor Nat. League for Nursing, N.Y.C.; chair Cambria/Somerset Coun. for Health Profls., Inc., Johnstown, 1984-89, Cambria/Somerset Mgmt. Com., 1994-96. Recipient Tribute to Women award for excellence in edn., YWCA, 1988, Sch. Nursing Dean's Disting. Tchg. award, 2001. Mem.: Soroptomist Internat. (pres. 1994—96), Sigma Theta Tau. Lutheran. Avocations: calligraphy, art. Home: 810 Linden Ave Johnstown PA 15902-2856 Office: U Pitts 141 Biddle Hall Johnstown PA 15904 Office Phone: 814-269-2947. Business E-Mail: ngrove@pitt.edu.

GROVE, VIRGINIA A., science educator; AS, Lake Mich. Coll., 1967; BS, Western Mich. U., 1969, MA in Tchg. of Secondary Sci., 1975. Sci. tchr. Lakeshore Pub. Sch. Sys., 1969—83, Tapp Mid. Sch., Powder Springs, Ga., 1983—84, St. Joseph Pub. Sch. Sys., Mich., 1985—87, Lake Mich. Cath. Mid. Sch./HS, St. Joseph, 1988—91, 1993—. Mem. study skills com. St. Joseph HS, mem. tchrs. self-esteem com., mem. sci. curriculum com.; co-chair sci. curriculum com. Lakeshore Pub. Schs.; mem. steering com. Lakeshore Career Edn.; adv. Equestrian Club, Jr. High Student Coun., Future Medic's Club, Jr. Class Environ. Club, Sci. Olympiad, Leeianau Outdoor Ctr. Vol. tchr., adult edn. courses Lakeshore Pub. Schs.; vol. tchr. Winning, Inc. Reading Recovery with Benton Harbor Schs., Boys & Girls Club; vol. Emergency Room Link Crisis Intervention Ctr., Tree of Life Ministries: Rosebud Sioux Indian Resevatio, SD. Recipient LMC Tchr. of Yr., 2003. Home: 2209 Paw Paw Ave Benton Harbor MI 49022

GROVER, PENELOPE H., singer, music educator; b. Glen Cove, NY, Apr. 11, 1953; d. Gilbert Robert Herdt and Clara Burling Roesch; m. Anthony Hilton Grover, Oct. 24, 1981; children: Corin Adriel, Evan Peris, Taryn Ephraim, Knaishia Paloma. MusB, Boston U, 1976. V.p. A Small Co. In Am., Deer Park, NY, 1981—; chorus tchr. Waldorf Sch. of Garden City, NY, 2002—; prof. voice Five Towns Coll., Dix Hills, NY, 2005—. Pvt. voice tchr., NY, 1978—; soprano soloist First Ch. of Christ, Levittown, NY, 1988—, Cmty. Synagogue Sands Point, NY, 1999—. Actor: Nuts; prodr., actor: more than 100 theatrical shows, musicals, plays. Morgan Pk. Music scholar, 1974. Mem.: Nat. Assn. Music Edn. Avocation: yoga. Home: 211 Sammis Ave Deer Park NY 11729 Office: A Small Company In America (ASCIA) 211 Sammis Ave Deer Park NY 11729 Office Phone: 516-686-7894. Personal E-mail: phgrover@hotmail.com.

GROVER, ROSALIND REDFERN, oil and gas company executive; b. Midland, Tex., Sept. 5, 1941; d. John Joseph and Rosalind (Kapps) Redfern;m. Arden Roy Grover, Apr. 10, 1982; 1 child, Rosson. BA in Edn. magna cum laude, U. Ariz., 1966, MA in History, 1982; postgrad. in law, So. Meth. U. Libr. Gahr H.S., Cerritos, Calif., 1969; pres. The Redfern Found., Midland, 1982—89; ptnr. Redfern & Grover, Midland, 1986—; pres. Redfern Enterprises Inc., Midland, 1989—. Chmn. bd. dirs. Flag-Redfern Oil Co., Midland. Sec. park and recreation commn. City of Midland, 1969-71, del. Objectives for Convocation, 1980; mem., past pres. women's aux. Midland Cmty. Theatre, 1970; chmn. challenge grant bldg. fund, 1980, chmn. Tex. Yucca Hist. Landmark Renovation Project, 1983, trustee, 1983-88; chmn. publicity com. Midland Jr. League, Midland, Inc., 1972, chmn. edn. com., 1976, corr. sec., 1978; 1st v.p. Midland Symphony Assn., 1975; chmn. Midland Charity Horse Show, 1975-76; mem. Midland Am. Revolution Bicentennial Commn., 1976; trustee Mus. S.W., 1977-80, pres. bd. dirs., 1979-80; co-chmn. Gov. Clements Fin. Com., Midland, 1978; mem. dist. com. State Bd. Law Examiners; mem. bd. visitors Hockaday, 2001-03; trustee Midland Meml. Hosp., 1978-80, Permian Basin Petroleum Mus., Libr. and Hall of Fame, 1989-98, Midland Cmty. Theatre, 2005—. Recipient HamHock award Midland Cmty. Theatre, 1978. Mem. Ind. Petroleum Assn. Am., Tex. Ind. Producers and Royalty Owners Assn., Petroleum Club, Racquet Club (Midland), Horseshoe Bay (Tex.) Country Club, Phi Kappa Phi, Pi Lambda Theta. Republican. Office: PO Box 2127 Midland TX 79702-2127 Office Phone: 432-683-9137. E-mail: rozgrover@aol.com.

GROVES, B. C., educational consultant, writer; d. James Alvis Cowan and Jean Maxine Wilkinson; m. Winford E. Groves, Dec. 16, 1955; 1 child, Cheryl J. BA, North Tex. State U., 1962; MS, Okla. State U., 1976. Cert. tchr. Tex., Okla., 1966. Tchr. Carrollton (Tex.) ISD, 1966—74; supr. Right to Read, Stillwater, Okla., 1974—75; writing tchr. Dallas County Cmty., 1976—78, Dallas C.C., El Centro Coll.; tchg. asst. Tex. A&M, Coll. Sta., 1979—82; real estate broker self-employed, Dallas and Denton, 1982—90; mayor City of Lewisville (Tex.), 1991—93; author, cons. self-employed, Oreg., 1994—. Bd. dirs. Crimestoppers, Denton, Tex., 1989—91. Contbg. author: Reflections on the Umpqua, 1999; co-author: Keeping Christmas, 2002; author: Heros of Lively County, 2003; contbr. articles to profl. jours., local newspapers. Mem. Dallas Crime Commn., 1989—90; precinct chair Denton County Rep., Lewisville, Tex., 1990—93; precinct person Douglas County Rep. Party, Oreg., 2004—. Recipient Outstanding Woman, Dallas Times Herald, 1972. Mem.: AAUW, DAR (com. chair 2003—05, 2nd vice regent Umpqua chpt. 2003—05), Tex. State Tchrs. (life). Republican. Episcopalian. Avocations: hiking, gardening, travel. Personal E-mail: greyfeather2006@yahoo.com. Business E-Mail: pennypublication@hotmail.com.

GROVES, BERNICE ANN, retired elementary and secondary school coordinator, educator; b. Bklyn., Feb. 5, 1928; d. Charles and Mary (Silverman) Lichtenstein; m. Stuart Weiss, June 5, 1949 (div. June 1978); children: Joel Weiss, Patricia Weiss Levy; m. Sidney Groves, July 30, 1978 (dec. May 2000). MA, Adelphi U., 1971; MS in Edn., Coll. of New Rochelle, 1975. Cert. adminstr., supr., N.Y. K-6th grade tchr., reading tchr. Ossining (N.Y.) Schs., Byram Hills Schs., Armonk, NY, Bedford (NY) Schs., 1964—84; reading specialist The Hallen Sch., Mamaroneck, NY, 1984-88, coord. testing and curriculum New Rochelle, NY, 1988—2001; ret., 2002. Mgr. nutrition ctr. GNC, Scarsdale, NY, 1981—82; mem. curriculum adv. coun. Lower Westchester BOCES, 1988—2001. Pres. Mineola (N.Y.) Elem. Sch. PTA, 1962-63. Mem. ASCD, Lower Hudson Coun. Adminstrv. Women in Edn., Westchester Reading Coun., Orton Dyslexia Soc., Am. Mensa Ltd. Avocations: tennis, gourmet cooking, nutrition.

GROVES, CHARLA M., secondary school educator; b. Jacksonville, Fla., July 4, 1973; d. Errol I. and Arlene B. Matthews; m. Brian S. Groves, Apr. 6, 1998; 1 child, Ellison O'Neal. BS in Elem. Edn., Coll. of Charleston, S.C., 1996; MEd in Elem. Adminstrn. and Supervision, Charleston So. U., S.C., 2005. Tchr. Berkeley County Sch. Dist., Ladson, SC, 1996—. Adept evaluator Berkeley County Sch. Dist., Ladson, 2000—; proteam curriculum trainer S.C. Ctr. for Educator Recruitment, Retention, and Advancement, Rock Hill, SC, 2002—04; policy bd. mem. S.C. Ctr. for Educator Recruitment, Retention, and Advancement., Rock Hill, 2003—05; cons. S.C. Dept. of Tchr. Quality, Columbia, 2003; co-chairperson Berkeley County Tchr. Forum, Berkeley County Sch. Dist., Moncks Corner, SC, 2003—04, chairperson, 2004. Leader 6th grade youth group Bethany United Meth. Ch., Summerville, SC, 2002—04. Named Berkeley County Tchr. of the Yr., Berkeley County Sch. Dist., 2003—04, Coll. Pk. Mid. Sch. Tchr. of the Yr., Coll. Pk. Mid. Sch., 2003—04. Mem.: SC. Mid. Sch. Assn., Berkeley County Tchr. Forum, S.C. Tchr. Forum (life), Phi Mu (membership chairperson 1993—94), Alpha Delta Kappa. Office: College Park Mid Sch 713 College Park Rd Ladson SC 29456 Office Phone: 843-553-8300. Business E-Mail: grovesc@berkeley.k12.sc.us.

GROVES, LIZABETH A., accountant, network administrator; b. Muncie, Ind., June 21, 1964; d. Gary Michael and Pamela Kay Groves; m. Monti Klayman, Oct. 21, 1990. AA in Bus. Adminstrn., Brookdale C.C., Lincroft, N.J., 1993; BS in Acctg. summa cum laude, Kean U., Union, N.J., 1996. CPA, N.J. Bookkeeper Bonanza Motel, Wildwood Crest, N.J., 1982-83, Colts Head (N.J.) Vet., 1983-85; para-profl. Aronson & Thoma, Red Bank, N.J., 1985-94; acct. Withum, Smith & Brown, Red Bank, 1994-96, sr. acct., 1996-97, sr. acct., LAn adminstr., 1997—. Cons. AT&T Labs., Somerset, N.J., 1996-97; QuickBooks profl. advisor, 1999—. Mem. AICPA, N.J. Soc. CPAs, Assn. Cert. Fraud Examiners (assoc.), Phi Kappa Phi. Republican. Avocations: hiking, kayaking, travel. Office: Withumsmith Brown 331 Newman Spgs Rd Ste 125 Red Bank NJ 07701-6765 E-mail: lklayman@withum.com.

GROVES, SHARON SUE, elementary school educator; b. Springfield, Mo., Apr. 25, 1944; d. William Orin Jr. and Ruth M. (Jones) Hodge; m. Donald L. Groves, July 20, 1963. BA, Drury Coll., 1966, MEd, 1969. Cert. life elem. tchg.; Psychol. Examiners Cert. Adminstrn. Elem. tchr. Springfield Pub. Schs., 1966-96; asst. instr. individual testing Drury Coll., Springfield, 1969-76; asst. instr. enhancing math. S.W. Mo. State U., Springfield, 1991-94; parent resource educator, title I tech. support Springfield Pub. Schs., 1998—. Sr. leader MAP 2000 (Mo. Assessment Project) Class I. Author: Modeling Effective Practices: Geometry and Computation. Active Springfield's Curriculum Coun.; mem. Tchg. Cadre, Strategic Planning Team; hon. life mem. PTA; chmn. adminstrv. coun. Hood United Meth. Ch.; children's coord., math. workshops.; sr. leader Mo. Assessment Project, 1993—. Recipient Extra Mile award, 1989; named Fremont Tchr. of the Yr., 1988, 93. Mem. ASCD, Internat. Reading Assn., Assn. for Childhood Edn., Nat. Coun. Tchrs. Math., Mo. Coun. Tchrs. Math., Mo. State Tchrs. Assn. (pres. S.W. dist. 1994-95, Educator of Yr. 1989), Springfield Edn. Assn. (pres. 1989-90, 93-96, Leader of Yr. 1990, pres. Scholarship corp. 1998-2000), Delta Kappa Gamma (1st v.p., pres. 2000-2002, state 2nd v.p. 2005—). Home: 8076 W Farm Road 144 Springfield MO 65802-8782

GROWNEY-SEALS, SHARON ANN, literature and language professor, department chairman; b. Omaha; d. John T. and Gertrude Growney; m. Larry D. Seals, Mar. 18, 1984; children: Catherine S. Seals, John B. Seals. BA in English, U. St. Mary, Leavenworth, Kans., 1983; MA in Lit., Mich. State U., East Lansing, 1985; EdD in Higher Edn. Leadership & English Edn., Nova Southeastern U., Ft. Lauderdale, Fla., 2005. English grad. asst. Mich. State U., 1983—85; English instr. Midlands Tech., Columbia, SC, 1985—86; learning ctr. coord. Am. Tech. Inst., Ft. Jackson, 1986—87; English instr. U. S.C., Columbia, 1985—89, U. Ark., Little Rock, 1991—97, Ouachita Tech., Malvern, 1997—. Pres. Port Adventure, Inc., Sheridan, 1996—. Author poetry. Recipient Tchr. of Yr. award, 1998, 2001; grantee, 2004, NEH, Walden, Mass., 2006. Mem.: Ark. Chairs English Depts. (mem. content specialist team 2005—). Office: Ouachita Tech Coll 1 College Cir Malvern AR 72104 Business E-Mail: sseals@otcweb.edu.

GRUBE, DEBORAH JEAN, special education educator, science educator; b. Landsdowne, Pa., Feb. 27, 1963; d. Paul Wesley and Mary Ann Ware; m. Brian Dudley Grube, June 2, 1984; children: Joshua Dale, Jonathan Douglas. BS in Med. Tech., Okla. State U., Stillwater, 1985; MEd in Learning Disabilities with honors, U. Ctrl. Okla., Edmond, 1998. Cert. tchr. in learning disabilites, mentally handicapped, anatomy, physiology, biology, chemistry, phys. sci., mid. sch. sci. Med. technologist St. Francis Hosp., Tulsa, Okla., 1985—86, Meth. Hosp., Dallas, 1986—88, Alexian Bros., San Jose, Calif., 1989—91, Okla. U. Med. Ctr., Okla. City, 1991—95, Presbyn. Hosp., Okla. City, 1994—95; spl. edn. tchr. Okla. City Pub. Sch. Dist., El Reno, 1998—2000; spl. edn./sci. tchr. El Reno Pub. Sch. Dist., Okla., 2000—. Grantee, El Reno Found., Inc., 2003, El Reno Pub. Sch. Found., Inc., 2004, 2005. Mem.: Nat. Sci. Tchr. Assn. Avocations: reading, swimming, water sports. Office: El Reno Pub Sch Dist PO Box 580 El Reno OK 73036 Business E-Mail: dgrube@elreno.k12.ok.us.

GRUBE, REBECCA SUE, elementary school educator, consultant; b. Lancaster, Pa., June 27, 1945; d. Warren Landis and Ruth Rebecca (Hackman) Newcomer; m. Terry Wayne Grube, Aug. 27, 1966; children: T. David, Joy Lynn, Matthew Warren. Student, Juniata Coll., 1963-65; BA, Franklin and Marshall Coll., 1976; MEd, Millersville U., 1979; postgrad., Temple U. Cert. spl. edn., neurolinguistic programmer. Grad. asst. Millersville U., Pa., 1978-79; tchr. gifted and learning disabled Sch. Dist. of Lancaster, 1979-80; tchr. pvt. sch. Lancaster, 1980-81; elem. tchr. Lancaster Country Day Sch., 1981-85, tchr. resource room, 1985-90, chmn. elem. lang. arts curriculum, 1985-88, mem. curriculum com., 1986-87, tchr. psychology, 1989—, dir. spl. projects, 1990-91, head lower sch., 1991—. Instr. Franklin and Marshall Coll., 1991; pvt. practice ednl. cons., tutor, Lancaster, 1981—; dir. program Tchg. Talented and Outstanding Pupils for Success, 1987, 88—; instr. Performance Learning Systems, 1987—, Wilkes Coll., 1987—; mem. faculty Inst. Student Leaders, NAIS, 2006.; faculty inst. student leaders Nat. assn. Ind. Schs. Conf., 2006. Contbr. articles to profl. quars.; author rsch. report. Pres. bd. dirs. Contact Lancaster, 1986, chairperson support workers, 1987-88; mem. Listening Ear, Parents of Adoptive Children Orgn., 1981-85, Martin Luther King Scholarship Fund, Janus L.D. Sch.; mem. Leadership Pa., 1990. Fellow Christa McAuliffee U.S. Dept. Edn., 1988-89, Leadership Lancaster, 1989; recipient award Lancaster Assn. Retarded Citizens, 1978-79, cert. of appreciation AFL-CIO Cmty. Svcs., 1983, CONTACT award City of Lancaster, 1988, Literacy award for Tchg. Talented and Outstanding Pupils for Success, Lancaster-Lebanon Reading Coun., 1988. Mem. Assn. Supervision and Curriculum, Orton Dyslexia Soc., Assn. for Children with Learning Disabilities (past bd. dirs. Lancaster Lebanon chpt.), Pa. Assn. for Gifted Children, Coun. Exceptional Children, Nat. Assn. for Gifted Children, Ctrl. Pa. Friends of Jazz, Pi Lambda Theta (chmn. Lehman Home Project 1984-86), Delta Kappa Gamma. Republican. Lutheran. Avocations: tennis, walking, piano, drums, reading. Home: PO Box 4036 Lancaster PA 17604-4036 Business E-Mail: grubeb@e-lcds.org.

GRUBIN, SHARON ELLEN, lawyer, former federal judge; b. Newark, Feb. 9, 1949; d. Harold and Blanche (Dultz) G. AB with honors, Smith Coll., 1970; JD with honors in Legal Writing and Analysis, Boston U., 1973. Bar: N.Y. 1974, U.S. Dist. Ct. (so. and ea. dists.) N.Y. 1974, U.S. Ct. Appeals (2nd cir.) 1974. Litigator White & Case, N.Y.C., 1973-84; judge U.S. Dist. Ct. (so. dist.) N.Y., N.Y.C., 1984-2000; gen. counsel Metroplitan Opera, N.Y.C., 2000—. Chair 2d Cir. Task Force on Gender, Racial and Ethnic Fairness in the Cts.; lectr. NYU Sch. Law, Yale Law Sch., Bklyn. Law Sch., N.Y. Law Sch.; dir., sec., exec. com. Lawyers' Com. on Violence, Inc. Author: (with others) Advocacy-The Art of Pleading a Cause, 1985, Removal, Federal Civil Practice, 1989, and supplement, 1993; spkr. seminars in field. Mem. ABA (chair spl. projects com. 1996-97, nat. conf. fed. trial judges, jud. adminstrn. divsn.), Nat. Assn. Women Judges (chair fed. gender bias com., publicity and pub. affairs com., newsletter com.), Fed. Bar Coun. (trustee, exec. com., chair nominating com. 1994, v.p. 1990-94, award com. 1988-94, com. on 2d cir. cts. 1982-96, long-range planning com. 1992-96), N.Y. State Bar Assn. (exec. com., nominations com., fed. cts. task force, comml. and fed. litig. sect.), N.Y. State Assn. Women Judges (bd. dirs.), Assn. of Bar of City of N.Y. (long-range planning com., chair nominating com. 1995—, chair spl. com. on legal history 1994-96, chair spl. com. on Orison S. Marden Meml. lectrs., chair 1994-96, exec. com. 1990-94, spl. com. on gender bias in fed. cts. 1991-94, coun. on jud. adminstrn. 1986-90, prof. and jud. ethics com. 1986-89, nominating com. 1984-85, 95-96, com. on jud. 1982-83, chair young lawyers com. 1979-81, com. on entertainment law, 2001-), Am. Judicature Soc. (editl. com. 1994-97). Office: Metropolitan Opera Lincoln Ctr New York NY 10023

GRUCCI BUTLER, DONNA, fireworks company executive; d. Felix and Concetta Grucci; m. Philip Butler; children: Jeffrey, Danielle. Pres. Fireworks by Grucci, Brookhaven, NY, 2001—. Prodr.: (firework prodn.) Bi-Centennial Celebration on Charles River for Arthur Fielder's Boston Pops, 1976, Six consecutive Presdl. Inaugurations, 1981, 1985, 1989, 1993, 1997, 2001, Bklyn. Bridge, 1983, Centennial Celebration of Statue of Liberty, 1986, Wedding of Prince Abu Dhabi, Olympics, 1981, 1985, 2002, World's Fair, 1982, 1984, 1993; spokesperson for firework tours Wisk Bright Nights, Lever Brothers', Merit Harbor Lights, Philip Morris. Tchr. Cath. religious edn. classes to 1st graders; mem. local C. of C. events, local Head Start Programs; vol. fundraiser Am. Heart Assn.; established two scholarships Bellport H.S., 1992. Recipient Gold medal, Monte Carlo Internat. Fireworks Competition, 1979, Ellis Island medal of Honor for Outstanding Achievements in Arts and Entertainment Field, Nat. Ethnic Coalition Orgns., 1995. Avocations: gardening, reading. Office: Fireworks By Grucci 1 Grucci Ln Brookhaven NY 11719 E-mail: info@grucci.com.

GRUDESKI, JENNIFER ANNE, elementary school educator; b. Lake Worth, Fla., June 5, 1970; d. John and Johanna Mae Green; m. Richard Joseph Jr. Grudeski, Nov. 11, 1989; children: Cassandra Lynn, Alexandra Marie, Richard Joseph III. BS, East Stroudsburg U., Pa., 1993, MEd, 2002. Cert. tchr. Pa. Tchr. North Pocono Sch. Dist., Moscow, Pa., 1994—. Lutheran. Home: PO Box 1161 Gouldsboro PA 18424 Office: North Pocono Mid Sch 701 Church St Moscow PA 18444 Office Phone: 570-842-4588. Business E-Mail: jgrudeski@npsd.org.

GRUEBEL, BARBARA JANE, retired internist, pulmonologist; b. Honolulu, May 12, 1950; d. Robert William and Elenor Jane (Perry) G. BS, Stephen F. Austin State U., 1977; MD, Baylor Coll. Medicine, 1974. Diplomate Nat. Bd. Med. Examiners. Intern in internal medicine U. Rochester, 1974-75, resident in internal medicine, 1975-77; pulmonary fellow U. Mich., 1977-79; mem. med. staff Anthony L. Jordan Health Center, Rochester, N.Y., 1976-77, Univ. Health Service, Ann Arbor, Mich., 1978-79; med. dir. progressive respiratory care unit Meth. Med. Ctr., 1979-80; asst. prof. medicine U. Tex. Health Sci. Center, Dallas, 1979-80; cons. in pulmonary disease Dallas, 1980-93; pvt. practice of pulmonary medicine, 1993—99, Nacogdoches, Tex., 1999—. Clin. asst. prof. medicine U. Tex. Health Sci. Center, 1980-97; nat. affiliate faculty Am. Heart Assn.; mem. faculty First Internat. Conf. Women's Health, Beijing, 1993; lectr. in field. Mem. TEXPAC. Recipient award for gen. excellence in pediatrics, 1974, Stanley W. Olson award for acad. excellence, 1974, John Richard Fox award, 1974, Stuart A. Wallace award in pathology, 1974; named one of Am.'s Top Physicians, Consumers Rsch. Coun. Am., 2004-05; Welch Found. grantee, 1970; Am. Lung Assn. tng. fellow, 1977-79; Robert Wood Johnson Found. scholar; Coll. Women's Club scholar. Fellow Am. Coll. Chest Physicians (named Young Pulmonary Physicians of Future 1979); mem. Am. Med. Women's Assn. (scholastic excellence award 1974), Am. Thoracic Soc., Am. Lung Assn., AMA, Am. Coll. Physicians, Dallas County Med. Soc., Tex. Med. Soc., Dallas Internist Assocs., Dallas Acad. Internal Medicine, Am. Cancer Soc., Dallas C. of C., Dallas Mayors Outstanding Women of Dallas, Oak Cliff C. of C., Alpha Omega Alpha, Beta Beta Beta. Office Phone: 936-462-7602. E-mail: bjgruebel@cox.net.

GRUEN, MARGARET, actress; b. N.Y.C., July 24, 1949; d. Arno G. and Judith (Goldstein) Milenbach. Student, Yale Sch. Drama. Actress. Writer, performer (theatre) Tanya Talks: The Last Jew, 1997, The Young Sophisticate, 1994, What A Wonderful World, 1990, Dracula, 1970; one-woman show: Grenfell's Eccentric Characters; appeared in theatre, TV, and radio prodns., including Uncle Vanya, Garcia Lorca's New York; mem. comedy team The Chamansky Sisters. Mem. Am. Fedn. Television & Radio Artists, Actors Equity Assn., Screen Actors Guild. Office Phone: 917-968-3662. Personal E-mail: gruen_margaret@yahoo.com.

GRUEN, SHIRLEY SCHANEN, artist; b. Port Washington, Wis., Dec. 2, 1923; d. William Frank Schanen and Laura Thien Leffingwell; m. Gerald A. Gruen, Feb. 1, 1947; children: Gerald Jr., Lorelei Hosler, Lorna Nagler. BS in Art Edn., U. Wis., 1945; postgrad., Art Ctr. Sch., L.A., 1945—47, Cardinal

Stritch U., 1970—90. Instr. portrait and watercolor Milw. Area Tech. Coll., 1972—80; owner Shirley Gruen Art Gallery, Port Washington, 1972—. Bd. mem., curator Port Washington Hist. Soc.; publicity chmn. Eghart House Mus., Port Washington. One-woman shows include West Bend (Wis.) Gallery Fine Arts, 1981, Water Street Gallery, Milw., 1984, exhibitions include Neville Mus., Green Bay, Wis., 1991, 1995, New Visions Gallery, Marshfield, Wis., 2002, exhibitions include many others. Represented in permanent collections Ozaukee Bank, Port Washington, Wis., Holiday Inn, Heritage Ins., Sheboygan, Wis., West Pub. Co., St. Paul, Milw. Art Commn., West Bend Fine Arts Gallery, West Bend Mut. Ins. Co., Wausau (Wis.) Hosp. Ctr., many others. Named Citizen of Yr., Port Washington C. of C., 2003; recipient Legis. citation, Wis. Assembly, 2003. Mem.: Wis. Watercolor Soc., Wis. Painters and Sculptors. Democrat. Roman Catholic. Avocations: piano, sailing.

GRUENBECK, LAURIE, librarian; b. Sebewaing, Mich., Mar. 4, 1936; d. Ernest R. and Gertrude M. (Dierks) G. BA, Valparaiso (Ind.) U., 1961; MS in Libr. Sci., Our Lady of the Lake U., 1971. Deaconess Zion Luth Ch., Oklahoma City, 1961-62, Caracas, Venezuela, 1962-64; 3rd and 4th grade tchr. Zion Luth. Sch., Hemlock, Mich., 1964; 4th grade tchr. Saginaw Pub. Schs., 1965-67; substitute, cataloger San Antonio Pub. Libr., 1967-72, cataloger, 1972-77, br. mgr., 1977—98; ret., 1998. Adminstr. of adult edn. classes Bazan Br. Libr., San Antonio, 1983-96. Mem. ALA, Internat. Reading Assn., Tex. Libr. Assn., Hymn Soc. U.S. and Can. Democrat. Roman Catholic. Avocations: collecting christmas carol memorabilia, mexican cookbooks. Home: 3103 Saunders Ave San Antonio TX 78207-4050 Personal E-mail: gruenbeck652@hotmail.com.

GRULIOW, AGNES FORREST, artist, educator; b. Davenport, Iowa, July 5, 1912; d. James Lindsay and Agnes (Johnston) F.; m. Leo Gruliow, Sept. 25, 1945; children: Frank Forrest, Rebecca Agnes Lindsay. BA, Antioch Coll., Yellow Springs, Ohio, 1938; student, Art Students League, N.Y.C., 1963-66. Resident dir. Am. Peoples Sch., N.Y.C., 1937-41; asst. nat. sec. Nat. Fedn. Settlements, N.Y.C., 1941-43; assoc. pers. dir.,asst. prof. Antioch Coll. Extramural Sch., Yellow Springs, 1943-45; index designer-editor Current Digest of Soviet Press, Washington and N.Y.C., 1949-53; freelance editor N.Y.C., 1954-57; tchr. art City & Country Sch., N.Y.C., 1966-68; hostess Am. Friends Svc. Com. Internat. Seminar, Oestgeest, Netherlands, 1960, Poughkeepsie, NY, 1961; sr. vis. fellow Woodrow Wilson Found., 1977-80; proprietor art studio N.Y.C., 1961-69, Worthington, Ohio, 1970-72; art therapy asst. Harding Hosp., Worthington, 1970-72. One-woman show at Antioch Coll., 1967; group shows Herndon Gallery, Yellow Springs, Ohio, 2000, Northwood Art Space, Columbus, Ohio, 2003. Pres. Columbia U. Greenhouse Nursery Sch., NYC, 1954-59; bd. mem. Open Door Day Care Ctr., NYC, 1954-59; mem. founding bd. East Harlem Tutoring Program, NYC, 1965-73; mem. bd. Columbus Area Internat. Program, 1970-72, 79-87, edn. sec., 1981, pres., 1982-85, chair adv. bd., 1983-87; del. Nat. Bd. Coun. Internat. Programs, Cleve., 1981-83; mem. bd. Cmty. Svc., Inc., Yellow Springs, 1981-99. Mem. Columbus Meml. Soc., Columbus Mus. Art, UNA, UNICEF, World Federalist Assn. Ctrl. Ohio (membership sect. 1987-94), Crichton Club (Columbus), Order Eastern Star. Home: 163 E Lane Ave Columbus OH 43201-1212

GRUMAN, JESSIE CHRISTINE, not-for-profit developer; b. Berea, Ky., Dec. 7, 1953; d. Lawrence Lowell and Eleanor Angell (Weekes) Gruman; m. Richard Peter Sloan, June 21, 1984. BA, Vassar Coll., 1975; PhD in Social Psychology, Columbia U., 1984. Counselor, cmty. organizer Greenwich House Counseling Ctr., N.Y.C., Greenwich Settlement House, N.Y.C., 1979—84; mgr. employee health promotion AT&T Comm., Basking Ridge, NJ, 1984—86; nat. dir. pub. edn. Am. Cancer Soc., N.Y.C., 1986—88; project officer Nat. Cancer Inst. NIH, Bethesda, Md., 1988—92; pres., founding exec. dir. Ctr. Advancement Health, Washington, 1992—. Bd. mem. Public Health Inst. Mem. editl. bd. Annals Family Medicine, 2003—; contbr. articles to profl. jours. Chair adv. panel Health Care Financing Adminstrn. Evidence Report and Evidence-Based Recommendations: Health Risk Appraisals and Medicare, 2001; trustee Mind Brain Body and Health Initiative, Galveston, Tex., 2001—; mem. adv. bd. U.S. Cochrane Ctr., 2003—; trustee Sallan Found., 2004—. Fellow: Soc. Behavioral Medicine; mem.: APA, Nat. Orgn. Tobacco Use Rsch. Funders, Pub. Health Inst., Am. Psychosocial Oncology Soc., Nat. Adv. Coun., Nat. Health Coun. Office: Ctr Advancement Health 2000 Florida Ave NW Ste 210 Washington DC 20009-1231 E-mail: jgruman@cfah.org.

GRUMBACH, KATHERINE ELIZABETH, science educator; b. Middleburg Hts., Ohio, Dec. 1, 1981; d. David and Martha Grumbach. BE, Ohio U., Athens, 2000—04. Cert. tchr. Ohio Dept. Edn., 2004. Rsch. asst. Ohio U., 2003—04; secondary sci. tchr. Teays Valley HS, Ashville, Ohio, 2004—. Mem.: Kappa Phi (editor, historian, publicity chair 2000—04), Kappa Delta Pi. Achievements include research in the understanding of scientific concepts at the college level. Home: 10858 Meadow Trail Strongsville 44149 Afghanistan

GRUMET, PRISCILLA HECHT, fashion specialist, consultant, writer; b. Detroit, May 11, 1943; d. Lewis Maxwell and Helen Ruth (Miller) Hecht; m. Ross Frederick Grumet, Feb. 24, 1968; 1 child, Auden Lewis. AA, Stephens Coll., 1963; student, Ga. State Coll., 1983-85. Buyer Rich's Dept. Store, Atlanta, 1963-68; instr. fashion retail Fashion Inst. Am., Atlanta, 1968-71; pres., lectr., cons. Personally Priscilla Personal Shopping Svc., Atlanta, 1971—; retail and customer svc. cons. By Priscilla Grumet, Atlanta, 1989—; instr. Cont. Edn. Program Emory U., Atlanta, 1976—; fashion merch. coord. Park Pl. Shopping Ctr., Atlanta, 1979-83; writer Atlanta Bus. Mag., 1984—; cons., buyer Greers-Regensteins Store, Atlanta, 1986-87; writer Atlanta Mag., 1994—; owner antiques bus. Personally, Priscilla, 2004—. Guest lectr. Fashion Group of Am., Rancho La Puerta Resort, Tecate, Mex., 1985—; bus. cons. Atlanta Apparel Mart, 1992—; adv. bd. Bauder Fashion Col., 1986—, Atlanta Apparel Mart, 1992—; fashion panel judge Weight Watchers Internat., 1981; columnist Marquee mag., Atlanta, 1992—; lectr. on customer svc. Rhodes Furniture, Marriott Corp., So. Bell, Lady Love Cosmetics, Atlanta Retail Stores, others, 1994—; presenter profl. seminars on bus. etiquette, 1996—; lectr. on profl. etiquette corps.; special events planner, Fusebox Restaurant, Atlanta, 2000, Emory U. Continuing Edn. program, 1996—; panel leader Americasmart, Atlanta; owner Personally Priscilla Antique Shop, Buckhead, Atlanta, 2004—; spkr. in field. Author: How to Dress Well, 1981; reporter Women's Wear Daily, 1976-90; columnist Atlanta Scene Mag.; contbr. articles to mags. and publs. including Atlanta, Seventeen, Nat. Jeweler's (Editor's Choice award The Nat. Libr. of Poetry 1995), The Old Farmer's Almanac, Bus. Seminars Profl. Etiquette, Performance Plus, 1996—. Pub. rels. dir., Atlanta Jewish Home Aux., 1986-89, 90-95; admissions advisor, Stephens Coll., 1979—. Mem. Fashion Group, Inc., Women in Comm., Nat. Coun. Jewish Women, Atlanta Press Club, Buckhead Bus. Assn., Temple Sisterhood (spkr., spl. events com. 1983—). Avocations: antiques, aerobics. Home and Office: Apt 606N 2500 Peachtree Rd NW Atlanta GA 30305-5611

GRUNBERG, NANCY R., lawyer; b. Mankato, Minn., Sept. 26, 1953; BA with distinction, Stanford U., 1975; JD, Columbia U., 1979. Bar: Pa. 1979, DC 1983, Md. 1996. Litigation assoc. Davis Polk & Wardwell, Washington, 1981—88; atty. securities, banking and commercial litigation priv. practice, Washington, 1992—96; lead trial atty., enforcement div. US Securities and Exchange Commn., 1996—99, litigation counsel, office of internat. affairs, 1999—2000, asst. dir., div. of enforcement, 2000—02; ptnr. Venable LLP, Washington, 2002—. Mem.: ABA, Md. Bar Assn., DC Bar Assn. Office: Venable LLP 575 7th St NW Washington DC 20004 Office Phone: 202-344-4730. Office Fax: 202-344-8300. Business E-Mail: nrgrunberg@venable.com.

GRUNDISH, LEE ANNE, small business owner, writer; b. Kalamazoo, Mich., Apr. 13, 1959; d. Allen Grundish and Jeane Gratop. BA in Psychology, U. Toledo, 1984. Bus. owner, pres. Grafix Svcs./Achieve Success!, Toledo, 1989—. Bus. develp. mktg. cons., 1985—89. Lyricist (song) Love Is What We Need; writer: numerous resumes in resume guides including Expert Resumes for Baby-Boomers, Barron's Designing the Perfect Resume, Best Resumes and Letters for Ex-Offenders, others. Parent counselor Family and Child Abuse Prevention Ctr., Toledo, 1984, fundraising vol., 1998; youth mentor Big Bros. & Big Sisters, Toledo, 1990—91, fundraising vol., 1995—98, Arts Commn. of Greater Toledo, 1998; voters' rights vol. Nat. Voice, Toledo, 2004. Mem.: ASCAP, ACA, Nat. Resume Writers Assn., Nat. Employment Counselors Assn. Democrat. Avocations: poetry, politics. Home: 2242 Portsmouth Ave Toledo OH 43613 Office: 2149 Evergreen Rd Toledo OH 43606 Office Phone: 419-534-2709. Business E-Mail: grafixservices@aol.com.

GRUNNET, MARGARET LOUISE, retired pathologist, educator; b. Mpls., Feb. 20, 1936; d. Leslie Nels and Grace Harriet (Thomson) Grunnet; m. Irving Noel Einhorn, Mar. 10, 1972; stepchildren: Jeffrey Allan, Franne Ruth, Eric Carl, Stanley Glenn. BA summa cum laude, U. Minn., Mpls., 1958; MD, U. Minn., 1962; MS, Ohio State U., 1969. Resident in psychiatry U. Pa. Sch. Medicine, Phila., 1963-64; resident anatomic pathology Presbyn.-U. Pa. Med. Ctr., Phila., 1965-66; fellow neuropathology Phila. Gen. Hosp., 1967, Ohio State U. Hosp., Columbus, 1968-69; instr. Ohio State U., 1969; asst. prof. U. Utah Sch. Medicine, Salt Lake City, 1970-76, assoc. prof., 1976-80; assoc. prof. pathology U. Conn. Sch. Medicine, Farmington, 1980-90, prof., 1990—2006, prof. emeritus, 2006—. Contbr. articles to profl. jours. Mem. Am. Med. Women's Assn., Internat. Soc. Neuropathology, Conn. Soc. Pathologists, World Muscle Soc., Am. Assn. Neuropathologists, Phi Beta Kappa, Alpha Omega Alpha. Mem. Ch. of Christ. Avocations: reading, music, travel. Office: U Conn Health Ctr Dept Pathology Farmington CT 06032 Home: 275 Steele Rd B415 West Hartford CT 06117-2805 Business E-Mail: grunnet@nso1.ucnc.edu.

GRUTMAN, JEWEL HUMPHREY, lawyer, writer; b. N.Y.C., Mar. 13, 1931; d. Robert and Gladys Humphrey; m. Robert W. Bjork, June 26, 1954 (div. Apr. 22, 1975); 1 child, Bruce Bjork; m. Roy Grutman, Oct. 30, 1975 (wid. 1994); m. Fredrick Yonkman, July 4, 1998. BA magna cum laude, Mt. Holyoke Coll., 1952; LLB, Columbia U., 1955. Bar: N.Y., U.S. Dist. Ct. (So. Dist.) N.Y. 1971, U.S. Dist. Ct. (ea. dist.) N.Y. 1974, U.S. Dist. Ct. Conn. 1984, U.S. Supreme Ct. 1983. Atty. Debevoise & Plimpton, N.Y.C., 1954-60; ptnr. Eaton Van Winkle, N.Y.C., 1976-79, Grutman Greene & Humphrey, N.Y.C., 1979—. Co-author: (with CD-ROM) The Ledgerbook of Thomas Blue Eagle, 1994 (Christopher award 1995, Internat. Reading Assn. award), The Sketchbook of Thomas Blue Eagle, 2001, (CD-ROM) The Journey of Thomas Blue Eagle, 1995 (Best Project award Intermedia, Asia, 1995, Creative NGee ANN Disting. award 1995, EMMA award best visual content 1996); asst. prodr., editor (ednl. film on art) Where Time is a River (1st prize Women's Film Festival); contbr. photograph illustrations: The Reforming Power of the Scriptures, 1996; developer series of designs based on Native Am. art; contbr. articles to mags. and newspapers. Dir. Inwood Ho., N.Y.C., 1970-80; past mem. various coms. Mt. Holyoke Coll.; mem. com. sr. advisors N.Y. Commn. for Internat. Bus. and UN, 1997; past chmn. com. to establish Barbara Black Fellowship at Columbia U. Law Sch.; past pres. 85th St. Playground Assn., N.Y.C.; active supporter The Children's Storefront, Harlem, N.Y.C., N.Y. Jr. League. Mem.: Assn. Bar City N.Y., Coral Ridge Country Club (Ft. Lauderdale, Fla.), The Stanwich Club (Greenwich, Conn.). Avocations: opera, golf, tennis, poetry. E-mail: bijou203@optonline.net, bijou203@bellsouth.net.

GRUVER, NANCY, publishing executive; Founder, pub. New Moon Pub., Duluth, Minn., 1992—. Author: How To Say It To Girls, 2004; prodr. (mag.) New Moon: The Magazine for Girls and Their Dreams, 1992—. Office: New Moon Publishing 2 W 1st St Ste 101 Duluth MN 55802-2062 Office Phone: 218-728-5507. Business E-Mail: nancyg@newmom.org.

GRZESIAK, KATHERINE ANN, primary school educator; BS, Ctrl. Mich. U., 1968; MA in Tchg., Saginaw Valley State U., 1975; postgrad., various univs., 1975—. 6th grade tchr. Buena Vista Sch. Dist., Saginaw, Mich., 1968-69, 70-71; tchr. Carrollton Pub. Schs., Saginaw, 1972-80, St. Peter and Paul Elem. Sch., Saginaw, 1981-84, Sch. Dist. of City of Saginaw, 1984-90; instr. Ctr. for Innovation in Edn., Saratoga, Calif., 1989—; tchr. Midland (Mich.) Pub. Schs., 1991—; 5th grade tchr. Eastlawn Elem., Midland. Adj. faculty Saginaw Valley State U., University Center, Mich., 1976-80, 88-90; presenter in field. Contbr. articles to profl. jours. Recipient Presdl. award for Excellence in Sci. and Math. Tchg., 1994, Top Tchr. in Mich. Met. Woman mag., 1997, Nat. Educator award Milken Family Found., 1998; named Mich. Tchr. of Yr., 1998. Home: 3115 McGill St Midland MI 48642-3928 Office: Eastlawn Elem Sch 115 Eastlawn Dr Midland MI 48640-5561 Office Phone: 989-923-7112. E-mail: grzesiakka@mps.k12.mi.us.

GUADAGNO, CHRISTINE ELLEN, social studies educator; d. George M. and Eleanor A. Anderson; m. Gary Michael Guadagno, May 3, 1986; children: Glen Michael, Michael George. Master's, St. John's U., N.Y., 1977. Lic. tchr. N.Y., 1977. Tchr. Fransican H.S., Lake Mohegan, NY, 1977—80, Maria Regina H.S., Hartsdale, NY, 1980—84, Albert Leonard Jr. H.S., New Rochelle, NY, 1985—86, Hendrick Hudson H.S., Montrose, NY, 1984—87, tchr. social studies, 1996—. Instrnl. leader social studies Hendrick Hudson H.S., 2003—. Home: 12 Hamilton Rd Hopewell Junction NY 12533 Office: Hendrick Hudson HS 2166 Albany Post Rd Montrose NY 10548 Office Phone: 914-736-5250. Business E-Mail: cguadagno@henhud.k12.ny.us.

GUARDO, CAROL J., association executive; b. Hartford, Conn., Apr. 12, 1939; d. C. Fred and Marion (Biase) G. BA, St. Joseph Coll., 1961; MA, U. Detroit, 1963; PhD, U. Denver, 1966. Asst. prof. psychology Eastern Mich. U., Ypsilanti, 1966-68; assoc. prof., staff psychologist U. Denver, 1968-73; assoc. prof., dean coll. Utica Coll. of Syracuse U., Utica, N.Y., 1973-76; prof., dean Coll. Liberal Arts, Drake U., Des Moines, 1976-80; provost, prof. U. Hartford, 1980-85; pres. R.I. Coll., Providence, 1986-90, Great Lakes Colls. Assn., Ann Arbor, Mich., 1990—. Mem. Iowa Humanities Bd., 1976-80, pres., 1978-80; bd. dirs. Am. Coun. Edn., People's Bank. Author: The Adolescent As Individual: Issues and Insights, 1975; contbr. articles to profl. jours. Trustee St. Joseph Coll., Monmouth Coll., Colby-Sawyer Coll., Cabrini Coll. NSF fellow, 1964, NIMH fellow, 1964-66. Mem. Am. Assn. Higher Edn., Assn. Am. Colls. (vice chair 1987, chair 1988), Am. Psychol. Assn., Assn. Gen. and Liberal Studies (pres. 1979-81), Soc. Rsch. in Child Devel., Greater Providence C. of C., Phi Beta Kappa. Office: Great Lakes Colls Assn 2929 Plymouth Rd Ste 207 Ann Arbor MI 48105-3206

GUARINO, DANITA CRONIN, special education educator; b. Morristown, N.J., Sept. 4, 1951; d. Daniel Joseph Jr. and Rita (Reichert) Cronin; m. Ronald Joseph Guarino, July 28, 1973; children: Kristen, Kerry Anne. BA in Edn., Coll. of St. Elizabeth, 1973. Cert. spl. edn. educator, nursery sch. educator, CPR instr. Tchr. Brookside (N.J.) Sch. Twp. Bd. of Edn., 1973-75, Sussex (N.J.)-Wantage Bd. of Edn., Eatontown (N.J.) Bd. of Edn.; staff edn. instr. Centra State Med. Ctr., Freehold, N.J., 1988—; tchr. spl. edn. East Windsor Bd. of Edn., Hightstown, N.J., 1988—. Ctrl. Jersey grant emergency med. svc. tng. com. N.J. Dept. Transp., Trenton, N.J., 1989—; sci. assessment com. Tchr. Prep Program, Princeton (N.J.) U., 1993—; tchr. connection steering com. Liberty Sci. Ctr., Hoboken, N.J., 1994—. Co-author: (guidebook) Quest, A Teacher's Guide, 1994, (manual) A Learning-Based Model for Assessing Elementary Science Learning, 1995. Capt., line officer Englishtown Manalapan (N.J.) First Aid, 1987—; critical inciden stress debriefing team mem. Emergency Med. Svcs., Central, N.J., 1988—; CPR instr. trainer Centra State Hosp., Freehold, N.J., 1988—. Recipient Geraldine Dodge fellowship Dodge Found., 1993, N.J. Gov.'s award State of N.J., 1993-94, Presdl. award for Excellence in Elem. Sci. Teaching, NSF, 1994; named Dist. Tchr. of Yr., East Windsor Regional Schs., 1994. Fellow Merck Inst. of Sci. (summer faculty 1993—); mem. ASCD, NSTA, Coun. for Elem. Sci. Internat., N.J. Sci. Suprs. Assn., N.J. Tchrs. Assn. Office: E Windsor Regional Sch Dist Ethel McKnight Sch 58 Twin Rivers Dr S East Windsor NJ 08520

GUARNERE, JOANNE, protective services official; b. Rochester, N.Y., May 6, 1952; d. Paul and Betty Jane Guarnere. BSW, SUNY, Brockport, 1974; MS in Edn., Nazareth Coll., 1990. Cert. police instr., firearms cert. N.Y. State Bur. Mcpl. Police. Caseworker Monroe County Dept. Social Svcs., Rochester, N.Y., 1975-79; adminstrv. coord. City of Rochester, 1979-84; sr. probation officer County of Monroe, Rochester, 1984—; group facilitator Genesee Mental Health Ctr., Rochester, 1995—. Bd. mem. Domestic Violence Consortium, Rochester, 1994-96, Monroe County-City of Rochester Victims Task Force, 1994—; adj. prof. Monroe C.C., Rochester, 1996—. Literacy tutor Vols. Am., Rochester, 1999—; probation co-chair Heart Assn.-Heart Walk, Rochester, 1999. Mem. Am. Probation and Parole Assn., Civil Svc. Employees Assn. (pres. probation sect. 1996-99, v.p. 1999—), N.Y. State Probation Officers Assn., Monroe County Probation Officers Assn. Avocations: bicycling, hiking, photography, travel, literature. Office: Monroe County Office Of Probation 33 Fitzhugh St N Rochester NY 14614-1210

GUARNIERI, ALBINA, Canadian legislator; b. Faeto, Italy, June 23, 1953; BA, MA, McGill U. Solicitor Gen., Can., 1980; liberal leader1981 election; press sec. Mayor of Toronto, Ont., Can.; M.P. Ho. Commons, 1988—; parliamentary sec. to min. Canadian heritage Govt. of Can., Ottawa, 1993—96, assoc. min. nat. defense, 2003—, min. state (civil preparedness), 2003—, min. VA, 2005—. Office: House of Commons Rm 450 Confederation Bldg Ottawa ON Canada K1A OA6

GUARNIERI, ROBERTA JEAN, elementary school educator, consultant; d. Robert S. Norte and Zenda Giffin Higdon; m. Michael Wayne Guarnieri, May 27, 1967; children: Andrea Nicole Thornton, Aimee Michele. Degree in home econ., Calif. State U., LA, 1968. Cert. tchr. Calif. 7th grade tchr. Our Lady of Guadalupe, LA, 1996—97, 5th grade tchr., 1997—98; 4th-5th grade tchr. Kentwood Elem. Sch., LA, 1998—99, 5th grade tchr., 1999—. Advisor People to People Leadership Program, Spokane, 2003—. Pres. Sandpipers, Hermosa Beach, Calif., 1997—98. Named Eddy Awards Tchr. of Yr., Westchester-Playa del Rey C. of C., 2004; recipient Poetic Achievement award, Creative Communication, 2003—05; Environ. grantee, Playa Vista Found., 1999—2000, Sch. Yard Habitat grantee, Calif. Cmty. Found., 2004—06, Tchr. grantee for Habitat, Rotary Club of Westchester, 2004—05, Colonial Williamsburg scholar, Williamsburg Tchr.'s Inst., 2003. Mem.: NEA, NSTA, Calif. Teachers Assn., Nat. Coun. Tchrs. Math., Delta Zeta (life; rush chmn. 1966—67, Pres.' award 1966). Office: Kentwood Elem Sch 8401 Emerson Ave Los Angeles CA 90045 Office Phone: 310-670-8977.

GUBBIN, BARBARA ASHLEY BRENDON, library director; b. Calcutta, India, Jan. 9, 1952; d. Richard F.B. and Rosemarie A. (Walker) G.; m. J. Sidney Cunningham, Aug. 16, 1975. BA, U. Birmingham, 1972; diploma in library sci., U. London, 1976, MA, 1977. Librarian Fawcett Library, London, 1976-77; reference librarian San Antonio Pub. Lib., 1977-79; collection devel cons. San Antonio Area Library System, 1979-80, coordinator, 1980-85, Houston Area Library System, 1985-89; asst. dir. Houston Pub. Libr., 1989-95, dir., 1995—2004, Jacksonville Pub. Libr., Fla., 2004—. Bd. dirs. Tex. Coun. for the Humanities, 1993—, treas., 1996; bd. dirs. Houston READ Commn., 1995—, sec.; OCLC Users Coun. del., 1993—, mem. exec. com., 1996—. Mem. ALA, Tex. Libr. Assn. (pres. 1996, Outstanding New Libr. 1983). Office: Jacksonville Pub Libr 303 N Laura St Jacksonville FL 32202*

GUBBIOTTI, CHRISTINE M., lawyer; b. Pittston, Pa., Nov. 1, 1968; d. Thomas Joseph and Patricia Ann Gubbiotti; m. Joseph A. O'Boyle, Feb. 1, 2003. BS in Polit. sci., U. Scranton, 1990, MA in History, 1990; JD, Dickinson Sch. Law, 1993. Bar: Supreme Ct. Pa. 1993. Staff atty. Blue Cross of Northeastern Pa., Wilkes-Barre, 1994—98, corp. counsel, 1998—2000; gen. counsel Geisinger Health Plan, Danville, Pa., 2000—04, v.p., Legal Svcs., 2004—, Geisinger Quality Options, Inc., Danville, Pa., 2005—. Asst. sec. Geisinger Health Plan, 2000—, Geisinger Indemnity Ins. Co., 2000—. Mem. various coms., advisory bds. Am. Health Ins. Plans, Washington, 2000—; bd. dirs. Arthritis Found. of NEPA, Wilkes-Barre, 2000—. Victims Resource Ctr. Mem.: Pa. Bar assn. (health, in-house counsel com. 1993—), Am. Health Lawyers Assn., Wilkes-Barre Law Libr. Assn. (health law com. 2000—). Democrat. Roman Catholic. Office: Geisinger Health Plan 100 N Academy Ave Danville PA 17822 Office Phone: 570-271-7389. Office Fax: 570-271-5268. Business E-Mail: cmgubbiotti@thehealthplan.com.

GUBEN, JAN K., lawyer; b. Balt., Md., Nov. 11, 1942; BA, Tusculum Coll., 1964; LLB, U. Balt., 1967. Bar: Md. 1967, DC 2001. Ptnr., real estate law Venable LLP (formerly Venable, Baetjer and Howard), Balt., chair. bus. div., 1995—2001. Lectr. real estate Johns Hopkins U., 1986-95, deleg. US Agy. Internat. Devel., 1997. Mem. ABA, Md. State Bar Assn., Bar Assn. Balt. City. Office: Venable LLP 1800 Mercantile Bank & Trust Bldg 2 Hopkins Plz Baltimore MD 21201 Office Phone: 410-244-7624. Office Fax: 410-244-7742. Business E-Mail: jkguben@venable.com.

GUCKERT, NORA JANE GASKILL, medical/surgical nurse, hospice nurse, holistic consultant; b. Pitts., June 17, 1945; d. James E. and Nora L. (McAllister) Gaskill; m. Ray H. Guckert, Aug. 1, 1964 (div. May 2001); children: Brian K. Sr., Bruce M., Brenda L. Jansen. LPN, C.C. Allegheny County, Pitts., 1976, AS in Nursing, 1982; BS, Clayton Coll. Holistic Med., 1998, MS, 1999, PhD, 2001. Staff nurse St. Margaret's Meml. Hosp., Aspinwall, Pa., 1976-86; vis. nurse Personal Touch Home Care, Pitts., 1986-87, Norfolk, Va., 1995-98; pvt. practice, 1988—; staff nurse Kimberly Quality Home Care/Portsmouth (Va.) Naval Hosp., 1988-90; liason Sentara Home Health, 1992; cons. Holistic Health of Tidewater, Inc., Va., 1995-99; dir. nursing Med. Staff Svcs., Inc., Va. Beach, 1997-98; hospice dir. Personal Tech Home Care, 1997—99; home health nurse Tender Loving Care/Staff Builders Inc., 2000—02; dir. nursing edn. Virginia Beach, Newport News and Richmond campsuses Med. Careers Inst., 2000—03; home health nurse Comfort Care Home Health, 2003—; cons. Holistic Health of Virginia Beach Cons. Svc., 1997—. Dir. 1st holistic conf. by profls., Virginia Beach, 1997; cons. Holistic Health of Va. Beach Cons. Svc., 1997—. Author materials on nutritional needs. Vol. Chesapeake Indigent Care Clinic. Home: 3280 Winterberry Ln Virginia Beach VA 23453-5910 Personal E-mail: nonniejphd@cox.net.

GUDE, NANCY CARLSON, lawyer; b. Kane, Pa., Aug. 5, 1948; d. Edward Walter and Theo Alberta (Herzog) Carlson. BA in History, Pa. State U., 1969; MS in Computer Sci., U. Central Fla., 1981; JD, Thomas M. Cooley Law Sch., 2001. Bar: Fla. 2001, U.S. Dist. Ct. (no. and so. dists.) Fla. 2003. Programmer Group Hospitalization, Inc., Washington, 1969-70; programmer analyst Space Age Computer Sys., Washington, 1970-73, Ky. Fried Chicken, Louisville, 1973-75; sys. analyst Sentinel Comm. Co., Orlando, Fla., 1975-77, programming supr., 1977-78, sys. and programming mgr., 1978-80, asst. dir. data processing, 1980, mgr. staff devel., 1981-82; mgmt. info. svcs. mgr. Sun-Sentinel Co., Ft. Lauderdale, Fla., 1982-83, v.p., dir. info. sys., 1983-94, sys. cons., 1994-98; assoc. atty. Walton Lantaff Schroeder & Carson, Ft. Lauderdale, 2002—04. Adj. instr. U. Ctrl. Fla., Orlando, 1981—82. Participant Leadership Broward X; chair LBX Artserve Intervention Group. Recipient Thomas M. Cooley Leadership Achievement award, 2001. Mem.: Broward County Bar Assn., Fed. Bar Assn., The Fla. Bar, Pa. State U. Alumni Assn. (Ft. Lauderdale chpt., treas. 1990—92, v.p. 1992—93, pres. 1993—95). Presbyterian. Home: 9 NE 20 Ave Pompano Beach FL 33060

GUDENZI-RUESS, IDA CARMEN V., music educator, artist; b. Bronx, NY, Nov. 4, 1926; d. Hamlet G. and Dolores Gudenzi; m. Raymond Edmond Ruess, Aug. 20, 1965; 1 child, Raida. AA, Columbia-Greene C.C., Hudson, NY, 1994; studied drawing and sculpture, Arts Student League, NYC; studied with NYC concert pianist Vladzia Mashke. Montessori tchg. cert. Bergamo, Italy, 1973. Tchr. piano and sculpture, NY. Sculptor (bust) WWII Marine Corps Comdt. Gen. Holland Meade Smith, Hawaii, 1966. Mem.: Phi Theta Kappa. Home: 12 Eldridge Ln Red Hook NY 12571 Office Phone: 845-758-9560.

GUDGEON, VALERIE A., school system administrator; d. LeRoy and Patricia Gudgeon. BS, St. Louis U., 1976, MA, 1977. Cert. administrator Ill., dir. spl. edn. Ill., tchr. spl. edn. Ill. Tchr. spl. edn. Spl. Edn. Dist. Lake City, Gurnee, Ill., 1977—80, supr. spl. edn., 1980—90, North Suburban Spl. Edn.

Dist. 181, Highland Pk., Ill., 1990—2000; dir. spl. edn. Hinsdale (Ill.) Elem. Dist. 181, 2000—01, Evanston (Ill.) and Skokie Sch. Dists., 2001—04; asst. dir. Ctr. Spl. Edn. Niles Township H.S., Morton Grove, Ill., 2004—05; dir. student svcs. Aurora (Ill.) East Dist. 131, 2005—. Mem.: Coun. Exceptional Children, Ill. Alliance Adminstrs. Spl. Edn. Avocations: reading, tennis, travel. Office: Aurora East Sch Dist 131 Child Svc Ctr 231 E Indian Tr Rd Aurora IL 60505

GUDMUNDSON, BARBARA ROHRKE, ecologist; b. Chgo. d. Lloyd Ernest and Helen (Bullard) Rohrke; m. Valtyr Emil Gudmundson, June 14, 1951 (dec. Dec. 1982); children: Holly Mekkín Leighton, Martha Rannveig. BA, U. Tenn., 1950; MA, Minn. State U., 1965; PhD, Iowa State U., 1969. Microbiologist Hektoen Inst. & Ill. Ctr. Hosp., Chgo., 1950-52; immunologist Jackson Meml. Lab., Bar Harbor, Maine, 1952-54; dist. ecologist Corps of Engrs., St. Paul, 1971-72; sr. ecologist North Star Rsch. Inst., Mpls., 1972-76; staff engr. Met. Waste Control Commn., St. Paul, 1976-77; pres., prin. ecologist Ecosystem Rsch. Svc./Upper Midwest, Mpls., 1978-99. Pvt. practice as cons. ecologist, Des Moines and Mpls., 1968-70; mem. Citizens League Task Force on the Mississippi Riverfront, 1973-74; mem. adv. com. Mpls. Lakes Water Quality, Mpls., 1974-75; river ecologist Mississippi River Canoe Expdn., Coll. of the Atlantic, Bar Harbor, 1979; mem. Minn. Interfaith Campaign Climate Change, 2001-04. Author: V. Emil Gudmundson: Icelandic Canadian Unitarian, A Personal Biography, 1991; editor-in-chief The Icelandic Unitarian Connection, 1984; contbr. articles to profl. jours. Mem. from 61st dist. Dem.-Farmer-Labor Ctr. Com., Minn., 1978-80; mgr. Minnehaha Creek Watershed Dist., 1979-83, sec., 1982-83; mem. Capital Long-Range Improvement Com., Mpls., 1981; mem. steering com. Nokomis East Neighborhood Assn., 1995-97, bd. dirs. 1997-2003. Recipient Leadership award Izaak Walton League, 1982; River Basin Ecology grantee Iowa Acad. Scis., Cedar Falls, 1976, Mississippi River Ecology grantee Freshwater Biol. Rsch. Found., Navarre, Minn., 1979; Fulbright Sr. Rsch. grantee USA/Iceland Fulbright Commns., Washington, Reykjavik, 1986, 92. Mem. NOW (Minn. state bd. 1989-96, Anita Hill Courage and Justice award Twin Cities chpt. 1994, Minn.-NOW's Charlotte Striebel Long Distance Runner award 1998), Ecol. Soc. Am. (pres. Minn. chpt. 1971-75), Geol. Soc. Minn. (pres. 1981), Phycological Soc. Am., Internat. Assn. Diatom Rsch., Icelandic Am. Assn. Minn., Hekla Icelandic Club (pres. 1977), Fulbright Assn., Sigma Xi, Phi Kappa Phi, Sigma Delta Epsilon-Grad. Women in Sci. (nat. mem. com. 1990-93, chmn. 1991-93). Unitarian Universalist. Achievements include discovery of diatom genus Biddulphia in the state of Iowa; establishment of Diatom Herbarium of Iceland. Home: 5505 28th Ave S Minneapolis MN 55417-1957

GUDNITZ, ORA M. COFEY, secondary school educator; b. Crawfordsville, Ark., Jan. 24, 1934; d. Daniel S. and Mary (Oglesby) Cofey; children: Ingrid M. Hunt, Carl Erik, Katrina Beatrice. BA, Lane Coll., Jackson, Tenn., 1955; MEd, Temple U., 1969; student, U. Copenhagen, 1957; MA in Theol. Studies, Ea. Bapt. Theol. Sem., Pa., 1995, Eastern Bapt. Theol. Sem., 1995. Cert. permanent English, social studies and French tchr., Pa. Tchr. English, chmn. dept. Sayre Jr. High Sch., Phila.; tchr. English, Overbrook High Sch., Phila. Founder, exec. dir. Young Communicators Workshop, Inc.; lectr., Denmark. Contbr. articles to newspapers, poetry to anthologies. Recipient award Chapel of Four Chaplains, 1976, Women in Edn. award, 1988; grantee Haas Found., 1977, also others. Mem. Nat. Coun. Tchrs. English, Assn. for Ednl. Communication and Tech., Phi Delta Kappa, Delta Sigma Theta.

GUENGERICH, RUTH LAPP, counselor; d. John Edwin and Edith R. Nyce Lapp; m. Ronald Dean Guengerich, Sept. 4, 1967; children: Paul Thomas, Catherine Alisa Hart. BA, Ea. Mennonite U., 1968; MEd, James Madison U., 1983. Nat. cert. counselor Nat. Bd. Cert. Counselors, 1984, lic. profl. counselor State of Ohio Counselor and Social Worker Bd., 1998. Dir. student life Hesston Coll., Kans., 1983—86; counselor Hutchinson CC, Kans., 1986—96, Charter Behavioral Health, Defiance, 1997—2000, Sauder Woodworking EAP, Archbold, Ohio, 1999—, Shalom Ministries, Archbold, 1999—. V.p. Fairlawn Aux. Bd., Archbold, 2005, pres., 2006. Mem.: ACA. Home: 1100 Lindau St Archbold OH 43502 Office Phone: 419-445-1552.

GUENTNER, GAIL MARIE, software engineer; b. Milw., Apr. 17, 1961; d. Theodore Edward and June Dolores (Carlson) G. BS in Computer Sci., U. Wis., 1985. Software engr. Norland Corp., Ft. Atkinson, Wis., 1986—87; software support engr. Heurikon Corp., Madison, Wis., 1987—89, mgr. tech. support, 1989—90, software engr., 1990—93; software support mgr. Neuro-Concepts, Inc., Madison, 1993; software engr. cons. Insight Ind., Platteville, Wis., 1993—94; sys. analyst Telephone and Data Sys., Madison, 1994—96; sr. software engr. GE Spacenet-Tridom, Marietta, Ga., 1996—97; sys. integrator Lockheed Martin, Marietta, 1997—. Mem.: World Wildlife Fund, Assn. Computing Machinery, Soc. Women Engrs. Avocations: downhill skiing, camping, hiking, volleyball, photography. Office: Lockheed Martin EIS 86 S Cobb Dr Marietta GA 30063 Office Phone: 770-793-0301. Personal E-mail: gailg17@acm.org.

GUERINOT, MARY LOU, biology professor; B in Biology, Cornell U., 1975; PhD in Biology, Dalhousie U., Can., 1979. Postdoctoral rschr. U. Md., Mich. State U.-Dept. Energy Plant Rsch. Lab.; asst. prof. Dartmouth Coll., Hanover, NH, 1985—91, assoc. prof., 1991—97, prof., 1997, Ronald and Deborah Harris prof. dept. biol. scis. Chair dept. biol. scis. Dartmouth Coll., 1994—98, assoc. dean faculty of scis., 1998—2001, vice provost, 2001—04; bd. dirs. The Arabidopsis Info. Resource. Contbr. articles to profl. jours.; assoc. editor: Plant Molecular Biology. Office: Dept Biol Scis Dartmouth Coll 6044 Gilman Rm 304 Hanover NH 03755-3526 E-mail: Mary.Lou.Guerinot@Dartmouth.edu.*

GUERRA, EDNA, pharmacist; b. Kingsville, Tex., Dec. 4, 1952; d. Fidel and Rebecca Rodriguez; m. R. David Guerra, Aug. 16, 1975; children: Omar D., Sara Elena. BS in Elem. Edn., Tex. A&I U., 1975; BS in Pharmacy, U. Tex., 1981. Cert. tchr., Tex.; registered pharmacist, Tex. Tchr. Bishop (Tex.) Consol. Ind. Sch. Dist., 1975-76, N.E. Sch. Dist., San Antonio, 1976-77; cmty. pharmacist Laredo, Tex., 1981-90, McAllen, Tex., 1990-93. Mem. adv. bd. McAllen Internat. Mus., 1994—; bd. dirs. McAllen Ednl. Found., 1999—; co-chair United Way of Hidalgo County, McAllen, 1995, mem. allocation com., 1996, 98, 99; vol. Milam Elem. Sch. PTSA, McAllen, 1990, Gonzalez Elem. Sch. PTSA, McAllen, 1991-95; docent McAllen Internat. Mus., 1991-93, coll. fundraiser admittance chair, 1996, mem. com. 1997, coll. fundraiser, 1998-99; bd. dirs. Arthritis Found. Rio Grande Valley, McAllen, 1993-94, Rio Grande Valley Pharm. Assn., Mcallen, 1991-94; v.p. Young Women's Book Rev. League, McAllen, 1995-96; CCD instr. Our Lady of Sorrows Cath. Ch., McAllen, 1991; gala admittance chair Easter Seals Assn., McAllen, 1997; adminstr. Fidel Rodriguez Family Scholarships, Bishop Consol. Ind. Sch. Sch. Dist., 1996—; vol. Nat. Hispanic Scholarship Fund, McAllen, 1996, South Tex. Symphony Assn. fundraiser, McAllen, 1998, 99, Valley Alliance of Mentors for Opportunities and Scholarships, McAllen, 1998, Food Bank, Corpus Christi, Tex., 1999. Recipient Vol. of Yr. award Easter Seals, 1997. Mem. U. Tex. Ex-Students' Assn., Tex. Pharm. Assn. Roman Catholic. Avocation: reading.

GUERRA, JAMEE ELIZABETH RUND, music educator; b. San Diego, Dec. 19, 1980; d. James Robert and Elizabeth Ann Rund; m. Mario Humberto Guerra, Sept. 20, 2005. B in Music Edn., Rider U., Princeton, NJ, 2003. Cert. music tchr. grades K-12 NJ, 2003. Music tchr., organist St. Mary's Sch., Valley, Virgin Gorda, British Virgin Islands, 2003—04; music tchr. Purnell Sch., Pottersville, NJ, 2004—. Choir and band dir. Purnell Sch., Pottersville, 2004—. Home: Box 500 51 Pottersville Rd Pottersville NJ 07979 Personal E-mail: jrund@purnell.org.

GUERRA, MAYRA, insurance company executive; b. N.Y.C., Aug. 3, 1968; d. Israel and Eloisa (Marquis) Anta; m. Jose Antonio Guerra, Feb. 8, 1992; children: Tony Scott, Elle Frances. Lic. prodr., Kovats Sch. Ins., Paramus, N.J., 1989. Customer svc. ins. rep. Muller Agy., Hoboken, N.J., 1988-90, Scirocco Assocs., North Bergen, N.J., 1990-96, Carle & Christie, Englewood Cliffs, N.J., 1996-99. Mem. Nat. Assn. Ins. Women No. (chair safety com. 1998-99). Office: Gulfshore Ins Inc 4100 Goodlette Rd N Ste 100 Naples FL 34103-3303 E-mail: mgu@gulfshoreinsurance.com.

GUERRANT, MARY THORINGTON, music educator; b. Taft, Tex., May 7, 1925; d. William Lord Thorington and Mary Guerrant Burnett; m. William Barnett Jr., Sept. 3, 1946; 1 child, William B. Guerrant III. BA in English, Austin Coll., 1946; MusM in Piano, Tex. Tech. U., 1971, PhD in Fine Arts, 1976. Piano instr. Austin Coll., Sherman, Tex., 1957-58; assoc. prof. piano and composition Tunghai (Taiwan) U., 1976-77, vis. prof., 1984-86; vis. scholar (piano) Hong Kong Bapt. Coll., 1986-88. Adjudicator Nat. Guild of Piano Tchrs., Sherman and Lubbock, Tex., 1966-84, Lubbock Music Tchrs. Assn. Solo piano recitals include First United Meth. Ch., Albuquerque, 1995, U. N.Mex., 1992, Hong Kong Bapt. Coll., 1988, St. John's Cathedral, Hong Kong, 1988, and others; composer (chamber opera) The Shepherds, 1976, (ensemble) Pecos Ruins, 1974; contbr. articles to profl. publs. Vol. Cmty. Concerts, Sherman, 1954-66, Albuquerque Literacy Program, 1988-90, Meals on Wheels, Albuquerque, 1989; bd. dirs. Friends of Music, Albuquerque, 1991, 92. Heard fellowship in English Austin Coll., 1945-46, Disting. Alumni award, 1979. Mem. Music Tchrs. Nat. Assn. (cert. master tchr.), Profl. Music Tchrs. of N.Mex., Albuquerque Music Tchrs. Assn., Alpha Chi, Pi Kappa Lambda. Avocations: travel, camping, hiking, foreign language study, tennis. Home: 14217 Turner Ct NE Albuquerque NM 87123-1836

GUERRERO, DONNA MARIE, sales executive; b. L.A., Apr. 27, 1964; d. Henry Joseph Guerrero and Dolores Catherine Veiga. BA, Whittier Coll., 1985; MPA, Harvard U., 1988. Presdl. intern, pub. rels. mgr. U.S. EEOC, Washington, Houston, 1988—98; profl. sales & leasing cons. Moss Bros. Toyota, Moreno Valley, Calif., 2002—. Bd. mem. Nat. Hispanic Media Coalition, L.A., 1994—98. Adv. bd. League of United Latin Am. Citizens, Houston, 1995—97. Recipient Heroes of Reinvention Award, V.P. Al Gore's Nat. Performance Rev., 1994. Roman Catholic. Avocations: christian devotional/spirituality, holistic health, sports memorabilia/collectibles. Home: 11037 Le Grand Ln Moreno Valley CA 92557 Personal E-mail: dguerrero@tmo.blackberry.net.

GUERRERO, LISA (LISA GUERRERO-COLES), former sports reporter; b. Chgo., Apr. 8, 1964; m. Scott Erickson, Feb. 3, 2004. Cheerleader Los Angeles Rams; dir, choreographer Atlanta Falcons Cheerleaders, New England Patriots; reporter Extra, 1994; co-host Sports Geniuses, 2000; reporter The Best Damn Sports Show Period!, FoxSportsNet, 2000—03; sideline reporter Monday Night Football, ABC, 2003—04. Actress: (films) Batman Returns, 1992; Love Potion No. 9, 1992; Fire Down Below, 1997; (TV series) Wild West Showdown, 1994; Sunset Beach, 1998—99. Vol. Salvation Army, Cedar Sinai Med. Ctr. Achievements include appearing in over 200 commercials and the covers of Maxim and FHM.

GUERRINI, ANITA, historian, educator; b. Torrington, Conn., May 23, 1953; d. Armando Severino Guerrini and Rita Lillian Greco; m. Michael Andrew Osborne, Aug. 13, 1983; children: Paul Andrew Osborne, Henry Severino Osborne. BA, Conn. Coll., New London, Conn., 1975; MA, Oxford U., England, 1977; PhD, Ind. U., Bloomington, Ind., 1983. From asst. prof. to prof. history and environ. studies U. Calif., Santa Barbara, Calif., 1995—2004; Mellon postdoctoral fellow Am. Philos. Soc. Libr., 1984—85; vis. asst. prof. history of medicine and history of sci. U. Minn.-Twin Cities, 1985—88; lectr. dept. history U. Calif., Santa Barbara, 1989—95, prof. history and environ. studies, 2004—. Fellow, Ctr. Nat. Sci. Rsch., 1999—2000; grantee, NSF, 1999—2000, NEH, 2003—. Mem.: Am. Soc. Eighteenth-Century Studies (exec. bd. 1995—98), History Sci. Soc. (coun. 1995—98), Am. Hist. Assn. Avocations: travel, hiking, music. Office: University of California Santa Barbara Department of History 9410 Santa Barbara CA 93106-9410 Office Phone: 805-893-8827.

GUERRY, PAULA MARY, school nurse practitioner; b. Paterson, NJ, Feb. 19, 1951; d. Paul John and Mary Julia Grusczynski; m. Ronald Dennis Guerry, June 4, 1987 (div. May 14, 1999); 1 child, Nicole Noelle; m. Stevean Wayne Reynolds, Oct. 16, 1971 (div. June 1, 1987); 1 child, Jamie Beth Reynolds. Diploma, Albany Med. Ctr., 1980; AA in Natural Scis., Napa Coll., Calif, 1976. RN 1980. Staff nurse Albany Med. Ctr., 1980—80, Norwich State Hosp., Conn., 1981—84; acting charge nurse Va. Ctr. Psychiatry, Portsmouth, 1984—85; staff nurse Naval Hosp. Portsmouth, 1985—89, Naval Hosp. Beaufort, 1989—91, Sc Dhec, 1991—2001; sch. nurse Dept. Def., 2001—; staff nurse Beaufort Meml. Hosp., 2005—. Staff nurse USN, Portsmouth, Va., 1985—88, Beaufort, SC, 1988—91, Beaufort County Health Dept., 1991—2001; clinic coord. USNR, North Charleston, 2000—05; sch. nurse Dept. Def., Beaufort, 2001—. Weatherwatcher NOAA. Lt. comdr. USN, 1969—91. Decorated Nat. Def. Svc. medal USN, Meritorious Unit citation, Humanitarian Svc. award; recipient Michael Jarret award, Sc Dhec, 1998. Mem.: Navy Nurse Corps Assn., AMVETS (life), MENSA. Conservative. Roman Catholic. Avocations: beachcombing, reading, cooking, collecting cook books. Home: 65 Evergreen Lane Beaufort SC 29906 Office: Dod _ Galer Elementary School 1516 Cardinal Lane Beaufort SC 29906 Office Phone: 843-846-9571. Office Fax: 843-846-1860. Personal E-mail: paula_guerry@yahoo.com. E-mail: paula.guerry@am.dodea.edu.

GUESON, EMERITA TORRES, obstetrician, gynecologist; b. Angeles City, The Philippines, Jan. 4, 1942; came to U.S., 1964; d. Lina (Torres) Gueson. AA, U. Sto. Tomas, Manila, Philippines, 1958, MD, 1963. Resident in ob-gyn. Phila. Gen. Hosp., 1966-71; attending physician Nazareth Hosp., Phila., 1973—, Holy Redeemer Hosp., Meadowbrook, Pa., 1983—. Bd. dirs. Physicians Who Care; lectr. healthcare issues to consumer groups, Phila. Author: Doctors Under Fire, 1989, Scales of Justice: Exploring the Wilderness of Health Care and Society's Moral Conscience, 1992, Do HMO's Cut Costs.and Lives, 1997, Survival Guide for HMO Patients, 1997; pub. ThereseVision Publs.; also med. writer, screenplay writer, line dir., prodr. Hon. co-chair physicians adv. bd. Republican Nat. Com. Fellow ACOG, ACP; mem. AMA, Pa. Med. Soc., Philadelphia County Med. Soc., Pro-Life Ob.-Gynecologists (charter). Avocations: writing, painting, refinishing furniture. Office: 3336 Aldine St Philadelphia PA 19136-3802 E-mail: therese44@aol.com.

GUESS, AUNDREA KAY, accounting educator; b. Seth, W.Va., Feb. 7, 1953; d. Hobert and Inez Elizabeth (Howell) Adams; children: Renae, Rhonda. BBA, Baylor U., Waco, Tex., 1988; MBA, Auburn U., 1989; PhD, U. North Tex., 1993. CPA, Ala., Fla. Co-owner Stevenson (Ala.) All-Mart, 1967-94; grad. rsch. asst. Auburn (Ala.) U., 1988-89; teaching fellow U. North Tex., Denton, 1989-90, lectr., 1990-93; prof., dir. acctg. program Samford U., Birmingham, Ala., 1993—97, dir. new masters of acctg. degree program; prof. U. Tex., 1997—; dir. acctg. MBA profram St. Edwards U., Austin, Tex., 1998—. Cons. Kay Guess Cons., Birmingham, 1993—, activity based costing Coca-Cola; presenter Southwestern Bus. Adminstrn. Conf., 1994; discussant, 1995 track chair for acctg. and fin. Southwestern Case Rsch., pres. 2003—; owner Kay's Designer Dresses, Stevenson; prof. St. Edwards U., 2003; bd. dir. N.Am. Case Rsch. Assn. Contbr. pubs. to various jours. Recipient Fin. Execs. Inst. award, 1987, 89; Rsch. grantee Samford U.Heloise Brown Canter scholar Am. Women's Soc. CPA and Am. Soc. Women Accts., 1992. Mem. AICPA, Am. Acctg. Assn., Am. Soc. Women CPAs (South Birmingham chpt., Laurel scholar 1992, scholar 1989), Fla. Inst. CPAs, Inst. Mgmt. Accts. (bd. dirs. 1994—, dir. tech. meetings 1994—), Acad. Acctg. Historians, Inst. Internal Auditing, Phi Theta Kappa, Alpha Kappa Psi, Beta Alpah Psi (treas. Auburn chpt. 1989), Phi Kappa Phi, Beta Gamma Sigma. Baptist. Avocations: sewing, cake decorating, running. Home: 651 Martin Rd Dripping Springs TX 78620-3506

GUEST, SUZANNE MARY, adult education educator, artist; b. Monroe, Mich., Sept. 24, 1935; d. Hubert George Guest and Lola Viola Anne Pfeffer. BA, Marygrove Coll., 1957; MFA, U. Notre Dame, 1969. Chmn. art dept. Marian H.S., Birmingham, Mich., 1960—66, St. Mary H.S., Akron, Ohio, 1966—68, Am. Sch., London, 1971—91; adult educator Wordens World of Art, Pompano, Fla., 1994—, Ft. Lauderdale (Fla.) H.S., 1994—, First Presbyn. Ch., Pompano, 1999—; mem. sisterhood Immaculate Heart of Mary, Detroit, 1957—69. Freelance artist Alan Kent Design Group, London, 1970; presenter workshops in field; calligraphy sabbatical Oreg. Sch. Arts and Crafts, Portland, 1988—89. Author: Calligraphy for Those Who Are Young at Heart, 1988; contbr. Ency. Calligraphy Techniques, 1990; exhibitions include various schs., restaurants, art stores, chs. Recipient Outstanding Svc. in Secondary Edn. award, European Coun. Internat. Schs., London, 1977—90, Calligraphy award, Soc. Scribes and Illuminators, London, 1991. Mem.: So. Fla. Watercolor Soc., Mus. for Women in Arts, Humane Soc. Democrat. Roman Catholic. Avocations: music, meditation, watercolor. Home: 3051 NE 48th St Apt 104 Fort Lauderdale FL 33308-4903

GUEVARA, ROXANNA, elementary school educator, gifted and talented educator; BS in Edn., Tex. Christian U., Ft. Worth, 1999; MA, Nova Southeastern U., Fla., 2002. Cert. elem. early childhood edn. Tex., ESL tchr. Tex. ESL and gifted tchr. Ft. Worth Ind. Sch. Dist., 1999—2001; 5th grade bilingual tchr. El Paso Ind. Sch. Dist., 2001—02, sci., gifted tchr., 2002—. Vol. Jr. League, El Paso, 2002—06, Tex. Neurofibromatosis, 1980—2006. Office: El Paso Ind Sch Dist Vilas Elem 220 Lawton El Paso TX 79902 Office Phone: 915-351-3240. Personal E-mail: roxannaguevara@sbcglobal.net. Business E-Mail: rgueva13@episd.org.

GUFFEY, BARBARA BRADEN, retired elementary school educator; b. Pitts., Aug. 10, 1948; d. James Arthur and Dorothy (Barrett) Braden; 1 child, William Butler Guffey III. BA in Elem. Edn., Westminster Coll., New Wilmington, Pa., 1970; MEd in Elem. Edn., Slippery Rock State Coll., 1973; postgrad., U. Pitts., Duquesne U., Pitts., Westminster Coll. Cert. tchr., elem. and secondary history and govt. edn, elem. prin. Tchr. Shaler Area Sch. Dist., Glenshaw, Pa., 1970—2005, lang. arts area specialist, 1988—91, 1992—93, grad. level chmn., 1991—92, curriculum support math./sci., 1994—2005, mem. instrnl. support team, 1995—2005; ret., 2005; student tchr. supr. Duquesne U., 2006. Mem. Shaler Area Stretegic Planning Core Team, 1992-2005; mem. A.S.S.E.T. Leadership Team, 1995-2005; condr. seminars and workshops in field Pres. alumni coun. Westminster Coll., 1993—97, 2004—, v.p., 1995—96, chmn. homecoming all-alumni luncheon, 1991—93, chmn. homecoming, 1995—96, trustee, 1999—, mem. sesqicentennial com., 2002, mem. enrollment mgmt., ednl. policy and student affairs com., vice chmn. instl. advancement com., 2003—06, mem. exec. com., 2006—; chair Westminster Fund, 2003—; active Burchfield Elem. Sch. PTA; chmn. publicity Shaler Area Choir Parents Assn., 1996—2000; vice chair Child Care Adv. Bd., 2006—; elder, chair Christian edn. com. Glenshaw Presbyn. Ch., 1995—2001, mem. Presbyn. Women. Mem.: NEA, Shaler Area Edn. Assn. (mem. at large, negotiator, former rec. sec., v.p., bldg. rep., editor newsletter), Pa. Edn. Assn., Nat. Geneal. Soc. (local arrangements chair Pitts. conf. 2003), Armstrong County Hist. and Mus. Soc., Ind. County Geneal. and Hist. Soc., Western Pa. Geneal. Soc. (bd. dirs. 1992—, chair 25th Anniversary 1999, pres. 1999—2000, publicity 2000—03, pres. 2002—03, editor newsletter 2004—, recording sec. 2004—, chair Gen. Conf. 2006—), Perry Historians, Juniata County Hist. Soc., First Families of Western Pa. (charter mem.), Westminster Coll. Women's Club Pitts. (pres. 1975—76, treas. 1994—99, pres. 2001—03, v.p., sec., chair ways and means, pres. 2006—), Kappa Delta Pi. Personal E-mail: guffeyb@verizon.net.

GUGEL, MERILYNN SUE, artist; b. Van Wert, Ohio, Nov. 22, 1938; d. Merlin Harvey Smith and Margaret Ann Louise Miller; m. Lorenz Walter Gugel, Dec. 28, 1959 (dec. 1980); children: Scott, Craig, Kristina. Studied with David Humphreys Miller, 1957; student, U. N.Mex., 1965-67, U. Alaska, 1967-71. Tchr. art therapy ARC, El Paso; art tchr. Shiva Paint Co., El Paso, 1972-74, Officers Club, El Paso, Fairbanks, Alaska, 1975-80, Umpqua C.C., 1975—; art tchr. spl. arts, disabilities Umpqua Valley Arts Ctr. One-woman shows include Tolly's Art and Antiques, Oakland, Oreg., Art Mill Gallery, Roseburg, Oreg., Vision Gallery, Sutharlin, Umpqua Valley Art Ctr., Roseburg, 2004, Roseburg Art Ctr., 2004, Bend City Hall, Oreg., 2003, exhibited in group shows at Rickerts Gallery, Newport, Oreg., Fischer Galleries, Washington, Represented in permanent collections Bapt. State Conv. Bldg., Anchorage, Pioneer Hall of Fame, Burrough Pub. Libr., Fairbanks, Alaska, Roseburg Forest Products, Trent Colls., Wash., Oreg., Starfire Lumber, Marsha Leaptrout Collection, Ford Found., others. Charter mem. Nat. Mus. Women in the Arts. Mem. Fairbanks Art Assn. (pres., award), Umpqua Valley Arts Assn. (pres., award), Nat. Soc. Lit. and the Arts, Willamette Ve. Artists Assn. Republican. Avocations: music, politics. Home: 550 S State St Apt 33 Sutherlin OR 97479 E-mail: lindaf@teleport.com.

GUGINO, CARLA, actress; b. Sarasota, Fla., Aug. 29; Studied acting, with Gene Bua. Appearances include (TV series) Falcon Crest, 1989-90, Spin City, 1996, Chicago Hope, 1999-2000, Karen Sisco, 2003-04, Threshold, 2005-, (TV movies) Murder Without Motive, 1992, A Private Matter, 1992, Motorcycle Gang, 1994, A Seaspm for Miracles, 1999, Mermaid Chronicles Part 1: She Creature, 2002, (TV miniseries) The Buccaneers, 1995, (films) Troop Beverly Hills, 1989, Welcome Home, 1990, Son-in-Law, 1993, Miami Rhapsody, 1995, Homeward Bound II: Lost in San Francisco, 1996, Michael, 1996, Red Hot, 1996, The War at Home, 1996, Wedding Bell Blues, 1996, Lovelife, 1997, Snake Eyes, 1998, Spy Kids, 2001, Spy Kids 2: Island of Lost Dreams, 2002, The Singing Detective, 2003, Spy Kides 3-D: Game Over, 2003, Life Coach: The Movie, 2005, Sin City, 2005; (broadway) After the Fall, 2004, (Theatre World award, 2005), Suddenly Last Summer, 2006. Avocations: yoga, travel. Office: William Morris Agy 151 S El Camino Dr Beverly Hills CA 90212-2704*

GUGLER, MARY DUGAN, composer, music educator; d. Richard Franklin and Lucile Shoger Dugan; m. Bruce Terry Gugler, Apr. 2, 1977 (dec.); children: Benjamin Franklin II, Mark Alan. MusB in Edn., Va. Commonwealth U., 1968, MusM in Edn., 1977. Cert. collegiate profl. Va. Dept. of Edn., 2001. Band dir. Churchland Jr. HS, Portsmouth, Va., 1968—78, Manor HS, 1978—81, Churchland HS, 1981—92, Churchland Mid. Sch., 1992—. Asst. dir. Young Razzcals Jazz Project, Norfolk, 2002—03. Composer: (music composition) Virginia, From Mountains To The Sea, Lake Gaston Suite. Parent adv. bd. Va. Governor's Sch. For The Arts, Norfolk, Va., 2004—05; vol. Va. Arts Festival Rhythm Project, 1998—2005, ARC, 2003—05, Meals On Wheels, 2003—05. Named Outstanding Young Educator, Portsmouth JAYCEES, 1976, Tchr. of Yr., Churchland Mid. Sch., 2005, Mid. Sch. Tchr. of Yr., Portsmouth Pub. Schs., 2005; grantee, Learn & Serve Am., 2002—03; scholar, Va. Dept. Edn., 1963—66. Mem.: NEA, Va. Edn. Assn., Va. Band & Orch. Directors Assn. (dist. chmn. 1976—78), Va. Music educators Assn., Music Edicators Nat. Conf., Ladies Aux. VFW (life), Phi Kappa Lamda, Alpha Delta Kappa, Delta Omicron. Avocations: computers, music, crafts, sewing, fishing, camping. Office Phone: 757-686-2512 44123.

GUGLIELMI, RHONDA E., nursing administrator; b. Columbus, Ohio, July 20, 1959; d. Richard Earl Harris and Linda Kay Dillion; m. Richard Lewis Baxter (div.); children: Michael Shane Miller, Eric Robert Miller; m. Gary Robert Guglielmi, Aug. 5, 2000. Lic. nurse, Columbus Pub. Sch. Nursing, 1994. In-home care provider Elder Care, London, Ohio, 1984—91; nursing asst. Arbors, London, 1991—92; charge nurse Sharonview Nursing Rehab., South Vienna, Ohio, 1994; clin. nurse mgr. Arlington Ct. Nursing Rehab., Columbus, 1994—2001. Contbr. short stories to anthologies. Named Ohio Job Tng. Partnership Act Participant of Yr., Madison County Tecumseh Consortium, 1995; recipient Success Is a Journey award, Gov. Voinovich, State of Ohio, 1995, State Hon. award, Gen. Assembly, Ohio Senate, 1995, Award of Excellence, Arlington Ct. Nursing Rehab., 1998. Mem.: Reflex Sympathetic Dystrophy Assn. (co-chairperson 2004—). Avocations: painting, writing, playing piano, violin, mandolin. Home: 1915 N Devon Rd Columbus OH 43212 Personal E-mail: rhondabg2000@yahoo.com.

GUHL, GABRIELLE V., music educator; b. Bournemouth, Eng., Apr. 28, 1934; d. James Herbert and Eugenie Victoria (Biermer) Clegg; m. Hans Joachim Herzog, Mar. 15, 1962 (div. 1982); children: Teddy Michael Herzog, Karl Frederic Herzog, Heidi Elisabeth Herzog, Bruno Wilhelm Herzog; m. Gerhard Hermann Guhl, Apr. 15, 1988. AD in Musik, Mozarteum, Salzburg,

Austria, 1950; BA in Music Performance, Conservatoire De Musique, Paris, 1952; MA in Music Performance, Musikhochschule, Hamburg, Germany, 1958; BS in Music Edn., Skidmore Coll., 1973. Cert. music tchr., N.Y. Music tchr. St. Peters Sch., Saratoga Springs, N.Y., 1969-76, ch. organist, choir dir., 1969-76; music tchr. St. Clements Sch., Saratoga Springs, 1976-80, ch.organist, folk group leader, 1976-79; ch. organist, choir dir. St. Matthews Ch., Greenwich, N.Y., 1979-80; chorus coach, tchr., dir. Herzog Music Sch., Del Mar, Calif., 1980-87; music tchr. St. John's Sch., Encinitas, Calif., 1982-85; music tchr., dir. Guhl Music Studio, Houston, 1987-90, Santa Barbara, Calif., 1990—. Trainer neuroassociative conditioning Robbins Rsch. Internat., San Diego, 1983-96; co-founder Saratoga Springs Suzuki Music Festival, 1972; co-founder, music dir. Schuylerville Cmty. Theater, 1976. Driver, caregiver Meals on Wheels, Barbados, W.I., 1961. Recipient priz a l'unanimité Conservatoire de Music, Paris, 1952, Best Spkr. award Toastmasters Am., 1984, Best Humourous Speech award, 1992. Mem. LWV, Nat. Assn. Investment Clubs (bd. dirs. Channel Islands chpt.), Vivace Investors of Santa Barbara (ednl. v.p. 1998-99, pres. 1996-98), Model Club. Avocations: exercise, yoga, playing the piano, making music in a group.

GUICHARD, SUSAN WEIL, dietician, consultant; b. Cleveland, Ohio, May 9, 1954; d. Alexander and Ruth Weil; m. Peter James Guichard, Aug. 2, 1952. BS, Miami U., Oxford, Ohio, 1976; Dietetic Internship, Barnes Hosp., St. Louis, Mo., 1976—77. Registered dietitian Am. Dietetic Assn., 1977, Bd. Cert. Specialist in Renal Nutrition Commn. on Dietetic Registration, Am. Dietetic Assn., 2001. Renal dietitian UCLA Med. Ctr. Kidney and Pancreas Transplant Program and UCLA DaVita Dialysis Ctr., Los Angeles, Calif., 1979—; speakers' bur. Amgen, Inc., Thousand Oaks, Calif., 2003—; renal dietitian U. Hospitals of Cleve., Cleveland, Ohio, 1977—79; clin. instr. of nutrition edn. program Gen. Internal Medicine Residency Tng. Program, UCLA Sch. of Medicine, L.A., Calif., 1982—92, co-ordinator of nutrition edn., 1990—92. Cons. (temp.) Amgen, Inc., Thousand Oaks, Calif., 2004—04; cons. Nephrology Ednl. Svcs. & Rsch., Inc., Tarzana, Calif., 2001—04. Author: (medical textbook on transplantation) Nutrition in the Kidney Tranplant Recipient, in Handbook of Kidney Transplantion, 1992, 2nd edit., 1996, 3rd edit., 2001, 4th edit., 2005, (textbook for dialysis nurses) Nutrition Management, in Review of Hemodialysis for Nurses and Dialysis Personnel, 1993, 6th edit., 1999; co-author: (interactive computer tchg. program) Renaltouch(TM); contbr. dietetics manual; co-author: Diet and Medications, in Living Well With Kidney Disease, 2006. Planning com. U.S. Transpl. Olympics Nat. Kidney Found., L.A., Calif., 1992; planning com. Gift of Life dinner Nat. Kidney Found. of So. Calif., L.A., Calif., 2004. Mem.: Coun. on Renal Nutrition, Nat. Kidney Found., Am. Dietetic Assn. Avocation: singing. Office Phone: 310-794-9687.

GUIDA, PAT, information broker, literature chemist; b. Highland Park, Mich. d. Mr. and Mrs. W.B. Graham; m. Edward Silvio Guida, 1965; children: Niels Bohr, Eric Bohr. Student, Regis Coll., 1946-48, Rutgers U., 1952-55; BS cum laude, Fairleigh Dickinson U., 1961. Asst. librarian Warner-Lambert Research Inst., Morris Plains, NJ, 1961-64; librarian Reaction Motors Div. Thiokol, Denville, 1964-69; mgr., info. ctr. Foster D. Snell Div., Booz Allen & Hamilton Inc., Florham Park, 1969-80; pres. Pat Guida Assocs., Fairfield, 1981—. Mem. sci. adv. bd. EPA, Washington, 1978-82, Library Com. Chemists Club, N.Y.C., 1983-89. Editor: Chemical Digest, 1971—74. Pres. PTA, Sparta, N.J., 1959-60. Avocations: theater, music, travel. Home and Office: 101 Madison Green Pompton Plains NJ 07444-2144 Office Phone: 973-831-0042.

GUIFFRE, JEAN ELLEN, shopping service company executive; b. Roseville, Va., July 15, 1942; d. Robert Nolan and Anna Mary (Kolarik) Fritter; m. LaBre Benedict Guiffre, June 20, 1959; children: Michael C., Suzette M., Anna C., Guy A. Ptnr. LaBre Assocs., College Park, Md., 1962-82; founder, exec. dir. Top Banana Home Delivered Groceries, Inc., Brandywine, Md., 1982—. Resource contact Prince Georges CC; cons. S.E. Top Banana; mem. Md. Food Com., mem. grants rev. com., mem. site visits com.; mem. Bus. Roundtable Prince George County, mem. edn. com.; mem. State Adv. Coun. Nutrition, 1996-2000. Inventor lightweight delivery cart system. Founding mem. Human Svcs. Coalition Prince George's County; co-founder Baden Cmty. Theater, 1967—72, prodn. mgr., 1967—72; mem., pres. PTA, 1965—77; hon. comdr. 79th surgical wing Andrew's Air Force Base, 2006. Recipient Best Practices award, HUD and Prince George's County, 2004, Hadassah award, 2005. Mem.: NAFE. Avocations: writing, dance, theater. Home and Office: 14100 Brandy Wine Rd Brandywine MD 20613

GUILBERT, FRANCES, mathematics educator; BS, U. Mass., Dartmouth. Cert. tchr. secondary math. Mass. Math tchr. Old Rochester Regional H.S., Mattapoisett, Mass., 2001—. Home: 25 Chime St New Bedford MA 02746 Office: Old Rochester Regional HS 135 Marion Rd Mattapoisett MA 02739

GUILFOYLE, NANCY JEAN, biology educator; b. Keokuk, Iowa, Nov. 6, 1950; d. Roscoe L. and Betty J. Beltz; m. Charles A. Guilfoyle, July 1, 1972; children: Stacey, Brian, Christina. BS Edn. Biology, Truman State U., Kirksville, Mo., 1972; postgrad., Mo. State U., Ctrl. Meth. U., Truman State U. Cert. lifetime tchr. Mo. Tchr. Biology Lewis County C-1 Sch., Ewing, Mo., 1977—. Judge sci. fair Lewis County C-1 Schs., Ewing, 1977—. Leader Bible Sch. First Bapt. Ch., LaGrange, Mo., 1982—. Named to Who's Who Among Am. Tchrs. Mem.: NEA, Cmty. Tchrs. Assn. (pres. 2000). Avocations: gardening, crocheting, sewing, reading. Home: PO Box 388 La Grange MO 63448

GUILFOYLE NEWSOM, KIMBERLY ANN, legal commentator; b. San Francisco, 1969; m. Gavin Newsom. BA, U. Calif., Davis; JD, San Francisco Law Sch. Asst. dist. atty. San Francisco Dist. Atty. Office; co-host Both Sides, Court TV, 2004—; legal commentator ABC's Good Morning Am., CNN's Anderson Cooper 360. Panalist USSF Hosp. Young Women's Health Conf., San Francisco. Mem.: ABA, La Raza Lawyers Assn., Calif. Dist. Attys. Assn., San Francisco Women's Polit. Caucus. Office: Court TV Network LLC 600 Third Ave New York NY 10016

GUILIANO, MIREILLE, consumer products company executive; b. Moyeuvre, France, Apr. 14, 1946; m. Edward Guiliano. Student, Sorbonne, Paris, Institut Supérieur d'Interprétariat et de Traduction; M in English and German; cert., interpreter/translator. Pres., CEO Clicquot, Inc., NYC, 1984—; and dir. Champagne Clicquot, Reims, France. Author: French Women Don't Get Fat, 2004 (Publishers Weekly bestseller list, NY Times bestseller list); contbr. articles to food, wine, lifestyle pubs. Mem.: Com. of 200.

GUILL, MARGARET FRANK, pediatrician, educator, medical researcher; b. Atlanta, Jan. 18, 1948; d. Vernon Rhinehart and Margaret N. (Tichenor) Frank; m. Marshall Anderson Guill III, July 6, 1974; children: Daniel Marshall, Laura Elizabeth. BA, Agnes Scott Coll., 1969; MD, Med. Coll. Ga., 1972. Diplomate Am. Bd. Pediatrics, Am. Bd. Pediatrics subbd. pulmonology, Am. Bd. Allergy and Immunology, Nat. Bd. Med. Examiners. Resident in pediatrics Kaiser Found. Hosp., San Francisco, 1976-78, fellow in allergy, 1978-79; staff physician Waipahu (Hawaii) Clinic, 1973-76; intern in internal medicine Med. Coll. Ga., Augusta, 1973, resident in pediatrics, 1974, fellow in allergy and immunology, 1979-80, from asst. prof. to prof. pediatrics, 1981—, also chief sect. pediatric pulmonology and dir. Asthma Ctr., dir. Cystic Fibrosis Ctr., 1990—, vice chair dept. pediat., 2000—, Dorothy A. Hahn chair pediats., 2001—. Pres. Physician Practice Group, 2001—04; pres. staff Childrens Med. Ctr. Hosp., 2000—01; spkr. in field. Host Healthwatch weekly program WJBF-TV, 1982-83; contbr. articles to profl. jours. Active Reid Meml. Presbyn. Ch.; vol. tchr. Episcopal Day Sch., 1982-85; career day participant Acad. Richmond County, 1982, 83; med. advisor Augusta Area Allergy and Asthma Support Group, 1984-86; adv. bd. East Cen. br. Am. Lung Assn. Ga., 1985—, program of work com., 1987—, bd. dirs., 1987—, program coordinating com., 1990-91, exec. bd., 1989-91; med. staff Camp Breathe Easy, 1985—, med. dir., 1996-98. Recipient Mosby Book award, 1973; grantee rsch. grantee, BRSG, 1981—86, Del Labs., 1982, Merrell-Dow, 1983—84, Elan Pharms., 1986, Am. Lung Assn. Ga., 1986—87, Hollister-Stier, 1986, Fisons Corp., 1989, 1991—93, 1995, Med. Coll. Ga., 1989, Am. Heart Assn., 1991, Genentech, 1991—2005, Miles, 1992, Clintrials, 1990—95, PathoGenesis, 1995—2004, SmithKline Beecham, 1996, Kaleida Health, 2002, Chiron, 2002, Corus Pharma, 2005—06, Chiron, 2005—06, CF Found. Therapeutics, 2005—06. Fellow Am. Acad. Pediat., Am. Coll. Chest Physicians, Am. Acad. Allergy, Asthma and Immunology, Am. Coll. Allergy, Asthma and Immunology; mem. Med. Assn. Ga., Richmond County Med. Soc., Allergy and Immunology Soc. Ga., S.E. Allergy Assn. (Hal Davison award 1985), Ga. Thoracic Soc. (Med. Profl. of Yr. 1998), Am. Thoracic Soc., Alpha Omega Alpha. Home: 918 Littleton St Augusta GA 30904-4462 Office: Med Coll Ga Dept Pediatrics Augusta GA 30912 Office Phone: 706-721-2635. Business E-Mail: mguill@mail.mcg.edu.

GUILLERMO, LINDA, clinical social worker; b. Chgo., July 4, 1951; d. Triponio Pascua and Helen Elizabeth (Moskal) Guillermo. BA, U. Ill., Chgo., 1973, MSW, 1975, postgrad., 1980, Jane Addams Coll. Social Work, 1980—82. Diplomate in clin. social work, lic. real estate broker Ill. Mktg. rsch. interviewer Rabin Rsch. Co., Chgo., 1970—73; mktg. rsch. interviewer, coder Marcor Mktg. Rsch., Inc., Chgo., 1973—75; social work intern Child and Family Svcs., Chgo., 1973—74, Chgo. Bd. Edn., 1974—75; social worker, therapist child abuse and neglect, case investigator, case planning cons., social svc. program planner Ill. Dept. Children and Family Svcs., Chgo., 1975—78; social svc. program planner, contract negotiator, monitoring agt. Ctrl. Resources Contracts and Grants, 1978—79; real estate sales person Sentry Realty, Chgo., 1976—; social worker, therapist, program coord., casework supr. of child abuse assessment and intervention program, proposal writer Casa Ctrl., Chgo., 1979—82, casework cons. of child abuse assessment and intervention program, proposal writer, program dir. and casework supr. of early intervention program, 1979—85; social worker, clin. supr. Chgo. Bd. Edn., 1985—. Tng. specialist City Coll. of Chgo., 1980; adj. assoc. rschr. Asher Feren Law Office, Chgo., 1980—81. Treas. Greenleaf Condominium Assn., Chgo., 1980—81, sec., 1987—88, interim pres., 1988; regional rep. North Ill. Assn. of Sch. Social Workers, 1986—87; active various polit. campaigns, Chgo. Mem.: Ill. Cert. Lic. Social Workers, Nat. Assn. Cert. Social Workers (register clin. social workers), North Side Real Estate Bd. Home: 7405 N Kenneth Ave Skokie IL 60076 Office Phone: 847-763-0865.

GUILLERMO, TESSIE, foundation administrator; b. San Francisco; Grad., Calif. State U., Hayward, Gallup Leadership Inst. Founder, CEO Asian and Pacific Islander Am. Health Forum, 1987—2002; pres., CEO Community Tech. Found. of Calif., 2002—. Fellow Asian Pacific Am. Women's Leadership Inst., 1997; mem. President's Advisory Commn. on Asian Am. and Pacific Islanders, 2000; bd. mem. Catholic Healthcare W. Bd. dirs. Calif. Pan Ethnic Health Network; mem. Kaiser Arbitration Oversight Bd., Filipino Task Force on HIV/AIDS, Nat. Coalition of Asian Pacific Am.; bd. dirs. Calif. Endowment, 2003—; trustee Health Professions Edu. Found. Office: Community Tech Found of Calif One Rincon Ctr 101 Spear St Ste 218 San Francisco CA 94105*

GUILLILAND, MARTHA W., academic administrator; b. Pa. BS in Geology and Math., Catawba Coll., 1966; MS in Geophysics, Rice U., 1968; PhD in environ. engring./sys. ecology, U. Fla., 1973. Rsch. fellow sci. and pub. policy U. Mo., Kan. City, Mo., 1974—77; asst. prof. civil engring. and environment sci. U. Okla., 1975—77; exec. dir. Energy Policy Studies, Inc., El Paso, Tex., 1977—82; assoc. prof. civil engring. U. Nebr., Lincoln, 1988—90, dir. Ctr. Infrastructure Rsch., 1988—99; dean grad. sch. and asst. v.p. rsch. U. Ariz., 1990—93, vice provost academic affairs, 1993—95, academic v.p. info. and human resources, 1995—97, prof. hydrology and water resources, 1995—97; provost Tulane U., New Orleans, 1997—2000; pres. U. Mo., Kans. City, 2000—. Appointee Rsch. and Adv. Panel of Gen. Acctg. Office, Energy Engring. Bd. of Nat. Rsch. Coun., NAS Com. on Strategic Assessment of Dept. of Energy Coal Program, Nat. Inst. Global Change, Pres.'s Coun. of Advisors on Sci. and Tech., 2001. Author: (book) Energy Analysis: A New Public Policy Tool, co-author books; contbr. articles to profl. jours. Recipient Hubert H. Humphrey award, Policy Studies Orgn., 2002, Gov.'s award Excellence Total Qualty Efforts, Ariz.; fellow, W.K. Kellogg Found., 1985—88. Office: U Mo 5100 Rockhill Rd Kansas City MO 64110

GUILLIOT, VICKIE LEE, secondary school educator; b. Lake Charles, La., Feb. 21, 1958; d. Lee Robert Nunez, Jr. and Bobbye Jean Nunez; m. Albert Joseph Guilliot, July 23, 1994; 1 child, Alexa Gabrielle;children from previous marriage: David Lee Savoie, Andre Thomas Savoie. BS, McNeese U., 1980; cert. in spl. edn., U. La., 1999; MED, U. La., Lafayette, 2004. Tchr. home econs. Cameron (La.) Parish Sch. Bd., 1989—91; tchr. spl. edn. Lafayette (La.) Parish Sch. Bd., 1992; tchr. home econs. Iberia Parish Sch. Bd., New Iberia, La., 1993—95, St. Landry Parish Sch. Bd., Opelousas, La., 1995—97; tchr. spl. edn. St. Martin Parish Sch. Bd., St. Martinville, La., 1997—2001, tchr. home econs., 2001—; counselor St. Martinville Jr. High, 2004—. Pageant asst. dir., v.p. La. Fur and Wildlife Festival, Cameron, 1978—90; water safety instr. Red Cross, Creole, La., 1978—90. Recipient Tchr. Yr., La. Prostart, 2004. Avocations: swimming, cooking, home renovation. Home: 359 Market St Arnaudville LA 70512 Office: St Martinville Jr High 7190 Main Hwy Saint Martinville LA 70582

GUILLORY, JENNIFER LEE, secondary school educator; b. Tuscola, Ill., May 23, 1966; d. Joseph M. and Rena I. Tempel; m. Allen C. Guillory, Nov. 14, 1987; children: Katherine A., Zachary A. BA, U. Tex., Austin, 1988. Cert. tchr. secondary edn. Tex. Edn. Agy. Tchr. Deer Park Ind. Sch. Dist., Tex., 1990—. Curriculum writer Deer Park Ind. Sch. Dist., 2000—. Mem. edn. com. 1st Presbyn. Ch., Pasadena, 2005—06. Named Nat. Merit Scholar, 1984. Mem.: Tex. State Tchrs. Assn. Avocations: travel, reading, genealogy, camping. Office: Deer Park HS N 402 Ivy St Deer Park TX 77536 Office Phone: 832-668-7300.

GUILMET, GLENDA JEAN, artist; b. Tacoma, Mar. 28, 1957; d. Cody Calvin Black and Maria Isabel Rivera; m. George Michael Guilmet, May 24, 1980; children: Michelle Rene, Douglas James. BA in Bus. Adminstrn., U. Puget Sound, 1981, BA in Art, 1989; student, Clover Park Vocat. Tech. Inst., 1982—83. Freelance photographer, Tacoma and Blyn, 1976—; women's sports photographer U. Puget Sound, Tacoma, 1977-78, asst. photographer, 1978-79; visual artist Tacoma and Blyn, 1982—; photographic cons. Puyallup Tribe of Indians, Tacoma, 1984; on-call photographer Puyallup Tribal Health Authority, Tacoma, 1984-86. Instr. sculpture Tacoma Arts Commn., 1989; guest lectr. U. Puget Sound, 1990, 94; grants juror Artist Trust, Seattle, 1990; video festival juror Tacoma Mcpl. TV, 1990; photography competition juror Washington State PTA Reflections Com., 1995; art dir., Tacenda and Willo Trees Press, Eureka, Calif., 2004. Contbr. photographs to various publs.; one-woman shows include Stage Door Gallery, Tacoma Little Theatre, 1993, Seattle U. Women's Ctr., 1994, Inst. de Cultura Puertorriquena, Jayuya, Carolina and Caguana, PR, 1994—95, Galleria on Broadway, Tacoma, 1996, 1998, Sacred Cir. Gallery of Am. Indian Art, Seattle, 1996—97, 1999, Studio A and Studio B, Blyn, Wash., 2004, Daybreak Star Art Gallery, Seattle, 2005, exhibited in group shows at Nat. Mus. Women in the Arts, Washington, U. Puget Sound, Tacoma, 1989, Windhorse Gallery, Seattle, 1990, Chase Gallery, Spokane City Hall, 1990, Hanforth Gallery, Tacoma, 1990—91, Wash. State Capital Mus., Olympia, 1990, Foyer of the Okean Theater, Vladivostok, Russia, 1992, First Night Gallery, Tacoma, 1992, 1996—97, Sacred Cir. Gallery of Am. Indian Art, 1993, 1996, Cunningham Gallery U. Wash., 1993, Western Gallery, Western Wash. U., Bellingham, 1993, Seattle Art Mus., 1993, Bibliotheque Nat. de France, 1994, Street Level Photography Gallery, Glasgow, Scotland, 1995, Tacoma Art Mus., 1995, Park Ave. Armory, NYC, 1995, Westfalische Mus. fur Naturkunde, Munster, Germany, 1995—96, Iverness Mus., Scotland, 1997, Ione Gallery Highland Folk Mus., Kingussie, Scotland, 1997, U. Ariz. Mus. Art, 1997, Coos Art Mus., Coos Bay, Oreg., 1998, Pratt Fine Arts Ctr., Seattle, 2000, Wash. State Conv. and Trade Ctr., 2000, Port Angeles Fine Arts Ctr., 2005, Represented in permanent collections Steilacoom (Wash.) Tribal Mus., Bibliotheque Nat. de France, U. Puget Sound, Chief Leschi Schs., Puyallup Tribe of Indians, Seattle Art Mus., also pvt. and corp. collections; co-author: Shadow Dance, 2004. Recipient 1st pl. in photography Crosscurrents Art Contest, 1988, Hedgebrook Invitational Residency, Hedgebrook Found., Langley, Wash., 2000. Mem. Artist Trust, En Foco, Atlatl, Women's Caucus for Art, Nat. Mus. Women in the Arts. Home and Studio: 652 Old Blyn Highway Sequim WA 98382-9695 Office Phone: 360-582-9869. Personal E-mail: glendaguilmet@yahoo.com.

GUINIER, LANI, law educator; BA cum laude, Radcliffe Coll., 1971; JD, Yale U., 1974; MA (hon.), U. Pa., 1992; LLD (hon.), Northeastern U., 1994, Swarthmore Coll., 1996, Smith Coll., 1999, U. DC, 2001; D in Civil Law (hon.), Hunter Coll., 1994, Spelman Coll., 1998; LHD (hon.), U. RI, 1999. Bar: Mich. 1975, U.S. Supreme Ct. 1979, D.C. 1980, U.S. Ct. Appeals (5th, 6th, 8th and 11th cirs.). Law clk. to Hon. Damon J. Keith US Ct. Appeals 6th Cir., 1974—76; juvenile ct. referee Wayne County Juvenile Ct., Detroit, 1976—77; spl. asst. to asst. atty. gen. civil rights divsn. US Dept. Justice, 1977—81; asst. counsel NAACP Legal Def. and Ednl. Fund, Inc., NYC, 1981—88; assoc. prof. U. Pa. Law Sch., Phila., 1988—92, prof. law, 1992—98, Harvard Law Sch., Cambridge, Mass., 1998—2001, Bennett Boskey prof., 2001—. Adj. prof. NYU Sch. Law, 1985—89; of counsel NAACP Legal Def. Fund, Inc., 1988—91; trustee Phila. Cmty. Legal Svcs., 1989—90, Open Soc. Inst., 1996—; mem. adv. bd. com. on acad. freedom and tenure Assn. Am. Law Schs., 1992—93; mem. small grants adv. com. So. Regional Coun., 1992—95; founder, pres. Commonplace, Inc., 1994—99; vis. prof. Harvard Law Sch., 1996; mem. Penn Nat. Commn. on Soc., Cmty. and Culture, 1996—98; mem. vis. com. for diversity Brown U., 2000; presenter in field. Author: Lift Every Voice: Turning a Civil Rights Setback into a New Vision of Social Justice, 1987, The Tyranny of the Majority: Fundamental Fairness in Representative Democracy, 1994; co-author (with Michelle Fine and Jane Balin): Becoming Gentlemen: Women, Law Schools and Institutional Change, 1997; co-author: (with Susan Sturm) Who's Qualified: A New Democracy Forum on Creating Equal Opportunity in School and Jobs, 2001; co-author: (with Gerald Torres) The Miner's Canary: Enlisting Race, Resisting Power, Transforming Democracy, 2002; contbr. articles to profl. jours. Mem.: Am. Law Inst. Office: Harvard Law Sch 1563 Massachusetts Ave Cambridge MA 02138-2903 Office Phone: 617-496-1913. Office Fax: 617-495-4299. E-mail: lguinier@law.harvard.edu.

GUINN, JANET MARTIN, psychologist, consultant; b. Rapid City, SD, Aug. 16, 1942; d. Verne Oliver and Carolyn Yetta (Clark) Martin; m. David Lee Guinn, Oct. 27, 1962 (div. June 1988); children: Cynthia Gail, Kevin Scott, Garrett Lee. BS in Psychology, U. Alaska, 1980, MS in Counseling Psychology, 1983; PhD in Clin. Psychology, Calif. Sch. Profl. Psychology, 1988. Lic. psychologist, Alaska, Nev. Pvt. practice, Anchorage, 1988-93, Carson City and Reno, Nev., 1993—; clinician Behavior Medicine Cons., 1983-84; pvt. practice clinician, 1983-84; supr. Southcentral Counseling Ctr., Anchorage, 1984-85; cons. City/Borough of Juneau, Alaska, 1988; psychologist youth treatment program Alaska Psychiat. Inst., Anchorage, 1989-90; psychologist Nev. Mental Health Inst., Sparks, 1994-97. Cons. in field; cons. Alaska Small Bus. Coalition, Anchorage, 1990-92; reviewer Blors Corp. Contbr. articles to profl. jours. Active in politics. Mem. APA, Am. Coll. Forensic Examiners, Nev. Psychol. Assn., Internat. Neuropsychol. Soc., Rotary, Psi Chi. Republican. Avocations: skiing, gourmet cooking, dance. Office Phone: 775-887-4074.

GUINTHER, CHRISTINE LOUISE, special education educator; b. Chgo., Oct. 27, 1949; d. William Joseph and Olga (Sandul) Bacha; m. Paul H. Demper, July 22, 1972 (div. 1987); m. William Robert Guinther, June 25, 1988. BS in Edn., Ill. State U., 1971; MA in Exceptional Child Edn., Ohio State U., 1974. Cert. tchr., Mo. Resource tchr. for learning disabled students Palatine (Ill.) Community Consol. Sch. Dist. #15, 1971-72, Scioto-Darby City Schs., Hilliard, Ohio, 1972-76, Francis Howell Sch. Dist., St. Charles, Mo., 1976—. Mem. NEA (human rels. com. 1987-93, bd. dirs. 1993—), ACLU, ASCD, Nat. Staf devel. Coun., AAUW, Mo. NEA (bd. dirs. 1985-91, human rels. com. 1983—, exec. com. 1993—), Francis Howell Edn. Assn. (pres. 1981-82), NMSA, Delta Kappa Gamma. Methodist. Avocations: walking, music, needlecrafts, reading, Scrabble.

GUITRY, LORAINE DUNN, community health nurse; b. Bryan, Tex., Apr. 12, 1930; BS Elem. Edn., Paul Quinn Coll., 1954. Registered nurse U. Tex. Med. Br., Galveston, 1958—67, U.S. Pub. Health Svc., Galveston, 1967—. Home: 701 Chadley Ct Bryan TX 77803

GULAN, BONNIE MARION, writer, researcher; b. Kenosha, Wis., Feb. 27, 1922; adopted d. Matthew and Elizabeth Ummy Thomas; m. Edward J. Gulan, Nov. 26, 1949; children: John, Michael, Kathryn. Beauty cons. Globe Dept., Kenosha, Wis., 1950—54; inventor & pitch artist Beauty Blush Cosmetic Line, Waukegan, Ill., 1954—56; creator & founder Felture's Inc., Brookfield, Ill., 1956—59; gen. mgr. & designer Eichling's Flowers Inc., Skokie, Ill., 1960—64; founder, dir. An-Oix-Is In-home Youth Ministry, Winnetka, Ill., 1965—75; founder & ceo The Christmas Tree Story Ho. Mus., Multiple Locations, Ill., 1970—90; author & rschr. Milwaukee, Wis., 1990—98; author Saukville, Wis., 1998—. Founder, pres. World-Wide Women's Inventor's Orgn., Libertyville, Ill., 1961—65; creator, lectr. Miracle Thinking Lecture Series, Mundelein, Ill., 1965—69; spkr. in field. Author: (book) Family Miracles, 1981, Stories From The Christmas Tree Story House, 1981, The Great Bible Dig, 2001, The House of the Seven Cats - An Adventure, 2001, Lost Adventures-House of the 7 Cats, 2001, 7 Cats Promised Land Adventure, 2001, Over the Fence Non-Sense Tales, 2001, Lamp Of Hope, 2001, Back Yard Critter Tales, 2001, A Collection Of Mrs. Claus' Christmas Stories, 2001, The Master Toy Maker, 2001, Adventures Down Nursery Rhyme Lane, 2001, A Collection Of Nodding Off Stories, 2001, Christmas In Our Town, 2002, The Great Journey in Pursuit of Jesus' Way, Truth & Life, 2002; composer: (albums) Sounds of The Christmas Tree Story House, 1975. Founder, pres. & lectr. T.H.E Anti-Drug Youth Program, Winnetka, 1971—75. Home: 1053 South Main Street Saukville WI 53080 Office Phone: 262-268-1224. Personal E-mail: bmgulan@aol.com.

GULATI, GEETANJALI, psychologist; d. Baldev Raj and Sudesh Gulati. PsyD, Spalding U., 2000. Lic. Clinical Psychologist Ky. State Bd. of Psychology, 2001. Lic. psychol. assoc. Seven Counties Services, Louisville, 1998—2001, lic. psychologist, 2001—. Cons. on svc. rev. com. Brain Injury Trust Fund of Ky., 2003—04. Founding mem. Diversity Com. for Seven Counties Services, 2002—05. Mem.: Ky. Psychol. Assn. Liberal. Hindu. Achievements include development of risk assessment scale for domestic violence. Avocations: reading, travel. Office: Seven Counties Services 1512 Crums Ln Louisville KY 40216 Office Phone: 502-589-8920. Office Fax: 502-447-1967. E-mail: ggulati@sevencounties.org.

GULATI, MARTHA, health facility administrator, cardiologist; b. Lions Head, Ont., Can., May 14, 1969; BS summa cum laude, McMaster U., Hamilton, Can., 1991; MD, U. Toronto, 1995; MS in Health Studies for Clin. Profls., U. Chgo., 2002. Diplomate in internal medicine Am. Bd. Internal Medicine, in cardiology Am. Bd. Internal Medicine. Resident in internal medicine U. Chgo., 1995—98, fellow in cardiology, 1998—2001, clin. assoc. medicine, dept. medicine, divsn. cardiology, 2001—02; asst. prof. medicine and preventative medicine, divsn. cardiology Rush U., Chgo., 2002—05; asst. prof. medicine and preventative medicine, divsn. cardiology, assoc. med. dir. ctr. women's cardiovasc. health Feinberg Sch. Medicine, Northwestern Meml. Hosp., Chgo., 2005—. Named one of Chgo.'s Top 40 under 40 in Bus., Crain's Chgo. Bus., 2005; recipient Girls on the Run Inspiration award, 2005. Mem.: Am. Coll. Cardiology, Am. Heart Assn. (nominated mem. women in cardiology com., coun. clin. cardiology, go red for women com. mem.). Office: Bluhm Cardiovascular Inst of Northwestern 201 East Huron Ste 10-240 Chicago IL 60611 Office Phone: 312-695-4965, 312-695-0993.

GULBRANDSEN, NATALIE WEBBER, religious association administrator; b. Beverly, Mass., July 7, 1919; d. Arthur Hammond and Kathryn Mary (Doherty) Webber; m. Melvin H. Gulbrandsen, June 19, 1943 (dec. Feb. 23,

1991); children: Karen Ann Bean, Linda Jean Goldsmith, Eric Christian, Ellen Dale Williams, Kristin Jane Morgan. BA, Bates Coll., 1942, LLD (hon.), 1996; LHD (hon.), Meadville/Lombard Theol. Sch., Chgo., 1991. Social worker Bur. Child Welfare, Bangor, Maine. Leader Girl Scouts USA, Auburn, Maine, 1940—44, exec. dir. Belmont, Mass., 1943—45, leader Wellesley, Mass., 1952—65, leadership trainer, 1946—63, bd. dirs., 1950—63, pres., 1960—63; mem. Wellesle Town Meeting, 1967—91; trustee Unitarian Universalist Women's Fedn., 1971—81, pres., 1977—81, mem. commn. on appraisal, 1981—85; moderator Unitarian Universalist Assn., U.S. and Can., Boston, 1985—93; bd. dirs. Unitarian Universalist Ch. of the Larger Fellowship, 1992—98, chairperson bd. dirs., 1996—98, ch. search com., 1998—99, chair ministerial rels. com., 1999—2001; bd. dirs. Unitarian Universalist Women's Heritage Soc., 1994—2002, ch. bd., 2001—02; chair denominational affairs Unitarian Universalist Soc. Wellesley Hills, 2002—; bd. dirs. Wellesley program Am. Field Svc., 1964—70; mem. permanent sch. accomodations com. Wellesley, 1970—76; mem. Wellesley Youth Commn., 1968—70; trustee Wellesley Human Rels. Svc., 1964—76, pres., 1973—76; bd. dirs. Newton Wellesley Weston Needham Area Mental Health Assn., 1975—78; co-chairperson METCO Program of Wellesley, 1965—69. Co-recipient Wellesley Ctr. Cmty. award, 1981; recipient Unitarian Universalist Disting. Svc. award, 2002. Mem. AAUW, Boston Bates Alumnae Assn. (pres. 1966-69), Internat. Assn. Religious Freedom (mem. coun. 1981-90, v.p. 1990-93, pres. 1993-96, co-pres. U.S. chpt. 1997-2003, Clara Barton birthplace com. 1997-01). Unitarian Universalist. Home: 2251 Commonwealth Ave Auburndale MA 02466-1817

GULBRANDSEN, PATRICIA HUGHES, physician; b. May 9, 1940; d. Patrick Boland and Anne Hughes; m. Jon Alf Gulbrandsen, Mar. 6, 1972 (dec. Oct. 1984). BA, Cornell U., 1962; MD, U. Pa., 1967; MPH, Johns Hopkins U., 1980. Cert. Am. Bd. Disability Analysts; diplomate Am. Bd. Phys. Medicine and Rehab., Am. Bd. Occupl. Medicine. Rotating intern Chgo. Wesley Meml. Hosp., 1967-68; resident in neurology Pa. Hosp., Phila., 1968-69, Georgetown U. Hosp., Washington, 1972-74; fellow in gynecologic endocrinology Chelsea Hosp. for Women, London, 1969-71; resident in phys. medicine and rehab. Good Samaritan Hosp., Phoenix, 1974-76; commd. maj. U.S. Army, 1979, advanced through grades to lt. col., 1982; with Walter Reed Army Med. Ctr., Washington, 1979-81; occup. medicine officer U.S. Army/Army Environ. Hygiene Agy., Aberdeen Proving Ground, Md., 1981-83; resigned U.S. Army, 1983; med. dir. USN/Naval Surface Warfare Ctr., White Oak, Md., 1984-89, NASA Hdqs., Washington, 1990-93; acting chief med. officer Hdqs. FBI, Washington, 1995; med. officer Orgn. Am. States, Washington, 1999—2001; occupl. health phys., cons. Def. Intelligence Agy., Bolling AFB, Washington, 2001—03; NIOSH occupl. medicine physician Dept. Energy Worker Advocacy Program, 2004; pvt. practice Gulbrandsen Energy Medicine, LLC, 2006—. Occupl. medicine Profl. Occupl. Health Svcs., 1997-98; staff physiatrist, head consultation svc. New Eng. Med. Ctr. Hosps., Boston, 1977-78; instr. neurology and phys. medicine and rehab. Tufts U. Sch. Medicine, Boston, 1977-78; med. cons. Fairfax County (Va.) Health Dept., 1990, Hummer and Assocs., Cleve., 1990-93, Allied Med. Cons., Inc., Washington, 1994-95, AspenMed Svcs., Inc., 1995-96, 01-03, The Westwood Group, 2004, Gulbrandsen Energy Medicine, LLC, 2006—, Occu Save, Inc., Lanham, Md., 1996, staff privileges Drs. Cmty. Hosp., 1996-98, Hummer Whole Health Mgmt., 1998-99. Mem. Am. Coll. Preventive Medicine, Am. Coll. Occupl and Environ. Medicine, Montgomery County Med. Soc., Med. and Chirurg. Faculty Md. Office Phone: 301-585-6519. Office Fax: 301-585-6519. Personal E-mail: mddocg@yahoo.com.

GULDEN, LINDA LOBER, science educator; d. Harvey Gabriel Lober and Geraldine Anne Kovach; m. Michael U. Gulden, Mar. 23, 1974; children: Kristin Anne, Sarah Lynne, Katherine Marie, Benjamin Michael. BS in Chem. Engring., Northwestern U., Evanston, Ill., 1979; MEd in Curriculum and Instrn., George Mason U., 1993. Lic. tchr. State of Va. Assoc. engr. IBM, Rochester, Minn., 1983—86, staff engr. Manassas, Va., 1986—87; tchr. Linton Hall Sch., Bristow, Va., 1989—96, CD Hylton H.S., Woodbridge, Va., 1996—97, Internat. Sch. Stuttgart, Germany, 1997—2000, Forest Pk. H.S., Woodbridge, 2000—05; instr. LCPS Acad. Sci., Sterling, Va., 2005—. Bd. dirs. clean cmty. coun. Prince William County, Manassas; bd. dirs. adult literacy program Benedictine Ednl. Assistance and Outreach to Neighbors, Bristow, 2004—. Named Outstanding Educator, Va. Gov.'s Sch., 2005. Mem.: Nat. Sci. Tchrs. Assn., Am. Chem. Soc. Avocations: gardening, music, hiking. Office: Loudoun County Public Schools Acad Sci 21326 Augusta Dr Sterling VA 20164

GULIANA, BARBARA ANN, retired director; b. Phila., Pa., Nov. 7, 1943; d. Robert Pidgeon Kienzle and Monica Constance Kinney-Kienzle; m. Ronald T. Guliana, Dec. 28, 1963. B in Mktg., Del. State U., 1991, MBA, 1994; EdD, U. Del., 1999. Owner, sec., treas., bd. dir. Flat Rock (Mich.) Metal, 1981—83, Unicorn Travel, Trenton, Mich., 1983—89; adminstr. asst. to dean Del. State U., Dover, 1984—94; assoc. dir. Del. State U., Sussex County Program, Georgetown, 1994—97; acting dir. Del. State U., Georgetown, 1997—99, dir., 1999—2004; ret., 2004. Presenter Nat. and Internat. Mktg. Higher Edn. to the Non-Traditional Student.; vis. prof. Del. State U., 2005; adj. prof. Wesley Coll., Dover, Del., 2006. Coord. judges Sussex County Sci. Fair, Georgetown, 1995. Mem.: AAUW, Am. Coun. Women Higher Edn. (pub. rels. 2002—04), Am. Mktg. Assn., Alpha Chi, Delta Mu (pres. 1989). Avocations: skiing, sailing, weightlifting, reading, bicycling. Home: 10 Stuart Dr Dover DE 19901 Personal E-mail: barrongu@msn.com.

GULICK, DONNA MARIE, accountant; b. N.Y.C., Jan. 25, 1956; d. H.R. and M.G. Gulick. MBA, Fairleigh Dickinson U., 1981, MS, 1986. Programmer Wash. State U., Pullman, 1983; acctg. analyst IBM, Tarrytown, N.Y., 1983-89, program mgr., 1989-91, program mgr. long-term disability plan Purchase, N.Y., 1991-92, staff acctg. analyst labor charges Tarrytown, N.Y., 1992-94, project mgr. Somers, NY, 1994—97; staff acct. Somers, NY, 1997—2003; coverage lead EMEA Geography, Somers, 2002—. Mem. Assn. MBA Execs., ACM, Inst. of IEEE, Nat. Assn. Unknown Players, Delta Mu Delta. Roman Catholic. Avocations: flying, skiing, walking. Home: 395 State Route 28 Bridgewater NJ 08807-2471 Office: IBM Rt 100 Somers NY 10589 E-mail: cherokee-skyflight@yahoo.com.

GULLACE, MARLENE FRANCES, systems engineer, consultant; b. Ft. Belvoir, Va., Jan. 12, 1952; d. Amerigo Francis and Martha Arlene Guy; m. Gerald Lynn Tolley, June 26, 1970 (div. Nov. 1974); 1 child, Gerald Lynn Tolley Jr.; m. Salvatore Gullace, Nov. 19, 1976 (div. Apr. 1991). AA in Pre-Law, Cochise Coll., 1979; BA in Polit. Sci., U. Ariz., 1982; AA in Computer Sci. and Bus., Chaparral Coll., 1985. Realtor, entrepreneur, inventor, Sierra Vista, Ariz., 1977-84; ADP instr. Chaparral Coll., Tucson, 1985; model Barbizon, Tucson, 1986-87; clk. HUD/FHA, Tucson, 1987-88; computer programmer DOD Inspector Gen., Arlington, 1988-89; programmer analyst US Army Corps of Engrs., USAF, Washington, 1989-91, Calibre Sys. Inc., Falls Church, Va., 1991; cons., sys. analyst/programmer EDP, Vienna, Va., 1991-93; info. engr. Ogden/Anteon Corp., Vienna, 1993-96, Orkand Corp., 1996, SRA Internat., Inc., 1997-00, SRA Internat., 2000—01, SAIC, 2002—04, Lockheed Martin, 2004—. Patented toy, registered trademark. Realtor assoc. Cochise County Bd. Realtors, 1977-84. Mem. IEEE, Fed. Women's Program at SBA (sec. 1976). Methodist. Avocations: art, design, crafts, sewing. Home: 7829 Piccadilly Dr Warrenton VA 20186-8623

GULLETT, JULIA SHUPING, judge; b. Salisbury, N.C., Nov. 19, 1961; d. Bill Lee and Julia Ann (Benson) Shuping; m. Donald Alexander Gullett, Dec. 3, 1988; children: Courtney G. Campbell, Danielle Lynn, Amber Nicole, Michael Monroe. BA, Catawba Coll., Salisbury, 1984; JD, Campbell U. Sch. Law, Bucks Creek, N.C., 1988. Bar: N.C. 1988, cert.: N.C. (juvenile ct. judge) 2003; profl. lectr. law 1991. Asst. dist. atty., Statesville, NC, 1988—2001; adj. instr. Mitchell C.C., Statesville, 1990—94; dist. ct. judge Statesville, 2001—. Mem. Juvenile Crime Prevention Coun., Statesville, 2000—, Child Protection Task Force, Taylorsville, NC, 2000, Appropriate Punishment Options, Statesville, 2001—; foster parent Iredell County DSS, Statesville, 1994—2006; children's ministry dir. Westwood Bapt. Ch., Statesville, 2006; tchr. Sunday Sch. Cascasde Bapt. Ch., Mooresville, NC, 2004—05, Troutman Bapt. Ch., NC, 2000—04. Recipient Student of Yr., Catawba Coll., 1982—83, 1983—84, Pres.'s Svc. award, 1982—83. Mem.: N.C. Dist. Ct. Judges Assn. Southern Baptist. Office: Dist Ct Judges Office 220 Water St Statesville NC 28677 Office Phone: 704-878-4383.

GULLEY, JOAN LONG, banker; b. Balt., Sept. 10, 1947; d. Thomas F. and Florence (Waldron) Long; m. Philip Gordon Gulley, aug. 2, 1969; 1 child, Colin Jason. BA, U. Rochester, 1969; postgrad., Harvard U., 1985. Analyst U.S. Dept. Commerce, Washington, 1969-70, Fed. Res. Bd., Washington, 1970-74; sr. analyst 5, Washington, 1979-81; asst. v.p. Fed. Res. Bank Boston, 1975-79, v.p., 1981-83; sr. v.p. 5, 1983-86; exec. v.p. The Mass. Co., Boston, 1986-94, pres., CEO, 1994, also bd. dirs.; chmn., CEO PNC Bank New Eng., 1995-97; sr. v.p., mgr. strategic planning PNC Bank Corp., 1997-98, exec. v.p., dep. mgr. consumer bank, 1998—, dep. mgr. regional cmty. bank, 1999—2000; CEO PNC Bus. Banking, 2000—02, PNC Advisors, 2002—. Chmn. PNC Bank, New Eng., 1997-99. Mem. Allegheny Country Club, Nantucket Golf Club, Duquesne Club, Phi Beta Kappa. Office: PNC Bank Corp 1 PNC Plz 249 5th Ave Pittsburgh PA 15222-2709

GULLICKSON, NANCY ANN, art association administrator; b. Memphis, Jan. 7, 1942; d. Alfred John and Mildred Lucille (Houston) Bowen; m. John Charles Gullickson, June 25, 1966; children: Jay Weldon, Christine Lee. BFA, Miss. Univ. Women, 1964. Owner Yellow Awning Interiors, Lawrenceville, Ga., 1975-85; exec. dir. Gwinnett Coun. Arts, Inc., Duluth, Ga., 1983—. Pres. Ga. Assembly Cmty. Arts Agys., 1987, Alliance Children's Theatre, Atlanta, 1982-83, Lawrenceville Jr. Women's Club, 1977; trustee Woodruff Arts Ctr., Atlanta, 1982-83. Sec., bd. dirs. Gwinnett Conv. & Vis. Bur., 1992—; bd. dirs. Gwinnett Heart Assn., 1994—, Lawrenceville Downtown Devel. Authority, 1989-96; sustainer Gwinnett North Fulton Jr. League, 1985—. Recipient Gwinnett's Exceptional Women Leaders award League Women Voters, 1995. Avocations: boating, skiing, painting. Home: 373 Summit Ridge Dr Lawrenceville GA 30045-6041 Office: Gwinnett Coun Arts Inc 6400 Sugarloaf Pkwy Bldg 300 Duluth GA 30097-4091

GULLIKSON, ROSEMARY, lawyer; b. Chgo., Dec. 9, 1952; BS summa cum laude, No. Ill. U., 1974; JD cum laude, Northwestern U., 1994. Bar: Ill. 1994; RN Ill., 1974. Ptnr. Sonnenschein Nath & Rosenthal LLP, Chgo. Dir., pres. Tim & Tom Gullikson Found. Office: Sonnenschein Nath & Rosenthal LLP Sears Tower, Ste 8000 233 South Wacker Dr Chicago IL 60606 Office Phone: 312-876-8963. E-mail: rgullikson@sonnenschein.com.

GULSTONE, JACQUELINE, nurse; b. Georgetown, Guyana, Sept. 7, 1957; came to the U.S., 1985; d. Edward and Rachel (Gordon-Carryl) Billey; m. Basil Gulstone, June 7, 1986; children: Runako, Rufaro. BSN cum laude, Medgar Evers Coll. CUNY, N.Y.C., 1995; MSN, SUNY, Bklyn., 1998, bd. cert. family nurse practitioner, 1999; postgrad., Kennedy Western U., 2004—. Cert. perioperative operating room nurse, Assn. Operating Room Nurses; bd. cert. med./surg. nurse Am. Nurses Credentialing Ctr. RN, staff nurse Georgetown Hosp., 1979-82, RN, charge nurse, 1982-85; RN, staff nurse oper. rm. Downstate Med. Ctr., Bklyn., 1986-87; staff nurse All Care Registry, N.Y.C., 1987-92; staff nurse oper. rm. Brookdale U. Hosp., Bklyn., 1992—. Nursing supr. Menorah Nursing Home. Active comty. activities East 79th St. Block Assn., Bklyn., 1979—; mem. and vol. med. caregiver Health Edn. Relief Guyana, 1979—. Recipient Disting. Leadership award, 2005, Cmty. Svc. award, 2005. Mem. Assn. Oper. Rm., Medgar Evers Alumni Assn., Guyanese Nurses Am., Inc. (pres.), Caribbean Am. Nurses Assn., N.Y. State Nurses Assn.; Grammateus Omega Chi Avocations: reading, travel, music, athletics (track and field). Home: 574 E 79th St Brooklyn NY 11236-3135 Office: Brookdale Univ Hosp 1 Brookdale Plz Brooklyn NY 11212-3139

GULYAS, DIANE H., manufacturing executive; b. Chgo., 1956; BS in Chem. Engring., U. Notre Dame; advanced mgmt. program, Wharton Sch. Bus., 1994. Various sales, mktg., tech. and sys. devel. positions DuPont Polymers Bus. DuPont, Wilmington, Del., 1978, European bus. mgr. for Engring. Polymers Geneva, plant supt. Mechelen, Belgium, site, exec. asst. to chmn. bd. Wilmington, 1993—94, global bus. dir. Nylon Fibers New Bus. Devel. and Global Zytel Engring. Polymers, 1994—97, v.p., gen. mgr. DuPont Advanced Fiber Businesses Richmond, Va., 1997—2003, group v.p. DuPont Electronic and Comm. Techs. Platform Wilmington, Del., 2003—04, chief mktg. and sales officer, 2004—06, group v.p. DuPont performance materials, 2006—. Bd. dirs. Viasystems, St. Louis. Bd. dirs. Ministry of Caring; mem. strategic planning and advocacy com. Del. Nature Soc. Named one of 50 Most Powerful Women in Bus., Fortune mag., 2006. Office: DuPont Bldg 1007 Market St Wilmington DE 19898*

GUMAER, AMY ARNOLD, academic administrator; b. Hudson, NY, Apr. 30, 1963; d. Edward H. and Marion G. Arnold; m. Peter Tower Gumaer, June 1, 1991. BA cum laude in German, U. NH, 1985; MA in edn., SUNY Albany, 1989; ArtsD, SUNY, Albany, 2006. Dir. internat. lang. lab. Hudson Valley C.C., Troy, NY, 1991—2005, dir. internat. edn., 1995—2005, assoc. prof., 1995—2005; dir. pubs. Sch. Adminstr. Assn. of NY State, Albany, 1989—91; assoc. dean arts, humanities and social scis. Montgomery Coll., Takoma Park/Silver Spring, Md., 2005—. Member-at-large, bd. dirs. Coll. Consortium for Internat. Studies, Washington, 2003—05; mem., steering com. cross nat. project SUNY Office of Internat. Programs, Albany, 2005; mem., edn. & culture com. Albany-Tula: A Capital Region Alliance, 2004—05, mem., devel. com., 2004—05. Grad. fellowship to Wuerzburg U., Germany, U. at Albany, 1987—88, Challenger Award for Teachers, NY State Senate, 1986—87. Office: Montgomery Coll PF 220 7600 Takoma Ave Takoma Park MD 20912 Office Phone: 518-629-7500, 301-650-1380.

GUMBS, PAM, pharmacist; d. Sara Yancy and Gayton Yancy Sr.; m. John Gumbs, Apr. 21, 1971. PharmD, U. Calif., San Francisco, 1975, degree in geriatric clinical pharmacy, 1991. Clin. pharmacist Aseureth Med. Svcs., L.A., 1990—2006; CEO, clin. affairs Royal Med. Inc, Berkeley, Calif., 1996—. Mem. pharmacy and therapeutics com. Alameda Alliance For Health, Calif., 2004—, rep., 2004—06. Editor: (newsletter) Alameda County Pharmacists Assn. Newsletter, Pills & Potions (Trophy Winner for Commn. Excellence, 1987). Mem.: Am. Pharmacist Assn. (licentiate), Christian Pharmacists Fellowship Internat. (licentiate), Calif. Pharmacists Assn. (licentiate; pres. Alameda county chpt. 2002—03). Office: Royal Medical Inc 2929 Telegraph Ave Berkeley CA 94705 Office Phone: 510-843-3201. Office Fax: 510-843-0308. E-mail: drpam@consultwithdrpam.com.

GUMERSON, JEAN GILDERHUS, health foundation executive; b. Hayfield, Minn., Mar. 19, 1923; d. Nordeen Palmer and Mable Jeannette (Scharberg) Gilderhus; m. William Dow Gumerson Sr., Mar. 5, 1943 (dec. Jan. 1978); children: William Dow Jr., Ted Lee, Jon David. Student, U. Minn., 1941-42, U. Okla., 1961-62. Adminstrv. asst. to Rep. state party chmn., Oklahoma City, 1976-77; campaign coord. 1st dist. Paula Unruh for Congress, Tulsa, 1978; dir. pub. rels. C.R. Anthony Co., Oklahoma City, 1979-87; dir. human rels. Wilson Agy., Mass. Mut. Ins. Co., Oklahoma City, 1987; adminstrv. dir. Okla. Art Ctr., Oklahoma City, 1988-89; exec. dir. Children's Med. Rsch., Inc., Oklahoma City, 1989—; exec. dir., then pres. Presbyn. Health Found., Oklahoma City, 1989—2002, pres. emeritus, 2002—. Active exec. com. Pres.'s Com. on Mental Retardation, Washington, 1986-91; So. Govs. Conf. on Infant Mortality, Washington, 1987-92; chmn. City-County Health Dept. Bd., Oklahoma City, 1980-93; gov. appointee steering com. Healthy Futures, Oklahoma City, 1988-92; bd. dirs. Children's Med. Rsch. Inc., Okla. City 1982—; nat. bd. Contact U.S.A., Okla. City, 1992—. Recipient Gov.'s Arts award for community svc. Okla. Arts Coun., Woman of Yr. award Okla. Mental Health Assn., Humanitarian award Opportunities Indsl. Ctr., Outstanding Vol. Fund Raiser award Okla. chpt. Nat. Soc. Fund Raising Execs., 1988, Humanitarian award Nat. Conf. for Comty. and Justice, 1999; inducted to Okla. Hall of Fame, 1999; Jean Gumerson Endowed Chair in Pediat. Psychology established in his honor, 1999. Mem. AIA (hon.), Exec. Women in Govt., Charter 35, Econ. Club. Okla., Oklahoma City C. of C., Theta Sigma Phi. Presbyterian. Home: 6206 Waterford Blvd Apt 50 Oklahoma City OK 73118-1109

GUMINA, PAMELA RAY, municipal government administrator; b. Lamar, Colo., Nov. 2, 1954; d. James Dean and Elsie Ray Wilson; m. Kent B. Gumina, Dec. 16, 1978; children: Diane L., Anne E. AA, Lamar C.C., 1974; BA, Adams State Coll., 1977. Reporter, photographer Valley Courier, Alamosa, Colo., 1977-79; news editor Mid-Iowa Pub., State Center, Iowa, 1979-81; exec. dir. Sterling (Colo.) Urban Renewal Authority, 1983-90; cmty. devel. dir. City of Sterling, 1987-96, asst. to city mgr., 1996-2000, asst. city mgr., 2000—. Project mgr. depot renovation Sterling Downtown Improvement Corp., 1984-90; instr. non-profit grant writing, 1996; program mgr. mktg. campaign J. Harrigan Dialysis Ctr., 1995. Bd. dirs. cmty. edn. Northeastern Jr. Coll., Sterling, 1984-90; fundraiser St. Anthony's Sch., Sterling, 1991-96; mem. Colo. hist. grants com. Presbyn. Ch., Sterling, 1993-96. HUD grantee, 1995. Mem. Internat. City/County Mgmt. Assn., Am. Econ. Devel. Coun., Econ. Devel. Coun. Colo. (bd. dirs. 1994-97, Cmty. of Yr. award 1994)), Colo. Downtown Devel. Assn. (pres. 1990-91), Kiwanis (pres. 1990-91). Office: 421 N 4th St PO Box 4000 Sterling CO 80751-0400 E-mail: pgumina@ci.sterling.co.us.

GUMP, ABIGAIL MICHELLE, music educator; b. Columbus, Ohio, July 6, 1980; d. Robert Matthew and Marilyn Wilson Gump. BA in Music cum laude, We. State U., Gunnison, Colo., 2003. Lic. secondary tchg. Colo., cert. wilderness first responder Wilderness Medicine Inst., medication adminstrn. Gunnison, Colo., ropes course Adventure Experiences. Gymnastics coach Gunnison H.S., Gunnison, Colo., 2000—03; choral dir. Lyons Mid. and Sr. H.S., 2004—06; mng. mktg. dir. Am. Wilderness Outfitters Ltd., Augusta, Ga., 2006—. Sr. outdoor guide Adventure Experiences, Almont, Colo., 1999—2005, ropes course instr., 2003; track coach Lyons H.S., 2005; choral judge solo and ensemble, Longmont, Colo., 05. Nat. track competitor NCAA Divsn. II, 1999, 2003. Mem.: NEA, Colo. Music Edn. Assn., Am. Choral Dirs. Assn. Avocations: mountain climbing, backpacking, music, travel.

GUMPERT, CAROLYN L., secondary school educator; d. J. H. and Eva M. Shipman. BS in Edn., U. Cen. Ark., Conway, 1969. Cert. tchr. Mo., Tex. Secondary tchr. Gasconade R-II Schs., Owensville, Mo., 1969—74; adminstrv. sec. U. of Ark., Pine Bluff, 1974—78, Office of Pers. Mgmt., Little Rock, 1978—80, Dept. of the Navy, Virginia Beach, Va., 1982—85, Houston C.C., 1985—88; secondary tchr. Spring Ind. Sch. Dist., Houston, 1988—. Opres. Comty. Teachers' Assn., Owensville, Mo., 1973; pres. Officers' Wives Club, Virginia Beach, Va., 1984; dept. chair Spring Ind. Sch. Dist., Houston, 1990—. Summer missionary Bapt. Student Union, Monticello, Ark., 1968; tchr. Sunday sch. Oak Ridge Bapt. Ch., Houston, 2000—06; voting del. Mo. Teachers' Assn., Owensville, 1972; mem. campus improvement com. Wells Mid. Sch., Houston, 2002. Named Disting. Tchr., Spring Ind. Sch. Tchr., 2002. Mem.: NEA, Tex. State Tchrs. Assn., Parent Tchr. Orgn. Republican. Baptist. Avocations: tole painting, music, theater, reading.

GUMPERT, LYNN, gallery director; Student, Sorbonne, Paris, 1971-72; cert. completion first year, Ecole du Louvre, Paris, 1971-72; BA in History of Art with honors, U. Calif., Berkeley, 1974; MA in History of Art, U. Mich., 1977. Curatorial asst. The Jewish Mus., N.Y.C., 1978-80; curator The New Mus. Contemporary Art, N.Y.C., 1980-84, sr. curator, 1984-88; adj. curator Mus. Contemporary Art, L.A., 1988-89, We. States Arts Fedn., Santa Fe, 1988-89; coord. Eighth Biennale of Sydney Art Gallery N.S.W., Sydney, Australia, 1989-90; guest curator, adminstrv. dir. Amway (Japan) Ltd. and Setagaya Art Mus., Tokyo, 1989-91, Nat. Mus. Art, Osaka, Japan, 1989-91; cons. curator Gallery at Takashimaya, Inc., N.Y.C., 1992-95; guest curator, U.S. coord. ARC/Musée d'Art Moderne de la Ville de Paris, 1994-95; guest curator Grey Art Gallery, NYU, N.Y.C., 1996-97, dir., 1997—; interim dirl mus. studies program NYU, 1999-2000. Lectr. in field; juror in field; panelist in field; ind. curator/cons., 1988-97; mem. adv. com. Asia Soc. Galleries. Exhbns. include Grey Art Gallery, The New Mus. Contemporary Art, 1980, 81, 82, 84, 86, 89, Pitts. Ctr. Arts, 1983, Mus. Contemporary Art, Chgo., 1988, Galerie Ghislaine Hussenot, Paris, 1992, The Gallery at Takashimaya, N.Y.C., 1994, 95, numerous others; author: Christian Boltanski, 1993, reprint, 1996; editor: The Art of the Everyday: The Quotidian in Postwar French Culture, 1997. Decorated chevalier Order Arts and Letters (France); Univ. fellow U. Mich., 1975. Mem. Internat. Assn. Art Critics, ArtTable (N.Y.). Office: Grey Art Gallery NYU 100 Washington Sq E New York NY 10003-6688 Fax: 212-995-4024. E-mail: greygallery@nyu.edu.

GUND, AGNES, retired museum administrator; b. Cleve., Ohio; d. George Gund, Jr.; m. Daniel Shapiro, June 13, 1987; children: David, Catherine, Jessica, Anna. BA in art history, Conn. Coll., 1960; MA in art history, Fogg Mus., Harvard U., 1980; LHD (hon.), Case Western Reserve U., 1995, Brown U., 1996. Trustee Mus. Modern Art, N.Y.C., 1976—, v.p., 1988—91, pres., 1991—2002, pres. emerita, 2002—; chair Mayor's Cultural Affairs Adv. Commn., N.Y.C., 2003—. Bd. trustees Wexner Ctr. Found., 1997—; trustee Brown U., Aaran Diamond AIDS Rsch. Ctr., Inst. Advanced Study, Princeton, NJ, J. Paul Getty Trust, Calif.; mem. mus. coun. Cleve. Mus. Art. Named one of Top 200 Collectors, The ARTnews Mag., 2004; named to, 2006; recipient Women in the Arts award, Coll. Art Assn., Art Table award for Disting. Svc. to Arts, 1994, Montblanc de la Culture award, 1997, Nat. Medal Arts, 1997, Arts Edn. award, Am. for the Arts, 1999, Evan Burger Donaldson Achievement award, Miss Porter's Sch., 2003, Centennial Medal, Harvard U. Grad. Sch. Arts and Sciences, 2003. Fellow: Am. Acad. Arts and Sciences; mem.: Studio in a Sch. Assn. (founder, Gov.'s Art award, N.Y. 1988, Dorothy Freeman award, N.Y.C. 1988). Avocation: Collector of Contemporary, African, Chinese Art. Office: care Museum Modern Art 11 W 53rd St New York NY 10019-5401*

GUNDA, RAJESWARI, oncologist; b. India, Apr. 1, 1951; Lic. physician Mich., Ohio, diplomate Am. Bd. Internal Medicine with subspecialty in med. oncology. Resident in internal medicine St. Joseph Mercy Hosp., Pontiac, Mich., 1980—83; fellow in hematology and oncology Henry Ford Hosp., Detroit, 1984—87, staff physician dept. hematology, 1987—88; pvt. practice Blanchard Valley Med. Assocs., Findlay, Ohio, 1988—2003, Cancer Ctr. of N.W. Ohio, Findlay, 2003—. Office: Cancer Center of NW Ohio 2461 S Main St Findlay OH 45840-1167

GUNDECK, CAROLINE NYKLEWICZ, investment company executive; b. Paterson, NJ; BS econs., Marymount Coll. With Merrill Lynch, White Plains, NY, 1983, currently first v.p. investments, chair Adv. Com. to Mgmt. on Diversity, dir. Women's Bus. Devel., 2003—. Created No. NJ Women's Network for Financial Advisors. Mem. adv. com. Preservation and Use of Ellis Island appointed by Gov. Christine Todd Whitman; dir. Women Presidents' Orgn. Recipient Tribute to Women & Industry Award, YMCA, 1999, recognized for outstanding volunteerism, United Way of Passaic County, 2000. Office: 1300 Merrill Lynch Drive, 3rd Fl Pennington NJ 08534 E-mail: caroline_gundeck@ml.com.

GUNDERSEN, MARY LISA KRANITZKY, finance company executive; b. Schenectady, NY, July 20, 1955; d. Charles William Kranitzky and Shirley Ann (Thomas) Ballou. BS in Fin., U. Ala., 1982. Fin. specialist GE Co., Birmingham, Ala., 1981-83, supv. acctg. adminstrn. Atlanta, 1984-85, corp. auditor Schenectady, 1985-87; mgr. fin. analysis and auditing GE Constrn. Svcs., Burkville, Ala., 1988-90; mgr. fin. Manheim Auctions Inc., Atlanta, 1990-92; program fin. mgr. Latin Am. Sales Gen. Elec. Indsl. and Power Systems, Schenectady, 1992-94; dir. fin. GE Capital/PT Astra Sedaya Fin., Jakarta, Indonesia, 1995-97, GE Capital Asia Pacific, Hong Kong, 1997-99; comml. mgr. finance GE Energy Parts, Atlanta, 2000—. Bd. dirs. Birmingham Opera Theater, 1980—. Recipient Acad. Excellence medal, Fin. Execs. Inst., 1982, Disting. Alumni award, UAB Sch. Fin. Stephen M. Chazen, 2006. Mem.: Omicron Delta Epsilon, Phi Kappa Phi, Beta Gamma Sigma (named Alumni of Yr. U. Ala. Birmingham chpt. 2005, named U. Ala. Disting. Alumni 2006). Episcopalian. Avocations: music, water-skiing, reading, travel. Home: 2920 Perrington Ct Marietta GA 30066-8717 Office: GE Energy Parts 4200 Wildwood Pkwy Atlanta GA 30339-8402 Office Phone: 678-844-6785. E-mail: lisa.gundersen@ge.com.

GUNDERSON, JUDITH KEEFER, golf association executive; b. Charleroi, Pa., May 25, 1939; d. John R. and Irene G. (Gaskill) Keefer; m. Jerry L. Gunderson, mar. 19, 1971; children: Jamie L., Jeff S.; stepchildren: Todd G. (dec.), Marc W. Student pub. schs., Uniontown, Pa. Bookkeeper Fayette Nat. Bank, 1957-59, gen. leader bookkeeper, 1960-63; head bookkeeper 1st Nat. Bank, Broward, Fla., 1963-64; bookkeeper Ruthenberg Homes, Inc., 1966-69; bookkeeper, asst. sec.-treas. Peninsular Properties, Inc. subs. Investors Diversified, Mpls., 1969-72; conptr., pres. Am. Golf Fla., Inc. (doing bus. as Golf and Tennis World), Deerfield Beach, Fla., 1972-89, stockholder, 1972-92; sales assoc. Realty Brokers Internat., Inc., 1990; sec.-treas. Internat. Golf, Inc., 1974-89, stockholder, 1974-99; dir. Mary Kay Cosmetics, 1993-97; wellness cons. Nikken, Inc., 1997—; assoc. Travel Ptnrs. USA, 2002—06. Personal E-mail: jkgunde@aol.com.

GUNDICK, SINTHEA MARIE, assistant principal; b. Detroit, Mich., Apr. 14, 1965; d. George Donald and Carol Ann-Hall Valenti; m. Damian Gene Gundick, Aug. 6, 0198; children: Cody Hall, Alexis Helley. BS in Edn., Wayne State U., 1991; MS in Guidance and Counselling, Eastern Mich. U., 1994. Prin. Southgate Sch., Southgate, Mich., 2003—, athletic dir., 2003—, counselor, 1997—2003, sci. tchr., 1991—97, math tchr., 1991—97, asst. prin., 2003—. Com. mem. adv. bd. Southeast Mich. Health Alliance, 2002—; adv. bd. No. Ctrl. Accreditors, Mich.; pres. Sch. Develop. No. Ctrl. Accreditors, 2000—05. Adv. bd. St.Tim's Cath. Ch., 2005; mem. Bd. Athletic Dirs., 2003—; girl scout leader Girl Scouts, Trenton, 2006—; softball coach Trenton Baseball Assn., 2004—. Recipient Tchr. of Yr., Southgate Sch., 1994. Mem.: Career Ctr. for Credentialing and Edn., ASCD. Avocations: camping, travel, cooking, reading, rollerblading. Home: 4241 Westphol Trenton MI 48183 Office: Gerisch Mid Sch 12601 McCann Southgate MI 48195

GUNN, JOAN MARIE, health facility administrator; b. Binghamton, N.Y., Jan. 29, 1943; d. Andrew and Ruth Antoinette (Butler) Jacoby; m. Albert E. Gunn, Jr., May 18, 1968; children: Albert E. III, Emily Williams Gunn Hebert, Andrew R., Clare M. Berchelmann, Catherine A.B., Philip D. Diploma, Binghamton State Hosp., 1966; BS summa cum laude, Tex. Women's U., 1983; MSN, U. Tex., Houston, 1989. RN, NY, Tex., Va. Staff nurse Columbia/Presbyn. Med. Ctr., NYC, 1966-67; head nurse, ICU Montefiore Hosp. and Med. Ctr., NYC, 1967-68; staff nurse Nat. Orthopedic and Rehab. Hosp., Arlington, Va., 1972-73, Woman's Hosp. of Tex., Houston, 1976-80; staff nurse geriatrics St. Anthony's Ctr., Houston, 1985-86; charge nurse gero psychiatry Bellaire Gen. Hosp., Houston, 1986; from head nurse gero psychiat. unit to dir. patient svcs. Harris County Psychiat. Ctr. U. Tex., Houston, 1986—2001, dir. patient svcs. Harris County Psychiat. Ctr., 2001—. Mem. NRA, Nat. Soc. Colonial Dames of the XVII Century, Daus. of Union Vets. of Civil War, Sigma Theta Tau. Roman Catholic. Avocation: reading history. Home: 3514 Glen Haven Blvd Houston TX 77025-1306 Office: U Tex Harris County Psychiat Ctr 2800 S Macgregor Way Houston TX 77021-1032

GUNN, KAREN SUE, psychologist, educator; b. Detroit, May 7, 1951; d. Robert Leroy and Margaret Elizabeth (Glenn) G BA, Oakland U., Rochester, Mich., 1974; PhD, U. Mich., 1979. Cert. cmty. coll. instr., Calif.; cert. completion Intercultural Inst. Conf., 1995. Prof. Santa Monica Coll., 1985—; pres. Gunn Cons. Group, L.A., 1984—. Bd. dirs. Hollywood Sunset Cmty. Clinic, 1981-94; mem. adv. bd. Venice Family Clinic, 1994-2002, bd. dirs., 2002-04; chmn. behavioral studies dept. Santa Monica Coll., 1993-98; exec. asst. cmty. mental health psychologist L.A. County Dept. Mental Health, 1980-83 Author numerous papers on substance abuse, mental health, cmty. devel., and child abuse Commr. City of Santa Monica, Calif. Recipient Commendation for Dedicated Svcs. L.A. County, 1987, 92, Recognition for Outstanding Svc. to Cmty. Cert., 1984, Mayor's Cert. for Appreciation for Outstanding Efforts and Accomplishments, 1988, Profl. Achievement award, 1989, Recognition Cert., Calif. Legis. Assembly, 1988, Outreach Ministries Commendation Positive Role Model, 1992, Appreciation award Santa Monica Coll. Black Collegians, 1992, Appreciation award L.A. County Dept. Mental Health, appreciation cert. FAA Dept. Transp., 1994; named to Who's Who Among Am. Tchrs., 6th, 7th, 9th edits Mem. APA, ASTD (orgn. devel. bd. 1993-95), AAUW Democrat. Avocations: reading, bicycling, running, travel. Office: 4201 Wilshire Blvd Ste 617 Los Angeles CA 90010-3607 Home: Unit 504 2663 Centinela Ave Santa Monica CA 90405-3159 Office Phone: 323-939-1773.

GUNN, MARY ELIZABETH, retired language educator; b. Great Bend, Kans., July 21, 1914; d. Ernest E. and Elisabeth (Wesley) Eppstein; m. Charles Leonard Gunn, Sept. 13, 1936 (dec. Apr. 1985); 1 child, Charles Douglas. AB, Ft. Hays State U., Kans., 1935; BS in Edn., Ft. Hays State U., 1936, MA, 1967. Tchr. English Unified Sch. Dist. 428, Great Bend, 1963-80, Barton County C.C., Great Bend, 1977-84, tchr. adult edn., 1985-87, tchr. ESL, 1988-94; ret., 1994. Recipient Nat. Cmty. Svc. award, DAR, 1996; Conf. Am. Studies fellow, De Pauw U., 1969. Mem.: AAUW (outstanding mem. 1991), NEA, Bus. and Profl. Women (Woman of Yr. 1974), Kans. Adult Edn. Assn. (Master Adult Educator 1986), Kans. Assn. Tchrs. English, PEO, Delta Kappa Gamma, Alpha Sigma Alpha. Democrat. Mem. United Ch. Of Christ. Avocations: travel, driving, needlepoint, crossword puzzles, reading. Home: 3009 16th St Great Bend KS 67530-3705

GUNNING, CAROLYN SUE, dean, provost, nursing educator; b. Ft. Smith, Ark., Dec. 16, 1943; d. Laurence George and Flora Irene (Garner) G. BS, Tex. Woman's U., 1965; MS, U. Colo., 1973; PhD, U. Tex., Austin, 1981. RN, Tex. Clinician III Bexar County Hosp., San Antonio, 1968-71; instr. U. Tex. Sch. Nursing, San Antonio, 1973-74, asst. prof., 1974-83, asst. to dean, 1977-79, assoc. prof., asst. dean undergrad. programs, 1983-84, assoc. dean, 1984-88; dean Sch. Nursing Marshall U., Huntington, W.Va., 1988-90; dean Coll. Nursing Tex. Woman's U., Denton, 1991—2003, provost, v.p. academic affairs, 2003—04, 2005—, assoc. v.p. spl. projects, 2004—05. Accreditation site visitor Commn. on Collegiate Nursing Edn. Contbr. articles to profl. jours. Active Leadership San Antonio, 1978-79, Leadership Tex., 1992. Served to capt. Nurse Corps, U.S. Army, 1965-68; to lt. col. Army N.G., 1980-88. Decorated Army Commendation medal. Mem. ANA, Sigma Theta Tau, Kappa Delta Pi, Phi Kappa Phi. Office Phone: 940-898-3301.

GUNNING, MONICA OLWEN MINOTT, elementary school educator; b. Jamaica, W.I., Jan. 5, 1930; came to U.S., 1948; d. Reginald Minott and Gwendolyn (Spence) Morgan; m. Elon S. Gunning, Feb. 2, 1957 (div. 1982); children: Michael Anthony, Mark Elon. BS in Edn., CUNY, 1957; M in Edn., Mount St. Mary's Coll., 1971. Elem. tchr., 1959-87; tng. tchr. UCLA, U. So. Calif., 1969-72; bilingual tchr. 10th St Sch., L.A., 1974-76; ESL tchr. Union Are Sch., L.A.; dir. vacation ch. sch. Wilshire United Meth. Ch., L.A., 1977. Spkr. in field. Author: (poetry) Not A Copper Penny in Me House, 1993 (award 1994), Under the Breadfruit Tree, 1998 (Am. Studies award), Perico Bonito and the Two Georges, 1976. Active Friends of the Libr., 1974—; mem. So. Calif. Coun. of Lit. for Children and Young People, L.A., 1990—. Recipient Meritorious award Friends of the Libr., 1974—, Christian Edn. award Wilshire Meth. Ch., 1983. Mem. Soc. of Children's Book Writers and Illustrators, Toastmasters Beverly Hills Club (pres. 1990-91 Max Damm Outstanding Toastmaster 1995). Democrat. United Methodist. Avocations: gardening, travel, shopping flea markets, continuing education classes. Home: 30731 Paseo Del Niguel Laguna Niguel CA 92677-2306

GUNSEL, SELDA, chemical engineer, researcher; b. Istanbul, Turkey, Nov. 10, 1958; d. Nejat and Hikmet (Suntekin) G.; m. Donald Lee Pferdehirt, June 6, 1987; children: Melisa, Lara. BSc in Chem. Engring., Istanbul Tech. U., 1981; MSc in Chem. Engring., Pa. State U., 1983, PhD in Chem. Engring., 1986. Advanced rsch. engr. Pennzoil Prods. Co., The Woodlands, Tex., 1986-90, sr. rsch. engr., 1990-94, rsch. assoc., 1994-97, sr. rsch. assoc., 1997-98, dir. tech. devel., 1999-2000, v.p. tech. devel., 2000—02; bus. team mgr. automotive lubricants Shell Global Solutions (U.S.) Inc., Houston, 2002—. Editor: Current Research in Tribology in North Am., 1993; mem. editl. rev. bd. CRC Handbook Lubrication and Tribology, Vol. III; mem. editl. bd., Jour. of Lubrication Sci.; Assoc. editor, Lubrication Engrg. Jour., contbr. articles to profl. jours. Fellow Soc. Tribologists Lubncation Engr. (exec. com. 2000-); mem. Am. Chem. Soc., Am. Soc. Heating, Refrigeration, Air Conditioning Engrs., Soc. Automotive Engrs. (Excellence in Oral Presentation 1996, chmn. lubricant rsch. award bd. 1997-99), Soc. Tribologists and Lubrication Engrs. (Captain Alfred E. Hunt award 1998, bd. dirs. 1996—, instr. edn. courses 1990, 97, 99), Sigma Xi, Phi Lambda Upsilon. Achievements include patents for non-aqueous lamellar liquid crystalline lubricants, liquid crystal-surfactant technology; contributions in the field of lubrication science and tribology; leadership in the advancement of knowledge and application of science and lubrication and tribology; research in areas of thermal/oxidative stability of lubricants, friction/wear mechanisms in boundary and elastohydrodynamic lubrication, vapor-phase lubricants, liquid crystal lubricants, refrigeration lubricants. Office: Shell Global Solutions (US) Inc Westhollow Tech Ctr 3333 Hwy 6 S Houston TX 77082

GUNTER, LAURIE M., retired nurse educator; b. 1922; BS, Tenn A&I State U., 1948; MA, Fisk U., 1952; PhD in Human Devel., U. Chgo., 1959. Staff nurse George W. Hubbard Hosp., Nashville, 1943-44, 46-47, head nurse, 1945-46, supr., 1947-48; instr. Sch. Nursing, Meharry Med. Coll., Nashville, 1950-55, asst. prof., 1955-57, project dir. mental health tng., 1957-58, acting dean, 1957-58, dean, 1958-61; asst. prof. nursing UCLA, 1961-63, assoc. prof., 1963-65; prof. nursing Ind. U. Med. Ctr., Indpls., 1965-66; assoc. prof. U. Wash., Seattle, 1966-69, prof., 1969-71; head dept. nursing Pa. State U., 1971-75, prof., 1971-87, prof. emeritus, 1987. Author: Self-assessment of current knowledge in geriatric nursing: 1,311 multiple choice questions and referenced answers, 1976, Edn. for Gerontic Nursing, 1979; contbr. articles to profl. jour. Mem.: Inst. of Medicine, ANA. Home: 4008 47th Ave S Seattle WA 98118-1218

GUNTER-JUSTICE, TRACY D., psychiatrist, educator; b. Columbia, S.C., June 30, 1964; d. Paul Wilmer and Betty Foy (Rogers) Gunter; m. David A. Justice, June 15, 1990. BA, BS, U. S.C., 1985, MD, 1990. Diplomate Am. Bd. Psychiatry. Intern Spartanburg (S.C.) Regional Med. Ctr., 1990-91; resident U. S.C. Sch. Medicine/Hall Inst., Columbia, 1991-94, fellow in forensic psychiatry, 1994-95; tchr. psychiatry Hall Inst., Columbia, 1995-96; cons. psychiatrist Charter Rivers, Columbia, 1995-96, VA Hosp., Columbia, 1995-96; asst. prof. psychiatry U. S.C. Sch. Medicine, Columbia, 1995—, instr. family medicine, 1995—. Lectr. State Mental Health Forensic Dirs. Ann. Conf., 1996. Mem. AMA, APA, Am. Acad. Psychology and Law, Am. Soc. Addiction Medicine, S.C. Med. Assn., S.C. Psychiat. Assn. (sec. Midlands chpt. 1995-96, v.p. 1996-97, pres. 1997-98, newsletter editor 1996-97), Med. History Club. Avocations: hiking, travel. Office: Morris Village Alcohol and Drug Treatment Ctr Dual Diagnosis Program 601 Faison Dr Columbia SC 29203-3217 also: Univ Splty Clins 3444 Harden St Ext Columbia SC 29203-6835

GUNTHER, BARBARA, artist, educator; b. Bklyn., Nov. 10, 1930; d. Benjamin and Rose (Lev) Kelsky; m. Gerald Gunther, June 22, 1949; children: Daniel Jay, Andrew James. BA, Bklyn. Coll., 1949; MA, San Jose State U., 1975. Instr. printmaking, drawing, painting Cabrillo Coll., Aptos, Calif., 1976-93. Instr. lithography Calif. State U., Hayward, 1978-79; instr. studio arts Calif. State U., San Jose, summer 1977, 78, 80; co-founder San Jose Print Workshop, 1975. One-woman shows include include Palo Alto (Calif.) Cultural Ctr., 1981, Miriam Pearlman, Inc., Chg., 1984, D.P. Fong and Spratt galleries, San Jose, 1991—93, Branner/Spangenburg Gallery, Palo Alto, 1991, U. Calif., Santa Cruz, 1991, Cabrillo Coll., 1997, Frederick Spratt Galleries, San Jose, 1996, San Francisco, 2000, Triton Mus. of Art, Santa Clara, 2001, Represented in permanent collections San Jose Art in Pub. Places Program, Triton Mus., Santa Clara, Calif., Mus. City NY, Santa Clara Law Sch., Found. Press, Chrysler Motors. Recipient Purchase award Palo Alto Cultural Ctr., 1975, Judges' Merit award Haggin Mus., 1988. Mem. Calif. Printmakers Soc., San Jose Inst. of Contemporary Art. Studio: Cubberley Ctr 4000 Middlefield Rd Palo Alto CA 94303 Personal E-mail: bgunther@sbcglobal.net.

GUNTHORPE, KAREN ANN, elementary school educator; b. Paterson, N.J., July 23, 1961; d. Osborne and Lillie Mae Gunthorpe. BS, Morgan State U., Balt., 1983; MA, Montclair State U., N.J., 2006. Tchr. Newark Pub. Schs., 1985—. Mem.: Alpha Kappa Alpha. Home: 378 Orange Rd Montclair NJ 07042

GUNZBURGER, SUZANNE NATHAN, municipal official, social worker; b. Buffalo, July 12, 1939; d. Lawrence Emil and Ruth Lucille (Wohl) Nathan; m. Gerard Josef Gunzburger, Apr. l0, 1960; children: Ronald Marc, Cynthia Anne, Judith Lynn. BS in Edn., Wayne State U., 1959; MSW, Barry U., 1974. Tchr. pub. schs., Detroit, 1959-63, Trumbull, Conn., 1963-66, North Miami Beach, Fla., 1967-68, Broward County, Fla., 1968-72; pvt. practice clin. social work Hollywood, Fla., 1975—; vice mayor City of Hollywood, 1983-84, 85-87, city commr., 1982-92; commr. Broward County, 1992—, chair, 1994-95, 99-2000. Chmn. Met. Planning Orgn., Broward County, 1984—87, 1989, Statewide Human Rights Adv. Com., 1988—89; pres. Broward County Mental Health Bd., 1984; active Broward County Commn. Status Women, 1978—82, White House Conf. Families, Balt., 1980; del. Broward County League Cities, 1988—92; mem. adv. bd. Broward Homebound, 1991—; mem. Broward Children's Svc. Bd., 1988—92, Broward County Water Adv., 1992—94, 1997—98, Broward County Cmty. Redevel. Agy., 1992—, South Fla. Regional Planning Coun., 1992—94, 1998—99, treas., 1999; vice-chmn. Broward County Planning Coun., 1996—98, chair planning coun., 2000—01, Broward County Cultural Affairs Coun., 1996—; Broward chair Concert Assn. of Fla., Inc., 1996—; mem. Broward Children's Svc. Bd., 1998—; bd. dirs. Environ. Coalition Broward County, 1982—89, 1997—2000, Fla. Assn. of Counties, 1992—, Broward Alliance, 1992—2000, Broward Children's Svcs., 1997, Children's Svcs. Coun., 2001—. Named Broward County Woman of Yr., 1990, Humanitarian of Yr., David Posnack, Jewish Comty. Ctr., 1994, Environmentalist of Yr., Broward County Environ. Coalition, 1994, Polit. Leader of Yr., The Vanguard Chronicle, 1999, Woman of Valor, David Posnack JCC, 2003, First Lady Broward, Broward County Fair, 2004; recipient Woamn of Yr. in Govt. award Women in Comms., 1983, Disting. Achievement award Am. Jewish Congress, 1990, Fla. Philharm. Woman of Style and Substance, 1995, Woman of Distinction award March of Dimes, 1996, Heart award Children's Consortium, 1996, Disting. Alumni award Barry U., 1996, Jesse Portis Helms Dem. of Yr. award Dolphin Dem. Club, 1996, Gracias award Hispanic Unity, 1999, Polit. Alliance of Yr. award Dolphin Dem. Club, 1999, Cmty. Covenant award Broward Outreach Ctr., 2005, Com Leadership award Hispanic Unity, Women of Style and Substance, Social Activist award; inductee Broward County Women's Hall of Fame, 1995, Woman of Distinction award City of Hollywood, 1997, Women's Polit. Caucus, 1997, Encore award Art Serve, 2004; Jewish Mus. Fla., Queen Esther Court Honoree, 2004. Mem. Nat. Assn. Social Workers (diplomate clin. social work), Internat. Acad. Behavioral Med., Counseling and Psychotherapy (diplomate profl. psychotherapy), Am. Acad. Behavioral Med. (clin. mem.), Nat. Coun. Jewish Women (pres. 1980-82, Hannah G. Solomon award 1989), Met. Planning Orgn., Israel Bond Coun., Hollywood C. of C. (leadership devel. 1990—), Kiwanis. Democrat. Avocations: reading, swimming, travel. Office: Office Bd County Commrs Govtl Ctr Rm 412 115 S Andrews Ave Fort Lauderdale FL 33301-1818

GUO, SU, science educator; BS Bioengring., Fudan U., 1991; PhD Genetics & Devel., Cornell U., 1996. Postdoctoral fellow Harvard Med. Sch., 1996—97, Genentech, 1997—2000; asst. prof. biopharm. scis. U. Calif., San Francisco. Office: Sch Pharmacy 513 Parnassus Ave Box 0446 San Francisco CA 94143

GUPTA, MONA, lawyer; b. India, July 17, 1968; BS magna cum laude, Drexel U., 1991; JD, Rutgers U., Camden, 1994. Bar: Pa. 1995, US Dist. Ct. (ea. dist.) Pa., US Ct. Appeals (fed. cir.), US Ct. Appeals (3rd cir.). With Caesar, Rivise, Bernstein, Cohen & Pokotilow, Ltd., Phila., 1994—, now ptnr. Mem. Calendar Com. Hist. Soc., US Dist. Ct., Ea. Dist. of Pa. Mem.: South Asian Bar Assn., Am. Intellectual Property Law Assn., Phila. Intellectual Property Law Assn., Phila. Bar Assn. Office: Caesar, Rivise, Bernstein, Cohen & Pokotilow, Ltd 1635 Market St, 11th Fl Philadelphia PA 19103 Office Phone: 215-567-2010. Office Fax: 215-751-1142. E-mail: monagupta@crbcp.com.*

GUPTA, MONESHA, pediatrician, educator; arrived in U.S., 1993; d. Surendranath Kedarnath and Vijayalaxmi Gupta; m. Sanjay Malhotra, June 29, 2001. MBBS, Grant Med. Coll., Bombay, 1989. Diplomate in pediatrics and in pediatric cardiology Am. Bd. Pediatrics. Clin. instr. Mich. State U., Flint, 1993—96; pediatric cardiologist NY Presbyn. Hosp., NYC, 1996—99, U. Tex., Houston, 2002—. Cons. pediatric cardiologist U. Minn., Mpls., 2000—02, U. Tex., 2002—; adj. faculty Rockefeller U., NYC, 2001—02. Contbr. articles to profl. jours. Treas. Sci. of Spirituality, Naperville, Ill., 1989. Med. officer Signals Rgt. Indian Army, 1989—90. Fellow: Am. Coll. Cardiology, Am. Acad. Pediat. Avocations: painting, travel, volleyball. Office: Univ Texas Med Sch Houston Divsn Pediat Cardiology 6431 Fannin MSB 3 130B Houston TX 77030 Office Phone: 713-500-5743. Business E-Mail: monesha.gupta@uth.tmc.edu.

GUPTA, MONIKA, nephrologist, researcher; d. Krishna Devi and Vijay Kumar Gupta. MB, BChir, Maulana Azad Med. Coll., New Delhi, 1996. Diplomate Am. Bd. Internal Medicine, Am. Bd. Nephrology. Resident in internal medicine SUNY, Stony Brook, 1998—2001; fellow in nephrology, 2001—03; instr. medicine Med. U. SC, Charleston, 2003—05, asst. prof. medicine, 2005—. Med. dir. Dialysis Clinic Inc., Mount Pleasant, SC, 2003—06, Charleston, SC, 2006—; dir. continuous renal replacement therapies Med. U. SC, Charleston, 2004—. Contbr. articles to profl. jours. Recipient Distinction in Physiology award, Delhi U., 1992, Cert. of Achievement, Kidney and Urology Found. Am., 2003; grantee, Am. Soc. of Nephrology, 1999, Kidney and Urology Found. Am., 2002—03, Dialysis Clinic, Inc, 2006—. Mem.: ACP, SC Med. Assn., Nat. Kidney Found., Internat. Soc. Nephrology, Women in Nephrology, Am. Soc. Nephrology. Office: Med Univ SC CSB 826 96 Jonathan Lucas St Charleston SC 29425 Office Phone: 843-792-4123. Business E-Mail: guptam@musc.edu.

GUR, RAQUEL E., academic administrator; BS in Psychol., Mich. State U., 1971, PhD in Clinical and Develop. Psychol., 1974; MD, U. Pa., 1980. Resident assoc., neuropsychology Stanford U., 1973—74; postdoctoral fellow, Clinical Psychol. U. Pa., 1974—75, asst. prof., Dept. Psychiatry, 1975—87, resident, Dept. Neurology, 1980—84, resident, Dept. Psychiatry, 1984—86, dir. neuropsychiatry, Dept. Psychiatry Phila., 1984—, asst. prof., Depts. Psychiatry and Neurology, 1984—87, assoc. prof., Depts. Psychiatry and Neurology, 1987—89, prof., Depts. of Psychiatry, Neurology, and Radiology, 1989—. Contbr. articles to profl. jours. Mem.: Insat. of Medicine of NAS. Office: Univ Penn Sch Medicine 10 Gates Pavilion 3400 Spruce St Philadelphia PA 19104-4283

GURE, ANNA VALERIE, retired social worker, consulting psychotherapist; b. Kaunas, Lithuania, Jan. 5, 1921; came to U.S., 1948; d. Salomon and Maria (Kantorovich) Gurvich. BA, CUNY, 1962, MSW, 1965. Cert. social worker, N.Y.; diplomate in clin. social work Am. Bd. Examiners in Clin. Social Work. Psychiat. social worker N.Y. Mental Hygiene Dept., N.Y.C., 1963-64, 66-69; social worker N.Y.C. Housing Authority, N.Y.C., 1965-66; immigration social worker Svc. for Fgn. Born, N.Y.C., 1969-77; psychotherapist, N.Y.C., 1977-86; social worker N.Y.C. Bd. Edn., N.Y.C., 1979-86; cons. Cath. Charities, Bklyn., 1988-89. Mem. Acad. Cert. Social Worker, Delta Phi Alpha. Avocations: painting, classical music, golf, exercise. Home: 95 Christopher St New York NY 10014-6605

GURKE, SHARON MCCUE, career officer; b. Apr. 4, 1949; d. James Ambrose and Marion Denise (Coombs) McCue; m. Lee Samuel Gurke, Apr. 16, 1977; children: Marion Dawn, Leigh Elizabeth. BA, Molloy Cath. Coll., 1977. Lic. pilot; first female naval officer selected for aero. engring. tng. Commd. ensign USN, 1970, advanced through grades to capt., 1991; aircraft maintenance duty officer Orgn. Intermediate Maintenance Officer Comdr. Naval Air Force U.S. Pacific Fleet, Naval Air Sta., North Island, San Diego, 1974-77; head quality assurance divsn. Intermediate Maintenance Dept. Supporting Aircraft Naval Air Sta., Miramar, San Diego, 1977-78, avionics divsn. officer, 1978-80; officer in charge Naval Aviation Engring. Svc. Unit Pacific Naval Air Sta., North Island, 1980-82; aircraft Intermediate Maintenance officer Naval Air Sta., Alameda, Calif., 1982-84, Rota, Spain, 1984-86, Naval Air Sys. Command Aviation Maintenance Policy Br., 1986-88; asst. program mgr. NACOLMIS, 1987-88; dir. ops. Naval Aviation Depot, North Island, 1988-90, Dept. of Navy OP-514C, 1990-92; commdg. officer Naval Aviation Depot Co., Pensacola, Fla., 1994-96, chief of naval operation, indsl. facility policy head, 1996-99; mgr. corp. mktg./devel. Newport News Shipbuilding, 1999—. Interviewed by S.D. TV for Success Story. Decorated Legion of Merit (2), Naval Commendation medals (2), Meritorious Svc. medals (3). Mem. Ninety Nines, San Diego Naval Women Officers Network (chmn.). Office: 9336 Mt Vernon Cir Alexandria VA 22309-3219

GURKOW, HELEN J., retired physician; b. Lancaster, Wis., Feb. 15, 1926; d. Carl C. and Theresa (Zimmerman) Gurkow. BS in Physiology, U. Ill., Champaign, 1949; MS in Anatomy/Physiology, U. Wis., Madison, 1954, PhD, 1958; MD, U. Marquette, Milw., 1962. Pvt. practice, Plattenville, Wis., 1964—87. Flight surgeon Nat. Guard, 1982—90, field hosp. MD Nat. Guard, 1990—91, Saudi Arabia, state surgeon Ohio Nat. Guard, 1992—94, Columbus, ret. col. Army Nat. Guard, 1994. Avocations: photography, travel. Home: 1264 Deming Way #307 Madison WI 53717 Personal E-mail: lol4doc@tds.net.

GURLEY, RHONDA JEAN, special education educator, consultant; b. Somerville, Mass., Sept. 20, 1967; d. Luther Dean and Dorothy Ann Gurley. Assoc. Degree in Acctg., Fisher Coll., 1987; BS in Bus. Adminstrn./Acctg., Salem State Coll., 1989; M in Spl. Edn., Wheelock Coll., 1992. CEIS L/T cert. Asst. tchr., billing coord., adminstrv. asst. Tri City Mental Health, Medford, Mass., 1987—92; spl. edn. tchr. Cambridge/Somerville (Mass.) Early Intervention, 1992—2002; asst. dir. Just A Start Corp., Somerville, 2003—. Adj. faculty Wheelock Coll., Boston, 1999—; cons. Cerebral Palsy Assn. Ea. Mass., Inc., Lynn, 2002—. Office: Just A Start 16 Butler Dr Somerville MA 02145

GURNACK, ANNE MARIE, healthcare educator, consultant; b. Willimantic, Conn., June 13, 1945; d. William John Gurnack and Helene Pactwa. PhD, U. Tex., Arlington, 1980. Planner Ga. Dept. of Human Resources, Atlanta, 1971—76; vis. asst. prof. U. Tex., Arlington, 1978—80; mgmt. cons. U. Tex. Human Resources Ctr., Arlington; prof. U. Wis.-Parkside, Kenosha, 1980—; assoc. prof. and chair Calif. State U., Bakersfield, 1990—92. Cons. HHS, Washington DC, 1998—. Author (editor): (book) Drug Abuse in the Elderly, 2002, Older Adults Misuse of Alcohol, Medications, and Other Drugs, 1998; contbr. articles to profl. jours. Mem. Seawall Ltd., Racine, Wis., 2005—06. Mem.: Gerontol. Assn. of Am. (aging interest group founder and leader 1994—2006). Democrat-Npl. Catholic. Avocations: travel, silversmithing, basket weaving, writing. Home: 141 S Lakeshore Dr E-2 Racine WI 53403 Office: University of Wisconsin Parkside 268 Molinaro Kenosha WI 53141 Office Phone: 262-595-2069. Home Fax: 262-595-2120. Personal E-mail: anne.gurnack@uwp.edu.

GURTMAN, ALEJANDRA C., epidemiologist, research scientist; b. Buenos Aires, Oct. 14, 1960; MD, U. Buenos Aires Sch. Medicine, Buenos Aires, Argentina, 1983. Cert. Internal Medicine 1999. Resident Hosp. de Clinicas, U. Buenos Aires Sch. Medicine; fellow Mount Sinai Sch. Medicine, NY, asst. prof. medicine, divsn. infectious disease NY; clin. asst., divsn. infectious disease Mount Sinai Hosp., NY, attending physician, AIDS Ctr., founder, med. dir., Travel Health Program NY; prin. investigator AIDS Internat. Training Rsch. Program, Fogarty Internat. Ctr., NIH. Cons. on anthrax and smallpox City of NY; site dir. GeoSentinel, Divsn. Global Migration, Nat. Ctr. for Infectious Diseases, Ctr. for Disease Control and Prevention, Global Surveillance Network of the Internat. Soc. of Travel Medicine; med. dir.,

Hepatitis B vaccination program NYC Housing Authority. Contbr. articles to profl. jours. Achievements include research in HIV infection in women and emergent pathogens related to travel medicine; during the anthrax scare of 2001, she cared for two NYC patients stricken with the disease; served on an ad hoc bioterrorism adv. com. convened by then-mayor Rudolph Guiliani. Address: 263 Castle Dr Englewood Cliffs NJ 07632-1630 Office Phone: 212-241-9521. Office Fax: 212-876-1109. Business E-Mail: alejandra.gurtman@mssm.edu.

GURVIS, SANDRA JANE, writer; b. Dayton, Ohio, Jan. 23, 1951; d. Isadore R. and Regina Goldberg; children: Amy Lynn, Alexander Bryan. BS in Sociology/Psychology, Miami U., Oxford, Ohio, 1973. Job classification specialist Def. Constrn. Supply Ctr., Columbus, 1973-78; prodn. editor Charles Merrill Pub., Columbus, 1983-84; corr. People Mag., Columbus, 1981-96. Author: 30 Great Cities to Start Out In, 1997, Way Stations to Heaven: 50 Sites Where You Can Experience the Miraculous, 1996, America's Strangest Museums, 1996, 98, The Off-the-Beaten-Path Job Book, 1995, Careers for Non-conformists, 1999; author/editor: Swords Into Ploughshares: A "Home Front" Anthology, 1991. Author: 30 Great Cities To Start Out In, 1997, America's Strangest Museums, 1996, 1998, Careers for Nonconformists, 2000, The Well Traveled Dog, 2001, The Pipe Dreamers, 2001, Where have All The Flower Children Gone, 2006, others. Recipient Media award Ohio Optometric Assn., 1991. Mem. Am. Soc. Journalists and Authors, Ohioana Soc. Mem.: Am. Med. Writers Assn., Am. Soc. Journalists and Authors. Avocations: tennis, walking, travel, theater.

GURWITZ-HALL, BARBARA ANN, artist; b. Ayer, Mass., July 7, 1942; d. Jack and Rose (Baritz) Gurwitz; m. James M. Marshall III, Mar. 12, 1966 (div. 1973); m. William D. Hall, May 3, 1991; 1 child, Amanda Posner. Student, Boston U., 1960-61, Katherine Gibbs Sch., Boston, 1961-62. Represented by Wilde-Meyer Gallery, Scottsdale and Tucson, Ariz., Courtyard Gallery, New Buffalo, Mich., Joanne Coia Gallery, Delray, Fla., Tupelo Rd. Gallery, Taos, N.Mex. Artist-in-residence Desert House of Prayer, Tucson, 1989—91. One-woman shows include Henry Hicks Gallery, N.Y.C., 1971, Karin Newby Gallery, Ariz., 1989—99, CCGV Artist of Month, 1997, Martin and Roll Gallery, Durango, 1998, others, exhibitions include CG Rein Gallery, Santa Fe, 1986, Data Mus., Einhod, Israel, 1987, SCV/aa, 1997, Scharf Gallery, Santa Fe, N.Mex., 1998, Tucson Mus. of Art, 1998, 2000, 2002, 2004, 2006, Wilde-Meyer, Tucson, 2002, 2004, 2005, 2006, Los Cabaleros Mus., Wickerburg, Ariz., 2001, Craig Gallery, 2005, Tohono Chul Mus., 2002, Ponies del Pueblo a Tucson Pima Arts Project, 2002—03, Thono Chul Mus., 2003—, Phippen Mus., 2002—, Tucson Mus. Art, 2004—05, others, Deartrees Gallery, Harrison, Maine, 2006, exhibited in group shows at Santa Cruz Valley Art Assn., 1989—2000 (Best of Show award, 1989, award for excellence, 1992, Hon. Mention, 1990), NLAPW/GV, 1997 (2d prize, 1997, hon. mention, 1998, 2d prize, 1999), U. Tampa, 1998 (award of Honor, 1998), Represented in permanent collections Nat. Mus. Women in The Arts, Washington, Tucson Mus. Art, Goldman Sachs and Co., N.Y.C., Diocese of Tucson, Data Mus., Israel, Haiku Mus., Japan, Nat. Haiku Archive, Calif., Phippen Mus., Prescott, Ariz., Sheraton Corp., Saguaro Ranch Corp. Mem. Tubac Village Coun., 1979-86; bd. dirs. Pimeria Alta Hist. Soc., Nogales, Ariz., 1982-84; creator Children's Art Walk, Tubac Sch. Sys. and Village Coun., 1980; set designer, choreographer DeAnza Ann. Pageant, Tubac Ctr. Arts, 1982-97; bd. dirs. Cath. Found., 2003—. Mem. Nat. League Am. PEN Women (pres. pro tem Sonora Desert br. 1999-2000, pres. 2000-02), Tucson Mus. Art, Nat. Mus. of Women in Arts Washington, Mus. Contemporary Art Tucson, U. of A. Mus. of Art. Avocations: golf, theater, singing, travel. E-mail: gurwitzhal@mac.com.

GUSHÉE-MOLKENTHIN, ALLISON, financial advisor; b. Hartford, Conn., Apr. 6, 1962; d. Stephen Hale and Anne (Taylor) Gushée; m. Steven M. Molkenthin. BA in Mech. Engring. & Comparative Lit., Brown U., 1984; MBA, Insead, Fountainebleau, France, 1987. Assoc. Bankers Trust Co., N.Y.C., Paris, Milan, London, 1984-89; pres., COO UI-USA, Inc., N.Y.C., 1989-98; mng. dir. Bentley Assocs., LP, 1998—. Fulbright scholar U. Mohammed V, Rabat, Morocco, 1985. Mem. NAFE, Brown Club. Episcopalian. Avocations: french, italian, spanish, german and arabic languages. Home: 195 Hollow Tree Ridge Rd Darien CT 06820 Office Phone: 212-763-0349. E-mail: gusheemolkenthin@BentleyLp.com.

GUSKY, DIANE ELIZABETH, state agency administrator, planner; b. Orange, NJ, Mar. 4, 1948; d. Marvin Leonard and Mary Elizabeth (Frayne) Gusky; m. John Bertram Broster, May 21, 1983. B of Univ. Studies, U. N.Mex., 1981, M Cmty. and Regional Planning, 1984. Cert. cmty. planner. Cmty. planner Planning divsn. City Albuquerque, 1983-84; aviation planner Aeronautics office Tenn. Dept. Transp., 1985-88; chief planner Greater Nashville Regional Coun., 1988-90; sr. planner Buchart-Horn, Inc., 1990-92, Espey, Huston & Assocs. Inc., 1992-97; dep. dir. aeronautics divsn. Tenn. Dept. Transp., 1997-2000, asst. dir. Office Strategic Planning, 2000—03, dir. Office Strategic Planning, 2003—06; spl. asst. to commr. Tenn. Dept. Safety, 2006—. Mem. Title VI adv. bd. Tenn. Dept. Transp., 1998—, vice chmn., 2001-04. Co-author: Land Use Compatibility and Airports, A Guide for Effective Land Use Planning. Recreational therapist Assn. for Retarded Children, NJ and N.Mex., 1974-77; mem. Metro Greenways Citizens Adv. Com., Nashville, 1993—, chair planning and devel. com., 2000—; mem. Nat. Women's Polit. Caucus, bd. dirs. Greenways for Nashville, 2006-. Recipient So. Regional Adminstr.'s Top Flight award FAA, Atlanta, 1998; named to Outstanding Young Women of Am., 1983. Mem.: Am. Assn. Transp. and Hwy. Ofcls. (standing com. 2004—), Am. Inst. Cert. Planners, Rebuild Tenn. Coalition (chmn. 1997—98). Office: Tenn Dept Transp Office Strategic Planning 505 Deaderick St Ste 300 Nashville TN 37243 Office Phone: 615-532-3560. Business E-Mail: Diane.Gusky@state.tn.us.

GUSSACK, NINA M., lawyer; b. NYC, 1955; BA magna cum laude, MS magna cum laude, U. Pa., 1976; JD, Villanova U., 1979. Bar: Pa. 1979, NY 2000. Ptnr. litig. dept. Pepper Hamilton LLP, Phila., chair health effects litig. practice group, mem. firm exec. com., 1998—, vice chair firm exec. com., 2000—. Mem.: ABA, Internat. Assn. Def. Counsel, Product Liability Adv. Council, Def. Rsch. Inst. (chair drug and med. device com. 2003—), Phila. Bar Assn., Pa. Bar Assn. Office: Pepper Hamilton LLP 3000 2 Logan Sq 18th and Arch Streets Philadelphia PA 19103-2799 Office Phone: 215-981-4950. Office Fax: 215-981-4750. E-mail: gussackn@pepperlaw.com.

GUSSOW, SUE FERGUSON, artist, educator; b. Bklyn., Aug. 2, 1935; d. Samuel Nathan and May (Sheinin) Shapiro; m. Donald L. Gerard, Jan. 10, 1999. Student, Bklyn. Mus., 1956-57; Diploma in Fine and Graphic Arts, The Cooper Union, 1956; BS, Columbia U., 1960; MFA, Tulane U., 1964. Prof. The Cooper Union Sch. of Architecture, N.Y.C., 1970—2005, prof. emerita, 2003—. Asst. adj. prof. in painting and drawing NYU, 1973-81; assoc. adj. prof. dept. painting and sculpture, Columbia U., 1977-79; vis. asst. prof. in printmaking Manhattanville Coll., Purchase, N.Y., summer 1971; assoc. prof. printmaking Alfred U., summer 1971, others; vis. prof. The Frick Coll., 2002-2005; Pamela Djerassi Artist-in-Residence, Stanford (Calif.) U., 1982-83; vis. juror Yale U., 1987, 88, Newspace Gallery, Wilkinson Pl., New Orleans, 1977. Work exhibited in Cooper-Hewitt Mus./Smithsonian Inst., N.Y.C., Dalls Mus. of Fine Arts, Seattle Art Mus., New Orleans Mus. Art, New Orleans Jazz Mus., Phila. Free Libr., Mus. of Modern Art, N.Y.C., others; one-woman shows include New Orleans Mus. Art, 1966, Loyola Marymount U., L.A., 1983, Stanford U. Mus. Gallery, Calif., 1983, Marcelle Fine Arts, Southhampton, N.Y., 1989, 90, Hall of the Journalists, St. Petersburg, Russia, 1992, Window/Rm., Tokyo, 40-Yr. Retrospective at Houghton Gallery, Cooper Union, 1997, Houghton Gallery, Cooper Union, NY, 1997, others; represented in the pvt. collection of Dore Ashton, Eero Saarinen's C.B.S. Bldg., Van Deren Coke, Morley Safer, George and Mary Schmidt Campbell, others. Recipient scholarships Parsons Sch. Design, 1952, Pratt Inst., 1952-53, Bklyn. Mus., 1956-57, Columbia U., 1956-60, Tulane U., 1962-63; fellowships Columbia U., 1961, Tulane U., 1963-64; recipient purchase prizes The St. Paul (Minn.) Art Ctr., 1966, 1965 Artists of La., 1965, Isaac Delgado Mus., New Orleans, 1965, SUN Y, Potsdam, 1964, Olivet (Mich.) Coll. Festival of the Arts, 1963-64, others; recipient jurors spl. mention Ark. Art Ctr., Little Rock, 1964, 1st prize Dallas Mus. Fine Art, 1964. Office Phone: 212-219-8154.

GUST, ANNE BALDWIN, former retail apparel company executive; b. Grosse Pointe Farms, Mich., Mar. 15, 1958; d. Rockwell Thomas Jr. and Anne Elizabeth (Baldwin) G.; m. Jerry Brown, June 18, 2005 BA, Stanford U., 1980; JD, U. Mich., 1983. Bar: Calif. 1983, U.S. Dist. Ct. (no. dist.) Calif. 1983, U.S. Ct. Appeals (9th cir.) 1983. Assoc. Orrick, Herrington & Sutcliffe, San Francisco, 1983-86, Brobeck, Phleger & Harrison, San Francisco & Palo Alto, Calif., 1986—91; assoc. gen. counsel The Gap, Inc., San Francisco, 1991—94, sr. v.p., gen. counsel, 1994—98, exec. v.p., human resources, legal & corp. adminstrn., 1998—99, exec. v.p., human resources, legal, global compliance & corp. adminstrn., 1999—2000, exec. v.p., chief adminstrv. officer, 2000—05. Mem. bd. dirs., Jack in the Box Inc., 2003- Contbr. articles to labor trade jours. Mem. ABA (labor subcom.), Calif. Bar Assn.

GUST, JOYCE JANE, artist; b. Milw., June 5, 1952; d. Walter F. and Jane A. (Klappa) Stoelzel; m. Wayne C. Fitzner, Feb. 13, 1971 (div. 1979); 1 child, Mark Wayne; m. Melvin. R. Gust, June 24, 1983. BS, Marquette U., Milw., 1981; postgrad., U. Wis., Oshkosh, 1985-90. Registered med. technolgosit. One woman shows include Pinecotheca Gallery, Waupun, Wis., 1993, Blatz Gallery, Milw., 1994, Lazarro Signature Gallery Fine Art, Stoughton, Wis., 1994, Constance Lindholm Fine Art, Milw., 1995, 96, Pedestrian Arts, 1996, 99, 2001, Artworks Gallery, Green Bay, 1995; two person shows include Capitol Civic Ctr., Manitowoc, Wis., 1992, Globe Gallery, Oshkosh, Wis., 1997; exhibited in group shows at Signature Gallery, Stoughton, 1989, 91, Cudahy Gallery of Milw. Art Mus., 1989-92, Allen Priebe Art Gallery, Oshkosh, Wis., 1990, Jura Silverman Gallery, Spring Green, Wis., 1990, 99, 2000, Chimerical Gregg Art Gallery, La Puente, Calif., 1990, Peltz Gallery, Milw., 1991-92, Ariel Gallery, N.Y., 1990, Neville Mus., Green Bay, 1992, John Michael Kohler Art Ctr., Sheboygan, Wis., 1993, Paine Art Mus., Oshkosh, 1996, 99, 2000, 01, See Beck Gallery, Kenosha, Wis., 1999, 2000, Lawton Gallery, U. Wis.-Green Bay, 2000, others; represented in permanent collections Carroll Coll. Art Mus., Waukesha, Wis., Very Special Arts Wis. Permanent Artists Collection, Madison, Neville Pub. Mus., Green Bay, Sister Kenny Inst., Mpls., Aid Assn. for Lutherans Ins., others; featured artist Artworks Gallery, Green Bay, 1993; illustrator Angel Quest, 1996. Travel grantee Wis. Arts Bd., 1998. Recipient Jurors award 1st Ann. Wis. Artists Exhbn., 1992, purchase awards Parkside Nat. Print Exhbn., 1993, Galex Nat., Galesburg, Ill., 1993, Very Spl. Arts Wis. Purchase award, 1994, 96, 97, 1st Pl. Internat. award in Drawing, Sister Kenny Inst., 1995, 96, 97, 2004, 1st Pl. Mixed Media, 1996, 97; travel grantee Wis. Arts Bd., Mex., summer 1998. Mem. Wis. Painters and Sculptors (Jurors award 1992), Wis. Women in The Arts. Avocations: philosophy, theater, art restoration. Home: 7064 Jacobson Dr Winneconne WI 54986-9764 Personal E-mail: joyceeej@aol.com.

GUSTAFSON, ANNE-LISE DIRKS, lawyer, consul; b. Vejle, Denmark, Aug. 14, 1934; came to U.S., 1955; d. Hans and Edith Margerita Dirks; m. William L. Gustafson, June 23, 1958. BA cum laude, U. Miami, Fla., 1963, JD, 1971, LLM, 1973. Vice consul Nation of Denmark, Miami, Fla., 1973-76; consul, 1976—; assoc. atty. Aronovitz & Weksler, Miami, 1976-83; pvt. practice Miami, 1983—. Knighted by Queen of Denmark, 1976, 96. Mem. Fla. Bar Assn., Consular Corps Miami, Alpha Lambda Delta, Delta Phi Alpha, Kappa Delta Pi. Republican. Lutheran. Home and Office: 2655 S Le Jeune Rd Ph 1D Coral Gables FL 33134-5827 Fax: 305-448-4151, 305-448-9707.

GUSTAFSON, JUDITH, federal association administrator; b. Flint, Mich., May 16, 1938; d. Lorimer Bruce and Mildred Lucile (Carter) Gustafson. BA cum laude, Fairleigh Dickinson U., 1987. Asst. to dean of faculties and provost Columbia U., N.Y.C., 1958-65; adminstrv. sec. to exec. dir. Coun. on Fgn. Rels., N.Y.C., 1965-77, asst. to pres., 1977-87, asst. sec. of the corp., 1985-87, assoc. dir. studies, 1987-96, sec. of the corp., 1987—. Office: Coun on Fgn Rels 58 E 68th St New York NY 10021-5953 Home: 1 Corriedale Ln Cottekill NY 12419-5029

GUSTAFSON, MARDEL EMMA, secondary school educator, writer; b. Waukesha, Wis., June 10, 1922; d. Otto Robert and Emma Bertha (Steffan) Hoppe; m. Wayne Carroll Gustafson, Nov. 1, 1950; children: Faith, Keith, Richard, Wayne, John, Beverly. BS in Edn., U. Wis., 1946. Sec. Waukesha Motor Co., 1944—45, Wis. Gen. Hosp., Madison, 1945—46; tchr. Hannibal HS, Wis., 1946—49, St. John Pub. Sch., ND, 1949—50. Author: What Is Happening To Our Children? How to Raise Them Right, 1993, Why A Role Mother?, 2001, All My Love, 2001. Mem.: Wis. Alumni Assn., TOPS Club (sec. 1978—83). Lutheran. Avocations: sewing, knitting, crocheting, gardening, walking. Home: W289 S2915 County Rd DT Waukesha WI 53188-9581 Personal E-mail: waynemardel@aol.com.

GUSTAFSON, SALLY ANN, counselor, cosmetologist, educator; b. Olympia, Wash., Sept. 21, 1947; d. Thomas Buchanan and Dorothy May (Long) Ness; m. Douglas Carl Gustafson, Oct. 2, 1967; children: Troy Douglas, Tristan Suzan. Cert. cosmetologist, Mr. Roberts Beauty Coll., Tacoma, Wash., 1966; cert. counselor, Maranatha Inst., Oakley, Calif., 1994. Cosmetology instr. Calif. Beauty Coll., Pleasant Hill, 1969-70; mgr. Jafra Cosmetics, Antioch, Calif., 1970-84; cosmetologist J.C. Penney, Antioch, Calif., 1991—; counselor Pittsburg Christian Assembly, Calif., 1994—. Avocations: arts, crafts, tennis, camping, skiing. Office: Pittsburg Christian Ctr 1210 Stoneman Ave Pittsburg CA 94565-5458 Personal E-mail: sallyagus@yahoo.com.

GUSTAFSON, SANDRA LYNNE, retired secondary school educator; b. Phila., Mar. 8, 1948; d. William Henry Gustafson and Ruth Blossom (Berger) Watson. BS in Edn., Temple U., 1969. Tchr. Lincoln H.S., Phila., 1969—78, Germantown H.S., Phila., 1978—85, Lincoln H.S., Phila., 1985—88, Germantown-Lankenau Motivation H.S., Phila., 1988—98, dean of discipline, 1994—96; tchr. Germantown H.S., Phila., 1998—99, Saul H.S., Phila., 1999—2003; ret., 2003. Asst. to vice prin. Lincoln H.S., Phila., 1970-78; sponsor Nat. Honor Soc., Phila., 1989-92, 93-96, Peer Counselors and Peer Tutors, Phila., 1989-98, records mgr., testing coord. Germantown-Lankenau Motivation H.S., 1997-98; chaperone on choir's trip to Europe, Lincoln H.S., 1973, coord. Freshman Orientation Program, Phila., 1993-98. Sponsor Big Brother/Big Sister Program, 1994—98. Mem. MLA, Phila. Fedn. Tchrs. (del. to state conv. 1973, del. to nat. conv. 1973, 74), Phila. Area Spanish Educators, Sigma Delta Pi, Kappa Delta Epsilon. Democrat. Jewish. Avocations: theater, music, ballet, opera, reading. Personal E-mail: tigras03@verizon.net.

GUSTAFSON, SARAH, elementary school educator; b. Nashville, Jan. 3, 1959; d. John F. III and Mildred Ann (Vaughan) Baggett; children: Matthew, Nathan. BA, U. N.C., 1980; postgrad., Fla. Atlantic U. Cert. elem. tchr., early childhood tchr., Fla., N.C. Tchr. Okeechobee County Schs., Okeechobee, Fla., grade chmn., elem. tchr.; tchr. Chatham County Schs., Pittsboro, N.C., 1992-94, Wake County Schs., Raleigh, N.C., 1994—. Workshop tchr. Recipient Fla. Assoc. Master Tchr. award, 1985; named Fla. State Tchr. of Yr., 1990-91, Okeechobee County Tchr. of Yr., 1990. Mem. ASCD, Okeechobee Reading Coun. (v.p. 1983-84, pres. 1984-85), Fla. Reading Coun., Fla. Edn. Assn.-United, Fla PTA (hon. life). Office: Wake County Schs Apex Elem Sch Old Wake Forest Rd Raleigh NC 27502

GUSTAFSON-HAIGH, MARJORIE ANN, retired librarian; b. Murdo, SD, Mar. 15, 1944; d. Lawrence Raymond and Anna Marie Paulsen Gustafson; children: Rebecca, S. James(dec.), Elizabeth, Emelie. BS, No. State Coll., Aberdeen, SD, 1965. Remedial reading tchr. Lake Preston Pub. Sch., SD, 1966; libr. asst. Watertown Pub. Libr., SD, 1966—67; asst. libr. Mt. Marty Coll., Yankton, SD; social studies instr. St. Mary's Sch. Indian Girls, Springfield, SD; libr. Springfield Correctional, SD, 1984—90. Bd. dirs. Irene Cmty. Libr. Mem.: Bookends Book Club. Republican. Lutheran. Avocations: reading, writing, needlecrafts.

GUSTAFSSON, MARY BETH, lawyer; b. 1960; m. John Gustafsson; 1 stepchild, Christopher. BA, Boston U., 1981; JD, U. Mich., 1989. Bar: NY 1992. Atty. Hubbard & Reed, NYC, 1989—96; various positions including chief mergers and acquisitions counsel, chief counsel Honeywell Internat. Inc. (formerly AlliedSignal Inc.), 1996—2001; with Am. Standard Cos. Inc., Piscataway, NJ, 2001—, chief counsel Trane, sr. v.p., gen. counsel, sec. Office: Am Standard Cos Inc One Centennial Ave Piscataway NJ 08855-6820*

GUSTAVSON, CYNTHIA MARIE, social worker, writer; b. St. Paul, June 18, 1947; d. John Gustave Adolf and Dorothy Elvira (Knoblauch) Blomquist; m. Edward Ernest Gustavson, June 7, 1969; children: Britta Joy Gustavson, Kent Samuel. BS, Boston U., 1969; M in Social Work, La. State U., 1984. Lic. clin. social worker, Okla. Tchr. Plymouth River Sch., Hingham, Mass., 1969-70; dir. St. Croix Preschool, Stillwater, Minn., 1970-72; edn. dir. Mother Against Drugs, Shreveport, La., 1984-85; social worker, therapist Forest Lake (Minn.) Dr.'s Clinic, 1986-90; social worker St. Croix Family Svcs., Stillwater, 1990-94; instr., social worker La. State U. Children's Ctr., Shreveport, 1994-97; writer, 1997—; psychotherapist Ctr. for Counseling and Edn., Tulsa, Okla., 1999—. Author: Scents of Place: Seasons of the St. Croix, 1987, Re-Versing Your Life: A Poetry Workbook for Self-Discovery and Healing, 1995, Human Spirit, Holy Spirit, 2004, Re-Versing the Pain, 2006, Re-Versing the Numbers, 2006, Fe-Vers: Feeling Verses for Children, 2006, Fe-Vers: Feeling Verses for Teens, 2006, Conversing With God: Poetry Therapy for Spiritual Direction and Pastoral Counseling, 2006, Ruach, 2006, I Don't Write Love Poems, 2006, Beneath The Sick-A-War Tree, 2006, The Battle Within, 2006; songwriter Paul and Silas, 2005; contbr. articles to profl. jours. Chair pub. rels. Child Passenger Safety Assn., Shreveport, 1982-84, ARC, Stillwater, 1986-89; pres. Am Heart Assn., Stillwater, 1988-91, v.p., program chair, nominating chair; chair environ. ctr. com. Minn. Sch. Dist. 834, Stillwater, 1991; mem. Minn. State Commn. Caregiving, St. Paul 1993-94, Shreveport Regional Arts Coun. Writers Panel, 1995-97, Caddo Cmty. Action Mental Health Task Force, Shreveport, 1995-97, Caddo Cmty. Action Head Start Adv. Commn., 1996-97; coord. River Cities Writers Conf., Shreveport, 1995-97. Fellow Acad. Cert. Social Workers; mem. Nat. Assn. Pastoral Counselors, Nat. Assn. Social Workers, Nat. Assn. Poetry Therapy, Phi Kappa Phi. Democrat. Lutheran. Avocations: reading, writing, playing guitar, bike riding. Home: 2817 E 34th St Tulsa OK 74105-2919 Office Phone: 918-295-8692.

GUSTIN, BRENDA SUE, retired art educator, painter; b. Kenosha, Wis., July 22, 1949; d. Ralph Burt and Alene Margaret Robinson; m. John Julius Gustin, Mar. 25, 1972; children: Amy Beth Farr, John Andrew, Daniel Adam. BA, U. Wis. Parkside, Kenosha, 1971. Cert. unltd.life cert. State of Wis. Dept. Pub. Instrn., 1977, art tchr. grades K-8, secondary sch. tchr. grades 7-12. Art tchr. Kenosha Unified Sch. Dist. 1, 1974—2006, coord. art exhibit elem. children, 1991—2006, ret., 2006. Art coord., advertiser Animal Rehab. Kinship, Racine, Wis., 1987—91; coord. art exhibit Anderson Art Ctr., Kenosha, 2004, Bose Elem. Sch. Artist (exhibitions) local restaurants, Kenosha, 1969—71, U. Wis., Racine, Parkside Art Gallery, Kenosha, 1987, 1991, 1997, 1999, 2000, 2005, Anderson Art Ctr. Recipient Blue Ribbon, Kenosha County Fair, Wilmot, Wis., 1976, Cert. of Appreciation, Kenosha Unified Sch. Dist., 1999. Mem.: Kenosha County Ret. Educators Assn., Wis. Edn. Assn. Coun., Kenosha Edn. Assn., Kenosha Unified Twenty-Five Yr. Club. Independent. Lutheran. Avocations: collecting vintage dog figurines, travel, visiting Southwestern art galleries. Home: 1802 83rd St Kenosha WI 53143-1652

GUSTINA, LORI LAZENBY, music educator; b. Colubmus, Ohio, Sept. 3, 1963; d. Paul Eugene and Jacqueline Wishart Lazenby; m. Douglas John Gustina, Oct. 26, 1996. BA in Music Edn., Ohio State U., Columbus, 1995, MA, 2005. Music tchr. Bourbon County Schs., Paris, Ky., 1986—89, Hilliard City Sch.s, Ohio, 1989—98, Big Walnut Schs., Sunbury, Ohio, 1998—2000, Worthington City Schs., Ohio, 2000—. Mem. Worthington Hist. Soc., 2004—; adv. Aplastic Anemia Mylcopysic Syndrome Assn., Md. Mem.: Ohio Choral Dirs. Assn., Am. Choral Dirs. Assn., Ohio Music Educators Assn., Ctrl. Ohio Am. Orff-Schulwerk Assn. (bd. dirs.), Am. Orff-Schulwerk Assn. (bd. dirs.). Avocation: singing. Home: 850 Oxford St Worthington OH 43085 Office: Worthington Hills Elem Sch 1221 Candlewood Dr Columbus OH 43235

GUTENTAG, PATRICIA RICHMAND, social worker, family counselor, occupational therapist; b. Newark, Apr. 10, 1954; d. Joseph and Joan (Miller) Leflein; m. Herbert Norman Gutentag; children: Steven, Jesse. BS in Occupational Therapy, Tufts U., 1976; MSW, Boston Coll., 1979. Lic. family and marriage counselor, lic. clin. social worker, N.J.; diplomate Am. Bd. Examiners in Clin. Social Work; registered occupational therapist, N.J. Social worker Jewish Family Svc., Salem, Mass., 1979-82; pvt. practice family and marriage counselor Westfield and Red Bank, N.J., 1982—. Cons. high stress, Westfield and Red Bank, 1982—. Fellow N.J. Soc. for Clin. Social Work; mem. NASW, Am. Occupational Therapists Assn., Registered Occupational Therapists Assn., Soc. for Advancement Family Therapy in N.J., Am. Anorexia-Bulimia Assn., Am. Assn. Marriage and Family Therapy. Avocation: reading. Office: 200 Maple Ave Red Bank NJ 07701-1732

GUTHERY, GRACE MAXINE, retired secondary school educator; b. Aug. 24, 1934; d. Walker and Dora Belle (Chandler) McIntosh; children: James, Kenneth, Max. AA, Lees Jr. Coll., 1973; BA, McPherson Coll., 1978; Rank I, Morehead State U., 1990. Cook, sec. Oakdale Christian H.S., Jackson, Ky., 1969-75, tchr., adminstr., 1979-85; admissions sec., head resident Cen. Coll., McPherson, Kans., 1975-79; receptionist, dorm dir. Lees Coll., Jackson, Ky., 1986-88; tchr. English Owsley County H.S., 1989-97; ret., 1997. Author: (with Myrtle Anderson) The School in the Vale, 1985; contbr. poetry to Sparrow Grass Poetry Forum, Nat. libr. Poetry. Mem. Christian Writers Club. Democrat. Methodist. Avocations: reading, sewing, travel, loom crafts. Home: 681 Lower Twin Rd Jackson KY 41339-9765

GUTHRIE, DIANA FERN, nursing educator; b. NYC, May 7, 1934; d. Floyd George and A. May (Moler) Worthington; m. Richard Alan Guthrie, Aug. 18, 1957; children: Laura, Joyce, Tammy. AA, Graceland Coll., 1953; RN, Independence Sanitarium, Mo., 1956; BS in Nursing, U. Mo., 1957, MS in Pub. Health, 1969; EdS, Wichita State U., Kans., 1982; PhD, Walden U., 1985. Cert. diabetes educator, bd. cert. advanced diabetes mgmt.; RN Mo., Kans., cert. holistic nursing, RN advanced practitioner; lic. profl. counselor Kans., cert. stress mgmt. edn., clin. hypnosis, healing touch, lic. marriage and family therapist. Instr. red cross U.S. Naval Sta., Sangley Point, Philippines, 1961-63; acting head nurse newborn nursery U. Mo., Columbia, 1963-64, birth defect nurse dept. pediat., 1964-65, nursing dir. clin. research ctr., 1965-67, research asst., 1967-73; diabetes nurse specialist Sch. Medicine U. Kans., Wichita, 1973—, asst. then assoc. prof. Sch. Medicine, 1974-85, prof. dept. pediat. and psychiatry Sch. Medicine, 1985-99, prof. emeritus, 2000; prof. dept. nursing Kans. U. Med. Ctr., Wichita, 1985-99, ret., 1999. Nurse cons. diabetes Mo. Regional Med. Program, Columbia, 1970-73; nat. advisor Human Diabetes Ctr. for Excellence, Lexington, Ky., 1982-90, Phoenix, 1983-92, Charlottesville, Ky., 1990-95; adj. prof. Sch. Nursing Wichita State U., 1985—. Author: Nursing Management of Diabetes, 1977, 5th edit., 2002, The Diabetes Source Book, 1990, 5th edit., 2003, Alternative and Complementary Diabetes Case, 2000; contbr. articles to profl. jours. Health adv. bd. Mid-Am. All Indian Ctr., Wichita, 1978-80; bd. dirs. Wichita Urban Indian Health Clinic, 1980-82; bd. trustees Graceland U., Lamoni, Iowa, 1996-2001, bd. trustees emeritus, 2002—. Named Kans. Counselor of Yr., Kans. Counseling Assn., 2006. Fellow: Am. Acad. Nursing; mem.: APHA, ANA, Am. Assn. Med. Psychotherapists (profl. adv. bd. 1985—), Am. Assn. Diabetes Educators (Kans. area Disting. Svc. award 1999), Am. Diabetes Assn. (Kans. area prof. edn. and youth com. 1988—, affiliate bd. dirs. 1979—83, pres. Kans. affiliate 1980—81, 1990—91, Outstanding Educator award 1979, Regional Outstanding Svc. award 1984, South Ctrl. Kans. Counselor of Yr. 2006, Kans. Counselor of Yr. 2006), Sigma Theta Tau (Exemplary Recognition award Epsilon Gamma chpt. 1996). Democrat.

Mem. Cmty. Of Christ Ch. Avocations: harp, piano, painting, crafts, reading. Office: 200 S Hillside Wichita KS 67211-2127 Office Phone: 316-687-3100. Business E-Mail: dguthrie@kumc.edu.

GUTHRIE, HELEN A., nutritionist, educator, dietician; b. Sarnia, Ont., Can., Sept. 25, 1925; d. David and Helen Andrews; m. George Guthrie, June 4, 1949; children: Barbara, Jane, James. BA, U. Western Ont., 1946, DSc (hon.), 1982; MS, Mich. State U., 1948; PhD, U. Hawaii, 1968; DSc, U. Guelph, 1996. Registered dietitian, Pa. From instr. to prof. Pa. State U., University Park, 1949-73, chair dept., 1974-89, endowed prof. nutrition, 1989-91, prof. emerita, 1991—. V.p. Heinz Inst. Nutrition Sci., 1993—; nutrition cons. to industry, govt. and academia. Chmn. Bd. of Health, State College, Pa., 1977-82. Recipient Borden award Am. Home Econs. Assn., 1976, W.O. Atwater award USDA, 1989, Pacemaker award Pa. Nutrition Coun., 1994. Fellow Am. Inst. Nutrition (councillor 1982—, pres. 1987—, Elvehjhem award for pub. svc. 1989), Soc. Nutrition Edn. (pres. 1978-79, fellow, 1992), Internat. Life Sci. Inst.-Nutrition Found. (trustee 1979-92, v.p. nutrition 1986-89, editor Nutrition Today 1987-97, Philippine Assn. Nutrition and Dietetics (hon.). Office: Pa State U S-125 S Human Devel University Park PA 16802 Home: 5260 S Landings Dr Apt 907 Fort Myers FL 33919-4677 Business E-Mail: hag@psu.edu.

GUTHRIE, JANET, professional race car driver; b. Iowa City, Mar. 7, 1938; d. William Lain and Jean Ruth Guthrie. BS in Physics, U. Mich., 1960. Comml. pilot and flight instr., 1958-61; research and devel. engr. Republic Aviation Corp., Farmingdale, NY, 1960-67; publs. engr. Sperry Systems, Sperry Corp., Great Neck, NY, 1968-73; racing driver Sports Car Club Am. and Internat. Motor Sports Assn., 1963-86; profl. racing driver U.S. Auto Club and Nat. Assn. for Stock Car Racing, 1976-80; pres. Janet Guthrie Racing Enterprises Inc., 1978—2004; owner Guthrie Racing LLC, 2004—. Highway safety cons. Met. Ins. Co., 1980-87. Author: Janet Guthrie: A Life at Full Throttle, 2005. Named to Women's Sports Hall of Fame, 1980, Internat. Motorsports Hall of Fame, 2006; recipient Curtis Turner award, Nat. Assn. for Stock Car Racing-Charlotte World 600, 1976, First in class award, Sebring 12-hour, 1967, 1970. Mem. Madison Ave. Sports Car Driving and Chowder Soc., Women's Sports Found., Les Dames d'Aspen, Internat. Wine and Food Soc. Achievements include being the first woman to qualify for and race in Daytona 500, 1977, Top Rookie; first woman to qualify for and race in Indpls. 500, 1977, finished 9th, 1978; North Atlantic Road Racing Champion, 1973.

GUTHRIE, JUDITH K., federal judge; b. Chgo., July 13, 1948; d. David Curtis and Kathleen McAfee G.; m. John H. Hannah, Jr., May 9, 1992 (dec. 2003); m. Matthew Watson, May 28, 2006. Student, Ariz. State U., 1966—68; BA, St. Mary's U., 1971; JD cum laude, U. Houston, 1980. Bar: Tex. 1981, U.S. Dist. Ct. (ea. dist.) Tex. 1982, U.S. Ct. Appeals (5th cir.) 1982, U.S. Dist. Ct. (no. dist.) Tex. 1983, U.S. Dist. Ct. (we. dist.) Tex. 1984. Editor Am. Coun. Edn., Washington, 1972-73; exec. asst. Tex. Ho. Reps., Austin, 1973-75; lobbyist Bracewell & Patterson, Austin, 1975-80, assoc. Houston, 1980-81; briefing atty. Tex. Ct. Appeals, Tyler, 1981-82; ptnr. Hannah & Guthrie, Tyler, 1982-86; magistrate judge U.S. Dist. Ct. (ea. dist.) Tex., Tyler, 1986—. Instr. legal asst. program, Tyler Jr. Coll., 1986-87; apptd. Tex. Jud. Coun., 1991-97, gender bias task force, 1991-92; lectr. in field. Contbr. articles to profl. jours. Adv. bd. Main St. Project; legal asst. adv. bd. Tyler Jr. Coll., 1986—, chmn. adv. bd., 1996—; mem. Citizens Commn. Tex. Jud. Sys., 1992—93; bd. dirs. Habitat for Humanity, 2003—; former Dem. chmn. Smith County; former bd. dirs. Found. Women's Resources, Leadership Am., Leadership Tex. Mem.: ABA (Fed. trial judges legis. com. 1991—93), Smith County Bar Assn. (chmn. law libr. com. 1985—2001), State Bar Tex. (dist. 2A grievance com. 1990—, chmn. 1995—96), 5th Cir. Bar Assn., Fed. Magistrate Judges Assn., Am. Judges Assn. Office: US Dist Ct 300 Fed Bldg & US Ct House 211 W Ferguson St Tyler TX 75702-7212 Office Phone: 903-590-1077.

GUTHRIE, TERESA IRENE, pediatric nurse practitioner; b. Amityville, N.Y., Dec. 27, 1957; d. Anthony Arthur and Anita Gloria (Escorcia) Marino; m. Jay H. Guthrie, June 14, 1980; children: Derek Jay, Shannon Ashley. BSN, Adelphi U., 1980; MS, SUNY, Stony Brook, 1996. RN, N.Y. Staff nurse Sagamore Children's Hosp., Huntington, N.Y., 1980, Brunswick Hosp. Ctr., Amityville, 1980-85, charge nurse in orthopedic unit, 1985-90, staff nurse, 1990-94, Lewin Svcs., Inc., Riverhead, N.Y., 1994-95, West Sayville (N.Y.) Children's Med. Svcs., 1996—. Avocations: crafts, reading, outdoor sports. Home: 58 Newport Beach Blvd East Moriches NY 11940-1577

GUTIERREZ, GABRIELLA, architecture educator; b. Albuquerque; Grad., U. N.Mex., 1984; MArch, Columbia U., 1988. Lic. arch., Tex. Archtl. intern Antoine Predock Archs., Albuquerque, 1983—87, I.M. Pei and Ptnrs., N.Y.C.; ptnr. Morris Gutierrez Archs., Houston, 1991—98; asst. prof. U. Houston, Coll. Arch., 1991—98; assoc. prof. U. N.Mex., Albuquerque, 1998—, assoc. dean Sch. Arch. and Planning, 2001—. Vis. critic Cath. U. Am., Summer Inst. Arch., 1997. Recipient Tau Sigma Delta Silver Medal award, U. Houston, Houston Educator award, AIA, ACSA/AIAS New Faculty award, 1996. Office: Univ NMex Sch Arch and Planning 2414 Central Ave SE Albuquerque NM 87131

GUTIERREZ, JONI MARIE, landscape architect, political organization worker; BS in Horticulture, N.Mex. State U.; MLA in Landscape Arch., U. Ariz. Founder, prin. Gutierrez Borowski Assocs., Las Cruces, N.Mex.; vice chmn. Dem. Party, N.Mex., 2003, acting chmn., 2003. Office: Democratic Party Chmn 1301 San Pedro NE Albuquerque NM 87110

GUTIÉRREZ, MARY CARMEN, artist; b. Villarro Bledo, La Mancha, Spain, Sept. 13, 1946; came to U.S., 1965; d. Francisco Gutiérrez and Asuncion Maroto; children: Ann Frances, Carol Stephanie. BA in Spanish, Visual Arts, Ctrl. U. Langs., Madrid, 1962. Tchr. arts and crafts Annunciation Pvt. Sch., Cleve., 1971-75; mgr., nat. sales dir. Murfoley Internat. Creations Inc., Manhattan, N.Y., 1975-79; graphic design dir. Lloyderson Internat., Ltd., Lancaster, Pa., 1979-95; ind. artist/designer, muralist San Remo, Fla., 1995—; owner One King St. Gallery, St. Augustine, Fla., 1998, Salon Art Boutique, St. Augustine, 1999; ofcl. translator City of St. Augustine, 1998. One-woman exhbns. include King St. Gallery, St. Augustine, Fla., Franklin and Marshall Coll. Square/Dioh's, Lancaster, Pa. State Coll. Ctr., Lancaster, Homestead Village Ctr., Lancaster, House of Lloyderson, Manhattan, N.Y., Lancaster County Art Assn., Byers/Basciano Phys. Therapy and Rehab. Ctr., Lancaster, Twin Brook Winery, Gap, Pa., Art Walk Week-End, Lancaster, Willow Valley Manor, Lancaster; group exhbsn. include Weber House Gallery, Springfield, Ill., Rosseti's, St. Augustine, St. Augustine Art Ctr., Galerie 110, Harrisburg, Pa., Lebanon (Pa.) Campus C.C., Pa. Acad. Music, Lancaster, Art Assn. Harrisburg, Mus. Art, Lancaster, Lancaster Dispensing Co., Heritage Ctr. at Penn Square, Lancaster, Artworks at Donecker's, Ephrata, Pa., Art Sundays, Lancaster, Lancaster Mus. Art, Art Walk, Lancaster, Arts Celebration Downtown Pub. Libr., Cleve., Barefoot in the Park, Cleve., Three Rivers Festival, Pitts.; designed and coordinated mural for Downtown Lancaster; designer, painter 3 murals for City Festival, 1999, flags and banners, 2000, permanent collection, Lancaster (Pa.) General Hosp.; illustrator numerous books, 1998-2001. Bd. dirs. Lancaster County Art Assn., Red Rose Ctr. for Arts, Spanish Profls. Am., Countdown New Yr. Celebration, Lancaster, Lancaster Mus. Art, Art Assn. Harrisburg, Nat. Mus. Women in Arts, Washington; bd. advisors Spain-U.S. C. of C., N.Y.C.; mem. St. Augustine Art Assn., Fla.; advisor Bd. of St. Augustine Textile Art Guild; coach/chmn. Art Walks; instr. All Around the World, Heritage Ctr., Lancaster; day camp dir. Summer Youth Ctr., Ohio; apptd. hon. vice-consul Jacksonville and St. Augustine representing Spain, 2002; advisor, assessor sister cities Aviles, Spain and Island of Menorca, Spain, 1999-2002. Recipient Michael Angel award, 1993. Mem. Lancaster County Art Assn., Lancaster Mus. Art, Art Assn. Harrisburg, Springfield Art League, Lloyderson Internat. Gallery, N.Y., Nat. Mus. Women in Arts, Catharine Lorillard Wolfe Art Club, St. Augustine Art Assn., Textile Art Guild; Historic Preservation and Heritage Tourism, 1999-02, St. Augustine Historical Soc., 1999-02. Office: La casa Del Hidalgo 35 Hypolita St Saint Augustine FL 32084

GUTIERREZ, YVONNE SOLIZ, school system administrator; b. Laredo, Tex., Apr. 6, 1951; d. Roberto and Estela (Segovia) Soliz; m. Juan F. Gutierrez, Jr., Oct. 30, 1971 (div. June 1992). BS in Edn. magna cum laude, Laredo State U., 1979, MS in Edn., 1982; postgrad., Our Lady of the Lake U., 1999—. Tchr. Laredo Ind. Sch. Dist., 1979-83, counselor, 1983-86, vice prin., curriculum facilitator, 1986-95, ctrl. office adminstr., 1995—. Mem. conduct site visits Tex. Sch. Improvement Initiative, Austin, 1996—. Contbr. Teen Forum Column Laredo News Newspaper, 1986, Parent to Parent Column Fed. Focus Parent Newsletter, 1996. Mem. Tchr. Corps U.S. Dept. Edn., Laredo, 1977; pres. Freedom's Found. of Valley Forge, Laredo, 1994; past sec. Laredo Commn. Women, 1995—; mem. Domestic Violence Coalition, 1998-99; bd. dirs. Casa de Misericordia Shelter for Battered Women, 1999—; mem. adv. bd. Safe and Drug Free Schs., Laredo, 1995—, Jr. Achievement, Laredo, 1998—. Recipient Paul Harris award Rotary Internat., 1995. Mem. AAUW, Laredo Adminstrs. and Suprs. Assn. (chaplain 1987-88), Princess Pocahontas Coun. (bd. dirs., sec. 1988—), A & M Mothers Club (v.p. Laredo 1993-95), Delta Kappa Gamma (Alpha Nu chpt.). Democrat. Roman Catholic. Avocation: writing. Home: 1309 Hibiscus Ln Laredo TX 78041-3320 Office: Laredo Ind Sch Dist 1702 Houston St Laredo TX 78040-4906 E-mail: yvonnesg@surfus.net.

GUTIN, MYRA GAIL, communications educator; b. Paterson, NJ, Aug. 13, 1948; d. Stanley and Lillian (Edelstein) Greenberg; m. David Gutin, Sept. 5, 1971; children: Laura, Sarah, Andrew. BA, Emerson Coll., 1970, MA, 1971; PhD, U. Mich., 1983. Asst. prof. comm. Cumberland County Coll., Vineland, N.J., 1972-80, Rider U., Lawrenceville, N.J., 1981-88, prof., 1989—. Adj. instr. Essex County Coll., Newark, 1971-72, Nassau C.C., Garden City, N.Y., 1972, Trenton (N.J.) State Coll., 1981-84; adj. asst. prof. Rider U., 1981-85; lectr. in field. Author: The President's Partner The First Lady in the 20th Century, 1989; contbr. articles to profl. jours. Officer Emerson Coll. Nat. Alumni Bd., 1994—2002, pres., 1998—2000; bd. dirs. Harry B. Kellman Acad., 1999—2002, vice chair bd. dirs., 1998—2000, chair bd. dirs., 2000—02; bd. dirs. Jewish Cmty. Relations Coun., 2003—, bd. sec., 2006—. Recipient Alumni Achievement award, Emerson Coll., Boston, 1991. Mem.: Ctr. for Study of the Presidency, Nat. Comm. Assn., Ea. Comm. Assn. Avocations: travel, theater. Home: 119 Greenvale Ct Cherry Hill NJ 08034-1701 Office Phone: 609-895-5568. Business E-Mail: mgutin@rider.edu.

GUTMAN, LUCY TONI, social worker, educator; b. Phila., July 13, 1936; d. Milton R. and Clarissa (Silverman) G.; divorced; children: James, Laurie. BA, Wellesley Coll., Mass., 1958; MSW, Bryn Mawr Coll., Pa., 1963; MA in History, U. Ariz., Tucson, 1978; MEd, Northwestern State U., Natchitoches, La., 1991, MA in English, 1992; postgrad., U. So. Miss., Hattiesburg, 1992—. Cert. sch. social work specialist, Nat. Bd. Cert. Counselor; diplomate in clin. social work; cert. secondary tchr., La.; cert. counselor, La.; cert. Acad. Cert. Social Workers, La. Bd. Cert. Social Workers. Social worker Phila. Gen. Hosp., 1963-65; sr. social worker Irving Schwartz Inst. Children and Youth, 1965-66; sr. psychiat. social worker Child Study Ctr. Phila., 1966-68; chief social worker Framingham (Mass.) Ct. Clinic Juvenile Offenders, 1968-72; dir. clinic, supr. social work Tucson East Cmty. Mental Health Ctr., 1972-74; coord. spl. adoptions program Cath. Social Svcs. So. Ariz., Tucson, 1974-75; social worker Met. Ministry, 1983; supr. social work Leesville (La.) Mental Health Clinic, 1984; sch. social worker Vernon Parish Sch. Bd., Leesville, 1984—. Cons. Nashua Cmty. Coun., NH, 1969-72; adj. instr. English, sociology, Am. and European history Northwestern State U., Ft. Polk, La., 1984-1994; counselor River North Psychol. Svcs., Leesville, 1989-92; presenter in field. Contbr. articles to profl. jours. Nat. Soc. Colonial Dames scholar, 1978-79; fellow Pa. State, 1961-62, NIMH, 1962-63. Mem. NASW (diplomate), La. Hist. Assn., So. Hist. Assn., So. Assn. Women Historians, Gamma Beta Phi, Phi Alpha Theta, Phi Kappa Phi. Home: 2004 Allison St Leesville LA 71446-5104 Office: Spl Edn Svcs Vernon Parish Sch Bd 201 Belview Rd Leesville LA 71446 Office Phone: 337-239-1689.

GUTMANN, AMY, academic administrator, political science and philosophy educator; b. Bklyn., Nov. 19, 1949; m. Michael Doyle, 1976; 1 child: Abigail. BA magna cum laude, Harvard-Radcliffe Coll., 1971; MSc in polit. sci., London Sch. Economics, 1972; PhD in polit. sci., Harvard U., 1976. Asst. prof. politics Princeton U., NJ, 1976—81, assoc. prof. politics NJ, 1981—86, prof. politics NJ, 1987—2004, Andrew W. Mellon Professor NJ, 1987—90, dir. grad. studies dept. politics NJ, 1986-88, dir. polit. philosophy program NJ, 1987-89, dir. ethics and pub. affairs program NJ, 1990-95, NJ, 1997—2000, founding dir. U. Ctr. for Human Values NJ, 1990—95, NJ, 1998—2001, dean faculty NJ, 1995-97, academic advisor to pres. NJ, 1997—98, Laurance S. Rockefeller U. Prof. of Politics and the U. Ctr. for Human Values NJ, 1990—2004, provost NJ, 2001—04; pres. U. Pa., Phila., 2004—. Visitor Inst. for Advanced Study, Princeton U., 1981-82; vis. Rockefeller Faculty Fellow, Ctr. for Philosophy and Pub. Policy, U. Md., 1984-85; vis. prof., Kennedy Sch. Govt., Harvard U., 1988-89, adv. coun., 1996-2001; Tanner lectr., Stanford U., 1994-95; academic adv. bd. Inst. Human Sciences, Vienna, 2001-; mem. bd. dirs., exec. com., Centers for Advanced Study in Behavioral Sciences, Stanford U., 1998-, Princeton U. Press, 1996-; secondary faculty appointment Annenberg Sch. for Comm., 2004—; bd. dirs, The Vanguard Group, 2006- Author: Liberal Equality, 1980, Democratic Education, 1987, 2nd edit., 1999; co-author: (with Dennis Thompson) Democracy & Disagreement, 1996, (with Anthony Appiah) Color Conscious, 1996 (award N.Am. Soc. Social Philosophy), Identity in Democracy, 2003, (with Dennis Thompson) Why Deliberative Democracy? 2004; editor: Democracy and the Welfare State, 1988, Multiculturalism, 1992, Freedom of Association, 1998, U. Ctr. for Human Values Series, Princeton U. Press, 1992-; co-editor: (with Dennis Thompson) Ethics and Politics, 3d edit., 1997; mem. editl bd. Teachers' Coll. Record, 1990-95, Cambridge Studies in Philosophy and Pub. Policy, 1991-, Raritan, 1995-, Jour. Polit. Philosophy, 1995-, Handbook of Polit. Theory, 1999-, Annual Reviews, 2001-05; internat. adv. bd. Ethnicities, 2000-. Trustee Carnegie Corp., 2005—. Fellowship, NEH, 1977, Am. Coun. Learned Societies, 1978-79, U. Hong Kong, 1998-99; Grant, Spencer Found., 1995-98, Sr. Scholar Award, 1999-2003; recipient Gustavus Myers Ctr. for Study of Human Rights in N.Am. Award, 1997, N.Am. Soc. for Social Philosophy Book Award, 1996-97, Ralph J. Bunche Award, Am. Polit. Sci. Assn., 1997, Bertram Mott Award, Am. Assn. Univ. Profs., Rider Coll., 1998, President's Disting. Tchg. Award, 2000, Centennial Medal, Harvard U., 2003, others. Mem. Assn. Practical and Profl. Ethics (exec. com., 1990-), Am. Soc. Political and Legal Philosophy (pres. 2001-04); fellow Am. Academy of Arts and Sciences, Nat. Academy of Edn., Am. Academy Polit. and Social Sci. Office: Univ Pa 100 College Hall Philadelphia PA 19104-6380*

GUTOWSKI, KATHLEEN SULLIVAN, special education educator; b. Evanston, Ill., Sept. 2, 1948; d. John Emmett and Marguerite Avis Sullivan; m. Richard Zenon Gutowski, Aug. 8, 1970; children: John Richard, Rory Zenon, Darina Kathleen. BA, St. Mary's Coll., 1970; MS in Edn., U. Kans., 1970; cert. advanced study, Fairfield U., 1978. Cert. profl. educator State of Conn. Spl. edn. tchr. Louisville Pub. Sch., 1970—71, Norwalk (Conn.) Pub. Sch., 1971—. Mem.: Norwalk Fedn. Tchrs. (maternity liaison 1978—). Roman Catholic. Avocations: travel, exercise, needle work, reading. Office Phone: 203-846-3600 3105.

GUTREUTER, JILL STALLINGS, financial consultant, financial planner; b. Chgo., Mar. 25, 1937; d. C.G. and Ann (Subject) Stallings; m. Robert L. Gutreuter, June 5, 1971; 1 child, Julia E. BA, U. Ill., 1967; postgrad., Chgo.-Kent, 1968-69, Coll. Fin. Planning, Denver, 1994. Staff dir. ABA, Chgo., 1969-71; trust officer Peoples Trust/Summit Bank, Ft. Wayne, Ind., 1980-87; fin. cons. Merrill Lynch, Ft. Wayne, Ind., 1987—2003; 2d v.p. investments Smith Barney, Ft. Wayne, Ind., 2003—. Fin. planning tchr., continuing edn. divsn. Ind. U.-Purdue U., Ft. Wayne, 1990—2000. Bd. dirs., mem. fin. com. YWCA, Ft. Wayne, 1997—2003; pres. Art League, Ft. Wayne Mus. Art, 1992—93; trustee Episcopal Diocese of North Ind. Found., South Bend, 1995—2000; bd. dirs. Girl Scouts of the Limberlost, No. Ind., 1997—2000, 2003—. Recipient Women of Achievement award YWCA, Ft. Wayne, 1994. Mem.: Inst. CFPs, Altrusa Internat. (pres. Ft. Wayne chpt. 1992—94), DAR, Rotary Internat. Episcopalian. Avocations: swimming, walking, painting, knitting. Home: 2312 Forest Park Blvd Fort Wayne IN 46805-3619 Office: Smith Barney One Summit Sq 20th Fl Fort Wayne IN 46869-3429

GUTTMACHER, SALLY JEANNE, education educator; d. Alan Frank and Leanore Florence Guttmacher; 1 child, Benjamin Alan Guttmacher Holtzman. PhD, MPhil, Columbia U., 1975. Prof. NYU, 1990—. Hon. staff mem. med. rsch. coun. South African Health Sys., Cape Town, South Africa; hon. lectr. U. Cape Town Sch. Pub. Health; dir. MPH program NYU. Author: The Role of Community Based Health Organizations in the Provision of Health Care in the US, 2005. Bd. mem. Pub. Health Assn. of N.Y.C., 1972. Grantee Rsch., NIH, 1998—2000. Mem.: Pub. Health Assn. of N.Y.C. (pres. 1996—99). Achievements include research in Cmty. based health promotion and disease prevention interventions and evaluations. Home: 15 Claremont Ave (#83) New York NY 10027 Office: New York Univ Pub Health Rm 515 726 Broadway New York NY 10003 E-mail: sg2@nyu.edu.

GUTTMAN, HELENE NATHAN, biomedical consultant, transpersonal counselor; b. N.Y.C., July 21, 1930; d. Arthur and Mollie (Bergovoy) Nathan. BA, Bklyn. Coll., 1951; AM, Harvard U., 1956; MA, Columbia U., 1958; PhD, Rutgers U., 1960. Registered and cert. profl. past-life regression therapist; bd. cert. nutrition specialist; bd. cert. and registered hypnotherapist; registered and cert. transpersonal counselor; cert. and registered neurolinguistic therapist. Rsch. technician Pub. Health Rsch. Inst., N.Y.C., 1951-52; control bacteriologist Burroughs-Wellcome, Inc., Tuckahoe, NY, 1952-53; vol. rschr. Haskins Labs., N.Y.C., 1952-53, rsch. asst., 1953-56, rsch. assoc., 1956-60, staff microbiologist, 1960-64; lectr. dept. biology Queens Coll., N.Y.C., 1956-57; rsch. collaborator Brookhaven Nat. Labs., Upton, L.I., NY, 1958; guest investigator Botanisches Institut der Technisches Hochschule, Darmstadt, Germany, 1960; rsch. assoc. dept. biol. scis. Goucher Coll., Towson, Md., 1960-62; vis. asst. rsch. prof. dept. medicine Med. Coll. Va., Richmond, 1960-62; asst. prof., then assoc. prof. dept. biology NYU, 1962-67; from assoc. prof. to prof. dept. biol. scis. U. Ill.-Chgo., 1967-75, prof., 1969-75; prof. dept. microbiology U. Ill. Med. Sch., 1969-75; assoc. dir. for rsch. Urban Systems Lab. U. Ill., 1975; expert Office of Dir. Nat. Heart, Lung and Blood Inst., NIH, Bethesda, Md., 1975-77, coord. rsch. resources Office Program Planning and Evaluation, 1977-79; dep. dir. Sci. Adv. Bd., Office of Adminstr., EPA, 1979-80; program coord., post-harvest tech., food safety and human nutrition, sci. and edn. adminstrn. USDA, 1980-83, assoc. dir. Beltsville (Md.) Human Nutrition Rsch. Ctr., Agrl. Rsch. Svc., 1983-89; pres. HNG Assocs., 1983—; nat. animal care coord. Nat. Program Staff Agr. Rsch. Svc./USDA, Beltsville, 1989-95. Bd. advisors The Monroe Inst., 1993—. Sr. author: Experiments in Cellular Biodynamics, 1972; co-editor (procs.) First Joint USA-USSR Joint Symposium on Blood Transfusion, Moscow, 1976, DHEW Publ. No. (NIH) 78-1246, 1978; editl. bd. Jour. Protozoology, 1972-75, Jour. Am. Med. Women's Assn., 1978-81, Methods in Cell Sci., 1994-2004; sr. editor: Science and Animals: Addressing Contemporary Issues, 1989; editor: Guidelines for Well-being of Rodents in Research, 1990, Rodents and Rabbits: Current Research Issues, 1994; (with others) Rodents and Rabbits: Addressing Current Issues, 1994; contbr. articles to profl. jours. Mem. edn. com. Ill. Commn. on Status Women, 1974-75; cons. EPA, sci. adv. bd., 1974-79; bd. dirs. Du Page County Comprehensive Health Care Agy., 1974-75. Andelot fellow Harvard U., 1956, Rutgers scholar Rutgers U., 1960; recipient Thomas Jefferson Murray prize Theobald Smith Soc., 1959; spl. award for work in Germany Deutscher Forschungs Gemeinschaft, 1960; Fellow Dazian Found., 1956; rsch. grantee. Fellow: AAAS, N.Y. Acad. Scis., Am. Acad. Microbiology, Am. Inst. Chemists (chmn. com.); mem.: Univ. and Coll. Women Ill. (past v.p.), Fed. Orgn. Profl. Women (past chmn. task force, past pres.), Assn. Women in Sci., Soc. Protozoology (past mem. exec. com., past com. chmn.), Am. Soc. Clin. Nutrition, Am. Soc. Cell Biology (past com. chmn.), Am. Soc. Microbiologists, Neuroscis. Soc., Am. Soc. Biol. Chemistry and Molecular Biology, Tissue Culture Assn. (com. chmn. Nat. Capital Area br. 1988—90), Soc. Sci. Exploration, Soc. for In Vitro Biology (chmn. constn. and bylaws com. 1994—2002, Disting. Svc. award 1995, 1999), Assn. for Transpersonal Psychology (profl. mem.), Soc. Am. Bacteriologists (pres.'s fellow), Internat. Assn. Regression Therapies (life profl.), Am. Running and Fitness Assn. (bd. dirs., mem. editl. bd., mem. bd. advisors 1993—95), Sigma Xi, Sigma Delta Epsilon (past coord. regional ctrs.). Home and Office: 5607 Mclean Dr Bethesda MD 20814-1021

GUY, ELEANOR BRYENTON, retired writer; b. Pitts., Sept. 6, 1930; d. Lloyd Charles and Verda Eleanor (Hooper) Bryenton; m. Daniel Sowers Guy, Dec. 22, 1962; children: Stanley, Sharon. BA, Ohio Wesleyan U., 1953. Program dir. Lakewood Br. Cleve. Met. YWCA, Lakewood, Ohio, 1953-56, ctr. dir., 1956-57; residence dir., mem. faculty St. Luke's Hosp. Sch. Nursing, Shaker Heights, Ohio, 1957-59; pers. asst., counselor Acacia Mutual Life Ins. Co., Washington, 1959-62; admissions counselor Ohio No. U., Ada, 1963-64; freelance writer, photographer Kenton (Ohio) Times, 1984-88, Ada Herald, 1988-96; coord. external affairs, editor the Writ, Pettit Coll. of Law, Ohio No. U., 1995-96, ret., 1996. Sec. bd. trustees, chmn. pub. rels. com. Ada Pub. Libr., 1982—86; mem. pub. rels. com., bd. dirs. Hardin County Alcohol and Drug Abuse Ctr., Kenton, 1989—92; chmn. publicity Town and Gown Planning Com., Ada, 1988; tchr., mem. co-chair edn. com., mem. missions com., mem., sec. adminstrv. coun., mem. centennial com., publicist United Meth. Ch., 1985—2003, lay dist. del. to West Ohio Ann. conf., 1998—2004, 2006. Mem. AAUW (pres. local br. 1978-80), Ohio No. U. Women (parliamentarian, pub. rels. chair Christmas Arts Festival 1990-96), P.E.O. (v.p. 1994-96, sec. 1998-99), Twice Ten Art Club (pres. 1984-85, 90-91, 97-98, sec. 1988-89, 99-01, mem. v.p. 2000-05), United Meth. Women (dist. spiritual growth coord. 2000-03, chmn. publicity and pub. rels. 2006). Methodist. Avocations: photography, travel, music.

GUY, JASMINE, actress; b. Boston; m. Terrence Duckette, Aug. 22, 1998; 1 child, Imani. Actress: (TV series) A Different World, 1987-93, Dead Like Me, 2003-04, (films) School Daze, 1988, Harlem Nights, 1989, Boy Meets Girl, 1993, Kla$h, 1995, (voice) Cat's Don't Dance, 1997, Madeline, 1998, Lillie, 1999, Guinevere, 1999, The Law of Enclosures, 2000, Diamond Men, 2000, Dying On the Edge, 2001, (TV films) At Mother's Request, 1987, Runaway, 1989, A Killer Among Us, 1990, Stompin' at the Savoy, 1992, American Dream, 1996, Perfect Crime, 1997, Carrie, 2002, (TV miniseries) Queen, 1993, A Century of Women, 1994; appeared in Broadway musicals Leader of the Pack, The Wiz (revival), Grease, 1997 and Off-Broadway prodn. Beehive; regional theatre The Fourposter, 2005; TV credits include Fame, A Killer Among Us; TV Spl. Stompin' at the Savoy, 1992; writer short stories, poems; author: (book) Evolution of a Revolutionary, 2004.

GUY, MARY (PENNY) WHYTLAW, secondary school educator, school librarian; b. Santa Rita, N.Mex., May 8, 1947; d. Theodore Henry Schroeter and Lula Ann Clark; m. Peter M. Guy, Mar. 4, 2006; m. David G. Whytlaw (dec.); children: Thomas D., Brian T. BA summa cum laude, Ea. N.Mex. U., Portales, 1969; MA, U. Tex., Odessa, 1992. Cert. tchr. Tex., sch. libr. Tex. Tchr. Midland H.S., Tex., 1969—71, Goddard Jr. H.S., Midland, 1976—81, head libr., 1981—87; tchr. Bohnham Jr. H.S., Odessa, Tex., 1987—2002, Eng. dept. chair, 1989—96; head libr. Odessa H.S., 2002—05. Contbr. articles to profl. jours., essays and poems to pubs. Grantee, Ednl. Found., Odessa, 2005. Meth. Avocations: reading, writing, kayaking, crew.

GUY, SALLIE T., artist; b. N.Y.C., Dec. 17, 1928; d. Julius Paul Turner and Bessie Alice Cohen; m. John K. Mount, Dec. 24, 1949 (dec.); children: Deborah Akins, Daniel, Laurel, Paul; m. Carroll W. Guy, Dec. 1, 1966; stepchildren: Patricia Funk, Peggy Panter. BA with high honors in History, U. Rochester, 1950. Juried mem. Ky. Dept. Art, Frankfort, 1984; bd. mem. Midwest Weavers Assn., 1981—86; mem. stds. com. Ky. Guild Artists and Craftsmen, Berea, 1982—83, Berea, 1987—90; chair new bylaws com. Complex Weavers, 1994—95. Author, instr.: instrnl. video Tips, Tricks & Problem Solvers for the Handweaver, 1989, Warping and Loom Preparation, 1997; contbr. articles to profl. jours. Pres. LWV, Murray, 1980, Friends of Oakhurst, Murray State U., 1995, Murray Civic Music Assn., 1996—97; elder, trustee First Presbyn. Ch., Murray; staff, mem. evaluation com. Synod of the Covenant; chair divsn. presbytery resourcing Synod of Living Waters, 1988—90, chair comm. com., 1996—2000; moderator Presbytery Western Ky., 1980—81. Mem.: Murray Art Guild (treas. 2002—04, Artist of Yr. 2004), Handweavers Guild Am. (state rep. Ky. 1978—81, bd. dirs. 1981—89, sec. 1983—85, third v.p. 1985—86, first v.p. 1986—88). Democrat. Presbyterian. Avocations: watercolor, knitting, photography. Home: 424 Moser Ln Murray KY 42071-5029 E-mail: kenlake2@aol.com.

GUY, SANDRA, journalist, telecommunications writer; b. Bristol, Tenn., Jan. 7, 1961; d. William Clinton and Ruby Jeannette Guy. BA in Mass. Comms. cum laude, Emory & Henry Coll., 1983. Staff writer The Coalfield Progress, Norton, Va., 1983-84; Sullivan County bur. reporter Kingsport (Tenn.) Times-News, 1984-88; polit. writer The Times of N.W. Ind., Munster, Ind., 1988-93, West Lake editor, 1993-95; news editor to mng. ed. Telephony mag., Chgo., 1995-98; news editor (mag. supplement) Internet Edge, 1997; bus. and tech. editor Am. Med. News, Chgo., 1998-99; freelance writer The Writing Experts, Chgo., 1999—; bus. writer Chgo. Sun-Times, 1999—. Child life vol. La Rabida Children's Hosp., Chgo., 1998-99. Mem. Art Inst. Chgo., 1988—. Fellow Knight Ctr. for Specialized Journalism, 1996; recipeint Meeman Found. award for Pub. Svc. Tenn. Press Assn., 1985, 1st pl. Best News Story, 1985, 2d Pl. In-Depth Writing award Va. Press Assn., 1984, News Media award N.W. Ind. Jewish Fedn., 1994. Mem. NAFE, Assn. for Women Journalists (web site coord. 1998—), Soc. Profl. Journalists, Investigative Reporters and Editors, Chgo. Women in Pub., Nat. Mus. Women in the Arts. Lutheran. Avocations: tennis, tae bo, reading, volunteer work. Office: Business Writer Chgo Sun-Times 401 N Wabash Ave Chicago IL 60611-5642

GUYER, HEDY-ANN KLEIN, special education educator; b. Phila., Dec. 25, 1947; d. Edward Chuck Klein and Gladys Selma (Shapiro) Sussman; m. Eugene August Guyer, Aug. 24, 1980 (div. Mar. 2002). BS in Secondary Edn., St. Joseph's U., Phila., 1981; MEd in Spl. Edn., Arcadia Univ., 1996. Cert. in social studies, elem. edn., spl. edn. of mentally and/or physically handicapped, Pa. Tchr. spl. edn. Sch. Dist. Phila., 1996—. Mem. ASCD, Women in Edn., George Washington H.S. Alumni Assn., B'nai B'rith (educators unit), Coun. Exceptional Children. Home: 1033 Bloomfield Ave Philadelphia PA 19115-4829 Office: Sch Dist Phila William Penn HS Broad and Master Sts Philadelphia PA 19122-4097

GUYETT, ANNE ELGAR, performing arts educator; b. Wash., Mar. 17, 1949; d. Robert Campbell and Elgar Sherman (Jones) Gilmore; m. David Fairfield Pratt Guyett, Aug. 28, 1971; 1 child, Justin Fairfield Pratt. BA, St. Lawrence U., Canton, N.Y., 1971; MAT, Nat. Louis U., Evanston, Ill., 1973; doctoral work in dance and related arts, Tex. Women's U., Denton, Tex. Tchr. (4th grade) Hardey Prepatory Sch., Chgo., 1973—75; tchr. (6th grade), TAG pub. schs., Bend, Oreg., 1975—80; tchr. (4th, 5th grades, middle sch.) Akiba Academy, Dallas, 1986—89, 1990—91; tchr. (5th grade) mid. sch. composition, movement arts, drama (preschool-grade 5) Oak Hill Academy, Dallas, 1991—2003; tchr. (3d, 5th grades) Dallas Internat. Sch., 2003—. Freelance cons., presenter, tchr., performer movement arts connected to lang. devel. local, state, nat. schs., colls., various orgns., 1970—; choreographer/tchr. pub. and pvt. schs. and theatre groups, Md., N.Y., Ill., Oreg., Tex.; tchr.-movement to enhance bilingual edn. Dallas Ind. Schs., Kramer Elem., 2004—. Author: (book) A Marriage of Music and Dance: The Partitas of J.S. Bach. Recipient Excellence in Edn. award, Internat. Dyslexia Assn., Dallas, 2003. Mem.: Dance Coun., Am. Alliance Health, Phys. Edn., Recreation and Dance, Kappa Delta Pi. Christian Scientist. Achievements include development of an extensive movement arts curriculum (ages 3-10) to enhance language skills, with emphasis on special populations. Avocations: classical music, dance, literature, visual arts, attending workshops, exhibits, lectures, symposiums on the arts. Personal E-mail: aelgar@sbcglobal.net.

GUYETTE, DIANA, minister; b. South Porcupine, Ont., Can., Oct. 18, 1942; d. Arthur and Marie Louise Doiron; 1 child, Susie Marie Florence Ordner. MDiv, Emory U., 1996. Ordained elder United Meth. Ch., 1998. Assoc. pastor Mulberry United Meth. Ch., Macon, Ga., 2000—02; dir. Hannibal (Ohio)-Clarington United Meth. Parish, 2002—05; pastor West Farmington (Ohio) United Meth. Ch., 2005—. Chair Savannah (Ga.) Dist. Coun. on Ministries of the United Meth. Ch., 1998—99; mentor St. Clairsville Dist. of the East Ohio United Meth. Conf., Hannibal, 2003—; participant Pastors of Excellence program Ashland (Ohio) Theol. Sem., 2004—05. Literacy tutor Chatham County Libr., Savannah, 1985—87; lectr. Ga. Coun. on Child Abuse, Savannah, 1986—88; co-facilitator incest survivor group Army Cmty. Svc., Savannah, Ga., 1988—89; bd. dirs. East Ohio conf. bd. ordained ministry United Meth. Ch., 2005—; lectr. Candler Sch. Theology, Atlanta; bd. dirs. Tri-County Help Ctr., Inc., St. Clairsville, Ohio, 2005—. Margaret Adger Pitts fellow, Andrew Coll., 1996. Methodist. Avocations: leading retreats, cross stitch, crocheting. Home: PO Box 93 West Farmington OH 44491 Office Phone: 330-889-3345. Personal E-mail: dguyette@neo.rr.com.

GUZE, SANDRA LEE, secondary school educator; b. Hartford, Conn., Feb. 24, 1956; Student, Hartford (Conn.) Art Sch., 1974-75; BS, Ctrl. Conn. State Coll., 1980; MA in Liberal Studies, Wesleyan U., Middletown, Conn., 1994. Cert. profl. educator, Conn. Art instr., dept. head Bolton (Conn.) High Sch., 1985-91; art instr. Conard High Sch., West Hartford, Conn., 1991-92; visual arts mentor, instr. Ctr. for Creative Youth Wesleyan U., Middletown, Conn., 1993—98; art instr. Farmington (Conn.) High Sch., 1994-95, Rocky Hill (Conn.) High Sch., 1995—. Exhibited in shows at Wesleyan U., Middletown, 1993, 94, 95, Artspace, New Haven, 1993, 94, Pump House Gallery, Hartford, 1993, Artworks Gallery, Hartford, 1993, 94, Discovery Mus., Bridgeport, Conn., 1994, Guilford (Conn.) Handcrafts Ctr., 1994, McKillop Gallery, Newport, R.I., 1995, U. Conn., 1996, Fourth Floor Gallery, N.Y.C., 1996, Eleftherias Park Art Ctr., Athens, Greece, 1996, Pump House Gallery, Hartford, Conn., 1998, Bartholomew St. Hartford, 1999, Soho 20, NYC, 2000, New Britain Mus. Am. Art, Conn., 2001, Real Art Ways, 2001, John Jay Coll., NYC, 2003. Recipient 1st Pl. award Artworks Gallery, 1993, Conn. Celebration Excellence award, 2000; named Tchr. of Yr., Rocky Hill H.S., 2001 Mem. Nat. Assn. Women Artists, Conn. Art Edn. Assn., Nat. Art Ed. Assn., Artworks Gallery. Avocation: working in mixed media.

GUZMAN, CAROLE L., small business owner; b. Bklyn., N.Y., July 10, 1955; d. Carol Helen (Lipp) and Nicasio Guzman. Assoc. prodr. In The Life TV, N.Y.C., NY, 1992—93; asst. dir. pub. affairs Crosswalks TV, N.Y.C., NY, 1993; 2d asst. dir. 10 Benny, Montclair, NJ, 1994, Ed's Next Move, N.Y.C., NY, 1994; asst. dir. The Truth of Human Life, N.Y.C., NY, 1994, The Dinner Party, N.Y.C., NY, 1994; office mgr. September Music, N.Y.C., NY, 1995; exec. asst. New Sch. U., N.Y.C., NY, 1995—98; supr. Bus. and Legal Reports, Old Saybrook, Conn., 1998—2001; bus. owner Video Movietime, Westbrook, Conn., 2003—. Cons. Ms. Found. for Women, N.Y.C., NY, 1998. Author: (play) Pack My Bags.I'm Goin' to Heaven. Activist Act Up, N.Y.C., NY, 1982—92. Recipient IBM Means Svc., IBM Corp., 1988. Mem.: Women Make Movies.

GUZMAN, KATHLEEN MCFADDEN, antiques appraiser, auctioneer; b. N.Y.C., Dec. 31, 1955; d. Walter Michael and Mary Ann (Plummer) McFadden; m. Wilfredo Guzman, Sept. 3, 1977; 1 child, Caitlin. A degree, Finch Coll., 1975; BA, Manhattanville Coll., 1977; MA in Art History, Queens Coll., 1979; exec. program (hon.), Columbia U., 1989. Auctioneer Plaza Art Galleries, N.Y.C., 1979-80; dir. Art Deco Christie's, N.Y.C., 1981-84, mgr., 1984-90; pres. Christie's East, N.Y.C., 1990—2000; ind. appraiser, 2000—. Lectr. in field; regular featured appraiser PBS' Antiques Roadshow. Bd. mem. Heaven on Earth, Dixon Pl.; auctioneer Make-a-Wish, Juvenile Diabetes, Am. Craft Mus. Avocation: restoring old homes. Office: 200 E End Ave New York NY 10128

GUZMAN, MARTHA PATRICIA, science educator; b. Mexicali, Mexico, Apr. 24, 1978; arrived in U.S., 1989; d. Jose Alfredo and Andrea Concepcion Guzman. BA, Columbia Union Coll., 2002, BS in Phys. Edn., 2003. Spanish tchr. John Nevins Andrews Sch., Takoma Park, Md., 2001—03, Sligo Adventist Sch., Takoma Park, 2001—03; sci. tchr. YSA Montgomery Coll., Takoma Park, 2003—04, Spencerville Adventist Acad., Silver Spring, Md., 2003—. Mem. acad. evaluation team Columbia (Md.) Union Office of Edn., 2006. Mem.: NSTA. Seventh-Day Adventist. Office: Spencerville Adventist Acad 15930 Good Hope Rd Silver Spring MD 20905

GUZY, CAROL, photojournalist; b. Bethleham, PA, Mar. 7, 1956; ADN, Northampton County Area C.C., Pa., 1978; AAS in Photography, Art Inst. Ft. Lauderdale, 1980. Staff photographer The Miami Herald, 1980-88, The Washington Post, 1988—. Named Newspaper Photographer of Yr., Nat. Press Photographer Assn., 1989, 1992, 1996, Photographer of Yr., White House News Photographers Assn., 1991, 1993, 1994, 1995, 1996, 1997, 1997, 1998, 2000; recipient Best Portfolio Award, Atlanta Seminar Photojournalism, 1982, 1985, 1990, Robert F. Kennedy award, 1984, Excellence Citation, Overseas Press Club, 1986, Leica Excellence medal, 1994, Pulitzer Prize in spot news photography, 1986, 1995, Pulitzer Prize in feature photography, 2000. Office: The Washington Post 1150 15th St NW Washington DC 20071-0002 Office Phone: 202-334-6000.

GUZZO, JESSICA ANN, music educator; b. Pittsfield, Mass., Sept. 10, 1979; d. Joseph Olin and Donna Linda Guzzo. BS in Music Edn., Coll. St. Rose, Albany, 2001. Music dir. Lisbon Ctrl. Sch., 2001—03, Springfield Ctr. Sch., Springfield, 2004—05; performing arts tchr. BArt Charter Sch, Adams, Mass., 2005—06, dir. musicals and plays, 2001—06; music dir., vocal Pittsfield Pub. Sch., 2006—. Condr. Seaway Valley Sr. High Chorus, Ogdensburg, NY, 2003. Carol choir dir. First United Meth. Ch., 2004—. Recipient Employee of Month, Lisbon Sch., 2002. Mem.: Shakespeare and Co., Berkshire Boch Soc., Town Players Pittsfield. Office: Taconic High Sch 96 Valentine Rd Pittsfield MA 01201 Office Phone: 413-448-9634. Business E-mail: jguzzo@pittsfield.net.

GUDMUNDSDÓTTIR, BJÖRK **See BJÖRK**

GWALLA-OGISI, NOMSA, education educator; arrived in U.S., 1972; d. Johannes Peter and Clarice Thoko Gwalla; 1 child. BA, U. Zululand, Empangeri, South Africa; MSEd, So. Ill. U., 1975, PhD, 1980. Divsn chair devel. of spl. edn. U. Zululand, South Africa, chair and sch. guidance dept.; asst. prof. Missouri Valley Coll., Marshall, Mo., Ind. State U., Terre Haute, 1987—88; assoc. prof. U. Wis., Whitewater, 1988—. Cons. numerous sch. dists. in Wis., Ill. and Ind. Contbr. chapters to books, articles to numerous profl. jours., scientific papers to confs. and jour. Fund raiser YMCA, 1979. Mem.: Internat. Assn. for Spl. Edn. (past pres.), Coun. for Exceptional Children Internat., Coun. for Children with Behavior Disorders, Phi Delta Kappa. Avocations: tennis, racquetball, flower arranging, gardening, travel. Office Phone: 262-472-5807. E-mail: gwallan@unw.edu.

GWILLIM, ALLISON LEE, conductor, music educator, department chairman; b. Binghampton, NY, July 7, 1972; d. Fred John and Donna Jean Murray. B in Music Edn., Marywood U., Scranton, Pa., 1995; M in Ednl. Leadership with Prin. Certification, Wilkes U., Wilkes Barre, Pa., 2004. Cert. instrnl. II Pa., 2006. Daycare dir. United Neighborhood Centers, Scranton, 1996—98; elem. gen. music and 4th grade strings Abington Heights Sch. Dist., Clarks Summit, Pa., 1998—2000, chairperson of the music dept., 2004—; orch. dir. Abington Heights H.S., Clarks Summit, 2000—. Mem. Marywood Campus Choir, Scranton, 2006—. Mem.: PSEA, NEA (mem.), Music Educators Nat. Conf., Pa. Music Educators Assn. Office: Abington Heights School District 222 Noble Rd Clarks Summit PA 18411 Office Phone: 570-585-5325.

GWINN, HELEN H., artist, educator; b. Sanco, Tex., Feb. 2, 1940; d. Herman H. Carwile and Verna A. Thomason; m. Allen C. Gwinn, Aug. 24, 1963; children: Jenifer Kristen, Allen IV. Student, Tex. Christian U., 1959, student, 1960; BA, Tex. Tech. U., 1962; postgrad., U. Tex., El Paso, 1976—78. Cert. secondary sch. tchr. Tex. Secondary tchr. Houston Ind. Sch. Dist., 1963—68; presch. tchr. Escuela de Valle, El Paso, 1973—76; pvt. art instr. Puzzletree Fine Art Studio, Carlsbad, N.Mex., 1980—98. Workshop presenter in field; juror, judge art exhbns. Midland (Tex.) Fine Arts, 1999, N.Mex. Arts and Crafts, Albuquerque, 2000, Masterworks of N.Mex., Albuquerque, 2001. Contbr. articles to mags.; exhibitions include Loggia di Pallazzo Gazzoli, Terni, Italy, Nat. Acad. Design, N.Y.C., Nat. Watercolor Okla., Omniplex, Internat. Soc. Exptl. Artists, Muncie, Ind., Fine Art Mus., N.Mex., First Frontier Coll. Soc., Austin, Tex., Trail Painted Ponies, Santa Fe, Watercolor Art Soc. Houston, Mill Atelier Gallery, Weems Artfest, Western Fedn. Watercolor Socs., SoQ Exhibit, N. Mex. Mus. Fine Art, 2004, Florence Biennale, Italy, 2005, Gov.'s Gallery, Santa Fe, 2006. Mus. sch. art tchr. City Spirit, Carlsbad, 1978—82; pres. Carlsbad Area Art Assn., 1980—82. Mem.: Western Fedn. Watercolor Socs. (signature), The Pecos River Artists (exhibiting artist 1991—), West Tex. Watercolor Soc., Kans. Watercolor Soc. (signature), N.Mex. Watercolor Soc. (signature). Methodist. Avocations: stitchery, reading, writing, walking, swimming. Home: 608 W Riverside Dr Carlsbad NM 88220 Studio: The Puzzletree Fine Arts Studio 608 W Riverside Dr Carlsbad NM 88220 E-mail: hgwinn@zianet.com.

GWINN, MARY ANN, newspaper reporter; b. Forrest City, Ark., Dec. 29, 1951; d. Lawrence Baird and Frances Evelyn (Jones) Gwinn; m. Richard A. King, June 3, 1973 (div. Jan. 1981); m. Stephen E. Dunnington, June 10, 1990. BA in Psychology, Hendrix Coll., 1973; MEd in Spl. Edn., Ga. State U., 1975; MA in Journalism, U. Mo., 1979. Tchrs. aide DeKalb County Schs., Decatur, Ga., 1973—74, tchr., 1975—78; reporter Columbia (Mo.) Daily Tribune, 1979—83, Seattle Times, 1983—, internat. trade and workplace reporter, 1992—96, asst. city editor, 1996—98, book editor, 1998—. Instr. ext. divsn. U. Wash., Seattle, 1990; instr. journalism Seattle U., 1994. Recipient Edn. Reporting award, Charles Stewart Mott Found., 1980, Enterprising reporting award, C.B. Blethen Family, 1989, Pulitzer Prize for Nat. Reporting, 1990. Mem.: Newspaper Guild. Avocations: writing, gardening, reading, camping. Office: Seattle Times PO Box 70 Seattle WA 98111-0070

GWOZDZ, KIM ELIZABETH, interior designer, furniture designer; b. Spokane, Wash., June 10, 1958; d. Myron Marcus and Marilyn Kay (Alsterlund) Westerkamp; children: Ryan Marcus, Lauren Taylor. Student, U. Florence, Italy, 1979; BFA in Graphic Design, Illustration and Art History, U. Ariz., 1980. Interior designer Pat Bacon & Assocs., 1983-88; prin, interior designer Kim E. Gwozdz/Provenance, Phoenix, 1988—. Prin., designer Marcus Taylor Furniture. Contbr. articles to profl. jours. Mem. Mt. Cavalry Luth. Ch., Phoenix, 1981-96, trustee, 1993-96; mem. Christ Luth. Ch., Phoenix, 1996-2002; Jr. League of Phoenix, 1989—, HIV/AIDS com., 1994-2000; mem. Orpheum Theater com., 1989-94, vice chmn., 1990-91, chmn., 1992-2002, Gift Mart com. Design Decorations, 1991-92, chmn., 1991, exec. com. Orpheum Theatre Found., 1989-91, bd. dirs., 1992—; active annual gala com. Am. Cancer Soc., 1993-94, 94-95, 95-96, 97-98, 98—, March of Dimes Gourmet Gala, 1991, 93, 95, 97; design affiliate Nat. Trust for Hist. Preservation, 1986—. Recipient 1st place award Ann. Wool Rug Design Competition, Edward Fields, Inc., 1989, 2d place award, 1990, 3d place award, 1991; Internat. Illumination design awards, 1998, Cutler award, 1998, Lumen award, 1998. Mem. Am. Soc. Interior Designers (assoc. Ariz. North chpt., significant interiors survery com. 1975-91, chmn. 1990-91, Phoenix Home and Garden com. 1989-90, Herberger Theatre com. 1989-91, awards com. 1989, 91, chmn. 1990, competitions com. 1991, 96, chmn. 1989-90, Rosson House Christmas chmn. 1986-91, hist. preservation chmn. 1988-91, directory chmn. Designers Market 1991, project designer, 1996, 97, mem. nominating com. 1991-92, 98, mktg. com. 1995, 3d place award Ariz. North 1987, 96, 2d place award 1987, 88, 92, 95, 1st place award Nat. 1989, 94, 95, 97). Republican. Lutheran. Avocations: art, gardening, cooking. Home: 4820 E Merrell St Phoenix AZ 85018 Office: 2415 E Camelback Rd Ste 700 Phoenix AZ 85016-4245 Office Phone: 602-912-8552.

GYENIZSE, DEBBIE LINDA, communications educator; b. Passaic, N.J., Mar. 29, 1944; d. Chaim and Bessie Furman; life ptnr. George Morejon; children: Lisa Ann Lacourse, Karen Amy Betsy, Charles Louis, Alexander Karl. AA, Miami-Dade Coll., Fla., 1998; BA in English, Fla. Internat. U., Miami, 2000, MA, 2004. Instr. freshman composition Fla. Internat. U., 2001—, Miami-Dade Coll. Kendall, 2005—. Recipient Excellence in Tchg. award, Acad. for the Art of Tchg., Fla. Internat. U., 2002, Adj. Excellence in Tchg. award, 2005. Mem.: Grad. English Assn. (founding mem. 2002—04), Fla. Internat. Alumni Assn., Phi Theta Kappa, Golden Key Honor Soc. (life), Sigma Tau Delta (life; sr. mem. 1998—2000). Democrat. Jewish. Avocation: travel. Home: 7415 SW 23 St Miami FL 33155-1416 Office: Fla Internat Univ University Park Blvd Miami FL 33199 Office Phone: 305-348-2874. Office Fax: 305-348-3878. Business E-Mail: gyenizse@fiu.edu.

GYER, JANE E., artist, educator; b. San Francisco, June 13, 1925; d. Raymond Bruce Linganfield and Amy Elizabeth Dunaway; m. Basil Eugene Judd, May 1949 (div. 1970); children: Kenneth Eugene Judd, Robin Judd Rodrigues; m. Jack Gyer, Oct. 24, 1971. Artist in residence, Yosemite Nat. Park, 1981, 93, Rocky Mt. Nat. Park, 1985; BA, Emerson Inst., 1997, MS, 1999. Art editor Sierra Star, Oakhurst, Calif., 1957-69; freelance artist The Jays, Oakhurst, 1969—; art tchr. Vision Acad. Arts, Oakhurst, 1989—; art instr. Emerson Inst., Oakhurst, 1997—. Bd. dirs. Timeberline Gallery, Oakhurst; lectr. in field. Executed numerous murals, 1975—; illustrator Discovering Sierra Trees, 1972 (NPS Director's award); exhibited in numerous shows, including Kings Art Ctr., Hanford, 2002; represented in pvt. and pub. collections. Bd. dirs. Vision Acad. of Arts, Oakhurst, 1995—. Avocation: singing. Home: 50137 Sunset Dr # C Coarsegold CA 93614-9709 Office: The Jays PO Box 456 Oakhurst CA 93644-0456

GYLLENHAAL, MAGGIE, actress; b. NYC, Nov. 16, 1977; d. Stephen Gyllenhaal and Naomi Foner; 1 child, Ramona. BA in English, Columbia U., 1999. Actor: (TV series) Shake Rattle and Roll: An American Love Story, 1999; (TV films) Shattered Mind, 1996, The Patron Saint of Liars, 1998, Resurrection, 1999, Strip Search, 2004; (films) Waterland, 1992, A Dangerous Woman, 1993, Homegrown, 1998, The Photographer, 2000, Cecil B. Demented, 2000, Pornographer: A Love Story, 2000, Donnie Darko, 2001, Riding in Cars with Boys, 2001, Secretary, 2002, 40 Days and 40 Nights, 2002, Adaptation, 2002, Confessions of a Dangerous Mind, 2002, Casa de los babys, 2003, Mona Lisa Smile, 2003, Criminal, 2004, Happy Endings, 2005, The Great New Wonderful, 2005, Trust the Man, 2005, Sherrybaby, 2006, Paris, je t'aime, 2006, World Trade Center, 2006, (voice) Monster House, 2006. Office: Creative Artists Agy 9830 Wilshire Blvd Beverly Hills CA 90212*

GYORKY, SUSAN MEINIG, medical/surgical nurse; b. Reading, Pa., June 11, 1947; d. Hans Richard and Elsie Marian (Miller) Meinig; m. Attila Istvan Gyorky, Aug. 22, 1970; 1 child, Robert Stephan. Student, East Stroudsburg State Coll., 1965-67; diploma, Reading Hosp. Sch. Nursing, 1970. RN, Pa.; CNOR; cert. laser safety officer Rockwell Inst. Evening charge nurse Monroe County Hosp., East Stroudsburg, Pa., 1970-71, Community Gen. Hosp., Reading, Pa., 1973-74; oper. rm. staff nurse Reading Hosp. and Med. Ctr., 1971-73, 74-77, head nurse oper. rm., 1977-88, head nurse laser surgery, 1986-89, asst. supr. ambulatory surgery, 1988-94, supr., head dept. ambulatory surgery, 1994—2006; ret., 2006. Presenter at profl. confs. Bd. dirs. Reading Hosp. and Med. Ctr. Fed. Credit Union, 1974-88; mem. CAP, Reading, 1990-91. Mem. Assn. Oper. Rm. Nurses (cert., pres. Tri-County chpt. 1983-87, bd. dirs. 1987-89, workshop chmn. 1987). Lutheran. Avocations: golf, creative writing, calligraphy, drawing, reading. Home: 7432 Brimway Ln Reading PA 19606-9727 Office: Reading Hosp and Med Ctr 6th and Spruce Sts West Reading PA 19612

HAACK, ALLISON KAYE, music educator; b. Cedar Rapids, Iowa, Dec. 9, 1980; d. David Ellis and Marcia Ann Reid; m. Ryan Lee Haack, June 22, 2002. BA in Music Edn., Mount Mercy Coll.; student, U. Hawaii, 2005—. Elem. sch. music tchr. Marion Ind. Schs., Iowa, 2003—04, middle sch. music tchr., 2004—05, Lone Tree (Iowa) Sch., 2005—. Piano tchr. West Music Co., Coralville, Iowa, 2003—04; musician/mem. worship team Our Redeemer Ch., Iowa City, 2005. Active Rep. Party, Johnson County, Iowa, 2002—. Mem.: NEA, Music Educator's Nat. Conf., Am. Choral Dirs. Assn. Republican. Christian-Evangelical. Avocations: acting, singing, travel. Home: 3562 Vista Park Dr Iowa City IA 52245 Office: Lone Tree School 303 S Devoe St Lone Tree IA 52755 Personal E-mail: allie4him@hotmail.com.

HAAG, JENNIFER LYNN, music educator; b. Buffalo, N.Y., May 6, 1978; d. Walter E. and Linda S. Kempa; m. Paul M. Haag, Aug. 10, 2002. B of Music Edn., Baldwin-Wallace Coll., Berea, Ohio, 2000; MusM, SUNY, Fredonia, 2003. Orch. tchr. West Clermont Local Sch. Dist., Cin., 2000—01, Hamburg Cen. Sch. Dist., Hamburg, NY, 2001—. Violinist Orchard Park Symphony Orch., NY, 2001—. Mem.: Erie County Music Educators Assn. (chair jr. high south orch. 2004—06), Am. String Tchrs. Assn. Home: 4479 Richwood Dr Hamburg NY 14075 Office: Union Pleasant Elem Sch 150 Pleasant Ave Hamburg NY 14075

HAAGEN, ELAINE K., psychiatrist; b. Lancaster, Pa., Nov. 16, 1944; d. Conrad Hess and Marian Nelson Haagen; m. David L. Fisher, July 11, 1998; 1 child from previous marriage, Jed. BA, Oberlin Coll., Ohio, 1966; MD, Albert Einstein Coll. Medicine, Bronx, N.Y., 1970. Resident Albert Einstein Coll. Medicine, Bronx, 1973—75, fellow, 1975; med. dir. Assoc. Mentally Ill Children, Briarcliff, NY, 1975—. Dir. child nursery Clearview Day Treatment Met. Hosp., N.Y.C., 1975—77, dir. pediat. liason, 1975—77. E-mail: ekhmd@earthlink.net.

HAAHEIM, PATRICIA JANE DANDO, pastor, consultant; b. Abington, Pa., May 29, 1947; d. Eion Ephraim and Jean Barbara (Wilson) Dando; m. Robert James Thompson, July 11, 1981 (div. July 26, 1994); 1 child, Zachary Eion Dando-Thompson; m. Dale Robert Haaheim, Oct. 4, 1996. BA, U. Calif., Davis, 1969; tchg. credential, San Jose State U., 1970; MDiv, Bethel Theol. Sem., 1979; specialty in social change, Twin Cities Consortium of Sems., 1980. Tchg. credential Calif., Oreg. Tchr. McKenzie Elem. Sch., Blue River, Oreg., 1971—74; pvt. tchr., governess Selsdon Park Hotel, Sanderstead, England, 1974—75; pastor People's Congl. Ch., Bayport, Minn., 1981—84; missionary Nat. Assn. Congl. Christian Chs., Taiwan, 1985; founding pastor Promise Congl. Ch., Apple Valley, Minn., 1991—99; cons. revitalization pastor Nat. Assn. Congl. Christian Chs., Milw., 2000—. Adviser comty. edn Bldg. Youth Assets Dist. # 196 Comty. Edn., Apple Valley, 1992—95; comty. leader drug abuse prevention Searsport (Maine) Schs. and Comty., 1986—89; mem. adv. bd. Family Shelter Ministry S.O.M.E., Santa Rosa, Calif., 1989—91; co-founder Family Violence Network. Author: (booklet/Bible study guide) Saying Yes to God, 1987; contbr. articles to profl. jours. Recipient Founders award for prevention of family violence, Family Violence Network, 2001, Comty. Svc. award, Comty. Edn. Dist. # 196, 1995, Project award alcohol and drug prevention, Comty. Edn., 1988. Mem.: Internat. Congregation Fellowship (vice-chair youth commn. 2002—04), Minn. Fellowship Congregationalists (vice-chair 2002—03, chair 2003—04), Nat. Assn. Congl. Christian Chs. (mem. exec. com. 1999—2003). Congregationalist. Avocations: reading, travel, community work. Home: 13302 Ellice Ct Apple Valley MN 55124-8118 E-mail: revpatti@yahoo.com.

HAAKE, DOROTHY MAY, secondary school educator; b. Champaign, Ill., Mar. 31, 1963; d. Forrest Tom Neilson and Nancy Victoria Cooper; m. Henry Charles Haake, June 12, 1998. BE with honors, U. Ill., Champaign, 1981—86; MA in Ednl. Adminstrn., No. Ill. U., DeKalb, 1991—93. Cert. athletic trainer Nat. Athletic Trainer's Assn. Head athletic trainer Conant HS, Hoffman Estates, Ill., 1986—87, health & phys. edn. tchr., 1987—88, Shaumburg HS, Ill., 1988—89; health & phys. edn. tchr., driver's edn. tchr. Glenbard W. HS, Glen Ellyn, Ill., 1989—. Head girls gymnastics coach

Glenbard W. HS, 1989—99, asst. athletic dir., 1993—; gymnastics judge Ill. HS Assn., 1999—2002. Mem. U. Ill. Women's Gymnastics Team, 1981—83. Mem.: Nat. Athletic Trainer's Assn. (athletic trainer 1986—). Avocations: running, golf.

HAAS, BEVERLY JEAN, secondary school educator, coach; b. Janesville, Wis., June 15, 1950; d. Marie Elizabeth Elliott. BS of Edn. in Biology & General Sci., U. Wis., Whitewater, 1973, MS in Tchg., 1992. Tchr., coach volleyball Turner HS, Beloit, Wis., 1973—97, tchr., coach softball, 1988—91. Named Volleyball Coach of the Yr., Rock Valley Conf., 1996. Mem.: Wis. Soc. Sci. Office Phone: 608-364-6370.

HAAS, CAROLYN BUHAI, elementary school educator, publisher, writer, consultant; b. Chgo., Jan. 1, 1926; d. Michael and Tillie (Weiss) Buhai; m. Robert Green Haas, June 29, 1947 (dec. June 30, 1984); children: Andrew Robert, Mari Beth, Thomas Michael, Betsy Ann, Karen Sue. BEd, Smith Coll., Northampton, Mass., 1947; postgrad., Nat. Coll. Edn., Evanston, Ill., 1956-59, Art Inst. Chgo., 1958-59. Tchr. Francis W. Parker Sch., Chgo., 1947-49; tchr. art Glencoe (Ill.) Pub. Schs., 1967-68, substitute tchr., 1964-72. Co-founder PAR Leadership Tng. Found., Northfield, Ill., 1969-81; pres., editor CBH Pub., Inc., Northfield, 1979-92; cons., writer, adv. bd. The Learning Line; cons. presch. sci. program Mus. Sci. and Industry, Chgo.; adv. bd. My Own Mag.; cons. in field. Author: (with Ann Cole and Betty Weinberger) I Saw a Purple Cow, 1972, A Pumpkin In A Pear Tree, 1974, Children Are Children Are Children, 1976, Backyard Vacation, 1978, Purple Cow to the Rescue, 1982, Recipes for Fun and Learning, 1982, Recetas Para Divertirse, 1997; (with A.C. Friedman) My Own Fun, 1990, The Big Book for Recipes for Fun, 1979, Look at Me: Activities for Babies and Toddlers, 1985; co-editor: Know Your Town/East Hampton League Women Voters of the Hamptons, 1993; contbr. articles to profl. jours. Pres. West Sch. PTA, Glencoe, Jr. Bd. Scholarship and Guidance, Chgo.; bd. dirs. Family Counseling Svc. of Glencoe, Glencoe Human Rels. Com.; pres., sec, bd. dirs. Glencoe Pub. Libr.; pres. Friends of Glencoe Pub. Libr.; co-founder Glencoe Patriotic Days Com.; co-chair Frank Lloyd Wright Bridge Com., Glencoe; pres., bd. dirs. Chgo. League Smith Coll.; mem. women's bd. Northwestern U.; bd. dirs. Chgo. chpt. Am. Jewish Com.; mem. women's com. Chgo. Symphony Orch. Clubs; bd. dirs. Art Resources in Tchg.; vol. Parish Art Mus., The Retreat; vol. Children's Mus. of Santa Fe. Mem. AAUW, LWV (bd. dirs.), Internat. Reading Assn., Soc. Children's Bookwriters, Children's Reading Roundtable, Nat. Assn. Edn. Young Children, Assn. Childhood Edn. Internat., NEA, Artists Alliance of East Hampton (bd. dirs.), Ladies Village Improvement Soc. (bd. dirs.). Democrat. Jewish. Avocations: art, reading, sports, travel. E-mail: cbhpub@aol.com.

HAAS, EILEEN MARIE, homecare advocate; b. Pitts., Feb. 27, 1948; d. Michael Joseph and Bridget Agnes (Connolly) McNulty; m. Jerry Albert Haas, July 19, 1975; 1 child, Melissa. Student, York Coll. of Pa., 1975-78, Messiah Coll., Grantsville, Pa., 1978-80. Clk. Exch. Bur. Pitts., 1966-67; debt. collector Nat. Account Sys., Pitts., 1967-71; preadoptive advocate Hershey, Pa., 1983-84, Phila., 1984-85; homecare advocate Dillsburg, Pa., 1985-88, Deer Lodge, Mont., 1988-92, Gibsonia, Pa., 1992—. Interpreter svcs. St. Victors Ch., Bairdsford, Pa., 1992—; presenter Harrisburg (Pa.) Area C.C., 1985, Pa. Soc. Respiratory Therapy, Ctrl. Pa. chpt., 1985; co-presenter Coun. Exceptional Children, Salt Lake City, 1997; rschr. in pulmonary rehab. With USN, 1971-74. Mem. DAV, Am. Soc. Deaf Children, Coun. Exceptional Children, Assn. Severe Handicaps, Profl. Networking for Excellence in Svc. to Deaf and Hard of Hearing. Republican. Roman Catholic. Avocations: deaf education research, dysphagia research, writing, needlepoint, knitting. Home: 90 Kaufman Rd Gibsonia PA 15044-7950

HAAS, GRETCHEN, literature and language professor; PhD, U. Minn., Twin Cities, 2006. Project mgr., bus. analyst U.Minn., Mpls., 1999—2005; asst. prof. Minn. State U., Mankato, 2005—. Grantee, Minn. State U., 2005—06. Mem.: Nat. Comm. Assn., Assn. Tchrs. of Tech. Writing, Rhetoric Soc. Am., Soc. Tech. Comm. Office: Minn State Univ Mankato 230 Armstrong Hall Mankato MN 56001 Office Phone: 507-389-5506.

HAAS, INGRID ELIZABETH, physician; b. Portland, Oreg., June 5, 1953; d. Fred F. and Anastasia Haas; children: Kristen, Lauren. BS, Oreg. State U., 1975; MD, U. Oreg., 1978. Diplomate Am. Bd. Ob.-Gyn. Physician CIGNA Healthplan, Phoenix, 1982-84, chief of staff, 1984-85; pvt. practice Scottsdale, Ariz., 1985—. Chmn. ob.-gyn. dept. Scottsdale Meml. Hosp. North, 1987-88, chief of surgery, 1988-89, chmn. laser com., 1990—; adv. bd. Scottsdale Meml. Office Community Health Edn., 1990—, chmn. perinatal subcom. 1992; proctor Mentor Corp. for Advanced Pelvic Surgery; spkr. in field; cons. in field. Trustee SMH Found.; physician mem. Ariz. Med. Bd. 2002-05, med. cons. 2005—; mem. aux. bd. Desert Found; chmn. Honor Ball. Recipient Best Doctors in Am., 2004, Best Drs. in Am., 2005—06, Ind. Best Drs., 2005—06, Scottsdale 101 Best Dr. of Yr., Best Drs., Phoenix mag., 2005, 2006. Mem. Am. Coll. Ob-Gyn., Am. Assn. Gynecologic Laparascopists, Ariz. Med. Assn., Maricopa County Med. Soc., Am. Fertility Soc. Independent. Lutheran. Avocation: skiing. Office: 10617 N Hayden Rd Ste 102 Scottsdale AZ 85260-5577 Office Phone: 480-483-9011. Personal E-mail: heydoc2025@aol.com.

HAAS, JUDITH, elementary school educator; b. New Rockford, N.D., Jan. 27, 1949; d. Norman E. Braaten and Audrey Nuella O'Hare; m. Duane Darryl Haas, Oct. 7, 1988. BS in Elem. Edn., Mayville (N.D.) State U., 1971. Cert. tchr., N.D. 6th and 3d grade tchr. Minnewaukan (N.D.) Pub. Sch., 1971-76; 5th grade tchr. St. John (N.D.) Pub. Sch., 1976-87; 6th grade tchr. Little Flower Sch., Rugby, N.D., 1987-88. Pres. N.D. Tchr.'s Assn., 1985-87; vol. tchr. religious edn., Minnewaukan, 1974-76, St. John, 1980-82, Dunseith, N.D., 1995-99; leader Girl Scouts U.S.A., Minnewaukan, 1974-76 Republican. Roman Catholic. Avocations: reading, painting, drawing. Home: HC 2 Box 15A Saint John ND 58369-9712

HAAS, MARLENE RINGOLD, special education educator; b. Pitts., June 14, 1950; d. Rita Weisbrode and Irwin Mark Ringold; children: Melissa Beth, Ilyssa Meg, Seth Ringold. B in K-8 Elem. Edn. and K-12 Spl. Edn., Case Western Res. U., 1972; M in Spl. Edn., Duquesne U., 1975. Cert. spl. edn. K-12 Pa. Spl. edn. tchr. Pitts. Pub. Schs., 1972—. Home: 4244 Saline St Pittsburgh PA 15217 Office: Reizenstein Mid Sch 129 Denniston Ave Pittsburgh PA 15206

HAAS, SHEILA JEAN, secondary school educator; b. Rock Island, Ill., Sept. 26, 1947; d. Marcel Henry and Ida Germaine Vroman, Catherine Honora Vroman (Stepmother); m. David Joseph Haas, May 10, 1996; children: Laura, Joshua, Elena. BA, Bradley U., Peoria, Ill., 1971; MA, North Cen. Coll., 1998; postgrad., No. Ill., DeKalb, 2000. Cert. tchr., adminstr. Ill. English aide North Jr. High, Crystal Lake, Ill., 1987—88; substitute tchr. Sch. Dist. 155, Crystal Lake, 1989—90; social sci. tchr. South HS, Crystal Lake, 1990, Cen. HS, Crystal Lake, 1991—96, Prairie Ridge HS, Crystal Lake, 1997—, social sci. dept. chair, 2000—. Curriculum facilitation staff Sch. Dist. 155, Crystal Lake, 2002—, AP adv. com., 2004—06. Active Dem. Party, Lake Zurich, Ill., 2004—06. Mem.: NEA, Ill. Coun. for Social Sci., Nat. Coun. for Social Sci. Democrat. Jewish. Avocations: travel, cooking, classical music, art, reading. Home: 206 Parkview Dr Wauconda IL 60084 Office: Prairie Ridge High Sch 6000 Dvorak Dr Crystal Lake IL 60012

HAAS, SUZANNE ALBERTA, elementary school educator, secondary school educator; b. Perrysburg, Ohio, Nov. 29, 1934; d. Albert Joseph and Mary Elizabeth (Gurtzweiler) Haas; m. Robert Chester Kemp (dec.). BA, Xavier U., 1961; MS, Eastern Mich. U., 1975; attended, Mary Manse Coll., 1956—64, Toledo U., 1963, George Peabody U., 1964—65, St. Louis U., 1967, Bemidui U., 1979. With Religious Sisters of Mercy, Cin., 1952—68; tchr. St. Catherine Cath. Sch., Toledo, 1956—57, 1961—62, St. Peter Cath. Sch., Upper Sandusky, Ohio, 1957—58, St. Anne Cath. Sch., Fremont, Ohio, 1958—59, St. Rita Cath. Sch., Cin., 1959—61, St. Vincent de Paul Sch., Toledo, 1962—63, St. Mary Cath. Sch., Vermilion, Ohio, 1963—64, St. Polycarp Cath. Sch., Pleasure Ridge, Ky., 1964—65, Mother of Mercy Acad., Louisville, 1965—66, Mercy HS, Louisville, 1966—68, Rosarian Acad., W. Palm Beach, Fla., 1968—69, Howell Watkins Jr., Sr. High, Palm Beach Gardens, Fla., 1969—71, Brighton Jr. High, Brighton, Mich., 1972—76, St. Mary Mission Sch., Red Lake, Minn., 1977—82, Groveland NY State Prison, Attica, NY, 1989—92, Attica NY State Prison, Attica, 1993—95, Wyo. NY State Prison, Attica, 1995—. Sunday sch. tchr. Parochial Sch., Fort Knox Mil. Base, Fort Knox, Ky., 1966, St. John Fischer, W. Palm Beach, 1969. Author (poetry): Treasured Poems of America, 1993—2004, Poetic Voices of America, 1993—2004, Irish Wolfhound Quarterly, 2005. Recipient Honorary Boy Scout award, Boy Scouts of Am., 1999; grantee, NSF, 1964—65. Mem.: Employee Assistance Program, State Employee Fund Assn., Profl. Educator Fedn. Republican. Roman Catholic. Avocations: showing Irish Wolfhounds, birdwatching, writing, gardening, butterfly watching.

HAAS, TERRI LEIGH, music educator; b. Amityville, NY, Apr. 14, 1954; d. Robert and Connie Haas (Stepmother), Joyce Ryan; m. George Gelish, July 30, 1983; 1 child, Stephanie Gelish. BS in Music Edn., CUNY Hunter Coll., NYC, 1984; MA in Tchr. Edn. Program, CUNY Hunter Coll., 1991. Orff Certification Level I Hofstra U., NY, 1989, Orff Certification Level II Hofstra U., NY, 1990, Gordon Learning Theory Level I Hartt Coll. Conn., 1998. Music tchr. NYC Bd. of Edn., 1984—87; choir dir. St. Luke Luth. Ch., Dix Hills, NY, 1990—2000; music tchr. Portledge Sch., Brookville, NY, 1991—93, NYC Bd. of Edn., 1993—94, South Huntington UFSD, Huntington Sta., NY, 1993—. Guest lectr. C.W. Post U., Greenvale, NY, 2004—; guest condr. Suffolk County Music Educators Music Festival, NY, 2005; profl. vocalist Various, 1974—. Mem. Huntington Choral Soc., NY, 1989. Recipient Anders Emile Choir award, CUNY Hunter Coll., 1984, 1984; scholar Charlotte Newcombe Found. scholarship, 1982; Alice Minnie Hertzinger scholarship, 1984, Leubsdorf scholarship. Mem.: ACDA, Music Educators Nat. Conf., SCMEA. Avocations: travel, creative arts, gardening, music. Office: South Huntington UFSD Weston St Huntington Station NY 11746 Office Phone: 631-425-5432. E-mail: thaas@shufsd.org.

HAASE, LAUREN, mathematics educator; d. Raymond and Barbara Mottola; m. Thomas Haase, May 23, 2003. MS, Molloy Coll., Rockville Centre, N.Y., 2003. Tchr. math. Herricks H.S., New Hyde Park, NY, 1998—. Office: Herricks HS 100 Shelter Rock Road New Hyde Park NY 11040 Office Phone: 516-248-3140. Business E-Mail: lhaase@herricks.org.

HAASER, PAULA MARLENE, language educator; b. Garden Grove, Calif., Apr. 17, 1959; d. Paul Clinton Becker and Georgia Marlene Schaefer; m. Barry Alan Haaser, Sept. 21, 1885; children: Mitchell Alan, Alexandra Catherine. BA in English, San Jose State U., Calif, 1989; MA in Edn., San Jose State U., Calif., 2006. Preliminary adminstrn. credential Calif. State Credentialing, 2006. Tchr. English Andrew P. Hill, San Jose, Calif., 1998, Live Oak H.S., Morgan Hill, Calif., 1999—. Mid. sch. tchr. Windmill Springs Sch., San Jose. Advisor Live Oak H.S. Patriot Club. Recipient Dorothy Wright English award, San Jose State U., 2004, 2005. R-Consevative. Protestant. Avocations: travel, reading, swimming. Home: 17431 Lakeview Dr Morgan Hill CA 95037 Office: Live Oak HS 1505 E Main Av Morgan Hill CA 95037 Office Phone: 408-210-6100 2122. Personal E-mail: phaaser@verizon.net. Business E-Mail: phaaser@liveoak.mhu.k12.ca.us.

HABACHY, SUZAN SALWA SABA, economist, not-for-profit developer; b. Cairo, July 15, 1933; came to the U.S., 1952; d. Saba and Gameela (Gindy) H. BA, Bryn Mawr (Pa.) Coll., 1954; MA, Harvard U., Cambridge, Mass., 1956. Teaching fellow Ohio U., Athens, 1957-58; economist Mobil Oil Co., N.Y.C., 1959-64; reporter, editor Petroleum Intelligence Weekly, N.Y.C., 1964-65, McGraw Hill News Bur., London, England, 1965-68; program officer UN, N.Y.C., 1969-75, section chief, 1975-88; focal point for women UN Office of Pers., N.Y.C., 1988-93; exec. dir. The Trickle Up Program, N.Y.C., 1994-2001. Avocations: theater, travel, reading. Home: 1056 5th Ave New York NY 10028-0112

HABBERSTAD, AMY RENAE, secondary school educator; b. Gooding, Idaho, May 27, 1975; d. Edwin Lee and Cheryl Leslie Stevens; m. Scott Thomas Habberstad, Sept. 26, 1998; 1 child, Catheryne Grace. BA in English Edn., Boise State U., 1998; EdM in Curriculum and Instrn., Reading Splty., U. Alaska, Anchorage, 2006. English/yearbook tchr. Ketchikan H.S.-KGBSD, Alaska, 1998—2001; English tchr. Anchorage Sch. Dist., 2001—. Republican. Avocations: art, travel, photography. Office: South Anchorage High School 13400 Elmore Rd Anchorage AK 99516 Office Phone: 907-742-6200. Personal E-mail: amy_habberstad@hotmail.com.

HABEL, WENDY JO, elementary school educator; b. Chgo., Apr. 30, 1953; d. Marjorie Katherine and Donald Henry Sieg (Stepfather); m. Gary Arthur Habel, July 20, 1974; children: Joshua Michael, Mathew Daniel. BS in Edn., We. Ill. U., Macomb, Ill., 1974; MS in Edn., No. Ill. U., DeKalb, Ill., 1992. Tchr. Maywood Sch. Dist. 89, Melrose Park, Ill., 1974—. Leader ednl. team Stevenson Sch. Jr. H.S., Melrose Park, Ill., 1992—, sponsor svc. club, 1986—, coord. students, 1986—96; chmn. various coms. Maywood Sch. Dist. Contbr. book revs. Active devel. and restoration of local prairie Westmont Pk. Dist., Westmont, Ill., 2000—02; chmn. fund raising United Way Maywood Sch. Dist., Maywood, Ill., 1995—96; bd. dirs. christian edn. Burr Ridge United Ch. Christ, Ill., 1992—2002. Mem.: Ill. Environ. Edn. Assn. Avocations: skiing, hiking, scuba diving. Office: Maywood School Dist 89 906 Walton Melrose Park IL 60160 Office Phone: 708-450-2053. Office Fax: 708-344-1356. Business E-Mail: whabel@maywood89.org.

HABER, CATHERINE S., medical/surgical nurse, nursing administrator; b. Chgo., Oct. 20, 1942; d. John D. and Emily (Markus) Faber; m. George F. Haber Jr., Nov. 21, 1959; children: Elizabeth Ann, Amy Lucille, Rachel Marie. AA, Wright Jr. Coll., Chgo., 1977; BSN, U. Ill., Chgo., 1980. Staff nurse Evanston (Ill.) Hosp., nurse clinician; mgr. clin. unit Edgewater Hosp., Chgo.; nurse mgr. MacNeal Hosp., Berwyn, Ill.; asst. dir. nursing Bethesda Home and Retirement Ctr., Chgo.; dir. nursing Whitehall Convalescent Home; dir. nursing svcs. St. Joseph Home Chgo., St. Joseph Village Chgo. Mem. Assembly on Nursing Practice Ill. Nurse's Assn., 2005. Recipient Nurse Mgr. Adminstr. award, Ill. Nurse's Assn., 2005. Mem. Orgn. Nurse Execs., Chgo. Nurses Assn. (past pres., bd. mem.), Sigma Theta Tau. Home: 2623 N New England Ave Chicago IL 60707-1732

HABER, SUSAN C., history professor; b. Miami; m. Tony Haber; children: Allison, Jonathan. MA in History, San Diego State U., 1971. History prof. Cuyamaca Coll., El Cajon, Calif., 1990—. Condr. workshops in field; lectr. in field. Vol. presenter various women's clubs and orgns., San Diego, 1985—2006. Named Tchr. of the Yr., Faculty of Cuyamaca Coll., 1996. Mem.: Colonial Williamsburg Found. (assoc.), Orgn. of Am. Historians (assoc.), San Diego Hist. Soc. (assoc.). Avocations: travel, reading, visiting museums. Office: Cuyamaca College 900 Rancho San Diego Pkwy El Cajon CA 92019 Office Phone: 619-660-4212. E-mail: susan.haber@gcccd.edu.

HABERL, VALERIE ELIZABETH, physical education educator, small business owner; b. N.Y.C., July 6, 1947; d. William Anthony and Rose Mary (Hoholecek) H. BS, So. Conn. State U., 1969, postgrad., 1979. Cert. elem. tchr., Conn. Tchr. phys. edn. West Haven (Conn.) Bd. Edn., 1969—. Pres. Creative Studio, 1992—; inventory control specialist, 1997-2001. Mem. Conn. Assn. Health, Phys. Edn., Recreation and Dance. Republican. Roman Catholic. Office Phone: 203-934-8918. E-mail: vhaberl@comcast.net.

HABERMAN, LOUISE SHELLY, consulting company executive; b. N.Y.C. d. Harry Martin and Rebecca (Binstock) H.; m. Gordon Joel Schochet. BA, Cornell U., 1971; PhD, Princeton (N.J.) U., 1984. Mem. faculty numerous colls. and univs., 1975-84; researcher pub. policy U.S. Dept. Commerce, 1976; prin. investigator pub. policy study State of N.J., Trenton, 1979-80; pvt. practice cons. Highland Park, N.J., 1984-86; head regional bank svcs. Multinational Strategies, Inc., N.Y.C., 1986-90; pres. Haberman Assocs., Inc., Edison, N.J., 1990—. Author: (monograph) Regional Banks: International Strategies for the Future, 1987; editor: (with Paul Sacks) Ann. Rev. of Nations, 1988; contbr. articles to profl. jours. Issues advisor selected polit. candidates and civil liberties causes. Avocations: gardening, painting. Office: Haberman Assocs Inc 315 N 8th Ave Edison NJ 08817-2914

HABERMANN, HELEN MARGARET, botanist, educator; b. Bklyn., Sept. 13, 1927; AB, SUNY, Albany, 1949; MS, U. Conn., 1951; PhD, U. Minn., 1956. Asst. botanist U. Conn., Storrs, 1949-51; asst. U. Minn., Mpls., 1951-53, asst. plant physiologist, 1953-55, head residence counselor, 1955-56; rsch. assoc. U. Chgo., 1956-57; rsch. fellow Hopkins Marine Sta. Stanford (Calif.) U., 1957-58; from asst. prof. to prof. biol. scis. Goucher Coll., Towson, 1958—82, chmn. dept. biology, 1963-66, 68, 78-79, Lilian Welsh prof. biol. scis., 1982-92; prof. emeritus, 1992—. Co-author Biology: A Full Spectrum, 1973, Mainstreams of Biology, 1977. NIH spl. rsch. fellow Rsch. Inst. Advanced Study, Balt., 1966-67. Fellow AAAS; mem. Phytochem. Soc. N.Am. (sec. 1987-93), Am. Soc. Plant Physiologists, Am. Soc. Hort. Sci., Soc. Devel. Biology, Am. Soc. Photobiology, Am. Inst. Biol. Scis., Scandinavian Soc. Plant Physiology, Internat. Soc. Plant Molecular Biology, Japanese Soc. Plant Physiology, Soc. Exptl. Biology and Medicine, Am. Camellia Soc., Pioneer Camellia Soc. (pres. 1994-95, sec. 2000-01), Am. Hort. Soc., Sigma Xi. Personal E-mail: hhabermann@wans.net.

HABLUTZEL, NANCY ZIMMERMAN, lawyer, educator; b. Chgo., Mar. 16, 1940; d. Arnold Fred Zimmerman and Maxine Lewison (Zimmerman) Goodman; m. Philip Norman Hablutzel, July 1, 1980; children: Margo Lynn, Robert Paul. BS, Northwestern U., 1960; MA, Northeastern Ill. U., 1972; JD, Ill. Inst. Tech. chgo.-Kent Coll. Law, 1980; PhD, Loyola U., Chgo., 1983. Bar: Ill. 1980, U.S. Dist. Ct. (no. dist.) Ill. 1980, U.S. Supreme Ct. 1995; ordained deacon 4th Presbyn. Ch. Chgo., 2000. Speech therapist various pub. schs. and hosps., Chgo. and St. Louis, 1960—63, 1965—72; audiologist U. Chgo. Hosps., 1963—65; instr. spl. edn. Chgo. State U., 1972—76; asst. prof. Loyola U., Chgo., 1981—87; adj. prof. Ill. Inst. Tech. Chgo.-Kent Coll. Law, 1982—, Lewis U., 1990—92; lectr. Loyola U., Chgo., 1990—98; legal dir. Legal Clinic for Disabled, Chgo., 1984—85, exec. dir., 1985—87; of counsel Whitted & Spain P.C., 1987—89; prin. Hablutzel & Assocs., Chgo., 1989—94, 1997—. Hearing officer Cir. Ct. of Cook County, 1994—96, supervising hearing officer, 1995—97; faculty No. Ill. U., 1997—2003; advisor Ill. Dept. Children and Family Svcs., 1997—2003; hearing officer Ill. State Bd. Edn., 1999—2005; asst. prof. Coll. Edn. U. St. Francis, Joliet, Ill., 2003—05. Co-author (with B. McMahon): Americans with Disabilities Act: Access and Accomodations, 1992; contbg. editor: Nat. Disability Law Reporter, 1991—92. Mem. Ill. Gov.'s Com. on Handicapped, 1972—75; mem., faculty moderator student divsn. Coun. for Exceptional Children, 1982—87; mem. adv. com. for disabled Ill. Atty. Gen., 1985—; mem. adv. com. Scouting for People with Disabilities, Chgo. Area Boy Scouts Am., 1988—92. Grantee Loyola-Mellon Found. grantee, 1983. Fellow: Ill. Bar Found. (sec. fellows 1992, vice chair fellow 1993, chair 1994), Chgo. Bar Found. (life); mem.: ABA, Chgo. Hearing Soc. (bd. dirs. 1992—94, Marion Goldman award 1988), Chgo. Bar Assn. (corp. law com., exec. com. 1984—94, chmn. Divsn. IV 1988—91, sec. 1991—92, vice chair 1992—93, chair 1993—94), Ill. Bar Assn. (Inst. Pub. Affairs 1985—, assoc., standing com. on juvenile justice, sec. 1986—87, vice chmn. 1987—88, chmn. 1988—89, legis. com. 1991—, mem. juvenile justice sect. coun. 1994—, standing com. on leg. 1995—, com. on cable tv programs 1999—, com. lon legal edn., adminstrn. to bar and competency 2002—, edn. law sec. coun. 2005—), Nat. Coun. of Juvenile and Family Ct. Judges (permanency planning com., continuing jud. edn. com. 1994—99). Avocations: sailing, travel, cooking, swimming. Office: 19 S LaSalle St Ste 1300 Chicago IL 60603

HACH, PHILA RAWLINGS, small business owner, writer; b. Nashville, Tenn., June 13, 1926; d. Arthur Lee and Sophia Shadow Rawlings; m. Adolf K. Hach (dec.); 1 child, Joe K.; m. Sallie B. Hach; children: Joseph, Carter, Liza. BA, Peabody-Vanderbilt U., 1949.

HACKEL-SIMS, STELLA BLOOMBERG, lawyer, former government official; b. Burlington, Vt., Dec. 27, 1926; d. Hyman and Esther (Pocher) Bloomberg; m. Donald Herman Hackel, Aug. 14, 1949; children: Susan Jane, Cynthia Anne; m. Arthur Sims, Aug. 28, 1980. Student, U. Vt., 1943-45; JD cum laude, Boston U., 1948. Bar: Vt. 1948, Mass. 1948, D.C. 1979, Va. 1982. Individual practice law, Burlington, 1948-49, Rutland, Vt., 1949-59, 73—; city prosecutor City of Rutland, 1957-63; commr. Vt. Dept. Employment Security, 1963-73; treas. State of Vt., 1975-77; dir. U.S. Mint, Dept. Treasury, Washington, 1977-81. Chmn. Vt. Municipal Bond Bank, 1975-77 Mem. Vt. Adv. Com. on Mental Retardation, Interdept. Council on Aging, Commn. on Status Women, Human Resource Inter-Agency Com., Emergency Resource Priorities Bd., Info. Planning Council, Legis. Council Equal Opportunity Com., Vt. Indsl. Devel. Authority, Vt. Housing Fin. Agy., Vt. Claims Commn., Vt. Tchrs. Retirement Fund. Bd., Vt. Home Mortgage Guaranty Bd.; chmn. Vt. State Employees Retirement Fund; ex-officio mem. Nat. Manpower Adv. Com., 1971-72, Fed. Adv. Council on Unemployment Ins., 1971-72; Pres. Rutland Girl Scouts Leaders Assn., 1949-50, Rutland League Women Voters, 1951-52, Rutland Council Jewish Women, 1955-56; chmn. womens div. Rutland Community Chest Dr., 1952, Rutland County-Vt. Assn. for Blind, 1953-56; pres. Rutland County Democratic Women's Assn., 1956-63; treas. Rutland City Dem. Com., 1957-63; former rep. office women's activities Dem. Nat. Com., Regional Council I., Women's CD Councils; mem. Vt. bd. Girl Scouts USA; chmn. Arlington County Tenant-Landlord Commn., Va., 1986—; citizen police review bd. City of Naples, Fla., 2006-. Mem.: LWV, AAUW (pres. Rutland County br. 1961—62), Interstate Conf. Employment Security Agys. (v.p. region I 1966—68, legis. com. 1969, sr. v.p. 1970—71, pres. 1971—72), Am. Soc. Pub. Adminstrn., Vt. Coun. Social Agys., Bus. and Profl. Women's Club, Rutland County Bar Assn. (pres. 1973), Vt. Bar Assn., Emblem (dir. 1960-63), Woodmont Country; Internat. (Washington), Moorings Country Club (Naples, Fla.) (bd. dirs. 2003—), Emblem Club (dir. 1960—63), Delta Phi Epsilon. Personal E-mail: stellahs@earthlink.net.

HACKENAST, SHERRI, race track owner, former race car driver; b. Frankfort, Ill., Jan. 17, 1975; d. Frank and Michelle. Owner, promoter Kentucky Lake Speedway, Calvert City; promoter Kankakee Speedway, Ill.; CEO A-Reliable Auto Parts. Named one of 40 Under 40, Crain's Chgo. Bus., 2005. Avocations: camping, racing. Mailing: Sherri Hackenast Racing 2247 West 139th St Blue Island IL 60406 Office Phone: 708-641-9999. Office Fax: 708-824-9128. E-mail: raceteam99@aol.com, sherriheckenast@aol.com.*

HACKENBERG, BARBARA JEAN COLLAR, retired advertising and public relations executive; b. Venango County, Pa., Apr. 15, 1927; d. Guy Lamont and Marion Leona (Kingsley) Collar; m. George Richardson, June 13, 1953; children: Kurt Edward, Kim Ellen, Caroline Kingsley. BA, Grove City (Pa.) Coll., 1948; ML, U. Pitts., 1949. Advt. dir. The Halle Bros. Co., Erie, Pa., 1950-52, advt. and sales promotion dir. Pa. divsn., 1952-54; exec. dir. Wyomissing (Pa.) Inst. Fine Arts, 1970-74; dir. and cmty. liaison Freedman Gallery, Albright Coll., Reading, Pa., 1976-78; selling supr. Pomeroy's Children's Dept., Wyomissing, Pa., 1981-83; pub. rels. account exec. Wentworth Assocs., Lancaster, Pa., 1983-84; exec. dir. World Affairs Coun., Reading, 1987—97; owner The WRITE Place, Reading, 1979—. Vice pres. Harrisburg (Pa.) Foreign Policy Assn., 1964-67; various fund-raising activities, 1954-70; pub. rels.chmn. Erie World Affairs Ctr., 1957-60; mem. mil. affairs com. Berks County chpt. ARC, 1998—, mem. internat. com., 2003—; apptd. to Parks and Recreation Bd., Twp. of Cumru, 1998—; mem. internat. com. YMCA, Berks County, Pa., 1999—. Mem. Women in Communications, Inc. (pub. relations chmn. ctrl. Pa. chpt., 1984-87, sec. ctrl. Pa. chpt., 1986-87). Avocations: writing, theater, art, concerts, bicycling. Home and Office: 1334 Welsh Rd Reading PA 19607-9334 Office Phone: 610-775-3832.

HACKENSON, ELIZABETH, information technology executive, telecommunications industry executive; BS, NY State U. IT mgmt. positions EDS, Computech, TRW, Grumman and Sperry; with UUNET, Concert Communication, MCI Inc., Ashburn, Va., 1997—2006, exec. v.p., chief info. officer, 2004—06; chief info. officer Lucent Technolgies, Murray Hill, NJ, 2006—.

Bd. dir. Serena Software, Inc., San Mateo, Calif., 2006—. Named one of Top 200 female executives, Washington Post, 2004, Premier 100 IT Leaders, Computerworld, 2006. Office: Lucent Technolgies 600 Mountain Ave New Providence NJ 07974 Fax: 601-460-8269.*

HACKER, COLLEEN MARIE, physical education educator, consultant, dean; b. Lancaster, Pa. d. Garth and Kathryn Hacker. BS in Health, P.E. and Recreation, Lock Haven U., 1978; MS in Sport and Exercise Sci., U. Ariz., 1980; PhD in Human Movement Studies, 1992. Co-author: (book) Catch Them Being Good, 2002. Recipient Tchg. Excellence award, Pacific Lutheran U., President's medal, APA. Office: Pacific Lutheran U Olson Ave Tacoma WA 98447

HACKERMAN, ANN E., psychotherapist; d. Kenneth S. Hackerman and Carola L. Kisber-Hackerman. BA, Christian Bros. Coll., 1989; MS, Memphis State U., 1993. Lic. Bd. Profl. Counseling and Marriage and Family Therapists, Tenn., 1997, cert. Nat. Bd. Cert. Counselors, Inc., 1996, Commn. on Rehab. Counselor Cert., 1993, Nat. Bd. Cognitive Behavioral Therapists, 1995. Mental health counselor Parkwood Hosp., Olive Branch, Miss., 1993—96; intake coord., psychotherapist Meth. Family Counseling Ctr., Memphis, 1996—98; career counselor, psychotherapist Clovernook Ctr. for the Blind, Memphis, 1998—2000; adult clin. team supr., psychotherapist Comprehensive Counseling Network, Memphis, 2001—. Author: Street Gangs: An Inside Look: A Guide for Professionals and Others Concerned with the Epidemic Plaguing the United States; contbr. articles to profl. jours., chapters to books. Mem.: Tenn. Counselors Assn. (assoc.), Am. Counseling Assn. (assoc.). Business E-Mail: annh@ccnmemphis.org.

HACKETT, CAROL ANN HEDDEN, physician; b. Valdese, NC, Dec. 18, 1939; d. Thomas Barnett and Zada Loray (Pope) Hedden; m. John Peter Hackett, July 27, 1968; children: John Hedden, Elizabeth Bentley, Susanne Rochet. BA, Duke U., 1961; MD, U. N.C., 1966. Intern Georgetown U. Hosp., Washington, 1966—67, resident, 1967—69; clinic physician DePaul Hosp., Norfolk, Va., 1969—71; chief spl. health svcs. Arlington County Dept. Human Resources, Va., 1971—72; gen. med. officer USPHS Hosp., Balt., 1974—75; pvt. practice family medicine Seattle, 1975—. Mem. staff, chmn. dept. family practice Overlake Hosp. Med. Ctr., 1985-86; clin. asst. prof. Sch. Medicine U. Wash. Bd. dirs. Mercer Island (Wash.) Presch. Assn., 1977-78; coord. 13th and 20th Ann. Inter-profl. Women's Dinner, 1978, 86; trustee Northwest Chamber Orch., 1984-85. Fellow Am. Acad. Family Practice; mem. King County Acad. Family Practice (trustee 1993-96, pres.-elect 1997-98, pres. 1998-99), King County Med. Soc. (chmn. com. TV violence), Wash. Acad. Family Practice, Wash. State Med. Assn., DAR, Bellevue C. of C., N.W. Women Physicians (v.p. 1978), Seattle Symphony League, Eastside Women Physicians (founder, pres.), Seattle Yacht Club, Sigma Kappa. Episcopalian. Home: PO Box 3098 Bellevue WA 98009-3098 Office: 1380 112th NE Ste 100 Bellevue WA 98004 Office Phone: 425-454-8191. Home Fax: 425-462-5313.

HACKETT, KAREN L., medical association administrator; Exec. v.p., COO Am. Coll. Healthcare Execs., Chgo. Office: Am Coll Healthcare Execs One N Franklin St Ste 1700 Chicago IL 60606-3491

HACKETT, MARY J., lawyer; b. Pitts., Sept. 8, 1962; m. Arlie R. Nogay; children: Walter, Robert. BA in economics & politics, Mt. Holyoke Coll., 1984; JD with honors, U. Pitts., 1987. Bar: Pa. 1987, US. Dist. Ct. We. Dist. Pa., US Ct. Appeals 3rd Cir., US Ct. Appeals 4th Cir., US Ct. Appeals 6th Cir., US Ct. Appeals 8th Cir. Law clk. to. Judge Donald E. Ziegler US Dist. Ct. We. Dist. Pa., 1989—90; chief counsel-litig. PNC Fin. Services Group Inc., 1998—2001; assoc. Reed Smith LLP, Pitts., 1987—89, 1990—96, ptnr., 1996—98, 2001—, practice group leader fin. services litig. group, 2003—. Mem.: ABA, Allegheny County Bar Assn., Pa. Bar Assn. Office: Reed Smith LLP 435 Sixth Ave Pittsburgh PA 15219 Office Phone: 412-288-3250. Office Fax: 412-288-3063. Business E-Mail: mhackett@reedsmith.com.

HACKETT, MOLLY LYNN, small business owner, consultant; b. Lakewood, Ohio, Oct. 10, 1934; d. John Wilson and Marion Harriet (Shepard) Duffell; m. Benjamin Prescott Hackett, June 25, 1961 (div. 1981); children: Scott, Bruce. Student, Coll. of Wooster, 1952-55; BA, U. Mont., 1956, MA, 1957. Editor U. Chgo. Press, 1957-59; tchr. Stevensville (Mont.) Pub. High Sch., 1959-61; co-owner cattle ranch Sweathouse Creek Ranch, Victor, Mont., 1961-81; owner, operator The Frame Shop, Hamilton, Mont., 1981—. Editor: Montana Genesis, 1971; garden columnist Missoulian and Ravalli Republic, 1994—. Mem. Rural Conservation and Devel. Com., Hamilton, 1970-72; sec. Hamilton County Planning Bd., 1973-77; founder Friends Afar; bd. mem. Habitat for Humanity, Ravalli County, Mont., 2003—. Mem. Profl. Picture Framers Assn. Lodges: Soroptimist (chairperson com. 1982—), Order of Eastern Star (matron 1975-76). Presbyterian. Avocations: birdwatching, gardening, playing recorder.

HACKLER, RHODA E. A., retired historian; b. NYC, Nov. 7, 1923; d. William Campbell and Rhoda Elizabeth Armstrong; m. Windsor Gregory Hackler, Mar. 31, 1951; 1 child, Jeffrey Madison. BA, U. Hawaii, 1970, MA, 1972, PhD, 1978. Adminstrv. asst. US Embassy Japanese Lang. Sch., Tokyo, 1955—56; with J.F. Begg Real Estate, 1962—65; lectr. history U. Hawaii, Honolulu, 1972—91; project dir. Hawaiian Hist. Soc., 1978—79; rsch. assoc. territory Hawaii history project San Jose State U., Calif., 1980—82; ret., 1982. Lectr. in field. Contbr. articles to profl. jours.; editor: (newsletter) Friends of East-West Center Newsletter, 1973—77, Friends of Iolani Palace Newsletter, 1976—88. Vol. Motor Corps., DC, 1941—42, Lennox Hill Hosp., NYC, 1946—47; chmn. historic rsch. on Iolani Palace Jr. League Honolulu, 1965—68; mem. restoration com. Friends of Iolani Palace, 1969—77, ops. & interpretation com., 1978—96, edn., publs. com., 1978—96, com. mem. Palace Shop, 1978—96; mem. Bishop Mus. Assn. Coun., 1982—86; mem. Liberal Arts Adv. Coun. Hawaii Pacific U., 1988—; mem. Bishop Mus. Assn. Coun., 1993—96; dir. Hawaii Opera Theatre & Edn., 1980—2006; mem. vestry Ch. Holy Nativity, Honolulu, 1987—89, 1993—, chair outreach com., 1992—93, chair United Thank Offering, Women Outreach, 1993—94; mem. Diocese Coun. Diocese Hawaii, 1989—92, mem. Campus Min., 1989—93, mem. Commn. Ministry, 1992—96, mem. Standing Com., 1997—2000, chair Nurture & Edn. Com., 2003—, diocesan coun., 2003—; bd. dirs. Friends of Iolani Palace, Honolulu, 1968—. Sgt. U.S. Army, 1943—45, lt. USAR, 1949—57, 2d lt. USAR, 1951—54. Mem.: Caledonia Soc. Hawaii (sec. 2003—05), Hawaii Army Mus. Soc. (trustee 2001—), Soc. Asian Arts Hawaii (v.p. 1998—99, pres. 1999—2001), Kahala Cmty. Assn. (dir. 1995—96), Assn. Hawaiian Archivists, Hawaii Mus. Assn., Hawaiian Hist. Soc. (life; pres. 1977—79). Home: 4389 Malia St #515 Honolulu HI 96821

HACKLEY, CAROL ANN, public relations educator, consultant; b. Sacramento, Mar. 20, 1940; d. Charles Peter and Alice Marian (Schmidt) Cusick; m. William E. Hall, Sept. 1, 1966 (dec. Aug. 1991); children: Kevin Dennis Hall, Kimberlee Marian Hall Floyd; m. T. Cole Hackley, Apr. 10, 1993. BA, Calif. State U., Sacramento, 1961; MA, Ohio State U., 1984, PhD, 1985. Pub. rels. dir., tchr. Lincoln Unified Schs., Stockton, Calif., 1961-63; advt. promotion copy writer, columnist Hawaii Newspaper Agy., Legis. Bur., Honolulu Star-Bull., 1964; instr. U. Nebr., Lincoln, 1964-66, Ohio State U., Columbus, 1972-80, 82-85; exec. dir. Jour. Assn. Ohio Schs., Columbus, 1974-80, 82-85; asst. prof. U. Hawaii, Manoa, 1980—82; prof. pub. rels. comm. dept. U. Pacific, Stockton, 1985—, chair comm. dept., 1992-94, intern coord., 1985—, experiential edn. dir. comm. dept., 2006; pub. rels. cons. Hackley Ent. Inc., 1995—; owner, pub. rels. and sr. cons. Pacific Pub. Rels., 1999—. Pub. rels. cons. Hall & Hall Prescriptive Pub. Rels., Stockton, 1987—91; prof.-in-residence Edelman Pub. Rels. Worldwide, Syndey, London, San Francisco, 1990—92; dir. mktg. and univ. rels. U. of Pacific, Stockton, San Francisco, Sacramento, 1997—98; adj. prof. Benerd Sch. Edn. Co-author: Wordsmithing: The Art and Craft of Writing for Public Relations, 2006. Chmn. bd. dirs. Mountain Valley Multiple Sclerosis, Stockton, 1989—91. Fellow: Pub. Rels. Soc. Am. (v.p. Oakland/East Bay chpt. 1994, educators sect., internat. sect., mem. internat. pub. rels. exec. com. 1995, del. nat. assembly 1995—97, pres.-elect 1997, pres. 1998, del. nat. assembly 2001—03, ethics officer 2001—03); mem.: Assn. Edn. Journalism and Mass Comm., Internat. Comm. Assn., Stockton C. of C. (edn. task force 1996—99), Navy League US (life; pres. Stockton coun. 1997—98, chair nat. pub. affairs com. 1997—99, nat. dir. 1997—, nat. v.p. pub. rels. 2001—02, mem. steering com. spl. adv. pub. rels. 2003—04, mem. Puerto Vallarta coun., pres. amb. to Mex. 2003—05, nat. v.p. pub. rels. 2004—05, Pacific Ctrl. region v.p. PR 2005, Nat. Pres. award 2004). Avocations: singing, cooking, travel. Home: 2618 Sheridan Way Stockton CA 95207-3246 Office: Univ of the Pacific 3601 Pacific Ave Stockton CA 95211-0197 Office Phone: 209-946-3046. E-mail: tchackley@yahoo.com.

HACKMAN, (MARY) JUDITH DOZIER, university administrator, researcher; b. Springfield, Ill., Dec. 30, 1940; d. John Burrel and Elva Hannah (Smith) Dozier; m. (John) Richard Hackman, Sept. 1, 1962; children: Julia Beth, Laura Dianne. Attended, MacMurray Coll., 1959—62; BA, U. Ill., 1963; MS, So. Conn. State U., 1970; postgrad., Yale U., 1979—80; PhD, U. Mich., 1983. Tchr. Oakwood H.S., Fithian, Ill., 1963—66; rschr. Yale U., New Haven, 1966—71, dir. criteria study, 1971—73, spl. projects, 1974—79, assoc. dir. instl. rsch., 1979—82, dir. instl. rsch., 1982—87; assoc. dean Yale Coll., 1987—. Cons. Edn. Rsch. Assocs.; guest lectr. numerous univs. Contbr.: articles to profl. jours. Bd. dirs. Info. and Counselling Svc. for Women, New Haven, 1972-77, 79-80, New Careers for Women, New Haven, 1974-80, Bethany Cmty. Schs., Conn., 1978-79; mem. Town Dem. Com., Bethany, 1984-89, Greater New Haven Cmty. Loan Fund, 1988-, pres. 1993; moderator, ch. coun. Battell Ch. of Christ in Yale, New Haven, 1985-86; vice chair United Way Greater New Haven, 2004—. Recipient Outstanding Alumnus award, So. Conn. State U., 1983, Vol. Yr., United Way Greater New Haven, 2006. Mem. Assn. Instl. Rsch. (forum panel com. 1985-86, nominating com. 1986-87, publs. bd. 1987-89), North East Assn. Instl. Rsch. (program chmn. 1984-85, pres. 1985-86, chmn. nominating com. 1986-87), Assn. Study Higher Edn. (program vice chmn. 1984-85, program chair 1987, mem. bd. dirs. 1988-, pres.-elect 1989-90, pres. 1990-91, past pres. and chair nominating 1991-92), New Eng. Assn. Schs. and Colls. (accreditation liaison officer for Yale 1983-, Coll. Bd. adv. bd. Washington office 1987-89), Soc. Coll. and Univ. Planning (editl. bd. 1986-). Avocation: playing baritone horn. Home: 109 Sperry Rd Bethany CT 06524-3519 Office: Yale Coll Yale Ave # 1604A New Haven CT 06515

HACKMAN, VICKI LOU, physician; b. Lancaster, Pa., Nov. 11, 1952; d. Harry Eugene and Marian Ruth (Miller) Hackman; m. James Roger Begley, June 3, 1989 (dec.). BS cum laude, Lebanon Valley Coll., 1974; MD, Med. Coll. of Pa., 1978. Resident St. Margaret Meml. Hosp., Pitts., 1978—81; family practitioner Norlanco Med. Assoc., Elizabethtown, Pa., 1981-84; physician KRON Med. Corp., Chapel Hill, NC, 1984—88; hosp. based family practice Mary Breckenridge Hosp., Hyden, Ky., 1988—90; pvt. family practice Medway (Maine) Family Practice, 1990—94; physician Intermountain Health Care, South Jordan, Utah, 1995—99, Berea (Ky.) Primary Care, 1999—. Active staff Millinocket (Maine) Regional Hosp., 1990—94, Cottonwood Hosp., Salt Lake City, 1995—99, Berea Hosp., 1999—; cons. Elizabethtown (Pa.) Hosp. and Rehab. Ctr., 1982—84. Mem.: Am. Acad. Family Practice. Republican. Methodist. Avocations: horses, farming. Home: 1080 College Hill Rd Waco KY 40385-9735 Office Phone: 859-985-1415. E-mail: vichac@msn.com.

HACKNEY, MARCELLA WICHSER, biology professor; b. New Orleans, La., Sept. 29, 1947; d. Celeste George Wichser and Lucille Eileen Leach; m. William Philip Hackney, Dec. 28, 1968; children: Amy Hackney Blackwell, Philip, Madeleine, Ryan. BS in Sci. Edn., U. New Orleans, 1968; MNS in Natural Scis., La. State U., Baton Rouge, 1984; PhD in Curriculum Instrn., La. State U., 1999. Type A 049885 gen. sci., biology, chemistry, academically gifted La. Tchr. biology and chemistry Dominican H.S., New Orleans, 1969—70; tchr. life sci. Istroma Mid. Magnet, Baton Rouge, 1985—86; tchr. biology Scotlandville Magnet H.S. and H.S. for Engring., Baton Rouge, 1986—2000; asst. prof. biology Baton Rouge C. C., 2000—. Presenter in field. Co-author: The Power of Analogy: Teaching Biology with Relevant Classroom-Tested Activities, 2002; contbr. articles to profl. jours. Mem., docent, sec., pres. Patrons of La. State U. Mus. Natural Sci., Baton Rouge, 1983—90. Recipient Tchg. Excellence award, NISOD, 2003, LCTCS, 2003. Mem.: Nat. Assn. Biology Tchrs. (presenter, Outstanding Biology Tchr. 1990), Phi Kappa Phi. Avocations: travel, reading, gardening. Home: 7450 Oak Hollow Dr Baton Rouge LA 70810 Office: Baton Rouge C C 5310 Florida Blvd Baton Rouge LA 70806

HACKNEY, VIRGINIA HOWITZ, lawyer; b. Phila., Jan. 11, 1945; d. Charles Rawlings and Edith Wrenn (Pope) Howitz; m. Barry Albert Hackney, Feb. 15, 1969; children: Ashby Rawlings, Roby Howison, Trevor Pope. BA in Econs., Hollins Coll., 1967; JD, U. Richmond, 1970. Bar: Va. 1970. Assoc. Hunton & Williams, Richmond, Va., 1970-77, ptnr., capital fin., real estate, 1977—, also dep. gen. counsel. Pres. Am. Acad. Hosp. Attys. Chgo., 1992-93. Mem. agy. evaluation com. United Way of Greater Richmond, 1981-86; sustainer Jr. League of Richmond; mem. and fellow Am. Health Lawyers Assn. (pres. 1992-93, bd. dirs. 1988-94). Recipient Women of Achievement award, Met. Richmond Women's Bar Assn., 1998, Distinction award Va. Women Attys. Assn., 2006; named Outstanding Woman in Field of Law, YWCA, Richmond, 1981. Fellow Am. Health Lawyers Assn.; mem. ABA (forum com. health law 1982—), Va. State Bar (long range planning com. 1985-90, chmn. standing com. lawyer discipline 1986-90, exec. com. 1988-90, Bar Coun. mem. 1984-90). Avocations: book tapes, reading, boating, jogging/walking. Office: Hunton & Williams Riverfront Plz East Tower 951 E Byrd St Richmond VA 23219-4074 Office Phone: 804-788-8263. Office Fax: 804-788-8218. Business E-Mail: vhackney@hunton.com.

HADAS, ELIZABETH CHAMBERLAYNE, editor; b. Washington, May 12, 1946; d. Moses and Elizabeth (Chamberlayne) H.; m. Jeremy W. Heist, Jan. 25, 1970 (div. 1976); m. Peter Eller, Mar. 21, 1984 (div. 1998). AB, Radcliffe Coll., 1967; postgrad., Rutgers U., 1967—68; MA, Washington U., St. Louis, 1971. Editor U. N.Mex. Press, Albuquerque, 1971-85, dir., 1985-2000, spl. acquisitions editor, 2000—. Bd. dirs. N.Mex. Humanities Coun., 2001—. Mem. Assn. Am. Univ. Presses (pres. 1992-93). Democrat. Home: 2900 10th St NW Albuquerque NM 87107-1111 Office: U New Mexico MSC 04 2820 Albuquerque NM 87131-0001 E-mail: ehadas@unm.edu.

HADAS, RACHEL, poet, educator; b. NYC, Nov. 8, 1948; d. Moses and Elizabeth (Chamberlayne) H.; m. Stavros Kondilis, Nov. 7, 1970 (div. 1978); m. George Edwards, July 22, 1978; 1 child, Jonathan. BA in Classics, Radcliffe Coll., 1969; MA, Johns Hopkins, 1977; PhD, Princeton U., 1982. From adj. to assoc. prof. Rutgers U., Newark, 1981-92, prof., 1992—, Bd. Govs. Prof., 2002—; adj. prof. Columbia U., N.Y.C., 1992-93. Vis. prof. Hellenic studies program Princeton U., 1995. Author: (poetry) Slow Transparency, 1983, A Son From Sleep, 1987, Pass It On, 1989, Living in Time, 1990, Mirrors of Astonishment, 1992, Other Worlds Than This, 1994, The Empty Bed, 1995, The Double Legacy, 1995, Halfway Down the Hall: New and Selected Poems, 1998, Indelible, 2001, Laws, 2004, The River of Forgetfulness, 2006, (criticism) Merrill, Cavafy. Poems and Dreams, 2001. Recipient award Am. Acad. Inst. Arts and Letters, 1990; Guggenheim fellow in poetry, 1988-89. Fellow Am. Acad. Arts and Scis.; mem. MLA, Poets, Essayists and Novelists. Democrat. Avocation: reading. Home: 838 W End Ave Apt 3A New York NY 10025-5365 Office Phone: 973-353-5279 ext. 520. Business E-Mail: rhadas@rutgers.edu.

HADDA, JANET RUTH, language educator, lay psychoanalyst; b. Bradford, Eng., Dec. 23, 1945; arrived in US, 1948; d. George Manfred and Annemarie (Kohn) H.; m. Allan Joshua Tobin, Mar. 22, 1981; stepchildren: David, Adam. BS in Edn., U. Vt., 1966; MA, Cornell U., 1969; PhD, Columbia U., 1975. Rsch. psychoanalyst So. Calif. Psychoanalytic Inst., LA, 1988—, tng. and supervising analyst, 1995—, Inst. Contemporary Psychoanalysis, 1993—; prof. Yiddish emerita UCLA, 2004—. Author: Yankev Glatshteyn, 1980, Passionate Women, Passive Men: Suicide in Yiddish Literature, 1988, Isaac Bashevis Singer: A Life, 1997, with New Introduction, 2003; contbr. articles to prof. jours. Mem. MLA, Assn. Jewish Studies, Am. Psychoanalytic Assn., Inst. Contemporary Psychoanalysis, So. Calif. Psychoanalytic Inst., Phi Beta Kappa.

HADDAD, COLLEEN, marketing executive; b. Hackensack, N.J., Feb. 24, 1969; d. Charles Ross and Joan Chinni; m. Robert Edward Haddad, Sept. 9, 1995. BS, Northeastern U., Boston, 1992. Cert. NASD. Ops. mgr. Prudential Securities, N.Y.C., 1992-94, assoc. mgr. internal sales Newark, 1994-97; sr. regional sales PaineWebber, Inc., Weehawken, N.J., 1997-98; v.p. sales and mktg. Mitchell Hutchins, Weehawken, 1998—2000; v.p. mktg. The Dreyfus Corp., 2001—. Office: 200 Park Ave New York NY 10166 E-mail: Haddad.C@Dreyfus.com.

HADDAD, LISA R., lawyer; BBA cum laude, U. Mass., Amherst, 1993; JD magna cum laude, Harvard U., 1996. Bar: Mass. 1996. Ptnr. Bus. Law Dept. Goodwin Procter LLP, Boston. Office: Goodwin Procter LLP Exchange Place 53 State St Boston MA 02109 Office Phone: 617-570-8311. E-mail: lhaddad@goodwinprocter.com.*

HADDADY, SHIRIN, medical educator; b. Tehran, Iran, June 14, 1967; d. Nayereh Pezeshk and Hamid Haddady; m. Farshid Alizadeh-Shabdiz, June 17, 1993; children: Pardis Alizadeh-Shabdiz, Sarah Alizadeh-Shabdiz, Jasmin Alizadeh-Shabdiz. MD, Tehran U., 1992. Resident Tehran U., Georgetown U., Washington, 1999—2002; fellow U. Mass., Worcester, 2002—05, instr., 2005—. Rsch. asst. Walter Reed Army Med. Ctr., Wash. Hosp. Ctr., Washington, 1998—99; rschr. U. Mass., 2002—. Contbr. articles to profl. jours. Recipient Appreciation for Quality of Patient Care, 1994, Best Poster Presentation, 2001, 2002. Mem.: AMA, Internat. Soc. Clin. Densitometry, Am. Assn. Clin. Endocrinologists, Am. Soc. Reproductive Medicine, Endocrine Soc. Avocations: travel, cooking. Office Phone: 508-856-1128.

HADDAWAY, JANICE LILLIAN, psychotherapist, consultant; b. Lexington, Ky., Oct. 26, 1941; d. James L. and Della A. (Mattingly) Evans; children: Chuck, Jennifer, Jeanni, Jim, Rich, Alex, Donna. BS, U. Ky., 1967; MA, We. Ky. U., 1981, Rank I, 1992. Cert. tchr. grades 6-12; lic. marriage and family therapist. Tchr. Ninth Bapt. Acad. and S.W. Christian Sch., Louisville, Ky., 1980-89; dir. guidance counseling S.W. Christian Sch., Louisville, 1983-92; pvt. practice Louisville, 1991—. Originator, developer support groups for children of incarcerated parents Jefferson County Pub. Schs., Louisville, 1995—, early childhood mental health cons. Ky. Head Start, South Ctrl. Ky., 1995—. Named Hon. Ky. Coll. for work with children, State Govt. Mem. Am. Assn. Marriage and Family Therapists (clin.), Nat. Bd. Cert. Counselors (clin.), Ky. Assn. Marriage and Family Therapists (clin.). Republican. Baptist. Home: 8006 Rush Ct Hardwood Forest Louisville KY 40214

HADDY, THERESA BREY, pediatrician, educator, hematologist, oncologist; b. Wabasso, Minn., Feb. 27, 1924; d. Francis William and Elizabeth Katherine (Daub) Brey; m. Francis John Haddy, Sept. 21, 1946; children: Richard Ian, Carol Haddy Froelich, Alice Haddy Hellen. BS, U. Minn., 1944, MB, 1946, MD, 1948. Diplomate in pediatrics and in pediatric hematology/oncology Am. Bd. Pediatrics. Intern Mpls. Gen. Hosp., 1947—48; resident in pediat. U. Minn., Mpls., 1950—52; fellow in hematology U. Okla., 1962—64; practice medicine, specializing in gen. pediatr. Des Plaines, Ill., 1954—61; asst. prof., dir. pediat. hematology oncology U. Okla., Oklahoma City, 1961—66; chief child health Mich. Dept. Pub. Health, Lansing, 1966—69; assoc. prof., dir. pediat. hematology oncology Mich. State U., East Lansing, 1969—76; expert in blood diseases NIH, Bethesda, Md., 1977—79; assoc. prof., dir. pediat. hematology oncology Howard U., Washington, 1979—87, prof., 1987—89, prof. emeritus, 1989—. Guest rschr. pediat. oncology br. NIH, NCI, Bethesda, 1989-2001; mem. acad. adv. staff Children's Nat. Med. Ctr., Washington, 2000—. Author: (book) Country Doctor and City Doctor: Father and Daughter, 2006; contbr. over 100 articles to profl. jours. Mem. Am. Soc. Hematology, Am. Soc. Pediat. Hematology/Oncology (publs. com. 2002-04), Nat. Hypertension Assn. (adv. bd. 2002—), Am. Soc. Clin. Oncology, NIH Alumni Assn. Episcopalian. Personal E-mail: tbhaddy@aol.com.

HADLEY, CHARLINE A., protective services official; b. Coffeyville, Kans., Aug. 8, 1947; d. Charles Wesley and Geraldine Virginia (Bates) Clithero; children: Melissa Reneé (Hadley) Dos Santos, Kimberly Dawn (Hadley) Mominah, George Edward. AA, Tulsa CC, 2002. Cert. notary pub. Sec. State Okla. Purchasing agt. Wagone County Okla., Wagoner, Okla., 1982—84; regional fin. officer Okla. Dept. of N.E. Dist. Corrections, 1996—2002, adminstv. programs office, 2002—. Fin. com. So. States Correctional Assn., 1994—. Treas. St. James Espic. Ch., Wagoner, 1985—92. Recipient Employee of Yr., Okla. Dept. Corrections, 1986, 1990, 1991, 2000, 2001. Mem.: Coun. for Exceptional Children, Okla. Edn. Assn., Nat. Edn. Assn., Okla. Corrections Assn., Am. Corrections Assn., So. States Corrections Assn. Democrat. Episcopalian. Avocations: reading, travel. Office: Okla Dept Corrections NE Dist Cmty Corrections 70015 Azalea Pack Dr Wagoner OK 74467

HADLEY, JANE FRANCIS, family nurse practitioner; b. Fort Knox, Ky., Oct. 15, 1953; d. Richard Aloyisius and Mary Elizabeth (Davis) Walsh; m. P.C. McNamara, Dec. 20, 1975 (div. Jan. 1986); children: Joel, Heather; m. William Melvin Hadley, Oct. 13, 1990 BSN, U. N.Mex., 1977; MSN, U. Tex., El Paso, 1986; cert. family nurse practitioner, Tex. Tech U. Health Scis. Ctr., 1995. RN, N.Mex.; cert. nurse practitioner, Ariz.; cert. advanced oncology nurse practitioner. Staff nurse U. N.Mex. Hosp., Albuquerque, 1978—81; faculty Maternal Child U. Albuquerque, 1980; staff nurse Step-down Unit Presbyn. Hosp., Albuquerque, 1981; faculty clin. pediat. Luna Vocat.-Tech. Inst., Las Vegas, N.Mex., 1982; from diabetes educator to rsch. coord. Lovelace Med. Ctr., Albuquerque, 1982—88; pharmacology faculty Diabetes Ctr. U. Va., Charlottesville, 1989; clin. educator St. Joseph's Med. Ctr., Albuquerque, 1989—90; clin. nurse specialist Post Traumatic Stress Disorder VA Med. Ctr., Albuquerque, 1990—93, nurse mgr. Acute Psychiat., 1993—95; family nurse practitioner Primary Care Clinic, 1995—98; nurse practitioner Cancer Rsch. and Treatment Ctr. U. N.Mex., 1998—99; advanced nurse practitioner Gastrointestinal Oncology program H. Lee Moffitt Cancer Ctr., Tampa, 1999—2000; cons. patient care, nurse cons. Schering Oncology/Biotech, 2000—01; nurse practitioner Digestive Disease Cons., 2001—04; nurse practitioner radiation oncology Mayo Clinic Ariz., Scottsdale, 2004—06; nurse practitioner hematology and oncology Mayo Hosp., Ariz., 2006—. Grantee U.S. Govt., 1979-81 Mem. ANA (cert. family nurse practitioner, clin. nurse specialist, psychiat. adult mental health nurse, grantee 1994-95), Am. Assn. Diabetes Educators (chpt. coun. chair 1986-87, bd. dirs. 1987-90, fin. com. chair 1987-90), Oncology Nursing Soc., Zia Assn. Diabetes Educators (pres. 1985-86), N.Mex. Nurses Assn. (com. 1992-94, bd. dirs. 1995-96), Sigma Theta Tau Avocations: raising yellow labrador retrievers, music, gardening. Home: 42406 N 9th Ave Phoenix AZ 85086-7198 Office: Mayo Clinic Arizona 13400 E Shea Blvd Scottsdale AZ 85259 E-mail: jfhadley724@aol.com.

HADLEY, LEILA ELIOTT-BURTON (MRS. HENRY LUCE III), writer; b. NYC, Sept. 22, 1925; d. Frank Vincent and Beatrice Boswell Eliott Burton; m. Arthur T. Hadley, II, Mar. 2, 1944 (div. Aug. 1946); 1 child, Arthur T. III; m. Yvor H. Smitter, Jan. 24, 1953 (div. Oct. 1969); children: Victoria C. Van D. Smitter Barlow, Matthew Burton Smitter Eliott, Caroline Allison F.S. Nicholson; m. William C. Musham, May 1976 (div. July 1979); m. Henry Luce III, Jan. 1990 (dec. Sept. 8, 2005). MD, St. Timothy's Sch., 1943; LLD (hon.), Mount St. Mary's Coll., Newburgh, NY, 2006. Author: Give Me the World, 1958, reprinted, 1999, Give Me the World, 2003, How to Travel with Children in Europe, 1963, Manners for Children, 1967, Fielding's Guide to Traveling with Children in Europe, 1972, rev., 1974, 1984, Traveling with Children in the U.S.A., 1974, Tibet-20 Years After the Chinese Takeover, 1979; author: (with Theodore B. Van Itallie) The Best Spas: Where to Go for Weight Loss, Fitness Programs and Pure Pleasure in the U.S. and Around the World, 1988, rev., 1989; author: A Journey with Elsa Cloud, 1997, paperback edit. with afterword, 2003, Give Me the World, 1999, A Garden by the Sea, 2005; assoc. editor Diplomat mag., N.Y.C., 1964—65, Saturday Evening Post, 1965—67, contbg. editor ICON: World Monuments Mag.; contbg. editor: Tricycle, the Buddhist Rev., 1991—; editl. cons. TWYCH, N.Y.C., 1985—87, book reviewer Palm Beach Life, Fla., 1967—72, consulting editor Tricyle, The Buddhist Rev., 1991—, garden columnist Fishers Island Gazette; contbr. articles to various newspapers, mags. Bd. dirs. Wings World Quest, Inc., 1992, Tibet House, 1995, Fishers Island Conservancy, 1995, Donald & Shelley Rubin Cultural Trust, 2001, Bd. Helike Found. Recipient Norman Vincent Peale award, 2002. Fellow Royal Can. Geog. Soc. (hon.); mem. Acad. Am. Poets, Soc. Woman Geographers, Authors Guild, Nat. Writers Union, Nat. Press Club, PEN, Explorers Club, Central Park Conservancy, Ocean Conservancy, N.Y. Acad. Medicine (guest bd.), The Kitchen Ctr. Haleakala, Inc., Nat. Arts Club, Lansdowne Club (Eng.). Office Phone: 212-759-8640. E-mail: leilahadleyluce1@aol.com.

HADLOW, VIVIAN JEAN, elementary school educator, retired principal; b. Scottdale, Pa., June 5, 1934; d. Harry and Martha Pearl (Dailey) Wigley; m. Clarence Eugene Hadlow, Dec. 5, 1953 (dec.); children: Martin Lee, Patrick Donn, John Michael. B in Elem. Edn., Cleve. State U., Ohio, 1972; M in Adminstrv. Supervision, Baldwin Wallace Coll., Berea, Ohio, 1984. Cert. tchr. Ohio, 1984. Tchr. Avon Local Schs., Ohio, 1965—92, prin., 1988—89; tchr. Pearl River County Schs., Carriere, Miss., 1998—2005; ret. Chairperson Task Force to Update Curriculum, Avon, 1979—80. Recipient Martha Holden Jennings Scholar Plate, Martha Holden Jennings Found., Cleve., 1987—88. Republican. Methodist. Achievements include incorporating DARE program into Avon East Elementary School. Avocation: antiques. Home: 201 Marianne Cir Sulphur Springs TX 75482

HADSELL, NANCY ANN, music educator; b. Savannah, Ga., Dec. 11, 1950; d. William Valentine, Jr. and Ann McGillicuddy Hadsell; 1 child, Kathryn Diane Howard. PhD, U. Kans., Lawrence, 1985. Cert. Music Therapist Cert. Bd. for Music Therapists, 1985. Asst. prof. music therapy Tenn. Technol. U., Cookeville, 1977—81; music prof. Tex. Woman's U., Denton, 1984—. Dir., bd. dirs. Cert. Bd. for Music Therapists, Downingtown, Pa., 2000—03; pres. Southwestern Region, Am. Assn. for Music Therapy, Silver Spring, Md., 2003—05. Dissertation Fellowship, U. Kans., 1983—84. Mem.: Am. Music Therapy Assn. (assembly del. 2000—06, Spirit of Unification 1998). Liberal. Mem. Cmty. Of Christ Ch. Avocations: listening to books on ipod, exercise. Office: Tex Woman's Univ PO Box 425768 TWU Station Denton TX 76204 Home Fax: 940-898-2494. Personal E-mail: singsongtx@mac.com.

HADYK-WEPF, SONIA MARGARET, artist, real estate manager; b. May 30, 1931; d. Albert and Margaret Wepf; m. Walter Hadyk, Feb. 14, 1957 (div.June 1976); 1 child, W. Gordon Hadyk. BS in Art Edn., Pratt Inst., 1954. Tchr. art Midland Park (N.J.) Jr. H.S., 1954-55, Lyncourt (N.Y.) Pub. Sch., 1969-70; staff artist Norcross Greeting Cards, N.Y.C., 1955-56, Spencer Advt. Art, Union City, N.J., 1956-58, L.W. Peckham Advt., Syracuse, N.Y., 1958-59; freelance artist Syracuse, 1959-74; mgr. jewelry dept. Naum's, DeWitt, N.Y., 1974-75; owner Hadyk House of Gem Design, Syracuse, 1974—; mgr. Walter Hadyk Rental Homes, Syracuse, 1993—. Guest lectr. Carrier Women's Club, Syracuse, 1972, Nat. League Pen Women, Syracuse, 1972; juror Arts and Crafts Festival, Camillus (N.Y.) Hist. Soc., 1973. Designer, craftsman (cultured pearl necklace) Golden Claws, 1971, (bracelet) Bubbles, 1971, (ring) Elipses, 1983; designer, goldsmith numerous pieces including All Done With Mirrors, 1980 (Judges prize for Most Creative); designer, platinumsmith (earrings) Snowflake, 1982 (1st Runner-up). Recipient numerous awards Diamond Info. Ctr., N.Y.C., 1973, DeBeers Mines, N.Y.C., 1977, 1st prize award Jewelers' Circular Keystone, Radnor, Pa., 1979; finalist in color catalog of winning designs "Colored Gemstone Design award 2000,"; sponsored by Signity N.Y. Ltd., Stuller, Jewelers of Am., Nat. Jeweler Mag.; numerous others. Mem. Real Estate Investors Ctrl. N.Y., Gem and Mineral Soc. Syracuse Inc. Unitarian-universalist. Avocations: gem carving, gardening. Office: 102 Dewey Ave Fayetteville NY 13066-1607

HAEBERLE, ROSAMOND PAULINE, retired music educator; b. Clearwater, Kans., Oct. 23, 1914; d. Albert Paul and Ella (Lough) H. BS in Music Edn., Kans. State U., 1936; MusM, Northwestern U., 1948; postgrad., Wayne State U., 1965-66. Profl. registered parliamentarian. Tchr. sch. dist., Plevna, Kans., 1936-37, Esbon, Kans., 1937-41, Frankfort, Kans., 1941-43, Garden City, Kans., 1943-44, music supr. Waterford Twp., Mich., 1944-47, tchr. Pontiac, Mich., 1947-80, ret., 1980. Pres. Pontiac Fedn. Tchrs., 1961-63. Bd. dir. Pontiac Oakland Town Hall; adv. coun. Waterford Sr. Citizens, chmn., 1990-93; pres. Oakland County Pioneer and Hist. Soc., 1992-94. Recipient Tchrs. Day award, Mich. State Fair, 1963. Mem.: Mich. DAR (parliamentarian state, Excellence in Cmty. Svc. award 1995), DAR (regent 1983—85, Gen. Richardson chpt., libr. and parliamentarian), AAUW (pres. Pontiac br. 1970—72, founds. chair Pontiac br.), Mich. Assn. Retired Sch. Persons, Pontiac Area Ret. Sch. Pers. (pres. 1981—84, parliamentarian), Louise Saks Parliamentary Unit, Mich. Registered Parliamentarians (pres. Louise Saks unit 1990—92), Pontiac Area Fedn. Women's Club (pres. 1976—78, 1981—84), Detroit Women's Club, Waterford-Clarkston Bus. and Profl. Women's Club (bylaws and parliamentarian), Bloomfield Rep. Women's Club (parliamentarian 1999—2003), Mich. Bus. and Profl. Women's Club (dir. dist. 10 1965—67, Honored Recognition award 2000, Citations award 2000), Mich. Fedn. Music Clubs (pres. Tuesday musicale of Pontiac 1984—86, pres. S.E. dist. 1986—90, state pres. 1993—95, chair Northeastern Region Nat. Music Week 1996—99, chmn. Music for the Blind Northeastern region 2000—, parliamentarian 2001—, chmn. state bylaws and citations com.), Mich. Fedn. Bus. And Profl. Women's Club (Woman of Achievement award dist. IX 1994), Pontiac Bus. and Profl. Women (pres. 1959—61, Woman of Yr. award 1974), Ea. Star (60 yr. award 2004), Zeta Tau Alpha, Mu Phi Epsilon (70 yr. award), Beta Sigma Phi (life). Republican. Methodist. Avocations: travel, playing piano, reading, bell ringing, dance.

HAEGELE, PATRICIA, publishing executive; b. Wheeling, W.Va., Dec. 19, 1950; d. Thomas J. and Marcella (Kissell) Cook. Student, W. Liberty Coll., 1970-71, Brevard Community Bus. Coll., 1973-74, Rollins Coll., 1974-76. Retail advt. rep. Coca Today/Gannett Co., Cocoa, Fla., 1973-76, Tampa Tribune Co., Tampa, Fla., 1976-79; corp. advt. rep. Washington Post Co. Inc., Washington, 1979-82; corp. advt. mgr. USA Today/Gannett Co. Inc., NYC, 1982-84, div. sales mgr., 1984-85, v.p., eastern sales mgr., 1985, v.p., advt. dir., 1985-86; v.p., advertising dir. USA Weekend, NYC, 1986-88, pub., 1988; sr. v.p. advt. USA Today, NYC, 1988—91; pub. Travel Holiday mag. (Gannett Co.), 1991—94; pres. gen. mgr. Newspaper Nat. Network, 1994—97; sr. v.p., pub. Good Housekeeping, 1997—. Selected to YWCA's Acad. of Women Achievers, 1988; profiled On The Rise column Fortune mag., Aug., 1988. Mem. Am. Newspapers Pubs. Assn., Internat. Newspaper Advt. Mktg. Assn., Am. Mktg. Assn. Republican. Roman Catholic. Avocations: running, biking, body tng. Office: Good Housekeeping 250 West 55th St New York NY 10019*

HAEGER, GAYLE MIGNON, biology educator; b. Ardmore, Okla., Apr. 21, 1942; d. James Woodrow and Wilda Mignon Wilson; m. Gerald Gene Haeger, Sept. 8, 1963; children: Eric Edward, Marta Ann Haeger Beaubien, Hans Jonathan. BS, Paficic Union Coll., Angwin, Calif., 1964; MA, Andrews Univ., Berrien Springs, Mich., 1968; MPH, Loma Linda Univ., Loma Linda, Calif., 1979. Cert. state profl. secondary tchr. Wash. Coll. sci. tchr. Peruvian Union Coll., Lima, Peru, 1974—77; health educator Health Edn. Ctr., Victoria, BC, 1979—82; exec. dir. Adventist Health Network-Vancouver, Vancouver, BC, 1983—86, Adventist Health Network-Spokane, Spokane, Wash., 1986—88; jr. H.S. tchr. Spokane Adventist Sch., Spokane, Wash., 1988—91; chemistry tchr. Walla Walla Valley Acad., Coll. Pl., Wash., 1991—95; biology tchr. Upper Columbia Acad., Spangle, Wash., 1995—. K-12 curriculum com. North Pacific Union Edn., Portland, Oreg., 2004—; curriculum com. Upper Columbia Acad., Spangle, Wash., 1998—. Recipient Alma McKibben award, N. Pacific Union Edn. Dept., 1993, Don Keele Excellence in Edn. award, 2001, 2005. Mem.: NSTA, Adventist Sci. Tchrs. Assn. (commn. dir. 1999—). Avocations: scuba diving, archaeology, travel, misson trips, ornithology. Office Phone: 509-245-3693.

HAENDIGES, ANNE R., marriage and family therapist; d. James A. and Anne P. Bohan; m. Roger H. Haendiges, Nov. 25, 2000; m. Donald J. Rudolph (dec.); children: Anne O'Donnell, Donald J. Rudolph, Lisa A. Haig. RN, NYU, 1957; BSN, Columbia U., 1960; MSc, Russell Sage Coll., 1975; PhD, Walton U., Coral Gables, Fla., 1977. RN N.Y.; cert. sex therapist, sex educator, sexual diplomat Am. Bd. Sexuality. Nurse Bellevue Hosp., N.Y.C., 1957—59; tchg. nurse Albany Manpower Tng. Program, 1963—69; asst. prof. SUNY, Albany, 1969—80; instr. Albany Med. Sch., 1970—75; pvt. practice as sex therapist Clifton Park, NY, 1970—2000. Sec. faculty SUNY, Albany; lectr. on human sexuality. Recipient fed. grant, Russell Sage Coll., 1969; scholar, Tchrs. Coll., Columbia U., 1958. Fellow: Am. Assn. Sex Counselors, Educators, and Therapists (cert.); mem.: N.Y. Nurses Assn. (mem. adv. bd.). Republican. Roman Catholic. Avocations: golf, swimming, walking. Home: 1011 Park Ave N Winter Park FL 32789 Office Phone: 407-622-7648. Personal E-mail: ahaendiges@cfl.rr.com, adlrud@aol.com.

HAENSLY, PATRICIA ANASTACIA, psychology professor; b. Kronenwetter, Wis., Dec. 4, 1928; d. Paul Frank and Valeria (Woyak) Banach; m. William E. Haensly, 1954; children: Paul, Robert, Thomas, James, John, David, Mary, Katherine. BS, Lawrence U., 1950; MS in Genetics, Iowa State U., 1953; PhD in Ednl. & Devel. Psychology, Tex. A&M U., 1982. Histo technique specialist dept. vet. pathology Iowa State U., Ames, 1958-63; asst. prof. dept. ednl. psychology Tex. A&M U., College Station, 1982-97; instr. Blinn Jr. Coll., College Station; prin. Investigator Project Mustard Seed, U.S.D.O.E. Javits Grant, 1993-96; assoc. dir. programs Inst. for Gifted and Talented Tex. A&M U., College Station, dir. summer presch. program Minds Alive, 1987-95. Mem. adj. faculty psychology Western Wash. U., Bellingham, 1996—2006. Contbg. editor Roeper Rev., 1996—; mem. editl. bd. Gifted Child Quar., 1996—, Gifted Child Today, 1997—; guest editor: (spl. issues) Gifted Teachers/Teachers of Gifted Learners, Parenting the Gifted; contbr. articles to profl. jours., chpts. to books. Alt. U.S. del. World Coun. Gifted and Talented Children, 1997-99, 2001-02, del., 1999-2001; del. People to People amb. program Pacific N.W. Initiative to the People's Rep. of China., 1998. Recipient Outstanding Woman award AAUW, 1980, Govt. Rsch. Javits grante, 1993-96 Mem. Tex. Assn. for Gifted and Talented (1st v.p. 1988, 89, editor news mag. 1988, 89), Nat. Assn. Gifted Children (co-chmn. rsch. and evaluation com. 1985-87, John Curtis Gowan Rsch. award 1981, program chair Conceptual Found. divsn. 1997-99, chair 2000-01), World Coun. for Gifted and Talented Children, Inc., Soc. for Rsch. in Child Devel., Coun. for Exceptional Children, Assn. for Childhood Edn. Internat., Am. Creativity Assn. (charter), Am. Psychol. Soc., Phi Kappa Phi. Home: Eagle's Trace 102 Pecan Grove Apt 216 Houston TX 77077 Personal E-mail: patricia1015@earthlink.net.

HAERBIG, ALAINA BETH, elementary school educator; d. A. Wesley and Lora Skinner Carr; m. Chris Haerbig, Apr. 15, 1995; 1 adopted child, Brenda children: Matthew, Nathan. BSEd, U. Del., Newark, 1991; MSEd, Johns Hopkins U., Balt., 1996. Spl. educator Howard County Pub. Schs., Ellicott City, Md., 1991—95, gifted educator, 1995—2005, Carroll County Pub. Schs., Westminster, Md., 2005—. Foster parent Carroll County Dept. Social Svcs., Westminster, 2001—; tchr. Lifepoint Ch., Reisterstown, Md., 1999—, missions worker, 2004—. Mem.: Md. Educators Gifted Studies. Avocations: quilting, reading.

HAERI, NILOOFAR M., linguist, educator; d. Jamaleddin Mazandarani Haeri and Behjat Sadat Altoma; m. Thomas Philip Porteous, June 19, 2004; 1 child, Daniel Haeri Porteous. PhD in Liguistics, U. Pa., Phila., 1979—91. Prof. Johns Hopkins U., Balt., 1990—. Fellow Radcliffe Inst. for Advanced Study, Harvard U., 1999—2000. Office: Johns Hopkins Univ 3400 N Charles St Baltimore MD 21218 Home Fax: 410-516-6080; Office Fax: 410-516-6080. Business E-Mail: haeri@jhu.edu.

HAFER, BARBARA, state official; b. LA, Aug. 1, 1943; m. Jack Pidgeon; 4 children, John, Kelly, Bethany, Regan. BS, Duquesne U., Pitts., 1969; postgrad., U. Pitts., U. London. Founder, exec. dir. Allegheny County Ctr. for Victims of Violent Crime, 1973—79; account exec. Sautel Agency, 1979—82; employee relations mgr. South Hills Health System, 1982—83; auditor gen. State of Pa., Harrisburg, 1989-96, state treas., 1997—. Commr. Allegheny County bd. commissioners, 1984—89; mem. Del. River Port Authority, 1989—, Pa Partnership for Econ. Edn., 1997—, Pa. Pub. School Employees Retirement System Bd., 1996—. Office: State of Pennsylvania Treasury Dept 129 Finance Building Harrisburg PA 17120-0018 E-mail: barbarahafer@patreasury.org.

HAFETS, CLAIRE M., assistant principal; b. N.Y.C., Mar. 24, 1951; d. Morton and Pearl Judith Margolis; m. Richard Jay Hafets, June 18, 1972; children: Brooke, Amy. BA in History cum laude, Am. U., Washington, 1973; MS in Reading, Johns Hopkins U., Balt., 1978; postgrad., Loyola Coll., Balt., 2000. Cert. advanced profl. cert. in reading. Social studies and psychology tchr. Wooton H.S., Rockville, Md., 1973—79; English and reading tchr. Wilde Lake Mid. Sch., Columbia, Md., 1993—95; reading specialist, reading tchr. Elkridge Landing Mid. Sch., Elkridge, Md., 1995—2001, 8th grade team leader, 1996—2001; instr. for staff devel. Howard County Pub. Schs., Ellicott City, Md., 1999—; instr. Towson U., Md., 2002—; asst. prin. Bonnie Branch Mid. Sch., Ellicott City, 2001—. Lectr. in field. Pres. PTSA, Savage, Md., 1991—93, rec. sec. Columbia, Md., 1993—2000. Named Merit Educator of the Yr., Howard County C. of C., 1998; recipient Equity award, Black Student Achievement Program, 1994. Mem.: ASCD, Nat. Assn. for Secondary Sch. Prins., Howard County Adminstrs. Assn. Avocations: reading, hiking, skiing, cycling. Home: 7346 Narrow Wind Way Columbia MD 21046

HAFFEY, DEBORAH BUSH, communications educator; d. Samuel Bush and Juanita Cissne; m. David Allen Haffey, 1969. BA, Cedarville U., 1968; MA, Ohio State U., 1969; PhD magna cum laude, Ohio State U., Columbus, 2002. Tchr. Walkerton Pub. Schs., Ind., 1969—72; prof. Cedarville U., Ohio, 1986—, dir. comm. studies divsn. comm. arts, 2003—. Profl. spkr.; debate coach. Co-dir. Women of Vision Internat. Named Faculty Mem. of Yr., Cedarville U., 1998; named one of Outstanding Young Women Am., 1984; recipient Disting. Educator award, Cedarville U., 2006, Debate Coach of Yr., Nat. Edn. Debate Assn., 1991—92, 1993—94, 1995—96, Debate Program of Yr., 1999; fellow, Ohio State U., 1968; grantee, Cedarville U., 1999. Mem.: Midwest Am. Pub. Opinion Rsch., Nat. Comm. Assn., Internat. Comm. Assn., Phi Kappa Phi. Office: Cedarville Univ 251 N Main St Cedarville OH 45314 Office Phone: 937-766-7962.

HAFFNER, MARLENE ELISABETH, internist, public health administrator; b. Cumberland, Md., Mar. 22, 1941; Student, Western Res. U., 1958—61; MD, George Washington U., 1965; MPH, John Hopkins U., 1991. Intern Geroge Washington U., Washington, 1965-66; fellow in dematology Columbia-Presbyn. Med. Ctr., N.Y.C., 1966-67; resident in internal medicine St. Luke's Hosp., N.Y.C., 1967-69; fellow in hematology Albert Einstein Coll. Medicine, Bronx, 1969-71; vis. asst. attending Bronx Mcpl. Hosp. Ctr. (N.Y.), 1969-71; clin. assoc. in family, cmty. and emergency medicine U. N.Mex. Sch. Medicine, Albuquerque, 1974-83; asst. clin. prof. medicine Albert Einstein Coll. Medicine, Bronx, 1971-73; clin. assoc. dept. med., 1974-83; acting clin. dir. Gallup Indian Med. Ctr. (N.Mex.), 1973-74; chief adult outpatient dept., 1971-74; chief dept. internal medicine, 1971-74; dir. Navajo Area Indian Health Svc. Indian Health Svc., Window Rock, Ariz., 1974-81; assoc. dir. for health affairs Bur. Med. Devices, FDA, Rockville, 1981-82; dir. Office Health Affairs Ctr. for Devices and Radiol. Health, 1982-87; dir. office of orphan products devel. FDA, 1987—; adj. prof. preventive medicine/biometrics. Clin. prof. dept. medicine Uniformed Svcs. U. Health Scis., Bethesda, Md., 2003—. Advanced through grades to rear admiral; U.S. Pub. Health Svc. Fellow: Royal Coll. Physicians (London), Am. Coll. Physicians. Office: Orphan Products Devel FDA HF 35 5600 Fishers Ln Rockville MD 20857-1750 Office Phone: 301-827-3666. Business E-Mail: marlene.haffner@fda.hhs.gov.

HAFNER, CATHERINE COURTNEY, retired physics educator; b. N.Y.C., Nov. 14, 1946; d. Patrick Brendon and Mary Teresa (Feeley) Courtney; m. Carl John Hafner, June 15, 1968; children: Lisa Ann, Steven David. BS, Fordham U., 1968; MA in Sci. Edn., Columbia U., 1969. Cert. secondary tchr., N.Y., N.J. Physics, math., earth sci. tchr. Mother Cabrini High Sch., NYC, 1969-70; sci. tchr. Cardinal Spellman High Sch., Bronx, NY, 1970-71; physics and earth sci. tchr. Monroe-Woodbury Sr. High Sch., Central Valley, NY, 1984—2005. Leader Sarah Wells Council Girl Scouts USA, Middletown, N.Y., 1981-84, service team chmn., 1982-84. Research grantee NSF, SUNY at Stony Brook, 1985-88. Mem. Am. Assn. Physics Tchrs., N.Y. State Sci. Tchrs., N.Y. State United Tchrs. Avocation: reading. Office: Monroe-Woodbury Sr High Sch 155 Dunderberg Rd Central Valley NY 10917 Home: 19 Robert Ln Rensselaer NY 12144-5401

HAFNER, MARGOT ANNETTE, music educator, voice educator; b. Cedar Rapids, Iowa, Nov. 25, 1950; d. Harold Lloyd and Helen Mae Santon; m. Derald Dean Hafner, July 9, 1977; children: Brandon, Brock, Nina, Nathan. BS in Music Edn., U. Iowa, Iowa City, 1975. Cert. Tchg. NC, Iowa. Music tchr. Cedar Rapids Comm. Schs., Cedar Rapids, Iowa, 1975—76, North Scott Cmty. Sch., Eldridge, Iowa, 1976—77, Calvary Christian Sch., Louisburg, NC, 1996—98, Granville Sch., Oxford, NC, 2000—06. Piano and voice instr. pvt., Granville County, 1998—, Music Acad. South, Wake Forest, NC, 2004—, choir dir., 2004—. 4H leader, v.p., sec. county and state chpts. 4H, Granville County, NC, 1990—96; vol. elder care; sec. Granville County Rep. Party, 1992—94; bd. mem. Granville Little Theater, 2005—06; mem. Grass Roots N.C., Raleigh, 2006. Recipient Outstanding 4H leader, NC State 4H, 1998. Mem.: Nat. Assn. Tchrs. Singing, Music Educators Nat. Conf., Music Tchrs. Nat. Assn. Republican. Baptist. Avocations: gardening, sewing, singing, swimming. Office: West Oxford Elem Sch 412 Ivey Day Rd Oxford NC 27565 Office Phone: 919-693-9161. E-mail: marghafner@yahoo.com.

HAFNER-EATON, CHRIS, medical researcher, educator; b. N.Y.C., Dec. 9, 1962; d. Peter Robert and Isabelle (Freda) Hafner; m. James Michael Eaton, Aug. 9, 1986; children: Kelsey James, Tristen Lee, Wesley Sean. BA, U. Calif., San Diego, 1986; MPH, UCLA, 1988, PhD Health Svcs. Rsch./Policy Analysis, 1992. Cert. health edn. specialist; internat. bd. cert. lactation cons. Cons. dental health policy UCLA Schl. Dentistry, 1989; grad. teaching asst. UCLA Sch. Pub. Health, 1987-92; health svcs. researcher UCLA, 1987-92; cons. health policy U.S. Dept. Health & Human Svcs., Washington, 1988—; analyst health policy The RAND/UCLA Ctr. Health Policy Study, Santa Monica & L.A., 1988-94; asst. prof. health care adminstrn. Oreg. State U. Dept. Pub. Health, Corvallis, 1992-95; pres. Health Improvement Svcs. Corp., 1994—2003; dir. rsch. rev. La Leche League Internat., 1996-99. Adj. faculty pub. health Linn-Benton Coll., 1995—, Natural Health Improvement Svcs., 2003—; bd. dirs. Benton County Pub. Health Bd., Healthy Start Bd.; mem. Linn-Benton Breastfeeding Task Force, Samaritan Mother-Baby Dyad Team., Am. Public Health Assn. (sect. Council Med. Care). Peer reviewer for NIH jours., others; contbr. articles to profl. jours. including JAMA, Midwifery Today, Jour. Ambulatory Care Mgmt.; other numerous lay publs. such as Mothering Mag. Rsch. grantee numerous granting bodies, 1988—. Mem. AAUW, NOW, Internat. Lactation Cons. Assn., La Leche League Internat. (area profl. liaison for Oreg.), Am. Pub. Health Assn. (med. care sect. coun., women's caucus), Am. Assn. World Health, Oreg. Pub. Health Assn., Oreg. Health Care Assn., Assn. Health Svcs. Rsch., Soc. Pub. Health Edn., Physicians for Social Responsibility, UCLA Pub. Health Alumni Assn. (life), Pub. Health Honor Soc., Delta Omega. Office Phone: 949-701-0602. Personal E-mail: dr.hafner-eaton@centurytel.net. Business E-Mail: drmom@proaxis.com.

HAFT, GAIL KLEIN, pediatrician; b. NYC, Mar. 5, 1938; d. Herbert and Pearl (Mittleman) Klein; m. Jacob I. Haft, Mar. 27, 1964; children: Bethanne, Ian. AB in Chemistry, Vassar Coll., 1959; MD, U. Rochester, 1963. Diplomate Nat. Bd. Med. Examiners, Am. Bd. Pediatrics. Intern Albert Einstein Coll. Medicine, N.Y.C., 1963-64, resident, 1964-65, Mt. Sinai Hosp., N.Y.C., 1967-68; pediatrician Dept. Health, Staten Island, NY, 1965-67, Head Start, Englewood, NY, 1969-71, Dept. Health, Hackensack, NJ, 1970-71; utilization rev. physician Hosp. Corp., N.Y.C., 1973-76; pediatrician Westchester County Health Dept., NY, 1974-76; sch. physician Bd. Edn., Yonkers, NY, 1974-76; bus. mgr. Heartronics, Newark, 1980-94; chief med. officer Bergen County Spl. Svcs., Paramus, NJ, 1984—; physician Tenafly (N.J.) Sch. Bd. Edn., 1990-94. Mem. Tenafly Bd. Edn., 1983-89, pres., 1986-88.

HAFTER, RUTH ANNE, library director, educator; b. NYC, Apr. 18, 1935; BA in History and Econs. cum laude, Brandeis U., 1956; cert. Bus. Adminstrn., Harvard-Radcliffe U., 1957; MLS, Columbia U., 1963; PhD in Libr. and Info. Studies, U. Calif., Berkeley, 1984. Supr. sch. librs. Halifax County, N.S., Can., 1965-66; asst. edn. libr. Harvard U., Cambridge, Mass., 1967-68; univ. libr. St. Mary's U., Halifax, N.S., Can., 1969-75; libr. dir. Sonoma State U., Rohnert Park, Calif., 1978-86, San Jose (Calif.) State U., 1986-91, prof. div. libr. and info. sci., 1987-99, prof. emeritus, 1999—. Instr. St. Mary's U., 1972-75, Sonoma State U., 1982-85, U. Calif., Berkeley, 1975-78, 85-86; cons. Ministry of State Urban Affairs, Can., 1975, Sonoma County Hist. Records, 1979-80; coord. Geysers Info. Project., 1980-81; project humanist Calif. Coun. for Humanities, 1981-83; dir. Indochinese Cultures project Nat. Endowment for Humanities, 1983-84, Videodisc Work Shop Calif. State U., 1987—, Online Pub. Catalog Implementation, 1989; pres. Beethoven Ctr. San Jose State U., 1987-88. Author: Academic Librarians and Cataloging Networks: Visibility, Quality and Professional Status, 1986, (with George Rawlyk) Acadian Education in Nova Scotia, 1970; contbr. articles to profl. jours. Mem. Mayor Feinstein's com. on Teaching of Holocaust, San Francisco, 1986, adv. com. Foothill Coll. Libr. Tech. Asst. Program, 1987—, San Jose Pub. Libr. Found., 1987—, bd. govs. 1987-89, exec. bd. Friends of San Jose Pub. Libr., 1989—, Calif. State Libr. Networking Task Force, 1989—, adv. bd. dirs. Frances Gullard Child Devel. Ctr., 1990—; pres. alumni bd. Sch. Libr. and Info. Sci, U. Calif., Berkeley, 1993-94. Inst. Ethnography grantee Dept. Edn., 1994-95. Mem. ALA (com. on accreditation, field site vis. bd. 1982—, libr. career resource network 1987—, program com. reference and adult svcs. div. 1989—), Coop. Libr. Agy. Systems and Svcs. (bd. govs. 1988—, acad. librs. rep.), Calif. Acad. and Rsch. Librs. (pres. 1983-84), Calif. Libr. Assn. (legis. network 1988—, chair continuing edn. com. 1997), North Bay Coop. Assn. (exec. com. 1984-85), Phi Beta Kappa, Phi Kappa Phi. Home: 177 19th St Apt 1E Oakland CA 94612-4653 E-mail: rhafter@earthlink.net.

HAGAN, DALIA LAPATINSKAS, library director; b. Chgo., Apr. 20, 1953; d. Vytautas V. and Alice Lapatinskas. BA, U. Wash., 1974; MS, Drexel U., 1979. Cataloger, info. specialist Air Products & Chems., Allentown, Pa., 1979—82; cataloger Aurora U., Ill., 1983—84; head tech. svcs. St. Charles Pub. Libr., Ill., 1984—86, Tacoma Pub. Libr., 1986—88; libr. dir. St. Martin's Coll., Lacey, Wash., 1988—2005, Whitman Coll., Walla Walla, Wash., 2005—. Faculty pres. St. Martin's Coll., 2001—02. Editl. bd. (mag.) Choice, 2006—. Trustee Olympia Timberland Libr. Bd., Wash., 1989—97. Recipient Outstanding Student award, Spl. Libr. Assn., Phila. Chpt., 1979. Mem.: ALA (lama bes member-at-large 2004—), N.W. Commn. on Colls. and Univs. (evaluator 2004—), Lithuanian-Am. Assn., Seattle Chpt. (member-at-large 2001—05), Orbis Cascade Alliance, NW Assoc. Pvt. Coll. & U. Libraries (chair 2002—03), Daughters of Lithuania, NW Chpt. (sec. 2000—), Beta Phi Mu (Alice B. Kroeger award 1979). Office: Whitman Coll 345 Boyer St Walla Walla WA 99362 Office Phone: 509-527-5193.

HAGAN, DIANA LYNN, elementary school educator; b. Clark AFB, Philippines, May 28, 1969; d. John and Diane George (Stepmother), David (Stepfather) and Barbara Kearney; married, Aug. 26, 2005; children: Jonathan, Matthew, Andrew. AS, Onondaga CC, Syracuse, NY, 1989; BS, SUNY, Cortland, 1992; MS, SUNY, Albany, 1999. Cert. elem. and early secondary edn. tchr. NY. Sci. tchr. Albany City Sch. Dist., 1997—. Home: 174 County Rt 405 South Westerlo NY 12083 Office: Albany City Sch Dist 700 Wasington Ave Albany NY 12203 Personal E-mail: dl826gh@verizon.net.

HAGAN, JUDITH ANN, social worker; b. Chgo., May 7, 1943; d. Glenn Dean and Laura May Phillips; m. George Leonard Hagan, Nov. 13, 1993; children from previous marriage: Stephen L. Curtis, Michael L. Curtis. AA with highest distinction, Scottsdale (Ariz.) CC, 1978; BS magna cum laude, Ariz. State U., 1979, MSW, 1985. LCSW Ariz.; cert. critical incident stress mgmt. FEMA. Bus. assoc. Am. Express, Phoenix, 1980-89; client svcs. rep. Pharm. Card Sys., Scottsdale, 1986-87; case mgr. Child Protective Svcs., State of Ariz., Phoenix, 1985; dir. social svcs. S.W. Adoptions, Scottsdale, 1989-92; employee assistance profl. Ariz. Dept. Transp., Phoenix, 1992-96, program and projects specialist procurement staff, 1996—; pvt. practice psychotherapy; owner, operator Complete Counseling Svcs., Phoenix; mobil therapist Terros Behavioral Health Agy., Phoenix, 2002—03; counselor II Valle Del Sol, Inc., 2003; counselor sex offender treatment New Horizons Counseling Svc., 2003—05; pvt. practice Desert View Counseling and Cons., 2005—. Presenter programs on reconstituted families, relationships and mental health, drug abuse, stress mgmt.; freelance writer, editor. Writer, editor: Ariz. Dept. Transp. Women's Resource Group newsletter; editor: pub. newsletter Procurement Update, 1997—2002; author, dir. (pub. tng. film) Panorama County Svcs. Mgrs., 1984; author: Ariz. Dept. Transp. Intellectual Properties Drug Abuse Program, 1993; column writer: Moon Valley Tattler, 1999—2003. Activist Green Peace, LA, 1971, NOW, 1980, Civil Rights, Sumter, SC, 1962, Citizens Against Cockfighting, 1998, Yr. of Humane Child, 2000; vol. cmty. devel. Battered Women's and Children's Shelter Maricopa County, Phoenix, 1979. Recipient seal, Acad. Cert. Social Workers, 1996—97. Mem.: Ariz. Counselors Assn. (policy com., editor newsletter, editor newsletter 2003—), Women Mil. Svc. Am. (charter), Phi Theta Kappa. Avocations: healthy gourmet cooking, yoga, public speaking. Address: 11361 N 99th Ave # 106 Peoria AZ 85345 Office Phone: 602-291-4646.

HAGANS, VALERIE MAE GEE, special education educator; b. San Antonio, Mar. 23, 1966; d. George Francis and Mae (Smith) Gee; m. Danny Franklin Hagans, June 24, 1989. Bachelors in Early Childhood Edn., Meth. Coll., 1988; MA in Edn.-Spl. Edn., Fayetteville State U., 1993. Cert. tchr., N.C.; nat. bd. cert. tchr. Spl. educator Cumberland County Pub. Schs., Fayetteville, N.C., 1989—. Mem. Alpha Delta Kappa (Gamma Sigma chpt.), Coun. for Exceptional Children, Omicron Delta Kappa. Methodist. Home: 171 Water Ridge Ln Stedman NC 28391 Office: Warrenwood Elem Sch 4618 Rosehill Rd Fayetteville NC 28311 Office Phone: 910-488-6609. E-mail: valeriehagans@ccs.k12.nc.us.

HAGARTY, WENDY L., music educator; b. Worcester, Mass., Apr. 27, 1962; d. James and Thalia Oosterman; m. Ted Hagarty, July 20, 1990; 1 child, Caitlin M. MusB, Berklee Coll. of Music, Boston, 1984. Cert. tchr. Mass., 1984. Elem. music tchr. Millis Pub. Schs., Mass., 1984—89, Framingham Pub. Schs., Mass., 1989—. Colorguard coach Foxborough Pub. Schs., Mass., 1989—93; assoc. dir. music Medway Cmty. Ch., Mass., 1997—2001. Mem. ch. praise team; mem. charity fund raising bicycle ride Cystic Fibrosis. Dunning Video Diary grantee, Framingham Edn. Found., 1997. Mem.: Mass. Teacher's Assn., Tech. Inst. Music Educators, Mass. Music Educator's Nat. Conf. Independent. Avocations: skiing, reading, travel. Office: CA Dunning Elem Sch 48 Frost Street Framingham MA 01701 Office Phone: 508-626-9156. Personal E-mail: twch@verizon.net.

HAGBERG, KAREN L., lawyer; b. Cleve., 1953; BA, SUNY Binghamton, 1977; JD cum laude, Cornell U., 1984. Bar: N.Y. 1985, Japan (Gaikokuho-Jimu-Bengoshi) 1999. Law clk. to Hon. Miriam Goldman Cedarbaum U.S. Dist. Ct., So. Dist. N.Y., 1986—87; assoc. Morrison & Foerster LLP, N.Y.C., 1987—92, ptnr., 1992—97, ptnr.-Tokyo office, 1997—2002, mng. ptnr.-N.Y. office, 2002—. Office: Morrison & Foerster LLP 1290 Avenue of Americas New York NY 10104-0185 Office Phone: 212-468-8032. Office Fax: 212-468-7900. Business E-Mail: khagberg@mofo.com.

HAGBERG, VIOLA WILGUS, lawyer; b. July 3, 1952; d. William E. and Jean Shelton (Barlow) Wilgus; m. Chris Eric Hagberg, Feb. 19, 1978. BA, Furman U., Greenville, SC, 1974; JD, U. SC, 1978, U. Tulsa, 1978; diploma (hon.), DOD Army Logistics Sch., Ft. Lee, Va., 1981—82. Bar: Okla. 78, U.S. Ct. Appeals (4th cir.) 79. With Lawyers Com. for Civil Rights, Washington, 1979; pub. utility specialist Fed. Energy Regulatory Commn., Washington, 1979—80; contract specialist U.S. Army, C.E., Ft. Shafter, Hawaii, 1980—81; contract officer/supervisory contract specialist Tripler Army Med. Ctr., Hawaii, 1981—83; supervisoty procurement analyst and chief policy Procurement divsn. USCG, Washington, 1983; contracts officer and chief Avionics Engrng. Contracting Br., 1984; procurement analyst office of sec. Dept. Transp., 1984—85; contracting officer Naval Regional Contracting Ctr., Long Beach, Calif., 1985—87; chief acquisition rev. and policy Hdqrs. Def. Mapping Agy., Washington, 1987—92, dir. acquisitions Fairfax, Va., 1992—93, dir. acquisition policy, 1994—96; dir. acquisition policy, tech. and legis. programs Nat. Mapping and Imagery Agy., 1996—97, dep. assoc. and sr. counsel for adminstrv. law and litigation; dir. acquisition policy, tech. and legis. programs Office Gen. Counsel, Nat. Geospatial Intelligence Agy., Bethesda. Mem.: ABA (law student divsn. liaison 1977—78), Okla. Bar Assn., Va. State Bar Assn., Nat. Contract Mgmt. Assn., Kappa Delta Epsilon, Phi Alpha Delta. Home: 9810 Meadow Valley Dr Vienna VA 22181-3215 Office: Nat Geospatial Intelligence Agy Office Gen Counsel 4600 Sangamore (MS-D-10) Bethesda MD 20816

HAGE, CHRISTINE LIND, library administrator; b. Detroit, Nov. 26, 1949; d. Richards I. and Letizia L. (Majorana) Lind; m. Robert M. Hage, Aug. 21, 1971; children: Paul R., Andrew M. BA in English, Oakland U., Rochester Hills, Mich., 1970; MLS, U. Mich., 1971. Cert. libr., Mich. Head of adult and circulation svcs. Troy (Mich.) Pub. Libr., 1971-77; dir. Shelby Twp. (Mich.) Libr., 1977-81; head of adult svcs. Rochester Hills Pub. Libr., 1981-88, dir., 1988-99, Clinton-Macomb Pub. Libr., Mich., 1999—2005, Rochester Hills Public Libr., Mich., 2006—. Chair Detroit Suburban Librs. Roundtable, 1981, 92; chair Oakland County Union List of Serials, 1989. Editor: Public Library Policy Resource Manual, 1987, Michigan Associations Directory, 1987. Bd. dirs. Greater Rochester Area Cmty. Found., 1994-98. Recipient Rose award AAUW, Utica, Mich., 1980; named Mich. Libr. of the Yr., 1997. Mem. Am. Libr Assn. (councilor), Pub. Libr. Assn. (bd. dirs. 1990-94, pres. 1998-99), Mich. Libr. Assn. (chair numerous units 1971—), Mount Clemens Rotary. Lutheran. Home: 1893 Ludgate Ln Rochester Hills MI 48309-2965 Office: Clinton Macomb Public Library 40900 Romeo Plank Rd Clinton Township MI 48038-2955 E-mail: christine@cmpl.org.*

HAGE, MADELEINE COTTENET, French language educator; b. Metz, France, Sept. 22, 1933; came to U.S., 1966; d. Jean Auguste-Albert and Germaine (Spiegelstein) Cottenet; m. Jerald Hage, Jan. 27, 1966; children: Martin, Rebecca Guyot. Agrégation, U. Paris, 1965; D. U. Nancy (France) II, 1974. Prof. Lycée Technique, Cachan, France, 1960-66; Fulbright-Hays cons. Wis. Dept. Pub. Instrn., Madison, 1966-67; prof. Madison Area Tech. Coll., 1967-75; prof. English, Inst. Tech., Cachan, 1975-78; prof. French, U. Md., College Park, Md., 1978—2001, prof. emeritus, 2001—. Author: Gisèle Prassinos ou le Désir du lieu intime, 1988, also other books; co-editor: Dictionnaire Littéraire des Femmes écrivains de langue Française, 1996; contbr. articles to profl. jours. and anthologies. Decorated chevalier des Palmes Académiques (France); Fulbright scholar, 1961-62, Fulbright-Hays scholar, 1966-67. Mem. MLA, Am. Assn. French Tchrs. Avocations: music, tai-chi, hiking. Office: U Md French And Italian Dept College Park MD 20742-0001

HAGEDORN, DOROTHY LOUISE, librarian; b. McKeesport, Pa., Sept. 4, 1929; d. Emil and Catherine (Middlemiss) H. BA, Seton Hill Coll., 1950; MS, Fordham U., 1952, Columbia U., 1957. Tech. info specialist Lawrence Radiation Lab., Berkeley, Calif., 1961-64; libr. New Orleans Pub. Libr., 1964-71, Tulane U., New Orleans, 1971—. Mem. ALA, La. Library Assn. Office: Tulane U Howard-Tilton Meml Libr 7001 Freret St New Orleans LA 70118-5549

HAGEN, JOANNE R., elementary school educator; b. Sparta, Wis., Aug. 14, 1967; d. Maynard B. and Marie A. Hagen. BA, Coll. St. Scholastica, Duluth, Minn., 1989; MA, Viterbo U., LaCrosse, Wis., 2003. Tchr. presch., primary child care Wee Welcome Inn Child Ctr., Sussex, Wis., 1989—95; substitute tchr. Sparta (Wis.) Area Schs., 1995—97, tchr. title I, 1997—99, tchr. 5th grade, 1999—. Nominee Disney Tchr. of Yr.; recipient 3d pl. WebFair Competition award, U. Wis.-Stout, 2002. Mem.: Delta Kappa Gamma Alpha Upsilon (chpt. women educators). Avocations: reading, walking, crocheting, sports, computers. Home: PO Box 34 Sparta WI 54656 Office: Sparta Area Schs 506 N Black River St Sparta WI 54656 Business E-Mail: jhagen@spartan.org.

HAGEN, LINDA RENEE, secondary school educator; b. Pomona, Calif., Aug. 16, 1958; d. Sarah Ann and Oral Venson Foster; m. John William Hagen, June 18, 1983; children: Sierra Dawn, Christopher John. BA, BS, Calif. Bapt. Coll., Riverside, 1980. Cert. pre-advanced placement/advanced placement Ark. Dept. Edn., 2000, English lang. learner Ark. Tech U., 2001. Tchr., coach Goldenwest Christian Sch., Westminster, Calif., 1980—82; tchr., coach, athletic dir. Leffingwell Christian Sch., Norwalk, Calif., 1982—92; tchr. Coleman Jr. H.S., Van Buren, Ark., 1995—. Mem. Friends of Van Buren (Ark.) Pub. Libr., 2006, Concord Bapt. Ch., Van Buren/Alma, Ark., 2000—06; com. chmn. Parent Involvement Com., Van Buren, 2004—06. Baptist. Avocations: reading, music. Office Phone: 479-471-3160.

HAGEN, WENDY W., public relations executive; Grad., Georgetown U. Exec. v.p./chief mktg. officer Arnold Worldwide; now exec. v.p. Porter Novelli, Washington. Mem. bd. trustees The Robert Wood Johnson Found., Princeton, NJ, 2001—. Office: Porter Novelli 1909 K St NW Washington DC 20006 Office Phone: 202-973-5800. Office Fax: 202-973-5858.

HAGER, BEULAH ELIZABETH, lay worker; b. Marlette, Mich., Mar. 10, 1929; d. Kent J. and Hazel Fern Hager. BA, Bob Jones U., Greenville, S.C., 1950; MA, U. P.R., Rio Piedras, 1980. Tchr. jr. high Emmanuel Christian Sch., Pontiac, Mich., 1950—51; missionary Bapt. Mid-Missions, Hato Mayor and Santo Domingo, Dominican Republic, 1951—75, San Juan and Cayey, PR, 1975—84, Greenville, SC, 1984—. Founder, dir. Primary Sch. Bapt. Mid-Missions, Hato Mayor, 1953—65. Author (textbook): Spanish I for Christian Schools, 1993, Spanish II for Christian Schools, 1995; author: Coleccion de Lecciones Objetivas, 1989; translator: Formula Para La Unidad Familiar, 1989. Recipient Recognition 50 Yrs. Outstanding Svc., S.C. Ho. Rep., 2002, Recognition Missionary Svcs. Dominican Republic, Assn. Bapt. Churches, 2006, Plaque for Founding Schs. in Dominican Republic, Colegio Bautista Dominicano, 2006. Republican. Avocations: reading, cooking, travel. Home: 3400 Edwards Rd Taylors SC 29687

HAGER, ELIZABETH SEARS, state legislator, social services administrator; b. Washington, Oct. 31, 1944; d. Hess Thatcher and Elizabeth Grace (Harper) Sears; m. Dennis Sterling Hager, Sept. 3, 1966; children: Annie Elizabeth, Lucie Caroline. BA, Wellesley Coll., 1966; MPA, U. N.H., 1979. Prin. Philbrook Ctr., Concord, NH, 1970-71; rep. N.H. Gen. Ct., Concord, 1973-76, 85-94, 1996—; del. N.H. Constitutional Conv., Concord, 1974, 84; campaign coord. Anderson for Pres. Rep. Primary, NH, 1980; mem. Concord City Coun., 1982-90; mayor City of Concord, 1988-90; exec. dir. United Way of Merrimack County, Concord, 1996—. Bd. dirs. Lincoln Fin. Variable Funds, TD Banknorth, NH. Pres. Greater Concord United Way, 1980-81; campaign chair United Way of Merrimack County, Concord, 1986. Republican. Episcopalian. Office: 46 N Main St Concord NH 03301-4913 Home: 5 Pleasant View Ave Concord NH 03301-2555

HAGER, LOUISE ALGER, retired chaplain; b. Spokane, Wash., Dec. 15, 1923; d. Russel S. and Thelma Ella (Geib) Alger; m. Bernard Coe, Nov. 16, 1945 (dec. July 1965); children: Cynthia W., Marjorie L.; m. Onslow B. Hager, Jan. 16, 1970 (dec. Dec. 1983). BEd, Nat. Coll. Edn., 1946; M of Theol. Studies, St. Paul Sch. Theology, 1997. Kindergarten tchr. Edgewater Park Bd. Edn., Beverly, NJ, 1946-47, 59-83; pres. bd. mgrs. Cinnaminson (N.J.) Home, 1985-88; chaplain Rsch. Med. Ctr., Kansas City, Mo., 1986-88; assoc. chaplain John Knox Village, Lee's Summit, Mo., 1988-98; ret., 1998; vol. chaplain, psychogeriatric inpatient unit Sheppard Pratt Health Sys., 1999—; vol. chaplain Hollowell and Taylor Halls health care units Inpatient Nursing Svcs. at Broadmead Retirement Cmty., 1999—. Mem., ethics com. Sheppard Pratt Health Sys., 2004—05. Chaplain vol. Burlington County Hosp., Mt. Holly, N.J., 1987-88; lay minister; mem. Sheppard Pratt Ethics Com., 2004—. Recipient Disting. Alumni award, Nat. Louis U., 2002, Vol. Impact award for extrordinary svc., Sheppard Pratt Health Hosp., 2002. Mem. NEA, Lee's Summit Ministerial Soc., Coll. Chaplains, Am. Soc. on Aging, Mid-Am. Congress on Aging, Sheppard Pratt 1853 Soc. Democrat. Mem. Soc. Of Friends. Avocations: reading, piano playing, singing, sewing, walking. Home: Broadmead 13801 York Rd Apt M1 Cockeysville MD 21030-1891

HAGER, MARIA LYNNE, music educator; b. Natrona Heights, Pa., Aug. 31, 1952; d. Joseph Frank and Anna Suitek Brim; m. Patrick K. Hager, June 8, 1974; children: Elizabeth, Sara, Daniel, Timothy. BA in Music Elem. Edn., Edinboro State Coll., Pa., 1973; M Reading, St. Bonaventure U., NY, 1998. Music tchr., substitute tchr. Pioneer Ctrl. Sch., Yorkshire, NY, 1974—93; music tchr. Holland Ctrl. Sch., NY, 1993—. Choir dir. St. Mary's Parish, Strykersville, Pa., 1974—. Named Tchr. of Yr., Holland Tchrs. Assn., 2005. Mem.: St. Mary's Altar Rosery Soc. (pres. 2002—05), Delta Kappa Gamma. Roman Catholic. Avocation: baking. Home: 898 Geer Rd Arcade NY 14009 Office: Holland Ctrl Sch Holland NY 14080

HAGER, MARY HASTINGS, nutritionist, educator, consultant; b. Upland, Calif., Mar. 27, 1948; d. Howard Benjamin and Miriam Agnes Hastings; m. Douglas Francis Hager, Jan. 4, 1982; children: Marghet Janet, Bettina Miriam. BS in Foods and Nutrition, U. Del., 1971; MS in Nutrition and Dietetics, U. Calif., Davis, 1973, PhD in Nutrition, 1978. Registered dietitian. Nutritionist U. Calif. Sch. Medicine, Davis, 1973-74; staff scientist Procter and Gamble Co., Cin., 1978-83, devel. staff, 1986-87; asst. prof. Coll. Mount St. Joseph, Cin., 1983-85, Tex. Christian U., Ft. Worth, 1987-89; vis. lectr. Rutgers U., New Brunswick, NJ, 1989-90; assoc. prof. Coll. of St. Elizabeth, Morristown, NJ, 1991-96, prof., assoc. dean, 1996-2000; scientist Entelos, Inc., Menlo Park, Calif., 2000—03; dir. Hope House, Dover, NJ, 2003; sr. mgr. for regulatory affairs Am. Dietetic Assn., 2004—. Cons. IGA Grocers, Cin., 1984-85, Hoffman-LaRoche Corp., Nutley, N.J., 1989-90, Procter and Gamble Co., Cin., 1990—; dietetic internship site visitor. Contbr. articles and abstracts to profl. publs. Chmn. bd. dirs. Greater Cin. Nutrition Coun., 1985-86; mem. edn. task force Am. Heart Assn., Ft. Worth, 1988-89; pub. edn. com. Am. Cancer Soc., Ft. Worth, 1988-89; mem. Health Care Reform Adv. Bd., 11th Congl. Dist., 1993-94. Grad. fellow Procter and Gamble Co., 1975-78; Amy Rextrew scholar U. Del., 1970; grantee Tex. Christian U. Rsch. Fund, 1988. Fellow Am. Dietetic Assn; mem. Am. Inst. Nutrition (rsch. award 1978), Am. Soc. Enteral Parenteral Nutrition Soc. for Nutrition Edn., N.J. Dietetic Assn. (pres.-elect 1996-97, pres. 1997-98, ho. dels. 1998—), Mortar Bd., Sigma Xi. Democrat. Episcopalian. Avocations: swimming, walking. Home: 12 Kings Ridge Rd Randolph NJ 07869-2743 Office: American Dietetic Assn Ste 480 1120 Connecticut Ave NW Washington DC 20036 Office Phone: 202-775-8277 ext. 6007. Business E-Mail: mhager@eatright.org.

HAGERTHEY, GWENDOLYN IRENE, retired music educator; b. Sheffield, Eng., Sept. 28, 1937; arrived in U.S., 1938; d. Colin Clifford and Dorothy Abbott Oldfield; m. George Robert Hagerthey, June 23, 1962; children: Wendy Lee Hagerthey Canfield, Scot Edward. BS in Music, Trenton State Coll., 1959. Tchr. music Northfield Pub. Schs., NJ, 1959—64, 1971—74, Enfield Pub. Schs., Conn., 1974—78, Mt. Olive Twp. Pub. Schs., Budd Lake, NJ, 1978—99; ret., 1999. Organist, choir dir. various chs. including Stanhope (N.J.) Meth. Ch., 1950—98; camp music dir. Willow Lake Day Camp, Lake Hopatcong, NJ, 1985—97. Vol. Shore Meml. Hosp., Somers Pt., NJ, 1999—, Meadowview Nursing Home, Northfield, 1999—; dir. Atlantic County Hist. Soc., Somers Pt., 1999—. Named Rookie of Yr., Shore Meml. Hosp., 2000; recipient Govs. award for Outstanding Tchg., 1991. Mem.: AAUW (1st v.p. 1959—61). Home: 26 E Meyran Ave Somers Point NJ 08244

HAGGARD, GERALDINE LANGFORD, primary school educator, adult education educator, consultant, writer; b. Wellington, Tex., Dec. 12, 1929; d. Frank and Zelma Dell (Edmondson) Langford; children: Colby, Sarah, Mary. MEd, Tex. Women's U., 1973, EdD, 1980; Cert. in Reading Recovery, Ohio State U., 1989. Elem. sch. tchr. Denton County (Tex.) Schs., 1949-62, Plano (Tex.) Ind. Sch. Dist., 1963-69, reading tchr., reading dir., 1999-2001. Vis. prof. Tex. Woman's U.; cons. for sch. dists. Editor and author lang. arts texts; contbr. articles to profl. jours.; author: Teaching and Assessing Comprehension Strategies Grades 3, 4 and 5, 2003. Sunday Sch. tchr. Prairie Creek Baptist Ch., Plano, 1994—; vol. facilitator Journey of Hope program for grief counseling. Named Hero Plano ISD centennial celebration, 1998, Dreamers, Doers and Unsung Hero Real Estate Found.; recipient Outstanding Edn. Vol. of Yr. award, 2006. Mem. N.Am. Coun. Reading Recovery (bd. mem. 1995-99), Internat. Reading Assn., Tex. State Coun. Reading, Tex. Assn. Improvement of Reading, Coalition Reading English Suprs. Tex. (sec. 1994-97), Tex. Ret. Tchrs. Assn. (Plano chpt.), Alpha Delta Kappa, Delta Kappa Gamma, Phi Delta Kappa. Home: 2017 Meadowcreek Dr Plano TX 75074-4663

HAGGERTY, GRETCHEN R., accounting and finance executive; BS in Acctg., Case Western Reserve U., Cleveland; JD, Duquesne U., Pitts. CPA. V.p. acctg. and fin. U.S. Steel Group, Pitts., tax assist., 1977—80, leasing analyst, 1980—82, sr. financial analyst, 1982—84, corp. finance mgr., 1984—85, dir. plant and gen. acctg. USS Chemicals Div., 1985—86, gen. tax atty., dir. taxes, 1987—88, assist. treasurer corp. finance, 1988—89, assist. comptroller corp. acctg., 1989—91; v.p. and treasurer USX Corp., Pitts., 1991—98; v.p. acctg. and finance U.S. Steel Group, Pitts., 1998—2002, sr. v.p. and controller, 2002, sr. v.p. and treasurer, 2002—03, exec. v.p., treasurer, CFO, 2003—. Chmn. U.S. Steel and Carnegie Pension Fund; mem. exec. com. Pa. Bus. Roundtable; bd. dir. Highmark Inc. Bd. mem. Civic Light Opera, United Way Allegheny County. Mem.: Allegheny County Bar Assoc. Office: US Steel 600 Grant St Pittsburgh PA 15219-2800*

HAGGETT, ROSEMARY ROMANOWSKI, academic administrator; BA in Biology, U. Bridgeport, 1974; PhD in Physiology, U. Va., 1979. Postdoctoral fellow Northwestern U., Evanston, Ill., 1979-82; asst. prof. biology Loyola U. Chgo., 1982-87; from program dir. to divsn. dir. animals and nutrition USDA, 1988-94, dep. assoc. adminstr., 1988-94; prof. animal and vet. sci. W.Va. U., Morgantown, 1994—, dean Coll. Agr., Forestry and Consumer Scis., 1994-99, assoc. provost acad. programs, 1999—2003; dir. divsn. undergrad. edn. NSF, 2003—; acting dep. asst. dir. EHR, 2005—. Office: EHR NSF Ste 805 4201 Wilson Blvd Arlington VA 22230 Office Phone: 703-292-8600. Business E-Mail: rhaggett@nsf.gov.

HAGGIS, MARY RIPLEY, nurse, genealogist; b. Ellsworth, Ohio, July 13, 1934; d. Sehon Miller and Hazel Emma (Hoyle) Ripley; m. William Campbell Haggis, Aug. 7, 1955; children: Cheryl Rene, William Campbell II. Grad., Salem City Hosp. Sch. Nursing, Ohio, 1955. RN Ohio. RN, surgical nurse operating room Mercy Hosp., Springfield, Ohio, 1955—57; RN gen. duty Good Samaritan Hosp., Zanesville, Ohio, 1959—60; RN gen. duty and intensive care unit Ohio Valley Hosp., Steubenville, Ohio, 1968—72; RN Family Practice Office of Dr. Paul W. McFadden, Dover, Ohio, 1979—99. Leader Steubenville Brownies, 1968, Jr. Girl Scouts, Steubenville, 1969, Cub Scouts, Steubenville, 1970—71; sec. Dover Band Boosters, Ohio, 1976—78; pres. Arts Coun. Tuscarawas, Dover, Ohio, 1979—84; stats. sec. Ctrl. Conf. Ohio United Luth. Ch. Women, Columbus, Ohio, 1961; tchr. Grace Luth. Ch., 1984—97, deacon, 1990—98; bd. mem. Young Women's Christian Assn., Steubenville, 1966—67, Personal and Family Counseling, Dover, 1974—75. Recipient Surg. Nurse award, Salem City Hosp. Sch. Nursing, 1955, Founder's Day award, Grace Luth. Ch., 1997. Mem.: DAR, Settlers and Builders of Ohio, Ohio Ea. Star, Pioneer Families of Trumbull County, Pioneer Families of Mahoning County, Soc. Civil War Families, First Families of Ohio, South Ctrl. Pa. Geneal. Soc., Tuscarawas County Geneal. Soc., New Eng. Hist. and Geneaology Soc., Order St. Luke the Physician, Trumbull County Geneal. Soc., Mahoning County Geneal. Soc., Ohio Geneal. Soc. Republican. Lutheran. Avocations: genealogy, travel, bible study. Home: 827 E 4th St Dover OH 44622-1319 Personal E-mail: mbhaggis@tusco.net.

HAGIN, NANCY, printmaker, painter; b. Elizabeth, NJ, 1940; BFA, Carnegie-Mellon U., 1962; MFA, Yale U., 1964. Prof. Maryland Inst. Coll. Art, Balt., 1964—73, Pratt Inst., NYC, 1973—74, 1985, RI Sch. of Design, 1974, Fashion Inst. Tech., NYC, 1974—, Cooper Union, NY, 1982—92, SUNY Purchase, NY, 1994, U. Arts, Phila., 1999. One-woman shows include Alpha Gallery, Boston, 1972, 1976, 1974, 1979, 1982, 1985, 1992, 1995, 2000, U. Md., 1973, Terry Dintenfass Gallery, NY, 1975, 1978, Fischbach Gallery, NY, 1981, 1982, 1985, 1987, 1989, 1991, 1993, 1995, 1998, 1999, 2002, 2004, exhibited in group shows at Balt. Mus. Ann. Exhbn., 1965—70, IFA Gallery, Washington DC, 1968—73, Allen Frumkin Gallery, NY, 1971, Smithsonian Inst., Washington DC, 1974, Indpls. Mus. Art, 1976, Butler Inst., Ohio, 1977, Lehigh U., Pa., 1979, Nassau County Mus. Art, Roslyn, NY, 1980, New Britain Mus. Am. Art, Conn., 1982, Rahr-West Mus., Wis., 1983, Fitchburg Art Mus., Mass., 1984, William Sawyer Gallery, San Francisco, 1985, C. Grimaldis Gallery, Balt., 1986, Fay Gold Gallery, Atlanta, 1989, Nat. Acad. Design, NY, 1989—90, Rice U., Tex., 1993, NJ Ctr. Visual Arts, 1994, Lizan Tops Gallery, NY, 1995, AAAL, NY, 2001, Doran Gallery, Tulsa, 2002, 323 West Gallery, NY, 2003, DeCordova Mus. & Sculpture Pk., Mass., 2003—04. Recipient Yale/Norfolk award, 1961, Purchase award, Fashion Inst. Tech., 1976, Butler Inst. Tech., 1977, Emil & Dines Carlsen award, Nat. Acad. Design, 1989; Fulbright Grant, Rome, 1966—67, McDowell Colony Fellowship, 1974, 1979, 1982, Creative Artists Pub. Svc. Grant, 1975, Artist in Residence, Palisades Interstate Pk., NY, 1975, NEA Grant, 1982, 1991. Mem.: Nat. Acad. Design, NY, 1992. Mailing: c/o Fischbach Gallery 210 11th Ave New York NY 10001

HAGIN, ROSA A., psychologist, educator; b. Elizabeth, N.J., June 14, 1921; d. William N. and Jennie B. (Smith) H BS, Trenton State Coll., 1941; MA, NYU, 1944, PhD, 1955. Diplomate: Am. Bd. Profl. Psychology. Dir. spl. svcs. Roselle Bd. Edn., NJ, 1951—58, Irvington Bd. Edn., NJ, 1958—61; fellow clin. psychology NYU Med. Ctr., 1948—51, instr., 1961—64, asst. prof., 1964—69, rsch. assoc. prof. psychology, 1969—76, rsch. prof., 1976—79, co-dir. learning disorders unit, 1964—83; prof. divsn. psychol. and ednl. svcs. Fordham U. at Lincoln Center, N.Y.C., 1979—90; prof. emeritus Fordham U., 1990—; pvt. practice psychology N.Y.C., 1955—95. Contbr. articles to profl. jours Fellow APA; mem. NEA (life), N.J. Psychol. Assn Home: 14 Witherwood Dr Hamburg NJ 07419-1274

HAGINS, BARBARA J., pharmaceutical consultant; b. Johnstown, Pa., Mar. 29, 1953; d. Jack H. and Katherine E. Hagins; 2 children. BSN, U. Pitts., 1976, AD in Psychology, 1976. RN Pa., Ill. RN U. Pitts. Med. Ctr., 1976—87; unit coord. Med. Coll. Va. Hosp., Richmond, 1987—89; QA cons. Albany (N.Y.) Med. Ctr., 1989—91; assoc. dir. regulatory affairs Abbott Labs., Abbott Park, Ill., 1991—2003; pres., prin. cons. Barbara Hagins & Assoc., Inc., Gurnee, Ill., 2003—. Mem.: Drug Info. Assn., Food and Drug Law Inst. Office: 4756 Kings Way N Gurnee IL 60031

HAGLUND, BERNICE MARION, elementary school educator; b. Negaunee, Mich. d. Paul and Bernice Cody; m. Charles Haglund; children: Christopher C., Mary. BA, No. Mich. U., 1971, MA, 1978. Tchr. Arnold Elem. Sch., Mich. Center Schs., Mich. Social sec., v.p., pres. Mich. Ctr. Jr.

Child Study Group, 1979-83, com. mem. sci. com., dept. head to curriculum counsel, 1993—. V.p., treas., social sec. Commonwealth Wives, Jackson, 1971-82. Mich. State grantee U.S. Optical soc., 1993. Mem. AAUW (sec. social edn. area), ASCD, Bus. and Profl. Women (sec. 1969-71, coord. study group 1972—, sec., social, contact edn. chair, woemn's issues), Orton Soc. (workshop trainer), Mich. Dyslexia Inst., Mich. Sci. Tchrs. Assn., Nat. Sci. Tchrs., Acad. Orton Gillingham, Phi Delta Kappa. fellow, of Orton Gillingham Soc., Delta Kappa Gamma. Roman Catholic. Home: 1840 Noon Rd Jackson MI 49201-9154

HAGMANN, LILLIAN SUE, violin instructor; b. Fontana, Calif., Mar. 10, 1931; d. Riley Royston and Winifred Lillian (Humphry) Green; m. Armand P. Oueilhe, Dec. 17, 1950 (div. 1971); children: Ellen Lynne Oueilhe Keene, Karen Sue Oueilhe Stanton, A. Louis Oueilhe (dec. 1971), Gregoire Pierce Oueilhe; m. Rolf Hagmann, May 19, 1971. AA, Chaffey Coll., 1951; Travel Counselor, Internat. Travel Tng., Chgo., 1974; student, Suzuki Violin Tchr. Tng. Inst., Guelph, Can., 1992, Suzuki Violin Tchr. Tng. Inst., Forest Grove, Oreg., 1993, 97, Occidental Coll., Eagle Rock, Calif., 1994, Suzuki Violin Tchr. Tng. Inst., Stevens Point, Wis., 1995, Suzuki Violin Tchr. Tng. Inst., Aspen, Colol., 1998, Suzuki Violin Tchr. Tng. Inst., Chgo., 2000. Pricer MacNall Bldg. Materials, Santa Barbara, Calif., 1964-67; office mgr. Laguna Blanca Sch. Devel. Program, Santa Barbara, 1968; pub. rels. asst. to mgr. Goleta (Calif.) Savs. and Loan, 1969-71; travel counselor Around The World Travel, Palatine, Ill., 1974-77; travel mgr./dir. pub. rels. Newport Area Travel, Newport Beach, Calif., 1977-80; travel counselor Cresenta Valley Travel, La Crescenta, Calif., 1981; violin instr. Arise Acad. Arts, Pomona, Calif., 1989-94, U. Redlands (Calif.) Cmty. Sch. Music, 1994—2003, Arts Encounter, Rowland Heights, Calif., 1996—97. Del. 1st Stringed Instrument Edn. Del., China, 1997. Mem. The Fandango Chamber Group. Violinist Santa Barbara Symphony, 1962-70, Riverside (Calif.) City Coll. Symphony, 1990-97; judge Search for Talent contest Riverside Exch. Clubs, 2000-02; active Adams Sch. PTA, Santa Barbara, 1967—; bd. dirs. Calif. Congress PTA; organizer, pres. Assn. for Neurologically Handicapped Children, 1970-71; choir Corona Cmty. Ch., 1995-97; mem. five piece ensemble Evang. Free Ch. of Corona, 2004-05, mem. Praise Orch.; organizer violin concerts for children including Master of Ceremonies, Orange County Suzuki Strings Festival, 2002-05. Mem.: Music Tchrs. Assn. Calif. Democrat. Avocations: gardening, artist. Home: 1143 Via Santiago Corona CA 92882-3950 E-mail: mrbeethoven@prodigy.net.

HAGOPIAN-GRANTZ, HOLLY ANN, elementary school educator; b. Katonah, N.Y., Nov. 21, 1955; d. Gregory Augustus and Jacqueline Reed (Waite) Hagopian; m. Anthony Ashley Grantz, June 11, 1983; children: Mark Anthony, Jacqueline Ann. BA, U. Colo., Boulder, 1977; MSc, Mt. St. Mary's Coll., L.A., 1979. Tchr. Corpus Christi Cath. Sch., Pacific Palisades, Calif., 1979—83, Holy Trinity Cath. Sch., Colo. Springs, Colo., 1983—84, Divine Redeemer Cath. Sch., Colo. Springs, 1984—87, Colo. Springs Dist. 11, 1987—. Mem.: Colo. State Edn. Assn. Avocations: bicycling, swimming, running, reading.

HAGUE, ANGELA L., artist, consultant, art gallery director; b. New Bedford, Mass., Mar. 16, 1941; d. Anthony and Alyce M. (Fraga) Perry; m. Ronald T. Hague, Sept. 29, 1962; children: Erica Hague MacNaught, Ronald J. Jr., Keith A., Ross J. Student, Cape Cod C.C., Barnstable, Mass., 1971-75, Cape Mus. Fine Arts, Dennis, Mass., 1986, R.I. Sch. Design, 1987, U. Mass., Brewster, 1988, Indian River C.C., St. Lucie, Fla., 1991; DFA (hon.), London Inst. Applied Rsch., 1994. Underwriter, claims mgr. Jacques Ins. Agy., New Bedford, 1959-62; underwriter, claims Frank Thacher Ins. Agy., Huannis, Mass., 1963-65; fin. mgr. The Hague Cos., Dennis, 1969-92; gallery sales Spectrum Gllaery Am. Art, Brewster, 1991-92; studio artist Create-A-Vision Studio Arts, Fla., also Dennis, 1991-95; art dir., tchr., art cons. Self Discovery Learning Ctr., Jensen Beach, Fla., 1994; art cons., mgr. Rose of Creede Art Gallery, Creede, Colo., 1995—; exec. dir., art workshop leader Adobe Arispace on the Silverthread, Colo., 2002—. Adj. faculty Indian River C.C., Port St. Lucie West, 1993. Curator art exhibits at galleries; display mgr. art shows and auctions; paintings and other artwork represented in pvt. collections in U.S. Mem. steering co. Earth Keeping Conf., 1989-90; rec. sec. Cape Mus. Fine Arts, 1988-89, Dennis Babe Ruth League, 1974-76; bd. dirs. Creede Repertory Theater, 1995-99; chair com. Bachelor Loop Audio Tour, 1998. Mem. Creede Arts Coun. (v.p. 1995-99), Creede-Mineral County C. of C. (bd. dirs.), Colo. Coun. on Arts, Western States Art Fedn. Avocations: interior and architectural design, floral arrangement and landscape design, theater, horticulture. Home: PO Box 40 Creede CO 81130-0040

HAGUE, DEBBIE LOU TUCKER, secondary school educator; b. Norfolk, Va., Mar. 8, 1966; d. Warren Deitrick and Betty Brimmer Tucker; m. Jeffrey Blanton Hague, Nov. 4, 1989; children: William Baxter, James Tucker, Parkerson Bruner. BA in Geography, George Mason U., Fairfax, Va., 1988, MA in Edn. Curriculum and Instrn., 1993. Tchr. Fairfax County Pub. Schs., 1989—93, Virginia Beach City Pub. Schs., Va., 1993—. Mem. stds. of learning com. Bias in History, Va., 2005—06. Active First Colonial H.S. PTA, Virginia Beach, 1993—2006, Linkhorn Park Elem. PTA, Virginia Beach, 2001—06, Youth Leadership Initiative, Charlottesville, Va., 2002—06; mem. alter guild Ea. Shore Chapel, Virginia Beach; life mem. Virginia Beach Beautification; exec. bd. Va. Coun. Social Studies, 1991—, pres., 2000—02. Named First Colonial Tchr. of Yr., First Colonial H.S. Mem.: ASCD, NEA, Va. Edn. Assn., Virginia Beach Edn. Assn., Va. Geog. Alliance, Va. Hist. Soc., Va. Coun. for the Social Studies (pres. 2000—02, awards chair, conf. exhibit chair 2001, 2002, 2003, 2004), Nat. Coun. for the Social Studies (voting del. gen. assembly 2000—03), Alpha Omicron Pi. Episcopalian. Office: First Colonial HS 1272 Mill Dam Rd Virginia Beach VA 23454 Business E-Mail: debbie.hague@vbschools.com.

HAGY, TERESA JANE, elementary school educator; b. Bristol, Va., Nov. 1, 1950; d. Don Houston and Mary Garnett (Yeatts) Hagy. AA in Pre-Edn., Va. Intermont Coll., 1970, BA in Elem. Edn., 1972; MEd, U. Va., 1976, postgrad., Radford U. Cert. technology cert. U. Va., tchr. Va., Tenn. Tchr. 1st and 4th grades St. Anne's Demonstration Sch., Bristol, Va., 1972-75; tchr. 1st, 3d, 4th, 5th and 6th grades Washington Lee Elem. Sch., Bristol, 1975—. Clin. instr. edn. Va. Intermont Coll., Bristol, 1972-75; coordinator gifted and talented program Bristol Schs., 1980-82; condr. workshops; developer tests to evaluate reading progress. Pres. women's circle Cen. Christian Ch., Bristol, Tenn., also v.p., sec. women's fellowship, libr. chmn., mem. ch. choir, dir. music for Bible Sch., 1992, Tchr. of Yr., Rotary, 2000. Mem.: AAUW (sec. 1976—79, v.p. 1981—86), NEA, Va. State Reading Assn., Internat. Reading Assn., Bristol Edn. Assn. (sec. 1978—80, chmn. Am. Edn. Week 1993, v.p. membership chair 1994—95, sch. renewal steering com. 1994—99, chair staff and personal com. 1994—99, comm. rep. 1995—97, faculty rep. 1996—98, comm. rep. 2000—, 2001—, faculty rep. 2005—), Va. Edn. Assn., Nat. Trust for Hist. Preservation, U. Va. Alumni Assn., Va. Intermont Coll. Alumni Assn. (nat. pres. 1987—89), U. Va. Alumnae Assn., Phi Theta Kappa, Delta Kappa Gamma (chpt. v.p. 1986—88, pres. 1988—90, coordinating coun. chmn. 1990—92). Republican. Avocations: singing, piano, stitchery, walking, reading. Home: 820 Virginia Ave Bristol TN 37620-3935 Office: Washington Lee Elem Sch Washington Lee Dr Bristol VA 24201 Office Phone: 840-821-5800. Business E-Mail: thagy@bristolvaschools.org.

HAHN, BEATRICE A., education educator; B, U. of Regensburg, W. Germany; MD, U. of Munich, Med. Sch., 1981. Post doctoral fellowship R.C. Gallo at the Nat. Cancer Inst., Bethesda, Md., 1982—85; prof. of medicine and microbiology U. of Ala., Dept. of Medicine, 1985—. Achievements include research in human retroviruses and associated diseases. Office: University of Alabama at Birmingham Dept of Medicine and Microbiology 720 20th St South Kaul 816 Birmingham AL 35294

HAHN, DEBORAH KAY, nurse, consultant; b. Waco, Tex., Apr. 11, 1958; d. Edwin Arthur and Melva Irene (Michelsen) H. BS in Nursing, Baylor U., 1980. Lic. R.N., Tex. Staff nurse Providence Hosp., Waco, Tex., 1980-81, head med. nurse, 1981-85; dir. svcs. All Svc. Health Care, Waco, Tex., 1985-86; office mgr. Gastrology Office, Waco, 1986-98; dir. surgical svc. Hillcrest Baptist Med. Ctr., Waco, 1998-2001; dir. home care and hospice svcs. Hillcrest Health Sys., 2001—. Instr., mem. Am. Heart Assn., 1984—. Recipient Outstanding Young Women Am. award, 1984. Mem. Central Tex. Zool. Soc., Am. Nurses Assn., Tex. Nurses Assn. (bd. dirs. 1984—, v.p. 1986-87, pres. 1988-90), Baylor U. Nursing Alumni (treas. 1987—), Soc. Gastroenterology Nurses Assn., Alpha Tau Delta (nat. v.p. 1981-83, pres. 1983-85), Sigma Theta Tau, Baylor U. Alumni Assn. (life). Lutheran. Avocations: travel, needlework, music, travel. Home: 4800 Lake Arrowhead Dr Waco TX 76710-2927 Office: 3000 Herring Ave Waco TX 76708

HAHN, ELLEN R., elementary school educator; b. Binghamton, N.Y., July 22, 1950; d. William Richard and Mary Elizabeth Phinney; m. Gary Edward Hahn, Aug. 14, 1998; children: Jennifer, Anndrea. BS, SUNY, Plattsburg, 1971; MS, SUNY, Albany, 1974; PhD, U. Wash., 1980. Cert. tchr. N.Y., Wash. Basic skills instr. Lakewood (Ohio) CC, 1974—75; basic skills tchr. Highline CC, Midway, Wash., 1975—82; reading tchr. Pierce Coll., Tacoma, 1982—84, baskic skills coord., 1984—85; adj. instr. reading U. Wash., Seattle, 1983; grant writer self-employed cons., 1985—94; elem. reading/math. tchr. Wilkeson Elem., Buckley, Wash., 1994—. Home: 25305 153d St Ct E Buckley WA 98321-9063 Office Phone: 360-829-6132. E-mail: ehahn@whiteriver.wednet.edu.

HAHN, HELENE B., former motion picture company executive; b. NYC; BA, Hofstra U.; JD, Loyola U., Calif., 1975. Bar: Calif. 1975. V.p. bus. affairs Paramount Pictures Corp., L.A., sr. v.p. bus. affairs, 1983-84; sr. v.p. bus. and legal Walt Disney Studios, Burbank, Calif., 1984-87, exec. v.p., 1987-94; co-COO Dreamworks SKG, Glendale, Calif., 1994—2003, COO, 2003—04, cons., 2004—05. Recipient Frontrunner award in bus. Sara Lee Corp., 1991, Big Sisters Achievement award, 1992, Clairol Mentor award, 1993, Women in Bus. Magnificent Seven award, 1994.

HAHN, JOAN L., art educator, artist; b. Orange City, Kans., June 21, 1930; d. Rudolph R. and Lilly E. Frager; m. Richard R. Hahn, May 23, 1953; children: David, Carol, Donald, Kathleen. BFA, Bethany Coll., Lindsborg, Kans., 1952; MS in Art Edn., Kans. State U., Manhattan, 1955. Tchr. art Clay Ctr. Elem. Schs., Kans., 1952—55; art instr. Kans. State U., Manhattan, 1955—57, Plainview H.S., Tex., 1962—64; cons. pvt. art studio, 1964—. Vol. artist layouts Children's Christian Concern Soc., Topeka. One-woman shows include, 1962—2003. Mem. bd. Heart Assn., Decatur, Ill., Emergency Shelter, Manhattan, Raymer Soc. Recipient Alumni award of Merit, Bethany Coll., 2003. Lutheran. Home: 1200 Sharingbrook Dr Manhattan KS 66503

HAHN, LORNA, political organization executive, author; b. Phila., June 16; d. Charles William and Belle Herman; m. Walter F. Hahn; 1 child, Randolph P. BA, Temple U.; MA, U. Pa., PhD in Internat. Rels., 1962. Instr. Temple U., Phila.; researcher Spl. Ops. & Rsch. Office, Washington; rsch. coord. Hist. Evaluation & Rsch. Orgn., Washington; dir. Masters program Am. U., Washington; exec. dir. Assn. Third World Affairs, Washington, 1968—. V.p. Internat. Fedn. for Protection of Religious, Linguistic & Ethnic Minorities, Washington, 1987—; pub. Third World Forum, 1976—; advisor Save Cambodia, Inc.,Washington, 1980—; lectr. Cath. U., Washington, 1965-66, Howard U., Washington, 1971-73, 82-83. Author: North Africa: Nationalism to Nationhood, 1960, Undergrounds in Insurgency, Revolutionary and Resistance Warfare, 1964, Morocco: Old Land, New Nation, 1966, An Historical Dictionary of Libya, 1981; author numerous monographs, articles and reviews; frequent guest on talk shows. Advisor Dem. candidates. Recipient Scholarship medal Phi Gamma Mu. Mem. Dems. 2000. Mem. Unitarian Ch. First woman to lecture at U.S. Nat. War Coll. and other mil. staff colls. Office: Assn Third World Affairs 1629 K St NW Washington DC 20006-1602

HAHN, MARGARET CATHERINE, secondary school educator; d. Herbert and Margaret Levery Hahn. BS, U. Houston, 1965; MS, Tex. A&M U., College Sta., 1978. Tchr. Houston Ind. Sch. Dist., 1965—70, LCISD, Rosenberg, Tex., 1970—2006. Recipient Tchr. of Yr., LCISD, 2003.

HAHN, MARY DOWNING, writer; b. Washington, Dec. 9, 1937; d. Kenneth Ernest and Anna Elisabeth (Sherwood) Downing; m. William Edward Hahn, Oct. 7, 1961 (div. 1977); children: Katherine Sherwood, Margaret Elizabeth; m. Norman Pearce Jacob, Apr. 24, 1982. BA in Fine Arts and English, U. Md., 1960, MA in English, 1969. Asst. libr. children's sect. Prince George's County (Md.) Meml. Libr. System, 1975-91; instr. English U. Md., College Park, 1970-74; free-lance illustrator PBS/WETA, Arlington, Va., 1973-75. Author: The Sara Summer, 1979, The Time of the Witch, 1982, Daphne's Book, 1983 (William Allen White Children's Choice award 1985-86), The Jellyfish Season, 1985, Wait Till Helen Comes: A Ghost Story, 1980 (11 Children's Choice awards), Tallahassee Higgins, 1987, Following the Mystery Man, 1988, December Stillness, 1988 (Book award Child Study Assn. 1989, Calif. Young Readers' medal 1990-91), The Doll in the Garden, 1989 (Md. Children's Book award 1990-91, 7 Children's Choice awards), The Dead Man in Indian Creek, 1990 (4 Children's Choice awards), The Spanish Kidnapping Disaster, 1991, Stepping on the Cracks, 1991 (Scott O'Dell Hist. Fiction award 1992, ALA notable 1991, Joan G. Sugarman award, Hedda Seisler Mason award, Children's Choice awards), The Wind Blows Backward, 1993 (ALA Best Books for Young Adults), Time for Andrew, 1994 (7 Children's Choice awards), Look for Me by Moonlight, 1995 (Yalsa Quick Picks for Reluctant Readers), The Gentleman Outlaw and Me-Eli, 1996, Following My Own Footsteps, 1996, As Ever, Gordy, 1998, Anna All Year Round, 1999, Promises to the Dead, 2000, Anna on the Farm, 2001, Hear the Wind Blow, 2003, The Old Willis Place, 2004, Janey and the Famous Author, 2005 Recipient Scott O'Dell award for hist. fiction, 1992, author's award Md. Libr. Assn., 1997. Mem. Soc. Children's Book Writers, Washington Children's Book Guild. Personal E-mail: mdh12937@aol.com.

HAHN, MOIRA ELIZABETH, artist, educator; b. Boston, June 14, 1956; d. William and Margaret Mary (Ronayne) Hahn; m. Mark Alan Hotchkiss, June 14, 1991. BFA, Md. Inst. Coll. Art, 1977; MFA, Calif. State U., Fullerton, 2000. Adj. faculty Coastline CC, Westminster, Calif., 1989—90, Costa Mesa, Calif., 1996, 1997, Santa Ana (Calif.) Coll., 1990, 1995, 1997, Calif. State U., Fullerton, 1999, Long Beach, 1999, Long Beach City Coll., 2003; instr. Riverside (Calif.) CC, 2000—01; asst. prof. Santiago Canyon Coll., Orange, Calif., 2001—, assoc. prof., 2005—. One-woman shows include Koplin del Rio Gallery, LA, 2005, Roq La Rue Gallery, Seattle, 2005, others, The New Yorker, 1994, Time Mag., 1995, prin. works include mag. cover, 1996. Pro-bono graphic artist Save Puvungna Coalition, Long Beach, 1990—94; mem. archeol. task force Seal Beach, Calif., 1991—93; mem. archeol. adv. com., 1993—97. Fellow, Art Matters, 1992; grantee, Art Alliance Tribute Fund, 1997; scholar, Calif. State U., Fullerton, 1998. Avocations: travel, dance, hiking, cultural preservation, dogs. Office: Santiago Canyon Coll 8045 E Chapman Orange CA 92869

HAHN, SHARON LEE, city official; b. Kenosha, Wis., Sept. 22, 1939; d. Vincent B. and Mary Lee (Vaux) McCloskey; 1 child, John V. Calhoun. Student, Kent State U., 1983. Cert. mcpl. clk., notary pub., Ohio. Sec. Simmons Bedding Co., Columbus, Ohio, 1960-61; exec. sec. Westinghouse, Columbus, 1962-68; legal sec. Bricker Law Firm, Columbus, 1969-70; asst. to prosecutor Whiteleather Law Firm, Columbia City, Ind., 1970-77; legal sec. Metz, Bailey & Spicer, Westerville, Ohio, 1977-80; clk. of coun., sec. to city mgr. City of Westerville, 1981-87, clk. of coun., records mgr., 1981—99. Deputy registrar Franklin County Bd. Elections. Pres. Meadowlake Assn., 1991-94. Mem. Am. Assn. Records Mgrs. and Adminstrs., Nat. Assn. Govt. Archives and Records Adminstrs., Internat. Inst. Mcpl. Clks. (records mgmt. com. 1986-94, CMC award 1984), Ohio Mcpl. Clks. Assn. (bd. dirs. 1984-86, 91-94, asst. treas. 1994-95). Home: 358 Lake Way Oldsmar FL 34677 E-mail: shahn3@verizon.net.

HAHN, VIRGINIA LYNN, reservations agent; b. Wharton, Tex., Oct. 27, 1951; d. Conrad E. and Verna Mae (Ammons) H. Student, Sam Houston State U., 1974. Reporter Pasadena (Tex.) Citizen Newspaper, 1975-97; reservations agt. Continental Airlines, 1997—. Mem. Tex. Press Women, 1976-86, Nat. Fedn. Press Women, 1976-86; condr. workshop Christian Writer's Conf., Pasadena, 1992. Bd. dirs. San Jacinto Day Found., Pasadena, 1990—2006; mem. pub. rels. com. Am. Cancer Soc., Pasadena, 1996—; vol. Restoration of USS Tex., Pasadena, 1992-94; former mem. Am. Heart Assn., Pasadena, 1990-92; docent Houston Mus. Natural Sci., 1998—. Recipient awards Nat. Fedn. Press Women, 1985—, Tex. Press Women, 1985-90, Harris County Med. Soc., 1991-94. Mem. Am. Cancer Soc. (com. mem.), Pasadena Hist. Soc., Rotary, Pasadena Kiwanis Club (hon.), Alpha Rho (sec., pres. preceptor 1998), Beta Sigma Phi. Democrat. Mem. Church of God. Avocations: reading, visiting museums, cooking, embroidery.

HAHNE HOFSTED, JANET LORRAINE, artist; b. Bklyn., Apr. 1, 1948; d. Lawrence Henry and Dorothy Lorraine Meyer; m. Ronald Charles Hahne, Nov. 22, 1976 (div. Oct. 1983); children: Jackson Noah, Carlena Amanda; m. Jolyon Gene Hofsted, Dec. 7, 1985. BS, SUNY, New Paltz, 1971. Dir., founder Maverick Art Ctr., Woodstock, N.Y., 1997—. Lectr. in field. One-woman shows include Fletcher Gallery, 1997, Kleinart Gallery, Woodstock, N.Y., 2004, Maverick Art Ctr., Woodstock, N.Y., 2005; group shows include Kingston (N.Y.) City Hall, 1986, Gracie Mansion Mus. Store, N.Y.C., 1986, Woodstock Artists Assn., 1986, 88, Hawthorn Gallery, 1988, Rage, Kingston, 1990, Helio Gallery, N.Y.C., 1986, Dome Gallery, N.Y.C., 1990, Fletcher Gallery, Woodstock, N.Y., 1996, 2002, Sky's the Limit Gallery, Kingston, 1997, Maverick Art Ctr., Woodstock, 1997, 2000, Marcuse, Kingston, 1998, Period Gallery, Nebr., 2001, Macy Gallery, Columbia U., N.Y.C., 2001, Family of Woodstock, Kingston, N.Y., 2002, Kleinart Gallery, Woodstock, 2003, Klapper Hall, Queens Coll. CUNY, 2003 Mem. Woodstock Artists Assn. Home: 157 Maverick Rd Woodstock NY 12498-2500 Office: Maverick Art Ctr 163 Maverick Rd Woodstock NY 12498-2500

HAIDOSTIAN, ALICE BERBERIAN, concert pianist, volunteer, not-for-profit fundraiser; b. Highland Park, Mich., Sept. 21, 1925; d. Harry M. and Siroun Vartabedian Berberian; m. Berj H. Haidostian, Oct. 1, 1949; children: Cynthia Esther Haidostian Wilbanks, Christine Rebecca Haidostian Garry, Dicran Berj. MusB, U. Mich., 1946, MusM, 1949. Pvt. piano tchr., 1946-48; tchr. music Detroit Pub. Sch., 1953; dir. vocal trio The Haidostians, 1959—71; dir. youth choral group Cultural Soc. Armenians from Istanbul, 1965—72. Chmn. adv. coun. Armenian Studies Program, U. Mich., 1984-99. Initiator (Operas) Anoush, Mich. Opera Theatre, 1981—82, 2001—02, Transparent Anatomical Manikin exhibit, Detroit Sci. Ctr., 1976. Initiated Centennial Celebration U. Mich. Sch. Music, Detroit, 1980; mem. Armenian Gen. Benevolent Union Alex Manoogian Sch., 1981—91, Detroit chpt. core group com., 1992—; chmn. Marie Manoogian group Armenian Gen. Benevolent Union Alex Manoogian Sch, 1993—; active Detroit Women's Symphony Orch, Mich. Opera; bd. trustees Mich. Opera Theatre, 1982—; active Oakway Symphony Orch.; mem. Save Orch. Hall women's divsn.Project HOPE, 1964—, pres., 1995—96, Detroit Armenian Women's Club, 1957—; active women's chpt. Armenian Gen. Benevolent Union, Detroit, 1944—93; bd. dirs. Childhelp USA Greater Detroit Aux., 1998—; active Detroit Sci. Ctr., 1976—, bd. trustees, 1999—; organist, choir dir. Armenian Congl. Ch., Detroit, 1946—48; mem. Chancel Choir Westminster Ch. Detroit, 1965—80; bd. dirs. Detroit Symphony Orch., 1986—88. Recipient Spirit of Detroit award, 1980, Heart of Gold award United Found. City Detroit, 1981, Nat. Svc. citation U. Mich. Alumnae Coun., 1980, Disting. Alumni Svc. award U. Mich., 1981, Leadership plaque Detroit Symphony Orch., 1988, Magic Flute award Internat. Found. Mozarteum, Salzburg, Austria, 1989, Lifetime Achievement award Outstanding Woman Mich. Project HOPE, 1998, Cmty. Svc. award Wayne County Med. Soc. Alliance, 2000; named Armenian Mother of Yr., Internat. Inst. Detroit, 1981. Mem. Detroit Assn. Univ. Mich. Women (pres. 1969-71), Mich. Fedn. Music Clubs, Mich. State Med. Soc. Alliance, Wayne County Med. Soc. Aux. (pres. 1975-76), Pro Mozart Soc. Greater Detroit (pres. 1982-02, pres. emeritus 2002-, Cert. Appreciation 2002), Pro Musica Detroit (sec. 1969-90, 1st v.p. 1990—), Tuesday Musicale Detroit (pres. 1970-72), Univ. Mich. Alumni Assn. (chmn. alumnae coun. 1977-79), Univ. Mich. Sch. Music Alumni Soc., Women's Assn. Detroit Symphony Orch. (pres. 1986-88, vol. coun. Detroit Symphony Orch.), U. Mich. Alumni Assn. (bd. dirs.), U. Mich. Emeritus Club (pres. 1997-98). Avocation: piano. Home: 6838 Valley Spring Dr Bloomfield Hills MI 48301-2845

HAIG, SUSAN, conductor; BA in Music Theory and Composition, Princeton U.; DMA in Orchestral Conducting, MM in Orchestral Conducting, MM in Piano, State U. N.Y., Stony Brook; PhD in Humanities (hon.), U. Windsor, 1998. Coaching/conducting fellow Juilliard Am. Opera Centre, 1981—83; assistant conductor Minnesota Opera, 1983—84, New York City Opera, 1984—86, Santa Fe Opera, 1986; resident coach and conducting assistant Canadian Opera Co., 1986—88; resident staff conductor Calgary Philharmonic Orch., 1988—91; artistic dir. and principal conductor Windsor Symphony Orch., 1991—2001; music dir. S.D. Symphony Orch., 2001—02; assoc. conductor Fla. Orch., Tampa, 2003—. Recipient Heinz Unger Conducting award, 1992, Mayor's award for excellence in the performing arts, 1999. Mailing: c/o Michael Gerard Mgmt Group 192 Catherine St E PO Box 22 Callander ON P0H 1H0 Canada

HAIGH, JENNIFER, writer; b. Barnesboro, Pa., Oct. 1968; B, Dickinson Coll.; MFA in Fiction Writing, Iowa Writers' Workshop. Lectr. creative writing Boston U. Author: Mrs. Kimble, 2003 (PEN/Hemingway award for outstanding first fiction), Baker Towers, 2005, (short stories) Good Housekeeping, Hartford Courant, Alaska Quarterly Rev., Va. Quarterly Rev., others. Fulbright Scholar, James A. Michener Fellowship, 2002. Mailing: c/o Wm Morrow Publishers HarperCollins Inc 10 E 53rd St New York NY 10022

HAIGHT, CAROL BARBARA, lawyer; b. Buffalo, May 3, 1945; d. Robert H. Johnson and Betty R. (Walker) Hawkes; m. H. Granville Haight, May 28, 1978 (dec. Nov. 1983); children: David Michael, Kathleen Marie. BSW summa cum laude, Widener U., Chester, Pa., 1980, BA in Psychology summa cum laude, 1980; JD cum laude, Widener U., Wilmington, Del., 1984. Assoc. Pepper, Hamilton & Scheetz, Phila., 1985-88, Hodgson, Russ, Andrews, Woods & Goodyear, Buffalo, 1988-90; pvt. practice Boca Raton, Fla., 1990—2004; corp. counsel Eilink Corp, Fremont, Calif., 2000. Arbitrator Am. Arbitration Assn., 1989—; Fla. Supreme Ct. cert. mediator, mediation instr.; founding dir. Mediation Ednl. Svc.; pro bono spkr. and counsel Hospice, 1988-2004. Contbr. articles to profl. jours. Mem. Pa. Bar, Fla. Bar, Phi Kappa Phi Hon. Soc., Phi Alpha Delta, Phi Gamma Mu. Republican. Episcopalian. Avocations: scuba diving, skiing, tennis, sailing, ballroom dancing, flying. Home: 9385 E Maiden Ct Vero Beach FL 32963 Office Phone: 561-362-9100. Personal E-mail: cbhaight@yahoo.com.

HAIGHT, GERI L., lawyer; b. 1970; BA, SUNY, Plattsburgh, 1992; JD, Northeastern U., 1997. Bar: Mass. 1998, NY 1998, US Ct. Appeals (1st Cir.), US Ct. Appeals (Fed. Cir.), US Dist. Ct. (Dist. Mass.). Spl. asst. dist. atty. Middlesex County Dist. Attorney's Office, 2002; ptnr. Litig. Sect. and Intellectual Property Sect. Mintz, Levin, Cohn, Ferris, Glovsky and Popeo PC, Boston. Recipient Nat. Ally of Justice award, 2000. Mem.: Internat. Trademark Assn., Am. Intellectual Property Law Assn., Women's Bar Assn., Boston Bar Assn., Mass. Bar Assn. Office: Mintz, Levin Cohn Ferris Glovsky and Popeo PC One Financial Center Boston MA 02111 Office Phone: 617-348-1675. Office Fax: 617-542-2241. E-mail: GLHaight@mintz.com.*

HAIG NICOL, TERESA IMINTA, choreographer, educator; b. NYC, June 23, 1958; d. Edward Haig Jr. and Sarah Gloria Haig; m. Dawood Haig Nicol, July 9, 2005. BS, Brockport U., NY, 1980. Tchr. h.o.t.s. Franklin County Sch. Sys., Carnesville, Ga., 1996—2001; tchr. dance Albany City Sch. Dist., NY, 2003—. Tchr. dance EBA Dance Theatre, Albany, 2003—. Activist Citizens Action, Albany, 2002—06. Democrat. Office: Albany City Sch Dist 315 Northern Blvd Albany NY 12220 Personal E-mail: danzer623@yahoo.com.

HAIJ, KARLA MARIE, secondary school educator; b. Pipestone, Minn., Apr. 6, 1954; d. Clayton Morley and Elaine Clarice Haij; children: Brett Elizabeth Collins, Corbin Lee Collins, Erik Anthony Collins. BA, Augsburg Coll., Mpls., 1976; MS, St.Cloud State U., Minn., 1996. Cert. tchr. Minn. Tchr. Anoka-Hennepin Ind. Sch. dist. #11, Coon Rapids, Minn., 1977—. Dir.: (plays) Kiss Me Kate, Midsummer Night's Dream, Music Man, The Matchmaker, Footloose, Diary of Anne Frank, Oaklahoma, You Can't Take it with You, The King and I, Godspell, the Fantastiks, Christmas Carol, and numerous one -act play. Dfl. Lutheran. Avocations: gardening, reading, travel. Office: Coon Rapids HS 2340 Northdale Blvd Coon Rapids MN 55433 Office Phone: 763-506-7329. Business E-Mail: karla.haij@anoka.k12.mn.us.

HAIL, KAREN L., bank executive; Founding exec. officer MidSouth Bancorp, 1984—, bd. dirs., 1988—, sr. exec. v.p., COO; CFO, dir. MidSouth Bank (subsidiary of MidSouth Bancorp). Mem. technology com. Independent Community Bankers of Am. Named one of 25 Women to Watch, US Banker mag., 2005. Office: Midsouth Bancorp 102 Versailles Blvd Lafayette LA 70501*

HAILE, LISA A., lawyer; BA in Biology, Rollins Coll., 1982; PhD in Microbiology & Immunology, Georgetown U. Sch. Medicine, 1987; JD, Calif. Western Sch. Law, 1991. Bar: Calif. 1992, cert.: US Patent and Trademark Office. Postdoctoral fellow La Jolla Cancer Rsch. Found., NIH, 1987—89; ptnr. Gray, Cary, Ware, & Freidenrich, 1999—2004; ptnr., co-chmn. Life Sciences practice group DLA Piper Rudnick Gray Cary, San Diego, 2005—. Adj. prof. patent law Calif. Western Sch. Law; mem. BIOCOM Sci. and Tech. Com., 2004. Bd. mem. Am. Liver Found., Athena; mem. Sci. & Tech. com. BIOCOM. Named one of Top 45 Attorneys Under 45, The Am. Lawyers, 2003. Mem.: ABA, Licensing Exec. Soc., Am. Intellectual Property Law Assn., Calif. Bar Assn., San Diego Bar Assn., San Diego Intellectual Property Law Assn. (pres. 1997—99), Ass. for Women in Sci. Office: DLA Piper Rudnick Gray Cary 4365 Executive Dr San Diego CA 92121 Office Phone: 858-677-1456. Office Fax: 858-677-1401. Business E-Mail: lisa.haile@dlapiper.com.

HAILEY, KATHLEEN WILSON, elementary school educator; b. Porterville, Calif., Sept. 24, 1947; d. Kenneth Carmel and Margaret Elenor (Worthen) Wilson; m. John David Hailey, Feb. 7, 1970; children: Jonathan David, Carolyn Elizabeth. AA, Porterville Coll., 1967; BA, St. Mary's Coll. of Calif., Moraga, 1979. Profl. clear tchg. credential 2d grade tchr. Calif. 2nd grade tchr. Terra Bella (Calif.) Union Sch. Dist., 1968-69; 1st grade tchr. Hughson (Calif.) Elem. Sch. Dist., 1984-85, 2nd grade tchr., 1985-88, 5th grade tchr., 1988-89, 6th grade tchr. Emilie J. Ross Mid. Sch., 1989—. Adult sch. night tchr. Ceres (Calif.) Adult Sch., 1985—94; mem. program quality rev. team Stanislaus County Schs., Modesto, Calif., 1992—; mem. Stanislaus UniServ Bd., 1996—2001, sec., 1997—98, treas., 1998—2000, v.p., 2000, pres., 01; treas. Hughson Elem. Educator/CTA, 1991—94, pres., 1995—2001, chief negotiator, 1996—2003; tchr., trainer Calif. Arts Project, 1999—; trainer I Can Do It/I Have Done It, CTA, 2001—; vice chair Stanislaus Svc. Ctr. Coun./CTA, 2002, mem. steering com., 03, treas., 2004—. Editor: (anthology) Thoughts Beneath the Tower, 1993, Facts, Faces, Fiction and Fantasy, 1995; contbr. chapters to books. Mem. Persephone Guild, Ceres, 1994—95; bd. dirs., den leader cub scouts Boy Scouts Am., 1981—84; bd. dirs. Ceres Cmty. Found., 1995—96; troop leader Girl Scouts U.S., 2005—. Named Mentor Tchr., Hughson Elem. Sch. Dist., 1994. Mem.: Internat. Order Job's Daus. (Bethel guardian 1990—95, dep. grand guardian 1992—, Grand 2d messenger 2000), Delta Kappa Gamma (rec. sec. 2002, 2006—). Democrat. Bah'A'I. Avocations: sailing, sewing, reading, travel. Home: 2817 Joy Ave Ceres CA 95307-2810 Office: Emilie J Ross Mid Sch PO Box 189 Hughson CA 95326-0189 Office Phone: 209-883-4425. Personal E-mail: ladykat000@aol.com.

HAILEY, V. ANN, retail executive; Sr. v.p., CFO Pillsbury Co., 1994—97; exec. v.p., CFO Limited Brands Inc., Columbus, Ohio, 1997—, bd. dir., 2001—. Bd. dir. Fed Reserve Bank of Cleveland, 2004—. Office: Limited Brands Inc 3 Limited Pkwy Columbus OH 43230-1467*

HAILPARN, DIANA FINNEGAN, psychotherapist, writer; b. Newark, Jan. 25, 1949; d. Thomas Patrick Finnegan and Aurora Floyd Durden; m. Michael Hailparn, May 10, 1973. BA, William Paterson U., 1971; MA, Fairleigh Dickinson U., 1973; MS, Columbia U., 1975. LCSW, diplomate Clin. Social Work Assn. Psychotherapist Clifton Mental Health Clinic, NJ, 1975—79, Diana Assoc., Mahwah, NJ, 1979—. Cons. in field, 1979—. Author: Fear No More: A Psychotherapist's Guide to Overcoming Anxiety and Panic, 2000; contbr. articles to profl. publs. Mem.: NASW (licentiate). Avocations: travel, art, fine dining, design, writing. Home: 19 North Bayard Ln Mahwah NJ 07430 Office: Diana Assoc 19 N Bayard Ln Mahwah NJ 07430-2236 Office Phone: 201-934-6295. Personal E-mail: leaurore@yahoo.com.

HAILS, BARBARA GELDERMANN, artist; b. NYC, Mar. 15, 1944; d. Edward Joseph and Helena Monica (McCann) Geldermann; m. Robert Louis Hails Sr., July 2, 1966; children: Robert Louis Jr., Charlotte Lynne. BA, Catholic U. Am., Washington, 1965. Freelance artist Hails Studio, Gathersburg-Olney, Md., 1965—. Speaker Montgomery Coll., Rockville 1987; exhibition juror Md. Fedn. Art, Annapolis 1987. Work exhibited in Capricorn Galleries, Bethesda, Md. 1982—, Cudahy's Gallery, Richmond, Va. 1981—, McBride Gallery, Annapolis, Md. 1985— Hails Fine Art Gallery, Olney, Md., 1994—; one-woman shows include Capricorn Galleries, 1984, 87, Art Expo, NY, 1986-2005, DecorExpo, Atlanta, 1986—; artist in residence City Rockville, Md. 1975; publ. Dimensional Aesthetics Inc., Olney 1985; contbr. articles to profl. jours. Fundraiser Parks and History Assn., Great Falls, Md. 1987, Sandy Spring Mus., Olney 1984. Recipient grant Montgomery County Arts Council, Rockville 1986; named Outstanding Artist Yr. Nat. League Am. Penwomen, Chevy Chase, Md. 1983; invited exhibitor Société Des Pastellistes de France, Lille 1987. Mem. Pastel Soc. Am., Md. Pastel Soc., Artists Equity Assn. Avocations: photography, travel. Office: Dimensional Aesthetics 18319 Georgia Ave Olney MD 20832-1435 Office Phone: 301-774-6249.

HAIMBACH, MARJORIE ANNE, music educator; b. Abington, Pa., Feb. 9, 1927; d. Charles Albert and Laura Adeline (Hungerford) Haimbach. BA in Music, Ursinus Coll., Collegeville, Pa., 1948. Pvt. piano tchr., Langhorne, Pa., N.Y.C. Mem.: Soc. of Mayflower Descendants, Am. Coll. Musicians, Pa. State Music Tchrs. Assn., Nat. Guild of Piano Tchrs., Bucks County Assn. of Piano Tchrs. Home: 113 W Maple Ave Langhorne PA 19047

HAINES, CARYL, retired medical/surgical nurse; b. Addison, N.Y., Nov. 8, 1939; d. Carl Ward and Phoebe Anna (Cotton) Hamilton; m. Gale Swinter Haines, Dec. 31, 1964. Diploma, Arnot Odgen Meml. Hosp., Elmira, N.Y., 1960; student, Elmira Coll.; BS in Profl. Arts, St. Joseph's Coll., 2001. Cert. nurse adminstr. Staff nurse Arnot Ogden Meml. Hosp., 1960—61, head nurse med. surg. unit, 1961—92, dir. unit pediats. and child life dept., 1992—2001, dir. unit obstetrics, labor and delivery, newborn nursery, childbirth edn., 1996—2001; ret., 2001. Mem. ANA, N.Y. State Nurses Assn. Home (Summer): 62 Maple St Addison NY 14801-1124 Home (Winter): 2421 S Conway Ave Lot 757 Mission TX 78572-1560

HAINES, CYNTHIA WEBER FARAH, photographer, publisher; b. Long Island, N.Y., June 2, 1949; d. Andrew John and Aria Emma (Jelnikova) Weber; m. James Clifton Farah, Jan. 12, 1974 (div. 1992); children: Elise, Alexa; m. James S. Haines, Apr. 13, 2001. BA in Comms., Stanford U., 1971; MA, U. Tex., 1992. Mem. prodn. staff Sta. KDBC-TV, El Paso, Tex., 1971-73; film critic El Paso Times, 1972-77; v.p. Sanders Co. Advtsg., El Paso, 1973-74; freelance photographer, 1974—; lectr. film studies U. Tex., 1995-98, asst. prof., 1998—2004, assoc. prof., 2004—05; ret., 2005. Pres. CM Pub., El Paso, 1981-89. Author: Literature and Landscape: Writers of the Southwest, 1988, Colors on Desert Walls: The Murals of El Paso, 1997, Showtime! From Opera Houses to Picture Palaces in El Paso, 2006; co-author, photographer: Country Music: A Look at the Men Who've Made It, 1982; film critic St. KTEP, 1993-2005, Sta. KVIA-TV, 1997-2003, KCUR-FM. Bd. dirs. N.Mex. State U. Mus. Adv. Bd., Las Cruces, 1982-90; dir., vice-chmn. Shelter for Battered Women, El Paso, 1981-86; active Jr. League, 1977-90, sustaining mem., 1990—, C.of C. Leadership El Paso Program, 1983-84; mem. El Paso County Hist. Commn., 1984-89, vice chmn., 1986, 87; mem. El Paso County Hist. Alliance, vice chmn., 1986-88; trustee El Paso Cmty. Found., 1984-89; mem. adv. bd. El Paso Arts Resources dept., 1987-93, chmn., 1991-93; mem. adv. bd. Tex. Film Alliance, 1991, Tex. Ctr. for the Book, 1987-2000; mem. lit. adv. panel Tex. Commn. on Arts, 1991-93, media adv. panel, 1997-98; mem. adv. coun. El Paso Bus. Com. for Arts, 1988-90, Harry Ransom Humanities Rsch. Ctr. U. Tex., Austin; mem. Tex. Com. Humanities Bd., 1993-98; mem. lit. panel Cultural Arts Coun. Houston, 1993; mem. adv. com. Tex. Book Fair, 1996-99; ct. apptd. Spl. Adv. Children, 2005-; mem. Gov.'s Film Undustry Task Force, 2005-, Kans. Film Commn. CASA, 2005-06, mem. exec. com. Kans. State Hist. Soc. Bd., 2006-. Recipient J.C. Penny Golden Rule award, 1989, Vol. Svc. award El Paso Bur. United Way, 1989, Clara Barton Medallion ARC, 1979, Conquistador award City of El Paso, 1991; named Outstanding Active Mem. Jr. League, 1987-88, Outstanding Sustaining Mem., 1993-94; named to El Paso Women's Hall of Fame, 1992. Mem. U. Tex. at El Paso Libr. Assn. (v.p. 1987-88, pres. 1989-91), Modern Assn., Stanford U. Alumni Assn., Soc. Cinema Studies, Broadcast Film Critics Assn. Episcopalian. Address: 984 N 1800 Rd Lawrence KS 66049-9021 E-mail: cfarahhaines@aol.com.

HAINES, JOYBELLE, retired elementary school educator; b. Geronomo, Okla., Oct. 20, 1930; d. William Tommie and Ruby Dell Heffington; m. Meredith C. Haines, Aug. 22, 1953; children: Cynthia Elaine, Stephen Michael, Lisa Joy. Grad., Asbury Coll., Wilmore, Ky.; postgrad., Ball State Tchrs. Coll., Calif. State U. Missionary tchr., Seoul, Republic of Korea, 1954—56; tchr. Hartford City, Ind., 1956—65, Muncie, Ind., 1965—66, Stockton (Calif.) Unified Sch. Dist., 1966—2000; ret., 2001. Cons. new tchrs., tutor, Stockton, 1999—. Mem.: AAUW, Rep. Women's Club. Baptist. Home: 8853 Bainbridge Pl # 2 Stockton CA 95209-4845

HAINES, KATHLEEN ANN, pediatrician, educator; b. NYC, July 28, 1949; d. George Raymond and Gertrude Ann (Driscoll) H.; m. Emil Claus Gotschlich, May 24, 1975; 1 child, Emily Claire. BA, CUNY, 1971; MD, Albert Einstein Coll. Medicine, 1975. Diplomate Am. Bd. Pediatrics, Am. Bd. Allergy and Immunology. Intern, resident NY Hosp./Cornell U., NYC, 1975-77, fellow in allergy/immunology, 1977-80; from instr. in pediatrics to assoc. prof. Sch. Medicine NYU, NYC, 1980—91, assoc. prof. clin. pediatrics and medicine Sch. Medicine, 1991—2005, adj. assoc. prof. Sch. Medicine, 2005—; dir. pediat. rheumatology Hosp. Joint Diseases/NYU Med. Ctr., 1994—2002; dir. clin. immunology lab. Hosp. Joint Diseases, 1995—2002; sect. chief pediat. immunology Hackensack U. Med. Ctr., NJ, 2002—; assoc. prof. pediat. U. Medicine and Dentistry NJ/NJ Med. Sch., 2005—. Mem. rsch. coun. NY Heart Assn., 1988-90; program com. Am. Coll. Rheumatology, 2000-03, vis. prof., 2001. Contbr. articles to profl. jours., chpts. to books in field. Med. and Scientific Com. N.Y.C. chpt. Arthritis Found., 1993-99. Grantee, N.Y. Arthritis Found., 1990, 1996, NIH, 1993—98. Fellow Am. Acad. Allergy and Immunology, Am. Acad. Pediatrics (mem. exec. com. rheumotology sect., 2003—); mem. Am. Fedn. Med. Rsch., Allergy, Asthma and Immunology Soc. of Greater N.Y. (sec. 1995-97, pres.-elect 1997-98, pres. 1998-99), Harvey Soc., Soc. Pediatric Rsch., Clin. Immunology Soc. Office: Hackensack U Med Ctr 30 Prospect Ave Hackensack NJ 07601 Office Phone: 201-996-5306. Business E-Mail: khaines@humed.com.

HAINES, MARTHA MAHAN, lawyer; b. Detroit, Feb. 4, 1952; d. Albert F. and Martha M. (Sager) Mahan; divorced; children: Ella Catherine, Emily Martha. Student, U. Utah, 1970-72; BA magna cum laude, Wayne State U., 1974; JD, U. Mich., 1977. Bar: Ill. 1978, U.S. Dist. Ct. (no. dist.) Ill. 1982. Assoc. Chapman and Cutler, Chgo., 1978-82, jr. ptnr., 1982-86; of counsel Altheimer & Gray, Chgo., 1986-90, ptnr., 1990-97, Barnes & Thornburg, Chgo., 1997-99; chief Office Mcpl. Securities, SEC, Washington, 1999—; asst. dir. divsn. mkt. regulation SEC, 2000—. Office: Office Mpcl Securities SEC 100 F St NE Washington DC 20549-1001 Office Phone: 202-551-5681. Business E-Mail: hainesm@sec.gov.

HAINES, RANDA, film director; b. L.A., Feb. 20, 1945; Studied with Lee Strasberg; student, Am. Film Inst. Bd. advisors F.O.C.U.S. Inst. Film. Dir.: (TV films) Under the Sky, 1979, (PBS) The Jilting of Granny Weatherall,(TV movie) Something About Amelia, 1984 (Emmy award nomination for director of a limited series or spl.), Alfred Hitchcock Presents, 1985, The Ron Clark Story, 2006, (TV episodes) Hill St. Blues, 1982, (films) Children of a Lesser God, 1986, (DGA nomination best dir.), The Doctor, 1991, Wrestling Ernest Hemingway, 1993, Dance with Me, 1998; prodr.: A Family Thing, 1996; dir., exec. prodr. (TV film) The Outsider, 2002, prodr. (film) Antwone Fisher, 2002; exec. prodr. Los Zafiros: Music from the Edge of Time, 2004. Recipient Franklin J. Schaffner award, Am. Film Inst., 1993. Mem. Dirs. Guild Am. Office: Dirs Guild Am 7950 W Sunset Blvd Los Angeles CA 90046-3307 also: FOCUS-LA # 200 600 Corporate Pointe Ste 200 Culver City CA 90230-7658 Address: care Elliott Web Broder/Webb/Chervin/Silbermann 9242 Beverly Blvd Ste 200 Beverly Hills CA 90210*

HAINING, JEANE, psychologist; b. Camden, N.J., May 2, 1952; d. Lester Edward and Adina (Rahn) H. BA in Psychology, Calif. State U., 1975; MA in Sch. Psychology, Pepperdine U., 1979; MS in Recreation Therapy, Calif. State U., 1982; PhD in Psychology, Calif. Sch. Profl. Psychology, 1985. Lic. clin. psychologist 1987, lic. ednl. psychologist 1982. Crisis counselor Calif. State U., Northridge, 1973-74; recreation therapist fieldwork Camarillo (Calif.) State Hosp.-Adolescent/Children's Units, 1974; Intern recreation therapist UCLA Neuropsychiatric Inst., L.A., 1975-76; substitute tchr./recreation therapist New Horizons Sch. for Mentally Retarded, Sepulveda, Calif., 1976-79; sch. psychologist Rialto (Calif.) Unified Sch. Dist., 1979-82; clin. psychologist field work San Joaquin County Dept. Mental Health, Stockton, Calif., 1982-83; intern clinical psychologist Fuller Theol. Sem. Psychology Ctr., Pasadena, Calif., 1984-85; clin. psychologist U.S. Dept. Justice, Terminal Island, Calif., 1985-86; cmty. mental health psychologist L.A. County Dept. Mental Health, 1987-89; clin. psychologist Calif. Dept. Corrections, Parole Outpatient Clinic, L.A., 1990—, Mary Magdeline Project, Commerce, Calif., 1992-2000. Adv. bd. Camarillo (Calif.) State Hosp., 1994-97, vice-chmn. adv. bd., 1996-97; examiner Lic. Ednl. Psychologist Oral Examinations, Calif. Bd. Behavioral Sci. Examinations, Sacramento, 1985. Recipient award Outstanding Achievement Western Psychology Conf., Calif., 1974. Mem. APA, Forensic Mental Health Assn. (con. planning com. 1993). Democrat. Lutheran. Avocations: rock climbing, skiing, skating, tennis, piano.

HAINSWORTH, MELODY MAY, library and information scientist, researcher; b. Vancouver, B.C., Can., May 13, 1946; m. Robert John Hainsworth, Jan. 6, 1968; children: Kaleeg William, Shane Alan. BA with honors, Simon Fraser U., 1968; MLS, Dalhousie U., 1976; PhD, Fla. State U., 1992. Libr. Dept. Edn. of Tanzania, Mbeya, 1969—72, Dept. of Edn. of Zambia, Mwinilunga, 1972—74; law libr., deptl. libr. Dept. of Atty. Gen. of N.S., Halifax, 1975—77; regional libr. Provincial Ct. Librs. Dept. of Atty. Gen. of Alta., Calgary, 1977—80, So. Alta. Law Soc. libr., 1980—89; dir. librs. Keiser Coll., Tallahassee, 1992—93; v.p. info. resources and svcs. Internat. Coll., Naples, Fla., 1993—2005; with HMSMG Mgmt. Group, Coquitlam, B.C., Canada, 2005—; census mgr. Stats. Can., 2005—. Census mgr. Stats. Can., 2005—; adj. instr. Sch. Libr. and Info. Studies Fla. State U., Tallahassee, 1990-91, libr. cons., 2004—; spkr. in field; co-founder Naples Free-Net, pres. 1993—; co-founder World Class Acad., rschr. law and info. sci.; mem. faculty Practising Law Inst.; active Women's Polit. Caucus; evaluator SACS/COC, 1999—; mem. external rev. panel ALA/COA, 1999—; spkr. Practising Law Inst. Contbr. articles to profl. jours. Co-chair adv. com. edn. and tech. com. Fla. State Bd. Ind. Colls. and Univs., 1993-2001; founding mem. Pub. Access to Law of Fla., 1990—; mem. exec. bd. Calgary Legal Guidance, 1985-89, vice chmn., 1988-89, hon. life mem.; tech. grant com. Collier County Edn. Found., 1994-96, sec./webmaster World Class Collier, supt. search com., 1998; chair edn. com. East Naples Civic Assn., 1998; bd. dirs. Seacrest Country Day Sch., 1996-2002; mgr. local census office Statistics Can. Census, 2006. Student Leader Bursaries Simon Fraser U. scholar, 1966-68; H.W. Wilson scholar Dalhousie U., 1974; recipient Woman of Distinction award AAUW, 1999, Women of Distinction, Tempo Internat., Naples, 2005, Woman of Style, 2005. Mem. Spl. Librs. Assn (pres. 1994-95), Assn. Online Profls., Fla. State Ct. and County Librs. Assn., Tallahassee Law Librs. Assn., Fla. Libr. Assn., Assn. Libr. and Info. Sci. Edn., Alta. Legal Archives Soc. (hon. life), Collier County Bar Assn., Women's Polit. Caucus (webmaster 1999—), Tempo Internat. (bd. dirs., Named Woman of Distinction 2005), Naples Press Club (bd. dirs.), Women in Bus. Vancouver Avocations: squash, hiking, travel. Home: 472 Alouette Dr Coquitlam BC Canada V3C 4Y8 Office Phone: 604-666-0470, 604-763-2057. Business E-Mail: melody@hmsmg.ca.

HAIR, DINA MARIE, geriatrics services professional; d. Robert Earl and Shirley Baxter Hair. AA in Human Svcs., Piedmont Tech. Coll., Greenwood, SC, 1982; BS, Presbyn. Coll., Clinton, SC, 1984; MEd in Counseling, Clemson U., SC, 2000. Dir. activities & environ. svcs. Martha Franks Bapt. Retirement Ctr., Laurens, SC, 1985—86, dir. activities & vol. svcs., 1986—93, dir. resident svcs., 1993—2001, dir. resident svcs. & cmty. rels., 2001—. Bd. dirs. YMCA, Laurens, 2005—. Recipient Disting. Alumni award, Piedmont Tech. Coll., 1993, Outstanding Young Women award, Presbyn. Coll., 2000. Mem.: Nat. Cert. Coun. Activity Profls., Am. Counseling Assn., Chi Sigma Iota. Baptist. Avocations: exercise, reading, gardening, photography. Office: Martha Franks Bapt Retirement Ctr 1 Martha Franks Dr Laurens SC 29360

HAIR, KITTIE ELLEN, secondary school educator; b. Denver, June 12, 1948; d. William Edward and Jacqueline Jean (Holt) H. BA, Brigham Young U., 1971; MA in Social History, U. Nev., Las Vegas, 1987, cert. paralegal, 1995. cert. tchr., Nev. Health educator Peace Corps, Totota, Liberia, 1971—72; tchr. Clark County Sch. Dist., Las Vegas, Nev., 1972—77, chair dept. social studies, 1993—95; missionary Ch. Jesus Christ Latter-Day Saints, Alta., Canada, 1977—79; tchr. Clark County Sch. Dist., Las Vegas, 1979—, chair social studies dept., 2005—. Assessor Nat. Bd. Profl. Tchg. Stds. Recipient Outstanding Faculty award U. Nev./Southland Corp., Las Vegas, 1991, State Champion Coach, Nev. HS, 2006; named Educator of Yr. Kiwanis Club, 1998-99. Mem.: Nev. HS Mock Trial Bd. (chmn. 2003—04), Phi Alpha Theta, Phi Kappa Phi. Democrat. Avocations: collecting western and Native American art, gardening, cooking. Office: Advanced Technologies Acad 2501 Vegas Dr Las Vegas NV 89106-1643 Business E-Mail: kehair@interact.ccsd.net.

HAIRALD, MARY PAYNE, retired secondary school educator; b. Tupelo, Miss., Feb. 25, 1936; d. Will Burney and Ivey Lee (Berryhill) Payne; m. Leroy Utley Hairald, May 31, 1958; 1 child, Burney LeShawn. BS in Commerce, U. Miss., 1957, M in Bus. Edn., 1963; postgrad., Miss. Coll., 1964, Miss. State U., 1970, U. So. Miss., 1986-88, 90, U. Calif., Davis, summer 1997, Babson Coll., summer 1998. Bus. edn. tchr. John Rundle High Sch., Grenada, Miss., 1957-59; youth recreation leader City of Nettleton, Miss., summers 1960-61; tchr. social studies Nettleton Jr. High Sch., 1959-70; tchr.-coord. coop. vocat. edn. program Nettleton High Sch., 1970—2005; area mgr. World Book, Inc., Chgo., 1972-84; local coord. Am. Inst. for Fgn. Study, Stamford, Conn., 1988—. Instr. bus. Itawamba C.C., Tupelo, 1975-80; coord. Program of Acad. Exch. (PAX), 1998—; advisor DECA, Nettleton, 1985-2005, area rep. Career Cultural Exchange 2004—, DECA state officers' advisor, 1995-01; apptd. adv. coord. mem. Miss. Coop. Edn.-State Dept. Edn. Contbr. articles on coop. edn. to newspapers. Co-organizer Nettleton Youth Recreation Booster Club; fundraiser Muscular Dystrophy Assn.; Sunday sch. tchr. coll. and career class Nettleton United Meth. Ch. Recipient 1st place Nat. Newsletter award Nat. DECA, 1988, 1989, 1990, 2+92, Excellence in Supervision award Am. Inst. for Fgn. Study, 1992, Excellence award Pub. Edn. Forum, 1997; named Star Tchr., Miss. Econ. Coun., 1978, 1995, Tchr. of Yr., Wal-Mart, 1997, Outstanding Tchr. of Yr., Tech. Edn. Air Force, 2005; finalist award Miss. Mfrs. Assn., 1997, 1998, 2002. Mem. AAUW (charter), Am. Vocat. Assn. (Region IV New and Related Svcs. Tchr. of Yr. 1986, 96, Region IV Mktg. Edn. Tchr. of Yr. 1988, Region IV Outstanding Vocat. Tchr. of Yr. 1996, Nat. Tchr. of the Yr. 1997), Coop. Work Experience Edn. Assn., Miss. Assn. Vocat. Educators (dist. sec., pres. 2001-02), Miss. Assn. Coop. Vocat. Edn. Tchrs. (v.p. 1980-83, pres. 1983-84, Miss. Tchr. of Yr. 1984, 1987, 1995), Miss. Assn. Mktg. Educators (Dist. II Tchr. of Yr. 1993, 1994), Mktg. Edn. Assn., Jim Bowers/DECA Found. (charter, life), Nettleton Ladies Civitan Club (charter), DECA (hon., life, adv. 1985—, adv. state newsletter 1987-92, Nat. Newsletter award 1988-90, 92, named Adv. of Yr. Dist. II Miss. Assn. 1990, 1993, 2000, State Adv. of Yr. 2000, Alumni of Yr. 1998, named to Nat. Hall Fame 1996), Phi Delta Kappa (Phi Delta Kappa Kappan of Yr. 1998, found. rep.) Democrat. Methodist. Home: PO Box 166 Nettleton MS 38858-0166 Office Phone: 662-963-7405. Personal E-mail: grandmaymay2005@yahoo.com.

HAIRRELL, ANGELA RENEE, humanities educator, researcher; b. San Antonio, Jan. 17, 1970; d. Edmund G. and Lenora A. Sebesta; m. Brad Hairrell, Jan. 6, 1990; children: Cullen, Deanna. BS Interdisciplinary Studies, Tex. A&M U., College Station, 1991; MEd Curriculum and Instrn., Tex. A&M U., 1994. Cert. ESL Master Reading Tex. Tchr. 1st grade Snook Ind. Sch. Dist., Tex., 1992—98, tchr. 5th grade, 1998—2001, tchr. 3d grade, 2001—02, coach reading, 2002—05; rschr., project dir. Tex. A&M U., 2005—. Sec. Snookfest Com., 1994—; Helper Lodge 9 Yacht Club, Snook, 1999—; v.p. 4-H Adult Leader Assn.; mgr. Snook 4-H Club, 2002—; dir. Snook Brethren Ch., 1992—. Named Outstanding Coll. Edn. Grad., Tex. A&M U., 1991. Avocation: reading. Home: 11482 PM 2155 Somerville TX 77879

HAIRSTON, GERALDINE, mathematics educator; BS in Edn., U. Emporia, Kans., 1971; MEd, U. Kans., Lawrence, 1976. Cert. learning disabilities tchr. Kans., 1974, Va., 1977, math. tchr. Va., 1988. Tchr. spl. edn. Kansas City Pub. Schs., Kans., 1971—73, lead tchr. learning disabilities, 1973—74, tchr. learning disabilities, 1975—77, Fairfax County Pub. Schs., Springfield, Va., 1977—89, tchr. math., 1990—. Mem.: Fairfax County Tchrs. of Math., Nat. Coun. of Tchrs. of Math. Office: Washington Irving Mid Sch 8100 Old Keene Mill Rd Springfield VA 22152 Office Phone: 703-912-4500.

HAISTEN, JUDY AURICH, language educator; b. Clark AFB, The Philippines, Sept. 26, 1959; d. Edwin David and Jean Morris Armbruster; m. Craig Alan Aurich, Dec. 1977 (div. Apr. 1986); children: Jennifer Aurich, Craig A. Aurich, Jalynn Aurich, Andrea Aurich, Steven Aurich; m. Phil Haisten, Nov. 19, 1993. BA in Edn., U. N. Fla., 1988; MA in Edn., U. Fla., 1992. Tchr. H.S. English and Spanish Union County H.S., Lake Butter, Fla., 1989—94; asst. prof. Ctrl. Fla. C.C., Ocala, 1994—; instr. Command Spanish, Ocala, Fla., 1999—. Judge Fla. Spanish Competition, Orlando, 1997—2000; co-advisor Hispanic Student Orgn., Ocala, Fla., 2000—01; mem. adv. bd. Project Reward, Ocala, 1994—96. Named to Tchr.'s Honor Role, Arrid Corp., 1992. Mem.: Fla. Fgn. Lang. Instrs. in C.C. (sec. 1998—), Fla. Assn. C.C.'s, Fla. Fgn. Lang. Assn. (Fla. C.C. Fgn. Lang. Tchr. of Yr. 2001). Mem. Lds Ch. Avocations: crafts, reading, church volunteering. Home: 15701 S Hwy 475 Summerfield FL 34491 Office: Ctrl Fla CC PO Box 1388 Ocala FL 34478

HAIZLIP, VIOLA, medical/surgical nurse; b. Albany, NY, Mar. 16, 1969; d. William and Viola Augusta Haizlip; life ptnr. Sean Glaze, Nov. 28, 2004; 1 stepchild, Devon Glaze. BSN, Coll. New Rochelle, 1991; postgrad., HSI Sch. Intuitive Abilities, 2004—. RN NY. Nurse St. Peter's Hosp., Albany, NY, 1990—2000, N.E. Nursing, Glenmont, NY, 1992—2003; nurse care mgr. Value Options, Troy, NY, 2003—05; pub., owner Vix Pub. Co.; coord. inpatient care Capital Dist. Physicians Healthplan, 2005—. Author: (children's book) Kitty of My Heart, 2004. Active Helping Healing Program, Schenectady, NY, 2004. Recipient award, Intl. Libr. Poetry, 1999, 2001, 2002. Home: 1115 6th Ave Watervliet NY 12189 Office: Vix Pub Co PO Box 692 Glenmont NY 12077 Office Phone: 518-253-9341. Business E-Mail: vixpub@yahoo.com.

HAJEK, MELISSA DAWN, elementary school educator; d. Thomas Carroll and Kathryn Ann Walker; m. Randall Ray Hajek, Jan. 12, 1985; children: Jessica Dawn, Joshua Randall. BS in Elem. Edn., Valley City State U., Valley City, N.D., 1985; MS in Elem. Edn., Minot State U., N.D., 2002. Relief postmaster U.S. Postal Svc., Horace, ND, 1987—97; choral dir. Horace Luth. Ch., ND, 1985—; tchr. grade 5 West Fargo Sch. Dist./Horace Elem. Sch., West Fargo, ND, 1997—. Exec. bd. mem., v.p. Valley Reading Coun., Fargo/West Fargo, 2005—; singer Cool Reign, 2000—; supervising tchr. for student-tchrs. Contemporary worship leader Horace Luth. Ch., 1999—, worship and music bd. dirs., 1986—. Mem.: NEA, West Fargo Edn. Assn., Valley Reading Assn., Internat. Reading Assn. Lutheran. Avocations: singing, piano, walking, reading. Office: Horace Elementary School 110 3rd Ave N Horace ND 58047 Business E-Mail: hajek@west-fargo.k12.nd.us.

HAJNIK, GENEVIEVE L., accountant; b. Pitts., Apr. 17, 1981; d. Joseph V. Hajnik and Carole J. Hoag, Richard D. Hoag (Stepfather). BS in Acctg., Villanova U., 2003, BS in Fin., 2003. CPA Pa. Mem. tax staff Deloitte Tax LLP, Pitts., 2003—05; tax acct. HJ Heinz Co., Pitts., 2005—. Mem.: Pa. Inst. CPAs (assoc.; young CPA com.), Mensa (assoc.; young Mensan coord. 2004—06). Office: HJ Heinz CO WHQ PO Box 57 USSB -7 Pittsburgh PA 15230-0057 Office Phone: 412-456-1765.

HAKALA, KAREN LOUISE, retired real estate specialist; b. Lansing, Mich., Dec. 8, 1941; d. Herod Maxson and Flora Belle (Barton) Mitchell; m. Paul Kenneth Hakala, June 24, 1959 (div. Nov. 1972); children: Chris, Craig. BS, No. Mich. U., Marquette, 1986. Real estate specialist Cleve.-Cliffs Iron Co., Ishpeming, Mich., 1967-99; ret., 1999. Mediator Cmty. Resolution Resource Ctr., 2002—. Mem. devel. com. Planned Parenthood No. Mich., Marquette, 1996—99; bd. dirs. Marquette Symphony Orch., 1998—2000, treas., 1999—2000; mem. planning commn. City of Negaunee, Mich., 2001—, sec., 2001—02, 2005—. Mem.: LWV (bd. dirs. Marquette County 2002—06), AAUW (pub. policy rep. Marquette County chpt. 1995—99, pres. 1999—2001), Ret. Sr. Vol. Program.

HAKKI, AYESHA, editor-in-chief; BA in Journalism & Mass Media, Rutgers U. Asst. editor Men's Club mag., Pakistan; editor NJ Goodlife/Home Design mag., Ladies Home Journal, NYC, photo editor, special interest pub.; art dir. Jupiter Comm., NYC, Compaq Corp., Houston; founder Alias Art, NYC; now editor & publisher Bibi Mag., Hoboken, NJ. Recipient Achievement award, Asia Houston Network, Bronze medal, Art Dirs. Club, Golden Web award, 2003. Office: Bibi Mag 66 Willow Ave Hoboken NJ 07030

HALABY, MARGARITA GONZALEZ, marketing professional, communications executive; m. Dominique Halaby; children: Austin C., Cameron R. BJ, U. Tex., 1997. Asst. placement dir., editor, photographer U. Tex. Grad. Sch. Libr. and Info. Sci., Austin, 1993—94; portrait photographer Lifetouch Portrait Studios, Austin, 1995—96; editl. asst. Constrn. Data News Constrn. Data Corp., Austin, 1996—97; staff writer The Brownsville (Tex.) Herald; Freedom Comm. Inc., 1997—98; reporter Valley Morning Star; Freedom Comm. Inc., Harlingen, Tex., 1998—99; mktg. comm. coord. Brownsville Pub. Utilites Bd., 1999—2000; mktg. and comm. mgr. Brownsville Pub. Utilities Bd., 2000—. Mktg. and pub. rels. cons. Importante Inc., Brownsville, 1998—2000. Bd. mem. BBB of South Tex., Weslaco, 2001—, Am. Cancer Soc. - So. Cameron County Chpt., Brownsville, 1999. Recipient Team award for Newspaper Series - Border Govs. Conf., Assn. Profl. Mng. Editors, 1999, Group Study Exch. to Finland, Rotary Internat., 2000, Ann. Report award of merit, Am. Pub. Power Assn., 2000. Mem.: Tex. Assn. Municipal Info. Officers Assn., Am. Mktg. Assn. (assoc.), Pub. Rels. Soc. Am. (assoc.), Tex. Pub. Power Assn. (mktg. and customer svc. com. mem.), Sunrise Rotary Club. Office: Brownsville Public Utilities Board 1425 Robinhood Dr Brownsville TX 78521-4230 E-mail: mhalaby@brownsville-pub.com.

HALABY, NOELLE M., lawyer; BA, UCLA, 1993; JD, Southwestern Univ., 1996. Bar: Calif., US Dist. Ct. Ctrl. Calif., US Ct. Appeals Ninth Cir., cert.: Calif. (Family Law Specialist). Ptnr. Moore, Halaby & Associates, Pasadena, Calif.; assoc. Lisa Helfend Meyer & Associates, Century City, Calif.; prin., family law private practice Glendale, Calif., 2003—. Family Law Judge Pro Tem LA Superior Ct., mediator, Family Law dept. Named a Rising Star, So. Calif. Super Lawyers, 2006. Mem.: State Bar Calif., LA County Bar Assn., Beverly Hills Bar Assn., Century City Bar Assn., Calif. Assn. Family Law Specialists, Woman Lawyers LA, Am. Bus. Women Assn. Office: Noelle M Halaby Ste 200 130 N Brand Blvd Glendale CA 91203 Office Phone: 818-502-3939. Office Fax: 818-502-3999. Business E-Mail: noelle@noellehalaby.com.*

HALAS, CYNTHIA ANN, business information specialist; b. Norristown, Pa., July 24, 1961; d. George and Maria (Mitrik) H. Student, Temple U., 1979-80; AS in Bus. Adminstrn., Montgomery County Coll., Blue Bell, Pa., 1993; student, Springhouse Computer Sch., Exton, Pa., 1994-95. Columnist, corr. The Recorder, Conshohocken, Pa., 1980-81; claims supr. Liberty Mut. Ins. Co., Blue Bell, 1980-84; claims svc. rep. Met. Property & Liability Ins. Co., Wayne, Pa., 1984-87; model Frank James Assocs., Phila., 1986-87; auditor/tng. coord. Coresource, Inc., Wayne, 1987-94; sys. support analyst Del. Valley Fin. Svcs., Inc., Berwyn, Pa., 1994-95; sys. support coord. Aetna Inc., Blue Bell, Pa., 1995—. Active Nat. Arbor Day Found. Mem. NAFE, U.S. Fencing Assn. Byzantine Catholic. Avocations: golf, fencing, horseback riding, needlepoint, travel. Office: Aetna Inc 1425 Union Meeting Rd Blue Bell PA 19422-1959

HALAS, NAOMI J., nanoscale science and engineering educator; b. New Eagle, Pa., Aug. 1, 1957; d. Frank P. and Mary A. (Monthey) H.; m. Peter J. A. Nordlander, Aug. 1, 1986. BA in Chemistry, LaSalle Coll., 1980; MA in Physics, Bryn Mawr Coll., 1984, PhD in Physics, 1987. Grad. tchg. asst. Bryn Mawr Coll., Phila., 1980-83; grad. student/rsch. assoc. IBM T.J. Watson Rsch. Ctr., Yorktown Heights, NY, 1983-86; postdoctoral assoc. Vanderbilt U., 1987, AT&T Bell Labs., Holmdel, NJ, 1987-89; asst. prof. Rice U., Houston, 1989—94, assoc. prof., 1994-99, prof., dept. elec. and computer engring., 1999—2001, prof., dept. chemistry, 1999—, Stanley C. Moore prof. in elec. and computer engring., 2001—, founder, dir., Lab. for Nanophotonics, 2004—. Founding mem. Nanospectra Biosciences, Inc.; mem. scientific review bd., materials sci. and tech. divsn. Los Alamos Nat. Lab.; mem. vis. adv. bd. Penn. State Materials Rsch. Science and Engring. Ctr.; mem. adv. bd. Nanobusiness Alliance; mem. NSF review panels, 1992—2000; external review panel interviewee Tex. Advanced Tech. Program, 1994; mem. NSF grad. fellowship evaluation com., physics and astronomy, 96; spkr. in field. Contbr. articles to perr-reviewed jours.; reviewer Optic Letters, Optics Communications, Applied Physics Letters, Jour. Chem. Physics, Phys. Review, Langmuir, Jour. Phys. Chemistry B, Nanoletters, Nature Materials, Science, Advanced Materials, Jour. Biomedical Optics. Recipient Young Investigator award NSF, 1992, Hershel M. Rich Invention awards (for C60 Purification Method, 1993, for Metal Nanoshells, 1998, for Photothermal Nanoshell-Polymer Drug Delivery Materials, 2001, for Optically Active Nanoparticles for use in Therapeutic and Diagnostic Methods, 2003), Chevy Trucks Lone Star Hero, 2003, Breast Cancer Rsch. Program Innovator award, US Army Med. Rsch. and Material Command, Congessionally funded med. rsch. programs, dept. def., 2003, Nanotechnology Now's Best Discovery of 2003, 2004; co-recipient CRS-Cygnus award for Outstanding Grad. Student Rsch., 2000; finalist Small Times Magazines' Best Researcher of 2004. Fellow AAAS, Am. Phys. Soc. (laser sci. topical group, student travel grant awards com., 1993-96, exec. com. divsn. laser sci. 1996-98, exec. com. Tex. sect. 1996-98, divsn. laser sciences, chair, undergraduate summer rsch. grants awards com., 1996-98), Optical Soc. Am.; mem. Am. Chem. Soc., IEEE (sr. mem.) Achievements include patents in field. Office: Halas Nanophotonics Group Dept Elec and Computer Engring Rice U Abercrombie Lab A235 6100 Main St MS 366 Houston TX 77005-1892 Office Phone: 713-348-5611. Office Fax: 713-348-5686. E-mail: halas@rice.edu.*

HALBERSTAM, MALVINA, law educator, lawyer; b. Kempno, Poland, May 2, 1937; came to U.S., 1947; d. Marcus and Pearl (Halberstam) H.; m. Wolf Z. Guggenheim (dec. 2002); children: Arye, Achiezer. BA cum laude, Bklyn. Coll., 1957; JD, Columbia U., 1961, MIA, 1964. Bar: N.Y. 1962, U.S. Dist. Ct. (so. dist.) N.Y. 1963, U.S. Ct. Appeals (2d cir.) 1965, U.S. Supreme Ct. 1966, Calif. 1968. Law clk. Judge Edmund L. Palmieri Fed. Dist. Ct. (so. dist.) N.Y., 1961-62; rsch. assoc. Columbia Project on Internat. Procedure, 1962-63; asst. dist. atty. N.Y. County, 1963-67; with Rifkind & Sterling, L.A., 1967-68; sr. atty. Nat. Legal Program on Health Problems of the Poor, L.A., 1969-70; prof. Sch. Law Loyola U., L.A., 1970-76; prof. Benjamin N. Cardozo Sch. Law Yeshiva U., N.Y.C., 1976—. Vis. prof. Gould Law Ctr., U. So. Calif., L.A., 1972-73, U. Va. Sch. Law, 1975-76, U. Tex. Sch. Law, summer 1974, Hebrew U., Jerusalem, 1984-85; counselor on internat. law U.S. State Dept. Office of Legal Adviser, 1985-86; cons., 1986-92. Author (with De Feis): Women's Legal Rights: International Agreements An Alternative to ERA?, 1987; articles and rev. editor Columbia Law Rev., 1960—61, reporter Am. Law Inst. Model Penal Code Commentaries, 1977—81, mem. editl. bd. Jour. Nat. Security Law and Policy, 2005—; contbr. articles, commentary, book revs. to profl. jours. Mem. Bklyn. Coll. Alumni Adv. Bd. on Women's Career Devel. and Leadership Program.; adv. com. to standing com. on law and nat. security, ABA; study group on shape Arab-Israeli settlement, humanitarian, and demographic issues Coun. on Fgn. Rels. Kent scholar (2x); Stone scholar; recipient Jane Marks Murphy prize. Mem.: Am. Assn. Law Schs. (chair sect. internat. law 2002—03, co-vice chmn. sect. nat. security law 2003—04, co-chmn. elect nat. security law sect. 2004—05, mem. exec. com. 2005—), Am. Assn. Jewish Lawyers and Jurists (bd. govs.), Internat. Law Assn. (Am. br. exec. com., human rights com.), Assn. Bar City of N.Y. (coun. on internat. affairs 1998—2004), Am. Soc. Internat. Law, Am. Law Inst. (life), Columbia Law Sch. Alumni Assn., Phi Beta Kappa. Home: 160 Riverside Dr New York NY 10024-2106 Office: Benjamin N Cardozo Sch Law Yeshiva U 55 Fifth Ave New York NY 10003-4391 Office Phone: 212-790-0394. E-mail: halbrstm@yu.edu.

HALBREICH, KATHY, museum director; b. N.Y.C., Apr. 24, 1949; d. Irwin and Betty Ann (Stoll) H.; m. John Kohring; 1 child, Henry. BA, Bennington Coll., 1971; postgrad., Skowhegan Sch. Painting and Sculpture, Maine, 1965, Am. U., Mexico City, 1966. Adminstr. spl. programs Bennington (Vt.) Coll., 1975-766; dir. teaching seminar Assn. Collegiate Schs. Architecture, Washington, 1977; v.p. programs, trustee Artist Found., Boston, 1979-84; dir. com. on visual arts Hayden Gellery, List Visual Arts Ctr., MIT, Cambridge, Mass., 1976-86; ind. curatorial cons., 1986-88; curator contemporary art Mus. Fine Arts, Boston, 1988-90; dir. Walker Art Ctr., Mpls., 1991—. Cons. St. Louis Art Mus., Artists Space, N.Y.C., Capp St. Project, San Francisco, Mus. Modern Art, N.Y.C., Seattle Arts Commn., Southeastern Ctr. for Contemporary Art, Louis Comfort Tiffany Found., Beacon Cos., Frito-Lay Inc., New Eng. Gen. Svcs. Adminstrn. Art-in-Architecture Program, Nat. Endowment for Arts, VA Art-in-Architecture Program; trustee MA Coun. on the arts and Humanities; advisor Pub. Art Policy Project and Publ., Nat. Endowment for Arts, 1987; mem. nat. com. P!ub. Art in Am. Conf., Phila., 1987. Trustee Twin Cities Pub. TV, 1992. Mem. Assn. Art Mus. Dirs., Andy Warhol Found. for Visual Arts Inc. (bd. dirs. 1992), Mpls. Club. Office: Walker Art Ctr 1750 Hennepin Ave Minneapolis MN 55403-1138

HALDEY, OLGA, music educator; b. Moscow, Aug. 18, 1972; d. Boris and Elvira (Entina) Haldey. PhD in Musicology, Ohio State U., Columbus, 2002. Asst. prof. music history U. Mo., Columbia, 2002—06; asst. prof. musicology U. Md., College Park, 2006—. Contbr. articles to profl. jours. Fellow Alvin H. Johnson fellow, Am. Musicological Soc., 2001; Presdl. fellow, Ohio State U., 2001, Rsch. grant, Paul Sacher Stiftung, Switzerland, 2003. Mem.: Coll. Music Soc., Am. Musicological Soc., Phi Kappa Phi, Pi Kappa Lambda. Office Phone: 301-405-4389. Business E-Mail: ohaldey@umd.edu.

HALE, CAROL JEAN, teacher, city commissioner; b. Ann Arbor, Mich., July 2, 1942; d. Ward Karcher and Evelyn May (Gillson) Parr; m. Jan Raymond Hale, Aug. 21, 1964; children: David Dart, Matthew Joseph. BA in English and History, U. Mich., 1964, MA in Russian History, 1970. Cert. tchr., Mich. Tchr. Livonia (Mich.) Pub. Schs., 1965-69; civic worker Traverse City, Mich., 1970-88; exec. dir. Downtown Traverse City Assn., 1984-86; tchr. govt., history Traverse City area pub. schs., 1986—; city commr. City of Traverse City, 1977-85, 87—, mayor, 1983-84. Pres. Ctrl. Neighborhood Assn., Traverse City, 1976; sec. Grand Traverse Dept. Pub. Works, Traverse City, 1977-88; mem. Friends of the Capitol, 1982-84, Downtown Devel. Authority, Traverse City, 1985, Traverse City Planning Commn., 1986-89; treas. chmn. Grand Traverse Commons, 1990—; docent Dennos Mus., 2004—. Recipient Rotary Red Rose award, 1984, Dist. Service award Traverse City C. of C., Mich. Historic Preservation Network Lifetime award, 2004. Mem. Michigan State Boundary Commn., Mich. Mcpl. League, LWV (local pres. 1975). Lodges: Zonta (Woman of Yr. 1984), Record Eagle (Most Influential Community mem. 1984). Methodist. Home: 439 6th St Traverse City MI 49684-2415

HALE, CHERYL WRIGHT, marketing professional; b. San Jose, Calif., Oct. 1954; d. Edward James Wright, Uva Estelle Wright. BS in Animal Sci., Calif. Poly. State U., San Luis Obispo, 1975; MS in Mass. Comm., San Jose State U., 1978. V.p. Bank of Am., San Francisco, 1985—87; sr. mgr. Deloitte & Touche, San Francisco, 1987—92; mgr. info. resource audit Sun Microsystems, Inc., Palo Alto, Calif., 1992—94, strategic mktg. mgr., 1994—96, profl. svcs. mktg. dir., 1996—99, bus. devel. mgr., 1999—2001; prin. Cheryl Wright Mktg. Consulting, Incline Village, Nev., 2001—02; v.p. mktg. MuseGlobal, Salt Lake City, 2002—. Instr. info. tech. Golden Gate U., San Francisco, 1987—88. Contbr. chapters to books, articles to profl. jours. Vol. Tahoe Women's Svcs., Incline Village, 2001—01. Mem.: Tahoe Rim Trail Assn., AAUW. Avocations: skiing, hiking, kayaking. Personal E-mail: cheryl@cherylhale.net.

HALE, CYNTHIA LYNETTE, religious organization administrator; b. Roanoke, Va., Oct. 27, 1952; BA, Hollins Coll., 1975; MDiv, Duke U., 1979; D in Ministry, United Theol. Sem., Dayton, Ohio, 1991; DD (hon.), Bethany Coll., N.W. Christian Coll. Ordained Disciples of Christ Ch., Va., 1977. Head resident Hollins (Va.) Coll., 1975-76; intern to minister St. Mark's United Meth. Ch., Charlotte, N.C., 1976; undergrad. counselor Office of Minority Affairs Duke U., Durham, N.C., 1976-77; intern to minister Staunton Meml. Ch., Pittsboro, N.C., 1977-78; coordinating counselor summer transitional program Duke U., Durham, N.C., 1978; chaplain Fed. Correctional Instn., Butner, N.C., 1978-83; chaplain, instr. staff tng. acad. Fed. Prison System, Glynco, Ga., 1983-85; pastor, developer Ray of Hope Christian Ch., Decatur, Ga., 1986—; 1st vice moderator Christian Ch. (Disciples of Christ), U.S. and Can., 1993—. Bd. dirs. Coun. on Christian Unity, 1978-81; bd. trustees Disciples Nat. Convocation, 1980-86, pres. 1982-84, pres. ministers' fellowship, 1990—; task force on Renewal and Structural Reform, Disciples of Christ, 1980-87, adminstrv. com. 1982-87, gen. bd., 1982-88; bd. dirs. Disciples Divsn. Higher Edn., St. Louis, 1986-89; bd. trustees Lexington (Ky.) Theol. Sem., 1990—; bd. dirs. Disciples' Nat. Evangelic Assn., 1991—. Mem. Project Impact-Dekalb, South Dekalb Ch. Coalition; bd. dirs. Beulah Heights Bible Coll., Destiny Atlanta.com; mem. governing bd. Nat. Coun. Chs., 1978—83, panel on bio-ethical concerns, 1980—82. Named Outstanding Ga. Citizen and Goodwill Amb., Sec. of State, 2001, Chaplain of the Day, Ho. of Reps., 2004; recipient Liberation award, Disciples Nat. Conv., 1984, Religion award, DeKalb Br. NAACP, 1990, Religious award for dedicated svc., Ninety-Nine Breakfast Club, award, Martin Luther King's Bd. of Preachers, 1993, Chosen award, Atlanta Gospel Choice, 1998, Profiles of Prominence award, Nat. Women Achievement, 2000, Gospel Honor award, 2000, Youth V.I.B.E. award for outstanding contbns. to the cmty., 2003, James H. Costen award in religion, 2004. Mem. Christian Ch. Office: Ray of Hope Christian Ch 2778 Snapfinger Rd Decatur GA 30034-2439 E-mail: kingdominfo@rayofhope.org.

HALE, JANE ALISON, literature and language professor; b. Washington, Sept. 29, 1948; BA in French magna cum laude, Coll. William and Mary, 1970; MST in Edn., U. Chgo., 1974; MA in French, Stanford U., 1981; postgrad., Ecole Normale Supérieure de Jeunes Filles, Paris, 1981-82; PhD with distinction, Stanford U., 1984. Student tchg. supr., counselor Peace Corps Tng. Program, Ft. Archambault, Chad, 1971; tchr. French, cross-cultural coord. Peace Corps Tng. Ctr., St. Thomas, British Virgin Islands, 1972; Peace Corps vol., tchr. English as fgn. lang. Lycée Franco-Arabe, Abéché, Chad, 1970-72; tchr. 2d grade Pleasant Grove Union Elem. Sch., Burlington, NC, 1974-77; tchg. fellow in French Stanford U., 1982-83; tchr. French Inst. Intensive French, U. Fla., 1986-88; asst. prof. French and comparative lit. Brandeis U., Waltham, Mass., 1985-91, assoc. prof. French and comparative lit., 1991—. Presenter Internat. Conf. on TV Drama at Mich. State U., 1985, Samuel Beckett at 80 at U. Stirling, Scotland, 1986, Internat. Colloquium on Raymond Queneau, Thionville, France, 1990, Internat. Vian-Queneau-Prévert Colloquium at U. Victoria, Can., 1992, Internat. Symposium on Beckett in the 1990s, The Hague, 1992, MLA, N.Y.C., 1992, West Africa Rsch. Assn. Internat. Symposium, Dakar, Senegal, 1997, African Literature Assn., Fès, Morocco, 1999, Internat. Colloquium on Feminist Rsch. in French, Dakar, Senegal, 1999. Author: The Broken Window: Beckett's Dramatic Perspective, 1987, The Lyric Encyclopedia of Raymond Queneau, 1989; contbr. chpts. to books and articles to profl. jours. French Govt. scholar, 1981-82, Fulbright Sr. scholar, Senegal, 1993-94; Whiting fellow in the humanities, 1983-84, Dana faculty fellow Brandeis U., 1985-90, Bernstein faculty fellow Brandeis U., 1989, Marion and Jasper Whiting fellow, 1994-98; NEH travel grantee, 1988, Mazer grantee for faculty rsch. Brandeis U., 1990; recipient Lerman-Neubauer prize for excellence in tchg. and counseling, 2001. Mem. Samuel Beckett Soc. (exec. bd. dirs. 1989-92), Les Amis de Valentin Brû, Phi Beta Kappa. Office: Brandeis U Dept Romance & Comp Lit MS 024 Waltham MA 02454 E-mail: jhale@brandeis.edu.

HALE, LOIS J., retired mathematics educator; b. Oakland, Calif., Mar. 17, 1942; d. Edward Everett and Frances Elizabeth Hale. Student, U. Calif., Berkeley, 1959—63; BA, Calif. State U., Hayward, 1964; MA, U. San Francisco, 1978. Tchg. credential secondary, elem., adminstrv. svcs., math. Tchr. Chatom Union Sch. Dist., Turlock, Calif., 1966—67, Ballico-Cressey Sch. Dist., Calif., 1967—2004; ret. Mem.: Stanislau Math. Coun. (mem.-exec. bd., sec. 2003—05), Calif. Math. Coun. (sec. 2000—02, 2006—08, pres.-elect 2002—04, pres. 2004—06, George Polya award 2000). Avocations: needlecrafts, golf, spectator sports, gardening. Home: 3105 Liquid Amber Dr Denair CA 95316 Personal E-mail: loishale@aol.com.

HALE, MARGARET SMITH, insurance company executive, educator; b. Browning, Mont., May 10, 1945; d. Stephen Howard and Evelyn Sarah (Beer) Smith; m. Lawrence L. Hale, Apr. 25, 1970 (div. Jan. 1984); children: Katherine Moore, Laura Ellen. BSBA, Boston U., 1967; AS in Risk Mgmt., Ins. Inst. Am., 1986. Underwriter Chubb & Son, Inc., N.Y.C., 1967-70, br. mgr., asst. v.p. Boston, 1970-80; asst. v.p., account exec. Marsh & McLennan Inc., Boston, 1980-84; sr. v.p. Frank B. Hall, Boston, 1984-87; resident v.p. Warwick Ins. Co., Needham, Mass., 1987-90; pres. Smith & Hale Assocs., Inc., South Orleans, Mass., 1990—. Lectr. Risk and Ins. Mgrs. Soc., Boston, 1975—85; mem. fin. divsn. Babson Coll., Wellesley, Mass., 1987—. Bd. dirs. Lupus Erythematosus Assn., Boston, 1975-78, Parker Hill Med. Ctr., Boston, 1978-80; tchr. Congl. Ch. Sch., Needham, Mass., 1982—; chmn. ins. adv. com. Town of Needham, 1982-95; pres. Interfaith Coun. for the Homeless, 1999—. Mem. Ins. Mgrs. Assn. (treas. Boston 1971-80), Ins. Library Assn. (dir. 1980-82). Office: Smith & Hale Assocs PO Box 136 South Orleans MA 02662-0136 Home: 7 Markham RD #20 East Hampton CT 06424-1640 Office Phone: 508-237-3723. Personal E-mail: smithhale@bigplanet.com.

HALE, MARIE STONER, artistic director; b. Greenwood, Miss. Student in Piano, U. Miss., Hattiesburg; studied with Richard Ellis, Christine du Boulay, Jo-Anna Kneeland, David Howard. Tchr. Ellis/du Boulay Sch., Chgo., Jo-Anna Kneeland Imperial Studios, Palm Beach County, Fla.; co-founder Ballet Arts Found., West Palm Beach, Fla., 1973-86; founder, artistic dir. Ballet Fla., West Palm Beach, 1986—. Office: Ballet Florida 500 Fern St West Palm Beach FL 33401-5726*

HALE, MARSHA BENTLEY, journalist, photographer, real estate rehabilitator, song writer, mannequin historian, b. Santa Monica, Calif., Dec. 23, 1951; d. Marvin Addison Kempf and Margery Edith Hale; m. Douglas Eugene Marx. Student, UCLA, 1977-79; BFA in Film and Video, Calif. Inst. Arts, 1981; postgrad. Calif. Inst. Arts, 2003-, postgrad. in Mythological Studies, Pacifica Grad. Inst., 2005-06. Co-owner Designer's Workshop, Beverly Hills, Calif., 1972-75, The Latticemakers, Westwood, Calif., 1975-76; owner Nat. Design Cons., 1976-86; mannequin historian, 1978—; CEO Vidi Vici, Inc., 1986-2003; contbg. writer FashionWindows.com, 2000-; animation archivist Amblin Entertainment, MCA Universal, 20th Century Fox, Dreamworks SKG, 1995-96; with Landworks Restoration & Design, Malibu, Calif., 1995-2000; songwriter Bentley Hale Prodns. (now Whirlwind Music LLC), 1996—; contbr. articles to profl. jours. Avocations: ocean, mountains, travel, cultural arts. Office: PO Box 97493 Las Vegas NV 89193-7493 E-mail: writingpen@aol.com.

HALE, MARTHA LARSEN, librarian; b. Pitts., Nov. 30, 1942; d. Olaf and Corinne (Carlson) Larsen; m. Frank A. Hale, Dec. 26, 1964 (div. 1976); children: Matthew, Jennifer. BA, U. N.H., 1965; MLS, Syracuse U., 1977; PhD, U. So. Calif., 1983. Dean libr. sci., Emporia, Kans. Democrat. Presbyterian. Office: 1200 Commercial St Emporia KS 66801-5057

HALE, MIGNON S. PALMER-FLACK, elementary school educator, educator; b. Silver Spring, Md., July 09; d. Lawrence Henry and Dorothy Elizabeth (Still) Scott; m. Harley Eugene Flack (dec. Mar. 1998); children: Oliver S. Palmer II, Michael Scott Palmer; stepchildren: Harley E. II, Christopher F.; m. Frank W. Hale Jr., July, 2003. BS, D.C. Tchrs. Coll., 1966; MS, Johns Hopkins U., 1977. Cert. tchr., Md. Elem. tchr. D.C. Pub. Schs., Washington, 1968-71; dir. Home Day Care Ctr., Columbia, Md., 1973-77; from elem. tchr. to resource tchr. gifted and talented Howard County Pub. Schs., Columbia, Md., 1977-90; elem. tchr. Cherry Hill (N.J.) Pub. Schs., 1990-94. Lang. arts rep. Howard County Pub. Schs., Columbia, 1977-86, student tchr. coord., 1984-90, tchr. recruiter, 1986-90; cons., tutor Village Reading Ctr., Columbia, 1986-90. Bd. trustees Children's Mus. Dayton, Ohio, 1995—, Opera Guild Dayton, 1995—, Muse Machine, Dayton, 1995—, Dayton Mus. Natural History, 1996; planning com. Centennial Flight-Yr. 2003, 1995—; first lady of Wright State U., Dayton. Recipient Cmty. Svc. award United Way Ctrl. Md., 1982; named Outstanding Supt., Breath of Life Ch., 1981, First Lady of Wright State U., 1994-98. Mem. AAUW, Nat. Assn. State U. and Land Grant Colls., Am. Assn. State Colls. and U., Wright State Orgn. for Women, Phi Delta Kappa, Alpha Lambda Delta. Avocations: reading, travel, music, cooking, entertaining. Home: 9222 Snow Shoe Ln Columbia MD 21045-1826

HALE, SUE A., editor; Reporter, metro editor, city editor, news editor Daily Oklahoman, Oklahoma City, asst. mng. editor, 1989—96, gen. mgr. Connect Okla., Inc. subs., 1996—2000, exec. editor, 2000—. Named one of Heroes of the 50 States, State Open Govt. Hall of Fame, Soc. Profl. Journalists/Nat. Freedom of Info. Coalition, 2003. Office: Daily Oklahoman 9000 N Broadway PO Box 25125 Oklahoma City OK 73125

HALE, SUZANNE K., ambassador; m. Hunter Hale; 2 children. Attended, Columbia U., Internat. Christian U., Tokyo, Beloit Coll. Mem. trade policy staff USDA, Washington, 1978—81; agrl. attaché to agrl. trade officer Embassy in Tokyo, 1981—88; dir. AgExport Svcs. Div. Fgn. Agrl. Svc., 1990—96; min.-counselor for agrl. affairs US Embassy in Beijing, 1997—2000, Embassy in Tokyo, 2000—04; US amb. to Federated States of Micronesia US Dept. State, 2004—. Office: US Embassy 4120 Kolonia Washington DC 20521-4120

HALE, VICTORIA G., chemist, pharmaceutical executive; m. Ahvie Herskowitz. BS, Univ. Md., 1983; PhD pharmaceutical chemistry, Univ. Calif., San Francisco, 1990. Sr. reviewer U.S. FDA, 1990—94; scientist Genentech Inc., 1994—97; co-founder, chief sci. officer Axum Biomedical

Inc., 1999—2000; founder, chmn., CEO Inst. for OneWorld Health, San Francisco, 2000—. Adj. assoc. prof. biopharmaceutical sciences Univ. Calif., San Francisco, 2002—; mem. indsl. adv. bd. Calif. Quantitative BioMedical Rsch. Group; adv. WHO; expert reviewer NIH. Named one of Most Outstanding Social Entrepreneurs, Schwab Found. Switzerland, 2004; recipient Exec. of the Yr., Esquire mag., 2005, Innovation award for social & econ. innovation, The Economist mag., 2005, Skoll award for social entrepreneurship, Skoll Found., 2005; fellow, Ashoka Innovators for the Public, 2006; MacArthur Fellow, John D. and Catherine T. MacArthur Found., 2006. Office: Inst for OneWorld Health Ste 500 50 California St San Francisco CA 94111*

HALES, JACQUELINE A., grant writer, elementary school educator; b. Hattiesburg, Miss., Feb. 10, 1964; d. Namon and Cordelia Hales. MS, Chgo. State U., 1993; MA magna cum laude, Spalding Coll., Louisville, 2004. Cert. learning and behavior specialist Ky., 2004. Writer Office of Mayor, Chgo., 1985—86; mgr. devel. Advocate Charitable Found., Chgo., 1998—2000; resource tchr. Jefferson County Pub. Schs., Louisville, 2001—05, Chgo. Pub. Schs., 2005—. Office Phone: 773-535-5000.

HALE SINGLETON, LORI T., special education educator; b. Washington, Nov. 6, 1970; d. Samuel W. and Gloria M. Hale; m. Robert Singleton; children: Janasia Rene' Taylor-Singleton, Jalisia Rachelle Talyor-Singleton, Chazzyn Reche' Singleton. MA, Ctrl. Mich. U., 2004. Emotional behavioral disorders tchr. Springfield Dist. 186, Springfield, Ill., 1999—2000; behavior specialist City Sch. Decatur, Ga., 2000—05, Atlanta Pub. Schs., 2005—06. Tchr. 1st St. Peter AME Ch., Stone Mountain, Ga., 2004—05.

HALEY, JENIFER JO, science educator; b. Boise, Idaho, Oct. 23, 1978; d. Barbara June and Robin Emanuel Holmquist; m. Byron Eugene Haley, June 5, 2000. BA Chemistry Edn., NW Nazarene U., Nampa, 2000. Tchr. sci. Caldwell H.S., Idaho, 2000—01, Horseshoe Bend H.S., Idaho, 2001—. Caravan scout leader Ch. of Nazarene, Emmett, Idaho, 2004—06. Grantee, Idaho Forrest Products Commn., 2003—04; Sci. and Tech. Grant, Idaho Nat. Lab., 2005—06, Rangelands Grant, Idaho Range land Resource Commn., 2002—03. R-Liberal. Nazarene. Avocations: hunting, fishing, horseback riding. Home: 300 Scenic Drive Emmett ID 83617 Office: Horseshoe Bend HS Horseshoe Bend ID Personal E-mail: behaley1@msn.com.

HALEY, JOHNETTA RANDOLPH, music educator; b. Alton, Ill., Mar. 19; d. John A. and Willye E. (Smith) Randolph; children from previous marriage: Karen, Michael. MusB in Edn., Lincoln U., 1945; MusM, So. Ill. U., 1972. Cert. cons. 1995. Vocal and gen. music tchr. Lincoln H.S., East St. Louis, Ill., 1945-48; vocal music tchr., choral dir. Turner Sch., Kirkwood, Mo., 1950-55; vocal and gen. music tchr. Nipher Jr. H.S., Kirkwood, 1955-71; prof. music Sch. Fine Arts So. Ill. U., Edwardsville, 1972—, dir. East St. Louis Campus, 1982—. Adjudicator music festivals; area music cons. Ill. Office Edn., 1977-78; program specialist St. Louis Human Devel. Corp., 1968. Interim exec. dir. St. Louis Coun. Black People, summer, 1970; bd. dirs. YWCA, 1975-80, Artist Presentation Soc., St. Louis, 1975, United Negro Coll. Fund, 1976-78; bd. curators Lincoln U., Jefferson City, Mo., 1974-82, pres., 1978-82; chairperson Ill. Com. on Black Concerns in Higher Edn.; mem. Nat. Ministry on Urban Edn. Luth. Ch.-Mo. Synod, 1975-80; bd. dirs. Coun. Luth. Chs. Stillman Coll.; pres. congregation St. Phillips Luth. Ch.; bd. dirs. Girls, Inc.; mem. Ill. Aux. Bd., United Way; v.p. East St. Louis Cmty. Fund, Inc.; trustee emeritus Stillman Coll., Ala., 2005. Recipient Cotillion de Leon award for Outstanding Cmty. Svc., 1977, Disting. Alumnae award Lincoln U., 1977, Disting. Svc. award United Negro Coll. Fund, 1979; SCLC, 1981; recipient Cmty. Svc. award St. Louis Drifters, 1979, Disting. Svc. to Arts award Sigma Gamma Rho, Nat. Negro Musicians award, 1981, Sci. Awareness award, 1984-85, Tri Del Federated award, 1985, Martin Luther King Drum Maj. award, 1985, Bus. and Profl. Women's Club award, 1985-86, Fred L. McDowell award, 1986, Vol. of Yr. award Inroads Inc., 1986, Woman of Achievement in Edn. award Elks, 1987, Woman of Achievement award Suburban Newspaper of Greater St. Louis and Sta. KMOX-Radio, 1988, Love award Greeley Cmty. Ctr., Sammy Davies Jr. award in Edn., 1990, Yes I Can award in Edn., 1990, Merit award Urban League, 1994, Legacy award Nat. Coun. Negro Women, 1995, Diversity award Mo. ARC, 2001, St. Louis Coun. of Govts. Outstanding Achievement award, 2006; named Disting. Citizen St. Louis Argus Newspaper, 1970, Dutchess of Paducah, 1973; Johnetta Haley Scholars Acad. minority scholarship named in her honor So. Ill. U., Lifetime Achievement award, East West Coun., 2006. Mem. AAUP, Music Educators Nat. Conf., Nat. Choral Dirs. Assn., Nat. Assn. Negro Musicians, Coll. Music Soc., Coun. Luth. Chs., Ill. Music. Educators, Jack and Jill, Inc., Women of Achievement in Edn., Friends of St. Louis Art Mus., The Links, Inc. (nat. parliamentarian, chair constnl. and by-laws com.), Las Amigas Social Club, Alpha Kappa Alpha (internat. parliamentarian, dir. 17th ctrl. region 1970-74, Golden Soror award 1995, Grad Svcs. award 2001), Mu Phi Epsilon, Pi Kappa Lambda. Lutheran. Home: 1926 Bennington Common Dr Saint Louis MO 63146-2575 Personal E-mail: johnethaley@aol.com.

HALEY, PATRICIA ANN, psychiatric therapist, school counselor, administrator; b. Waxahachie, Tex., Jan. 17, 1951; d. Bob A. and Gertie M. (Graham) H. BA, Tex. Woman's Univ., 1973, postgrad. in deaf edn., 1978; MEdin counseling and student svcs., U. North Tex., 1994. Lic. profl. counselor. Tchr. Ennis (Tex.) Ind. Sch. Dist., 1985-93; counselor Ferris (Tex.) Ind. Sch. Dist., 1994—; PRN, psychiat. therapist HCA Med. Ctr.; co-owner Jasmine's Gifts. Owner Poetic Perspectives, Waxahachie, 1988—, Jasmine's. Editor (poetry) Family Tributes, 1989, Therapeutic Poetry, 1990, Heroes and Heroines, 1991; contbg. poet (cassette) The Sound of Poetry, 1993. Mem. prof. women's adv. bd. Am. Biog. Inst. Recipient Tex. Counseling Assn. Profl. Devel. award, 1996. Fellow AAUW (interviewee cable TV show 1994); mem. ACA, Tex. Counseling Assn. (Ednl. Endowment award 1996, Profl. Devel. award 1996), Poetry Soc. of Tex., Tex. Play Therapy Assn., Tex. Sch. Counselors Assn., Kappa Delta Pi, Phi Delta Kappa, Pi Lambda Theta, Chi Sigma Iota. Avocations: singing, acting, reading, poetry, swimming.

HALEY, PRISCILLA JANE, printmaker; b. Boston, June 22, 1926; d. Arthur Benjamin and Jessamy (Fountain) H.; m. Tadeusz Bilous, May 21, 1961. BA, Oberlin Coll., Ohio, 1948; postgrad., Bklyn. Mus. Sch., 1955. Resident artist Yaddo Found., Saratoga Springs, NY, 1957. One-man show Village Art Ctr., N.Y.C., 1960; 3-man show Islip Art Mus., 1975; represented in permanent collection N.Y. Pub. Libr., Nat. Acad. Galleries, Bklyn. Mus., Libr. of Congress, Bowdoin Coll. Art Mus., Oberlin Coll., Addison Gallery art, Wesleyan U. Libr., Portland (Oreg.) Mus. Art, others; portfolio of prints and poems by Maine poets, The Island, 1961. Recipient Medal of Honor Audubon Artists, 1957, 1st prize Bablyon Arts Coun. Juried Exhbn., 1992; Louis Comfort Tiffany Found. grantee, 1959. Mem. Soc. Am. Graphic Artists, York Art Assn. Home: 79 York St York ME 03909

HALEY, ROSLYN TREZEVANT, educational program director; b. Washington, July 23, 1955; d. Morti Trezevant and Sara Roslyn Kebe; m. Darrell D. Haley, July 30, 1988; children: Jessica, Darrell Jr., Donald, Anthony, Krystal. BA in History, S.C. State U., 1976; MPA, Calif. State U., L.A., 1983; EdD, UCLA, 1999. Cert. tchr. Calif., adminstr. Calif. Admissions evaluator UCLA, 1979-81, counselor Sch. Pub. Health, 1981-83, head counselor dept. theater, 1983-93; dir. student, counseling, and recruitment svcs. UCLA Sch. Theater, Film and TV, 1993—2005; faculty chair gen. studies Univ. Coll., 2005—. Adult edn. tchr. LA Unified Sch. Dist., 1984-93; assoc. prof., faculty area chair. U. Phoenix, Costa Mesa, Calif., 1996—; bd. dirs. Palmdale (Calif.) HS, Visual and Performing Arts Acad., 1999; co-founder, adminstr. Jesus is Lord Christian Ch.; state coord. Calif. March for Jesus, 2005. Author of poetry. March organizer March for Jesus, L.A., 1994, Antelope Valley, 1995-02; adminstr. Command Ctr., Convoy of Hope, Palmdale, 1998; sch. site coun. Palmtree Elem. Sch., Palmdale, 1998-99; recruiter Boy Scouts Am. Western L.A. Coun. Bd., 1998-99; campaign chair Antelope Valley YMCA, 2001; adminstr. Jesus is Lord Christian Ch.; state coord. March of Jesus, Calif. Recipient Outstanding Svc. award March for Jesus, L.A., 1994, Outstanding Svc. award First Missionary Bapt. Ch., Littlerock, Calif., 1997, Outstanding Svc. award Jesus Day, Antelope Valley. Mem. Am. Assn. Ednl. Rsch. Avocations: reading, swimming, horseback riding, bicycling. Home: 37518 Larchwood Dr Palmdale CA 93550-6037 Office: UCLA Sch TFT 405 Hilgard Ave Los Angeles CA 90095-9000 Fax: 310-825-3383. Office Phone: 661-274-0889. Personal E-mail: drrozhaley@yahoo.com. E-mail: rhaley@tft.ucla.edu.

HALEY, SHIRLEY JEAN, piano educator, photographer; b. Yakima, Wash., Dec. 8, 1932; d. Clayton Emry and Jean Montana (Kimball) Roberts; m. Oliver Louis Kienholz, May 5, 1952 (div. Oct. 1973); children: Clayton Louis Kienholz, Nancy Jean Kienholz, Linda Diane Wilson; m. James William Haley, June 15, 1974. Cert. Nat. Music Tchrs. Assn. Pvt. practice piano tchr., Pullman, Wash., 1946-57, Puyallup, Wash., 1957-71, Burlington, Wash., 1971—. Pvt. practice photographer, Big Lake, Wash. Mem. Skagit Art Assn. (sec. 1994-96, pres. 1996-2000), Tacoma Music Tchrs. Assn. (pres.), Puyallaup Music Tchrs. Assn. (pres.), Mt. Vernon Music Tchrs. Assn. (pres.). Avocations: hiking, mountain climbing, backpacking, botany, writing. E-mail: topshots@wavecable.com.

HALFPAP, KAYLA JEAN, special education educator; b. Iowa Falls, Iowa, Aug. 21, 1962; d. Richard Raymond and Shirley Kathleen Hankom; m. Douglas Dean Halfpap, June 6, 1992; 1 child, Colin Richard. BS, Iowa State U., Ames, 1985. Lic. std. tchr. State of Iowa Bd. Ednl. Examiners, 1985. Spl. edn. tchr. early childhood Area Edn. Agy. 2, Clear Lake, Iowa, 1985—97, Charles City Pub. Schs., 1997—2000, Washington Early Childhood Ctr., Mason City, Iowa, 2000—. Actor Mason City Cmty. Theatre, Iowa, v.p., 2000—. Office Phone: 641-421-4418.

HALIL, SUSAN TERRELL, dental hygienist; b. Bessemer, Ala., June 23, 1949; d. Jack Ingram Terrell and Betty May Hardiment; m. Donald William Halil, Sr., Sept. 29, 1972; children: Donald William, Douglas Winston, Melissa Marie. AS, Pensacola Jr. Coll., 1969. Registered dental hygienist Fla. Bd. Dentistry. Dental hygienist Dr. Maxwell de la Rua, Pensacola, Fla., 1969—70, Dr. Reuben Groom, Jacksonville, Fla., 1970—72, Dr. A.J. Bauknecht, Jacksonville, 1972—86; new patient orientation/dental hygienist Dr. Bruce Kanehl, Jacksonville, 1986—87; periodontal dental hygienist Dr. Lamar Pearson, Jacksonville, 1987—89; ins. assoc. Capital Ins. Agy., Jacksonville, 1989—91; dental hygienist Dr. Eric Townsend, Ponte Vedra, Fla., 1991—2001, new patient coord., dental hygienist, 2003—, Dr. Joseph Barton, Jacksonville, 2001—02. Presenter in field. Newsletter editor:. Pres. San Jose Cath. Parish Coun., Jacksonville, 2003—04, San Jose Cath. Women's Guild, Jacksonville, 1983—84. Recipient Svc. award, N.E. Dist. Dental Hygienists' Soc., 1971, 1980. Mem.: N.E. Fla. Dental Hygiene Assn. (first v.p. 1972—73, pres. 1973—74, newsletter editor 1973—74, 1980—81, Achievement award 1995), Fla. Dental Hygiene Assn. (N.E. Fla. rep. coun. on govtl. affairs 1991—97, N.E. Fla. del. 1992—97, v.p. 1994—95, pres. elect 1995—96, pres. 1996—97, immediate past pres. 1997—98, mem. nominating com. 1997—, Disting. Svc. award 2002, Component Outstanding Mem. award 2002, 2004), Am. Dental Hygienists' Assn. (alt. del. 1970—71, nat. del. 1971—73, 1994—97, chairperson nat. del. 1996—97, liaison Inst. for Oral Health 1998—99). Republican. Roman Catholic. Avocations: gardening, walking, bicycling, dance, yoga. Home: 7104 St Augustine Rd Jacksonville FL 32217 Office Phone: 904-285-7711. Personal E-mail: shalil@bellsouth.net.

HALL, ADRIENNE A., international marketing communications executive, consultant, life balance coach; b. LA; d. Arthur E. and Adelina P. Kosches; m. Maurice Hall; children: Adam, Todd, Victoria, Stefanie; adopted children: Joe Hibbitt, Kim Hibbitt, Joe Kwan, Georgina Kwan, Carlos Moreno, Miriam Moreno. BA, UCLA. Founding ptnr. Hall & Levine Advt., L.A., 1970-80; vice chmn. bd. Eisaman, Johns & Laws Advt. Inc., L.A., Houston, Chgo., N.Y.C., 1980-94; pres., CEO The Hall Group, Beverly Hills, Calif., 1994—. Co-founder, chair, bd. dirs. Women, Inc.; chair bd. dirs. Women's Pres. Orgn., 1999—, co-chair, State Econ. Network, 2000—; chmn. Eric Bovy Inc., 1986-89, Hall Partnership, Venture Capital; bd. dirs. Calif. Mfrs. Assn., Calif. Life Corp., Inc.; mem. adv. bd. Global Asset Mgmt., The Edison Co., Sempra Energy, The Gas Co., Nestle, Merrill Lynch. Trustee UCLA; bd. regents Loyola-Marymount U., 1990—, Natl. Bus. Counc., Wash. D.C.; mem. The Founders of Music Ctr., Save the Children, Vietnam and Haiti.; mem., chair women's leadership bd. Kennedy Sch. Govt., Harvard U.; commr. L.A. County Arts Commn.; commr. Calif. Gov.'s Commn. on Econ. Devel., task force Rebuild L.A.; chair Leading Women Entrepreneurs of the World; bd. dirs. United Way, ARC, Exec. Svc. Corps, The Com. of 200, Shelter Partnership; trustee Nat. Health Found., Women's Enterprise Devel. Corp.; gov. Town Hall; mem. adv. coun. Girls' Clubs Am.; mem. adv. bd. Girl Scouts U.S., Asian Pacific Women's Adv. Bd., Coalition of 100 Black Women, Nat. Network of Hispanic Women, Women of Color, Women in Bus., Downtown Women's Ctr. and residence, Leadership Am., Washington, L.A., Food Bank; mem. exec. bd. Greater L.A. Partnership for Homeless, Recipient Nat. Headliner award Women in Comm., 1982, Profl. Achievement award UCLA Alumni, 1979, Award for Cmty. Svc., 1994, Asian Pacific Network Woman Warrior award, 1994, Woman of the Yr. award Am. Advt. Fedn., 1973, Ad Person of West award Mktg. and Media Decisions, 1982, Bus. Woman of Yr. award Boy Scouts Am., 1983, Women Helping Women award Soroptimists Internat., 1984, 1st ann. portfolio award for exec. women, 1985, Communicator of Yr. award Ad Women, 1986, Leader award YWCA, 1986, L.A. Women's Found. Mentor award, 1997, Leading Women Entrepreneurs of World award, 2003; named Bus. Leader of Yr., L.A. Bus. Coun., 1999, NAW Legal Defense/Edn. Fund. award, 2001, Cosmo award, Women's Leadership Exch., 2006; named NAWBO Hall of Fame, 2002, Hall of Fame Enterprising Women Mag., NY, 2004; Adrienne Hall Women's Mentorship Fund established in her honor, Kennedy Sch. Govt., Harvard U., 2005. Mem. Internat. Women's Forum (Woman Who Made a Difference award 1987), Am. Assn. Advt. Agys. (bd. dirs. 1980, chmn. bd. govs. western region), Western States Advt. Agys. Assn. (pres. 1975), Hollywood Radio and TV Soc. (dir.), Nat. Advt. Rev. Bd., Overseas Edn. Fund, Com. 200 (western chmn.), Women in Communications, Orgn. Women Execs., Calif. Women's Forum (founder, chmn. The Trusteeship), Rotary (L.A. 5 chpt.), Internat. Bus. Fellows (mem. adv. bd.), Women's Econ. Alliance, Nat. Assn. Women Bus. Owners (adv. bd.), L.A. Area C. of C. (chmn., alumni dir.). Clubs: Calif. Yacht; Stock Exchange, Los Angeles Advt. (pres.) (Los Angeles). Lodges: Rotary. Achievements include having the Harvard University and Kennedy School of Government Leadership Board establish the Adrienne Hall Women's Mentorship Fund in perpetuity in her honor in 2006; founding the first advertising agency in the nation headed by women. Personal E-mail: aahall@earthlink.net.

HALL, AMI S., elementary school educator, actress; b. Englewood, Colo., Dec. 7, 1973; d. Patti Shoup; m. Steven H Hall, Aug. 7, 1999. BA, Luther Coll., Decorah, Iowa, 1996; MA in Edn. Arts Integration, Lesley U., Boston, 2006. Fifth grade tchr. Sheridan Sch. Dist., Sheridan, Colo., 1997—99, performing arts tchr., 1999—. Artistic dir. Ascot Theatre. Fundraiser ADA. Mem.: Phi Beta Kappa (life). Avocations: singing, writing, reading, cycling, travel. Office Phone: 720-833-6670.

HALL, AMY MATTHEWS, science educator; b. Shreveport, La., Dec. 7, 1941; d. James William and Annie Ruth (Brown) Matthews; m. Jon H. Hall, June 19, 1962; children: Jon William, Elizabeth Anne May. BS in Edn., Centenary Coll., 1967. Fifth grade tchr. Caddo Parish Schools, Shreveport, La., 1968—71; sci. tchr. Agnew Town and Country Sch., Shreveport, 1971—72, Southfield Sch., Shreveport, 1972—86, Caddo Mid. Magnet, Shreveport, 1986—. Mem. exec. bd. Caddo Fed. Tchrs. and Support Pers. Author: (books of poetry) Coll. Anthology of Poetry, 1960, rev. sci. curriculum, rev. Caddo Parish Discipline policy. Named Master Tchr., So. Assn. Ind. Sch., 1985. Mem.: Caddo Fedn. Tchrs. (exec. bd.), La. Mid. Sch. Assn., Nat. Biology Tchr. Assn., Paw Prints Club. Republican. Meth. Avocations: antiques, gemology, needlecrafts. Home: 9815 E Trails End Shreveport LA 71118 Office: Caddo Mid Magnet Sch 7635 Cornelius Lane Shreveport LA 71106

HALL, ANNA CHRISTENE, retired government official; b. Tyler, Tex., Dec. 18, 1946; d. Willie B. and Mary Christine H. BA in Polit. Sci., So. Meth. U., 1969. Clk.-stenographer Employment and Tng. Adminstrn., U.S. Dept. Labor, Dallas, 1970, fed. rep., 1970-80, program analyst Washington, 1980-84, div. chief, 1984-87, exec. asst., 1987-88, office dir. Dallas, 1988—2001; ret., 2002. Part-time cons. DTI Assocs., 2004—. Mem. Partnership for Employment and Tng., Nat. Honor Soc. Democrat. Presbyterian. Avocations: reading, theater, playing piano. Home: 603 Kingfisher Ln Arlington TX 76002-3456 Office Phone: 214-237-9111 ext. 254. E-mail: annachall@juno.com.

HALL, BARBARA, television producer; b. Danville, Va. d. Ervis and Flo Hall; m. Paul Karon; 1 child, Faith. BA summa cum laude in English, James Madison U., 1982. Author: Skeeball and the Secret of the Universe, 1987, Dixie Storms, 1990, Fool's Hill, 1992, House Across the Cove, 1995, A Better Place, 1994, Close to Home, 1997, Summons to New Orleans, 2000; Writer (TV series) include, Family Ties, Newhart, Anything But Love, Northern Exposure, I'll Fly Away, ER, Chicago Hope, New York News, Writer, prodr. Moonlighting, Writer, exec. prodr., developer Judging Amy, 1999—2002, cons. prodr. Northern Exposure, Chicago Hope, Judging Amy, 2002—, Creator, writer, exec. prodr. Joan of Arcadia, 2003—; singer: (band) The Enablers. Recipient Humanitas award, Golden Laurel, Prodrs. Guild of Am., awards, Am. Libr. Assn., award, Children's Def. Fund. Office: CBS/Sony Productions 10202 W Washington Blvd Tracy West Culver City CA 90232

HALL, BARBARA LOUISE, interior designer, artist; b. Tulsa, Jan. 24, 1936; d. Paul Martin and Nell (Coy) Bolley; m. Denton Lee Richey, 1955 (div. 1970); m. William Volker Longmoor, 1971 (dec. 1981); m. Robert Leroy Hall, Sept. 11, 1984; 1 child, Christina Lee Edwards. BFA, U. Kans., 1975. Interior designer Pat O'Leary Assoc., Fairway, Kans., 1974-78, Jack Rees Interiors, Kansas City, Mo., 1978-83; interior designer, owner, pres. The Studio, Inc., Prairie Village, Kans., 1983-86; prin. Barbara Hall Interiors, Sun Lakes, Ariz., 1984—. Mem. Nat. Oil and Acrylic Painters Soc., Am. Soc. Interior Design (profl.), Ariz. Watercolor Assn. (juried mem.). Home and Office: 10915 E Twilight Dr Sun Lakes AZ 85248-7927

HALL, BEVERLY ADELE, nursing educator; b. Houston, Aug. 19, 1935; d. Leslie Leo and Lois Mae (Pesnell) H. BS, Tex. Christian U., 1957; MA, NYU, 1961; PhD, U. Colo., 1974. RN, Tex., N.Y. With Ft. Worth (Tex.) Dept. Health, 1957-59; asst. prof. U. Mass., Amhurst, 1961-65; chief nurse N.Y.C. Med. Coll., 1965-67; asst. prof. U. Colo., Denver, 1967-70; assoc. prof. U. Washington, Seattle, 1974-80; prof., chmn. dept. U. Calif., San Francisco, 1980-84; Denton Cooley prof. nursing U. Tex., Austin, 1984-2001, prof. emeritus, 2001—, mem. grad. faculty Sch. Biomed. Sci. Galveston; disting. prof. Coll. Art & Scis., Akachi, Japan, 1999-2000. Pres. med. svcs. Bd. Dir. Project Transitions; disting. prof. Coll. Nursing, Arts and Scis., Hyogo, Japan; mem. NIH Study Group; cons. HIV/AIDS Internat. Coun. fo Nurses. Author: Mental Health and the Elderly, 1985 (Book of Yr.); mem. editl. rev. bd. Advances in Nursing, Archives Psychiat. Nursing, Qualitative Health Rsch., Rsch. in Nursing and Health, Nursing Outlook, Jour. Profl. Nursing, Jour. of the Am. Psychiat. Nurses Assn.; contbr. articles to profl. jours., chpts. to books. Served to capt. U.S. Army, 1962-66. Recipient Tex. Excellence Teaching award U. Tex. Ex-Students Assn., 1994. Fellow Am. Acad. Nursing (governing bd., mem. fellowship selection com.), Am. Coll. Mental Health Adminstrn.; mem. ANA (divsn. gerontological practice), Coun. Nurse Rschrs., Am. Inst. Life Threatening Illness and Loss, So. Nursing Rsch. Soc. Office: U Tex 1700 Red River St Austin TX 78701-1412 Office Phone: 512-232-4704, 512-471-7913.

HALL, BEVERLY BARTON, librarian; b. Cin., July 15, 1918; d. Clarence Earl Barton and Maude Ethel Wedmore; m. Randolph Van Lew Hall, Apr. 26, 1947; children: Barton M., Martha H. Kern, Patricia H. Pellerin. BA, Middlebury Coll., 1940; BS, Columbia U., 1941; MS, So. Conn. State Coll., 1975. Cert. tchr./libr. grades K-12, Conn. Libr. Wellesley (Mass.) Coll., 1941-42, Great Neck (N.Y.) Pub. Libr., 1942-44, Yale U. Sch. Law, New Haven, 1944-50, Amity Regional H.S., Woodbridge, Conn., 1967-80. Author: Secret of the Lion's Head, 1995; also short stories. Founder, bd. dirs. Orange (Conn.) Pub. Libr., 1956-63; founder, head libr. St. John's Ch. Libr., Naples, Fla., 1993—; active Collier County Geneal. Soc., Collier County Hist. Soc., Collier County Friends of the Libr. Mem. Ch. and Synagoge Libr. Assn. (sec. 1999-2000). Republican. Episcopalian. Avocations: water aerobics, counted cross-stitch, crocheting, music. Home: Apt 107 49 High Point Circle South Naples FL 34103

HALL, BEVERLY JOY, police officer; b. St. Paul, Minn., Dec. 31, 1957; d. Kenneth Ray and Harriet Kathleen (Fuller) H.; m. Charles Alan Neuman, Feb. 14, 1956. AAS in Law Enforcement, North Hennepin C.C., Brooklyn Park, Minn., 1977; grad., FBI Nat. Acad., 1993; BA in Law Enforcement Mgmt., Met. State U., St. Paul, 1999. Lic. peace officer, Minn. Officer cmty. svc. Brooklyn Park Police Dept., 1977—79; police officer St. Paul Police Dept., 1979—86, police sgt., 1986—95, police lt., 1995—2000, police comdr., 2000—. Hostage negotiator, St. Paul Police Dept., 1991-92, hostage negotiating team coord., 1992-96. Mem. Internat. Assn. Women Police (regional coord. 1988-94, bd. dirs.), Nat. Assn. Women Law Enforcement Execs. (2d. v.p. 2000-01), Minn. Assn. of Women Police (pres. 1982-86), Assn. Tng. Officers of Minn., FBI Nat. Acad. Assocs. Avocations: gardening, jogging, reading. Office: Saint Paul Police Dept 367 Grove St Saint Paul MN 55101-2296

HALL, BEVERLY L., school system administrator; b. Montego Bay, Jamaica; m. Luis Hall, Dec. 22, 1973; 1 child, Jason. BA in English, Bklyn. Coll., 1970, MA in Guidance and counseling, 1973; PhD in Adminstrn., Fordham U., 1990. English tchr. Jr. H.S. 265, Bklyn., 1970—76; asst. prin. Satellite West Jr. H.S., Bklyn., 1977—83; prin. Pub. Sch. 282, Bklyn., 1983—87, Jr. H.S. 113, Bklyn., 1987—92; supt. Cmty. Sch. Dist. 27, Queens, NY, 1992—94; dep. schs. chancellor for instrn. N.Y.C. Pub. Schs., 1994—95; supt. Newark City Schs., 1995—99, Atlanta Pub. Schs., 1999—. Office: Atlanta Pub Schs 130 Trinity Ave SW Atlanta GA 30303 Office Phone: 404-802-2820.

HALL, BREDA FAYE KIMBROUGH INMAN, counselor, educator; d. Byron C. and Vera J. Kimbrough; m. Charles Roland Inman (dec.); m. James Webster Hall (div.); 1 child, Rachel Lauren Hall Clark. BS, U. Ala., Birmingham, 1984; MA, U. N.D., Grand Forks, 1987. Nat. cert. counselor Nat. Bd. for Cert. Counselors, Inc., lic. profl. counselor N.Mex. Counseling and Therapy Practice Bd., clin. mental health counselor N.Mex. Grad. asst. learning svcs. U. N.D., Grand Forks, 1985—86, practicum counseling ctr., 1986; counseling intern St. Luke's Hosp. Chaplaincy and Radiation Oncology, Fargo, ND, 1986—87; counselor, instr., dir. student svcs. U. N.Mex., Los Alamos, 1987—90, practicum instr. human svcs. Valencia, 1990—91, counselor/sr. counselor with grief intervention program Office Med. Investigator Albuquerque; therapist Gulf Coast Mental Health, Gulfport, Miss., 1994—97. DHSR mem., mental health profl. The ARC; spkr. in field; developed grief ctr. for children. Author: A Manual for the American Voter, Personality Development from the Biblical Perspective. Vol. paraprofessional Rape Crises Ctr., Birmingham; vol. Civitan's Spl. Olympic's, Los Alamos; vol. paraprofessional McDonough Ho., Birmingham. Recipient Psychology Rsch. award, U. Ala., Birmingham, 1984. Mem.: Ala. Counseling Assn., Am. Counseling Assn. (assoc.). Achievements include research in severity of illness and emotional relationships with patients in tri-state area of ND, SD, MN (UND); development of interactive grief support groups between parents and teenagers suffering loss of child (or sibling) between ages of 0-18; research in difference between cognitive and emotional intake of information in recruiting Apheresis Donors. Avocations: reading, movies, gardening, skiing, water-skiing. Home: PO Box 1643 Brandon MS 39043-1643 Personal E-mail: bredaihall@yahoo.com.

HALL, CAROL ANN, music educator; b. Lamar, Colo., Dec. 22, 1952; d. Raymond Dewey and Hazel Vera Morrow; m. Charlie Merle Hall, Apr. 21, 1979 (dec. Oct. 10, 2001); 1 child, Charlie Walter. AA, Lamar C.C., 1972; BA in Elem. Edn., BA in Music Edn. K-12, Adams State Coll., Alamosa, Colo., 1974. 4th grade tchr. Springfield Elem. Sch., 1974—75, tchr. K-6 music,

1990—; tchr. K-6 music Parkview Elem. Sch., Lamar, 1975—78; tchr. K-12 music Vilas Sch., 1986—88. Piano tchr., Vilas, 1986—88; voice tchr., Pritchett, Vilas and Springfield, Colo.; performer, recorded composed song Goldband records, 2002—03. Music leader, mem. Tri Ch. Trio Springfield Bapt. Chapel. Recipient award, Am. Women of Who's Who, 2002—03. Mem.: Springfield Elem. Tchrs. Assn., Music Educators Nat. Conf. Baptist. Avocations: bowling, composing.

HALL, CHARLOTTE HAUCH, editor; b. Washington, Sept. 30, 1945; d. Charles Christian and Ruthadele Bertha (LaTourrette) H.; m. Robert Lindsay Hall, June 8, 1968; 1 child, Benjamin H. BA, Kalamazoo Co., 1966; MA, U. Chgo., 1967. Reporter, news editor The Ridgewood (N.J.) Newspapers, 1971-74; copy editor, news editor The Record, Hackensack, N.J., 1975-76; asst. mng. editor The Boston Herald Am., 1977-78; dep. met. editor The Washington Star, 1979-80; copy chief, met. editor, Nassau editor Newsday, Melville, NY, 1981—86, Washington news editor, 1986—88, asst. mng. editor for Long Island, 1988-94; mktg. dir. Newsday, Inc., Melville, NY, 1994-96, mng. editor, 1997-99, v.p., mng. editor, 1999—2003, v.p. planning, 2003—04; v.p., editor Orlando Sentinel, Fla., 2004—. Trustee Kalamazoo Coll. Recipient Robert G. McGruder Awards for Diversity Leadership award, Am. Soc. Newspaper Editors, 2003. Mem. Am. Soc. Newspaper Editors (bd. dirs.), Newspaper Assn. Am., Phi Beta Kappa. Office: Orlando Sentinel 633 N Orange Ave Orlando FL 32801-1349

HALL, CYNTHIA HOLCOMB, federal judge; b. LA, Feb. 19, 1929; d. Harold Romeyn and Mildred Gould Holcomb; m. John Harris Hall, June 6, 1970 (dec. Oct. 1980). AB, Stanford U., 1951, JD, 1954; LLM, NYU, 1960. Bar: Ariz. 1954, Calif. 1956. Law clk. to judge U.S. Ct. Appeals 9th Cir., 1954—55; trial atty. tax divsn. Dept. Justice, 1960—64; atty.-adviser Office Tax Legis. Counsel, Treasury Dept., 1964—66; mem. firm Brawerman & Holcomb, Beverly Hills, Calif., 1966—72; judge U.S. Tax Ct., Washington, 1972—81, U.S. Dist. Ct. for Ctrl. Dist. Calif., L.A., 1981—84; cir. judge U.S. Ct. Appeals (9th cir.), Pasadena, Calif., 1984—, sr. judge, 1997—. Lt. (j.g.) USNR, 1951—53. Office: US Ct Appeals 9th Cir 125 S Grand Ave Pasadena CA 91105-1621

HALL, DENISE, special education educator; b. L.A., Sept. 15, 1960; d. Willie Mae and Curtis Coleman; children: Lanneau L. White Iv, Joshua L. White. BA, U. Tex., San Antonio, 1999. Cert. spl. edn. Com. officer U. Tex. at San Antonio Police Dept., San Antonio, 1995—98; tchr. sci. and english spl. edn. Northside Alternative HS, San Antonio, 1999—2002. Mentor Northside Ind. Sch. Dist., San Antonio, 1999—2002. Grantee Edn., U. Tex. at San Antonio, 1997—99. Home: 11218 Taylor Crest San Antonio TX 78249 Office: Northside Alternative HS 144 Hunt Ln San Antonio TX 78245-1102 Personal E-mail: Dhall915@aol.com.

HALL, DORIS SPOONER, music educator; b. New Orleans, Dec. 27, 1949; d. Henry and Geneva (Battley) Spooner; m. Morris D. Hall, Aug. 4, 1973; 1 child, Amy Evon. B of Music Edn., La. State U., 1971, M of Music Edn., 1972, postgrad., ALA A&M U., 1991. Cert. tchr. Ala., La. Band dir. Shreveport (La.) City Schs., 1972-73; asst. band dir. Ala. A&M U., Normal, 1973-74, asst. prof. music, 1974-79, aux. coord. marching units, 1979-87, prof. music, 1980—. Lectr. music U. Ala., Huntsville, 1980-89, Oakwood Coll., Huntsville, 1980-90; clinician Ala. Sch. System, Birmingham, 1989-92; cons. in field. Active Huntsville Sympjony Orch., 1975-79, 86-92; recitals U. Ala. and Ala. A&M U., 1990-92. Named Outstanding Young Women, 1982; recipient Outstanding Achievers awards, 1983. Mem. AAUP, Nat. Flute Assn., Nat. Woodwinds Assn., Music Educators Nat. Conf., Ala. Edn. Assn., Tau Beta Sigma, ALpha Kappa Alpha. Roman Catholic. Avocations: dance, reading, skating. Home: 12000 Bell Mountain Dr SW Huntsville AL 35803-3406

HALL, ELIZABETH MURCHIE, retired special education educator, consultant; b. Jan. 14, 1945; BA in Philosophy, Sarah Lawrence Coll., 1967; MEd in Spl. Edn., Ala. A&M U., 1977; PhD in Spl. Edn., Peabody/Vanderbilt U., 1981. Tchr. English Brevard County schs., Melbourne, Fla., 1972-75; tchr. spl. edn., program coord. Huntsville (Ala.) City Schs., 1977-80; prof. Athens (Ala.) State Coll., 1980-98; owner, cons. Skills for Success, Huntsville, 1999—; owner Lewiston Hall Properties Devel. of Afordable Housing, Huntsville, Ala., 2004—. Office: Lewiston Hall Properties Devel of Affordable Housing 1428 Weatherly Rd Ste 201 Huntsville AL 35803 Office Phone: 256-881-5959.

HALL, ELLA TAYLOR, clinical school psychologist; b. Macon, Miss., Nov. 30, 1948; d. Essex and Mamie (Roland) Taylor; children: Banyikaai Monique (dec.), Motiqua Shante. BA, Fisk U., 1971, MA, 1973; PhD, George Peabody Coll., 1978. Mental health specialist behavioral sci. divsn. Meharry Med. Coll., Nashville, 1976-77; assoc. psychologist Bronx (N.Y.) Psychiat. tr., 1979; clin. psychologist Wiltwyck Residential Treatment Ctr., Ossining, N.Y., 1979-81; clin. cons. Abbott House, Irvington, N.Y., 1982-85; sch. psychologist Abbott Union Free Sch. Dist., 1985—. Cons. psychologist Youth Theater Interactions, Inc., N.Y.; rschr in the field. Author: (poetry) Double Twister, Somebody, Clinging Tears, 1994, Maple Tree at Dawn, 1995, Down My Three Rows, 1995, Mama Sis, 1995, These Times, 1995, Ordinary, 1996, Young Wilted Flower, 2000, Secret Garden, 2000, Blood Silence, 2000; (art) In My Mind, 1994, Picking Cotton, 1995. Lay reader, acolyte Episcopal Ch.; mem. Com. on Spl. Edn. NIMH tng. grantee, Kendall grantee; Crusade fellow. Mem. Schomburg Ctr. for Rsch., N.Y. State Psychol. Assn., N.Y. Bot. Soc., Wildlife Conservation Soc., Delta Sigma Theta. Avocation: photography.

HALL, FRANCES BENN, writer, retired theater educator; b. Waukegan, Ill., June 17, 1918; d. Clinton Claude Benn and Bessie Beulah Harn; m. E. James Hall, Jan. 1, 1942 (dec. May 1982); children: Parnell, Terrence, Caitlin. BA, U. Wis., 1940, MA, 1941; postgrad., Oxford (Eng.) U., 1988, Yeats Summer Sch., 1989-92, Synge Summer Sch., Wicklow, Ireland, 1995, Trinity Coll., Dublin, Ireland, 1997, Univ. Coll., Dublin, 1998, Cambridge (Eng.) U., 1999, U. Limerick, Ireland, 2000. Theater dir., tchr. Windsor Mt. Sch., Lenox, Mass., 1947-75; theater tchr. Berkshire C.C., Pittsfield, Mass., 1982—2000; ret., 2000. Dir., play prodr. Lenox Cultural Coun., 1989—2000. Author: Ezra's Noh for Willie, 1996, Pasternak's Boots, 2006. Mem.: Am. Coun. Irish Studies, Yeats Soc. N.Y., Yeats Soc. Boston (founding mem.). Democrat. Avocations: travel, Irish studies. Home: 80 Hawthorne St Lenox MA 01240-2403 Personal E-mail: yearsnoh@yahoo.com.

HALL, GEORGANNA MAE, elementary school educator; b. St. Louis, June 4, 1951; d. George Winfred and Judith Lou (Wheatley) H. BS in Edn., Stephen F. Austin U., 1973; MS in Edn., U. Houston, 1979. Cert. elem., early childhood and kindergarten edn. tchr., Tex.; cert. mid mgmt. adminstr. Elem. educator Lamar Consol. Ind. Sch. Dist., Rosenberg, Tex., 1973-94; part-time campus coord. Houston C.C., 1994; regional dir. Sylvan Learning Ctrs. Pasadena Ind. Sch. Dist., Tex., 1994—2004, dyslexia intervention specialist, 2004—05; secondary reading specialist Ft Bend Ind. Sch. Dist., 2005—. Mem. Smith Elem. Improvement Task Force, Richmond, Tex., summers 1988-90, active mem., summer 1991. Mem. choir St. John's Meth. Ch., Richmond. Mem. Tex. Classroom Tchrs. Assn., Nat. Assn. for the Edn. Young Children, Assn. Curriculum and Supervision, Celebration Ringers, Delta Kappa Gamma, Sigma Kappa. Avocations: needlecrafts, crafts, doll collecting. Home: 2923 Pasture Ln Sugar Land TX 77479

HALL, JANE ANNA, writer, model, artist; b. New London, Conn., Apr. 4, 1959; d. John Leslie Jr. and Jane Dezzie (Green) H. Grad. model, Barbizon Sch., 1976; grad., Westbrook H.S., 1977. Model Barbizon Agy., New Haven, 1977; employed by dir. of career planning Wesleyan U., Middletown, Conn., 1985-86; free lance writer, poet, 1986—; artist, 1989—. Poetry contest judge Saybrook 25th Anniversary Celebration, Acton Pub. Libr., 1992; group poetry reader Literacy Vols. Valley Shore, Westbrook, 1995, Russell Libr., Middletown, Conn., 1999, 2000. Author: Cedar and Lace, 1986, Satin and Pinstripe, 1987, Fireworks and Diamonds, 1988, Stars and Daffodils, 1989, Sunrises and Stone Walls, 1990, Mountains and Meadows, 1991, Moonlight and Water Lillies, 1992, Sunsets and Beaches, 1993, New and Selected Poems 1986-94, 1994, Under Par Recipes, 1994, New and Selected Poems for Children 1986-95, 1995, Butterflies and Roses, 1996, Hummingbirds and Hibiscus, 1997, Swans and Azaleas, 1998, Damsel Flies and Peonies, 1999, Egrets and Cattails, 2000, Doves and Rhododendron, 2001, Bluebirds and Mountain Laurel, 2002, Beach Poems, Vol. I, 2002, Cardinals and Maples, 2003, Spring Poems Vol. I, 2003, Summer Poems Vol. I, 2003, Autumn Poems Vol. I, 2003, Winter Poems Vol. I, 2003, Sandpipers and Drift Wood, 2004, Wedding Poems Vol. I, 2004, Emeralds and Gardenias, 2005, Dragonflies and Pearls, 2006; cover designer (books), 1986—, founder, editor (newsletter) Poetry in Your Mailbox, 1989—; contbr. poetry The Bell Bouy, Expressions I and II, The Pictorial Gazette, Conn. chpt. Romance Writers of Am. Newsletter, others; (one-woman shows) Westbrook (Conn.) Pub. Libr., 1989—99, Russell Libr., Middletown, 2000, 2002; one-woman shows include Russell Libr., 2003—04, 2004, 2006; (one-woman shows) Guilford (Conn.) Free Libr., 2001; one-woman shows include Deep River Pub. Libr., 2003, 2005, Brainerd Meml. Libr., Haddam, Conn., 2003, 2005, Conn. Action Pub. Libr., Old Saybrook, Conn, 2006;, author poems, The Full Moon Looks Like, 2002; contbr. articles Conn. chpt. Romance Writers Am. Newsletter; reader (group poetry), Conn. Sunday sch. tchr. 1st Congl. Ch., Westbrook, 1977-90, asst. supt., mem. bd. Christian edn., 1979-84; poetry reader Congl. Ch., Broad Brook, Conn., 1988; vol. ch. fair Westbrook Congl. Ch.; group poetry reader and displayer Westbrook Pub. Libr., 1989, 91, reader Night of Thousand Stars readathon, 1990; group poetry displayer Acton Pub. Libr., Old Saybrook, Conn., 1990, judge poetry contest 25th anniversary celebration, 1992; vol. 1st Congrl. Ch. Fair, Westbrook, Conn. Recipient 2d prize Conn. Poetry Soc., 1983-86, 3d hon. mention, 1996, chapbooks added to Soc. permanent archives at Housatonic Cmty. Tech. Coll., 1995; cert. of merit for disting. svc. to cmty., 1989, cert. world leadership, 1989. Mem. Internat. Platform Assn., Romance Writers Am. (book cover bd. designer Conn. chpt. 1991-93), Conn. Poetry Soc. (pres. Old Saybrook chpt. 1989-91, world poetry chmn. 1989; poetry reader 20th anniversary celebration at Russell Libr. Middletown, Conn. 1994, group poetry reader, Waterbury 2001). Avocations: interior decorating and design, postcard collecting, tennis, gardening, photography. Address: PO Box 629 Westbrook CT 06498-0629

HALL, JOAN LORD, language educator, literature educator; d. John Lord and Mary Urmson Leay; m. Clifton Dale Hall, Dec. 21, 1977 (dec. 2001); 1 child, Alison Jane. BA Honors, U. Coll. London, 1968; M Lit., Girton Coll. Cambridge, Eng., 1971. Lectr. English Lang. and Lit. U. Lancaster, Lancashire, England, 1971—78; lectr. English U. Colo., Boulder, 1979—2000, instr. writing and rhetoric, 1986—. Lectr. in english lang. and lit. U. of Lancaster, Lancashire, England, 1971—78. Author: (lit. criticism) Four Guides to Shakespeare (Henry V, Othello, Antony and Cleopatra, The Winter's Tale, The Dynamics of Role-Playing in Jacobean Tragedy. Mem.: MLA (chair Shakespeare panel Rocky Mountain chpt. 2004). Home: 3958 Bosque Court Boulder CO 80301 Office: Program of Writing and Rhetoric University of Colorado Boulder CO 80304 Personal E-mail: hallj123@juno.com.

HALL, JO(SEPHINE) MARIAN, editor; b. Aberdeen, S.D., July 12, 1921; d. Charles Martin Sykes and Deedie Mae (Keiser) Gruett; m. Winston Hall, Dec. 4, 1940 (dec.); children: Wendy Diane, Willis Edward. Student, U. Colo., 1958, U. S.D., 1976. With advt. dept. Mobridge (S.D.) Reminder, 1955-61, columnist, 1956-61; with advt. dept., columnist Mobridge Tribune, 1961-67, 93—, news editor, photographer, 1968-81, editor people page, 1981—. Airway observer U.S. Weather Bur., Mobridge, 1939-84; sec. bd. dirs. Klein Mus., Mobridge, 1976-80; chpt. pres. Am. Field Svc., 1972-82; vol. Mobridge Regional Hosp., 1990—; organist, dir. choir, sr. warden of vestry St. James Episcopal C., Mobridge; mem. S.D. Episcopal Diocesan Coun., 1993-99; grand marshal Sitting Bull Parade and Rodeo, Mobridge, S.D., 2003. Recipient numerous state and nat. awards for feature stories, news stories, columns, obituaries, photography, spl. sects. headlines, 1959—, including Herbert Bayard Swope award, 1978; 1st place award for newspaper editing Nat. Fedn. Press Women, 1979, for spl. edit., 1982; Honored 50 Yrs. as Journalist Mobridge Tribune, 2006; Golden Quill award S.D. Press Women, 1988; named S.D. State Homefront Hero of WW II, 2002. Democrat. Avocations: water aerobics, swimming, reading, cooking, gardening. Home: 910 3rd Ave W Mobridge SD 57601-1605 Office Phone: 605-845-3646. E-mail: hallenterprises@weatriv.com.

HALL, JUDITH ANN, artist, printmaker; b. Cape Giradeau, Mo., July 30, 1940; d. Earl Wayne and Frances Ione (Bryan) H.; m. Marvin Eugene Cloves, Oct. 7, 1972 (div. Aug. 1982); m. Leslie Ray Manzer, Apr. 23, 1988; stepchildren: Michael Leslie, David Walter, Barbara Elizabeth Manzer. Student, Wesleyan Coll., 1958-59, U. Tenn., Memphis, 1961-62. Owner, gallery dir. Hall Galleries, St. Simons Island, Ga., 1970-82; artist, printmaker Judith Hall Etchings, St. Simons Island, Ga., 1998—. Art editor: Islander Newspaper, St. Simons Island, 1973-80; represented in permanent collections at U. Miss., Oxford, Brenau, Gainesville, Walt Disney Enterprises, Calif. Sponsor Christian Children's Fund, 1981—. Mem. Nat. Wildlife Fedn., Quinlan Art Assn., Coastal Art Alliance, Coastal Ctr. for Arts, Audubon Soc., World Wildlife Fund. Home: 1912 Demere Rd Saint Simons Island GA 31522-2805

HALL, KAREN JANNA, pediatrics nurse, critical care nurse; b. Battle Creek, Mich., Mar. 13, 1944; d. Isa Paul and Mary Jane Bushouse; life ptnr. Edith Elsa Fobe, Feb. 23, 1994; m. Bruce Stanley Hall (div.). Diploma in Nursing, Bronson Meth. Hosp. Sch. Nursing, 1965. RN. Nurse Intensive Care Unit Borgess Hosp., Kalamazoo, 1967—68; nurse Open Heart Intensive Care Unit Mt. Sinai Hosp., N.Y.C., 1966—67; nurse Coronary Care Intensive Care Unit St. Francis Hosp., San Francisco, 1968—70; from nurse Med. Surg. Intensive Care Unit to nurse Newborn Intensive Care Unit Childrens Hosp., San Francisco, 1970—81, nurse Newborn Intensive Care Unit, 1981—. Mem. com. Gay Lesbian Parade, San Francisco, 1974—2005; vol. mayoral campaign Art Agnos for Mayor, San Francisco, 1976. Mem.: ANA, Nat. League Nursing, Calif. Nurses Assn. (mem. negotiations com. 1976—88). Democrat. Avocations: cars, kids, cooking, cabernet. Home: 762 Bellevue Daly City CA 94015 Office: Cal Pac Med Ctr Sutter Health 3700 Calif St San Francisco CA 94120

HALL, KATHLEEN YANARELLA, financial executive; b. Beacon, N.Y., Feb. 21, 1957; d. Joseph R. and Mary Jane Reilley Yanarella; m. John Curtis Hall, Apr. 1, 1995. BS in Acctg., Marist Coll., 1979; MBA in Fin., Pace U., 1983. Acct. Alfa-Laval AB, Poughkeepsie, N.Y., 1979-81; bus. ops. mgr. IBM, Somers, Poughkeepsie, NY, 1981-96, fin. consol. mgr. Research Triangle Park, NC, 1996—2002, dir. fin. Somers, 2002—. Dir. Raleigh (N.C.) Ensemble Players. Recipient Salute to Women and Industry award YWCA, Dutchess County, N.Y., 1994. Mem. Inst. Mgmt. Accts. (cert. fin. mgr., cert. mgmt. acct., sec., dir. employment 1979-82). Avocations: theater, arts, reading. Office: IBM Rte 100 Somers NY 10589 Home: PO Box 4 Sherman CT 06784-0004 E-mail: kyhall@us.ibm.com.

HALL, KATHRYN H., public relations executive; b. Douglas, Sept. 5, 1944; m. Steve Hall (div. 2003); children: Stephen, Scott, Stuart, Justin. Student, Casper Jr. Coll., Wyo., Nebr. Tchrs. Coll., Mesa State Coll., Grand Junction, Colo. Owner, v.p. Well Servicing Equipment and Supply, Grand Junction, 1979—85; dir. western office U.S. Sen. William Armstrong, Grand Junction, 1985—90, Sen. Hank Brown, Grand Junction, 1990—93; loan officer El Paso Mortgage Co., Grand Junction, 1993—95; br. mgr. Am. Rockies Mortgage Co., Grand Junction, 1995; commr. Mesa County Commn., Grand Junction, 1995—2003; owner Kathy Hall/Pub. Rels., Grand Junction, 2003—. Chair Dept. Human Svcs., Grand Junction, Cmty. Air Svc. Task Force, Grand Junction; chair legis. com. Colo. River Water Conservation Dist. Bd., Grand Junction, 1996—. Contbr. numerous articles to profl. jours. Co-chair United Way, Mesa County, 2003—; mem. Gov.'s Task Force on Welfare Reform, Gov.'s Task Force on Civil Justice Reform, Gov.'s Child Welfare Reform Task Force; chmn. legis. com. Colo. River. Conservation Dist.; mem. Colo. West Mental Health Adv. Com.; steering com. Colo. Benefits Mgmt. System; past chmn., treas. Assoc. Govts. of N.W. Colo.; mem. Riverfront Commn., Pvt. Industry Coun.; pres. Marillac Clinic; mem. Parks Improvement Adv. Bd.; active numerous other civic coms., subcoms., bds.; chmn. bd. Mesa County Commrs., Grand Junction, 1997—99, 2001—02. Recipient Elizabeth Prebich Disting. Leadership award, 2001. Republican. Methodist. Home: 2305 Pheasant Run Grand Junction CO 81506-4877 Office: Kathy Hall Pub Rels 743 Horizon Ct Ste 100C Grand Junction CO 81506

HALL, KATHRYN MARIE, elementary school educator; d. Murray Hall and Mary Nielsen. AS, Snow Coll., 1981; BS, Weber State U., 1997. Cert. tchr. Utah State Bd. Edn., 1997. Tchr. 3d grade Ogden City Sch. Dist., 1999—. Vol. Jordan Sch. Dist., Riverton, Utah, 1992—97; tchr. Utah State U.; profl. devel. trainer Ogden City Sch. Dist.; master tchr., presenter State Office Edn., Utah State U., 2005—; presenter in field. Mem. Cmty. Sch. Council; coach Spl. Olympics, Salt Lake City, 1999—2003. Mem.: Core Acad. (master tchr.), Ogden Edn. Assn. (licentiate). Conservative. Mem. Lds Ch. Avocations: skiing, travel, history, art, music.

HALL, KATHY, health facility administrator; b. Covington, Ky., Feb. 15, 1953; d. Joseph B. and Mary Louise (Weindel) Dusing; m. Harold G. Hall, Oct. 6, 1973; children: Becky, Amy, Sarah. AA, Eastern Ky. U., 1973, BS in Nursing, 1978; MS in Nursing, Bellarmine U., 1999. Med.-surg. staff nurse Good Samaritan Hosp., Lexington, Ky., 1973; infection control nurse Pattie A. Clay Hosp., Richmond, Ky., 1975-93, orientation instr., 1978-82, quality assurance dir., 1982-93; nurse epidemiologist U. Ky. Chandler Med. Ctr., Lexington, 1993—99; edn. dir. Shriners Hosp. for Children, Lexington, 1999—2002; dir. continuing edn. and devel. Coll. Health Sci. Ea. Ky. U. Mem.: NNSDO, KNA, ANA, Ctrl. KY Staff Devel. Group, Sigma Theta Tau. Office: CHS Continuing Edn and Devel 202 Perkins Bldg Ea Ky U 521 Lancaster Ave Richmond KY 40475-3102 Office Phone: 859-622-1826. E-mail: Kathy.Hall@eku.edu.

HALL, LEE, artist, educator, writer; b. Lexington, NC, Dec. 15, 1934; d. Robert Lee and Florence (Fitzgerald) H. BFA, U. N.C., 1955; MA, N.Y. U., 1959, PhD, 1965; postgrad., Warburg Inst. U. London, 1965; DFA (hon.), U. N.C.-Greensboro, 1976. Asst. prof. N.Y. State U. Coll., Potsdam, 1958-60; assoc. prof., chmn. art dept. Keuka Coll., 1960-62; assoc. prof. art Winthrop Coll., 1962-65; asst. prof., chmn. art dept. Drew U., Madison, NJ, 1965-67, assoc. prof., chmn. art dept., 1967-70, prof., chmn. art dept., 1970-74; dean visual arts State U. N.Y. Coll. at Purchase, 1974-75; pres. R.I. Sch. Design, Providence, 1975-83; sr. v.p., dir. div. arts and communications Acad. for Ednl. Devel., N.Y.C., 1984-92. Dir. rsch. on Pres. Kennedy's image in recent art, John F. Kennedy Meml. Library; panelist NEH, 1972-80. Exhibited in group shows in London, N.Y.C., Winston-Salem, Eugene, Oreg., others; author: Wallace Herndon Smith: Paintings, 1987, Ale Ajay, 1989, Betty Parsons: Artist, Dealer, Collector, 1991; Common Threads: A Parade of American Clothing, 1992; Elaine and Bill (de Kooning), 1993, Olmsted's America, 1994, Athena: A Biography, 1994; contbr. articles to profl. jours. Recipient research grant Am. Philos. Soc., 1965, 68; Childe Hassam Purchase award Am. Acad. Arts and Letters, 1977; RISD Athena medal, 1983 Home: 14 Silverwood Ter South Hadley MA 01075-1237 Personal E-mail: tobybrowndog@comcast.com.

HALL, LINDA KAYE, music educator; d. Dorothy and Eugene Kee. BS, U. Memphis, 1972, MEd, 1974. Tchr. music Memphis City Schs., Memphis, 1972—2006. Composer: They're Out Of Sight (Doing More Than Is Expected award, 2005), Energy Crisis; composer: (arranger) Johnny Has Gone For A Soldier, Arkansas Traveler. Mem. Ch. of Harvest, Memphis, 1989—2005. Grantee, Rotary Found. Memphis, 1970; scholar, U. Memphis, 1970, 1971, 1972. Mem.: Am. Orff Schulwerk Assn. (former pres.), Kappa Delta Pi. Avocations: piano, gardening, guitar, fishing. Office Phone: 901-416-2148.

HALL, LISA GERSH, broadcast executive, lawyer; m. John Hall; 2 children. JD, Rutgers U., 1983. Atty. Debevoise & Plimpton, LLP; founding ptnr. Friedman, Kaplan & Seiler, LLP, NYC; co-founder Oxygen Media, Inc., NYC, 1998—, chief adminstrv. officer and gen. counsel, 1998—99, COO, 1999—, pres., 2004—. Office: Oxygen Media Inc 7th Fl 75 9th Ave New York NY 10011

HALL, LOIS BREMER, secondary school educator, volunteer; b. Oak Park, Ill., July 27, 1923; d. Frederick Statler and Mabel (Forbes) Bremer; m. Bruce Hall, Sept. 9, 1955 (dec. Mar. 1981); children: Donald, Richard, Barbara. B in Music Edn., U. Mich., 1946. Cert. elem., secondary tchr. Mich., Ky.; ordained elder Presbyn. Ch. Tchr. handbell ringing Elm St. Recreation Ctr., Atlantic Recreation Ctr. Handbell ringer AARP, Osprey Village and Quality Health, Bapt. Hosp., 1st Presbyn. Ch. Fernandina Beach; dir. Amelia Handbell Choir; singer Amelia Island Chorale, Meml. United Meth. Ch., Amelia Plantation Chapel, Amelia Bapt. Ch., St. Peter's Episcopal Ch., tenor Amelia Island Cmty. Corale. Mem. com. Peck Ctr.; founding mem., vol. coord. CROP Walk, 1989—99; vol. Michah's Place (abused women refuge); player Praise Band, 2000—04; vol. Abused Women Shelter, 2003—04; mem. New Horizon Band, 2004; vol. advocate Abused Women's Shelter, 2004—06; mem. exec. bd. Meml. United Meth. Ch.; vol. Church World Svc., Fernandina Beach, Synod of South Atlantic Coun., 1989; mem. Presbytery of St. Augustine Coun., 1984—97, music coord. of handbell and choral workshops, 1990—98; mem. hunger com. Presbyn. Gen. Assembly, 1992—96; vol.-in-mission New Hope Meth. Presbyn. Ch., N. Pole, Alaska, 1991—94, 1996; bass, clarinet Ch. Choirs; mem. Meth Ch. Handbell Choir, 2002—06; dir., pres. Ch. Handbell Choir, 2004; dir. Presbyterian Ch. Handbell Choir, 2004—06; bd. dirs. Amelia Arts Acad., 1994—2003, Ann. Fernandina Beach Talent Show, 2001—02. Recipient award for cultural enrichment, City of Fernandina Beach, 2001. Mem.: AARP (bd. dirs.), Woman's Club Fernandina Beach (pres. 1983—84, 1991—92, Outstanding New Mem. 1980—81, Cmty. Svc. award 1987—88), Rose Garden Club (treas. 1998—2002), Alpha Omicron Pi, Delta Omicron. Republican. Home: 607 Goldenrod Way Saint Marys GA 31558

HALL, LULA, retired special education educator; b. Eastman, Ga., Oct. 11, 1942; d. Lawrence and Lizzie Jackson Hall. BS, postgrad., Tuskegee U. Cert. spl. edn. tchr. Ga. Tchr. Ga. Dept. Juvenile Justice, Eastman, Dodge County Bd. Edn., Eastman; ret., 1997. Author poetry; contbr. articles to local newspaper. Sec. United Concerned Citizens of Dodge County, Eastman, 1994—99; vol. Dodge County Hosp. Aux./Pink Ladies, 1997—; actove civil rights projects and cmty. improvement. Recipient cert. of appreciation, Dodge County chpt. NAACP, Eastman, 1990. Baptist. Home: PO Box 844 Eastman GA 31023-0844

HALL, MADELON CAROL SYVERSON, elementary school educator; b. Kerkhoven, Minn., Dec. 27, 1937; d. Reuben C. and Hattie C. (Anderson) Syverson; m. Lewis D. Hall, June 13, 1959 (dec. 1984); children: Warren L., Charmaine D. BA, Trinity Bible Coll., Chgo., 1959; MEd, U.Cin., 1973. Cert. tchr., Ohio. Dir. admissions, asst. registrar Trinity Bible Coll., 1959-62; supr. elem. music edn. Dist. 80 Cook County Schs., Norridge, Ill., 1962-65; tchr. Rockford (Ill.) City Schs., 1966-67; tchr. music elem. grades Boone County Pub. Schs., Florence, Ky., 1970-72, Oak Hills Local Sch. Dist., Cin., 1972—. Also bldg. career coord., Jr. Achievement coord., safety patrol sponsor; mem. sch. improvement team, character/citizenship team, profl. devel. team. Composer: Seven Ways to Grow for Children's Mus., 1991. Dir. Summer Safety Village Program, 1987-91, Cin. May Festival Chorus, 1991-1993. Recipient Spl. Projects award Great Oaks Career Devel., 1992; named Tchr. of Yr. Oak Hills Sch. Dist, 1990-91, Ptnr. with PTA award, 2002-03. Mem. NEA, Ohio Edn. Assn., Music Educators Nat. Conf., Career Edn. Assn. (Tchr. of Yr. Ohio unit 1989-90), The Hunger Project, Just Say No Club. Methodist. Avocations: vocal music, piano, composing. Home: 1685 Towerwoods Dr Cincinnati OH 45224 Office Phone: 513-922-1485.

HALL, MARCIA JOY, non-profit organization administrator; b. Long Beach, Calif., June 24, 1947; d. Royal Waltz and Norine (Parker) Stanton; m. Stephen Christopher Hall, Mar. 29, 1968; children: Geoffrey Michael,

Christopher Stanton. AA, Foothill Coll., 1967; student, U. Oreg., 1967-68; BA, U. Washington, Seattle, 1969. Cert. contracts count presenter 2005. Instr. aide Glen Yermo Sch., Mission Viejo, Calif., 1979—80; market rsch. interviewer Rsch. Data, Framingham, Mass., 1982—83; instr. adult edn. Community Sch. Use Program, Milford, Mass., 1982—83; coord. career info. ctr. Milford High Sch., 1983—86; dir. corp. rels. Sch. Vols. for Milford, Inc., 1985—86; coord. N.E. area YWCA of Annapolis and Anne Arundel County, Severna Park, Md., 1987—89; exec. dir. West Anne Arundel County C. of C., Odenton, Md., 1989—2001, also exec. dir. Found., Inc., 1999—2001; coord. bus. and entrepreneurship continuing profl. edn. and outreach Anne Arundel C.C., Arundel Mills, Md., 2001—03, lead instr. nonprofit leadership devel., 2003—; pres., CEO, cert. contracts ct. presenter Marcia Hall & Assocs., LLC, Severna Park, Md., 2003—. V.p. Corridor Transp. Corp., 1997-99; bd. dirs. Entrepreneur's Exch.; cert. Contacts Count! presenter, 2005—. Pres. PTO, Mission Viejo, 1979-80, Milford, 1981-84; consumer assistance vol., Calif. Pub. Interest Rsch. Group, 1977-78; chmn. grant com. 21st Century Edn. Found., Ann Arundel Pub. Schs., Leadership Anne Arundel. Mem.: Nat. Speakers Assn., Md. Assn. C. of C. Execs. (pres. 1999—2000), Toastmasters (treas. 1988—, pres. 1989—). Avocations: piano, music composition, bridge, reading. Home: 507 Devonshire Ln Severna Park MD 21146-1017 Office Phone: 410-987-0857.

HALL, MARIAN M., retired music educator; b. York, Pa., June 22, 1932; d. Thomas Adrian and Olive Murray Martin; m. John H. Hall, June 1, 1953; children: Debra Grey, Cindy Dolen, Michael, Daniel. BA, Western Md. Coll., 1953; M Equivalence, Towson State U., 1972. Music tchr. Balt. City Schs., 1971—95; ret., 1995. Organist, choir dir. Rocklin Meth. Ch.; with Beth Ifiloh Summer Camp, Pikesville, Md.; piano tchr. Jason's Music Store, 1990—. Mem.: Suzuki Assn., Music Educators Nat. Conf. Avocations: music, camping, hiking, boating, swimming. Home: 4600 Lincoln Dr Baltimore MD 21227 E-mail: thehalldurnfamily@comcast.net.

HALL, MARTHA ANNE, elementary school educator; d. Ronald C. and Mary Anne Kittle; m. Thomas Wesley Kittle, July 21, 2001. M in Music Edn., Ea. Ky. U., Richmond, 1990. Cert. tchr. Ky. Band dir. Leslie County HS, Hyden, Ky., 1990—2001; gen. music tchr. New Haven (Ky.) Sch., 2001—. Mem.: Ky. Music Edn. Assn., Delta Omicron. Office: New Haven Sch 489 High St New Haven KY 40051 Office Phone: 502-349-7232. Business E-Mail: mhall@nelson.k12.ky.us.

HALL, MAXINE P., minister; b. Columbus, Miss., Sept. 10, 1945; d. James and Beatrice Moore; m. Johnny Hall, Jr., Dec. 21, 1985; children: Mildred, Jackie, Calrol, Trina. Degree in Cosmetology, Mary Holmes Jr. Coll., 1983; degree in Bible Interpretation, Rhoma Bible Coll., 1993. Pastor Full Gospel Ministry, Columbus, Miss., 1991—. Named Power Woman of Yr., WACR Radio Sta., 1991; named one of Most Influential Leader of 500, Am. Biog. Inst., 1991. Fellow: Internat. Assn. (life; dep. gov.); mem.: Spkr. Platform Associated, Women With a Cause Internat. (pres. S.W. region 1994—2005). Avocations: flower arranging, painting, crossword puzzles. Home: 1414 3 1/2 Ave No Columbus MS 39701 Office: Full Gospel Ministry 1504 19th St No Columbus MS 39701

HALL, MITZY DELAINE, chemistry educator; b. Newport, Tenn., Oct. 28, 1966; d. Ivan Warren and Ima Jane Hall; m. James Mardis Lichlyter, Aug. 21, 1993; children: Brittany Nicole Wright, Miranda LeAnne Wright, James MorganDakota Lichlyter. BS inChemistry, East Tenn. State U., Johnson City, 1993; MA, Tusculum Coll., Greeneville, Tenn., 2002; EdS, Lincoln Meml. U., Harrogate, Tenn., 2003; doctorate, Trevecca Nazarene U., Nashville, 2006. Cert. profl. educator Tenn. Tchr. Cocke County Schs., Newport, 1994—, Walters State CC, Morristown, Tenn., 2000—. Mem.: Cocke County Edn. Assn. (assoc.; pres. 1997—98), Lions Club (pres. 2001—02). Democrat. Nazarene. Avocations: swimming, cross stitch, travel. Office: Cocke County HS 216 Hedrick Dr Newport TN 37821 Office Phone: 423-623-8718 150. Home Fax: 423-523-1213; Office Fax: 423-623-1213. Personal E-mail: mitzy_h@hotmail.com. Business E-Mail: hallm@mail.cocke.k12.tn.us.

HALL, MOLLY J., psychiatrist, educator; b. Princeton, N.J., Mar. 27, 1951; 4 children. BS magna cum laude, Yale Coll., 1973; MD, Cornell U., 1977. Bd. cert. psychiatry and neurology. Intern N.Y. Hosp., 1977—78; resident psychiatry N.Y. Hosp.-Payne Whitney Clinic, 1978—81; psychiatry residency tng. dir. integrated civilian-mil. program Wright Patterson AFB-Wright State U., 1988—95; chief outpatient svcs., staff psychiatrist to dept. mental health USAF Med. Ctr., Wright-Patterson AFB; staff psychiatrist Miami Valley Hosp., Dayton, Ohio, 1993—95; staff Malcolm Grow Med. Ctr., Washington, 1995—; assoc. prof. psychiatry Uniformed Svcs. U. Health Scis., 2001—. Examiner Am. Bd. Psychiatry and Neurology, 1989—, sr. examiner, 1995—; psychiat. cons. Astronaut Selection Bd., 1990—; v.p. mil. dist. br. Soc. Uniformed Svcs. Psychiatry, 1994, 95, 96; splty. cons. psychiatry USAF Surgeon Gen., 1995—99; flight comdr. Mental Health Flight 89th Med. Group, Andrews AFB, 1995—98; chief clin. quality mgmt. divsn. Bolling AFB Office Surgeon Gen., 1998—2000; mem. nat. adv. coun. Substance Abuse and Mental Health Svcs. Adminstrn., Ctr. for Mental Health Svcs. Contbr. articles to profl. jours. Col. USAF. Decorated Air Force Commendation medal, Air Force Meritorious Svcs. medal with three oak leaf clusters, Nat. Def. Svc. medal; recipient first ann. Excellence in Med. Edn. award, Am. Psychiat. Assn., 1991, Career Woman of the Yr. award, Dayton YWCA, 1992. Mem.: Alpha Omega Alpha. Office: Malcolm Grow Med Ctr 89MDOS/SGOH 1050 W Perimeter Dr Andrews Air Force Base MD 20762

HALL, NANCY KAY, music educator; b. Texas City, Tex., Mar. 29, 1951; d. Gerald Taylor and Modine (Griffith) Ramsey; m. David Earl Railey, July 20, 1974 (div. Sept. 1983); 1 child, Rachel Michal; m. Michael Mabray Hall, Oct. 13, 1984. BS, Houston Bapt. U., 1973; postgrad., Southwestern Bapt. Theol. Sem., Ft. Worth, 1974. Pvt. piano tchr., Houston, 1970-73, Ft. Smith, Ark., 1977-84, Wharton, Tex., 1984-88, The Woodlands, Tex., 1988—; tchr. Kindermusik of Wharton, Tex., 1987-88, Kindermusik of The Woodlands, 1988—; studio and music store owner Hall's Family Musik, The Woodlands, 1994—. Mem. Nat. Assn. Music Tchrs., Nat. Guild Piano Tchrs. (cert., local chmn. 1997—), Am. Coll. Musicians, Early Childhood Music and Movement Assn. (Level 3 cert.), Kindermusik Educators Assn. (master tchr. cert., maestro 2000-), Conroe Music Tchrs. Assn. (v.p. 1994-96, pres. 1996-98, Tchr. of Yr. 1996). Republican. Avocations: boating, fishing, snorkeling. Home: 64 Eagle Rock Cir The Woodlands TX 77381-4343 Office: Hall's Family Musik and Kindermusik of The Woodlands 25210 Grogans Park Dr The Woodlands TX 77380-2175

HALL, NANETTE H., adult education educator; d. John Harvey Pruden and Jeanette Anita Holms; children: Dane Philip Mariott, Allan W. BBA, Nat. U., San Diego, 1988. Cert. tchr. Calif., Utah. Legal sec. various law firms, Washington and Beverly Hills, Calif., 1971—79, Pima County Pub. Defender, Tucson, 1979; adminstrv. asst. to presiding judge Pima County Cts., Tucson, 1979; adult edn. HS completion tchr., tchr., dir. Unitah Basin Applied Tech. Ctr., Roosevelt, Utah, 1993—2001; adult edn. HS completion tchr., tchr., coord. Ute Indian Tribe, Fort Duchesne, Utah, 2001—. Project dir. Family Literacy Grant, Ute Tribe, Fort Duquesne, 2002—. Mem. bd. rev. Boy Scouts Am., Vernal, Utah, 2000—03, merit badge counselor, 2004. Republican. Mem. Lds Ch. Home: 1945 E 3050 S Vernal UT 84078

HALL, OCEOLA S., federal agency administrator; BS with highest honors, Southern U., Baton Rouge, La. Agencywide fed. women's program mgr. NASA, 1974—78, dir. discrimination complaints div., 1978—96; dep. assoc. adminstr. NASA Office of Equal Opportunity Program, 1996—. Recipient Exceptional Svc. medal, NASA, Outstanding Leadership medal, Equal Opportunity medal, Meritorious Rank award, Presdl. Rank award. Office: NASA Hdqrs Mail Code E 300 E St SW Washington DC 20546

HALL, PAMELA ELIZABETH, psychologist; b. Jacksonville, Fla., Sept. 10, 1957; d. Gary Curtiss and Ollie (Banko) H. BA, Rutgers U., 1979; MS in Edn., Pace U., 1981, D in Psychology, 1984. Lic. psychologist, N.Y., N.J., Calif., Conn. Psychology extern St. Vincent's Med. Ctr., N.Y.C., 1981—82; intern in clin. psychology Elizabeth (N.J.) Gen. Med. Ctr., 1982—83, staff psychologist, 1983—85, J.F.K. Med. Ctr., Edison, NJ, 1985-87; pvt. practice Summit and Perth Amboy, NJ, 1985—; sr. supervising psychologist Muhlenberg Med. Ctr., Summit, 1987—90; prof. psychology Nyack Coll., Nyack, NY, 2001—. Rsch. affiliate, internat. lectr. NIMH field trials on assessment of dissociative disorders Yale U., New Haven, 1990—; adj. prof. psychology Pace U., NYC, 1979-99; exec. bd. dir. Nat. Coun. on Alcoholism and Drug Dependence of Middlesex County, 2000-02. Active Mayor's Com. on Substance Abuse, Perth Amboy, 1987; bd. trustees Nat. Coun. Alcoholism and Drug Dependence, 2000—. Henry Rutgers scholar, 1979; named to Perth Amboy High Sch. Hall Fame, 2005. Mem. Am. Soc. Clin. Hypnosis, Internat. Soc. for Study of Dissociation (founder, pres. NJ chpt. 1988—, dir. component socs.), Pace U. Alumni Assn., Rutgers U. Alumni Assn., Psi Chi. Avocations: crew, swimming, fine arts, weightlifting. Home: PO Box 1820 Perth Amboy NJ 08862-1820 Office: 12 Kent Place Blvd Summit NJ 07901-1907 Office Phone: 908-277-2383. Personal E-mail: dr.pamelahall@comcast.com.

HALL, PAMELA S., environmental services administrator; b. Hartford, Conn., Sept. 4, 1944; d. LeRoy Warren and Frances May (Murray) Sheely; m. Stuart R. Hall, July 21, 1967 (dec.). BA in Zoology, U. Conn., 1966; MS in Zoology, U. N.H., 1969, BSBA summa cum laude, 1982; postgrad., Tufts U., 1986-90. Curatorial asst. U. Conn., Storrs, 1966; rsch. asst. Field Mus. Natural History, Chgo., 1966-67; tchg. asst. U. N.H., Durham, 1967-70; program mgr. Normandeau Assocs. Inc., Portsmouth, NH, 1971-79, marine lab. dir., 1979-81, programs and ops. mgr. Bedford, NH, 1981-83, v.p., 1983-85, sr. v.p., 1986-87, pres., 1987—. Mem. Conservation Com., Portsmouth, 1977-90, Wells, Estuarine Rsch. Res. Rev.Commn., 1986-88, Great Bay (N.H.) Estuarine Rsch. Res. Tech. Working Group, 1987-89; trustee Trust for N.H. Lands, 1990-93; trustee N.H. chpt. Nature Conservancy, 1991—, chair 1995-99, chair emeritus, 1999, trustee, 2000—, incorporator N.H. Charitable Fund, 1991-99; bd. advisors Vivamos Mejor, USA, 1990—; bd. dirs. Environ. Bus. Coun. New England, 1995—, treas. 1997—; bd. emeritus Ecosystems Inst., 1997—; commr. N.H. Land and Heritage Commn., 1998-99; bd. advisers N.H. Corp. Wetlands Restoration Partnership, 2003—; bd. dirs. Seacoast Sci. Ctr., Rye, N.H., 2004—. Recipient Environ. Leadership award Environ. Bus. Coun. New Eng., 1998; Graham Found. fellow, 1966; NDEA fellow, 1970-71. Mem. Nature Conservancy, Soc. of the Protection NH Forests, Nat. Audubon Soc., Audubon Soc. NH, Am. Mgmt. Assn., Phi Sigma, Sigma Xi. Office: Normandeau Assocs Inc 25 Nashua Rd Bedford NH 03110-5500 Office Phone: 603-472-5191. Personal E-mail: phall@normandeau.com.

HALL, PENELOPE COKER, editor, writer; b. Charlotte, NC, Mar. 19, 1932; d. James Lide and Elizabeth (Boatwright) Coker; m. William Parmenter Wilson, Sept. 6, 1964 (div. 1971); 1 child, Eliza Wilson Ingle; m. Mortimer Waddhams Hall, Dec. 8, 1972; stepchildren: Dorothy, Margaret, Mary Howland, Matthew. Student, Sarah Lawrence Coll., Bronxville, NY, 1954; DHL (hon.), Coker Coll., Hartsville, S.C., 2006. Sr. editor, biographer Cleveland Amory's Celebrity Register, NYC; prodr., commentator Wrap-Up with Mike Wallace, NYC; co-prodr., interviewer for series of hr. long spls. NBC-TV, NYC; co-host 10 Around Town Channel 10 TV, Phila.; co-host The New Yorkers Channel 5 TV, N.Y.C., 1968-70; reporter, Sunday anchor 10 O'Clock News, Channel 5, NYC, 1970-73; host cable cooking show Millbrook, NY, 1976—; editor-in-chief Dutchess Mag., NYC, 1993—99, editor-at-large, columnist Millbrook, 1998—. CEO Alpacalypse Hall LLC, 2005—. Contbr. numerous articles to profl. jours.; author: Fancy and the Cement Patch, 1966, The Wish Bottle, 1967, Riding High, 1990. Bd. trustees Spoleto Festival, Charleston, SC, 1997—, Coker Coll., Hartsville, SC, 2000— Mem. Authors League, Nat. Trust for Hist. Preservation Nat. Trust Coun., Sandanona Beagles, Millbrook Hounds, Century Assn., Millbrook Golf and Tennis Club (bd. dirs. 1989-93), Cosmopolitan Club. Democrat. Episcopalian. Avocations: painting, horseback riding, boating. Home: PO Box 516 Millbrook NY 12545-0516

HALL, SARA Y., retired music educator; b. Bardstown, Ky., Oct. 10, 1944; d. Glenn and Marian Hampton Yarbrough; m. Larry B. Hall, Mar. 26, 1966; children: Larissa, Larry B. Jr. B in Music Edn., Georgetown Coll., 1966; postgrad., U. Ky., 1975; postgrad., Amarillo Coll., 1986. Music tchr. grades K-8 Harrison (Ohio) Schs., 1966—67; music tchr. grades K-5 Wesleyan Day Sch., Sandy Springs, Ga., 1976—78; music tchr. grades 6-12 Dumas (Tex.) Ind. Schs., Dumas, 1984—87; music tchr. grades K-12 Artesia (N.Mex.) Sch. Sys., 1987—94, Las Cruces (N.Mex.) Sch. Sys., 1994—2002; music tchr. grades 6-9 Rio Rancho (N.Mex.) Schs., 2002—04; ret., 2004. Mem. Atlanta Symphony Chorus and Chamber Chorus, 1976—78; dir. Dumas Cmty. Choir, 1985—86, Mesilla Valley Chorale, Las Cruces, 2000—02; accompanist Treble All-State Choirs, Albuquerque, 1989—2003; coord., accompanist All-City Mid-High Choirs, Las Cruces, 1996—99; dir., mem. Artesia Cmty. Chorus, 1990—92; mem. Georgetown Choral Soc., Ky., 2005—, Lexington Singers, Ky. Named Tchr. of Yr., Lynn Middle Sch., 2000. Mem.: Ky. Choral Dirs., Ky. Music Educators, N.Mex. Music Educators, Music Educators Assn., N.Mex. Choral Dirs., Am. Choral Dirs. Assn., Delta Kappa Gamma, Delta Omicron. Avocations: reading, cross stitch, cooking, walking. Home: 112 Josie Trail Georgetown KY 40324

HALL, SHARON GAY, retired language educator, artist; b. Centralia, Ill., Oct. 2, 1942; d. Leon Lucene and Olyve Elizabeth Hall. BS, So. Ill. U., 1966, MS, 1984; postgrad., Ea. Ill. U., 1985—90. Cert. secondary tchr. Ill. English tchr. Webber Twp. H.S., Bluford, Ill., 1966—67, Mt. Vernon (Ill.) H.S., 1967—99, ret., 1999. Artist-in-residence Cedarhurst Art Guild, Cedarhurst Mus., 1974—. Treas. bd. dirs. Bus. and Profl. Women's Club, Mt. Vernon, 1966—76; mem. Jefferson County Hist. Soc., 2000—. Recipient Recognition award, Cedarhurst Mus., 2000. Mem.: NEA, AAUW, Ill. Edn. Assn., Mt. Vernon Edn. Assn. (sec., treas., bd. dirs. 1967—99), Phi Delta Kappa, Phi Theta Kappa, Alpha Delta Kappa. Republican. Avocations: raising exotic animals, handspinner, weaver, fiber artist, seamstress. Home: 11384 E Idlewood Rd Mount Vernon IL 62864

HALL, SUSAN, author, film producer; d. Isaac Davis and Marion (Dalton) H.; 1 child, David. Grad., Milton Acad., Mass. Past film writer, prodr. Harvest Films, ABC; ind. prodr., N.Y.C.; films include Summer's Children, The Smartest Kid in Town, Helping Hands, Cosmopolis, Children's Games; prodr. Chess Starts Here!, 1998; books include Encounter series, On and Off the Streets, Down Home, Street Smart, Gentleman of Leisure, Ladies of the Night, Out of Left Field, Top Form with Pat Etcheberry (Vancouver Film Festival award, Am. Film Festival award, San Francisco Film Festival award, Am. Inst. Graphic Arts award, Gold medal Venice Film Festival); text editor: Pictures Under Discussion, Amphoto, Mural With a Blue Brushstroke, Abrams, Cat Who Came for Christmas; contbr. articles to mags. Mem. Authors Guild. Office: PO Box 844 New York NY 10016 E-mail: susanhallbooks@gmail.com.

HALL, SUSAN LAUREL, artist, educator, writer; b. Point Reyes Station, Calif., Mar. 19, 1943; d. Earl Morris and Avis Mary (Brown) H. BFA, Calif. Coll. Arts and Crafts, Oakland, 1965; MA, U. Calif., Berkeley, 1967. Mem. faculty Sarah Lawrence Coll., Bronxville, NY, 1972—75, Sch. Visual Arts, NYC, 1981—92, Skowhegan Sch. of Painting and Sculpture, Maine, 1981, U. Colo., Boulder, 1981, Art Inst. Chgo., 1981, U. Tex., Austin, 1993, San Antonio, 1995, San Francisco Art Inst., 1996. One-woman shows include San Francisco Mus. Art, 1967, Quay Gallery, San Francisco, 1969, Phillis Kind Gallery, Chgo., 1971, Henderson Mus. U. Colo., Boulder, 1973, Paule Anglim Gallery, San Francisco, 1975—83, Nancy Hoffman Gallery, N.Y.C., 1975, U. R.I. Gallery, Kingston, 1976, Harcus Krakow Rosen Sonnabend Gallery, Boston, 1976, Hal Bromm and Getler-Pall Galleries, N.Y.C., 1978, Helene Shlien Gallery, Boston, 1978, Hamilton Gallery, N.Y.C., 1978—79, 1981, 1983, Ovsey Gallery, L.A., 1981—82, 1984, 1987, 1989, 1991, Ted Greenwald Gallery, N.Y.C., 1986, Trabia Macafee Gallery, 1988—89, Wyckoff Gallery, Aspen, Colo., 1990—92, Milagros Contemporary Art, San Antonio, 1995, Brendan Walter Gallery, L.A., 1995, U. Tex., San Antonio, 1996, Jan Holloway Gallery, San Francisco, 1997, Phillis Kind Gallery, Chgo., 1998, San Francisco Mus. Art Gallery, 1998, Gail Harvey Gallery, L.A., 1999, 2001, Frank Lloyd Wright Civic Ctr., San Rafael, 1999, Jernigan Wicker Gallery, San Francisco, 1999, Bolinas (Calif.) Mus., 2002, Tobys Gallery, Point Reyes Sta., Calif., 2005, exhibited in group shows at Whitney Mus. Am. Art, one-woman shows include Whitney Mus., N.Y.C., exhibited in group shows at San Francisco Mus., 98 Greene St. Loft, N.Y.C., Oakland Mus., Balt. Mus., Inst. Contemporary Art, Phila., Hudson River Mus., Bklyn. Mus., Nat. Mus. Women in the Arts, Mus. Fine Arts, Boston, Aldrich Mus. Contemporary Art, G.W. Einstein Gallery, Blum Helman Downtown, Leo Castelli Gallery Uptown, Graham Modern, N.Y.C., Kunstmus., Luzern, Switzerland, Landesmus., Bonn, Ranches and Rolling Hills, Nicasio, Calif., 2001, 2002, 2003, 2004, 2005—06, Represented in permanent collections pub. collections Whitney Mus., San Francisco Mus., Bklyn. Mus., Carnegie Inst., St. Louis Mus., Nat. Mus. Women in the Arts, others; author: Painting Point Reyes, Susan Hall, 2003, Home Before Dark Color Plates of Painting, 2005. Nat. Endowment Arts fellow, 1979-87, Adolph Gottlieb Found. fellow, 1995; grantee: Pollack Krasner Found., N.Y. State Coun. on Arts; recipient Marin Arts Coun. Bd. Dirs. award, 1999.

HALL, TELKA MOWERY ELIUM, retired assistant principal; b. Salisbury, NC, July 22, 1936; d. James Lewis and Malissa (Fielder) Mowery; m. James Richard Elium III, June 20, 1954 (div. 1961); 1 child, W. Denise Elium Carr; m. Allen Sanders Hall, Apr. 15, 1967 (div. 1976). Student, Am. Inst. Banking, 1955—57, Mary-Hardin Baylor Coll., Waco, Tex., 1957; BA, Catawba Coll., Salisbury, 1967; MEd, Miss. U. for Women, Columbus, 1973; EdS, Appalachian State U., Boone, N.C., 1975; postgrad., U. N.C., Greensboro, 1977; EdD, U. N.C., Chapel Hill, 1990; postgrad., Ind. U., 1998. Cert. early childhood, intermediate lang. arts and social studies tchr., curriculum specialist, adminstr., supr., supt., NC; notary pub., NC; cert. in CPR and first aid and safety, ARC. Bookkeeper, teller Citizens & So. Bank, Spartanburg, SC, 1955-56; bookkeeper lst Nat. Bank, Killeen, Tex., 1956-58; bookkeeper, savs. teller Exch. Bank & Trust Co., Dallas, 1958-61; acct. Catawba Coll., 1961-65; floater teller bookkeeping and proof depts. Security Bank & Trust Co., Salisbury, 1965-68, 71; tchr. Rowan County Sch. System, Salisbury, 1967-70, 71-72, 1973-82; asst. prin. North Rowan Elem. Sch., Spencer, NC, 1982-94, Rockwell Elem. and China Grove Elem. Sch., NC, 1994-96, ret. NC, 1996; part-time asst. prin. of curriculum China Grove Elem., 1996-99, also part-time outside observer for Ctrl. Office, 1996, asst. prin. curriculum, 1996-99, ret., 1999. Receptionist H & R Block, Salisbury, 1979-83; Chpt. I reading tchr. Nazareth Children's Home, Rockwell, NC, 1979-81. Author: The Effect of Second Language Training in Kindergarten on the Development of Listening Skills, 1990, Celebrate the Journey: History of Franklin Presbyterian Church, 1829-2004, 2005. Active Salisbury Cmty. Chorus, 1951—52, Hist. Salisbury Found., Inc., Salisbury Concert Choir, 1981—83; foreperson Rowan County Grand Jury, 1991; cons. Dial HELP, Salisbury, 1981—83; charter mem. bd. dirs. Old North Salisbury Assn., 1980—2000; past mem. Children's Literacy Guild, ARC; bd. dirs. Hanford-Dole chpt. ARC, 2004—, disaster action team, 2002—; charter choir mem. Franklin Presbyn. Ch., 1947—, pianist, 1952—55, moderator women of ch., 1964—65, choir dir., 1974—87, adult class Sunday sch. tchr., 1979—80, deacon, 1980—83, elder, 1991—92, clk. of session, 1992, elder, nursery Sunday sch. tchr., 1996—99, clk. of session, 1996—98, co-moderator women of ch., 1999—2002, elder, 2001—04, clk. of session, substitute Sunday sch. adult class tchr., 2002—04, moderator, 2003—04; active Magnify Christian Concert Choir, 1999—2004. Civitan Music scholar, 1954, Kiwanis Acad. scholar, 1966, Catawba Coll. Acad. scholar, 1965-67, Mary Morrow Ednl. scholar NC Assn. Educators, 1966, Miss. U. for Women Scholars, 1972-73. Mem. NEA, NCAE, AARP, AAUW (v.p. 1985-87, 91-94, 2001-04), AARP, ARC (vol.), NC Ret. Govt. Employees' Assn., Rowan-Salisbury Ret. Pers., Salisbury Hist. Assn., Kappa Delta Pi, Theta Phi (pres. 1992-93). Avocations: photography, genealogy, calligraphy, singing, gardening. Home: 105 Sharon Ct Salisbury NC 28146-7241

HALL, TENNIEBEE M., editor; b. Bakersfield, Calif., May 21, 1940; d. William Elmer and Lillian May (Otis) Hall; m. Harold Robert Hall, Feb. 20, 1965. BA in Edn., Fresno State Coll., 1962; AA, Bakersfield Coll., 1960. Cert. tchr., Calif. Tchr. Edison (Calif.) Sch. Dist., 1962-65; substitute tchr. Marin and Oakland Counties (Calif.), Berkeley, 1965-66; engring. asst. Pacific Coil Co., Inc., Bakersfield, 1974-81; editor United Ostomy Assn., Inc., Irvine, Calif., 1986-91. Co-author: Treating IBD, 1989, Current Therapy in Gastroenterology, 1989; author, designer: Volunteer Leadership Training Manuals, 1982-84; editor: Calif. Parliamentarian, 1999-2003, 04—; contbr. articles to Ostomy Quar., 1973-2005. Mem. Pacific Beach Town Coun., San Diego, 1977-2006; campaign worker Maureen O'Connor (1st woman mayor of city), San Diego, 1986; mem. Nat. Digestive Diseases Adv. Bd., NIH, Washington, 1986-91; mem. planning and devel. bd. Scripps Clinic and Rsch. Found. Inflammatory Bowel Disease Ctr., San Diego, 1993-2003; various vol. activities, 1966-74, 81-86. Recipient Outstanding Svc. award VA Vol. Svc., Bur. of Vets. Affairs, Washington, 1990. Mem. Nat. Assn. Parliamentarians, United Ostomy Assn. Inc. (regional program dir. 1980-84, pres. 1984-86, Sam Dubin award 1983, Industry Adv. award 1987), Crohn's and Colitis Found. Am. (nat. trustee 1986-95, nat. v.p. 1987-92). Avocations: travel, volunteerism. Home and Office: 8585 Via Mallorca Unit 7 La Jolla CA 92037-2585

HALL, TERESA JOANNE KEYS, manufacturing engineer, educator; b. Chanute, Kans., 1954; d. William Milton and Mary Joanne (Greve) Keys; m. Douglas Wayne Hall, Jan 31, 1986; 1 child, Benjamin Alan. BA in Industry, U. No. Iowa, 1988, MA in Tech., 1991; PhD in Indsl. Edn. and Tech., Iowa State U., 1997. Cert. mfg. engr. Dept. mgr. Cooks Inc., Waterloo, Iowa, 1974-76; grounds maintenance City of Waterloo, 1976-77; trades mechanic Deere & Co., Waterloo, 1977-79, foundry maintenance planner, 1979-82, metals analyst, 1982-84, sr. maintenance planner, 1984-87; pvt. practice Waterloo, 1988-91; instr. U. Northern Iowa, Cedar Falls, 1992-96, asst. prof., 1997-00, assoc. prof., 2001—03, mfg. program coord., 1998—2003; prof. S.D. State U., Brookings, 2003—, dept. head engring. tech. and mgmt., 2003—, dir. Polytechnic Ctr., 2003—. Expert witness mfg. fabrication and safety issues, 1999—2000; panel reviewer NSF, 1999—2000; dir. Polytech. Ctr. S.D. State U., Brookings, 2003—04. Tech. editor, Am.Jour. Undergrad. Rsch., 2003—;contbr. articles to profl. jours. Grantee NSF, 1996, 98, Tchr. Edn. Alliance, 1997. Mem. AAUW, Soc. Mfg. Engrs. (faculty advisor 1993-2001, Region 9 exec. bd. 1998—, chair chpt.186, 2003, chmn. certification oversight and appeals bd. 2004—, President's award 2000, Internat. award of merit, 2003), Am. Mensa Ltd., Nat. Assn. Indsl. Technologists (Outstanding Prof. of Yr. for Region 2, reviewer Jour. Indsl. Tech.), Epsilon Pi Tau. Avocation: gardening. Office: SD State U Dept Engring Tech & Mgmt Brookings SD 57007-0092

HALL, TERESA RUTH, publishing executive; b. Sunnyvale, Calif., May 8, 1969; d. Brent Peter and Maria Lucia Delia Yolanda Fabbi; m. James Joseph Hall, May 16, 1994; children: Cameron James, Mackenzie Victoria. BS in Secondary Edn. with distinction, U. Nev., Reno, 1995. Math. instr. Truckee Meadows C.C., Reno, 1996—97; math. lectr. U. Nev., Reno, 1997—98; math. instr. Edgewood Coll., Madison, 1998; edn. program specialist Wis. Dept. Pub. Instrn., Madison, 2000—02; devel. mgr. CTB/McGraw-Hill, Monterey, Calif., 2002—. Active mem. Country View Elem. Parent Tchr. Assn., Verona, Wis., 2002—; treas. Ridge Oak Dr. Homeowners Assn., Madison, 2001—02; mem. Hawthorne Elem. Parent Tchr. Assn., Madison, 1999—2002. Recipient Team Mem. award, CTB/McGraw-Hill, 2003. Mem.: Nat. Orgn. Female Execs. Avocations: gardening, reading, Latin ballroom dancing, travel.

HALL, TERRY, accountant; b. Champaign, Ill., Dec. 10, 1949; d. Albert L. and Catherine A. (Comstock) Hall; m. Thomas F. Johnston, Sept. 27, 1971 (div. Jan. 1979); 1 child, Daniel K. Johnston. BA, Barat Coll., Lake Forest, Ill., 1984. CPA Ill. Acct. Terry Hall, CPA, PC, Gurnee, Ill., 1985—; treas., CFO Facilitec USA, Inc., 2004—, Nat. Fire Svcs., LLC, 2004—. Bd. dirs. Lake Forest Profl. Women's Round Table, Ill. Bd. dirs. YWCA of Lake County, Waukegan, Ill., 1987-89; bd. dirs. Women in Dir.'s Chair, Chgo., 1989-96, Stage Two Theater Co., 1991-2003; mem. alumni coun. Lake Forest Acad., 1986-98. Mem. AICPA, ABA (assoc.), Nat. Assn. Tax Preparers, Nat.

Soc. Tax Profls., Ill. Soc. CPAs (mem. faculty, mem. state litigation com. 1988-95), Wis. Inst. CPAs (state litigation com. 1989-92), Chgo. Soc. Women CPAs, Lake County Estate Planning Coun., CPAs for the Pub. Interest (Outstanding Vol. 1991). Avocation: travel. Office: 5250 Grand Ave Ste 14 Gurnee IL 60031 Office Phone: 847-623-3025.

HALL, WANDA JEAN, mental health professional, consultant; b. Miami, Okla., July 3, 1943; d. Max Calvin Kinnaman and Dorothy D. (Peck) Fadler; m. James Marvin Hall, Apr. 10, 1964 (div. Feb. 1965); m. George Edward Hall, Mar. 21, 1973; children: Heather Renata, Samuel. AA, Stephens Coll., Columbia, Mo., 1963; BS, Kans. U., Pittsburg, 1965; MS, New Sch. for Social Rsch., N.Y.C., 1991. Asst. psychologist Parsons (Kans.) State Hosp., 1966-67; hosp. care investigator N.Y. Dept. Social Work, N.Y.C., 1968-70; social worker Drug Abuse Program, Amsterdam, The Netherlands, 1970-74; dir. Washington Park Co-op Presch., N.Y.C., 1974-75; project dir. Manhattan Devel. Ctr., N.Y.C., 1975-77; pvt. practice human devel. specialist human devel. specialist, N.Y.C., 1978-81; cmty. rels. coord. Orange County Dept. Mental Health, Goshen, N.Y., 1981-97, Flagler Coll., St. Augustine, Fla., 1998—. Parenting cons. Teens Exploring Parenting, Inc., Middletown, N.Y., 1990-94; instr. Orange County C.C., Middletown, 1990-97, Mt. St. Mary Coll., Newburgh, N.Y., 1993-96. Producer, host radio talk show Conversation on Epilepsy, Radio Sta. WGNY, 1981; dir, narrator mental health skits Forum Players, 1980; producer, host 6 TV series Love from the 26, 000 Club, 1983. Bd. dirs. Orange County Coalition for Choice, Warwick, N.Y., 1981-97, Orange County Task Force on Child Abuse/Neglect, 1984-89, Ct. Apptd. Spls. Assts., 1987-96, Bandwagon Cmty. Ctr., chair, 1990-95; mem. Planned Parenthood, Orange County, 1989-97, Safe Homes, Orange County, 1987-97, Middletown Coun. Cmty. Agys., 1980-96, Interagy. Coun. Child Sexual Abuse; co-founder Orange County Parenting Coalition., 1990-97. Recipient DWI Alcohol Safety award N.Y. State Alcohol Bur., Albany, 1986, Cmty. Svc. award Youth Bur. Goshen, 1987, Zonta scholar award, 1989, Cmty. Svc. award Otisville (N.Y.) State Correction, 1989, Nat. Assn. Counties award Confident Parenting Program, 1993, Hospice Orange Vol. award, 1993, The Gilbert award, 1995, Human Rights award Orange County Human Rights Commn., 1995, faculty award Assn. for Gerontology in Higher Edn., 2003, Gold award Internat. Chinese Martial Arts Championship, 2005; named to Wall Tolerance, Civil Rights Meml. Ctr., Montgomery, Ala., 2005, 2006. Mem. NAACP. Methodist. Avocations: tai chi, swimming, piano, horseback riding.

HALLADAY, LAURIE ANN, public relations consultant, food products executive; b. Monroe, Mich., Aug. 18, 1945; d. Alvin John and Florence (Lowrey) Kohler; m. Edward L. Howell, Aug. 27, 1966; m. 2d Fredric R. Halladay, May 24, 1980. BJ, U. Mo., 1967. Reporter, staff writer Copley Newspapers, L.A., 1967-69; account exec. Furman Assocs., L.A., 1969-71, v.p., 1971-74; account supr. Bob Thomas & Assocs., L.A., 1974-76, v.p., 1976-78; v.p., sr. ptnr. Fleishman-Hillard, Inc., St. Louis, 1980-84; owner, operator McDonald's, Portland, Oreg., 1984-87, McDonald's McStop of Mid.-Mo., Kingdom City, 1988-92. Chmn. press ops. for Budweiser/G.I. Joe's Portland 200 Indy Car Race, 1984-87; mem. advt., promotions com. Hollywood Boosters, 1986. Bd. dirs. Waterman Place Assn., St. Louis, 1983; mem. pub. rels. com. Winston Churchill Meml., Fulton, 1988-92. Recipient Merit award Calif. Press Women, 1969, Lulu award Los Angeles Women's Ad Club, 1976, McDonald's Outstanding Store award, 1985, 86, 89, 90, 91. Mem. PRSA (Prism award 1977), Soc. Am. travel Writers (assoc. 1981-84), Women in Comm. (dir. St. Louis 1980-82), Nat. Tour Assn., Mo. Travel Coun., Delta Delta Delta (alumna adviser 1989, 90, v.p. Delta Xi House Corp. 1991, collegiate dist. officer 1991, 94, regional program chmn. 1994, program resource team pub. rels. specialist 1995-96, nat. chmn. pub. rels. 1996, cons. pub. rels. chpt. 1998-2000). Address: 1602 Alabama Dr 304 Winter Park FL 32789 Personal E-mail: halladayl@yahoo.com.

HALLAM, BEVERLY (BEVERLY LINNEY), artist; b. Lynn, Mass., Nov. 22, 1923; d. Edwin Francis and Alice (Linney) Hallam Murphy. BS in Edn, Mass. Coll. Art, 1945; postgrad., Cranbrook Acad. Art, Mich., 1948; MFA, Syracuse U., 1953. Chmn. dept. art Lasell Jr. Coll., Auburndale, Mass., 1945-49; assoc. prof. Mass. Coll. Art, 1949-62. Bd. dirs. Barn Gallery Assocs., Inc., Ogunquit, Maine. One-person shows include Joe and Emily Lowe Art Center, Syracuse U., 1953, DeCordova Mus., Lincoln. Mass., 1954, Shore Galleries, Boston, 1959, 62, 68, 73, 74, Witte Meml. Mus., San Antonio, 1968, U. Maine, 1969, Lamont Gallery, Exeter, N.H., 1969, Addison Gallery, Andover, Mass., 1971, Fitchburg Art Mus., 1972, Fairweather Hardin Gallery, Chgo., 1972, Hobe Sound (Fla.) Galleries, 1973, Inst. Contemporary Art, Boston, 1977, PS Galleries, Maine, 1981, Payson-Weisberg Gallery, N.Y.C., 1984, Farnsworth Mus., Rockland, Maine, 1984, 98, Midtown Galleries, N.Y.C., 1988, Francesca Anderson Gallery, Boston, 1988, Hobe Sound Galleries North, Portland, Maine, 1988, Evansville (Ind.) Mus. Arts and Sci., 1990, Sheldon Swope Mus., Terre Haute, Ind., 1990, Art Mus. S.E. Tex., Beaumont, 1990, Bergen Mus. Art and Sci., Paramus, N.J., 1990, Polk Mus. Art, Lakeland, Fla., 1991, Farnsworth Art Mus., 1998, Ogunquit Art Assn., 1999, Mass. Coll. Art, Boston, 2000, U. New England, 2000, Berkshire C.C., Pittsfield, Mass., 2003, River Tree Ctr. for the Arts, Kennebunk, Maine, 2003, George Marshall Store Gallery, York, Maine, 2005; two-person show, Inst. Contemporary Art, Boston, 1956, numerous group shows including Barn Gallery, 1954-2005, Busch-Reisinger Mus., Harvard U., 1956, 59, 60, Portland Mus., 1959, 84, 92, 93, 97, 2004, Mus. Fine Arts, Boston, 1960, Inst. Contemporary Art, Boston, 1960, 63, 68, 77, Pace Gallery, Boston, 1962, DeCordova Mus., 1963, 64, 68, 69, 70, 71, 75, Ward-Nasse Gallery, N.Y.C., 1971-72, Ogunquit (Maine) Mus. Am. Art, 1964, 70, 71, 78, 80, 84, 89, 91-93, 95, 98, 00, 03, River Tree Ctr. Arts, 2004, R.I. Arts Festival, 1966, Smithsonian Instn., Washington, 1966, Am. Water Color Soc. Traveling Exhbn., 1967, Watercolor U.S.A., Springfield, Mo., 1968, Maine State Mus., 1976, 04, Maine Coast Artists, 1974, 75, 77, 83, 89, 92, 93, Joan Whitney Payson Gallery of Art, Maine, 1980, Farnsworth Art Mus., 1982, 87, 92, 95, 96, Bowdoin Coll. Mus. Art, 1984, 92, Midtown Payson Galleries, N.Y.C., 1985, 87, 90, 92, Expo '92, Seville, Spain, Barbara Scott Gallery, Bay Harbor Island, Fla., 1993, Fitchburg (Mass.) Art Mus., 1994, Monmouth (N.J.) Mus., 1995, Evansville Mus. Arts and Sci., 1996, U. New England, 2000, 05, Francesca Anderson Fine Art, Lexington, Mass., 2002, Addison Gallery Am. Art, Andover, Mass., 2003, River Tree Ctr. for Arts, Kennebunk, Maine, 2004, Ctr. Maine Contemporary Art, Rockland, 2006, Greenhut Galleries, Portland, 2006; represented in permanent collections Rose Art Mus. Brandeis U., Fogg Art Mus., Cambridge, Mass.; Corcoran Gallery Am. Art, Washington, Witte Meml. Mus., San Antonio, DeCordova Mus., Lincoln, Addison Gallery, Andover, Bowdoin Coll. Mus. Art, Fitchburg Art Mus., Ogunquit Mus. Am. Art, Portland Mus., Colby Coll., U. Maine, Currier Gallery Art, Manchester N.H., Farnsworth Library and Art Mus., Rockland, Maine, U. N.H. Art Galleries, Durham, Everson Mus., Syracuse, First Nat. Bank, Boston, Ernst and Ernst, Chgo., Carnegie Corp., N.Y., Nat. Mus. Women in the Arts, Washington, Gouws Capital Mgmt., Inc., Portland, Maine, Marion Koogler Art Mus., San Antonio, Tex., others, also, pvt. collections, U.S. Can., Paris, Switzerland; Publ. Beverly Hallam, Paintings, Drawings and Monotypes, 1956-71, 1971; subject of book and video Beverly Hallam: The Flower Paintings, 1990, Beverly Hallam: An Odyssey in Art, 1998, (by Carl Little) One Hundred Works From the 20th Century at Colby College Museum of Art, 1996, Maine In America, Farnsworth Art Mus., 2000, On Paper: Masterworks From The Addison Collection, 2003, others. Recipient Pearl Safir award Silvermine Guild Artists, New Canaan, Conn., 1955, Painting prize Boston Arts Festival, 1957, Blanche E. Colman Found. award, 1960, Hatfield awards Boston Soc. Watercolor Painters, 1960, 64, 1st prize Edwin Webster award, 1962, Am. Artist Achievement award, 1993, Disting. Alumna award Mass. Coll. Art, 2000, Maine Coll. Art award for Visual Artist Achievement, 2001. Mem. Ogunquit Art Assn. (past pres.), Archives Am. Art. Avocations: photography, digital abstractions. Home: 30 Surf Point Rd York ME 03909-5053

HALL-BARRON, DEBORAH, lawyer; b. Oakland, Calif., Oct. 7, 1949; d. John Standish Hall and Mary (Swinson) H.; m. Eric Levin Meadow, Feb. 1973 (div. June 1982); 1 child, Jesse Standish Meadow Hall; m. Richie Barron, 1997. Paralegal cert., Sonoma State U., Rohnert Park, Calif., 1984; JD, John F. Kennedy U., Walnut Creek, Calif., 1990. Bar: Calif. 1991. Paralegal Law Offices Marc Libarle/Quentin Kopp, Cotati, Calif., 1983-84, MacGregor & Buckley, Larkspur, Calif., 1984-86, Law Offices Melvin Belli, San Francisco, 1987-88, Steinhart & Falconer, San Francisco, 1988; mgr. Computerized Litigation Assocs., San Francisco, 1986; law clk. Morton & Lacy, San Francisco, 1989-91, assoc., 1991-96; atty. Law Offices of Charlotte Venner, San Francisco, 1996-97, Plastiras & Terrizzi, San Francisco, San Rafael, Calif., 1998, Bishop, Barry, Howe, Haney & Ryder, San Francisco, 1998-99, McLemore, Collins and Toschi, Oakland, Calif., 1999-2000, Nevin Levy, LLP, Walnut Creek, 2000—01, Curtis & Arata, Modesto, Calif., 2001—03, Parker Sommers, Sacramento, 2003—05, Law Offices of Deborah Barron, Sacramento, 2005—. Atty. Vol. Legal Svcs., San Francisco, 1991-96; judge San Francisco Youth Ct., 1995-97; com. chmn. Point Richmond (Calif.) coun., 1994-96. Recipient Whiley Manuel Pro Bono award State Bar Calif., 1993. Mem. Nat. Assn. Ins. Women, Def. Rsch. Inst., Bar Assn. San Francisco (del. 4th world conf. on women 1995, chair product liability com.), Internat. Com. Lawyers for Tibet (litigation com. 1991-97, co-chair women's com.), Ins. Claims Assn. (chmn. membership com. 1994-96), Hon. Order of Blue Goose Internat., Queen's Bench (chmn. employment com. 1994-97, bd. dirs. 1996—, newsletter editor and webmaster 1999), BASF intellectual property/entertainment law), Sacramento Blues Soc. (pres. 2004). Democrat. Avocations: human rights advocate, boating. Home: 2411 Tuscano Ct Rancho Cordova CA 95670-3836 Office Phone: 916-486-1712. Business E-Mail: deborah.barron@lawbarron.com.

HALLECK, DONNA P., piano educator; b. South Boston, Va., July 16, 1955; d. Edward Nathaniel and Joyce Fears Peade; m. Allen Duaine Halleck, July 23, 1977; children: Nathaniel, Stephen, Paul, Mark. BA, Bob Jones U., 1977. Tchr. 3rd grade, piano Thrifthaven Bapt. Ch. Sch., Memphis, 1977-79, Denbigh Bapt. Ch. Sch., Newport News, Va., 1979-84; tchr. Sunday sch., piano Ft. Washington, Mo., 1984-89; tchr. piano Chesapeake, Va., 1989—. Tchr. Sunday Sch., Chesapeake, Va.; active Nursing Home Min., Sentara Nursing Care, Chesapeake; poll worker Rep. Party of Md., Ft. Washington. Mem.: Tidewater Music Tchr. Forum (scholarship treas. 1999—2003). Avocation: reading. E-mail: allen-donnahalleck@juno.com.

HALLENBECK, LINDA S., elementary school educator; m. Theodore R. Hallenbeck; 2 children. BS, Kent State U., 1974, MEd, 1976, postgrad. Cert. tchr. K-3, K-8, computer sci., math., Ohio Ohio, Nat. bd. cert. Grad. asst. Kent State U., Ohio, 1974—76; tchr. 3d grade Hudson Elem. Sch., Ohio, 1976—77; tchr. 1st grade Evamere Sch., Hudson, 1977—86; tchr. 5th grade J.P. McDowell Elem. Sch., Hudson, 1986—92, East Woods Sch., Hudson, 1992—2001; tchr. Hudson Mid. Sch., 2001—03; rsch. assoc. NSF, 2002—03, Mich. State U., 2003—04. Cons. NSF, Washington, 1989-95, tchr. in residence Office of Gov. Bob Taft, 1999-2001; tchr. Presdl. Acad. for Excellence in Tchg. Math. at Princeton and Northwestern U., Middle Sch. Math. State Trainer, Math Acad., 2001—; mem. exec. bd. Ohio Math./Sci. Coalition. Recipient Presdl. award for excellence in teaching sci. and math. NSF, 1993, Govs. Edn. leadership award, 1998, Ohio Pioneer in Edn award, 2000. Mem. Nat. Coun. Tchrs. Math., Ohio Coun. Tchrs. Math. (pres. 2004—), Ohio Math. Edn. Leadership Coun Avocations: skiing, gardening, sewing, decorating. Home: 7615 Oxgate Ct Hudson OH 44236-1877 Office Phone: 330-650-4912.

HALLENBECK, RACHEL KIRSTEN, music educator, director; b. Jackson, Calif., Nov. 1, 1965; d. Ronald K. and Martha Lou Grabke; children: Kirsten Elizabeth, Brianna Ruth. BSc in Music Edn., Ea. Nazarene Coll., 1989, MEd in Elem. Edn., 1999, MEd in Adminstrn., 2000. Music specialist Braintree Pub. Schs., 1989—2000, dir. music, 2000—. Soloist Boylston Congl. Ch., Boston, 1990—, Town of Braintree, 1990—; accompanist Quincy Pub. Schs., 1998—, vocal dir. performing arts workshops, 2004—; condr. Braintree Choral Soc., 2001—02; musical dir. Harmony Youth Chorus and No Place for Hate Project, 2004—05. Singer: Boston (Mass.) Symphony Orch., 1989—; dir.: Quincy (Mass.) Dinner Theater, 1990—93; singer: (albums) The Boston (Mass.) Pops Orch., The Boston (Mass.) Symphony Orch. Republican. Avocations: singing, choreography, piano. Office: Braintree Public Schools 128 Town St Braintree MA 02184

HALLER, MARCIA SMITH, art educator; children: Jessica Hutton, Sylvia. BA in Art Edn., Kean Coll., Union, N.J., 1972, MA in Art Edn., 1986. Tchr. art Watching Hills Regional H.S., Warren, NJ, 1988—89, North Brunswick Regional H.S., 1989—90, North Plainfield H.S., 1990—91, Roselle Mid. Sch., 1992—93, South River H.S., 1993—. EARTH Club advisor South River H.S., 1993—, Nat. Honor Soc. advisor, 1994—99. Drawings selected in mag., Earthwatch, 1991, paintings featured on Earthwatch website, 1977, exhibitions include photographs Liberty Sci. Ctr., Jersey City, enamel, Newark Mus., 1995. Named Tchr. of Yr., South River Sch. Dist., 1999—2000; fellow, Internat. Crane Found., 1994; grantee, N.J. Edn. Assn. A+ Kids, 1993; E.R. Dodge fellow, Earthwatch, 1990. Avocations: photography, travel. Office: S River HS 11 Montgomery St South River NJ 08882 Office Phone: 732-613-4014.

HALLEY, DIANE ESTHER, artist; b. Jasper, Ind., May 14, 1939; d. John and Esther Margaret (Kruse) Darden; m. Norman B. Halley, May 21, 1966; 1 child, William Tull. BS in Elem. Edn., Ind. State U., 1961. Tchr. 4th grade, New Albany, Ind., 1961, Seymour, Ind., 1962-64, Westminster, Colo., 1964-68; portrait artist Arvada, Colo., 1979—. Juror fall exhbn. Colo. Watercolor Soc., 2002. Paintings included in books, Colo., 1990—, Denver Art Mus., Best of Watercolor-Painting Textures, 1997, Splash Six-The Magic of Texture, 2000; one-woman shows include Denver Nat. Bank, 1983, Foothills Art Ctr., Golden, Colo., 1984, Nat. Ctr. Atmospheric Rsch., Boulder, Colo., 1991, Colo. Christian U., 2000, exhibitions include Lincoln Ctr., Ft. Collins, Colo., 2003, Challenge of Champions, Watercolor Art Soc. Houston, 2003, 53rd Nat. Exhibition of Contemporary Realism in Art, Acad. Artists Assn., 2003, Artists Who Happen to be Women, Tex. A&M U., 2004, Watercolor Mo. Nat., Winston Churchill Meml. Libr., 2004 (Bd. Dirs. award, 2004), Great 8 Exhbn., Kans. Watercolor Soc., Wichita Art Mus., 2004, 2006, 50th Anniversary Mem. Exhbn., Colo. Watercolor Soc., 2004, Small Works Exhbn., Attleboro Art Mus., 2005, Brand Libr. and Art Ctr., 2006, Karpeles Libr. Mus., 2006, exhibitions include Ports of Call Gallery, 2006. Pres. Clear Creek Valley Med. Aux., Lakewood, Colo., 1973—74, 1991—92. Recipient Founder's award, Colo. Watercolor Soc., 1992, Pres.'s award, 1994, Best in Show award, Colo. Watercolor Soc. 50th Ann. Exbn., 2004, Grumbacher award, Pikes Peak Watercolor Soc., 1995, Cash award, Lakewood Arts Coun., 2001, Award of Distinction, Mo. Nat. Watercolor Exhbn., 2003, Westminster Cmty. Artist Series award, 2003. Mem.: Mo. Watercolor Soc. (signature mem.), Kans. Watercolor Soc. (signature mem., Am. artist cash award 1999), Rocky Mountain Nat. Watermedia Soc. (signature mem.), Nat. Watercolor Soc. (signature mem., Del Mar Coll. award 1981), Nat. Assn. Women Artists (signature mem., Cecil Shapiro Meml. award 1998), Catherine Lorillard Wolf Art Club (signature mem., Adriana Zahn award 1985, Cynthia Goodgal award 1986). Avocations: Bible study, bridge, gardening. Home: 6631 Osceola Ct Arvada CO 80003-6426

HALLEY, JANET E., law educator; BA in English Lit., summa cum laude, Princeton U., 1974; PhD in English Lit., UCLA, 1980; JD, Yale U., 1988. Mem. English faculty Hamilton Coll., Clinton, NY, 1980—85; law clk. to Chief Judge Gilbert Merritt US Ct. Appeals 6th Cir., 1988—89; assoc. Skadden, Arps, Slate, Meagher & Flom, Boston, 1989—91; assoc. prof. Stanford Law Sch., 1991—95, prof., 1995—2000; prof. law Harvard Law Sch., Cambridge, Mass., 2000—. Vis. prof. law Harvard Law Sch., 1999. Author: Don't: A Reader's Guide to the Military Anti-Gay Policy, 1999. Named Robert E. Paradise Faculty Scholar for Excellence in Teaching and Rsch., Stanford Law Sch., 1996. Office: Harvard Law Sch 1563 Massachusetts Ave Cambridge MA 02138 Office Phone: 617-496-0182. Office Fax: 617-496-4947.

HALLIDAY, KRISTEN LEE, language educator; b. Winchester, Mass., May 27, 1981; d. Michael Robert and Barbara Jane Halliday; m. John Michael Tinsley, July 15, 2006. BS English, SW Bapt. U., Bolivar, Mo., 2003. Cert. Tchr. Mo., 2003. Tchr. Timberland H.S., Wentzville, Mo., 2003—. Curriculum writer Wentzville R-IV Sch. Dist., 2005—06. Scholar Betty Gipson Outstanding Writer award, SW Bapt. U., 2002. Mem.: Mo. State Tchrs. Assn. (assoc.). R-Consevative. Baptist. Office: Wentzville School District One Campus Drive Wentzville MO 63385

HALLIDAY, NANCY RUTH, scientific illustrator; b. Chgo., Mar. 30, 1936; d. Stuart Ernest and Ruth (Yehl) Halliday. Student, Coll. for Creative Studies, Detroit, 1956—57; BS in Zoology, U. Okla., 1962; MA in Geography and Environ. Studies, Northeastern Ill. U., Chgo., 1988. Receptionist, lectr. The Mus., Mich. State U., East Lansing, 1957—60; summer asst. Mus. of No. Ariz., Flagstaff, 1963; artist, office of exhibits Smithsonian Instn., Washington, 1966—70; sci. illustrator Fla. State Mus., Gainesville, 1973—81; artist, naturalist Forest Preserve Dist. of Cook County, Ill., 1989—2003. Instr. bot. art and illustration cert. program The Morton Arboretum, Lisle, Ill., 1995—, adv. bd. in establishing cert. program, 1994; biol. illustration curriculum com. U. Fla., Gainesville, 1978—81; condr. workshops in field; artist resident Ill. Arts Coun., 1986, 89, 91; lectr. in field. Illustrator (12 watercolor plates) Mammals of North America, 2002, Atlas of Breeding Birds in Pennsylvania, 1992; author: Illustrating Birds, Guild Handbook of Scientific Illustration, 2d edit., 2003; one-woman shows include Thomas Ctr. for the Arts, Gainesville, Fla., 1982, two-person shows, Mus. Arts and Scis., Macon, Ga., 1982, exhibited in group shows at Smithsonian Instn., Washington, 1969, 1978, 1996, Bell Mus., Mpls., 1971, 1994, Acad. Natural Scis., Phila., 1981—82, Denver Mus. Natural History, 1982, Leigh Yawkey Woodson Art Mus., Wausau, Wis., 1983, Chgo. Bot. Garden, Glencoe, Ill., 1995, King Dom Manuel's Palace, Évora, Portugal, 2000, Denver Mus. Nature and Sci., 2003, Ariz.-Sonora Desert Mus., Tucson, 2004—05 (Curator's Choice for Mammalogy). Active Bicycle Adv. Bd., Gainesville, 1975—78; environmental concerns com. Ill. Yearly Meeting of Friends (Quakers), 1991—; natural resources commr. Village of Glenview, Ill., 2006—. Recipient 2d prize for watercolor, Nat. Wildlife Fedn., 1983, Purchase prize, Visual Arts Gallery, Pensacola Jr. Coll., 1983. Mem.: Am. Soc. Bot. Artists, Soc. Animal Artists, Guild of Natural Sci. Illustrators (historian 1995—, 1st prize for color 1979). Avocations: canoeing, bicycling, birdwatching. Home: 1156 Pine St Apt 4 Glenview IL 60025

HALLIGAN, FREDRICA ROSE, clinical psychologist; b. Greenwich, Conn., Sept. 21, 1938; d. Wilmer Herman and Eunice Rose (Wixon) Greul; m. John Francis Halligan, Apr. 8, 1961 (dec. Apr. 1987); children: Patricia Ann Schumacher, Michael Edward, Stephen Frederick. BA in Math. summa cum laude, Hollins Coll., 1959; MA in Counseling and Psychology, Fairfield U., 1975, cert. advanced studies, 1980; PhD in Clin. Psychology, Fordham U., 1985. Cons. Yale U. Med. Sch., New Haven, 1976-77; counselor, dir. guidance Sacred Heart Acad., 1977-78; counselor Fairfield (Conn.) U., 1978-80; psychology intern VA Med. Ctr., Northport, N.Y., 1984-85; post-doctoral fellow, lectr. Rehab. Inst. Chgo. Northwestern U. Med. Sch., 1985-86; cons. Albert Einstein Coll. Medicine, N.Y.C., 1982-88; pvt. practice Riverside, Conn., 1987-96; assoc dir. Counseling Ctr. Fordham U., Bronx, NY, 1986-95; sr. psychologist Life Span Devel. Sys., 1995-96; assoc. dir. psychology, religion St. Louis Behavioral Medicine Inst., 1996-99. Vis. assoc. prof. Fordham U., 1999-2002; adj. faculty Fordham U., Iona Coll., Washington U., St. Louis U. Med. Sch., Fairfield U., Coll. New Rochelle, Mercy Coll., Northwestern U. Med. Sch, Western Conn. State U.; co-host Cafh Found. Spirit Seminars, N.Y.C., 1991-96, St. Louis, 1996-99; co-tchr. Cape Cod Inst., Albert Einstein Coll. Medicine, Wellfleet, Mass., 1991-93; tchr. C.G. Jung Inst., N.Y.C., 1992; dir. counseling ctr. Western Conn. State U., 2002-. Author: The Art of Copying, 1995, Listening Deeply to God: Exploring Spirituality in an Interreligious Age, 2005; co-editor: The Fires of Desire: Erotic Energies and the Spiritual Quest, 1992; contbr. chpts. to books, numerous articles to profl. jours., papers to profl. confs. Active in civic and ch. programs. Recipient Rotary Club scholarship, Schering-Plough fellowship, 1985. Mem. APA, Am. Bd. Med. Psychotherapists, Conn. Psychol. Assn., New Eng. Assn. Specialists in Group Work, Sigma Xi, Phi Kappa Phi, Pi Epsilon Mu. Avocation: writing. Office: The Mind-Body-Spirit Inst 2289 Bedford St Unit G19 Stamford CT 06905-3977 Office Phone: 203-837-8693.

HALLIMAN, TINA LYNETTE, special education educator; b. Harvey, Ill., June 6, 1971; d. Lenore and Leo Edward Guyton (Stepfather); m. Collin Hugh Halliman, Dec. 20, 1998; children: Madison Lynette, Matthew Moses. MS in Spl. Edn. with honors, Dominican U., River Forest, 1999; MSW, Aurora U., Ill., 2000; PhD in Edn., Loyola U., Chgo., 2006. Cert. sch. social worker Ill.; gen. adminstrn. Ill., learning behaviour specialist Ill. Crisis intervention coord. Dist. 130 Pub. Schools, Blue Island, Ill., 1996—97; spl. edn. tchr. Chgo. Pub. Schools, 1997—2000; clin. coord. Infinity Schs. Chgo., 2000—01; devel. therapist Dept. of Human Svcs., Chgo., 2000—04; resource coord., sch. social worker, staffing coord. Homewood Flossmoor HS, Flossmoor, Ill., 2001—05, dean of students, 2005—06, dir. spl. edn., 2006—. V.p. bd. dirs. Youth First Connections, Inc., Calumet Park, Ill., 2003—; diversity trainer Seeking Ednl. Equity and Diversity, Ill., 2005—; fellow Diversifying Faculty and Higher Edn. Institutions/Loyola U. Chgo., 2003—06. Spl. edn. profl. del. to South Africa People to People Ambassador Program. Recipient Human and Civil Rights award, Ill. Edn. Assn.; George Williams Sch. of Social Work scholar, Aurora U., 1999—2000. Mem.: Tender Loving Care (founding mem., parent adv. com., sec. 2003—05), Coun. for Exceptional Children (sub-com. coun. adminstrs. in spl. edn. and tchr. edn. divsn.), Phi Delta Kappa Internat., Alpha Kappa Alpha (sec.). Avocations: travel, exercise. Home: 22707 Maddeline Ln Frankfort IL 60423 Office Phone: 708-385-6800. Home Fax: 815-464-2229. Personal E-mail: cthalliman@aol.com.

HALLINAN, MAUREEN THERESA, sociologist, educator; BA, Marymount Coll., 1961; MS, U. Notre Dame, 1968; PhD, U. Chgo., 1972. Prof. U. Wis., Madison, 1980-84; with U. Notre Dame, Ind., 1984—, William P. and Hazel B. White prof. arts and letters dept. sociology, dir. Ctr. Rsch. Ednl. Opportunity. Author: The Structure of Positive Sentiment, 1974; editor: Sociology of Edn., 1981—86, The Social Context of Instruction: Group Organization and Group Processes, 1983, The Social Organization of Schools: New Conceptualizations of the Learning Process, 1987, Change in Societal Institutions, 1990, Restructuring Schools: Promising Practices and Policies, 1995, Handbook of the Sociology of Education, 2000, Handbook of the Sociology of Education, Chinese edit., 2004; co-editor: Stability and Change in American Education: Structure, Process and Outcomes, 2003, School Sector and Student Outcomes, 2006; assoc. editor: Social Forces, 1977—80, Sociology of Edn., 1979—81, 1991—2001; contbr. articles to profl. jours. Mem.: Nat. Acad. Edn. (v.p. fellows 2001—05), Sociol. Rsch. Assn. (sec.-treas. 1999—2000, pres. 2000—01), Am. Sociol. Assn. (session organizer 1980, 1984, sec.-treas. 1988—90, session organizer 1989, chmn. sociology edn. sect. 1991—92, chmn. 1991—92, session organizer 1992, pres. 1995—96, session organizer 1996—2001, Willard Waller award 2004), Phi Beta Kappa. Office: U Notre Dame Dept Sociology Notre Dame IN 46556 Business E-Mail: pauley.1@nd.edu.

HALLINGBY, JO DAVIS, arbitrator; b. N.Y.C. d. Irwin and Ruth Davis; m. Paul Hallingby Jr., Nov. 17, 1994. BA, Boston U., 1966; JD cum laude, Bklyn. Law Sch., 1973. Bar: N.Y. 1974, U.S. Ct. Appeals (2nd cir.) 1974. Legal intern counsel to chmn. N.Y.C. Planning Commn., summer 1972; law clk. Hon. John R. Bartels U.S. Dist. Judge Ea. Dist. N.Y., 1973; law clk. Hon. William C. Conner U.S. Dist. Judge So. Dist. N.Y., 1974; staff atty. Criminal Appeals Bur., Legal Aid Soc., 1974-77; asst. U.S. atty. Ea. Dist. N.Y., 1978-83; assoc. Kass, Goodkind, Wechsler & Labaton, 1977-78; litigation counsel CBS, Inc., 1983-84; N.Y. counsel Kaye, Scholer, Fierman, Hays & Handler, 1984-93; arbitrator Nat. Assn. Securities Dealers, N.Y. Stock Exch., 1994—. Mem. U.S. Commn. on Civil Rights-N.Y. State Adv. Com., 1984-86; jud. com. Assn. of the Bar of the City of N.Y., 1984-90, fed. cts. com., 1990-94; dir. Riverside Park Fund, 1986-93; ct. adv. group com. on civil litigation U.S. Dist. Ct. Ea. Dist. N.Y., 1990-95; dir. Landmarks Preservation Found., 1995—; spkr. in field. Notes editor Bklyn. Law Rev., 1972-73. Office: Nat Assn Securities Dealers NY Stock Exch 1 Sutton Pl S New York NY 10022-2471

HALLMAN, CECILIA ANN, real estate consultant; d. James Cecil and Lillie Mae Hallman. Certificate in dentistry, Midland Tech. Coll., Columbia, S.C., 1972; student, U. S.C., Aiken, 1993; MBA in Essentials 1 Cert., Tulane U., 2004; Art certificate, Oxford U., 2005. Lic. real estate S.C., Ark. Property mgr. Wyatt Devel. Co., Inc., Aiken, 1987—89, The Keenan Co., Columbia, 1989—90; co-owner, mgr. Aiken Indsl. Supply, Inc., 1990—92; office adminstr. Dr. Rocky L. Napier, Aiken, 1992—96; dir. of mem. svcs. Wyatt Devel./Sage Valley Golf Club, Aiken, SC, 1996—2002; dir. mem. svcs. Stephens Inc./The Alotian Club, Little Rock, 2002—04. Author, pub.: The Memphis Kingmaker, 2006. Vol. Am. Cancer Soc., Aiken, 1990—92. Mem.: Woodside Plantation Country Club (assoc.), Green Boundary Club (assoc.), Rotary. Home and Office: 223 Forest Pines Rd Aiken SC 29803 Office Fax: 803-642-8023. Personal E-mail: irgllc@gforcecable.com.

HALLMAN, CINDA A., management consultant; BSc in Math., U. So. Ark. With DuPont, 1981—2001; CEO Spherion Corp., Ft. Lauderdale, Fla., 2001—. Bd. dirs. Toys "R" Us, Catalyst, United Way Am., Christiana Care Health Sys.; bd. trustees Christiana Care. Named CIO of Yr., Info. Week, 1995; named one of Most Influential Info. Tech. Execs. of Decade, CIO Mag., 1997; recipient Visionary award, Comm. Week, 1996.

HALLMAN, JANELLE M., psychotherapist, educator; b. Tacoma, Oct. 8, 1956; d. Frank Jay and Margo Zelle Winzeler; m. R. Kelly Burleson, July 29, 2000; 1 child from previous marriage, Jenae Kaleen. BA in Econ. with distinction, U. Colo., Denver, 1985; MA in Counseling with honors, Denver Seminary, Colo., 1995. Cert. paralegal Denver Paralegal Inst., lic. profl. counselor Colo. Dept. Regulatory Agy. Paralegal Saunders, Snyder, Ross and Dickson, Denver, 1980—83; leg. asst. Colo. House Reps., Denver, 1984; v.p. Sellect Designs, Denver, 1985—90; staff counselor Where Grace Abounds, Denver, 1990—94; pvt. practice Denver, 1995—. Adj. faculty Colo. Christian U., Denver, 1998—2001; regional rep. Exodus Internat., 1998—2001; adj. faculty Denver Seminary, 2003—. Campaign mgr. Colo. State Rep., 1984, 1986. Named Top Student, U. Colo., 1983, Outstanding Grad., 1985; named to Nat. Dean's List, 1985. Mem.: Nat. Assn. Rsch. and Therapy of Homosexuality (bd. mem. at large 2003—), Am. Counseling Assn., Am. Assn. Christian Counselors. Avocations: travel, skiing, hiking, cooking, gardening. Office: 8771 Wolff Ct 110 Westminster CO 80031 Office Phone: 303-273-2877. Business E-Mail: janellehallman@juno.com.

HALLMAN, LINDA D., medical association administrator; b. Wash., DC; BA in Music Edn., Indiana U.; MS in Orgnl. Mgmt., George Wash. U. COO Am. Coll. Heathcare Adminstrs., Alexandria, Va.; dir. profl. svcs. Am. Coll. Healthcare Adminstrs., 1989—94, dir. member svcs., 1989—94; pres. Am. Hort. Soc., Alexandria, Va., 1997—2002; exec. dir. Am. Med. Women's Assn., Alexandria, Va., 2002—. Mem.: Assn. Fundraising Professionals, Am. Soc. Assn. Executives. Office: AMWA Ste 400 801 N Fairfax St Alexandria VA 22314*

HALLMAN, PATRICIA L., music educator, musician; d. Robert A. and Theda E. Laubach; m. Donald L. Hallman, June 3, 1967; children: Jonathan A., Katherine E. BS in Music Edn., Susquehanna U., Selinsgrove, Pa., 1966. Cert. tchr. Pa. Jr. HS music tchr. Quakertown Cmty. Sch. Dist., Pa., 1966—69; elem. music specialist Upper Merion Area Sch. Dist., King of Prussia, Pa., 1968—. Musician, substitute musician Trinity Luth. Ch., Ft. Washington, Pa., 1965—; dir. children's summer history camp Hope Lodge State Hist. Site, Ft. Washington, 1986—96; accompanist Philomusica Chorale of Delaware Valley, Phila., 1984—. Transcriber, writer, arranger (musical for children) The Bubble Gum Mayor, 1994. Sunday sch. tchr., choir mem.; bd. dirs., sec. Laubach Family Assn. Named Friend of Libr., Upper Merion Twp. Libr., 2004; named to Wall of Fame, Upper Merion Area Sch. Dist., 1995. Mem.: NEA, Upper Merion Area Edn. Assn., Pa. State Edn. Assn., Pa. Music Educators' Assn., Music Educators' Nat. Conf., Sigma Alpha Iota. Lutheran. Avocations: reading, travel. Home: 609 Hartranft Ave Fort Washington PA 19034 Office: Caley Elem Sch 725 Caley Rd King Of Prussia PA 19406 Office Phone: 610-205-3665. Business E-Mail: phallman@umasd.org.

HALLOCK MORRIS, MARY THERESA, education educator; d. Charles Raymond Hallock and Judith Mary Brooks, Bonnie Parkison (Stepmother); m. Gerald William Morris, Feb. 16, 1991. BS, Defiance Coll., Defiance, Ohio, 1991; MA, McGregor Sch. of Antioch U., Yellow Springs, hio, 1997; PhD, Ind. U., Bloomington, 2004. News editor Mercer County Chronicle, Coldwater, Ohio, 1991—96; life quality specialist So. Mut. Help Assn., New Iberia, La., 2001—02; tchg. fellow Ind. U., New Albany, 2002—03; asst. prof. U. So. Ind., Evansville, 2003—. Adj. staff So. Mut. Help Assn., New Iberia, 2002—. Editor: (journal) Indiana Jour. of Political Sci. Recipient Katherine C. Greenough Dissertation award, Ind. U. Dept. of Polit. Sci., 2004; Excellence through Engagement Summer Rsch. Fellowship, U. So. Ind., 2006. Mem.: So. Polit. Sci. Assn., Ind. Polit. Sci. Assn. (pres. 2006—), LWV, Women of the Moose. D-Conservative. Cath. Avocations: hiking, travel. Office: Univ of Southern Ind 8600 University Blvd Evansville IN 47712 Office Phone: 812-461-5207. E-mail: mhmorris@usi.edu.

HALLORAN, JEAN M., human resources specialist; b. NY; B in History, Princeton U.; MBA, Harvard U. Various positions in human resources, mfg., and strategic planning med. products group Hewlett-Packard, 1980—93, personnel mgr. measurement sys. orgn., 1993—97, dir. corp. edn. and devel., 1997—99; sr. v.p. human resources Agilent Technologies, Palo Alto, Calif., 1999—. Office: Agilent Technologies Inc 395 Page Mill Rd Palo Alto CA 94306 Office Phone: 650-752-5633. Office Fax: 650-752-5633.

HALLORAN, KATHLEEN L., retired gas industry executive, accountant; b. Sandwich, Ill., July 19, 1952; d. Oscar L. and Gertrude L. Huber. BA in Acctg., Lewis U., 1974; MBA, No. Ill. U., 1979. CPA Ill. With NICOR, Inc., Naperville, 1974-84; asst. sec. No. Ill. Gas subs. NICOR, Inc., Naperville, 1983-84, asst. contr., 1984; sec., treas. NICOR Inc., Naperville, 1984-87; sec., contr. NICOR, Inc., Naperville, 1987-89, v.p., sec., contr., 1989-92, v.p. info. svcs. and gen. acctg., 1992-94; v.p. info. svcs. and rates No. Ill. Gas, Aurora, 1994-95, v.p. info. svcs., rates and human resources, 1995-96, sr. v.p. info. svcs., rates and human resources, 1996-98, sr. v.p. adminstrn., 1998-99, exec. v.p. fin. and adminstrn., 1999—2004; ret., 2004. Bd. dirs. Ctrl. DuPage Health, Voices Am.'s Children, Ill. Children's Healthcare Found.; mem. com. dirs. Voices Ill. Children; trustee Lewis U. Mem.: Chgo. Network. E-mail: khallor@nicor.com.

HALLORAN-BARNES, JILL, secondary school educator; d. Delphine and Matthew Jerrry Halloran; m. Scott Alan Barnes. BS in Bus., Ind. U., South Bend, 1990, MS in Secondary Edn., 2002. Cert. tchr. Ind. Math tchr. Oreg. Davis HS, Hamlet, Ind., 1997—2001; math and computer tchr. Elkhart Ctrl. HS, Ind., 2001—. Avocations: dance, ballet, jazz. Office Phone: 574-295-4700.

HALLSTRAND, SARAH LAYMON, denomination executive; b. Nashville, Oct. 25, 1944; d. Charles Martin and Lillian Christina (Stenberg) Laymon; m. John Peter Hallstrand, July 6, 1974; 1 child, Lillian Johanna. BA cum laude, Fla. So. Coll., 1966; ThM, Boston U., 1971; D of Ministry, McCormick Theol. Sem., 1985; grad., Coll. for Fin. Planning, Denver, 1990. Ordained Am. Baptist Ch., 1976; cert. ret. counselor; CFP. Dir. Christian edn. Trinity United Meth. Ch., Bradenton, Fla., 1968-70, Univ. United Meth. Ch., Syracuse, N.Y., 1971-73; assoc. min. First Bapt. Ch., Syracuse, 1973-78; pastor Oneida (N.Y.) Bapt. Ch., 1978-80; midwest rep. Mins. and Missionaries Benefit Bd., Am. Bapt. Chs., Oak Park, Ill., 1981—2002; pastor First United Meth. Ch., Tellico Plains, Tenn., 2002—03; cons. MMBB, 2002—04; interim exec. min. ABCCONN, 2004, ABC of Greater Indpls., 2005—. Leader ret. planning seminars Am. Bapt. Assembly, Green Lake, Wis., 1985-02, AutumnQuest Ret. Sems., Midwest Ministry Devel. Svc., 1994—, bd. dirs., 1987-01, chair, 1993-96; mem. rep. Midwest Ministerial Leadership Commn., Valley Forge, Pa., 1985-02; adj. prof., pastoral care McCormick Theol. Sem., Chgo., 1986-01; adj. prof. retirement planning The Divinity Sch., Rochester, N.Y., 1994; vis. scholar Am. Bapt. Bd. Ednl. Ministries, Valley Forge, 1986-87; bd. dirs. The Gathering Place Retreat Ctr., Gosport, Ind., 1988-95; mem. program com. and women in ministry rep. Roger Williams Fellowship, 1988-95; mem. nat. continuing edn. team Am. Bapt. Chs., Valley Forge, Pa., 1991-98; mem. strategic planning com. The Celebration of a New Bapt. Covenant, 2006—; conf. leader for women's spiritual renewal weekends; mem. strategic planning com. The Celebration of a New Bapt. Covenant, 2006; spkr. in field. Contbg. author: Songs of Miriam: A Women's Book of Devotions, 1994; contbr. articles to profl. jours. including The Inclusive Pulpit Jour. Mem. Fin. Planning Assn., Alpha Gamma Delta. Democrat. Home and Office: 126 Santee Way Loudon TN 37774 E-mail: sh4406@hotmail.com.

HALLY, JANE ELOISE, religious organization administrator, social worker; b. Boston, May 28, 1943; d. James Thomas and Pauline Rice; m. William Donald Smith (div.); 1 child, Claire Hally Smith. AB, Vassar Coll., 1964; student, Duke U., 1971—74; MDiv, Candler Sch. Theology, 1982; MSW, U. Ga., 2000. Ordained deacon 1982, priest 1983; LCSW. Deacon, priest, asst. to rector Ch. of the Atonement, Sandy Springs, Ga., 1982—84; asst. to rector, pastoral counselor St. Bartholomew's Ch., Atlanta, 1986—90, founding dir. Emmanuel ctr. pastoral counseling, 1991—95; pastoral counselor Care and Counseling Ctr., Ga., 1995—. Deacon interns, supr., 1986—89; staff rep. to bd. trustees Care and Counseling Ctr., Ga., 2004—; owner Nature of Clay Studio and Showroom, Avondale Estates, Ga., 2005—. Contbr. chapters to books, articles. Vol. Peace Corps, 1964—66. Fellow: Am. Assn. Pastoral Counselors; mem.: Soc. St. Anna the Prophet, Nat. Assn. Social Workers. Democrat. Episcopal. Avocations: painting, gardening, swimming. Office: Cathedral Counseling Ctr 2744 Peachtree Rd NW Atlanta GA 30305 Office Phone: 404-841-4953, 404-636-1457 x. Personal E-mail: jehally@mindspring.com. Business E-Mail: ehally@cccgeorgia.org.

HALM, NANCYE STUDD, retired academic administrator; b. Jamestown, N.Y., Mar. 26, 1932; d. Thomas Howerton and Margaret Hazel (LeRoy) Neathery; m. David Philip Mack, Aug. 25, 1951 (div. 1972); children: Margaret, Jennifer, Geoffrey, Peter; m. Loris L. Studd, July 6, 1974; m. James Richard Halm, Aug. 30, 1991 (dec. 2005). BS in Edn., SUNY, Fredonia, 1954, postgrad., 1954—68, St. Bonaventure U., 1970, postgrad., 1981. Tchr. Morning Sun (Iowa) Consolidated Schs., 1956-57, Panama (N.Y.) Cen. Schs., 1958-65, Jamestown (N.Y.) Pub. Schs., 1967-69, Olean (N.Y.) Pub. Schs., 1969-72, Jamestown Pub. Schs., 1972-73; pers. mgr. F.W. Woolworth Co., Lakewood, N.Y., 1972-79; dir. Nat. Conf. Christians & Jews, Jamestown, 1979-86; counselor N.Y. State Div. for Youth, Jamestown, 1979-89; exec. rep. Am. Bapt. Found., Valley Forge, Pa., 1989-94; adminstr. New Castle Christian Acad., 1996—2002; ret., 2002. Pastor West Pitts. United Meth. Ch., 2003—04, Ellington United Meth. Ch., 2004—. V.p. Chautauqua County Am. Bapt. Women, 1981—90; pres. Falconer Bapt. Women, 1986—90; love gift chmn. Pitts. Bapt. Assn., 1990—91; trustee, chair endowment fund Chautauqua Bapt. Union at Chautauqua Inst., 1982—; pres. ch. coun. Wesley United Meth. Ch., 2001—03; mem. nat. bd. dirs. Am. Bapt. Chs. U.S.A., Valley Forge, Pa., 1988—89. Recipient Cert. of Merit, Cassadaga Job Corp, 1984. Mem. Rebekah. Democrat. Avocations: reading, crafts, quilting. Home: 60 Morgan St Falconer NY 14733

HALNON, FAITH E., elementary school educator; b. Boston, Apr. 1, 1970; d. Michael C. and Linda E. Higgins; m. Timothy P. Halnon, July 10, 1993; 1 child, Shannon E. B, Castleton State Coll., Vt., 1992, M, 2003. Cert. permanent tchg. N.Y. State. Tchr. preschool Alphabet Ho., Rutland, Vt., 1993—95; asst. spl. needs Wells Village Sch., 1995—96; classroom asst. Wallingford Elem. Sch., 1996—97; substute tchr. Vt., NY, 1997—99; tchr. Granville Elem. Sch., NY, 1999—. Mentor Granville Ctrl. Sch. Dist., NY, 2005—; mem. leader team ATLAS cmties. Pathway Leadership Team, 2005—. Supporter 4-H. Mem.: Granville Tchrs. Assn. (mem. grievance com). Avocations: gardening, reading, horseback riding, scrapbooks. Home: 1070 South St Castleton VT 05735-9251 Office: Granville Elem Sch 61 Quaker St Granville NY 12832

HALPER, JUNE, medical center director; Pres. Consortium Multiple Sclerosis Ctrs., 1995—97, exec. dir., 1997—; found exec. dir. Internat. Orgn. Multiple Sclerosis Nurses; founder, exec. dir. Gimbel Multiple Sclerosis Ctr., 1989—. Editor: Comprehensive Nursing Care in Multiple Sclerosis, Advanced Concepts of Nursing Care in Multiple Sclerosis; co-editor: Staying Well with Multiple Sclerosis: A Self-Care Guide. Recipient First June Halper award for Excellence in Nursing Multiple Sclerosis, Inter. Orgn. Multiple Sclerosis Nurses. Fellow: Am. Acad. Nursing; mem.: Am. Acad. Nurse Practitioners. Office: Gimnel Multiple Sclerosis Ctr 718 Teaneck Rd Teaneck NJ 07666

HALPERN, CHERYL F., federal agency administrator; BA in Political Sci., Barnard Coll.; MBA in Finance, NYU. Prodr. news and classic music programs Sta. WKCR-FM, N.Y.C.; mem. Bd. for Internat. Broadcasting U.S. Info. Agy.; apptd. mem. bd. govs. Internat. Broadcasting Bur. U.S. Info. Agy., 1995—. Coalitions chair N.J. Rep. Com.; chair Nat. Jewish Coalition; bd. dirs. Washington Inst. for Near East Policy, N.J.-Israel Commn. Mem. Anti-Defamtion League (mem. N.J. adv. bd.), Ctr. for Pub. Policy. B'nai B'rith.

HALPERN, DIANE F., psychology educator, professional association executive; b. Phila. BA in psychology, U. Penn., 1969; MA in psychology, Temple U., 1973, U. Cin., 1977, PhD in psychology, 1979. Tchg. assistantship U. Cin., 1977—78, cons. behavioral scis. lab., 1978—79; lectr., dept. psychology U. Calif., Riverside, 1979—81; asst. prof. dept. psychology Calif. State U., San Bernardino, 1981—84, assoc. prof. dept. psychology, 1984—86, prof. dept. psychology, 1986—2001, chair, dept. psychology, 1996—99; dir. Berger Inst. for Work, Family, and Children Claremont McKenna Coll., 2001—, prof. psychology, 2001—. Named Scholar-in-Residence, Rockefeller Found., 1995; recipient Prof. Yr. award, C. of C., 1986, Silver Medal, Coun. Advancement and Support Edn. (CASE), 1986, Ednl. Equity award, Assn. Black Faculty and Staff, 1987, Outstanding Alumni award, U. Cin., 1988, Birkett Williams Meml. Lecture award, Ouachita Baptist U., 1992, Fulbright Scholar award, 1994, Arthur Moorefield Meml. award, 1997, Disting. Vis. Scholar award, James Madison U., 1998. Fellow: Western Psychological Assn. (pres. 1999—2000, Outstanding Tchg. award 2002), Am. Psychological Soc. (charter mem.); mem.: APA (pres. 2004, named G. Stanley Hall Lecture 1991, Disting. Career Contbns. to Edn. and Training 1996—97, Eminent Women in Psychology 1998, Am. Psychological Found. award for disting. tchg. 1999—99, fellow divsn. 1, 2, 3, 35 1989), Psychonomic Soc., Am. Assn. Higher Edn. Office: Berger Inst Work, Family, and Children Claremont McKenna Coll Dept Psychology 850 Columbia Ave Claremont CA 91711: APA Pres's Office 750 First St NE Washington DC 20002-4242 Office Phone: 202-336-6074. Office Fax: 909-607-9647, 909-607-9672, 202-336-6157. Business E-Mail: diane.halpern@claremontmckenna.edu.

HALPERN, NORA R., museum director, curator; b. NYC, Dec. 5, 1960; d. Ben and Lois Jule (Gordon) H.; m. Kerry Bryan Brougher, Aug. 9, 1987; children: Emily Clara Brougher, Julia Gordon Brougher. BA, UCLA, 1983, MA, 1990. Curator Frederick Weisman Collections, L.A., 1983-90; founding dir. Frederick R. Weisman Mus. Art, Malibu, Calif., 1992-94; dir. fine arts, Los Angeles; asst. v.p. Sothebys, Beverly Hills, Calif., 1995-97; thesis adv. in art history Oxford Univ., England, 1997—2001; v.p. leadership advancement Americans for the Arts, Washington, 2001—. Adj. prof. Pepperdine U., Malibu, 1992-97; art cons., lectr., writer, critic L.A., 1983-97. Editor: Frederick R. Weisman Foundation of Art, Vol. II, 1985, Selections from Frederick R. Weisman Art Foundation, 1987, Dynaton, Before and Beyond, 1992; author catalog essay; co-curator Street Scenes, a series of installations, Washington, 2006. Trustee L.A. Inst. Contemporary Art, 1983-87; bd. mem. Santa Monica Mus. Art, 1994-97; mem. adv. bd. Frederick R. Weisman Art Found., 1996-2001; nat. chair Advocacy for Arttable. Recipient LA Mayor's award of merit; Helena Rubenstein fellow Whitney Mus. Am. Art, 1981-82. Office: Americans for the Arts 6th Fl 1000 Vermont Ave NW Washington DC 20005 Office Phone: 202-371-2830. Business E-Mail: nhalpern@artsusa.org.

HALPIN, ANNA MARIE, retired architect; b. Murphysboro, Ill., July 24, 1923; d. John William and Anna Christina (Weilmuenster) Halpin. BS in Architecture, U. Ill., 1948. Designer, project arch. various firms, San Francisco, Rome, N.Y.C., 1948-67; editorial dir. Sweet's div. McGraw-Hill, Inc., N.Y.C., 1967-88; freelance cons., 1988-98; ret., 1998. Rep. to constrn. industries coordination com. Am. Nat. Metric Coun., 1974—80. Mem.: AIA (treas., bd. dirs. N.Y. chpt. 1974—78, coll. fellows 1976, nat. bd. dirs. 1977—79, nat. v.p., dir. Found. 1980, Richard Upjohn fellow 1991), Alliance Women Architecture, Constrn. Specifications Inst., Women's Equity Action League (pres. N.Y. 1976—77). Home: Apt 401 1404 NW 122nd St Oklahoma City OK 73114-8052

HALPRIN, ANNA SCHUMAN (MRS. LAWRENCE HALPRIN), dancer; b. Wilmette, Ill., July 13, 1920; d. Isadore and Ida (Schiff) Schuman; m. Lawrence Halprin, Sept. 19, 1940; children: Daria, Rana. Student, Bennington Summer Sch. Dance, 1938-39; BS in Dance, U. Wis., 1943; PhD in Human Services (hon.), Sierra U., Riverside, Calif., 1987; PhD (hon.), U. Wis., 1994, Santa Clara U., Calif.; student, Calif. Arts Coll., Calif., 2003; PhD (hon.), Art Inst. of San Francisco, Calif., 2003. Presenter opening invocation State of the World Forum by spl. invitation from Mikhail S. Gorbachev. Author: Moving Toward Life, Five Decades of Transformative Dance, Dance as a Healing Art, A Teachers' Guide and Support Manual for People with Cancer; dancer: at Kennedy Ctr., Washington, Yerba Buena Ctr. for Arts, San Francisco, Joyce Theatre, NYC, 2001—, d'Autumne Festival Paris, Pompidou Theatre, 2004, Cowell Theatre, Returning Home (1st prize Film Dance Festival N.Y.C., 2004), (film) Moving with the Earth Body, Learning Lessons in Life, Loss & Liberation, 2003, Intensive Care, Reflections on Death and Dying, 2003, Jewish Cmty. Ctr. Kinball Theatre, 2006, San Francisco, Jewish Cmty. Ctr., 2006, others. Bd. dirs. East West Holistic Healing Inst.; mem. Gov.'s Coun. on Phys. Fitness and Wellness. Recipient award Am. Dance Guild, 1980, Guggenheim award, 1970-71, Woman of Wisdom award Bay Area Profl. Women's Network, Tchr. of Yr. award Calif. Tchrs. Assn., 1988, Lifetime Achievement award in visual and performing arts San Francisco Bay Guardian newspaper, 1990, Women of Achievement, Vision and Excellence award, 1992, Balasaraswati/Joy Ann Dewey Bieneke chair for disting. tchg. Am. Dance Festival, 1996, Lifetime Achievement in Modern Dance award Am. Dance Festival, 1997, Lifetime Achievement award Calif. Arts Coun., 2000, Breast Cancer Watch, 2001, Dance Mag. N.Y.C. award, 2004; Person of Yr. in field of Dance award Ballet-ranz, Berlin; named to Isadora Duncan Hall of Fame, Bay Area Dance Coalition, 1986; Nat. Endowment Arts Choreographers grantee, 1976, NEA choreography grantee, 1977, San Francisco Found. grantee, 1981, Calif. Arts. Coun. grantee, 1990—; inductee Marin Women's Hall of Fame, 1998, lifetime achievement award Marin Arts Coun., Sustained Achieve. award Am. Theatre Edn. Assn., 2005, award Healing Arts Network, 2006. Fellow Am. Expressive Therapy Assn.; mem. Assn. Am. Dance, Conscientious Artists Am., San Francisco C. of C. Home and Office: 15 Ravine Way Kentfield CA 94904-2713 Office Phone: 415-461-5362. Personal E-mail: anna@annahalprin.org.

HALSALL, MARY E., biology educator; d. Ernest and Blanche Katarski. BS, Ariz. State U., 1967; MS, UCLA, 1970. Cert. in secondary edn. Ohio, 1990, in young adult/adolescent sci. Nat. Bd. for Profl. Tchg. Standards, 1998. Sci. tchr. Hughes HS, Cin., 1990—98; biology tchr. Mariemont HS, Cin., 1998—; rsch. assoc. Oak Ridge Nat. Labs., Oak Ridge, Tenn.; cooperating tchr. tchr. tng. No. Ky. U., 2005—, Xavier U., 2005—, Miami U., Cin., 2005—. Recipient Gov.'s Ednl. Leadership award, State of Ohio, 1998; grant, CUSI/NSF, 1996-1998. Mem.: NSTA (assoc.), Nat. Assn. Biology Tchrs. (assoc.). Office: Mariemont HS 3812 Pocahontas Ave Cincinnati OH 45227 Office Phone: 513-272-7600. Business E-Mail: mhalsall@mariemontschools.org.

HALSBAND, FRANCES, architect; b. NYC, Oct. 30, 1943; d. Samuel and Ruth H.; m. Robert Michael Kliment, May 1, 1971; 1 child, Alexander H. BA, Swarthmore Coll., 1965; MArch, Columbia U., 1968. Registered architect, N.Y., N.J., Mass., Conn., Ohio, Va., N.H., Pa., D.C., N.C., Ill., Miss., La., Fla.; cert. Nat. Coun. Archtl. Reg. Bds. Arch. Mitchell/Giurgola Archs., N.Y.C., 1968-72; ptnr. R.M. Kliment & Frances Halsband Archs., N.Y.C., 1972—. Vis. critic archtl. design Columbia U., 1975-78, 87, N.C. State U., 1978, Rice U., 1979, U. Va., 1980, Harvard U., 1981, U. Pa., 1981, U. Calif., Berkeley, 1997; dean Sch. Architecture, Pratt Inst., 1991-94; Freidman prof. U. Calif., Berkeley, 1997; Emens Disting. prof. Ball State U., 1998; Kea prof. U. Md., 2000; mem. N.Y.C. Landmarks Preservation Commn., 1984-87; lectr. U. So. Calif., U. Va., Temple U., Washington U., Tulane U., Harvard U., U. Oreg., U. Washington. Projects include: computer Sci. Bldg., Columbia U. (AIA Nat. Honor award 1987), Gilmer Hall addition U. Va., Town Hall, Salisbury Conn., Computer Sci. Bldg., Princeton U. (AIA Nat. Honor award 1994), Case Western Res. Adelbert Hall restoration (AIA Nat. Honor award 1994), Alvin Ailey Am. Dance Theater Found., N.Y.C., hdqs. Marsh & McLennan Co., Ind. Bank Hdqs., Bklyn. Coll. Master Plan, Entrance Pavillion L.I. Rail Rd. Penn Sta. (AIA Nat. award), U.S. Courthouse and Post Office, Bklyn., Yale Div. Sch., Dartmouth Roth Ctr. for Jewish Life, U.S. Courthouse, Gulfport, Miss.; works exhibited in Cooper-Hewitt Mus., Bklyn. Mus., Nat. Acad. Design, Deutsches Architekturmuseum, Frankfourt; author: Annotated Bibliography of Technical Resources for Small Museums, 1983. Trustee Nat. Inst. Archtl. Edn., 1988-93; mem. archtl. rev. panel Fed. Res. Sys., 1993—; mem. U.S. Dept. State Office Fgn. Bldgs. Ops. Archtl. Adv. Bd., 1998—; U.S. Gen. Svcs. Adminstrn. Nat. Register Peer Profls., 1998—. Fellow AIA (exec. bd. N.Y.C. chpt. 1979, pres. N.Y.C. chpt. 1991-92), Century Assn.; mem. Archtl. League N.Y. (exec. bd. 1975—, v.p. arch. 1981-85, pres. 1985-89), Assn. Collegiate Schs. Architecture (N.E. regional dir. 1993-95). Office: RM Kliment & Frances Halsband 255 W 26th St New York NY 10001-8001

HALSEY, JEAN MICHELE, nursing educator; b. St. Louis, Oct. 16, 1949; d. Martha Idabelle Halsey and George Orlander Johnson; 1 child, Rene' Erle Jordan. Diploma, St. Louis Mcpl. Sch. of Nursing, 1972. RN Mo., 1972, Wyo., Calif., 1979, Fla., Okla., 1982, Wash., 2004. Staff nurse St. Louis City Hosp., 1972—75, St. Louis U. Hosp., 1975—78; travel nurse Comprehensive Nursing Svcs., St. Louis, 1979; staff nurse Cedar Sinai Med. Ctr., LA, 1979—82; critical care instr. Los Altos Hosp., Long Beach, Calif., 1981—82; staff nurse City of Faith, Tulsa, Okla., 1982—83, St. Mary's Hosp., West Palm Beach, Fla., 1983—85, PRN Nursing Agy., Clearwater, Fla., 1985—. Vol. nurse educator Am. Heart Assn., West Palm Beach, Fla., 1982—85. Prayer ptnr. City of Faith, Tulsa, Okla., 1982—83. Republican. Achievements include research in the effects of intravenous inderal on the outcome of post myocardial infarction patient; the effects of streptokinase, urokinase and tissue plasminogen activator on myocardial infarction patients; the effects of intravenous nitroglycerine, intravenous amiodarone, intravenous dopamine, intravenous dobutrex, and intravenous nitropresside on the outcomes of cardiogenic shock patients; the use of angioplasty on post myocardial infarction patients; the use of various types of Swan Ganz catheters in the treatment of myocardial infarction patients. Avocations: domestic and European travel, gardening, reading, gourmet cooking. Home: 731 Park Pl West Palm Beach FL 33401 Office: PRN Nursing Agy Ste 102 13575 58th St N Clearwater FL 33760 Office Phone: 727-443-4443. Office Fax: 727-538-4258. Personal E-mail: jhals3@aol.com.

HALSEY, MARTHA TALIAFERRO, Spanish language educator; b. Richmond, Va., May 5, 1932; d. James Dillard and Martha (Taliaferro) H. AB, Goucher Coll., 1954; MA, U. Iowa, 1956; PhD, Ohio State U., 1964. Asst. prof. Spanish Pa. State U., University Park, 1064—1970, assoc. prof., 1970—79, prof., 1979—95, prof. emeritus, 1995—. Vis. Olive B. O'Connor prof. lit. Colgate U., Hamilton, NY, 1983. Author: Antonio Buero Vallejo, 1973, Dictatorship to Democracy: the Recent Plays of Buero Vallejo (La Fundación to Música cercana), 1994; editor: Madrugada, 1969, Hoy es fiesta, 1978, Los inocentes de la Moncloa, 1980, El engaño, Caballos desbocaos, 1981, (with Phyllis Zatlin) The Contemporary Spanish Theater: A Collection of Critical Essays, 1988, Entre actos: Diálogos sobre teatro español entre siglos, 1999, Estreno, 1992-98; gen. editor Estreno Contemporary Spanish Plays, 1992-98, Estreno Studies in Contemporary Spanish Theater, 1998—; mem. editl. bd. Modern Internat. Drama, 1968-75, Ky. Romance Quar.,

1970-76, Annals Contemporary Spanish Lit., 1991—, Tesserae: Jour. Iberian and Latin Am. Studies, 1997—; contbr. articles to profl. jours. Grantee Am. Philos. Soc., 1970, 78, Inst. for Arts and Humanistic Studies, 1977, Program Cultural Coop. Between Spanish Ministry Culture and U.S. Univs., 1992, 94-95. Fellow Hispanic Soc. Am. (hon.); mem. MLA, N.E. MLA, Am. Assn. Tchrs. Spanish and Portuguese, Fellowship of Reconciliation, War Resisters League, Phi Beta Kappa, Phi Sigma Iota, Sigma Delta Pi. Democrat. Episcopalian. Home: 500 E Marylyn Ave Apt I-140 State College PA 16801-5248 Office: Pa State U Dept Spanish University Park PA 16802 Office Phone: 814-238-0270.

HALSNE-BAARDA, ALANA MICHELLE, secondary school educator; b. Park Ridge, Ill., Nov. 18, 1971; d. Howard Osmund and Karen Diane Halsne; m. Brent Eric Baarda, May 31, 2002. BS, Ariz. State U., 1993; MA, Northeastern Ill. U., Chgo., 1998; EdD, Loyola U. Chgo., 2002. Cert. tchr., sch. adminstr. Ill. Tchr. Wickenburg HS, Ariz., 1994—95, Warren Twp. HS Dist. 121, Gurnee, Ill., 1995—; summer sch. tchr. Adlai E. Stevenson HS, Lincolnshire, Ill., 1996—2002, Dist. 211/Palatine HS, Ill., 2003; adj. prof. Am. Intercontinental U., Hoffman Estates, Ill., 2003—, Coll. of Lake County, Grayslake, Ill., 1997—. Textbook reviewer Thomson Pub., Mason, Ohio, 2002—. Contbr. articles to profl. jours. Dance tchr. Granwood Pk. Dist., Gurnee, 1996—97; swim coach Gurnee Pk. Dist., 1996—; Sun. sch. tchr. St. Gilbert Ch., Grayslake, 2000. Mem.: ASCD, Nat. Bus. Edn. Assn., Phi Delta Kappa. Republican. Roman Catholic. Avocation: scuba diving. Office: Warren Twp HS Dist 121 34090 Almond Rd Gurnee IL 60031 Office Phone: 847-599-4324. Personal E-mail: abaarda@wths.net.

HALSTEAD, REBECCA S., career military officer; b. Willseyville, NY; d. Richard and Betty Jeanne Halstead. Grad., U.S. Military Acad., 1981; M in Military Art and Sci., Command and Gen. Staff Coll.; M in Nat. Resource Strategy, Nat. Def. U. Advanced through ranks to gen. US Army; platoon leader 69th Ordinance Co., 559th Artillery Group, Vicenza, Italy, ops. officer, exec. officer; comdr. Hdqs. Co., 63rd Ordinance Co.; materiel officer 80th Ordinance Battalion, Fort Lewis, Wash.; exec. officer battalion and support ops. 101st Airborne Divsn., Fort Campbell, Ky.; comdr. 325th Forward Support Battalion, 25th Infantry divisn., Shofield Barracks, Hawaii, 10th Mountain Divsn Support Command, Fort Drum, NY; exec. asst. to combatant comdr. U.S. So. Command, Miami; dep. commdg. gen. 21st Theater Support Command, Kaiserslautern; comdr./comdt. Army Ordinance Ctr. and Schools Aberdeen Proving Ground, Md., 2006—. Decorated Def. Superior Svc. Medal, Legion of Merit, Meritorious Svc. Medal with five oak leaf clusters, Army Commendation Medal with oak leaf cluster, Army Achievement Medal, Air Assault Badge, Army Staff Badge. Achievements include becoming first female West Point graduate to achieve the rank of general. Office: US Army Aberdeen Proving Ground 2201 Aberdeen Blvd Aberdeen Proving Ground MD 21005-5001*

HALSTED, MARGO, music educator, carillonneur; b. Bakersfield, Calif., Apr. 24, 1938; d. Anthony Charles and Rose Louise (Buzan) Armbruster; m. A. Stevens Halsted, Sept. 12, 1959 (div. 1987); children: Suzanne, Christopher; m. Peter LeSourd, July 21, 2002. BA, Stanford U., Calif., 1960, MA, 1965, U. Calif., Riverside, 1975; diploma, Netherlands Carillon Sch., 1981. Cert. tchr. Calif. Assoc. carillonneur Stanford (Calif.) U., 1967—77; lectr. U. Calif., Riverside, 1977—87; from asst. prof. to prof. emeritus U. Mich., Ann Arbor, 1987—2003, prof. and carillonneur emeritus, 2003—. Cons. in field. Musician: various recitals internationally. Recipient Berkeley medal, U. Calif., 1959, Bell and Citation awards, World Carillon Fedn., 1986, 2003. Mem.: Guild of Carillonneurs in N.Am. (sec., com. chmn., del., Extraordinary Svc. cert. 1997), American Guild Organists, Coll. Music Soc., Am. Musicological Soc. Achievements include discovery of 2 historic carillon manuscripts in Belgium. Avocations: skiing, languages, hiking. Home: 330 Cordova St # 324 Pasadena CA 91101-3602

HALTER, CASSANDRA J., elementary school educator; b. St. Louis, Oct. 20, 1954; d. William W. Hendley Jr. and Billie Jean Hendley; m. Lawrence M. Halter, June 28, 1975; children: Brandon H., Wesley R., Larah N. Richard. A (hon.), St. Louis CC, Florissant Valley, Mo., 1990; BS (hon.), St. Louis U., 1992; MEd, Maryville U., St. Louis, 1999. Tchr. Ferguson Florissant Sch. Dist., Mo., 1989—, sci. fair coord. Mo., 1994—. Com. mem. Boys Scouts Am., St. Louis, 1985—99, Girl Scouts Am., St. Louis, 1985—99; vol. Jump Rope for Heart, Florissant, 1985—2006, Light the Night, St. Louis, 2005. Grantee, Ferguson-Florissant Sch. Dist., 1998. Mem.: NEA, Internat. Reading Assn. Avocations: reading, sports.

HALTERMAN, KAREN ANNIE, psychologist; b. Council Bluffs, Iowa, Nov. 12, 1952; d. Kenneth Harvey Rasmusen and Elinor Anne Clark; m. David Leo Halterman, June 14, 1991; 1 child, Kathryn Jacqueline;children from previous marriage: Kelly Michelle Schlueter, Bruno Arnold Schlueter. AA, Western Wyo. Cmty. Coll., 1981; BA in elem. edn., U. Wyo., 1981. Educational Specialist and Psychologist U. Nebr., 1990. Head tchr. K-8 Sparks Sch. Dist., Nebr., 1982—83; tchr. Kewanee Elem., Cherry County, Nebr., 1983—84, Lake View Elem., Tedd County, SD, 1984—89; sch. psychologist Todd County Schools, SD, 1989—91, Sweetwater County Schools, Rock Springs, Wyo., 1991—97, Box Elder County Schools, Brigham County, Utah, 1997—. Early childhood specialist Sweetwater Children's Ctr., Rock Springs, Wyo., 1992—2003; autism team specialist Box Elder County, Brigham City, Utah, 2004—05. Mem. tag team Communities that Care, Brigham City, Utah, 2004—. Mem.: Utah State Autism Team, Utah Assn. Sch. Psychologists (county rep. 1997—2005), Nat. Assn. Sch. Psychologists. Latter Day Saints. Avocations: sewing, genealogy, gardening. Office: Box Elder County Schools 960 So Main Brigham City UT 84302

HALVORSON, JUDITH ANNE (JUDITH ANNE DEVAUD), elementary school educator; b. Bethesda, Md., Apr. 28, 1943; d. Henri J. and Mary L. (Baumgart) Devaud; m. Peter L. Halvorson, Feb. 4, 1964; 1 child, Peter Chase. BS in Edn., U. Cin., 1965; MA in Edn., U. Conn., Storrs, 1974, Cert. Advanced Grad. Study in Edn., 1980, postgrad. in French, 2000—. Tchr. Greenhills-Forest Park City Schs., Ohio, 1965-67, Weld County Schs., Greeley, Colo., 1969-70, Chaplin Elem. Sch., Conn., 1970-2000; ret., 2000. Mentor Beginning Educator Support program State of Conn. and Chaplin Elem. Sch., 1988-2000; supr. student tchrs. East Conn. State U., U. Conn., U. No. Colo., 1969-2000. Past vice-chmn., past chmn., past sec. Coventry Bd. Edn., Conn., 1981-95; chmn. Coventry Sch. Bldg. com., 1981-92, Coventry Parks and Recreation Com., 1980-82, chmn., 1982; mem. Dem. Town Com. Coventry, 1973-98. Grantee, Nat. Sci. Edn. project, 1977-78; named Outstanding Elem. Tchr. Am., 1974; recipient Citation for Cmty. Leadership, Nat. Women's History Month, 1991; recognized for svc. to pub. edn. in Conn., Conn. Assn. Bds. of Edn., 1993-95, for contbns. to Conn., Beginning Educator Support and Tng. program Conn. State Dept. Edn., 1991-93, for svc. to cooperating tchr. programs Ea. Conn. State U., 1993, 95, for Outstanding Svc. to Pub. Edn., State of Conn., 1995. Mem. NEA (life), Conn. Edn. Assn. (life), Chaplin Edn. Assn. (past pres., v.p., chmn. negotiations 1970-2000), Assn. Ret. Tchrs. Conn., Pi Lambda Theta (past pres., v.p., chmn. membership Beta Sigma chpt. 1974—), Phi Delta Kappa. Episcopalian. Avocations: skiing, French language and culture, leisure/educational travel, watersports, classical music concerts. Home: 90 David Dr Coventry CT 06238-1320 Personal E-mail: jandphalvorson@msn.com.

HALVORSON, MARY ELLEN, education educator, writer; b. Salem, Ohio, Apr. 23, 1950; d. Robert J. and Betty June (Bear) Batzli; m. Thomas Henry Halvorson, June 10, 1972; children: Christine Lynn, Matthew Thomas, Rebecca Lynn. BS in Edn. with distinction, No. Ariz. U., 1972, postgrad., 1973-92, U. Ariz., 1974-76, Ariz. State U., 1975-76, U. Phoenix, 1989-90; PhD in Edn., Calif. Coast U., 2001. Cert. Supt. Ariz., 2001, elem. tchr. libr. Ariz. Tchr. Prescott (Ariz.) Unified Schs., 1972-77, dir. community nature ctr., 1978, reading tutor, 1985-88, family math. tchr., 1989-90, part-time libr., 1991-92; dir. Prescott Study Ctr., 1987-90; writer ednl. materials Herald House, Independence, Mo., 1994—; instr. Yavapai C.C., 1994-96; edn. coord. Yavapai Prescott Indian Tribe, 1996-98; tchr. Prescott Unified Sch. Dist., 1998—99; supt. Tri-City Coll. Prep. H.S., 1999—. Guest speaker Abia Judd Young Authors, Prescott, 1992; math. enthusiast instr. Ariz. Dept. Edn., Prescott, 1989-92; asst. instr. outdoor edn. Ariz. State U., Prescott, 1977-78; tutor English grammar No. Ariz. U., Flagstaff, 1971-72; presenter, U. Oxford (Eng.) Round Table, 2003. Co-author: Arizona Bicentenial Resource Manual, 1975; contbr. book rev. column to Prescott Courier, 1993, also articles to profl. publs. Adult instr. Temple Sch., Independence, Mo., 1985—; sec., bd. dirs. Whispering Pines, Prescott, 1989-93; music docent Prescott Symphony Guild, 1982-85; state Christian edn. dir. Cmty. of Christ. Ch., Ariz., 1977-82, elder, counselor to pastor, 1993—; spokesperson Franklin Heights Homeowners, Prescott, 1985; leader Prescott Pioneers 4-H Club, 1989—, Christian Youth Group, 1985—; fundraiser Graceland Coll., 1993; craft demonstrator Sharlott Hall Mus.; master of ceremonies Prescott Summer Pops Symphony, 1995, 97; pres., founder Mary Ellen Halvorson Edn. Found., 1999—. Recipient 4-H Silver Clover Svc. award, 1995; named Outstanding Young Educator, Prescott Jaycees, 1976, Outstanding Young Women of Am., 1985. Mem. Phi Kappa Phi, Kappa Delta Pi, Sigma Epsilon Sigma. Avocations: piano, sewing, painting. Home: 2965 Pleasant Valley Dr Prescott AZ 86305-7116 Personal E-mail: mary_halvorson@hotmail.com. Business E-Mail: Dr.H@tricityprep.org.

HALWIG, NANCY DIANE, banker; b. Rochester, NY, Sept. 17, 1954; d. Norman Charles and Elizabeth Marie (Callemyn) Graupman; m. John Michael Halwig, June 14, 1975; children: Courtney Elizabeth, John Christopher. BA in Elem. Edn. with honors, Goucher Coll., 1975; M in Fin. Mgmt., Northwestern U., 1979. Br. adminstrv. mgmt. trainee Md. Nat. Bank, Balt., 1975-76; comml. banking officer Am. Nat. Bank, Chgo., 1976-80; v.p. relationship mgr. Citicorp USA, Chgo., 1980-85; v.p. team leader Citicorp N. Am., Atlanta, 1985-89, v.p. region credit officer, 1986-90; v.p. regional mgr. Kredietbank, Atlanta, 1990-95; regional v.p. Bank of Am., FSB, Atlanta, 1995-96, sr. v.p., 1996-98; sr. v.p. regional mktg. mgr. Congress Fin. Corp., Atlanta, 1999—2003; mng. dir. Dovebid Valuation Svc., 2004—. Contbns. com. Citicorp, Chgo., Atlanta, 1984-90; sec. S.W. Cobb Allergy and Asthma, P.C., 1989-97. Fin. com. Big Bros./Big Sisters, Atlanta, 1987-91; leadership forum Scottish Rite Hosp., Atlanta, 1988-92; contbns. contact Scitrek Mus., Atlanta, 1988-90, pres.'s coun., 1990-91; steering com. N.W. Ga. Girl Scouts Friendship Cir., 1993-94, active Friendship Cir., 1993-2003, Juliette Low assoc., 1998-2003; troop treas. Girl Scouts U.S., 1994-96; sustainer Atlanta Women's Fund, 1995—; co-chair Atlanta Women in Fin., 1999. Named one of Atlanta Women to Watch, Atlanta Bus. Chronicle, 1988, Women Looking Ahead News Mag.'s WLA 100's List of Ga.'s Most Powerful Women in Banking & Fin., 1999, 2000, 2001. Mem. Fin. Women Internat. (Paragon Cir., futures com. 1996-97, nominating com. 1997-98), Nat. Assn. Bank Women (found. trustee 1984-85, treas. found. 1985-86, bd. dirs., chmn. fin. com. 1987-88, chmn. task force on child care financing alternatives, restructuring task force 1988-89, nat. conf. program chmn. 1991-92), Aux. Am. Coll. Allergy, Asthma and Immunology, Women's Fin. Exch. (founding bd. dirs.), Atlanta C. of C. (bd. advisors), Atlanta Venture Forum, Assn. Corp. Growth (bd. dirs. Atlanta chpt. 2000—, pres. 2003-04, chpt. pres. dir., 2005—, chair Atlanta capital connection conf. 2003, branding task force 2003-04, exec. planning com., 2004—, global awards chair 2004—), Turnaround Mgmt. Assn., Comml. Fin. Assn. (bd. dirs. 2002-03), Northwestern U. Club Atlanta, Vinings Village Women's Club (pres. 2000-01), Phi Beta Kappa Republican. Avocations: strength training, swimming, running. Home: 4400 Woodland Brook Dr NW Atlanta GA 30339-5365 Office: Dovebid Valuation Svcs Inc 1203 Roberts Blvd Ste 150 Kennesaw GA 30144 Office Phone: 770-590-9200 109. Personal E-mail: ndhalwig@aol.com. Business E-Mail: nhalwig@dovebid.com.

HAM, JILL MARIE, mathematician, educator; b. Waco, Tex., July 28, 1979; d. Earl and Mary Broadway; m. Justin Douglas Ham, July 12, 2003. B of Math., Tex. Tech U., Lubbock, 2001. Tchr. math. Cy-Fair Ind. Sch. Dist., Houston, 2001—04, Midland Ind. Sch. Dist., 2004—. Mem.: Jr. League Midland.

HAMAMOTO, PATRICIA, school system administrator, educator; b. Honolulu, Sept. 30, 1944; BA in History, Calif. State Coll., Long Beach, 1967, profl. tchg. diploma, 1967; education administrator's cert., U. Hawaii M, 1985. Social studies tchr. Fountain Valley H.S., Calif., 1967—72; social studies tchr., dept. chair Iiima Intermediate Sch., Ewa Beach, Hawaii, 1976—81; tchg. grad. asst. geography dept. U. Hawaii at Manoa, 1981—83; tchr. guidance/math. Pearl City H.S., Hawaii, 1985; vice prin. Maui H.S., Kahlui, Hawaii, 1983—85, Nanakul H.S. and Intermediate Sch, Nanakuli, Hawaii, 1985—87; prin. Pearl City Highlands Elem. Sch, Hawaii, 1987—89; pers. specialist ii Office Personnel Svcs. Contract Adminstrn., Honolulu, 1989—91; prin. Pres. William McKinley H.S., Honolulu, 1992—99; dep. supt. Hawaii Dept. Edn., Honolulu, 1999—2001, interim supt., 2001; supt. of edn. Hawaii Dept Edn., Honolulu, 2001—. Mem.: ASCD, Pacific Resources for Edn. and Learning, Coun. of Chief State Sch. Officers, Nat. Assn. Secondary Sch. Prins. Avocations: golf, reading, travel, walking. Home: 1767 Puowaina Dr Honolulu HI 96813 Office: Hawaii Dept Edn PO Box 2360 Honolulu HI 96804-2360 Office Phone: 808-586-3310. E-mail: patricia_hamamoto@notes.k12.hi.us.

HAMBLETON, BETTY BEALL, public health administrator; b. Washington, Dec. 6, 1941; d. Lawrence Edwin Beall Sr. and Edith Emma Donaldson; m. Robert Henry DeGroot, June 6, 1962 (div. Dec. 1980); children: Kimberly Harrell, Nicole Halkyard; m. Neal Hambleton, Aug. 13, 1983; stepchildren: Terry Langmead, Dawn Shreve. AA, Montgomery Coll., 1981; BS cum laude, U. Md., 1986. Program analyst Bur. Health Professions, USPHS, Hyattsville, Md., 1977-81; program specialist Office of Family Assistance Social Security Adminstrn., Washington, 1981-84; program analyst Bur. Health Professions, USPHS, Rockville, Md., 1984-87, pub. health analyst, 1987-90, supervisory pub. health analyst, 1990-95; sr. advisor womens health Health Resources Svcs. Adminstrn. U.S. Dept. Health & Human Svcs., Rockville, 1996—. Mem. nat. adv. com. breast and cervical cancer program Ctrs. for Disease Control and Prevention, Atlanta, 1997—; mem. nat. adv. coun. women's health quality initiative Nat. Assn. Women's Health, Chgo., 1999. Mgr. combined fed. campaign U.S. Dept. Health & Human Svcs., Washington, 1998-99; mem. Washington area Women's Found., 1997—. Recipient Md.'s Gov.'s citation-Woman of Yr., Bus. and Profl. Women's Clubs, 1982. Mem. APHA, Am. Med. Women's Assn., Nat. Acad. Women's Health, Jacobs Inst. for Womens Health, Nat. Acad. Women's Health Med. Edn., Nat. Assn. Women's Health, U. Md. Alumni Assn., Alpha Sigma Lambda. Avocations: fitness walking, golf, gardening. Office: Health Resources & Svcs Adminstrn 5600 Fishers Ln Rm 14 Rockville MD 20857-0001 E-mail: bhambleton@hrsa.gov.

HAMBLIN, SUSAN ANNETTE, elementary school educator; b. Eau Claire, Wis., June 5, 1947; d. Hector Thomas and Catherine (Pattison) Mayheu; m. Gary Harold Hamblin, May 2, 1970; children: Erica, Mark, Bridget. BS, U. Wis., Eau Claire, 1969; MS, U. Wis., Milw., 1973. Tchr. 1st through 8th grades, Chippewa Falls, Eau Claire, Wis., 1970—71, Sussex-Hamilton, Wis., 1971-79, Madison, Wis., 1996—2006; social studies resource tchr. kindergarten through twelfth grade, 2006—. Sales assoc. Casual Corner, 1989—97, 2001—06. Alderperson City of Madison, 1991-2001, coun. pres., 1993-94, acting mayor, 1994. Named One of 25 Most Influential Madison Mag., 1994. Roman Catholic.

HAMBRICK, ERNESTINE, retired colon and rectal surgeon; b. Griffin, Ga., Mar. 31, 1941; d. Jack Daniel and Nannie (Harper) Hambrick Rubens. BS, U. Md., 1963; MD, U. Ill., 1967. Diplomate Am. Bd. Colon and Rectal Surgery, Am. Bd. Surgery. Intern in surgery Cook County Hosp., Chgo., 1967-68, resident in gen. surgery, 1968-72, fellow colon and rectal surgery, 1972-73, attending surgeon, 1973-74, part-time attending surgeon, 1974-80; pvt. practice colon and rectal surgery Chgo., 1974-97; pres. med. staff Michael Reese Hosp., Chgo., 1990-92, chief surgery, 1993-95; founder, chmn. STOP Colon/Rectal Cancer Found., 1997—. Mem. Nat. Colorectal Cancer Round Table, 1997—, steering com. 2000—. Contbr. articles to profl. jours. Trustee Rsch. and Edn. Found., Michael Reese Med. Staff, Chgo., 1994-98, treas., 1994-98. Fellow ACS, Am. Soc. Colon and Rectal Surgeons (v.p. 1992-93, trustee Rsch. Found. 1992-98), Am. Coll. Gastroenterology. Avocations: travel, photography, scuba diving, flying, writing. Office: PMB 133 47 W Division St Chicago IL 60610 Office Phone: 312-944-4636. Personal E-mail: ehcrsone@aol.com.

HAMBRUSCH, SUSANNE, computer engineering educator; MS in Computer Sci., Tech. Univ. of Vienna, 1977; PhD in Computer Sci., Penn. St. Univ., 1982. Prof., Dept. Computer Sci. Purdue Univ., Ind., Ind. Contbr. articles to numerous profl. jours. Fellow: IEEE (mem. tech. com. parallel processing). Achievements include Outstanding Engring. Alum award, UPenn, 2003; TechPoint Mira Edn. award, 2004. Office: Purdue Univ Computer Sci Dept 250 No Univ St West Lafayette IN 47907-2066 Office Phone: 765-494-1831. Office Fax: 765-494-0739. E-mail: seh@cs.purdue.edu.*

HAMBURG, MARGARET ANN (PEGGY HAMBURG), public health administrator; b. Chgo., July 12, 1955; d. David Alan and Beatrix Ann (Mc Cleary) H.; m. Peter Fitzhugh Brown, May 23, 1992; children: Rachel Ann Hamburg Brown, Evan David Addison Brown. BA magna cum laude, Harvard/Radcliffe Coll., 1978; MD, Harvard, 1983. Diplomate Am. Bd. Internal Medicine, Nat. Bd. Med. Examiners. Intern, resident in internal medicine The N.Y. Hosp., Cornell Med. Coll., N.Y.C., 1983-86; spl. asst. to the dir., office of disease prevention and health promotion, office of the asst. sec. for health U.S. Dept. Health and Human Svcs., Washington, 1986-88; spl. asst. to the dir. Nat. Inst. Allergy and Infectious Diseases, NIH, Bethesda, Md., 1988-89, asst. dir., 1989-90; deputy commr. Family Health Svcs., N.Y.C. Dept. Health, N.Y.C., 1990-91; commr. of health N.Y.C. Dept. Health, N.Y.C., 1991-97; asst. sec. planning and evaluation U.S. Dept. HHS, Washington, 1997—2001; v.p. biological programs Nuclear Threat Initiative, Washington, 2001—. Guest investigator The Rockefeller U., N.Y.C., 1985-86; clin. instr. dept. medicine Georgetown U. Sch. Medicine, Washington, 1986-90; asst. prof. clin. pub. health Columbia U. Sch. Pub. Health, N.Y.C., 1991-97; adj. asst. prof. medicine Cornell U. Med. Coll., N.Y.C., 1991-97; scholar Pub. Health Leadership Inst. Ctr. for Disease Control U. Calif., 1992; bd. dirs. N.Y.C. Health Systems Agy., Med. and Health Rsch. Assn., Health Hosps. Corp, Nat. Coun. on Women's Health, Primary Care Devel. Corp.; steering com. women and aids NIH, 1991; bd. govs. Greater N.Y. Hosp. Assn., 1991-97; mem. bd. sci. advisors. Nat. Pub. Radio, 1992-97; com. mem. on substance abuse mental health issues in aides rsch., 1993; advisory bd. mem. Medunsa Trust, Inc., Med. U. So. Africa, 1993-97; mem. defense sci. bd. task force on Gulf War Syndrome U.S. Dept. Defense, 1993—; bd. mem. sci. counselors Nat. Ctr. Infectious Diseases, U.S. Ctrs. for Disease, 1994-97. Editorial bd. mem. Jour. N.Y. Acad. Sci., 1992-97, The Bull. of N.Y. Acad. Medicine, 1992-97, Current Reviews in Pub. Health, 1993-97; contbr. to numerous profl. jours. Vol. attending physician The Washington Free Clinic, Washington, 1988-90; coun. fgn. rels. bd. overseers Harvard U., 1999—; trustee Rockefeller Found. Recipient commendation Pub. Health Svc., 1988, 90, Spl. Recognition award Pub. Health Svc., 1990, cert. of Honor The Women's Club of N.Y., 1993, N.Y. Rotary Club award, 1993, Robert F. Wagner Pub. Svc. award NYU, 1993. Fellow AAAS (med. scis. section com. 1989—), ACP; mem. APHA, Am. Med. Women's Assn., Nat. Acad. Scis., Coun. on Fgn. Rels., Health Care Exec. Forum, N.Y. Acad. Medicine, Pub. Health Assn. N.Y.C., Inst. Medicine, Soc. Social Biology, Women in Health Mgmt., Med. Office: Nuclear Threat Initiative 1747 Pennsylvania Ave NW 7th Fl Washington DC 20006*

HAMBURGER, MARY ANN, management consultant; b. Newark, Aug. 25, 1939; d. Herman and Sylvia (Strauss) Marcus; div. June 1966; children: Bruce David, Marc Laurence. AA, U. Bridgeport, 1960. Office mgr., Millburn, NJ, 1970—84; propr., mgr. Mary Ann Hamburger, Assocs., Maplewood, NJ, 1984—. Tchr. adult edn. South Orange Maplewood Bd. Edn., 1975-83; profl. physician recruiter, NY, NJ; broker med. practices. Mem.: NAFE. Democrat. Jewish. Avocations: reading, music, needlepoint, theater, sports. Home and Office: 74 Hudson Ave Maplewood NJ 07040-1403 Office Phone: 973-763-7394. Personal E-mail: mahassoc@hotmail.com.

HAMBURGER, SUSAN, librarian; b. Newark, Feb. 22, 1949; d. Francis Leo Murphy, Mildred Marie Schultz; m. Joseph Victor Hamburger. AB, Rutgers U., 1975, MLS, 1976; MA, Fla. State U., 1985, PhD, 1994. Cert. archivist. Assoc. univ. libr. Fla. State U., Tallahassee, 1981—89; archivist, head description sect. Va. State Libr. and Archives now Libr. of Va., Richmond, 1989—92; manuscripts cataloger U. Va., Charlottesville, 1992—93, Va. Hist. Soc., Richmond, 1993—94; manuscripts cataloging libr. Pa. State U., University Park, 1994—. Contbr. Book A Guide to the History of Florida, 1989, Book The American Civil War, A Handbook of Research and Literature, 1996 (One of Choice's 625 Outstanding Academic Books of 1997, 1998), Book Encyclopedia of Rural America: The Land and People, 1997 (One of Library Journal's 30 Best Reference Sources 1997, 1998), Book American Book and Magazine Illustrators to 1920 (Dictionary of Literary Biography, vol. 188), 1998, Multi-volume book American National Biography, 1999 (Dartmouth medal, 1999), Book Before the New Deal: Southern Social Welfare History, 1830-1930, 1999, Book Biographical Dictionary of Literary Influences: The Nineteenth Century, 1800-1914, 2001, Book Encyclopedia of New Jersey, 2004, Book Historical African Americans in Sports, 2004, Book Dictionary of Literary Influences: The Twentieth Century, 1914-2000, 2004; author: Out of The Shadows: A Biographical History of African American Athletes, 2006. Mem.: So. Assn. Women Historians, Fla. Hist. Soc., N.Am. Soc. for Sport History (conf. co-mgr. 1998—99), Soc. Am. Archivists (liaison to ALA com. on cataloging: description and access 2000—04, Am. Archivist editl. bd. 2004—), Mid-Atlantic Regional Archives Conf. (chair publs. com. 1995—99, webmaster 1996—2005, Svc. award 1999, 2000, 2004), Phi Alpha Theta, Alpha Sigma Lambda. Avocations: organic gardening, guitar, selling vintage clothes, reading, cats. Office: Pa State Univ 126 Paterno Libr University Park PA 16802 Office Phone: 814-865-1755. Office Fax: 814-863-7293. Business E-Mail: sxh36@psulias.psu.edu.

HAMBY, BARBARA JEAN, writer, poet; b. Chico, Calif., Apr. 20, 1929; d. Frank Llewellyn Fairfield and Grace Ellen Mann (deceased); children: Gail D. Wilson Anderson, Kurt E. Deutscher. Student, U. Wash., 1947-48, Clark Coll., 1990—2001, Portland CC, 2002—. Author: My Muse Has Many Moods, 1995, Trilogy: Love Lines, Life Lines, Laugh Lines, 1998, Find Romance in Later Life, 2003. Named Golden Poet, World of Poetry, 1987, 91, Silver Poet, 1989, People to People Amb. to South Africa, Women Writers, 1998. Mem. Willamette Writers League, Oreg. State Poetry Assn. (2nd prize 1995). Democrat. Unitarian Universalist. Avocations: swimming, travel. E-mail: musebjh@aol.com.

HAMBY, KRISTIE LYNNE, director; b. Wilkesboro, Nc, Dec. 19, 1971; d. Danny Lee and Judith Redmond Hamby. MusB in Edn., Appalachian State U., Boone, N.C., 1995. Dir. bands anson county sch. Anson H.S. Band, Wadesboro, NC, 1995—. 911 communicator Anson County Govt., Wadesboro, NC, 2000—. Recipient Dir. of Honors Band, Wingate U., 1999. Mem.: NC Music Educators Assn. (licentiate). R-Liberal. Meth. Avocations: travel, music, theater. Home: 2839 Nc Hwy 109 N Wadesboro NC 28170 Office: Anson H S Hwy 74 West Wadesboro NC 28170 Office Phone: 704-694-7445. Business E-Mail: kristieb28@hotmail.com.

HAMBY, SHERRY LYNNE, psychologist, researcher; m. Carl Albert Bardi, Apr. 1, 1995; children: Lynnaya, Julian. BS, Coll. William and Mary, 1985, MA, 1989; PhD, U. N.C., 1992. Registered Nat. Register Health Svc. Providers Psychology, lic. clin. psychologist N.C. Rsch. scientist U. N.H., Durham, 1998—99, rsch. asst. prof., 1999—2001; clin. & rsch. psychologist San Carlos (Ariz.) Apache Tribe, 1996—98; rsch. assoc. prof. U. N.C., Chapel Hill, 2002—. Invited prof. U. Lausanne, Dept. Criminology, Switzerland, 2006. Co-author: (book) In Sickness and in Health: The Status of Women's Health in North Carolina, 1993, Out of the Darkness: Contemporary Rsch. Perspectives on Family Violence, 1997, Partner Violence: A Comprehensive Rev. of 20 years of Rsch., 1998, Violence Against Women: A Physician's Guide to Identification and Mgmt., 2003, The Conflict Tactics Scales Handbook, 2003; contbr. articles to profl. jours.; mem. editl. bd.

PsycCritiques, 2005—. Treas. People Helping People, San Carlos, 1998—99; sec. Domestic Violence & Rape Crisis Ctr. of Scotland County, Laurinburg, NC, 2002—03, v.p., 2003—04. Recipient Alfred M. Wellner Meml. award, Nat. Register Health Svc. Providers Psychology, 1998; grantee, Office Environ. Health, Indian Health Svcs., U.S. Dept. of Interior, 1997, Nat. Ctr. Health Stats., Ctrs. Disease Control, 1998—99, L'Office Fédéral de la Formation Professionelle et de la Technologie, La Confédération Suisse, 2001—02, USAF and the Nat. Network Family Resiliency, Pro Juventute. Geneva, Switzerland, 2002—03; Merit fellow, U. N.C., 1987—88, NIMH fellow, U. N.H., 1994—96. Mem.: APA, Nat. Coun. Family Rels., Soc. Psychology Women, Soc. Cmty. and Action (chair rural interest group 1998—2001, S.E. regional coord. 2005—). Avocations: genealogy, travel. Home: 12780 Stratford Dr Laurinburg NC 28352 Office: Possible Equalities P O Box 772 Laurinburg NC 28353

HAMDANI, ZUBEDA A., elementary school educator; b. Bombay, Oct. 23, 1930; arrived in U.S., 1969, naturalized; d. Fazlehusen K. Lakdawala and Amtabai Bokha; m. Abbas H. Hamdani, June 4, 1961; children: Sumaiya, Amal(dec.). BA, U. Bombay, 1954; cert. modern math., Hamilton Coll., Clinton, N.Y., 1967; BS Elem. Edn., U. Wis. Milw., 1974, MS Elem. Edn., 1983. Cert. tchr. K-6, ESL Wis. Dept. Edn. Tchr. St. Josephs Convent Sch., Nagdur, India, 1954—56, Rajkumar Coll., Rajkot, India, 1956—61, Post Said Sch., Cairo, 1962—67, Cairo Am. Coll., 1967—69; substitute tchr. Milw. Pub. Schs., 1974—76, tchr., 1976—94; ret., 2001. Trainer new tchrs. Milw. Pub. Schs., 1976—94; vol. tchr. Adult Learning Ctr., Milw., 1974—76, Milw., 2001—06. Mem.: AAUW (corr. sec. Milw. br. 2001—), Whitefish Bay Women's Club (scholarship com. Milw. br. 2001—). Avocations: swimming, camping. Home: 1729 E Cumberland Blvd Milwaukee WI 53211-1146

HAMECS, FRANCELLA CHESLOCK, secondary school educator; b. Hazleton, Pa., Mar. 7, 1947; d. Richard Mark and Helen (Zanfofski) Cheslock; m. Robert Thomas Hamecs; children: Bryan Robert, Daniel Raphael. BS, Pa. State U., State College, 1969; MA, Fairleigh Dickinson U., Teaneck, NJ, 1978. Tchr. Warminster Schs., Pa., 1969—70, Wayne Bd. Edn., NJ, 1970—. Counselor London Police, 1986—88; chmn. Focus Orgn., London, 1986—88. Leader Team Tobago, Wis., 2004—06. Named Tchr. of Yr., Pa. State U., 2006; recipient Gov.'s award, State of NJ, 2002, Honor award, USMC, 2003. Mem.: NEA, Wayne Edn. Assn. (rep. 2001—06), Pa. State Alumni Assn. Business E-Mail: fhamecs@wayneschools.com.

HAMED, MARTHA ELLEN, government administrator; b. Washington, Jan. 14, 1950; d. Rockford Norris and Dorothy Hope Hamed. AA, George Washington U., 1985, BA in Psychology and Sociology, 1989; MS in Adminstrn., Ctrl. Mich. U., 1999. Command fed. women's program mgr. U.S. Atlantic Fleet, Norfolk, Va., 1978-79; fed. women's program mgr. Naval Ordnance Sta., Indian Head, Md., 1979-80; pers. mgr., Equal Employment Opportunity course dir. Naval Civilian Pers. Command, Arlington, Va., 1980-83; dep. Equal Employment Opportunity officer, site mgr. Ship R&D Ctr., Bethesda, Md., 1983-85, Naval Surface Weapons Ctr., Silver Spring, Md., 1985; command fed. women's program mgr. Naval Sea Sys. Command, Washington, 1985-87, mgr. command tng. programs, 19987-88, asst. dir. awards and performance appraisal programs, 1988-89; asst. mgmt. analysis Office of Insp. Gen., 1989-92; project mgr. Office of Under Sec. of Def., 1992—98; ret. fed. govt., 2005; owner Spiral Path - Women's Empowerment Cir. Chief interag. bus. integration divsn. Def. Human Resource Office Under Sec. Def., 1998—2005. Comnr Anne Arundel County Women's Commn., 1990—92. Named to Oustanding Young Women Am, US Jaycees, 1983; recipient V P Hammer Award Bus Processing Re-Eng, 1995, Commendation Award, VA Vets Benefits Admin, 1996, Award and Medal, Pres's Comn Y2K, 2000, Commendation Award Y2K Transition, Secy Def, 2000. Mem.: AAUW, NOW (life), Fed. Exec. Inst. Alumni Assn., Nat Assn. Ret. Fedn. Employees, Federally Employed Women. Democrat. Avocations: natural history, cats, salt-water fishing. Office Phone: 252-489-9202.

HAMEL, ESTHER VERAMAE, author; b. Circle, Mont., May 20, 1922; d. Frank Max and Catherine (Mahlstedt) Knopp; m. Robert Joseph Hamel, Mar. 16, 1941; children: Kathryn Dee Hamel Kelly, Dennis R. (dec.). Grad. high sch., Ronan, Mont. Co-owner Chalimar Farms, St. Ignatius, Mont., 1942—; lectr. Nat. Coun. State Garden Clubs, 1951—; owner, mgr. Ponderosa Pubrs., St. Ignatius, 1965—; v.p. Rings 'n Things Inc., Missoula, Mont., 1966-72; chief exec. officer, pres. Hamelly Internat., Inc., St. Ignatius and L.A., 1972—. Instr. flower show schs., 1969-80; chmn. landscape licensing bd. State of Mont., 1975-83; dir. fin. orgns. Author: Creative Design with Dried and Contrived Flower, 1971, Gestalt.Flower Show Judging, 1975, Educational Exhibits Explained, 1976, Executive Think Link (TM), 1991, The Quirky World of Intuitive Gambling, 2006; co-author: House of Termites, 1972, Dried Flower Designs, 1973, Feeling Dreams, 1992; editor Mont. Gardens mag., 1956; editor/author newsletters: Judge's Contacts, 1963-65, Nat. Awards News, 1965-69, For Land's Sake, 1971-75; patentee in field. Co-author Bill to Revise Mont. Tax Structure, 1990; bd. dirs. Nat. Teenage Found. Named Golden Poet, Wide World of Poetry, 1990; named Spl. Woman Zonta Internat., 1974, Woman of the Yr. Bus. and Profl. women, 1968, Gardener of the Yr. Mont. Fedn. Garden Clubs, 1958. Mem. Nat. Coun. State Garden Clubs (nat. awards chmn. 1965-69, nat. landscape critics chmn. 1971-75). Office: 1369 Blue Lake Cir Punta Gorda FL 33983-5951

HAMEL, LORIE ANN, psychologist; b. Greenville, S.C., Oct. 23, 1957; d. Francis Joseph and Jessie Pearl (Spoone) Boniface; m. Adrian Paul Cooper, Aug. 7, 1977 (dec. July 1990); children: Paul, Philip, Andrew; m. Loren B. Hamel, Oct. 21, 1995; stepchildren: Chad, Matthew, Jason, Angela BS Elem. Edn., So. Adventist U., Collegedale, Tenn., 1979; MA Cmty. Counseling, Andrews U., Berrien Springs, Mich., 1994; PhD Counseling Psychology, Andrews U., 1997; DMin Formational Counseling, Ashland Theol. Sem., Ohio, 2006. Missionary Ctrl. African Union, Bujumbura, Burundi, 1979—82, Adventist U. Ctrl. Africa, Gisenyi, Rwanda, 1982—90; psychologist U. Med. Specialties, Berrien Springs, Mich., 1994—. Cons., psychologist Adventist Frontier Missions, 1994—2005. Recipient Sirrine scholarship, Greenville, 1975, Steele scholarship, Berrien Springs, 1992, 94, Weniger scholarship, 1994 Mem. APA, Am. Acad. Experts in Traumatic Stress, Internat. Soc. Traumatic Stress Studies, Phi Kappa Phi Seventh-day Adventist. Avocations: travel, birdwatching, skiing. Office: Univ Med Ctr Berrien Springs MI 49103

HAMEL, SUZANNE PATRICE, lawyer; b. Haverhill, Mass., Dec. 8, 1972; BS magna cum laude, Lesley Coll., 1994; JD, George Washington U., 1997. Bar: Mass. 1998, Md. 1998, Conn. 1998, DC 1999. Intern Equal Employment Opportunity Commn.; law clk. to Hon. David S. Tatel US Ct. Appeals (DC Cir.); assoc. Wilmer Cutler Pickering Hale and Dorr LLP, Edwards Angell Palmer & Dodge LLP, Boston. Mem.: Mass. Bar Assn., Boston Bar Assn. Avocations: travel, home design, independent films. Office: Edwards Angell Palmer & Dodge LLP 111 Huntington Ave Boston MA 02199 Office Phone: 617-951-3374. Office Fax: 617-227-4420. E-mail: shamel@eapdlaw.com.*

HAMID, SUZANNE L, academic administrator; d. B A and Helen Hamid. Ed. D (ABD), U. of Tenn., Knoxville, TN, 1997—2002. Dir., student events Lee U., Cleveland, Tenn., 1992—95, dir., first-year programs, 1996—. Workshop facilitator Wadsworth Pub. Co, Belmont, Calif., 2000—. Editor: (monograph) Peer Leadership: A Primer On Program Essentials. Supportor of fgn. missions. Grantee Strengthsfinder Project, Fipse In Conjunction With Cccu, 2001. Mem.: Aahe, Noda. Achievements include research in Peer Leadership. Home: 408 Barberry Drive Cleveland TN 37312 Office: Lee University 1120 N Ocoee St Cleveland TN 37312 Personal E-mail: shamid2leeuniversity.edu. E-mail: shamid@leeuniversity.edud.

HAMIL, BURNETTE WOLF, science educator; d. Jessie Lang and Stella Posey Wolf; m. James G. Hamil; 1 child, Olivia Hamil Penrod. BS in Edn., Miss. Coll.; MS in Curriculum and Instrn., U. So. Miss., Hattiesburg, PhD, 1994. Cert. secondary sci. tchr. Miss. Dept. Edn., 1970. Tchr. sci. Hawkins Mid. Sch., Forest, Miss., 1970—92; assoc. prof. Miss. State U., 1996—. Sci. program improvement reviewer NSTA, Arlington, Va., 2005—06; reviewer Nat. Coun. for Accreditation of Tech. Edn. Author: (grant) Preparing Teachers to Deliver Technology-Rich, Problem-Based Learning Experiences. Del. NSTA, Arlington, 2001—04. Named to Wall of Fame, Hawkins Mid. Sch., 2005. Mem.: Miss. Sci. Tchrs. Assn. (pres. 2003—04, Outstanding Coll. Sci. Tchr. 2002), Mind, Brain and Edn. Soc., Phi Kappa Phi, Phi Delta Kappa (Outstanding Rsch. award 2002). Methodist. Achievements include research in problem solving perception in education. Office Phone: 662-325-7109.

HAMILTON, AMELIA WENTZ (AMY WENTZ), elementary school educator; b. Elizabethtown, Ky., Mar. 31, 1970; d. Willard Mason and Judith Parr Wentz; m. Brian Joseph Hamilton; children: Clinton, Levi, Samuel Jewell. B in Music Edn., Morehead State U., 1993, BA in Edn., 1994; MA in Edn., Western Ky. U., 1997. Rank I in edn. adminstrn. (elem. principalship). Music tchr. Flaherty Elem. Sch., Ekron, Ky., 1995—, extended sch. svc. tchr., 1995—. Testing cons. Ky. Instrnl. Results Info. Sys. Stewart Pepper Mid. Sch., Brandenburg, Ky., 1995; substitute tchr. Meade County Bd. Edn., Brandenburg, 1995; test scoring Ky. Instrnl. Results Info. Sys. Advanced Sys., Lexington, 1993—94; mem. scholarship com. Flaherty Elem. PTO, Ekron, 2001—. Named to All-Collegiate Band, Ky. Music Educators Nat. Conv., 1992, 1993; recipient 18 Outstanding Salesperson awards, The Castle, 1993—95. Mem.: Mothers of Preschoolers, Am. Orff-Schulwerk Assn., Meade County Edn. Assn., Ky. Edn. Assn., Ky. Music Educators Nat. Conf., Ky. Orff-Schulwerk Assn., Meade County Women's Dem. Club, Pi Kappa Phi, Gamma Beta Phi, Sigma Alpha Iota (life), Chi Omega (life). Baptist. Avocations: vocal music, reading. Home: 326 Homeview Dr Brandenburg KY 40108 Office: Flaherty Elem Sch 2615 Flaherty Rd Ekron KY 40117 Personal E-mail: brianamy@bbtel.com.

HAMILTON, ANN HOLLINGSWORTH, library director; b. Bessemer, Ala., Feb. 6, 1947; d. Evelyn Virginia and Alonzo Ray Hamilton. BA, Ala. Coll., Montevallo, 1968; MA, Miss. State U., Starkville, MS, 1970; M.Librarianship, Emory U., Atlanta, 1971; Diploma for Advanced Study in Librarianship, Emory U., 1988. Cert. archives adminstr. Ga. Dept. of Archives and History, 1971. Ref. libr. (asst. prof.) Birmingham-Southern Coll., Birmingham, Ala., 1971—85; libr. dir. Va. Intermont Coll., Bristol, 1985—87; head, circulation dept. (assoc. prof.) U. of Ala. Librs., Tuscaloosa, 1987—92; assoc. dir. librs., assoc. prof. Ga. So. U., Statesboro, 1992—94, assoc. libr., assoc. prof., 1994—2001, assoc. dean of the libr. and assoc. u. libr. (prof.), 2001—. Contbr. chapters to books. Bd. dir. Birmingham Internat. Ednl. Film Festival, Birmingham, Ala., 1984—85; acad. and instrnl. support adv. com. mem. Va. Highlands C.C., Abingdon, Va., 1987—89; libr. adv. bd. Ogeechee Tech. Inst., Statesboro, Ga., 1994—95; Ga. hist. records adv. bd. Ga. Heritage Planning Com., Atlanta, 1999—2000; mem. Spl. Olympics Ga., 2001—, area thirteen mgmt. team and sec., 2001—05. Grantee Vis. Prof. with Birmingham City Coun., Kellogg Found., 1978, Sabbatical grantee, Mellon Found., 1981; scholar Grad. Tchg. Assistantship - Dept. of History, Miss. State U., 1969—70, Grad. Assistantship, Emory U., 1970—71. Mem.: Ala. Libr. Assn., Ga. Libr. Assn. (pres. 1998—99, Bob Richardson awrd for significant contbns. 2003), Southeastern Libr. Assn. (sec. 1992—94, treas. 1994—96, pres. 2002—04, Mary Utopia Rothrock award 2006), ALA (governing coun. 2001—, chair, chpt. rels. com. 2005—06), Bulloch County Hist. Soc. (life), Kappa Mu Epsilon, Phi Alpha Theta, Beta Phi Mu (pres. beta kappa chpt. 1979—80). Democrat-Npl. Episcopalian. Avocations: reading, photography, cross stitch. Home: 211 Wendwood Dr Statesboro GA 30458-5075 Office: Georgia Southern University Zach S Henderson Library Box 8074 Statesboro GA 30460-8074 Office Phone: 912-681-5115. Office Fax: 912-681-0093. E-mail: ahamilton@georgiasouthern.edu.

HAMILTON, ANN KATHERINE, artist; b. Lima, Ohio, June 22, 1956; d. Robert S. and Elizabeth B. Hamilton; m. Michael John Mercil, Nov. 1993; 1 child, Emmett Moore Mercil. BFA in Textile Design, U. Kans., 1979; MFA in Sculpture, Yale Sch. Art, 1985; PhD (hon.), RI Sch. Design, 2002. Prof. Ohio State U., 2003—. Asst. prof. U. Calif., Santa Barbara, 1985-91. One woman shows include Santa Barbara Contemporary Arts Forum, Calif., 1985, The Mus. Contemporary Art, LA, 1988, San Diego Mus. Contemporary Art, La Jolla, Calif., 1990, 21st Internat. Sao Paulo Bienal, 1991, Louver Gallery, NYC, 1991, Tate Gallery, Liverpool, 1994, Mus. Modern Art, NYC, 1994, Ruth Bloom Gallery, Santa Monica, Calif., 1994, Inst. Contemporary Art, Phila., 1995, Wexner Ctr. for the Arts, Columbus, Ohio, 1996, Venice Biennale, Italy, 1999, Akira Ikeda Gallery, Japan, 2001, Irish Mus. Modern Art, Dublin., 2002, Wanas Found., Sweden, 2002 others. Exhibited in group shows at The Exit Gallery, Banff, Alta., Can., 1981, Walter Phillips Gallery, Banff, Alta., Can., 1981, Twining Gallery, NYC, 1983, 84, 90, Oakland Mus., Cleve. Inst. Art, 1987, Carl Solway Gallery, Cin., 1987, Whitney Mus. Am. Art, Philip Morris, NY, 1987, Santa Barbara Mus. Art, Calif., 1988, Nat. Mus. Modern Art, Kyoto, 1990, BMW Gallery, NYC, 1990, New Orleans Mus. Art, 1990, Carnegie Mus. Art, Pitts., 1991, Hayward Gallery, South Bank Ctr. London, 1992, Stux Gallery, NYC, 1992, Whitney Mus. Am. Art at Equitable Ctr., NY, 1991, Mus. Modern Art, NYC, 1993, Cleve. Ctr. Contemporary Art, 1994, Art Inst. Chgo., 1995, others. Commissioned projects Mess Hall, Headlands Ctr. for the Arts, Sausalito, Calif., 1989-90, San Francisco Pub. Libr. Commn., Arts Commn. San Francisco, 1990-93; contbr. articles to profl. jours. Recipient Bessie award NY Ann. award in the performing arts, creator category, 1988, Guggenheim Meml. Fellowship, 1989, Louis Comfort Tiffany Found. award, 1990, CAA Artist award, 1992, Skowhegan medal for Sculpture, 1992, NEA Visual Arts Fellowship, 1993, MacArthur Fellowship, 1993. Office: Ohio State U Dept Art 146 Hopkins Hall 128 N Oval Hall Columbus OH 43210

HAMILTON, BARBARA DENISE, computer science educator; d. Travis Jean Cooper and Bobbie Lois Roach; m. Coltis Demonz Hamilton, Dec. 17, 2004; 1 child, Sharbrodric Demarte Young. BBA, So. Ark. U., Magnolia, 1996; MBA, Tex. A&M U., Texarkana, 2003. Microsoft officer user specialist Microsoft. City ct. clk. Eldorado Police Dept., Ark., 1997—99; family svc. adviser FACT, Inc., Eldorado, Ark., 1999—2000; computer support specialist So. Ark. U., Magnolia, 2000—03; instr. So. Ark. U. Tech., Camden, 2003—. Adviser Phi Beta Lambda, Camden, 2005—. Mem. Leadership Magnolia, 2004—05. Recipient NISOD Excellence award, 2006. Mem.: AAWTYC (assoc.), Sigma Gamma Rho (assoc.). Office: So Ark U Tech 100 Carr Rd Magnolia AR 71753 Office Phone: 870-574-4466. Office Fax: 870-574-4474. Business E-Mail: bhamilto@sautech.edu.

HAMILTON, BEVERLY LANNQUIST, investment executive; b. Roxbury, Mass., Oct. 19, 1946; d. Arthur and Nancy Lannquist. BA cum laude, U. Mich., 1968; postgrad., NYU, 1969-70. V.p. Auerbach, Pollak & Richardson, N.Y.C., 1972-75, Morgan Stanley & Co., N.Y.C., 1975-80, United Techs., Hartford, Conn., 1980-87; dep. comptr. City of N.Y., 1987-91; pres., ret. ARCO Investment Mgmt Co, L.A., 1991-2000. Bd. dirs. Oppenheimer Funds, Am. Fund's Emerging Markets Growth Fund; trustee The Calif. Endowment, Monterey Inst. Internat. Studies, Cmty. Hosp. Monterey, Middlebury Coll.; investment coms. U. Mich. Trustee Hartford Coll. for Women, 1981-87, Stanford Univ. Mgmt. Co., 1991-99; bd. dirs. Inst. for Living, 1983-87. Mem. NCCJ (bd. dirs. 1987-91). Address: 5485 Quail Meadows Dr Carmel CA 93923-7971

HAMILTON, CANDIS LEE, counselor; b. Saratoga, N.Y., Apr. 8, 1942; d. Harry Lee Van Arnam and Lois Carey Pickett; m. Woodbury Rogers Hamilton, Apr. 16, 1963; children: Sonya Ann Thaysen, David Sean, Lise Carey Hamilton-Hall, Paul Tate. Student, Brockport Coll., Tavistock Inst., Harvard U., Moreno Inst., 1976—80, U. Rochester, 1974—78, Sisters of St. Joseph Spirituality Ctr., Rochester, NY, 1986—90, St. Bernard's Inst., 1991. Founder, co-pres. Penfield Learning Disabilities Assn., NY, 1971—78; program designer, facilitator, instr. Designs for Anti- Racism, Rochester, 1973—81; program facilitator Sisters of St. Joseph Spirituality Ctr., Rochester, 1992—2000, spiritual dir., adj. staff, 1995—. Author: Who am i; Who are U; Who are we?, Woman's Workbook on Mark's Mosaic of Daily Disciple-ship. Facilitator Wellsprings, Rochester, 1991—96; facilitator, instr. Rochester Jungian Soc., 1990—98; team coord. Sisters of St. Joseph Spirituality Ctr., 1998—2001. Recipient certs. and letters of appreciation, various individuals and local ch. groups, 1971—2003. Democrat. Roman Catholic. Avocations: snorkeling, trampoline, recycling. Home: 844 Whalen Rd Penfield NY 14526

HAMILTON, DAGMAR STRANDBERG, lawyer, educator; b. Phila., Jan. 10, 1932; d. Eric Wilhelm and Anna Elizabeth (Sjöström) Strandberg; m. Robert W. Hamilton, June 26, 1953; children: Eric Clark, Robert Andrew Hale, Meredith Hope. AB, Swarthmore Coll., 1953; JD, U. Chgo. Law Sch., 1956, Am. U., 1961. Bar: Tex. 1972. Atty. civil rights divsn. U.S. Dept Justice, Washington, 1965-66; asst. instr. govt. U. Tex., Austin, 1966-71; lectr. Law Sch. U. Ariz., Tucson, 1971-72; editor, rschr. Assoc. William O. Douglas U.S. Supreme Ct., Washington, 1962-73, 75-76; editor, rschr. Douglas autobiography Random House Co., 1972-73; staff counsel Judiciary Com. U.S. Ho. of Reps., 1973-74; asst. prof. L.B. Johnson Sch. Pub. Affairs U. Tex., Austin, 1974-77, assoc. prof., 1977-83, prof., 1983—, assoc. dean, 1983-87. Interdisciplinary prof. U. Tex. Law Sch., 1983—; vis. prof. Washington U. Law Sch., St. Louis, 1982, U. Maine, Portland, 1992; Godfrey Disting. vis. prof. U. Maine Law Sch., 2002; vis. fellow U. London, QMW Sch. Law, 1987—88; vis. prof. U. Maine, Portland, 2002; vis. fellow U. Oxford Inst. European & Comparative Law, 1998. Contbr. to various publs. Mem. Tex. State Bar Assn., Am. Law Inst., Assn. Pub. Policy Analysis and Mgmt., Swarthmore Coll. Alumni Coun. (rep.), Kappa Beta Phi (hon.), Phi Kappa Phi (hon.). Democrat. Mem. Soc. Of Friends. Home: 403 Allegro Ln Austin TX 78746-4301 Office: U Tex LBJ Sch Pub Affairs Austin TX 78713 Office Phone: 512-232-4019. Business E-Mail: dagmar.hamilton@mail.utexas.edu.

HAMILTON, ELAINE H., retired nurse, artist; b. Osage, Iowa, Sept. 22, 1923; d. Maurice Marshel Hudson and Pearl Baker; m. Thomas R. Hamilton (div.); children: Maxine M., Ann E. Reynolds. RN, St. Lukes Meth. Sch. Nursing, Cedar Rapids, Iowa, 1944; AA, San Francisco City Coll., 1984; BA in Art Printmaking, San Francisco U., 1988; MA in Liberal Studies, U. Maine, 1992. Workshop art tchr., Bango, Maine, 1992—98, Orono, Maine, 1998—2000; RN, 1944—88. 2d lt. U.S. Army, 1945—49. Mem.: Nat. Mus. of Women in Arts, Banger Art Assn., Calif. Printmaker Assn. Democrat. Methodist. Home: 5008 Ingrsoll Ln 3A Des Moines IA 50312

HAMILTON, HILDA WINGO, elementary school educator; b. Washington, Oct. 8, 1962; d. Granville Ross and Margaret Soper Wingo; m. Scott T. Hamilton, Sept. 13, 1986; children: Kara Marie, Laura Kate. BS, Appalachian State U., Boone, NC, 1984, MA in Edn., 1990. Lic. tchr. NC, 1984, cert. early adolescent generalist Nat. Bd. Profl. Tchg. Stds., 1994, Nat. Bd. Profl. Tchg. Stds., 2004. Grade 6 tchr. A.L. Stanback Jr. H.S., Hillsborough, NC, 1984—85; grade 9 tchr. C. W. Stanford Jr. H.S., Hillsborough, 1895—1986; grade 7 tchr. Miller Creek (NC) Intermediate Sch., 1986—92; grades 6-8 tchr. Mabel Elem. Sch., Zionville, NC, 1992—97; grade 8 tchr. Rugby Mid. Sch., Hendersonville, NC, 1997—. Pvt. practice edn. cons., Hendersonville, NC, 1994—; Nat. Bd. Profl. Tchg. Stds. candidate support group co-dir. Henderson County Schs., 1999—; NC master tchr. bd. mem. Prentice Hall, Hollywood, Fla., 2003—04. Ptnr. Watauga Youth Network, Boone, NC, 1988; hunger walk student coun. sponsor Rugby Mid. Sch., Hendersonville, 1999; youth group advisor First Presbyn. Ch., Boone, NC, 1991. Named Tchr. of Yr., Millers Creek Intermediate Sch., 1990, Rugby Mid. Sch., 2004, NC Region 8 Mid. Sch. Team of Yr., NC Mid. Sch. Assn., 2005; named one of, Outstanding Young Women Am., 1987; recipient C.B. Eller Excellence in Tchg. award, C.B. Eller Found., 1990, Outstanding Young Educator Disting. Svc. award, Henderson County Lion's Club, 1997; grantee, Wilkes County Edn. Found., 1990. Mem.: NEA, NC Assn. Educators, Alpha Delta Kappa. Independent. Avocations: travel, reading, photography. Home: 114 White Cedar Ln Hendersonville NC 28791 Office: Rugby Middle School 3345 Haywood Rd Hendersonville NC 28791 Office Phone: 828-891-6566.

HAMILTON, JANE, writer; b. 1957; Author: The Book of Ruth, 1988 (PEN/Ernest Hemingway Found. award, 1989), The Frogs Are Still Singing, 1989, A Map of the World, 1994, The Short History of a Prince, 1998 (Heartland prize for fiction), Disobedience, 2000, short stories. Office: Doubleday Pubs 1540 Broadway New York NY 10036

HAMILTON, JANET RENEE, protective services official; b. Oklahoma City, Sept. 22, 1959; d. Elvert L. Newton and Jelila M. Ramay; m. Jerry A. Hamilton, Oct. 14, 1995; children: Janette M. Sierra L. AA, Rose State Coll., 1985. Emergency Number Professional Nat. Emergency Number Assn., Fla., 2002. Account clk. Okla. Health Dept., Oklahoma City, 1985—88; constrn. sec. T A Forsberg, Punta Gorda, Fla., 88—91; 911 dir. Charlotte County Sheriffs Office, 1992—. Mem. Ams. with Disability Adv. Com., Port Charlotte, Fla., 2001—03, Fla. 911 Legis. Com., 2003—04, Nat. Emergency Number Assn. Pub. Edn., 2003—04. Republican. Presbyterian. Avocations: travel, crafts, boating. Office Phone: 941-575-5339. Office Fax: 941-575-5335. E-mail: hamilton@ccso.org.

HAMILTON, JEAN See CHAUDOIR, JEAN

HAMILTON, JEAN, financial services executive, software executive; BS in Comms., U. Ill.; MBA in Fin. and Acctg., U. Chgo. Sr. v.p., head N.E. banking First Nat. Bank Chgo. (now Bank One Corp.); pres. Prudential Capital Group, Prudential Asset Sales and Syndicates, 1988—95, Prudential Diversified Group, 1995—98; exec. v.p. Prudential Fin., Newark, 1998—2002; CEO Prudential Instl. Prudential Ins. Co. Am., 1998—2002; CEO Broadstairs Capital, 2002—, Xonos.com, Inc., 2006—; mem. Brock Capital Group, LLC, 2005—. Bd. mem. Renaissance Re Holdings, LTD, First Eagle Funds and First Eagle Variable Funds, Four Nations, Grad. Sch. Bus., U. Chgo.; former bd. mem. The Prudential Found.; bd. mem. Prudential Investment & Mgmt. Svcs., Prudential P&C Holdings, Pruco Life, The Prudential Bank & Trust Co., The Prudential Savings Bank, The Ind. Coll. Fund NJ, Rewards Plus, The Women's Econ. Roundtable, Standing Tall, Glass Roots, Nat. Urban League; with Women's Forum NY, Women's Forum Edn. Fund; mem. adv. bd. Hudson Opera House. Named one of Bus. Ins. Top 100 Women in Ins., Risk Mgmt. and Employee Benefits; named to Who's Who in NJ Bus. Leader List, NJ Star Ledger's 10 Most Powerful Women in Bus. List, Women Bus. Leaders list, Bus. News, NJ. Mem.: Com. of 200, Internat. Women's Forum, Cosmopolitan Club, Econ. Club NY.

HAMILTON, JEAN CONSTANCE, judge; b. St. Louis, Nov. 12, 1945; AB, Wellesley Coll., 1968; JD, Washington U., St. Louis, 1971; LLM, Yale U., 1982. Atty. Dept. of Justice, Washington, 1971-73, asst. U.S. atty. St. Louis, 1973-78; atty. Southwestern Bell Telephone Co., St. Louis, 1978—81; judge 22d Jud. Circuit State of Mo., St. Louis, 1982-88; judge Mo. Ct. Appeals (ea. dist.), 1988-90, U.S. Dist. Ct. (ea. dist.) Mo., 1990—, chief judge, 1995—2002. Office: US Courthouse 111 S 10th St Saint Louis MO 63102

HAMILTON, JEANNE MARIE, retired librarian; b. Richmond, Va., Aug. 2, 1944; d. Charles Gilbert and Regina Elizabeth Barrett; m. Leslie Clark Hamilton. BA, Wheeling Jesuit U., 1966. Congl. rsch. specialist Libr. of Congress, Wash., DC, 1966—2000; ret. Mem. Rep. Nat. Com., 2000—; vol. White House. Mem.: SW Fla. Med. Res. Corp. Found, S W Fla. Med. Res. Corps., Garage Sisters. Republican. Cath. Avocation: tap dancing. Home: 1332 Sand Castle Rd Sanibel FL 33957

HAMILTON, JOAN NICE, editor-in-chief; b. Chgo., 1948; d. William and Dorothy Nice. Grad., Pomona Coll., 1970. Former editor High Country News; editor Climbing Mag.; editor-in-chief Sierra Mag., San Francisco. Contbr. articles to Audubon, Defenders, Nat. Wildlife Mags. Office: Sierra Mag 85 2nd St San Francisco CA 94105-3459

HAMILTON, LAURELL K., writer; b. Heber Springs, Ark., 1963; Author: Guilty Pleasures, 1993, The Laughing Corpse, 1994, Circus of the Damned, 1995, The Lunatic Cafe, 1996, Bloody Bones, 1996, The Killing Dance, 1997, Burnt Offerings, 1998, Blue Moon, 1998, Obsidian Butterfly, 2000, A Kiss of

Shadows, 2001, Narcissus in Chains, 2002, A Caress of Twilight, 2003, Seduced By Moonlight, 2004, Incubus Dreams, 2004 (Publishers Weekly Bestseller). Office: c/o Author Mail Berkley Pub Penguin Group 375 Hudson New York NY 10014

HAMILTON, LINDA, actress; b. Salisbury, MD, Sept. 26, 1956; m. Peter Horton, 1979 (div. 1980); m. Bruce Abbott Dec. 19, 1982 (div. 1989); 1 child, Dalton Abbott; m. James Cameron, July 26, 1997 (div. 1999); 1 child, Josephine Archer. Appeared in plays Looice, 1975, Richard III, 1977, The Night of the Iguana, 2006; films include T.A.G.: The Assassination Game, 1982, Children of the Corn, 1984, The Stone Boy, 1984, The Terminator, 1984, Black Moon Rising, 1986, King Kong Lives!, 1986, Mr. Destiny, 1990, Terminator 2: Judgment Day, 1991, Silent Fall, 1994, The Shadow Conspiracy, 1996, Dante's Peak, 1997, The Secret Life of Girls, 1999, Skeletons in the Closet, 2001, Wholey Moses, 2003, Jonah, 2004, Smile, 2005, Missing in America, 2005, The Kid and I, 2005; TV series include The Secrets of Midland Heights, 1980-81, King's Crossing, 1982, Beauty and the Beast, 1987-89 (Golden Globe award nomination 1988, 89), (voice) Hercules, 1998, Thief, 2005-; TV movies include Reunion, 1980, Rape and Marriage - The Rideout Case, 1980, Country Gold, 1982, Secrets of a Mother and Daughter, 1983, Secret Weapons, 1985, Club Med, 1986, Go Toward the Light, 1988, The Way to Dusty Death, 1995, A Mother's Prayer, 1995, On The Line, 1998, Point Last Seen, 1998, Resuers: Stories of Courage - Two Couples, 1998, The Color of Courage, 1999, (voice) Batman Beyond: The Movie, 1999, Sex and Mrs. X, 2000, Bailey's Mistake, 2001, Silent Night, 2002. Office: United Talent Agency 5th Floor 9560 Wilshire Blvd Fl 5 Beverly Hills CA 90212-2400*

HAMILTON, LINDA HELEN, psychologist; b. NYC, Dec. 2, 1952; d. Peter and Helen (Casey) Homek; m. Terrence White, Aug. 10, 1974 (div. 1983); m. William Garnett Hamilton, Dec. 29, 1984. BA summa cum laude, Fordham U., 1984; MA, Adelphi U., 1986, PhD, 1989. Lic. psychologist NY. Dancer N.Y.C. Ballet, 1969-88; clin. psychologist Fair Oaks Hosp., Summit, N.J., 1989-90, Miller Inst. for Performing Artists, N.Y.C., 1989-95; pvt. practice N.Y.C., 1991—. Rsch. assoc. Miller Inst. Performing Artists, NYC, 1987-95; chair dance com. MedArt U.S.A., NYC, 1990-92; cons. psychologist Sch. Am. Ballet, NYC, 1991—, Alvin Ailey Am. Dance Ctr., NYC, 1996—; wellness cons. NYC Ballet, 2003-06, psychologist, 2006-; advice columnist Dance Mag., 1992—, sr. editor, 1997—; adj. assoc. prof. Fordham U., 1998-2002; co-leader Performing Arts Medicine Delegation to Russia and Ea. Europe, 1992; co-designer Wellness Program, N.Y.C. Ballet, 2001—. Author: The Person Behind the Mask: A Guide to Performing Arts Psychology, Advice for Dancers; featured in: (documentaries) by European Media Support; Dying to be Thin (Nova), 2001. Mem. exec. com. BFA Dance Program, Fordham U., 1997—. Miller Inst. Performing Artists grantee, 1987. Mem. APA (Daniel E. Berlyne award 1993), Fordham Psychological Assn. (outstanding achievement award for alumna), 2004, Internat. Assn. Dance Medicine and Sci. (mem.-at-large 2003-, chair media com. 2003—), Performing Arts Medicine Assn., Dance Profls. Assocs. (bd. dirs. 1997—2002), Psi Chi. Avocations: travel, reading, opera, ballet. Office: 2000 Broadway New York NY 10023-5028 Office Phone: 212-362-8308. Personal E-mail: lindahamilton1@msn.com.

HAMILTON, LISA GAY, actress; b. LA, Mar. 25, 1964; d. Ira and Tina. Grad., Juilliard Sch., 1988. Appeared in films: Krush Groover, 1985, Reversal of Fortune, 1990, Naked in New York, 1994, Drunks, 1995, Palookaville, 1995, Twelve Monkeys, 1995, Palookaville, 1995, Nick and Jane, 1997, Lifebreath, 1997, Jackie Brown, 1997, Drunks, 1997, Beloved, 1998, True Crime, 1999, Ten Tiny Love Stories, 2001, The Sum of All Fears, 2002, The Truth About Charlie, 2002, Nine Lives, 2005; TV appearances include Homicide, 1993, Way Cool, 1991, Naked In NY, 1993, Homicide: Life on the Street, 1993, New York Undercover, 1994, All My Children, 1994, Law & Order, 1995, Clarissa, 1995, Murder One, Chicago Hope, The Practice, 1997-2003, One Life to Live, 1996, The Defenders: Choice of Evils, 1998, Ally McBeal, 1998, Swing Vote, 1999, A House Divided, 2000, Hamlet, 2000, Sex and the City, 2002, The Practice, 2003, The L Word, 2004, ER, 2005, Law & Order, Special Victims Unit, 2006; dir., prodr. Beah: A Black Woman Speaks, 2003; on Broadway plays include The Piano Lesson; (off Broadway) Measure for Measure, N.Y.C., Valley Song (Obie award, Clarence Derwent award, Drama Desk nominee). Office: Writers Artists 360 N Crescent Dr Bldg North Beverly Hills CA 90210-6818

HAMILTON, MARCELLA LAURETTE, social worker; b. Charleston, SC, Jan. 24, 1964; d. Lawrence and Dorothy Hamilton; children: Kayla Marie, Marcella Laurette Jr. BSW, NC State U., 1994; MSW, U. NC, Chapel Hill, 1996. Lic. Master Social Worker SC, 2002. Youth leadership coord. Bldg. Together Ministries, Raleigh, NC, 1996—98; vis. lectr., rschr. NC State U., Raleigh, 1998—99; foster care coord. Haven Ho., Raleigh, 1999; clin. therapist Med. U. SC, Charleston, 1999—2004; clin. social worker Oasis Christian Counseling, Moncks Corner, SC, 2001—. Bd. dirs. Friends Program, Raleigh, 1996—99, One World Market, Raleigh, 1997—99, HALOS, Charleston, 2002—. Author, project coord. (tng. manual) Child Welfare Pre-Service Training/BSW Curriculum Review Project. Foster parent Dept. Social Svcs., North Charleston, 2000; parent vol. Midland Pk. Elem., North Charleston, 2003; cmty. vol. ARC, Charleston, 2002. E-4 U.S. Army, 1990—91, Ft. Bragg. Named Collegiate of Yr., Zeta Phi Beta Sorority, 1994. Mem.: NASW, Am. Assn. Black Christian Counseling, Am. Assn. Christian Counseling. Home: 2551 Realm St North Charleston SC 29406 Office: Oasis Christian Counseling 117 E Main St Moncks Corner SC 29461 Office Phone: 843-899-4949. Home Fax: 843-899-7224; Office Fax: 843-899-7224. Personal E-mail: celham2@netscape.net. E-mail: oasischristiancounseling@yahoo.com.

HAMILTON, MAXINE KEITER, retired physician; b. Wilmington, Ohio, Mar. 8, 1920; d. Joseph Wesley and Georgia (McKay) Keiter; m. David Hamilton; children: Catherine, David, Thomas. BS, Wilmington Coll., 1945; MD, U. Cin., 1949. ER physician Cin. Gen. Hosp., 1950—51; pvt. practice Wilmington, 1951—87; ret., 1987. Resident Cin. Gen. Hosp.; chief staff Clinton Meml. Hosp., Wilmington. Mem. Met. Housing Bd., Soil Conservation Bd., Clinton County Park Bd. Named Outstanding Woman, Clinton County, 2006. Republican. Avocations: farming, gardening. Home: 276 Larish Wilmington OH 45177

HAMILTON, NANCY BETH, data processing executive; b. Lakewood, Ohio, July 22, 1948; d. Edward Douglas and Gloria Jean (Blessing) Familo; m. Thomas Woolman Hamilton, June 10, 1970; children: Susan Elizabeth, Catherine Anne. BA, Denison U., 1970. Cert. secondary edn. tchr., Fla. Tchr. Orange County (Fla.) Bd. Edn., 1970-71; registrar Jones Coll., Orlando, Fla., 1971-72; mgr. service dept. Am. Lawyers Co., Cleve., 1972-79, mgr. data processing dept., 1980-95, corp. sec.-treas., 1995—. Mem. bd. assoc. editors Comml. Law Jour., 1991—, mem. bd. editors, 1994—, vice chair, 2002—. Trustee, treas. Westshore Montessori Assn., Rocky River, Ohio, 1988—94; bd. dirs. Holly Lane PTA, Westlake, Ohio, 1988—94, treas., 1992—94; bd. dirs. Parkside PTA, Westlake, 1991—97, treas., 1994—96, Westlake Coun. PTAs, 1999—2001, Westlake H.S. PTA, 1995—98, pres., 1998—2000. Mem. Comml. Law League Am. (chmn. com. 1989-94, membership chmn. 1994-96, com. chair 1997—, Award of Distinction 2005), Comml. Law League of Am. (Midwestern dist. rec. sec. 1997—), Assn. Law List Pubs. (treas. 1998—), Alpha Phi (pres. Cleve. Westshore chpt. alumnae 1986-88). Republican. Methodist. Avocations: skiing, travel. Office: Am Lawyers Co 853 Westpoint Pky Ste 710 Cleveland OH 44145-1532

HAMILTON, PARKER, library director; m. J. Mauri Hamilton. BA, MLS, U. Ill., Urbana. Libr. Champaign Pub. Libr., Ill., Evanston Township HS; branch mgr. Long Branch and Davis librs. Montgomery County Pub. Librs. (MCPL), Rockville, Md., pub. svc. adminstr. for human resources, 1993—2001, acting dir., 2005, dir., 2005—; asst. chief adminstrv. officer Montgomery County, 2001—05. Office: Montgomery County Pub Librs 99 Maryland Ave Rockville MD 20850 Office Phone: 240-777-0002. Office Fax: 240-777-0014.*

HAMILTON, PATRICIA ROSE, art dealer; b. Phila., Oct. 21, 1948; d. William Alexis and Lillian Marie (Sloan) Hamilton. BA, Temple U., Phila., 1970; MA, Rutgers U., New Brunswick, N.J., 1971. Sec. to curator Whitney Mus., NYC, 1971-73; sr. editor Art in Am., 1973; curator exhbns. Crispo Gallery, 1974-75; dir. Hamilton Gallery, 1976-84; artist's agt., 1984—2002; art dealer, 2002—. Democrat. Avocations: tennis, swimming, cooking. Home and Office: 6753 Milner Rd Los Angeles CA 90068-3214 Office Phone: 323-512-4737. Personal E-mail: hamiltonpatricia@sbcglobal.net.

HAMILTON, PRISCILLA, mathematics educator; b. Amherst, Ohio, Sept. 14, 1948; d. Paul and Lena White; m. Neal Hamilton, Aug. 24, 1968; children: Andrew, Cherith Codispoti. BA, Kent State U., 1968—72, BS, 1982—85, Med, 1986—89. Cert. tchr. Ohio, 1985. Math. tchr. Brunswick Christian Sch., Ohio, 1981—84, Cuyahoga Valley Christian Acad., Ohio, 1985—. Mem.: NCTM, Greater Akron Math. Educators Soc. (assoc.). Avocations: travel, skiing. Office: Cuyahoga Valley Christian Acad 4687 Wyoga Lake Rd Cuyahoga Falls OH 44224 Office Phone: 330-929-0575 111. E-mail: phamilton@cvcaroyals.org.

HAMILTON, RHODA LILLIAN ROSÉN, retired guidance counselor, language educator, consultant; b. Chgo., May 8, 1915; d. Reinhold August and Olga (Peterson) Rosén; m. Douglas Edward Hamilton, Jan. 23, 1936 (div. Feb. 1952); remarried, Aug. 1995 (dec. 1997); children: Perry Douglas, John Richard Hamilton. Grad., Moser Coll., Chgo., 1932-33; BS in Edn., U. Wis., 1953, postgrad., 1976; MAT, Rollins Coll., 1967; postgrad., Ohio State U., 1959-60; postgrad. in clin. psychology, Mich. State U., 1971, 76, 79, 80; postgrad., Yale U., 1972, Loma Linda U., 1972; postgrad. in computer mgmt. sys., U. Okla., 1976; postgrad. in edn., U. Calif., Berkeley, 1980. Exec. sect. to pres. Ansul Chem. Co., Marinette, Wis., 1934-36; pers. counselor Burneice Larson's Med. Bur., Chgo., 1954-56; adminstrv. asst. to Ernst C. Schmidt Lake Geneva, Wis., 1956-58; assoc. prof. fin. aid Ohio State U., 1958-60; tchr. English to spkrs. of other langs. Istanbul, Turkey, 1960-65; counselor Groveland (Fla.) H.S., 1965-68; guidance counselor, psychol. cons. early childhood edn. Dept. Def. Overseas Dependents Sch., Okinawa, 1968-85; instr./lectr. early childhood Lake Sumter Jr. Coll., Leesburg, Fla., 1986-88; pres. Hamilton Assocs., Groveland, Fla., 1986; ret. Vis. lectr. Okla. State U., 1980; co-owner plumbing, heating bus., Marinette, 1943-49; journalist Rockford (Ill.) Morning Star, 1956-58, Istanbul AP, 1960; lectr. Lake Sumter C.C., 1989, Lake Sumter Jr. Coll., 1989. Author poetry on Middle East, 1959-64; Career Awareness, 1978; Listen Up, 1997-98. Vol. instr. U.S. citizenship classes, Okinawa, 1971-72; judge Gold Scholarships Okinawa Christian Schs., 1983, 84. Mem. Am. Fedn. Govt. Employees, Fla. Retired Educators, Order Ea. Star (organist; life mem. Shuri One in Okinawa and Trillium 208 in Wis.), Marinette Woman's Club (Wis., pres. 1949-51), Groveland Woman's Club (Fla.), Phi Delta Gamma. Episcopalian.

HAMILTON, STEFANIE MARIE, mathematics educator; b. Washington, Pa., Dec. 10, 1981; d. Kimberly Marie and Richard Hamilton. Degree in Applied Math., Robert Morris U., Moon Twp., Pa., 2004. Cert. profl. tchg. Pa., Fla., 2004. Math. tchr. Pitts. Pub. Sch. Dist., 2004—05, Hendry County Sch. Dist., Clewiston, Fla., 2005—. Named Tchr. of Yr., Pitts. Pub. Sch. Dist., 2004—05. Office: Hendry County Sch Dist 1501 S Francisco Street Clewiston FL 33440 Office Phone: 863-983-1520.

HAMILTON, VIRGINIA VAN DER VEER, historian, educator; b. Kansas City, Mo., Sept. 7, 1921; d. McClellan and Dorothy (Rainold) Van der Veer; m. Lowell S. Hamilton, Aug. 4, 1946; children: Carol, David. AB, Birmingham Coll., Ala., 1941, MA (Ford Found. Fund Adult Edn. fellow), 1961; PhD, U. Ala., 1968, LittD, 1992. Staff writer AP, Washington, 1942—46, Birmingham News, 1948—50; asst. prof. history U. Montevallo, Ala., 1951—55; asst. prof., asst. to pres. pub. rels. Birmingham-So. Coll., 1955—65; lectr. in history U. Ala., Birmingham, 1965—68, asst. prof., 1968—71, assoc. prof., 1971—75, prof., 1975—87, prof. emerita, 1987—. Author: Hugo Black: The Alabama Years, 1972, Alabama: A History, 1977, The Story of Alabama, 1980, Your Alabama, 1980, Seeing Historic Alabama, 1982, rev. edit., 1996, Lister Hill: Statesman from the South, 1987, Looking For Clark Gable and Other 20th Century Pursuits, 1996; editor: Hugo Black and the Bill of Rights, 1978. Faculty Rsch. grantee U. Ala. at Tuscaloosa, 1969, U. Ala. at Birmingham, 1973-74, 74-75. Mem. So., Am. hist. assns., Orgn. Am. Historians, Soc. Am. Historians, Ala. Assn. Historians, Ala. Hist. Soc.

HAMILTON, WENDY J., foundation administrator; b. N.Y. m. Lawrence Hamilton; children: Kaitlin, Ryan, Greer. Student, Genesee C.C., Batavia. Mem. Ind. chpt. MADD, 1984—, mem. nat. bd. dirs., 1995—, v.p. victim issues, v.p. field issues, nat. pres., 2002—, founder Ill. chpt., founder N.Y. chpt., N.Y. state chair, 1990—94, 1997—98, pub. policy liaison Md. chpt., 1998—2002.

HAMILTON JACKSON, MARILYN J., dancer, educator, choreographer; d. Albert Arthur Jr. and Gwendolyn Aenid Atkinson; m. Kenneth D. Hamilton (div.); 1 child, Kalik Damione Hamilton. BA, CUNY, 1973; MA, Columbia U., 1984. Dance tchr. ElmCor Youth and Adult Activities, Inc., East Elmhurst, NY, 1975—76; dance dir. Langston Hughes Libr., Corona, NY, 1976—82; tchr. Harbor Sch. (now Tito Puente Performing Acad.), NYC, 1977—, asst. dir., 1982—83; owner, dir. Encore! Dance Sch., Corona, 1982—92. Mentor Joyce Theater Dance Edn. Program, NYC, 1998—; mem. Sammy Davis Jr. Internat. Tour, 1968—69. Dancer Alvin Ailey II Dance Co., 1972, (Broadway plays) Raisin, 1973—76, Seesaw, 1973, Images Performing Ensemble, 1980—82; TV appearances: Hollywood Palace; Jerry Lewis Telethon. Named Tchr. of Yr., Harbor Sch. Performing Arts, 1998—99; recipient cmty. svc. award, ElmCor Youth and Adult Activities, Inc., 1987, cert. of appreciation, Langston Hughes Cmty. Libr., 1992, proclamation, Office of Mayor Dinkins, NYC, 1992, Recognition and Appreciation cert., Assn. Black Educators, 2002, Excellence in Tchg. award, Union Settlement Assn., 2004; Am. history fellow, NY State Dept. Edn., 2001—02. Avocations: reading, Scrabble, travel, crocheting. Office: Tito Puente Performing Acad 240 E 109th St New York NY 10029

HAMLETT, TIFFANY, psychologist, educator; m. Geremy Hamlett. M in Child Devel., Tex. Woman's U., Denton, 2004. Adj. instr. child devel. Tarrant County Coll., Hust, Tex., 2004—. Contbr. articles to profl. jours.

HAMLIN, HARRIETT E., educational consultant; BS, Tuskegee U., 1977—81; MS, Queens Coll., 1986—89. Advanced Profl. Tchr. Cert. Md. Dept. Edn., 1993, Lower Elem. Montessori Cert. Tchr. Am. Montessori Soc., Md., 1996, cert. Ednl. Tech. Goucher Coll., 2005. Elem./secondary academic instr. N.Y.C. Pub. Schs., Bklyn., 1987—92; elem. academic instr. Prince George's County Pub. Schools, Md., 1992—2000; mid. sch. sci. specialist Montgomery County Pub. Schs., Md., 2000—. Weather edn. resource tchr. Am. Meteorol. Soc., Forestville, 1999—; chairperson Sch. Liaison Collaborative Com., Montgomery County, 2000—02; teacher's assn. rep. Montgomery County Educators Assn., 2000—02; mid. sch. advisor Math., Engring., And Sci. Achievement, Montgomery County, 2004—. Presenter (exhbn.) Fetal Alcohol Syndrome. Mem. Bapt. Career Women, Washington, 2003—05. Mem.: Md. Assn. of Sci. Tchrs., Md. Assn. for Adult, Cmty. and Continuing Edn., Kappa Delta Pi, Zeta Phi Beta. Avocations: bowling, tennis, reading, travel.

HAMLIN, SONYA B., communications specialist; b. NYC; d. Julius and Sarah (Saltzman) Borenstein; m. Bruce Hamlin (dec. 1977); children: Ross, Mark (dec. 1992), David. BS, MA, NYU; HLD (hon.), Notre Dame Coll., 1970. Host arts program Sta. WHDH-TV, Boston, 1963-65; host, prodr., writer (syndicated PBS program) Meet the Arts Sta. WGBH-TV, Boston, 1965-68; cultural reporter Sta. WBZ-TV, Boston, 1968-71, TV host, producer The Sonya Hamlin Show, 1970-75; host, producer Sunday Open House program Sta. WCVB-TV, Boston, 1976-80; host, producer, writer Speak Up and Listen program Lifetime Cable Network, N.Y.C., 1982-84; pres. Sonya Hamlin Communications, Boston and N.Y.C., 1977—, Different Drummer Prodns., N.Y.C., 1982-86. Pvt. comm. cons., U.S., Can., and Europe, 1977—; adj. lectr. Harvard Grad. Sch., Edn., Cambridge, Mass., 1974-76, Harvard Law Sch., 1977-81, Kennedy Sch. Govt., Harvard U., 1978-79; adj. asst. prof. Boston U. Med. Sch., 1977-80; mem. faculty Nat. Inst. Trial Advocacy, South Bend, Ind., 1977—, U.S. Dept. Justice, Washington, 1979-87, ABA, Chgo., 1979—; chmn. Law/Video Co., N.Y.C. and Waltham, Mass., 1987-92; comm. cons., weekly and weekend performer Today in NY (NBC), 1995—; daily panelist O.J. Today (Fox), 1995-96. Author: What Makes Juries Listen, 1982, How to Talk So People Listen, 1988, What Makes Juries Listen Today, 1998, How to Talk So People Listen: Connecting in Today's Workplace, 2006; prodr., dir., writer (films) China" Different Path, 1979 (Emmy nominee), Paul Revere: What Makes a Hero, 1976, others; contbr. articles to numerous profl. jours. Active Gov. Commn. Status of Women, Mass., 1973-83; campaign co-chair Mass. ERA Campaign, 1975-76; cons. Gov. Michael Dukakis, 1978, Dem. Nat. Party, Washington, 1979; bd. dirs. mem. Nat. Vol. Action com. United Way, Washington, 1986-91; bd. dirs. Taubman Ctr. Kennedy Sch. Harvard U., 1989-95; mem. adv. bd. Martha Graham Dance Co., 1997—, Shakespeare & Co.; mem. Women's Leadership Bd., Kennedy Sch. Govt., Harvard U., 1999—. Recipient Best Program award for Meet the Arts Internat. Ednl. TV Assn., Tokyo, 1969, Ohio State Cultural Reporting award, 1970; named Outstanding Broadcaster New Eng. Broadcasters, Boston, 1973; Sonya Hamlin Day named in her honor Mayor of Boston, 1974.; archive of her works established Boston U. Library, 1983. Mem.: NATAS (two Emmy nominations), Internat. Women's Forum, Am. Fedn. TV and Radio Artists. Avocations: skiing, tennis, piano, dance, museums. E-mail: sonyaham@aol.com.

HAMM, MIA (MARIEL MARGARET HAMM), retired professional soccer player; b. Selma, Ala., Mar. 17, 1972; m. Christian Corry, 1994 (div. 2001); m. Nomar Garciaparra, Nov. 22, 2003. BS in Polit. Sci., U. NC, 1994. Forward U.S. Women's Nat. Soccer Team, 1987—2004; profl. soccer player Washington Freedom, 2001—03. Mem. US Women's Soccer Team, Athens Olympic Games, 2004. Author: Go for the Goal: A Champions Guide to Winning in Soccer and Life, 1999. Founder Mia Found., 1999. Named US Soccer Female Athlete of Yr., 1994—98, MVP, US Women's Cup, 1995, Best Female Athlete of Yr., ESPY, 1998, 2000, Women's World Player of Yr., FIFA, 2001, 2002; named to Pele's 100 greatest living soccer players list; recipient Soccer Player of Yr. Award, ESPY, 2000, 2001, Best Female Soccer Player, 2004. Achievements include being a member of U. NC NCAA National Championship teams, 1989-93; having number retired, U. NC, 1994; being a member of US Women's Soccer Gold Medal Team, Atlanta Olympics, 1996, Athens Olympic games, 2004; being a member of US Women's Soccer World Cup Championship Team, 1999; being a member of US Women's Soccer Silver Medal Team, Sydney Olympics, 2000; being the all-time leading international goal scorer for men and women. Office: US Soccer Fedn US Soccer House 1801 S Prairie Ave Chicago IL 60616-1319

HAMM, SUZANNE MARGARET, psychologist; b. Port Washington, Wis., June 28, 1943; d. Raymond and Margaret (Ernster) Hubing; m. Fred Joseph Hamm, July 28, 1973. BA, Dominican Coll., Racine, Wis., 1966; MS, U. Wis., Whitewater, 1972; PhD, U. Denver, 1986. Nationally cert. sch. psychologist; lic. psychologist. Sch. tchr. St. Charles Elem. Sch., Burlington, Colo., 1966-71; sch. psychologist Denver Public Sch., 1972—; part-time pvt. practice Denver, 1987—. Counselor Shelter for Battered Women, Denver, 1986-88; psychologist Shelter for the Homeless, Denver, 1987—; advisor Schs. for Urban Neighborhoods, Denver, 1989—; chair bd. trustees Mackintosh Acad., 2005—. Recipient Sch. Psychol. of the Year, Colo. Assoc of Sch. Psychol, 1990. Mem. Am. Psychol. Assn., Colo. Psychol. Assn. (bd. mem. 2005—), Nat. Assn. Sch. Psychologists, Colo. Assn. Sch. Psychologists, Western Psychol. Assn., Nat. Ednl. Assn. Roman Catholic. Avocations: gardening, travel. Office: 3540 S Poplar St Denver CO 80237-1360 Home: 773 Rangeview Dr Golden CO 80403-8735

HAMME, MARTA DENISE, elementary school educator; d. James C. and M. J. Nelson; m. Randall L. Hamme, July 27, 1981; children: Jessica, Katelyn. B in Secondary Edn., Pa. State U., 1976. Grade 10 world cultures tchr. W. Shore Sch. Dist., New Cumberland, Pa., 1978—80, grade 8 history tchr., 1981—. Mem. ch. coun. Grace Evang. Luth. Ch., Camp Hill, 2004—. Recipient Acclaim award, W. Shore Sch. Dist., 2005. Mem.: Pa. Coun. Social Studies Tchrs., Nat. Mid. Sch. Assn., Nat. Coun. Social Studies Tchrs. Republican. Lutheran. Home: 800 Nissel Ln New Cumberland PA 17070 Office: Lemoyne Mid Sch 701 Market St Lemoyne PA 17043

HAMMEL, ALICE MAXINE, music educator; b. Tampa, Fla., May 7, 1965; d. Nelson Dodge and Alice Maxine King; m. Bruce Ray Hammel, Feb. 6, 1993; children: Hannah Elizabeth, Hollie MaryAlice. BME, Shenandoah U., 1987; MME, Fla. State U., 1989; DMA, Shenandoah U., 1999. Band, choral dir. Trinity Cath. Sch., Tallahassee, 1987-89; choral dir. Hanover County Schs., Ashland, Va., 1990-93; ind. educator music Richmond, Va., 1989—; staff adjudicator Music Festivals, Birdsboro, Pa., 1989—; instr. U. Richmond, 1998—2002, dir. ednl. programs Musicate, 2002—05; adj. asst. prof. music James Madison U., 2004—; music tchr. Stony Point Sch., 2004—. Vis. asst. prof. U. Richmond; cons. and presenter in field; networking rsch. mentor Music Educators Nat. Conf., 2002—, nat. spokesperson. Musician (flutist): Music of Allan Blank, 1999; contbr. articles to profl. jours. Patriotic edn. chair Daus. Am. Colonists, Richmond, 1999—2001; dist. good citizens chair DAR, Richmond, 1998—2001, music chmn., 1997. Recipient Young Career Achievement award, Shenandoah U., 2000. Mem.: Coll. Music Soc., Va. Assn. Gifted, Am. Coun. Exceptional Children, Va. Music Educators Assn. (chamber music chair 1990—98, sight reading chair 1998—, spl. learners chair 1998—), Music Tchrs. Nat. Assn. (keynote spkr. 2001, woodwind rep. 2002), Music Educators Nat. Conf. (networking mentor rschr.), Sigma Alpha Iota (Nat. Leadership award 1987). Democrat. Baptist. Home: 3131 E Weyburn Rd Richmond VA 23235 E-mail: alice@hammel.us.

HAMMEL, SABRINA IRENE, political scientist, educator; adopted d. Edwin Dickson and d. Bobbie Winn; m. Roger L. Hammel, Feb. 14, 1987; children: R. J. Eckard, Shawna S. Oper, Morgan A. MA Interdisciplinary Studies, Tex. State U., San Marcos, 1997, BS Polit. Sci., 2005; MA Polit. Sci., Internat. Rels. and M Pub. Admin., St. Mary's U., San Antonio, 2006—06. Adj. instr. NW Vista Coll., San Antonio, 2002—. Instr. govt. and econs. Wayland Bapt. U., San Antonio, 2002—; instr. govt. U. Incarnate Word, San Antonio, 2005—, St. Mary's U., San Antonio, 2006—. Promote student activity in politics Dem. Party, San Antonio, 1989—2006. Named to Who's Who of Am. Tchrs., Who's Who, 2005; recipient Instrnl. Innovation award, U. Tex., 2004, Excellence in Tchg. award, NW Vista Coll., 2003; Instrnl. Innovation Grant, 2005. Democrat-Npl. Avocation: motorcycling.

HAMMER, BONNIE, broadcast executive; m. Dale Huesner. BA in Edn., Boston U., MA in Media and New Tech. With WGBH, Boston; dir. devel. Dave Bell Associates, LA; programming exec. Lifetime Television Network; v.p. current programs USA Networks, N.Y.C.; sr. v.p. Sci-Fi programming and USA org. productions NBC Universal, 1998—99; exec. v.p., gen. mgr. Sci-Fi Channel (subsidiary of USA Networks), 1999, pres. Universal City, Calif., 2001; pres. USA Network, Sci-Fi Channel NBC Universal, 2004—. Recipient Lillian Gish award, Women in Film. Office: Sci-Fi Channel c/o Vivendi Universal 100 Universal City Plaza Universal City CA 91608-1002*

HAMMER, DEBORAH MARIE, librarian, paralegal; b. Bronx, NY, Nov. 16, 1947; d. Ben and Helen (Lorenz) Halprin; m. Mark Stewart Hammer, May 30, 1976; 1 child, Joshua Robert. BA, CCNY, 1968; MLS, Rutgers U., 1969. Cert. libr. NY. Gen. asst. info. tel. ref. divsn. Queens Borough Pub. Libr., Jamaica, NY, 1969-71, gen. asst. popular libr., 1972-80, asst. div. head history, travel & biography, 1972-81, divsn. head history, travel & biography, 1981-92, div. mgr. social scis., 1992-98; fee conciliation coord., computer systems mgr. Nassau County Bar Assn., Mineola, NY, 1999—. Democrat. Avocations: reading, cooking, handcrafts, camping. Office: 15th and West Sts Mineola NY 11501 E-mail: halimer@juno.com.

HAMMER, LINDA See LINDROTH, LINDA

HAMMER, STEPHANIE ANN, elementary school educator; b. New Orleans, Jan. 2, 1969; d. Kathleen and Terry Bruce; m. Todd Alan Hammer, Feb. 2, 1992; 1 child, Hayden. BS with honors, McMurry U., Abilene, Tex., 1991. Cert. tchr. Tex. 6th grade English tchr. Madison Mid. Sch., Abilene, Tex., 1992—2000, 8th grade English tchr., 2000—. Mem.: ATPE. Office: Madison Mid Sch 3145 Barrow St Abilene TX 79605 Office Phone: 325-692-5661.

HAMMERMAN, SUSAN FRANCES WEISSFELD, lawyer; b. N.Y.C., Nov. 20, 1961; d. Jerold C. and Mary (Solak) Weissfeld; m. Jan L. Hammerman, June 1, 1986; children: Laura, Tamara. BA with honors, Johns Hopkins U., 1984; JD, Columbia U., 1985; BS summa cum laude, U. Colo., 2005. Bar: N.Y., 1986, Colo., 1987, D.C., 1989. Assoc. Phillips, Nizer, Benjamin, Krim and Ballon, N.Y.C., 1985-86, Sherman and Howard, Denver, 1986—88; sr. atty. Resolution Trust Corp., Denver, 1990—94; corp. counsel, asst. corp. sec. Gates Corp., Denver, 1999—. Colo. chpt. chair ABA Publs. Subcommittee, sect. Real Property, Probate & Trust Law, 1995—98; dir. Assn. Corp. Counsel, 2003—, v.p. ops., 2004—; conf. spkr. in field. Mng. editor Columbia-VLA Jour. of Art and Law, 1984-85; contbr. articles to profl. jours. Pres. Columbia Advs. for the Arts, N.Y.C., 1984-85; chair black tie gala Colo. chpt. Assn. Corp. Coun., 2005. Recipient Outstanding Achievement award, Colo. chpt. Assn. Corp. Coun., 2006. Mem. ABA, Internat., Am., Colo. Bar Assns., Pi Sigma Alpha. Avocations: skiing, piano. Office: Tomkins Law Dept Gates Corp 1551 Wewatta St MC 10 A5 Denver CO 80202 Office Phone: 303-744-5642.

HAMMERSMITH, NITA MARIE, writer; b. Paris, Tex., Aug. 31, 1948; d. Tommie Hugh and Sadie Mae Denson; m. Richard Robert Hammersmith, Nov. 15, 1953; children: Bobby Joe Stamps, Marleen Annette Stamps, Sharon Latrice King. AA, Mesa Coll., 2000; student, San Diego State U., 2005—06. Waste Water Technology Calif., 1981. Author Nita Hammersmith Ministries, San Diego, 1989—; free lance writer Christian Woman Mag., Phoenix, 2000—; writer Sisterhood Newsletter, Atlanta, 2001—; free lance writer Christian Mirror Internet Mag., Tex., 2002—. Author: (bible study & devotional work book) Lessons To Live By, (bible story for children) Benny & Michael & Jonah & The Big Fish, (biblical book for teenagers) How To Choose A Mate For Life, (bible study) Help Me Lord. Commencement spkr. Mesa Coll. Graduation, San Diego, 2000; keynote spkr. Ch. Christ, 1990—2005, Flint, Mich., 2001, Mpls., 2002, San Diego, 2004, Sisterhood Rally, Atlanta, 2003; facilitator Ch. Christ, 1991—. Recipient Jane Nelson Meml. award, San Diego State U., 2002. Mem.: Phi Theta Kappa (life). Office: Nita Hammersmith Ministries for Women 2196 Fenton Pky #107 San Diego CA 92108 Office Phone: 619-640-2846. Personal E-mail: nitarichnita@san.rr.com.

HAMMETT, DORIS BIXBY, retired pediatrician; b. Wichita, May 26, 1924; d. Benjamin Parker Bixby and Ruth V. Wickham; m. James Frank Hammett, July 3; children: Karen Marie, James Frank III, Kristen Irene. BA, U. Kans., Lawrence, 1945, MD, 1948. Home: 400 Wesley Dr Apt 58 Asheville NC 28803-2003

HAMMOND, ANN P., retired elementary. high school and college educator, poet; b. Worthing, Great Britian, June 11, 1936; arrived in U.S., 1964; d. Sydney Martyn Hammond and Elizabeth Mathewson. BS, Adelphi U., Garden City, N.Y., 1973, MA, 1974. Cert. permanent tchr. N.Y., 1974. Dir. phys. edn. Pipers Corner Sch., High Wycombe, England, 1958—60, Arundel Sch., Harare, Zimbabwe, 1960—64, East Woods Sch., Oyster Bay, NY, 1964—74; health educator East Hampton Sch. Dist., East Hampton, NY, 1974—96. Pres. Assn. of Women in Phys. Edn., N.Y., 1976—80; cons. Bklyn. Coll., N.Y., 1973—74, Adephi, N.Y., 1974. Contbr. poems to lit. publs. and anthologies. Avocations: writing, sailing, swimming, golf, reading. Personal E-mail: annhammonda@excite.com.

HAMMOND, BRENDA HINES, elementary school educator; b. Wilson, N.C., Oct. 27, 1943; d. Carl Wendell and Ruth (Johnson) Hines; m. Thomas A. Hammond Jr.; 1 child, Thomas A. III. BA, Fisk U., 1965; MA, George Washington U., 1969, EdD, 1982. Tchr. Montgomery County Pub. Schs., Silver Spring, Md., 1965—2006. Avocation: reading. Office: Montgomery County Pub Schs Dept Math Rockville MD 20012

HAMMOND, DEBORAH LYNN, lay worker; b. Olney, Md., Feb. 12, 1958; d. Cornelius Dennis Sr. and Beverly Laura (Dunn) H. AA in Gen. Studies, Catonsville C.C. Sec. Mt. Zion United Meth. Ch., Ellicott City, Md., 1980-95; data entry clerk Balt. Gas Electric Co., Pasadena, Md., 1994-95; sec. The Md. Correctional Instn. for Women, Jessup, Md., 1995-97; instr. computer & typing Milford Mill Acad., Randallstown, Md., 1996—2003; ch. sec. Trinity United Meth. Ch., Catonsville, Md., 1997—2003; adminstrv. ch. office mgr. Falls Rd AME Ch., Balt., 1996—; with Rees Sci. and Tech. Ltd., Balt., 1997—2004; legal asst. Currant and O'Sullivan P.C., 2003—. Chaplain, vol. activity coord. sec. Md. Correctional Instn. Women, 1995; choir dir. Falls Road AME Ch., 1995—; instr. adult edn. Milford Mill Acad., 1996—; bookkeeper Balt. Subway, 2002. Mem.: Order of the Eastern Star (Myra, Balt. chpt.). Home: 1 Sulky Ct Apt 101 Randallstown MD 21133-3149 Office: Currant and O'Sullivan PC Ste 302 8101 Sandy Spring Rd Laurel MD 20707 also: Falls Rd AME Ch 2145 Pine Ave Baltimore MD 21244-2827 Personal E-mail: deborah5909@aol.com.

HAMMOND, HARMONY, artist, educator; b. Chgo., Feb. 8, 1944; d. William Joseph and Harmony R. (Jensen) H.; m. Stephen Clover, May 1963 (div. 1970); 1 child, Tanya Hammond. BA, U. Minn., 1967. Prof. art dept. U. Ariz., Tucson, 1988—2005. Vis. artist Phila. Coll. Art, Rutgers U., Art Inst. Chgo., U. N.Mex., Tyler Sch. Fine Art, Santa Fe Art Inst., Anderson Ranch, Vt. Studio Ctr.; co-founder Heresies Mag., A.I.R. Gallery. Author: Wrappings: Essays on Feminism, Art and the Martial Arts, 1984, Lesbian Art in America: A Contemporary History, 2000; one-woman shows include A.I.R. Gallery, N.Y.C., 1973, 1982, 1984, Lerner-Heller Gallery, 1982, Matrix Gallery, Wadsworth Atheneum, Hartford, Conn., 1984, Luise Ross Gallery, N.Y.C., 1984, Bernice Steinbaum Gallery, N.Y.C., 1986, Trabia-MacAffe Gallery, N.Y.C., 1987, Etherton-Stern Gallery, Tucson, 1987, 1994, Linda Durham Gallery, Galisteo, N.Mex., 1988, Tucson Mus. Art, 1993, Linda Durham Gallery, Santa Fe, 1998, Site Santa Fe, 2002, Mus. Contemporary Art, Tucson, 2002, Dwight Hackett Projects, Santa Fe, 2004, Ctr. Contemporary Arts, Santa Fe, 2005, others, Represented in permanent collections Dwight Hackett Projects. Recipient award, Nat. Endowment of Arts-Sculpture, 1979, Nat. Endowment for Arts-Graphics, 1983; grantee, Pollock-Krasner Found., 1989, Guggenheim Found., 1991, Rockefeller Found. Bellagio, 1994, Adolph and Ester Gottlieb Found., 1995, Joan Mitchell Found., 1998, Andrea Frank Found., 2000; CAPS grantee, NY State Coun. of Arts-Sculpture, 1982. Mem. Coll. Art Assn. Avocation: Aikido.

HAMMOND, JANE PAMELA, adult education educator; b. Flint, Mich., Aug. 10, 1951; d. Duane Aurther and Norine Janet Moore; m. Larry Duane Hammond, June 22, 1974; children: Jason Duane, Joel Brady. BA in Sociology, Olivet Nazarene U., 1973; postgrad., U. Mich., 1973—74. Lic. real estate Mich. Line supr. Tex. Instruments, Lubbock, Tex., 1976—78; elem. tchr. United Meth. Ch. Sch., Tampa, Fla., 1979—80; adult edn. and substitute tchr. Mt. Morris (Mich.) Consol. Schs., 1981—85, substitute tchr., 1992—99; automobile sales person Hobson Ford Dealership, Clio, Mich., 1985—86; real estate salesperson Century 21, Clio and Flint, Mich., 1987—92; tchr. adult and alternative edn. Clio Area Schs., 1999—. Career pathways rep. Clio Area Schs. Cmty. Edn., 2000—; substitute tchr. Marshall Schs. Mem. exec. com. Genesee County Reps., Flint, 2000—; sustaining mem. Mich. State and Nat. Rep. Coms., 2000—; Sunday sch. tchr. Ch. of the Nazarene, Mt. Morris, Flint, 1986—. Jr. Miss Vocal scholar, House of Harmony, 1967. Mem.: Clio Area C. of C. (Enhancement award 2002), Clio Common Grounds (lifelong learning and arts and recreation com.), Mich. Hist. Soc., Clio Hist. Soc., Mich. Farm Bur., VFW Ladies Aux. Avocations: interior decorating, flower arranging, antiques, camping. Home: 16624 F Dr North Marshall MI 49068

HAMMOND, JANE REBECCA, artist; b. Bridgeport, Conn., 1950; BA in Art cum laude, Mount Holyoke Coll., 1972; postgrad., Ariz. State U., 1973-74; MFA, U. Wis., 1977. Prin. works exhibited in numerous one-person and group shows including Cin. Mus. Art, 1993, Orlando, (Fla.) Mus. Art, 1994, Jose Freire Fine Art, N.Y.C., 1993, Brooke Alexander Gallery, N.Y.C., 1993, Bobbie Greenfield Gallery, Venice, Calif., 1993, Wetterling Gallery, Stockholm, 1993, Colgate U., Hamilton, N.Y., 1993, Greg Kucera Gallery, Seattle, 1993, Feigenson-Preston Gallery, Birmingham, Mich., 1993, many others; represented in numerous pub. collections including Albertina, Vienna, Austria, Albright-Knox Gallery, Buffalo. Recipient Louis Comfort Tiffany award, 1989, Sponsored Work award N.Y. State Coun. on Arts, 1989; grantee in painting N.Y. Found. for Arts, 1989, NEA grantee, 1987, Mellon grantee Md. Inst., 1986, grantee in painting Ludwig Vogelstein Found., 1985; NEA fellow, 1989. Home: 75 Grand St Apt 4E New York NY 10013-2289

HAMMOND, LOU RENA CHARLOTTE, public relations executive; b. Muenster, Tex. d. Louis Martin and Regina L. (Schoech) Wolf; m. Christopher Weymouth Hammond, Sept. 6, 1964; 1 child, Stephen. BA, U. Houston, 1962. Rep. pub. rels. Pan Am. Airways, N.Y.C., 1968-76, mgr. pub. rels., 1977-79, dir. pub. rels., 1980-81, dir. pub. affairs, 1981; pres., ptnr. Taylor and Hammond, N.Y.C., 1981-84; prin., pres. Lou Hammond and Assocs., N.Y.C., 1984—. Editor: (calendar) Avenue mag., 1976-79. Recipient Matrix award in pub. rels., 1992, Winthrop W. Grice award Hotel Sales and Mktg. Assoc. Internat., 1992, Inside PR Mag.'s All-Star award, 1992, Circle of Excellence award Public Relations, Internat. Furnishings and Design Assn (IFDA). Mem. Soc. Am. Travel Writers, Fashion Group, Assn. Better N.Y., Les DAmes de Escoffier, Women's Forum, Spoletto USA, Women Execs. in Pub. Rels., Doubles Club. Roman Catholic. Avocations: bridge, tennis, 18th century antiques. Office: Lou Hammond & Assocs Inc 39 E 51st St New York NY 10022-5916 Office Phone: 212-308-8880. Personal E-mail: louh@lhammond.com.

HAMMOND, MARIE S., psychology educator, researcher, consultant; d. Robert T. and Dorothy A. Dekutoski; m. Michael G. Hammond, Dec. 31, 1985. BME, Olivet Coll., 1978; MA in Counseling & Personnel Svcs., U. Mo.-Columbia, 1980, PhD in Counseling Psychology, 1999. Cert. counselor nat., 1985, master career counselor 2003, lic. profl. counselor Mo., 1987, psychologist, health svcs. provider Okla., 2001, Tenn., 2004. Rsch. specialist, instr. Lincoln U., Jefferson City, Mo., 1981—85; adj. instr., field rep. City Colls. Chgo., Karlesruhe, Germany, 1986—87; job tng. specialist I Job Tng. Partnership Agy., Jefferson City, Mo., 1987—88; rsch. analyst Missouri Senate, Jefferson City, 1988—90; dir. career planning & placement William Woods Coll., Fulton, 1990—93, dir., instl. rsch., 1993—95; instr., rschr., lab asst. U. Mo.-Columbia, 1995—98; pre-doctoral intern Salt Lake City Veteran's Affairs Med. Ctr., 1998—99; staff psychologist, career counselor U. Tulsa, 1999—2003; asst. prof. Tenn. State U., Nashville, 2003—. Cons. Summit Info. Svcs., Holts Summit, Mo., 1995—98. Flautist Jefferson City Orchestra, Mo., 1981—85. Mem.: APA, Am. Evaluation Assn., Soc. for Vocat. Psychology, Southeastern Psychological Assn., Nat. Career Devel. Assn. (PR, chair 2002—03). Catholic. Avocations: reading, horseback riding, dog training, music. Office: Tenn State U Dept Psychology 3500 John A Merritt Blvd Nashville TN 37209 Office Phone: 615-963-5191. Business E-Mail: mhammond1@tnstate.edu.

HAMMOND-KOMINSKY, CYNTHIA CECELIA, optometrist; b. Sept. 1, 1957; d. Andrew and Angeline (Laorno) Kominsky; m. Theodore Glen Hammond, Sept. 21, 1985. Student, Oakland U., Rochester, Mich., 1976—77; OD magna cum laude, Ferriss Coll. Optometry, 1981. Lic. optometrist Mich., cert. diagnostic and therapeutic pharm. agt. Intern Optometric Inst. and Clinic of Detroit, 1980, Ferris State Coll., Big Rapids, Mich., 1980, Jackson (Mich.) Prison, 1981; assoc. in pvt. practice Warren, Mich., 1981—82; optometrist Pearle Vision Ctr., Sterling Heights, Mich., 1982—87, K-Mart Optical Ctr., Sterling Heights, 1982—87, Royal Optical, Sterling Heights, 1988—. Provided eye care to nursing homes, Mt. Clemens, Mich. Head vol. caregivers and organ donation programs St. Therese of Lisieux Ch., Shelby Twp., Mich. Achievements include invention of binocular low vision aid device. Avocations: music, sports, decorative painting, gardening, antique crystal. Home: 47626 Cheryl Ct Shelby Township MI 48315-4708 Office: Royal Optical Lakeside Mall 14300 Lakeside Cir Sterling Heights MI 48313-1326

HAMMONTREE, MARIE GERTRUDE, writer; b. Jefferson County, Ind., June 19, 1913; d. Harry Clay and Hattie Agnes (Means) H. BA, Butler U., 1949. Sec. Bobbs-Merrill Co., Indpls., 1934-42, Ind. U. Med. Ctr., Indpls., 1942-48, Travel Enterprises, Inc., N.Y.C., 1949-50, U.S. Dept. Justice (FBI), Indpls., 1950-75; bookkeeper, purchasing agt. Office of William H. Hudnut, III/ Mayor of Indpls., 1978-92; ret. Author: (children's books) Will and Charlie Mayo: Doctor's Boys, 1954, A.P.Giannini: Boy of San Francisco, 1956, Albert Einstein: Young Thinker, 1961, Mohandas Gandhi: Boy of Principle, 1966, Walt Disney: Young Movie Maker, 1969. Active in campaigns of Mayor William H. Hudnut, III and Ind. State Reps., Indpls., 1975-92. Mem. Nat. League Am. Pen Women (pres. Indpls. chpt. 1978-80), Women in Comms., Soc. of FBI Alumni, Inc. (treas. Indpls. chpt. 1990-98), Sigma Tau Delta, Phi Kappa Phi. Republican. Presbyterian. Avocations: travel, writing for children. Home: 8140 Township Line Rd Apt 5213 Indianapolis IN 46260-5866

HAMMOUD, CATHERINE LOUISE, special education educator; b. Toledo, Ohio, Oct. 9, 1951; d. M. Samuel and Anne (Mohammed) Adray; m. M-Nazih Hammoud, Apr. 21, 1979; children: Rima Deal, Abrar. MEd, Purdue U., W. Lafayette, Ind., 1981. Cert. Ohio Profl. Standard Ohio Dept. Edn. Tchr. Am. Sch. Kuwait, 1975—77, Toledo Pub. Schools, 1977—79, Internat. Coll. Beirut, 1982—88; spl. edn. tchr. Lafayette Sch. Corp., Ind., 1979—81, Wood County ESC, Bowling Green, Ohio, 1989—2001, Erie-Huron-Ottawa ESC, Genoa, Ohio, 2001—. Chair bd. trustees Islamic Sch. Greater Toledo, Perrysburg, 2003—. Recipient Team Award, Erie-Huron-Ottawa Ednl. Svc. Ctr., 2004; grantee New Horizons. Mem.: Phi Delta Kappa. Moslem. Avocations: cross stitch, cooking, crossword puzzles. Home: 28848 Starlight Rd Perrysburg OH 43551 Office: Erie Huron Ottawa Ednl Svc Ctr 310 Main St Genoa OH 43430 Office Phone: 419-855-3589. E-mail: nhammoud@wcnet.org.

HAMNER, ROME, social services administrator; b. 1974; Grants mgr. Our Family Services, Inc. Co-founder Odaiko Sonora. Vol. grant reviewer Tucson Pima Arts Coun. Named one of 40 Under 40, Tucson Bus. Edge, 2006. Mem.: Arizona Commn. on Arts Roster of Artists, Southern Ariz. Alliance of Nonprofits, Japan Am. Soc. of Tucson (bd. dir.), OTO Dance Studios. Avocation: Taiko drumming. Office: c/o Tucson Pima Arts Council 10 E Broadway 106 Tucson AZ 85701*

HAMNER, SUZANNE LEATH, retired history educator; b. Ft. Worth, Feb. 29, 1940; d. Roland Martin and Mabel Lois (Hall) Leath; m. W. Easley Hamner, June 18, 1961; children: Janine Suzanne, Michael Edward. BA summa cum laude, Meredith Coll., Raleigh, N.C., 1961; MA, Tulane U., New Orleans, 1964. Tchg. asst. Tulane U., New Orleans, 1963-66; instr. history Coll. Liberal Arts Northea. U., Boston, 1966-71, lectr. history Univ. Coll., 1972-75; lectr. history Coll. Arts and Scis., Univ. Coll., Boston, 1985—2002, ret., 2002—. Sr. lectr. U. Coll., 1985-2002. Contbg. editor Reclaiming Our Global Heritage, Vol. I and Vol. II, 1990. Mem. adv. com. Follow Through Program, Cambridge (Mass.) Sch. Dept., 1977-79; treas., v.p. adv. bd. Parents Assn., Buckingham Browne and Nichols Sch., Cambridge, 1980-86; clk., bd. dirs., adv. bd. Cambridge Civic Assn., 1976-95; treas. Alice Wolf Election Com., City Coun., Cambridge, 1979-96; advisor Wolf Campaign for State Rep., 1996, 98; overseer Handel and Haydn Soc., Boston, 1989—; trustee Chorus pro Musica, 1993-95; adv. com. Meml. Ch., Harvard U., 1992-94; vice co-chair leadership com. United Way Cambridge, 1997, co-chair, 1998-2001, com. 1997-; incorporator The Cambridge Homes, 1999—, bd. dirs, 2004-, v.p., 2005—; mem. grants com. Meml. Ch., Harvard U., 1998-2000; reader Rec. for the Blind and Dyslexic, 2002—. Woodrow Wilson Found. fellow, Princeton, N.J., 1961-62; Tulane U. scholar, 1962-64. Mem. Am. Hist. Assn., New England Hist. Assn., Mass. Hist. Soc., Cambridge Club (pres. 2005-2006), Phi Alpha Theta. Democrat. Avocations: music, reading, travel, politics. Home: 3 Ellery Sq Cambridge MA 02138-4227

HAMOLSKY, TINA LORMAN, special education educator; b. Lowell, Mass., Aug. 31, 1956; d. Richard Edwin and Janet Ellen (Clark) L.; m. David James Hamolsky, July 21, 1985; children: Johnathan Charles, Ginny Lynn. BS, Fitchburg State, 1978; MEd in Learning Disablities, Keene State Coll., 1998. Cert. elem. and spl. edn. tchr., Mass., N.H. Tchr. reading chpt. I Groton (Mass.) Elem., 1978-79; spl. educator Spl. Needs Ednl. Collaborative, Shirley/Pepperell, Mass., 1979-82, P.L.U.S. Co., Nashua, N.H., 1982-84; workshop supr. Manchester (N.H.) Assn. for Retarded Citizens, 1984; spl. educator Jaffrey-Rindge Sch. Dist., Rindge, N.H., 1984-88; preschool spl. educator Jaffrey-Rindge Spl. Needs Preschool Program Conant High Sch., 1988—, preschool cons., 1990—; resource rm. special edn. tchr. Marlborough Elem., Marlborough, NH, 2000—02; intensive learning ctr. tchr. Jaffrey Rindge Mid. Sch., 2002—05. Cons. in field; special Olympics coord. Jaffrey Rindge Sch. Dist., 2003—05; adj. tchr. of tchg. special need students Franklin Pierce Coll., 2003—04. Coord. Spl. Olympics, Nashua, 1983-84. Mem. ASCD, NEA,Coun.for Exceptional Children. Avocations: aerobic walking, cross-stitch, crossword puzzles. Office Phone: 603-532-8122. E-mail: t.hamolsky@aol.com.

HAMOND, KAREN MARIE KOCH, secondary school educator; b. Arlington, Mass., Dec. 12, 1954; d. James Walter and Dorothy Mary (Buchanan) Koch; m. Norman Roy Hamond, Oct. 9, 1976; children: Jeremy Michael, Jason Matthew, Jillian Marie, Jennifer Margaret. BA, Salem (Mass.) State Coll., 1976; MS, Lowell (Mass.) U., 1983; Cert. Advanced Studies, Harvard U., 1992. Cert. secondary math. tchr. Mass., secondary maths. tchr. N.H. Tchr. St. Mary's High Sch., Lawrence, Mass., 1976-77, Peabody (Mass.) Vets. Meml. High Sch., 1977-78, Triton Regional High Sch., Byfield, Mass., 1978—99, math. team advisor, 1980-91; prof. math. Western New Eng. Coll., Springfield, Mass., 1992—99; head math. dept. Timberlane Regional HS, Plaistow, NH, 1999—2001; head math. and bus. dept., head math./tech. dept. Everett (Mass.) HS, 2001—; math dept. coord., 1995—99. Tchr. summer sch. Gov. Dummer Acad., Byfield, Mass., 1993-99. Mem ASCD, Nat. Coun. Tchrs. of Maths., Math. Assn. Am., NEA, Mass. Tchrs. Assn. Am. Math. Soc. Avocations: camping, skiing, travel. Home: 14 Riverview Dr Newbury MA 01951-1807 E-mail: hamond@comcast.net.

HAMOY, CAROL, artist; b. NYC, May 22, 1934; d. Morris David and Selma (Essex) Cohen. Student, Newark (N.J.) Sch. Fine Art, 1952-54, Art Students League, N.Y.C., various yrs. Lectr., spkr. in field. Solo exhibitions include USMA/West Point, NY, 1978, Katonah (NY) Gallery, 1983, Lower Manhattan Cultural Coun., NYC, 1986, May Mus./Lawrence, NY Ceres, NYC, 1992, MTA-Arts for Transit, NYC, 1993, Robert Kahn Gallery, Houston, 1993, Temple Judea Mus., Elkins Park, Pa., 1993, Univ. Art Ctr., Shreveport, La., 1994, Ceres, NYC, 1995, 98-99, 2001, Goldman Art Gallery, Rockville, Md., 1996, Nat. Mus. Am. Jewish History, Phila., 1996, Broadway Windows, NYC, 1997, Ellis Island Immigration Mus., NYC, 1997, Mizel Mus., Denver, 1997, Breman Heritage Mus., Atlanta, 1998, Eldridge St. Project, NYC, 1998, Inter-Am. Gallery, Miami, Fla., 1998, Skirball Mus., Cincinnati, 1999, Franklin Marshall Coll., Lancaster Pa., 1999, Margolis Gallery, Houston, 1999, Lower East Side Tenement Mus., NY, 2000, The Neuberger Mus., Purchase, NY, 2000, Ceres, NYC, 2001, Dacotah Prarie Mus., Aberdeen, S.D., 2002, Azarian/McCullough Gallery, Sparkill, NY, 2002, Futernick Gallery, Miami, 2003, Longyear Mus., Hamilton, NY, 2005, Hebrew Union Coll. Mus., NYC, 2005—, Mizel Mus., Denver, 2005—, Kansas City Jewish Mus., Overland Pk., Kans., 2006, Catherine Murphy Gallery, St. Paul, Minn., 2006; exhibited in group shows at Pelham (NY) Art Ctr., 1988, U. Ky., Lexington, 1989, HUC, NYC, 1989, Kentuck Mus., Northport, Ala., 1989, Clough Hansen Gallery, Memphis, 1989, JRC Gallery, Evanston, Ill., 1992, Soho 20, NYC, 1993, Charach-Epstein Mus., West Bloomfield, Mich., 1994, 97, Nat. Jewish Mus., Washington, 1995, Fine Arts Rosen Mus., Boca Raton, Fla., 1995, Right Brain Gallery, Atlanta, 1999, Miss. Univ. for Women, 1999, Skirball Mus., Cin., 1999, Neuberger Mus., Purchase, NY, 2000, Ellipse Arts Ctr., Arlington, Va., 2000, Contemporary Crafts, Pitts., 2000, Ceres, 2000, The Joseph Gallery Mus, NYC, 2000-01, Moving On/Frauen Mus., Bonn, Germany, John Jay Coll., 2001—, Joseph Gallery, NY, 2000-01, Frauen Mus., Bonn, Germany, 2001-02, Detritus Show John Jay College, NY, 2001-02, Judaica Mus., Riverdale, NY, 2001-02, Kommunale Galerie Wilmersdorf, Berlin, 2001-02, Ctr. for Visual Art & Culture, Stamford, Conn., 2002, Am. Craft Mus., NY, 2002-03, Joseph Gallery, NYC, HUC Mus., NYC, 2003—, 2005-06, Jewish Mus. Md., Balt., 2004, Alper Art Gallery, Miami, Fla., 2004, Wain Ling Art Ctr., Haverford, Pa., 2005, Futernick Gallery, Miami, 2005, Rutgers U., Camden, N.J., 2005, Gotthelf Gallery, La Jolla, Calif., 2006, others; permanent collections include Nat. Mus. Women in the Arts, Nat. Jewish Mus., Washington, Frauen Mus., Bonn, Duke U., Durham, NC, Ringling Sch. Art, Sarasota, Fla., others. Nominee, Joan Mitchell Found., 2000; grantee Va. Ctr. for Creative Arts, Sweet Briar, Va., 1980, Artists' Space, NYC, 1981, Hillwood Art Mus., NY State Coun. for Creative Arts, 1992, MTA-Arts for Transit, NYC, 1993, Lucius N. Littauer Found. Bessemere Trust Co. N.A., 1997, Meml. Found./Jewish Culture Artists' Fellowship, Inc. of NYC, 1999, Pollock-Krasner Found., 2005. Studio: 340 E 66th St New York NY 10021-6821

HAMPER, ANIETRA, news anchor; BA in Comm. and Polit. Sci., Heidelberg Coll., 1995. Programming asst. Sta. WSYX-TV, Columbus, Ohio; anchor, reporter, prodr. Sta. WHEI-TV, Tiffin; prodn. asst. The McLaughlin Group, Washington; news asst. Sta. KARK-TV, Little Rock; anchor, reporter, dir. cmty. affairs Sta. WTTE-TV, Columbus; reporter Sta. WSYX-WTTE-TV, 1996—98, WKEF-TV, Dayton, 1998—99; anchor, reporter Sta. WRGT-TV, 1998—99; reporter Sta. WCMH-TV, Columbus, 1999—2001, anchor, 2001—. Recipient YWCA Women of Achievement award, U.S. Congrl. award, JC Penny Golden Rule award, Jefferson award. Mem.: Nat. Assn. Television Arts and Scis. Office: WCMH-TV 3165 Olentangy River Rd Columbus OH 43202 Office Phone: 614-261-4497. E-mail: anietra.hamper@nbc.com.

HAMPLE, JUDY G., academic administrator; BA in Speech Comm. and Secondary Edn./French, David Lipscomb U.; MA and PhD in Comm., Ohio State U. Univ. fellow, asst. dir. intercollegiate debate Ohio State U.; faculty dept. speech comm. U. Ill., Champaign-Urbana; divsn. dir. dept. comm. arts and scis. Western Ill. U., assoc. dean for budget and pers. Coll. Arts and Scis.; dean Coll. Liberal Arts and Scis. Emporia (Kans.) State U., 1983—86; dean Coll. Arts and Scis. Ind. State U., 1986—93; sr. v.p. acad. affairs U. Toledo, 1993; chancellor Pa. State Sys. of Higher Edn., Harrisburg, 2001—; vice chancellor planning, budget and policy analysis, vice chancellor and chancellor bd. regents State Univ. Sys. Fla., 1998—2001. Cons.-evaluator North Cen. Accreditation Assn.; pub. cons.-evaluator ABA. Co-editor: Teaching in the Middle Ages, 3 vols.; editor: Studies in Medieval and Renaissance Teaching; contbr. articles to profl. jours. Office: Pa State Sys of Higher Edn Dixon Univ Ctr 2986 N 2d St Harrisburg PA 17110 Office Phone: 717-720-4010.

HAMPTON, CAROL MCDONALD, priest, educator, historian; b. Oklahoma City, Sept. 18, 1935; d. Denzil Vincent and Mildred Juanita (Cussen) McDonald; m. James Wilburn Hampton, Feb. 22, 1958; children: Jaime, Clayton, Diana, Neal. BA, U. Okla., 1957, MA, 1973, PhD, 1984; cert. individual theol. study, Episcopal Theol. Sem. of S.W., 1998; MDiv summa cum laude, Phillips Theol. Sem., 1999. Ordained to Episcopal Transitional Diaconate, 1999, ordained priest, 1999. Tchg. asst. U. Okla., Norman, 1976—81; instr. U. Sci. and Arts Okla., Chickasha, 1981—84; coord. Consortium for Grad. Opportunities for Am. Indians U. Calif., Berkeley, 1985—86; trustee Ctr. of Am. Indian, Oklahoma City, 1981. Vice chmn. Nat. Com. on Indian Work, Episc. Ch., 1986; field officer Native Am. Ministry of Episc. Ch. (Nat.), 1986-94, sec., co-chmn., advising elder, prin. elder coun., 1994-96; field officer for Congl. Ministries of Episc. Ch. (Nat.), 1994-97; mem. nat. coun. Chs. Racial Justice Working Group, 1990-97, co-convenor, 1991-93, convenor, 1993-95; officer Multicultural Ministries of Episc. Ch.

(Nat.), 1994-97; (hon.) canon of St. Paul's Cath., Oklahoma City, 2001—. Mem. editl. bd.: First Peoples Theology Jour.; contbr. articles to profl. jours. Trustee Western History Collections, U. Okla., Okla. Found. for the Humanities, 1983-86; mem. bd. regents U. Sci. and Arts Okla., 1989-95; bd. dirs. Okla. State Regents for Higher Edn., mem. adv. com. on social justice; mem. World Coun. of Chs. Program to Combat Racism, Geneva, 1985-91; bd. dirs. Caddo Tribal Coun., Okla., 1976-82; accredited observer Anglican Consultative Coun. UN 4th World Conf. on Women, 1995; v.p. Nat. Conf. Cmty. Justice, 1999-2002; bd. dirs. Ctrl. Okla. Human Rights Alliance, 1999—; dir. Planned Parenthood of Ctr. Okla. Bd., 2002—; mem. Okla. Coun. Indian Ministry, 1998—, co-chair, 2006—. Recipient Okla. State Human Rights award, 1987; Francis C. Allen fellow Ctr. for the History of Am. Indian, 1983. Mem.: Okla. Coun. Indian Ministy (co-chair 2006—), Okla. Conf. Chs. (bd. dirs. 2000—), Indigenous Theol. Tng. Inst. (bd. dirs. 2000—), Jr. League (Oklahoma City), Am. Assn. Indian Historians (founding mem. 1981—), Okla. Hist. Soc., Am. Hist. Assn., Orgn. Am. Historians, Western Social Sci. Assn., Western History Assn. Democrat. Episcopalian. Avocation: travel. Home: 1414 N Hudson Ave Oklahoma City OK 73103-3721 Office Phone: 405-235-3436. E-mail: cjchampton@sbcglobal.net, champton@stpaulsokc.org.

HAMPTON, MARGARET FRANCES, counselor; b. Gainesville, Fla., May 12, 1947; d. William Wade and Carol Dorothy (Maples) H.; m. Kenneth Lee Kauffman (dec.); 1 child, Robert Lee. BA in French summa cum laude, Fla. State U., 1969; postgrad., U. Nice, France, 1969; MBA in Fin. (Alcoa Found. fellow), Columbia U., 1974. Fin. analyst, economist Bd. Govs. Fed. Res. Sys., Washington, 1974—75; asst. v.p. corp. fin. Mfrs. Hanover Trust Co., N.Y.C., 1975—76; v.p., dir. corp. planning and fin., asset and liability mgmt. and strategic planning coms. Nat. Bank Ga., Atlanta, 1976—81; sr. v.p. corp. planning and devel. Bank South Corp., Atlanta, 1981—85; mng. ptnr. Hampton Mgmt. Cons., Atlanta, 1985—97; pres., bd. dirs. Ascent Enterprises, Inc., Atlanta, 1983—97; agt. Steward Internat. Trade and Fin., 1997—99; counselor Eagle's Wings Ministry (ministry to the emotionally wounded), 2003—. Nat. trustee Leukemia Soc. Am., 1986-90; trustee Ga. chpt. Leukemia Soc., 1980-94, treas., 1981-82, 1st v.p., 1982-84, sec., 1991-92, hon. bd. dirs., 1994—; dir. Combined Health Appeal Ga., 1991—, sec., 1992—. Named Trustee of Yr., Leukemia Soc., 1982, 85; recipient Gold Key, Fla. State U. Hall of Fame. Mem. Aglow Internat., Planning Execs. Inst., Atlanta Venture Forum, Am. Inst. Banking, Inst. of Fin. Edn., Am. Fin. Assn., Downtown Atlanta C. of C. (govt. affairs subcom. 1976-77), Atlanta C. of C. (high tech. task force 1982-83), Ga. Women's Forum (sec./treas., bd. dirs. 1985-86), Ga. Exec. Women's Network (sec. 1982-83, dir. 1982-84), Bus. and Tech. Alliance, Mortar Bd., Alliance Française, Kappa Sigma Little Sisters (pres., treas., sweetheart), Women's Commerce (charter mem., steering com. 1985-86), Northside Athletic Club, Oxford Club (life), Phi Beta Kappa, Beta Gamma Sigma, Phi Kappa Phi, Alpha Lambda Delta, Pi Delta Phi, Alpha Delta Pi. New Life Christian. Abundant Life Christian.

HAMPTON, MARTA TORUNO, dermatologist, educator; b. Managua, Nicaragua, Jan. 27, 1958; arrived in U.S., 1960; d. William and Teresa Toruno; m. Archibald A. Hampton, Dec. 20, 1980; children: Sara, Ben, Joe. BS, U. Fla., Gainesville, 1982; MD, U. Fla., Gainesville, 1985. Asst. prof. Med. U. S.C., Charleston, 1990—93; dermatopathology fellowship, 1992—93; physician pvt. practice Charleston, SC, 1994—. Clin. assoc. prof. dermatology Med. U. S.C., 1990—. Fellow: Women's Dermatologic Soc.; mem.: Am. Acad. Dermatology, Am. Soc. Dermatolopathology (assoc.), Alpha Omega Alpha, Phi Beta Kappa. Republican. Catholic/Methodist. Achievements include research in outpatient dermatology clinical research trials. Mailing: PO Box 31757 Charleston SC 29417 E-mail: 5sayle@bellsouth.net.

HAMPTON, SHELLEY LYNN, hearing impaired educator; b. Muskegon, Mich., Nov. 27, 1951; d. Donald Henry and Ruth Marie (Heinanen) Tamblyn; m. John Pershing Hampton Jr., Aug. 10, 1985; 1 child, Sarah Elizabeth. BA, Mich. State U., 1973, MA, 1978. Cert. tchr., Wash., Mich., N.Y. Tchr. presch. thru 3d grade N.Y. State Sch. for Deaf, Rome, 1973-78; cons. Ingham Intermediate Sch. Dist., Lansing, Mich., 1978-81; hearing impaired coord. Shoreline Sch. Dist., Seattle, 1981—. N.W. rep. Bur. of Edn. Handicapped, N.Y.C., 1978; N.Y. del. Humanities in Edn., 1977; adv. bd. State Libr. for the Blind, Lansing, 1980-81; adj. prof. Mich. State U., 1979-81, Seattle Pacific U., 1984-86; participant World Cong. Edn. and Tech., Vancouver, B.C., 1986; computer resource technician Spl. Programs, 1988-92, collegial team leader, 1992-95; rep. Site-Based Mgmt. Coun., Seattle, 1992-95. Writer: Social/Emotional Aspects of Deafness, 1983-84. Del. N.Y. State Assn. for Edn. of Deaf, N.Y.C., 1974-78; N.Y. del. Humanities in Edn., 1977; mem. bd. Plymouth Congl. Ch., Seattle, 1983-87; coord., Kids on the Block puppet troupe, 1999-2003. Recipient Gov.'s Plaque of Commendable Svc., State of Mich., 1981; grantee State of Wash., 1979, 82, Very Spl. Arts Festival, 1979-81; recipient Outstanding Svc. award Mich. Sch. for the Blind, 1980. Mem. NEA, Wash. State Edn. Assn., Shoreline Edn. Assn., Alexander Graham Bell Assn., Regional Hearing Impaired Coop. for Edn., Internat. Orgn. Educators of the Hearing Impaired, Auditory-Verbal Internat., U.S. Pub. Sch. Caucus, Conf. Ednl. Adminstrs. Serving the Deaf. Home: 14723 62nd Dr SE Everett WA 98208-9383 Office: Shoreline Hearing Program 16516 10th Ave NE Seattle WA 98155-5904 Office Phone: 206-361-4271.

HAMRICK, ELIZA CARNEY, secondary school educator, consultant; b. Mt. Vernon, Ohio, Nov. 7, 1961; d. James D. and Eliza Macaulay Carney; m. Michael F. Hamrick, June 21, 1987; children: Eliza Singleton, Thomas Joseph. BA in Secondary Edn., U. Ariz., Tucson, 1985; MA in Edn., Adams State Coll., Alamosa, Colo., 2002. Lic. tchr. Colo., 1986. Adult edn. instr. Aurora Pub. Schs., Colo., 1986—88; instr. Libr. Congress, Washington, 2000—02, Cherry Creek Sch. Dist.-Overland H.S., Englewood, Colo., 1986—. Editor on-line newsletter Libr. Congress, Washington, 2003. Author: (online lesson) Women, Their Rights and Nothing Less. County organizer U.S. Senate Campaign, Colo., 2004. Named Colo. Tchr. of Yr., DAR, 2002, Never Be Forgotten Tchr. of Yr., Denver Found., 2005; fellow, Libr. Congress, 1999. Mem.: ACLU, NEA. Democrat. Lutheran. Avocations: running, reading. Home: 6477 S Jericho Way Centennial CO 80016 Office: Overland High School 12400 E Jewell Ave Aurora CO 80012 Office Phone: 720-747-3728. Business E-Mail: ehamrick@cherrycreekschools.org.

HAMRICK, LINDA L., secondary school educator; b. Fort Wayne, Ind., Feb. 14, 1954; BS in Edn., Ball State U., 1977, EdD in Ednl. Leadership, 1991; MS in Edn., Ind. U., 1980. Cert. tchr., sch. adminstr., supt. Ind. Tchr. Fort Wayne (Ind.) Cmty. Schs., 1978—; adminstrv. intern Ft. Wayne (Ind.) Cmty. Schs., 1997—; educator-YIC Whitley County Probation, Columbia City, Ind., 1997—. Assoc. faculty Ind. U., 1987, 88; sch. supt. internship N.W. Allen County Schs., Fort Wayne, 1990-91. Site dir. youth basketball Ft. Wayne YMCA, 1982-86; site supr. Ft. Wayne Park Dept., 1980-85. Mem. AAPHERD, Ind. Middle Level Educators Assn., Internat. Reading Assn., Am. Endurance Ride Conf., Internat. Arabian Horse Assn., Upper Midwest Endurance Ride Conf. Avocations: horse riding endurance, snowmobiling, downhill skiing, boating, water-skiing. Office: South Side HS 3601 S Calhoun St Fort Wayne IN 46807-2006 Office Phone: 260-467-2600. Business E-Mail: linda.hamrick@fwcs.k12.in.us.

HAMSTRA, CHRISTINE JOSEPHINE, social worker; b. Wyandotte, Mich., July 28, 1953; d. Joseph and Stefania (Karolczyk) Baran; m. Jeffrey William Hamstra, July 18, 1987; children: Kathryn, Stephan. BA, Ea. Mich. U., 1975; MSW, U. Mich., 1983. Lic. social worker, Tex. Mental health worker Ypsilanti (Mich.) Area Community Svcs., 1975-76; program assoc. 4-H Youth Programs, Wayne, Mich., 1978-79; child care worker Yorkwood's Ctr., Ypsilanti, 1979-81; youth therapist Bridgeway Ctr., Inc., Jackson, Mich., 1983-84; adolescent therapist Care Unit Hosp. of Dallas/Ft. Worth, Ft. Worth, 1984-88; chem. dependency therapist Psychiat. Inst. of Ft. Worth, 1988-89; pvt. practice, prin. Daigle & Assocs., Hurst, Tex., 1989-91; pvt. practice Dr. Saleem & Assocs., Hurst, 1991—. Mem. NASW. Avocations: outdoors, aerobics, reading, travel, running. Office: Dr Saleem & Assocs 500 Goldhawk Bedford TX 76022 Office Phone: 817-285-0333. Personal E-mail: hamstracj@aol.com.

HAMTPTON, JACQUELYN DANA, principal; b. Cleve., Jan. 26, 1971; d. Franklin B. and Peggy Ann Hampton. Secondary Edn., Ohio State U., Columbus, 1994; Master's Degree, Ashland U., Ohio, 1999, Ednl. Adminstrn., 2003. Cert. adminstrn. Ashland U., Ohio, 2003. English tchr. Shaw H.S., East Cleveland, Ohio, 1994—2003, small sch. tchr. leader, 2003—04, small sch. prin., 2004—. Active Calvary Ministries Internat., Youngstown, Ohio, 2005—06. Mem.: Nat. Assn. Secondary Sch. Prins. (assoc.), Ohio Assn. Secondary Sch. Adminstrs. (assoc.). Office Phone: 216-268-7938. Personal E-mail: jackied29@hotmail.com.

HAMURA, KAORI, artist; b. Fukuoka, Japan, Mar. 9, 1970; d. Shoei Yoh and Kimiko H. AA, Sophia Jr. Coll., Tokyo, 1990; BFA, Parsons Sch. Design, 1993. Character designer MTV Network, N.Y., 1993—, dir., animator, 1995; illustrator N.Y. Press, Interview, Timeout, Mademoiselle, New Yorker, N.Y., 1995—, Clark Kent Co., Tokyo, 1988-90; artist Artist's Space, N.Y.C., 1992—, Drawing Center, N.Y.C., 1994—. Artist: Hotwired Pop Gallery, 1996. Recipient Poster Design award Harajuku Police Station, 1988; scholarship Parsons Sch. Design, 1990-93. Mem. N.Y. Found. Arts. Office: MTV Network 1633 Broadway Fl 31 New York NY 10019-6708

HAMWI, BONNIE L., education educator, consultant; b. Corbin, Ky., Apr. 10, 1949; d. Raymond and Dorothy Adams; m. Richard Hamwi, June 26, 1998; 1 child, Michele L. Alsip. BSc magna cum laude, Cumberland Coll., Williamsburg, Ky., 1992, M in Spl. Edn. summa cum laude, 1993; EDS-Education Specialist, Argosy U., Sarasota, Fla., 2005. Cert. instrnl. II Pa. State Bd. Edn., 1996, spl. edn. N.Y. State Bd. Edn., 1996, tchr. Ky. State Bd. Edn., 1992. Elem. spl. edn. tchr. Jesse D. Lay Elem. Sch., Barbourville, Ky., 1993—96; elem. learning support tchr. W.R. Croman Elem., Troy, Pa., 1996—99; adj. faculty Mercyhurst Coll., Erie, Pa., 1999—2000; adminstr. St. Matthew's Luth. Sch., Erie, 2000—01; asst. prof. Gannon U., Erie, 2001—04; instr., supr. student tchrs. Albright Coll., Reading, Pa., 2004—, Millersville U., Pa., 2005. Spl. edn. cons. Albright Coll., 2005—. Sponsor student coun. Exceptional Children, Erie, 2003—05. Named Educator of Yr., Kappa Delta Pi, 2003; recipient scholarship, Lambda Chpt. Delta Kappa Gamma, 1992. Mem.: Pa. Edn. Assn., NEA, Erie Arts Coun., Coun. for Exceptional Children, ASCD (assoc.). Avocations: acrylic and watercolor painting, travel, camping, needlepoint. Home: 1506 College Ave Reading PA 19604 Office Phone: 814-490-6653. Personal E-mail: bonniehamwi@msn.com. Business E-Mail: bhamwi@alb.edu.

HAN, HEE-WON, professional golfer; b. Seoul, South Korea, June 10, 1978; m. Hyuk Son. Attended, Rukoku U. Winner Wendy's Championship for Children at Tartan Fields, 2003, Sybase Big Apple, 2003, Safeway Classic, 2004. 48 victories as amateur; mem. Nat. Conf. Team, 1992—97; silver medallist Hiroshima Asia Games, 1994. Recipient Louise Suggs Rolex Rookie of Yr., 2001. Avocation: quilting. Office: c/o LPGA 100 International Golf Dr Daytona Beach FL 32124-1092*

HANAMEY, ROSEMARY T., nursing educator; b. Detroit, May 16, 1937; d. Albert Edward and Catherine Margaret (Shaheen) Hanamey. BSN, Mercy Coll., Detroit, 1959; MS, Boston Coll., 1963; postgrad., U. Mich., 1982. RN Mich., 1959. Staff nurse Mt. Carmel Mercy Hosp., Detroit, 1959—60, Mass. Gen. Hosp., Boston, 1960—63; instr. nursing Mercy Coll., Detroit, 1963—65, asst. prof., 1967—69; asst. exec. sec. Mich. Nurses Assn., Lansing, 1965—67; exec. sec. Mich. Conf. AAUP, Detroit, 1969—70; instr. nursing Madonna Coll., Livonia, Mich., 1972—76; asst. prof. nursing Ea. Mich. U., Ypsilanti, 1976—80; vol. parish nurse St. Joseph Cath. Ch., Dexter, Mich., 1997—. Mem. careers com. Mich. League Nursing, Detroit, 1977—97; cons. Detroit Practical Nurse Ctr., 1980—85; mem. parish nurse partnership St. Joseph Mercy Health Sys., Ann Arbor, Mich., 1997—. Author: (videotape) Intravenous Therapy: Monitoring and Problem Solving, 1977 (2nd place, 1978), Intravenous Therapy: Basic Concepts, 1977 (3rd place, 1978). Precinct del. Dem. Party, Detroit, 1966—69. Grantee, USPHS, 1961—62; scholar, Marygrove Coll., Detroit, 1955—56. Mem.: AAUP, Cath. Med. Assn. Avocations: swimming, walking. Home: 8074 Huron St Unit 1 Dexter MI 48130-1053 Office Phone: 734-426-8483.

HANAWAY, CATHERINE LUCILLE, prosecutor; b. Schuyler, Nebr., Nov. 8, 1963; m. Christopher; children: Lucy, Jack. BA, Creighton U., 1987; JD, The Catholic U. of Am., 1990. Owner, atty. Hanamore Solutions, LLC; atty. Peper, Martin, St. Louis, 1990—93; campaign mgr. Bredemeier for Atty. Gen., 1996; dist. dir. Senator Kit Bond, 1993—96, 1996—98; polit. advisor Missourians for Kit Bond, 1998; mem. Mo. State Ho. of Reps., 1998—2004, spkr., 2002—04; exec. dir. Mo. Bush/Cheney, 2002; US atty. (ea. dist.) Mo. US Dept. Justice, St. Louis, 2005—. Mem. Housing Adv. Bd.; bd. dirs. Hope House, Foster and Adoptive Care Coalition. Mem.: Mo. Bar Assn., St. Louis Junior League, St. Louis Jaycees (past pres.). Republican. Roman Catholic. Office: US Attys Office 111 S 10th St 20th Fl Saint Louis MO 63102 Office Phone: 314-539-2200.*

HANCE, LAURIE ANN, biology educator; b. Somerville, N.J., Apr. 4, 1975; d. Linda Marie and Jerry T. Kowal; m. William James Hance, June 19, 1972. BS in Sci., Trenton State Coll., N.J., 1998; MS, East Stroudsburg U., Pa., 2005. Biology tchr. Voorhees H.S., Glen Gardner, NJ, 1998—. Mem.: N.J. Forensic Sci. Assn., Biology Tchrs. Assn., Holland Twp. Woman's Club (v.p. 2006). Home: 227 Church Rd Milford NJ 08848 Office: Voorhees HS 256 County Rd 513 Milford NJ 08848 Office Phone: 908-638-2199 2073. Personal E-mail: bioteacher@verizon.net. Business E-Mail: lhance@nhvweb.net.

HANCOCK, BEVERLY J., retired counseling consultant, secondary school educator; b. Bridgeton, N.J., Dec. 16, 1943; m. J. Everett Hancock, Jr., Aug. 9, 1969; children: J. Michael, Faith Lynn. BE, Montclair State U., 1966; MEd in Counseling, Temple U., Phila., 1972. Cert. Social Studies Tchr. N.J. Dept. Edn., 1966, Sch. Counselor N.J. Dept. Edn., 1972, Nat. Bd. Cert. Counselors, 1983, lic. Profl. Counselor Bd. of Marriage and Family Therapy Examiners of N.J., 1999, nat. cert. counselor, nat. cert. sch. counselor. Tchr. English and social studies Burlington Twp. (N.J.) HS, 1966—69, Burlington County Inst. Tech., Westhampton, NJ, 1969—72, guidance counselor, 1972—93, student resource ctr. counselor, 1993—98, guidance counselor, 1998—2002, cons. counselor, English instr., 2002—04; ret., 2004. Staff coord. Student-Supr. Liason Com., 1988—90; cons. N.J. Statewide Non-Traditional Career Assistance Ctr., 1992—. Author: Work Resource Handbook, 1986, Student Leadership Handbook, 1989; editor: The Source Guidance Bull. Co-developer Burlington County Job Fair for HS Srs. Mem.: NEA, N.J. Sch. Counselors Assn. (Counselor of Yr. 1990), N.J. Edn. Assn., Burlington County Sch. Counselors Assn., Am. Sch. Counselor Assn., Delta Kappa Gamma, Chi Sigma Iota. Episcopalian. Achievements include created and distributed wallet size Human Services CARE (help number) Cards to county schools and organizations. Avocations: crafts, carpentry, reading. Home: 1419 Noreen Dr Burlington NJ 08016

HANCOCK, CAROLE PATRICIA, academic administrator; b. Taylor, Tex., Dec. 4, 1939; d. Wellington Lorenzo and Bennie Louise Hancock. BS, Lincoln U., Jefferson City, Mo., 1960; MA in Tchg., Webster U., St. Louis, 1971. Cert. edn. adminstrn. specialist U. Mo. Tchr. St. Louis Pub. Schs., 1963—96, dept. head, coach, 1975—96, adminstr., 1996—2002; dir. City Divsn. Recreation, St. Louis, 1964—75; counselor, athletic coord. Upward Bound, Webster U., 1976—79; drug edn. specialist St. Louis CC at Forest Park, 1989—95, coach, adj. faculty, 1994—97; ofcl. Nat. Fedn. HS Ofcls., St. Louis, 1987—, Tex. Assn. Sports Ofcls., Wichita Falls, 2002—. Advisor, reviewer Health Edn. Curriculum, St. Louis, 1996—99; mem. Harvard Prins. Ctr., 1997—2002; facilitator Leadership Acad., Jefferson City, Mo., 1998—2002; edn. amb. People to People Internat., Kansas City, Mo., 2000—; adj. faculty St. Charles County CC, 2001. Vol. Am. Stroke Assn., St. Louis, 2001—04; mem., participant Susan G. Komen Found., Wichita Falls, Tex., 2002—; active Nat. Com. to Conserve Social Security, Washington, 2004—. Named Coach of Yr., Inner City Athletic Assn., 1981, 1982, 1987, Wall of Tolerance honoree, So. Poverty Law Ctr., 2004; recipient Humanitarian award, St. Louis Am., 1996; scholar, Mo. Leadership Acad., 1998, 1999. Mem.: ASCD, AARP, Mo. State H.S. Athletic Assn., Nat. Assn. Sports Ofcls., Nat. Health and Wellness Club, Am. Fitness Assn., Delta Sigma Theta. Democrat. Baptist. Avocations: walking, jogging, weightlifting, reading, singing. Home: 1420 N Rosewood Ave Wichita Falls TX 76301-1413

HANCOCK, DONNA, secondary school educator; b. Crosset, Ark., Oct. 28, 1942; d. Mady Lee and Verna Marie (Hicks) Watts; m. James Weldon Hancock, Feb. 21, 1966; children: Terrence Ray, James Weldon. BS, Kent State U., 1965; MA, U. Louisville, 1975. Cert. tchr. secondary edn. English tchr. Gary (Ind.) Ind. Schs., 1965-69; English and bus. edn. tchr. Jefferson County Schs., Jeffersontown, Ky., 1970-71, 72-78; English tchr. Tyler (Tex.) Pub. Schs., 1978-81; counselor battered women Waukesha (Wis.) Women's Ctr., 1981-82; expeditor, buyer GE Co., Waukesha, 1982-85; English tchr., yearbook adv. South Milwaukee Pub. Schs., 1985-89; English tchr. Greenville County Schs., Greenville, S.C., 1989-99. Minority cons. S. Milw. Pub. Schs., 1987-89. Contbr. poetry to poetic jours. Rep. outstanding minority students in Wis. Minority Leadership Forum, 1985-86; mem. state bd. min. affairs com. Wis. State Tchrs. Assn., 1986-87; mem. bd., sec. NAACP, Waukesha, 1986-88. Mem. Greenville County Mus. Art, Am. Assn. Univ. Women (pub. policy chmn. 1996-98, bd. dirs. 1996-99), Emrys Art Found. (bd. dirs. 1996-, sec. 1999-2000) Avocations: writing, playing the piano, theater, travel. Home: 109 Coventry Rd Greenville SC 29615-3203 E-mail: jimhancock@msn.com, jimhancock@bellsouth.net.

HANCOCK, ELLEN MARIE, communications executive; b. N.Y.C., Apr. 15, 1943; d. Peter Joseph and Helen Gertrude (Houlihan) Mooney; m. W. Jason Hancock, Sept. 17, 1971. BA, Coll. New Rochelle, 1965; MA, Fordham U., 1966. With IBM, 1966—, programmer Armonk, NY, 1966-81, dir. communications programming sect., communication products div. Raleigh, NC, 1981-83, v.p. communications programming sect., communication products div., 1983-84, asst. group exec. systems devel. info. systems and storage group Armonk, NY, 1985, v.p. telecommunication systems communication prodn. div., 1985-86, pres. communications products div., 1986-88, v.p., gen. mgr. communication system Somers, NY, 1988-91, v.p., gen. mgr. networking systems Staines, England, 1991-92, sr. v.p., 1992—95; exec. v.p., COO Nat. Semiconductor Corp., 1995—96; exec. v.p. R&D, chief tech. officer Apple Computer. Inc., Cupertino, Calif., 1996-97; pres. Exodus Comm., Inc., 1998—2000, CEO, 1998—2001, chmn., 2000—01; co-founder, pres., COO, CFO, sec., bd. dir. Acquicor Tech. Inc., Irvine, Calif., 2005—. Bd. dirs. Aetna, Inc., Colgate-Palmolive, Watchguard Technologies, Inc., Electronic Data Systems Corp., Inst. for Advanced Catholic Studies Trustee Marist Coll., Poughkeepsie, Santa Clara Univ. Council on Fgn. Rels., Pacific Council of Internat. Policy Roman Catholic. Office: Acquicor Tech Inc 4910 Birch St Ste 102 Newport Beach CA 92660*

HANCOCK, JANE SYERS, music educator; d. James Douglas and Sue Mills Syers; m. Thomas Walter Hancock, Dec. 30, 1976; children: Brianne, John Syers, Mark Thomas. BA in Music Edn., summa cum laude, Murray State U., 1978. Music tchr. St. Margaret Mary Sch., Wichita, Kans., 1978—80, Mrs. Ronda's Montessori Sch., Huntsville, Ala., 1987—93; accompanist Holy Family Sch., Huntsville, 1988—96, Westminster Christian Acad., Huntsville, 1998—2003, choir dir., 2003—. Baritone Sweet Adelines, Madison, Ala., 1998—2000. Pres. Holy Family Sch. Parent-Tchr. Assn., 1988—91, 1995—96; co-founder, sec. Holy Family Sch. Athletic Boosters, 1991—96; concessions chmn. Westminster Christian Acad. Athletic Boosters, 1998—2003, mem., 1994—2003; clinic vol. Am. Red Cross, Holy Family Sch., 1988—94; vol. Am. Red Cross, 1998—99; accompanist St. John Cath. Ch., Madison, Ala., 1981—92, Grace United Meth. Ch., Huntsville, 2003—04, Our Lady Queen of Universe Cath. Ch., Huntsville, 2004—, music liturgy, 2003—. Mem.: Madison County Choral Dirs. Assn. (founding mem. 2003—), Ala. Vocal Assn., Nat. Assn. Music Edn., Rainbow Mountain Homemakers, Alpha Delta Pi, Sigma Alpha Iota. Avocations: reading, sewing. Office: Westminster Christian Acad 1400 Evangel Dr Huntsville AL 35816

HANCOCK, KATHLEEN J., political science professor; b. Denver, Colo., 1960; d. James Hancock and Josephine Southgate Martin; m. John DeRose; children: Jamie Min Hancock DeRose, Willa Jun Hancock DeRose. BA, U. Calif., Santa Barbara, 1982; MA, George Washington U., Washington, 1988; PhD, U. Calif., San Diego, 2001. Analyst Congl. Rsch. Svc., 1988; sr. analyst GAO, Washington, 1988—93; prof. U. Tex., San Antonio, 2002—. Contbr. articles to profl. jours. Bd. mem. Families with Children from China, San Antonio. Recipient Excellence Tchg. award, UCSD Polit. Sci. Dept., 1996, Honors Alliance Tchg. award, U. Tex. San Antonio, 2003, Award for Outstanding Tchg. in Polit. Sci., Am. Polit. Sci. Assn., 2004, Faculty Excellence award, U. Tex., San Antonio Students, Disability Svcs., 2004; Exxon Corp. fellowship, George Wash. U., 1988-89, fellowship, Inst. Global Conflict, Cooperation, MacArthur, 1996-97, Profl. Devel. fellowship, Inst. Internat. Edn., 1996-97, fellowship, Inst. Global Conflict, Cooperation, 1997-1998. Mem.: Am. Polit. Sci. Assn., Internat. Studies Assn. (bd. dirs.), Sigma Kappa Upsilon. Office: U Texas San Antonio 501 W Durango Blvd San Antonio TX 78207

HANCOCK, MELINDA BOWNE, minister; d. Stephen C. and J. Elaine Bowne; m. Joshua David Hancock, May 22, 2004. BA in Religion, Olivet Nazarene U., 2003. Lic. min. Ch. of the Nazarene, 2001. Grad. asst. Olivet Nazarene U., Bourbonnais, Ill., 2003; edn. asst. Nazarene Compassionate Ministries, Kansas City, Mo., 2003—05, spl. projects adminstr., 2006—; sr. pastor Trinity Ch. of the Nazarene, Kansas City, Mo. Tutor Kansas City Urban Youth Ctr., 2006. Pres. scholar, Olivet Nazarene U., 1999—2003. Avocations: piano, singing. Home: 4117 Adams Kansas City KS 66103 Office: Trinity Ch of the Nazarene 4413 Rainbow Blvd Kansas City KS 66103 Office Phone: 816-333-7000, 913-384-1919. Personal E-mail: mindyb1020@hotmail.com.

HANCOCK, PATRICIA ANN, artist; b. Columbia, SC, Apr. 1, 1956; d. William Edwards and Joan Marie (Moore) H. Student, Queens Coll., 1973-75; BFA, U. Ga., 1979; postgrad., Va. Commonwealth U., 1980-81. Art tchr. Thornwell Sch., Clinton, S.C., 1979-80. Author, illustrator: Rupert, The Fantastic Flamingo, 1989; exhibited works in C&S Bank Show, 1991, 92, Florence Mus., 1998, Chapel Hill Mus., 1999. Mem. DAR, Nat. Soc., Jr. League (sustaining). Presbyterian. Avocations: sewing, jogging.

HAND, ANGELA RENE, singer; b. Springfield, Mo., June 26, 1960; d. Charles Eugene and Nieta Lee (Routh) Hand. B Music Edn., S.W. Bapt. U., 1982; MusM in Vocal performance, Memphis State U., 1987; DMA in Vocal performance, U. Tex., 2000. Cert. level I Orff Schulwerk music specialist. Orff music specialist Memphis City Schs., 1988—90; tchr. music Walter Sundling Jr. H.S., Palatine, Ill., 1990—94; tchr. pvt. voice Westlake H.S., Austin, Tex., 1995—99; tchg. asst. voice U. Tex., Austin, 1995—99, asst. instr. voice, 1998—99; asst. prof. Augustana Coll., Rock Island, Ill., 1999—2005. Co. mgr. City Opera of Quad Cities, Davenport, Iowa, 2005—. Singer: (Operas) (various roles) Opera@Augustana, 1999—2004, Genisius Guild, Lincoln Park Series, 2003, Opera Theatre, 1994—99, So. Opera Theatre, 1984—89, Opera Memphis, 1986, So. Ohio Light Opera, 1990—94; soprano soloist Handel Oratorio Soc., 2001—02; soprano soloist: Tarrytown United Meth. Ch., 1996—99, Chy. of Good Shepherd, 1994—96, Buntyn Presbhn. Ch., 1984—90, various area chs., chief writer, contbr.: Pop Hits tchg. guides, 1992—96. Judge musical convs., competitions in field; mem. Rep. Nat. Com., 1985—, Bettendorf Mission, Iowa, 2000—. Scholar, Getty Found., 1998; Annie Giles Barnhart scholar, 1994. Mem.: NRA, Coll. Music Soc., Nat. Assn. Tchrs. Singing, Nat. Opera Assn., Tau Beta Sigma. So. Baptist. Avocations: target shooting, writing science fiction, gardening, riding. Office: Augustana Coll Bergendorf Fine Arts 639 38th St Rock Island IL 61201 Office Phone: 309-794-7425. Business E-Mail: muhand@augustana.edu.

HAND, ANTOINETTE MARIE, accountant; b. St. Louis, Mo., Mar. 1, 1962; d. John Anthony and Patricia Ann Garanzini; m. William David Hand II, June 16, 1989; children: Gabriella Michelle, Krystal Alisha, Avery Tygre, Casey Orion. BS in Acctg. summa cum laude, Strayer U., 1999. Fin. officer Dept. State, Washington, 1989-98, CIA, Washington, 1983—88, 1998—, budget officer, dep. CFO, 1999-2000, CFO, 2000—04, sys. acct., 2004—. Mem., troop leader Girl Scouts Am., 1998—. Mem. Phi Beta Lambda (pres. Sierra Vista Chpt. 1981-82, state v.p. Ariz., 1982). Avocations: reading, needlecraft, walking, travel. Home: 14529 William Carr Ln Centreville VA 20120

HAND, JONI MARIE, art educator; b. Bedford, Ohio, May 29, 1964; d. Vincent Michael Stenger and Sherry Ann Anulies; m. Scott Emory Garlock, June 3, 1989 (div. Sept. 1994); m. Kevin Curtis Hand, June 19, 2000. BA, Kent State U., 1989; MA, Bradley U., 1997; MA in Art History, Hunter Coll., 2004; PhD, CUNY, 2004. Chair art dept. Havana H.S., Ill., 1992—97; art instr. Homewood-Flossmoor H.S., Ill., 1997—2000, Tappan Zee H.S., Orangeburg, NY, 2000—; adj. prof. Hunter Coll., 2003—, St. Francis Coll., Bklyn., 2004. Adj. art instr. Prairie State Coll., Chicago Heights, Ill., 1997—2000; set designer, instr. Summerstage, Orangeburg, NY, 2000. Co-author: Creating Democratic Classrooms, 1996. Mem.: Coll. Art Assn., N.Y. Road Runners Club. Home: 514 Bayridge Parkway Apt 3A Brooklyn NY 11209 E-mail: JoniH@nyc.rr.com.

HAND, MARY JANE, artist, poet, educator; b. St. Cloud, MN, Oct. 3, 1947; d. Lloyd and Delores (Hand) Wahlberg; children: Amy Beth, Emily Jane, Chelsea Jo. BS in Art Edn., U. Minn., 1972; postgrad., Am. Acad. Dramatic Arts, 1984—85; MA in Human Devel./Arts Adminstrn., St. Mary's U., 2000. Cert. tchr. art edn., K-12 Minn. Adminstrv. asst. L.J. Graham Advt., N.Y.C., 1984—85, Augsburg Pub., Mpls., 1986, World Congress of Women, Moscow, 1987, Inst. Cultural Affairs; CNA Augsburg, Ebeneezer, Fairview, Margaret Hamm and James E. Kelly Estate. Asst. chef Grain Country Restaurant, San Diego, 1990; personal asst. to Meridel Lesueur, Hudson, Wis., 1991—. Fundraiser Mpls. Pk. and Recreation, Pine Ridge Reservation, SD, Minn. Orch., Minn. Sinfonia, Mpls. Children's Theatre Co., Minn. Battered Women's Movement, 1982—; fundraiser CTC, 2000; with project Leon Educators For Peace Minn., Nicaragua, 1989; del. leadership Hennepin County Children's Mental Health Adv. Coun., 2004—05; vol. Art in Bloom, Mpls. Inst. Art, 2003—, Women of Vision and Action Conf., Washington, 1995; vol. Am. Experience Corp., Mpls., 2006—, Women's Art Inst./MCAD, Mpls. Coll. Art and Design, 2006. Home: 2110 Clinton Ave Apt 1 Minneapolis MN 55404-2649 Office Phone: 612-871-6169.

HAND, MARYANNE KELLY, artist, educator; b. Augusta, Ga., Apr. 15, 1955; d. Issac Marvin and Dorothy Whaley Kelly; children: Jill Estes Tatum, Micah Kelly. AA in Graphic Design/Visual Comm., Art Inst. Atlanta, 1974; postgrad., Ga. So. U., Statesboro, Ga. State U., Atlanta. Tchr. Episcopal Day Sch., Augusta, 1984—91; tchr. art Augusta State U., 1993—2000; pvt. tchr. sales and design Transatlantic Antiques, Augusta, 2002—; freelance artist. Exhibitions include Phipps Plz., Atlanta, The Historic Cotton Exch., Augusta Mus. History, Ga. Welcome Ctr., Augusta Mayor's Office, Barnes and Noble, Augusta, Sacred Heart Cultural Ctr., Hawg Wild and Big Iron Saloon, Snug, Vallarte Restaurant, Augusta, Villa, Southern Design Trans Atlantic Antiques, Atlanta, Cottage Collection, The Blue Door, Pastel, Eclectics of the South, Debris, Atlanta, Represented in permanent collections Augusta Mus. History, coverpiece, SASS mag. Named to Nat. Archives Women Artists; recipient Hon. Mention, Manhattan Arts. Mem.: S. Ea. Pastel Soc. Avocations: interior decorating, painting, dance, woodcarving. Office: Transatlantic Antiques 840 Broad St Augusta GA 30901-1215 Office Phone: 706-339-5916, 704-821-1787. E-mail: makart@comcast.net.

HANDA, EUGENIE QUAN, graphic designer; b. Oakland, Calif., Oct. 18, 1957; d. Eugene Ernest and Ruby Quan; children: Sharice Quan, Chaz Quan. BFA in Graphic Design with distinction, Calif. Coll. Arts and Crafts, 1979. Graphic artist Bemis Corp., Union City, Calif., 1979-80; graphic designer Hubbert, Ltd. Advtsg., Santa Clara, Calif., 1980-81, Darien, Russell & Hill Advtsg., San Jose, Calif., 1981-82, KNTV, Inc.-Channel 11, San Jose, 1982-83; owner, graphic designer Quanda Design, San Jose and Danville, Calif., 1983—. Vol. graphic designer, cons. Sycamore Valley Elem. Sch., Danville, Calif., 1994-2003, Charlotte Wood Mid. Sch., Danville, 1999-2006, San Ramon Valley H.S., Danville, 2002—. Work includes design for No. Calif. Hyatt Hotels, 1983-88, Lifescan Quality Awards Program, 1984-87, Hewlett-Packard Collateral, 1987-2002, Jadtec Computer Group Collateral, 1987-95, Am. Med. Writer's Assn. Booklets, 1993-94, others. Art dir. fundraiser East Valley Ednl. Found., San Jose, Calif., 1986; adv. sch. bond Sycamore Valley PTA, Danville, Calif., 1995-98; legis. rep. San Ramon Valley Unified Sch. Dist., Sacramento, 1997-99, 2001-03; standing com. PTA, newsletter and directory chmn., 1995-97; troop team mem., designer, coord. sibling care San Francisco Bay coun. Girl Scouts USA, 1996-97; fundraiser com. chair Sycamore Valley Ball, 1997-2001, Charlotte Wood Charger Classic, 1999-2002; selected interview team mem. for middle sch. prin. San Ramon Valley Unified Sch. Dist. 2001. Recipient Sam Seagull award Advtsg. Club Monterey Peninsula, 1982, Outstanding Vol. award San Francisco Bay Girl Scout Coun., 1997, Charlotte Wood Mid. Sch. Svc. award, 2002, 04. Mem.: Calif. Coll. Arts and Crafts Alumni, PTA. Avocation: volunteering for children's education.

HANDELSMAN, JO, plant pathologist, educator; BS in agronomy, Cornell Univ., Ithaca, NY; PhD in molecular biology, U. Wis.-Madison. Asst. prof. to prof. U. Wis.-Madison, 1985—, dir. Inst. Pest & Pathogen Mgmt., 1997—99, Clark Lectr. Soil Biology, 2002—. Co-author: Biology Brought to Life, 1997. Grantee professorship, Howard Hughes Med. Inst., 2002—. Achievements include establishing Women in Sci. & Engring. Leadership Inst. Office: Dept Plant Pathology U Wisconsin-Madison 1630 Linden Dr Madison WI 53706 Office Phone: 608-263-8783. Office Fax: 608-265-5289.

HANDLER, CAROLE ENID, lawyer, city planner; b. NYC, Dec. 23, 1945; d. Milton and Marion Winter (Kahn) Handler; m. Peter U. Schoenbach, May 30, 1965 (div. Sept. 1979); children: Alisa, Ilana. AB, Radcliffe Coll., 1957; MS, U. Pa., 1963, JD, 1975. Bar: Pa. 1975; Calif. 1987; U.S. Dist Ct. Ea. Pa. 1976, N.J. 1979, Ctrl. Calif. 1987, So. Calif. 1990, So. N.Y. 1990, No. Calif. 1991, Ea. Calif. 1993, Mid. & So. Fla. 1994; U.S. Ct. Appeals 3d cir. 1976, 9th cir. 1988, 2d cir. 1989, 11th cir. 1992; Pa. Supreme Ct.; U.S. Supreme Ct. Planner Boston Redevel. Authority, 1959-61; head gen. plans sect. Phila. City Planning Commn., 1963-66; ednl. facilities planning cons. Phila. Sch. Dist., 1966-67, coordinator and dir. policy planning, 1967-69; instr. U. Sao Paulo, Rio de Janeiro, 1970-71, Cath. U., Rio de Janeiro, 1970-71; law clk. to Hon. Edmund B. Spaeth Jr. Pa. Superior Ct., Phila., 1975-76; assoc. Goodman & Ewing, Phila., 1976-78, Schnader, Harrison, Segal & Lewis, Phila., 1978—; sr. v.p., gen. counsel MGM/UA Distbn. Co., Los Angeles, 1985-87; ptnr. Le Boeuf, Lamb, Leiby & MacRae, L.A., 1987-89, Proskauer Rose Goetz & Mendelsohn, L.A., Alschuler Grossman Pines, L.A., Kaye Scholer Fierman Hays & Handler, L.A., 1997—2000, O'Donnell & Shaeffer, L.A., 2000—04, Thelen Reid & Priest, L.A., 2004—05, Foley & Lardner, LLP, Century City, Calif., 2005—. Adj. prof. Univ. So. Calif. Bd. dirs. St. Peter's Sch.; former bd. dirs. Soc. Hill Synagogue, LA Chamber Orch., 1990—, Public Counsel 1999-; exec. bd. Am. Jewish Congress 2004-; mem Bet Tzedek Legal Svcs. Named one of Top 50 Women Litigators in Calif., Daily Journal Extra, 2002—04. Mem. Phila. Vol. Lawyers for the Arts (v.p.), ABA, Fed. Bar Assn., Pa. Bar Assn., N.Y. Bar Assn., Beverly Hills Bar Assn., L.A. County Bar Assn. (chair antitrust sect. 1992-93), Assn. Bus. Trial Lawyers, Copyright Soc., Calif. Women's Law Ctr. Jewish. Office: Foley & Lardner LLP Ste 3500 2029 Century Park East Los Angeles CA 90067-3021 Office Phone: 310-975-7860. Business E-Mail: chandler@foley.com.

HANDLER, EVELYN, consultant, former university president; b. Budapest, Hungary, May 5, 1933; U.S. citizen; m. 1965; two children. BA, Hunter Coll., 1954; MSc, NYU, 1962, PhD in Biology, 1963; LHD (hon.), Rivier Coll., 1982, U. Pitts., 1987, Hunter Coll., 1988. Rsch. assoc. Sloan-Kettering Inst., 1958-60, Merck Inst. Therapeutic Rsch., 1958-60; lectr. Hunter Coll., 1962-64, from asst. to prof. biol. sci., 1965-80, dean sci. and math., 1977-80; pres. U. N.H., 1980-83, Brandeis U., 1983-91; exec. dir. Calif. Acad. Scis., San Francisco, 1994-98; pres. Merrimack Consultants LLC, Bow, NH, 1999—2004. Vis. scientist Karolinska Inst., 1971-72; evaluator Com. Higher Edn., Middle States Assn., 1972—; vice chmn. univ. faculty senate CUNY, 1974-76; generalist, mem. Am. Coun. Pharm. Edn., 1978-83; bd. dirs. New Eng. Life Ins. Co., Student Loan Corp. Trustee Bay Area Biosci. Ctr., 1995—, Mills Coll., 1995—. Sr. fellow Carnegie Found. Advanced Tchg., 1990-92; scholar in residence Harvard U., 1991-92, assoc. in edn. 1992-93; rsch. grantee NIH, 1964-69, 73-76, NSF, 1965-67, 70-72, CUNY, 1972-74. Fellow AAAS, N.Y. Acad. Sci.; mem. Internat. Soc. Hematology, Harvey Soc. Office: Student Loan Corporation Board of Directors 750 Washington Blvd Stamford CT 06901

HANDLEY, LOUISE PATRICIA, artist; b. Portland, Oreg., Apr. 9, 1938; d. Willard Alan and Dorothy Davis Johnson; m. Richard Dale Handley, June 7, 1957; children: Beth, Richard Jr., Jennifer, Michael. Studied, Lewis & Clark Coll., Portland, Oreg., 1957. Tchr. decorative painting Handleycrafts, Bandon, Oreg., 1973—86. Author: Fabric Silhouettes-Quilted Treasures from the Family Album, 2006. Mem.: Designing Women, Nat. Soc. Decorative Painters (cert.). Democrat. Home: 640 8th St SW Bandon OR 97411 Personal E-mail: louiseh@mycomspan.com.

HANDLEY, MARGIE LEE, manufacturing executive; b. Bakersfield, Calif., Sept. 29, 1939; d. Robert E. and Jayne A. (Knoblock) Harrah; children: Steven Daniel Lovell, David Robert Lovell, Ronald Eugene Lovell; m. Leon C. Handley, Sr., Oct. 28, 1975. Grad. H.S., Willits, Calif. Lic. gen. engring. contractor. Owner, operator Shasta Pallet Co., Montague, 1969-70, Lovell's Tack 'n Togs, Yreka, Calif., 1970-73; v.p. Microphor, Inc., Willits, 1974-81; pres. Harrah Industries, Inc., Willits, 1981—. Gen. ptnr. Madrone Profl. Group, Willits, 1982—; pres. Hot Rocks, Inc., Willits, 1983-89; co-ptnr. Running Wild Ostriches, 1994—; bd. dirs. N-Tech, Nat. Bank of the Redwoods, NBR Mortgage Co., Howard Found., Willits Electronics Assembly, Inc., Redwood Empire Bancorp.; active State of Calif. Employment Tng. Panel, 1993-95, coord. State Calif. Timber Transition, 1994-95; apptd. mem. State of Calif. Econ. Strategy Panel, 1995-2000, mem. Selective Svc. Sys., Local Bd. State of Calif., 2002. Sec. Willits Cmty. Scholarships, Inc., 1962; trustee Montague Meth. Ch., 1966-73; sec. Montague PTA, 1969; clk. bd. trustees Montague Sch. Dist., 1970-73; del. Calif. State Conf. Small Bus., 1984; alt. del. Rep. Nat. Conv., Kansas City, Detroit, 1976, 80; 3d dist. chmn. Mendocino County Rep. Ctrl. Com., 1978-84; mem. Calif. State Rep. Ctrl. Com., 1985—; Rep. nominee for State Senate Calif. 2nd Senate Dist., 1990, 93; mem. Rep. Congl. Leadership Coun., 1980-82; Mendocino County chmn. Reagan/Bush, 1980, 84; Mendocino County co-chmn. Deukmejian for Gov., 1982; mem. Region IX Small Bus. Adminstrn. Adv. Coun., 1982-93; mem. Gov.'s Adv. Coun., 1983-90; Rep. nominee State Assembly 1st Assembly Dist.; del., asst. sgt. of arms Rep. Nat. Conv., Dallas, 1984, del., New Orleans, 1988, Houston, 1992, San Diego, 1996, Phila., 2000, NYC, 2004; chmn. Mendocino County Rep. Ctrl. Com., 1985-2004; active Calif. Transp. Commn., 1986-90; state dir. North Bay Dist. Hwy. Grading and Heavy Engring. divsn., 1986; dir. Lit. Vols. Am.; mem. Calif. Rural Devel. Coun., 1998-2000; dir. Mendocino County Employer's Coun., 1999—; North Coast reg. chair George W. Bush for Pres., 1999-2000; mem. Calif. Rural Devel. Coun., 1998—; State vice-chair, Simon for Gov., 2001-2002; chmn. Mendocino County Scwarzenegger for Gov., 2006. Named Mendocino 12th Dist. Fair Woman of the Yr. 1987. Mem. No. Coast Builders Exch., Soroptimist Internat., Willits C. of C. (hon.), Rotary (dir. 2001-2006, pres. 2004-05). Home: PO Box 1329 Willits CA 95490-1329 Office: Harrah Industries Inc 42 Madrone St Willits CA 95490-4206 Personal E-mail: margiehandley@adelphia.net.

HANDLEY, SIOBHAN A., lawyer; BA cum laude, Coll. of the Holy Cross, 1990; JD, NYU Sch. Law, 1994. Bar: NY, US Dist. Ct., NY (Ea. & So. Dist.). Assoc. Orrick, Herrington & Sutcliffe LLP, NYC, ptnr., product liability litigation, 2003—. Mem.: NY State Bar Assn. Office: Orrick, Herrington & Sutcliffe LLP 666 Fifth Ave New York NY 10103-0001 Office Phone: 212-506-5000. Office Fax: 212-506-5151. Business E-Mail: shandley@orrick.com.

HANDLEY, TILLIAN MARIE ROSE, lawyer; b. May 1, 1961; d. Herman and Catherine Goeman; m. Arthur Handley, Dec. 29, 1989; children: Audrey, Thomas, Theodore, Ava, Amelia. BA in History summa cum laude, U. Mich., Ann Arbor, 1978; JD, U. Penn., 1981. Bar: (Pa.) 1981. Assoc. attorney Barnes and Wheeler LLP, Phila., 1981—91, Meriks Gramer Frazier LLP, Scranton, Pa., 1991—2000, sr. assoc., 2000—. Vol. Scranton Women's Shelter, Pa., 1992—96; fundraising coord. St. Thomas Ch., Scranton, Pa., 1999—2004; bd. dirs. Scranton Sch. Dist. Parents Assn., Pa., 2000—. Mem.: Bar Assn. Pa., Phi Beta Kappa. Office: Meriks Gramer Frazier LLP 120 Franklin Ave #125 Scranton PA 18503-1927 Business E-Mail: handley@meriksgramerfrazier.net.

HANDLY, HILDA ANN, gifted and talented educator; d. James M. and Sarah Jane Higgins; m. David Allen Handly, July 15, 1978; 1 child, Sara Kate. BS in Elem. Edn., Ctrl. Mo. State U., 1978, MS in Counseling, 1987. Cert. gifted edn. Mo. Dept. Edn., counselor Mo. Dept. Edn., spl. edn. Mo. Dept. Edn., elem. edn. Mo. Dept. Edn., sch. pscyhol. examiner Mo. Elem. tchr. Shawnee R-III Sch., Clinton, Mo., 1978—79; spl. edn. tchr. Windsor (Mo.) R-I Schs., 1979—80; elem. tchr. Higginsville (Mo.) C-I Schs., 1980—84, Warrensburg (Mo.) R-VI Schs., 1984—89, elem. counselor/gifted tchr., 1991—94, gifted tchr. - k-5, 1994—; instr. gifted edn. Ctrl. Mo. State U., Warrensburg, 2004—. Conf. presenter Mo. Sch. Counselors Assn., 1993; profl. devel., Love and Logic group leader Warrensburg R-VI Schs., 2001—03; cons., curriculum author Ctrl. Mo. State U., Warrensburg, 2004—05. Mem. Travel and Tourism Bd., Warrensburg, 2001—02. Recipient Spl. Svc. award, VFW, 1999; grantee Co-author of Counseling grantee, State Dept. Edn., 1994. Mem.: NEA (local chpt. pres. 1997—99), Gifted Assn. Mo. (dist. rep. 1994—96, conf. presenter), PEO (sec. 1995—97). Avocations: reading, travel, exercise. Home: 1101 Kismet Dr Warrensburg MO 64093 Office: Warrensburg R VI Sch Dist 522 East Gay Warrensburg MO 64093 Office Phone: 660-747-7478.

HANDSCHU, BARBARA ELLEN, lawyer; b. Buffalo, June 28, 1942; d. Joseph and Rose H. BA, NYU, 1963; JD, U. Mich., 1966. Bar: N.Y. 1967, U.S. Dist. Ct. (ea., so. and we. dists.) N.Y., U.S. Supreme Ct. Hearing examiner Erie County Family Ct., Buffalo, 1981-82; lectr. SUNY, Buffalo, 1983; pvt. practice Buffalo; spl. counsel Mayerson Stutman, N.Y.C. Contbr. articles to legal publs. Mem. Buffalo Housing Ct. Adv. Bd., 1981-84; pres., bd. dirs. Neighborhood Legal Svcs., Buffalo, 1981-85. Recipient proclamation Buffalo City Coun., 1983, Women Helping Women award NOW, Buffalo, 1986. Fellow Internat. Acad. Matrimonial Lawyers; mem. ABA (co-chmn. custody com. 1987—), NY State Bar Assn. (chair family law sect. 1990-92), Am. Acad. Matrimonial Attys. (pres. 2004-05, v.p. 1997-2003, pres. NY chpt. 1995-97, bd. mgr. NY State chpt. 1986—, editor-in-chief jour. 1995-97), Phi Beta Kappa. Democrat. Jewish. Office Phone: 716-885-8005. E-mail: bhandschu@mayersonstutman.com.

HANDY, DANETTE FARMER, coach; b. Winston-Salem, NC, Aug. 18, 1978; d. Raymond Lendell and Shirley Goins Farmer; m. Jeremiah Patterson Handy, Mar. 3, 2001. BS in Sports Medicine, High Point U., NC, 2000. Atc-L NATABOC/NC. Phys. edn. tchr., coach Carver HS, Winston-Salem, 1996—2005; athletic trainer, coach Salem Acad. and Coll., Winston-Salem, 2005—. Mem.: NATA, Kappa Delta Pi. Office: Salem Acad and Coll PO Box 10548 Winston Salem NC 27108 Office Phone: 336-705-0556. Home Fax: 336-721-2733; Office Fax: 336-721-2733. Business E-Mail: handy@salem.edu.

HANE, LAURIE S., lawyer; BA phi beta kappa & summa cum laude, Knox Coll., 1981; JD, Northwestern U., 1984. Bar: Calif. 1984. Law clk. to Hon. Robert F. Peckham U.S. Dist. Ct., No. Dist. Calif., 1984—85; assoc. Morrison & Foerster LLP, 1985—91, ptnr., co-mng. ptnr. ops. Office: Morrison & Foerster LLP 425 Market St San Francisco CA 94105-2482 Office Phone: 415-268-7092. Office Fax: 415-268-7522. Business E-Mail: lhane@mofo.com.

HANES, DARLENE MARIE, marketing professional; b. St. Mary's, Pa., Mar. 24, 1956; d. Donald Frank and Martha Mary (Krug) H. CLU degree, Am. Coll., Bryn Mawr, Pa., 1986, chartered fin. cons. degree, 1988. CLU. Underwriter N.Y. Life Ins. Co., Concord, Calif., 1980-87; v.p. East Bay Fin. Ctr., Concord, 1987-96, v.p. agy. devel., 1988-91; v.p. brokerage ops. Ruckart Assocs., Murfreesboro, Tenn., 1990-96; with Allstate Life Inst., Nashville, 1996-99; fin. planner Nat. Brokerage Co., Nashville, 2000—. Pres. Am. Cancer Soc. League, 1984-86, bd. dirs.; bd. dirs. Airport Commn., St. Mary's, 1975, Nashville Assn. CLU and ChFC Soc., Hosp. Hospitality House, 1995-96, Friends of Watkins Inst., 1996-97; active Jr. League. Named Person of Day, Am. Heart Assn., 1985. Mem. Nat. Assn. Life Underwriters (Nat. Quality award 1985, 86, 87, Pres.'s Trophy 1986), Mt. Diable Assn. Life Underwriters (bd. dirs. 1982—, pres. 1986-87), East Bay CLU Soc. (v.p. 1989), Calif. Assn. Life Underwriters (regional coord. 1987—), Gen. Agts. and Mgrs. Assn., Hosp. Guild (sec. 1989-90), Palm Beach Assn. Ins. and Fin. ADvisors (bd. dirs.), Palm Beach County chpt. Fin. Svc. Profls. (bd. dirs.), Jr. League. Republican. Roman Catholic. Avocations: water-skiing, skydiving, water-skiing, para sailing. Office Phone: 561-252-1061. E-mail: dmcduchfc@adelphia.net.

HANEWICH DURANCZYK, DEBORAH A., art therapist, educator; b. Detroit, May 8, 1955; d. Peter Valery and Ann (Fosha) Hanewich; m. Edward Frank Duranczyk Jr.; 1 child, Alexandra Ann Catherine. BS in Spl. Edn., Ea. Mich. U., 1982; MEd with honors, Wayne State U., 1988. Cert. spl. edn. educator Mich; registered art therapist. Spl. edn. tchr. Washtenaw Intermediate Sch. Dist., Ann Arbor, Mich., 1982—. Art educator in various programs in prisons, summers programs and art shows, Mich., 1981—. Exhibited in group shows at Plymouth Art Fair, 1977, Sixth Ann. Women's Work Art Exhibit, Bay City, Mich., 1988, Mich. Edn. Assn. 24th Ann. Art Exhibit, Lansing, 1988, Stockbridge Spring Art Show, Mich., 1991—; represented in permanent collections in Mich., N.Y., Tex., Washington. Friend Very Spl. Arts Mich., 1994; judge 4-H Youth Programs, Washtenaw County, 1990, 91, Ingham County, Mich., 1992. Mem. Am. Art Therapy Assn., Mich. Assn. Art Therapy (legis. chair 1989-91), Nat. Art Edn. Assn., Mich. Art Edn. Assn. (Purchase award for Watercolor Collage 1990), Stockbridge Coun. for the Arts. Democrat. Avocations: art, crafts, travel. Office: Washtenaw Intermed Sch Dist PO Box 1406 1819 S Wagner Rd Ann Arbor MI 48103-9715

HANEY, MARLENE CAROL, music educator; b. Spokane, Wash., Dec. 10, 1952; d. Edward Nishan and Myrtle Anne (Jenkins) Getoor; m. Dennis Lee Haney, June 14, 1975; children: Mark Phillip, Stephanie Ann. BA, Whitworth Coll., 1975. Cert. Music Tchrs. Nat. Assn., 97, Wash. State Music Tchrs. Assn., 1998. Prin., owner Grand M Studio, Spokane, 1980—. Adv. bd. Music Fest N.W., Spokane, 1995—; adjudicator sonatina/sonata festival Ctrl. Wash. U., 2003. Adjudicator Sonatina/Sonatina Festival Ctrl. Wash. U., 2003. Mem.: Spokane Music Tchrs. Assn. (pres. 1995—97), Wash. State Music Tchrs. Assn., Music Tchrs. Nat. Assn., Mu Phi Epsilon. Nazarene. Avocations: rose gardening, travel.

HANFLING, SUE CAROL (SUKI HANFLING), social worker; b. N.Y.C., Dec. 22, 1945; d. Seymour Leonard and Arline Jocelyn (Marcus) H.; 1 child, Michael Ian. BA magna cum laude, U. Rochester, 1968; BA, U. Chgo., 1969; MSW, Boston Coll., 1973. Cert. sex therapist, diplomat Am. Assn. Sex Educators, Counselors, and Therapists. Dir. Walnut St. Ctr. for Retarded Adults, Somerville, Mass., 1970-71; pvt. practice Belmont, Mass., 1976—; adminstrv. social worker McLean Hosp. Adult Outpatient Clinic, Belmont, 1977—2002. Founder, dir. Human Sexuality program McLean Hosp., Belmont, 1985—, co-founder, dir. McLean Inst. for Couples and Families, 1985—; cons. Watertown Multi-Svc., 1980-90, founder/dir. The Inst. for Sexuality and Intimacy, 2002—; lectr. in field. Recipient award for outstanding contbns. to the field of sex therapy as a therapist, tchr., and supr., New Eng./N.Y. divsn. Am. Assn. Sex Educators, Counselors and Therapists, 2001. Mem. Am. Assn. for Sex Educators, Am. Assn. Sex Therapists (cert.), Phi Beta Kappa. Democrat. Jewish. Avocations: photography, piano, working out. Home: 4A Locust Ln Watertown MA 02472-1733 Office: 73 Trapelo Rd Belmont MA 02478-1048 Office Phone: 617-489-7592. Personal E-mail: sukihanfling@aol.com.

HANFORD, GRAIL STEVENSON, writer; b. Far Rockaway, NY, Apr. 10, 1932; d. Warren Day and Agnes Beatrice (Kane) Hanford. BA, Smith Coll., 1954. Reporter Tustin (Calif.) News, 1955; newspaper editorial asst. The Register, Santa Ana, Calif., 1955; assoc. editor Am. Mercury Mag., N.Y.C., 1956-59; freelance writer N.Y.C., 1959-60; editor Royal Ins. Cos., N.Y.C., 1960-62; book editor/copy editor Am. Legion Mag., N.Y.C., 1962-75, sr. editor Washington and Indpls., 1976-82, asst. editor Indpls., 1982-83; sr. writer Writers For Bus., Indpls., 1983-88, Tampa, Fla., 1988—. Contbr. articles to profl. jours. Bd. dirs. Cathedral Sch. of St. Mary, Garden City, N.Y., 1967-71, pres. Alumna Assn., 1967-69; bd. dirs. Hort. Soc. Indpls. Mus. of Art, 1981-86; pres. Smith Coll. Club Indpls., 1982-84. Mem. Fla. Motion Picture and TV Assn., Nat. Book Critics Cir., Indpls. Press Club (bd. dirs. 1980), Am. News Women's Club, West Fla. Smith Coll. Club (v.p. 1992-94, pres. 1996-99), Ivy League Club of Tampa Bay (bd. dirs. 1989-96, sec. 1990, v.p. 1991). Republican. Roman Catholic. Home and Office: Writers For Bus 4141 Bayshore Blvd Tampa FL 33611-1803

HANFT, RUTH S. SAMUELS, economist, consultant; b. N.Y.C., July 12, 1929; d. Max Joseph and Ethel (Schechter) Samuels; m. Herbert Hanft, June 17, 1951; children: Marjorie Jane, Jonathan Mark. BS, Cornell U., 1949; MA, Hunter Coll., 1963; PhD, George Washington U., 1989; ScD (hon.), U. Osteo. Med & Health Scis., 1993. Cons. Urban Med. Econs. Project, Hunter Coll., N.Y.C. and D.C. Dept. Health, 1962—63; health economist Office of Rsch. and Stats., Social Security Adminstrn., Washington, 1964—66; chief grants mgmt. health div. Office Econ. Opportunity, Washington, 1966—68; sr. health analyst Office of Asst. Sec. Planning and Evaluation HEW, Washington, 1968—71, spl. asst., asst. sec. health, 1971—72, dep. asst. sec. for health policy, rsch. and stats. Office of Asst. Sec. for Health, 1977—79, dep. asst. sec. for health rsch., stats. and tech., 1979—81; health care cons., 1981—88; cons., rsch. prof. dept. health svcs. mgmt. and policy George Washington U., Washington, 1988—91, prof., 1991—95; cons., 1995—. Vis. prof. Dartmouth Med. Sch., 1976—; sr. rsch. assoc. Inst. Medicine NAS, Washington, 1972—76; adj. Ctr. for Bioethics, U. Va., 1999—; mem. exec. adv. coun., adj. prof. James Madison U., 2004—. Contbr. articles to profl. jours. Mem. Med. Assistance Svc. Bd. Commonwealth Va., 1984—89; trustee Meharry Med. Coll., 1989—94; mem. adv. bd. Inst. on Innovation in Health and Human Svcs., James Madison U., 2004—; bd. dirs. N.W. Va. Health Sys., 2003—. Fellow: Acad. Health Svcs. Rsch., Hastings Ctr., Nat. Acad. of Social Ins. (charter mem.); mem.: NAS, Inst. Medicine, Cosmos Club. Jewish. Home: 3340 Brookside Dr Charlottesville VA 22901-9566 Personal E-mail: hrhanft@earthlink.net.

HANKENS, DEBORAH JANE, secondary school educator; b. Minot, N.D., Jan. 8, 1951; d. Thomas Hubert and Jean Theresa (Neil) Miller; m. Richard Stephen Hankens, June 1, 1974; children: Jeffrey Andrew, Kevin William. Bs in Secondary Edn., Dakota State U., Madison, S.D., 1973; MA in Edn., Morningside Coll., Sioux City, Iowa, 1995. Cert. tchr., coach Iowa Dept. Edn. Tchr., coach Cherokee Cmty. Schs., 1980—; tchr. Western Iowa Tech. CC, Sioux City, 1981—2002. Mem., past pres. AAUW, Cherokee, 1975—82, EE P.E.D., Cherokee, 1978—, T.T.T. TV, Cherokee, 1984—. Named All Am., Track & Field Assn. Am., 1981, Iowa Dist. Coach of Yr., Iowa HS Athletic Assn., 1991, 2002; recipient Women's Masters Champion award, Drake Relays Marathon, 1981. Mem.: Cherokee Edn. Assn., Alpha Delta Kappa. Avocations: triathalon, ironman. Office: Washington HS 600 W Buff St Cherokee IA 51012 Business E-Mail: dhank@cherokee.k12.ia.us.

HANKIN, ELAINE KRIEGER, psychologist, researcher; b. Scranton, Pa., Oct. 17, 1938; d. Maurice and Beatrice (Blumberg) Krieger; m. Abbe Hankin, Dec. 22, 1957; children: Susan Hankin-Birke, Elyse Rae Burton. BA, Temple U., 1979, MEd, 1980; PhD, Bryn Mawr Coll., 1984. Therapist Comac Youth Service Bur., Willow Grove, Pa., 1975-76; therapist, supr. interns Aldersgate Youth Service Bur., Willow Grove, 1975-84; staff psychologist, coord. diagnostic testing Buck's County Guidance Ctr., Doylestown, Pa., 1981-84; psychologist, clin. dir. Abington (Pa.) Psychol. Assocs., 1984-99; v.p., adminstr. dir. Corp. Devel. Systems, Abington, 1984-86; supervisor psychology interns Friends Hosp., Abington, 1996—99; pvt. practice psychology, 1985—. Mem. adj. staff Huntington Hosp., Willow Grove, Pa., 1986-98, Eugenia Hosp., Ft. Washington, 1986-99, Progression Inst., Ft. Washington, 1986-90, Westmeade Ctr., 1990-95, Friends Hosp., 1996-99. Mem. adv. bd. for Women and Minority Bus. President's scholar Temple U., 1979, Alumnae scholar Bryn Mawr Coll., 1982. Fellow Pa. Psychol. Assn., Phila. Soc. Clin. Psychologists (mem. membership com.); mem. AAUW, Am. Psychol. Assn., Nat. Coun. on Family Rels., Pa. Coun. on Family Rels., Pa. Soc. Behavioral Medicine and Biofeedback, Phila. Folk Song Soc., Phi Beta Kappa, Psi Chi. Home: 242 Ironwood Cir Breyer Woods Elkins Park PA 19027 Office: York Rd & Twp Line Rd One Abington Plz Ste 403A Jenkintown PA 19046 Office Phone: 215-887-1113.

HANKINS, ELIZABETH AYLMER, orchestra director; b. Lansing, Mich., Sept. 30, 1967; d. Dan Edgar Hankins and Christine Aylmer Newton. BA in Music Edn., Oberlin Conservatory, Ohio, 1989; MEd, Baldwin Wallace Coll., Berea, Ohio, 2003. Cert. tchr. Ohio, 1989. Orch. dir. Lakewood City Schs., Lakewood, Ohio, 1990—. Clinican Am. String Tchrs. Assn., Dallas, 2003; clinician Ohio Music Edn. Assn., Cleve., 2006; orch. dir. Baldwin Wallace Summer String Camp, Berea, 2003—; founder/orch. dir. ROCK ON String Camp, Lakewood, Ohio, 2005—; orch. dir. Ohio String Tchrs. Assn., Columbus, 2005—. Named PTA Tchr. of The Yr., Lakewood H.S. PTA, 2003. Mem.: Ohio String Tchrs. Assn., NEA (assoc.), Ohio Music Edn. Associaion (assoc.; pres. 2006—, N.E. region chair elect 2006—), Am. String Teachers Assn. (assoc. Ohio String Tchr. of the Yr. 2002). Office: Lakewood High School 14100 Franklin Blvd Lakewood OH 44107 Office Phone: 216-227-5990. Office Fax: 216-529-4459. E-mail: elizabeth.hankins@lakewood.k12.oh.us.

HANKINS, SHERLENE LASALLE, mathematician, educator; d. Elloise Hickman Hankins. Degree in Math. Edn., NC Ctrl. U., Durham, 1995. Cert. Educator N.C. Dept Instrn., 1993. Educator Durham Pub. Schools, 1993—97, 1999—; tchr. math. Brunswick County Schools, Bolivia, NC, 1997—99; instr. math. Brunswick C.C., Supply, NC, 1997—99. Mem.: ASCD, NAACP (life; Raleigh-Apex br.), N.C. Coun. Tchrs. Math. Democrat-Npl. Baptist. Avocations: travel, reading, skating, exercise. Office: Durham Public Schools 2905 Fayetteville Street Durham NC 27707 Office Phone: 919-560-3944. Office Fax: 919-560-3489.

HANKLA, CATHRYN, language educator, writer; b. Richlands, Va., Mar. 20, 1958; d. Alden Staley and Joyce Hankla. BA, Hollins Coll., Roanoke, Va., 1980; MA, Hollins Coll., 1982. Prof. English Hollins U., Roanoke, 1983—. Lectr. fiction writing U. Va., Charlottesville, 1985; writer-in-residence Randolph Macon Woman's Coll., Lynchburg, Va., 1987; vis. asst. prof. English Washington and Lee U., Lexington, Va., 1989-91 Author: Phenomena, 1983, Learning the Mother Tongue, 1987, A Blue Moon in Poorwater, 1988, Afterimages, 1991, Negative History, 1997, Texas School Book Depository, 2000, Poems for the Pardoned, 2002, Emerald City Blues, 2002, The Land Between, 2003, Last Exposures, 2004; contbr. articles to profl. jours Mem. Acad. Am. Poets, Authors Guild, PEN Am. Ctr., Phi Beta Kappa, Omicron Delta Kappa Office: Hollins Univ PO Box 9677 Dept English Roanoke VA 24020-1673 Office Phone: 540-362-6278. Business E-Mail: chankla@hollins.edu.

HANKS, ROBIN, rehabilitation nurse; b. 1968; PhD from Dept. Psych., Wayne State U., 1996. Postdoctoral fellow U. Washington Sch. of Medicine; project dir. Southeastern Mich. Traumatic Brain Injury System; dir., Tng. predoctoral and postdoctoral tng. prog., Clinical Psych.; assoc. prof., Phys. Medicine and Rehab. Wayne State U. Sch. of Medicine; adj. prof., Psych. Wayne State U. Sch. of Sci.; chief of Rehab Psych. & Neuropsychology Rehab. Inst. Mich., 1999—. Named one of 40 Under 40, Crain's Detroit Bus., 2006. Office: Rehabilitation Institute of Michigan 261 Mack Ave Detroit MI 48201 Office Phone: 313-745-1203.*

HANLEY, ALLISON ANNE, federal agency administrator; b. Glenridge, N.J., Oct. 31, 1964; d. Michael Joseph Hanley and Carole Helen Matosin. AA in Bus., Abraham Baldwin U., 1984; BSc in Edn., Western Ill. U., 1989; MA, Seton Hall U., 2000. Mil. police sgt. U.S. Army, 1990—96; canine enforcement officer U.S. Customs, Newark, 1997—2001, supr. canine officer Washington, 2001—02; program mgr. Anti-Terrorism Divsn. Customs and Border Protection Dept. Homeland Security, Washington, 2002—05, program mgr. Anti-Terrorism Divsn. Customs and Border Protection, 2005—. Nat. recruiter U.S. Customs, Newark, 1998—2001, Washington, 1998—2001; nat. K-9 evaluator Customs and Border Protection, mem. def. tactics and baton. Sgt. U.S. Army, 1991—96, discharged U.S. Army, 1996. Decorated NATO medal U.S. Army, Expeditionary award. Mem.: Women in Fed. Law Enforcement, Nat. Women's History Mus., Seton Hall U. Hon. Soc. Republican. Roman Cath. Avocations: sports, reading, fishing. Office: Dept Homeland Security Customs and Border Protection 1300 Penn Ave Office Tng and Devel Washington DC 20229

HANLEY, DEBORAH ELIZABETH, meteorologist, wildland firefighter; b. Liverpool, NS, Canada, Nov. 5, 1967; d. Richard Joseph and Nancy Elizabeth (Payzant) Hanley; m. Philip Cunningham, Dec. 30, 1994; children: Catherine Elizabeth Cunningham, Victoria Anne Cunningham. BSc with honors, Dalhousie U., Halifax, NS, 1990, diploma in Meteorology, 1991, MS, 1993; PhD, SUNY, Albany, 1999. Cert. wildland firefighter Fla. Postdoctoral rsch. assoc. Fla. State U., Tallahassee, 2000—02; meteorologist Fla. Divsn. Forestry, Tallahassee, 2002—. Reviewer Holt, Rinehart and Winston, Austin, Tex., 2003—04. Contbr. articles to profl. jours. Mem.: Internat. Assn. Wildland Fire, Am. Geophys. Soc., Am. Meteorol. Soc., Big Bend Parents of Twins Club. Roman Catholic. Achievements include research in effect of upper-tropospheric troughs on the intensification of hurricanes in the Atlantic basin. Avocations: racquetball, golf, sewing, reading. Office: Florida Divsn Forestry 3125 Conner Blvd Tallahassee FL 32399 Office Phone: 850-413-7172. E-mail: hanleyd@doacs.state.fl.us.

HANLEY, KATHERINE KEITH, state official; b. Columbia, Mo., Mar. 5, 1943; d. Everett E. and Anna Catherine (Blanchard) Keith; m. Edward John Hanley, Aug. 6, 1966; children: Cecelia Anne, Patrick Keith. BA in French Civilization, BSin Secondary Edn., U. Mo., 1965; MA in Tchg., Harvard U., 1966. Tchr., guidance counselor City of Falls (Va.) Church Pub. Schs., 1966-78; owner, operator Manor Home Ctr., Mt. Lake Park, Md., 1976-79; counselor U. Mo.; mem., Providence Dist. rep. Fairfax County Bd. Supervisors, Fairfax, Va., 1986-95, chmn., 1995—2006; sec. of commonwealth Commonwealth of Va., 2006—. Chmn. human svcs. subcom., chmn. info. tech. subcom., chmn. audit com. Fairfax County Bd. Suprs.; pres.-elect Va. Mcpl. League; mem. exec. com. Transp. Coordinating Coun.; mem., past chmn. No. Va. Transp. Commn.; mem. No. Va. planning Dist. Commn., 1987—, chmn. legis. com.; bd. dirs., mem. transp. planning bd., mem. bd. vision planning steering com., past mem. met. devel. policy com. Met. Washington Coun. Govts.; mem. regional mobility panel Washington Met. Area Transit Authority; mem. adv. bd. Va. Inst. of Govt. Mem. exec. com. Greater Washington Initiative; mem. State Supt.'s Cmty. Adv. Com., Dulles Airport Regional Econ. Study Commn., Dulles Corridor Rail Study Policy Com.; mem. Commn. on State and Local Govt. Responsibility and Taxing Authority, mem. subcom. on devolution; past bd. dirs. Urban Partnership; past trustee Fairfax Hosp. Sys.; past mem. Commn. to Study Efficiency in Use of Pub. Edn. Funds, Task Force on Tchg. as a Profession, Fairfax County Child Care Adv. Coun., Citizens' Com. on Changing Enrollment in Secondary Schs., Fairfax County Cmty. Action Adv. Bd., other civic orgns.; past vice chmn. Fairfax County Supt.'s Cmty. Adv. Coun.; past pres. Holmes Run Woods and Crossing Civic Assn. Named Pub. Servant of Yr., Greater Merrifield Bus. Assn., 1992; award recipient Mental Health Assn. No. Va., 1995. Mem. Va. Assn. Counties (immediate past pres.), Phi Beta Kappa. Democrat. Office: Office Sec of Commonwealth PO Box 2454 Richmond VA 23218 Office Phone: 804-786-2441. Office Fax: 804-371-0017.*

HANLON, BARBARA JEAN, family and consumer sciences educator; b. Johnstown, Pa., July 17, 1953; d. Bernard Charles and Jean Rigo; m. Robert S. Hanlon, Aug. 20, 1988; children: Jennifer, Gina Kessler, Charles. BS in Home Econs. Edn., Ind. U. Pa., 1974; MEd in Secondary Edn., West Chester U., 1981. Tchr. home econs. Phoenixville Area Sch. Dist., Phoenixville, Pa., 1978—89; instr. early childhood Chester County Intermediate Unit, 1989—2005, cooperative edn. coord., 2005—. Advisor Family Career & Cmty. Leaders Am., 1989—2006, Key Club advisor, 2005—; mem. Future Dirs. Family & Consumer Scis. Task Force, Pa. Dept. Edn., Harrisburg, 2003—. Pres. bd. dirs. Phoenixville Area Children's Learning Ctr., 2000—, Phoenixville Area Violence Prevention Network. Mem.: NEA, Pa. Early Childhood Educators Assn., Nat. Child Care Assn., Assn.Career and Tech. Edn., Chester County Assn. Family and Consumer Scis., Pa. Assn. Family and Consumer Scis., Am. Assn. Family and Consumer Scis., Pa. Assn. Coop. Edn., Nat. Assn. Edn. Young Children, Kappa Omicron Nu. United Methodist. Avocations: reading, sewing, camping, swimming. Office: Ctr Arts & Tech Pickering Campus 1580 Charlestown Rd Phoenixville PA 19460 Office Phone: 610-933-8877. E-mail: barbha@cciu.org.

HANN, LUCY E., radiologist, educator; b. 1946; MD, Harvard Med. Sch., 1971. Cert. diagnostic radiology 1977. Resident U. Pa. Hosp., Mass. Gen. Hosp.; radiologist, dir. ultrasound Meml. Sloan-Kettering Cancer Ctr., N.Y.C.; prof. radiology Weill Med. Coll., Cornell U. Office: Meml Sloan-Kettering Cancer Ctr 1275 York Ave Rm C278 New York NY 10021

HANNA, ANNE MARIE, artist; b. Bloomington, Ind., Mar. 16, 1938; d. August de Belmont Hollingshead and Carol Evaleen Dempsey; m. Gary E. Hanna, June 10, 1961; children: Haldee Calore, Mark H., Scot E. Student, Cen. Sch. Art, London, 1958—59; BA, BS, Ind. U., 1961. Mgr. art dept. Curry's Coll. Bookstore, Ind. U., Bloomington, Ind., 1961—65; nursery sch. tchr. Powder Mill Village, Beltsville, Md., 1965—67; art tchr. Prince Georges County Schs., Laurel, Md., 1973—89; dir. Savage Mill Galleries Savage Mill Corp., Savage, Md., 1989—96; artist Mid-Atlantic region, 1980—. Pres. Laurel Art Guild, 1973—74; lectr. art film series South Coastal Lab., Bethany Beach, Del., 2003—; grad. sculpture instr. Ind. U., 1960; chair vol. program JHES/Prince Georges County Schs., 1972—86; docent Rehobeth Art League, 1998—. Represented in permanent collections Am. Founders of Scouting, portaits, Boy Scouts Am., Qoro LLC, Internat. Art Expo NY Javits Ctr., 2004. U.S. rep. Citizen Amb. Program to China, 1993; ofcl. portrait artist Nat. Capital Area Coun. Boy Scouts Am., Washington, 1984—2000; leader Girl Scouts Am., Prince Georges County, Md., 1968—76, Boy Scouts Am., Washington, 1974—94, leader Sea Scout, 1986—94, dist. tng. chair Patuxent dist., 1984—89, woodbadge instr., 1984—94. Named one of Top 10 Artists to Track, Del. Beach Life Mag., 2006; recipient Best in Show award, Rehobeth Art League, 2002, 2004, Zwanfendael Art Gallery, Nat. Landscape Show, 2003, Silver Beaver award, Boy Scouts Am., 1986, Sea Badge award, 1992, Best in Show award, Rehoboth Art League, 2002, 2004, 2005, Best in Show, Bethany Beach Watercolor, 2006; Individual Artist Opportunity grantee, Del. State Arts Divsn. Mem.: Gallery One Co-Op, Del. Watercolor Soc. (Biggs Mus. award 2005, Best in Show 2006), Nat. League Am. Pen Women, Nat. Portrait Soc., Potomac Valley Watercolorists, Balt. Watercolor Soc. (life), DAR (historian Laurel chpt. 1981—95). Home: 143 Riverview Dr Dagsboro DE 19939 Personal E-mail: artfoxag@msn.com.

HANNA, ANNETTE A., artist, art educator; d. Lucien Adrianowski and Kazimiera Adrianowska; m. David A. Dawley, Dec. 21, 2002; children from previous marriage: Mark, Cliff, Scott, Tod, Tracy. BFA, Centenary Coll., 1997. Mem. faculty Morris County Art Assn., Morristown, NJ, 1997—, Centenary Coll., Hackettstown, NJ, 1998—99, Somerset Art Assn., Bedminster, NJ, 2001—. Pres. Blackwell St. Ctr. Art, Dover, NJ, 1998—2005; bd. dirs. Morris County Art Assn., 2004—. Author: How to Paint Portraits in Oil, 1992. Chmn. com. Arts Coun. Morris Area, Morristown, 2000, 2002, 2004, 2006. Named winner nat. painting competition, Winsor-Newton; recipient Gold medal, Grumbacher, NY, 1988. Fellow: Am. Artist's Profl. League (medal of honor 2000); mem.: Pastel Soc. Am. (signature mem.), Catherine Lorillard Wolfe Club (signature mem., medal of honor 1995). Home: 6 Overlook Rd Boonton NJ 07005

HANNA, CAROL ANN, nursing educator; b. Pine Grove, Pa., Sept. 21, 1942; d. Arthur and Emma Mae (Nye) Potts; m. Paul Joseph Hanna (dec.); 1 child, Kelly Erin. BA, Villanova U., Pa., 1974; MA in Health Edn., St. Joseph's U., Phila., 1977; MSN, Gwyneso-Mercy Coll., Pa., 1989; D Nursing Sci., Widener U., Chester, Pa., 2000. RN Pa., 1964. Staff nurse, head nurse Hahnemann Hosp., Phila., 1963—68, assoc. prof., 1978—97; nurse, relief supr. Pocopson Home, West Chester, Pa., 1980—; mem. faculty Delaware County CC, Media, Pa., 1998—; staff nurse Riddle Meml. Hosp., Media, 2003—. Adj. faculty mem. Immaculata U., Pa., 1998—2001, Widener U., 1999—; cons., mem. exam. com. Commn. Grad. Fgn. Schs. Nursing, Phila., 1996—. Vol. Chester County Cancer Ctr., West Chester, 1999—2001. Mem.: Hahnemann Nurse's Alumni Assn. (treas., Edn. award 1996), Nat. League Nursing (mem. program evaluation com.), Sigma Theta Tau (pres. 1998—2000, Rsch. award 1998). Democrat. Lutheran. Avocations: travel, needlecrafts, gardening, crafts. Home: 425 Merrick Ln Kennett Square PA 19348 Office: Delaware County CC 901 S Media Line Rd Media PA 19063

HANNA, EMMA HARMON, architect, small business owner, mayor; b. Sharpsville, Pa., Apr. 29, 1939; d. James McKarney Supplee and Anne (Woods) Thompson; m. William Hayes Harmon, Sept. 1, 1962 (div. 1984); 1 child, James McKarney Harmon; m. Hugh Allen Hanna, Mar. 21, 1992. BArch, Kent State U., Ohio, 1962. Drafter W.H. Harmon Architects, Orlando, Fla., 1970-73; pres., owner The Plan Shop, Inc., Orlando and Palm Bay, Fla., 1973-87, The Plan Place, Inc., Palm Bay, 1987-97; pres. Engring. & Design Concepts, Palm Bay, 1986-97; owner, pres. The Hanna Studio, Inc., 1997—. Vice chmn. Palm Bay Utility Corp.; vice chmn. substance abuse program Broken Glass, Valkaria, Fla. Mem. coun. City of Palm Bay, 1989-91, dep. mayor, 1991-92; treas. League of Cities, Brevard County, Fla., 1989-92, East Ctrl. Fla. Planning Coun., Orlando, 1989-90; mem. Federated Rep. Women, South Brevard County, 1989-91; mem. exec. com. Brevard County Reps.; mem. Panther Athletic Assn. bd. Fla. Inst. Tech., 1990—, pres., 1995-96, women's locker room bd., 1997-2000; mem. open campus adv. coun. Brevard C.C., Holmes Regional Hosp. Devel. Coun., 1991-04, bd. dirs. 1998—; bd. dirs. Holmes Regional Found., 2002-05; mem. Health First Women's Adv. Coun. Bd., 1997-2000, pres., 1999, found. bd. dirs. 2002-03; mem. Brevard County Commn. on Aging, 2000-04; chair devel. coun. Palm Bay Hosp., 2001-03; bd. dirs. Fla. Inst. Tech. Sch. Psychology, 2002—. Mem.: Greater South Brevard C. of C. (mem. govt. affairs com., bd. dirs. 1991—93, 1998—2001), Palm Bay C. of C., Bldg. Ofcls. Assn. Brevard County (assoc., Assoc. of Yr. 1989), Home Builder and Contractors Brevard County (assoc., bd. dirs. 1993—97, 2nd v.p. 1994—95, Assoc. of Yr. 1995), Drafters Guild (organizer), Zonta Club Melbourne (bd. 1997—2001, sec. 1999—2001, Zontian of Yr. 1998), Exch. Club (chpt. pres., charter pres.). Avocations: bridge, walking. Home and Office: The Hanna Studio 1482 Meadowbrook Rd NE Palm Bay FL 32905-5007 Office Phone: 321-726-8485. E-mail: hannastudio@megabits.net.

HANNA, JULIET MARIE, lawyer; b. Englewood, Colo., May 28, 1970; d. Bruce Edward and Kanchana Kosiyasthit Hanna; m. Michael James Reilly, Sept. 18, 1999. BA in Linguistics and Anthropology, UCLA, 1992; JD, Columbia U., 1998. Bar: Colo. 1998, U.S. Dist. Ct. Colo. 1998. Assoc. Gibson Dunn & Crutcher, LLP, Denver, 1998—2003, 2005—; atty. Greenberg Traurig, LLP, Denver, 2004—05. Author: (screenplay) Off Center, 2001 (film festival finalist, 2002); contbr. articles to profl. jours. Vol. Denver Pub. Schs., 1998—. Fulbright scholar, Inst. Internat. Edn., Cologne, Germany, 1993—94, European law fellow, Columbia U., 1996—97. Mem.: ABA, Denver Bar Assn., Colo. Bar Assn., Internat. Bar Assn. Avocations: reading, writing, skiing, scuba diving, travel. Office: Gibson Dunn & Crutcher LLP 1801 Calif St Ste 4200 Denver CO 80202 Business E-Mail: hannaj@gtlaw.com, jhanna@gibsondunn.com.

HANNA, KATHRYN LURA, university administrator; b. Fairmont, Minn., Jan. 23, 1947; d. Russell George and Dorothy Jane (Buchner) Hanna; m. Jeffrey R. Hoelmer, June 10, 1968 (div. Dec. 1980). BA, Hamline U., 1969; MA, Mankato State U., 1971; PhD, U. Minn., 1999. Instr. biology U. Minn., Waseca, 1971-77, asst. prof., 1977-86, assoc. prof., 1986—, dir. arts & scis., 1990, vice chancellor acad. affairs, 1990-93, asst. dean Coll. Biol. Scis. St. Paul, 1993—99, assoc. dean Coll. Biol. Scis., 2000—01, dir. biology colloquium program, 2001—. V.p. membership Grad. Women in Sci., Mpls., 1993-97; mem. Commn. on Women, U. Minn., Mpls., 1988-97. Author: The New Bio Book, 1984; co-author: The Bio Book Too, 1984. Bd. dirs. Mpls. Coll. of Art and Design Assocs., 1991—, Minn. Acad. Sci., 2001--. Recipient Svc. award Sigma Delta Epsilon, 1989; named Outstanding Educator Adminstr. South Cen. Edn. Assn., 1991. Mem. AAAS, Assn. for Study of Higher Edn. Office: U Minn Coll Biol Scis 123 Synder Hall 1475 Gortner Ave Saint Paul MN 55108-6172 Home: 1816 Commerce Blvd Mound MN 55364-1127

HANNA, MARSHA L., artistic director; b. Tiffin, Ohio, Nov. 27, 1951; d. Willis Leondadis and Frances Lucille (Neeley) H. BS, Bowling Green State U., 1980. Drama specialist City of Dayton, Ohio, 1975-80; gen. mgr. Illumination Theatre, 1978-85; product analyst Lexis/Nexis, 1980—86; instr. Sinclair C.C., 1986—; freelance stage dir., 1986—; resident dir. Human Race Theatre Co., 1986—, artistic dir., 1990—. Dir.: Equus, 1981, Beyond Therapy, 1983, The Diviners, 1984, Amadeus, 1985,Getting Out, 1987, Orphans, 1988, Fool for Love, 1989, A Shayna Maidel, 1990, A Christmas Carol, 1991, Closer Than Ever, 1993, The Good Times Are Killing Me, 1994, Cloud Nine, 1995, Three Tall Women, 1996, The Cherry Orchard, 1996, Quilters, 1997, Taking Sides, Stonewall Jackson's House, 1998, On Golden Pond, 1999, Three Days of Rain, 1999, Art, 2000, Resident Alien, 2001, I Hate Hamlet, 2002, The Dazzle, 2003, Odd Couple, 2004, Every Good Boy Deserves Favour (with Dayton Philharmonic), Johnny Appleseed, Copenhagen, 2005, The Elephant Man, Moonlight and Magnolias, 2006. Office: The Human Race Theatre Co 126 N Main St Ste 300 Dayton OH 45402-1766 E-mail: Marsha@humanracetheatre.org.

HANNA, NOREEN ANELDA, adult education educator, consultant; b. Napa, Calif., Nov. 28, 1939; d. Thomas James and Eileen Anelda (Jordan) H.; m. Leon O'bine Gotcher, Aug. 14, 1971 (div. Nov. 1980); children: John Allen, Tamara Kay. BA, San Francisco State U., 1963; postgrad., Sonoma State U., 1974-81, Ctr. for Leadership Devel., 1982-83; MA, U. San Francisco, 1989. Cert. gen. elem., specialist in reading, gen. adminstrv. svcs. Classroom tchr. Ullom Elem. Sch., Las Vegas, Nev., 1963, J. L. Shearer Elem. Sch., Napa, 1963-78, reading resource tchr., 1978-80; asst. prin. Napa Valley Adult Sch., Napa, 1980-81, acting prin., 1981-82; prin. El Centro Elem. Sch., Napa, 1982-83; adminstr. J.T.P.A./Gain Programs, Napa, 1983-90; prin. Napa Valley Adult Sch., Napa, 1983-99, ret., 1999; inst., curriculum for adult learners U.C. Berkley, 2001—. Commn. mem. Calif. Post Secondary Edn., 1987-89; adv. bd. dir. Ctr. for Adult Edn., San Francisco State U., 1988-95, Immigration Reform & Control Act, Sacramento, 1989-92; presenter, cons. in field. Exec. bd. dir. Leadership Napa Valley, 1985-93; sec. Leadership Napa Valley Found., 1988-99. State Edn. scholar Calif. PTA, 1976, Grad. Edn. scholar Delta Kappa Gamma, Napa, 1977; recipient Cmty. Leadership award Napa Valley Unified Sch. Dist., 1988, George C. Mann Discing. Svc. award Calif. Coun. for Adult Edn., 1994; named Outstanding Adult Edn. Adminstr., Calif. Adult Edn. Adminstrs. Assn., 1998. Mem. ASCD, Am. Assn. Adult and Continuing Edn., Assn. Calif. Sch. Adminstrs. (chair to state adult edn. com. 1988-1991, 93—95, state rep. assembly del. 1989-92, state adult edn. com. chairperson 1989-92, Adult Edn. Adminstr. of Yr. award 1992), Calif. Coun. Adult Edn. (North Coast chpt. bd. dir. 1988-99), Napa C. of C. (bd. dir. 1985-88, edn./bus. com. 1985-99, others), Correctional Educators Assn., Soroptimist Internat. of Napa, Napa Valley Historical Soc. (pres. 1999-01), Napa Valley Geneological and Bio. Soc. (chart. mem.), Phi Delta Kappa, Delta Kappa Gamma. Democrat. Roman Catholic. Avocations: needlepoint, reading, sailing, swimming, hot air ballooning. Office Phone: 707-252-7433. Personal E-mail: napalady1139@sbcglobal.net.

HANNA, WANDA SIMMONS, secondary school educator; b. Whiteville, NC; BA, Winthrop Coll., Rock Hill, SC, 1974; MEd, Winthrop Coll., Francis Marion Coll., Florence, SC, 1974. Cert. in art, elem. edn. and adminstrn. SC. Tchr. South Florence HS, SC, 1974—. Home: 819 Hamilton Dr Florence SC 29505 Office: S Florence HS 3200 S Irby St Florence SC 29505 Office Phone: 843-664-8190. Personal E-mail: whanna@fsd1.org.

HANNAFORD, JANET KIRTLEY, software administrative manager; b. Seattle, June 25, 1940; d. Vernon Augustus and Dorothy Kathryn (Jenns) Kirtley; m. Norman Kenneth Christie, July 1, 1960 (div. 1978); children: Linda Jean, Norman Bruce; m. Robert John Hannaford, Dec. 26, 1981. BA magna cum laude, U. Wash., 1984. Adminstrv. sec. Baylor Coll. of Medicine, Houston, 1976-78; asst. to pres. Weems & Co., Inc., Houston, 1978-79; adminstrv. asst. Seattle Trust & Savs. Bank, 1979-82; cons. Fred Hutchinson Cancer Rsch. Ctr., Seattle, 1985-88. Mktg. cons. Lifetime Learning Ctr., seattle, 1987. Editor newsletter AAUW Bull., 1987. Site dir., chmn. Expanding Your Horizons in Math. and Sci., Seattle Cen. Community Coll., 1990-92; founder, 1st pres. SMARTgirls, Inc., 1996-99. Mem. AAUW (1st v.p. 1989-90, task force chmn. 1990-92), Beta Gamma Sigma, Phi Beta Kappa. Avocations: creative needlework, folk dancing, reading, volunteering, electronic puzzles and card games. Home: 7550 40th Ave NE Seattle WA 98115-4926 E-mail: janhanna2@aol.com.

HANNAH, DARYL, actress; b. Chgo., Dec. 3, 1960; d. Don and Sue Hannah. BA, U. So. Calif.; student, Goodman Theater Co., Chgo. Ind. actress, 1978—. Films include The Fury, 1978, The Final Terror, 1981, Hard Country, 1981, Summer Lovers, 1982, Blade Runner, 1982, Reckless, 1984, Splash, 1984, The Pope of Greenwich Village, 1984, The Clan of the Cave Bear, 1986, Legal Eagles, 1986, Roxanne, 1987, Wall Street, 1988, High Spirits, 1988, Steel Magnolias, 1989, Crimes and Misdemeanors, 1989, Crazy People, 1990, At Play in the Fields of the Lord, 1991, Memoirs of an Invisible Man, 1992, Grumpy Old Men, 1993, The Little Rascals, 1994, A Hundred and One Nights, 1995, The Tie that Binds, 1995, Grumpier Old Men, 1995, Two Much, 1996, The Last Days of Frankie the Fly, 1996, the Real Blonde, 1997, Gun, 1997, The Gingerbread Man, 1998, Hi-Life, 1998, Tripwire, 1999, Wild Flowers, 1999, Hearts and Bones, 1999, Speedway Junky, 1999, My Favorite Martian, 1999, Enemy of My Enemy, 1999, Dancing at the Blue Iquand, 2000, Diplomatic Siege, 1999, Cord, 2000, Cowboy Up, 2001, Jackpot, 2001, A Walk to Remember, 2002, Run for the Money, 2002, Bank, 2002, Northfork, 2003, The Job, 2003, The Big Empty, 2003, Casa de los babys, 2003, Kill Bill: Volume 1, 2003, Kill Bill: Volume 2, 2004, Silver City, 2004, Careful What You Wish For, 2004, Lucky 13, 2005; (TV films) Paper Dolls, 1982, Attack of the 50 Foot Woman, 1993, The Last Don, 1997, The Last Don II, 1998, Rescuers: Stories of Courage: Two Families, 1998, Addams Family Reunion (voice), 1998, Rear Window, 1998, Hard Target, 2000, Jack and the Beanstalk: The Real Story, 2001; prodr, dir.(feature films), Strip Notes, 2001; (short films) The Last Supper (Jury award for Best Short, Berlin Internat. Film Festival, 1994), 1994. Office: c/o UTA 9560 Wilshire Blvd #500 Beverly Hills CA 90212

HANNAH, JUDY CHALLENGER, private education tutor; b. Balt., Oct. 8, 1948; d. John Thomas and Doris Rose (Etherington) Diehl; m. Brian Challenger, Apr. 15, 1968 (div. Dec. 1994); children: John Joseph, Jennifer Elizabeth; m. W. P. Hannah, Oct. 6, 2001. AA, Arlington Bible Coll., 1985; BS, Liberty U., Lynchburg, Va., 1991; M in Edn., Mt. St. Mary's Coll., 1996; Diploma, Inst. of Children's Lit., 1997; postgrad., Regent U., 2005—, Oxford U., 2006. Cert. elem. tchr. Md., 1996. Tchr., K-4 Mill Valley Sch., Owing Mills, Md., 1984—85, Arlington Bapt. Sch., Balt., 1985—86, Mill Valley Sch., 1986—87; bookkeeper, sec. Challenger Engr., Inc., Finksburg,

1987—92; dir. B/A child care ABC Care Inc., 1992—95; tchr. internship Thurmont Elem. Sch., Md., 1995—96; tutor/office mgr. Learning Resources, Westminster, Md., 1996—97; pvt. tutor, owner A Lesson Learned, Inc., Union Bridge, Md., 1997—; dir. edn., ednl. psychology studies Regent U., Va. Mem. delegation People to People Amb. Programs, China, 2001, Global Peace Mission, People to People Internat., Egypt, 2003. Vol. Crisis Hotline, Balt., 1972, leader/tchr. Pioneer Girls Internat., Arlington Bapt. Ch., 1975-78. Recipient Plato award, Internat. Biog. Ctr. Eng., 2006. Mem. Md. Emmaus, Internat. Dyslexia Assn., Smithsonian Inst., Vol. in Missions, Pi Lamba Theta, People To People Internat. Republican. Avocations: writing, hiking. Home: 48 Bucher John Rd Union Bridge MD 21791-9527 Personal E-mail: judyhannah@verizon.net.

HANNAMAN, ALBERTA ANNA, artist; b. Passaic, NJ, Dec. 11, 1932; d. Henry George and Alice Edith Hannaman. Student, Newark Sch. Fine & Indsl. Art, 1950-53. Offset stripper Screenline Photo, N.Y.C., 1956-84, Verilen Graphics, N.Y.C., 1984-87; offset stripper inhouse printing dept. DDB Needham Worldwide, N.Y.C., 1987-88, Screen Images, N.Y.C., 1988-91. Poet, artist: Prince of Flowers, 1987; contbr. articles to poetry anthologies; exhibited in group shows at Del Bello Gallery, Toronto, Ont., Can., 1988-91, The Miniature Painters, Sculptors and Gravers Soc., Washington, 1990, 91, 98-05 Long Beach Island Art Gallery, Surf City, NJ, 1990, 91, 98, 03-05.

HANNEGAN, REBECCA ANN, retired elementary school educator; b. Orange, Tex., Dec. 31, 1946; d. Donald Martin and Helen Ernestine Jeansonne; m. Ivan Vincent Hannegan, June 23, 1967; children: Julie Waldo, Grant. BS in Edn., Lamar U., Beaumont, Tex., 1967. Tchr. Sims Elem., Bridge City, Tex., 1972—2003; ret., 2003. Workshop presenter Tchr. Tutors Sci., Orange, 1995—2006. Lifetime mem. PTA. Mem.: Sci. Tchrs. Assn. Tex., Nat. Sci. Tchrs. Assn. Home: 9162 Pepper Rd Orange TX 77630-0138

HANNER, JEAN P., retired nursing administrator, art gallery owner, religious organization administrator; b. Toronto, Ontario, Can., July 19, 1940; arrived in US, 1953; d. Joseph William and Dorothy (Tootell) Candy; m. Frank M. Beverley (dec.); m. Charles L. Hanner (dec.); 1 child, Anthony David. AS in Nursing, Chaffey Coll., 1978; BA in Pub. Admin., Calif. Poly., 1982, BS, 1970. RN Calif., Fla. Dir. psychiat. nursing edn. Lanterman Devel. Ctr., Pomona, Calif., 1964—2004; owner Pat Hanner Art Gallery, Ontario, Calif., 1964—; pres. Hanner Gallery, Inc., Mesquite, Nev., 2004—. Bd. dirs. Pacific Fed. Credit Union, Pomona, membership chair; bd. dirs., founder Here We Grow Child Care Ctr., Pomona. Author: Ontario City Sewer System, 1980, A Miracle in the Making, 1993. Donor Boystown, Parkinsons Resource Ctr., Palm Springs, Calif. Named Employee of the Month, Lanterman Devel. Ctr., 2003, Employee of the Yr., 2003. Avocations: art, computers, Web surfing. Home and Office: Pat Hanner Art Gallery 911 W Rosewood Ct Ontario CA 91762 Office Phone: 909-983-2304. Personal E-mail: phannerl@excite.com.

HANNIGAN, ALYSON, actress; b. Washington, Mar. 24, 1974; m. Alexis Denisof, Oct. 11, 2003. Actor: (films) My Stepmother Is an Alien, 1988, Dead Man on Campus, 1998, American Pie, 1999, Boys and Girls, 2000, American Pie 2, 2001, Beyond the City Limits, 2001, American Wedding, 2003, Date Movie, 2006; (TV films) Switched at Birth, 1991, The Stranger Beside Me, 1995, A Case for Life, 1996, For My Daughter's Honor, 1996, Hayley Wagner, Star, 1999; (TV series) Free Spirit, 1989—90, Buffy the Vampire Slayer, 1997—2003, How I Met Your Mother, 2005—; guest star Picket Fences, 1992, Roseanne, 1988, Touched by an Angel, 1994, The Torkelsons, 1991. Office: c/o Innovative Artists 1505 10th St Santa Monica CA 90401*

HANNON, LAURA L., accountant, educator; b. Plattsburg, N.Y., May 26, 1965; d. John Calvin and Christine H. Hannon; life ptnr. Andy Plair. BBA in Acctg., U. Ga., Athens, Ga., 1987. Bookkeeper Ins. Unlimited, Tifton, Ga., 1995—. Adj. instr. Moultrie Technical Coll., Tifton, Ga., 1999—. Home: 28 Cedar Ridge Drive Tifton GA 31794 Office: Moultrie Technical College 52 Tech Drive Tifton GA 31794 Office Phone: 229-391-2600. Home Fax: 229-386-0124; Office Fax: 229-391-2626. Business E-Mail: lhannon@moultrietech.edu.

HANNON, PATRICIA ANN, library director; b. Passaic, NJ, Jan. 1, 1947; d. L. Robert and Frances Laurent Hannon. BA in Math., Caldwell Coll., 1968; MLS, L.I. U., 1972. Libr. Hackensack Pub. Libr., NJ, 1968-75; dir. Wood-Ridge Pub. Libr., NJ, 1975-81, Wanaque Pub. Libr., NJ, 1983-84, Oakland Pub. Libr., NJ, 1984-88, Emerson Pub. Libr., NJ, 1988—2005, W. Milford Twp. Libr., NJ, 2005—. Pres. St. Joseph's Parish Coun., E. Rutherford, NJ, 1979, Regency Pk. Condominium Assn., Ramsey, NJ, 1990-91. Named Outstanding Young Women of Am., 1977. Mem.: Highlands Regional Libr. Coop. (pres. 1999—2001), Bergen County Libr. Coop. Sys. (pres. 1988, 1997), NJ Libr. Assn. (pres. 2003—04), Emerson C. of C. (sec. 1992—94, 1997—2002), Beta Phi Mu. Avocations: guitar, needlepoint houses. Office: Director W Milford Township Libr West Milford NJ 07480 Office Phone: 973-728-2824. Business E-Mail: hannon@wmtl.org.

HANNON, SHERRILL ANN, artist; d. Helen Lorraine Hartley and Frederick Henry White; m. Frederick Daniel Hannon Jr., July 21, 1973; 1 child, F. Daniel III. BA, U. N.H., 1972; student, Paul Ingbretson Studio of Drawing and Painting, Manchester, N.H., 1995—99. RN Mass. RN Newton-Wellesley Hosp., Newton Lower Falls, Mass., 1978—83; real estate salesperson Prudential, DeWolfe and Delta Real Estate, Westwood/Medfield, Mass., 1983—95; fine artist Tripp St. Studios, Framingham, Mass., 2000—. Artist demonstrator Everett (Mass.) Art Assn., 2003—. Exhibited in group shows at Salmagundi Club Grand Nat. Exhbn., 2000, Am. Artists Profl. League 73d Grand Nat. Exhbn., 2001, Am. Artists Profl. League 75th Grand Nat. Exhbn., 2003, Acad. Artists Assn. 52d Nat. Exhbn., 2002, Harvard Club, 2002, 2004, Boston Guild Artists Exhbn., 2002, 2004, Rockport Art Assn., 2003, 2004, 2005, Powers Gallery, 2004, 2005. Housing adv. mem. Greater Boston Interfaith Orgn., Boston, 2001, nursing home advocate mem., 2004—; v.p. LWV, Westwood, 1986—87; local coord. Bread for the World, 1985—87. Recipient Ampersand Art award, Copley Art Soc., Boston, 1999, 1st prize, Neponset River Watershed Assn. Canton, Mass., 2000. Mem.: Nat. Academic Artists Assn., Portrait Soc. Am., Rockport Art Assn. (Francis S. Butler Meml. award 1998), Am. Artists Profl. League, Catharine Lorillard Wolfe Art Club (assoc.). Avocations: skiing, reading, gardening. E-mail: sherrillhannon@hotmail.com.

HANOVER, DONNA ANN (DONNA ANN KOFNOVEC), radio personality, actress, journalist; b. Oakland, Calif., Feb. 3, 1950; d. Bob and Gwen Kofnovec; m. Stanley Hanover (div.); m. Rudolph Giuliani (div.); children: Caroline, Andrew; m. Edwin Oster. BA in Polit. Sci., Stanford U.; MA in Journalism, Grad. Sch. Journalism, Columbia U. Former anchor WPIX Channel 11, NYC; co-host, The WOR Morning Show WOR 710 AM Radio, NYC, 2006—. Host (TV series) House Beautiful; actor: (films) The Intern, 2000, Keeping the Faith, 2000, Series 7: The Contenders, 2001, Someone Like You, 2001, Just a Kiss, 2002; (TV films) Another Woman's Husband, 2000, Jenifer, 2001; (TV series) Another World, 1997, As the World Turns, 1999, All My Children, 1999, One Life to Live, 2000, (guest appearances) Law & Order, The Practice, Ally McBeal, Family Law, Sex and the City; author: (books) My Boyfriend's Back, 2005; actor: (plays) The Vagina Monologues, 2000.*

HANRATH, LINDA CAROL, librarian, archivist; b. Chgo., Aug. 22, 1949; d. John Stanley and Victoria (Fraint) Grzesiakowski; m. Richard Alan Hanrath, Nov. 1, 1980; 1 child, Emily BA History, Rosary Coll., 1971, MLS, 1974. Tchr. social studies Notre Dame HS, Chgo., 1971—75; outreach libr. Indian Trails Pub. Libr., Wheeling, Ill., 1975—76, Arlington Heights Meml. Libr., Ill., 1976—78; corp. libr. William Wrigley Jr. Co., Chgo., 1978—. Mem. Spl. Librs. Assn. (chmn. libr. jobline com. 1981-83, 86-87, food agrl. and nutrition divsn. 1988-89, sec. Ill. chpt. 1984-86, pres.-elect 1993-94, pres. Ill. chpt. 1994-95, conf. bd. info. svcs. adv. coun. 1990—, winner Outstanding Achievement award 1997), Assn. Records Mgrs. and Adminstrs., Soc. Am. Archivists, Midwest Archives Conf., Beta Phi Mu Avocations: needlecrafts, skiing, reading, gourmet cooking, tap dancing. Home: 715 E Devon Ave Roselle IL 60172-1461 Office: William Wrigley Jr Co 410 N Michigan Ave Chicago IL 60611-4213 E-mail: lhanrath@wrigley.com.

HANRATTY, CARIN GALE, pediatric nurse practitioner; b. Dec. 31, 1953; d. Burton and Lillian Aleskowitz; m. Michael Patrick Hanratty, May 22, 1983; children: Tyler James, Alison Erin. BSN, Russell Sage Coll., 1975; postgrad., U. Calif., San Diego, 1980, St. Joseph's Cool., 2002—. Cert. CPR instr.; cert. NALS; cert. specialist ANA. PNP day surgery unit Children's Med. Ctr., Dallas, 1981-85; clin. mgr. pediatrics Trinity Med. Ctr., Carrollton, Tex., 1985-86; pediatric drug coord. perinatal intervention team for substance abusing women and babies Parkland Meml. Hosp., Dallas, 1990-97; sch. nurse practitioner Dallas Ind. Sch. Dist., 1997-98; head nurse Lewisville Ind. Sch. Dist. Colony H.S., 1998—2002; nurse Agape Clinics of Tex., 2003—04, Healthcare Med. Assocs., 2400—. Guest talk show Morning Coffee, Sta. KPLX-FM, various TV programs. Rep. United Way, 1988-97, blood donor chair Parkland Hosp., 1990-97, chair March of Dimes, 1992-97; bd. dirs., med. cons. KIDNET Found. Mem. ARC (profl., life), Nat. Assn. PNPs (v.p. Dallas chpt. 1982-83), Tex. Nurses Assn. Avocations: sewing, swimming. Personal E-mail: caring1231@comcast.net.

HANS, PAULA, television producer; Student, U. Nebr., Kearney, 1994—98. TV news prodr., reporter NTV-KHGI, Kearney, 1995—2000; TV news reporter, anchor KSN, Wichita, Kans., 2000—02; TV news prodr. KMTV, Omaha, 2002—03, FOX-31, Denver, 2003—04, KMGH, Denver, 2004—. Recipient Best Feature award, Nebr. Broadcast Assn., 2000, Best Newscast award, Kans. Assn. Broadcasters, 2001, Best Spot News award, 2001. E-mail: paula_hans@kmgh.com.

HANSBURG, FREDA B., psychologist, mental health consultant; b. N.Y.C., Apr. 18, 1950; d. Leon M. and Muriel L. (Goldstein) Forman; m. Frederick Kelner (div. 1984); m. Daniel Hansburg, Jan. 19, 1985 AB magna cum laude, Barnard Coll., 1972; MSW, Bryn Mawr Grad. Sch. Social Work, 1977; PhD, Temple U., 1988. Cert. trainer in psychiat. rehab.; lic. psychologist. Social worker N.E. Cmty. Mental Health Ctr., Phila., 1977—78, Cmty. Life Svcs., Darby, Pa., 1978—79; assoc. Ctr. for Integrated Therapy and Edn., Devon, Pa., 1978—79; dir. program Intercommunity Action, Inc., Phila., 1980—82; coord. Bridgeway House Tech. Assistance Ctr., Monmouth Junction, NJ, 1982—88; dir. IMPACT, asst. prof. dept. mental health scis. Hahnemann U., Phila., 1988—92; psychologist, cons. N. Phila. Health Sys., 1992—93; dir. Tech. Assistance Ctr. U. Medicine Dentistry N.J., Piscataway, 1993—2000; v.p. Active Tng., Berkeley Heights, NJ, 2000—. Psychologist Affiliated Psychotherapists, Long Valley, NJ, 1993—2006, Summit Psychol. Svcs., NJ, 2006—. Co-author: PeopleSmart, 2000, Working PeopleSmart, 2004. Mem. APA, N.J. Psychol. Assn Home: 3 Meadowview Ln Berkeley Heights NJ 07922-1369 Office Phone: 908-273-5558.

HANSELL, SUSAN, writer, educator; b. Stockton, Calif., May 8, 1956; d. Jack Aaron Smuck and Jane Hansell Lewis; m. Gerald Prindaville Uyeno, Oct. 21, 2005. BA with high honors, U. Calif., Berkeley, 1981; MA, San Francisco State U., 1987; MFA, CUNY, Bklyn. Coll., 1996. Lectr. San Francisco State U., 1987-88, Calif. State U., Northridge, 1989-92, Loyola Marymount U., L.A., 1990-91, Bklyn. Coll.-CUNY, 1994—2000, Calif. State U., Long Beach, Calif., 2000—. Represented in permanent collections It Means Dick; author: (plays) Am. Rose, 1997, Rollover Othello, 1996, Affair on the Air, 1998, My Medea, 1995, Drop It, 1988, 14 Ladies in Hats, 1988, Pink Rope, 1986, Mary Mary, 1996, Little Kings, 2001, What Do We Have Here?, 2002, We Are All Dick 3, 2003, I Am Not This Story, 2006. Recipient E.A. Biderman poetry prize Grey Panthers, 1985. Mem. Dramatists Guild, Theatre Comms. Group. Avocation: swimming. Office: CSULB Dept English 1250 Bellflower Blvd Long Beach CA 90840 Office Phone: 562-985-4216. Business E-Mail: shansell@csulb.edu.

HANSEN, ANNE KATHERINE, poet; b. Coulter, Iowa, Oct. 29, 1928; d. Carl Christian and Else Katherine (Paulsen) H. BA, Chapman U., 1958; MA, U. Redlands, 1971. Life credential, Calif. Elem. tchr. Bloomington (Calif.) Schs., 1958-60, San Bernardino (Calif.) Unified Sch. Dist., 1960-87; ret., 1987. Pub.: book of poetry Listen To My Heart, 1999; contbr. poetry to anthologies. Recipient Golden Poet award World of Poetry, 1988, 89, 90, 91, 92, Poet of Merit award Internat. Soc. Poets, plaque, 1993, 94, 96, medallion, 1996. Home: 1371 Parkside Dr Apt 230 San Bernardino CA 92404-5356

HANSEN, BARBARA CALEEN, physiologist, science educator; b. Boston, Nov. 24, 1941; d. Reynold L. and Dorothy (Richardson) Caleen; m. Kenneth Dale Hansen, Oct. 8, 1976; 1 child, David Scott. BS, UCLA, 1964, MS, 1965; PhD, U. Wash., 1971. Asst. prof. then assoc. prof. U. Wash., Seattle, 1971—76; prof., assoc. dean U. Mich., Ann Arbor, 1977—82; assoc. v.p. acad. affairs and research, dean grad. sch. So. Ill. U., Carbondale, 1982—85; v.p. for grad. studies and research U. Md., Balt. and Balt. County, 1985—90, prof. physiology, dir. obesity and diabetes rsch. ctr., 1990—. Mem. adv. com. to dir. NIH, Washington, 1979—83; mem. joint health policy com. Assn. Am. U., Washington, 1982—86, Nat. Assn. State U. and Land-Grant Colls., Washington, 1982—86, Am. Coun. on Edn., Washington, 1982—86; mem. nutrition study sect. NIH, 1979—83; mem. program com. Inst. Medicine-NAS, Washington, 1982—84; mem. Armed Forces Epidemiology Bd., 1991—95; mem. bd. sci. counselors NIEHS, 1992—94, NIH, 1992—94, mem. nat. toxicology bd., 1992—94, NIEHS, 1992—94; mem. search com. Office of Rsch. Integrity, NIH, 1992—93. Author: The Commonsense Guide to Weight Loss for People with Diabetes, 1998, The Metabolic Syndrome X, 1999; co-editor: Controversies in Obesity, 1983, editor chpts. on physiology; contbr. articles to profl. jours.; co-editor: Insulin Resistance and Insulin Resistance Syndrome, 2002. Mem. adv. com. Am. Bur. Med. Advancement China, NYC, 1982—85; mem. adv. bd. African-Am. Inst., 1987—91; mem. adv. com. Robert Wood Johnson Found., Princeton, NJ, 1982—91. Fellow Nueroscis. fellow, U. Pa., 1966—68. Mem.: Internat. Assn. Study of Obesity (pres. 1986—90), Nat. Assn. State U. and Land Grant Colls. (chmn. coun. on rsch. policy and grad. edn. 1986—87), N.Am. Assn. Study of Obesity (pres. 1984—85, 1986—), Am. Soc. for Clin. Nutrition (pres.-elect 1994—95, pres. 1995—96, v.p.), Am. Soc. for Nutritional Scis., Inst. Medicine of NAS, Am. Physiol. Soc., Phi Beta Kappa (Arthur Patch McKinley scholar 1964). Republican. Presbyterian. Achievements include discovery of of periodic (10-14 min.) cycling pattern of pancreas insulin secretion; identification of the pattern of progressive defects in insulin secretion and insulin action preceeding overt clinical type 2 diabetes mellitus; showed prevention of obesity prevents most type 2 diabetes. Office: U Md-Balt Sch Medicine Obesity-Diabetes Rsch Ctr 10 S Pine St MSTF 600 Baltimore MD 21201-1116

HANSEN, BARBARA SOPHIE, elementary school educator; b. Detroit, Mar. 31, 1942; d. Theodore Marion and Cecelia Pearl Lowe; m. Henry Christian Hansen, Jr., July 25, 1964; children: Diane Catherine, Gail Ann. BA in History, Mich. State U., East Lansing, 1964; Cert. in Elem. Edn., U. Mich., 2002. Cert. tchr. Mich. Tchr. St. Thomas Aqunas Sch., Detroit, 1994—95; profl. asst. reading program Dist. #7 Schs., Dearborn Heights, Mich., 1995—97; tchr. 1st grade St. Sabina Sch., Dearborn Heights, Mich., 1997—98; tchr. 2d grade St. Pascal Sch., Taylor, Mich., 1997—2000; tchr. 5th and 6th grades Mt. Hope Luth. Sch., Allen Park, Mich., 2000—01; tchr. K-6 Dearborn Schs., Mich., 2001—. Hist. presenter Greenfield Village, Dearborn, Mich., 1996—; mem., pub. rels. Wayne County Reading Coun., Westland, Mich., 1996—. Vol. Charilty Golf Tournament for PAL, Dearborn, Mich., 1996—2002, Detroit Super Bowl XL, 2006, Show Train Intercontinental Railway, North Freedom, Wis., 2006. Mem.: Wayne County Reading Coun., Mich. Reading Assn. (vol. conv. 2004), Pi Lambda Theta, Epsilon Sigma Alpha. Avocations: playing the accordion, researching, reading, sharing information, writing. Home: 3147 Roosevelt St Dearborn MI 48124 E-mail: barbarasophiehansen@hotmail.com.

HANSEN, CAROL DIANNE, professor; b. Memphis, Oct. 15, 1948; d. Stanley Frederick and Rheba (Elizabeth) H. BS, U. Ill., 1970, MA, 1972; PhD, U. N.C., 1985. Tchr. various schs., Switzerland and U.S., 1970-75; research asst. Internat. Program for Tng. in Health, Chapel Hill, N.C., 1981-83; sr. instructional designer Arthur Andersen & Co., Washington, 1983-85; asst. prof. Sch. Edn. Am. U., Washington, 1985; br. chief tng. design and evaluation svcs. U.S. Dept. State, Washington, 1986-89; assoc. prof. human resource devel. Ga. State U., Atlanta, 1990—. Cons., asst. project dir. AIDS Technician Tng. Rsch. Ctr. Disease Control, Atlanta, 1992—; dir., author USIA-funded grant between Ga. State U. and Ministry of higher Edn. (Ivory Coast) for creation of Ivorian HRD Ctr. Co-author: (with Wallace Hannum) Instructional Systems Development in Large Organizations, Educational Technology, 1988 (A.E.C.T. award for excellence 1990); contbr. rsch. articles to profl. jours. including Human Rels., HRD Quar., HRM Rev. Fulbright-Hay scholar, 1973. Mem. ASTD, Am. Ednl. Rsch. Assn., Nat. Soc. for Performance and Instrn., Alliance Francaise, Am. Evaluation Assn., Acad. for Human Resource Devel. (founding mem.). Episcopalian. Avocations: travel, photography. Office Phone: 404-651-1653.

HANSEN, CAROL LOUISE, literature and language professor; b. San Jose, Calif., July 17, 1938; d. Hans Eskelsen and Thelma Josephine (Brooks) Hansen; m. Merrill Chris Davis, July 17, 1975 (div.). BA in English, San Jose State U., 1960; MA in English Lit., U. Calif., Berkeley, 1968; PhD in English Lit., Ariz. State U., 1975. Asst. prof. English City Coll. San Francisco, Calif., 1985—, Coll. San Mateo, Calif., 1987—, De Anza Coll., 1998-99; lectr. expository writing U. San Francisco, 2001; prof., dean of journalism Olivet U., San Francisco, 2005—. Writing coord. Calif. State U., Monterey Bay, 1996; mem. rsch. com. Conf. on Coll. Composition and comm., 2001; presenter in field. Author: Woman as Individual in English Renaissance Drama, 1993, 2d edit., 1995, 3d edit., 2000, The Life and Death of Asham: Leonard and Virginia Woolf's Haunted House, 2000, Beyond Evil: Cathy and Cal in East of Eden, 2002; contbr. articles to profl. jours. Active Grace Cathedral, San Francisco. Fellow NDEA. Mem.: MLA (chair exec. com. discussion group on two-yr. colls. 1999), Virginia Woolf Soc. Episcopalian. Office: City Coll San Francisco 50 Phelan Ave San Francisco CA 94112-1821 Office Phone: 415-452-7068. Personal E-mail: carhansen@sbcglobal.net.

HANSEN, ELAINE TUTTLE, academic administrator; m. Stanley Hansen; children: Emma, Isla. AB with greatest distinction cum laude, Mt. Holyoke Coll., 1969; MA, U. Minn., 1972; PhD, U. Wash., 1975. Asst. editor Mid. English dictionary U. Mich., 1975-77, assoc. rsch. editor, 1977—78; asst. prof. dept. English Hamilton Coll., NY, 1978—80, Haverford Coll., Pa., 1980—86, assoc. prof., 1986—90, chair, 1989—92, prof., 1991—2002, provost, 1995—2002; pres. Bates Coll., Lewiston, Maine, 2002—. Lectr. in field. Author: The Solomon Complex: Reading Wisdom in Old English Poetry, 1988, Chaucer and the Fictions of Gender, 1992, Mother Without Child: Contemporary Fiction and the Crisis of Motherhood, 1997; mem. editl. bd. Coll. Lit.; reader manuscripts for jours. and univ. presses; contbr. articles to profl. jours., also revs. and papers. NEH Summer stipendee, 1981; Mellon grantee for faculty devel. in humanities, 1983-84, Whitehead grantee for faculty in the humanities, 1987-88; Am. Coun. Learned Socs. fellow, 1993-94. Mem. MLA (mem. Chaucer divsn. exec. com. 1995-99, divsn. rep. to del. assembly 1996-99, com. on acad. freedom and profl. rights and responsibilities 1997-2000), Am. Coun. Learned Socs. (prescreener Cen. Fellowship Program), Medieval Acad., New Chaucer Soc., Nat. Women's Studies Assn., Soc. for Feminist Medieval Scholarship (pres. 1993-95). Office: Bates College Office of the Pres Lane Hall Rm 204 Lewiston ME 04240 Office Phone: 207-786-6100. E-mail: president@bates.edu.*

HANSEN, ELIZABETH ANN, education educator; b. Des Moines, Iowa, May 13, 1977; d. Fred Ernst and Susan Mary Koch; m. Ryan Allen Hansen, June 9, 2001. BS, U. No. Iowa, Cedar Falls, 1999; MS, U. Iowa, Iowa City, 2001, PhD, 2006. Tchg./rsch. asst. U. Iowa, 1999—2006; prof. Western Ill. U., Macomb, 2006—. Recipient Allen T. Craig award for Outstanding Tchg. Asst., U. Iowa, 2003.

HANSEN, ELIZABETH (BETH) STEVENS, human resources consultant; b. Muskegon, Mich., Jan. 3, 1961; d. C. Leigh Stevens II and Ruth Stephens Stevens; m. J. Mark Hansen; children: Helen, Hannah. BS in Mgmt. Sci., So. Meth. U., 1983. Systems engr. Procter & Gamble, Dallas, 1982—89, customer svc. logistics mgr. Sherman, Tex., 1989—91; regional customer svcs. mgr. Procter & Gamble Distbg., Dallas, 1992—94; juice ops. mgr. Procter & Gamble, Sherman, 1994—99, site human resources mgr., 1999—2002; pres. HansenHR, Inc., Fairview, Tex. Founding pres. Found. Lovejoy Sch., Allen, Tex.; bd. dirs. Cross Timbers Youth Orch., McKinney, 2003—, pres., 2005—06; bd. dirs. Heard Natural Sci. Mus., McKinney, Tex., 1994—99, Dallas Symphony Innovators, Dallas, 1986—92, McKinney Symphony Orch., McKinney, Tex., 2000—02. Mem.: Texoma Human Resource Mgmt. Assn. (pres. 2001). Congregationalist. Avocations: swimming, gardening, music, travel. Office: HansenHR Inc 500 Lakewood Dr Fairview TX 75069 Office Phone: 214-893-6826.

HANSEN, JANET M., bank executive; b. Sioux Falls, S.D., June 5, 1943; d. Edward Woodrow and Ruth Lillian Hansen. Student, Nettleton C.C., Sioux Falls, 1961; BS, U. Minn., 1983; JD, William Mitchell Coll. Law, 1987. Bar: Minn. 1988. Tchr. Nettleton Coll., 1961-65; dep. clk. U.S. Dist. Ct., Sioux Falls/Rapid City, S.D., 1965-78; paralegal East River Legal Svcs., Vermillion, S.D., 1978-80; legal sec. Faegre & Benson, Mpls., 1980-86, law clk., 1986-87; trust acct. mgr. Norwest Bank Minn., Mpls., 1987-91, trust dept. mgr., 1991-97; regional trust mgr. pvt. client svcs. Wells Fargo, Las Vegas, 1997—99; sr. regional trust mgr. Wells Fargo Pvt. Client Svcs. Ctr., 1999—. Team capt. United Way, Mpls., 1996, Las Vegas, 1997-98. Recipient Leader Lunch award YWCA, 1986. Mem. Minn. Bar Assn., Hennepin County Bar Assn., Minn. Women Lawyers, Fin. Women Internat., So. Nev. Estate Planning Coun., So. Nev. Golf Assn. for Bus. Women (pres. 1999-2000), Women's So. Nev. Golf Assn. (v.p. 2002-03, pres. 2004-2005). Avocations: golf, reading, theater, movies, fishing. Office: Wells Fargo Ste 200 3300 W Sahara Ave Las Vegas NV 89102 E-mail: Hansenjm@wellsfargo.com.

HANSEN, JEAN MARIE, mathematics educator, computer educator; b. Detroit, Mar. 8, 1937; d. Harvey Francis and Ida Marie (Hay) Chapman; m. Donald Edward Hansen, Aug. 29, 1968; children: Jennifer Lynn, John Francis. BA, U. Mich., 1959, MA, 1960. Cert. Secondary Sch. Tchr. Tchr. Detroit Pub. Schs., 1959-60, Newark Sch. Dist., Calif., 1960-65, Dept. Def., Zweibruken, Germany, 1965-67, Livonia Pub. Schs., Mich., 1967-69; instr. Ford Livonia Transmission Plant, 1990—. Trustee, pres. Northville Bd. Edn., Mich., 1981-97; trustee Northville Dist. Libr., 1999—, pres. bd., 2003. Author: California People and Their Government, 1965, Voices of Government, 1969-70. Named Disting. Bd. Mem., Mich. Assn. Sch. Bds., 1991, Citizen of Yr., Northville C. of C., 1991. Mem. AAUW (v.p. Northville bd. 1982-86, pres. 1987-89, Mich. chpt. Agt. of Change award, edn. area 1985), LWV, Kiwanis, Northville Women's Club. Republican. Avocations: weaving, basket weaving, skiing, golf, travel. Home: 229 Linden St Northville MI 48167-1426 E-mail: jhansen@comcast.net.

HANSEN, JEANNE, music educator; b. Spokane, Wash., Jan. 20, 1942; m. Edward Henry Weisman, June 16, 1968; children: Marc Richard, Beth Adair. BA, Whitman Coll., 1964; MA, Syracuse U., 1967. Lectr. SUNY, Cortland, N.Y., 1968-69; piano tchr. Ohio, 1970—; instr. Andover Educators, Portland, Oreg., 1998—. Cons. editor FJH Music Inc., Ft. Lauderdale, Fla., 1990—. Editor (music publ.) Developing Artist, 1990, Achievement Skill Sheets Nos 1-6, 1995, Achievement Skill Sheets Nos. 7 and 8, 1997. Mem. Music Tchrs. Nat. Assn. (adjudicator 1980—), Suzuki Assn. Ams., Nat. Guild Piano Tchrs. (adjudicator 1975—).

HANSEN, JO-IDA CHARLOTTE, psychology professor, researcher; b. Washington, Oct. 2, 1947; d. Gordon Henry and Charlotte Lorraine (Helgeson) H.; m. John Paul Campbell. BA, U. Minn., 1969, MA, 1971, PhD, 1974. Asst. prof. psychology U. Minn., Mpls., 1974-78, assoc. prof., 1978-84, prof.,

1984—, dir. Ctr. for Interest Measurement Rsch., 1974—, dir. counseling psychology program, 1987—, dir. Vocat. Assessment Clinic, 1997—, prof. human resources and indsl. rels., 1997—, assoc. dean for grad. studies Coll. Liberal Arts, 2005—. Author: User's Guide for the SII, 1984, 2d edit., 1992, Manual for the SII, 1985 2d edit. 1994; editor: Measurement and Evaluation in Counseling and Development, 1993-2000; editor Jour. Counseling Psychology, 1999-2005; contbr. over 150 articles to profl. jours., chpts. to books. Recipient early career award U. Minn., 1982, E.K. Strong, Jr. gold medal, 1984. Fellow APA (coun. reps. 1990-93, 97-99, pres. divsn. counseling psychology 1993-94, chmn. joint com. testing practices 1989-93, com. to revise APA/Am. Ednl. Rsch. Assn. nat. coun. measurement evalation testing stds. 1993-99, exam. com. Assn. State Provincial Psychology Bds. 1996-99, bd. sci. affairs, 2003-05, chair coun. of editors 2003-04; Leona Tyler award for rsch. and profl. svc. 1996); mem. ACA (extended rsch. award 1990, disting. rsch. award 1996), Assn. for Measurement and Evaluation (pres. 1988-89, Exemplary Practice award 1987, 90). Avocations: golf, theater, music, water and downhill skiing, spectator sports. Office: U Minn Dept Psychology Ctr Interest Measurement 75 E River Rd Minneapolis MN 55455-0280 Business E-Mail: hanse004@umn.edu.

HANSEN, JULIA ANN, elementary school educator; b. St. Joseph, Mo., Nov. 24, 1954; d. Jule Holmes and Beverly Jean (Brown) T.; m. Jess Hansen, June 2, 2001. BS in Elem. Edn., N.W. Mo. State U., 1976, MEd, 1980. Tchr. learning disabilities Nodaway-Holt, Maitland, Mo., 1976-79, Lexington (Mo.) R-V, 1979-84, classroom tchr., 1984—2005; ret., 2005. Mem. Young Citizens for Jerry Litton, Chillicothe, Mo., 1972, 76; mem. PTO, 1984-2005, historian, 1993-94, 94-95, 95-96; mem. Leslie Bell Tchr. Support Team, 1995-96, 96-97, Level II Math. Com., 1984-2005. Named Tchr. of Yr., Leslie Bell Elem., 2005; recipient Ernestine Seiter Meml. award, 2005. Mem. Mo. State Tchrs. Assn., Comty. Tchrs. Assn. (sec. 1992-93, bldg. rep. 1999-2005, prin. adv. com. mem., 2003-2005, tchr. mentor, 1998-99, 2003-2004), Order Ea. Star, Delta Kappa Gamma (chair personal growth and svcs. com. 1996-1998, 2000-, 2d v.p. 1998-2000). Baptist. Avocations: reading, playing piano, walking, travel.

HANSEN, KAREN THORNLEY, accountant; b. Chgo., June 1, 1945; BA, Marycrest Coll., Davenport, Iowa, 1967. CPA, N.Y.; cert. med. technologist. Med. staff tech. Mercy Hosp., Davenport, Iowa, 1967-68, St. Joseph Hosp., Chgo., 1968, Spl. Hematology, Wilford Hall, USAF Hosp., Lackland AFB, Tex., 1973-78; staff acct. Lewittes & Co., Poughkeepsie, N.Y., 1980-81; sr. acct. Urbach, Kahn & Werlin, Poughkeepsie, 1981-82; ptnr. Hansen & Dunn, CPA's, Poughkeepsie, 1982-94, Hansen & Arnold, Poughkeepsie, 1995-2000, Sedore & Co., CPA, 2001—. Bd. dirs., sec. United Way Dutchess County, Poughkeepsie, 1988—94; mem. Jr. League Poughkeepsie, 1979—; mem. membership com. and econ. devel. com. Poughkeepsie Partnership, Inc.; trustee St. Martin de Porres Ch.; bd. dirs. YMCA Dutchess County, Girl Scouts U.S.A., 1983—87, Mid-Hudson Civic Ctr., Inc., 1993—95, Civic Properties, Inc., 1992—, Poughkeepsie Inst., 1999—, Am. Heart Assn. Dutchess and Ulster Counties. Mem. AICPA, N.Y. State Soc. CPAs, Greater Poughkeepsie Area C. of C. (bd. dirs. 1986—, 1st vice chair 1996, chair, 1997, sec. exec. com. 1991, Amrita Club (bd. dirs. 1982-92, pres. 1990), Poughkeepsie Tennis Club. Republican. Roman Catholic. Home: 2678 South Rd Poughkeepsie NY 12601-5254

HANSEN, LINDA MARIE, small business owner; b. Ottawa, Ill., June 5, 1953; d. Orville H. and Delphine M. (Waggoner) Smith; m. James D. Hansen, Oct. 8, 1970 (div. July 1994); children: Gary, Larry, Tyee. Student, Sauk Valley Coll., Dixon, Ill., 1988. Cert. cosmetologist, Ill. Stylist Total Look, Dixon, 1984, Ahead Time, Dixon, 1985-89; color technician ind. contractor, Dixon, 1989-94; owner, operator A Head of Times, Dixon, 1995—. Color cons., 1995—. Supporter girls athletic programs, Dixon, 1995—; fundraiser Muscular Dystrophy Assn., Dixon, 1997; make-up artist for drama group, Dixon, 1989. Mem. Am. Home Garden Club, Cath. Women's Club. Avocations: landscaping, flower gardening. Office: 1116 Carondelet Rd Dixon IL 61021-9368

HANSEN, LOUISE HILL, music educator, retired application developer; b. Claudville, Va., Oct. 28, 1936; d. James Hobert Hil and Ruth Hubbard Hill; m. Gary George Hansen, Mar. 2, 1958; 1 child, Ricky Allen. AA, Sandhill CC, 1969; BA in History, West Chester State U., Pa., 1971; cert., Assumption Montessori Tchrs. Sch., 1972; student in Music, Lincoln U., 1977—95; MPA, U. Mo., 1984. Cert. tchr. 1996. Clk. The Pentagon USAF, Washington, 1955—57; tchr. Libertyville (Ill.) Montessori Sch., 1972—75; adminstrv. asst. Office Gov. Joseph Teasdale, Jefferson City, Mo., 1977—81; programmer analyst Dept. Social Svcs., Jefferson City, 1981—96; prin., owner Hansen Music Studio, Waupaca, Wis., 1997—. Organist Crystal Lake Ch., Waupaca, 2000—. Mem.: DAR, Nat. Guild Piano Tchrs., Wis. Music Tchrs. Assn., Suzuki Assn. Am. (tchr. tng. 1996, 1997, 1999—2001, 2003—04). Democrat. Avocations: exercise, travel. Home and Office: Hansen Music Studio N2237 Smith Rd Waupaca WI 54981

HANSEN, MATILDA, former state legislator; b. Paullina, Iowa, Sept. 4, 1929; d. Arthur J. and Sada G. (Thompson) Henderson; m. Robert B. Michener, 1950 (div. 1963); children: Eric J., Douglas E.; m. Hugh G. Hansen (dec.). BA, U. Colo., 1963; MA, U. Wyo., 1970. Tchr. history Englewood (Colo.) Sr. H.S., 1963-65; dir. Albany County Adult Learning Ctr., Laramie, Wyo., 1966-78, Laramie Plains Civic Ctr., 1979-83; treas. Wyo. Territorial Prison Corp., Laramie, 1988-93, also bd. dirs. Bd. dirs. Wyo. Territorial Pk. Author: (textbooks) To Help Adults Learn, 1975, Let's Play Together, 1978, Clear Use of Power, A Slice of Wyoming Political History, 2002. Legislator Wyo. Ho. of Reps., Cheyenne, 1975-95, minority whip, 1987-88, asst. minority leader, 1991-92, 93-94; mem. mgmt. coun. Wyo. State Legislature, Cheyenne, 1983-84; chair Com. for Dem. Legislature, Cheyenne, 1990-94, Wyo. State Dems., 1995-99; clk. Wyo. Soc. of Friends meeting, 2003-. GE fellow in econs. for high sch. tchrs., 1963; named Pub. Citizen of Yr., Wyo. Assn. Social Workers, 1980-81. Mem. LWV Wyo. (v.p. 1966-68), LWV Laramie (bd. dirs. 1966-72, Nat. Conf. State Legislators (vice chair human resources 1983, nat. exec. com. 1990-94), Laramie Area C. of C., Laramie Women's Club, Faculty Women's Club. Democrat. Avocations: gardening, mountain climbing, quilting. Home and Office: 1306 E Kearney St Laramie WY 82070-4142

HANSEN, MICAELA L., assistant principal; d. Michael J and Melva M Persinger; m. Larry D Hansen, Mar. 20, 1995; children: Michael R Kastning, Gina L Kastning-Navarrette. PhD, U.S.D., Vermillio7, 1997. Prin. Everett Accelerated Elem. Sch., Sioux City, Iowa, 1998—2003; assoc. prin. Sioux City West H.S., 2003—. Cons. Excel Ednl. Svcs., South Sioux City, Nebr., 1993—99. Mem.: Sch. Adminstrs. of Iowa (assoc.). Office: Sioux City West HS Casselman IA 51103 Office Phone: 712-279-6655. E-mail: hansenm@sioux-city.k12.ia.us.

HANSEN, MICHELE SIMONE, communications executive; b. Nashua, N.H., Feb. 19, 1947; d. Real Louis and Eleanore Marie (Desbiens) Bujold; widowed; 1 child, Karl Alexander BA cum laude, Rivier Coll., 1968, MA cum laude, 1988. Cert. tchr., N.H. Reporter, editor Nashua Telegraph, 1968—70; editor USAF Cmty. Newspaper, Izmir, Turkey, 1972—74, USAF Wives Mag., Ramstein, Germany, 1975—78; tchr. journalism and English Nashua Sr. H.S., 1980—2004; ret., 2004; proofreader Merrimack News, 2005—. Chair publicity Adopt-A-Sch. Com., Nashua, 1985-95; mem., treas. St. Joseph's Choir, 1982-97; bd. dirs. Yankee Pen, 1992— Named N.H. Journalism Tchr. of Yr., Union Leader, 1992, Young Career Woman of Yr., Nashua Bus./Profl. Women's Club, 1968 Mem. Nat. Coun. Tchrs. English, N.H. Coun. Tchrs. English, Journalism Edn. Assn. (N.H. state dir. 1998-2004), Ret. Officers Assn., DAV Aux., USCG Acad. Parents Assn., Rivier Coll. Alumni Assn. (bd. dirs. 1980-84) Democrat. Roman Catholic. Avocations: travel, singing. Office: Nashua Sr High Sch 36 Riverside Dr Nashua NH 03062-1312

HANSEN, NANCY C. URDAHL, retired special education educator, small business owner; b. Tacoma, May 17, 1940; d. Arthur Selmer and Doris Lavina (Perry) Urdahl; m. John Raymond Hansen, Apr. 2, 1966 (div.); children: John Raymond, Julia Amy. BA, U. Puget Sound, 1969; postgrad., Gov.'s State U., 1972-73; AA, Seattle C.C., 1978; MEd, U. Wash., 1979. Cert. spl. edn. tchr., Wash. Tchr. Grace Migrant Sch., Park Forest, Ill., 1970-71, Rainbow Valley Child Care Ctr., Seattle, 1977-78; tchr. aide Highline Pub. Schs., Seattle, 1978, Experimental Edn. Unit U. Wash., Seattle, 1978; vol. coord. Camp Fire Inc., Seattle, 1979-80; rschr. Mott Rehab. Svcs., Mountlake Ter., Wash., 1980-82; tchr. South Kitsap Sch. Dist., Port Orchard, Wash., 1980-82, resource rm. tchr., 1982—2004; advisor, tchr. Micro-Society (econ. model for sch.), 1994-96; ret., 2004; owner Glenwood Gardens, Port Orchard, Wash., 2006—. Interviewer King County Interagy. Project U. Wash., Seattle, 1978-80; sec. Queen Anne Juvenile Ct. Conf. Com., Seattle, 1976-78. Contbr. articles to profl. jours. Mem. citizen adv. group Piecre County Comprehensive Plan, Tacoma, 1992; co-coord. Keep Wash. Liveable, Tacoma, 1990; sec., co-founder Peninsula Neighborhood Assn., Gig Harbor, Wash., 1988-91, bd. dirs., 1992; coord. & co-founder Peninsula Stream Monitors, Gig Harbor, 1992-95. Mem. Wash. Edn. Assn., South Kitsap Edn. Assn., Learning Disabilities Assn. Wash., Alpha Phi Sorority. Avocations: gardening, reading.

HANSEN, RAE LAVONE, secondary school educator; b. Des Moines, Feb. 22, 1964; d. Raymond Keith and Helen Lenore Gartin; life ptnr. Michael D. Larson; children: Sydni Helen, Jesse Lee. BS, Iowa State U., 1986; MA, Jones Internat. U., 2006. Cert. Nat. Bd. Profl. Tchg. Standards, 2000. Tchr. english Pierce (Nebr.) H.S., 1986—88, Webster (Iowa) City H.S., 1988—. Office: Webster City High School 1001 Lynx Avenue Webster City IA 50595 Office Phone: 515-832-9210. Business E-Mail: rhansen@webster-city.k12.ia.us.

HANSEN, ROBYN L., lawyer; b. Terre Haute, Ind., Dec. 2, 1949; d. Robert Louis and Shirley (Nagel) Wieman; m. Gary Hansen, Aug. 21, 1971 (div. 1985); children: Nathan Ross Hansen, Brian Michael Hansen; m. John Marley Clarey, Jan. 1, 1986; 1 child, John Zender Clarey. BA, Gustavus Adolphus, 1971; JD cum laude, William Mitchell Coll. Law, 1977. Bar: Minn. 1977, U.S. Dist. Ct. Minn. 1977. Atty. Briggs and Morgan P.A., St. Paul, 1977-93, Leonard, Street and Deinard, Mpls., 1993—. Trustee Actors Theatre, St. Paul, 1980—88, Minn. Mus. Am. Art, 1994—97; active Minn. Inst. Pub. Fin., 1987—93, bd. dirs., 1993—95, pres., 1995; bd. dirs. St. Paul Downtown Coun., 1985—93, St. Paul Area Conv. and Vis. Bur., 1995—2005, chair, 1999—2001; trustee Met. State U. Found., 1993—2005, chair, 2000—02; bd. dirs. Capital City Partnership, 1997—, Pk. Sq. Theatre, 2003—, St. Paul Found., 2005—; mem. River Ctr. Conv. and Visitors Authority, 2005—06, Minn. State Fair Found., 2005—, Amherst H. Wilder Found., 2006—. Mem. ABA, Minn. Bar Assn., Ramsey County Bar Assn., Nat. Assn. Bond Lawyers, St. Paul Area C. of C. (bd. dirs., exec. com. 1997-99). Office: Leonard Street and Deinard 150 S Fifth St Minneapolis MN 55402 Office Phone: 612-335-1987. Business E-Mail: robyn.hansen@leonard.com.

HANSEN, RUTH LUCILLE HOFER, business owner, consultant; b. Wellman, Iowa, Feb. 8, 1916; d. Harve Hiram and Frances Ada (Fitzsimmons) Hofer; m. Donald Edward Hansen, June 26, 1937 (dec. Feb. 1996); children: James Edward, Sandra Kaye. Student, Upper Iowa U., 1958, U. Northern Iowa, 1959. Co-founder, v.p. H & H Distbg. Co., West Union, Iowa, 1946-59, cons.; v.p., gen. ptnr., sec., treas. Don E. Hansen Family Partnership Ltd. Pres. United Presbyn. Women of Bethel Presbyn. Ch., West Union, Iowa, 1967—, mem. comty. planning and devel. commn.; pres. Lakes & Prairies Presbyterial, Cedar Rapids, Iowa, 1972-75; elder Bethel Presbyn. Ch., West Union, 1960-63; v.p., program chmn., camp dir., leader Camp Wyo. Ch. Camp; dist. Wapsipinicon coun. Girl Scouts, 1972-75; tchr. Vacation Bible Sch., Ch. Sch. for Adults, 1970; rep. John Knox Presbytery. Mem. Bus. and Profl. Women (pres.). Avocations: community plays, sewing, dance, golf, bridge. Home (Summer): 601 N Vine St West Union IA 52175-1033

HANSEN, SHERRI M., psychiatrist; b. Royal Oak, Wis., Mar. 7, 1965; d. Altan Hansen and Mary Katharine Bogart. BS, Mich. State U., East Lansing, 1987; MD, U. Mich., Ann Arbor, 1991. Diplomate gen. psychiatry Am. Bd. Psychiatry and Neurology, 1996. Pvt. practice psychiatrist, Capitol Assocs., LLC, Madison, Wis., 2000—. Clin. asst. prof. dept. psychiatry U. Wis. Med. Sch., Madison, 2000—. Contbr. chapters to books, articles to profl. jours. Active Wis. United for Mental Health, Madison, 2006—06. Recipient George Sternberg medal for Excellence in Preventative Medicine, U. Mich. Med. Sch., 1991, William Herdman award for Resident Tchr. of Yr., U. Mich. Med. Sch., Dept. Psychiatry, 1994, 1995, Med. Edn. Devel. and Leadership Program award, U. Wis. Med. Sch., 2000; Academic fellow, Academic Psychiatry, 1996. Mem.: State Med. Soc. Wis., Am. Psychiat. Assn. Lutheran. Avocations: Christian composer and musician, knitting, yoga. Office: Capitol Associates LLC Ste 200 440 Science Dr Madison WI 53711 Office Phone: 608-238-5176. Office Fax: 608-238-2727. Business E-Mail: sherrihansen@tds.net.

HANSEN-DABERKOW, MICHELLE LEN, elementary school art educator; d. Gene Dale and Janet Kay Hansen; m. James Lowell Daberkow, Dec. 20, 1997; 1 child, Callum Hanz Daberkow. BA in Art Tchg., Bethany Coll., Lindsborg, Kans., 1991; MS in Art Edn., Wayne State U., Nebr., 1996. K-12 art educator Beemer Pub. Schs., Nebr., 1991—94, Stanton Cmty. Schs., Nebr., 1993—96; k-5 art specialist Lincoln Pub. Sch., Nebr., 1996—. Tchr. adult classes Norfolk (Nebr.) Arts Ctr., 1993—94; artist in residence Stone House Gallery, Fredonia, Kans., 1991. Co-leader, chair after sch. program United Luth. Ch., Lincon, 1998—2002. Recipient award, Berry Co., Lincon, 2004. Mem.: Nat. Art Edn. Assn., Nebr. Art Tchr. Assn., Guild Natural Sci. Illustrators. Republican. Lutheran. Avocations: bicycling, quilting, gardening, writing, cello. Office: Lincoln Pub Schs Kahoa Elem 7700 Leighton Ave Lincoln NE 68507

HANSEN-KYLE, LINDA L, counselor, nursing educator; b. Selma, Calif, Aug. 24, 1947; d. Ernest L. and Mary Hansen; m. Kenton L. Kyle, Feb. 16, 1974. BA in History summa cum laude, Humboldt State, 1969, MA in Psychology, 1972; ASN, Saddleback Coll., 1976; MS in Human Resources and Mgmt. Devel., Chapman U., 1993; MSN, Calif. State U., Dominguez Hills, 2000; postgrad. in nursing, U. San Diego, 2001—. Cert. case mgr.; RN Calif. ICU nurse supr. Scripps Clinic and Rsch., San Diego, 1978-81; asst. dir. nursing Mari Coll., San Diego, 1980-85; mgr. of ops. United Healthcare, San Diego, 1985—97; adj. instr. nursing Grossmont CC, 1999—. Adj. instr. U. San Diego, 2003—. Mem.: ANA, Gase Mgmt. Soc. Am., Western Inst. Nursing Rsch., Phi Kappa Phi, Sigma Theta Tau.

HANSON, JANE, newscaster; married; 1 child. BA in Broadcast Journalism, U. Minn. Reporter Sta. KSFY-TV, Sioux Falls, Iowa; from gen. assignment reporter to anchor Sta. WMT-TV, Cedar Rapids, Iowa; corr., anchor WNBC, N.Y.C., 1979—, co-anchor Today in New York, 1988—2003, host Jane's New York, 2003—. Adj. prof. Stern Coll., L.I. Chmn. March of Dimes Walk-Am.; hon. chair Susan B. Koman Found.'s Race for the Cure, N.Y.C.; bd. dirs. Graham Windham, N.Y.C., NY. Named Corr. of the Yr., N.Y. Police Detectives, N.Y. Firefighters, Outstanding Mother of the Yr., Nat. Mother's Day Com., 1995; recipient Emmy Outstanding Morning News Program, 1996, 1997, 2000. Mem.: NATAS (trustee, bd. govs. N.Y. chpt.). Office: WNBC 30 Rockefeller Plz New York NY 10112

HANSON, JANICE CRAWFORD, artist; b. Norwalk, Conn., Oct. 8, 1952; d. Arthur James and Jean Alice (MacKinnon) Crawford; m. Jeffrey Becker Hanson, May 29, 1976; children: Forrest James, Shane Crawford. BA, Wellesley Coll., 1974; MBA, U. Denver, 1979. CFA. Sec. to assoc. dean Yale Sch. of Music, New Haven, Conn., 1975-76; adminstrv. asst. to dir. of internships Inst. Policy Scis. Duke U., Durham, N.C., 1976-78; fiscal analyst Denver Water Bd., 1979-84; fin. analyst Englewood, Colo., 1984; part-time fin. analyst Jeffrey B. Hanson M.D., P.C., Granger, Ind., 1989-92; part-time watercolorist Englewood, Colo., 1989—. Exhibitions include group shows Watercolor West Exhbn., Riverside, Calif., 1995, 1999, Western Colo. Watercolor Soc. Nat. Juried Exhbn., Grand Junction, Colo., 1994—96, 2000, 2004—06, Rocky Mountain Nat. Watermedia Exhbn., Golden, Colo., 1996, 1998, 2002, 2006, Pikes Peak Watercolor Soc. Internat. Exhbn., Colorado Springs, Colo., 1997, 1998, 2000, Colorado Springs, 2003, Am. Women Artists Nat. Juried Competition, Taos, N.Mex., 1999, Nat. Watercolor Soc. Annual Exhbn., Brea, Calif., 2001, 2002, Western Fedn. Watercolor Soc., 2002, 2003, 2005, 2006. Vol. Denver Dumb Friends League, 1986-88, Cherry Creek Schs., Englewood, Colo., 1992-2006. Recipient Best of Show awards Nat. Greeley Art Mart, 1994, Steamboat Springs Art Coun. Summer Art, 2003, others; Platinum award, Nat. Greeley Art Mart, 1995, Dean Witter award for originality Colo. Watercolor Soc. State Juried Exhbn., 1996, Exec. award, 2004; WinsorNewton Merchandise award Am. Women Artists, 1999, Daler-Rowney award Pikes Peak Watercolor Soc. Internat. Exhbn., 2000, Betty Simpson award Rocky Mountain Nat. Watermedia Exhbn., 2002; Am. Women Artists scholar, 1999. Mem.: Rocky Mountain Nat. Watercolor Soc. (signature mem.), Western Fedn. Watercolor Socs. (signature), Denver Soc. Security Analysts, Western Colo. Watercolor Soc. (signature), Colo. Watercolor Soc. (bd. mem. 2005—, signature, Exec. award 2004), Watercolor West (juried assoc.), Assn. for Investment Mgmt. and Rsch., Nat. Watercolor Soc. (signature). Avocations: running, fiber arts, needlecrafts, photography.

HANSON, JEAN ELIZABETH, lawyer; b. Alexandria, Minn., June 28, 1949; d. Carroll Melvin and Alice Clarissa (Frykman) Hanson; children: Catherine Jean, Benjamin Colman (twins). BA, Luther Coll., 1971; JD, U. Minn., 1976. Bar: NY 1977, U.S. Dist. Ct. (so. dist.) 1977. Probation officer Hennepin County, Mpls., 1972-73; law clk. Minn. State Pub. Defender, Mpls., 1975-76; assoc. Fried, Frank, Harris, Shriver & Jacobson, N.Y.C., 1976-83, ptnr., 1983-93, 94—. Gen. counsel U.S. Treasury, Washington, 1993—94; mem. bd. regents Luther Coll., Concordia Coll.; mem. bd. visitors Law Sch. U. Minn. Recipient Disting. Svc. award Luther Coll., 1991, Outstanding Achievement award U. Minn., 1999. Mem. ABA, N.Y. State Bar Assn., Assn. of Bar of City of N.Y. (securities regulation com. 1991-98, mem. task force women in the profession 1995-98), U. Minn. Law Alumni Assn. Democrat. Lutheran. Office: Fried Frank Harris Shriver & Jacobson One New York Plaza New York NY 10004 Office Phone: 212-859-8198. E-mail: jean.hanson@friedfrank.com.

HANSON, JO, artist, educator, writer; b. Carbondale, Ill. d. Thomas A. and Carrie M. H. MA in Art, San Francisco State U.; MA in Edn, U. Ill. Past instr. sculpture U. Calif., Berkeley, Calif. Coll. Arts and Crafts, Oakland. Participant art panels Women's Caucus for Art and Coll. Art Assn., 1979, 81, 89, 91, 93, 99, Exploratorium Symposium, "Rising Above Our Garbage", San Francisco, 1994; co-curator Living in Balance, San Francisco Internat. Airport and Richmond Art Ctr., 1993, 94, Dear Mother Earth, Marin County Civic Ctr., 1998; moderator Bioneers Conf. panels on art and ecology, 1999—; presenter Soc. for Ecol. Restoration, 1999; subject of "Life Messages" book by Josephine Carleton, Andreus McMeel, 2002. Author: Artists' Taxes, The Hands-on Guide, 1987; co-prodr. Women Environment Artists Directory, 1996—; contbr.: Women, Art and Technology, MIT Press, 2003; one-woman shows of sculpture and installations include, Corcoran Gallery Art, Washington, 1974, Pa. Acad. Fine Arts, Phila., 1976, Utah Mus. Fine Arts, Salt Lake City, 1977, San Francisco Mus. Modern Art, 1976, 80, Internat. Sculpture Conf., San Francisco, 1982, Internat. Conf. Healthy Cities, San Francisco, 1993, Dublin (Calif.) Civic Ctr., 1994, Fresno Art Mus., 1998; exhibited in group shows at San Francisco Mus. Modern Art, 1978, Museau de Arte Contemporanea da U. de São Paulo, Brazil, 1980, Pratt Manhattan Center, N.Y.C., 1981, Auckland City Art Gallery, N.Z., 1985, Municipal Art Soc., N.Y. 1990, John F. Kennedy U., San Francisco, 2001, Yerba Buena Ctr., San Francisco, 2002, Thoreau Ctr., 2005; represented in permanent collections including Herbert F. Johnson Mus. Cornell U., Fresno (Calif.) Art Mus., Mills Coll., Oakland, Calif., Oakland Mus. of Art, San Francisco Arts Commn., San Francisco Mus. Modern Art, Knoxville Mus. Art, Tenn., Fine Arts Museums of San Francisco; numerous pvt. collections. San Francisco Arts commr., 1982-89; adv. bd. artist-in-residence Exploratorium, San Francisco, 1983-91; originator, advisor artist-in-residence program San. Fill Co., San Francisco, 1989—; advisor art and ecology Bioneers Conf., 1999—, EarthLight Mag., 1999—. Recipient citation San Francisco Bd. Suprs., 1980, San Francisco mayor, 1989, Honor award Bioneers Conf., 2000, Honor award Calif. Lawyers for the Arts, 2004; named Disting. Woman Artist of Yr., Fresno (Calif.) Art Mus., 1998; Nat. Endowment for Arts fellow, 1977, grantee, 1980. Mem. Coll. Art Assn. (co-chair panel art and ecology 1999), Women's Caucus for Art (Regional Lifetime Achievement award 1992, Nat. Lifetime Achievement award 1997), Pacific Rim Sculptors Group. Office Phone: 415-864-7139.

HANSON, JODY ELIZABETH, special education educator; b. Milw., Mar. 28, 1958; d. Alfred Herbert and Barbara Ann Bopp; m. Bryan Richard Hanson, Oct. 20, 1979; children: Keith Richard, Melissa Beth. BS in Edn., U. Wis., Whitewater, 1980, M in Spl. Edn., 1990, lic. SLD, 1994. Tchr. spl. edn. grades 9-12 Waterford Union H.S., Wis., 1989—. Mem. acad. stds. com. Waterford (Wis.) Union H.S. Staff, 1998—; adviser Students Against Destructive Decisions, Waterford, 1993—. Pres., softball coach Mukwonago (Wis.) Comty. Athlete Assn., 1974—2002. Mem.: CEC, Wis. Divsn. for Learning Disabled (Tchr. of Yr. 2003), Wis. Coun. for EBD, Wis. Coun. for Exceptional Children, Coun. for Children with Behavioral Disorders. Avocations: camping, golf, reading, motorcycling. Office: Waterford Union H S 100 Field Dr Waterford WI 53185-4116 Business E-Mail: JHanson@waterforduhs.k12.wi.us.

HANSON, KAREN NOBLE, financial holding company executive; b. Rochester, N.Y., June 17, 1943; d. Joseph L. and Kathryn C. Noble; children by previous marriage: Tammy C. Tobin, Scott R. Tobin, Robert L. Tobin; m. Thomas L. Hanson, May 7, 1977; step: Timothy. BA cum laude, U. Rochester, 1970, postgrad., 1972; LHD, St. Augustine's Coll., 1986; attended, Dept. Agr. Sr. Exec. Svc. Devel. Program, 1981. Tchg. fellow U. Rochester, 1971, grad. tchg. asst., 1971—72; dir. agrl. manpower Cornell U., 1972—73; exec. dir. Program Funding, Inc., Rochester, 1973—77; dir. Farmer's Home Adminstr., U.S. Dept. Agr., N.Y. and U.S. V.I., 1977—81, spl. asst. to adminstr. Wash., 1981; v.p. Genesee Mgmt., Inc. (mgmt. holding co. for Wilmorite, Inc.), Rochester, 1981—99; canon, CFO Episcopal Diocese of Rochester, 1999—. Trustee U. Rochester; bd. mem. N.Y. Job Devel. Authority, N.Y. Ch. Ins., Mon County Cultural Ctr. Commn. Recipient Disting. Svc. award, United Way/Rochester, 1976, Special Svc. award, Nat. Assn. Farm Workers, 1982, Athena award, Rochester C of C, 1994. Democrat. Episcopalian. Office: Episcopal Diocese 935 East Ave Rochester NY 14607 Office Phone: 585-473-2977. E-mail: knhanson@aol.com.

HANSON, LINDA N., academic administrator, educator; d. Pierce R. Nesbitt and Miriam B. Brinson; m. J. Laird Hanson; 1 child, J. Pierce Hanson. B English, Speech, So. Nazarene U.; M Ednl. Adminstrn., Seattle U., EdD Ednl. Leadership. Tchr. Savannah Christian Prep. Sch.; English tchr. secondary sch. Atlanta pub. schs.; tchr. Sch. Edn. and Inst. Pub. Svc. Seattle U.; asst. provost exec. edn. Seattle U.; v.p. U. Rels. Seattle U.; pres. Coll. Santa Fe, 2001—. Pres. Ind. Colls. Wash.; v.p. devel. Tex. A&M U., Corpus Christi. With Assn. of Coll., U. and Cmty. Arts Adminstrs., Tex. Commn. on Arts Peer Rev., Rotary IV, others; mem. Santa Fe Chamber Music Festival's Adv. Bd., Santa Fe C. of C., Pres.'s Leadership Group, Higher Edn. Ctr. Alcohol and other Drug Prevention; exec. dir. Paramount Theatre for Performing Arts. Mem.: N.Mex. Women's Forum, Nat. Assn. Ind. Colls. and Us., Roundtable. Office: Coll Santa Fe 1600 St Michael's Dr Santa Fe NM 87505

HANSON, MARGARET, social worker; b. Liverpool, Eng., July 6, 1933; d. Joseph and Catherine Agnes (Bergin) H BA, Coll. St. Rose, 1956; MA, Cath. U., 1967; MSW, Marywood Sch. Social Work, 1977. Cert. social worker, N.Y.; diplomate Am. Bd. Examiners in Clin. Social Work. Tchr. Latin and English h.s. Cath. Schs. of Diocese Syracuse, Binghamton and Rome, NY, 1957—69; clin. social worker Cath. Social Svcs., Binghamton, 1969—75, Alch. Ctr. Broome City, Binghamton, 1975—78, PROBE, Inc., Binghamton, 1978—79, Binghamton Psychiat. Clinic, 1979—81, Binghamton Gen. Hosp.,

1981—2004, Samaritan Counseling Ctr., Endicott, NY, 2005—. Bd. dirs., pres. PROBE, Inc., Binghamton Bd. dirs. Ladies of Charity USA, Binghamton chpt., 1993-2002, pres. 2003-04 Roman Catholic. Avocations: gardening, woodworking, ballet.

HANSON, MARLENE KAY, music educator; b. Malta, Mont., Aug. 22, 1956; d. Melvin Leo and Hazel Odessa Hanson. MusB, U. Mont., 1980; MA in music edn., U. St. Thomas, 2001. Teaching Certification State of Mont. Contbr. articles. Choir sch. condr. Christian Ctr., 1982—86, music festival adjudicator. Mem.: Treasure State Orff Chpt. (pres. 1996—98), Mont. Music Educators Assn., Nat. Assn. for Music Edn., Orgn. Am. Kodaly Educators, Schulwerk Assn. Avocations: water-skiing, hiking, golf, tennis, sewing. Home: 376 Ponderosa St Kalispell MT 59901 Office: Columbia Falls Sch Dist #6 21 Sixth St W Columbia Falls MT 59912

HANSON, NORMA HALMAGYI, priest; b. Welch, W.Va., Jan. 6, 1937; d. Anthony and Mildred Evelyn (Crane) Halmagyi; m. Stephen Martin Hanson, June 2, 1996; m. Hawthorne A. Davis (div.); children: Ellen D. Filer, Jessica D. Hege, Andrea D. Hill, H. Anthony Davis. AB, Randolph Macon Women's Coll., Lynchburg, Va., 1958; MS, U. Va., Charlottesville, 1960; MDiv, Lancaster Theol. Seminary, Pa., 1994; D in Ministry, Luth. Theol. Seminary, Phila., 2004. Rsch. assoc. U. Va. Sch. Medicine, Charlottesville, 1960—62, Dupont Exptl. Station, Wilmington, Del., 1963; instr. biology Lenoir Cmty. Coll., Kinston, NC, 1973—87; farm program mgr. Del. Nature Ctr., Hockessin, Del., 1988—90; chaplain Christina Hosp., Newark, Del., 1995—97; rector Christ Episc. Ch., Del. City, 1997—2004; assoc. Trinity Episc. Ch., Asheville, NC, 2004—05, ret., 2005. Contbr. articles to jour. Recipient Phi Sigma for Rsch. Biol. Scis., U. Va., 1960. Mem.: Order of St. Luke (convener 1985—86), Assn. Profl. Chaplains, Assembly Episc. Hosp. and Chaplains. Episcopal.

HANSON, NORMA LEE, farmer; b. Brainerd, Minn., Feb. 3, 1930; d. Fred Christian Kruckow and Lena Belle Sawyer; m. Lynn Curtis Hanson; 1 child, Michael Lynn. Student, Mpls. Sch. Bus., 1949—50; grad., Northland C.C., 1972. File clk. and predetermining mortgage payments Investors Diversified Svcs., Mpls., 1949—53; social reporter Thief River Falls Times, 1954—63; office mgr. Kiewel Products Co., 1963—70; lobbyist Minn. Farmers Union, St. Paul, 1970—72, columnist, 1973—76; asst. farm mgr. Good-Vue Ayr Farms, Goodridge, 1976—. Chmn. Senate Dist. 1, Minn., 1990—, Northwest Minn. Women's Fund, 2001—. Mem.: NW Minn. Dairy Assn. (sec., treas. 2000—), Am. Dairy Assn. (pres. 1986—2001), Midwest Dairy Assn. (bd. dirs. 1995—2000, sec., treas. N.W. Minn. chpt. 2000—), Am. Agrl. Women (chmn. dairy com. 1999—), Hort. Soc. (pres. 13th dist. 2000—), Goodridge Area Hist. Soc. (pres. 1980—, founder). Democrat. Lutheran. Avocations: horticulture, horseback riding, reading, writing, snowmobiling. Home: 21625 330th Ave NE Goodridge MN 56725

HANSON, PAULA, sports association executive; B.Journalism, U. Colo. Dir. promotions Denver Nuggets, v.p. mktg., v.p., asst. gen. mgr.; v.p. team svcs. NBA, 1985—96, sr. v.p. team ops., 1996—99; sr. v.p., COO WNBA, N.Y.C., 1999—2003, sr. v.p. Team Business Operations, 2003—.

HANSON, PEG, gemstone dealer, psychic, graphic designer, writer; b. Detroit, Sept. 14, 1946; d. Heber C. and Kathryn (Shields) Hizar; children: Peter Christopher. Student, Cranbrook Art Inst., 1958—60, Universidad de Mex., 1963, Mich. State U., 1964—67. Writer, illustrator, designer Leisure mag., Bauston Spa, NY, 1974—75; designer Van de Car DePoor & Johnson Advt., Albany, NY, 1975; prodn. mgr. Children's Design Ctr., Saratoga Springs, NY, 1975; creative dir. Kellert Advt., Albany, 1975—77; ad mgr. Higerson Bury & Sons, Bennington, Vt., 1977—86; owner Peg Hanson & Assoc., Albany, 1996—; dir. mktg. United Way Northea. N.Y., 1987—90; mgr. graphic arts Elliot Publs., Inc., 1990—91; owner Peg Hanson Visual Comm., 1991—. Mem. Rensselaerville (N.Y.) Hist. Soc., 1989—; pub. rels. com. Ronald McDonald House; bd. dirs. Rensselaerville Libr. Howard and Bush grantee; recipient Strathmore Paper Graphics award. Mem. Internat. Assn. Bus. Comm., Internat. House Printing Craftsmen, Nat. Assn. Desktop Pub Avocations: fine art, piano, composing. Home: PO Box 17 Rensselaerville NY 12147-0017

HANSON, POLLY (PAULINE) MAE EARLY, librarian; b. Danville, Ill., Sept. 20, 1927; d. Jesse Alonzo and Mamie Viola Mapes Early; m. Carl Ludwig Hanson, June 18, 1950; children: Eric Alan, Wendy Sue Hanson Martin, Julie Marie Hanson-Geist. BA in English Lit., U. Mich., 1949; MLS, U. Wash., Seattle, 1967. Asst. children's libr. Seattle Pub. Libr., 1950—51; children's libr. King County Libr. Sys., Wash., 1967, Mercer Island, Wash., 1967—71, br. mgr. Wash., 1971—75; asst. libr. dir., pub. services Whatcom County Libr. Sys., Wash., 1975—78, libr. dir., 1978—83; founding libr. dir. NW Indian Coll., Lummi Indian Nation, Wash., 1985—95; owner-mgr. West Shore Farm Bed & Breakfast, Lummi Island, Wash., 1984—. Founder Skyway Br. Libr. King County Libr. Sys. Author: (newspaper column) Skyway Community Column, Renton News Record. Founding bd. mem. Parent Coop. Nursery Sch., Skyway, Wash., 1954—56, Lummi Island Conservancy, 1988—2002; elected cemetery bd. commr. Lummi Island Cemetery Dist., Wash., 1995; bd. dirs. Lummi Island Cmty. Land Trust, 1998—2005; mem. Lummi Island Subarea Plan, Whatcom County, Wash., 2000—04; Lummi Island precinct com. officer Whatcom County Democrats, 2000—04; mem. Dem. Ctrl. Com., Whatcom County, Wash., 1990, Whatcom County Democrats, 2000—04, chair, 2000—04; bd. mem. Young Women's Christian Assn., Bellingham, Wash., 1980—82; founding bd. mem. Lummi Island Hist. and Preservation Soc., 1978. Recipient Photographer award, Seattle Pub. Libr., 1995, 10-yr. svc. wall plaque, NW Indian Coll., 1995. Mem.: Uppity Women's Book Club and Writing Cir. (life). D-Liberal. Unitarian Universalist. Achievements include first to development of natural childbirth breast feeding movement leading to Childbirth Education Association; Mercer Island environmental committee that re-designed Highway I-90 on Mercer Island to meet community and environmental needs. Avocations: organic and native plants, birdwatching, tai chi, gardening. Home: 2781 West Shore Dr Lummi Island WA 98262 Office: WestShore Farm Bed and Breakfast 2781 West Shore Dr Lummi Island WA 98262-8715 Office Phone: 360-758-2600. Personal E-mail: westshorefarm@msn.com.

HANSON, TAMARA W., accountant; b. Lewiston, Idaho, Oct. 23, 1948; d. Brooks E. and Dona J. (Rogers) O'Kelley; m. Thomas J. Hanson Jr., 1 son, Stewart Alan. BBA cum laude, North Tex. State U., 1976. Securities lic., ins. lic.; CPA, Tex. Staff acct. James C. Beach CPA, Carrollton, Tex., 1972-76, Deloitte, Haskins & Sells, CPA, 1976-77; CFO Comm. Sys., Inc. (name changed to Scott Cable Comm. 1983), Irving, Tex., 1977-84; pvt. practice acctg. Dallas, 1984-93; treas., v.p. FTS Life Ins. Agy., Inc., 1993—. Author: Mastering the Dance, 2004. Active St. Andrews United Meth. Ch. Mem. AICPA, Tex. Soc. CPA (former Dallas chpt. ethics com.), Beta Alpha Psi.

HANSON, TENA LORAYN, finance educator; b. Aberdeen, Idaho, Aug. 8, 1973; d. James Rodney and Bonadyn Prestidge; m. Jeffrey Allyn Hanson, Aug. 30, 1997; children: Randi Leigh, Jessica Ann, Tanner James. BS in Edn., Mayville State U., 2001; MSc U. ND, 2006. Bus./tech. tchr. Fisher Pub. Sch., Minn., 2001—; outreach and innovation instr. Northland Cmty. Tech. Coll., Thief River Falls, Minn., 2003—. Cmty. edn. instr. Fisher Pub. Sch., 2001—, yearbook adv., 2001—, nat. honor soc. adv., 2004—. Sunday sch. tchr. New Hope Luth. Ch., Alvarado, Minn., 2005—06, Sunday sch. supt., 2001—03. Mem.: NEA, ASCD, Delta P.Epilson. Avocations: reading, gardening. Home: 20337 450th Ave NW Alvarado MN 56710 Office: Fisher Pub Sch 313 Park Ave Fisher MN 56723

HANSON, VIRGINIA A., human services administrator; b. Mpls., Apr. 26, 1935; d. Edwin Fred Wahl, Elsie (Johnson) Wahl; m. Marshall Richard Hanson, Mar. 10, 1956; children: Bruce M., Christopher, Brian(dec.). Student, St. Olaf Coll., 1953—55, Mpls. Sch. Art, 1955—56, U. Cin., 1974. Cert. activity dir. Nat. Certification Coun. for Activity Profls. Fashion artist Daytons, Mpls., 1956—57, Maurice L. Rothchild-Young Quinlan, Mpls., 1957—58; activity dir. Beechknoll Woods, Cin., 1975—81; tchr. art, recreational counselor New Horizons for Developmentally Disabled, Millbrook, NY, 1983—91; tchr. therapeutic recreation art Waterside Retirement Estates, Sarasota, Fla., 1996—2001, Sarasota Bay Club, 2002—06. Developed unique style archtl. gouache painting, 1984—. Recipient 1st pl. in Watercolor, Kent Art Assn., 2001, Critics Choice award, Pindar Art Gallery, 1990. Mem.: Womens Resource Ctr., Therapeutic Recreation Assn. (v.p. 1976—80), Women Contemporary Artists (Merit award 1982). Home: 5172 Marshfield Ln Sarasota FL 34235

HANTHORNE, CAROL, elementary school educator; b. Des Moines, Aug. 5, 1950; d. Bernard R. and Jean Anne (Jarnagin) Seagren; m. James E. Hanthorne, Nov. 20, 1971. BA, Morningside Coll., Sioux City, Iowa, 1972, MA in Teaching, 1987. Cert. permanent profl. tchr., Iowa. Elem. tchr. Ayrshire (Iowa) Community Schs., 1974-81, Spencer (Iowa) Community Schs., 1981—. Lead tchr. CSR Grant; reading curriculum coord. Dist. Lang. Arts Spencer Cmty. Schs., Iowa, dist. leadership team, dist. literacy team. Connie Belin fellow U. Iowa. 1989. Mem. NEA, Iowa Edn. Assn. Home: 1115 W 8th St Spencer IA 51301-3037 Office: Lincoln Elem Sch 615 4th Ave SW Spencer IA 51301-6209 Office Phone: 712-262-3752. Personal E-mail: jchan@ncn.net. Business E-Mail: chanthorne@spencer.k12.ia.us.

HANTUCHOVA, DANIELA, professional tennis player; b. Poprad, Slovakia, Apr. 23, 1983; d. Igor and Marianna. Profl. tennis player WTA Tour, 1999—. Named Most Improved Player of Yr., WTA Tour, 2002. Mem.: Slovak Republic Fed. Cup Team. Achievements include Winner singles titles: Indian Wells, 2000; Winner doubles titles: (with Habsudova) Bratislava, 2000, (with Bovina) Luxembourg, 2001, (with Sanchez-Vicaro) New Haven, 2002, Amelia Island, 2002; Winner mixed doubles titles: (with Friedl) Wimbledon, 2001, (with Ullyett) Australian Open, 2002. Office: WTA Tour 1 Progress Plz Ste 1500 Saint Petersburg FL 33701-4335

HANZALEK, ASTRID TEICHER, public information officer, consultant; b. N.Y.C., Jan. 6, 1928; d. Arthur Albin and Luise Gertrude (Funke) Teicher; m. Frederick J. Hanzalek, Nov. 11, 1955. A, Concordia Coll., 1947; BA, U. Pa., 1949. Cons., Suffield, Conn., 1960—; state rep. Conn. Gen. Assembly, Hartford, 1970-80, asst. majority leader, 1973-74, asst. minority leader, 1975-80. Corporator Conn. Childrens Med. Ctr., 1986—95; bd. dirs. Conn. Water Co., Clinton; mem. Conn. Nitrogen Credit Adv. Bd., 2001—. Contbr. articles to profl. jours. Mem. Conn. State Coun. Environ. Quality, Hartford, 1980—93; chmn. Conn. State Ethics Commn., Hartford, 1985—93; commr. New Eng. Interstate Water Pollution Control Commn., 1993—; mem. Conn. Greenways Commn., 1992—; mem., chair history com. Conn. Commn. on Culture and Tourism, 2003—; trustee Priscilla Maxwell Endicott Scholarship Fund, 1972—; vice chmn. Bd. State Acad. awards, 1996—; chmn. Conn. Energy Found., Hartford, 1986—96; vice-chmn. Bradley Internat. Airport Commn., 1972—2002, Greater Hartford chpt. ARC, 1975—82; mem. Conn. Inter Agy. Libr. Planning Com., Hartford, 1975—85; bd. dirs. Riverfront Recapture, Inc., 1986—; chmn. Conn. River Watershed Coun., Greenfield, Mass., 1980—92; pres. Conn. Sr. Intern Program, Bridgeport, 1980—90; sec. Conn. Humanities Coun., Middletown, 1980—92. Named Panelist of the Yr., Auto. Consumer Action Panel, 1975—85; recipient Man of the Yr. award, Conn. Jaycees, 1972, Suffield Citizenship award, 1996. Mem.: Nat. Order Woman Legislators, Suffield Land Conservancy (bd. dirs. 1965—98, founder), Conn. Coun. Environ. Quality, Conn. Forest and Pk. Assn. (v.p., bd. dirs. 1975—), Antiquarian and Landmarks Soc. (v.p. 1974—95, pres. 1996—2002, bd. dirs., sec. 2003—). Republican. Lutheran. Avocations: musical activities, sports, culinary arts. Home: 31 Abraham Ter Suffield CT 06078-2167

HAPNER, JOANNA SUE, humanities educator; b. Richmond, Ind., Mar. 30, 1956; d. Marne Dalton Fox, Martha Marie Yount; m. David Scott Hapner, June 19, 1976 (div.); children: Justin David, Clare Dennise. BA in English, U. South Fla., 1999. Tchr. pre-sch. Trinity Children's Ctr., Bradenton, Fla., 1985—95; tchr. Booker Mid. Sch., Sarasota, Fla., 2000—. Mem. youth bd. Trinity United Meth. Ch., Bradenton, 2000. Named Tchr. of Yr., Baker Mid. Sch., 2004—06. Mem.: AAUW, Fla. Coun. Tchrs. English (Tchr. of Yr. 2004—05), Visual and Performing Arts Network. Avocations: reading, theater, art museums, fishing, hiking. Home: 708 30th St W Bradenton FL 34205 Office: Booker Mid Sch 2250 Myrtle Ave Sarasota FL 34234 E-mail: joa99grad@yahoo.com.

HAPNER, MARY LOU, securities trader, writer; b. Ft. Wayne, Ind., Nov. 9, 1937; d. Paul Kenneth Brooks and Eileen (Summers) H. BS with honors, Ariz. State U., 1966, MS, 1967. Stockbroker Young, Smith & Peacock, Phoenix, 1971-76, v.p., 1976-89, Peacock, Hislop, Staley & Given, Phoenix, 1989-90, 1st v.p., 1990—. Author: Career Courage, 1984; (poems) The Power of Forgiveness, 1995, Take Someone's Hand, 1997, Cherubs, 1997, Self Portrait, 1998, Vision, 1999, Millenium, 2000, Walk with Me, 2001, Lullabies at Night, 2004. Chmn. March of Dimes, Sun City, Ariz., 1983; trustee St. Lukes, Phoenix, 1978; mem. fin. com. YWCA, Phoenix, 1975; mem. dean's coun. of 100, Ariz. State U. Coll. Bus., 2000-03; chair budget com. Ch. of Beatitudes, Phoenix, mem. exec. coun., 1991; bd. dirs. Ariz.'s Children Found., 1998; founder Ariz. Biltmore Country Club Women's Orgn., 1976, champion 1976-83. Recipient Spirit of Philanthropy award, 1997, Impact award for Enterprising Women, 2001, Arthritis Angel award, 2002, Rookie of Yr. award Arthritis Found., 2003. Mem. Charter 100 (chair membership 1979-81, pres. 1980, pres. 1982, v.p. 1981, treas., membership chair 1995, v.p. 2003—, chair 25th Anniversary 2004). Republican. Lutheran. Avocations: golf, singing with concert choirs, poetry. Office Phone: 602-952-6803. Business E-Mail: mlhapner@phs&g.com.

HAQUE, MALIKA HAKIM, pediatrician; b. Madras, India; arrived in US, 1967; d. Syed Abdul and Rahimunisa (Hussain) Hakim; m. C. Azeez Haque, Feb. 5, 1967; children: Kifizeba Haque Akbar, Masarath Haque Khan, Asim Zayd Haque. MBBS, Madras Med. Coll., 1967. Diplomate Am. Bd. Pediatrics. Rotating intern Miriam Hosp. Brown U., Providence, 1967-68; resident in pediatrics N.J. Coll. Medicine Childrens Hosp., 1968-70; fellow in devel. disabilities Ohio State U., 1970-71; acting chief pediat. Nisonger Ctr., 1973-74; staff pediatrician Children and Youth Project Children's Hosp., Columbus, Ohio; clin. asst. prof. pediatrics Ohio State U., 1974-80, clin. assoc. prof. pediatrics, 1981-99, clin. assoc. prof. dept. internat. health Coll. Medicine, 1993-99, clin. prof. pediatrics and internat. health Coll. Medicine, 1999—. Pediatrician Children's Hosp. Physician Health Ctrs. Children's Hosp., Columbus, 1982—; dir. Pediat. Academic Assn., 1992-2002; cons. Ctrl. Ohio Head Start Program, 1974-79; med. cons. Bur. Rehab. and Devel. Disabilities for State of Ohio, 1990—. Contbr. articles to profl. jours. and newspapers. Charter founder Ronald Reagan Rep. Ctr.; trustee Asian Am. Health Alliance Network, Columbus, 1994-2001. Recipient Physician Recognition award, AMA, 1971—86, 1988—99, 2002—05, Gold medals in surgery, radiology, pediat. and ob-gyn., Presdl. medal of Merit, Pres. Ronald Reagan, 1982, Nat. Leadership award, Nat. Rep. Congl. Com., 2001, Physician of the Yr. award, 2003. Fellow Am. Acad. Pediatrics; mem. Islamic Med. Assn., Am. Assn. of Physicians of Indian Origin, Pediat. Acad. Assn. (dir. 1992-2002), Ambulatory Pediat. Assn., Ctrl. Ohio Pediatric Soc. Achievements include research on enuresis and tumors caused by human papilloma viruses. Home: 5995 Forestview Dr Columbus OH 43213-2114 Office: 700 Childrens Dr Columbus OH 43205-2664 Office Phone: 614-722-4955.

HARA-ISA, NANCY JEANNE, graphics designer; b. San Francisco, May 14, 1961; d. Toshiro and Masaye Hara; m. Stanley Takeo Isa, June 15, 1985. Student, UCLA, 1979-82; BA in Art and Design, Calif. State U., L.A., 1985. Salesperson May Co., L.A., 1981; svc. rep. Hallmark Cards Co., L.A., 1981-83; prodn. artist Calif. State U., L.A., 1983, Audio-Stats Internat. Inc., L.A., 1983; prodn. asst. Auto-Graphics Inc., Pomona, Calif., 1984-85, lead supr., 1985-86; art dir., contbg. staff writer CFW Enterprises, Burbank, Calif., 1987-88; graphic designer, prodn. mgr. Bonny Jularbal Graphics, Las Vegas, Nev., 1988-90; graphic designer Weddle Caldwell Advt., Las Vegas, 1990-92; owner Nancy Hara-Isa Designs, 1992—; graphic artist Regional Transp. Commn. of Clark County, Las Vegas, 1993-98; mgmt. analyst, graphic artist Clark County Dept. Aviation, Las Vegas, 1998—. Freelance designer Caesars Palace. Writer Action Pursuit Games mag. Parade asst., mem. carnival staff Nisei Week., L.A., 1980-84; asst. mem. Summit Orgn., L.A., 1987—; mem. selection com. United Way; alumni grad. Clark County Leadership Forum, 1996; mem. pub. policy com. Alzheimers Assn. So. Nev. Mem. NAFE, Women in Profl. Graphic Svcs. (acting 1st v.p. 1990, 2d v.p. 1991), Women in Comms., Green Valley Rep. Women's Club (1st v.p. 2000, treas. 2003), Am. Soc. Pub. Adminstrs. (coun. mem. 1998-99). Avocations: photography, swimming, horseback riding, shooting, scuba diving. Home: 1803 Dalton Dr Henderson NV 89014 E-mail: haraisa@earthlink.net.

HARALSON, KERI TEMPLE, prosecutor; b. Flowood, Miss., Jan. 11, 1979; d. Lacey Marshal and Norma Dale (Sadka) Haralson; 1 child, Brett Benton. BA, Miss. Coll., 2001; JD, Miss. Coll. Sch. of Law, 2004. Intern Hinds County Pub. Defender, Jackson, 2002; law clk. Miss. Supreme Ct., Jackson, 2004—05; assoc. atty. Southern Legal Clin. PLC, Brandon, Miss., 2005—. Treas. Law Student Bar Assn., Jackson, 2003—04. Contbr. articles to profl. jours. Recipient Excellence in Criminal Law, John Collette, 2004. Mem.: ABA, Assn. of Trial Lawyers of Am., Phi Delta Phi. Republican. Southern Bapt. Avocations: travel, singing, horseback riding, swimming. Office: Southern Legal Clin PLLC 106 Town Square Brandon MS 39042 Office Fax: 601-825-6464.

HARALSON, LINDA JANE, communications executive; b. St. Louis, Mar. 24, 1959; d. James Benjamin and Betty Jane (Myers) N.; married. BA summa cum laude, William Woods Coll., 1981; MA, Webster U., 1982. Radio intern Stas.-KFAL/KKCA, Fulton, Mo., 1981; paralegal Herzog, Kral, Burroughs & Specter, St. Louis, 1981-82; staffing coord. then mktg. coord. Spectrum Emergency Care, St. Louis, 1982-85, mktg. mgr., 1985-87; dir. mktg. and recruitment Carondelet Rehab. Ctrs. Am., Culver City, Calif., 1987—. Mktg. dir. outpatient and corp. svcs. Calif. Med. Ctr., L.A., 1987-88; mktg. dir. Valley Meml. Hosp., Livermore, Calif., 1988-89; account exec. Laurel Comm., Medford, Oreg., 1989-91; cmty. rels. dir. Rogue Valley Med. Ctr., Medford, 1991-95; cmty. pub. rels. dir. Rogue Valley Manor, Medford, 1995-97; pvt. practice in comms. and mktg., 1997—. Party chmn. Heart Assn., St. Louis, 1982—; bd. dirs. Am. Lung Assn. Oreg. Recipient Flair award Advt. Fedn. St. Louis, 1984, Hosps. award Hagen Mktg. Rsch. and Hosps. mag., 1984; Presdl. Acad. scholar William Woods Coll., Fulton, 1977-81. Mem. AAUW, Britt Music Festivals, Alpha Phi Alumnae Assn. (pres. chpt. 1985-87). Republican. Avocations: running, travel, sports, french, needlepoint. Home and Office: 1550 NW Patrick Ct Albany OR 97321 Office Phone: 541-928-0027. E-mail: joelindaharalson@comcast.net.

HARARI, ZARALEYA KURZWEIL, psychologist, psychotherapist; b. Bklyn., Dec. 30, 1926; d. Phillip and Goldie (Simon) Kurzweil; m. Lawrence H. Strear, Aug. 24, 1947 (div. Sept. 1969); children: Peter Mark, Marcy Jana De Luca, Karen Jody Cucolo; m. Carmi Harari, Dec. 31, 1979; stepchildren: Karen Tarnofsky, Michelle Chino. BA, Bklyn. Coll., 1948; MS, CUNY, 1961; EdD, Yeshiva U., 1969. Lic. psychologist, sch. psychologist; nat. cert. sch. psychologist; nat. cert. health svc. provider psychology. Psychologist Wyandanch (N.Y.) Pub. Schs., 1961-63, Uniondale (N.Y.) Pub. Schs., 1963-69; pvt. practice N.Y.C. and Rockland County, 1969—; asst. prof. CUNY, 1970-75; mem. field faculty grad. program Goddard Coll., N.Y.C., 1977-78; consulting psychologist Greer-Woodycrest Children's Svcs., Pomona, NY, 1980-82; psychologist East Ramapo Ctrl. Sch. Dist., Spring Valley, NY, 1982-91. Lectr. Nassau C.C., Garden City, N.Y., 1967-69, Coll. of New Rochelle, N.Y., 1977-78, Rockland C.C., Suffern, N.Y., 1977-80; lectr. spkr.'s bur. Rockland County Mental Health Assn., Pomona, 1977—; cons. drug rehab. Topic House, L.I., N.Y., 1965-69; clin. dir. homosexual walk-in ctr. Identity House, N.Y.C., 1972-76; bd. dirs. women's issues divsn. Humanistic Psychology Ctr. of NY, N.Y.C.; pres. Women Unltd.; med. staff Nyack (N.Y.) Hosp., 1974—; presenter in field over 50 countries, 1972—. Editor: (Bklyn. Coll. Yr. Book) Brocklundian, 1947; contbr. articles to profl. jours., chapters to books; creator Zaraleya Psychoenergetic Technique, 1972, Zaraleya Semester Based Self-Actualization Psychotherapy; Exhibited in group shows at Arts Coun. Rockland (NY), 1997, 1999, Rockland Ctr. for Arts, 1998. Parent seminar leader New City (N.Y.) Libr., 1981; conf. presenter E. Ramapo Ctrl. Sch. Dist., 1982, 1984, 1987; newsletter editor Rockland Ctr. for the Arts, Nyack, NY, 1986—88. Recipient Gold Key award Bklyn. Coll., 1947. Mem.: APA (exec. bd. divsn. humanistic psychology, newsletter editor 1977—79, svc. award 1977), Internat. Assn. Cross-Cultural Psychology, Internat. Assn. Applied Psychology, Internat. Coun. Psychologists (chair com. libr. subscription devel.), Nat. Register Health Svc. Providers in Psychology, Nassau and Suffolk Psychol. Assn., Rockland County Psychol. Soc. (chairperson clin. com. 1981, 1982), N.Y. Soc. Clin. Psychologists, Nat. Assn. Sch. Psychologists. Avocations: writing, drawing, painting, travel.

HARATANI, JOAN MEI, lawyer; b. Redwood City, Calif., Aug. 2, 1957; d. Donald R. Chambers and Claire Meiko Haratani Chambers; m. Ralph Gregory Latza, Jan. 6, 2002. BA in Philosophy, St. John's Coll., 1979; JD, U. Calif.-Davis, 1984. Bar: all Calif. state cts., no. and ctrl. fed. cts. 1985. Assoc. Crosby Heafey Roach & May, Oakland, Calif., 1984—90, ptnr., 1990—2002, Shook Hardy & Bacon, San Francisco, 2002—05, Morgan, Lewis & Bockius, 2005—. Chair The Asian Pacific Fund, San Francisco, 1999—; sec. Lawyers Commn. of Civil Rights, 1999; mem. bd. Leukemia & Lymphoma Soc., 2006—; pres. Bar Assn. of San Francisco, 2004—06; past pres. Asian Am. Bar Assn. of the Greater Bay Area, 2000; mem. Claremont Resort. Named a Super Lawyer of No. Calif., San Francisco mag., 2004, 2005, 2006; named one of 500 Most Influential Asians in Am., Ave. Asia mag., 2003; recipient Top Rainmaker, Calif. Law Bus., 1996—97, 1999, Advocate of Yr. Joe Morozumi award, Asian Am. Bar Assn of No. Calif., 2001, Female Litigator on the Rise, Diversity & the Bar (publ. of Minority Corp. Counsel Assn.), 2004. Mem.: Bar Assn. San Francisoc, Nat. Asian Pacific Am. Bar Assn., Assn. Managing Counsel. Achievements include completing Ironman triathlon race, 2000. Avocations: triathlete, cooking, reading. Office Phone: 415-442-1000. Office Fax: 415-442-1001. Business E-Mail: jharatani@morganlewis.com.

HARAYDA, JANICE, newspaper book editor, author; b. New Brunswick, N.J., July 31, 1949; d. John and Marel (Boyer) H. BA cum laude, U. N.H., 1970. Editl. asst. Mademoiselle mag., N.Y.C., 1970; asst. to travel editor Saturday Rev., N.Y.C., 1971; sr. editor, contbg. editor Glamour mag., N.Y.C., 1971-78; editl. dir. Boston mag., 1978-81; freelance writer Boston, 1981-87; book editor Plain Dealer, Cleve., 1987-98; editor-in-chief N.J. Life mag., Lambertville, 1998, Princeton (N.J.) Alumni Weekly, 1999. Lectr. Radcliffe Pub., Cambridge, Mass., 1979, 80, Cath Conf., among others; instr. writing Marymount Manhattan Coll., N.Y.C., 1977; instr. journalism Boston U. Sch. Pub. Comm., 1979; adj. journalism Fordham U., N.Y.C., 2005; freelance writer. Author: The Joy of Being Single, 1986; contbg. author: Rooms with No View, 1974, Titters, 1979, Women: A Book for Men, 1979, The Accidental Bride, 1999, Manhattan on the Rocks, 2004. Adminstrv. bd. Park Ave. United Meth. Ch., N.Y.C., 1975-78, active civic, corp. and religious groups, 1988—. Recipient award for Excellence in Journalism Cleve. Press. Club, 1994; named guest editor Mademoiselle mag., 1970. Mem. Am. Authors Guild, Nat. Book Critics Cir. (bd. dirs. 1997—, v.p. awards 1998-99), Royal Scottish Country Dance Soc., Clan Donald USA. Avocations: opera, theater, ballet, travel, dancing with scottish country dance troupes. Office: 41 Watchung Plz #99 Montclair NJ 07042

HARBAUGH, JANICE M., counselor, consultant; b. Carroll, Iowa, Aug. 17, 1949; d. Robert William and Bernice Kuehl; m. Gaylon L. Harbaugh, Feb. 10, 1973. BSc in Edn., Drake U., 1971, MSc in Edn., 1973, EdS, 1979, EdD, 1984. Lic. Tchr. Iowa, 1971. Tchr. Iowa State Tng. Sch., Mitchellville, 1972—82, Colfax-Mingo Cmty. Sch., Iowa, 1982—98; with psychology dept. Woodward State Hosp. Sch., Iowa, 1982; pvt. counseling practice Newton, Iowa, 2001—. Chairperson Foster Care Rev. Bd., Des Moines, 1987—88; ct. apptd. spl. adv. 5th Jud. Dist., Iowa, 1988; cons. HomeSch. Unlimited, Newton, Iowa, 2005—. Author: (children's book) Captain Duffy and the Kid Who Threw Eggs, 1985, (play) Put On Your Brand New Bonnet, 1995;

publisher: ednl. materials Down Home Press, 1985—90. Founder Weaver St. Irregulars, Colfax, 1986—98; entertaining as Tapper T. Bear, 1991—; lay eucharistic min. Iowa Women's Correctional Facility, Mitchellville, 2002—03; spl. edn. adv. in pvt. practice, Iowa, 1995—. Recipient Gov.'s Vol. award, Iowa, 1988. Mem.: US Chess Fedn. Episcopalian. Achievements include research in the use of bibliotherapy with female juvenile delinquents; and archiving of materials concerning James Baird Weaver. Avocations: chess, piano. Office Phone: 515-669-6984.

HARBERT MITCHELL, KAREN (KAREN ALDERMAN HARBERT MITCHELL), government agency administrator; Bachelors, Rice Univ., Tex. Dir. Latin Am. Caribbean programs Internat. Republican Inst.; mgr. mktg. communications K&M Group; dep. asst. admin. for Latin America and Caribbean U.S. Agy. Internat. Devel.; asst. sec. policy and internat. affairs U.S. Dept. Energy. Office: US Dept Energy 1000 Independence Ave SW Washington DC 20585 Office Phone: 800-342-5363. Office Fax: 202-586-4403.

HARBOUR, PAMELA JONES, commissioner, lawyer; m. John Harbour; 3 children. BMus, Ind. U., Bloomington, 1981; JD, Ind. U., 1984. Asst. counsel NY State Dept. Trans., Albany, NY; atty. antitrust bur. NY State Atty. Gen., 1987—96, dep. atty. gen. pub. advocacy, 1997—99; ptnr. litig. dept. Kaye Scholer LLP, NY, 1999—2003; commr. FTC, Washington, 2003—. Recipient Antitrust Section Svc. award, NY State Bar Assn., 2005. Office: FTC 600 Pennsylvania Ave. NW Washington DC 20580

HARCOURT, MARION GOLDTHWAITE, retired social worker; b. Indpls., Aug. 18, 1928; d. John Louis and Helen (Whitehead) Goldthwaite; m. Robert Shaw Harcourt, Apr. 1, 1955 (div. Nov. 1979); children: Katherine, Shirley, John, Beth, David. BA, DePauw U., Greencastle, Ind., 1950; MS, Purdue U., 1953; MSW, Ind. U., 1976. Cert. clin. social work. Med. soc. worker Pub. Health Nursing, Indpls., 1977-78, Pub. Health Marion County, Indpls., 1978-81; family therapist Family Growth Ctr., Indpls., 1983-86; psychiat. social worker, family therapist Midtown Community Mental Health Ctr., Indpls., 1986—97; ret., 1997. Author: (chpt.) Child Sexual Abuse, 1986; contbr. articles to profl. jours. Disaster Svc. Humane Resource Am. Red. Cross, 1997—, supervisor Disaster Mental Health; docent Historic Landmarkers of Ind., 1995—; pres. Ind. chptr. U.S. China Peoples Friendship Assn., 2003—; clerk, coun. mem. First Congregational Ch., United Ch. Christ, 2001—; nat. bd. U.S. China Peoples Friendship Assn., 1992—98. Mem. DAR (mgmt. bd. 2005-), Nat. Assn. Social Workers (chair com. on ethics Ind. chpt. 1985-87), Internat. Transactional Analysis Assn. (cert.), Am. Assn. Marriage and Family Therapists (clin.), Acad. Family Mediators, Acad. Cert. Social Workers, Mensa (exec. com. cntrl. ind. 1992-98), Intertel, Mediation Assn. of Ind. (sec., bd. dirs. 1988-89). Avocations: travel, photography, genealogy. Home: 8426 Viburnum Ct Indianapolis IN 46260-2277

HARDAGE, PAGE TAYLOR, elementary school educator; b. Richmond, Va., June 27, 1944; d. George Peterson and Gladys Odell (Gordon) Taylor; 1 child, Taylor Brantley. AA, Va. Intermont Coll., Bristol, 1964; BS, Richmond Profl. Inst., 1966; MPA, Va. Commonwealth U., Richmond, 1982. Cert. tchr., Va. Competent toastmaster, dir. play therapy svcs. Med. Coll. Va. Hosps., Va. Commonwealth U., Richmond, 1970-90; dir. Inst. Women's Issues, Va. Commonwealth U., U. Va., Richmond, 1986-91; adminstr. Scottish Rite Childhood Lang. Ctr. at Richmond, Inc., 1991-99. Bd. dirs. Richmond Bus. Coun. Math. and Sci. Ctr. Found., Richmond, Emergency Med. Svcs. Adv. Bd., Richmond. Treas. Richmond Black Student Found., 1989—90, Leadership Metro Richmond Alumni Assn.; group chmn. United Way Greater Richmond, 1987; bd. dirs. Maggie L. Walker Hist. Found., Richmond YWCA, 1989—91, Capital Area Health Adv. Coun.; commr. Mayors Commn. of Concerns of Women, City of Richmond. Mem.: ASPA, NAFE, Va. Assn. Fund Raising Execs., Va. Recreation and Park Soc. (bd. dirs.), Internat. Mgmt. Coun. (exec. com.), Adminstrv. Mgmt. Soc., Rotary Club of Hanover. Unitarian Universalist. Avocations: bridge, target shooting, aerobics.

HARDCASTLE, MARCIA E. (MARCIA E. TEMME), retired journalist; b. Oakland, Calif., Nov. 28, 1945; d. Charles Frederick and Lillian Callita (Johnson) Temme; children: Glenn Arthur Hardcastle, Jason Roger Hardcastle. BA, San Jose State U. Society editor Los Altos (Calif.) News, 1967-70; reporter, lifestyle editor Santa Maria (Calif.) Times, 1979-82; adminstrv. asst. sr. Diablo Canyon Nuclear Power Plant, Calif., 1983-86; lifestyle editor 5-Cities Times Press Recorder, Arroyo Grande, Calif., 1987-98; arts and entertainment features editor Pulitzer Cmty. Newspapers, 1998-2000. Chair bd. dirs. publicity Am. Heart Assn., San Luis Obispo, Calif.; freelance photographer, writer, artist. Co-author: poetry.com. Press sec. Assemblyman Eric Seastrand, Calif.; co-founder Five Cities Women's Network, 1987; mem. Girl Scouts Am. Recipient Cmty. Svc. award Santa Maria Mental Health Assn., 1980, Media award Calif. Mental Health Assn., 1980, Hon. Mention award Nat. Newspaper Assn., 1989, 2d Place award Best Lifestyle/Family Life Pages Calif. Newspaper Assn., 1991, Editor's Choice award for outstanding achievement in poetry Internat. Libr. Poetry, 2003. Mem.: Bus. and Profl. Women, Internat. Order Rainbow for Girls (worthy advisor), Theta Sigma Phi. Avocations: photography, painting, travel. E-mail: marcia_hardcastle@yahoo.com.

HARDEN, ANNETTE C., recreation director; b. Peoria, Ill., July 17, 1976; d. D. Michael and Peggy A. Hutchison, Suzan Hutchison (Stepmother); m. Kenneth L. Harden Jr., July 27, 2002; 1 child, Kennedi C. BS in Sport Adminstrn., U. Indpls., 1998; MS in Sport Mgmt. with honors (hon.), Ind. State U., Terre Haute, 2000. Customer svc. mgr. Ind. U.-Purdue U. Indpls., 2000—02; asst. recreation dir. intramurals Butler U., Indpls., 2002—; sales assoc. Wooden Key Hallmark Gold Crown, Indpls., 1999—. Mem.: AAHPERD (Excellent Student Profl. award 1998), Nat. Intramural Recreation Sport Assn. Avocations: shopping, swimming. Office: Butler University 330 W 49th St Indianapolis IN 46208 Office Phone: 317-940-8514. E-mail: aharden@butler.edu.

HARDEN, MARCIA GAY, actress; b. LaJolla, Calif., Aug. 14, 1959; m. Thaddaeus D. Scheel, 1996; children: Eulala Grace Scheel, Hudson Harden Scheel, Julitta Dee Harden Scheel. BA in Theatre, U. Tex., 1980; MFA, NYU. Actor: (plays) Simpatico, 1994, Angels in America: Millennium Approaches/A Gay Fantasia on National Themes, 1993 (Tony nomination); (films) The Imagemaker, 1986, Miller's Crossing, 1990, Crush, 1992, Used People, 1992, Safe Passage, 1994, The Spitfire Grill, 1996, The Daytrippers, 1996, Spy Hard, 1996, The First Wives Club, 1996, Far Harbor, 1996, Flubber, 1997, Desperate Measures, 1998, Meet Joe Black, 1998, Curtain Call, 1999, Space Cowboys, 2000, Pollock, 2000 (Acad. award for best supporting actress, N.Y. Film Critics Circle award for best supporting actress), Gaudi Afternoon, 2001, Mystic River, 2003 (Acad. Award nomination for best supporting actress, 2004), Casa de los babys, 2003, Mona Lisa Smile, 2003, Just Like Mona, 2003, Welcome to Mooseport, 2004, Bad News Bears, 2005, Am. Dreamz, 2006; (TV films) Kojak: None So Blind, 1990, In Broad Daylight, 1991, Fever, 1991, Sinatra, 1992, Talking with, 1995, Convict Cowboy, 1995, Path to Paradise: The Untold Story of the World Trade Center Bombing, 1997, Labor of Love, 1998, Spenser: Small Vices, 1999, Thin Air, 2000, See You In My Dreams, 2000, From Where I Sit, 2000, Walking Shadow, 2001, King of Texas, 2002, She's Too Young, 2003; (TV series) The Education of Max Bickford, 2001; (TV miniseries) Guilty Hearts, 2002. Office: Creative Artists Agy 9830 Wilshire Blvd Beverly Hills CA 90212-1825

HARDEN, NEVA NINETTE, writer, consultant; d. Fred Newell and Annette Ida Stevens; children: Paul M., Janelle E., Eric N. BA, Mich. State U., 1948; MA, U. Denver, 1962. Instr. So. Colo. State Coll., Pueblo, Colo., 1964—66; assoc. prof., adv. fgn. students Adams State Coll., Alamosa, Colo., 1966—76; coord. Ctr. Handicapped San Luis Valley, 1970—71; prin., owner Horizon Comms., Albuquerque, 1982—; exec. dir. Recreation, Health and Occupl. Ctr., 1994. Writer and cons. in juvenile corrections, 2005—. Author: Survival Skills: A Job Finding Guide, 1998, rev. edit., 2006, Grantsmanship: Taming the Beast, 2001, rev. edit., 2005; editor and publisher: Blacks in the Workforce, 1987, Architecture and Children, 1991, The Era of Allan R. Phillips: A Festscrift, 1997, Ola Anfenson: Pioneer Photographer, 1997, publisher: Wildlife Rehabilitation Coloring and Activity Book, 1995. Presbyterian. Home and Office: Horizon Communications 2710 San Diego SE Albuquerque NM 87106

HARDEN, OLETA ELIZABETH, literature educator, academic administrator; b. Jamestown, Ky., Nov. 22, 1935; d. Stanley Virgil and Myrtie Alice (Stearns) McWhorter; m. Dennis Clarence Harden, July 23, 1966. BA, Western Ky. U., 1956; MA in English, U. Ark., 1958, PhD, 1965. Teaching asst. U. Ark., Fayetteville, 1956-57, 58-59, 61-63; instr. S.W. Mo. State Coll., Springfield, 1957-58, Murray (Ky.) U., 1959-61; asst. prof. English Northeastern State Coll., Tahlequah, Okla., 1963-65; asst. prof. Wichita (Kans.) State U., 1965-66; asst. prof. English Wright State U., Dayton, Ohio, 1966-68, assoc. prof., 1968-72, prof., 1972-93, asst. chmn. English dept., 1967-70, asst. dean, 1971-73, assoc. dean, 1973-74, exec. dir. gen. univ. services, 1974-76, pres. of faculty, 1984-85, prof. emerita, 1993—. Author: Maria Edgeworth's Art of Prose Fiction, 1971, Maria Edgeworth, 1984; editor: The Extension, 1999—. Grantee, Ford Found., 1971. Mem. MLA, AARP (impact alliance leader Ohio, 2001—), AAUP, Coll. English Assn., Women's Caucus for Modern Langs., Am. Conf. for Irish Studies (presenter 1989, 91, 94, 95), Wright State U. Retiree Assn. (pres. 1995-96), Elizabeth McWhorter Harden Forensics Alumni Assn. (founder, pres. We. Ky. U. chpt. 2004—). Office: Wright State U Dept English 7751 Colonel Glenn Hwy Dayton OH 45431-1674 Home: 2618 Big Woods Trl Dayton OH 45431-8704 Office Phone: 937-775-3136. Personal E-mail: oharden@aol.com.

HARDEN, OLETA J., lawyer, utilities executive; m. Phillip Harden. BA, MA, U. Ala.; JD, U. Calif. Sch. of Law, 1979. Atty. Federal Trade Commn., Wash., DC, 1979, Allstate Insurance Co., NJ; asst. public defender N.J. Dept. of Public Advocate; joined N.J. Resources, Wall, NJ, 1984, sr. v.p., sec., 1987—, gen. counsel, 1996—. Mem. bd. trustees Monmouth U.; bd. mem. N.J. Manufacturers Insurance Co. Mem.: ABA, N.J. State Bar Assn., Am. Soc. of Corp. Secretaries, Am. Gas Assn. (mem. legal com.). Office: NJ Resources 1415 Wyckoff Rd Wall NJ 07719

HARDER, WENDY WETZEL, communications executive; b. Oceanside, Calif., Feb. 14, 1951; d. Burt Louis and Marjorie Jean (Evans) W.; m. Peter N. Harder, Dec. 1, 1984; 1 child, Jonathan Russell. AA, Palomar Coll., 1971; BA in Comm., U. So. Calif., 1973; MBA, Pepperdine U., 1988. Pub. rels. dir. Orange County Cmty. Devel. Coun., Santa Ana, Calif., 1975-76; assoc. prodr. Sta. KOCE-TV, Huntington Beach, Calif., 1976-77, reporter, 1977-79, anchor, assoc. prodr., 1979-82; sr. adminstr. comm. Mission Viejo (Calif.) Co., 1983-84, mgr. corp. affairs, 1984-85, dir. corp. affairs, 1985-91, v.p. corp. affairs, 1991-93, v.p. mktg. and corp. comm., 1993-97; dir. cmty. rels. Soka Univ. Am., 1998—. 1st v.p. Aliso Viejo (Calif.) Cmty. Found., 1988-93, 03-04, pres., 1993-97, Saddleback Coll. Found., Mission Viejo, 1989-94; co-chmn. The Ctr. on Tour-Schs. Com., Orange County, Calif., 1989-92; v.p. Found. for Vocat. Visions, 1996-02, pres., 2000-03; bd. dirs. Dunaj Internat. Dance Ensemble, Orange County, 1985-00; den leader Pack 709 Cub Scouts, 2001-05; mem. troop com. 1602 Boy Scouts Am., 2005—, asst. scout master, 2006-; bd. dirs. Mt. of Olives Found., 2003-. Co-recipient Golden Mike award, Radio & TV News Assn., 1979; recipient, 1981. Mem. Pub. Rels. Soc. Am. (co-recipient Best Spl. Event award 1986), Aliso Viejo C. of C. (bd. dirs. 2002-2005), Laguna Niguel C. of C. (bd. dirs. 2006-), Anaheim/Orange County Conv. & Visitors Bur., Orange County Press Club (Best Feature Release award 1983), Phi Beta Kappa. Republican. Lutheran. Avocations: folk dancing, reading. Office: Soka Univ Am 1 University Dr Aliso Viejo CA 92656 Office Phone: 949-480-4081. Business E-Mail: wwharder@soka.edu.

HARDIN, BRIDGETTE EVERHART, educational research analyst; d. Arnold Alonzo and Twyla Gale Everhart; m. Eric Robert Hardin, Aug. 30, 1992. BA in Psychology, Met. State Coll. Denver, 1992, BA in Comm., 1992; MS in Occupl. Career Tng. Devel., Tex. A&M U., Corpus Christi, 2002. State master PRIDE train the trainer Tex. Dept. Protective and Regulatory Svcs., 1999, works welfare advisor Dept. Human Sevcs., Tex., 1996; cert. mgmt. devel. Governer's Ctr. Mgmt. Devel., Tex., 2003. Social worker Tex. Dept. Human Svcs., Corpus Christi, 1996—99; adj. psychology prof. Del Mar C.C., Corpus Christi, 1997—99; foster, adopt master pride trainer Tex. Dept. Protective and Regulatory Svcs., Corpus Christi, 1999—2002, leadership devel. coord., 2002—03; rsch. analyst, cons. Tex. A&M U., Corpus Christi, 2003—; pres. South Tex. Consortium for Instnl. Rsch., 2005—. Author: (children's story) Zachary's Special Gift; contbr. assessment guide. Named to V.P. George Bush's Honor Roll, US Dept. Edn., 1989—92; recipient Thinking Out of the Box award, Tex. Dept. Protective and Regulatory Svcs., 2000, Dean of Senate Collegiate Recognition award, State of Tex. Sen. Carlos Truan, 2002, State of Tex. Commendation award, Gov. and State of Tex. through Tex. Dept. Protective and Regulatory Svcs., 2003, Above and Beyond medallion, Tex. A&M U., Corpus Christi, 2004, Celebrating Excellence medallion, EEOC- Tex. A&M U., Corpus Christi, 2004; scholar, Coll. Edn., Tex. A&M U., Corpus Christi, 2005; Youth Leadership Devel. grantee, Ctr. for Edn. Devel. and Edn. Rsch., 2005. Mem.: Am. Soc. Tng. Devel. (assoc.), South Tex. Consortium Instl. Rsch. (assoc.), Tex. Assn. Instl. Rsch. (assoc.). Achievements include design of Texas state employee wellness program; motivation organization model for Texas state employees. Office Phone: 361-825-5989.

HARDIN, JANET BECKER, gifted and talented educator, music educator; b. Knoxville, Tenn., Oct. 26, 1952; d. M. Carl and Mary Evelyn (Carruth) Becker; m. Richard Vardry Hardin, Aug. 3, 1974; children: Patrick Vardry, Richard Nathaniel, Michael Joseph. MusB, Carson-Newman Coll., Jefferson City, TN, 1974; MA in Elem. Edn., Furman U., Greenville, SC, 2002. Cert. music edn. K-12 SC, elem. edn. SC, gifted edn. SC. Math asst. A.R. Lewis Elem. Sch., Pickens, SC, 1993—94; tchr. music and gifted and talented Ambler Elem. Sch., Pickens, SC, 1994—, tchr. art, 1995—98, sch. web mgr., 1998—; gifted and talented tchr. Holly Springs Elem., Pickens, SC, 1998—99; choral dir. Lakes and Mountains Sch. Arts, Pickens, SC, 2005—. Editor, author (oral history collection) Ambler Elementary School: Our Heritage, Ambler Elementary School: Our Legacy. Publicity chmn. PTO Ambler Elem. Sch., Pickens, 1991—92, pres. PTO, 1992—94; co-dir. Arts and CATS Spring Arts Festival, Pickens, 1995—2005; dir. children's choir Saluda Hill Bapt. Ch., Cleveland, SC, 1974—81, adult choir dir., 1974—, ch. pianist, 1974—. Named Tchr. of Yr., Ambler Elem. Sch., 2002; grantee, Humanities Coun. SC, 2004—05; Robinson grantee, Constl. Rights Found., 2003—04. Mem.: SC Music Educators Assn., Music Educators Nat. Conf., SC Consortium for Gifted Edn. Achievements include discovery of Ambler's history. Office: Ambler Elem Sch 838 Ambler Sch Rd Pickens SC 29671 Office Phone: 864-898-5588. Home Fax: 864-836-5282; Office Fax: 864-898-5589. E-mail: hardinjb@pickens.k12.sc.us.

HARDIN, MARTHA LOVE WOOD, civic leader; b. Muncie, Ind., Aug. 13, 1918; d. Lawrence Anselm and Bonny Blossom (Williams) Wood; m. Clifford Morris Hardin, June 28, 1939; children: Susan Hardin Wood, Clifford Wood, Cynthia Hardin Milligan, Nancy Hardin Rogers, James Alvin. Librarian U. Chgo., 1939-40. Co-author Genealogy: Ancestors of Lawrence Anselm Wood, Genealogy Ancestors of Bonny Williams Wood; contbr. articles to profl. jours. Chair Nebr. Heart Fund, 1967; vol. worker Lincoln Gen. Hosp., 1965, Clarkson Hosp., 1966; hon. chair Symphony Ball, Washington, 1970; met. bd. YWCA, Washington, 1969-71, St. Louis, 1973-95; women's com. Pres.'s Com. on Employment of Handicapped, 1970-91, bd. dirs., 1970—; co-chmn. nat. fund-raising campaign U. Nebr. Found., 1977-80. Mem. DAR, PEO, Soc. Mortar Bd., Lincoln Country Club, Wednesday Club, Phi Beta Kappa, Pi Beta Phi. Home: 6525 Lone Tree Dr Lincoln NE 68512-2405

HARDIN, MARY L., interior designer; d. William Alexander and Mary Louise (Murphy) Prosser; m. R. McCurdy, 1954 (dec.); children: Terry L. McCurdy, Lynn R. McCurdy; m. O. Hardin, 1977 (dec.). BS, Clayton Coll., 2000. Missionary oblates, Ill., 1970; mem. presdl. task force U.S. Govt, Wash., DC, 1987, 1991. Mem.: Nat. Writers Club, Sierra Club, Lourdes Prayer League, Peale Ctr. for Christian Living, World Wildlife Fund, Dinshah Health Soc., Natural Resource Def. Coun., Nat. Trust for Historic Preservation, Nat. Mus. Women in the Arts, Nat. Pks. Conservation Assn., Acad. Am. Poets, Nat. Arbor Day Found., Defenders of Wildlife, Smithsonian Instn., The Oxford Club (life). Avocations: writing, painting, poetry, antiques.

HARDING, FANN, retired science administrator; b. Henderson, Ky., Jan. 29, 1930; d. James Hilary and Lucy (Caldwell) H. Student, Western Coll., Oxford Ohio, 1947-48; AB in Biology, Coker Coll., Hartsville, S.C., 1951; MS in Anatomy, Med. U. S.C., Charleston, 1954, PhD, 1958. Research and teaching asst. dept. anatomy Med. U. S.C., 1951-53, teaching fellow, 1953-55, research fellow, 1955-58; analyst pub. health research program, research and tng. grants br. Nat. Heart Inst., Bethesda, Md., 1958-61, scientist adminstr. research and tng. grants br., 1961-64, chmn. nat. adv. heart council statements com., 1961-64, sr. health scientist adminstr. research grants br. (sect. chief), 1964-69, sr. health scientist adminstr. thrombosis and hemorrhagic diseases br. (acting chief), extramural program, also arteriosclerosis program, 1969-72; mem. Nat. Heart Inst. (Fellowship Bd.), 1966-68; sr. health scientist adminstr. thrombosis and hemorrhagic diseases program (acting chief), div. blood diseases and resources Nat. Heart and Lung Inst. (name changed to Nat. Heart, Lung and Blood Inst. 1976), Bethesda, 1972-74; asst. to dir. div. blood diseases and resources Nat. Heart, Lung and Blood Inst., 1974—, program dir. extramural research tng. and career devel. in blood diseases and transfusion medicine, exec. sec. blood diseases and resources adv. com., 1974-95; asst. coordinator U.S.-USSR Health Exchange Program, 1974-95; ret., 1996; sculptor, 1996—. Women's Action Program adv. coun. HEW, 1971-72; cons. James H. Mitchell Found., Washington, 1962-67, Washington VA Hosp., 1968-70; environ. cons. Henderson (Ky.) Citizens Com., 1974-76; initiated and implemented concept of transfusion medicine, 1982—; adv. bd. Psychoceramic Found., 2001—. Editorial bd.: Lupus News, 1988—. Organizer NIH Orgn. for Women, 1970; bd. dir. Assn. Women in Sci. Edn. Found., 1973-77, Lupus Found. Am., 1985-88; bd. visitors Coker Coll., 1974-78; bd. dir., sec., treas. Nat. Children's Choir, Washington, 1981-91; bd. advisors Psychoceramie Found., 2002; mem. Women's Nat. Dem. Club, 2004. Recipient Ruth Patrick award, 1951, NIH sustained performance award, 1973, Nat. award Fedn. Orgns. for Profl. Women, 1977, Disting. Svc. award Transfusion Medicine Acad. Award Program, Am. Assn. Blood Banks, 1990, Disting. Alumni award Coker Coll., 1992, award of Merit, NIH, 1993, Founder's award, Fedn. Orgns. for Profl. Women, 1995, Foremother award, Nat. Rsch. Ctr. Women and Children, 2005. Fellow Sigma Delta Epsilon; mem. AAAS (panel on women in sci. 1973-77), Nat. Women's Polit. Caucus (charter), Assn. Women in Sci. (founding mem. 1971, exec. bd. 1973-75), Fedn. Orgn. Profl. Women (founding pres., exec. bd. 1972—), Nat. Microcirculatory Soc. (charter), Reticuloendothelial Soc. (charter), Am. Assn. Blood Banks, Internat. Soc. Thrombosis & Haemostasis, Internat. Soc. Blood Transfusion, Internat. Soc. Lymphology, Womans Party Sewell-Belmont Ho. and Mus. (bd. dir. 1981-2005, corr. sec. 1989-91, rec. sec. 1991-96, chair audit com. 2005), Woman's Nat. Dem. Club. Home: 1661 Crescent Pl NW Apt 305 Washington DC 20009-4066 Home Fax: 202-265-3267. Personal E-mail: ffharding@aol.com.

HARDING, LINDA KRISTINA, special education educator; b. Queens, N.Y., July 23, 1964; d. George J. and Lucille D. Coleman; m. Timothy Joseph Harding, Aug. 17, 1991; children: Rebecca, Troy, Caitlin. BS in Elem. Edn., Psychology, Molloy Coll., Rockville Ctr., N.Y.; MS in Spl. Edn., Hofstra U., Uniondale, N.Y. Cons. tchr. grade 4 Binghamton City Sch. Dist., Binghamton, NY, cons. tchr. grade 5, cons. tchr. K-2, self contained spl. edn. tchr.; 2nd grade tchr. North Bellmore Sch. Dist., NY; tchr. asst. Garden City Sch. Dist., NY. Mem. diversity com. Binghamton City Sch. Dist., spl. edn. reading specialist, child study coord. Leader Girl Scouts U.S., Vestal, NY; coach Odyssey of the Mind, Vestal and Binghamton; talent show coord. Clayton Ave. PTO. Mem.: Binghamton Area Reading Coun. Home: 417 Clayton Ave Vestal NY 13850

HARDING, MARIE, ecological executive, artist; b. Glen Cove, NY, Nov. 13, 1941; d. Charles Lewis and Marie (Parish) H.; m. John P. Allen, Jan. 29, 1965 (div. Oct., 1991); 1 child, Eden A. Harding. BA, Sarah Lawrence Coll., 1964; postgrad., Arts Students League, N.Y.C., 1965. Founder Synergia Ranch Ctr. for Innovation, Retreats and Confs., Santa Fe, 1969; founding mem., actress Theater of All Possibilities, Santa Fe, 1971-86; founding mem., dir. Inst. Ecotechnics, Santa Fe, also London, 1974—; bd. dirs., founding mem. Savannah Systems Pty., Ltd., Kimberly region, Australia, 1976—, Outback Sta. Pty. Ltd., Kimberly region, Australia, 1976-94; chair, dir. EcoWorld, Inc., Santa Fe, 1982-94; dir., founding mem., CFO Space Biospheres Ventures, Biosphere 2, Ariz., 1984-94; chair, CEO Oceans Expdns., Inc., 1986-92; pres. ecol. and biosphere R&D/implementation project Global Ecotechnics Corp., Santa Fe, 1994—; pres. Decisions Team, Inc. Ecol. Project Mgmt., Ariz., 1994—, Silver Hills Ranch Homeowners Assn., 1996—2006; pres., mng. mem. Synergia Ranch, LLC, Santa Fe; mem. San Marcos Dist. Planning Co., 2004; chmn. Tropic Seas Rsch. Co., 2006—, sec., 2006—. Participant in constrn. and fin. Capt. R. Heraclitus Rsch. Vessel, Oakland, Calif., 1974; bd. dirs. Synergetic Press, London and Ariz.; chmn., sec. Tropic Seas Rsch. Co., 2006. Exhibitions include Biosphere 2, Ariz., 1979-93, Biosphere 2, October Gallery, London, 1996, 2003-04, Berlin, 2003, Peoples Bank N.Mex., 2003; project dir., artist mural project History of Jazz, Dance, Theater, Ft. Worth, 1982-83, San Marcos Studio Tours, 1999-2004; prodr., dir. (films) Bryon Gysin Loves ya, Project Charlie, The Search, Planet Earth Conf Vol. Swallows, Madras, India, 1964, Project Concern, Vietnam, Hong Kong, 1964-65; artist, founder, trustee October Gallery Trust, London, 1979; pres. Short Hills Ranch Homeowners Assn., 1996—. Mem.: Silver Hills Reach Homeowners Assn. (pres. 1996—). Avocations: painting, gardening. Home and Office: 26 Synergia Rd Santa Fe NM 87508-4438 Office Phone: 505-471-2573.

HARDING, NANCY ELIZABETH, language educator; b. Baxter Springs, Kans., Mar. 26, 1965; d. Kenneth Gibson and Beverly Ann Molloy; m. Michael Robert Harding, Oct. 1, 1988. BA in Edn., U. Mo., Kansas City, 1993; BSBA, Mo. So. State U., Joplin, 1987. Store mgr. Fashion Gal, Joplin, 1987—88; sys. trainer Child Craft, Overland Park, Kans., 1991—93. Profl. cons. Step Up to Writing, Las Vegas, 2004—. Named Disting. Educator, Clark County Sch. Dist. SE Region, 2001. Fellow: So. Nev. Writing Project. Avocation: painting. Office: Silverado High School 1650 Silver Hawk Las Vegas NV 89123 Office Phone: 702-799-5790. E-mail: nehardin@interact.ccsd.net.

HARDIN-PIERCE, MELANIE G., nursing educator; Prof. U. Ky., Lexington, 1991—; nurse practitioner U. Ky. Med. Ctr. Office: University of Kentucky 760 Rose Street Lexington KY 40536 Office Phone: 859-323-5658. Home Fax: 859-323-1057; Office Fax: 859-323-1057. Personal E-mail: mhpier00@uky.edu.

HARDISON, CYNTHIA ANN STOLTZE, hematologist, retired oncologist; d. Norris Sanborn Stoltze and Frances Willard Virtue; m. Joseph Hammond Hardison, Jr., Apr. 8, 1961; children: Joseph III, Sanborn Stoltze, Anna Katharine. BS, Stanford U., Calif.; MS, U. Minn., Mpls.; MD, Northwestern U., Evanston, Ill. Intern Evanston Hosp., Ill., 1954—55; fellow Mayo Clinic, Rochester, Minn., 1955—59, cons. in hematology, 1959—64; founder and prin. Raleigh Internal Medicine Assoc., NC, 1964—89; ret., 1989. Cons. Jour. AMA, 1964—69. Bd. dir. N.C. Symphony Found., 1983—86. Mem.: Am. Coll. Gastroenterology Auxilliary (pres. 1981), Monday Luncheon and Literacy Soc., Olla Podrida Book Club. Republican. Presbyterian. Avocations: painting, travel. Home: 1612 Oberlin Rd 7 Raleigh NC 27608

HARDT, NANCY SISSON, pathology and laboratory medicine educator; b. Ill., May 17, 1952; married; 2 children. BA in Modern Lang. (magna cum laude), Sweet Briar Coll., Va., 1974; MD, Loyola U. Stritch Sch. Medicine, Ill., 1977. Cert. of added qualification in cytopathology Am. Bd. Pathology, 1990, diplomate Am. Bd. Pathology in Anatomic and Clin. Pathology, 1989, Am. Bd. Obstetrics/Gynecology, 1984, cert. Am. Registry of Diagnostic Med.

Sonographers, 1983. Intern, obstetrics/gynecology U. Ky., Coll. Medicine, 1977—78, resident, obstetrics/gynecology, 1978—81; clin. fellow, divsn. maternal/fetal medicine, dept. obstetrics/gynecology U. Fla., Coll. Medicine, 1981—83, med. dir., reproductive ultrasound lab., dept. obstetrics/gynecology, 1983—86, asst. prof., obstetrics/gynecology, 1983—86, resident, anatomic and clin. pathology, dept. pathology, 1986—89, fellow, gynecologic pathology and cytopathology, 1989—90, asst. prof., pathology and lab. medicine, 1990—93, assoc. prof., obstetrics/gynecology, 1993—2000, assoc. prof. with tenure, pathology and lab. medicine, 1993—2000, prof., obstetrics/gynecology, 2000—02, prof. with tenure, pathology and lab. medicine, 2000—02, adj. prof., dept. obstetrics/gynecology, 2002—06, adj. prof., dept. pathology, 2002—06, clin. prof. pathology and lab. medicine, 2006—; prof., dept. obstetrics/Gynecology U. Tenn. Coll. Medicine, 2004—06, prof. with tenure, dept. preventative medicine, 2002—06; dir., Inst. for Women's Health U. Tenn. Health Sci. Ctr., 2002—05, Methodist Endowed chair for women's health, 2002—05; med. dir., physician services LabDoc, 2006—. Mem. admissions com. Loyola U., Stritch Sch. Medicine, 1975—77; mem. phase B curriculum com., dept. pathology U. Fla. Coll. Medicine, 1991—98, mem. surgical case review com., 1991—94, faculty coun. rep., 1992—94, faculty coun. v.p., 1993—94, chair faculty coun. task force on the office for faculty develop., 1993, women faculty assn. pres., 1993—94, mem. search com. for chair of anatomy and cell biology, 1994—95, faculty coun. pres., 1994—95, mem. curriculum com. task force on integration reproductive services, 1994, mem. assoc. prof. promotion and tenure com., 1995—96, past pres., faculty coun., 1995—96, mem. faculty capital campaign steering com., 1995, mem. Dean's task force on early retirement, 95, mem. Dean's task force on diversity and comm., 95, mem. dept. pathology and lab. medicine, variable compensation com., 1996—2002, mem. contract adv. com., dept. pathology, managed care, 1996—2001, mem. faculty group practice bd. dirs., 1996, mem. faculty compensation mem., 1996—97, co-chair, cash collections and billing design team, adminstrv. reassignment, 1996—97, rep. to the Health Sci. Ctr. Libr. adv. bd., 1996—97, assoc. med. dir., cytopathology, dept. pathology, immunology and lab. medicine, 1997—98, mem. faculty group practice ops. com., 1997, mem. faculty group practice bd. dirs., 1998—2002, mem. exec. com., dept. pathology, 1998—2002, com. mem., chair faculty compensation, 1998—99, asst. dean, clin. affairs and managed care, 1998—99; coord. Chancellor's hours U. Tenn., 2004—05, mem. bd. dir. com. on Outreach, 2003—05; mem. student conduct standards com. U. Fla., Health Sci. Ctr., 1996—2002, co-dir., Ctr. for Rsch. on Women's Health, 1998—2002, faculty senate mem., edn. policy com., 2003—, faculty senate chair legis. resource com., 2003—04; assoc. chair for Step 3 computer-based case simulation com. Nat. Bd. Med. Examiners, 1999, mem. Step 3 com., 2001—, bd. dir., 2001—, mem. fin. com., 2001—, chair, Step 3 Test Material Develop. Com. for computer- based case stimulations, 2001—05, group leader for scripting for the step 3 computer-based case stimulation com., 2000—05; coord. Memphis City Schools Svc. Learning Project, 2002—05, Mini Med. Sch., 2003, 04, 05; mem. State Tenn. SIDS Advisory, 2004—, Governor's TennCare Advisory, 2003—04, Women's Health Adv. Com. State Commr. of Health, 2003—06; spkr. in field; invited lectr. in field. Guest editor Jour. Fla. Med. Assn.; contbr. articles to profl. jours., chapters to books. Chair, health com. New Pathways, 2004—06, bd. dir., 2003—06; co-chair, rsch. com. Cmty. Inst. for Early Childhood, 2003—04; regional health coun. mem. 0-5 Com., 2002—06; chair, Infant Mortality Prevention Com. Regional Health Coun., 2002—06, mem. exec. com., 2002—04; bd. chair Memphis Challenge, 2004—06; mem. Memphis Area Women's Coun. Bd., 2002—06, pres., 2005—06. Named one of 50 Women Who Make a Difference (Memphis), 2005; recipient Young Investigators award, Am. Acad. Pediatrics Perinatal Pediatrics Sect., 1983, Gender Equity award, Am. Med. Writers Assn., 1997, Alachua and Bradford Counties (Fla.) Women of Distinction award, 1998, Great Apple award, Memphis City Schools, 2005, Disting. Svc. award, Nat. Bd. Med. Examiners, 2006; Am. Cancer Soc. Nat. Clin. Oncology fellowship, 1989—90, Robert Wood Johnson Health Policy Fellow, IOM, 2006. Fellow: Am. Coll. Obstetrics and Gynecology, Coll. Am. Pathologists (First prize, Residents Rsch. Competition (awarded jointly with Anatomic Pathology Divsn. Am. Soc. Clin. Pahtology) 1988); mem.: Alachua County Med. Soc., Am. Inst. Ultrasound in Medicine, Am. Soc. Clin. Pathologists, US and Canadian Acad. Pathology (Residents Rsch. Competition, Stowell Orbison award 1989), Internat. Soc. Gynecological Pathologists, Am. Assn. Med. Colleges (women liason officer 1994—2001), AMA (coll. medicine delegate 1995), Exec. Leadership in Academic Medicine (adv. bd. 1997—99), Am. Coll. Physician Executives, Med. Group Mgmt. Assn., Soc. for Exec. Leadership in Academic Medicine (fellow 1995—96, pres. 1997—99, bd. dir. 1997—2001), Soc. for Women's Health Rsch. (mem. steering com., Women's Health Rsch. Coalition 1999—), Phi Beta Kappa, Alpha Sigma Nu. Achievements include co-inventing Surface Modified Silicone Drug Depot. Office: U Fla Coll Medicine Dept Pathology Immunology & Lab Medicine Rocky Point Lab Rm 1153 4800 SW 35th Dr Gainesville FL 32607 also: Dept Pathology Immunology & Lab Medicine U Fla Coll Medicine PO Box 100275 Gainesville FL 32610-0275 Office Phone: 352-265-0111 ext 7-2054. Office Fax: 352-265-9901. Business E-Mail: hardt@pathology.ufl.edu.*

HARDWICK, ELIZABETH, writer; b. Lexington, Ky., July 27, 1916; d. Eugene Allen and Mary (Ramsey) H.; m. Robert Lowell, July 28, 1949 (div. Oct. 1972); 1 child, Harriet. AB, U. Ky., 1938, MA, 1939; postgrad., Columbia U., 1939-41. Adj. assoc. prof. Barnard Coll. Author: The Ghostly Lover, 1945, The Simple Truth, 1955, A View of My Own, 1962, Seduction and Betrayal, 1974, Sleepless Nights, 1979, Bartleby in Manhattan, 1983, Sight Readings, 1998, Herman Melville, A Life, 2000; editor: The Selected Letters of William James, 1960; adv. editor: NY Rev. Books Recipient George Jean Nathan award for dramatic criticism, 1966, Gold medal for criticism, Am. Acad. Arts and Letters, 1993; Guggenheim fellow, 1947. Mem. Am. Acad. and Inst. Arts and Letters, Acad. Arts and Scis. Home: 15 W 67th St New York NY 10023-6226

HARDWICK, MELINDA S., writer; b. Belleville, Ill., July 31, 1970; d. Charles Thomas Hardwick and Susan Glenn Lampe. BA, St. John Fisher Coll., 1993; MEd, Lesley U., 2001; MFA in Writing for Children, Vt. Coll., 2005. Cert. tchr. Wash. HS tchr. Chrysalis Sch., Woodville, Wash., 2001—04; writer Seattle, 2004—. Cons. Tutor Hall, Everett, Wash., 2004—. Contbr. articles to profl. publs. Vol. Children's Mus., Everett, 2004—. Grantee, Centrum, 2002, Children's Mus., 2002, Nat. Book Found., 2002. Mem.: AAUW, Nat. Tutoring Assn. Democrat. Mem. Unity Ch. Avocations: weaving, swimming, reading.

HARDWICKE, CATHERINE HELEN, film director, set designer; b. McAllen, Tex., 1955; d. John Benjamin III and Jamee Alberta (Bennett) H. BArch with highest honors, U. Tex., 1979; postgrad., UCLA. Prodn. designer: (films) Tapeheads, 1988, I'm Gonna Git You Sucka, 1988, Martins Go Home, 1990, Passed Away, 1992, Posse, 1993, Freaked, 1993, Tombstone, 1993, Car 54, Where Are You, 1994, Tank Girl, 1995, 2 Days in the Valley, 1996, SubUrbia, 1996, Mad City, 1997, The Newton Boys, 1998, Three Kings, 1999, Antitrust, 2001, Vanilla Sky, 2001, Laurel Canyon, 2002, (theatre) Carnage, Methusalem, Alagazam--After the Dog Wars; dir.: (films) Thirteen, 2003 (also writer), Lords of Dogtown, 2005; art dir.: (films) Hunk, 1987, Mr. Destiny, 1990 Recipient Carl Walker Animation award Disney Studios, 1984, Nissan Focus award, 1984, Joseph Jefferson award Chgo. Non-Equity Theatre, 1990, others.

HARDY, DORCAS RUTH, business and government relations executive; b. Newark, N.J., July 18, 1946; d. C. Colburn and Ruth (Hart) H.; m. Samuel V. Spagnolo. BA, Conn. Coll., 1964-68; MBA, Pepperdine U., 1976. cert. sr. advisor. Legis. rsch. asst. U.S. Senator Clifford P. Case, Washington, 1970; spl. asst. White House Conf. Children and Youth, Washington, 1970-71; exec. dir. Health Svcs. Industry Commn., Cost of Living Coun., Washington, 1971-73; asst. sec. Calif. Dept. Health, Sacramento, 1973-74; assoc. dir. U. So. Calif. Ctr. Health Svcs. Rsch., 1974-81; asst. sec. human devel. svcs. HHS, Washington, 1981-86; commr. Social Security Washington, 1986-89; pres. Dorcas R. Hardy & Assocs., Spotsylvania, Va., 1989—; exec. v.p. Pub. Issue Mgmt., Washington, 2001—03. Chmn. bd. dirs., and CEO Work Recovery, Inc., Tucson, 1996-98; bd. dirs. First Coast Svc. Options, Inc., Wright Investors Svc. Managed Funds; Social Security Advisory Bd.; chmn. vocat. rehab. and employment task force VA, 2003-04; chmn. com. 2005 White House Conf. on Aging Policy, 2004-06. Author: Social Insecurity: The Crisis in America's Social Security System and How to Plan Now for Your Own Financial Survival, 1992. Mem. Girl Scouts USA, Va. Bd. Rehab. Svcs., 1998-2002; bd. dirs. Com. on Developing Am. Capitalism; former chmn. Pres.'s Task Force on Legal Equity for Women. Mem. Soc. Cert. Sr. Advisors. Office: Washington Metro Office 11407 Stonewall Jackson Dr Spotsylvania VA 22553-4608

HARDY, GRACE HERVEY, elementary guidance counselor, language arts educator; b. Coffeeville, Miss., Feb. 3, 1940; d. Amos and Louella (Brown) Hervey; m. Willie Hardy, July 13, 1978; 1 child, Victor Kermit. B.A. magna cum laude, Miss. Indsl. Coll., 1961; M.Ed., Memphis State U., 1974. Tchr. English, Sand Flat High Sch., Mount Pleasant, Miss., 1961-62; sec. bus. edn. Tate County High Sch., Coldwater, Miss., 1963-73; tchr. Tate County Attendance Ctr., Coldwater, 1973-76; tchr. lang. arts, guidance counselor Coldwater Elem. Sch., 1976-84, tchr. French and lang. arts, guidance counselor, 1984—; sch. guidance counselor, computer lab. monitor, migrant tchr./recruiter grades K-6, Tate County Schs. 1985-95; profl. sch. counselor, Memphis City Schs., 1995-2002; served numerous coms. and worked with curriculum coords., suprs., prins., faculty, parents, cmty. and other leaders in using innovative methods for enhancing student learning. Counselor, club leader Goodwill Boys Club, Memphis, 1974; mem. N.W. Miss. Regional Screening Team for Spl. Edn. Students, Hernando, Miss., 1977-81; mem., cons. to bd. dirs. for GED Test, N.W. Miss. Jr. Coll., Senatobia, 1984—; asst. sec. Truckers Caucus Assn., Memphis, 1979—; asst. sec. Rocky Mountain M.B. Ch., Water Valley, Miss., 1960-78; mem. Christian edn. bd., dir. Red Circle Missionary Soc.; pres. Improvement Circle, Sunday sch. tchr. Mt. Joyner M.B. Ch. Recipient Outstanding Performance award Mercury Bus. League of Rust Coll., Holly Springs, Miss., 1960; mem. Christ United Bapt. Ch., dir./organizer of ch. ministries, tchr. ch. mem.'s class, participant in ministries: Mission, Mothers, Sisters, In-Christ, Scholarship, Bible Study and Trustee. Mem. Tate Assn. Educators, Miss. Assn. Educators, NEA, N.W. Miss. Counseling Assn., Miss. Counseling Assn. Democrat. Baptist. Clubs: Memphis State U. Alumni; Le Cercle Francais (sponsor 1984-85). Avocations: traveling; interior decorating; reading. Home: 137 Sullivan Cv Memphis TN 38109-4545

HARDY, JANE ELIZABETH, communications educator; b. Fenelon Falls, Ont., Can., Mar. 27, 1930; came to U.S., 1956, naturalized, 1976; d. Charles Edward and Augusta Miriam (Lang) Little; m. Ernest E. Hardy, Sept. 3, 1955; children: Edward Harold, Robert Ernest. BS with distinction, Cornell U., 1953. Garden editor and writer Can. Homes Mag., Maclean-Hunter Pub. Co., Ltd., Toronto, Ont., 1954-55, 56-62; contbg. editor Can. Homes, Southam Pub. Co., Toronto, Ont., 1962-66; instr. Cornell U., 1966-73, sr. lectr. in comm., 1979-96. Provost's adv. com. on status of women Cornell U., 1977—81, coun. mem., 2003—; lectr., condr. workshops on writing. Author: Writing for Practical Purposes, 1996; editor pro-tem Cornell Plantations Quar., 1981-82; author numerous publs. including brochures, slide set scripts, contbr. articles to popular mags. Bd. dirs. Matrix Found., 1998—2005, chmn. bd. dirs., 1998—2003. Mem.: Assn. Women Comms. (nat. bd. dirs. 1997—2000), Women in Comms., Inc. (faculty advisor 1977—95, liaison 1986—94, chair, adv. mem. 1988—90), Cornell Assn. Class Officers (exec. bd., v.p. 2005—), Ithaca Women's Club, Ithaca Garden Club (pres. 2005—), Royal Hort. Soc., Alpha Omicron Pi, Phi Kappa Phi, Pi Alpha Xi. Home: 215 Enfield Falls Rd Ithaca NY 14850-8797

HARDY, JANICE AUDREY NEUBERT, retired elementary school educator; b. Chester, Pa., Aug. 2, 1936; d. Arthur Bruno and Bertha May (Lawton) Neubert; m. Thomas Leon Hardy, Mar. 31, 1955; children: Cynthia Lou Hardy Blake, Timothy Kent (dec.), Amy Lee Hardy Hollenbeck. BA magna cum laude, Glassboro State Coll., 1982; AS, Delaware County CC, 1978. Cert. elem. tchr., N.J. Elem. tchr., Aston, Pa., 1967-77; elem. tchr. Somers Point, N.J., 1977-99, math. and testing coord., ret., 1999. Active Girl Scouts U.S.A.; sec. Notre Dame Aux.; Eucharistic minister St. Joseph Ch., Somers Point, 1984—; extraordinary minister Shore Meml. Hosp. Named Lay Tchr. of Yr. St. Josreph coun. K.C., 1998. Mem. N.J. Coun. Math. Tchrs., Nat. Cath. Educators Assn. Republican. Roman Catholic. Avocations: poetry, sewing, porcelain dolls, quilting, greeting card designer. Home: 301 Bliss Ave Somers Point NJ 08244-2203 Office Phone: 609-927-0108. Personal E-mail: janhardy@aol.com.

HARDY, JENNIFER BETH, lawyer; b. 1969; BA in Sociology, Boston Coll., 1991; JD, New England Sch. Law, 1996. Bar: Mass. 1996, US Dist. Ct. (Dist. Mass.). Jr. ptnr. Melick, Porter & Shea, LLP, Boston. Mem.: Women's Bar Assn., Mass. Bar Assn. Office: Melick Porter & Shea LLP 28 State St Boston MA 02109 Office Phone: 617-523-6200. Office Fax: 617-523-8130. E-mail: jhardy@melicklaw.com.*

HARDY, LINDA LEA STERLOCK, media specialist; b. Balt., Aug. 15, 1947; d. George Allen and Dorothy Lea (Briggs) Sterlock; m. John Edward Hardy III, Apr. 25, 1970; 1 child, Roger Wayne. BA in History, N.C. Wesleyan Coll., 1969; MEd in History, East Carolina U., 1972, MLS, 1990. Cert. tchr. NC. History tchr. Halifax (N.C.) County Schs., 1972-83, learning lab tchr., 1983-91, computer lab tchr., 1990-95; media specialist Nash-Rocky Mount (N.C.) Schs., 1995—. Part-time history instr. Nash C.C., 1993. Mem. AAUW (pres. Rocky Mount br. 1993-95, sec. 1997-99, Named Gift award 1987), Bus. and Profl. Women (pres. Rocky Mount chpt. 1986-87, 90-91, 2003-05, treas. 1992-97, 2000-03, 2005—, sec.-treas. dist X 1989-90, state election chmn. 1989-90, 93-95, state credentials chmn. 1997-98, sec.-treas. dist. 6 1997-98, 2006—, Girl Friday award 1981, 98, Woman of Yr. award 1986, 97, 2002, state found. fin. chair 1996-97, state treas. 1999-2001, state sec. 2001-02, dist. VI dir. 2002-03, state membership chair 2003-04, trustee 2003-06, state found. bd. 2005—), Nat. Assn. Educators, N.C. Assn. Educators, Nash/Rocky Mount Assn. Educators (faculty rep. 1995-2005). Methodist. Avocations: reading, travel, needlepoint, computers. Office: Red Oak Middle School 3170 Red Oak Battleboro Rd Battleboro NC 27809-9284 Office Phone: 252-451-5500. Personal E-mail: llshardy@netscape.net. Business E-Mail: lhardy@nrms.k12.nc.us.

HARDY, MELANIE ANN WALKER, secondary school educator, science educator; d. Bruce Walker and Karol Metevia, Joseph Metevia (Stepfather). BS, Mich. State U., East Lansing, 1999. Tchr. sci. Grandville H.S., Mich., 1999—2000, Collins Hill H.S., Suwanee, Ga., 2000—. Office Phone: 770-682-4100.

HARDY, SANDRA VANESSA, elementary school educator; d. Junius Irvin and Lorean Burk Hardy; 1 child, Brandon. BS, St. Paul's Coll., Lawrenceville, Va., 1982; MS in Edn., Old Dominion U., 2002. Weaver Burlington Industries, South Hill, 1982—98; tchr. Brunswick County Pub. Schs., Lawrenceville, 1994—. Mem.: Brunswick Edn. Assn. Avocations: reading, gardening. Home: 477 Fresh Medow Rd Lawrenceville VA 23868

HARDY, SARALYN REECE, museum director; m. Randall Hardy; children: Stephen, Thomas, William. BA, U. Kans., 1976, MA in Am. studies, 1994. Project coord. Helen Foresman Spencer Mus. Art, U. Kans., Lawrence, 1977—79, dir., 2005—, Salina Art Ctr., Kans., 1986—2002; dir. mus. and visual arts Nat. Endowment for Arts, Washington, DC, 1999—2002. Recipient Women of Achievement award, Salina YWCA, Kansas Gov.'s Art Award, 1995. Mem.: Inst. Mus. and Libr. Svcs., Mus. Trustee Assn., Am. Assn. Mus., Am. Fedn. of Arts Mus. Dirs., Getty Leadership Inst. Office: Spencer Mus Art U Kans 1301 Mississippi St Lawrence KS 66045-7500

HARDY, SHARON ARLENE, elementary school educator, small business owner; b. Pitts., Aug. 26, 1946; d. Andrew Sylvester and Dorothy Faye Mark; children: Mark David, Michael James. BS in Edn., Indiana U. Pa., 1968; MS in Edn., U. South Fla., Tampa, 1983. Tchr. Hazleton (Pa.) Area Sch. Bd., 1968—79, Desoto County Sch. Bd., Arcadia, Fla., 1979—. Leader Boy Scouts Am., Port Charlotte, Fla., 1993—2004. Mem.: MENC, Delta Kappa Gamma, Delta Omicron (life), Alpha Omicron Pi (life). Avocations: travel, reading, music, gardening. Home: 20352 Astoria Port Charlotte FL 33952 Office: Desoto County Sch Bd 530 Lasalona Ave Arcadia FL 33821 Office Phone: 863-494-3155.

HARDY, VICTORIA ELIZABETH, finance educator; b. Marion, N.C., Feb. 26, 1947; d. Milton Victor Roth and Bertha Jean (Norris) R.; m. Michael Carrington Hardy, June 19, 1983 (div. 1993); 1 child, Christopher. BS in Edn., U. Mo., 1970; postgrad., So. Ill. U., 1974-75; postgrad. Mgmt. Devel. Program, Stanford U., 1980-81; MA in Mgmt., Aquinas Coll., 1999. Cert. facility mgr. Pub. sch. tchr. English and Theater, 1970-75; gen. mgr. Miss. River Festival, Edwardsville, Ill., 1975-77; dir. events and svcs. Stanford (Calif.) U., 1977-83; exec. dir. Meadowlands Ctr. for the Arts, Rutherford, N.J., 1983-87; pres., chief exec. officer Music Hall Ctr. for the Arts, Detroit, 1987-89; prin. AMS Planning & Rsch., Conn., 1989-94; prof. facility mgmt. Ferris State U., Big Rapids, Mich., 1994—2003; acad. dept. head Wentworth Inst. Tech., Boston, 2003—. Contbr. to various publs. Mem. USICA study team to China, 1981; bd. dirs. Internat. Facility Mgmt. Assn., 1994-97, standing coms. recognition and profl. devel.; mem. People to People facilities del. to Australia and New Zealand, 1996; bd. dirs., chair IFMA Found., 1998-2004. Named Disting. Educator of Yr., Internat. Facility Mgmt. Assn., 2001, Disting. Mem. of Yr., 2005, Educator of Yr., Boston Internat. Facility Mgmt. Assn., 2005; named to Creativity in Business Doubleday, 1986; recipient Gold medal for Cmty. Programs, Coun. for Advancement and Support of Edn., Stanford, 1985. Mem. League of Hist. Am. Theaters (pres. bd. dirs. 1987-89). Democrat. Avocations: skiing, gardening. Office: Acad Dept Head Design & Facilities Wentworth Inst Tech 550 Hungtington Ave Boston MA 02115 Office Phone: 617-989-4050.

HARDYMAN, LISA W., music educator, elementary school educator; b. Rigby, Idaho, Apr. 27, 1957; d. B. Wayne and Delores E. (Labrum) Wood; m. Paul B. Hardyman, June 6, 1986; children: Nathan, Megan. BA, Brigham Young U., 1979, MusM, 1987. Tchr. Sch. Dist. #251, Rigby, Idaho; music specialist Provo (Utah) Sch. Dist.; grad. asst. music Brigham Young U., Provo; tchr. Provo Sch. Dist.; music tchr. Rigby HS. Mem.: Music Tchrs. Nat. Assn. Home: 134 S 3rd W Rigby ID 83442-1343

HARE, ELEANOR O'MEARA, computer scientist, educator; b. Charlottesville, Va., Apr. 6, 1936; d. Edward King and Eleanor Worthington (Selden) O'Meara; m. John Leonard Ging, Feb. 4, 1961 (div. 1972); 1 child, Catherine Eleanor Ging Huddle; m. William Ray Hare, Jr., May 24, 1973. BA, Hollins Coll., 1958; MS, Clemson U., 1973, PhD, 1989. Rsch. asst. cancer rsch. U. Va. Hosp., Charlottesville, 1957-58; rsch. specialist rsch. labs. engring. sci. U. Va., Charlottesville, 1959-64; tchr. Pendleton (S.C.) High Sch., 1964-65; vis. instr. dept. math. sci. Clemson (S.C.) U., 1974-79, instr. dept. computer sci., 1979-83, lectr. dept. computer sci., 1983-90, asst. prof. dept. computer sci., 1990-98, assoc. prof. dept. computer sci., 1998—. Contbr. articles to profl. jours. Bd. dirs. LWV of the Clemson Area, 1988-96; chmn. nursing home study LWV of S.C., 1988-92; oboe and English horn player Anderson (S.C.) Symphony, 1980—. Fellow Inst. Combinatorics and its Applications; mem. AAUP. Office: Clemson U Dept Computer Sci Clemson SC 29634-0001

HARE, ESTER ROSE, physician; b. St. Catherine, Jamaica, Apr. 15, 1952; came to U.S., 1979; d. Emcle and Lovina (Lee) H. BSc with honors, U. West Indies, Jamaica, 1975; PhD in Biochemistry, Dalhousie U., Halifax, Can., 1984; MD, U. Conn., 1990. Diplomate Am. Bd. Internal Medicine. Intern U. Hosp. Cleve., 1990-91; resident Med. U. Hosp., Charleston, SC, 1992-94; pvt. practice Orangeburg (S.C.) Med. Assn., 1994—. Mem. bd. health Women's Christian Orgn., Orangeburg, 1995—. Mem. ACP, AMA, Nat. Med. Assn., Am. Soc. Internal Medicine, S.C. Med. Assn., Sigma Psi. Avocations: gardening, aerobics. Office: Orangeburg Med Assocs 1291 Glen Gloria Orangeburg SC 29118

HARE, MOLLY KAY, physical education educator; d. David and Mary Sue Hare. BS, Bowling Green State U., Ohio, 1991; MS in Pedagogical Kinesiology, U. Ill., Urbana-Champaign, 1998, PhD in Pedagogical Kinesiology, 2000. Phys. edn. tchr. Holy Cross Sch., Champaign, 1992—99; tchg. asst. U. Ill., 1992—99, instr., 1998—99; asst. prof. Ind. State U., Terre Haute, 2000—06, assoc. prof., 2006—. Home: 624 Monterey Ave Terre Haute IN 47803-2552

HARE, NORMA Q., retired school system administrator; b. Dadeville, Mo., July 10, 1924; d. James Norma and Mary Delia (Blakemore) Quarles; m. John Daniel Hare, June 27, 1944 (dec.); children: J. Daniel, Thomas C. BA, Calif. State U. Fresno, 1958, MA, 1963. Cert. tchr., sch. adminstr. Elem. tchr. Parlier Sch. Dist., Calif., 1956-57, Sanger Sch. Dist., Calif., 1958-66, S. San Francisco Schs., 1966-67, elem. edn. specialist, 1967, elem. sch. principal, 1967-81. Dir. Title I, Spruce Sch. ESEA, El Rancho Sch. Early Childhood edn. program, sch. dist. mgmt. negotiator, S. San Francisco Schs., 1977-79. Author: (books) Who is Root Beer, 1977, Wish Upon A Birthday, 1979, Mystery at Mousehouse, 1980, Puritans, Pioneers and Planters, 1995; co-author: (book) The Magatagans, 1998. Mem.: DAR, AAUW, Colonial Dames XVII Century (treas. 1995—98, pres. Sierra de Santa Lucia chpt. 2003—05), Soc. Mayflower Descs. (gov. San Francisco/Peninsula colony 1983—86, govs. award 1988, 1992). Avocations: genealogy, travel. Personal E-mail: nghare@aol.com.

HAREN, ELIZABETH GAYE, counselor; b. Port Hueneme, Calif., Dec. 7, 1970; d. Larry Dale and Cecilia Gay Haren; m. Ted Shelton, Jan. 15, 1999. BA, Emory U., 1993; MA, East Tenn. State U., 1998. Lic. profl. counselor mental health svc. provider Tenn., 2003, nat. cert. counselor Nat. Bd. Cert. Counselors, 1999. Pub. rels. staff Preferred Internet, Blountville, Tenn., 1996—98; dir. support svcs. Tri-Cities Online, Blountville, 1997—98; mobile crisis response therapist Frontier Health, Gray, Tenn., 1998—, crisis response supr., 2001—, clin. liaison frontier mobile crisis response, 2003—. Cert. applied suicide intervention skills trainer Tenn. Suicide Prevention Network/Living Works, Nashville, 2002—; cert. QPR trainer Tenn. Suicide Prevention Network, Nashville, 2004—, apptd. mem. adv. com., 2004, chair N.E. region, Johnson City, 05; critical incident stress debriefer Internat. Critical Incident Stress Found., Ellicott City, Md., 2003—; team mem. Tenn. Pub. Safety Network, Gray, 2003. Recipient NE Tenn. Suicide Prevention award, Tenn. Suicide Prevention Network, 2005, Cert. Appreciation For Support Work During Ops. Desert Shield and Dessert Storm, US Dept. Army, 1991. Mem.: Am. Psychotherapy Assn., Assn. for Specialists in Group Work, Internat. Assn. Addictions and Offender Counselors, Am. Counseling Assn., Internat. Critical Incident Stress Found., Registry Interpreters for the Deaf (assoc.), Kappa Delta Pi, Phi Kappa Phi (life). Avocations: scuba diving, camping, music, art, photography. Office Phone: 423-232-4153.

HAREZI, ILONKA JO, medical technology research executive; b. Princeton, Ind., Jan. 17, 1949; d. Joseph and Helen Marie Fullop; m. John O. Schofield, Dec. 14, 1971 (div. Dec. 1982); 1 child, Franceska; m. Courtland Reeves, Nov. 26, 1986; children: Bryan, Katharine. PhD, Chgo. Sch. Design, 1969. Mktg. ptnr. Fullop and Assocs., 1983-85; founder, sec., treas. Kinetic Energy Ltd., 1985-90; freelance set designer Ilonka Creative Environments, 1974-84; founder, v.p. Harezi Internat., 1980-84; founder, sec., treas. Elf Cocoon Corp., 1984-86; founder, pres., chmn. Elf Cocoon Internat. Ltd., 1985-92; founder, pres. Elfworks, Inc., 1991-94, Elfworks, Nev., 1994-96; pres., dir. Allied Fund for Capital Appreciation, Inc., 1994—98; v.p. Phillip Stein Teslar, 2001—; pres. Nanogy, Inc., 2003—, Biotelemetric Signaling, Inc., 2004—. Interviewed by radio, TV, and newspapers on design and extremely low frequency electromagnetic tech.; presenter tech. sems. on ELF, the Quantum and scalar phenomena. Author: The Resonance in Residence; contbr. articles to profl. jours. Bd. dirs. Inst. for Higher Human Learning Potential, Phila., 1979. Fellow N.Y. Acad. of Sci.; mem. NAFE, ACLU, AAAS, Am. Inst. Interior Designers, Women's Internat. League for Peace and Freedom, Nat. Assn. Against Health Fraud, Nat. Narcotics Officers Assns.

Coalition, N.Y. Acad. Sci., UN-USA Bus. Coun., Knights of Malta (dame), Knights of Africa (dame), U.S. Acad. Polit. Sci., Am. Craft Coun. Achievements include patents pending for transdermal pump and teslar chip. Office: Teslar Global Tech St Rt 1 Saint Francisville IL 62460 also: 169 E Flagler 17th Fl Miami FL 33101 also: 17555 Collins 2705-06 Sunny Isles Beach FL 33160 Office Phone: 618-948-2393, 305-398-7690, 305-373-0037, 305-933-6768. Personal E-mail: ilonkaharezi@aol.com.

HARF, PATRICIA JEAN KOLE, syndicated columnist, clinical and behavioral psychologist, educational consultant, marriage and family therapist, lecturer; b. Berea, Ohio, Oct. 14, 1937; d. Paul Frederic and Mena (Labordes) Kole. BS in Edn. with honors, Baldwin-Wallace Coll., Berea, Ohio, 1959; MS in Edn. with honors, U. Akron, 1966; D in Edn. cum laude, Ariz. State U., 1972; PhD, London Inst. Applied Rsch., 1995; HHD, World Acad., 1994; PhD, London Inst. Applied Rsch., 1995. Rsch. Ednl. Rsch. Coun. Am., 1967-69; tchr. Berea City Schs., Cleve. and Parma, Ohio, 1969-73; asst. prof. Cleve. State U., 1975—; corr., columnist, freelance writer, syndicated columnist Universal PressChronicle-Telegram, Elyria, Ohio, 1986-89; owner Harf Family Counselors, Berea, Ohio, 1993—. Ednl. cons. State of Ohio Bd. Edn. and Gov., 1997—; syndicated columnist Universal Press, Cleve. Plain Dealer; diagnostician of reading difficulties; trustee Coalition for Children's Media; cons. learning disabilities; guest lectr.; TV guest appearances; court appointed spl. cons. for juveniles, 1996-97; mem. Reading Enrichment for Adult Devel.; mem. Coun. of Higher Learning; cons., adult juror Kids First Coalition for Quality Children's Media; advisor, cons. to Juvenile Cts. of Clyahoga County. Author teaching materials and tchr. and children's texts; contbr. articles to profl. jours.; also advisor to book pubs. and magazines. Pres. Berea Hist. Soc., World Found. Successful Women; mem. Cleve. Orch. Women's Com., Nat. Mus. Women in Arts, Coun. Exceptional Children, Ohio Town Forum, Ohio Arts Festival, com. 500 Project READ; advisor Cleve. Radio and TV Coun.; tutor Project Learn, Cleve.; mem. Berea Rep. Precinct Com.; founder Preventive Parenting; dep. senator Internat. Parliament Safety & Peace Italy; mem. Children's TV Workshop, 1995-96; trustee United Meth. Childrens Found. and Home, 1996-97, Berea Children's Home. Named Intellectual Woman of Yr., 1991-92, Emminent fellow in Universe of Mankind, 1994, Ohio Ednl. Woman of Yr., Ohio Educator of Yr. and Outstanding Educator, Outstanding Citizen Berea C. of C., Outstanding Berea High Grad. awd., 1997; Ohio Edn. Woman of Yr., 1991, Most Admired woman of Yr., 1993, Lifetime Fellow and Hon. Prof. Australian Inst. for Coordinated Rsch., 1995; recipient Women's Inner Cir. of Achievement award, 1992, Woman of Yr. commemorative medal Order of Internat. Fellowship, 1994, Excellence in Journalism award 1990-93, World Lifetime Achievement award, 1996, Gold Star award Am. Soc. for Outstanding Volunteerism, 1995; named baroness Royal Order Bohemian Crown, 1994. Mem. NEA, NOW, AAUW, LWV, Am. Writers Assn, Am. Women in Radio and TV, Inc., Soc. Profl. Journalists (Excellence in Journalism award 1990, Ohio Live, Woman Source directory 1998-00), Women in Journalism, Assn. Tchrs. of Learning Disabilities, Am. Assn. Women in Bus., Berea C. of C. (Outstanding Citizen 1965), Bus. Profl. Women Assn., Australian Inst. Coordinated Rsch. (fellow, hon. prof.), Berea Hist. Soc., Berea Bus. and Profl. Women, Women in Comm. Inc., Internat. Women's Media, Internat. Reading Assn. (cons. and writer for reading tchrs.), Ohio Edn. Assn. (Woman of Yr. in Comms. 1991), Internat. Platform Assn., World Found. of Successful Women, Nat. Assn. Women (Internat. Leaders in Achievement award 1996), Profl. Educators Assn., Learning Disability Assn., Nat. Assn. Psychologists, Ohio Assn. Psychologists, Nat. Assn. Women in the Arts, Western Res. Rep. Women's Assn., S.W. Women Rep. Assn., Kiwanis (sec., v.p.), Berea Rep. Club (Mayoral Volunteerism award 1987), Press Club of Cleve. (award 1996), Cleve. Women's City Club, Cleve. Orch. Women's Soc., U. Akron Alumni Assn., Berea H.S. Alumni Assn., Berea Town Forum, Berea C. of C., Baldwin Wallace Alumni Assn., Baldwin Wallace Women's Club, Berea Town Forum. Republican. Methodist. Avocations: reading, golf, flower arranging, politics, crafts. Home: PO Box 811164 Cleveland OH 44181-1164

HARGITAY, MARISKA MAGDOLINA, actress; b. LA, Jan. 23, 1964; d. Mickey Hargitay and Jayne Mansfield; m. Peter Hermann, Aug. 28, 2004; 1 child, August Miklos Friedrich Hermann. Student, UCLA. Actor: (films) Ghoulies, 1985, Welcome to 18, 1986, Jocks, 1987, Mr. Universe, 1988, The Perfect Weapon, 1991, Strawberry Road, 1991, Hard Time Romance, 1991, Bank Robber, 1993, Leaving Las Vegas, 1995, Lake Placid, 1999, Perfume, 2001; (TV films) Finish Line, 1989, Blind Side, 1993, Gambler V: Playing for Keeps, 1994, The Advocate's Devil, 1997, Plain Truth, 2004; (TV series) Downtown, 1986—87, Falcon Crest, 1988, Tequila and Bonetti, 1992, Can't Hurry Love, 1995—96, Prince Street, 1997, Law & Order: Special Victims Unit, 1999— (Golden Globe award for best actress TV series - drama, 2005, Emmy award for outstanding lead actress in a drama series, 2006); (TV miniseries) Night Sins, 1997, (TV appearances include) Falcon Crest, 1984, In the Heat of the Night, 1988, Freddy's Nightmares, 1988, Baywatch, 1989, Wiseguy, 1990, Thirtysomething, 1990, Booker, 1990, Gabriel's Fire, 1990, Key West, 1993, Seinfeld, 1993, Hotel Room, 1993, All-American Girl, 1995, Ellen, 1996, The Single Guy, 1996, Cracker, 1997, ER, 1997—98. Office: Law and Order SVU NBC 30 Rockefeller Plaza New York NY 10112

HARGRAVE, SARAH QUESENBERRY, consulting company executive, public relations executive; b. Mt. Airy, NC, Dec. 11, 1944; d. Teddie W. Quesenberry and Lois Knight Quesenberry Stout. Student, Radford Coll., 1963-64, Va. Poly. Inst. and State U., 1964-67. Mgmt. trainee Thalhimer Bros. Dept. Store, Richmond, Va., 1967-68; Cen. Va. fashion and publicity dir. Sears Roebuck & Co., Richmond, 1968-73, nat. decorating sch. coord. Chgo., 1973-74, nat. dir. bus. and profl. women's programs, 1974-76; v.p., treas., program dir. Sears-Roebuck Found., Chgo., 1976-87, program mgr. corp. contbns. and memberships, 1981-84, dir. corp. mktg. and pub. affairs, 1984-87; v.p. personal fin. svcs. and mktg. Northern Trust Co., Chgo., 1987-89; pres. Hargrave Consulting, 1989—. Spkr., seminar leader in field. Bd. dirs. Am. Assembly Collegiate Schs. Bus., 1979-82, mem. vis. com., 1979-82, mem. fin. and audit com., 1980-82, mem. task force on doctoral supply and demand, 1980-82; mem. Com. for Equal Opportunity for Women, 1976-81; chmn., 1978-79, 80-81; mem. bus. adv. coun. Walter E. Heller Coll. Bus. Adminstrn., Roosevelt U., 1979-89; co-dir. Ill. Internat. Women's Yr. Ctr., 1975. Named Outstanding Young Women of Yr. Ill., 1976; named Women of Achievement State Street Bus. and Profl. Woman's Club, 1978 Mem. ASTD, Profl. Women's Network, Profl. Coaches and Mentors Assn. Home and Office: 34 Fairlawn Ave Daly City CA 94015-3425 Personal E-mail: shargrave@earthlink.net.

HARGROVE, LINDA, professional basketball coach; m. Ed Hargrove; children: Brian, Tara. BS magna cum laude, Southwestern Coll., 1975; MEd, Wichita State U., 1985. Head coach Cowley County Cmty. Coll. Tigers, 1972-89, Wichita State U. Shockers, 1989-98; head coach, dir. player pers. Colo. Xplosion, Am. Basketball League, Denver, 1998—99; head coach Portland Fire, WNBA, 1999—2002; scout Washington Mystics, Washington, 2003, asst. coach, 2004—, gen. mgr., 2005—. Asst. coach 1990 U.S. Sr. Nat. Women's Team, 1989, 1992 U.S. Olympic Team; cons. WNBA Orlando Miracle; mem. USA Basketball Sr. Nat. Team Com. Inductee Southwestern Coll. Athletic Hall of Fame, 1992. Mem. Women's Basketball Coaches Assn. (bd. dirs., Midwest divsn. I rep.). Office: Washington Mystics MCI Ctr 601 F St NW Washington DC 20004 E-mail: lhargrove@washsports.com.

HARGROVE, SANDRA LEIGH, financial planner; b. Hillsboro, Oreg., Dec. 1, 1946; d. William Paul and Hazel Hannah Burgher; m. Larry Burke Hargrove, Nov. 25, 1977; m. John Anthony Coleman, July 13, 1964 (div. May 0, 1977); children: Tereasa Kay Taylor, Deborah Leigh Coleman. Student, Clatsop County C.C., Astoria, Oreg., 1983—85. Mgr. Columbia Ins., Knappa, Oreg., 1973—75; office supply and mail rm. staff Crown Zellerbach Corp Wauna Mill, Clatskanie, Oreg., 1975—76; switchboard operator/receptionist Crown Zellerbach Wauna Mill, Clatskanie, 1976—78, acct. #1 & 2 paper machines, 1978—80; gen. ledger acct. Crown Zellerbach/James River Corp. Wauna Mill, Clatskanie, 1980—84; fin. mgr. James River Corp. Wauna Mill, Clatskanie, 1984—89; co-owner S & K Images, Svenson, Oreg., 1996—98; relief postmaster USPS Oysterville (Wash.) Post Office, 2002—. Originator of project concept & manager (historical/genealogical research) The Lewis & Clark Descendant Project. Treas. Immanuel Luth. Ch., Knappa, 1996—98. Mem.: Pacific County Wash. Geneal. Soc. (pres. 1999—2001), Clatsop County Oreg. Geneal. Soc. (pres. 1998—2001). Democrat. Lutheran. Avocations: walking, genealogy. Personal E-mail: shargrov@pacifier.com.

HARING, ELLEN STONE (MRS. E. S. HARING), philosophy educator; b. L.A., 1921; d. Earl E. and Eleanor (Pritchard) Stone; m. Philip S. Haring, Dec. 1942 (div. June 1951). BA, Bryn Mawr Coll., 1942; MA, Radcliffe Coll., 1943, PhD (AAUW fellow), 1959. Adminstrv. worker ARC, Boston, 1943; mem. faculty Wheaton Coll., Norton, Mass., 1944-45, Wellesley Coll., 1945-72, assoc. prof., 1958-64, prof. philosophy, 1964-72, U. Fla., Gainesville, 1972-93, prof. emerita, 1993—, chmn. dept., 1972-80. Mem.: Am. Philos. Assn., Metaphys. Soc. Am. E-mail: ellenharing@netzero.net.

HARIRI, GISUE, architect, educator; b. Abadan, Iran, May 16, 1956; came to U.S., 1974; d. Karim Hariri and Behjat (Isphahani) Saboonchi. BArch, Cornell U., 1980. Apprentice Jennings and Stout, San Francisco, 1980-82; Paolo Soleri, Arcosanti, Ariz., 1982-83; apprentice Paul Segal Assocs. Architects, N.Y.C., 1983-85; ptnr. Hariri & Hariri, N.Y.C., 1986—. Lighting and furniture designer, 1993—; participant in Urban Housing Festival, The Hague, The Netherlands, 1991; lectr. in field. Work exhibited in Mus. Modern Art, 1999, Storefront for Art and Architecture, N.Y.C., 1988, Parson Sch. Design, N.Y.C., 1988, Princeton (N.J.) U., 1988, Archtl. League N.Y., 1990, Kent (Ohio) State U., 1991, Richard Anderson Gallery, N.Y.C., 1993, Cornell U., Ithaca, N.Y., 1993, Contemporary Arts Ctr., Cin., 1993, others, also in various profl. publs.; Monograph: Hariri & Hariri Work in Progress, 1996, Kliczkowski Casas Internat., 1997. Recipient Young Architects Forum award Archtl. League N.Y., 1990. Mem. Internat. Interior Design Assn. Media Stars, 1998. Office: Hariri & Hariri 18 E 12th St New York NY 10003-4458

HARITON, JO ROSENBERG, psychotherapist, educator; b. Albany, N.Y., June 12, 1948; d. Irving H. and Madeline P. Rosenberg; m. Frank J. Hariton; 2 children. BA, Goucher Coll., Towson, Md., 1970; MS, Columbia U., 1973; PhD, NYU, 1992; postgrad., Postgrad. Ctr. Mental Health, N.Y.C., 1979. Cert. psychoanalyst. With maternal and child health dept. Bronx (N.Y.) Mcpl. Hosp. Ctr., 1973-76, coord. emergency svcs. children's dept. child psychiatry, 1976-79; field work instr. NYU Sch. Social Work, 1977-79; sr. psychiat social worker divsn. child and adol. psychiatry Westchester divsn. N.Y. Hosp.-Cornell Med. Ctr., White Plains, N.Y., 1979-82, social work coord., 1982-98; mem. faculty Cornell U. Med. Sch., 1982—; pvt. practice psychoanalysis and psychotherapy N.Y.C. Co-head ADHD Svc. Line, 1996—. Contbr. articles on group therapy to profl. jours. Fellow N.Y. State Soc. Clin. Social Work Psychotherapists; mem. NASW, Acad. Cert. Social Workers, Am. Group Psychotherapy Assn. Home: 1065 Dobbs Ferry Rd White Plains NY 10607-2212 Office: NY Presby Hosp Westchester Divsn 21 Bloomingdale Rd White Plains NY 10605-1596 Office Phone: 914-997-5957. E-mail: jhariton@med.cornell.edu.

HARITON, LORRAINE JILL, information technology executive; b. NYC, Nov. 7, 1954; d. Martin and Barbara (Jaffee) H.; m. Stephen Alan Weyl June 17, 1979; children: Eric, Laura. BS in Math Sci., Stanford U., 1976; MBA, Harvard U., 1982. Sales rep. IBM, N.Y.C., 1977-80, regional rep. San Francisco, 1982-84, sales mgr. Oakland, Calif., 1984-86; mgr. pricing Rolm, Santa Clara, Calif., 1986-87, adminstrv. asst. to v.p. sales, 1987-88, br. mgr., 1988-90, product line mgr., 1990-92; dir. mktg. Verifone, Inc., Redwood City, Calif., 1992-93; v.p. mktg. Network Computing Devices, Mountain View, Calif., 1993—99; pres., CEO Beatnik Inc., San Mateo, Calif., 1999—2003, chmn., 2003—; pres., CEO Apptera, Inc., San Bruno, Calif., 2003—05. Business E-Mail: chariton@applera.com.

HARKER, VICTORIA D., electric power industry executive; b. NYC, Oct. 24, 1964; d. Paul A. and Mary Ellen (Duva) Dux; m. Drew Alan Harker, June 24, 1989; children: Zachary Paul, Ethan, Benjamin. BA, U. Va., 1986; MBA, Am. U., 1990. Fin. analyst Arnold & Porter, Washington, 1986-89; from fin. mgr. to sr. mgr. bus. analysis & devel. MCI, 1990, dir. mass markets bus. analysis and planning, v.p. fin. mass markets, 1996; CFO MCI Group WorldCom Inc., 1998—2000; various mgmt. positions including acting CFO, sr. v.p. corp. fin. and treas. MCI; exec. v.p., CFO AES Corp., 2006—. Mem. Mt. Vernon Coll. Inst. on Women in Work, Washington, 1992-94; adv. Am. U. MBA Alumni Coun., Washington, 1993-94. Mem. Am. Mgmt. Assn., Women's Golf Assn., Jr. League Assn. No. Va. (chair placement com. 1991-93). Avocations: golf, reading, travel. Office: AES Corp 4300 Wilson Blvd 11th Fl Arlington VA 22203*

HARKIN, ANN WINIFRED, elementary school educator, psychotherapist; b. Glasgow, Scotland, Oct. 14, 1951; came to US, 1956; d. John Joseph and Mary W. Leavy H.; 1 child, Julia A. Wilkinson. BA in Psychology cum laude, Immaculata Coll., 1973, MA in Counseling Psychology summa cum laude, 1999. Instrnl. II permanent cert. elem., secondary sch. tchr., Pa. Tchr. grade 3 St. Anastasia, Newtown Square, Pa., 1973-78; tchr. grade 1 Mother of Divine Providence, King of Prussia, 1979-89, St. Aloysius Acad., Bryn Mawr, Pa., 1989—; legal asst. Elizabeth R. Howard, Esquire, 2001—. Counselor Paoli Addictions Ctr., Pa. Mem. APA, ACA, Nat. Cath. Educators Assn., Diamond Rock Schoolhouse Assn., Donegal Soc. Phila., Chi Sigma Iota. Avocations: horticulture, animals, hiking, swimming, drawing. Home: 738 Cedar Dr Phoenixville PA 19460-3606

HARKIN, RUTH R., lawyer; b. Vesta, Minn. d. Walter Herman and Virginia (Coull) Raduenz; m. Tom Harkin, July 6, 1968; children: Amy, Jenny. BA in English, U. Minn., 1966; JD, Cath. U., 1972. With Dept. Army, Korea, 1966-67, Polk County Social Svcs., Des Moines, 1968; clk. Lawyers Com. Civil Rights under Law; elected county atty. Story County, Iowa, 1972-76; spl. prosecutor Polk County, 1977-78; dep. gen. counsel Dept. Agriculture, Washington, 1979-81, Akin, Gump, Strauss, Hauer & Feld, LLP, Washington, 1983-93; pres., chief exec. officer Overseas Pvt. Investment Corp., Washington, 1993—97; sr. v.p. internat. affairs, gov. relations United Tech. Corp., Hartford, Conn., 1997—; chair United Tech. Internat., 1997—. Bd. mem. ConocoPhillips, Nat. Assoc. of Mfr., U.S.-Russia Bus. Council. Mem. Iowa Bar Assn., D.C. Bar Assn. Democrat. Lutheran. Office: United Tech Corp One Financial Plz Hartford CT 06101

HARKINS, ANN M., federal agency administrator; b. Phila., Apr. 8, 1952; BA in History, Cath. U. Am., 1974, MA in Latin Am. History, 1977; JD, Georgetown U., 1982. Bar: D.C. Staff mem. for Sen. Patrick J. Leahy Senate Com. on Jud. U.S. Congress, 1979-82; assoc. Davis, Polk & Wardwell, 1982-86; minority gen. counsel subcom. on patents copyrights, 1986-87; chief counsel subcom. on tech. and law Sen. Com. on Jud., 1987-94; sr. v.p. Podesta Assocs., 1994-95; dep. asst., prin. dep. asst., acting asst. atty. gen. Office of Legis. Affairs U.S. Dept. Justice, Washington, 1995-98, dep. chief of staff, counselor to atty. gen., 1998-99, chief of staff, counselor to atty. gen., 1999—2001; staff mem Sen Jay Rockefeller (D-WV) U.S. Congress, Washington, 2001—. Mem. ABA, D.C. Bar Assn. Roman Catholic. Avocations: travel, reading, walking, church choir. Office: Off of Sen Jay Rockefeller 217 West King St Ste 307 Martinsburg WV 25401-3211

HARKLEROAD, ASHLEY, professional tennis player; b. Rossville, Ga., May 2, 1985; d. Danny and Tammy. Profl. tennis player, 2001—. Recipient Ranked #52, WTA, Ranked #9 Among U.S. Players, Winner Wimbledon Doubles Title, 2001, Highest Season Ending Single's Ranking #115, 2002, Top Ranked Am. Jr. Player at # 14 Internat., 2002, 2 Women's Circuit Singles Titles, ITF. Office: WTA Tour Corporate Headquarters One Progress Plz Ste 1500 Saint Petersburg FL 33701

HARKLEROAD, JO-ANN DECKER, special education educator; b. Wilkes-Barre, Pa., Oct. 22, 1936; d. Leon Joseph Sr. and Beatrice Catherine (Wright) Decker; m. A. Dwayne Harkleroad; 1 child, Leon Wade. AS, George Washington U., 1960, BS in Health, Phys. Edn. and Recreation, minor in Spl. Edn., 1968, MA in Spl. Edn. and Ednl. Diagnosis and Prescription, 1969, postgrad., 1997-99. Recipient Appreciation cert. Fairfax County (Va.) Police Dept., 1987, Meritorious Svc. medal Pres. Com. on Employment of People with Disabilities, 1988. Instr. Cath. U. Am., Washington, 1960-61; tchr. Bush Hill Day Sch., Franconia, Va., 1961-63; ednl. diagnostician Prince William County Schs., Manassas, Va., 1969-71, supr. title I, 1971-72; writer, editor Sta. WNVT-TV, Fairfax, Va., 1980-82; dir. spl. edn. Highland County Schs., Monterey, Va., 1987-90. Author: (novels) Horse Thief Trail, 1981, 3d edit., 1986, Blood Atonement, 2004, Ketch Colt, 2005; columnist op-ed page The Recorder; radio broadcaster Sta. WVMR, Frost, W.Va. Ruling elder Presbyn. Ch., McDowell, Va., Clifton, Va.; mem. divsn. Faith in Action Hunger com. Shenandoah Presbytery; dir. McDowell Presbyn. Ch. Choir; rotating dir. Highland County Cmty. Choir; past pres. Highland County Pub. Libr. Bd. Mem.: Presbyn. Women (life), Stonewall Women's Club (past pres. 1990—92). Avocations: hiking, camping, rifleshooting, reading, gardening. Home: Windy Ridge Farm HC 33 Box 60 Mc Dowell VA 24458-9704

HARKNESS, MARY LOU, librarian; b. Denby, S.D., Aug. 19, 1925; d. Raleigh Everette and Mary Jane (Boyd) Barker; m. Donald R. Harkness, Sept. 2, 1967. BA, Nebr. Wesleyan U., 1947; AB Libr. Sci., U. Mich., 1948; MS, Columbia U., 1958. Jr. cataloger U. Mich. Law Library, 1948—50; asst. cataloger Calif. Poly. Coll., 1950—52; asst. cataloger, then head cataloger Ga. Inst. Tech., 1952—57; head cataloger U. South Fla., Tampa, 1958—67, dir. libraries, 1967—87, dir. emeritus, 1987—. Cons. Nat. Library Nigeria, 1962—63. Bd. dirs. Southea. Libr. Network, 1977—80. Recipient Alumni Achievement award Nebr. Wesleyan U., 1972 Mem. ALA, Fla. Library Assn., Athena Soc. Democrat. Presbyterian. Home: 12401 N 22d St Apt E-104 Tampa FL 33612-4623 E-mail: marylouh@tampabay.rr.com.

HARKNESS, NANCY P., lawyer; b. 1959; BA in Economics, Cornell U., 1980; JD, Fordham U., 1985. Bar: NY, Calif. With Internat. Broadcasting, LA; cons. Olympic Regional Devel. Authority, Lake Placid; head bus. & legal affairs dept. Motown Record Co. LP, 1995—97; named v.p. bus. & legal affairs Universal Studios Consumer Products Group, 1997; sr. v.p. bus. affairs Digital Entertainment Network Inc.; sr. counsel Akin, Gump, Strauss, Hauer & Feld, LLP; of counsel Sonnenschein Nath & Rosenthal, LA. Office: Sonnenschein Nath & Rosenthal LLP 601 S Figueroa St, Ste 1500 Los Angeles CA 90017 Office Phone: 213-892-5151. Office Fax: 213-623-9924. Business E-Mail: nharkness@sonnenschein.com.

HARLAN, CARMEN, television journalist; b. Detroit; married; 2 children. BA in Speech, U. Mich., 1975. Anchor, reporter, pub. affairs dir. Sta. WWWW-FM, 1975—78; gen. assignment reporter, noon anchor Sta. WDIV-TV, Detroit, 1978—81, evening newscaster, 1981—. Named Best Anchor, Hour Mag.; named one of Top 2 Anchorwomen in Country, Ladies Home Jour., 1991, Detroit's 100 Most Influential Women, Crain's Detroit Bus., 2002; recipient Emmy nominee, Child Advocacy award, Starr Commonwealth, Media award, So. Christian Leadership Conf. Office: WDIV-TV 550 W Lafayette Blvd Detroit MI 48226

HARLAN, M. ANN, lawyer; BA, Skidmore Coll.; JD, Case Western Reserve U. Ptnr. Calfee, Halter & Griswold LLP; asst. gen. counsel J.M. Smucker Co., gen. counsel, asst. sec., 2002—, v.p., gen. counsel, sec., 2005—. Office: JM Smucker Co 1 Strawberry Lane Orrville OH 44667

HARLAN, MEGAN, journalist, poet; b. Burlington, Vt., Jan. 1, 1970; d. Neal MacLaren and Sherry (Yandle) Harlan; m. Matthew Thomas Culligan, July 28, 2001. BA, Tufts U., 1991; MFA, NYU, 1993. Freelance book critic The N.Y. Times, N.Y.C., 1996—; freelance journalist Elle mag., N.Y.C., 1997—2000; freelance travel writer The N.Y. Times, N.Y.C., 1999—; freelance book critic The San Francisco Chronicle, 2001—. Contbg. writer, book critic Entertainment Weekly, NYC, 1995—2003. Author short stories, numerous poems. Recipient Writers fellowship, NYU GSAS, 1991—93. Mem.: PEN West (assoc.), Nat. Book Critics Cir. (assoc.). Liberal. Personal E-mail: meg@meganharlan.com.

HARLAN, REBECCA, secondary school educator, social sciences educator; b. Dallas, Aug. 29, 1949; d. Paul Young and Rebecca Forbis Harlan; m. John Orifici, Aug. 9, 1997. BA, Muskingum Coll., New Concord, Ohio, 1971; MA, Rutgers U., Camden, NJ, 1993; MA ini Tchg., Marygrove Coll., Detroit, 1996. Tchr. social studies Atlantic City H.S., 1973—80, Mainland Regional H.S., Linwood, 1984—. Recipient Tchr. Yr. award, 1996, 2000, 2006. Mem.: NEA. Avocations: travel, reading, crossword puzzles, swimming, weightlifting. Office: Mainland Regional High School 1301 Oak Avenue Linwood NJ 08221 Business E-Mail: rharlan@mainlandregional.net.

HARLAN, SHIRLEY, protective services official, videographer; b. Cleve., Oct. 14, 1929; d. Max and Golda (Schecter) Dorf; m. Herbert Graves Harlan (dec.); 1 child, Lyn; 1 child, Larry. BA, Flora Stone Mather, 1952. Policewoman Redland Police Dept., Redlands, Calif., 1956—; welfare worker San Bernardino Co., Redlands, 1952; dir. Las Amigas Probation and San Bernardino, 1960; ret., 1989. Prodr.: (documentaries) Older Women's League, 2005, Envisioning the Future, 2004, (conf.videos). Mem.: NOW, Older Women's League, San Bernardino Dem. Luncheon Club. Democrat. Jewish. Home: PO Box 2276 San Bernardino CA 92406 Personal E-mail: vldy@aol.com.

HARLEM, SUSAN LYNN, librarian; b. LA, Oct. 1, 1950; d. Frank Joseph and Esther Frances (Bomell) H.; m. Anthony Stephen Hacsi, Aug. 31, 1990. BA, UCLA, 1972, MLS, 1976. Libr. U. Md., College Park, 1976-79, U.S. Dept. Edn., Washington, 1979-82, GSA, Washington, 1982-87, NLRB, Washington, 1988—. Tutor Washington Lit. Coun., 1992—. Co-author: Washington on Foot, 1984. Office: NLRB Libr 1099 14th St NW Washington DC 20570-0001 Business E-Mail: susan.harlem@nlrb.gov.

HARLEMAN, ANN, literature educator, writer; BA in English, Douglass Coll., 1967; PhD in Linguistics, Princeton U., 1972; MFA in Creative Writing, Brown U., 1988. Asst. prof. dept. English, Rutgers U., New Brunswick, NJ, 1973-74, U. Wash., Seattle, 1974-79, assoc. prof., 1979-84; vis. assoc. prof., rsch. affiliate writing program MIT, Cambridge, 1984-86; vis. scholar program in Am. civilization Brown U., Providence, 1986—; Cole disting. prof. Wheaton (Mass.) Coll., 1992-93; prof. English, RISD, Providence, 1994—. Fulbright-Hays lectr., 1980-81. Author: Graphic Representation of Models in Linguistic Theory, 1976, (with Bruce A. Rosenberg) Ian Fleming: A Critical Biograhy, 1989, Happiness, 1994, Bitter Lake, 1996; translator: Mute Phone Calls, 1992; contbr. over 50 articles to scholarly publs., transls. and revs., poems and short stories to lit. mags. Recipient Raymond Carver prize, 1986, Nelson Algren runner-up award Chgo. Tribune, 1987, 3d prize Judith Siegal Pearson award, 1988, Chris O'Malley fiction prize Madison Rev., 1990, Judith Siegal Pearson award, 1991, syndicated fiction award PEN, 1991, Iowa short fiction award, 1993, spl. mention, Pushcart prize, 1998, Zoetrope Fiction award, 2002, O'Henry prize, 2003, Goodheart prize, 2004, Rona Jaffe Writer's award, 2004; Guggenheim fellow, 1976-77, fellow Huntington Libr., 1979-80, MacDowell Colony, 1988, 99, 2004, Am. Coun. Learned Socs., 1992, Wurlitzer Found., 1992, R.I. Coun. Arts, 1989, 97, 2006, Berlin fellowship in Lit., 2000, Civitella Ranieri fellowship 2006; sr. scholar Am. Coun. Learned Socs./IREX, 1976-77; grantee NEH, 1988, Rockefeller Found., 1989, Bogliasco Found., 1998, 2004, Civitella Ranieri, 2006. Mem. PEN Am. Ctr. Address: 18 Imperial Pl #5 Providence RI 02903 Office Phone: 401-272-7987. E-mail: ann_harleman@brown.edu.

HARLESS, KATHERINE J., telecommunications industry executive; m. Skip Harless; children: Skip Jr., Ely, Bill. B in Acctg., U. Tex., 1972. With GTE, 1973—, regional pres. telephone ops. Tex. and Mexico, 1994-96, pres. airfone, 1996—2000; pres. info. services Verizon Communications, 2000—. Vice chmn. Yellow Pages Assn., 2005—06, chmn., 2002, 2006—; bd. dir. Toro Co. Mem. adv. bd. McCombs Sch. Bus. Univ. Tex. Mem. Com. of 200 (tres. com. 200 found. bd.), Chgo. Network, Internat. Women's Forum, Execs. Club Chgo., Barbara Bush Found. (mem. celebration of reading com.), Leadership Am. Mailing: Verizon Info Systems PO Box 619810 Dallas TX 75261-9810*

HARLEY, NAOMI HALLDEN, radiologist, educator, environmental scientist; b. NYC, Aug. 4, 1932; d. Carl Edward and Ida Wilson (Palmer) Hallden; m. John Henry Harley, Sept. 11, 1964. BS, Cooper Union U., N.Y.C., 1959; MS, NYU, 1967, PhD, 1971, Advanced Profl. Cert., 1983. Phys. scientist U.S. AEC, N.Y.C., 1951-65; rsch. prof. environ. medicine NYU, 1965—; coun. mem., sci. com. chmn. Nat. Coun. on Radiation Protection and Measurement, Washington, 1982—. Contbr. articles to profl. jours. Adviser to UN Sci. Com. on Effects of Atomic Radiation (UNSCEAR), 1989—. USPHS fellow, 1988. Fellow: AAAS, Health Physics Soc. Democrat. Office: NYU Sch of Medicine Dept Environ Medicine 550 1st Ave New York NY 10016-6402 Office Phone: 212-263-5287. E-mail: naomi.harley@med.nyu.edu.

HARLEY, RUTH, artist, educator; b. Phila. children: Peter W. Bressler, Victoria Angela. Student, Pa. State U., 1941; BFA, Phila. Coll. Art, 1945; postgrad., U. N.H., 1971, Hampshire Coll., 1970. Instr. Phila. Mus. Art, 1946-59; art supt. Ventnor (N.J.) City Bd. Edn., 1959-61. Art tchr. Print Club, Phila., Allens Ln. Art Ctr., Phila., Suburban Ctr. Arts, Lower Merion, Pa., Radner (Pa.) Twp. Adult Ctr., 1949—59, Atlantic City Adult Ctr., 1959—60. One-woman shows include Dubin-Lush Galleries, Phila., 1956, Contemporary Art Assn., 1957, Vernon Art Exhbns., Germantown, Pa., 1958, Detroit Inst. Arts, 1958, Phila. Mus. Art, 1957, 1959, Moore Inst., Phila., 1962—68, Greenhill Galleries, 1974, Phila. Civic Ctr., 1978, Natal Rio Grande du Norte, Brazil, 1979, Galerie Novel Esprit, Tampa, Fla., 1992—95, Mind's Eye Gallery, St. Petersburg, Fla., 1993, Ga. Tech. Art Ctr., 1998, Robert Ferst Ctr. for Arts Ga. Inst. Tech., 1998—99, exhibited in group shows at Group 55, Phila., 1955, Print Club, 1955, Nat. Tours, 1956—59, Pa. Acad. Fine Arts, 1957, Vernon Art Exhbns., 1958, Detroit Inst. Arts, 1958, Phila. Mus. Art, 1959, Moore Inst., 1962, Phila. Civic Ctr. Mus., 1975, Galerie Nouvel Esprit Assemblage Russe, 1992, Kenneth Raymond Gallery, Boca Raton, 1992—93, Mind's Eye Gallery, 1993, Polk Mus. Art, Lakeland, Fla., 1993, Don Roll Gallery, Sarasota, Fla., 1994—95, Las Vegas (Nev.) Internat. Art Expo, 1994, Heim Am. Gallery, Fisher Island, Fla., 1996, McLean Gallery, Malibu, Calif., 1997—99, Robert Ferst Ctr. for Arts Ga. Inst. Tech., 1998—99, Christina Gallery, Atlanta, 1999, Adrian Howard Gallery, St. Petersburg, 2000—02, 2004, Melrose (Fla.) Bay Art Gallery, 2001, Red River Valley Mus., Vernon, Tex., 2001, Kirkpatrick Mus., Okla., 2001, Airport, Gainesville, Fla., 2001, In Celebration of Art, 2004, Represented in permanent collections U. Villanova (Pa.) Mus., Temple U. Law Sch., Pa., Woodmere Mus., Phila.; included in Art in Am. Ann. Guide, 2000—01, 2002; commd. sculpture, Phila. Re-Devel. Authority. Contbr. art prize Ventnor N.J. Sch. Sys. Home: 5000 SW 25th Blvd Unit 3117 Gainesville FL 32608-8931 Personal E-mail: harleyruth@aol.com.

HARLIN, MARILYN MILER, marine botany educator, researcher, consultant; b. Oakland, Calif., May 30, 1934; d. George T. and Gertrude (Turula) Miler; m. John E. Harlin II, Oct. 25, 1955 (dec. Feb. 1966); children: John E. III, Andrea M. Harlin Cilento. AB, Stanford U., 1955, MA, 1956; PhD, U. Wash., 1971. Instr. Am. Coll. Switzerland and Leysin, 1964-66; asst. prof. Pacific Marine Sta., Dillon Beach, Calif., 1969; asst. prof. marine biology U. R.I., Kingston, 1971-75, assoc. prof., 1975-83, prof., 1983-2000, prof. emerita, 2000—, chair botany dept., chair dept. biol. scis. Guest scientist Atlantic Regional Lab., Halifax, N.S., Can., 1973-78; hon. vis.prof. LaTrobe U., Bundoora, Victoria, Australia, 1984; resource person R.I. Coastal Resource Mgmt. Coun., 1980-2000, R.I. Dept. Environ. Mgmt., 1980; cons. Applied Sci. Assocs., Narragansett, R.I., 1988-98, Western Australia Water Authority, Perth, 1994; rsch. assoc. U. Calif., Santa Cruz, 1993. Co-editor: Marine Ecology, 1976, Freshwater and Marine Plants of Rhode Island, 1988. Bd. dirs. Westminster Unitarian Ch., East Greenwich, R.I., 1987; bd. govs. Women's Ctr., Kingston, 1989-90. Grantee NOAA, 1975-81, Dept. Environ. Mgmt./EPA, 1989-91, U.S. Fish and Wildlife, 1995. Mem. Internat. Phycological Soc., Phycological Soc. Am. (editor newsletter 1982-84, editorial bd. 1988-90), Union Concerned Scientists (nat. adv. bd. 2004—), N.E. Algal Soc. (exec. com.), Sigma Xi (pres., sec. 1979-82). Avocations: yoga, hiking, reading, writing, gardening. Personal E-mail: mharlin@macforcego.com.

HARLING, BARBARA JEAN, social worker; b. Raleigh, N.C., July 21, 1939; d. Edwin Alexander and Margaret Brice Harling; 1 child, Christopher Parr Addams. BA in History, Wilson Coll., Chambersburg, Pa., 1961; MA in Am. History, Seton Hall U., South Orange, N.J., 1967; MSW, Cath. U., Washington, 1973; DSW, Cath. U., 1988. LCSW D.C., diplomate in psychotherapy Am. Assn. for Psychotherapy, 1998. Caseworker Cath. Charities, Washington, 1960—75; clin. dir. Ctr. for Mental Health Inc., Washington, 1973—2004; psychotherapist in pvt. practice Washington, 1976—; clin. dir. Anchor Mental Health, Washington, 2004, Woodley House Behavioral Healthcare Svc. Cons., mentor Clin. Social Wk. Inst., Inc., Washington, 1999—; instr. for advanced supervision course Greater Washington Soc. for Clin. Social Wk., 1989—; tchg. affiliate Va. Commonwealth U.; adj. clin. asst. prof. U. Md., Balt.; lectr., presenter in field; condr. seminars in field. Mem. Dupont Cir. Citizens Assn., Washington, 1968—86, Glover Park Citizens Assn., Washington, 1990—; mem. grandparent initiative adv. group AARP, 2003. Named Outstanding Practitioner/Supr., Chi Sigma Iota, Rho Theta chpt., 1999—2000. Mem.: NASW (diplomate in clin. social wk. 1993—), Internat.l Soc. for Psychol. Treatment of Schizophrenias and Other Psychoses, Am. Group Psychotherapy Assn., Nat. Alliance for the Mentally Ill, Am. Psychotherapy Assn., Coun. on Social Wk. Edn., Greater Washington Soc. for Clin. Social Wk. (tchr. 1980—), Nat. Network for Social Work Mgrs. Democrat. Avocations: reading, music, needlepoint. Home and Office: 2221 38th St NW Washington DC 20007 Office Phone: 202-337-9219. Business E-Mail: bharling@woodleyhouse.org.

HARLOW, ELIZABETH SNELL, physical education educator; b. Huntsville, NC, Apr. 10, 1979; d. Michael Lawrence and Kim Sandridge Snell; m. Mason Edwards Harlow, May 20, 2000. AA in Edn., Reinhardt Coll., Waleska, Ga., 2000; BS in Phys. Edn., U. NC, Wilmington, 2002. Cert. phys. edn. tchr. K-12 NC. Dance and phys. edn. tchr. Northwoods Park Mid. Sch., Jacksonville, NC, 2002—05; dance tchr. Step Ahead Gym, Jacksonville, 2005—. Mem.: Nat. Dance Educators. Home: 110 Grantham Ln Jacksonville NC 28546 Office Phone: 910-382-6769. E-mail: eharlow@ec.rr.com.

HARLOW, RUTH, lawyer; b. 1961; AB, Stanford U.; JD, Yale U. Bar: 1988. Atty. ACLU, NJ, Am. Civil Liberties Union, Lambda Legal Def. and Edn. Fund, 1996—2000, legal dir., 2000—03; atty. pvt. practice, 2003—. Recipient Lawyer of the Year, Nat. Law Journal, 2003. Office: 120 Wall St Ste 1500 New York NY 10005

HARMAN, CAROLE MOSES, retired art educator, artist; b. Bklyn. BFA in Art Edn., R.I. Sch. Design, 1965, MA in Art Edn., 1969; PhD of Pedagogy (hon.), R.I. Coll., 2002. Tchr. art Fairfield (Conn.) Pub. Schs., 1965-68; chair dept. art Hope H.S., 1969—78, Central H.S., 1978—99; critic tchr., dept. art edn. R.I. Sch. Design, Providence, 1969—99; ret., 1999. Lectr. R.I. Inst. Secondary Edn., Brown U., 1989—99; adj. tchr. art edn. dept. R.I. Coll., 1999—, coll. supr. art student tchrs., 1999—; cons. to the arts Providence Sch. Dept., 2000—; bd. dirs. New Urban Arts; trustee R.I. Sch. Design, 2002—. Exhbns. include Providence Art Club, Diva Gallery, Providence, R.I. Sch. Design, R.I. Art Educators, Salon de Refuse AS220, Providence, others. Active John Hope Settlement House; co-chair bus. edn. partnership Citizens Bank and Central H.S., 1989-99; trustee R.I. Sch. Design, 2002—. Recipient Proclamation citation and Key to the City awarded by Mayor Vincent Cianci for Outstanding Svc. to schoolchildren of Providence, Tchr. of Yr. award Providence Sch. Dept., 1982-83, Milken Family Found. Nat. Edn. award, 1993, Excellence in Edn. tchr. award Pub. Edn. Fund, 1998; grantee Pub. Edn. Fund, 1992-96. Mem. R.I. Sch. Design Alumni Assn. (pres. 1994-96, v.p. 1992), R.I. Art Edn. Assn. (exec. bd.). Address: 158 10th St Providence RI 02906-2922

HARMAN, JANE, congresswoman; b. NYC, June 28, 1945; d. A. N. and Lucille (Geier) Lakes; m. Sidney Harman, Aug. 30, 1980; children: Brian Lakes, Hilary Lakes, Daniel Geier, Justine Leigh. BA, Smith Coll., 1966; JD, Harvard U., 1969. Bar: D.C. 1969, U.S. Ct. Appeals (D.C. cir.) 1972, U.S. Supreme Ct. 1975. Spl. asst. Commn. of Chs. on Internat. Affairs, Geneva, 1969-70; assoc. Surrey & Morse, Washington, 1970-72; chief legis. asst. Senator John V. Tunney, Washington, 1972-73; chief counsel, staff dir. Subcom. on Rep. Citizen Interests, Com. on Judiciary, Washington, 1973-75; adj. prof. Georgetown Law Ctr., Washington, 1974-75; chief counsel, staff dir. Subcom. on Constl. Rights, Com. on Judiciary, Washington, 1975-77; dep. sec. to cabinet The White House, Washington, 1977-78; spl. counsel Dept. Def., Washington, 1979; ptnr. Manatt, Phelps, Rothenberg & Tunney, Washington, 1979-82, Surrey & Morse, Washington, 1982-86; of counsel Jones, Day, Reavis & Pogue, Washington, 1987-92; mem. US Congress from 36th Calif. dist., 1993—99, 2001—; mem. nat. security com., intelligence com. 103rd-105th Congresses; mem. energy and commerce com., intelligence com. 107th Congress, 2001—; mem. Nat. Commn. on Terrorism, 1999—2000. Regents prof. UCLA, 1999-2000; mem. vis. coms. Harvard Law Sch., 1976-82, Kennedy Sch. Govt., 1990-96. Vice-chmn. Ctr. for Nat. Policy, Washington, 1981—90; trustee Smith Coll.; counsel Dem. Platform Com., Washington, 1984; chmn. Dem. Nat. Com. Nat. Lawyers' Coun., Washington, 1986—90; bd. dirs. Planned Parenthood, 1998—2000, Venice (Calif.) Family Clinic, 1998—2000. Mem. Phi Beta Kappa. Democrat. Office: US Ho Reps 2400 Rayburn Ho Office Bldg Washington DC 20515-0536 also: Dist Office Ste 3270 2321 Rosecrans Ave El Segundo CA 90245-4932

HARMAN, MARYANN WHITTEMORE, artist, educator; b. Roanoke, Va., Sept. 13, 1935; d. John Weed and Clifford Kelly Whittemore; m. Roger Walke, Aug. 25, 1984; children: Mary Kelly, John Whittemore, Phillip Mears. BA, Mary Washington Coll., 1955; MA, Va. Poly. Inst., 1974. Faculty Va. Poly. Inst., Blacksburg, 1963—, prof. art, 1981—2001, prof. emeritus, 2001—. Guest artist Emma Lake Art Workshop, U. Sask., 1985. One-woman shows include Andre Emmerich Gallery, N.Y.C., 1976, 78, Rubiner Gallery, Detroit, 1977-78, 90, Meredith Long Gallery, N.Y.C., 1980, Theodore Haber Gallery, N.Y.C., 1981-82, 84-85, Osuna Gallery, Washington, 1982, 84, 87, 91, Wade Gallery, L.A., 1986-87, 89, 91, Ulysses Gallery, 1990, 94, Martha Mabey Gallery, 1994, Gallery K, Washington, 1996, Armory Art Gallery VATECH, Va., 1997, 2002, Art Pannonia, Va., 2003, Va. Commonwealth U. Anderson Gallery, 2004; exhibited in group shows at Va. Mus. Art, Richmond, 1973-75, 80-81, Southeastern Ctr. for Contemporary Art, Winston Salem, N.C., 1963, 65, 67, 71, 76, Boston Mus. Fine Arts, 1981, 84, Roanoke (Va.) Mus., 1963-79, Butler Inst. Contemporary Art, Youngstown, Ohio, 1969, 72, Anita Shapolsky Gallery, N.Y.C., 1988, C.S. Schulte Gallery, East Orange, NJ, 1998-06, Lee Hansley Gallery, Raleigh, NC, 2001-06, Sandy Carson Gallery, Denver, 1995-06, Gallery One, Toronto, 1990-06, Studios in the Sq., Va., 2000-06, So. Landscape Ptnrs. Group Show, 2006; represented in permanent collections Boston Mus., Gen. Motors, Detroit, Hunter Mus., Chattanooga, Roanoke Mus., Phillip Morris Corp., Richmond and N.Y.C., Mfrs. Hanover Trust, N.Y.C., Am. Can Corp., N.Y.C., Shawmut Bank of Boston, Mint Mus., CSX Corp., Ethyl Corp., Capital One, others. Mem. Coll. Art Assn., Nat. Hon. Art and Architecture Soc., Tau Sigma Delta. Episcopalian. Personal E-mail: maryannwalke@mindspring.com.

HARMATUK, FRANCES A., retired psychiatrist, anesthesiologist; d. William Harmatuk and Frances Koleczek; m. Nicholas W. DiMinno, Jan. 19, 1961 (dec.). AB magna cum laude, Syracuse U., 1937, MD cum laude, 1941. Diplomate Am. Bd. Anesthesiology, Am. Bd. Psychiatry and Neurology in Psychiatry and in Child Psychiatry. Rotating intern Meadowbrook Hosp., Hempstead, NY, 1941—42; resident in anesthesiology Bellvue Hosp., NYC, 1942—44; resident in psychiatry Bellevue Hosp., NYC, 1958—61; anesthesiologist St. Clares Midtown Hosp, NYC, 1944—57; child psychiatrist Flower Fifth Ave. Hosp., NYC; chief psychiatrist Cath. Charities Guidance Clinic, Bronx, NY, Holy Cross, Imperial Point Coral Ridge Hosp., Ft. Lauderdale, Fla., 1974—77; psychiatrist Henderson Clinic, Pompano Beach, Fla., 1975—76, Valley Psychiat. Hosp., Chattanooga, 1978—79; pvt. practice Virginia Beach, Va., 1979—90; ret., 1990. Clin. instr. psychiatry NY Med. Coll., 1972—74; dir. dept. anesthesiology Midtown Hosp., NYC, 1952—58. Founding mem. Wood Libr. Mus. Anesthesiology. Fellow: Am. Acad. Child Psychiatry, NY Acad. Medicine; mem.: AMA, Soc. Med. Jurisprudence, Am. Soc. Anesthesiologists, NY County Med. Soc., NY State Med. Soc., NY Soc. Clin. Psychiatry, Phi Kappa Phi, Bus. and Profl. Women's Club, Phi Beta Kappa. Avocation: organ. E-mail: frha@cox.net.

HARMEL, HILDA HERTA See PIERCE, HILDA

HARMELINK, RUTH IRENE, marriage and family therapist, writer; b. Rock Valley, Iowa, Aug. 22, 1945; d. Gerritt Harmelink and Rena Miedema; m. John Bruce Kragt, Aug. 14, 1964 (div. June 1980); children: Daniel John, Thomas Dean, Michele Renae Kersten; m. Dennis Oliver Kaldenberg, May 23, 1982; 1 child, Sarah Ruth. AA, Iowa Lakes C.C., 1976; BA magna cum laude, Buena Vista Coll., Storm Lake, Iowa, 1978; MA, Drake U., Des Moines, 1983; PhD, Iowa U., 1985. Extension specialist Iowa State U., Ames, 1985—86; asst. prof. S.D. State U., Brookings, 1986—87, Oreg. State U., Corvallis, 1987—89; pvt. practice Corvallis, 1985—86, 1989—96; prof., dir. marriage & family therapy masters program Northwest Christian Coll., Eugene, Oreg., 1991—96; therapist pvt. practice Ind., 1997—2000; adjunct prof. Notre Dame U., South Bend, 2000—01. Approved supr. Lutheran Family Svc., Portland, Oreg.; organizational cons. Tng. Inst., South Bend, 1997—; therapist Chapin Street Clinic, South Bend, 2000—. Author (and editor): (videotape) Lenders: Working Through the Farmer and Lender Crisis!, 1986. Elder Presbyn. Ch., Corvallis. Oreg. and South Bend, Ind., 1989—; bd. dirs., counselor Story County Sexual Assault and Care Ctr., Ames, Iowa, 1983—85. Recipient Pearl S. Swanson fellowship, Coll. Home Econs, Iowa State U., 1983. Mem.: Am. Assn. Marriage and Family Therapists. Democrat. Presbyterian. Avocations: gardening, knitting, reading, sewing, quilting. Home: 52471 Sunfield Loop Granger IN 46530 Personal E-mail: rihdok@comcast.net.

HARMENING, GAIL JOAN, craft pattern designer; Craft pattern designer www.quiltingoutlet.com, 1991-98; ind. NEWAYS distbr. www.havemoreincome.com/owner/gail1316, 1992—; entrepreneur craft patter designs; distbr. personal care products NEWAYS Internat., 1992—. Designer clown doll Clancey, (quilted wall-hanging patterns) Gail's Mini Quilt Patterns; author: Clancey the Clown Gets a New Look, children's stories; clown doll, bean bag bird. Recipient award for best original design, Del Mar (Calif.) Fair, 1995, Del Mar Fair, 1995. Republican. Avocations: reading, walking, swimming.

HARMER, NICOLE CHRISTINE, science educator; b. Brainerd, Minn., Oct. 16, 1972; d. John Thomas and Rebecca Jo Tanner; m. Bart William Harmer, May 27, 1995; children: Cole, Camille. BS, Bemidji State U., Minn., 1995; BS in Tchg., St. Cloud State U., Minn., 1997. Lic. tchr. life sci. grades 7-12, gen. sci. grades 5-9, chemistry grades 10-12. Sci. tchr. Brainerd H.S., Minn., 1997—. Mem., event treas. Brainerd Jaycees, 1996—2000; mem., various vols. activities Lord of Life Ch., Baxter, Minn., 2000—. Mem.: Sci. Mus. Minn., Minn. Sci. Tchrs. Assn., Nat. Sci. Tchrs. Assn. Avocations: reading, outdoor sports, gardening, travel, digital media. Home: 5854 Parkwood Ct Baxter MN 56425-7432

HARMON, ANGIE (ANGIE SEHORN), actress; b. Dallas, Aug. 10, 1972; d. Larry and Daphne Harmon; m. Jason Sehorn, June 9, 2001; children: Finley Faith, Avery Grace. Actor: (TV series) Baywatch Nights, 1995-97, C-16: FBI, 1997-98, Law & Order, 1998-2001, Inconceivable, 2005-, (TV films) Video Voyeur: The Susan Wilson Story, 2002, Sudden Fear, 2002, (films) Lawn Dogs, 1997, Good Advice, 2001, Agent Cody Banks, 2003, The Deal, 2005, Fun with Dick and Jane, 2005. Office: c/o Creative Artists Agy 9830 Wilshire Blvd Beverly Hills CA 90212*

HARMON, ELIZABETH OAKWOOD, school system administrator; b. Evanston, Ill., Feb. 12, 1938; d. Harland William and Maybelle Minnie (Kuelzow) Oakwood; m. Bernard Leonard Harmon, Apr. 27, 1963; children: Anne Elizabeth, Matthew James. BS, U. Ill., 1960; MS, Nova U., 1982, EdD, 1990. Cert. health edn. specialist. Tchr. Western Springs (Ill.) Pub. Schs., 1960-62, River Forest (Ill.) Pub. Schs., 1962-65; dept. chairperson Lee County Sch. Dist., Ft. Myers, Fla., 1970-82, dist. adminstr., 1982—. Cons. WHO, Dominica, W.I., 1989-90; bd. dirs. Health Kids Corp., Tallahassee. Author: Life Management Skills, 1988. Bd. dirs. Am. Cancer Soc., Ft. Myers., Fla., 1982—, Lee County, 1985—, Lee County Coalition for a Drug Free, Ft. Myers, 1989—. Recipient Recognition award State of Fla., 1990. Mem. AAHPERD, Fla. Assn. Profl. Health Educators (pres. 1988-89), Am. Advancement Health Edn., Fla. Assn. Sch. Adminstrs., Phi Delta Kappa. Republican. Methodist. Avocations: music, art, tennis, gardening. Home: 1592 Covington Cir E Fort Myers FL 33919-2004 Office: Lee County Sch Dist 2055 Central Ave Fort Myers FL 33901-3916

HARMON, JACQUELINE BAAS, minister; b. Kalamazoo, Mich., Oct. 23, 1934; d. Jacob and Ethyl (Zuidema) Baas; m. Robert E. Davis, Aug. 21, 1955 (div. July 1979); children: Robert J. Davis, Sarah Jane Davis, James E. Davis; m. W. R. Harmon, Jan. 5, 1985 (dec. Nov. 2001). BS, Western Mich. U., 1955; postgrad., U. Iowa, 1961; MLS, U. Tex., Austin, 1978; MDiv, Asbury Theol. Sem., 1997. Cert. tchr. Mich., Tex., Iowa. Dir. info. svcs. Motorola, Inc., Austin, 1978-83; mgmt. and sys. specialist Lockheed Missiles and Space Corp., Austin, 1983-84; corp. libr. Microelectronics and Computer Tech. Corp., Austin, 1984-98; pastor Lone Oak (Tex.) United Meth. Ch., 1998—2000, Keltys United Meth. Ch., Lufkin, Tex., 2001—. Contbr. articles to profl. jours. Pres. Austin Libr. Commn., 1978—89, Sta. KLRN Adv. Bd., Austin, 1979, Ctrl. Tex. Libr. Sys. Bd., Austin, 1986—88; v.p. Internat. Hospitality Commn., Austin, 1976—88; mem. bd., commr. Meth. Children's Home, Waco, Tex., 2003—; mem. adv. coun. U. Tex. Libr. Sch., 1984—89. Mem.: ALA, IEEE, Tex. Libr. Assn., Am. Assn. Artificial Intelligence. Home: 508 McMullen St Lufkin TX 75904 Office Phone: 936-634-3950. Personal E-mail: j-wr-harmon@juno.com.

HARMON, JANE, theater producer; With Jane Harmon Assocs., N.Y.C. Prodr. The Last Night of Ballyhoo (by Alfred Uhry), Tony award Best Play, Driving Miss Daisy (by Alfred Uhry, Pulitzer prize), also nat. and internat. tours and Broadway, Buried Child (by Sam Shepard), A Life in the Theatre (by David Mamet), The Robber Bridegroom (by Waldman/Uhry); co-prodr. Asinamali!, Beloved Friend. Bd. dirs. Young Playwrights Inc.; mem. League of Am. Theatres and Prodrs. Inc., Off Broadway Theatre League, League of Profl. Theatre Women. Office: Jane Harmon Assocs One Lincoln Plaza Ste 280 New York NY 10023 Office Phone: 212-362-6836.

HARMON, MONICA RENEE, music educator; b. Greenville, Ohio, June 3, 1960; d. William Neil Harmon and Julie Ann Erk; m. Ronald Burk Lummis, Apr. 3, 1999. MusB magna cum laude, Morehead State U., 1983; BS, W.Va. State Coll., 1986; MusM, U. Miami, 1996. Profl. Tchr. Cert. Nat. Bd. for Profl. Tchg. Stds., 2002. Permanent substitute tchr. South Charleston (W.Va.) Jr. High, 1987—88; music tchr. Coconut Grove (Fla.) Elem., 1988—90; music dir. George Wash. Carver Mid. Sch., Miami, Fla., 1990—, dept. head electives, 1996—. Children's choir dir. Coral Gables (Fla.) Congl. Ch., 1991—94, Plymouth Congl. Ch., Coconut Grove, 1995—96; vocalist Coral Gables Chamber Symphony and Opera Co., 2003—, Polyphony, Renaissance Ensemble, 2004—. Choir mem. St. Thomas Episc. Parish, 2002—. Mem.: Am. Choral Dirs. Assn., Fla. Orch. Assn., Fla. Vocal Assn., Fla. Bandmasters Assn., Music Educators Nat. Conf. Home: 9720 SW 146th St Miami FL 33176 Office: George Washington Carver Middle School 4901 Lincoln Dr Miami FL 33133 Office Phone: 305-444-7388. Personal E-mail: harmonlummis@yahoo.com. E-mail: harmonm@gwcm.dadeschools.net.

HARMON, PEGGY W., electronics engineer; AAS in Electronics Tech., Thomas Nelson C.C., Hampton, Va., 1980. Cert. level B instr. high reliability soldering and electronics discharge control. Apprentice NASA Langley Rsch. Ctr., 1973—78, head electronics instrumentation devel. sect., tng. coord. electronics tech. br. Tech. rep. NASA Assurance Stds. With U.S. Army.

HARMON, PHYLLIS DARNELL, mortgage banker; b. Kingsport, Tenn., May 24, 1937; d. Kelly R. Darnell and Leah Viola Denny; m. John L. Harmon, Sept. 26, 1958; 1 child, Mark Darnell. Credit mgr. Givner's, Inc., Lorain, Ohio, 1955-59; traffic mgr. Sta. WQTE-AM-FM, Monroe, Mich., 1959-61; accounts receivable mgr. Dundee (Mich.) Cement Co., 1961-65; owner, operator Grosse Pointe (Mich.) Mortgage Co., 1984—. Prospects and clerical chmn. United Found., Detroit, 1965-68; bd. dirs. Wayne County (Mich.) Spl. Edn. Adv. Bd., 1978-87, State Mich. Bd. Licensing and Regulation, Lansing, 1980-85; dir. corp. bd. dirs. United Cerebral Palsy Assn., Detroit, 1984-89. Office: Grosse Pointe Mortgage Co 1263 Berkshire Rd Grosse Pointe Park MI 48230-1034 Office Phone: 313-885-4060. Fax: 313-884-3131. E-mail: phyllisharmon1@sbcglobal.net.

HARMON, TERESA WILTON, lawyer; b. 1968; BS, U. Ala., 1990, MBA, 1991; JD, U. Chgo., 1994. Bar: Ill. 1994. Clk. for Hon. Phyllis Kravitch, U.S. Ct. Appeals (11th cir.), 1994; with Sidley Austin LLP, Chgo., 1995—, ptnr., 2003—. Adj. prof. U. Ill. Coll. Law. Mem.: ABA (sect. bus. law and uniform comml. code com.), Chgo. Bar Assn. (co-chair comml. fin. and transactions com.). Office: Sidley Austin LLP Bank One Plz One S Dearborn St Chicago IL 60603

HARMON BROWN, VALARIE JEAN, hospital laboratory director, information systems executive; b. Peoria, Ill., June 21, 1948; d. Donald Joseph and Frances Elizabeth (Classen) Harmon; m. James Roger Brown, Aug. 21, 1982 (dec. May 1994). BSMT, Northwestern U., Chgo., 1970. Med. tech. Evanston (Ill.) Hosp., 1970-71, chief tech., 1971-75; med. tech. II M.D. Anderson Hosp., Houston, 1975-76; dir. lab. Physicians Ref. Lab., Houston, 1978-81, Med. Ctr. Hosp., Conroe, Tex., 1981-91, Palo Pinto Gen. Hosp., Mineral Wells, Tex., 1993-94; sales mgr. Long Beach (Calif.) Meml. Med. Ctr., 1995-96; quality assurance/regulatory affairs mgr. Consol. Med. Labs., Lake Bluff, Ill., 1996-97; adminstrv. dir. Bio-Diagnostics Labs., Torrance, Calif., 1997-2000; asst. dir. lab. Parkview Cmty. Hosp. Med. Ctr., Riverside, Calif., 2000—01; regional mgr. Memphis Antech Diagnostics, Southaven, Miss., 2001—03; lab. mgr. Doctor's Data, Inc., St. Charles, Ill., 2003—04, Idexx Labs., Elmhurst, Ill., 2004—. Lab. cons. Texaco Chem. Wellness Program, Conroe, 1989; health career sponsor Willis Ind. Sch. Dist., Tex., 1989, 90; mem. adv. bd. Med. Lab. Technician program Weatherford Coll., 1994. Coord. blood drive Gulf Coast Region Blood Ctr., 1986-91; sponsor colon cancer screening Montgomery County Health Fair, 1986; sponsor Camp Sunshine/Lions Club, 1988; sponsor cholesterol screening Med. Ctr. Hosp. Health Fair, 1989. Mem. NAFE, Am. Soc. Clin. Pathologists, Am. Soc. Med. Technologists, Clin. Lab. Mgmt. Assn. Republican. Roman Catholic. Avocations: embroidery, reading, antiques. Home: 313 Larsdotter Ln Geneva IL 60134 Office Phone: 630-516-7966. Business E-Mail: valarie-brown@idexx.com.

HARMS, CORA BEENHOUWER, music educator; b. White Plains, NY, Apr. 23, 1956; d. Herbert and Bernice Beenhouwer, Susan McGreevy (Stepmother); m. Leon Herman Harms, Aug. 18, 1979; children: Ariel Bernice, Rena Frances. MusB in Edn., U. N.Mex, 1981, MusM in Conducting, 1994. Music educator Santa Fe Pub. Schs., 1986—; instr. music Santa Fe CC, 1997—. Dir./mem. High Desert Chpt. Sweet Adelines Internat., Santa Fe, 1987—97; dir. Coro de Camera Chamber Choir, Los Alamos, 1998—2003, Santa Fe Youth Symphony Choir, 2002—05, Santa Fe Desert Chorale Children's Choir, 2004—. Author: (curriculum design) Humanities Course (1st Pl. N.Mex Ednl. Rsch., 1989). Mem. artistic bd. Santa Fe Youth Symphony, 2002—05. Recipient Recognition award, Santa Fe Pub. Schs., 1995, 1999—2001, Nat. Found. for Advancement in the Arts, 2001. Mem.: NEA, Chorus Am., Am. Choral Dirs. Assn., Chorus Am., Music Educators

Nat. Conf., Kumusha Marimba Ensemble. Avocations: chamber music pianist, gardening, knitting, crocheting. Home: 21 Rockridge Rd Cerrillos NM 87010 Office: Santa Fe Pub Schs 610 Alta Vista Santa Fe NM 87505 Office Phone: 505-467-2000.

HARMS, DEBORAH GAYLE, psychologist; b. Ft. Worth; d. Raymond O. Smith and Billie (Allen) Greenwade; m. Joel Randall Harms; children: J. Christopher, Ryan R., Catherine R. BA with honors with high distinction, Wayne State U., 1977; MA in Clin. Psychology, U. Detroit, 1979, PhD in Clin. Psychology, 1984. Lic. psychologist. Trainee in psychology Henry Ford Hosp., Troy, Mich., 1978-79; intern in psychology Detroit Psychiat. Inst., 1979-82; staff psychologist Eastwood Clinic, Harper Woods, Mich., 1983-86; pvt. practice Harms and Harms, PC, Birmingham, Mich., 1985—; staff psychologist Dominican Consultation Ctr., Detroit, 1986-89; sr. psychologist Oakland County Probate Ct., Pontiac, Mich., 1990; candidate Mich. Psychoanalytic Inst., 2003—. Teaching fellow U. Detroit, 1978-79. Mem. APA, Am. Psychoanalytic Assn. (affiliate), Nat. Register Health Care Providers in Psychology, Mich. Psychol. Assn., Mich. Psychoanalytic Soc., Mich. Women Psychologists, Mensa, Phi Beta Kappa. Avocations: reading, ballet. Home: 21783 Corsaut Ln Beverly Hills MI 48025-2607 Office: Harms and Harms PC 31815 Southfield Rd Ste 19 Beverly Hills MI 48025 Office Phone: 248-258-5102.

HARMS, ELIZABETH LOUISE, artist; b. Milw., May 26, 1924; d. Frederick George and Veva (Sanderson) H.; m. Douglas Derwood Craft, Sept. 8, 1951. Diploma, Sch. Art Inst. Chgo., 1950, BFA, 1963, MFA, 1964. One-man shows: 55 Mercer St., N.Y.C., 1980, Fischbach Gallery, N.Y.C., 1975, Carnegie Inst. Mus. Art, 1969, Condeso/Lawler, 1982, 84, 85, 86, 90, 93, Gallery Jupiter, Little Silver, N.J., 1987, Jersey City Mus., 1988, Paul McCarron, N.Y.C., 2001, DVA, Narrowsberg, N.Y., 1996, 2002; group shows include Moravian Coll., Bethlehem, Pa., 1978, Jersey City Mus., 1980, 86, North of New Brunswick, South of N.Y., Rutgers-Newark, 1981, Coll. of New Rochelle, 1982, T. Bell Invitational, Condeso/Lawler, 1985, Montclair (N.J.) Art Mus., 1984, 86, Robeson Mus., Rutgers, Newark, 1988, Invitational Acad. & Inst. for Arts & Scis., N.Y.C., 1992, Skidmore Coll., Saratoga Springs, N.Y., 1993, So. Allegheny Mus. Art, Loretto, Pa., 1994, NAD Invitational, N.Y.C., 2004. Recipient Armstrong prize, Art Inst. Chgo., 1962; grantee, Tiffany Found., 1977. Home: PO Box 245 Jeffersonville NY 12748-0245

HARMS, JANET BERGGREN, music educator; b. Kearny, N.J., Feb. 19, 1947; d. Herbert L. Berggren and Evelyn R. Bellbach; m. Paul Harms (div.); m. Gerard Krellwitz (div.); children: Jacquelyn Joy, Jonathan. BSM, Northeastern U., Essex Fells, N.J., 1968; MusM, Am. Conservatory, Chgo., 1972; EdD, Columbia U., N.Y.C., 1981. Prof. music Nyack (N.Y.) Coll., 1972—81, Azusa (Calif.) Pacific, 1982—86, 1997—, Redlands (Calif.) U., 1992—95, Calif. Poly, Pamona, Calif., 1997—. Dir.(founder): Windsong Southland Chorale, 1995—; musician: (albums) The Nordic Sound, 1995. Mem.: Am. Guild Organists. Avocations: water-skiing, painting. Home: 1551 Hillerest Dr Pomona CA 91768 Personal E-mail: Awindsong@aol.com.

HARMS, MICHELE GAIL, director; d. Richard J. and Gail W. Harms. AS, Jamestown C.C., 1987; BS, SUNY, Fredonia, 1989; cert. in med. tech., Rocherster Gen. Hosp., N.Y., 1990; MS, SUNY, Fredonia, 1995. Cert. med. technologist Am. Soc. Clin. Pathology, 1990. Med. technologist Women's Christian Assn. Hosp., Jamestown, NY, 1990—2002, program dir. Sch. Med. Tech., 2002—. Sec. Allegany Region Missions, Randolph, NY, 2002. Mem.: Am. Soc. Clin. Lab. Scientists (assoc.), Am. Soc. Clin. Pathology (assoc.). Office: WCA Hosp Sch Med Tech 207 Foote Ave Jamestown NY 14701 Office Phone: 716-664-8484. Business E-Mail: michele.harms@wcahospital.org.

HARMS, NANCY ANN, nursing educator; d. Orval M. and Ruth Marie (Nelson) H.; m. Gerhart J. Wehrbein. Diploma, Bryan Meml. Hosp., 1971; BS in Natural Sci., Nebr. Wesleyan U., 1971; BSN, U. Nebr., 1975, MSN, 1977, PhD, 1988. RN, Nebr. Staff nurse, asst. supr., ins. coord. Brewster Hosp., Holdrege, Nebr., 1971-72; instr. Immanuel Sch. Nursing, Omaha, 1972-75; coord. nursing care plan devel. Hosp. Info. Sys. U. Nebr. Med. Ctr., Omaha, 1975; asst. chair dept. Coll. St. Mary, Omaha, 1975-80; curriculum coord. Midland Luth. Coll., Fremont, Nebr., 1980-88, chair nursing divsn., 1988—. Mem. ANA (mem. Ho. of Dels.), Nebr. Nurses' Assn. (Nurse Excellence award, Excellence in Writing award jour., adv. Nebr. Student Nurses Assn., mem. various coms.), Nat. League Nursing, Sigma Theta Tau (theta omega, gamma pi chpts.).

HARNEDY, JOAN CATHERINE HOLLAND, retired systems analyst; b. Hackensack, NJ, May 31, 1936; d. John Joseph and Marion Rita (Sexton) Holland; m. Edmund Richard Harnedy, Dec. 29, 1962; children: Richard J., Julia Ann. BS, Coll. New Rochelle, 1957. Adminstrv. asst. Ford Found. funded, Rockefeller Found. funded, 1957—59; sys. analyst IBM, White Plains, NY, 1960—65; publicity chair YWCA, White Plains, NY, 1966—69; ret., 1969. Travel cons., photographer, White Plains, 1970—92. Mem.: NAFE, NY Pub. Libr., Children's Cancer Soc., Wildlife Fedn., Defenders Wildlife, Nat. Audubon Soc., Nature Conservancy, Nat. Parks Conservancy, Met. Mus. Art, Phi Chi. Avocations: writing, gardening, art history, photography, gourmet cooking.

HARNER, CATHY J., social worker, educator; b. Lebanon, Pa., Oct. 15, 1954; d. Richard H. and Dorothy J. Harner. PhD, U. Ill., Champaign-Urbana, 1991. Prof. Taylor U., Upland, Ind., 1992—2006, dir. social work edn., 2004—06. V.p. St. Martin De Porres, Marion, Ind., 1998—2006. Society Of Friends. Avocations: music, travel, tennis. Office: Taylor University 236 W Reade Avenue Upland IN 46989-1001 Office Phone: 765-998-5209. Office Fax: 765-998-4930. Personal E-mail: ctharner@taylor.edu.

HARNER, KATHRYN DENISE, music educator; b. Waynesboro, Va., Aug. 9, 1980; d. David Allen and Velma Kathryn Harner. BA, Bridgewater Coll., 2002. Lic. tchr. Va. Music dir. Guy K. Stump Elem. Sch., Stuarts Draft, Va., 2002—05. Home: 47-360 Hui Iwa St Apt B Kaneohe HI 96744-4445

HARNER, WILLA JEAN, librarian; b. Millersburg, Ohio, Jan. 23, 1943; d. Wilson Eugene and Maxine Bennett Spencer; m. Philip Balch Harner, June 9, 1964; children: Heather Jean Harter, Ariana Karen. BA, Coll. Wooster, 1964; MLS, Kent State U., 1987. Jr. dept. aide Tiffin-Seneca Pub. Libr., Ohio, 1979—84, ref. asst., 1984—87, ref. libr., 1987—90, head, jr. dept., 1990—2005; ret., 2005. Pres. FISH, Tiffin, 1974—75, Presbyn. Women, 1999—2000, 2004—06. Mem.: LWV (sec. 1993—97), U.S. Bd. Books Young People, Ohio Libr. Assn. Presbyterian. Avocations: travel, gardening, art, music. Home: 30 Elmwood St Tiffin OH 44883 Office Phone: 419-447-3751. Office Fax: 419-447-3045. E-mail: willajeanh@yahoo.com.

HARNETT, LILA, retired publishing executive; b. Bklyn., Oct. 4, 1926; d. Milton Samuel and Claire S. (Merahn) Mogan; m. Joel William Harnett. BA, CUNY, 1946; postgrad., New Sch. for Social Rsch., 1950. Pers. exec. Walter Lowen Agy., N.Y.C., 1947-52; pub. Bus. Atomics Report, N.Y.C., 1953-63; weekly columnist N.Y. State Newspapers, 1964-74; fine arts editor Cue Mag., N.Y., 1975-80; founder, contbg. editor Phoenix Home & Garden mag., 1980—, assoc. pub., 1988—, editor, 1996-99. Pub. Scottsdale (Ariz.) Scene mag., 1992-98. Trustee Phoenix Art Mus., 1999—. Mem.: ArtTable, Inc. (founder 1979—). Home: 4523 E Clearwater Pkwy Paradise Valley AZ 85253 E-mail: lharnett@qwest.net.

HARNOIS, VERONICA, psychologist, educator; d. John Joseph and Vera Shannon D'Urso; children: Kent, Kathleen Duquette, Sheila Foley, Carol Recor, Jeanne, John. BA, Merrimack Coll., North Andover, Mass., 1957; MEd, Am. Internat. Coll., Springfield, Mass., 1971, D of Edn., 2003. Cert. sch. psychologist Mass., lic. ednl. psychologist Mass. Substitute tchr., tchr. Springfield Pub. Schs., 1958—69; co-dir., cons., tchr. Miss Barker's Sch., 1969—75; ednl. dir., tchr. Osborn Day Sch., Agawan, 1975—83; vocat. counselor, examiner Urban League, Springfield, 1984—85; clin. specialist, sch. psychologist Kolburne Sch., New Marlborough, 1986—94; dir. sch. program Brightside, Inc., Springfield, 1994—96; cons., psychol. examiner May Inst., West Springfield, 1997—98; sch. psychologist Springfield Pub. Schs., 1998—. Instr. psychology spl. edn. Am. Internat. Coll., 1991—. Author: The Harnois Program, 1994. Mem.: Pioneer Valley Reading Coun. (bd. dirs. 1988—), Nat. Assn. Sch. Psychologists, Western Mass. Counseling Assn., Delta Kappa Gamma. Roman Catholic. Avocation: reading. Home: 38 Nassau Dr Springfield MA 01129 Office: Springfield Pub Schs 195 State St Springfield MA 01103

HAROLD, CONSTANCE CAMMILLE, theater educator, artist; d. Lillian Evelyn Southern and Harold James; 1 child, Jason Harold Haynes. Courtroom sketch artist WKBD-TV, Detroit, 1986—87; writer, coord. ARC Anne Arundel County, Annapolis, Md., 1992—2002; mktg. projects adminstr. Morgan State U., Balt., 2002—03; cons. City of Annapolis, 2004—05; dir. devel. Howard U. TV, Washington, 2004—. Continuing edn. instr. theater Anne Arundel C.C., 2001—; dramaturge Balt. Playwrights Festival, 2001—02; writer Balt. Playwrights Festival - Staged Readings, 2003, Inside Annapolis Mag., Annapolis, 2004—, Four Seasons Playwrights' Cir., Annapolis, Md., 2004—; creator, host Radio Clay St., Annapolis, 2004—. Author: (play) What Remains., Coming Forth By Day (Md. State Arts Coun. Individual Artist Award in Playwrighting, 2003), (children's play) Frederick Douglass: Somebody's Child (Produced by Pumpkin Theatre, 1999), (play) Eggs and Bones (Monologue Pub. in More Monologues for Women by Women, Heinemann Press, 1997), Another New Year's Eve (Produced by Colonial Players of Annapolis, 1995), (poetry) Torn Asunder From the Skies (Third Pl. Poetry Award, Md. Writers' Assn., 1997). Adv. bd. Kunta Kinte-Alex Haley Found., Annapolis, 2001—04. Mem.: Md. Writers' Assn., Women in Film & Video, Four Seasons Playwrights' Cir. (founding mem. 2004—05), Dramatists Guild (assoc.). Avocations: philosophy and religious studies, walking. Office Phone: 202-860-3017.

HAROON, NASREEN, artist; b. Karachi, Pakistan, Dec. 10, 1952; arrived in U.S., 1980; d. Ahmad and Amina (Dada) Adaya; m. Haroon Haji Husein, Apr. 29, 1972; children: Omar, Sana. BA in Psychology, Philosophy and History, St. Josephs Coll., Karachi, 1972. Design cons. Shangri-La Hotel, Santa Monica, Calif., 1983—; spkr. on cultural, ethnic, religous diversity, 1991—. Exhibited oil paintings in numerous exhbns., 1992—; featured in premier issue Zarposh Mag., 1997; appeared regularly on Adelphia Cable TV program God Squad; participant Muslim Jewish Dialogue; paintings selected for Art In Embassies program, displayed at U.S. Embassy, Pakistan, Senegal and United Arab Emirates. Bd. dirs. Islamic Ctr. So. Calif., 1999-2002, pres. women's assn., 1991, Pakistan Arts Coun. of Pacific Asia Mus., Pasadena, Calif., 1994-96, v.p., 1997-99, Devel. in Literacy, L.A., 1996-97, Santa Monica (Calif.) Bay Interfaith Coun., 1994—; co-chmn. Muslim Jewish Dialogue; bd. dirs. Cornerstone Theater Prodns. Co. Recipient award for planning Youth Day, Westside Interfaith Coun., 1998. Democrat. Moslem. Avocations: reading, gardening, jewelry design, photography, travel. Office: Shangri-La Hotel 1301 Ocean Ave Santa Monica CA 90401-1010

HARP, DIANE CHRISTINE, librarian, educator; b. Spokane, Wash. d. David Arnold Ries and Patricia Marie Robertson; m. William Raymond Harp, July 11, 1989; 1 child, Casey Winston. MA in Edn., Ea. Wash. U., Cheney, 1998. Cert. tchr. Idaho, 2005. Tchr. Plummer Worley Sch. Dist., Plummer, Idaho, 1994—, dist. libr., 2005—. Nat. honor soc. advisor Plummer Worley Sch. Dist., 2003—, sr. projects dir., 2003—. Blood dr. coord. Nat. Honor Soc., Plummer, 2003—06, clean-up organizer for adopt -a-highway, 2004—06; cubmaster Tekoa Cub Scouts pack 597, Tekoa, Wash., 2001—06. Recipient First Pl. Poem Mom's Art book, Whitman County Libr., 2000, NISTAR Tchr. Recognition, Student Selection, 2006. Mem.: Inland NW Coun. of Tchrs. of English (assoc.). Office: Plummer Worley School District PO Box 130 Plummer ID 83851 Office Phone: 208-686-2152.

HARPEN, SHAWN M., lawyer; BA, Univ. Toledo, 1990, JD, 1998. Bar: Calif. Ptnr., bus. litigation McDermott Will & Emery, Irvine, Calif. Named a Rising Star, So. Calif. Super Lawyers, 2004—06. Mem.: ABA, Calif. Bar Assn., Fed. Bar Assn., LA County Bar Assn., Orange County Bar Assn., Order of the Coif. Office: McDermott Will & Emery Ste 500 18191 Von Karman Ave Irvine CA 92612 Office Phone: 949-757-6061. Office Fax: 949-851-9348. Business E-Mail: sharpen@mwe.com.*

HARPER, DIANE MARIE, retired corporate communications specialist; b. Harrisburg, Pa., Oct. 22, 1938; d. Harry Paull Rineard and Berneice Marie (Westhafer) Gerhardt; m. William Irvin Harper, Nov. 17, 1957 (div. Aug. 1981); children: Dawn Michelle, Steven Lee, William Madison; 1 stepson: William Lee. Telephone operator United Telephone Pa., Carlisle, 1956-59, keypunch operator Harrisburg, 1960-61, Safety Sales & Svc., Harrisburg, 1967-70; keypunch operator, lead data entry operator Kinney Shoe Corp., Camp Hill, Pa., 1970-84; data entry operator First Health, Harrisburg, 1984-92; resolution analyst Electronic Data Systems, Camp Hill, 1992-97; comms. retailer Electronic Data Sys., Rossmoyne, 1997-99, ret., 1999. Part-time cashier KMart, 2000-01; Stephen min. of Evang. Luth. Ch., Stephen min. tng. leader, 2003; reporter, writer pubs. com. Electronic Data Systems, 1996-97, human resources coord. corrective action com., 1993-96, social coord. 2d shift Pa. XIX staff, 1993-96. Committeeperson 4th Ward, Carlisle, Pa., 1959-61, 1st Ward, Mechanicsburg, 1997—; minority insp. polls, Carlisle, 1959-61; pres. Mothers of DeMolay, Carlisle, 1976-78, Mechanicsburg Area Dem. Club, 1998-99, pres. emeritus, 1999, v.p., 2000; Halloween parade assoc. City of Mechanicsburg; mem. coun., chair witness and outreach com. St. Paul's Evang. Luth. Ch., Carlisle, Pa., 2000-04, also lay minister, mem. choir, home visitation and communion lay min., 2005; del. to Fedn. Pa. Dem. Women's Clubs' Convs., 2005, 06. Mem. NOW, Nat. Abortion and Reproductive Rights Action League, Nat. Pks. and Conservation Assn., Nat. Resources Def. Coun., Nat. Arbor Day Found., Pa. Sheriff's Assn. (hon.), Pa. Chiefs of Police Assn., Mechanicsburg Mus. Assn., Legal Assts. Club, Friends Dauphin County Libr., Friends Mechanicsburg Libr., Little Theatre Mechanicsburg (v.p. 1962-63, pres. 1963-67), Nat. Trust for Hist. Preservation, Carlisle Women's Dem. Club (chaplain 2004-2005, pres., 2006—), Mechanicsburg Dem. Club, Dem. Nat. Com., Blues Soc. Ctrl. Pa., Red Hat Soc. Democrat. Avocations: theater, reading, travel, cooking. Home: 306 S Market St Mechanicsburg PA 17055-6326

HARPER, DONNA MARIE, elementary education and performing arts educator, consultant, special education educator; b. Quantico, Va., Apr. 26, 1952; d. Robert Thomas Jr. and Frances Earl (Ellis) Hanifin; m. James Carl Harper, Mar. 22, 1975 (div. June 19, 2003); children: Kathleen Marie, James Robert. BA in Eng., Art, San Diego State U., 1974; MS in Ednl. Adminstrn., Nat. U., Vista, Calif., 1996. Cert. elem. tchr., Calif.; cert. physically handicapped, learning handicapped, severely handicapped, Crosscultural Lang. and Acad. Devel., Calif. Elem. tchr. Vista Unified Sch. Dist., Calif., 1974-78, elem. phys. handicapped educator Calif., 1978-80, H.S. trainable mentally retarded Calif., 1981-83, resource specialist Calif., 1985-86, spl. day class tchr. Calif., 1986-87, elem. tchr. Calif., 1987-95, vivual performing arts tchr. Calif., 1995—2002, special day class-learning handicapp and austistic, 2002—. Mentor Vista (Calif.) Unified Sch. Dist., 1990-91, 94-95; ednl. cons. Metrolink, Los Angeles, 1995-97, Haikow (China) Mid. Sch., 1999; rschr. Vista cmty. history. Author, editor: View of Vista, 1991. Pres. Friends of Vista Libr., 1980—, v.p., sec., parliamentarian, bd. dirs, editor; mem., sec. Children's Home Soc. - Niños Precious, Vista, 1987-98; founding mem., docent Rancho Guajome Adobe, Vista, 1991—. Recipient leadership award Friends of Vista Libr., 1988, 89, svc. award Children's Home Soc., Vista, 1991, svc. to sch., cmty. award Vista Masonic Lodge #687, 1997; writer grantee Calif. Schs. Tech. Senate Bill 1510, 1990, 94. Mem. NEA, AAUW, Calif. Tchrs. Assn., Vista Tchrs. Assn., Assn. for Supervision and Curriculum Devel., Gamma Phi Beta, Pi Lambda Theta. Democrat. Roman Catholic. Avocations: art, writing, volunteering, travel, golf. Office: Vista Unified Sch Dist 1234 Arcadia Ave Vista CA 92084-3404 Home: 1266 Phillips St Vista CA 92083-7117

HARPER, DONNA WALLER, secondary school educator; b. Nashville, May 31, 1950; d. Eugene William and Louise Parker Waller; m. James Alan Harper, Nov. 9, 1974 (div. Sept. 2, 1981); children: Kimberly Jade, Jacob Anthony. BA in English History, Austin Peay State Coll., Clarksville, Tenn., 1973, MA in History, 1975; ArtsD in English, Mid. Tenn. U., Murfreesboro, 1991. Cert. tchr. Tenn. Dept. Edn. Tchr. North HS, Nashville, 1975—78, Maplewood HS, Nashville, 1978—91; adj. Mid. Tenn. State U., Murfreesboro, 1991—2002; tchr. Hillwood HS, Nashville, 2002—, IB coord., 2005—06. Bd. mem. Popular Culture Assn. in South Program, 1992—; chair Popular Culture Assn.- Am. Culture Assn., 2002—. Contbr. chapters to books. Coord., religious edn. St. Ignatious, Nashville, 1981—89, mem. parish coun., 1997—99. Recipient Tch. of Yr. award, Maplewood/Hillwood, 2006, Women in Global Perspective award, NEH, 2000—. Roman Catholic. Avocations: needlecrafts, reading. Home: 2948 Cherry Hills Dr Antioch TN 37013 Office: Hillwood HS 400 Davidson Rd Nashville TN 37205 Business E-Mail: donna.harper@mnps.org.

HARPER, ELIZABETH SCOTT, academic administrator, retired literature educator; b. Norfolk, Va., Mar. 16, 1943; d. S. Dale Scott, Sr.; m. Jim Buchanan (div.); 1 child, June Buchanan Vance. BS in Secondary Edn., Old Dominion U., 1965; MA in Edn. and Guidance Counseling, U. N.C., 1973. Tchr. Henrice County Schs., Va., 1965—66, Va. Beach (Va.) City Pub. Schs., 1966—67; tchr. mid. sch. Fort Bragg Schs., Fayetteville, NC, 1967—68; tchr. H.S. Charlotte (N.C.) Mockelenburg Schs., 1970—72; tchr., dir. tchg. measurement Charlotte Latin Sch., Matthews, NC, 1973—77; instr., coord. developmental studies Carteret C.C., Marchead City, NC, 1978—2001. Fellow, Kellog Found., 1995—96. Republican. Methodist. Home: 4514 Rivershore Dr New Bern NC 28560

HARPER, GLORIA JANET, artist, educator; b. Idaho; children: Dan, Janet. Student, Famous Artists Sch., 1967-69, 69-71; A in Comml. Art, Portland C.c., 1981; postgrad., Valley View Art Sch., Lewis & Clark, 1982, Carrizzo Art Sch., 1983, Holdens Portrait Sch., 1989; studied with Daniel Greene, 1989, postgrad. in paralegal studies; B in Art, Lewis & Clark, 1982. Cert. art educator. Artist, art instr. Art By Gloria, 1980—; owner Art By Gloria Art Sch. and Gallery, Pendleton, Oreg., 1991—. Lectr., workshop presenter in field, 1980—. Paintings and prints included in various mags. Mem.NAFE, Water Color Soc. Am., Nat. Mus. Women in Arts, So. Career Inst. Profl. Legal Assts. (area rep.), Northwest Pastel Soc., Profl. Legal Assts., Pendleton C. of C. Avocations: photography and art of nature, hiking, gardening, learning. Office Phone: 541-276-0911.

HARPER, JANE ARMSTRONG, college administrator, consultant; b. Paris, Tex., Oct. 19, 1942; d. David Lewis and Martha Christine (Speegle) A.; m. Bobby Drake Harper, Aug. 5, 1962 (div.); 1 child, Bradley Drake. BA, East Tex. State U., 1963, MA, 1966, PhD, 1971. Proprietor Inside Corner Boutique, Arlington, Tex., 1970-74; ptnr. Harper and Felmet Clothing Store, Caddo Mills, Tex., 1974-76; ptnr., v.p. United Data Systems, Arlington, 1978-80; instr. in French Greenville (Tex.) Sr. High Sch., 1963-64, U. Tex., Arlington, 1966-68; grad. teaching asst. in French East Tex. State U., Commerce, 1965-66; asst. prof. French Tarrant County Jr. Coll. Northeast Campus, Ft. Worth, 1968-69, asst. prof., chair fgn. langs. dept., 1969-70, assoc. prof., chair fgn. langs. dept., 1970-73, chair humanities div., 1986—2006, prof., chair. fgn. langs. dept., 1973-86, dean of humanities, 2006—; ptnr. Harper and Lively Edn. Svcs., 1987—. Mem. coun. on instnl. effectiveness Tarrant County Jr. Coll., 1990—93, chair dist. self-study com. on instnl. effectiveness, 1990—93, mem. dist. self-study for So. Assn. Colls. and Schs. steering com., 1990—93, chair instnl. effectiveness com. for SACS study, 2000—03; chair Vision and Assessment Ctr. for Instrnl. Tech., 1993—96, dist. academic computing com., 1988—89; mem. devel. edn. task force, 1988; minority retention com., 1985—86; pres.'s branding iron com., 1985; many others; vis. asst. prof. Coll. Edn. Dept. Higher Edn. Tex. Tech U., Lubbock, 1973; adj. asst. prof. Sch. Edn. Dept. Secondary and Higher Edn. C.C. Ctr. East Tex. State U., 1973—77; cons., spkr. numerous sch. systems; participant numerous workshops and seminars; mem. acad. adv. coun. on world lang. Coll. Bd., 2002—06. Author (with M. Lively): HOTStuff for Teachers of Foreign Languages: A Manual of Unites of Instruction Incorporating Higher Order Thinking Skills, 1989, HOTStuff for Teachers of French: A Manual of Units of Instruction Incorporating Higher Order Thinking Skills, 1989, HOTStuff for Teachers of German: A Manual of Units of Instruction Incorporating Higher Order Thinking Skills, 1989, HOTStuff for Teachers of Spanish: A Manual of Units of Instruction Incorporating Higher Order Thinking Skills, 1989; author: (with others) Liens: en Parole, 1994; author: (with M. Lively and M. Williams) Thèmes, 2000; author: The Yellow Pages, 2003; contbr. numerous articles to publs.; editor (with M. Lively and M. Williams): The Coming of Age of the Profession, 1998. Bd. govs. Trinity Arts Coun., Hurst-Euless-Bedford, Tex., 1988-90; mem. Arlington Choral Soc., 1976-88, Touch of Class, Arlington, 1980-88. Edn. for Econ. Security Act Grantee, 1987, 88, 89. Mem. AAUP, MLA, ASCD, Am. Ednl. Scis. Assn., Am. Assn. for Higher Edn., Am. Assn. tchrs. of French, Tex. Jr. Coll. Tchrs. Assn. (vice chair fgn. langs. sect. 1971-72, chmn. fgn. langs. sect. 1972-73, 81-82), Tex. Assn. Depts. of Fgn. Langs. (pres.-elect 1979-81, pres. 1981-83, planning team for Seminar West 1984), Tex. Fgn. Lang. Assn. (polit. task force 1982-84, chmn. French sect. fall conf. 1983, local arrangements com. spring conf. 1983, coun. com. on oral proficiency testing 1984, v.p. 1989-90, Tex. French Tchr. Yr. award 1982), S.W. Conf. on Lang. Tchg. (bd. dirs. 1987-89, acting sec. bd. dirs., mem. adv. coun.), Ctrl. States Conf. on Tchg. of Fgn. Langs. (adv. coun.), Ft. Worth Fgn. Lang. Educators, Cmty. Coll. Humanities Assn., South Ctrl. MLA, S.W. Conf. on Lang. Tchg., Tex. Coun. Arts in Edn., tex. Tchrs. English for Spkrs. of Other Langs., Tex. Assn. Supervision and Curriculum Devel., Assn. dept. Fgn. Langs. (exec. coun. 1992-94), Cap and Gown, Pi Theta Kappa, Kappa Delta Pi, Phi Alpha Theta, Phi Delta Kappa, Alpha Chi. Presbyterian. Avocations: music, reading, travel. Office: Tarrant County Jr Coll 828 W Harwood Rd Hurst TX 76054-3219 E-mail: jane.harper@tccd.edu.

HARPER, JANET SUTHERLIN LANE, retired educational administrator, writer; b. La Grange, Ga., Apr. 2, 1940; d. Clarence Wilner and Imogene (Thompson); m. William Sterling Lane, June 28, 1964 (div. Jan. 1981); children: David Alan, Jennifer Ruth; m. John F. Harper, June 9, 1990. BA in English and Applied Music, LaGrange Coll., 1961; postgrad., Auburn U., 1963; MA in Journalism, U. Ga., Athens, 1979. Music and drama critic The Brunswick News, Brunswick, Ga., 1979-99; info. asst. Glynn County Schs., Brunswick, 1979-82; adj. prof. Brunswick Coll., Ga., 1981-87; dir. pub. info. and publs. Glynn County Schs., Brunswick, 1982-99, dir. grant writing and rsch., 1999-2000; ret., 2000. Contbg. editor Ga. Jour., 1981-84; editor, writer GAEL Conf. Jours., 1987-89. Mem. Golden Isles Arts and Humanities Bd., 1997—2000, sec., 1998—2000; organist St. Simons United Meth. Ch., 1981—; bd. dirs. Jekyll Island Music Theatre, 1994—2001, pres., 1994—97; bd. dirs. Am. Cancer Soc., 1998—2001. Recipient award of excellence in sch. and cmty. rels. Ga. Bd. Edn., 1984, 92, Edn. Leadership award, Ga., 1989, disting. svc. award Ga. Sch. Pub. Rels. Assn., 1991. Mem.: Ga. Sch. Pub. Rels. Assn. (exec. bd. 1981—87, pres. 1985—86, exec. bd. 1996—2000), Brunswick Press-Advt. Club (award of excellence in pub. rels. 1992), Ga. Assn. Ednl. Leaders (media rels. 1983—2001), Nat. Sch. Pub. Rels. Assn. (Golden Achievement award 1985, 2 awards 1988, 1990, 3 awards 1991, 1992, 1994, 1998), Mozart Soc. E-mail: harpermail@bellsouth.net.

HARPER, JANICE, anthropologist, educator; b. Lansing, Mich., July 23, 1958; d. Clifton Harper and Neela Rumsey Anderson; 1 child, Mira Kalina Skladany. PhD, Mich. State U., Lansing, 1999. Asst. prof. U. Houston, 2000—04, U. Tenn., Knoxville, 2004—. Author: (ethnography) Endangered Species: Health, Illness and Death Among Madagascar's People of the Forest; editor: (book) Women and International Development Annual, Volume III, Women and International Development, Volume IV, (book series) Legacies of Warfare; contbr. articles to profl. publs. Pres. Mothers for Clean Air, Houston, 2002—04. Fellow fellow land degradation and resource mgmt. in Madagascar, J. William Fulbright Found., 1995—96; rsch. fellow in Madagascar and France, Social Sci. Rsch. Coun., 1992—93, fellow area studies in France, Madagascar and Malagasy lang., U.S. Dept. Edn., Fgn. Lang. and Area

Studies, 1992—95, deforestation and medicines in Madagascar grantee, NSF, 1995. Mem.: Soc. Applied Anthropology, Am. Anthrop. Assn. Office: U Tenn 250 S Stadium Hall Knoxville TN 37996 Office Phone: 865-974-2912. Business E-Mail: harper@utk.edu.

HARPER, KAREN, writer; b. Ohio, 1945; m. Don Harper; children: Sharon, Bill, Nancy. High sch. English tchr., Columbus, Ohio; instr. English Ohio State Univ. Author: (novels) Island Ecstasy, 1982, Passion's Reign, 1983, Sweet Passion's Pain, 1984, Rapture's Crown, 1985, Midnight Mirage, 1985, One Fervent Fire, 1987, Tame the Wind, 1988, Eden's Gate, 1989, The Firelands, 1990, Almost Forever, 1991, Circle of Gold, 1992, Wings for Morning, 1993, River of Sky 1994, Promises to Keep, 1994, Dark Road Home, 1996, Black Orchid, 1996, Dawn's Early Light, 1997, Empty Cradle, 1998, Liberty's Lady, 1998, The Baby Farm, 1999 (RITA award nominee, 1999), Poyson Garden, 1999, Tidal Poole, 2000, Down to the Bone, 2000, Shaker Run, 2001, Twilight Tower, 2001, Queene's Cure, 2002, Stone Forest, 2002, Falls, 2003, Thorne Maze, 2003, Queene's Christmas, 2003, Dark Harvest 2004, Fyre Mirror, 2005, Dark Angel, 2005 (Simon & Schuster-Mary Higgins Clark award Mystery Writers Am., 2006), The Last Boleyn, 2006, Hurricane, 2006, Fatal Fashione, 2006. Mailing: Author Mail Random House 1745 Broadway New York NY 10019 Home: Columbus OH also: Naples FL*

HARPER, LAURA LEE, principal; b. Apr. 22, 1959; d. M. Herman and Mary Jo Walters; m. Greg Noel Harper, Dec. 25, 1959. BA, Fort Lewis Coll., Durango, Colo., 1989; MA, N. Mex. State U., Las Cruces, 1995. Tchr. Kirtland (N.Mex.) Ctrl. Sch., 1989—95; vice prin. Aztec H.S., 1995—98, prin., 1998—2004, Dolores (Colo.) Secondary Sch., 2004—. Mem. adv. bd. Sch. to Career Program, Farmington, N.Mex., 1997—2000; bd. mem. San Juan Family Preservation, 1989—2004; cons. Svc. Learning, Dolores, Colo., 2004—, Continuous Improvement, 2004—. Recipient Prin. of Yr., 2000, Quality N. Mex. Piñon recognition, Quality N. Mex. Road Runner recognition. Mem.: Kiwanis, Rotary. Office: Dolores Secondary 1301 Ctrl Ave Dolores CO 81323 Office Phone: 970-882-7289.

HARPER, MARGARET MILLS, educator; b. Chapel Hill, N.C., Nov. 30, 1957; d. George Mills and Mary Jane (Hughes) H.; children: Pierce Rayvon IV, Margaret Grace, George Christian. BA summa cum laude, Fla. State U., 1978; MA, U. N.C., 1981, PhD, 1986. Mgn. editor Algonquin Books of Chapel Hill, 1982-84; asst. prof. Ohio State U., Marion, 1986-89; from asst. to full prof. Ga. State U., Atlanta, 1989—. Author: (book) The Aristocracy of Art: Joyce and Wolfe, 1990, Wisdom of Two: The Spiritual and Literary Collaboration of George and W.B. Yeats, 2006; co-editor: (book) Yeats's Vision Papers, 1991, 2001; contbr. articles to profl. jours. Grantee, NEH, 1997, Queen's U., Belfast, 2002. Mem. MLA, Am. Conf. Irish Studies, South Atlantic Modern Lang. Assn., Internat. Assn. Study Irish Lit., James Joyce Found., Phi Kappa Phi, Phi Beta Kappa. Democrat. Mem. Soc. Of Friends. Office: Ga State U English Dept 1 University Ave SW Atlanta GA 30303

HARPER, MARSHA WILSON, retired religious organization administrator; b. Wilmington, Del., Apr. 14, 1942; d. Woodrow and G. Lucille (Watson) Wilson; m. Conrad Kenneth Harper, July 17, 1965; children: Warren Wilson, Adam Woodburn. BA, Boston Coll. (formerly Newton Sacred Heart), 1964; student, NYU, New Sch. Social Rsch., 1966—67. Cert.: (mediator); paralegal. Jr. caseworker Boston Redevel. Authority, 1964—65; caseworker F. Shervier Home Hosp., Riverdale, NY, 1965—68; exec. dir. Westchester Putnam chpt. ACLU, White Plains, NY, 1971—76; cons., conf. planner Westchester County Women's Ctr.-Minority Women's Conf.; devel. cons. Congregations Linked Urban Strategy Effect Renewal, Yonkers, NY, 1979—81, assoc. dir., 1981, exec. dir., 1982—87; cons., 1987—93; Diocesan deployment officer Episcopal Diocese Washington, 1993—96; faculty CREDO Inst., 1997—. Bd. dir. Assn. Episcopal Colls., N.Y.C., 1988—92; interim cons. Diocese N.Y., 1991—93, transition cons., 1996—2005, trainer, 1996—2005, former chair social concerns com.; bd. dir. Episcopal Ch. Office Deployment, 1994—99; trustee Va. Theol. Sem.; vestry St. Barnabas Episcopal Ch., Irvington, NY, 1986—90, Ch. Epiphany, N.Y.C., 2006—. Mem. NAACP. Mem.: Jane Austen Soc. N.Am., Bronte Lit. Soc., Edith Wharton Lit. Soc. Democrat. Episcopalian.

HARPER, MARY SADLER, financial consultant; b. Farmville, Va., June 15, 1941; d. Edward Henry and Vivien Morris (Garrett) Sadler; m. Joseph Taylor Harper, Dec. 21, 1968; children by previous marriage: James E. Hatch III, Mary Ann Hatch Czajka. Cert., Fla. Trust Sch., U. Fla., 1976. Registered securities rep., Fla., gen. securities prin., fin. and ops. prin., options prin., mcpl. securities prin., investment mgmt. advisor, wealth adv. specialist. Dep. clk. Polk County Cts., Bartow, Fla., 1964-67; rep. Allen & Co., Lakeland, Fla., 1967-71; with First Nat. Bank, Palm Beach, Fla., 1971-89, sr. v.p., 1984-86, S.E. Bank N.A., Palm Beach, 1986-89, 1st United Bank, 1997-98; pres., CEO Palm Beach Capital Svcs., Inc., 1986-88; mng. dir. Investment Svcs., Palm Beach Capital Svcs. Divsn., 1988; v.p. investments, trustee J.M. Rubin Found, Palm Beach, 1983—; v.p. sec., sr. v.p. investment divsn. Island Nat. Bank & Trust Co., 1989-97; chair, dir., pres., CEO Island Investment Svcs., Inc. (A Wachovia Co.), Palm Beach, 1989-98; also bd. dirs., mng. exec., sr. v.p. Wachovia Investments, Palm Beach, 1998-2000; sr. v.p. Wachovia Bank N.A., 1999-2000; sr. v.p., investment mgmt. advisor Wachovia Securities, Inc., 2000—05; sr. v.p. investments, wealth adv. specialist Legg Mason, Wood, Walker, Inc., 2000—05; dir. pvt. banking Credit Suisse Securities, LLC, 2005—. Adv. coun. Nuveen, 1987-99, pres.'s coun., 2001, chmn.'s coun., 2002-05; adv. bd. Kidsanctuary, Inc. Adv. panel Palm Beach County YWCA, 1985, mem. endowment com., 1990—93; mem. pres.'s club Jupiter Med. Ctr. Found., 1989—; life mem. Juno Beach Civic Assn.; profl. endowment com. Rehab. Ctr. for Children and Adults, 1998—2002; chmn. Palm Beach adv. bd. Palm Beach Nat. Bank & Trust Co., 2000—01; dir., v.p. Friends of Abused Children, 2001—03; mem. Fla. History Mus.; dir. Ctr. for Family Svcs., 2003—; bd. dirs. Biomotion Found., 2002—05, pres., 2004—05; mem. Palm Beach Hist. Soc., 2004—. Mem. Inst. CFPs (assoc.), Nat. Assn. Securities Dealers (dist. com. 1995-98), Fin. Planners Assn., Fin. Women Internat., Fla. Securities Dealers Assn., Exec. Women of Palm Beaches (fin. com. 1985-92), Internat. Soc. Palm Beach (treas., trustee 1986—), Jupiter Med. Ctr. Found. (pres.'s club 1989—), Loxahatchee Hist. Soc. (bd. dirs. 1991-93, chair devel. com. 1992-93), Sebring, Fla. Hist. Soc. (life), Jupiter/Tequesta C. of C. (assoc.), United Daus. of Confederacy, Gov.'s Club, Pub. Securities Assn. (exec. rep.), Jonathans Golf Club, Rotary (Palm Beach Found. com. 1990—, bd. dirs. 1992-94, 2001-, co-chair, 1997, chair Rotary Internat. Found., Palm Beach 1998-2006, Paul Harris fellow 1992), Lighthouse Ctr. for the Arts (life), Norton Art Mus. (patron), Palm Beach Yacht Club, Ritz Carlton Spa and Club (Jupiter), Palm Beach County Hist. Soc., Palm Beach Preservation Found. Democrat. Baptist. Avocations: reading, history. Home: 800 Ocean Dr PH 4 Juno Beach FL 33408-1730 Office: Credit Suisse 420 Royal Palm Way Ste 200 Palm Beach FL 33480 Office Phone: 561-366-2501. Home Fax: 561-626-7978. Business E-Mail: mary.harper@credit-suisse.com.

HARPER, PATRICIA NELSEN, psychiatrist; b. Omaha, July 25, 1944; d. Eddie R. and Marjorie L. (Williams) Nelsen. BS, Antioch Coll., Yellow Springs, Ohio, 1966; MD, U. Nebr., 1975; grad., Topeka Inst. Psychoanalysis, 1997. Cert. psychiatrist. Psychiatric residency Karl Menninger Sch. of Psychiatry, Topeka, 1975-78; staff psychiatrist The Menninger Clinic, Topeka, 1978-98; chmn. dept. mental health Park Nicollet Clinic, 2004—. Faculty mem. Karl Menninger Sch. of Psychiatry, Topeka, 1982-98. Program dir. Addictions Recovery Program C.F. Menninger Meml. Hosp., Topeka, 1987-98. Mem. Am. Psychiatric Assn., Am. Med Women Assn., Am. Psychoanalytic Assn. Office: Pk Nicollet Clinic 3800 Park Nicollet Blvd Minneapolis MN 55416-2527 Office Phone: 952-993-3307.

HARPER, SANDRA REYNOLDS, music educator; b. Greenville, NC, Aug. 9, 1951; d. Wilson Thomas and Mary Frances Reynolds; m. Steven Konrad Harper, Feb. 3, 1973; children: William Barton, Carrie Elizabeth, Robert Thomas. BA in English and Am. Lit. and Lang., U. of Tenn., Chattanooga, 1973. Teacher of English grades 6-12; gifted in field State of Ga., 1989. Tchr. of english grades 8 and 9 Ooltewah H.S., Tenn., 1973—76; tchr. of vocat. improvement program Ctrl. H.S., Chattanooga, 1980—82; 4th grade tchr. Brainerd Bapt. Sch., 1986—87, music tchr., 1987—88; tchr. of adj. devel. english Chattanooga State Tech. C.C., 1988—89; tchr. of h.s. english Ringgold H.S., Ga., 1989—. English dept. chair Ringgold H.S., Ga., 2002—05. Christian. Avocations: reading, piano, travel. Office: Ringgold HS 29 Tiger Trail Ringgold GA 30736 Office Phone: 706-935-3986. E-mail: sharper.rhs@catoosa.k12.ga.us.

HARPER, SANDRA STECHER, academic administrator; b. Dallas, Sept. 21, 1952; d. Lee Roy and Carmen (Crespo) Stecher; m. Dave Harper, July 6, 1974; children: Justin, Jonathan. BS in Edn., Tex. Tech. U., 1974; MS, U. N. Tex., 1979, PhD, 1985; grad. mgmt. devel. program, Harvard U., 1992. Speech/reading tchr. Nazareth H.S., Tex., 1974-75; speech/English tchr. Collinsville H.S., Tex., 1975-77, Pottsboro H.S., Tex., 1977-79; instr. comm. Austin Coll., Sherman, Tex., 1980-82; rsch. asst. U. N. Tex., Denton, 1982-84; from asst. prof. to assoc. prof. comm. McMurry Coll., Abilene, Tex., 1985-95; dean Coll. Arts and Scis. McMurry U., Abilene, 1990-95, asst. dir. NEH univ. core curriculum project; v.p. for acad. affairs Oklahoma City U., 1995-98; provost, v.p. for acad. affairs Tex. A&M U., Corpus Christi, 1998—2006, prof. comm., 1998—2006; pres. Our Lady of the Lake Coll., Baton Rouge, 2006—. Vis. instr. comm. Austin Coll., Sherman, 1985; CIES mentor for Russian adminstr. from Moscow State U., Ulyanovsk, 1995-96; mem. adv. bd. Coll. Am. Indian Devel., 1995-98; critic judge Univ. Interscholastic League, Austin, 1980-93; mem. adv. bd. Univ. Rsch. Consortium, Abilene, 1990-95; mem. formula adv. com., mem. instrn. and operation formula study com. Tex. Higher Edn. Coordinating Bd., 1999-2004, mem. adv. com. AA in Tchg., 2003-04; mem. working group Am. Assn. State Colls. and Univs. Am. Democracy Project, 2002-06; mem. La. Student Fin. Assistance Commn. and La. Tuition Trust Authority, 2006—. Contbr. articles to profl. jours.; author: To Serve the Present Age, 1990; co-author U.S. Dept. Edn. Title III Grant; mem. editl. bd. Soc. for the Advancement of Mgmt. Jour., 1999—. Planner TEAM Abilene, 1991; del. Tex. Commn. for Libr. and Info. Svcs., Austin, 1991; chair Abilene Children Today: Life and Cmty. Skills Task Force, 1994-95; del. Oklahoma City Ednl. TV Consortium, 1997-98; bd. dirs. South Tex. Pub. Broadcasting, 1998-2004, Leadership Corpus Christi; mem. gov.'s exec. devel. program Class XVIII, LBJ Sch. Pub. Affairs, U. Tex., Austin, 1999, S. Tex. Regional Leaders Forum, 2001-02. Media Rsch. scholar Ctr. for Population Options, 1989; recipient Corpus Christi YWCA Women in Careers Secondary Edn. award, 2000. Mem. Nat. Comm. Assn., Am. Assn. Higher Edn., Tex. Pub. Univ. Chief Acad. Officers Assn. (v.p. 2003-04, pres. 2004-05), Soc. for Advancement of Mgmt. (Mgmt. Excellence award 2005). Democrat. Roman Catholic. Office: Our Lady of Lake Coll 7434 Perkins Rd Baton Rouge LA 70808 Office Phone: 225-768-1710. E-mail: sandra.harper@ololcollege.edu.

HARPER, SHIRLEY FAY, nutritionist, educator, consultant, lecturer; b. Auburn, Ky., Apr. 23, 1943; d. Charles Henry and Annabelle (Gregory) Belcher; m. Robert Vance Harper, May 19, 1973 (dec. Mar. 2000); children: Glenda, Debra, Teresa, Suzanna, Cynthia. BS, Western Ky. U., 1966, MS, 1982. Cert. nutritionist and lic. dietitian, Ky. Dir. dietetics Logan County Hosp., Russellville, Ky., 1965-80; cons. Western State Hosp., Hopkinsville, Ky., 1983-84, instnl. dietetic adminstr., 1984-88; dietitian Rivendell Children's Psychiat. Hosp., Bowling Green, Ky., 1988-90; instr. nutrition Western Ky. U., Bowling Green, 1990-92. Cons. Auburn (Ky.) Nursing Ctr., 1976-95, Belle Meade Home, Greenville, Ky., 1980—, Brookfield Manor, Hopkinsville, 1983—, Sparks Nursing Ctr., Ctrl. City, Ky., 1983—, Muhlenberg Cmty. Hosp., Greenville, 1989-2000, Russellville Health Care Manor, 1978-83, 92-, Westlake Cumberland Hosp., Columbia, Ky., 1993-, Franklin-Simpson Meml. Hosp., Franklin, Ky., 1993-2003, Lakeview Health Care Ctr., Morgantown, Ky., 2001-03, Morgantown Care and Rehab. Ctr., 2003-, Trigg County Personal Care Home, Cadiz, 2002-, Gainsville Manor, Hopkinsville, 2002-; nutrition instr. Madisonville (Ky.) C.C., 1995-98. Mem. regional bd. dirs. ARC of Ky., Frankfort, 1990-96; vice chair ARC of Logan County, 1992-93, chmn., 1993-96, 97—; bd. dirs. Logan County ARC United Way, 1993—; co-chair adv. coun. devel. disabilities Lifeskills, 1992-93, adv. coun. Lifeskills Residential Living Group Home, 1993-2000, human rights adv. coun., 1994-2000; chair Let's Build our Future Campaign; nutrition del. Citizen Am. Program to USSR, 1990; adv. chair for vocat. edn., Russellville; mem. adv. coun. for home econs. and family living, We. Ky. U., 1990-93; bd. dirs. ARC of Logan County for United Way, 1993—; del. 24th Internat. Congress on Arts and Comm., Oxford (Eng.) U., 1997. Recipient Outstanding Svc. award Am. Dietetic Assn. Found., 1993, Outstanding Svc. award Barren River Mental Health-Mental Retardation Bd., 1987, Svc. Appreciation award Logan-Russellville Assn. for Retarded Citizens, 1987, Internat. Woman of Yr. award for contbn. to Nutrition and Humanity, Internat. Biog. Assn., 1993-94, World Lifetime Achievement award Am. Biog. Inst., 1995; inaugurated Lifetime Dep. Gov., Am. Biog. Rsch. Bd., 1995, Pres.'s award ARC of Logan County, 1996, award of excellence Oxford, Eng. Internat. Congress on Arts and Comm., Internat. Sash of Acad., Am. Biog. Inst., 1997. Mem. Am. Dietetic Assn., Nat. Nutrition Network, Ky. Dietetic Assn. (pres. Western dist. 1976-77, Outstanding Dietitian award 1984), Bowling Green-Warren County Nutrition Coun., Nat. Ctr. for Nutrition and Dietetics (charter), Ky. Nutrition Coun., Logan County Home Economist Club (sec. 1994-95, 1999-2000, v.p. 1995-96, 2000-01, pres. 1996-97, 2001—), Internat. Biog. Assn., Internat. Platform Assn., Diabetes Care and Edn., Dietitians in Nutrition Support, Cons. Dietitians in Health Care, Phi Upsilon Omicron (pres. Beta Delta alumni chpt. 1994-96, Outstanding Alumni award 1997). Avocations: music, drawing and art, poetry, reading, cake decorating. Home and Office: 443 Hopkinsville Rd Russellville KY 42276-1286

HARPHAM, VIRGINIA RUTH, violinist; b. Huntington, Ind., Dec. 10, 1917; d. Pyrl John and Nellie Grace (Whitaker) Harpham; m. Dale Lamar Harpham, Dec. 25, 1938; children: Evelyn, George. AB, Morehead State U., 1939. Violinist Nat. Symphony Orch., Washington, 1955-90, prin. of second violin sect., 1964-90; mem. Lywen String Quartet, 1960-69, Nat. Symphony String Quartet, 1973-82. Named to Hall of Fame, Morehead State U., 2003. Episcopalian. Home: 5354 43d St NW Washington DC 20015-2008 E-mail: veeharp@tidalwave.net.

HARPLE, ERIN H., music educator; d. William F. and C. Lynette Harple. EdB, NW U., Kirkland, Wash., 1999. Classroom music tchr. Tudor Elem., Anchorage, 2000—. Co-dir. Mini Music Machine!, Anchorage, 1991—2006. Children's choir co-dir. Muldoon Cmty. Assembly, Anchorage, 2001—05. Mem.: Alaska Orff Soc. Independent. Assemblies Of God. Avocations: reading, singing, travel.

HARR, GALE ANN, school psychologist; b. Youngstown, Ohio, June 21, 1955; d. William Brown and Marilyn Jean (Pratt) Roberts; m. Richard Kenneth Harr, Oct. 8, 1977; children: Brandon Scott, Brittany Lee. BA, Mount Union Coll., 1977; MEd, Kent State U., 1979, EdS, 1981, PhD, 1998. Cert. and lic. sch. psychologist, secondary tchr. pupil personnel, Ohio. Substitute tchr. Summit County (Ohio) Schs., 1978-80; intern in sch. psychology Stow (Ohio) City Schs., 1980-81; sch. psychologist Maple Heights (Ohio) Schs., 1981-85, coordinator spl. pupil services, 1985-88, dir. instruction, 1988-94; dir. student svcs. and spl. edn. Brunswick City Schs., 1994—. Columnist Maple Heights Press, 1982-86. Organizer, leader Chem. Abuse Reduced by Edn., Maple Heights, 1981—. Mem. ASCD, Nat. Assn. Sch. Psychologists, Ohio Sch. Psychologists Assn. (planning com. 1986-87, newsletter editor 1987—, pres. 1989-90, past pres. 1990-91), Cleve. Assn. Sch. Psychologist (program com. 1986-88), Kent-Akron Assn. Sch. Psychologists, Ohio Assn. of Pupil Svcs. Adminstrs. Avocations: reading, cooking, gymnastics, outdoor sports, music. Home: 2918 Chautauqua Dr Silver Lake OH 44224-3839 Office: Brunswick City Schs 3643 Center Rd Brunswick OH 44212-3619

HARR, LUCY LORAINE, public relations executive; b. Sparta, Wis., Dec. 2, 1951; d. Ernest Donald Harr and Dorothy Catherine (Heintz) Harr Vetter BS, U. Wis., Madison, 1976, MS, 1978. Lectr. U. Wis., Madison, 1977-82; from asst. editor to editor Everybody's Money Everybody's Money Credit Union Nat. Assn., Madison, 1979-84, mgr. ann. report, 1984-92, v.p. pub. rels., 1984-93, sr. v.p. credit union devel., 1993-96, sr. v.p. consumer rels. and corp. responsibility, 1996-97; owner Providing Solutions, Stoughton, Wis., 1997—; ptnr. Fourth Lake Comm., LLP. Dir. consumer appeals bd. Ford Motor Co., Milw., 1983-87. Author: Credit Union Basic Guide to Retirement Planning, 1998. Bd. dirs. Madison Area Crimestoppers, 1982-84; Midwest coord. of ofcls. USA Triathlon, 2003. Recipient Clarion award, 1982. Mem. Women in Comm. (pres. Madison profl. chpt. 1982-83, nat. v.p. programs 1986-87, vice-chair/sec. nat. interim bd. 1996-97, chair nat. bd. dirs. 1997-2001), Internat. Assn. Bus. Communicators (program chair dist. meeting 1981), Am. Soc. Assn. Execs. (Gold Circle award 1984) Avocations: bicycling, reading. E-mail: lharr@providing-solutions.com.

HARRALL, NEVA ANN, elementary school educator; b. Aurora, Mo., Aug. 9, 1957; d. Billy Ray and Shirley Jean Rinker; m. Edward Henry Harrall, Feb. 3, 1978; children: Misty Lynn, Jami Marie, Zachary Edward. BS in Edn., Mo. So. U., Joplin, 1995; M in Adminstrn., William Woods U., Fulton, Mo., 2006. Jr. high, hs tchr. Verona (Mo.) Sch. Dist., 1997—.

HARRELL, FLORENCE LOUISE, elementary school educator; b. Eure, N.C., Mar. 24, 1954; d. Lillian and Florence (Nowell Morings; m. Robert Leon Harrell Jr., Aug. 15, 1977; 1 child, Kenya LaCole. BS, Norfolk State U., Va., 1976; MEd, U. Va., 1987. Tchr. Gates County Schs., Gatesville, N.C., 1976-79, Hertford County Schs., Ahoskie, N.C., 1979-82, Suffolk (Va.) City Schs., 1982—. Bd. dirs. Vacation Bible Sch., Drum Hill, N.C., 1986. Mem. Edn. Assn. of Suffolk (bldg. rep. 1987—). Democrat. Pentacostal Ch. Avocations: reading the bible, cooking, tropical fish. Home: 410 White Oak Rd Eure NC 27935-9731 Office: Robertson Elem Sch 132 Robertson St Suffolk VA 23438-9705

HARRIEL, MARCY, actress; b. NJ, Aug. 06; m. Rob Grad., The Boston Conservatory, Carnegie Mellon U. Actress (regional plays) Company, Lucky Duck, HMS Pinafore, Candide, A Chorus Line, A Sondheim Celebration, Little Fish, Weird Romance, Compleat Female Stage Beauty, West Side Story, Blood Brothers, (Off-Broadway plays) Jigsaw, Outlaws, The Capeman, Mask, Was, Sorrow & Rejoicing, Wicked, (Broadway plays) Rent, Lennon, 2005, (TV series) Law & Order, Queens Supreme, Ed.

HARRIELL, KYSHA, athletic trainer, educator; b. Washington, July 25, 1973; d. Fred and Patricia Ann Harriell. BS in Athletic Tng., U. Pitts., 1996; MS in Edn. in Sports Medicine, U. Miami, 1999, MS in Edn. in Sports Adminstrn., 2001. Cert. athletic trainer Nat. Athletic Tng. Assn. BOC, lic. Fla. Asst. athletic trainer U. Miami, Coral Gables, Fla., 1997—, adj. prof., 1999—2005. Mem. Ethnic Diversity Adv. Coun., Dallas, 1997—2004. Mem.: Amnesty Internat., Delta Sigma Theta (assoc.). Democrat. Avocations: travel, sports, reading. Home: 7355 SW 82d St # 7 Miami FL 33143 Office: U Miami 5821 San Amaro Dr Coral Gables FL 33146 Office Phone: 305-284-4131. Office Fax: 305-284-3008. Personal E-mail: harriell@bellsouth.net. E-mail: kharriell@miami.edu.

HARRIFF, SUZANNA ELIZABETH BAHNER, media consultant; b. Vicksburg, Miss., Dec. 30, 1953; d. David S. and F. Suzanne (McElwee) Bahner; m. James R. Harriff, Sept. 10, 1977; 1 child, Michael James. BA summa cum laude, SUNY-Fredonia, 1976; postgrad., Cornell U. Law Sch., 1981; MDiv with distinction, Colgate Rochester Div. Sch., 1995. Ordained to ministry Am. Bapt. Chs. USA, 1995. Media asst. Comstock Advt., Syracuse, N.Y., Buffalo, 1976-77; media buyer/planner G. Andre Delporte, Syracuse, 1979-81; media dir. Roberts Advt., Syracuse, 1982; dir. media svcs. Signet Advt., Syracuse, 1982-84; owner, pres. MediaMarCon, Syracuse, 1984—. Interim dir. mktg. and comm. Onondaga CC, 1998—99; adj. prof. Newhouse Sch. Syracuse U., 2001—02; pub. rels. cons. Syracuse Symphony Orch., 2000—01, 2005. Singer: Aspen Dreams, 1996—2005. Vol. pub. TV auction drive, chair media divsn. Sta. WCNY-TV, 1986—97, 2004, gen chair, 1994, chair media divsn., 1986—97, 2004—06; Pheresis donor ARC, 1987—2005; accompanist musicals and chorus Manlius-Pebble Hill Sch., 1991—96; resource devel. chair Winterfest, Syracuse, 1992; cmty. liason Cmty. United Way, 2000—01; media panelist Hugh O'Brien Youth Leadership Conf., 2003, 2004; bd. dirs. Westminster Manor, 2004—06; music dir., pianist Manlius (N.Y.) United Meth. Ch., 1983—92, youth dir., 1983—85; co-chair St. Nicholas Ecumenical Festival, 1992—98, Am. Bapt. Ch. Nat. Biennial Conf., 1995; dir. music First Bapt. Ch., Manlius, 1993—96; assoc. pastor Andrews Meml. United Meth. Ch., 1996—99; workshop leader United Meth. Ch., 1997—; interim pastor Oswego First United Meth. Ch., 2000; pastor Apulia and Onativia United Meth. Chs., 2000—02; interim pastor Hannibal (N.Y.) Cmty. Ch., 2003—04; tchr. Am. Bapt. Chs. N.Y. state lay studies program Bethel Bible Inst., Syracuse. Recipient 500 Hour Svc. pin, WCNY, 1996, Gold Medallion of Excellence, Upstate N.Y. Dist., 1999, Bronze and Silver Paragon awards, Nat. Coun. Mktg. and Pub. Rels., 2000, Women in Bus. award, 2001. Mem.: NAFE, Irish-Am. Cultural Inst. Syracuse, Syracuse Advt. Club (bd. dirs. 1985—88, program chair 1986—88, pres. 1988—89), Phi Beta Kappa. Democrat. Avocations: music, theater. Home: 8180 Bluffview Dr Manlius NY 13104-9740 Office Phone: 315-423-0226. Business E-Mail: sharriff@mediamarcon.com.

HARRIGAN, ROSANNE CAROL, medical educator; b. Miami, Fla., Feb. 24, 1945; d. John H. and Rose (Hnatow) Harrigan; children: Dennis, Michael, John. BS, St. Xavier Coll., 1965; MSN, Ind. Univ., 1974, EdD in Nursing and Edn., 1979. Staff nurse, recovery rm. Mercy Hosp., Chgo., 1965, evening charge nurse, 1965—66; head nurse Chgo. State Hosp., 1966—67; nurse practitioner Health and Hosp. Corp. Marion County, Indpls., 1975—80; assoc. prof. Ind. U. Sch. Nursing, Indpls., 1978—82; nurse practitioner devel. follow up program Riley Hosp. for Children, Indpls., 1980—85; prof. Ind. U. Sch. Nursing, Indpls., 1982—85; chief nursing sect. Riley Hosp. Child Devel. Ctr., Indpls., 1982—85; chmn., prof. maternal child health Loyola U., Niehoff Sch. Nursing, Chgo., 1985—92; dean sch. nursing U. Hawaii, Honolulu, 1992—2002; nurse practitioner Waimanalo Health Ctr., Hawaii, 1998—2002; Frances A. Matsuda chair women's health John A. Burns Sch. Medicine U. Hawaii Manoa, Honolulu, 2000—, assoc. dean, 2002—, chair complementary and alternative medicine dept., 2002—, prof. pediat., 2003—. Lectr. Ind. U. Sch. Nursing, 1974-75, chmn. dept. pediat., family and women's health, 1980-85; adj. prof. of pediat. Ind. U. Sch. Med., 1982-85; editl. bd. Jour. Maternal Child Health Nursing, 1984-86, Jour. Perinatal Neo-natal, 1985—, Jour. Perinatology, 1989—, Loyola U. Press, 1988-92; adv. bd. Symposia Medicus, 1982-84, Proctor and Gamble Rsch. Adv. Com. Blue Ribbon Panel; sci. rev. panel NIH, 1985; mem. NIH nat. adv. coun. nursing rsch., 2000-; cons. in field. Contbr. articles to profl. journals. Bd. dir. March of Dimes Ctrl. Ind. Chpt., 1974-76, med. adv., 1979-85; med. and rsch. adv. March of Dimes Nat. Found., 1985—, chmn. Task Force on Rsch. Named Nat. Nurse of Yr. March of Dimes, 1983; faculty rsch. grantee Ind. U., 1978, Pediatric Pulmonary Nursing Tng. grant Am. Lung Assn., 1982-85, Attitudes, Interests, and Competence of Ob-Gyn. Nurses Rsch. grant Nurses Assn. Am. Coll. Ob-Gyn., 1986, Attitudes, Interests, and Priorities of Neo-natal Nurses Rsch. grant Nat. Assn. Neonatal Nurses, 1987, Biomedical Rsch. Support grant, 1988; Doctoral fellow Am. Lung Assn. Ind. Tng. Program, 1981-86. Mem. AAAS, ANA (Maternal Child Nurse of Yr. 1983), Assn. Women's Health, Obstetrical and Neonatal Nursing (chmn. com. on rsch. 1983-86), Am. Nurses Found., Nat. Assn. Neo-natal Nurses, Nat. Perinatal Assn. (bd. dir. 1978-85, rsch. com. 1986), Midwest Nursing Rsch. Soc. (theory devel. sect.), Ill. Nurses Assn. (commn. rsch. chmn. 1990-91), Ind. Nurses Assn., Hawaii Nurses Assn., Ind. Perinatal Assn. (pres. 1981-83), N.Y. Acad. Sci., Ind U. Alumni Assn. (Disting. Alumni 1985), Sigma Xi, Pi Lambda Theta, Sigma Theta Tau (chpt. pres. 1988-90). Business E-Mail: harrigan@hawaii.edu.

HARRINGTON, ANNE WILSON, medical librarian; b. Phila., June 18, 1926; d. Edgar Myers and Jean Gould (DeHaven) Wilson; m. James Paul Harrington, June 11, 1948; children: Barbara Gould Harrington Murphy, Ian Edgar, Eric Bradley. BA, U. Pa., Phila., 1948; MS in Libr. Sci., Villanova U., 1977. Clk. Princeton U., 1948-51; CEO, ptnr. Teesdale Co., Kennett Square, Pa., 1954—2005; libr. asst. Franklin Inst., Phila., 1974-76; med. staff libr. The Chester County Hosp., West Chester, 1977-99. Mem., treas., chmn. sub-com. Consortium Health Info., Chester, 1977-99. Trustee, sec., com. chmn.

Wilmington (Del.) Friends Sch., 1963—72, 1989; bd. dirs., subcom. chmn. cmty. bd. Kendal Corp. Continuing Care Retirement Cmty., Kennett Square, Pa., 1973—98; treas. com. on edn. Phila. Yearly Meeting Soc. Friends, 1980—91; mem., rep. Friends Coun. on Edn., Phila., 1991—96; overseer Quaker Info. Ctr., Phila., 1992—96, Phila. Yearly Meeting Soc. Friends, libr. svcs. group, 1999—2003, publ. working group, 2000—. Mem. AAUW, Acad. Health Info. Profls. (sr.), Phila. Area Med. Library Assn., Lake Paupac Club (chmn. environ. com., bd. dirs. 1990-96), Friends Med. Soc. Democrat. Avocations: music, reading, walking, sailing, tennis. Home: 234 Crosslands Dr Kennett Square PA 19348 E-mail: libawh@aol.com.

HARRINGTON, CAROL A., lawyer; b. Geneva, Ill., Feb. 13, 1953; d. Eugene P. and M. Ruth (Bowersox) Kloubec; m. Warren J. Harrington, Aug. 19, 1972; children: Jennifer Ruth, Carrie Anne. BS summa cum laude, U. Ill., 1974, JD magna cum laude, 1977. Bar: Ill. 1977, U.S. Dist. Ct. (no. dist.) Ill. 1977, U.S. Tax Ct. 1979. Assoc. Winston & Strawn, Chgo., 1977-84, ptnr., 1984-88, McDermott, Will & Emery, 1988—. Adv. com. Heckerling Inst. Estate Planning; speaker in field. Co-author: Generation-Skipping Tax, 1996, Generation-Skipping Transfer Tax, Warren, Gorham & Lamont, 2000. Fellow Am. Coll. Trusts and Estate Coun. (bd. regents 1999-2005); mem. ABA (chmn. B-1 generation skipping transfer com. 1987-92, coun. real property, probate and trust law sect. 1992-98), Ill. State Bar Assn., Chgo. Bar Assn., Chgo. Estate Planning Coun. Office: McDermott Will & Emery 227 W Monroe St Ste 3100 Chicago IL 60606-5096 Office Phone: 312-984-7794.

HARRINGTON, CHESTEE MARIE, artist, sculptor; b. New Iberia, La., Dec. 5, 1941; d. Herschel F. Harrington, Sr. and Vivian M. Haydel; m. J. R. Minvielle, 1959 (div. 1974); m. M. R. Aubin, Jr., 1978 (div. 1996); children: Stephen D. Minvielle, Brian A. Minvielle, Theadore L. Minvielle, Katherine H. Minvielle, Jeann'e L. Aubin, Cle'lie C. Aubin. Student, Famous Artist Sch., West port, Conn., 1962—66; Assoc. Degree, Art Students League, N.Y.C., 1985, Woodstock Art Sch., NY, 1985. Tchr. drawing Iberia Parish Pk. Svc., New Iberia, La., 1966—68; cultivated Sch. Spiritual Expressionism, St. Francisville, La., 1995—. One-woman shows include Festival Internat., Lafayette, La., 1998, Jean Lafitte, National Park, La., 1999, Mus. of the Gulf Coast, Port Arthur, Tex., 1999, over 35 group shows including most recently, exhibited in group shows at The Shadows on the Teche, Nat. Trust, NILA, 2004, The Cigar Factory, Charleston, S.C., 2005, Brimstone Mus., Sulphur, La., 2006, Represented in permanent collections La. State U., Baton Rouge, Hist. New Orleans Collection, NOLA, The McIlhenny Collection La., Art Ctr. for S.W. La., Lafayette, The White House, Washington, The Vatican, Rome, Touro Hosp., 53 exhibns. Avocations: storytelling, music, gardening, dance, poetry. Home and Office: 1065 West Main Street New Iberia LA 70560 also: 212 North St New Iberia LA 70560 Office Phone: 337-560-4393. Personal E-mail: chestee@chestee.com.

HARRINGTON, DIANE, librarian, writer; d. G. Robert and Jane Coupe Harrington; m. Bradley Kent Purvis, Mar. 21, 1981; 1 child, Megan Susan Purvis. BA in English, Wellesley Coll., 1968; MA in English, Columbia U., 1971. Cert. adminstr. Fordham U., 1981, lib. media specialist Palmer Sch. Info. Sci., 1999. Sr. fellow, instr. Columbia U., NYC, 1971—73; media specialist, lead tchr. New Rochelle Sch. Dist., NY, 1973—75; instr. CUNY, 1975—77, adj. instr., 1977—79; spl. specialist Office of Chancellor NYC Pub. Schs., 1984; ednl. writer United Fed. Tchrs., 1986—91; adj. instr. Westchester CC, NY, 1993—95; English tchr. Nyack HS, 1995—96; lib., media specialist White Plains HS, NY, 1996—2005; libr. media specialist Rye HS, NY, 2005—. Edl. cons., 1980—96; freelance writer, editor, 1980—. Co-author (with Laurette Young): School Savvy, 1993, lib. website; developer HS rsch. handbook; contbr. articles to. profl. jours. Unitarian Universalist. Avocations: singing, reading. Office: Rye HS Parsons St Rye NY 10580

HARRINGTON, E.B., art dealer; b. N.Y., May 2, 1953; d. Robert Charles and Clarice (Garrett) Barbato.; m. Mark Garland Harrington, June 3, 1978 (div. May 1986); 1 child: Alexandra Harrington; m. Peter Ridgway Barker, June 5, 1992; 1 child: Robert Brinton Barker. BS, Finch Coll., 1975. Asst. dir. Richard L. Feigen & Co., N.Y., 1975-78; pres. E.B. Harrington & Co., N.Y., 1978—. Art cons. Procter & Gamble, Cin., Ohio, 1986—, James D. Wolfensohn, N.Y., Washington, D.C., 1988—, BT Wolfensohn, N.Y., 1997-99. Mem. (student) Appraiser's Assn. Am. Avocations: painting, drawing, tennis, cooking. Home and Office: 1500 Lexington Ave #B New York NY 10029-7301 E-mail: ebh-art@pipeline.com.

HARRINGTON, JEAN PATRICE, academic administrator; b. Denver; d. James Michael and Katherine Ann (Holl) H. BA, Coll. Mt. St. Joseph, 1953; MA, Creighton U., 1958; PhD, U. Colo., 1967; LHD (hon.), Xavier U., 1983, Ohio Dominican Coll., 1988; LLD (hon.), St. Thomas Inst., Cin., 1985, Coll. Mt. St. Joseph, 1988, Hebrew Union Coll., 1990; D. Tech. Studies (hon.), Cin. Tech., 1988; LLD (hon.), No. Ky. U., 1996, U. Dayton, 1999. Joined Sisters of Charity of Cin., 1940; prin. St. Rose of Lima, Denver, 1953-56; tchr. Cathedral H.S., Denver, 1956-58, prin., 1958-68; dir. instl. rsch. Coll. Mt. St. Joseph, Cin., 1968-69, pres., 1977-87; exec. dir. Cin. Youth Collaborative, 1988-90; interim pres. Cin. State Coll., 1997. Bd. dirs. Penrose Hosp., Colorado Springs, 1976-86, St. Mary Corwin Hosp., Pueblo, Colo., 1972-80, Cin. Bicentennial Commn., 1982-89, Samaritan Health Resources, Inc., 1983-96, St. Rita Sch. for Deaf, 1983-86, United Appeal Cabinet, 1983, Cin. Cmty. Chest, 1988-95, Dan Beard coun. Boy Scouts Am., 1988-91; trustee Good Samaritan Hosp. and Health Ctr., Dayton, Ohio, 1978-80, 89-97, bd. dirs., 1989-96; trustee Miami U., 1989-97, chmn. 1994-97; bd. dirs. Coll. of Mt. St. Joseph, 1995-2002; trustee U. Dayton, 1999-2002. Recipient Disting. Svc. citation NCCJ, 1987, Women Helping Women award Soroptimist Internat., 1990, Statesman award Cin. Assn. Execs., 1988, St. Francis award Friars Club, 1994, Daniel Ransahoff Initiative award, 1994, Lincoln award No. Ky. U., 1994, Gt. Living Cincinnatian award C. of C., 1996, Svc. to Edn. award Ohiana Libr. Assn., 1998, Children's Advocate award Beech Acres; named Career Woman of Achievement YWCA, 1981, Disting. Bus. and Profl. Woman of Yr., 1982; inductee Hall of Excellence of Ohio Fedn. of Ind. Colls., 1990, Ohio Women's Hall of Fame, 2000, Pres.' award Children's Def. Fund, 2003. Mem. Nat. Assn. Ind. Colls. and Univs., Assn. Cath. Colls. and Univs. (bd. dirs.), Ohio Found. Ind. Colls., Greater Cin. Consortium Colls. and Univs. (vice chmn. 1980-82), Coun. Ind. Colls. (bd. dirs. 1981-85), Cin. C. of C. (bd. dirs. 1978-84, trustee 1981-85, sec. 1979-85, named Great Living Cincinnatian 1996). Roman Catholic. Personal E-mail: jphsc@juno.com.

HARRINGTON, JOAN KATHRYN, counselor; b. Harvey, Ill., Dec. 21, 1934; d. Roy W. and Thelma (Hedlund) H. BA, Gordon-Barrington Coll., 1967; MPS, Alliance Theol. Sem., 1984; MEd, William Paterson State U., 1986; PhD, Calif. Grad. Sch. Theology, 1995; LittD, Jacksonville (Fla.) Theol. Sem, 1997. Cert. counselor; ordained Bapt. min. Rural Bible tchr. New Eng. Fellowship Evangs., Boston, 1960-62; co-dir. Children's Haven Inc., East Douglas, Mass., 1962-78; dir. edn. Calvary Gospel Ch., Newark, 1975-80; min. edn. Northside Community Chapel, Paterson, N.J., 1980-85; dir. guidance Eastern Christian High Sch., North Haledon, N.J., 1985-87; counselor Passaic County C.C., Paterson, 1987-89; counselor activities, social svcs. Palm Shores Retirement: The Colonnade, St. Petersburg, Fla., 1989-91; mental health therapist sr. support svcs. Suncoast Ctr. for Cmty. Mental Health, St. Petersburg, Fla., 1990-93; prof., asst. dean students St. Petersburg Theol. Sem., 1992-98; prof. Jacksonville Theol. Sem., Tampa; pres. Atlantic So. Bible Coll., 2003—. Urban coord. Africa Inland Mission, Newark, Paterson, 1975-82; vis. prof. Alliance Theol. Sem., Nyack, N.Y., 1986-88; min. parish witness First Bapt. Ch., Paterson, 1987-89; min. counseling Am. Bapt. Ch. of Beatitudes, St. Petersburg, 1990-95; clin. dir. Life Mgmt. Counseling Svcs., 1994-95; founder, dir. The Care Ctr., Crossover Internat., Inc., 1995-98. Author: (poetry) Deep Rivers, 1981; script writer, producer Haven Radio Club, 1962-78. Family Selection com. Habitat for Humanity, Paterson, 1985; bd. dirs. Urban Ministries of A.I.M., Newark, Children's Haven, Inc. (clk. 1962-77); mem. Paterson Clergy Assn., Paterson, 1980-85; pastor counseling and edn. Safe House, Atlanta, 1998—; profl. counselor Ch. in the Now, 1999—. Mem. ACA, Am. Assn. Christian Counselors, Assn. Specialists in Group Work, Am. Mental Health Counselor's Assn., Assn. for Spiritual, Ethical and Religious Values in Counseling, Nat. Assn. Alcoholism and Drug Abuse Counselors, Christian Assn. Psychol. Studies, Pi Lambda Theta. Independent. Avocations: reading, writing, music. Home: 418 Smith Store Rd Covington GA 30016-4272 Office Phone: 678-520-4247. E-mail: Revdrjoan@aol.com.

HARRINGTON, JOYCE D., music educator; d. Ramond C. and Mary D. Harrington; m. Gregory G. Washburn, Dec. 20, 1997. BA, Edinboro U., Pa., 1983; MusM, New Eng. Conservatory of Music, Boston, 1988. Cert. tchr. Mass. Dept. Edn., 1985. Band dir., music tchr. Abington Pub. Sch., Mass., 1984—2004; dir. music Abington Pub. Sch, Mass., 2004—. Free lance musician, 1986—. Founder, conductor, music dir. Abington Cmty. Band. Mem.: Am. Fedn. Musicians, Mass. Music Educators Assn., Music Educators Nat. Conf., Am. Band Providence (pres. 1996—97), Blue Moon Orch. Home: 34 Morrow St Mansfield MA 02048 Office: Abington High Sch 201 Gliniewicz Way Abington MA 02351 Office Phone: 781-982-2160.

HARRINGTON, MARY EVELINA PAULSON (POLLY HARRINGTON), writer, educator; b. Chgo. d. Henry Thomas and Evelina (Belden) Paulson; m. Gordon Keith Harrington, Sept. 7, 1957; children: Jonathan Henry, Charles Scranton. BA, Oberlin Coll., 1946; postgrad., Northwestern U., Evanston, Ill., Chgo., 1946-49, Weber State U., Ogden, Utah, 1970s, 80s; MA, U. Chgo.-Chgo. Theol. Sem., 1956. Publicist Nat. Coun. Chs., N.Y.C., 1950-51; mem. press staff 2d assembly World Coun. Chs., Evanston, Chgo., 1954; mgr. Midwest Office Communication, United Ch. of Christ, Chgo., 1955-59; staff writer United Ch. Herald, N.Y.C., St. Louis, 1959-61; affiliate missionary to Asia, United Ch. Bd. for World Ministries, N.Y.C., 1978-79; freelance writer and lectr., 1961—; corr. Religious News Svc., 1962—. Prin. lectr. Women & Family Life in Asia series to numerous librs., Utah, 1981, 1981—82; pub. rels. coord. Utah Energy Conservation/Energy Mgmt. Program, 1984—85; tchr. writing Ogden Cmty. Schs., 1985—89; adj. instr. writing for publs. Weber State U., 1986—; instr. Acad. Lifelong Learning, Ogden, 1992—95, Eccles Cmty. Art Ctr., Ogden, 1993—94; dir. comm. Shared Ministry, Salt Lake City, 1983—97; chmn. comm. Intermountain Conf., Rocky Mountain Conf. Utah Assn. United Ch. of Christ, 1970—78, 1982—, Ind. Coun. Chs., 1960—63, United Ch. of Christ, Ogden, 1971—; dir. comm. United Chs., 1971—78, Christ Congl., Ogden,, 1980—; chmn. comm. Ch. Women United Utah, 1974—78, Ogden rep., 1980—, hostess Northern Utah, 1998. Editor: Sunshine and Moonscapes: An Anthology of Essays, Poems, Short Stories, 1994; (booklet) Family Counseling Service: Thirty Years of Service to Northern Utah, 1996; contbr. articles to profl. jours. Pres. T.O. Smith Sch. PTA, 1976-78, Ogden City Coun. PTA, 1983-85; assoc. dir. Region II, Utah PTA, Salt Lake City, 1981-83, mem. State Edn. Commn., 1982-87; chmn. state internat. hospitality and aid Utah Fedn. Women's Clubs, 1982-86; v.p. Ogden dist., 1990-92, pres. Ogden dist., 1992-96, state resolutions com., 1996—; trustee Family Counseling Svc. No. Utah, Ogden, 1983-95, emeritus trustee, 1995—; Utah rep. to nat. bd. Challenger Films, Inc., 1986—; state pres. Rocky Mountain Conf. Women in Mission, United Ch. of Christ, 1974-77, sec., 1981-84, vice moderator Utah Assn., 1992-94; chair pastor-parish rels. com. United Ch. of Christ Congl., Ogden, 1999-03, chair search com., 1995-96, mission com., 2002—, chmn. mission com., 2006—; Interfaith Works!, rep. Interfaith Cmty., North Utah. Recipient Ecumenical Svc. citation Ind. Coun. Chs., 1962, Outstanding Local Pres. award Utah PTA, 1978, Outstanding Latchkey Child Project award, 1985, Cmty. Svc. award City of Ogden, 1980-82, Celebration of Gifts of Lay Woman Nat. award United Ch. of Christ, 1987, Excellence in the Arts in Art Edn. award Ogden City Arts Commn., 1993, Spirit of Am. Woman in Arts and Humanities award Your Cmty. Connection, Ogden, 1994, Heart and Hand award United Ch. of Christ, Ogden, 2001; Utah Endowment for Humanities grantee, 1981-82. Mem. Nat. League Am. Penwomen (chmn. Utah conv. 1973, 11 awards for articles and essays 1987-95, 1st pl. news award 1992, 1st pl. short stories 1997, 3d pl. articles 1997), AAUW (state edn. rep. 1982-86, parliamentarian Ogden br. 1997—, membership v.p. Ogden br. 2003—, Disting. Woman award 2006), League of Utah Writers (Publ. Quill award 1998). Democrat. Home and Office: 722 Boughton St Ogden UT 84403-1152 E-mail: gkharrington1@comcast.net.

HARRINGTON, MICHAELE MARY, artist, educator; b. Boston, June 27, 1946; d. William Gerard and Jadwiga (Jerasonek) H.; m. Jeffrey Fancher Nicoll, Sept. 12, 1970 (div. July 24, 2002); children: Heather Anne, James Craig William. BFA, Mass. Coll. Art, 1968; MFA, Md. Inst., 2000. Prodn. mgr. R.H. Stearns Co., Boston, 1968-69; layout artist Grossman's, Braintree, Mass., 1971-72, Bradlee's, Braintree, 1973; asst. art dir. Canton (Mass.) Advt. Agy., 1973-78; watermedia and collage artist, graphic designer, illustrator Hyattsville, Darnestown, Balt., Md., 1978-88; represented by The Franklin St. Gallery, Hagerstown, Md., 1988—92. Faculty Rockville Arts Pl., 1990—92; demonstrator, studio and workshop tchr., 1988—; design cons. KBL Group, Silver Spring, Md., 1986—92; book illustrator Denlinger Publs., Ltd., Fairfax, Va., 1986; set designer, tech. asst. Ridgeview Mid. Sch., Gaithersburg, Md., 1994—96; adj. continuing studies Md. Inst., Coll. Art, 1999—2005; adj. prof. art Montgomery Coll., Rockville, Md., 2000—; adj. Balt. City CC, 2001—02; faculty Black Rock Arts Ctr., Germantown, Md., 2002—05. Exhibited in group shows at So. Watercolor Soc., Pensacola, Fla., 1982, Am. Watercolor Soc., N.Y.C., 1983, 90, Catherine Lorillard Wolfe Arts Club, N.Y.C., 1983-84 (Gold medal 1984), Midwest Watercolor Soc., Davenport, Iowa, 1983, Mid-Atlantic Regional, Balt., 1983-84, 86-87, 89, 91, New Orleans Art Assn. (2d pl. award), 1984, Dundalk Coll., Md., 1985, San Diego Watercolor Soc., 1990, North Coast Collage Soc., Pitts., Watercolor Soc. (Zeber Exptl. award), Rocky Mountain Nat., 1991, Rock Creek Gallery, Washington, 1993, The Art Barn, Washington, 1993, Ariz. Aqueous IX, Tubac, 1994 (Merit award), Three Rivers Art Festival, Pitts., 1994, Strathmore Hall, Rockville, Md., 1995-2000 (award of merit 2000), Kensington Gallery, Md., 1996, Md. Inst., Coll. of Art, Balt., 1997-99, Friendship Heights Gallery, Chevy Chase, Md., 2000, Paul Peck Art Gallery, Montgomery Coll., Rockville, Md., 2000—; one-woman shows include Montpelier Cultural Arts Ctr., Laurel, Md., 1982, Friendship Gallery, Chevy Chase, Md., 1990, Artshowcase Gallery, Balt., 1991-92, Strathmore Hall Arts Ctr., Rockville, Md., 1999, Unicorn Gallery, Lutherville, Md., 2002, Ozmosis Gallery, Bethesda, Md., 2004; represented in permanent collections Washington Health Ctr., Coast Guard Art Collection of Smithsonian Instn., Washington. Juror art in pub. places program Md.-Nat. Capital Parks and Planning Commn., Hyattsville, Md., 1980-81, assorted Washington area art assns.' regional exhbns., 1990—. Recipient Jurors Choice award Md. Fedn. Art, 1982, Abstract award Md. Nat. Found., 1989. Mem. Potomac Valley Watercolorists (juried, v.p. 1993-97), Strathmore Hall Artists, Coast Guard Artists Program. Avocations: gardening, reading women's studies, science, science fiction, psychology, mythology, comparative religion. Personal E-mail: michaeleha@hotmail.com.

HARRINGTON, PATTI, school system administrator; BA, MEd, Brigham Young U.; PhD in Ednl. Adminstrn., U. Utah. Prin. Provo HS, Utah; asst. supt. Provo; supt., 2001; assoc. supt. State of Utah, 2002—04, supt. of pub. instrn., 2004—. Recipient Secondary Sch. Prin. of Yr., 1997. Office: Utah Office of Edn 250 E 500 S PO Box 144200 Salt Lake City UT 84114-4200 Office Phone: 802-538-7500. Office Fax: 801-538-7768.

HARRINGTON, TERRI ANN, retired elementary school educator; b. Watsonville, Calif., Aug. 15, 1947; d. Theodore Norville and Mary Nell (Crippen) Prather; m. James Leo Harrington Jr., Apr. 4, 1971; children: Matthew Lee, Andrew James. BA in Sociology with honors, U. Calif., Santa Barbara, 1969. Cert. elem. tchr., Calif. Tchr. Evergreen Sch. Dist., San Jose, Calif., 1970-74, Bethany Presbyn. Kindergarten, Grants Pass, Oreg., 1978-85, Grants Pass Sch. Dist., 1985—2004. Chairperson Children's Festival, Grants Pass, 1983-84. AAUW Ednl. Found. Named Gift honoree, 1987-88. Mem. AAUW. Democrat. Methodist.

HARRIS, ALICE, linguist, educator; b. Columbus, Ga., Nov. 23, 1947; d. Joseph Clarence and Georgia (Walker) H.; m. James Vaughan Staros, Aug. 7, 1976; children: Joseph Vaughan, Alice Carmichael. BA, Randolph-Macon Woman's Coll., 1969; MA, U. Essex, Eng., 1972; PhD, Harvard U., 1976. Tchg. fellow linguistics Harvard U., Cambridge, Mass., 1972-74, 75-76, lectr. linguistics, 1976-77, rsch. fellow linguistics, 1977-79; rsch. asst. prof. linguistics Vanderbilt U., Nashville, 1979-84, assoc. prof. linguistics, 1985-91, assoc. prof. anthropology, 1986-92, prof. linguistics, 1991—2002, prof. anthropology, 1992—2002, chair dept. Germanic, Slavic langs., 1993—2002; prof. linguistics SUNY, Stony Brook, 2002—. Chair faculty coun. Coll. Arts and Scis., 1995-96; vice chair grad. faculty coun., 1993-94, sec. faculty senate, 1993-94; assoc. rsch. U. Tbilisi, USSR, 1974-75; tutor linguistics Dunster House, Harvard U., Cambridge, 1975-77; cons. to Simon and Schuster; Erskine vis. prof. U. of Canterbury, Christchurch, New Zealand, 1999; adv. bd. Pubs. MLA, 1995-98. Author: (book) Georgian Syntax, 1981, Diachronic Syntax, 1985, The Indigenous Languages of the Caucasus, 1991, Endoclitics and the Origins of Udi Morphosyntax, 2002; co-author: Historical Syntax in Cross-Linguistic Perspective, 1995 (Leonard Bloomfield book award, 1998); assoc. editor (jour.) Language, 1988—89, mem. editl. bd. Diachronica, 1994—2002, Natural Language and Linguistic Theory, 1987—90, Linguistic Typology, 2003—; contbr. articles to profl. jours. Sinclair Kennedy fellow Harvard U., 1974-75, NSF Nat. Needs Postdoctoral fellow, 1978-79; grantee Internat. Rsch. and Exch. Bd., 1973, 74-75, 77, 81, 89, 92, Linguistic Soc. Am., 1981, NSF 1980-83, 81-83, 83-85, 85-89, 97-99, 2001-03, 2003-06, NEH, 1990-91, Deutscher Adademischer Austausch Dienst, 1994; scholar Harvard U. 1972-73, Georgetown U., 1973; recipient Mellon Found. Regional Faculty Devel. award 1981, ACLS travel award, 1988, venture fund Vanderbilt U., 1987, 92, 94, Earl Sutherland prize for rsch. Vanderbilt U., 1998. Mem. Internat. Soc. Hist. Linguistics (mem. exec. com. 1995-01), Linguistic Soc. Am. (cons., com. status women in linguistics, nominating com.), Southeastern Conf. Linguistics, Soc. for Study of Caucasia (exec. coun. 1990-98), Societas Caucasologica Europaea (v.p. 1990-92, exec. com. 1992-94, 1994-2000), Phi Beta Kappa. Office: SUNY Dept Linguistics Stony Brook NY 11794-4376 Office Phone: 631-632-7758. Business E-Mail: alice.harris@stonybrook.edu.

HARRIS, ANN BIRGITTA SUTHERLAND, art historian; b. Cambridge, Eng., Nov. 4, 1937; came to U.S., 1965, naturalized, 1996; d. Gordon B.B.M. and Gunborg Elizabeth (Wahlström) Sutherland; m. William Vernon Harris, July 13, 1965 (div. Oct. 1999); 1 son, Neil William Orlando Sutherland. BA with 1st class honours, Courtauld Inst., U. London, 1961, PhD, 1965. Asst. lectr. U. Leeds (Eng.), 1964-65; asst. prof. art history Columbia U., N.Y.C., 1965-71, Hunter Coll., N.Y.C., 1971-73; assoc. prof. SUNY, Albany, 1973-77; chmn. for acad. affairs Met. Mus. Art, N.Y.C., 1977-80; part-time faculty Juilliard Sch., N.Y.C., 1978-84; prof. U. Pitts., 1984—. Founder, 1st pres. Women's Caucus for Art, 1973-76; disting. vis. prof. U. Tex.-Arlington, fall 1982; Mellon prof. history of art U. Pitts., spring 1984; vis. prof. history of art So. Meth. U., Dallas, fall 1993. Author: Andrea Sacchi, 1977, Selected Drawings of Gian Lorenzo Bernini, 1977, Seventeenth Century Art and Architecture, 2004; co-author: Die Zeichnungen von Andrea Sacchi und Carlo Maratta, 1967, Women Artists: 1550-1950, exhbn. catalogue, 1977, Landscape Painting in Rome, 1575-1675, exhbn. catalogue, 1985, Italian, French, English and Spanish Drawings and Watercolors in the Detroit Institute of Arts, 1992. Fellow Guggenheim Found., 1971, Ford Found., 1975-76, NEH, 1981-82, rsch. fellow Getty Mus. Art, 1988. Mem. Coll. Art Assn., Women's Caucus for Art. Office: U Pittsburgh Dept History of Art Pittsburgh PA 15260 Office Phone: 412-648-2408. Business E-Mail: ash6@pitt.edu.

HARRIS, ANNE ELDREDGE, artist, educator; b. Pensacola, Fla., May 5, 1918; d. Inman Fowler Eldredge and Callie Agatha Landrum; m. Edward Hooper Harris, Mar. 28, 1937 (dec. July 22, 1982); children: Mark, Christopher Robin, Benjamin Hooper. Student, U. Ala., Tuscaloosa, 1935—37, Newcomb Art Sch., New Orleans, La., 1955—67, Newcomb Art Sch., 1975—81. Mem. Napoleon Gallery, New Orleans, 1964—72; vol. art tchr. St. Paul's Episcopal Sch., New Orleans, 1960—67, Newark (Del.) Ctr. for Creative Learning, 1983—87, Cokesbury Village Memory Impaired, Hockessin, Del., 1987—93; mem. Art On The Net Art.net, 1995—. Editor: Landrum-Eldredge Collection Tulane Library; one-woman shows include Napoleon Gallery, 1966, exhibited in group shows at Newcomb Art Gallery, 1976—81, Gallery 21, Newark, Del., 1982, numerous others; contbr. art and writings to numerous books on aging;, author numerous self published books. Children's art show organizer ann. Newark Days festival, Newark, Del., 1984—87; vol. art tchr. Cuban refugee children, New Orleans, 1958—66, neighborhood youth, Bay St. Louis, Miss., 1977—83; vol. coord. Transp. City Blind Thru Christ Ch. Cathedral, New Orleans. Mem.: Descendants of Mayflower Soc. (life; editor LYNES 1992—95). Episcopalian. Avocations: astronomy, sewing, reading. Home: 726 Loveville Rd A44 Hockessin DE 19707 Personal E-mail: anne1918@comcast.net.

HARRIS, ARLENE, lawyer; b. Buffalo, Dec. 29, 1944; d. Yetta (Kerner) Cramer; m. Ira S. Harris, Dec. 25, 1971; children: Elliot, David, Sara. BA cum laude, Bklyn. Coll., 1965; JD, NYU, 1968. Bar: NY 1969. Assoc. trusts and estates dept. Paul, Weiss, Rifkind, Wharton & Garrison, 1968-75; asst. atty. gen. NY State Dept. Law, 1975-76; law asst.-referee NY County Surrogate's Ct., 1976-78, chief law asst., 1978-90; ptnr. trusts and estates dept. Shea & Gould, NYC, 1990-93; spl. counsel, chair Wills & Estates Dept. Kaye, Scholer LLP, NYC, 1993—. Mem. Internat. Acad. of Estate and Trust Law, Estate's Discussion Groups; bd. dirs. Estate Planning Coun.; adj. prof. law St. John's U. Sch. Law, 1984-92; instr. NYU Sch. Continuing Edn., 1991—; lectr. on estate planning, trusts and estates ABA Nat. Inst., World Trade Inst., NY County Lawyer's Assn., Acad. Trial Lawyers, United Jewish Appeal Ann. Estates Conf., Practising Law Inst. Contbr. chpt. to book, articles to legal publs. and procs. Bd. dirs. East Bay Civic Assn., Inc., 1974-87. John Norton Pomeroy scholar NYU, 1968. Fellow Am. Coll. Trusts and Estate Counsel; mem. NY State Bar Assn. (chmn. legislation com., former mem.-at-large trusts and estates sect., lectr. trusts and estates law sect., chmn. trusts and estates law sect.), Assn. of Bar of City of NY (mem. trusts, estates and surrogate's cts. com. 1979-81, 2005—), Order of Coif. Avocations: gardening, reading, boating. Office: Kaye Scholer LLP 425 Park Ave New York NY 10022-3506 Business E-Mail: aharris@kayescholer.com.

HARRIS, AUDRA BRISSON, education educator; m. Jason Gates Harris; 1 child, Morgan. MBA, U. NC, Pembroke, 2002. Instr. Robeson C.C., Lumberton, NC, 2003—. Contbr. articles to profl. jours. Co-adv. Nat. Tech. Honor Soc., Lumberton, NC, 2005—06. Office: Robeson Cmty Coll PO Box 1420 Lumberton NC 28359 Office Phone: 910-272-3454. Business E-Mail: aharris@robeson.cc.nc.us.

HARRIS, BARBARA S., publishing executive, editor-in-chief; BS in Phys. Edn., Fla. State U., 1978; Masters, N.E. Mo. State U. Editor-in-chief Weider Publ., Woodland Hill, Calif., 1987—2003; exec. v.p. Am. Media, Woodlands Hills, 2003—. Current advisor Calif. Gov.'s Coun. on Phys. Fitness and Sports; past chmn. bd. dirs. Am. Coun. on Exercise; mem. adv. bd. Fitness Cert. program U. Calif., LA; nat. women's wellness expert and presenter. Appearances on Oprah, Today Show, CNN, MSNBC, Access Hollywood, Entertainment Tonight. Achievements include climbing 20,000 foot mountain in the Bolivian Andes, Mt. Rainier and Mt Kilimanjaro. Avocations: running, weight training, kayaking, photography, rock climbing. Office: Am Media 21100 Erwin St Woodland Hills CA 91367-3712 Business E-Mail: bharris@weiderpub.com.

HARRIS, BETH A., lawyer; b. NYC, 1953; m. Duncan Harris; children: Jennifer, Andrew, Katherine. BA in Human Devel., U. Chgo., 1974; M in Psychology, U. Houston, 1978; JD, Northwestern U., 1980. Bar: 1980. Assoc. gen. counsel U. Chgo Hosps.; assoc. gen. coun. U. Chgo., 1995—2001, gen. counsel, v.p., 2001—. Bd. dirs. U. Chgo. Charter Sch. Bd. Pres. Hyde Park Sch. Ballet. Mem.: Chgo. Network. Office: U Chgo 5801 S Ellis Ave 503 Chicago IL 60637 Office Phone: 773-702-7243. Office Fax: 773-702-0934. E-mail: bharris@uchicago.edu.

HARRIS, BETTY JEAN, social sciences educator; d. Miles Harris and Ella Jessie Estill-Harris; children: Lynn Kathryn, Robert Michael. MA in Sociology, U. Ill., Chgo., 1972, MSW Jane Addams Sch. of Social Work, 1996. Prof. sociology Harold Wash. Coll./City Colls. Chgo., 1972—. Pres. bd. Third

Unitarian Ch., Chgo., 1991—2000. Recipient Disting. Prof., City Colls. Chgo. Mem.: Phi Delta Kappa (assoc.; pub. rels. 2001). Office: Harold Washington Coll 30 E Lake St Chicago IL 60601

HARRIS, BONNIE, psychological education specialist; b. Dayton, Ohio, Apr. 10, 1950; d. Joseph Boniface and Virginia May Myers; m. Gordon Harris, Oct. 17, 1978; children: Curtis, Hallie, Ashley. BS, Bowling Green State U., 1972, MS, 1974; postgrad., Wright State U., 1979, U. Dayton, 1974—76. cert. elem. edn, learning and behavior disorders. Tchr. Napoleon Schs., Ohio, 1972-74; psychol. edn. specialist Akron Child Guidance, Ohio, 1974-76; class therapist S. Cmty. MH, Dayton, 1976-78; psychol. edn. specialist Gordon A. Harris & Assocs., Dayton, 1978—. Spkr. numerous workshops. Mem. Councel Exceptional Children, Orton Dyslexic Soc. Home: 7320 Wastler Rd Clayton OH 45315-9777 Office: Gordon A Harris Assocs 5400 N Main St Dayton OH 45415-3453 E-mail: ionafarm@aol.com.

HARRIS, CARLA ANN, investment company executive; m. Victor Adrian Franklin, Aug. 11, 2001. BA in economics, Harvard U., 1984, MBA, 1987. Joined Morgan Stanley, NYC, 1987, mergers, acquisitions, and restructuring dept., 1987—91, joined equity capital markets dept., 1991, mng. dir. global capital markets, head equity pvt. placements and retail capital markets. Singer: (albums) Carla's First Christmas, 2000, Joy is Waiting, 2005. Funded Carla Harris Scholarship at Harvard U. and Bishop Kenny H.S., Jacksonville, Fla.; exec. bd. Food for Survival, NYC Food Bank, St. Charles Borromeo Cath. Sch., Sponsors for Ednl. Opportunities, A Better Chance Inc.; bd. dirs. Boy Scouts Am., Manhattan; bd. mem. Apollo theater. Named Most Powerful African Am., Fortune Mag.; recipient Bethune Award, Nat. Coun. Negro Women, Ron Brown Trailblazer Award, St. John's U. Sch. Law, Women of Distinction Award, Girl Scouts of Greater Essex and Hudson Counties, Frederick Douglass Award, NY Urban League, 2003. Office: Morgan Stanley 1585 Broadway New York NY 10036 Office Phone: 212-761-5375. Business E-Mail: carla.harris@morganstanley.com.*

HARRIS, CAROL LYNN, elementary school educator; b. Topeka, Dec. 14, 1952; d. Earl Rogers and Billie Lavonne (Mears) McLaughlin; m. Jerry Lee Harris, Nov. 25, 1972; children: Cari Lynn, Juston Lee, Casey Lane. AA, Claremore Jr. Coll., Okla., 1973; postgrad., Northeastern State Coll., Tahlequah, Okla., 1972—74; BA, U. Okla., Norman, 1988, MEd, 1993. Cert. tchr. Okla. Dir., tchr. Kindercare, Norman, 1980—88; tchr. Norman Pub. Schs., 1989—. Presenter in field. Named Tchr. of Yr., Whittier Mid. Sch., Norman, 1998—99. Mem.: Okla. Edn. Assn., Nat. Sci. Tchr. Assn., Order Ea. Star. Baptist. Avocations: genealogy, camping, fishing, reading. Office: Whittier Mid Sch 2000 W Brooks Norman OK 73169

HARRIS, CAROLE RUTH, education educator, researcher, consultant; b. N.Y.C., Nov. 29, 1933; d. Erwin and Fay (Fisher) Marks; m. Donald Schulkind, Jan. 23, 1955 (div. Oct. 1980, dec.); children: Laura Margaret, Heidi Elyse; m. John Nathaniel Harris, May 19, 1983. BA in English, Hunter Coll. CUNY, 1955; MA in English, Adelphi U., 1966; EdD in Gifted Edn., Columbia U., 1987; postgrad., SUNY, Stony Brook and Albany; postgrad. various specialized edn. studies, Empire State Coll., U. So. Calif. Los Angeles, U. Hawaii. Tchr. English N.Y.C. Pub. Schs., 1955-57; instr. dept. English Adelphi U., Garden City, N.Y., 1966-68; teaching asst. SUNY, Stonybrook, 1968-70, supr. elem. undergrad. student teaching, 1970-72; master tchr., cons. creative writing and humanities BOCES Inst. Gifted and Talented Youth, 1972-76; instr. gifted edn. U. Hawaii, Honolulu and Marshall Islands, 1977-81; prin. investigator Research Corp. of the Univ. of Hawaii, Marshall Islands, 1977-81; dir. Creatively Gifted Devel. Cons., Inc., Honolulu, 1981-83; researcher dept. spl. edn. Tchrs. Coll., Columbia U., N.Y.C., 1984-88; assoc. in edn., dept. of human devel. Harvard Grad. Sch. of Edn., Harvard U., Cambridge, Mass., 1989—; mem. faculty Sch. of Edn. grad. div. U. Mass., Lowell, 1990-99, also rsch. assoc.; prof. edn. Northeastern U., Boston, 1999—. Instr. English, Nassau C.C., 1973, gifted edn. Three-Village Schs., Setauket, N.Y., 1974; dir. Leadership Tng. Ctr., Marshall Islands, 1977-81; dir. pre-Kindergarden-Grade 8 program, Ebeye, Marshall Islands, 1984-85; fed. evaluator Magnet Schs. Lowell; mem. Nat. Task Force on the Culturally Different Gifted; dir. Gifted and Talented Edn. Svcs. Rsch. and Evaln.; spkr. in field; cons. in field. Contbr. articles to profl. jours.; author: (poetry) Mountain Image at Gruyere, 1976, other poems in lit. mags. and jours.; author: (with others) Worldwide Perspectives on Disadvantaged Gifted, 1993, Diversity in Gifted Education, 2005; (with Mervin Lynch) Fostering Creativity for Children K-8: Theory and Practice, 2000; (chpt.) Kaleidoscope, 1995, others; editor Proc. N.Y. NOW Conf. on Feminist Edn., 1973. Grantee Research Corp. U. Hawaii, 1977-81. Fellow Nat. Acad. Ednl. Rsch. (governing bd. 1997—); mem. APA, Council Exceptional Children (TAG div.), Nat. Assn. Gifted Children (chair subcom. Asian/Pacific populations. nat. task force on diversity, other coms., John C. Gowan award), Nat. Assn. Asian and Pacific Am. Edn., World Council Gifted and Talented Children (mem. gifted child internat. network), Am. Ednl. Rsch. Assn., Ea. Ednl. Rsch. Assn. (chmn. gifted), Assn. Advancement Ednl. Rsch. (dir. symposiums), Mass. Assn. Gifted Edn., Comparative and Internat. Edn. Soc., Kappa Delta Pi, Sigma Tau Delta. Jewish. Avocations: painting, crewel, hawaiian quilting, storytelling. Office: GATES Rsch and Evaluation PO Box 302 Winchester MA 01890-0302 Office Phone: 781-729-4283. Business E-Mail: harris@gates-edu.com.

HARRIS, CAROLYN LOUISE, librarian; b. Austin, Tex., Nov. 17, 1947; d. Elmer L. and Betty L. Hixson BA, U. Tex., 1969, M.L.S., 1970. Librarian Southwestern U., Georgetown, Tex., 1970-71; librarian United Services Automobile Assn., San Antonio, 1971-72; manuscript cataloger Humanities Research Ctr. U. Tex., Austin, 1973-80; asst dir. for preservation Columbia U. Libraries, N.Y.C., 1981—. Intern Council on Library Resources, 1984-85; cons. Assn. Research Libraries/Office Mgmt. Studies; mem. adv. bd. N.E. Document Conservation Ctr., 1983— Mem. ALA Office: Columbia Univ Libraries 535 W 114th St New York NY 10027-7035

HARRIS, CHRISTINE, dance company executive; b. Milw. Mktg. dir. Milw. Symphony Orch., 1984-90, head Arts in Cmty. Edn. program, 1990-95; with Inst. Music, Health and Edn., Mpls., 1996-97; exec. dir. Milw. Ballet, 1997—2002; pres. United Performing Arts Fund, 2002—. Office: United Performing Arts Fund 929 N Water St Milwaukee WI 53202

HARRIS, CORA LEE, science educator, small business owner; b. Huntsville, Ala., Apr. 26, 1939; d. Dnaiel and Orell (Draper) Barley; m. William Anderson Harris; children: William J., Coral A. BS, U. Memphis, 1969, MS, 1970; PhD, Goring Beauty Sch., 1999. Cosmetologist Goring Beauty Coll., Tenn., 1961; nailologist Mid-South Beauty Sch., Tenn., 1970; biology tchr. Memphis City Schs., 1967-84; owner Coral's Bazaar, Memphis, 1984—; biology and chemistry tchr. Shelby State C.C., 1993-96; biology tchr. Creigmont H.S., Memphis, 1999—. Mem. cosmetology bd. Hamilton H.S., Memphis; sci. fair coord. Memphis City Schs.; sales agt. Celebrity Fashion Gems; coord. trade shows, beauty pageants. Fashion editor Memphis City Newspaper; contbr. poetry to lit. publs. Bd. dirs. YWCA, Memphis, 1983; vol. food distbn. Dismas House, Memphis, 1989; judge city and state beauty pageants. Recipient Cert. of Appreciation, Sr. Svcs., 1996, Vol. Svc. award Girls Inc. Memphis, 1991, Cert. of Recognition Memphis Light Gas and Water Divsn., 1993; grantee Faith Brent U., 1999. Mem. NAACP (mem. Afro-Acad. cultural tech. sci. olympics 1979), Nat. Coalition of 100 Black Women (v.p.), Nat. Coun. Negro Women (fundraiser, social chair), Ladies of Distinction, Inc., Eta Phi Beta (pres.), Phi Delta Kappa, Delta Sigma Theta (social action chair, Delta of Yr. 1993, Cert. of Appreciation 1982). Democrat. Home: 4345 Hillbrook St Memphis TN 38109-5476 Office: Coral Bazaar 1515 Victor St Memphis TN 38106-5612

HARRIS, CRYSTAL STONE, science educator, coach; b. Flint, Mich., Aug. 30, 1962; d. Billy Gene and Rose Marie Stone; m. Robert Allen Harris; children: Jordan Shianne Brown, Madison Breanne. BSc, Appalachain State U., Boone, N.C., 1987. Cert. tchr. sci. grades 7-12 N.C., 1987. Tchr. sci., dept. chair Iredell- Statesville Sch., NC, 1987—. Achievements include discovery of an illegal dump in our community, leading to a county transfer station to be built. Office: Irsdell-Statesville Schs 303 Watermelon Rd Statesville NC 28625 Office Phone: 704-873-2887. Office Fax: 704-881-0581. Business E-Mail: csharris@iss.k12.ns.us.

HARRIS, CYNTHIA VIOLA, principal; b. San Francisco, Aug. 18, 1948; d. Gilbert and Mary Lee (barnes) H. BA in Speech, San Francisco State U., 1970, MA in Counseling, 1975; EdD, Nova U., 1987. Cert. tchr., adminstr., Calif. Tchr. Martin L. King Elem. Sch., Oakland, Calif., 1971-74; tchg. v.p. Peralta Yr. Round Sch., Oakland, 1974-80, prin., 1980-86, coord. staff devel., 1986-90, dir. staff devel., 1990-91, coord. recruitment, 1991—, asst. coord. to supt. cmty., parents, bus. ptnrships, 1992—; prin. Nystrom Magnet Sch., 2003—06; regional supt. Portland Pub. Sch., Oreg., 2006—. Mgmt. cons. year-round educ., leadership; guest lectr. Mills Coll., LaVerne U; coord. Community, Parents and Bus. Partnership; coord. coaches West Contra Costa Unified Sch. Dist., 2002-03; devel. dir. Help Other People Evolve; mem. Head Start commn. panel City of Oakland. Author: (tchg. manual) All About Us, 1980. Bd. dirs. Wiley Manuel Law Found., Charles Harrison Mason Scholarships; chair minority caucus New Oakland Com. Nominated Outstanding Woman of Am., Alpha Kappa Alpha, 1981; recipient Capwell's Networker award, 1985; named Outstanding Youth Leader, Nat. Bus. and Profl. Bd., 1981; named to Alameda Edn. Hall of Fame, 2001. Mem. Nat. Assn. Female Execs., Nat. Assn. Prins., Nat. Ch. of God in Christ Bus. and Profl. Women, United Adminstrs. Oakland, Alliance Black Educators, Black Summit (internat. enrollment mgr.), Glamor Working Women's Panel, Coalition of 100 Black Women, Phi Delta Kappa. Democrat. Mem. Pentacostal Ch. Home: The Merrick 1231 NE Martin Luther King Blvd #509 Portland OR 97232 E-mail: harriscynthiaharris@hotmail.com.

HARRIS, DALE HUTTER, retired judge; b. Lynchburg, Va., July 10, 1932; d. Quintus and Agnes (Adams) Hutter; m. Edward Richmond Harris Jr., July 24, 1954; children: Mary Fontaine, Frances Harris Russell, Jennifer Harris Haynie, Timothy Edward. BA, Sweet Briar Coll., 1953; MEd in Counseling and Guidance, Lynchburg Coll., 1970; JD, U. Va., 1978; LLD (hon.), Wilson Coll., 1988; LHD (hon.), Lynchburg Coll., 2002. Bar: Va. 1978, U.S. Dist. Ct. (we. dist.) Va. 1978, U.S. Ct. Appeals (4th cir.) 1978. Admissions asst. Sweet Briar Coll. (Va.), 1953-54; caseworker Winchester/Frederick Dept. Welfare, Va., 1954-55; vis. lectr. Lynchburg Coll., Va., 1971; assoc. Davies & Peters, Lynchburg, 1978-82; substitute judge 24th Dist. Gen. Dist., Juvenile and Domestic Rels. Dist. Ct., Va., 1980-82; judge Juvenile and Domestic Rels. Dist. Ct., Lynchburg, 1982—2003; ret., 2003. Judge Family Ct. Pilot Project, Va., 1990—91; lectr. law U. Va. Law Sch., 1986—98; pres. Va. Coun. Juvenile and Family Ct. Judges, 1994—96; mem. panel of experts and adv. com. Child Protection and Custody Resource Ctr., 1994—2001; mem. Commn. on Future of Va.'s Jud. Sys., 1987—89; mem. adv. bd. Hilton Project on Model State Laws about Family Violence. Vice chmn. bd. dirs. Sweet Briar Coll., 1976-86; vol. coord. vols. in probation with Juvenile and Domestic Ct., 1971-73; chmn. steering com. for establishment Youth Svc. Bur., Lynchburg, 1972-73; chmn. bd. dirs. Lynchburg Youth Svcs., 1973-75; mem. adv. bd. Juvenile Ct., 1957-60, 62-68, sec., 1966-68; bd. dirs. Family Svc. Lynchburg, 1967-69; Lynchburg Fine Arts Ctr., 1965-67, Seven Hills Sch., 1966-73, Greater Lynchburg United Fund, 1963-65, Lynchburg Assn. Mental Health, 1960-61, Miller Home, 1980-82, Lynchburg Gen.-Marshall Lodge Hosps., Inc., 1980-82; v.p. Lynchburg Mental Health Study Commn., 1966; bd. dirs. Lynchburg Sheltered Workshop for Mentally Retarded Young Adults, 1965-69; bd. dirs. Lynchburg Guidance Ctr., 1959-61, v.p., 1970, pres., 1961; bd. dirs. Hist. Rev. Bd. Lynchburg, 1978-82; adv. bd. study of effectiveness of civil protection orders Nat. Ctr. State Cts., 1994-97; chair Va. State Bar Access to Legal Svcs. com., 2006-. Mem.: ABA, Am. Prosecutors Rsch. Inst., Nat. Coun. Juvenile and Family Ct. Judges (mem. child custody edn. com. 1993—98, chair family violence commn. 1998—2000, trustee 1998—2001, chair custody com. 1999—2001), Lynchburg Bar Assn., Va. State Bar (bd. govs. criminal law sect. 1988—90, bd. govs. family law sect. 1989—91, chair access to legal svcs. spl. com. 2006—), Va. Bar Assn., Phi Beta Kappa.

HARRIS, DEANNA LYNN, special education educator, writer; b. Granite City, Ill., Feb. 25, 1948; d. Robert Eugene and Emma Lee Harris; m. George Thomas Aebel, May 6, 1967 (div. Apr. 28, 1983). BS, So. Ill. U., 1973, MS, 1986; degree, Inst. of Children's Lit., 1989. Cert. tchr. Madison County, Ill., 1973, Camden County, Mo., 1985. Adminstrv. sec. So. Ill. U., Edwardsville, Ill., 1966—69; elem. tchr. St. Boniface Sch., Edwardsville, 1973—77, Wolf Ridge Edn. Ctr., Bunker Hill, Ill., 1977—85; spl. edn. tchr. Camdenton R-III Sch. Dist., Mo., 1985—2006, ret., 2006; propr. Heron Ho. Pub. Co., Linn Creek, Mo., 1996—. Pvt. tutor, Camdenton, 1985—2006. Author: God's Gift, 1995 (Editor's Choice award The Nat. Libr. of Poetry, 1995), Taters of the Ozarks, The Feud, 1996, 101+ Tater Jokes, 1996, The Man, 1998; editor: (newsletter) Foxtales, 1986—88. Recipient English award, St. Elizabeth Sch., 1962, Presdl. Sports award, President's Coun. on Phys. Fitness, 1988, 1993, 1996; grantee, State of Ill., 1972—73; scholar, 1969—73. Master: Red Hat Soc. (queen mother 2003); mem.: Coun. for Exceptional Children (assoc.), Learning Disabilities Assn. (assoc.), Mo. State Tchrs. Assn. (assoc.), Nat. Honor Soc., Quill and Scroll Journalism, Holy Childhood Assn. Republican. Roman Catholic. Avocations: travel, gardening, water sports, pets, reading. E-mail: tatertown1996@yahoo.com.

HARRIS, DEBORAH A., psychotherapist, consultant; d. Robert Lee and Adele Harris; m. Jonathan W. Sims, 0000. BS in Psychology, Northwestern State U., Natchitoches, La., 1996; MS in Behavioral Sci. Psychology, Cameron U., 1998; MA in Counseling, Webster U., 2002; PhD in Psychology, Capella U., 2006. Clinically cert. behavior therapist Nat. Assn. Forensic Counselors, lic. profl. counselor I S.C. Exec. dir., founder Hopes for Higher Edn., Washington, 2001—, academic dean, 2006—. Clin. dir. Ramsey Youth Svcs., 2001—02; regional dir. Family Preservation Svcs., 2002—03. Mem. mayor's com. permanency for children, 2005; bd. dirs. New Pathways, 2006., Sallie Mae/ USA Group scholar, 2001—05. Mem.: APA, Alpha Kappa Alpha, Order Ea. Star, Psi Chi. Personal E-mail: dharris_aka@msn.com.

HARRIS, DEBORAH ANN, science educator; b. Jacksonville, Fla., Oct. 9, 1951; d. William Wendell and Rose Nell Neinast; m. John William Harris, Dec. 28, 1974; children: Andrew William, Brett Nelson. BS, Tex. Tech U., 1973. Registered microbiologist 1978, cert. tchr. 1995, mid. sch. sci. 2001. Quality control microbiologist Illes Co., Dallas, 1973—74; rsch. assoc. Baylor Coll. Medicine, Houston, 1975—84; tchr. Chapelwood Day Sch., Houston, 1989—95; tchr. sci. Houston Ind. Sch. Dist., 1995—2002, St. Francis Episc. Sch., Houston, 2002—. Mem. adv. bd. Academics Alive, Houston, 2001—. Chmn. sci. dept. St. Francis Episcopal Sch. Recipient Lawrence Scadden award, N.Mex. State U., 2002, Crystal award of Outstanding Tchg., Houston Chronicle, 2001. Mem.: NSTA, Am. Soc. Clin. Pathologists, Sci. for Students with Disabilities (adv. bd. 2002—), Am. Soc. Microbiologists. Methodist. Avocations: travel, reading. Office: St Francis Episc Day Sch 335 Piney Point Houston TX 77024 Office Phone: 713-458-6426.

HARRIS, DEBRA CORAL, physical education educator; b. Portland, Oreg., Feb. 4, 1953; d. Raymond Dale and Kathleen Caroline (Himpel) H. AA, Cen. Oreg. Community Coll., 1974; BS in Health and Phys. Edn., So. Oreg. State Coll., 1976, MST in Health Edn., 1982. Tchr. phys. edn., coach Franklin High Sch., Portland, 1976-79; instr. health, phys. edn., tennis coach Mt. Hood Community Coll., Gresham, Oreg., 1979-80; health and phys. edn. specialist, coach Inza R. Wood Middle Sch., Wilsonville, Oreg., 1980-86; tchr. health and phys. edn. West Linn (Oreg.)High Sch., 1986—. Mem. planning com. Seaside Health Conf., Oreg. Dept. Edn., 1985-87; writer AIDS curriculum, 1987-88; cons. health edn. textbooks Glenco Pub. Co., 1987-88. Mem. AIDS subcom. ARC, Portland, 1988-89, safety svcs. com. 1988—, sex edn. coalition com. Planned Parenthood, Portland, 1988-90, com. women's sport leadership network U. Oreg., Eugene, 1988—. Recipient Vol. of Month award ARC, 1984, Profl. Leadership award Oreg. Gov's. Coun. for Health Phys. Edn. Fitness & Sport, 1986, Outstanding Health/Phy. Edn. award Portland State U., 1988, Nat. High Sch. Physical Educator of the Year award, 1993. Mem. Am. Alliance Health, Phys. Edn., Recreation & Dance (nat. pub. affairs & legis. com. 1987—), Oreg. Alliance Health, Phys. Edn., Recreation & Dance (pres. 1984-85), Oreg. Assn. Advanced Health Edn. (pres. 1987-89), AAUW, Oreg. Edn. Assn. (uniserv treas. 1985-86), Kappa Delta Pi. Avocations: swimming, skiing, tennis, travel. Office: West Linn High Sch 5464 W A St West Linn OR 97068-3199

HARRIS, DIANA KOFFMAN, sociologist, educator; b. Memphis, Aug. 11, 1929; d. David Nathan and Helen Ethel (Rotter) Koffman; m. Lawrence A. Harris, June 24, 1951; children: Marla, Jennifer. Student, U. Miami, 1947-48; BS, U. Wis., 1951; postgrad., U. Oxford, Eng., 1968-69. Advt. and sales promotion mgr. Wallace Johnston Distbg. Co., Memphis, 1952-54; welfare worker Tenn. Dept. Pub. Welfare, Knoxville, Tenn., 1954-56; instr. sociology Maryville (Tenn.) Coll., 1972-75, Fort Sanders Sch. Nursing, Knoxville, 1971-78, U. Tenn., Knoxville, 1967—; series editor Garland Pub., Inc., 1989—. Author: Readings in Social Gerontology, 1975; author: (with Cole) The Elderly in America, 1977; author: The Sociology of Aging, 1980, 2d edit., 1990; co-author: Sociology, 1984, Annotated Bibliography and Sourcebook: Sociology of Aging, 1985, Dictionary of Gerontology, 1988, Teaching Sociology of Aging, 1991, 4th edit., 1996, 5th edit., 2000, Maltreatment of Patients in Nursing Homes: There Is No Safe Place, 2006; co-editor: Encyclopedia of Ageism, 2005; aging series editor Garland Pub., Inc., 1989—; contbr. articles to profl. jours. Chmn. U. Tenn. Coun. on Aging, 1979—; organizer Knoxville chpt. Gray Panthers, 1978; mem. Govnr.'s Task Force on Preretirement Programs for State Employers, 1973, White Ho. Conf. on Aging, 1981; bd. mem. Knoxville-Knox County Coun. on Aging, 1976, Sr. Citizens Info. and Referral, 1979, Sr. Citizens Home-Aide Svc., 1977; del. E. Tenn. Coun. on Aging, 1977. Recipient Meritorious award Nat. U. Continuing Edn. Assn., 1982, Pub. Svc. award Nat. Alumni Assn., 1992, Appreciation award Assn. Gerontology in Higher Edn., 1994, Appreciation award for excellent scholarly contbn. to ednl. gerontology lit. Ednl. Gerontology jour., 1996; grantee Retirement Rsch. Found., 1997—. Mem. Am. Sociol. Assn., AAAS, Gerontol. Soc. Am., Popular Culture Assn., So. Sociol. Soc., So. Gerontol. Soc. (pres.'s award 1984), N. Central Sociol. Assn., London Competitor's Club, Nat. Contest Assn., Knoxville Kontestars. Home and Office: U Tenn Dept Sociology PO Box 50546 Knoxville TN 37950-0546 Business E-Mail: dharris@utk.edu.

HARRIS, DIANE CAROL, merger and acquisition consulting firm executive; b. Rockville Centre, NY, Dec. 25, 1942; d. Daniel Christopher and Laura Louise (Schmitt) Quigley; m. Wayne Manley Harris, Sept. 30, 1978. BA, Cath. U. Am., 1964; MS, Rensselaer Poly. Inst., 1967. With Bausch & Lomb, Rochester, NY, 1967-96, dir. applications lab., 1972-74, dir. tech. mktg. analytical systems divsn., 1974-76, bus. line mgr., 1976-77, v.p. planning and bus. programs, 1977-78, v.p. planning and bus. devel. Soflens divsn., 1978-80, corp. dir. planning, 1980-81, v.p. corp. devel., 1981-96; v.p. RID-N.Y. State, 1980-83; pres. Hypotenuse Enterprises, Inc., 1994—. Mem. adv. bd. Merger Mgmt. Report, 1986—92; internat. bd. dirs. Assn. Corp. Growth, v.p. corp. mem. affairs, 1993—94, v.p. internat. expansion, 1994—95, pres.-elect, 1996—97, pres., 1997—98, immediate past pres., 1998—99; bd. dirs. Flowserve Corp., chmn. audit com., 2001—04, mem. fin. com., 2004—; bd. dirs. Monroe Fund, Venture Capital Group. Contbr. articles to profl jours. Pres Rochester Against Intoxicated Driving, 1979—83, chmn polit action comt, 1983, 1986; bd dirs, chmn long range planning comt Rochester area Nat Coun Alcoholism, 1980—84; mem Stop DWI Adv Panel to Monroe County Legis, 1982—87, NY State Coalition for Safety Belt Use, 1984—85; mem. key exec. group Rensselaer Poly. Inst., 1993—96; mem. Com. 200, 1993—2002; mem ACG Speakers Bur, 1993—; mem adv comt Catalyst, 1995; bd dirs Rochester Rehab Ctr, 1982—84, Friends of Bristol Valley Playhouse Found, 1983—87. Named one of 50 Women to Watch in Corp Am, Bus Week Mag, 1987, 1992, 100 Women to Watch, Duns Bus Rev, 1988; recipient Distinguished Citizen's Award, Monroe County, 1979, Tribute to Women in Indust and Serv Award, YWCA, 1983, Pres's 21st Century Leadership Award, Women's Hall of Fame, 1995; grantee NSF, 1963. Mem.: Assn. Corp. Growth (Meritorious Svc. award 1995), Internat. Alliance Com. and Rochester Women's Network (com. of 200 1993—2002), Nat. Assn. Women Bus. Owners, Fin. Execs. Inst., Am. Mgmt. Assn., C. of C. (pub safety com. Rochester area chpt, task force on hwy. safety 1981—86, High Tech. Rochester adv. panel 1989—91, 1999—2000), Phi Beta Kappa, Delta Epsilon Sigma, Sigma Xi. Home: 60 Mendon Center Rd Honeoye Falls NY 14472-9363 Office: Hypotenuse Enterprises Inc 1545 East Ave Rochester NY 14610-1614 Office Phone: 585-473-7799. E-mail: harris@hypot.com.

HARRIS, DOLORES M., retired academic administrator, adult education educator; b. Camden, NJ, Aug. 5, 1930; d. Roland Henry, Sr. and Frances Anna (Gatewood) Ellis; m. Morris E. Harris, Sr., 1948 (div. 1987); children: Morris E. Jr., Sheila Davis, Gregory M. Sr. BS, Glassboro (NJ) State Coll., 1959, MA, 1966; EdD, Rutgers U., 1983. Tchr., reading specialist Glassboro Bd. Edn., 1958-68, dir. aux. svcs., 1968-70; supr. adult edn. Camden Welfare Bd., summer 1968; Head Start dir. Glassboro SCOPE, summer 1969-70; assoc. dir. Jersey City State Coll., summer 1971; dir. adult edn. Glassboro State Coll., 1970-74, dir. continuing edn. dept., 1989-90, acting assoc. v.p. acad. affairs, 1989-91; ret., 1991. Cons. Mich. State Dept. Edn., Lansing, 1973; examiner N.Y. State Civil Svc. Commn., 1976—; chmn. adv. bd. Women's Ednl. Equity Comm. Network Project, San Francisco, 1977—78; cons. crossroads project Temple U., Phila., 1977; bd. dirs. Glassboro State Coll. Mgmt. Inst.; cons. corrections project Va. Commonwealth U., Richmond; vice-chmn. comm. Accrediting Coun. Continuing Edn. and Tng., Richmond, 1985—89, chmn., 1989—. Author: (book) How to Establish ABE Programs, 1972; author: (with others) Black Studies for ABE and GED Programs in Correction, 1975; founding editor: newsletter For Adults Only, 1970; contbr. articles to profl. jours. Founder, trustee, chair bd. trustees Glassboro Child Devel. Ctr., 1974—87; bd. dirs. Gloucester County United Way, NJ, 1977—, sec. bd. dirs. NJ, 1980, pres. bd. dirs. NJ, 1983—85; charter mem., bd. dirs. Glassboro Glass Mus., 1979—87; vice chair, chair, mem. Gloucester County Commn. Women, NJ, 1983—87; trustee Frederick Douglas Meml. and Hist. Assn., 2000—. Named Woman of the Yr., Gloucester County Bus. and Profl. Women's Club, 1985, Woman of Achievement, Gloucester County Commn. Women, 1987, Counselor of Yr., Svc. Corps Ret. Execs., 2003; named one of Outstanding Citizens, Holly Shores Girl Scouts U.S., 1987, 100 Most Influential Black Ams., Ebony Mag., 1989—92; named to Legion of Honor, Chapel of Four Chaplains, 1983; recipient Disting. Alumnae award, Glassboro State Coll., 1971, Disting. Svc. award, Camden County, 1974, Holly Shores Girl Scouts U.S., 1979, N.J. Woman of Achievement award, 1991. Mem.: AAUW (v.p. membership com. Gloucester County chpt. 1986—87), NEA, Ea. Montgomery County Svc. Corps Ret. Execs. (chair seminars, workshop programs 2001—, Counselor of Yr. 2003), NJ Edn. Assn., Women Greater Phila. (bd. dirs.), Soc. Docta (bd. dirs. 1987—), N.J. Adult Edn. Assn. (life; pres. 1973—74), South Jersey Links Club (v.p. 1982—84, pres. 1984—86), Links Club, Nat. Assn. Colored Women's Clubs, Inc. (pres. 1988—92), Northeastern Fedn. Women's Clubs (v.p.-at-large 1983—85, parliamentarian 1985—), NJ State Fedn. Colored Women's Clubs (pres. 1976—80). Presbyterian. Avocations: reading, fitness exercises.

HARRIS, DOROTHY D., residential treatment therapist; d. Vernell R.L. and Desiree L. Harris. BA magna cum laude, Cardinal Stritch U., 2001; MA, Marquette U., 2004. Bd. eligible cert. nat. counselor Nat. Cert. Counselors Assn. Paralegal Bankruptcy Law Office of Richard A. Check, Milw., 1998—2004; intern Audobon Mid. Sch., Milw., 2000; lead therapist Wis. Early Autism Project, Wauwatosa, 2000—01; grad. intern AIDS Resource Ctr., Milw., 2003—04; residential treatment therapist Lad Lake, Inc., Dousman, 2004—. Recipient Multicultural Image award, Cardinal Stritch award, 2000. Fellow: Delta Epsilon Sigma. Avocations: bowling, reading, exercise, horseback riding. Office: Lad Lake Inc PO Box 158 Dousman WI 53118

HARRIS, ELAINE K., medical consultant; b. N.Y.C., Mar. 17, 1924; d. Julius and Bertha (Wecker) Kirschbuam; m. Herbert Harris, Aug. 1, 1948; children: Gail, Linda, Geoffrey. AB Bus. Economics cum laude, Hunter Coll.; AM Bus. Edn., Columbia U. Lic. tchr. bus. NY. Founder, pres. Sjogren's Syndrome Found., 1983-91, exec. dir., 1991-94. Cons. in field; v.p. exec. bd.

Nat. Alliance for Oral Health; developer Sjogren's Syndrome Ednl. Symposia for lay and profls., nat. and internat. support group network. Editor: Moisture Seekers Newsletter, 1984-94, Sjogren's Syndrome Handbook: An Authoritative Guide for Patients, 1989; editor: The New Sjogren's Syndrome Handbook, 1998; contbg. author: Sjogren's Syndrome: Clinical and Immunologic Aspects, 1987, Self-Help, Concepts and Applications, 1992; contbr. articles to profl. jours. Founded Nassau-Suffolk Chpt. Hunter Coll. Alumni Assn., 1949; past treas. Youth Employment Svc., Great Neck (N.Y.) Pub. Schs., former chair Broader Horizons Com., PTA, Great Neck Pub. Sch., others; active Jewish communal field. Recipient Women's Living Legacy, Women's Internat. Ctr., 1994, Third Internat. Conf. on Sjogren's Syndrome, Greece, 1991; elected to Hunter Coll. Hall of Fame, 1989. Mem. Pi Lambda Theta. Avocations: gardening, baking, photography, duplicate bridge. Personal E-mail: elaine.hh@verizon.net.

HARRIS, ELLEN GANDY (MRS. J. RAMSAY HARRIS), civic worker; b. Spokane, Wash., Jan. 9, 1910; d. Lloyd Edward and Helen (George) Gandy; m. J. Ramsay Harris, Jan. 20, 1936; children: Sue Ellen, Hayden Henry. Student, U. Wash.; grad., Smith Coll., 1930. Mem. U.S. com. UNICEF, 1948-66; mem. Def. Adv. Com. Women in Service, 1951-54; nat. co-chmn. Citizens for Eisenhower, 1953-54; Republican candidate U.S. Congress from Denver, 1954; mem. Internat. Devel. Adv. Bd., 1955- 57; nat. co. chmn. Com. Internat. Econ. Growth, 1958-60; regional chmn. Met. Opera Council, 1958-66; mem. Gov. Colo.'s Local Affairs Commn., 1963-66; pres. Colo. Consumers Council, 1965-67; dir. Nat. Safety Council, 1958-60; mem. Nat. Adv. Council on Nurse Tng., HEW, 1969-73; pres. The Park People, 1975-79. Mem. Gov.'s Commn. on Status Women, 1970-75 Trustee 4 Mile Historic Park, The Park People. Mem. Assn. Jr. Leagues Am. (bd. dirs. 1947-50), Colonial Dames Am. Episcopalian.

HARRIS, EMILY LOUISE, special education educator; b. New London, Conn., Nov. 16, 1932; d. Frank Sr. and Tanzatter (McCleese) Brown; m. John Everett Harris Sr., Sept. 10, 1955; children: John Everett Jr., Jocelyn E. (dec.). BS, U. Conn., 1955; MEd, Northeastern U., 1969. Cert. tchr. elem. spl. subject sci., Mass., spl. subject reading, secondary prin., elem. prin. Tchr. New Haven Sch. Dept., 1957-59, Boston Sch. Dept., 1966-68, Natick (Mass.) Sch. Dept., 1969-72; cert. nurse's asst. The Hebrew Rehab. Ctr., Roslindale, Mass., 1973-75; spl. edn. educator Boston Sch. Dept., 1975-76, 78—, support tchr., 1976-78. Site coord. Tchr. Corps., 1977-81; leader, co-leader Harvard U. Student Tchrs. at Dorchester H.S. Sem., 1995—; tchr. adviser Future Educators Am. Dorchester H.S. Editor, compiler: Cooking With the Stars, 1989. Mem.-del. Mass. Fedn. Tchrs., Boston, 1993-96; elected rep. AFL-CIO (Boston Tchrs. Union), 1986-96; registrar of voters Dorchester (Mass.) H.S., 1986—; adv. bd. New England Assn. Schs. and Colls., 1980-93; 1st v.p., bd. dirs. League of Women for Comty. Svcs., Boston, 1976-80, Cynthia Sickle-Cell Anemia Fund, Boston, 1976-80. Recipient Tchg. award Urban League Guild Mass., 1993. Mem. AAUW, Zeta Phi Beta (Zeta of Yr. 1994), Alpha Delta Kappa, Kappa Delta Pi, Order Ea. Star (past worthy matron Prince Hall chpt. 1983-84), Delta Omicron Zeta, Phi Delta Kappa. Baptist. Avocations: reading, sewing. Home: 36 Dietz Rd Hyde Park MA 02136-1134

HARRIS, EMMYLOU, singer; b. Birmingham, Ala., Apr. 2, 1947; d. Walter and Eugenia; children: Hallie, Meghann. Student, U.N.C.-Greensboro. Singer, 1967; assisted Gram Parsons on album GP, Grievous Angel, 1973; toured with Fallen Angels Band, performed across Europe and U.S.; recording artist on albums for Reprise Records, Warner Bros. Records., Electra/Asylum Records; appeared in rock documentary The Last Waltz, 1978; albums include The Gliding Bird, 1969, Pieces of the Sky, 1975, Elite Hotel, 1976 (Grammy award), Luxury Liner, 1977, Quarter Moon In A Ten Cent Town, 1978, Profile: Best of Emmylou Harris, 1978, Blue Kentucky Girl, 1979, Light of the Stable, 1979, Evangeline, 1981, Last Date, 1982, White Shoes, 1983, Profile II: Best of Emmylou Harris, 1984, The Ballad of Sally Rose, 1985, Thirteen, 1986, Trio (with Dolly Parton, Linda Ronstadt), 1987 (Grammy award), Angel Band, 1987, Bluebird, 1988, Duets, 1990, Cowgirl's Prayer, 1993, Songs Of The West, 1994, Wrecking Ball, 1995 (Grammy award 1996), Spyboy, 1998, The Horse Whisperer, 1998, Singin' with Emmy Lou Harris, Vol. 1, 2000, Vol. 2, 2003, Red Dirt Girl, 2000, Anthology: The Warner-Reprise Years, 2001, Nobody's Darling But Mine, 2002, Stumble Into Grace, 2003, The Very Best of Emmylou Harris: Heartaches & Highways, 2005 (Grammy award 2006 for The Connection); co-writer, co-prodr.: (with Paul Kennerley) The Ballad of Sally Rose, 185. Pres. Country Music Found., 1983. Recipient of 12 Grammy awards, 1979, 80, 81, 84, 87, 92, 96, 98, 99, 2000, 2001, 2006, Orville H. Gibson Lifetime Achievement award, 1996, Patrick J. Leahy Humanitarian award-Americana Music awards Lifetime Achievement Performer, 2002; named Female Vocalist of Yr., Country Music Assn., 1980; co-recipient (with Dolly Parton and Linda Ronstadt) Album of Yr. award Acad. Country Music, 1987; named to Ala. Music Hall of Fame, 2003. Office: Vector Management 1607 17th Ave S Nashville TN 37212-2875

HARRIS, GAYLE ELIZABETH, bishop; b. Cleve., Feb. 12, 1951; m. Peter W. Peters; 3 children. BA in history, Lewis and Clark Coll., Portland, 1978; MDiv, Ch. Div. Sch. of the Pacific, Berkeley, Calif., 1981. Ordained deacon, 1981, priest, 1982; priest-in-charge Holy Communion Ch., Washington, 1984—92; rector St. Luke and Simon Cyrene, Rochester, NY, 1992—2002; consecrated bishop, 2003; bishop suffragen Episcopal Diocese of Mass., Boston, 2003—. Episcopalian. Office: Episcopal Diocese of Mass 138 Tremont St Boston MA 02111

HARRIS, GRACE E., academic administrator; BS with highest honors, Hampton Inst., 1954; postgrad., Boston U., 1954-55; MA, U. Va., 1974, PhD, 1975; DHL (hon.), Va. Union U., 1995. Caseworker Dept. Pub. Welfare, Hampton, Va., 1955-57; caseworker, supr. Va. Dept. Welfare and Instns., Richmond, Va., 1957-63; exec. dir. Friends' Assn. Children, Richmond, Va., 1963-66; asst. dir. Richmond Cmty. Action Program, 1966-67; asst. prof. sch. social work Va. Commonwealth U., Richmond, 1967-76, dir. student affairs, 1975-76, assoc. prof. sch. social work, 1976-80, assoc. dean sch. social work, 1978-90, prof. sch. social work, 1981-90, dean sch. social work, 1982-90, vice provost continuing studies & pub. svc., 1990-93, provost, v.p. acad. affairs, 1993—, acting pres., 1995, 98. Bd. dirs. Richfood Holdings, Inc.; bd. trustees U. Richmond, 1992—; cons., presenter in field. Mem., trustee Coun. United Way Svcs., 1998, bd. dirs., 1982-89, 90-93; dir. Ctrl. Va. Ednl. Telecomm. Corp., 1997—, trustee World Affairs Coun. Greater Richmond, 1997—; mem. Richmond City Charter Commn., 1995, Richmond Cmty. Criminal Justice Bd., 1995—; bd. dirs. Christian Children's Fund, Inc.; vice chmn. State Bd. Family and Children's Trust Fund; mem. adv. com. spl. edn. Richmond Pub. Schs., 1981-86; mem. adv. bd. health professions Va. Union U., 1979-83; bd. dirs. Met. YMCA, 1979-82; mem. search com. Asst. City Mgr. Human Resources, 1979; mem. adv. bd. State Divsn. Volunteerism, 1979-83; Va. del. Rosalynn Carter's Cmtys. Plan Employment, 1978; bd. dirs. Womens Bank, 1976-84; active Cmty. Mental Health and Mental Retardation Svcs. Bd., 1976-82, chair, 1979; mem. task force Devel. Sch. Gifted/Disadvantaged Children, 1976; mem. com. Richmomd Area Cmty. Coun., 1972-73, day care com., 1971-72; client involvement com. State Dept. Weldare and Instns., 1971-72; bd. dirs. Young Women's Christian Assn., 1970-74; mem. adv. com. Richmond Redevel. & Housong Authority, 1967-69; bd. dirs. St. Gerard's Maternity Home, 1963-66. Recipient Alumna of Yr. award, Va. Comopnwealth U., 1989, Educator of Yr. award, Nat. Coalition 100 Black Women, 1990, Flame Bearer Edn. award, United Negro Coll. Fund, 1995, Va. Power Strong Men and Women Excellence in Leadership award, 1997, Coun. Va. Mus. Fine Arts Va. Women Style and Substance award, 1998, Presdl. award Cmty. Multicultural Enrichment and Riese-Melton award, Va. Commonwealth U., 1999; United Negro Coll. Fund fellow, Boston U., 1954-55, Phelps Stokes fellow U. Va., 1972-74, Ford Found. fellow, 1972-74, Am. Coun. Edn. fellow Am. Adminstrn. Va Commonwealth U., 1980-81; Va. Dept. Pub. Welfare grad. scholar, 1959-60. Mem. NASW (Knee/Whitman award 1991), Nat. Acads. Practice, Coun. Social Work Edn., Lychnos Hon. Soc., The Forum Club, Phi Beta Sigma, Alpha Kappa Mu. Office: Va Commonwealth U 901 W Franklin St PO Box 842527 Richmond VA 23284-2527

HARRIS, HARRIET, actress; b. Ft. Worth, Jan. 8, 1955; Grad., Juilliard. Actor: (TV series) The Five Mrs. Buchanans, 1994, Union Square, 1997—98, Stark Raving Mad, 1999, The Beast, 2001, It's All Relative, 2003, Desperate Housewives, 2005; (plays) Hamlet, 1986—, Four Baboons Adoring the Sun, 1992, Jeffrey, 1993—, The Man Who Came to Dinner, 2000, The Dining Room, 2005, (Broadway musical) Thoroughly Modern Millie, 2002— (Tony award, 2002); (films) Memento, 2000, Nurse Betty, 2000.

HARRIS, HAZEL LYNN, medical/surgical nurse; b. Taylor, Tex., Apr. 29, 1953; d. L.B. Clark, Doris Evelyn Clark; m. James Paul Harris; 1 child, Jonathan. BSN, Tex. Woman's U., 1974. RN Tex., cert. orthopedic nurse. Student nurse Parkland Health & Hosp. Sys., Dallas, 1973—74, staff nurse, 1974—80, unit mgr., 1982—. Clin. instr. Am. Tng. Ctr., Dallas, 1988—90; mem. nursing peer rev. Parkland Health & Hosp. Sys., Dallas, 1999—99. Contbr. Book Decision Making in Medical / Surgical Nursing, 1990. Polit. action com. Am. Heart Assn., Dallas, 2000—03. Finalist Tex. Nurses Excellence award Cmty. Svc., Nurseweek, 2000; named one of Great 100 Nurses, Dallas/Ft. Worth Hosp. Coun. and Dists. Three and Four of Tex. Nurses Assn., 1998. Mem.: ANA, Tex. Nurses Assn., Nat. Assn. Orthopedic Nurses (treas. Dallas chpt. 1982—90), Nat. Coun. Negro Women (life; rec. sec. Greater Trinity sect. 1999—2003), Chi Eta Phi Sorority- Xi Phi Chapter (Tamiochus 2001—03, Basileus 2003). Methodist. Avocations: shopping, travel, walking. Home: 5606 Shady Crest Trail Dallas TX 75241-1803 Office: Parkland Health & Hosp Sys 5201 Harry Hines Blvd Dallas TX 75235 Home Fax: 214-374-0823. Personal E-mail: hazelharrisrn@aol.com. Business E-Mail: hlharr@parknet.pmh.org.

HARRIS, JACQUELINE MYERS, speech pathology/audiology services professional; b. Phila., Oct. 22, 1949; d. Murray Irving Myers and Gladys Markovitch; m. Joseph Steven Harris, Dec. 31, 1994. BA, L.I. U., 1971; postgrad., U. South Fla., 1973—75, Nova U., 1980—81. Cert. speech/lang. therapy Fla., hearing correction Fla. Sec. Sch. Adv. Bd., Hollywood, Fla., 1995—97; lead speech pathologist Hollywood Hills Speech Zone, 2002—06; peer rev. mem. So. Assn. Colls. and Schs., Fla., 2003—05; founder Children Helping Children food drive Broward City Schs., 1993—94, founder Student Ct. for Elem. Schs., 1997—98, founder Hard Bound Book Program for Speech/Lang. Students, 2001—04. Co-author: Manual for Conflict Mediation in the Elementary Schools, 1992—93, The Slide Therapy Technique for Fluency, 2005; author: If I Could Change the World, 1998, I'll Love You Forever Today, 2005. Founding mem. bd. dirs. Maestro Broward Philharmonic, Ft. Lauderdale, Fla., 1992—93; com. mem. Winterfest, Ft. Lauderdale, 1993—95; active Haddasah, Davie, Fla., 1994—2004; vol. Boca Raton (Fla.) Mus. Art, 2003—. Mem.: Broward Tchrs. Union, Am. Found. Suicide Prvention (bd. mem. 2001—). Avocations: dance, art, music, charitable projects. Office: Stoneman Douglas HS 5901 Pine Island Rd Parkland FL 33076 Office Phone: 754-321-3400. Business E-Mail: jacqueline.harris@browardschools.com.

HARRIS, JENNY LOU, elementary school counselor; b. Washington, Sept. 29, 1948; d. James Stockley and Jennie Mae (Lewis) Williams; m. David Jonathan Harris, June 3, 1972 (div.); children: David Jeremy, Jami Danielle. BA, Ottawa U., Kans., 1970; MEd, Northeastern State U., Tahalequah, Okla., 1990; EdD in Tchr. Leadership, Walden U., 2006. Cert. elem. tchr., counseling in elem. edn., Okla. Respiratory technician Washington Hosp. Ctr., 1971-72; office mgr. Moton Health Ctr., Tulsa, 1976-77; sch. sec. Tulsa Pub. Schs., 1981-86, elem. tchr., 1986-90, elem. sch. counselor, 1990-97, mem. polit. action com., 1986—, mid. sch. counselor, 1995—. Adj. instr. Langston U., S.W. CC, 2000-04; conductor presentations and workshops in Tulsa Pub. Schs., Phi Delta Kappa, Inc. Usher bd., sec. nat. renewal project, bd. Christian edn., missionary soc., Mt. Olive C.M.E. Ch., Memphis. Mem. NEA, AACD, NAACP, West Tenn. Counseling Assn., West Tenn. Reading Assn., Okla. Assn. Counseling and Devel., Okla. Edn. Assn., Tulsa Assn. Counseling and Devel., Am. Multicultural Counseling Assn., Am. Sch. Counselors Assn., Tenn. Counseling Assn., Tenn. Multicultural Counseling Assn. (pres.-elect), Jack 'n Jill Clubs Am., Urban League Guild, Alpha Kappa Alpha, Phi Delta Kappa (African-Am. Male Coalition, sponsor Kudo Youth Group). Avocations: reading, bowling, swimming, tutoring. Home: 6983 Cobbleston Dr Memphis TN 38125 Office Phone: 901-416-3189. Personal E-mail: jennyharris@bellsouth.net.

HARRIS, JEWELL BACHTLER, social worker; b. Aug. 30, 1948; BA, Skidmore Coll., 1970; MSW, Simmons Sch. Social Work, 1973; D Social Work, U. Ala., 1990. LCSW Idaho, 1991. Psychiat. social worker Philbrook Ctr. for C&Y Svcs., Concord, NH, 1973—78, Cmty. Coun. Nashua, NH, 1978—79, dir. C&Y Svcs., 1979—84, 1987—90; social work cons. Rolfe and Rumford Home, Concord, 1974—81; social worker Pierre O. Durand, M.D., P.A., Bedford, NH, 1990—91, Family and Children's Mental Health Svcs., Pocatello, Idaho, 1991—93, pvt. practice, Pocatello, 1993—; clin. supr., clin. social worker Valley Med. Shoppe, Pocatello, 2001—03; adj. prof. social work Idaho State U., Pocatello, 2003—04, vis. faculty social work, 2004—06. Mem. N.H. Project on the Health Care of Foster Children, Manchester, 1988—90, N.H. divsn. Mental Health Task Force Mental Health of Children, Concord, 1977—84; sec. Pocatello Human Rels. Adv. Com., 2005—; Bd. dirs. Big Bros./Big Sisters, Nashua, 1988—91, sec., 1991. Scholarship Simmons Coll. Sch. Social Work, 1971-73 Mem. NASW, Acad. Cert. Social Workers (diplomate), Nat. Alliance Mentally Ill, Internat. Dyslexia Soc

HARRIS, JOAN WHITE, foundation administrator; b. Mar. 9, 1931; d. Louis and Martha (Rahm) White; m. Gerald Baumann Frank, Feb. 12, 1953 (div. 1974); children: Daniel Bruce, Jonathan White, Louise Blodgett; m. Irving Brooks Harris, June 19, 1974. BA, Smith Coll., 1952; degree (hon.), Knox Coll., 1996, U. Ill., Chgo., 2001, Erikson Inst., 2002. Editl. asst. Oxford U. Press, N.Y.C., 1952-53, Ency. Brit., Chgo., 1953-54; TV prodr. Chgo., 1976, 1978, 1980; pres. Chgo. Opera Theater, 1977—84, chair, 1984—87; trustee Harris Found., Chgo., 1976—. Panelist and cons. NEA, 1980—85; chair nat. bd. Aspen Music Festival, Colo., 1998—2002, chair bd. trustees, 2002—05, trustee, 1990—; mem. adv. bd. U.S. China Arts Exch., 1985—93. Bd. dir./trustee Mus. Contemporary Art, Chgo., 1976-2000, vice chmn., 1989-97, Hampshire Coll., Amherst, Mass., 1977-84, Chgo. Symphony Orch., 1978—, Nat. Inst. Music Theater, Washington, 1982-87, Ind. Sector, Washington, 1983-89; pres. Ill. Art Alliance, 1990-97, Chgo. Music and Dance Theater, 1992—, chmn., 2004—; trustee Columbia Coll., 1994-2002; bd. dir. Ill. Ctr. Book, 1990-94, Northwestern Program Performing Artists, 1986-90, Am. Coun. Arts, 1990-96, Nat. Cultural Alliance, 1991-96, Sculpture Chgo., 1991-96, Chgo. Inst. Architecture & Urbanism, 1992-94; commr. cultural affairs City of Chgo., 1987-89, Nat. Pub. Radio, 1991-97, Young Women's Leadership Sch. of Chgo., 1999—; mem. People American Way, 2000-, Am. Friends, Israel Philharm. Orch., 1993-2005. Home and Office: 191 N Wacker Dr 1500 Chicago IL 60606

HARRIS, JUDITH E., lawyer; b. Apr. 28, 1945; AB, Mount Holyoke Coll., 1967; JD, Howard U., 1970. Bar: Pa. 1971. City solicitor City of Phila., 1992-93; ptnr. Morgan, Lewis & Bockius LLP, Phila. Office: Morgan Lewis & Bockius LLP 1701 Market St Philadelphia PA 19103-2903 Office Phone: 215-963-5028. Business E-Mail: jeharris@morganlewis.com.

HARRIS, JULIE (JULIE ANN HARRIS), actress; b. Grosse Pointe Park, Mich., Dec. 2, 1925; d. William Pickett and Elsie (Smith) Harris; m. Jay I. Julien, Aug. 12, 1946 (div. 1954); m. Manning Gurian, Oct. 21, 1954 (div. 1967); 1 child, Peter; m. Erwin Carroll, Apr. 26, 1977 (div. 1982). Student, Perry Mansfield Theatre Work Shop, 1941-43, Yale Drama Sch., 1944-45. Theater debut in It's a Gift, N.Y.C., 1945; appeared in plays Playboy of the Western World, 1946, Oedipus, 1946, Henry IV-Part II, 1946, Alice in Wonderland, 1947, We Love A Lassie, 1947, Macbeth, 1948, Sundown Beach, 1948 (Theatre World award 1949), The Young and Fair, 1948-49, Magnolia Alley, 1949, Montserrat, 1949, The Member of the Wedding, 1950-51 (Donaldson award 1950), I Am a Camera, 1951-52 (Tony award 1952, Donaldson award 1952, Variety-N.Y. Drama Critics Poll 1952), Mademoiselle Colombe, 1954, The Lark, 1955 (Tony award 1956), The Country Wife, 1957, The Warm Peninsula, 1959, Little Moon of Alban, 1960, Romeo and Juliet, 1960, King John, 1960, A Shot in the Dark, 1961, Marathon 33, 1964 (Tony nomination 1964), Hamlet, 1964, Ready When You Are, C.B, 1964, The Hostage, 1965, Skyscraper, 1965 (Tony nomination 1969), A Streetcar Named Desire, 1967, Forty Carats, 1968 (Tony award 1969, Antoinette Perry award for best actress), The Women, 1970, And Miss Reardon Drinks A Little, 1971-72, Voices, 1972, The Last of Mrs. Lincoln, 1972 (Tony award 1973, Antoinette Perry award for best actress), The Au Pair Man, 1973 (Tony nomination 1974), In Praise of Love, 1974, Break a Leg, 1979, On Golden Pond, 1980, Mixed Couples, 1980, Under the Ilex, 1983, Tusitala, 1988, (nat. co.) Driving Miss Daisy, Love Letters, 1989, The Belle of Amherst, 1977 (Grammy award 1977, Tony award 1977), Currier Bell, Glass Menagerie, 1994, Ellen Foster, 1997, Love is Strange, 1999, Fossils, 2001; one-woman theater presentations include Lucifer's Child, 1991; film debut in The Member of the Wedding, 1952 (Acad. award nomination); other films include The East of Eden, 1955, I Am A Camera, 1955, The Truth About Women, 1958, Poacher's Daughter, 1960, Requiem for a Heavyweight, 1962, The Haunting, 1963, The Moving Target, 1966, You're a Big Boy Now, 1966, Harper, 1966, Reflections in a Golden Eye, 1967, Tarzan and the Perils of Charity Jones, 1967, Tarzan and the Four O'Clock Army, 1968, The Split, 1968, Journey into Midnight, 1968, The People Next Door, 1970, The Hiding Place, 1975, Voyage of the Damned, 1976, The Bell Jar, 1979, The Prostitute, 1980, The Nutcraker: The Motion Picture, 1986, Gorillas in the Mist, 1988, Housesitter, 1992, The Dark Half, 1993, Little Surprises, 1995, Carried Away, 1996, Bad Manners, 1997, Gentle into the Night, 1998, The Way Back Home, 2005; TV series include Thicker Than Water, 1973, The Family Holvak, 1975, Knots Landing, 1979-87; TV movies include Wind From the South, 1955, The Good Fairy, 1956, The Lark, 1957, Johnny Belinda, 1968, Little Moon of Alban, 1958 (Emmy award 1959), A Doll's House, 1959, Victoria Regina, 1961 (Emmy award 1962), The Power and the Glory, 1961, The Heiress, 1961, Pygmalian, 1964, Hamlet, 1964, The Holy Terror, 1965, Anastasia, 1967, The House on Green Apple Road, 1970, How Awful About Alan, 1970, Home for the Holidays, 1972, The Greatest Gift, 1974, The Belle of Amherst, 1976, The Last of Mrs. Lincoln, 1976, Stubby Pringle's Christmas, 1978, Backstairs at the White House, 1979, The Gift, 1979, The Christmas Wife, 1979, The Annihilator, 1986, The Woman He Loved, 1988, Too Good To Be True, 1988, Single Women, Married Men, 1989, They've Taken Our Children: The Chowchilla Kidnapping Story, 1993, When Love Kills: The Seduction of John Nearn, 1993, One Christmas, 1994, Scarlett, 1994, Little Surprises, 1995, Secrets, 1995, The Christmas Tree, 1996, James Dean: A Portrait, 1996, Carried Away, 1996, Bad Manners, 1997, Ellen Foster, 1997, The First of May, 1998, Love is Strange, 1999, (voice) Frank Lloyd Wright, 1998; author: (with Barry Tarshis) Julie Harris Talks to Young Actors, 1971. Recipient Nat. Medal of the Arts, 1994, Tony award for lifetime achievement in theatre, 2002, Drama Desk Career Achievement award for commitment to excellence in theatre, 2005, Kennedy Ctr. Honor, John F. Kennedy Ctr. for Performing Arts, 2005. Office: William Morris Agy c/o Samuel Liff 1325 Avenue of the Americas New York NY 10019*

HARRIS, KAMALA D., prosecutor; b. Oakland, Calif., 1964; BA, Howard U.; JD, U. Calif. Bar: 1990. Dep. dist. atty. Office Dist. Atty., Alameda County, Calif., 1990—98, mng. atty. career criminal unit San Francisco, 1998—2000, head city atty.'s divsn. on families and children, 2000—04, dist. atty., 2004—. Co-chair Lawyers' Com. Civil Rights; pres. bd. dirs. Partners Ending Domestic Abuse; founder mentoring program San Francisco Mus. Modern Art; founder Coalition to End Exploitation of Kids. Named Child Advocate of Yr., San Francisco Child Abuse Prevention Coun., 2004; named one of Top 20 Young Lawyers Calif., Daily Journal, 1998; recipient award, Crime Victims United, County Counsel Assn. Calif., Thurgood Marshall award, Nat. Black Prosecutors Assn., 2005. Office: San Francisco Dist Attys Office 850 Bryant St Rm 322 San Francisco CA 94103*

HARRIS, KARI K., lawyer; BA in English Lit., Boston U., 1991; JD cum laude, Boston Coll., 1998. Bar: Mass. 1998. Assoc. Corp. Dept. Ropes & Gray LLP, Boston, 1998—. Mem. Bull Terrier Club of New England. Mem.: ABA, Mass. Bar Assn., Boston Bar Assn. Office: Ropes and Gray LLP One International Place Boston MA 02110-2624 Office Fax: 617-951-7983, 617-951-7050. E-mail: kari.harris@ropesgray.com.*

HARRIS, KATHERINE, congresswoman; b. Key West, Fla., Apr. 5, 1957; m. Anders Ebbeson. Student, U. Madrid, 1978; BA in History, Agnes Scott Coll., 1979; MPA in Internat. Trade, Harvard U., 1996. Senator 24th dist. Fla. State Legislature, 1994—98; sec. of state State of Fla., 1999—2002; mem. US Congress from 13th Fla. dist., 2003—. Vice chmn. banking and ins. com. Fla. State Senate, vice chmn. govtl. reform and oversight com., chmn. commerce and econ. opportunities com. Congl. intern U.S. Senate and U.S. Ho. of Reps., 1978; vice chmn. Sarasota County Legis. Del.; mem. Supreme Ct. Gender Bias Commn.; vice chmn. Fla. Am. Legis. Exch. Coun.; mem. arts and tourism com. Nat. Conf. State Legislators; former mem. adv. coun. Mote Marine Lab., Women's Resource Ctr., Sarasota County Arts Coun.; mem. Leadership Sarasota, Leadership Tampa; former vice chmn. bd. trustees Ringling Mus.; mem. nominating com. Pub. Svc. Commn.; active Habitat for Humanity, New Coll., Fla. Rep. Exec. Com. Recipient Disting. Leadership Alumni award, Leadership Sarasota, 1994, Arts Advocacy award, Sarasota County Arts Coun., 1995, Best Govt. Ofcl. award, Sarasota Mag., 1995—2002, Legislator of Yr. award, Sarasota Opera, 1996, Ind. Funeral Dirs. of Fla., 1996, Fla. Optometric Assn., 1996, Legis. Appreciation award, Dept. Labor and Employment Security, 1996. Mem. Sarasota C. of C. (Disting. Leadership Alumni award 1994), Englewood C. of C., Charlotte C. of C., Venice C. of C., Jaycees. Republican. Presbyterian. Avocations: reading, sailing, painting, skiing, skeet shooting. Office: US House Reps 116 Cannon House Office Bldg Washington DC 20515-0913 also: Dist Office Ste 181 1991 Main St Sarasota FL 34236

HARRIS, KATHERINE SAFFORD, speech and hearing educator; b. Lowell, Mass., Sept. 3, 1925; d. Truman Henry and Katherine (Wardwell) Safford; m. George Harris, Oct. 2, 1952; children: Maud White, Louise. BA, Radcliffe Coll., 1947; PhD, Harvard U., Cambridge, Mass., 1954. Rsch. assoc. Haskins Labs., New Haven, 1952-85, v.p., 1985—; prof. CUNY, N.Y.C., 1970—, disting. prof., 1982—. Active U.S./Israeli Speech Program Littauer Found., N.Y.C., 1986. Author: (with Borden and Raphael) Speech Science Primer, 1970, 4th edit., 2002, (with Baer and Sasaki) Phonatory Control, 1986. Active U.S./Israeli Speech Program Littauer Found., N.Y.C., 1986. Nat. Inst. Deafness and Other Comm. Disorders grantee. Fellow AAAS, Acoustical Soc. Am. (pres. 2000-01, Silver medal in speech commn. 2006, Rossing prize in acoustics edn. 2006), Am. Speech Hearing Assn., N.Y. Acad. Scis. Office: CUNY Grad Sch 415 5th Ave New York NY 10016 Personal E-mail: loumau2003@yahoo.com.

HARRIS, KATHRYN A.Z., internist; b. Tacoma, Wash., May 14, 1953; d. Dwight Judson and Emilie Elizabeth Zulauf; m. Geoffrey Webb Harris, Sept. 11, 1977; children: Morgan W., Adrian L., Erin G. BA in Chemistry and Biology, Pacific Luth. U., Tacoma, 1975; MD, U. Wash., Seattle, 1979. Resident in internal medicine R.I. Hosp., Providence, 1979—82; pvt. practice Seattle, 1982—. Chmn. continuing med. edn. com. Northwest Hosp., Seattle, 1998—2005. Mem.: King County Med. Soc. (trustee 2002—04). Avocations: swimming, reading, music. Office: Northwest Hosp # 207 1560 N 115th St Seattle WA 98133 Office Phone: 206-362-8337.

HARRIS, KRISTINE, historian, educator; b. New York, July 10, 1964; d. Robert and Ingrid H.; m. Robert Polito, June 27, 1987. BA, Wellesley Coll., 1986; MA, PhD, Columbia U., 1997. Instr. New Sch. Social Rsch., N.Y.C., 1995; asst. prof. history SUNY, New Paltz, 1996—2003, dir. Asian studies program, 2000—, assoc. prof. history, 2003—. Contbr. articles to profl. jours. and books, collections. Fulbright Found. fellow, 1992-93, Am. Coun. Learned Socs. fellow, 1993, 98; grantee Pacific Cultural Found., 1994-95. Mem. Am. Hist. Assn., Assn. Asian Studies. Office: Dept History State U New York New Paltz NY 12561 E-mail: harrisk@newpaltz.edu.

HARRIS, LANI M., theater educator; b. LA, June 8, 1951; d. Charles Edward and Lucy Rosetta McDonald; m. Thomas Lee Langkau, Sept. 30, 1980; children: Aeryn Paige Howard, Joseph Thomas Travis Langkau. AA, Coll. of the Redwoods, 1972; BA, Humboldt State U., 1976; MFA, U. So. Calif., L.A., 1980. Instr. Shasta Coll., Redding, Calif., 1983—90; lectr. Calif. State U., Chico, 1990—93, guest artist lectr. Bakersfield, 1993; asst. prof. U. Ala., Tuscaloosa, 1994—97; assoc. prof. U. Ctrl. Fla., Orlando, 1997—, provost's fellow in acad. affairs, 2005—06. Artistic dir. RCT Theatre, Redding, 1983—91. Contbr. chapters to books Stage Directions Guide to Auditions, 1998, 50 Great Directors of the Twentieth Century, 2003; prodr.: Air Born, 1995. V.p. Shasta County Arts Coun., Redding, 1986—91; chair coll. univ. divsn. Southeastern Theatre Conf., Greensboro, NC, 2001—04; bd. dirs. ACLU, Orlando, 1999—2002. Recipient Women's Rsch. award, U. Ctrl. Fla., 2005; grantee, Fulbright-Hays Grant Program, 2003; Sr. fellow, U. Ctrl. Fla. Mem.: Kennedy Ctr. Am. Coll. Theatre Festival (dir. of plays 1991—). Avocations: horseback riding, constitutional law. Office: U Ctrl Fla PO Box 162372 Orlando FL 32816-2372 E-mail: lharris@mail.ucf.edu.

HARRIS, LENNA RAE, music educator; d. William S. and Ruth L. Harris. B Music Edn., George Peabody Coll., Nashville, Tenn., 1973. Tchr. Hickman County Schs., Tenn., 1973—75, Green Acres Sch., Rockville, Md., 1979—83, Knowlton Twp. Elem. Sch., Delaware, NJ, 1985—; pvt. music instr. Ctr. for Performing Arts, Gaitersburg, Md., 1975—80, Nazareth Music, 1993—. Presenter in field; master tchr. NJ Symphony Orch., Newark, 1995, Newark, 2001. Composer, arranger: choral ch. music. Dir. Nazareth Area Cmty. Chorus, 2001—, St. John's Brass, 2005—; mem. Heritage Brass Quintet. Named Outstanding Young Woman Am., 1974; recipient Gov.'s award for excellence in tchg., 1995. Mem.: NJ Music Educators Assn., NJ Edn. Assn. Lutheran. Avocations: travel, reading, concerts.

HARRIS, LUCILLE SAWYER, retired music educator, musician, volunteer; b. New Bern, NC, Aug. 26, 1926; d. James Henry and Ida Cahoon Sawyer; m. Carl Vernon Harris, Aug. 6, 1955. AA, Mars Hill Coll., Mars Hill, NC, 1944; AB, Meredith Coll., Raleigh, NC, 1946; Mus B, Meredith Coll., 1947. Tchr. piano Mars Hill Coll., 1947—50, Gov. Morehead Sch. for Blind, Raleigh, NC, 1950—55, U. Wis., Platteville, Wis., 1956, Wake Forest U., Winston-Salem, NC, 1957—91, prof. emeritus, 1991—2006. Organist Mars Hill Bapt. Ch., Mars Hill, NC, 1947—50, Fairmont Meth. Ch., Raleigh, NC, 1950—52. Mem.: Am. Assn. Univ. Women, Music Tchrs. Nat. Assn., NC Music Tchrs. Assn., Alliance Bapts., Kappa Nu Sigma. Avocations: reading, music.

HARRIS, MAIA H., lawyer; b. Cleve., 1974; BA magna cum laude, U. Rochester, 1995; JD, Harvard U., 2000. Bar: Mass. 2001, US Dist. Ct. (Dist. Mass.) 2001. Student intern Robinson & Cole; assoc. Nixon Peabody LLP, Boston. Office: Nixon Peabody LLP 100 Summer St Boston MA 02110 Office Phone: 617-345-1213. Office Fax: 866-947-1794. E-mail: mharris@nixonpeabody.com.*

HARRIS, MARCELITE JORDAN, retired career officer; b. Houston, Jan. 16, 1943; d. Cecil Oneal and Marcelite Elizabeth (Terrell) Jordan; m. Maurice Anthony Harris, Nov. 29, 1980 (dec. Jan. 1996); children: Steven Eric, Tenecia Marcelite. BA, Spelman Coll., 1964; postgrad., Ctrl. Mich. U., 1973-75, crwa. State U., 1975-76, Chapman Coll., 1979-80; BS, U. Md., Okinawa, Japan, 1986. Tchr. Head Start, Houston, 1964-65; commd. 2d lt. USAF, 1965, advanced through grades to maj. gen., 1965-97; student Squadron officers Sch., 1975; with Hdqrs. USAF, Pentagon, 1975; comdr. 39 Cadet Squadron, USAF Acad., Colorado Springs, Colo., 1978, Air Refueling Wing, McConnell AFB, Kans., 1980, Avionics Maintenance Squadron, McConnell AFB, 1981, Field Maintenance Squadron, McConnell AFB, 1982; dir. maintenance Pacific Air Forces Logistics Support Ctr., Kadena Air Base, Japan, 1982; student Air War Coll., 1983; dep. chief maintenance Tech. Tng. Ctr., Keesler AFB, Miss., 1986, wing comdr., 1988; student Harvard U.Sr. Officers Course, 1988, Capstone Flag and Gen. Officers Course, 1990; vice comdr. Oklahoma City Air Logistics Ctr., Tinker AFB, 1990-97; dir. tech. tng. USAF, Randolph AFB, Tex., 1993-97, dir. of maintenance, 1994, ret., 1997. Cabinet mem. United Way, Oklahoma City, 1991; mem. adv. bd. Salvation Army, Oklahoma City, 1991—; bd. dirs. U.S. Automobile Assn., 1993—, 5 Who Care, 1992, Urban League. Decorated Bronze star, D.S.M.; named one of Top 100 Afro-Am. Bus. and Profl. Women, Dollars and $ense Mag., 1989, named Most Prestigious Individual, 1991, One of Top 100 Most Influencial People, City News, N.J., 1997; recipient Ellis Island Medal of Honor award, 1996, Living Legacy award 1998. Mem. AAUW, Air Force Assn. (life), Tuskegee Airmen Inc. (life), Maintenance Officer Assn., Retired Officer Assn., Ret. Officer Assn., Delta Sigma Theta.

HARRIS, MARGARET T., school system administrator; b. Boston, Feb. 22, 1944; d. Michael Cotter and Margaret Murnane; m. James M. Harris Jr., May 28, 1966; children: Troy, Jason, Damien, Gillian. BSEd, U. Mass., Boston, 1966; MLS, Boston U., 1973; MSc, Syracuse U., 1989; EdD, U. Mass., Amherst, 2003. Cert. tchr. Nat. Bd. Edn., 2003. Tchr. Boston Schs., 1966—67; tchr. history and social studies Martha's Vineyard Schs., Oak Bluffs, Mass., 1976—2003, dir. curriculum and instrn. Tisbury, Mass., 2003—04, head history dept., 1980—2003, asst. supt. curriculum, 2004—. Contbr. articles to profl. publs. Mem. Martha's Vinehard Libr. Commn., Oak Bluffs, 1977—80, Martha's Vineyard Conservation Commn., Oak Bluffs, 1978—82. Fulbright fellow, Brazil, 1993, Japan, 1997, South Africa, 2001. Mem.: AAUW, Orgn. Am. History (mem. various coms.), Phi Beta Kappa. Democrat. Avocations: dogs, music, dance, reading, knitting, walking. Business E-Mail: margaret_harris@fc.mv.k12.ma.us.

HARRIS, MARIAN S., social work educator; b. Tallahassee; d. Leo and Ida Mae Hoskin; 1 child, Trina S. Madison. BA, Fla. A&M U., 1964; MSW, Fla. State U., 1977; PhD, Smith Coll., 1997. Cert. social worker, diplomate in clin. social work, lic. ind. clin. social worker Wash., lic. clin. social worker Ill. Program dir. Ctrl. Bapt. Family Svcs., Chgo., 1990—93; postdoctoral fellow U. Wis.-Madison, 1997—99; rsch. adv. Smith Coll. Sch. for Social Work, Northampton, Mass., 1996—, adj. asst. prof., 1997—; asst. prof. U. Ill., Chgo., 1999—2002; faculty assoc. Chapin Hall Ctr. for Children U., Chgo., 2002—; asst. prof. U. Wash., Tacoma, 2002—; pvt. practice Tacoma, 2004—. Cons. reviewer U.S. Children's Bur., Washington, 2002—; expert witness O'Callaghan & Colleagues, PC, Chgo., 2002—05; cons. FAST Program, Madison, 2003; commr. Coun. Social Work Edn., Alexandria, Va., 1999—2005; pvt. practice social work, 2004—. Cons. editor: AFFILIA Jour. Women and Social Work, 2003—08. Chair Children's Alliance Pub. Policy Coun., Seattle, 2005—; bd. dirs. Children's Alliance, Seattle, 2005—. Recipient SAMHSA Clin. Tng. award, Coun. Social Work Edn., 1994—97, Social Work Educator of Yr., Wash. State Chpt., Nat. Assn. Social Workers, 2004; fellow, NIMH, 1997—99; grantee, U. Wash., 2003, Inst. Ethnic Studies U.S. U. Wash., 2005, 2006. Mem.: ACLU, So. Poverty Law Ctr., Pub. Policy Coun. (chair 2005—), Soc. Social Work and Rsch., Coun. Social Work Edn. (commn. role and status of women 1994—2005), Social Welfare Action Alliance, Alpha Kappa Alpha. Democrat. Roman Catholic. Avocations: tennis, swimming, jogging, travel, music. Office: U Wash 1900 Commerce St Tacoma WA 98402-3100 also: 2412 N 30th St Ste 102 Tacoma WA 98407 Business E-Mail: mh24@u.washington.edu.

HARRIS, MARION HOPKINS, retired federal official, academic administrator; b. Washington, July 27, 1938; d. Dennis Cason and Georgia (Greenleaf) Hopkins; 1 child, Alan E. MPA, U. Pitts., 1971; M in Mgmt. Sys., U. So. Calif., 1984, D Pub. Adminstrn., 1985. Dir. program planning Rochester (NY) Urban Renewal Agy., 1971—72; exec. dir. Fairfax County Redevel. and Housing Authority, Fairfax, Va., 1972—73; dep. dir. housing mgmt. HUD, Detroit, 1973—75; pres, mng. auditor GAO, Washington, 1979—80, sr. field officer housing, 1979—89; dir. evaluation divsn. USHUD, 1989—91; prof. Sch. Bus. Bowie State U., Md., 1991—, acting v.p. fin. and adminstrn. Md., 2005—; pres. Leo Group Mgmt. Cons., 1995—; prof. Grad. Sch. Mgmt. and Tech. U. Md. U. Coll., 1997—. Bd. dirs. S.W. Neighborhood Assembly Commn., Washington, 1979—80; commr. S.W. Adv. Neighborhood Commn., Washington, 1986; pub. adv. com. Washington Coun. Govts., 1985—87; mem. consumer adv. bd. Wash. Suburban Sanitation Com., 1989—; bd. dirs. Bowie State U. Found., 1991—; mem. Md. Gov.'s Workforce Investment Bd., 1996—; mem. charter commn. Howard County, Md., 2003—; mem. transition team Gov. State of Md., 1995. Recipient Outstanding Performance award, HUD, 1984, travel-study award, Ford Found., 1970; Carnegie-Mellon mid-career fellow, 1970. Mem.: LWV (exec. bd. Washington 1983—84), U. So. Calif. Doctoral Assn., Am. Acad. Soc. and Polit. Sci. Roman Catholic. Avocations: ballroom dancing, foreign travel, swimming. Home: 10229 Rutland Round Rd Columbia MD 21044-2727 Office Phone: 301-806-5837. Personal E-mail: mhharris@erols.com.

HARRIS, MARY LYNN, science educator, consultant; b. Kalamazoo, Mich., July 20, 1949; d. Robert Eugene and Margaret Marie Coe; m. William Arthur Harris, June 19, 1971; children: Jennifer Lynn, Jonathan William. BA in Biology and Chemistry, No. Mich. U., Marquette, 1971. Student tchr. No. Mich. U., Marquette, 1967—71; substitute tchr. Escanaba (Mich.) Area Pub. Schs., 1971—73, 1978—84, Gladstone (Mich.) Area Pub. Schs., 1971—73, 1978—84, Bark River (Mich.)-Harris Pub. Sch., 1971—73, 1978—84, Holy Name Cath. Sch., Escanaba, 1973—84; adult edn. tchr. North Cen. Area Schs., Powers, 1988—92; sci. tchr. grades 8-12 Nah-Tah-Wahsh Pub. Sch. Acad., Wilson, Mich., 1984—86, 1988—. Mem. environ. protection com. Hannahville Indian Comty., Wilson, 1988—92; sci. edn. adviser Delta-Schoolcraft Ind. Sch. Dist., Escanaba, 1988—2006; sci. coord. K-12 Nah Tah Wahsh PSA, Wilson, 1990—2001; coord., coach Native Am. Sci. Bowl Team, 1999—2004; grantwriter in field. Named Sci. Tchr. of Yr., No. Mich. Univ. chpt. Sigma Xi, 1998, Outstanding Conservation Tchr., Menominee Conservation Soc., 1998; recipient Native Am. Cultural award, Hannahville Indian Sch., 1998, Beyond the Books Outstanding Educator award, 1990—91, 1997—98. Mem.: VFW, Native Am. Sci. and Engrng. Soc., Mich. Sci. Tchrs. Assn. (presenter cof. 1999—2000), Nat. Wildlife Fedn. Avocations: gardening, travel, crocheting, birdwatching. Home: 1005 Lake Shore Dr Escanaba MI 49829 Office: Nah-Tah-Wahsh Pub Sch Acad N 14911 Hannahville B-1 Rd Wilson MI 49896

HARRIS, MELBA IRIS, elementary school educator, secondary school educator, state agency administrator; b. Cullman, Ala., Aug. 8, 1945; d. Karl and Leona Christine (McDowell) Budweg; m. James Allen Harris, Apr. 17, 1965 (div. June 1981); 1 child, James Allen II BS Home Econs., U. Ala., 1970, MA Elem. Edn., 1977, EdS, 1982; BS Elem. Edn. magna cum laude, St. Bernard Coll., 1975. Instr. Cullman City Schs., Ala., 1966—68, Ft. Payne City Schs., Ala., 1974—99, Gwinnett County Schs., Ga., 1999—. Curriculum developer Ala. State Dept. Edn., Montgomery, 1987—89; coord. aerospace edn. Ala. State Dept. Aeronautics, Montgomery, 1987—89. V.p. Ft. Payne Civettes, 1979 Recipient commendations Ala. Gov. George C. Wallace, 1985, 86, Gov. Guy Hunt, 1987, Ft. Payne City Coun., 1987, Ft. Payne City Bd. Edn., 1987, CAP Albertville Composite Squadron, 1987, Ala. State Bd. Edn., 1987, Ala. State Excellence in Edn. award FAA, 1987, Stewart G. Potter award Nat. Aircraft Distbrs. and Mfrs. Assn., 1988, Nat. Frank G. Brewer Meml. Aerospace Edn. award CAP, 1989, Aviation Edn. Excellence award Nat. Gen. Aviation Mfrs. Assn., 1989, NEWEST award NASA, 1995, Achievement in Edn. award Optimist Club, 1999, Tchrs. as Leaders Inc. award, Gwinnett County Bd. Edn., 2001; named A. Scott Crossfield Nat. Aerospace Educator of Yr., 1987, The Nat. Aerospace Edn. Tchr. of Yr., 1987; Christa McAuliffe fellow, 1987, Tchr. of Yr. Meml. award, 1991; named to Ala. Aviation Hall of Fame, 1991 Mem. NEA, NSTA, Ala. Edn. Assn. (state aerospace edn. coord. 1992—), Ft. Payne Edn. Assn. (pres. 1985-86), Air Force Assn. (life), Ala. Aviation Assn., Exptl. Aircraft Internat. (Maj. Achievement award 1988), Exptl. Aircraft Chpt. 683 (sec., treas. 1987, pres. 1988), Internat. Ninety-Nines, Inc., Kappa Delta Pi Home: PO Box 681174 Fort Payne AL 35968-1613 Office: Bethesda Sch 525 Bethesda School Rd Lawrenceville GA 30044-3509 Office Phone: 770-921-2000. Business E-Mail: fanflight@comcast.net.

HARRIS, MERLE WIENER, college administrator, educator; b. Hartford, Conn., July 25, 1942; d. Irving and Leah (Glasser) Wiener; m. David R. Harris, June 23, 1963; children: Jonathan, Rebecca. BS, Ctrl. Conn. State U., 1964, MS, 1973; EdD, U. Mass., 1988. Clk., edn. com. Conn. Gen. Assembly, Hartford, 1971-72; career edn. coordinator Bloomfield (Conn.) Pub. Schs., 1973-78; asst. to commr. Dept. of Higher Edn., Hartford, Conn., 1978-82, asst. commr., 1982-88, deputy commr., 1988-89; pres. Charter Oak State Coll., New Britain, Conn., 1989—; exec. dir. Bd. for State Acad. Awards, New Britain, Conn., 1989—; interim pres. Cen. Conn. State U., 1995-96. Cons.on career edn. U.S. Dept. Edn., Washington, 1974; fellow Inst. for Ednl. Leadership, 1980; bd. dirs. Old State House, 1996—2003, Conn. Hist. Soc., 2003—, Conn. Literacy Vols., 1991—98, Conn. Humanities Coun., 1991—97, Conn. Acad. for Edn. in Math., Sci. and Tech., 2000—, vice chmn., 2002—05, chmn., 2005, Joint Com. Ednl. Tech., 1991—98; mem. Conn. Commn. Ednl. Tech., 2000—. Mem. New Eng. Assn. Schs. and Colls. (bd. dirs. 1997-2003), Am. Coun. on Edn. (commr. on ednl. credit and credentials 1995-98). Democrat. Jewish. Avocations: gardening, cooking. Office Phone: 860-832-3875. Business E-Mail: mharris@charteroak.edu.

HARRIS, MICALYN SHAFER, lawyer, educator, arbitrator, consultant, mediator; b. Chgo., Oct. 31, 1941; d. Erwin and Dorothy Shafer. AB, Wellesley Coll., 1963; JD, U. Chgo., 1966. Bar: Ill. 1966, Mo. 1967, US Dist. Ct. (ea. dist.) Mo. 1967, US Supreme Ct. 1972, US Ct. Appeals (8th cir.), 1974, NY 1981, NJ 1988, US Dist. Ct. NJ, US Ct. Appeals (3d cir.) 1993. Law clk. US Dist. Ct., Mo., 1967-68; atty. May Dept. Stores, St. Louis, 1968-70, Ralston-Purina Co., St. Louis, 1970-72; atty., asst. sec. Chromalloy Am. Corp., St. Louis, 1972-76; pvt. practice St. Louis, 1976-78; atty. CPC Internat., Inc., 1978-80; divsn. counsel CPC N.Am., 1980-84, asst. sec., 1981-88; gen. counsel S.B. Thomas, Inc., 1983-87; corp. counsel CPC Internat., Englewood Cliffs, NJ, 1984-88; assoc. counsel Weil, Gotshal & Manges, NYC, 1988-90; pvt. practice, 1991; v.p., sec., gen. counsel Winpro, Inc., 1991—. Arbitrator Am. Arbitration Assn., NYSE, NASD; adj. prof. Lubin Sch. Bus. Pace U.; expert cons., mediator. Mem.: ABA (Ctr. Profl. Responsibility, bus. law sect., past chair corp. counsel com., past chair subcom. counseling mktg. function, mem. securities law com., tender offers proxy statements subcom., chair task force e-mail privacy, task force electronic contracting, task force conflicts interest, ad hoc com. tech., profl. responsibility com., profl. conduct com. task force on revised code of jud. conduct), Am. Law Inst. (mem. consultative groups restatement of agy. 3d intellectual property, prins. governing jurisdiction & judgements, internat. enforcement of judgements), NYC Bar Assn. (mediation coach), NJ Bar Assn. (computer law com.), NY State Bar Assn. (securities regulation com. and legis. com., past chair internet tech. law com., past chair subcom. on licensing, task force shrink-wrap licensing, electronic comm. task force). Mailing: 625 N Monroe St Ridgewood NJ 07450-1206

HARRIS, MICHELLE RENEÉ, pastor; b. Metairie, La., Jan. 22, 1975; d. Delvin Max and Jane Ruth (Schmaltz) McGough; m. Steven Paul Harris, Mar. 8, 2003; children: Coleman Luke, Clay Matthew. BA in Bible, Ctrl. Bible Coll., Springfield, Mo., 1996. Program mgr. Accadiana Teen Challenge, St. Martinsville, La., 1997—98; tchr. Northside Christian Sch., Crowley, La., 1998—2003; worship pastor Northside Assembly of God, Crowley, 1999—. Clean-up com. mem. Strive Interface Youth Ministries, Crowley, 2000—02; mgr. program Acadiana Teen Challenge; dir. bell choir 9-11 Acadia Parish Meml.; youth sponsor Interface Youth Ministries, Crowley, 1998—2002; com. mem. Nat. Day of Prayer, Crowley, 2001—02; bell choir dir. 911 Arcadia Parish Meml., Crowley, 2002. Republican. Assemblies Of God. Avocations: cooking, music, violin. Home: 115 Queens Row Crowley LA 70526 Office: Northside Assembly of God Ch 809 E Northern Ave Crowley LA 70526 Office Phone: 337-783-3620.

HARRIS, MILDRED CLOPTON, clergy member, educator; b. Chgo., May 27, 1936; d. Jordan and Willa Mildred Clopton; m. Herbert Curlee Harris, Feb. 4, 1928. BA, DePaul U., 1957; MA, Columbia U., 1963, Governors State U., 1975; MPS, Loyola U., Chgo., 1985; D in Min., Bible Inst. Sem., Plymouth, Fla., 1985. Ordained to ministry Ind. Assemblies of God. Tchr. Gary (Ind.) Pub. Schs., 1957-93; founder, pres. God First Ministries, Chgo., 1978—. Organizer Chgo. March for Jesus, 1995-97. Author: Traits of an Intercessor, 1991, Educating Your Child God's Way, 1991, The Productive Prayer Guide, 1991; exec. prodr. (cassette) tribe of Judah En Danse, 1995-96 (ASCAP award); host (TV show) Born Again, (radio show) WYCA 92.3, WCFJ 1470 AM. Bd. dirs. Midwestern U., Chgo., 1989-97, Goodman Theater, Chgo., 1994—, Make a Wish Found., Chgo., 1994-97, Windows of Opportunity, Chgo., 1997—; mem. exec. adv. com. Chgo. Housing Authority, 1995-99, commr., 1999—; overseer Gary (Ind.) Educators for Art, 1990—; adv. bd. mem. to Lisa Madigan Atty. Gen. Ill.; adv. bd. mem. to Daniel Hynes Comptr., Ill. Recipient CHANCE award Chgo. Housing Authority, 1998, Seniors-Gladys Reed award, 1998; Mary Herrick scholar Du Sable H.S. Alumni, 1998, Jefferso TV award, NBC, 2005. Mem. ASCAP, Nat. Soc. Fundraising Execs., Religious Conf. Mgmt. Assn., Nat. Coun. Negro Women (life), Union League Club Chgo., Chgo. Ill. Links Inc. Avocations: travel, interior decorating. Home: 7246 S Luella Ave Chicago IL 60649-2514

HARRIS, MILDRED STAEGER, retired broadcast executive; b. Newark, Oct. 18, 1917; d. Henry Ernest and Louise Sheffick Staeger; m. William Finlaw Harris, Oct. 20, 1945 (dec. Nov. 1963); children: Steven Alan, Sandra Louise, Douglas William. Prof. designation in bus. mgmt., UCLA, 1980. Mgr. fixed assets ABC, L.A., 1971-76, mgr. adminstrn., 1976-80, tech. mgr., 1980-85. Children's libr. counselor Kings County Literacy Coun., Hanford, Calif., 1990, bd. dirs., 1991—; coord. Am. Women in Radio and TV, L.A., 1979-84. Named Businesswoman of Yr., YWCA Coun., 1973; recipient Emmy award for Summer Olympics, NATAS, 1985. Mem. Calif. Sheriffs Assn., Literacy Vols. Am., Libr. of Congress. Avocations: history, language, reading, genealogy. Office: Kings Literacy Coun 505 W Cameron St Hanford CA 93230-3615

HARRIS, NANCY LEE, special education educator, behavior analyst; b. West Point, NY, Dec. 25, 1955; d. Richard Lee and Joan Patricia (Corbett) Sandison; 1 child. Student, Lesley Coll., 1975—78; AA, Cape Cod Cmty. Coll., Barnstable, Mass., 1976; BS, U. Mass., Boston, 1987; postgrad., Salem State, 1992. Cert. elem. edn. and learning disabilities and emotionally disturbed Fla., N.C., elem. disabilities and learning and mentally and physically challenged Pa., nat. bd. cert. assoc. behavior analyst, cert. elem. edn. and learning disabilities Mass. Spl. edn. tchr. St. Anne's Home, Methuen, Mass., 1987, Mass. Cerebral Palsy, Methuen, 1988, IFFL, Danvers, Mass., 1989—91; LD tchr. Janus Sch., Lancaster, Pa., 1991—93; ED/LD tchr. PS Jones Mid. Sch., Washington, NC, 1993—97, Devereux Viera, Fla., 1998—2001, Milestones Charter Sch., Palm Bay, Fla., 2002—; with Indian River County Schs., Fla., 2002—. Home: 1115 18th Ave SW Vero Beach FL 32962-5364 Office Phone: 772-913-0604. Personal E-mail: nancileeh@yahoo.com.

HARRIS, NANCY LEWIS, home economics educator; b. Muhlenberg, Ky., Nov. 29, 1939; d. Clarence Martin and Dorothy Louise (Lile) Lewis; m. Ralph Norman Harris, Feb. 11, 1962; children: Ronald Norman Harris, Sarah Elizabeth Harris. BS, Murray State Coll., 1961; MS, U. Ky., 1962; 6 yr. cert., Furman U., 1977. Cert. tchr., N.C. Tchr. Nolan Jr. High Sch., Killen, Tex., 1962-64, Pinellas County Bd. Edn., Safety Harbor, Fla., 1964-68, 69-71, P.K. Younge Lab. Sch., Gainesville, Fla., 1971-73, Greenville (S.C.) Schs., 1973-78, Statesville (N.C.) Schs., 1978—. Tchr. recruiter Statesville H.S., 1988-91. Mem. Am. Assn. Family and Consumer Scis. (home econs. edn. N.W. regional mgmt. team 1994-97), Am. Vocat. Assn., P.E.O. (pres. 1984-86), Alpha Delta Kappa (Fidelis Tau chpt. pres. 2006—), Gamma Alpha (pres. 1990-92). Democrat. Presbyterian. Avocations: reading, walking, crafts, rug hooking. Home: 167 Upper Oak Dr Statesville NC 28625-8856

HARRIS, PATRICIA ANN BRADY, principal, educational consultant; b. Asheboro, N.C., Apr. 21, 1947; d. Joseph Graham and Mary Louetta (Coltrane) Brady; m. Norman Lee Harris, Feb. 17, 1968; children: Joseph Troy, William Chadwick. B in Music Edn., U. N.C., 1971, MusM, 1978, M in Edn. Adminstrn., 1985, D in Edn. Adminstrn., 1990. Tchr. Randolph County Schs., Liberty, NC, 1972—85; tchr., asst. prin. Chatham County Schs., Pittsboro, NC, 1985—90; prin. Nottaway (Va.) County Schs., 1990—96, Smithfield (N.C.) Mid. Sch., 1996—2001, W. Johnston HS, Benson, NC, 2001—. Adminstrv. mentor, evaluator cert., Va., 1992; cons., 1996—2003. Recipient Chatham 2000 Citizen award, Chatham County, N.C., 1989, Pub. Svc. award, VFW, 1994—96; grantee, U.S. Govt., 1991—95. Mem.: NSSE, ASCD (Lighthouse award 2001), NEA, N.C. Assn. Educators, Phi Delta Kappa. Avocations: bridge, flowers, reading. Home: 502 W Wellons St Smithfield NC 27577-3865

HARRIS, REBECCA SUE, mathematics educator; b. Greencastle, Ind., Oct. 12, 1951; d. Willis Waldo and Opal Regina Ader; m. Arthur Ray Harris, Nov. 21, 1992. BS in Math., Ind. State U., Terre Haute, 1973, MS in Math., 1975. Lic. life tchg. Ind. H.s. math. tchr. Western Boone Cmty. Sch. Corp., Thorntown, Ind., 1973—. Mem. honor soc. selection com. Western Boone Jr-Sr H.S., Thorntown, 1985—, mem. sch. improvement team, Thorntown, 1994—, chairperson math. dept., 1984—; adj. staff math. dept. Ind. U., Bloomington, 1986—. Vice precinct com. person Dem. Party. Named Del. to Govs.' Talks with Tchrs., Western Boone Sch. Corp., 1984, Panel Mem. for Hugh O'Brien Youth Leadership, 2001, Boone County Tchr. of Yr., Union Fed. Bank, 2005, Outstanding Treas., Indian State Tchrs. Assn., 1999; recipient Ind. Acad. All-Stars Cert. of Merit, Ind., 1988, Tandy Tech. Scholars Program Outstanding Tchg. award, Tandy Corp., 1991—92. Mem.: NEA (assoc.), Western Boon Tchrs. Assn. (assoc.; treas. 1985—2005, Outstanding Treas. award 1999). Home: 999 E Co Rd 325 N Greencastle IN 46135-8025 Office: Western Boone Jr- Sr H S 1205 N State Rd 75 Thorntown IN 46071 Office Phone: 765-482-6143 ext. 3206. Office Fax: 765-482-6146. Personal E-mail: aharris@link2000.net. Business E-Mail: rebecca.harris@webo.k12.in.us.

HARRIS, ROSALIE, psychotherapist, clinical counselor, Spanish language professional and multi-linguist, English as second language educator; b. N.Y.C., Dec. 9, 1937; d. Herman and Lilly (Hyman) H.; children: Attila, Steven. BA in Psychology, Hunter Coll., 1967, MA in ESL, 1973; MS in Community Mental Health, L.I. U., 1990; advanced cert. in marriage and family counseling, Queens Coll., 1992; primary cert., Inst. for Rational Emotive Therapy, N.Y.C., 1995, advanced cert., 1996. Adminstr., supr. N.Y.C. Bd. Edn., 1967-79, tchr., 1967-88; social worker Bur. Child Welfare, N.Y.C., 1967-69; lectr. Queens Coll., Flushing, N.Y., 1979-86; mental health counselor Copay, Great Neck, N.Y., 1989-90; marriage and family counselor Aspects, Ozone Park, N.Y., 1990—. Bilingual counselor Copay, Great Neck, 1989-90; multi-lingual specialist, 1967—. Mem. Nassau County Bd. of Elections. Mem. NASW, Am. Assn. Marriage and Family Therapy (clin.), N.Y. State Assn. Marriage and Family Therapy (L.I. chpt.), N.Y. State Assn. Counseling and Devel., N.Y. State Assn. Tchrs., ESL, L.I. Mental Health Counselors Assn., Kappa Delta Pi Hon. Soc., Assn. for Asian Studies. Avocations: multi-linguist, world traveler, dancer, stained glass artist. Home and Office: 67 Bayview Ave Great Neck NY 11021-1731

HARRIS, ROSE M., academic administrator; b. Shreveport, La., Oct. 26, 1967; d. Artis T. Harris, Sr. and Lessie B. Hardman Harris. BA in Polit. Sci., So. U., Baton Rouge, La., 1989; MA in Polit. Sci., Howard U., Washington, 1991; PhD, Rutgers U., New Brunswick, N.J., 1999. Part-time lectr. Rutgers U., New Brunswick, NJ, 1993—95; coord. of planning and devel. So. U., Shreveport, La., 1996; vis. scholar U. of Houston, 2000—01; chancellor's post-doctoral fellow and adj. asst. prof. of polit. sci. U. of Ill. at Champaign-Urbana, Champaign, Ill., 2001—02; asst. prof. Ohio State U., Columbus, 1997—2002; dir. The La. Ctr. for Women and Govt. at Nicholls State U., Thibodaux, La., 2002—. Assoc. program dir. (head staff, staff mem. and counselor) La. Girls State, Baton Rouge, 1984—98. Editor: (book) Women in Louisiana Politics: Essays on Race, Gender and Politcs in the Bayou State, Louisiana's Political Women, 1930-2006, The African American Political Woman: A Reader. Apptd. by the gov. as a commn. mem. (former vice-chair of the commn.) La. Women's Policy & Rsch. Commn., Baton Rouge, 2003, 2004; co-founder The Assn. for the Study of Black Women in Politics, Thibodaux, La. Named a 2005 Pacesetter as a Proven Woman Leader, Stennis

Ctr. Pub. Svc.; recipient Houston's Prominent Woman Table Talk, U. of Houston, Women's Studies, 2001; fellow NSF Minority Grad. fellow, The NSF, 1990—91, 1992—94, Excellence fellow, Rutgers U., 1994—96. Mem.: Nat. Conf. of Black Polit. Scientists (Sammy D. Young Award 1989), Women's Caucus for Polit. Sci., So. Polit. Sci. Assn., Am. Polit. Sci. Assn. Non-Denominational Christian. Avocations: bible study and bible teaching, reading, running. Office: The Louisiana Center for Women & Govt PO Box 2062 Nicholls State University Thibodaux LA 70310 Office Phone: 985-448-4770. Office Fax: 985-448-4771. E-mail: lcwg-info@nicholls.edu.

HARRIS, ROSEMARY ANN, actress; b. Ashby, Eng., Sept. 19, 1930; d. Stafford Berkley and Enid (Campion) Harris; m. Ellis Rabb, Dec. 4, 1959 (div. 1967); m. John Ehle, Oct. 21, 1967; 1 child, Jennifer Ehle. Degree, Royal Acad. Dramatic Art, 1951-52; doctorate (hon.), Smith Coll., 1969, Wake Forest U., 1978. Actress (plays) Winter Sunshine, 1948, The Climate of Eden, 1952, Seven Year Itch, 1953, Much Ado About Nothing, Man and Superman, Pygmalion, Troilus and Cressida, 1957, Interlock, 1958, The Disenchanted, 1958, Peter Pan, 1958—59, The Tumbler, 1960, You Can't Take It With You, 1965, The Lion in Winter, 1966 (Tony award, best actress in a play, 1966, Antoinette Perry award, 1966), The School for Scandal, 1966, Right You Are If You Think You Are, 1966, We, Comrades Three, 1966, The Wild Duck, 1967, War and Peace, 1967, Old Times, 1971, The Merchant of Venice, 1973, A Streetcar Named Desire, 1973, The Royal Family, 1975, The New York Idea, Three Sisters, 1977, The Seagull, 1981, All My Sons, 1981, Heartbreak House, 1983, Pack of Lies, 1984 (Antoinette Perry award, 1984), Hay Fever, 1985, Lost in Yonkers, 1992, An Inspector Calls, 1994, A Delicate Balance, 1996, Waiting in the Wings, 1999, The Other Side, 2005, (films) Beau Brummell, 1954, The Shiralle, 1956, Uncle Vanya, 1963, A Flea in Her Ear, 1968, The Boys From Brazil, 1978, The Ploughman's Lunch, 1983, To The Lighthouse, 1983 (Locarno Film Festival award, 1983), Crossing Delancey, 1988, The Delinquents, 1989, The Bridge, 1992, Tom & Viv, 1994, Hamlet, 1996, Dark Side of the Moon, 1998, My Life So Far, 1999, Sunshine, 1999, The Gift, 2000, Blow Dry, 2001, Spider-Man, 2002, Spider-Man 2, 2004, Being Julia, 2004, (TV films) Othello, 1955, Twelfth Night, 1957, (voice TV films) Eh, Joe?, 1966, (TV films) Blithe Spirit, 1966, The Royal Family, 1977, Tales From the Hollywood Hills: The Old Reliable, 1988, Strange Interlude, 1988, Death of a Salesman, 1996, The Little Riders, 1996, Belonging, 2004, (TV miniseries) Notorious Woman, 1974, Holocaust, 1978 (Golden Globe award), The Chisholms, 1980, The Camomile Lawn, 1992. Recipient Vernon Rice award, 1962, Theatre World award, 1953, Obie award, 1961, 1965, Delia Austrian Drama League award, 1967, Whitbread award, 1965—67, London Evening Standard award, 1969, Outer Critics Circle award, 1972, Drama Desk award, 1971, 1972, 1976, Emmy award, 1976. Mem.: Screen Actors Guild, AFTRA, Actors Equity Assn., Royal Acad. of Dramatic Art (assoc.). Address: c/o Johnnie Planco Parseghian Planco 23 E 22nd St New York NY 10010-5300*

HARRIS, RUBY LEE, realtor; b. Booneville, Miss., Mar. 5, 1939; d. Carl Jackson and Gladys (Downs) Hill; m. Lee Kelly Harris, Apr. 21, 1962; children: Lee Kelly Jr., Bradford William. Student, N.E. Miss. Jr. Coll., Booneville, 1957-58, U. Ala., Tuscaloosa, 1958-59. Lic. realtor, Calif. Agt. Forest E. Olson, Lake Forest, Calif., 1974-76, Coldwell Banker, Mission Viejo, Calif., 1976-78, Associated Realtors, Mission Viejo, 1978—. Mem. Children's Home Soc. Calif., Mission Viejo, 1985-88, Boys and Girls Club Am., San Clemente, Calif., 1989-91, Capistrano, 1994-95; mem. election com. Orange County, Mission Viejo, 1974—. Mem. Nat. Assn. Realtors, Calif. Assn. Realtors, Saddleback Valley Bd. Realtors (bd. dirs. 1989). Republican. Avocations: bicycling, gardening. Office: Associated Realtors 25350 Marguerite Pkwy Ste B Mission Viejo CA 92692-2993 Office Phone: 949-300-1332.

HARRIS, SHELLEY FOLLANSBEE, business development professional; b. Quantico, Va., Oct. 20; d. Lawrence Peyton and June Maynard (Trout) H. Student, Western Carolina U., 1967-69; BS in Fine Arts, Towson State U., 1973. Surgeon's asst. Drs. Bennett, Johnson & Eaton, P.A., Balt., 1979-82; mgr. human resources Morino Assocs., Inc., Vienna, Va., 1983-88; account exec. Snelling & Snelling, Vienna, 1988-89; acct. exec. Forbes Assocs., Inc., Annandale, Va., 1989-90; contracts adminstr., legal affairs Electronic Data Sys. Corp., Herndon, Va., 1991—95; bus. devel. prof. EDS, Herndon, 1995—2000, client sales exec., 2000—03; bus. devel. profl. Capgemini Govt. Solutions LLC, 2004—. Author: stories and poetry. Vol. scuba instr. asst.; vol. for various cmty. and career-related efforts. Recipient regional awards for paintings, regional and nat. awards for sales and mktg., also awards for community contbns. Mem. Artist's Equity. Episcopalian. Avocations: fine arts, painting, sculpting, printmaking, scuba diving. Home: Lansdowne on the Potomac 19188 Greystone Sq Lansdowne VA 20176 Office: 2250 Corporate Park Dr Ste 410 Herndon VA 20171 Business E-Mail: shelley.harris@capgemini-gs.com.

HARRIS, SHIRLEY, elementary school educator, secondary school educator, adult education educator; b. Chgo., Aug. 14, 1945; BA in Behavioral Sci., Nat. Louis U., 1985; MS in Edn., Chgo. State U., 1993. Cert. in curriculum and instr. Legal sec. Friedman/Rochester, Chgo. and Portland, Oreg., 1974; supr., clerical positions Model Cities, Chgo. and Portland, Oreg., 1973-75; bd. sec. Portland Comm., 1976-78; tchr., clerical positions Portland O.I.C., 1975-76; tchr., juvenile/youth counselor Yaun Youth Ctr., Portland, 1978-80; pres. Flexible Temps, Chgo., 1980—. Part-time prof. Wright Jr. Coll., 1999, Northeastern Ill. U., 1999—, Robert Morris Coll., 2000, DeVry Inst. Tech., 2000; adj. prof. U. St. Francis, Chgo., 2005; cons. in field, Chgo., 1983; typing tchr., Chgo., 1983; pers. recruiter, Chgo., 1974-75. Author: (poetry and lyrics) True Covenant Not Mine; contbr. poetry to anthologies. Bd. dirs. Operation Probe, Chgo., 1990-93. Mem. NAFE, ASCD, Internat. Platform Assn. Baptist. Home: 28 E Jackson Blvd Ste 5805 Chicago IL 60604 Office Phone: 312-375-9522. E-mail: harris590405@yahoo.com.

HARRIS, SKILA, government agency administrator; b. Bowling Green, Ky. d. Skiles Browning and Dorothy (Lester) Harris; m. Fred Graham. BS in Polit. Sci., Western Ky. U.; MS in Legis. Affairs, George Washington U. V.p. devel. and compliance Steiner-Liff Iron and Metal Co., Nashville, 1989—92; spl. asst. V.P. Al Gore, 1993—97; chief of staff Tipper Gore, 1993—97; with U.S. Dept. Energy, Washington, U.S. Synthetic Fuels Corp.; exec. dir. U.S. Sec. of Energy Adv. Bd., 1997—99; dir. TVA, Knoxville, 1999—. Bd. dirs. Nuclear Elec. Ins. Ltd.; vice chair2002 Consumer Energy Coun. Am.'s Forum on Energy Security and Electric Industry Restructuring. Grad. Leadership Knoxville, 2001. Office: TVA 400 W Summit Hill Dr Knoxville TN 37902-1499 Office Phone: 865-632-3871.

HARRIS, SUSAN V., lawyer; b. 1961; BA, Oberlin Coll., 1983; JD, U. Chgo., 1992. Bar: Ill. 1992. With Sidley Austin Brown & Wood, Chgo., ptnr., 2000—. Mem.: ABA. Office: Sidley Austin Brown and Wood Bank One Plz 10 S Dearborn St Chicago IL 60603

HARRIS, TAMMY DOTSON, elementary school educator; b. Hebron, Ky., Dec. 8, 1967; d. Gaines Stallard and Opal Mae (White) Dotson; m. Richard Paul Harris, Apr. 2, 1993; children: Sara, Noah, Jonah. BS, Cumberland Coll., Williamsburg, Ky.; MA in Edn., No. Ky. U., Highland Heights, postgrad. Cert. tchr. grades k-5, self-contained language arts 6-8, rank I instructional leadership. Elem. sch. tchr. Kenton County Bd. Edn., Ft. Wright, Ky., 1990—. Kindergarten Sunday sch. tchr. Kentoboo Bapt. Ch., Florence, Ky. Mem.: ASCD. Republican. Baptist. Avocations: reading, bicycling, gardening. Home: 981 Mt Zion Rd Independence KY 41051 Office: Piner Elem Sch 2845 Rich Rd Morning View KY 41063 Business E-Mail: tammy.harris@kenton.kyschools.us.

HARRIS, THERESA, lawyer; b. Bronx, NY, July 25, 1957; BSN, Coll. Mt. St. Vincent, Riverdale, NY, 1979; JD, Pace U., 1995. Bar: NY 1995, NJ 1995, US Dist. Ct. Ea. Dist. NY, US Dist. Ct. So. Dist. NY. Ptnr. Wilson, Elser, Moskowitz, Edelman & Dicker LLP, NYC. Mem.: ABA, NY State Bar Assn. Office: Wilson Elser Moskowitz Edelman & Dicker LLP 23rd Fl 150 E 42nd St New York NY 10017-5639 Office Phone: 212-490-3000 ext. 2776. Office Fax: 212-490-3038. Business E-Mail: harrist@wemed.com.

HARRIS, TINA, science educator; b. Marion, Ind., Mar. 23, 1961; d. Robert Andrew and Phyllis Pauline West; m. Douglas Irving Harris, Dec. 12, 1982 (div. June 1988); children: Megan, Erin. BS, Purdue U., 1983; MA, Ball State U., 1990; postgrad. in Edn., Ind. U. Cert. earth/space, phys. and gen. sci. tchr. Sci. tchr. Anderson (Ind.) Cmty. Sch. Corp., 1986—, home sch. tutor, 1986-88, 99, chmn. Sci. Dept., 1994—2002, computer svc. technician, 1998, 2002; assoc. instr. Ind. U., 2002—04. Mem.—2002, Ind. State Sci. Stds. Com., Dept. of Edn., Indpls., 1997—2000; tutor Ivy Tech. CC, 2002—04; workshop presenter in field; adj. faculty Ind. U., 2006. Leader Wapehani Girl Scout Coun., Daleville, Ind., 1985—98, day camp dir., 1990; vol. Park Elem. Sch., Fairmount, Ind., 1990—2002. Recipient awards. Mem.: AAUW, ASCD, Ind. Earth Sci. Tchrs. Assn., Geol. Soc. Am., Assn. Sci. Tchr. Edn., Nat. Assn. Rsch. Sci. Tchg., Nat. Mid. Level Sci. Tchrs. Assn., Ind. Earth Sci. Tchrs. Assn. (sec. 2001—), Hoosier Assn. Sci. Tchrs. (bd. dirs. 2002—05, 2006—, presenter), Nat. Earth Sci. Tchrs. Assn., Nat. Sci. Tchrs. Assn. (presenter), Am. Fedn. Tchrs., Pi Lambda Theta. Avocations: swimming, reading, camping, travel, rock collecting. Office: East Side Middle Sch 2300 Lindberg Rd Anderson IN 46012 Personal E-mail: taharris79@yahoo.com.

HARRIS, TOMIKA TANTRICE, lawyer; d. Burnell and Dyann Harris. BA, U. So. Miss., Hattiesburg, Miss., 1997; MA, Miss. State U., Starkville, 1999; JD, U. Miss., Oxford, 2002. Guardian Ad Litem: Miss. Jud. Coll. 2005. Law clk. Judge Lamar Pickard, Hazlehurst, Miss., 2002; assoc. Byrd & Assocs. PLLC, Jackson, Miss., 2002—04; atty. Gibbs & Martin, PLLC, Jackson, 2004—06, Tomika T. Harris - Atty. at Law, Ridgeland, Miss., 2006—. Active mem. Jr. League of Jackson; vol. tutor Barksdale Reading Inst., Jackson; active mem./asst. announcer Pine Grove Bapt. Ch., Fayette, Miss. Mem.: Magnolia Bar Assn. (sec. 2006—), Order Ea. Star. Democrat-Npl. Baptist. Office Phone: 601-899-9886. Business E-Mail: tomikaharris@jam.rr.com.

HARRIS, VENITA VAN CASPEL, retired financial planner; b. Sweetwater, Okla. d. Leonard Rankin and Ella Belle (Jarnagin) Walker; m. Lyttleton T. Harris IV, Dec. 26, 1987. Student, Duke, 1944-46; BA, U. Colo., 1948, postgrad., 1949-51, N.Y. Inst. Fin., 1962. CFP. Stockbroker Rauscher Pierce & Co., Houston, 1962-65, A.G. Edwards & Sons, Houston, 1965-68; founder, pres., owner Van Caspel & Co., Inc., Houston, 1968—87, Van Caspel Wealth Mgmt.; owner, mgr. Van Caspel Planning Svc., Van Caspel Advt. Agy.; sr. v.p. investments Raymond James and Assocs., 1987-95; ret., 1995. Moderator PBS TV show The Money Makers and Profiles of Success, 1980; 1st women mem. Pacific Stock Exchange. Author: Money Dynamics, 1978, Money Dynamics of the 1980's, 1980, The Power of Money Dynamics, Money Dynamics for the 1990's, 1988; editor: Money Dynamics Letter. Bd. dirs. Horatio Alger Assn.; trustee Northwood U.; founding mem. Com. of 200. Recipient Matrix award Theta Sigma Phi, 1969, Horatio Alger award for Disting. Americans, 1982, Disting. Woman's medal, Northwood Univ., 1988, George Norlin award U. Colo. Alumni Assn., 1987. Mem. Internat. Assn. Fin. Planners, Inst. Cert. Fin. Planners, Phi Gamma Mu, Phi Beta Kappa. Presbyterian. Home: 4 Saddlewood Estates Dr Houston TX 77024-6841 Office: 6524 San Felipe St Ste 102 Houston TX 77057-2611

HARRIS, VIRGINIA SYDNESS, religious organization administrator, publisher; m. G. Reed Harris; children: G. Richard, Donald Thomas, Steven Jeffrey. Student, Mills Coll., 1964—66; BA in Polit. Sci. and Edn., Moorhead State U., 1967; C.S.B., Mass. Metaphys. Coll., 1982. Asst. to presdl. interpreter U.S. Dept. State, Washington, 1967-68; sec. sch. tchr. Fargo (N.D.) Pub. Schs., 1968-70; TV host, prodr. Pub. Broadcast Sys., Fargo, 1968-70; Christian Sci. practitioner, 1979—; Christian Sci. tchr., 1982—; Christian Sci. lectr., 1983-89. Bd. dirs. LWV, 1969-74; faculty mem. Healing & Spirituality Symposium Harvard Med. Sch. and Mind/Body Inst., Boston, 1995—; clk. The First Ch. of Christ Scientist, 1986-90; bd. dirs. The Christian Sci., 1990—, chmn. bd. dirs., 1992—. Pub. The Writings of Mary Baker Eddy, 1992—. Mem., treas., bd. dirs. Nat. Found. Women Legislators, Inc., Washington, 1994-2001; fellow George H. Gallup Internat. Inst., 1998-; chmn bd. trustees The Mary Baker Eddy Libr. for the Betterment of Humanity, 2000—, Dr.'s Coun. Harvard Divine Sch.'s women's studies in religion program, 2000—; adv. bd. Drucker Found., 2001-; bd. overseers Boston Symphony Orch., 2003-. Mem. Coun. Women World Leaders Founders Fund Inaugural Cir., City Club Washington, Internat. Women's Forum (lectr., spkr., contbr. to profl. jours.). Avocations: skiing, reading, golf.

HARRIS, WENDY TAKE, psychologist, educator; b. Havelock, N.C., Apr. 10, 1966; d. Seiko Harris; 1 child, Phoebe Florence. BA in Behavioral Sci., Nat. U., 1998; MA, Arusa Pacific U., 2000, cert. in Sch. Psychology, 2002; student in Ednl. Psychology, Capella U., 2005—. Mgr. Jenny Craig Inc., Redland, Calif., 1997—2000; psychologist, tchr. Total Edn. Solutions, Sacramento, 2002—; sch. psychologist Hollister (Calif.) Sch. Dist., 2005—. Cons. in field. Recipient Leadership award, Nat. U., 1997. Mem.: Nat. Assn. Sch. Psychologists, Calif. Assn. Sch. Psychologists, Pi Lambda Theta. Democrat. Avocations: reading, travel, languages. Office: Hollister Sch Dist 2690 Cienega Rd Hollister CA 95023

HARRIS, YOLANDA, newscaster; b. Columbus, Ohio; married. BS in Broadcast Journalism, Bowling Green U. Reporter Call & Post Newspaper, Columbus, Ohio; with promotions, Kids Club dept. Sta. WSYX/WTTE-TV, reporter, 1996—99, weekend anchor, 1999—2002, main anchor, 2002—. Office: WSYX/WTTE-TV 1261 Dublin Rd Columbus OH 43215 E-mail: yharris@sbgnet.com.

HARRIS-BARBER, DAISY, elementary school educator; d. Mable Harris and Edward Harris, Sr.; m. Craig Barber; children: Brandi J. Barber children: Cory Cormier. BA, So. U., Baton Rouge, La., 1977; postgrad., McNeese U., Lake Charles, La., 1983. Tchr. 1st grade tchr., Lake Charles, La., 1977—2002, 7th grade tchr., 2002—. E-mail: d82455@cox-internet.com.

HARRIS-LEWIS, TAMELA SUZETTE, social studies educator, tax specialist; b. Oak Ridge, Tenn., Nov. 30, 1968; d. Henry Thomas and Helen Virginia Harris; m. Alvin Godfrey Lewis, June 24, 2000; children: Dameon Marello Harris, Alvin Zacchеus Lewis. BS in Elem. Edn. (hon.), S.C. State U., Orangeburg, 1993. Cert. elem. edn. tchr., middle level social studies tchr. S.C. Tchr. Millwood Elem. Sch., Sumter, SC, 1993—94; dir. aviation one summer youth program Wia/ Hi Tek Learning Systems, Sebring, Fla., 1994—2003; social studies tchr. Tanglewood Mid. Sch., Greenville, SC, 1994—, social studies dept. chair, 2003—, Black history mo. coord. Office mgr./tax analyst H.T. Harris Income Tax Svc., Mauldin, SC, 1995—. Mem. Redemption World Outreach Ctr., Greenville, SC, 2006; CPR responder ARC, Greenville, SC, 2005. Mem.: Alpha Kappa Alpha. Home: 153 Perigon Ct Greenville SC 29607 Office: Tanglewood Middle School 44 Merriwoods Dr Greenville SC 29611 Office Phone: 864-355-4548. Home Fax: 864-234-6766; Office Fax: 864-355-4512. Personal E-mail: tlewis@aol.com. E-mail: tlewis@greenville.k12.sc.us.

HARRIS-OFFUTT, ROSALYN MARIE, counselor, consultant, mental health nurse, writer; b. Memphis; d. Roscoe Henry and Irene Elnora (Blake) Harris; 1 child, Christopher Joseph. RN, St. Joseph Cath. Sch. Nursing, Flint, Mich., 1965; student, Hurley Med. Ctr. Sch. of Anesthesia, 1970; BS in Wholistic Health Scis., Columbia-Pacific U., 1984, postgrad., 1985—. RN; cert. registered nurse in anesthesia; nat. bd. cert. addiction counselor; cert. psychiat. nursing Kalamazoo State Hosp.; lic. profl. counselor, N.C.; cert. detoxification acupuncturist; bd. cert. med.-legal nurse cons. Staff nurse anesthetist, clin. instr. Cleve. Clinic Found., 1981-82; pvt. practice psychiat. nursing and counseling; assoc. counselor human svcs. Shaker Heights, Ohio, 1982-84; ind. contractor anesthesia Paul Scott & Assocs., Cleve., 1984, Via Triad Anesthesia Assocs., Thomasville, NC, 1984-85; sec. Cons. Psychology Counseling, P.A., 1984-86; pvt. practice psychiat. nursing and counseling Greensboro, NC, 1984-86; pvt. practice psychiat. nursing, counseling, psychotherapy UNA Psychol. Assocs., 1986—; staff cons. Charter Hills Psychiat. Hosp. in Addictive Disease, 1991—98. Nat. resource cons. Am. Assn. Nurse Anesthetists on Addictive Disease; cons. Ctr. for Substance Abuse Prevention, also advisor to assoc. and clin. med. dir. Ctr. Substance Abuse Prevention. Contbr. chpt. to book, also articles and columns in health field. Co-sponsor adolescent group Jack and Jills of Am., Inc., Bloomfield Hills, Mich., 1975; co-sponsor Youth of Unity Ctr., Clevelend Heights, Ohio, 1981-84; vol. chmn. hospitality Old Greensboro Preservation Soc., 1985; bd. dirs. Urban League, Pontiac, Mich., 1972; apptd. mem. gov's. coun. on alcohol and other drug abuse State of N.C., 1989—, gov's. coun. women's issues of addiction, 1991—; apptd. advisor to assoc. clin., med. dir. Ctr. for Substance Abuse Prevention, Dept. Health and Human Svcs. U.S., 1991—, nat. spkrs. bur., 1991—, cons.; apptd. legis. com., mental health study commn. on child and adolescent substance abuse State of N.C., 1992—; lay speaking min. United Meth. Ch.; mem. Triad United Meth. Native Am. Ch. Mission. Columbia-Pacific U. scholar, 1983. Fellow Soc. Prevention Nutritionists; mem. Am. Assn. Profl. Hypnotherapists (registered profl. hypnotherapists, adv. bd.), Am. Assn. Nurse Anesthetists (cert.), Nat. Alaska Native Am. Indian Nurses Assn., Assn. Med. Educators and Rsch. in Substance Abuse, Nat. Acupuncture Detoxification Assn., Am. Assn. Counseling and Devel., Assn. for Med. Edn. and Rsch. in Substance Abuse, Am. Assn. Clin. Hypnotists, Am. Assn. Wholistic Practitioners, Am. Acad. Experts Traumatic Stress, Am. Nurse Hypnotheray Assn. (state pres. 1992-93), Am. Nurse Assn., Am. Holistic Nurses Assn. (charter mem.), Guilford Native Am. Assn., Negro Bus. and Profl. Women Inc. (v.p., parliamentarian 1961-83, 2001-03), Oakland County Coun. Black Nurses (v.p. 1970-74), Assn. Med. Educators (rschr. substance abuse, ad hoc com. mem. cultural diversity 1994—), Zeta Phi Beta (Nu Xi Zeta chpt. 2d anti-basilevs 1992-93, Beta Nu Zeta chpt. Greensboro). Republican. Avocations: music, nature, reading, egyptian history, metaphysics. Office: UNA Psychol Assocs and Prima Med-Legal Nurse Cons 620 S Elm St Ste 371 Greensboro NC 27406-1398 Office Phone: 336-370-0655. E-mail: rharrisoffutt@cs.com.

HARRISON, ANGELA EVE, manufacturing executive; b. Little Rock, Apr. 9, 1967; d. Stephen E. and Donie E. (Brown) H.; m. Petey King, Sept. 19, 1998; children: Haven Harrison King, Ashton Harrison King. BA in Psychology, U. Ark., 1989. Clin. specialist Nutri-Sys., Little Rock, 1990-91; sec., trea. Welsco, Inc., Maumelle, Ark., 1991-94, pres., CEO, 1994—. Co-chairperson Humane Soc., Pulaski County, Ark., 1996-98. Recipient Ark. Bus. Exec. Yr. Ark. Bus., 1997, named Top 100 Women Ark., 1996, 97, 98, 99, Top 500 Women Owned Cos. Working Women Mag., 1998, 99, 2000, 2001. Mem.: Internat. Oxygen Mfg. Assn. (bd. dirs. 1996—2000), Nat. Welding Supply Assn. (regional chmn. 1996—2000), Nat. Assn. Women Bus. Owners (Woman Bus. Owner of Yr., Ark. chpt. 1998), Young Pres.'s Assn. Avocation: golf. Office: Welsco Inc 9006 Crystal Hill Rd North Little Rock AR 72113-6693 Business E-Mail: mail@welsco.com.

HARRISON, BETTY CAROLYN COOK, retired education educator, administrator; b. Cale, Ark., Jan. 11, 1939; d. Denver G. and Minnie (Haddox) Cook; m. David B. Harrison, Dec. 31, 1956; children: Jerry David, Phyllis Lynley. BSE, Henderson State Tchrs. Coll., Arkadelphia, Ark., 1961; MS, U. Ark., 1971; PhD, Tex. A&M U., 1975. Tchr. secondary schs., McCrory, Ark., 1962-64, Taylor, Ark., 1964069, Shongaloo, La., 1969-73, Minden, La., 1974-76, 77-80; adminstrv. intern La. Dept. Edn., 1974; cooperating tchr., supr. student tchrs. Grambling (La.) State U., 1974-76, La. Tech. U., Ruston, 1974-76, 78-80; asst. prof. vocat. edn. Va. Poly. Inst. and State U., Blacksburg, 1976-77; asst. prof. vocat. edn. Coll. Agr., La. State U., Baton Rouge, 1980-85, assoc. prof. Sch. Vocat. Edn., 1985-90, prof. vocat. edn., 1990—2001, prof. emeritus, 2001. Prof. career devel. specializing in instrnl. methodologies and brain-based learning, edn. and tng., edn. educator, sect. leader home econs. edn. La. State U., 1982-85, head dept. home econs. edn. and bus. edn., 1985-87, dir. La. Job Link Ctr., 1988-91, mem.grad. coun., 1990-96, dir. Sch. Edn., 1993-94, courses and curriculum sch. and coll., 1989-92. Contbr. articles to profl. jours. HEW fellow, 1973; grantee Future Homemakers Am., 1956, Coll. Acads., 1956, Ark. Edn. Assn., 1966-69, Internat. Paper Co., 1966-68, La. Dept. Edn., 1972, others. Mem. NEA (nat. assembly del.), ASTD (v.p. comm. 1991-92, sec. 1993-94), Am Vocat. Assn., Nat. Assn. Vocat. Spl. Needs Pers., Am. Vocat. Edn. Rsch. Assn., Am. Home Econs. Assn., La Home Econs. Assn. (bd. dirs., pres.-elect), La. Vocat. Assn. (bd. dirs.), La. Assn. Vocat. Home Econs. Tchrs. (pres.), Nat. Assn. Vocat. Home Econs. Tchrs., Nat. Assn. Vocat. Home Econs. Tchr. Educators, (newsletter editor), Home Econs. Edn. Assn. (regional dir., nat. v.p., editor and chair publs. 1987-93), Family Rels. Coun. La. (edn. chmn. officer) Phi Delta Kappa, Delta Kappa Gamma (chpt. v.p., rsch. chair 1978-86), Gamma Sigma Delta (historian, sec., treas. 1984-93). Democrat. Baptist. Home: 37 Broadmoor Dr Magnolia AR 71753-4381

HARRISON (INGLE), BETTYE (BETTYE INGLE), real estate company executive; b. Chattanooga, Mar. 9, 1924; d. Merle Roy and Irene (Ayers) Ingle; m. George K. Harrison Sr.; children: Elwynn Harrison, George K. Harrison Jr. Grad., Tenn. Realtors Inst. Cert. real estate brokerage mgr. CRB designation; cert. residential specialist CRS designation. Prin. broker E. Cecil Phillips Agy., Chattanooga, 1964—77; sr. v.p. Gloria Sutton Realtors, 1977—87; broker Developers Mktg., 1987—89; pres. Bettye Harrison & Assocs., Chattanooga, 1990, Realty Execs., Chattanooga, 1993—. Pres. Tenn. Real Estate Edn. Found., 1982-83. Mem. Chattanooga Assn. Realtors, pres., 1983 and 1998, Tenn. Assn. Realtors, Nat. Assn. Realtors, bd. dirs., 1987, Women's Council Realtors, nat. pres., 1986, regional v.p., gov. and state chpt. pres., 1987, Tenn.'s Women's Council Realtors, Pilot Internat., Realty Execs., Internat. Franchise, 1992. Meth. Office: Corporate Office 6505 Lee Highway Chattanooga TN 37421-1196 Office Phone: 423-894-3020. E-mail: bettyeharrison2000@yahoo.com.

HARRISON, CAROL LOVE, fine art photographer; b. Washington, Mar. 4, 1950; d. Hunter Craycroft and Margaret Varina (Edwards) H.; m. Gregory Grady, Feb. 25, 1978; children: Olivia Love Harrison, Blake McGregor, Harrison Edwards. BS in Fgn. Svc., Georgetown U., 1973; MFA, U. Md., 1983. Guest lectr. art George Mason U., 1986, 87, Shephard Coll.,1987, 96, No. Va. C.C., 1986; participant creative program Fairfax County Coun. of Arts, 1990-92; participant artist workshop program Va. Mus. Fine Arts, Richmond, 1988-89; tchr. visual arts faculty tchg. photography The Bullis Sch., 2005-06; co-dir. Creative Camp, 2006. One-woman shows include Rizzoli Internat. Bookstore and Gallery, Washington, 1982, Arnold and Porter, Washington, 1983, Covington and Burling, Washington, 1983, Crowell and Moring, Washington, 1984, Nat. Strategy Info. Ctr., Washington, 1984, Swidler and Berlin, Washington, 1985, Reynolds Minor Gallery, Richmond, Va., 1987, Peninsula Fine Arts Ctr., Newport News, Va., 1989, Georgetown U., Washington, 1994, Sam Gilliam + Olivia, The Kathleen Ewing Gallery, Washington, 2005; exhibited in group shows at The Barrie Gallery, Marymount U., 2003, The Swedish Am. Mus., Chgo., 2001, Touchstone Gallery, 1999, Rockville Arts Place, 1999, Mus. Contemporary Art, Contemporary Mus., Balt., 1999—, Balt.'s Festival of the Arts, Rockville Arts Place, 1999, Photography Exhibit, 2001, Joan Kuyper Farver Art Gallery, Pella, Iowa, Art Gallery U. Md., Smithsonian Instn., Washington Women's Art Ctr., including Washington Project for Arts, 1981, Beijing Inst., 1985, Art Inst. Pitts., 1986, Kathleen Ewing Gallery, 1986-89, 2004, Mus. Contemporary Art, Washington, 1996, 98, 99, 2003, Dallas Mus. Art, 1997, Washington Arts Coun. Gallery, 1997, 98, 99, 2000, Snapshot, The Contemporary Mus., Balt., 1999—, Mus. Contemporary Art, Washington, 1998, 99, 2000, Aldrich Mus. Contemporary Art, Ridgefield, Conn., 2002, Arcadia U. Art Gallery, Glenside, Pa., 2002, Barrie Gallery Marymount U., 2003, The Reedville Fishermen's Mus., 2005; represented in permanent collections at Corcoran Gallery Art, Washington, Va. Mus. Fine Arts, Richmond, Arnold and Porter, Williams Cos., Tulsa, Covington and Burling, United Va. Bank, Touchstone Gallery, 1999, Mus. of Contemporary Art, Washington, 1999-00, Artscape, Balt., 1999, U.S. Holocaust Meml. Mus., Am. Ctr. Polish Culture, Washington, Embassy of Poland, Washington, Nat. Gallery Art, Nat. Portrait Gallery, Addison Gallery Am. Ar.; pub. in Antietam Rev., Washington Rev., Photo Rev., Washingtonian, Profiles, Kalliope; Honorarium, Fla. Dept. Cultural Affairs, 1998; represented by Reynolds Gallery. Vol. Our Lady of Victory

Sch., Washington, 1995—96, Westminster Sch., Annandale, Va., 1996—2003; mem. women's com. Nat. Symphony Orch., 1998—. Recipient honorarium Fla. Dept. Cultural Affairs, 1998, Cash award for black and white photography Westmoreland Art Nats., LaTrobe, Pa., 1998. Mem. Nat. Mus. Women in Arts (women's com. 1997—), No. Va. Fine Arts Assn. (artist mem.), Congl. Country Club, Langley Swim and Tennis Club. Episcopalian. Avocations: films, swimming. Home and Office: 666 Live Oak Dr Mc Lean VA 22101-1569 Personal E-mail: photoclh@aim.com.

HARRISON, DIANE B., elementary school educator; d. John Paul and Wanda Veronica Barnoski; m. Jeffrey B. Harrison, Apr. 21, 1979; 1 child, Jonathan B. BS, U. Bridgeport, 1976; MS, Fairfield U., Conn., 1986. Ednl. paraprofl. Fairfield Pub. Schs., 1977—78, remedial reading tchr., 1978—79, elem. educator, 1987—, St. Thomas Sch., Fairfield, 1979—81, St. Ann Sch., Bridgeport, 1984—87. Mem. Elem. Sch. Bldg. Com., Fairfield, 2001—05; founder, sec. Tunxis Hill Village Neighborhood Improvement Assn., Fairfield, 1990—95; mem. Holy Family Rosary Guild, Fairfield, 2004—, People in Emmaus, Fairfield, 2004—; advisor McKinley Sch. Quilt Team, Fairfield, 1995—. Recipient Celebration of Excellence award, State of Conn. and So. New Eng. Tel. Co., 1991; Instrnl. Improvement grantee, Fairfield Pub. Schs., 2005—. Mem.: NEA, Victoria's Quilters, Delta Kappa Gamma (membership chmn. 1994—95), Phi Delta Kappa (corr. sec. 1986—88). Democrat. Roman Catholic. Avocations: quilt design, swimming, boating, reading, gardening.

HARRISON, ESTHER M., elementary school educator, state representative; b. Columbus, Miss. Attended, Alcorn State U., Miss. State U. for Women. Tchr. Miss. State Schs.; adminstr. Minority Bus., Jackson, Miss.; rep. Ho. of Reps., Jackson, Miss., 2000—. Mem. Constitution, Edn., Juvenile Justice, Labor and Mil. Affairs coms. Ho. Reps., Jackson, Miss., 2000—. Mem.: Helping Hands, Lowndes County League of Voteers, NAACP (life), Zeta Phi Beta. Democrat. African Meth. Episcopalian. Home: 914 S 7th St Columbus MS 39701 Office: PO Box 1018 Jackson MS 39215-1018

HARRISON, FAYE VENETIA, anthropologist, educator, writer; b. Norfolk, Va., Nov. 25, 1951; d. James and Odella Blount (Harper) Harrison; m. William Louis Conwill, May 17, 1980; children: Giles Harrison-Conwill, L. Mondlane Harrison-Conwill, Justin Harrison-Conwill. AB, Brown U., 1974; MA, Stanford U., 1977, PhD, 1982. Asst. prof. anthropology U. Louisville, 1983-89; assoc. prof. U. Tenn., Knoxville, 1989-97, prof., 1999—2004; prof., grad. dir. women's studies U. S.C., Columbia, 1997-99; prof. anthropology and African Am. studies U. Fla., Gainesville, 2004—. Editor, contbg. author: Black Folks in Cities Here and There, 1988, Decolonizing Anthropology, 1991, 2d edit., 1997, W.E.B. DuBois and Anthropology, 1992, American Anthropologist Contemporary Forum: Race and Racism, 1998, African-American Pioneers in Anthropology, 1999, Resisting Racism and Xenophobia, 2005, assoc. editor: Urban Anthropology, 1992—99, cons. editor: Women and Aging, 1990—96, Identities: Global Studies of Culture and Power, 1992—99; mem. editl. com. Critique of Anthropology, 1995—99, Annual Rev. Anthropology, 1995—2000, Am. Anthropologists, 2000—05, mem. editl. bd. U. Tenn. Press, 1996—97, mem. adv. com. Womanist Theory and Research, Transforming Anthropology, 1990—2004; author, performer: (one woman show) The Other Side of Paradise; Three Women; One Struggle; contbr. articles to profl. jours. Mem. Nat. Alliance Against Racist and Polit. Repression, 1970—, Black Women Organized for Power, Lousiville, 1984—86, Alliance Against Women's Oppression, Lousiville, 1988—89, E. Tenn. Coalition Against State Killing, 1995—97, 1999—2004, So. Human Rights Organizers Network, 2000—; organizer Ky. Rainbow Coalition, Lousiville, 1987—89; mem. adv. bd. Sister Song Reproductive Health & Rights Collective, 2002—, Knoxville Roman Cath. Diocese's Justice, Peace, Integrity of Creation, 1996—97. Recipient cert. of Merit, U. Louisville Pres. Office, 1989, Phi Beta Kappa U. Tenn. chpt., 1993, Hardy Liston, Jr. Symbol of Hope award for Promotion Cultural Diversity, U. Tenn. Commn. Blacks, 2003, award for Disting. Contbn. to Study of N.Am., Soc. Anthropology N.Am., 2004; Ford Found. fellow, 1987—88. Mem.: Internat. Union Anthrop. and Ethnol. Scis. (co-chair commn. anthropology women 1993—98, chair commn. anthropology women 1998—), Assn. Black Anthropologists (pres. 1989—91), Am. Anthrop. Assn. (exec. bd. dirs. 1990—91, 1999—2001). Office: Univ Fla Turlington Hall Gainesville FL 32611 Office Phone: 352-392-1020. Personal E-mail: fevenetia@yahoo.com.

HARRISON, GAIL G., public health educator; M in Nutritional Scis., Cornell U.; PhD in Biol. Anthropology, U. Ariz. Mem. faculty Coll. Medicine, founding dir. program in internat. health, prof. family and cmty. medicine U. Ariz., 1976—92; chair, prof. dept. cmty. health scis. UCLA Sch. Pub. Health, 1992—; asst. program dir. program for health and at-risk populations UCLA/Jonsson Comprehensive Cancer Ctr. Mem. Food and Nutrition Bd., Nat. Acad. Scis./Inst. Medicine; cons. WHO, UNICEF. Mem.: Inst. Medicine. Office: UCLA Ctr for Health Policy Rsch Ste 1550 10960 Wilshire Blvd Los Angeles CA 90024 Business E-Mail: gailh@ucla.edu.

HARRISON, GLORIA JEAN, retired music educator; b. Watertown, S.D., Mar. 11, 1947; d. Alvin Oliver Solum-Nuttbrock and Elenor Jean Solum-Nuttbrock; m. Loren Duane Harrison, Oct. 5, 2001; children: Jonathan James Brandt, David Royal Brandt. BA in Vocal Performance, Dakota Wesleyan U., 1969. Cert. tchr. S.D. Music specialist Rapid City Area Schs., SD, 1969—74, 1980—2003, ret., 2003. Artistic dir., dir. edn. and devel. Rapid City Children's Chorus, SD, 1986—2004; vocal dir. SD Amb. of Excellence, Vermillion, SD, 1989; exec. dir., founder S.D. Jr. Honor Choir, 1993—; world music drumming instr. Arts Edn. Inst., BHSU, Spearfish, 2003—; instr. Arts Edn. Inst., SDSU, Brookings, SD, 2006. Recipient Encore award, S.D. Am. Choral Dirs. Assn., 1997, Lifetime Achievement award, 2005, Disting. Svc. to Music award, S.D. Music Educators Assn., 2003. Mem.: Orgn. Am. Kodaly Educators, Am. Choral Dirs. Assn. (chair jr./mid. sch. repertiore and stds. 1993—96, co-chair summer conf. 1995). Avocations: gardening, woodworking, drums. Home: 24295 Rushmore Ranch Rd Keystone SD 57751

HARRISON, HOLLY A., lawyer; b. 1958; BA, U. Denver, 1981; JD, Boston U., 1984. Bar: Mass. 1984, Ill. 1985. Law clk. to Hon. Raymond J. Pettine, U.S. Dist. Judge Dist. R.I., 1984—85; with Sidley Austin Brown & Wood, Chgo., 1985—, ptnr., 1992—. Office: Sidley Austin Brown and Wood Bank One Plz 10 S Dearborn St Chicago IL 60603

HARRISON, JUDITH ANNE, human resources executive; b. N.Y.C., Aug. 15, 1954; d. William Russell and Lucille Kathlene Harrison; m. Brian Taylor Jarvis, Sept. 18, 1993. BA, CCNY, 1976. Bus. mgr. creative svcs. Burson-Marsteller, N.Y.C., 1976-80; creative ops. mgr. mktg. and comm. Arthur Young, N.Y.C., 1981-84; dir. collateral svcs. advt. and promotion CBS, N.Y.C., 1984-86; dir. mktg. comm. Media Gen., N.Y.C., 1986-87; pres. J.A. Harrison Comm., N.Y.C., 1988-92; v.p. The Fry Group, N.Y.C., 1992-96; v.p. human resources Ruder Finn, N.Y.C., 1997-99, s.r. v.p., 1999; chairwoman HR Roundtable/Coun. of Pub. Rels. Firms, 2000—. Mem.: World Studio Found. (bd. dirs. 1998—), Am. Women in Radio and TV (bd. dirs. N.Y. chpt. 1990—91), Soc. Human Resource Mgmt., Pub. Rels. Soc. Am., Women in Comms.

HARRISON, KATHERINE GORDON, tennis coach; b. Austin, Tex., Nov. 14, 1934; d. Thomas Perrin Harrison, Jr. and Katherine Evelyn Boone. BA, U. Tex.-Austin, 1956, MA, 1968. Singles and doubles ranked amateur US Tennis Assn. Women's tennis coach U. N.C., Chapel Hill, 1976—98. Asst. profl., faculty staff recreation assn. U. N.C., 1973—79; asst. profl. Hollow Rock Racquet & Swim Club, 1974—78; com. mem. Assn. Intercollegiate Athletics Women, 1976—80; com. mem. univ. accreditation regarding athletics, 1995. Author: (monograph for genealogy) Leftwich Hist. Assn., 1999, 2002. ESL tchr., 1998—2000; v.p. Leftwich Hist. Assn., 2006—08. Named to N.C. Tennis Hall of Fame, N.C. Tennis Found., Greensboro, 2004. Mem.: U.S. Tennis Assn., Philanthropic Ednl. Orgn., Nat. Sr. Women's Tennis Assn. (life), Phi Beta Kappa, Kappa Kappa Gamma. Episcopalian. Avocations: travel, reading, walking, writing (genealogical rsch.). Home: 404 Mimosa Dr Chapel Hill NC 27514

HARRISON, LIZETTE MARIE, language educator; b. Mayaguez, P.R., Feb. 19, 1961; d. Carl Eugene and Luz Anilda Shoemaker; children: Jeremy Lynn Thayer, Devon J. Byers, Payton Jean. BS, N.Mex State U., Las Cruces, 1983; MS, U. Nev., Las Vegas, 1993. Tchr. theatre Boulder City H.S., Nev., 1983—89, Basic H.S., Henderson, Nev., 1989—93, Durango H.S., Las Vegas, Nev., 1993—94; tchr. English Bonanza H.S., Las Vegas, Nev., 1994—. Dir. Nev. State Thespians, Las Vegas, Nev., 1990—99. Bd. dirs. Trinity Meth. Ch., Las Vegas, 1994—97. Mem.: Thespians. Democrat-Npl. Avocations: travel, reading. Office: Bonanza High School 6665 W Del Rey Las Vegas NV 89146 Office Phone: 1-702-799-4000. E-mail: lmh452@interact.ccsd.net.

HARRISON, LOIS SMITH, hospital executive, educator; b. Frederick, Md., May 13, 1924; d. Richard Paul and Henrietta Foust (Menges) Smith; m. Richard Lee Harrison, June 23, 1951; children: Elizabeth Lee Boyce, Margaret Louise Wade, Richard Paul. BA, Hood Coll., 1945, MA, 1993, Columbia U.; LHD (hon.), Hood Coll., 1993. Counselor CCNY, 1945-46; founding adminstr., counselor, instr. psychology and sociology Hagerstown (Md.) Jr. Coll., 1946-51, registrar, 1946-51, 53-54, instr. psychology and orienta, 1954-56; registrar, instr. psychology Balt. Jr. Coll., 1951-54; bus. mgr., acct. for pvt. med. practice Hagerstown, 1953-2000; trustee Washington County Hosp., Hagerstown, 1975-97, chmn. bd., 1986-88, 95—; mem. bd. Washington County Health Sys. Inc., 1997—. Chmn. Home Fed. Savs. Bank, Hagerstown, 1997-99; chmn. acute care Health Sys. Bd., 1997—; chmn. bd. dirs. Home Fed. Savs. Bank, 1998-2000, emeritus, 2001—; spkr. ednl. panels, convs. hosp. panels and seminars Author: The Church Woman, 1960-65, With Courage and Vision: Christ's Reformed Church Celebrate 150 Years, 2004. Trustee Hood Coll., Frederick, 1972—, chmn. bd., 1979-95; mem. Md. Gov.'s Commn. to Study Structure and Ednl. Devel. Commn., 1971-75; pres. Washington County Coun. Ch. Women, 1970-72; appointee Econ. Devel. Commn., County Impact Study Commn. Bd.; bd. dirs. Md. Hosp. Assn., 1988-98, Md. Chs. United, 1975—; chmn. bd. dirs. Md. Hosp. Edn. Inst., 1978-98; mem. Christ's Reformed Ch., 1935—; pres. Ch. Consistory; chmn. Chesapeake Healthcare Forum, 1995-97; chmn. Centennial Celebration, Washington County Hosp. Bd. Recipient Alumnae Achievement award Hood Coll., 1975, Washington County Woman of Yr. award, AAUW, 1984, Md. Woman of Yr. award, 1984, Md. Woman of Yr. award Francis Scott Key Commn. for Md.'s 350th Anniversary, 1984; named one of top 10 women Tri-State area, Herald-Mail Tri-State newspaper, 1990, Zonta Internat. Woman of Yr., 1994, Outstanding Woman of the Yr., Woman At the Table award, 2002. Mem. Hagerstown C. of C. Republican. Home: 12835 Fountain Head Rd Hagerstown MD 21742-2748 Office: Washington Cty Hosp Off Chmn Bd Hagerstown MD 21740 Office Phone: 301-790-8107. Personal E-mail: lorichco@aol.com.

HARRISON, MARGIE ANN, nursing educator, emergency nurse practitioner; b. Somerset, Pa., Mar. 18, 1949; d. David Allen and Thelma Irene (Rhodes) Barron; m. Charles Wesley Harrison, Nov. 16, 1969; children: Christine Marie Harrison McClung, Michael Barron. LPN, Somerset Area Practical Nursing Sch., Pa., 1968; AAS, Shenandoah U., Winchester, Va., 1992; MSN, Georger Mason U., Fairfax, Va., 2003. RN Va., 1992, cert. ACLS, Va., 1994, BCLS, Va., 1982, TNCC, Va., 1996, PNCC, Va., 1998. Emergency dept. nurse Winchester Med. Ctr., Va., 1981—; prof. nursing Lord Fairfax C.C., Warrenton, Va., 2003—. Mem. Emergency Nurses Cancel Alcohol Related Emergencies, Winchester, Va., 1999—2003. American Independent. Methodist. Avocations: travel, camping, cooking, swimming. Office: Lord Fairfax CC 6480 College St Warrenton VA 20187 Office Phone: 540-351-1559. Office Fax: 540-351-1540. Business E-Mail: mharrison@lfcc.edu.

HARRISON, MARSHA YARBERRY, volunteer; b. Pine Bluff, Ark., Feb. 12, 1949; d. Randle A. and Sara Ann (Lee) Yarberry; m. Preston E. Harrison Jr., June 24, 1971; children: Kristofer Lee, Robert Randle. BS in Therapeutic Recreation, Tex. Woman's U., 1970. Cert. recreation therapist. Activities dir. Treemont, Dallas, Albert Schweitzer Homes, Mpls. Bd. mem. Jr. League Tyler, ARC, Tyler, Discovery Sci. Pl., Tyler, 1986—, Boy Scouts of East Tex., Tyler, 1993—, United Way Tyler, 1992—, campaign chair 2006; pres. City Coun. PTA, Tyler, 1996—. Named Outstanding Vol., Jr. League of Tyler, 1990; recipient Graduate Benton HS award Heart of Gold, Smith County Med. Soc., 2006, Outstanding Vol., Tyler City, 1991. Mem. PTAs (life). Avocations: gardening, decorating, handbells. Home: 2104 Parkway Pl Tyler TX 75701-4753

HARRISON, NICOLE MARIE, special education educator; b. Cooperstown, NY, Oct. 7, 1980; d. Lou Ann and Bruce Harrison. B in Elem. Edn., SUNY, Oneonta, 2002; M in Spl. Edn., U. Albany, NY, 2003. 4th and 5th grade spl. edn. tchr. Del. Acad. and Ctrl. Sch. Dist., Delhi, NY, 2003—. Republican. Methodist. Avocations: cross stitch, travel. Office Phone: 607-746-2105.

HARRISON, PATRICIA DE STACY, broadcast executive, former federal agemcy administrator; b. NYC; m. Emmett Bruce Harrison; 3 children. BA, Am. U., 1968; MA, George Mason U.; PhD (hon.), Am. U., 2002. V.p. Holly Realty Co., Arlington, Va., 1965-69; co-founder, ptnr. E. Bruce Harrison Co., Washington, 1973—96; former pres. AEF/Harrison Internat., Washington; asst. sec. edn. & cultural affairs U.S. Dept. State, Washington, 2001—05, acting sec. pub. diplomacy & pub. affairs, 2004; pres., CEO Corp. for Pub. Broadcasting, Washington, 2005—. Keynote spkr. U.S. Dept. Labor del. to Israel and Greece, Indsl. Devel. Authority of Ireland Conf./Women Execs. in Mgmt., U.S. Info. Agy./WorldNET program for entrepreneurs via satellite to 7 countries, Export Expo '90, Seattle, Nat. Govs. Conf., U.S. SBA Fin. Mgmt. Conf. in 9 states, mgmt. and tng. program for women entrepreneurs Budapest, Hungary (Alliance Decade for Democracy series); guest lect. Thomas Colloquium on Free Enterprise, 1989; trustee Guest Svcs., Inc.; mem. adv. coun. Avon Products, Inc. Author: Inside and Out: The Story of a Hostage, 1981, (with Margaret Mason, editor) The Washington Post Pocket Style Plus, 1983-84, America's New Women Entrepreneurs, 1986. Bd. dirs. Med. Coll. Pa. Recipient Librs.' and Tchrs.' award for play produced at Kennedy Ctr., 1980, Del. award Insieme per La Pace, Rome, 1988, Disting. Woman award Northwood Inst., 1991; named Washington Woman of Yr., Washington Women Mag., 1985, Entrepreneur of Yr., Washington, Arthur Young Co. and Venture mag., 1988, Women of Enterprise award. Mem. Nat. Women's Econ. Alliance Found., Pres.'s Export Coun., SBA Nat. Adv. Coun. (co-chmn., exec. com.), SBA Women's Network for Entrepreneurial Tng. (adv. coun.), Nat. Coal Coun. (exec. com.), Women in Internat. Trade, Nat. Fedn. Press Women (ex-officio, communication award 1979, bus. communicator of yr. 1988), Capital Press Women (ex-officio, named bus communicator of yr. 1988, journalist award for non-fiction 1988), Pub. Rels. Soc. Am. (counsellors acad.), Internat. Pub. Rels. Assn. Office: Corporation Public Broadcasting 401 Ninth St NW Washington DC 20004-2129 Office Phone: 202-879-9600.

HARRISON, RACHEL, artist; b. NYC, 1966; One-woman shows include Posh Floored as Ali G Tackles Beck, Galerie Arndt & Ptnr., 2004, Brides & Bases, Oakville Galleries, Can., 2002, Look of Dress-Separates, Greene Naftali Gallery, NYC, 1997, Should Home Windows, Arena Gallery, Bklyn., 1996, exhibited in group shows at Dreams & Conflicts: Dictatorship of Viewer, La Biennale di Venezia, Venice, 2003, Experimenters, Lombard-Freid Fine Arts, NYC, 1997, Rachel Harrison & Michael Lazarus, Feature, NYC, 1996, Space, Mind, Place, Andrea Rosen Gallery, NY, 1996, Summer Exhbn., Greene Naftali Gallery, NY, 1996, Sex, Drugs & Explosives, New London Art Forms, London, 1996, Sculpture Incorporating Photog., Feature Gallery, NY, 1996, Post Hoc, Stark Gallery, NY, 1996, Facing the Millennium: The Song Remains the Same, Arlington Mus., Tex., 1996, Oy, 121 Greene St., NY, 1995, High Anxiety, 66 Crosby, NY, 1995, Looky Loo, Sculpture Ctr., NY, 1995, Dark Room, Stark Gallery, NY, 1995, Unsuccess, 479 Broome St., NY, 1994, Tight, Tannery Gallery, London, 1994, Dirty, John Good Gallery, NY, 1994, I Could Do That, 109 Spring St., NY, 1994, Poverty Pop: Aesthetics of Necessity, Exit Art, NY, 1993, Resurrections, William Benton Mus. Art, U. Conn., 1993, Benefits for Four Walls Gallery, David Zwirner Gallery, NY, 1993, Shooting Blanks, 81 Greene St., NY, 1993, 1920: Subtlety of Subversion, Continuity of Intervention, Exit Art, NY, 1993, Simply Made in Am., Aldrich Mus. Contemporary Art, 1993, I Was Born Like This, Mulberry St. Gallery, NY, 1993, Morality Cafe, Postmasters Gallery, NY, 1993, Unlearning, 142 Greene St., NY, 1991, Open Bar, Flamingo East, NY, 1991. Mailing: c/o Greene Naftali Gallery 526 West 26th St New York NY 10001

HARRISON, VIRGINIA M., federal agency administrator; b. Cheverly, Md., Oct. 14, 1954; d. John Emory and Josephine (Holiday) H. AA in Bus. Mgmt., Prince George's C.C., Largo, Md., 1986; BRE, Washington Saturday Coll., 1992, MRE, 1993; PhD in Christian Edn., Faith Bible Coll., Plymouth, Fla., 2005. Ordained minister. Corr. clk. typist Passport Office Dept. of State, Washington, 1972-75; passport/visa clk. typist US Army Svc. Ctr. for Armed Forces Dept. of Army, Washington, 1975-77, passport agt./adminstrv. asst. Nat. Def. U., 1977-79, tng. coord. Automation Support Detachment, 1979-81, mgmt. asst. Mil. Pers. Command Alexandria, Va., 1981-82, mgmt. analyst Adj. Gen. Ctr. Washington, 1982-84, mgmt. analyst Cmty. and Family Support Ctr., 1984-89; mgmt. analyst Bur. Naval Pers. Dept. of Navy, Washington, 1989-97; founder, pastor Kingdom of God Ministries, 1993; supervising mgmt. analyst USMC Resource and Mgmt. Analysis Office, Arlington, Va., 1997-99; equal employment opportunity specialist Equal Opportunity Office, Dulles, Va., 1999—. Spkr. seminars, retreats, radio talk programs; with Def. Threat Reduction Agy., Ft. Belvoir, Va., 2000—04, Office of Adminstrv. Asst. to Sec. of Army, Arlington, Va., 2004—; founder Virginia Harrison Ministries. Author: Wedding Vows for Christians, 1992, 1993. Founder, pastor Kingdom of God Ministries, 1993. Named Outstanding Club Pres., Toastmasters Internat., 1991. Mem. Toastmasters Internat. (Disting. toastmaster). Democrat. Avocations: travel, reading. Home: 11006 Penny Ave Clinton MD 20735-3937 Office: Def Threat Reduction Agy Equal Opportunity Office Arlington VA 22202-3905 Office Phone: 703-602-0615.

HARRISON, (HILDE), artist; b. Wallduern, Baden, Germany, Mar. 16, 1936; came to U.S., 1953; d. Heinz Lennartz and Hilde Lennartz-Klein; m. Charles E. Harrison Jr., Jan. 31, 1959; children: Charles, Marianne, Andrea, Pete, Bianca. Assoc. BS, Lord Fairfax Coll., 1989; BFA, Shepherd U., 1994; MA, NYU, Venice, 2001. Tchr. Pavan, Winchester, Va., 1998; pvt. lessons Front Royal, Va., 1999—; lectr. Frederick County Sch. Sys., Va., 1999—. Lectr. Culpeper (Va.) Art League, Manasas (Va.) Art League, Lurray (Va.) Art League. One-woman shows include Blue Ridge Arts Coun., Front Royal, 1984, Wallduern, Germany, 1992, Presina, Italy 1999, Venice, Italy, 1999, 2000, N.Y.C., 2001. Pres. Assn. for Children with Learning Disability, West Chester, Pa., 1972; founder, pres. Warren County Assn. for Children with Learning Disability, Front Royal, 1975; chair Warren County Sch. Bd. Spl. Edn., Front Royal, 1980, Vacation Bible Sch., Front Royal. Recipient Corning Glass award, 1980, Wheat Security award, 1984, 1st pl. Regional Show, Blue Ridge Arts Gallery, 2002, 2d pl., 2003. Mem. Women Arts, Va. Watercolor Assn., Blud Ridge Arts Coun. (docent), Shenandoah Valley Art Assn., Shenandoah Arts Coun. Avocations: reading, hiking, cooking, swimming, crafts. Home: 381 Windy Ridge Rd Front Royal VA 22630-7207

HARRISON-BRIDGEMAN, ANN MARIE, claims adjuster; b. St. Louis, Aug. 11, 1942; d. James W. and G. Marie Harrison; m. Loren JC Bridgeman, Apr. 10, 1961 (div. Feb. 1979); children: Michael, Mitchell, Michelle. AA, Belleville (Ill.) Area Coll., 1970; AS, San Antonio Coll., 1979; BS, S.W. Tex. State U., San Marcos, 1984, MS, 1999; postgrad., Okla. U., Norman, 1999—. Lic. sr. claims law assoc. Asst. chief acct. St. Mary's U., San Antonio, 1977-80; instr. acctg. and computers Reedley (Calif.) Jr. Coll., ABC Bus. Coll., Fresno, Calif., 1985; asst. to head acct. Hanford (Calif.) Cmty. Hosp., 1985-86; claims rep. acctg. USAA Ins. Co., San Antonio, 1980-85, policy svc. rep., 1987-99, 1980-82, acctg. tech., 1982-85, claims adjuster, 1987-96, total loss/salvage adjuster San Antonio & Okla. City, 1996-99; sr. total loss/slavage rep. U.S. Automobile Assn. Ins. Co., Oklahoma City, 1999—. Vol Olympic Games, 1993, others, 1990-96. With USN, 1960-62. Mem. AAUW, Smithsonian Instn., Nat. Geog. Soc., Am. Assn. Ret. Persons, Phi Theta Kappa. Roman Catholic. Office: USAA 212 S Quadrum Dr Oklahoma City OK 73108-1114

HARRISS, CYNTHIA THERESE (CYNTHIA THERESE CLARKE), retail executive; b. Huntington, W. Va., June 12, 1952; d. Forbes Richard and Arlene (Will) Clarke. Buyer Scripps McCartney, Canton, Ill., 1972—73; store mgr. Paul Harris Stores, Cin., 1973—75, dist. mgr. St. Louis, 1975—77, regional mgr. Chgo., 1977—82, v.p. stores operation Indpls., 1982—85, v.p. div. mdse. mgr., 1985—89; sr. v.p. sales, Walt Disney Stores The Walt Disney Co., Glendale, Calif., 1992—97; sr. v.p. park ops. Disneyland Resort, The Walt Disney Co., Glendale, Calif., 1997—99, exec. v.p., 1999, pres., 1999—2003; pres., Gap Outlet stores The Gap Inc., San Francisco, 2004—05, pres., Gap Brand, 2005—. Bd. trustees Laguna Beach Playhouse. Recipient Internat. Disting. Leadership award, Jewish Nat. Fund, Tree of Life award, 2000. Mem.: Women's Leadership Bd., Harvard U., JFK Sch. Govt. Roman Catholic. Office: Gap Inc Two Folsom St San Francisco CA 94105*

HARROD, AUDREY HUNTER, retired executive secretary; b. Raleigh, N.C., Dec. 30, 1928; d. Wade Hampton and Katie Clarke Hunter; m. Elias Edward Harrod (dec.); children: Glenn Denise Logan Scott, Rodney Karl Logan(dec.). BA, St. Augustine's Coll., Raleigh, 1950; postgrad., N.C. State U., 1954—55. Head teller, sec. Mechanics & Farmers Bank, Raleigh, 1958—67; tchr. N.C. State Sch. Blind & Deaf, Raleigh, 1967—69; exec. sec. Office Pres. Howard U., Washington, 1969—91; ret., 1991. Mediator Rappahonnock Mediation Ctr., Fredericksburg, Va., 1993—2005. Bd. dirs. United Way, Fredericksburg, 1998—2000, ARC, Fredericksburg, 2004—; founder Lunch Bunch Pinochle Club, 1994—; Ch. of the Messiah Sec. to Vestry, 1996—98; bd. mem. Am. Red Cross. Recipient Appreciation Pres.'s award, Rappahonnock Mediation Ctr., 1999, Tenacity in Fundraising, ARC, Fredericksburg, 2002, Appreciation award, 2004. Mem.: Va. Mediation Network, St. Clares Guild, Alpha Kappa Alpha. Democrat. Episcopalian. Avocations: collecting miniature shoes, pinochle, travel. Home: 4002 Norris Dr Fredericksburg VA 22407-6864

HARRON, PHOEBE ZASLOVE, investment banking executive; b. Knoxville, Tenn., June 12, 1953; d. Herbert James and Jean (Butler) Zaslove; m. Michael Fralinger Harron, Aug. 25, 1984. BA in Journalism, U. Ky., 1973; BSM in Piano, Sch. Fine Arts, Boston U., 1975; postgrad., Inst. Fin., 1978—79. Registered rep., SEC, all exchanges Nat. Assn. Securites Dealers. Instl. option sales trader First Boston, N.Y.C., 1978—80; prin. stockholder, head domestic and internat. instl. option arbitrage Morgan Stanley & Co., Inc., N.Y.C., 1980—. Recipient Swiss Govt. Tibor Varga Festival scholar, Sione, Switzerland, 1975—76. Mem.: Nat. Option and Futures Soc. (dir. 1979—80), N.Y. Option Soc., Concert Artists Guild (dir. 1982—84). Episcopalian. Achievements include concert performances throughout New Eng., N.Y. and Europe, 1969-76. Office: Morgan Stanley & Co 1585 Broadway New York NY 10036-8200

HARRY, DEBORAH ANN, singer; b. Miami, Fla., July 11, 1945; d. Richard Smith and Catherine (Peters) H. AA, Centenary Coll., 1965. Singer, songwriter rock group Blondie, 1975-83. Albums include Blondie, 1976, Plastic Letters, 1977, Parallel Lines, 1978, Eat to the Beat, 1979, Autoamerican, 1979, The Best of Blondie, 1981, The Hunter, 1982; (solo) Koo Koo, 1981, Rockbird, 1981, Def, Dumb & Blond, 1989, Debravation, 1993, Blonde and Beyond, 1993, Jazz Passengers - In Love, 1994, Rapture, 1994, The Platinum Collection, 1994, Virtuosity, 1995, Los Fabulosos Caillacs-Rey Azucar, 1995, Blodie-Atomic, 1995, Rockbird, 1996, Der Einziger Weg, 1999; songs include Heart of Glass, 1978 (ASCAP award), Call Me, Tide is High, Rapture, 1980; film appearances include Union City Blues, 1980, Videodrome, Roadie, 1980, Hairspray, 1988, Tales From the Darkside: The Movie, 1990, Joe's Day, 1999, Zoo, 1999, Six Ways to Sunday, 1999, Ghost Light, 2000, Dueces Wild, 2000, Red Lipstick, 2000; TV appearances include Saturday Night Live, The Muppet Show, Tales from the Darkside, Wiseguy; appeared on Broadway Teaneck Tanzi, The Venus Flytrap, 1983; (movie) Satisfaction, New York Stories, 1989, Wigstock: The Movie, 1995, Heavy, 1995, Copland, 1997.

Recipient Gold, Silver and Platinum records; named to Rock and Roll Hall of Fame, 2006. Mem. ASCAP, AFTRA, Screen Actors Guild, Equity. Office: c/o 10th St Entertainment Ste G410 700 San Vicente Blvd West Hollywood CA 90069*

HARRYMAN, KATHLEEN A., board administrator; b. Balt., Feb. 12, 1950; d. Michael A. and Catherine A. (White) Wagner; m. Steven L. Fader, Sept. 13, 1970 (div. Jan. 1976); m. Michael Andrew Harryman, July 17, 1981; 1 child, Tyler Andrew. Clk. typist Md. State Hwy. Adminstrn., 1968-71, stenographer, 1971-72, office sec., 1972-73, office sec. for met. dist./utility engr. Brooklandville, 1973-76, exec. sec. for met. dist. engr., 1976-84, asst. MIS coord., computer divsn. Balt., 1984-90; asst. exec. dir. Md. State Bds. Barbers and Cosmetologists, Balt., 1990-92, adminstr., 1992—. Mem. task force on exam. process Md. Higher Edn. Commn., Annapolis; mem. cosmetology program adv. bd. Md. Divsn. Rehab. Svcs., Balt., 1992—. Chair clerical study com. Md. Classified Employees Assn., Balt., 1980; rep. Nat. Interstate Coun. Cosmetology. Avocations: crafts, writing poetry and children's stories. Office: Md State Bd Barbers and Cosmetologists 500 N Calvert St Baltimore MD 21202-3651

HARSANYI, JANICE, retired soprano, educator; b. Arlington, Mass., July 15, 1929; d. Edward and Thelma (Jacobs) Morris; m. Nicholas Harsanyi, Apr. 19, 1952; 1 son, Peter Michael. BMus, Westminster Choir Coll., 1951; postgrad., Phila. Acad. Vocal Arts, 1952-54. Voice tchr. Westminster Choir Coll., Princeton, NJ, 1951-63, chmn. voice dept., 1963-65; lectr. music Princeton Theol. Sem., 1956-63; voice tchr. summer sessions U. Mich., 1965-70; artist-in-residence Interlochen Arts Acad., 1967-70; voice tchr. N.C. Sch. Arts, Winston-Salem, 1971-78; music faculty Salem Coll., 1973-76; condr. voice master classes, choral clinics various colls., 1954—; prof. voice Fla. State U., Tallahassee, 1978—, chmn. dept., 1979-83; ret., 2005. Concert singer, 1954—, debut, Phila. Orch., 1958; appearances with, Am., Detroit, Houston, Minn., Nat., Symphony of Air orchs., Bach Aria Group, 1967-68, maj. music festivals, U.S., 1960—; toured with, Piedmont Chamber Orch., 1971-78, concerts and recitals, in major U.S. cities, also in Belgium, Eng., Ger., Italy, Switzerland and Sweden; rec. artist, Columbia, Decca, CRI records. Mem. Nat. Assn. Tchrs. Singing, Music Tchrs. Nat. Assn., Coll. Music Soc., Riemenschneider Bach Inst., Sigma Alpha Iota, Pi Kappa Lambda. Home: 2116 Trescott Dr Tallahassee FL 32308-0732

HARSE, CONSTANCE BRADFORD, retired social worker; b. Birmingham, Ala., Sept. 19, 1941; d. Nathaniel Gouveaneur Bradford and Constance (Malone) Brown; m. Donald Albert Harse (div.); children: John Harold Clark, Jessica Flame Harse Moore. BA, Tulane U., New Orleans, 1963. LCSW Ohio. Social investigator NYC Welfare Dept., 1963—64; caseworker Erie County Welfare Dept., Buffalo, 1965—66; market rschr. AC Nielsen Co., NYC, 1966—77; caseworker, quality control reviewer Athens County Dept. Jobs and Family Svcs., Athens, Ohio, 1982—2001; ret., 2001. Home: 10800 Peach Ridge Rd Athens OH 45701-9765

HARSH, ALEXIS GOODSELL, middle school educator; b. Omaha, Apr. 21, 1974; d. Nancy Guile and Timothy Gerard Goodsell; m. Lucas Oliver Harsh, Aug. 15, 1998; children: Mason Oliver, Hunter Keith. B, Emory U., Atlanta, 1996, MA in Tchg., 1999, diploma in Advanced Study in Tchg., 2005. Tchr. Gwinnett County Pub. Sch., Lawrenceville, Ga., 1999—2006. Home: PO Box 1263 Lawrenceville GA 30046 Office Phone: 770-338-4714. Personal E-mail: alexisharsh@yahoo.com. E-mail: alexis_harsh@gwinnett.k12.ga.us.

HARSH, ANTOINETTE MOLLETT, investor; b. Glendale, Calif., Nov. 21, 1946; d. Byron Hendrix Mollett and Margaret Louise Hunter; children: Casey, Brent, Troy, Danielle. Student, Cambridge U., 1967; BS cum laude in History, U. So. Calif., 1968, MS in Edn., 1969. Edn. asst. L.A. County Mus. Natural History, 1968—70; tchr. Washoe County Sch. Dist., Reno, 1970—72; ptnr. Valley Bldg. Co., Glendale, Calif., 1975—, bd. dir., 1st v.p., 2002—. Owner Profl. Filing Svcs., Reno, 1989—2000; sr. v.p. Kirby-Smith and Assocs., Quarreyville, Pa., 1998—2001. Mem. Human Resources Consortium, Reno, 2002—04; Fin. Adv. Bd. Reno, 1998—2000; bd. dirs. Reno Regional Govt., 2002—04; liason Arts and Culture Commn., Reno, 2000—04, Hist. Resources Commn., Reno, 2000—04, Parks & Rec. Commn., Reno, 2000—04; liaison Urban Forestry Commn., Reno, 2002—04, Citizens Traffic Adv. Com., Reno, 2002—04; pres. Vorces Truckee Meadows, PAC, 2004—; coun. mem. Reno City Coun., 2000—04; pres. Truckee Meadows Heritage Trust, Reno, 1999; mem. Reno Sr. Aux. Vol. Effort, 2004—05, bd. dirs. Ret. and Sr. Vol. Program, 2005—; vice-chmn. Salvation Army, Reno, 2005—; bd. dirs. Scenic Nev., 2005—, Reno Tahoe Winter Games Com., 2005—. Recipient Hero award, Scenic Nev., 2003. Mem.: U. So. Calif. Alumni, Delta Delta Delta (pres. Reno chpt. 1996—98). Republican. Avocations: history, rafting. Address: PO Box 2327 Reno NV 89505 Office Phone: 775-846-1910. Personal E-mail: tonihars@charter.net.

HARSH, MITZI ANN, language educator, coach; b. Bartlesville, Okla., July 19, 1967; d. Charles Daniel and Norma Joy Houser; m. John Bryan Harsh, Mar. 23, 1991; 1 child, Brett Daniel. BA in Secondary English Edn., Okla. Wesleyan U., Bartlesville, 1989. Cert. secondary tchr. English Okla. & Kans., 1985. Tchr. English, girls' basketball coach Copan H.S., Okla., 2004—; adj. instr. Okla. Wesleyan U., Bartlesville, 2005—. Mem.: Okla. Basketball Coaches Assn. D-Conservative. Wesleyan. Avocations: softball, writing, reading. Home: 394391 W 900 Rd Copan OK 74022 Office: Copan HS 527 Hornet Lane Copan OK 74022 Office Phone: 918-532-4344. Business E-Mail: mharsh@copan.k12.ok.us.

HART, ANN WEAVER, academic administrator; b. Salt Lake City, Nov. 6, 1948; d. Ted Lionel and Sylvia (Moray) Weaver; m. Randy Bret Hart, Sept. 12, 1968; children: Kimberly, Liza, Emily, Allyson. BS in History, U. Utah, 1970, MA in History, 1981, PhD in Ednl. Adminstrn., 1983. Tchr. pub. schs., Salt Lake City, 1970-73, 80-81; jr. high sch. prin. Provo Pub. Schs., Utah, 1983-84; prof. ednl. adminstrn. U. Utah, Salt Lake City, 1984—98, assoc. dean Grad. Sch. Edn., 1991-93, dean Grad. Sch., 1993—98; provost, v.p. acad. affairs Claremont Grad. U., Calif., 1998—2002; pres. U. NH, Durham, 2002—06, Temple U., Phila., 2006—. Bd. dirs. Citizens Bank N.H. Author: Principal Succession: Establishing Leadership in Schools, 1993, The Principalship, 1996, Designing and Conducting Research, 1996; editor: Ednl. Adminstrn. Quar., 1990-92; contbr. articles to profl. jours. Grantee U. Utah, State of Utah, U.S. Dept. Edn. Mem. Am. Ednl. Rsch. Assn., Am. Coun. on Edn., Phi Beta Kappa, Phi Kappa Phi. Avocations: skiing, backpacking, hiking, kayaking, bicycling. Office: Temple Univ Office of Pres 200 Sullivan Hall 1330 W Berks St Philadelphia PA 19122 Office Phone: 215-204-7405. Business E-Mail: president@temple.edu.

HART, BETTY MILLER, artist; b. East Orange, N.J., Apr. 15, 1918; d. John Erwin and Frances Louise (Hockett) M.; m. Harold Harmon Hart Jr., Mar. 8, 1947; children: John David, Harold Harmon 3d, Judith Hockett, Mary Elizabeth Vail. Student, Syracuse U., 1936-38, Newark Coll. Engring., 1941-42. Mech. designer L.S. Brach, Newark, 1941-43; pvt. worker Bur. Ships, Washington, 1942-43; mech. designer Laurence Engring. and Rsch., Linden, N.J., 1943-45, Phila. Arsenal, 1945, Heyer Industries, Belleville, N.J., 1945-48; pvt. clothing designer Little Silver, N.J., 1950-53; instr. drawing Home Studio and Guild Creative Art, Little Silver, Shrewsbury, N.J., 1959-85; artist, 1965—. Founder, mem., past pres. Guild Creative Art, Shrewsbury, N.J., 1957-82; founder, 1st pres. Art Aux. Monmouth Med. Ctr., Long Branch, N.J., 1970-75; mem. Arts Club Washington, 1989-92. One woman shows include Old MIll Gallery, Tinton Falls, N.J., 1952, Guild Creative Art, Shrewsbury, N.J., 1964, 67, Capricorn Galleries, Bethesda, Md., 1975, 83, 93; group shows, Newark Mus., 1968, 79, Pa. Acad. Fine Arts, 1969, Phila. Art Mus., 1970, N.J. State Mus., 1967-73, Nat. Acad. Design, N.Y.C., 1978, Rutgers U., N.J., 1980, Boulder Ctr. Visual Arts, 1982, Salmagundi Club, N.Y.C., 1984, 85, (The Drawing award 1981), Butler Inst. Am. Art, Youngstown, Ohio, 1987, Nat. Arts Club N.Y., 1992. Vol. Instructing Handicapped to Draw, Redbank, N.J.; bd. dirs. Monmouth Workshop Handicapped, 1960-65; spkr. in field. Recipient purchase award Monmouth Coll. Festival Arts West Long Branch, N.J., 1976, N.J. State Mus., Princeton, 1978, Philip Desind Collection, Washington, 1976, 83, 85, 87, John R. Marsh Meml. award Hunterdon Art Ctr., N.J., 1973, Merit award Monmouth Coll. Festival Arts, 1973, Bee Co. award Jersey City Mus., 1974, 1st place mixed media St. James Commons Art Exhibition, Newark, 1978, Arts Coun. Suburban Essex Seton Hall Univ., South Orange, N.J., 1980, merit award Nat. Arts Club, N.Y.C., 1985, honorable mention 1984, Gumbacker award Ocean County Artist Guild, 1988, others. Mem. Mus. Art and Sci., Greater Daytona Kappa Kappa Gamma Alumnae Assn., Daytona Beach Area Alumnae Panhellenic. Republican. Roman Catholic. Achievements include patents in field. Avocations: gardening, wildlife, opera, big band, dance. Home: 738 Five Mile Dr # 2 Ithaca NY 14850-9354 Office: Carpicorn Galleries 10236 River Rd Potomac MD 20854-4905

HART, BRENDA REBECCA, retired gifted and talented educator; b. West Point, Ga., Aug. 29, 1941; d. Howard William Godfrey, Sarah Will Clegg; m. William Samuel Hart, Mar. 26, 1961 (dec. Oct. 1971); 1 child, Keith Samuel. BA in Social Studies, La Grange Coll., 1977, MEd in History, 1979. Tchr. gifted and talented State Dept. Edn., Atlanta, 1998—2003, ret., 2003. Collector data State Dept. Edn., Atlanta, 1985—, advance placement, 1998—. Home: 1702 Rosemont Ave West Point GA 31823 Personal E-mail: bghart@knology.net.

HART, CHERIE ANN, music educator; b. L.A., May 11, 1964; d. Jon Kenneth and Carol Ann Hart. MusB, U. Minn., Mpls., 1988; MusM, U. Wis., Madison, 1991. Tchr. music pvt. practice, Mpls., 1987—, Washington County, Wis., 1987—; dir. music St. Paul's U.C.C., Menomonee Falls, 1998—; coach gymnastics La Fleurs Gymnastics, 1998—; coach flute Washington County Youth Orch., West Bend, 2006—. Mem. com. Sch. Nutrition Team, Hartford, Wis., 2006. Author: (children's book) Day of the Moon, 2005. Mem.: Mensa, Alliance Francaise Milw. Avocations: astronomy, tennis, languages.

HART, CLAIRE-MARIE, secondary school educator; b. Lawrence, Mass., Dec. 6, 1942; d. Roderick P. and M. Claire (Sullivan) H. BS in Edn., Bridgewater State Coll., 1964; MA, U. R.I., 1968; MAT, Salem State Coll., 1985. Tchr. English B.M.C. Durfee H.S., Fall River, Mass., 1964—68, Beverly H.S., Mass., 1968—. Adj. prof. English No. Shore C.C., Danvers, Mass., 1970—, Endicott Coll., Beverly, 1997—; mentor cons. Beverly Sch. Dist., 1996—; cons., presenter in field. Mem. subcom. Beverly Sch. Com., 1998-2000; mem. Local Religious Ch. Orgn., Beverly, 1978—, Dem. City Com., Beverly, 1978—. Recipient Outstanding Educator award, Harvard U., Cambridge, Mass., 2000, Mass. Mentor of Yr. award, 2004, Tchr. of Yr. Rotary Club, 2005, Inspirational Tchr. award Boston Globe, 2006; NEH grantee, 1986, 88. Mem. NEA, MLA, Nat. Coun. Tchrs. English, Dante Soc. Am., New Eng. Assn. Tchrs. English, Mass. Tchrs. Assn. Roman Catholic. Avocations: reading, antiques, gardening, theater. Home: 5 Cornell Rd Beverly MA 01915-1611 Office: Beverly High Sch 100 Sohier Rd Beverly MA 01915 Personal E-mail: cmhdante@aol.com.

HART, CLARE, information company executive; b. Morristown, NJ, Sept. 22, 1960; m. Greg Baer. BS in Finance and Computer Systems Mgmt., Drexel U., 1983; MBA, Rider U., 1986. Programmer, analyst applications dept. Dow Jones & Co., 1983—90, sr. programming analyst to program mgr. advanced systems group; joined Desktop Data (renamed NewsEdge in 1998), Mich., 1991—92; regional sales dir. US Central region and Canada Dow Jones & Co., Mich., 1992, dir. corp. news products Dow Jones Interactive NYC, 1995, dir. enterprise mktg., 1996, exec. dir. enterprise products, 1999; v.p., dir. Global Sales Dow Jones Reuters Business Interactive LLC (now Factiva), 1999; pres., CEO Factiva, 2000—06, chmn. bd., 2006—; exec. v.p. Dow Jones & Co., 2006—; pres. Dow Jones Enterprise Media Group, 2006—. Recipient NY Ten Awards, Exec. Coun., 2005. Mem.: Special Libraries Assn., Soc. Competitive Intelligence Professionals (bd. dirs. 1999—2000), Software and Info. Industry Assn. (bd. dirs.). Avocations: horseback riding, theater. Office: Dow Jones & Co 1 World Financial Ctr 200 Liberty St New York NY 10281*

HART, DEBORAH RACHEL, mathematical biologist, marine biologist; d. Philmore J and Adelle Hoffman Hart. BS, U. of Chgo., 1978; PhD, Calif. Inst. of Tech., Pasadena, 1983. Rsch. sceintist Tel Aviv U., 1995—99; ops. rsch. analyst NOAA NE Fisheries Sci. Ctr., Woods Hole, Mass., 1999—. Mem., sea scallop plan and devel. team New Eng. Fisheries Mgmt. Coun., Newburyport, Mass., 1999—. Author: (book) Calculus Problems for a New Century; contbr. articles to profl. jours.l. Avocations: duplicate bridge, tennis. Office: NOAA Northeast Fisheries Science Center 166 Woodland Trail Woods Hole MA 02543 Office Phone: 508-495-2369. E-mail: deborah.hart@noaa.gov.

HART, DIONNE A., physician; b. Harvey, Ill., Dec. 5, 1970; d. Morris John Hart Sr. and Everline Hart; m. Patrick Sean Kimbrough Sr., June 18, 1989 (div. Dec. 23, 1992); children: Brandon Orlando Kimbrough, Patrick Sean Kimbrough Jr., Candice Kiara Kimbrough. AB, U. Chgo., 1992. Lic. physician Minn., 2004. Physician Mayo Clinic, Rochester, Minn., 2003—. Social chair person Mayo Fellows Assn., Rochester, Minn., 2005—. Recipient The 24 Hour Woman award, R.E.A.C.H: Rallying the Entertainment and Athletic Communities to Help, 1999, MJ Martin award, Mayo Clinic Dept. of Psychiatry and Psychology, 2004-2005. Mem.: AMA, Minn. Med. Assn., Assn. of Women Psychiatrists, Am. Acad. of Child and Adolescent Psychiatrists (Outstanding Psychiatry Resident award 2005), Am. Psychiat. Assn. (Shire fellowship 2005—06), Alpha Kappa Alpha. Roman Catholic. Office: Mayo Clinic 200 First St SW Rochester MN 55906 Office Phone: 507-284-0324.

HART, ELIZABETH ANN, foundation administrator; b. Moulton, Ala., Sept. 14, 1942; d. Maburn L. Bertie Hale and Julia Mae Evans; m. Bruce Burleson Hart, Dec. 19, 1964; 1 child, Alexandra Natasha Burleson Hart. Diploma in Nursing, Brigham & Women's Hosp., Boston, 1963; BA in Psychology and English, George Washington U., Washington, 1971; postgrad. in business, Le Tourneau U., Longview, Tex., 1999—. RN, N.Y. Co-therapist Psychiatric Inst., Washington, 1969—72; staff nurse NIMH, Bethesda, Md., 1966—67; instr. biology Vernon Ct. Jr. Coll., Newport, RI, 1965—66; chmn., CEO Susan G. Komen Breast Cancer Found., Dallas, 1994—95; pres., CEO Hart Internat., Dallas, 1995—, Easter Seals Rehab. Svcs., Dallas, 1999—, Easter Seals Greater Dallas, 2002. Instr. biology and gen. sci. Miramar Sch. Girls, Newport, R.I., 1965-66; cons. Nat. Cancer Inst., Bethesda, 1993—, Ctr. Non-Profit Mgmt., Dallas, 1995—, Cancer Cube, 1996—, Dept. Defense, Washington, 1997-99; cons. U.S. Army Breast Cancer Rsch. Program, 1993-97, consumer evaluation subcom., writing group, 1994, exec. com. integration panel, 1994-95, exec. com. liaison subcom., 1995-96; adv. coun. sch. nursing U. Tex., Austin, 1994-99; patient adv. com. NSABP/BCPT, 1995, subcom. clin. ctr. performance evaluation, 1995; bd. dirs. Nat. Cancer Policy Bd., Bethesda, 1997-99; data safety and monitoring com. Internat. Breast MRI Consortium. Exec. prodr. (film) Women's Lives Dialogues on Breast Cancer, 1996; prodr. (video) Building for the Future, 2001. Pres. Women's Guild United Cerebral Palsy, 1985, Presbyn. Women, 1994-99; active Nat. Plan on Breast Cancer, Washington, 1995-2000; v.p. devel. Yellow Rose Found., 1996, v.p. cmty. outreach, 1997, Dallas Action Symphony Orch. League, Friends of Timberlawn. Recipient Vol. of Yr. award United Cerebral Palsy Assn. Met. Dallas, 1983, 101% Vol. award, 1983. Mem. Dallas-Ft. Worth Internat. Soc. Republican. Avocations: reading, mountain climbing, painting. Home: 9051 Oak Path Ln Dallas TX 75243 Office: Easter Seals Rehab Svcs 4443 N Josey Ln Carrollton TX 75010 E-mail: hart.elizabeth@worldnet.att.net, ehart@easterseals.com.

HART, ELLEN, writer; b. Mpls., Aug. 10, 1949; d. Herman Charles and Marjory Rowena (Anderson) Boehnhardt; life partner Kathleen Linda Kruger; children: Shawna Kruger Gibson, Bethany Kruger. BA, Ambassador U., 1972. Tchr. The Loft, Mpls., 1995-96, U. Minn. Compleat Scholar Program, Hamline U. Author: Hallowed Murder, 1989, Vital Lies, 1991, Stage Fright, 1992, A Killing Cure, 1993, A Small Sacrifice, 1994, This Little Piggy Went to Murder, 1995, For Every Evil, 1995, Faint Praise, 1995, Robbers Wine, 1996, The Oldest Sin, 1996, Murder in the Air, 1997, Wicked Games, 1998, Death on a Silver Platter, 2003, Immaculate Midnight, 2002, An Intimate Ghost, 2004 (Goldie Award, 2005), No Reservations Required, 2005, The Iron Girl, 2005. Recipient Lambda Lit. award (3), Minn. Book award (2). Mem. Sisters in Crime. Avocation: gourmet cooking. Mailing: Publicity Dept St Martin's Press 175 Fifth Ave New York NY 10010 E-mail: ellenhart@earthlink.net.

HART, JANET MARILYN, writer, lecturer; b. Dublin, Tex., Sept. 13, 1940; d. Nathan L. and Minnie (Novit) Siegel; m. Charles Benjamin Hart, June 4, 1961; children: Deborah Leigh, Katherine Helaine, David Wolf. AA, Lon Morris Jr. Coll., Jacksonville, Tex., 1973. With Beall's Dept. Store, Jacksonville, 1972-73, Jacksonville Pub. Libr., 1974-76, Rippon Middle Sch., Woodbridge, Va., 1976-77; sec. Camp Fire, Inc., Temple, Tex., 1978-80; sec./adminstrv. asst. Scott & White Hosp., Temple, 1980-82; salesperson Century 21, Temple, 1984-86, Charles B. Hart, Broker, Temple, 1986—. Author: (children's books) Hanna, the Immigrant, 1991, The Many Adventures of Minnie, 1992; More Adventures of Minnie, 1994. Active Contemporaries, Temple, Tex. Jewish Hist. Soc.; bd. dirs. Chisholm Trail Chorus of Sweet Adelines, Inc., 1980-91, Temple Civic Theatre, 1978, Tex. Commn. On Arts Touring Arts Program, 2001-05 Avocations: acting, singing, walking, bridge, travel.

HART, KAREN JEAN, special education educator; b. Elizabeth, NJ, July 6, 1952; d. Santo Joseph and Florence (Machrone) Materia; m. Thomas Raymond Hart, June 28, 1975; children: Brian, Kimberly. BA, Kean Coll. of N.J., 1974, MA, 1981. Cert. elem. tchr. of reading, reading specialist, tchr. of handicapped and learning disabilities, supr. Elem. tchr. Harding Sch., Kenilworth, N.J., 1970-74; adj. faculty Kean Coll., Union, N.J., 1981-87; supplemental instr. Bridgewater (N.J.) -Raritan, 1987-91; tchr. of the handicapped Somerset County Vo-Tech, Bridgewater, 1991—2005; learning disabilities tchr. cons. Somerset County Vocat. Tech., NJ, 2005—. Yearbook fin. advisor Sch. Yearbook, 1993-95; advisor Vocat. Indsl. Clubs Am.; state officer team mgr. N.J. Skills USA, 2000—. Den leader Boy Scouts Am., Bridgewater, 1989-91, cubmaster, 1991-92, advancement chair, Martinsville, 1993-97; sec., cultural arts chair PTO, Bridgewater, 1991—. Recipient Citation State Legis., State of N.J., 1992. Mem. Coun. of Exceptional Children, Assn. Learning Cons., Kappa Delta Pi, Phi Delta Kappa, Epsilon Pi Tau Home: 282 Carber St Bound Brook NJ 08805-1529 Office: Somerset County VoTech HS North Bridge and Vogt Bridgewater NJ 08807 Office Phone: 908-526-8900. Business E-Mail: khart@scettc.org.

HART, KITTY CARLISLE, performing arts association administrator; b. New Orleans, Sept. 3, 1910; d. Joseph and Hortense (Holtzman) Conn; m. Moss Hart, Aug. 10, 1946 (dec. 1961); children: Christopher, Cathy. Student, London Sch. Econs., Royal Acad. Dramatic Arts; DFA (hon.), Coll. New Rochelle; DHL (hon.), Hartwick Coll.; LHD (hon.), Manhattan Coll., Amherst Coll., Curtis Inst. Music. Chmn. emeritus N.Y. State Council on the Arts. Former panelist: TV show To Tell the Truth; actress on stage and in films including The Marx Brothers A Night at the Opera, 1936; Broadway theatre appearance in On Your Toes, 1983-84; singer, Met. Opera; one woman show on Great Performances My Broadway Memories, 1999; TV moderator and interviewer; author: (autobiography) Kitty, 1988; contbr. book revs. to jours. Assoc. fellow Timothy Dwight Coll. of Yale U., NYU, Skidmore Coll.; bd. dirs. Empire State Coll.; formerly spl. cons. to N.Y. Gov. on women's opportunities; mem. vis. com. for the arts MIT Recipient Nat. medal of Arts from Pres. Bush, 1991.

HART, MARGARET ROGENE, b. Amsterdam, N.Y., Dec. 26, 1913; d. Edmond James and Rogene Margaret (Dougherty) H. BA, U. Albany, 1934; MA, Syracuse U., 1935. Lic. tchr. h.s., N.Y. Instr. Collegiate Ctr. Syracuse U., Rome, N.Y., 1936; tchr. Rome Pub. Schs., 1937-45; reporter Daily Sentinel, Rome, 1946-51, copyeditor, 1952-79, libr. cons., 1981-94. Editing cons. 5 books on harness horse racing, 1969-81; editing cons. book on Adirondacks, 1982. Playwright: Wednesday Is the Best Day of the Week, 1992; author: (book sect.) Centennial History of Rome, N.Y., 1970; contbr. poetry to anthologies. Bd. dirs. United Way, Rome, 1985-88, Dollars for Scholars, Rome, 1990-96; trustee Rome Hist. Soc., Rome, 1984-87; tutor Literacy Vols. of Am., Utica and Rome, 1988-94. Recipient Gold award for svc. Rome United Way, 1989, commendation Civil Def. Coun., 1967. Mem. Nat. League Am. Pen Women (nat. chmn. grants for mature women 1992), Bus. and Profl. Women's Club (charter, Rose of Challenge 1977), Wednesday Morning Club Rome (pres. 1987-89). Roman Catholic. Avocations: public speaking, theater, antiques. Home: 611 E Garden St Rome NY 13440-5305

HART, MARY, television talk show host; b. Sioux Falls, SD, Nov. 8, 1951; m. Burt Sugarman, Apr. 8, 1989; 1 child. BA, Augustana College, 1972. Co-host, prodr. Danny's Day, Oklahoma City, Iowa; co-host PM Mag., LA, 1978, The Regis Philbin Show, NYC, 1981-92, Entertainment Tonight, Hollywood, 1982—; co-owner Customer's Last Stand. Host: Tournament of Roses Parade, Macy's Thankgiving Day Parade; other TV appearences include (miniseries) Hollywood Wives, 1985, Circus of the Stars, Good Morning America, Blossom, Coach; exec. prodr., host Mary Hart Presents: Love in the Public Eye, 1990, Mary Hart Presents: Power in the Public Eye, 1990; musical debut Dolly, ABC-TV; headliner, dancer, singer, Las Vegas debut Golden Nugget, 1988, Resorts Internat., Atlantic City; videos include: Shape Up with Mary Hart, 1989, Mary Hart: Fit and Firm, 1990. Office: Paramount TV 5555 Melrose Ave Los Angeles CA 90038-3112*

HART, MARY T., lawyer; BA, Georgetown U., 1991; JD, Fordham U., 1995. Bar: NY, US Dist. Ct. So. Dist. NY, US Dist. Ct. Ea. Dist. NY. Ptnr. Wilson, Elser, Moskowitz, Edelman & Dicker LLP, NYC. Mem.: Assn. of the Bar of the City of NY. Office: Wilson Elser Moskowitz Edelman & Dicker LLP 23rd Fl 150 E 42nd St New York NY 10017-5639 Office Phone: 212-490-3000 ext. 2113. Office Fax: 212-490-3038. Business E-Mail: hartm@wemed.com.

HART, MAXINE BARTON, education educator; b. Gladewater, Tex., Nov. 23, 1934; d. David Allen and Lillie Mae (Beard) Barton; m. Clyde Hart Jr., Feb. 3, 1934; children: Greg Patterson, Scott Barton. BBA, Baylor U., 1956; MEd, U. Ark., 1963; EdD, U. Houston, 1979. Bus. tchr. North Little Rock (Ark.) High Sch., 1957-63, Robinson High Sch., Waco, Tex., 1965-66, Univ. High Sch., Waco, 1966-68; bus. instr. McLennan Community Coll., Waco, 1968-71; prof. bus. Baylor U., Waco, 1971—. Contbr. articles to profl. jours. Mem. coms. 1st Bapt. Ch., Waco, Community Devel., Waco, 1976. Mem. Am. Bus. Communication Assn., Nat. Bus. Edn. Assn., Tex. Bus. Edn. Assn. (Tchr. of Yr. Waco chpt. 1975, 84), Nat. Records Mgrs. Assn., S.W. Adminstrv. Svcs. Assn. (chmn. 1988), Data Processing Assn., Beta Gamma Sigma, Delta Pi Epsilon, Phi Gamma Nu. Avocations: reading, watching sports. Office: Baylor U Dept Info Systems BU Box 8005 Waco TX 76712

HART, MELISSA ANNE, congresswoman; b. Pitts., Apr. 4, 1962; d. Donald P. and Albina Simone Hart. BA, Washington & Jefferson Coll., 1984; JD, U. Pitts., 1987. Mem. Pa. State Senate, 1990-2000, US Congress from 4th Pa. dist., 2001—, mem. ways and means com., 2005—, mem. standards of ofcl. conduct com. Bd. trustees Washington & Jefferson Coll., U. Pitts, CC Allegheny County, Vietnam Vets. Leadership Prog., Pitts. Film Office, Pitts. Ballet Theatre. Named Guardian of Small Bus., Nat. Fedn. Ind. Bus.; recipient Hero of the Taxpayer award, Ams. for Tax Reform, Legislator of Yr. award, Am. Legis. Exch. Coun., Eagle award, Associated Builders and Contractors, Pres.'s medal, Chatham Coll., Thomas Jefferson award, Food Distbrs. Internat., Advocacy award, Nat. Epilepsy Assn., Spirit of Enterprise award, US C. of C., People Leading Change award, Pa. Leadership Coun., Status of Women award, Zonta Internat., Women of Spirit award, Carlow Coll. Mem.: North Suburban Builders Assn., Allegheny County Bar Assn., Pa. Bar Assn. Republican. Office: US Ho Reps 1024 Longworth Ho Office Bldg Washington DC 20515 Office Phone: 202-225-2565.*

HART, MELISSA JOAN CATHERINE, actress; b. Smithtown, N.Y., Apr. 18, 1976; m. Mark Wilkerson, July 19, 2003; 1 child, Mason Walter. Appeared in TV series, including Clarissa Explains It All, Sabrina The Teenage Witch; appeared in TV movies, including Kane and Able, Christmas Show, The Tale of the Frozen Ghost, Family Reunion, Twisted Desire, Sabrina The Teenage Witch, Two Came Back, Sabrina Goes to Rome, Silencing Mary; appeared in feature film Can't Hardly Wait, Drive Me Crazy, 1999, Recess: School's Out (voice), 2001, Hold On, 2002, Rent Control, 2002, Jesus, Mary and Joey, 2003; appeared in plays, including Besides Herself, Imagining Brad, The Crucible; actress (TV movie) The Voyage to Atlantis: The Lost Empire, 2001; actress, prodr. (TV movie) Sabrina, Down Under, 1999. Office: Creative Artists Agy 9830 Wilshire Blvd Beverly Hills CA 90212

HART, NAN SUSAN, counselor; b. Springfield, Mo., Dec. 31, 1948; d. Dan Merle and Dorothy Orline Booker; m. Lynn Alvin Morris (div.); 1 child, Mandy Lynn Jones; m. David Eugene Hart, July 23, 1988. BA, Southwest Mo. State U., Springfield, 1987; MSc, Mo. State U., Springfield, 2005. Lic. nursing home adminstr. 1991. Adminstr. nursing home Foster Healthcare Group, Springfield, 1989—91; adminstr. retirement living Creekside Elfindale, Springfield, 1995—97; bereavement coord. Cmty. Hospices of Am., Springfield, 1993—. Mem. cmty. adv. bd. Cox Coll. Nursing, Springfield, 1998—. Vol. Alzheimer's Assn., Springfield, Relay for Life, Springfield. Named Top Masters Class, Mo. State U., 2005. Mem.: DAR. Democrat. Presbyterian. Avocations: bicycling, reading, jogging, tennis, travel. Office: Ozarks Counseling Ctr 1550-A E Battlefield Springfield MO 65804 E-mail: dsharte@mchi.com.

HART, NANCY DIANE, family nurse practitioner, educator, consultant, writer, mental health nurse; b. Miami, Sept. 23, 1953; d. Gus Richard and Billie Mae (Mills) H.; 1 child, Adam J. Teichner. ASN, Palm Beach Jr. Coll., 1976; BS in Health Adminstrn., Fla. Atlantic U., Boca Raton, Fla., 1978; MS in Counseling Psychology, Nova U., Ft. Lauderdale, Fla., 1989; MSN, U. South Ala., 1995. Cert. family nurse practitioner; cert. psychiat. and mental healthnurse; cert. alcohol and drug abuse counselor; cert. substance abuse counselor; cert. neonatal intensive care nurse. NICU level III/emergency rm. Good Samaritan Hosp., West Palm Beach, Fla., 1980-85; rehab. supr. Employee Rehab. Svcs., West Palm Beach, 1985-87; pediatric oncology nurse Hematology/Oncology Assn., Atlantis, Fla., 1987-90; IV therapist/mental health nurse Homecare, Atlantis, 1990-93; enlisted USAF, 1993; advaned through grades to capt., 1993; mental health and substance abuse nurse Eglin AFB, 1993-95; med. edn. and quality assurance officer, 1995-97; family nurse practitioner Rural Health Clin., Crestview, Fla., 1997—. Guest spkr. Am. Cancer Soc., Ft. Walton Beach, 1992-94, profl. edn. adv. bd., 1993-94; guest spkr., adv. bd. Leukemia Soc., West Palm Beach, 1988-91; adj. prof. MSN and family nurse practitioner program U. S. Ala. Author: Reducing Cardiovascular Disease in Diabetic Women, 1997. Violinist N.W. Fla. Symphony, Ft. Walton Beach, 1994-95; oboeist/English horn Palm Beach Atlantic Symphony, West Palm Beach, 1991-94 Mem. ANA, Fla. Nurses Assn., Fla. Pediatric Oncology Nurses, Oncology Nursing Soc., Am. Cancer Soc. Avocation: classical musician. Home: 7473 Sandstone Rd Navarre FL 32566-7613 Office: Crestview Rural Health Clin Fort Walton Beach FL 32547

HART, PAMELA HEIM, banker; b. Chgo., July 14, 1946; d. Gordon Theodore and Leah Almira (Gardner) Heim; m. William Richard Hart, July 8, 1972 (div. 1979); 1 child, Elizabeth Alyson. BA, DePauw U., 1968; MA in Tchg., Washington U., St. Louis, 1970; M in Mgmt., Purdue U., 1982. Chartered bank auditor; cert. bank compliance officer. Tchr. history University City (Mo.) H.S., 1969-74; tchg. asst. Purdue U., Hammond, Ind., 1980-82, guest faculty, 1983-84; auditor Continental Bank NA, Chgo., 1984-86, legal and regulatory compliance specialist, 1986-88, asst. auditor, 1988-92, sr. portfolio risk analyst, 1992-94; with asset securitization group Bank of Am. (formerly Continental Bank NA), Chgo., 1994-98; v.p. capital raising products Bank of Am., Chgo., 1994-99, v.p. pvt. bank strategic planning and projects, 1999-2000, sr. audit mgr., 2001—. Trustee Forest Ridge Acad., Schererville, Ind., 1987-88, Wash. U. Eliot Soc.; mem. vestry St. Paul Episc. Ch., Munster, Ind., 1982-92, jr. warden, 1998, 99; active LWV. Mem. Chartered Bank Auditors Assn., Chicagoland Compliance Assn. (bd. dirs., treas. 1987-88), Cert. Bank Compliance Officer Assn. (exam. com. mem. 1992-96), P.E.O, Washington U. Eliot Soc. Avocations: needlecrafts, travel, reading. Home: 910 Ridge Rd Munster IN 46321-1750 Office: Bank of Am 231 S La Salle St Chicago IL 60604-1407 E-mail: hartpamela55555@aol.com.

HART, PAMELA WALKER, artist; d. Frank Patton Jr. and Beatrice Caroline Cox Walker; m. Donald H. Hart, Feb. 12, 1972. BA in Fashion Merchandising, Fla. State U., 1965; BS in Art Edn. with honors, U. Nebr., 1978; MS in Edn. with honors, Elmira (N.Y.) Coll., 1989. Cert. tchr. art K-12, N.Y., Wis. Dept. mgr. Maas Bros., Tampa, Fla., 1965-67; regional office mgr. Cole of Calif., Atlanta, 1968-70; art tchr. grade K-12 various pub. schs., Rome, N.Y., Madison, Wis., 1979-88; artist, writer, owner LookGlas Images, Westernville, NY, 1989—. Spkr., presenter Munson Williams Proctor Art Inst., Utica, NY, 2001, Rome (NY) Club, 2001, Multi-Media Creative Thinking Program, Town of Western Libr., NY, 2005, Brantingham-Greig Cmty. Libr., NY, 2005, Wednesday Morning Club, Rome, NY, 2005 One-woman shows include Gannett Gallery, SUNY, Marcy, 1989, 1992, Mohawk Valley Ctr. for Arts, Little Falls, N.Y., 1995, 2005, Library Gallery, Westernville, N.Y., 2001, Rome Club, N.Y., 2001, Art and Cmty. Ctr., Rome, NY, 2003, 2005, exhibited in group shows at Nat. Acad. Mus., NYC, 2000, Hiestand Gallery, U. Miami, Oxford, Ohio, 2001, Gallery of Contemporary Art, U. Colo., Colo. Springs, 2001, Van Vechten-Lineberry Art Mus., Taos, N.Mex, 2001, Nat. Arts Club, NYC, 2001, Art Assn. Galleries, Cooperstown, 2001, 2003, Fifth Ave. Gallery, Nat. Assn. Women Artists, N.Y.C., 2003—05, Kirkland Art Center, Clinton, N.Y., 2003, Ctrl. N.Y. Cmty. Arts Coun., Utica, 2003, 2006, Chapman Gallery Cazenovia Coll., NY, 2004, Onondaga County Libr. Galleries, Syracuse, N.Y., 2004, Liebig Gallery, Mystic, Conn., 2004, Peninsula Fine Arts Ctr., Newport News, VA., 2005, McQuade Gallery, North Andover, Mass., 2005, Represented in permanent collections Lib. Nat. Mus. Women in the Arts, Washington; author and artist: Mother Wisdom, 2004; art reproduced in Best of Sketching and Drawing, 1999, The Art of Layering: Making Connections, 2004; cover art, Women in Motion mag., 2004—05; contbr. articles to popular mags. Commr. Commn. of the Arts, Rome, NY, 2005. With USAF, 1970—74, col. USAFR, 1974—95. Recipient Golden Poet award World of Poetry, 1991, 1st prize SUNY, Marcy, 1995, 99, Merit award East Wash. Watercolor Soc., 1999, Adolph and Clara Obrig prize Nat. Acad. Mus., NYC, 2000, Watermedia prize Cooperstown Art Assn., 2001. Mem.: AAUW, Nat. League Am. Pen Women, Acad. Am. Poets, Nat. Assn. Women Artists, Nat. Women's History Mus., Nat. Mus. Women in the Arts, Soc. Layerists in Multi-Media, Ctrl. N.Y. Watercolor Soc. Office: LookGlas Images PO Box 337 Westernville NY 13486

HART, VOLEEN VICTORIA, music educator; b. Jonesborough, Tenn., July 21, 1958; BA in Music, U. Tenn., 1980. Lic. tchr. Tenn., 1980. Music tchr. White Pine Sch., Tenn., 1981—86, Rock Springs Elem. Sch., Morristown, Tenn., 1986—99; tchr. Meriks Charter Sch., Kingsport, Tenn., 1999—. Asst. track coach Morristown Catholic HS, Tenn., 1990—97; track coach Meriks Charter Sch., Kingsport, Tenn., 2000—. Choir dir. Kingsport Baptist Ch., 2000—. Mem.: Music Tchrs. Nat. Assn., Tenn. Edn. Assn. Avocations: piano, running, needlepoint, painting. Office: Meriks Charter Sch 1205J N Eastman Rd #207 Kingsport TN 37664-3145

HART-DULING, JEAN MACAULAY, clinical social worker; b. Bellingham, Wash. d. Murry Donald and Pearl N. (McLeod) Macaulay; m. Richard D. Hart, Feb. 3, 1940 (dec. Mar. 1973); children: Margaret Hart Morrison, Pamela Hart Horton, Patricia L. Hart-Jewell; m. Lawrence Duling, Jan. 20, 1979 (dec. May 1992); children: Lenora Daniel, Jayne Munch. BA, Wash. State U., 1938; MSW, U. So. Calif., 1961. Lic. clin. social worker, Calif.; accredited counselor, Wash. Social worker Los Angeles County, 1957-58; children's svc. worker Dept. Children's Svcs., L.A., 1958-59; program developer homemakers svcs. project Calif. Dept. Children's Svcs., L.A., 1962-64; developer homemaker cons. position State of Calif., L.A., 1964-66; supr. protective svcs. Dept. Children's Svcs., L.A., 1966-67; dep. regional svc. adminstrn. Dept. Los Angeles County Children's Svcs., 1967-76; adminstr. Melton Home for Developmental Disability, 1985-86; pvt. practice pro bono therapy Calif. and Wash. Therapist various pro bono cases. Mem. Portals Com., L.A., 1974, Travelers Aid Bd., Long Beach, Calif. 1969. Recipient Nat. award work in cmty., spl. award for work with emotionally disturbed Com. for Los Angeles, 1974. Mem. AAUW, NASW, Acad. Cert. Social Workers, Calif. Lic. Clin. Soc. Workers, Wing Point Golf and Country Club (Bainbridge Island, Wash.), Los Angeles County Retirement Assn. Republican. Congregationalist. Avocations: golf, bridge.

HARTEN, ANN M., relocation services executive; married; 1 child. BA in Indsl. Psychology, Indiana U. of Pa. With Boise Cascade, 1987—2000, dir. integrated supply, 1999—2000; v.p., chief info. officer US ops. SIRVA, Westmont, Ill., 2000—. Office: SIRVA 700 Oakmont Ln Westmont IL 60559

HARTER, CAROL CLANCEY, former academic administrator, English language educator; m. Michael T. Harter, June 24, 1961; children: Michael R., Sean P. BA, SUNY, Binghamton, 1964, MA, 1967, PhD, 1970; LHD, Ohio U., 1989. Instr. SUNY, Binghamton, 1969-70; asst. prof. Ohio U., Athens, 1970-74, ombudsman, 1974-76, v.p., dean students, 1976-82, v.p. for adminstrn., assoc. prof., 1982-89; pres., prof. English SUNY, Geneseo, 1989-95; pres. U. Nev., Las Vegas, 1995—2006. Co-author: (with James R. Thompson) John Irving, 1986, E.L. Doctorow, 1990; author dozens of presentations and news columns; contbr. articles to profl. jours. Bd. dirs., mem. exec. com. NCAA, 2000—; mem. exec. com. Nev. Devel. Authority, 2001—; bd. dirs. Nev. Test Site Devel. Corp., 2000—; trustee Associated Western Univs., 2001—. Office: U Nev Office Pres 4505 S Maryland Pkwy # 1001 Las Vegas NV 89154-1001 E-mail: harter@ccmail.nevada.edu.

HARTER, JACQUELINE A., social worker, educator; d. Paul Gregg; children: Abigain, Gregg. BS in Social Work, Bowling Green State U., Ohio, 1984; MSW, Ohio State U., Columbus, 1995. Foster care and adoption social worker Williams County Dept. Human Svcs., Bryan, 1984—87; clin. social worker Cath. Charities Diocese Toledo, Defiance, Ohio, 1988—98, Inner Peace Homes, Bryan, 1998—; dir. residence svcs. Pk. View Nursing Ctr., Edgerton, Ohio. Instr. NW C.C., Archbold, Ohio. Ch. lay leader/spkr. Farmer United Meth. Ch., Ohio, 2002—06. Democrat. Methodist. Avocations: reading, gardening, volunteering. Office Phone: 419-630-0127.

HARTER, LONNA, city manager; b. Bucyrus, Ohio, Oct. 15, 1940; d. Ernest Alfred and Letona Marie Rice; m. John Fredrick Harter, Mar. 14, 1969. BA cum laude, Ohio State U., 1995. Actuarial asst. Nationwide Ins., Columbus, Ohio, 1958-69; legal sec. Laughbaum & Assoc., Galion, Ohio, 1969-76; mayors adminstrv. sec. City of Galion, 1976-80, income tax mgr., 1980-91, dep. fin. dir., 1991-01. Sec. SSI, Inc.-User Group, Lebanon, Ohio, 1994, v.p., 1995. Bd. sec. St. Mark's United Meth. Ch., 1981-83. Mem. Golden Key Nat. Honor Soc., Women of the Moose, Valley View Golf League (v.p. 1999—), New Winchester Golf League. Avocations: golf, painting, reading, pets, cooking. Office: City of Galion PO Box 790 115 Harding Way E Galion OH 44833-1902 Home: 14 Charles Dr Winter Haven FL 33880-4906

HARTFORD, CATHY JEANETTE, elementary school educator; b. Independence, Mo., May 28, 1954; d. Edward Arthur and Peggy Jeanette (Goth) Richeson; m. Michael Winfield Hartford, Apr. 12, 1975; children: Rachel, Ian. BA, U. Mo., Kansas City, 1977, MA, 1982. Cert. tchr., Mo. Kindergarten tchr. Cordill-Mason Elem. Sch., Blue Springs, Mo., 1985-88, Thomas Ultican Elem. Sch., Blue Springs, 1984-85; tchr. 6th grade math. and lang. Georgeff-Baker Mid. Sch., Blue Springs, 1995—96; tchr. 6th grade Moreland Ridge Mid. Sch., Blue Springs, Mo., 1977-84, 88-95, 1996—. Presenter workshop in field. Mo. Dept. Elem. and Secondary Edn. grantee, 1989-90. Mem. ASCD, Nat. Coun. Tchrs. English, Nat. Writing Project, Greater Kansas City Writing Project. Avocations: needlepoint, gardening, reading. Office: Moreland Ridge Mid Sch 900 SW Bishop Blue Springs MO 64015

HARTFORD, MAUREEN A., academic administrator; m. Jay Hartford. BA in French and History, U. N.C., Chapel Hill, MA in coll. tchg.; EdD in higher edn. adminstrn., U. Ark. Dean of student affairs Case Western Res. U., Cleve., 1982—86; vice provost student affairs Wash. State U., 1986—92; v.p. student affairs U. Mich., Ann Arbor, 1992—99; pres. Meredith Coll., Raleigh, NC, 1999—. Faculty Ctr. Study of Higher and Post-Secondary Edn., Ann Arbor, Mich., 1992—99. Mem. governing bd. LeaderShape; bd. trustees Wake Edn. Partnership; bd. dir. Greater Raleigh C. of C., N.C. Triangle United Way; bd. of governors Capital City Club. Recipient Women in Bus., Bus. Jour., 2002, Dist. Scholar award, N.C. Coll. Pers. Assn., 2002. Office: Meredith Coll 3800 Hillsborough St Raleigh NC 27607

HARTGER, BARBARA J., marketing professional; b. Grand Rapids, Mich., June 14, 1950; d. Harold Vos Hartger and Marjorie Hartger Bjork. AA, Pine Manor Jr. Coll., 1970; BFA, Sch. of Art Inst. Chgo., 1974; MBA, Baylor U., 2006. Animator, audio-visual dir, tech. dir. Wernecke Studios, Greyhound Exposition Svcs., Chgo., 1974—79; comm. specialist Briefing Ctr. IBM, 1979—83, staff comm. specilist Rochester, Minn., 1983—89, sr. mktg. support rep. Software Group Dallas, 1999—2003. Pres. Country Villas Homeowners Assn., Carrollton, Tex., 2002—; pub. info. chmn. United Way of Olmsted County, 1982—83. Recipient Gold award, United Way Am., 1980, Vol. Recognition award, State of Minn., 1983, cert. of appreciation, Dallas County Juvenile Dept., 1988, Appreciation award, Rochester Area C. of C., 1979. Mem.: Leadership Tex., Frank Reaugh Art Club. Episcopalian. Avocations: theater, travel, symphony, choral music, skiing. Personal E-mail: hartger@comcast.net.

HARTIG, KAREN JOYCE, psychotherapist, social worker; b. N.Y.C., July 22, 1957; d. Thomas and Phyllis (Green) H.; m. Carlos Castrillo, June 10, 1990 (div. 2003). BA, Queens Coll., 1979; MSW, Adelphi U., 1982. Cert. clin. social worker. Staff therapist South Bronx Mental Health Ctr., Bronx, N.Y., 1982-83, Coney Island Hosp., Bklyn., 1983-84; dir. Queens (N.Y.) Rape Counseling Ctr., 1985—; staff therapist New Hope Guild, Queens, 1987-88, Washington Square Inst., N.Y.C., 1988-92, N.Y. Psychotherapy and Counseling Ctr., Bklyn., 1985-87; pvt. practice, 1985—. Contbr. articles in field to newspapers. Mem. Nat. Assn. Social Workers. Democrat. Avocations: skiing, tennis, acting, bicycling. Office: Queens Rape Counseling Ctr 71-49 Loubet St Forest Hills NY 11375-6720

HARTIGAN, KARELISA VOELKER, classics educator; b. Stillwater, Okla., Mar. 5, 1943; d. Charles Henry and Elsie Florence Voelker; m. Barry Hartigan, Apr. 21, 1966 (div. Feb. 1978); 1 child, Timothy Lawrence; m. Kevin Michael McCarthy, Dec. 22, 1992. BA in Classics, Coll. of Wooster, 1965; AM in Classics, U. Chgo., 1966, PhD in Classics, 1970. Asst. prof. St. Olaf Coll., Northfield, Minn., 1969-73; asst. prof., assoc. prof. Greek studies U. Fla., Gainesville, from 1973, prof., 1991—, co-dir. Ctr. for Greek Studies, 1980—, assoc. dir. honors program, 1989-95. Author: The Poets and the Cities, 1979, Ambiguity and Self-Deception, 1991, Greek Tragedy on the American Stage, 1995, Myths Behind Our Words, 1998, Muse on Madison Avenue, 2001; editor Text and Presentation jour., 1983-94; editor spl. issues Classical and Modern Lit.; Classical Reflections, 1980. Recipient Excellence in Tchg. award Am. Philol. Assn., 1985; Disting. Alumni Prof. award U. Fla., 1987-89, Univ.-Wide Tchg. award, 1990, Tchg. award, 1994, Disting. Prof. award, 2001. Mem. Modern Greek Studies Assn. (sec. 1983-1986), Classical Assn. Mid. West and South (pres. so. sect. 1986-88, nat. pres. 1992-93). Avocations: bicycling, swimming, travel, cooking, dogs. Office: University of Florida Ctr Greek Studies PO Box 117435 Gainesville FL 32611-7435 E-mail: kvhrtgn@classics.ufl.edu.

HARTIL, KIRSTEN, research scientist; b. Irvine, Scotland, Dec. 8, 1974; d. John Davidson and Jean Adams Hartil. BSc, Aberdeen U., Scotland, 1996; PhD, Cambridge U., Eng., 2000. Rsch. assoc. Albert Einstein Coll. Medicine, Yeshiva U., Bronx, NY, 2001—. Mem.: Am. Diabetes Assn. (Menor Based fellow), NY Acad. Sci. (assoc.), Am. Heart Assn. (assoc.). Office: Albert Einstein Coll Medicine 1300 Morris Park Ave Bronx NY NY104 Office Phone: 718-430-2853. Office Fax: 718-430-8676. E-mail: khartil@aecom.yu.edu.

HARTINGER, PATRICIA BERNARDINE, retired elementary school educator; b. Monterey, Calif., Sept. 16, 1935; d. John George and Myra Hall Curran; m. Walter Hartinger, Nov. 14, 1959; children: Maureen, John. AA with honor, Monterey Peninsula Coll., 1955; BA with great distinction, San Jose State U., 1958; postgrad., U. Calif., Santa Cruz, U. Santa Clara. Cert. life sch. libr., jr. high sch., child devel. Libr. San Jose (Calif.) State Coll., 1956-58, Milpitas (Calif.) Sch. Dist., 1960-62, Alma Coll., Los Gatos, Calif., 1963-65, Santa Clara (Calif.) Pub. Libr., 1966-69; tchr. Westerner Schs., Los Gatos, 1975-82, Town & Country Pre-Sch., San Jose, Calif., 1982-83, Diocese of San Jose, 1982—2004. Curriculum writer in field; spkr. in field. Author: Earthquake of Apr. 18, 1906 in the Santa Clara Valley, 1973 (cash award), History of Santa Clara Valley Handweavers Guild, 1988; contbr. articles on Peace Edn. to various pubs., recipes to Sunset Mag. Vol. tchr. Lyceum of Santa Clar County for Gifted Children, San Jose, 1974-80; vol. libr. Santa Clara Valley Med. Ctr., San Jose, 1962-63, Los Gatos Elem. Sch. Dist., 1968-75; tchr. of religion pre-sch. Diocese of San Jose, 1971-80; vol. tchr. Don Edwards Nat. Wildlife Refuge, 2004—; tchr. trainer Jason Expdn., 2004—. Scholar Kiwanis Club, 1956, Delta Delta Delta Sorority, 1957-58, Angel Island Immigration Sta., Found. Tchrs. Fellows Program, 2001-02, Gilder Lehrman Inst. Am. History, 2003. Mem. Calif. Coun. Social Studies, Santa Clara County Reading Coun., Santa Clara Valley Handweavers (founding), mem. Nat. Audubon Soc., Nature Conservancy, Sierra Club, Lewis and Clark Trail Heritage Found., San Jose State U. Key Club, Phi Alpha Theta, Phi Kappa Phi, Lewis and Clark Trail Heritage Found. (v.p. Calif. Chpt.). Democrat. Avocations: weaving, reading, travel. Home: 16155 Jacaranda Way Los Gatos CA 95032-3627 E-mail: shadowcat16155@yahoo.com.

HARTLAUB, MAXINE LOUISE, literature educator; b. Gettysburg, Pa., Nov. 23, 1950; d. Joseph L. and Anna J. Hess; m. Randy L. Hartlaub, Sept. 5, 1970; children: Eric, Brian. BS, Shippensburg U., Pa., 1972; MEd, Shippensburg U., 1983. Tchr. St. Francis Xavier Sch., Gettysburg, 1972—76; reading specialist Upper Adams Sch. Dist., Biglerville, Pa., 1981—88, tchr., 1988—. Battlefield guide Gettysburg Nat. Military Park, 1991—. Mem.: Adams County Hist. Soc., Gettysburg Civil War Round Table, Assn. Battlefield Licensed Guides, Delta Kappa Gamma. Home: 243 Friendship Ln Gettysburg PA 17325 Office: Upper Adams Sch Dist Main St Biglerville PA 17307 Business E-Mail: mrhartlaub@superpa.net.

HARTLEY, CELIA LOVE, nursing consultant, writer, retired nursing educator, nursing administrator; b. Colfax, Wash., Oct. 25, 1935; d. Thomas Warren and Ella Marie (Kerkman) Love; m. Lawrence Dosser (div.); children: Laurie Denise Draper, Byron Garth Dosser; m. Gordon E. Hartley, Dec. 17, 1972. Diploma, Deaconess Hosp. Sch. Nursing, Spokane, Wash., 1956; BSN, U. Wash., Seattle, 1965, MSN, 1968. RN, Wash., Calif. Staff nurse Deaconess Hosp., Spokane, 1956-62; charge nurse Northgate Gen. Hosp., Seattle, 1963-65; hosp. supr. Stevens Meml. Hosp., Edmonds, Wash., 1965-66; prof. nursing Shoreline C.C., Seattle, 1967-73, dir. nursing edn., asst. div. chmn. health occupations, 1973-92; chair health sci. divsn. Coll. of the Desert, Palm Desert, Calif., 1992-99, prof. emerita, 1999—; nursing curriculum cons. Pres. Coun. on Nursing Edn. in Wash. State, 1992; adv. com. Antioch West and Seattle U., 1979-81, Nursing Edn. Com. Higher Edn. Coordinating Bd., 1990, Western Wash. U. Nursing, 1984, Seattle Pacific U. Nursing, 1992; other coms. various orgns., 1979—; presenter in field. Author: (with Janice Ellis) Nursing in Today's World; Challenges, Issues, and Trends, 1980, 8th rev. edit., 2004, Managing and Coordinating Patient Care, 1991, 4th edit., 2005, (book chpt.) Fundamentals of Nursing, 1992; mem. editl. bd. Assoc. Degree Nurse, 1987-91, Jour. Nursing Edn., 1991—; contbr. articles to profl. jours. Mem. Nat. League of Nursing (bd. dirs. 1981-84, appeal panel Coun. AD Programs 1988-91, 95-98, chmn.-vice chmn. various coms.), Wash. Constituent League (v.p. 1986-87, chmn. nominating com. 1984-85, chmn. membership com. 1985-86), Sigma Theta Tau. Methodist. Home: 3234 Mabana Rd Camano Island WA 98282 Office Phone: 360-387-0822. Personal E-mail: cegohart@wavecable.com.

HARTLEY-LONABAUGH, KAREN LEE, critical care nurse; b. Clearwater, Fla., July 28, 1958; d. William Joseph and Nancy Ann (Partridge) L.; m. William Edward Hartley, Nov. 22, 1997. ASN, St. Petersburg Jr. Coll., 1981, AS in Human Svcs., 1985; postgrad., St. Leo Coll. CCRN; cert. BLS, ACLS, cert. basic trauma life support, neonatal advanced life support, PALS, PALS Instr. Critical care coord. Lake Seminole (Fla.) Hosp., 1986-89; cardiac rehab. counselor Palm Harbor (Fla.) Cardiac Rehab., 1988-89; head nurse intensive care Univ. Gen. Hosp., Seminole, 1989-90, house supr., 1990-91; hosp. staffing pool ICU, cardiopulmonary rehab. Suncoast Hosp., Largo, Fla., 1991-95; dir. clin. svcs. MedTrans, AMR-West Fla., 1995—; clin. hosp. rep. Genentech, Emerald Coast Divsn., 1997—. Cardiovascular cons., preceptor, Hudson, Fla., 1991-97. Mem. AACN, Fla. Neonatal Transport Network, Fla. Nurses Assn. Episcopalian. Avocations: scuba diving, hiking, football, biking, arts and crafts, horses. Address: 24537 Evaline St Brooksville FL 34601-4912

HARTLINE, REBECCA SUE, secondary school educator; b. Canton, Ohio, May 3, 1958; d. Clyde Robert and Lucille May Boyd; m. Neil Edward Hartline, Dec. 1, 1979; 1 child, Nathan Paul. BA in English, Malone Coll., Canton, BS in Psychology, 1980. English tchr. Massillon (Ohio) Christian Sch., 1980—, chairperson English dept., psychology/sociology tchr., 1987—. Nat. honor soc. advisor Massillon Christian Sch., 1980—, girls basketball coach, 1986—91, 2005—, girls volleyball coach, 1988—2005. Mem. orch. Massillon Bapt. Temple, 1969—2006, from tchr. to toddler I supt., 1975—2006, 1st and 2d grade youth group, 1978—90. Republican. Avocations: sports, reading, piano, exercise. Office: Massillon Christian Sch 965 Overlook Ave SW Massillon OH 44647

HARTMAN, CAROL LEE, art educator, reading specialist; d. Charles Downes and Mary Ann Sokol; m. Darryl Richard Hartman, Dec. 23, 1993; m. Joseph Alfred Oliva (div.); 1 child, Joseph Richard Oliva. AS in Biology and Chemistry, Bronx C.C., 1975; BA in Psychology, Lehman Coll., Bronx, 1977; MA in Devel. Psychology, SUNY, Buffalo, 1981; MA in Leadership, Coll. Notre Dame, Balt., 2003; postgrad., Buffalo State Coll., SUNY, Buffalo. Cert. art tchr. Md., 2002, Pa., 2005, elem. edn. Md., 1999, spl. educator Md., 1999, reading specialist Pa., 2005, elem. education Pa., 2005. Counselor Christian Counseling Svcs., Lancaster, NY, 1987—90; psychology instr. child, adolescent and adult devel. and aging Niagara County C.C., Sanborn, 1987—93; educator Everywoman Opportunity Ctr., Buffalo, 1990—94; counselor, educator Oakview Treatment Ctr., Columbia, Md., 1995—96; tchr. Balt. City Pub. Schs., 1996—2004, Balt. County Pub. Schs., Parkton, 2004—05; tchr. art, comm. edn. So. York County Sch. Dist., Glen Rock, Pa.; reading specialist Hanover Mid. Sch., 2005—; freelance artist. Initiated and supported women's spiritual growth group Amherst Presbyn. Ch., 1988—90; pres. Williamsville Art Soc., NY, 1987—88. Recipient award Excellence Chemistry, Bronx C.C., 1975. Mem.: York Art Assn., Pa. Watercolor Soc. (assoc.), Kappa Delta Pi, Psi Chi, Mensa (assoc.). Avocations: gardening, antiques, reading, interior decorating, art. Office: Hanover Mid Sch 300 Keagy Avenue Hanover PA 17331 Office Phone: 717-637-9000.

HARTMAN, JOAN EDNA, retired literature educator, provost; b. Bklyn., Oct. 5, 1930; d. H. Graham and Edna (Kuebler) H. BA, Mt. Holyoke Coll., 1951; MA, Duke U., 1952; postgrad., Oxford U., 1958-59; PhD, Radcliffe Coll., 1960. Instr. Washington Coll., Chestertown, Md., 1952-54, Wellesley Coll., 1959-62, asst. prof., 1962-63, Conn. Coll., New London, 1963-66, CUNY-Queens Coll., Flushing, 1967-70, CUNY-S.I. C.C., 1970-72, assoc. prof., 1972-76; prof. CUNY-Coll. S.I., 1976-98, acting dean humanities and social scis., 1995-98; ret., 1998. Vis. prof. Am. U. of Rome, 1991, 99, 2001, 03, acting provost, 2005—. Editor: Women in Print I, II, 1982, (En)Gendering Knowledge, 1991, The Norton Reader, 2000; contbr. articles to profl. jours. Fellow, AAUW, NEH, Mellon Found., Folger Shakespeare Libr. Mem.: MLA,

Women's Caucus for the Modern Langs., Soc. Study of Early Modern Women, Nat. Arts Club. Home: 201 E 21st St Apt 17C New York NY 10010-6423 Personal E-mail: hartman@mail.csi.cuny.edu.

HARTMAN, JOAN EVANS, educational consultant; b. Gibson, Tenn., Sept. 30, 1935; d. William Slaton and Helen (Mann) Evans; children: John Scott, Edwin Evans, Mary Lane Hartman McKinney. BA, Lambuth U., Jackson, Tenn., 1957; MA, Vanderbilt U., 1958; EdD, Memphis State U., 1991. Tchr. Davidson County Schs., Nashville, 1958-60, pvt. kindergartens, Memphis and Ripley, Tenn., 1971-74, Lauderdale County Schs., Ripley, 1982-90, supr. fed. projects, 1990—2006. Mem. evaluation teams So. Assn. Coll. and Schs., Memphis, 1985-88. Author: Sam's Special Cookie, 2006. Recipient Grad. Rsch. Symposium award Memphis State U., 1989, Career Ladder III Tenn. State Dept. Edn., Nashville, 1988-2006. Mem. Western Tenn. Edn. Assn. (v.p. 1985-88), Tenn. Edn. Assn., NEA, ASCD, Tenn. Assn. for Supervision and Curriculum Devel., Kappa Delta Pi. Methodist. Avocations: reading, needlepoint, travel. Address: 111 Lankford Dr Ripley TN 38063 Personal E-mail: hartbeat@bellsouth.net.

HARTMAN, KATHRYN ROSE, elementary school educator; b. Cleve., Feb. 20, 1954; d. Joseph James and Nellie Rose (Pitts) H. BS in Edn., Cleve. State U., 1977, Masters in Edn., 1989. Cert. tchr., Ohio. Tchr. Corpus Christi Sch., Cleve., 1977-86, Buhrer Elem. Sch., Cleve., 1986-92; peer advisor Cleve. Pub. Schs., 1992—. Vol. Mt. Alverna Nursing Home, Cleve., 1983—. Martha Holden Jennings scholar, 1991. Mem. Alpha Delta Kappa. Avocations: reading, travel, music. Home: 2885 Pease Dr Apt 105 Rocky River OH 44116-3232

HARTMAN, LEE ANN WALRAFF, secondary school educator, consultant; b. Milw., Apr. 21, 1945; d. Emil Adolph and Mabelle Carolyn (Goetter) Walraff; m. Patrick James Hartman, Oct. 5, 1968; children: Elizabeth Marie, Suzanne Carolyn. BS, U. Wis., 1967; postgrad., U. R.I., 1972—73, Johns Hopkins U., 1990, Trinity Coll., 1996. Cert. tchr., Wis., Md. Secondary educator Port Wash. Bd. Edn., Wis., 1967-68; instr. ballet YWCA, Wilmington, Del., 1977-78; tutor Md. Study Skills Inst., Columbia, 1984-86; tchr. Howard County Bd. Edn., Columbia, 1985—. Contbr. articles to profl. jours. Bd. dirs. Columbia United Christian Ch., 1980-83; mem. Gifted and Talented Com., Columbia, 1980—, Lang. Arts Com., 1985—, USCG Officers Wives Club, 1970-72, Hosp. Aux. Bay St. Louis, 1970-72; troop leader Girl Scouts U.S., Columbia, 1980-91, Hospice; exec. bd. PTA, 1990-2000. Recipient Life Achievement award, Internat. Biog. Ctr., 1994, Woman of Yr. award, Am. Biog. Inst., 1994, Shirley Mullinex Tchr. of Yr. award, 1997, State of Md. Home/Hosp. Tchr. of Yr. award, 2001—02. Mem.: NAFE, AAUW (exec. bd. 1985—, v.p. Howard County br. 1990—92, pres. Howard County br. 1998—2000, membership chair 2003—05), Home/Hosp. Tchrs. Assn. Howard County (pres. 2005—), Internat. Platform Assn. (mem. citizen's adv. com. 1995—), Home Hosp. Tchrs. Assn. Md. (chair pub. rels., sec. 1994—98, v.p. 1998—99, pres. 1999—2002), Beaverbrook Homemakers Assn. (pres. 1995—97). Avocations: reading, swimming, skiing, ballet. Home: 5070 Durham Rd W Columbia MD 21044-1445 Office: Howard County Bd Edn Rte 108 Columbia MD 21044 Personal E-mail: hartmanlus@yahoo.com. E-mail: hartmanl@netzero.net.

HARTMAN, MARILYN D., English and art educator; b. Denver, May 2, 1927; d. Leland DeForest Henshaw and Evelyn Wyman Henshaw; m. James Hartman, Oct. 7, 1949 (dec. Dec. 1989); children: Charles, Alice, Mary Hale. Student, U. Denver, 1947; BA, U. Colo., 1958; MA, UCLA, 1965, EdD in English Edn., 1972. Calif. life std. tchg. credential English and art, Colo. secondary English and art. Tchr. Denver Pub. Schs., 1959—65; asst. prof. San Fernando Valley State U., Northridge, Calif., 1970—72, San Diego State U. Mem., presenter Am. Ednl. Rsch. Assn., L.A., 1965-72; mem. Nat. Coun. Tchrs. English, L.A., 1965-72; officer Pi Lambda Theta-Alpha Delta chpt., L.A., 1970-72; with Ctr. for the Study Dem. Instns., L.A., 1970-72; tchg. asst., 1964, discussion leader linguistics; tchr. evaluator UCLA, 1970-72, Iliff Sch. Theology, Denver U.; cons. Dept Edn., Riley, 1992-2000, State Dept., 1992-2000, to Pres. Clinton, 1992-2000. Author: Linguistic Approach to Teaching English, 1965, Two Letters and Some Thoughts, 1968, Sound and Meaning of BE Speech, 1969, Teaching a Dialect, 1970, Contrastive Analysis: BE and SE Teaching, 1972, Touch the Windy Finger, 1980, Under the Hand of God, 2000; author: (with Bill Kirton) (short stories) O God, 1970, On Her Own: To Know and Not Know, 2002; author: The Luckiest People, 2002. Chmn. Denver Metro Area Food Drive, 1985, Interfaith Alliance; mem. Dem. Nat. Com., 1992—2002. Mem.: VFW, NOW, AAUW, Women in the Arts, Interfaith Alliance, Nat. Philatelic Soc., Am. Philatelic Assn., Common Cause, Sierra Club, Franciscan Missions, Natural Resources Def. Coun., Kempe Children's Found., Colo. Fedn. Dem. Women's Clubs, Inc. (officer 2001). Avocations: singing, painting, writing, teaching, counseling.

HARTMAN, MARY MARGARET, secondary school educator; b. Kenton, Ohio, Nov. 13, 1925; d. Willis and Lillian Mary (Couts) Walker; m. Maurice A. Hartman, Aug. 3, 1947; children: Mark W., Marsha L., Margaret A. BS in Edn., Defiance Coll., Ohio, 1972. Cash acct. N. Elec. Mfg. Co., Kenton, Ohio, 1948-50; kindergarten tchr. VGanWert City Schs., Ohio, 1959-69, Paulding Exec. Village Schs., Ohio, 1970-74; learning disabilities tchr. Mt. Vernon U., 1979—81, Mt. Vernon City Schs., Ohio, 1981-89. Mem. AAUW, Kappa Delta Phi, Dappa Delta Pi, Phi Kappa Phi. Republican. Methodist. Avocations: sewing, reading, music. Home: 312 Wendy Ln Waverly OH 45690-1558

HARTMAN, MARY SUSAN, historian, educator; b. Mpls., June 25, 1941; married. BA, Swarthmore Coll., 1963; MA, Columbia U., 1964, PhD, 1970. From instr. to asst. prof. Rutgers U., 1968-75; from assoc. prof. to prof. history Douglass Coll., Rutgers U., 1975—; dean Douglas Coll. Rutgers U., 1982-94; dir. Inst. for Women's Leadership Douglass Coll., 1994—; prof. Rutgers U., 1994—. Author: Clio's Consciousness Raised, 1974, Victorian Murderesses, 1978; editor: Talking Leadership: Conversations with Powerful Women, 1999, The Household and the Making of History: A Subversive View of the Western Past, 2004. Office: 162 Ryders Ln New Brunswick NJ 08901-8555 Office Phone: 732-932-1463 ext. 648.

HARTMAN, NANCY LEE, physician; b. Philipsburg, Pa., July 29, 1951; Grad., Barbizon Sch. Modeling, 1970; AA Med. Tech., Harcum Jr. Coll., 1971; BA Biology and Med. Tech., Lycoming Coll., 1974; MS Med. Biology, L.I. U., 1977; MD, Am. U. Caribbean, Plymouth, Montserrat, W.I., 1981. Cert. med. technologist. Med. technologist Lock Haven Hosp., Pa., 1971—72, Williamsport Hosp., Pa., 1972—73, Renovo Hosp., Pa., 1974; med. technologist microbiology Jersey Shore Hosp., Pa., 1974; microbiologist N.Y. Hosp. and Cornell Med. Ctr., N.Y.C., 1974—75, Drekter and Heisler Labs., N.Y.C., 1975, North Shore Labs., Inc., Syosset, NY, 1976—78; lab. technician North Shore Hosp., Manhasset, NY, 1981—82, Nat. Health Labs., Inc., Bethpage, NY, 1982; resident internal medicine program Interfaith Med. Ctr., Bklyn., 1983—84; med. cons. Shapiro & Baines, Mineola, NY, 1985—88; resident pathology program Lenox Hill Hosp., N.Y.C., 1986—87; resident clin. pathology Beth Israel Med. Ctr., N.Y.C., 1988—89; resident internal medicine Lenox Hill Hosp., 1990; med. specialist, pres. Advt. Ltd., Glenwood Landing, NY, 1990—92. Med. cons. Leader Mfg., Inc., Quebec, Can., 1988-89, Meiselman, Boland, Reilly and Pittoni, Mineola, 1988-92, Law Office Sybil Shainwald, N.Y.C., 1989-91, Reichenbaum and Silberstein, Great Neck, N.Y., 1990-92, Audio Visual Med. Mktg., Inc., N.Y.C., 1990-92, Law Office Peter D. Kolbrener, Westbury, N.Y., 1990-92, Siben & Siben, Bayshore, N.Y., 1990-92, 93-94, Whiteman & Gorray, Uniondale, N.Y., 1990-92, Law Office Jed Neil Kirsch, Mineola, 1990-92, Gandin, Schotsky & Rappaport, Melville, N.Y., 1990-92, Doniger, Garland & Engstrand, N.Y.C., 1991-92, Law Office Steven Miller, Mineola, 1991-92, Law Office Harry Organek, Westbury, 1991-92, Law Office Michael Flomenhaft, N.Y.C., 1991-92, Damashek, Godosky & Gentile, N.Y.C., 1991-92, Easton & Clark, Levittown, N.Y., 1991-92, Tomas, Simonhoff, O'Brien, and Adourian, Haddonfield, N.J., 1993-94, Med. Surveillance, Inc., Westchester, Pa., 1993-94; rsch. fellow Rockefeller U., N.Y.C., 1996, med. cons., 1996— Author: The Pocket Handbook of Infectious Agents and Their Treatments, 1987; contbr. articles to profl. jours. Mem. Rep. Presdl. Task Force. Allied Health Professions Traineeship grant, 1975—77. Mem. AMA, Am. Med. Women's Assn., Am. Soc. Clin. Pathologists (registered med. technologist), Internat. Platform Assn., Am. Soc. Microbiology. Avocations: jogging, scuba diving, flying, tennis, golf. Home: PO Box 374 Roslyn NY 11576-0374

HARTMAN, ROSEMARY JANE, retired special education educator; b. Gainesville, Fla., Aug. 24, 1944; d. John Leslie and Irene (Bowen) Goddard; m. Alan Lynn Gerber, Feb. 1, 1964 (div. 1982); children: Sean Alan, Dawn Julianne Silva, Lance Goddard; m. Perry Hartman, June 27, 1992. BA, Immaculate Heart Coll., 1967; MA, Loyola U., 1974. Cert. resource specialist. Tchr. L.A. Unified Schs., 1968-78; resource specialist Desert Sands Unified Sch. Dist., Palm Desert, 1978-83, Palm Springs Unified Schs., 1983-99, ret., 1999. Facilitator Phobics Anonymous World Svc. Ctr. Author: Jesus, My Higher Power, 2005; co-author: The Twelve Steps of Phobics Anonymous, 1989, One Day At A Time in Phobics Victorious, 1992, The Twelve Steps of Phobics Victorious, 1993; founder Phobics Victorious, 1992. Mem. Anxiety Disorders Assn. Am. Office: Phobics Victorious PO Box 695 Palm Springs CA 92263-0695 Business E-Mail: rosemaryjane@dc.rr.com.

HARTMAN, RUTH CAMPBELL, director, educator; b. Galion, Ohio, Aug. 18, 1938; d. Richard Lewis and Florence Evelyn (Ireland) Campbell; m. Richard Louis Hartman, Jan. 14, 1956; children: Jeffery Lee, Marsha Elaine, Jerry Steven. BS, Ohio State U., 1970; MEd, U. LaVerne, 1976, postgrad., 1985, U. Akron, 1977—85. cert. tchr., Ohio. Tchr. Willard City Schs., Ohio, 1964—65; educator Mansfield City Schs., Ohio, 1966—, home tutor, 1971—81, faculty advisory com., 1990—2001, young authors coord., 1991—92, co-coord. career edn., 1991—97; owner, dir. Hope Sch., Plymouth, Ohio, 2002—. Cons. Ohio State U., Ashland (Ohio) Coll., Mt. Vernon (Ohio) Nazarene Coll., 1976—. Co-author: Handbook for Student Teachers, 1983; contbr. to Norde News. Dir. constrn. Hope Sch. Mem NEA, Ohio Edn. Assn., North Ctrl. Ohio Tchrs. Assn., Mansfield Edn. Assn. Republican. Methodist. Avocations: reading, travel, tennis, music. Home: RR 1 Plymouth OH 44865-9801 Office: Hope School 4200 Opdyke Rd Plymouth OH 44865- Office Phone: 419-687-7507.

HARTMAN-ABRAMSON, ILENE, medical educator; b. Detroit, Nov. 8, 1950; d. Stuart Lester and Freda Vivian (Nash) Hartman; m. Victor Nikolai Abramson, Oct. 24, 1941. BA, U. Mich., Ann Arbor, 1972; MEd, Wayne State U., Detroit, 1980; PhD in Higher Edn., Wayne State U., 1990. Cert. continuing secondary tchr., Mich. Program developer and instr. William Beaumont Hosp., Royal Oak, Mich., 1972—74; vocat. counselor for emigres Jewish Vocat. Svc. and Cmty. Workshop, Detroit, 1974—81; program developer and cons. Detroit Psychiat. Inst., 1982; instr. for foreign students Oakland C.C., Farmington Hills, Mich., 1983-99. Mem. adv. bd. Mich. Dept. Edn., Detroit, 1981; lectr. Internat. Conf. Tchrs. English to Speakers of Other Langs., 1981; guest presenter Wayne State U., Lawrence Tech. U., 1991, U. Mich. Anxiety Disorders Program, 1993; presenter rsch. presentations Nat. Coalition for Sex Equity in Edn., Ann Arbor, Mich.; presenter at seminar on learning anxiety Interdisciplinary Studies program Wayne State U., 1995; chair profl. stds. and measures com. Mich. Devel. Edn. Consortium, editor newsletter, 1997; mem. rehab. adv. coun. State of Mich.; guest lectr. med. edn./residency tng. initiatives Detroit Med. Ctr. Hutzel Hosp., Providence Hosp., Beaumont Hosp., Detroit Med. Ctr., Harper Hosp.; adj. faculty Wayne State U., 2000; adj. prof. internat. comms. Lawrence Tech. U., 2000—. Mem. editl. bd. Mensa Rsch. Jour.; contbr. articles to prof. jours. Mem. Am. Acad. on Physician and Patient, Am. Mensa (rsch. rev. com.). Jewish. Avocations: self-defense for women, Karate. Office: Lawrence Tech U 21000 W Ten Mile Rd Southfield MI 48075-1058 Personal E-mail: ihabramson@aol.com. Business E-Mail: abramson@ltu.edu.

HARTMEIER, GINA MARIE, psychiatrist; b. Independence, Mo., Sept. 9, 1958; d. Joseph Robert and Irene Helen (Blair) Hartmeier; m. Alan Antill Jr. (div.); 1 child, Benjamin Blair Hartmeier Antill. BA in Biology, BA in Chemistry, MD, U. Mo., Kansas City, 1984; BFA in Painting, Sch. Vusian Arts, NYC, 1999. Diplomate Am. Bd. Psychiatry and Neurology. Psychiatrist Manhattan Psychiat. Ctr., NYC, 1994—99; co-dir. Gouverneur Hosp. Project HELP and Mobile Crisis Team; psychiatrist Newark Behavioral Med. Ctr., 1999—2000; pvt. practice Hoboken and Jersey City, NJ, 2000—; psychiatrist Jersey City Med. Ctr., 2002—04; ER, in-patient psychiatrist Englewood (NJ) Hosp., 2005—; psychiatrist NYC Human Resources Adminstrn., Customized Assistive Svcs., 2006—. One-woman shows include (pottery and ceramics) Jersey City, 2002. Asst. coach Jersey City Youth Soccer; mem. Clearwater Environ. Orgn. Mem.: Assn. NJ Psychiatrists, NJ Psychiat. Assn., Am. Psychiat. Assn, Sierra Club. Green Party. Unitarian Universalist. Avocation: fine arts. Office Phone: 212-495-2910.

HARTSBURG, JUDITH CATHERINE, entrepreneur; b. Terre Haute, Ind., June 16, 1955; d. Ferris Lee and Mary Ann (Tully) Roberson; m. Donald Matthew Seprodi, Aug. 1, 1972 (div. Oct. 1994); children: Antoinette Seprodi, Jacob Seprodi, Brooklyn Seprodi; m. Joseph Wayne Hartsburg, Feb. 14, 1998. AA, Ivy Tech., 1990; grad., Dale Carnegie Course. Lic. property/casualty ins. agt.; notary pub. Sec. Equifax, Oklahoma City, 1975-76; ins. clk. Northside Family Medicine, Del City, Okla., 1976; office mgr. Dick Clark Ins., Terre Haute, 1981, Simrell's, Terre Haute, 1981-85; ADC acctg. clk./typist V Vigo County Welfare, Terre Haute, 1985-86, head ADC acctg., clk./typist IV, 1986-87; purchasing agt. Bruce Fox, Inc., New Albany, Ind., 1987-88; acctg. mgr. Terre Haute Coke and Carbon, 1988-96, acting sec. bd. dirs., 1989; ptnr., owner Thistlehare; office mgr. Terre Haute Truck Ctr., 1996; internet programmer, webmaster Advanced Microelectronics, Inc., Vincennes, Ind., 1997—2001; ptnr., entrepreneur Ceilings, Walls & All, 2000—. Bookkeeper Seprodi Constrn., Terre Haute, 1989—; grad. asst. Dale Carnegie Inst.; owner Take-A-Letter; online entrepreneur Compubear on ebay.com. Author: (poetry) Between Darkness and Light, In-Between Days. Coach, bd. dirs. Terre Haute Youth Soccer Assn., 1979—82; player N. Tex. Women's Soccer Assn., Plano, 1977—78. Recipient Dale Carnegie Highest award for Achievement. Mem.: NAFE, Profl. Bookkeepers Assn., Am. Notary Assn., Am. Inst. Profl. Bookkeepers, Vigo County Taxpayers Assn. Democrat. Roman Catholic. Avocations: gardening, camping, sewing, piano, antiques. Home: PO Box 323 Sandborn IN 47578-0323 E-mail: stocksnbears@tds.net.

HARTSHORN, BRENDA BEAN, elementary school educator; b. Randolph, Vt., June 23, 1962; d. David Anthony and Reta Mae (Jones) Bean; children: Tyler Anthony, Caitlyn Elizabeth. BA, Vt. Coll., 1985; MEd, St. Michael's Coll., 1990. Teaching prin. aide Moretown (Vt.) Elem. Sch., 1984-85, 1-3 grade tchr., 1985—. Cons. math. & assessment, Waitsfield, Vt., 1993—; assoc. in math. Inst. for Math. Mania, Montpelier, Vt., 1994—, specialist for Vt. Dept. Edn. and Univ. of Vt., Early Literacy Intervention, 1999-2001. Contbr. articles to jours. Forums with state legis., Vt. NEA, 1985—; Justice of the Peace, 1998-. Recipient Sallie Mae Outstanding First Yr. Tchr. award Sallie Mae, 1985-86, Outstanding Tchr. of Yr. award, 1993-94, Presdl. award in Math. Nat. Sci. Found., 1994-95. Mem. NEA, Nat. Coun. of Tchrs. Math., Vt. Coun. on Reading, Assn. Supervision & Curriculum Devel. Democrat. Avocations: quilting, reading, writing, outdoor sports, travel. Home: 1192 Crossett Hill Waterbury VT 05676 Office: Moretown Elem Sch Rt 100B Moretown VT 05660

HARTSOCK, LINDA SUE, retired management consultant; b. St. Joseph, Mo., Feb. 20, 1940; d. Waldo Emerson and Martha (Skelkop) H. BS, Ctrl. Meth. Coll., Fayette, Mo., 1962; EdM, Pa. State U., 1965, EdD, 1971. Cert. assn. exec. Am. Soc. Assn. Execs. Tchr. Jr. High Sch. (North Kansas City (Mo.) Pub. Sch. Sys.), 1962; sr. resident Pa. State U., 1963—64, asst. coord. residence halls, 1964—65, residence hall coord., 1965—66, asst. dean women, 1966—68, asst. dean students, 1968—71; rschr. Ctr. for Study Higher Edn., 1971, dir. new student programs, 1971—72; nat. dir. program AAUW, 1972—76; exec. dir. Adult Edn. Assn., 1976—80; now ret. CEO Integrated Options, Inc., assn., edn. and mgmt. svcs., Greenbackville, Va.; designer tng. and ednl. programs for various orgns. and assns. V.p. fin. Com. for Full Finding Edn., 1979; first adv. panel convened future directions of a learning soc. project Coll. Entrance Exam. Bd., 1978, planning group for Course-By-Newspaper exam. project, 1979; bd. dirs. Coalition Adult Edn. Orgns., 1976; mem. White House Conf. on Aging Com., 1979; nat. adv. bd. Nat. Ctr. Higher Edn. Mgmt. Sys. Project to Develop a Taxonomy for the Field of Adult Edn., 1978; nat. adv. coun. on adult edn. Futures and Amendments Project, 1977; adv. Collection of Census Data, Nat. Ctr. Ednl. Stats., 1977; pub. policy com., program com. chmn. Adv. Coun. Nat. Orgns. to Corp. for Pub. Broadcasting, 1976; adv. devel. New Mediated Programs, Office Instructional Resources, Miami Dade C.C., 1976; innovative awards com. Nat. Univ. Ext. Assn., 1977; field reader U.S. Dept. Edn. Title III Grants, 1981-83 Mem. editl. bd. Off to Coll. mag, 1972-74; contbr. articles to profl. jours. Active Greenbackville Va. Fire Dept. Women's Aux., 2000—02; instr. water exercise Lower Shore YMCA, Pocomoke City, Md., 2002—; tour guide Chincoteague Nat. Wildlife Refuge, 2002—06; chair family coun. Hartley Hall Nursing Home; bd. mgrs. Lower Shore YMCA, 2004—, chair fin. devel. com., 2005—06. Recipient Disting. Alumni award Ctrl. Meth. Coll., 1978. Mem. Am. Soc. Assn. Execs. (individual membership coun. 1979-81, edn. com. 1985-88, 92-94, univ. affairs commn. 1989-92, awards com. 1991), Washington Women's Forum (budget, program and exec. coms. 1978-82), Alumni Soc. Coll. Edn. Pa. State U. (bd. dirs., chairperson strategic planning com. 1986, Outstanding Alumni award). E-mail: ioinc@dmv.com.

HARTSOUGH, CHERYL MARIE, recreation director, nutritionist; b. Phila., Dec. 30, 1959; d. Edward Joseph and Anna Marie (Hansell) Hartsough; children: Katrina Raspa, Hannah Rose. BS in Dietetics, U. Fla., 1985. Dietitian U. South Fla., Tampa, 1985-87; lead nutritionist Doral Saturnia Internat. Spa, Miami, 1987-90; cons. nutritionist Turnberry Isle, Aventura, Fla., 1991-92; dir. nutrition PGA Resort & Spa, Palm Beach Gardens, Fla., 1991-96; dir. wellbeing Aspen (Colo.) Club, 1996-98; dir. wellness Nemacolin Woodlands Resort & Spa, Farmington, Pa., 1999-2000; spa dir. Gurney's Inn Resort & Spa, Montauk, NY, 2001—. Lectr. Gatorade Speakers Network, Chgo., 1991—; nutrition cons. YMCA, Tampa, Fla., 1985-87; instr. Hillsborough C.C., Tampa, 1986-87. Author: Anti-Cellulite Diet, 1991, Doral Cookbook, 1991; editor: Gov.'s Coun. of Sports, 1987. Sec. nutrition com. Am. Heart Assn., Tampa, 1986-87. Recipient Gov.'s award State of Fla., 1987. Mem. Am. Cancer Soc., Am. Dietetic Assn. Found. (chairperson 1988-90, chairperson southeast sports and cardiovascular nutrition 1987-91, Young Recognized Dietetian 1989), DAR. Republican. Avocations: hiking, water and snow skiing. Office: Gurney's Resort & Spa 290 Old Montauk Hwy Montauk NY 11954 Office Phone: 631-668-1742. E-mail: cherylhartso@aol.com.

HARTSOUGH, GAYLA ANNE KRAETSCH, management consultant; b. Lakewood, Ohio, Sept. 16, 1949; d. Vernon W. and Mildred E. (Austin) Kraetsch; m. James N. Heller, Aug. 20, 1972 (div. 1977); m. Jeffrey W. Hartsough, Mar. 12, 1983; 1 child, Jeffrey Hunter Kraetsch. BS, Northwestern U., Evanston, Ill., 1971; EdM, Tufts U., Medford, Mass., 1973; MEd, U. Va., Charlottesville, 1978; PhD, U. Va., 1978. Vol. VISTA, Tenn., 1970-71; asst. tchr. Perkins Sch. for the Blind, Watertown, Mass., 1971-72; resource tchr. Fairfax (Va.) County Pub. Schs., 1972-76; asst. dir. ctr. U. Va., Charlottesville, 1976-78; sr. program officer Acad. Edn. Devel., Washington, 1978-80; mng. cons. Cresap/Towers Perrin, Washington, LA, 1980-86; pres. KH Consulting Group, LA, 1986—. Mem. nat. adv. coun. Sch. Comm. Northwestern U., Evanston, Ill., 1992—2005. Contbr. articles to profl. jours. Co-founder LA Higher Edn. Roundtable, 1987—94; mem. nat. adv. coun. Northwestern U., 1992—2005, mem. coun. of 100, 1999—. Recipient Outstanding Women of Achievement award, Century City C. of C., 1991. Mem.: BTW (bd. dirs.), Orgn. Women Execs. Home: 15624 Royal Ridge Rd Sherman Oaks CA 91403-4207 Office: KH Consulting Group 1901 Ave Of Stars Ste 1900 Los Angeles CA 90067-6020 Office Phone: 310-203-5417. Office Fax: 310-203-5419. Personal E-mail: khcggak@aol.com.

HARTWELL-IVINS, VICKY ROSE, office manager, medical/surgical nurse; b. Holden, Mo., Nov. 19, 1954; d. Donald Lee and Myrtle Ann (Williams) Hartwell; m. Gregory K. Ivins, Dec. 13, 1980; children: Melissa Nicole, Stephanie Danielle. BSN, U. Mo., 1976, MSN, 1981. Cert. AACN. Staff nurse Clin. Rsch. Ctr., Columbia, Mo., 1978-79, VA Hosp., Columbia, 1979-81; clin. instr. SUNY, Buffalo, 1981-84; office mgr. for gen. surgeon Fulton, Mo., 1984—; clin. coord. gen. orthop. surgeon, 1990—. Tchr. med.-surgery and developed slide program sect. NCLEX Rev. for Nursing Transition. Author: (with others) Adult Health Nursing Text, 1984. Mem. AACN, Nat. Assn. Orthopedic Nurses, Oncology Soc. Home: 3891 State F Rd Fulton MO 65251

HARTWIG, RHONDA DEAN, secondary school educator; b. Ft. Walton Beach, Fla., Apr. 20, 1958; d. Dwight Moody and Wanda Lea Skinner; 1 child, Brittany JoAnn. BA, Southwestern Okla. State U., Weatherford, 1980. Drama tchr. Yukon H.S., Okla., 1987—; asst. dir. Summer Spectacular, Putnam City, Okla., 2000—. Drama dir. Counter Pointe, Putnam City, 2000—. Avocations: mentoring, travel. Office Phone: 405-354-6661. Personal E-mail: rhondahartwig@cox.com.

HARTZ, JILL, museum director; b. Montreal, Que., Can., July 25, 1950; Undergrad. study, Oberlin U., 1969-71; MA in English Lang. and Lit. with honors, U. St. Andrews, Scotland, 1973; student, Cornell U., 1989-94. Mgr. Tompkins County Arts Coun., Ithaca, 1981-82, Grapevine Graphics, Ithaca, 1982-83; co-editor Grapevine Weekly Mag., Ithaca, 1983-84, Living Publs., Ithaca, 1984-86; coord. exhbns., asst. to dir. Herbert F. Johnson Mus. of Art, Cornell U., 1976-81, dir. pub. rels. and publs. Ithaca, 1986-93; asst. to chair, dept. of art Cornell U., Ithaca, 1993-94; coord. pub. rels. and spl. programs Coun. for the Arts, Cornell U., Ithaca, 1993-94; dir. comm. Arts & Scis. Devel. Office, U. Va., Charlottesville, 1994-97; interim dir. U. Va. Mus. Art (Bayly Art Mus.), Charlottesville, 1997, dir., 1997—. Co-curator Agnes Denes exhbn., 1991-92, editor monograph; co-founder, ptnr. LunaMedia pub. rels. co., Ithaca, 1993-94. Mem. Am. Assn. Museums, Nat. Cultural Alliance. Office: U Va Mus Art 155 Rugby Rd Charlottesville VA 22903 Fax: 804-924-6321.

HARTZELL, IRENE JANOFSKY, retired psychologist; d. Leonard S. and Annelies Janofsky. BA, U. Calif., Berkeley, 1963, MA, 1965; PhD, U. Oreg., 1970. Psychologist Lake Washington Sch. Dist., Kirkland, Wash., 1971-72; staff psychologist VA Med. Ctr., Seattle, 1970-71, Long Beach, Calif., 1973-74; dir. parent edn. Children's Hosp., Orange, Calif., 1975—78; clin. psychologist Kaiser Permanent, Woodland Hills, Calif., 1979—94; clin. instr. pediats. Coll. Medicine U. Calif., Irvine, 1975—78; ret., 1994. Author: The Study Skills Advantage; contbr. articles to profl. jours. Intern Oreg. Legis., 1974—75. U.S. Vocat. Rehab. Adminstrn. fellow, U. Oreg., 1966—67, 1969. Personal E-mail: drijh@earthlink.net.

HARTZLER, BELINDA SUE, social studies educator; b. South Bend, Ind., Mar. 4, 1966; d. Richard Allan and Rosemany Emma Stutzman; m. Jeffrey Scott Hartzler, June 4, 1988; children: Audrey Elise, Alexander James. BS, Ind. U., Bloomington, 1988; EdM, U. Minn., St. Paul, 1991. Lic. tchr. Minn., 1989. Social studies tchr. Anoka Hennepin, Coon Rapids, Minn., 1989—94; 9th grade social studies tchr. Hopkins #270, Minnetonka, Minn., 1994—. Test writer Harcourt Brace, Tex., 1998—2000; dist. coord. Project Citizen: Ctr. for Legal Edn., St. Paul, 2003—06. Nominee Tchr. of Yr., Ashland Oil, 1990. Mem.: Nat. Mid. Sch. Assn. (assoc.). Avocations: scuba diving, water-skiing, billiards, travel, walking. Home: 14109 Brandbury Walk Minnetonka MN 55345 Office: Hopkins #270 3830 Baker Rd Minnetonka MN 55345 Office Phone: 952-456-1223. Business E-Mail: belinda_hartzler@hopkins.k12.mn.us.

HARVARD, RITA GRACE, real estate agent, volunteer; b. Aurora, Ill., June 28, 1929; d. Walter Scott Fredenhagen and Grace Lucille Towsley-Fredenhagen; m. Anton Castagnoli (div. Mar. 10, 1978); children: Susan G., Jodie A., Thomas A.; m. John Francis Harvard. BA, Monmouth Coll., 1951. Educator 5th grade Dixon (Ill.) Pub. Sch., 1951—53; real estate mgr. Naperville (Ill.) Prince Castles Co., 1972—85; sec.-treas. Naperville Creamery Co., 1985—2000. Part-time vol. asst. tchr. Naperville Pub. Sch. Sys., 1968. Trustee North Ctrl. Coll., 1982—; mem. instnl. rev. bd. Edward Hosp.,

Naperville, 1992—; active Bd. Fire and Police Commr., City of Naperville, Ill., 1996—; trustee Naperville YMCA, 1996—; active Naperville Century Walk Bd., 1999—; trustee Monmouth Coll., Ill., 1974—81; hon. chmn. annual benefit Naperville United Way, 1988; bd. mem. Grace Meth. Ch. Found., 1993—, Naperville Heritage Soc., 1970—75, 1980—85, Grade Sch. and Jr. High Home and Sch. Assns., 1965—75, DuPage County Hist. Soc., 1975—78, Original Naperville Recycling Ctr., 1970—75, Edward Hosp. Aux., 1955—61. Named Outstanding Woman Leader of DuPage County, YWCA/DuPage, 1995; recipient Disting. Svc. award, Naperville Jaycees, 1993, Gael D. Swing award for meritorious svc., North Ctrl. Coll., 1995, Naperville Family Spirit award, 1997, Crystal award, Citibank Naperville, 1997, Outstanding Alumna award, Naperville Ctrl. H.S., 1998. Mem.: LWV, AAUW (Woman of Yr. award Naperville br. 1988), PEO, Naperville Heritage Soc. (Outstanding Svc. award 1999—2000), Rep. Women's Club, Rotary Club Naperville (chmn. membership devel. 1992—2000, cmty. svc. and membership devel. com. 1998—2002, past pres. 1994—95, Rotarian of Yr. award 1995). Methodist. Home: 439 LeProvence Cir Naperville IL 60540

HARVELL, GAYLE MARIE, cardiovascular technologist; b. Tulsa, July 9, 1955; d. John L. and Margaret L. (Drouhilet) Rodgers; children: Stefan Blaine, Adam Brian. Student, Tex. A&M U., 1973-77, N.Mex. State U., 1982-85. Registered vascular technologist, diagnostic cardiac sonographer. Vascular technologist Noninvasive Vascular Lab., Roswell, N.Mex., 1985-88; tech. dir. Southwest Cardiology Assocs., Roswell, 1988—. Internship dir. ENM Sch. Radiology, Roswell, 1992-93; vis. lectr. N.Mex. Mil. Inst., Roswell, 1994. Fellow Am. Coll. Angiobiology (affiliate); mem. Am. Soc. Echocardiology, Soc. Vascular Tech., N.Mex. Soc. Vascular Technologists. Republican. Office: Southwest Cardiology Assocs 405 W Country Club Rd Roswell NM 88201-5209

HARVEY, ALLISON CHARMAINE, chemist; b. Port-of-Spain, Trinidad and Tobago, Oct. 11, 1961; d. Clyde Francis and Frances Hosanna Harvey. BA, U. Ill., Champaign-Urbana, 1984. Cert. hazardous waste site worker EPA. Biologist/organic data reviewer Lockheed-Martin, Contractor to USEPA, Chgo., 1990—2001; assoc. chemist Alion Sci. and Tech., Contractor to USEPA, Chgo., 2001—06; sr. organic data reviewer Techlaw, Contractor to USEPA, Chgo., 2006—. Home: 1858 W 82nd St Chicago IL 60620-4640 Office: Techlaw Environ Consultants 536 S Clark St Chicago IL 60605 Office Phone: 312-353-2960. Office Fax: 312-353-8307. Personal E-mail: trinicharm@earthlink.net. E-mail: aharvey@techlawinc.com.

HARVEY, CHRISTINE LYNN, publishing executive; b. Bklyn., Dec. 7, 1962; AS in Liberal Arts, Nassau C.C., 1982; BA in Comm. Arts, Adelphi U., 1985. Cert. EMT, 1983-86. Franchise mgr. N.Y. Daily News, Mineola, 1981-84; copywriter, vido prodr., 1984-85; pub. rels. assoc. King Features Syndicate, N.Y.C., 1986; account exec. Promotional Broadcasting Svc., Babylon, NY, 1986-87; sr. account mgr. L.I. Bus. News, Ronkonkoma, NY, 1987-91; sr. ptnr. Karen Saeger Assocs., Stony Brook, NY, 1990—; editor The Steuben News, Ridgewood, NY, 1992—; founder, pub., editor-in-chief New Living, Stony Brook, 1991—; pub. rels. cons. Am. Health Found., Valhalla, NY, 1994—96; radio prodr./dir./host New Living Prodns., Stony Brook, 1997—98. Clin. hypnotherapist, Reiki master, 1999; TV prodr. Outlook Mag., 1985; TV news reporter, field prodr. LI News Tonite, 1984. Avocations: running, swimming, bicycling, hiking, golf. Office: New Living 1212 Route 25A Ste 1B Stony Brook NY 11790-1919

HARVEY, ELEANOR JONES, museum curator; b. Washington, Sept. 20, 1960; d. Charles Roy Jr. and Margaret McChesney (Jeffries) Jones; m. Stephen Jay Harvey, Oct. 10, 1992. BA with distinction summa cum laude, U. Va., 1983; MA, Yale U., 1985, MPhil, 1987, PhD, 1998. Asst. curator Am. paintings Mus. Fine Arts, Boston, 1989-91; assoc. curator Am. art Dallas Mus. Art, 1992-98, cons. curator Am. art, 1996—99; curator Am. art, 1999—2002; cons. curator Nat. Mus. Wildlife Art, 1996—99; curator Luce Foundation Center for American Art, Washington, 2003; chief curator Smithsonian American Art Museum, Washington, 2003—. Lectr. in field. Author: The Painted Sketch: American Impressions from Nature, 1830-1880, 1998, In Context: Painting in Dallas 1889-1945, 1999, Thomas Moran and the Spirit of Place, 2001, The Voyage of the Icebergs: Frederic Church's Arctic Masterpiece, 2002, An Impressionist Sensibility: The Halff Collection, 2006; co-author: Albert Pinkham Ryder, 1990, The Lure of Italy, 1992, Dallas Museum of Art: A Guide to the Collection, 1996, Cosmos: From Romanticism to the Avant Garde 1801-2001, 1999, Hudson River School Visions Landscapes of Sanford R. Gifford, 2003; contbr. articles to profl. jours. Bd. dirs. Wood Turning Ctr., Phila., 1998—; mem. ann. giving adv. coun. U. Va.; mem. U. Va. Assocs. of Libr., 1998—. Henry S. McNeill fellow in Am. decorative arts Yale U., 1985-87, Smithsonian predoctoral fellow Nat. Mus. Am. Art, 1988-89; Henry Luce Found. grantee, 1987-88. Mem. Am. Assn. Mus., Am. Craft Guild, Coll. Art Assn. Office: Smithsonian American Art Museum MRC 970 PO Box 37012 Washington DC 20013-7012 Office Phone: 202-275-1503. Business E-Mail: harveye@si.edu.

HARVEY, ELINOR B., child psychiatrist; b. Boston, Jan. 11, 1912; d. William and Florence (Maysles) H.; m. Donald K. Freedman, July 2, 1936; children: Peter, F. Kenneth. BS cum laude, Jackson Coll., 1933; MD, Tufts U., 1936. Diplomate Am. Bd. Psychiatry and Neurology, Nat. Bd. Med. Examiners. Intern New Eng. Hosp. Women and Children, Roxbury, Mass., 1936-37; resident Sea View Hosp., Staten Island, N.Y., 1937-39; adminstrv. and indsl. physician Assoc. Hosp. Svc. N.Y., 1939-41; house physician, resident Henry St. Settlement House, N.Y.C., 1939-41; pvt. practice Arlington, Va., 1941-43; pvt. practice as pediatrician Newport News, Va., 1943-46; clinician Westchester County Health Dept., White Plains, N.Y., 1947; pediatrician Arrowhead Clinic, Duluth, Minn., 1947-48; resident in psychiatry VA Hosp., Palo Alto, Calif., 1949-52; resident in child psychiatry child guidance clinic Children's Hosp. San Francisco, 1952-53, fellow in child psychiatry, 1953-54; pvt. practice as child and family psychiatrist Berkeley, Calif., 1954-68, Juneau, Alaska, 1968-77. Instr. Am. Univ. Washington, 1941—43; clinician prenatal clinics Arlington County Health Dept., Arlington, 1941—43; clinician Planned Parenthood, Wash., 1941—43; mem. adv. bd. emergency maternal and infant care program C's. Bur., Wash., 1942—48; instr. pediatrics schs. nursing Buxton and Riverside Hosps., 1943—46; consult pediatrician Community Hosp. and Clin, Two Harbors, Minn., 1947—48; mem. courtesy staff Herrick Hosp., Berkeley, Calif., 1955—68, Bartlett Mem. Hosp., Juneau, 1968—77; consult. US Bur. Indian Affairs Dept. Educ., Alaska, 1968—76, Southeast Regional Mental Health Clin., Juneau, 1975—77, Mars & Kline Psychiat. Clin. and Hosp., Port-Au-Prince, Port-Au-Prince, Haiti, 1977—78, Navajo Area Indian Health Serv., Gallup, N.Mex., 1980—, Brookside Hosp., San Pablo, Calif., 1980—84, San Pablo, 1984—; instr. mental health and mental illness Alaska Homemaker-Home Health Aide Servs., Juneau C.C., 1968—77, 1984—99; coord. State Alaska Program Continuing Educ. Mental Health, 1974—76; clin. assoc. prof. dept. psychiat. and behavioral scis. Univ. Washington, 1976—77; vol. child and family psychiatrist Baptist Mission, Fermathe, Haiti, 1977—79; instr. child develop. Mars and Kline Pscychiat. Clin and Hosp., 1977—78; mem. hosp. staff Gallup (NM) Indian Med. Cent., 1980—; consult. Brazelton neonatal behavioral assessment Navajo Area Indian Health Serv., 1982—; consult. infant-parent program Brookside Hosp., 1984—; demonstrator Brazelton neonatal behavioral assessment scale Cent. Recursos Educatius Deficients Visuals Catalunya, Barcelona, 1992; active Child Protection Agency, Juneau; mem. planning bd. Coordinated Child Care Cent., Juneau; presenter in field. Author: (with others) Annual Progress in Child Psychiatry and Child Development, 10th ann. edit., 1977, Expanding Mental Health Intervention in Schools, Vol. I, 1985, Psychiatric House Calls, 1988, The Indian Health Service Primary Care Provider, 1991; contbr. articles to profl. jours. Mem. comprehensive health planning coun. City and Borough of Juneau. Grantee NIMH, 1958-63. Fellow Am. Psychiat. Assn. (life), Am. Acad. Child and Adolescent Psychiatry (life, mem. task force Am. Indian children); mem. No. Calif. Psychiat. Assn. (Outstanding Achievement award 1996), Internat. Assn. Child Psychiatry, World Fedn. Mental Health, Internat. Assn. Circumpolar Health, Soc. Reproductive and Infant Psychology, Phi Beta Kappa. Home: 4220 Viscount Cir Anchorage AK 99502-4282

HARVEY, GLORIA-STROUD, physician assistant; b. Washington, D.C., Apr. 16; d. Robert W. and Ruth Elizabeth (Brown) Stroud; m. Jimmy Lawrence Harvey; children: Dana, Daman, Byron, Justin. BS, U. Md., 1968; physician asst. cert., Howard U., 1977. Physician asst. Weaver Clinic, Ahoskie, N.C., 1977-80, Western State Hosp., Staunton, Va., 1980-84, Walter Reed Army Med. Ctr., Washington, 1984-91, John Amsted Hosp., Butner, N.C., 1991—, U. N.C., Chapel Hill, 1991—. Physician asst. Aroyga, Durham, N.C., 1992—, Maria Parham Hosp., Henderson, N.C. Bd. dirs. Unique Builders, Henderson N.C., 1994-95, Cultural Initiatives, 1995. Mem. Am. Bus. Women's Assn., N.C. State-Employed Physician Assts.' Assn. (chmn. 1994), Triangle Assn. for Physician Assts., N.C. Assn. for Physician Assts. Methodist. Home: 2693 Hidden Spring Ln Oxford NC 27565-6146

HARVEY, JANE HULL, church administrator; BA with high honors, Scarritt Coll., Nashville, 1958; MA in Spl. Edn. with highest honors, Columbia U., 1972; grad., Tokyo Sch. Japanese Lang., 1966; Tchg. Cert., Sogetsu Japanese Ikebana Inst., Tokyo, 1969. Tchr. remedial English lang. arts Englewood (N.J.) Pub. Schs.; tchr. Head Start learning disabled children Ctrl. Harlem, N.Y.C.; person in mission United Meth. Ch., Korea, Japan, Okinawa, 1958-60, 64-69, 1975-80; office mgr. ednl. TV office Pub. Broadcasting Svc., Washington, 1980-81; program coord., asst. dir. dept. social/econ. justice Gen. Bd. Ch. and Soc. of United Meth. Ch., 1981-86, program coord. Justice for women project, 1986-88, dir. dept. human welfare, 1988-92, asst. gen. sec., 1992—. Lectr. in field. Contbr. articles to profl. jours.; asst. to editor Japan Christian Activity News, Tokyo, 1975-79; editl. asst. AMPO Mag., Tokyo, 1975-79. Chair bd. dirs. Interfaith IMPACT for Justice and Peace, 1995—; chair Washington Interreligious Staff Cmty., 1983-85, 89-91; co-chair Interreligious Coalition on Smoking or Health, 1992—; founding mem. World Alliance for Breast-feeding Action, Internat. Conf., Penang, Malaysia, 1990—; liaison to Gen. Comm. on Status and Role of Women, 1988—; chief staff Infant Formula Task Force, 1988-94; advisor Korean Legal Aid Ctr. for Family Rels., 1980-87; co-chair religion and race com. Dumbarton United Meth. Ch., Washington, 1986-88; founding mem., advisor Co-Madres, 1982; bd. dirs. Ptnrs. for Global Justice, 1982-87, Ctr. for Reproductive and Sexual Health, N.Y.C., 1973-75; co-founder Judson Health Project for Working Women, N.Y.C., 1973-75; adult counselor Youth March Against Hunger, Englewood, 1972-74; vol. adminstrv. asst. Greater Englewood Housing Authority, 1972-74; co-coord. United Farm Workers Boycott, Englewood, 1972-74; campaign coord., speech writer Dem. Mayoral Campaign, Englewood, 1972; co-dir. McGovern for Pres. campaign, Englewood, 1972. Office: United Meth Ch Gen Bd Ch Soc 100 Maryland Ave NE Washington DC 20002-5625

HARVEY, JANE R., retired investment company executive; b. Tarrytown, N.Y., Oct. 13, 1945; d. Fred W. and Margaret (White) Rosenbauer. Student, U. Ariz., Iona Coll., Coll. Fin. Planning; BA, Pace U., 2001. Lic. ins. counselor; registered fin. cons. Registered rep. KMS Fin. Svcs., Inc., Tucson, acct. exec., 1994—2002; ret., 2002. Contbr. articles to profl. jours. Active Resources for Women. NAFE, Internat. Assn. Fin. Planning (past bd. dirs., pres. 1993—, So. Ariz. chpt. v.p. membership, chpt. pres., 1983-2000), Internat. Assn. Registrd Fin. Planners (bd. govs., speaker conv.), Internat. Assn. Registered Financial Cons. (bd. dirs. 1995—), Am. Bus. Womens Assn., Am. Assn. Individual Investors, Tucson C. of C., Nat. Assn. Women Bus. Owners (So. Ariz. chpt. v.p., chpt. pres., Woman Bus. Owner of Yr. 2000). Office Phone: 520-270-6141. E-mail: Jharvey102@aol.com.

HARVEY, JOAN CAROL, psychologist; b. Clinton, Mass., June 2, 1943; d. Andrew Edward and Dorothy M. (Follansbee) Shusta; children: Stephen C., Daniel J. BA, U. Mass., 1967; MA, Temple U., 1977, PhD, 1981. Licensed clin. psychologist. Fellow in clin. psychology Dept. Psychiatry U. Pa., Phila., 1981-83; gen. practice psychology Phila., 1983-88; pvt. practice psychology Newark, Del., 1985-95. Clin. inst. dept. psychiatry U. Pa. Med. Sch., Phila., 1983-85, clin. assoc., 1985-88; affiliate staff mem. Med. Ctr. of Del., Wilmington, 1988-95. Author: If I'm So Successful, Why Do I Feel Like a Fake?: The Impostor Phenomenon, 1985, Families in Search of Love, 1996, Aging in America, 1997, Grownups Can Read Mother Goose, 1998. Mem. APA. Avocations: bicycling, boating, swimming, gardening, dogs. Home: 1730 Walnut Ave Winter Park FL 32789-2038

HARVEY, JUDITH GOOTKIN, elementary school educator, real estate agent; b. Boston, May 29, 1944; d. Myer and Ruth Augusta (Goldstein) Gootkin; m. Robert Gordon Harvey, Aug. 3, 1968; children: Jonathan Michael, Alexander Shaw. BS Edn., Lesley Coll., Cambridge, Mass., 1966; MS Edn., Nazareth Coll., Rochester, NY, 1987. Tchr. kindergarten Williams Sch., Chelsea, Mass., 1966—69; owner, tchr. Island Presch., Eleuthera, The Bahamas, 1969—70; substitute tchr. Brighton Ctrl. Sch., Rochester, NY, 1985—95; agt. Prudential Rochester Realty, Pittsford, NY, 1994—98. Author, dir.: (plays) The Parrot Perch, 1991. Bd. dir. in charge pub. rels. George Eastman Ho. Coun., mem. award steering com. honoring Lauren Bacall, 1990, chmn. gala celebration honoring Audrey Hepburn, 1992, mem. steering com. honoring Ken Burns, 1995; mem. art in bloom steering com. for fashion show Meml. Art Gallery, 1994; co-chmn. Fashionata, Rochester Philharm. Orch., 1990; mem. steering com. of realtors Ambs. to arts; mem. Parrot Players Acting Group, 1990—; mem. steering com. Reels and Wheels Antique Car Festival, 1995, 1996; bd. dir. Birmingham Bloomfield Newcomers, 2000—03, in charge spl. events, 2000—02; com. mem. Birmingham Antiques Festival, 2000—02; co-chair World of James Bond Gala and the Spring Fashion Show, 2001, Saturday Night Fever.Live It! Gala and Spring Fashion Show, 2002; historian Birmingham Bloomfield Newcomers, 2002—03; mem. Dow Jones Investment Group, 2002—, rec. ptnr., 2004—05, 2006—; mem. Cranbrook Tables Com., 2004. Mem.: Birmingham Country Club, Genesee Valley Club, Chatterbox Club. Avocations: acting, directing, gardening, writing, bridge. Personal E-mail: hcsailor@aol.com.

HARVEY, JULIE L., artist; d. Julian Tobey and Marie Teresa Harvey. BFA magna cum laude, Va. Commonwealth U., 1985; MFA, Parsons Sch. of Design, N.Y.C., 1987. Artist Featured artwork in films and TV shows such as Sex And The City and Spin City, N.Y.C., NY, 1992—; artist-lectr., series Governor's Magnet Sch. for the Gifted, Norfolk, Va., 1988; scenic painter for film,TV, and photography Harvey Backdrops, N.Y.C., NY, 1986—92; lectr. -sr. seminar lecture series Va. Commonwealth U., Richmond, Va., 1998. Prin. works include public art design Liberty Mural, N.Y.C. (First Pl., Wall St. Dist. Mural Competition, 1996), In the Garden, sculpture, Cubes (Mitsubishi Chem. Am. Project Grant, 1995), Red Hall (First Pl., Gallery '81, Norfolk VA, 1981). Grantee, ED Found., 2002, Mitsubishi Chem. Am., 1995—, 9-11 Arts Recovery Fund, 2002. Mem.: NOW, Guggenheim Mus., Whitney Mus. of Am. Art, Mus. of Modern Art, Soc. of Mayflower Descendents. Achievements include patents for bonding artist's material to archtl. panels. Avocations: dance, yoga, music, films. Office: Julie Harvey 174 Fifth Ave #201 New York NY 10010 Office Phone: 212-924-1992. E-mail: inquiries@julieharvey.com.

HARVEY, KATHERINE ABLER, civic worker; b. May 17, 1946; d. Julius and Elizabeth (Engelman) Abler; m. Julian Whitcomb Harvey, Sept. 7, 1974. Student, La Sorbonne, Paris, 1965-66; AAS, Bennett Coll., 1968. Asst. libr. McDermott, Will & Emery, Chgo., 1969-70; libr. Chapman & Cutler, Chgo., 1970-73, Coudert Freres, Paris, 1973-74. Adv., organizer libr. Lincoln Park Zool. Soc. and Zoo, Chgo., 1977-79, mem. soc.'s women's bd., 1976—; chmn. libr. com., 1977-79, sec., 1979-81, mem. exec. com., 1977-81; mem. jr. bd. Alliance Francaise de Chgo., 1970-76, treas., mem. exec. com., 1971-73, 75-76, mem. women's bd., 1977-80, 95—; trustee Chgo. Acad. Scis., 1986-88; adv. coun. mem. program for performing artists Northwestern Meml. Hosp., 1986-94, mem. exec. com., 1992—, bd. treas., 1992—; pres., bd. dirs. William Ferris Chorale, 1988-89; mem. Fred Harvey Fine Arts Found., 1976-78, Phillips Acad. Alumni Coun., Andover, Mass., 1977-81, mem. acad.'s bicentennial celebration com. class celebration leader, 1978, co-chmn. for Chgo. acad.'s bicentennial campaign, 1977-79, mem. student affairs and admissions com., 1980-81. Mem. aux. bd. Art Inst. Chgo., 1978-88; mem. Know Your Chgo. com. U. Chgo. Extension, 1981-84; mem. guild Chgo. Hist. Soc., 1978—, bd. dirs., 1993—; mem. women's bd. Lyric Opera Chgo., 1979—, chmn. edn. com., 1980, mem. exec. com., 1980-84, 88—, treas. women's bd., 1983-84, 1st v.p. 1988-90; mem. women's bd. Northwestern Meml. Hosp., 1979—, treas., chmn. fin. com., 1981-84, 92-94, mem. exec. com., 1981-88, 92—, devel. com. 1995-97, 2d v.p. 1996-97, 1st v.p. 1997—, founding chair pres. com. 1993—, pres. 1999—, dir. Northwestern Meml. Hosp., 1999—, pres. women's bd. 1999—, 1st v.p. 1997-99; vis. com. Sch. Music Northwestern U., 1995—; bd. dirs. Found. Art Scholarships, 1982-83; bd. dirs. Glen Ellyn (Ill.) Children's Chorus, 1983-90, founding chmn. pres.'s com., 1983—; mem. women's bd. Chgo. City Ballet, 1983-84; bd. dirs. Grant Park Concerts Soc., 1986-92; chmn. pres. com. Chgo. Children's Choir, 1991-93. Mem. Antiquarian Soc. of Art Inst. Chgo. (life), Guild of Chgo. Historical Soc., Arts Club Chgo. (dir. 1996—), Chgo. Symphony Soc. (life), Friday Club (corre. sec. 1981-83), Casino Club (gov. 1982-88, sec. 1984-85, 1987-88, 1st v.p. 1985-86, 2d. v.p. 1986-87), Cliff Dwellers Club. Home: 1209 N Astor St Chicago IL 60610-2314

HARVEY, LYNNE COOPER, broadcast executive, civic worker; b. near St. Louis; d. William A. and Mattie (Kehr) Cooper; m. Paul Harvey, June 4, 1940; 1 child, Paul Harvey Aurandt. DHL (hon.), Rosary Coll., 1996; D (hon.), Washington U., 1988. Broadcaster ednl. program KXOX, St. Louis, 1940; broadcaster-writer women's news WAC Variety Show, Ft. Custer, Mich., 1941-43; gen. mgr. Paul Harvey News ABC, 1944—. Pres. Paulynne Prodn., Ltd., Chgo., 1968—, exec. prodr. Paul Harvey Comments, 1968—; pres. Trots Corp., 1989—; editor, compiler The Rest of the Story. Pres. women's bd. Mental Health Assn. Greater Chgo., 1967-71, v.p. bd. dirs., 1966—; pres. woman's aux. Infant Welfare Soc. Chgo., 1969-71, bd. dirs., 1969—, benefits hon. chmn., 1994, 96; mem. Salvation Army Woman's Adv. Bd., 1967; reception chmn. Cmty. Lectures; women's com. Chgo. Symphony, 1972—; pres. Mothers Coun., River Forest, 1961-62; charter bd. mem. Gottlieb Meml. Hosp., Melrose Park, Ill.; mem. adv. bd. Nat. Christian Heritage Found., 1964—; mem. USO woman's bd., 1983, woman's bd. Ravinia Festival, 1972—; trustee John Brown U., 1980—; bd. dirs. Mus. Broadcast Comms., 1987—; adv. coun. Charitable Trusts, 1989—; mem. Joffrey Ballet Com.; chmn. Brookfield Zoo Whirl, 2000. Named to, Mus. Broadcast Comm.-Radio Hall of Fame; recipient Heritage of Am. award, 1974, Little City Spirit of Love award, 1987, Salvation Army Others award, 1989, disting. friend award, NCPCA, disting. alumni award, Washington U., Friske Meml. award, USO, 2000, Lynne Harvey scholarship named in her honor, Musicians Club of Women.

HARVEY, MICHELLE MAUTHE, researcher, consultant; b. Bethesda, Md., Dec. 29, 1954; d. Benjamin Camille and Lelia Anne (Webre) Mauthe (dec.); m. Don Warren Harvey, Mar. 31, 1979; children: Elise Brandner, Benjamin Casimir. BS in Forestry, U. South, 1976; MBA, Duke U., 1989. Forester Internat. Paper Co. Inc., Natchez and Brandon, Miss., 1976-80; framer, mgr. Frame Workshop, Lexington, Ky., 1981-83; mgr., dir. Country Stitchery Frameshop, Raleigh, N.C., 1984; dir. found. rels., placement and internship Sch. Forestry & Environ. Studies Duke U., Durham, N.C., 1984-90; dir. Am. Forest Found., Washington, 1990-92; mgr. planning and devel. Am. Forest Coun., 1990-92; dir. Environ. Partnership Initiative-MEB, Washington, 1993; v.p. programs Nat. Environ. Edn. and Tng. Found., Washington, 1994-98, v.p. edn., 1998-99; dir. sci. and edn. Soc. of Am. Foresters, 2000—04; cons. pvt. practice, 2004—. Mem. N.Am. Waterfowl Mgmt. Plan Implementation Bd., 1990—92; chair Animal Inn Nat. Partnership, 1992; mem. Project WILD program com., 1996—2000; mem. nat. adv. bd. CDC-Nat. Ctr. for Environ. Health, 1997—2002; mem. Project Learning Tree Program com., 1999—. Bd. dirs. Wake County Literacy Coun., Raleigh, 1984-88, Soc. Preservation Hist. Oakwood City Lights Ball, 1988, Ctr. Children's Environ. Lit., 1994-00; trustee SAF Ins. Trust, 1995-2000. Mem. Soc. Internat. Practical Tng. (mem. regional com. 1985-90), Soc. Am. Foresters (cert., trustee Ins. truste 1995-2000, mem. nat. task force on forestry edn. 1991-93, sec. human resources working group 1993-94, rep. social scis. to Forest Sci. and Tech. Bd. 1995-97, chair nat. capital chpt. 1995-96, mem. nat. leadership conf. steering com. 1990-93, mem. nat. com. on women and minorities 1984-88), Assn. Found. Group (co-chair program planning 1991-93, dean tng. workshops 1991-93), Washington Ethical Soc. (mem. steering com. nat. helping hands craft sale 1992, teen youth leader 1993-97, newsletter editor 1998-2000, bd. trustees, treas. 2000—). Democrat. Avocations: historic restoration, stained glass, gardening, photography.

HARVEY, NANCY MELISSA, media specialist, art educator; b. Atlanta, Mar. 31, 1934; d. Alfred Alonzo and Helen Rosella (Puntney) Ettinger; m. Dale Gene Harvey, Aug. 23, 1957; children: Howard Russell, Andrew Dale, Renee Jeannine. BA, U. Mont., 1957; M in Human Svcs., Coll. of Gt. Falls, Mont., 1987. Cert. tchr., Mont. Media specialist, libr. Flathead H.S., Kalispell, Mont., 1971-79; libr., art tchr. Cut Bank (Mont.) H.S., 1979-94. Author: (poetry collection) Bluffs, 2000; contbr. poetry to Arts in Mont., Mont. Arts mag., Poetry Today quar., Today's Poets anthology. Recipient Mary Brennan Clapp Poetry awrd Mont. Arts Found., 1973; grantee Mont. Com. for the Humanities, 1985, 87. Mem. AAUW (life), Mont. Genealogy Soc. (treas. Tangled Roots chpt. 1990—), Delta Kappa Gamma (chpt. pres. 1994-96), Phi Kappa Phi. Democrat. Presbyterian. Avocations: music, painting, creative writing, photography. E-mail: nmhbluffs@centurytel.net.

HARVEY, PATRICIA A., school system administrator; BS in elem. edn., Lincoln U.; MA in sch. admin., Roosevelet U. Prin. Hefferan Elem. Sch., Chgo., Idaho; exec. asst. to gen. supt. Chgo. Schs., 1994—95, chief accountability officer, 1995—97; sr. fellow dir. urban edn. Nat. Ctr. Edn. and Econ., Wash., DC, 1997—99; supt. Saint Paul Pub. Schs., Saint Paul, Minn., 1999—. Office: Saint Paul Pub Sch 360 Colborne St Saint Paul MN 55102

HARVEY, PATRICIA JEAN, retired special education services professional; b. Newman, Calif., Oct. 27, 1931; d. Willard Monroe and Marjorie (Greenlee) Clougher; m. Richard Blake Harvey, Aug. 29, 1965; children: G. Scott Floden, Timothy P. BA, Whittier Coll., 1966, MA, 1971. Resource specialist Monte Vista High Sch. and Whittier (Calif.) High Sch., 1977-98; dept. chair spl. edn. Whittier (Calif.) High Sch., 1982-94; ret., 1998. Author: (tchrs. manual) The Dynamics of California Government and Politics, 1970, 90; co-author: Meeting The Needs of Special High School Students in Regular Education Classrooms, 1988. Active Whittier Fair Housing Com., 1972; pres. Women's Aux. Whittier Coll., 1972-73, sec., 1971-72; historian Docian Soc. Whittier Coll., 1963-64, pres. 1965-66. Democrat. Episcopalian. Home: 424 E Avocado Crest Rd La Habra Heights CA 90631-8128 Office: The Learning Advantage Ctr 13710 Whittier Blvd Ste 206 Whittier CA 90605-4407

HARVEY, SHEILA MCCAFFERTY, lawyer; b. Ridgewood, NJ, June 28, 1954; AB summa cum laude, Bryn Mawr Coll., 1976; JD, Univ. Mich., 1979. Bar: DC 1979. Ptnr., co-chmn. Environ. Land Use & Natural Resources practice Pillsbury Winthrop Shaw Pittman, Washington. Mem.: ABA, Environ. Law Inst. Office: Pillsbury Winthrop Shaw Pittman 2300 N St NW Washington DC 20037-1128 Office Phone: 202-663-8224. Office Fax: 202-663-8007. Business E-Mail: sheila.harvey@pillsburylaw.com.

HARVEY, VIRGINIA SMITH, psychologist, educator; b. Bradford, Pa., Oct. 23, 1950; d. Robert Kinsel and Mary Ring (Olinger) Smith; m. Marshall L. Harvey, Dec. 27, 1971 (div. 1997); 1 child, Karen; m. Timothy Dawson, Jan. 1, 2003. BA, Smith Coll., 1972; MS, Ind. U., 1974, PhD, 1979. Cert. psychologist N.H., lic. sch. psychologist Mass., cert. nat. sch. psychologist. Social worker Sweet Brook Nursing Home, Williamstown, Mass., 1972; child care worker Sleighton Sch. Farm for Girls, Media, Pa., 1971; asst. instr. Ind. U., Bloomington, 1974-75; child care worker Develtl. Tng. Ctr., Bloomington, 1972-74; psychometrist Hammond Pub. Schs., Ind., 1976-79, psychologist Ind., 1979-81; chief psychologist Nashua Pub. Schs., NH, 1981-93; psychologist Counseling Ctr., Nashua, 1990-92; instr. Rivier Coll., Nashua, 1992; assoc. prof. dept. counseling and sch. psychology U. Mass., Boston, 1993—, dir. Sch. Psychology program, 1996—, chair, dept. counseling & sch. psychology, 2002—05, assoc. dean grad. coll. edn., 1997—2001, acting dean, 2000—. Cons. Clear Way, Nashua, 1981-85. Author: Effective Supervision in School Psychology, 2000, School Psychology Self Evaluation, 1992; contbr. articles to profl. jours. Smith Coll. scholar, 1968-72; Ind. U. Dept. Edn.

grantee, 1976. Mem. APA, Nat. Assn. Sch. Psychologists, N.H. Assn. Sch. Psychologists (Sch. Psychologist of Yr. 1989, pres. 1990-91), Mass. Sch. Psychology Assn. Democrat. Avocations: art, music. Office: Univ Mass Grad Coll Edn Wheatley Hall 100 Morrissey Blvd Boston MA 02125-3393

HARVIE, JESSICA GRANGER, performing company executive; b. Houma, La., Mar. 5, 1975; d. Jerry W. and Bethany Bourg Granger; m. Michael Lee Harvie, Nov. 13, 2004. BA in French, Nicholls State U., Thibodaux, La., 2000. Cert. dance tchr. S & S Sch. Dance, La., 1993. Student instr., tchg. certification intern S & S Sch. Dance, Inc., Houma, La., 1990—93; studio owner, bus. mgr., dance instr., artistic dir., choreographer Studio 48 Sch. Fine Arts Dance Acad., Bourg, La., 1994—2000; dance dir., choreographer Dance, Inc., A Performance and Prodn. Dance Co., Bourg, 1994—2000; dance educator, dir. dance dept. Davenport Sch. Arts, Fla., 2000—; artistic dir., choreographer Davenport Dancers, A Performance and Prodn. Dance Co., 2000—; site coord., site admin. 21st Century Grant Afterschool Programs, Mi Casa Su Casa Grant, Davenport Sch. Arts, 2005—; dance educator, dir. dance dept. Ridge Cmty. H.S., Davenport, 2006—. Dir.: (dance concert prodn.) Opening Night, All That Jazz, A Tribute to Anything and Everything Disney, A Evening of Praise and Worship through Dance, A Tribute to Dance, Music Explosion, Songs of Inspiration, Dance, Dance, Dance, Dance Extravaganza, Gotta Dance; co-dir.: Dance Concert 2005, 6th Annual Student Dance Concert 2006. Recipient Sch. Wide Creative Ticket award, The Kennedy Ctr., 2004, Sch. Wide Arts Achieve award, State Fla. Gov., 2004. Mem.: Fla. Dance Educators Orgn. (state bd. mem., fin. com. chair 2005—06).

HARVILLE, MYRA M., psychologist, educator; b. Grenada, Miss., Mar. 10, 1961; BS in Edn., Delta State U., Cleveland, Miss., 1981, MEd, 1984; PhD, Columbia Pacific U., Calif., 1995. Spl. edn. tchr. Parks Elem. Sch., Bolivar Sch. Dist, Cleveland, 1983—84; psychology instr. Holmes C.C., Grenada, 1987—. Named Outstanding Tchr., Grenada C. of C., 2001—02. Home: 1012 Highway 51 South Grenada MS 38901 Office: Holmes CC 1060 Avent Dr Grenada MS 38901 Office Phone: 662-227-2322. Business E-Mail: mharville@holmescc.edu.

HARWELL, DENISE, researcher; BA in Psychology, U. Ala., Huntsville, 1992, MA in Psychology, 1996. Rsch. asst. U. Ala., 1992, 1993; psychiatric tech. Crestwood Hosp., Huntsville, 1995—97; resident asst. Morningside of Madison, 2001—04; patient care tech. Huntsville Hosp., 2004—. Rsch. asst. U. Ala., Huntsville, 1993. Named Assoc. of the Quarter, Morningside, 2003; recipient Angel on Earth award, 2003. Mem.: Nat. Inst. Mental Health, Alzheimer's Assn., Ala. Psychological Assn. (assoc.), Am. Psychological Assn. (assoc.). Personal E-mail: 102740.1756@compuserve.com.

HARWELL, JOANNE BRINDLEY, music educator; b. Columbia, Tenn., June 29, 1935; d. Hugh Payne and Edna Doris (Bradford) Brindley; m. A. Brantley Harwell, June 18, 1957. BA in Music, Howard Coll., 1957; MEd in Elem. Edn., U. West Ga., 1980, EdS in Mid. Grades, 1983, MusM in Voice Performance, 1986. Tchr. Pritchard (Ala.) Jr. High, 1957—58, Lamar County Schs., Barnesville, Ga., 1974—76; min. music 1st Bapt. Ch., Barnesville, 1973—76; tchr., choral dir. Carrollton (Ga.) City Schs., 1976—88; tchr. Clayton County Schs., Morrow, Ga., 1988—95; tchr., choral dir. Henry County Schs., McDonough, Ga., 1995—98; music dir. St. James Episcopal Ch., Clayton, Ga., 2001—, Tallulah Falls (Ga.) Sch., 2002—. Coord. coun. mem. Cooperate Bapt. Fellowship, Macon, Ga., 2001—04, nominating com., 2004—, edn. com., 2001—04, mem. nat. coord. coun., 2004—, mem. personnel com. Mem.: Music Educators Nat. Conf., Macon Morning Music Club (sec.), Am. Guild of English Handbell Ringers, Macon Piano Tchrs. Guild (pres. 1970), Ga. Bapt. Mins. Wives (pres. 1986, program chair, chair nominating com.), Ga. Music Edn. Assn., Chorister's Guild (mem. Atlanta chpt.), Kappa Delta Pi, Phi Kappa Phi, Phi Delta Kappa (Student Rsch. award 1984), Delta Omicron (life; pres. Omicron Gamma chpt., Sr. award Omicron Gamma chpt.). Democrat. Baptist. Avocations: hiking, travel, reading. Home: 143 Valley Croft Rd Otto NC 28763 Personal E-mail: jharwell143@alltel.net.

HARWELL, LINDA WAITES, medical/surgical nurse; b. Columbia, S.C., Dec. 30, 1957; d. H.A. and Doris Harwell; children: Matthew, Grace. ADN, Midlands Tech. Coll., 1987. RN, S.C. Staff nurse oncology unit McLeod Regional Med. Ctr., Florence, S.C., nurse, staff float nurse med. and surg. units.

HARWICK, BETTY CORINNE BURNS, sociology educator; b. L.A., Jan. 22, 1926; d. Henry Wayne Burns and Dorothy Elizabeth (Menzies) Routhier; m. Burton Thomas Harwick, June 20, 1947; children: Wayne Thomas, Burton Terence, Bonnie Christine, Beverly Anne Carroll. Student, Biola, 1942-45, Summer Inst. Linguistics, 1945, U. Calif., Berkeley, 1945-52; BA, Calif. State U., Northridge, 1961, MA, 1965; postgrad., MIT, 1991. Prof. sociology Pierce Coll., Woodland Hills, Calif., 1966-95, pres. acad. senate, 1976-77, pres. faculty assn., 1990-91, chmn. dept. for philosophy and sociology, 1990-95, co-creator, faculty advisor interdisciplinary program religious studies, 1988-95. Chmn. for sociology L.A. C.C. Dist., 1993-95; occasional cmty. guest lectr. religious studies and sociology, 1995—. Author: (with others) Introducing Sociology, 1977; author: Workbook for Introducing Sociology, 1978. Faculty rep. Calif. C.C. Assn., 1977-80. Alt. fellow NEH, 1978. Mem. Am. Acad. Religion, Soc. Bibl. Lit., Am. Sociol. Assn. Presbyterian. Home: 2661 Tallant Rd MW515 Santa Barbara CA 93105

HARWOOD, ELEANOR CASH, retired librarian; b. Buckfield, Maine, May 29, 1921; d. Leon Eugene and Ruth (Chick) Cash; m. Burton H. Harwood, Jr., June 21, 1944 (div. 1953); children: Ruth (Mrs. William R. Cline), Eleanor, James Burton. BA, Am. Internat. Coll., 1943; BS in Libr. Sci., New Haven State Tchrs. Coll., 1955. Libr. Rathbun Meml. Libr., East Haddam, Conn., 1955-56; asst. libr. Kent (Conn.) Sch., 1956-63; cons. Chester (Conn.) Pub. Libr., 1965-71. Author: (with John G. Park) The Independent School Library and the Gifted Child, 1956, The Age of Samuel Johnson, LLD, Remember When, 1987, (essay) Growing Up in Chester, 1993, Moosley Yours, 1996, Chester, Years Ago, 2002. Mem. United Ch. Lt. (j.g.) USNR, 1944—46, WWII. Named Women of 20th and 21st Century, 2000, Eleanor C. Harwood prize in her honor, Rev. Jacob Meml. Christian Coll., India, Libr. Named in Her Honor, 2003, New Chapel Alter Named in Her Honor, 2005; recipient medal, Am. Theater-Victory. Mem. ALA, Conn. Libr. Assn., Chester Hist. Soc. (trustee 1970-72), Nat. Fedn. Blind, Am. Fedn. Blind, DAV, Am. Legion, Am. Legion Aux., Soc. Mayflower Descs., Appalachian Mountain Club. Home: 10 Maple St Chester CT 06412-0255

HARWOOD, SANDRA STABILE, lawyer, state representative; b. June 25, 1950; BBA, Kent State U., 1988; JD, Univ. Akon Sch. of Law, 1991. State rep. dist. 65 Ohio Ho. of Reps., Columbus, 2002—, mem. judiciary, ranking minority mem. civil and comml. law, econ. devel. and environ. health. Democrat. Office: 77 S High St Columbus OH 43215-6111 Office Phone: 614-466-3488.

HARWOOD, VIRGINIA ANN, retired nursing educator; b. Lawrenceville, Ohio, Nov. 5, 1925; d. Warren Leslie and Ruth Ann (Wilson) H.; m. Kenneth Dale Juillerat, Dec. 21, 1946 (div. 1972); children: Rozanne Augsburger, Vicki Anderson, Carol Mann, Karen Albaugh. RN, City Hosp. Sch. Nursing, Springfield, Ohio, 1946; BSN, Ind. U., 1968; MS in Edn., Purdue U., 1973, PhD, 1982. Cert. psychiat./mental health nurse, ANA. Staff nurse various hosps., 1946-60; pub. health nursing supr. Whitley County Health Dept., Columbia City, Ind., 1960-65; nursing supr., coordinator staff devel. Ft. Wayne (Ind.) State Hosp., 1965-69; faculty sch. nursing Parkview Hosp., Ft. Wayne, 1969-74; faculty dept. nursing Ball State U., Muncie, Ind., 1974-77; dir. nursing program Thomas More Coll., Ft. Mitchell, Ky., 1977-79; faculty sch. nursing Purdue U., West Lafayette, Ind., 1979-80; dean sch. nursing Ashland (Ohio) Coll., 1980-83; retired, 1983-86; charge nurse admission psychiat. unit VA Med. Ctr., Marion, Ind., 1986-93, ret., 1994—. Active Rep. Nat. Com., 1978—, U.S. Senatorial Club, 1984—; ch. coun. Grace Luth. Ch., Gas City, Ind., 1993-96; bd. dirs. Luth. Ctr., Ball State U., Muncie, Ind., 1994-96; bd. mgrs. Covington Creek Condominium Assn., 1997-2001; vol. Foellinger-Freeman Bot. Conservatory, 1993—. With Cadet Nurse Corps, 1944—46. Mem. Am. Nurses Found., Ohio State Nurses Assn. (pres. Mohican dist. 1981-83), Mensa, Intertel, Sigma Theta Tau, U.S. Amateur Ballroom Dancing Assn. (bd. dirs. Ft. Wayne chpt. 1998-2001, v.p. 2000, pres. 2001. Avocations: travel, reading, dance, orchid culture. Home: 6611 Quail Ridge Ln Fort Wayne IN 46804-2875

HARZOFF, ELIZABETH GAIL, special education educator; b. Cleve., Aug. 24, 1952; d. Willard and Charlotte Rosenberg Harzoff; m. Conrad Michael Eberle, June 19, 1982; children: Max Matthias Eberle, Louise Dana Eberle. BA in Liberal Studies, Hampshire Coll., 1975; MA in Folk Studies, Western Ky. U., 1981; MS in Human Ecology, Ohio State U., 1994. Cert. pre-kindergarden tchr. Ohio Dept. of Edn., 1993, early edn. of handicapped Ohio Dept. of Edn., 1995, early intervention specialist Ohio Dept. of Mental Retardation and Devel. Disabilities, 1995. Tchr. Ohio State U., Nisonger Early Childhood Edn., Columbus, Ohio, 1994—, practicum supr., 2001—, resource coord., 2004—. Cons. folklorist, Ohio, 1977—; in-service trainer, Ohio, 1992—. Bd. dirs. BalletMet Columbus Parents' Assn., 2000—05; troop leader Girl Scouts Am., Seal of Ohio Coun., Columbus, Ohio, 1992—2005, trainer, 2001—05; v.p. North Broadway Childrens' Ctr., Columbus, 2000—04. Recipient Outstanding Leader award, Girl Scouts Am., Seal of Ohio Coun., 1998, Outstanding Vol. award, 2000; fellow, Western Ky. U., 1977—79, Ohio State U., 1993—94. Mem.: Coun. Exceptional Children, Nat. Assn. for Edn. of Young Children. Avocations: costume design and construction, jewelry design, artist-in-education, Jai Alai. Home: 44 E Longview Ave Columbus OH 43202 Office: Ohio State Univ-Nisonger Ctr 1581 Dodd Dr Columbus OH 43210 Office Phone: 614-292-9605. Business E-Mail: eharzoff@wowway.com.

HASALONE, ANNETTE LEONA, research and development company executive; d. Glenn Allen Greene and Betty Leona Palmer; m. Mark Joseph Eve, Sept. 24, 2002; m. Cipriano Ramirez, May 24, 1977 (div. Sept. 0, 1985); children: Elizabeth Leona Ramirez, Dominic Earl Ramirez, Jerrod Emmett Ramirez. D in Naturopathy, Trinity Coll. Natural Healing, Warsaw, Ind.ana, 2003. Pres. Elemental Rsch., LLC, Post Falls, Idaho, 1999—; R&D cons. Eniva Corp., Blaine, Minn., 1999—2003. Case mgr. Homeless Mental Health Program, Oroville, Calif., 1984—86; account clk. I GAIN, Woodland, Calif., 1986—88; drug and alcohol specialist Health and Human Svcs., Woodland, 1988—89; DUI edn. counselor AK Bean Found., Fairfield, Calif., 1988—89; mgr./cons. WaterOz, Grangeville, Idaho, 1997—99; radio talk show host WGTG, Ga., 1998—2000, WHJM, Knoxville, Tenn., 1998—2000; product knowlege liaison Shagoi/Lanea Rx Larrea Corp., 2005. Author: (educational book) Mono-Atomic Minerals Information and Reference Guide, 1999, Off Balance, 2003, (educational booklet) Essential Information Booklet, (audio tape) Naturally Healthy With Mono-Atomic Minerals, (protocols for natural healing) Protocols Booklet. Campaign mgr. Ted Gunderson for Pres., Las Vegas, Nev., 1996—96. Recipient Outstanding Achievement in Poetry award, Internat. Libr. Poetry and Poetry.com, 2001, Outstanding Contbn. award, Enira Corp., 2001. Mem.: NAFE (assoc.), Internat. Ozone Soc. (assoc.). Republican. Achievements include invention of proprietary process for cell ready, ionic, liquid, water-soluble mineral supplements. Avocations: skiing, art, research and development, guitar, poetry. Office: Elemental Research LLC 4353 E Poleline Ave Post Falls ID 83854 Office Phone: 800-314-2884. Business E-Mail: annette@elementalresearchllc.com. E-mail: ahasalone@gmail.com.

HASELL, MARY JOYCE (JO), architecture educator; BS in Interior Design, U. N.C., Greensboro, 1967, MS in Interior Design, 1971; DArch, U. Mich., 1983. Registered interior designer, Fla. Interior design faculty U. Fla., Gainesville, 1988—, dir. PhD program, prof. Coll. Design, Constrn. and Planning, grad. coord. Master of Interior Design. Co-author: Accessible Design Review Guide: ADAAG Compliance in Building and Site Plans and Specifications; chair publ. bd.: Jour. Interior Design, mem. editl. rev. bd.:. Named Tchr. of Yr., 1992; recipient Tchg. Improvement award, 1994. Office: Univ Fla Coll Design Constrn and Planning 362 Architecture PO Box 115705 Gainesville FL 32611-5701

HASELOFF, CYNTHIA, fiction writer; d. Henry T. and Virginia Haseloff. PhD, U. Mo., Colombia, 1971; JD, U. Ark., Fayetteville, 2003. Tchr. journalism Springdale High Sch., Ark., 1976-80; tchr. gifted students Central Jr. High, Springdale, 1984-86. Author: (novels) Ride South!, 1980, A Killer Comes to Shiloh, 1981, Marauder, 1982, Bad Man, 1983, Dead Woman's Trail, 1984, The Chains of Sarai Stone, 1995, Anthologized Short Stories in the Western Story, 1995 (ed. Jon Tuska), Man Without Medicine, 1996, The Kiowa Verdict, 1997, The Morrow Anthology of Great Western Short Stories, 1997 (ed. Jon Tuska and Vicki Piekarski), Satanta's Woman, 1998, Changing Trains, 2000 (Western Writers Am. Spur award, 1998). Mem. ABA, Western Writers of Am., Ark. Bar Assn., Okla. Bar Assn. Home and Office: PO Box 161 Springdale AR 72765-0161

HASELTINE, FLORENCE PAT, obstetrician, gynecologist, medical association administrator; b. Phila., Aug. 17, 1942; d. William R. and Jean Adele Haseltine; m. Frederick Cahn, Mar. 12, 1964 (div. 1969); m. Alan Chodos, Apr. 18, 1970; children: Anna, Elizabeth. BA in Biophysics, U. Calif., Berkeley, 1964; PhD in Biophysics, MIT, 1969; MD, Albert Einstein Coll. of Medicine, 1972. Diplomate Am. Bd. Ob-Gyn., Am. Bd. Reproductive Endocrinology. Intern U. Pa.; resident Brigham and Women's Hosp., Boston; asst. prof. dept. ob-gyn. and pediatrics Yale U., New Haven, 1976—82, assoc. prof. dept. ob-gyn. and pediatrics, 1982—85; dir. Ctr. for Population Research, Nat. Inst. Child Health and Human Devel. NIH, Bethesda, Md., 1985—; founder Haseltine System, Inc., Products for the Disabled, 1995—. Founding sr. editor Jour. Women's Health. Co-author: Woman Doctor, 1976, Magnetic Resonance of the Reproductive System, 1987; co-editor: 25 books on reproductive scis. Bd. dirs. Older Women's League, 1998—, Am. Women in Sci., 1998—. Fellow: AAAS; mem.: Soc. Cell Biology, Soc. for Women's Health Rsch. (founder 1990, bd. dirs.), Soc. Gynecol. Investigation, Inst. of Medicine. Office: NIH/NICHD Ctr Population Rsch Executive Bldg Rm 8B07 6100 Executive Blvd Bethesda MD 20892-7510 Office Phone: 301-496-1101. E-mail: haseltif@mail.nih.gov.*

HASELY-HARSHMAN, TRACY, nurse; b. New Castle, Pa., May 28, 1963; d. Louis Charles and Muriel (French) H.; children: William Steven, Michael Hasely, Morgan Muriel. BSN, W.Va. Wesleyan Coll., 1985. RN. Staff nurse Hardee Meml. Hosp., Wauchulla, Fla., 1985, Manatee Meml. Hosp., Bradenton, Fla., 1986, asst. dir. nursing, 1986-87; staff nurse Wyo. Med. Ctr., Casper, 1987-89; occupational health nurse Amoco Corp., Chgo., 1989-92; wellness coord. Converse County Meml. Hosp., Douglas, Wyo., 1992-93; dir. student health Casper Coll., 1993—. ACLS instr. 1988—; cert. occupational hearing conservationist, 1989—; neonatal resuscitation instr., 1992—; trainer, drug and alcohol Concorde, Inc., Phila. & Casper, 1994—. Mem. Nat. League Nursing, Am. Coll. Health Assn., Am. Assn. Occupational Health Nurses. Republican. Methodist. Avocations: rock/ mountain climbing, rapelling, racquetball, volleyball, hunting, fishing. Home: 3920 S Oak St Casper WY 82601-6016 Office: Casper Coll 125 College Dr Casper WY 82601-4612

HASENJAGER, TANYA, music educator; b. Manitowoc, Wis., May 24, 1974; d. Lloyd August and Leatrice Clara Liermann; m. Trevor Jon Hasenjager, June 17, 2000; 1 child, Abigail Lynn (dec.). BA in Music Edn., Carthage coll, 1996; MA in Music Edn., Vander Cook Coll., 2003. Music tchr. St. Joseph High, Kenosha, Wis., 1997—. Pvt. tchr., Kenosha, Wis., 1996—. Mem.: Music Educators Nat. Conf. Avocation: running. Business E-Mail: thasenjager@kenoshastjoseph.com.

HASHIM, ELINOR MARIE, librarian; b. Pittsfield, Mass., Dec. 13, 1933. B.A., U. Vt., 1955; M.S., So. Conn. State U., 1970. Engring. asst. United Techs. Research Ctr., East Hartford, Conn., 1956-58, tech. research asst., 1958-63, supr. engring. aides and assts., 1963-68; head reference dept. Mary Cheney Library, Manchester, Conn., 1968-71; head circulation dept. New Britain (Conn.) Pub. Library, 1971-72, head bus., sci. and tech. depts., 1972-73, head reference dept., 1973-75; dir. Welles-Turner Meml. Library, Glastonbury, Conn., 1975-81; supr. reference and tech. services Perkin-Elmer Corp., Norwalk, Conn., 1981-85; program dir. spl. libraries Online Computer Library Ctr., Dublin, Ohio, 1985-90, govt. rels. officer, 1990-93, legis. analyst, 1993—; mem., chmn. Nat. Commn. on Libraries and Info. Sci., Washington, 1982-86, chmn. emeritus, 1986—; apptd. Conn. State Library Bd., 1974, chmn., 1976-82. Recipient Disting. Alumni award So. Conn. State U., 1982. Mem. ALA (pub. library assn. membership com. 1979-80, councilor Conn. chpt. 1980-82, councilor-at-large 1987-88, com. on legis. 1987-89, resolutions com. 1989-91, standards com. 1991-95), Conn. Library Assn. (chmn. legis. com. 1971-73, chmn. nominations com. 1975-76, rep. to ALA 1980-82, Librarian of Yr. award 1982), Spl. Libraries Assn. (fellows designation 1987, gov. rels. com. 1987-91), New Eng. Libr. Assn. (pres. 1977-78, Emerson Greenaway award 1989).

HASKELL, BARBARA, curator; b. San Diego, Nov. 13, 1946; d. John N. and Barbara (Freeman) H.; m. Leon Botstein; children: Clara Haskell Botstein, Maxim Haskell Botstein. BA, UCLA, 1969. Asst. registrar Pasadena (Calif.) Art Mus., 1969, curatorial asst., 1970, asst. curator, 1970, assoc. curator, 1970-72, curator painting and sculpture, 1972-74, Whitney Mus. Am. Art, N.Y.C., 1975—. Author: Arthur Dove, 1974, Marsden Hartley, 1980, Milton Avery, 1982, Blam! The Explosion of Pop, Minimalism and Performance 1958-64, 1984, Georgia O'Keefe: Works on Paper, 1985, Ralston Crawford, 1985, Charles Demuth, 1987, Red Grooms, 1987, Donald Judd, 1988, Burgoyne Diller, 1990, Agnes Martin, 1992, Joseph Stella, 1994, The Am. Century: Art and Culture 1900-1950, 1999, Edward Steichen, 2000, Elie Nadelman, 2002, Oscar Bluemner, A Passion for Color, 2005. Recipient award for scholarly excellence in field of Am. art history Archives of Am. Art, 2003; named Woman of Yr., Mademoiselle mag., 1973. Office: Whitney Mus Am Art 945 Madison Ave New York NY 10021-2701 Office Phone: 212-570-3606. Business E-Mail: barbara_haskell@whitney.org.

HASKELL, CHERYL MONA, telecommunications industry executive; b. Cheyenne, Wyo., Apr. 23, 1946; d. Bernard William and Ferne Adele Payne; children: Brian Dean, Brad Allen, Monica Lyn. BS in Stats., U. Wyo., 1967, BS in Math Edn., 1977. Dir. fiscal and statis. acctg. Wyo. State Govt., Cheyenne, 1970—75; tactical planner Mountain Bell, Cheyenne, 1978—84; statis. forecaster US West, Denver, 1984—94; tactical planner Qwest, Littleton, Colo., 1994—. Mem.: Gamma Phi Beta (fin. v.p. 2004—). Home: 3062 E Peakview Cir Centennial CO 80121 Personal E-mail: cheryl_haskell@msn.com.

HASKELL, ELIZABETH MCKNIGHT, not-for-profit developer, educator; b. Proctor, Vt., May 27, 1945; d. John Thomas and Phyllis Irene (Creaser) Conway; m. James Brian McKnight, June 6, 1964 (div. 1983); m. Charles T. haskell, December 26, 1996 (dec. 1998). BS with honors, Northeastern U., 1975; cert., Doscher Sch. Photography, Woodstock, Vt., 1976; MA in Environ. Affairs, Clark U., 1978. Reporter AP, Boston, 1974-75; tchr. journalism and environ. sci. Lawrence Acad., Groton, Mass., 1975-78; publs. mgr. Zellars-Williams, Inc., Lakeland, Fla., 1978-79; photographer, writer E.C. McKnight, Burlington, Vt., 1979-81; communications and mktg. mgr. Dufresne-Henry, Inc., North Springfield, Vt., 1981-82; gen. mgr. Assoc. Cons., Inc., Londonderry, Vt., 1982-85; dir. ops. Group Design Architects, Rutland, Vt., 1986-90; co-leader Rio Roosevelt Expedition, 1991-92, Livingstone's Last Journeys Expedition, 1993; founder, dir. New Century Conservation Trust Inc., 1991—. Freelance photographer, writer. Co-prodr. (documentaries for PBS' New Explorers): The River of Doubt, 1992, In the Footsteps of Dr. Livingstone, 1993; prodr. and host: (interactive television series) Living Classroom. Chairwoman citizens adv. com. Rutland County (Vt.) Solid Waste Dist., 1989-90; mem. Rutland Mayor's Com. on Volvo Site Selection, 1989; cons. Rutland Partnership, 1988-90, interim dir., mem. exec. com., 1989-90; bd. dirs. Merrymeeting AIDS Support Svcs., 1991-95; mem. Brunswick planning bd., 1995-96; mem. Brunswick Zoning Devel. Task Force, 1995-96; pres. New Century Conservation Trust. Recipient Theodore Roosevelt Disting. Svc. medal Theodore Roosevelt Assn., 1992. Fellow Explorers Club; mem. Royal Geog. Soc., Soc. Woman Geographers (Outstanding Achievement award 1996). Avocations: environmental conservation, photography, writing, lecturing, exploration. Home: PO Box 75 Dresden ME 04342 E-mail: ehaskell@midmaine.com.

HASKELL, JANE ZIRINSKY, artist, educator; b. Cedarhurt, N.Y., Nov. 24, 1923; d. Louis I. Zirinsky and Birdie Levy; m. Edward Norton Haskell (dec.); children: Anne Frances, Patricia Jane, Judith Lee. BS, Skidmore Coll., Saratoga Springs, N.Y., 1944; MA in History of Art, U. Pitts., Pa., 1961. Lectr. art history Duquesne U., Pitts., 1968—78. Lectr. in field. Prin. works include color and light environ., Platform Level Steel Plaza Subway Sta., Pitts., ltd. edit. print, Brandywine Graphics Workshop, Phila., The Atrium, Vista Internat. Hotel, Pitts., neon installation, William Pitt Student Union, U. Pitts., wall installation, YMCA, Pitts., wall installation, Everbrite Electric Sign Co., Greenfield, Wis., light installation, Intelligent Tech. Group, Pitts., neon installation, Ctrl. Parking Garage, Logan Airport, Boston., fluoorescent light installation, Birmingham Pl., Pitts., fluoorescent light installation, Pitts. Cultural Trust, fiber optic installation, Delta Terminal Ft. Lauderdale Airport, stairwell installation, Pressure Chem., Inc., Pitts., neon installation, Pitts. Ctr. Arts, fluorescent light installation, Heinz U.S.A., Inc., Pitts., sculpture, Pitts. Symphony Soc., numerous shows since 1980 including most recently, one-woman shows include A.I.R. Gallery, N.Y., N.Y., 1988, 1990, 1992, Westmoreland Mus. Am. Art, 1996, Chilimark Libr., Mass., 2003, exhibited in group shows at Gallery 707, Pitts., 2005, Concept Gallery, 2006, Pitts. Ctr. Arts, 2006, Represented in permanent collections Mead Art Mus., Amherst Coll., Mass., Carnegie Mus. Art, Pitts., Milw. Art Mus., Skidmore Coll., Saratoga Springs, N.Y., U. Pitts., Westmoreland County Mus. Art, Greensburg, Pa.; contbr. articles to catalogues and mags. Many other coms., bds. in the cmty.; bd. dirs. Winchester Thurston Sch., Pitts., 1980—88, Carnegie Mus. Art, Pitts., 1999—, mem. adv. bd. women's com., 1999—; mem. panel visual arts Pa. Coun. Arts, Harrisburg, Pa., 1985—88; mem. art adv. com. Pitts. Cultural Trust, 1990—2000; mem. art com. Jewish Cmty. Ctr., Pitts., 1992—; bd. dirs. Jewish Residential Svcs., Pitts., 1989—95. Named Artist of Yr., Pitts. Ctr. Arts, 2006, Citizen of Yr., Squirrel Hill Urban Coalition, 2003; recipient Purchase award, Carnegie Mus. Art, 1979, Pitts. Highlights award, Three Rivers Arts Festival, Pitts., 1987, Westinghouse Purchase award, 1987, Purchase award, Friends Art Pitts. Pub. Schs., 1992, Distinction award, Persad Ctr., Inc., 1995, A Tribut to Women award, YWCA, 2003. Mem.: Internat. Soc. Sculptors, Soc. Sculptors (adv. bd., Patrons prize 1979, Juror's award 1996, 1997, 1997, grantee 1980, Nat. Torchtip award 1986), Associated Artists Pitts. (adv. bd., sec. 1961—64, bd. dirs. 1961—64, Small Show award 1980, Juror's award 1982, 2006, Ann. Sm. Show award 1980). Avocations: tennis, theater, reading, travel.

HASKELL, MOLLY, writer; b. Charlotte, N.C., Sept. 29, 1939; d. John Haskell and Mary Clark; m. Andrew Sarris, May 31, 1969. BA, Sweet Briar Coll.; student, U. London, England, Sorbonne, Paris. Pub. rels. assoc. Sperry Rand; writer, editor French Film Office, N.Y.C.; film critic Village Voice, Viva, New York Magazine, Vogue, 1969-74, 74-80; film reviewer "Special Edition" Pub. TV; film reviewer "All Things Considered" Nat. Pub. Radio; assoc. prof. film Barnard Coll., N.Y.C., 1990; adj. prof. film Columbia U., N.YC., 1992—95, Sarah Lawrence Coll., 2004; writer. Artistic dir. Sarasota French Film Festival. Author: From Reverence to Rape: The Treatment of Women in the Movies, 1973, rev. edit., 1987, Love and Other Infectious Diseases: A Memoir, 1990, Holding My Own in No Man's Land, 1997; (plays) The Last Anniversary, 1990; contbr. articles and essays to jours. Decorated chevalier Order Arts and Letters (France); recipient Nat. Bd. Review of Motion Pictures award, 1989, Disting. Alumna award Sweet Briar Coll., 1994. Mem. N.Y. Inst. for the Humanities, Authors Guild (coun. 2000-03), The Century Club, Phi Beta Kappa.

HASKETT, DIANNE LOUISE, retired mayor, lawyer, consultant; b. London, Ont., Can., Mar. 4, 1955; d. Allan Douglas and Frances Shirley (Crone) Haskett; m. Jack Kotowicz; 1 child, Annie Kotowicz. BA, U.

Waterloo, Ont., 1974; LLB, U. Western Ont., 1977; LLM, London Sch. Econs., 1979, George Washington U., 2005. Bar: DC 2005. Lawyer Law Soc. Upper Can., Ont., 1980—; founding ptnr. Haskett, Menear Assoc., Law Firm, 1980—94; speechwriter, internat. cons., and pub. rels. advisor Washington Contact, 2001—; estate and bus. coord. Living Trust Atty. Ltd., Fairfax, Va.; Senate and Congl. campaign advisor. V.p. London Urban Alliance Race Rels. Contbr. articles to profl. jours. Founder Open Homes Can., London, 1992; founding mem. London Citizens Com., 1980—84; v.p. Ark Aid St. Mission Inc., London, 1986—88; city councillor London City Coun., 1991—94; mayor City of London, 1994—2000. Recipient Pericles award, Am. Hellenic Ednl. Prog. Assn., 1999; Grad. scholar, Rotary Internat., 1978—79, Paul Harris fellow, Rotary Club London, 1998. Mem.: Law Soc. Upper Can. Avocations: journalism, speech making. Home: 2970 Kildare Ln Fairfax VA 22031

HASKINS, DEBRA MAY, academic administrator, educator; d. John Albert and Norma W. Haskins; m. Lee Mead; children: Julia, Kerry, Donna, Gavin, Jacqueline. BA, SUC Cortland, NY, 1975; MA, SUNY, Stony Brook, 1991; student, Coll. New Rochelle, NY, 1992—94, St. John's U., Jamaica, NY, 1995—2005. Cert. social studies educator, grades 7-12, sch. dist. adminstr. Pub. rels. position Taylor Wine Co., Hammondsport, NY, 1973—75; realtor Carriage Home Realty, Smithtown, NY, 1979—81; social studies tchr. Baldwinsville Acad., NY, 1975—79, Sachem Schs., Holbrook, NY, 1983—84, Huntington Unified Sch. Dist., NY, 1981—83, 1984—98, chair-person social studies, 1998—. Exec. bd. tchr. ctr. Huntington Tchr. Ctr., 1999—; exec. bd. mem. Long Island Coun. Social Studies, NY, 2001—03. Women's advocate Chosin Few, L.I., 1996—2003. Mentoring Grant for Tchrs., Huntington, NY, 1999—2002, Art and Architecture grant, NEA, 2002—04, Taft scholar, Freedoms Found. Mem.: ASCD, Nat. Coun. Social Studies. Independent. Avocations: painting, writing, reading, travel, dream interpretation. Home: 96 Summit Dr Smithtown NY 11787 Personal E-mail: debhaskins@aol.com.

HASKINS, LINDA L., language educator; b. Beaver Falls, Pa., Aug. 31, 1947; d. Henry Griffin and H. Elizabeth Haskins. BA in English, Del. State U., 1969; MA in English, Seton Hall U., 1971; MA in Film, West Chester State U., 1983; postgrad., U. Del., 1988-91. Instr. Capitol Sch. Dist., Dover, Del., 1971-72, U. Del., Newark, 1972-75; asst. prof. Del. State U., Dover, 1975—. Contbg. editor: Succeeding Despite the Odds; editor Tangled Roots, 2005 Recipient NEH award, 1983. Mem. AAUP, AAUW, Nat. Coun. Tchrs. of English, NAACP, Alpha Kappa Mu, Alpha Kappa Alpha. Avocations: reading, gardening, singing. Office: Del State U 1200 N Dupont Hwy Dover DE 19901-2277 Office Phone: 302-857-6575.

HASKO, JUDITH ANN, lawyer; b. Waterbury, Conn., Feb. 11, 1964; BA, Vassar Coll., 1986; MPhil, U. Sussex, Brighton, Eng., 1988; JD, U. Wis., 1994. Bar: Wis. 1995, Calif. 1995, US Patent and Trademark Office 1998. Rsch. assoc. Genentech Inc., South San Francisco, Calif., 1988-92; ptnr. Cooley Godward, Palo Alto, Calif., 1994—2006, Latham & Watkins, Menlo Park, Calif., 2006—. Articles editor Wis. Law Rev., 1993-94. Mem.: ABA. Office Phone: 650-463-3065. Business E-Mail: judith.hasko@lw.com.

HASLACH, PATRICIA M., ambassador; m. David Herbert; children: Shereen, Kiran. BA, Gonzaga U.; MA in Internat. Affairs, Columbia U. With Fgn. Svc., US State Dept., 1986—, agrl. attaché New Delhi, polit. officer US Mission to the European Union, resource fficer Lagos, Nigeria, and Jakarta, Indonesia, dir. Office for Afghanistan, US amb. to Lao People's Dem. Republic, 2004—. Recipient Sinclaire Award, 1997, Herbert Salzman Award for Excellence in Internat. Econ. Performance, 1999, Dir. Gen.'s Award for Impact and Originality in Reporting, 2002. Office: US Embassy of Lao People's Dem Republic 4350 Vientiane Pl Washington DC 20521-4350

HASLETT, RHONDA LORRAINE, elementary school educator; b. Peoria, Ill., May 4, 1969; d. Ned Allan and Andrea Kay Pendleton; m. Larry Dale Haslett, June 12, 1993; children: Brett Lawrence, Megan Leanne. B, Bradley U., Peoria, Ill., 1989—91; MEd, Ill. State U., Normal, 1995—2001. Tchr. Peoria Heights CUSD #325, Ill., 1991—. Office: Peoria Heights Grade Sch 500 E Glen Peoria Heights IL 61616 Business E-Mail: rhaslett@phcusd325.net.

HASS, LISA M., freelance/self-employed counselor; b. Nashville, Sept. 4, 1953; d. Raymond Alonzo Palmer and Anne Michelle (Jones) Davies; m. Joseph Monroe Hass, Jr. BSBA, Belmont U., 1975; AA in Interior Design, Internat. Fine Arts Coll., 1977; postgrad., Tenn. State U., 1991-98; grad., Citizen Police Acad., 1997; postgrad., Westbrook U., 1998—. Interior designer Lisa Palmer Interior Designs, Nashville, 1977-84; sec. to pres. Hermitage Elect. Supply Corp., Nashville, 1981-83; sec. to dir. Tenn. Dept. Mental Health and Mental Retardation, Nashville, 1984-86; transp. planner Tenn. Dept. Transp., Nashville, 1986—99; pvt. practice wholistic lifestyle counselor Madison, Tenn., 1999—. Recipient cert. of appreciation Tenn. Dept. Mental Health and Mental Retardation, 1986; named Hon. Mem. Tenn. Ho. of Reps., 1990. Mem.: NRA, Mensa. Republican. Mem. Christian Ch. (Disciples Of Christ). E-mail: chachaqueen@comcast.net.

HASS, VICTORIA YUSIM, psychogeriatrics services professional, consultant; b. Chgo., Feb. 20, 1957; d. Sheldon Phillip Yusim and Sharon Friedman; m. Jeffrey Elliot Hass, Apr. 21, 1985; children: Matthew, Avi. BA in Polit. Sci., U. Wis., 1979; MA in Social Svc. Adminstrn., U. Chgo., 1983; PhD in Clin. Psychology, Northwestern U., 1995. Lic. clin. psychologist, Ill., clin. social worker, Ill. Cmty. supr. ret. sr. vol. program Hull House Assn., Chgo., 1979-81; social worker Coun. for Jewish Elderly, Lieberman Geriat. Health Ctr., Skokie, Ill., 1983-85; clin. psychologist Psychol. Assessments, Chgo., 1996-97; clin. dir. IN-PSYTE, Chgo., 1996-97; pvt. practice in psychogeriat. Wilmette, Ill., 1997—; mng. ptnr. Praxis Cognitive Rehab. Assocs., Skokie, 1999—. Psychol. cons. Coun. for Jewish Elderly Lieberman Ctr., Skokie, 1998—. Presenter at industry confs. V.p. Solomon Schechter Day Sch. Parent Orgn., Skokie, 1996—, Dorit chpt. Na'amat USA, Skokie, 1996—; v.p. ways and means Beth Hillel Synagogue, Wilmette, 1999—; bd. dirs. Bd. of Jewish Edn., Northfield, Ill., 1998—. Scholar Northwestern U., 1985-88. Mem. APA, NASW, Am. Group Psychotherapy Assn., Ill. Psychol. Assn., Internat. Psychogeriat. Assn. Avocation: psychology and religion in literature and film. Home: 720 Lamon Ave Wilmette IL 60091-2018 Office: 3612 Lake Ave Wilmette IL 60091-1000

HASSELBALCH, MARILYN JEAN, retired state official; b. Omaha, Jan. 2, 1930; d. Paul William and Helga Esther (Nodgaard) Campfield; m. Hal Burke Hasselbalch, June 13, 1954 (div. 1973); children: Kurt Campfield, Eric Burke, Peter Nels, Ane Catherine Hasselbalch McBride. BA with high distinction, U. Nebr., 1951. Cert. secondary tchr., Nebr. Pub. sch. tchr., Omaha and Long Beach, Calif., 1951-55; staff asst. U.S. Congressman Charles Thone, Lincoln, Nebr., 1973-78, Gov. of Nebr., Lincoln, 1978-82; exec. asst. Nebr. State Treas., Lincoln, 1983-86; sr. asst. Nebr. Gov. Kay A. Orr, Lincoln, 1987-91; exec. dir. Nebr. Appraiser Licensing Bd., Lincoln, 1991—2005; ret., 2005. Pres. Kempa Investment Properties, 2005—. Mem. camp bd. dirs. YMCA, Nebr., 1969-70; mem. Nebr. Edn. Policies Commn., 1982; state conv. del. Rep. Party Nebr., 1986, 88; gov.'s rep. Nebr. State Hist. Soc., Lincoln, 1987-89; del. Edn. Commn. on States, Balt., 1988; participant strategic leadership for gubernatorial execs. Duke U., 1988; sr. advisor Mission bd. Christ Luth. Ch., 1993-2005; treas. Danish Sisterhood #90, 1995—. Named to Outstanding Young Women Am., 1961, Woman of Yr., Rho Epsilon, 2000. Mem.: Assn. Appraiser Regulatory Ofcls. (bd. dirs. 1995—2002, publs. com. 1998—2002), Lancaster County Rep. Women (exec. bd. 1988), Nat. Fedn. Rep. Women, Danish Sisterhood Am., Am. Legion Aux., Phi Beta Kappa, Kappa Tau Alpha, Theta Sigma Phi. Lutheran. Avocations: reading, writing, travel, history, entertaining. Home and Office: 4705 South St Lincoln NE 68506-1257 Office Phone: 402-489-1793. Personal E-mail: marilynhas@msn.com.

HASSELMAN, SAN D., secondary school educator; b. Bklyn., Apr. 22, 1949; m. Kurt Hasselman, Apr. 6, 1972. BA in Fine Arts, Montclair State U., 1971; MA in Liberal Arts, Kean Coll., 1993. Cert. secondary sch. tchr., N.J. Tchr. art, English, gifted Union County Reg. Dist. #1, Springfield, NJ, 1976—97; secondary sch. tchr. art puppetry, English, gifted Arthur L. Johnson HS, 1997—, tchr. leader art and music, 2001—. Costumer (Villager Theater) The Lion in Winter, 1992; actress (Stony Hill Players) The Skin of Our Teeth, 1996. Avocations: poetry, theater, fine arts, puppetry. Home: 976 Mountain Ave Berkeley Heights NJ 07922-2357 Office: Arthur L Johnson HS 365 Westfield Ave Clark NJ 07066-1706 Office Phone: 732-382-0910.

HASSELMEYER, EILEEN GRACE, medical researcher; b. Bklyn., May 23, 1924; d. Edwin Allen and Margaret Grace (Cody) H. RN, Bellevue Sch. Nursing, 1946; BS, NYU, 1954, MA, 1956, PhD, 1963. Mem. staff Pediatric Metabolic and Nutritional Rsch. Svc., NYU Children's Med. Svc., Bellevue Hosp., N.Y.C., 1946-56, study coord., 1951-56; rsch. nursing supr. Met. Hosp., N.Y.C., 1951; lectr. pediatric nutrition rsch. U. Tex. Sch. Nursing, 1952-53; nursing dir. nutritional rsch. studies Children's Hosp. of John Seely Hosp. (U. Tex. Med. Br.), Galveston, 1952-53; lectr. and nursing rsch. assoc. nutritional svc. pediat. dept. Hosp. Infantile, Mexico City, 1953; nursing dir. rsch. unit Willowbrook State Sch., S.I., 1953-54; commd. USPHS, 1956, advanced through grades to asst. surgeon gen.-rear adm., 1981; ret. 1989; nurse cons. Divsn. Nursing Resources, Bur. Med. Svcs., USPHS, Washington, 1956-59; prin. investigator Handling and Premature Infant Behavior project, NYU, N.Y.C., 1961-63; sr. nurse cons. Div. Nursing, Bur. State Svcs., USPHS, Washington, 1963; spl. asst. for prematurity Office of Dir., Nat. Inst. Child Health and Human Devel., Bethesda, Md., 1963-66, acting dir. perinatal biology and infant mortality program, extramural programs, 1967-68, dir., 1969-74, asst. to dir. for perinatology, 1974-80; chief pregnancy and infancy br. Ctr. for Rsch. for Mothers and Children, 1974-79, acting chief clin. nutrition and early devel. br., 1979-80; assoc. dir. for sci. rev. Office of Dir., 1979-89; spl. asst. to dir. N.C. for Nursing Rsch., 1986-89; exec. dir. Uniform Svcs. U. Health Sci., Fed. Coll. Nursing Feasability Study Task Force, 1989-92. Annie W. Goodrich vis. prof. Yale U. Sch. Nursing, New Haven, 1968-69; asst. surgeon gen. USPHS, Dept. Health and Human Svcs., 1981-89, chmn. interagy. panel on sudden infant death syndrome, 1974-82, others. Contbr. articles to profl. jours. Recipient NICHD Recognition of Outstanding Performance, 1973, plaque for 25 yrs. dedicated svc., 1987, Chief Nurse Officer's medal USPHS, 1989; USUHS Commendable Svc. medal, 1990; USPHS Surgeon Gen.'s Cert. of Appreciation, 1990; HEW-USPHS Commendation medal, 1975; recipient Perinatal Research Soc. award, 1979; NYU Sch. Edn., Health, Nursing and Arts Professions Creative Leadership award, 1980; Achievement award Nat. Sudden Infant Death Syndrome Found., 1987, Eileen G. Hasselmeyer Disting. Sci. Achievement award Sudden Infant Death Syndrome Alliance, 1990; Outstanding Performance award NCNR, 1987, Meritorious Svc. medal HHS-USPHS, 1989; cert. appreciation NIH-NCNR, 1989; Nat. League for Nursing Commonwealth fellow, 1959-62; NIH fellow, 1962-63; Am. Nurses Found. grantee, 1962-63; State of Conn. Maternal and Infant Program grantee, 1969; Sigma Theta Tau research grantee, 1969-71; Yale U. Sch. Nursing developmental grantee, 1969; disting. alumnae award Bellevue Alumnae Assn., 1997. Mem. Pub. Health Svc. Commd. Officers Assn., Bellevue Alumnae Assn.

HASSELMO, ANN HAYES DIE, executive recruiter, consultant, psychologist, educator, retired academic administrator; b. Baytown, Tex., Aug. 15, 1944; d. Robert L. and Dorothy Ann (Cooke) Hayes; 1 child, Meredith Anne. BS with highest honors, Lamar U., 1966; MEd, U. Houston, 1969; PhD, Tex. A&M U., 1977. Lic. psychologist. Asst. prof. dept. psychology Lamar U., Beaumont, Tex., 1977—82, assoc. prof., dir. Psychol. Clinic, 1982—86, Regents prof. psychology, 1986, dir. grad. programs in psychology, 1981—86, pres. faculty senate, 1985—86; pvt. practice clin. psychology Beaumont, 1979—87; prof. Tulane U., New Orleans, 1988—92, dean Newcomb Coll., 1988—92, assoc. provost, 1991—92; pres., prof. psychology Hendrix Coll., Conway, Ark., 1992—2001, pres. emerita, 2001—; v.p., ptnr. higher edn. practice A.T. Kearney, Inc., Alexandra, Va., 2001—02; mng. dir. Acad. Search Consultation Svc., Washington, 2002—. Adminstr. adolescent residential unit Mental Health/Mental Retardation S.E. Tex., 1979-80, mem. cmty. adv. com., 1981-87; cons. in field; coordinating bd. Tex. Coll. and Univ. Sys. Internship, 1986, chair, bd. dirs. Ednl. and Instl. Ins. Adminstrs., 2000-02; bd. dirs. Nat. Merit Scholarship Corp., Acxiom Corp., Found. for Ind. Higher Edn., Air U., USAF. Contbr. articles to profl. jours. Mem. cmty. adv. com. Beaumont State Ctr. Human Devel., 1981-88; chair So. Collegiate Athletic Conf., 1996-97; participant Nat. Identification Program for Women, Am. Coun. on Edn., 1985, mem. govt. rels. commn., 1993-96, chmn., 1994-96, chmn. coun. of fellows, 1995-96, bd. dirs., 1997-2000; bd. dirs. Beaumont Civic Opera, Lamar U. Wesley Found., Tulane U. Wesley Found.; bd. govs. Isidore Newman Sch., 1991-92; trustee Robert Morris Coll., 1990-98, chmn. edn. com., 1990-94, chmn. pers. com., 1994-98; mem. univ. senate United Meth. Ch., 1993-01, chair commn. on instnl. rev., 1997-01; 1st v.p. Nat. Assn. Schs. & Colls. United Meth. Ch., 1996, pres. 1997-98; bd. dirs. Ouachita coun. Girl Scouts U.S., 1996-2000; mem. bd. visitors Air U., 1999—; mem. Internat. Women's Forum, 1995—, Ark. Women's Leadership Forum, 1999-02, pres. 2000-01; mem. Ark. Commn. to Streamline State Govt., 1996-98; mem. pres. commn. NCAA, 1997-01, chmn. div. III, 1999-2001, mem. exec. com. 1999-2001; chair Assoc. Coll. of the South, 1997-99; bd. dirs. Ark. Repertory Theatre, 2000-01, United Way of Faulkner County, 2000-01. Am. Coun. Edn. fellow Coll. William and Mary, 1986-87; recipient Regents Merit award, 1979, Coll. Health and Behavioral Sci. Merit award, 1982, Lamar U.; named one of Top 100 Women in Ark., Ark. Bus., 1995-99. Mem. APA, Southwestern Psychol. Assn., Family Svcs. Assn. (bd. dirs. 1988-89), Tex. Psychol. Assn. (dir. divsn. acad. psychologists 1986), S.E. Tex. Psychol. Assn. (treas. 1978-80, pres. 1983), Mental Health Assn. Jefferson County, Nat. Register Health Svc. Providers in Psychology, Nat. Assn. Ind. Colls. and Univs. (bd. dirs., vice chmn. 1995, chair 1996). Address: 5960 E Placita Alta Repasa Tucson AZ 85750

HASSELSTROM, LINDA MICHELE, writer, rancher; b. Houston, July 14, 1943; d. John and Florence Mildred (Baker) H.; m. George Randolph Snell, Mar. 10, 1979 (dec. Sept. 7, 1988). BA in English and Journalism, U. S.D., 1965; MA in Am. Lit., U. Mo., 1969. Pub. Lame Johnny Press and Ind. Pub. Svcs., 1971-85; rancher Windbreak Ho. Retreat, Hermosa, SD, 1953—. Condr. numerous writing workshops and seminars, including Minot (N.D.) State U., Moorhead (Minn.) State U., U. Minn., Duluth, others; participant numerous rev. panels and readings, at profl. confs.; former cons. pub. schs. Author of numerous poems; editor: Journal of a Mountain Man: James Clyman, 1984; co-editor: Leaning Into the Wind: Women Write from the Heart of the West, 1997; contbr. poems and essays to numerous jours., anthologies and collections; featured in many mags. and jours., including S.D. Rev., Bloomsbury Re., S.D. Mag., others. Judge numerous lit. contests, spkr. various orgns. NEA fellow, 1984; featured in Ms. Mag., 1975; named Author of Yr., S.D. Coun. Tchrs. of English, 1997, West River Notable, Rapid City (S.D.) Jour., 1992; recipient Distinguished Achievement awrd, S.D. Newspaper Assn., 1996, Gov.'s award in creative distinction/arts, S.D. Gov.'s Office, 1989. Mem. The Authors Guild, Inc., Poets & Writers, S.D. Artists' Network, Mari Sandoz Heritage Soc., The Land Inst., Assn. Study of Lit. and the Environ., Great Plains Native Plant Soc., S.D. Grassland Coalition. Avocations: reading, riding horseback, photography and albums, walking. Office: Windbreak House Retreat PO Box 169 Hermosa SD 57744 E-mail: info@windbreakhouse.com.

HASSER, JULIA M., mathematics educator; b. Paterson, N.J., Apr. 15, 1958; d. James Norbert and Eunice Marie Hasser. MEd, Rutgers U., New Brunswick, N.J., 1992. Cert. tchr. math. grades K-12 Dept. Edn., N.J., 1989. Tchr. Gt. Oaks Career Ctrs., Cin., 2000—01, Hillsborough Twp. Bd. Edn., NJ, 2001—. Mem. Planning Bd., Rocky Hill, NJ, 2004—06. Airman 1st class USAF, 1976—78. Office: Hillsborough HS 466 Raider Blvd Hillsborough NJ 08844 Office Phone: 908-874-4200. Business E-Mail: jhasser@hillsborough.k12.nj.us.

HASSETT, PATRICIA, university administrator; BA in Psychology with honors, CUNY, 1973; MA, Columbia U., 1974. Admissions counselor lesley Coll., Cambridge, Mass., 1974-75; asst. to dir. offfice admission sevcs. CUNY, 1975-77, dir. admissions and fin. aid Baruch Coll., 1980-85, dir. admissions CCNY, 1977-80; v.p. adminstrn. Fairleigh Dickinson U., Teaneck; v.p., chief compliance officer, special assistant John W. Rowe, Mt. Sinai/NYU Health; joined AETNA Inc., 2000, v.p., chief of staff, 2002—. Cons. in field. Adv. bd. Gateway Inst.; co-founder, Grad. Sch. Polit. Mgmt. George Washington U. Office: AETNA Inc 151 Farmington Ave Hartford CT 06156

HAST, ADELE, historian, editor, writer; b. NYC, Dec. 6, 1931; d. Louis and Kate (Miller) Krongelb; m. Malcolm Howard Hast, Feb. 1, 1953; children: David Jay, Howard Arthur. BA magna cum laude, Bklyn. Coll., 1953; MA, U. Iowa, 1969, PhD, 1979. Rsch. assoc. Atlas Early Am. History Project, Newberry Library, Chgo., 1971-75; assoc. dir. Atlas Great Lakes Indian History Project, 1976-79, Hist. Boundary Data File Project, 1979-81; editor in chief Marquis Who's Who, Inc., Chgo., 1981—86; survey dir. Nat. Opinion Rsch. Ctr., U. Chgo., 1986-89; rsch. fellow Newberry Libr., Chgo., 1989-95, scholar in residence, 1995—; exec. editor St. James Press, Chgo., 1990-92; mng. editor Hist. Ency. of Chgo. Women U. Ill., Chgo., 1991-93, dir., editor Hist. Ency. of Chgo. Women project, 1993-2001, sr. rsch. assoc. Ctr. for Rsch. on Women and Gender, 1999—2002. Mem. faculty Newberry Libr. Summer Inst. Cartography, 1980; cons. NEH planning grant Addams' Hull-House Mus., 2006. Author: Loyalism in Revolutionary Virginia, 1982, American Leaders Past and Present: The View from Who's Who in America, 1985; compiler: Iowa, Missouri, vol. 4 of Historical Atlas and Chronology of County Boundaries, 1788-1980, 1984; editor: International Directory of Company Histories, vols. 3-5, 1991-92, Women Building Chicago 1790-1990: A Biographical Dictionary, 2001; assoc. editor: Atlas of Great Lakes Indian History, 1987; curator exhibit on Chgo. history Spertus Inst. of Jewish Studies, 2002-03; contbr. articles to profl. jours. Mem. profl. adv. grad. program pub. history Loyola U., 1986—; treas., bd. dirs. Chgo. Map Soc., 1980-81, 93-95; mem. New Trier Twp. H.S. Bd. Caucus, 1972-74; mem. acad. coun. Am. Jewish Hist. Soc., 1985—; pres. Chgo. Jewish Hist. Soc., 1980-81, bd. dirs., 1977—. Recipient Alumna of Yr. award Bklyn. Coll., 1984, Colonial Williamsburg Found. grantee-in-aid, 1975, Brit. Acad. rsch. fellow, 1979; Am. Coun. Learned Socs. grantee-in-aid, 1980; NEH rsch. grantee, 1985, 87, 93-95, 97-98, fellow Jewish Women's Archive, 2003-04. Fellow Royal Hist. Soc., Phi Beta Kappa, Kappa Delta Pi; mem. Am. Hist. Assn., Orgn. Am. Historians, Chgo. Area Women's History Coun. (sec., treas. 1994-2004, bd. dirs. 1990—), Caxton Club (coun. 1990-93, 2003—, v.p. 2005—). Office: Newberry Library 60 W Walton St Chicago IL 60610-3380

HASTINGS, DEBORAH, bass guitarist; b. Evansville, Ind., May 11, 1959; d. Mortimer Winthrop Hastings and Margaret Hooper (Smith) Zimmerman. Student music, U. Wis. Bass guitarist, N.Y.C. and Madison, Wis., 1975—; freelance photographer Madison, 1976-81; band leader Bo Diddley, 1992—; founder A/Prompt Computer Telepromting Svcs., Inc., 1994—. Featured bassist with Duck Dunn for Bush inauguration, performing with Billy Preston, Dr. John, Koko Taylor, Willie Dixon, Carla Thomas, Eddie Floyd, Ron Wood, Steve Cropper, Bo Diddley, Jerry Lee Lewis, Chuck Berry, Joe Louis Walker; has also performed with Ben E. King, Little Anthony, Sam Moore, John Lee Hooker, Mick Fleetwood, Al Kooper, James Cotton; TV shows include Legends of Rock and Roll Live from Rome; appeared on David Letterman Show, 2003; subject of PBS Spl., 2003. Bass player TV shows Joan Rivers, 1987, Classics of Rock and Roll, 1988, Gunslingers tour Live from the Ritz with Ron Wood & Bo Diddley, 1988, Live from the Ritz, 1989, Legends of Rock and Roll (live from Australia), Legends of Guitar from Seville, Spain, 1991, Showtime at the Apollo, 1992, N.Y. at Night, 1992; performed Into The Night, 1991 (TV show) Nashville Now, 1991, American Musicshop, 1991, Johnny Carson Show, 1990, Pat Sajak Show, 1990, Carla Thomas, 1991, Arts & Entertainment Revue, 1990, (Madison Sq. Garden) Tribute to John Lee Hooker, 1990, Richard Nader's 25th Anniversary Show, 1994, Conan O'Brien Show, 1996; recordings include Bo Diddley's Grammy Nominated Album "A Man Amongst Men", 1996; performer in concert video "A Man Amongst Men", 1996; tours in Europe, Australia and Japan; performed at inaugurations of Pres. George Bush, 1989, Pres. Bill Clinton, 1997; performed with Bo Diddley opening of Seattle Music Experience Mus., 2000, Edgar Winter, 2003, Buffy Saint-Marie, 2003, Rock n'Roll Hall of Fame, 2005, with Eric Clapton, Robbie Robertson, Bo Diddley. Fundraiser, bassist polit. campaigns, Madison. Recipient numerous awards for pottery, award Arts Coun., Madison, Arts Coun., Ann Arbor, Mich.; played at Rock and Roll Hall of Fame Mus. Johnnie Johnson in Buenos Aires, Argentina, 2003. Mem. Musicians Union (local 802). Democrat. Avocations: computers, photography, graphics design, video. Office: Talent Cons Internat 1560 Broadway Ste 1308 New York NY 10036-1518 Office Phone: 212-730-2701.

HASTINGS, L(OIS) JANE, architect, educator; b. Seattle, Mar. 3, 1928; d. Harry and Camille (Pugh) H.; m. Norman John Johnston, Nov. 22, 1969. B.Arch., U. Wash., Seattle, 1952, postgrad. in Urban Planning, 1958. Architect Boeing Airplane Co., Seattle, 1951-54; recreational dir. Germany, 1954-56; architect (various firms), Seattle, 1956-59, pvt. practice architecture, 1959-74; instr. archtl. drafting Seattle Community Coll., part-time 1969-80; owner/founder The Hastings Group Architects, Seattle, 1974—; lectr. design Coll. Architecture, U. Wash., 1975; incorporating mem. Architecta (P.S.), Seattle, 1980, pres., from 1980. Mem. adv. bd. U. Wash. YWCA, 1967—69; mem. Mayor's Com. on Archtl. Barriers for Handicapped, 1974—75; chmn. regional public adv. panel on archtl. and engrng. services GSA, 1976; mem. citizens adv. com. Seattle Land Use Adminstrn. Task Force, 1979—; AWIU guest of Soviet Women's Con., 1983; spkr. Pacific Rim Forum, Hong Kong, 1987; guest China Internat. Conf. Ctr. for Sci. and Tech. of the China Assn. for Sci. and Tech., 1989; mem. adv. com. Coll. architecture and urban planning U. Wash., 1993; mem. accreditation team U. Oreg. Coll. Architecture, 1991, N.J. Inst. Tech. Sch. Architecture, 1992; juror Home of the Yr. ann. award AIA/Seattle Times, 1996; mem. architect selection com. Wash. State capital carillon project, Pratt Art Ctr. new bldg., 2001. Design juror for nat. and local competitions, including Red Cedar Shingle/AIA awards, 1977, Current Use Honor awards, AIA, 1980, Exhibit of Sch. Architecture award, 1981; Contbr. to: also spl. features newspapers, articles in profl. jours. Sunset mag. Mem. bd. Am. Women for Internat. Understanding, del. to, Egypt, Israel, USSR, 1971, Japan and Korea, 1979, USSR, 1983; mem. Landmarks Preservation Bd. City of Seattle, 1981-83; mem. Design Constrn. Rev. Bd. Seattle Sch. Dist., 1985-87; mem. mus. con. Mus. History and Industry, 1987—; leader People to People del. women architects to China, 1990. Recipient AIA/The Seattle Times Home of Month Ann. award, 1968; Exhbn. award Seattle chpt. AIA, 1970; Environ. award Seattle-King County Bd. Realtors, 1970, 77,; AIA/House and Home/The American Home Merit award, 1971, Sp. Honor award Wash. Aggregates and Concrete Assn., 1993, Prize bridge Am. Inst. Steel Contrn., 1993; Honor award Seattle chpt. AIA, 1977, 83; Women Achievement award Past Pres. Assembly, 1983, Washington Women and Trading Cards, 1983; Nat. Endowment for Arts grantee, 1977; others; named to West Seattle High Sch. Hall of Fame, 1989, Woman of Achievement Matrix Table, 1994; named Woman of Distinction, Columbia River Girl Scout Coun., 1994. Fellow AIA (pres. Seattle chpt. 1975, pres. sr. coun. 1980, state exec. bd. 1975, N.W. regional dir. 1982-87, Seattle chpt. found. bd. 1985-87, Bursar Coll. Fellows 1989-90, Coll. of Fellows historian 1994—, internat. rels. com. 1988-92, vice chancellor 1991, chancellor 1992, Seattle chpt. medal 1995, Northwest & Pacific region Medal of Honor 2002, Leslie N. Boney Spirit of Fellowship award 2003, Richard Upjohn Fellows medal), Internat. Union Women Architects (v.p. 1969-79, sec. gen. 1985-89, del. UIA Congress, Montreal 1990), Am. Arbitration Assn. (arbitrator 1981—), Coun. of Design Professions, Assn. Women Contrs., Suppliers and Design Cons., Allied Arts Seattle, Fashion Group, Tau Sigma Delta, Alpha Rho Chi (medal).

HASTINGS, MARY JANE, minister; b. N.Y.C., July 23, 1949; d. Lucy Lake and Charles Thomas Hastings. BS in Bus. Administrn., Caldwell Coll., 1998; MDiv, Luth. Theol. Sem., Phila., 2002. Sec. TV Bur. Advt., N.Y.C., 1968—72; exec. asst. to pres. TeleRep, Inc., 1972—80; v.p. ops. TV Program Enterprises divsn. TeleRep, Inc., 1980—93; exec. v.p. and ptnr. Al Masini

Productions, 1993—94; dir. sales and mktg. The Mediacenter, 1994—96; pastor St. Mark Luth. Ch., Morristown, 2002—. V.p. Morris Area Clergy Coun., Morristown, 2003—. Writer (short drama) The Trial of Judas, The Sacrificing Samaritan, Second Chance, The Wives of the Disciples, Mary Magdalene - A Personal Reflection. Recipient Tracy L. Maul award, Luth. Theol. Sem., Phila., 1999. Mem.: Delta Epsilon Sigma, Kappa Gamma Pi, Alpha Chi. Lutheran. Avocations: travel, walking, old movies, exercise, reading. Home: 100 James St Morristown NJ 07960 Office: St Mark LuthCh 100 Harter Rd Morristown NJ 07960 Office Phone: 973-538-3939. Office Fax: 976-538-6223. Personal E-mail: mjhast50@aol.com.

HASTINGS, MARY LYNN, real estate broker; b. Carthage, N.Y., Jan. 16, 1943; d. Floyd Albert and Mary Frances (Schack) Neuroth; m. Ronald Anthony Casel, Nov. 28, 1963 (div. Nov. 1977); children: Mark, Steven, Glen; m. Charles F. Hastings, Apr. 27, 1991 (dec. 1998). Grad., Harper Method, Rochester, N.Y., 1961. Lic. real estate broker. Owner M.L. Salon, Rochester, N.Y., 1962-72; splty. tchrs.-aide Broward County, Ft. lauderdale, Fla., 1973-77; office mgr. Broward County Voter Registration, Margate, Fla., 1977-82; real estate salesperson Pelican Bay, Daytona Beach, Fla., 1982-84, broker, 1984—; broker, owner Mary Lynn Realty, Daytona Beach, Fla., 1989—. Mem. adv. bd. Dem. Club, Margate, 1977-82. Mem. NAFE, Nat. Assn. Realtors, Fla. Home Builders Assn., Nat. Home Builders Assn., Daytona Beach Home Builders Assn., Daytona Beach Bd. Realtors, Ft. Lauderdale Bd. Realtors, Nat. Assn. Women in Constrn. (v.p. 1988-89, pres.-elect 1989—, pres. 1990—), Sales and Mktg. Coun. Democrat. Episcopalian. Avocations: travel, round and square dancing, theater, real estate investments. Home: 112 Marsh Wren Ct Daytona Beach FL 32119-8707 Office: Mary Lynn Realty 1301 Beville Rd Ste 21 Daytona Beach FL 32119-1503 E-mail: marylynn@marylynnrealty.com.

HASTINGS, SUSAN C., lawyer; b. Mpls., 1959; BA, U. Iowa, 1980, JD with distinction, 1985. Bar: Ohio 1985, registered: US Dist. Ct. (No. Dist.) Ohio, US Ct. Appeals (6th cir.). Ptnr. Squire, Sanders & Dempsey LLP, Cleve., chmn., Labor & Employment Practice Group. Mem.: ABA (Labor & Employment Law Sect.), Ohio State Bar Assn. (Labor & Employment Law Sect.), Nat. Sch. Bd. Assn., Ohio Coun. of Sch. Bd. Attys. Office: Squire Sanders & Dempsey LLP 4900 Key Tower 127 Public Sq Cleveland OH 44114-1304 Office Phone: 216-479-8723. Office Fax: 216-479-8780. Business E-Mail: shastings@ssd.com.

HASTINGS, VIVIEN N., lawyer; b. Havana, Cuba, Dec. 22, 1951; BA, U. Conn., 1973; JD, Wash. U., 1977. Bar: Ill. 1977, Fla. 1990. Assoc. Winston & Strawn, 1977—82; v.p., co-gen. counsel Merrill Lynch Hubbard, Inc., 1982—89; various positions WCI Communities Ltd. Partnership, sr. v.p., gen. counsel; sr. v.p., gen. counsel, sec. WCI Communities, Inc., Bonita Springs, Fla. Office: WCI Communities Inc 24301 Walden Ctr Dr Bonita Springs FL 34134 Office Phone: 239-947-2600. Office Fax: 239-498-8277.

HASTY, JENNIFER ELEANOR, anthropologist, educator; b. Springfield, Mo., Dec. 3, 1967; d. Ralph Lee and Mary June (Dalrymple) Hasty. BA in Anthropology, UC Berkeley, Calif.; PhD in Cultural Anthropology, Duke U., NC. Asst. prof. anthropology Pacific Luth. U., Tacoma; rsch. affiliate, Inst. African Studies U. Ghana-Legon, 1996—97; polit. reporter The Ghanaian Independent, 1996—97, Public Agenda, 1996—97, Ghanian Chronicle, 1996—97, Ghana News Agy., 1996—97, Daily Graphic, 1996—97; rsch. assoc. Ctr. Africa and Media Africa News Svc., Durham, NC, 1998; program dir. Summer Abroad Program Duke U., Ghana, 1999; rsch. fellow Ctr. Democracy and Devel., Accra, Ghana, 2004—05; asst. prin. investigator Serious Fraud Office, Accra, Ghana, 2004—05. Author: The Press and Political Culture in Ghana, 2005; contbr. articles various profl. jours. Recipient Regency Scholars award, Pacific Luth. U., 2001; Predoctoral fellowship, Andrew W. Mellon Found., 1997—98, Summer Rsch. grant, 2002, Individual Rsch. grant, Wenner-Gren Found., 2004—05. Progressive. Buddhist. Avocations: swimming, dance, cooking, kayaking. Home: c/o MJ Hasty 2155 E Richmond St Springfield MO 65804 Business E-Mail: hastymj@plu.edu.

HATCH, BARBARA JEAN, secondary school educator; b. Alton, Ill., Aug. 30, 1950; d. Paul John Van Buren and Loretta Barbara Wardein; m. John Spencer Hatch, Nov. 27, 1982; children: Joshua Spencer, Adam Michael. BA magna cum laude, Loyola U., Chgo., 1972; M, No. Ariz. U., Flagstaff, 1996. Cert. tchr. Ariz. TOEFL tchr. CEG Escale (Peace Corps), Thies, Senegal, 1972—75, Imperial Iranian Navy, Rasht, Iran, 1975—76; tchr. history and English St. Croix Country Day Sch., Christiansted, VI, 1977—90, Judson Sch., Scottsdale, Ariz., 1990—2000; tchr. history Sonoran Prep, Glendale, Ariz., 2000—01, Cactus Shadows HS, Cave Creek, Ariz., 2001—. Advisor Ariz. Heritage Project, Cave Creek, Ariz., 2003—06. Named one of Top 10 Ariz. Tchrs. of Yr., 2005; recipient Tchr. of Yr., St. Croix Country Day Sch., 1986—90, Character award, Judson Sch., 1996. Mem.: Ariz. Humanities Coun., Ariz. Geog. Alliance, Nat. Coun. Econ. Edn., Ariz. Coun. Social Studies, Nat. Coun. Social Studies. Avocations: travel, languages, quilting. Home: 4233 E Redfield Rd Phoenix AZ 85032 Office: Cactus Shadows HS Box 426 Cave Creek AZ 85327 Office Phone: 480-575-2562. Personal E-mail: bhatch12@cox.net. E-mail: bhatch@ccusd93.org.

HATCH, MARGARET OENONE, secondary school educator; b. Johannesburg, May 28, 1946; d. Eustace and Jean Stuart (Wallis) Duncan; m. Thomas Phillips Hatch, Apr. 3, 1987; m. Colin Martin Eisenstein, Mar. 10, 1972 (div. Nov. 1, 1982); children: Natasha Jane van der Linde, Clare Justine Eisenstein. MD, U. Witwatersrand, Johannesburg, South Africa, 1970; MA in Tchg., U. Memphis, Memphis, Tenn., 1994. Registered med. practitioner South African Med. and Dental Coun., 1971, Gen. Med. Coun., London, U.K., 1976; lic. tchr. Tenn. Dept. Edn., 1998. Physician and sr. med. officer Soweto (South Africa) Clinics Baragwanath Hosp., 1972—76, physician, designer, tchr. Primary Care Program RNs, 1976—79, prin. physician supr. primary health care tng. and supervision Soweto (South Africa) Clinics, 1979—80; physician rschr. South African Inst. Med. Rsch., Johannesburg, 1980—86; adj. asst. prof. biology lab. Christian Bros. U., Memphis, 1988; asst. prof. physiology lab. So. Coll. Optometry, Memphis, 1988—90; tchr. Memphis (Tenn.) City Schs., 1994—. Contbr. scientific papers, articles to profl. jours. Vol. reading tutor Memphis (Tenn.) Literacy Coun., 1989—93. Mem.: Memphis Educators Assn. Avocations: travel, reading, crossword puzzles, photography. Home: 3643 Oak Branch Cove Bartlett TN 38135 Office: Memphis City Schools-Cordova High School 1800 Berryhill Road Cordova TN 38016 Office Phone: 901-416-4540. Office Fax: 901-416-4545. Personal E-mail: mohatch@hotmail.com. Business E-Mail: hatchmagareto@mcsk12.net.

HATCH, SALLY, science educator; b. Westbrook, Maine, Oct. 27, 1976; d. Brenda Gherardi and George Gherardi, Jr.; m. Timothy Hatch, Oct. 3, 2004. B in Biology, St. Joseph's Coll., Standish, Maine, 2000. 7th grade life sci. tchr. Lake Region Sch. Dist., Naples, Maine, 2000—04; h.s. phys. sci. tchr. Gorham Sch. Dept., Gorham, Maine, 2004—. Sci. dept. team leader Gorham H.S., Maine, 2004—. Recipient Innovative Tchg. of Biology, St. Joseph's Coll., 2000.

HATCH, SALLY RUTH, foundation administrator, writer, consultant; b. Grand Rapids, Mich., Apr. 16, 1935; d. George and Evangeline (Boerma) Meyer; m. S. John Byington, Nov. 27, 1964 (div. Dec. 1988); children: Nancy Lee Rhodes, Barbra Ann Byington; m. Robert C. Hatch, Sept. 20, 2003. BA, Western Mich. U., 1957; MA, U. Md., 1962. Cert. tchr. K-8 Md. Grad. asst. U. Md., College Pk., 1959-60; tchr. U. Chgo. Lab. Sch., 1963-64, Grand Rapids, 1957-59. 64-65, Montgomery County Pub. Schs., Rockville, Md., 1961-63; learning specialist Endeavor Learning Ctr., Rockville, 1987-88; asst. to pres. Women in Mil. Svc., Arlington, Va., 1988-89; exec. asst. Korean War Vets. Meml. Adv. Bd., Washington, 1989-91; pub. safety cons., civic activist, 1991—2000. Cons. Children Early Edn. Program, Bur. Edn. Handicapped, Dept. Edn., Washington, 1975—80; pvt. practice diagnostician. Author: (book) Marriage Through Divorce and Beyond. Vol. Fairfax County Pub. Schs. Enrollment Study, 1985; coord. Capital Hill Cmty. Policing Coun.; mem. MPD's Chief Police Citizens Adv. Coun.; project dir. Guns into Plowshares Sculpture Project; mem. Ward 6 Crime Task Force; mem. coun. Neighbors Who Care DC; exec. bd. dirs. MidNortheast Family Strengthening Collaborative; active Balt. County Orgn. Neighborhoods; coord. Antictam Creek Watershed Alliance; mem. Citizens Protection Washington County; pres. Greater Springfield Rep. Women's Club, Va., 1980, v.p., 1980; dir. Fairfax County Rep. Com., 1988. Recipient Vol. Recognition award, Fairfax Pub. Schs., 1985; fellow, Metro Urban Concerns Ministry. Mem.: LWV (study rep. 1980), Capital Hill Restoration Soc. (pub. safety issues chair). Avocations: reading, writing poetry and music, active sports, church activities. Home and Office: 1201 Jefferson Blvd Hagerstown MD 21742 Office Phone: 301-790-0378. E-mail: bob.hat@worldnet.att.net.

HATCHELL, SYLVIA, basketball coach; b. Gastonia, N.C., Feb. 28, 1952; m. Sammy Hatchell; 1 child, Van. B.Phys. Edn. cum laude, Carson-Newman Coll., 1974; MS, U. Tenn., 1975. Coach jr. varsity women's team U. Tenn.; head coach Francis Marion Coll.; head women's basketball coach U. N.C., Chapel Hill, 1986—. Asst. coach U.S. World Univ. Games team, 1983, 85; ct. coach U.S. Olympic basketball try-outs, 1984, 92; basketball events taff Olympic Games, L.A., 1984; asst. coach U.S. team 1988 Olympic Games, Goodwill Games and World Championships; coach USA team World Univ. Games, Fukuoka, Japan, 1995, R. william Jones Cup, 1994. Named Nat. Coach of the Yr., USA Today, 1994, Coll. Sports Mag., 1994, Converse NAIA Reg. Coach of the Yr., 1986, AMFVoit Championship Coach, 1986, Coll. Basketball Coach of the Yr., Athletes Internat. Ministries, 1995, Carson-Newman Disting. Alumnus of the Yr., 1994; inductee Francis Marion U. Athletic Hall of Fame, 1993. Mem. Women's Basketball Coaches Assn. (pres. 1996-97, past bd. dirs.), Amateur Basketball Assn. of U.S. (women's games com.).*

HATCHER, BARBARA A., lawyer; BA, Univ. N.H., 1977; JD, Wake Forest Univ., 1980. Atty. Squire, Sanders & Dempsey, Washington; asst. gen. counsel Burlington Industries; v.p., gen. counsel GNB Technologies Inc.; group counsel transp. bus. group Exide Technologies, Alpharetta, Ga., 2000—04, dep. gen. counsel, asst. sec., 2004—06, exec. v.p., gen. counsel, 2006—.*

HATCHER, BEVERLY J., pastor; d. Roy Early and Hattie Francis Long; m. Raymond Wayne Hatcher, June 25, 1972; children: Tiffany Chanel Southern, Jeremy Wayne. BA, High Point U., 1997; MDiv, M. Christopher White Sch. of Div., 2000; D of Ministry, M.Christopher White Sch. of Div., 2006. Certificate of Ordination Pfafftown Bapt. Ch./ Pilot Mountain Bapt. Assn., 2000, Certificate of License New Beginning Bapt. Ch., 1994, Certificate of Completion Am. Bapt. Churches, U.S.A/ Ch. Planter's Inst., 2003, Clinical Pastoral Education Wake Forest U. Bapt. Med. Ctr., 2000. Cert. dental asst. Dr. Mark L. Meyer, Winston-Salem, NC, 1993—95; co-pastor New Beginning Bapt. Ch., King, NC, 1997—98; children's min. Pfafftown Bapt. Ch., NC, 1998—2001; pastor Covenant Cmty. Faith, Salisbury, NC, 2001—06. Mem./ treas. Rowan Ministerial Assn., Salisbury, NC, 2001—05. Recipient Parker-Locke award for Academic Excellence, High Point U., 1997. Home: 612 Brookford Pl Ct Winston Salem NC 27104 Office Phone: 704-637-3009. Personal E-mail: bhatcher@bellsouth.net. Business E-Mail: lifeofcovenant@bellsouth.net.

HATCHER, CAROLYN JOYNER, school nurse; d. William Earl and Mary Sue Stephens; m. Marcus Hamilton Hatcher, May 6, 2000; m. William T. Joyner (dec.); children: Celeste Joyner, Susan Joyner. BSN, U. South Ala., Mobile, 1999. RN S.C. Dialysis nurse Med. Ctr. Clinic, Pensacola, Fla., 1984—86; dialysis nurse-peritonea Nephrology Ctr. Pensacola, Fla., 1986—89; dialysis nurse Tidewater Dialysis Ctr., Norfolk, Va., 1989—90; cmty. health nurse USN Family Svc. Ctr., West Ruislip, London, 1990—92; dialysis nurse FMC Easley Dialysis, SC, 1992—94; sch. nurse Wren Elem. Sch., Piedmont, SC, 2003—. Mem.: S.C. Assn. Sch. Nurses (conf. agenda com. 2003—), Sigma Theta Tau. Republican. Baptist. Avocations: reading, piano. Office: Wren Elem Sch 226 Roper Rd Piedmont SC 29673 Office Phone: 864-850-5950. Office Fax: 864-850-5951.

HATCHER, TERI, actress; b. Sunnyvale, Calif., Dec. 8, 1964; d. Owen and Esther Hatcher; m. Marcus Leithold, June 4, 1988 (div. 1989); m. Jon Tenney, May 27, 1994 (div. Mar. 2003); 1 child, Emerson Rose. Student, Deanza Jr. Coll., Am. Conservatory Theater. Spokeswoman Clairol Nice 'n Easy hair color. Actor: (films) Tango and Cash, 1989, The Big Picture, 1989, Soapdish, 1991, Straight Talk, 1992, Heaven's Prisoners, 1996, Two Days in the Valley, 1996, Dead Girl, 1996, Tomorrow Never Dies, 1997, Since You've Been Gone, 1998, Fever, 1999, Spy Kids, 2001, The Chester Story, 2003; (TV films) Dead in the Winter, 1991, The Brotherhood, 1991, Running Mates, 2000, Jane Doe, 2001, Say Uncle, 2001, Momentum, 2003; (TV series) The Love Boat, 1985-86, Capitol, 1986-87, Karen's Song, 1987, Lois and Clark: The New Adventures of Superman, 1993-97, Desperate Housewives (Golden Globe Award for best actress in a TV series - musical or comedy, 2005, Screen Actors Guild Award for outstanding performance by a female actor in a comedy series, 2005, Screen Actors Guild Award for outstanding performance by an ensemble in a comedy series, 2005, 2006), 2004-; Author: Burnt Toast: And Other Philosophies of Life, 2006 Named one of The Most 10 Fascinating People of 2005, Barbara Walters Special. Address: Desperate Housewives Touchtone Television 100 Universal City Plaza Bldg 2128 Ste G Universal City CA 91608

HATFIELD, BARBARA SCOTT, academic administrator; d. Jim Seth and Marie Miller Scott; m. Steven Hunter Hatfield, Dec. 28, 1985. BS, Miss. State U., 1971; MEd, U. So. Miss., 1976; EdS, Miss. State U., 1980; PhD, U. Ky., 1991. Tchr. math. grades 7, 9, 11, and 12 Meridian Pub. Sch., Miss., 1971—83; mem. adj. faculty Meridian C.C., 1981—82; Va Felder vis. instr. U. So. Miss., Hattiesburg, 1982—83; tchg. asst., fellow U. Ky., Lexington, 1983—90; rsch. assoc. U. Utah, Salt Lake City, 1989; asst. prof. U. Rio Grande, Ohio, 1990—94, assoc. prof., 1994—98, prof. math., 1998—, chair, Sch. Scis., 1997—99, coord. semester conversion, 1999—2002, interim dean, Coll. Liberal Arts and Scis., 2002—04, dean, Coll. Liberal Arts and Scis., 2004—05, interim provost, v.p. acad. affairs, 2005—. Co-coord. title III grantee Rio Grande CC, 2003—06; leadership team SE Ohio Ctr. Excellence in Math. and Sci., Athens, 2004—06; module devel. Ohio Math. Acad. Program Math Sci. Learning Network, Columbus, 2004—06. Named Tchr. of the Week, U. So. Miss. Student Newspaper, 1982; recipient Donna Chen Women's Equity award, Ohio U., 2000. Mem.: Am. Conf. Acad. Deans, Assn. Am. Colls. and Univs., Nat. Coun. Tchrs. English, Math. Assn. Am., Delta Kappa Gamma (pres. 1997—2002, Beta Alpha chpt., internat. scholar 1985), Phi Alpha Theta, Delta Gamma (treas. 1968—70). Achievements include founding co-director of Girls Emerging in Math and Science program. Office: U Rio Grande Office Academic Affairs 218 N Coll Ave PO Box 500 Rio Grande OH 45674 Office Phone: 740-245-7215. Business E-Mail: hatfield@rio.edu.

HATFIELD, C. MAILE, lobbyist; b. Exeter, N.H., Sept. 16, 1971; d. Harris Harding and Virginia Holmes (Brodhead) Hatfield. BA in English, William Smith Coll., Geneva, N.Y., 1993. Registered lobbyist, U.S. Congress. Rep. govt. affairs Grocery Mfrs. Am., Washington, 1995-98, mgr. fed. affairs, 1998—. Mem. Pub. Affairs Coun. Washington, 1998—. Chair United Way Campaign, Grocery Mfrs. Am., Washington, 1999; chair D.C. phonathon Emma Willard Sch., Troy, N.Y., 1999. Mem. The Food Group. Republican. Avocations: skeet/sporting clays, travel, music, philanthropy, architecture. Office: Grocery Mfrs Am 1010 Wisconsin Ave NW Ste 900 Washington DC 20007-3673 Home: 62 Frustuck Ave Fairfax CA 94930-1950

HATFIELD, ELAINE CATHERINE, psychology professor; b. Detroit, Oct. 22, 1937; d. Charles E. and Eileen (Kalahar) H.; m. Richard L. Rapson, June 15, 1982. BA, U. Mich., 1959; PhD, Stanford U., 1963. Asst. prof. U. Minn., Mpls., 1963-64, assoc. prof., 1964-66; asso. prof. U. Rochester, 1966-68, U. Wis., Madison, 1968-69, prof., 1969-81; now prof. U. Hawaii, Honolulu, chmn. dept. psychology, 1981-83. Author: Equity: Theory and Research, 1978, Mirror, Mirror: The Importance of Looks in Everyday Life, 1986, Psychology of Emotions, 1991, Love, Sex and Intimacy, 1993, Emotional Contagion, 1994, Love and Sex: Cross-cultural Perspectives, 1996, Rosie, 2000; contbr. articles to profl. jours. Recipient Disting. Scientist award Soc. Exptl. Social Psychology, 1993. Fellow APA; mem. Soc. Sci. Study of Sex (pres., Disting. Scientist award 1996, Alfred Kinsey award 1998). Home: 3334 Anoai Pl Honolulu HI 96822-1418 Office: U Hawaii 2430 Campus Rd Honolulu HI 96822-2216 Office Phone: 808-956-6276. E-mail: elaineh1@aol.com.

HATFIELD, JULIE STOCKWELL, journalist; b. Detroit, Mar. 22, 1940; d. William Hume and Ruth Reed (Palmer) Stockwell; m. Philip Mitchell Hatfield, Aug. 1, 1964 (div. 1979); children— Christian Andrew, Juliana, Jason David; m. Timothy Leland, Nov. 23, 1984; stepchildren— Christian Bourso, London Chamberlain BA, U. Mich, 1962. Staff reporter Women's Wear Daily, NYC, 1962-64; freelance feature writer Bath-Brunswick Times, Wis. State Jour., 1964-68, Quincy Patriot Ledger, Mass., 1968-77; freelance music critic, fashion editor Boston Herald, 1977-79; fashion editor Boston Globe, 1979-95, living/arts writer, 1995-96, soc. columnist, 1996-2001, travel writer, 2001, bus. columnist, 2005—; freelance travel writer, 2001—. Author: (with others) Guide to the Thrift Shops of New England, 1982, Felix, 2004; contbg. editor The Boston (Mass.) Courant, The Lawrence Eagle - Tribune, AAA Horizons mag.; contbr. columns to newspapers. Recipient Lulu award, Men's Fashion Assn., 1985, Atrium award for Outstanding Writing on Fashion, U. Ga., 1987, 1992; Nat. Endowment Arts grantee, 1973. Mem.: Soc. of Am. travel writers. Episcopalian. Avocation: piano. Office Phone: 781-934-2624.

HATFIELD, MARY LOU, nurse, paramedic; b. Kenosha, Wis., June 18, 1951; d. Jeanie (Galle) Hatfield; children: Anthony Bellantonio, Theresa Bellantonio. ADN, Gateway Tech. Coll., 1986. LPN, 1977-86; RN; cert. emergency nurse, Wis.; trauma nurse specialist; nat. registered emergency med. technician-paramedic. Staff nurse Kenosha Meml. Hosp., 1970-85, 87-89, St. Luke's Hosp., Milw., 1989-91; EMT I Arcadia (Wis.) Ambulance, 1991-97; flight nurse Gundersen Luth., La Crosse, Wis., 1991—; dep. med. examiner La Crosse County, 1993-2000; chief dep. med. examiner, 2000—; paramedic Tri-State Ambulance, La Crosse, 1996—. Mem. Internat. Forensic Nurse Assn., Air Surface Transport Nurse Assn., Emergency Nurse Assn., Air Surface Transport Nurse Assn. (edn. chair 1999-2000), Western Wis. Emergency Nurse Assn. (sec. 1995-97, pres. 1999-2000), North Ctrl. Nurse Assn. (Wis. rep. 1997-99, 2000—, pres.-elect 1999, pres. 2000), Wis. Coroners & Med. Examiners Assn. Avocations: cross-stitching, reading, biking, photography. Office: Gundersen Luth Med Ctr 1910 South Ave La Crosse WI 54601-5467 Home: 3832 Azalea Dr Las Cruces NM 88005-1027 E-mail: chopperRN@aol.com, mlhatfie@gundluth.org-w.

HATFIELD, RENEE S.J., music educator; b. Worcester, Mass., July 15, 1962; d. Raymond S.Y. and Ramona Mok Chin; m. Jeffery Allen Hatfield, Oct. 5, 1986; children: Aria Jenee, Tyler Allen. B in Music Edn., Campbellsville Coll., Ky., 1985; M of Creative Arts in Learning, Lesley U., 2006. Lic. tchr. pre K-12 Mass. Gen. music tchr. Jacob Hiatt Magnet Sch. Blue Ribbon, Worcester, 1985—. Chair Campbellville Coll. Handbook, 1984—86; sec. student found. Campbellsville Coll., 1983—84. Singer: Campbellsville Coll., 1982—83. Mem. Campbellsville Handbell Choir, 1980—85, Campbellsville Coll. Singer, 1982; ch. pianist, worship leader, diversity leader First Bapt. Ch., Shrewsbury, Mass., 1970—; ch. pianist, worship leader Faith Bapt. Ch., Auburn, Mass., 2003—. Mem.: Orgn. Am. Kodaly Educators, Music Educators Nat. Conf. Home: 33 Neptune Rd Worcester MA 01605 Office: Jacob Hiatt Magnet Sch Worcester Pub Sch Systems 772 Main St Worcester MA 01610 Office Phone: 508-799-3601 x3602. Personal E-mail: hatfieldrenee33@verizon.net. E-mail: hatfieldrenee@hotmail.com.

HATFIELD, STACEY, elementary school educator; d. Curt and Susan Franz; m. Jason Hatfield, June 19, 1999; 1 child, Jaron. BS in Multidisciplinary Studies, Tex. Tech U., Lubbock, 1996. Provisional tchg. cert. Tex., 1996. 5th grade math., sci. and social students tchr. Lamesa Elem. Sch., Tex., 1997—98; 6th grade math. Blalack Mid. Sch., Carrollton, Tex., 1998—2000; 6th grade gifted and talented and 7th grade pre advanced placement math. Ruth Dowell Mid. Sch., McKinney, Tex., 2000—. Mem.: Assn. Tex. Profl. Educators.

HATFIELD, STACIE H., professional pianist; b. Shreveport, La., Mar. 12, 1967; d. Roger Dorion and Rita (Jasura) Haneline; m. Scott Andrew Hatfield, Aug. 14, 1993; children: Justin Edward, Veronica Cecilia. BMusic, Converse Coll., Spartanburg, S.C., 1989; MMusic, Manhattan Sch. Music, 1992. Dir. music St. Vincent's Acad., Savannah, Ga., 1991-93; pianist Honolulu Chorale, 1996-98; asst. pianist Hawaii Opera, Honolulu, 1996-98; pianist Hawaii Vocal Arts, Honolulu, 1996-98; tchr. Newport News, Va., 1998—. Freelance pianist; substitute organist Our Lady of Mt. Carmel, Newport News; accompanist, U. Norfolk, Christopher Newport U., Canberra, Australia; mem. Internat. Flabours Concert Series, Canberra. Mem. Va. Piano Tchrs. Assn., Am. Embassy Women's Assn. (co-chair hospitality), Women's Internat. Club. Home: 14206 S 30th Ave Bellevue NE 68123-2695 E-mail: Staciehh@bigpond.net.

HATFIELD, SUSAN WILLIAM, school psychologist; b. Sioux City, Iowa, June 12, 1932; d. Keith Eugene Strange and Victorine Jessie (Williams) Strange Bridenbaugh; m. Robert Eugene Hatfield, Aug. 16, 1958 (div. Sept. 1973); children: Heidi Hatfield Fagerquist, Rex Hatfield. Student, Smith Coll., 1950-52; BA, U. N.Mex., 1955, MA, 1958; postgrad., U. Minn., 1974; EdD, U. S.D., 1976. Cert. sch. psychologist, Iowa. Camp swimming counselor Sioux Trails for Girl Scout Camp, Sioux City, 1951; grad. asst. in psychology U. N.Mex., Albuquerque, 1955-56; dist. dir. Sioux Trails Girl Scout Coun., Sioux City, 1958; part owner, mgr. Hatfield Apt. Bldg., Sioux City, 1958-68; psychologist Goodwill Industries, Sioux City, 1961-62; census taker, office worker U.S. Census Bur., Sioux City, 1970; life ins. agt. Bob Hatfield Ins. Co., Sioux City, 1970-73; psychologist Dr. Richard Satterfield, Sioux City, 1973-76; rsch. asst. U. S.D., Vermillion, 1974-76; pvt. practice Sioux City, 1976—; sch. psychologist Western Hills Area Edn. Agy., Sioux City, 1976-99; ret., 1999. Cons. to lawyer, Sioux City, 1982; cons., psychologist Goodwill Industries, Sioux City, 1990-94, Vocat. Rehab. Dept., Sioux City, 1993—; workshop presenter U. N.Mex., Albuquerque, 1980; participant/dir. rsch. projects in reading, written lang., math. for sch. children; grad. Sioux City Police Dept. Citizens Acad. IX, 1999. Contbr. papers to profl. jours. Mem. Jr. League, Sioux City, 1959-66, Found. Bd. for Family Planning, 1988—, Planned Parenthood of Greater Iowa, 1968—, St. Luke's Hosp. Aux., 1996—, PEO, Sioux City, 1955-73; bd. dirs. Sioux Trails Girl Scout Coun., Sioux City, 1959-62; vol., case aide for returnees from mental health instns. ARC, Sioux City, 1961-66; bd. dirs., v.p., regional rep., pres. Planned Parenthood, Sioux City, 1968-74, 84-97; bd. dirs., pres. Siouxland Drug Abuse Coun., Sioux City, 1974; Sunday sch. tchr. 1st Congl. Ch., Sioux City, 1964-68; leader Brownie troop, Girl Scout troop, Cub Scout troop, 1966-70; mem., chairperson Iowans for Med. Control of Abortion, Sioux City, 1968-73; mem., workshop presenter Women's Polit. Caucus, Sioux City, 1973-80; com. mem. for youth seminar Morningside Coll., Sioux City, 1973; mem., precinct chairperson, del. Dem. Party, Sioux City, 1980-94, vol. St. Luke's Hosp., Sioux City, 2001; bd. trustees 1st Unitarian Ch., Sioux City, 1973-74, ERA, 1973-90; mem. bd. dirs. Am. Internat. Profl. Inst. (S.C. Chpt.), 2004—, co-v.p., 2005-06, 06-; bd. mem. PFLAG, 2004—, co-v.p., program chmn., 2005-06, co-pres., 2006-. Recipient Award of Honor We. Hills Area Edn. Agy., 1999. Mem. NOW, Nat. Assn. for Sch. Psychologists, Portfolio Club. Democrat. Unitarian Universalist. Avocations: swimming, reading, travel, fine arts, dance. Home and Office: 17 Congress Ave Sioux City IA 51104-4053 E-mail: suehat17@aol.com.

HATFIELD, VICKI D., secondary school educator; b. Chillicothe, Ohio, Jan. 11, 1953; d. Robert Eugene and Edna Robertie White; m. Jack E. Hatfield, Aug. 1, 1988; 1 child, Wendy Ann Adams. BFA, Ohio U., Athens, 1975; MA, Ohio State U., Columbus, 1986. Substitute tchr. Chillicothe City

Schs., Ohio, 1980—81, tchr. art, home econs., 1981—87; tchr. art, reading, English Beechcroft HS, Columbus, 1987—. Adj. educator art Kenyon Coll., Gambier, Ohio, 1999—. Grantee, Roeloff Found., Gambier, 2005; Martha Holden Jennings scholar, Gambier, 2002. Mem.: Phi Delta Kappa. Office: Beechcroft HS 6100 Beeahcroft Rd Columbus OH 43229

HATHAWAY, ANNE, actress; b. Bklyn., Nov. 12, 1982; d. Gerard Hathaway and Kate McCauley. Actor: (TV series) Get Real, 1999—2000; (films) The Princess Diaries, 2001, The Other Side of Heaven, 2001, (voice) The Cat Returns, 2002, Nicholas Nickleby, 2002, Ella Enchanted, 2004, The Princess Diaries 2: Royal Engagement, 2004, (voice) Hoodwinked, 2005, Havoc, 2005, Brokeback Mountain, 2005, The Devil Wears Prada, 2006. Office: William Morris Agy One William Morris Pl Beverly Hills CA 90212*

HATHAWAY, JUANITA, medical and surgical nurse; AAS, San Antonio Coll., 1971. RN, Tex. Charge nurse Gonzales Warm Springs Rehab. Hosp., Edgar B. Davis Hosp., Luling, Tex., oper. room supr., DON; staff nurse, nurse mgr. Guadalupe Valley Hosp., Seguin, Tex., Gonzales Mel. Hosp.

HATHAWAY, LYNN MCDONALD, education advocate, administrator; b. N.Y.C., Mar. 28, 1939; d. William Douglas IV and Dorothy Edna (Homan) McDonald; m. Earl Burton Hathaway II, July 7, 1962; children: Earl Burton III, Amanda McDonald. BA, Bryn Mawr Coll., 1960. Editl. asst. Mademoiselle mag., N.Y.C., 1960-61; adminstrv. asst. Peace Corps office Nat. Coun. Chs., N.Y.C., 1961-62; vice chmn. cmty. rsch. N.Y. Jr. League, 1969-70; editor, chmn. N.Y. Entertains cookbook, 1973-74; edn. chair London Svc. League, 1979-80; pres., dir. London Svc. League, Jr. League, 1980-82; ind. writer, editor London, 1983. Bd. dirs. Friends of Ferguson Libr., Stamford, Conn., 1988, mem., rec. sec., v.p., pres., 1988-95, trustee, 1996-01, sec. bd. trustees, 2000—, citizen adv., 2001—, continuing chair student life com.; trustee, mem. exec. com., chair student life com. Conn. State U. Sys., 1991—, sec. bd. trustees, 1999—. Mem. Bryn Mawr Alumnae Assn. (pres. London 1983-86, internat. councillor 1988-90). Episcopalian. Home: 7 Oakmont Dr Falmouth ME 04105-1157 Fax: 203-359-2511. E-mail: lynnhath@aol.com.

HATHAWAY, ROBIN, writer; married; 2 children. BA in English, Smith Coll. Owner Barnhouse Press. Author: (novels) (Dr. Fenimore series) The Doctor Digs a Grave, 1998 (Malice Domestic Agatha award for best first novel, 1998), The Doctor Makes a Dollhouse Call, 2000, The Doctor and the Dead Man's Chest, 2001, The Doctor Dines in Prague, 2003, The Doctor Rocks the Boat, 2006, (Jo Banks series) Scarecrow, 2003, Satan's Pony, 2004. Mailing: Author Mail St Martin's Minotaur 175 Fifth Ave New York NY 10010 Business E-Mail: robdoneit@aol.com.*

HATHCOCK, BONITA CATHERINE (BONNIE HATHCOCK), managed health care company executive; b. Chambersburg, Pa., Oct. 30, 1948; d. John McGillis Gentry and Lola Vaneda (Showaker) Wood; m. Lindsay Levoy Hathcock, Apr. 14, 1984. BS in Bus., Shippensburg State U., 1971; MBA, Nova Southwestern U., 1989; grad. Exec. Human Resource Program, Stanford U. Instr. bus. Cen. Pa. Bus. Sch., Summerdale, 1972-75; with Xerox Corp., various locations, 1975-84, product planning mgr. Dallas, 1982-84; dir. mktg. edn. Datapoint Corp., San Antonio, 1984-85, sr. dir. corp. edn., 1985, sr. dir. worldwide edn., 1985-87; various positions including dir. corp. tng. and v.p. human resources Siemens-Rolm, Boca Raton, Fla.; v.p. human resources U.S. Airways; joined Humana Inc., Louisville, 1999, now sr. v.p., chief human resources officer. Prin. bcG Enterprises (profl. awareness tng. co.) Dallas, 1982-84. Avocations: cooking, swimming, reading, walking, writing. Office: Humana Inc The Humana Bldg 500 W Main St Louisville KY 40202

HATHORNE, GAYLE GENE, musician, family historian; b. Concordia, Kans., Sept. 3, 1953; d. Richard and R. Virginia (Huscher) Hathorne; 1 child, Amanda Kimberly. BMusic, Manhattan Sch. Music, N.Y.C., 1976; Artist's Diploma, Karajan Akademie, Berlin Philharm. Orch., 1980. Backstage hornplayer Bayreuth Festival, 1977; 3d/1st solo hornist Stadt. Orch., Solingen, Germany, 1980-88; genealogy instr. Blue Ridge C.C., 1999—2002; dir. membership, office mgr. N.Y. Geneal. and Biog. Soc., 2002—05; adminstrv. asst. Legal Lang. Svs., Leawood, Kans., 2006—. Substitute tchr. music and German, Henderson County Pub. Schs., 1988-98; pvt. horn tchr., Hendersonville, 1989— Sr. editor Tarheel Tattler, 1994-96, River Ramblings, 1994-96; editor Kuykendall Gazette, 1996-97; performer on CDs/cassettes; extra in film 28 Days, 1999, The Departed, 2006. Nat. Fedn. Music Clubs nat. scholar, 1971. Mem. DAR (state pub. rels. N.C. Soc. 1997-99, organizing regent Abraham Kuykendall chpt. 1996), Children of Am. Revolution (organizing sr. pres. French Broad River Soc. 1992, state libr. 1996-98). Democrat. Avocations: genealogy, photography, travel, writing, listening to opera. Personal E-mail: gaylegenehath@yahoo.com.

HATLER, PATRICIA RUTH, lawyer; b. Las Vegas, Nev., Aug. 4, 1954; d. Houston Eugene and Laurie (Danforth) Hatler; m. Howard A. Coffin II; children: Sloan H. D. Coffin, Laurie H. M. Coffin. BS, Duke U., 1976; JD, U. Va., 1980. Bar: Pa. 1980, Ohio 2002. Assoc. Dechert, Price & Rhoads, Phila., 1980-83; assoc. counsel Independence Blue Cross, Phila., 1983-86, sr. v.p., gen. counsel, corp. sec., 1987-99; exec. v.p., chief legal, gov. officer Nationwide, Columbus, 1999—. Home: 17 N Parkview Ave Bexley OH 43209-1427 Office: Nationwide One Nationwide Plaza Columbus OH 43215 Office Phone: 614-677-8754. E-mail: hatlerp@nationwide.com.

HATT, JOYCE LYNN, peri-operative nurse; b. Berkeley, Calif., Aug. 29, 1959; d. William John and Patricia Louis (Waller) Stirton; 1 child, Justin. BS in Nursing, San Diego State U., 1982; MSN, Calif. State U., Dominquez Hills, 1999. Cert. operating rm. nurse. Staff nurse Vets. Affairs Med. Ctr., San Diego, 1981-84; staff nurse operating rm. French Hosp., San Francisco, 1985-86, Vets. Affairs Med. Ctr., Martinez, Calif., 1986-91; head nurse operating rm. VA Med. Ctr., Fresno, Calif., 1991—99; surgical nurse practitioner Vets. Ctrl. Calif. Health Care Sys., Fresno, Calif., 1999—. Laser safety officer Vets. Affairs Med. Ctr., Martinez. Mem. Assn. Operating Rm. Nurses, San Joaquin Health Ministries Assn., Assn. Perioperative Reg. Nurses, San Joaquin Health Ministries Assn.

HATTAB, HELEN NATHALIE, philosophy professor; b. Seoul, Republic of Korea; d. Stephan and Gerda Andel; m. Jamal Jim Hattab. PhD, U. Pa., Phila., 1998. Vis. asst. prof. philosophy Va. Tech, Blacksburg, 1998—99; asst. prof. philosophy So. Ill. U., Carbondale, 1999—2002; vis. asst. prof. philosophy Wabash Coll., Crawfordsville, Ind., 2002—03; asst. prof. philosophy and honors coll. U. Houston, 2003—. Contbr. articles to profl. jours. Fellow, NEH, 2000, 2001; Dibner Libr. fellow, Smithsonian Inst., 2004, Herzog Aug. Bibliothek grantee, German Academic Exch. Svc. and Herzog Aug. Libr., 2005. Mem.: History of Sci. Soc., Internat. Soc. Intellectual History, Am. Philos. Assn. Office: U Houston Dept Philosophy Agnes Arnold 513 Houston TX 77030 Office Phone: 713-743-4147. E-mail: hnhattab@mail.uh.edu.

HATTAR, JACQUELINE, lawyer; b. Yonkers, N.Y., Sept. 24, 1967; BA cum laude, Fordham U., Bronx, NY, 1988; JD, Pace U., White Plains, NY, 1991. Bar: NY 1992, US Dist. Ct. (ea. and so. dists.), NY 1993, US Ct. Appeals (2d cir.) 1993. Asst. dist. atty. Bronx (N.Y.) County Dist. Atty.'s Office, 1991—97; sr. trial atty. Goodman & Jacobs, NYC, 1997—2001; in-house counsel Frontier Ins. Co., Rock Hill, NY, 2001; atty. Wilson, Elser, Moskowitz, Edelman, Dicker, LLP, White Plains, NY, 2001—. Mem. CPLR com. NY Bar Assn., 2002—. Mem.: ABA, NY State Trial Lawyers, Westchester County Bar Assn., Westchester County Women's Bar Assn., NY County Lawyers Assn., NY State Bar Assn. (civil practice law and rules com., stds. atty. conduct com., tort, ins. & compensation law sect.). Cath. Avocations: reading, art, theater, sailing. Office: Wilson Elser Moskowitz Edelman & Dicker LLP 3 Gannett Dr White Plains NY 10604-3407 Office Phone: 914-323-7000. Office Fax: 914-323-7001. Business E-Mail: jacqueline.hattar@wilsonelser.com.

HATTAWAY, KAREN ANN, literature and language professor; d. William N. and Hildur A. Kennett; m. David R. Hattaway, Jan. 20, 1968; children: Elizabeth Ann, William David. BA, U. Mo., Columbia, 1966; MA, U. Okla., Norman, 1967; PhD, Rice U., Houston, 1981. Cert. online instr. Virtual Coll. of Tex., 2004. Prof. of English San Jacinto Coll. N., Houston, 1968—. Grant dir. Eisenhower grant: count on reading, Houston; gearup grant profl. devel. coord. and tchr. trainer San Jacinto Coll. N., Houston; reaffirmation self-study chair San Jacinto Coll. Dist., 1987—89, interim planning dir., 1989—95, chair, core-curriculum rev., 2002—04; divsn. chair, lang. arts San Jcinto Coll. N., 1987—98. Musician handbell choir dir. Coun. on ministries, mem. bd. of edn. Houston East Dist. of the Tex. Conf. of the United Meth. Ch. Named Outstanding Tchr., Nat. Inst. for Orgn. and Staff Devel., 2000, 2006, Nat. Inst. for Staff and Orgnl. Devel., 2000—06, 2006; fellow summer tchr. inst. at UC Santa Cruz: Dickens the Crisis Years, NEh, 2004; grantee Co-Dir. Reacher Quality: Mid. Sch. Math, Tex. Higher Edn. Coordinating Bd., 2004—05, Dir. Tchr. Quality: Inquiry Learning Beats the Word Problem Blues, 2003—04, Eisenhower grantee, 2000—03. Mem.: Phi Beta Kappa, Delta Kappa Gamma (chpt. pres. 1980—82, chpt. achievement award 1985). Democrat-Npl. Methodist. Achievements include first to Learning community instruction pairing developmental reading and developmental mathematics. Avocations: quilting, gardening, piano. Office: San Jacinto College North 5800 Uvalde Road Houston TX 77049 Office Phone: 281-458-4050 7212. Office Fax: 281-459-7602. E-mail: karen.hattaway@sjcd.edu.

HATTERY, ANGELA JEAN, sociologist, educator; d. Robert Ralph and Diane Sittler Hattery; children: Travis Mathew Freetly, Emma Elise Freetly. PhD, U. Wis., Madison, 1996. Asst. prof. Ball State U., Muncie, Ind., 1996—98; assoc. prof. Wake Forest U., Winston-Salem, NC, 1998—. Author: (book) Women Work and Family: Balancing and Weaving. Mem. Darryl Hunt Project for Freedom and Justice, Winston-Salem, 2006—. Zachary T. Smith Reynolds fellow, Wake Forest U., 2004—. Democrat.

HATTON, BARBARA R., academic administrator; b. La Grange, Ga., June 4, 1941; d. William H. and Katye (Tucker) H.; 1 child, Kera M. Washington. BS, Howard U., 1962; MA, The Atlanta U., 1966; MEA, Stanford U., 1971, PhD, 1976. Assoc. dir. Stanford (Calif.) U., 1970-72, asst. prof. edn. adminstrn. and policy studies, 1976-79; chair Dept. Adminstrn. & Supervision, acting assoc. dean The Atlanta U., 1979-80; dean, prof. Tuskegee U., Ala., 1984-88; dep. dir. The Ford Found., N.Y., 1988; scholar-in-residence So. Edn. Found., Atlanta, 1992—; pres. S.C. State U., Orangeburg, 1993—, Knoxville Coll., 1997—. Mem. adv. com. Tchr. Edn. Project Assn. Am. Colls.; mem. review panel Fifth Yr. Non-Trad. Edn. Programs Ala. Dept. Edn.; mem. futures task force Am. Assn. Colls. for Tchr. Edn.; noms. com. New Deans Orientation Com. Trainer New Dean's Inst. Am. Assn. of Colls. of Tchr. Edn.; commn. on ednl. quality So. Regional Edn. Bd.; mem. Math. Standardization Com. Atlanta Pub. Schs.; reader Jour. Ga. Ednl. Rsch. Assn.; chmn. subcommittee on provisional certification and reciprocity, exec. com. Bd. Regents and State Bd. of Edn., State of Ga. Mem. S.C. Humanities Coun., Orangeburg C. of C.; bd. dirs. Assn. Presbyn. Colls. and Univs., Tenn. Rsch. Valley, Knoxville Symphony; active Met. Drug Com., Coll. Bds. Equity 2000 Project. Fellow NDEA, EPDA; recipient The Rose award U. S.C., 1993, Drum Major for Justice awards, 1993. Mem. Am. Ednl. Rsch. Assn., Am. Assn. Sch. Adminstrs., Exec. Women's Assn., Rotary Knoxville, Alpha Kappa Alpha Sorority Inc., Phi Chi Hon. Soc., Phi Delta Kappa Hon. Soc. Office: Knoxville Coll 901 College St Knoxville TN 37921-4724 Office Phone: 865-524-6511. Business E-Mail: bhatton@knoxvillecollege.edu.

HATTON, LAURIE, elementary school educator; d. Tom and Donna Hatton. BA, U. No. Colo., Greeley, 1991. Tchr. Woodland Pk. Mid. Sch., Colo., 1993—, track coach, 1999—2000, basketball coach, 2004—06. Freshmen girls basketball coach Woodland Pk. H.S., Woodland Park, Colo., 1992—96; track coach Manitou Mid. Sch., Manitou Springs, Colo., 1999—2000. Mem.: Colo. Coun. Internat. Reading Assn. Republican. Avocations: reading, sports, movies, travel.

HAUBEGGER, CHRISTY, media consultant, publishing executive; b. Houston, Tex. adopted d. David and Ann Haubegger. BA in philosophy, U. Tex., Austin, 1989; JD, Stanford U., 1992. Owner Alegre Enterprises, Inc.; founder, pub., CEO Latina Mag., N.Y.C., 1996—2001; bd. dirs. Latin Media Ventures, N.Y.C., 1996—; founder Latina Mag., N.Y.C., 2001—; cons. Hispanic-related initiatives Creative Artists Agy., 2003—. Assoc. prodr. (films) Chasing Papi, 2003. Bd. dirs. New Am. Alliance; mem. governing bd. Mgmt. Leadership for Tomorrow. Named to Am. Advt. Fedn. Advt. Hall of Achievement, 1999; David Rockefeller Fellow, N.Y.C. Partnership, 2002. Office: Latin Media Ventures 1500 Broadway Ste 700 New York NY 10036

HAUCH, VALERIE CATHERINE, historian, educator; b. Washington, May 20, 1949; d. Charles Christian and Ruthadele Bertha (LaTourrette) H.; life ptnr. Jacquelyn Farrow. BA in History, Kalamazoo Coll., 1971; MA in Medieval Studies, Western Mich. U., 1977; grad. cert. C.C. Teaching, U. St. Thomas, St. Paul, 1995. Social sci. analyst congl. rsch. svc. Libr. Congress, Washington, 1971-72; ind. contractor Minn. Hist. Soc., St. Paul, 1987-88, adminstrv. asst., 1990—; cmty. edn. tchr. Mpls. Pub. Schs., 1990—; instr. Minn. Sch. Bus., 1999—2004. Instr. Fla. C.C., Jacksonville, 2003—. Mem. Am. Hist. Assn., Am. Assn. Mus., Phi Beta Kappa. Home: 3540 33rd Ave S Minneapolis MN 55406-2725 E-mail: valeriehauch@msn.com.

HAUFT, AMY GILBERT, artist; b. Cin., Apr. 9, 1957; d. Neil Edward and Eleanor (Snyder) H. BFA, U. Calif., Santa Cruz, 1980; postgrad., Skowhegan Sch. Painting, Maine, 1981; MFA, Art Inst. Chgo., 1983. Prof. Tyler Sch. Art, Phila., 1989-2004, sculpture dept. chair, prof. Va. Commonwealth U. Sch. Arts, Richmond, Va., 2004—; vis. lectr. Princeton (N.J.) U., 1989; mem. vis. faculty Calif. Inst. Arts, Valencia, 1988. One-Woman shows include P.S.I. Mus., L.I., 1987, New Mus., N.Y.C., 1989, Contemporary Arts Forum, Santa Barbara, Calif., 1990, Ctr. for Arts Wesleyan U., Middletown, Conn., 1990, Berland/Hall Gallery, N.Y.C., 1991, Andrea Rosen Gallery, N.Y.C., 1993, Quint/Krichman Gallery, San Diego, 1993, Pub. Art Fund, N.Y.C., 1993-94, Lipton Owens Co., N.Y.C., 1994, Galeria Wschodnia, Lodz, Poland, 1997, Derek Eller Gallery, N.Y.C., 1998, Beaver Coll. Art Gallery, Phila., 1998, Am. Acad. Rome, 1999, Cooper Union, N.Y.C., 1999, Art Container Project, N.Y.C., 2001, Alcott Gallery, U. NC., Chapel Hill, 2006; exhibited in group shows at Mus. Contemporary Art, Chgo., 1987, ArtPark, Lewiston, N.Y., 1988, Bklyn. Mus., 1990, Internat. Artists Mus., Lodz, Poland, 1993, John Michael Kohler Arts Ctr., Sheboygan, Wis., 1995, Neuberger Mus., SUNY Purchase, 1995, 2003, Katonah (N.Y.) Mus., 1996, Gallery Joe, Phila., 2001. Grantee Flintridge Found., 1989, Artmatters, Inc., 1989, 88, ArtPark, 1988, N.Y. State Coun. Arts, 1987, Pub. Art Fund, 1993; Civitella Ranieri Found. fellow, 1995, N.Y. Found. fellow, 1995-96, Howard Found. fellow, 1995-96, Artslink grantee, 1997, Phila. Exhbns. Initiative, Pew Charitable Trust, 1998, Saint-Gaudens Meml. fellow, 1998-99, N.Y. Found. fellow, 2000-01.

HAUGAN, GERTRUDE M., clinical psychologist; b. New Richland, Minn. d. Henry Albert and Ella Pauline (Gardson) H. BA, George Washington U., 1952, MA, 1956; PhD, U. Md., 1970. Lic. psychologist, D.C., Md. Research psychologist New Eng. Med. Ctr., Boston, 1959-62; intern clin. psychology Hall Psychiat. Inst., Columbia, SC, 1968-69; fellow in pediatrics Sch. Medicine Johns Hopkins U., Balt., 1970-71; clin. psychologist adloescent program Devel. Services Ctr., Washington, 1971-72, chief children's unit, 1972-85; chief Devel Services Ctr., Washington, 1986-94. Cons. in psychology Ea. Shore State Hosp., Cambridge, Md., 1969-71, in child psychology Ctr. for Spl. Edn., Annapolis, Md., 1972-76; instr. in child psychology Montgomery Coll., Rockville, Md., 1977-78. Contbr. articles to profl. jours. Mem. profl. adv. council Easter Seal Soc. for Disabled Children and Adults, Washinton, 1987. Mem. APA, D.C. Psychol. Assn., Am. Assn. on Mental Retardation, Phi Beta Kappa. Home: 4720 S Chelsea Ln Bethesda MD 20814-3720 Personal E-mail: trudyhaugan@aol.com.

HAUGEN, CHRISTINE, plastic surgeon; b. Newport Beach, Calif., Aug. 20, 1968; d. Bjorn Hugo and Margit Haugen; m. Frederick Martin Haddad, Sept. 20, 2003; 1 child, Hunter Haugen Haddad. Student, U. So. Calif., 1986—87; AB in English Lit. cum laude, Bryn Mawr Coll., 1990; MD Med. Coll. Pa., 94. Diplomate Am. Bd. Plastic Surgery. Resident in gen. surgery Brown U., Providence, 1994—97; resident in plastic surgery U. Miami, Fla., 1998—2000; plastic surgeon Advanced Cosmetic Laser Ctr., Ft. Lauderdale, Fla., 2000—01; pvt. practice Ft. Lauderdale, 2001—03; med. dir. Med. Spa Ft. Lauderdale, 2003—04, Radiance Med. Spa, Palm Beach Gardens, Fla. Contbr. articles to profl. jours. Active Hospice Hundred, Ft. Lauderdale, 2002—, Goodwill Amb., Ft. Lauderdale, 2004—. Hannah E. Longshore Meml. scholar, Bryn Mawr Coll., 1990. Mem.: Am. Soc. Plastic Surgeons. Avocations: skiing, surfing, travel. Office: 6600 N Andrews Ave Ste 555 Fort Lauderdale FL 33309 Office Phone: 954-343-5304.

HAUGEN, JANET B., corporate financial executive; B in Econ. magna cum laude, Rutgers U. Ptnr. Ernst & Young LLP; corp. v.p., contr. Unisys Corp., Blue Bell, Pa., 1996—2000, corp. sr. v.p., CFO, 2000—. Mem.: Conf. Bd. Coun. of CFOs, Fin. Exec. Inst., Forum Exec. Women. Office: Unisys Corp Unisys Way Blue Bell PA 19424

HAUGEN, MARGARET ELLEN, daycare administrator; b. Butte, Mont., June 14, 1948; d. W. Stewart and Margaret Anne (Murphy) Zeigler; children: Cherie Anne, Alek Hemmel Spach. Student, Scranton Coll., 1983—84. Dental asst. Dr.Stephen Jones, Butte, 1967—69; religious edn. tchr. St. Patrick's Ch., Butte, 1963—70; daycare provider, 1970—. Vol. tutor Lit. Program, Butte; vol. Butte Rescue Mission Thrift Store. Named to Wall of Tolerance, Nat. Campaign for Tolerance, 2002, 2005; recipient Cert. Appreciation, Wall of Tolerance, 2005. Home: 626 W Galena St Butte MT 59701-1508

HAUGEN, MARY MARGARET, state legislator; b. Camano Island, Wash., Jan. 14, 1941; d. Melvin Harry and Alma Cora (Huntington) Olsen; m. Basil Badley; children: Mary Beth Fisher, Katherine Heitt, Richard, James. Mem. Wash. Ho. Reps., Olympia, 1982-1992, past mem. natural resources com., transp. com., mem. joint legis. com. on criminal justice system; mem. Wash. Senate, Dist. 10, Olympia, 1993—, chair transp. com., mem. rules com. Mem. LWV, Stanwood Camano Soroptomists. Lodges: Order Ea. Star. Democrat. Methodist. Avocations: fishing, reading, collecting antique clothing. Office: Wash Senate Legis Bldg PO Box 40482 Olympia WA 98504-0482 E-mail: haugen_ma@leg.wa.gov.

HAUGHT, JUDY C., language educator; b. Hollis, Okla., Nov. 22, 1952; d. Albert Shirley Atkinson and Bertha Ethel Calloway; m. Floyd Douglas Haught, Jan. 1, 1973; children: Lauren Shelton, Shannon, Keenan. BA in English, Southwestern Okla. State U., Weatherford, Okla., 1975; MEd in English, Southwestern Okla. State U., 1982. Instr. gen. studies program Southwestern Okla. State U., Sayre, 1988—. Mem. Goal One Com., Weatherford, 2005—06; pres. Friends of the Libr., Elk City, 2005—; mem. youth coun. United Meth. Ch., Elk City, 2006. Recipient Let's Talk About It grant, Okla. Humanities Coun., 2002. Mem.: Okla. Coun. Tchrs. English, Nat. Coun. Tchrs. English, Phi Delta Kappa. Democrat. Methodist. Avocations: travel, reading, antiques. Office: Southwestern Okla State Univ 409 E Mississippi Ave Sayre OK 73662-1236 Office Phone: 580-928-5533.

HAUGHTON, MARY L., elementary school educator; b. Ferriday, La., Sept. 27, 1951; d. John J. and Ethel Virginia McFarland; m. Frederick Wade Haughton (div.); 1 child, Gentry Lee; m. Ken Lee Tate, June 11, 1992. BA, La. STate U., Shreveport, 1991. Tchr. Vivian (La.) Mid. Sch., Stoner Elem., Shreveport, Hollywood Mid. Sch., Shreveport, A.C. Steere Elem. Sch., Shreveport. Mem. writing process com. Caddo Parish Writing Process, Shreveport, 1993—94. Mem.: Associated Profl. Educators of La. Office: A C Steere Elem Sch 4009 Youree Dr Shreveport LA 71105

HAUGNER, CAROLYN M., elementary school educator; b. Appleton, Wis., Aug. 16, 1948; d. Joseph A. and Rosemary A. (Probst) Suess; m. John C. Haugner Jr., June 22, 1974; children: Krista Haugner Sieg, John C. III. BA in Elem. Edn., St. Norbert Coll., West De Pere, Wis., 1970; MS in Edn., U. Wis., Oskkosh, 1976. Tchr. grades 3-4 Hilbert Pub. Schs., Wis., 1970—71; tchr. grades 4-6 Hortonville Pub. Schs., 1971—74; tchr. grade 1 Kettle Moraine Schs., Delafield, 1974—86, reading specialist, 1986—. Bd. mem. St. Bruno Sch. Com., Dousman, Wis., 1992—96, 2002—06; vol. St. Bruno Parish, 1974—. Recipient Leadership award, Kettle Moraine Sch. Dist., Wales, Wis., 1990; fellow, Herb Kohl Ednl. Found., Wis., 2005. Mem.: NEA, Internat. Reading Assn. (Celebrate Literacy award 2006), Wis. State Reading Assn., Wis. Edn. Assn., Waukesha County Reading Coun. (pres. 1998—99, 2001—02, sec. 2004—06). Roman Catholic. Avocations: travel, reading. Home: S15 W37060 Willow Springs Dr Dousman WI 53118 Office: Cushing Sch 227 Genesee St Delafield WI 53018

HAULENBEEK, ANDREA B., music educator, farmer; d. Lyle Taylor and Myrtle Carter Baldwin; m. Fred Haulenbeek, Feb. 21, 1994; children from previous marriage: Brian Gerry, Stacy Prall, Joy Amao, Grace Amao. BS in Music Edn., U. Vt., Burlington, 1969; postgrad., CSSU, New Britain, Conn., 2000. Cert. tchr. Vt. Classrom and instrumental music tchr. Hinesburg Elem. Sch., Vt., 1984—86; choral, theory and piano tchr. Mount Mansfield Union HS, Jericho, Vt., 1987—2003; choral and classroom tchr. Williston Ctrl. Sch., Vt., 2003—. Freelance musician; ch. musician. Composer, arranger: various secular and sacred musical compositions. Founder string program for children Mountain Strings, 1999. Named Tchr. of Yr., Mount Mansfield Union HS, 2003—04. Mem.: Vt. Music Edn. Assn., Am. Choral Dirs. Assn., Vt. Assn. Arts Edn. (Arts Educator 2003).

HAUPT, CAROL MAGDALENE, retired elementary school educator; b. New Britain, Conn., Aug. 3, 1945; d. Richard Henry and Alfrieda (Sitz) Haupt. BS in Edn., Wagner Coll., Staten Island, N.Y., 1967, MS, 1969; EdD, Rutgers U., 1984. Elem. sch. tchr. N.Y.C. Bd. Edn., 1969—2004, ret., 2004. Mem. PTA of P.S. 69R (Tchr. Recognition Day award N.Y.C. Bd. Edn. 1981). Named to Outstanding Young Women of Am., 1972; recipient Alumni Svc. award, Wagner Coll., 1982, Cert. of Commendation, N.Y. Alliance for Pub. Schs., 1988, N.Y. City Regional Reading Coun. award, 1995. Mem. AARP, AAUW (life, pres. S.I. chpt. 1985-87, past membership chair, past v.p.), Internat. Reading Assn., S.I. Reading Assn. (pres. 1992-94), Archaeology Soc. S.I. (pres. 1987-2005, past treas., sec., v.p., membership chmn.), Archaeological Inst. of Am., Wagner Coll. Alumni Assn. (past treas., v.p. S.I. chpt.), NYS United Tchrs., United Fedn. Tchrs., Am. Fedn. Tchrs., Delta Kappa Gamma (world fellowship chair 1992-93, personal growth chair 1993-94, legis. chair 1994-95), Belles Lettres Soc.(v.p. 2006—), Smithsonian Instn., Nat. Trustee for Historic Preservation, Zeta Tau Alpha (life). Republican. Lutheran. Avocations: travel, reading, gardening. Home: 66 Seneca Ave Staten Island NY 10301-4224

HAUPT, PATRICIA A., principal; Diplome du premier cycle, U. Strasbourg, France, 1969; dipome des etudes superieures, U. Montpellier, France, 1971; BA summa cum laude, St. Francis Coll., 1972; MA in French, Middlebury Coll., 1976; prin.'s cert. summa cum laude, Western Md. Coll., 1984; EdD in Adminstrn. and Leadership, Temple U., 1986. Cert. instrnl. II Pa., prin. Pa., asst. supt.'s letter of eligibility Pa., supt.'s letter of eligibility Pa. Die casting machine operator Doehler-Jarvis Internat., Pottstown, Pa., 1972—74; tchr. French Palmyra (Pa.) Area H.S., 1973—84; real estate agt. Jack Gaughen Realtor, Hershey, Pa., 1979—84; dir. pupil pers. svcs. K-12 So. Lehigh Sch. Dist., 1985—89; asst. prin. So. Lehigh Mid. Sch., 1984—89; prin. Fleetwood Area Mid. Sch., 1989—92, Bala Cynwyd (Pa.) Mid. Sch., Bala Cynwyd, 1992—. Lectr. and presenter in field; co-facilitator Lang. Immersion Program; coord. Tri-Dist. Consortium; mem. Gov.'s Task Force for Fgn. Langs.; ednl. liaison Kutztown Area C. of C. Recipient Leadership award, Am. Legion, ednl. scholarship for study abroad. Mem.: ASCD, Nat. Mid. Schs. Assn., Pa. Sch. Bds. Assn., Nat. Assn. Secondary Sch. Prins., Am. Assn. Sch. Adminstrs., Delta Epsilon Sigma, Delta Kappa Gamma (pres. Delta chpt.). Avocations: playing classical organ and piano, reading, swimming.

HAUPTLI, BARBARA BEATRICE, foundation administrator; b. Glenwood Springs, Colo., Sept. 20, 1953; d. Frederick James and Evelyn June (rood) Hauptli. BBA, Western State Coll., 1975. Contract specialist USA-TACOM, Warren, Mich., 1981-86; contract buyer Martin Marietta Orlando (Fla.) Aerospace, 1986; purchasing expediter Moog, Inc., Clearwater, Fla., 1986-89; subcontract adminstr. Olin Ordnance, St. Petersburg, Fla., 1989-91, sr. subcontract adminstr., 1991-93; reimbursement specialist Tod. K. Allen, Inc., 1993-96; program mgr. Nat. Rsch. Tech. Contract Mfg., Tallahassee, 1997-2000; payroll mgr. Worldwide Flight Svcs., Eagle, Colo., 2000—01; customer svc. rep. United Parcel Svc., Glenwood Springs, Colo., 2001—04; underwriter Total Merchant Svcs., Basalt, Colo., 2004—06; office mgr. McMillan Claim Svc., Glenwood Springs, 2006—. Avocations: reading, travel, gardening. Office: McMillan Claim Svc 813 Colorado Glenwood Springs CO 81601 Home: 50627 Hwy 6 No 1 Glenwood Springs CO 81601

HAUS, JUDITH ANN, elementary school educator; b. Pitts., Feb. 6, 1937; d. Albert Alphonse and Margaret Louise (Reiland) Pschirer; m. Richard Frederick Boland, Feb. 9, 1957 (div. 1971); children: Richard Frederick, Jr., David Todd; m. Lloyd Wesley Merritt, Feb. 18, 1984 (div. 1996); m. Fran Haus, Jr., July 1998. BS, Indiana U. of Pa., 1963; MS, Pa. State U., 1976. Tchr. Millvale Sch. Dist., Pitts., 1963-68, Shaler Area Sch. Dist., Glenshaw, Pa., 1968-96, curriculum support tchr., 1995-96, ret., 1996. Subject area specialist in social studies, 1987-88, 89, 90-91, 92-93; mem. tchr.'s adv. panel Peoples Natural Gas Co., Pitts., 1990-92. Mem. Carnegie Inst. Soc., Pitts., 1982-84, 87-88, Pitts. History Landmarks Soc., 1985—. Carlow Coll. grantee, 1985, grantee Duquesne Light Duquesne U. Cmty. Alliance, 1992-93, 94, Fulbright-Hayes grantee, 1992 Mem. NEA, Pa. State Edn. Assn., Shaler Area Edn. Assn. (bldg. rep. 1984-96, mem-at-large 1985-88), Hobe Sound Golf Club, Golf Club of Amelia Island. Avocation: golf. Home: 11466 SE Plandome Dr Hobe Sound FL 33455-7901 Personal E-mail: judyhaus@aol.com.

HAUSE, EDITH COLLINS, retired academic administrator; b. Rock Hill, S.C., Dec. 11, 1933; d. Ernest O. and Violet (Smith) Collins; m. James Luke Hause, Sept. 3, 1955; children: Stephen Mark, Felicia Gaye Hause Friesen. BA, Columbia Coll., SC, 1956; postgrad., U. NC, Greensboro, 1967, U. SC, 1971—75. Tchr. Richland Dist. II, Columbia, 1971—74; dir. alumnae affairs Columbia Coll., 1974—82, v.p. devel., 1984—89, v.p. alumnae affairs, 1989—99; ret., 1999. Named Outstanding Tchr. of Yr., Richland Dist. II, 1974; recipient Disting. Svc. award, Columbia Coll. Alumae Assn., 2003, Columbia Coll. Medallion, 2003. Mem.: Nat. Soc. Fund Raising Execs., Coun. for Advancement and Support Edn., Columbia Network for Female Execs., SC Advocates for Women on Bds. and Commrs. (bd. dirs.), SC Assn. Alumni Dirs. (pres. 1996—98). Republican. Methodist. Home: 92 Mariners Pointe Rd Prosperity SC 29127-7674

HAUSELT, DENISE ANN, lawyer; BS, Cornell U., 1979, JD, 1983. Bar: N.Y. 1984, Ill. 1984, U.S. Dist. Ct. (we. dist.) N.Y. 1984, U.S. Bankruptcy Ct. 1984. Summer assoc. Wildman, Harrold, Allen & Dixon, Chgo., 1982; assoc. Nixon Peabody LLP, Rochester, N.Y., 1983-86; asst. counsel Corning (N.Y.) Inc., 1986-93, divsn. counsel, 1993-99, asst. gen. counsel, 1999-2000, asst. gen. counsel, asst. sec., 2000—01, corp. sec., 2001—. Adv. coun. Cornell Law Sch.; sec. Corning Inc. Found., Corning Mus. of Glass. Recipient Am. Jurisprudence Constl. Law prize, Cornell U., 1981. Mem.: ABA, Soc. Corp. Secs. and Governance Profls., Cornell Law Assn., Assn. Corp. Counsel. Republican. Avocations: sailing, skiing. Office: Corning Inc Riverfront Plz Mp Hq E2 Corning NY 14831-0001

HAUSER, ANNE LYNN, music educator, director; b. Menomonee Falls, Wis., Aug. 25, 1975; d. John Robert and Susan Romberg Jaeckel; m. Jonathan Michael Hauser, Aug. 21, 1999. BA in Music Edn., Augustana Coll., Rock Island, Ill., 1997; MusM in Music Edn., U. Wis., Milw., 2003. Cert. tchr. instrumental music K-12 Ill., 1997, tchr. instrumental music 6-12 Wis., 1997, Assn. Christian Schs. Internat., 2005. Tchr. instrumental music The Luth. H.S. Assn. of Greater Milw., Greendale, Wis., 1998—2005; hornline instr. Pioneer Drum and Bugle Corps, Milw., 2002—05; band dir. Aurora Christian Sch., Ill., 2005—; colorguard instr. Marmion-Rosary H.S. Band, Aurora, 2006—. Mem. brass ensemble Immanuel Luth. Ch., Batavia, Ill., 2006—. Mem.: Music Educators Nat. Conf. Lutheran. Avocations: music, cross stitch, drums. Office Phone: 630-892-1551.

HAUSER, JEAN, theater educator, theater director; b. Altadena, Calif., Aug. 18, 1947; d. Leslie King and Orabelle Arlene Sobetzer; m. John Michael Hauser, May 10, 1970; 1 child, Erin Kathleen. BA, U. Calif. Santa Barbara. Instr. theater and English, theater chair, dir. Cordova Sr. H.S., Sacramento, 1970—80; co. mgr., assoc. dir./prodr., artistic dir. Gaslamp Quarter Theatre Co., San Diego, 1980—89; instr. theater, debate and speech, dept. chair fine arts, theater dir./designer/prodr. U. San Diego High, 1989—99; instr./coord. theater arts, prodr./dir. theatre arts Santa Margarita Cath. H.S., Rancho Santa Margarita, Calif., 2000—. Involved with downtown revitalization San Diego Gaslamp Dist., 1980—90. Mem.: Nat. Forensics League, Calif. Speech Assn., Nat. Educators English, ETA, Calif. Ednl. Theatre Assn. Avocation: bicycling. Office: Santa Margarita Cath HS 22062 Antonio Pkwy Rancho Santa Margarita CA 92688 Business E-Mail: hauserj@smhs.org.

HAUSER, JOYCE ROBERTA, marketing professional; b. NYC; d. Abraham and Helen (Lesser) Frankel; divorced; children: Mitchell, Mark, Ellen BA, SUNY, 1976; PhD, Union Inst. and U., 1987. Editor Art in Flowers, 1956-58; pres. Joyce Advt., 1958-65; ptnr. Hauser & Assocs., Pub. Rels., 1966-75; dir. broadcasting Bildersee Pub. Rels., 1973-75; pres. Hauser & Assocs., Inc., Pub. Rels., 1975-78; COO, pres. Hauser-Roberts, Inc., Pub. Rels./Mktg., N.Y.C., 1978—85; pres. Mktg. Concepts & Communications Inc., N.Y.C., 1985-92; moderator show Perceptions Sta. WEVD, 1975-77, Speaking of Health Sta. WNBC, 1977-89, 97 Health Line, Sta. WYNY, 1980-83, Conversations with Joyce Hauser, Sta. WNBC, 1975-86, What's on Your Mind, Sta. WYNY, 1983-84, Talk-Net, 1983-90; entertainment critic Sta. NBC, 1986-92. Instr. Baruch Coll., CCNY, 1980—85; assoc. prof. NYU, 1987—, prof. edn., 1992—. Sr. editor Art & Leisure News Svc., 1988—; editor-in-chief N.Y. State Comms. Annual, 1999—; contbg. editor Alive, 1976-77; author: Good Divorces, Bad Divorces: A Case for Divorce Mediation, 1995; contbr. 70 articles to profl. jours., chpts. to books. Mem. Citywide Health Adv. Coun. on Sch. Health, 1970-88, treas., 1980-92; mem. adv. bd. degree programs NYU Sch. Continuing Edn.; mediator/arbitrator Victim Svcs. Agy., 1986-87, Inst. Mediation and Conflict Resolution, 1985-86. Named one of 10 Top Successful Women, Cancer Soc., 1976, Tchr. of Yr., Zeta Beta Tau, 1989-90, one of 20 Top Women in Pub. Rels., 1981, Prof. of Yr. Sch. of Edn., 1999, Prof. of Yr., NYU Sch. Edn., 1999-2000; recipient Professionalism award Sta. WNBC, 1980; John E. Wilson fellow, 1996-97. Mem. AFTRA, Pub. Rels. Soc. Am., Nat. Assn. Communicators, Nat. Assn. Scholars, NY State Communicators (treas., v.p. 1996, pres. 1997), NY State Comms. Assn. (editor annual 1998), Acad. Family Mediators, Soc. Am. Travel Writers, Soc. Profl. Dispute Resolutions, Drama Desk (bd. dirs. 2004), Outer Critics Cir., NY Press Club. Office Phone: 212-772-1625.

HAUSER, LYNN ELIZABETH, eye surgeon; b. Cleve., Apr. 11, 1951; d. Cavour Herman and Ruth Natalie (Lageman) H.; B.S. in Medicine, Northwestern U., 1974, M.D., 1976; m. Neil L. Ross, June 20, 1975; children—Michael Hauser Ross, Benjamin Hauser Ross. Resident in ophthalmology Northwestern U., 1976-80; practice medicine specializing in cataract surgery, Sycamore, Ill., 1980—; clin. asst. prof. ophthalmology U. Ill., Chgo.; lectr. in ophthalmology Northwestern U.; project ophthalmologist Nat. Eye Inst. Early Treatment Diabetic Retinopathy Study, 1982. Diplomate Am. Bd. Ophthalmology. Fellow ACS, Am. Acad. Ophthalmology, mem. AMA, Dekalb County Med. Soc., Ill. Assn. Ophthalmology, Ill. Med. Soc., LWV. Office: 2240 Gateway Dr Sycamore IL 60178-3113

HAUSER, RITA ELEANORE ABRAMS, lawyer; b. NYC, July 12, 1934; d. Nathan and Frieda (Litt) Abrams; m. Gustave M. Hauser, June 10, 1956; children: Glenvil Aubrey, Ana Patricia. AB magna cum laude, CUNY Hunter Coll., 1954; D in Polit. Economy with highest honors, U. Strasbourg, France, 1955; Licence en Droit, U. Paris, 1958; student, Harvard U., 1955-56; LLB with honors, NYU, 1959; LLD (hon.), Seton Hall U., 1969, Finch Coll., 1969, U. Miami, Fla., 1971, Colgate U., 1995. Bar: D.C. 1959, N.Y. 1961, U.S. Supreme Ct. 1967. Atty. U.S. Dept. Justice, 1959-61; pvt. practice N.Y.C., 1961-67; ptnr. Moldover, Hauser, Strauss & Volin, 1968-72; sr. ptnr. Stroock & Stroock & Lavan, N.Y.C., 1972-92, of counsel, 1992—; pres. The Hauser Found., N.Y.C., 1990—; apptd. mem. fgn. intelligence bd. Pres., 2001—04. Handmaker lectr., Louis Brandeis Lecture Series, U. Ky. Law Sch.; lectr. internat. law Naval War Coll. and Army War Coll.; lectr. St. Anthony's Coll., Oxford (England) U., 2002; Mitchell lectr. in law SUNY, Buffalo; USIA lectr. constl. law Egypt, India, Australia, New Zealand; U.S. chmn. Internat. Ctr. for Peace in Middle East, 1984-92; bd. dirs. Internat. Peace Acad., chair 1993—; U.S. pub. del. to Vienna follow-up meeting of Conf. on Security and Cooperation in Europe, 1986-88; mem. adv. panel in internat. law U.S. Dept. State, 1986-92, Am. Soc. Internat. Law Award to honor Women in Internat. Law; mem. Pacific Coun. on Internat. Policy, 1998-2000; bd. dirs. The Rand Corp., Internat. Inst. Strategic Studies, London, The Lowy Inst. Internat. Policy, Sydney, The Ctr. Internat. Governance Innovation, Can.; chair internat. adv. bd. The Internat. Crisis Group, 2004—. Contbr. articles to profl. jours. U.S. rep. to UN commn. on Human Rights, 1969-72; mem. U.S. del. to Gen. Assembly UN, 1969; vice chmn. U.S. Adv. Com. on Internat. and Cultural Affairs, 1973-77; mem. N.Y.C. Bd. Higher Edn., 1974-76, Stanton Panel on internat. info., edn., cultural rels. to reorganize USIA and Voice of Am., 1974-75, Mid. East Study Group Brookings Inst., 1975, 87-88, U.S. del. World Conf. Internat. Women's Yr., Mexico City, 1975; co-chair Com. for Re-election Pres., 1972, Presdl. Debates project LVW, 1976, Coalition for Regan/Bush; adv. bd. Nat. News Coun., 1977-79; bd. dirs. Bd for Internat. Broadcasting, 1977-80, Internat. Peace Acad., The Aspen Inst., The RAND Corp.; chair internat. adv. bd. Internat. Crisis Group; trustee Lincoln Ctr. Performing Arts; adv. bd. Ctr. For Law and Nat. Security, U. Va. Law Sch., 1978-84; vis. com. Ctr. Internat. Affairs Harvard U., 1975-81, John F. Kennedy Sch. Govt., Harvard U., 1992—, chair adv. bd. Hauser Ctr. for Non-Profit Orgns. at Harvard U.; co-chair dean's bd. advisors Harvard Law Sch., 1996—, vice-chair, nat. co-chair univ. fund-raising campaign, 1997-2000, vice chmn. com. on univ. resources, 2002-; bd. advisors Mid. East Inst., Harvard U.; bd. trustees NYU Law Sch.; bd. visitors Georgetown Sch. Fgn. Svc., 1989-94; chmn. adv. panel Internat. Parlimentary Group for Human Rights in Soviet Union, 1984-86; mem. Lawyers Com. for Human Rights, 1995—; mem. spl. refugee adv. panel Dept. State, 1981; bd. fellows Claremont U. Ctr. and Grad. Sch., 1990-94; former trustee Internat. Legal Ctr., Legal Aid Soc. N.Y., Freedom House; mem. Lawyers Comm. Human Rights, 1996—. Fulbright grant U. Strasbourg, 1955; Intellectual Exch. fellow Japan Soc.; recipient Jane Addams Internat. Women's Leadership award, 1996, Women in Internat. Law award Am. Soc. Internat. Law, 1995, Fulbright award for Fulbright Alumni, 1997, Servant of Justice award, Legal Aid Soc. N.Y., 2000, Vanderbilt medal NYU Law Sch., 2004, Albert Gallatin medal, NYU, 2006. Fellow ABA (life, mem. standing coms. on law and nat. security 1979-85, standing com. on world order under law 1969-78, standing com. on jud. selection, tenure, compensation 1977-79, coun. sect. on ind. rights and responsibilities 1970-73, advisor bd. jour. 1973-78); mem. Am. Soc. Internat. Law (v.p. 1988—, mem. exec. com. 1971-76), Am. Fgn. Law Assn. (bd. dirs.), Am. Arbitration Assn. (past bd. dirs.), Ams. Soc. (bd. dirs. 1988—), Coun. Fgn. Rels. (bd. dirs.), Internat. Inst. for Strategic Studies (London, bd. dirs. 1994—), Internat. Adv. Bd., Jaffee Ctr. for Strategic Studies, Tel Aviv Univ. (1999—), Am. Coun. on Germany, The Atlantic Coun. U.S., Friends of the Hauge Acad. Internat. Law (bd. dirs.), Assn. of Bar of City of N.Y., Catalyst (bd. dirs. 1989-96). Republican. Office: Stroock & Stroock & Lavan 180 Maiden Ln Fl 17 New York NY 10038-4937 also: The Hauser Found Office of Pres 712 5th Ave New York NY 10019-4108

HAUSERMAN, JACQUITA KNIGHT, management consultant; b. Donalsonville, Ga., Apr. 23, 1942; d. Lendon Bernard and Ressie Mae (Robinson) Knight; m. Mark Kenny Hauserman, July 8, 1978 (div. Mar. 1998). BS in Math., U. Montevallo, Ala., 1964; MA in Tchg. Math., Emory U., 1973; MBA in Fin., Ga. State U., 1978. Fin. analyst Cleve. Electric Illuminating Co., 1982-83, gen. supr. employment svc., 1983-85, sr. corp. planning advisor, 1985-86, dir. customer svc., 1986-88, v.p. adminstrn., 1988-90; v.p. customer svc. & cmty. affairs Centerior Energy Corp., Independence, Ohio, 1990-93, v.p. customer support, 1993-95, v.p. bus. svcs., 1995-97; v.p., chief devel. officer Summa Health Sys., Akron, Ohio, 1999-2000; prin. Arcadia Consulting, Pepper Pike, Ohio, 2000—. Home and Office: 2901 Greenflower Ct Bonita Springs FL 34134-4387 E-mail: jhauserman@johnrwood.com.

HAUSMAN, HARRIET SECELEY, administrator; b. Chgo., Apr. 8, 1924; d. Samuel and Lena Rubin; m. Martin C. Hausman, June 30, 1946 (dec. Apr. 1988); children: Daniel, Barbara. Student, U. Ill., 1941—42, Northwestern U., 1943—45; BS, Rosary Coll., 1972. Asst. tchr. Winfield (Ill.) Sch., 1945; psych testing Hines Vet. Hosp., Maywood, Ill., 1972-74; social worker Cook County Hosp., Chgo., 1973; pres. Power Parts Co., Chgo., 1947-87, CEO, 1987-92. Author: Reflections, A History of River Forest, 1975. Trustee River Forest (Ill.) Twp., 1978-90; bd. dirs. ACLU, 1988—, v.p.; bd. dirs. Jewish Childrens Bur., pres. 1970-92, v.p., 1992—; v.p., bd. dirs. Bldg. Better Futures (BBF), 1992-96, v.p. BBF Scholarship Bd., 1997-; vice chmn. scholarship com., 1998-; adv. bd. Bus. and Proff. People for Pub. Interest, 1999—; plannig commn. Oak Pk. Temple, 2001—. Named Woman Entrepreneur of Yr., 1992, U.S. Transp. Cmty. Svc. award Oak Park and River Forest, 1980, 96, 90, 92, 96, 99, Carl Winter Svc. award, 1972, Lifetime Achievement award, 2005. Democrat. Jewish. Achievements include one of 4 who est. River Forest Cmty. Ctr. Avocations: symphony, opera, drama, gardening, travel.

HAUVER, CONSTANCE LONGSHORE, lawyer; b. Abington, Pa., Oct. 9, 1938; d. Malcolm Rettew and Margaret Evans (Lyon) L.; m. Arthur R. Hauver, 1962 (div. Mar. 1979); 1 child, Sian; m. Giles Toll, 1990. BA with high honors, Swarthmore Coll., 1960; MA, UCLA, 1962; JD magna cum laude, U. Denver, 1967. Bar: Colo. 1968, U.S. Dist. Ct. Colo. 1968, U.S. Tax Ct. 1970. Libr. Friends Com. on Nat. Legis., Washington, 1960-61; lectr. U. Hawaii, Honolulu, 1963-64; assoc. Sherman & Howard, Denver, 1968-73, ptnr., 1973-91; vol. naturalist Lookout Mountain Nature Ctr., 1998—. Mem. grievance com. Colo. Supreme Ct., 1981—86. Co-contbr. legal articles. Trustee Rocky Mountain Women's Inst., Denver, 1987-90, Swedish Med. Ctr. Found., Denver, 1978-85; bd. dirs. Women's Forum Colo. Inc., Denver, 1988-89, Girls Count, Denver, 1995-2000, pres., 1996-97. Named New Vol. Naturalist of Yr., Lookout Mountain Nature Ctr., 1998, Vol. Naturalist of Yr., 2001; recipient Athena award, Alliance Profl. Women, 1987. Fellow Am. Coll. Probate Counsel; mem. Colo. Bar Assn. (chair probate and trust law sect. 1982-83), Denver Bar Assn. (del. to ABA Ho. of Dels. 1986-88), Rocky Mountain Estate Planning Coun. (pres. 1980-81). Democrat. Mem. Soc. Of Friends. Avocations: mountain climbing, kayaking, skiing, reading, learning Spanish.

HAVENS, CANDACE JEAN, urban planner, consultant; b. Rochester, Minn., Sept. 13, 1952; d. Fred Z. and Barbara Jean (Stephenson) H.; m. Bruce Curtis Mercier, Feb. 22, 1975 (div. Apr. 1982); 1 child, Rachel; m. James Arthur Renning, Oct. 26, 1986; children: Kelsey, Sarah. Student, U. Calif., San Diego, Darmouth Coll., 1970-72, Am. U., Beirut, 1973-74; BA in Sociology, U. Calif., Riverside, 1977; MPA, Harvard U., 1994. Project coord. social svc. orgn. Grass Roots II, San Luis Obispo, Calif., 1976-77; planner City San Luis Obispo, 1977-86, city parking, spl. projects mgr., 1986-88; spl. asst. to city adminstr. City of San Luis Obispo, 1989, planning cons., mediator, 1991—; mgmt. rsch. specialist Bank of Boston, 1995-96; owner Office Suites, San Luis Obispo, Calif., 1997-2000, ADR Collaborative, 1997—. Past pres. Nat. Charity League, Riverside; mem. San Luis Obispo Med. Aux., 1986-93, San Luis Obispo Arts Coun., 1986—; pres. bd. dirs. San Luis Obispo Children's Mus., 1990-91, CFO, 1993; mediator in Newton (Mass.) Cts., 1996, San Luis Obispo, 1997; pres. Underwood Elem. PTO, 2000-01; chmn. traffic coun., City of Newton, 2002—; mem. comprehensive plan adv. com. City of Newton; mem. task force Newton (Mass.) Ctr., 2004—. Mem.: AAUW, Inst. Transp. Engrs., Mass. Assn. Mediation Profls. and Practitioners, Am. Planning Assn., Am. Inst. Cert. Planners, Assn. Conflict Resolution, Toastmasters (sec. 1986—87, v.p. 1987—88, pres. 1989—90, treas. 1991—92). Avocations: photography, running, arts, cooking, travel, languages. Office: 25 Hunnewell Ave Newton MA 02458-2214

HAVENS, PAMELA ANN, academic administrator; b. Plattsburgh, N.Y., Nov. 30, 1956; d. Thomas L. and MaryAnn (Zalen) Romeo; m. Stephen L. Havens, Aug. 9, 1986; children: Stephanie Leigh, Skylar Lucas. BA, Eisenhower Coll., 1978; MA summa cum laude, SUNY, Plattsburgh, 1987; AAS summa cum laude, Cayuga C.C., 1999. VISTA vol. Retired Sr. Vol. Program, Plattsburgh, 1978-79; copywriter, newsperson Stas. WEAV-AM/WGFB-FM, Plattsburgh, 1979-83; traffic clk. Sta. WCFE-TV, Plattsburgh, 1983-84, pub. info. coord., 1984-85; coll. rels. officer Clinton C.C., Plattsburgh, 1985-89; dir. publs. and comm. Cayuga C.C., Auburn, NY, 1989-2001; dir. donor rels. Hamilton Coll., Clinton, NY, 2001—. Mem. adv. bd., vice-chair St. Mary's Sch. PTA, Clinton, NY, 2002—04. Leader Girl Scout Troop, 2004—. Named Young Careerist Alternate Bus. and Profl. Women's Club, 1986; recipient award ACC/CCC Alumni Assn., 2000. Mem.: CASE, AAUW, Assn. Donor Rels. Profls. (v.p. 2005—), Nat. Coun. Mktg. and Pub. Rels. (Pro Devel. award 1999, Disting. Svc. award 2000), Eisenhower Coll. Aumni Assn. (bd. dirs. 1990—97, chmn. bd. 1992—95, dir. emeritus 2004—, chmn. bd. 2006—), Phi Theta Kappa. Avocations: fiction and poetry writing, doll and bear collecting, olympic pin collecting, tap dancing. Office: Hamilton Coll 198 College Hill Rd Clinton NY 13323 Office Phone: 315-859-4673. Business E-Mail: phavens@hamilton.edu.

HAVER-ALLEN, ANN, communications director; d. Vivian Faye Haver; m. William Allen, June 21, 1986; children: Jason Allen, Summer Allen. BA in Journalism, Thomas Edison State Coll., Trenton, N.J. Reporter Angleton Times, Tex., 1985—86; mng. editor Princeton Packet Group, NJ, 1986—90, Engel Pub. Ptnrs., West Trenton, NJ, 1990—92; dir. engrng. comm. Princeton U., NJ, 1992—2004; dir. pub. rels. and mktg. Prescott Coll., Ariz., 2004—05; founder aha Creative Ink, 2005—; mng. editor The Rim Country Gazette, 2006—. Editor: EQuad News at Princeton U., Transitions at Prescott Coll. Commr. Red Heart Coastal Mvskoke Clan, Robertsdale, Ala., 2001—; bd. dirs. Cmtys. for Compassion and Justice, Prescott. Recipient APEX award for publ. excellence, 2002—04, Communicator award, 2002, Communicator award design/logo, 2004, Award of Merit, Internat. Assn. Bus. Communicators, 2002, 2004, Silver Quill award, Assn. Bus. Communicators, 2003, Crystal Award of Excellence, 2003, Clarion award, Assn. Women Comm., 2003—04, Magnum Opus Gold award in Best Rewrite category, Mo. Sch. Journalism and industry comm. profls., 2004, Merit award, Dalton Pen Comms., 2004. Mem.: NAFE, N.J. Press Assn. (hon. mention), Nat. Newspaper Assn. (Blue Ribbon Excellence 1988), Internat. Assn. Bus. Communicators (IRIS Award of Excellence 2002, IRIS award 2004), Women in Comm., Ednl. Press Assn. Am., Coun. for Advancement and Support of Edn. Office Phone: 928-717-2412, 928-717-2412. Personal E-mail: aha_prescottcollege@yahoo.com, editoraha@yahoo.com. Business E-Mail: aha@ahacreativeink.com.

HAVERLAND, MURIEL JEAN, speaker, career management consultant; b. Bklyn., Nov. 9, 1946; d. Jerry Isaac and Blossom (Markowitz) Negrie; m. Neal Savitt, Apr. 29, 1967 (div. Jan. 1973); children: Gary, Jason, Matthew Keysor; m. Sevket Yilmazcetin, Apr. 4, 1982 (div. Aug. 1993), m. Willard D. Haverland, Jan. 16, 2004 BA in Anthropology, Calif. State U., Northridge, 1968; MA in Applied Psychology, U. Santa Monica, 1991. Owner, pres. Mentor, Inc., Severna Park, Md., 1990-93; v.p. outplacement divsn. Dinte Resources, Inc., McLean, Va., 1992-96; pres. Mentor, Inc., 1996—2004; v.p. human resources adminstrn. PermitsNow.com, 2000—01; chair TEC, 2001—; facilitator Women Presidents Orgn., 2001—03; dir. CEO programs Boardroom Bound, 2001—; pres. Mentor Dynamic, Inc., 2004—, Prescott Connections, 2004—, Citizens Water Adv. Group2005, 2005—. Author: Untangling Your NOTS, 1997; radio talk show host. Pres. Am. Seminar Leaders Assn., Nat. Capital area, Greenbrook Village Homeowners Assn., 1997-2001; vol. Women's Ctr.; sec., bd. dirs. Literacy Vols. of Am., Nat. Capital Area; mem. Greater Washington Alliance of Coaches, 1997-2001; pres. Citizens Water Advocacy Group, 2005—; bd. United Way Yavapai County, 2005—. Mem. Soc. Human Resource Mgmt., Am. Bus. Women (com. chmn. 1991, v.p. 1992), Dulles Soc. Human Resource Mgmt. (dir. 1996, treas. 1994-96), Women in Tech., Tower Club (mem. coun. 1997-2000), Women in Comms., Nat. Capital Speakers Assn., Women Bus. Owners Assn., Nat. Speakers Assn., Internat. Coaching Fedn. Avocations: travel, reading, psychology, spirituality in business, personal development. Office: 786 Panicum Dr Prescott AZ 86305 Office Phone: 928-443-5353. Personal E-mail: muriel@murielspeaks.com.

HAVERLY, PAMELA SUE, nursing administrator; b. Huntingburg, Ind., Aug. 14, 1955; d. Robert Ray Reckelhoff and Shirley Ann Reister; children: Aaron, Madison. ADN, Marion Coll., Indpls., 1985; BSN, Ind. U., Indpls., 1994. RN Ind., cert. CLCP, CCRN, ACLS. Nurse various depts. Wishard Meml. Hosp., Indpls.; AIDS home nurse VA, Indpls.; liaison nurse Family Home Health, Indpls.; managed care specialist Rehab. Profls., Louisville, Ellis & Assocs., Chgo., Zurich North Am., Indpls.; clin. nurse cons. Venetec Internat., San Diego. Bd. dirs. Kid's Chance, Indpls Vol. Gennerstreet Free Clinic, Indpls.; vol. trauma nurse Police & Firemen's Games, Indpls., 2000—01; active various other civic/charitable orgns.; del. to People's Republic of China Ind. U. Sch. Nursing, 1999. Mem. Ind. Workmen's Compensation Inst., ANA, Ind. State Nurses Assn. (peer rev. com. 1986—99, del. 1985—), Sigma Theta Tau, Kappa Kappa Sigma. Roman Catholic. Avocations: reading, gardening. Home: 8127 Tanager Ct Indianapolis IN 46256-1775 Office: Eli Lilly Indianapolis IN 46206

HAVILAND, KAY LYNN (KADE HAVILAND), mental health services professional; b. Deer Lodge, Mont., July 16, 1952; d. Jackson C. and Juanita Maxine (Voelkel) Price; children: Jesse Jean, Kelsey Ann, Molly Claire. BA in English Lit., Mont. State U., 1976; MA in Counseling Psychology, Adams State Coll., 1994. Cert. addictions counselor III Colo., lic. profl. counselor Colo. Cert. addictions counselor, outpatient therapist Arapahoe House Denver Outpatient Clinic, Denver, 1996—2005; dept. human svcs. on-site substance abuse evaluator, 1998—2001; addictions counselor, trainer State of Colo. Alcohol Drug Abuse divsn. Health and Hosps., Denver, 2001—04, 2004—, Odyssey Training Ctr., 2002—06; pvt. practice in eating disorders and substance abuse, 2004—. Asst. therapist, CORE obesity project, Weight Choice Program dept. pediatrics U. Colo., 1999—2001. Author, editor: (mag.) Human Interest, 1987-88 (1st place award 1989); contbr. articles to profl. jours. Mem.: Am. Counseling Assn., Eating Disorder Found., Eating Disorder Profls. of Colo., Lambda Iota Tau, Pi Beta Phi. Office Phone: 303-250-5251. E-mail: kadhavi@yahoo.com.

HAVILAND, MARLITA CHRISTINE, elementary school educator; b. Moses Lake, Wash., Sept. 4, 1952; d. Marvin Curtis and Delita F. (Grout) McCully; m. James A Haviland, June 18, 1971. BS in Edn., So. Nazarene U., Bethany, Okla., 1973; MA in Edn., No. Ariz. U., 1987. Cert. elem. tchr., Ariz., Colo., ESL, basic edn., spl. edn. tchr., c.c., Ariz., early childhood edn., Colo.; cert. libr./media specialist. Elem. tchr. St. Paul (Ark.) Pu. Sch., Twin Wells Indian Sch., Sun Valley, Ariz., Navajo Gospel Mission, Kykotsmovi, Ariz., Shonto (Ariz.) Boarding Sch. (now Shonto Prep Sch.). Instr. Northland Pioneer Coll., Diné Coll.; coord. Sch. Wide Book Fair.; coach Accelerated Schs. Coord. Children Inc., Shonto; local chair, North Ctrl. Assn., amb. Mem. Nat. Fedn. Fed. Employees (past pres., sec.-treas., steward), Am. Libr. Assn., Internat. Reading Assn., Alpha Nu, Phi Kappa Phi. Home: PO Box 7427 Shonto AZ 86054-7427 E-mail: mchaviland@yahoo.com.

HAWES, BESS LOMAX, retired folklorist; m. Baldwin Hawes; children: Corey, Naomi, Nicholas. BA, Bryn Mawr U., 1941; MA, U. Calif., 1970; PhD (hon.), Kenyon Coll., 1994, U. N.C., 1995. With music divsn. N.Y. Pub. Libr.; prof. anthropology Calif. State U., Northridge, 1963—74, Smithsonian Instn., 1974—76; dir. Folk Arts Program Nat. Endowment for Arts, 1977—92; ret., 1992. Recipient Nat. Medal of Arts, Pres. Clinton, 1993. E-mail: bess.hawes@csun.edu.

HAWES, GRACE MAXCY, archivist, retired writer; b. Cumberland, Wis., Feb. 4, 1926; d. Clarence David and Mabel Hannah (Erickson) Maxcy; m. John G. Hawes, Aug. 28, 1948 (dec.); children: Elizabeth, John D., Mark- (dec.), Amy; m. E. Zumbrunnen, 1993. Student, U. Wis., 1944—46; BA, San Jose State U., 1963, MA, 1971. Libr. asst. NASA, Langley, Va., 1948—49; archival specialist Hoover Archives, 1976—80, adminstrv. asst., 1980—82; archival specialist Hoover Inst., 1982—89, rsch. archivist, 1989—93, 1997—. Author: The Marshall Plan for China: Economic Cooperation Administration, 1948-1949, 1977. Address: 925 Ponselle Ln Capitola CA 95010 Home: 15864 NW Ryegrass St Portland OR 97229-9217

HAWK, PAULETTA BROWNING, elementary school educator; b. Gilbert, W.Va., Aug. 10, 1952; d. Walter Browning and Gracie Tyner; children: Clifford Thompson III, Angie Thompson AA, Cen. Fla. Community Coll., Ocala, 1988; BS in Elem. Edn., U. Cen. Fla., 1991; MEd in Curriculum and Instrn., Nat. Louis U., 1996. Med. receptionist Bluefield (W.Va.) Clinic, 1975-76; ins. clk. Bristol (Tenn.) Meml. Hosp., 1976-78; med. sec. Inter-Mountain Pathology Assn., Bristol, Tenn., 1978-80; substitute tchr. Citrus County Sch. Bd., Inverness, Fla., 1980-81, guidance sec., 1981-85, acct. I, 1990-91; office mgr. Victor Nothnagel, O.D., Inverness, 1985-87; tchr. Inverness Primary, 1991—99, Banyan Elem., Sunrise, Fla., 1999—2002, Brooksville (Fla.) Elem., 2002—03, Homosassa (Fla.) Elem. Sch., 2003—. Vol. Nat. Arthritis Found., 1988-89, Inverness Primary Sch., Citrus County Sch. Bd., 1989. Mem. Phi Theta Kappa. Democrat. Baptist. Avocations: reading, swimming, bicycling, gardening, clay modeling. Home: 5066 E Backner Ln Inverness FL 34452-8314

HAWKES, CAROL ANN, academic administrator; b. NYC; d. Howard N. and Lavinia M. (Lally) H. BA, Barnard Coll., 1943; MA, Columbia U., 1944, PhD, 1949. Dir. acad. English liberal arts div. Katharine Gibbs Sch., N.Y.C., 1950-57; prof. English, chmn. dept. English and comparative lit. Finch Coll., N.Y.C., 1957-75; v.p. for ednl. affairs, dean of coll. Hartwick Coll., Oneonta, NY, 1975-80; pres. Endicott Coll., Beverly, Mass., 1980-87; assoc. v.p. for acad. affairs, founding dean Sch. Visual and Performing Arts Western Conn. State U., Danbury, 1987—. Trustee Norwich U., Hartwick Coll. Author: Master's Degree Programs and the Liberal Arts College, 1968. Harvard Sch. Dental Medicine fellow. Mem. MLA, LWV, Modern Humanities Rsch. Assn., Princeton Club (N.Y.C.), Columbia U. Club New Eng., Phi Beta Kappa. Office: Western Conn State U Academic Affairs Danbury CT 06810 Office Phone: 203-837-8851. Business E-Mail: hawkesc@wcsu.edu.

HAWKINS, ALIA ELAINE, dancer, small business owner; b. Chgo., June 6, 1977; d. Calvin DeLee and Lennie Elaine Hawkins. BA, St. Mary's Coll., Notre Dame, Ind., 1999; MBA, U. Phoenix, Phoenix, Ariz., 2003. Dance instr., choreograhper Mirror Image Dance Acad., Valparaiso, Ind., 1999—2003; prin., owner Beachfront Dance Sch., Gary, Ind., 2003—. Dir.: High Priest (Gold award Am. Dance Awards, 2006), Dancing in My Dreams, A Trip to the Theatre, Gettin' Good At Bein' Bad (High Silver award Am. Dance Awards, 2006), I Can't Stand the Rain (High Silver award Am. Dance Awards, 2006); dancer Performance, Forrest Gump Medley. Mem.: Dance Masters Am. (assoc.), Dance Educators Am. (assoc.). Republican. Roman Catholic. Avocations: travel, swimming, tennis, sewing, cooking. Office Phone: 219-938-0366.

HAWKINS, ANGELA, music educator; b. Murray, Ky., June 11, 1971; d. James Winston Houser and Sharon Kaye Filbeck; m. Roy Hawkins, May 25, 1996; 1 child, Nicolas. MusB in Edn. magna cum laude, Murray State U., 1994, M in Music Edn. summa cum laude, 2003. Music tchr. Paris (Tenn.) Spl. Sch. Dist., 1994—. Mem. exec. bd. Christian Student Ctr. Alumni and Friends, Murray, Ky., 2000—, newsletter editor, 2001—04; tech. coach and webmaster W.G. Rhea Elem. Sch., Paris, 2000—04. Dir. family bible sch. Ch. of Christ, Murray, Ky., 2001—04. Mem.: Music Educators Nat. Conf., Sigma Alpha Iota (songleader Iota Beta chpt. 1993—94). Democrat. Avocations: computers, travel, collecting Disney memorabilia. Office: Paris Special School District 115 South Wilson Paris TN 38242 E-mail: hawkins@wgr.k12.tn.us.

HAWKINS, ANN R., educator, researcher; d. Harold R. and Mary Wagliardo Hawkins; m. Miles A. Kimball. PhD, U. Ky., Lexington. Asst. prof. Tex. Tech U., Lubbock, 2002—. Editor: Venetia by Benjamin Disraeli, Victims of Society by Countess of Blessington, Teaching Bibliography, Textual Criticism and Book History, Henrietta Temple by Benjamin Disraeli. Bd. mem. TTU Ctr. SW, 2005—. Fellow, Folger Shakespeare Libr., 2001, Rare book Sch., 2003, Rare Book Sch., 2005, NEH, 2005; grantee, Helen Jones Found., 2005—06. Mem.: Nat. Coll. English Assn. (pres. 2005—06), North Atlantic Soc. Study Romanticism, Assn. Documentary Editing, Soc. Textual Scholarship, Internat. Byron Soc., Soc. History Authorship, Reading and Pub. Office: Department of English Texas Tech University Lubbock TX 79409 Office Phone: 806-742-2500.

HAWKINS, BARBARA JANE, small business owner, writer; b. Detroit, Apr. 23, 1938; d. Roland L. and Kathryn Elizabeth Ebaugh; m. George Edward Hawkins, Mar. 23, 1957; children: Daniel, Debbie, David. BE, Mich. State Univ., East Lansing, Mich., 1959, MA, 1967. Cert. elem. edn. K-8 Mich. Elem. tchr. Bath Pub. Sch., Bath, Mich., 1959—61, Dickinson Sch., Dickinson, ND, 1962—64, Croswell Lexington Sch., Croswell, Mich., 1969—2002; founder, mgr. Little House Site Tours LLC., Mich., 2001—. Edn. cons. Discovery Toys, Mich., 1987—2006; presenter at confs. World Congress on Reading, Aukland, New Zealand, 2000, Internat. Reading Assn., 2000. Author: 100 Verses About Laura Ingalls Wilder, 2005, (video) Visiting the Homesites of Laura Ingalls Wilder, 2001. Mem.: Mich. Edn. Assn. for Young Children, Internat. Reading Assn., Nat. Coun. for Social Studies, Mich. Reading Assn. Avocations: photography, travel.

HAWKINS, BARBARA REED, mental health nurse; b. Burghettstown, Pa., July 20, 1945; d. John Francis Reed and Iona Eleanor Spring; m. Hal Kenneth Hawkins, Sept. 6, 1969; children: David, Heidi, Brian, Russell. BS in Nursing, Duke U., 1968; MSN, U. N.C., 1973; postgrad., Houston Montessori Ctr., 1992—95. RN N.C., 1968. Staff nurse pediatrics Duke U. Med. Ctr., 1968—69; psychiatric nurse, group co-therapist Durham County Mental Health Ctr., 1971—72; counselor Durham Crisis and Suicide Ctr., 1972—73; lectr. psychiat. nursing U. N.C., Sch. Nursing, Chapel Hill, 1972; lectr. U. N.C., 1972—73, instr., 1973—77; therapist Psychiat. Assocs. Chapel Hill, 1975—79; head nurse, nursing supr., acting unit dir. Ga. Mental Health Inst., 1979—80; coord. career devel. Emory U. Hosp., 1980—81; tchr. Sugar Creek Children's Montessori Sch., Sugarland, Tex., 1992—95. Cons. in field. Contbg. author Patterson Family Favorites, 1998. Vol. Tex. Wildlife and Rehab. Ctr., 1983—2004; vol. cons. in counseling crisis intervention, 2000—. Avocations: shell collecting, gourmet cooking, gardening, interior decorating, crafts. Home: 5500 N Braeswood Blvd Apt 198 Houston TX 77096

HAWKINS, CYNTHIA, artist, educator; b. N.Y.C., Jan. 29, 1950; d. Robert D. Hawkins and Elease Coger; m. Steven J. Chaiken, Feb. 5, 1977 (div. Aug. 1985); m. John Edward Owen, Aug. 24, 1985; children: Ianna, Zachary. BA, Queens Coll., Flushing, N.Y., 1977; MFA, Md. Inst. Coll. Art, 1992. Tchg. asst. Md. Inst. Coll. of Art, Balt., 1990-92; adj. instr. Rockland C.C., Suffern, N.Y., 1993-96, Parsons Sch. Design, N.Y.C., 1996, The Coll. at New Paltz, SUNY, 1996-98, Ramapo Coll. of N.J., 1998-99; dir. galleries Cedar Crest Coll., Allentown, Pa., 2000—03; curator Rush Art Gallery, 2003—; ind. curator African Am. Printmakers: The Legacy Continues traveling exhbn., 2003—; ind. curator jat Aljina Ctr. for Contemporary Art, 2005. Mentor Empire State Coll., Nyack, N.Y., 1994; artist-in-residence The Studio Mus. Harlem, N.Y., 1987-88, Va. Ctr. for Creative Arts, Sweet Briar, Va., 1995-96, Exptl. Printmaking Inst., Lafayette Coll., Pa., 2005; vis. artist Round House Press, Hartwick Coll., Oneonta, N.Y., 1994; curator Rockland Ctr. for Arts, art dept. Rockland C.C., Nyack, 1994-95, The Rotunda, 1994-95; vis. lectr. Forman Gallery, Hartwick Coll., Oneonta, 1994, Rockland C.C., Suffern, 1994-95; presenter in field. One-woman shows include, Paul Klapper Libr., Queens Coll., N.Y., 1974, Just Above Midtown/Downtown Gallery, N.Y.C., 1981, Frances Wolfson Art Ctr., Miami (Fla.)-Dade C.C., 1986, Cinque Gallery, N.Y.C., 1989, Essex (Md.) C.C., 1991, Queens Coll. Art Ctr., Benjamin S. Rosenthal Libr., Queens Coll., CUNY, Trinity Luth. Ch., New Milford, Conn., 1993, Wilmer Jennings Gallery, N.Y., 2004, exhibited in group shows at Queens Coll. Gallery, N.Y.C., 1973, 2004, Emily Lowe Gallery, Hempstead, N.Y., 1979, Jamie Szoke Gallery, N.Y.C., 1984, Grace Borgenicht Gallery, N.Y.C., 1986, Aljira Gallery, Newark, 1989, Dome Gallery, N.Y.C., 1990, Decker Gallery, Balt., 1991, Kromah Gallery, Balt., 1992, Arts Alliance Haverstraw, N.Y., 1993, Nabisco Gallery, East Hanover, N.J., 1994, Artist Space, N.Y.C., 1993, Bronx Mus. Arts, 1994, U. Notre Dame at Balt., 1995, No. Westchester Ctr. for Arts, Mt. Kisco, N.Y., 1996, Hopper House, Nyack, 1996, Rush Art Gallery, N.Y., 1999, Foxglove Gallery, Stroudsburg, Pa., 2002, Wilmer Jennings Gallery, N.Y., 2004, Represented in permanent collections, The Bronx Mus. of Arts, N.Y.C., Trinity Luth. Ch., New Milford, Dept. of State, Washington, The Printmaking Workshop, Chevron Corp., Calif., Cameron and Colby, N.Y.C., C.D. Walsh Assocs., Conn., Brooks Sausage Co., Kenosha, Wis., The Habitat Co., Chgo., Brown Mgmt., Balt.; art works featured in pubs. including N.Y. Times, Village Voice, 25 Years of African American Women Artist, Home Mag. Mem. com. Art in Pub. Places, Rockland County, 1999—2001. Recipient 2d pl. award for mixed media Atlanta Life Ins. Co. exhbn. and competition, 1984; fellow Va. Ctr. for Creative Arts, 1996, The Studio Mus. in Harlem, 1987-88, Patricia Robert Harris fellow U.S. Dept. Edn., 1990-92. Democrat. Episcopalian. E-mail: hawkins.cynthia@gmail.com.

HAWKINS, DALANA MARIE, social studies educator; b. Beaver, Okla., Dec. 20, 1977; d. David Wayne Brooks and Deitra Sue Rock, Tracey Diane Brooks (Stepmother); m. Jason Dean Hawkins, Apr. 6, 1996; children: Jaden Darnay, Daylan Wayne. AA, Redlands C.C., El Reno, Okla., 2000; B in Social Studies Edn., U. Ctrl. Okla., Edmond, 2003; postgrad., Southwestern Okla. State U. Lic. secondary tchr. Okla. State Dept. Edn., 2003. Social studies tchr. Ponca City (Okla.) H.S., 2003—. Vol. Americorps, Kingfisher, Okla., 2002—03. Republican. Avocations: coaching youth community sports (softball, t-ball, basketball, etc.), academic team coach.

HAWKINS, DIANA WENDELLIN, elementary school educator; b. Leonard, Mo., June 16, 1950; d. Chester Glen and Mary Margaret McEwen; m. Kenneth Kyl Cooper (div.); children: Christopher Scott Cooper, Angel Christin Cooper; m. James Michael Hawkins, 1993. Completion cert., Art Instrn. Sch., Mpls., Minn., 1967; BS in Edn. magna cum laude, Hannibal LaGrange Coll., Mo., 1991. Cert. elem., art tchr. Mo. 5th/6th grade tchr.'s aide Shelby County R-IV, Clarence, Mo., 1992; 1st grade tchr.'s aide Shelby County C-I, Shelbyville, Mo., 1992—93; 3rd grade tchr. Paris R-II, Mo., 1993—97; 2nd and 3rd grade tchr. FFL Christian Sch., Mo., 1998—99; art and Title I math tchr. Mid. Grove C-1, Madison, Mo., 1998. Baptist. Avocations: singing, reading, poetry writing, flower gardening, watercolor painting. Home: 514 Cooper Ave Paris MO 65275 Office: Mid Grove C-1 11476 Rte M Madison MO 63463 E-mail: iluv2teach123abc@yahoo.com.

HAWKINS, ELINOR DIXON (MRS. CARROLL WOODARD HAWKINS), retired librarian; b. Masontown, W.Va., Sept. 25, 1927; d. Thomas Fitchie and Susan (Reed) Dixon; m. Carroll Woodard Hawkins, June 24, 1951; 1 child, John Carroll. AB, Fairmont State Coll., 1949; BS in Libr. Sci., U. N.C., 1950. Children's libr. Enoch Pratt Free Libr., Balt., 1950-51; head circulation dept. Greensboro (N.C.) Pub. Libr., 1951-56; libr. Craven-Pamlico Libr. Svc., New Bern, N.C., 1958-62; dir. Craven-Pamlico-Carteret Regional Libr., New Bern, N.C., 1962-92. Storyteller children's TV program Tele-Story Time, 1952-58, 63—; bd. dirs. Triangle Bank of New Bern. Mem. New Bern Hist. Soc., 1973—, Tryon Palace Commn., 1974—; mem. adv. bd. Salvation Army. Mem. N.C. Assn. Retarded Children, Pilot Club (pres. 1957-58, v.p. 1962-63). Baptist. Home: PO Box 57 Cove City NC 28523-0057 Personal E-mail: msclaus6@cconnect.net.

HAWKINS, EMMA B., humanities educator; b. Ardmore, Okla., July 28, 1946; d. Bernard C. and Occie E. (Morris) H. BA, Okla. Bapt. U., 1968; MDiv, Southwestern Bapt. Theol. Sem., 1976; MA, U. North Tex., 1990, PhD in English (Medieval), 1995. Instr. U. North Tex., Denton, 1990-95; lectr. Lamar U., Beaumont, 1995-97, asst. prof., 1997—2002, assoc. prof., 2003—. Chair program and arrangements South Cen. Conf. on Christianity and Lit., 1999, mem. exec. bd., 1999-2004; presenter numerous papers at profl. confs. Contbr. chpt. to book, articles to profl. jours. Recipient Go the Extra Mile award, 1997. Mem. MLA (sec. Old and Mid. English sect. South Ctrl. chpt. 1997, chair Old and Mid Eng. sect. chpt. 1998), Tex. Medieval Assn., Conf. on Coll. Tchrs. English (CCTE award best paper Brit. Lit., 2004), South Ctrl. Conf. Christianity and Lit. (chair various sessions, James Sims award 2000), Phi Kappa Phi (pres. chpt. 95), Sigma Tau Delta. Office: Lamar U PO Box 10023 Beaumont TX 77710-0023

HAWKINS, FRANCES PAM, business educator; b. Woodland, Ala., Dec. 2, 1945; d. Lowell M. and Bernice E. Mcmanus; children: Scott Cummings, Veronica Lovvorn. AS in Bus., Southern Union C.C., 1989; BS in Bus. Edn., Auburn U., 1990, MEd, 1992. Ptnr. C & S Pharmacy, Roanoke, Ala., 1974—90; bus. office tech. instr. West Ga. Tech. Coll., Lagrange, Ga., 1991—. Bus. tech., divsn. chair West Ga. Tech. Coll., Lagrange, 1999—2003, bus. office tech. adv. com. mem., 1992—, chairperson libr. com., 2001—; mem. tech. in edn. com. Ga. Dept. Edn., Atlanta, 2001—. Team leader March of Dimes, LaGrange, 1998—. Mem.: Ga. Bus. Edn. Assn., So. Bus. Edn. Assn., Nat. Bus. Edn. Assn. (com. mem. 2001), Auburn Alumni Assn., Phi Beta Lambda (local advisor 1992—, sec. 1997—2001, pres. Ga. Found. Inc. 1998—, state advisor 1999—2005, nat. bd. dirs. future bus. leaders Am. 2001—, exec. dir. 2005—). Methodist. Office: West Ga Tech Coll 303 Fort Dr Lagrange GA 30240 Office Phone: 706-837-4222. Business E-Mail: phawkins@westgatech.edu.

HAWKINS, IDA FAYE, elementary school educator; b. Ft. Worth, Dec. 28, 1928; d. Christopher Columbus and Nannie Idella (Hughes) Hall; m. Gene Hamilton Hawkins, Dec. 22, 1952; children: Gene Agner, Jane Hall. Student, Midwestern U., 1946-48; BS, North Tex. State U., 1951; postgrad., Lamar U., 1968-70; MS, McNeese State U., 1973. Tchr. DeQueen Elem. Sch., Port Arthur, Tex., 1950-54, Tyrrell Elem. Sch., Port Arthur, Tex., 1955-56, Roy Hatton Elem. Sch., Bridge City, Tex., 1967-68, Oak Forest Elem. sch., Vidor, Tex., 1968-91; ret., 1991. Elementary school educator; b. Ft. Worth, Dec. 28, 1928; d. Christopher Columbus and Nannie Idella (Hughes) Hall; m. Gene Hamilton Hawkins, Dec. 22, 1952; children: Gene Agner, Jane Hall. Student Midwestern U., 1946-48; BS, N. Tex. State U., 1951; student Lamar U., 1968-70; MS, McNeese State U., 1973. Tchr. DeQueen Elem. Sch., Port Arthur, Tex., 1950-54, Tyrrell Elem. Sch., Port Arthur, 1955-56, Roy Hatton Elem. Sch., Bridge City, Tex., 1967-68, Oak Forest Elem. Sch., Vidor, Tex., 1968-91, ret. 2d v.p. Travis Elem. PTA, 1965-66, 1st v.p., 1966-67; corr. sec. Port Arthur City coun. PTA, 1966-67; Sunday sch. tchr. Presbyn. Ch., 1951-53, 60-66. Named Tchr. of Yr., Oak Forest Elem., 1984-85. Mem. NEA, Tex. State Tchrs. Assn. 2d v.p. Travis Elem. PTA, 1965-66, 1st v.p., 1966-67; corr. sec. Port Arthur City Coun. PTA, 1966-67; Sunday sch. tchr. Presbyn. Ch., 1951-53, 60-66. Named Tchr. of Yr., Oak Forest Elem., 1984-85. Mem. NEA, Tex. State Tchrs. Assn. Home: 5415 Brisvalley #820 Houston TX 77096 Personal E-mail: hawkinsshi@aol.com.

HAWKINS, JACQUELYN, elementary and secondary education educator; b. Russell Springs, Ky., Apr. 30, 1943; d. J.T. Hawkins and Maudie Bell Crew. BS, Andrews U., 1969; MEd, Xavier U., 1976. Cert. elem. tchr., Ohio, reading tchr. elem. and high sch., Ohio. Tchr. Cin. Pub. Schs., 1969-99, Cummins Sch., Cin., 1971-81, Windsor Sch., Cin., 1982-83, 1983-89, acting contact tchr. chpt. 1 reading program, 1989-93, reading recovery tchr. Cin., 1993-99; ret., 1999; pvt. child care worker, 2002—. Rep. Cin. Coun. Educators, 1986-89, 91-92, 92-93, mem. book com.; mem. sch. improvement program Windsor Sch., 1982-84; mem. Sch. Improvement Program Cin. Chairperson United Way at Windsor Sch. Cin., 1986-89, 90-92, United Negro Coll. Fund Cin., 1986-89, ARC, Windsor Sch., Cin., 1986-89, 90-92; rep. Fine Arts Fund Cin., 1986-88; co-leader 4-H Club, Cin., 1987-88; leader Girl Scouts U.S., Cin., 1988-93; tutor Tabernacle Bapt. Ch., 1989; co-chairperson Windsor ARC, 1991-92. Recipient Cert. Achievement Cummins Sch. Cin., 1978 Democrat. Avocations: travel, reading, needlecrafts.

HAWKINS, JAMESETTA See JAMES, ETTA

HAWKINS, JOELLEN MARGARET BECK, nursing educator; b. Harvey, ND, Dec. 15, 1941; d. Charles Joel and Gertrude Adelaide (Waits) Beck; m. Charles Albert Watson, June 27, 1964 (div. 1978); children: John Charles, Andrew Bruce; m. David Gene Hawkins, Oct. 4, 1978. Student, Oberlin Coll., 1959—61; diploma, Chgo. Wesley Meml. Hosp. Sch. of Nursing, 1964; BSN, Northwestern U., Chgo., 1964; MS, Boston Coll., 1969, PhD, 1977. Cert. women's health nurse practitioner. Staff nurse Sheboygan (Wis.) Meml. Hosp., 1964-65; instr., staff Boston Lying in Hosp., 1965-66, 68-69; staff nurse Brookline (Mass.) Vis. Nurse Assn., 1968, Guy's Hosp., London, 1968; campus nurse Roger Williams Coll., Bristol, RI, 1969-70; instr. Salve Regina Coll., Newport, RI, 1970-74; faculty Roger Williams Coll., Bristol, RI, 1974-75; prof. U. Conn., Storrs, 1978-83; asst., assoc. prof. William F. Connell Sch. Nursing Boston Coll., Chestnut Hill, Mass., 1975-78, prof., 1983—. Women's health nurse practitioner Crittenton Hastings House, 1984-2000, U. Conn. Student Health Women's Clinic, 1978-83, Sidney Borum Health Ctr., 2000—, Pine St. Inn Women's Clinic, 2000—. Author: Maternal-Newborn Nursing: Pretest Self-Assessment and Review, 1978, Clinical Experience in Collegiate Nursing Education: Selection of Clinical Agencies, 1981, Health Care of Women: Gynecological Assessment, 1982, Women and the Menopause, 1983, Linking Nursing Education and Practice: Collaborative Experiences in Maternal Child Health, 1987, Dictionary of American Nursing Biography, 1988, Nursing and the American Health Care Delivery System, 4th edit., 1993, Nurse-Social Worker Collaboration in Managed Care: A Model of Community Case Management, 1998, The Advanced Practice Nurse: Current Issues, 5th edit., 2000, Guidelines for Nurse Practitioners in Gynecologic Settings, 8th edit., 2004— (Book of Yr. award Am. Jour. Nursing, 2004); editor: Linking Nursing Education and Practice, 1987 (Book of Yr. award Am. Jour. Nursing, 1988), Clin. Excellence for Nurse Practitioners: Internat. Jour. of NPACE, 1996—2005, Diversity in Health Care Research: Strategies for Multisite, Multidisciplinary, and Multicultural Projects, 2003; nursing editor: Taber's Medical Dictionary, 2005—; contbr. articles to profl. jours., chapters to books. Recipient Disting. Alumni award North H.S., North St. Paul, Minn., 1989, Miriam Manisoff award Planned Parenthood Fedn. Am., 1997, Disting. Alumna award Chgo. Wesley Meml. Hosp. Sch. Nursing, 1999; named Nurse Practitioner of Yr. Am. Acad. of Nurse Practitioners, 1995. Fellow Am. Acad. Nursing, Am. Acad. Nurse Practitioners; mem. ANA, Mass. RNs Assn. (Disting. Nurse Rschr. award 1984, Lucy Lincoln Drown Nursing History award 1994), Internat. Coun. Women's Health, Nat. Acads. Practice (Nicholas A. Cummings award 2006), Am. Assn. History Nursing (nominating chair 1989), Assn. Women's Health Obstetric and Neonatal Nurses, Sigma Theta Tau (Elizabeth Russell Belford Founder's award 1993) Democrat. Unitarian Universalist. Home: 151 Stanton Ave Auburndale MA 02466-3005 Office: Boston Coll William F Connell Sch Nursing 140 Commonwealth Ave Chestnut Hill MA 02467 Office Phone: 617-552-4252. Business E-Mail: hawkinsj@bc.edu.

HAWKINS, KATHERINE ANN, hematologist, educator, lawyer; b. Teaneck, N.J., Oct. 25, 1947; d. Howard Robert and Helen Ann (Foley) Hawkins; m. Paul Jonathan Chrzanowski, June 29, 1974; children: Eric, Brian. AB, Manhattanville Coll., Purchase, N.Y., 1969; MD, Columbia U., 1973; JD, Fordham U., Sch. of Law, 2002. Intern Presbyn. Hosp., N.Y.C., 1973, Roosevelt Hosp., N.Y.C., 1974-75, resident, 1975-77; fellow NYU, 1977-79; attending hematologist Sickle Cell Ctr. St. Luke's Hosp., N.Y.C., 1985-87; assoc. attending physician St. Luke's - Roosevelt Hosp. Ctr., N.Y.C., 1989—; asst. clin. prof. medicine Columbia U., N.Y.C., 1987-94, assoc. clin. prof., 1994—96; assoc. dir. dept. medicine, dir. med. edn. St. Luke's Hosp., N.Y.C., 1991-96; assoc. residency program dir. Beth Israel Med. Ctr., N.Y.C., 1996—; assoc. prof. clin. medicine Albert Einstein Coll. Medicine Yeshiva U., N.Y.C., 1996—. Mem. attending staff Beth Israel Hosp., N.Y.C., St. Luke's-Roosevelt Hosp. Ctr., N.Y.C. Contbr. articles to profl. jours. Fellow ACP; mem. ABA, Am. Soc. Hematology, Am. Soc. Clin. Oncology, Am. Coll. Legal Medicine Roman Catholic. Office: Gair Gair Conason Steigman and Mackauf 80 Pine St New York NY 10005 Office Phone: 212-943-1090.

HAWKINS, LINDA PARROTT, school system administrator; b. Florence, SC, June 23, 1947; d. Obie Lindberg Parrott and Mary Francis (Lee) Evans; m. Larry Eugene Hawkins, Jan. 5, 1946; 1 child, Heather Nichole. BS, U. S.C., 1969; MS, Francis Marion Coll., 1978; EdS in Adminstrn., U. S.C., 1994; PhD in Ednl. Adminstrn., U. SC, 2002. Tchr. J.C. Lynch HS, Coward, SC, 1973—80; tchr., chair bus. dept. Lake City (SC) HS, 1980—89, assoc. prin., 1989—98; dir. Florence County Sch. Dist. 3, Lake City, 1998—2002, sr. dir. accountability, 2002—. Mem. Williamsburg Tech. Adv. Coun., Kingstree, S.C., 1985-90; adv. coun. Florence-Darlington (S.C.) Tech., 1981-87; co-chair Pee Dee Tech Prep consortia steering com.; co-chmn. allied health adv. com., 1990-93; spkr., presenter in field. Editor: Parliamentary Procedure Made Easy, 1983; contbr. articles to profl. jours. State advisor Future Bus. Leaders of Am., Columbia, S.C., 1978-86; treas. S.C. State Women's Aux., 1983-93; sec.-treas. J.C. Lynch Elem. Sch. PTO. Mary Eva Hite scholar, 2001; named Outstanding Advisor SC Future Bus. Leaders of Am., 1985, Tchr. of Yr., SC Bus. Edn. Assn., 1988-89, Secondary Tchr. of Yr., Nat. Bus. Edn. Assn., 1989-90, Educator of Yr. SC Trade & Indsl. Edn. Assn., 1993, SC Asst. Prin. of Yr., 1995, 2020 Vision Dist. Adminstr. award, 2000, Leadership award Nat. Assn. Fed. Program Adminstrs., 2005 Mem. Profl. Secs. Internat., Nat. Bus. Assn. (S.C. chpt. membership dir. 1986-89, so. region membership dir. 1989-92, secondary program dept. dir. 1991-92), SC Bus. Edn. Assn. (jour. editor 1985-86, v.p. for membership 1986-87, treas. 1987-88, pres. elect 1988-89, pres. 1989-90), Am. Vocat. Assn., SC Vocat. Assn. (parliamentarian 1985-86, v.p. 1989-90, treas. 1991-92), SC Assn. of Title I Admin. (pres. elect 2003-2004, pres. 2004-2005), Internat. Soc. Bus. Educators, Lake City C. of C., Kappa Kappa Iota, Delta Kappa Gamma. Democrat. Baptist. Avocations: cross stitch, reading, softball. Office: Florence County Sch Dist 3 PO Box 1389 Lake City SC 29560-1389 Office Phone: 843-374-8652 ext. 1115. Business E-Mail: lhawkins@florence3.k12.sc.us.

HAWKINS, LORETTA ANN, retired secondary school educator, playwright; b. Winston-Salem, N.C., Jan. 1, 1942; d. John Henry and Laurine (Hines) Sanders; m. Joseph Hawkins, Dec. 10, 1962; children: Robin, Dionne, Sherri. BS in Edn., Chgo. State U., 1965; MA in Lit., Governor's State U., 1977, MA in African Cultures, 1978; MLA in Humanities, U. Chgo., 1998. Cert. tchr., Ill. Tchr. Chgo. Bd. Edn., 1968—2002; lectr. Chgo. City Colls., 1987-89; tchr. English, Gage Park H.S., Chgo., 1988—2002; ret., 2002. Mem. steering com. Mellon Seminar U. Chgo., 1990; tchr. adv. com. Goodman Theatre, Chgo., 1992, mem. cmty. adv. coun., 1996—; spkr. in field; creator 5-4-3-2-1- Essay Writing Method, 1997. Author: (reading workbook) Contemporary Black Heroes, 1992, (plays) Of Quiet Birds, 1993 (James H. Wilson award 1993), Above the Line, 1994, Good Morning, Miss Alex, (work books) 5-4-3-2-1 ESSAY!: A Holistic Writing Program Book 1 & 2; contbr. poetry, articles to profl. publs.; featured WYCC-TV-Educate, 1996. Mem. Chgo. Tchg. Connections Network, DePaul U. Ctr. Urban Edn., 2001; mem. Chgo. Pub. Schs. Mentoring and Induction of New Tchrs. Program. Fellow Santa Fe Pacific Found., 1988, Lloyd Fry Found. 1989, Andrew W. Mellon Found., 1991, Ill. Arts Coun., 1993; grantee Cmty. Arts Assistance Program Award, Chgo. Dept. Cultural Affairs; recipient Feminist Writers 3d pl. award NOW, 1993, Zora Neale Hurston-Bessie Head Fiction award Black Writer's Conf., 1993, Suave Tchr. Plus award, 2002; numerous others. Mem. AAUW, Nat. Coun. Tchrs. English (spkr. conv.), Am. Fedn. Tchrs., Women's Theatre Alliance, Dramatists Guild of Am., Internat. Women's Writing Guild. Avocations: films, coins, reading, walking. Home: 8928 S Oglesby Ave Chicago IL 60617-3047

HAWKINS, MARY ELIZABETH, obstetrician, gynecologist, educator; b. New Orleans, July 6, 1936; d. Ralph Acey and Pauline Blane Hawkins. BS, Miss. U. for Women, Columbus, 1957; MD, La. State U. Sch. Medicine, New Orleans, 1963. Lic. La. and Miss., 1969. Pvt. practice ob/gyn, Jackson, Miss.,

1967—99; asst. prof. U. Miss. Med. Sch., Jackson, 2001—. Chief staff Women's Hosp., Flowood, Miss., 1983—84. Fellow: Am. Coll. Ob/Gyn. Presbyterian. Avocations: coin collecting/numismatics, genealogy, horse farming. Home: 255 Lake Tr Flora MS 39071 Office: Univ Miss Med Ctr Ob/Gyn Dept 2500 N State St Jackson MS 39216 Personal E-mail: docmeh@aol.com.

HAWKINS, MARY ELLEN HIGGINS (MARY ELLEN HIGGINS), retired state legislator, public relations executive; b. Birmingham, Ala., Apr. 18, 1923; m. James H. Hawkins, Feb. 13, 1960 (div. 1971); children: Andrew Higgins, Elizabeth, Peter Hixon. Student, U. Ala., Tuscaloosa, 1945-47. Congl. aide to several mems. U.S. Ho. Reps., 1950-60; instr. art Sumter County Schs., Americus, Ga., 1971-72; staff writer Naples (Fla.) Daily News, 1972-74; prin. Daniels-Hawkins, Naples, 1982-84; mem. Fla. Ho. Reps., Tallahassee, 1974-94; vice chmn. BancFlorida Fin. Corp., Naples, 1979-91, pres., CEO, 1991-92, chmn., 1991-93, also. bd. dirs. Columnist, contbr. articles to local newspapers. V.p. Naples Philharm., 1984-91; life mem., vice chair Big Cypress Basin bd. South Fla. Water Mgmt. Dist., 1999-05; mem. adv. com. Lower Gulf Coast Water Supply Plan, 1999; trustee CREW Land and Water Trust, 2002-, treas., 2004-; vice chair Fla. Children's Campaign, 1997—; various offices Rep. Party Ga., Americus, 1965-71; literacy vol., 2005—. Mem. Zonta Internat. Avocation: painting. Office Phone: 239-262-4932. Personal E-mail: mhawk26249@aol.com.

HAWKINS, NAOMI RUTH, nurse; b. Ft. Smith, Ark., Mar. 8, 1947; d. William Oscar and Sallie Inez (Reynolds) H. BS in Nursing, U. Cen. Ark., 1974. RN, Ark.; cert. pediatric nurse practitioner, Ark.; cert. family nurse practitioner. Nurse practitioner Booneville (Ark.) Med. Clinic, 1975-78; lic. practical nurse Greenhurst Nursing Home, Charleston, Ark., 1967-73, RN, 1973-75; pediatric nurse practitioner Ark. Dept. Health, Paris, Ark., 1978—. Fellow Nat. Assn. Pediatric Nurse Assocs. and Practitioners; mem. Ark. Assn. Pediatric Nurse Assocs. and Practitioners, Am. Assn. Christian Counselors, Pub. Health Nurses Assn. Ark., Ark. State Employees Assn. Democrat. Baptist. Avocations: photography, counted cross stitch. Home: 11111 Hwy 41 Charleston AR 72933-9418 Office: 102 E Academy St Paris AR 72855-4432

HAWKINS, PAMELA KAY, entertainer, writer; m. Edward Campbell Hawkins, Feb. 9, 1990. BA in English, Hist., Journalism, U. Okla., Norman, 1982, MA in Journalism, 1984. Freelance entertainer, Oklahoma City and Tulsa, 1984—; pres. Rocking Chair Enterprises, LLC, Tulsa, Okla., 1999—. Pres. Tuesday Writers, Tulsa, 1993—95. Composer (lyricist): (children's cd) Rockin' the Day Away; author: Two Minute Bible Stories. Bible tchr. St. Luke's Meth. Ch., Oklahoma City, Okla., 1985—90. Mem.: ASCAP, Soc. Childrens Book Writers and Illustrators. R-Consevative. Avocations: watercolor painting, reading, piano, bridge. Office: Rocking Chair Enterprises LLC 4328 South Dogwood Ave Broken Arrow OK 74011-1524 Office Phone: 918-455-3744. Office Fax: 918-451-7491. Business E-Mail: phaw842897@aol.com.

HAWKINS, PEGGY ANNE, veterinarian; b. Omaha, Dec. 9, 1956; d. Robert Leon and Karen Lynne Hawkins. BS, Iowa State U., 1982, DVM, 1991, MS, 1992. Vol., h.s. tchr. U.S. Peace Corps, Lesotho, 1982-85; lab. technician Iowa State U., Ames, 1986-87, tchg. asst., 1990-92; veterinarian, swine practitioner White Oak Mills/ProGenetics, Elizabethtown, Pa., 1992-94; tech. svcs. veterinarian Pfizer, Animal Health Group, Lee's Summit, Mo., 1994-96, global product devel. vet. advisor N.Y.C., 1996—2001, vet. med. mgr., 2001—02; health svcs. vet. Monsanto Choice Genetics, St. Louis, 2002—06; dir. vet. svcs. Minitube Am., Verona, Wis., 2006—. Vol. tchr. Jr. Achievement, N.Y.C. Pub. Schs., 1999. Recipient Swine Proficiency award Purina Mills, Inc., 1991; Iowa State U. scholar. Mem.: AVMA, Iowa Vet. Med. Assn., Am. Assn. Swine Veterinarians (Found. fellow 1998—), Iowa State U. Alumni (life), Toastmasters Internat. Avocations: travel, photography, hiking. Office: Minitube Internat Ctr for Biotechnology PO Box 930187 Verona WI 53593 Office Phone: 508-437-1902 ext. 2617.

HAWKINS, VIVIAN AGATHA, mental health nurse, educator; b. N.Y.C., NY, Dec. 18, 1917; d. Joseph Emanuel Williams and Naomi Adorcus Wallace; m. William Hawkins, Dec. 13, 1949 (dec.). BSN, M Sociology, M Cmty. Health, L.I. U.; cert. in group therapy, Washington Sq. Inst. Psychotherapy, 1982. Lectr., clin. instr. fundamental nursing NY Tech. Coll., Bklyn., 1972—77; clin. instr. psychol./med. surg. nursing Kings County Sch. Nursing, Bklyn., 1972—77; supr. psychiatry partial hospitalization and cmty. outreach Met. Hosp. Ctr., N.Y.C., 1977—79; psychiat. nurse clinician Kings County Hosp. Ctr., Bklyn., 1979—82; clin. group psychiatrist Washington Sq. Inst. Psychotherapy and Mental Health, 1982—86; adj. prof. Manhattan C.C., N.Y.C., 1985—86; clin. nurse instr. Clara Barton H.S., Bklyn., 1988—91; supr. Sheepshead Nursing Home, Bklyn., 1992—94; PMR surveyor First Mental Health Inc., Nashville, 1994—95; adj. prof. clin. psychiatry Borough of Manhattan C.C., 1995. Author, actor: (video) Remotivation Technique, 1984. Grief counselor Project Liberty. Mem.: Am. Group Psychotherapy Assn. (cert.). Avocations: travel, reading, cooking, sports, knitting. Home: 801 E 52d St Brooklyn NY 11203-5913 E-mail: vivaga@aol.com.

HAWKINS BLANCHARD, KELLEE M., mental health services professional; b. Indpls., Nov. 26, 1965; d. William M. Hawkins, Sr. and Laura C. Hawkins; children: Imani B. Blanchard, Nia M. Blanchard. BA, Ind. U., 1987, MSW, 1992; PsyD, U. Indpls., 2003. Sch. social worker Met. Sch. Dist. Decatur Twp., Indpls., 1992—96; med. social worker Wishard Meml. Hosp., Indpls., 2001—04; supr. Midwest Psychological Ctr., Inc., Indpls., 2004—. Cons. Midwest Psychological Ctr., Inc., Indpls., 2003—; adj. prof. Marion Coll., Indpls., 2003. Cmty. Svc. grant, Pfizer Pharm., 2004. Mem.: Nat. Coalition of Negro Women, Nat. Assn. Social Worker, Am. Psychological Assn. Meth. Avocations: travel, exercise, reading, jazz, sports. Office Phone: 317-923-3930. E-mail: kmh9699@aol.com.

HAWKINSON, LORRAINE A., librarian; b. Stoughton, Wis., Oct. 2, 1922; d. Parker Lynn and Myrtle A. Lee; m. Carroll Stanley Hawkinson, July 20, 1941; children: Dennis, Donna Hawkinson Ross. Student, U. Wis., Whitewater, 1958—59, U. Wis., Madison. Writer on staff Stoughton Courier-Hub, 1954—59; asst. libr. Stoughton H.S. Libr., 1959—61; libr. technician U. Wis. Meml. Libr., Madison, 1961—88; libr., rschr. Vesterheim Geneal. Ctr. and Naeseth Libr., Madison, 1991—. Questionnaire editor U.S. Census, Madison, 1990; freelance writer, photographer, 1955—. Columnist: Stoughton Courier-Hub, 1955—60. Mem. Town of Dunn Planning Commn., Dane County, Wis., Sr. Ctr. Commn. on Aging, Stoughton, 1995—. Recipient Gov.'s Spl. award for 27 yrs. svc. to state of Wis., Notable Norwegian award, Norwegian Am. Fest, 1998, Local History award of merit, Wis. State Hist. Soc., 1997, Winning Entry award, Wis. Sesquicentennial Com., 1998, Com. Appreciation award, Stoughton City, 1996, Stewardship award, Town of Dunn. Mem.: Norwegian-Am. Hist. Assn., Wis Regional Writers Assn. (historian 1980—, Svc. award 1993). Democrat. Lutheran. Office: Vesterheim Geneal Ctr and Naeseth Libr 415 W Main St Madison WI 53703

HAWKINS-SNEED, JANET LYNN, school psychologist, human resources administrator, small business owner; b. July 3, 1956; d. James Crawford Jr. and Oberia (Aiken) H. BS in Spanish and Psychology, Furman U., 1978; MEd in Secondary Edn., Converse Coll., 1981; EdS in Counseling and Sch. Psychology, Wichita State U., 1986. Tchr. Spartanburg Sch. Dist. 5, Duncan, S.C., 1979-80, Wichita (Kans.) Sch. Dist., 1982-85; psychology intern Mulvane (Kans.) Sch. Dist., 1985-86; sch. psychologist Sch. Dist. Greenville (S.C.) County, 1986-93; with Dyslexia Resource Ctr., Greenville; with benefits dept. Suitt Constrn. Co., Greenville, 1997—98, human resources coord., 1998—99; owner, CEO Mystic Gifts, Williamston, SC. Presenter at profl. confs. Chancellor, Upstate S.C. Ch. of Wicca. Mem. NOW, Coun. Exceptional Children, Nat. Assn. Sch. Psychologists, Sierra Club, Nat. Wildlife Fedn., Phi Kappa Phi. Avocations: music, art, nature, equestrian, breeder of beagles. Office: PO Box 455 Williamston SC 29697

HAWLEY, ANNE, museum director; b. Iowa City, Nov. 3, 1943; d. Marshall Newton and Leone Ardith (Wilson) Hawley; m. Bruce Ivor McPherson, Sept. 4, 1977; 1 child, Katherine Black. BA, U. Iowa, 1966; MA, George Washington U., 1969; LHD (hon.), Lesley Coll, 1987; LHD (hon.), Williams Coll., 1989, Babson Coll., 1990, sr. exec. prog., Kennedy Sch. Govt, Harvard Univ., Intern in edn., Washington, 1967-69; research assoc. Nat. Urban League, Washington, 1969-71, Ford Found. Study Leadership in Pub. Edn., Washington, 1971-73; exec. dir. Cultural Edn. Collaborative, Boston, 1974-77, Mass. Council Arts/Humanities, Boston, 1977-89; mus. dir. Isabella Stewart Gardner Mus., Boston, 1989—; resident Nat. Hist. Soc. 1993—; adv. com. Nat. Trust of Historic Preservation, 1993—; vis. com. Fitchburg Art Mus., 1992-94. Bd. dirs. New Eng. Found. for Arts, 1978-89, Nat. Assembly/State Arts Agencies, Washington, 1981-83, Greater Boston Arts Fund, 1984-89, Boston Archtl. Found., 1986-89, Nat. Art Stabilization Fund, 1990-95, Boston Fenway Program, 1990-93. Trustee Inst. Contemporary Art, Boston, 1990—, Old Sturbridge Village, 1991-94; vis. comm. Sch. Mus. Fine Arts, Boston, 1989—, adv. bd. Mass. Coll. Art, 1979-81. Fulbright scholar, 1986; recipient Design Travel Grant, Women's Travel Club, Boston, Mass., 1982, Polaroid travel grant, 1987, Fund for Mutual Understanding travel grant to USSR, 1988, Art award Mass. Coll. Art, 1987, Lyman Ziegler award Commonwealth of Mass., 1988. Mem. Nat. Endowment for Arts (mus. panel 1978-81, task force on trng. and devel. of artists and art edu., 1978, dance panel 1982-84, design panel 1978-81, 88—, Pres. Clinton's transition team for arts and humanities, 1992-93), Boston Soc. Architecture (hon. mem. 1989); Radcliffe Alumnae Career Svcs. (adv. comm. 1974). Office: Isabella Stewart Gardner Mus 280 The Fenway Boston MA 02115-5807*

HAWLEY, KIMRA, computer company executive; BS in Psychology, Pitts. State U. Founding prin. MarketBound, Inc., Silicon Valley, Calif.; various mktg. mgmt. positions Amdahl Corp.; imaging mktg. dir. Action Point Software (formerly Cornerstone Imaging), 1992-96, gen. mgr. software divsn., pres., CEO, chmn. bd., 2001—04; interim CEO, pres. iUniverse, Inc., 2004, bd. dirs., 2005—. Office: iUniverse Inc 2021 Pine Lake Rd Ste 100 Lincoln NE 68512 Office Phone: 402-323-7800. Office Fax: 402-323-7824.

HAWLEY, NANCI ELIZABETH, professional society administrator; b. Detroit, Mar. 18, 1942; d. Arthur Theodore and Elizabeth Agnes (Fylling) Smisek; m. Joseph Michael Hawley, Aug. 28, 1958; children: Michael, Ronald, Patrick (dec.), Julie Anne. Pres. Tempo 21 Nursing Svcs., Inc., Covina, Calif., 1973-75; v.p. Profl. Nurses Bur., Inc., L.A., 1975-83; owner, CEO Hawley & Assocs., Covina, 1983-87; exec. v.p. Glendora (Calif.) C. of C., 1984-85; dir. membership West Covina (Calif.) C. of C., 1985-87; exec. dir. San Dimas (Calif.) C. of C., 1987-88; mgr. pub. rels. Soc. for Advancement of Material and Process Engrs., Covina, 1988-92; small bus. rep. South Coast Air Quality Mgmt. Dist., 1992-94; bus. counselor Commerce and Trade Agy., Small Bus. Devel. Ctr., 1994; exec. v.p. Ontario (Calif.) C. of C., 1994-97; CEO, RMH Elec. Contractors, Colorado Springs, Colo., 1997-98; exec. v.p. Teen Resources, Inc., Colorado Springs, 1998; meetings mgr., registrar Am. Birding Assn., Colorado Springs, 1999—2006; co-owner, pres. 719 Day Spa and Salon, Colorado Springs, 2006—. V.p. Sangabriel valley chpt. Women in Mgmt. Recipient Youth Motivation award Foothill Edn. Com., Glendora, 1987. Mem. NAFE, Colo. Assn. Nonprofit Orgns., Pub. Rels. Soc. Am., Soc. Nat. Assn. Publs., Am. Soc. Assn. Execs., Nat. Assn. Membership Dirs., Profl. Communicators Assn. So. Calif., Profl. Conf. Mgrs. Assn., West End Bus. Assn. (pres. 1997-99), Western Assn. Chamber Execs. (Spl. merit award for mag. pub. 1995), Profl. Conv. Mgrs. Assn., Bus. Network Internat., eWomen Network, Kiwanis (sec. 1989-90, pres. West Covina 1990-91, Kiwanian of Yr. 1989), Rotary. Avocations: reading, walking, painting, gardening, birdwatching. Office: 719 Day Spa and Salon # 205 5969 N Academy Blvd Colorado Springs CO 80918 Office Phone: 719-535-9300. Personal E-mail: nanmick58@aol.com. E-mail: dayspa719@aol.com.

HAWLEY, SUZANNE, psychologist, researcher; MPH in Biostatistics, Loma Linda U., Calif., 1999, PhD in Clin. Psychology, 2002. Lic. psychologist Kans., 2003. Program dir. U. Kans. Sch. Medicine, Wichita, 2002—, asst. prof., 2003—, dir. Recipient Spl. Svc. award, Kans. Pub. Health Assn., 2004. Mem.: Women in Sci. and Medicine (Wichita rep. 2004—05), Kans. Psychol. Assn., Kans. Pub. Health Assn., APHA (assoc.). Office: Univ Kansas Schf Medicine 1010 N Kansas St Wichita KS 67214 Office Phone: 316-293-2627.

HAWN, GOLDIE, actress; b. Washington, Nov. 21, 1945; d. Edward Rutledge and Laura (Steinhoff) H.; m. Gus Trinkonis, May 16, 1969 (div. 1976); m. Bill Hudson, July, 1976 (div. 1979); children: Oliver, Kate; 1 child (with Kurt Russell), Wyatt Russell. Student, Am. U.; Ph.D (hon.), Loyola Marymount U., 2004. Co-head (with Kurt Russell, Kate Hudson, Oliver Hudson) Cosmic Entertainment, 2003—. Profl. dancer, 1965; profl. acting debut in Good Morning, World, 1967-68; mem. company TV series Laugh-In, 1968-70; film appearances include: The One and Only Genuine Original Family Band, 1968, Cactus Flower, 1969 (Acad. award best sup. actress, 1969, Golden Globe best sup. actress, 1969), There's A Girl In My Soup, 1970, $ (Dollars), 1971, Butterflies Are Free, 1971, The Sugarland Express, 1974, The Girl from Petrovka, 1974, Shampoo, 1975, The Duchess and the Dirtwater Fox, 1976, Travels with Anita, 1978, Foul Play, 1978, Seems Like Old Times, 1980, Lovers and Liars, 1981, Best Friends, 1982, Swingshift, 1984, Overboard, 1987, Bird on a Wire, 1989, Deceived, 1991, Housesitter, 1992, Death Becomes Her, 1992, Crisscross, 1992, The First Wives Club, 1996, Everyone Says I Love You, 1996, The Out of Towners, 1999, Town and Country, 1999, The Banger Sisters, 2002; actor, exec. prodr. (films) Private Benjamin, 1980, Protocol, 1984, Wildcats, 1986; exec. prodr.(films) My Blue Heaven, 1990, Something to Talk About, 1995; exec. prodr. (TV films) When Billie Beat Bobby, 1991, The Matthew Shepard Story, 2002; exec. prodr., dir. (TV films) Hope, 1997; host TV spl. Pure Goldie, 1970, Goldie Hawn Special, 1978, Goldie and Liza Together, 1980, Goldie and Kids: Listen to Us!, 1982; Author: (memoir) Goldie: A Lotus Grows in the Mud, 2005 (NY Times Bestseller list, 2005). Named Woman of the Year, Hasty Pudding Theatricals, 1999; recipient Women in Film Crystal award, 1997. Office: 9465 Wilshire 6th fl Beverly Hills CA 90212

HAWN, MOLLY KER, not-for-profit developer; d. Michael Ker and Irene A. Tabet; m. Matthew T. Hawn, Dec. 21, 2002; 1 child, Sterrett Katherine. BA with honors, Cambridge U., England, 1992. V.p. ops. Agency.com, London and NYC, 1998—2001; nat. programs dir. Children's Book Coun., NYC, 2001—05. Bd. dirs. Us Bd. on Books for Young People, Newark, 2004—. Mem. jr. com. Prospect Park Alliance, Bklyn.; trustee Old Stone Ho., Bklyn., 2001—03; mem. adv. bd. Soldier', Sailors', Marines' and Airmen's Club. Recipient Martha Washington medal, SAR, 2002. Mem.: DAR (regent Peter Minuit chpt. 2001—03, nat. chmn. pub. rels. com. 2004—). Democrat.

HAWTHORNE, BARBARA L., anthropologist, educator; b. Denver, Colo., Mar. 13, 1949; d. Virgil James Moore and Doris Ann Matteson-Moore; m. H. Douglas Hawthorne, Mar. 9, 1990. MA in Anthropology, Colo. State U., 1995, cert. with hons. in Women's Studies, 2005, PhD with hons. in Edn. and Anthropology, 2005. Prin., owner Moss Bay Design, Inc., Kirkland, Wash., 1985—95; tchr. Lake Wash. Vocat. Sch., Kirkland, 1990—95; prof. U. No. Colo., Greeley, Colo., 2003—. Dir. Kaplan-Hoover Archaeology Preserve, Windsor, Colo., ptnr.; prof. Front Range C.C., Ft. Collins, Colo., 2005—06, Aims C.C., Greeley, Colo., 1998—; instr. Lake Wash. VoTech, Kirkland, Wash., 1990—95. Contbr. articles to profl. jours. Named Most Influential Tchr., U. No. Colo., 2006; recipient Disting. Tchg. award, Aims C.C., 2004, 2005, 2006, Excellence in Tchg. award, 2006; Patsy Boyd scholarship, Women's Studies Colo. State U., 2004. Mem.: AAUW (assoc.), Windsor-Severance Hist. Soc. (pres.), High Plains Applied Anthropology Assn., Archaeology Conservancy (assoc.), Colo. Hist. Soc. (assoc.), Visual Anthropology Assn. (assoc.), Am. Anthropology Assn. (assoc.). Avocations: drawing, photography, swimming, nature, bicycling. Home: 401 Locust Street Windsor CO 80550 Office: University of Northern Colorado Greeley CO Business E-Mail: barbara.hawthorne@unco.edu.

HAWTHORNE, SARAH BECK, reading educator; b. Macon, Ga. d. James Edward Beck, Sr. and Margaret (Wall) Beck; m. W. Fleming Hawthorne, Jr.; 1 child, Jennifer Smith. BA, Mercer U., 1964; MEd, U. Ga., 1972, EdD, 1985. Tchr. Houston County Schs., Warner Robins, Ga., 1964—66; tchr./ reading specialist Gainesville City Schs., 1970—75; reading specialist Bibb County Schs., Macon, 1975—79, dir. regional assessment ctr., 1980—91; curriculum dir. Wilkinson County Schs., Irwinton, Ga., 1993—96; pres. AlphaSkills, Inc., Jeffersonville, Ga., 1997—. Adj. prof. Mercer U., 1980—89. Author: (tchr. tng. materials) Read with Sarah, Modeled Comprehension Strategies, I Tri Tutoring, Language, Listening and Literacy Learning: Birth to Five. Chairperson downtown devel. authority City of Jeffersonville, 2004—05; mem. Macon Jr. Womans Club; counselor Stake Relief Soc.; primary pres. LDS Ch., Macon; mem. Macon Arts Alliance. Named an Outstanding Young Women of Am., 1978; recipient Tchr. of the Yr., Runner Up, Ga. Dept. of Edn., 1975, Reading Tchr. of Yr., Ga. Coun. of Internat. Reading Assn., 1978, Annette P. Hopson Svc. award, 1983. Mem.: Internat. Reading Assn. (com. mem.), Delta Kappa Gamma (v.p.), Phi Delta Kappa (v.p.), Ga. Reading Assn. (pres. 1982—83), Chi Omega. Achievements include development of guided reading program for kindergarten through ninth grade; one-to-one tutoring program for kindgarten through fifth grade; literacy program for children from birth to five years old; Alpha Skills Family Literacy Program. Office: AlphaSkills Inc PO Box 188 Jeffersonville GA 31044 Office Phone: 478-945-3915.

HAWTHORNE, SHELBY MYRICK, reading specialist; b. Washington, June 20, 1945; d. James Franklin and Mildred Elizabeth (Myrick) Smith; m. Randall Stone Hawthorne, June 17, 1967. BA Elem. Edn., Coll. William and Mary, 1967, MA in Edn., 1975. Tchr. Norge (Va.) Elem. Sch., 1967-75, reading specialist, 1975-89, Clara Byrd Baker Elem. Sch., Williamsburg, Va., 1989—. Bd. dirs. Spiked Shoe Soc., Williamsburg, Va., 1976—; participant People to People Internat., 1993. Mem. Internat. Reading Assn., Delta Kappa Gamma (chpt. pres. 1988-90), Phi Delta Kappa (chpt. v.p. 1994-95, pres. 1995-97). Office: Clara Byrd Baker Elem Sch 3131 Ironbound Rd Williamsburg VA 23185-2320 Home: 106 Millneck Rd Williamsburg VA 23185-3418 Office Phone: 757-221-0949. Business E-Mail: hawthornes@wjcc.k12.va.us.

HAWTHORNE, TERRI, director; m. John Charles Hawthorne. BA, Met. State U., St. Paul; MS, Minn. State U., Mankato. Faculty Met. State U., Twin Cities, Minn., 1989—, dir. women svcs., 1997—2001. Film prodr. Laughlin & Hawthorne Prodns., Twin Cities, 1999—. Mem. Minn. Battered Women's Coalition. Mem.: Minn. Women's Consortium, Nat. Women Studies Assn.

HAY, ELIZABETH DEXTER, embryologist, educator; b. St. Augustine, Fla., Apr. 2, 1927; d. Isaac Morris and Lucille Elizabeth (Lynn) H. AB, Smith Coll., 1948; MA (hon.), Harvard U., 1964; ScD (hon.), Smith Coll., 1973, Trinity Coll., 1989; MD, Johns Hopkins U., 1952, LHD (hon.), 1990. Intern in internal medicine Johns Hopkins Hosp., Balt., 1952-53; instr. anatomy Johns Hopkins U. Med. Sch., Balt., 1953-56, asst. prof., 1956-57, Cornell U. Med. Sch., N.Y.C., 1957-60, Harvard Med. Sch., Boston, 1960-64, Louise Foote Pfeiffer assoc. prof., 1964-69, Louise Foote Pfeiffer prof. embryology, 1969—, chmn. dept. anatomy and cellular biology, 1975-93; prof. dept. cell biology, 1993—. Cons. cell biology sect. NIH, 1965-69; mem. adv. coun. Nat. Inst. Gen. Med. Sci., NIH, 1978-81; mem. sci. adv. bd. Whitney Marine Lab., U. Fla., 1982-86; mem. adv. coun. Johns Hopkins Sch. Medicine, 1982-96; chairperson bd. sci. counselors Nat. Inst. Dental Rsch., NIH, 1984-86; mem. bd. sci. counselors Nat. Inst. Environ. Health Sci., NIH, 1990-93. Author: Regeneration, 1966; (with J.P. Revel) Fine Structure of the Developing Avian Cornea, 1969; editor: Cell Biology of Extracellular Matrix, 1981, 2d edit., 1991; editor-in-chief Developmental Biology Jour., 1971-75; contbr. articles to profl. jours. Mem. Scientists Task Force of Congressman Barney Frank, Massach, 1982-92. Recipient Disting. Achievement award N.Y. Hosp.-Cornell Med. Ctrl. Alumni Coun., 1985, award for vision rsch. Alcon, 1988, Excellence in Sci. award Fedn. Am. Socs. Exptl. Biology. Mem. Soc. Devel. Biology (pres. 1973-74, E.G. Conklin award 1997), Am. Soc. Cell Biology (pres. 1976-77, legis. alert com. 1982—, E.B. Wilson award 1989, chair 40th anniversary 2000), Am. Assn. Anatomists (pres. 1981-82, legis. alert com. 1982—, Centennial award 1987, Henry Gray award 1992), Am. Acad. Arts and Scis., Johns Hopkins Soc. Scholars, Nat. Acad. Sci., Inst. Medicine, Internat. Soc. Devel. Biologists (exec. bd. 1977, keynote spkr. 1st Australian EMT conf. 2003), Boston Mycol. Club. Home: 14 Aberdeen Rd Weston MA 02493-1733 Office: Harvard Med Sch Dept Cell Biology 220 Longwood Ave Boston MA 02115-5701 Office Phone: 617-432-1651. Business E-Mail: ehay@hms.harvard.edu.

HAY, JANISANN, secondary school educator; b. New London, Conn., Sept. 17, 1957; d. James Cahill Hay and Ruth Ann Anderson; children: Justyne Alison Sewell, Jennifer Elaine Sewell. BA in Art History, Hood Coll., 1979. Cert. tchr. Md., 2001, highly qualifed/secondary edn. Md., 2005. Payroll/tax acct. M/A Com Atlanthus Corp., Rockville, Md., 1980—84, Planning Rsch. Corp., McLean, Va., 1985—87; antiquarian, weekend mgr. The Chase Ltd, Middleburg, Va., 1988—98; tchr. history and social studies Montgomery County Pub. Schs., Rockville, 1999—. Tchr. fellow Smithsonian Folklife and Heritage, Washington, 2002; silk rd. festival educator Smithsonian Instn., Ctr. for Folklife and Cultural Heritage, Washington, 2002, festival educator Meml. Day Vets. Reunion on the Mall, 04, festival educator First Ams. Festival, 05. V.p. Belmont Elem. Sch. PTA, Olney, Md., 1997—99; pres. Rosa Parks Mid. Sch. PTA, Olney, 2001—03; girl scout troop leader Nat. Coun. For Girl Scouts, Olney, 1993—98; citizen rep. Fairfax City Coun. for the Arts, Va., 1983—85; membership chair Olney Mill Swim Club, 2000—02. Recipient Achievement of Excellence/Certification Honors, Princeton Rev., 2005. Mem.: NEA (corr.), Md. State Tchrs. Assn. (corr.), Nat. Coun. for Social Studies (corr.), Assn. Payroll Accts. (assoc.), Corcoran Sch. Art and Mus. (assoc.), Smithsonian Inst. (assoc.). Democrat. Episcopalian. Avocations: historical research, swimming, gardening, travel. Office: White Oak Middle School 12201 New Hampshire Ave Silver Spring MD 20904 Office Phone: 301-989-5748. Personal E-mail: janisann_hay-sewell@mcpsmd.org.

HAY, NANCY ELIZABETH, social worker; b. Balt., Nov. 25, 1941; d. Joshua Wilson and Nancy Dulaney Rowe; m. Erroll Baldwin Hay, III, June 30, 1962; children: Marjorie Lott, Cornelia McKenna. BA in Psychology, Goucher Coll., Balt., 1963; MSW, U. Md., Balt., 1992. LCSW-Clin. Md., 1994. Rsch. asst. Balt. County Ct. Psychiatrist, Towson, Md., 1963—64; asst. dir. admissions Goucher Coll., Balt., 1974—78; assoc. dir. admissions St. Timothy's Sch., Stevenson, Md., 1978—81; dir. admissions Garrison Forest Sch., Owings Mills, Md., 1981—90; clin.l social worker U. Md. Cancer Ctr., Balt., 1991—95, Hospice of Balt., Towson, 1995—2001; group facilitator, clin. social worker Hope Well Cancer Support, Brooklandville, Md., 2001—. Bd. dirs. The Wellness Cmty., Balt., 1992—95; bd. trustees Goucher Coll., Balt., 1980—93; bd. govs. Ruxton-Riderwood Improvement Assn., Towson, 1977—86, pres., 1979—80; Eudowood bd. Johns Hopkins Med. Instn., Balt., 1985—; bd. dirs. Jr. League of Balt., 1971—79, Goucher Coll. Alumnae Assn., 1971—83, pres., 1975—76. Fellow, Am. Cancer Soc., 1991—92. Mem.: Assn. Oncology Social Workers (Oncology Social Worker of the Yr. 1994), Phi Kappa Phi.

HAYDEN, CARLA DIANE, library director, educator; d. Bruce Kenard and Colleen (Dowling) Hayden. BA, Roosevelt U., 1973; MA in Libr. and Info. Sci., U. Chgo., 1977, PhD, 1987; LHD (hon.), U. Balt., 2000, Morgan State U., 2001. Children's and young adult libr. Chgo. Pub. Libr., 1973-81; asst. prof. Sch. Libr. and Info. Sci. U. Pitts.; libr. svcs. coord. Mus. Sci. and Industry, Chgo., 1982-87; mem. faculty Sch. Libr. and Info. Sci., Pitts., 1987-91; 1st dep. commr., chief libr. Chgo. Pub. Libr., 1991-93; exec. dir. Enoch Pratt Free Libr., Balt., 1993—. Adj. prof. U. Md., College Park, 1995—; faculty mem. L.I. U., NY, 1994, Columbia U., NYC, 1990, 91. Contbr. numerous articles to profl. jours. Bd. dirs. Md. African Am. Mus. Corp., Balt. City Hist. Soc., Balt. Reads, Goucher Coll., Md., Greater Balt. Cultural Alliance, Franklin and Eleanor Roosevelt Inst. and Libr., NYC, Balt., Md. Pub. Broadcasting Commn., Mercy Hosp., mem. adv. bd. Women's Ctr., Nat. Aquarium, mem. nat. adv. bd., Balt., PALINET, Sinai Hosp., U. Pitts. Sch. Info. Scis. Named Libr. of Yr. Libr. Jour., 1995, One of Md.'s Top 100

Women Warfield Bus. Record 1996, Daily Record, 2003, Woman of Yr. Ms. mag., 2003; recipient Legacy of Literacy award DuBois Cir., 1996, Torch Bearer award Coalition of 100 Black Women, 1996, Andrew White medal Loyola Coll., 1997, Pres.'s medal Johns Hopkins U., 1998, Pro Urbe award Coll. Notre Dame Md., 2004, Whitney M. Young Jr. award Greater Balt. Urban League, 2004, Leader award YWCA, Balt, 2004, Medal of Distinction Barnard Coll., 2005. Mem.: Md. Libr. Assn., Pub. Libr. Assn., ALA (pres.-elect 2002—03, pres. 2003—04, immediate past pres. 2004—05, chmn. com. on accreditation and spectrum initiative). Office: Enoch Pratt Free Library 400 Cathedral St Baltimore MD 21201-4401*

HAYDEN, DOLORES, author, architecture educator; b. NYC, Mar. 15, 1945; d. J. Francis and Katharine (McCabe) H.; m. Peter Horsey Marris, May 18, 1975; 1 child, Laura Hayden Marris. BA, Mt. Holyoke Coll., 1966; diploma in English studies, Cambridge (Eng.) U., 1967; LHD (hon.), Mt. Holyoke Coll., 1987; MArch, Harvard U., 1972; MA (hon.), Yale U., 1991. Registered architect. Lectr. U. Calif., Berkeley, 1973; assoc. prof. MIT, Cambridge, 1973-79; prof. UCLA, 1979-91, Yale U., New Haven, 1991—. Author: Seven American Utopias, 1976, The Grand Domestic Revolution, 1981, Redesigning the American Dream, 1984 (notable book award ALA, 1984, award for outstanding publ. in urban planning Assn. Collegiate Schs. of Planning 1986), rev. edit., 2002, The Power of Place: Urban Landscapes as Public History, 1995 (Assn. Am. Pubs. award), Playing House, 1998, Line Dance, 2001, Building Suburbia, 2003, A Field Guide to Sprawl, 2004, American Yard, 2004; also articles (Best Feature Article award Jour. Am. Planning Assn. 1994). Guggenheim fellow, 1981, Rockefeller Humanities fellow, 1980, ACLS/Ford fellow, 1989, Nat. Endowment for the Humanities fellow; recipient Radcliffe Grad. Soc. medal, 1991, Preservation award L.A. Conservancy, 1986, Vesta award Woman's Bldg., L.A., 1985, Design Rsch. award Nat. Endowment for the Arts, Feminist scholarship in the arts, The Writer/Emily Dickinson award Poetry Soc. Am., 2001, Boyle Farber award New Eng. Poetry Club, 2004. Mem. Am. Studies Assn., Orgn. Am. Historians, Am. Planning Assn. (Diana Donald award 1987, various awards L.A. and Calif. chpts.), Urban History Assn. (dir. 1991-93), Soc. Am. City and Regional Planning History. Avocations: travel, poetry. Office: Yale Univ Sch Architecture PO Box 208242 180 York St New Haven CT 06520-8242 Office Phone: 203-432-4782. E-mail: dolores.hayden@yale.edu.

HAYDEN, I. JILL, secondary school educator; d. Vernon Thomas and Vonna May Anderson; m. Phillip G. Hayden, Aug. 8, 1980. BA in Secondary Edn. Math., N.W. Nazarene Coll., 1973. Cert. tchr. Oreg. Tchr. Mountain Home (Idaho) AFB Jr. High, Idaho, 1973—83, Crook County Middle Sch., Prineville, Oreg., 1983—98, The Dalles (Oreg.) Middle Sch., 1998—, math. dept. head, mem. various coms., 1998—; bookkeeper, corp. sec. Juniper Heating, Inc., The Dalles, 2003—. Mem. State Math Content and Assessment Panel, Oreg., 2003—. Coord. PJ's Childrens Ministries, The Dalles, 1984—. Finalist Presdl. Math. and Sci. Tchg. Excellence award, Abimai Sci. Found., 1998; named Tchr. of Yr., Mountain Home Sch. Dist., 1979. Mem.: NEA, Dalles Edn. Assn. (bldg. rep. 1998—2003), Oreg. Coun. Tchrs. Math., Oreg. Math. Tchrs., Nat. Coun. Tchrs. Math., Oreg. Edn. Assn., Fellowship Christian Magicians. Republican. Avocations: balloon creations, walking, camping. Office: The Dalles Middle Sch 1100 E 12th St The Dalles OR 97058 Office Phone: 541-296-4616. Business E-Mail: haydenj@nwasco.k12.or.us.

HAYDEN, JENNIFER B., elementary school educator; d. Ginley and Allen; m. Todd A. Hayden, Nov. 27, 1977. Cert. tchr. Ohio. Tchr. Fremont City Schs., Ohio, 2001—06. Sci. Conf. grant, Martha Holden Jennings Found. Office Phone: 419-332-5569.

HAYDEN, KAREN BOONE, history educator; d. Edward G. and Sandra S. Boone; m. Erik Hayden, Mar. 10, 2001. BA, Sarah Lawrence Coll., Bronxville, N.Y., 1997. Cert. tchr. Tex., 2002. U.S. history tchr. Stockdale Jr. High, Tex., 2002—04; U.S. history tchr., history dept. chair Dahlstrom Mid. Sch., Buda, Tex., 2004—. Mem.: Nat. Com. History Educators (assoc. spkr. nat. conf. 2006). Office: Dahlstrom Mid Sch 3700 Fm 967 Buda TX 78610 Office Phone: 512-268-8441. Personal E-mail: haydenk@hayscisd.net.

HAYDUK, SONNA A.S., secondary school educator, department chairman; b. Farmington, Me., Sept. 1, 1966; d. Robert H. Sween and Constance W. Jack. BA, U. Vt., Burlington, 1988; MS, Hofstra U., N.Y., 2000. Cert. tchr. biology, chemistry, gen. sci. N.Y. Dept. Edn. Sci./math. tchr. Cheshire Acad., Conn., 1988—90; sci. tchr. Hopkins Sch., New Haven, Conn., 1990—94, Berkeley Carroll Sch., Bklyn., Parkslope, NY, 1994—96; sci. tchr., dept. head Portledge Sch., Locust Valley, NY, 1996—. PTA com. chairperson Landing Sch., Glen Cove, NY, 2005—. Mem.: NSTA, PTA. Office: Portledge Sch 355 Duck Pond Rd Locust Valley NY 11560

HAYEK, CAROLYN JEAN, financial consultant, retired judge; b. Portland, Oreg., Aug. 17, 1948; d. Robert A. and Marion L. (DeKoning) H.; m. Steven M. Rosen, July 21, 1974; children: Jonathan David, Laura Elizabeth. BA in Psychology, Carleton Coll., 1970; JD, U. Chgo., 1973; webmaster cert., Lake Washington Tech. Coll., 2000. Bar: Wash. 1973. Assoc. Jones, Grey & Bayley, Seattle, 1973-77; pvt. practice Federal Way, Wash., 1977-82; judge Federal Way Dist. Ct., 1982-95; ret., 1995. Task force Alternatives for Wash., 1973-75; mem. Wash. State Ecol. Commn., 1975-77; columnist Tacoma News Tribune Hometown Sect., 1995-96; bus. law instr. Lake Washington Tech. Coll., 2000-01; exec. dir. People's Meml. Assn., Seattle, 2002-03; owner Hayek Svcs., 2003-. Bd. dirs. 1st Unitarian Ch., Seattle, 1986-89, vice-chair 1987-88, pres. 1988-89; ch. adminstr. Northlake Unitarian Universalist Ch.; treas. Eastshore Unitarian Universalist Ch. Women's Perspective, 2001-02; den leader Mt. Rainier coun. Boy Scouts Am., 1987-88, scouting coord., 1988-89; bd. dirs. Twin Lakes Elem. Sch. PTA; v.p. Friends of the Libr. Kirkland, 2000-05; mem. City of Kirkland Planning Commn., 2002—, chair, 2005—06. Recipient Women Helping Women award Fed. Way Soroptimist, 1991, Martin Luther King Day Humanitarian award King County, 1993, Recognition cert. City of Fed. Way Diversity Commn., 1995. Mem.: ABA, AAUW (pres. Federal Way br. 1978—80, chair state level conf. com. 1986—87, pres. Federal Way br. 1990—92, diversity com. 1991—98, state bd. 1995—97, co-pres. Kirkland-Redmond br. 1999—2000, co-v.p. Lake Washington br. 2001—03, Wash. State pres. 2004—06, dir. ESL project), Nat. Assn. Women Judges (dist. bd. dir. 1984—86, chmn. rules com. 1988—89, chmn. bylaws com. 1990—91, nat. bd. dir.), Elected Wash. Women (dir. 1983—87), King County Dist. Ct. Judges Assn. (treas. exec. com. 1990—93, chair and rules com. 1990—94), Wash. State Bar Assn., Wash. Women Lawyers, Plz. on State Owners Assn. (pres. 1997—99, bd. dir. 1997—2000, sec. 1999—2000, webmaster 2000—), Eliot Inst. (bd. dir. 1996—2000, vice chair 1998—99, bd. chair 1999—2000, webmaster 1999—2002), Unitarian Universalist Women's Fedn. (chair bylaws com. 1996), Greater Federal Way C. of C. (dir. 1978—82, sec. 1980—81, v.p. 1981—82), Fed. Way Women's Network (bd. dir. 1984—91, pres. 1985, program co-chair 1989—91, bd. dir. 1995—97, co-editor newsletter), Wash. Women United (bd. dir. 1995—97), Rotary (Sunrise Fed. Way chpt.) (membership com. 1991—96, youth exch. officer 1994—95, comty. svc. chair, bd. dir.). Office Phone: 425-822-2794. E-mail: chayek@verizon.net.

HAYEK, SALMA, actress; b. Coatzacoalcos, Veracruz, Mexico, Sept. 2, 1968; d. Sami Hayek Domingues and Diana H. Television work includes: Un Nuevo amanecer, 1988, Teresa, 1989, The Sinbad Show, 1993, Roadracers, 1994, El Vuelo del aguila, 1996, The Hunchback, 1997, In the Time of the Butterflies (also exec. prod.), 2001; Television appearances: Dream On, 1992, Nurses, 1992, Action, 1999. Films include Mi Vida Loca, 1993, Four Rooms, 1995, Desperado, 1995, Fair Game, 1995, From Dusk Til Dawn, 1996, Fled, 1996, Fools Rush In, 1997, Follow Me Home, 1997, Breaking Up, 1997, Sister Diastole, 1997, The Velocity of Gary, 1998, The Faculty, 1998, 54, 1998, Dogma, 1999, Wild Wild West, 1999, No One Writes to the Colonel, 1999, Shiny New Enemies, 2000, Frida, 2000, Timecode, 2000, Chain of Fools, 2000, Living It Up, 2000, Traffic, 2000, Hotel, 2001, Frida (also prod.), 2002, Spy Kids 3-D: Game Over, 2003, Once Upon a Time in Mexico, 2003, After the Sunset, 2004, Sian Ka'an, 2005, Ask the Dust, 2006; dir, exec. prod.: The Maldonado Miracle, 2003. Named one of 25 Most Influential Hispanics, Time Mag., 2005. Office: Creative Artists Agy 9830 Wilshire Blvd Beverly Hills CA 90212*

HAYES, ALICE BOURKE, academic administrator, biologist, researcher; b. Chgo., Dec. 31, 1937; d. William Joseph and Mary Alice (Cawley) Bourke; m. John J. Hayes, Sept. 2, 1961 (dec. July 1981). BS, Mundelein Coll., Chgo., 1959; MS, U. Ill., 1960; PhD, Northwestern U., 1972; DSc (hon.), Loyola U., Chgo., 1994; HHD (hon.), Fontbonne Coll., 1994; LHD (hon.), Mount St. Mary Coll., 1998; DSc (hon.), St. Louis U., 2002; EdD (hon.), Providence Coll., 2004; DLH, LHD, U. San Francisco, 2006. Rschr. Mcpl. Tb San., Chgo., 1960-62; faculty Loyola U., Chgo., 1962-87, chmn. dept., 1968-77, dean natural scis. divsn., 1977-80, assoc. acad. v.p., 1980-87, v.p. acad. affairs, 1987-89; provost, exec. v.p. St. Louis U., 1989-95; pres. U. San Diego, 1995—2003, pres. emerita, 2003—. Mem. space biology program NASA, 1980—86; mem. adv. panel NSF, 1977—81, Parmly Hearing Inst., 1986—89; del. Bot. Del. to South Africa, 1984, to People's Republic of China, 1988, to USSR, 1990; reviewer Coll. Bd. and Mellon Found. Nat. Hispanic Scholar Awards, 1985—86; bd. dirs. Jack-in-the-Box, ConAgra; mem. Ill. Bd. Higher Edn., 2004; trustee Edn. Systems Exch. Co-author books; contbr. articles to profl. publs. Campaign mem. Mental Health Assn. Ill., Chgo., 1973-89; trustee Chgo.-No. Ill. divsn. Nat. Multiple Sclerosis Soc., 1981-89, bd. dirs., 1980-88, com. chmn., sec. to bd. dirs., vice chmn. bd. dirs.; trustee Regina Dominican Acad., 1984-89, Civitas Dei Found., 1987-92, Rockhurst Coll., Loyola U., Chgo., San Diego Found.; trustee St. Ignatius Coll. Prep. Sch., bd. dirs., 1984-89, sec., vice chmn.; bd. dirs. Urban League Met. St. Louis, St. Louis Sci. Ctr., 1991-95, Cath. Charities St. Louis, 1992-95, St. Louis County Hist. Soc., 1992-95, Cath. Charities San Diego, 1996—2003, San Diego Hist. Soc., 1996—2003; bd. dirs., trustee Old Globe Theater, 1996—2003. Named to Tchrs.' Hall of Fame Blue Key Soc.; fellow in botany U. Ill., 1959-60; fellow in botany NSF, 1969-71; grantee Am. Orchid Soc., 1967; grantee HEW, 1969, 76; grantee NSF, 1975; grantee NASA, 1980-85. Mem. AAAS, AAUP (corp. rep. 1980-85), Am. Assn. for Higher Edn., Am. Assn. Univ. Adminstrs. (mem. program com. nat. meeting 1988), Am. Soc. Gravitational and Space Biology, Assn. Midwest Coll. Biology Tchrs., Am. Soc. Plant Physiology, Bot. Soc. Am., Am. Inst. Biol. Scis. Acad., Chgo. Network, Soc. Ill. Microbiologists (edn. com. 1969-70, Pasteur award com. 1975, pub. rels. com. 1974, chair speakers' bur. 1974-79), Chgo. Assn. Tech. Socs. (acad. liaison 1982-85, awards com. 1984-89), Am. Coun. on Edn. (corp. rep. higher edn. panel), Ctr. Rsch. Librs. (nominating com. 1986), N.C. Assn. Colls. and Schs. (cons., evaluator Commn. on Higher Edn. 1984-95, commr.-at-large 1988-94), Mo. Women's Forum Club, North Ctrl. Assn. Schs. and Colls., Western Assn. Schs. and Colls., N.W. Assn. Schs. and Colls., Sigma Xi, Delta Sigma Rho, Sigma Delta Epsilon, Phi Beta Kappa, Alpha Sigma Nu. Roman Catholic. Home: 6801 N Loron Chicago IL 60646 Personal E-mail: alicehayes@sbcglobal.net.

HAYES, ALLENE VALERIE FARMER, government executive; b. Sept. 23, 1958; d. Thomas Jonathan and Allena V. (Joyner) Farmer; m. Thomas Gary Hayes; children: Tommia Chanel, Alle Victoria. Student, Richmond Coll., London, 1980; BA, Clark U., 1980; cert., U. Oxford, England, 1981; MLS, U. Md., 1986. Libr. asst. NUS Corp., Gaithersburg, Md., 1981—82; cataloger Libr. of Congress, Washington, 1982—84, copyright specialist, 1984—85; congl. fellow Ho. of Reps. Com. on D.C., Washington, 1985—. English tutor, writer Natural Motion, Washington, 1983-84; intern, archivist Howard U., Washington, 1985; intern Libr. Congress Intern Program, 1991-92. Compiler: Single Mother's Resource Directory, 1984; compiler, editor: Policy Research, 1985; author booklet: D.C. Statehood Issue, 1986. Mem. U. Md. Coll. Park Black Women's Coun., 1984; vol. Congl. Black Caucus Found., Washington, 1985 (fellow 1985). Recipient Fgn. Study award Am. Inst. for Fgn. Study, 1981. Mem. NAACP, ALA, Libr. of Congress Profls. Assn., Daniel A.P. Murray Afro-Am. Culture Assn. of Libr. of Congress (mem. exec. bd., newsletter editor, pres. 1994—), D.A.P. Murray African Am. Culture Assn. (pres. 1994-96), Delta Sigma Theta (tutor 1986). Avocations: travel, writing, dance, drama, tennis. Home: 2405 17th St NE Washington DC 20018-2051 Office: Libr of Congress 101 Independence Ave SE Washington DC 20540-0002

HAYES, ANN CARSON, computer company executive; b. Hamlin, Tex., Apr. 25, 1941; d. Fred Elbert and Nona Faye (Riddle) Carson; m. James Russell Brown, May 7, 1959 (div. July 1973); children: James Allen Brown, Daniel Russell Brown, Robert Anthony Brown, Debra Faye Brown; m. Robert Lee Hayes, Nov. 15, 1975. AAS, Howard Coll., Tex., 1972; student, Regents Coll., N.Y.C., 1986. Lic. ins. agt. Nat. Assn. Self-Employed. Freelance artist, Big Spring, Tex., 1956-76; real estate agt. Century 21, Littleton, Colo., 1976-78, Huntsville, Ala., 1978-79; art dir. Hayes and Co., Splendora, Tex., 1979—; CEO Hayes Enterprises, New Caney, Tex., 2000—. Executor Hayes Tax Svc., New Caney, 1992. Mem.: NAFE. Democrat. Episcopalian. Avocations: sculpting, glass etching. Home and Office: 20152 Split Oak Dr New Caney TX 77357-3565 Personal E-mail: achayes1@yahoo.com.

HAYES, AUDIMARIE, medical/surgical and critical care nurse; b. Ft. Worth, Sept. 12, 1956; d. Audy Lee and Marie Jo (Raifsnider) Knox; m. Ronnie Ray Hayes, Feb. 19, 1982 (div.); children: Rashonda Marie, Cori Ray. AS, Cooke County Coll., Gainesville, Tex., 1978; BSN, U. Tex., Arlington, 1981. ACLS. LVN instr. Cooke County Coll.; nurse Cooke County Ambulance Svc., Gainesville, N. Tex. Med. Ctr., 1978—. Mem. AACCN. Home: 1325 Muenster Rd Forestburg TX 76239-9768

HAYES, BRENDA SUE NELSON, artist; b. Rockford, Ill., May 26, 1941; d. Reuben Hartvick and Mary Jane (Pinkston) Nelson; m. John Michael Hayes, Jan. 26, 1964; 1 child, Amy Anne. BFA in Graphic Design, U. Ill., 1964. Exec. officer JMH Corp., Indpls., 1971—. Exhibited at Art Source, Bethesda, Md., The Corp. Collection, Kansas City, Mo., The Hang Up Gallery, Sarasota, Fla., Dean Johnson Gallery, Indpls., Ind., Art Phase I, Chgo., SJ Doyle-Designer Builder, Indpls., JMH Gallery, Indpls., Swan Coach House Gallery, Atlanta, Arnot Art Mus., Elmira, N.Y., Indpls. Mus. Art, Pindar Gallery, Soho, N.Y., Franklin (Ind.) Coll.; represented in permanent collections at Anson Group, Indpls., Holy Family Hosp., Des Plaines, Ill., Lilly Endowment, Dow Venture Ctr. Internat. Hdqs., Wishard Hosp., Indpls., Deloitte Touche, Inc., USA Group, Indpls., Am. Trans. Airlines, Indpls., Indpls. Art Ctr., IBM, AT&T, U.S. Sprint, NWS Corp., Chgo., Meth. Hosp., Indpls., Eli Lilly Corp., Indpls. and Chgo., Hewlett-Packard, Trammell Crow, Dow Consumer Products, Melvin Simon & Assocs., Dow Elanco Corp. Hdqs., Ikon Inc., Support Net, Bank One, All Steel, L.A., Verizon/Cellular One, NBD Bank Processing Ctr. Lobby, Indpls., Mckinney Processing Bank Ctr., Indpls., Cellular One Regional Offices, Nat. City Plaza, Riley Children's Hosp., Indpls., Anson Group, Indpls., 250 pvt. collections. Bd. dirs. Contemporary Art Soc. for Indpls. Mus. Art, 1993—, sec., 1992-94; charter mem. Nat. Mus. Women in Arts, Habitat for Humanity, Wall of Tolerance, Ctr. for Tolerance, Birmingham, Ala. Lydia Bates scholar U. Ill., 1961-63, Ill. Found. of Study scholar, 1963-64, resident schoar, 1960-64; recipient Panhellenic award for Study U. Ill., 1963-64, Gallery Exhbn. awards. Mem.: Nat. Women's History Mus. (charter mem. 2006), Nat. Mus. Women in the Arts (charter mem.), Gamma Alpha Chi (Outstanding Woman in Journalism 1964). Home: 157 E 71st St Indianapolis IN 46220-1011 Office Phone: 317-255-3400.

HAYES, CAMELA PAIGE, psychologist; b. Eugene, Oreg., Jan. 4, 1970; d. Craig Powell Hayes and Sandra Lee Wenzl. BA, We. Wash. U., Bellingham, Wash., 1994; MA, Ea. Ill. U., Aratleston, Ill., 1997; student, Antioch U., Seattle, Wash. Cert. sch. psychologist Wash. Test standardizer Riverside Pub., Chgo., 1996; intern sch. psychology Berwyn (Ill.) Sch. Dist., 1996—97; sch. psychologist Maywood (Ill.) Sch. Dist., 1997—98, Auburn (Wash.) Sch. Dist., 1998—. Office: Sch Psychologist 1813 19th Ave Apt 202 Seattle WA 98122

HAYES, CANDACE ASHMORE, elementary school educator; d. James and Ruth Ashmore; m. Wayne Lee Hayes; children: Phillip, Alyson. BS in Edn., Winthrop U., Rock Hill, SC, 1973; M, Gardner Webb U., Boiling Green, SC, 1988. Tchr. grades 1-8 Gaston County Schs., Gastonia, NC, 1973—, gifted edn. program specialist, 1998—2002. Presenter in field, 1997—. Mem.: NC Tchrs. Math. Baptist. Avocations: music, travel.

HAYES, CYNTHIA ANN (C.A. HAYES), writer; b. L.A., Sept. 11, 1954; d. Lafayette and Verna (O'Gee) H.; 1 child, LaLaunie Charisse. Student, U. Calif., L.A., 1972-75. Author: The My Family Collection, 1985, That Lovely Piece of Art, 1997, The Death of Lillie Maroe, 1998, The Night Aunt Ives Went to Sleep, 1999. Donor The Brotherhood Crusade, The Donor's Welfare Plan. Mem. U. Calif. L.A., The Duvall Found. Democrat. Baptist. Avocations: sewing, creating graphic designs, sailing, bicycling, attending concerts and theater.

HAYES, CYNTHIA ANN, music educator; d. Robert and Nancy Waltman; m. Brent Hayes, Dec. 20, 1997; children: Sky, Alex. BA in Music, Calif. State U. Stanislaus, Turlock, 1994. Cert. music tchr. Calif., NC. Band tchr. Rivera Mid. Sch., Merced, Calif., 1996—2003; music tchr. Broadway Elem. Sch., NC, 2003—. Children's ch. tchr. Glad Tidings Ch., Dunn, NC, 2004—06. Mem.: Profl. Educators NC.

HAYES, CYNTHIA LANE, secondary school educator; b. West Plains, Mo., Dec. 7, 1956; d. Rillis Vergene and Donna Lane Hayes. BAE, S.W. Mo. State U., Springfield, 1979; MEd, U. Mo., Kansas City, 1985. Tchr. Turner HS, Kansas City, 1980—99, Bonner Springs HS, 1999—. Character edn. instr. St. Mary's Coll., Overland Park, Kans., 2003—. Active Jr. League of Kansas City, 1995—98. Grantee Woodrow Wilson grant, Princeton, 1995. Mem.: NSTA, NEA. Avocations: travel, teaching dance, reading.

HAYES, DANIELLE DAWN, counselor; d. Edwin and Sheila Hayes, Darlene Hayes (Stepmother); m. Christopher Allen Slee, Nov. 21, 1992 (div. Feb. 26, 2003); children: Cassandra Slee, Katrina Slee, Sydney Slee, Christian Slee. BS in Psychology, Ohio State U., Columbus, 2004, MA in Phys. Activity and Edn. Svcs. and Cmty. Counseling, 2006. Lic. profl. counselor Ohio, 2006. Intern counselor Maryhaven, Columbus, Ohio, 2005, Harding Adult Partial Hospitalization Program Ohio State u., 2005—06. Contbr. articles to profl. jours. Day sch. com. mem. and chair Trinity Luth. Ch., Marysville, Ohio, 1996—2000. Named Outstanding MA Cmty. Counseling Student, Ohio State U. Cmty. Counseling Program, 2006. Mem.: OCA, ACA.

HAYES, DEBORAH, musicology educator, college administrator; b. Miami, Fla., Dec. 13, 1939; d. Lauffer Truby Hayes and Margaret Hayes Parsons. AB, Oberlin Coll., 1960; AM, Stanford U., 1961, PhD, 1968. From instr. to prof. U. Colo., Boulder, 1968—95, prof. musicology, 1995—2000, prof. emeritus, 2000—. Author: Peggy Glanville-Hicks: A Bio-Bibliography, 1990, Peter Sculthorpe: A Bio-Bibliography, 1993; contbr. articles to profl. publs.; feature editor Internat. Alliance for Women in Music, 1993—; contbr. articles to profl. jours. Mem. Am. Musicological Soc. Home: 3290 Darley Ave Boulder CO 80305-6412

HAYES, JANET GRAY, retired management consultant, retired mayor; b. Rushville, Ind., July 12, 1926; d. John Paul and Lucile (Gray) Frazee; m. Kenneth Hayes, Mar. 20, 1950; children: Lindy, John, Katherine, Megan. AB, Ind. U., 1948; MA magna cum laude, U. Chgo., 1950. Psychiat. caseworker Jewish Family Svc. Agy., Chgo., 1950-52; vol. Denver Crippled Children's Service, 1954-55, Adult and Child Guidance Clinic, San Jose, Calif., 1958-59; mem. San Jose City Coun., 1971-75, vice mayor, 1973-75; mayor San Jose, 1975—82; co-chmn. com. urban econs. U.S. Conf. Mayors, 1976-78, co-chmn. task force on aging, mem. sci. and teck task force, 1976-80, bd. trustees, 1977-82; bd. dirs. League Calif. Cities, 1976-82, mem. property tax reform task force, 1976-82; chmn. State of Calif. Urban Devel. Adv. Com., 1976-77; mem. Calif. Commn. Fair Jud. Practices, 1976-82; client-community relations dir. Q. Tech., Santa Clara, Calif., 1983-85; bus. mgr. Kenneth Hayes MD, Inc., 1985-88; CEO Hayes House, Book Distbr., 1998—. Mem. Dem. Nat. Campaign Com., 1976; mem. Calif. Dem. Commn. Nat. Platform and Policy, 1976; del. Dem. Nat. Conv., 1980; bd. dirs. South San Francisco Bay Dischargers Authority; chmn. Santa Clara County Sanitation Dist.; mem. San Jose/Santa Clara Treatment Plant Adv. Bd.; chmn. Santa Clara Valley Employment and Tng. Bd. (CETA), League to Save Lake Tahoe adv. bd., 2000—; past mem. EPA Aircraft/Airport Noise Task Group; bd. dirs. Calif. Center Rsch. and Edn. in Govt, Alexian Bros. Hosp., 1983-92; bd. dirs., chmn. adv. council Public Tech. Inc.; mem. bd. League to Save Lake Tahoe, 1984-2000; pres. bd. trustees San Jose Mus. Art, 1987-89; founder, adv. bd. Calif. Bus. Bank, 1982-85; polit. advisor Citizens Against Airport Pollution, 2003—. AAUW Edn. Found. grantee. Mem. Assn. Bay Area Govts. (exec. com. 1971-74, regional housing subcom. 1973-74), LWC (pres. San Francisco Bay Area chpt. 1968-70, pres. local chpt. 1966-67), Mortar Bd., Phi Beta Kappa, Kappa Alpha Theta. Office Phone: 408-295-3609. Personal E-mail: janetgrayhayes@sbcglobal.net.

HAYES, JOYCE MERRIWEATHER, retired secondary school educator; b. Bay City, Tex., Aug. 29, 1943; d. Calvin and Alonia (Harris) Merriweather. BS, Wiley Coll., Tex., 1967; postgrad., U. N.Y., Stony Brook, 1968; MS in Guidence Counseling, Ea. Mich. U., 1974; postgrad., Mercy Coll., 1991-92, Ea. Mich. U., 1991-92; MEd, U. Detroit, 1992. English tchr. Terrance Manor Mid. Sch., Augusta, Ga., 1968-69, Longfellow Jr. H.S., Flint, Mich., 1969-81, No. H.S., Flint, 1981—2002, chmn. English dept., 1992—2002; edn. cons. Ventures Edn. Systems Corp., N.Y.C., 2000—02, ret., 2002. English and speech tchr. Jordan Coll., Flint, 1989-91; adult edn. tchr. Mott Adult H.S., Flint, 1978-80, on-state content stds. com.; presenter workshops in field.; motivational spkr. Composer 3 gospel songs. Vol. Second Ward City Coun., Flint, 1989, Cmty. Coun., Flint, 1992-93, Cmty. Wide Assn. Coun., Flint, 1993; intercessory prayer warrior, 1995—; area dir. Home Ministry new mem. class tchr., Grace Emmanuel Bapt. Ch., co-coord. spl. svc. for Nat. Coun. Tchr. of Eng. Conv. Detroit, 1997; prayer warrior, decision counselor, new mem. coord. Covenant Glen UMC. Named Saginaw Valley Tchr. of Yr., 2001, No. Alumni Tchr. of Yr., 2001. Mem. NEA, Nat. Coun. Tchrs. English (chair workshops 1992-93, mem. nominating com. 1994), Mich. Edn. Assn., United Tchrs. of Flint (in-svc. com., Flares-English tchrs.), Phi Delta Kappa (Xinos advisor, del. to conf. 1999, past pres., textbook selection com.). Home: 1201 Dulles Ave Apt 6105 Stafford TX 77477-6105 Personal E-mail: silverfoxhayes@aol.com.

HAYES, JUDITH, psychotherapist, educator; b. Lumberton, N.C., June 28, 1950; d. Eugene Lennon and Ada Margaret (Regan) Hayes; m. Jonathan Lafayette II Cutrell (div. Jan. 1979); 1 child, Jonathan L. Cutrell III; m. William Evans Hannon. BA, Augusta Coll., 1973; MA summa cum laude, U. N.C., Charlotte, 1996. Cert. tchr. midl sch. exceptional children. Tchr. Horry County (S.C.) Schs., 1973-77, Alexander County Schs., Taylorsville, N.C., 1978-83, Iredell County Schs., Statesville, N.C., 1983-94; with Charter Pines Behavioral Health, Charlotte, N.C., 1996-97; counselor Brawley Mid. Sch., Mooresville, N.C., 1997—. Bd. dirs. Statesville Dogwood Festival, 1981-82; ch. organist Fair Bluff (N.C.) Bapt., 1974-78. Fellow Phi Kappa Phi; mem. ACA (rep. N.C. Assn. Educators 1993-94), Mu Tau Beta chpt. Chi Sigma Iota. Avocations: reading, music, research.

HAYES, JULIA MORIARTY, retired science educator; b. Manchester, Conn., Aug. 14, 1934; d. Matthew Michael and Julia Sheridan Moriarty; m. David Vincent Hayes, June 22, 1957; children: David M., Brian J., Mary Hayes Siegrist, John Marc. BA, Albertus Magnus Coll., New Haven, Conn., 1957; diploma, Alliance Francaise, Paris, 1966; MA, Conn. Coll., New London, 1974. Treas., acct. reviewer Moriarty Brothers, Inc., Manchester, 1957—61; sci. tchr. Manchester H.S., 1974—76, E. Cath. H.S., Manchester, Conn., 1976—2001, chemistry coord., 1982—86, sci. dept. head, 1986—99. Author: French Cooking for People Who Can't, 1979; contbr. articles to newspapers. Bd. dirs., treas. Cmty. Child Guidance Clinic, Manchester, 1970.

Mem.: Conn. Sci. Suprs. Assn. (bd. dirs. 2000—02, treas. 2005—06). Avocations: gardening, travel, walking, cooking, writing. Home: PO Box 509 Coventry CT 06238 Fax: 860-742-7687. Personal E-mail: dvhayes@snet.net.

HAYES, LINDA MARIE, coach; b. Honolulu, Mar. 9, 1957; d. Jerome Donald and Rose Marie (Davalos) H. Student, Southwest Tex. State U., 1975-80, George Mason U., 1987—. Swim coach Prince William Swim Club, Dale City, Va., 1986—. Instr. ARC, Fla., Tex., Va., 1982—. With USN, 1980-86, mem. Res. Mem. Am. Swimming Coaches Assn., U.S. Swimming Assn., AAHPER and Dance, Am. Running and Fitness Assn., Va. Edn. Assn., Kappa Delta Pi, Delta Psi Kappa. Baptist. Avocations: rugby, fencing, music, poetry, reading. Office: Prince William Swim Club 14751 Danville Rd Woodbridge VA 22193-1924

HAYES, MAUREEN A., psychotherapist, consultant; b. Nashua, NH, Sept. 3, 1962; d. Donald Lee and Joan Barbara (Soucy) Hayes; m. Norman Paul Letourneaux (dec.). AS, Rivier Coll., NH, 1983, BS, 1987, MA, 1998. Bd. mem. Anthem BC/BS, Manchester, NH, 2001—02; mem. NHMHCA, 2000—. Vol. Girls Inc., Nashua, 1998, Red Cross, Nashua, NH, 2001. Mem.: Am. Acad. Bereavement (cert. bereavement counselor), Am. Mental Health Counselors. Democrat. Roman Catholic. Office: Cmty Council of Nashua NH Inc 440 Amherst St Nashua NH 03060 E-mail: hayesm@ccofnashua.org.

HAYES, MAXINE DELORES, public health service officer, physician, pediatrician; b. Nov. 29, 1946; children: Leon Williams, Kevin Williams. AB in Biology, Spelman Coll., 1969; MD, SUNY Buffalo, 1973; MPH, Harvard U., 1977; DSc (hon.), Spelman Coll., 2000. Intern pediat. Vanderbilt Hosp., Nashville, 1973-75; resident Children's Hosp., Boston, 1975-76; dir. Divsn. Parent-Child Health Svcs., Olympia, Wash., 1988-90, asst. sec., 1990-93, Cmty. and Family Health, Olympia, 1993-2000, acting health officer, 1998-2000; state health officer Wash. State Dept. Health, 2000—. Pres. Assn. Maternal and Child Health Programs, Washington, 1995-97; nat. program dir. Robert Wood Johnson Child Health Initiative, 1994-97; chair, Comprehensive Health Edn. Found. Bd. Dir., Seattle Recipient Outstanding Contbns. in Field of Pub. Health award Wash. State Pub. Health Assn., 1994, Guardian of Women's Health award Aradia Women's Health Ctr., 1996, Stockton Kimball award for medicine SUNY, Buffalo, 2000, Dr. Nathan Davis award AMA, 2002, Richard P. Nelson Lecture Series award Iowa Pub. Health Assn., 2002, Lifetime Achievement award Wash. Health Found., 2003. Fellow Am. Acad. Pediatrics; mem. APHA. Avocations: opera, art, science. Office: Wash State Dept Health PO Box 47890 Olympia WA 98504-7890 Office Phone: 360-236-4018. Business E-Mail: maxine.hayes@doh.wa.gov.

HAYES, MELANIE, secondary school educator; b. Dallas, June 30, 1957; d. James Weldon and Marshalleen Shafer Mitchell; m. Douglas Keith Hayes, Aug. 27, 1976; children: Melissa Dianne Cox, Laurel Elizabeth Warren, Ashton Leigh. BS in Edn., Tex. Tech., Lubbock, 1978. Tchr. Wellman (Tex.) Ind. Sch. Dist., 1988—89, Dawson Ind. Sch. Dist., Welch, Tex., 1989—. Office Phone: 806-489-7461.

HAYES, PAMELA M., music educator; b. Garden City, Mich., Nov. 14, 1966; m. Lennis James Hayes, Oct. 16, 1993; children: Emily C., Anne M. BME, Ea. Mich. U., Ypsilanti, 1992. Cert. Tchr. Mich., 1992. Music educator Reese Pub. Schs., Mich., 1992—94, Fenton Area Pub. Schs., Mich., 1994—. Author: (curriculum) FAPS Music Curriculum. Mem. Mich. Sch. Band and Orch. Assn., 1992—2006. Office: Fenton Area Public Schools 404 West Ellen Street Fenton MI 48430 Office Fax: 810-591-8305. E-mail: phayes@fenton.k12.mi.us.

HAYES, PATRICIA ANN, health facility administrator; b. Binghamton, NY, Jan. 14, 1944; d. Robert L. and Gertrude (Congdon) H. BA in English, Coll. of St. Rose, 1968; PhD in Philosophy, Georgetown U., 1974. Tchr. Cardinal McCloskey H.S., Albany, NY, 1966-68; tchg. asst. Georgetown U., Washington, 1968-71; instr. philosophy Coll. of St. Rose, Albany, 1973-75, instr. bus., 1981, adminstrv. intern to acad. v.p., 1973-74, dir. admissions, 1974-78, dir. adminstrn. and planning, 1978-81, v.p. adminstrn. and fin., treas., 1981-84; pres. St. Edward's U., Austin, Tex., 1984-98; exec. v.p., COO Seton Healthcare Network, Austin, 1998—2001, 2003—, interim pres., CEO, 2001—02. Bd. dirs. Tex. Assn. Pub. and Nonprofit Hosps., Topfer Family Found. Roman Catholic. Office: Seton Med Ctr 1201 W 38th St Austin TX 78705-1006 Office Phone: 512-324-1102. Business E-Mail: phayes@seton.org.

HAYES, PATRICIA THORNTON, music educator, retired director; m. Raymond S. Hayes, Jr., Nov. 28, 1959; children: Rhett S., Amber. BA, W.Va. U. Inst. Tech., 1956; MS in Edn., Old Dominion U., 1970. Dir. music Clendenin H.S. Kanawha County Schs., Charleston, W.Va., 1956—57; dir. music Shelton Pk. Elem. Sch., Va. Beach, Va., 1957—58, Suburban Pk. Elem. Sch., Norfolk, Va., 1958—60, Bayview Elem. Sch., Norfolk, 1958—60; tchr. music and spl. edn. Mt. Zion Elem. Sch., Suffolk, Va., 1970—71; dir. choral and orch. Portsmouth (Va.) City Schs., 1973—96; specialist music Portsmouth (Va.) Diagnostic Ctr., 1993—2005, ret., 2005. Dir. music programs, festivals, theater prodns. various schs., Va. Composer: (songs) We're Supporting You All The Way Student - Farrah Fale, 1991; dir.: (chorus) Mayor's Breakfast, Seawall Festival, Manor H.S. Award Banquet, NAVSEA and CG. Recipient Proclamation award, Fine Arts Commn., Chesapeake, Va., 1981—89, Oustanding Music Works awards, Portsmouth (Va.) City Sch. Bd., 1992.

HAYES, PAULA FREDA, federal agency administrator; b. Apr. 5, 1950; d. Ario Louis and Elena Marguerite (Gentile) Freda; m. Robert J. Hayes, Sept. 6, 1975; children: Brendan Michael, Lauren Ann. BA magna cum laude, R.I. Coll., 1972; MPA, Syracuse U., 1973. Criminal justice planner City of Syracuse, NY, 1973—75, asst. coord. crime control, 1975—77; specialist supervisory grants Nat. Endowment Arts, Washington, 1977—78; analyst criminal justice program Dept. Justice, Washington, 1978—79, mgr. arson discretionary grant program, 1979—80, sr. analyst mgmt., 1980—81; dir. legis. and analysis divsn. Office of Insp. Gen., Dept. Agr., Washington, 1981—89, asst. insp. gen. for policy devel. and resources mgmt., 1989—2003, asst. insp. gen. for planning and spl. projects, 2003—04, asst. insp. gen. for mgmt. USAID, 2004—05, acting dep. insp. for gen. USAID, 2005—06, asst. insp. mgmt., 2006; asst. dean, dep. dir. IG Inst. George Mason U., 2006—. Roman Catholic. Office: IG Inst George Mason Univ Washington DC 20253-2004 Office Phone: 703-248-4519. Business E-Mail: phayes@iginstitute.gov.

HAYES, REBECCA EVERETT, gifted and talented educator; d. Charles and Faye Everett; m. Keith Hayes, June 13, 1992; 1 child, Katherine Fei. BS, Miss. U. for Women, Columbus, 1989; MS, Miss. State U., Starkville, 1993. Cert. tchr. Miss., Nat. Bd. cert. tchr. 4th grade reading/lang. tchr. Wilson Elem./Noxubee County Schs., Brooksville, Miss., 1989—91; 6th grade self-contained tchr. Annunciation Cath. Sch., Columbus, Miss., 1991—94, 2nd-6th grade gifted edn. tchr., coord., 1994—99; 8th grade gifted edn. tchr. Lee Mid. Sch., Columbus, 1999—2000; 7th and 8th grade gifted edn. tchr. New Hope Mid. Sch., Columbus, 2000—03; 2nd and 3d grade gifted tchr. New Hope Elem. Sch., 2003—. Presenter in field. Mem.: ASCD, Miss. Assn. for Gifted Children, Miss. Profl. Educators (bldg. rep. 1989—), Kappa Kappa Iota (empathy reporter 2003—). Baptist. Avocations: reading, journaling. Office: New Hope Elementary School 199 Enlow Dr Columbus MS 39702

HAYES GLADSON, LAURA JOANNA, psychologist; b. Winnebeau, N.C., Mar. 26, 1943; d. Victor Wilson and Pansy Lorraine (Springsteen) Hayes; m. Jerry Allen Gladson, June 20, 1965 (div. Mar. 1992, remarried Dec. 27, 1997); children: Joanna Kaye, Paula Rae. BA, So. Coll., 1965; MEd, U. Tenn., Chattanooga, 1977; EdD, Vanderbilt U., 1985. Lic. psychologist, Ga. Psychol. intern Lakeshore Mental Health Inst., Knoxville, Tenn., 1985-86; counselor, psychologist Tara Heights Enterprises, Atlanta, 1986—; psychologist, owner Assoc. Psychol. Svcs., Inc., Ringgold, Ga., 1990—. Bd. dirs. Theraplay, Inc., Ringgold; founder Abused Children in Therapy, Inc., 1997. Mem. APA, Christian Assn. for Psychol. Studies, Ga. Psychol. Assn. Democrat. Home: 327 Homestead Cir Kennesaw GA 30144-1335 Office: Assoc Psychol Svcs Box 700 479 Cotter St Ringgold GA 30736-5149 Office Phone: 706-937-5180.

HAYGOOD, ALMA JEAN, elementary school educator; d. John Thomas and Alma Perry Haygood. BS, Ala. A&M U., 1978; MA, George Mason U., 2001. Kindergarten tchr. Talladega (Ala.) County Pub. Schs., 1978—80; adult edn. tchr. Ft. Carson (Colo.) Mil. Base, 1980—82; day care ctr. tchr. KinderCare Learning Ctrs., Colorado Springs, Colo., 1982—84; child care ctr. dir. Open Hands Preschool, Colorado Springs, Colo., 1984—85; preschool tchr. Gum Springs Child Devel. Ctr., Alexandria, Va., 1985—87; tchr. Fairfax County Pub. Schs., Springfield, Va., 1987—. Cons., tutoring-mentoring program Lomax Ch., Arlington, Va., 1989—95. Sch. union rep. Fairfax Edn. Assn., Fairfax, Va., 2001—. Tchr. tng. grantee, Fairfax Edn. Assn., 2003. Mem.: Kappa Delta Pi (assoc.; mem. 2002—). Democrat. Baptist. Avocations: piano, singing, exercise. Home: 5318 Harbor Court Dr Alexandria VA 22315-3934 Office: Mount Vernon Woods Elem Sch 4015 Fielding St Alexandria VA 22309 Personal E-mail: hhaggard86@aol.com. E-mail: Alma.Haygood@fcps.edu.

HAYGOOD, EITHEL MARINELLA, artist, educator; b. Ohio County, Ky., Nov. 18, 1926; d. Lloyd Urbin and Alma Alice (Simpson) Miller; m. James Richard Haygood, June 12, 1955; children: James Steven, Russell Alan, Marcus Llyod, Susan Marinella. BA, Ark. State Coll., 1952. Art and speech tchr. Bell City (Mo.) Consol., 1952—54; art and English tchr. Lamar Consol. Ind. Sch. Dist., Rosenberg, Tex., 1954—55, 1964—88. Founding mem. Visual Arts Coun. Scholar, Ark. State Coll., 1949. Mem.: Tex. Ret. Tchrs. Assn., Tex. State Tchrs. Assn., Nat. Mus. Women in Arts, Ret. Tchrs. Assn., S.W. Artisans Soc. (founding mem.), Art Exchg. Baptist. Avocations: singing, gardening, photography, birdwatching, reading. Home: 1423 Gardenia Cir Rosenberg TX 77471

HAYGOOD, THERESA, science educator, medical technician; b. Andrews AFB, Md., May 27, 1964; d. Rufus Donald and Mabel Martin Haygood. BS in Med. Tech., Med. Coll. Ga., Augusta, 1986; MEd, U. W. Ga., Carrollton, 1996. Med. technologist ASCP. Med. technologist Kennestone Hosp., Marietta, Ga., 1986—; sci. eductor Gordon County Schs., Calhoun, 1991—. Sponsor, ecology club Telban Elem. Sch., Resana, Ga., 2002. Recipient Tchr. of Yr., Gordon County Schs., 2004. Mem.: NSTA, Am. Soc. Clin. Pathologists, Pi Lambda Theta. Avocations: gardening, bowling. Home: 59 Shinall-Gaines Rd Cartersville GA 30121 Office: Gordon County Schs Calhoun GA

HAYMAN, HELEN FEELEY, retired nursing director; b. Rahway, N.J., June 9, 1918; d. John J. and Margaret (Crahan) Feeley; 1 child, Richard J. Hayman. Nursing Diploma, All Souls Hosp., Morristown, 1939; BA, Trenton Coll., 1963. RN, N.J., Conn. Pvt. duty nurse Muhlenberg Hosp., Plainfield, N.J., 1939, staff nurse pediatrics, 1940-42, pvt. duty nurse, 1944-57; office nurse Westfield, N.J., 1939-40; indsl. nurse Nat. Pneumeonic, Rahway, N.J., 1942-44; dir. sch. nursing Bd. of Edn., Plainfield, N.J., 1957-67, dir. presch. health, 1967-73, dir. nurses health program, 1973-80, ret., 1980. Past mem. Town Coun.; vol. Jerry Lewis Labor Day Telethon Muscular Dystrophy; commr. Trumbull Sr. Citizens, Conn. State Dept. Aging; pres. Stern Village Residents Assn., 2000. Mem. Am. Cancer Soc. (Jail and Bail award), Nat. Assn. Ret. Educators, Trumbull Ct. (commr., chmn. vial of life), Greater Bridgeport Ret. Tchr. (exec. bd.), Trumbull Women's Club. Democrat. Roman Catholic. Home: 5316 Bradenbury Ct Charlotte NC 28215-5358

HAYMAN, LINDA C., lawyer; b. Morgantown, W.Va., 1947; BS, Ohio State U., 1969; MA, U. Colo., 1973; JD, Capital U., 1979. Bar: Ohio 1979, NY 1982. Ptnr. Skadden, Arps, Slate, Meagher & Flom, L.L.P., N.Y.C. Liaison to permanent editl. bd. Uniform Comml. Code, 1994—2000. Editor: e-Source; editl. bd. The Business Lawyer. Mem.: TriBar Opinion Com., Am. Coll. Comml. Fin. Lawyers (bd. regents), Am. Coll. Investment Counselors, Am. Bar Found., Am. Law Inst., ABA (sec., Bus. Law Sect.). Office: Skadden 4 Times Sq New York NY 10036-6522 Office Phone: 212-735-2637. Office Fax: 917-777-2637. E-mail: lhayman@skadden.com.

HAYMOND, PAULA J., psychologist, diagnostician, hypnotherapist; b. Warsaw, Ind., Sept. 29, 1949; d. George Milton and Phyllis (Freeman) H. BA, Butler U., 1971, MS, 1973; EdD, Ind. U., 1982. Lic. psychometrist, Ind.; lic. psychologist, Tex. Sr. asst. psychology dept. Butler U., Indpls., 1970-71; behavioral clinician I psychology dept. Ind. Boys Sch., Plainfield, 1973-75, behavioral clinician II diagnostic unit, 1975-78, Ind. Girls Sch., Indpls., 1978-80; human factors cons. Lund Cons. Inc., N.Y.C., 1981-82; adminstr. DePelchin Children Ctr./Bayou Pl., Houston, 1982-85; diagnostician Larry Pollock PhD & Assoc., Houston, 1985-88; ptnr. Montrose Psychotherapy P.C., Houston, 1988—; vol. CEO Noah's House, Houston, 1998—. Biofeedback therapist Teresa A. Atkinson RPT, Houston, 1989-91; psychology supr. Larry Pollock PhD & Assocs., Houston, 1990-91; instr. Wharton County Jr. Coll. Police Acad., 1990-99; presenter S.W. Women's Conf., Houston, 1990, 5th Internat. Congress on Ericksonian Approaches to Hypnosis and Psychotherapy, 1992; seminar instr. Inst. Group and Family Psychotherapy, Moscow, Russia, 1994. Presenter U. Tex. Dental Sch., Houston, 1990, 91. Recipient Symbol of Excellence award, Goodwill Industries, 1999, Rehab. Profl. of Yr. award, Tex. Rehab. Assn., 2001. Mem. APA, AACD, Am. Soc. Clin. Hypnosis, Nat. Bd. Crt. Clin. Hypnotherapists, Biofeedback Soc. Tex., Exec. and Profl. Assn. Houston (bd. dirs., comty. affairs com. 1993-96, bd. trustees 1996-98), Delta Delta Delta, Kappa Kappa Kappa. Avocations: dressage, show jumping. Office: Haymond Rappaport & Assocs 310 South Mason Rd #303 Katy TX 77450 E-mail: mppc@houston.rr.com.

HAYNES, IRIS FITZGERALD, music educator; m. Thomas Rogers Haynes, Aug. 21, 1982; children: Roger Morris, Gerald Spencer. BS, Hampton U., Va., 1976; MusM Edn., Va. Commonwealth U., Richmond, 1981. Band and orch. dir. Richmond Pub. Schs., Va., 1977—82; gen. music tchr. Saginaw Pub. Schs., Mich., 1983—87, Cin. Pub. Schs., 1988—90; gen. music and asst. band dir. Lawrence Twp. Pub. Schs., Indpls., 1990—93; asst. band dir., orch. dir., gen. music tchr. Pike Twp. Schs., Indpls., 1993—96; instrumental and gen. music tchr. Saginaw Pub. Schs., Mich., 1996—99; orch. dir. White Pine Mid. Sch., Saginaw, 1999—. Named Mich. Sch. Band and Orch. Tchr. of Yr., Outstanding Orch. Dir., 2003; grantee, Saginaw Cmty. Found., 1999, Saginaw Cmty. Found. and White Pine Parent Coun., 2003. Mem.: Alpha Kappa Alpha (pres. Mu Alpha Omega chpt. 2003—05). Office: White Pine Mid Sch 505 N Center Rd Saginaw MI 48638 Office Phone: 989-797-1814 3239. Business E-Mail: ifhaynes@stcs.org.

HAYNES, KAREN SUE, academic administrator, educator; b. Jersey City, July 6, 1946; d. Edward J. and Adelaide M. (Hineson) Czarnecki; m. James S. Mickelson; children: Kingsley Eliot Mickelson, Kimberly Elizabeth Mickelson, David Mickelson. BA in Social Work, Goucher Coll., 1968; MSW, McGill U., 1970; PhD in Social Work, U. Tex., 1977. Dir., social work divsn., sociology dept. Mary Hardin-Baylor Coll., Tex.; faculty mem. S.W. Tex. State U., San Marcos, Tex.; cons. Inst. Nat. Planning, Cairo, 1977-78; asst. prof. Ind. U., Indpls., 1978-81, assoc. prof., 1981-85; prof. social work U. Houston, 1985-95, dean, 1985-95; pres. U. Houston-Victoria, Tex., 1995—2004, Calif. State, San Marcos, 2004—. Founding presdl. sponsor Tex. Network Women Higher Edn.; formula adv. com. Tex. Coord. Bd. Higher Edn. Author: (book) Sage Publications, 1984, Longman, 1986, 1996, Springer, 1989, Allyn and Bacon, 2000, 2003; contbr. articles to profl. jours. Mem.: NASW, Leadership Houston, Leadership Tex., Leadership Am., Nat. Alliance Info. and Referral (pres. 1983—87), Internat. Assn. Schs. Social Work, Coun. Social Work Edn., Am. Coun. Edn. Network (mem. exec. bd. dirs.), Am. Assn. State Colls. and Univs. (sec.-treas., mem. exec. bd. dirs. 2003—). Avocation: poetry. Office: Calif State U 333 S Twin Oaks Valley Rd San Marcos CA 92096-0001

HAYNES, LINDA ANN, health information management administrator; b. Rochester, N.Y., May 11, 1955; d. Gerald Joseph and Ida (Bartell) Bonadanna; 1 child, Thomas Gerald; m. Brian P. Cunliffe. AAS, Monroe C.C., 1975. Dir. med. records Lakeshore Nursing Home, Rochester, 1975; utilization rev. coord. Genesee Valley Med. Found., Rochester, 1975-76; MCE coord. Genesee Region PSRO, Inc., Rochester, 1976-78; dir. med. records and splty. practice Westside Health Svcs., Rochester, 1978-81; office mgr. Northeastern Scanning Svc., Rochester, 1981-85; dir. med. records Westgate Nursing Home, Rochester, 1986-88, Rochester Friendly Home, 1988-93; mgr. health info. mgmt./secretarial support Genesee Region Home Care, 1993—. Mem. adv. bd. health info. mgmt. tech. Monroe C.C., Rochester, 1991—; cons. to long term care orgns., Rochester, 1978—; adj. instr. health info. mgmt. tech. Monroe C.C., 1991—. Mem. Am. Health Info. Mgmt. Assn. (sec. long term care sect. 1991-92), N.Y. Health Info. Mgmt. Assn. (chair long term care sect. 1989-92), Rochester Regional Info. Mgmt. Assn. (chair edn. 1979-80). Avocations: reading, cooking. Office: Genesee Region Home Care 3111 Winton Rd S Rochester NY 14623-2905

HAYNES, LINDA ROSE, medical/surgical nurse; d. Floyd George Hilbers, Sr. and Mildred Ann Hilbers; children: Jinny Marie Millican, Thomas Baird. ADN, Vernon Regional Coll. Am. Nurses Credentialing Ctr., RN Tex. Dir. of patient care Outreach Health Svcs., Wichita Falls, 2002—, RN case mgr., 1994—2002. Mem.: Am. Diabetic Assn. (diabetic educator), Phi Theta Kappa (Omega Kappa). Roman Catholic. Avocations: crafts, reading. Office: Outreach Home Health Ste 3 1411 13th St Wichita Falls TX 76301

HAYNES, PATRICIA L., psychologist, researcher; d. Henry W. and Carolyn J. Haynes; m. David A. Glickenstein, Sept. 5, 2004. BA, U. Mo., Columbia, 1992—96; MS, San Diego State U., Calif., 1997—2001; PhD, U. Calif., San Diego, 1997—2003. Intern Southwest Consortium Predoctoral Psychology Internship, Albuquerque, 2002—03; postdoctoral fellow U. Ariz., Tucson, 2003—05, rsch. asst. prof., 2005—. Faculty career devel. program Am. Sleep Medicine Found. Contbr. articles to profl. pubs. Grantee Nat. Rsch. Svc. award, NIH, 2002—03, Pilot Grant Program, Inst. for Mental Health Rsch., 2006—. Mem.: APA, Assn. Behavioral and Cognitive Therapies, Sleep Rsch. Soc. Office Phone: 520-626-1855.

HAYNES, RUTH ELAINE, accountant; b. Cranesville, Pa., Sept. 21, 1943; d. Jack and Viola Emma (Drury) Gelvin; m. Jim D. Haynes, Aug. 26, 1962 (div. July 1974); children: Christine Haynes-Rollins, Jim Michael. AA summa cum laude, Del Mar Coll., 1973; BBA summa cum laude (Warren Found. scholar), Tex. A&I U. Corpus Christi, 1976; MBA summa cum laude, Corpus Christi State U., 1977; PhD in Fed. Taxation, U. Tex., Arlington, 1995. CPA Tex. Tax acct. Tex. Comptroller Public Accounts Dept., Ft. Worth, 1976—83; supr. Chgo., Ill. State Tex. Audit Office, 1983—84, Ft. Worth Audit Office, 1984—86; pvt. practice acctg. Richland Hills, Tex., 1986—. Grad. assoc. U. Tex., Arlington, 1988—93; adj. instr. Tarrant County Jr. Coll., 1980—83, 1985—88, Dallas Bapt. U., 1993—95; spkr. ind. bus. seminars. Mem. Am. Inst. CPAs, Mid Cities Assn. CPAs, Am. Soc. Women in Acctg. (legis. chair Tarrant County br.), Altrusa (corresponding sec. Arlington chpt.), Network Exec. Women, Phi Theta Kappa, Ft. Worth Girls Club (bd. dirs.). Democrat. Lutheran. Avocations: reading, swimming, camping, travel, art. Office: 7232 Glenview Dr Richland Hills TX 76180-8612 Office Phone: 817-590-0300. Personal E-mail: rhaynes262@aol.com.

HAYNES, VICTORIA F., science administrator; Chief tech. officer, v.p. Advanced Tech. Group, BFGoodrich Co., 1992—99; pres., CEO Rsch. Triangle Inst., Research Triangle Park, NC, 1999—. Bd. dir. Ziptronix Bd., Lubrizol Corp., Nucor Corp., MCNC, N.C. Biotech. Ctr., N.C. Bd. Sci. and Tech., PPG Ind.; appt. to Kans. Bioscience Authority, 2004—. Office: c/o Rebecca Switzer Rsch Triangle Inst Internat PO Box 12194 Research Triangle Park NC 27709-2194

HAYNES, YVETTE, nurse, science educator; b. Jamaica, W.I., May 3, 1960; d. Reginald and Hazel Haynes; children: Christina, Rovetta. BSN, CCNY, 1983; postgrad., Health Sci. Ctr., Bklyn., 1993, Medgar Evers Coll., 1987-88. RN, N.Y. Staff nurse MCH and oncology Mt. Sinai Hosp., N.Y.C., 1984—. Sci. tchr. Stephen DeCatur Jr. High Sch., Bklyn., 1989-91. Mem. ANA, N.Y. State Nurses Assn.

HAYNIE, BETTY JO GILLMORE, personal property appraiser, antiques dealer; b. Jackson, Ala., July 3, 1937; d. Joe McVey and Mary Elizabeth (Bolen) Gillmore; m. William T. Haynie Jr., Aug. 21, 1960; children: Virginia Elizabeth, Mary Allison. BA, U. Ala., 1959, MA, 1960, postgrad., U. So. Miss., U. Ala., Birmingham; grad. Paris program, Parsons Sch. Design, 1992; grad., Winter Inst., Winterthur, Del., 1994. Tchr. Demopolis (Ala.) Elem. Sch., 1960-61; instr. in history U. Livingston, Ala., 1961-64; tchr. history for jr. high Brooke Hill Sch. for Girls, Birmingham, Ala., 1965; instr. in history Jefferson State Jr. Coll., Birmingham, 1965-67; tchr. history and govt. Mt. Brook High Sch., Birmingham, 1970-71; instr. history U. Ala., Birmingham, 1971-72, Jefferson Davis Jr. Coll., Gulfport, Miss., 1978-81, Faulkner Jr. Coll., Fairhope, Ala., 1983-86; instr. spl. courses U. South Ala., Mobile, 1988—2003, instr. Elderhostel programs, 1990—99. Owner Crown and Colony Antiques, Fairhope, Ala., 1982—92, Antiques and Fine Art, Fairhope, Ala., 1997—; co-owner Gillmore Plantation, Jackson, Ala., Ala., 1987—, and other properties. Contbr. articles to historical mags. Mem.: DAR, Internat. Soc. Appraisers, Clarke County Hist. Soc., Nat. Trust for Hist. Preservation. Presbyterian. Avocations: tennis, creative writing, travel. Home: PO Box 485 Montrose AL 36559-0485

HAYNIE, SUZANNA KENNEDY, secondary school educator; d. Robert Edmond and Patricia Henslee Kennedy; m. Jeffery Stephen Haynie, Nov. 5, 1994; children: Robert John, Kennedy Stephen. AS, East Ctrl. C.C., Decatur, Miss., 1988; BS in Biol. Engring., Miss. State U., 1990; MS in Biol. and Agrl. Engring., U. Ark., Fayetteville, 1992. Cert. Ga. profl. educator T-5 Level Ga. Profl. Stds. Commn., 2005. Sci. tchr. Madison County Schs., Danielsville, Ga., 1995—96; chemistry tchr. Clarke County Schs. - Cedar Shoals H.S., Athens, Ga., 1996—. Seed sower Gt. News Network, Athens, 2005—06. Named Target Winning Tchr., 1998; 21st Century Classroom Tech. grantee, Clarke County Sch. Dist., 2005—06. Mem.: Ga. Assn. Educators. Avocations: reading, needlecrafts. Office Phone: 706-546-5375.

HAYNOR, PATRICIA MANZI, nursing educator, consultant; children: Kelly Christine, Craig; m. Donald C. Maaswinkel. Diploma in nursing, Grasslands Hosp., Valhalla, N.Y.; BSN, Fairleigh Dickinsn U., l967; MSN in Nursing Adminstrn., U. Pa., l969; D Nursing Sci., Widener U., 1989. RN, Pa., N.J., N.Y., Del. Asst. dir. surg. nursing Thomas Jefferson U. Hosp., Phila., 1972-74; asst. dir. nursing care depts. Our Lady of Lourdes Hosp., Camden, NJ, 1974-76; assoc. dir. nursing West Jersey Hosp., Camden, 1976-79; dir. nursing West Jersey Health System, Camden, 1979-81, corp. dir. nursing, 1981-82; v.p. nursing Crozer-Chester (Pa.) Med. Ctr., 1982-85; coord. nursing adminstrn. program, asst. prof. Widener U., Chester, 1985-87; v.p. for nursing St. Francis Med. Ctr., Trenton, NJ, 1987-90; asst. prof. U. Del. Coll. Nursing, 1990-92; assoc. prof. Villanova (Pa.) U. Coll. Nursing, Phila., 1992—. Cons. Nurse Assocs., West Deptford, N.J., 1985—; spkr. in field. Contbr. articles to profl. pubs. Mem. Am. Orgn. Nurse Execs., Am. Coll. Healthcare Execs., S.E. Pa. Orgn. Nurse Leaders. Office: Villanova U Coll Nursing Villanova PA 19085 Home: 301 Lentz Rd Thorofare NJ 08086 Office Phone: 610-519-7751. E-mail: patriciahaynor@villanova.edu.

HAYS, ANNETTE ARLENE, secondary school educator; b. Dallas, Jan. 22, 1951; d. Ogle Winifred and Loretta Lavelle Hatfield; m. William Ned Hays, Aug. 7, 1971; children: Quincy Merritt, Gretchen Laurel. BS in Home Econ. Edn., U. Ark., Fayetteville, 1973. Office asst. dept. entomology U. Ark., Fayetteville, 1970—71; sales assoc. Hunt's Dept. Store, Fayetteville, 1971—72, Singer Sewing Co., Joplin, Mo., 1972—76, instr., 1974—76; home econ. tchr. Parkwood HS, Joplin, 1976—80; family & consumer sci. tchr. Acorn Sch., Mena, Ark., 1988—. Owner Hatfield, Honey & Sorghum, Pine Ridge, Ark., 1980—; Family, Career and Cmty. Leaders Am. advisor

Acorn Sch., 1988—, mem. personnel policy com., developer tech-prep/transition program; trainer Ark. Workplace Readiness, 1993—; apptd. by gov. Ark. Workforce Commn., 1997—98; grantwriter; spkr. in field; bd. dirs., chair Healthy Connections, Mena, Ark., 2001—. Mem. Oden Sch. Bd., 1986—98, past sec., past v.p.; choir mem First Presbyn. Ch., Mena, del. to Peacemaking Conf., 1996. Recipient Tchr. of Yr., Ark. Assn. Family & Consumer Scis., 2003. Mem.: Am. Assn. Family and Consumer Scis., Ark. Assn. Family Consumer Scis. (bd. dirs. 2001—), Ark. Assn. Career and Tech. Educators (bd. dirs. 1999—2001, Tchr. of Yr. 2005), Assn. Career & Tech. Educators (Region IV Tchr. of Yr. 2005), Ark. Assn. Tchrs. Family & Consumer Scis. (pres. elect 1999—2000, pres. 2000—01, past pres. 2001—02, Polk County Tchr. of Yr. 2002, Tchr. of the Yr. 2003, Nat. Tchr. Yr. finalist 2004, Star Edn. award 2006), Delta Kappa Gamma. Presbyterian. Avocations: hiking, reading, landscaping. Home: 38 Honey Bear Ln General Delivery Pine Ridge AR 71966 Office Phone: 479-394-2101. Business E-Mail: haysa@acorn.dmsc.k12.ar.us.

HAYS, CLARE A., veterinarian, biologist, educator; b. Denver, Nov. 15, 1957; d. Morton and Judy G. Hoffman. BS in Zoology, Colo. State U., Ft. Collins, 1979, DVM, 1983. Veterinarian in pvt. practice, Golden, Colo., 1983—88; prof. dept. biology Met. State Coll., Denver, 1988—. Author: Caring for Llamas and Alpacas, 1988, 2006. Office: Metropolitan State College PO Box 173362 Denver CO 80217

HAYS, EDITH H., mathematics professor; d. Edward and Valerie Haight; m. Thomas R. Hays, July 26, 1963; children: Victoria Mitchell, Geoffrey. BBA, So. Meth. U., Tex.; MS, TWU, Tex. Lectr. Tex. Woman's U., Denton, 1989—2001, sr. lectr., 2001—, dir. Learning Assistance Ctr., 1995—2004, dir. Math. and Tech. Success Ctr., 2005—. Foster puppy raiser Paws with a Cause, Denton, 2003—04. Mem.: Tex. Assn. Suprs. Math., Tex. Coun. Tchrs. Math., Nat. Coun. Suprs. Math., Nat. Coun. Tchrs. Math., Phi Kappa Phi (assoc.; scholarship and awards officer 2005—06). Episcopalian. Office: Texas Womans University 1200 Frame St Denton TX 76204 Office Phone: 940-898-2905. Office Fax: 940-898-2179. Business E-Mail: ehays@twu.edu.

HAYS, JUDY MEYER, music educator; b. Fairbury, Ill., Feb. 2, 1957; d. Jean Ellyn Meyer; children: Nathan P., Aaron J., Ella J. BA, Carthage Coll., 1979; MEd, U. Ill., 1986. Cert. tchr. Ill. Music tchr. choral and guitar Kennedy Mid. Sch., Germantown, Wis., 1979; music tchr. K-8 Sch. Dist. 123, Oak Lawn, Ill., 1979—80, Sch. Dist. 135, Orland Park, Ill., 1980—83; early childhood music instr. Palatine and Elk Grove Village Pk. (Ill.) Dists., 1983—93; founder, dir. Palatine Children's Chorus, 1986—93; music tchr. K-6 Schaumburg (Ill.) Sch. Dist. 54, 1992—. State clinician Ill. Music Educators' Assn., Mokena, 2004—05. Vol. Prince of Peace Luth. Ch., Schaumburg, 1995—2005. Finalist Golden Apple award, 2000; recipient Lois Bailey Glenn award for tchg. excellence, Nat. Music Found., 2004, 2005, Amb. for Excellence award, Schaumburg Sch. Dist. 54, 2005, 2006, Te@ch award, Best Buy, 2006; grantee, Schaumburg Twp. Found., 1998, 1999, 2000, 2001; Competitive Tech. grantee, Schaumburg Sch. Dist. 54, 2000. Mem.: Music Educators Nat. Conf. Home: 1521 Fairfield Ln Hoffman Estates IL 60195 Office: Armstrong Sch 1320 S Kingsdale Ln Hoffman Estates IL 60194 Office Phone: 847-357-6719. E-mail: judyhays@sd54.org.

HAYS, LOUISE STOVALL, retail fashion executive; b. Crenshaw, Miss., Aug. 30, 1916; d. Ernest Sydney and Anne Mary (Ray) Stovall; m. James Marion Klaer, June 30, 1938 (dec. Jan. 1962); m. Samuel Jackson Hays, Apr. 29, 1965 (dec. March 14, 2001); stepchildren: Elizabeth Razee, Samuel Jackson III, Carruthers Donelson. Grad., Memphis Sch. of Commrce; student, U. Memphis. Sec. Goldsmith's, Memphis, 1938, exec. sec., 1939, fashion coord., 1941-47, fashion dir., 1947-50, dir. fashion promotions and spl. events, 1950-74. Cons. Mademoiselle mag., 1964. Bd. dirs. Am. Heart Assn., 1960s, Memphis Arts Coun., 1964, Brooks Mus. Art, Memphis, 1989; chmn. Memphis Heart Gala, 1978. Named Vol. of Yr., Brooks Mus. League, 1987, Memphis Brooks Mus., 1989. Republican. Episcopalian. Avocations: art, poetry writing, travel. Home: 1701 Village Ridge Pl Collierville TN 38017-8700

HAYS, MARGUERITE THOMPSON, nuclear medicine physician, educator; b. Bloomington, Ind., Apr. 15, 1930; d. Stith and Louise (Faust) Thompson; m. David G. Hays, Feb. 4, 1950 (div. 1975); children: Dorothy Adele, Warren Stith Thompson, Thomas Glenn. AB cum laude, Radcliffe Coll., 1951; postgrad., Harvard U. Med. Sch., 1954; MD, UCLA, 1957; ScD (hon.), Ind. U., 1979. Diplomate Am. Bd. Internal Medicine, Am. Bd. Nuc. Medicine. Intern UCLA Sch. Medicine, 1957-58, resident, 1958-59, 61-62, USPHS postdoctoral trainee, 1959-61, USPHS postdoctoral fellow, 1963-64, asst. prof. medicine, 1964-68, SUNY-Buffalo, 1968-70, asst. prof. biophys. sci., 1968-74, assoc. prof. medicine, 1970-76, clin. assoc. prof. nuc. medicine, 1973-77; asst. chief nuc. medicine VA Med. Ctr., Wadsworth, Calif., 1967-68; chief nuc. medicine Buffalo VA Med. Ctr., 1968-74, assoc. chief of staff for rsch., 1971-74; dir. med. rsch. svc. VA Ctrl. Office, Washington, 1974-79, asst. chief med. dir. for R & D, 1979-81; chief of staff Martinez VA Med. Ctr., Calif., 1981-83; prof. radiology Sch. Medicine U. Calif., Davis, 1981-93, prof. medicine and surgery, 1983-91, assoc. dean, 1981; clin. prof. radiology Stanford U. Sch. Medicine, 1990—; assoc. chief of staff for rch. Palo Alto (Calif.) VA Med. Ctr., 1983-97, staff physician, 1997-99, cons., 1999—2001. Vis. rsch. scientist Euratom, Italy, 1962-63; chmn. radiopharm. adv. com. FDA, 1974-77; co-chmn. biomedicine com. Pres.'s Fed. Coun. on Sci., Engrng. and Tech., 1979-81; mem. rsch. restructuring adv. com. Va. R & D Office, 1995-96, chair task group to restructure R & D Career Devel. Program, 1996-97; chmn. coop. studies evaluation com., Med. Rsch. Svc., VA, 1990-93; mem. sci. rev. and evaluation bd. Health Svcs. Rsch. and Devel. Svc., VA, 1988-91, chmn. career devel. com., 1991-99, chmn. career devel. com. Rehab. Rsch. and Devel. Svc., 1997-2003. Rsch. grantee VA, 1968-2003. NIH grantee, 1964-71; recipient Exceptional Svc. award Sec. Vets. Affairs, 2000. Fellow ACP; mem. Soc. Nuc. Medicine (chmn. publs. com., trustee, v.p. 1983-84), Am. Thyroid Assn. (bd. dirs. 1993-96), Endocrine Soc., Western Assn. Physicians. Home: 270 Campesino Ave Palo Alto CA 94306-2912 Office: 3801 Miranda Ave Palo Alto CA 94304-1207 E-mail: ritahays19@yahoo.com.

HAYSBERT, JOANN WRIGHT, academic administrator; b. Kingstree, SC; d. Norwood and Lillie Mae (Scott) Wright; m. Barral Stanley Hershel Haysbert; children: Andre, Nineveh, Nazareth, Jordan, Samaria. BA, Johnson C. Smith U., Charlotte, N.C., 1969; MEd, Auburn U., 1974, EdD, 1978. Coordinator rsch. and program planning Macon County Pub. Sch. System, Tuskegee, Ala., 1971-76; title IX coordinator Auburn (Ala.) U., 1976-78; instr. psychology Alexander City (Va.) State Jr. Coll., 1977-78; asst. prof. edn. Va. State U., Petersburg, 1978-80, prin. lab. sch., 1979-80; dir. women and minorities program Hampton (Va.) U., 1981-82, asst. v.p. acad. affairs, dir. summer session, various positions including asst. provost, provost, prof. and dean, acting pres., 2003—04; pres. Langston U., Langston, Okla., 2005—. Cons. in field. Author ednl. materials. Mem. Va. Nat. Identification Program for Advancement of Women in Higher Edn. Adminstrn. Ford Found. fellow, 1973. Mem. Nat. Assn. Women Deans, Adminstrs. and Counselors, Nat. Assn. Summer Sessions (chmn. com. 1986-88), Assn. Univ. Summer Sessions, AAUW, Phi Delta Kappa. Avocations: reading, music. Office: Langston Univ PO Box 907 Langston OK 73050 Office Phone: 405-466-3201. Office Fax: 405-466-3461. E-mail: jwhaysbert@lunet.edu.

HAYSLETT-WALLACE, JEANETTE, music educator; d. John and Mattie Hilda Hayslett; m. Clarence Wallace, Dec. 20, 1952; children: Clarence Michael Wallace, Charnette Michelle Wallace-Simmons. BS, Va. State Coll., 1952; MA, Columbia U., 1962. Music tchr. Norfolk County and Chesapake Schools, Va., 1952—90; counselor Va. Music Camp, Massanetta Springs, Harrisonburg, Va., 1970—87. Music tchr. forum judge Tidwater Music Tchr. Hymn Festival, Chesapeake, Va., 1990—2000. Rep. Dist. IV State Bd. Music Edn., Chesapeake, Va.; bd. mem. Chesapeake Cmty. Services Bd., Va. Recipient Tidewater Area Musician award, 1992. Home: 615 Leonard Ave Chesapeake VA 23324

HAYT, THERESE D., newspaper executive; With Time-Life Books; deputy photo editor Sports Illustrated, NYC; photo editor San Diego Union-Tribune, Calif.; sports photo editor Newsday, NYC; photo editor Orlando Sentinel, Fla.; with mktg. and advt. divsn. The Walt Disney Co., Orlando; dir. photography Ariz. Daily Star, 2000—02, asst. mng. editor presentation, 2002—04, mng. editor, 2004—. Office: Ariz Daily Star 4850 S Park Ave Tucson AZ 85714

HAYWARD, FRANCES CRAMBERT, retired dietician; b. Shelbyville, Ky., June 3, 1936; d. Allen Sanford and Anna Fletcher (Shipman) Wilson; m. Albert Clark Crambert, Oct. 18, 1958 (dec. Nov. 1985); m. David C. Hayward, Nov. 13, 1994; children: Anna Crambert Klune (dec. Nov. 1995), Rebecca Frances; m. Darryl Reiter, Feb. 11, 1996. BA, DePauw U., 1958. Registered dietitian. Clin. dietitian Delaware County Meml. Hosp., Drexel Hill, Pa., 1978-88; dietitian Diabetes Treatment Ctr. Met. Hosp., Springfield, Pa., 1988-89; dietitian Food Mgmt. Svcs., Inc., Charter Fairmount Inst., Phila., 1989-91, The Wood Co., 1991-94. Mem.: Am. Assn. Diabetes Educators. Democrat. Methodist. Home: PO Box 5372 Lancaster PA 17606-5372 E-mail: haywarddf@aol.com.

HAYWARD, JEAN, artist, musician, interior designer, performance artist; b. L.A., Apr. 4, 1917; d. Herbert Hastings Eastwood and Irma Isabel Arundell; m. William Hayward (dec.); m. George R. Collins (dec. Sept. 26, 1939); children: Julia Ann, Stephen, George, Mark. BA, U.C.L.A., L.A., 1938. Mime story telling with orchestras, all around the world; designer clothing line of denim for Bullock's Willshire; architecture and design houses, Santa Barbara. Contbr. articles to profl. jour.;, performer symphony soloist. Vol. Jr. League, Santa Barbara, Calif., 1946—70. Mem.: Birnam Wood Golf Club. Republican. Episcopalian. Avocation: horseback riding. Home: 300 Hot Springs Rd Santa Barbara CA 93108

HAYWARD, OLGA LORETTA HINES (MRS. SAMUEL ELLSWORTH HAYWARD), retired librarian; b. Alexandria, La. d. Samuel James and Lillie (George) Hines; m. Samuel E. Hayward, July 12, 1945; children: Anne Elizabeth, Olga Patricia (Mrs. William Ryer). AB, Dillard U., 1941; BSLS, Atlanta U., 1944; MALS, U. Mich., 1959; MA in History, La. State U., 1977. Tchr. Marksville (La.) H.S., 1941-42; head libr. Grambling (La.) Coll., 1944-46; br. libr. br. nine New Orleans Pub. Libr. System, 1947-48; reference libr. So. U. Baton Rouge, 1948-73, libr. bus. and social scis. libr., 1973-84, libr. collection devel. consent decree program, 1984-86, chairwoman dept. reference, 1986-88, ret., 1988. Author: Graduate Theses of Southern University, 1959-71, A Bibliography of Literature By and About Whitney Moore Young Jr., 1929-71, 1972, The Influence of Humanism on Sixteenth Century English Courtesy Texts, 1977; also other bibliographies. Bd. dirs. La. Diocese Episcopal Cmty. Svcs., 1972-78; mem. banquet com. Baton Rouge chpt. Nat. Conf. Christians and Jews, 1981-2000, Nat. Conf. for cmty. and Justice, 2001-02. Recipient recognition, La. LIbr. Assn., 2003. Mem. life, La. Libr. Assn. (chair-elect subject specialists divsn. 1986-87, chairwoman subject specialists sect. 1987-88, Lucy B. Foote award subject specialists sect. 1990), Spl. Librs. Assn. (pres. La. chpt. 1978-79, Roll of Honor award 1995). Episcopalian. Home: 2539 Olive St Baton Rouge LA 70806-5457

HAYWOOD, ANNE MOWBRAY, pediatrician, educator; b. Balt., Feb. 5, 1935; d. Richard Mansfield and Margaret (Mowbray) H. BA in Chemistry, Bryn Mawr Coll., 1955; MD, Harvard U., 1959. Cert. Am. Bd. Pediat. Intern U. Calif. Med. Ctr., San Francisco, 1959-60; fellow biochemistry dept. Columbia U., N.Y.C., 1961-62; fellow divsn. biology Calif. Inst. Tech., Pasadena, 1960-61, 62-64; asst. prof. microbiology, microbiology dept. Northwestern U. Med. Sch., Chgo., 1964-66, Yale U. Med. Sch., New Haven, 1966-73; resident in pediat. U. Wash., Seattle, 1974-75, pediat. infectious disease fellow, 1975-76, Vanderbilt U., Nashville, 1976-77; assoc. prof. Dept. Pediat. and Microbiology U. Rochester, NYC, 1977—. Vis. asst. prof. Rockefeller U., N.Y.C., 1971-72; vis. scientist biophysics unit Agrl. Rsch. Coun., Cambridge, Eng., 1972-74, Inst. for Immunology and Virology, U. Zürich, Switzerland, 1987; vis. assoc. prof. dept. zoology U. Calif., Davis, 1986; vis. assoc. prof. McArdle Lab. for Cancer Rsch., U. Wis., 1999-2000; adj. scientist Nat. Inst. Child Health and Human Devel., NIH, 2004-05. Co-author: Practice of Pediatrics, 1977, Infections in Children, 1982, Liposome Letters, 1983, Practice of Pediatrics, 1987, Molecular Mechanisms of Membrane Fusion, 1988, Membrane Fusion, 1991, Encyclopedia of Human Biology, 1991, 2d edit., 1997, Cell and Model Membrane Interactions, 1991, Infections of the Central Nervous System, 2004. Fogarty Internat. Ctr. Sr. fellow NIH, 1987, European Molecular Biology Orgn. fellow, 1973-74, NIH Spl. fellow, 1971-73, Am. Cancer Soc. Postdoctoral fellow, 1960-62; Harvard Med. Sch. scholar, 1955-59, Harriet Judd Sartain scholar, 1955-59, N.Y. Alumnae scholar Bryn Mawr Coll., 1951-55. Mem. Biophys. Soc., Am. Soc. for Cell Biology. Democrat. Office: U Rochester Med Ctr Dept Pediatrics PO Box 777 Rochester NY 14642-8777 Office Phone: 585-275-7945. Business E-Mail: ahyw@mail.rochester.edu.

HAYWOOD, B(ETTY) J(EAN), anesthesiologist; b. Boston, June 1, 1942; d. Oliver Garfield and Helen Elizabeth (Salisbury) H.; m. Lynn Brandt Moon, Aug. 29, 1969 (div. Aug. 1986); children: Kaylin, Kristan, Kelly, Kasy R BSc, Tufts U., 1964; MD, U. Colo., 1968; MBA, Oklahoma City U., 1993; Grad., Air War Coll., 1997. Intern Wilford Hall AFB, San Antonio, 1968-69; resident in pediatrics U. Ariz., Tucson, 1971-72, resident in anesthesiology, 1972-74; dir. anesthesia dept. Pima County Hosp., Tucson, 1975-76; staff anesthesiologist South Community Hosp., Oklahoma City, 1977—, Moore (Okla.) Mcpl. Hosp., 1981-94, chief of anesthesia, 1990-94; staff anesthesiologist St. Anthony Hosp., Oklahoma City, 1982—; instr. dept. anesthesia U. Okla. Health Sci. Ctr., Oklahoma City, 1999—; col. USAF, active duty for Op. Enduring Freedom Wilford Hall Med. Ctr., Lackland AFB, Tex., 2001—02. Chief of ethics com. S.W. Med. Ctr., 1996. Bd. dirs. N.Am. South Devon Assn., Lynnville, Iowa, 1978—86; mem. med. com. Planned Parenthood Okla., 1992—; col. USAFR, 1968—. Mem. ASA, World South Devon Assn. (U.S. rep. 1985, 88), Tufts U. Alumni Assn. (rep.), Chi Omega (treas. 1963-64) Republican. Presbyterian. Avocations: skiing, sailing. Home: 705 NW 144th St Edmond OK 73013-1878 Personal E-mail: Beej1942@sbcglobal.net.

HAYWORTH, LAURA, banker, real estate analyst; b. Atlanta, July 28, 1948; d. Robert Edward Hayworth and Georgia Mabel Coffee; m. Randy Bruce Marrs, Feb. 19, 1977 (div. June 1980). BA in Psychology, Ga. State U., 1970, MS in Real Estate, 1984. Cert. property mgr. Asst. mgr. real property ops. Trust Co. Bank, Atlanta, 1978-80; 1st level officer real estate ops. So. Bell Telephone, Atlanta, 1980-81; v.p., trust officer C&S Nat. Bank, Atlanta, 1981-89; comml. loan workout officer FDIC, Atlanta, 1989-92; market analyst Mortgage Guaranty Ins. Corp., Atlanta, 1992; real estate and loan analyst Berkshire Mortgage Fin., Atlanta, 1993, contract real estate and loan analyst, 1994-97; asset mgr. retail portfolio Branch and Assocs., Atlanta, 1993-94; market rsch. assoc. Amresco Rsch., Atlanta, 1996-97; asst. v.p. and trust officer personal trust real estate ops. SunTrust Bank, Atlanta, 1997—. Pres. Emory Garden Condominium Assn., Decatur, Ga., 1984-86; bd. mem. Maple Bend Condominium Assn., Chamblee, Ga., 1987-93, Dunwoody (Ga.) Club Townhomes Condominium Assn., 1993—; mem. Assistance League Atlanta, Chamblee, 1996—. Home: 4101 Dunwoody Club Dr Apt 41 Atlanta GA 30350-5215 Office: Sun Trust Bank Trust and Investment Svcs 25 Park Pl NE Atlanta GA 30303-2900

HAZAN, MARCELLA MADDALENA, writer, educator, consultant; b. Cesenatico, Italy, Apr. 15, 1924; d. Giuseppe and Maria (Leonelli) Polini; m. Victor Hazan, Feb. 24, 1955; 1 child, Giuliano. Dr. in Natural Scis., U. Ferrara, 1952, Dr. in Biology, 1954. Rschr. Guggenheim Inst., 1955-58; prof. math. and biology Italian State schs., 1963-66; founder Sch. of Italian Cooking, N.Y.C., 1969-94, Marcella Hazan Sch. of Classic Italian Cooking, Bologna, Italy, 1976-94, Master Classes in Classic Italian Cooking, Venice, Italy, 1986-98. Pres. Hazan Classic Enterprises, Inc., 1978-99. Author: The Classic Italian Cookbook, 1973, More Classic Italian Cooking, 1978, Marcella's Italian Kitchen, 1986, Essentials of Classic Italian Cooking, 1992, Marcella Cucina, 1997, Marcella Says, 2004. Decorated knight Presdl. Order Star of Italian Solidarity. Roman Catholic. Address: 1211 Gulf Of Mexico Dr # 109 Longboat Key FL 34228 Fax: (941) 387-0183.

HAZARD, LYNN MARCHETTI, occupational therapist; b. Detroit, Feb. 7, 1956; d. Giacomo and Josephine Marchetti. BS, Western Mich. U., 1978, MA in Blind Rehab., 1981; MAEd, U. Ala., Birmingham, 1993. Lic. occupl. therapist, Ala.; bd. cert. pediats. Spl. edn., visully impaired occupl. therapist Postsecondary Edn., Montgomery, Ala., 1995—. Mem. Am. Occupl. Therapy Assn. (cert.), Ala. State Occupl. Therapy Assn., World Fedn. Occupl. Therapists, Ala. Edn. Assn. (alt. del. 1999—). Office: Wallace State Cmty Coll-Hanceville PO Box 2000 801 Main St Hanceville AL 35077

HAZBOUN, VIVECA, psychiatrist; b. Ramallah, Jordan, Nov. 2, 1949; arrived in U.S., 1966; d. Albert Anthony and Helen Hazboun. BS in Chemistry, Immaculate Heart Coll., L.A., 1970; MD, U. So. Calif., 1976. Diplomate in adult psychiatry Am. Bd. Psychiatry and Neurology, 1980, in child psychiatry Am. Bd. Psychiatry and Neurology, 82. Tchg. asst. Grad. Sch. U. So. Calif., L.A., 1970—72; intern in internal medicine Huntington Meml. Hosp., Pasadena, Calif., 1976—77; resident in adult psychiatry Los Angeles County-U. So. Calif. Med. Ctr., 1977—79, fellow in child and adolescent psychiatry, 1979—81, chief child resident, 1980—81, asst. prof. clin. psychiatry, 1981—85, clin. instr., 1980—81; practice adult, child and adolescent psychiatry L.A., 1980—; supr. mental health UN Relief and Work Agy., 1990—95; dir. adult and child psychiatry and neurology Guidance and Tng. Ctr., 1994—. Ward chief children's inpatient Los Angeles County-U. So. Calif. Med. Ctr. Psychiat. Hosp., 1981—85; cons. staff Edgemont Psychiat. Hosp., L.A., 1982—85; cons. Medecins sans Frontieres, Jerusalem, Medecins du Monde, Jerusalem; project dir. World Vision; founder Guidance and Tng. Ctr. for the Child and Family, 1994—, dir., 1994—. Contbr. articles to med. jours. Recipient Papal award, Rome, 1968, recognition awards Child Guidance Clinic, 1980, Women in Data Processing, 1983; fellow Child Guidance Clinic, 1980. Mem. WHO (steering com., thematic group, 2003—), Am. Acad. Child Psychiatry, So. Calif. Psychiat. Soc., So. Calif. Soc. Child Psychiatry, Internat. Assn. Child and Adult Psychiatry (sci. com.), Ea. Mediterranean Child and Adult Psychiatry Assn. (ethics com.), Am. Arab Univ. Grads. Office: PO Box 51399 Jerusalem Israel Office Phone: 011-97252 2770 0489. Office Fax: 011-972522519867. Business E-Mail: gtc@p_ol.com.

HAZEL, MARY BELLE, university administrator; b. Orange, NJ, May 30, 1932; d. Morris M. Sr. and Robena (Brinkley) Thomas; m. James H. Hazel, Sept. 28, 1958 (div. Sept. 1976); children: Sharon Marie Hazel-Griggs, James Thomas. BSBA, Seton Hall U., South Orange, NJ, 1992, MA in Edn. cum laude, 1998. Publs. asst. advt. and pub. rels. dept. Foster Wheeler Corp., NYC, 1969-87; ind. contractor, 1987-92; adminstrv. coord. dean's office Univ. Medicine and Dentistry NJ Sch. Health Related Professions, Newark, 1992—. Elder Elmwood United Presbyn. Ch. Mem. AAUW, NAFE, Smithsonian Nat. Assn., Soc. Allied Health Professions NJ, YWCA, NJ Performing Arts Ctr., Jersey Ednl. Opportunity Fund Profl. Assn., Newark Mus. Assn., YWCA of Essex and West Hudson (NJ).

HAZELIP, LINDA ANN, musician, small business owner, executive assistant; b. El Campo, Tex., Oct. 20, 1952; d. Al Gareth and Annabelle (Black) Braswell; m. Richard Chris Hazelip, July 28, 1972 (div. Aug. 30, 1984). Diploma in computer programming and data processing, Massey Bus. Coll., 1972. Cert. tchr. progressive series intermediate level piano St. Louis Conservatory Music, 1971. Tchr. basic music and piano, 1971—79; bookkeeper Millar Instruments, Houston, 1973—74; sec. St. Andrew's United Meth. Ch., Houston, 1975—79; various positions as exec. asst., mgmt. asst., exec. sec., adminstr., and other adminstrv. positions Houston, 1979—; bus. owner, organist/choirmaster, pianist, vocalist sacred occasions, select secular spl. occasions Met. Area, Houston, S.E. Tex., 1986—; dir., exec. sec. Exponet Trading Co., Houston, 1983—86; exec. sec. InterFirst Bank Post Oak, Houston, 1986; sec., adminstr., mgmt. asst. Halliburton Energy Svcs., Houston, 1991—96; tchr. voice, organ, piano, 2000—. Organist, vocalist, pianist, children's music dir. Faith United Methodist Ch., South Houston, 1972—77; organist, vocalist, children's music dir. Old River Ter. United Methodist Ch., Channelview, Tex., 1978—80; organist, vocalist, music dir. St. John's United Methodist Ch., Baytown, Tex., 1980—84; organist, vocalist St. Stephens United Methodist Ch., Houston, 1983—85; organist, choir dir., vocalist Parker Meml. United Methodist Ch., Houston, 1984—85; choir dir., vocalist Reid Meml. United Methodist Ch., Houston, 1985, Covenant United Methodist Ch., Houston, 1985—86. Vocalist, pianist Open Door Mission, Houston, 1997—; mem. First United Meth. Ch., Houston, 1986—. Mem.: NAFE, Chorister's Guild, Houston Area League PC Users, Am. Bus. Women's Assn. (Skyscraper chpt., Woman of Yr. 1993—94), Am. Guild Organists, Nat. Honor Soc., Nat. Math. Honor Soc. Republican. Methodist. Avocation: holy land study tours. Office: 2501 Westridge 241 Houston TX 77054-1519 Office Phone: 713-668-2248. Business E-Mail: lhazelip@hal-pc.org.

HAZELTINE, JOYCE, former state official; b. Pierre, SD; m. Dave Hazeltine; children: Derek, Tara, Kirk (dec.). Student, Huron Coll., SD, No. State Coll., Aberdeen, S.D., Black Hills State Coll., Spearfish, S.D. Former asst. chief clk. SD Ho. of Reps.; former sec. SD State Senate; sec. of state State of SD, Pierre, 1987—2003. Bd. dirs. S.D. Bankers Found.; chair SD Bankers Found., 2004—05; bd. dirs. Chiesman Ctr. Democracy, Black Hills Playhouse. Adminstrv. asst. Pres. Ford Campaign, SD; Rep. county chmn. Hughes County SD; state co-chair Phil Gramm for Pres., 1996; mem. Custer Co. Rep. Women; bd. dirs. Black Hills Playhouse. Mem. Nat. Assn. Secs. of State (exec. bd., pres.), Women Execs. in State Govts. (bd. dirs.). Republican.

HAZELTON, CATHERINE LYNETTE, elementary school educator; b. Augusta, Ga., Jan. 27, 1969; d. James Allen Hazelton and Dearia Ann (Ratliff) Davis. BA in Edn., N.C. Ctrl. U., 1991. Cert. elem. edn. tchr., N.C. Office mgr., enrichment coord. N.C. Ctrl. U., Durham, 1988-94; tchr. Guilford County Schs., Greensboro, N.C., 1991—. Cons., workshop presenter, facilitator, assessor N.C. Tchg. Fellows Program, Raleigh. Mem. N.C. Assn. Educators, Guilford County Assn. Edns. Avocations: poetry, listening to music.

HAZELTON, JUANITA LOUISE, librarian; b. Glendale, Calif., June 12, 1942; d. James Chester and Eddith Pearl (Henson) McCrain; m. Merrill Edward Hazelton, Apr. 27, 1968; children: Larry Scott, James Edward. BA in Arts and Letters, U. Oreg., 1964; MLS, U. Tex., 1970; tchg. cert., Tex. Woman's U., 1984. Cert. county libr., 1997. Librarian Dallas Pub. Libr., 1966-69; libr. asst. Austin Coll., Sherman, Tex., 1974-75; tchr., librarian Gunter Ind. Sch. Dist., Tex., 1984-94; librarian Plano Pub. Libr., Tex., 1994-95; libr. dir. Van Alstyne Pub. Libr., Tex., 1995—. Contbg. author: Telling Our Stories-Texas Family Secrets, 1997 (Gold Star award 1997); Bookshelf columnist Van Alstyne Leader, 1995—. Recipient Libr. of Yr., N.E. Tex. Libr. Sys., 1996; named Bus. Citizen of Yr. Van Alstyne C. of C., 1998, named to Tall Texans, 2003. Mem. Tex. Libr. Assn. (treas. dist. 5, 2000-01), TALL Tex., Toastmasters Internat. Republican. Mem. Ch. of Christ. Avocations: amateur storytelling, computers, genealogy, writing poetry and family history. Office: Van Alstyne Pub Libr PO Box 629 117 N Waco Van Alstyne TX 75495 Office Phone: 903-482-5991. Business E-Mail: jhazelton@vanalstynepl.lib.tx.us.

HAZELTON, PENNY ANN, law librarian, educator; b. Yakima, Wash., Sept. 24, 1947; d. Fred Robert and Margaret (McLeod) Pease; m. Norris J. Hazelton, Sept. 12, 1971; 1 child, Victoria MacLeod. BA cum laude, Linfield Coll., 1969; JD, Lewis and Clark Law Sch., 1975; M in Law Librarianship, U. Wash., 1976. Bar: Wash. 1976, U.S. Supreme Ct. 1982. Assoc. law libr., assoc. prof. U. Maine, 1976-78, law libr., assoc. prof., 1978-81; asst. libr. for rsch. svcs. U.S. Supreme Ct., Washington, 1981-85, law libr., 1985, U. Wash., Seattle, 1985—, prof. law, assoc. dean libr. and computing svcs., 1985—. Tchr. legal rsch., law librarianship, Indian law; cons. Maine Adv. Com. on County Law Librs., Lawyers Coop. Pub., 1993-94, Marquette U. Sch. Law,

2002, Georgetown U. Law Ctr., 2004. Author: Computer Assisted Legal Research: The Basics, 1993; author: (with others) Washington Legal Researcher's Deskbook, 3d edit., 2002; contbr. articles to legal jours.; gen. editor Specialized Legal Rsch. (Aspen). Recipient Disting. Alumni award U. Wash., 1992. Mem. ABA (sect. legal edn. and admissions to bar, chair com. on libs. 1993-94, vice chair 1992-93, 94-95, com. on law sch. facilities 1998—), Am. Assn. Law Schs. (com. law librs. 1991-94), Law Librs. New Eng. (sec. 1977-79, pres. 1979-81), Am. Assn. Law Librs. (program chmn. ann. meeting 1984, exec. bd. 1984-87, v.p. 1989-90, pres. 1990-91, program co-chair Insts. 1983, 95), Law Librs. Soc. Washington (exec. bd. 1983-84, v.p., pres. elect 1984-85), Law Librs. Puget Sound, Wash. State Bar Assn. (chair editl. adv. bd.), Wash. Adv. Coun. on Librs., Westpac. Office: U Wash Marian Gould Gallagher Law Libr William H Gates Hall Box 353025 Seattle WA 98195 Office Phone: 206-543-4089. Business E-Mail: pennyh@u.washington.edu.

HAZELWOOD, CHRISTY STAMPS, elementary school educator, small business owner; d. Foy C. and Betty B. Stamps; m. Andy R. Hazelwood, Dec. 21, 1984; 1 child, William Andrew. BS, David Lipscomb College(now Lipscomb U.), Nashville, 1983. Cert. tchr. Tenn. Tchr. Tullahoma City Schs., Tenn., 1983—; adj. faculty Motlow State C.C., Lynchburg, Tenn., 1984—89. Mem. youth and worship com. Cedar Ln. Ch. of Christ, Tullahoma, 1989—. Named Tullahoma City Schs. Tchr. of Yr., Tullahoma City Sch. Bd., 1988, Tullahoma's Best Mid. Sch. Tchr., Tullahoma News, 2004; Tenn. Tech. grantee, State of Tenn. Dept. Edn. Mem.: Tenn. Edn. Assn. (state rep. 1991—93), Tullahoma City Edn. Assn. (salary com., rep. 1997—2004), Nat. Coun. Tchrs. Math. Home: 109 Provins Dr Tullahoma TN 37388 Office: East Mid Sch 908 Country Club Dr Tullahoma TN 37388 Office Phone: 931-454-2632. Personal E-mail: chazelwood@hotmail.com.

HAZLEWOOD, JUDITH EVANS, retired librarian; b. McKenzie, Tenn., Mar. 30, 1930; d. Henry Bascom and Bertie (Harvey) Evans; m. Bob J. Hazlewood, June 11, 1955; children: Jeffrey E., Amy H. McAtee. BS in English, Memphis State U., 1952; MA in English, Vanderbilt U., 1954; MA in Libr. Sci., George Peabody Coll., 1959. Sec. bus. office Memphis State U., 1951-53; tchr. English and home econs. Messick High Sch., Memphis, 1954-57; statis. clk. office v.p. U. Fla., 1957-58; English tchr. Hume-Fogg High Sch., Nashville, 1958-59; cataloger Nashville Pub. Libr., 1962-63; acquisitions libr. Lambuth U., Jackson, Tenn., 1964-74, libr. dir., 1974-95. Part-time English instr. Bethel Coll., McKenzie, 1960-62. Mem. Tenn. Libr. Assn. (sec. for educators, nominating com., chair honors awards com., chair staff devel./recruitment com., membership com.), West Tenn. Libr. Assn., West Tenn. Acad. Libr. Consortium, Tenn. Archivists, Delta Kappa Gamma, Kappa Delta Pi. Methodist. Avocations: sewing, cake decorating, reading, travel. Office: Lambuth U 705 Lambuth Blvd Jackson TN 38301-5296

HAZZARD, MARY ELIZABETH, nursing educator; b. Evansville, Ind., Mar. 2, 1941; d. John Waven and Lucille Elizabeth (Theobold) H.; 1 child, Mary Lucille. BSN, Nazareth Coll., 1963; AM, NYU, 1965, PhD, 1970; family nurse practitioner, U. Tenn., 1997. Cert. min.; cert. family nurse practitioner. Staff nurse Caldwell County War Meml. Hosp., Princeton, Ky., 1962, staff nurse supr., 1963, 65; asst. nurse St. Joseph's Hosp., Louisville, 1962-63; teaching fellow NYU, 1966, instr., 1966-68; nursing sister-in-charge Meru (Kenya) Dist. Hosp., 1966; asst. prof. U. Va. Sch. Nursing, Charlottesville, 1968-70, assoc. prof., 1970-74, dir. learning resources, 1971-74; assoc. prof. Sangamon State U., Springfield, Ill., 1974-79; prof. Western Ky. U., Bowling Green, 1979-99; prof. emeritus, 1998; prof. Nat. U., LaJolla, Calif., 1998—. Head dept. nursing Western Ky. U., Bowling Green, 1979-96; adj. assoc. prof. U. Ky., Lexington, 1983-94; curriculum cons. MacMurray Coll., Jacksonville, Ill., 1978, U. Louisville, 1981; pres. So. Coun. on Collegiate Edn. in Nursing, 1993-95; nurse practitioner Cmty. Health Care Plus, Brownsville, 1997-98, St. Vincent DePaul Med. Clin. Homeless, San Diego, 1998—. Author: Review of Med-Surg Nursing, 1976, Nursing Outline Series: Critical Care Nursing, 1978; also articles; mem. edit. rev. bd. Health Care for Women Internat., 1984—. Pres. So. Coun. on Collegiate Edn. in Nursing, 1993-95. Fellow Am. Acd. Nursing; mem. ANA, Ky. Nurses Assn. (pres. 1986-87), Ky. Assn. Baccalaureate and Higher Degree Programs (sec. 1986-87), Ky. Cols., Sigma Theta Tau, Pi Lambda Theta. Democrat. Roman Catholic. Office: Nat U 11255 N Torrey Pines Rd La Jolla CA 92037-1011 Office Phone: 858-642-8361. Business E-Mail: mhazzard@nu.edu.

HAZZARD, SHIRLEY, author; b. Sydney, Australia, Jan. 30, 1931; d. Reginald and Catherine (Stein) Hazzard.; m. Francis Steegmuller, Dec. 22, 1963 (dec. Oct. 1994). Student, Queenwood Sch., Sydney, 1946. With Spl. Ops. Intelligence, Hong Kong, 1947—48, U.K. High Commr. Office, Wellington, New Zealand, 1949—50, UN (gen. svc. category), NYC, 1952—61. Boyer lectr., Australia, 1984, 88. Author: Cliffs of Fall and other stories, 1963; (novels) The Evening of the Holiday, 1966, People in Glass Houses, 1967, The Bay of Noon, 1970, The Transit of Venus, 1980, History Defeat of an Ideal: A Study of the Self Destruction of the UN, 1973, History Countenance of Truth, 1990; (novel) The Great Fire, 2003 (Nat. Book award, 2003); (memoir) Greene on Capri, 2000. Trustee N.Y. Soc. Libr. Named Hon. Citizen Capri, 2000, Libr. Lion, N.Y. Pub. Libr., 2005; recipient Lit. Award, Nat. Inst. Arts and Letters, 1966, First prize, O. Henry Short Story Awards, 1976, Cir. Award for Fiction, Nat. Book Critics, 1981, Clifton Fadiman Medal for Lit., 2001, Nat. Book Award for Fiction, 2003, Medal of Honor, Nat. Arts Club Lit., 2004, Mary McCarthy award, Bard Coll., 2004, Miles Franklin award, Australia, 2004; Guggenheim Fellow, 1974. Fellow Royal Soc. Lit.; mem. AAAL (William Dean Howells medal 2005), Nat. Arts and Sci., Century Club N.Y.C. Address: 200 E 66th St Apt C1705 New York NY 10021-9187

HCINTOSH, ELAINE HOUSEHOLDER, physical education educator; d. James Ashley and Julia Pancoast Householder; m. Gilbert Weston McIntosh, June 26, 1982; 1 child, James Hunter. BS, Tenn. Techoln. U., Cookeville, 1975; MA, Tenn. Technol. U., Cookeville, 1981. Tchr. phys. edn. Pi Beta Phi Elem. Sch., Gatlinburg, Tenn., 1975—. Mem. adv. com. City of Pigeon Forge, Tenn., 1998—2000; coord. Jump Rope for Heart Am. Heart Assn., Gatlinburg, 1990—2006; mem. Family Readiness Group, Ft. Gillem, Ga., 2001—06; mem. steering com. Dr. Robert F. Thomas Found., Sevierville, Tenn., 2002—03. Named Mid. Sch. Tchr. of Yr., Sevier County Sch. Bd., 2001—02, Co-Tennis Educator of Yr., U.S. Tenn. Tennis Assn., 2004—05. Mem.: DAR, Alpha Delta Pi, Delta Kappa Gamma (state area dir. 2005—07, Order of the Rose 2004). Avocations: water-skiing, reading, walking, tennis. Office: Pi Beta Phi Elem Sch 125 Cherokee Orchard Rd Gatlinburg TN 37738

HEACKER, THELMA WEAKS, retired elementary school educator; b. Lakeland, Fla., Nov. 27, 1927; d. Andrew Lee and Stella Dicy (Hodges) Weaks; m. Howard V. Heacker, Aug. 21, 1947; children: Victor, Patricia, Paula, Jonathan, Johannah; m. V.L. Brown, Mar. 31, 1991. BA, Carson-Newman Coll., Jefferson City, Tenn., 1949; MA, Tenn. Technol. U., 1980; postgrad., U. Tenn. Cert. elem. and secondary tchr., Tenn.; cert. secondary tchr., Ga. Elem. tchr. Hamblen County Pub. Schs., Morristown, Tenn., 1949; secondary tchr. Morgan County-Coalfield High Sch., Coalfield, Tenn., 1986-87, Roane County-O. Springs High Sch., Oliver Springs, Tenn., 1949-71; elem. tchr. Morgan County-Petros-Joyner Sch., Oliver Springs, 1975-93. Vol. Keystone Elder Day Care, 2000—. Named Tchr. of Yr., 1986. Mem. NEA, Tenn. Edn. Assn., Ea. Tenn. Edn. Assn., Morgan County Edn. Assn., RCTA, HCTA Home: 102 Ulena Ln Oak Ridge TN 37830-5237 Office: Petros Joyner Elem Sch Petros-Joyner Rd Oliver Springs TN 37840-9700

HEACOCK, LIZBETH LEE, elementary school educator; d. Milton J. and Laurabell F. Urick; m. Patrick J. Heacock, Oct. 13, 1973; children: Kurt M., Matthew W. BS, San Diego State U., Calif., 1975; M in Edn., Calif. State U., San Bernardino, 2002. Standard Elementary Teaching Credential State of Calif., 1976. Elem. sch. tchr. Tulelake Basin Joint Unified Sch. Dist., Calif., 1981—84; mid. sch. tchr. Moreno Valley Unified Sch. Dist., Moreno Valley, Calif., 1984—. Mentor tchr. Moreno Valley Unified Sch. Dist., Calif., social sci. subject adv. com., 2002—06, dist. curriculum coun., 2002—06. Edn. commn. chair Moreno Valley United Meth. Ch. Recipient Tchr. of Yr., Moreno Valley Unified Sch. Dist., 2002, Leader in Edn., Calif. State U., San Bernardino Edn. Dept., 2002. Mem.: Phi Delta Kappa. Methodist. Avocations: travel, reading. Office: Landmark Mid Sch 15261 Legendary Dr Moreno Valley CA 92555 Home: 951 Ave Carmel #A Laguna Woods CA 92637 Office Phone: 951-571-4220. E-mail: lheacock@mvusd.k12.ca.us.

HEAD, ELIZABETH, lawyer, arbitrator, mediator; b. Rochester, Minn., Dec. 17, 1930; d. Walter Elias and Ruth Winnogene (Evesmith) Bonner; m. C. J. Head, Dec. 30, 1950; 1 child, Alison Elizabeth. BA, U. Chgo., 1949, JD, 1952. Bar: Ill. 1952, Calif. 1955, N.Y. 1958, U.S. Supreme Ct. 1963, DC 1978. Atty. Nat. Labor Rels. Bd., Washington, 1953-54; assoc. Johnston & Johnston, San Francisco, 1954-56; atty. Aminoil Inc., San Francisco, 1956-57; tchg. assoc. Law Sch. Columbia U., N.Y.C., 1957-58, gen. counsel, 1989-97; assoc. Skadden Arps, N.Y.C., 1958-60; atty. Coca-Cola Corp., N.Y.C., 1961-65; assoc. Kaye Scholer, N.Y.C., 1965-72, ptnr., 1973-82; mem. Hall & Estill, Tulsa, 1983-87; vis. fellow antitrust analysis Fed. Energy Regulatory Commn., Washington, 1987-89; arbitrator, mediator N.Y. Stock Exch., Nat. Assn. Securities Dealers, 1998—; mediator fed. cts. Trustee Mary Baldwin Coll., Staunton, Va., 1983—87. Mem.: ABA (mem. standing com. dispute resolution 1983—90), Assn. Bar City of N.Y. (mem. non-profit orgns. com. 1989—90, chair 1992—95, mem. health law com. 1997—2000), Century Assn., Phi Beta Kappa, Order of Coif. Avocations: travel, music, art, theater. Home and Office: 303 E 57th St 47F New York NY 10022-2947 Personal E-mail: elizabethhead@nyc.rr.com.

HEAD, LORI J., performing arts educator; b. Elko, Nev., Sept. 30, 1956; d. George Jukich and Edna Mae McGown; m. John M. Head, Aug. 16, 1981; children: Alex, Lacey. BS, Boise U., Idaho, 1978; MA, Ariz. State U., Tempe, 1981; PhD, U. Idaho, Idaho Falls, 2003. Dir. owner Lori J. Head Sch. Dance & Pilates, Twin Falls, Idaho, 1988—99; asst. prof. choreography Idaho State U., Picatello, 1997—. Bd. dirs. Animal Humane Soc., Pocatello, 2003—. Mem.: Am. Alliance Health, Phys., Recreation & Dance. Roman Catholic.

HEAD, MELVA ANN, artist; b. St. Louis, July 9, 1937; d. Melvin G. and Muriel J. (Hall) Irwin; m. Fred L. Head, Dec. 15, 1956; children: Allan L., Shawn M. Studied with, Thelma DeGoede Smith, 1973—83, Kwok Wai Lau, 1983—. V.p. gallery La Habra (Calif.) Art Assn., 1986-88, v.p. membership, 1988-89, v.p. programs, 1989-91, pres., 1991-92, dir., 1992-95. One person shows, including La Habra (Calif.) Art Assn., 1986, 90; exhibited in group shows at L.A. Art Assn., Chevron Oil and Field Rsch., La Habra, 1991, Long Beach (Calif.) Arts, 1994-2002, 05-06, Palm Springs (Calif.) Desert Mus., 1994, 97, 2000, 02-06, Gallery 825, L.A., 1995-2004, Pasadena (Calif.) Presbyn. Ch., 1995-97, Guggenheim Gallery, Chapman U., Orange, Calif., 1997-98, Hollywood Los Feliz Jewish Cmty. Ctr., L.A., 1997, San Bernardino County Mus., 2000, Women Painters West, 2001, 03-06, Orange County Ctr. for Contemporary Art, 2001, San Diego Watercolor Soc., 2003, 05, 06, City of Brea (Calif.) Gallery, 2005 Mem. Artists Coun. Palm Springs, L.A. Arts, Long Beach Arts, La Habra Art Assn., Whittier Art Assn., Women Painters West, San Dieo Watercolor Soc. (signature mem.). Avocations: sewing, reading. Personal E-mail: ma.head@spamex.com.

HEAD, REBECCA ANN, mathematics professor; d. Constance Myrtle Smith; m. Rick L. Head, July 23, 1983; children: Shauna Diane, Christopher Lee, Jennifer Lynne. BS, U. Colo., Boulder, 1983; MS in Math., Calif. State U., Northridge, 1995. Prof. math. Bakersfield Coll., Calif., 1996—. Recipient Sam McCall Tchr. Yr., Bakersfield Coll. Student Body, 2001. Mem.: Math. Assn. Am. (sect. vice chair 2005—06, Disting. Coll. Tchg. award 2004). Avocations: bicycling, travel.

HEADDEN, SUSAN M., editor; Formerly reporter Indpls. Star, Indpls.; sr. editor to asst. mng. editor, spl. projects U.S. News & World Report, Washington, mng. editor, spl. projects, 2004—. Recipient Pulitzer prize for investigative reporting, 1991. Office: US News and World Report 1050 Thomas Jefferson St NW Washington DC 20007 Office Phone: 202-298-0485.

HEADLEY, DEBBIE MARCIA, music educator; b. St. John's, Antigua and Barbuda, Feb. 7, 1969; d. Glenn B. and Adalia M. Samuel; m. Mark Stephen Headley, June 21, 1992; children: Lanae Marcia, Felicia Adalia, Leah D'Mar, Lydia Valretta. B Music Edn., Westminster Choir Coll., Princeton, NJ, 1991. Music specialist Roland Pk. Sch., Balt., 1991—92, Fuller Mid. Sch., Little Rock, 1993—94, Wilbur D. Mills HS, Little Rock, 1993—96, Cloverdale Magnet Mid. Sch., Little Rock, 2002—03, Baseline Elem., Little Rock, 2003—; pvt. voice and piano tchr. Ctr. Stage Music, Ark., 1993—96. Profl. devel. leader Profl. Devel. for Music Educators Grant, Little Rock, 2003—. Choral dir., performer Seventh-Day Adventist, Little Rock, 1993—99. Mem.: Music Educators Nat. Conf., Am. Orff-Schulwerk Assn. (v.p. 2006—). Office: Little Rock Sch Dist 810 W Markham Street Little Rock AR 72201 Office Phone: 501-447-3700. Personal E-mail: arwccmom@sbcglobal.net. Business E-Mail: debbie.headley@lrsd.org.

HEADLEY, HEATHER A., actress; b. Trinidad, W.I., 1974; came to U.S., 1990; d. Iric and Hannah H. Student, Northwestern U., Evanston, Ill. Profl. acting roles include: (Broadway and other plays) Ragtime, 1996, The Lion King, 1997, Aida, 1998, 2000, (Tony nomination for 2000 performance, Drama Desk award for Outstanding Actress in a Musical, Tony for Actress in a Musical), Do Re Mi, 1999; discography contbns. include: The Lion King/Disney Records, 1998, Return to Pride Rock: Songs Inspired by 'The Lion King II: Simba's Pride, 1998, From the Soul of a Man, 1998, Do Re Mi: 1999 Original Cast Recording, 1999, Elton John and Tim Rice's Aida/Rocket Records, 1999; (films) Dirty Dancing: Havana Nights, 2004; (video) Elmos' Magic Cookbook, 2001; solo albums: This is Who I Am, 2002, In My Mind, 2006. Studio: RCA Records 1540 Broadway New York NY 10036*

HEADLEY, JOANNA EVONNE, mental health services professional, researcher; b. NYC, Dec. 27, 1972; d. John Stokeley and Monica Elaine Headley. AA, Miami Dade Coll., Fla., 1993; BA in Psychology, Fla. Internat. U., Miami, 1995; MS in Mental Health, Nova Southeastern U., Miami, 1998; PhD, Barry U., Miami, 2006. Lic. mental health counselor Fla., 2001. Rsch. asst. Fla. Internat. U., Miami, 1994—95; intern Agape Women's Ctr., 1996—98; counselor coll. reach out program Barry U., 1999—2005; mental health counselor Children's Psychiat. Ctr., 2000—. Mem. adv. bd. Coll. Reach Out Program, Miami, 2002—05. Contbr. chapters to books. Mem.: APA, Am. Counseling Assn., Kappa Delta Pi. Democrat. Roman Catholic. Avocations: badminton, reading, drawing, music. Office: Childrens Psychiat Ctr 9380 SW 72d St Miami FL 33176

HEADLEY, LUNETTA FORSYTH, retired librarian; b. Conshohocken, Pa., Apr. 15, 1925; d. William Robinson and Olive Augusta (Zug) Forsyth; m. William Kenneth Headley, June 26, 1948; 1 child, Lisa Jane Headley Guglielmino. BA, Wilson Coll., 1947; MS of Libr. Scis., Villanova U., 1975. Cert. sch. librarian K-12, Pa., cert. jr. and sr. high sch. English and history, Pa. Tchr. Souderton Jr.-Sr. High Sch., Pa., 1947-48; circulation libr. Haverford Coll., Pa., 1948-54; dir. curriculum lab. Eastern Coll., St. Davids, Pa., 1970-77; coord. edn. Resource Ctr. Rosemont Coll., Pa., 1977-82; med. libr. Bryn Mawr Hosp., Pa., 1983—2005; ret. Mem. AAUW (v.p. 1981-83, ednl. found. gift honoree Valley Forge br. 1975, co-pres. 2001-2003), Wilson Coll. Alumnae Assn. (bd. dirs. 1971-73), Wilson Coll. Club of Phila. (pres. 1968-70), Paoli Woods Homeowner's Assn. (v.p., 2001-2003).

HEADRICK, LISA HUGHES, biologist, educator; d. Verlon E. and Patsy R. Hughes; m. Johnny Dewayne Headrick, May 14, 1988. BS, Miss. Coll., Clinton, 1983; MS, U. So. Miss., Hattiesburg, 1989. Instr. sci. Rankin County Sch. Dist., Puckett, Miss., 1988—89; inst. biology Jones County Jr. Coll., Ellisville, 1989—. Music dir. Ctr. Hill Bapt. Ch., Raleigh, Miss., 1999—2006. Recipient Lamplighter Tchr. award, Jones County Jr. Coll. Adminstrn., 2000. Mem.: Miss. Assn. Biology Educators, Miss. Sci. Tchr. Assn., Human Anatomy and Physiology Soc. Office: Jones County Junior College 900 South Court St Ellisville MS 39437 Office Phone: 601-477-4066.

HEAGARTY, MARGARET CAROLINE, retired pediatrician; b. Charleston, W.Va., Sept. 8, 1934; d. John Patrick and Margaret Caroline (Walsh) H. BA, Seton Hill Coll., 1957; BS, W.Va. Sch. Medicine, 1959; MD, U. Pa., 1961; DSc honoris causa, Iona Coll., 1989. Diplomate: Am. Bd. Pediatrics. Intern Phila. Gen. Hosp., 1961—62; resident in pediatrics St. Christopher's Hosp. for Children, Phila., 1962—64; dir. pediatric ambulatory care services N.Y. Hosp.-Cornell Med. Ctr., N.Y.C., 1969—78; dir. pediatrics Harlem Hosp. Ctr. Columbia U., N.Y.C., 1978—2000, prof. pediatrics coll. physicians & surgeons, 1987—2000, prof. emerita coll. physicians and surgeons, 2000—. Cons. Dept. HEW Promotion of Child Health, Washington; mem. Com. Community Oriented Primary Care Inst. Medicine, Washington; mem. Robert Wood Johnson Found. Program for Prepaid Managed Health Care, 1984; mem. governing council Inst. Medicine, Nat. Acad. Scis., 1986 Author: Changing the Medical Car System-Report of an Experiment, 1974, Medical Sociology: A Systems Approach, 1975, Child Health: Basics for Primary Care, 1980. Grantee Commonwealth Found., 1981, Robert Wood Johnson Found., 1983, Ctr. for Disease Control, 1985, Health Rsch. and Svc. Adminstrn., 1988, Nat. Inst. Allergy/Infectious Disease, 1988. Fellow Inst. Medicine (steering group for nat. forum on future of children and their families 1987—); mem. Ambulatory Pediatric Assn. (pres. 1976-77), Soc. Pediatric Research, Am. Pediatric Soc., Am. Acad. Pediatrics (com. on hosp. care 1988—), Assn. Pediatric Program Dirs., Nat. Bd. Med. Examiners. Home: 2520 Kingsland Ave Bronx NY 10469-6108 E-mail: mheagarty@aol.com.

HEAGY, LORRAINE MARY, office manager; b. Lancaster, Pa., Aug. 19, 1935; d. Ralph Long and Ella Ruth Shreiner; m. John Franklin Heagy, Oct. 15, 1960 (dec. 1979); children: John Franklin III, Loralie Leslie, Michael David. Grad. high sch., Lititz, Pa. Clk. typist Woodstream Corp., Lititz, 1953-54, Lititz Mut. Ins. Co., 1955-56; sec. Warner Lambert Co., Lititz, 1956-61; adminstrv. asst. Elam G. Stoltzfus, Jr., Lancaster, Pa., 1973-84; mgr. office support dept. Lancaster Labs., 1984-99; ret., 1999. Democrat. Avocations: reading, travel, sewing.

HEALD, PATRICIA ANNE, middle school educator; b. Cleve., Aug. 7, 1944; d. Carl Gernie and Ruth Ida Elizabeth (Samuelson) Lindquist; m. James William Heald, July 23, 1966; children: David Carl, Kristen Marie. Student, Edinboro State Coll., Warren, Pa., 1962-64; BA in Math., Ea. Nazarene Coll., Quincy, Mass., 1966; student, Pa. State U., 1969-71; MAT in Math., U. N.C., 1994. Cert. tchr., Pa., N.C. Tchr. math. Minot Pub. Schs., ND, 1966-68, Bellefonte Pub. Schs., Pa., 1968-72; tchr., math. specialist Githens Mid. Sch., Durham, NC, 1988-98; math. tchr. Ligon GT Mid. Sch., Raleigh, NC, 1998—; ret., 2006. Bd. dirs. Durham Math. Coun.; coach Math Counts, 2001—. Mem. Nat. Coun. Tchrs. Math., N.C. Coun. Tchrs. Math. Nazarene. Office Phone: 919-856-7929. Business E-Mail: pat@thehealds.org.

HEALEY, KERRY MURPHY, lieutenant governor; b. Omaha, Apr. 30, 1960; d. Edward Morris and Shirley (Cumming) M.; m. Sean Michael Healey, Dec. 28, 1985; children: Alexander Edward, Averill Adair. AB in Govt., Harvard Coll., 1982; PhD in Law and Polit. Sci., Trinity Coll., Dublin, Ireland, 1991. Proctor freshman dean's office, vis. reseacher Law Sch. Harvard U., Cambridge, Mass., 1985—86; legal policy analyst ABT Assocs., Inc., Cambridge, 1986—87; pub. policy cons. Bklyn. and Boston, 1990—99; mem. Mass. Rep. State Com., 1999—; chmn. Mass. Republican Party, 2001—02; lt. gov. State of Mass., 2003—. Del. UN NGO assembly, 1994-95 Author: State and Local Experience with Drug Paraphernalia Laws, 1987, Victim and Witness Intimidation: New Developments and Emerging Responses, 1995; co-author: Compendium of Federal Justice Statistics, 1989, Handbook of Drug Control in the United States, 1990, Prosecutorial Response to Heavy Drug Case Loads, 1993. Bd. dirs., Mass. Women's Polit. Caucus, 1999-2001; bd. dirs., North Shore C.C. Found., Danvers, Mass., 1999-2002, Friends of Beverly (Mass.) Hosp., 1999-2001; co-chair North Shore United Way Campaign, Beverly, 2001, bd. dirs. YWCA, N.Y.C., 1992-95, mem. YWCA World Svc. Coun., 1992—. Grad. fellow Rotary Internat., 1983-84; rsch. grantee Mark DeWolfe Howe Fund of Harvard Law Sch., 1986. Mem. Coun. on Fgn. Rels., Harvard Club N.Y.C. (mem. schs. com. 1987-95), N.Y. Jr. League (rep. N.Y.C. ednl. priorities panel 1992-95), Cosmopolitan Club (N.Y.C.), Union Club (Boston). Republican. Office: State House Office of the Governor Room 360 Boston MA 02133 Office Phone: 617-725-4000.

HEALY, ALICE FENVESSY, psychology professor, researcher; b. Chgo., June 26, 1946; d. Stanley John and Doris (Goodman) Fenvessy; m. James Bruce Healy, May 9, 1970; 1 child, Charlotte Alexandra. AB summa cum laude, Vassar Coll., 1968; PhD, Rockefeller U., 1973. Asst. prof. psychology Yale U., New Haven, 1973-78, assoc. prof. psychology, 1978-81, U. Colo., Boulder, 1981-84, prof. psychology, 1984—. Rsch. assoc. Haskins Labs., New Haven, 1976—80; com. mem. NIMH, Washington, 1979—81; co-investigator rsch. contract USAF U. Colo., 1985—86, prin. investigator rsch. contract U.S. Army Rsch. Inst., 1986—; prin. investigator rsch. contract Naval Tng. Sys. Ctr., 1993—94; rsch. grant prin. investigator U.S. Army Rsch. Office U. Colo., 1995—2002, 2005—; rsch. grant prin. investigator NASA, 1999—. Co-author: Cognitive Processes, 2d edit., 1986; editor: Memory and Cognition, 1986—89, Experimental Cognitive Psychology and its Applications, 2005; co-editor (with S. M. Kosslyn and R. M. Shiffrin): (Essays in Honor of William K. Estes) From Learning Processes to Cognitive Processes Vol I, 1992; co-editor: (with S.M. Kosslyn and R.M. Shiffrin) From Learning Theory to Connectionist Theory: Essays in Honor of William K. Estes, Vol. II, 1992; co-editor: (with L.E. Bourne Jr.) Learning and Memory of Knowledge and Skills: Durability and Specificity, 1995, Foreign Language Learning: Psycholinguistic Studies on Training and Retention, 1998; co-editor: (with R. W. Proctor) Experimental Psychology, 2003; assoc. editor: Jour. Exptl. Psychology, 1982—84; contbr. articles to profl. jours. and chpts. to books. Recipient Sabbatical award, James McKeen Cattell Fund, 1987—88; grantee, NSF, 1977—86, 2003—, Spencer Found. Rsch., 1978—80. Fellow: AAAS (nominating com. 1988—91, chair nominating com. 1991, chair psychology sect. 1995—96), APA (chair membership com. 1992—93, exec. com. divsn. 3 2001—04, pres. 2004—05), Soc. Exptl. Psychologists; mem.: Soc. for Applied Rsch. in Memory and Cognition, Cognitive Sci. Soc., Rocky Mountain Psychology Assn. (pres. 1994—95), Soc. Math. Psychology, Psychonomic Soc. (governing bd. 1987—92, publs. com. 1989—93), Univ. Club, Sigma Xi, Phi Beta Kappa. Avocation: French pastries. Home: 840 Cypress Dr Boulder CO 80303-2820 Office: U Colo Dept Psychology 345 UCB Boulder CO 80309-0345 Office Phone: 303-492-5032. Business E-Mail: healy@colorado.edu.

HEALY, BERNADINE P., physician, educator, former federal official; b. NYC, Aug. 2, 1944; d. Michael J. and Violet (McGrath) Healy; m. Floyd Loop, Aug. 17, 1985; children: Bartlett Anne Bulkley, Marie McGrath Loop. AB summa cum laude, Vassar Coll., 1965; MD cum laude, Harvard Med. Sch., 1970. Diplomate Am. Bd. Med. Examiners, Am. Bd. Cardiology, Am. Bd. Internal Medicine, lic. physician Md., Ohio. Intern in medicine Johns Hopkins Hosp., Balt., 1970—71, asst. resident, 1971—72; staff fellow sect. pathology Nat. Heart, Blood & Lung Inst., NIH, Bethesda, Md., 1972—74; fellow cardiovascular div. dept. medicine Johns Hopkins U. Sch. Medicine, Balt., 1974—76, fellow dept. pathology, 1975—76, asst. prof. medicine and pathology, 1976—81, assoc. prof. medicine, 1977—82, asst. dean postdoctoral programs and faculty devel., 1979—84, assoc. prof. pathology, 1981—84, prof. medicine, 1982—84, dean Coll. Med. and Pub. Health, 1995—99, prof. internal medicine, physiology, 1995—99; active staff medicine and pathology Johns Hopkins Hosp., 1976—, dir. CCU, 1976—84; pres. ARC, 1999—2001; advisor on weapons of mass destruction & bioterrorism White House, Washington, 2001—; med. & healthcare columnist, sr. writer U.S. News & World Report, 2002—. Dep. dir. Office Sci. and Tech. Policy Exec. Office of Pres., White House, Washington, 1984—85; chmn. Rsch. Inst. The Cleve. Clinic Found., 1985—91, sr. health and sci. policy advisor, 1994—95; dean Med. Sch. Ohio State U., 1995—97; dir. NIH, Bethesda, Md., 1991—93; vice-chmn. Pres.' Coun. Advisers on Sci. and Tech., 1990—91; mem. Spl. Med. Adv. Group, Dept. Vet.'s Affairs, 1990—91, chmn. adv. panel for Basic Rsch. for 1990s, Office Tech. Assessment, 1990—91, mem. NHLBI Task Force on Atherosclerosis, 1990; mem. Vis.

Com. Bd. Overseers Harvard Med. Sch. and Sch. of Dental Medicine, Boston, 1986—91; councillor Harvard Med. Alumni Assn., 1987—90; mem. Nat. Adv. Bd. Johns Hopkins Ctr. for Hosp. Fin. and Mgmt., 1987—91, Bd. Overseers Harvard Coll., 1989—; chmn. Office of Tech. Assessment Panel New Devels. in Biotech., U.S. Congress, 1986—87; mem. U.S.-Brazil Panel on Sci. and Tech., 1987, White House Sci. Coun., 1988—89; cons. Nat. Heart, Lung and Blood Inst., NIH, 1976—91; mem. adv. com. to dir. NIH, 1986—91; chmn. steering com. Post-CABG Clin. Triai, 1987—91; bd. dirs. Medtronic, Inc., Mpls., Nat. City Corp., Cleve., Nova Pharms., Balt.; mem. adv. bd. Bayer Fund for Cardiovasc. Rsch., N.Y.C., 1987—89; trustee Edison BioTech. Ctr., Cleve., 1990—; chmn. Ohio Coun. on Rsch. and Econ. Devel., 1989—91; bd. dirs. Nat. City Corp., 1989—90, 1995—2001, 2003—. Editl. cons. numerous jours.; abstract reviewer:, editl. bd.: Jour. Cardiovasc. Medicine, 1980—91, Am. Jour. Cardiology, 1981—82, Circulation, 1981—, Jour. Am. Coll. Cardiology, 1982—84, Am. Jour. Medicine, 1986—91; contbr. articles to profl. jours. Recipient Nat. Bd. Ann. award for Medicine, Med. Coll. Pa., 1983; fellow Eloise Ellery fellow, 1965—66, Stetler Rsch. fellow, 1976—77; scholar Matthew Vassar scholar, 1962—65, Harvard Nat. scholar, 1965—70. Mem.: ACP, Inst. Medicine NAS, Am. Bd. Internatl Medicine (bd. dirs. 1983—87, bd. govs. 1986—), Am. Soc. Clin. Investigation, Assn. for Women in Sci., Am. Med. Women's Assn., Internat. Acad. Pathology, Assn. Am. Med. Colls., Am. Coll. Cardiology (bd. govs. 1979—82), Am. Heart Assn. (fellow coun. on clin. cardiology, coun. on circulation, dir. 1983—84, pres. 1988—89, award 1983—84, 1990), Am. Fedn. Clin. Rsch. (pres. 1983—84), Johns Hopkins U. Soc. Scholars, Alpha Omega Alpha, Phi Beta Kappa.

HEALY, BRIDGET M., lawyer; b. Clinton, Iowa, Feb. 14, 1955; AB with honors, Brown U., 1976; JD magna cum laude, Georgetown U. Law Ctr., 1982. Assoc. Davis, Polk & Wardwell; ptnr. Strook & Strook & Lavan; atty. Becton, Dickinson & Co., Franklin Lakes, NJ, 1995—97, v.p., sec., 1997—, gen. counsel, 2000—. Mem.: Am. Soc. Corp. Sec. Inc., Am. Corp. Counsel Assn., ABA. Office: Becton Dickinson Co One Becton Dr Franklin Lakes NJ 07417-1880 Home: 601 Tenth St Brooklyn NY 11215 Office Phone: 201-847-6800. Office Fax: 201-847-6475.

HEALY, JANE ELIZABETH, newspaper editor; b. Washington, May 9, 1949; d. Paul Francis and Connie (Maas) H.; children: Randall, Kevin. BS, U. Md., 1971. Copy clk. N.Y. Daily News, Washington, 1971-73; met. reporter Orlando (Fla.) Sentinel, 1973-81, editorial writer, 1981-83, chief editorial writer, 1983-85, assoc. editor, 1985-92, mng. editor, 1993—2001, editl. page editor, 2001—. Recipient Pulitzer Prize, Columbia U., 1988, Sigma Delta Chi Disting. Service award, 1988. Mem. Am. Soc. Newspaper Editors. Office: Orlando Sentinel 633 N Orange Ave Orlando FL 32801-1349

HEALY, JOYCE ANN KURY, banker, marketing professional; b. Pitts., Sept. 23, 1947; d. Andrew G. and Mary Jane (Jacobs) Kury; m. Donall Healy, May 17, 1969; children: Brian, Mary Caitlin. Student, U. Toronto, 1965—68; BA in Sociology, U. Pitts., 1969; MA in Urban Studies, Boston U., 1973; postgrad., NYU and N.Y. Inst. of Fin., 1974—75. Analyst Boston Model Cities Adminstrn., 1969—71; mktg. research analyst Mfrs. Hanover Trust, 1971—72, sr. mktg. rsch. analyst, 1972—73, asst. sec., 1973—74, asst. v.p. 1974—75, v.p., 1975—81, sr. v.p., 1981—. Speaker in field. Contbr. articles to prof. jours. Trustee YMCA Greater N.Y. Named Woman of the Yr., Nat. Kidney Found., 1984. Mem.: Bank Mktg. Assn. (exec. com.). Avocations: bicycling, community activities.

HEALY, KAREN, automotive executive; B in Journalism, Mich. State U., 1976. With GM, 1976—95, staff pub. rels. fisher guide divsn., 1985—86, mgr. employee comm. Buick-Oldsmobile-Cadillac group, 1986, sr. adminstr. pub. affairs, dir. media comm. Delphi Corp. (formerly auto. components group worldwide), 1993—95; dir. comm. Delphi Corp., Troy, Mich., 1995—96, exec. dir. comm., 1997, v.p. corp. affairs, 1998—, v.p. mktg. comm. and facilities, 2000—. Trustee Music Hall Ctr. Performing Arts, Detroit; bd. visitors Oakland U. Bus. Sch.; bd. dirs. Forgotten Harvest, North Suburban Figure Skating Club. Named Businesswoman of Yr., Detroit News, 2000; named one of 100 Leading Women in Auto. Industry, Auto. News, 2000, Most Influential Women S.E. Mich., Crain's Detroit Bus., 2001. Mem.: Automotive Women's Alliance, Arthur Page Soc., Pub. Rels. Coun., Troy C. of C. (bd. dirs.). Office: 5725 Delphi Dr Troy MI 48098-2815

HEALY, MARGARET MARY, retail marketing executive; b. Bklyn., Dec. 31, 1938; d. Nicholas Joseph and Margaret Marie (Ferry) H.; m. Robert L. Parker, 1979 (div. 1988); 1 child, Nicole Parker. BA, Manhattanville Coll., 1961; cert., NYU, 1967, Columbia U., 1971. Account exec. Geer, DuBois & Co., Inc., N.Y.C., 1965-71; dir. mktg. comm. Dry Dock Savs. Bank, N.Y.C., 1971-72; oper. v.p. Bloomingdales, N.Y.C., 1972-79; owner, pres. Healy & Pratts, Inc., N.Y.C., 1979-88; mgr. corp. pub. rels. J.C. Penney Co., Dallas, 1988-92; owner, pres. PH Network, Dallas, 1992—; co-owner, mng. dir. Network Assocs. Internat., Dallas, 1997-98. Mem. bd. advisors North Fork Bancorp, Melville, N.Y., 1997-99. Co-author: Salute to Italy Celebrity Cookbook, 1984, Salute to America Celebrity Cookbook, 1986; contbg. editor Dallas Home Mag. Bd. dirs. Dallas Children's Theater, 1989-2000. Recipient Cmty. Svc. award VFW, 1978. Roman Catholic. Avocations: Mexican culture, travel, reading Irish literature. Office Phone: 516-652-9218. Personal E-mail: phnetwork@earthlink.net.

HEALY, MARY (MRS. PETER LIND HAYES), singer, actress; b. New Orleans, Apr. 14, 1918; d. John Joseph and Viola (Armbruster) H.; m. Peter Lind Hayes, Dec. 19, 1940 (dec. Apr. 1998); children: Peter Michael, Cathy Lind. Degree (hon.), St. Bonaventure U. With 20th Century Fox, Hollywood, Calif. Author: Twenty-five Minutes from Broadway, 1961; pictures and others, 1937-40; Broadway prodns. Around the World, 1943-46; (with husband) TV series Inside U.S.A, 1949, Peter and Mary Show, Star of the Family, 1952, Peter Lind Hayes Radio show, CBS, 1954-57; Broadway prodn. Who Was That Lady, 1957-58, Peter Lind Hayes show, ABC-TV, 1958-59, Peter and Mary, ABC-Radio, 1959—, Peter and Mary in Las Vegas; TV-film; Star (with husband) WOR radio show, 6 yrs; TV film series Fin. Planning for Women; (with husband) Film The 5000 Fingers of Dr. T, 1953; Appeared in: (with husband) Film Peter Loves Mary, 1960, When Television Was Live, 1975; films: You Ruined My Life, 1986, Looking To Get Out with Jon Voight, 1985. Mem. Pelham Country Club. Roman Catholic. Home: Canyon Gate 8641 Robinson Ridge Dr Las Vegas NV 89117-5807

HEALY, SONDRA ANITA, consumer products company executive; b. 1939; married; 3 children. BFA, Goodman Sch. Drama, 1963; MA, Nat. Coll., 1964. Owner, chair Turtle Wax, Chgo., 1973—. Office: Turtle Wax 5655 S 73rd Ave Chicago IL 60638

HEALY, STEPHANIE LEMME, hospital organization administrator; b. 1972; Pres. Hosp. Coun. Southern Ariz. Mem. Southern Ariz. AIDS Found.; hostess Silver and Turquoise Ball; bd. mem. Juvenile Diabetes Rsch. Found.; bd. dir. Pledge-A-Job. Named one of 40 Under 40, Tucson Bus. Edge, 2006. Mem.: Pima Assn. (Governments Population Planning Com.), Ariz. Assn. for Econ. Devel., Armory Park Neighborhood Assn. Office: Southern Arizona Leadership Council 4400 E Broadway Ste 307 Tucson AZ 85711*

HEALY, THERESA ANN, retired ambassador; b. Bklyn., July 14, 1932; d. Anthony and Mary Catherine (Kennedy) H. BA, St. John's U., 1954, LLD (hon.), 1985. Tchr. elem. and secondary schs., N.Y.C., 1951-55; with U.S. Fgn. Svc., 1955-94, amb. to Sierra Leone, 1980-83; with Ctr. for Internat. Affairs, U. South Fla., Tampa, 1983-84; faculty Nat. Def. U., Washington, 1984-86; with pers. and mgmt. policy bur. U.S. Dept. State, 1986-92; with Office of Freedom of Info., 1992-94; ret., 1994. Cons. Dept. State, 1996—, Office of Freedom Info., 1997—; arbitrator dispute resolution Nat. Assn. Security Dealers, 1999—. Mem. Am. Fgn. Svc. Assn., Diplomatic and Consular Officers Ret. Roman Catholic. Home: 6800 Fleetwood Rd Apt 1002 Mc Lean VA 22101-3610

HEANUE, ANNE ALLEN, retired librarian; b. Ft. Oglethorpe, Ga., Feb. 7, 1940; d. James Edward and Mary (Dennean) Allen; m. Kevin E. Heanue, July 20, 1963; children: Mary, Brian, Patricia. BA cum laude, Dunbarton Coll., 1962; MA, Georgetown U., 1966; MS in Libr. Sci., Cath. U. Am., 1976. Libr. Deloitte Haskins and Sells, Washington, 1977—79; asst. to dir. ALA, Washington, 1979—81, asst. dir., 1981—84, assoc. dir., 1984—98; ret., 1998. Bd. dirs. Alexandria (Va.) LWV, 1967-78; chmn. Alexandria Spl. Edn. adv. com., 1978-79; mem. Alexandria Gypsy Moth Control Commn., 1991-96; vol. White House, 1999—; trustee Freedom to Read Found., 2003—; mem. cancer care com. Inova Alexandria Hosp. Found., 2003—. Recipient Fed. Librs. Round Table Achievement award, 1988. Mem. ALA, Hist. Soc. Washington D.C., Va. Hist. Soc., Rappahannock Hist. Soc., D.C. Libr. Assn. (bd. dirs. 1994-97), Beta Phi Mu, Pi Gamma Mu. Roman Catholic. Avocations: reading, travel, theater.

HEAP, JOAN S., elementary school educator; b. Ogden, Utah, July 13, 1944; d. Ralph William Spackman and Reita Anone Ward; m. Brent Aaron Heap, Sept. 3, 1965; children: Amie Nicole, Aaron Robert, Ethan Trevor, Tucker Justin, Tyler Brent, Morgan Katie Zavala, Kellie Joan. BS, Weber State U., Ogden, Utah, 1965. Lang. arts tchr. Walhquist Jr. High, Harrisville, Utah, 1965—66, Rocky Mountain Jr. High, West Haven, 1994—99; lang. arts tchr., dept. chair N. Ogden Jr. High, Ogden, 1999—. Adv. Nat. Jr. Honor Soc., Ogden, 1999—; team mem. Utah Behavior Intervention, Salt Lake City, 2003—, Student at Risk Intervention, Ogden, 2003—. Active Cmty. Coun., 1994—. Recipient Tchr. of Yr., Weber Sch. Dist., Ogden, 2005, Utah Tchr. of Yr. award, 2006. Mem.: NEA, UCTE, WEA, Utah Edn. Assn. Republican. Mem. Lds Ch. Avocations: hiking, skiing, mountain biking, marathoner. Office: North Ogden Jr High 575 E 2900 N North Ogden UT 84414

HEAPHY, JANIS BESLER, newspaper executive; b. Kalamazoo, Oct. 10, 1951; d. Elvin Julius and Margaret Louise (Throndike) Olson; m. Douglas R. Dern, Aug. 15, 1980 (div. Nov. 1985); m. Robert Thomas Heaphy, Feb. 11, 1989; 1 child, Tanner. BS, Miami U., 1973, MEd, 1976. Tchr. Edgewood Jr. H.S., Seven Mile, Ohio, 1973—75; acct. exec. L.A. Times, 1976—79, sr. acct. exec., 1986—87, ea. mag. mgr., 1987—89, nat. advt. mgr., 1989—92, retail advt. mgr. then sr. v.p. advt./mktg., 1992—97; acct. exec. L.A. Mag., 1979—82; mgr. L.A. Omni Mag., 1982—86; pub. Sacramento Bee, 1997—, pres. Co-editor: Secrets of the Master Sellers, 1987. Mem.: Advt. Club L.A. Avocations: home decorating, reading, swimming, music. Office: Sacramento Bee 2100 Q St Sacramento CA 95852 Mailing: Sacramento Bee PO Box 15779 Sacramento CA 95852 Office Fax: 916-321-1109. E-mail: jheaphy@sacbee.com.*

HEARD, BARBARA MUSE, business owner; b. Raleigh, NC, Apr. 10, 1958; d. Robert Hartman and Patricia (Hoskins) Muse; m. James Kenneth Heard, Sept. 12, 1990; children, James Daniel, Catherine Jean. AA, Valencia Community Coll., Orlando, Fla., 1978; BS, Fla. State. U., 1981. Sr. designer Drexel Heritage Furnishings, Drexel, N.C., 1981-84; showroom designer Hickory Chair Co., Hickory, N.C., 1984-87; textile coord., designer Baker Furniture, Chgo., 1987-89; creative dir. Robert Allen Div. of Masco Home Furnishings, Boston, 1989-91; owner Heavy Metal Hardware, Boston, 1991—93, Interior Cons., Boston and Oakton, Va., 1990—. Editor: The Valencian, 1978. Vol. Rep. Party, Chgo., 1988. Recipient Literary Scholarship Valencia Community Coll., 1977, Marshal Hamilton Acad. Scholarship Fla. State U., 1978-81. Republican. Methodist. Avocations: outdoor sports, travel, photography, writing.

HEARN, BEVERLY JEAN, education educator; b. Lexington, Tenn., Sept. 10, 1953; d. James Lawrence and Marie (Sparks) Kee; m. Larry Joseph Hearn, June 15, 1973; children: Matthew Joseph, David Andrew. BA, Union U., 1974; MLS, George Peabody Coll. for Tchrs., 1975; EdD, Memphis State U., 1991. Acqusitions librarian Union U., Jackson, Tenn., 1975-80, reference librarian, 1980-86; tchr. Madison County Bd. Edn., 1986—2004; dir. reading ctr., asst. prof. reading U. Tenn., Martin, 2004—. Instr. Memphis State U., 1990-95, Jackson State C.C., 1992-97; freelance cataloger, 1978-86; multicultural edn. cons., 2004—. Grantee Fulbright Hayes Group Projects Abroad, US govt., 2000, 2002. Mem. TESOL, Tenn. TESOL (pres. 2004-06), Internat. Reading Assn., Assn. for Curriculum Devel. Democrat. Baptist. Home: 558 Wallace Rd Jackson TN 38305-2839 Office Phone: 731-881-7197. Business E-Mail: bhearn@utm.edu.

HEARN, CYNTHIA ANN, education educator; b. Harrison, Ark., Sept. 6, 1962; d. Raymond Eugene Stills, Ann Etta Stills; m. Jeff Hearn, Aug. 9, 1980; children: Rebekah, Hannah. BA, Harding U., 1982, MEd, 1991; Ednl. Specialist, U. Ark., 2000, DEd, 2002. Cert. ednl. adminstr., Title I Specialist. Educator Harrison Pub. Schs., Harrison, Ark., 1984—2000, Title I Specialist, 2000—02; cons. Hearn and Assocs., Harrison, Ark., 1990—2002. Mem. Harding U. Pres.'s Devel. Coun. Author: (integrated ednl. program) MoveN'Learn, 1998, (ednl. program) KidNews, 1999; contbr. literacy program Camp Read-A-Lot, 2001. Recipient Roy G. Miller award, U. Ark., 2001; grantee, Harrison Pub. Schs. Found., 1998, 1999, Entergy, 2001. Mem.: AAUW, ASCD, NEA, Tchrs. Ark. Students Coun., Nat. Coun. Tchrs. English, Ozark Reading Coun., Internat. Reading Assn., Ark. Reading Assn., Harrison Edn. Assn., Ark. Edn. Assn., Phi Delta Kappa. Avocations: travel, music, literature, hiking, target/skeet. Office: Harrison Pub Schs 500 N Chestnut Harrison AR 72601 Personal E-mail: cynthia@alltel.net.

HEARN, JOYCE CAMP, retired state legislator, educator, consultant; b. Cedartown, Ga. d. J.C. and Carolyn (Carter) Camp; m. Thomas Harry Hearn; children: Theresa Hearn Potts Bailey, Kimberly Ann Johnson, Carolyn Lee Becker. Student, U. Ga.; BA, Ohio State U., 1957; postgrad., U. S.C. Former h.s. tchr.; dist. mgr. U.S. Census, 2d Congl. Dist., 1970; mem. S.C. Ho. of Reps., 1975-89. Asst. minority leader, 1976-78, 86-89; chmn., commn. alcohol beverage control, 1989-91; pres., cons. Hearn & Assocs., Columbia, S.C., 1995—. Mem. Richland County Planning Commn., 1974-76; bd. dirs. Meml. Youth Ctr. and Stage South; chmn. Sexual Assault Awareness Week; vice chmn. Dist. Rep. Com., 1968; Rep. chmn. 2d Congl. Dist., 1969; Rep. chmn. Richland County, 1972; del., platform com. Rep. Nat. Conv., 1980, 84; moderator Kathwood Bapt. Ch., 1979-80, former asst. Sunday Sch. tchr.; bd. dirs. Small Bus. Devel. Ctr., S.C., Columbia Coll. Bd. Vis., Columbia Urban League, Fedn. of Blind; trustee Columbia Mus. Art; apptd. to Alcohol Beverage Control Bd., 1989, apptd. chmn. commn., 1990-92, commr., 1991-94; bd. dirs. Lupus Found., 1990—; chair nat. adv. com. Occupl. Safety and Health, 1980-88. Recipient Outstanding Citizen award Columbia Rape Coalition, 1977, Disting. Svc. award Claims Mgmt. Assn., S.C., 1977, Nat. Fedn. Blind S.C., 1978, Columbia Urban League, 1983, MADD, 1985, Outstanding Legislator of Yr. award Alcohol and Drug Abuse Assn., 1980, Retarded Citizens Assn., 1982, S.C. Rehab. Assn., 1984, S.C. Assn. of Deaf, 1987, Legislator of Yr., Fedn. of Blind, 1988, Disting. Legislator, DAV, 1989; honoree Easter Seals, 1989; numerous other awards. Mem. Nat. Order of Women Legislators (v.p., pres.), Order of the Palmetto, S.C. Women's Club, Columbia Women's Club (bd. dirs.), Larkspur Garden Club, Spring Valley Country Club Golf Assn. (pres. 1973, 97), Spring Valley Country Club. Office Phone: 803-256-7255. E-mail: jchearn@bellsouth.net.

HEARN, MELISSA PATE, geriatric administrator; b. Dennison, Tex., July 30, 1960; d. Carroll M. and Nellie Alice (Hightower) Pate; m. William M. Hearn Jr., Oct. 10, 1992; children: Frank W. IV, William M. III. BSN, Auburn U., 1982. Charge nurse East Ala. med. Ctr., Opelika; staff nurse Phoebe Putney Meml. Hosp., Albany, Ga., Athens (Ala.)-Limestone Hosp.; dir. nursing Athens Convalescent Ctr.; dir. nursing, now resident care adminstr. Limestone Health Facility. Named Dir. of Nursing of Yr., Ala. Nursing Home Assn., Inc., 1990.

HEARN, ROBIN KIM, secondary school educator; b. Dallas, Oct. 1, 1956; d. Jack and Patty Hearn; children: Luke Cheatham, Brian Cheatham. BS, Tex. Woman's U., Denton, 1982. Secondary dance tchr. Tex., cert. secondary English tchr. Tex., comms. tchr. Tex. Owner Showtime Dance Studio, Denton, 1981—96, Denton Costume and Danceworld, 1980—96; classroom tchr. NW Ind. Sch. Dist., Justin, Tex., 1997—. Mem.: United Educators Assn. Office: Northwest Ind Sch Dist 2209 Texan Dr Justin TX 76247 Office Phone: 817-215-0200.

HEARON, HOLLY ELIZABETH, religious studies educator; d. William Montgomery and Barbara Olsen Hearon; life ptnr. Lorna Shoemaker, Aug. 31, 1991. BA, Wellesley Coll., Mass., 1978; D.Min., Union Theol. Sem., Richmond, Va., 1983; PhD, Grad. Theol. Union, Berkeley, Calif., 1998. Assoc. min. Westminster Presbyn. Ch., Pasadena, 1984—86; assoc. for women's program Presbyn. Ch. (USA), Kansas City, Mo., 1987—89; assoc. prof. N.T. Christian Theol. Sem., Indpls., 1999—. Author: (scholarly monograph) The Mary Magdalene Tradition: Witness and Counter-Witness in Early Christian Communities (First Pl. Award for First Time Author, Cath. Press Assn., 2005); contbr. articles to profl. jours. Participant in travel to Nicaragua Witness for Peace, 1984; mem. of adv. bd. Religion and Faith Program, Human Rights Campaign, Washington, 2006; mem. com. on ministry Presbytery of the Redwoods, Calif., 1993—95; mem. com. on preparation for ministry Presbytery of the Heartland, 1989; mem, task force on Ctrl. Am. Synod of So. Calif. and Hawaii, 1986; chair com. on peacemaking Presbytery of San Gabriel, 1985—86, mem. ch. and soc. com., 1985—86; bd. mem. Martin Luther King Multi-Svc. Ctr., Indpls., 2000—05. Mem.: Cath. Bibl. Assn., Soc. of Bibl. Lit. Office: Christian Theological Seminary 1000 W 42nd St Indianapolis IN 46208 Office Phone: 317-931-2333.

HEARON, SHELBY, writer, educator; b. Marion, Ky., Mar. 18, 1931; d. Charles Boogher and Evelyn Shelby (Roberts) Reed; m. William Halpern, Aug. 19, 1995; children from previous marriage: Anne Rambo, Reed. BA, U. Tex., 1953. Disting. vis. prof. U. Ill., Chgo., 1993, Colgate U., 1993, U. Miami, Fla., 1994, U. Mass., Amherst, 1994-96, Middlebury Coll., 1996-98. Author: Armadillo in the Grass, 1968, The Second Dune, 1973, Hannah's House, 1975, Now and Another Time, 1976, A Prince of a Fellow, 1978, Painted Dresses, 1981, Afternoon of a Faun, 1983, Group Therapy, 1984, A Small Town, 1985, Five Hundred Scorpions, 1987, Owing Jolene, 1989, Hug Dancing, 1991, Life Estates, 1994, Footprints, 1996, Ella in Bloom, 2001; mem. editl. bd. Am. Literary Rev., The Writer Mag.; contbr. articles, short fiction and book revs. to various publs. Pres. Tex. Inst. Letters, 1980; chair lit. panel Tex. Commn. on Arts, 1980; mem. lit. panel N.Y. Coun. on Arts, 1985. Named to, Tex. Lit. Hall of Fame, 2004; recipient Syndication prize, NEA/PEN, 1984—85, 1985, 1987, 1988, Lit. award, Am. Acad. Arts and Letters, 1990, Lifetime Achievement award, Tex. Book Festival, 2003; fellow, Guggenheim, 1982, Nat. Endowment Arts, 1983; grantee, Ingram Merrill, 1987. Mem.: PEN, Associated Writing Programs, Tex. Inst. Letters (Fiction award 1973, 1978), Poets and Writers Inc., Authors Guild. Democrat. Presbyterian. Home: 246 S Union St Burlington VT 05401-4514

HEARTT, CHARLOTTE BEEBE, university official; b. N.Y.C., Nov. 12, 1933; d. Stacey Kile and Charlotte Beebe; m. William Hollis Peirce, 1954 (div. 1960); children: Daniel Converse, William Kile; m. Stephen Heartt, 1962 (div. 1968); children: Thomas Beebe, Sarah Lincoln. BA, Wellesley Coll., 1954. Intern Office of V.p. Richard Nixon, Washington, 1953; asst. Computing Numerical Analysis Lab. U. Wis., Madison, 1954-56; dir. fund raising Boston Arts Festival, 1961; asst. to dean coll. rels. Radcliffe Coll., Cambridge, Mass., 1961-62; sec. to chmn. dept. city planning Harvard U., Cambridge, 1962; Fulbright program adviser, study abroad adviser Brandeis U., 1966-71, dir. office internat. programs, 1971-76, dir. found. and corp. rels., 1976-79; dir. corp. rels., asst. dir. devel. Smith Coll., Northampton, Mass., 1979-81, dir. devel., 1981-95, dir. prin. gifts, 1995-98; ind. cons., 1999—. Mem. Commonwealth Task Force on the Open Univ., 1973; bd. dirs. Coun. on Internat. Ednl. Exch., 1973-77, mem. exec. com., 1975-77; bd. dirs. Boston Area Seminar for Internat. Students, 1973-76; mem. adv. com. New England Colls. Fund, 1981-95; trustee Berkshire Sch., 1989-98, trustee emerita, 1999—; bd. dirs. Hampshire Cmty. United Way, 1996-2000; mem. devel. com. Belmont Day Sch., Belmont, Mass., 2000-04, Boston (Mass.) Leadership Gift Com. Wellesley Coll., 2002—, chmn. spl. gifts 50th reunion, 2000-04. Mem. Sect. on U.S. Study Abroad (nat. sec., regional rep. 1972-74), Nat. Assn. Fgn. Student Affairs (nat. commr. liaison), Nat. Assn. Women Deans, Adminstrs. and Counselors (internat. students and programs com. 1974-76), Nat. Soc. Fund Raisers, Coun. for Advancement and Support Edn. Home: 11 Carver Rd Wellesley MA 02481-5351 E-mail: c.heartt@comcast.net.

HEATH, ALICE FAIRCHILD, retired mental health services professional; b. Normal, Ill., Jan. 18, 1931; d. Forrest Clark and Eunice Jane (Dooley) Fairchild; m. Robert Winfield Heath, June 14, 1952; children: Katharine Ann, Nancy Diane. BA in Sociology and Psychology, Ill. Wesleyan U., 1952; postgrad., Jane Addams Sch. Social Work, 1976—77; postgrad., No. Ill. U., 1990—91. Vol. svcs. coord. H.D. Singer Mental Health and Develop. Ctr., Rockford, Ill., 1979—99. Adv. curriculum com. human svc. dept. Rock Valley Coll., 1980—84; adv. com. student svc. learning Rockford Coll., 1993—98; mem. vol. svc. dept. human svc. State of Ill., 1990, policy manual rev. com. dept. human svc., 1995—97; steering com. Conf. Vol. Adminstrs., Ill., 1995—96. Steering com. Rockford Coalition for Homeless, 1985—86; co-chair planning com. Forward Rockford Congress, 1970; mem. Rockford Bd. Edn., 1972—75; mem. United Way, Rock River Valley, 1978—84; bd. dirs. YWCA, 1960—65, 1969—75; pres. Bloom Sch. PTA, Rockford, 1965—67; brownie leader Girl Scouts Am., 1960—66; mem. Winnebago County Bd. Health, 1990—99; co-chair fundraising event Rockford Area Lit. Coun., 1990, 1994; chair No. Ill. Cmty. Health Found., 1999—2001, vice-chair, 2001—; pres. Rockford chpt. Lyric Opera Chgo., 1991—93; steering com. Women's History Week, 1978—79, 1980; mem. Stephen minister Westminster Presbyterian Ch., Rockford, 1995—, former deacon & elder. Mem.: AAUW (edn. chair 1966—68), Ctr. for Learning in Retirement, Archaeology Inst. Am., Rockford Network, League Women Voters (pres. 1969—70), Winnebago-Boone Geneal. Soc., Alabet Temple Daughters of Nile, AARP, Kappa Kappa Gamma. Presbyterian. Avocation: community service. Home: 1017 Lundvall Ave Rockford IL 61107 E-mail: aheath1017@aol.com.

HEATH, AUDREY MARY, artist, jewelry designer; b. Providence, Mar. 1, 1956; d. Alfred Peter Venditto, Jr. and Loretta Ann Rice; m. Carmine Imbriglio III, Apr. 16, 1978 (div. July 1981); m. Michael Alfred Heath, May 4, 1998; one child, Michael Alfred II. Grad., C.C. R.I., 1983; BFA, Jewelry Inst. R.I., 1987. Cert. nursing asst. Artist and jewelry designer, R.I., 1987-98. Activity therapist, coord., psychiat. therapist R.I. State Med. Ctr. Pres. Jr. Achivement of R.I. Roman Catholic. Avocations: art, music, jewelry design.

HEATH, BERTHANN JONES, educational association administrator; b. Dallas, May 4, 1938; d. James Lafayette and Allie Mae (Hudson) Jones; m. John Willie Heath, Jr., July 14, 1963 (div. 1975); 1 child, John William, III. BS cum laude, Pepperdine U., 1959; MS, UCLA, 1960. Instr. cert. family and consumer scientist. Tchr., dept. chair L.A. Unified Sch. Dist., 1960—69, tchr. dist. resource, 1972—75; counselor L.A. H.S., 1968—72; regional supr., home econ. edn. Calif. State Dept. Edn., 1975—85; program mgr., sch.-to-career transition San Diego City Sch., 1985—2000; cons., 2000—; owner Berthann's Enterprises, 2000—. Trustee Consumer Credit Counselors of San Diego and Imperial Counties, Calif., 1986-2000; mem. adv. com. Calif. State Dept. Edn. Home Econs. and Health Careers, Sacramento, 1985-98; mem. articulation team SDUSD and San Diego C.C.s, 1987-2000. Author, contbr. to curriculum guides, pamphlets and leaflets. V.p. San Diego chpt. The Links, Inc., 1995-97; presenter TV-8 Looks at Learning and Inside San Diego, 1985-95. Recipient Appreciation/Commendation award Calif. Dept. Edn., 1987, Nat. Gourmet Cook award Nat. Assembly, Links, Inc., 1996, Fin. Literacy Program Svc. award Consumer Credit Counselors of San Diego and Imperial Counties, 1996, Am. Assn. Family and Consumer Scis. Nat. Leader of Yr. award, 1998; named Woman of Distinction, Women, Inc., 1999. Mem. Am. Vocat. Assn. (bylaws chair family and consumer scis. edn. divsn. 1993-97), Nat. Assn. Local Suprs. of Family and Consumer Scis. (pres. 1992-93), Am. Vocat. Assn. (policy and planning com. 1991-97), Calif. Assn. Family and Consumer Scis. (San Diego chpt., chair secondary edn. 1985-95, state chair edn. com. 1989-90, ex-officio mem. articulation com. 1989-96), So. Calif. Biotech. Consortium (charter 1994-96), Links, Inc., Alpha Rho Tau, Delta Sigma Theta, Kappa Omicron Nu, Phi Delta Kappa. Avocations: food design and recipe experimentation, writing, elder care research and development. Office: Berthann's Enterprises PO Box 10823 Marina Del Rey CA 90295

HEATH, EMILY B., interior designer; b. Balt., Feb. 18, 1953; children: Aaron Brodsky Health, Allison Brodsky Health. BFA in Interior Design, Md. Inst. Coll. Art, 1975. V.p., mkg. design dir. Michael Asner Assocs. Inc., 1975—91; pres. Heath Design Group Inc., 1991—. Bd. dirs. Md. Permanent Bank. Mem. leadership cabinet Greater Balt. Com., 1992—93; Mem. devel. com. Park Sch., 1996—98; chair, bd. dirs. United Jewish Appeal Leadership Cabinet, 1992—98; bd. dirs. Network 2000, 1995—, Associated Women's Dept., 1990—98, Associated Jewish Coll. Svcs., 1994—99, Girl Scouts Cen. Md., 1996—99, Associated Jewish Cmty. Fedn. Balt., 1992—94. Named one of Md.'s Top 100 Women, Daily Record, 1997, one of Top 200 Design Firms in Interior Design Mag., 1994; recipient Urban Enterprise 25 award for Balt.'s Fastest-Growing Cos., 1999, Bldg. Congress and Exch. Craftsmanship award, Johns Hopkins Bayview Physicians, Merritt Park Facility Project, 1999, Merit award, Associated Builders and Contractors Excellence in Constrn., 1999, ASID Design award, 1995, 1997, 1994, Harry Greenstein Young Leadership award for leadership and cmty. svc., 1992. Office: Ste 200 316 N Charles St Baltimore MD 21201

HEATH, JAYNE MARIE, music educator; b. Denver, Feb. 23, 1955; d. Harold Edward and Alice Clara Walker; m. William B. Heath, Aug. 28, 1976; children: James, Jared, Jessica. B.Mus.Edn., U. No. Colo., 1976, MA, 1980. Lic. tchr. Colo. Music tchr. Cherry Creek Sch. Dist., Centennial, Colo., 1976—; mus. dir. Stage Eleven, Centennial, 1984—96, Young Actors Theatre, Centennial, 1996—. Mem.: Music Educators Nat. Conf. Avocations: softball, reading, gardening, scrapbooks. Office: Walnut Hills Elementary Sch 8195 E Costilla Blvd Centennial CO 80112

HEATH, JOSEPHINE WARD, foundation administrator; b. San Jose, Calif., Sept. 5, 1937; d. James Hugh and Adella Ward; m. Stratton Rollins Heath Jr.; children: Stratton, Kristin Heath-Colon, Joel. BS, Ea. Oreg. State U., 1959; MS, U. Wis., 1960. Commr. Boulder (Colo.) County, 1982-90; tchg. fellow John F. Kennedy Sch. of Govt., Harvard U., Cambridge, Mass., 1991; spl. asst. to the dir. White Ho. Office of Nat. Svc., Washington, 1993; pres. Jurismonitor, Boulder, 1993-95; tchr., project liberty John F. Kennedy Sch. Govt., Harvard U., Cambridge, 1994-98; pres. The Cmty. Found., Boulder, 1995—. Tchr. Bad Kreuznach, Germany, 1966-67, El Paso, Tex., 1963-64, Appleton, Wis., 1961-62; regional dir. ACTION, Denver, 1977-79. Editor: Alternative Work Patterns, 1977. Candidate U.S. Senate, Colo., 1992, 1990; commr. Met. Baseball Stadium Dist., Maj. League Colo. Rockies, 1991—; county commr. Boulder County, 1982-90; co-founder Women's Found. of Colo., 1987; trainer for elected offcls. in Ctrl. Europe, 1994-98. Named to Colo. Women's Hall of Fame, 2000; recipient William Funk award for Statewide Cmty. Leadership, Colo. Assn. Non Profits, 2004. Mem. Internat. Women's Forum (bd. dirs. 1986-89), Women's Forum of Colo. (pres. 1991), Internat. Com. Coun. on Founds. Democrat. Avocations: skiing, hiking, sports. Home: 2455 Vassar Dr Boulder CO 80305-5728 Office: The Cmty Found 1123 Spruce St Boulder CO 80302-4001 Office Phone: 303-442-0436. Personal E-mail: JosieHeath@aol.com.

HEATH, LIA KATHRYN, apparel designer; b. Oakland, Calif., Oct. 19, 1975; d. William Horn and Barbara Jean Ramsey; m. Thayer Ashley Heath, May 14, 2005. BSc in Mass Comm. magna cum laude, UCLA, 1997; AA in Design, Fashion Inst. Design & Merchandising, 2000. Sr. designer, pres., owner The North Face. Named one of Top Designers Under 30, San Francisco Design Ctr., 2002. Mem.: Fashion Inst. Design and Merchandising Alumni Assn., Phi Beta Kappa. Personal E-mail: divaplanet_lia@yahoo.com.

HEATH, MARIWYN DWYER, writer, legislative staff member; b. Chgo., May 1, 1935; d. Thomas Leo and Winifred (Brennan) Dwyer; m. Eugene R. Heath, Sept. 3, 1956; chilren: Philip Clayton, Jeffrey Thomas. BJ, U. Mo., 1956. Mng. editor Chemung Valley Reporter, Horseheads, N.Y., 1956-57; freelance writer, platform spkr., editor Tech. Transls., Dayton, Ohio, 1966—. Cons. Internat. Women's Commn., 1975-76; ERA coord. Nat. Fedn. Bus. and Profl. Women's Clubs, 1974-82, 92—; polit. and mgmt. coms. ERAmerica, 1976-82, exec. dir., 1982-88; pres. Miami Valley Regional Transit Authority, 1986-88; chair Regional Transit Coalition, 1991-94. Author: 75 Years and Beyond-BPW/USA, 1994. Active Gov. Ohio Task Force Credit for Women, 1973, Ohio Womens Commn., 1990-98, vice-chair, 1993-96, chair, 1996-98; midwest regional adv. com. SBA, 1976-82; task force Women Ohio Bicentennial Commn., 1999—; pres. Dayton Pres. Club, 1973-74; chmn. Ohio Coalition ERA Implementation, 1974-75; appt. joint civilian orientation conf. U.S. Dept. Def., 1988. Recipient Legion of Honor award Dayton Pres. Club, 1987, Keeper of Flame award Ohio Sec. of State, 1990; named one of 10 Outstanding Women of World Soroptimist Internat., 1982; named to Ohio Womens Hall of Fame. Mem. AAUW (dir. Dayton 1965-72, Woman of Yr. award Dayton 1974), Nat. Fedn. Bus. and Profl. Womens Clubs (pres. Dayton 1967-69, Ohio 1976-77, nat. polit. action com. 1985-98, chmn. 1988-98), Miami Valley Mil. Affairs Assn. (bd. dirs.), Ohio Women (v.p. 1983-86, bd. dirs. 1977-89), Assn. Women Execs., Women in Comm. Republican. Roman Catholic. Home: 145 Huffman Ave Dayton OH 45403-1915

HEATH, PATTI, art educator, musician; b. Syracuse, N.Y., Nov. 10, 1956; d. Maryann Clark; m. Steven Heath; 1 child, Sarah. MusB cum laude, Hartt Sch., Hartford, Conn., 1974—78; MusM, Manhattan Sch. Music, N.Y.C., 1978—79. Prin. clarinet Festival of the Americas, San Jose, Costa Rica, 1984, Palm Beach Opera, West Palm Beach, 1984—93, Palm Beach Symphony, West Palm Beach, 1984—93; techg. artist Young Audiences of South Fla., West Palm Beach, 1990—93; tchg. artist Syracuse Inst. Aesthetic Edn., 1995—; artist in residence Blodgett Sch., Syracuse, 2002—05; instrumental music/visual arts tchr. St. James Sch., Syracuse, NY, 2004—, dir. after sch. programs, 2005—. Recipient Applied Music award for Outstanding Musical Achievement, Hartt Sch., 1978. Mem.: Americans for the Arts. Avocations: travel, building traditional folk instruments.

HEATH-PSYD, PAMELA B. WASSERMAN, psychologist; b. Queens, N.Y., Nov. 20, 1967; d. Jerry A. and Donna L. Wasserman; m. Jeffrey A. Heath, Nov. 7, 1998; 1 child, Leah Heath. BA magna cum laude, L.I. U., 1989; D of Clin. Psychology, Ill. Sch. Profl. Psychology, 1995. Lic. clin. psychologist Ill., N.Y. Psychologist VA Med. Ctr., Denver, 1995; clin. supr. Greenwood Care, Inc., Evanston, Ill., 1995—97; clin. psychologist Evanston, 1997—99; clin. psychologist, dir. tng., clin. supr. St. Francis Hosp., Evanston, 1999—2000; psychologist Brookville, NY, 2001—. Assoc. faculty mem. Ill. Sch. Profl. Psychology, Rolling Meadows, 1996—99; cons. Greenwood Care, Inc., Evanston, 1995—99, Denver, 1993, Chgo., 92. Mem.: APA, N.Y. Psychol. Assn., Psi Chi. Republican. Jewish. Avocations: tennis, swimming. Office: 4 Quaker Ridge Rd Glen Head NY 11545

HEATON, JANET NICHOLS, artist, art gallery director; b. Miami, Fla., May 27, 1936; d. Wilmer Elwood and Katherine Elizabeth (Rodgers) Nichols; children: Benjamin Nichols Heaton, Nancy Elizabeth Breedlove. Student, Fla. State U., 1954-56. Artist Heaton's Studio & Gallery, Lake Park, Fla., 1976—, dir., 1979—. One woman show Comercia Bank Trust, Palm Bch. Gardens, Fla., 1999; Exhibited in group shows at Leigh Yawkey Woodson Art Mus., Wausau, Wis., 1988-89, 91-93, 95-97, 99, Norton Gallery Art, West Palm Beach, Fla., 1989, 92, Mt. Kenya Safari Club, Kenya, East Africa, 1989, 92, Prestige Gallery, Toronto, Can., 1989, Kimball Art Ctr., Park City, Utah, 1990-91, Grand Cen. Gallery, N.Y.C., 1990, Gallery Fine Arts, Ft. Myers, Fla., 1990, Cornell Fine Art Mus., Winter Park, Fla., 1990, Cen. Park Zoo Gallery, N.Y.C., 1991, The Art League Marco Island, Fla., 1993, 96, Washington State Hist. Soc. Mus., Tacoma, 1993, Old Sch. Sq. Cultural Arts Ctr., Delray Beach, Fla., 1993, 94, The Salmagundi Club, N.Y.C., 1994, J.N. Bartfield Galleries, N.Y.C., 1994, Pt. Royal Gallery, Naples, Fla., 1994, Brookfield Zoo, Chgo., 1994, Ward Mus. Wildfowl Art, Salisbury, Md., 1995, Easton (Md.) Waterfowl Festival, 1995, Sarasota (Fla.) Visual Art Ctr., 1995, Shenandoah Art Ctr., North Wainsboro, Va., 1996, Village Gallery, Venice, Fla., 1997, The Hiram Blauvelt Art Mus., Oradell, N.j., The Mus. of Hounds and Hunting, Leesburg, Va., 1997, Nat. Arts Club Grand Gallery, N.Y.C., 1997, Fort Hayes Met. Edn. Ctr., Columbus, Ohio, 1997, Nat. Arts Club, N.Y.C., 1997, Leigh Yawkey Woodson Art Mus., Wausau, 1997, Wendell Gilley Mus., Southwest Harbour, Maine, 1996, Tampa (Fla.) Mus. Art, 1998, Village Gallery, Venice, Fla., 1998, 99, Disney's Animal Kingdom, Orlando, 1998, Smithsonian Instn.'s Conservation & Rsch. Ctr. & Noah's Network, Front Royal, Va., 1998, 99, Comercia Bank Trust, Palm Bch. Gardens, 1998, The Nature Gallery, West Boylston, Mass., 1998, Mus. Sci. and Scpace Transit Planetarium, Miami, 1998, Ambleside Gallery, Groose Points, Mich., Bigfork Art & Cultural Ctr., Bigfork, Mont., 1998, Holland and Holland Function, N.Y.C., 1999, Leigh Yawkey Woodson Art Mus., Wausau, Wis., 1999, John L. Wehle Gallery at Genesee County Mus., Mumford, Fla., 1999, Cleve. Mus. Natural Hist., Cleve., 1999, Comerica Bank & Trust, Palm Beach Gardens, Fla., 2000, Leigh Yawkey Woodson Art Museum, Wausau, Wisc., 2000-03, Feline Fine: Art of Cats Exhibition Tour, The Arts and Science Ctr., Pine Bluff, AR, 2002, Jouh D. MacArthur Beach State Park, North Plam Beach, Fla., 2003; numerous others; numerous exhbns. including most recently John D. MacArthur Beach State Pk., North Palm Beach, Fla., 2003, Ackley Hall Mus. Natural History, N.Y., 2003, Hiram Blauvelt Art Mus., Oradell, N.J., 2003, Geoffrey C. Smith Galleries, Stuart, Fla., 2003, Art League of Marco Island Gallery, Fla., 2004, Animals in Art, Miami Metro-Zoo, 2004, Hiram Blauvelt Art Mus., Oradell, 2004, Geoffrey C. Smith Galleries 2d Annual Christmas Show, Fla., 2004, Nev. State Mus., Carson City, 2005, Soc. Animal Artists 45th Annual Nat. Mus. Tour, 2005; represented in permanent collections Leigh Yawkey Woodson Art Mus., State House, Nairobi, Kenya, PGA Nat., Palm Beach Gardens, Fla., also numerous pvt. collections; subject numerous art jours.; represented by J.N. Bartfield Gallery, N.Y.C. Mem.: Catherine Lorillard Wolfe Art Club (Signature), Outdoor Writers Assn., Fla. Watercolor Soc. (Signature), Pastel Soc. Am. (Signature), Soc. Animal Artists (Signature). Avocation: photography. Office: Heatons Studio and Gallery 1169 Old Dixie Hwy Lake Park FL 33403-2311 Office Phone: 561-844-3415. Personal E-mail: heatonstudio@aol.com.

HEATON, JEANNE ALBRONDA, psychologist; b. San Francisco, Mar. 25, 1944; d. Henry Frederick and Mildred Perry Albronda; m. David Marlin Heaton, June 19, 1976; children from previous marriage: Shannon O'Leary, Kevin Moore-O'Leary, Alan O'Leary. BS, U. Oreg., Eugene, 1966; MEd, Ohio U., Athens, 1972, PhD, 1975. Dir., psychologist Counseling & Psychol. Svcs., Athens; pvt. practice. Author: Turning in Trouble, 1995, Building Basic Therapeutics, Talking to Eating Disorders, 2005. Mem.: APA, Am. Assn. Univ. and Coll. Counseling. Avocations: walking, gardening, dog training. Home: 66 Briarwood Athens OH 45701 Office: Ohio U Hudson Health Ctr Athens OH 45701 Office Phone: 740-593-1616. Business E-Mail: heaton@ohio.edu.

HEATON, KATHLEEN HOGE, realtor; b. Flint, Mich., Mar. 3, 1948; d. Paul L. and Isabel Evelyn (Martin) Hoge; m. Joel Brion Heaton, Sept. 14, 1968; children: Paul Brion, Todd Erin. Student, Ohio U., 1966-67, U. Hawaii, 1969; grad., Realtors Inst. Va., 1987. Cert. residential specialist, Ill., 1991; lic. broker assoc., Va., 1990; cert. residential broker. Pub. rels. specialist USN Commissary and Exch., Pearl Harbor, Hawaii, 1969-71; asst. configuration mgr. Ball Rsch. Corp., Boulder, Colo., 1972; realtor assoc. Welbourne & Purdy Realty, Saratoga Springs, N.Y., 1979-82, Nancy Chandler Assocs., Norfolk, Va., 1982—2002. Bd. dirs. Little Theatre Norfolk, 1985-90; mem. Maltese Cross Circle Children's Hosp. of Kings Daus., Norfolk, 1982-2002; pres. Lochhaven Civic League, 1998-2002; Mem. Greater Hampton Rds. Realtors Assn. (mem. cir. excellence, 1995-2003, mem. grievance com., 2003), Navy League U.S. (treas. Norfolk Women's Coun. 1987-90), Lochhaven Civic League. Republican. Episcopalian. Avocations: golf, bridge, travel. Home: 7431 Muirfield Rd Norfolk VA 23505-1753 Office: Nancy Chandler Assocs 701 W 21st St Norfolk VA 23517-1920 E-mail: kheaton@nancychandler.com.

HEATON, PATRICIA, actress; b. Bay Village, Ohio, Mar. 4, 1958; d. Chuck and Pat Heaton; m. David Hunt Oct. 10, 1990; children: Sam, John Basil, Joseph Charles, Daniel Patrick. BA in Theater, Ohio State U., 1980. Spokesperson Albertsons, Inc. supermarkets. Actor (stage) The Johnstown Vindicator, 1987, Don't Get God Started, 1987-88, Miracle in the Woods, 1997, (TV series) Room for Two, 1992-93, Someone Like Me, 1994, Women of the House, 1995, Everybody Loves Raymond, 1996—2005 (Best Actress in Quality Comedy Viewers for Quality TV award 1998, Outstanding Lead Actress in Comedy Series Emmy award, 2000 and 2001); (TV movies) Shattered Dreams: The Charlotte Fedders Story, 1990, Miracle in the Woods, 1997, A Town Without Christmas, 2001, The Goodbye Girl, 2004, The Engagement Ring, 2005 (also exec. prodr.), (films) Beethoven, 1992, Memoirs of an Invisible Man, 1992, The New Age, 1994, Space Jam, 1996; TV appearances include Alien Nation, 1989, Thirtysomething, 1989-91, Matlock, 1990, DEA, 1991, Party of Five, 1996, The King of Queens, 1999, (voice) Danny Phantom, 2004; author (book): Motherhood and Hollywood, 2003. Hon. chairperson Feminists for Life. Mem.: Delta Gamma. Office: United Talent Agency 9560 Wilshire Blvd Ste 500 Beverly Hills CA 90212*

HEBARD, BARBARA ADAMS, conservator; b. Fort Dodge, Iowa, July 26, 1951; d. George D. and Bonnie J. Adams; m. Christopher G. Hebard, Jan. 10, 1981. B. U. Mass., 1975. Handbinder cert. North Bennet St. Sch., Mass., 1990. Book conservator Boston Athenaeum, 1990—. Chair alumni steering com. North Bennet St. Sch., Boston, 1998—2002, mem. corp., 2002—04, overseer, 2004—. Author: (catalogue) Boston Athenaeum Conservation Dept. Finishing Tools; exhibitions include Roundup: Rocky Mountain chpt. Guild of Book Workers, 9th Wexford Artist Books Exhbn., Book Explorations, Arts Iowa City: Multiple Talents, Heaven on Earth: Lone Star Chapter of the Guild of Book Workers, Essence: The Art of Simplicity, Society of Arts and Crafts: Centennial Edn., Planet Dada Show, The Nurtured Spirit: Rocky Mountain Chapter of the Guild of Book Workers Exhibit, NE School of Art and Design exhibit, Bound Together: Ten Years of Bookbinding at N. Bennet St. Sch., Boston Athenaeum Mems., New England Vignettes: NE Chapter of Guild of Book Workers, Leap of Faith, 2004, 2005, 1st Internat. Collage, 2d Internat. Collage, N. Bennet St. Sch. Juried Show of Grad. Work, 2000—, San Diego Book Artists Nat. Juried Exhibit, 2006, Chgo. Pub. Libr., 2006; contbr. articles to profl. jours. Mem. parish coun. St. Paul Ch., Cambridge, Mass., 2003—06. Andrew Oliver Wellspring fellow. Fellow: Internat. Inst. Conservation Hist. and Artistic Works; mem.: New Eng. Conservation Assn. (bd. mem.), Assn. Coll. and Rsch. Librs., Am. Inst. Conservation Hist. and Artistic Works (assoc.), Guild Book Workers (coord. NE chpt. exhbn.), Cultural Emergency Mgmt. Team, Ticknor Soc. Achievements include design of design binding, Grace Raymond Hebard scrapbook purchased by the Marriott Rare Book Library at the University of Utah. Office: Boston Athenaeum 10 1/2 Beacon St Boston MA 02108 Office Phone: 617-720-7632. Business E-Mail: hebard@bostonathenaeum.org.

HEBENSTREIT, JEAN ESTILL STARK, religion educator, practitioner; d. Charles Dickey and Blanche (Hervey) Stark; m. William J. Hebenstreit, Sept. 4, 1942; children: James B., Mark W. Student Conservatory of Music, U. Mo. at Kansas City, 1933-34; AB, U. Kans., 1936. Authorized C.S. practitioner, Kansas City, 1955—; bd. dirs. 3d Ch., Kansas City, 1952-55, chmn. bd., 1955, reader, 1959-62; authorized C.S. tchr. C.S. Bd., 1964—, bd. dirs. Boston, 1977-83, chmn., 1981—82. Mem. Christian Sci. Bd. of Lectureship, Christian Sci. Bd. Edn.; bd. trustees The Christian Sci. Pub. Soc., bd. dirs. First Ch. Christ.Scientist, 1977-83, chmn., 1981-82. Contbr. articles to C.S. lit. Pres. Mother Ch., The First Ch. of Christ, Scientist, 1999. Mem. Art of Assembly Parliamentarians (charter, 1st pres.), Pi Epsilon Delta, Alpha Chi Omega (past pres.), Carriage Club. Home: 310 W 49th St Ste A-2 Kansas City MO 64112-2425 Office: 310 W 49th St Apt A-3 Kansas City MO 64112-2425

HEBERLEIN, ALICE LATOURRETTE, healthcare educator, physical education educator, coach; b. L.A., Mar. 7, 1963; d. Louis and Jean Marie LaTourrette; m. Dave Heberlein, Mar. 20, 1993. BA, Idaho State U., 1985, MA, 1987. Tchr., coach Pocatello (Idaho) H.S., 1985—93; head women's volleyball coach Idaho State U., Pocatello, 1993—95; tchr., coach Pocatello H.S., 1995—99, Century H.S., Pocatello, 1999—, chair health dept., 2001—, chair phys. edn. dept., 2003—. Mem. nursing adv. bd. Vo-Tech H.S., Pocatello, 1995—2001; bd. dirs. Idaho Tennis Assn., Boise, 1998—99. Named Coach of Yr., Idaho H.S. Activity Assn., 1990—91, Jour. Coach of Yr., Idaho State Jour., 1999, Region 5 Coach of Yr., 1986—87, 1989—90, 1991—2000, Region 4-5-6 Coach of Yr., 2001. Mem.: Pocatello Edn. Assn. Achievements include coaching volleyball teams, 1989, H.S. state champions, 1990, 4th pl. State of Idaho, 2000, 2d pl. State of Idaho, 2001. Avocations: cross country skiing, hiking, tennis, snow shoeing, skate skiing. Office: Century HS 7801 Diamondback Dr Pocatello ID 83204 Home: 838 Spy Glass Pt Pocatello ID 83204-4478

HEBERT, MARGARET BURNS, social worker; b. Houston, June 29, 1947; d. Albert Leroy Jr. and Margaret Stewart (Forristall) Burns; m. James Byron Hebert, Apr. 18, 1970; children: Margaret, Miia, Mary Grace, Madeleine. BA, Tulane U., 1969; MA, U. S.W. La. (now U. La. Lafayette), 1972; MSW, La. State U., 1977. Welfare technician Vermilion Parish Div. of Family Svcs., Abbeville, La., 1974; foster care caseworker Lafayette (La.) Office of Community Svcs., 1974-75, Vermilion Parish Office of Community Svcs., Abbeville, 1977-78, social work supr., 1978-82; sch. social worker Vermilion Parish Sch. Bd., Abbeville, 1982-85, 95—; sch. counselor Mt. Carmel Elem. Sch., Abbeville, 1985-88; pvt. practice Abbeville, 1988—2002. Regional del. Dem. Caucus, Thibodeaux, La., 1972; foster parent Lafayette Area Office of Family Svcs., 1980-82; bd. dirs. Vermilion Parish Milk Fund, Abbeville, 1975-78, Acadiana Symphony Assn., Lafayette, 1989; bd. dirs. Family Tree, Lafayette, 1999—; mem. Abbey Players Community Theatre; facilitator Family Life Community, 1979-89. Democrat. Roman Catholic. Mem. NASW (bd. dirs. La. chpt. 1984-86), Assn. for Social Work Vendorship (bd. dirs. 1988-89), La. Social Svc. Suprs. Assn. (founder Lafayette chpt. 1980-82), La. Sch. Social Work Network (chair La. chpt. 1985, Lafayette region rep. 1999-2004), Confrerie de l'Omelette Geante (bd. dirs. 1995-99, chevalier 1997—, treas. 2003—). Avocations: needlecrafts, sewing. Home: 108 N Louisiana St Abbeville LA 70510-5117 Office: Vermilion Parish Sch Bd PO Box 520 Abbeville LA 70511 Office Phone: 337-898-5759. E-mail: megbhebert@bellsouth.net.

HEBERT, MARY OLIVIA, retired librarian; b. Nov. 11, 1921; d. Arthur Frederick and Clara Marie (Golden) Meyer; m. N. Hal Hebert, Sept. 9, 1943 (dec. Mar. 1969); children: Olivia, Stephen (dec. 1989), Christina, Deborah (dec. 1999), Beth, John, James. Secretarial positions in advt., 1942-43; v.p. Hebert Advt. Co., 1955-66; adminstrv. asst. comms. Blue Cross, St. Louis, 1966-69, libr., 1969-91; ret., 1991. Part-time archivist Cathedral Basilica of St. Louis, 1999. Mem. Spl. Librs. Assn. (pres. St. Louis Metro chpt. 1984), St. Louis Med. Librs., St. Louis Regional Libr. Network (coun. 1986-89). Roman Catholic. Personal E-mail: claramyrtle@aol.com.

HEBERT, MONA MILLIMAN, elementary school educator; b. Abbeville, La., Aug. 29, 1953; d. Joseph Charles and Darnella LeBlanc Milliman; m. Carl Wayne Hebert, Nov. 18, 1972; children: Kristina Hebert Adams, Adrienne Michelle. BA, U. La., 1976, MEd, 1984. Cert. supr. student tchrs. U. La., Lafayette, 1986, ESOL U. La., Lafayette, 1985. Tchr. Vermilion Parish Sch. Bd., Abbeville, La., 1976—2000, 2002—04, reading first coach, 2004—; program coord. La. Dept. Edn., Lafayette, 2000—02. Reading, math, tech. workshop presenter Vermilion Parish Sch. Bd., La. Dept. Edn.; coord. Learning Intensive Networking Cmtys. for Success, Region IV La. Dept. Edn., 2000—02, facilitator online courses, 2001—03; presenter various profl. confs. Named Tchr. of Yr., Meaux Elem., 1994, Tchr. of Yr., 1999, Vermilion Parish, 1994, Educator of Yr., Abbeville C. of C., 1999, Outstanding Alumni, Coll. Edn., U. La., Lafayette, 2002; recipient Tchr. of Yr., Vermilion Parish, 1999. Mem.: NEA, La. Assn. Computer Using Educators, La. Reading Assn., Vermilion Edn. Assn., La. Edn. Assn., Phi Delta Kappa, Beta Sigma Phi (pres., v.p., sec., Girl of Yr. 1987, 1995, 1999, Beta Lambda Sweetheart 2000, 2006). Roman Catholic. Home: 8838 Eastwood Dr Abbeville LA 70510 Office: James A Herod Elem Sch 120 Odea St Abbeville LA 70510 Personal E-mail: monah@vrml.k12.la.us.

HECETA, ESTHERBELLE AGUILAR, retired anesthesiologist; b. Cebu City, Philippines, Jan. 1, 1935; came to U.S., 1962, naturalized, 1981; d. Serafin Aquilar and Elsie (Nichols) Aguilar; m. Wilmer G. Heceta, Apr. 5, 1962; children: W. Cristina, W. Elgine, Wuela E. BS in Chemistry cum laude, Silliman U., Dumaguete City, Philippines, 1955, BS cum laude, 1956; MD cum laude, U. East Ramon Magsaysay, Quezon City, Philippines, 1961. Diplomate Am. Bd. Anesthesiology, Philippine Bd. Anesthesiology. Intern Youngstown (Ohio) Hosp. Assocs., 1962-63, resident in anesthesiology, 1963-66; anesthesiologist Salem (Ohio) City Hosp., 1967, St. Joseph's Hosp., Manapla, Philippines, 1967-72; instr. dept. anesthesiology U. Tenn., Memphis, 1972-74; staff anesthesiologist Ohio Valley Med. Ctr., Wheeling, W.Va., 1974—, Bellaire (Ohio) City Hosp., 1975—, East Ohio Regional Hosp., Martins Ferry, 1989—. Jt. conf. com. for profl. affairs, exec. com., sec.-treas. med. dental staff Ohio Valley Med. Ctr., 1992-96, pres.-elect, 1993-94, pres. med. dental staff, 1994-95; physician reviewer Anesthesiology W.Va. Med. Inst., 1992-96. Claims rev. panel W.Va. Med. Assn., 1990-95; vol. med.-surg. mission to Philippines, 1982-90. Fellow Am. Coll. Anesthesiology; mem. AMA, Am. Soc. Anesthesiologists, Ohio Valley Phillipine Med. Assn. (pres. 1988-90), Tri-State Phillipine-Am. Assn. (pres. 1991-92), Assn. Philippine Physicians in Am., Philippine Soc. Anesthesiologists in Am., W.Va. Soc. Anesthesiologists, Internat. Anesthesia Rsch. Soc., Am. Med. Womens Assn. (organizer, pres. 1983, regional gov. region IV 1987-89), W.Va. Med. Soc., Ohio County Med. Soc. Presbyterian. Home and Office: 15 Holly Rd Wheeling WV 26003-5656

HECHE, ANNE (ANNE CELESTE HECHE), actress; b. Aurora, Ohio, May 25, 1969; d. Donald Heche; m. Coley Laffoon, Sept. 1, 2001; 1 child, Homer Heche Laffoon. Actress (films) An Ambush of Ghosts, 1993, The Adventures of Huck Finn, 1993, A Simple Twist of Fate, 1994, Milk Money, 1994, I'll Do Anything, 1994, The Wild Side, 1995, Pie in the Sky, 1995, Walking and Talking, 1996, The Juror, 1996, Volcano, 1997, Donnie Brasco, 1997, Wag the Dog, 1997, I Know What You Did Last Summer, 1997, Return to Paradise, 1998, Six Days Seven Nights, 1998, Psycho, 1998, The Third Miracle, 1999, Auggue Rose, 2000, Prozac Nation, 2001, John Q., 2002, Timepiece, 2003, Birth, 2004; (TV movies) O Pioneers!, 1992, Against the Wall, 1994, Girls in Prison, 1994, The Investigator, 1994, Kingfish: A Story of Huey P. Long, 1995, If These Walls Could Talk, 1996, Wild Side, 1996, SUBWAYStories: Tales from the Underground, 1997, One Kill, 2000, Gracie's Choice, 2004, The Dead Will Tell, 2004, Sexual Life, 2005, Silver Bells, 2005, Fatal Desire, 2006; (TV series) Another World, 1987-91, Murphy Brown, 1991-92, Ally McBeal, 2001, Ellen, 1998, Everwood, 2004-05, Men in Trees, 2006-; (stage) Getting Away with Murder, 1991-92; (Broadway plays) Proof, 2002-03, Twentieth Century, 2004- (Tony nom. best actress in a play, 2004); actor, prodr. (TV movies) The Dead Will Tell, 2004; dir. (films) Reaching Normal, 2001; dir., writer (TV films) On the Edge; dir.(TV movies) If These Walls Could Talk 2, 2000; writer (short film) Stripping for Jesus, 1998; author: (autobiography) Call Me Crazy: A Memoir, 2001. Recipient Emmy award Another World; named one of the 50 Most Beautiful People in the World, People, 1998.*

HECHT, MARJORIE MAZEL, editor; b. Cambridge, Mass., Dec. 21, 1942; d. Mark and Theresa (Shuman) Mazel; m. Laurence Michael Hecht, July 2, 1972 BA cum laude, Smith Coll., 1964; postgrad., London Sch. Econs., 1964-65; MSW, Columbia U., 1967. Dir. Forest Neighborhood Service Ctr., N.Y.C., 1967-70, Wiltwyck Sch. for Boys, Bronx Center, NY, 1970-73; mng. editor Fusion Mag., Washington, 1977-87, 21st Century Sci. & Technol. Mag., Washington, 1987—; sci. editor Exec. Intelligence Rev., Washington, 1997—. Co-author: Beam Defense: An Alternative to Nuclear Destruction, 1983 (Aviation and Space Writers award 1983); editor: Colonize

Space! Open the Age of Reason, 1985, The Holes in the Ozone Scare: The Scientific Evidence That the Sky Isn't Falling, 1992. Press rep. LaRouche Campaign, N.Y.C., 1984 Democrat. Jewish. Avocation: astronomy. Office: 21st Century Sci & Technol Mag PO Box 16285 Washington DC 20041-6285 Office Phone: 703-777-6943. E-mail: editorial@21stcenturysciencetech.com.

HECHT, SUSANNA BETTINA, adult education educator, writer; b. Salt Lake City; d. Hans Helmut and Ilse Hecht. BS, U. Chgo., 1973; PhD, U. Calif., Berkeley, 1983. Prof. UCLA, LA. Author: Fate of the Forest, 1990, Lost Paradise of Enceddes des Curla, 2001. Avocation: horseback riding. Office: UCLA 405 Hilgard AVe #915636 Los Angeles CA 90095

HECK, DEBRA UPCHURCH, information technology, procurement professional; b. Valparaiso, Fla., Nov. 4, 1956; d. Robert P. and Sallaine S. (Sledge) Upchurch; m. Robert J. Heck, May 31, 1980; children: Andrew W., Jennifer A. BS in Math., Purdue U., 1978, MS in Mgmt., 1980. Analyst mgmt. sci. Monsanto Corp. Mgmt. Sci., St. Louis, 1980-81; sys. analyst Monsanto Agr. Group, St. Louis, 1981-82, sr. sys. analyst, 1982-84; sr. analyst mgmt. sci. Monsanto Polymer Products Group, St. Louis, 1984-86; total quality fundamentals instr. Monsanto Co., St. Louis, 1985-86; project mgr. Monsanto Chem. Co., St. Louis, 1986-88; group leader Monsanto Corp. MIS, St. Louis, 1988-92, sr. group leader, 1992-95; info. tech. dir. Monsanto Bus. Svcs. Fin. & Procurement, St. Louis, 1995—97, dir. strategic sourcing procurement strategic initiatives, 1997—2000; exec. dir. global procurement Pharmacia, St. Louis, 2000—03; exec. dir. global sourcing Pfizer, 2003—04; v.p. corp. procurement Express Scripts, St. Louis, 2005—. Trustee, chair fall gathering, doubles, social com. Ethical Soc., St. Louis, 1982—; mem. sci. adv. com., PTO bd. Parkway Sch. Dist., St. Louis, 1992—; vol. St. Louis Assn. for Retarded Citizens, 1978-85. Recipient Leader award, YWCA Monsanto Corp., 1999. Mem. Nat. Assn. Purchasing Mgmt., Human Resource Sys. Profls., Leadership Am. Alumni (award 1994), Winning Women. Avocations: travel, sports. Personal E-mail: debrauheck@aol.com.

HECK, JENNIFER LEIGH, neonatal/perinatal nurse practitioner, educator; b. Tulsa, Okla., May 17, 1977; d. Alfred Lee and Carol Ann Tibbs; m. Allan Shane Heck, Dec. 31, 2004. BSN, U. Okla., 1999, MSN, 2004. RN Okla. Bd. of Nursing, cert. level III NICU, Nat. Certification Corp. Student nurse technician VA Med. Ctr., Oklahoma City, 1998—99; nurse Hillcrest Med. Ctr., Tulsa, 1999—, mem. unit coun. com., 2002—04, primary dayshift preceptor, 2003—04, mem. pain adv. com., 2004; nurse NormanRegional Hosp., Okla., 2005; asst. prof. nursing Bacome Coll., Muskogee, Okla., 2006—. Recipient Advanced Edn. Nurse Traineeship grant, U. Okla. Coll. of Nursing, 2000—03. Mem.: Acad. Neonatal Nursing, Assn. Women's Health, Obs. and Neonatal Nurses (scholarship Okla. sect. 2003), U. Okla Alumni Club, Sigma Theta Tau. Democrat. Baptist. Avocations: reading, travel, cooking. Office: Bacone Coll Dept Nursing 2299 Old Bacone Rd Muskogee OK 74403

HECKATHORNE, DEBORAH KATHRYN, mathematics educator, supervisor; b. Oil City, Pa., May 25, 1951; d. John William and Kathryn Margaret Garmong; m. Robert Kenton Heckathorne, June 19, 1976; children: Amy Leah, Andrew Joseph. MA, Edinboro U., Pa. Lic. supr. Pa, 2001. Tchr. Oil City (Pa.) Area Sch. Dist., 1973—, supr. math, 2001—. Tchr. adv. coun. Casio, Dover, NJ, 2006—. Mem. NCTM. Mem.: Pa. Coun. Tchrs. Math., PCSM, Nat. Coun. Tchrs. Math. Roman Catholic. Avocations: travel, reading. Home: 216 Oak Rd Oil City PA 16301 Office: Oil City Area School District 10 Lynch Blvd Oil City PA 16301 Office Phone: 814-676-2771. Business E-Mail: dheckathorne@mail.ocasd.org.

HECKENAST, SHERRI, auto parts executive, sports association executive; b. 1975; Sales mgr., wholesale divsn. A Reliable Auto Parts, Blue Island, Ill., 1996—98, gen. mgr., 1998—2003, CEO, 2003—; owner Kentucky Lake Motor Speedway, Ill., 2004—. Named one of 40 Under Forty, Carin's Bus. Chgo., 2005. Office: A Reliable Auto Parts 2247 W 139th St Blue Island IL 60406 Office Phone: 708-385-5955.*

HECKMAN, CAROL A., biology educator; b. East Stroudsburg, Pa., Oct. 18, 1944; d. Wilbur Thomas and Doris (Betts) H. BA, Beloit (Wis.) Coll., 1966; PhD, U. Mass., Amherst, 1972. Rsch. assoc. Yale U. Sch. Medicine, New Haven, 1973-75; staff mem. Oak Ridge (Tenn.) Nat. Lab., 1975-82; adj. assoc. prof. U. Tenn.-Oak Ridge Biomed. Grad. Sch., 1980-82; assoc. prof. Bowling Green (Ohio) State U., 1982-86, prof. biology, 1986—. Cons. NSF, Washington, 1977-80, NIH, Rockville, Md., 1996-98; dir. EM facility Bowling Green State U., 1982—; NSF trainee, Amherst, 1967-70; vis. prof. Univ. Coll. London. Contbr. articles to profl. jours., chpts. to books. Internat. Cancer Rsch. Tech. fellow Internat. Union Against Cancer, 1980, Heritage Found. fellow, 1982, guest rsch. fellow, Uppsala, Sweden, 1989-90; grantee NSF, 1981-84, 90-92, NIH, 1987-88, 98-2001, Dept. of Def., 2000-02. Mem. Am. Assn. Cancer Rsch., Am. Soc. Cell Biology, Microscopy Soc. Am., N.W. Ohio Microscopy (sec.-treas. 1986-90, pres. 1990-94), Soc. In Vitro Biology, Mid-Am. Drug Devel. (pres. 1999), Ohio Acad. Sci., Sigma Xi. Episcopalian. Achievements include research evaluation and development of in vitro antícarcinogens. Office: Bowling Green State U Dept Biol Scis Bowling Green OH 43403-0001 Office Phone: 419-372-8218. Business E-Mail: heckman@bgnet.bgsu.edu.

HECKMAN, JYOTSNA (JO) L., bank executive; married; 2 children. With Denali State Bank, Fairbanks, Alaska, 1986—, pres., CEO, 2003—. Named One of 25 Women to Watch, U.S. Banker Mag., 2003. Office: Denali State Bank 119 N Cushman PO Box 74568 Fairbanks AK 99707-4568

HECKMAN, LUCY T., librarian; b. Queens, N.Y., June 9, 1954; d. Charles and Ruth Heckman. BA in English, St. John's U., Jamaica, N.Y., 1976, MLS in Libr. Info. Sci., 1977; MBA, Adelphi U., 1981. Catalog libr. St. John's U. Libr., Jamaica, 1977—82, reference libr., 1982—2001, head reference, 2002—. Author: Franchising in Business, 1989, The New York Stock Exchange, 1992, Nasdaq, 2001, Damascus, 2004. Mem.: ALA (sec. bus. ref. and svcs. sect. 1998—), Beta Phi Mu. Avocations: photography, antiques. Home: 100-50 223 St Queens Village NY 11429 E-mail: heckmanl@stjohns.edu.

HECTOR-SKINNER, VICKI L., artist; b. Highland Park, Ill., Nov. 6, 1945; d. William Joseph and Agnes Mary Hector; m. Roger J. Skinner, Aug. 20, 1999. BA, Calif. State U.-Northridge, 1980, Spl. Edn. Art Credential Credit, 1996. Lic. realtor Calif. State Bd. Realtors, 1990. Owner V-ELLE and BDI's Paint Beads by V-ELLE, Arleta, Calif., 1977—; store mgr., retail sales GNC, Woodland Hills, Calif., 1980—81; regional sales mgr. Alvin Last, Inc., Yonkers, 1984—89; realtor James Gary, Inc., Woodland Hills, 1990—98. Pvt. tchr. V-ELLE, West Hills, Calif., 1977—96. Exhibitions include tactile paint sculpture A Body of Work, 1990—; contbr. art instrn. manuals, autobiographical material and recipes. Mem.: Am. Craft Coun., Beta Sigma Phi. Achievements include development of tactile paint sculpture. Avocations: music appreciation, cultural activities, gourmet and health cooking, sculpting, dogs. Office Phone: 818-892-3236.

HEDGE, CHRISTINE MARLE, science educator; arrived in U.S., 1962; d. William John and MaryAnn Chichwak; m. Kenneth Eugene Hedge, Aug. 6, 1983; children: Carrie Ann, Matthew, Kendra. B, Purdue U., West Lafayette, Ind., 1985. Med. tech. Am. Soc. Clin. Pathology, Indpls., 1987—; tchr. Western Boone Sr. HS, Thorntown, 2004—. Pres. PTO, Sheridan, Ind., 1995—96, Sheridan H.S. Athletic Booster Club, 2004—. Recipient Hamilton County Literacy award, Hamilton County Reading Coun., Ind., 2002. Mem.: NEA, Nat. Sci. Tchrs. Assn., Am. Soc. Clin. Pathology. Republican. Avocation: reading. Home: 6705 E 400 N Lebanon IN 46052

HEDGE, NANCY, secondary school educator; d. Kenneth D. and Katherine D. Swank; m. Jack Hedge, Nov. 26, 1980; 1 child, Kristen. BS in Elem. Edn., Okla. State U., 1978. Lic. tchr. Okla. Dept. Edn., 1978. Educator Will Rogers Jr. HS, Claremore, Okla., 1978—, chmn. dept., 1997—, leader academic team; dist. gifted dir. Adv. com. gifted students Claremore Schs., Okla., 1992—, vertical team leader sci., 1995—. Team leader Bowl for Kids Sake, Claremore, 2000—02; bldg. rep. Am. Heart Assn., Claremore, Okla., 1997—99. Named Tchr. of Yr., Will Rogers Jr. HS, 2000, 2004; grantee, Claremore Schs., 2004. Mem.: Supporting the Emotional Needs of Gifted, Nat. Sci. Tchr. Assn., Paralyzed Vets. Am., Rotary (vol. bluegrass and chili fesitval 2005), Delta Kappa Gamma. Office: Will Rogers Junior High 1915 N Florence Ave Claremore OK 74017 Office Phone: 918-341-7411. Business E-Mail: nhedge@claremore.k12.ok.us.

HEDGES, EDITH RITTENHOUSE, retired nutrition and family and consumer sciences educator; b. Oakland, Calif., Mar. 15, 1937; d. Lloyd Lee and Florence Muriel (McCurdy) Rittenhouse; m. Frank Hill Hedges III, Dec. 16, 1967. BS in Nutrition/Dietetics, U. Nev., Reno, 1960; MS in Nutrition Rsch., U. Wis., 1962; postgrad., Purdue U., 1971-75, U. Ill., 1975-78. Rsch. asst., cmty. nutritionist U. Wis., Madison, 1960-62; nutritionist Nat. Sch. Lunch program USDA Regional Office, N.Y.C., 1962-64; nutritionist, home economist Am. Friends Svc. Com., Mex., 1964-66; instr. English pub. secondary sch., Tonatico, Mex., 1965-66; from instr. to asst. prof. Eastern Ill. U., Charleston, 1966-93, prof. emeritus, 1993—. Cons. nutritionist Coles County Mental Health Dept., 1982-85, 97. Mem. Coles County Arts Coun., Charleston, 1990—; vol. Ptnrs. in Adult Literacy, Ill. Recipient Rehab. Achievement award Mercy Hosp. Rehab. Ctr., Urbana, Ill., 1987; named Woman of Achievement Women's Studies Coun., Eastern Ill. U., 1994, Outstanding Vol. Docent, Tarble Art Ctr., 1984, 85, 86. Mem. LWV (Coles County pres. 2002-2004), Ea. Ill. U. Annuitants Assn.(editor newsletter 1995-2005), Zonta (chair various coms.), Handweavers Guild Am. (prs. local guild 1983-85), Coalition of Citizens with Disabilities in Ill. Mem. Soc. Of Friends. Avocations: photography, watercolors, camping, birdwatching. Home: 21324 E County Road 400N Charleston IL 61920-9077

HEDGES, JESSICA DIANE, lawyer; b. Spencer, W. Va., May 8, 1972; BA summa cum laude, Boston Coll., 1994; JD, Northeastern U., 1999. Bar: Mass. 2000, US Dist. Ct. (Dist. Mass.) 2003, W. Va. 2004. Law clk. Superior Ct. Mass.; ptnr. Hrones, Garrity & Hedges, Boston. Instr. criminology Boston Coll., 2002—. Mem.: Nat. Police Accountability Project, Nat. Lawyers Guild, ACLU, Mass. Assn. Criminal Defense Lawyers, Phi Beta Kappa. Office: Hrones Garrity & Hedges Lewis Wharf Bay 232 Boston MA 02110 Office Phone: 617-227-4019. Office Fax: 617-227-3908. E-mail: Hedges@masscriminallawyer.com.*

HEDGES, KAMLA KING, library director; b. Covington, Va. d. John Wilton and Rhoda Alice (Loughrie) K.; m. Harry George Hedges, July 24, 1988. AB, Coll. of William and Mary, 1968; MLS, Vanderbilt U., 1969. Law and legis. reference libr. Conn. State Libr., Hartford, 1969-74; dep. law libr. Steptoe and Johnson, Washington, 1974-78; law libr. Wilkinson, Cragun and Barker, Washington, 1978-83; corp. libr. The Bur. of Nat. Affairs, Inc., Washington, 1983-94, dir. libr. rels., 1995—. Compiler: (directories) BNA's Directory of State and Federal Courts, Judges, Clerks, 1995, BNA's State Administrative Codes and Registers, 1995; contbr. chpt. to law manual. Bd. dirs. Friends of the Law Libr. of Congress, 2000—05. Mem. Am. Assn. Law Librs. (exec. bd. dirs. 1984-87), Spl. Libr. Assn. Episcopalian. Home: 4331 Embassy Park Dr NW Washington DC 20016-3607 Office: Bur Nat Affairs Inc 1231 25th St NW Washington DC 20037-1197

HEDGES, MARIETTA, performing arts educator, actor; b. Balt., Apr. 11, 1961; d. William Leonard and Elaine Catherine Hedges. BA, NYU, N.Y.C., 1986; MFA, Columbia U., N.Y.C., 2001. Lectr. U. North Tex., Denton, 2003—04; asst. prof. Cath. U. Am., Washington, 2004—. Actor, author: (plays) Fear Up. Grantee, Cath. U., 2005. Mem.: SAG, Am. Fed. TV and Radio Artists, Actors' Equity Assn. Office: Catholic University America 3801 Harewood Rd NE Washington DC 20017 Office Phone: 202-319-5362. Business E-Mail: hedges@cua.edu.

HEDGES, NORMA ANN, retired secondary education educator; b. Depue, Ill., May 21, 1941; d. Memford Euing and Louise Gertrude (Krueger) H. BA, Knox Coll., 1963; MEd, U. Ill., 1973. Camp sec. Pilgrim Park Camp, Princeton, Ill., 1961-64; English tchr., counselor Malden (Ill.) H.S., 1963-78, Morris (Ill.) H.S., 1978-93; ret., 1993. History of Depue, Illinois, 1976. Vol. Morris Hosp. Gift Shop, 1993—; driver We Care, 1993—2003. Mem. Grundy County Retired Tchrs.(regional dir. 2001-2005, state nominating com. 2005, area rep., 2006—), Ill. Ret. Tchrs. Assn., Delta Kappa Gamma (state scholarship com. 2001-05, area rep., 2006—). Republican. Congregationalist. Avocations: reading, antiques, genealogy, travel.

HEDGPETH, KIM ROBERTS, trade association administrator; m. Gilbert W. Hedgpeth. BA, Harvard U.; JD, Georgetown U. Bar: Calif., NY. Contract adminstr., asst. exec. dir./house counsel, co-exec. dir. AFTRA, NYC, 1981—86, exec. dir. San Francisco, 1987—92, asst. nat. exec. dir. news and broadcast, 1992—97, assoc. nat. exec. dir., 1997—2005, nat. exec. dir., 2005—. Dir. labor and employee rels. Harvard U.; v.p. human resources Safe Horizon. Mem.: Associated Actors and Artists Am. (exec. sec.). Office: AFTRA 260 Madison Ave New York NY 10016-2401 Office Phone: 212-532-4219.

HEDIN, ANNE MILLER, editor, writer, software marketing professional; b. Cambridge, Mass., Mar. 9, 1944; d. William H. and Margaret (Cahill) Miller; m. Ray Hedin, Sept. 1969 (div. May 1977); 1 child, Mark A.; m. John A Curry, Jan 22, 1980. BA, Emmanuel, 1965; MA, Columbia, 1967; PhD, U. Va., 1974. Instructor Bishop Coll., Dallas, 1967-69; asst. prof. Ind. U., Bloomington, 1974-82; editor Great Books Found., Chgo., 1982-83; editor in chief Systems 3X/400 Mag., Des Plaines, Ill., 1984-90, IBM Bus. Partner Newsletter, Chgo., 1990-91; cons. IBM Midrange Co., 1990—92; software mktg. System Software Assocs., Chgo., 1992—94, Computer Assoc., Chgo., 1996—99; dir. Comm. Maestro Commerce, 1999—2000; global web content mgr. Frontrange Solutions, Colo. Springs, 2000—01; pres. Hedin Comm., Bloomington, 2001—. Sec. Am. Soc. Bus. Press Editors, Chgo., 1987-89. Contbr. articles to profl. jours. Editor newsletter Bucktown Community Orgn., Chgo., 1991; organizer local sch. coun. elections, Chgo., 1989. Recipient Woodrow Wilson fellowship and internship, Woodrow Wilson Found., Princeton, N.J., 1965-69; Gov.'s Fellowship U. Va., Charlottesville, 1971-74. Mem. Feminist Writers Guild (sec.). Avocations: reading, bicycling, gardening. Office Phone: 812-323-7485.

HEDLUND, ELLEN LOUISE, state agency administrator, educator; b. Omaha, Feb. 17, 1943; d. Edwin Hugo and Olga Josephine Parrish; m. Ronald David Hedlund, Aug. 22, 1964; children: Karen Marie, David Peter. BA, Augustana Coll., 1965; MA, U. Iowa, 1966; PhD, U. Wis. Milw., 1989. Cert. life cert. in guidance and counseling Wis. Dept. Pub. Instr., 1977. Counselor Clear Creek Cmty. Schs., Oxford, Iowa, 1966—67; counselor, tchr. Nicolet H.S., Glendale, Wis., 1967—72, 1979; tchr. asst., project mgr. U. Wis., Milw., 1982—89, proposal writer, 1989; cons. R.I. Coll., Providence, 1990; adj. prof. U. R.I., Kingston, 1991; assessment coord. R.I. Dept. Edn., Providence, 1991—. Ptnr., cons. Wis. Pub. Opinion Mktg. Rsch., Milw., 1976—89. Adv. bd. U. Wis., Milw. Coll. for Kids, 1980—89; Sunday sch. supr. Bay Shore Luth., Whitefish Bay, Wis., 1987—89; congl. pres. Luth. Ch. of the Good Shepherd, Kingston, RI, 1996. Named Viking of Distinction, North HS, Omaha, Nebr., 2003. Mem.: Am. Edn. Rsch. Assoc., Assoc. for Supervision and Curriculum Devel., R.I. Assoc. Supervision and Curriculum Devel. Lutheran. Avocations: reading, gardening, home decor, stained glass. Office: RI Dept Elem Secondary Edn 255 Westminster St Providence RI 02903

HEDRICK, JOAN DORAN, writer, university educator; b. Balt., May 1, 1944; d. Paul Thomas and Jane (Connorton) Doran; m. Travis K. Hedrick, Aug. 26, 1967; children: Jessica, Rachel. AB, Vassar Coll., 1966; PhD, Brown U., 1974. Instr. Wesleyan U., Middletown, Conn., 1972-74, asst. prof. English, 1974-80; prof. history Trinity Coll., Hartford, Conn., 1994—, also dir. women's studies program, 1987-98. Vis. asst. prof. Trinity Coll., Hartford, 1980-81, vis. assoc. prof., 1981-82. Author: Solitary Comrade: Jack London and His Work, 1982, Harriet Beecher Stowe: A Life, 1994 (Pulitzer Prize for biography 1995); editor: The Oxford Harriet Beecher Stowe Reader, 1999. Mem. MLA, Am. Studies Assn., Org. Am. Historians, Soc. Am. Historians. Office: Trinity College Dept of History 300 Summit St Dept Of Hartford CT 06106-3186

HEDRICKS, PHYLLIS, secondary school educator; BS in Edn., Baylor U., Waco, Tex., 1978; M in Ednl. Adminstrn., U. Tex., Tyler, 1991. Cert. tchr. Tex. Edn. Agy., 1978, ednl. adminstr. Tex. Ednl. Agy., 1991. Tchr./social studies dept. chair John Tyler H.S., Tyler, 1999—. Avocations: travel, reading. Office Phone: 903-262-2850.

HEEG, PEGGY A., lawyer, former gas industry executive; b. Louisville, June 25, 1959; BA with honors, U. Louisville, 1983, JD, 1986. Bar: Ky. 1986, DC 1987, Tex. 1987. Various Tenneco Energy, El Paso Corp., Houston, 1996—97, v.p., assoc. gen. counsel regulated pipelines, 1997—2001, sr. v.p., dep. gen. counsel, 2001, exec. v.p., gen. counsel, 2002—04; ptnr. Fulbright & Jaworski L.L.P., 2004—. Legal advisor to commr. Charles Stalon Fed. Energy Regulatory Commn., 1988; bd. dirs. El Paso Tenn. Pipeline Co. Mem.: ABA, Interstate Natural Gas Assn. Am., DC Bar, State Bar Tex., Ky. Bar Assn., Energy Bar Assn. Office: Fulbright & Jaworksi LLP 1301 McKinney Ste 5100 Houston TX 77010-3095 Office Phone: 713-651-5151.

HEER, CAROL LYNNE, special education educator; b. Wauseon, Ohio, Dec. 8, 1948; d. Richard and Lois (Gentit) H. BA in Edn., Adrian Coll., 1970; MEd, Bowling Green State U., 1987. Cert. elem. tchr., Ohio. Tchr. Millcreek-West Unity (Ohio) Schs., 1970—, Title I tchr., 1987—; admissions dir. Sauder Farm and Craft Village, Archbold, Ohio, 1978—. Supt. United Meth. Ch., West Unity, 1992-94, lay reader, 1989-90, Sunday sch. tchr., 1986-95, style show coord., 1993-95. Mem. Ohio Reading Assn., Internat. Reading Assn. Methodist. Avocations: reading, travel. Office: Millcreek West Unity Schs S Defiance St West Unity OH 43570

HEERE, KAREN R., astrophysicist; b. Teaneck, NJ, Apr. 9, 1944; d. Peter N. and Alice E. (Hall) H. BA summa cum laude, U. Pa., 1965; MA, U. Calif., Berkeley, 1968; PhD, U. Calif., Santa Cruz, 1976. Rsch. assoc. NRC NASA Ames Rsch. Ctr., Moffett Field, Calif., 1977—79; rsch. astronomer NASA Ames Rsch. Ctr., U. Calif., Santa Cruz, 1979—86, sr. analyst, 2004—; assoc. prof. San Francisco State U., 1986-87; scientist Sci. Applications Internat. Corp., Los Altos, Calif., 1974-76, 87-93; rsch. specialist Sterling Software, Redwood City, Calif., 1993-98; sr. scientist Raytheon, Moffett Field, 1998—2003, mgr. space and earth sci., 2001—03. Vis. scientist TATA Inst. for Fundamental Rsch., Bombay, 1984. Contbr. articles to profl. jours. Mem.: Am. Astron. Soc. Avocations: hiking, travel. Home: PO Box 2427 El Granada CA 94018-2427 Office Phone: 650-604-6524.

HEESSEL, ELEANOR LUCILLE LEA, retired state agency administrator; b. Diller, Nebr., Nov. 6, 1916; d. Edward Richard and Gertrude (Loock) Henrichs; m. Stanley Guy Lea, Mar. 6, 1936; children: Dianna Evenson, Cylesta Peters, Jeffrey, Chad; m. William H. Heessel, May 28, 1997. Student, Fairbury State Coll. Owner Modern Furniture Store, Fairbury, Nebr., 1945-80; dist. mgr. Field Enterprises, Chgo., 1966-80; libr. resource person Fairbury Pub. Libr., 1982-85; job coord. Blue River Area Agy. on Aging, Lincoln, Nebr., 1985-87; ret., 1987. Bd. mem. Operation ABLE, Lincoln, 1987-92, Nat. Grandparent Program, Beatrice, Nebr., 1985-87. Pres., dist. v.p. United Meth. Women; Sunday Sch. supt. Meth. Ch., Fairbury; v.p. sch. bd. Fairbury Pub. Sch. Bd., 1956-62; bd. mem. Girl Scouts U.S.A., 1950-56. Mem. Toastmasters (v.p. pub. rels. Lincoln 1992-94). Republican. Avocations: reading, skiing. Home: 7641 Tahiti Ln #104 Lake Worth FL 33467 Personal E-mail: eleanhss1@aol.com.

HEESTAND, DIANE ELISSA, medical educator; b. Boston, Oct. 9, 1945; d. Glenn Wilson and Elizabeth (Martin) Heestand. BA, Allegheny Coll., 1967; MA, U. Wyo., 1968; edn. specialist, Ind. U., 1971, EdD, 1979. Asst. prof. communication Clarion (Pa.) State Coll., 1971; asst. prof. learning resources Indiana U. of Pa., 1971-72; asst. prof. communication U. Nebr. Med. Ctr., Omaha, 1972-74; assoc. prof. learning resources Tidewater Community Coll., Virginia Beach, Va., 1975-78; ednl. cons. U. Ala. Sch. Medicine, Birmingham, 1978-81; dir. learning resources, assoc. prof. med. edn. Mercer U. Sch. Medicine, Macon, Ga., 1981-88; asst. dean ednl. devel. and resources Ohio U. Coll. Osteopathic Medicine, 1989-90; assoc. prof. clin. med. edn., dir. biomed. communications U. So. Calif. Sch. Medicine, L.A., 1990-95, acting chair dept. med. edn., 1992-95; prof., dir. office ednl. devel. U. Ark. for Med. Scis., Little Rock, 1995—. Cons. Lincoln (Pa.) U., summer, 1975; vis. fellow Project Hope/China, Millwood, Va., summer, 1986. Author (teleplay) Yes, 1968 (award World Law Fund 1968); producer, dir. (slide tape) Finding a Way, 1980 (1st Pl. award HESCA 1981, Susan Eastman award 1981). Rsch. sect. chair So. Group on Ednl. Affairs, 1998—2000. Grantee, Porter Found., 1984, Ark. Dept. Higher Edn., 1996—97, UAMS Spl. Devel., 1997—99; Family and Preventive Medicine fellow, Health Resources and Svcs. Adminstrn., 2003—. Mem. Health Scis. Comm. Assn. (bd. dirs. 1982-86, pres.-elect 1987-88, pres. 1988-89, Spl. Svc. award 1990), Assn. Ednl. Comm. and Tech. (pres. media design and prodn. div. 1985-86), Assn. Biomed. Comm. Dirs. (bd. dirs. 1993-95), Soc. of Dirs. of Rsch. in Med. Edn. (steering com. 2000—, chair-elect 2002, chair 2003), Generalists in Med. Edn. (steering com. 1998-2001, chmn. 1999-2000). Democrat. Presbyterian. Avocations: tennis, gardening, golf. Office Phone: 501-686-5720. Business E-Mail: heestanddianee@uams.edu.

HEFFERAN, COLIEN JOAN, economist; b. Mpls., May 13, 1949; d. Bernard and Rosemary Arnsdorf; m. Hollis Spurgeon Summers, Oct. 14, 1987; 1 child, Margaret Vimont Summers. BS, U. Ariz., 1971; MS, U. Ill., 1974, PhD, 1976. Asst. prof. Pa. State U., University Park, 1975-79; econ., rsch. leader Agrl. Rsch. Svc., USDA, Hyattsville, Md., 1979-88; adminstr. Coop. State Rsch., Edn. and Ext. Svc., 1988—. Adj. prof. U. Md., University Park, 1982-88; chmn. Ctr. for Family, Washington, 1985-87; vis. fellow Australian Nat. U., Canberra, NSW, 1989-91. Mem. editl. bd. Jours.-Family Econ. Issues, 1987—. Recipient Outstanding Citizen award U. Ariz., 1985, Outstanding Alumni award U. Ill., 1986, Presdl. Rank award as Disting. Fed. Exec., 2000. Mem. Am. Econ. Assn., Am. Coun. on Consumer Interests. Democrat. Roman Catholic. Office Phone: 202-720-4423. Business E-Mail: chefferan@csrees.usda.gov.

HEFFERNAN, DEBRA JANE, administrator; b. Milw., Nov. 30, 1953; d. Joseph Jacob and Marjorie Christine (Stadler) Anheier; m. John William Heffernan, Oct. 19, 1974; 1 child, Justin Bryant. BS, U. Wis., Milw., 1979; MEd, U. Ill., Chgo., 1984; adminstrv. cert., Govs. State U., 1989; postgrad., Chgo. State U., 1990—; EdS, No. Ill. U., 2005. Cert. adminstr. Tchr. Guardian Angel Day Treatment Program, Joliet, Ill., 1981-86, Joliet Twp. Adult Edn. Program, 1982-84; instr. DeVry Inst. of Tech., Lombard, Ill., 1989; bldg. prin. Ann Rutledge Therapeutic Sch. Lincoln Way Area Spl. Edn. Coop., Frankfort, Ill., 1986—2000; spl. svcs. dir. Lincoln-Way HS, 2000—06; prin Martin P. MacKay Edn. Ctr., New Lenox, Ill., 2006—. Mem., sec., bd. dirs. Head Start, Joliet, 1985-89; adv. bd. Groundwork, Joliet, 1990—. Mem. Coun. for Exceptional Children, Ill. Coun. of Adminstrs. of Spl. Edn., Delta Kappa Gamma Soc. Internat. (v.p., 1998-2000, pres., 2002-04, 2006-). Avocations: arts and crafts, music, reading. Office: Martin P Mackay Edn Ctr 516 S Cedar New Lenox IL 60451 Office Phone: 815-463-8068.

HEFFLEFINGER, CLARICE THORPE, retired real estate broker; b. Oregon, Ill., Oct. 5, 1937; d. Ralph Wayne and Wyota Anita (Nashold) Thorpe; m. Jack Kenneth Hefflefinger, Jan. 24, 1970; children: Kenneth, Jack, Deborah, Kevin. AA, Coll. Sequoias, Visalia, Calif., 1967; B of Pub. Adminstrn., U. San Francisco, 1987. Various positions in banking and ins., 1956—76; real estate broker Hefflefinger Realty, Tulare, Calif., 1977—. Substitute tchr. Tulare City Schs., 1979—. Vol. tchr. local vets. orgns.; past chmn. Tulare County SSS Draft Bd.; mem. para-legal bd. dirs. Coll. of Sequoias, Visalia. Named Realtor of Yr., Tulare Bd. Realtors, 1983. Mem.:

Tulare Bd. Realtors (bd. dirs., pres. 1982), Calif. Assn. Realtors (bd. dirs.), Nat. Assn. Realtors, Tulare C. of C. (dir. crime scope), AMVETS Aux. (life; pres. 1982). Home and Office: Space 77 2459 N Oaks St Tulare CA 93274-1363

HEFFRON, JUDITH ANN, music educator; b. Platteville, Wis., Jan. 14, 1952; d. James Arthur and Mabel Marie (Runde) Bass; m. Thomas James Heffron, Aug. 24, 1974; children: Catherine Lynne, Jennifer Laura. BA in Music Edn., U. Wis., Oshkosh, 1974. Cert. tchr. Nat. Bd. Profl. Tchrs., 2003. Elem. music tchr. Freedom Pub. Schs., Wis., 1974—76, Waterloo Pub. Schs., Wis., 1976—78, Beaver Dam Unified Schs., Wis., 1986—; 2d grade tchr. Immaculate Conception Sch., Morris, Ill., 1978—85. Sec. Friends of Libr., Beaver Dam, 1992—96; concert master Beaver Dam Area Orch., 1986—; liturgist, musician, bd. dirs. St. Patrick's Ch., Beaver Dam, 1986—2000. Named Tchr. of Yr., Beaver Dam Unified Sch., 1996; recipient Kohl Tchr. award, Sen. Kohl, Wis., 1996. Mem.: Nat. Edn. Assn., Wis. State Music Assn., Wis. Edn. Assn., Music Educators Nat. Conf. Roman Catholic. Avocations: sewing, painting, reading, gardening, travel. Home: 112 Washington St Beaver Dam WI 53916 Office: Beaver Dam Unified Sch Dist 600 Grove St Beaver Dam WI 53916

HEFNER, CHRISTIE ANN, publishing executive; b. Chgo., Nov. 8, 1952; d. Hugh Marston and Mildred Marie (Williams) H. BA in English and Am. Lit., summa cum laude, Brandeis U., 1974. Freelance journalist, Boston, 1974-75; spl. asst. to chmn. Playboy Enterprises, Inc., Chgo., 1975-78, v.p., 1978-82, bd. dirs., 1979—, vice chmn., 1986-88, pres., 1982-88, COO, 1984-88, chmn., CEO, 1988—. Bd. dirs. Playboy Found., Mag. Pubs. Assn. Bd. dirs. Creative Coalition, Rush Med. Ctr., Canyon Ranch, Bus. Com. for the Arts, NCTA Diversity Com. Named Advocate of Yr., AIDS Legal Coun., 1998, Friend for Life, Howard Brown Med. Ctr., 1998; named one of 100 Most Powerful Women in World, Forbes mag., 2005—06; named to Today's Chgo. (Ill.) Woman Hall Fame, 2002; recipient Agness Underwood award, L.A. chpt. Women in Comm., 1984, Founders award, Midwest Women's Ctr., 1986, Human Rights award, Am. Jewish Com., 1986, Harry Kalven Freedom of Expression award, ACLU, Ill., 1987, Spirit of Life award, City of Hope, 1988, Eleanor Roosevelt award, Internat. Platform Assn., 1990, Will Rogers Meml. award, Beverly Hills C. of C. and Civic Assn., 1993, Humanitarian award, Rainbow/PUSH Coalition, 1998, Corp. Leadership award, AIDS Pastoral Care Network, 1998, Exec. Leadership award, Nat. Soc. Fundraising Execs., 1998, Champion of Freedom award, ADL, 2000, Spirit of Hope award, John Wayne Cancer Ctr., 2001, Bettie B. Port Humanitarian award, Mt. Sinai, 2001, Christopher Reeve 1st Amendment award, Creative Coalition, 2001, Bette B. Port Humanitarian award, Sianai Health Sys., 2001, Vanguard award, Nat. Cable & Telecommunications Assn., 2002, Philanthropic Innovator Luminary award, Com. of 200, 2002, Family Bus. Coun. Leadership award, U. Ill., Chgo., 2003, Friends of Cmty. award, Diversity Healthcare, Inc., 2005, Lifetime Achievement award, 25-Yr. Club, 2005. Mem. Nat. Cable and Telecom. Assn. (Vanguard award 2002, Interlochen's Path of Inspiration award 2003), Mus. of TV and Radio Media Ctr., Brandeis Nat. Women's Com. (life), Com. of 200, World Pres. Orgn., Chgo. Network, Sierra Club, Emilys List, Phi Beta Kappa. Democrat. Office: Playboy Enterprises Inc 680 N Lake Shore Dr Chicago IL 60611-4455

HEFTER, SHOSHANA, psychologist; d. Gavriel and Ottilie Pollak; m. Malkiel Hefter, Apr. 6, 1978; children: Chanina, Moshe Chaim, Yeshaya, Tzvi Menachem, Gavriel. BA, Notre Dame Coll., Cleve., 1980; MEd, John Carroll U., 2004. Cert. tchr. Beth Jacob Jerusalem, lic. sch. psychologist Ohio. Tchr. Yeshiva of Bklyn., 1974—76, Beth Rivka, 1976—78, Hebrew Acad. of Cleve., 1978—2004; student tchg. coord. Yavne Teachers Coll., 2002—05; sch. psychology intern CH-UH Dist., 2004—05; sch. psychologist Hebrew Acad. of Cleve., 2005—. Pres. Hebrew Acad. of Cleve. PTA, 1989—91. Vis. scholar Regent scholar, NY State, 1973. Mem.: Ohio Sch. Psychologists Assn., Nat. Assn. Sch. Psychologists. Jewish. Avocations: reading, puzzles, swimming, biking. Home: 3558 Bendemeer Rd Cleveland Heights OH 44118 Office: Hebrew Acad Cleveland 1860 S Taylor Rd Cleveland Heights OH 44118 Home Fax: 216-371-1413. Personal E-mail: shanih@hotpop.com.

HEGEL, CAROLYN MARIE, farm management extension agent; b. Lagro, Ind., Apr. 19, 1940; d. Ralph H. and Mary Lucile (Rudig) Lynn; m. Tom Lee Hegel, June 3, 1962. Student pub. schs., Columbia City, Ind. Bookkeeper Huntington County Farm Bur. Co-op, Inc., Ind., 1959-67, office mgr. Ind., 1967-70; twp. woman leader Wabash County (Ind.) Farm Bur., Inc., 1970-73, county woman leader, 1973-76; dist. woman leader Ind. Farm Bur., Inc., Indpls., 1976-80, 2d v.p., bd. dirs., 1980—, chmn. women's com., 1980—, exec. com., 1988—. Farmer Andrews, Ind., 1962—; dir. Farm Bur. Ins. Co., Indpls., 1980—, exec. com., 1988—, audit com., 2000—, chmn. audit com., 2003—; bd. dirs., spkr. in field, bd. mem. Country Way Ins., 2002—. Women in the Field columnist Hoosier Farmer mag., 1980—. Mem. rural task force Gt. Lakes States Econ. Devel. Commn., 1987—88; mem. Ind. Farm Bur. Svc. Co., 1980—; active Leadership Am. Program, 1988; Sunday sch. tchr., bd. dirs. children's activities Bethel United Meth. Ch., 1965—; pres. Bethel United Meth. Women, Lagro, 1975—81; bd. dirs. Ind. Farm Bur. Found., Indpls., 1980—, Ind. Inst. Agr., Food and Nutrition, Indpls., 1982—, Ind. 4-H Found., Lafayette, 1983—86; mem. Ind. Rural Health Adv. Coun., 1993—96, Hoosier Homestead Award Cert. Com., Indpls., 1980—; organizer farm divsn. Wabash County Am. Cancer Soc. Fund Dr., 1974; bd. dirs. N.E. Ind. Kidney Found., 1984—, Nat. Kidney Found. of Ind., 1985—89. Named Big Sister of Yr., Wabash County, Ind., 2003; named one of Outstanding Farm Woman of Yr., Country Woman Mag., 1987; recipient State 4-H Home Econs. award, Ind. 4-H, 1960. Mem.: Am. Farm Bur. Fedn. (midwest rep. to women's com. 1986—93), Producers Mktg. Assn. (bd. dirs. 1980—94), Ind. Agrl. Mktg. Assn. (bd. dirs. 1980—94), Women in Comm., Inc. Republican. Home: 3330 N 650 E Andrews IN 46702-9616 Office: Ind Farm Bur Inc PO Box 1290 225 S East St Indianapolis IN 46202-4058 Office Phone: 317-692-7830. E-mail: chegel@infarmbureau.com.

HEGENDERFER, JONITA SUSAN, public relations executive; b. Chgo., Mar. 18, 1944; d. Clifford Lincoln and Cornelia Anna (Larson) Hazzard; m. Gary William Hegenderfer, Mar. 12, 1971 (dec. 1978). BA, Purdue U., 1965; postgrad., Calif. State U., Long Beach, 1966-67, Northwestern U., 1969-70. Tchr. English, Long Beach (Calif.) Schs., 1965-68; editl. asst. Playboy Mag., Chgo., 1968-70; comms. specialist AMA, Chgo., 1970-72; v.p. Home Data, Hinsdale, Ill., 1972-75; mktg. mgr. Olympic Savs. & Loan, Berwyn, Ill., 1975-79; sr. v.p. Golin/Harris Comms., Chgo., 1979-89; pres. JSH & A, Chgo., 1989—. Bd. dirs. Chgo. Internat. Film Festival, 1989, 90, 2005, 06. Author: Slim Guide to Spas, 1984, (video) PR Guide for Chicago LSCs, 1991; editor: Financial Information National Directory, 1972; contbr. articles to profl. jours. Co-chmn. pub. rels. com. Am. Cancer Soc., Chgo., 1984; mem. com. March of Dimes, Chgo., 1986; mem. pub. rels. com. Girl Scouts Chgo., 1989-90, bd. dirs., 1994-95; bd. dirs. Greater DuPage Women's Bus. Coun., 1992-93, Girl Scouts U.S. DuPage County, 1994—; vol. ctr. adv. com. United Way, Chgo., 1990-93; mem. cmty. svc. com. Publicity Club Chgo., 1990—. Recipient 5 Golden Trumpet awards Publicity Club Chgo., 1983, 96, 94, Silver Trumpet awards, 1984, 86, 88, Spectra awards Internat. Assn. Bus. Communicators, 1984, 85, 87, Gold Quill aard, 1985, Bronze Anvil award Pub. Rels. Soc. Am., 1985, award Nat. Creativity in Pub. Rels. award, 1995; named Influential Woman in Bus., 1998. Mem. Am. Mktg. Assn., Publicity Club Chgo., Pub. Rels. Soc. Am., Chgo. Women in Pub., Nat. Assn. Women Bus. Owners, DuPage Area Assn. Bus. Tech. (bd. dirs. 1997), Coun. on Fgn. Rels., Met. Women's Forum, Cinema Chgo. (bd. dirs. 1988-89, 2005-). Avocations: travel, photography. Office: JSH & A Ltd 2 Transam Plaza Dr Ste 450 Oakbrook Terrace IL 60181-4290 Office Phone: 630-932-4242. Business E-Mail: jonni@jsha.com.

HEGERTY, NANNETTE H., police chief; b. Milw. m. George Hegerty; stepchildren: Suzanne, Scott. BS in Edn., U. Wis., 1972; MS in Mgmt., Cardinal Stritch Coll., 1985; student, FBI Nat. Tng. Acad., 1988. From officer to chief police Milw. (Wis.) Police Dept., 1976—2003, chief of police, 2003—; head Ea. Dist. Office U.S. Marshals Svc., 1994—2002. Office: Milwaukee Police Adminstrn Bldg 749 W State St Milwaukee WI 53233

HEGGENESS, JULIE FAY, foundation administrator, lawyer; b. Long Beach, Calif., Nov. 9, 1959; d. Clark Richard Heggeness, June Lorraine Heggeness; 1 child, Thaddeus. BFA, U. So. Calif., 1982; JD, Western State U., 1998. Cert. specialist planned giving. Dir. Long Beach Meml. Med. Ctr., Long Beach, 1995—99, Meml. Med. Ctr. Found., Long Beach, 1999—. 1st v.p. Camp Fire U.S., Long Beach, 1999—2001; Leadership Long Beach Class of 2003 estate planning and trust coun., bd. mem. at large; mem. Nat. Coun. Planned Giving. Mem.: Long Beach (Calif.) Bar Assn., Assistance League Long Beach, Cameo Profl. Aux. Republican. Roman Catholic. Avocations: golf, gardening, skiing. Office: Meml Med Ctr Found 2801 Atlantic Ave Long Beach CA 90806 Personal E-mail: jheggeness@memorialcare.org.

HEGGER, SAMANTHA LYNN, social studies educator; b. Cambridge, Mass., Feb. 24, 1980; d. Joyce and James Guelli. BA in History, U. N.H., Durham, 2002, MA in Tchg., 2003. Cert. secondary social studies tchr. N.H. Tchr. 7th grade social studies Rochester Mid. Sch., NH, 2003—. Avocations: yoga, travel, hiking, reading. Home: 53 Rustic Shores Rd Alton NH 03809 Office: Rochester Mid Sch 47 Brock St Rochester NH 03867 Personal E-mail: hegger.rms@rochesternh.net.

HEGLER, ELLEN MARIE, retired language educator, small business owner; b. Dryden, Oreg., Dec. 16, 1916; d. George Westley Van Buskirk and Marie Frances Mineo; children: Brian Neils, Rollin Grant, Gary Mark. BA in English cum laude, So. Oreg. Coll., 1959, MA in English, 1963; postgrad., UCLA, 1969-70. Cert. secondary tchr., Calif., Oreg. Prodr., announcer Radio Program KYSC, Yreka, Calif., 1947-48; v.p., sec. Carl Hegler Logging Inc., Ashland, 1951-59; social worker Jackson County Pub. Welfare Commn., 1959-60; English tchr. Sr. H.S., Medford, Oreg., 1961-62; fashion editor May Co., L.A., 1963-64; asst. prof. English So. Oreg. Coll., Ashland, 1964-70, Calif. State U., L.A., 1971-72; owner Hegler Enterprises Ltd., Ashland, Medford, 1976—. Contbr. articles to profl. publs. Sec. Ashland Meml. Hosp. com., 1956-58; pub. rels. dir. Sch. Bond Issues, Ashland, 1958; sec., exec. bd. Ashland Hosp. Found., 1981-83; co-founder Nat. Literary Hon. Fraternity, 1958. Avocation: writing.

HEGYELI, RUTH INGEBORG ELISABETH JOHNSSON, pathologist, federal official; b. Aug. 14, 1931; came to U.S., 1963; d. John Alfred and Elsa Ingeborg (Sjogren) Johnsson; m. Andrew Francis Hegyeli, July 2, 1966 (dec. June 1982). BA in Scis., U. Toronto, 1958, MD, 1962. Intern Toronto Gen. Hosp., 1962-63; sr. rsch. pathologist Battelle Meml. Inst., Columbus, Ohio, 1967-69; med. officer Nat. Heart and Lung Inst., 1969-73; chief program devel. and evaluation Nat. Heart, Lung and Blood Inst., Bethesda, Md., 1973-76, acting dir. office program planning, 1975-76, asst. dir. internat. rels., 1976-86, assoc. dir. internat. rels., 1986—2005. Mem. sci. adv. bd. Giovanni Lorenzini Found., Inc., N.Y.C., Milan, 1982—. Coord. editor: Jour. Soviet Rsch. in Cardiovasc. Diseases, 1979-86; editor: Christopher Columbus Commemorative Book on Discovering New Worlds in Medicine, 1992, Internat. Position Paper: Women's Health and Menopause, A Comprehensive Approach, 2002, also 11 sci. books; contbr. poetry to nat. and internat. anthologies. Mem. nat. adv. bd. Nat. Mus. Women in Arts. Named Hon. Mem. Eagle Tribe of Haida Indians, Queen Charlotte Islands, B.C., Can., 1961; named to, Internat. Poetry Hall of Fame, 1997; recipient German Friendship award, German Ministry Rsch. and Tech., 1988, Nicolaus Copernicus medal, Academica Medica, 1988, Superior Svc. award, HEW, 1975, DHHS, 1991, Outstanding Achievement award in Poetry, 2003, Internat. Peace prize, 2004, Exemplary Svc. award, Surgeon Gen., 2005, Fogarty Scholar Gold medal, 2005. Fellow Acad. Medicine, Toronto; mem. Soc. Geriatric Cardiology (founding mem.), Am. Soc. Artificial Internat. Organs, N.Y. Acad. Scis., Acad. Am. Poets, Internat. Soc. Poets, World Literary Acad., Fed. Exec. Alumni Assn. Republican. Avocations: poetry, writing, art, music, travel. Home: 24301 Hanson Rd Gaithersburg MD 20882-3501 Personal E-mail: johnelsa@verizon.net.

HEICHEL, PAULA, investment company executive, financial consultant; b. Phila., Apr. 26, 1949; d. Francis Stephen Heichel and Dorothy Pauline O'Brien. BA in Bus., Rutgers U., Camden, N.J., 1971; MS in Consumer Econs., U. Mo., 1973. Vista vol. Neighborhood Legal Svc. Corp., Washington, 1973-75; dep. dir. Legal Svcs. for the Elderly/AARP, Washington, 1975-80; 1st v.p. investments, fin. cons. Smith Barney, Washington, 1981—. 1st soprano Alexandria (Va.) Singers, 1995—; mem. dean's coun. Rutgers U., Camden. Mem. Exec. Women Internat. (program dir. 1985-86). Avocations: dog training, scuba diving. Office: Smith Barney 1050 Connecticut Ave NW Ste 800 Washington DC 20036-5349 E-mail: paula.heichel@smithbarney.com.

HEID, MARY KATHLEEN, mathematics educator; b. Erie, Pa., Mar. 13, 1948; d. Frederick F. and Mary Alice (Kuhn) Heid Schultz. BA, Cath. U., 1970; MA, U. Md., 1974, PhD, 1984. Tchr. Prince George County Schs., Upper Marlboro, Md., 1970-79; asst. instr. U. Md., College Park, 1980-84; from asst. prof. to prof. Pa. State U., U. Pk., Pa., 1984—2005, disting. prof., 2005—. Author: (supplemental materials) Mathcounts; contbr. articles to profl. jours. Grantee, NSF, 1987—95, 1997—, Mid Atlantic Ctr. Math., Tchg. and Learning, 2000—. Mem.: Nat. Coun. Tchrs. Math. (bd. dirs. 2003—06), Math. Assn. Am. (bd. govs. 1998—2003). Office: Pa State U 271 Chambers Bldg University Park PA 16802-3205

HEIDBREDER, JESSICA LOU, music educator; m. William Edward Heidbreder, July 27, 2002. MusB, Northwestern U., Evanston, Ill., 1992; MusM in Edn., U. Ill., Champaign-Urbana, 2001. Dir. bands Notre Dame H.S., Burlington, Iowa, 1992—93, Johnston H.S., 1993—2000; tchg. asst. U. Ill., Champaign-Urbana, 2000—01; dir. band Johnston H.S., 2001—. Pvt. instr. horn, Des Moines, 1992—; tour advisor Iowa Ambassadors Music, 1998—2000. Recipient John and Clara Beattie award Outstanding Work Music Edn., Northwestern U., 1992; Theodore Presser Found. scholar, 1991. Mem.: South Ctrl. Iowa Bandmasters Assn. (assoc.; chair pub. rels. 2006—, chair honor band 1994—98, pres. 2005—06). Office: Johnston High School 6501 NW 62nd Avenue Johnston IA 50131 Office Phone: 515-278-0449.

HEIDELBERGER, KATHLEEN PATRICIA, physician; b. Bklyn., Apr. 13, 1939; d. William Cyprian and Margaret Bernadette (Hughes) H.; m. Charles William Davenport, Oct. 8, 1977. BS cum laude, Coll. Misericordia, 1961; MD cum laude, Woman's Med. Coll. Pa., 1965. Intern Mary Hitchcock Hosp., Hanover, N.H., 1965-66, resident in pathology, 1966-70; mem. faculty U. Mich., Ann Arbor, 1970—, assoc. prof. pathology, 1976-79, prof., 1979—2002; ret., 2002. Mem. Am. Soc. Clin. Pathologists, U.S.-Can. Acad. Pathology, Soc. for Pediatric Pathology, Coll. Am. Pathologists.

HEIDEN, CARA, mortgage company executive; Joined Norwest Bank Iowa, 1981, CFO, 1988—92, Norwest Mortgage, 1992—94, head, servicing and post closing, 1994—97, head, mktg. and retail direct client services, 1997—98, head, nat. consumer lending, 1998—2004; div. pres., nat. consumer & institutional lending Wells Fargo Home Mortgage (division of Wells Fargo Bank, N.A.), Des Moines, 2004—. Pres. Norwest Housing Found., 1996—99. Named one of 25 Women to Watch, US Banker mag., 2005. Office: Wells Fargo Home Mortgage 405 SW 5th St Des Moines IA 50309*

HEIDENREICH, LORI JEAN, music educator; b. Sparta, Wis., June 16, 1956; d. Jacque Andrews and Audrey Mae Walker; children: Steven, Avery. MusB, U. Wis., Whitewater, 1980, M in Choral Edn., 2001. Instr. tchr. gen. music, instrumental music Fontana Elem. Sch., Wis., 1981—83; tchr. vocal music, gen. music, instrumental music Whitewater Unified Schs., Wis., 1983—. Music dir. Whitewater 4-H, 1983—97; octagon advisor Whitewater Octagon Club, 1986—; pres., treas. publicity Whitewater Jaycees, 1987, 1989, 1993; governing bd. Wis. Alliance for Arts Edn., 1993—99; sec. Wis. Assn. for Music Suprs., 1993—98; stds. com. Dept. Pub. Instrn., 2004—. Recipient Outstanding Student Condr. award, Wis. Choral Dirs. Assn., 1981. Mem.: Am. Choral Dirs. Assn., Music Educators Nat. Coun., Wis. Sch. Music Assn. (adjudicator mus. events), Delta Omicron (pres., music dir.). Achievements include choir chosen to perform with Mil. Symphony Orch., 2006. Avocations: golf, volleyball, tennis, travel, reading. Home: 630 S Janesville St Whitewater WI 53190 Office: Whitewater HS 534 S Elizabeth St Whitewater WI 53190 Office Phone: 262-472-8174. E-mail: lheidenreich@wwusd.org.

HEIDKAMP, PATRICIA JEAN, librarian; b. Chgo., July 31, 1951; d. Howard Henry and Rosemary Frances (Stegmeyer) Luecke; m. Michael Francis Heidkamp, Aug. 4, 1979. BA, Mundelein Coll., Chgo., 1973; MA, No. Ill. U., 1989. Tchr. Notre Dame HS for Girls, Chgo., 1973-74, Resurrection HS, Chgo., 1974-75; libr. tech. asst. Roosevelt U., Chgo., 1975-82; mgr. info. cen. Ill. CPA Soc., Chgo., 1982-87; ref. libr. Sidley & Austin, Chgo., 1987-88; info. assoc. McMillan/Doolittle, Chgo., 1988-90; lead rschr. The Boston Cons. Group, Chgo., 1990—. Assoc. editor Who Owns That Store?, 1990; editor: Partners' Weekly Retail Summary, 1990; contr. to Bus. Info. Alert, 1990-93, ICPAS News Jour., 1984-87, Informant, 1991. Ill. Gen. Assy. legis. scholar, 1989. Mem. Spl. Librs. Assn., Am. Libr. Assn., No. Ill. U. Alumni Assn., Smithsonian Assocs., Beta Phi Mu. Democrat. Avocations: doll collecting, british mysteries, bowling. Office: The Boston Cons Group Inc 200 S Wacker Dr Chicago IL 60606-5829

HEIDLAGE, PATSY JO, physical education educator; b. Chickasha, Okla., Oct. 21, 1937; d. Harry James and Esther Victoria Gibson; m. Robert Frederick Heidlage Sr., Aug. 9, 1959; children: Robert Frederick Heidlage Jr., Vickie Ann Heidlage-Williams, Charles James. BS, Okla. Coll. for Women, Chickasha, 1955; MEd, Northeastern State U., Tahlequah, Okla., 1991. Cert. tchr. phys. edn., sci., counseling Okla., 1959. Phys. edn. tchr. Claremore H.S., Okla., 1973—75; tennis instr. and coach Rogers State U., Claremore, 1975—77; phys. edn. tchr. Westside Elem. Sch., Claremore, 1977—. Cmty. tennis camp dir. Claremore Parks Dept., 1968—; elem. counselor Westside Sch., Claremore, 2004—; bd. dirs. Title 1 Com. / Westside Elem., Claremore, 2005—; bd. mem. and sec. Claremore Pk. Bd., 1975—81. Jump rope for heart coord. Am. Heart Assn., Claremore, 1985—2006; choir mem. Claremore Cmty. Chorus, 1995—2006; sec. Rogers County Bd. Adjustment, Claremore, 1975—80; bd. dirs. U. Sci. and Arts, 1966—, Claremore United Way, 1997—. Recipient Claremore Pub. Schs. Tchr. of the Yr., Claremore Classroom Tchrs. Assn., 1987. Mem.: AAHPERD, Okla. Tennis Coaches Assn. (pres., dir. 1998—2003, Tennis Coach of the Yr. 1998), Delta Kappa Gamma (sec. 1995—97, Scholarships 1989, 1990 and 1991), Okla. Edn. Assn., Okla. Assn. Health Phys. Edn. and Recreation, NEA. D-Conservative. Catholic. Avocations: tennis, restoration, gardening. Home: P O Box 781 Claremore OK 74018 Office: Westside Elementary School 2600 Holly Rd Claremore OK 74017 Office Phone: 918-341-3511. Home Fax: 918-343-6338; Office Fax: 918-343-6338. Personal E-mail: pheidlage@claremore.k12.ok.us.

HEIDRICK, KATHY JO, medical technician, educator; b. Dodge City, Kans., May 6, 1954; d. Floyd G. and Bonnie Lee Loughrige; m. Paul L. Heidrick, July 30, 1977; children: Alan James, Julie Lynn, Lori Michelle. AS, Dodge City C.C., 1974; B in Med. Tech., Kans. State U., Manhattan, 1976. Generalist Ctrl. Kans. Med. Ctr., Great Bend, 1976—77; hematology staff Hays Pathology Lab., Kans., 1977—78, head microbiology, 1978—80; med. lab. technician instr. Barton County C.C., Great Bend, 1980—98, 2001—, computer svcs. staff, 1998—2001. Mem. Med. Lab. Technician Adv. Bd., Great Bend, 1980—98, Great Bend, 2001—, Health Adv. Bd., Great Bend, 1992—98. Softball and basketball coach; mem. evangelism, edn. and adv. coms. Foundry Meth. Ch. Mem.: SW Assn. Clin. Microbiologists, Am. Soc. Microbiology. Home: 1611 Warner Rd Great Bend KS 67530 Office: Barton County CC 245 NE 30th Rd Great Bend KS 67530

HEIDT, AMY R., science educator; b. Wuertzburg, Germany, Mar. 21, 1954; arrived in U.S., 1955; d. Paul Wilmer and Daisy Louise Heidt; m. Paul Edward Sumner, Dec. 27, 1979; children: Shelly Anne Sumner Schmeisser, Elliot Paul Sumner. BS cum laude, U. Ga., 1977, MS, 1979; MEd, Valdosta State Coll., 1991, EdS, 1994. Cert. T-4 Valdosta State Coll., PBT-5, PBT-6, gifted endorsement. Sci. tchr. grades 8-12 Fitzgerald H.S. Ben Hill County Schs., 1985—91, life sci. tchr. grade 7 Ben Hill County Schs., 1991—93; team leader, life sci. tchr. grade 7 J.T. Reddick Mid. Sch. Tift County Sch. Sys., 1993—96, chair sci. dept. 7 J.T. Reddick Mid. Sch., 1994—96, sci. tchr. grades 8-9 Tift County Jr. H.S., 1996—98, sci. tchr. grades 8-9 Northeast Mid. Sch., 1997—98, sci. tchr. grade 9 Northeast Mid. Sch., 1998—, head sci. dept. N.E. campus Tift County H.S., 2000—. Presenter in field. Named Tchr. of Yr., TCHS, Northeast Campus, 2001; recipient Cub Scout Leader award, S.W. Ga. coun. Boy Scouts Am., 1998, Dist. Award of Merit, 1998, Scout Tng. award, 2000, 10 Yr. Pin, Girl Scouts of Am., 2001, grants in field, Silver Beaver award, Boy Scouts of Am., 2003. Mem.: NEA, Ga. Assn. Educators, Ga. Sci. Tchrs. Assn., Nat. Sci. Tchrs. Assn. Avocations: dog training, bicycling, camping, hiking. Office: Tift County H S NE Campus 3021 Fulwood Rd Tifton GA 31794

HEIFNER, CAROL JOAN, social work educator; b. Sioux Falls, SD, July 10, 1940; d. Cecil Leonard Byg and Violet Irene (Miller) Noller; m. Dennis Roy Heifner, June 3, 1960; children: Janine, Renee, Denise. AA, S.D. State U., 1960; BSW, Briar Cliff Coll., 1978; MSW, U. Iowa, 1980; PhD, Case Western Res. U., 1999. County coord. Upper Des Moines Opportunity, Emmetsburg, Iowa, 1974-75; caseworker, family therapist Harmony Youth Home, Orange City, Iowa, 1980; coord. Woodbury County Ct. Referral Svc., Sioux City, Iowa, 1977; outside evaluator Florence Crittendon Home, Sioux City, 1980-81; sch. social worker Area Edn. Agy. 4, Sioux Center, 1980-87; instr. Dordt Coll., Sioux Center, 1987-91. Team evaluator Area Edn. Agy. 3, Cylinder, Iowa, 1984; co-tchr. in teen conflict N.W. Iowa Tech. Coll., Sheldon, Iowa, 1989; grant co-author REACH Team, Sioux Center, 1984, 85; mem. workshop Nursing Home Activity Dirs., N.W. Iowa, 1989; part-time instr. St. Mary's Coll. of Minn., Winona, 1991, Mandel Sch. Applied Social Scis./Case Western Res. U., 1991-93; cons. for curriculum devel. Babes-Bolyai U. Club-Napoca, Romania, 1993; lectr. U. Wis. LaCrosse, 1998-99, adj. faculty, 1999; part-time instr. sociology Viterbo Coll., LaCrosse, 1999; Fulbright lectr. U. Ion Cuza, Iasi, Romania, 1995-1996; curriculum cons. clin. pastoral edn. program Franciscan Skemp Med. Ctr., 2001; ind. rschr.; facilitator Conflict Resolution Workshop. Founding mem. Sioux County Multidisciplinary Tream, Orange City, 1980-83; founding bd. dirs. Children's World Day Care Ctr., Sheldon, 1974; founding bd. dirs., chair Domestic Violence Aid Ctr., Inc., Sioux Center, 1982-86; bd. dirs. Plains Area Mental Health, LeMars, Iowa, 1978-80. Mem.: Soc. for Romanian Studies. Avocations: sewing, painting, furniture refinishing, reading, music.

HEIGHT, DOROTHY I., former foundation administrator; b. Richmond, Va., Mar. 24, 1912; d. James Edward and Fannie (Burroughs) Height. BA, MA, NYU. Mem. nat. staff YWCA of the U.S.A., 33 yrs.; caseworker NYC Welfare Dept., 1934; dir. Ctr. Racial Justice YWCA, 1946; nat. pres. Nat. Coun. Negro Women Inc., 1957—97, pres. emeritus, 1998—. With Dept. Def. Adv. Com. Women, 1952—55; mem. N.Y. State Social Welfare Bd., 1958—68; bd. govs. ARC, 1964—70; pres.'s com. Employment Handicapped; mem. ad hoc com. Pub. Welfare Dept. Health Edn. and Welfare; dir. Ctr. Racial Justice YMCA. Pres. Nat. Coun. Negro Women, 1957—; hon. mem. nat. bd. dirs. YWCA of the U.S.A. Recipient Disting. Svc. award, Nat. Conf. Social Welafre, 1971, William L. Dawson award, 1974, Citizens Medal award, 1989, Camille Cosby World Children award, 1990, Amb. award, YWCA of the USA, 1993, Presdl. Freedom medal, 1994, Congl. Gold Medal, 2004, 100 Most Influential Black Americans, Ebony mag., 2006. Office: Pres Emerita Nat Coun Negro Women 633 Pennsylvania Ave NW Washington DC 20004*

HEIGL, KATHERINE MARIE, actress; b. Washington, DC, Nov. 24, 1978; d. Paul and Nancy Heigl. Actor: (films) That Night, 1992, King of the Hill, 1993, My Father the Hero, 1994, Under Seige 2: Dark Territory, 1995, Wish Upon a Star, 1996, Prince Valiant, 1997, Stand-ins, 1997, Bug Buster, 1998, Bride of Chucky, 1998, The Tempest, 1998, 100 Girls, 2000, Valentine, 2001, Descendant, 2003, Zyzzyx Rd., 2005, Side Effects, 2005, The Ringer, 2005, Caffeine, 2006; (TV series) Roswell, 1999—2002, Grey's Anatomy, 2005—, (guest appearance) The Twilight Zone, 2002,; (TV films) Vegas Dick, 2003, Love Comes Softly, 2003, Evil Never Dies, 2003, Critical Assembly, 2003, Wuthering Heights, 2003, Love's Enduring Promise, 2004, Romy and

Michele: In the Beginning, 2005. Office: c/o Grey's Anatomy Los Feliz Tower, 4th Fl 4151 Prospect Ave Los Angeles CA 90027 also: c/o Paradigm 360 N Crescent Dr, N Bldg Beverly Hills CA 90210*

HEIKE, MELISSA, secondary school educator; d. Ronald and Deborah Sawicki; m. Bruce Heike, Apr. 8, 2006. BS Math. and Secondary Edn., Seton Hall U., South Orange, NJ, 2000. Cert. tchr. NJ. Tchr. math., drama dir. Roxbury HS, Succasunna, NJ, 2000—. Office: Roxbury High Sch 1 Bryant Dr Succasunna NJ 07876 Office Phone: 973-584-1200 ext 624.

HEILBRUNN, LORRAINE JUDITH, psychologist, educational administrator; b. Bklyn. BA magna cum laude, SUNY, Buffalo, 1968, PhD, 1973. Lic. psychologist, Mass. Intern Judge Baker Guidance Ctr., Boston, 1972-73; psychologist Boston Univ., Boston, 1973-79; faculty mem., dir. admissions Mass. Sch. Profl. Psychology, Boston, 1979—99; pvt. practice Brookline, Mass., 1975—. Mem. Nat. Register of Health Providers. Avocations: skiing, swimming, aerobics, tennis, dance. Office: Mass Sch Profl Psychology 1752 Beacon St Brookline MA 02445

HEIM, DIXIE SHARP, family practice nurse practitioner; b. Kansas City, Kans., Feb. 28, 1938; d. Glen Richard and Freda Helen (Milburn) Stanley; m. Theodore Eugene Sharp, Aug. 12, 1960 (dec. Apr., 1972); children: Diane Yvonne Price, Andrew Kirk, Bryan Scot; m. Roy Bernard Heim, June 14, 1979. Diploma nursing, St. Luke's Hosp. Sch. Nursing, Kansas City, Mo., 1959; family practice nurse clinician, Wichita State U., 1974. Cert. advanced registered nurse practitioner, Kans. Nurse surg. ICU Staff Kaiser Found. Hosp., San Francisco, 1959-61; oper. rm. supr. St. Luke's Hosp., Kansas City, Mo., 1962-63; emergency rm., oper. rm. supr. Lawrence (Kans.) Meml. Hosp., 1963-72; nurse clinician various doctors, Lawrence, 1973-81; nursing supr. spl. projects St. Francis Hosp. and Med. Ctr., Topeka, 1981-94; primary health care giver Health Care Access, Lawrence, 1992-94; nurse practitioner Dr. Glen Bair, Topeka, 1990-94; advanced registered nurse practitioner Dr. Jerry H. Feagan, Topeka, 1994, McLouth (Kans.) Med. Clinic, 1994—, Jefferson County Meml. Hosp., Winchester, Kans., 1995-96; family practice nurse practitioner Robert E. Jacoby II., M.D., Mathew Bohm M.D., Topeka, Kans., 1995-2000. Preceptor nurse practitioner program U. Kans., 1993-2001, registered nurse program Washburn U., 1996-2001; primary health care provider Jefferson County Law Enforcement Ctr., Oskaloosa, Kans., 1995-96. V.p. Am. Bus. Women. Assn. Lawrence chpt., 1969, sec. 1968; vol. Children's Hour, Lawrence, 1965-72, Comty. Resource for Career edn., 1975-76; adv. bd. E. Ctrl. Kans. Econs. Opportunity Corp., Lawrence, 1993-95; mem. Rep. Women Douglas County, Lawrence, 1994-2004. Recipient Nursing the Heart of Health Care award Kaiser Permanente, 1994. Mem. ANA, Am. Acad. Nurse Practitioners (cert.), Kans. State Nurses Assn. (v.p. 1958, chairperson fund raising campaign 1994, bd. dirs. 1996). Home: 540 Arizona St Lawrence KS 66049-2100 Office: Flannery & McBratney MDs PA 3550 S 4th St # 10000 Leavenworth KS 66048 Personal E-mail: DKtrDixie@aol.com.

HEIM, HAZEL, nurse; b. Courtland, Miin. d. Frederick William H. and Augusta Marie Georgius. Diploma, Meth. Kahler Sch. Nursing, 1929. Charge nurse St. Mary's Hosp., Rochester, Minn.; vol. nurse Red Bird Mission Hosp., Beverly, Ky.; pvt. duty nurse Kahler Hosp., Rochester. Republican. Methodist.

HEIM, KATHRYN MARIE, psychiatric nurse; b. Milw., Sept. 29, 1952; d. Lester Sheldon Wilcox and Laura Dora (Corpie) Wilcox Sears; m. Vincent Robert Gouthro, June 30, 1970 (div. 1976); 1 child, Robert Vincent; m. George John Heim, Sept. 17, 1977 (div. 1988). AS in Nursing, Milw. Area Tech. Coll., 1983; BS in Nursing, NYU, 1986; MS in Mgmt., Cardinal Stritch Coll., 1988; PhD in Human Behavior, Newport U., 1997. Cert. psychiatric and mental health nurse, AMA. Staff geriatric nurse Clement Manor, Greenfield, Wis., 1983; nurse, health educator Milw. Boys Club, 1983-84; nurse mgr. Milw. County Mental Health Complex, 1984—2002, mem. gero-psychiat. inpatient adv. com., 1986-87, mem. joint practice com., guest rels. com., 1999-2001; hospitality com., 1999-2000; RN Psychiat. Acute Care Day Hosp., 1992—2002, cmty. support RN case mgr., 2002, Milw. County Dept. Aging, 2002—, quality assurance RN, 2005—. Cons. Positive Perspectives, 1999-2000; rschr. on loneliness/mental health, 1989-92. Contbr. articles to profl. jours. Mem. wellness task force Milw. County Mental Health Complex, 1988-89, chairperson sensory deficit com. Geropsychiatry, 1989-90; active Boy Scouts Am., Milw., 1978-80. Mem. ANA (cert. gerontol. nurse), NAFE (network dir. Milw. chpt. 1982-92), Wis. Nurses Assn., Nat. Marfan Found. (Wis. network group leader), NYU Alumni Assn., Cardinal Stritch Alumni Assn. (class rep. 1986-88), Milw. Area Tech. Coll. Alumni Assn. Avocations: yoga, jogging, reading, writing. Home: 226 N 63rd St Milwaukee WI 53213-4137 E-mail: kheim2000@yahoo.com.

HEIMANN, JANET BARBARA, volunteer trail consultant; b. Santa Cruz, Calif., Dec. 18, 1931; d. John Louis and Charlotte Lucina (Burns) Grinnell; m. Richard Frank Gustav, July 10, 1953; children: David Robert, Gary Alan, Kathleen Janet. BS, U. Calif., Berkeley, 1954. Vol. trail rschr. Monterey County Pks. Dept.; appointee Carmel Valley Trail Adv. Com., 1993-99. Pres. Folsom Freedom Trails, Placer County, Calif., 1980-83; chmn. Adopt-a-Trail, Folsom Lake Trail Patrol, Placer County, 1986-88; bd. dirs. Loomis Basin Horseman Assn., Placer County, 1986-87. Republican. Home: 11565 McCarthy Rd Carmel Valley CA 93924-9239

HEIMANN-HAST, SYBIL DOROTHEA, literature and language professor; b. Shanghai, May 8, 1924; arrived in U.S., 1941; d. Paul Heinrich and Elisabeth (Halle) Heimann; m. David G. Hast, Jan. 11, 1948 (div. 1959); children: Thomas David Hast, Dorothea Elizabeth Hast-Scott. BA in French, Smith Coll., Northampton, Mass., 1946; MA in French Lang. and Lit., U. Pitts., 1963; MA in German Lang. and Lit., UCLA, 1966; diploma in Spanish, U. Barcelona, Spain, 1972. Cert. German, French and Spanish tchr. Calif. Assoc. in German lang. UCLA, 1966-70; asst. prof. German Calif. State U., L.A., 1970-71; lectr. German Mt. St. Mary's Coll., Brentwood, Calif., 1974-75; instr. French and German, diction coach Calif. Inst. of Arts, Valencia, 1977-78; coach lang. and diction UCLA Opera Theater, 1973-93, ret., 1993, lectr. dept. music, 1973-93; interviewer, researcher oral history program UCLA, 1986-93; dir., founder ISTMO, Santa Monica, Calif., 1975—. Cons. interpreter/translator LA Music Ctr., U.S. Supreme Ct., LA, J. Paul Getty Mus., Malibu, Calif., Warner New Media, Panorama Internat. Prodn., Sony Records, 1986—; voice-over artist; founder, artistic dir. Westside Opera Workshop, 1986—94. Author: numerous poems. Mem. KCET Founder Soc. Grantee, UCLA, 1990—91. Mem.: AFTRA, SAG, MLA, AAUP, German Am. C. of C., Sunset Succulent Soc. (v.p., bd. dirs., reporter, annual show chmn.). Avocations: performing arts, literature, history, plants, designing and knitting sweaters. Home and Office: River's Edge 111 Dekoven Dr Apt 606 Middletown CT 06457-3463

HEIMBOLD, MARGARET BYRNE, publisher, educator, consultant, realtor; came to U.S., 1966, naturalized, 1973; d. John Christopher and Anne (Troy) Byrne; m. Arthur Heimbold, Feb. 26, 1984; children: Eric Thomas Gordon, Victoria Byrne Heimbold BA, Queens Coll.; MA, Georgetown U., 2003; cert., Dale Carnegie, 1977, Psychol. Corp. Am., 1981, Wharton Sch., 1983, Stanford U., 1989. Mgr. group advt. N.Y. Times, N.Y.C., 1978—85; pub. Am. Film, Washington, 1985—86; v.p., pub. Nat. Trust for Hist. Preservation, Washington, 1986—90; pres. Summerville Press, Inc., Washington, 1990—; realtor Long and Foster, Washington, 2005—. Pub. Metro Golf, 1992—; advisor Mag. Pubs.; mentor Women's Ctr. Va.; judge various publ. competitions; judge various mags, awards programs Trustee Nat. Mus. Women in Arts, Choral Arts Soc. Washington, Kidsave Internat., Irish Peace Inst. Office Phone: 202-944-8400, 202-812-2750. Business E-Mail: margaret.heimbold@longandfoster.com. E-mail: summervillemedia@erols.com.

HEIMBUCH, BABETTE E., bank executive; b. 1948; BS in Math Summa Cum Laude, U. Calif., Santa Barbara, 1972. Sr. v.p., CFO FirstFed. Bank Calif., Santa Monica, 1982—85, exec. v.p., CFO, 1985—87, dir., 1986—, FirstFed. Fin. Corp., 1987—; sr. exec. v.p., CFO FirstFed. Fin. Corp. & FirstFed Bank Calif, 1987—88, pres., COO, 1989—97, pres., CEO, 1997—2002, chmn., pres., CEO, 2002—. Bd. dirs. Water Pik Technologies Inc., 2002—, Scape Industries. Chair bd. advisors Santa Monica-UCLA Med. Ctr.; fin. oversight com. Santa Monica/Malibu Unified Sch. Dist. Named one of 25 Women to Watch, US Banker Mag., 2003. Office: First Fed Bank Calif 401 Wilshire Blvd Santa Monica CA 90401-1416

HEIMES, CHARMAINE MARIE, elementary school educator, poet, writer; b. Detroit, June 28, 1960; d. Charles M. and Mary Patricia (Allen) H. BA, Olivet Coll., Mich., 1982. Cert. tchr. Tex., nat. cert. abstinence educator, cert. USA track & field ofcl. 2005. Substitute tchr. Charlotte (Mich.) Pub. Schs., 1982-84; coach jr. varsity volleyball Charlotte High Sch., 1983-84, coach jr. varsity softball, 1984; tcrh. phys. edn., coach Cigarroa Mid. Sch., Laredo, Tex., 1984—, head phys. edn. dept., 1988—. Asst. field hockey coach Olivet (Mich.) Coll., 1982-83; abstinenece master tchr. 1999-; Tex. Bess mentor, 2004-; Quest mentor Tex. A&M Internat. U., 2000-. Avocations: coin collecting/numismatics, plates, poetry, writing, Elvis memorabilia. Office: Cigarroa Mid Sch 2600 Palo Blanco St Laredo TX 78046-8232 Office Phone: 956-795-3706. E-mail: laredomac@hotmail.com.

HEIN, KAREN KRAMER, pediatrician, epidemiologist; b. NYC, Feb. 2, 1944; d. Irving W. and Ruth (Eisenberg) Kramer: m. Ralph Dell, Aug. 28, 1983; children: Ethan, Molly. BA, U. Wis., 1966; B of Med. Sci., Dartmouth Med. Sch., 1968; MD, Columbia U., 1970. Intern Bronx Mcpl. Hosp., Bronx Mcpl. Hosp. Ctr., 1970, resident, 1971-73; dir. adolescent AIDS program Montefiore Med. Ctr., NYC, 1987-94; prof. pediat. Albert Einstein Coll. Medicine, NYC, 1991—, prof. epidemiology and social medicine, 1993—, clin. prof. pediat., epidemiology and population health, 1995—; exec. officer Inst. Medicine NRC, Washington, 1995—98; pres. William T. Grant Found., NYC, 1998—2003. Cons. NYC Dept. Health, 1980-85, NYC Bd. Edn., 1987-93; bd. dirs. Dartmouth Med. Sch., Hanover, NH; bd. mem. Consumers Union, 1998-, Childfund Internat., 2005-, Internat. Rescue Com., 2005-. Author: AIDS: Trading Fears for Facts Consumer Reports Books, 1989. Named Outstanding Physician, Dept. Health and Human Svcs., 1989, Adminstrs. Citation award, 1993. Fellow Am. Bd. Pediat.; mem. Am. Pediatric Soc., Soc. for Pediatric Rsch., Am. Acad. Pediat., Soc. for Adolescent Medicine (pres. 1992-93). Address: Box 607 Jacksonville VT 05342

HEINECKE, MARGARET THERESA, librarian; b. N.Y.C., Sept. 13, 1923; d. William and Mary Ellen (O'Callaghan) Brand; m. Heinrich Heinecke, Mar. 10, 1962 (div. Feb. 1991); 1 child, Fredrich Heinrich. BA, Coll. St. Elizabeth, 1945; MA in History, Columbia U., 1949, MLS, 1954. Instr. history, libr. Panzer Coll., East Orange, N.J., 1954-57; libr. Watchung Hills (N.J.) Regional H.S., 1957-59; libr. GS 11 USAF Europe, Germany, 1959-66; dep. county libr. San Diego County, 1967-82. Vol. Proposition 13, San Diego, 1978, America's Cup, San Diego, 1992; puppeteer San Diego Opera, 1993-97, mem. outreach, 1995-97. Mem. AAUW. Avocations: rockhounding, travel, reading. Home: 3338 S Bonita St Spring Valley CA 91977-3020

HEINEMAN, HELEN L., retired academic administrator; m. John L. Heineman; 4 children. BA summa cum laude, Queens Coll., 1958; MA in English, Columbia U., 1959; PhD, Cornell U., 1967. Prof., chair English Dept. Cardinal Cushing Coll., Brookline, 1964-73; fellow Bunting Inst. Radcliffe Coll., 1973-92; dept. chair Framingham State Coll., 1974, acad. v.p., interim pres., provost, 1996-99, pres., 1999—2006. Recipient Woodrow Wilson fellowship, AAUW fellowship. Office: Framingham State Coll 100 State St PO Box 9101 Framingham MA 01701-9101*

HEINICKE, JANET LOUISE, educator, artist; b. Richmond, Ind., June 11, 1930; d. Homer Stroud and Mary DeMaris (Way) Hart; m. Herbert Raymond Heinicke, June 15, 1955; children: Peter, John, Mary Elizabeth, Mark, Sarah. BS, Wittenberg U., 1952; MS, U. Wis., 1955; MFA, EdD in Edn. Adminstrn., MFA, EdD in Edn. Adminstrn., No. Ill. U., 1977; postgrad., Syracuse U. Supr. elem. art Goshen (Ind.) Pub. Sch., 1952-54; tchr. art Shaker Heights (Ohio) Pub. Sch., 1954-55; asst. prof. art Judson Coll., Elgin, Ill., 1960-62, 69-74; program coordinator Kankakee (Ill.) Community Coll., 1977-82; chmn. fine arts divs., dir. Farnham Galleries Simpson Coll., Indianola, Iowa, 1986—2001; prof. emeritus Simpson Coll., 2001—. Guest artist, lectr. S.W. C.C., Creston, Iowa, 1985, Indian Hills C.C., Ottumwa, Iowa, 1986; guest artist, critic Iowa Amateur Artists Assn., Chariton, 1985; mem. edml. exch. to USSR, 1990, head del., 1992, 94; mem. del. to Heibei Province, China, 1993; vis. scholar Fukuoka Jo Gakuin Coll., Japan; edml. cons. Pedagogical Inst., Riga, Latvia; chmn. Iowa sister States-Stavropol Commn.; vis. artist, Terengandu, Malaysia; judge Iowa Amateur Artists Assn., 1994, 95; guest lectr. U. Dan-es. Salaam, Tanzania, 2006; instr. Des Moines Art Ctr. Mus. Sch., Des Moines Higher Edn. Consortium. Dir. Judson Coll. Art Gallery, 1969-74; chmn. faculty growth and devel. com. Kankakee (Ill.) C.C., 1977-82, chmn. campus beautification com., 1977-79; chmn. womens network group Simpson Coll., 1983-85; chmn. bldg. and planning com. Redeemer Luth. Ch., Indianola, 1984-86; mem. adv. panel cmty. devel. Iowa Arts Coun., 1986-90. Recipient Faculty Rsch. award Simpson Coll., 1994, Faculty Svc. award, 1994, Outstanding Alumni, Wittenberg U., No. Ill. U. Coll. Edn., Alumni award Coll. Edn., No. Ill. U., Alumni citation Wittenberg U., Springfield. Mem. ASCD, AAUW (regional v.p. N.E. ctrl. region 1977-79, chmn. nat. com. structural change 1979-81, pres. Indianola bd. 1984-86, bd. dirs. Iowa divsn., 1986—, Iowa pres. 2006—, Fellowships award panel 1993-95), Art Edn. Assn., Chgo. Artists Coalition, Coll. Art Assn., Nat. Assn. Art Adminstrs., Nat. Assn. Women Deans and Counselors, Delta Kappa Gamma (pres. 1988-90), Pi Lambda Theta, Alpha Lambda Delta (pres. Iowa Sister States). Home: 1302 W Boston Ave Indianola IA 50125-2166

HEINRICHS, APRIL, soccer coach; b. Charlottesville, Va., Feb. 27, 1964; BA in Radio, TV and Motion Pictures, U. N.C., 1986. Lic. U.S. Soccer Federation "A" coaching license. Player U.S. Nat. Team, 1986—91; profl. soccer player Prato, Italy, 1987—92; head coach Princeton U., 1990, U. Md., 1991—95, U. Va., 1996—99; full time asst. U.S. Women's Nat. Team, 1995—97; mem. coaching staff 1995 Women's World Cup, 1995, 1996 Olympic Women's Soccer Team, 1996; head coach U.S. U-16 Nat. Team, 1997—2000; head coach, tech. dir. U.S. Women's Nat. Team, 2000—. Mem. NCAA Championship Team, 1983, 84, 86. Recipient U.S. Soccer Female Athlete of Yr. award, 1986, 89; voted female player of the 1980s Soccer America Magazine; first female inducted into Nat. Soccer Hall of Fame, 1998; named First Team All-American U. N.C. (3 times); inaugural recipient NSCAA Women's Com. award of Excellence, 2000. Achievements include coached U.S. Women's Soccer Team to Silver Medal, Sydney Olympic Games, 2000. Office: US Soccer House 1801-1811 S Prairie Ave Chicago IL 60616

HEINS, DIANNE C., lawyer; b. Newark, N.J., Nov. 28, 1948; d. John and Alice Mary Hogg; children: Madeleine, Nora Anne. BA, Mary Washington Coll., Fredericksburg, Va., 1970; JD, U. Minn., Mpls., 1973. Counsel Minn. State Senate, St. Paul, 1973—78; pvt. practice Mpls., 1978—89; pro bono counsel Fargre & Benson LLP, Mpls., 2000—. Mem. Minn. Supreme Ct. Juvenile Rules Com., St. Paul, 2000—, Hennepin Co. Childrens Justice Initiative, Mpls., 2001—. Pres., bd. dirs. Friends of Children Found., Mpls., 2003—, Childrens Law Ctr. Minn., St. Paul, 2000—02. Office: Faegre & Benson LLP 2200 Wells Fargo Ctr 90 S 9th St Minneapolis MN 55402

HEINS, ESTHER, artist, illustrator; b. Bklyn, Nov. 10, 1908; d. Israel and Margaret (Brown) Berow; m. Harold Heins; Sept. 8, 1929 (dec. 1987); children: Marilyn Heins, Judith Leet. BS in Edn., Mass. Coll. Art, 1929. Freelance artist, Boston, 1930-60; bot. artist, illustrator plant introductions Arnold Arboretum, Boston, 1960—. Contbr. bot. illustrations to profl. jour.; one-woman shows include Graham Arader Gallery, NYC, Harvard Radcliffe Hilles Libr., Arnold Arboretum, Boston Pub. Libr., Schlesinger Libr., Cambridge, Mass.; group shows include Hunt Inst. for Bot. Documentation, Pitts., Arnold Arboretum, Munich, Germany, Smithsonian, Washington, Oakland, Calif., others; represented in permanent collections at Mus. Fine Arts, Boston, Hunt Inst. for Bot. Documentation, Schlesinger Libr., Radcliffe Coll., Arnold Arboretum, Boston Pub. Libr., Fogg Mus., Cambridge, and numerous others in pvt. collections; illustrator, contbr. essay: (book) Flowering Trees and Shrubs: The Botanical Paintings of Esther Heins, 1987; illustrator many covers Jour. AMA., the most recent 2002. Mem. Guild of Natural Sci. Illustrators. Avocations: attending concerts of Boston Symphony, gardening. Home: 8 Mitchell Rd Marblehead MA 01945-1130

HEINTSCHEL, RUTHANN M., school system administrator; d. Vincent Henry Heintschel and Florence Minnie Yenzer. BA, Mary Manse Coll., 1967; MEd, U. Toledo, 1973, PhD, 1978. Cert. sch. adminstr. Ohio, ednl. adminstrv. asst. Ohio, supt. Ohio, supr. Ohio. Classroom tchr. Toledo Diocesan Schs/, 1964—73, Columbus (Ohio) Diocesan Schs., 1974—76; cons. and asst. dir. of tchr. edn. Ohio Dept. of Edn., Columbus, Ohio, 1978—84; mem. faculty, asst. v.p., interim v.p. Notre Dame Coll. of Ohio, South Euclid, Ohio, 1984—97; mem. facult, asst. chmn. divsn. edn. Baldwin Wallace Coll., Berea, Ohio, 1997—2004; adminstr., curriculum coord. Office Cath. Edn., Columbus, 2004—. Co-founder, pres. Profl. Endeavors Network, Inc., Middleburg Heights, Ohio, 1997—; cons. Am. Cash Flow, Middleburg Heights, 1999—; rep. ACN, Inc., Middleburg Heights, 2004—. Named Outstanding Sci. Tchr., Ohio Acad. Sci., 1974; recipient Krecker award for outstanding sci. dept., 1972, 1974. Mem.: ASCD, Assn. Tchr. Educators, Phi Delta Kappa (Outstanding Educator award 2004, Outstanding Svc. to Edn. award 2002). Office: Office Cath Edn 1404 East 9th St Cleveland OH 44114 Office Phone: 216-696-6525 3240. Office Fax: 216-579-9655. Business E-Mail: rheintschel@dioceseofcleveland.org.

HEINTZ, CAROLINEA CABANISS, retired home economist, retired educator; b. Roanoke, Va., Jan. 19, 1920; d. Luther Bertie and Emblyn Bird (Jennings) Cabaniss; m. Howard Elmer Smith, Dec. 19, 1942 (div. Aug. 1975); children: Emblyn Davis, Cynthia Shannon, Cheryl Peterson, Melyssa Sexton; m. Raymond Walter Heintz, May 21, 1977; 1 stepchild, James. BS in Home Econ. Edn., U. Ala., Tuscaloosa, 1941; vocat. home econ. degree, Montevallo Coll., 1941. Cert. vocat. home econs. tchr. Swimming instr. Camp Mudjekeewis, Centerlovel, Maine, summer 1940; home econs. tchr. Roanoke Pub. Schs., 1941-43; dietitian U. Va., Charlottesville, 1943; nutrition edn. specialist Liberty Health Ctr. Svcs., Liberty Center, Ohio, 1974-80; home economist Dayton Hudson Dept. Store, Toledo, 1980-84; splty. food instr., continuing edn. U. Toledo, 1984-85. Pres., mem. Greater Toledo Nutrition Coun., 1966-98; pres. Sunset House Aux., 1999-2001, bd. dirs., 2001-06. Co-editor ch. cookbook Loaves and Fishes and Other Dishes, 2000. Spkr. United Way, Toledo, 1965-90; founder, pres. Mobile Meals Toledo, Inc., 1968-71, mem. adv. bd., 1988-2006, bd. dirs., 2005, chmn. pub. rels., 1997-99, nominating com., 2000-04, mem. long-range planning com., 2005-06, Spirit of Mobile Meals award, 1998; affiliate mem. Arts Commn., Toledo, 1976-77; chmn. Saphire Ball, Toledo Symphony Orch., Toledo Opera, 1978; adminstrv. coord. Feed Your Neighbor program Met. Chs. United, Toledo, 1979-86; deacon Collingwood Presbyn. Ch., 1969-71, elder, 1972-74, 77-79, 97-99, 2001-05, trustee, 1984-86, elder, clk. of session, 1991-94, stewardship chmn., 1996-97, del. to Maumee Valley Presbytery, 1991-99; mem. steering com. Interfiath Hospitality Network, 1992-94, bd. dirs., 1993-94; alt. del. Gen. Assembly Presbyn. Ch. U.S.A., 1993, del.-commr., 1994. Recipient Woman of Toledo award St. Vincent Hosp. and Med. Ctr. Guild, 1967, 80, Outstanding Community Svc. award United Way, 1987, Henry Morse vol. award, Greater Toledo award United Way, 1998, runner-up Nat. Vol. of the Year award Project Meal Found., Reynolds Metal Co., 1998. Mem. AAUW (bd. dirs. 1974-76, 94-96, 97-98, chmn. mem. gourmet group 1966-99, 2001, 03, edn. found. chmn. 1994-96, book sale chmn. 1998, chmn. nominating com. 2005-06), Ohio Med. Aux. (1st v.p. 1973-74), Aux. Acad. Medicine (pres. 1967-68, chmn. edn. gourmet group 1966-99, 2001-03, Health Care award 1974), Indian Trails Garden Club (pres. 1997-98), Sigma Kappa (various alumni offices). Republican. Avocations: volunteering, gourmet cooking, travel, bridge. Home: # 108 4030 Indian Rd Toledo OH 43606-2225

HEINZ, LEE, actress, educator; d. Edward Riel and Ruth (Milligan) Heinzman. BA, Vassar Coll., Poughkeepsie, NY; cert. French studies, U. Neuchatel, Switzerland; cert. in drama, Yale U., New Haven. Actor Broadway Theatre Assn., NYC, 1980—, Centennial Theatre Co., Simsbury, Conn., 2002; tchr. Neighborhood Playhouse, NYC, 1998—, Chautauqua Spl. Studies, NY, 2000—. Cons. in field. Author: Next! The Peril of Auditioning, 1991, (play) The Secret Society, 2006. Recipient James Kisicki award, Detroit Free Press, 1991. Mem.: SAG, Am. Assn. TV and Film, Actors Equity Assn. Office Phone: 212-414-5380.

HEINZELMAN, KRIS F., lawyer; b. Monroe, Wis., Jan. 9, 1951; AB, Brown U., 1973, MA magna cum laude, 1973; JD, Yale U., 1976. Bar: N.Y. 1977. Assoc. Cravath, Swain & Moore, N.Y.C., 1976—83, ptnr., corp. dept, 1983—. Named one of 12 Dealmakers of the Yr., The Am. Lawyer, 2004. Mem.: ABA, Am. Coll. Investment Counsel, Assn. of the Bar of the City of N.Y., N.Y. State Bar Assn. Office: Cravath Swain & Moore Worldwide Plz 825 8th Ave Fl 38 New York NY 10019-7475 also: 1 Chase Manhattan Plz New York NY 10005-1401 Office Phone: 212-474-1336. Office Fax: 212-474-3700. Business E-Mail: kheinzelman@cravath.com.

HEINZ KERRY, TERESA F. (MARIA TERESA THIERSTEIN SIMOES-FERREIRA), foundation administrator; b. Mozambique, Oct. 5, 1938; d. Jose Simoes Ferreira and Irene Thierstein; m. John Heinz, 1966 (dec. 1991); children: John, Andre, Christopher; m. John Kerry, 1995; stepchildren: Alex, Vanessa. BA in Romance Langs., Lit., U. Witwatersrand, Johannesburg, South Africa, 1960; grad., U. Geneva, 1963; PhD (hon.), Beloit Coll., Wis., Bank ST. Coll. Edn., N.Y., Drexel U., Pa., Med. Coll. Pa. Cons. UN Trusteeship, NYC; chmn. Heinz Family Found., Pitts., Howard Heinz Endowment; trustee Vira I. Heinz Endowment; founder Women's Inst. for Secure retirement, 1996—. Endowed creation of professorship environ. mgmt. Harvard Bus. Sch., chair environ. policy John F. Kennedy Sch. Govt.; vice chair Environ. Def.; past mem. external adv. bd. Inst. Biospheric Studies, Yale U.; mem. adv. bd. Earth Comm. Office; founder Second Nature; co-founder, bd. dirs. Alliance to End Childhood Lead Poisoning; bd. dirs. Carnegie Corp., Family Comm.; trustee Brookings Inst.; former bd. dirs., trustee Phillips Exeter Acad., St. Paul's Sch., Georgetown U.; co-founder Nat. Coun. Families TV; featured speaker Dem. Nat. Convention, Boston, 2004. Founding mem., co-chair Congl. Wives Soviet Jewry; trustee governing bd. Yale Art Gallery; mem. trustees coun. Nat. Gallery Art; bd. dirs. Carnegie Inst., Pitts. Women's Leadership award, Save the Children Found., 2003, World Ecology award, Internat. Ctr. for Tropical Ecology, U. Mo., 2003, Albert Schweitzer Gold medal for Humanitarianism, John Hopkins U., 2003. Fellow: Am. Acad. Arts and Sciences. Avocation: art collecting. Office: The Heinz Family Office 1101 Pennsylvania Ave NW Ste 350 Washington DC 20004-2532

HEINZL, CAROLYN BARBARA, school system administrator; b. Pitts., Mar. 26, 1949; d. Carl and Apollonia Heinzl. BA in Music, Carlow Coll., 1973, M Ednl. Leadership, 1994. Cert. tchr., prin. Pa. Music tchr. Pitts. Pub. Schs., 1980—97, adminstr., 1997—. Elder, mem. exec. bd. Beechview United Presbyn. Ch., Pitts., 1995—. Mem.: ASCD, Nat. Assn. Elem. Sch. Prins., Nat. Assn. Secondary Sch. Prins., Pa. Assn. Secondary Sch. Prins., Music Educators Nat. Conf., Pa. Interscholastic Athletic Assn., Nat. Assn. Sports Ofcls., US Tennis Assn., Andrew Carnegie Athletic Assn. Avocations: swimming, tennis, reading, lacrosse, photography. Home: 219 Flack St Pittsburgh PA 15210

HEINZMAN, BARBARA K., educational consultant; d. Gladys J. Kosztowniak; m. Dale M. Heinzman, Nov. 26, 1977; children: Andrew D., Eric W. BS, Medaille Coll., Buffalo, 1969; postgrad., Elmira coll., NY, 1970—74. Tchr. elem. sch. Geneva City Schs., NY, 1970—2003; ednl. cons. Silver Strong and Assocs., Ho-Ho-Kus, NJ, 1990. Staff developer Geneva City Schs., 1990—. Grantee, Wayne- Finger Lakes BOCES, 2002. Mem.: Delta Kappa Gamma (chair ceremonies 2006).

HEISE, DOROTHY HILBERT, retired librarian, retired government agency administrator; b. Erie, Pa., June 17, 1945; d. George William and Annette Genevieve (Forrester) Hilbert; m. Charles W. Heise, June 29, 1968 BSL.S., Edinboro State U., Pa., 1968; postgrad., Catholic U., 1971-72; MLS, U. Md., 1987. Cert. sch. librarian, N.J., Va., Md. Librarian Toms River Intermediate Sch., N.J., 1968-70; librarian Prince George's County Schs., Md., 1970-72, Congl. Sch., Falls Church, Va., 1972-75, Consumer Product Safety Commn., Washington, 1976-77; tech. info. specialist Raytheon Service Co., Crystal City, Va., 1977-79, U.S. Dept. Agr., Washington, 1979—, head Econ. Research Service Reference Ctr., 1981—85; rsch. libr. Nat. Agr. Libr., 1985—2005; ret., 2005. Recipient award for contbn. to Econ. Research Service Reference Ctr., U.S. Dept. Agr., 1985, award for contbn. to sci.gov website, 2001, award for contbn. to InvasiveSpecies.gov, 2001, award for NAL's Kids' Sci. website, 2001. Mem. ALA, Gamma Sigma Sigma. Lutheran. Avocations: needlecrafts, painting. Home: 8569 Tyrolean Way Springfield VA 22153-2241

HEISE, MARILYN BEARDSLEY, public relations company executive, publishing company executive; b. Cedar Rapids, Iowa, Feb. 26, 1935; d. Lee Roy and Angeline Myrtle Beardsley; m. John W. Heise, July 9, 1960; children: William Earnshaw, Steven James, Kathryn Kay Benninghoff. BA, Drake U., 1957. Prodn. mgr. Vend Mag., 1958—59; account exec. The Beveridge Orgn., Chgo., 1959—62; editor, pub. The Working Craftsman mag., Northbrook, Ill., 1971-78; columnist Chgo. Sun-Times, 1973-78; pres. Craft Books, Inc., Northbrook, 1978-84; v.p. Sheila King Pub. Rels., Chgo., 1984-87, Aaron D. Cushman, Inc., Chgo., 1987-88; pres. Creative Cons. Assocs., Inc., Glencoe, Ill., 1989—91, Heartfelt Charity Cards, 1991—2003. Mem. adv. panel Nat. Crafts Project, Ft. Collins, Colo., 1977; mem. adv. panel and com. Nat. Endowment for Arts, Washington, 1977; mem. editl. adv. bd. The Crafts Report, Seattle, 1978-86. Recipient achievement award Women in Mgmt., 1978. Mem. Pub. Rels. Soc. Am. (accredited).

HEISKELL, MARIAN SULZBERGER (MRS. ANDREW HEISKELL), newspaper executive, civic worker; b. NYC, Dec. 31, 1918; d. Arthur Hays and Iphigene (Ochs) Sulzberger; m. Orvil Eugene Dryfoos, July 8, 1941 (dec. May 1963); children: Jacqueline Hays, Robert Ochs, Susan Warms; m. Andrew Heiskell, Jan. 30, 1965 (dec. 2003). Grad., Frobeleague Kindergarten Tng. Sch., N.Y.C., 1941; LL.D. (hon.), Poly. Inst. N.Y., 1974, Dartmouth Coll., 1975. Dir. N.Y. Times Co., 1963—; Bd. dirs. N.Y.C. Partnership; chmn. Council on Environment N.Y.C.; bd. dirs. Regional Plan Assn., Inc.; bd. mgrs., exec. com. N.Y. Bot. Garden; mem. State Park and Recreation Commn. for City N.Y.; bd. dirs. Nat. Audubon Soc.; trustee Parks Council, Consol. Edison Co. N.Y., Inc.; co-chmn. We Care About N.Y., Inc. Dir. Ford Motor Co., 1976-89, Merck & Co., Inc. Chmn. New 42d St., NYC. Recipient Mrs. Lyndon B. Johnson ann. award Keep Am. Beautiful, 1974; (with husband) Disting. Service award Citizens Union, 1975

HEISS, ALANNA, museum director; b. Louisville, Ky. married; 1 child. Degree, Lawrence U., Wis. Founder Inst. Art and Urban Resources (now Inst. for Contemporary Art), N.Y.C., 1971; dir. Clocktower Gallery, 1972—, PS1 Mus. (affiliate of Mus. Modern Art), N.Y.C., 1976—; dep. dir. Mus. Modern Art, 2000—; founder, exec. prodr. WPS1 online radio station, 2004—. Co-author (with John Wesley): Paintings: 1961-2000, 2001; co-author: (with Janet Cardiff) (foreward) A Survey of Works, Including Collaborations with George Bures Miller, 2002. Recipient award given by Mayor Koch, N.Y.C., 1980, Chevalier of Arts and Letters, France, 1987, Skowhegan award, 1989. Achievements include being knighted by the Swedish government in 1984; direction of over 500 shows. Office: PS1 Contemporary Arts Ctr 22-25 Jackson Ave Long Island City NY 11101

HEISS, MARY WYNNE, artist; b. Martinsville, Va., May 14, 1954; d. Robert Wayne and Ruth Elizabeth (Midkiff) H. AA, Montgomery Coll., 1975; BA, U. Md., 1978; MFA, George Washington U., 1984. Prodn. asst. Pyramid Atlantic, Riverdale, Md., 1992. Demonstration artist ann. Discover Graphics Day, Nat. Mus. Am. Art, Smithsonian Instn., 1978. One and two woman shows at Prince George's C.C., Largo, Md., 1987, C. Alden Phelps Gallery, Reisterstown, Md., 1989, Clin. Ctr. Galleries, NIH, Bethesda, Md., 1991, Arnold and Porter Law Firm, Washington, 1992; exhibited in group shows at Rose Art Mus., Brandeis U., Waltham, Mass., 1985, Trenton (N.J.) State Coll., 1988, Internat. Monetary Fund Art Soc. Gallery, Washington, 1989, Minot (N.Dak.) State U., 1989, Rockland Art Ctr., Ellicott City, Md., 1989, Somerstown Gallery, Somers, N.Y., 1990, Queensborough C.C., Bayside, N.Y., 1991, Museu de Gravura Citade De Curitiba, Rio de Janeiro, 1991, Acad. Arts, Easton, Md., 1992, Soc. Am. Graphic Artists, N.Y.C., 1993; represented in permanent collections including Trenton State Coll., Freddie Mac Corp., Vienna, Va., Nassau C.C., Garden City, N.Y., The State Dept., Washington, So. Utah U., Cedar City, Alexandria (La.) Mus. Art. Recipient Purchase award Nassau C.C., 1989, 1st place and Purchase award Riverwalk Art Festival and Juried Exhbn., York, Pa., 1989, 90, 3d Place and Cash award Clary-Miner Gallery, 1991, Hon. Mention award Stockton (Calif.) Nat. Print and Drawing Exhbn., 1990, Cash award San Bernardo County Mus., Redlands, Calif., 1989. Mem. L.A. Printmaking Soc. (Purchase award 1990), Md. Printmakers.

HEIST, KAREN GARTLAND, elementary school educator; b. Pennsacola, Fla., Apr. 11, 1950; d. Frithiof N. and Anne (Monihan) Sagerholm; m. J. Donald Gartland III, Sept. 12, 1970 (dec.); children: J. Donald IV, G. Taylor; m. Thomas H. Heist III, Oct. 17, 1987; stepchildren: Thomas, Amanda, Kristina, John. AA, Briarcliffe Coll., 1970; BA, Beaver Coll., 1972. 2nd grade tchr. Pennsbury Sch. Dist., Fallsington, Pa., 1972-74; 1st grade tchr. Delran (N.J.) Sch. Dist., 1974-78; dist. sales mgr. C.R. Jolly Couture Sales, Edgefield, S.C., 1982-85; mgr. Crossings Motor Inn, Ocean City, N.J., 1985-88; salesperson Monihan Realty, Ocean City, 1988-90; substitute tchr. Ocean City Sch. Dist., 1989-90, basic skills instr., 1990-91, 1992—, 3rd grade tchr., 1993—. Bd. dir. Ocean City Humane Soc., Atlantic City Med. Ctr. Aux., Found. Spina Bifida; mem. Miss Am. Hostess Com.; youth activities chairperson Ocean City Yacht Club; soccer coach Ocean City Recreation Ctr.; bd. sec. Ocean City Free Pub. Libr. Named Outstanding Young Woman of Am., 1980, Role Model, Sun Newspaper, 1989. Mem. Ruth Newman Shapiro Cancer Soc., Ocean City Yacht Club (bd. dirs.). Republican. Episcopalian. Avocations: reading, skiing, walking, motorcycling. Home: 501 Waverly Blvd Ocean City NJ 08226-4749 Office: Ocean City Primary Sch 5th St and West Ave Ocean City NJ 08226 E-mail: heistski@hotmail.com.

HEIT, MARNY, lawyer; b. Miami, Fla., Nov. 22, 1976; BA, Syracuse Univ., 1998; JD, Emory Univ. Sch. Law, 2001. Bar: State of Ga. 2001. Atty., divsn. traffic and DUI Chestney-Hawkins Attys., 2001—, now ptnr. Spkr. in field. Recipient Best Speaker award, Irving R. Kaufman National Securities Moot Court Competition, 2000. Mem.: Ga. Assn. Women Lawyers, Ga. Assn. Criminal Defense Lawyers, Bar Ga. Ct. Appeals. Office: Chestney-Hawkins 448 East Paces Ferry Road Atlanta GA 30305*

HEITKAMP, THOMASINE LEA, social work educator; b. Breckneridge, Minn., Nov. 25, 1953; d. Raymond Bernard and Doreen LaVonne (Berg) H.; m. Alvin O'Niel Boucher, Oct. 1, 1983; children: Evan, Luke. BS in Social Work, U. N.D., 1975; MS in Social Work, U. Wis., 1980. Lic. cert. social worker, ind. social worker. Social Worker II Grand Forks Area Social Svc. Ctr., ND, 1975-77, social worker III ND, 1977-79, Burleigh County Social Svc. Bd., Bismarck, ND, 1980-82; devel. disabilities case mgr. West Cen. Human Svc. Ctr., Bismarck, 1982-83; instr., asst. prof., assoc. prof., dept. chair U. N.D., Grand Forks, 1983—. Policy bd. mem. Luth. Social Svcs. ND, 1989—; adv. bd. mem., vice chair N.D. Dept. Human Svcs., 1989—, total quality mgmt. implementation com. 1992—; bd. dirs. Regional Adolescent Treatment Facility for Emotionally Disturbed Youth, N.E. Human Svc. Ctr., Grand Forks, 1987—. Author: (with Leola Furman and Myrna Haga) Learning Contracts, 1986; editorial bd. mem. The Clin. Supervisor; contbr. articles to profl. jours. Bd. dirs. N.D. Children's Trust Fund; com. mem. Witnesss and Victims of Crime Commn., 1985-87. Grantee N.D. Dept. Human Svcs., 1986, 87, 88, U. N.D. Women's Equity Com., 1987. Mem. NASW, N.D. Mental Health Assn., N.D. Conf. Social Welfare (chair edn. com. 1985, 30 Yr. Svc. award), Grand Forks Food Coop. (bd. dirs. 1985). Democrat. Roman Catholic. Avocations: running, politics. Home: 1805 Chestnut St Grand Forks ND 58201-7353 Office: Univ ND Dept Social Work PO Box 8171 Grand Forks ND 58202-8171

HEITLAND, JULIE ANN, school librarian; d. Joseph Ambrose and Bernadette Anita Ryan; m. Arthur LuVerne Heitland, Apr. 28, 1984; children: Philip Kyle, Benjamin Ryan. AA, Kirkwood C.C., 1978; BA, U. No. Iowa, 1980, MA, 1994. Media specialist k-12 Postville (Iowa) Cmty. Sch., 1994—. Com. mem. Taste of Postville, 2000, Boys Scouts Am., Postville, 1995—2005; edn. rep. Workforce Devel. Bd., Iowa, 2003; tchr., musician St. Bridgets Ch., Postville, 2000. Mem.: Postville Edn. Assn. (pres., sec., com. chair 2000—01), Iowa Assn. Sch. Libr., Club of Hour (pres., v.p., sec. 2000—05). Independent. Roman Cath. Office: Postville Cmty Sch 312 W Post PO Box 717 Postville IA 52162 Office Phone: 563-864-7651. Office Fax: 563-864-7659.

HEITLER, SUSAN MCCRENSKY, clinical psychologist; b. Alton, Ill., July 17, 1945; d. Harold A. and Mary (Gordon) McCrensky; m. Bruce F. Heitler, June 6, 1971; children: Abigail, Sara, Jesse, Jacob. BA, Harvard U., 1967; MEd, Boston U., 1968; PhD, NYU, 1975. Lic. psychologist, Colo. Pvt. practice clin. psychology, Denver, 1977—. Author: David Decides About Thumbsucking, 1985, From Conflict to Resolution, 1990, (audiotape) Working With Couples in Conflict, 1992, The Power of Two, 1997, The Power of Two Workbook, 2003. Founder, pres., mem. KOHELET. Mem. APA, Soc. for Exploration Psychotherapy Integration, Radcliffe Alumne Assn. (regional dir.), Harvard Club of the Rocky Mountains (pres.), Green Gables Country Club, Denver Tennis Club, JCC Tennis Club. Democrat. Jewish. Avocations: skiing, tennis, violin. Home: 170 S Dexter St Denver CO 80246-1053 Office: 4500 E 9th Ave Ste 660S Denver CO 80220-3926

HEITSCH, LEONA MASON, artist, writer; b. Pontiac, Mich., Jan. 6, 1931; d. Russell Leonard and Margaret M. (Arnold) Mason; m. Charles Weyand Heitsch, July 5, 1952; children: Russell, Carrie, Grace, Charles, Irene. BA in chemistry, U. Mich., 1952. Edn. asst. Spl. Sch. Dist., St. Louis County, Mo., 1969-81. Commentator Sta. KUMR, Rolla, Mo., 1996—. Author: (pvt. printing) Echoes of the Ridge, 1985, Get Him to St. Louis, 1983; contbg. author: (poem anthology) Seasons of the Ozarks, 1998, Missourians Write About Reading, 2002, Apples, Apples Everywhere; contbr. poetry, articles to various publs. Sec., activist Mo. Assn. Children with Learning Disabilities, St. Louis, 1973-75; fundraising, writing Friends of Foster-Dolbeer Farm, Walled Lake, Mich., 1996—; contbg. poet Wis. Breastfeeding Coalition, Lac du Flambeau, 1996—; activist Poets Against the War, 2003. Recipient honorable mention Mo. Writers Week award for poetry, 1992, 94, grand prize Artists Embassy Internat., San Francisco, 1997, Editors Challenge award Internat. Soc. Authors and Artists, Abilene, Tex., 1997, included in Memories and Memoirs, Anthology of Mo. authors, 2000; featured in Grandmother Earth IX, 2003, Grist, Mo. State Poetry Soc., 2003. Mem. St. Louis Poetry Soc., Rolla Area Writers Guild. Home and Office: Ridge Orchards 13321 Hwy N Bourbon MO 65441-9305 E-mail: clheitsc@fidnet.com.

HEITZENRODER, WENDY ROBERTA, elementary school educator; b. Erie, Pa., Nov. 14, 1948; d. Robert Walfred and Ruth Wilhelmena (Sandberg) Gustavson; m. Frederick Charles Heitzenroder, June 20, 1970; 1 child, Matthew Frederick. BA, Thiel Coll., Greenville, Pa., 1970; MA, W.Va. U., 1980, EdD, 1988. Caseworker Philadelphia County, Phila., 1970-71; spl. edn. tchr. John E. Davis Sch., East. Pa. Psychiat. Inst., Phila., 1971-77, Marion County Schs., Fairmont, W.Va., 1977-90, Fox Chapel Area Schs., Pitts., 1990—. Instr. spl. edn. W.Va. U., Morgantown, 1989-90; cons. Marion County Bd. Edn., Fairmont, 1989-90. Mem. Jr. League of Fairmont, 1980s; mem. choir Salem Luth. Ch., 1990—, mem. bell choir, 1990—. Jr. League of Fairmont grantee, 1989; Excellence for Edn. grantee, Pitts., 1991, 92; Thanks to Tchrs. finalist Giant Eagle award, 1994-95; recipient, Silver award Tchr. Excellence Found., 2001, 2002. Mem. Phi Delta Kappa. Avocations: reading, swimming, tennis, needlecrafts. Office: Fox Chapel Area Sch Dist 611 Field Club Rd Pittsburgh PA 15238-2406 Home: 510 Poplar Dr Greensburg PA 15601

HEIVILIN, DONNA MAE, retired government executive; b. Clear Lake, Iowa, May 12, 1937; d. Nels Oliver Ouverson and Nellie Bernice (Humphrey) Ouverson-Loats; m. Thomas Stuart Heivilin, Dec. 26, 1961 (div. Dec. 1971); children: Vincent Stuart, James Edward. Student, Iowa State U., 1956-57; BA, U. Minn., 1959; MPA, George Washington U., 1974, DPA, 1988. Assoc. dir. Navy issues, nat. security and internat. affairs U.S. Gen. Acctg. Office, Washington, 1985-88, dir. logistics issues, nat. security and internat. affairs, 1988-93, dir. def. mgmt., NASA issues, 1993-95, vice chair job process reengring. team, 1995-96, dir. planning & reporting, nat. security & internat. affairs, 1996-99, dir. quality and risk mgmt., 1999-2000, dir. applied rsch. and methods, 2000—04; ret., 2004. Pres. Nat. Coun. Assn.'s Policy Scis., Washington, 1980-83. Profiler editor Pub. Budget and Fin. Jour, 1985-98. Vol. Fin. Svcs. Vol. Corps, 2006. Mem. Exec. Women in Govt. (pres. 1996-97), Am. Assn. Budget and Programming Analysts (bd. dirs. 1980-83, 98-99), Coun. Logistics Mgrs., Soc. Logistics Engrs., World Future Soc. US Nat. Capitol (region chpt., bd. dirs. 2006-), Profl. Futurists Assn., Nat. Capitol Region Futurists (bd. dirs. 2006-), The Internat. Alliance for Women (bd. dirs. 1997—, treas. 1998, 1st v.p. 1999, pres. 2000-01, amb. at large 2004-05), Phi Kappa Phi. Avocations: recreational walking, plays, shakespeare, country music. Home: 5330 36th St N Arlington VA 22207-1816 Office Phone: 703-532-0610. Personal E-mail: donna.heivilin@verizon.net.

HELD, KAREN LEE, science educator; b. Allentown, Pa., May 24, 1956; d. Bruce Held and Peggy Ann Anderson; m. John Montoya, Aug. 9, 1995. BS, U. N.Mex., Albuquerque, 1979. Cert. tchr. N.Mex., 1983. Tchr. math., health Nyfarkollie Jr. H.S., Zowienta, Liberia, 1980—81; tchr. math., sci. Menaul H.S., Albuquerque, 1983—86, Del Norte H.S., Albuquerque, 1986—94; tchr. sci. Highland H.S., Albuquerque, 1994—. Chair dept. math. Menaul H.S., Albuquerque, 1984—86. Logo designs. Mem.: Albuquerque Gem and Mineral Club, Jim Hawkes Karate, N.Mex. Trials Assn. Office Phone: 505-265-2711 26256.

HELD, LILA M., art appraiser; b. Cleve., Oct. 5, 1925; d. Mark and Edythe H. (Dobrin) Bloomberg; m. Jacob Herzfeld, Oct. 20, 1946 (div. 1964); children: Garson Herzfeld, Michael Herzfeld; m. Merle Donald Held, Feb. 19, 1966 (dec. 1997); children: Joanne, Barbara. Student, Coll. William and Mary, 1945—46, Ohio State U., 1943—44, Case Western Res. U., 1944—45, postgrad., 1962—66; student, Akron U., 1960—61; BS in Art Edn., Kent State U., 1961—62; M in Valuation Sci., Lindenwood Coll., 1989. Instr. art Canton (Ohio) YMCA, 1965, Beachwood (Ohio) Bd. Recreation, 1967-68; substitute tchr. art, art history Cleveland Heights, Ohio, 1967-68; freelance artist, writer, researcher, 1940—; art cons., appraiser Art Consultants Assocs., Englewood, Colo., 1985—. Curatorial aid Denver Art Mus., 1985—89; fine arts appraiser, Cleve., 1989—; spkr. in field; judge art shows. Mem. Cleve. Artists Found., Akron (Ohio) Art Mus., Butler Inst. Am. Art, Cleve. Mus. Natural History, Western Res. Hist. Soc., Toledo Mus. Art, Temple Mus., Mus. Am. Folk Art, Albright-Knox Mus., Buffalo; sec. coun. Cleve. Ctr. Contemporary Art; active Allen Meml. Art Mus.; bd. dirs. Contemporary Art Soc. Cleve. Mus. Art; mem. Nat. Coun. Jewish Women; active Continuing Edn. Assn. Case-Western Res. U. Mem.: Art Alliance Contemporary Glass, Ohio Contemporary Glass Alliance, Am. Soc. Appraisers (sr. cert. fine arts). Avocations: reading, travel, theater, music, literature. Home and Office: 16695 Chillocothe Rd Chagrin Falls OH 44023 Office Phone: 440-708-1767. Personal E-mail: artvalue@earthlink.net.

HELD, NANCY JEAN, academic administrator, educator; b. Winnipeg, Man., Can., Oct. 27, 1932; d. Harry Earl and Lucy Gladys (Fie) Graffam; m. Charles Holborn Held, Mar. 25, 1967; children: Heidi Alice, Kirstin Lucretia. Student, Iowa State U., 1950; BS in Edn., Drake U., 1954, MS in Edn., 1955; postgrad., Mich. State U., 1962—; LHD, Albion Coll., 2006. Dir. vis. edn. tchr. Northbrook (Ill.) Pub. Sch., 1954-56; tchr. Deerfield (Ill.) Pub. Sch., 1956; assoc. prof. edn. and psychology, head dept. elem. edn. Iowa Wesleyan Coll., Mt. Pleasant, 1957-60; dir. edn. program, prof. edn. Albion (Mich.) Coll., 1961-93. Mem. AAUW (life), Phi Kappa Phi, Phi Beta Kappa, Alpha Chi Omega, Kappa Delta Pi, Delta Kappa Gamma. Republican. Presbyterian. Avocation: woodworking. Home: 1155 River Bend Dr Albion MI 49224-2246

HELDER, KAREN FAY, social worker; b. Grand Rapids, Mich., Mar. 18, 1952; d. John Sidney and Gertrude (Diekevers) H BA, Dordt Coll., Sioux Center, Iowa, 1974; MS Clin. Psychology, Ea. Mich. U., 1975; MSW, U. Iowa, 1985. Cert. social worker. Therapist Wedgwood Christian Svcs., Grand Rapids, 1976—79, dir. profl. svcs., 1984—2001; dir. regional ops. Bethany Christian Svcs., Grand Rapids, 2001—; counselor, instr. social work Dordt Coll., Sioux Center, 1979—84. Part-time therapist Bethesda Midwest, Orange City, Iowa, 1980-84; cons. Bethany Christian Svcs., Orange City, 1980-84 Bd. dirs. Kent County Coun. for Prevention of Child Abuse and Neglect, Grand Rapids, 1985-88, Partners Worldwide; bd. trustees Reformed Bible Coll., 1996-2005; mem. chaplain com. Christian Reformed Ch., Grand Rapids, 1986-89; ch. liaison Grand Rapids Area Ctr. for Ecumenism, 1989-91. Mem. Christian Assn. for Psychol. Studies, Nat. Assn. Christians in Social Work Avocations: reading, volunteer church work, speaking engagements, walking, travel. Home: 2452 Village Dr SE Grand Rapids MI 49506-5455 Office: Wedgwood Christian Young and Family Svcs PO Box 88007 Grand Rapids MI 49518-0007 Office Phone: 616-224-7610.

HELDMAN, BETTY LOU FAULKNER, retired health facility administrator; b. Washington, NC, June 3, 1937; d. Basil Frank Faulkner and Willie Mae Rose; m. Arthur Charles Heldman Jr., Aug. 23, 1959; children: Ruth Victoria, Andrew Basil. BS in Biology, Davis and Elkins Coll., Elkins, W.Va., 1959; MS in Med. Biology, C.W. Post Coll., 1978. Cert. eye bank technician Eye Bank Assn. Am. Lab. asst. Portsmouth (Va.) Gen. Hosp., 1954—58; lab. technician Johnson & Johnson Rsch., New Brunswick, NJ, 1959—62; med. assoc. Brookhaven Nat. Lab., Upton, NY, 1973—86; adminstrv. dir. Lions Eye Bank for L.I., Great Neck, NY, 1986—97; ret. Presenter in field; pres., v.p. exec. bd. Brookhaven Women in Sci., 1979—86; chairperson United Fund Brookhaven Nat. Lab., 1983—84; elected mem. lectr. com. Brookhaven Lab., 1978—84. Author, pub.: Faulkner, Cannon, Rose, Brickell-Families of Eastern North Carolina, 2003; contbr. rsch. papers to profl. jours. Recipient Outstanding Svc. in Sci. award, Town of Islip, 1985, Plaque of Appreciation, Lions and Lioness Clubs, 1991, Disting. Recognition award, Knights of the Blind, 2004. Mem.: Assn. for Women in Sci. Home: 2146 Seaton Springs Rd Sevierville TN 37862 E-mail: bheldman@bellsouth.net.

HELFAND, TOBY SCHEINTAUB, retired dermatologist; b. NYC, Aug. 5, 1931; d. David and Pauline Shapiro Scheintaub; m. Isidore Helfand, Mar. 22, 1953; children: Jerry, Gloria, Robert, Rita. BA, Antioch Coll., Yellow Springs, Ohio, 1952; MD, Western Res. U., Cleve., 1957. Diplomate Am. Bd. Dermatology. Med. intern Cleve. Clinic, Cleveland, Ohio; resident in dermatology U. Hosps., Cleve., 1964—68; mem. dermatology staff U. Hosps. Cleve., 1968—95; chief of dermatology Ohio Permanente Med. Group, Cleve., 1969—90; dermatologist U. Dermatologists Inc., Cleve., 1993—95. Clin. assoc. prof. Case Western Res. U., Cleve., 1968—2001, emerita clin. assoc. prof., 2001—06. Mem.: Cleve. Dermatol. Soc. (treas. 1985—87). Home: 2734 Brainard Hills Dr Pepper Pike OH 44124 Personal E-mail: thelfand@pol.net.

HELFANT, ANN M., history educator; d. Rex and Mariann Helfant. BA in History, Rowan U., Glassboro, N.J., 2000; MLitt, Drew U., Madison, N.J., 2004; post grad. in Ednl. Adminstrn., Caldwell Coll., N.J., 2004—. Cert. secondary edn. N.J., secondary supr. N.J. Tchr. history Ridge H.S., Basking Ridge, NJ, 2000—. Softball coach Ridge H.S., Basking Ridge, NJ, 2001—03, class advisor, 2003—05. Mem.: ASCD, NEA, Nat. Coun. Social Studies, N.J. Edn. Assn. Office: Ridge HS 268 S Finley Ave Basking Ridge NJ 07920 Office Phone: 908-204-2585 4239.

HELFER, RICKI TIGERT, banking consultant; b. N.C., Feb. 4, 1945; m. Michael S. Helfer; 1 child, Matthew. BA with honors, Vanderbilt U.; MA, U. N.C.; JD with honors, U. Chgo. Law. clk. to hon. John Minor Wisdom U.S. Ct. Appeals; counsel to Jud. Com. U.S. Senate, Washington, 1978-79; assoc., ptnr. Leva, Hawes, Symington, Martin and Oppenheimer, 1979-83; sr. counsel internat. fin. Treasury Dept., Washington; chief internat. lawyer Fed. Reserve Bd., 1985-92; ptnr. Gibson, Dunn & Crutcher, Washington, 1992-94; chmn. FDIC, Washington, 1994-97; nonresident sr. fellow The Brookings Inst., Washington, 1998-99; prof. law, dir. fin. instns. program Washington Coll. Law, Am. U., Washington, 2000—; cons. Am. Cmty. Bankers, Washington, 2000—. Bd. govs., chmn. audit com. Phila. Stock Exch., 1997-99; cons. internat. banking and fin. regulation. Bd. dirs. Girl Scouts U.S., 1995-99, Life Pt. Hosps., Inc., 1999—; mem. vis. com. U. Chgo. Law Sch., 1989-92, 94-97. Mem. ABA (former chair internat. banking and fin. com.), Am. Law Inst., Coun. Fgn. Rels., Washington Fgn. Law Soc. (past pres.), Basle Com. Banking Supervision.

HELFGOTT, GLORIA VIDA, artist; b. NYC, May 25, 1928; d. Charles and Anna (Cohen) Wolff; m. Roy B. Helfgott; 1 child, Daniel Andrew. Grad. in fine arts, Cooper Union, 1948. Faculty mem. Ctr. for Book Arts, N.Y.C., 1989-98, San Francisco Ctr. for the Book, 1998-, Brookfield (Conn.) Craft Ctr., 1988—, Art New Eng. at Bennington (Vt.) Coll., 1992, Womens Studio Workshop, Rosendale, N.Y., 1992, Long Beach Art Mus., 1997-98. Solo and group exhbns. include P.S.I., L.I., N.Y., 1979, Handin Hand Gallery, N.Y.C., 1985, Grad. Ctr. for the Arts, W.Va. U., Morgantown, 1988, Berkshire Mus., Pittsfield, Mass., 1988, Ctr. for the Arts, Avado, Colo., 1989, Hoffman Gallery, Portland, Oreg., 1990, Granary Books, N.Y.C., 1990, Ted Cronin Gallery, N.Y.C., 1990, Boca Raton (Fla.) Mus., 1991, Sazama Gallery, Chgo., 1992, Harper-Collins Exhbn. Space, N.Y.C., 1993, 1998, 2000, Istvan Kiraly Mus., Hungary, 1994,1996, 1998, 2006, Meml. Art Mus., Ormond Beach, Fla., 1994, Brown U., 1995, Nexus Gallery, Phila., 1995, Ctr. for Book Arts, 1996, 2002, 2005, UCLA Art Libr., 1997; traveling exhbn. U.S. State Dept., 1996-98, San Francisco Libr., 1999, 2001, 2006, U. Judaism, L.A., 2004; represented in permanent collections Ruth and Marvin Sackner Archive of Concrete and Visual Poetry, Miami Beach, Fla., Nat. Mus. Women in the Arts, Washington, Victoria and Albert Mus., London, Bklyn. Mus., Stanford U., UCLA, Swarthmore Coll., Oberlin Coll, U. of Alberta, LIU; curator, So Called Books, 1999-2002, San Francisco, NYC, Salt Lake City, Los Angeles; Beyond the Page, 1995, NYC; Metafiction, 1992, Kent, Conn. Mem. Guild of Book Workers. Home: 764 Jacon Way Pacific Palisades CA 90272

HELGENBERGER, MARG, actress; b. Fremont, Nebr., Nov. 16, 1958; m. Alan Roseberg Sept. 9, 1989; 1 child, Hugh. BS, Northwestern U., 1982. Appeared in TV series Ryan's Hope, 1984-86, The Shell Game, 1987, China Beach, 1988-91 (Emmy award; named Primetime Programming Individual Outstanding Supporting Actress in Drama Series, 1990, 91), CSI:Crime Scene Investigation, 2000-; co-host of New Year's Rockin' Eve, 1988, Home, 1989, (TV movies) Blind Vengence, 1990, Death Dreams, 1991, In Sickness and In Health, 1992, Through the Eyes of a Killer, 1992, When Love Kills: The Seduction of John Hearn, 1993, Stephen King's The Tommyknockers, 1993, Where Are My Children?, 1994, Lie Down with Lions, 1994, Partners, 1994, Perfect Murder, Perfect Town: Jon Benet and the City of Boulder, 2000; appeared in films Always, 1989, After Midnight, 1989, Crooked Hearts, 1991, Desperate Motive, 1993, The Cowboy Way, 1994, Bad Boys, 1995, Species, 1995, Erin Brockovich, 2000, In Good Company, 2004; TV appearances include Spenser: For Hire, 1986, Matlock, 1987, Thirtysomething, 1987, Tales from the Crypt, 1991, The Larry Sanders Show, 1995, ER, 1996, Frasier, 2000, (voice) King of the Hill, 2004.

HELKE, CINDA JANE, pharmacology and neuroscience educator, researcher, academic administrator; b. Waterloo, Iowa, Feb. 27, 1951; d. Gerald and Lorna (Smith) Pieres; m. Joel Edward Helke, Aug. 10, 1974. BS in Pharmacy, Creighton U., 1974; PhD, Georgetown U., 1978. Staff fellow NIH, Bethesda, Md., 1978-80; asst. prof. dept. pharmacology Uniformed Svcs. Univ. of the Health Scis., Bethesda, 1980-85, assoc. prof. dept. pharmacology,

1985-88; prof. dept. pharmacology Uniformed Svcs. Univ. Health Scis., Bethesda, 1988—, prof. neurosci. program, 1991—2001, dir. neurosci. program, 1993—2002, assoc. dean for grad. edn., 2001—. Mem. adv. panel Am. Heart Assn., 1984-87, NIH, Bethesda, 1987-91; mem. oversight rev. panel NSF, 1986, pharmacology test com. Nat. Bd. Med. Examiners, 1992-94. Editl. bd. Synapse, Pharmacology; contbr. chapters to books, articles to profl. jour. NIH grantee, 1981. Mem. AAAS, Am. Soc. Pharmacology and Exptl. Therapeutics (sec.-treas. elect 2002—, Soc. for Neurosci. Women in Sci., Women in Neurosci., Soc. for Neurosci. (sec.-treas. Washington chpt. 1985-87). Avocations: piano and choral music, aerobics, photography, travel. Office: Uniformed Svcs U Health Sci 4301 Jones Bridge Rd Bethesda MD 20814-4712 Office Phone: 301-295-1104. Office Fax: 301-295-6772. E-mail: chelke@usuhs.mil.

HELLER, ELLEN DISTILLER, gifted and talented educator; b. Balt., Dec. 31, 1942; d. E. Melvin and Florence (Fox) Distiller; children: Dana Beth, William Morris. BA, Western Md. Coll., 1963; MS, Nova U., 1982. Tchr. French, Altoona (Pa.) Schs., 1966-68; tchr. English and creative writing and ESOL and gifted Dade County Schs., Miami, 1963-66, 78—; chair for gifted edn. Region IV, Miami Dade County Pub. Schs., 1995—. Lectr. and workshop presenter Dade County Schs. and other orgns., Miami, 1983—; ednl. rsch. and dissemination local site coord. AFT, Miami, 1987—; supt. creative writing Dade County Youth Fair, 1990—. Vol. Campaign to Elect Dante Fascell, Miami, 1963-91, Kennedy Libr. exhibit, Miami, Campaigns to Elect Johnson, Carter, Dukakis, Clinton, Miami; sec. Young Dems., Miami, 1964-65; active mem. Dade County Reading Coun. Recipient Impact II award, Tchr. of Yr., 1991-92; NDEA fellow U. Ky., 1965. Mem. Internat. Reading Assn., Nat. Coun. Tchrs. English, Fla. Coun. Tchrs. English, Dade County Coun. Tchrs. English, Tchrs. and Writers Collaborative, U. Miami Writing Inst. (assoc.), Book Rev. Club (pres. 1988-89), Phi Delta Kappa (bd. dirs. 1988—), Alpha Delta Kappa (sgt. at arms 1986-88, historian 1988—, rec. sec. 1992—), Delta Kappa Gamma. Jewish. Avocations: reading, writing, needlecrafts, sporting events, theater. Office: Cutler Ridge Elem Sch Gifted Ctr 20210 Coral Sea Rd Miami FL 33189-1532 Home: 8820 SW 85th St Miami FL 33173-4519 Office Phone: 305-235-4611. Personal E-mail: ellenhelle@bellsouth.net.

HELLER, ESTHER A., writer, educator; b. Malden, Mass., Nov. 14, 1947; d. Eugene Gregory and Goldie (Stern) Heller; m. Nicholas A. Corsano, Sept. 4, 1971. BA with honors, Brandeis U., 1969; MS, Stanford U., 1971; postgrad., U. Calif., Davis, 1979. Cert. diversity trainer Equity Inst., 1995. Engr. DCA Reliability, Sunnyvale, Calif.; firmware engr. ISS/Sperry-Univac, Cupertino, Calif., 1979-81; hardware engr. Hewlett-Packard, Cupertino, 1981-86, software engr., 1986-95; ind. cons., trainer and diversity coach self employed, Menlo Park, Calif., 1995—. Author diversity columns, 1996—; staff writer Voices of New Bridges-Connections in Judaism, 1999-2003. Bd. dirs. San Francisco Bay coun. Girl Scouts U.S.A., 1988—95, troop leader, 1972—2003; trainer San Francisco Bay coun. Girls Scouts U.S.A., 1982—, subchair capital campaign, 1997—98; founding mem. Silicon Valley Partnership, 1999, co-chair, 2001—02, 2005—; mem.-at-large Jewish Cmty. Rels. Coun., San Francisco area, 2000—; bd. dirs. Keddem Congregation, 2002—, 1st v.p., 2006—. Recipient Thanks badge San Francisco Bay coun. Girl Scouts U.S.A., Ora award Nat. Jewish Girl Scout Com., 1997, Maude Whalen award, 2003. Mem.: Profl. and Tech. Diversity Network of Bay Area (founding mem.), Soc. Women Engrs. (chair Santa Clara Valley sect. diversity com. 1996—, mem. nat. multicultural com. 2000—, chair nat. Girl Scout com. 2000—, leadership coach 2003—). Jewish. Avocations: needlecrafts, orienteering, photography. Office: Ind Cons and Trainer 665 Gilbert Ave Menlo Park CA 94025-2731 E-mail: esther@galarc.com.

HELLER, JANET SEIP, retired secondary school educator; b. Easton, Pa., Jan. 29, 1929; d. Joseph Herbert Seip and Irene May Clader; m. Warford Harris Heller, Sept. 1, 1956 (dec.); children: Tracy, Wade Hampton. BA in English, Ohio U., 1949; MA in English, U. Pa., 1955. Cert. secondary English tchr. Pa. Proofreader Mack Printing Co., Easton, Pa., 1949—51; reporter Easton Express, 1951—53; rsch. assoc. Pa. Dept. Internal Affairs, Harrisburg, 1955—56; English tchr. Easton Area H.S., 1963—89; assoc. dir. Coll. Bd., Phila., 1989—98. AP exam. reader Ednl. Testing Svc., Princeton, NJ, 1975—85; vis. assoc. English U. Ill., Champaign-Urbana, 1983—84. Author: (books and lyrics, mus. comedy) Paragon, 1976, Busy Bodies, 1977, Seedy by the Sea, 1977. Pres. bd. dirs. Mary Meuser Libr., Easton, 1959—67; treas. Philly Walks, Phila., 1999—; mem. George Pepper Soc. Phila. Libr., Phila., 2002—; v.p. LWV, Easton, 1958—72. Mem.: Phi Beta Kappa. Democrat. Avocations: travel, theater, concerts, writing, museums. Home: 1801 Buttonwood St # 1613 Philadelphia PA 19130

HELLER, LOIS JANE, physiologist, educator, researcher; b. Detroit, Jan. 4, 1942; d. John and Lona Elizabeth (Stockmeyer) Skagerberg; m. Robert Eugene Heller, May 21, 1966; children: John Robert, Suzanne Elizabeth. BA, Albion Coll., 1964; MS, U. Mich., 1966; PhD, U. Ill., Chgo., 1970. Instr. med ctr. U. Ill., Chgo., 1969-70, asst. prof., 1970-71, U. Minn., Duluth, 1972-77, assoc. prof., 1977-89, prof., 1989—. Author: Cardiovascular Physiology, 5th edit., 2003; contbr. numerous articles to profl. jours. Mem. Am. Physiol. Soc., Am. Heart Assn., Soc. Exptl. Biology and Medicine, Internat. Soc. Heart Rsch., Sigma Xi. Avocation: birding. Home: 9129 Congdon Blvd Duluth MN 55804-0005 Office: Univ Minn Sch of Medicine Duluth MN 55812

HELLER, MARY WHEELER, photographer; b. Sterling, Ill., Mar. 4, 1928; d. LeRoy Coe and Gladys (Lawrence) Wheeler; m. Peter Seton Heller, June 30, 1956; 1 child, Kate Heller O'Reilly. B in Philosophy, U. Chgo., 1947; BA, U. Ariz., 1950; student, Internat. Ctr. Photography, N.Y.C., 1979-81, Maine Photographic Workshop, 1980. Editl. asst. The New Yorker, N.Y.C., 1951-56, reporter, 1957-60; art photographer N.Y.C., 1970—. Stock photographer Getty Images, 1985—; com. mem. Internat. Ctr. Photography, 1990—. One-woman shows include James Hunt Barker Gallery, Nantucket, Mass., 1979, Siasconset Bookstore, Nantucket, 1984, Studio Gallery, Siasconset, 1982, 1986—88, 1990, Ledel Gallery, N.Y.C., 1990, X Gallery, Nantucket, 1992—95, Lisa Steinmetz Gallery, Clayton, Mo., 1997, U.S. Embassy, Yemen, 1998, Old Spouter Gallery, Nantucket, 1998, New Gallery, 1999, Artists Assn. Nantucket, 2000, 2002, Century Assn., 2000, exhibited in group shows at Vision Gallery, San Francisco, 1987—88, Ledel Gallery, N.Y.C., 1987—88, Main St. Gallery, Nantucket, 1987—91, 1996—98, U.S. Embassy, Oman, 1997, One Pleasant St. Art Ctr., Nantucket, 1996—97, Artists' Assn. Nantucket, 1998—2006, Gallery N., Setauket, N.Y., 1999, Photo Dist. Gallery, N.Y.C., 2003, Phillips Mill Gallery, New Hope, Pa., 2005, Cork Gallery, Lincoln Ctr., NYC, 2006, others. Trustee N.Y.C. Sch. Vol. Program (now named Learning Leaders), 1961—, classroom tutor, 1961—62, chmn. bd. trustees, 1967—72, chmn. search com. for new exec. dir., 1976; bd. dirs. Pub. Edn. Assn., N.Y.C., 1966—74, pres. bd. dirs., 1972—74; co-chmn. edn. com. N.Y. Philharm, N.Y.C., 1970—80; bd. dirs. Chamber Music Soc. Lincoln Ctr., N.Y.C., 1975—91, chmn. exec. com., 1979—82, pres. bd. dirs., 1988—91; bd. dirs. Nantucket Land Coun., 1986—; v.p. bd. dirs. MacDowell Colony, Peterborough, NH, 1975—79, chmn. search com. for new dir., 1977. Mem.: Profl. Women Photographers, Am. Soc. Media Photographers. Episcopalian. Avocations: reading, visual and performing arts, travel, golf, tennis. E-mail: photocomp@earthlink.net.

HELLINGS, JESSICA ALICE, psychiatrist, educator; arrived in US, 1989; d. Jan Eise Hellings and Nora Dooley-Hellings; children: Terry Baynes, Richard Baynes. MB, BChir, Witwatersrand U., Johannesburg, 1978. Diplomate Am. Bd. Psychiatry and Neurology. Resident in gen. psychiatry Johannesburg Hosp., 1984—88, staff physician emergency rm., 1980—84, attending psychiatrist, 1989; chief of psychiatry Hillbrow Hosp., Johannesburg, 1988; asst. clin. prof. U. Kans. Med. Ctr., Kansas City, 1992—96, asst. prof., 1996—2001, assoc. prof., 2001—. Founder, dir. neurodevel. psychiatry for children, adolescents and adults U. Kans. Med. Ctr., Kansas City, 1992—; advisor Abbott Pharms.; reviewer Kans. Found. for Med. Care, Topeka, 1993—, Kans. State Bd. Healing Arts, NIMH, 2001—. Co-prodr.: videos, DVDs and manuals Dual Diagnosis Series: 5 Titles in Developmental Disabilities, 1999—. Mem. com. Women in Medicine and Sci. U. Kans. Med. Ctr., 2000—. Named one of Top Psychiatrists, Consumer's Rsch. Coun. Am., Washington, 2004; recipient Career Devel. award, NIMH, Washington, 1998, You Make a Difference award, Lake Mary Ctr., Paola, Kans., 2004. Mem.: AAUW, Am. Acad. Child and Adolescent Psychiatry (pres. Greater Kansas City Regional Coun. 2005—), South African Coll. Medicine, Am. Psychiat. Assn. (women's caucus). Avocations: swimming, gardening, dance, music. Office: U Kans Med Ctr 3901 Rainbow Blvd Kansas City KS 66160 Office Phone: 913-588-1800. Office Fax: 913-588-1305.

HELLMAN, FRANCES, physics professor; b. Croyden, G.B., Oct. 28, 1956; came to U.S. 1957; d. Frederick Warren and Patricia Christina (Sander) H. BA, Dartmouth Coll., 1978; PhD in Applied Physics, Stanford U., 1985. Rsch. asst. Stanford U., 1978-85; postdoctoral mem. tech. staff AT&T Bell Labs., Murray Hill, N.J., 1985-87; asst. prof. physics U. Calif., San Diego, 1987—2005, assoc. faculty mem., Ctr. for Magnetic Recording Rsch., full prof. physics Berkeley, Calif., 2005—, joint appt. in material sci. and engring. dept. and material sci. divsn. Lawrence Berkeley Lab. Mem. adv. bd., Los Alamos Neutron Scattering Ctr; head of U. Calif., San Diego Physics Dept. NSF-REU site Program; mem. several sci. bds.: NSF adv. bd. on Math and Phys. Sciences, NRC bd. on physics and astronomy, Inst. for Complex Adaptive Matter, Elementary Inst. Sci., San Diego Edn. Found, San Diego Found. Sci. and Tech. Working Group; mem. state adv. bd. Calif. State Summer Sch. for Math. and Sci. (COSMOS), 2005-; lectr. in field. Editl. bd. mem. Review of Scientific Instruments, Contbr. articles to profl. jours.; patentee in field. Mentor Faculty Mentor Programs for Women and Minority Students, U. calif., San Diego, 1988-91. IBM predoctoral fellow 1980-82; NSF grantee, 1989-91, Air Force Office Sci. Rsch. grantee, 1989-91, Univ.-wide Energy Rsch. Group grantee, 1989-91. Fellow Am. Phys. Soc. (chair, topical group on magnetism and its applications, 2000 chair exec. com., divsn. materials physics, 1997, program chair, com. on the status of women in physics, 2003-04, mem, 2000-05, Keithley award, 2006); mem. Am. Vacuum Soc., Matls. Rsch. Soc., NAS (mem. bd. physics and astronomy, adv. com., mem., solid state sciences com., adv. com.), Phi Beta Kappa. Avocations: soccer, backpacking, movies. Office: 317 Birge Dept Physics U Calif Berkeley Berkeley CA 94720 Office Phone: 510-642-6135. Business E-Mail: fhellman@berkeley.edu.*

HELLSTRÖM, INGEGERD, medical researcher; b. Stockholm; permanent resident, US, 1966, US citizen, 1996; m. Karl Erik Hellström; children: Katarina Elisabet, Per Erik. MD of Medicine, Karolinska Inst. Med. Sch., Stockholm, 1964, PhD of Medicine (Tumor Biology), 1966. Rsch. assoc. (docent), dept. Tumor Biology Karolinska Inst. Med. Sch., Stockholm, 1959-66, asst. prof. dept. tumor biology, 1966; asst. prof. microbiology U. Wash., Seattle, 1966—, rsch. assoc. prof. microbiology, 1969-72, prof. microbiology/immunology, 1972—85, adj. prof. pathology, 1972—85, affiliate prof. pathology, 1985—; mem. and program head, divsn. tumor immunology Fred Hutchinson Cancer Rsch. Ctr., Seattle, 1975—83; sr. scientist Oncogen, Seattle, 1983—85, lab. dir., 1985—86; v.p. Oncogen/Bristol-Myers Squibb, Seattle, 1986-90; v.p. immunological diseases Bristol-Myers Squibb Pharm. Rsch. Inst., Seattle, 1990—97; pron. investigator Pacific Northwest Rsch. Inst., Seattle, 1997—2004. Patents in the field: 17 US patents and 1 UK Patent; mem. editl. adv. bd., Jour. of Nat. Cancer Inst.; assoc. editor, Cancer Research, 1980-87, 1988-93, 1995-; mem. editl. bd., Anticancer Research; mem. gen. assembly, GM Cancer Rsch. Found.; mem. external adv. com, Specialized Ctr. for Cancer Rsch., U. Ill. at Chgo., Coll. Medicine, 1991-; contbr. to 450 sci. publs. Recipient Lucy Wortham James award, Ewing Soc., 1971, Matrix Table award, 1972, Pap award Outstanding Contbn. Cancer Rsch., Papanicolaou Cancer Rsch. Inst., 1973, Am. Cancer Soc. Nat. award 1974, RNO (Knight of Northern Star, First Class Swedish Order of Merit), 1976, Humboldt award to Sr. US Sci., Humbolt Stiftung Bonn, W. Germany, 1980. Mem. AMA, Am. Assn. Immunologists, Am. Fedn. Clin. Rsch., Am. Assn. Cancer Rsch., Soc. Biol. Therapy. Office: Harborview Med Ctr Box 359939 325 Ninth Ave Seattle WA 98104-2499 Office Phone: 206-341-5908. Business E-Mail: ihellstrom@u.washington.edu.

HELLUMS, LORI ROBERTS, elementary school educator; d. Van Douglas and Judy Harbin Roberts; m. Jack Dewayne Hellums, Sept. 2, 2000; 1 child, Jackson. BSc, U. North Ala., Florence, 1994; MEd, U. North Ala., 2003. Tech. prep. reading tchr. Bevill State C.C., Hamilton, Ala., 1995—96; tchr. 1st grade Marion County Sch. Sys. Phillips Elem. Sch., Bear Creek, Ala., 1996—2005; tchr. 6th grade Madison City Sch. Sys. Madison Elem., Ala., 2005—06, tchr. kindergarten, 2006—. Sec., treas. Marion Edn. Assn., Hamilton, Ala., 2001—03. Mem.: NEA, Internat. Reading Assn., Ala. Edn. Assn., Kappa Delta Pi, Alpha Theta Chi. Democrat. Ch. Of Christ. Avocations: reading, travel, shopping. Office: Madison Elem 17 Coll St Madison AL 35758

HELLWEGE, NANCY CAROL, special education educator; b. Bridgeport, Conn., Dec. 28, 1933; d. Emil and Dorothy Alma (Sell) Rosenoch; children: Michael, Christie, Patricia. BS with distinction, Ind. U., Ft. Wayne, 1972, MS, 1977; EdS, Ball State U., 1984. Tchr. 1st grade Luth. Schs., Ft. Wayne, Ind., 1962—66; coord. Head Start, Ft. Wayne, 1967—68; tchr. kindergarten Luth. Schs., Ft. Wayne, 1968—78; tchr. resource rm. East Allen County Schs., New Haven, Ind., 1978—81; cons. N.E. Colo. BOCES, Haxtun, 1982—84; strategist South Ctrl. BOCES, Pueblo, Colo., 1984—86; supr. Mt. BOCES, Leadville, Colo., 1986—87; coord. Broward County Schs., Ft. Lauderdale, Fla., 1987—88; pres. Learning Power, Inc., 1988—; prin., owner Sch. for Learning Disabled Christi Acad., 2000—. Author handbooks: Helping Children Reach Their Potential, 1991, Different Strokes/Different Folks, 1990. Mem.: NAFE, Phi Delta Kappa. Avocations: swimming, reading, camping. Office Phone: 954-597-0645. Business E-Mail: n.hellwege@christiacademy.org.

HELLYER, CONSTANCE ANNE (CONNIE ANNE CONWAY), writer, musician; b. Puyallup, Wash., Apr. 22, 1937; d. David Tirrell and Constance (Hopkins) H.; m. Peter A. Corning, Dec. 30, 1963 (div. 1977); children: Anne Arundel, Stephanie Deak Cunningham; m. Don W. Conway, Oct. 12, 1980 (dec. 2005) BA with honors, Mills Coll., 1959. Grader, rschr. Harvard U., Cambridge, Mass., 1959-60; rschr. Newsweek mag., NYC, 1960-63; author's asst. Theodore H. White and others, NYC, 1964-69; freelance writer, editor Colo., Calif., 1970-75; writer, editor Stanford U. Med. Ctr., 1975-79; comm. dir. No. Calif. Cancer Program, Palo Alto, 1979-82, Stanford Law Sch., Palo Alto, 1982-97; vocalist String of Pearls Band, 1991—, co-leader China tours, 1999, 2001, 2002; percussionist North Coast Symphonic Band, North Oreg. Coast Symphony, 2005—. Bd. mem. North Coast Symphonic Bd., 2006—. Founding editor (newsletters) Insight, 1978-80, Synergy, 1980-82, Stanford Law Alum, 1992-95; editor (mag.) Stanford Lawyer, 1982-98; contbr. articles to profl. jours. and mags. Recipient silver medal Coun. for Advancement and Support Edn., 1985, 89, award of distinction dist. VII, 1994. Mem. Nat. Assn. Sci. Writers, Phi Beta Kappa. Democrat. Home: PO Box 828 Cannon Beach OR 97110 Personal E-mail: conniepearl@yahoo.com.

HELM, DOROTHY DAWN, nurse; b. Decatur, Ill., Oct. 12, 1965; d. Robert Lee and Wanda Kathleen (Parker) H. Diploma, Decatur Area Vocat. Sch., 1984; ADN, Moberly Area Jr. Coll., 1986; BSN, U. Mo., 1997. RN, Mo.; cert. breast feeding educator. Nurse Loch Haven Nursing Home, Macon, Mo., 1984-85; staff nurse Moberly Regional Med. Ctr., Mo., 1986—2004; nurse Randolph County Health Dept., Moberly, 1989-90; staff nurse, breast feeding educator Moberly Regional Clinics, 1997—. Instr. nursing education Moberly Area CC, Mo., 2002-; spkr. in field. Co-developer Ob-Gyn. Amish Clinic, 1996. Mem. Mo. Nurses Assn., Internat. Child Birth Educators Assn. Home: 805 Holman Rd Moberly MO 65270-1247 Office: MACC 101 E College Ave Moberly MO 65270 Office Phone: 660-263-4110 ext. 369. E-mail: ddhelm@sbcglobal.net.

HELM, JUDITH, retired clergywoman; b. Washington, Nov. 1, 1939; d. Walter Scott and Marian Florence (Pyles) Beck; m. Neil Richard Helm, June 2, 1962 (div. July 1981); 1 child, Karl Andrew. BA, Dickinson Coll., 1960; MDiv, Luth. Theol. Sem., Gettysburg, Pa., 1985. Ordained to ministry Luth. Ch., 1985. Editor William R. Hamilton & Staff, polls, market surveys, Washington, 1968-79; pastor Zion Lehigh Luth. Ch., Alburtis, Pa., 1985-90, Nativity Luth. Ch., Allentown, Pa., 1991—2003; ret., 2003. Author: Tenleytown, DC, 1981, 2d edit., 2000. Democrat.

HELM, MONICA M., elementary school educator, psychotherapist, secondary school educator; b. Edgemont, Ill., Sept. 3, 1967; d. Eddie and Mildred Helm. BA in Comm., Ea. Ill. U., 1990. Comm. cons. Bd. Edn., East St. Louis, Ill., 1990—92, tchr., 1992—96, mental health therapist, 1997—98, tchr. Cahokia, 1998—99, 2001—; mgr.-in-training customer rels. ATT, Manchester, Mo., 1999—2001. Cons. in field, Belleville, Ill., 2001—. Charter mem. Nat. Women's History Mus., Washington, US Libr. Congress, 2001, 2005. Named one of Great Women of the 21st Century, U.S. Libr. of Congress, 2001, 2005. Mem.: NAFE, U.S. Libr. Congress, Nat. Women's History Mus. Republican. Avocations: reading, aerobics, tennis, bowling, writing.

HELMAN, IRIS BARCA, elementary school educator, consultant; b. Kenosha, Wis., May 21, 1930; d. Alphonse and Rosalie (Russo) Barca; divorced; 1 child, Gabriel Heidi. BS in Edn., U. Wis., 1955; MS in Edn., U. Wis., Milw., 1971; Student, U. Wis., Kenosha, 1980-82, Carthage Coll., 1972-74. Cert. elem. tchr. Wis. Sec. USN, Great Lakes, Ill., 1950-53; tchr. Kenosha Unified Sch. Dist. #1, 1955—92; student tchr. supr. U. Wis. Sys. Cons. in field. Author: Now What Do I Do?, 1980, Primer on Gifted Education, 1982; co-author: Shapers of Wisconsin, 1998; contbr. articles to profl. jours. Chmn. Democratic Com., Kenosha, 1977; legisl. chmn. City of Kenosha, 1979-80, harbor commr., 1987-90; pres. Wis. Orgn. for Gifted and Talented, 1977-79; chmn. Wis. Coun. for Gifted and Talented, 1979-80; bd. dirs. AFL-CIO Coun., Kenosha, 1980—; vice-chmn. City Plan Commn., 1992-98, 2000—. Named Outstanding Labor Person, City of Kenosha, 1989, County of Kenosha, 1989. Democrat. Roman Catholic. Avocations: reading, skiing, sailing, tennis, politics. Home: 6207 7th Ave Apt 22 Kenosha WI 53143-4565

HELMAR-SALASOO, ESTER ANETTE, language and literature educator, researcher; b. Subiaco, W.A., Australia, Oct. 26, 1956; came to U.S., 1987; d. Harald R. and Liana M. (Kikas) H.; m. Lembit Salasoo, Jan. 2, 1988; children: Imbi, Markus, Kristjan. BA, U. W. Australia, Perth, 1977, Diploma in Edn., 1978; MS, SUNY, Albany, 1988, PhD in Edn., 2001. Tchr. English, lit. Pub. Schs. W. Australia, 1978-85; ESL tchr. Tuart Coll., W. Australia, 1986; teaching asst. SUNY, Albany, 1988, rsch. asst., 1989-90; facilitator instrnl. and profl. devel. Nat. Rsch. Ctr. on English Learning and Achievement, SUNY, Albany, 2001—03; tchr. ESL Amsterdam H.S., N.Y., 2004. Cons. Nat. Javits Project for Lang. Arts Rsch., Washington, 1992. Author: (reports) A National Study of States' Roles in Choosing Reading and Literature for Second Language Learning, 1993, (with Kahn S.) Collegial Support and Networks Invigorate Teaching: The Case of the Marsha Slater, 1999. Home: 2280 Berkley Ave Schenectady NY 12309-2726

HELMER, M(ARTHA) CHRISTIE, lawyer; b. Portland, Oreg., Oct. 8, 1949; d. Marvin Curtis and Inez Bahl (Corwin) H.; m. Joe D. Bailey, June 23, 1979; children: Tim Bailey, Bill Bailey. BA in English magna cum laude, Wash. State U., 1970; JD cum laude, Lewis & Clark Coll., 1974; LLM in Internat. Law, Columbia U., 1998. Bar: Oreg. 1974. Assoc. Miller Nash, Portland, 1974-81, ptnr., 1981—. Adj. prof. Lewis & Clark Law Sch., 1999—; guest lectr. Xiamen U. Law, China, 1995; mem. Oreg. Bd. Bar Examiners, Portland, 1978-81; del. 9th Cir. Jud. Conf., 1984-87, mem. exec. com., 1987-90. Author: Arrest of Ships, 1985, Has China Adopted the UCC?, 1999. Mem.: ABA (internat. and litig. sections), Internat. Bar Assn., Maritime Law Assn., Oreg. Bar Assn. (bd. govs. 1981—84, treas. 1983—84, ho. of dels. 2003—), World Affairs Coun. (chair bd. dirs.), Multnomah Athletic Club, Phi Beta Kappa. Avocations: antiques, travel, fashion. Office: Miller Nash 111 SW 5th Ave Ste 3500 Portland OR 97204-3699 Office Phone: 503-205-2464. Business E-Mail: chris.helmer@millernash.com.

HELMER, NICOLE M., lawyer; b. Massena, N.Y., Jan. 3, 1978; d. Michaeloral and Toni Marie Helmer. BS in Acctg., Le Moyne Coll., Syracuse, N.Y., 2000; JD, Union U., Albany, N.Y., 2003. Bar: N.Y. 2004, U.S. Dist. Ct. (no. dist.) N.Y. 2004, cert.: N.Y. (law guardian) 2005. Summer assoc. Law Office of Michael V. Almasian, Massena, NY, 2001; jud. intern Albany County Surrogate Ct., NY, 2002; assoc. atty. Poissant, Nichols & Grue, PC, Malone, NY, 2003—05, Tully, Rinckey & Assocs., Pllc, Albany, NY, 2005—. Home: 31 Wembley Ct Albany NY 12205-3830

HELMETAG, DIANA, music educator; b. Bryn Mawr, Pa., 1965; d. Charles and Ruth Helmetag; m. Steven Glanzmann, 1993; children: Amanda, Anna Marie. BS in Music Edn. cum laude, Duquesne U., 1987; MusM, Pa. State U., 1990. Instr. Sch. Music Pa. State U., University Park, 1988, 90, lectr. Delaware County campus Media, 1991-95; music tchr. Radnor (Pa.) Twp. Sch. Dist., 1993-94, 95, 96; piano accompanist Villanova (Pa.) Voices Villanova U., 1995-99; instr. Delaware County C.C., Media, 1996; orch. dir. Upper Merion Area Sch. Dist., King of Prussia, Pa., 1996—, subject area leader, 1997—2001, pit orch. dir., 1997, 1998, 2001—; choir dir., chamber music coach and children's orch. dir. Strings Internat. Music Festival Bryn Mawr (Pa.) Coll., 2001—. Pianist, violinist Mu Phi Epsilon recitals, Phila., 1991, 92, 94; orch. dir. Schuylkill Valley Area Orch. Festival, Wayne, Pa., 1996—; founding mem. Montgomery County Honors String Orch. Festival, host dir., 2005; music dir. King of Prussia Players, 2000; guest condr. Bucks County String Day, 2003-04. Orch. dir., pianist, violinist Narberth (Pa.) Cmty. Theatre, 1997—. Recipient grad. assistantship Pa. State U., 1987-90. Mem. Am. String Tchrs. Assn. with Nat. Sch. Orch. Assn., Music Educators Nat. Conf., Music Tchrs. Nat. Assn., Coll. Music Soc., Pa. Music Educators Assn. (host. dist. 11 orch. festival 1998, orch. dir. and presiding chair in-svc. conf. 2001, host all-state orch. festival 2002, chamber group selected to perform for All-State Conf., 2005), Phi Kappa Phi, Pi Kappa Lambda. Office: Upper Merion Area Sch Dist 435 Crossfield Rd King Of Prussia PA 19406 Business E-Mail: dhelmetag@umasd.org.

HELMICK, GAYLE JOHNSTON, retired elementary education educator; b. Beaver Falls, Pa., July 22, 1936; d. Dwight Edward and Helen Ruth (Reed) Johnston; m. Wayne W. Helmick, Sept. 26, 1959; children: Susan, Kristen Helmick-Nelson, Kathleen. BS in Edn., Geneva Coll., 1961; M in Reading, Slippery Rock State U., 1983. Cert. reading specialist, Pa. Tchr. 5th grade Rochester (Pa.) Area Schs., 1960-61; reading specialist, learning advisor Beaver (Pa.) Area Schs., 1977—2001. Team mem. Devel. Thinking Presentation Team of Beaver Schs., Beaver, 1986—; fellow Wester. Pa. Writing Project, Pitts., 1990—. Active Cmty. Bible Study; past pres. Beaver Jr. Women's Club; vol. Beaver Mus. Mem.: MENSA, Beaver Literacy Soc., Keystone State Reading Assn., Pa. State Edn. Assn., Internat. Reading Assn., Beaver County Ret. Tchrs. Assn., Leotta Hawthorne Reading Coun. (v.p. 1992—93, pres. 1993—94, sec. 2005—), Pa. State Ret. Tchrs. Assn., Beaver Area Heritage Soc., Beaver Area Libr. Brown Bag Book Club, Delta Kappa Gamma (sec. Zeta chpt. 1992—). Episcopalian. Avocations: reading, collecting signed first editions of books. Home: 440 Bank St Beaver PA 15009-2701

HELMOND, KATHERINE, actress; b. Galveston, Tex., July 5, 1928; d. Patrick Joseph and Thelma Louise (Malone) H.; m. George N. Martin (div.); m. David Christian, 1962. Pres. Taur Can Prodns., Hollywood, Calif., 1979— Appeared as Jessica Tate in TV series Soap, 1978-81 (Emmy award best actress, 1978, 79, 80, 81, Golden Globe award 1980); co-star TV series Who's The Boss?, 1984-92, Coach, 1995—97; appearances in TV series and in TV movies including Dr. Max, 1974, Larry, 1974, Locusts, 1974, The Autobiography of Miss Jane Pittman, 1974, The Legend of Lizzie Borden, 1975, The Family Nobody Wanted, 1975, Cage Without a Key, 1975, The First 36 Hours of Dr. Durant, 1975, James Dean, 1976, Wanted: The Sundance Woman, 1976, Little Ladies of the Night, 1977, Getting Married, 1978, miniseries Pearl, 1978, Diary of a Teenage Hitchhiker, 1979, Scout's Honor, 1980, miniseries World War III, 1982, For Lovers Only, 1982, Rosie: The Rosemary Clooney Story, 1982, When Will I Be Loved, 1990, The Perfect Tribute, 1991, Deception: A Mother's Secret, 1991, Grass Roots, 1992, Liz: The Elizabeth Taylor Story, 1995, Ms. Scrooge, 1997, Providence, 1999, Strong Medicine,

2000, How to Marry a Billionaire: A Christmas Tale, 2000, Mr. St. Nick, 2002, Everybody Loves Raymond, 1996, 1998-04; film appearances include: The Hospital, 1971, The Hindenberg, 1975, Baby Blue Marine, 1976, Family Plot, 1976, Time Bandits, 1981, Brazil, 1986, Shadey, Overboard, 1987, Lady in White, 1988, Inside Monkey Zetterland, 1993, Amore!, 1993, The Spy Within, 1994, Fear and Loathing in Las Vegas, 1998, The Perfect Nanny, 2000, Living in Fear, 2001, Black Hole, 2002, (voice) Cars, 2006; stage appearences include House of Blue Leaves, 1971 (N.Y. Drama Critics Variety award 1971, Clarence Derwent award 1971, L.A. Drama Critics award 1972), Great God Brown, 1973, Quartermaine's Terms, 1984, Mixed Emotions, 1993; appeared with numerous repertory theatres including Associated Producing Artists, N.Y.C., Trinity Sq. Repertory Co., R.I., Hartford Stage, Phoenix Repertory, N.Y.C. Mem. Screen Actors Guild, AFTRA. Roman Catholic. Office: William Morris Agy care Lee Stollman 151 S El Camino Dr Beverly Hills CA 90212-2775*

HELMS, BELVA ELIZABETH, secondary school educator, mathematician; b. Tuscaloosa, Ala., Mar. 11, 1968; d. Loather Paul and Cressie Lucille Helms. MEd in Math., U. Ala., Birmingham, Ala., 2001. Cert. tchr. Nat. Bd. Cert. Tchrs., 2000. Tchr. math. Jefferson County Sch. Dist., Birmingham, Ala., 1997—2003, Murray (Utah) Sch. Dist., 2003—. Advisor Nat. Honor Soc., Murray, 2003—. Named Concurrent Enrollment Tchr. of Yr., Salt Lake C.C., 2005. Republican. Mem. Lds Ch. Avocations: tennis, travel. Home: 45 E 820 South Centerville UT 84014 Office: Murray High School 5440 South State Street Murray UT 84107 Office Phone: 801-264-7460. Personal E-mail: bhelms@mury.k12.ut.us.

HELMS, CAROL DOROTHY, elementary school educator; b. Yankton, S.D., Sept. 8, 1959; d. Joseph F. and Marcella M. (Schramm) Kotalik; m. John W. Helms, June 18, 1983; children: Tiffany M., J.W. BS in Elem. Edn., No. State Coll., Aberdeen, S.D., 1981. Tchr. 4th-8th grades Harding County Sch., Buffalo, SD, 1981—83, tchr. 4th grade, 1983—89, tchr. 2d grade, 1989—95; tchr. Title I Reva Sch., 1995—2002, tchr. 3d-5th grades, 2002—03; tchr. 1st-3d grades Camp Crook Sch., SD, 2003—04, tchr. kindergarten, 3d-4th grades, 2004—05, 2005—06, tchr. kindergarten-2d grade, 2006—. Mem. Internat. Reading Assn. Home: PO Box 143 Buffalo SD 57720-0143

HELMS, DORIS R., academic administrator; BA, Bucknell Univ.; PhD, Univ. Ga. Joined Clemson (S.C.) U., 1973—, provost, 2002—, also vice-pres. academic affairs. Office: Clemson Univ Office VP and Provost 206 Sikes Hall Clemson SC 29634

HELMS GUBA, LISA MARIE, nursing administrator; b. Sioux City, Iowa, Nov. 24, 1962; d. Dean Edward and Betty Lou Victoria (Guenther) H. BA in Nursing, Carroll Coll., Helena, Mont., 1986; postgrad., Calif. State U., Sacramento, 1990-92; MSN, Incarnate Word Coll., 1996. Cert. pediatric nurse. Enlisted U.S. Army, 1981, advanced through grades to lt. col., 2004, nurse San Francisco, 1986-90, Calif. Nat. Guard, San Francisco, 1990-92, Rio Linda (Calif.) Union Sch. Dist., 1990-92; enlisted USAF, 1992; mem. A.F. Nurse Corps Wilford Hall Med Ctr., Lackland AFB, Tex., 1992-96; asst. nurse mgr. and critical care aeromed. transp. team nurse dir. Malcolm Grow Hosp., Andrews AFB, Md., 1996-2000; dir. Nurse Triage Ctr., 2001—03; nursing exec. Internal Medicine and Women's Health, Dover AFB, 2003—03, case mgr., 2004—06; nurse mgr. multi svcs. unit Malcolm Gaw Med. Ctr., Andrews AFB, Md., 2006—. Deployed to Guantanamo Bay, Cuba, July to Oct. 1994 for Operation Sea Signal, Operation Safe Haven; provider med. care to Haitian/Cuban migrants. Mem. AACN. Roman Catholic. E-mail: lisaguba@sprintmail.com.

HELMSTETTER, WENDY LEE, librarian; b. Port Arthur, Ont., Can., Aug. 31, 1947; came to U.S., 1960; d. Estyn Lloyd and Vera Gertrude (Derwa) Edwards; m. Glenn Charles Grisetti, June 17, 1967 (div.); 1 child, Lee Glenn Grisetti; m. Charles Edward Helmstetter, July 1, 1988. BA in Psychology summa cum laude, SUNY, Buffalo, 1985; MLS, U. South Fla., 1994. Adminstrv. asst. to libr. dir. Roswell Pk. Cancer Inst., Buffalo, 1973-89; reference libr. Fla. Inst. Tech., Melbourne, 1994—96, academic info. svcs. libr., 1996—2002, asst. libr. dir., 2002—05, dir. resources and svcs., 2005—. Bd. dirs. Friends of Evans Libr., Melbourne, 1996-98. Recipient Excellence Scholarly Achievement award SUNY/Buffalo, 1986. Mem. ALA, Assn. Coll. and Rsch. Librs. (instrn. sect., policy com. 1996-98, sci. and tech. sect., univ. librs. sect., membership com. 1996-98), Libr. Adminstrn. and Mgmt. Assn., Reference and User Svcs. Assn., Fla. Inst. Tech. Faculty Senate (chmn. faculty excellence awards com. 2005—), Fla. Libr. Assn., Libr. Assn. Brevard (continuing edn. com. 1994-95), Ctrl. Fla. Libr. Cooperative (del.), Phi Kappa Phi, Beta Phi Mu, Alpha Sigma Lambda. Home: 854 Hawksbill Island Dr Satellite Beach FL 32937-3850 Office: Fla Inst Tech 150 W University Blvd Melbourne FL 32901-6975 E-mail: whelmste@fit.edu.

HELMS-VANSTONE, MARY WALLACE, anthropology educator; b. Allentown, Pa., Apr. 15, 1938; d. Samuel Leidich and Mary (Wallace) Helms; divorced. BA, Pa. State U., State College, 1960; MA, U. Mich., 1962, PhD, 1967. Instr. Wayne State U., Detroit, 1965-67; asst. prof. Syracuse (N.Y.) U., 1967-68; lectr. Northwestern U., Evanston and Chgo., Ill., 1969-79; prof. U. N.C., Greensboro, 1979—2004, prof. emerita, 2004—, head dept. anthropology Greensboro, 1979-85. Author: Asang: A Miskito Community, 1971, Middle America, 1975, Ancient Panama, 1979, Ulysses' Sail, 1988, Craft and the Kingly Ideal, 1993, Creations of the Rainbow Serpent, 1995, Access to Origins, 1998, The Curassow's Crest, 2000; contbr. articles to profl. jours. Fellow: Am. Anthrop. Assn.; mem.: Medieval Acad. Am., So. Anthrop. Soc. (pres. 1980—81, procs. editor 1982—94), Am. Ethnological Soc., Am. Soc. Ethnohistory (pres. 1976). Avocations: travel, painting, musical activities, crafts. Office: Univ NC Dept Anthropology PO Box 26170 Greensboro NC 27402-6170

HELOISE, columnist, writer; b. Waco, Tex., Apr. 15, 1951; d. Marshal H. and Heloise K. (Bowles) Cruse; m. David L. Evans, Feb. 13, 1981. BS in Math. and Bus, S.W. Tex. State U., 1974. Owner, pres. Heloise, Inc. Asst. to columnist mother, Heloise, 1974-77, upon her death took over internationally syndicated column, 1977; author: Hints from Heloise, 1980, Help from Heloise, 1981, Heloise's Beauty Book, 1985, All-New Hints from Heloise, 1989, Heloise: Hints for a Healthy Planet, 1990, Heloise from A to Z, 1992, Household Hints for Singles, 1993, Hints for All Occasions, 1995, In The Kitchen With Heloise, 2000, Heloise Conquers Stinks & Stains, 2002, Get Organized with Heloise, 2004; contbg. editor Good Housekeeping mag., 1983, Speaker for the House; co-founder, 1st co-pilot Mile Pie in the Sky Balloon Club. Mem. Good Neighbor Coun. Tex.-Mex.; sponsor Nat. Smile Week. Recipient Mental Health Mission award Nat. Mental Health Assn., 1990, The Carnegians Good Human Rels. award, 1994. Mem. AFTRA, SAG, Women in Comm. (Headliner 1994), Tex. Press Women, Internat. Women's Forum, Women in Radio and TV, Confrerie de la Chaine des Rotisseurs (bailli San Antonio chpt.), Ordre Mondial des Gourmets De'Gustateurd de U.S.A., Death Valley Yacht and Racket Club, Zonta. Home: PO Box 795000 San Antonio TX 78279-5000

HELSEL, ELSIE DRESSLER, retired special education educator; b. Butler, Pa., July 10, 1915; d. Adolph and Nelle Simpson Dressler; m. Robert Griffith Helsel, Sept. 2, 1939; children: William Griffith Waring, Robert Griffith Helsel, Jr., Marjorie Lynn. AB in Biology and Pre-Medicine magna cum laude, Chatham Coll., 1937; MS in Genetics, U. Pitts., 1939, PhD in Genetics, 1942; MA in Spl. Edn., Ohio State U., 1962. Biology tchr. Wilkinsburg (Pa.) H.S., 1937—41; instr. human genetics dept. zoology Ohio State U., Cole, 1951—53; cons. med. and sci. dept. United Cerebral Palsy Assn., N.Y.C., 1955, dir. Washington, 1968—74; coord. spl. edn. Ohio U. Coll. Edn., Athens, 1974—77, prof. emeritus, 1981—; dir. Ohio U. Affiliated Ctr. for Human Devel., 1975—81. Asst. dir. divsn. spl. studies Am. Assn. Mental Deficiency, 1964—68; project coord. Protective Svcs. Project Ohio Dept. Mental Health and Mental Retardation, 1967—69; chairperson Ohio Devel. Disabilities Planning Coun., 1993—98; mem. govs. vision com. Dept. Mental Retardation and Devel. Disabilities, 1997—99. Contbr. articles to profl. jours. Mem. govtl. activities com. United Cerebral Palsy Assn., 1965—97, bd. dirs., 1976—94, mem. cmty. svcs. com., 1995—97; Ohio coun. rep. Nat. Assn. Devel. Disabilities Couns., 1985—87, mem. policy com., 1995—97; bd. dirs. United Cerebral Palsy Ohio, 1955—76, 1990—96, v.p., 1977—83, vol. exec. dir., 1991—97; chairperson cmty. svcs. programs Ohio U. Coll. Medicine, 1995—98.

HELSENE, AMY L., lawyer; b. Austin, Minn., June 21, 1973; BA cum laude, U. Minn., Mpls., 1995; JD, U. Minn. Law Sch., Mpls., 1998. Bar: Minn. 1998. Clk. to Hon. James T. Swenson Hennepin County Dist. Ct.; assoc. Larkin, Hoffman, Daly & Lindgren, Ltd., Mpls. Contbr. articles to profl. jours. Named a Rising Star, Minn. Super Lawyers mag., 2006. Mem.: Vol. Lawyers Network, Douglas K. Amdahl Inns of Ct., Minn. Women Lawyers, ABA, Minn. State Bar Assn., Hennepin County Bar Assn., Phi Beta Kappa. Office: Larkin Hoffman Daly & Lindgren Ltd 1500 Wells Fargo Plz 7900 Xerxes Ave S Minneapolis MN 55431 Office Phone: 952-896-3326. E-mail: ahelsene@larkinhoffman.com.*

HELSTEIN, IVY RAE, communications executive, psychotherapist, writer; d. Harold and Celia Weintraub Markowitz; children: Hilary, Eden, Flyn. BA, Queens Coll., 1958; MA in Human Behavior, Goddard Coll., Plainfield, Vt., 1979. Founder, pres. Comm. Dynamics, Great Neck, NY, 1973—. Creator Practical Spiritualism; instr., lectr. classroom mgmt. skills various sch. dists., N.Y., 1976; instr. assertiveness tng., conflict mgmt., adult continuing edn. Hofstra U., Hempstead, N.Y., 1976, C.W. Post U., Brookville, N.Y., 1979; adj. faculty Nassau C.C., Garden City, 1977—. Author: Great Persuaders: Sales Training, 1984, Great Communicators II, 1987, Infinite Abilities: Living Your Life on Purpose, 1999. Trainer N.Y. State Child Protective Svcs., 1995—, Suffolk County (N.Y.) Dept. Labor, 1997. Mem. Nat. Spkr. Assn. (profl., past pres., Chpt. Mem. of the Yr. award 1986), Tri-State Nat. Spkrs. Assn. (pres. 1985-86), Authors Guild, Inc. Avocation: world travel. Home and Office: 27 Georgian Ln Great Neck NY 11024-1615 Personal E-mail: IHelstein@aol.com.

HELTON, JANE MARIE, literature and language educator; b. Fort Wayne, Ind., Mar. 6, 1959; d. Frederick Lewis and Marilyn Lee Rentschler; m. Bill Ray Helton, July 28, 1983; children: Wesley Frederick, Christie Faith. BA, U. Evansville, Ind., 1981; MS, Ind. U., Ft. Wayne, 1987. Tchr. English Eastside H.S., Butler, Ind., 1981—88; guidance counselor Garrett H.S., 1988—89; instr. English Purdue U., West Lafayette, 1989—90; tchr. English West Lafayette H.S., 1990—. Head English dept. West Lafayette H.S., 2003—. 2003—; reader AP English lit. and composition exam Coll. Bd./Ednl. Testing Svc., 1999—. Mem. choir St. James Luth. Ch., Lafayette; mem. sch. bd. com. St. James Luth. Sch. Recipient English Tchg. award, Purdue U., Dept. English, 1989—90, Golden Apple Tchg. award, Greater Lafayette C. of C., 2000. Mem.: NEA, West Lafayette Edn. Assn., Ind. State Tchrs. Assn., Nat. Coun. Tchrs. English. Lutheran. Avocations: singing, reading, writing poetry. Home: 10 Rawlings Court Lafayette IN 47905 Office: West Lafayette High School 1105 North Grant Street West Lafayette IN 47906 Office Phone: 765-746-0400. E-mail: heltonj@wl.k12.in.us.

HELTON, KAREN JOHNSON, college administrator; b. Cin., May 20, 1947; d. James C. and Ruth (Lee) Payne; m. Malcolm Helton, June 29, 1995; children: Terence, Traci, Tina. BA, Ohio U., 1969; MSW, Atlanta U., 1976; postgrad., U. Mich., 1978, Tex. A&M U., 1992. Social worker Hamilton County, Cin., 1969-74; dir. planning LeMoyne-Owen Coll., Memphis, 1976-82; fed. programs officer Mary Holmes Coll., West Point, Miss., 1982-85; v.p. devel. Tex. Coll., Tyler, 1985-87; asst. to pres. Wiley Coll., Marshall, Tex., 1987—95, dir. sponsored programs, 2005—06, v.p. for instnl. advancement, 2005—. Chmn. Higher Edn. and Campus Ministry, 1992-94; bd. dirs. United Way of Harrison County, 1997-2000; mem. East Tex. Chapter The Links Inc, 2004—; mentor Rotary Internat., 2005—; bd. mem. Boys and Girls Club, 2005—. Recipient Disting. Svc. award U.S. Dept. Edn., 1996. Mem. NAFE, Zonta (pub. rels. com. 1989-92), Zeta Phi Beta (3d v.p. 1990-94). Democrat. Methodist. Avocations: photography, interior decorating. Office: Wiley College 711 Wiley Ave Marshall TX 75670-5199 Home: PO Box 118 Marshall TX 75671-0118 Office Phone: 903-926-1043. Business E-Mail: kheltone@wileyc.edu.

HELTON, KATHLEEN JACOBSON, neuroradiologist; d. Gerald Jacobson and Mary Margaret Fitzgerald; m. Stephen Lane Helton, June 7, 1981. MSN, U. of Tenn. Coll. of Nursing, 1979—80; MD, U. of Tenn. Coll. of Medicine, 1986—91. Radiologist Am. Bd. of Radiology, 1996. Neuroradiology fellow Vanderbilt U. Med. Ctr., Nashville, 1996—98, clin. instr., neuroradiology, 1998; neuroradiologist St Jude Children's Rsch. Hosp., Memphis, 1999—. Interim dir. mri St. Jude Children's Rsch. Hosp., 2003—. Recipient Achievement Citation for Scholastic Achievement, Janet M. Glasgow Meml. Fund, 1991; Josephine Cir. scholarship, U. of Tenn. Sch. of Nursing, 1975—77. Mem.: Am. Soc. of Neuroradiology, Am. Soc. of Pediatric Neuroradiology (assoc.), Southeastern Neuroradiological Soc. (assoc.), Am. Coll. of Radiology (assoc.), Alpha Omega Alpha Soc. (assoc.). Avocations: swimming, travel, music. Office: St Jude Children's Rsch Hosp 332 N Lauderdale St Memphis TN 38105 Office Phone: 901-495-2412. E-mail: kathleen.helton@stjude.org.

HELTON, PATRICIA BETH, realtor; b. Paintsville, Ky., Sept. 5, 1954; d. Oscar Jr. and Chloteen (McFarlan) Wheeler; m. John Keith Helton, Mar. 8, 1975. BS in Edn., Ea. Ky. U., 1975; MS, St. Cloud State U., 1983; grad. realtors inst., Nat. Realtors Inst., 1991. Cert. residential specialist. Med. sec. Willard (N.Y.) State Psychiat. Ctr., 1975-76; adminstrv. asst. Leo Payne Automotive Plaza, Denver, 1976-77; tchr. elem. edn. Aroka (Minn.)-Hennepin Schs., 1977, Naperville (Ill.) Sch. Dist., 1983-85; realtor, real estate instr. Coldwell Banker Real Estate, Westlake Village, Calif., 1985—, estates dir., 1988—, corp. property specialist, 1989—. Co-author: (history book) Profiles of Women, 1993. Trustee St. Matthews Meth. Ch., Newbury Park, Calif., 1987; mem. Nat. Women's Polit. Caucus, Thousand Oaks, Calif. Mem. AAUW (dir. univ. rels. 1993-94, v.p. edn. found. 1985-94, Gift Honoree 1991), Calif. Assn. Realtors, Women's Coun. Realtors (speker 1985-92), Order of Ea. Star. Republican. Methodist. Avocations: skiing, biking, canoeing, hiking, swimming. Office: Coldwell Banker Real Estate 171 E Thousand Oaks Blvd Thousand Oaks CA 91360-5712

HELTZEL, KATHLEEN LASSALLE, elementary school educator; b. Greenville, Pa., May 19, 1945; d. Fredric William Lassalle and Elizabeth Davis; m. John Herald Heltzel, Oct. 7, 1989; children: Susan, Courtney, John Raymond. BS in Elem. Edn., Edinboro U., Pa., 1967. Tchr. Huntingdon Area Schs., Pa., 1967—68, Adelphi Coll. Pk. Woods Preschool, Md., 1970—72, Lakeview Area Schs., Stoneboro, Pa., 1977—2006. Presenter in field. Mem.: Lakeview Edn. Assn. (chmn. flower com., mem. playground com., grade leader, reading selection com.), Pa. State Edn. Assn., Red Hat Soc., Atlantic Friends and Flower Club, Delta Kappa Gamma. Avocations: reading, gardening, rollerblading, photography, kayaking. Home: 5225 Sandy Lake Rd Cochranton PA 16314

HELWICK, AMBER, science educator; d. George and Rhonda Ritzhaupt; m. Shaun Helwick. BS in Biology, Northeastern State U., Tahlequah, Okla., 2001, MS Edn., 2003. Cert. sci. tchr. Okla. Sci. tchr. Muskogee HS, Okla., 2002—03, Hilldale Mid. Sch., Muskogee, 2003—, cheerleading coach, 2004—06. Cheerleading coach Muskogee All Starz, Okla., 2005—06; youth leader, math. tutor Boys and Girls Club, Tahlequah, Okla., 2001—02. Mem. Svc. League, Muskogee. Recipient Light of the Lamp award, Delta Zeta, Character First award, Hilldale Mid. Sch., Citation for Outstanding Leadership, Hilldale Pub. Schs. Bd. Edn., Florence Hood Miner award, Delta Zeta, Regional Collegiate Coord. award; scholar, Indian Health Svc., Collegiate Scholars, Northeastern State U.; Tsa-La-Gi Trail of Tears scholar, Cherokee Nation, OKAMP-SEM Minority Sci. and Math scholar, Ctr. for Tribal Studies. Mem.: NEA, Math and Sci. Tchr. Enhancement Project, Hilldale Assn. Classroom Tchrs. (negotiations team mem. 2005—06), Okla. Edn. Assn., Order of Omega. Achievements include design of. Avocation: scrapbooks. Office: Hilldale Mid Sch 400 E Smith Ferry Rd Muskogee OK 74403 Office Phone: 918-683-0763.

HELWICK, CHRISTINE, lawyer; b. Orange, Calif., Jan. 6, 1947; d. Edward Everett and Ruth Evelyn (Seymour) Hailwood; children: Ted C., Dana J. BA, Stanford U., 1968; MA, Northwestern U., 1969; JD, U. Calif., San Francisco, 1973. Bar: Calif., U.S. Supreme Ct. U. S. Ct. Appeals (9th cir.), U.S. Dist. Ct. (no., ctrl., so. and ea. dist.) Calif. Tchr. history New Trier Twp. High Sch., Winnetka, Ill., 1968-69; sec. to the producer Flip Wilson Show, Burbank, Calif., 1970; assoc. Crosby, Heafey, Roach & May, Oakland, Calif., 1973-78; asst. counsel litigation U. Calif., Oakland, 1978-84, mng. univ. counsel, 1984-94, counsel Berkeley campus, 1989-94; gen. counsel Calif. State U. Sys., 1994—. Lectr. in field. Mem. instnl. rev. bd. Devel. Studies Ctr., Oakland, 1990—; mem. Alameda County Fee Arbitration Panel. Mem. Nat. Assn. Coll. and Univ. Attys. (bd. dirs. 1995-98, 2000-2004, pres. 2002-03), Nat. Assn. Coll. and Univ. Bus. Officers (bd. dirs. 2002—), State Bar Calif. (exec. com. 1980-83, Leadership Calif. 1998), dirs. 1977), Alameda County Bar Found. (adv. trustee 1988-90, bd. dirs. 1991), Order of Coif. Episcopalian. Office: Calif State U 401 Golden Shore 4th Fl Long Beach CA 90802-4275

HELWIG, ANNETTE L., retired elementary school educator; b. Burlington, N.J., Dec. 18, 1926; d. William and Jesselyn V. Cox; m. Edward O. Helwig, Aug. 20, 1949; children: Lyn M., Keith W. BS in Edn., SUNY, Buffalo, 1948. Elem. tchr. North Tonawanda (N.Y.) Bd. Edn., Cedar Grove (N.J.) Bd. Edn.; ret., 1993. Cooperating tchr. for student tchrs. William Paterson State Coll., Caldwell Coll.; now chair program Ptnr. Vols. Vol. leader, tchr. Elem Schs. Help the Tchrs. Group, Cedar Grove, NJ, 2004—. Named N.J. Tchr. of Excellence, 1986, 90. Mem. NEA,NJBEA, N.J. Edn. Assn., Essex County Edn. Assn., Cedar Grove Edn. Assn. (sec., 2d v.p., chmn., rep.), VFW Aux. (v.p.). Home: 20 Pine Dr Cedar Grove NJ 07009-1036

HELWIG, JANET, computer science educator; d. Dudley and Alice Rolla; m. Curtis Helwig, Aug. 21, 1982; children: Sarah, Claire. BS, Miami U., Oxford, Ohio, 1978; MS, DePaul U., Chgo., 1986. Prof. Dominican U., River Forest, Ill., 1987—; project mgr. Arthur Andersen & Co, Chgo., 1979—91. Mem.: ACM. Office: Dominican University 7900 W Division St River Forest IL 60305 Office Phone: 708-524-6451. E-mail: jhelwig@dom.edu.

HEMBY, TINA MARIE, elementary school educator; d. Ray H. and Eyvonne H. Wright; m. Robert M. Hemby, June 17, 1995; children: Kayla S., Kiara B. BS in Elem. Edn., S.C. State U., Orangeburg, 1994, MEd, 2001. Cert. in early adolescent math. Tchr. William J. Clark Mid. Sch., Orangeburg, Robert E. Howard Mid. Sch., Orangeburg; adj. prof. Claflin U., Orangeburg. Cons. Math Strategies, Orangeburg. Named Tchr. of the Yr., Reading Coun., 2000. Mem.: S.C. Educators Assn. (v.p 1994), Nat. Coun. Tchrs. Math. Avocations: reading, tennis, computers. Office: W J Clark Mid Sch 919 Bennett St Orangeburg SC 29115-4213

HEMBY-GRUBB, VIRGINIA, education educator, consultant; b. Brookhaven, Miss., Mar. 8, 1960; d. James Ray and Fannie Mae Hemby; m. Robert E Grubb; 1 child, Matthew Winston Jackson. BS, U. So. Miss., 1988—91, MEd, 1991—92, PhD, 1992—95. Assoc. prof. Ind. U. of Pa., Indiana, Pa., 1995—2004, Mid. Tenn. State U., Murfreesboro, Tenn., 2004—. Co-author: Effective Communication Skills for Criminal Justice Professionals, Instructor's Manual and Test Bank for Law Enforcement in the 21st Century; contbr. articles to profl. jours. Recipient Post-Secondary Educator award, Pa. Bus. Edn. Assn., 2002, Golden Pen award, Miss. Bus. Edn. Assn., 1996. Mem.: ASTD (assoc.), Tenn. Bus. Edn. Assn. (assoc.), Assn. Career and Tech. Edn. (assoc.; editor Bus. Edn. Digest 2004), Assn. Bus. Comm. (assoc.), Nat. Bus. Edn. Assn. (assoc.; comm. sect. editor Bus. Edn. Forum 2002—05), Orgnl. Systems Rsch. Assn. (assoc.; exec. v.p. 2004—05, pres. 2005—), So. Bus. Edn. Assn. (assoc.; chair tour com. 2005), Ea. Bus. Edn. Assn. (assoc.; sec. 2002—03), Nat. Assn. Tchr. Educators in Bus. Edn. (assoc.; sec. 2001—03), Beta Gamma Sigma (assoc.), Pi Omega Pi (assoc.), Golden Key (assoc.), Phi Kappa Phi (assoc.), Epsilon Pi Tau (assoc.), Delta Pi Epsilon (assoc.; chair nat. membership com. 2003—05, nat. v.p. 2006—). Avocations: reading, travel, public speaking. Office: Middle Tenn State Univ BMOM Dept Box 40 Murfreesboro TN 37132 Office Phone: 615-898-2369. Office Fax: 615-898-5438. E-mail: kvhemby@mtsu.edu, drhembygrubb@comcast.net.

HEMISH, CAROL MARIE, liturgist/spiritual director, musician; b. Canby, Minn., June 12, 1950; d. Richard Joseph and Mathilda Rose (Mihm) H. BA in Music Edn., Piano Performance, Mt. Mary Coll., Milw., 1973; MA in Liturgical Studies, St. John's U., Collegeville, Minn., 1985; MA in Human Developmental Biospirituality, St. Mary's U. of Minn., 2000. Cert. spiritual dir. Dir. music, liturgy and spiritual renewal St. Mary's Parish, Willmar, Minn., 1981-84; dir. music ministries Epiphany Parish, Coon Rapids, Minn., 1984-87; liturgy dir. Marquette U., Milw., 1987-90, St. Benedict Ctr., Madison, Wis., 1990-92; assoc. dir. Archdiocesan Spirituality Ctr., New Orleans, 1992-93; coord. Ctr. for Liturgy at St. Louis U., 1994—2001; conf. ctr. coord. Good Counsel Hill, Mankato, Minn., 2003—05; ministry team mem. King's House, Buffalo, Minn., 2005—. Retreat dir. Sacred Heart Retreat House, Sedalia, Colo., 1989-2000; liturgy cons. various religious congregations, dioceses, parishes, 1980—. Mem. Sch. Sisters Notre Dame, Nat. Pastoral Musicians, Assn. Contemplative Sisters, Spiritual Dirs. Internat. Avocations: vegetarian cooking, creative sewing. Home: 1404 2nd Ave 5 Apt 8 Buffalo MN 55313-3205

HEMLOCK, ROBERTA LEIGH, veterinary technician; b. Chgo., Aug. 24, 1946; d. John Nolan and Gertrude Mathilda (Lahti) Hemlock. AA, Chgo. City Coll., 1966; BFA, Art Inst. Chgo., 1970; AAS, Bel-Rea Inst., 2001. Intelligence analyst State Dept., England, 1972—73; pres. Hemlock, Hemlock & Others, Chgo., 1973—80, design dir., 1973—80; prof. Colo. Inst. Art, Denver, 1980—93; v.p. ops. and design Design Prodns., Inc., Denver, 1993—94; v.p. ops., editor Syber Media Group, Denver, 1994—96; pvt. practice tech. grantwriter Denver, 1996—2000; vet. technician Huron Animal Hosp., Denver, 2001—03; vet. technician/surgery Erie Animal Hosp., Colo., 2003—04, Church Ranch Vet. Wellness Ctr., Denver, 2004—06, practice mgr., 2005—06; supr. surg. svcs. Alameda East Animal Hosp., 2006—. Mem. adv. bd. CCD of Denver, 2001—. Founding exec. dir. Le Musée du Renaissance Mus. of Print Art, 2006. Recipient Honoree Wall of Tolerance, Nat. Civil Rights Meml., Montgomery Ala., 2005. Mem.: AAUW (cons. 2001—), NAVTA, Colo. Assn. Cert. Vet. Technicians (state pub. rels. dir. 2001—04, cert.), Internat. Assn. U. Women (cons. 2001—), Denver Gardens. Avocations: photography, conceptual writing, publishing, collecting early Renaissance art. Home: 10648 Huron St #1505 Northglenn CO 80234-4022 Personal E-mail: rhemlock@excite.com.

HEMM, CYNTHIA JEAN, music educator; b. Belle Plaine, Iowa, Sept. 17, 1956; d. Dean Harold and Eleanor Jean McLeod; m. Stephen C. Hemm, June 14, 1980. MusB in Ch. Music, Drake U., Des Moines, 1978, B Music Edn., 1978. Cert. tchr. Iowa. Music instr. Sheffield-Chapin Cmty. Sch., Iowa, 1978—98, 2001—, substitute tchr., 1998—2000, spl. edn. asst., 2000—01; music instr. Meservey-Thornton Cmty. Sch., Thornton, Iowa, 2002—. Organist Zion St. John Luth. Ch., Sheffield, 1978—, adult choir dir., 1982—; accompanist, dir. Philharm. Music Cmty. Group, Sheffield. Participant Relay for Life event Am. Cancer Soc., Sheffield, 2006. Mem.: NEA, Sheffield-Chapin Edn. Assn. (pres. 1997—98), Am. Choral Dirs. Assn. Avocations: travel, cats, concerts. Office: Sheffield-Chapin Sch 5th and Park Sts Sheffield IA 50475 also: Meservey-Thornton Sch 110 N 5th St Thornton IA 50479

HEMMASI, HARRIETTE ANN, university librarian; b. Sherman, Tex., July 10, 1947; d. John Melvin and Evelyn Mae (Walden) Hall; 1 child, Farzaneh. MusB, Baylor U., 1965; MusM, Ind. U., 1971; M Libr Info Sci, U. Calif., Berkeley, 1989. Instr. music Shiraz U., Iran, 1972-80; libr. asst. Humboldt State U., Arcata, Calif., 1984-87; libr. asst. music libr. U. Calif.,

Berkeley, 1988-89; head tech. svcs. music libr. Rutgers U., New Brunswick, NJ, 1989—98, interim assoc. univ. libr. tech. and automated svcs., 1998—2000; dean of libraries Ind. U., Bloomington, 2003—05; univ. libr. Brown U., Providence, 2005—. Adj. instr. Rutgers U., New Brunswick, 1991-92; dir. Music Thesaurus Project at Rutgers U., New Brunswick, 1991—. Contbr. articles to profl. jours., chpt. to book. Vol. Am. Diabetes Assn., Highland Park, N.J., 1993; mem. Cantabile Chorus, Bound Brook, N.J., 1992. Recipient State Merit award State of Calif., 1987. Coop. Rsch. Grant Coun. Libr. Resources, 1991-92. Mem. ALA (subcom. on Music Thesaurus Project 1993—), Music Libr. Assn. (chair subject access subcom. 1988-93, Gerboth award 1993). Avocations: singing, piano playing, walking, reading. Office: Brown U Univ Libr Providence RI 02912 Office Phone: 401-863-2162. E-mail: Harriette_Hemmasi@brown.edu.*

HEMMINGER, PAMELA LYNN, lawyer; b. Chgo., June 29, 1949; d. Paul Willis and Lenore Adelaide (Hennig) H.; m. Robert Alan Miller, May 14, 1979; children: Kimberly Anne, Jeffrey Ryan, Eric Douglas. BA, Pomona Coll., 1971; JD, Pepperdine U., 1976. Tchr. Etiwanda (Calif.) Sch. dist., 1971-74; law clerk Gibson Dunn & Crutcher, Newport Beach, Calif., 1974-76, assoc. L.A., 1976-84, ptnr., 1985—. Contbg. author Sexual Harassment, 1992, Employment Discrimination Law, 3d edit. and supplements, 1996, Employment Litigation, Calif. Practice Guide; contbr. articles to profl. jours. Mem. Comparable Worth Task Force Calif., Sacramento, 1984, Pepperdine U. Sch. of Law Bd. Visitors, 1990—, Calif. Law Revision Commn., 1998-99, 2005-; mem., bd. dirs. Dispute Resolution Svcs., 1998—. Named alumnus of yr. Pepperdine Sch. Law, 1996; listed in Best Lawyers in Am., 1998--. Mem. L.A. County Bar Assn. (chair, labor and employment sect. 1996-97), Calif. C. of C. (employment rels. com. 1984—). Republican. Lutheran. Office: Gibson Dunn & Crutcher Ste 4921 333 S Grand Ave Los Angeles CA 90071-3197

HEMMINGS, DIANNE SMITH, artist, educator; b. Beaufort, SC, June 7, 1956; d. Med Cleveland and Neva M. Smith; m. Paul Hemmings, Nov. 25, 1989; children: Jennifer Loren Pitts, Jason Keith Pitts. AA, Gordon Coll., Barnesville, Ga., 1990; MusB, Columbus (Ga.) State U., 1994, MusM in Edn., 1995. Music tchr. Lamar County Bd. Edn., Barnesville, 1996—98, Beaufort County Bd. Edn., SC, 1998—2005; tchg. artist Beaufort, 2005—. Named Tchr. of Yr., Lamar County Elem. Sch., 1998, Beaufort Elem., 2002—03. Mem.: SC Alliance for Arts Edn., Music Educators Nat. Conf., Kappi Delta Pi. Personal E-mail: dshemmings@journeyintorhythm.org.

HEMMINGS, MADELEINE BLANCHET, management consultant, not-for-profit administrator, media consultant; b. Bryn Mawr, Pa., Aug. 14, 1942; d. Wilfred Loyola and Feroline (Sissenere) Blanchet; m. Richard B. Hemmings, Mar. 14, 1970; 1 child, Laurie Cornwall Hemmings Stull. Cert. in lang. and linguistics, U. Fribourg, Switzerland, 1961; BS in Indsl. and Labor Rels., Cornell U., 1976. Owner Hallmark Pers. of Pa., Harrisburg, Pa., 1964-70; assoc. dir. human resources Cornell U., Ithaca, NY, 1972-77; policy dir. employee benefits NAM, Washington, 1977-79; policy dir. edn., employment and tng. C. of C. U.S., Washington, 1979-83; v.p. policy Nat. Alliance Bus., Washington, 1983-85; pres. W.Va. Roundtable, Charleston, 1985—96; exec. dir. Nat. Assn. State Dirs. Careers Tech. Edn., Washington, 1987-96; mng. dir. Nat. Telelearning Network, Inc., Washington, 1996-98; pres. Hemmings Assocs., Inc., 1998—2002; grants coord. Wayne-Finger Lakes Bd. of Coop. Edn. Svcs., Newark, NY, 2002—. Select adv. com. to asst. sec. edn., 1989—93; pres. adv. com. Fed. Office Vocat. Edn. Performance Stds., 1992—95; adv. bd. Ctr. Edn. and Work, U. Wis., 1992—96, Nat. Ctr. Rsch. Vocat. Edn., Berkeley, Calif., 1993—96. Author: (book) The New Job Training Partnership Act, 1982, Economic Development Plan, State of West Virginia, 1987, Education for a Working America, 1994, (newsletter) The Techocrat, 1988—95. Exec. dir. Nat. Vocat. Tech. Edn. Found., 1987—96; campaign mgr. Connie Cook for Congress, Ithaca, 1984; sponsor U.S. Pony Club, Olney, Md., 1987—96. Mem.: Greater Washington Soc. Assn. Execs. (chief exec. coun. 1989—98), U.S. C. of C. (edn. com. 1987—96), Cornell Pres.' Club. Avocations: thoroughbred breeding and racing, combined training, painting. Home: 111 Lea Dr Newark NY 14513 Office: Wayne-FInger Lakes BOCES 131 Drumlin Ct Newark NY 14513 Fax: 301-570-9104. Office Phone: 315-332-7379. E-mail: mhemmings@wflboces.org.

HEMMINGSEN, BARBARA BRUFF, retired microbiologist; b. Whittier, Calif., Mar. 25, 1941; d. Stephen Cartland and Susanna Jane Bruff; m. Edvard Alfred Hemmingsen, Aug. 5, 1967; 1 child, Grete. BA, U. Calif., Berkeley, 1962, MA, 1964; PhD, U. Calif., San Diego, 1971. Lectr. San Diego State U., 1973-77, asst. prof., 1977-81, assoc. prof., 1981-88, prof., 1988—2004; ret., 2004. Vis. asst. prof. Aarhus U., Denmark, 1971—72; cons. AMBIS, Inc., San Diego, 1984—85, Woodward-Clyde Cons., 1985, 1987—91, Novatron, Inc., 2000—06. Author (with others): (book) Microbial Ecology, 1972; contbr. articles to profl. jours. Mem. Planned Parenthood, San Diego. Mem.: AAAS, San Diego Assn. Rational Inquiry (sec. 1998—2001, treas. 2002—), Am. Women Sci., Am. Soc. Microbiology, Phi Beta Kappa (corr. sec. Nu chpt. Calif. 1994—2002, past pres., historian 2003—), Sigma Xi. Democrat.

HEMPERLY, REBECCA SUE, publishing manager; b. Reading, Pa., June 17, 1966; d. Kenneth Jay and Ann Rebecca (Riehl) H. BA, Wheaton Coll., 1988; MA, Emerson Coll., 1992. Editl. asst. Coll.-Hill Press/Little, Brown, Boston, 1988-90, Little, Brown and Co., Boston, 1990, contracts coord., 1990-92, asst. mgr. contracts, 1992-96, mgr. contracts, 1996-98; paralegal WGBH Ednl. Found., Boston, 1998-99, pub. contracts cons., 1998-99, v.p. client svcs., 2000; client svcs. mgr. Database Pub. Group, Cambridge, Mass., 1999-2000; contracts mgr. Candlewick Press, Cambridge, 2000—05, contracts dir., 2006—. Del. 1st Amendment Congress, 1997; spkr. rights and permissions Assn. Am. Pub., Washington, 1996; mem. diversity task force Little, Brown and Co., Boston, 1993-98. Contbr. essays: The Book Group Book, 3d edit., 2000, Teaching Contemporary Theory to Undergraduates, 1995. Team capt. AIDS walk-a-thon Little, Brown and Co./AIDS Action Com., Boston, 1995-97; phone coord. GLOW, Watertown, Mass., 1989-98; mem. Rails to Trails Conservancy, 1995—. Mem. Women in Publishing, Nat. Writers' Union, Bookbuilders of Boston, Phi Beta Kappa (scholar 1988). Avocations: gardening, bicycling, Karate, photography.

HEMPFLING, LINDA LEE, nurse; b. Indpls., July 28, 1947; d. Paul Roy and Myrtle Pearl (Ward) H. Diploma, Meth. Hosp. Ind. Sch. Nursing, 1968; postgrad., St. Joseph's Coll. Cert. med. audit specialist, 2000. Charge nurse Meth. Hosp., Indpls., 1968; staff nurse operating rm. Silver Cross Hosp., Joliet, Ill., 1969; charge nurse oper. rm. Huntington (NY) Hosp., 1969-73; night supr. oper. rm., post anesthesia care unit Hermann Hosp., Houston, 1973-76, unit mgr., purchasing coord. oper. rms., 1976-83; RN med. auditor, quality improvement, tng. coord. Nat. Healthcare Rev., Inc., Houston, 1984—98; RN med. auditor Per Se Technologies, 1999—. Future Nurses Am. scholar, 1965, Nat. Merit scholar, 1965. Mem.: Am. Assn. Med. Audit Specialists, Tex. Med. Auditors Assn., Assn. PeriOperative Registered Nurses. Office: 9401 SW Freeway # 631B Houston TX 77074

HEMPLEMAN, BARBARA FLORENCE, archivist; b. Bellevue, Pa., Mar. 3, 1925; d. Warren Wilson and Florence Permelia (Firth) Hampe; m. David William Hempleman, Aug. 4, 1956; children: Warwick, Terence. BA, Coll. of Wooster, 1947; MA, NYU, 1953; MLS, Atlanta U., 1973. Dir. Christian edn. Calvary Reformed Ch., Reading, Pa., 1951-52; libr. asst. Duke U., Durham, N.C., 1957-59; asst. prof. history Warren Wilson Coll., Asheville, N.C., 1948-51, 54-56, 66-69, libr. dir., 1978-86, archivist, 1986-98, adj. prof. women's history, 1983-96; vis. prof. libr. sci. Emory U., Atlanta, 1973-74; adj. prof. libr. sci. Atlanta U., 1973, 78, reference libr., 1974-78. Contbr. numerous articles to Owl and Spade mag. Bd. dirs. YWCA, Asheville, 1978-79; libr. developer, adminstr. Black Mountain (N.C.) Correctional Ctr. for Women, 1997—. Nat. Assn. Fgn. Student Affairs grantee, 1975. Mem. Women's History Club Asheville (historian 1996—). Democrat. Presbyterian. Avocations: travel, reading. Personal E-mail: firthhampe@aol.com.

HENARD, ELIZABETH ANN, controller; b. Providence, Oct. 9, 1947; d. Anthony Joseph and Grace Johanna (Lokay) Zorbach; m. Patrick Edward Mann, Dec. 18, 1970 (div. July 1972); m. John Bruce Henard Jr., Oct. 19, 1974; children: Scott Michael, Christopher Andrew. Student, Jacksonville U., Fla., 1966. Sec. So. Bell Tel. & Tel., Jacksonville, 1964-69; office mgr. Gunther F. Reis Assocs., Tampa, Fla., 1969-71; exec. sec. Ernst & Ernst, Tampa, 1971-72; exec. sec. to pres. Lamalie Assocs., Tampa, 1972-74; exec. sec. Arthur Young & Co., Chgo., 1975; adminstrv. asst. Irving J. Markin, Chgo., 1975; contr., v.p., corp. sec. Henard Assocs., Inc., Dallas, 1983-92; realtor Coldwell Banker Residential Real Estate, Tampa, 1999—; contr. Meridian Ptnrs., Tampa, 2003—. Mem. Dallas Investors Group (treas. 1986-91), Tampa Palms Country Club. Republican. Roman Catholic. Avocations: photography, crafts, golf, reading. Home: 5014 Wesley Dr Tampa FL 33647-1375 E-mail: eahenard@aol.com.

HENCE, JANE KNIGHT, interior designer; b. Pitts., June 27, 1937; d. Luther and Doris (Ayers) Knight; m. Carleton Campbell Hence, May 12, 1962 (div. 1975); children: Kyle Fitz-Randolph Hence, Maxson Bentley Hence, Juliellen Hence Casey. Grad., Emma Willard Sch., Troy, N.Y., 1955; student, Skidmore Coll., Saratoga Springs, N.Y., 1955—58; Grad., Traphagen Sch. of Design, N.Y.C., 1960; student, Yale U., 1986—90, R.I. Sch. of Design, 1988—90. Owner various bus. ventures including Bed and Breakfast, catering bus., free-lance interior design, 1982—; owner, prin. JKH Design, 1989—; consulting assoc. and designer Michael McKinley & Assocs., Stonington, Conn., 1993—2001. Mem. Westerly Sch. Facilities Com., Westerly, R.I., 1993-96, Westerly Sch. Bldg. Com., 1992-93; mem. Bd. S.E. Mus., Brewster, N.Y., 1970-74; photographer, interviewer Green Light, Newport Designer over 50 bldgs., renovations and additions in New Eng.; co-designer overn 40 bldgs. in R.I. and Conn.; interior designer, 1998—; painter various media in collections in Midwest, South, N.Y. and New Eng.; photographer, interviewer Green Light Quar. bulletin, Newport. Alt. Westerly Zoning Bd., RI, 2000—02. Avocations: travel, reading, opera, theater. Home and Office: 73 Washington St Newport RI 02840-1533 Office Phone: 401-847-3767. Personal E-mail: rockbound@earthlink.net.

HENDERSHOTT, ANNA LORRAINE, educational director; d. Luis Aguirre Cordova and Hortensia Petra Warner, William Alfred Warner (Stepfather); m. David Anthony Hendershott, May 12, 1979; children: David William, Jeffrey Alexander, Julie Anna. BS in Elem. Edn. and Spanish, Grand Canyon U., 1979; MA in Ednl. Leadership, No. Ariz. U., 1997. Tchg. cert. Ariz. Dept. Edn., supervisor cert. Ariz. Dept. Edn., adminstrv. cert. Ariz. Dept. Edn. Bilingual and ESL tchr. Peoria (Ariz.) Unified Sch. Dist., 1980—96, staff devel. specialist, 1994—96, instrnl. program specialist, 1996—98; lang. acquisition dir. Paradise Valley Unified Sch. Dist., Phoenix, 1998—, title VII project devel. and implementation grant dir., 1999—2002. Refugee grant dir. Paradise Valley Unified Sch. Dist., Phoenix, 1999—, grant dir. Indian edn., 2000—; Peoria power play writing and drama project Peoria Unified Sch. Dist., 1995—98; mem. adj. faculty grad. edn. in tchr. edn. Ariz. State U. West, Phoenix, 1997—98; mem. adj. factulty grad. edn. in gifted edn. Ottawa U., Phoenix, 1999—2000; mem. adj. faculty grad. edn. in ESL, gifted edn. and math. Chapman U., Phoenix, 2002—04. Recipient Pride of Peoria Outstanding Employee of Yr. award, Peoria Unified Sch. Dist., 1996; grantee, U.S. Dept. Edn., 1999—2002, 2000—03, 2001—04, 2001—04; scholar, Grand Canyon U., 1975—79, Concordia U., Lang. Villages Tchr. Seminar, Peoria Unified Sch. Dist., 1998. Mem.: Ctrl. Ariz. Bilingual Consortium (pres. elect 2001—02), Ariz. Assn. for Gifted and Talented (bd. dirs. 1998—2005, conf. chair 2001—03, pres. elect 2003—03, pres. 2004—04), Nat. Assn. for Gifted Child, Nat. Staff Devel. Coun., Assn. for Supervision and Curriculum Devel., Ariz. Dept. Edn. Structured English Immersion Task Force (rep. 2003—04), Ctrl. Ariz. Bilingual Consortium (pres. 2003—04), ELL Connections (founding mem. 2004—05), Learning Connections Consortium, Interclub Coun. Ariz. (del. 1989—96), Delta Kappa Gamma (parliamentarian 1989—91, pres. 1992—94, v.p. 1987—89). Republican. Roman Catholic. Avocations: ballet folklorico, painting, crafts, sewing, reading.

HENDERSHOTT LOVE, ARLES JUNE, marketing professional; b. Rockford, Ill., Oct. 22, 1956; d. Eugene Bourden and Rose Marie (Erickson) Hendershott; m. Joseph William Love, Sept. 20, 1986. BS with high honors, Ill. State U., Normal, 1979; postgrad., U. Mo., Columbia, 1992. Reporter Sta. WTVO-TV, Rockford, 1979-82, news prodr., 1982-83; news assignment editor Sta. WIFR-TV, Rockford, 1983-86, news dir., 1986-97; dir. cmty. rels. Benedek Broadcasting Corp./WIFR-TV, 1997—2004; dir. resource devel. Milestone, Inc., 2005—. Speaker Rockford Pub. Schs., 1980-83, 97—. Producer news story Pee Wee Explosion, 1985 (AP award 1986). Bd. dirs. Rockford Airshow, 1994-95; mem. com. YWCA, Rockford, 1987, Westminister Presbyn. Ch., Rockford, also tchr. Sunday Sch., 1983-2000; bd. dirs. No. Ill. chpt. March of Dimes, 1980-84, NW Ill. chpt. Spl. Olympics, Rockford, 1986-2004, Discovery Ctr. Mus., Rockford, 1987-90, N.W. Ill. Alzheimer & Related Disorder Assn., 1991, Rockford CrimeStoppers, 1992—; active YWCA Leader Luncheon Coun., 1992-93, leader Lunch Coun., 1994-95; bd. dirs. YWCA Rockford, 1997-99, Am. Lung Assn. Winnebago County, 1997-05, Rockford Boys and Girls Club, 1997—; pres. bd. dirs. Am. Hearth Assn. Winnebago County 1999-2002, bd. dirs. 1997-2002. Recipient Leadership award Ken-Rock Cmty. Ctr., Rockford, 1980, Presdl. award of honor Rockford Jaycees, 1986, Dist. award Zonta Pub. Rels. Campaign, 1990, Leader Luncheon award YWCA, 1991, Recognize the Abilities Cmty. Svc. award, 1999, Congl. Cert. for Cmty. Svc., 1999, Midwest Affiliate Am. Heart Assn. Spl. Heart award, 1999, Crimestopper of Yr. award Rockford, 1996, 2000, Disting. Svc. award Am. Heart Assn., 2000, award of merit Ill. Pub. Health Assn., 2000, Kiwanis Touch A Life award, 2003. Mem. AAUW (bd. dirs. 1982-84), NAFE, Radio-TV News Dirs. Assn. (TV state coord. for Ill. 1989-96), Ill. News Broadcasters Assn., Soc. Profl. Journalists, Am. Mgmt. Assn., Archeology Inst. Am., Rockford C. of C. (pres. club 1993-05, public policy com. 1997—, amb. 1997—), Univ. Chgo. Oriental Inst., Ill. Assoc. Press (exec. com. 1989—, pres.-elect 1990, pres. 1991), Lens & Shutter Club (pres. 1983-85, others), Zonta. Avocations: travel, photography. Office: Milestone Inc 4450 N Rockton Rockford IL 61103 Business E-Mail: arles@milestone-inc.org. E-mail: jwl-ajh@worldnet.att.net.

HENDERSON, ALMA, religious studies educator; b. Milw., Mar. 19, 1920; d. Gotthieb and Matilda (Zielke) Siewert; m. George Henderson, Sept. 28, 1946 (dec. May 1997); adopted many African and Chinese young people. Grad., Flight Sch., 1945; BA, Tocoa Falls Coll., 1946; MA, U. Ga., 1973. Missionary tchr. N.Am. Bapt., Cameroon, West Africa, 1947-70; tchr. Athens (Ga.) Christian Sch., 1973-83, U. Ga., Athens, 1983-99. Baptist. Avocations: african and chinese culture, foreign student affairs, theological studies.

HENDERSON, CONNIE CHORLTON, retired city planner, artist, writer; b. Cedar Rapids, Iowa, July 16, 1944; d. Robert Brown and Lorraine Madeline (Marquardt) Chorlton; m. Dwight Franklin Henderson, Dec. 24, 1966; 1 child, Patricia BA, Anderson U., 1966; MA Edn., St. Francis Coll., Ft. Wayne, Ind., 1972; MPA, U. Tex. San Antonio, 1987. Art coord. Ft. Wayne Cmty. Schs., 1966—67; tchr. art East Allen County Schs., New Haven, Ind., 1968—71, 1974—79; instr. Manchester Coll., North Manchester, Ind., 1971—72; rsch. assoc. Tremar Real Estate Rsch., San Antonio, 1983—84; vol. planning asst. City of San Antonio, 1985—88, planner I, 1988—89, project mgmt. specialist, 1990, coord. conservation edn., 1990—91; planner II San Antonio Water Sys., 1991—96, 2003—, coord. water edn., 1996—97, coord. spl. events., 1998—2002; youth edn. specialist, 2003—05; coord. spl. events, 2006; ret., 2006. Docent (vol.) San Antonio Mus. Assn.; rsch. mgr. N. San Antonio C. of C., 1988 Artist: numerous paintings and fiber sculptures in juried and invitational shows, 1966-80; poetess: (2d prize Iowa Poetry Day Assn., 1961) Bd. dirs. Tex. Soc. to Prevent Blindness, San Antonio, 1981-83; v.p. U. Tex. at San Antonio Women's Club, 1981-82, pres. 1983-84; mem. San Antonio Conservation Soc., 1985—, mem. Assistance League of San Antonio, 1988—, liason Thrift House, San Antonio, 1995-96; co-pres. River Gardens Family and Friends, 1993-94, sec., 1995-96; sec. Rebuilding Together San Antonio, 2005-2006 Mem. Am. Planning Assn. (cert. planner, asst. dir. San Antonio sect. 1990, dir., 1991-93), U. Tex. San Antonio Alumni Assn Avocations: travel, reading, landscape design, swimming, music. Home: 18222 Redriver Sky San Antonio TX 78259 Office Phone: 210-233-3634. Business E-Mail: chenderson@saws.org.

HENDERSON, CYNTHIA, medical librarian; d. Donald and Frances Henderson. BS in Ednl. Psychology cum laude, Alcorn State U., 1987; MS in Info. and Libr. Sci., U. Mich., 1991. Asst. prof. Iowa State U., Ames, 1991—92; asst. dir. libr. svcs. Charles R. Drew U. Medicine and Sci., L.A., 1992—95; asst. prof. U. Ill., Chgo., 1995—97; dir. John A. Graziano Meml. Libr. Samuel Merritt Coll., Oakland, Calif., 1997—2000; asst. prof. health and human sciences program Samuel Merritt Coll., 1997—2000; dep. dir. multi-media ctr. academic med. libr. Morehouse Sch. Medicine, Atlanta, 2000—04, dir. multi-media ctr. academic med. libr., 2004—. Spl. collections and collections devel. libr. Iowa State U., Ames, 1991—92; health sciences libr. U. Ill., Urbana, 1995—97; reviewer Jour. AMA. Contbr. articles to Bull. Med. Libr. Assn. Mem.: Med. Libr. Assn. Mem. Ame Ch. Avocations: reading, writing, cooking, dancing, sewing. Office: Morehous Schole Medicine 202 Rotherhithe Ln Nw Marietta GA 30066-3492 Office Phone: 404-752-1531. Office Fax: 404-752-1049. E-mail: chenderson@msm.edu.

HENDERSON, CYNTHIA ANNE, theater educator, actress; b. Mobile, Ala., May 11, 1966; d. Geraldine D. P. Henderson and Bobbie R. Henderson, Sr.; 1 child, Justin C. Baldessare. BS, Troy State U., 1994; MFA, Pa. State U., 1997. Asst. prof. Ithaca (N.Y.) Coll., 1999—. Actor: stage, film and TV (Best Supporting Actress in Musical, European Tournament of Plays, 1991). Demonstrator, Washington, 2003. Fulbright Scholar, CIES - Fulbright, 2003—. Mem.: Actor's Equity Assn. Avocations: hiking, camping, poetry, pastels, travel. Office: Ithaca Coll Dept Theatre 201 Dillingham Ctr Ithaca NY 14850 Personal E-mail: chenderson@ithaca.edu.

HENDERSON, DEIRDRE HEALY, foundation administrator; b. Chgo., Nov. 10, 1942; d. Laurin Hall and Patricia (Kelly) H.; m. Duncan Yeandle, Sept. 27, 1969; children: Allison Dow, Duncan Dylan. AA, Briarcliff Coll., 1962; BA, Conn. Coll., New London, 1964. Editorial asst. Commerce Clearing House, San Francisco, 1964-65; tchr. Harris Sch., Chgo., 1966-67; stockbroker Dominick and Dominick, E.F. Hutton, Chgo., 1968-70; ptnr. Park West Interiors, Chgo., 1976-88; founder, pres. Franklin and Copley, Ltd., Chgo., 1987-98; coord. gun control com. San Francisco Gen. Hosp. Trauma Found., 1998—. V.p., bd. mem., Com. for Handgun Control, Chgo., 1976-84, organizer G.A. Ranney for U.S. Senate, Donald Haider for Mayor, Chgo., 1985-87. Mem. events com Coro No. Calif., 1997—, San Francisco Gen. Hosp. Found., 1998—2000; trustee Chgo. Hist. Soc., 1990—93, Westover Sch., Middlebury, Conn., 1990—96; officer, bd. dirs. Women's Bd. Rehab. Inst., Chgo., 1073—1985, Women's Bd. Rush-Presbyn., St. Luke's Hosp., Chgo, 1973—84; mem. steering com. U. Chgo. Women's Bd., Field Mus. Women's Bd., 1989—93, Antiquarian Soc. of the Art Inst.; mem. bd. dir. The Trauma Found., San Francisco, 2003—; devel. com. bd. dir. The Bell Campaign; bd. trustees Penobscot Marine Mus., Searsport, Maine, 1998—, officer, 2001—; bd. dir. Coro No. Calif., 2000—02. Mem. Chgo. Hist. Soc. Guild (officer, bd. dirs., chmn. 1985-93), Chgo. Acad. of Scis. (bd. dirs. 1984-93), Chgo. Found. for Edn. (bd. dirs. 1985-92), Friends of Lincoln Park (bd. dirs. 1985-92), Seven Seas Cruising Assn. (transatlantic sailor), Woman's Athletic Club (officer bd. dirs. 1975-81), Friday Club (officer bd. dirs. 1985-91), Children's Theatre Assn. (bd. dirs. 2000-02), Calif. Tennis Club, San Francisco Golf Club. Episcopalian. Avocations: tennis, sailing, golf, photography, biking.

HENDERSON, DONA LEE, mathematics educator; b. Columbus, Nebr., May 27, 1951; d. Jerome and Dorothy Mae (Heibel) Luckey; divorced; children: Jennifer, Lori. BS, Kearney State Coll., 1972, MS, 1977; postgrad., Okla. State U., 1986-88; EdD, U. S.D., 1995. Instr., math. Kearney State Coll., SD, 1978-83, U. S.D., Vermillion, 1983—86, 1988—95, McCook CC, Nebr., 1995—. Asst. leader, Girl Scouts Am., Vermillion, 1985, 86, 88—. Mem. Nat. Coun. Tchrs. Math., Math. Assn. Am., S.D. Coun. Tchrs. Math.

HENDERSON, E. SUZANNE, elementary school educator; b. Champaign, Ill., Nov. 18, 1947; d. Donald Albert Fackler and Fiana B. Warfel Hardig; m. William Arthur Henderson, Aug. 17, 1968; children: Holly Janel, Rachel Eileen. BS, So. Ill. U., 1968; MEd, U. Ill., 1976. Tchr. grade 4 Pulaski County Spl. Sch. Dist., Jacksonville, Ark., 1968-70; tchr. grade 5 Tuscola Cmty. Unit Sch. Dist., Tuscola, Ill., 1970—. Recipient Presdl. Award for Excellence in Teaching of Math. and Sci., 1994. Mem. NEA, Ill. Edn. Assn., Tuscola Edn. Assn. (v.p. 1994-95), Nat. Coun. Tchrs. Math., Ill. Coun. Tchrs. Math. Avocations: flower gardening, golf. Home: 105 E Scott St Tuscola IL 61953-1834 Office: Tuscola Sch Dist 409 S Prairie St Tuscola IL 61953-1770 Business E-Mail: shenderson@net66.com.

HENDERSON, ELMA MAE, singer, composer, educator, dancer, actress; b. St. Louis, Mo., Jan. 6, 1928; d. Elliott Brian and Wilma Marie Henderson; m. David A. Donnan, 1950 (div. 1963); children: David E. Donnan, Laurel E. Slater, Linda Anne Jessop, Rollin A. Donnan. MusB, U. Ariz., 1949, MusM, 1950, Cert. in Secondary Edn., 1964; Cert. in Elem. Edn., Ariz. State U., 1965. Cert. Calif. Life Credential 1966, Calif. Basic Ednl. Skills Test 2000. Tchr. Nev., Ariz. Calif. Schs., 1961—2005; self employed music tchr. Elma Mae's Music Studio, Redlands and Stockton, Calif., 1989—; nursing asst. Loma Linda (Calif.) U. Med. Ctr., 1971—73; childcare attendent, tchr. YMCA Faith Luth. Cypress, Redlands, Calif., 1980—89; house dir. Residential Life and Housting U. Pacific, Stockton, 1996—99; instr., prescriber Sylvan Learning Ctr., 2003—. Performer, singer Stockton Chorale, Prelude Ensemble; singer, dancer, actress Stockton Civic Theatre. Composer: (music books) In the Beginning Books 1 and 2, 1990; actor: (Operas) Carmen, Hansel and Gretel, Little Red Riding Hood, The Marriage of Figaro, Amahl and the Night Visitors, (musicals) My Fair Lady, Kiss me Kate, Annie Get Your Gun, Sound of Music, Footloose, Here's Love, Music Man, Guys and Dolls, Anything Goes; contbr. articles to profl. jours. Performer Sunflower Entertainers Stockton Retirement Facilities, 1999—; singer, performer Stockton Civic Theatre, 2000—03; singer, section leader, libr. Chorale, 2004—. Recipient Pres. Recognition award, Stockton Chorale, 2004, St. Louis Symphony Soc. Young Artist Competition. Mem.: Phi Kappa Phi, Internat. Music Fraternity, Alpha Phi (Panhellenic pres. 1949—50, v.p., pledge trainer), Mu Phi Epsilon (1st. v.p. 1998—2003). Independent. Home: 1222 Stratford Cir #110 Stockton CA 95207 Office: Sylvan Learning Ctr 6385 Pacific Ave Stockton CA 95207 Office Phone: 209-477-7720. E-mail: emsmusic@sbcglobal.net.

HENDERSON, ERIN F., lawyer; b. 1969; BA, Williams Wood Coll., 1991; JD, Villanova U., 1995. Bar: Pa., NJ. Law clk. to Hon. Linda Wallach Miller Ct. of Common Pleas, Monroe County, Pa., 1995—96; assoc. Rawle & Henderson LLP, Phila. Lectr. in field. Office: Rawle & Henderson LLP Widener Bldg One S Penn Sq Philadelphia PA 19107 Office Phone: 215-575-4311. Office Fax: 215-563-2583. E-mail: ehenderson@rawle.com.*

HENDERSON, FLORENCE, actress, singer; b. Dale, Ind., Feb. 14, 1934; d. Joseph and Elizabeth Elder H.; m. Ira Bernstein, Jan. 9, 1956 (div.); children: Barbara, Joey, Robert Norman, Elizabeth; m. John Kappas, Aug. 4, 1987. Attended, St. Francis Acad., Owensboro, Ky; studied at, Am. Acad. Dramatic Arts. Broadway and stage debut in Wish You Were Here, 1952; on tour in Oklahoma!, 1952-53, at N.Y.C. Ctr., 1953, Fanny, 1954, The Sound of Music, 1961, in revival of Annie Get Your Gun, 1974; appeared in The Great Waltz, Los Angeles Civic Light Opera Assn., 1953, on Broadway in The Girl Who Came to Supper, 1963, in revival of South Pacific, 1967, in revival The Sound of Music, Los Angeles Civic Light Opera Assn., 1978, Bells are Ringing, Los Angeles Civic Light Opera Assn., 1979; appeared in Oldsmobile indsl. shows, 1958-61; actress: (movies) Song of Norway, 1970, Shakes The Clown, 1991, Naked Gun 33 1/2: The Final Insult, 1994, The Brady Bunch Movie, 1995, Holy Man, 1998, Get Bruce, 1999; appeared on TV in Sing Along, 1958, The Today Show, 1959-60, The Brady Bunch, 1969-74, The Brady Bunch Hour, 1977, The Brady Girls Get Married, 1981, A Very Brady Christmas, 1988, The Bradys, 1990, Fudge-A-Mania, 1995, (host) Bradymania, 1993; numerous other TV appearances include The Love Boat, 1976, 83, The Brady Brides, 1981, Hart to Hart, 1981, Fantasy Island, 1981, 83, Alice, 1983, Murder She Wrote, Dean Martin TV Series; hostess Country Kitchen; appeared in TV spl. Just a Regular Kid; guest appearances It's Garry Shandling's Show, Wil Shriner Show, Jay Leno Family Spl.; first female host of The Tonight Show; co-host: Later Today, 1999-2000; writings, A Little Cooking, A Little Talking, and A Whole Lotta Fun; films include: Speaking of Women's Health, Lifetime. Recipient Sarah Siddons award Office: Don Buchwald and Assoc 6500 Wilshire Blvd Ste 2200 Los Angeles CA 90048 Office Phone: 310-479-0612. E-mail: askflo@flohome.com.

HENDERSON, FRANCES J., lawyer; b. Glasgow, Scotland, Feb. 17, 1957; LLB with honors, U. Glasgow, Scotland, 1978; LLM, U. Va., 1979; JD, U. Minn., 1984. Bar: DC 1985. Of counsel Graham & James, Washington; ptnr. Sonnenschein Nath & Rosenthal, Washington, 1998—. Office: Sonnenschein Nath & Rosenthal LLP Ste 600, E Tower 1301 K St NW Washington DC 20005 Office Phone: 202-408-6357. Office Fax: 202-408-6399. Business E-Mail: fhenderson@sonnenschein.com.

HENDERSON, GLADYS EDITH, retired social welfare examiner; b. Black River, N.Y., Jan. 17, 1928; d. Lynn Bruce and Ina Marion (Carey) Scott; m. Vern V. Leeder, May 4, 1947 (dec. Oct. 1950); children: Linda Leeder McCarthy, Thomas Leon. AS in Criminal Justice, Jefferson C.C., 1977; BA in Pub. Justice, SUNY, Oswego, 1979. Sec.-receptionist Delavan Warehouse, Syracuse, N.Y., 1968-69; self employed cosmetologist Black River, 1970-74; receptionist N.Y. State DEC, Watertown, 1979-80; social welfare examiner Jefferson County Dept. Social Svcs., Watertown, 1980-90, ret., 1990. Author of poetry. Mem. Civil Svc. Employees Assn., Watertown, 1980—, sec., 1986—89; treas. ladies' group Watertown Bapt. Temple, 1993—97. Recipient Pres.' award for lit. excellence Nat. Authors Registry, 1996, 98, 2000; inductee Internat. Poetry Hall of Fame, www.poetry.com. Mem.: Black River Valley's Writers Club. Republican. Avocations: antiques and collectibles, crochet, embroidery, writing. Home: 432 Glenn Ave Watertown NY 13601-1825

HENDERSON, HARRIET, librarian, director; b. Pampa, Tex., Nov. 19, 1949; d. Ervin Leon and Hannah Elizabeth (Yoe) H. AB, Baker U., 1971; MLS, U. Tex., 1973. Sch. libr. Pub. Sch. Sys., Pampa, 1971-72; city libr. City of Tyler, Tex., 1973-80, City of Newport News, Va., 1980-84, dir. librs. and info. svcs. Va., 1984-90; dir. Louisville Free Pub. Libr., 1990-97, Montgomery County (Md.) Pub. Librs., 1997—2005, Richmond Pub. Libr., Va., 2005—. Del. White House Conf. Librs. and Info. Svcs., 1991; mem. Leadership Louisville, 1991—97, Alliant Health Sys. Adult Oper. Bd., 1991—97; mem. adv. com. dept. edn. Spalding U., 1991—95; mem. Md. Adv. Coun. on Librs., 2001—05; diaconate Hiddenwood Presbyn. Ch., Newport News, 1983—85; bd. dirs. Tex. Libr. Sys. Act adv. bd., 1979—80, Peninsula Women's Network, Newport News, 1983—85. Recipient Tribute to Women in Bus. and Industry, Peninsula YWCA, Newport News, 1984. Mem.: ALA (councillor 2001—05), Pub. Libr. Assn. (v.p. 1998, pres. 1999), Va. Libr. Assn. (chmn. legis. com. 1981—84, v.p. 1985, pres. 1986), Ky. Libr. Assn. (chair pub. libr. sect. 1995, Outstanding Pub. Libr. Svc. award 1997). Office: Richmond Pub Libr 101 E Franklin St Richmond VA 23219

HENDERSON, HAZEL, economist, writer; b. Bristol, Somerset, U.K., Mar. 27, 1933; arrived in US, 1957, naturalized, 1962; d. Kenneth and Dorothy May (Jesseman) Mustard; m. Carter Henderson (div. 1981); 1 child, Alexandra Leslie Camille Henderson Cassidy; m. Alan F. Kay, 1996 Baccalaureate, Clifton Sch., Bristol, U.K., 1950; ScD hon., Worcester Poly. Inst., Mass., 1975; ScD (hon.), Soka U., Tokyo, 2000, U. San Francisco, 2001. Freelance writer, various locations, 1967—. Vis. regent's lectr. U. Calif., Santa Barbara, 1979, Horace Albright chair dept. forestry, Berkeley, 82; advisor Calvert Social Investment Funds, 1982—2005; ptnr. Calvert-Henderson Quality of Life Indicators, 2000—; internat. adv. bd. Inst. Ethos, São Paulo, Brazil; dir. Worldwatch Inst., 1975—2001; guest Today Show, AM Am., Bill Moyers's Jour.; prodr. Sunrise Semester series, CBS, 1977, 78, informative series, PBS, 1984; founder Ethical Markets Media LLC; cons., lectr., presenter in field. Author: Creating Alternative Futures: The End of Economics, 1978, The Politics of the Solar Age: Alternatives to Economics, 1981, 1988, Paradigms in Progress, 1991, 1995, Building a Win-Win World, 1996, Beyond Globalization, 1999; co-author: Planetary Citizenship, 2004, Ethical Markets Growing the Green Economy, 2006; editor: The United Nations: Policy and Financing Alternatives, 1996; syndicated columnist InterPress Svc., LA Times-Mirror Syndicate; contbr. articles to Christian Sci. Monitor, US News and World Report, Time, NY Times, InterPress Svc., to anthologies; mem. editl. bd. Futures U.K., Foresight U.K., Futures Rsch. Quar., Future Survey, Resurgence; prodr.: informative series, PBS, 1984, co-exec. prodr.: PBS series Ethical Markets, 2005—06. Adv. coun. US Congress Office Tech. Assessment, Washington, 1974-80; adv. Com. on Future Fla. State Legislature, Tallahassee, 1984-86; internat. adv. bd. Forum 2000, Prague, 1995-2000; Rsch. Applied to Nat. Needs com. NSF, 1975-78; Pub. Engring. Policy com. Nat. Acad. Engring., 1976-79. Named Citizen of Yr. NY Med. Soc., 1967; awardee UN Environ. Program; co-winner Global Citizen award, 1996 Fellow: Findhorn Found., World Futures Study Fedn., World Bus. Acad., World Wisdom Coun., Club of Rome (hon.), Club Budapest (hon.). Avocations: bicycling, gardening, swimming. Office: PO Box 5190 Saint Augustine FL 32085-5190 Office Phone: 904-826-1381.

HENDERSON, JANET E. E., lawyer; b. 1956; BA, U. Okla., 1978; JD, Columbia U., 1982. Bar: Okla. 1982, U.S. Dist. Ct. (no. dist.) Okla. 1982, Ill. 1986, U.S. Dist. Ct. (no. dist.) Ill. 1986. With Sidley & Austin, Chgo., 1985—, ptnr., 1990—. Lectr. on lender liability issues and bankruptcy to legal orgns., including Midwest Assn. Secured Lenders. Harlan Fiske Stone scholar Columbia U., 1982. Mem. ABA, Chgo. Bar Assn., Am. Bankruptcy Inst., Phi Beta Kappa. Office: Sidley & Austin Bank One Plz 10 S Dearborn St Chicago IL 60603 Fax: 312-853-7036.

HENDERSON, JANET LYNN, small business owner; b. Chgo., Sept. 14, 1943; d. Howard Charles and Lucille Laura (Lambrecht) Harris; m. Todd Dierks Nelson, Jan. 30, 1965 (div. May 1997); children: Erik Nelson, Brooks Nelson, Jessica Nelson, Jillian Nelson; m. Phil M. Henderson, Dec. 26, 1997. BS in Bus. Adminstrn., Elmhurst Coll., 1966. Lic. real estate broker. Career counselor Employee Svcs., Inc., Chgo., 1966-67; acctg. mgr. Ins. Mgmt., Inc., Milw., 1967-70, Hosp. Coun. Greater Milw., 1970-84; broker assoc. Klein & Heuchan, Inc., Clearwater, Fla., 1994-99; pres., owner Weddings On Water, Clearwater, Fla., 2003—. Mem. leadership tng. coun. Nat. League Cities, Washington, 1999—2002; mem. internat. com. Fla. League Cities, Tallahassee, 1999—2002. Pres. Dunedin Youth Guild, 1993—; chair Relay for Life, 2003, Pinellas County Heart Ball, 2000, Tour of Kitchens, 2005—06, Krewe of Venus Debutante Ball, 2005—06; co-chair Tour of Kitchens, 2006—; v.p. Arms of Venus, 2006—; city commr. City of Dunedin, Fla., 1997—2002, vice mayor, 1999, 2002; bd. dir. Childrens Svc. Soc., 1983—86, Ruth Eckerd Hall Found., Clearwater, Fla., 1998—2004, Pinellas Planning Coun., Clearwater, Fla., 1998—2002, Lighthouse for Pinellas, 1999—2006; bd. dirs. Leading Ladies, 2001—06, Bowman Meml. Scholarship Fund Com., 2003—06; vice chair Lighthouse for Pinellas, 2005—06; active Pinellas County Cmty. Found., 2006; v.p. Dunedin Hist. Soc., 2004—05; bd. dir. Dunedin C. of C., 2003—06, vice-chair membership, 2005—; chmn. steering com. Women in Philanthropy, 2004; active Leadership Pinellas, 1993—2006; vice-chair gov. affairs Dunedin C. of C., 2006; vice-chair gov. affairs found. bd. Upper Pinellas County Fla. Assn. Retarded Citizens, 2006—. Ill. State scholar, 1962. Mem.: Dunedin Hist. Soc., Friends Libr., Jr. League (mem. cmty. adv. bd. 2004—06), Rotary. Republican. Office: Weddings on Water Inc 200 Seminole St Clearwater FL 33755 Office Phone: 727-466-0969. Business E-Mail: janet@weddingsonwater.com.

HENDERSON, JOANN H., social worker, consultant; b. Broadway, Va., Feb. 12, 1957; d. Reaford Ezra and Vira Gladys (Miller) Hershberger; m. James S. Henderson, Sept. 1, 1979; children: Anna Catherine, Max Elliot. AAS magna cum laude, Blue Ridge C.C., Wayers Cave, Va., 1977; BSW magna cum laude, Va. Commonwealth U., Richmond, 1979. Residential provider Pleasant View Homes Inc., Broadway, Va., 1977—82, Henrico Co., Richmond, 1982—84; dir. social svcs. Franklin Co. DSS, Malone, Va., 1984—86; counselor outreach svcs. Harrisonburg Rockingham Cmty. Svcs. Bd., Va., 1986—88, supr. MR svcs. Va., 1988—90; behavioral cons. Va. Dept. MHMR, Richmond, 1996—98, residential provider Broadway, 1998—, pastoral care specialist, 2006—. Bd. mem. Harrisonburg Rockingham Cmty. Svcs. Bd., 1999—2002; vol. Rockingham Co. Pub. Schs., 1991—; mem. Rockingham Dem. Com., Broadway, 2003—06; congregational leadership, lay minister Zion Mennonite Ch., Broadway, 1986—; del. USA Mennonite Ch., Elkhart, Ind., 2005. Mem.: Am. Assn. Pastoral Counselors. Democrat. Mennonite. Avocations: reading, writing, pastoral counseling. E-mail: jjhenders@msn.com.

HENDERSON, KAREN LECRAFT, federal judge; b. Oberlin, Ohio, 1944; BA, Duke U., 1966; JD, U. N.C., 1969. Ptnr. Wright & Henderson, Chapel Hill, NC, 1969—70, Sinkler, Gibbs & Simons, P.A., Columbia, SC, 1983—86; asst. atty. gen. Columbia, 1973—78; sr. asst. atty. gen., dir. of spl. litigation sect., 1978—82; deputy atty. gen., dir. of criminal div., 1982; judge U.S. Dist. Ct. S.C., Columbia, 1986—90, U.S. Ct. Appeals (D.C. cir.), Washington, 1990—. Apptd. Dist. Ct. Adv. Com. Mem.: ABA (litigation sect. and urban, state and local government law sect.), Am. Law Inst., Supreme Ct. Hist. Soc., Fed. Judges Assn., Fed. Am. Inn of Ct., Am. Judicature Soc., SC Bar Assn. (government law sect., trial and appellate practice sect., fed. judges assn.), NC Bar Assn. Office: US Ct Appeals 333 Constitution Ave NW Washington DC 20001-2802*

HENDERSON, LILLIAN MILBRA, educator, librarian, clergyperson; b. Sacramento, Aug. 2, 1945; d. Henry Chuck and Milbra (Fobbs) Cooper; m. Harry Anthony Henderson. BS, BLS, Grambling State U., La., 1969. Cert. tchr. English and library sci., La. Librarian McEvans High Sch., Shaw, Miss., 1969-70, Biloxi (Miss.) High Sch., 1970-73; tchr. Helen Cox Middle Sch., Harvey, La., 1973-76, Jefferson Parish Adult Edn., Marrero, La., 1976-77, Marrero (La.) Middle Sch., 1978-84, Alcee Fortier High Sch., New Orleans, 1984—; pastor Army of God Bapt. Ch., New Orleans, 1984—. Recipient personal evangelism award West Bank Revival Ctr., Gretna, La., 1978, cert. of appreciation Alcee Fortier High Sch., 1987. Mem. Jefferson Fedn. Tchrs., Jefferson Library Chpt., Am. Fedn. Tchrs., ALA, United Tchrs. and Librarians of New Orleans, Clearview Christian Edn. Assn. (recording sec. 1984—). Clubs: Path Finders (New Orleans), Young Ladies Soc. Democrat. Avocations: writing, reading, piano, bible research. Home: PO Box 3053 Harvey LA 70059-3053

HENDERSON, MADELINE MARY (BERRY HENDERSON), chemist, researcher, consultant; b. Merrimac, Mass., Sept. 3, 1922; d. Burton B. and Irene R. (Murphy) Berry; m. Richard S. Henderson, Nov. 5, 1957; children: Anne M., Matthew R., Katherine M., Laura J. AB in Chemistry, Emmanuel Coll., Boston, 1944; MPA, Am. U., Washington, 1977. Chemist E.I. DuPont, Gibbstown, NJ, 1944—45, MIT, Cambridge, Mass., 1946—52; info. specialist Battelle Meml. Inst., Columbus, Ohio, 1953—55; rsch. assoc. NSF, Washington, 1956—62; computer specialist Nat. Bur. Standards, Washington, 1964—79; cons. Bethesda, 1980—. Chmn. Gordon Rsch. Conf. on Sci. Info. Problems, 1972. Author, co-author, editor books on info. sci.; co-author, author papers, articles on info. sci., standards, and libr. automation. Dept. of Commerce Sci.-Tech. fellow, 1971-72; Am. U. Key Exec. scholar, 1975-77. Fellow AAAS (sec. sect. info. scis. 1978-85); mem. Am. Chem. Soc., Am. Soc. Info. Sci. & Tech. (mem. publs. com. 1983-87, chmn. pub. affairs com. 1987-89, Watson Davis award 1989), Pi Alpha Alpha (nat. honor soc. pub. adminstr.). Office: 7401 Willow Rd #425 Frederick MD 21702-2500

HENDERSON, MAUREEN MCGRATH, medical educator; b. Tynemouth, Eng., May 11, 1926; arrived in U.S., 1960; d. Leo E. and Helen McGrath Henderson. MB BS, U. Durham, Eng., 1949, DPH, 1956. Prof. preventive medicine U. Md. Med. Sch., 1968—75, chmn. dept. social and preventive medicine, 1971—75; assoc. epidemiology Johns Hopkins U. Sch. Hygiene and Pub. Health, 1960—75; prof. epidemiology and medicine U. Wash. Med. Sch., 1975—96, prof. emeritus epidemiology and medicine, 1996—, asst. v.p. and assoc. v.p. health scis., 1975—81, head cancer prevention rsch. program Fred Hutchinson Cancer Rsch. Ctr., 1983—94; mem. Nat. Inst. Environ. Health Scis. Adv. Coun., 1994—97. Chmn. epidemiology and disease control study sect. Nih, 1969—82; chmn. clin. trial rev. com. Nat. Heart Lung and Blood Inst., 1975—79; mem. Nat. Cancer Adv. Bd., 1979—84; mem. bd. Robert Wood Johnson Health Policy Fellowship, 1989—93; bd. radiation effects rsch. NRC, 1991—97. Assoc. editor Hour. Cancer Rsch., 1984—88, mem. editl. bd. Jour. Nat. Cancer Inst., 1988—, mem. editl. adv. bd. Cancer Detection and Prevention, 1992—. Decorated Order of Brit. Empire; recipient John Snow award, Am. Pub. Health Assn., 1990; scholar Luke-Armstrong, 1956—57, John and Mary Markle, Acad. Medicine, 1963—68. Mem.: Nat. Rsch. Coun. (mem. report rev. com. 1996—2002, mem. com. rsch. priorities for airborne particulate matters 1998—2000), Am. Epidemiol. Soc. (pres. 1990—91), Internat. Coun. Cancer Rsch. (sci. adv. bd. 1989—92), Soc. Epidemiol. Rsch. (chmn. 1969—70), Assn. Tchrs. Preventive Medicine (pres. 1972—73), Am. Coll. Epidemiology, Inst. Medicine N.A.S. Home: 5309 NE 85th St Seattle WA 98115-3915 E-mail: mhenders@w-link.net.

HENDERSON, MAXINE, writer; b. Rusk, Tex., May 30, 1926; d. A.J. and Johnnie I. (Lewis) Ralson; widowed; children: Kenneth, Gerald, Richard, Nancy, Sally. BS, U. Denver. Registered med. technologist. Med. technologist, Denver and Ypsilanti, Mich., 1947-85. Author: Country Cuisine from Maxine, 1989, Snax from Max, 1996. Gourmet cook AAUW Study Group, Ypsilanti, 1979—. Mem. AAUW, Am. Soc. Clin. Pathology. Methodist. Home: A 105 1740 S Grove St Ypsilanti MI 48198-6658

HENDERSON, MAXINE OLIVE BOOK (MRS. WILLIAM HENDERSON III), foundation executive; b. Rush, Colo., Apr. 22, 1924; d. Jesse Frank and Olive (Booth) Book; m. William Henderson III, Apr. 10, 1948 (dec. May 1983); children: William IV, Meredith. BA, U. Colo., 1945. Personnel adminstr. GE Co., Schenectady, N.Y.C., 1945-54; asst. dir. placement Katherine Gibbs Sch., N.Y.C., 1967-70; v.p., dir. William Henderson Cons., Inc., N.Y.C., 1969-83, pres., dir., 1983-86; dir. recruitment Girl Scouts U.S.A., N.Y.C., 1973-78, dir. human resources, 1978-82, dir. career devel., 1982-91, adminstr. human resources, 1991-93; pres., adminstr. World Found., 1993-2000. Pres. Goddard-Riverside-Trinity Sch. Thrift Shop, N.Y.C., 1964-65, Trinity Sch. Mothers' Orgn., N.Y.C., 1965-66, Trinity Sch. Parents Assn.; treas. Brearley Sch. Parents Assn., N.Y.C., 1966-67; mem. L.I. Mus., Met. Mus. Art, N.Y.C. Mem. North Suffolk Garden Club, Nissequogue Beach Club. Episcopalian. Home: 606 W 116th St New York NY 10027-7011

HENDERSON, NANCY GRACE, marketing executive, technical documentation executive; b. Berkeley, Calif., Oct. 23, 1947; d. John Harry and Lorraine Ruth H. BA, U. Calif., Santa Barbara, 1969; MBA, U. Houston, 1985; teaching credential, UCLA, 1971; MLA, Naropa U., 2002. Chartered fin. analyst. Tchr. Keppel Union Sch. Dist., Littlerock, Calif., 1969-72, Internat. Sch. Prague, Czechoslovakia, 1972-74, Sunland Luth. Sch., Freeport, Bahamas, 1974-75; tchr., dept. head Internat. Sch. Assn., Bangkok, 1975-79; exec. search Diversified Human Resources Group, Houston, 1979-82; data processing analyst Am. Gen. Corp., Houston, 1982-83, personnel and benefits dept., 1983-85, investment analyst, 1985-86, equity security analyst/quantitative portfolio analyst, 1986-87; dir. mktg. and communications Thomson Corp., San Francisco, 1987-90, dir. tech. writing, 1990—. Tchr. English as Second Language program Houston Metro. Ministries, 1980-81. Pres., bd. dirs. Home Owners Assn., Walnut Creek, Calif., 1988-90; tchr. English to refugees Houston Metro Ministries, 1982; exec. dir. Internat. Child Abuse Prevention Found., 1989; ch. choir, session, fundraising and com. chmn. Presbyn. Ch.; active Crisis Hotline, 1978-79, 92-93; dir. project Working in Networks for Good Shelter, 1993-95. Named a Notable Woman of Tex., 1984-85. Mem. CFA Inst., Toastmasters (pres. Houston chpt. 1983, v.p. 1982-83) Avocations: tennis, skiing, hiking, photography, writing short stories and essays. Office: Thomson Financial 425 Market St Fl 6 San Francisco CA 94105 Office Phone: 415-344-6025. E-mail: nancy.henderson@thomson.com.

HENDERSON, RITA BEATRICE, county official; b. Clinton, S.C., May 23, 1952; d. William D. and Mattie D. (Williams) Taylor; m. Curtis Henderson, Apr. 6, 1974; 1 child, Tori Rodshida. AS, Piedmont Tech. Coll., 1990; student, So. Wesleyan U., 1997—. Billing clk. Ithaca, Inc., Clinton, S.C., 1973-86; adminstrv. asst. United Way Laurens County, Clinton, S.C., 1990-91; head payroll dept. B.F. Shaw Fabricating Co., Laurens, S.C., 1991-92; dir. Laurens County Registration/Elections, 1993—. Screener Good Shepherd Free Clinic, Laurens, 1994-98. Methodist. Avocations: reading, piano, cooking, travel. Home: 118 Paul St Laurens SC 29360-7544 Office: Laurens County Registration/Elections 3 Catherine St Laurens SC 29360-1745

HENDERSON, ROBERTA MARIE, librarian, educator; b. Mosinee, Wis., July 27, 1929; d. Roy H. and Marie Helena (Dittman) H. BS, Ctrl. State Tchrs. Coll., Stevens Point, Wis., 1951; MS, U. Wis., 1958; MA, No. Mich. U., 1975; Cert. of Adv. Studies, U. Denver, 1980. Librarian Wiesbaden (Ger.) Am. High Sch., 1954-55, Ashland (Wis.) High Sch., 1955-56; tchr./librarian Clark AFB, Philippines, 1956-57; librarian Prescott (Ariz.) Jr. High Sch., 1958-59, Frankfurt (Ger.) Am. High Sch., 1959-63; tchr./librarian Zama Am. High Sch., Camp Zama, Japan, 1963-66; librarian Ankara (Turkey) Am. High Sch., 1966-68; tutor Nkozi Tchr. Tng. Coll., Mpigi, Uganda, 1968-70; ref. librarian/prof. No. Mich. U., Marquette, 1971-93; retired, 1993; cons. No. Mich. U. and Pub. Librs., 1993—. Coord. faculty workshops No. Mich. U., 1986-88; cons. Escanaba (Mich.) Pub. Libr., 1987, 90, 92; Master tchr. Mich. State U. Extension, 2003—. Author slide/tape: Locating Materials in Periodicals and Documents, 1977, Library Materials for Literature Students, 1979. Mem. libr. com. Marquette County Hist. Soc., 1981—; mem. Upper Peninsula Environ. Coalition, Houghton, 1985—; host Marquette-Japan Sister Coalition City Program, 1988, mem. Marquette Sister City adv. bd., 2005—, No. Ctr.Lifelon Learning bd., 2003— Title II-B fellow, U. Denver, 1979-80; Human Resources Dept., No. Mich. U. grantee, 1986, 87; recipient Disting Faculty award No. Mich. U., 1988. Mem. ALA, AAUP, Libr. Instrn. Roundtable, Phi Kappa Phi (chpt. treas. 1987-91), Marquette Century Club, No. Mich. U. Women Avocations: interior decoration, gardening, hiking, cats. Home: 515 E Ridge St Marquette MI 49855-4216 E-mail: rhenders@nmu.edu.

HENDERSON, ROBYN LEE, health program executive director; b. Hastings, Nebr., Apr. 3, 1960; d. Darrel Franklin and Bonnalynne Beulah Henderson. BS, Nebr. Wesleyan U., Lincoln, 1982; MHS, Johns Hopkins U., Balt., 1996. Aide to spkr. Nebr. Legis., Lincoln, 1981-82; program instr. Close Up Found., Arlington, Va., 1982-84; legis. aide Sen. Jim Exon, Washington, 1984-91; legis. rep. Am. Thoracic Soc., Washington, 1991-94; rsch. assoc. Nat. Health Policy Forum, Washington, 1994-96; govt. policy analyst Nat. Rural Electric Coop. Assn., Arlington, Va., 1996-98; v.p. program svcs. Nat. Rural Health Assn., Kansas City, 1998—2003; project mgr. U. Nebr. Pub. Policy Ctr., Lincoln, 2003—05; asst. dir. Rural Health Edn. Network, Omaha, 2005—06; exec. dir. Southeast Nebr. Area Health Edn. Ctr., Beatrice, 2006—. Chair govt. rels. Affinity Group Nat. Health Coun., Washington, 1993-94, Rural Renaissance Network, Washington, 1996-98. Pres. Nebr. Wesleyan U. Alumni Coun., 2005—; bd. govs. Nebr. Wesleyan U., 2005—, co-chair presdl. search com., 2006—. Recipient Young Alumna Loyalty award Nebr. Wesleyan U., 1980; named one of Outstanding Young Women Am., 1984, 87. Mem. Women in Govt. Rels., Am. Soc. Assn. Execs., Nat. Rural Health Assn., Nebr. Rural Health Assn., Pub. Health Assn. Nebr., Kansas City Soc. Assn. Execs., Phi Alpha Theta. Avocations: reading, history, music. Home: 6409 Boxelder Dr Lincoln NE 68506 Office: # 408 5109 W Scott Rd Beatrice NE 68310 Office Phone: 402-228-9094. E-mail: rhenderson@se-ahec.org.

HENDERSON, ROGENE FAULKNER, toxicologist, researcher; b. Breckenridge, Tex., July 13, 1933; d. Philander Molden and Lenoma (Rogers) F.; m. Thomas Richard Henderson II, May 30, 1957; children: Thomas Richard III, Edith Jeanette, Laura Lee. BSBA, Tex. Christian U., 1955; PhD, U. Tex., 1960. Diplomate Am. Bd. Toxicology. Research assoc. U. Ark. Sch. Med., Little Rock, 1960-67; from scientist to sr. scientist and group supr. chemistry and toxicology Lovelace Inhalation Toxicology Research Inst., Albuquerque, 1967—; deputy dir. Nat. Environ. Respiratory Ctr. Lovelace Respiratory Rsch. Inst., Albuquerque, 1998—. Mem. adv. com. Burroughs Wellcome Toxicology Scholar award, 1987-89, NIH toxicology study sect., 1982-86, Nat. Inst. Environ. Health Scis. adv. coun., 1992-95, EPA scientific adv. bd. environ. health commn., 1991-95; mem. bd. sci. counselors EPA, 2002—; mem. Com to Assess the Sci. Base for Tobacco Harm Reduction, adv. group Am. Cancer Soc.on Cancer and the Environment, 1999—, Health Effects Inst. Rsch. Com., 1997—; vice chmn. US Environ. protection Agy. Bd. of Sci. Counselors, 2001—; chmn. clean air sci. adv. com. U.S. EPA, 2004—. Assoc. editor Toxicology Applied Pharmacology, 1989-95, Jour. Exposure Analysis and Environ. Epidemiology, 1991-95; contbr. articles to profl. jours. Named Woman on the Move YWCA, Albuquerque, 1985; grantee NIH, 1958-60, 1960-62, 1986—. Mem. AAAS, NAS (bd. on environ. studies and toxicology 1998—), Am. Chem. Soc. (chmn. ctrl. N.Mex. sect. 1981), Soc. Toxicology (pres. Mountain-West Regional chpt. 1985-86, pres. inhalation specialty sect. 1989—), N.Y. Acad. Scis., Nat. Acad. Scis. (com. toxicology 1985-98, chair 1992-98, com. epidemiology of air pollution 1983-85, com. biol. markers 1986—, com. on risk assessment methodology 1989-92, bd. environ. studies and toxicology 1998—), Nat. Acad. (nat. assoc.) Presbyterian. Home: 5609 Don Felipe Ct SW Albuquerque NM 87105-6765 Office: Lovelace Respiratory Rsch Inst 2425 Ridgecrest Ave SE Albuquerque NM 87108 Office Phone: 505-348-9464. Business E-Mail: rhenders@lrri.org.

HENDERSON, (RUEJENUIA) SECRET, social worker; d. Johnnie Henderson, Sr. and Mary Lula Henderson; children: Steven O'Neal, Reginald Patrick. BA in Social Work, Tex. So. U., 1994. LCSW; cert. state cert. HIV antibody testing counselor, state cert. HIV ptnr. elicitation and notification counselor, AIDS/HRAP adolescent tng. trainer, Assn. Drug Abuse Prevention and Treatment, Facing HIV/AIDS in the Deaf Cmty., Toward Healthy Sexuality, Montrose Clinic HIV Update Conf., Regional VII Client Coun. Clk. social work dept., chemistry dept. Tex. So. U., Houston, 1986—89; sec. State of Tex. Client Coun. and Regional VII Client Coun., Austin, Tex., 1988—; case mgr., HIV counselor, st. outreach worker Montrose Clinic, Houston, 1986—98; case mgr. Donald R. Watkins Meml. Found., Houston, 1999—2000; outreach case mgr. St. Hope Found., Houston, 2001; HIV case coord. Harris County Sheriff's Office, Houston, 2001—. Pres. State of Tex. Client Coun., 2001; v.p. Lone Star Legal Svc., 2002. Vol. client coun. mem., sec., pres., bd. dirs. Gulf Coast Legal Found., Houston, 1972—. Mem.: NASW, Assn. Black Social Workers (Outstanding Student award 1992), Tex. So. U. Social Work Club, Tex. So. U. Sociology Club. Democrat. Church Of Christ. Avocation: helping others. Home: PO Box 8454 Houston TX 77088-8454 Office: Harris County Sheriff's Office 1200 Baker St Houston TX 77002 Office Phone: 713-755-9252.

HENDERSON, SHIRLEY ELIZABETH, minister; b. Phila., Apr. 13, 1954; d. Clyde Elinwood Wright and Ellen Smith; m. Harry Warren Henderson (dec. July 4, 2001). Gen. equivalency diploma, Internat. Corr. Sch., Scranton, Pa., 1988. Lic. min. Emmanuel Tabernacle Bapt. Ch. of the Apostolic Faith, Ohio, 1968, ordained apostle Praise Ministries, Inc., Orlando, 1994, ordained min. Tabernacle Enlightened Ch. of God, Fla., 1989. Electronic assembler Western Electric, Roanoke, Va., 1973—75; min. of music E. C. Cannon Evangelistic Crusade, Inc., Charlotte, NC, 1975—83; founder and pastor Praise Ministries Deliverance Ctr., Inc., Raleigh, NC, 1994—; religious instr. Pilgrim Assemblies of the World, Bklyn., 1985—88; founder and pastor Praise Ministries Inc., Orlando, Fla., 1989—94. Chief apostle, sr. pastor Praise Ministries Family Worship Ctr., Inc., Raleigh, NC, 1995—; chief exec. officer/dir.CEO, dir. Project Help Cmty. Devel. Ctr., Inc., Garner, NC, 1995—, cons., 1995—. Author: The Power of Worship and Praise, 1986 (Spl. Recognition award, 2000), Victory, 1989, Who's Doing the Talking, 2001, Male and Female Created He Them, 2003; composer: Apostle Shirley E. Henderson and the PMI Apostolic Company Present the Power of Worship and Praise, 2000; prodr.: (songs/live recording) LaNore's Music (Trophy, 1997); composer: (songbook) The Power of Worship and Praise for Ch. Services, 1996, The Power of Worship and Praise Songbook for Choirs, 1999. Dir. Praise

Ministries Inc. Food Bank, Orlando, Fla., 1990—94; cmty. involvement vol. Project Help Cmty. Devel. Ctr., Inc., Garner, NC, 1996—99, interior decorator/painter, 1995; presenter/supporter N.C. Assn. of Educators-Education Rally, Raleigh, NC, 2003; dir./presenter of music entertainment Nat. Computer Tech. Conf., Orlando, Fla., 1993. Recipient Letter of Recognition, City of Raleigh, 2001. Democrat. Avocations: cooking, interior decorating, painting, singing, writing. Home: 2208 Hawkins St Raleigh NC 27610 Personal E-mail: apostlepmdc@yahoo.com. Business E-Mail: projcthelp@yahoo.com.

HENDERSON HALL, BRENDA FORD, computer company executive; d. Frances Long and adopted d. Johnny Dell Ford, William Alfred Randall; m. Joseph Aubrey Hall, Jan. 1, 2001. BS in Acctg., U. NC, 1981; MBA, U. N.C., 1985. Six Sigma Green Belt 2003. Bookkeeper, transit operator Wachovia Bank, Wilmington, NC, 1968—73; cost acctg. technician, staff reliever E I du Pont de Nemours and Co., Inc., Wilmington, NC, 1973—86; systems engr. Electronic Data Systems, Dallas, 1986—87; mgr. edp Potomac Savs. Bank, Silver Spring, Md., 1987—88; sr. systems analyst Maxima Corp., Lanham, Md., 1988—94; account mgr., developer, analyst The Maxim Group, Reston, Va., 1995—97; sr. mem. tech. staff Computer Scis. Corp., Falls Church, Va., 1994—95, prin. cons., 1997—2002, sr. mem. exec. staff Lanham, Md., 2002—04, sr. cons. engr. Hanover, Md., 2004—. Instr. acctg. Shaw U., Wilmington, NC, 1985—86; v.p. Fin. Comm. Sys. Svcs. Inc., Clinton, Md., 1987—89; instr. acctg. Prince George C.C., Largo, Md., 1990—93; pres. Your Efficient Tax Svc., Oxon Hill, Md., 1992—93; team leader, developer, analyst Maxim Group, Reston, 1997; acct. exec. - fed. sector Computer Scis. Corp., Lanham, 2003—04. Charter mem. Williston Alumni Assn., Wilmington, NC, 1974—78; pres. -master of bus. adminstrn. assn. U. NC, 1983—85; bd. mem. DuPont's Cape Fear Employees' Credit Union, Wilmington, NC, 1979—80; charter mem. Nat. Assn. Accountants U. NC, 1980—81. Mem.: NAFE, AAUW. D-Liberal. Baptist. Achievements include facilitated the effort that resulted in the achievement of the first software acquisition capability maturity model level 3 rating. Avocations: travel, swimming, reading, philanthropic activities, writing. Office: Computer Scis Corp 7231 Parkway Dr Hanover MD 21076 Office Phone: 443-445-8809. Personal E-mail: bhall540@comcast.net. Business E-Mail: bhall25@csc.com.

HENDLEY, EDITH DI PASQUALE, physiology and neuroscience educator; b. N.Y.C., Sept. 5, 1927; d. Michael and Rose (Parillo) Di Pasquale; m. Daniel Dees Hendley, Apr. 21, 1952; children: Jane Alice, Joyce Louise, Paul Daniel. AB, Hunter Coll., N.Y.C., 1948; MS, Ohio State U., 1950; PhD, U. Ill., Chgo., 1954. Instr. U. Chgo., 1954-56; asst. lectr. U. Sheffield, England, 1956-57; instr., rsch. assoc. Johns Hopkins U. Sch. Medicine, Balt., 1963-72; sr. investigator Friends Med. Sci. Rsch. Ctr., Balt., 1972-73; from assoc. prof. to prof. U. Vt. Coll. Medicine, Burlington, 1973-94, prof. emeritus, 1994—. Co-author: 6 books; contbr. articles to profl. jours. Rsch. grantee NIH, 1974-95, NSF, 1986-98, Vt. affiliate Am. Heart Assn., 1982-83, The Sugar Assn. Inc., 1984-85. Mem. AAAS, Am. Physiol. Soc., Am. Soc. Pharmacology and Exptl. Therapeutics, Soc. for Neurosci. (exec. com., treas. Vt. chpt. 1978-84), Assn. for Women in Sci. (treas. 1972-74, exec. com., long-range planning com. 1974-76). Avocations: music, opera, theater, cinema. Home: 10 Highland Ter South Burlington VT 05403-7601 Office: U Vt Coll Medicine Dept Molecular Phys Bi Burlington VT 05405-0001 Business E-Mail: hendley@physiology.med.uvm.edu.

HENDRA, BARBARA JANE, public relations executive; b. Watertown, N.Y. d. Frederick R. and Irene J. H. BA, Vassar Coll., 1960. Dir. publicity Fawcett World Libr., N.Y.C., 1961—69; v.p., dir. publicity and pub. rels. Pocket Books-Simon & Schuster, N.Y.C., 1969—77; corp. dir. publicity and pub. rels. Putnam Pub. Group, N.Y.C., 1977—79; pres. Barbara J. Hendra Assocs., Inc., N.Y.C., 1979—91, The Hendra Agy. Inc, Bklyn., 1991—. Adj. prof. NYU, 1981. Contbg. author: Trade Book Marketing, 1983, The Encyclopedia of Publishing, 1995. Mem. Pubs. Publicity Assn. (bd. dirs. 1977-81, pres. 1979-81), Publicity Club N.Y., Soc. Profl. Journalists, Women's Media Group, Nat. Book Critics Cir., Vassar Club, Regency Whist Club. Home: 140 Sterling Pl Brooklyn NY 11217-3307 Office: The Hendra Agy Inc 142 Sterling Pl Brooklyn NY 11217-3307 Office Phone: 718-622-3232.

HENDRICK, ZELWANDA, drama and psychology educator; b. Rusk, Tex., Nov. 28, 1925; d. Lloyd Irvin and Viola Alice (McGuire) Hendrick; AA, Lon Morris Coll., 1945; BS, N. Tex. U., 1947; MA, So. Meth. U., 1958. Tchr. theatre arts Overton HS, Tex., 1947-49, Nacogdoches HS, Tex., 1949-50, Boude Storey Sch., Dallas, 1950-53, Kimball HS, Dallas, 1953-62; tchr. theatre arts H. Grady Spruce HS, Dallas, 1962-78, chmn. fine arts dept., 1963-77, ret., 1978; drama and psychology tchr. Alexander Sch., 1978—; substitute tchr. Highland Park HS, Dallas, 1980—; part-time tchr. John Robert Powers Finishing Sch., 1951—; tchg. fellow N. Tex. U., 1964-65; ptnr. Adventure II Miniature Horse Ranch, Rusk, Tex., 1985—; co-dir. Adventure II Miniature Horse Show, Lufkin, Tex., 1987—. Active, Tyler Civic Symphony, Tex., 1949-50, Tyler Civic Theatre, 1949-50, Dallas Theatre Center, 1960-61; guest dir. Cherokee Civic Theatre, Rusk, 1983, pres. 2002—; mem. adv. com. Smithsonian Instn., 1975; co-sponsor US Inst. Tech. Theatre; del. Democratic Dist. Conv., 1980; candidate Tex. State Legislature, 1980; chmn. Dallas County Transp. Bd., 1982—; mem. Friends of the Neches River-Wild Life Refuge; life mem. First United Meth. Ch. (bd. mem.), Rusk. Mem. Internat. Thespians (state dir.), Tex. Speech Assn. (sec. 1973—), Am. Assn. Ednl. Theatre, Am. Miniature Horse Registry, Friends of the Railroad, Dallas Ednl. Drama Assn. (governing bd.), Tex. Tchrs. Assn., Nat. Forensic League, AAUW, Classroom Tchrs. Dallas, Internat. Platform Assn., Ednl. Arts Assn., Tex. Congress Parent Tchr. Assn. (hon. life), DAR, Daus. Republic of Tex., N. Texas Collie Club, Nat. Assn. Royalty Owners, Tex. Ind. Producers and Royalty Owners Assn., Tex. Farm Bur., Am. Miniature Horse Assn., Friends of the Tex. State RR, Paws of E. Tex., Delta Kappa Gamma. Club: Order Eastern Star. Contbr. to A Guide to Student Teaching in Music, 1968-70. Home: 204 E 4th St Rusk TX 75785-1308 Office: Adventure II Miniature Horse Ranch Hwy 84 W Rusk TX

HENDRICKS, MARILYN LOUISE, small business owner; b. Juneau, Alaska, Feb. 24, 1952; d. Tarleton Friend and Doris Jean (Gregg) Smith; m. John Leland Hendricks, Mar. 28, 1970; 1 child, Debbie Pruett. Student, Griffin Bus. Coll., Seattle, 1969-70, Midway Adult Sch., San Diego, 1970-71, Bellingham (Wash.) Vocat. Tech. Inst., 1977. Circulation mgr. La Jolla (Calif.) Light Newspaper, 1972-74; sec., receptionist The Petersburg (Alaska) City Manager, 1976; owner Northwest Off-Road Specialties, Inc., Bellingham, Wash., 1978—, Marilyn's Yarn, Inc., Bellingham, 2005—. Coordinator Toyota Jamboree, British Columbia. Republican. Avocations: needlecrafts, gardening, travel, trout fishing, raising ferrets. Office: NW Off-Rd Specialties 1999 Iowa St PO Box 1617 Bellingham WA 98227-1617 also: Marilyn's Yarn! Inc 3110 Northwest Ave Bellingham WA 98225 Office Phone: 360-676-1300.

HENDRICKS, SHASAREE, dean, music educator; d. William Anthony Anderson and Debra M. Reddick; m. Bernard D. Anderson, Sept. 1, 2001; children: Destini D., Bernard D. B in Music Edn., Fla. A&M U., Tallahassee, 2000. Cert. music edn. grades K-12 Fla., 2002. Music tchr. Orange County Pub. Schs., Orlando, Fla., 2001—06, adminstrv. dean, 2006—. Office Phone: 407-532-7930.

HENDRICKSON, ELIZABETH ANN, retired secondary school educator; b. Bismarck, N.D., Oct. 21, 1936; d. William Earl and Hilda E. (Sauter) Hinkel; m. Roger G. Hendrickson, Apr. 18, 1960; 1 child, Wade William. BA, Jamestown Coll., 1958; postgrad., U. Calif., Davis, 1962, Calif. State U., Sacramento, 1964, U. San Diego, 1985-88, Ottawa U., 1986-88. Cert. tchr., Calif. Tchr. Napoleon (N.D.) High Sch., 1958-59, Kulm (N.D.) High Sch., 1959-61, Del Paso Jr. High Sch., Sacramento, 1961, Mills Jr. High Sch., Rancho Cordova, Calif., 1961-97; ret., 1997. Mem. sch. attendance rev. bd. Folsom-Cordova Unified Sch. Dist. Mem.: AAUW, NEA, Sacramento Area Gifted Assn., Folsom Cordova Ret. Tchrs. Assn. (sec., mem. steering com., mem. newsletter com.), Calif. Ret. Tchrs. Assn., Calif. Tchrs. Assn., Calif. Assn. for Gifted, N.G. Aux., Sgt. Maj. Assn. of Calif. Aux. Enlisted Assns., Soroptimists (news editor Rancho Cordova 1985). Democrat. Lutheran. Home: 2032 Kellogg Way Rancho Cordova CA 95670-2435

HENDRIE, ELAINE, public relations executive; b. Bklyn. d. David and Pearl Kostell; m. Joseph Mallam Hendrie; children: Susan, Barbara. Asst. acct. exec. Benjamin Sonnenberg Pub. Rels., N.Y.C., 1953-57; pub. rels. cons., writer, editor, dir. pub. rels. and media Religious Heritage of Am., Washington, 1973-75; nat. media coord. NOW, Washington, 1978; media dir. Am. Speech-Lang.-Hearing Assn., Washington, 1979-80; pub. info. officer, head media and mktg. Dept. Navy, Washington, 1980-81; pres. Hendrie & Pendzick, 1982-92, Elaine Hendrie Pub. Rels., 1992—. Prodr., interviewer radio program, sta. WRIV, WALK AM/FM, L.I., N.J., Westchester County, N.Y., Conn., 1974-77; exec. dir. Women in New Directions, Inc., Suffolk County, N.Y., 1974-77, cons., 1981—; resource person for media Nat. Commn. on Observance of Internat. Women's Yr., 1977; cons. Multi-Media Prodns. Inc., N.Y.C., 1978—; adv. bd. Women's Edn. and Counseling Ctr., SUNY, Farmingdale. Mem. Bellport-Brookhaven Hist. Soc. (trustee 1999—). Home: 50 Bellport Ln Bellport NY 11713-2736

HENDRIX, CHRISTINE JANET, retired government agency administrator, retired small business owner, volunteer; b. Corry, Pa., Dec. 3, 1939; d. Merle Alvin and Janet May Besson; m. Alfred E. Hendrix, Mar. 27, 1965; 1 child, Lee Andrew. BS in Edn., Clarion State Teacher's Coll., Pa., 1961. Tchr. Montour Schs., McKees Rocks, Pa., 1961—62, Newcomerstown (Ohio) Exempted Schs., 1962—65; welcome wagon hostess Welcome Wagon Internat., Newcomerstown, 1965—71; mgr. Amos Placement Bur., New Phila., Ohio, 1972—75; paralegal Pros. Atty.'s Office, New Phila., 1976—79; small bus. coowner Child Care Alternatives, New Phila., 1980—85; dir. Tuscarawas County Sr. Ctr., Dover, Ohio, 1985—89; relocation agt. Ohio Dept. of Transp., Fairlawn, Ohio, 1989—98; assignment commr. Mcpl. Ct., New Phila., 1998—2000, ret., 2000. Editor: Child Care Alternatives Newsletter, 1980—85. Vol. Cats N Us, Dover, Ohio, 2002, Ret. Sr. and Vol. Program, New Phila., 2003; ctr. and exec. com. Tuscarawas County Dem. Party, New Phila., 1980; various offices New Phila. (Ohio) Dem. Club, 1994—2001; mem. Bd. of Zoning Appeals, New Phila., 1979—89; rep. sr. citizens United Way, New Phila., 1983—85; mem. Domestic Violence Orgn., New Phila., 1987—89; various offices NOW, New Phila., 1974—79; vol. COMPASS Inc., New Phila., 2000. Democrat. Protestant. Avocations: genealogy, antiques. Home: 183 Wabash Avenue NW New Philadelphia OH 44663 Personal E-mail: cjhendrix@wilkshire.net.

HENDRIX, DIANNE ROBERSON, artist, writer; b. Atlanta, Jan. 12, 1946; d. Thomas Glenn Roberson and Ella Mae Smith; children: Tinara Dyan, Angelean Oedra. AS in Tech. Illustration and Design, Tarrant County Coll., Tex., 1979. Artist Art of the No. Lights, Palmer, Alaska, 1966—; writer Free Lance, Palmer, Alaska, 1998—. Alaska Art, Aurora Connection (KAKM PBS TV 25 anniversary artist, 2004). Mem.: Bonanaza Book Club. Conservative. Office: Artworld Plus PO Box 4983 Palmer AK 99645 Office Phone: 907-745-7311. Personal E-mail: akwriter@polar.mtaonline.net.

HENDRIX, MARY ELIZABETH, language educator, researcher; b. Tuscaloosa, Ala., Mar. 17, 1973; d. Lawrence Thomson and Evelyn Jacobs Hendrix. BA in English & Dance cum laude, U. Ala., Tuscaloosa, 1998, MA in Secondary Edn., 2000, postgrad., 2005—. Coord. Am. reads program U. Ala., Tuscaloosa, 1999—2000; tchr. English Meadow Creek High Sch., Lawrenceville, Ga., 2000—01, The Capitol Sch., Tuscaloosa, 2001—02, Shelton State C.C., 2001—04; rsch. asst. U. Ala., 2003—; English tchr. Mem. adv. bd. cmty. svc. & vol. U. Ala., 1999—2000. Mem. Ala. Citizens Constl. Reform, Tuscaloosa, 2004—, Ala. Arise, Birmingham, 2005—06; ctrl. region coord. Constl. Reform Edn. Campaign Greater Birmingham Ministries. Recipient Eddy Fulks award, The Elliott Soc., U. Ala., 1997; scholar, U. Ala., 2005. Mem.: Southeast Philosophy Edn. Soc., Nat. Coun. Tchrs. English, Am. Ednl. Studies Assn., Am. Ednl. Rsch. Assn., The Blackburn Inst., Alpha Epsilon Lambda, Sigma Tau Delta, Kappa Delta Pi, Phi Delta Kappa. Democrat. Achievements include patents in field. Avocations: writing, dance, exercise, reading, theater. Home: 2706 31st Ave Way Northport AL 35476-3610 Office: U Ala Coll Edn 210 Wilson Hall Box 870302 Tuscaloosa AL 35487 Office Phone: 205-826-5549. Personal E-mail: ehendrix@cobra.simplecom.net, ehendrix1105@bellsouth.net.

HENDRIX, SUSAN CLELIA DERRICK, civic worker; b. McClellanville, S.C., Jan. 19, 1920; d. Theodore Elbridge and Susan Regina (Bauknight) Derrick; m. Henry Gardner Hendrix, June 5, 1943; children: Susan Hendrix Redmond, Marilyn Hendrix Shedlock. BA, Columbia Coll., 1941; MA, Furman U., 1961; EdD (hon.), Columbia Coll., 1985. Cert. tchr. SC. Tchr. Whitmire Pub. Schs., 1941-43, Greenville (S.C.) Pub. Schs., 1944-46, 58-63, dir. Reading Clinic, 1965-68; counselor Greenville County Sch. Dist., 1965-68, dir. pub. rels., 1968-83; grad. instr. Furman U., 1967-69. Cons. Nat. Seminar on Desegregation, 1973. Author (with James P. Mahaffey): Teaching Secondary Reading, 1966, Communicating with the Community, 1979, History of Robert Morris Class, 1995; editor: Communique, 1968—83, Celebrating Our Legacy--Oral Interviews, 2001; mem. United Meth. Gen. Conf. editl. and revision com.: Book of Discipline, 1996, 2000; contbr. articles to profl. jours. and mags. Trustee Columbia Coll., 1958—70, chair, 1968—70; chmn. Greenville County Rehab. Bd., 1974—76; vice chmn. bd. Jr. Achievement, Greenville, 1978—79; mem. S.C. Commn. on Women, Columbia, 1979—88, chmn., 1982—88; pres. United Meth. Women Buncombe St. Ch., Greenville, 1956—57; mem. adminstrv. bd. Buncombe St. Ch., 1968—2004, trustee, 1980—88; mem. endowment fund bd. trustees, 1994—, chmn., 2001—03, co-chair ch. bldg. com., 1999, lay del. to S.C. Ann. Conf., 1986—2003, mem. commn. on Archives and History, 2001—; mem. United Meth. Ch. Southeastern Jurisdictional Coun. on Ministries, 1980—88, Southeastern Jurisdictional Commn. on Archives and History, 1984—88; chmn. S.C. Conf. Coun. on Ministries United Meth. Ch., 1980—88, del. gen. conf., 1980, 1984, 1988, 1992; mem. S.C. Conf. Commn. Com., 1995—97; chmn. S.C. Conf. Budgeting Task Force, 1996—97; mem. S.C. Conf. Ann. Fund Com. Camps and Retreats, 1998—2001; mem. strategic planning com. Columbia Coll., 1996—97, class agt., 2000—, mem. com. of 150, 2003, mem. Sesquicentennial com., 2003—05; mem. Bd. Global Ministries United Meth. Ch., 1972—80, chmn. fin. com., 1976—80; mem. gen. ch. commn. study of ministry United Meth. Ch., 1984—92, mem. gen. ch. coun. ministries, 1988—96, mem. gen. conf. agys. staff and site location com., 1988—96, rschr. missions project West Africa West Africa, 1986, chmn. gen. ch. com. legis., 1992—96, chmn. gen. ch. com. on inter-agy. legis., 1992—96, gen. ch. mission agy. site location com., 1993—96, gen. ch. structure com., 1992—96; mem. S.C. Conf. Africa U. Task Force, 2000—01; charter mem. Nat. Mus. Women in Arts, 1978—. Recipient medallion, Columbia Coll., 1980, Alumnae Disting. Svc. award, 1983, Disting. Achievement award, Women's History Week, Greenville, 1984, S.C. Woman of Achievement award, 1988, Clelia D. Hendrix endowment Archives and History at Buncombe St., United Meth. Ch., 2000; established Clelia D. Hendrix Endowed Scholarship, Columbia Coll., 1988. Mem. S.C. PTA (life), Columbia Coll. Alumnae Assn. (life), Dem. Women, S.C. Women in Govt. (bd. dirs. 1985-87), Alpha Delta Kappa (pres. 1970-72, 90-91). Home and Office: 309 Arundel Rd Greenville SC 29615-1303

HENDRY, JEAN SHARON, psychopharmacologist; b. Hanover, Pa., June 2, 1947; d. Clarence Richard and Frances Lee (Manger) Shaver; 1 child, Robert Andrew. BA, Hunter Coll., 1976; MA, Princeton U., 1978; PhD, 1980. Rsch. asst. Hunter Coll., N.Y.C., 1974-75; asst. instr. Princeton U., Princeton, NJ, 1976-78; post doctoral fellow Med. Coll. Va., Richmond, 1979-82; psychology instr. U. Richmond, 1985-86, Pa. State U., Media, Pa., 1987-88. Guest reviewer various psychological and pharmacological jours. Contbr. numerous articles to profl. jours. Active Arts Coun. of Moore County, World Wildlife Assn.; v.p. Women of Weymouth Ctr. Arts and Humanities. Mem.: APA, Nat. Wildlife Fedn., Am. Psychol. Soc., Nat. Audubon Soc., Assn. Princeton Grad. Alumni (bd. mem.), Nature Conservancy, Sigma Xi, Phi Beta Kappa (v.p.). Avocations: exercise, reading, dog training.

HENEHAN, GINA L., history educator; b. Inglewood, Calif., Dec. 23, 1965; d. Eddie R. Bozarth and Diana Rodgers; m. Brian A. Henehan; children: Ryan, Brett Webber, Krista, Katherine. BA in History, Chapman U., Orange, Calif., 1994; MA in Edn., Chapman U., 1998. Tchg. credential Calif. Tchrs. Commn., CLAD Calif. Tchrs. Commn. History tchr. Tustin Unified Sch. Dist., Santa Ana, Calif., 1996—2003, Acalanes HS Dist., Walnut Creek, Calif., 2003—05, Monte Vista HS, Danville, Calif., 2005—. Nominee Tchr. of Yr., Foothill HS, 2003; named Tchr. of Millennium, 2000. Avocation: family heritage. Office: Monte Vista HS 3131 Stone Valley Rd Danville CA 94526 Office Phone: 925-552-5530. Office Fax: 925-743-1744. E-mail: ghenehan@mvhigh.net.

HENES, DONNA, artist, writer; b. Cleve., Sept. 19, 1945; d. Nathan and Adelaide (Ross) Trugman. Student, Ohio State U., 1963-66; BS, CCNY, 1971, MS in Art Edn., 1972. Prodr. series pub. participatory celebratory events in parks, museums and univs., 100 cities in 9 countries, 1970—. Designer Olympic Medalist Tickertape Parade, N.Y.C., 1984; ednl. cons. New Wilderness Foundation, N.Y.C., 1985; judge Jane Addams Peace Assn. Children's Book Award, N.Y.C., 1983-89; ritual cons. Mama Donna's Tea Garden. Author, designer Dressing Our Wounds in Warm Clothes, 1982, Noting the Process of Noting the Process, 1977, Celestially Auspicious Occasions, 1996, The Moon Watcher's Companion, 2004, The Queen of My Self, 2005, author, performer (CD) Reverence to Her: Part I Mythology, the Matriarchy & Me, 1998, pub., editor quar. Always in Season: Living in Sync with the Cycles, columnist United Press Internat. Religion & Spirituality Forum; editor: Celebration News, 1986—92; internationally syndicated columnist; contbr. numerous articles to profl.jours. Co-founder, pres. STAND (Stand Together Affirmative Neighborhood Devel.), N.Y.C.; composer Chants for Peace/Chance for Peace, Sta. WNYC, first peace message in space, 1982. Fellow Nat. Endowment for Arts, 1982, interarts, 1983, N.Y. Found. for Arts, 1986, 90; grantee N.Y. State Coun. on Arts, N.Y.C. State Bicentennial Commn., Com. for Visual Arts, Money for Women, Beard's Fund, Jerome Found., Ctr. for the Media Arts; recipient Citation award Mayor of N.Y.C. David Dinkins. Mem. Internat. Ctr. for Celebration (bd. dirs., co-founder). Avocations: dance, travel, reading, walking, swimming. Office Phone: 718-857-1343. Personal E-mail: cityshaman@aol.com.

HENEVELD-STORY, CHRISTY JEAN, educational researcher; b. San Jose, Calif., June 30, 1967; d. Sally Jean Dudley and Robert Michael Heneveld, Charles Gustav Sieloff (Stepfather) and Barbara Leech Heneveld (Stepmother); m. Robert David Duis, July 22, 1992; children: James Michael Story, Charles David Story, Christopher Robert Story. PhD, U. Calif., 1998. Lectr. U. Calif., Santa Cruz, 1999—2000; rschr. Ctr. for Study of Law and Soc. - UC Berkeley, 2000—02; tchr. Castilleja Sch., Palo Alto, Calif., 2002—. Internship coord. Castilleja Sch., Palo Alto, Calif., 2002—04. Sec. Ladera Cmty. Assn., unincorporated San Mateo County, Calif., 1999—2002; tutor Los Lomitas Sch. Dist., Atherton, Calif., 2001—04. Fellow, UC Regents, 1991-1992; Post Doctoral fellow, Ctr. for Study of Law and Soc., 2001-2002, Rsch. fellow, Ctr. for Study of Russia and Soviet Union, Moscow, Russia, 1996. Mem.: Western Assn. Women Historians, Am. Assn. Women in Slavic Studies, Am. Hist. Assn. D-Liberal. Avocations: scuba diving, travel, cooking. Home: 170 Pecora Way Portola Valley CA 94028 Office: Castilleja Sch 1310 Bryant St Palo Alto CA 94301 Office Phone: 650-328-3160. Personal E-mail: story@alum.vassar.edu.

HENG, SIANG GEK, communications executive; b. Singapore, Dec. 4, 1960; came to U.S., 1984. m. G.J. Sturgis, 1991. BSEE with honors, Nat. U. Singapore, 1983; MSEE in Computer Engring., U. So. Calif., 1985; MS in Engring. Mgmt., Nat. Technol. U., 1993. Cisco cert. design profl., cert. network profl. Rsch. engr. Nat. Univ. Singapore, 1983—84; sys. mgr. LinCom Corp., LA, 1985—87; fin. planner NY Life Ins. Co., LA, 1987—88; mem. tech. staff AT&T Bell Laboratories, Holmdel, NJ, 1988—96; sr. mem. tech. staff AT&T, Holmdel, NJ, 1996—2000, prin. tech. staff mem., 2000—04, sr. tech. specialist, 2004—. Freelance computer and comm. cons., N.J., 1987-94. Contbr. articles to profl. jours.; patentee in field. Avocations: music, kickboxing, swimming, reading, weightlifting. Office: AT&T Rm A2-2F34 200 S Laurel Ave Middletown NJ 07748-1998 E-mail: sgheng@att.com.

HENGEN, NANCY L., lawyer; b. NYC, Oct. 1, 1951; BA, Swarthmore Coll., 1973; JD, Harvard Univ., 1976. Bar: NY 1977. Ptnr., maritime law, comml. fin. Holland & Knight LLP, NYC. Contbr. articles to profl. journals. Mem.: Am. Coll. Comml. Fin. Lawyers, Maritime Law Assn. (proctor), Internat. Bar Assn. Office: Holland & Knight LLP 195 Broadway New York NY 10007 Office Phone: 212-513-3255. Office Fax: 212-385-9010. Business E-Mail: nancy.hengen@hklaw.com.

HENINGTON, CARLEN, psychologist, educator; d. Carl Frank and Betty Jean Votapka; m. William Leonard Henington, 1978; children: Blake Leonard, Robin Leonard, Brianne Marie. PhD, Tex. A&M U., Coll. Sta., Tex., 1991—96. Cert. Sch. Psychol. NASP, 1996. Asst. prof. Miss. State U., 1996—2000, assoc. prof., 2000—. Cons. Miss. Early Intervention Program, Jackson, Miss., 1997—2003. Children's adv. Statewide Sch. Districts, Miss., 1994—2003. Mem.: APA, Behavior Spl. Interest Group - NASP (sec. 1999—2001), Nat. Assn. Sch. Psychol. (Miss. state del. 2005—, Miss. com. chmn.). Office: Mississippi State University 508 Allen Hall Box 9727 Mississippi State MS 39762 Office Phone: 662-325-7099. E-mail: cdh@colled.msstate.edu.

HENIN-HARDENNE, JUSTINE, professional tennis player; b. Liège, Belgium, June 1, 1982; d. Jose and Francoise Henin. Winner, Roland Garros French Open Grand Slam, 2003, 2006, US Open, 2003, German Open, 2003, Medibank Internat., 2006, Dubai Duty Free Women's Open, 2006, Hastings Direct Internat. Championships, 2006, Pilot Pen Tennis, 2006. Office: WTA Tour 1 Progress Plz Ste 1500 Saint Petersburg FL 33701-4335*

HENKE, JANICE CARINE, educational software developer, marketing professional; b. Hunter, N.D., Jan. 28, 1938; d. John Leonard and Adeline (Hagen) Hanson; children: Toni L., Tom L., Tracy L. BS, U. Minn., 1965; postgrad., misc. schs., 1969—. Cert. elem. tchr., Minn., Iowa. Tchr. dance, 1953-56; tchr. kindergarten Des Moines Pub. Schs., 1964-65; tchr. elem. Ind. Sch. Dist. 284, Wayzata, Minn., 1969-93; pvt. bus. history Wayzata, 1978—; marketer, promoter health enhancement Jeri Jacobus Cosmetics Aloe Pro, Am. Choice Nutrition, Multiway, KM Matol, Wayzata, 1978—; developer ednl. software, marketer of software Computer Aided Teaching Concepts, Excelsior, Minn., 1983—; Edn. Minn. authorized rep. with Midwest Benefit Advisers, Excelsior, 1993—. Developer, author drug edn. curriculum, Wayzata, 1970-71; mem. programs com. Health and Wellness, Wayzata, 1988-93; chmn. Wayzata Edn. Assn. Ins. Com., 1991-93; mem. Staff Devel. Adv. Bd., Wayzata, 1988-93; coach Odyssey of the Mind, 1989-93. Author, developer computer software; contbr. articles to newspapers. Fundraiser Ind. Reps. Wayzata, 1976-79; mem. pub. rels. com. Lake Minnetonka (Minn.) Dist. Ind. Reps., 1979-81, fundraising chmn., 1981-82; chmn. Wayzata Ind. Reps., 1981-82; sec. PTO, Wayzata, 1981-82. Mem. NEA, Minn. Edn. Assn., Wayzata Edn. Assn. (bd. mem., ins. chairperson). Lutheran. Avocations: swimming, skiing, travel, reading, learning. Office: Henke Services Inc 20380 Excelsior Blvd Excelsior MN 55331-8733

HENKE, TRACY ANN, former federal agency administrator; b. Moscow Mills, Mo., 1969; BS in Polit. Sci., U. Mo.-Columbia. Sr. policy adv. to Senator Christopher S. Bond from Mo. US Senate, Washington; prin. dep. asst. atty. gen., Office Justice Programs US Dept. Justice, Washington, 2001—03, acting asst. atty. gen. Office Justice Programs, dep. asst. atty. gen., 2003—05; asst. sec., Office Grants & Tng. US Dept. Homeland Security, Washington, 2006.*

HENKEL, KATHRYN GUNDY, lawyer; b. West Columbia, Tex., Oct. 16, 1952; d. Louis Ory Jr. and Patricia Dolores (Fields) Gundy. BA cum laude, Rice U., 1973; JD cum laude, Harvard U., 1976. Bar: Tex. 1976, U.S. Dist. Ct. (no. dist.) Tex. 1982, U.S. Ct. Appeals (5th cir.) 1994, U.S. Tax Ct. 1981,

U.S. Supreme Ct. 1983; bd. cert. estate planning and probate law, Tex. Bd. Legal Specialization. Ptnr. Hughes & Luce, L.L.P., Dallas, 1982—. Author: Estate Planning and Wealth Preservation: Strategies and Solutions, 1997. Mem. adv. coun. Cmtys. Found. Tex. Inc., 1982—; mem. planned giving adv. com. Children's Med. Ctr., Dallas; trustee Dallas Opera. Fellow Am. Coll. Trust and Estate Counsel; mem. ABA (vice chair sect. real property, probate and trusts com. on generation-skipping transfers 1992-95, chair sect. of taxation com. on estate and gift taxes 1993-95, coun. dir. sect. taxation 1996-99, co-chair sect. real property, probate and trust law estate planning study com. on law reform), State Bar Tex. (chair sect. taxation 1992-93), Dallas Bar Assn. (past chair sect. taxation), Tex. Bar Found. Roman Catholic. Avocations: reading, travel.

HENKEL, KATHY, composer; b. L.A., Nov. 20, 1942; d. Norman Nicholas and Lila Rhea (Lee) Henkel; m. Michael Eric Manes (div.). BA in hist., UCLA, 1965; BM in music, Calif. State U., Northridge, 1976, MA in music, 1982. Music rschr. Paramount Pictures, L.A., 1978—81; music reviewer L.A. Times, 1979; scriptwriter, prod. KUSC-FM, L.A., 1984—89; program annotation, edn. cons. Chamber Music/LA, 1987—95; program annotation L.A. Chamber Orch., 1988—98, edn. cons., 1998—; liner note writer Pro Piano Records, N.Y.C., 1994—2003; composer, owner Sign of the Silver Birch Music, L.A., 2004—. Adv. bd. Los Angeles City Coll. Music Dept., 1994—. Composer various chamber music, song cycles. Recipient Commn. for Music award, State of Alaska, 1994. Mem.: Nat. Acad. Rec. Arts and Scis., Profl. Musicians Local 47, Phi Beta Kappa Alumni, Phi Beta Women's Profl. Fraternity. Avocation: hiking Cornwall coastal path. Home: 2367 Creston Dr Los Angeles CA 90068

HENKIN, TINA M., science educator, researcher; PhD in Genetics, U. Wis., 1984. Joined Ohio State U., 1995—, prof. dept microbiology. Spkr. in field. Contbr. articles to profl. jours. Recipient Award in Molecular Biology, NAS, 2006, Disting. Scholar award, Ohio State U., 2004. Fellow: Am. Acad. Microbiology. Office: Ohio State U Dept Microbiology 484 W 12th Ave Columbus OH 43210-1292 Office Phone: 614-688-3831. Office Fax: 614-292-8120. Business E-Mail: henkin.3@osu.edu.

HENLE, MARY, retired psychology educator; d. Leo and Pearl Henle. AB, Smith Coll., Northampton, Mass., 1934, AM, 1935; PhD, Bryn Mawr Coll., Pa., 1939; LHD (hon.), New Sch. U., 1983. Rsch. assoc. Swarthmore Coll., Pa., 1939—41; instr. U. Del., Newark, 1941—42, Bryn Mawr Coll., 1942—44; mem. faculty Sarah Lawrence Coll., Bronxville, NY, 1944—46; from asst. prof. to assoc. prof. psychology New Sch. Social Rsch., N.Y.C., 1946—54, prof., 1954—83; prof. emerita, 1983—. Cons. Ednl. Svcs., Cambridge, Mass., 1965—67; vis. prof. Cornell U., fall, 1981. Author: 1879 and All That, 1986, numerous articles, chpts.; editor: (book) Documents of Gestalt Psychology, 1961, Selected Papers of W. Köhler, 1971, others. Fellow, J.S. Guggenheim Meml. Found., 1951—52, 1960—61; rsch. fellow, Harvard U., Cambridge, 1963—64, sr. scholar, Ednl. Svcs., Cambridge, 1964—65. Fellow: AAAS, APA (pres. divsn. 26 1971—72, pres. divsn. 24 1974—75); mem.: Ea. Psychol. Assn. (pres. 1981—82). Democrat. Avocations: old houses, reading. Home: 3300 Darby Rd Apt 5212 Haverford PA 19041-7706

HENLEY, DARL HEATHCOTT, librarian, educator; b. Dyersburg, Tenn., Dec. 23, 1944; d. Hobert Valentine and Martha Erle (McClearn) Heathcott; m Paul N. Herron III, June 6, 1964 (div. Sept. 1987); m. James Robert Henley, Feb. 20, 1988; children: Dawn Michele Herron, Mark Heathcott Herron. BS in Elem. Edn. and Libr. Sci., Murray (Ky.) State U., 1966; postgrad., U. Ky., 1970-71. 6th grade tchr. Weaverton Elem. Sch., Henderson, Ky., 1966-68; substitute tchr. Henderson City Schs., 1970; libr., remedial tchr. Henderson City High, 1971-73; 6th grade tchr. Marion (Ky.) Elem., 1980-81, Crittanden County Elem. Sch., Marion, 1980-84, elem. libr., 1984—2001; ret., 2001. Past state pres. Kappa Kappa Iota Nat. Tchrs. Sorority. Mem. Cumberland Presbyn. Women Fellowship. Democrat. Avocations: reading, walking, fishing, travel, cooking. Home: 6208 Us Highway 60 W Marion KY 42064-7015

HENLEY, DEBORAH S., newspaper editor; City editor New York Newsday, N.Y.C.; exec. editor The News Journal, New Castle, Del.; asst. mng. editor, Long Island Newsday, mng. editor, 2005—. Office: Newsday 235 Pinelawn Rd Melville NY 11747

HENLEY, PATRICIA JOAN, consultant, former superintendent; b. Harrison, Ark., Dec. 30, 1944; d. Durward Milford and Nola V. (Foresee) Ellis; m. Robert Lee Henley; children: Robert, Kevin, Laura. BA, Wichita State U., 1968; MS, Pittsburg (Kans.) State U., 1973, EdS, 1976; PhD, Kans. State U., 1980. Tchr. Wichita (Kans.) Pub. Schs., 1968-70; tchr. Oswego (Kans.) Pub. Schs., 1970-73; elem. prin. Aurora (Mo.) Schs., 1973-77; grad. teaching asst. Kans. State U., Manhattan, 1977-78; asst. supt. Turner Unified Sch. Dist. #202, Kansas City, Kans., 1978-82; supt. Platte County Schs., Platte City, Mo., 1982-89; dep. supt. Kansas City (Mo.) Schs., 1989-91; founding dir. Mo. Ctr. for Safe Schs., 1995—2000; elem. prin. Ft. Osage Schs., Independence, Mo., 1991—95; supt. Univ. Acad., 2000—06; cons., 2006—. Asst. rsch. prof. grad. courses U. Mo. Kansas City; assessor, supt. mem. Mo. Dept. Elem. and Secondary Edn. Spl. Edn. Panel; founding dir. Mo. Ctr. Safe Schs., 1995-2000; prin., CEO U. Acad., 2000—. Recipient Outstanding Leadership award Jackson County Inter-Agy. Coun., 1995, Heroes in Edn. award Reader's Digest, 1995; named Bus. Woman Yr. Townsend Publs., 1989. Mem. Nat. Assn. Elem. Sch. Prins. (Nat. Disting. prin. 1994), Mo. Assn. Elem. Sch. Prins., Kansas City Suburban Assn. Elem. Sch. Prins., Rotary. E-mail: henleyp@sbcglobal.net.

HENLEY, RITA DARBY, biology educator; b. Batesville, Miss., June 11, 1954; d. Richard Price and Bobbie Nell (Thomas) Darby; m. Harris Brand Henley, Jr., Dec. 31, 1976; children: Hap, Price, Richard. BS in Biology, U. Miss., Oxford, 1975, M.Combined Sci., 1977. Faculty chemistry and biology N.W. Miss. Jr. Coll., Senatobia; tchr. math Horn Lake H.S., Miss.; tchr. biology Copiah Linconna Jr. Coll., Wesson, Miss.; tchr. math, gifted Crystal Springs Elem. Sch., Miss.; tchr. math, biology Copiah Acad., Gallman, Miss. Mem.: MPSFA (dist. dir. 2004—05, v.p. 2005—06, pres. 2006—). Home: 1118 Henley Cir Hazlehurst MS 39083 Office: Copiah Academy PO Box 125 Gallman MS 39077-0125 E-mail: brhenley@bellsouth.net.

HENNEBERGER, JUDITH NOLEN, retired music educator; b. Bassett, Va., Mar. 13, 1942; d. Aaron Dove Nolen, Gladys Young Nolen; m. John Edwin Henneberger; 1 child, John. BS in Music Edn., Bridgewater Coll., 1964; MA in Edn., Va. Tech, 1987. Cert. Orff Schulwerk tchr. Min. music Ch. of the Brethren, Arlington, Va., 1966—78; tchr. Fairfax County Pub. Schs., 1971—90, music supr., 1990—98; univ. supr. James Madison U., Harrisonburg, Va., 1999—; writer music curriculum McGraw-Hill Pub., 2004—. Music cons. Kennedy Ctr. Performing Arts, Washington, 1998—; presenter regional, nat. music edn. confs.; guest condr. choral festivals. Author: (book) Musical Games and Activities to Learn By, 1976, Stepping Stones Choral Curriculum, 1997; editor: (music book) The Little Music House, The Giant Music House, (book) The High School Music Sampler, (book) The Middle School Music Curriculum. Mem.: Music Educators Nat. Conf., Va. Music Educators Assn., Am. Choral Directors Assn., Am. Orff-Schulwerk Assn. (mem. adv. bd.), Choristers Guild (bd. dirs. 1993—99), Bridgewater Coll. Alumni Assn. (bd. dirs. 1996—2004). Avocations: travel, gardening. Personal E-mail: hennberg@aol.com.

HENNESSY, ELLEN ANNE, lawyer, financial analyst, educator; b. Auburn, N.Y., Mar. 3, 1949; d. Charles Francis and Mary Anne (Roan) H.; m. Frank Daspit, Aug. 27, 1974. BA, Mich. State U., 1971; JD, Cath. U., 1978; LLM in Taxation, Georgetown U., 1984. Bar: D.C. 1978, U.S. Ct. Appeals (D.C. cir.) 1978, U.S. Supreme Ct. 1984. Various positions NEH, Washington, 1971-74; atty. office chief counsel IRS, Washington, 1978-80; atty.-advisor Pension Benefit Guaranty Corp., Washington, 1980-82; assoc. Stroock & Stroock & Lavan, Washington, 1982-85, Willkie Farr & Gallager, 1985-86, ptnr. Washington, 1987-93; dep. exec. dir. and chief negotiator Pension Benefit Guaranty Corp., Washington, 1993—98; sr. v.p. and dir. Actuarial Sci. Assoc. Holdings Inc., 1998—2000; sr. v.p. Aon Cons. Inc., Washington, 2000—03; pres. Fiduciary Counselors, Inc., 1999—. Adj. prof. law Georgetown U., Washington, 1985—; mem. com. on continuing profl. edn. Am. Law Inst./ABA, 1994—97; dir. Women's Inst. for a Secure Retirement, Nat. Women's Law Ctr. Mem. ABA (supervising editor taxation sect. newsletter 1984-87, mem. standing com. on continuing edn. 1990-94, chair joint com. on employee benefits 1991-92, mem. standing com. on tech. and info. sys. 2002—, mem. task force on corp. responsiblity, 2002-03), Worldwide Employee Benefits Network (pres. 1987-88), D.C. Bar Assn. (mem. steering com. tax sect. 1988-93, chair continuing legal edn. com. 1993-95), Am. Coll. Employee Benefits Counsel (bd. govs. 2000-03). Democrat. Avocation: whitewater canoeing. Home: 1926 Lawrence St NE Washington DC 20018-2734 Office: Ste 700 700 12th St NW Washington DC 20005-3949 Office Phone: 202-558-5141. Business E-Mail: nell.hennessy@fiduciarycounselors.com.

HENNING, JOAN DENISE, secondary school educator; d. Edward John and Pelagia Duesbout; m. James Ronald Henning, June 22, 1985; children: Matthew James, Mark Michael. BS, Ctrl. Mich. U., Mt. Pleasant, MS in Tchrs. Biology, 1984. Cert. tchr. Mich. Tchr. Carson City (Mich.)-Crystal Area Schs., 1985—, sci. dept. chairperson, 1986—. Mem.: Internat. Curly Horse Orgn., Am. Bashkir Curly Registry. Office Phone: 989-584-3175. Business E-Mail: jhenning@carsoncity.k12.mi.us.

HENNING, LILLIAN JOYCE, special education educator; d. Walter Orville and Betty Wyvetta Roberts; m. Douglas D. Henning, Mar. 19, 1966; children: Scott, Matthew. BS, Western Oreg. U., 1966; MEd, Mid Am. Nazarene U., 1993; postgrad., Kans. State U., 1996; cert. in learning disabilities, U. Kans., 2000; postgrad., Cambridge U., Eng., 2002, U. Kans., 2002. Cert. learning disabilities K-9 Kans., Colo., elem. edn. K-8 Kans., Wash., Oreg., social studies, natural scis. K-8 Wash. Kindergarten tchr. Clover Creek Elem., Spanaway, Wash., 1987—88; 2d grade tchr. Camas Prairie Elem., Spanaway, 1988—91; 3d grade tchr. Hilltop Elem., Spring Hill, Kans., 1991—2000, spl. edn. tchr., 2003—, Spring Hill Unified Sch. Dist. 230, 2000—01, instrnl. facilitator, 2001—02; dean of students, tchr. European Nazarene Coll., Busingen, Switzerland, 2002—03; with Prairie Creek Elem., Olathe, Kans. Nominee Tchr. of Yr., Spring Hill Unified Sch. Dist. 230, 1994—95; Grace M. Phinney scholar, U. Kans., 1998—99. Mem.: NEA. Office: Prairie Creek Elem Sch 17077 W 165th St Olathe KS 66062 Office Phone: 913-592-7255 ext. 7179. Personal E-mail: joyhenn@yahoo.com. E-mail: henningj@usb230.com.

HENNING, RONI ANITA, printmaker, artist; b. Bklyn., Mar. 19, 1939; d. Margaritis George Michos and Jane Eliza Duggan; m. John Henry Henning, Dec. 28, 1958 (dec. May 18, 1992); children: Dawn, Diane. Cert. in fine art, Cooper Union Sch. Art and Arch., 1970. Dir., masterprinter, tchr. screenprint workshop N.Y. Inst. Tech., Old Westbury, NY, 1977—95; dir., masterprinter Henning Screenprint Workshop, Bklyn., 1994—. Leader screened monotype workshop Rutgers U., New Brunswick, NJ, 1998, New Brunswick, 2000, Lower Eastside Printshop, N.Y.C., 1998—2003, Hunterdon Art Mus., Clinton, NJ, 1999—2001; cons. Photographys Changing Image Frontiers of Photography, Time Life Book, N.Y.C., 1972; cons. waterbased screen printing U. of the West of Eng., Bristol, 1999; leader children's printmaking workshop Goddard-Riverside Cmty. Ctr., N.Y.C., 1990. Author: Screenprinting: Water-based Techniques, 1994; exhibitions include The Art of Women Printmaker, The Womens Mus., Washington, 1991, Represented in permanent collections Lang Comm., NIH, Bethesda, Md. Active print project for Save the Children Columbia Tchrs. Coll., N.Y.C., 1985. Scholar, Cooper Union Sch. Art and Arch., N.Y.C., 1966—70. Achievements include development of quality non-toxic water-based screenprinting system as an alternative to the traditional solvent-based one. Avocations: gardening, travel, protecting wildlife and their environment. Home: 7908 Ridge Blvd Brooklyn NY 11209 Office: Henning Screenprint Workshop 7908 Ridge Blvd Brooklyn NY 11209

HENNINGS, DOROTHY GRANT (MRS. GEORGE HENNINGS), education educator; b. Paterson, N.J., Mar. 15, 1935; d. William Albert and Ethel Barbara (Moll) Grant; m. George Hennings, June 15, 1968. AB, Barnard Coll., 1956; EdM, U. Va., 1959; EdD, Columbia U., 1965. Tchr. Pierrepont Elem. Sch., Rutherford, NJ, 1956-58, Thomas Jefferson Jr. H.S., Fair Lawn, NJ, 1959-64; prof. edn. Kean U. of N.J., Union, 1965-99, disting. prof. edn., 1999—2002, disting. prof. emeritus, 2002—. Author citation N.J. Inst. Tech., Divsn. Continuing Edn., 1982; author: (with B. Grant) Teacher Moves, 1971; Content and Craft: Written Expression in the Elementary School, 1973; Smiles, Nods and Pauses: Activities to Enrich Children's Communication Skills, 1974; Mastering Classroom Communication: What Interaction Analysis Tells the Teacher, 1975; (with G. Hennings) Keep Earth Clean, Blue and Green: Environmental Activities for Young People, 1976; Words, Sounds, and Thoughts: More Activities to Enrich Children's Communication Skills, 1977; Communication in Action: Teaching the Language Arts, 1978, 8th edit. 2002 (with D. Russell) Listening Aids Through the Grades, 1979; (with G. Hennings) Today's Elementary Social Studies, 1980, 2d edit., 1989; Written Expression in the Language Arts, 1981; Teaching Communication and Reading Skills in the Content Areas, 1982; (with L. Fay) Star Show, 1989, Grand Tour, 1989, Previews, 1989, Reading with Meaning: Strategies for College Reading, 1990, 6th rev. edit., 2004, Poets Journal, 1991, Beyond the Read Aloud: Learning to Read Through Listening to and Reflecting on Literature, 1992, Vocabulary Growth: Strategies for College Word Study, 2001, Words Are Wonderful: An Interactive Approach to Vocabulary, books 1 and 2, 2003, book 3, 2004, book 4, 2005; contbr. articles to Edn., The Record, Lang. Arts, Sci. Tchr., The Reading Tchr., Jour. of Adolescent & Adult Lit., Jour. of Reading, Tchr. to Tchrs., Sci. and Children, Early Years, Reading Rsch. and Instrn., New Eng. Jour. of History, Jour. Reading Edn., others. Mem. Unitarian Ch., Summit, NJ; trustee Kean U. Found., 2005—. Recipient Edn. Press award, 1974, Outstanding Article award, 1999, Bldg. named in Her Honor, Kean U., 2005; NSF Acad. Yr. Inst. grantee, 1959, Field Enterprise grantee, Columbia U., 1965. Mem. Nat. Coun. Tchrs. English, N.J. Reading Assn. (Disting. Svc. to Reading award 1993), Internat. Reading Assn. (Outstanding Tchr. Educator in Reading award 1992), Suburban Reading Coun., Phi Beta Kappa, Phi Delta Kappa, Phi Kappa Phi, Kappa Delta Pi. Home: 21 Flintlock Dr Warren NJ 07059-5014 Personal E-mail: hennings@verizon.net.

HENNION, CAROLYN LAIRD (LYN HENNION), investment executive; b. Orange, Calif., July 27, 1943; d. George James and Jane (Porter) Laird; m. Reeve L. Hennion, Sept. 12, 1964; children: Jeffrey Reeve, Douglas Laird. BA, Stanford U., Calif., 1965; grad. in Securities Industry Inst., Wharton Sch., U. Pa., Phila., 1992. CFP, fund specialist; lic. ins. agt.; registered gen. securities prin. Portfolio analyst Schwabacher & Co., San Francisco, 1965-66; adminstrv. coord. Bicentennial Commn., San Mateo County, Calif., 1972-73; dir. devel. Crystal Springs Uplands Sch., Hillsborough, Calif., 1973-84; tax preparer Household Fin. Corp., Foster City, Calif., 1982; freelance, 1983-87; sales promotion mgr. Franklin Distbrs., Inc., San Mateo, 1984-86, v.p. and regional sales mgr. of N.W., 1986-91, v.p. Mid-Atlantic, 1991-94; v.p. Viatech, Inc., 1986-92; propr. Buncom Ranch, 1990—; v.p. Keypoint Svcs. Internat., 1992—2002; pres. Brock Rd. Corp., 1993—; v.p. Strand, Atkinson, Williams & York, Medford, Oreg., 1994—2004, sr. v.p., 2004—; asst. treas. Allamar Techs., Inc., 2004—. Editor: Lest We Forget, 1975. Pres. South Hillsborough Sch. Parents' Group, 1974—75; sec. Vol. Bur. San Mateo County, Burlingame, Calif., 1975; chmn. Cmty. Info. Com., Town of Hillsborough, 1984—86, mem., subcom. chmn. fin. adv. com., 1984—86; mem. adv. com. Rogue Valley Internat. Airport, 1996—2003, chair, 2001—03; mem. coun. Town of Buncom, Oreg., 1990—; chmn. Jackson County Applegate Trail Sesquicentennial Celebration, 1995—97; founding dir. So. Oreg. Hist. Soc. Found., 1995—2005, sec., 1995—98, pres., 1998—2001; sec., treas. Oreg. Shakespeare Festival Endowment Fund, 1997—98, pres., 1998—2000; dir. Rogue Valley Manor Cmty. Svcs., 1996—, vice-chair, 1997—2006, chair, 2006—; dir. Craterian Performances Co., 1997—2004, pres., 2001—03; dir. So. Oreg. Estate Planning Coun., 1997—2003, pres., 1998—99; dir. Oreg. Cmty. Found., 2002—; chmn. Oreg. Cmty. Found. So. Oreg. Leadership Coun., 2002—; dir. Applegate Valley Rural Fire Protection Dist. #9, 2004—, sec./treas., 2004—; dir. Pacific Retirement Svcs., 2006—; bd. dirs. Pacific N.W. Mus. Natural History, 1995—96, Providence Cmty. Health Found., 1996—2003, sec., 1998—2000, v.p., 2000—01, pres., 2001—02; bd. dirs. Chamber of Medford, Jackson Co., 1997—2000, v.p., 1999—2000; bd. dirs. Oreg. Shakespeare Festival, 2002—, OR529 Coll. Savs. Network, 2005—. Recipient Coun. for Advancement and Support of Edn. award, 1981, Exemplary Direct Mail Appeals Fund Raising Inst. award, 1982, Golden Mic award Frederic Gilbert Assocs., 1993, White Rose award March of Dimes, 2004, Heritage award, So. Oreg. Hist. Soc., 2004; named Wholesaler of Yr., Shearson Lehman Hutton N.W. Region, 1989, one of Top 300 Fin. Advisors, Worth Mag., 1998, Top 250 Fin. Advisors, 1999, 2001, one of 10 Outstanding Brokers Registered Rep. Mag., 2000, named to Am. Best Fin. Planners Consumers Rsch. Coun., 2005-06. Mem. So. Oreg. Estate Planning Coun., Buncom Hist. Soc., Oreg. Shakespeare Festival, Britt Festivals, So. Oreg. Hist. Soc., Jr. League, Medford Rogue Rotary, Craterian Performances Co. Republican. Home: 3232 Little Applegate Rd Jacksonville OR 97530-9303 Office: Strand Atkinson Williams & York 2495 E Barnett Ste A Medford OR 97504 Business E-Mail: lhennion@strandatkinson.com.

HENNUM, SUSANNA SHELLY, art history educator; b. Iquique, Chile, Jan. 14, 1928; came to U.S., 1935; d. William A. and Geneva E. (Lewis) Shelly; m. Paul R. Hennum, May 15, 1955; children: Ruth Eileen Hennum Fowler, Eric Lawrence. BA, DePauw U., 1950; MA, Wichita (Kans.) State U., 1970. Registrar, curatorial asst. to dir. Wichita Art Mus., 1970-74; instr. art history and women's studies Clark Coll., Vancouver, Wash., 1977-89, dir. index gallery, 1980-81; instr. art history Marylhurst (Oreg.) Coll., 1988—. Lectr. art history Tabor Coll., Hillsboro, Kans., 1970, Wichita State U., 1969-70; docent Portland Art Mus., 1989—. Mem. mayor's com. Pick Out Art for City Hall, Vancouver, 1985; mem. women's com. Reed Coll., Portland, 1983-87; arts panel moderator Evergreen State Coll., Vancouver, 1980; docent trainer Nihonga Art Exhibit, Vancouver, 1985-86; bd. dirs. Columbia Bus. Commn. for the Arts, Vancouver, 1983-86. Recipient Commendation, Assn. Students Clark Coll. Bd. Commrs., 1983. Mem. AAUW (pres. Vancouver br. 1983-85, Grantee 1985). Avocations: spinning, sewing, travel, reading, weaving. Home: 2800 NE 113th St Vancouver WA 98686-4236

HENOCH, REVA, elementary school educator; d. Pery and Patty Bailey. BS in Edn., Hannibal-LaGrange Coll., Mo., 1992. Tchr. Keokuk Mid. Sch., Iowa, 1997—. Dir., actress, singer Great River Players. Named Outstanding tchr., Belin & Blank Inst. for Gifted Edn. Office: Keokuk Middle School 2002 Orleans Keokuk IA 52632 Office Phone: 319-524-3737.

HENRETTA, DEBORAH A., consumer products company executive; m. Sean Murray; 3 children. Grad., St. Bonaventure U., 1983; MA, Syracuse U. Brand asst. Procter & Gamble, Cin., 1985, v.p., 1999—; gen. mgr. global baby care Proctor & Gamble, Cin., 1999—2001; pres. global baby care Procter & Gamble, Cin., 2001—. Bd. dirs. Sprint Corp., 2004—. Mem. adv. com. Newhouse Sch. Pub. Comm., Syracuse U. Named one of 50 Most Powerful Women in Bus., Fortune, 2002. Office: Procter & Gamble Procter & Gamble Plaza Cincinnati OH 45202

HENRI, JANINE JACQUELINE, librarian; b. Washington, Aug. 16, 1955; d. Victor Philippe and Christine (Leuschner) H.; m. David Theron Sanford, July 24, 1982; 1 child, Geoffrey K. Sanford. AB, San Diego State U., 1979; postgrad., UCLA, 1979—82; M of Libr. Info. Sci., U. Calif., Berkeley, 1996. Res. supr. bus. and social sci. libr. U. Calif., Berkeley, 1982-87, monographs, res. supr. environ. design libr., 1987-89, head tech. svcs. environ. design libr., 1989-91; art libr. fine arts libr. U. Tex., Austin, 1991—95, head libr. architecture and planning libr., 1995—. Author: The Library and the Accreditation Process in Design Disciplines: Best Practice, 2003; Compilor 1986-88 Bibliography of South Asian Art, 1990; contbr. articles to profl. jours. Mem. ALA, Art Libraries Soc. North Am. (exec. bd. 1996-97), Am. Com. for South Asian Art, Assn. Architecture Sch. Libr.

HENRICKSON, BONNIE, women's college basketball coach; BS in Phys. Edn., St. Cloud (Minn.) U., 1986; MS in Phys. Edn., Western Ill. U., 1988. Asst. coach U. Ia., 1995-97, Big 10 regular season conf. champions, 1995-96, Big 10 tournament conf. champions, 1996-97; asst. coach Va. Poly. U. Hokies, Blacksburg, Va., 1988-95, head coach, 1997—2005, Atlantic 10 tournament champions, 1997-98; head coach U. Kans., Lawrence, 2005—. Office: Athletic Dept U Kans 1502 Iowa St Lawrence KS 66045

HENRICKSON, MARTHA MARIE, trade association administrator; b. Austin, Minn., Nov. 11, 1976; d. Laurence Andrew and Rena Jane Langowski; m. Charles Eugene Henrickson, May 17, 2003. BA, St. Mary's U. Minn., 1999; MA, Coll. St. Scholastica, St. Paul, 2003. Pers. dir. Mid-America Festivals, Shakopee, Minn., 1999—2000; human resources profl. Low Voltage Contractors, Edina, Minn.; asst. chpt. mgr. Nat. Elec. Contractors Assn., Mpls., 2002—. Chmn. South Ctrl. Minn. JATC, Rochester, Minn., 2005—06; sec south ctrl. MInn. elec. joint apprenticeship tng. com. Minn. Statewide Ltd. Energy, Fridley, Minn., 2003—06. Named Mgmt. Student of Yr., St. Mary's U. Minn., 1999; St. Thomas Moore scholar, St. Mary's U., 1995. Mem.: Am. Mensa. Office: Minneapolis NECA Ste 365 5100 Gamble Dr Minneapolis MN 55416 Office Phone: 952-591-1800. Personal E-mail: mhenrickson@mplsneca.org.

HENRIKSEN, EVA HANSINE, retired anesthesiology educator; b. Petaluma, Calif., Jan. 1, 1929; d. Peder Henrik Boas and Karen (Nielsen) Henriksen; m. Daniel Edward MacLean, Aug. 25, 1957 (dec. Dec. 1981); children: Elizabeth, Mary Ann. AA, U. Calif., Berkeley, 1948, BA, 1950; MD, Yale U., 1954. Diplomate Am. Bd. Anesthesiology. Intern, resident Los Angeles County Hosp., L.A., 1954-57; from instr. to asst. prof. anesthesia Loma Linda U. (formerly Coll. Med. Evangelists), L.A., 1957-68; from instr. to assoc. prof. surgery anesthesiology Sch. Medicine U. So. Calif., L.A., 1957-94, assoc. prof. anesthesiology emeritus, 1994—. Anesthesia cons. L.A. Coroner's Office, 1992—. Mem. governing coun. Angelica Luth. Ch., 1992—2000, 2002—06. Democrat. Avocation: patchwork quilt making. Home: 957 Arapahoe St Los Angeles CA 90006-5703

HENRION, ROSEMARY PROVENZA, psychotherapist, educator; b. Greenville, Miss., Oct. 2, 1929; d. Vincent and Camille (Portera) Provenza; m. Albert Joseph Henrion, Sept. 8, 1956 (dec.); 1 child, Albert Joseph Jr. BSN, U. Tex., 1963; MSN in Psychiat./Mental Health Nursing, Vanderbilt U., 1972; MS in Secondary Edn., U. So. Miss., 1974. RN Tex.; cert. logotherapist. Psychotherapist St. Mary's Hosp., Galveston, Tex., 1951—52, office and pvt. duty surg. nurse, 1952—53; supr. ob-gyn. nursing Greenville Gen. Hosp., 1954—56, head nurse, ob-gyn. and med.-surg. nursing, 1953—54; instr. nursing Providence Hosp. Sch. Nursing, Waco, Tex., 1957—59; dir. inservice edn., asst. dir. nursing svc. Meml. Hosp., Gulfport, Miss., 1966—67, dir. nursing svc., 1967—68; psychiat. clin. nurse specialist Biloxi VA Med. Ctr., Miss., 1972—89, in-house cons., 1975—92, assoc. chief nursing svc., 1989—92; clin. nurse specialist VA Outpatient Ctr., Pensacola, Fla., 1992—98; adj. clin. prof., psychiat.-mental health nursing La. State U., New Orleans, 1975—76; adj. clin. prof. grad. nursing program U. So. Miss., Hattiesburg, 1983—92; faculty V.F. Inst. Logotherapy, Berkeley and San Jose, Calif., 1983—92, Abilene, Tex., 1993—; clin. instr. grad. nursing program U. So. Ala., 1998—99. Internat. bd. dirs. V. F. Inst. of Logotherapy, 1992—; guest lectr. internat. program on logotherapy U. South Africa, Pretoria, 2005; co-founder The Inst. Meaningful Living, 2003—. Co-author: The Power of Meaningful Intimacy: Key to Successful Relationships, 2004; contbg. author: Favorite Counseling and Therapy Techniques, 1998, Favorite Counseling and Therapy-Homework Assignments, 2001, International Forum for Logotherapy, 2004, 2006; contbr. articles to profl. jours. Mem. Pope John Paul II Cultural Ctr. Mem.: AAUW, Menninger Soc., Nat. Women's History Mus. (charter 2004), Women's Mus., Miss. Bd. Nursing (pres. 1977—79),

Smithsonian Instn., Vanderbilt Alumni Assn., The Wilson Assocs. (assoc.), Sigma Theta Tau Internat. (Iota chpt. 1972—). Home and Office: 19 Wenmar Ave Pass Christian MS 39571-3144 Office Phone: 228-343-4240. Personal E-mail: ahenrion@cableone.net.

HENRIQUES, DIANA BLACKMON, journalist; b. Bryan, Tex., Dec. 17, 1948; d. Lawrence Ernest and Pauline (Webb) Blackmon; m. Laurence Barlow Henriques, Jr., June 7, 1969. BA with distinction, George Washington U., 1969. Editor Lawrence Ledger, Lawrenceville, NJ, 1969-71; reporter Asbury Park Press, NJ, 1971-74; copy editor Palo Alto Times, Calif., 1974-76; investigative reporter Trenton Times, NJ, 1976-82; bus. writer The Phila. Inquirer, 1982-86; writer Barron's Fin. Weekly, NYC, 1986-89; investigative reporter NY Times, 1989—. Vis. fellow, cons. Woodrow Wilson Sch., Princeton U., NJ, 1981-82, Guggenheim Found., NY, NJ, 1981-82. Author: (books) The Machinery of Greed, 1986, Fidelity's World, 1995, The White Sharks of Wall Street, 2000; contbr. articles to profl. jours. Mem. internat. coun. Elliott Sch. Internat. Affairs George Washington U. Recipient Bell Prize N.J. Press Assn., 1977, Investigative Reporting prize Deadline Club, 1997, George B. Polk award for military reporting, 2005; co-recipient Loeb award Deadline Reporting, 1999. Mem. NY Fin. Writers Assn., Phi Beta Kappa, Lectr. Am. Press Inst. Avocations: walking, reading. Office: The New York Times 229 W 43rd St New York NY 10036-3959

HENRY, ANN RAINWATER, retired education educator; b. Okla., Nov. 2, 1939; d. George Andrew and Opal Norma (Cohea) Rainwater; m. Morriss M. Henry, Aug. 1, 1964; children: Paul, Katherine, Mark. BA, U. Ark., 1961, MA, 1964, JD, 1971. Bar: Ark. 1971. Pvt. practice law, Fayetteville, Ark., 1971—72; instr. Coll. Bus. Adminstrn. U. Ark., Fayetteville, 1976—78, asst. prof., 1979—84, assoc. prof., 1984—99, asst. dean, 1984—86, assoc. dean, 1986—89, faculty chair, 1989—91; ret., 1999. Bd. dirs. City of Fayetteville, 1977-83, 91-92, Arvest Bank Bd., Fayetteville; chmn. cert. com. Ark. Tchrs. Evaluation, 1984-85; mem. Ark. Local Svcs. Adv. Bd., 1980-88, Ark. Gifted and Talented, 1989—, Ark. State Bd. Edn., 1985-86, Kids for Health Bd., 2000-, Cancer Challenge, 1996-2004, Fayetteville Cmty. Found., 2003-06; mem. bd. Ark. Nature Conservancy, trustee, 2006—; Dem. nominee 3d Dist. Ark. U.S. Ho. Reps., 1996 Mem. U. Ark. Alumni Assn. (bd. dirs., asst. treas. 1989-93), Fayetteville C. of C. (bd. dirs. 1983-85), Ark. Bar Assn. (chmn. ethics com. 1986-87) Democrat. Methodist. Avocations: reading, sailing, needlepoint, gardening. Home: 2465 Township Common Dr Fayetteville AR 72703-3568 Business E-Mail: ahenry@uark.edu.

HENRY, BARBARA ANN, publishing executive; b. Oshkosh, Wis., July 23, 1952; d. Robert Edward and Barbara Frances (Aylesworth) Henry BJ, U. Nev., 1974. With Gannett Co., 1974—; reporter Reno Gazette-Jour., 1974—78, city editor, 1978-80, mng. editor, 1980-82; asst. nat. editor USA Today, Washington, 1982-83; exec. editor Reno Gazette-Jour., 1981-86; editor, dir. Rochester (N.Y.) Dem. and Chronicle and Times-Union, 1986—91; pub. Great Falls (Mont.) Tribune, 1992-96; pres., pub. Des Moines Register, 1996—2000, The Indianapolis Star, 2000—; pres. Ind. Newspaper Group, 2002—. Recipient Publisher of the Year, Gannett Newspaper Group, 2001. Mem. Soc. Profl. Journalists, Associated Press Mng. Editors, Am. Soc. Newspaper Editors Avocation: skiing. Mailing: Indianapolis Star PO Box 145 Indianapolis IN 46206-0145

HENRY, BARBARA ANN, finance company executive, director; b. Norwalk, Conn., Apr. 12, 1965; d. Robert Lee and Azalene (Crowder) Henry; children: Tamika, Taylor. AS Accounting, Norwalk C.C., 2003. Supr. acctg. Decker Corp., Norwalk, Conn., 1986—97; asst. dir. fin. Conn. Renaissance, Inc., Bridgeport, 1997—. Bd. dirs. Crestwood Housing Corp., Norwalk, Conn., 2000—, Carver found, Norwalk, Conn., 2004—. Avocations: reading, travel. Office: Conn Renaissance 350 Fairfield Ave Bridgeport CT 06604 Office Phone: 203-336-5225. Office Fax: 203-336-2851. E-mail: bahenry@optonline.net.

HENRY, CLARICE RUTH, librarian; b. N.Y.C., Mar. 25, 1921; d. Jacob Marx and Esther Skurka Zinaman; m. Paul Henry, Nov. 9, 1947; children: Loraine, Alan. BA in Romance Lang., Queens Coll., N.Y.C., 1972, MA in Art History, 1974, MLS, 1973. Art reference libr. Hewlett-Woodmere Pub. Libr., Hewlett, NY, 1975—90. Active Dem. Com. Nassau County, NY, 1966—68; pres. Garden City Jewish Ctr. Sisterhood, 1965—67; bd. mem. Long Island Hort. Soc., 1995—, program chmn.; bd. mem. Long Island Craft Guild, 1988—90, recording sec. Democrat. Jewish. Avocations: horticulture, jewelry. Home: 790 Garden Dr Franklin Square NY 11010

HENRY, DEBBIE CHERYL, elementary school educator; b. Des Plaines, Ill., Oct. 12, 1949; d. Don and Tommye Auch; children: Patrick, Erin. BS in Elem. Edn., N.Mex. State U., 1972; AA, Ea. N.Mex. U.; postgrad., Calif. State U., U. N.Mex., Santa Fe C.C. Elem. sch. tchr. Poudre Sch. Dist., Ft. Collins, Colo., 1972—78, Santa (N.Mex.) Pub. Schs., 1978—88; mid./elem. sch. tchr. Roswell (N.Mex.) Ind. Sch. Dist., 1988—. Named N.Mex. Secondary Edn. Conservation Tchr. of Yr., 1995—96, N.Mex. Mid. Sch. Tchr. of Yr., 1994—95, S.W. Regional Secondary Edn. Conservation Tchr. of Yr., 1995—96; recipient Presdl. award for excellence in sci., 1995, award, Milken Family Found., 1995, Laureate award, 1994. Mem.: NEA, Roswell Edn. Assn. Home: 117 E Mescalero Apt 9 Roswell NM 88201 also: 800 Marion Richards Rd Roswell NM 88201 Office Phone: 505-627-2775. E-mail: junk4deb@aol.com.

HENRY, DEBORAH EPSTEIN, lawyer; b. Scarsdale, NY, 1967; married; 3 children. BA, Yale U., 1989; JD cum laude, Bklyn. Law Sch., 1994. Bar: Conn. 1994, NY 1995, Pa. 1997, NJ 1997. Law clerk to Hon. Jacob Mishler U.S. Dist. Ct. NY (ea. dist.), 1994—96; litigation assoc. Patterson, Belkap, Webb & Tyler, LLP, NYC, 1996—97, Schnader Harrison Segal & Lewis, Phila., 1997—2002, of counsel, 2002—. Founder Flex-Time Lawyers, LLC, Phila., 1999—; bd. trustees Bklyn. Law Sch.; spkr. in field. Contbr. articles to profl. jours. Mem.: Phila. Bar Assn., Pa. Bar Assn. Office: Schnader Harrison Segal & Lewis LLP 1600 Market St Ste 3600 Philadelphia PA 19103 Office Phone: 215-751-2159. E-mail: dehenry@flextimelawyers.com.

HENRY, DONNA EDWARDS, elementary school educator; b. Washington, Oct. 1, 1949; d. Conard Paul and Jean Marie (Kemp) E. BS, D.C. Tchrs. Coll., 1971; MA, Columbia U., 1974. Cert. tchr., Md. Tchr. Binghamton Sch. Sys., NY, 1971—73; group tchr., supr., acting dir. N.Y.C. Coll. Day Care Ctr., 1974—76; tchr., supr. student tchrs. Balt. City Schs., 1976—87, Prince George's County Schs., Laurel, Md., 1987—, Bowie, Md., 1996—, Mitchelleville, 2004—. Asst. volley-ball coach Binghamton Sch. System, 1973; project dir. Fund for Ednl. Excellence, Balt., 1986-87 (ednl. grant); participant Gov.'s Acad. Sci., Math., and Tech. Towson (Md.) State U., 1991. Contbr. articles and photographs to mags.; co-writer nat., state, nat. and local awards. Coach Balt. City Volleyball League, 1979-80; vol. Balt. Neighborhoods, Inc., 1980-87. Winner Washington Post Grants for Edn., 1995; named Bowie Tchr. Yr., 1999. Mem. NEA (vol. conv. comms. com., del. Prince George's County chpt.). Avocations: photography, racquetball, volleyball. Business E-Mail: borntoplay@msn.com.

HENRY, ELAINE OLAFSON, artist, educator; b. Marshall, Minn., Aug. 25, 1945; d. Norman Jonas and Isfold Sigurdur (Josefson) Olafson; m. James Edward Henry, Sept. 30, 1967 (div. Dec. 1978); children: Julie Lynn, Cheryl Anne Henry Fields; m. Richard Story Garber, July 25, 1992. BFA, U. Wyo., 1992; MFA, So. Ill. U., 1995. Mktg. coord. Cannon Design, Inc., Grand Island, N.Y., 1978-82; mktg. cons. Mpls., 1982-83; mktg. dir. Campbell City C. of C., Gillette, Wyo., 1983-86; owner J&J Awards and Ad Concepts, Gillette, 1986-89; grad. asst. So. Ill. U., Carbondale, 1992-95; asst. prof. Emporia (Kans.) State U., 1996—2002, chair dept. art, 2000—, assoc. prof., 2002—. Pres. Nat. Coun. on Edn. for the Ceramic Arts, Erie, Colo., 2002-04, past pres., 2004-06; pres. Emporia Arts Coun., 1997-99; pres. Kans. Artist Craftsman Assn., 1999-2000; adv. bd. Ceramics: Art & Perception Mag., Sydney, Australis, 2005— Featured artist/sculptor Ceramics: Mastering the Craft, 2001, Studio Potter Mag., 1999, Ceramic Design Book, 1998, World Famous Ceramic Artists Studios, vol. II, 2004; featured artist and author Ceramics Monthly Mag., 1996. Named Artist of Yr., Emporia Arts Coun., 2005; grantee Emporia State U., 1997, 99 Mem. Kans. Artist Craftsmen Assn. (pres. 1999). Avocations: travel, books, gardening. Office: Emporia State U Campus Box 4015 1200 Commercial St Emporia KS 66801-5087 Office Phone: 620-341-5246.

HENRY, FRANCES ANN, retired journalist, educator; b. Denver, July 23, 1939; d. Lewis Byford and Betsy Mae (Lancaster) Patten; m. Charles Larry, June 28, 1963 (div. May 1981); children: Charles Kevin, Tracy Diane. BA in English, Carleton Coll., 1960; MA in Social Sci., U. Colo., Denver, 1988; MA in Journalism, Memphis State U., 1989. Cert. tchr. Lang. arts tchr. Rolla (Mo.) Pub. Schs., 1963-66; journalism/English tchr. Douglas County Pub. Schs., Castle Rock, Colo., 1976-99, retired, 1999, chmn. English dept., 1992-98; asst. prof. Memphis State U., 1991-92; mng. editor Douglas County News-Press, Castle Rock, 1986-87; editor Fourth World Bulletin, 1988; exec. editor Daily Helmsman Memphis State U., 1988-89, gen. mgr. Daily Helmsman, 1991-92; sole proprietor The Editor's Desk, 1997—. Contbr. articles to profl. jours. Recipient Gov.'s award for excellence in edn. Colo. Endowment for Humanities, 1997. Mem. ACLU, Colo. H.S. Press Assn. (sec. 1981-83, pres. 1983-91, bd. dirs., named Colo. Journalism Tchr. of Yr. 1985), Mensa, Kappa Tau Alpha. Democrat. Episcopalian. Personal E-mail: fhenry1@comcast.net.

HENRY, JULIE L., orthopedist, surgeon; BS, Miami U., Oxford, Ohio, 1988—91; MD, Med. U. Ohio, Toledo, 1991—95. Lic. Mich., 1998. Post doctorate residency U. Mich., Ann Arbor, 1995—2000; orthopaedic surgeon St. John Hosp. and Med. Ctr., Detroit, 2000—, Bon Secours Cottage Hosp., Grosse Pointe, Mich., 2000—. Mem. Jr. League of Detroit, Grosse Pointe, Mich., 1996—2006. Republican. Office: Julie L Henry MD PC 27721 Schoenherr Rd Warren MI 48088 Office Phone: 586-754-4417.

HENRY, KAREN LEE, writer, educator; b. Grand Rapids, Mich., Feb. 20, 1944; d. Leo John and Mary Alice (Mallick) Henry. AS with high honors, Davenport Coll., 1983; BA, U. Mich., 1989. Writer Palestine Human Rights Campaign, Chgo., 1984-85; journalist Al Fajr, Jerusalem, 1985-86; dir. activities Villa Maria Retirement Cmty., Grand Rapids, Mich., 1990-93; libr. asst. Grand Rapids Pub. Libr., 1994—2000; freelance writer, lectr. Grand Rapids; exec. dir. dept. justice Weed & Seed, 2000—. Ednl. cons. on Mid. East Inst. for Global Edn., Grand Rapids, 1983—, bd. dirs., 1995—. Contbr. articles to profl. jours. Apptd. Housing Bd. Appeals, Grand Rapids, 1984; spl. projects dir. Econ. Devel. Corp., Grand Rapids, 1983; active Grand Rapids AIDS Task Force, 1986-92, Coop Am., Feminist Majority, Am. Ednl. Trust, New Jewish Agenda, Am. Arab Anti-Discrimination Com., YWCA, Nat. Humane Soc., Expressions for Women; bd. dirs. YWCA, Grand Rapids, 1996-97, Am. Friends Svc. Com. of Great Lakes Region, 1996-2002; pres., founding mem. Women's Action Network, Grand Rapids, 1993—; mem. pediat. oncology resource team Butterworth Hosp., 1998—, Racial Justice Inst., 1999-, Grand Rapids Inst. Info. Democracy, 1998—; chmn. task force Project Safe Neighborhood, 2002; bd. dirs. Pediat. Oncology Resource Team, 2003—; gov. appointee Arab Am. Affairs Commn.; U.S. atty. appointee Bldg. Respect in Diverse Groups to Enhance Sensitivity; founder, Women's Empowerment Network, 2003; charter mem., Progressive Women's Alliance, 2004; mayoral appointee, Cmty. Relations Commn., 2004. Recipient Appreciation cert. Econ. Devel. Corp., 1983, Housing Appeal Bd., 1985, Chicago House, 1987, Civil Libertarian of the Yr., ACLU of West Mich., 2004, Equality award, Women's Resource Ctr., 2005. Mem. AAUW, Nat. Assn. Arab Am. Women, Nat. Mus. Women in Arts, Am. for Mid. East Understanding, Union Palestinian Women's Assn., Progressive Women's Alliance, Gilda's Club. Avocations: hiking, discussing books. Home and Office: 29 Wallinwood Ave NE Grand Rapids MI 49503-3719

HENRY, KATHLEEN CLOHERTY, lawyer; b. 1972; BA magna cum laude, Boston U., 1995; JD, Northeastern U., 2000. Bar: Mass. 2001, US Dist. Ct. (Dist. Mass.) 2001. Assoc. Litig. Dept. and Ins. & Reinsurance Litig. Practice Group Choate, Hall & Stewart LLP, Boston, 2000—. Alumni bd. dirs. Northeastern U.; pro bono atty. Political Asylum & Immigration and Refugee Project, Women's Bar Found. Family Law Project for Battered Women. Mem.: Women's Bar Assn., Boston Bar Assn. (pub. svc. com., mem. pub. interest leadership program 2003), ABA. Office: Choate Hall & Stewart LLP Two International Place Boston MA 02110 Office Phone: 617-248-4702. Office Fax: 617-248-4000. E-mail: khenry@choate.com.*

HENRY, KATHLEEN MARIE, marketing executive; b. Stillwater, Okla., Sept. 24, 1950; d. Irl Wayne and Hulda Mary Henry. BS, U. Cen. Okla., Edmond, 1972. Community relations dir./account exec. Lowe Runkle Advt., Oklahoma City, 1972-74, account coordinator, 1975; sales promotion cons. McDonald's Corp., Houston, 1974, regional advt. supr. Southfield, Mich., 1975, regional advt. mgr., 1976-78, local store mktg. mgr. Oak Brook, Ill., 1978-80, staff dir., store mktg./sales promotion, 1980-82, home office dir. store mktg./sales promotion, 1982-83, dir. nat. sales promotion, 1983-84, internat. mktg. dir., 1984-85; mktg. dir. McDonald's System France, 1985-86, McDonald's System Europe, 1985-88, v.p. mktg., 1988-97; pres. Henry Jamieson Assocs., Tulsa, Okla., 1997—, Zepper Entertainment, Tulsa, 2004—. Publicity chmn. Keep Okla. Beautiful, 1973-74; publicity chmn. Muscular Dystrophy Assn. Am., Okla. chpt., 1973-74; bd. dirs. Southfield Arts Coun., Mich., 1976-78; commr. Lake Keystone Planning and Zoning Commn., 1999—; bd. dirs. Perry High Sch. Alumni Assn., 1999-; bd. dirs. sec. Keystone Peninsula Property Owners Assn., 1998—; commr. State of Okla. Film and Music Commn. Recipient Chgo. YWCA Leadership award, 1978, Disting. Former Student award U. Ctrl. Okla., 1979, Bronco award U. Ctrl. Okla. Centennial, 1991; named Outstanding Sr. Woman U. Ctrl. Okla., 1972, Outstanding Greek Woman, 1972. Mem. U. Ctrl. Okla. Alumni Assn. (dir. 1974, 1998-2002, found. bd. dirs. 1999—), U. Ctrl. Okla. Centennial Commn., Sigma Kappa. Office: Henry Jamieson Assocs Rte 3 Box 150A Cleveland OK 74020

HENRY, KATHLEEN SUE, minister; b. St. Louis, July 24, 1943; d. Millard Harris and Helen Roberta Murray; m. Robert Earl Henry, Feb. 27, 1965 (dec.); children: Shawn Robert, Seth Elbert. BA summa cum laude, Drew U., 1965; MEd, Harvard U., 1967; MDiv, Andover Newton Theol. Sch., 1981, D of Ministry, 1993. Ordained min. United Ch. of Christ, 1982. Tchr. Schenectady (NY) City Schs., 1968—70; min. Park Pl. Congl. Ch., Pawtucket, RI, 1981—86, United Ch. of Assonet, 1987—94; sr. interim min. East Congl. Ch., Milton, Mass., 1994—95, United Ch. of Canton, 1995—97; sr. min. 1st Congl. Ch., Bristol, RI, 1997—2002; sr. interim min. Trinitarian Congl. Ch., Norton, Mass., 2003—05; interim min. Dennis UnionCh., 2005—. Cert. supr. student ministries Andover Newton Theol. Sem., 1986—, chaplain, 1990—93; mem. RI conf. United Ch. of Christ. Coach Barrington Little League, RI, 1979—85; pres. YMCA of Greater Fall River, Mass., 1993—96; founder Cancer Info. Svc. Am. Cancer Soc., RI; writing group leader Amherst Writers and Artists, Mass.; bd. dirs. Interfaith Counseling Ctr., 2003—05. Named Woman of Yr., Girl Scouts Am., Bristol, RI, 1998. Democrat. Avocations: writing, leading international religious tours, coaching, theater, fishing. Home: 394 New Meadow Rd Barrington RI 02806 Office Phone: 508-385-3543. Personal E-mail: ksmhenry@cox.net.

HENRY, LIDIA AGNIESZKA, elementary school educator; b. Rzeszow, Poland, July 10, 1976; arrived in U.S., 92, permanent resident, 95; d. Franciszek and Wladyslawa Brzuska; m. Francis Joseph Henry, Aug. 2, 2003. BS magna cum laude, Ctrl. Conn. State U., New Britain, 2006. Cert. mid. sch. math. Conn., 2006. Polish lang. tchr. Polish Saturday Sch., Hartford, Conn., 1996—; math. tchr. Woodrow Wilson Mid. Sch., Middletown, Conn., 2002—. Office: Woodrow Wilson Mid Sch 1 Wilderman's Way Middletown CT 06457 Office Phone: 860-347-8594.

HENRY, LOIS HOLLENDER, psychologist; b. Phila., Jan. 19, 1941; d. Edward Hubert and Frances Lois (Nesler) Hollender; m. Charles L. Henry, Oct. 24, 1964 (div. 1971); children: Deborah Lee, Randell Huitt, Andrew Edward. BA, Thomas A. Edison Coll., 1979; MSW, Fordham U., Bronx, N.Y., 1981; PhD in Indsl. Psychology, City U. L.A., 1992. Diplomate cert. neurofeedback provider; cert. social worker, Ariz., N.Y., N.J., EEG Biofeedback Practitioners; lic. svc. profl., career counselor, Ariz. Pers. asst., sec. IBM, Paterson, N.J., St. Louis, 1964-66; min.'s asst. Grace Luth. Ch., St. Cloud, Fla., 1966-68; adminstr., tchr. Fla. Finishing Acad., St. Cloud, 1968-70; adminstv. asst. Newark Book Ctr., 1972-77; intern, med. social worker Jersey City Med. Ctr., 1979-80; intern, psychiat./med. social worker VA Med. Ctr., Lyons, N.J., 1980-81; sch. social worker Lakeview Learning Ctr., Budd Lake, N.J., 1981-82; mgr. human resources Terak Corp., Scottsdale, Ariz., 1982-85; v.p. counseling and bus. devel. Murro & Assocs., Phoenix, 1985-88, exec. v.p. cons., 1988-91; prin. career cons. Henry & Assocs., Scottsdale, 1982-97; staff psychologist Nelson O'Connor & Assocs., Phoenix, 1993-97; v.p. dir. profl. svcs. Lee Hecht Harrison, Phoenix, 1997-98; cert. neurotherapist Forensic Psychol. Svcs., Phoenix, 1995-96; career cons., individual, family counselor, psychotherapist, neurotherapist, spkr. Henry & Assocs., Scottsdale, 1982-97. Adj. prof. Ottawa U.; mem. employers com. Ariz. Dept. Econ. Security; cons. in field. Coord.-vol. Job-A-Thon, Phoenix, 1983. Fellow Am. Orthopsychiat. Assn., Internat. Assn. Outplacement Profls. (treas. Ariz. region 1992-95, assoc. editor Internation Jour. Neuronal Regulation), Nat. Registry of Soc. Neuronal Regulation (diplomate, charter mem.); mem. NASW, Soc. Human Resource Mgmt., Am. Assn. Psychophysiology.

HENRY, LYNN J., youth church administrator; b. Ridgeway, S.C., Aug. 14, 1954; d. Tillman and Geneva Jones; 1 child, Albert Henry. BS in Speech Lang. Pathology, Columbia Union Coll., Takoma Park, Md., 1997; MS in Nutritional Scis., S.C. State U., Orangeburg, 1994. Cert. med. missionary tng.; money mgmt., comm. skills, sch. text evaluator, Christian counseler. Parade coord. S.C. Mental Retardation, Columbia, 1978; master guide Youth Pathfinder Adventist Youth Soc., youth leader Seventh-Day Adventist Ch., Columbia, 1991, comty. svc. coord., 1992, women's ministry leader, 2002—04, youth ch. coord., 2006—. Mem. parent luncheon com. Gwinnett County Schs., Lawrenceville, Ga., 2005—06, mem. sch.-wide title I com., 2004—, mem. crisis mgmt. com., 2005—06. Mem.: Gwinnett Reading Coun., Internat. Reading Assn. Avocations: debates, reading, travel, entertaining, cooking. Home: 1870 Crowell Rd Conyers GA 30094-4018

HENRY, MAURINE DALE, elementary school educator; b. Manchester, N.H., Aug. 24, 1950; d. Henry A. and Mary Barbara St. Laurent; m. Terry L. Henry, July 24, 1971; children: James, Stephen BEd, Keene State Coll., N.H., 1972; MEd, Keene State Coll., 2000. Parent trainer Keene State Coll., 1981—86; tchr. kindergarten Gilsum Elem. Sch., NH, 1987—2003, asst. prin., 2003—. Staff devel. presenter Supervisory Union # 38, Swanzey, N.H., 1996-2001; webmaster Gilsum Elem. Sch., N.H., 2002—, technology mentor, 2002—. Author: (book) Thematic Mother Goose Activities, 1999 Coach Spl. Olympics, Keene, 1988-95; v.p. individual devel. N.H. Jaycee Women, 1984-85, mgr. state speakup program, 1983-84, treas., 1981-82, chpt. pres., 1980-81 Recipient U.S. Jaycee Women Congress # 01337 award, 1985 Mem. Delta Kappa Gamma (v.p. 2000-2006, state webmaster 2003—, pres. Alpha chpt. 2006—) Home: 118 Old Walpole Rd Keene NH 03431 Office: Gilsum Elem Sch Box 38 Rte 10 Gilsum NH 03448 E-mail: mohenry@maurineh.com.

HENRY, MICHELE FERREE, music educator, elementary school educator, language arts educator; b. Ft. Wayne, Ind., Apr. 9, 1973; d. Delbert Dan Surfus, Sr. and Lou Eda Surfus; m. David James Henry, May 27, 1995; children: Alexander David, Emma Hope Michele, Elise Gabriele. BS in Elem. Edn., Ind. Wesleyan U., Marion, 1996, MEd in Curriculum Design, 2002. Cert. in lang. arts edn. Ind., 1996, in music edn. Ind., 1996, lic. in state tchg. Ind., 1996, in tchg. Assn. Christian Schs. Internat., 1997. Third grade tchr. Lakeview Christian Sch., Marion, 1996—2000, tchr. in curriculum writing, 1998—, kindergarten-twelfth grade music/choir, 2000—03, presch. and elem. music tchr., 2003—04, 2004—, fourth grade lang. arts tchr., 2004—. Supervising tchr. Ind. Wesleyan U., 1998—2002, adj. prof., 2002—, tchr. observation, 2003—04. Mem. Brookhaven Wesleyan Ch., Marion, 1991—2006; dir. Ind. North Dist. Wesleyan Ch. Teens and Talent Competition, Marion, 1998—2005; youth sponsor Brookhaven Wesleyan Ch., Marion, 2003—06. Mem.: Assn. Christian Schs. Internat., Ind. Reading Assn. (assoc.; treas. 2003—05). R-Consevative. Avocations: music, art, travel, camping. Office: Lakeview Christian Sch 5318 S Western Ave Marion IN 46953

HENRY, MURIEL BOYD, retired social worker; b. Chgo., Feb. 17, 1927; d. Thomas Alexander and Muriel Alice (Engelhard) Boyd; m. Gerrit V. Henry Jr., Nov. 24, 1971; children by previous marriage: Janet Spangler, Carl Thomas Peterson, JoAnne Peterson. BA in Sociology, U. Wash., 1974, MSW, 1977. Social worker Travelers Aid Soc., Seattle, 1978-81; med. social worker Overlake Hosp., Bellevue, Wash., 1981—91; ret., 1991. Mem. Evergreen Stroke Assn., Seattle, 1983-85, pres., 1984. Dir. of residential campaign United Way of King County, Seattle, 1969-73. Mem. Nat. Assn. Social Workers, Acad. Cert. Social Workers (cert.). Avocation: sailing.

HENRY, ROLANNE, law educator; b. Newark, 1942; d. Roland Frederick and Ann Catherine Henry. AB, Rutgers U., New Brunswick, NJ, 1964; PhD, Columbia U., NYC, 1972; JD, Rutgers U., Newark, NJ, 1978; LLM, NYU, 1980. Bar: NJ. 1979, NY 1982. Asst. prof. Rutgers U., Newark, 1972—75, vis. asst. prof. Sch. Bus., 1977—78, asst. dir. Small Bus. Devel. Ctr., 1978—78; clk. and officer mgr. US Ct. Appeals (2d cir.), NYC, 1979—80; pvt. practice law NJ, 1980—91; lectr. NJ. Inst. Tech., Newark, 1995—. Elder Presbyn. Ch. Madison, NJ, 1972. Recipient Phi Beta Kappa, Rutgers U. (Douglass Coll.), 1964. Mem.: Am. Assn. U. Women, NJ. State Bar Assn., Phi Beta Kappa. Avocations: photography, painting, golf. Office: New Jersey Inst Tech University Heights Newark NJ 07102-1982 Office Phone: 973-596-5608. Business E-Mail: henry@adm.njit.edu.

HENRY, RUTH SWINDLE, dancer, educator; d. Elro Marlin and Doris Mildred Swindle; m. Thomas Cleveland Henry, July 4, 1991. BA in Dance, Butler U., Indpls., 1976, MA in Dance, 1980; cert. movement specialist, New Sch., N.Y.C. Instr. Huntingdon Coll., Montgomery, Ala., 1976—79; assoc. dir. Montgomery Civic Ballet, 1976—79; adj. prof. U. Ala., Tuscaloosa, 1979, Birmingham, 1980; prof. Birmingham So. Coll., 1981—. Choreographer Linly Heflin Scholarship Unit, Birmingham, 1979—; bd. dirs. Ala. Dance Coun., Brimingham, 2003—. Recipient Obelisk award, Birmingham Obelisk Com., 1986. Office: Birmingham So Coll Box 549015 900 Arkadelphia Rd Birmingham AL 35254

HENRY, SALLY, academic administrator; b. Elyria, Ohio; d. Robert A. and Dorothy M. Eskins; m. James M. Henry (dec.); children: Ronald, Gregory, Mark, Tammy, Gary. A in Liberal Arts, Lorain County C.C., Elyria, 1978; B in Elem. Edn., U. Ky., 1980, M in Elem. Edn., 1981, EdD, 1987. Cert. tchg. and leadership Ky., tchg., leadership and ESOL Fla. Tchr. mid. sch. St. Peter Sch., Lexington, Ky., 1983—85; adj. instr. Lexington C.C., 1985—88; grad. asst. U. Ky., 1985—87; curriculum cons. Harcourt Brace, Orlando, Fla., 1988—89; tchr., educator Polk County Schs., Bartow, Fla., 1989—95; program specialist Collier County Schs., Naples, Fla., 1995—99, asst. prin., 1999—2004; supr. Fla. Gulf Coast U., 2004—. Facilitator, chair Sch. Adv. Coun., Everglades City, Fla., 1995—2004; coord. vol. program, Everglades City, 1995—, Ptnrs. in Edn., Everglades City, 1995—. Recipient Kids Count award, First Union Bank, Naples, 1996, Environ. award, Dept. Environ. Edn., Tallahassee, Fla., 1997—2001; grantee Great Gator Reading grant, Collier County Edn. Found., Naples, 1996, Creative Writing grant, United Arts Coun., Naples, 2000. Mem.: AAUW, Fla. Reading Coun., Phi Beta Kappa. Avocations: reading, rose gardening, decorating, shopping, collecting manatee memorabilia. Home: 348 Nassau Ct Marco Island FL 34145 E-mail: shenryphd@aol.com.

HENRY, SALLY MCDONALD, lawyer; b. Durham, N.C., Aug. 1, 1948; d. John Frederick and Mary Frances (McDonald) Henry. BA, Duke U., 1970; MA in Anthropology, SUNY, Binghamton, 1973; JD, NYU, 1982. Bar: U.S. dist. ct. (ea. dist.) N.Y. Tchr. Endicott (N.Y.) Pub. Schs., 1971-75, Monticello (N.Y.) Pub. Schs., 1975-79; clk. U.S. Bankruptcy Ct., Bklyn., 1982-83; assoc.

Skadden, Arps, Slate, Meagher & Flom L.L.P., N.Y.C., 1983-91, ptnr., 1991—. Author: Ordin on Contesting Confirmation, 1998; editor articles Rev. Law and Social Change, 1981-83; contbr. numerous articles to profl. jours. Mem. rules com. Ea. dist. N.Y. bar, Bklyn, 1984. Home: 395 Riverside Dr Apt 6A New York NY 10025-1843 Office: Skadden Arps Slate Meagher & Flom 4 Times Sq Fl 24 New York NY 10036-6595

HENRY, SHERRYE P., political advisor, radio personality; b. Memphis, July 13, 1935; Grad. magna cum laude, Vanderbilt U.; MBA, Fordham U. Asst. adminstr. Office Women's Bus. Ownership SBA; sr. advisor to Congresswoman Louise M. Slaughter, 2000—. Vice-chair interagy. com. on women's bus. enterprise. Author of 2 books including The Deep Divide: Why American Women Resist Equality; contbr. numerous articles to nat. mags.; creator, host Woman! program on Sta. WCBS-TV, N.Y.C.; ind. prodr., broadcaster Sherrye Henry Program WOR Radio, N.Y.C. Active Group for the South Fork, eastern end of L.I., N.Y., Fedn. Protestant Welfare Agys. N.Y., The Retreat, East Hampton, N.Y. Mem. Women's Forum N.Y. (founding mem.).

HENRY, SUSAN ARMSTRONG, biology professor, dean; b. Alexandria, Va., June 27, 1946; d. Frederic Sylvester and Frederica Ann (Thompson) A.; m. Peter Edward Henry, July 20, 1968; children: Rebecca Alice, Joshua Armstrong. BS in Zoology, U. Md., 1968; PhD in Genetics, U. Calif., Berkeley, 1971. Postdoctoral fellow Brandeis U., Waltham, Mass., 1971-72; asst. prof. genetics, molecular biology Albert Einstein Coll. Medicine, Bronx, NY, 1972-77, assoc. prof. genetics and molecular biology, 1972-82, prof., 1972-87, dir. Sue Golding grad. div., 1983-87; prof. biol. scis. Carnegie Mellon U., Pitts., 1987-2000, head dept. biol. scis., 1987-91, program dir. undergrad. biol. scis. edn. initiative, Howard Hughes Med. Inst., 1989-2000, dean Mellon Coll. Sci., 1991-2000; dean Coll. of Agrl. and Life Sci. Cornell U., Ithaca, NY, 2000—. Mem. nat. adv. gen. med. scis. coun. NIH, 1995-98, adv. com. rsch. on minority health, 1998-00, chmn., 1999-00; co-dir. W.M. Keck Ctr. Advanced Tng. Computational Biology, 1992-97; bd. dirs. Agrium, Inc. Contbr. over 100 articles to profl. jours. Mem. N.Y. Farm Bur. Recipient Merit award NIH, 1991, 95, Career Devel. award, 1975-80, Irma T. Hirschl Faculty award Hirschl Found., 1980-85; rsch. grantee NIH, 1972—. Fellow AAAS (mem. com. coun. affairs 2004—, sect. biol. scis. coun. del. 2004—); mem. Genetics Soc. Am., Am. Soc. Biol. Chemists, Am. Soc. Microbiologists (grad. microbiology tchg. award nominating com. 2003-), Nat. Acads. (nat. rsch. coun. com. sci. and tech. to support health care, sustainability, and other aspects of devel. assistance 2004-05). Office: Office of the Dean CALS Cornell U 260 Roberts Hall Ithaca NY 14853-5905 Office Phone: 607-255-2241. E-mail: sah42@cornell.edu.

HENSCHEL, LEONORE KATHERINE, elementary educator; b. Milw. d. Max and Elisabeth (Mattern) Oettmeier; m. James H. Henschel, June 14, 1958; children: Mark, Lynda, Marylynn. BA, U. Wis., 1959, MS, 1963. Cert. elem. and Jr. coll. tchr., Wis., Fla. Tchr., St. Francis and New Berlin, Wis., 1958-62, Oakland Park, Fla., 1972-76, Pompano Beach, Fla., 1976—99. Bd. dirs. edn. Christ Meth. Ch., Ft. Lauderdale, 1984-87, Stephen minister, 1988—; sec. Coral Ridge Homeowners Assn., Ft. Lauderdale, 1987-99. Mem. Broward Tchrs. Union, Jaycees (aux.), Coral Ridge Jr. Woman's Club, Coral Ridge Jr. Woman's Assn. (editor newspaper 1967-71), Alpha Delta Kappa. Republican. Avocations: music, reading, travel. Home: 2334 S Cypress Bend Dr Apt 301 Pompano Beach FL 33069-4488

HENSCHEL, SHIRLEY MYRA, licensing agent; b. N.Y.C., Dec. 18, 1932; d. Joseph and Leah Rose (Cooper) Henschel. BA, Barnard Coll., N.Y.C., 1954. Pub. rels., sales promotion exec. Louis Marx & Co., Inc., N.Y.C., 1954-59; acct. exec. Harold J. Siesel Co., N.Y.C., 1959-62; pres. U.S. Motor Sport Promotions, Inc., N.Y.C., 1962-66; v.p. Flora Mir Candy Corp., N.Y.C., 1966-71, Marden-Kane, Inc., N.Y.C., 1971-79; pres. Alaska Momma, Inc., N.Y.C., 1979—. Mem. Licensing Industry and Merchandisers Assn. (charter mem. Achievement award 1988), Women Inc., Women in Toys (charter mem.). Democrat. Jewish. Avocations: cooking, travel, reading, theater, investing. Office Phone: 212-369-8124. E-mail: smh1218@aol.com.

HENSCHKE, CLAUDIA INGRID, physician, radiologist; b. Berlin, Mar. 3, 1941; d. Ulrich Konrad and Gisela Franziska H. BA in French, So. Meth. U., 1962, MS in Math. Stats., 1966; PhD in Stats., U. Ga., 1969; MD, Howard U., 1977; Radiologist, Harvard U., 1981. Diplomate Am. Bd. Radiology. Internship, residency dept. radiology Harvard Med. Sch./Brigham and Women's Hosp., 1977-81, clin. fellow in radiology, 1977-81; rsch. fellow in radiology Brigham and Women's Hosp., 1981-82, Harvard Med. Sch., Boston, 1981-82; rsch. fellow in epidemiology Harvard Sch. of Pub. Health, 1981-82; assoc. radiologist Brigham and Women's Hosp., 1982-83, co-dir. Thoracic Divsn., 1983; asst. attending radiology to assoc. radiologist The N.Y. Hosp. - Cornell Med. Ctr., 1983-87, 87-92, sect. chief, chest imaging to chief of divsn., 1988-92, 92-95, attending radiologist, 1992—, chief, Divsn. of Health Care Policy and Tech. Assessment, 1995—, chief, Divsn. of Chest Imaging, 1995—. Various acad. positions to prof. radiology, Cornell U. Med. Coll., 1992—; cons. Rockefeller U., 1986—, Med. Billing Program Devel. and Med. Computer Systems Planning, 1986—; lectr. in field; mem. numerous coms. in field; vis. prof. numerous univs., including Columbia U., 1999, Roy Castle Internat. Ctr. for Lung Cancer Rsch., Liverpool, Eng., 1999, Washington U., 1999, Clinica U., Pamplona, Spain, 1999, U. Rochester, N.Y., 1999, others. Mem. editl. bd. Complications in Surgery, 1995—, Investigative Radiology, 1990-94, Clin. Imaging, 1988—, Acad. Radiology, 1994—, others; reviewer Am. Jour. Cardiology, 1982—, Chest, 1992—, Radiology, 1993—, Jour. of Computed Assisted Tomography, 1995—, Am. Jour. of Radiology, 1995—, others; contbr. numerous books, including: Women's Complete Handbook, 1994, Introduction to Statistics and Computer Programming, 1975, Instructions for General Purpose Program Package, 1971, First and Second Biomedical Computing Symposium 1965 and 1966, 1967; contbr. numerous articles to profl. jours. and publs. Named Ky. Col. by Gov. of Ky., 1963; grantee in field. Mem. Am. Statis. Soc., Am. Assn. Women Radiologists (Marie Curie award/2d place 1994), Radiol. Soc. N.Am., Am. Coll. Radiology, Soc. Thoracic Radiology, Sigma Xi, Phi Kappa Phi. Office: New York Hosp/Dept Radiol Cornell Med Ctr New York NY 10021 Business E-Mail: chensch@med.cornell.edu.

HENSEL, NANCY H., academic administrator; 1 child. BA, MA, Calif. State U., San Francisco; EdD, U. Ga., 1973. Prof. early childhood edn., Calif., Ohio; dean coll. of edn., health and rehab. U. Maine, Farmington, 1992—95, provost and v.p. academic affairs, 1995—99; pres. U. Maine at Presque Isle, 1999—. Named to Fourteenth Maine Women's Hall of Fame, 2003.

HENSINGER, MARGARET ELIZABETH, real estate, horticultural and agricultural advertising and marketing executive; b. Jackson, Mich., Aug. 31, 1950; d. John Kenneth and Inez Estelle (McVay) H.; m. William C. Pixley, Apr. 26, 1985; children: William Christopher, Patrick Edward. BS, Eastern Mich. U., 1973. Lic. realtor-broker, Fla. Salesperson Hunter Pub. Co., Winston-Salem, N.C., 1974-76, Josten's-Am., Topeka, 1976-77; editorial asst. Mich. Dept. Agriculture, Lansing, 1977-80, U. Fla., Apopka, 1981-82; pres. Country Carousel, Inc., Mt. Dora, Fla., 1983—; editor, pres. Green Pages Ltd., Mt. Dora, 1984-88; owner, pres. Sunbelt Mktg. Services, Inc., Mt. Dora, 1982-99; pub. Fax-It-Green The Hort Fax Directory, 1987-98; pres., treas. Duragreen Mktg. Stars Realty USA, Inc., Mt. Dora, 1990-99; broker Coldwell Banker, 1999—. Comptr. Adventure Yacht Harbor, Inc., Daytona Beach, Fla., 1999-2005; mem. 5th dist. com. for unlicensed practice of law Fla. Supreme Ct., 2001-2004 Mem. Leadership Am., Fairfax, Va., 1990; pres. Our Turning Point Ranch, Inc.; mem. adv. coun. Citizens for a Sound Economy, Lake and Sumpter Counties, 2001—. Mem. Nat. Assn. Women in Horticulture (v.p., past pres., organizer), Am. Soc. of Advt. Promotion, Mt. Dora C. of C. (exec. bd., bd. dirs., sec. 1988-89, v.p. 1989-95, pres. 1996), Golden Triangle Federated Rep. Women's Club (pres. 2003-2004). Republican. Avocations: reading, travel, gardening, motorcross. Home: PO Box 1483 Mount Dora FL 32756-1483 Office: Coldwell Banker All Stars 3949 S Peninsula Dr Port Orange FL 32127-6510 also: 600 N Donnelly St Mount Dora FL 32757 Office Phone: 386-756-7703, 352-735-4433.

HENSLER, DEBORAH ROSENFIELD, law educator; b. Syracuse, NY, May 23, 1942; d. Nathan and Vivian (Feller) Rosenfield; m. Carl Peter Hensler, May 23, 1965; children: Benjamin, Rebecca. AB in Polit. Sci. summa cum laude, CUNY, 1963; PhD in Polit. Sci., MIT, 1973. Asst. to dir., mgr. tech. ops. Survey Rsch. Ctr. UCLA, 1969-73; social scientist RAND Corp., Santa Monica, Calif., 1973—80, sr. social scientist, 1980—98, dir. survey rsch. group, 1975—85, assoc. head social sci. dept., 1975-80, rsch. dir. Inst. Civil Justice, 1986—90, dir. Inst. Civil Jusice, 1993—98, mem. faculty grad. sch., 1980—93, sr. fellow, 1998—2001; prof. law and social sci. U. So. Calif. Law Ctr., 1993—98; Judge John W. Ford. prof. dispute resolution Stanford Law Sch., 1998—; dir. Stanford Ctr. on Conflict & Negotiation, 2000—. George E. Allen Chair U. Richmond Law Sch., spring 1990; scholar-in-residence U. So. Calif. Law Sch., LA, fall 1990, vis. prof. social sci. in law, 1991-93; vis. prof. U. Chgo. Law Sch., spring 1991; presenter in field, 1970—; mem. law and social sci. adv. panel NSF, 1991-94; mem. study com. of Fed. Employers' Liability Act, Nat. Transp. Bd., 1992-93; mem. steering com. Nat. Conf. Lawyers and Scientists AAAS-ABA, 1994; mem. editl. bd. Pub. Opinion Quarterly, 1988-91, Law & Soc. Rev., 2000-03; cons. editor Psychology, Pub. Policy, and Law. Bd. dirs. Calif. Supreme Ct. Hist. Soc., 1998-. Recipient Achievement Award Soroptomist Club, LA, 1977, Woman of Yr. Award YWCA, Santa Monica, 1980; named to Hunter Coll. Hall of Fame, CUNY, 1985; Woodrow Wilson Fellow, 1963-64, Woodrow Wilson Dissertation Fellowship, 1965, NSF Fellowship, 1966-67, Stouffer Fellowship Harvard-MIT Joint Ctr. for Urban Studies, 1966-67, NSF Dissertation Rsch. Fellowship, 1967-68. Fellow Am. Acad. Polit. and Social Sci.; mem. Am. Judicature Soc. (bd. dirs. 1993-99), Law and Soc. Assn. (bd. trustees 1993-96, chmn. nominating com. 1993-94), Am. Arbitration Assn. (bd. dirs. 1990-95), Soc. for Profls. in Dispute Resolution (pub. policy com. 1990-94), Am. Assn. for Pub. Opinion Rsch. (chmn. stds. com. 1982-84), Am. Inns of Ct. (leadership coun., 1997-2001), Phi Beta Kappa, Pi Sigma Alpha. Office: Stanford Law Sch Crown Quadrangle 559 Nathan Abbott Way Stanford CA 94305-8610 Office Phone: 650-723-0146. E-mail: dhensler@stanford.edu.

HENSLEY, ELIZABETH CATHERINE, nutritionist, educator; b. Mpls., Feb. 27, 1921; d. Erich Christian and Lulu Mabel (Elliott) Selke; m. Eugene B. Hensley, June 10, 1954 (dec. 1992). BS in Edn., U. N.D., 1942; MS, Cornell U., 1944, postgrad., 1950-51. Instr. food and nutrition U. Del., 1944-47; asst. prof. Okla. A&M U., 1947-50; mem. faculty U. Mo., Columbia, 1951—, prof. food and nutrition, 1954-84, prof. emeritus, 1984—, chmn. dept. home econs., 1954-55, head dept. food and nutrition, 1955-65, co-chmn. dept. human nutrition, 1973-76. Author: Basic Concepts of World Nutrition, 1981. Mem. Am. Home Econs. Assn., Nutrition Today Soc., Mo. Home Econs. Assn., Boone County Hist. Soc., PEO, Pi Lambda Theta, Omicron Nu, Phi Upsilon Omicron, Gamma Sigma Delta, Kappa Alpha Theta Mem. Christian Ch. (Disciples Of Christ). Home: 802 Greenwood Ct Columbia MO 65203-2841

HENSLEY, MARY KAY, dietician; b. Dodge, Nebr., June 2, 1946; d. Joseph Leo and Sally H. (Fangman) Klitz; m. Charles Hensley, Feb. 4, 1978 (div. Dec. 30, 1985). BSc, Coll. of St. Mary, 1967, U. Nebr., 1970; MSc, Gov.'s State U., 1982. Registered dietician Am. Dietetic Assn., cert. specialist in renal nutrition. Therapeutic dietician ARA Hosp. Food Mgmt., Omaha, 1968—75, food prodn. mgr., 1975—77, renal dietician Hammond, Ind., 1977—92, Comprehensive Renal Care, Gary, Ind., 1992—99, Total Renal Care/Davita (now Davita), Gary, 1999—. Chmn. Coun. Renal Nutrition, 1986, 89. Editor: CRN Quarterly, 1983—85; contbr. articles to profl. jours.; mem. editl. bd.: Jour. Renal Nutrition, 1990—95. Named Outstanding Nephrology Profl., Tri-State Renal Network, 1990, Dietitian of Yr., Ill. Coun. Renal Nutrition, 1999; recipient Recognized Renal Dietitian award, Coun.on Renal Nutrition, 1990. Mem.: Am. Dietetic Assn. (specialty cert. panel 1997—), Nat. Kidney Found. Ind. (sec. 1991, 1998—2000, pres. 1993—95). Roman Catholic. Home: 20 Spruce Ct Schererville IN 46375 Office: Comprehensive Renal Care Davita 4802 Broadway Gary IN 46408

HENSLEY, NOEL M. B., lawyer; b. LA, Dec. 25, 1944; BS magna cum laude, North Tex. State U., 1975; JD cum laude, So. Meth. U., 1978. Bar: Tex. 1978. Law clk. to Hon. Robert W. Porter US Dist. Ct. (No. Dist.) Tex., 1978-80; mem. Haynes & Boone LLP, Dallas, 1980—, ptnr., Bus. Litig. Arbitrator Nat. Assn. Securities Dealer, 1986—; instr. Nat. Inst. Trial Advocacy, 1989—, So. Meth. U. Sch. Law, 1990—92. Editor: Southwestern Law Jour., 1977—78. Rsch. fellow, Southwestern Legal Found. Fellow: Tex. Bar Found., Dallas Bar Found.; mem.: Am. Law Inst., State Bar Tex. (Litig. Sect.), ABA (Litig. Sect.), Order of Coif. Office: Haynes & Boone LLP 3100 NationsBank Plz 901 Main St Ste 3100 Dallas TX 75202-3789 Office Phone: 214-651-5631. Office Fax: 214-200-0470. Business E-Mail: noel.hensley@haynesboone.com.

HENSLEY, PATRICIA DRAKE, principal; BLS in Liberal studies, St. Louis U., Mo., MA in Edn., PhD in Edn. Adminstrn. Cert. use of tech. in sch. setting Tech. Leadership Acad. Tchr. grades 7 and 8 math. and sci., 1976—82; prin. St. Mary Magdalen, St. Louis, 1982—86; vice-prin. St. Elizabeth Acad., St. Louis, 1986—91; prin. St. Francis of Assisi, St. Louis, 1991—95; acad. adviser grad. programs Webster U., St. Louis, 1990—2002; prin. Ursuline Acad., St. Louis, 1995—. Adj. instr. math. and computer sci. Webster U., St. Louis, 1986—; nat. media cons. FM radio stas.; fellow St. Louis Prin. Acad., 1994; state prin. assessor NASSP, 1994; grant reviewer U.S. Dept. Edn., 2002. Mem. Archdiocesan Com. for Rev. of H.S. Admissions, 1997—99; bd. dirs., co-chair ednl. policies com. DeSmet Jesuit H.S., 1998—; bd. dirs. Vianney H.S., 1999—. Office Phone: 314-966-4556 ext. 212. Personal E-mail: pdrakehensley@hotmail.com.

HENSON, ANNA MIRIAM, retired otolaryngologist, retired medical educator; b. Springfield, Mo., Nov. 7, 1935; d. Bert Emerson and Esther Miriam (Crank) Morgan; m. O'Dell Williams Henson, Aug. 1, 1964; children: Phillip, William. BA, Park Coll., Parkville, Mo., 1957; MA, Smith Coll., 1959; PhD, Yale U., 1967. Instr. Smith Coll., Northampton, Mass., 1960-61; rsch. assoc. Yale U., New Haven, 1967-74; instr. U. N.C., Chapel Hill, 1975-78, rsch. asst. prof., 1978-83, rsch. assoc. prof., 1983-86, prof. Sch. Medicine dept. otolaryngology, 1986—2001; ret., 2001. Mem. study sect. on hearing rsch. NIH, Bethesda, Md., 1990-93. Contbr. articles to profl. jours. Fulbright scholar, Australia, 1959-60; NIH grantee, 1975—2003. Mem. Assn. for Rsch. in Otolaryngology, Sigma Xi. E-mail: mmhenson@med.unc.edu.

HENSON, GLENDA MARIA, newswriter; b. Marion, NC, June 17, 1960; d. Douglas Bradley and Glenda June (Crouch) H. BA in English cum laude, Wake Forest U., 1982. Reporter Ark. Dem., Little Rock, 1982-84; bur. reporter Tampa Tribune, Crystal River, Fla., 1984; statehouse reporter Ark. Gazette, Little Rock, 1984-87, bur. chief Washington, 1987-89; editl. writer Lexington (Ky.) Herald-Leader, 1989-94; editl. writer, columnist The Charlotte (N.C.) Observer, 1994-98; dep. editl. page editor Austin (Tex.) American-Statesman, 1998-2001, asst. mng. editor enterprise, 2001—04; dep. editl. page editor Sacramento Bee, Calif., 2004—. Lectr. journalism, Indonesia, 2001; juror Nat. Headliner Awards, 2002—04, ASNE Writing Awards, 2001—03, Nieman Fellowship Selection Com., 2004. Editor: Pulitzer Prize Series, 2005. Mem. Wake Forest Presdl. Scholarship Com., Ky., 1992, Wake Forest Bd. Visitors, 1995-99; Pulitzer Prize juror, 1994, 95, 99, 2000. Nieman fellow Harvard U., 1993-94, Found. Am. Comm. Econs. fellow, 1997; recipient Pulitzer prize, 1992, Walker Stone award Scripps Howard Found., 1992, Ky. Press Assn. award, 1992, N.C. Press Assn. award, 1995-96, Leadership award Duke U., 1995, Nat. Headliner award, 1996; named Wake Forest Woman of Yr., 1992 Mem. Soc. Profl. Journalists (Sigma Delta Chi award 1991, Green Eyeshade award Atlanta chpt. 1992), Nat. Conf. Editorial Writers, Investigative Reporters & Editors Assn., Am. Soc. Newspaper Editors, Omicron Delta Kappa. Avocations: skiing, bicycling, swimming, travel, rafting. Office: Sacramento Bee 2100 Q St Sacramento CA 95816 Office Phone: 916-321-1907. Business E-Mail: mhenson@sacbee.com.

HENSON, JANE ELIZABETH, information management professional, adult education educator; b. Ft. Wayne, Ind., Dec. 1, 1946; d. Robert Eugene and Lucile Catherine (Feeney) Tucker; m. Phillip Likins Henson, Aug. 23, 1971; 1 child, Robert Likins. BS in Edn., Ind. U., 1970, MS in Edn., 1973, MLS, 1976. Tchr. pub. schs., Ft. Wayne, 1970-71, Nevada, Mo., 1971-72; libr., cataloger Ctrl. Conn. State U., New Britain, 1976-77; libr. numeric data U. Wis., Madison, 1978-80; adj. prof. libr. Navy Safety Sch. Ind. U., Bloomington, 1981-83, reference libr. Vocat. Edn. Project, 1984-86; asst. dir. ERIC Clearinghouse, Bloomington, 1988-95, assoc. dir., 1995-98, co-dir., 1999—2003; assoc. dir. Social Studies Devel. Ctr., Bloomington, 2004—. Co-author: Rising Expectations: A Framework for ERIC's Future in the National Library of Education, 1997; editor: Libraries Link to Learning: Final Report on the Indiana Governor's Conference on Libraries and Information Services, 1990. Chair ERIC tech. com. U.S. Dept. Edn. ERIC Program, Washington, 1990-2003, mem. ERIC exec. com., 1990-2003 Mem. Am. Soc. Info. Sci. (dept. dir. SIG cabinet 1993, chair behavioral and social sci. SIG 1994, cert. of appreciation 1993). Roman Catholic. Avocations: reading, travel. Office: Social Studies Devel Ctr 2805 E 10th St Ste 140 Bloomington IN 47408-2698 Office Phone: 812-855-3838. Business E-Mail: henson@indiana.edu.

HENSON, JOY KAY, special education educator; b. Jacksonville, Tex., Feb. 6, 1951; d. Jack Raymond and Elbie Arthena Lovett; children: Brian Keith, Jeffrey Raymond. BS, East Tex. Bapt. U., 1973; MEd, Stephen F. Austin U., 1980. Cert. in spl. edn. Tex., 2002, ESL Tex., 2003. Tchr. Sky View Bapt. Kindergarten, Memphis, 1982—84, First Bapt. Christian Sch., Claremore, Okla., 1985—86, 1988—89; legal asst. Eldred Smith, Atty., Longview, Tex., 1994—2001; tchr. Houston Ind. Sch. Dist., 2001—, Jack 'n Jill Day Sch., Longview, Tex., 1976—79. Youth dir. asst. Macedonia Bapt. Ch., Longview, Tex., 1975—80, Sky View Bapt. Ch., Memphis, 1980—84, Trinity Bapt. Ch., Claremore, Okla., 1985—91. Recipient Spl. Edn. Tchr. of the Yr. Ctrl. Dist., Houston Ind. Sch. Dist., 2004. Mem.: Coun. for Exception Children with Behavior Disabilities, Coun. for Exceptional Children.

HENSON, PAMELA TAYLOR, secondary education educator; b. Mobile, Ala., Aug. 31, 1958; d. Richard Dowdy and Martha Jo (Hanson) Taylor; m. Thomas Baird Henson III, Mar. 7, 1987; 1 child, Joshua Taylor. BS in Secondary Edn./Biology, U. South Ala., 1983; MS in Secondary Edn./Biology, U. Mobile, 1989, Adminstrv. Cert., 1990; Edn. Specialist Adminstrn., Ala. State U., 1995; postgrad., U. West Fla. Cert. secondary edn. educator. Sci. tchr. Fairhope (Ala.) Middle Sch., 1984-91, Foley (Ala.) H.S., 1991-97; sci. supr., grant writer Baldwin County Schs., 1994—. Christa McAuliffe fellow State Dept. of Edn., 1994, Outstanding Biology tchr. Nat. Assn. Biology Tchrs., 1994, Outstanding Instr. in Environ. Edn., Legacy Found., 1995, Outstanding Sci. Supr. award, 2002, Mobile Bay NEP award, 2002, YWCA Woman of Profl. Achievement award, 2002; recipient Presdl. award NSTA, 1994, Melvin Paul Jones award Tuskegee U., Outstanding Svc. to Edn. award. Mem. NSTA, Nat. Assn. Biology Tchrs., Ala. Sci. Tchrs. Assn., Nat. Marine Educators Assn., Baldwin County Assn. Profl. Educators (pres. 1994—), Alpha Delta Kappa (treas. 1994-96). Republican. Baptist. Avocations: travel, walking, outdoor summer sports. Home: PO Box 1676 810 Juniper Ct Daphne AL 36526-4358

HENSON, PATRICIA LOU, elementary school educator; d. Howard William and Dorothy Marie Birkholz; children: Jason Donald, Jillian Patrice Wilson, Joshua Donald. BS, U. Wis., Oshkosh, 1970; M in Tchg., Aurora U., Ill., 2000. Registered phys. edn. tchr. State of Ill., 1970. Tchr. Egin Sch. Dist. U-46, Ill., 1970—1778, Ctrl. Sch. Dist. 301, Burlington, 1991—92; tchr. physical edn. Sch. Dist. U-46, Elgin, 1991—. Tchr. SAFE, Elgin, 1995—2006, Adult Edn., 1995—2006. Mem.: IAHPERD (assoc.). Office Phone: 847-888-5000.

HENSON SCALES, MEG D(IANE), artist, writer, publisher; b. Portland, Oreg., Oct. 16, 1953; d. Kenneth Jack and Jessie Louise (Mott) Henson; m. Jeffrey Charles Henson Scales, Dec. 16, 1985; 1 child, Coco Tigre Roja. Student, San Francisco State U., 1972-73, 74-75, Friends' World Coll., Guatemala, 1974. Founding mem. Black Edn. Ctr., Portland, Oreg., 1970-71; mng. editor Woman's Bldg., L.A., 1979-81; pvt. investigator Kleinbauer Investigations, L.A., 1981-83; tchr. CUNY, N.Y.C., 1987-89, Mindbuilders, Bronx, NY, 1987-89; painter, writer, strategist Henson Scales Prodns., N.Y.C., 1989—; founder Com. for Rational African Americans Against the Parade, N.Y.C., 1995; pub., editor The Harlem Howl, N.Y.C., 1995—; freelance photographer N.Y. Times, The Oregonian, The Internat. Herald Tribune, The LA Weekly, 2001—; freelance writer N.Y. Times, 2001—. Commn. Sacred banners for Grace Methodist Ch., Wilmington, Del., 1997; spkr. in field. Author: The Book of Love, 1988, Melisma, 1989 (Deming award 1989); co-creator, performer Tragedy in Black and White/A Race Record in One Act, 1981; dir., prodr. video documentary Class, 1989, Action/Reaction, 1998; prodr., dir. videos Who's Your Daddy, 2003, You Slay Me, 2004; author essays Tenderheaded; Man, God and the Okey-Doke; Be/Held; contbg. author: Divine Mirror: The Maddonna Revealed, 2001, Tenderheaded, 2001, Internat. Rev. of African Am. Art, 2001, Davis Mus./Wellesley Coll., 2000; illustrator: (children's book) Freer by the Dozen, 2005-2006, one-woman show U. Fla. at Gainesville Univ. Gallery, 1998, Smithsonian Anacostia Mus. and Ctr. for African Am. History and Culture, 1999; contr. articles to profl. rsch. papers. Founding mem. African Am. Against Violence, N.Y.C., 1995. Recipient N.Y. Found. Arts fellowship, N.Y.C., 1989. Avocations: creation myths, prayers, piano, flute. Personal E-mail: mhensons@yahoo.com.

HENTGES, HARRIET, not-for-profit developer; m. Wayne Allan Koonce, 1985. BS, Coll. St. Catherine, St. Paul; MS in Internat. Rels. and Econs., Am. U., Washington; PhD in Internat. Econs., Johns Hopkins U., Balt. Aide Sen. Mark O. Hatfield; spl. asst. Dep. Spl. Rep. for Trade Negotiations; economist policy planning staff U.S. Dept. State, Washington; exec. dir. LWV, 1978—81; v.p. planning and rsch. Sears World Trade, Inc.; mng. ptnr. Clifton Investment Group LP, Arlington, Va.; chair Balkans Initiative U.S. Inst. of Peace, Washington, 1994—99, exec. v.p., COO, 1999—. Trustee Coll. of St. Catherine, St. Paul. Office: US Inst of Peace 1200 17th St NW Washington DC 20036

HENTHORN, SUSAN KAY, school librarian; d. Robert Eugene Henthorn and Gene Lois Gibbs. MusB in Edn., Otterbein Coll., 1978; MLS, Kent State U., Ohio, 1989. Sales Stanton's Sheet Music, Columbus, Ohio, 1978—88; libr. Ashland Chem., Dublin, Ohio, 1990—90; libr. reference and instrn. Berea (Ky.) Coll., 1990—2001, coord. electronic svcs., 2001—. Player, libr., bd. mem. Adv. Brass Band, Danville, Ky., 1995—; player and bd. mem. Lexington Brass Band, Lexington, Ky., 2004—. Author: (website) Bibliographic Instruction Program Evaluation. Recipient Alumni Achievement award, Mortar Bd., 1995. Mem.: ALA, Ky. Libr. Assn. (sec. academic sect. 2002—04), Assn. Coll. and Rsch. Libraries, Mensa, Beta Phi Mu, Mortar Bd., Delta Omicron (life). United Methodist. Avocations: brass bands, reading, travel. Office: Berea College Hutchins Library Berea KY 40404 Office Phone: 859-985-3268.

HENTZ, SUSAN MARIE, private school educator, consultant; b. Somerset, N.J., May 2, 1961; d. Donald George and Susan Elizabeth Hentz. BA, Glassboro State Coll., 1983; MA, U. So. Fla., 1995; EdS in Ednl. Leadership, Nova Southeastern U., 2001. Cert. tchr. Fla., 2001. Exceptional student edn. tchr. Sarasota (Fla.) Bd. of Edn., 1989—2004; pres., owner Valuable Innovative Ednl. Wisdom (VIEW), Inc., Sarasota, 2003. Contbg. author: (textbooks) Early Childhood Education Today, Teaching in America, 2004. Mem. Adv. for Better Hearing, Inc.; bd. dirs. Sarasota County Leadership Acad. Named ESE Model Demonstration Classroom Tchr., 1993, Sarasota County Model Classroom Tchr., 1997, Tchr. of the Year, Sarasota County Coun. for Exceptional Children, 2002; recipient PRSE Recognition award, 2000. Mem.: Fla. Spkrs. Bureau, Coun. for Exceptional Children (pres. 1998—99, named Marjorie Crick Tchr. of the Yr., Fla. br. 2002, Award of Excellence 1999). Home and Office: VIEW Inc 750 N Tamiami Trail Ste 902 Sarasota FL 34236 E-mail: susan@viewinc.net.

HENZEL, ROBYN ELLEN, artist; b. N.Y.C., Sept. 23, 1962; d. Anne Palmer Schneider. BA, CUNY, 1989; JD, Yeshiva U., 1992; Cert. Programming Software Devel., Columbia U., 1999. Bar: (N.Y.) 1994. One-woman shows include Jadite Galleries, N.Y.C., 2004, exhibited in group shows at Woman Made Gallery, Chgo., 2002, contbg. artist, Pink Ladies Series, Art"O"Mat, 2004. Mem.: EBSQ Plus Self Representing Artists Group (Juror's awards 2002—03), Woman MADE Gallery (Chgo.), Art Students League N.Y. Avocations: yoga, boating, gardening. Home: PO Box 262 Lake Clear NY 12945 Office: 142 W End Ave # 12R New York NY 10023

HEPBURN, JEANETTE C., family practice nurse practitioner; b. Provo, Utah, Nov. 7, 1952; d. George Blaine Clay, Sr. and E. Joan Clay; m. David Smiley, Feb. 15, 1975 (div. Aug. 1991); children: Peter David, Paul William, Adam George; m. Moller Boon, June 10, 1994 (dec. Sept. 1994); m. Charles Raymond Hepburn, June 3, 2000. Diploma, Crouse Irving Meml. Hosp. Sch. Nursing, Syracuse, N.Y., 1972; BSN, Rockhurst Rsch. Coll., Kansas City, Mo., 1997; MSN, Bowie State U., 2004. RN, APRN, BC, cert. tech., ARC Disaster Health Svcs. Nursing asst. Crouse-Irving Meml. Hosp., Syracuse, NY, 1970—72; nurse RR, emergency rm., ICU Tompkins County Hosp., Ithaca, NY, 1972—75; ICU staff nurse II George Washington Hosp., Washington, 1975—78; ICU staff nurse Prince William Hosp., Manassas, Va., 1978—79; office nurse Romaker & Assocs., Kansas City, Mo., 1992—95; home health nurse Glen Burnie, Md., 1995—2004; served with disaster relief Anne Arundel County, 2001—04, ARC disaster nurse Balt., 1998—2003, served with disaster relief Pentagon Hyattsville, Md., 1998—2003; nurse practitioner Intermountain Surgery and Pain Ctr., Providence, Utah, 2005—06. Assisted in treating patients Cache County Cmty. Clinic, 2005. Sem. tchr. Ch. LDS, Adelphi, Md., 1999—2000, relics soc. counselor Adelphi, Glen Burnie, Md., 1996—98, relief soc. counselor, 2000—01. Scholar Senatoral scholar, Md., 2001—03. Mem.: Bowie Student Nurses Assn., Phi Sigma Tau. Mem. Lds Ch. Avocations: cross stitch, dog training, swimming, skiing. Home: 3285 South 250 West Nibley UT 84321 Office: 284 N Gateway Dr Ste 201 Logan UT 84321 Personal E-mail: crhepburn@msn.com.

HEPLER, JANE A., secondary school educator; b. Lebanon, Pa., Aug. 7, 1964; d. Harvey H. and Anne Marie Hepler; 1 child, Cyja J. BS, Lebanon Valley Coll., Annville, Pa., 1986; MEd, Temple U., Phila., 1997. Psychiat. asst., social work Philhaven Hosp., Lebanon, Pa., 1985—89; tchr. Cedar Crest H.S., 1990—. Pres. Lebanon County Edn. Coun., 1996—; learning focused schs. trainer Cornwall Lebanon Sch. Dist., 2001—; chair PSEA Intergroup Rels. Commn., Harrisburg, 1995—2002. Drama team leader United Meth. Ch. Good Shepherd, Lebanon, 2005—06. Named WalMart Tchr. Yr., 2000. Mem.: NEA (commn. chair, com. mem. 1990—2006), Pa. Sci. Educators Assn. Liberal. Office: Cedar Crest High School 115 East Evergreen Road Lebanon PA 17042 Office Phone: 717-272-2033.

HEPP, JODY, music educator; b. Smyrna, Tenn., July 17, 1967; d. Dan Berry and Judy Sargent; m. Joseph Hepp, Aug. 3, 1991; children: Josy, Daniele. B of Music Edn., Ohio State U., Columbus, 1990, MA, 2001. Cert. tchr. Ohio Dept. Edn., 2004. Tchr. vocal music Pike-Delta-York Schs., Ohio, 1990—95, Bryan City Schs., 1995—97, Bexley City Schs., 1997—2003, Jefferson Local Schs., West Jefferson, 2003—. Praxis assessor Ohio Dept. Edn., Columbus, 1999—; praise, worship leader Hilliard United Meth. Ch., 2005—. Mem.: Ohio Music Educator's Assn. (adjudicator 1998—). Home: 1791 Jupiter Ave Hilliard OH 43026 Office: Jefferson Local Schools 1 Roughrider West Jefferson OH 43162 Office Phone: 614-879-8345. Personal E-mail: jodyhepp@yahoo.com. E-mail: jhepp@west-jefferson.k12.oh.us.

HEPPE, KAROL VIRGINIA, lawyer, educator; b. Vinton, Iowa, Mar. 14, 1958; d. Robert Henry and Audry Virginia (Harper) Heppe. BA in Law and Society, U. Calif., Santa Barbara, 1982; JD, People's Coll. Law, 1989. Cmty. organizer Oreg. Fair Share, Eugene, 1983; law clk. Legal Aid Found. L.A., summer 1986; devel. dir. Ctrl. Am. Refugee Ctr., L.A., 1987-89; exec. dir. Police Watch-Police Misconduct Lawyer Referral Svc., L.A., 1989-94; instr. People's Coll. Law, L.A., 1992-94; dir. alternative sentencing project Ctr. Juvenile and Criminal Justice, 1994-95; cons. Bay Area Police Watch, 1996; investigator Office Citizen Complaints City and County of San Francisco, 1998—. Vol. law clk. Legal Aid Found. L.A., 1984—86, Lane County Legal Aid Svc., Eugene, 1983. Editor: (newsletter) NLG Law Students Action, 1986, Ctrl. Am. Refugee Ctr., 1986—89, Prison Break, 1994. Mem. Coalition Human Immigrants Rights, 1991—92, So. Calif. Civil Rights Coalition, 1991—92; bd. dirs. Nat. Police Accountability Project Adv. Bd., 1999—2003, People's Coll. Law, 1985—90, Law Student Civil Rights Rsch. Coun., N.Y.C., 1986. Scholar, Kramer Found., 1984—88, Law Students' Civil Rights Rsch. Coun., 1986, Davis-Putter Found., 1988, Assn. Cmty.-Based Edn. Prudential, 1988. Avocations: reading, gardening. Business E-Mail: karol_heppe@sfgov.org.

HEPPER, CAROL, artist, educator; b. McLaughlin, SD, Oct. 23, 1953; d. Adolph and Lavern Hepper. BS, S.D. State U., 1975. Instr. drawing Standing Rock C.C., Ft. Yates, NC, 1980-82, Sch. Visual Arts, N.Y.C., 1984. Vis. lectr. RISD, Providence, 1986-88, Md. Art Inst., Balt., 1988, SUNY, Purchase, 1989, U. Mass., Amherst, 1989, Princeton (NJ), 1989, 2005, U., Williams Coll., Williamstown, Mass., 1992, U. Colo. Boulder, 1990, Brandeis U., Waltham, Mass., 1992, Cranbrookl Acad. Art, Birmingham, Ala., 1992, Worcester Art Mus., Mass., 1992, Portland (Oreg.) State U., 1993, Harvard U., 1999. One-woman shows include Inst. for Art and Urban Resources, Queens, NY, 1982, Rosa Esman Gallery, NYC, 1988-89, 91, Worcester (Mass.) Art Mus., 1992, Miss. Mus. Art, Jackson, 1995, Orlando (Fla.) Art Mus., 1995, Portland Inst. for Contemporary Art, 1996, Hopkins Ctr. Dartmouth Coll., Hanover, NH, 2000, Md. Inst. Coll. Art, Balt., 2002, Burapha U., Chonburi, Thailand, 2003, others; exhibited in group shows at Contemporary Art Ctr., Cin., 1987, Sculpture Ctr., NYC, 1987, Art Gallery Western Australia, Perth, 1986, Art Gallery NSW, Sidney, 1986, Guggenheim Mus., NYC, 1987, Aldrich Mus. Art, Ridgefield, Conn., 1988, Walker Art Ctr., Mpls., 1989, Phillips Collection, Washington, 1992, Portland Art Mus., 1993, Decordova Mus., and Sculpture Park, Lincoln, Mass., 1993-94, Laumeier Sculpture Park, St. Louis, 1995—, White House Sculpture Garden, Washington, 1995, Neuberger Mus. Art, Purchase, NY, 1997, Mead Art Mus., Amherst Coll., Mass., 2006; represented in permanent collections Walker Art Ctr., Minn., Guggenheim Mus., NYC, Mus. Contemporary Art, Chgo., SD Meml. Art Ctr., New Sch. Social Rsch., NYC, Met. Mus., NYC, NY Pub. Libr., Hood Mus., Hanover, N.H., Detroit Inst. Arts, New Sch. for Social Rsch., NYC, ND Mus. Art, Grand Forks, Newark Mus., Portland Art Mus., Detroit Inst. Arts, Orlando (Fla.) Art Mus., NY Pub. Libr., Am. Telephone and Telegraph, NY, Phoenix Art Mus., NYC, Champion Paper, Stanford Conn., Aterrana Found., Vaduz, Leichtenstein, Mus. Modern Art, NY Betty Brazil meml. sculpture grantee, 1981, Louis Comfort Tiffany Found. sculpture grantee, 1984, Pollock-Krasner Found. sculpture grantee, 1986, N.Y. Found. for Arts sculpture grantee, 1989, Nat. Endowment for Arts grantee, 1990. Office Phone: 212-619-8108. E-mail: carolhepper@yahoo.com.

HEPPLER, ROBIN LEE, project manager; b. Detroit, Aug. 12, 1953; d. Warren G. and Maurida (Tillie) Heppler. Student, Glendale CC, 1971-74, 82, Ariz. State U., 1975, 81, U. Wis., 1981. Various positions Valley Nat. Bank, Phoenix, 1971-78; project bus. regional dir. Jr. Achievement, Inc., Phoenix, San Jose, Atlanta, 1978-81; asst. v.p., ctr. mgr. 1st Tenn. Bank, Memphis, 1981-83; customer svc. mgr., ops. analyst Wells Fargo Credit Corp., Phoenix, 1983-84; officer Citibank, Ariz., Phoenix, 1984-85; ops. mgr., asst. v.p. MeraBank, Phoenix, 1985-89; lending officer, policy analyst 1st Interstate Bank, Phoenix, 1989; project mgr. Colo. Nat. Bank, 1991-93; project mgr. Ctr. of Excellence for Project Mgmt. US West Techs., Denver, 1993—2000; lotus notes developer and project mgr. EDS at Western Union, Englewood, Colo., 2000—. Active Fiesta Bowl Parade Com., 1983—92; sec. bd. dirs. Ariz. Easter Seal Soc., Phoenix, 1989—90, Human Svcs. Inc., Denver, 1991—95; bd. dirs. Ctrl. Ariz. Arthritis Found., Phoenix, 1989—90, chmn. jingle bell run, 1989; chmn. jail-athon Am. Cancer Soc., 1989; fundraiser Fiesta Bowl Com., Tempe, Ariz., 1990—92; chmn. Festival of Kites, Denver, 1992; chmn. champagne and chocolate black tie silent auction, 1994; chmn. Denver Jr. League, 1994—2000, chair holiday mart solicitations, 1996; coporate teams chair Safehouse Denver 5K Run, 1994, 1995; precinct bd. Maricopa County Election Dept., Phoenix, 1990; coord. Andre Ho. Diocese of Phoenix, 1987—90. Named one of Outstanding Young Women Am., 1979; recipient award for outstanding contbn., Arthritis Found., 1990, award for outstanding achievement, Am. Cancer Soc., Phoenix, 1989. Mem.: Soc. Tech. Comm., Fin. Women Internat. (bd. dirs. 1988—90). Avocations: calligraphy, guitar, skiing, hot air ballooning. Home: 3635 S Carr St Denver CO 80235-1801

HEPPNER, GLORIA HILL, health facility administrator, educator; b. Gt. Falls, Mont., May 30, 1940; d. Eugene Merrill and Georgia M. (Swanson) Hill; m. Frank Henry Heppner, June 6, 1964 (div. 1975); 1 child, Michael Berkeley. BA, U. Calif., Berkeley, 1962, MA, 1964, PhD, 1967. Damon Runyon postdoctoral fellow U. Wash., Seattle, 1967—68; asst. and assoc. prof. Brown U., Providence, 1969-79, Herbert Fanger meml. lectr., 1988; chmn. dept. immunology, dir. labs., sr. v.p. Mich. Cancer Found., Detroit, 1979-91; dir. breast cancer program Karmanos Cancer Inst., 1991—2003, dep. dir., 1994—2003; assoc. chair for rsch. dept. internal medicine Wayne State U. Sch. Medicine, Detroit, 1991—2001, asst. dean cancer program, 2002—03, spl. asst. to dean, Karmanos Cancer Inst., 2003, assoc. v.p. rsch., 2003—. Mem. external adv. com. basic sci. program M.D. Anderson Hosp. and Tumor Clinic, Houston, 1984-94; mem. external adv. com. Case Western Res. U. Cancer Ctr., Cleve., 1988—, Roswell Park Meml. Inst., Buffalo, 1991-98; Sarah Stewart meml. lectr. Georgetown U., Washington, 1988; bd. sci. counselors Nat. Inst. Dental Rsch., 1993-97. Editor: Macrophages and Cancer, 1988; mem. editl. bd. Cancer Rsch., 1989-93, Jour. Nat. Cancer Inst., 1988, Sci., 1988-92; contbr. over 200 articles to sci. jours. Bd. dirs. Lyric Chamber Ensemble, 1996-99, Detroit Symphony Orch., 2005-. Recipient Mich. Sci. Trail-Blazer award State of Mich., 1987; fellow Damon Runyon-Walter Winchell Found., 1967-69. Mem. AAAS, Am. Assn. for Cancer Rsch. (bd. dirs. 1983-86, chmn. long-range planning com. 1989-91), Am. Assn. Immunologists, Metastasis Rsch. Soc. (bd. dirs. 1985-89), Women in Cancer Rsch. (nat. pres.), Internat. Differentiation Soc. (v.p. 1990-92, pres. 1992-94), LWV (bd. dirs. Grosse Pointe, Mich. 1989-95). Democrat. Avocations: music, theater. Office: 5057 Woodward Detroit MI 48201 Office Phone: 313-577-8848. E-mail: heppnerg@wayne.edu.

HERALD, CHERRY LOU, medical researcher, educator; b. Beeville, Tex., 1940; m. Delbert Leon Herald, Jr., July 31, 1964; children: Heather Amanda, Delbert Leon, III. BS, Ariz. State U., 1962, MS, 1965, PhD, 1968. Faculty rsch. assoc. Cancer Rsch. Inst. Ariz. State U., Tempe, 1973-74, sr. rsch. chemist, 1974-77, asst. to dir. and sr. rsch. chemist, 1977-83, asst. dir., assoc. rsch. prof., 1984-88, assoc. dir., rsch. prof., 1988—. Co-author: Biosynthetic Products for Cancer Chemotherapy, vols. 4, 5, & 6, 1984, 85, 87, Anticancer Drugs from Animals, Plants & Microorganisms, 1994; contbr. articles to sci. jours. Mem. Am. Soc. Pharmacognosy, Am. Chem. Soc. Office: Ariz State U Cancer Rsch Inst Tempe AZ 85287-2404 Business E-Mail: cherald@asu.edu.

HERBERT, BARBARA RAE, librarian, educational media specialist; b. Neptune, N.J., Apr. 1, 1955; d. Raymond Louis and Grace Caroline (Freiermuth) Swan; m. Edward O. Herbert, Jr., June 7, 1986. AA cum laude, Ocean County Coll., 1974; BA, Georgian Court Coll., 1976; MLS, Rutgers U., 1982. Ednl. media specialist, N.J., 1983. Substitute tchr. Brick Twp. Schs. (N.J.), 1976-77; dir. Instructional Media Ctr. Georgian Ct. Coll., Lakewood, N.J., 1977-88, audio-visual libr. instructional materials, 1988-89, lending svcs. libr., 1989-1992, instrnl. media libr., 1993-98, behavioral scis. libr., 1998-; media cons. Lakewood Learning Ctr., 1980-81; video reviewer Video Rating Guide Librs., 1990-94. Brick Twp. Fine Arts Guild drama scholar, 1972. Mem. Ocean County Coll. Alumni Assn., M.I. Hummel Club, Ocean County Alumnae Club Georgian Court Coll., Gamma Sigma Sigma, Phi Alpha Theta. Republican. Presbyterian. Office: Sr Mary Joseph Cunningham Libr Georgian Ct Univ 900 Lakewood Ave Lakewood NJ 08701-2697 Office Phone: 732-987-2428.

HERBERT, ELIZABETH ANNE, elementary school educator; b. Nofolk, Va., Feb. 7, 1979; d. Henry Edgar and Jean Davis Herbert. BA in History, U. Va., Charlottesville, 2001; MA in Elem. Edn., East Carolina U., Greenville, N.C., 2004. Fifth grade tchr. Northside Elem.- Warren County Pub. Schs., Warren County, NC, 2001—03; tutor (reading, math, and test prep.) Sylvan Learning Ctr., Greenville, NC, 2003—04; third grade tchr. Dreamkeepers Acad., Norfolk, 2004—. Choreographer Encore Dancers of Chesapeake, Va. (multiple awards at various dance competitions, 2006). Corps mem. (tchr.) Teach For Am. (an Americorps program), Raleigh, 2001—03. Recipient Induction into the Nat. Honor Soc. for Edn., Kappa Delta Pi (Eta Chi Chpt. of East Carolina U.), 2004. Office: Dreamkeepers Academy 2600 E Princess Anne Rd Norfolk VA 23504 Office Phone: 757-628-2555.

HERBERT, KATHY J., retail executive; MBA, Lake Forest Grad. Sch. Mgmt., 1985. Dir. personnel tng. Jewel-Osco divsn. Am. Stores Co., 1996—98, v.p. human resources, 1998—2001; exec. v.p. human resources Albertson's, Inc., Boise, 2001—. Chair Jewel-Osco United Way Campaign; bd. dirs. Chgo. Sinfonietta, Kohl's Childrens Mus. Office: Albertsons Inc 250 Parkcenter Blvd PO Box 20 Boise ID 83706 Office Phone: 208-395-6200. Office Fax: 208-395-6349.*

HERBERT, LINDA R., military officer; b. St. Paul, Sept. 19, 1961; d. Edker Henry and Jean Ruth Cherrier; m. Jeffrey H. Herbert. BA, Hamline U., St. Paul, 1985; MSc, Ctrl. Mich. U., Mt. Pleasant, 1993; MSc in Program Mgmt., Naval Postgrad. Sch., Monterey, Calif., 1995; MEd in Counseling, Wayne State U., Detroit, 1999. Nat. cert. counselor NBCC, Inc., N.C., 2000, lic. profl. counselor Mich., 2000, certification of ordination: clergy Christian Internat. Network of Chs., Fla., 2003. Commd. U.S. Army, 1985, comdr. 4-26 Inf. Ft. Dix, 1989—90, bridage S-4, dep. G-4, 1991—93, asst. product mgr. PEO Tactical Wheeled Vehicle, 1996—99; chief acquisition Policy, Pentagon, 2000—03; comdr., product mgr. Forward Looking Infrared U.S. Army, Ft. Belvoir, Va., 2003—. Author: (book) The Pentagon Miracle: An Eyewitness Account, 2002; co-author: (article) The Day I'll Never Forget, 2004. Charitable guest spkr. 9-11 cmty. events. Decorated Iraqi Campaign Medal, Noble Patron of Armor Medal; nominee Product Mgr. of Yr., Program Exec. Office Intelligence, Warfare and Sensors, 2005. Mem.: Am. Counseling Assn., Mil. Officers Assn. Am. Business E-Mail: linda.r.herbert@us.army.mil.

HERBERT, MARY KATHERINE ATWELL, writer; b. Grove City, Pa., Dec. 9, 1945; d. Stewart and Luella Irene (Brown) Atwell; m. Roland Marcus Herbert; children: Stephen Todd, Amy Elizabeth, Jill Anne. BA, Ariz. State U., 1968, MA, 1973; film cert., U. So. Calif., 1978. Film writer Scottsdale Daily Progress, 1976-79; dir. pub. relations Phoenix Theatre, 1980-85; script analyst, 1985-86; exec. asst. to v.p. prodn. DeLaurentiis Entertainment Group, 1986; producer's assoc. film TRAXX, 1986-87; dir. of devel. Devin/DeVore Prodns., 1988-89; free-lance script analyst and writer Glendale, Calif., 1989-97. Chmn. motion picture TV dept. Scottsdale (Ariz.) Coll., 2000—. Script writer: (TV shows) Trial By Jury, Dick Clark Prodn., (feature films) Dry Heat, Blind Desire, others; author: Writing Scripts Hollywood Will Love, 1994, 2d edit., 2000, Selling Scripts to Hollywood, 1999, The Perfect Screenplay, Writing It and Selling It, 2006. Mem. bd. mgrs. Hollywood-Wilshire YMCA, 1992-96. Mem. Authors Guild, Soc. Southwestern Authors. Personal E-mail: kathherb@cox.net.

HERBERT, PHYLLIS SYDNEY, social worker; b. Providence, Mar. 23, 1928; d. Alton M. and Celia Marian (Robrish) T.; m. Edward Herbert, June 8, 1946; 1 child, Edward Aaron. Registered clin. social worker, Oreg.; lic. clin. social worker. Instr. U. Oreg., Eugene, 1965-66; social worker Eugene Pub. Sch., 1966-67, Child Care, Inc., Eugene, 1967-68, social worker Crippled Children div., 1968-70; trainee drug addition NIMH Boston State Hosp., Mattapan, Mass., 1970—71; pvt. practice social work Eugene and Portland, 1980—. Vol. Aslan House, Eugene, 1978-80, William Temple House, Portland, 1986—; mem. Lane County Drug Adv. Com., Eugene, 1971-72, mem. Bur. Land Mgmt. Adv. Com., Eugene, 1980-82; alt. Oreg. State Water Quality Policy Adv. Com., 1978. Mem. Nat. Assn. Social Workers (cert.), LWV (bd. dirs.), Audubon Soc. (bd. dirs.), Oreg. Shores Conservation Coalition. Democrat. Episcopalian. Avocation: environmentalist.

HERBIG, JOAN E., information technology executive; BA in French, U. Louisville; MS in Computer Sci., U. Ky. Customer support IBM Corp.; sr. product line mgr. Digital Comm. Assoc., 1987—95; with XcelleNet, 1995—2005, CEO, Cambia, 2005—. Bd. dirs. AeA, Tech. Assn. Ga.; bd. adv. Atlanta CEO Coun. Recipient Woman of Yr. Tech., (WIT) Women in Tech., 2001. Mem.: Women in Tech. Internat. (Women Forging the Future award 2001), Ga. 100 Mentoring Program, Ga. Exec. Women's Network. Office: Cambia Ste 675 11675 Rainwater Dr Alpharetta GA 30004*

HERBOLD, PATRICIA LOUISE, ambassador; BA, Edgecliff Coll.; JD, No. Ky. Mayor, Montgomery, Ohio; v.p., gen. counsel Bank One; mem. Taft, Stettinius & Hollister; commr. Wash. State Gambling Commn., 1997—2000; chmn. Rep. party King County, Wash.; U.S. amb. to Singapore US Dept. State, 2005—. Bd. dirs. Wash. Policy Ctr. Office: 4280 Singapore Pl Washington DC 20521*

HERBST, JANE ELIZABETH, school librarian; b. NYC, Sept. 14, 1950; d. John Joseph Abritis and Helen Elizabeth Heath; m. Mitchell J. Maushay, Aug. 30, 1986 (dec. Aug. 14, 1990); m. Thomas Michael Herbst, June 26, 1993; children: Elizabeth Channan, Daniel Baoanthi. BA in Humanities, Dowling Coll., Oakdale, NY, 1972; MS in Libr. and Info. Sci., LI U., Greenvale, NY, 1986. Chief copy editor Phys. Rev. D, Am. Inst. Physics, Upton, NY, 1973—76; tech. editor Data Comm., Melville, 1976—80; publications mgr. Inst. Advanced Studies World Religions, Stony Brook, 1980—86; children's libr. Sachem Pub. Libr., Holbrook, 1984—2000; instr. Palmer Sch. Libr. and Info. Sci., LI U., Greenvale, 1986—88; sch. libr. media specialist Silas Wood Early Childhood Ctr., South Huntington, 1988—92, Babylon Junior-Senior H.S., Babylon, 1992—. Instr. NY State United Tchrs., Effective Tchg. Program, Albany, 2001—. Author (editor): (poetry anthology) Peel Me a Banana, Baby, I'll Be Home By Twelve. Warden St. Mary's Episcopal Ch., Ronkonkoma, NY, 1990—93; policy bd. mem. Suffolk's Edge Tchr. Ctr., Wheatly Heights, 1992—. Recipient Outstanding Contbn. Sch. Libr. Media Profession, Suffolk Sch. Libr. Media Assn., 2006; grantee, NEH, 2005. Mem.: ASCD, ALA, Am. Assn. Sch. Librs., NY Libr. Assn., Suffolk Sch. Libr. Media Assn. (past pres. 2005—), Beta Phi Mu. Episcopalian. Avocations: acting, singing, travel. Office: Babylon Junior-Senior High School 50 Railroad Avenue Babylon NY 11702 Office Phone: 631-893-7910. E-mail: jherbst@babylonsd.org.

HERBSTMAN, LORETTA, sculptor, painter; b. Bklyn., June 14; d. Berardino and Sabina (Senelli) Guicciardini; m. Martin Herbstman, Aug. 28; children: Jason, Dana. Instr. stone sculpture J. Reid Sch. Art, Buford, Ga.; instr. art Brimarsh Acad., Roswell, Ga. Sculptor in stone, cast bronze, cast resins and wire mesh; exhbns. include galleries throughout Manhattan, L.I., Staten Island, Ga., Fla. and shown on Joe Franklin TV Show, as well as Smithtown Art Coun. Mill Pond House, C.W. Post U. Hutchins Gallery, Gallery North, Suffolk County Bald Hill Cultural Ctr., Falconaire's Gallery, N.Y. Design Ctr.; jewelry designer/maker. Founder, pres. Farmingville (N.Y.) Improvement Coun.; mem. East End Arts Coun., Huntington Town Art League, Smithtown Art League, Westhampton Cultural Consortium. Recipient 1st prize for sculpture in a mixed-media juried show East Islip Arts Coun., numerous others. Mem. Nat. Sculpture Soc., Ga. Artists Registry. Home: 1490 S Orlando Ave Cocoa Beach FL 32931-2334

HERBSTREITH, YVONNE MAE, primary school educator; b. Wayne County, Ill., Aug. 18, 1942; d. Daniel Kirby and Rizpah Esther (Harvey) Smith; m. Bobbie L. Cates, Oct. 18, 1964 (div. 1969); 1 child, Shawn L.; m. Jerry Carrol Herbstreith, Sept. 15, 1979. BS, So. Ill. U., 1964. Cert. elem. tchr., Ill. Kindergarten tchr. Beardstown (Ill.) Elem., 1964-65, Pekin (Ill.) Pub. Schs. # 108, 1966-94. V.p. Pekin Friends of 47, 1986-91, pres. 1991-93, pres. Rebecca-Sarah Cir. 1st United Meth. Ch., Pekin, 1988—; trustee Sta. WTVP-TV, Peoria, Ill., 1990-91; active PTA, 1965-94, treas. 1992-93. Recipient Louise Alloy award Sta. WTVP, 1995. Mem. NEA (life), AAUW, Ill. Edn. Assn., Pekin Edn. Assn., Pekin Friends of Libr., Tazewell County Ret. Tchrs., Alpha Delta Kappa, Alpha Theta (chpt. pres. 1986-88, state sgt. at arms 1990-92, state chaplain 1992-94, state pres.-elect 1994-96, state pres. 1996—). Democrat. Methodist. Avocations: mystery books, reading, ceramics, crafts, photography, travel. Home: 1922 Quail Hollow Rd Pekin IL 61554-6351

HERDER, SUSAN HIDEKO, secondary school educator; d. Robert Elliott and Yasuko Kiyota Kulp; m. Gregory John Herder, Apr. 13, 1996; 1 child, Ciara Michiko. AB, Bryn Mawr Coll., 1992; MS, U. NC, 1995. Cert. secondary tchr. Minn. Mid. sch. sci. tchr. Highview Mid. Sch., New Brighton, Minn., 1999—; mid. sch. sci. resource tchr. Mounds View Pub. Schools, Shoreview, Minn., 2004—. Mem.: ASCD, NSTA, Nat. Mid. Sch. Assn. Dfl. Office Phone: 651-633-8144.

HERDMAN-FISHER, CAROLYN A., music educator; b. Johnstown, Pa., Mar. 30, 1980; d. Francis Paul and Barbara Ann Herdman; m. Thomas P. Fisher, June 19, 2004. BS Music Edn., Clarion U. Pa., Clarion, Pa., 2002. Cert. Md.Tchg.(Music K-12) Md., 2002, Pa. Tchg.(Music K-12) Pa., 2002, Kindermusik Kindermusik Internat., 2003. Musician The Mountain Playhouse, Jennerstown, Pa., 1998—; choral dir. Charles County Pub. Schs., Waldorf, Md., 2002—. Pvt. music instr., Waldorf, Md., 2002—; adjudicator Md. All-State Band and Chorus, 2002—; clinician (woodwind), Pa., 2002—, Md., 2002—; summer reading tchr. Charles County Pub. Schs., Reading Acad., Bryons Road, Md., 2003—; musician St. Ignatius Cath. Ch., Port Tobacco, Md., 2004—. Mem.: NEA, Md. Music Educators Assn., So. Md. Music Educators, Edn. Assn. of Charles County, Am. Fedn. of Musicians, Music Educators Nat. Conf., Order of Ea. Star. Roman Cath. Avocations: jogging, travel. Home: 5028 Skylark Dr La Plata MD 20646 Office Phone: 301-535-5949. Personal E-mail: tomandcarolynfisher@hotmail.com.

HERGE, DONNA CAROL, secondary school educator; b. Rockford, Ill., Nov. 11, 1948; d. William Carl and Grace Wilma Kling; m. John Arthur Herge, June 9, 1973; 1 child, Thomas William. BA in Math. and Philosophy, Rockford Coll., 1970; MS in Math., Wright State Univ., 1973; PhD and MS in Stats., Fla. State Univ., 1992. Commd. 2d lt. USAF, 1971, advanced through grades to lt. col., 1989, comdr. Detachment 1, 6th Weather Squadron Kelly AFB, Tex., 1974—75, contract monitor 16th Surveillance Squadron Shemya AFB, Alaska, 1975—76, asst. prof. math USAF Acad. Colorado Springs, Colo., 1976—80, comm.-electronics br. chief Offutt AFB, Nebr., 1980—83, stats. br. chief Air Force Inst. Tech. Wright Patterson AFB, Ohio, 1986—91; dir. rsch. and analysis AF Quality Inst., Maxwell AFB, Ala., 1991—95; ret. USAF, 1995; math tchr. Cath. H.S., Montgomery, Ala., 1996—. Adj. prof. stats. Troy State U., Montgomery, 1995—96, Auburn U., Montgomery, 1995—96. Editor: (book) Process Improvement Guide: Tools for Today's Air Force, 1992. Alto St. Bede Ch. Adult Choir, Montgomery, 1995—. Decorated Commendation medal USAF, Meritorious Svc. medal; recipient Comm. Electronics Profl. Achievement award, Aerospace Def. Command, 1976. Mem.: Am. Soc. for Quality, Am. Statis. Assn., Phi Beta Kappa (hon.). Business E-Mail: d_herge@knights.pvt.k12.al.us.

HERGENHAN, JOYCE, public relations executive; b. Mt. Kisco, N.Y., Dec. 30, 1941; d. John Christopher and Goldie (Wago) H. BA, Syracuse U., 1963; MBA, Columbia U., 1978. Reporter White Plains Reporter Dispatch, 1963-64; asst. to Rep. Ogden R. Reid Washington, 1964-68; reporter Gannett Newspapers, 1968-72; with Consol. Edison Co. of N.Y., Inc., N.Y.C., 1972-82, v.p., 1977-79, sr. v.p. pub. affairs, 1979—82; v.p. corp. pub. relations General Electric Co., Fairfield, Conn., 1982—98; pres. GE Found., 1998—. Trustee Syracuse U., 1996-; bd. dirs. Civilian Pub. Affairs Coun.,

U.S. Mil. Acad. at West Point, 1990-, Jackie Robinson Found. 2001, Conn. Audubon Soc., Inner City Found. for Edn. and Charity; past chmn. Pub. Rels. Seminar. Recipient Lifetime Achievement award, Women in Communications, 1999.

HERGO, JANE ANTOINETTE, music educator, composer; b. Dayton, Ohio, Apr. 16, 1946; d. Frank Gustav and Antoinette Rosalyn (Jean) Hergo. BMus, U. Dayton, 1968, BS in Music Edn., 1975; MMus, Wright State U., 1980. Cert. music tchr., Ohio. Kindergarten tchr., Englewood, Ohio, 1971; elem. tchr. Dayton, Ohio, 1976—77, 1978—81; class piano instr. Sinclair C.C., Dayton, Ohio, 1981, piano accompanist for ballet and modern dance, 1983—84; ind. piano tchr. Dayton, Ohio, 1984—. Composer (book) Five Finger Frolics, 1988, Keyboard Confections, 1992 (sheet music) Gems on the Lake, 1991 (Ohio Music Tchrs. Assn. award 1990), Skeleton Skedaddle, 1993 (hon. mention award composition contest), Forest in the Rain (hon. mention award composition contest), Jazz Spooks (hon. mention award composition contest), Ghostly Gathering, 1991, Chilipeppers, 1998, Snowswirls, 2002 (hon. mention award composition contest). Piano soloist Dayton Philharm. Designer Show House, 1985, 87; adjudicator Jr. Music Club Festivals, Dayton, 1989—. Recipient Jr. Composer award Ohio Fedn. Music Club, 1998, Piano Compositions awards Key Piano Mag., 1990, 93, Merit award Nat. Fedn. Music Clubs, 1990. Mem. ASCAP, Music Tchrs. Nat. Assn. (nat. cert.), Ohio Music Tchrs. Assn. (officer student composition sect. Western dist. 1988-90, composition panel 1989, state conv. 1992), Jr. Music Club, Dayton Music Club (composer), Sigma Alpha Iota. Avocations: emboidery, drawing, sewing, reading, flower gardening.

HERING, DORIS MINNIE, dance critic; b. N.Y.C., Apr. 11, 1920; d. Harry and Anna Elizabeth (Schwenk) H. BA cum laude, Hunter Coll., 1941; MA, Fordham U., 1985. Freelance dance writer, 1946-52; assoc. editor, prin. critic Dance mag., N.Y.C., 1952-72; exec. dir. Nat. Assn. for Regional Ballet, N.Y.C., 1972-87; adj. assoc. prof. dance history NYU, 1968-78; freelance dance writer, lectr., cons., 1987—. Mem. dance panel NEA, 1972-75, cons., 1991—; mem. dance panel N.Y. State Coun. Arts, 1992-96, program auditor, 1997—; bd. dirs. Walnut Hill Sch., 1975—, Internat. Ballet Competition, 1981—; hon. bd. dirs. Phila. Dance Alliance, 1980—; cons. Regional Dance Am.; adj. assoc. prof. dance history NYU Grad. Sch. Edn. Author: 25 Years of American Dance, 1950, Dance in America, 1951, Wild Grass, 1965, Giselle and Albrecht, 1981; sr. editor Dance mag., 1989—. Howard D. Rothschild Rsch. fellow Harvard U., 1991-93; recipient 33d ann. Capezio Dance Found. award for lifetime svc., 1985, Award of Distinction Dance mag., 1987, Sage Cowles Land Grant chair in dance U. Minn., 1993, Sr. Critics tribute Dance Critics Assn., 2002, Annual award, Martha Hill Dance Fund, 2002; named to Hunter Coll. Alumni Hall of Fame, 1986. Mem. Dance Critics Assn., Assn. Dance History Scholars, Phi Beta Kappa, Chi Tau Epsilon (hon.). Office Phone: 212-787-3834.

HERL, SONYA, elementary school educator; b. Hays, Kans., Apr. 21, 1965; d. Robert Frances and Dolores (Helget) Dreiling; m. David Alan Herl, Oct. 11, 1991. BS in Elem. Edn., Fort Hays State U., 1987. Tchr. elem. St. Marys Parochial Sch., Ellis, Kans., 1987-90, O'Loughin Elem. Sch., Hays, Kans., 1990—. Cons. Social Studies Assessment Kans. State Bd. Edn., Hays, 1994—. Recipient Presdl. award NSF, 1995, Excellence in Tchg. award Kans./Am. Med. Assn., 1995. Office: O'Loughin Elem Sch 1401 Hall St Hays KS 67601-3753

HERLEY, DAVEEN DOROTHY, art educator, artist; arrived in U.S., 1965; d. Stewart Barker and Elizabeth Gladys Hodges; m. Patrick James Herley (dec.). BA, Rhodes U., 1955, edn. diploma, 1956, EdB, 1959; Masters Degree, Adelphi U., 1975. Cert. elem. edn. and art edn. N.Y. Lectr. art, prof. edn. Grahamstown (South Africa) Tng. Coll., 1957—60; H.S. art tchr. Woodbury Down Comprehensive, London, 1961—64; elem. tchr. South Haven (N.Y.) Sch. Dist., 1972—89, South Country Sch. Dist., East Patchogue, NY, 1989—2002; adj. prof. Suffolk County C.C., Selden, NY, 1972—. Chair ednl. problems com. Bellport Tchrs. Assn., East Patchogue, NY, 1990—93; workshop leader in field. Author: Art Through Your Child's Eyes, 1975; exhibitions include, Brookhaven, Smithtown and East Hampton, N.Y., St. James, 1972—. Mem. Smithtown Arts Coun., East End Arts Coun. Recipient Recognition award, Bellport Tchrs. Assn., 1990, 1991, 1992, 1993, Cert. Spl. Recognition, South Country Sch. Dist., 2001, 2002. Mem.: SAEYC (pres. 1975—77), NAEYC, Internat. Dyslexia Soc., Movable Book Soc. Avocations: collecting movable books, gardening, golf, antiques. Personal E-mail: herley67@aol.com.

HERLIHY, JENNIFER BOYD, lawyer; b. Doylestown, Pa., Nov. 17, 1971; BA in Journalism, cum laude, Boston U., 1993; JD, Suffolk U., 1997. Bar: Mass. 1997, US Dist. Ct. (Dist. Mass.) 1998, RI 2003. Ptnr. Adler, Cohen, Harvey, Wakeman & Guekguezian LLP, Boston. Mem.: RI Bar Assn., Mass. Bar Assn. Office: Adler Cohen Harvey Wakeman & Guekguezian LLP 75 Federal St Boston MA 02110 Office Phone: 617-423-6674. Office Fax: 617-423-7152. E-mail: jbh@achwg.com.*

HERLIHY, MAURA ANN, medical technician; b. Yokohama, Japan, July 13, 1953; d. Joseph Brendan and Margaret Cecilia (Corrigan) H. AA in Liberal Arts, Middlesex Community Coll., 1973; BA in Elem. Edn., Rivier Coll., 1975, MA in Counseling, 1986. Sub. tchr. Bedford (Mass.) Pub. Schs., 1975-76; sec. Instrumentation Labs., Lexington, Mass., 1976-77, Electronized Chems. Corp., Burlington, Mass., 1977-78, Digital Equipment Corp., Bedford, Mass., 1978-80; sales clk. Lord and Taylor, Burlington, 1979-81; sec. Dept. VA, Bedford, 1980-89, psychology technician, 1989—. Mem.: DAV Aux, Women Affirming Life, Inc., Nat. Right to Life Assoc., North Am. Bluebird Soc., Mass. Audubon Soc., Feminists for Life of Am., Mass. Bluebird Assoc., Am. Birding Assoc., Sierra Club, Applachian Mountain Club. Roman Catholic. Avocations: reading, sewing, piano, music. Home: 426 Great Elm Way Acton MA 01718-1005 Office: Dept Vet Affairs 200 Springs Rd Bedford MA 01730-1114

HERLIHY-CHEVALIER, BARBARA DOYLE, retired mental health nurse; b. Cambridge, Mass., June 28, 1935; d. William A. and Aloyse V. (Mahoney) Doyle; m. Timothy J. Herlihy, Aug. 20, 1955 (dec. Oct. 1983); children: Michael, Ann-Marie, Sharon, Ellen, Stephen, Kathleen, James; m. Robert J. Chevalier, May 28, 1994 (dec. Oct. 1995); 1 stepchild, Ron. RN, Mass. Gen. Hosp., 1956; BS in Human Svcs., N.H. Coll./So. N.H. U., 1983; MS in Nursing, Anna Maria Coll., 1987. Nat. cert. instr. and coord. remotivation therapy. Pvt. duty nurse N.E. Bapt. Hosp., MGH, Boston, 1956, St. John's Hosp., Lowell, Mass., 1966—70; charge nurse Tewksbury (Mass.) Hosp. Mass. Dept. Pub. Health, 1970—76; coord. remotivation therapy Danvers (Mass.) State Hosp., 1976—79; registered community mental health nurse Mass. Dept. Mental Health, Lawrence, 1979—91; mental health nurse Lowell (Mass.) Adult Day Treatment, 1991—94. Fellow Nat. Remotivation Therapy Orgn. (nat. instr., coord., Dorothy Hoskins Smith honorarium 2001); mem. Internat. Adv. Coun. Remotivation Therapy, Nat. Remotivation Therapy Orgn., Inc., Bay State Remotivation Coun. Home: 142 Trull Rd Tewksbury MA 01876-1705 Office Phone: 978-851-7977. Personal E-mail: barbhc851@aol.com.

HERMAN, ALEXIS M., retired labor union administrator; b. Mobile, Ala., July 16, 1947; Student, Edgewood Coll. Sacred Heart, 1966—67; BA, Xavier U., New Orleans, 1969; Ph.D (hon.), Lesley Coll. Community worker Interfaith, Inc., Mobile, Ala., 1969; social worker Catholic Social Svc., Mobile, Ala., 1969—72; consult., supr. Recruitment & Training Program Inc., NYC, 1973—74; nat. dir. Minority Women's Employment Program, Washington, 1974—77; dir., founder, Women's Bur. US Dept. Labor, Washington, 1977-81; v.p., co-founder Green, Herman & Associates, 1981—85; founder, pres., CEO A.M. Herman & Assocs., Washington, 1985—93; chief staff, then dep. chair Dem. Nat. Conv. Com., Washington, 1989—91, CEO, 1991-92; dep. dir. Clinton-Gore Presdl. Transition Office, Washington, 1992-93; asst. to Pres., pub. liaison dir. The White House, Washington, 1993-96; sec. U.S. Dept. Labor, Washington, 1997-2001; chmn., CEO New Ventures, Inc., Washington, 2001—; chairperson Coca-Cola Human Resources Diversity Task Force, Ga., 2001—; chmn. Toyota N Am. Diversity Bd., 2002—. Mem. bd. dirs. Entergy Corp., 2003—, Cummins Inc., President Life Insurance Co., MGM Mirage. Recipient Outstanding Young Person in Atlanta award, 1974, Atlanta's First Woman award, 1976, Dorothy I. Height Leadership award, Ctrl State U., Sara Lee Front Runner award, 1999. Mem. Atlanta Black Woman's Coalition, Am. Soc. Bus. & Profl. Women, Diocesan Commn. Social Justice, Internat. Personnel Mgmt. Assn., Nat. Coun. Negro Women, Delta Sigma Theta. Democrat.

HERMAN, ALICE GERTRUDE, retired nursing educator; b. West Milton, Pa., Dec. 6, 1925; d. Mark Artley and Alice (Harman) Herman. BSN, Case We. Res. U., 1963; cert. in Midwifery, Frontier U., 1958; MS in Nursing, U. Ky., 1972; PhD, U. London, 1988. RN Pa., Ky., England, Wales. Asst. instr. Geisinger Med. Ctr., Danville, Pa., 1955—56; dist. nurse midwife Frontier Nursing Svc., Hyden, Ky., 1956—60; instr. Berea Coll., Ky., 1965—67; project nurse midwife Maternal-Inpant Care Project, McCreary Co., Ky., 1967—69; supervising pub. health nurse Montour, Snyder, Union, Northumberland Co., Pa., 1969—73; asst. prof. U. Ky., 1973—75; asst. prof. clin. nursing Bloomsburg U., Pa., 1975—77; asst. prof. Morehead State U., Ky., 1978, Albright Coll., Reading, Pa., 1978—79; coord. perinatal nurse edn. Dept. Ob-gyn. U. Louiseville, Ky., 1979—82; chmn. Dept. Nursing Prestonsburg C.C., Ky., 1982—83; assoc. dir. hosp. edn. Warne Clinic Pottsville Hosp., Pa., 1983—84; asst. prof. nursing Pa. State U., Hershey, 1984—87; coord. tng. Cmty. Health Aide Program Bristol Bay Area Health Corp., Dillingham, Alaska, 1988—92; support personnel U.S. Forest Svc., Jackson, Wyo., 1993—94; pvt. practice nurse-midwife Lewisburg, Pa., 1994—96; ret., 1996. Chmn. med. adv. com. Columbia/Montour Home Health Svcs.; mem. dist. adv. coun. State Health Plan Pa.; mem. various coms. U. Ky., Bloomsburg (Pa.) State Coll., Albright Coll., U. Louiseville; lectr. in field. Contbr. articles to profl. jours. 1st lt. nurse corps. U.S. Army, 1960—64. Recipient award, Commr. Health, Dept. Health, Ky., 1968, Kiwanis, Danville, Pa., 1969, Cmty. Svcs. Pa., 1971, Oustanding Svc. award, Am. Cancer Soc., 1975, award, Columbia-Montoner Home Health Svcs., Merit cert., U.S. Dept. Agr., U.S. Forest Svc., 1994. Mem.: Am. Legion, Sigma Theta Tau. Episcopalian. Avocations: gardening, reading, music, mushing. Home: 543 Kennedy Bridge Rd Harrodsburg KY 40330

HERMAN, ANDREA MAXINE, newspaper editor; b. Chgo., Oct. 22, 1938; d. Maurice H. and Mae (Baron) H.; m. Joseph Schmidt, Oct. 28, 1962. BJ, U. Mo., 1960. Feature writer Chgo.'s Am., 1960-63; daily columnist News Am., Balt., 1963-67; feature writer Mainichi Daily News, Tokyo, 1967-69; columnist Iowa City Press-Citizen, 1969-76; music and dance critic San Diego Tribune, 1976-84; asst. mng. editor features UPI, Washington, 1984-86, asst. mng. editor news devel., 1986-87; mng. editor features L.A. Herald Examiner, 1987-91; editor/culture We/Mbl Newspaper, Washington, 1991—. Recipient 1st and 2d prizes for features in arts James S. Copley Ring of Truth Awards, 1982, 1st prize for journalism Press Club San Diego, 1983. Mem. Soc. Profl. Journalists, Am. Soc. Newspaper Editors, AP Mng. Editors, Women in Communications. Avocations: music, art. Office: We Mbl Newspaper 1350 Connecticut Ave NW Washington DC 20036-1722 Office Phone: 858-459-3625. Business E-Mail: jdschmidt@ucsd.edu.

HERMAN, DOROTHY, real estate broker; b. Bklyn., May 10, 1953; d. Joseph Edward and Louise (Dicerbo) D'Ambrosio; m. Jay Herman; 1 child, Christine. BA, Adelphia U., 1983. Cert. fin. planner. Mgr. Merrill Lynch Realty, L.I., NY, 1982-84, regional v.p., 1985-87, pres. L.I., 1988-90; co-owner, pres. Prudential L.I. Realty (aquired Douglas Elliman), 1990—2003; co-owner, pres., CEO Prudential Douglas Elliman Real Estate, NYC, 2003—. Mem. faculty N.Y. Inst. Tech., 1988— Contbr. weekly article to Newsday, 1990. Mem. Internat. Assn. of Fin. Planners (cert. fin. planner), L.I. Bd. Realtors, Columbia Soc. Real Estate Appraisers. Avocation: racquetball. Office: Prudential Douglas Elliman 575 Madison Ave 4th Fl New York NY 10022 also: 110 Walt Whitman Rd Ste 106 Huntington Station NY 11746 Office Phone: 212-891-7695.*

HERMAN, EDITH CAROL, journalist; b. Edgewood, Md., July 1, 1944; d. Herbert R. and Thirza E. (Simmons) H.; m. Leonard Wiener. BA, Purdue U., 1966. Reporter Hollister Newspaper Chain, Wilmette, Ill., 1966-68, Chgo. Tribune Newspaper, 1968-79, edn. editor, 1971-74, feature writer, 1976-79; sr. editor TV Digest Inc., 1980-83; pub. rels. mgr. AT&T, 1983-90; pub. rels. cons. Bethesda, 1990—93, Warren Comm., 1994—, assoc. mng. editor, 2001—. Bd. dirs. Sigma Delta Chi Found. of Washington, 1990—92. Recipient Journalism award Ill. Edn. Assn., 1969-70; Editorial award Ill. Automatic Merchandising Council, 1977 Mem.: Soc. Profl. Journalists. Home: 5501 Burling Ct Bethesda MD 20817-6309 E-mail: eherman@warren-news.com.

HERMAN, JOAN ELIZABETH, health insurance company executive; b. NYC, June 2, 1953; d. Roland Barry and Grace Gales (Goldstein) Herman; m. Richard M. Rasiej, July 16, 1977. AB, Barnard Coll., 1975; MS, Yale U., New Haven, 1977. Actuarial student Met. Life Ins. Co., NYC, 1978-82; asst. actuary Phoenix Mut. Life Ins. Co., Hartford, Conn., 1982-83, assoc. actuary, dir. underwriting rsch., 1983-84, 2nd v.p., 1984-85, v.p., 1985-89, sr. v.p., 1989-98; pres. splty. bus. WellPoint Health Networks, Woodland Hills, Calif., 1998, grp. pres., 1999—2001, pres. splty., sr. and state sponsored progs. divsn., 2002—04; pres., CEO, splty. sr. and state sponsored bus. divsn. WellPoint, Inc., Indpls., 2004—. Bd. dirs. PM Holdings, Inc., Phoenix Grp. Holdings, Inc., Phoenix Am. Life Ins. Co., Emprendimiento Compartido, S.A.; v.p. BC Life & Health Co., Profl. Claims Svcs. Inc., Proserv., MEDIX. Contbr. articles to profl. jours. Bd. dirs. Health Ins. Assn. Am., 2002—03; capt. fundraising team Greater Hartford Arts Coun., Hartford, 1986; bd. dirs. Children's Fund Conn., 1992—98, My Sister's Pl. Shelter, Hartford, 1989—94, Western Mass. Regional Nat. Conf. Conn., 1995—98, Greater Hartford Arts Coun., 1997—98, Hartford Ballet, 1989—95, corporator, 1995—98; bd. dirs. Leadership Greater Hartford, 1989—94, chmn. bd. dirs., 1993—94; bd. dirs. So. Calif. Leadership Network, 2003—; mem. bd. founders Am. Leadership Forum Hartford, 1991—98; corporator Hartford Sem., 1994—98; bd. dirs. Hadassah, Glastonbury, Conn., Temple Beth Hillel, South Windsor, Conn., 1983—84. Fellow: Soc. Actuaries (chairperson health sect. coun. 1994—95); mem.: Am. Leadership Forum, Am. Acad. Actuaries (bd. dirs. 1994—97). Jewish. Avocations: reading, swimming, bicycling, jogging, aerobic dancing, hiking. Office: WellPoint Inc 1 Wellpoint Way Thousand Oaks CA 91362-3893 Office Phone: 805-557-6333. Business E-Mail: joan.herman@wellpoint.com.

HERMAN, JONI MARIE-VICTOR, artist; b. L.A., Jan. 13, 1963; d. Victor Herman and Joan Marie DiPirro. Cert., U. Jerusalem, 1980, Rocky Mountain Painting, Salt Lake City, 1995. Lic. contractor Calif. Owner Renaissance Studios, Orange County, Calif., 1984—. Group leader SGI-USA, Orange County, 1981—; vol. art instr. Orange County Dept. Edn., 1999—; mem. Violence Prevention Coalition, Orange County, 2001—. With USAR, 1980—81. Named Vol. of Yr., Vol. Ctr. Dept. of Edn., Orange County, 2000; recipient Amb. of Peace award, Violence Prevention Coalition, 2001. Buddhist. E-mail: joniherman1@aol.com.

HERMAN, KIMBERLY B., lawyer; b. 1969; BA cum laude, Northeastern U., 1992; JD, Western New England Coll., 1995. Bar: Mass. 1995, US Dist. Ct. (Dist. Mass.) 1995, US Ct. Appeals (Fed. Cir.) 1996. Reporter Boston Globe; corp. counsel PerkinElmer, Inc.; assoc. Intellectual Property & Tech. Practice Group Goodwin Procter LLP; counsel Intellectual Property Group and Corp. Dept. Sullivan & Worcester LLP, Boston; assoc. gen. counsel FairMarket Inc. Instr. intellectual property law Suffolk U. Law Sch. Mem.: Computer Law Assn., Internat. Trademark Assn., Mass. Bar Assn., Boston Bar Assn. Office: Sullivan & Worcester LLP One Post Office Square Boston MA 02109 Office Phone: 617-338-2943. E-mail: kherman@sandw.com.*

HERMAN, MARY ELIZABETH, educator; b. Hugo, Okla., Dec. 19, 1943; d. Artie Hern and Frankie Mae (McCasland) H. BS in Edn., Southeastern Okla. State U., 1965, MEd, 1971; postgrad., S.W. Mo. State U., 1991—. Elem. tchr. Altus Pub. Schs., Okla., 1965-71; asst. prof. Bapt. Bible Coll., Springfield, Mo., 1971-81, prof. edn., chair elem. edn. dept., 1981—2002; tchr. travelling internat to train Sun. sch. tchrs. Bapt. Bible Fellowship Internat. (BBFI), 2002—. Contbr. articles to jours. Mem. Internat. Reading Assn., Mo. Reading Assn., Tchr. Educators Assn. Baptist. Avocations: painting, gardening, travel. Home: 7962 N Springhill Ln Springfield MO 65803-8093 Office: Bapt Bible Fellowship Internat PO Box 191 Springfield MO 65803

HERMAN, MARY MARGARET, neuropathologist; b. Plymouth, Wis., July 26, 1935; d. Elmer Fredolein and Esther Lydia (Bross) H.; m. Lucien Jules Rubinstein, Jan. 31, 1969. BS in Med. Sci., U. Wis., 1957, MD, 1960. Diplomate Nat. Bd. Med. Examiners, Am. Bd. Anatomic Pathology, Am. Bd. Neuropathology. Intern Mary Hitchcock Meml. Hosp., Hanover, NH, 1960-61; resident in neurology U. Wis. Hosps., 1961-62; intern in pathology Yale U., New Haven, 1962-63, asst. resident in pathology, 1963-64, fellow in neuropathology, 1964-65, rsch. assoc. pathology, 1967-68; fellow in neuropathology Stanford U., Palo Alto, Calif., 1965-66, fellow, acting instr. neuropathology, 1966-67, asst. prof. pathology, 1967-74, assoc. prof., 1974-81; prof., co-dir. divsn. neuropathology U. Va. Sch. Medicine, Charlottesville, 1981-91, prof. clin. pathology, 1991-92; spl. expert neuropathology in clin. brain disorders br. NIMH, Washington, 1991-96, sr. staff scientist, 1996—; neuropathologist NIMH Brain Collection, 1992—, Stanley Fund Brain Collection, 1992—2002. Vis. asst. prof. Albert Einstein Coll. Medicine, Bronx, NY, 1971—72; mem. program project rev. com. Nat. Inst. Neurol. and Communicative Diseases NIH, 1973—77; cons. lab. svc. VA Hosp., Salem, Va., Ctrl. Va. Tng. Ctr., Lynchburg, 1982—92, ad hoc mem. pathology A study sect., 1986—91; cons. neuropathologist DC Med. Examiner's Office, Washington, 1992—, Med. Examiner's Office, No. Va. Dist., Fairfax, 2000—, DC Gen. Hosp., 1992—2002; mentor scientist NIH Intramural Rsch. Tng. award, Fogarty Fellows, Howard Hughes Med. Inst./MCPS/NIH student and tchr. internships program, Stanley Found. scholar's program. Mem. editl. bd.: Jour. Neuropathology and Exptl. Neurology, 1989—93, 2001—; contbr. over 200 articles to profl. jours. Recipient Rsch. Career Devel. award, NIH, 1967—72, Staff Recognition award, 2000—06, Faculty Devel. award, Merck Found., 1969. Mem.: AAAS, AMA, Am. Assn. Anatomists, Soc. Biol. Psychiatry, Am. Assn. Neuropathologists (Weil award 1974), Am. Soc. for Investigative Pathology, Soc. for Devel. Biology, Internat. Soc. Neuropathology, Am. Soc. Cell Biology (rsch. fellowship program, mentor scientist summer tchr. 1994), Internat. Acad. Pathology, Soc. In Vitro Biology, Soc. Neurosci. Achievements include research in neuropathology of major mental disorders, neurodegeneration and aluminum neurotoxicity, and embryonal tumors of the CNS. Avocations: tennis, gardening, music. Home: 10008 Stedwick Rd Apt 304 Montgomery Village MD 20886-3718 Office: Clin Brain Disorders Br NIMH NIH Msc 9402 5625 Fisher Ln Rm 4N03 Bethesda MD 20892-9402 Office Phone: 301-480-0042. E-mail: mh230t@nih.gov.

HERMAN, MICHELLE, writer; b. Bklyn., Mar. 9, 1955; d. Morton and Sheila Marcia (Weiss) Herman. BS, Bklyn. Coll., 1976; MFA in English, U. Iowa, 1986. Manuscript editor Van Nostrand Reinhold Co., N.Y.C., 1976; reporter Assoc. Press, City Desk, N.Y.C., 1977; freelance editor various pubs., N.Y.C., 1977-84; instr. U. of Iowa, Iowa City, 1984-86; prof. English Ohio State U., Columbus, 1988—. Author: (novel) Missing, 1990 (Harold U. Ribdow award Hadassah 1990), (stories) A New and Glorious Life, 1998, Dog, 2005, (novel) The Middle of Everything: Memoirs of Motherhood, 2005; short stories; playwright: Tyler and Althea, 1980; editor (lit. mag.) The Journal. NEA fellow, 1986; recipient Tchg.-Writing award U. Iowa, 1985, 86, James Michener award 1987, Ohio Arts Coun. awards, 1989, 99, 2004. Democrat. Jewish. Office Phone: 614-292-5767.

HERMAN, MINDY, broadcast executive; d. Leonard and Flora Herman. BS in Economics, Wharton Sch. Bus., U. Penn, 1982; JD, MBA, UCLA; student, London Sch. Economics. With News Corp., 1990—98; v.p. bus. affairs Twentieth Century Fox, 1990—93; sr. v.p. bus. affairs FX Networks, 1993—95; exec. v.p. bus. ops. Tele-TV, 1995—97; exec. v.p. Fox Television Studios, 1997—99; pres., CEO Viewer's Choice (renamed In Demand, 2000), 1999—2000, E! Networks, N.Y.C., 2000—04. Recipient Women of Vision in Cable award, 2002, Larry Stewart Leadership and Inspiration award, Prism Awards, The Entertainment Industries Coun., 2004. Office: E! Networks 11 W 42d St Fl 19 New York NY 10036

HERMAN, SARAH ANDREWS, lawyer; b. Fargo, ND, June 20, 1952; BA magna cum laude, U. N.D., 1974; JD, U. Mich., 1977. Bar: N.D. 1977, U.S. Dist. Ct. N.D. 1978. With Nilles, Hansen & Davies, Ltd., Fargo, ND, 1977—94, bd. dirs.; ptnr., trial and labor and employment practice groups Dorsey & Whitney LLP, ptnr. in charge Fargo office, 1997—, co-head labor employment group, 1996—2000, group head, mgmt. comm. mem. for regulatory group, 2000—05. Mem. Fed. Practice Com., 8th Cir. Gender Task Force. Co-chair N.D. Gender Fairness, 1993-94. Mem. ND State Bar Assn. (pres. 2000), Cass County Bar Assn. Office: Dorsey & Whitney LLP Ste 402 Dakota Ctr 51 N Broadway Fargo ND 58102 Office Phone: 701-235-6000. Office Fax: 701-235-9969. Business E-Mail: herman.sarah@dorsey.com.

HERMANCE, BETTY JEAN, special education educator; b. Chgo., Mar. 20, 1940; d. Louis and Helen (Minnick) Matalin; m. Duane Edward Heinen, Dec. 8, 1958; children: Thadeus Heinen, Susan Heinen; m. Steve Arthur Hermance, Nov. 5, 1988. AA, Rock Valley Coll., Rockford, Ill., 1980; BS in Child Devel., Rockford Coll., 1982, postgrad., 1984; student, U. Va./Longwood Coll., 1994. Spl. educator for severely emotionally disturbed The Pines Treatment Ctr., Portsmouth, Va., 1991-94; spl. edn. tchr. Dolan Ednl. Ctr., Durand, Ill., 1994-2000, Sch. Dist. 205, Rockford, Ill., 2000—.

HERMANN, MILDRED L., artist; b. Bklyn., Mar. 8, 1920; d. Philip and May Atkin Lipskin; m. Arthur E. Hermann, June 27, 1942; children: Laurie Schwartzer, Elizabeth Schoenfeld, Jane Simons. Student, Bklyn. Coll., 1937—40, Artists in Am. Sch. Painting. One-woman shows include over 21 solo shows, Represented in permanent collections Albright-Knox Gallery, Buffalo, N.Y., Norton Mus. Art, West Palm Beach, Fla. Recipient Childe Hassam Purchase award, Am. Acad. Arts and Letters, 1978. Mem.: Audubon Artists (Mixed Media Painting award 1981), Nat. Assn. Women Artists. Address: c/o Denise Bibro Fine Art 529 W 20th St 4th Fl New York NY 10011 Office Phone: 212-647-7030.

HERMANN, SHARON BETH BETSY, music educator; b. West Reading, Pa., June 27, 1952; d. Norman Ernest Klopp and Mary Elizabeth Lowman. BA in Music Edn., Ind. U. Pa., 1970—74; MS in Music Edn., U. Ill., Champaign Urbana, 1987—88. Cert. tchr. Va. Organist, choir dir. Bethel Luth. Ch., Manassas, Va., 1981—2004; choral music tchr. Manassas Pk. City Schs., Va., 1982—87; vocal music tchr. Fred Lynn Mid. Sch., Woodbridge, Va., 1988—90; choral dir. Osbourn Pk. HS, Manassas, 1990—. Recipient Tchr. of Yr., Osbourn Pk. HS, 2001. Mem.: Nat. Edn. Assn., Music Educators Nat. Conf., Am. Choral Dirs. Assoc., Phi Delta Kappa, Delta Omicron Honoray Music (life). Lutheran. Avocations: genealogy, racquetball. Home: 8458 Willow Glen Ct Manassas VA 20110 Office: Osbourn Park HS 8909 Euclid Ave Manassas VA 20111 Business E-Mail: hermansb@pwcs.edu.

HERMINGHOUSE, PATRICIA ANNE, foreign language educator; b. Melrose Park, Ill., Mar. 13, 1940; m. 1964; 2 children. BA, Knox Coll., 1962; MA, Washington U., 1965, PhD in German, 1968. Asst. prof. German U. Mo.-St. Louis, 1966-67, vis. lectr., 1968-69; asst. prof. Washington U., St. Louis, 1967-78, assoc. prof. German, 1978-83; Fuchs prof. German studies U. Rochester, NY, 1983—, chmn. dept. fgn. langs., lits. and linguistics NY, 1983—89. Lectr. German, Fontbonne Coll., 1965-66. Internat. Research & Exchanges Bd. ad hoc grantee, 1976. Editor or co-editor: Literatur der DDR in den siebziger Jahren, 1983, Literatur und Literaturtheorie in der DDR, 1976, Frauen im Mittelpunkt, 1987, Gender and Germaness, 1997, Ingeborg

Bachmann and Christa Wolf, 1998, German Feminist Writings, 2000; editor GDR Bull., Newsletter Lit. and Culture in German Dem. Republic, 1975-83; co-editor: Women in German Yearbook, 1994-2002. Recipient Susan B. Anthony Lifetime Achievement award, 2003; grantee Fulbright German Studies Summer Seminar, 2005; sr. fellow, NEH, 1991. Mem. MLA, Am. Assn. Tchrs. German (exec. coun. 1979-81), German Studies Assn. (exec. com., v.p./pres. 2001-02, pres. 2003-04), Coalition Women German (coord. 1974-75, nat. steering. com. 1976-79, 94-2002), Assn. Depts. Fgn. Langs. (exec. com.). Address: U Rochester Dept Modern Lang and Cultures Rochester NY 14627 Business E-Mail: pahe@troi.cc.rochester.edu.

HERMLE, LYNNE C., lawyer; b. New Haven, Conn., 1956; BA magna cum laude, U. Calif. Santa Barbara, 1978; JD, U. Calif., Hastings Coll., 1981. Bar: Calif. 1981. In house atty. AT&T; ptnr. Orrick, Herrington & Sutcliffe LLP, Menlo Park, mem. exec. com. Faculty mem. Nat. Ins. Trial Advocacy; co-editor in chief Start-up & Emerging Cos. Strategist Newsletter; Early Neutral Evaluator No. Dist. Calif., Fed. Ct. Co-author: Sexual Harassment in Workplace: Guide Law, 1994; author: Fuller: Intolerable Burden on Employers?, 1995, EAPs: Expert Roundtable Problems, Solutions, 1991. Named one of Am.'s top 50 women litigators, Nat. Law Jour. Mem.: ABA-labor & employment sect., State Bar Calif. Office: Orrick Herrington & Sutcliffe LLP 1000 Marsh Rd Menlo Park CA 94025 Office Phone: 650-614-7422. Office Fax: 650-614-7401. Business E-Mail: lchermle@orrick.com.

HERNANDEZ, ADRIANA, athletic trainer; b. San Antonio, Tex., Dec. 13, 1980; d. Luis and Terri Hernandez. BA, Tex. Luth. U., Seguin, 2002; MS, Angelo State U., San Angelo, Tex., 2004. Cert. Am. Coll. Sports Medicine Ind., 2005, Athletic Trainer Bd. of Certification Nebr., 2003. Personal trainer Spectrum Health Clubs, San Antonio, 2003—04; athletic trainer Alamo Heights Ind. Sch. Dist., San Antonio, 2005—. R-Consevative. Avocations: sand volleyball, international travel. Home: 2554 Ashley Oak Dr Schertz TX 78154 Office: Alamo Heights High School 150 E Fair Oaks Place San Antonio TX 78209

HERNANDEZ, AILEEN C(LARKE), urban consultant; b. Bklyn., May 23, 1926; d. Charles Henry and Ethel Louise (Hall) Clarke; divorced. AB in Sociology and Polit. Sci. magna cum laude, Howard U., 1947; MA in Pub. Adminstrn. with honors, Calif. State U., L.A., 1961; LHD (hon.), So. Vt. Coll., 1979. From organizer to dir. edn. and pub. rels. Internat. Ladies' Garment Workers' Union, Calif., 1950-61; asst. chief Calif. div. Fair Employment Practices, 1962-65; appointed commr. U.S. EEOC, Washington, 1965-66; prin. Aileen C. Hernandez Assocs., San Francisco, 1966—. Rsch. asst. dept. govt. Howard U., 1948; specialist in labor edn., lectr. U.S. Dept. State, 1960; mem. internat. conf. on minorities and the metropolis Konrad Adenauer Found./U.S. Dept. State, 1975; mem. Nat. Commn. on Study of People's Republic of China, 1978, Nat. Commn. on Am. Fgn. Policy Towards South Africa, 1981; advisor BART impact study com. Nat. Acad. Engring.; commr. Bay Vision 2020, 1990-93; vice chair San Francisco 2000; lectr. polit. sci. U. Calif., Berkeley, UCLA, San Francisco State U. Columnist Washington Tribune, 1946-47; contbr. commn. report South Africa: Time Running Out, 1981. Coord. Senator Alan Cranston's campaign for State Controller of Calif., 1961; chair Working Assets Money Fund; co-chair Nat. Urban Coalition, bd. dirs. Death Penalty Focus; vice chair nat. adv. couns. ACLU; coord. San Francisco African Am. Agenda Coun.; mem. adv. bd. Program for Rsch. on Immigration Policy; mem. nat. adv. coun. Nat. Inst. for Women of Color; bd. dirs. Ctr. for Women Policy Studies; mem. Citizens Commn. on Civil Rights; treas. Eleanor R. Spikes Meml. Fund; active San Franciscans Seeking Consensus, 1982—; founding mem., chair Coalition for Econ. Equity; chair Sec's. Adv. Com. on Rights and Responsibilities of Women; officer, bd. dirs. Mt. Zion Hosp.; bd. dirs. Westside Community Mental Health Ctr.; chair Calif. Coun. Humanities; founding mem. Nat. Women's Polit. Caucus, Black Women Organized for Action, Bay Area Black Women United, Nat. Hook-Up of Black Women; bd. dirs., project dir. Nat. Com. Against Discrimination in Housing; mem. housing com. Assn. Bay Area Govts.; chmn. Ctr. Common Good, Calif. Women's Agenda; bd. dirs. Wellesley Ctrs. for Rsch.; bd. Ctr. Govtl. Studies. Named Woman of Yr., Cmty. Rels. Conf. So. Calif. 1961, One of Ten Most Disting. Women in the San Francisco Bay Area, San Francisco Examiner, 1969, One of Ten Women Who Make a Difference, San Francisco LWV, 1985; recipient Disting. Postgrad. Achievement award Howard U., 1968, disting. svcs. to urban cmtys. award Nat. Urban Coalition, 1985, Bicentennial award Trinity Bapt. Ch., 1976, humanitarian svcs. award Glide Meml. United Meth. Ch., 1986, appreciation awards Nat. Inst. for Women of Color, 1987, Western Dist. Conf. of Nat. Assn. Negro Bus. and Profl. Women's Clubs, 1988, San Francisco Conv. and Visitors Bur., Parren J. Mitchell award San Francisco Black C. of C., 1985, Silver Spur award, Wise Woman award Ctr. for Women Policy Studies, Women of Achievement award, Vison and Excellence award, Earl Warren Civil Liberties award ACLU, 1989, others. Mem. NAACP (life), NOW (past nat. pres.), Ms. Found. for Women (bd. dirs.), Bay Area Urban League (past bd. dirs.), Urban Inst. (life trustee), Gamma Phi Delta (hon.), Alpha Kappa Alpha. Office: Aileen C Hernandez Assocs 818 47th Ave San Francisco CA 94121-3208 Personal E-mail: aileenfem@aol.com.

HERNANDEZ, ANTONIA, foundation administrator, lawyer; b. Torreon, Coahuila, Mexico, May 30, 1948; came to U.S., 1956; d. Manuel and Nicolasa (Martinez) H.; m. Michael Stern, Oct. 8, 1977; children: Benjamin, Marisa, Michael. BA, UCLA, 1971, JD, 1974. Bar: Calif. 1974, D.C. 1979. Staff atty. Los Angeles Ctr. Law and Justice, 1974-77; directing atty. Legal Aid Found., Lincoln Heights, Calif., 1977-78; staff counsel U.S. Senate Com. on the Judiciary, Washington, 1979-80; assoc. counsel Mexican Am. Legal Def. Ednl. Fund, Washington, 1981-83, employment program dir., 1983-84, exec. v.p., dep. gen. counsel Los Angeles, 1984-85, pres., gen. counsel, 1985—2004; pres., CEO Calif. Community Found., 2004—. Bd. dirs. Golden West Financial Corp., Automobile Club of So. Calif., Am. Charities. Contbr. articles to profl. jours. Active Inter-Am. Dialogue Aspen Inst., Nat. Com. Innovations in State and Local Govt., Nat. Endowment for Democracy, Pres.'s Commn. White House Fellowships; trustee Rockefeller Found. AAUW fellow, 1973-74. Mem. ABA, State Bar Calif., Washington D.C. Bar Assn., Mexican-Am. Roman Catholic. Avocations: gardening, outdoor sports. Office: Calif Community Fund 445 S Figueroa St Los Angeles CA 90071*

HERNANDEZ, GLORIA, mathematician, educator; d. Frank and Doris Parrino; m. Kenneth Earl Hernandez, Oct. 5, 1997; children: Jessica, Melissa. BS in Math., Northwestern State U., Natchitoches, La., 1996; MS in Math., La. State U. A&M, Baton Rouge, La., 1999. Student asst. Northwestern State U., 1992—96, instr., 1999; grad. asst. La. State U. A&M, Baton Rouge, 1996—97; substitute tchr. Mid. Lab. Sch. Natchitoches Parish Sch. Bd., 1999—2000; instr. La. State U., Eunice, La., 2000—. Recipient Outstanding Advisor award, La. State U. Edn.-Club, 2004; JOVE scholar, Northwestern State U., 1992—96, Leroy S. Miller scholar, Northwestern State U. Math. Dept., 1995—96. Mem.: Baton Rouge Area Tchrs. Math., La. Assn. Tchrs. Math., La. Miss. Math. Assn. Two-Yr. Colls. (sec. 2004, webmaster 2004), Nat. Academic Advising Assn., Math. Assn. Am., Nat. Coun. Tchrs. Math. Office: La State Univ Eunice PO Box 1129 Eunice LA 70535 Office Phone: 337-550-1237.

HERNANDEZ, IRIS N., clinical specialist; b. Arecibo, P.R., June 1, 1953; d. Israel Hernandez and Dolores Rodriguez; divorced; children: Zobeida Despiau, Jessica Despiau. ADN cum laude, Arceibo Regional Coll., 1972, BSN cum laude, 1982; MSN, U. P.R., 1985. RN, P.R., Md. Dir. nursing Manati (P.R.) Dr. Ctr. Hosp., 1985-87; emergency rm. nurse Md. Health Care Sys., Balt., 1987-88, clin. specialist in medicine, 1988-89, case mgr. medicine, 1989-90, nurse mgr., 1990-92, clin. specialist oncology, 1992—. Instr. UIC, Guatemala/Honduras, 1998, 2000. Instr. youth group Edgewood (Md.) Army Post, 1996—. Maj. U.S. Army, 1989—. Mem. NAFE, ANA, Nat. Oncology Nurses Assn. (membership award 1995), Greater Balt. Oncology Nurses. Avocations: dance, running, reading, friends, cooking. Home: 410 Sugarberry Ct Edgewood MD 21040-3555 Office: Md Health Care Sys 10 N Green St Baltimore MD 21201

HERNANDEZ, JO FARB, museum director, consultant; b. Chgo., Nov. 20, 1952; BA in Polit. Sci. & French with honors, U. Wis., 1974; MA in Folklore and mythology, UCLA, 1975; postgrad., U. Calif., Davis, 1978, U. Calif., Berkeley, 1978-79, 81. Registration Mus. Cultural History UCLA, 1974-75; Rockefeller fellow Dallas Mus. Fine Arts, 1976-77; asst. to dir. Triton Mus. Art, Santa Clara, Calif., 1977-78, dir., 1978-85; adj. prof. mus. studies John F. Kennedy U., San Francisco, 1978; grad. advisor arts adminstrn. San Jose (Calif.) State U., 1979-80; dir. Monterey (Calif.) Peninsula Mus. Art, 1985-93, cons. curator, 1994—2000; prin. Curatorial and Mus. Mgmt. Svcs., Watsonville, Calif., 1993—2000; dir. Natalie and James Thompson Art Gallery, San Jose State U., Calif., 2000—. Cons.SPACES (Saving and Preserving Art and Cultural Environ.), 2000—; panelist Creative Works Fund, 2001, 04; adj. prof. gallery mgmt. art dept. U. Calif., Santa Cruz, 1999—2000; cons. Archives Am. Art., 1998—2000; dir. Thompson Gallery, San Jose State U., 2000—; lectr., panelist, juror, panelist in field USIA, Calif. Arts Coun., Calif. Confedn. for Arts, Am. Assn. Mus., Western Mus. Assn., Am. Folklore Soc., Calif. Folklore Soc., Internat. Coun. on Mus., others; vis. lectr. U. Wis., 1980, U. Chgo., 1981, Northwestern U., 1981, San Jose State U., 1985, UCLA, 1986, Am. Cultural Ctr., Jerusalem, 1989, Tel Aviv, 89, Binational Ctr., Lima, Peru, 1988, Daytona Beach Mus. Art, 1983, UCLA, 1986, Israel Mus., 1989, Mont. State U., 1991, Oakland Mus., 1996, High Mus. Art, Atlanta, 1997, Mus. Am. Folk Art, NY, 1998, San Francisco Mus. Modern Art, 1998, U. Calif., 1998, Grinnell Coll., Iowa, 1999, Arts Coun. Silicon Valley, 2000, U. Calif., Santa Cruz, 2000, ICOM, Barcelona, 2001, Intuit Gallery, Chgo., 2004, Chgo., 04; guest curator San Diego Mus. Art, 1995—98; guest on various TV and radio programs. Author: (mus. catalogs) The Day of the Dead: Tradition and Change in Contemporary Mexico, 1979, Three from the Northern Island: Contemporary Sculpture from Hokkaido, 1984, Crime and Punishment: Reflections of Violence in Contemporary Art, 1984, The Quiet Eye: Pottery of Shoji Hamada and Bernard Leach, 1990, Alan Shepp: The Language of Stone, 1991, Wonderful Colors: The Paintings of August Francois Gay, 1993, Jeannette Maxfield Lewis: A Centennial Celebration, 1994, Armin Hansen, 1994, Jeremy Anderson: The Critical Link/A Quiet Revolution, 1995, A.G. Rizzoli: Architect of Magnificent Visions, 1997 (one of 10 Best Books in field Amazon.com), Misch Kohn: Beyond the Tradition, 1998, Fire and Flux: An Undaunted Vision/The Art of Charles Strong, 1998, Mel Ramos: The Galatea Series, 2000, Holly Lane: Small Miracles, 2001, Irvin Tepper: When Cups Speak/Life with the Cup, 2002; co-author: Sam Richardson: Color in Space, 2002, Marc D'Estout: Domestic Objects, 2003, Peter Shire: Go Beyond the Ordinary, 2004, Forms of Tradition in Contemporary Spain, 2005; mem. internat. editl. bd. Raw Vision Mag., 2001-; contbr. articles to profl. publs. Bd. dirs. Bobbie Wynn and Co. of San Jose, 1981-85, Santa Clara Arts and Hist. Consortium, 1985, Non-Profit Gallery Assn., 1979-83, v.p., 1979-80; mem. nat. adv. bd. The Fund for Folk Culture, Santa Fe, 1995-98; mem. founding and exec. bd. Alliance for Calif. Traditional Arts, 2002—; mem. founding internat. adv. bd. Friends of Fred Smith, 2002—. Recipient Golden Eagle award, Coun. Internat. Non-theatrical Events, 1992, Leader of Decade award, Arts Leadership Monterey Peninsula, 1992, merit award, N.Y. Book Show, 1997; Rsch. grantee, Calif. State U., 2001, 2002, 2003, Dean's grantee, 2001, 2005, Lottery Fund grantee, 2000, 2004. Mem.: Nat. Coun. for Edn. in Ceramic Arts, Western Mus. Conf. (bd. dir., exec. com. 1989—91, program chair 1990), Am. Folklore Soc., Art Table, Calif. Assn. Mus. (bd. dirs. 1985—94, v.p. 1987—91, chair nominating com. 1988, chair ann. meeting 1990, chair nominating com. 1990, pres. 1991—92, chair nominating com. 1993), Am. Assn. Mus. (lectr. 1986, mus. assessment program surveyor 1990, nat. program com. 1992—93, mus. assessment program surveyor 1994), Phi Beta Kappa. Office: School Art and Design San Jose State U One Washington Square San Jose CA 95192-0089 Office Phone: 408-924-4328, 408-924-4328. E-mail: jfh@cruzio.com.

HERNANDEZ, MARIA, Internet company executive; With IBM, 1985—, sales mktg., dir. e-business on demand bus. continuity solution. Founder, pres. Madrinas network for Hispanic women leaders; spkr. in field. Named to Elite Women, Hispanic Bus., 2005.

HERNANDEZ, MINERVA CUADRANTE, physician, consultant; d. Arsenio Francisco Cuadrante and Mercedes Rontas Relunia; m. Jose Yolando Balagtas Hernandez, Dec. 17, 1966; children: Jay, Myra, Maureen. MD, U. St. Tomas, Manila, 1962. Intern St. Clare's Hosp., Schenectady, NY, 1964—65; jr. resident Springfield Hosp., Mass., 1965—66; pediatric resident Trumbull Meml. Hosp., Warren, Ohio, 1966—69; resident, gen. pathology Allentown Hosp., Pa., 1969—70; staff physician Fla. State Hosp., Chattahoochee, 1974—78, Southwestern State Hosp., Thomasville, Ga., 1980—85; physician advisor Profl. Found. for Health Care, Tampa, Fla., 1985—89; staff physician Tricare Clinic, Atlantic Beach, Fla., 1993—97; med. dir. Spectrum Health Care Partnership, Cecil Field, Fla., 1995—96; physician Fla. State U., Thagard Student Clinic, Tallahassee, 1997—2004. Mem. Springtime Tallahassee, 1983. Fellow: Am. Bd. Disability (analyst), Am. Coll. Utilization Rev. Physicians; mem.: Panhandle Med. Soc., Assn. Am. Philippine Physicians, Am. Acad. Family Physicians. Avocations: ballroom dancing, creative writing, reading. Home: 3053 Carlow Cir Tallahassee FL 32309 Office: Fla State Univ Thagard Student Health Ctr Tallahassee FL 32309

HERNANDEZ, PEGGY SUE, science educator; children: Nadine, Johnny. BSc in Edn., Ill. State U., Normal, 1989; MA in Tchg. and Leadership, St. Xavier U., Chgo., 1997. Cert. tchr. early adolescents Nat. Bd. for Profl. Tchg. Standards, 2006. Tchr. kindergarten, grade 1 Sch. dist. U-46, Streamwood, Ill., 1991—94; tchr. sci. grade 8 Sch. Dist. U-46, Bartlett, Ill., 1994—. Office: Eastview Mid Sch 321 n Oak Ave Dundee IL 60118 Office Phone: 630-213-5550. Business E-Mail: peggyhernandez@u-46.org.

HERNANDEZ, THELMA QUINTANILLA, secondary school educator; b. Tuscon, Ariz., Nov. 6, 1963; d. Esmerardo Hinojosa and Dalia Bazan Quintanilla; m. Tomas Luis Hernandez, June 27, 1987; children: Monika Nikole, Gina Marie, Miranda Leigh. BS in Biology, Tex. A&I U., Kingsville, Tex., 1987, MS in Biology, 1990. Cert. tchr. Tex. Edn. Agy., 1987. Tchr. H. M. King H.S., Kingsville, Tex., 1987—. Tchr. Tex. A&M U., Kingsville, 1999—, rschr., 1999—, mentor, 1999—. Named Outstanding Biology Tchr. of Yr., Tex. A&M U., Kingsville; recipient Tchr. of Yr. award, Tex. Scholars Kingsville Ind. Sch. Dist. and Kingsville (Tex.) C. of C. Mem.: Soc. Advancement of Chicano and Native Americans in Sci. Democrat. Roman Catholic. Avocations: marine aquria, animals. Office: H M King HS/Texas A&M University 2210 So Brahma Blvd Kingsville TX 78363 Office Phone: 361-592-6401. Business E-Mail: thernandez@kvisd.esc2.net.

HERNDON, ALICE PATTERSON LATHAM, public health nurse; b. Macon, Ga., Dec. 18, 1916; d. Frank Waters and Ruby (Dews) Patterson; m. William Joseph Latham, July 21, 1940 (dec. Apr. 1981); children: Jo Alice Latham Miller, Marynette Latham Herndon, Lauruby Latham Herndon; 1 adopted child, Courtney Marie Herndon; m. Sidney Dumas Herndon, Apr. 26, 1985. Diploma, Charity Hosp. Sch. Nursing, New Orleans, 1937; student, George Peabody Tchrs. Coll., 1938-39; BS in Pub. Health Nursing, U. N.C., 1954; MPH, Johns Hopkins U., 1966. Staff pub. health nurse assigned spl. venereal disease study USPHS, Darien, Ga., 1939—40; county pub. health nurse Bacon County, Alma, Ga., 1940—41; USPHS spl. venereal disease project Glynn County, Brunswick, 1943—47, county pub. health nurse, 1949—51, Ware County, Waycross, 1951—52; pub. health nurse surp. Wayne-Long-Brantley-Liberty Counties, Jesup, 1954—56; dist. dir. pub. health nursing Wayne-Long-Appling-Bacon-Pierce Counties, Jesup, 1956—70; dist. chief nursing S.E. Ga. Health Dist., 1970—79, organizer mobile health svcs., 1973—. Founder, exec. dir. Wayne County Home Health Agy., 1968—80; exec. dir. Ware County Home Health Agy., 1970—79, mem. exec. com., 1978—85; mem. governing bd. S.E. Ga. Health Sys. Agy., 1975—82; organized and mem. governing bd. Health Dept. Home Health Agy., 1978—, also author numerous grant proposals; governing bd. Brunswick Civic Orch., 1993—97. Contbr. to state nursing manuals. Mem. adv. coun. Ware Meml. Hosp. Sch. Practical Nursing, Waycross, Ga., 1958; mem. Altar Guild St. Paul's Episc. Ch., 1979—86, vestrywoman, 1981—82; mem. Altar Guild St. Marks Episcopal Ch., Brunswick, Ga., 1994—2001; bd. dirs. Wayne County Mental Health Assn., 1959—61, 1981—82, Wayne County Tb Assn., 1958—62, a non-alcoholic organizer Jesup group Alcoholics Anonymous, 1962—63. Recipient recognition Gen. Svc. Bd., Alcoholics Anonymous, Inc. Fellow APHA; mem. ANA, 8th Dist. (pres. 1954-58, sec. 1958-60, dir. 1960-62, 1st v.p. 1962), Ga. Nurses Assn. (exec. bd. 1954-58, program rev. continuing edn. com. 1980-86, Dist. 21 Excellence in Nursing award 1994), Ga. Pub. Health Assn. (chmn. nursing sect. 1956-57), Ga. Assn. Dist. Chiefs Nursing (pres. 1976). Home: PO Box 859 Brunswick GA 31521-0859

HERNDON, ANNE HARKNESS, sales executive; b. Knoxville, Tenn., July 21, 1951; d. Alexander Jones and Mary Belle (Lothrop) Harkness; m. David S. Egerton, Apr. 21, 1972 (div. 1979); children: David, Mary; m. Morris Herndon, Nov. 26, 1993. Student, Agnes Scott Coll., Decatur, Ga., 1969-71, U. Tenn., 1971-73. Mktg., advt. mgr. Volunteer Realty, Knoxville, 1975-77; adminstrv. asst. nat. sales Creative Displays, Knoxville, 1977-81; salesperson Sta. WJXB Radio, Knoxville, 1981-86, sales mgr., 1988—; sales and mktg. mgr. Cellular One, Knoxville, 1986-87. Cons. nat. ourdoor advt. Berkline Corp., Morristown, Tenn., 1978-81, Knoxville C. of C.; speaker nat. convs. Contbr. articles to profl. jours. Bd. dirs. Knoxville Polit. Action Com., Knoxville Arts Coun., Knoxville Beautification Bd., Boy Scouts Fin. Com.; com. mem. Dogwood Arts Festival, United Way. Recipient Pres.'s award South Ctrl. Comm. Corp., 1991, 92, 93. Mem. Ad Club. Republican. Presbyterian. Avocations: water-skiing, hiking, boating. Office: WJXB 1100 Sharps Ridge Knoxville TN 37917-7112 Home: PO Box 1783 Crossville TN 38558

HERNDON, MERRI KATHLEEN, elementary school educator; b. Homestead AFB, Fla., Oct. 29, 1972; d. Conrad George and Gloria Ann Reich; m. Matt Allen Herndon, July 11, 1992; children: Mason Allen, Miller Jack. BS, U. Okla., Norman, 1998—2008. Cert. tchr. Okla. Dept. Edn., 1999. Employment tng. specialist Dale Rogers Tng. Ctr., Okla. City, 1993—95; tchr. Moore Pub. Schs., Okla., 1999—. Dist. staff devel. com. Moore Pub. Schs., Moore, 2005—, crisis mangagement team, 2005—; co-founder, v.p. Sooners Touching the Future, Inc., Okla. City, 1999—; edn. chair Challenger Learning Ctr. Devel. Team, Okla. City, 1999—. Named Tchr. of Yr., Winding Creek, 2005, Wal-Mart, 2005, Tchr. of Today, Masonic Frat., 2005; fellow Tchr. Workshop, TRIPS Program, 2003, Okla. Space Grant Consortium, 1998. Mem.: CAP, Okla. Reading Coun., Nat. Educator's Assn., Okla. Educator's Assn. Home: 14300 Sauna Lane Oklahoma City OK 73165 Office: Moore Public Schs/ Winding Creek Elem 1401 N E 12th St Oklahoma City OK 73160 Office Phone: 405-793-3270. Office Fax: 405-793-3273. Personal E-mail: mattherndon@sbcglobal.net. Business E-mail: merriherndon@mooreschools.com.

HERNSTADT, JUDITH FILENBAUM, city planner, real estate executive, broadcast executive; b. NYC, Nov. 18, 1942; d. Alex and Ruth Selena (Silberman) Filenbaum. BA, NYU, 1964, M Urban and Regional Planning, 1966; cert. smaller co. mgmt. program, Harvard Bus. Sch., 1977. With Office Planning Coordination, State of N.Y., 1966-68; ptnr. Devel. Planning Assocs., N.Y.C., 1967-68; with engring. scis. dept. Svc. Bur. Corp., N.Y.C., 1968-69; planning cons. Llewelyn-Davies Assocs., N.Y.C., 1969-71, Arlen Realty & Devel. Corp., N.Y.C., 1971-73; ptnr. Planning & Devel. Team, N.Y.C. and Las Vegas, 1974—; v.p. Sta. KVVU-TV Nev. Ind. Broadcasting Corp., Las Vegas, 1974-75, pres., 1976-77, Hernstadt Broadcasting Corp., 1978-81. Chmn. adv. bd. Internat. Film and TV Exch., Inc., 1996—2000; mem. coun. Rockefeller U., 1998—. Condr. TV interview programs. Bd. dirs. Nat. Com. on Am. Fgn. Plicy, Decorative Arts Trust, 1980—98, Eastside Internat. Cmty. Ctr., 1988—96; bd. advisors ACORN Found.; mem. fine arts com. U.S. Dept. State, 1976—; del. Fine Arts Fedn. N.Y., 1970—90; mem. Hudson Inst., 1980—92. Mem.: Nat. Inst. Social Scis., Women's Fgn. Policy Group, Hadji Baba Soc., Harvard Club (N.Y.C.), Lotos Club, Explorers Club. Home: 927 5th Ave New York NY 10021-2650

HEROLD, CASSANDRA ANN, music educator; b. Hazen, ND, Oct. 26, 1978; d. Bruce Richard and Rosalind Ann (Tidd) Herold. MB, Augsburg Coll., 2001. Instr. orchestra Willmar Pub. Schs., Minn., 2001—04, Edina Pub. Schs., Minn., 2004—. Violist Bloomington Symphony Orch., Minn., 2001—, bd. mem.-at-large, 2001—05. Performer (solo recital): St. Mary's Cath. Ch., 2003, 2004; performer: (duet recital) Augsburg Coll., 2005. Mem.: Minn. String and Orch. Tchrs. Assn. (membership coord. 2001—), Am. String Tchrs. Assn., Nat. Assn. Music Educators, Am. Viola Soc. Avocations: skiing, rollerblading, performing, travel, volunteering.

HEROLD, ROCHELLE SNYDER, early childhood educator; b. Bklyn., Oct. 6, 1941; d. Abe and Anna (Chazen) Snyder; m. Frederick S. Herold, May 7, 1966; children: David Marc, Caryn Michele. BA, Bklyn. Coll., 1963; MS, CCNY, 1968. Cert. tchr., N.Y.; cert. child-care provider, Fla. Tchr. N.Y.C. Pub. Schs., 1963-68; tchr., adminstr. Chanute AFB Pvt. Sch., Rantoul, Ill., 1970-72; dir. early childhood edn. Temple Solel, Hollywood, Fla., 1974-99, dir. social and ednl. programs for young couples, families and singles, 1995-99. Cons. bd. dirs. Temple Solel, 1982-99; nursery sch. com. PTO, 1982-89; lectr., coord. at tchr. seminars, parenting lecture series; freelance writer parenting mags. Author, illustrator: A Family Seder Through a Child's Eyes, 1984, Celebrating Shabbat in the Home, 1992, Perfect Parenting, 1994, Choosing Chessie, 2000, Baby Bear Learns to Share, 2001, A Bear in the Brook, 2001, Seven Secrets of P-E-R-F-E-C-T Parenting, 2004. Mem. AMA Aux., Fla. Med. Assn. Aux., Soc. Children's Book Writers and Illustators, Temple Solel Sisterhood. Avocations: ventriloquism, arts and crafts, interior design, directing children's musical productions. Personal E-mail: rsherold@aol.com, perfectparenting@aol.com.

HERRERA, ANA LUISA, news anchor, journalist, writer; b. Lima, Peru, Dec. 1, 1956; came to U.S., 1986; d. Alberto and Luisa (Jefferson) H.; m. Bruce Michael Baur, Sep. 12, 1993; children: Ana Jadira, José Alfredo. Masters in Journalism, Catholic U., Lima, 1975. Radio producer and anchor CIEN-FM, Lima, 1986; cultural reporter La Prensa newspaper, Lima, 1976-80; free-lance columnist El Comercio, Lima, 1984-86; news anchor Panamericana T.V., Lima, 1980-86; reporter El Nuevo Herald, Miami, Fla., 1987, Sta. WSCV, Miami, Fla., 1987-89; corr. Latin Am. and Caribbean Telemundo Network, Miami, Fla., 1989-91; news anchor Sta. KVEA, Los Angeles, 1992; news anchor internat. NBC Canal de Noticias, Charlotte, NC, 1993—98; Spanish sr. editor ZD Net LatinAm., 2000-2001; freelance Latin Am. corr., 2001—; editor Crystal Mag., Miami, 2002; assoc. editor El Sentinel Newspaper, 2002—. Avocations: tennis, classical music, theater, writing. Personal E-mail: ana_luisa_herrera@hotmail.com.

HERRERA, BETHANY SARA, social studies educator; b. Winfield, Ill., Jan. 6, 1982; d. Adrienne Carol and Gary Curtis Johnson; m. Paul William Herrera, July 30, 2004. B in Liberal Arts and Sci., U. Iowa, Iowa City, 2004. Educator Aurora West H.S., Ill., 2004—. Facilitator History Changing Lives, Aurora, 2005—06. Home: 130 Syril Dr Geneva IL 60134 Office: West Aurora High Sch 1201 W New York St Aurora IL 60506 Office Phone: 630-301-6613. Personal E-mail: bethanyherrera@sbcglobal.net. E-mail: bherrera@sd129.org.

HERRERA, BLANCHE MARIE, elementary school educator; b. El Paso, Tex., Nov. 14, 1958; d. Hector Alfonso Casillas and Sandra Lee Harris; m. Reinaldo Herrera, Dec. 27; children: Magdalena Luisa, Natalia Danielle. AA, El Paso CC; B in edn. and elem. sci., M in Edn. and Ind. Studies, UTEP, El Paso. Tchr. Alamo Elem. El Paso Sch. Dist.; tchr., tech. dir. St. Clement's Episcopal Parish Sch., El Paso; field registrar Ctrl. Tex. Coll.-Europe, Hanau Milcom, Germany. Home: 5736 Prince Edward Ave El Paso TX 79924-3415

HERRERA, CAROLINA, fashion designer; b. Caracas, Venezuela, Jan. 8, 1939; d. Guillermo and Maria Cristina Pacanina; m. Reinaldo Herrera, 1968; children: Mercedes, Ana Luisa, Carolina Adriana, Patricia. Founder, head designer Carolina Herrera, 1981—, launched bridal collection, 1987; opened Carolina Herrera / New York boutique, NYC, 2000. Released fragrance Carolina Herrera, 1988, Carolina Herrera for Men, 1991, Aqua Flore, 1995,

212 Carolina Herrera, 2003, 212 Men, 2004. Recipient Red Cross, 1979, Best Design Hall of Fame, 1980, Latin Am. Designer "Fashion award", 1987, Pratt Inst., 1990, Mary Ann Magnin awards, 1994, Special Distinction to a Career in the World of Design, Internat. Fashion Ctr. de New York, 1995, Reward to an enterprising spirit, Women's Div., Albert Einstein Coll. of Med. of Yeshiva U., 1996, Women with Heart award, Am. Aevet Assn., 2001. Office: 501 7th Ave Fl 17 New York NY 10018-5903 Office Phone: 212-944-5757. Office Fax: 212-944-7996.*

HERRERA, CHARLOTTE MAE, medical office administrator; b. Walla Walla, Wash., Dec. 15, 1945; d. Paul Donald and Doris Jean (Wells) Leonard; m. Hector Raul Herrera, Feb. 26, 1940; children: Elisa, David. A in Nursing, Monroe C.C., Rochester, N.Y., 1965. RN, N.Y. Nurse Rochester Gen. Hosp., 1965-72, head nurse, 1972-74; office mgr. Plastic Surgery Assoc., Rochester, 1981—. Pres., co-founder PTO Holy Trinity Sch., Webster, N.Y., 1985-87; pres. Aux. Monroe County Med. Soc., Rochester, 1990-92, 97-98, Coun. Meml. Art Gallery, 1994-96, chmn. numerous projects, 1985—, mem. bd. mgrs., 1997—. Home: 1195 Gatestone Cir Webster NY 14580-9142 Office: 1445 Portland Ave Rochester NY 14621-3036

HERRERA, G. SHIZUKO, theater educator; b. L.A., May 31, 1948; d. Carl Kazuo Kurata and Mary Yoshiye kurata Ohashi; children: Mitsuko Rachel, Yoshiko Margaret, Andersen Robert. MA in Theatre, Calif. State U., LA, 1991. Instr. LA City Coll., 1981—89; prof. theatre Calif. State U., 1989—. Mem.: US Inst. Theatre Tech., Am. Coll. Theatre Festival (corr.; design coord. - cir. 2 2003—06). Office: Calif State Univ LA 5151 State University Dr Los Angeles CA 90032-8103 Office Phone: 323-343-4120. Office Fax: 323-343-5567. E-mail: sherrer@calstatela.edu.

HERRERA, PALOMA, dancer; b. Buenos Aires, Dec. 21, 1975; d. Alberto Oscar and Diana Lia (Rube) H. Attended, Olga Ferri Studio, 1982, Ballet Sch. of Minsk, 1987, English Nat. Ballet, London, 1990, Sch. Am. Ballet, N.Y.C., 1991; diploma, Inst. Superior Art at The Colon Theatre, Buenos Aires, 1991. Soloist Am. Ballet Theatre, N.Y.C., 1992-95, prin. dancer, 1995—. Dancer (ballets) Don Quixote, 1987, 88, soloist La Bayadere, The Sleeping Beauty, Don Quixote, Met. Opera, N.Y.C., 1992, Etudes, The Sleeping Beauty, Swan Lake, Symphonie Concertante, Voluntaries, 1993, prin. Symphonie Concertatne, Symphonic Variations, 1993; prin. Peasant Pas de Deux in Giselle, Colon Theatre, Buenos Aires, 1992, La Bayadere, 1993; prin. Don Quixote, soloist Etudes, Voluntaries, Theme and Variations, Kennedy Ctr., Washington, 1993; prin. The Nutcracker, Dorothy Chandler Pavilion, L.A., 1993, Palace Theatre, Stamford, Conn., 1993; repertoire Met. Opera House Symphonic Variations, Theme and Variations, The Nutcracker, Cruel World, Symphonie Concertante, Gala Performance, 1994, La Bayadera, Don Quixote, Paquite, How Near Heaven, Les Sylphides, Cruel World, Tchaikovsky Pas de Deux, Romeo and Juliet, 1995; guest artist Ballet Gala, Toronto, 1993, Colon Theatre, Buenos Aires, 1993, Gala Ballet of Aix-En-Provence, France, 1993, New Generation Ballet, Moscow, Gala Tribute to Nureyev, Toronto, Le Gala des Etoiles, Montreal, Internat. Evenings of Dance, Vail, Colo., Don Quixote, Kremlin Palace, Moscow, 1995. Recipient First prize Latino Am. Ballet Contest, Lima, Peru, 1985, Coca-Cola Contest of Arts and Scis., 1986, Finalist diploma XIV Varna (Bulgaria) Internat. Competition of Ballet, 1990; scholar Colon Theatre Found., 1989; Dance scholar Antorchas Found., 1991. Home: One Lincoln Plz 20 W 64th St Apt F New York NY 10023-7129 also: Billinghurst 2553 10 Piso Dto CP 1425 Buenos Aires Argentina Office: American Ballet Theatre 890 Broadway Fl 3 New York NY 10003-1278

HERRERIAS, CARLA TREVETTE, epidemiologist, health science association administrator; b. Chgo., Apr. 8, 1964; d. Ludvik Frank and Carlotta Trevette (Walker) Koci; m. Jesus Herrerias, Feb. 25, 1989; children: Elena Mikele, Coco Trevette. BS in Med.Tech., Ea. Mich. U., 1987; MPH in Molecular and Hosp. Epidemiology, U. Mich., 1991. Med. clk. hydramatic divsn. GM, Ypsilanti, Mich., 1983-86; rschr., support staff dept. human genetics U. Mich., Ann Arbor, 1987-91; program mgr. Am. Acad. Pediat., Elk Grove Village, Ill., 1991-99, sr. health policy analyst, 1999—2003; clin. rsch. analyst Am. Coll. Chest Physicians, Northbrook, Ill., 2003—. Project mgr., contbr.: Clinical Practice Guideline: Otitis Media with Effusion in Young Children, 1994. Mem. APHA, Ill. Pub. Health Assn., Acad. Health Svcs. Rsch. and Health Policy, U. Mich. Alumni Soc., U. Mich. Club Chgo. Avocations: reading, biking, needlecrafts, horseback riding. Office: Am Coll Chest Physicians 3300 W Dundee Rd Northbrook IL 60062 Business E-Mail: cherrerias@chestnet.org.

HERRICK, DORIS A., elementary school educator; b. Brunswick, Maine, Jan. 3, 1950; d. Raymond J. and Gabrielle E. Favreau; m. Greg S. Herrick, Aug. 10, 1973; children: Jennifer L. Buckley, Angela J. BS, U. So. Maine, Gorham, 1972. 6-8 grade tchr. Poland Cmty. Sch., Maine, 1989—99; 7-8 grade math tchr. Whittier Mid. Sch., Poland, 1999—. Team leader Whittier Mid. Sch., 1999—, cert. com., 1999—, interim governance com., 1999—2001, roundtable coord., 2001—05. Mem. Poland Scholarship Com., 2005—06. Avocations: reading, crossword puzzles, gardening. Home: 299 Jackson Rd Poland ME 04274 Office: Whittier Mid Sch 1457 Maine St Poland ME 04274 Office Phone: 207-998-5400. E-mail: dherrick@poland-hs.u29.k112.me.us.

HERRICK, KATHLEEN MAGARA, retired social worker; b. Mpls., Oct. 18, 1943; d. William Frank and Mary Genevieve (Gill) Magara; m. John M. Herrick, Feb. 5, 1966; children: Elizabeth Jane, Herrick-Chapman, Kathryn Mary. BA in Social Work and French, Coll. St. Benedict, St. Joseph, Minn., 1965; MSW, Mich. State U., 1976. Cert. diplomate Am. Psychotherapy Assn., 1998; cert. Acad. Cert. Social Workers. Social worker II Carver County Social Svcs., Chaska, Minn., 1965—70; therapist St. Lawrence Cmty. Mental Health Ctr., Lansing, Mich., 1974—75; sch. social worker Ingham Intermediate Sch. Dist., Mason, Mich., 1975—76; home/sch. coord. Eaton Intermediate Sch. Dist., Charlotte, Mich., 1976—81; sch. social worker, 1994—2005; ret., 2004. Caseworker St. Vincent Home for Children, Lansing, 1979-80; tchr. cons. for severely emotionally impaired, 1981-83; behavior disorder cons., 1983-85; sch. social work cons., 1985-87, prevention specialist profl. and program svcs. region XIII SAPE, 1987-94. Chmn. bd. dirs. Eaton County Child Abuse and Neglect Prevention Coun., 1986—; Dem. precinct del.; bd. dirs. Cath. Social Svcs., Lansing. Recipient Eaton County Svc. to children award Eaton County Child Abuse and Neglect Prevention Coun., 1997; named Region E Sch. Social Worker of Yr., 2004; Mildred B. Erickson fellow Mich. State U., 1976. Mem.: NOW, NEA, NASW, Am. Psychotherapy Assn., Am. Orthopsychiat. Assn., Mich. Assn. Emotionally Disturbed Children, Mich. Assn. Sch. Social Workers, Mich. Edn. Assn., Nat. Women's Health Network, Amnesty Internat., Glasser Inst. Reality Therapy & Choice Theory, Mich. Assn. Suicidology, Phi Alpha, Phi Kappa Phi. Democrat. Home: 2113 Long Leaf Trl Okemos MI 48864-3210

HERRICK, SYLVIA ANNE, health facility administrator; b. Minot, ND, Oct. 5, 1945; d. Sylvester P. and Ethelina (Harren) Theis; m. Michael M. Herrick, Nov. 8, 1969; children: Leo J., Mark A. BSN, U. N.D., 1967; MS in Pub. Health Nursing, U. Colo., Denver, 1970; sch. nurse credential, San Jose State U., 1991; postgrad., Golden Gate U. RN Calif., cert. pub. health nursing, health svc., prof. in healthcare quality. Pub. health nurse Dept. Pub. Health City of Mpls.; instr. nursing San Francisco State U., 1975-88; cons. exec. search Med-Power Resources, Alameda, 1988; coord. health svcs. Alameda Unified Sch. Dist., 1988-91; team mgr. home care nursing and program devel. coord. Vis. Nurse Assn. and Hospice of No. Calif., 1991-99; mgr. disease mgmt. and health awareness East Bay Med. Network, Emeryville, Calif., 1999-2000, interim dir. med. mgmt., 2000; dir. utilization and quality mgmt. Children First Health Network, Oakland, Calif., 2001—. Spkr. in field; edn. com. mem. Mem.: Calif. Assn. Healthcare Quality, Nat. Assn. Healthcare Quality, Calif. Sch. Nurses Orgn. (bd. dirs., chair edn. Bay Coast sect.), Delta Kappa Gamma. Home: 1711 Encinal Ave Alameda CA 94501-4020 Fax: 510-450-5868. Office Phone: 510-428-3473. E-mail: sherrick@mail.cho.org.

HERRIDGE, CATHERINE, political correspondent; Bachelor's Degree, Harvard Coll.; Master's Degree in Journalism, Columbia U. Corr. ABC News, London; nat. corr. FOX News Channel, 1996—, Homeland Defense corr., 2001—. Corr. Fox Files, 1998; gen. field reporter The Pulse. Recipient Bronze World Medal, NY Festivals. Office: FOX News Channel 400 N Capitol St NW Ste 550 Washington DC 20001

HERRIDGE, ELIZABETH, museum director; Mng. dir. Guggenheim Hermitage Mus., Las Vegas, 2003—. Office: Guggenheim Hermitage Mus 3355 Las Vegas Blvd S Las Vegas NV 89109 Office Phone: 702-414-2002. E-mail: eherridge@guggenheim.org.

HERRIMAN, DARLEEN ANN, music educator; b. L.A., Aug. 19, 1951; d. Manuel Bibbins and Mathilda B. (Miljak) Diaz; m. Raymond James Herriman, Jan. 12, 1973; children: James, Rachel, Joseph, Michael, Matthew. AA, Palomar Coll., 1998; music cert., Biola U., 1999. Music specialist San Diego Schs., 1995—2000; choral dir. San Diego Childrens Choir, 2001—03; choral dir., music specialist Francisc Parker Sch., San Diego, 2003—. Youth choral dir. St. Michael Cath. Ch., Poway, Calif., 1993—; founder, dir. North County Interfaith Childrens Choir, Escondido, Calif., 2003—. Mem.: Am. Choral Dirs. Assn. Republican. Roman Catholic. Avocations: harp, piano, writing, attending concerts and musical theater. Office: Francis Parker Sch 4201 Randolph St San Diego CA 92103

HERRIMAN, JEAN ANN, elementary school educator; b. Charleston, W.Va., Aug. 14, 1953; d. John Charles and Dorothy Gwinn (Dearman) McIntosh; 1 child, John Phillip Raiford. BEd, Ga. So. Coll., 1981; early childhood endorsement, Tenn. Tech. U., 1984; M in Early Childhood, Piedmont Coll., 1997. Tchr. elem. Chickamauga (Ga.) City Sch. Sys., 1984-85, Whitfield County Sch. Sys., Dalton, Ga., 1985-86; tchr. Jackson County Schs., Jefferson, Ga., 1986—2005, Jackson (Ga.) County Schs., 1986—2005. Named Tchr. of Yr., 2000. Mem. Christian Motorcyclist Assn. Republican. Avocations: kayaking, horseback riding, guitar, piano, motorcycling. Office: Maysville Elem Sch 9270 Highway 82 Spur Maysville GA 30558-2101

HERRIN, KAREN PATRICIA, secondary school educator, singer, musician; b. Accrington, Lancashire, Eng., July 10, 1964; arrived in U.S., 1989; d. John Winston and Patricia Duxbury; m. William David Herrin, May 2, 1989; children: John Gregory Alexander, Nicholas James. BA, Trinity Coll. of Music, London, Eng., 1987; MM, Ga. State Univ., Atlanta, Ga., 1996; MEd, Montana State Univ., Bozeman, Montana, 2004. Lic. educator Mont., 2004. Freelance singer, piano accompanist, Atlanta, 1990—2000, Mont., 2000—; music dir. Mountain View United Meth., Marietta, Ga., 1990—93; opera career Atlanta Opera, Atlanta, 1995—99; music dir. Kirkwood Presbyn., Marietta, Ga., 1995—99; tchr. & music dir. Peerless K-12 Sch., Peerless, Mont., 2000—01, Nashua K-12 Sch., Nashua, Mont., 2001—03, Wolf Point Jr./Sr. HS, Wolf Point, Mont., 2003—. Finalist Region, Met. Opera, 1996; fellowship, Trinity Coll. of Music. London, Eng., 1988. Mem.: Music Educator Nat. Coun., Am. Guild of Musical Artists, Nat. Assn. of Tchrs. of Singing (State Winner, Ga. 1995). Avocations: genealogy, stamp collecting/philately, knitting. Home: HC66 Box 60 Lustre MT 59225 Personal E-mail: operaducky@aol.com.

HERRING, JOAN SANDERS, secondary school educator; b. St. Louis, Dec. 19, 1941; d. Eugene William Sanders and Ruth Chestine (Bailey) Williford; m. Whitley S. Ward, June 30, 1961 (div. 1987); children: Todd Ward, Susan Ward Wright; m. Charles E. Herring, May 19, 1990. BA in Chemistry, Emory U., 1963. Rsch. chemist Armour Agrl. Chem. Co., Atlanta, 1963-65; tchr. Alameda (Calif.) Unified Sch. Dist., 1966, 67, Naples (Fla.) Christian Acad., 1987—89. Mem. hosp. svc. league, Naples Community Hosp., 1969-71; Sunday sch. tchr., First Presbyn. Ch., Naples, 1973, 74, 76, tchr. vacation Bible sch., 1975; treas. Mothers Club, Naples Christian Acad., 1981-82. Mem. Phi Beta Kappa, Sigma Pi. Republican. Avocations: tennis, competitive ballroom dancing.

HERRING, SUSAN WELLER, dental educator, anatomist; b. Pitts., Mar. 25, 1947; d. Sol W. and Miriam (Damick) Weller; m. Norman S. Wolf, May 27, 1995. BS in Zoology, U. Chgo., 1967, PhD in Anatomy, 1971. NIH postdoctoral fellow U. Ill., Chgo., 1971-72, from asst. prof. to prof. oral anatomy and anatomy, 1972-90; prof. orthodontics U. Wash., Seattle, 1990—. Vis. assoc. prof. biol. sci. U. Mich., Ann Arbor, 1981; cons. NIH study sect., Washington, D.C., 1987-89; sci. gov. Chgo. Acad. Sci., 1982-90; mem. pub. bd. Growth Pub. Inc., Bar Harbor, Maine, 1982—. Mem. editl. bd. Cells, Tissues, Organs, 1989-2004, Jour. Dental Rsch., 1995-98, 2003—, Jour. Morphology, 1997—, Integrative Biology 2000—;, Archives of Oral Biology, 2003-; contbr. articles to profl. jours. Predoctoral fellow NSF, 1967-71; rsch. grantee NIH, 1975-78, 81—, NSF, 1990-92, 94-95. Fellow AAAS; mem. Internat. Assn. Dental Rsch. (dir. craniofacial biology group 1994-95, v.p. 1995-96, pres.-elect 1996-97, pres. 1997-98, Craniofacial Biology Rsch. award 1999), Soc. Integrated Comp. Biol.(chmn. vertebrate zoology 1983-84, exec. com. 1986-88), Am. Soc. Biomechanics, Am. Assn. Anatomists (chmn. Basmajian com. 1988-90), Soc. Vertebrate Paleontology, Internat. Soc. Vertebrate morphology (convenor 4th congress 1994, pres. 1994-97), Sigma Xi. Avocation: violin. Office: U Wash Box 357446 Seattle WA 98195-7446 E-mail: herring@u.washington.edu.

HERRINGER, MARYELLEN CATTANI, lawyer; b. Bakersfield, Calif., Dec. 1, 1943; d. Arnold Theodore and Corinne Marilyn (Kovacevich) C.; m. Frank C. Herringer; children: Sarah, Julia. AB, Vassar Coll., Poughkeepsie, N.Y., 1965; JD, U. Calif. (Boalt Hall), 1968; Exec. Program, Stanford Grad. Sch. Bus., 1994. Assoc. Davis Polk & Wardwell, N.Y.C., 1968-69, Orrick, Herrington & Sutcliffe, San Francisco, 1970-74, ptnr., 1975-81; v.p., gen. counsel Transamerica Corp., San Francisco, 1981-83, sr. v.p., gen. counsel, 1983-89; ptnr. Morrison & Foerster, San Francisco, 1989-91; sr. v.p. gen. counsel APL Ltd., Oakland, Calif., 1991-95, exec. v.p., gen. counsel, 1995-97; gen. counsel allied bus. Littler & Mendelson, San Francisco, 2000. Bd. dirs. World Savs. Bank, ABM Industries Inc., PG&E Corp., Pacific Gas and Electric Co., Golden West Fin. Corp., 1996-2006, Wachovia Corp., 2006-. Author: Calif. Corp. Practice Guide, 1977, Corp. Counselors, 1982. Regent St. Mary's Coll., Moraga, Calif., 1986-, pres., 1990-92, trustee, 1990-99, chmn., 1993-95; trustee Vassar Coll., 1985-93, The Head-Royce Sch., 1993-02, adv. com. Mills Coll., 1999-, The Benilde Religious & Charitable Trust, 1999-, Alameda County Med. Ctr. Hosp. Authority, 1998-02, U. Calif. Berkeley Art Mus., 2001-; bd. dirs. The Exploratorium, 1988-93. Mem. ABA, State Bar Calif. (chmn. bus. law sect. 1980-81), Bar Assn. San Francisco (co-chair com. on women 1989-91), Calif. Women Lawyers, San Francisco C. of C. (bd. dirs. 1987-91, gen. counsel 1990-91), Am. Corp. Counsel Assn. (bd. dirs. 1982-87), Women's Forum West (bd. dirs. 1984-87). Democrat. Roman Catholic. E-mail: mherringer@aol.com.

HERRMANN, CAROL, university administrator; b. Mt. Kisco, N.Y., Dec. 23, 1944; d. Eugene C. and Anne M. McGuire; m. Robert O. Herrmann; children: John Martin II, Nell Elizabeth. AB, Bucknell U., 1966; MA, Pa. State U., 1970. Bus. editor, writer Centre Daily Times Newspaper, State College, Pa., 1980-82; with Pa. State U., University Park, 1982—, exec. asst. to pres. for adminstrn., 1986-88, v.p. for adminstrn., 1988-94, sr. v.p. for adminstrn., 1994—. Bd. dirs. Mellon Bank, 1994—; bd. dirs. Woolrich, Inc. Bd. trustees Pa. Coll. Tech., 1989—; mem. Centre Regional Planning Commn., State Coll., 1973-80, chmn., 1974-76, borough planning commn., 1973-80; media coord. Common Cause 23d Congl. Dist., 1977-80; bd. dirs. United Way, Centre County, Pa., 1989-91. Mem. AAUW, Women in Communications, Kappa Tau Alpha, Phi Delta Kappa. Office: Pa State U 205 Old Main University Park PA 16802-1503 Home: 122 Abbott Ln State College PA 16801-7963

HERRMANN, ELSA MARIE, retired art educator; b. Staten Island, N.Y., Feb. 14, 1935; d. Karl Frederick James and Theodora (Townsend) Von Kökeritz; m. Siegfried Dieter Herrmann, Sept. 7. 1962; children: Peter Karl, Kristina Luisa. Student, U. Freiberg, Germany, 1955; BS, Skidmore Coll. Cert. art and German tchr. Tchr. art and German Sch. Dist. of Chathams, NJ, 1957—62, North Plainfield Bd. Edn., 1973—2001; ret., 2001. Mem. Am. Artists Profl. League, Somerset Art Assn., Raritan Valley Arts Assn., N.J. Water Color Assn., Ocean City Artists Guild, Manasquan River Group of Artists. Avocations: ice skating, languages. Home: 132 Jib Cir Brick NJ 08723-6719

HERRNKIND, HILDA MARIE, writer, military volunteer; b. Miami, Fla., Jan. 6, 1974; d. Jeanette Marie Herrnkind. A of Bus Admin. (hon.), Mt. Wachusett C.C., 1999. Cert. computer asst. acctg., Mt. Wachusett C.C., 1999; small bus. mgmt. Mt Wachusett C.C., 2000. Sales and svc. assoc. Bankboston, Gardner, Mass., 1996—99; writer Ind., 1999—. Coord. first investment seminar for customers Bankboston, Gardener, Mass., 1998, coord. first how-to banking program for H.S. students, 98. Contbr. (photos) A Moment in Time, In Enduring Textures, 2000, At the End of a Rainbow, In Chasing Dreams, 2000, Internat. Libr. Photography. Vol. USNG, Gardner, Mass., 2001; founder, pres. Make a Difference Found. in Memory of Jeanette Marie Herrnkind, 2004—; asst. to commdg. officer USNG, Gardner, Mass., 2001—02, asst. for N.Y. relief drive, 2001, mng. unit raffle, 2001—02. Decorated Unit Coin Vol. Svcs. USNG; named to Wall of Tolerance New Civil Right Meml. Ctr., Montgomery, Ala., 2004; recipient Svc. Stars for Intergrity and Teamwork, Bankboston, 1997—98. Mem.: USNG (hon.; auxliary mem. 2001), Alpha Beta Gamma (life Nat. Bus. Honor Soc. Cert. 1994). Avocations: reading, singing, travel, sports. Home: 61 Lake St Apt B205 Gardner MA 01440-3875 Personal E-mail: creativewriter2000@yahoo.com.

HERRON, BECKIE LEE, health service executive; b. Mar. 9, 1969; BA in Psychology, U. Louisville, 1991; MA in Health Svcs. Mgmt., Webster U., St. Louis, 1996. Cert. provider credentialing specialist. Trainer Sears Telecatalog, Louisville, 1989-91; mental health worker Caritas Peace, Louisville, 1991-92; intake coord. Ten Broeck Hosp., Louisville, 1992-93; dir. intake and provider rels. ACS/Managed Care Systems, Louisville, 1993-97; mgr. quality improvement Aperture Credentialing, Inc., Louisville, 1997—2000; dir. credentials TPI Health Sys., Louisville, 2000—. Mem. Nat. Assn. Med. Staff Svcs., Ky. Assn. Med. Staff Svcs. Office: TPI Health Sys 10300 Linn Station Rd Ste 100 Louisville KY 40223 Office Phone: 502-425-7000. Business E-Mail: bherron@tpihealth.net.

HERRON, BONNIE L., management consulting company executive; BA in Edn., U. Toronto, BA in Phys. Edn.; MBA, Mercer U. Dir. athletics, Ontario, Canada; gen. mgr. Datavue Corp.; dir. planning Quadram Corp., Intelligent Systems Corp., CFO, v.p. and corp. sec.; exec. dir. Gwinnett Innovation Pk. Chair Growth Capital SIG, Entrepreneurial SIG; adv. coun. Intellectual Capital Partnership Prog., Ga.; bd. dirs. Tech. Assn. Ga.; bd. dirs. southeast chpt. Am. Electronics Assn.; mem. steering com. Gwinnett Tech. Forum; bd. dirs., former chair Nat. Bus. Incubation Assn.; bd. dirs. Atlanta Venture Forum. Named Woman of Yr. Tech. (small/medium bus.), (WIT) Women in Tech., 2005. Office: Intelligent Systsems Corp 4355 Shackleford Rd Norcross GA 30093 Office Phone: 770-381-2900. Office Fax: 770-381-2808. E-mail: bherron@intelsys.com.*

HERRON, FLORINE PERNELL, retired music educator; b. Pitts., Mar. 14, 1951; d. Samuel Melvin and Sadie Leah Herron. BA in Music Edn., Duquesne U., Pitts., 1973; MA in Music Edn. and Performance, Ill. State U., 1975. Cert. tchr. Pa., Fla., Miss., La., Kans., Ill. Prof. music, chmn. dept. Donnelly Coll., Kansas City, Kans., 1983—84; min. music, clinician AME Ch., La., 1973—, chaplain Eighth Episcopal Dist. various locations, La., 2004—. Cons./clinician AME Ch., La., 1973—2003. Author: (piano/organ book) Harmonic Praise, (songbook - sacred and polit. music) In Thee O Lord Do I Put My Trust, (guitar method book) ProgressiveGuitar Melodies. Mem. La. Women's Legis. Caucus, La., 2003. Mem.: Am. Fedn. Of Tchrs., Nat. Coun. Of Negro Women, Connectional Music Com. (assoc. dir., keyboards 2000—03), Music Educators Nat. Conf., Women's Missionary Soc., Mu Phi Epsilon. African Methodist Episcopalian. Avocations: raising birds, composing and arranging music. Office: Florimusic Studios PO Box 1420 Slidell LA 70459 Personal E-mail: florineflorimusic@juno.com.

HERRON, GAYLE ANN, health facility administrator, forensic psychotherapist, consultant; b. L.A., Sept. 21, 1953; d. Robert Owen Sr. and Rachel Rebecca (Lemley) Colvin; m. Curtis William Sr. Herron, Feb. 14, 1997; children: Freddie, Brian, Ian, Abbi. AA in Psychology, Okla. City C.C., Oklahoma City, 1986; BS in Sociology, Okla. State U., 1989, BS in Psychology, 1990, MS in Counseling, 1992; postgrad., U. Okla., 1994—95, U. Nev., Las Vegas, 1995—96, SMSU, 2001. Lic. profl. counselor N.C., Mo., Nebr., bd. cert. master psychologist, cert. bd. cert. forensic clin. counselor. Adminstr., fin. cons. Security Fin. Cons., Oklahoma City, 1980-88; case worker Big Bros./Big Sisters, Stillwater, Okla., 1988-89; counselor Payne County Family Practices, Stillwater, 1989; social worker Dept. Human Svcs. Child Welfare, Stillwater, 1990-91; asst. to v.p. bus. and fin. Okla. State U., Stillwater, 1990-91; adj. instr. Langston (Okla.) U., 1992; cons. Christian Counseling Assocs., Stillwater, 1993-95; social worker U. Nev. Las Vegas Health Ctr., 1995, Clark County, Las Vegas, Nev., 1995—96; counselor Payne County Health Dept. Child Guidance Clinics, Stillwater and Cushing, Okla., 1992—95; clin. dir., clin. psychotherapist New Beginnings Clin. Svcs., Las Vegas, 1995—; clin. dir., masters psychologist/psychotherapist New Beginnings Diagnostic and Clin. Svcs., Brunswick City, NC, 1997—2005, clin. dir., psychotherapist Branson, Mo., 1999—2001; cons., clin. dir. Crisis Intervention Svcs., Branson, Mo., 2001—02; cons. adminstr., clin. liason Tri-Lakes Primary Care, Hollister, Mo., 2001—02; dir., forensic clin. counselor Ozark Child, Adolescent and Adult Counseling, Branson, 2002—04; clin. dir., forensic psychotherapist New Beginnings Family Counseling, Hollister, Mo., 2004—05. Vol. mental health clinician Crisis Incident Response Team, S.W. Mo., 2001-03; cons. Harron Enterprises, Branson, Miss., 2006—. Columnist Brunswick County News, 1997-98. Disaster vol. ARC, Oklahoma City, 1987-95; vol. disaster inquiry team, Oklahoma City, Las Vegas, 1995; vita site coord. IRS, Oklahoma City, 1982-84; emergency room EMT Hillcrest Hosp., Oklahoma City, 1984; EMT/intermediate paramedic Amcare Ambulance Svcs., 1984. Mem. ACA, APA, NASW, Am. Assn. for Christian Counselors, Nat. Assn. Social Workers, Okla. Psychol. Assn., Okla. Assn. Counseling and Devel., Assn. for Humanist Psychology, N.C. Assn. Lic. Counselors and Therapists, Am. Coll. Forensic Counselors, Mo. Mental Health Assn., Golden Key Soc., Phi Theta Kappa, Psi Chi. Democrat. Mem. LDS Ch., Roman Catholic. Avocations: travel, hiking, flying, sports. Address: PO Box 557 Hollister MO 65673-0557 Office Phone: 417-336-3444. Personal E-mail: gayleannherron@centurytel.net.

HERRON, HARRIETTE A., retired occupational health nurse; b. Barberton, Ohio, Dec. 25, 1940; d. Edward Francis Hone and Monica Beatrice Lustig; m. Richard Hagen (div.); children: John Hagen, Robin Hagen, David Hagen, Denise Hagen. RN, Akron Gen. Hosp., 1961; BS in healthcare, U. St. Francis, 1985; degree in cons. nurse paralegal, Nat. Inst. for Paralegal Arts and Sci., 1999. Cert. occupational health nurse Calif., 1985; CPR First Aid Am. Red Cross, 1992. RN, charge nurse Akron Children's Hosp., Ohio, 1968—70; first aid attendent, RN Motion Picture Industry, Calif., 1970—76; dept. head Walt Disney Prodn., Burbank, Calif., 1976—86; med. supr. UPS, L.A., 1986—93; med. svcs. and health safety UPS Corp. Office, Atllanta, 1993—2000, mgr. region occupl. health Laguna Hills, Calif., 2000—03; ret., 2003. Pres., dir. Southern Calif. Assn. Occupational Health Nurses, Los Angeles, Calif., 1986—88. Contbr. articles various profl. jours. Presenter, clin. session Annual Am. Assn. of Occupational Health Conf., 1985, 1986, Am. Soc. of Safety Engrs Nat. Conf., 1985, Calif. State Conf. Occupational Health Nurses, 1985; review com. NY libr., McNeil Consumer Products Co. "Worksite Wellsite", 1988; presenter US Dept. of Health and Human Svcs. "Health Objectives for the Nation", 1988; co-chair Calif. State Occupational Health Nurses Conf., 1988; presenter Annual Mtg. AHA, Savannah, Ga., 1995. Recipient Outstanding Vol. of Yr., YWCA, 1974. Mem.: Am. Heart Assn. Avocations: travel, dance. Home: 135 Hillside Ln Roswell GA 30076 Personal E-mail: haherron@bellsouth.net.

HERRON, HOLLY LYNN, critical care nurse, educator; b. Kirksville, Mo., Sept. 20, 1959; d. Rolland Edward Herron and Sonia Ann (Meisner) Bray; m. Robert Meader, June 20, 1992; children: Lauren Meader, Adam Meader. Diploma, Grant Hosp. Sch.Nursing, 1980; AAS, Otterbein Coll., 1980; BSN, Ohio U., 1984; MSN, Ohio State U., 1990. Charge nurse surg. ICU, preceptor, contingent staff Grant Med. Ctr., Columbus, Ohio, 1980-83, nurse open heart ICU, 1983-84, flight nurse, clin. coord., other positions for LifeFlight, 1984—, mgr. LifeLink outreach edn. program; instr. critical care & med.-surg. nursing Otterbein Coll., Westerville, Ohio, 1990—. Contbr. articles to profl. jours.and textbooks. Mem. AACN, ANA (Excellence in Nursing award 1990), Nat. Flight Nurses Assn. (pres. Ohio chpt. 1989-93, past v.p.), Assn. Air Med. Svcs. (edn. com.), Emergency Nurses Assn., ASTM, Sigma Theta Tau. Republican. Lutheran. Avocations: reading, rock collecting. Office: Grant Med Ctr 111 S Grant Ave Columbus OH 43215-4701

HERRON, JANET IRENE, retired industrial engineer; b. Zanesville, Ohio, Oct. 14, 1949; d. Lincoln and Freda Louise (Nolan) Estep; m. Wade Harold Herron, June 10, 1967; children: Toni Renee, Dawnise Renee. AAS, Muskingum Area Tech. Coll., 1978; BS, Ohio U., 1990. Elec., mech. designer Nat. Cash Register, Cambridge, Ohio, 1978—83; restructuring engr. Cooper Ind., Zanesville, Ohio, 1983—87; sr. product engr., quality mgr. Tomkins Ind., Malta, Ohio, 1990—93; pres., owner Herron Engring., Ltd., Chandlersville, Ohio, 1993—2004; co-owner Herron Renovations, Ltd., Chandlersville, Ohio, 1999—2004; ret., 2004. Engring. instr. Mid-East Ohio Joint Vocat. Sch., 1987-88, Ctrl. Ohio Tech. Coll., 1987-88, Muskingum Area Tech. Coll., 1990-2004; mfg. outreach engr. Edison Welding Inst. Columbus, Ohio, 1996-98; instr. CAD architecture Zane State Coll. 2004-. Mem. NAFE, AAUW, Am. Soc. Quality, Am. Soc. Home Inspectors, Inst. Indsl. Engr., Soc. Mfg. Engr., Soc. Engr. in Mfg., Soc. Women Engr., Mid-East Ohio Women's Entrepreneurs. Democrat. Presbyterian. Avocations: hosting fgn. exchange students, concerts, travel, home restoration. Home: 9945 Claysville Rd Chandlersville OH 43727-9765 Business E-Mail: herronengineering@sbcglobal.net.

HERROON, JOAN GEIGER, secondary school educator; b. Troy, Ohio, June 14, 1951; d. Paul B. and Katheryn Billingsley Geiger; m. Greg P. Herroon, July 24, 1971; 1 child, Mackenzie K. BS in Edn., Wright State U., 1973, MA in Edn., 2001. Tchr. Piqua (Ohio) City Schs., 1997—. Personal E-mail: gherroon@woh.rr.com.

HERSCHEL, ANDREA B., elementary school educator; b. N.Y.C., N.Y., June 12, 1948; d. John Clinton Herschel and Mary Pauline Fox; m. David L. Dreskin, June 20, 1981; children: Jessica M., Jeanne M. BA, Georgian Ct. U., Lakewood, N.J., 1970. Cert. tchr. art K-12 N.J. Dept. Edn., tchr. reading K-12 N.J. Dept. Edn. Tchr. art and lit. Sea Girt Bd. Edn., NJ, 1970—. Mentor young profls. Sea Girt Bd. Edn., 2002—. Mem.: NEA, Monmouth County Edn. Assn., N.J. Edn. Assn. Avocations: reading, needlecrafts, travel, writing. Home: 2833 Lakewood Allenwood Rd Howell NJ 07731 Office: Sea Girt Elem Sch Bell Pl Sea Girt NJ 08750

HERSETH, STEPHANIE MARIE, congresswoman, lawyer; b. Aberdeen, SD, Dec. 3, 1970; d. Ralph Lars and Joyce Herseth. BA summa cum laude in Polit. Sci. and Govt., Georgetown U., 1993, MA in Polit. Sci., 1996; JD, Georgetown U. Law Ctr., 1996. Bar: SD. Law clerk Staff of US Dist. Ct. Judge Charles Kornmann, Pierre, 1998—99, Staff of US 4th Cir. Ct. Appeals Judge Diana Gribbon Motz, Balt., 1999—2000; atty. Skadden, Arps, Slate, Meagher & Flom LLP, Washington, 2001; exec. dir. SD Farmers Union Found., 2003—04; mem. US Congress from SD at-large, 2004—, mem. Blue Dog Coalition, mem. agr. com., mem. resources com., mem. vets. affairs com., ranking minority mem. econ. opportunity subcommittee. Prof. Georgetown U. Law Ctr., 1997, Augustana Coll., 2003, SD State U., 2003; tchr. Fund for Am. Studies; counsel on energy and telecom. issues SD Pub. Utilities Commn., Pierre; bd. dir. First Nat. Bank, Brookings, SD. Sr. editor Georgetown U. Law Rev. Mem. Rotary Internat., Brookings, SD; co-chair Rural Working Grp.; legal counsel for the elderly. Recipient Small Bus. Adv., Small Bus. Survival Com., 2004. Mem.: SD Bar Assn., Phi Beta Kappa. Democrat. Lutheran. Achievements include traveling to the Czech Republic to teach classes on the American system of government to central and eastern European and Asian college students through The Fund for American Studies. Office: US Ho Reps 331 Cannon Ho Office Bldg Washington DC 20515-4101 Office Phone: 202-225-2801.*

HERSHAFT, ELINOR, space planner, interior designer; b. N.Y.C., Aug. 12, 1940; d. Solomon and Rose (Cohen) Klausner; m. Arthur Hershaft, June 21, 1959 (div. 1983); children: Karin, Peter; m. Alan J. Hoffman, Sept. 2, 1990. Student, Skidmore Coll., 1956-58; BA, N.Y.U., 1960; postgrad., N.Y. Sch. Interior Design, 1977-78. Lic. home improvement contractor, Conn. Interior designer Elinor Hershaft Interiors, Greenwich, Conn., 1979—. Major projects house constrn. with interior design, 1985-87, additions, 1982—; projects pub. in House Beautiful, 1988, Tile News, 1988, Kitchen and Bath Concepts, 1989; numerous comml. and residential interior design projects in Fairfield, Conn. and Westchester, N.Y. Counties, Mass., So. Fla., Boulder, Colo., Wilmington, N.C.; also custom furniture design and fabrication. Creative dir. Greenwich Jewish Fedn., 1983—86; creator logo Bobbie Silverman Inst. for Jewish Culture, Greenwich, Conn., 2001; developer design format, logo and calligraphy spl. fund raising campaign Temple Sholom, Greenwich, 1994—95; pro bono office design and space planning Jewish Cmty. Svcs. Recipient Svc. award Jewish Community Svcs. of Greenwich, 1985, Greenwich Jewish Fedn., 1983, 84, 85. Mem. ASID (allied mem.), Allied Bd. Trade, AIA (allied individual), AAF (allied individual). Jewish. Avocations: calligraphy, reading, swimming, piano. Studio: 115 Old Mill Rd Greenwich CT 06831-3015

HERSHENSON, MARTHA BRADFORD, history educator; b. Chgo., June 20, 1944; d. William Stephen Bradford and Barbara Hearn Kennedy; m. Loren Victor Hershenson, Sept. 4, 1988; 1 child, Holly Ann Boes. BA in History, Lake Forest Coll., 1966; M in Edn., Nat. Lewis U., 1971. Cert. K-8 edn. Ill., 6-12 edn. Ill. 6th grade educator Deerfield (Ill.) Grammar Sch., 1966—68, Woodland Intermediate Sch., Gages Lake, Ill., 1968—70; 4th-6th grade educator North Shore Sch. Dist., Highland Park, Ill., 1970—. Suicide phone worker Reed Zone Ctr., Chgo., 1973; supr. for student tchrs. North Shore Sch. Dist. 112, Highland Park, Ill., 1978—2002; mentor Lake Forest Coll.; 6th grade team leader Edgewood Mid. Sch., Highland Park, 2003—04. Bd. dirs. Highland Park Cmty. Orgn., 1995—97; mem. alumni bd. Lake Forest Coll., 1996—2000; mem. Youth, Edn. and Arts, Highland Park, 1998; sponsor trip to Ireland with h.s. students Rotary Internat. Project- Towards a Better Understanding (TABU), Highland Park, 1997; coll. scholarship sponsor Highland Park C. of C., 1992—2005. Named Best Tchr. on North Shore, Pioneer Press Survey of 17 Counties, 1994. Mem.: DAR (life), Ill. Fedn. Tchrs. (various edn. orgns. 1974—75), Maine Hist. Soc. (life), Descendants of Mayflower Soc. (life; bd. assts. for Ill. 2002—05), John Butler Civil War Soc. for Ill. (life), Highland Pk. Rotary Internat. (life). Avocation: genealogy. Home: 600 Beverly Pl Lake Forest IL 60045 Office: Edgewood Mid Sch 929 Edgewood Rd Highland Park IL 60035

HERSHENSON, MIRIAM HANNAH RATNER, librarian; b. Springfield, Mass., July 23, 1944; d. David and Thelma (Wasserman) Ratner; children: Trent M., Scott D. AB, Syracuse U., 1966; MS, Simmons Coll., 1967; postgrad., Nova U., 1987-89. Cert. tchr./librarian, Mass. Media specialist Quincy (Mass.) Pub. Schs., 1967-71, Virginia Beach (Va.) Pub. Schs., 1982-84, Portsmouth (Va.) Pub. Schs., 1984; regional children's coord. Broward County Libr., Ft. Lauderdale, Fla., 1985-88, br. liaison, 1988-89, br. librarian, 1989-93, regional br. supr., 1993-2001; head pub. svc. Nova Southeastern U./ Broward County Libr., 2001—03; pub. svc. adminstr. Broward County Libr., 2003—. Mem. ALA, Pub. Libr. Assn., Fla. Libr. Assn. (caucus chair 1990-91), Broward County Libr. Assn. (pres. 1994-95), Hadassah (life, chpt. pres. 1983-84), Nat. Coun. Jewish Women (life), Jewish Women Internat. (life), Brandeis Univ. Women (life). Office: Broward County Libr 100 South Andrews Ave Fort Lauderdale FL 33301 Office Phone: 954-357-7335. Business E-Mail: mhershen@browardlibrary.org.

HERSHEY, BARBARA (BARBARA HERZSTEIN), actress; b. Hollywood, Calif., Feb. 5, 1948; d. William H. Herzstein; 1 child, Tom; m. Stephen Douglas, Aug. 8, 1992 (div. 1995). Student public schs., Hollywood. Appearences include (TV series) The Monroes, 1966-67, From Here to Eternity, 1979, (mini-series) A Man Called Intrepid, 1979, Return to Lonesome Dove, 1993, Abraham, 1994; other TV appearances include Gidget, 1965, The Invaders, 1967, Daniel Boone, 1967, Love Story, 1973, Bob Hope Chrysler Theatre, 1967, High Chaparral, 1967, Kung Fu, 1973, CBS Playhouse, 1967, (TV movies) Flood, 1976, In the Glitter Palace, 1977, Just a Little Inconvenience, 1977, Sunshine Christmas, 1977, Angel on My Shoulder, 1980, The Nightingale, 1985, My Wicked, Wicked Ways.The Legend of Errol Flynn, 1985, Passion Flower, 1986, Killing in a Small Town, 1990 (Emmy award 1990, Golden Globe award 1991), Paris Trout, 1991 (Emmy award nomination), Stay the Night, 1992, Abraham, 1994, (films) With Six You Get Egg Roll, 1968, Last Summer, 1969, Heaven with a Gun, 1969, The Liberation of L.B. Jones, 1970, The Baby Maker, 1970, The Pursuit of Happiness, 1971, Dealing, 1971, Boxcar Bertha, 1972, Angela (Love Comes Quietly), 1974, The Crazy World of Julius Vrooder, 1974, Diamonds, 1975, You and Me, 1975, Dirty Night's Work, 1976, The Stunt Man, 1980, Take This Job and Shove It, 1981, The Entity, 1982, The Right Stuff, 1983, Americana, 1983, The Natural, 1984, Hoosiers, 1986, Hannah and Her Sisters, 1986, Tin Men, 1987, Shy People, 1987 (Best Actress Cannes Film Festival, 1987), A World Apart, 1988 (Best Actress Cannes Film Festival, 1988), The Last Temptation of Christ, 1988, Beaches, 1988, Tune in Tomorrow, 1989, Defenseless, 1991, The Public Eye, 1992, Falling Down, 1993, Swing Kids, 1993, Splitting Heirs, 1993, A Dangerous Woman, 1993, Last of the Dogmen, 1995, Portrait of a Lady, 1996 (nominated Golden Globe Best Supporting Actress, nominated Academy award Best Supporting Actress), The Pallbearer, 1996, A Soldier's Daughter Never Cries, 1998, Frogs for Snakes, 1998, The Staircase, 1998, Breakfast of Champions, 1999, Passion, 1999, Lantana, 2001, 11:14, 2003, Riding the Bullet, 2004; (theatre, Broadway) Einstein and the Polar Bear, 1981. Recipient Golden Palm award for best actress Cannes Film Festival, 1987, 1988. Office: Creative Artists Agy care Jenny Rawlings 9830 Wilshire Blvd Beverly Hills CA 90212-1804 also: Bymel O'Neill Mgmt care Suzan Bymel N Vista Los Angeles CA 90046

HERSHEY, LYNNE R., elementary school educator; b. Kingston, Pa. d. Thomas Arthur and Hilda Olwen James; m. Sylvan C. Hershey, June 9, 1973; children: Jonathan James, Eric Lee, Megan Elizabeth. BS in Health and Phys. Edn., Lock Haven U., Pa., 1973; degree in elem. tchg., Millersville U., Pa., 1987. Substitute tchr. Ephrata Area Sch. Dist., Pa., 1973—74; customer svc. Oxford U. Press, Fairlawn, NJ, 1974—79; tchr. nursery sch. Donna Reid's Child Devel. Ctr., Franklin Lakes, NJ, 1984—86; tchr. 5th and 6th grade Ephrata Area Sch. Dist., 1986—2001; tchr. 5th grade Warbrook Mid. Sch., Paramus, NJ, 2001—. Instr. tennis, gymnastics Ephrata Recreation Ctr., 1973—74; coord. adult edn. Ephrata Sch. Dist., 1986—88; advisor Reach (Rotary Club), Paramus, NJ, 2004—. Pres. Woman's Club Highland Meth. Ch., Allendale, NJ, 1982—84; mem. ch. coun. Meth. Ch., Ephrata, 1993—95. Mem.: Trout Unltd., NEA, Paramus Edn. Assn. Methodist. Avocations: reading, fishing, sewing. Home: 94 Medro Vista Dr Hawthorne NJ 07506 Office: West Brook Mid Sch 550 Roosevelt Blvd Paramus NJ 07652 Office Phone: 201-652-7800. E-mail: kisses5@optonline.net.

HERSHEY, NONA, artist, printmaker, educator; b. NYC, Oct. 31, 1946; d. Don and Rita (Meyrson) H.; m. Richard Akre Trythall, Jan. 19, 1972; (div. 1992). BFA, Temple U., 1967; MFA, Temple U., Rome, 1969; studied lithography, Istituto Statale d'Arte, Urbino, Italy, 1979, 80; studied woodcut and printing, Yoshida Hanga Acad., Tokyo, 1990-91. Asst. prof. drawing and printmaking Daeman Coll., Buffalo, 1972-73; mem. faculty studio art St. Stephen's Sch., Rome, 1973-79; lectr. studio art John Cabot Coll., Rome, 1979; asst. prof. printmaking Temple Abroad, Tyler Sch. of Art, Rome, 1979-90; vis. assoc. prof. drawing and printmaking Study Abroad Program, Temple U., Tokyo, 1990-91; vis. assoc. prof. printmaking Wesleyan U., Middletown, Conn., 1991-92; vis. assoc. prof. drawing and painting U. Iowa, Iowa City, 1992; assoc. prof. printmaking Mass. Coll. Art, Boston, 1993—. Vis. artist-critic Calcografica Nazionale, Rome, 1986, Istituto la Grafica, Latina, Italy, 1987, RI Sch. Design, Rome, 1987, 89, 90, 93, U. Conn., Storrs, 1992, 98, RI Sch. Design, Providence, 1998, 01, SUNY, Albany, 1993, Syracuse (NY) U., 1993, NY Grad. Sch. Figurative Art, NYC, 1993, Union Coll., Schenectady, NYC, 1994, U. Iowa, 1995, Cornell U., Ithaca, NY, 1997, Harvard U., Cambridge, Mass., 2003, Hartford Art Sch., Conn., 2005; artist-in-residence The MacDowell Colony, Peterborough, NH, 1989, 93, Ucross Found., Clearmont, Wyo., 1992, The Ballinglen Arts Found., County Mayo, Ireland, 2001, Asillah Forum Found., Morocco, 2002. One-woman shows include Jane Haslem Gallery, Washington, 1976, Laboratorio Artvisive, Foggia, Italy, 1979, 86, Villa Schifanoia Gallery, Florence, Italy, 1980, Il Patio Gallery, Ravenna, Italy, 1982, Galleria Il Ponte, Rome, 1985, 90, Mary Ryan Gallery, N.Y.C., 1983, 87, Dolan/Maxwell Gallery, Phila., 1987, Palazzo Sormani, Milan, 1993, RI Sch. Design, 1994, Miller/Block Gallery, Boston, 1995, 99, 02, 04, Robert Lehman Art Ctr., AIA, 2001, Soprafina Gallery, Mass., 2002, St. Botolph Club, Boston, 2003; group exhbns. include Smithsonian Inst., Washington, 1973, Honolulu Acad. Arts, 1973, USIS, Rome, 1973, Jane Haslem Gallery, 1974, 75, Mus. Fine Arts, Boston, 1975, Garden Gallery Modern Art, Raleigh, N.C., 1975, Met. Mus., Fla., 1977, USIS, Bucharest, Hungary, 1978, Am. Acad., Rome, 1978, Laboratorio Artivisive, 1981, 92, Rassegna di Grafica Contemporanea, Casalpusterlungo, Italy, 1982, Clark Gallery, Lincoln, Mass., 1983, Mary Ryan Gallery, 1983, 84, 85, 86, 88, 91, 92, Noyes Mus., N.J., 1984, Galleria Il Ponte, 1984, Dolan/Maxwell Gallery, 1985, Calcografia Nazionale, Rome, 1986, Palazzo Ducale, Pesaro, Italy, 1986, Bklyn. Mus., 1986, Walker Art Ctr., Mpls., 1986, Garton & Cooke Gallery, London, 1987, Istituto per la Grafica, Latina, Italy, 1987, Premio Sassoferrato, Italy, 1987, Premio Internazionale Biella per l'Incisione, Italy, 1987, Pa. Acad. Fine Arts, Phila., 1987, Premio Internazionale d'Arte Contemporanea, Campobello di Mazara, Italy, 1988, Greenville Mus. Fine Arts, N.C., Taipei Fine Art Mus., 1988, Dedalos Gallery, San Severo, Italy, 1990, Gallery Kabutoya, Tokyo, 1991, Art Multiple, Dusseldorf, Germany, 1992, G.W. Einstein Gallery, N.Y.C., 1993, Meml. Hall Ctr. for Arts, Vt., 1999, Atrium Mus., St. Louis, 1999, Rose Art Mus., Mass., 2000, ARTcetera, BCA, Boston, 2000, Hess Gallery, Mass., 2000, Corcoran Gallery of Art, Washington, DC, 2001, Nat. Acad. Design, NYC, 2001, John Elder Gallery, N.Y.C., Plum Gallery, Mass, 2002, Parchman Stremmel Gallery, San Antonio, 2002, Kochi Triennial Exhbn., Japan, 2002, Andersen Fine Art, Mass., 2003, Newton Art Ctr., Boston, 2003, Mass. Coll. Art, Boston, 2003, Emmerson Coll., Boston, 2004, Zimerli Art Mus., New Brunswick, NJ, 2005, Simmons Coll. Boston, 2006, Birckbottom Gallery, Somerset, Mass., 2006, The Schoolhouse Gallery, 2006, Danforth Mus. Art, 2006, Tufts U. Art Gallery, Mass., 2006; public collections include Met. Mus. Art, N.Y.C., Minn. Mus. Art, St. Paul, Pa. Acad. Fine Arts, Mint Mus., N.C., Nat. Print Cabinet, Rome, Civic Mus., Piacenza, Italy, Mcpl. Mus. Graphic Art, Caracas, Venezuela, Crakow Nat. Mus., Poland, Skopje Mus. Contemporary Art, Yugoslavia, Yale U. Art Gallery, S-E Banken, Stockholm, Mus. Fine Arts, Boston, Boston Pub. Library, Corcoran Mus. Art, Washington DC, Davison Art Ctr., NC, Wesleyan, U. Middletown, Conn., Fogg Art Mus., Mass., Free Library of Phila., Georgetown U., Washington DC, Haper Coll., Ill., Harvard U. Law Sch., Hunterdon Art Ctr., NJ, Library of Congress, Washington DC., Duke Mus. Art, NC, Georgetown U., Wash., Meml. Art Gallery, Rochester, NY, Decordoua Mus., Lincoln, Mass., Hartford Art Sch., Conn. Mass. Cultural Coun. grantee, 2004. Democrat. Office: Mass Coll Art 621 Huntington Ave Boston MA 02115-5801

HERSHKOFF, HELEN, law educator; b. 1953; AB, Radcliffe-Harvard Coll., 1973; BA, Oxford U., 1975, MA, 1979; JD, Harvard Law Sch., 1978. Bar: NY 1979. Assoc. Paul, Weiss, Rifkind, Wharton & Garrison, NYC, 1978—83; staff atty. The Legal Aid Soc. of NY, NYC, 1983—87; assoc. legal dir. ACLU, NYC, 1987—95; asst. prof. law NYU Sch. Law, 1995—98, assoc. prof., 1998—2000, prof., 2000—, co-dir. Arthur Garfield Hays civil liberties program. Cons. World Bank. Bd. dirs. Urban Justice Ctr., NYC. Office: NYU Sch Law Vanderbilt Hall Rm 334 40 Washington Sq S New York NY 10012-1099 Office Phone: 212-998-6285. E-mail: helen.hershkoff@nyu.edu.

HERSMAN, DEBORAH A. P., federal agency administrator; BA, Virginia Tech. U., 1992; MS, George Mason U., 1999. Staff dir., sr. legis. aide to senator of W. Va. US Senate, Washington, 1992—99, sr. profl. staff mem., Com. on Commerce, Sci. & Transp., 1999—2004; mem. Nat. Transp. Safety Bd. (NTSB), Washington, 2004—. Office: National Transportation Safety Board Rm 4401 490 L'Enfant Plaza East SW Washington DC 20594 Office Phone: 202-314-6662.*

HERSON, ARLENE, television producer, journalist, television personality, radio commentator; b. N.Y.C. d. Sam and Mollie (Friedman) Hornreich; m. Milton Herson, June 16, 1963; children: Michael, Karen. Student, Queens Coll., 1957, New Sch. for Social Rsch., N.Y.C., 1960. Exec. sec. Tex McCrary, Inc., N.Y.C., 1958—60; asst. to William L. Safire, Safire Pub. Rels., N.Y.C., 1960—62; columnist The Advisor, Inc., Middletown, NJ, 1974—78; prodr., host The Arlene Herson Show, N.Y.C., 1978—. Syndicated on Tempo TV, 1988, Channel Am., 1989-93, Boca Raton Ednl. TV, 2006; spokesperson Storer Cable TV, Monmouth County, 1989-91, Nutri/Sys., Monmouth and Ocean Counties, 1989-90; news anchor Nostalgia Cable TV Network at Rep. Nat. Conv., 1993; cons., talent coord. Super Annuities, 1993-94; moderator debate on capital punishment, 1998; moderator panel on assisted suicide, 1999; panelist radio program Fla. Forum NPR, 2004—; panelist, interviewer The Am. Sr. Side-WXEL-Nat. Pub. Radio, 1999-2004; co-host radio sta. WJNA, Lunch Bunch; entertainment chmn. Polo Club, 2001—; master of ceremonies Calvacade of Stars, 2004—, Wings of Memory Soc., 2005; mem. grievance com. Fla. Bar, 2003—06; presdl. appointee U.S. Holocaust Meml. Coun., 2004, mem. com. on conscience, 2006; mem. Fla. Film and Entertainment Adv. Coun., 2005—, vice chmn. membership, 2006; lectr., spkr. in field. Contbg. writer The Washington/Hampton Connection Dan's Papers, 1993-98, The Hill Newspaper, 1994-98; exec. producer The Magic Flute, conductor Victor Borge, DAR Constitution Hall, Washington, 1995, 1776, 1997; exec. producer, casting dir. (musical) 1776, DAR Constitution Hall, Washington, 1996, encore prodn., 1998; prodr. 1776 (featuring current mems. of Congress), 1998; interviewer Steven Spielberg's Shoah Found., 1997-99; host WXEL-TV Pledge Drive, 2000. 92d St. Y benefit com. Variety-The Children's Charity; active Women's Project and Prodns., 1992; com. mem. Children's Psychiat. Ctr., 1971-90, Monmouth Park Charity Fund, 1980-90; corp. exec. bd. Family and Childrens Svcs., 1985—90; life mem. N.Y. chpt. Brandeis U. Libr. Fund; dir.'s resource coun. Nat. Women's Econ. Alliance; social com. Westbridge Condominium; fin. chmn. Mike Herson for Congress, 1994, fin. com. March of Dimes, 1995; profl. women's coun. Nat. Mus. of Women in the Arts, 1994; com. mem. Vicent T. Lombardi Cancer Rsch. Ctr., 1994-98, Parkinson's Action Network, 1996; publicity chmn.exhbn. for Israel Tennis Ctrs. Excalibur Soc. of Lyn U., 1996—; adv. coun. to co-chmn. Rep. Nat. Com., 1997—2000; active Power of Women Effecting Renewal, 1997; 2d decade coun. Am. Film Inst., 1998; bd. dirs. A Healing Among Nations, 1999; active Soc. of 100, Fla. Philharm. Orch., 1999; benefit com. Caldwell Theatre, 1999; bd. dirs. Miami City Ballet; founder Israel Children's Ctrs., 2000; bd. dirs. Fla. Film and Entertainment Adv. Coun., 2001—; mem. com. Shaare Zedek Med. Ctr., 2001; honors bd. dirs. Miami City Ballet, 2000—05; com. mem. Ctr. for the Arts, 2001—03, Palm Beach Cultural Coun., 2001—03; corp. exec. com. Ctrl. Park Conservancy, Women of Washington; corp. exec. com. mentor program Women's Econ. Devel. Coun.; bd. dirs. Miami City Ballet Sch., 2001—03; exec. com. Cmty. Rels. Coun., 2001—03; leadership coun., exec. com. Rep. Jewish Coalition, 2002—; mem. Garnet Soc. PBS, NPR, 2004—05; life mem. Boca Raton cancer unit Papanicolau Corps for Cancer Rsch., 2002—; mem. Boca Raton Mus. Art, 2002—, coun. trustees, 2001—03; apptd. by Gov. Jeb Bush Fla. Film Entertainment Coun., 2004—; founder Lippy Leadership Soc., 2005; mem. com. on conscience U.S. Holocaust Mus., 2006; vice chmn. membership Fla. Film and Entertainment Adv. Coun., 2006; adv. coun., presdl. appointment Take Pride in Am., 1993; bd. dirs. women's activities campaign Sen. Jacob J. Javits, N.Y.C., 1968, Monmouth Mus., 1982—86, Will Rogers Inst., 1992—, Washington Symphony Orch., 1994—98, v.p., 1994; bd. dirs. Boca Raton Ednl. TV, 2001—, Palm Beach Internat. Film Festival, 2005—, Together Against Gangs, 2006. Recipient CAPE award for best talk show on Cable TV Network, 1984-93, Best Single Program with Suzanne Sommers, 1988, Woman of Achievement in Comm. award Adv. Commn. on Status of Women, 1986, Pub. and Leased Access (PAL) award for best talk show Paragon Cable TV, N.Y.C., 1988, spl. resolution N.J. Assembly, 1988, Willie award for outstanding svc. Will Rogers Inst., 1992; named Disting. Alumni mem. Waldorf Astoria, 1998; nominated Cable Ace award Best Talk Show nationwide The Arlene Herson Show, 1987, 89. Mem. NAFE, NATAS, Nat. Acad. Cable Programming, Nat. Assn. Profl. Women, Women in Comm., Women in Cable, Women in Film and Video, Am. Women in Radio and TV, Power Women Effecting Renewal, Internat. Radio and TV Soc., Internat. Newswoman's Assn., Rep. Gov's. Assn., Nat. Press Club, Friends for Life, Friars Club (house com. 1993, admissions com. 1994—), Bethesda Country Club, Lotos Club, East River Tennis Club, Excalibur Soc. of Lynn U., Seagate Beach Club, Boca Raton Rep. Club, Polo Club (cmty. rels. com. 1998-99, social com. 2000, entertainment chmn. 2001-2005), Palm Beach Rep. Club, Profl. Bus. Forum, Boca Raton Roundtable, Hadassah (life). Avocations: tennis, swimming, reading. Fax: 561-998-4776. E-mail: aherson123@aol.com.

HERTEL, HEATHER, artist; BFA magna cum laude, Syracuse U., N.Y., 1995, MS in Art Edn., 1998; MFA, Edinboro U. Pa., 2003; student, Santa Reparata Internat. Sch. Fine Art, Firenze, Italy, 2002. Student art tchr. Manlius Pebble Hill Sch., Dewitt, NY, 1997, Syracuse U., 1997, Durgee Jr. HS, Baldwinsville, NY, 1998, Fowler HS, Syracuse, 1998; art tchr. k-4 Charter Sch. of Excellence, Fort Lauderdale, Fla., 1999—2000; adult painting instr. Boat Yard Studio, Cocoa Beach, 2000; drawing & design instr. Edinboro U. Pa., 2004—06; lectr. Mercyhurst Coll., 2006. Lectr. in field. Exhibitions include Congressman Ridge Congl. Art Show, Edinboro U. Pa., 1991, Panorama Summer Arts Festival, Erie, Pa., 1993, Summer Art Show, Syracuse U., 1992, 1994, A Woman's Rowing Tale, Cummings Gallery, Mercyhurst Coll., Erie, Pa., 1995, Golden Key Art Show, Washington, D.C., 1996, Lowe Art Gallery Spring Show, U. Miami, 1996, Recent Works, Syracuse U., 1997, Grad. Art Exhibit, 1997, Sky-Clad: The Modern Nude, Urraro Gallery, Erie, Pa., 2000, Villa Maria Acad. 12th Ann. Art Exhibit, 2001, Mercyhurst Preparatory Alumni Show, Mercyhurst Coll., Pa., 2001, 2004, Contemporary Female Self Portraits, Edinboro U. Pa., 2001, Oct. Evenings Exhibit, Meadville Coun. Arts, Pa., 2002, Niagara Invitational Art Exhibit, Erie Maritime Mus., 2002, Celebration of the Arts, Montpelier Ctr., Va., 2003, Art of the State of Pa., State Mus., Greater Harrisburg Arts Coun., 2003, Self Portrait Show, Edinboro U. Pa., 2003, Edinboro U. Faculty Exhbn., 2004, Double Take, John Michael Kohler Arts Ctr., Sheboygan, Wis., 2004, Women Shine Through, Weave/Lylie Fisher of Art Harvest, Sacramento, Calif., 2005, Nat. Women's Exhbn., Impact Artists' Gallery, Buffalo, N.Y., 2005, Edinboro U. Faculty Exhbn., Bruce Gallery, Edinboro, Pa., 2005, one-woman shows include Heather Hertel: Glass Painting, Urraro Gallery, Erie, Pa., 2001, Trans Lumens, Meadville Coun. Arts, Pa., 2005, mural paintings, Hudson Bldg., Keystone Reality Bldg., Art Deco Dist., Miami Beach., Fla., 1996, Tu Tu Tango Rest., Coconut Grove, Fla., 1997, Map of the World, Multicultural Children's Ctr., Erie, Pa., 2005, art design, Neala-Julia, Inc., 2004. Coord. student art trips to N.Y.C. Syracuse U., 1994—95; field trip guide, group show fundraiser, drawing & painting club Edinboro U. Pa., 2005; participant numerous art auctions. Recipient athletic scholarships, 1991—95, Most Inspirational Artist award, Fish Commn., Erie, Pa. Cmty Project, 2001. Mem.: Northwestern Pa. Artist's Assn., Erie Art Mus., Nat. Mus. Women in Arts, Coll. Art Assn. Avocations: sailing, windsurfing.

HERTEL, JAIME S., lawyer; b. Smithtown, NY, 1977; BA cum laude, Brandeis U., 1999; JD, Northeastern U., 2002; LLM in Taxation, Boston U., 2003. Bar: Mass. 2002, NY 2003. Real estate assoc. Sherin and Lodgen LLP; assoc. Nixon Peabody LLP, Boston. Mem.: NY Bar Assn., ABA, Nat. Assn. Indsl. and Office Properties, Mass. Women's Bar Assn., Boston Bar Assn. Office: Nixon Peabody LLP 100 Summer St Boston MA 02110 Office Phone: 617-345-1238. Office Fax: 866-275-4096. E-mail: jhertel@nixonpeabody.com.*

HERTEL, SUZANNE MARIE, musician; b. Hastings, Neb., Aug. 8, 1937; d. Louis C. Hertel and W. Lenore (Cross) Budd. BA, Doane Coll., Crete, Nebr., 1959; MSM, Union Theol. Sem., 1961; postgrad., U. Hartford, 1966, U. Conn., 1975; MA, Merrill Palmer Inst., 1977; EdD, Boston U., 1982. Tchr. music Pub. Sch., Wethersfield, Conn., 1962—63; libr. serials Hartford Sem. Found., 1963—64; tchr. elem. Pub. Sch., Glastonbury, Conn., 1965—79; asst. prof. U. No. Iowa, Cedar Falls, 1979—81; tng. mgr. Focus Rsch. Sys. Inc., W. Hartford, Conn., 1982—89; pers. adminstr. City of Hartford, 1989—99; cons., 1999—2002. Mem. leadership educators program John F. Kennedy Sch. Govt., Harvard U., 1999; mem. Human Resource Mgmt. Del., Russia and Estonia, 1992, Initiative Edn., Sci. and Tech., South Africa, 1995. Recipient Maria Miller Stewart award, 1992. Mem.: Am. Guild Organists. Democrat. Personal E-mail: smher82@aol.com.

HERTING, CLAIREEN LAVERN, financial planner; b. Chgo., Sept. 7, 1929; d. Ernst and Louise Caroline (Wagner) Molzan; m. Robert L. Herting, June 5, 1954; 1 son, Robert L. Jr. BS, U. Ill.-Champaign, 1951; MBA, Northwestern U., Chgo., 1953; JD, John Marshall Law Sch., 1960. Bar: Ill. 1960; CPA Ill. With PricewaterhouseCoopers, L.L.P., Chgo., 1951—, audit sr., 1951-58, audit supr., 1959-64, tax supr., 1964-75, dir. personal fin. planning, 1974—85, tax mgr., 1985—. Adj. prof. Masters of Taxation program, John Marshall Law Sch., 1987-2001. Contbr. articles to profl. jours. Bd. dirs., sec., v.p., treas. Easter Seal Soc. Met. Chgo., 1974—; bd. dirs. Chgo. Soc. Contemporary Composers, 1979-84; sec., treas., v.p., mem. exec. com., bd. trustees John Marshall Law Sch., Chgo., 1984—; vice chmn. Ill. Dept. Registration and Edn., Springfield, 1984-94; mem. planned giving com. Art Inst. Chgo., 1990—; bd. dirs., treas. Free Arts for Abused Children, 1998—; bd. dirs. Ill. CPA Endowment Found., 1999-2003; chmn., mem. Ill. Bd. Examiners for CPA Exam., 2000— Recipient Disting. Svc. award John Marshall Alumni Assn., Chgo., 1983. Mem. ABA, AICPAs, Am. Soc. Women CPA, Ill. State Bar Assn., Ill. CPA Soc. (bd. dirs. 1974-75, 87-89, treas. 1987-89, hon. mem. 1993, Pub. Svc. award 1998), Chgo. Estate Planning Coun. (past pres., bd. dirs. 1976-84, Austin Flemin Disting. Svc. award 1990), Chgo. Bar Assn. (chmn. estate and gift taxation 1990-91, fin. trust law, fed. taxation com.), Am. Women Composers Midwest, Inc. (bd. dirs., treas. 1992-94), Nat. Assn. State Bds. Accountancy (regulatory structures and issues com. 2003—). Home: 618 W Edgemont Ln Park Ridge IL 60068 Office: PriceWaterhouseCoopers LLP 1 N Wacker Dr Chicago IL 60606 E-mail: claireen.l.herting@us.pwc.com.

HERTWECK, ALMA LOUISE, sociology and child development educator; b. Moline, Ill., Feb. 6, 1937; d. Jacob Ray and Sylvia Ethel (Whitt) Street; m. E. Romayne Hertweck, Dec. 16, 1955; 1 child, William Scott. AA, Mira Costa Coll., 1969; BA in Sociology summa cum laude, U. Calif., San Diego, 1975, MA, 1977, PhD, 1982. Cert. sociology instr., multiple subjects tchg. credential grades k-12, Calif. Staff rsch. assoc. U. Calif., San Diego, 1978—81; instr. sociology Chapman Coll., Orange, Calif., 1982—87; instr. child devel. Mira Costa Coll., Oceanside, Calif., 1983—87, 1988—89; instr. sociology U.S. Internat. U., San Diego, 1985—88; exec. dir., v.p. El Camino Preschools, Inc., Oceanside, 1985—2005. Author: Constructing the Truth and Consequences: Educators' Attributions of Perceived Failure in School, 1982; co-author: Handicapping the Handicapped, 1985. Mem. Am. Sociol. Assn., Am. Ednl. Rsch. Assn., Nat. Coun. Family Rels., Nat. ASsn. Edn. Young Children, Alpha Gamma Sigma. Avocations: foreign travel, sailing, bicycling. Home: 2024 Oceanview Rd Oceanside CA 92056-3104 Personal E-mail: ahertweck@cox.net.

HERTZ, JENNIFER L., lawyer; b. Missoula, Mont., Sept. 22, 1970; BA, Calif. Polytechnic State U., San Luis Obispo, 1995; JD, Suffolk U., 1999. Bar: Mass. 1999, US Dist. Ct. (Dist. Mass.), US Ct. Appeals (1st Cir.). Law clk. to Hon. Joan N. Feeney US Bankruptcy Ct. (Dist. Mass.), 1999—2001; assoc. Duane Morris LLP, Boston, 2001—. Mem.: Am. Bankruptcy Inst., Intern. Women's Insolvency and Restructuring Confederation, Boston Bar Assn. (co-chair young lawyers com., bankruptcy law sect.). Office: Duane Morris LLP Ste 500 470 Atlantic Ave Boston MA 02210 Office Phone: 617-289-9214. Office Fax: 617-289-9201. E-mail: JLHertz@duanemorris.com.*

HERTZIG, MARGARET E., psychiatrist; b. NYC, Feb. 9, 1935; d. Morris and Grace Koenig Hertzig; m. Herbert George Birch, Dec. 11, 1961 (dec. Feb. 5, 1973); children: Sarah Ellen Birch, Martin Lawrence Birch. AB, Vassar Coll., 1956; MD, NYU, 1960. Diplomate psychiatry Am. Bd. Psychiatry and Neurology, 1968, child psychiatry Am. Bd. Psychiatry and Neurology, 1977. Rotating intern Jewish Hosp. Bklyn., 1960—61, pediat. resident, 1961—62; psychiatric resident Bellevue Psychiat. Hosp., 1962—64; rsch. fellow NYU Sch. Medicine, 1964—66; assoc. prof. psychiatry Cornell U. Med. Coll., N.Y.C., 1977—95; assoc. attending psychiatrist N.Y. Hosp.-Cornell Med. Ctr., N.Y.C., 1977—95; dir. child and adolescent outpatient dept. Payne Whitney Clinic-N.Y. Presbyn. Hosp., N.Y.C., 1977—; prof. psychiatry Weill Med. Coll. Cornell U., N.Y.C., 1995—, interim vice-chair child and adolescent psychiatry, 2002—; attending psychiatrist N.Y. Presbyn. Hosp., Weill Cornell Med. Ctr., N.Y.C., 1995—. Cons. Spl. Citizens Inc., N.Y.C., 1980—. Fellow, NYU Sch. Medicine, 1964—66. Fellow: Am. Acad. Child and Adolescent Psychiatry. Office: Weill Med Coll Cornell Univ 525 East 68th St New York NY 10021 Office Phone: 212-746-5712. Business E-Mail: mehertzi@med.cornell.edu.

HERVEY, NINA FERN, retired church administrator, minister; b. Dunbar, W.Va., Aug. 16, 1924; d. Henry Jacob and Nova Aileen (Wilson) Hervey. BA cum laude, Asbury Coll., 1947; BDiv, Asbury Theol. Sem., 1952. Ordained to ministry Evang. Meth. Ch. 1980. Youth leader, pianist and Bible tchr. Lambert's Chapel Meth. Ch., Bryantsville, Ky., 1944—52; youth dir. and sec. First United Meth. Ch., Shamrock, Tex., 1952—56; pastor and youth worker Bible Meth. Ch., Shamrock, 1956—2002; ret., 2002. Sec. and organist Bible Meth. Ch., Shamrock, Tex., 1956—2002. Sec.-treas. Shamrock Ministerial Alliance; bd. dirs. Shamrock Good News Club, 1956—2002. Recipient Cert. Appreciation, Shamrock Ministerial Alliance, 1995, Honor award, 2001. Republican. Home: 607 N Choctaw St Shamrock TX 79079-2027 Office Phone: 806-256-2476.

HERVIEUX-PAYETTE, CÉLINE, Canadian senator; b. L'Assomption, Quebec, Can., Apr. 22, 1941; JD, U. Montreal, 1973. Cert.: Can. Investment Dealers Assn. Parliamentary sec. Solicitor Gen. Can., Min. State for Fitness and Amateur Sports, Min. State for Youth, 1979—85; senator The Senate of Can., Ottawa, 1995—. Dir. projects Premier Bourassa's Cabinet, 1973—78; dir. pub. rels. Steinberg Inc., 1978—79; v.p. bus. ventures SNC Group, 1985—89; exec. v.p., assoc. Donancy Ltd., 1990; v.p. pub. affairs Medycis, 1991; v.p. regulatory and legal affairs Fonorola Inc., 1991—95; counsellor Fasken, Martineau, Dumoulin, Montreal, 1995—. With Commonwealth Parliamentary Assn., 2001; pres. Can. Club Montreal, 2001, Can.-Mex. Friendship Group, 1996—. Named Woman of Yr., 1984; recipient Commemorative medal, Confederation of Can., 1993. Mem.: Interparliamentary Forum of the Ams. (pres. 2001—), FWA Que., Que. Bar Assn., Can. Bar Assn. Liberal. Office: The Senate of Canada 361-E Centre Block Ottawa ON Canada K1A 0A4

HERZ, IRENE LAUREL, web site design company executive, librarian; b. Bklyn., Apr. 26, 1948; d. Emanuel Albert Herz and Florence Jeanette Hirschberg; m. Duane Edward Tiemann, Oct. 5, 1985. BA, Barnard Coll., 1968; M in Libr. and Info. Sci., Pratt Inst., 1975. Sys. analyst Blue Cross/Blue Shield Conn., North Haven, 1985—88; sr. tech. project analyst Prodigy Svcs. Co., White Plains, NY, 1989—96; mgr., internet/intranet devel. ITT Industries, Upper Saddle River, NJ, 1996—2001; freelance Web designer Ossining, NY, 2001—04; pres. Aunt Reenee's Websites, Ossining, NY, 2004—. Co-founder Conn. RAMIS Users' Group, North Haven, 1986—88; chair ITT Web Devel. Ctr. Excellence, Upper Saddle River, NJ, 1997—2000. Author: Hey! Don't Do That!, 1978. V.p. voter svcs. LWV, Briarcliff, Ossining, Croton, Cortlandt, NY, 1993—95, membership dir., 1998—99; vol. database adminstr. Ossining Food Pantry, 2004—05; dist. leader Ossining Dem. Party, 2004—05; trustee Ossining Pub. Libr., 1995—2002. Mem.: Greater Ossining C. of C. (coord. village fair 2005, dir. comms. 2006), Rotary (bd. dirs. Ossining chpt. 2005—06, v.p. Ossining chpt. 2006—). Democrat. Jewish. Avocation: gardening. Office Phone: 914-941-7284. E-mail: ireneherz@auntreeneeswebsites.com.

HERZBERG, MARGARET ANN, orthopaedic nurse, researcher; b. Bellmore, N.Y., Dec. 11, 1957; d. Ernest Frederick and Ann Dorothy (Meehan) H. BS cum laude, Adelphi U., 1980, Masters Candidate Nursing Adminstrn., 1994—. RN, N.Y. Nurse, office mgr. East Side Sports Medicine Ctr., N.Y.C., 1980-81; staff nurse Nassau County Med. Ctr., East Meadow, N.Y., 1981-83; surg. nurse, office mgr. Otolaryngology/Cosmetic Surg. Ctr., Wantagh, N.Y., 1987-88; nurse, office mgr. Phys. Therapy Office, Merrick, N.Y., 1987-88; pvt. practice orthopedic nurse researcher North Bellmore, N.Y., 1988-94; dir. program devel. PRO-FORM Sports Medicine, P.C., St. James, N.Y., 1988-94; pvt. practice med./legal cons. North Bellmore, N.Y., 1993—; owner Creative Concepts Cons. Svcs., North Bellmore, 1993—. Coord. Nursing Resource Ctr. Skills Lab. and Computer Ctr., Adelphi U. Sch. Nursing, Garden City, N.Y. Mem. vol. med. staff Victory Games, U.S. Orgn. of Disabled Athletes, Uniondale, N.Y., 1990—. Mem. Nat. Assn. Orthopaedic Nurses (v.p. L.I. Orthopaedic Nurses 1994—), Nat. Athletic Trainers Assn. (assoc.), Nat. Assn. Strength and Fitness Profls. (nat. sec. 1990-91), Sigma Theta Tau (chpt. exec. bd., newsletter editor 1982-87, 88-89). Republican. Roman Catholic. Avocations: writing, water sports, art, physical fitness. Office: Adelphi U Sch Nursing Alumnae Hall Garden City NY 11530

HERZECA, LOIS FRIEDMAN, lawyer; b. July 7, 1954; d. Martin and Elaine Shirley (Rapoport) Friedman; m. Christian S. Herzeca, Aug. 15, 1980; children: Jane Leslie, Nicholas Cameron. BA with honors, SUNY-Binghamton, 1976; JD cum laude, Boston U., 1979. Bar: NY 1980, US Dist. Ct. (so. dist.) NY 1980, US Dist. Ct. (ea. dist.) NY 1980. Atty. antitrust div. U.S. Dept. Justice, Washington, 1979-80; assoc. Fried, Frank, Harris, Shriver & Jacobson LLP, NY, 1980-86, ptnr. NY, 1986—. Editor Am. Jour. Law & Medicine, 1978—79. Dir. Volunteers of Legal Svc., Children for Children Found. Mem.: Legal Aid Soc. (Cmty. Devel. Adv. Com.), Assn. Bar City NY, ABA. Office: Fried Frank Harris Shriver & Jacobson LLP 1 New York Plz Fl 22 New York NY 10004-1980 Office Phone: 212-859-8076. Office Fax: 212-859-4000. Business E-Mail: lois.herzeca@friedfrank.com.

HERZENBERG, CAROLINE STUART LITTLEJOHN, physicist; b. East Orange, N.J., Mar. 25, 1932; d. Charles Frederick and Caroline Dorothea (Schulze) Littlejohn; m. Leonardo Herzenberg, July 29, 1961; children: Karen Ann, Catherine Stuart. SB, MIT, 1953; SM, U. Chgo., 1955, PhD, 1958; DSc (hon.), SUNY, Plattsburgh, 1991. Asst. prof. Ill. Inst. Tech., Chgo., 1961-66, research physicist ITT Research Inst., 1967-70, sr. physicist, 1970-71; lectr. Calif. State U., Fresno, 1975-76; physicist Argonne (Ill.) Nat. Lab., Ill., 1977-2001. Prin. investigator NASA Apollo Returned Lunar Sample Analysis Program, 1967—71; disting. vis. prof. SUNY, Plattsburgh, 1991; mem. final selection com. Bower award and prize for Achievement in Sci., 1993—94, bd. adv.; mem. nat. panel advisors PBS TV Bill Nye the Sci. Guy, 1991—95; mem. steering com. Midwest Consortium Internat. Security Studies, 1994—95. Prodr., host (TV series) Camera on Science; author: Women Scientists from Antiquity to the Present: An Index, 1986; author: (with R. H. Howes) Their Day in the Sun: Women of the Manhattan Project, 1999; contbr. articles to profl. jours. Past chmn. NOW chpt., Freeport, Ill.; candidate for alderman Freeport, 1975. Finalist Am. Phys. Soc. Congl. Scientist Fellowship, 1976—77; recipient award in sci., Chgo. Women's Hall of Fame, 1989. Fellow: AAAS, Assnq. Women in Sci. (nat. sec. 1982—84, pres. 1988—90), Am. Phys. Soc. (past chmn. com., past sec.-treas. Forum Physics and Soc., chair elect, past exec. bd. Forum History Physics, mem. panel pub. affairs); mem.: Sigma Xi. Home and Office: 1700 E 56th St Apt 2707 Chicago IL 60637-5092 E-mail: carol@herzenberg.net.

HERZIG, RITA WYNNE, critical care nurse, soprano; b. N.Y., May 12, 1928; d. William and Pearl Edna Wynne; m. William Fred Herzig, June 29, 1950 (dec. Sept. 24, 2002). RN, Beth Israel Hosp., N.Y.C., 1951. RN N.Y., 1951. Singer Met. Opera, N.Y.C.; nurse Beth Israel Hosp., N.Y.C. Exec. dir. Doctors Orch., 1989—95. Prodr.: (TV series) Manhattan Cable Network; author: Final Exam, 2004; contbr. poetry to jours., articles to profl. jours. Vol. local police; vol. Mayoral Campaign, N.Y.C., 1990. Recipient Cable TV Silver award, Manhattan Cable, 1989. Mem.: Beth Israel Hosp. Nurse's Alumni Orgn. (bd. dirs.). Avocation: poetry. Home: One Gracie Terrace New York NY 10028

HERZLINGER, REGINA, economist, educator, writer; m. George Herzlinger. BS, MIT; Doctorate, Harvard Bus. Sch. Economist, Washington; v.p. Various Cons. Firms, Cambridge; asst. sec. Gov. Commonwealth Mass.; prof. Harvard Bus. Sch., Boston, 1971—. Pub. bd. dirs. 13 cos. Author: (books) Market-Driven Health Care, 2000, Consumer-Driven Health Care, 2004, 4 other books. Avocations: art, gardening, aerobics. Office: Harvard Bus Sch Soldier's Field Boston MA 02163 Business E-Mail: rherzlinger@hbs.edu.

HERZSTEIN, BARBARA See HERSHEY, BARBARA

HESS, CAROL, music educator; b. NY; d. Roland and Thelma Masters; m. David Hess, Dec. 26, 1975; 1 child, Allyson. MusB, Grove City Coll., Pa., 1973; MA, Marywood U., Scranton, Pa., 1978. Cert. music educator, libr. media specialist Pa. Music tchr. North Pocono Sch. Dist., Moscow, Pa., 1973—. Part-time organist Moscow United Meth. Ch., 1974—. Mem.: DAR (registrar 2001—), Daus. Union Vets. (chaplain 2005—06), Lehigh County Hist. Soc., Luzerne County Hist. Soc., Wyo. County Hist. Soc.

HESS, CONSTANCE J., mathematics educator; d. Robert H. and Monica F. Garrity; 1 child, Lauren M. BS, U. Pitts., 1972, MEd, 1975. Math. instr. U. Pitts., Pitts., CC Allegheny County, Pitts.; math. tchr. Fox Chapel Area Sch. Dist., Pitts., 1972—. Cheerleading coach Fox Chapel Area HS, Pitts. Vol. food bank, Bridgeville, Pa., 2001—06; hosp. vol. St. Clair Meml. Hosp., Pitts., John J. Kane Regional Hosp., Pitts. Fellow: Pa. State Edn. Assn. (assoc.; exec. bd. 2001—06). Democrat. Roman Catholic. Avocations: hiking, swimming, reading, bicycling, travel. Office Phone: 412 963-9600.

HESS, DARLA BAKERSMITH, cardiologist, educator; b. Valparaiso, Fla., June 4, 1953; d. James Barry and Irma Marie (Baker) Bakersmith; m. Leonard Wayne Hess, July 20, 1988; 1 child, Ever Marie. BS, Birmingham So. Coll., 1975; MD, Tulane U., New Orleans, 1979. Diplomate Am. Bd. Internal Medicine, Am. Bd. Cardiovascular Disease. Commd. ensign USNR, 1979, advanced through grades to lt. comdr., 1988; resident in internal medicine Portsmouth Naval Hosp., Va., 1979-82, cardiologist, head non-invasive cardiology Va., 1986-88; fellow in cardiology San Diego Naval Hosp., 1982-84; cardiologist, head med. officer in charge ICU Camp Lejeune Naval Hosp., N.C., 1984-85; dir. noninvasive sect. cardiology, dir. fetal echocardiography U. Mo., Columbia, 1991—99; asst. prof. medicine U. Miss. Med. Ctr., Jackson, 1988-91, asst. prof. ob/gyn., 1990-91; co-dir. fetal echocardiography U. Mo., Columbia, 1991—99, co-dir. Adult Congenital Heart Disease Clinic, 1991—99, assoc. prof. medicine, assoc. prof. ob/gyn., 1998—2001; cardiologist Leheigh Valley Heart Specialists, Pa., 2001—. Author: (with others) Obstetrics and Gynecology Clinics, 1992, Clinical Problems in Obstetrics & Gynecology, 1993, General Medical Disorders During, 1991; co-editor: Fetal Echocardiography, 1999; contbr. articles to So. Med. Jour., Ob/Gyn. Clinics N.Am., Soc. Perinatal Obs., Jour. Reproductive Medicine, others. Fellow Am. Coll. Cardiology, Fellow Am. Heart Assn. (fellow stroke coun.), Fellow Am. Soc. Echocardiography; mem. Am. Assn. Nuclear Cardiology, Phi Beta Kappa, Alpha Omega Alpha. Republican. Anglican. Home: 7945 Springhouse Rd New Tripoli PA 18066 Office Phone: 610-217-5753. E-mail: darlahess@aol.com.

HESS, EVELYN VICTORINE, medical educator; b. Dublin, Nov. 8, 1926; arrived in U.S., 1960, naturalized, 1965; d. Ernest Joseph and Mary (Hawkins) H.; m. Michael Howett, Apr. 27, 1954. MB, B.Ch, BAO, U. Coll., Dublin, 1949; MD, Univ. Coll., Dublin, 1980. Intern West Middlesex Hosp., London, Eng., 1950; resident Clare Hall Hosp., London, 1951-53, Royal Free Hosp. and Med. Sch., London, 1954-57; rsch. fellow in epidemiology of Tb Royal Free Med. Sch., London, 1955; fellow U. Tex. Southwestern Med. Sch., Dallas, 1958—59, asst. prof. internal medicine, 1960-64; assoc. prof. dept. medicine U. Cin. Coll. Medicine, 1964-69, McDonald prof. medicine, 1969—, dir. div. immunology, 1964-95. Sr. investigator Arthritis and Rheumatism Found., 1963-68; attending physician Univ. Hosp., VA Hosp.; cons. Children's Hosp., Cin., 1967—, Jewish Hosp., Cin., 1968—; mem. various coms., mem. nat. adv. coun. NIH; mem. various coms. FDA, Cin. Bd. Health. Contbr. articles on immunology, rheumatic diseases to jours., chpts. to books. Active Nat. Pks. Assn., Smithsonian Instn., others. Recipient award Arthritis Found., 1973, 78, 83, Am. Lupus Soc., 1979, Am. Acad. Family Practice, 1980, State of Ohio, 1989, Spirit of Am. Women, 1989, Daniel Drake medal U. Cin., 2001, Gold medal Lupus Found., 2004, Lifetime Hess Rsch. award Lupus Found., 2005; fellow Royal Free Med. Sch., Scandinavia, 1956; Empire Rheumatism Coun. travelling fellow, 1958-59. Master ACP (gov. Ohio chpt. 1999-2003, Master Tchr. award 1995); fellow AAAS, Am. Acad. Allergy, Royal Soc. Medicine, ACR (master, Disting. Rheumatologist award 1996); mem. Heberden Soc., Am. Coll. Rheumatology, Pan-Am. League Assns. for Rheumatology (Gold medal 2003), Ctrl. Soc. Clin. Rsch., Am. Fedn. Clin. Rsch., Am. Assn. Immunologists, Am. Soc. Nephrology, Am. Med. Womens Assn. (Local Hero award 2004), Am. Soc. Clin. Pharmacology and Therapeutics, N.Y. Acad. Scis., Soc. Exptl. Biology and Medicine, Rheumatological Soc. Colombia (hon.), Rheumatological Soc. Peru (hon.), Rheumatological Soc. Italy (hon.), Clin. Immunol. Soc. Japan (hon.), Cuban Soc. Rheumatology (hon.), Alpha Omega Alpha. Home: 2916 Grandin Rd Cincinnati OH 45208-3418 Office: U Cin Med Ctr ML 563 ML 563 MSB Cincinnati OH 45267-0001 Office Phone: 513-558-4701. Business E-Mail: hessev@email.uc.edu.

HESS, FRANCES ELIZABETH, retired secondary school educator, retired director; b. Trenton, N.J. d. George Alfred and Frances Randall Hess. BS in Edn., Temple U., 1956, MS in Edn., 1964. Tchr. Bd. Edn., Trenton, 1956—60, Fallsington, Pa., 1960—93, aquatics dir., 1981—97; ret., 1997. Mem. health & safety ARC, 1981—2006, instr., trainer, Pa., 1983—; tech. v.p. U.S. Synchronized Swimming, Indpls., 1999—2005, ofcls. v.p., 2004—. Nat. synchronized swimming judge, 1980—. Named to Hall of Fame, Temple U., 1983, Pennsbury Sch. Dist. Hall of Fame, 2004; recipient Lillian Mac Kellar Disting. Svc. award, U.S. Synchronized Swimming, 2003. Avocations: swimming, jigsaw puzzles, gardening. Home: 718 S Olds Blvd Fairless Hills PA 19030 Personal E-mail: bettyhess@verizon.net.

HESS, MARCIA WANDA, retired secondary school educator; b. Cin., Mar. 15, 1934; d. Edward Frederick Lipka and Rose (Wirtle) Lipka Stanley; m. Edward Emanuel Grenier, Aug. 9, 1952 (div.); m. Thomas Benton Hess, Mar. 25, 1960; children: Kathleen Ann, Cynthia Jean, Thomas Allen. Grad. high sch., Cin. Instr. asst. Cin. Pub. Schs., 1970-95, also mem. staff desegregation workshop and unified K-12 reading communication arts program staff tng. com.; ret., 1995. Contbr. tchr.-instr. asst. handbook, instr. asst. tng. film. Mem. Winton Place Vets of World War II Women's Aux. (pres. 1982-84, bd. dirs. 1982-86, 89-91, v.p. 1997-99). Republican. Roman Catholic. Avocations: travel, reading, needlepoint, photography, collecting first edition books. Home: PO Box 34 Perry Park KY 40363

HESS, MARGARET JOHNSTON, religious writer, educator; b. Ames, Iowa, Feb. 22, 1915; d. Howard Wright and Jane Edith (Stevenson) Johnston; m. Bartlett Leonard Hess, July 31, 1937; children: Daniel, Deborah, John, Janet. BA, Coe Coll., 1937. Bible tchr. Cmty. Bible Classes, Ward Presbyn. Ch., Livonia, Mich., 1959-96, Christ Ch. Cranbrook (Episcopalian), Bloomfield Hills, Mich., 1980-93, Luth. Ch. of the Redeemer, Birmingham, Mich., 1993-99. Co-author (with B.L. Hess): How to Have a Giving Church, 1974, The Power of a Loving Church, 1977, How Does Your Marriage Grow?, 1983, Never Say Old, 1984; author: Love Knows No Barriers, 1979, Esther: Courage in Crisis, 1980, Unconventional Women, 1981, The Triumph of Love, 1987, Lessons from Life's Journey, 2003; contbr. articles to profl. jours. Home: 15191 Ford Rd Apt 302 Dearborn MI 48126-4696

HESS, PATRICIA ANN, dietician; b. Washington, June 28, 1954; d. Robert Bruce Sr. and Kathryn Irene (Thomas) Black; m. Amos Christ Hess II, May 17, 1989; children: Hannah Ashley, Kenneth Andrew; stepchildren: Stephanie, Joshua. BS, U. Ky., 1978; MEd, U. Hartford, 1981. Registered dietician; cert. diabetes educator; bd. cert. advanced diabetes mgmt. Clin. dietician St. Joseph Hosp., Lancaster, Pa., 1989-99; dietician York Wellspan Endocrinology, York, Pa., 2000—. Cons. Nat. Nutrition, Inc., Lancaster, 1997. Sunday sch. tchr. St. Paul Ch., Millersville, Pa., 1990-93, Sunday sch. supt., 1992-93; mem. spkrs. bur. Lancaster Diabetes Assn., 1992—. Mem. Am. Dietetic Assn., Am. Soc. Parenteral and Enteral Nutrition, Am. Assn. of Diabetes Educators, Am. Nurse Credentialing Coun., Pa. Assn. of Diabetes Educators, Lancaster Assn. of Diabetes Edn. Lutheran. Avocations: teddy bear making, crosstitch, quilting, rollerblading, bicycling. Home: 9 N Duke St Millersville PA 17551-1601 E-mail: ThessRD@aol.com.

HESS, SUSAN IRENE, music educator; b. Cheyenne, Wyo., May 30, 1952; d. William Frank and Roberta Louise Rhodes; m. Elmer Davis Hess, Mar. 23, 1978; children: David Matthew, Karis Anne. B.Sacred Music, Bapt. Bible Coll. of Pa., Clarks Summit, 1974; MEd in Music, Edinboro U. of Pa., 1981. Choir dir. Bethel Bapt. Ch., Erie, Pa., 1981—93; music tchr. Bethel Christian Sch., Erie, 1979—95, Hollywood Christian Sch., Hollywood, Fla., 1995—99; instrumental instr. First Assembly Christian Acad., Erie, 1999—2002; elem. instrumental instr. Harbor Creek Sch. Dist., Pa., 1999—2003; owner, head tchr. Susan Hess Music Studio, Erie, 1999—. Organist, dir. traditional worship Wesley United Meth. Ch., Erie, 2000—. Performer, arranger (CD) One Holy Passion, 2004. Leader Women's Bible Studies, Erie, 2005—. Office: Susan Hess Music Studio 4023 Main St Erie PA 16511 Office Phone: 824-897-8136. E-mail: musicteacher@aol.com.

HESS, WENDI ELIZABETH, secondary school educator; b. Sheboygan, Wis. d. Ervin George and Marjorie Margarite Gutschenritter; m. A. Dean Hess, July 21, 1973. BS in Upper Elem. Edn., U. Wis., Oshkosh, 1973, MS in Edn. Reading, 1977, postgrad. Tchr. Peace Corps, Sierra Leone, 1973—74, Howard-Suamico Sch. Dist., Green Bay, Wis., 1974—. Cheerleading coach Howard-Suamico Sch. Dist., Green Bay, 2001—04, lang. arts com. sec., 1978—88, mem. social studies com., 1984—99, mem. cmty. linkage com., 2006. Bd. dirs. Brown County chpt. Izaak Walton League Am., Green Bay, 1990—2001; mem. decoration com. Village of Ashwaubenan, Wis. Recipient Robert Sanderson award, Izaak Walton League, 2000. Mem.: Howard-Suamico Edn. Assn., United N.E. Educators, Wis. Edn. Assn., Wis. State Reading Assn., U. Wis. Oshkosh Alumni Assn., Kappa Delta Pi.

HESS, WENDY K., curator, researcher, writer; b. Cleve., Aug. 9, 1961; d. Robert Sheldon and Linda Ruth Kendall; m. Julius Lewis Hess, Aug. 30, 1987; children: Maxwell Harrison, Theodore Lawrence. B in Philosophy, Miami U. of Ohio, 1983; MA, U. Minn., 1987. Art reviewer Rochester (Minn.) Post-Bull., 1988-89; asst. curator Akron (Ohio) Art Mus., 1989-95; art reviewer Cleve. Plain Dealer, 1996; freelance curator, writer Akron Art Mus., Acme Art Co. Gallery, 1996, Greater Columbus Arts Coun., 1996. Lectr. Cleve. Artists Found., Cleve., 1999, symposium discussant, presenter, 1993, 96; grant panelist Ohio Art Coun., Columbus, 1998; juror Women's Caucus for Art, Ohio chpt., Akron, 1993; vol. grant writer Revere Sch. Dist., 2000—. Author: Ohio Perspectives: Architectural Graphic and Industrial Design, 1991, The Art of William Sommer, 1993, (with others) Akron Art Museum: Art Since 1850, An Introduction to the Collection, 2000; contbr. articles to profl. jours. Vol. Children's Hosp. Doggie Brigade, Akron, 1995-99; vol. benefit com. Akron Zool. Park, 1992-95; com. chair City of Akron Holocaust Arts and Writing Competition, 1990-93. Recipient Achievement citation Ohio Gov. George Voinovich, 1994, Mus. Excellence award No. Ohio Live Mag., 1994. Mem. Am. Assn. Mus., Am. Craft Coun., Western Res. Kennel Club (com. chair 1999—). Avocations: travel, skiing, raising and showing dogs, collecting contemporary ceramics, reading.

HESSE, CAROLYN SUE, lawyer; b. Belleville, Ill., Jan. 12, 1949; d. Ralph H. Hesse and Marilyn J. (Midgley) Hesse Dierkes; m. William H. Hallenbeck. BS, U. Ill., 1971; MS, U. Ill., Chgo., 1977; JD, DePaul U., 1983. Bar: Ill. 1983, U.S. Dist. Ct. (no. dist.) Ill. 1983. Rsch. assoc. U. Ill., Chgo., 1974—77; tech. adviser Ill. Pollution Control Bd., Chgo., 1977—80; environ. scientist U.S. EPA, Chgo., 1980—84; assoc. Pretzel & Stouffer, Chartered, Chgo., 1984—87, Coffield Ungaretti Harris & Slavin, Chgo., 1987—88; ptnr. McDermott, Will & Emery, 1988—99; pvt. practice Chgo., 1999—2001; ptnr. Barnes & Thornburg, 2001—. Spkr. in field. Contbr. articles on environ. sci. to profl. jours. Mem. ABA, Chgo. Bar Assn. Office: Barnes and Thornburg 1 N Wacker DR # 4400 Chicago IL 60606-2807 Business E-Mail: chesse@btlaw.com.

HESSE, JULIA RUSH, lawyer; BA in Economics, with honors, Williams Coll., 1995; MS in Bioethics, U. Pa., 2001, JD, 2001. Bar: Mass. 2002, US Ct. Appeals (1st Cir.). Assoc. Health Care Practice Group Ropes & Gray LLP, Boston, 2005—. Office: Ropes & Gray One International Place Boston MA 02110-2624 Office Phone: 617-951-7624. Office Fax: 617-951-7050. E-mail: julia.hesse@ropesgray.com.*

HESSE, KAREN (KAREN SUE HESSE), writer, educator; b. Balt., Aug. 29, 1952; d. Alvin Donald and Frances Broth Levin; m. Randy Hesse; children: Kate, Rachel. BA, U. Md., 1975. Reference libr. U. Md., 1973-75, leave benefit coord., 1975-76; advt. sec. Country Journal mag., 1976-77, typesetter, proofreader, 1978-88; mental health care provider, 1989-91; children's lit. reviewer, 1993-94. Author: (children's books) Wish on a Unicorn, 1991 (Hungry Mind Rev. Children's Book of Distinction 1992), Letters From Rifka, 1992 (Nat. Jewish Book award 1993, IRA Children's Book award 1993, Christopher award 1992, Sydney Taylor Book award 1992, ALA Notable Book 1992, ALA Best Book for Young Adults 1992, Sch. Libr. Jour. Best Book of Yr. 1992, Horn Book Outstanding Book of Yr. 1992, Booklist Editors' Choice 1992, NY Pub. Libr. 100 Titles for Reading and Sharing 1992), Poppy's Chair, 1993 (Am. Booksellers Assn. Pick of List 1993), Lester's Dog, 1993 (Best Book of Yr. Sch. Libr. Jour. 1993, Notable Children's Trade Book in Field of Social Studies 1993), Lavender, 1993, Sable, 1994 (Sch. Libr. Jour. Best Book of Yr. 1994, NY Pub. Libr. 100 Titles for Reading and Sharing 1994, Boston Globe 10 Best Trade Books 1994, Parenting Mag. 40 Outstanding Children's Books 1994), Phoenix Rising, 1994 (Sch. Libr. Jour. Best Book of Yr. 1994, IRA Tchr.'s Choice 1995, NY Pub. Libr. Books for the Teenage 1995, Best Book for Young Adults ALA 1995, Notable Book, 1995, Wilson Libr. Bull. 33 Favorite Reads 1994 (S.C. Jr. Book award, 1996, others), A Time of Angels, 1995 (IRA Tchr's Choice 1996, IRA Young Adults' Choice, 1997, NY Pub. Libr. Books for the Teenager 1995), The Music of Dolphins, 1996 (Pub.'s Weekly Best Book of Yr. 1996, Best Book of Yr. Sch. Libr. Jour. 1996, Book Links, 100 Titles for Reading and Sharing NY Pub. Libr. Children's Book 1996, Best Books for Young Adults ALA, 1997, Golden Kite Honor Book, 1997), Out of the Dust, 1997 (Newbery medal 1998, Scott O'Dell award 1998), Just Juice, 1998 (100 Titles for Reading and Sharing NY Pub. Libr. 1998, Notable Children's Trade Book in the Field of Social Studies 1998), Come On, Rain!, 1999 (BCCB Blue Ribbon Book, NYPL 100 Books for Reading & Sharing, Jr. Library Guild selection, Book of the Month Club selection, Hon. Mention award, Columbus Internat. Film Fest., ALA Notable Video, 2004); contbr. When I Was Your Age, Vol. II, 1999 (2000 Books for the Teen Age), A Light in the Storm, 1999 (Notable Children's Trade Book in the Field of Social Studies 1999, Kennedy Ctr. Stage Adaptation, 2001), Stowaway, 2000 (SLJ Book of Yr., 2001, Capitol Choice Noteworthy Books for Children (10-14), 100 Titles for Reading and Sharing NY Pub. Libr., 2000, Jr. Libr. Guild Selection), Witness, 2001 (NY Pub. Libr. 100 Books for Reading and Sharing, ALA Notable Children's book, LA 100 Best Books 2001, 2002 IRA Notable 2002, CBC Choice 2002, Myers Award 2002, NCTE Notable 2002, Christopher award 2002, Parents Guide to Children's Media award); Aleutian Sparrow, 2003 (Jr. Libr. Guild selection 100 Titles for Reading and Sharing), The Stone Lamp, 2003 (NY Pub. Libr. 100 Titles, Assn. Jewish Librs. Notable), The Cats in Krasinski Square, 2004 (PW Best Book award 2004, Bologna Ragazzi Honorable Mention, Kirkus Editor's Choice 2004, N.Y. Pub. Libr. 100 Titles for Reading and Sharing, Parent Choice Gold award, Book Sense Children's Picks List for Winter 2004-05, ALA Notable, Koret Jewish Book award), The Young Hans Christian Andersen, 2005 (Notable Children's Trade Book in Field of Social Studies); contbr. articles to profl. jours. Chmn. Sch. Bd., 1989; sec. bd. dirs. Moore Free Libr., 1989-91; active Hospice, 1988—. MacArthur fellow, 2003—. Mem. Soc. Children's Book Writers and Illustrators, So. Vt. Soc. Children's Book Writers (leader 1985-92), Ctr. for Children's Environ. Lit., Author's Guild. Avocations: reading, hiking, cultivating friendships, music. Office: Scholastic 557 Broadway New York NY 10012-3919

HESSE, MARTHA O., gas industry executive; b. Hattiesburg, Miss., Aug. 14, 1942; d. John William and Geraldine Elaine (Ossian) H. BS, U. Iowa, 1964; postgrad., Northwestern U., 1972-76; MBA, U. Chgo., 1979. Rsch. analyst Blue Shield, 1964-66; dir. div. data mgmt. Am. Hosp. Assn., 1966-69; dir., COO SEI Info. Tech., Chgo., 1969-80; assoc. dep. sec. Dept. of Commerce, Washington, 1981-82; exec. dir. Pres.' Task Force on Mgmt. Reform, 1982; asst. sec. mgmt. and adminstrn. Dept. of Energy, Washington, 1982-86; chmn. FERC, Washington, 1986-89; sr. v.p. 1st Chgo. Corp., 1990; CEO Hesse Gas Co., Houston, 1990—2003. Bd. dirs. Pinnacle West Capital Corp., Ariz. Pub. Svc. Co., Mut. Trust Life, AMEC plc, Terra Industries, Enbridge Energy Prnrs. Home: 4171 Autumn Hills Dr Winnemucca NV 89445

HESSEL, MARIELUISE, art collector; b. Germany; m. Richard B. Black, Jan. 18, 1980 (div.). Contbr. over 1500 late 20th century artworks on permanent loan to the Center for Curatorial Studies at Bard College in New York. Named one of Top 200 Collectors, ARTnews, 2003—06. Mailing: 65 Avalanche Canyon Dr Jackson WY 83001-9009*

HESSELBEIN, FRANCES RICHARDS, foundation administrator, writer, editor; b. South Fork, Pa. d. Burgess Harmon and Anne Luke (Wicks) Richards; widowed, 1978; 1 child, John Richards. DHL (hon.), Buena Vista Coll., 1987, Juniata Coll., 1990, Hood Coll., 1991; D Mgmt. (hon.), GM Inst., 1990; LLD (hon.), Wilson Coll., 1991, Moravian Coll., 2000, U. St. Thomas, 2006; LHD (hon.), Marymount-Tarrytown Coll., 1993; DHL (hon.), Boston Coll., 1994, U. Nebr., Kearney, 1994, Lafayette Coll., 1995, Carroll Coll., 1996, Fairleigh Dickinson U., 1996, Muhlenburg Coll., 1996; D in Pub. and Internat. Affairs, U. Pitts., 2001; DHL (hon.), Mt. Mary Coll., 2002, Union Inst. and Univ., 2003, U. Cin., 2003. CEO Talus Rock Girl Scout Coun., Johnstown, 1970-74, Penn Laurel Girl Scout Coun., York, Pa., 1974-76, Girl Scouts U.S., N.Y.C., 1976-90; pres., CEO Peter F. Drucker Found. Nonprofit Mgmt., N.Y.C., 1990-99, chmn., 1999—2003, Leader To Leader Inst., N.Y.C., 2003—06. Chmn. Nat. Bd. Vols. Am., 2003-06; bd. dirs. Mut. of Am. Ins. Co., NYC; nat. bd. visitors Peter F. Drucker Grad. Mgmt. Sch. Claremont (Calif.) Grad. Sch., 1987—; chmn. bd. govs. Josephson Ethics Inst., 1989-99; adv. com. to bd. dirs. N.Y. Stock Exch., 1988-91; bd. govs. Ctr. for Creative Leadership, Greensboro, N.C., 1992-98; adv. bd. Harvard Bus. Sch.'s Initiative on Social Enterprise, Harvard's Kennedy Sch. Hauser Ctr. Nonprofit Policy and Leadership Program, Randall L. Tobias Ctr. Leadership Excellence Indiana U., 2005; chmn. Vols. Am., 2002-06, Leader to Leader Inst., 2003-. Editor-in-chief Leader to Leader; co-editor The Leader of the Future, The Organization of the Future, The Community of the Future, Drucker Found. Future Series, Leader to Leader Book, 1999, Leading Beyond the Walls, 1999, Leader of the Future 2, 2006, Be-Know-Do, 2004; author: Hesselbein on Leadership, 2002. Trustee Juniata Coll., Huntingdon, Pa., 1988—, Allentown (Pa.) Coll., 1988-97; mem. Pres.'s Adv. Com. on Points of Light Initiative Found., 1989; bd. dirs. Nat. Exec. Svc. Corps., N.Y., Commn. on Nat. and Cmty. Svc., 1991-94; adv. bd. The Leadership Inst., U. So. Calif., 1991, Harvard U.'s John F. Kennedy Sch. Govt. Nonprofit Policy and Leadership Program. Recipient Outstanding Achievement award Inter-Svc. Club Coun., Johnstown, 1976, Entrepreneurial Woman award Women Bus. Owners of N.Y., 1984, Nat. Leadership award United Way of Am., Washington, 1985, Disting. Cmty. Svc. award Mut. of Am. Ins. Co., 1985, Dir.'s Choice-award Nat. Women's Econ. Alliance, 1989, Pa. Soc. Disting. Citizen award, 1991, Wilbur M. McFeeley award, U. Pitts. Legacy Laureate award, 2000, Internat. Leadership award Athena Found., 2001, Henry Russo award Ind. U. Ctr., 2001, Dwight D. Eisenhower Series Nat. Security award, 2002, Leadership Devel. award, Boston U., 2003, Juliette award Women of Distincton Girl Scouts USA, 2004, Visionary award Am Soc. Assn. Execs., 2004; named to Bus. Hall of Fame, Johnstown, 1995; named Outstanding Exec., Savvy Mag., 1985, Disting. Alumni Fellow U. Pitts., 1999, Disting. Dau. of Pa., Gov. Ridge, 1999, Woman of Yr., Boy Scouts of Greater N.Y., Legacy Laureate, U. Pitts., 2000; on cover BusinessWeek, 1990, Presdl. Medal of Freedom, 1998; featured in Chief Exec. mag., 1995, Fortune, 1995-96, Chapel of Four Chaplains Gold Legion of Hon. medal, 1999, Athena Found.-Internat. Leadership award, 2001, Henry Rosso award for lifetime ethical fundraising Ind. U. Ctr., 2001-02, Marion Gisalon award Boston U., 2003, Juliette award Girl Scouts U.S., 2004, Visionary award A.S.A.E., 2004, Disting. Svc. award Columbia U. Tchrs. Coll., 2006, Disting. Leadership award Miss Hall's Sch., 2006, MCLC Frances Hesselbein Student Leadership Program award, 2006; Frances Hesselbein How To Be Leadership award for Ethical Leadership established at Jur. Achievement, 2003. Mem. Pa. Soc., Cosmos Club (Washington). Office: Leader to Leader Inst 320 Park Ave 3d Fl New York NY 10022-6815 Office Phone: 212-224-1154. Office Fax: 212-224-2508. Business E-Mail: frances@leadertoleader.org.

HESSELINK, ANN PATRICE, financial executive, lawyer; b. Tokyo, July 20, 1954; d. Ira John Jr. and Etta Marie (Ter Louw) H.; 1 child, Katherine Marie Hesselink Hicks. AB in Psychology, Hope Coll., 1975; JD, St. Johns U., 1980; advanced profl. cert. in fin., NYU, 1983. CPA NY; bar: NY 1981, Iowa 2004. Tax mgr. Coopers & Lybrand, N.Y.C., 1980—82; asst. v.p. Bankers Trust Co., N.Y.C., 1982—83; dir. internat. taxes PepsiCo, Inc., Purchase, NY, 1983—85; sr. v.p., dir. taxes Young & Rubicam Inc., N.Y.C., 1986—94; v.p. taxes, tax counsel AT&T Capital Corp., Morristown, NJ, 1994—97; cons., 1997—2002; dir. taxation Gentek Inc., Parsippany, NJ, 2002—03; 2d v.p. and counsel Prin. Fin. Group, Des Moines, 2004—. Trustee, v.p. Blue Rock Sch., Palisades, N.Y., 1987-89; treas., bd. dirs. Plays for Living, 1991-98; trustee New Brunswick Sem., 1993-98, Ctrl. Coll., 1999-2003, YWCA Greater DesMoines, 2004—. Mem.: ABA, AICPA, Am. Sch. in Japan Alumni Assn. Democrat. Home: 604 Liberty St #319 Pella IA 50219-1777 E-mail: hesselink.ann@principal.com.

HESSER, LORRAINE M., special education educator; d. Joseph V. Scolari III, Agnes E. McGovern; m. George W. Hesser III, June 1, 1979; children: Stephanie M., Matthew G. BA in Spl. Edn., Rowan U., 1996; AAS in Bus. Adminstrn., Mktg., Camden County Coll., 1977. Cert. Tchr. of Handicapped N.J., 1996, elem. tchr. N.J., 1997. Tchr. spl. edn. Vineland Pub. Schs., Vineland, NJ, 1998—, Ind. Child Study Teams, Jersey City, 1996—98. Mem. Salem County Bd. of Sch. Estimates, 2003—; chairperson Salem County Mental Health Bd., Salem, NJ, 1995—2003; bd. dirs., v.p. Salem County Spl. Svcs. Sch. Dist. Bd. Edn., Woodstown, NJ, 1996—, v.p., 2004—; parent adv. Phila. Child Guidance Ctr. Children's Hosp., 1994; organizer Girl Scouts Am., Medford, NJ, 1985—88. Mem.: NEA, Statewide Parent Adv. Network, N.J. Edn. Assn., Coun. for Exceptional Children (Learning Disabilities divsn., Culturally and Linguistically Diverse Exceptional Learners divsn., Spl. Educator award 2000). Avocations: music, travel, photography, gardening, reading. Home: 1065 Rainbow Cir Pittsgrove NJ 08318 Office: Vineland Board of Education 625 Plum St Vineland NJ 08360 Personal E-mail: lmhesser@aol.com.

HESSINGER, JILL A., art educator; b. Niagara Falls, N.Y., June 6, 1958; d. George and Janet A. Gunzelman; m. Philip M. Hessinger, Sept. 1, 1984; children: Kelly, Austen. AS in Fine Arts, Niagara County C.C., Sanborn, N.Y., 1990; BS in Art Edn., Buffalo State Coll., 1996, MS in Art Edn., 1999. Cert. art tchr. N.Y. Customer svc. rep. Marine Midland Bank, Niagara Falls, NY, 1979—93; art tchr. Kenmore (N.Y.) Ctrl. Sch. Dist., 1997—98, Niagara Wheatfield Ctrl. Sch. Dist., Sanborn, NY, 1998—. Contbr. articles. Grantee Niagara Orleans BOCES, 1999, 2000, 2001, Kenan Ctr., 1999, 2001, 2005; WOW grant, 2005. Mem.: N.Y. State Art Tchrs. Assn. Democrat. Avocations: painting, travel, visiting museums.

HESSLER, HELEN STOECKEL, social worker; b. Wilkes-Barre, Pa., Apr. 25, 1928; d. Harry Wellington and Rose (Dahn) S.; m. Earl Randolph Hessler, Jr., Aug. 26, 1961. BS in nursing edn., Wilkes U., 1956; AM, U. Chgo., 1960. Cert. social worker. Staff nurse Wilkes-Barre Gen. Hosp., Wilkes-Barre, 1949-50, Wyo. Valley Vis. Nurse Assn., Wilkes-Barre, 1950-51; social worker Lutheran Children's Bureau, Phila., 1951-61, State Dept. Pub. Welfare, Jackson, Miss., 1961-62, Tex. Dept. Pub. Welfare, San Angelo, Tex., 1962-64, Dept. Social Svcs., Baltimore, Md., 1968-69; dir. adoption svcs. Lutheran Social Svcs., Washington, 1969-83; social worker Hospice Of Northern Va., Arlington, 1983-88, 92-93; dir. social svcs. Tall Oaks Fellowship House, Reston, Va., 1988-91, asst. adminstr., 1991-92. Bd. mem. Pastoral Counselling & Consultation Svcs., Washington, 1972-74. Contbr. article to profl. jours. Lutheran. Avocations: travel, gardening, needlecrafts, reading. Home: 2672 Saint Paul Rd Chambersburg PA 17201-8191

HESTER, JULIA A., lawyer; b. L.A., Nov. 14, 1953; d. Robert William and Bertie Ella (Gilbert) Hester; children: Allison Hester-Haddad, Nancy Hester-Haddad. BA, Fla. Atlantic U., 1984; JD, Nova U., 1990. Bar: Fla. 1990, U.S. Dist. Ct. (mid. dist.) Fla. 1993. Asst. pub. defender Broward Pub. Defender, Ft. Lauderdale, Fla., 1990-93; atty., ptnr. Haddad & Hester, Ft. Lauderdale, 1993-95, 97—. Bd. dirs. St. Anthony Found., Ft. Lauderdale, Ft. Lauderdale Billfish Tournament, 1992—96; bd. dirs., mem. exec. bd. St. Thomas Aquinas Found.; mem. Sunrise Intercoastal Bd., Ft. Lauderdale, 1995; bd. dirs., officer Kids Inn Distress Aux., Ft. Lauderdale, 1984—87.

HESTER, LINDA HUNT, retired dean, counseling administrator, sociology educator, health and physical education educator; b. Winston-Salem, N.C., June 16, 1938; d. Hanselle Lindsay and Jennie Sarepta (Hunt) H. BS with honors, U. Wis., 1960, MS, 1964; PhD, Mich. State U., 1971. Lic. ednl. counselor, Wis. Instr. health and phys. edn. for women U. Tex., Austin, 1960—62; asst. dean women U. Ill., Urbana, 1964—66; dean of women, asst. prof. sociology and phys. edn. Tex. Woman's U., Denton, 1971—73; ret., 1973. Rsch. assoc. bur. higher edn. Mich. Dept. Edn., Lansing, 1969-70; vol. counselor Dallas Challenge and Dallas Ind. Sch. Dist., 1989-90. Friend of Kimbell Art Mus. com. of 1000 Philharmonic Ctr. for Arts, Naples, Fla.; mem. and donor Naples Mus. Art; founder Women's Mus., Dallas; founding mem. Dallas Ctr. Performing Arts; assoc. mem. Dallas Mus. Art, 1991—; Stradivarious mem. Dallas Symphony, 1991—; bd. dirs. Dallas Opera, 1986—; mem. Friends Art Dist., Dallas; mem. governing bd. Theatrical Arts Coordinating Assn., 2005—. Fellow, Coll. Edn. Mich. State U., 1968. Mem. ACA, Am. Coll. Pers. Assn., Nat. Assn. Women in Edn., Brookhaven Country Club, Wyndemere Country Club, Delta Kappa Gamma, Alpha Lambda Delta. Republican. Presbyterian. Achievements include listed in book, Texas Women, 2003. Avocations: golf, sailing, cooking, music, reading. Home: 7606 Wellcrest Dr Dallas TX 75230-4857

HESTER, NANCY ELIZABETH, county government official; b. Miami, Fla., Jan. 20, 1950; d. George Temple and Lorraine Patricia (Cluney) Hester. BA, Bucknell U., 1972; MIA, Columbia U., 1974; MBA, Fla. Internat. U., 1979; postgrad, Fla. Atlantic U., 2000—. Treasury rep. Westinghouse Electric Co., N.Y.C., 1974—76; adminstrv. officer serving in bldg. and zoning, gen. svcs. and corrections and rehab. depts. Metro Dade County, Fla., 1979—2000, bur. comdr. corrections and rehab. dept., 1990—2000. Adj. prof. Fla. Internat. U., Miami, 1980-83. Bd. dirs. YWCA Greater Miami, 1988-92, LWV Dade County, 1993-98; pres. bd. dirs., pres. bd. trustees edn. fund, 1994-96; mem. adv. bd. SafeSpace, 1995-2001, v.p. adv. bd., 2000, DAA, 2006. Mem.: DAR.

HESTON, BRIDGET L., vice principal, history educator; d. Suzanne Elizabeth Emanuel; m. David J. Carnemolla, Apr. 10, 2004. MEd, U. Bridgeport, Conn., 2001. History instr. State Conn. Doe, Bridgeport, 2001—03, dept. head Hamden, 2003—06, vice-prin. Hartford, 2006—; history & polit. sci. instr. Post U., Waterbury, Conn. Vol. St. Vincent DePaul Soc., Waterbury, 1999—. Mem.: Nat. Coun. Social Studies, Phi Kappa Phi.

HETHERINGTON, EILEEN MAVIS, psychologist, educator; b. Nov. 27, 1926; BA, U. B.C., 1947, MA, 1948; PhD in Psychology, U. Calif.-Berkeley, 1958. Clin. psychologist B.C. Child Guidance Clinic, 1948-51, sr. psychologist, 1951-52; clin. internship Langley Porter Clinic, 1956-57; instr. psychology San Jose State Coll., 1957-58; asst. prof. Rutgers U., 1958-60; from asst. prof. to prof. U. Wis., 1960-70; prof. psychology U. Va., Charlottesville, 1970-99, James Page prof. psychology, 1976-99, prof. emeritus, 1999—, dept. chmn., 1980-84. Editor Child Devel., 1971-77; rschr. in personality devel. and childhood psychopathology, the role of family process and parent characteristics on normal and deviant behavior in children, the effects of divorce and remarriage on families, parents and children. Bd. dirs. Found. for Child Devel. Recipient Disting. Scientist award Am. Assn. for Marriage and Family Therapy, 1988, Am. Family Therapy Assn., 1992, Burgess award Nat. Coun. on Family Rels., 2000. Mem. APA (pres. divsn. 7, 1978-79, Stanley Hall Disting. Scientist award 1987, Disting. Scientist award 1993), Soc. Rsch. in Child Devel. (pres. 1985-87, Disting. Scientist award 1995), Soc. Rsch. in Adolescents (pres. 1986-88, Disting. Scientist award 1988, William James Disting. Scientist award 1994), Am. Psychol. Soc. (Disting. Scientist award 2004). Address: The Terraces # 404 1'07 1st St S Charlottesville VA 22902

HETTICK, SANDRA ANN, literature and language educator; b. Ipswich, S.D., Aug. 7, 1955; d. Ivan Ervin and Arvella Jean Schumacher; m. Donald Earl Hettick, June 17, 1978; children: Christian Donald, Joshua John. BS, No. State U., Aberdeen, S.D., 1977. Tchr. English Timber Lake H.S., SD, 1977—78, Roscoe H.S., 1978—90, Edmunds Ctrl. H.S., 1990—. Pres. Roscoe Comml. Club, 2006. Mem.: S.D. Edn. Assn. Lutheran. Office: Edmunds Ctrl Sch PO Box 317 Roscoe SD 57471-0317

HETTMANSPERGER, SUE, artist; b. Akron, Ohio, Nov. 20, 1948; d. Hilton E. Hettmansperger and Dorothy E. Stone. Student, Yale U., New Haven, Conn., summer 1971; BFA in Lithography and Drawing cum laude, U. N.Mex., Albuquerque, 1972, MA in Lithography and Drawing, 1974. Grad. tchg. asst. U. N.Mex., 1972—74; instr. lithography, intaglio and drawing Pa. State U., State College, 1974—75; prof. painting and drawing U. Iowa, Iowa City, 1977—. Vis. lectr. U. N.Mex., Albuquerque, 1985; invited artist in residence in painting and drawing Roswell Art Mus., N.Mex., 1990; artist in residence in drawing U Cross Found., Wyo., 1992; curator of prints Tyler Graphics, Bedford Village, N.Y., 1976; nat. affiliate A.I.R. Gallery, N.Y.C., 1989—; lectr. in field. One-woman shows include, Frumkin & Struve Gallery Chgo., 1981, A.I.R. Gallery, NYC, 1990, 1994, 1999, 2003, CSPS Alternative Space, Cedar Rapids, Iowa, 1992, U. No. Iowa Gallery, Cedar Falls, 1994, Artemisia Gallery, Chgo., 1995, S.D. Sch. Mines and Tech., 2004, exhibited in group shows at Artemisia Gallery, Chgo., 1996, Arts Iowa City Gallery, 1998, Galeria Article 26, Carer de Ferlandina, Barcelona, Spain, 1999, U. Tex. San Antonio Gallery, 2002, Faulconer Gallery, Grinnell Coll., 2003, Bowling Green State U., 2005, No. Ariz. Univ. Mus., 2005, others, Represented in permanent collections; contbr. artwork to New Am. Paintings Midwest, 2006. MacDowel Colony Drawing fellow, 1977; NEA fellow in drawing, 1983; recipient Faculty Scholar award U. Iowa, 1997-99; arts and humanities interdisciplinary grantee U. Iowa, 2001, 06. Office: U Iowa Art Bldg W Riverside Dr Iowa City IA 52242

HETU, JOAN LAFFORD, nursing administrator, emergency nurse; b. Southbridge, Mass., Dec. 28, 1926; d. George William and Harriet (Delehanty) Tully; children: Christine Hamilton, George, Jennifer, Wendy, Martin. Diploma in Nursing, Meml. Hosp., Worcester, Mass., 1948; BS, Chapman Coll., Orange, Calif., 1984. RN, Calif., Mass. Asst. head nurse surg. unit Queen of Angels Hosp., L.A.; house supr. med./surg. units AMI Med. Ctr. of Garden Grove, Calif.; nursing adminstr., house supr. St. Jude Hosp., Yorba Linda, Calif.; clin. supr orthopedics, diabetes and neurology units, nurse recruiter Downey (Calif.) Community Hosp., 1993; safety/risk mgr. Pacifica Hosp. Care Ctr., Huntington Beach, Calif. Mem. NAFE, AAUW, Am. Orgn. Nurse Execs.

HEUER, BETH LEE, music educator, composer; b. Rockford, Ill., May 13, 1957; d. Stanton Lee and Gladys Mae Heuer. BA in Music, 1980, BFA in Music Edn., 1981, M in Music Edn., 2001. Vocal music tchr. Boylan Cath. H.S., Rockford, Ill., 1981—82, Pecatonica (Ill.) H.S., 1982—83; band dir. Boylan Cath. H.S., 1983—, chmn. dept. music, 1987—. Pvt. music tchr., Rockford, 1982—. Music arranger, composer, 1985—. Mem.: Ill. Music Educators Assn., Music Educators Nat. Conf., Internat. Jazz Educators Assn. Avocations: gardening, reading, traveling. Office: Boylan Cath HS 4000 St Francis Dr Rockford IL 61103 Office Phone: 815-877-0531.

HEUER, CATHERINE ANN, music educator; b. Oshkosh, Wis., Jan. 9, 1959; d. Walter Richard Dugolenski and Ruth Elizabeth Knaggs; m. William Michael Heuer, July 18, 1992. B in Music Edn., U. Wis., Oshkosh, 1981; Kodaly cert., Silver Lake Coll., 2002. Music tchr. Sts. Peter and Paul Sch., Kiel, Wis., 1982—84, St. Joseph Sch., Stratford, Wis., 1985—88, St. John Sch., Marshfield, Wis., 1988—2001, Marshfield Area Cath. Schs., 2001—. Music min. St. John the Bapt. Cath. Ch., Marshfield, 1994—; dir. Marshfield Area Recorder Ensemble, 1993—; mem. Ctrl. Chamber Chorale, Marshfield, 1995—2003. Mem.: Am. Recorder Soc., Music Educators Nat. Conf., Wis. Choral Dirs. Assn., Am. Choral Dirs. Assn., Orgn. Am. Kodaly Educators, Assn. Wis. Area Kodaly Educators (treas. 2002—). Avocation: aerobics.

HEUER, MARGARET B., retired microcomputer laboratory coordinator; b. Juneau, Alaska, Sept. 12, 1935; d. William George and Flora (Rusk) Allen; m. Joseph Louis Heuer; children: Leilani, Joseph (dec.), Daniel, Suzanne, Karen, Mark, Jerina. AA, San Bernardino Valley Coll., 1980. Cert. data processing, computer repair and maintenance, microcomputer support specialist. Coord. microcomputers lab. Oakton C.C., Skokie, Ill., 1981-93; ret., 1993; switchboard operator Coll. Am. Pathologists, 2000—06.

HEUER, MARILYN PATRICIA, operating room nurse, quality assurance nurse; b. Chgo., Mar. 24, 1930; d. Charles G. and Laura A. (Gould) Page; div.; children: James, Deborah. Diploma, Evanston (Ill.) Hosp., 1951; BS, Coll. St. Francis, Joliet, Ill., 1978. RN, Ill., Fla. Staff nurse in obstetrics and emergency room Evanston Hosp., 1951-66; dir. operating and recovery rms. Luth. Gen. Hosp., Park Ridge, Ill., 1966-79; mgr. utilization rev. and quality assurance Maxicare HMO, Chgo., 1980-83; dir. med. svcs. Luth. Gen. Health Plan, Park Ridge, 1983-93. Mem. Assn. Operating Room Nurses, Am. Coll. Utilization Rev. Physicians, Ill. Assn. Quality Assurance Profls. Home: 3851 Mission Hills Rd Northbrook IL 60062-5724

HEUERMANN-NOWIK, PATRICIA CALHOUN, theater director; d. William Royal Calhoun and Nancy Lee Griffitts; m. Eric Heuermann (div.); children: Beryl Lee, William Whitney, Lana Amanda, Linda Dilwara; m. Vete Nowik, Mar. 29, 1985. Grad., Curtis Inst. Music, 1951—55. Dir. opera theatre Emory U., Atlanta, 1968—75, Clark Coll., 1972—75; founder, artistic music dir. Atlanta Opera, 1975—80; mng. dir., touring ednl. program N.C. Opera, Charlotte, 1980—82; founder, artistic dir. Singers Theatre N.Y., N.Y.C., 1983—92; instr. stage artistry Am. Inst. Musical Studies, Graz, Austria, 1994—2001; dir. opera theatre Hofstra U., Hempstead, NY, 2000—06. Chair internat. opera singers competition Ctr. Contemporary Opera, 1990—94, chair artistic adv. bd., 1990—96. Mem.: Opera for Youth (bd. dirs. 2000—02, program chair nat. conf. 1995), N.Y. Singing Tchrs. Assn. (bd. dirs. 1998—99), Opera Am., Nat. Opera Assn. (N.E. regional gov. 1991—94, bd. dirs. 1991—95, v.p. resources 1995—98, v.p. programs 1998—2000, pres. 2000—02). Democrat. Avocations: cooking, reading, travel. Home: 20-49 48th St Astoria NY 11105 Office: Hofstra U Music Dept 112 Hofstra Univ Hempstead NY 11549-1120 Personal E-mail: patruschka@mindspring.com.

HEUKESHOVEN, JANET KAY, music educator; b. Mpls., Mar. 11, 1957; d. Burton O. and Bertha I. Norby; m. A. Eric Heukeshoven, June 17, 1979; children: Hans, Max. BS in Music Edn., U. Minn., 1979; MusM, Boston Conservatory, 1984; DMA, U. Wis., 1994. Assoc. prof. music, dir. band and orch. Coll. of St. Teresa, Winona, Minn., 1982—87; assoc. prof. instrumental music and music edn., band dir. St. Mary's U. of Minn., Winona, 1994—, chmn. dept. music, 1998—2004. Soloist, performer Minn. Amb. of Music, 2000—; performer, sect. leader Winona Mcpl. Band; performer, soloist recitals and chamber ensembles, 1984—; guest condr. various regional clinics and concerts, 1990—; flutist LaSalle Quintet Faculty Ensemble, St. Mary's U. Charter mem. Winona Fine Arts Commn., 1996—2002. Recipient R. Church Meml. Conducting award, U. Wis., 1994, Performance award, Sigma Alpha Iota, 1979. Mem.: Coll. Band Dirs. Nat. Assn. (chpt. sec. 2000—03), Minn. Music Educators Assn. Avocations: gardening, reading, cross country skiing. Office: Saint Mary's Univ of Minn 700 Terrace Heights #58 Winona MN 55987 Office Phone: 507-457-1675. Business E-Mail: jheukesh@smumn.edu.

HEUSCHELE, SHARON JO, dean; b. Toldeo, Ohio, July 12, 1936; BE, U. Toledo, 1965, MEd, 1969, PhD, 1973. Cert. elem., secondary tchr., Ohio. Asst. prof. Ohio Dominican Coll., Columbus, 1970-73, St. Cloud (Minn.) U., 1973-74; assoc. prof. Ohio State U., Columbus, 1974-79; dean instl. planning Lourdes Coll., Sylvania, Ohio, 1980—; chmn. sociology, econs. and polit. sci. dept. Cons. U. Hawaii, 1979, others. Bd. dirs. Trinity-St. Paul Inner City Program, Toledo, 1968; cons. Ohio Civil Rights Commn., 1972; active Dem. campaigns. U. Toledo fellow, 1967-69; recipient citation U. Toledo, 1979, Journalistic Excellence award Columbia Press Assn., N.Y.C., 1954. Mem. Am. Coun. Edn., Ohio Conf. Coll. and Univ. Planning, Soc. Coll. and Univ. Planning (com. 1984-85), Phi Theta Kappa, Phi Kappa Phi (citation 1973), U. Toledo Alumni Assn., USCG Aux. Roman Catholic. Avocations: fossil and mineral collecting, poetry, novel writing, horseback riding. Office: Lourdes Coll 6832 Convent Blvd Sylvania OH 43560-2891

HEUSER, MICHELLE S., manufacturing executive; d. Cortlan Ray Jr. and Jacalyn Faye Schupbach; m. Alan W. Heuser, Oct. 12, 1995; children: Audrey L., Alaina M. BSChemE, U. Okla., Norman, 1990; MBA, U. Houston, Clear Lake, 1997. Engr. Lyondell, Channelview, Tex., 1990—96, mkt. analyst Houston, 1996; planning analyst polymers Equistar, Houston, 1996—98, ops. supt. Channelview, 1998—2001; human resource mgr. Lyondell-Equistar, Houston, 2001—02, plant mgr. Victoria, Tex., 2002—03, Matagorda plant mgr. Bay City, Tex., 2003—. Pres. bd. Tex. Zoo, Victoria, 2002—03. Named Big Sister of Yr., Big Bros./Big Sisters Am., Houston, 1994. Mem.: Bay City C. of C. (bd. dirs. 2006).

HEUSSENSTAMM, FRANCES KOVACS, psychologist, artist; b. Cleve., Nov. 6, 1928; d. Fred Kovacs and Edna Jacqueline Reiter; m. Karl Alfons Heussenstamm, Aug. 25, 1948 (dec. Oct. 19, 1975); children: Paul Anthony, John Eric, Mark Ernest. BA, Whittier Coll., 1957, MA, 1960; PhD, U. So. Calif., 1968. Lic. clin. psychologist Calif. Prof. art and edn. Columbia U., N.Y.C., 1970—74; pvt. practice clin. psychologist Santa Monica, Laguna Beach, Calif., 1978—. Cons. U.S. Office Edn., Washington, 1966—80. Author: Blame It On Freud; contbr. articles to profl. jours.; paintings in pvt. and mus. collections in US and Australia. Rsch. grantee, various orgns., 1960—80. Mem.: APA (life). Democrat. Avocation: activist. Office: 668 N Coast Hwy Ste 260 Laguna Beach CA 92651 Personal E-mail: fkheuss@cox.net.

HEWITT, EMILY CLARK, federal judge, minister; b. Balt., May 26, 1944; d. John Frank and Margaret Genevieve (Gray) H. AB, Cornell U., 1966; MPhil, Union Theol. Sem., 1975; JD, Harvard U., 1978. Bar: Mass. 1978, US Dist. Ct. Mass. 1979, US Ct. Appeals (1st cir.) 1984, US Ct. Appeals (fed. cir.) 1999, U.S. Supreme Ct. 2003; ordained priest Protestant Episcopal Ch. 1974. Adminstr. Upward Bound Programs Cornell and Hofstra U., NYC, 1967-69; asst. min. St. Mary's Episcopal Ch., Manhattanville, NY, 1972-73; lectr. Union Theol. Sem., NYC, 1972-73, 74-75; asst. prof. Andover Newton Theol. Sch., Newton Centre, Mass., 1973-75; assoc. Hill & Barlow, Boston, 1978-85, ptnr., 1985-93; gen. counsel GSA, 1993-98; judge US Ct. of Fed. Claims, Washington, 1998—. Co-author: Women Priests: Yes or No?, 1973; contbr. works in field. Bd. dirs. Mass. Found. for Humanities and Pub. Policy, South Hadley, 1983-89. Mem.: Mass. Conveyancers Assn. (exec. com. 1990—93), New Eng. Women in Real Estate (dir. 1985—89), ABA (vice chair Bid Protest com. sect. pub. contract law 2000—02). Office: US Ct Fed Claims 717 Madison Pl NW Washington DC 20005

HEWITT, JACQUELINE N., astronomy educator; AB in Econs., Bryn Mawr Coll., 1980; PhD in Physics, MIT, 1986. Prof. physics MIT, 1989—; dir. MIT Kavli Inst. for Astrophysics and Space Rsch., 2002—. Recipient Annie Jump Cannon award in Astronomy, 1989; David and Lucille Packard fellow, 1990; Henry G. Booker prize award, 1993; Maria Goeppart-Mayer award Am. Phys. Soc., 1995; Alfred P. Sloan rsch. fellow, 1990. Fellow: Am. Phys. Soc. Office: MIT Dept Physics Room 37-241 Cambridge MA 02139 Business E-Mail: jhewitt@mit.edu.

HEWITT, JENNIFER LOVE, actress, singer; b. Waco, Tex., Feb. 21, 1979; d. Danny and Pat. Actor: (films) Munchie, 1992, Little Miss Millions, 1993, Sister Act 2: Back in the Habit, 1993, Little Miss Millions, 1993, House Arrest, 1996, Trojan War, 1997, I Know What You Did Last Summer, 1997, Can't Hardly Wait, 1998, Telling You, 1998, Zoomates (voice), 1998, I Still Know What You Did Last Summer, 1998, The Suburbans, 1999, Heartbreakers, 2001, The Devil and Daniel Webster, 2001, The Tuxedo, 2002, Garfield: The Movie, 2004, Garfield: A Tale of Two Kitties, 2006, (TV series) Kids Inc., 1989-91, Shaky Ground, 1992, The Byrds of Paradise, 1994, McKenna, 1994-95, Party of Five, 1995-99, Ghost Whisperer, 2005-, (TV films) The Audrey Hepburn Story, 2000, 100 Greatest Love Songs, 2002, A Christmas Carol, 2004; actor, prodr.: (films) If Only, 2004, (TV series) Time of Your Life, 1999-2000; actor, co-exec. prodr.: (TV movies) The Audrey Hepburn Story, 2000, In the Game, 2004, A Christmas Carol, 2004, (voice) The Magic 7, 2006. Prodr. (films) One Night, 2002. Singer: (albums) Let's Go Bang, 1995, Jennifer Love Hewitt, 1996, Love Songs, 1998, BareNaked, 2002. Office: William Morris Agy 151 S El Camino Dr Beverly Hills CA 90212-2775*

HEWITT, JUNE ANN, elementary school educator; b. Excelsior Springs, Mo., July 24, 1956; d. Clarence Jr. and Norma Ann (Parman) King; m. Roger C. Hewitt, June 19, 1982 (div. Nov. 1987); 1 child, Ryan. BS in Edn., William Jewell Coll., Liberty, Mo., 1978; MEd, Webster U., 1984. Tchr. 1st and 2d grades Excelsior Springs Pub. Schs., 1978—. Named Tchr. of Yr., Excelsior Springs Sch. Dist., 1993. Mem. NEA, Mo. Edn. Assn., Excelsior Springs Edn. Assn., Beta Sigma Phi, Delta Kappa Gamma (pres. chpt. 1987-90). Baptist. Avocations: reading, walking, piano. Office: Westview Elem Sch 500 N Jesse James Rd Excelsior Springs MO 64024-3614 Office Phone: 816-630-9260. E-mail: appleteacher@juno.com.

HEWITT, LISA CAROL (LISA CAROL VER HOEF), elementary school educator; b. Rock Rapids, Iowa, Oct. 7, 1963; d. Floyd Raymond and Carol Ann (Hollander) Ver Hoef; m. Douglas Ray Hewitt, July 22, 1995; 1 child, Mackenzie Ann Hewitt. BA summa cum laude, Buena Vista Coll., Storm Lake, Iowa, 1986. Cert. in elem. edn. and Spanish. Bilingual tchr. 2d grade Twombly Elem. Sch., Ft. Lupton, Colo., 1986—88; elem. tchr., technology trainer Rolling Green Elem. Sch., Urbandale, Iowa, 1988—. Jr. webmaster supr. Rolling Green Elem. Sch., 1988—, mem. bldg. assistance team, 1988—2004; new tchr. mentor, 2004—; math com. mem., 2002—. Mem. NEA, Iowa Edn. Assn., Urbandale Edn. Assn., Iowa Jaycees (state dir. 1989-90, mgmt. v.p. 1990-91, pres. 1991-92, dist. dir. 1992-93), Iowa Jaycee (adminstrv. v.p. 1993-94, region 7 regional dir. 1994-95). Methodist. Avocations: golf, travel, reading, swimming. Home: 5143 69th St Des Moines IA 50322-6907 Office: Rolling Green Elem Sch 8100 Airline Ave Urbandale IA 50322-2446 E-mail: hewittl@urbandale.k12.ia.us.

HEWITT, LOU, retired elementary school educator; b. Lincoln, Nebr., Mar. 15, 1944; d. Walter R. and Verna E. Powers; m. Darrell Dean Hewitt, July 1, 1942; children: Joseph Walter, Patrick Darrell. MusB in Edn., Nebr. Wesleyan U., Lincoln, 1966. Cert. tchr. Iowa, 1966. Tchr. music West Monona Cmty. Sch. Dist., Onawa, Iowa, 1966—2006; ret., 2006. Pres. Kiwanis, Onawa, Friends of Onawa Pub. Libr.; mem. boy scout troop com. Boy Scouts of Am., Onawa; mem. parish coun. St. John Ch., Onawa; pres. Cmty. Theater, Onawa. Democrat. Avocation: acting. Home: 1612 Lucas St Pl Onawa IA 51040

HEWITT, NANCY ARLENE, social worker; b. Chambersburg, Pa., July 13, 1946; d. Erskine Enoch and Phyllis Athelia (McLaughlin) H. BA, Thiel Coll., 1968; MSW, Simmons Coll., 1977. Lic. ind. clin. social worker. Clinician, supr. North Shore Community Mental Health Ctr., Salem, Mass., 1978-83; pvt. practice North Bay Counseling and Cons., Salem, 1981—; clinician, supr. Salem Hosp. Mental Health Ctr., 1983-89. Adj. asst. prof. Simmons Coll. Sch. Social Work, Boston, 1989-94. Mem. NASW, Pvt. Practice Colloquium. Office: Ste 322 70 Washington St Salem MA 01970-3520 Office Phone: 978-741-1167. E-mail: nahewitt@verizon.net.

HEWITT, PATRICIA HOPE, English government official, political scientist, researcher, announcer; b. Canberra, Australia, Dec. 2, 1948; arrived in U.K., 1967; d. Lenox and Hope (Tillyard) Hewitt; m. Julian Gibson-Watt, Aug. 8, 1970 (div. 1976); m. William Birtles, Dec. 17, 1981; children: Alexandra, Nicholas. BA, Newnham Coll., Cambridge, 1970; MA, Cambridge (Eng.) U., 1974, Oxford (Eng.) U., 1992. Gen. sec. Nat. Coun. Civil Liberties (now Liberty), England, 1974-83; press sec. to Leader of Opposition (Neil Kinnock), England, 1983-87; policy coord. Leader of Opposition, England, 1987-89; dep. dir. Inst. for Pub. Policy Rsch., England, 1989-94; dir. rsch. Andersen Consulting (now Accenture), England, 1994—97; mem. House of Commons, Parliament, 1997—, Sec. of State for Trade and Industry and Min. for Women, 2001—. Author: About Time: The Revolution in Work and Family Life, 1993. Bd. dirs. Internat. League for Human Rights, N.Y.C., 1983—; public relations officer, Age Concern, 1971-74, women's rights officer, 1973-74. Mem. Brit. Labour Party. Avocations: art history, gardening, cooking. Office: Dept Trade & Industry 1 Victoria St London SW1H OET England

HEWITT, RUTH PRICE, librarian, educator; b. Washington, May 17, 1948; d. Irby Lee Price and June Helen (Garrison) Price Kurze; m. Stephen Allen Hewitt, Oct. 17, 1981. BA in Elem. Edn., Newberry Coll., 1970; MLS, U. S.C., 1987; postgrad., Clemson U., N.C., LaVerne Coll., Furman U. Cert. elem. edn. Tchr. Laurel Creek Sch., Mauldin, SC, 1970—71, Sue Cleveland Sch., Piedmont, SC, 1971, Alexander Sch., Greenville, SC, 1971—73, Haynsworth Sch., Greenville, 1974—77; sub. tchr. Prince Georges Co. Schs., Upper Marlboro, Md., 1973—74, Greenville Co. Pub. Sch., 1977—80; libr., media specialist Ambler Elem. Sch., Pickens, SC, 1980—83; elem. tchr. Laurel Creek Sch., Mauldin, SC, 1970—71, Sue Cleveland Sch., Piedmont, SC, 1971, Alexander Sch., Greenville, SC, 1971—73, Haynsworth Pvt. Sch., Greenville, 1974—77; substitute tchr. Prince4 Georges County schs., Upper Marlboro, Md., 1973—74, Greenville County Pub. Schs., Trinity Luth. Sch., 1977—80; libr., media specialist Ambler Elem. Sch., 1980—83. Sch. rep. Assn. Classroom Tchrs., 1972—73. Chmn. tenant adv. com. Breckenridge Apts., 1976; vol. Alexander Elem., 2002—06, Laurel Creek Elem. Sch., 2001; sec. sch. bd. Our Saviour Luth. Ch., Greenville, 1982—85. Scholar Pres. scholarship, Newberry Coll., 1967—68. Mem.: Kappa Delta (chaplain 1968—69). Republican.

HEWITT, SARAH NICHOLE, educational consultant, researcher; b. Monroe, Wis., Nov. 20, 1980; d. James Daryl and Marsha Elaine Hewitt. BS in Biology, U. Miami, 2003, MS in Edn., 2005. With Sunshine Ace Hardware, Dunedin, Fla., 1999—2002; asst. to CEO Kane's Ace Hardware, Homosassa Springs, 2001—04; intern Helen Ellis Meml. Hosp. Emergency Rm., Tarpon Springs, 2002; rsch. asst. dept. pediatrics U. Miami, Coral Gables, 2002—03; intern Orthop. Specialists, Palm Harbor, 2000; rsch. asst. office spl. edn. U. Miami, 2000—05; tchr. Chgo. Pub. Schs., 2005—. Rsch. cons. office spl. edn. U. Miami, 2000—05; cons. Kane's Ace Hardware, Homosassa Springs, 2001—. Site leader Habitat for Humanity, Miami, 1999—2001; vol. Helen Ellis Meml. Hosp., Tarpon Springs, 2002—02; mem. v.p. adv. com. U. Miami, 2002—03; mem., vol. Miami Children's Hosp., 1999—2003; co-chair FunDay U. Miami, 1999—2003. Mem.: Coun. Exceptional Children, Pi Lambda Theta. Roman Catholic. Avocations: soccer, community service, travel, hiking, camping. Office: 1949 Spanish Oaks DR N Palm Harbor FL 34683 Office Phone: 727-560-3087. Personal E-mail: sarahnhewitt@gmail.com.

HEWITT, VIVIAN ANN DAVIDSON (MRS. JOHN HAMILTON HEWITT JR.), retired librarian; b. New Castle, Pa., Feb. 17, 1920; d. Arthur Robert and Lela Luvada (Mauney) Davidson; m. John Hamilton Hewitt, Jr., Dec. 26, 1949; 1 son, John Hamilton III. AB with honors, Geneva Coll., 1943, LHD, 1978; BSLS, Carnegie Mellon U., 1944; postgrad., U. Pitts., 1947-48. Sr. asst. libr. Carnegie Libr., Pitts., 1944-49; instr., libr. Sch. Libr. Sci. Atlanta U., Atlanta U., 1949-52; with Readers Reference Svc., Crowell-Collier Pub. Co., N.Y.C., 1953-55; libr. Rockefeller Found., N.Y.C., 1955-63; librarian Carnegie Endowment Internat. Peace, N.Y.C., 1963-83; librarian Mexican Agrl. Program, Rockefeller Found., summer 1958; dir. libr. and info. svcs. Katherine Gibbs Sch., N.Y.C., 1984-86; reference asst. Coun. on Fgn. Rels., 1986-89. Lectr. spl. librarianship at grad. schs. of L.S. and info. throughout U.S. and Can., 1968-88; condr. profl. seminars Am. Mgmt. Assn., 1968-69, UN Inst. Tng. and Rsch., 1973, 74, Grad. Sci. Libr. and Info. Sci., Rutgers U., 1986; mem. faculty Grad. Sch. Libr. and Info. Sci., U. Tex., Austin, summer 1985; SLA rep. to Internat. Fedn. Libr. Assns., 1970-73, 73-75, 75-77; mem. nat. adv. com. Ctr. for the Book, Libr. of Congress, 1979-84; mem. adv. bd. Who's Who Among African Ams., 1975—. Contbr. chpt. to: The Black Librarian in America, 1970, What Black Librarians Are Saying, 1972, New Dimensions for Academic Library Service, 1975, A Century of Service, 1976, Handbook of Black Librarianship, 1977, 2d edit., 2000, The Black Librarian in America Revisited, 1994, Notable Black American Men, 1999. Nat. historian Northeasterners, Inc., 1996—; bd. dirs. Graham-Windham, 1967, sec., 1980—87; bd. dirs. Laymen's Club, Cathedral Ch. of St.John the Divine, 1975—82, sec., 1986—93. Recipient Outstanding Cmty. Svc. awards, United Fund N.Y., 1965—77, Disting. Alumna award, U. Pitts.-Carnegie Mellon U. Alumni Assn., 1978, Merit award, Carnegie Mellon U. Alumni Assn., 1979, Leadership award, Carnegie Mellon U. Black Alumni, 2001. Mem.: ALA (Disting. Svc. to Librarianship award Black Caucus 1978, Leadership in Profession award Black Caucus 1992, Spirit Ctr. award 2005), Jack and Jill Am., Inc. (ea. regional dir. 1967—69), Spl. Librs. Assn. (rep. to Pacem in Terris Convocation 1965, rep. to White House Conf. Internat. Coop. Yr. 1965, pres. N.Y. chpt. 1970—71, nat. pres. 1978—79, Hall of Fame 1984, Leadership award 2001), Am. Soc. Order of St. John, Pierians, Inc. (hon.), Alpha Kappa Alpha, Tower Soc. Geneva Coll. Democrat. Episcopalian. Home: 862 West End Ave New York NY 10025-4959 E-mail: jhh2nyc@aol.com.

HEWLETT, CLOTHILDE, lawyer; BA with distinction, U. Calif., Berkeley, 1976, JD, 1979. Bar: Calif. 1980. Asst. dist. atty. City and County of San Francisco; police commr. San Francisco; Undersecretary of State and Consumer Svcs. Agency Calif., 1999; interim dir. Dept. Gen. Svcs. (DGS), 2002; ptnr. Preston Gates & Ellis LLP. Bd. dirs. Women's Found. Calif.; bd. trustees Calif. Sci. Ctr. Found. Mem.: Nat. Assn. Women Bus. Owners, Calif. Assn. Black Lawyers, Calif. Women's Leadership Forum. Office: Preston Gates & Ellis LLP Ste 1700 55 Second St San Francisco CA 94105-3493 Office Phone: 415-882-8026. Office Fax: 415-882-8220. E-mail: chewlett@prestongates.com.

HEWLETT, ELIZABETH M., county official; b. NYC, Apr. 4, 1955; BA in Polit. Sci., Tufts U., 1976; JD, Boston Coll., 1979; postgrad., John F. Kennedy Sch. Govt., Harvard U., 1998. Legal intern Dist. Attys. Office Queen's County, N.Y.C., 1978; legis. aide Prince George's County Coun., 1980—82; law clk. Prince George's County Atty.'s Office, 1982—84; litigation atty. Legal Aid Bur., Inc., 1984—86; assoc. atty. Meyers, Billingsley, Shipley, Curry, Rodell and Rosenbaum, 1986—88; assoc. gen. counsel Md. Nat. Capital Park and Planning Commn., 1988—95, chairwoman Prince George's County Planning Bd., 1995—. Apptd. mem. Gov.'s Drug and Alcohol Abuse Commn., 1989—95, Charter Com. of the Ct. Appeals Md., 1989—95, Md. State Bd. Law Examiner, 1995; chmn. Census Partnership in Prince George's County, 1999—2000; bd. dirs. Hospices of Nat. Capital Region, 1999—, Greater D.C. Cares, Inc., 1991—93, Pennvisions, 1992—97, Bowie Health Ctr. of Dimensions Health Corp., 1995—, Hospice Develop. Coun., 1996—98, Bowie Health Ctr. Found., 1997—99, YMCA Met. Washington, 1999—2001, Metropolitan Access Inc., 1999—. Named Heson Valley Montessori Sch. Honoree, 1998, 2000, Women of Yr., Prince George's Cmty. Found., 1998, Outstanding Bus. Achievement, Prince George's County/DC Minority Bus. Directory Inc., 1998; named one of Md. Top 100 Women, Daily Record, 1998, 2003; recipient Spl. Achievement award, Prince George's County Chpt. NAACP, 1995, Prince George's County, Gladys Noon Spellman award for Outstanding Govt. Svc., 1996, President's award, NCCJ, 1996, Women of Achievement in Md. History, 2002. Fellow: Md. Bar Found. Inc.; mem.: J. Franklyn Bourne Bar Assn. (pres., bd. dir., treas., banquet com. chmn. 1981—, mem. Partners in Edn. Com., chmn. fund raining com. 1981—), Nat. Forum for Black Pub. Adminstr. (mem. 1993—), Am. Planning Assn. (mem. 1995—), Nat. Coun. Negro Women (mem. 1999—), Doctor/Lawyer Edn. Partnership Program, Nat. Bar Assn. (life; affiliate chpt. pres. 1981—), Prince George's County Women Lawyers Caucus (mem. 1993—), Prince George's Bar Assn. (mem. corp. bd. dir. 1989—95, 1998—2000, bd. dir., membership com., med. liasion com., mem. outreach com., chair, adminstr. law com., mem. doctor/law partnership program, mem. banquet com.), Women's Bar Assn. Md. (mem. 1985—), Md. State Bar Assn. (mem. com. on jud. selection 1985—), Delta Sigma Theta Inc. (mem. 1977—). Office: Md Nat CapitalPk and Planning Commn 14741 Governor Oden Bowie Dr Upper Marlboro MD 20772 Business E-Mail: Elizabeth.Hewlett@ppd.mncppc.org.

HEWLETT, SANDRA MARIE, clinical consultant; b. Chgo., Jan. 28, 1959; d. Stanley Vincent and Angeline Sajkiewicz. BS, Rush U., 1988, MS, 1989; postgrad., U. Ill., Chgo., 1992-95, Tex. Woman's U., 1997—. RN, Ill.; cert. BLS instr. Am. Heart Assn.; cert. breast health awareness instr.; cert. advanced oncology nurse; cert. rehab. RN and advanced cardiac life support certification. Acct., comptr. McKinsey Steel Co., Inc., Forest Park, Ill., 1976-79; exec. dir. Adolescent Youth Svcs., Village of Stone Park, Ill., 1979-81; coord. Midwest Therapeutic Assocs., Morton Grove, Ill., 1981-83, adminstr., 1983-86; in-outpatient oncology nurse Rush North Shore Med. Ctr., Skokie, Ill., 1988-89; oncology resource nurse West Suburban Hosp. Med. Ctr., Oak Park, Ill., 1989-90; oncology clin. nurse specialist Holy Family Hosp., Des Plaines, Ill., 1990-92; oncology clin. specialist, dir. autologous transplant program N.W. Oncology, Hematology S. C., Elk Grove Village, Ill., 1992-95; dir. Breast Ctr. The Dr.'s Hosp., Dallas, 1996-97; cons. Schering Plough Pharms., Mansfield, Tex., 1997—2002; dir. patient care svcs., chief nurse exec. Healthsouth Rehab. Hosp., 2002—; clin. svc. line dir. Cancer Svcs. St. Mary's Health Ctr., 2005—. Asst. prof. Wright Coll., Chgo., 1990-95; profl. adv. bd. Rainbow Hospice, Park Ridge, Ill., 1990-93; profl. educator Ill. Cancer Pain Initiative, N.W. Suburban Cook County, Ill., 1991—. Author: AIDS-Facts & Myth, 1988, (cassettes) Chemo-Induced Sequelae, 1989, Lymphoscintigraphy and Sentinel Lymph Node Biopsy, 1999, Hepatitis C in the Hispanic Community, 2004. Rush U. scholar, 1987-88; recipient Luther Christman award and scholarship Rush U./Rush Presbyn. St. Lukes Med. Ctr., 1988, Excellence in Gerontol Nursing award, 1988, Spl. Project award, 1988. Mem. Oncology Nursing Soc. (pres. elect local chpt., chmn. com., continuing edn. approval panel bd. dirs. 1999—), Am. Cancer Soc. (nurses ednl. com. 1990—, profl. educator 1990—, Grad. scholar 1988-89, bd. dirs. unit 113 1992—), Soc. Otolaryngology and Head-Neck Nurses (treas. 1990-93, legis com. 1991, editor newsletter 1991), Gamma Phi chpt. Sigma Theta Tau. Republican. Roman Catholic. Avocations: reading, writing, travel, classical and jazz music. Home and Office: 12298A Dereks Way Holts Summit MO 65043 Personal E-mail: shewlett11@aol.com. Business E-Mail: sandra.hewlett@healthsouth.com.

HEWSON, MARY MCDONALD, civic volunteer; b. Larned, Kans., Nov. 5, 1922; d. William Michael and Bernice Ulata (Gregory) McDonald; m. Kenneth Dean Hewson, June 21, 1946; children: Rebecca Hewson Lewis, Roberta Hewson Grogan, Margaret Hewson Smith. BS in Edn. cum laude, Kans. State U., 1948, BS in Psychology, 1948. Cert. secondary edn. tchr. Freshman counselor Kans. State U., 1948-49; substitute tchr. Larned Unified Sch. Dist., 1958—, tchr. gifted program, 1988, vol. gifted tchr., 1997—, vol. grief counselor for secondary students, 1996—. At home tutor, 1938—; spkr. Nat. Fraternity Blue Key Kans. State U., 1995-1998; gifted coord. vol. secondary level, 1997—; bd. mem. Kans. State U. Trustee Kans. State U. Found., Manhattan, 1980—, trustee planning and funding com., 1996—; mem. Kans. Farmers Union, McPherson, 1982—, Help Eliminate Abuse Locally, Larned, 1982—, Mental Health Assn., Larned, 1982—; spokesperson 8 counties Pawnee County Health Resource, Kans., 1992—, Ctrl. Kans. Environ. Resource Planning Group, 1992—; chmn. Swim for Kids; mem. growth com. Pawnee County Fair, 1995, mem. bldg. com., 1996—; vol. gifted tchr. aide, 1996—; mem. exec. bd. 4-H Co., mem. completed 4-H Bldg; pres. Golden Key Club Kans State Univ. Alums, 1998; spkr. Kans. State U. Alums Family Weekend, 1998. Recipient Medallion award Kans. State U., 1986, Nat. Vol. of Yr. award Coun. for Advancement and Support of Edn., 1983; named to Nat. Women's Hall of Fame, 1996, Ret. Bus. Woman of Yr., 2001. Mem. AAUW (charter), DAR (officer), Kans. Press Women (life mem., patron ednl. support 1988), Patron Menninger Found., 1990—, YMCA (bd. dirs.), Philanthropic Ednl. Orng., Kans. State U. Alumni Assn. (bd. mem., strategic planning com., student rels. com.), Wildcats for Higher Edn. Program, Golden K Club (pres. 1998, spkr. family weekend 1998), Phi Alpha Mu. Avocations: reading, collecting antiques, collecting sports cards, writing, geneaology. Home: PO Box 102 Larned KS 67550-0102

HEYDE, MARTHA BENNETT, psychologist; b. New Bern, N.C., Jan. 31, 1920; d. George Spotswood and Katherine (McIntosh) Bennett; m. Ernest R. Heyde, Aug. 17, 1946. AB, Columbia U., 1941, MA, 1949, PhD, 1959. Instr. psychol. founds and svcs. Tchrs. Coll., Columbia U., N.Y.C., 1957-59, rsch. assoc., 1960-70, cons., 1970-73. Contbg. author: (rsch. monograph) The Vocational Maturity of Ningh Grade Boys, 1960, Floundering and Trial After High Sch., 1967; co-author: Vocational Maturity During the High School Years, 1979. Mem. Barnard Coll. alumnae coun. Columbia U., 1956-61, 69—, pres. class, 1956-61, trustee, 1974-79, hon. vice chmn. Barnard Coll. Centennial, 1987-89. Mem. APA, Sigma Xi, Kappa Delta Pi, Pi Lambda Theta. Home: 530 E 23rd St Apt 8E New York NY 10010-5030

HEYDECKER, JEANNE-ELISE MARIE, school district coordinator, traditional and web marketing executive; b. NYC, Sept. 8, 1960; d. Richard Creagh and Patricia Ann (Glynn) Heydecker; m. Steven Maurice Nunes, Jan. 8, 1984 (div. 1994); child: William Creagh, III. Student, Sch. Mus. Fine Arts, Boston, 1980-82. Asst. coord. arts in edn. program Cultural Edn. Collaborative, Boston, 1985-87; art dir. Winco Identification Corp., Tyngsboro, Mass., 1987-88; desktop publ. specialist Monroe Stationers & Printers, Boston, 1988—; ind. cons. Athena Design Sys., Inc.; com. dir. SEMAPHORE, North Andover, Mass., 1993—96; mktg. mgr. Telekol Corp. (NOKIA), Waltham, Mass., 1996—98; product mgr. traffic Tripod (Terra Lycos Network Property), Williamstown, Mass., 1998—99; mktg. com. mgr. MicroE Sys. Corp., Natick, Mass., 1999—2000; founder, v.p. BuzzBolt.com/BuzzBoltMEDIA.com (Forensicon), Chgo., 2000—02; dist. coord. web svcs. Indian Prairie Sch. Dist. 204, Aurora, Ill., 2002—06; dir. mktg. Forensicon, Chgo., 2006—. Owner, designer, GraphicAwareness, Nashua, N.H., 1985—; presenter and spkr. in field. Contbr. articles to profl. jours. Vol. Nat. Dance Inst. New Eng., Boston, 1985—88; rescue vol. Greyhounds Only former racer, 2002—; vol. other non-profit arts orgns., 1985—88. Recipient Award of Excellence website Ill. chpt. Nat. Sch. Pub. Rels. Assn.'s Comm.'s Contest, 2003, Gold award Am. Assn. Webmasters, 2004, Top Best of Web winner Nat. Sch. Pub. Rels. Assn. Ctr. Digital Edn.,

2005, Publs. and Electronic Media award. Mem. Foxboro Arts Coun. (charter). Avocations: arts, travel. Home: 177 Braxton Ln Aurora IL 60504 Office: Forensicon 226 South Wabash Chicago IL 60604

HEYDMAN, ABBY MARIA, academic administrator; b. Des Moines, June 1, 1943; d. Frederick Edward and Zeta Margaret (Harrington) Hitchcock; m. Frank J. Heydman, Dec. 20, 1967; 1 child, Amy Lee. BS, Duchesne Coll., 1967; MN, U. Wash., 1969; PhD, U. Calif., Berkeley, 1987. Registered nurse, Calif. Staff nurse Bergan Mercy Hosp., Omaha, 1964—65; student health nurse St. Joseph's Hosp., Omaha, 1965—66, instr. sch. nursing, 1966—68; staff nurse Ballard Community Hosp., Seattle, 1968—69; instr. Creighton U., Omaha, 1969—70, asst. prof., 1970—74, acting dean, 1971—72; chairperson nursing dept. St. Mary's Coll., Moraga, Calif., 1978—85; dean nursing program Samuel Merritt-Saint Mary's Coll., Oakland and Moraga, Calif., 1985—93; acad. dean Samuel Merritt Coll., Oakland, 1989—99, acad. v.p., provost, 1999—2002, spl. asst. to pres., 2002—04, prof. emeritus, 2004—; prof. St. Mary's Coll. of Calif., 2005—. Lectr. U. Calif., San Francisco, 1974-75. Contbr. articles to profl. jours. Chmn. Newman Hall Community Council, Berkeley, 1985-87; bd. dirs. Oakland YMCA, 1981-83. Mem.: ACAD, ANA, AAHE, Phi Kappa Delta, Sigma Theta Tau (pres.-elect 2001—03, pres. 2003—05, treas. 2005—). Roman Catholic. Avocations: swimming, writing, travel, reading. Home: 78629 Rainswept Way Palm Desert CA 92211 E-mail: aheydman@samuelmerritt.edu.

HEYDRON, JO ANN, writer; b. Sacramento, Sept. 2, 1953; d. Herman Heydron and Mary Faye Hill; m. Herbert Pluemer, Apr. 19, 1979 (div. Nov. 1984); 1 child, Alexander William Pluemer; m. Warren Kenneth Miller, Dec. 21, 1984; children: Victor Kenneth, Mary Lauren. BA in English, U. Calif., Berkeley, 1977; MA in English, San Jose State U., 1993. Tech. editor geophys. dept. Stanford (Calif.) U., 1978-95; pub. rels. profl. Advanced Micro Devices, Sunnyvale, Calif., 1983-85; prof. English Santa Clara (Calif.) U., West Valley Coll. and Foothill Coll., San Jose area, 1993-96; freelance writer, 1994—. Adj. prof. English Evergreen Valley Coll., 2002—. Contbr. short stories, poems and book revs. to literary and mainstream mag. Mem. Green Party. Presbyterian. Personal E-mail: JHeydron@aol.com.

HEYEN, BEATRICE J., psychotherapist; b. Chgo., June 23, 1925; d. Carl Edwin and Anna W. (Carlson) Lund; m. Robert D. Heyen, June 16, 1950 (dec. Feb. 1981); children: Robin, Jefferson, Neil; m. Robert Christiansen, Nov. 24, 1984. BS, U. Chgo., 1949. Instr. Boone (Iowa) Jr. Coll., 1959-64, Rochester (Minn.) Jr. Coll., 1967-68, Winona (Minn.) State Coll., 1965-68; dir. social svc. State Clinic, Kirksville, Mo., 1968-71; supr., dir. Family Counseling Agy., Joliet, Ill., 1971-85; pvt. practice Muskegon, Mich., 1985—. Cons. Homes for Aged, Programs for Aged, Winona, 1965-68, Spl. Programs and Individuals in Psychotherapy, Muskegon, 1984—; dir. Christiansen Fine Art Gallery, North Muskegon. Mem. Gov.'s Com. on Status of Women, Iowa, 1957-62, Gov.'s Com. on Aging, Minn., 1966-68; bd. mem. Mission for Area People, Muskegon, 1998. Grantee for Pilot Projects in Svc. to Women 1971-84. Mem. AAUW, NASW, Acad. Cert. Social Workers, C.G. Jung Inst. (Chgo.). Methodist. Avocations: ecological interests, day lily gardening, contemporary art. Home: 1610 N Weber Rd North Muskegon MI 49445

HEYER, STEPHANIE, science educator; b. Phoenix, Nov. 16, 1968; adopted d. John Edward and Marietta Pace Heyer; life ptnr. Stephanie Gonzales, Mar. 27, 1999. BS in Ecology and Evolutionary Biology, U. Ariz., 1991; MA in Secondary Edn., Calif. State U., 2005. Cert. sci. tchr. Calif. Commn. Tchr. Credentialling, 1996. Naturalist intern Clemmie Gill Sch. Sci. and Conservation, Springville, Calif., 1991—93; sci. club presenter Sci. Adventures, Huntington Beach, Calif., 1993—94; mid. sch. sci. tchr. Long Beach Unified Sch. Dist., Calif., 1996—, beginning tchr. support and assessment program mentor tchr., 2001—03, 2005—06; gifted and talented edn. dept. head Stanford Mid. Sch., Long Beach, 2003—06; summer enrichment program tchr. Long Beach Unified Sch. Dist., 2003—; mentor tchr. for student tchr. Calif. State U., 2003—. Curriculum cons. and workshop presenter Long Beach Unifed Sch. Dist., 1998—; workshop presenter Calif. Assn. for the Gifted, 2003—04, Calif. Sci. Tchrs. Assn., 2004, Nat. Assn. for the Gifted, Utah, 2004, Greater L.A. Tchrs. of Sci. Assn., 2005, Nat. Sci. Tchr. Assn., 2006. Mem. Human Rights Campaign, 2003—05, Equality Calif., 2002—05. Mem.: Nat. Assn. for Gifted Children, Calif. Assn. for the Gifted, Nat. Sci. Tchr. Assn., Phi Kappa Phi Honor Soc. (recipient chpt. scholarship 2004), Pi Lambda Theta Internat. Honor Soc. Christian. Avocations: reading, music, camping, travel, movies. Personal E-mail: scienceeduc8r@hotmail.com.

HEYMAN, RONNIE FEUERSTEIN, lawyer; b. NYC, 1948; m. Samuel J. Heyman, Nov. 1970; children: Lazarus, Eleanor, Jennifer, Elizabeth. BA magna cum laude, Harvard U. Radcliffe Coll., 1969; JD, Yale U., 1973. Bar: Conn. 1973. Ptnr. Heyman & Heyman; atty., prin. Heyman Properties, Westport, Conn. Pres. women's divsn. Albert Einstein Coll. Medicine, 1985—87, hon. pres. women's divsn.; dir. Ctr. Jewish Life Duke U. Established The Heyman Chair in Legal Ethics Yale Law Sch.; The Samuel and Ronnie Heyman Ctr. for Ethics, Pub. Policy and the Professions Duke U.; The Samuel & Ronnie Heyman Ctr. on Corp. Governance Yeshiva U., bd. trustees, bd. dirs. Benjamin N. Cardozo Sch. Law; trustee Barnard Coll.; exec. com. internat. directors' coun. Guggenheim Mus.; collectors' com. Nat. Gallery, Washington. Named one of Top 200 Collectors, ARTnews mag., 2000—06. Mem.: Yale Law Sch. Assn. Avocation: Collector modern and contemporary art, especially Miró, Léger, Gorky, Giacometti, and Dubuffet. Office: Heyman Properties 333 Post Rd W Westport CT 06880

HEYMANN, JENNIFER EDEN, elementary school educator; d. Gonzalez J. Jesse and Debbie M. Gonzalez; m. Michael S. Heymann, Oct. 14, 2000. BA in History, U. N.C., Charlotte, N.C., 1997. Cert. tchr. Nat. Bd. Profl. Tchg. Standards, N.J., 2005. Tchr. J.M. Alexander Mid. Sch. Charlotte-Mecklenburg Schs., Hunterville, NC, 1998—. Team leader J.M. Alexander Mid. Sch. Charlotte-Mecklenburg Schs., 2000—, faculty adv. coun. J.M. Alexander Mid. Sch., 2000—, new tchr. mentor J.M. Alexander Mid. Sch., 2004—, lead tchr. social studies, 2005—; validator Nat. Bd. for Profl. Tchg. Standards, 2005—, assessor, 2005—. Mem.: N.C. Mid. Sch. Assn. Office Phone: 980-343-3830.

HEYMOSS, JENNIFER MARIE, librarian; b. Detroit, Apr. 14, 1958; d. John Joseph and Virginia Marie (Kern) H. BA in English and German, Wayne State U., 1980, MS in Libr. Sci., 1981. Libr. asst. Wayne State U. Librs., Detroit, 1982-83; asst. libr. Plunkett & Cooney, Detroit, 1983-86, Henry Ford Mus. & Greenfield Village Rsch. Ctr., Dearborn, Mich., 1986-90, libr., 1990-92; asst. head tech. svcs. Flint (Mich.) Pub. Libr., 1992—. Literacy vol., 1987—. Mem. ALA. Spl. Librs. Assn. (various coms. 1988-92), Mich. Libr. Assn., Pub. Librs. Assn., Phi Beta Kappa, Beta Phi Mu. Democrat. Methodist. Avocations: reading, music. Office: Flint Pub Libr 1026 E Kearsley St Flint MI 48503-1994

HEYSE, PATRICIA LYNN, school psychologist; b. Evanston, Ill., Dec. 20, 1953; d. Howard Albert Alves and Alma Svea Krans; m. Donald Keith Heyse, July 1, 1978; children: Heather, Kevin, Erin. BA in Psychology, U. Colo., 1992; MS in Counseling Psychology, Colo. State U., 1996, PhD in Counseling Psychology, 2000. Lic. profl. counselor Colo., sch. psychologist Colo. Dept. Edn. Staff counselor Learning Assistance Ctr. Colo. State U., Ft. Collins, 1994—98; evaluator Adams Cmty. Mental Health, Brighton, Colo., 1999—2001; counselor Luth. Family Svcs., Ft. Collins, 1999—2001; sch. psychologist Poudre Sch. Dist., Ft. Collins, 2001—. Mem. social skills com. Bauder Elem., Ft. Collins, 1996—98; bd. mem. Ch. Women United, Ft. Collins, 2000—. Mem.: APA, Phi Beta Kappa. Mem. United Ch. Of Christ. Avocations: reading, gardening, hiking, choir member.

HEYSTEE, SUSAN, information technology executive; Degree in math. with dual concentration in computer sci. and bus. adminstrn. (with honors), U. Waterloo. Sr. positions with SSA Global; v.p. consulting practice Baan Americas, 1997, v.p., svcs., sr. v.p. field ops., pres., 2001—02, exec. v.p. worldwide solutions sales and delivery, 2002—04; v.p., area gen. mgr., Midwest area Novell, Inc., 2004—05, pres. Americas, 2005—, also mem. worldwide mgmt. com. Office: Novell Inc 404 Wyman Ste 500 Waltham MA 02451*

HEYWOOD, ANNE, artist, educator, author; b. Newport, RI, Sept. 15, 1951; d. Albert Paul and Eileen Frances (Laforest) Boretti; m. Ciro DiGiovanni, May 24, 1969 (div. 1980); 1 child, Carlo; m. Henry Robert Heywood, Nov. 9, 1985. BA in Art summa cum laude, Bridgewater (Mass.) State Coll. Tchr. drawing and pastels Silver Lake Reg. H.S. Adult Edn., Kingston, Mass., 1991—95; art educator pastels, drawing South Shore Art Ctr., Cohasset, Mass., 1996—; art educator pastels Fuller Mus. Art, Brockton, Mass., 1996—2003, Pastel Painters Soc. Cape Cod, Barnstable, Mass., 1997; art educator drawing Swinburne Sch., Newport, RI, 1995, Round Top Ctr. for Arts, Damariscotta, Maine, 1996, 2004; workshop instr. Northwest Pastel Soc., Gig Harbor, Wash., 2002. Pastel demonstrator, spkr. in field; artist residency Carillon Beach Inst., Panama City, Fla., 2002; juror Renaissance in Pastel, 1999; juror N.W. Pastel Soc., 2002, workshop instr., Wash., 02. Author: Pastels Made Easy, 2003; contbg. artist: Best of Pastel, 1996, Landscape Inspirations, 1997, Best of Sketching and Drawing 1999; one-woman shows include East Bridgewater (Mass.) Pub. Libr., 1992, 95, Mass. Audubon Soc., Marshfield, 1992, South Shore Natural Sci. Ctr., Norwell, Mass., 1993, Marion (Mass.) Art Ctr., 1994, Fuller Art Mus., Brockton, Mass., 1995, 2000, Passage Gallery, South Shore Art Ctr., Cohasset, Mass., 1996, 98, Sparrow House, Plymouth, Mass., 1997, 2000, 04, Landmark Bldg., Boston, 1999; exhibited in group shows at Duxbury Art Assn., Mass., 1993, Trenton (N.J.) State Coll., 1994, Bridgewater State Coll., 1994, Zullo Gallery, Medfield, Mass., 1995, 99, 2001, Maine Art Gallery, Wiscasset, 1995, Pastel Soc. Am., N.Y.C., 1995, 97, Internat. Assn. Pastel Socs., 1997, 99 (Convention Image award), Left Bank Gallery, Wellfleet, Mass., 1997, Gallery at C3TV, South Yarmouth, Mass., 1997, Salmagundi Club, N.Y. 1999 (George Inness Jr. Meml. award for pastel), Degas Soc., La. (La. Watercolor Soc. award of merit), Colo. History Mus., Fla. Pastel Soc., Soc. Western Artists, Mass., 1999, Pastel Soc. of the West Coast, 2001, Audubon Artists, 2001, Newington-Cropsey Found., N.Y., 2001, Attleboro Mus. Ctr. for Arts, 2003; pvt. collections; contbr. articles to profl. jours.; editor Pastel Painter's Soc. Cape Cod newsletter, 1998-99, bd. dirs. Sec. East Bridgewater Arts Coun., 1992-97, Artists Cir. at Fuller Mus., Brockton, Mass., 1995-97; juror Renaissance in Pastel, 1999, Northwest Pastel Soc., Harbor, Wash., 2002. Recipient 1st pl. drawing East Bridgewater Art Festival, 1991, 1st pl. awards Wickford (R.I.) Art Assn., 1992, Taunton (Mass.) Art Assn., 1993, South Shore Art Ctr. Blue Ribbon Members Show, Cohasset, 1994, Fuller Art Mus., Brockton, 1994, 1st pl. pastels Plymouth Guild May Members Show, 1994, award Providence Art Club, 1996, award of distinction All New Eng. Color Show, Cohasset, 1996; Vt. Studio Ctr. Residency fellow, 1999. Mem.: Copley Soc. (artist mem.), Nat. Assn. Women Artists (D.Wu and Elsie Jeck-Key Meml. award 2000), Oil Pastel Assn./United Pastellists Am. (signature mem.), Pastel Soc. Am. (signature mem., Holbein award 1995), Conn. Pastel Soc. (signature mem.), Pastel Painters Soc. Cape Cod (bd. dirs. 2000—, founding mem., signature mem., Canson-Talens award 1997), Allied Artists of Am., Associated Pastelists on Web (signature mem.), Am. Artists Profl. League, Internat. Assn. Pastel Socs. (bd. dirs. 2006—, Masters Cir. award 2005), Salmagundi Club. Roman Catholic. Avocations: reading, walking, biking, choir. Address: PO Box 651 East Bridgewater MA 02333 E-mail: aheywood@anne-heywood.com.

HEYWOOD, HARRIETT, lawyer, consultant; b. Durham, NC; d. Chester; m. James N. Washingtron, Sept. 1985; 1 child, James. BA, Johnson C. Smith U., 1969; JD, Howard U., 1972. Bar: NJ 1972, DC 1986. Office gen. counsel US Dept. Vet. Affairs, Washington, 1972—77, sr. atty., 1977—98, sr. atty., office discrimination complaints adjudication, 1998—2001, assoc. dir., ctr. women vets., 2001—04, coord. debt collection program, 1981—83, mgr., fed. womens program, 1996—97; atty., pvt. practice Silver Spring, Md., 2004—. Dist. ethics com. mem. Essex County Bar Assn., 1979—81; def. adv. com. women in svcs. mem. Dept. of Def., Pentagon, Arlington, Va., 2000—01. Vice chair, dist. 14 Montgomery county Dem. Club, Silver Sping, 2004—; bible study tchr. Peoples Cmty. Bapt. Ch., Silver Spring, 2000—. Named one of 25 Influential Black Women for 2003, The Network Jour. Mem.: Nat. Coun. Negro Women (Potomac Valley chpt.), DC Bar Assn., Delta Sigma Theta (chaplain 1995—, historian 2003—, Women with a Purpose award 2001). Baptist. Avocations: piano, reading, tennis.

HEYZER, NOELEEN, international organization official; b. Singapore; BA, MA, U. Singapore; PhD in Social Scis., Cambridge U., Eng. Former head, policy adviser, gender and develop. program Asian and Pacific Develop. Ctr.; former chair Sub-Group on Gender of UN Inter-agency Task Force on Women's Empowerment; exec. dir. UN Devel. Fund for Women (UNIFEM), 1994—. Sociology tutor U. Singapore; keynote spkr. for numerous univs. and orgns.; established Trust Fund in Support of Actions to Eliminate Violence Against Women, 1997; founding mem. DAWN, numerous Regional and Internat. Women's Networks; faculty mem. Salzburg Seminar Session 353, Sustainable Rural Cmty. Develop., 1998; bd. dir. internat. organizations working for social justice and gender equality. Author: Gender, Economic Growth and Poverty, The Trade in Domestic Workers, Working Women in South-East Asia. Recipient Global Tolerance award for humanitarian svc., Friends of the UN, 2000, Lifetime Achievement award, Inst. for Leadership Devel., 2000, Woman of Distinction award, NGO Com. on UN Commn. Status of Women, 2003, UNA-Harvard Leadership award, 2003, Leadership award, Ending Violence Against Women, Mt. Sinai Hosp., N.Y.C., 2004, UN Assn. Greater Boston-Harvard U. Kennedy Sch., 2004, Dag Hammarskjöld medal, 2004, Women Who Make a Difference award, Nat. Coun. Rsch. Women, 2005; fellow, Inst. Devel. Studies U. Sussex. Mem.: Isis Internat., Asia Pacific Women in Law and Devel., Devel. Alternatives with Women for a New Era. Achievements include playing a critical role in Security Council's adoption of Resolution 1325 on Women, Peace & Security & in ensuring that it's implemented in order to make a difference to women's lives on the ground. Office: UNIFEM 304 E 45th St 15th fl New York NY 10017

HIATT, FLORENCE ELLEN, musician; b. Elwood, Ind. d. Merrill Paul and Mildred Lenore (Knotts) H.; m. Frank Alvin Robertson, Sept. 1, 1948 (div. 1963); children: Lana Glynn, Bradley Reid. Attended, Cin. Conservatory Music, 1945—49; studied with Nadia Boulanger, Ecoles d'Art et Musique, Fontainebleau, France, 1961; MusB, Auburn U., Ala., 1964; MusM, Ind. U., Bloomington, Ind., 1972; postgrad., Fla. State U., Tallahassee, 1984—85. Mem. faculty piano and organ Auburn U., 1964-65; asst. mus. dir. then mus. dir. Lakewood Mus. Playhouse, Barnesville, Pa., 1971-72; mus. dir. Clinton Mus. Theatre, Conn., 1974-75; organist, choirmaster St. Thomas Episcopal Ch., Columbus, 1960—70; mus. dir. Springer Opera House, Springer Theatre, Springer Ballet and Sch. Theatre Arts, Columbus, 1971—84. Music dir. Temple Israel, Columbus, 1970—; mem. organ and harpsichord faculty Columbus Coll., 1982—86; keybd. specialist Columbus Symphony Orchestra, 1967—91; organist St. Luke United Meth. Ch., Columbus, 1984—99; archael. rschr. Budapest, Hungary, 1994. Author, composer choral, organ and vocal music. Wessex Theol. Coll. hon. fellow, Eng. Mem. Royal Coll. Organists, Am. Guild Organists (cert., past dean), Guild of Temple Musicians, Alliance Francaise, Mortar Bd. Soc. Home: 2801 Gardenia St Columbus GA 31906-2130 Personal E-mail: piperflo@charter.net.

HIATT, JANE CRATER, arts agency administrator; b. Winston-Salem, NC, May 26, 1944; d. Howard Rondthaler Jr. and Irene (Sides) Crater; m. K.W. Everhart Jr. (div. June 1973); m. Wood Coleman Hiatt, May, 1978; 1 child, Jonathan David. BA, U. N.C., 1966; MA, Wake Forest U., 1972. Eng. tchr. Winston-Salem (N.C.)/Forsyth County Schs., 1966-70; exec. dir. Tenn. Com. for the Humanities, Nashville, 1973-77; cons. various ednl. and cultural agys. Ocean Springs, Miss., 1978-80; asst. dir. Miss. Humanities Coun., Jackson, Miss., 1981-85; exec. dir. Arts Alliance of Jackson and Hinds County, Miss., 1985-89, Miss. Arts Commn., Jackson, 1989-95; interim dir. Miss. Mus. Art, 2001. Participant Arts Leadership Inst. of Humphrey Inst. for Pub. Affairs, Mpls., 1986, Leadership, Jackson, 1987; interim exec. dir. Miss. Mus. Art, 2001. Co-editor Peoples of the South, 1976; exec. producer (TV series) The South with John Siegenthaler, 1976; host, reporter Miss. Ednl. TV, Jackson, 1981-87. Active Miss. Econ. Coun., 1986—87, Miss. R&D Coun., 1984—88; pres. Mental Health Assn. of Hinds County, Jackson, 1986; treas. Miss. for Ednl. Broadcasting, 1987, 1988, 1989, Premier Class Leadership, Jackson, 1987, 1988; cmty. adv. coun. Jr. League of Jackson, 1995—; mem. representing Miss. Friends of Art and Preservation in Embassies Millennium Com.; bd. dirs. Miss. Mus. Art, 2000—, Friends of Univ. Press, 2004—; bd. dirs. Miss. state com. Nat. Mus. Women in Arts. Recipient Heritage award City of Biloxi, 1984. Mem.: Women's Fund (benefactor and steering com. 2002—), Greater Jackson Found. (bd. dirs. 1996—, chmn. 2002—03), Pub. Edn. Forum (bd. dirs. 1993—), Miss. Ctr. for Nonprofits (vice chmn., bd. dirs. 1993—96, adv. bd. 1997—), So. Arts Fedn. (bd. dirs. 1989—95), Nat. Assembly State Arts Agys. (bd. dirs. 1992—95, 2d v.p. 1995), Nat. Coun. on Arts, Nat. Assembly Local Arts Agys., Phi Beta Kappa. Home: 4 Waterstone Pl Jackson MS 39211-5987 E-mail: hiattw@bellsouth.net.

HIBBARD, CHRISTINE, psychotherapist, educator, minister; b. Chgo., July 5, 1948; d. George G. and Gudrun Curry; m. Harlan David Hibbard, Sept. 27; children: Ryan, Shannon. BA, U. Colo., 1974, MA, 1978; PhD, Sierra U., Costa Mesa, Calif., 1989. Cert. biofeedback therapist; ordained interfaith minister One Spirit Seminary, N.Y., 2005. Naturalist, rschr. U. Colo., Boulder, 1974—78, Boulder HS, Colo., 1976—79; co-mgr. Actualizations, 1979—80; dir. Louisville Biofeedback Clinic & Stress Mgmt. Clinic, Colo., 1980—; psychotherapist Family Med. Assocs., Louisville, Colo., 1980—. Prof. Naropa U., Boylaer, Colo., 2001—, Holos U., Mo., 2001—. Author: (book) In Progress, 2005. Trauma worker, tchr., Kosavo, 1999—, Israel, 1999—, Uganda, 1999—; hospice chaplain, bereavemnet counselor Boulder, 1982—; hosp. chaplain, 1982. Fellow: Biofeedback Cert. of Am. (pres. 1985—); mem.: ACCESS Counseling (bd.), ISSSEEM (pres. 1998—2002, bd. mem.). Avocations: birdwatching, hiking. Office: Family Med Assocs 1200 W South Boulder Rd Lafayette CO 80026-3546

HIBBARD, JENNIFER SPONHALTZ, mental health services professional; b. San Antonio, Tex., June 28, 1977; d. Burt E. and Joyce Budnik Sponhaltz; m. Mace Andrew Hibbard, June 1, 2002. MA in Profl. Counseling, SW Tex. State U., 2003. Cert. counselor Nat. Bd. Cert. Counselors, 2003, lic. profl. counselor Ga. Clinician GRN Cmty. Svc. Bd., Conyers, Ga., 2003—; mental health profl. Northside Psychiat., Conyers, Ga., 2004—. Mem.: ACA (assoc.). Office Phone: 770-918-6677. E-mail: sponhaltz@hotmail.com.

HIBBARD, JUDITH USHER, obstetrician; b. Chgo. m. Mark C. Hibbard. Studied, Edgewood Coll., Madison, Wis., 1966—68; BS in Secondary Edn., Gen. sci. & History, U. Wis., Madison, 1968—72, MS in sci. Edn., 1968—72; studied, Coll. of DuPage, Glen Ellen, Ill., 1977—78, Ill. Benedictine Coll., Lisle, 1978—79; MD, Loyola U., Maywood, Ill., 1979—82. Diplomate Nat. Bd. Med. Examiners, 1983, Am. Bd. Ob-Gyn., 1990, in Maternal-Fetal Medicine 1991. Sci. tchr. Verona Mid. Sch., Wis., 1970—72, Toledo Jr. H.S., Oreg., 1972—74; sci. and math. tchr. Mesquite H.S., Ridgecrest, Calif., 1975—77; resident, ob-gyn. U. Chgo., 1982—86, fellow, instr., maternal-fetal medicine, 1986—89, asst. prof., maternal-fetal medicine, 1989—96, acting dir., ob-gyn. ultrasound, 1999—2000, assoc. prof., clin. ob-gyn., 1996—2001, fellowship dir., maternal-fetal medicine, 2001—, prof., maternal-fetal medicine, 2001—, sect. chief, maternal-fetal medicine, 2003—. Reviewer for various jours. Recipient Hon. Sci. award, Bausch and Lomb, 1968, Scholastic Achievement award, Am. Med. Women's Assn., 1982, Young Investigator's award, Am. Diabetes Assn., 1988, Faculty Devel. Tng. award, Berlex Found., 1991, Young Investigator's Travel award, NIH, 1994. Mem.: Chgo. Soc. Perinatal Obstetricians, Chgo. Gyn. Soc., Ill. Perinatal Assn., Ctrl. Assn. of Ob-Gyn., Internat. Soc. of Ultrasound in Ob-Gyn., Internat. Soc. for Study of Hypertension in Pregnancy, Nat. Perinatal Assn., Soc. Obstetric Medicine, Soc. Maternal Fetal Medicine, Am. Coll. Ob-Gyn., Pi Lambda Theta, Alpha Omega Alpha. Office: Dept Ob-Gyn U Ill 820 S Wood St MC808 Chicago IL 60612

HIBBARD, SUSAN CLAYTON, secondary school educator; b. Trenton, NJ, Apr. 14, 1948; d. James John and Vincenza Spera Clayton; m. Peter Charles Hibbard, Mar. 24, 1973; children: Krista Suzanne Reddington, Stephen James. BA, Trenton State Coll., NJ, 1970; MS, U. Del., Newark, 1972. Cert. supr. NJ, tchr. NJ. Biology tchr. Upper Freehold Regional Bd. Edn., Allentown, NJ, 1970—78, St. Joseph HS, Toms River, NJ, 1978—82, Toms River Regional Sch. Dist., 1982—. Tchg. asst. U. Del., Newark, 1970—72. Pres. Ocean County area Zonta Internat., Toms River, 2004—06; tech. dir. Ocean County Citizens for Clean Water, Toms River, NJ, 1983—2006; deacon Presbyn. Ch. of Toms River, 2005—, choir mem., 1979—. Christa McAuliffe fellow, US Dept. Edn., 1990. Presbyterian. Avocations: quilting, needlecrafts, music, travel. Home: 12 Pine Fork Dr Toms River NJ 08755-5121 Office: Toms River HS South 55 Hyers St Toms River NJ 08753 Office Phone: 732-505-5735. Personal E-mail: udelstarfish@aol.com.

HIBBEN, BARBARA ANN PANDZIK, museum administrator, foreign service officer; b. North Island, Calif., Sept. 22, 1943; d. George Richard and Marguerite Elizabeth (Holzenberg) Pandzik; m. Stuart Galloway Hibben, May 29, 1994; children by previous marriage: Jessica Marguerite Hadley, Amanda Marie, Cara Elizabeth. BA, U. Nebr., 1965; postgrad., Yale U., 1966-67; MFA in Painting, George Washington U., 1980. Asst. to dir. The Phillips Collection, Washington, 1983-86, exec. asst. to dir., 1986-93; fgn. svc. officer U.S. Dept. State, Washington, 1993—. Artist paintings and drawings in numerous pvt. collections. Birdwatcher Md. Ornithol. Soc., Bethesda, 1990-93. Woodrow Wilson fellow, 1965-66. Mem. Diplomatic and Consular Officers Retired (assoc.), Phi Beta Kappa. Office: Am Embassy Cairo Unit 64900 # 7 APO AE 09839-4900

HIBBEN, CELIA LYNN, psychiatric mental health nurse practitioner; b. Birmingham, Ala., July 16, 1953; d. Kenneth Gordon and Bobbie Rae (Barnum) H. BSN, U. Tex., Tyler, 1990; postgrad., U. Tex., Arlington, 1993-97. Relief house supr. Glenoaks Hosp. (Psychiatric Hosp.), Greenville, Tex., 1990-92; coord. psychiat. nursing Tex. Longevity Healthcare Inst., Ft. Worth, 1992-93; case mgr., home health psychiat. cons. All Saints Hosp., Ft. Worth, 1993-97; collaborative practice with Dr. Robert Guzman, 1996; health care cons., 1996-97; sr. clin. devel. analyst Care Centric Solutions, Duluth, Ga., 1996—; corp. dir. profl. svcs. Guardian Health Care, 2002—. Vol. AIDS Outreach Ctr., Ft. Worth, 1991-96. Recipient Outstanding Clin. Achievement award U. Tex., Arlington, 1996; ANA scholar, 1990. Mem. Dallas Songwriters Assn., Sigma Theta Tau, Alpha Chi. Republican. Baptist. Avocations: guitar, writing and performing music. Home: PO Box 1451 Burleson TX 76097

HIBBS, DAWN WILCOX, elementary school educator; b. Buffalo, Sept. 30, 1940; d. Alfred and Helena Pavone; m. Leroy Wilcox, July 18, 1964 (div. June 1981); children: Brett Alan, Dana Lee; m. Harold Keith Hibbs, Dec. 27, 1986. Tchr. 5th grade North Tonawanda (N.Y.) Schs., 1961-63, Los Alamos (N.Mex.) Schs., 1963-64; tchr. 6th grade Kenmore (N.Y.) Schs., 1965-69; caseworker Erie County Dept. Social Svcs., Buffalo, 1980-84; elem. tchr. Lynwood (Calif.) Schs., 1986-88, Santa Ana (Calif.) Schs., 1988-96, intermediate tchr., 1996—2002, textbook advisor, grant writer, 1996-97; owner IDentaGLASS. Mentor new tchrs. Santa Ana Schs., 1991-92; instr. Reading to Learn programs, 1999-2000, tchr. cabinet rep., 1998-2000, mem. sch. site coun., 2000-2001; mem. Oreg. project, 2000-02. Patentee eyewear identification labels and design. Pres. Parents Without Ptnrs., Tonawanda, 1983; treas. Madame Helena Modjeska Chpt. of Guilds of Orange County Performing Arts Ctr., Calif., 2006—. Mem. AAUW (treas. 1995-96, EF fund prize chmn. 1997, membership v.p. 1997-2000, mem. membership com. Calif. 1998-2001, co-pres. Orange County Interbr. 1999-2000, tech. trek coord., 1999-2001, v.p. Mission Viejo-Saddleback Valley br. LAF 2000-2001, pres. 2003-2004), Class Act Investors (treas. 1999-2006).

HIBEL, EDNA, artist; b. Boston, Jan. 13, 1917; d. Abraham Bert and Lena (Rubin) H.; m. Theodore Plotkin, Jan. 7, 1940; children: Jon, Andy, Richard. Student, Boston Mus. Sch. of Fine Arts, 1938, 41-42; study abroad, Boston

Mus. Sch. of Fine Arts, Mexico, 1939; DHA (hon.), U. for Peace UN, 1988; LHD, Mt. St. Mary's Coll., 1988, Eureka Coll., 1995. Pvt. art tchr., Boston, 1957-58; art dir. Edna Hibel Gallery, Palm Beach, Fla., 1960—, owner, mgr. Boston and Palm Beach, Fla., 1960—; curator Hibel Mus. of Art, Palm Beach, Fla., 1977—. Prime organizer First Boston Arts Festival, 1954; judge statewide art competition, Tenn., 1983, Frances Hook Found. Scholarship Competition, Wis., 1985. Artist Soc. of the Little Flower, Darien, Ill., 1985-87; artist Lake Kezar Cookbook, Cordon Blue award, 1982; artist, author several art books; TV prodn.; Hibel's Russian Palette, on location in the Soviet Union, 1990, shown on PBS stas. across U.S.; commn. by Found. for Nat. Archives to Commemorate 75th Anniversary of ratification of 19th amendment to U.S. Constitution granting women the universal right to vote, 1995. Active Hibel Mus. Art. Recipient Woman of Yr. award State of N.J., 1979, Presdl. award Arts for the Handicapped, 1985, Spirit of Life award City of Hope, 1984, 94, Humanitarian of Yr. award, Boy's Town, Italy, 1994, Leonardo Da Vinci World award of arts, World Cultural Coun., 2001, Lifetime Achievement award, Women in Visual Arts, 2001; Ruth B. Sturtevant traveling fellow Boston Mus. Sch. Fine Arts, 1939. Fellow Royal Soc. of Art, World Acad. of Art and Sci. (first painter to be elected as such), Edna Hibel Soc. Lodges: B'nai B'rith (hon. founder Edna Hibel unit 1986). Democrat. Jewish. First fgn. woman artist to exhibit in People's Republic of China, 1986, and Yugoslavia, 1988; first Am. woman artist to exhibit porcelain art in United Kingdom, 1987, also first in Costa Rica, USSR, 1990; artwork selected for UN Commemorative Postal Issue, 1986; commd. by Found. for Nat. Archives, 1995.*

HIBNER, RAE A., risk management executive, medical/surgical nurse; b. Libertyville, Ill., Jan. 31, 1956; d. Richard Douglas (dec.) and Raelene Ann (Warren) Lyons; children: Kevin John, Thomas Ivan. Diploma, Luth. Gen. Hosp. Sch. Nursing, Park Ridge, Ill., 1979; BS in Nursing, U. Ill., Chgo., 1984; MS, No. Ill. U., 1987. RN. Staff nurse Cardiac Telemetry Luth. Gen. Hosp., 1979-81, staff nurse CCU, 1981-82; staff nurse coronary ICU U. Ill. Hosp., Chgo., 1982-83, asst. head nurse coronary ICU, 1983-86, head nurse coronary ICU, 1986-88, staff nurse coronary-med. ICU, 1988-90; coord. utilization rev. Parkside Health Mgmt. Corp., Chgo., 1989-91; asst. dir. utilization mgmt. U. Ill., Chgo., 1991-93; risk mgr. Rush-Presbyn.-St. Lukes Med. Ctr., Chgo., 1993-96; claims cons. CNA Ins. Cos., Chgo., 1996; dir. claims corp. accts. CNA Health Pro, Chgo., 1996-2001; claims cons. CNA, HealthPro, 2001—02; dir. risk mgmt. Loyola Univ. Med. Ctr., Maywood, Ill., 2002—05; sr. risk mgmt. cons. Zurich N.Am. Ins. Co., 2006—. Roman Catholic. Avocations: needlepoint, crochet, swimming, camping.

HICKCOX, LESLIE KAY, health educator, consultant; b. Berkeley, Calif., May 12, 1951; d. Ralph Thomas and Marilyn Irene (Stump) H. BA, U. Redlands, 1973; MA in Exercise Physiology, U. of the Pacific, 1975; MEd in Curriculum Teaching, Columbia U., 1979; MEd in Health Edn., Oreg. State U., 1987, MEd in Guidance & Counseling, 1988, EdD in Edn., 1991. Cert. Calif. State C.C. instr. (life). Phys. edn. instr., dir. intramurals SUNY, Stony Brook, 1981-83; instr. health edn. Linn-Benton C.C., Oreg., 1985-94; instr. human studies and comm. studies Marylhurst U., Portland, 1987-96, 2002—04; edn. supr., instr. Oreg. State U., Corvallis, 1988-90; health and phys. edn. instr. Portland C.C., 1994-95; instr. health edn. U. Auckland, New Zealand, 1991; instr., coord. dept. health, phys. edn. and recreation Rogue C.C., Grants Pass, Oreg., 1995-97; assoc. prof., coord. health and phys. edn. Western Mont. Coll., Dillon, Mont., 1997-99; asst. prof. health edn. Northeastern Ill. U., Chgo., 1999—2002; health edn. instr. Portland C.C., 2003—05; assoc. prof. health edn. West Liberty (W.Va.) State Coll., 2005—. Founder Experiential Learning Inst., 1992—, found., Lilly N.W. High Edn. Tchg. Conf., 1996; founding v.p. Home Health Diagnostics, Portland, Oreg., 1996, dir. health info., 1996-2003. Contbr. articles to profl. jours. Mem. ASCD, Am. Pub. Health Assn., Am. Sch. Health Assn., Am. Assn. Health Edn., Higher Edn. R&D Soc. Australasia, Coun. for Adult and Experiential Learning, Adult Higher Edn. Alliance, Kappa Delta Phi, Phi Delta Kappa. Home: 700 Northwood Ct Apt 102 Wheeling WV 26003-2683 Office Phone: 304-336-8132. Personal E-mail: lesliekayh@msn.com. Business E-Mail: lhickcox@westliberty.edu.

HICKEY, DELINA ROSE, retired education educator; b. N.Y.C., Mar. 25, 1941; d. Robert Joseph and Marie (Ripa) Hickey; m. David Andrews; 1 child, Jon Robert. BS in Edn., SUNY, Oneonta, 1963; MA, Manhattan Coll., Riverdale, N.Y., 1967; EdD in Counselor Edn. and Psychology, U. Idaho, Moscow, 1971; postgrad., Harvard U., Cambridge, Mass., 1995. Sch. tchr., counselor pub. schs., Westchester, NY, 1963-68; part-time instr. psychologist St. Thomas Aquinas Coll., Sparkhill, NY, 1971-72; asst. prof. edn. Nathaniel Hawthorne Coll., Antrim, NH, 1972-75; mem. faculty Keene (N.H.) State Coll., 1975—2000, assoc. prof. edn., 1978-87, prof., coord. faculty, 1987-2000, interim dean profl. studies, 1887, v.p. student affairs, 1990-2000; ret., 2000. Mem. adv. coun. Title IV, 1979—82; assoc. in edn. Harvard U., 1984—85, Inst. Ednl. Mgmt., 1995; chmn. curriculum Acad. Life Long Learning U. S.C., Aiken, SC, 2003—04; presenter in field. Contbr. articles to ednl. jours. Bd. trustees Hist. Aiken Found., 2002—04, Smart Growth Aiken, 2000—; pres., co-founder HMS Assocs. Ednl. Cons., 2002—; pres. Hist. Aiken Found., 2005—; mem. N.H. Ho. of Reps., 1981—85; v.p. Hist. Aiken Found., 2004—05; trustee Big Bros.-Big Sisters, Keene, 1978—80, Family Planning Svcs. S.W. N.H., 1976—85, Monadnock Family Svcs., 1995—97, Monadnock Hospice, 1994—96, chmn. pers. com.; mem. N.H. Juvenile Conf. Com., 1976—81; bd. dirs. Cheshire Med. Ctr.; trustee Cheshire Med. Assn., 1996—2001; pres. bd. dirs. CHESCO; trustee Home Health Care, 1998—2001. Fellow, Nat. Ctr. Rsch. in Vocat. Edn., 1984—85; grantee, Marion Jasper Whitney Found. Mem.: AAUW (vice chmn. programs 2002—), N.H. Assn. Student Pers. Adminstrs. (adv. bd.), N.H. Pers. and Guidance Assn., New Eng. Rsch. Orgn., New Eng. Assn. Tchrs. and Educators, Am. Vocat. Assn., Nat. Assn. Student Pers. Adminstrs. (adv. com. region I, editor, chief Net Results electronic mag. 1997-99), N.H. Order Women Legislators. Office: HMS Ednl Cons Aiken SC 29801 Personal E-mail: delhickey@bellsouth.net.

HICKEY, ENA VARNEY, elementary school educator; b. Cin., Feb. 29, 1956; d. Elster and Willa Dean (Mercer) Varney, Jr.; m. Daniel Thomas Hickey, July 31, 1987; children: Daniel Thomas Jr., William Joseph. BA, Miami U., 1977, MA. Cert. tchr., Ohio. Tchr., fourth grade N.W. Dist./Harrison (Ohio) Elem., 1977-78; tchr., second grade West Clermont dist./Withamsville Elem., Cin., 1978-93, tchr., kindergarten, 1993—98; tchr., thrid grade Williamsburg Elem., Ohio, 1998—. Mem. Ohio Edn. Assn., NEA, Internat. Reading Assn. Republican. Presbyterian. Avocations: crafts, cooking. Home: 3381 Twin Bridges Rd Williamsburg OH 45176-9699 Office: Williamsburg Elem 839 Spring St Williamsburg OH 45176

HICKEY, LADY JANE, librarian, minister; d. William Edgar and Betty Jane (Black) Hickey. BS in edn., U. Tulsa, 1969—71; MLS, Drexel U., Phila., Pa., 1981—85; MBA, St. Mary's U., San Antonio, Tex., 1995—98. Cert. Ordination Light Ho. Gospel Fellowship, 1969, Agape, Internat., 2001. Cataloging technician Messiah Coll., Grantham, Pa., 1979—86; catalog libr. St. Mary's U. Law Libr., San Antonio, 1986—2001; head cataloging unit Sam Houston State U., Huntsville, Tex., 2001—. Author: (reviews) Am. Reference Books Ann.; author: (reviewer) books and online jours.; co-author: (guides) Layperson's Guide to Legal Rsch.; reviewer: Choice; contbr. encyclopedia chpt. on social issues in Am., chpts. to encyclopedias. Mem.: ALA, AAUW, AAUP, Assn. of Christian Librians, Tex. Libr. Assn., Southwestern Assn. Law Librs., Assn. Libr. Collections and Tech. Svcs., North Am. Serials Interest Group, Am. Assn. Law Librs. Christian. Avocations: water aerobics, reading, dog obedience. Office: Sam Houston State U PO Box 2281 Huntsville TX 77341

HICKEY, WIN E(SPY), former state legislator, social worker; b. Rawlins, Wyo. d. David P. and Eugenia (Blake) Espy; children: John David, Paul Joseph. BA, Loretto Heights Coll., 1933; postgrad., U. Utah, 1934, Sch. Social Svc., U. Chgo., 1936; LLD (hon.), U. Wyo., 1991. Dir. Carbon County Welfare Dept., 1935—36; field rep. Wyo. Dept. Welfare, 1937—38; dir. Red Cross Club, Europe, 1942—45; commr. Laramie County, Wyo., 1973—80; mem. Wyo. Senate, 1980—90; dir. United Savs. & Loan, Cheyenne; active Joint Powers Bd. Laramie County and City of Cheyenne. Pub. Where the Deer and the Antelope Play, 1967; pres. Meml. Hosp. of Laramie County, 1986—88, Wyo. Transp. Mus., 1990—92; pres. county and state mental health assn., 1959—63; trustee U. Wyo., 1967—71; active Gov. Residence Found., 1991—93, Wyo. Transp. Mus., 1993—; trustee St. Mary's Cathedral, 1986—; active Nat. Coun. Cath. Women; pres., bd. dirs. U. Wyo. Found., 1986—87; chmn. adv. coun. div. cmty. programs Wyo. Dept. Health and Social Svcs.; chair Am. Heritage Assocs. of U. Wyo., 1992—96. Named Outstanding Alumna, Loretto Heights Coll., 1959, Woman of Yr., Commn. for Women, 1988, United Med. Ctr., Cheyenne, 1998, Legislator of Yr., Wyo. Psychologists Assn., 1988, Family of the Yr., U. Wyo., 1995, Person of Yr., United Med. Ctr., Cheyenne, Wyo., 1998. Mem.: Altrusa Club (Cheyenne).

HICKLE, SHALON R., physical therapist; d. Daniel R. and Cheryl A. Hickle. BS, High Point (NC) U., 2000; PhD in Phys. Therapy, Temple U., Phila., 2003. Lic. phys. therapist Pa., cert. Kinesio Taping Practitioner. Phys. therapist Lancaster Gen. Hosp., Pa., 2003—. Mem.: Nat. Athletic Trainers Assn. (cert.). Avocations: reading, travel, swimming, billiards. Office: Lancaster Gen Hosp 2100 Harrisburg Pike Lancaster PA 17601 Office Phone: 717-544-3103.

HICKMAN, ELIZABETH PODESTA, retired counselor; b. Livingston, Ill., Sept. 30, 1922; d. Louis and Della (Martin) Podesta; m. Franklin Jay Hickman, Mar. 17, 1944 (dec.); children: Virginia Hickman Hellstern, Franklin. BE summa cum laude, Ea. Ill. State U.; MA, George Washington U., 1966, EdD (Exxon Found.-Raskob Found. grantee), 1979; postgrad., U. Chgo., 1945, U. Va., 1964-66; postgrad. (fellow), Northeastern U., 1967-68. Lic. counselor, Va. Tchr. pub. schs., Ill., Ohio, Va., Naples, Italy, 1944-64; dir. coll. transfer guidance Maymount Coll. Va., Arlington, 1964-67, dir. Counceling Ctr., 1974-81, assoc. dean counseling and residence life, 1981-84; cmty. counselor Divsn. Mass. Employment Security, Newton, 1968-69; tchr. English conversation, Fuchu, Japan, 1969-73; placement dir., career counselor Coll. of Gt. Falls, Mont., 1973-74; assoc. rschr. George Washington U., Washington, 1986. Lectr. Far East divsn. U. Md., Fuchu, 1971-73; spl. advisor Internat. Ranger Camps, Denmark and Switzerland, 1974-81; spl. cons. Internat. Quaker Sch., Werkhoven, The Netherlands, 1959-63; mem. steering com. Pres.'s Com. on Employment of Handicapped, 1974-95. Vol., ARC, 1967-68, Family Svcs., 1954-75, White House Agy. Liaison, 1986—, Kennedy Ctr. Adminstrn., Washington, 1984—, Arlington Free Clinic, 2000-02. With WAVES, 1943-44. Recipient Disting. Alumnus award Ea. Ill. U., 1984. Mem. Brent Soc., Rose Soc., Potomac (Ill) Soc., Italian Am. Soc., Marymount U. Angels Soc., Women's Com. Nat. Symphony Orch., Washington Opera Guild, Delta Epsilon Sigma, Pi Lambda Theta. Roman Catholic. Home: 4708 38th Pl N Arlington VA 22207-2915

HICKMAN, JANET SUSAN, academic administrator, educator; b. Bklyn., Aug. 28, 1948; d. Richard and Frances J. (Falconer) Liberth; m. C. Kennedy Hickman, June 21, 1970; 1 child, Kennedy R. BSN cum laude, U. Bridgeport, 1970; MS, No. Ill. U., 1976; EdD, Temple U., 1987. RN, Ill., Ohio, Pa., Del., N.Y. Instr. St. Joseph Hosp., Joliet, Ill., 1974-77, Wright State U., Dayton, Ohio, 1977-78; asst. prof. Neumann Coll., Aston, Pa., 1979-81; assoc. dean health professions Ea. Coll., St. Davids, Pa., 1982-92; prof. West Chester U., 1992—, interim dean grad. studies, 2006. Author: Mental Health and Psychiatric Nursing, 1992, Health Assessment in Nursing, 1995; co-author: Nursing Theories, 5th edit., 2002, Fundamentals of Nursing, 2d edit., 2004, Faith Community Nursing, 2006; contbr. articles to profl. jours. Mem. Assn. Comty. Health Nursing Educators, Temple U. Alumni Assoc., Sigma Theta Tau Home: 1435 Clover Ln West Chester PA 19380-5906 Office: West Chester Univ Dept Nursing West Chester PA 19383-0001 Office Phone: 610-738-0547. Business E-Mail: jhickman@wcupa.edu.

HICKMAN, MARGARET CAPELLINI, advertising executive; b. Hartford, Conn., Sept. 21, 1949; d. Anthony Serafino Capellini and Mary Magdelan (Budash Capellini) Zanardi; m. Richard Lonnie Hickman, Nov. 6, 1982; children: Wilder A., Langdon B. BA, U. Conn., 1971. Mktg. asst. Advo Sys., Inc., Hartford, Conn., 1971-72, mktg. analyst, 1972-75; mktg. asst. Cinamon Assocs., Inc., Brookline, Mass., 1975-77, profn. supr., 1977-81, v.p. prodn., 1981-84, v.p. client svcs., 1984-85, 86; dir. client svcs. Bozell, Jacobs, Jenyon & Eckhardt, Boston, 1985-86; ptnr. Hickman & Hickman, Merritt Island, Fla., 1987; prodn. mgr. Direct Mktg. Aty., Stamford, Conn., 1988-90; v.p. prodn. Martin Direct, Glen Allen, Va., 1990-96, Martin Agy., Richmond, Va., 1996—. Mem.: Direct Mktg. Assn. (past sec., treas., v.p.), Cape Ann Child Devel. Programs (past dir.), Am. Legion Aux. Democrat. Roman Catholic. Home: 10717 Wellington St Fredericksburg VA 22407-1272 Office Phone: 804-698-8000. Business E-Mail: marge.hickman@martinagency.com.

HICKMAN, MARTHA WHITMORE, writer; b. Holyoke, Mass., Dec. 9, 1925; d. George Deming and Ruth Carr Whitmore; m. Hoyt Leon Hickman; children: Peter, John, Stephen, Mary. BA, Mount Holyoke Coll., 1947. Asst. editor Am. Baptist Publ. Soc., Phila., 1947—50; tchr. Lincoln St. Nursery Sch., New Haven, 1951—52; info. specialist United Meth. Ch., Nashville, 1974—80; freelance writer Nashville, 1980—. Tchr. writing for emotionally disturbed children Kennedy Sch., Erie, Pa., 1970—71; adj. instr. Tenn. State U., Nashville, 1978. Author: (fiction anthology) Days of Grass, 1965, (poetry in anthology) Images, 1976, (TV films) (script) Nativity, 1985, (books) How to Marry a Minister, 1968, Love Speaks its Voice: The Sights and Sounds of Middle Life, 1976, 2d edit., 1980, I Will Not Leave You Desolate: Some Thoughts for Grieving Parents, 1982, 2d edit., 1994, The Growing Season: The Sights and Sounds of Middle Life, Waiting and Loving: Thoughts Occasioned by the Illness and Death of a Parent, 1984, Prayers and Devotions for Teachers, 1989, Fullness of Time: Short Stories of Women and Aging, 1990, 2d edit., 1997, Healing After Loss, 1994, Daily Meditation for Working Through Grief, 1996, Such Good People, 1997, A Day of Rest: Creating Spiritual Space in Your Week, 1999, Wade in the Water: 52 Reflections on The Faith We Sing, 2003; Contbg. author (books) 365 Meditations for Women, 1989, 1993, contbg. author The Storyteller's Companion to the Bible, 1993; contbr. essays, fiction and poetry featured in Highlights, Christian Science Monitor, Good Housekeeping, Christian Century, Ms., Pastoral Psychology, Image, Weavings, Christian Herald, Pockets, others. Chair Citizens for Clark & Dilworth, Beaver Falls, Pa. Recipient Fiction award, Friends of Am. Writers, 1976, Assoc. Ch. Press, 1989. Mem.: Soc. Children's Book Writers & Illustrators, Authors Guild, Phi Beta Kappa. Democrat. United Methodist. Avocations: reading, travel, knitting, painting. Home: 373 Pine Ln Los Altos CA 94022 Personal E-mail: mjwhickman@aol.com.

HICKMAN, MATILDA COFFEY, principal; b. Lake Charles, La., Mar. 7, 1943; d. Robert Fagan and Evelyn Barton Coffey; m. Bennie Dewain Hickman, Jan. 24, 1965; children: Robert Coffey, Robin Hickman Fogle. BS in Secondary Edn., McNeese State U., Lake Charles, 1965; MA in English, McNeese State U., 1970. Cert. ednl. supr., tchr. gifted/talented, English Tex. Tchr. Beaumont (Tex.) Ind. Sch. Dist., 1971—73, 1979—91; English supr. Beaumont Ind. Sch. Dist., 1991—93; instr. La. State U., Baton Rouge, 1977—78; asst. prin. Odom Acad., Beaumont Sch. Dist., 1993—2000, prin., 2000—. Bd. dirs. Lamar-Orange (Tex.) Accelerated Cert., 2003—06. Editor: Lagniappe, A Little Something, 1983. V.p. Beaumont Heritage Soc., 1985—87; pres. Beaumont Symphony League, 1982; bd. dirs. Beaumont Symphony Soc., 1982—. Named Tchr. of Yr., Tex. A&M Club, Beaumont, 1984. Mem.: ASCD, Nat. Mid. Sch. Assn., Tex. Assn. Gifted/Talented (pres., v.p., sec.-treas., regional dir. 1994—2004). Office: Odom Acad 2550 W Virginia Beaumont TX 77706 Office Phone: 409-842-3217. Office Fax: 409-842-8604. Business E-Mail: mhickma@beaumont.k12.tx.us.

HICKMAN, TERRIE TAYLOR, administrator, elementary school educator; b. Rapid City, S.D., Dec. 2, 1962; d. William Adrian and Carolyn Gene (Habben) T.; children: Matthew, Kalie. BS, Okla. State U., 1985; MEd, Cen. State U., 1988. Cert. elem tchr., presch. tchr., Okla. Mktg. dir. Tealridge Manor, Edmond, Okla., 1989-90; owner Oxford Pointe Jazzercize, Edmond, Okla., 1989-90; adminstr. Retirement Inn at Quail Ridge, Oklahoma City, 1991-92, Country Club Square, Edmond, 1992-93; planner Areawide Aging Agency, Oklahoma City, 1992-97; elem. tchr. Edmond Pub. Sch., 2003—. Mem. adv. coun., co-chmn. Okla. Bus. and Aging Leadership Coalition, newsletter Networker editor; presenter in field; adv. coun. sr. companion planning com. State of Okla. Conf. on Aging; mem. Oklahoma City Reading Coun. Co-editor Sage Age; contbr. articles to various pubs. Co-chmn. media hosting party Olympic Festival, Norman, Okla., 1989; co-coord. jazzercize for hope Benefit for Hope Ctr., Edmond, The McGruff Safe House Program, Stillwater, Okla.; com. chmn. Coalition for Elderly Concerns, Oklahoma City; vol. Stillwater Domestic Violence Shelter, Payne County Employment Svcs., Stillwater; mem. renter's adv. bd. Okla. State U. Student Senate. Mem. ASCD, Women in Bus., Edmond Womens Club, Edmond Area C. of C., Okla. Bus. and Aging Leadership Coalition, Phi Kappa Delta, Alpha Gamma Delta, Sigma Phi Omega, Kappa Delta Pi, Delta Kappa Gamma. Republican. Lutheran. Avocation: biking. Personal E-mail: redhead2694@swbell.net.

HICKMAN, TRAPHENE PARRAMORE, retired library director, consultant; b. Dallas, Jan. 31, 1933; d. Redden Travis and Stella (Moore) P.; m. John Robert Hickman, June 9, 1950; children: Lynn Kleifgen, Laurie Ward AA, Mountain View C.C.; BA, U. Tex-Arlington; MLS, U. North Tex. Cert. libr., Tex. Libr. Cedar Hill (Tex.) Pub. Libr., 1959-77; dir. Dallas County Libr. Sys., Dallas, 1977-93; libr. cons. Dallas County, 1993-95; libr. High Pointe Elem. Sch. Cedar Hill Ind. Sch. Dist., 2003—. Chair leadership coun. and family ministries FUMC of Cedar Hill. Editor: History and Directory of Cedar Hill, 1976; editor News and Views newsletter Dallas county Employees, 1986-92. Chmn. Bicentennial Com., Cedar Hill, 1976; del. Dem. Nat. Conv. 9th Senate Dist., Tex., 1976; chmn. Sesquicentennial Com., Cedar Hill, 1984-86; Dallas County Dem. Forum; mem. Electoral Coll., 1988; chairperson Women's Bd. Northwood Inst., Cedar Hill; active Dallas County Sesquicentennial Com., 1996-; lay speaker United Methodist Ch., 2004. Recipient Newsmaker of Yr. award Cedar Hill Chronicle, 1976; named Amb. of Goodwill, State of Tex., 1976 Mem. ALA, Tex. Libr. Assn. (legis. com. 1984-95, councillor 1982-83, trustee com. 1987-95, pub. info. com. 1987-95), Pub. Libr. Adminstrs. of North Tex. (sec., v.p., pres. 1980, 87), Dallas County Libr. Assn., N.E. Tex. Libr. Sys. (legis. commn. 1978-95, Libr. of Yr. 1987), U. North Tex. Sch. Libr. and Info. Scis. Alumni Assn. (pres. 1987-88), Cedar Hill C. of C., Cedar Summit Book Club (officer), Dallas Area Storytelling Guild (pres. 1995-99) Democrat. Methodist. Avocations: writing, reading, storytelling, gardening, bridge, travel, square dancing. Home and Office: 421 Lee St Cedar Hill TX 75104-2697

HICKS, ANN NEUWIRTH, clinical social worker; b. Columbus, Ohio, Nov. 8, 1932; d. Willis A. and Luella (Knowlton) Neuwirth; children: Malcolm Lee, Geoff Cody. BA, Ohio State U., 1954; MA, West Tex. State U., 1980. Cert. social worker, Tex. Clin. social worker Amarillo State Ctr.; adoption and foster care social worker CAth. Family Svc., Amarillo, Tex.; social worker N.Mex. Health and Social Svcs., Clovis. Active community actitives. Mem. NASW (Nat. Assn. of Social Workers), League of Women Voters, Wildcat Bluff Nature Ctr. Home: 6301 Bayswater Rd Amarillo TX 79109-6503

HICKS, BETHANY GRIBBEN, judge, lawyer; b. NY, Sept. 8, 1951; d. Robert and DeSales Gribben; m. William A. Hicks III, May 21, 1982; children: Alexandra Elizabeth, Samantha Katherine. AB, Vassar Coll., Poughkeepsie, N.Y., 1973; MEd, Boston U., 1975; JD, Ariz. State U., Tempe, 1984. Bar: Ariz. 1984. Pvt. practice, Scottsdale and Paradise Valley, Ariz., 1984-91; law clk. to Hon. Kenneth L. Fields Maricopa County Superior Ct. S.E. dist., Mesa, 1991-93; commr., judge pro tem domestic rels. and juvenile depts. Maricopa County Superior Ct. Ctrl. and S.E. Dists., Phoenix and Mesa, Ariz., 1993-99; magistrate Town of Paradise Valley, Ariz., 1993-94; judge ctrl. dist. domestic rels. dept. Maricopa County Superior Ct., Phoenix, 1999-2000, presiding judge family ct. dept., 2000—02, judge S.E. dist. civil dept., 2002—04, judge Ctrl. Dist. criminal dept., 2004—. Dean Ariz. Jud. Coll., 2005. Mem. Jr. League of Phoenix, 1984-91; bd. dirs. Phoenix Children's Theatre, 1988-90; parliamentarian Girls Club of Scottsdale, Ariz., 1985-87, 89-90, bd. dirs., 1988-91; exec. bd., sec. All Saints' Episcopal Day Sch. Parents Assn., 1991-92, pres., 1993-94; active Nat. Charity League, 1995-99, Valley Leadership Class XIX, 1997-98; vol., Teach for Am., 1997-2001. Mem.: ABA, City Scottsdale Jud. Adv. Bd., Nat. Assn. of Women Judges, Assn. Family Ct. Conciliators (bd. dirs. 2001—03), Ariz. Women Lawyers' Assn. (steering com. 1998—2001), Maricopa County Bar Assn., State Bar Ariz. Democrat. Episcopalian. Office: 101/201 W Jefferson Phoenix AZ 85003 Office Phone: 602-506-2139. E-mail: bhicks@superiorcourt.maricopa.gov.

HICKS, BETTY HARRIS, real estate broker, real estate company executive; b. Tellico Plains, Tenn., May 5, 1946; d. Ellis Fay Harris and Dellie Elizabeth Lynn; m. Roy Edward Hicks, Oct. 8, 1981. Student, Hiwasse Coll., 1982; cert., Trees Real Estate Sch., 1983. Sewing machine operator Colonial Garments, Tellico Plains, 1965—79; owner, operator Garner's Beauty Salon, 1980—81; sec. Monroe County C. of C., Madisonville, Tenn., 1981—82; salesperson Norman Lee Real Estate, Madisonville, 1982—83, Wattenbarger Real Estate, Loudon, Tenn., 1983—84; broker, owner AApple Realty Co., Loudon, Tenn., 1984—91, Anchor Properties, Loudon, Tenn., 1992—; prin., owner Anchor Mortgage Co., Loudon, 2003—. Tchr. Tenn. Real Estate Sch., Knoxville, 1998; pres. Loudon County Bd. Realtors. Pres. Loudon C. of C., Loudon. Named Realtor of Yr., 1987; recipient Cert. of Appreciation, Loudon C. of C., 1988, City of Loudon, 1988. Mem.: Loudon County C. of C. Republican. Avocations: genealogy, gardening, cooking, reading, bird watching. Office: Anchor Properties 811 Mulberry St Loudon TN 37774 Office Phone: 865-408-0802. Personal E-mail: betty127@msn.com.

HICKS, CAROL ANN, small business owner, educator; b. Danville, Ill., Mar. 14, 1943; d. Hughie Jay Johnson and Doris N. Jean Bostwick; children: Beverly, Bobbi Ann, Sandra, Michael. AS, Danville (Ill.) Area C.C., 1985, AS in Desk Top Publ., 1996; B in Elem. Edn., Ea. Ill. U., 1988. Grain technician Danville Grain Inspection, 1981-91; tchrs. aide reading and phonics Honeywell Sch., Hoopston, Ill., 1985-88; substitute tchr. Hoopston (Ill.) Area Cmty. Schs., 1988—2000; mgr., asst. mgr. Casey's Gen. Store, Hoopeston, Gifford, Ill., 1994-98; owner, mgr. Carol's Corner and Genealogy Plus, Hoopeston, 1998—, Pape Meml. Home & Gardens, 2001—. Ct. reporter The Neighbor, Attica, Ind., 2001—04. Author: The Presley Family History, 1993, (newsletter) Presley Research Assn., 1993-99; editor: The Chronicle, Hoopeston, Ill., 2004—; contbr. columns to newspapers, 2000-04. Grant Twp. com. chmn. Dem. Party, Hoopeston, 1997—2000; hospice vol. USMC Logan Campus, Danville, 1991-96. Mem. Am. Legion Aux., Barbara Standish NSDAR (historian, regent 1991-95, 2000—), VFW Aux., Kappa Delta Pi (Beta Pi chpt.). Mem. Ch. LDS. Avocations: genealogy, research history, bowling, reading, travel. Home: 326 W Orange St Hoopeston IL 60942-1952 E-mail: chicks@advancenet.net.

HICKS, CHRISTY ANN, communications educator; b. Torrance, Calif., Feb. 19, 1970; d. James Robin and Sharon Ann (Crowe) H.; m. Gregory Lawrence Bowman, Sept. 2, 1996 BA History, Oakland U., 1997; MA in Youth Devel., Mich. State U., 2006; grad., New Detroit Multicultural Immersion Program, 2005, S.E. Asian Studies Summer Inst., 2005, New Generation Tng. Program. Cert. profl. facilitator 2006. Promotion dir. Metrogroup Promotions, Inc., Farmington Hills, Mich., 1987—90, CBS Radio, Inc., Southfield, Mich., 1990—92; instr. pub. speaking, coach forensics Cranbrook-Kingswood H.S., Bloomfield Hills, Mich., 1992—. Founder, coord. Oakland County Youth Leadership Inst., 2001-; supr. Madison Jr. H.S. Conflict Resolution Program, Pontiac, Mich., 1994-96; dir. Svc.-Learning Program, Pontiac and Oak Park, 1997—. Contbr. articles to profl. jours. Coord. workforce preparation program 4-H Youth Programs Mich. State U., 1994—; vol. Pres.'s Summit for Am's. Future, 1997, AmeriCorps Oakland, 1994, 95, AmeriCorps VISTA, 1996, Red Cross Disaster Action Team, Hands on Network Gulf Coast Hurricane Relief. Recipient Gov's. Cmty. Svc. award Gov. John Engler, Mich., 1996, Cmty. Svc. award Mich. Recreation and Park Assn., 1997, Pres. Clinton's Common Ground award The White House, Washington, 1999 Mem. Mich. Interscholastic Forensics Assn. (cert. judge), Oakland U. Honors Coll. Almuni Assn. (Odyssey award 2001), Internat. Assn.

Facilitators, LeadNet Cmty. Leadership Devel. Team, Assn. Psychol. Type, Americorps Alums, Oak Park Optimist Club, Phi Alpha Theta Office: Mich State U Extension 4-H Youth Programs 1200 N Telegraph Rd Dept 416 Pontiac MI 48341-0416 Office Phone: 248-858-0890.

HICKS, DEBRA CARTER, biology professor; b. Charleston, S.C., Feb. 11, 1955; d. Earl Reed Carter and Inell Garrison; m. William Lee Hicks, Sept. 26, 1992; children: Shane Hunter, Meta Hamby, Joseph Hamby. AS, N.W. Ala. C.C., Phil Campbell, Ala., 1976; BS in Edn., U. North Ala., Florence, 1988; MEd, U. Ala., Birmingham, 1991; EdD, Nova Southeastern U., Ft. Lauderdale, Fla., 1998. Cert. Nat. Bd. for Profl. Tchg. Stds., profl. educator Fla., Ala., Fla. Black Bear curriculum facilitator, Project Wild curriculum facilitator, Project Wet curriculum facilitator. Educator Birmingham Pub. Schs., 1989—92, Dist. Sch. Bd. Lake County, Tavares, Fla., 1992—2001; assoc. prof. Valencia C.C., Orlando, Fla., 1992—2001; asst. prof. Lake Sumter C.C., Clermont, Fla., 2000—. Instr. J.L. Scott Marino Edn. Ctr., Biloxi, Miss., 1991—92; mem. adv. com. Lake Sumter C.C. Fla. C.C. Consortium, Leesburg, 2005—; del. leader People to People Student Ambs., Spokane, Wash., 1995—; conf. leader World Leadership Forum, Washington, 2006. Named Griffin Mid. Sch. Tchr. of Yr., 2000; recipient Pittsburg Conf. Meml. Nat. Coll. grant, 2005, Ellen Onishuk Endowment award, 2005, Comty. Found. South Lake County grant, 2004. Mem.: Assn. Southeastern Biologists, Fla. Marine Sci. Educators Assn., Fla. Assn. Sci. Tchrs., Order of Ea. Star, Beta Beta Beta, Phi Delta Kappa, Phi Gamma Sigma. Avocations: hiking, gardening, travel. Office: Lake Sumter C C 1250 N Hancock Rd Clermont FL 34711

HICKS, DEBRA LEE, science educator; b. Pitts., Mar. 10, 1981; d. Warren and Patricia Parker; m. Jonathan Hicks, Dec. 28, 2004; 1 child, William. BS, Clarion U., 2004. Cert. Tchng. Va. Dept. Edn. Tchr. Hampton (Va.) City Sch., 2004—. Personal E-mail: lit_debbie@yahoo.com.

HICKS, ERICA C., mathematics educator; b. Lancaster, NH, Feb. 9, 1975; d. Kenneth Sears and Jay-Ann Roby Crane; m. Benjamin C. Hicks, Sept. 23, 2000; children: Haile Elizabeth, Tyler Benjamin. BS, Plymouth State Coll., NH, 1997. Waitress, bartender Jigger Johnson's, Plymouth, NH, 1995—98; dining rm. mgr. Seasonings Restaurant, Jefferson, 1998—2000. Peer outreach advisor White Mountains Regional H.S., Whitefield, NH, 1999—2000, class advisor, 2000—03, chair math. dept.; yearbook dedication class of 2006. Mem.: White Mountains Edn. Assn. (assoc.), Psi Chi, Kappa Delta Phi (assoc.). Home: 208 Old Cherry Mountain Road Jefferson NH 03583 Office: White Mountains Regional High School 127 Regional Rd Whitefield NH 03598 Office Phone: 603-837-2528. Personal E-mail: ehicks@sau36.org.

HICKS, HERALINE ELAINE, environmental health scientist, educator; b. Beaufort, S.C., Sept. 27, 1951; d. Heral and Ophelia Lillie (Albergottie) H. BA, Ohio Wesleyan U., 1973; MS, Atlanta U., 1978, PhD, 1980; postgrad., U. N.C., 1980-84. Rsch. assoc. Chapel Hill Dental Rsch. Ctr. U. N.C., 1980-81; NIH postdoctoral fellow Chapel Hill Dental Rsch. Ctr. Chapel Hill Dental Rsch. Ctr. and Dept. Surgery, 1982-84; guest scientist Naval Med. Rsch. Inst., Bethesda, Md., 1985-87; asst. prof. Chapel Hill Sch. Dentistry U. N.C., 1985-88; prof., dir. electron microscopy Morris Brown Coll., Atlanta, 1988-90; sr. environ. health scientist, dir. Cts. for Disease Control and Prevention/Agy. for Toxic Substances and Disease Registry, Atlanta, 1990—; program dir. Gt. Lakes Human Health Effects Rsch. Program, Agy. for Toxic Substances and Disease Registry. Mem. health profls. task force adv. bd. Internat. Joint Commn., Washington, 1995—. Author: (chpt.) Development and Diseases of Cartilage and Bone Matrix, 1987, Birth Defects and Reproductive Disorders, 1993; contbr. articles to profl. jours. Predoctoral traineeship NIH, 1977-79, Barnett F. Smith award for outstanding achievement Atlanta U., 1978; Acad. scholar Ohio Wesleyaan U., 1969-73, Josiah Macy Jr. scholar Woods Hole Marine Biol. Lab., 1979, Tuition scholar Atlanta U., 1979-80; postdoctoral fellow NIH, 1982-84, Notable Alumnus of Clark U., 1995; named one of Outstanding Young Women of Am., 1980. Mem. Am. Soc. for Cell Biology (Young Investigator fellowship 1990), Teratology (Young Investigator fellowship 1987), Microscopy Soc. Am., Biology Honor Soc., Beta Kappa Chi. Presbyterian. Avocations: reading, exercise, playing chess. Office: Ctrs for Disease Control and Prevention Mail Stop E29 1600 Clifton Rd NE Atlanta GA 30329-4018

HICKS, KAREN T., mathematician; b. L.A., Calif., July 7, 1957; d. William A. and Celia E. Smiley; m. Robert L. Hicks, Apr. 23, 2006; 1 child, Dorian O. Smiley. BS in Math., U. Calif., Irvine, 1994; MS in Math., U. Calif., Riverside, 1996. Adj. prof. Orange Coast Coll., Costa Mesa, Calif., 1996—2003; applied rsch. mathematician Dept. of Def., Savage, Md., 2003—. Mem.: Phi Beta Kappa. Office: Dept of Def Savage MD

HICKS, LINDA REONA, elementary school educator; b. Taloga, Okla., Oct. 14, 1949; d. Kenneth Merl and Ima Jean (Coyle) Hicks. BA, Southwestern Okla. State U., 1971, EdM, 1975; Reading Recovery cert., West Tex. A & M U., 2002; postgrad., Ft. Hays State U., 2004—05. Cert. reading specialist. Music and English educator Hardesty Pub. Schs., Okla., 1971—74, Tyrone Pub. Schs., Okla., 1974—2000; reading recovery educator Unified Sch. Dist. #480 - Lincoln Elem., Liberal, Kans., 2001—05; elem. music educator Unified Sch. Dist. McKinley Elem., Lincoln Elem., MacArthur Elem., 2005—. Chair Tyrone Tchrs. Inservice Com., 1996—97; mem. North Ctrl. Accreditation Steering Com. for Lincoln Elem., Liberal, Kans., 2001—05. Music dir. First Assembly of God, Liberal, 1988—, sec. bd., 2000—03, 2005—. Named Tchr. of Yr., Tex. County Edn. Assn., 1976, Tyrone Edn. Assn., 1998—99, Tchr. of Today, Masons, 1998—99. Mem.: Music Educators Nat. Conf., Internat. Reading Assn., Reading Recovery Coun. N.Am. (assoc.), Assn. Am. Educators (assoc.), Am. Choral Dirs. Assn. (life), Delta Kappa Gamma. Republican. Avocations: reading, scrapbooks, singing, playing musical instruments. Office: USD480 Liberal KS 67901 Business E-Mail: linda.hicks@usd480.net.

HICKS, MELINDA M., history professor; d. Clyde Garner and Nellie Marie Hicks. MA in History, Youngstown State U., Ohio, 2002; ABD, W.Va. U., Morgantown, 2006. Lectr. Pa. State U. Fayette, Uniontown, 2005—; lectr. Am. and world history W.Va. U., Morgantown, W.Va., 2002—. Dir. Rush Holt History Conf., Morgantown, W.Va., 2005; guest spkr. in field. Co-editor: Defending the Homeland: Historical Perspectives on Radicalism, Terrorism, and State Responses, 2007. Mentor and vol. Labor of Love Ministries, Morgantown, W.Va., 2005—06. Recipient Marion Blum Grad. Essay award, Dept. History Youngstown State U., 2002, Wesley Bagby III Meml. award, Dept. History W.Va. U. and Eberly Coll. Arts and Scis., 2004; fellow, Gilder-Lehrman Inst. Am. History, 2006; scholar, Colonial Dames of Am., 2005; Disting. Doctoral fellow, WVU Found., 2006. Mem.: Phi Alpha Theta (life). Avocations: music, reading, writing. Office Phone: 304-293-2421. E-mail: melindahicks@juno.com.

HICKS, PATRICIA J., secondary school educator; b. Harrisburg, Pa., Feb. 21, 1951; d. Joseph and Jean (Snyder) Agosta; m. David Hicks, Sept. 22, 1951; 1 child, Lindy. BA, U. West Fla., 1973, MEd, 1991. Tchr. Sch. Bd. Okaloosa County, Ft. Walton Beach, Fla., 1974—. Dept. chairperson Choctawhatchee HS, Ft. Walton Beach, 1975—. Mem.: Coun. for Exceptional Children (assoc.), Alpha Delta Kappa. Home: 362 Marie Circle Fort Walton Beach FL 32548 Office Phone: 850-833-3614. Personal E-mail: pjh47@yahoo.com.

HICKS, SHIRLEY E., director; b. St. Louis, Nov. 9, 1936; d. Joseph Alonzo and Thelma Elizabeth Hill; m. Sharon Lavert Hicks (div. Aug. 1978); children: Beth Ann Hargrove, Lynne Marie Catching. BA, Notre Dame Coll., Lemay, Mo., 1975; MA, Webster U., 1980. Program specialist/in-house coord. St. Louis Housing Authority; MEGASKILLS regional trainer Cooperating Sch. Dist., St. Louis; pres. S.E. Hicks and Assocs.; spl. svcs. educator Sch. Dist. City of Ladue, St. Louis. Chmn. mktg. and pub. rels. Mo. Coun. Women's Econ. Devel. Tng., State of Mo., 1988—93. Contbr. articles to profl. jours. Mem., com. chmn. Mo. Coun. on Women's Econ. Devel. and Tng., Jefferson City, St. Louis, 1988—93; mem. Grad. Class 13 Coro Found.-Women in Leadership, St. Louis. Recipient Leadership award, Chums, Inc., 1986, Excellence in Tchg. award, Urban League Met. St. Louis, 1993. Mem.: ASCD, Mo. State Tchrs. Assn. (pres. Ladue chpt. 1993—95), Red Hat Ladies Soc. (chap. founder 2005—), Chums, Inc. (nat. pub. rels. officer 1988—90, nat. v.p. 1990—94, Leadership award 1986), Zonta Internat. (St. Louis chpt.), Phi Delta Kappa (pres. 1992—94, Washington U.-Maryville chpt.). Avocations: travel, concerts, painting, reading. Home: Apt 217 3915 Olive St Saint Louis MO 63108-3157

HICKSON, JOYCE FAYE, counseling educator; b. Birmingham, Ala. d. Jesse Guy and Hazel Lonette (Streetman) Horton. BS, Troy (Ala.) State U., 1965; MA, Auburn U., 1965; EdD, Miss. State U., 1976. Instr. dept. comm. Auburn U., Ala., 1965-68; dir. Tyler Ednl. Ctr., Carbondale, Ill., 1968-70; head tchr., coord. Fairfax County Pub. Sch. System, Fairfax, Va., 1972-74; asst. prof. dept. counselor edn. Miss. State U., Starkville, 1976-85; grad. coord. dept. specialized edn. U. Witwatersrand, Johannesburg, 1985-91; prof., chmn. dept. counseling and clin. programs Columbus Coll., Ga., 1991—2003, mem. adv. bd. internat. studies program Ga., 1993—; v.p. Columbus Alliance for Battered Woman, 2003—; dir. SACS self study Columbus State U., 2003—05, dir. planning and spl. projects, 2006—. Cons. to sch. dists., Ill., 1968-70, Miss., 1976-85, Ga., 1991—. Author: Multicultural Counseling in a Divided and Traumatized Society, 1994; contbr. articles to profl. jours. Mem. ACA, Am. Sch. Counselors Assn. (so. regional rep. 1992), Ga. Sch. Counselors Assn. (at-large), Internat. Assn. for Spl. Edn. (editorial bd. 1992), AAUW. Democrat. Home: 7803 Edgewater Dr Columbus GA 31904-2109

HICKS-RAY, DENYSE, psychologist, commentator; d. Joe Louis and Elsie Hicks; m. Michael Anthony Ray; 1 child, Rashaan. BA, W.Va. State Coll., Institute, 1974; MA, U. South Fla., Tampa, 1982; PhD in Clin. and Forensic Psychology, U. Wis., Madison, 1987. Bd. cert. expert traumatic stress 2002, diplomate Acad. Traumatic Stress, 2004. Founder and CEO Trauma Svcs. Assoc., Charlotte, NC, 1999—. Talk show host The Not Just the Blues Show, Charlotte, 2001—; cons. Employee Svcs. Guardsmen & Reserve, 2005. Author: Mental Health: Culture Race, Ethnicity, 2001, The Pain Didn't Start Here: Trauma and Violence, 2004; contbr. articles to profl. jours. Exec. dir. African Am. Women's Mental Health Authority, Phila., 2000; founder DENRAH Found., 2001; active Mental Health Round Table; amb. Dr. Reginald A. Hawkins Legal Def. Fund; mem. Women's Leadership Coun. United Way Ctrl. Carolinas. Recipient Extraordinary Woman award, African Am. Women's Mental Health Authority, 2002; Hicks' scholar, Assn. Black Nurses. Fellow: Am. Acad. Experts in Traumatic Stress, Acad. Traumatic Stress; mem.: NAACP (life), Assn. Black Psychologists (nat. pub. rels. chairperson), Nat. Leadership Coun. on African Americans' Behavioral Health. Avocations: flying, reading, sailing, cooking, dancing. Office: Trauma Svcs Assoc LLC PO Box 680154 Charlotte NC 28216 Office Phone: 704-334-2225. Business E-Mail: dray@traumaservices.com.

HIDAKA, CHISA, medical researcher; b. Sasebo, Kyushu, Japan, June 25, 1964; d. Yoshiki and Kiyoko Hidaka. BA in Dance magna cum laude, Barnard Coll., 1986; MD, Cornell U., 1994. Intern in surgery NY Hosp., NYC, 1994—95; resident in orthopaedic surgery Hosp. Spl. Surgery, NYC, 1995—98, asst. scientist, 2001—. Dancer Vital Signs, St. Mark's Ch., NYC, 1991 (Bessie (to Marta Renzi), 1991). Recipient Marshall R. Urist resident rsch. award, Orthopaedics Rsch. and Edn. Found., 1999, Arthritis Investigator award, Arthritis Found., 2001—06, Russell S. Hibbs basic sci. award, Scoliosis Rsch. Soc., 2002; grantee, NIH, 2003—06. Mem.: Phi Beta Kappa, Alpha Omega Alpha. Achievements include patents for method to enhance bone density by co-transfer; patents pending for method for producing bone morphogenetic protein heterodimers. Avocations: dance education, singing, dance, choreography. Office Phone: 212-774-2384.

HIDAY, VIRGINIA ALDIGÉ, sociologist, educator; b. New Orleans, Jan. 28, 1939; d. Robert Joseph and Mary Boagni (Anding) A.; m. L.L. Hiday, Sept. 5, 1970 (div. June 2, 1997). AB, U. N.C., 1960, MEd, 1961, PhD, 1973. Asst. prof. U. Colo., Boulder, 1972-75; postdoctoral fellow Duke U. Med. Ctr., Durham, N.C., 1975-76; asst. prof., prof. N.C. State U., Raleigh, 1976—; rsch. asst. Sheps Ctr. Health Svcs. U. N.C., Chapel Hill, NC, 1990—. Vis. prof. U. N.C., Chapel Hill, 1974-75; referee for various sci. jours. in sociology, law, psychiatry; cons. N.C. Divsn. Mental Health, Raleigh, 1986, 89, Nat. Health Svc., London, 1999, Ont. Ministry of Health, Toronto, 2000. Mem. editl. bd. Contemporary Sociology, 1986-91, 98-2000, Rose Monograph Series, 1982-88, Jour. Health and Social Behavior, 2000-04, Internat. Jour. Law and Psychiatry, 2000—; contbr. numerous articles to profl. jours. Mem., com. AAUP, Boulder, Colo., 1972-75; worker Campaigns for local, state, nat. offices, Chapel Hill, 1966—, Habitat for Humanity, Chapel Hill, 1996-97; bd. dirs. Orange County Mental Health Assn., Chapel Hill, 1995-99. Named NIMH Postdoctoral fellow, Popultion Predoctoral fellow NICHD. Mem. Am. Sociol. Assn. (coun. mem. med. sect., sec., treas. mental health), So. Sociol. Soc. (coun. mem.), Internat. Acad. Law & Mental Health (coun. mem. 1993-2006), Soc. for Study of Social Problems, Am. Psychology and Law Assn., Phi Kappa Phi, Sigma Xi. Democrat. Episcopalian. Avocations: tennis, skiing, dance. Office: NC State U Dept Sociology/Anthropology PO Box 8107 Raleigh NC 27695-0001

HIDDEN-DODSON, NANCY, retired psychologist, consultant, educator; b. Everett, Mass., July 24, 1939; d. Frank Foster Thomas and Grace Evelyn Hickey; m. Edward Wesley Dodson, Dec. 21, 1985; m. Edwin William Hidden, Aug. 6, 1960 (div. Jan. 15, 1976); children: William Thomas Hidden, Glen Allen Hidden, Mark Samuel Hidden. BE in Sci. Edn., U. Alaska, 1970, M in Counseling Psychology, 1972; EdD, Seattle U., 1992. Cert. Tchr., Counselor Alaska, 1972, NH, 1974, CC Counselor and Instr. Calif., 1976, Counselor Nat. Bd. Cert. Counselors, 1985, Ednl. Staff Assoc., Counselor Wash., 1987, Ednl. Staff Assoc., Ednl. Psychology Wash., 1992, Ednl. Specialist in Ednl. Psychology Seattle U., 1992, lic. Mental Health Counselor Wash., 2001. Tchr. Tamworth Sch. Dist., NH, 1965—66, State Operated Schs., Northway, Alaska, 1971; sci. tchr. Conway Sch. Dist., 1972—74; instr. psychology Tanana Valley C.C., Fairbanks, 1974—86, counselor, coord. paraprofl. counseling program, 1977—81, student svcs. coord., 1978—81, dir. student svcs., 1981—82, dean students, 1982—85; mental health counselor Ctr. Family Counseling, Fairbanks, 1976—77, Peninsula Psychol. Ctr., Silverdale, 2001—03; ednl. counselor, psychologist Ocosta Sch. Dist., Westport, 1988—92; ednl. psychologist North Kitsap Sch. Dist., Poulsbo, 1992—2001. Dir. upward bound U. Alaska, Fairbanks, 1974—75; cons. Tanana Chiefs Counsel, Fairbanks, 1974—85, Maniilaq Assn., Kotzebue, 1975—85; cons. divsn. social and health svc. Wash., Wash., 1995—2003; dir., founder Interior Alaska Dispute Resolution Svcs., Fairbanks, 1985—86, Alaska Dispute Resolution Ctr., Fairbanks, 1985—87; mental health specialist Pudget Sound Mediation & Evaluation, Westport, Wash., 2000—05. Author: Musings Of A Women, 2004, Dancing with Nature, 2006; contbr. articles in field. Founder deeded land Hidden Hill Friends Ctr., Chena Ridge Friends Meeting, Fairbanks, 1980—2005. Recipient cert. Recognition, Boarding Home Program, Alaska, 1970, Fairbanks Head Start, 1976, Alaska State Police, 1980, Hospice Care, Fairbanks, 1984, Kingston Jr. High, 1993, 1994, 1995; scholarship, Pk. Coll., 1958-1960, Alaska, 1968-1970. Mem.: APA. Peace Party. Society Of Friends. Avocations: bicycling, poetry, crafts, sewing. Office Phone: 360-821-9048. Personal E-mail: nedodson@comcast.net.

HIDDLE, SUSAN K., music educator, musician; d. Lloyd C. Hiddle and Irma L. Hires-Hiddle. MusB, Ea. Ill. U., 1975, MA, 1977. Dir. music Steeleville (Ill.) Unit Dist. #138, 1975—76; band dir. Newton (Ill.) St. Thomas Cath. Sch., 1977—78; dir. bands Cumberland Unit Dist. #77, Toledo/Greenup, Ill., 1977—90; dir. vocal music Paris (Ill.) Union Sch. Dist. #95, 1990—2001, dir. band and vocal music, 2001—03, dir. vocal music, 1990—. Freelance flute soloist, Paris, 1990—; band dir. Paris City Band, 1999—; organist, sanctuary choir dir. First United Meth. Ch., Paris, 2001—. Mem.: NEA (assoc.), Am. Choral Dir. Assn., Ill. Music Educators Assn. (assoc.), Ill. Edn. Assn. (assoc.), Music Educators Nat. Conf. (assoc.), Nat. Flute Assn. (assoc.), Women Band Dir. Internat. (assoc.), Tau Beta Sigma (life; founding v.p. chpt. 1976—77). Methodist. Avocations: music performance, travel, animals. Office: Paris High Sch 309 S Main St Paris IL 61944 Office Phone: 217-466-1175. Business E-Mail: hiddles@paris95.k12.il.us.

HIDSON, PATRICIA DIANE, artist, educator; b. Edmonton, Alta., Can., Nov. 20, 1948; arrived in U.S., 1974; d. Albert John Hidson and Patricia Florence Ryland; m. James Wilfred Brozek, Feb. 14, 1991; m. Brian Peter Bentz, Jan. 16, 1974 (div. Oct. 1985); children: Paul Bentz, Meighan Bentz, Brian Bentz. BEd, U. Alta., Edmonton, 1975; postgrad., U. Wis., Milw., 1978—81, Cape Sch. Art, Provincetown, Mass., 1982—84, Milw. Inst. Art and Design, 1983—84, Peninsula Art Sch., 2004—. Dir., tchr. The Hidson Art Sch. and Studio, Milw.; prin., owner Pat Hidson Art Gallery, Milw., 2003—. Lectr., spkr. in field; mem. faculty Pa. Art Sch., Door County, Wis. One-woman shows include Regional Art Ctr., LaCrosse, Wis., 1998, Grace Chosy Gallery, Madison, Wis., 1998, 1995, 1993, Gruen Gallery, Chgo., 1997, 1990, Madison U. Med. Hosp., 1993, Tory Folliard Gallery, Milw., 1993, others, exhibited in group shows at Door County, Wis., 2001, Tory Folliard Gallery, 2000, 1999, 1998, Art Resources Gallery, St. Paul, 1998, Edmonton Art Gallery, 1997, Gallerie Stephanie, Chgo., 1995, Wustum Mus., Racine, Wis., 1985—97, Carolyn Ruff Gallery, Mpls., 1993, Banaker Gallery, San Francisco, 1993, San Miguel Allende, Mex., 1993, others, Wis. Artists Biennial, Anderson Art Ctr., Kenosha, 2005, Represented in permanent collections Walt Disney Corp., Quadracci Corp. Collection (Milw.), Associated Bank (Milw.), Marine Bank (Milw.), numerous others; featured and reviewed (numerous publs.). Episcopalian. Avocations: yoga, reading, wildlife rehabilitation. Home: 5730 N river Forest Dr Glendale WI 53209 Office: Hidson Art Sch Studio and Art Gallery 303-133 W Pittsburgh Ave Milwaukee WI 53204 Office Phone: 414-227-0991. E-mail: phidson@wi.rr.com.

HIEATT, CONSTANCE BARTLETT, English language educator; b. Boston, Feb. 11, 1928; d. Arthur Charles and Eleonora (Very) Bartlett; m. Allen Kent Hieatt, Oct. 25, 1958. Student, Smith Coll., 1945-47; AB, Hunter Coll., 1953, AM, 1957; PhD, Yale U., 1959. Lectr. City Coll., CUNY, 1959-60; from asst. prof. to assoc. prof. English Queensborough C.C., CUNY, 1960-65; from assoc. prof. to prof. St. John's U., Jamaica, NY, 1965-69; prof. English U. Western Ont., London, Canada, 1969-93, prof. emeritus, 1993—. Author: (with A.K. Hieatt) The Canterbury Tales of Geoffrey Chaucer, 1964, rev. edit., 1981, Spenser: Selected Poetry, 1970; The Realism of Dream Visions, 1967, Beowulf and Other Old English Poems, 1967, rev. edit., 1983, Essentials of Old English, 1968, The Miller's Tale By Geoffrey Chaucer, 1970; (with Sharon Butler) Pleyn Delit: Medieval Cookery for Modern Cooks, 1976, rev. edit., 1979; (with Brenda Hosington) rev. 2d edit., 1996, Karlamagnus Saga, Vols. I and II, 1975, Vol. III, 1980; (with Sharon Butler) Curye on Inglysch, 1985; An Ordinance of Pottage, 1988; (with Robin F. Jones) La Novele Cirurgerie, 1990; (with Minnette Gaudet) Guillaume de Machaut's Tale of the Alerion, 1994; (with Brian Shaw and Duncan Macrae-Gibson) Beginning Old English, 1994; (with Rudolf Grewe) Libellus de Arte Coquinaria, 2001, (with Terry Nutter and Johnna H. Holloway) Concordance of English Recipes: Thirteenth Through Fifteenth Centuries, 2006; also children books (with Hieatt) The Canterbury Tales of Geoffrey Chaucer, 1961, Sir Gawain and the Green Knight, 1967, The Knight of the Lion, 1968, The Knight of the Cart, 1969, The Joy of the Court, 1971, The Sword and the Grail, 1972, The Castle of Ladies, 1973, The Minstrel Knight, 1974. Yale U. fellow, and Lewis-Farmington fellow, 1957-59, Vis. fellow Yale U., 1985-86, 89-93; Can. Council and Social Sci. and Humanities Rsch. Coun. grant. Fellow Royal Soc. Can.; mem. MLA, Medieval Acad. Am., Internat. Soc. Anglo-Saxonists, Can Soc. Medievalists. Episcopalian. Home: 335 Essex Mdws Essex CT 06426-1526 Personal E-mail: constance.hieatt@yale.edu.

HIEBNER, AIDA CECILIA, secondary school educator, education educator; b. Quito, Ecuador, Aug. 18, 1946; arrived in U.S., 1975; d. Carlos Humberto Padilla Salazar and Zoila Amada Vallejo Diaz; m. Lauren Wayne, June 2; children: Andrey Johann, Diego Ryan. Elem. edn., Normal for Tchrs., 1965; BA in ESL, Ctrl. U. Quito, 1972, U. Nebr., 1987, MEd, 2001; postgrad., Inst. Children's Lit., 2001. Typist Dept. Civil Registry, Quito, 1965—69; exec. sec. Ecuadorian Ins. Co., Quito, 1969—73; sec. Def. Dept., Quito, 1973—75; tchr. Pvt. Sch., Quito, 1974—75; tchr. aide O'Neill Elem. Sch., Nebr., 1978—80; tchr. Page Pub. Sch., Nebr., 1989—92; tchr. art O'Neill Pub. Sch., 1993—. Tchr. art St. Mary's H.S., O'Neill, 1988—89, tchr. Spanish, 1993—; instr. Spanish I North East C.C., O'Neill, 2000—. Author (poem): Nat. Libr. Poetry, 1998 (Editor's Choice, 1998); Hispanic Art Show, Kearney, Nebr., 1986 (1st Pl., 1986), State Art Clubs, 1988 (Hon. Memtion), Ranchland Art Group, 1981—89 (Best of Show). Mem.: O'Neill Edn. Assn., Nebr. Assn. Art Clubs, Nebr. State Edn. Assn., Alpha Delta Kappa. Avocations: painting, travel, reading, photography, writing. Office: O'Neill Pub Sch PO Box 230 Oneill NE 68763

HIERHOLZER, JOAN, artist; BFA, U. Tex., Austin; MFA, Rutgers U.; m. Harlan B. Pratt; children: Charles Cooper Bennett, David Pine Bennett. Fashion illustrator, San Antonio; tchr. art Summit (N.J.) Art Ctr. and Pub. Schs.; one-woman shows of paintings include: Exxon Refinery, Linden, NJ, Marion Koogler McNay Art Mus., San Antonio, Summit Art Ctr., Ednl. Testing Svc., Princeton, NJ, Allied Chem. Corp., Morristown, NJ, AT&T Galleries, Basking Ridge, NJ, Phoenix Gallery, N.Y.C.; group shows include: Bodley Gallery, N.Y.C., Dallas Mus. Fine Arts, Equitable Life Assurance Co., N.Y.C., Fairleigh Dickinson U., Madison, NJ, Lever House, N.Y.C., Montclair (NJ) Art Mus., Mus. N.Mex., Santa Fe, Nabisco, NJ, Rutgers U. Art Gallery, New Brunswick, NJ, Witte Mus., San Antonio, NJ State Mus. Art, Trenton, Fed. Bldg., N.Y.C.; mem. Phoenix Gallery, N.Y.C.; represented in permanent collections: Westinghouse Elevator Co., Exxon Corp., Overlook Hosp., Summit, Schering Plough, Sentry Refining Inc., Chem. Bank., Juniata Coll., Pa., Hiram Coll., Ohio, Deloitte, Haskell & Sells, NJ, Diagnostic/Retrieval Systems, Inc., NJ, Schindler Corp., Jane Kimmerlie Art Mus., also pvt. collections. Fellow MacDowell Colony, Peterborough, N.H. Mem. Nat. Arts Club of N.Y.C., Nat. Assn. Women Artists, Artshowcase, Kappa Kappa Gamma. Republican. Address: 760 County Rd 513 Pittstown NJ 08867-9425 Personal E-mail: jhdachier@earthlink.net.

HIETALA, VALERIE GRACE, realtor, environmentalist, educator; d. Douglas Waldie Dill; m. Kaarlo John Hietala, July 27, 1999; children: Rachel, Kaarlo John, Ingrid, Amber, Sasha. BS in Agr., U. Wis., 1973; MS, U. Colo., 1991. Cert. edn. Fla., 1998, Fla. Assn. Realtors, 2002. Environ. educator Cheyenne Mountain Zoo, Colorado Springs, Colo., 1984—90; dir. Blue Belly Lizard, Los Olivos, Calif., 1993—96; environ. educator McIntosh Mid. Sch., Sarasota, Fla., 1996—2000; dir. Lucy Spoons Island Outfitters, Holmes Beach, 1998—2002; realtor, real estate sales Re/Max Gulfstream, 2000—. Environ. educator, cons. Butterfly Assn., Bradenton, Fla., 1999—. Jewelry, Non Titled (Longboat Key Art award, 2004). Edn. com. DAR, Anna Maria, Fla., 2003—04. Scholar, Longboat Key Art Ctr., 2004. Mem.: Selby Bot. (assoc.), Ringling Art Musuem (assoc.), DAR (assoc.). Achievements include research in Geneological research for Daughters of the American Revolution. Avocations: travel, swimming, photography, scuba diving, art. Personal E-mail: wawanuky@runbox.com.

HIGA, CHARMAINE KEALA, psychologist; d. William Higa and Charleen Ludden Marlow. BA in Psychology, U. Hawaii, 1999; MA in Clin. Psychology, U. Tulsa, 2001, PhD in Clin. Psychology, 2004. Resident clin. psychology U. Miss. Med. Sch., Jackson, 2003—04; clin. trial supr., project co-director U. Hawaii, Honolulu, 2004—. Adj. faculty Jackson (Miss.) State U., 2004, Argosy U., Honolulu, 2005; editl. asst. Jour. Abnormal Child Psychology, Honolulu, 2005—. Recipient Allen Chapman Grad. Scholar Presentation award, U. Tulsa, 1999-2002; Allen Chapman Faculty Devel. fellowship, 1999-2003, Student Rsch. grant, Office Rsch., U. Tulsa, 2000, 2002. Mem.: APA, Assn. Behavioral, Cognitive Therapies, Phi Beta Kappa.

HIGBEE, BETH, communications executive; b. 1971; B in Journalism, Pa. State U., 1992, B in French, 1992. Editor Rodale Press, founding mem., new media divsn.; dir. ops., entertainment websites NBCi, sr. product mgr.; co-founder Snap.com; v.p., new media Scripps Networks Interactive, 2000, sr. v.p. Named one of 40 Executives Under 40, Multichannel News, 2006. Mem.: Step Up Women's Network NY.*

HIGBEE, DONNA GOOD, writer, researcher; b. Cedar Rapids, Iowa, Feb. 28, 1947; d. Richard Vernon and Freda Lee Good; m. William Higbee, Sept. 23, 1989. BA in Dramatic Arts, Pasadena Playhouse Coll. Theatre Arts, Calif., 1967; AA in Psychology, Santa Barbara City Coll., Calif., 1982; BA in religious studies, U. Calif., Santa Barbara, 1985. Cert. clin. hypnotherapist Hypnosis Motivation Inst., 1994. Personal asst. to chancellor U. Calif., Santa Barbara, 1986—90; exec. asst., pub. rels. 2020 Group, Santa Barbara, 1993—94; pres. Daona Promotions, Santa Barbara, 1994—; dir. Contact Encounters Investigation Team, Santa Barbara, 1994—. Freelance writer, lectr., Santa Barbara, 1994—; counselor, lectr. Natural Alternative Medicine, Santa Barbara, 1996—. Actress: (films) The Girl Next Door, 2003; Shop Girl, 2003; Mrs. Harris, 2004; In Her Shoes, 2004; Chumscrubber, 2004; The Wedding Crashers, 2004; Monster-In-Law, 2005; (TV pilot) NYPD 2069, 2003; (TV movie) Turning Homeward, 2003; (TV series) Arrested Development, 2004; Wedding Chapel, 2005; author (children's book): Paula Pelican; contbr. articles to profl. jours. Involved in Katrina relief Am. Red Cross. Mem.: AFTRA, SAG, U. Calif. Alumni Assn., Pasadena Playhouse Alumni & Assocs. Avocations: music, dance.

HIGDON, LINDA HAMPTON, congressional staff; b. Athens, Tenn., Mar. 14, 1951; d. Lula Sue (Stiles) Hampton; a m. Donald Wayne Higdon, Dec. 20, 1973. BA, Tenn. Wesleyan Coll., Athens, 1973; MPA, U. Tenn., 1985. Cert. Am. Soc. Pub. Adminstrs., Knoxville, Tenn. Tchr. McMinn Co. Schs., Etowah, Tenn., 1973-75; dist. staff asst. U.S. Rep. John Duncan Jr., Athens, Tenn., 1975—. Adj. instr. Tenn. Wesleyan Coll., Athens, 1985-86. Former pres., McMinn Co. Young Rep., Athens, Tenn., McMinn Co. Rep. Women's Club; former GOP chmn. McMinn Co. Rep. Party, Athens, Tenn.; area 2 vice-chmn. Tenn. Fedn. Rep. Women State Bd.; program leader Athens Area C. of C. Leadership McMinn Program. Named Miss Tenn. Young Rep. State Yr-Fed, Nashville, 1972; recipient Lincoln award McMinn Co. Young Rep. Club, Athens, Tenn., 1992. Mem. ASPA. Republican. Methodist. Avocations: boating, gardening. Home: Kirkwood Est Englewood TN 37327 Office: US Rep John Duncan Jr 6 E Madison Ave Athens TN 37303-3697

HIGDON, PAMELA LEIS, writer; b. San Bernardino, Calif., Sept. 2, 1943; d. Stella Doss and Raymond Ellsworth Leis; m. Sherman Robert Higdon Jr., Aug. 29, 1964 (dec.); 1 child, Mary Katherine Christian. BS Edn., Tex. Technol. U., Lubbock, 1966. Cert. tchr. Tex., 1966. Tchr. elem. sch., sci. coord. for elem. sch., dist. lang. arts com. mem., after sch. computer instr. Arabian Am. Oil Co., Ras Tanura, Ea. Province, Saudi Arabia, 1978—86; editor/writer, Bird Talk Mag. and Birds USA Fancy Publs., Irvine, Calif., 1987—90; writer/editor, product developer, project mgr., acquisitions editor Ednl. Insights, Carson, Calif., 1990—94; freelance writer and editor PLH Writing/Editing, Castroville, Tex., 1994—. Author: (children's ednl. book) Science Notes: How Things Move; author, editor (pet care book) The Essential Cockatiel, The Essential Zebra Finch; editor: (prehospital med. booklet) The Life You Save: Community Defibrillation Programs & the Emergency Care Responder; author: (monthly newsletter Can. Paramedics) Jour. Emergency Med. Svcs.; editor (monthly periodicals) Journal of Emergency Medical Services, Fire Rescue Magazine, Clarity, EMS Insider, EMS M&S, EMS Best Practices, Caring for the Ages-for Long-Term Care Practitioners; author (with Julie Mancini): (bird watching book) Watching Backyard Birds; author: (children's ednl. book) Pattern Blocks (math series); author, project mgr. (computerized ednl. games) Geosafari & Geosafari Jr., assorted; author (with Katherine Christian): (ednl. book) Third Grade Review; writer, Nat. Wildlife Fedn. (interactive, wildlife, ednl.) Insects, Exotic Animals, Sea Life, Wild Animals, Dinosaurs; author (with Dr. David McCluggage): (animal care book) Holistic Care for Birds: A Manual of Wellness and Healing; author: (pet care book) Bird Care and Training, (bird care book) Happy Healthy Pets: The Quaker Parrot; writer, editor (pet care book) The Essential African Grey; copy editor: The Hospitalist. Vol. writer cmty. newsletter Mills Br. Village Bd. Dirs., Kingwood, Tex., 1996—2000; vol. writer, designer, pub. town newsletter Castroville, Tex., 2001—03; exec. bd., rec. sec. Meth. Ch., Castroville, 2003—04; past chair Landmark Hist. Preservation Commn., 2004—05. Recipient Cmty. Svc. award, Mills Br. Village Bd. Dirs., 1997. Mem.: DAR (life), Daus. Confederacy, Daus. Republic Tex. (rec. sec. 2002—04). Democrat. Avocations: mentoring children, quilting, reading, swimming, birdwatching.

HIGGINBOTHAM, DEBORAH WATTS, social worker; b. Charleston, W.Va., June 27, 1953; d. Michael Montgomery and Barbara Anne (Balderson) Watts; m. Gary R. Higginbotham, Sept. 4, 1951; children: Gary R., II, Amy Renee. BS, Alderson Broaddus Coll., 1974; MSW, Va. Commonwealth U., 1984; M in Divinity, Bapt. Theol. Seminary, Richmond, 2002. Lic. social worker, Va.; cert. massage therapist; registered play therapist/supr.; cert. in eye movement desensitization and reprocessing; ordained gospel min. Social worker Charles City County Dept. Social Svcs., Va., 1974-77, Chesterfield County Dept. Social Svcs., 1978-81; clin. social worker Ea. State Hosp., Williamsburg, Va., 1984-85, Am Masri, MD, Ltd., Petersburg, Va., 1985-88; dir. Ctr. Families and Children, Hopewell, Va., 1989—2003; pastoral counselor Kanawha Pastoral Counselling Ctr., 2004—. Cons. Commonwealth Health Care Home Health, Colonial Heights, Va., 1990—; chair Social Svcs. Adv. Bd., Hopewell, 1991-95; cons. adv. bd. Headstart, Hopewell, 1993—. Founder, dir. H.O.P.E., Hopewell, 1992-95; mem. cmty. svc. bd. Dist. 19, Petersburg, 1995-97. Mem. Nat. Assn. Social Work, Internat. Soc. Study Dissociation, Assn. Play Therapy (reg.). Democrat. Baptist. Achievements include first to first ordained woman in min. at First Bapt. Ch. St. Albans, W. Va. Avocations: travel, music, reading, gardening. Office: Kanawha Pastoral Counseling Ctr 16 Leon Sullivan Way Ste 300 Charleston WV 25306

HIGGINBOTHAM, EDITH ARLEANE, radiologist, researcher; b. New Orleans, Sept. 14, 1946; d. Luther Aldrich and Ruby (Clark) H.; m. Terry Lawrence Andrews (div. 1979); m. Donald Temple Ford (div. 1989). BS, Howard U., 1967, MS, 1970, MD, 1974. Diplomate Am. Bd. Radiology, Am. Bd. Nuclear Medicine. Intern St. Vincent's Hosp., N.Y.C., 1974-75, resident in diagnostic radiology, 1975-78, resident in nuclear radiology, 1978-79; asst. prof. radiology, chief nuclear medicine Howard U., Howard U. Hosp., Washington, 1979-82; assoc. prof. clin. radiology, dir. nuclear medicine U. Medicine and Dentistry N.J., Newark, 1982-90; locum tenens radiologist Sterling Med., Cin., 1991-94, Med. Nat., San Antonio, 1990-91; diagnostic radiologist Diagnostic Health Imaging Systems, Lanham, Md., 1994-95; locum tenens radiologist, 1995-97; radiologist, dir. radiology N.E. Wash. Med. Group, Colville, Wash., 1997—99; radiologist Mount Carmel Hosp., Colville, 1997-99, Barstow (Calif.) Cmty. Hosp., 1999, Queen of Peace Hosp., Mitchell, SD, 1999—2002, New Ulm Med Ctr., Minn., 2002—03, dir. radiology, 2003; radiologist Naeve Hosp., Albert Lea (Minn.) Med. Ctr., Mayo Health Sys., 2003—. Cons. Biotech. Rsch. Inst., Rockville, Md., 1989-94; profl. assoc. Ctr. for Molecular Medicine and Immunology, Newark, 1984-90; asst. prof. radiology George Washington U., Washington, 1990; counselor Am. Coll. Radiology, SD, 2001; presenter in field. Contbr. articles to profl. jours. Named Outstanding Working Woman, Glamour mag., 1981, Hon. Dep. Atty. Gen., State of La., 1982. Mem.: SD Med. Assn. (continuing med. edn. com. 2001), Freeborn County Med. Soc. (pres. 2005), Minn. Med. Assn. (continuing med. edn. com. 2005), Soc. Nuclear Medicine, Radiol. Soc. N.Am., Am. Coll. Radiology, Phi Delta Epsilon, Sigma Xi. Roman Catholic. Avocations: aerobics, reading, music, travel. E-mail: ehigginbothammd@charter.net.

HIGGINBOTHAM, EVE JULIET, ophthalmologist, educator, dean; b. New Orleans, Nov. 4, 1953; d. Luther Aldrich and Ruby Edith (Clark) H.; m. Frank Christopher Williams, June 7, 1986. BSChE, MS in Engring., MIT, 1975; MD, Harvard U., 1979. Intern Pacific Med. Ctr., San Francisco, 1979-80; resident La. State U. Eye Ctr., 1980-83; fellow Mass. Eye and Ear Infirmary, Boston, 1983-85; asst. prof. U. Ill., Chgo., 1985-90; assoc. prof. U. Mich., Ann Arbor, 1990-94; prof., chair dept. ophthalmology and visual sciences U. Md., Balt., 1994—2005; dean Morehouse Sch. Medicine, Atlanta, 2005—, sr. v.p. acad. affairs, 2005—. Co-editor: Management of Difficult Glaucoma, 1994, Clinician's Guide to Comprehensive Ophtholomology, 1998; contbr. articles to profl. jours; mem. editl. bd. Jour. of Glaucoma, 1990-93, Archives of Ophthalmology, 1994—; sect. editor: Glaucoma in Principles and Practice of Ophthalmology. Bd. dirs. Prevent Blindness Am., Schaumburg, Ill., 1990-97, chair publs. com., 1990-95, chair scientific adv. com., 1995—. Fellow Am. Acad. Ophthalmology (trustee 1992-95); mem. Women in Ophthalmology (bd. dirs. 1990-99), Assn. Univ. Profs. Ophthalmology, Assn. in Rsch. in Vision and Ophthalmology, Inst. Medicine, Md. Soc. Eye Physicians and Surgeons (v.p. 1997-99, pres. 2000—), Balt. City Med. Soc. (treas. 1999-00, v.p. 2000—). Avocations: golf, piano. Office: Office of Dean Morehouse Sch Medicine 720 Westview Dr SW Atlanta GA 30310-1495*

HIGGINBOTHAM, JOAN E., astronaut; b. Chgo., Aug. 03; BSEE, So. Ill. U., 1987; M in Mgmt., Fla. Inst. Tech., 1992, M in Space Sys., 1996. Payload elec. engr. divsn. ele. and telecomm. sys. NASA, Kennedy Space Ctr., Fla., 1987, lead orbiter experiments space shuttle Columbia, 1987, exec. staff asst. to dir. shuttle ops. and mgmt., backup orbiter project engr. space shuttle Atlantis, lead orbiter project engr. space shuttle Columbia; astronaut, mission specialist NASA, Johnson Space Ctr., Houston, 1996—. Named Disting. Alumni, Fla. Inst. Tech., 1997, So. Ill. U.; named one of 50 Disting. Scientists and Engrs., Nat. Tech. Assn.; recipient Key to City of Cocoa, Fla., Key to City of Rockledge, Presdl. Sports award in bicycling and weight training, Outstanding Woman of Yr. award, Exceptional Svc. Medal, NASA. Mem.: Links, Inc., Bronze Eagles, Delta Sigma Theta. Avocations: weightlifting, bicycling, music, motivational speaking. Office: Astronaut Office/CB NASA Johnson Space Ctr Houston TX 77058

HIGGINBOTHAM, WENDY JACOBSON, legislative staff member, writer; b. Salt Lake City, Oct. 23, 1947; d. Alfred Thurl and Virginia Lorraine (LaCom) Jacobson; m. Keith Higginbotham, July 12, 1969; children: Ann Elizabeth Morley, Ryan Keith, Laura Carol Hoopes. Student, Occidental Coll., 1965—66, U. Grenoble, France, 1967; BA cum laude with highest honors, Brigham Young U., 1969. Tchg. instr. Brigham Young U., Provo, Utah, 1969-70, editor univ. press, 1970-71; freelance editor Camarillo, Calif., 1971-78; freelance newspaper writer Vienna, Va., 1983-85; mem. profl. staff U.S. Senate Labor Com., Washington, 1985-86; exec. asst. U.S. Senator Orrin G. Hatch, Washington, 1986-88, legis. dir., 1988-91, chief of staff/adminstrv. asst., 1991-94, chief policy adviser, 1994-95; polit. adviser, freelance writer Washington, 1996—. Mem. Profl. Rep. Women, Phi Kappa Phi. Republican. Mem. Lds Ch. Avocations: travel, hiking. Home: 2022 Willow Branch Ct Vienna VA 22181-2972

HIGGINS, DIANE W., music teacher; b. Troy, N.Y., Jan. 19, 1949; d. Harris Arthur and Mary Agnes (Cochrane) Ward; m. Charles Royden Higgins, Jr., June 5, 1971; children: David Royden, Carolyn Ward. BMus, Salem Coll., 1971. Treas. N.C. Music Tchrs. Assn., 1986-89, v.p./scholarship, 1989-91, chair state piano tchrs., 1995-97, conv. chair, 1997-99, pres., 1999-2001; v.p. Charlotte Piano Tchrs. Forum, N.C., 1995-97, pres., 1997-99. Violinist Winston-Salem Symphony, 1967—71; founder, dir. Charlotte Music Career Fair, 1999—; piano instr. U. N.C.-Greensboro Summer Music Camp, 1996—2001. Solo pianist ASID Home Tour, Charlotte, N.C., 1986-2001, Holiday House Tour, Charlotte, 1989-2001, Fourth Ward Christmas Tour, Charlotte, 1989-99, Presbyn. Hosp., Charlotte, 1986-2001; mem. Salem Coll. Friends of Music, 2001; pres. Queens Coll. Friends of Music, 2001. Recipient violin scholarship Salem Coll., Winston-Salem, 1967-71. Mem.: Nat. Guild Piano Tchrs., Charlotte Music Tchrs. Assn. (sec. 1999—2001), Charlotte Piano Tchrs. Forum (pres. 1997—99), N.C. Music Tchrs. Assn. (pres. 1999—2001), Music Tchrs. Nat. Assn., Friends of Music at Salem Coll., Friends of Music at Queens Coll., Charlotte Civic Orch. (violinist 1987—), N.C. Fedn. Music Clubs (dist. chair 1981—84), Charlotte Music Club (sec. 1984—85). Home: 4625 Mullens Ford Rd Charlotte NC 28226-5040

HIGGINS, DOROTHY MARIE, dean, educator; b. Lawrence, Mass., May 1, 1930; d. John Daniel and Mary Jane (Herbertson) H. AB, Emmanuel Coll., Boston, 1951; MS, Cath. U., Wash., DC, 1961; PhD, Boston Coll., Mass., 1966. Assoc. prof. chemistry Emmanuel Coll., Boston, 1966-88, chair chemistry dept., 1974—85; divsn. chair math., sci., tech. Roxbury C.C., Roxbury Crossing, Mass., 1988—90; dean arts and scis. Teikyo-Post U., Waterbury, Conn., 1990—97; part-time instr. organic chemistry & gen. chemistry Naugatuck Valley C.C., 1998—, rsch. assoc., 1999—, instr. intro. to engring., 1998—, physics instr., 2004. Grant cons. N.E. Coll. Optometry, Boston, 1986; faculty cons. Zymark Corp., Hopkinton, Mass., 1982; rsch. assoc. U. Mass., Boston, 1975—84. Editor: (workbook) Geometry: Development Students, 1989; editor sci. newsletter, 1989; editl. adv. bd. Jour. Coll. Sci. Tchg., 1984-88, 2001-. Instrumentation grantee NSF, 1985, Chautauqua grantee NSF, 1981-82, Instrumentation grantee George Alden Trust, 1985, Boston Globe Found., 1985, Extramural Assoc. grantee NIH, 1984. Mem. Am. Chem. Soc., NSTA, New Eng. Chem. Tchrs., Soc. Coll. Sci. Tchg. Democrat. Roman Catholic. Avocations: needlecrafts, crocheting, cross country skiing. E-mail: dhiggins@snet.net.

HIGGINS, HARRIET PRATT, investment advisor; b. Cortland, N.Y., Dec. 18, 1950; d. Edward Frances and Adeline (Bostelmann) Higgins; children from previous marriage: John Higgins MacDonald, Peter Brewster MacDonald. BA, Wells Coll., 1972; MA, Middlebury Coll. Grad. Sch. Langs., 1973; MBA, Columbia U., 1977. Corp. fin. officer Bank Am., N.Y.C., 1978-80; asst. v.p. J. Henry Schroder Bank and Trust Co., N.Y.C., 1980-82; mgr. Royal Bank Can., N.Y.C., 1982-84, sr. mgr., 1984-94; v.p. pvt. client svcs. TCW Group, N.Y.C., 1994-99; mng. dir. Auda Advisor Assocs. LLC, 1999—2000; mgr., CEO Alyssa LLC, 1999—2000; pres. Mayflower Capital, 2000—04; mng. dir., ptnr. Fin. Net Boston, 2001—04; rep. Winston, Evans & Crocher, Boston, 2001—04; investment advisor Smith Barney/Citigroup, N.Y.C., 2005—. Adj. prof. econs. Pace U., N.Y.C., 1979—80, NYU, N.Y.C., 1983—84; chmn., CEO, pres. McGraw, NY, 1987—95; alumni bd. Columbia Bus. Sch., 1982—87; trustee, chair investment com. Wells Coll., 1998—. Mem. Commonwealth of Mass. Ctrl. Artery and Tunnel Commn.; vol., contbr. Rep. Nat. Com., N.Y.C., 1980—; trustee Boys and Girls Club, Newport County, 2000—. Fellow Carnegie Found., 1974—75. Mem.: Fin. Womens Assn., Preservation Soc. Newport County, Newport Hist. Soc., Desc. of the Mayflower Soc. Republican. Episcopalian. Avocations: skiing, tennis, violin. Office: Smith Barney Citigroup 284 Bellevue Ave Newport RI 02840

HIGGINS, ISABELLE JEANETTE, retired librarian; b. Evanston, Ill., Dec. 13, 1919; d. Frank LeRoy and Ada Louise (Wilcox) Heck; m. George Alfred Higgins, Jan. 23, 1945 (dec. Sept. 1994); children: Alfred Clinton, Donald Quentin, Heather Higgins Aanes, Laura Higgins Palmer, Carol Higgins. BS, Northwestern U., 1940; MLS, U. Md., 1971. Cert. libr., Md. With Liebermann Waelchli Co., Tokyo, 1940-41, Shanghai Evening Post, 1941-42; editl. asst. Newsweek mag., N.Y.C., 1944; wire editor FBIS/FCC, Washington, 1945—46; rsch. and analysis China desk CIA, Washington, 1946-49; supr. library vols. Westbrook Sch., Bethesda, Md., 1965-69; reference libr. Montgomery County Pub. Librs., Bethesda, 1969-83; libr. Brooks Inst. Photography, Santa Barbara, Calif., 1984-96, ret., 1996. Treas. Friends of Santa Barbara Pub. Libr., 1987-88. Mem. AAUW (bd. dirs. Santa Barbara br. 1988-94, del. nat. conv. 1989), Spl. Librs. Assn., Calif. Libr. Assn., Santa Barbara Little Gardens Club (pres. 1987-89), Floriade Garden Club (pres. 1990-91). Congregationalist. Avocations: reading, swimming, gardening. Home: 3775 Modoc Rd Apt 203 Santa Barbara CA 93105-4467 Personal E-mail: higginsij@aol.com.

HIGGINS, KAREN, television producer; BA in Liberal Arts and Scis., U. Ill., Urbana-Champaign, 1989; postgrad. diploma in film and TV, U. Bristol, Eng., 1993. Freelance tv prodr., Chgo., 1989—, L.A., 1997—; field prodr., internat. prodr. E! Networks, L.A., 1997—2001. Contbg. author: World Cinema: Diary of a Day, 1994. Ambassadorial scholar, Rotary Internat., 1992—93.

HIGGINS, KATHRYN O'LEARY (KITTY O'LEARY HIGGINS), federal agency administrator, former consulting firm executive; b. Sioux City, Iowa, Oct. 11, 1947; d. Paul C. and Mary Kathryn (Callaghan) O'Leary; widowed; children: Liam James, Kevan Paul. BS, U. Nebr., 1969. Manpower specialist US Dept. Labor, Washington, 1969-78; asst. dir. employment policy White House Domestic Policy, Washington, 1978-81; staff dir. minority U.S. Senate Labor & Human Resources Com., Washington, 1981-86; chief of staff U.S. Representative Sander Levin, Washington, 1986-93; chief of staff Sec. Robert Reich US Dept. Labor, Washington, 1993-95; asst. to Pres & sec. to cabinet The White House, Washington, 1995-97; dep. sec. US Dept. Labor, Washington, 1997-99; v.p. pub. policy Nat. Trust for Hist. Preservation, Washington, 1999—2004; pres., CEO TATC Cons. Firm, Washington, 2004—05; mem. Nat. Transp. Safety Bd. (NTSB), Washington, 2006—. Bd. dirs. Ignatian Vol. Corps. Democrat. Roman Catholic. Avocations: cooking, antiques, book club. Office: Nat Transp Safety Bd 490 L Enfant Plz SW Washington DC 20594 Office Phone: 202-314-6145.

HIGGINS, LARKIN MAUREEN, artist, poet, educator; b. Santa Monica, Calif. d. DuWayne and Mary Jean (Sampson) H. BA, Calif. State U., Long Beach, 1976; MA, Calif. State U., Fullerton, 1983; MFA, Otis Coll. Art and Design, 1995. Artist/poet resident Dorland Mountain Arts Colony, 2000, 2001, 2002; prof. art Calif. Luth. U., Thousand Oaks. Represented in numerous collections including Grunwald Collection-Armand Hammer Mus., Erie Art Mus., Pa., Laguna Beach Mus. Art, Calif. Mus. Photography, Laguna Beach Mus. Art, Calif. Mus. Photography; exhibited nationally in group and one-woman shows; art reviewed/ pub. in various pubs. including L.A. Times, Artweek, The Boston Globe, Genre, Antiques & The Arts Weekly, U-TURN, others; anthologies: Matchbook, Jitters: The Best of Southern California Coffee House Fiction and Poetry, So Luminous the Wildflowers: Anthology of California Poetry, Visiting Frost: Poems Inspired by the Life and Work of Robert Frost, 2005; contbr. poetry to mags. and jours Past. bd. dirs., past chairperson nat. photography exhbn. com. Westwood (Calif.) Ctr. for the Arts; past chairperson lecture com. L.A. Ctr. for Photographic Studies; founding mem. Women in Photography, L.A. Recipient cash award ASA Gallery, U. N.Mex., 1982, Purchase award Erie (Pa.) Art Mus., 1984; Hewlett Found. grantee, 1987-88, 2004, 06, Jones grantee, 1986. Mem. Modern Lang. Assn., Coll. Art Assn., Beyond Baroque Lit. Arts Ctr. Business E-Mail: higgins@clunet.edu.

HIGGINS, M. EILEEN, management consultant, educator; b. Dayton, Ohio, Apr. 4, 1943; d. Harold Elwood and Esther Marie (Kelly) Benjamin; m. James Edward Higgins (div.); children: Joseph Benjamin, James Timothy; m. Edward William Lavine, Jan. 1, 2000 (dec. Nov. 2006). BA in Psychology, Pa. State U., 1965; MBA, Frostburg State U., 1985; postgrad., U. Md., 2002—. Editl. asst. Signal Mag., Washington, 1965—66; publ. editor Nat. Coun. on Radiation Protection and Measurements, Washington, 1966—67; pvt. practice Montgomery Village, Md., 1967—78; sr. mng. editor Aspen Publ., Rockville, Md., 1978—88; prof. Frostburg (Md.) State U., 1989—. Trainer Georgetown U., Washington, 2000—; cons. in field; deans adv. panel, students adv. bd. U. Md., 2001—03. Editor: Editl. Experts, 1969—78; contbr. articles to profl. jours. Dir. publ. Am. Soc. Parenteral and Enteral Nutrition, Silver Spring, 1990—91. Mem.: Orgnl. Behavior Tchg. Soc., S.E. Decision Sci. Inst., Acad. Mgmt., Internat. Acad. Bus. Disciplines, Mgmt., Spirituality and Religion (sec.-treas. 2003—05), Frederick County C. of C. (spkrs. bur.), Am. News Women's Club. Avocations: reading, travel, yoga, hiking, music. Home: PO Box 383 Libertytown MD 21762 Office: Frostburg State Univ Univ Md System Bldg 32 W Washington St Hagerstown MD 21740 Office Phone: 240-527-2748. Personal E-mail: eileenbenj@aol.com.

HIGGINS, MARY CELESTE, lawyer, researcher; b. Chgo., Feb. 9, 1943; d. Maurice James and Helen Marie (Egan) H. AB, St. Mary-of-the-Woods Coll., Ind., 1965; JD, DePaul U., 1970; LLM, John Marshall Law Sch., Chgo., 1976; postgrad., Harvard U., 1981—82, MPA, 1982; MPhil, U. Cambridge (Eng.), 1983. Bar: Ill. 1970, U.S. Dist. Ct. (no. dist.) Ill. 1970. Pvt. practice, Chgo., 1970—72, 1979—80; atty. corp. counsel dept. Continental Bank, Chgo., 1972—76; asst. sec., asst. counsel Marshall Field & Co., Chgo., 1976—79; sr. atty. Mattel, Inc., Hawthorne, Calif., 1980—81; rsch. in revitalization and adjustment U.S. Industries in U.S. and World Mkts., 1981—83; legal cons., 1983—85; Midwest regional officer Legal Svcs. Corp., 1985—87, assoc. dir., 1986, acting dir. office of field svcs., 1986—87, dir., 1987—89, Meridian One Corp., Alexandria, Va., 1990—. Recipient Am. Jurisprudence award, 1966—70. Mem.: Ill. Bar. Assn. Home: 203 Yoakum Pky Apt 508 Alexandria VA 22304-3711 E-mail: mhiggins@meridianone.com.

HIGGINS, MARY ELLEN See HAWKINS, MARY

HIGGINS, OLEDA JACKSON, retired medical and surgical nurse; b. Thibodaux, La. d. Tillman and Bessie (Charles) Jackson; m. Samuel J. Higgins; 1 child, Sterling J. BSN, Dillard U., 1958. From staff nurse to nursing dir. Flint-Goodridge Hosp., New Orleans, 1958-78; staff nurse Jo Ellen Smith Med. Ctr., New Orleans, 1979-95; ret., 1995. Nursing home cons. Bapt. Faith Home, New Orleans, 1968-72. Mem. ANA, Nat. League for Nursing, Dillard U. Profl. Orgn. Nurses, Order Ea. Star, Chi ETa Phi (basileus Rho Chi chpt., chaplain 1976). Baptist. Avocations: singing, soft music, operas. Home: 4321 Macarthur Blvd New Orleans LA 70131-6843

HIGGINS, PAULINE EDWARDS, lawyer; b. Mandeville, Jamaica, W.I., Mar. 27, 1950; d. George Bazil and Doreen (Romans) Edwards; came to U.S., 1969; m. J. Aloysius Higgins, Aug. 10, 1973; children: Nicholas Alexander (dec.), Nathaniel Joseph. B.S., La. State U., 1977; JD, Tulane Law Sch., 1989, LLM, U. Houston, 1992 Audit mgr. Coopers & Lybrand, Houston, 1978-83; v.p., CFO, Benjamin Franklin Savs. Assn., Houston, 1983-86, chief of staff, counsel to Rep. Sheila Jackson Lee, US Congress, v.p., asst. gen. counsel, asst. corp. sec., JP Morgan & Chase Co., ptnr., chief diversity officer, Thompson & Knight LLP, Houston, 2006-; Author and editor tng. material for Coopers & Lybrand. Bd. dirs., asst. pres. Houston Women Employment and Edn., Inc., 1983 (Outstanding Fund Raiser award 1982); mem. Coalition 100 Black Women, Houston, 1983—; bd. dirs. Houston Area Women's Ctr., Episcopal Found. Tex. Mem. Am. Inst. C.P.A.s, Tex. Soc. C.P.A.s (savs. and loan com. 1983-84), Houston Soc. C.P.A.s, Fin. Mgrs. Soc., Nat. Assn. Female Execs. Club: Christian Profl. Women's Assn. (Houston); Recipient Rainbowmaker award, Monority Corp. Counsel Assn., 2004, Sarah T. Hughes award, State Bar Tex, Woman and Law section, 2005, Women on the Move award, Tex. Exec. Women, 2005; Named One of Tex. Top In-House Counsels, Tex. Lawyer mag., 2005 Office: Thompson & Knight LLP 333 Clay St Ste 3300 Houston TX 77002*

HIGGINS, RUTH ANN, social worker, family therapist; b. Rock Valley, Iowa, Sept. 23, 1944; d. Neal and Tillie (Feekes) Vonk; m. 1972 (div. Sept. 1986); children: Ashlie Kay, Steven Grant. BA, Northwestern Coll., 1966; MA, U. Colo., 1978; LCSW, U. Denver, 1983. Cert. profl. tchr., Colo., LCSW, Am. Bd. Social Work, 2004. Tchr. Adams County Dist. 12, Northglenn, Colo., 1967-69, Dept. Def., Clark AFB, The Philippines, 1969-70, Jefferson County Schs., Lakewood, Colo., 1970-75; social worker Boulder County Mental Health Ctr., Colo., 1977, Boulder Cmty. Counseling Ctr., 1979-81, Columbine Counseling Ctr., Broomfield, Colo., 1981—; sch. social worker Adams County Sch. Dist. 12, Northglenn, Colo., 1985—2005; clin. social worker Exempla Luth. Hospice Care, 2006—. Part time social worker Hospice of Metro Denver, 1984-85, Boulder Valley Pub. Schs., 1985, Lutheran Hospice Care, Wheatridge, Colo., 1985; bd. dirs. Health and Human Svcs. City and County Broomfield, Colo. Author, editor: Nothing Could Stop the Rain, 1976.

Counselor trainer for Up With People (Worldsmart), 1998-2000. Recipient Hon. Mention Counselor of Yr. award Colo. Sch. Counselors Assn., 1994; named finalist Alteria M. Bryant award Met. Denver Baha'i Ctr., 1996. Mem.: NASW (nat. bd. cert. diplomate in clin. social work 2004). Democrat. Avocations: stained glass, hiking, reading, music.

HIGGINS, SARAH JEAN, literature and language professor; b. Helena, Ark., Sept. 30, 1970; d. Charlie E. and Wanda J. Webb; m. Michael D. Higgins, July 7, 2003; children: Megan M. Webb, Amber I., Brittney D. BA in English, U. Ark., 1998, MA in Tchg., 1999. Lic. tchr. Ark. Dept. Edn., 1999. Tchr. Van Buren HS, Ark., 1999—2002; instr. N.W. Ark. CC, Bentonville, Ark., 2004—; tchr. Belle Point Ctr, Ft. Smith, Ark., 2005—, Fort Smith Pub. Schs., 2005—. Mem.: Nat. Coun. Tchrs. English, Am. Sch. Counselor Assn., Phi Delta Kappa (Secondary Tchr. of Yr. Western Ark. chpt. 2006), Chi Sigma Iota. Avocations: piano, reading, travel. Home: PO Box 529 West Fork AR 72774 Home Fax: 479-839-8293. Personal E-mail: sarah@arkansasusa.com.

HIGGINS, TARA A., lawyer; b. 1965; BA summa cum laude, St. John's U., 1985, JD cum laude, 1988. Bar: D.C. 1989, N.Y. 1988, N.J. 1989. Ptnr. Bingham McCutchen LLP, N.Y.C., co-chairperson project fin. practice group. Office: Bingham McCutchen LLP 399 Park Avenue New York NY 10022-4689 Office Phone: 212-705-7764. Office Fax: 212-752-5378. Business E-Mail: tara.higgins@bingham.com.

HIGGINS, SISTER THERESE, literature educator, former college president; b. Winthrop, Mass., Sept. 29, 1925; d. James C. and Margaret M. (Lennon) Higgins. AB cum laude, Regis Coll., 1947; MA, Boston Coll., 1959, DHL, 1993; PhD, U. Wis., 1963; DHL, Emmanuel Coll., 1977, Lesley Coll., 1991; postgrad. in lit. and theology, Harvard U., 1965-66; LLD (hon.), Northeastern U., 1982, Bentley Coll., 1992, Regis Coll., 1994. Joined Congregation of Sisters of St. Joseph, Roman Cath. Ch., 1947; asst. prof. English, Regis Coll., Weston, Mass., 1963-65, asst. prof., 1965-67, assoc. prof. English lit., 1968—, pres., 1974-92, also trustee, v.p. devel., 2003—05; cons., 1995—. Book reviewer Boston Globe, 1965—. Trustee Waltham (Mass.) Hosp., 1978—85, Cardinal Spellman Philatelic Mus., 1976—92; mem. Mass. Gov.'s Commn. on Status Women, 1977—79. U. Wis. rsch. grantee Eng. Mem. Nat. Cath. Ednl. Assn., AAUW, MLA, AAUP, Assn. Ind. Colls. and Univs. Mass. (exec. com.), New Eng. Colls. Fund, NEASC (commn.). Office: Regis Coll 235 Wellesley St Weston MA 02493-1505 E-mail: therese.higgins@regiscollege.edu.

HIGGINSON, JANE, environmental educator, biologist, conservationist; 1 child, Tyler Higginson Taylor. BS in Wildlife Sci., Utah State U., Logan, 1979; M in Environ. Planning, Wash. State U., Pullman, 1992; diploma in Permaculture Design, Permaculture Inst. Australia, 2000. Peace Corps trainer CHP Internat., Guatemala, Paraguay, 1974, Guatemala, Paraguay, 1977; cons. sustainable devel. Office of Emergency Projects, Guatemalan Ministry of Agr., Guatemala City, Guatemala, 1988; wildlife biologist U.S. Forest Svc., San Diego, 1989—92; coord. cmty. garden Sustainable Food Ctr., Austin Cmty. Gardens, Tex.; conservationist I Calif. Conservation Corps, San Diego, 2002—03; owner, co-dir. Snail Haven Farm and Sanctuary, El Cajon, 2004—; owner, dir. Archelonia, Ecol. and Permaculture, San Diego, 2005—. Adj. faculty Prescott Coll., Ariz., 1998—, Grossmont Coll., El Cajon, Calif., 2006, Design Inst. San Diego, 2006—; bd. dirs. San Diego Econ. Conversion Coun., Permaculture Ctr., 2004—, sec., 2004—. Author: Sea Turtle Hatchery Management, 1988. Vol. wildlife biologist Peace Corps, Guatemala, 1985—88. Recipient Beyond War award, 1987, Award of Merit for Conservation Efforts, U. San Carlos and Ministry Agr., Guatemala, 1989. Mem.: Xerces Soc. for Invertebrate Conservation. Achievements include starting system of community-operated sea turtle hatcheries in Guatemala. Avocations: meditation, nature. Home: PO Box 12027 El Cajon CA 92022

HIGH, (MARY) ELIZABETH HILLEY, retired art educator; b. Wilson, NC, Mar. 24, 1920; d. Howard Stevens Hilley and Maggie Tucker; m. Larry Allison High, May 12, 1940; children: Rebecca Elizabeth Tingen, Larry Allison, Robert Marshal, Margaret Almand Nowell. BA magna cum laude, Atlantic Christian Coll., 1939; MEd, East Carolina U., 1972. File clk. U.S. Army Depots, Richmond, Va., 1941—44, chief personnel; tchr. Nash County Schs., Rocky Mount, NC, 1966—82. Pres. Nash County Assn. Classroom Tchrs., Nashville, 1976—77. Mem. Planning Bd., Nashville, 1964—66; former chmn. NC Assn. Educators, Secondary Divsn.; former pres. NC Art Edn. Assn.; mem. acquisitions com. Nash County Arts Coun., 2001—03. Recipient Painting prize, Rocky Mt. Ann. Art Exhibit. Mem.: NC Mus. Art, Womens' Soc. Christian Svc., Barton Soc., Friends Cooley Libr., Friends Braswell Libr., Kappa Delta Pi, Delta Kappa Gamma. Meth. Home: 213 N Collins St Nashville NC 27856 Personal E-mail: lizhigh@earthlink.net.

HIGH, KEMBA M., special education educator; b. White Plains, NY, Jan. 6, 1972; d. Charles Anthony and Hannah Louise High. BS, Lincoln U., Pa., 1994; M in Elem. Edn., Lehman Coll., 2002, M in Spl. Edn., 2005. Spl. edn. tchr. NY City Bd. Edn., Bronx, 1998—2000, Yonkers Bd. Edn., 2000—; after sch. dir. White Plains Youth Bur., 1998—2000; early intervention Tender Care Agencies, Mt. Vernon, NY, 2004—. Democrat. Bapt. Home: 34 S Kensico Ave Apt 18 White Plains NY 10601

HIGHMAN, BARBARA, dermatologist; b. Washington; d. Benjamin and Helen (Wienshienk) H. Student, Northwestern U., 1960—63; MD, U. Mich., 1967. Diplomate Am. Bd. Dermatology. Intern Baylor U. Affiliated Hops., Houston, 1967—68; dermatology residency Henry Ford Hosp., Detroit, 1968—71; fellow in dermatology Johns Hopkins U., Balt., 1971—72; pvt. practice Laurel, Md., 1972—. Staff North Charles Hosp., Balt., 1972-77, Laurel Regional Hosp.; cons. in dermatology U.S. Army, Ft. Myer, Va., 1972-77. Fellow: Am. Acad. Dermatology (continuing med. edn. award given every 3 years 1978—); mem.: AMA (physicians recognition award given every 3 years 1971—), Prince George's Women's Med. Soc., Laurel Med. Soc., Med. and Chirugical Soc. State of Md., Anne Arundel County Med. Soc., Nat. Found. for Dermatology, Soc. for Investigative Dermatology. Office: 3335 Old Line Ave Laurel MD 20724-2234 Office Phone: 301-498-4682.

HIGHSMITH, WANDA LAW, retired medical association administrator; b. Cleveland, Mo., Oct. 25, 1928; d. Lloyd B. and Nan (Sisk) Law; 1 child, Holly. Student, U. Mo., 1954-56. Legal sec. firms in Mo. and D.C., until 1960; various staff positions Am. Coll. Osteopathic Surgeons, 1960-72, asst. exec. dir., conv. mgr. Alexandria, Va., 1974-94; ret., 1994. Mem.: Profl. Conv. Mgmt. Assn. (emeritus). Methodist. Home: 1500 S Fern St Apt 1106 Arlington VA 22202-2831 E-mail: w.highsmith@att.net.

HIGHTMAN, CARRIE J., telecommunications industry executive, lawyer; b. Ill., 1957; m. Harry Hightman; 2 children. BA, Univ. Ill.; JD, Fla. State Univ. Assoc. counsel Fla. Office of Public Counsel, 1983—86; staff counsel Fla. Public Svc. Commn., 1983—86; ptnr., energy, telecom., public utilities practice group Schiff, Hardin & Waite, Chgo., 1986—2001; pres. SBC Ill., Chgo., 2001—. Trustee Chgo. Symphony Orch., DePaul Univ.; mem. Ill. Bus. Roundtable; bd. dir. Lyric Opera, Chgo., 2001—, Chgo. Urban League, 2003—, Abraham Lincoln Presdl. Libr. Found., Chicagoland C. of C. Named one of 100 Most Influential Women, Crain's Chgo. Bus., 2004; recipient Women of Achievement award, Anti-Defamation League, 2004. Mem.: Chgo. Bar Found. (bd. dir.). Office: SBC Illinois 225 W Randolph Chicago IL 60606

HIGHTOWER, CAROLINE WARNER, arts management consultant; b. Cambridge, Mass., Feb. 22, 1935; d. William Lloyd and Mildred (Hall) Warner; children— Amanda Brantley, Matthew Lloyd Student, Northwestern U., 1953-54, Cambridge U., 1954-55; BA, Pomona Coll., 1958. Advt. mgr. U. Calif. Press, Berkeley, 1959-61; editor McGraw Hill, N.Y.C., 1961-64, Saturday Rev., N.Y.C., 1967-69; found. officer Carnegie Corp., N.Y.C., 1969-71; cons. Internat. Ctr. Photography, Children's TV Workshop, Rockefeller Found., Ford Found., N.Y.C., 1971-77; dir. Am. Inst. Graphic Arts, N.Y.C., 1977-94; cons. Am. Inst. Graphic Arts, Am. Soc. Media Photog. Found., Clio Awards, 1994—; dir. planning and programs Am. Numis. Soc., 2000—02. Vice chmn. creative artists pub. svc. program N.Y. State Coun. on Arts, N.Y.C., 1974-84; panelist Nat. Endowment Arts, Washington, 1979, 81, 83; scholarship juror Art Dept. Yale U., 1982, Nat. Inst. for the Deaf, RIT, 1988; commencement speaker, Art Ctr. Coll. of Design, Pasadena, 1987; moderator opening session Graphic Design in Am., Walker Art Ctr., Minn., 1989; vice chmn. bd. dirs. creative artists pub. svc. program N.Y. State Coun. on Arts, N.Y.C., 1974-84; bd. dirs. Pub. Ctr. for Cultural Resources, N.Y.C., 1984-89; mem. adv. bd. Documents of Am. Design, N.Y.C., Lubalin Ctr. Cooper Union, Ctr. for Book Libr. Congress, Innovative Design Fund, Coll. Applied and Fine Arts, Rochester Inst. Tech. Recipient medal, Am. Inst. Graphic Arts, NYC, 2004. Office: 333 Central Park W New York NY 10025-7145 Personal E-mail: chitower@aol.com.

HILB, JEANE DYER, community volunteer; b. Hutchinson, Kans., Apr. 8, 1921; d. Howard Emmons and Clara Riner Dyer; m. Frank Markel Swirles Jr. Oct, 24, 1942 (div. 1950); 1 child, Jeane Swirles MacClyment; m. Justin Mitchell Hilb, Oct. 6, 1979. BA, U. So. Calif., L.A., 1942; postgrad., Radcliffe Coll., 1943-45. Lifetime cert. tchr., Calif. Pres. Palm Springs Friends of Philharm., 1998—; mem. Coll. of the Desert Found., 1982—; founding pres. Coll. of the Desert Found. Aux., 1984-87, Ballet Guild of the Desert, 1985—. Recipient Disting. Svc. award Bd. Suprs. County of Riverside, 1998, day named in honor, 1998. Mem. Harvard-Radliffe Club of So. Calif, Phi Beta Kappa. Avocations: travel, theater, bridge. Home: 911 Juarez Ave Palm Springs CA 92262-4121

HILBERT, RITA L., librarian; b. Orange, N.J., Nov. 1, 1942; d. Ralph P. LaSalle and Arlene (Julian) Strobel; children: Toby Gayle Buchanan, Stacey Giordano, Joseph, Matthew. AA, NYU, 1988, BA, 1990; MLS, Rutgers U., 1992. Merchandising rsch. analyst Burrelle's, Livingston, NJ, 1975-82; teaching asst. Montessori Sch., Millburn, NJ, 1982-84; outreach specialist Rockwood Meml. Libr., Livingston, 1984-90, head spl. svcs., 1990-92; libr. dir. Lincoln Park (N.J.) Pub. Libr., 1992-94, Mount Olive Township Pub. Libr., 1994—. Mem. Adult Sch. Bd., Livingston, 1990—, Lincoln Pk. Bd. of Edn., 1995-98, chair policy com., 1997-98, negotiations com., 1997-98. Member Livingston Adv. Com. for the Handicapped, 1985—, Livingston Coun. for Sr. Citizens, 1985—, Region III Com. for Svcs. to Spl. Populations, sec., 1987-88; elected mem. Lincoln Park Bd. Edn., 1995-98, chair policy and negotiations coms., 1995-98; trustee Lincoln Park Libr., 1997-98. Recipient Founder's Day award NYU, 1990. Mem.: AAUW (scholarship 1987), ALA, Morris Automated Info. Network (sec. 1993—94, v.p. 1995, pres. 1996, rep. planning coun. 2004), NJ Assn. Libr. Assts. (pres. 1989—90, scholarship in her name 1994), NJ Libr. Assn. (scholarship 1990), Mt. Olive C. of C. (rec. sec. 2002—05, bd. dirs. 2005, v.p. 2006, Bus. Person of Yr. 2005), Mt. Olive Twp. Hist. Soc. (founding and charter mem.), Morris County 200 Club, Kiwanis (bd. dirs. 1999—), Alpha Sigma Lambda. Avocations: walking, painting, travel. Office: 202 Flanders-Drakestown Rd Flanders NJ 07836 Office Phone: 973-691-8686.

HILBURN, DAWN, special education educator; d. Donald Warner and Barbara Jane ODonnell, Douglas Darcy ODonnell (Stepfather); m. Douglas Hilburn, June 7, 1980; children: Kristopher, Brice. BS (with hons.), Fla. Internat. U., 1992. Cert. Tchr. Nat. Bd. Profl. Tchg. Standards, Profl. Educator Fla. Dept. Edn., English Spkrs. Other Lang. Sch. Bd. Broward County. Educator students with mild to moderate disabilities Sch. Bd. Broward County, Ft Lauderdale, Fla., 1992—2002, educator students with severe disabilities, 2002—. Mem.: Broward Tchrs. Union (assoc.). Office: Sch Bd Broward County 600 SE 3rd Ave Fort Lauderdale FL 33301 Business E-Mail: dawn.hilburn@browardschools.com

HILD, HEIDI, small business owner; b. Denver, Dec. 25, 1961; d. Leonard Gene and Marilyn Ann (Handrock) Hild; m. Samuel Ralph Boyer, Dec. 27, 1992 (div. 2004); children: Elliott Gene Boyer, Ryan Stuart Boyer. BA, Colo. State U., 1985. Sr. ptnr. H. Earhart & Assocs., Denver, 1987-90; dir. comm. Colo. Assn. Commerce and Industry, Denver, 1990; dir. legis. affairs Rocky Mountain Farmers Union, Denver, 1990-93; pres. Colo. Capitol Preservation Fund, Denver, 1995-98; state fin. dir. Norton for Gov., Denver, 1997-98; sr. ptnr. Sq. Root Gardens, 2002—. Rsch. assoc. Gov.'s Unified Housing Task Force, Denver, 1987; cons. Planned Parenthood Rocky Mountains, 1988, Gov.'s Task Force on Homeless, 1989; exec. dir. Denver Archtl. Found., 2004-06. Press sec. Sci. and Cultural Facilities Dist. Campaign, Denver, 1994; vol. Make-A-Wish Found., 1995-2000; mem. steering com. Colo. Open Lands, 1998—. Recipient Denver Post/Am. Newspaper Publs. Assn. Scholastic Journalist award, 1980. Mem. LWV, Inst. Internat. Edn., Colo. State U. Devel. Coun., Kappa Alpha Theta. Avocations: gardening, skiing, reading, travel.

HILDEBRAND, MARY SUE, elementary school educator, principal; d. Loyd F. and Genievive Nobile; m. Alan Hildebrand, July 23, 1983; children: Brackston, Erin. BSc, West Tex. A&M, Canyon, Tex., 1977; MEd, S.W. Tex. State U., San Marcos, Tex., 1998. Tchr., coach, Borger, Tex., 1977—82; tchr. spl. edn. Rockport, Tex., 1982—83; tchr., coach Austin, 1983—88; tchr. Lampasas, Tex., 1988—91, Goldthwaite, Tex., 1991—94, Liberty Hill, Tex., 1994—97; asst. prin. Lamposas (Tex.) Ind. Sch. Dist., 1997—2001; prin. Thornton Elem. Sch., Temple, Tex., 2001—. Mem.: Tex. Elem. Prins. and Suprs. (v.p. region XII 2003—06). Roman Catholic. Avocations: reading, shopping, travel. Office: Freeman Heights Acad Resource Ctr 300 S 27th St Temple TX 76502

HILDEBRAND, VERNA LEE, human ecology educator; b. Dodge City, Kans., Aug. 17, 1924; d. Carrell E. and Florence (Smyth) Butcher; m. John R. Hildebrand, June 23, 1946; children: Carol Ann, Steve Allen. BS, Kans. State U., 1945, MS, 1957; PhD, Tex. Women's U., 1970. Tchr. home econs. Dickinson County H.S., Chapman, Kans., 1945-46; tchr. early childhood Albany (Calif.) Pub. Schs., 1946-47; grad. asst. Inst. Child Welfare U. Calif., Berkeley, 1947-48; tchr. kindergarten Albany Pub. Schs., 1948-49; dietitian commons and hosp. U. Chgo., 1952-53; instr. Kans. State U., Manhattan, 1953-54, 59, Okla. State U., Stillwater, 1955-56; asst. prof. Tex. Tech U., Lubbock, 1962-67; from asst. prof. to prof. Mich. State U., East Lansing, 1967-97, prof. emeritus, 1997—. Legis. clk. Kans. Ho. of Reps., Topeka, 1955. Author: Introduction to Early Childhood Education, 1971, 6th edit., 1997, Guiding Young Children, 1975, 7th edit., 2004, Parenting and Teaching Young Children, 1981, 90, Management of Child Development Centers, 1984, 6th edit., 2006, Parenting: Rewards and Responsibilities, 1994, 7th edit., 2004, tchrs. annotated edit., 2003; co-author: China's Families: Experiment in Societal Change, 1985, Knowing and Serving Diverse Families, 1996, 2d edit., 1999. Mem. Nat. Assn. for the Edn. Young Children (task force 1975-77), Am. Home Econs. Assn. (bd. dirs., Leader award 1990), Women in Internat. Devel., Nat. Assn. Early Childhood Tchr. Edn. (award for meritorious and profl. leadership 1995).

HILDEBRANDT-WILLARD, CLAUDIA JOAN, banker; b. Ingelwood, Calif., Feb. 12, 1942; d. Charles Samual and Clara Claudia (Palumbo) Hildebrandt; m. I. LeRoy Willard, Nov. 5, 1993 (dec. Oct. 2001). BBA, U. Colo. Head teller First Colo. Bank & Trust, Denver, 1969—70; asst. cashier First Nat. Bank, Englewood, Colo., 1975—79, asst. v.p., 1979—83, v.p., 1983—92; owner CJH Enterprises, Inc., Breckenridge, Colo., 1980—, Garden Tea Shop, Georgetown, Colo., The Gifted Swan, Georgetown, Colo., 1982—92, Laudiac, Inc., Breckenridge, 1993—, Mgmt. for Ministry, 1993—. Mem.: Am. Inst. Banking, Am. Soc. Pers. Adminstrn., Fin. Women Internat. (pres.-elect 1989—92), Nat. Assn. Bank Women, Mile High Group. Roman Catholic. Home: PO Box 665 Georgetown CO 80444-0665 Office: 410 3d St Georgetown CO 80444

HILDENBRAND, JOYCE PLUHOWSKI, social work professional, marketing specialist; b. Pitts. m. Dennis J. Hildenbrand. B Social Work, U. Pitts., 1979, MSW, 1980. Lic. social worker, N.J. Social worker St. Francis Hosp., Pitts., 1980-81, Brackenridge Hosp., Austin, Tex., 1981-83, supr. social work, 1982-83; dir. provider rels. disabled children's svcs. Tex. Dept. Health, Austin, 1983-88; supr. social work and admissions coordination Rehab. Inst., at Morristown (N.J.) Meml. Hosp., 1988-90; dir. cmty. svcs., client svcs. Morristown (N.J.) Meml. Hosp., 1990—91; dir. social work svcs., vols., transp., pastoral care, ambulance transport Morristown Hosp., 1995—. Dir. Atlantic Health System Leadership Devel. Inst. 2000-03; mgr. customer rels. mgmt. info. sytems Atlantic Health System, 2002-03; prin. JHP Consulting, Morris Plains, N.J., leadership and bus. dvel., customer svc., 2003-; dir. bus. devel. and mktg. CareOne at Madison Ave., Morristown, N.J., 2004-05; mgr. bus. devel. and customer svc. Atlantic Ambulance, Atlantic Health Mgmt., 2005-; cons. on rehab., mktg., care articles to N.J. newspapers and profl. jours., 1989—. Contbr. articles to profl. jours. Mem. Soc. Social Work Adminstrs. in Healthcare (chmn. mktg. and pub. rels. com., mem.-at-large exec. com.), Nat. Soc. for Social Work Leaders in Healthcare, N.J. Soc. for Social Work Adminstrs. in Healthcare (pres.-elect 1996-97, pres. 1997, presenter nat. confs. 2000-, Leader of Yr. 2001). Avocations: scuba diving, golf. Office: Atlantic Ambulance Corp 120 Dorsa Ave Livingston NJ 07039 Office Phone: 201-572-7287.

HILE, MICHELE VERA, middle school educator; b. Bay City, Mich., July 8, 1950; d. Michael Kosa and Irene Mae Keene; m. Thomas Arthur Hile, Dec. 28, 1974; children: John Thomas, Allen Thomas. BSc, Mich. State U., 1972, MA, 1978. Cert. tchr. Mich. Dept. Edn., 1972. Tchr. Mid. Sch. Caro (Mich.) Cmty. Schs., 1972—. Insr. water aerobics WaterArt, Toronto, Canada, 2001—; pre-need funeral cons. Ransford Funeral Home, Caro, Mich., 2005—. Sec. Thumb Area Ctr. Arts, Caro, 1996—2004; chmn. lumanaria Tuscola County Relay for Life-ACS, Caro, 2002—; min. Universal Brotherhood, Margate, Fla., 2005—; treas. Watrousville United Meth. Ch., Caro, 1989—2005, lay leader, membership sec.; sec. Juniata Township Zoning Bd., Caro, 1972—76. Mem.: NEA, Mich. Edn. Assn., Caro Edn. Assn. (sec. 1996—). Avocations: reading, travel, theater, lawncare. Home: 1726 S Ringle Rd Caro MI 48723 Office: Caro Middle Sch 301 N Hooper St Caro MI 48723-1499 Office Phone: 989-673-3167. Personal E-mail: cen55375@centurytel.net.

HILEMAN, LINDA CAROL, elementary school educator; b. Aliquippa, Pa., Mar. 29, 1947; d. Charles Allen and Aurelia (Oprean) Cunningham; m. Hazen E. Hileman, June 11, 1971. BS, Clarion (Pa.) U., 1969, MEd, 1970; EdS, U. Wyo., 1977. Sci. tchr. Center Area Schs., Monaca, Pa., 1970-71; intermediate tchr. Purchase Line Schs., Commodore, Pa., 1971-72; tchr. 5th grade Carbon County #2 Schs., Medicine Bow, Wyo., 1972-73, team tchr. Saratoga, Wyo., 1973-80, prin. middle sch., 1980-83, tchr. math. and sci., 1983—. Adj. instr. U. Wyo., Laramie, 1988—; participant Marine Resource Inst., Key Largo, Fla., 1990, Nat. Radio Astronomy Obs., Green Bank, W.Va., 1992.; presenter in field. Co-author: First Women of Wyoming, 1990, Trek of the Mammoth II, 1993. Dir. Bible Sch. First Presbyn. Ch., Saratoga, 1985-87; moderator Presbyn. Women, Saratoga, 1988-92, vice moderator, 1992—; mem. Wyo. Commn. for Women, 1975-92. Named Tchr. of Yr., Saratoga Edn. Assn., 1977, Educator of Yr., Vets. Orgn., Saratoga, 1990, Wyo. Elem. Sci. Tchr. of Yr., Wyo. Sci. Tchrs. Assn., 1991; recipient Presdl. Award for Elem. Sci. Teaching, 1992, Predl. Award for Excellence in Teaching, 1993. Mem. Delta Kappa Gamma (pres. chpt. 1984-86). Republican. Avocations: hunting, hiking, bird watching, astronomy, observing nature. Home: PO Box 1322 Saratoga WY 82331-1322 Office: Saratoga Elem Sch 221 Spring St Saratoga WY 82331

HILER, MONICA JEAN, reading educator, sociology educator; b. Dallas, Sept. 3, 1929; d. James Absalom and Monica Constance (Farrar) Longino; m. Robert Joseph Hiler, Nov. 1, 1952; children: Robert, Deborah, Michael, Douglas, Frederick. BA, Agnes Scott Coll., Decatur, Ga., 1951; MEd, U. Ga., Athens, 1968; EdS, U. Ga., 1972, EdD, 1974. Social worker Atlanta Family and Children's Svcs., 1962-63; tchr. Hall County pub. schs., Ga., 1965-67; mem. faculty Gainesville Jr. Coll., Ga., 1968-87, prof. reading and sociology, 1975-87, chmn. devel. studies program, 1973-85, acting chmn. divsn. social scis., 1986-87, prof. emeritus reading and sociology, 1987—. Cons. So. Regional Edn. Bd., 1975-83, Gainesville Coll., 1987-95; apptd. spl. advocate Juvenile Ct. Union County, Ga., 1994-96; ch. organist, pianist, choir dir., 1964-82, 1988—. Pres. Ch. Women United, Ga., 1992—94. Named Ch. Woman of Yr, N.E. Ga., 2001, Woman of Yr., St. Francis of Assisi Ch., Blairsville, 1996. Mem. ASCD, Internat. Reading Assn., Ga. Sociol. Assn., Phi Beta Kappa, Phi Delta Kappa, Phi Kappa Phi. Avocations: piano, painting, sewing. E-mail: jeannbob1@alltel.net.

HILL, ALICE FAYE, secondary school educator; d. Elisha Alvin and Doris Louise Dooley; children: Vicky Faye (Hill) Warren, Bradford Rex. AS, Boise Jr. Coll., 1965; BA, Idaho State U., Pocatello, 1968. Tchr. phys. edn. Snake River Jr. High, Thomas, Idaho, 1968—70, W. Minico Jr. High, Paul, 1970—78, Minico HS, Rupert, 1978—86; tchr. social studies W Minico Jr. High, 1986—2006; tchr. health Mt. Harrison Alternative H.S., 2006—. E-mail: Alihill@hotmail.com.

HILL, ANITA FAYE, lawyer, educator; b. Lone Tree, Okla., July 30, 1956; d. Albert and Erma Hill. BS with honors in Psychology, Okla. State U., 1977; JD, Yale U., 1980; degree (hon.), Simmons Coll., 2001, Dillard U., 2001. Atty. Wald, Harkrader and Ross, Washington, 1980—81; asst. Office of Civil Rights, US Dept. Edn., Washington, 1981-82; mem. legal staff EEOC (reporting to Clarence Thomas), Washington, 1982-83; prof. Oral Roberts U., 1983-88, Coll. Law, U. Okla., Norman, 1986—96; prof. social policy, law, and women's studies Heller Sch. for Social Policy and Mgmt., Brandeis U., Waltham, Mass., 1997—. Spkr., lectr. on sexual harassment for colls. and orgns. Co-editor: Race, Gender and Power in America, 1995; author: Speaking Truth to Power, 1997; contbr. articles to law jours. Named Women of Yr., Glamour Mag., 1991. Baptist. Office: Brandeis U Heller 328 415 South St Waltham MA 02454-9110 Office Phone: 781-736-3896. E-mail: ahill@brandeis.edu.*

HILL, AUDRIANNE, English educator; b. Holland, Mich., Mar. 13, 1961; d. Roger Murray and Audrey Jean (Timmer) H. BS, Grand Valley State U., 1984, MA, 2004. Cert. tchr., Mich. English and journalism educator Grand Haven (Mich.) Area Pub. Schs., 1986—. Pub. rels. advisor Hope Summer Repertory Theatre, Holland, 1988-93. Contbr. poems to anthologies. Prodr. Ctrl. Park Players, Grand Haven, 1986. Mem. Mich. Edn. Assn., Grand Haven Edn. Assn. Democrat. Mem. Reformed Ch. Avocations: reading, writing, gardening, fleamarkets.

HILL, BARBARA BENTON, healthcare executive; b. Balt., May 28, 1952; d. George Stock and Charlotte (Russ) Benton; m. Charles David Hill, June 4, 1970 (dec. Oct. 1980); children: Gregory George, Douglas Charles; m. Ancelmo E. Lopes, May 9, 1987. BA, John's Hopkins U., 1973, MS, 1976. Counselor Planned Parenthood of Md., Balt., 1975-76, Hillcrest Clinic, Balt., 1977, dir. community rels., 1977-78, adminstr., 1978-80, exec. dir., 1980-83; pres. Hill & Ward Constrn. Co., Balt., 1980-81; exec. dir. East Balt. Med. Plan, Balt., 1983-84; v.p. John's Hopkins Health Plan, Balt., 1984-85, pres., 1985-91, Hopkins Preferred Network, Balt., 1986-91; v.p. mid-atlantic group ops. Prudential Ins. Co., Balt., 1991-93, v.p. health care policy Newark, 1993-94; pres. Aetna Health Plans of Midwest, Chgo., 1994-96, Rush Prudential Health Plans, Chgo., 1996—. Treas. Greater Balt. com., 1993-94, bd. dirs., 1991-94; mem. Mayor's Econ. Adv. Coun., 1993-94. Named Businessperson of the Yr., Balt. Bus. Jour., 1989. Mem. Ill. Assn. HMOs (v.p. 1994-96, pres. 1996—), Md. C. of C. (bd. dirs. 1993-94), Phi Beta Kappa. Office: Rush Prudential Health Plans 233 S Wacker Dr Ste 3900 Chicago IL 60606-6324

HILL, BEVERLEY JANE, physician assistant; b. Balt., May 19, 1938; d. Isaac Corbert Hill and Grace Vivian Bryant. BS in Phys. Edn., Western Md. Coll., Westminster, 1960, MEd, 1968; postgrad., Johns Hospkins Univ., 1972; cert. in physician asst., Essex Cmty. Coll., Balt., 1991. Lic. physician asst. Md., Va., Del., N.C. Tchr. phys. edn. Balt. County Sch. Sys., Towson, Md., 1960—65; tchr. John Carroll Sch., Bel Air, Md., 1965—86, dean of students,

1965—86, dir. of athletics, 1965—86; physician asst. Beebe Gen. Hosp., Lewes, Del., 1991—94, Johns Hopkins Hosp., Balt., 1992, San Carlos (Ariz.) Hosp., Apache Reservation, 1992; physician asst. Indian Health Svcs., Supai Indian Reservation, Grand Canyon, Ariz., 1992; physician asst. St. Agnes Hosp., Balt., 1993—94, EMSA, Ltd., Pax River, Md., 1994; ambulatory care Md. State Penitentiary, 1992—96; physician asst. Ft. Belvoir/Dewitt Army Hosp., 1996—97, Coastal Govt. Svcs., 1994—97, Profl. Occupl. Health, Lanhan, Md., 1997—98, Dept. of Def., Womack Army Med., Ft. Bragg, NC, 1998—, USN Acad., Annapolis, Md., 2001—02. Contbr. articles to profl. jours. Named to, Western Md. Coll. Sports Hall of Fame. Mem.: Phi Theta Kappa (mem. Nat. Deans list). Democrat. Avocations: running, walking, reading, writing.

HILL, BEVERLY ELLEN, medical educator; b. Albany, Calif., May 20, 1937; d. Bert E. and Catherine (Doyle) H. BA, Coll. Holy Names, 1960; MS in Edn., Dominican Coll., 1969; EdD, U. So. Calif., 1978. Producer, dir. Health Scis TV U. Calif., Davis, 1966-69, coordinator Health Scis. TV, 1969-73; asst. dir. IMS U. So. Calif., Los Angeles, 1973-76, asst. dir. continuing edn., 1976-80, dir. biocommunications, 1976-80; dir. Med. Ednl. Resources Program Ind. U. Sch. Medicine, Indpls., 1980—, acting asst. dean continuing med. edn., 1991-95. Presenter Cath. U. Nijmegen, Netherlands, 1980, 81, European Symposium on Clin. Pharmacy, Brussels, 1982, Barcelona, Spain, 1983. Contbr. articles to profl. jours. Pres. Indpls. Shakespeare Festival, 1982-83; mem. subcom. Ind. Film Commn., Indpls., 1984—. Recipient first place in rehab. category 4th Biannual J. Muir Med. Film Fest., 1980. Mem. Assn. Biomed. Communications (bd. dirs. 1985—), Health Scis. Com. Assn. (bd. dirs. 1976-79, First Place Video Festival, 1979), Assn. for Edn. Communications and Tech. Avocations: painting, travel, archaeology, music, tennis, swimming. Office: Med Ednl Resources Program BR 156 1226 W Michigan St Indianapolis IN 46202-5212 Home: 849 Michigan Blvd Pasadena CA 91107-5734

HILL, BONNIE GUITON, consulting company executive; b. Springfield, Ill., Oct. 30, 1941; d. Henry Frank and Elizabeth (Newman) Brazelton; m. Walter Hill Jr.; 1 child, Nichele Monique. BA, Mills Coll., 1974; MS, Calif. State U., Hayward, 1975; EdD, U. Calif., Berkeley, 1985. Adminstr. asst. to pres.'s spl. asst. Mills Coll., Oakland, Calif., 1970-71, adminstrv. asst. to asst. v.p., 1972-73, student svcs. counselor, adv. to resuming students, 1973-74, asst. dean of students, interim dir. ethnic studies, lectr., 1975-76; exec. dir. Marcus A. Foster Ednl. Inst., Oakland, 1976-79; adminstrv. mgr. Kaiser Aluminum & Chem. Corp., Oakland, 1979-80; v.p., gen. mgr. Kaiser CTR Inc., Oakland, 1980-84; vice chair Postal Rate Commn., Washington, 1985-87; asst. sec. for vocat. and adult edn. Dept. Edn., Washington, 1987-89; sec. State and Consumer Svcs. Agy. State of Calif.; spl. adv. to Pres. for Consumer Affairs, dir. U.S. Office Consumer Affairs, 1989-90; pres., CEO Earth Conservation Corps, Washington, 1990-91; sec. State and Consumer Svcs. Industry, State of Calif., 1991-92; dean McIntire Sch. Commerce U. Va., Charlottesville, 1992-97; v.p. The Times Mirror Co., 1997-2000; pres. B. Hill Enterprises, LLC, 2001—; COO Iconblue, Inc., LA Times, 2001—. Sr. v.p. comm. and pub. affairs L.A. Times, 1998—2001; pres., CEO The Times Mirror Found., 1997—2001; bd. dirs. The Home Depot Co., Hershey Foods Corp., AK Steele Corp., Yum Brands, Inc., Albertsons Inc., Calif. Water Svc. Co. Office: B Hill Enterprises LLC Ste 600 5670 Wilshire Blvd Los Angeles CA 90036 Office Phone: 323-634-5312.

HILL, CARLA LARSEN, physical education educator, gymnastics judge; b. Washington, May 28, 1951; d. Charles Arne and Clara (Kemp) Larsen; m Ronald Franklin Hill. Aug. 4, 1973; children: Michael Eric, Erin Michelle. AB in Math., Lenoir Rhyne Coll., 1973; MS in Computer Sci., Union Coll., 1979. Tchr. Wappingers Ctrl. Sch. Dist., Wappingers Falls, N.Y., 1974-75, substitute tchr., 1989-99; women's gymnastics judge USAG-N.Y. State, 1997—. Adj. lectr. Dutchess C.C., Poughkeepsie, N.Y., 1980—, Marist Coll., Poughkeepsie, 2000—. Troop leader Dutchess County coun. Girl Scouts U.S., 1984—; first aid instr. Dutchess County Red Cross, Poughkeepsie, 1978—; mem. com. Hudson Valley coun. Boy Scouts Am., 1984-99. Mem. AAUW, Girl Scouts U.S.A. (life; Nat. Appreciation award 1993, Nat. Honor pin 1997, 35-Yr. Pin 2003), Nat. Assn. Women's Gymnastics Judges. Lutheran. Avocations: reading, needlework. Home: 28 Bowdoin Ln Wappingers Falls NY 12590-3921 Office: Dutchess CC Pendell Rd Poughkeepsie NY 12601 E-mail: cmlhill@att.net.

HILL, CARLOTTA H., physician; b. Chgo., Apr. 8, 1958; d. Clarence Kenneth and Vlasta (Cizek) Hayes; m. Chester James Hill III, June 10, 1967 (div. 1974); m. Carlos A. Rotman, July 31, 1980; children: Robin Mercedes. BA magna cum laude, Knox Coll., 1969; MD with honors, U. Ill., 1973. Diplomate Nat. Bd. Med. Examiners, Am. Bd. Dermatology. Intern Mayo Sch. Medicine, Rochester, Minn., 1973-74; resident U. Ill., Chgo., 1975-78, asst. prof. clin. dermatology Coll. Medicine, 1978-93, assoc. prof. clin. dermatology Coll. Medicine, 1993—. Mem. U. Ill. Senate, Chgo., 1986-91, 99-2002; councilor Chgo. Med. Soc., 1990-96, 1999-2006. Contbr. articles to profl. jours. Bd. dirs. Summerfest St. James Cathedral, Chgo., 1986-91, YWCA, Lake Forest, Ill., 1995-, pres., 1998-2000; master gardner Chgo. Bot. Garden, Glencoe, Ill., 1994-98; bd. dirs. Lake Bluff Open Lands Assn., 1997-2006, Friends of Ryerson Woods, 2005—, Lake Forest/Lake Bluff Hist. Soc., 2006—; mem. Lake Bluff Libr. Bd., 2001-05. Recipient Janet Glascow award Am. Women's Med. Assn., 1973. Mem. Am. Acad. Dermatology, Herb Soc. Am. (ways and means No. Ill. unit 1992-94, treas. N. Ill. unit 1996-2000, vice chair 2000-02, chair 2002-04, ctrl. dist. steering com. 2004-06, nat. head garden com. 2006—), Ill. Dermatologic Soc., Phi Beta Kappa, Alpha Omega Alpha. Avocations: travel, cooking, gardening, reading. Office: Dept Dermatology 808 S Wood St Chicago IL 60612-7300 Office Phone: 312-996-6966. Business E-Mail: chhill@uic.edu.

HILL, CATHARINE BOND (CAPPY HILL), academic administrator, economics professor; b. Feb. 1954; m. Kent Kildahl; children: John, Thomas, Elizabeth. BA, Williams Coll., 1976; BA with 1st class honors, Oxford U., 1978; PhD, Yale U., 1985. With Congl. Budget Office, 1981—82, The World Bank, 1982—87; adv. for fiscal & trade policy, Ministry Fin. Govt. of Zambia, Lusaka, 1994—96; John J. Gibson prof. econ. Williams Coll., Williamstown, Mass., 1985—2006, chair dept. econs. and Ctr. for Devel. Econs., 1997—99, provost, John J. Gibson prof. econs., 1999—2006; pres. Vassar Coll., Poughkeepsie, NY, 2006—. Contbr. articles to profl. jours.; co-editor: Public Expenditure in Africa, 1996. Grantee, NSF, Coun. on Fgn. Rels., Am. Coun. Learned Socs. Avocation: golf. Office: Vassar Coll 124 Raymond Ave Poughkeepsie NY 12604*

HILL, CATHERINE LOUISE, secondary school educator; b. Lubbock, Tex., Apr. 17, 1966; d. Hollis and Charlotte Cain; m. Jonathan Wunder Hill; children: Joshua Cain, Rachel Catherine. MA in Math., Tex. Tech U., Lubbock, 1991. Instr. South Plains Coll., Levelland, Tex., 1991—95; tchr. Seminole HS, Tex., 2001—. Sunday sch. tchr. First Bapt. Ch., Seminole, Tex., 2003—06. Republican. Baptist. Avocations: reading, gardening, piano, writing. Office: Seminole HS 2100 NW Ave D Seminole TX 79360 Office Phone: 432-758-5873. Business E-Mail: chill@seminole.k12.tx.us.

HILL, CINNAMON MICHELLE, secondary school educator, director; b. Alamogordo, N.Mex., Jan. 1, 1978; d. David Dwight and Joyce Ann Hill. B in Music Edn., Baylor U., Waco, Tex., 2000, MEd, 2002. Cert. tchr., prin. Tex. Assoc. choral dir. Waco HS, 2000—. Mem.: Tex. Choral Dirs. Assn., Tex. Music Educators Assn.

HILL, CLARA EDITH, psychologist, educator; b. Shivers, Miss., Sept. 13, 1948; d. Fletcher Von and Anna (Teich) H.; m. James Gormally, May 25, 1974; children: Kevin, Katherine. BA, So. Ill. U., 1970, MA, 1972, PhD, 1974. Lic. psychologist, Md. Asst. prof. dept. psychology U. Md., College Park, 1974-78, assoc. prof. dept. psychology, 1978-85, prof. dept. psychology, 85—. Author: Therapist Techniques and Client Outcomes, 1989, Working with Dreams in Psychotherapy, 1996; author: (with K.M. O'Brien) Helping Skills: Facilitating Exploration, Insight and Action, 1999; author: Helping Skills: Facilitating Exploration, Insight and Action 2d edit., 2004, Helping Skills: The Empirical Foundation, 2001, Dream Work in Therapy: Facilitating Exploration, Insight and Action, 2004; editor: Jour. Counseling Psychology, 1994—99, Psychotherapy Rsch., 2004—. Recipient Outstanding Lifetime Achievement award, Soc. for Counseling Psychology, 2005; grantee, NIMH, 1983—92. Fellow APA (Leona Tyler award 2002, Disting. Psychologist award 2003); mem. Soc. Psychotherapy Rsch. (pres. N.Am. chpt. 1990, pres. internat. orgn. 1994-95), Assn. Study of Dreams, Soc. Exploration of Psychotherapy Integration. Avocations: reading, dining out, walking. Office: U Maryland Dept Psychology College Park MD 20742-0001 Business E-Mail: Hill@psyc.umd.edu.

HILL, DEBORA ELIZABETH, writer, journalist, screenwriter; b. San Francisco, July 10, 1961; d. Henry Peter and Madge Lillian (Ridgeway-Aarons) H. BA, Sonoma State U., 1983. Talk show host Rock Jour. Viacom, San Francisco, 1980-81; interviewer, biographer Harrap Ltd., London, 1986-87; editor North Bay Mag., Cotati, Calif., 1988; guest feature writer Argus Courier, Petaluma, Calif., 1993-95; concept developer BiblioBytes, Hoboken, NJ, 1994-95; feature writer The Econs. Press, 1996-97; film cons., editor United Film Prodns. Internat., 2003—. Assoc. prodr. White Tiger Films, 1995—; concept developer Star Trek: Voyager and Star Trek: Deep Space Nine, 1997—98; mem. MedioCom, 2001—03; script cons. Shadowhawk Prodns., Ireland, 2003—06; bd. dirs. United Film Prodn. Internat., 2004—06. Author: The San Francisco Rock Experience, 1979, CUTS from a San Francisco Rock Journal, 1982, Punk Retro, 1988, A Ghost Among Us, 2002, A Wizard By Any Other Name, 2004, (sequel) Jerome's Quest, 2003; author: (with Sandra Brandenburg) The Land of the Wand, 2006; author: numerous poems, short stories; co-writer, cons. prodr. The Danger Club; contbr.: Unconditional Love: Pet Tales By the Humans Who Love Them, 2004, Celebrations: Love Letters to my Mother, 2004; contbr. articles to profl. jours. Named Best Poet, Internat. Biographical Ctr., Cambridge, 2003. Mem.: FilmTies, ScriptNet, Film Industry Group. Democrat. Avocations: clothing design, cooking, internet, reading, interior design. Home and Office: Lost Myths Ink LLC 8312 Windmill Farms Dr Cotati CA 94931-4570 Office Phone: 707-792-7918. Personal E-mail: debhill@att.net.

HILL, DEBORAH ANN, special education educator; b. Dover, N.J., May 7, 1957; d. George Fred and Mary Ann (Marks) Lutz; m. Robert Charles Hill, Sept. 6, 1980. BS in Spl. Edn., Coll. Misericordia, Dallas, Pa., 1979. Cert. tchr., N.C. Tchr. Murdoch Ctr., Butner, N.C., 1979-87, Chapel Hill (N.C.) Carrboro City Schs., 1987—. Asst. leader Girl Scouts U.S., Wilkes Barre, Pa. 1978, Raleigh, N.C., 1985. Named Tchr. of Yr., Orange County Assn. Retarded Citizens, 1989-90; recipient Zora Rashkis Personal & Profl. Committment to Students & Staff award, 1995, Katherine Penn Spl. Edn. Tchr. award, Pub. Sch. Found. Chapel Hill, Carrkoro City Schs., 2005; Edn. grantee, 1989-90. Mem. ASCD, Am. Fedn. Tchrs. (N.C. chpt.), Coun. Exceptional Children, N.C. Mental Health Assn., Assn. Retarded Citizens. Democrat. Roman Catholic. Avocations: sewing, fishing, bicycling. Home: PO Box 25333 Durham NC 27702-5333 Office: Ephesus Elem Sch Ephesus Church Rd Chapel Hill NC 27514

HILL, DEBORAH NIXON, elementary school educator, minister; b. Norfolk, Va., Apr. 8, 1955; d. Joe Dancy and Gladys Jones Nixon; m. Fred Eugene Hill, July 4, 1975; children: Marcus Donnell, Calvin Dwayne, Alexis Evon. BS in Bus. Adminstrn. and Fin., Norfolk State U., 1973; M in Elem. Edn., Regent U., 1998. Operator/trainer AT&T Co., Norfolk, Va., 1978—92; tchr., child care coord. Norfolk Pub. Schs., 1992—. Lang. art tchr./coord. HOST, 1995—99; mem. Norfolk Pub. Sch. Tchr. Mentor Corp., Norfolk, 1998; site coord. Comer-Zigler, 1998—2003; mem. adv. bd. Ida Gray Yes 2 Children-Before/After Sch. Care, Norfolk, 2003. Mem.: NEA, Edn. Assn. Norfolk (bd. dirs.), Va. Edn. Assn. (state del. 2001—02), Internat. Reading Assn. (chaplain Alpha Chi chpt.), Nat. Coun. Negro Women, Iota Phi Lambda. Democrat. Apostolic. Avocations: reading, singing, walking. Home: 2121 Burnside Pl Chesapeake VA 23325

HILL, DIANE L., music educator; d. Jack M. and Marjory L. (Hoeksema) Hill. MusB, U. Cin., 1984; ME, Xavier U., 1998. Cert. Ohio. Music educator Williamsburg Local Schs., Cin., 1986—88, Ross (Ohio) Local Schs., 1988—91, Milford E.V. Schs., Cin., 1991—97, Dayton (Ohio) Pub. Schs., 1997—98, Cin. Pub. Schs., 1998—99, St. Martin's, Cin., 2002—. Presenter in field. Active May Festival Chorus, Cin., 1985—86. Mem.: Ohio Music Educators Assn., Music Educators Nat. Conf., U. Cin. Alumni Assn. Avocations: travel, running, reading. Home: 3579 Applewood Dr Amelia OH 45102-2194

HILL, DIANE LOUISE, educator; b. Niagara Falls, N.Y., June 10, 1951; d. Joseph A. and Margaret (Ditchkus) Heiman; m. James D. Hill, Sept. 27, 1975; children: Jennifer, Melanie. BS in Edn., Slippery Rock U., 1973; cert. in Chem. Tech., Brazosport Jr. Coll., 1978. Cert. elem. tchr., Pa., Tex. Spl. educator I Columbia Brazoria Ind. Sch. Dist., Tex., 1973-74; tchr. emotionally disturbed Brazosport Ind. Sch. Dist., Lake Jackson, Tex., 1974-78; dir., tchr. Creative Tchg., Lake Jackson, 1982—; chem. technician Dow Chem., Freeport, Tex., 1978-79; computer tech asst. bereavement program Meth. Hosp. Coordinator computer lab. Ney Elem. Sch., Lake Jackson, 1985-87. Coord. bereavement program Meth. Hosp.; voter registrar Brazoria County. Mem. Tex Computer Edn. Assn., Computer Using Educators, AAUW (dir. Sat. Morning enrichment 1987—, social newsletter 1984-86), Rotary Internat. Republican. Methodist. Home: 57 Oyster Creek Ct Lake Jackson TX 77566-4622

HILL, DONNA MARIE, writer, retired librarian; d. Clarence Henry and Emma Charlotte (Wirthlin) Hill. Student, Phillips Gallery Art Sch., 1940—43; BA, George Washington U., 1948; MS, Columbia U., 1952. Code clk. U.S. Embassy, Paris, 1949—51; asst. to librarian NY Pub. Libr., N.Y.C., 1952—59; instr. Hunter Coll., CUNY, N.Y.C., 1970—75, head tchrs. ctrl. lab., 1974—84, asst. prof., 1975—79, assoc. prof., 1980—84, prof. emeritus, 1984—. Established Donna Hill Collection Marriott Libr., U. Utah, Salt Lake City, 1994. Author: First Your Penny, 1985, Murder Uptown, 1992, Shipwreck Season, 1998 (Christopher award, 99); Exhibited in group shows at Paris, Washington, world tour, 1950—51. Recipient Cert. of Distinction, Alumni Assn. Ctrl. H.S., 1984. Mem.: Women's Nat. Book Assn. (membership chmn. N.Y.C. chpt. 1991—93), Am. Recorder Soc. (nat. sec. 1959—61, editor-in-chief 1962—63), Delta Kappa Gamma (Ruth Mack Havens award 1991), Phi Beta Kappa. Mem. Lds Ch. Avocations: opera, Baroque music, recorder playing, drawing, painting.

HILL, ELIZABETH ANNE, academic administrator, lawyer; b. NYC, Dec. 29, 1942; d. Harry Gerald and Grace Marie (Byrne) H. BA, St. Joseph's Coll., Bklyn., 1964; MA, Columbia U., 1965; JD, St. John's Law Sch., Jamaica, N.Y., 1978. Bar: N.Y. 1979, U.S. Dist. Ct. (ea. dist.) N.Y. 1979; cert. tchr. English and social studies K-12, N.Y. HS tchr. Acad. St. Joseph, Brentwood, NY, 1967-70, Bishop Kearney HS, Bklyn., 1970-71; co-dir. formation program Sisters of St. Joseph, Brentwood, 1971-76; atty. Cath. Migration Office, Bklyn., 1978-80; exec. asst. to pres. St. Joseph's Coll., Bklyn., 1980-97, pres., 1997—. Mem. bd. dirs. LI Assn., Commn. Independent Colls. and Univs., Ind. Savings Found., Myrtle Ave. Revitalization Project, Bklyn. C.of C.; mem. bd. trustees LI Reg. Adv. coun. Higher Edn. Mem. Bishop's Commn. on Pub. Policy, Bklyn., 1978-81; mediator Diocesan Mediation and Arbitration Panel, Bklyn., 1981—; bd. dirs. Independence Cmty. Found., Fort Greene Strategic Neighborhood Action Partnership, Fair Media Coun Mem. Nat. Assn. Coll. and Univ. Attys., Bklyn. C. of C. (bd. dirs.). Office: St Joseph's Coll 245 Clinton Ave Brooklyn NY 11205-3602 Office Phone: 718-636-6800. Business E-Mail: sehill@sjcny.edu.

HILL, ELIZABETH BETTY, retired secondary school educator; b. Thompson, Pa., Dec. 7, 1920; d. William Leroy Keeney and Kathryn Olive Echard; m. George Gardner Hill, June 21, 1947 (dec. May 20, 1988); children: George Gardner, Mildred Kathryn, Stephen Shuster. BA, Bluffton Coll., 1942; vocat. cert., Pa. State U., 1943; MA, U. Hartford, 1971. HS tchr. Congress schs., Ohio, 1942—43, Point Marion schs., Point Morlen, 1944; dir. feeding project Mennonite Ctrl. Com., Paraguay, 1945—47; home econs. tchr., 1947—48; tchr. child devel. Hartford HS, Conn., 1965—72; HS tchr. Norwalk (Conn.) schs., 1975—81. V.p. bd. dirs. Promoting Enduring Peace, New Haven; mem. outreach com., bible study mem. United Ch. of Christ, Hamden, Conn., 1998—. Democrat. Avocations: square dancing, indoor plants. Home: 167 Todd St Hamden CT 06518

HILL, ELIZABETH STARR, writer; b. Lynn Haven, Fla., Nov. 4, 1925; d. Raymond King and Gabrielle (Wilson) Cummings; m. Russell Gibson Hill, May 28, 1949 (dec. 1999); children: Andrea van Waldron, Bradford Wray. Student, Finch Jr. Coll., 1941-42, Columbia U., 1970-73. Freelance writer. Past dir. Princeton Creative Ctr.; tchr. writing Princeton Adult Sch. Author: (juvenile books) The Wonderful Visit to Miss Liberty, 1961, The Window Tulip, 1964, Evan's Corner, 1967, 91 (ALA Notable Book for Children), Master Mike and the Miracle Maid, 1967, Pardon My Fangs, 1969, Bells: A Book to Begin On, 1970, Ever-After Island, 1977, Fangs Aren't Everything, 1985, When Christmas Comes, 1989, The Street Dancers, 1991, Broadway Chances, 1992 (ABA Pick of the Lists), The Banjo Player, 1993, Curtain Going Up!, 1995, Bird Boy, 1999 (Outstanding Achievement in Children's Books award Parent's mag. 1999), Chang and the Bamboo Flute, 2002; contbr. articles to mags. including Reader's Digest, many others. Mem. Authors Guild Am., Authors League Am., Univ. Club Winter Park. Office: c/o Harold Ober Assocs Inc 425 Madison Ave New York NY 10017-0940

HILL, ELSA N., headmaster, literature and language educator, lawyer; m. Anthony Hill. AB, Smith Coll., Northampton, Mass.; MAT, Harvard U.; LLB, U. New S. Wales, Kensington, Australia. Head of sch. St. Mark's Sch., Southborough, Mass., 1994—. Office: St Mark's Sch 25 Marlborough Southborough MA 01772

HILL, EMITA BRADY, academic administrator, consultant; b. Balt., Jan. 31, 1936; d. Leo and Lucy McCormick (Jewett) Brady; children: Julie Beck, Christopher, Madeleine Vedel. BA, Cornell U., 1957; MA, Middlebury Coll., 1958; PhD, Harvard U., 1967. Instr. Harvard U., 1961-63; asst. prof. Western Reserve U., 1967-69; from asst. prof. to v.p. Lehman Coll. CUNY, Bronx, NY, 1970-91; chancellor, grad. faculty Ind. U., Kokomo, Ind., 1991-99, chancellor emerita, 1999—. Vis. advisor Salzburg Seminar Univs. Project; cons. in field. Trustee Am. U. in Central Asia; mem. Women's Forum of NY. Mem.: Internat. Assn. Univ. Pres., Phi Beta Kappa. Avocations: music, scuba diving, tennis. Business E-Mail: ehill@indiana.edu.

HILL, EMMA, apparel executive; b. Eng. Grad., Ravensbourne Coll. Design and Comm., London. Accessories designer Marc Jacobs; sr. designer for men's and women's accessories Calvin Klein, N.Y.C.; accessories designer Burberry, London; v.p. men's and women's accessories The Gap, Inc., San Francisco, 2002—.

HILL, EMMA LEE, education educator; b. Crane, Tex., Jan. 13, 1949; d. Howard Lee and Eddie Marie (Gill) H. BS, Hardin-Simmons. U., 1970; MEd, Abilene Christian U., 1974, postgrad., 1979. Cert. provisional elem. mentally retarded, lang./learning disabilities, bilingual tchr., profl. supr., profl. mid-mgmt., tchr. appraiser, Tex. Tchr. Kileen (Tex.) Ind. Sch. Dist., Harker Heights, 1970-71, Winters (Tex.) Ind. Sch. Dist., 1971-73, Abilene (Tex.) Ind. Sch. Dist., 1973—. Bldg. rep. Supt.'s Task Force on Schs. 5-Yr. Plan, Abilene, 1990-91; tchr. leader/dir. Coll. Connections, McMurray U., 1991—; sch. rep. Cleannn/Proud program. Illustrator: (book) Richard the Great, 1967. Mem. local election com. Tex. Tchrs. for Gov., Abilene, 1988; sec. Abilene PTA, 1980-82, Tex. PTA, 1980-82. Scholar Abilene C. of C., 1967-69. Mem. Assn. for Supervision and Curriculum Devel., Internat. Reading Assn., Tex. Assn. Bilingual Educators (pres. Abilene 1988-89), Tex. Classroom Tchrs. Assn., Assn. Tex. Profl. Educators (bldg. rep. 1980—, Outstanding Tchr. award 1989), AAUW, Internat. Soc. Poets (life), Nat. Honor Soc., Delta Kappa Gamma (treas. Abilene 1990-91). Avocations: watching professional sports, playing basketball and baseball, running, walking, movie classics. Home: PO Box 266 Tye TX 79563-0266 Address: 801 G Ave E Apt 3 Alpine TX

HILL, FAITH, musician; b. Jackson, Miss., Sept. 21, 1967; d. Ted and Edna Perry; m. Daniel Hill, 1988 (div. 1991); m. Tim McGraw, Oct. 6, 1996; children: Gracie, Maggie, Audrey. Grad., McLaurin H.S. With Warner Bros. Records, 1993—. Musician: (recordings) Take Me As I Am, 1993, It Matters To Me, 1995, Faith, 1998, Breathe, 1999 (ACM Video of YR., 2000, Billboard Hot 100 Airplay Track of Yr., 2000, Best Female Country Vocal Performance Grammy, 2001, Best Country Album, 2001, Top Selling Album, Can. Country Music Assn., 2001), Cry, 2002 (Best Female Country Vocal Performance Grammy, 2003, Hottest Female Video of Yr., CMT Flameworthy Video Music Awards, 2003), Firefly, 2005; contbr. to sound tracks: Pearl Harbour, How the Grinch Stole Christmas, Prince of Egypt, Practical Magic, Maverick, contbr. to TV sound track: King of the Hill; actor: (films) The Stepford Wives, 2004. Frounder Faith Hill Family Literacy Project, 1996. Named New Female Vocalist of Yr., ACM, 1993, Top Country Female Artist, Billboard, 1994, Female Star of Tomorrow, TNN/MCN, 1995, Female Vocalist of Yr., ACM, 1999, TNN/MCN, 2000, Female Country Artist of Yr., Country Weekly, 2000, Hot 100 Singles Female Artist of Yr., Billboard, 2000, Favorite Female Artist Country Music, AMA, 2001, Favorite Pop-Rock Female Artist, 2001, Female Vocalist of Yr., ACM, 2001, TNN/CTM Country Weekly Music Awards, 2001, Favorite Female Artist Country Music, AMA, 2002; recipient Single of Yr., Song of Yr., Video of Yr. for It's Your Love, ACM, 1998, Video of Yr. for This Kiss, CMA, 1998, Single of Yr. for This Kiss, ACM, 1999, Video of Yr. for This Kiss, 1999, Vocal Event of Yr. for Just To Hear You Say You Love Me, 1999, GNN/MCN, 1999, Song of Yr. for Just to Hear You Say That You Love Me, TNN/MCN, 1999, Sigle of Yr. for This Kiss, 1999, Video of Yr. for This Kiss, 1999, Best Country Collaboration with Vocals for Let's Make Lofe, Grammy Awards, 2001, Favorite Female Mus. Performer, People's Choice Awards, 2001, Favorite Country Album, AMA, 2001, 5 Platinum awards, Can. Rec. Industry Assn., 2001, Favorite Female Artist Country, AMA, 2003, Favorite Female Mus. Performer, People's Choice Awards, 2002, 2003, Best Country Collaboration With Vocals (with Tim McGraw), Grammy awards, 2006. Office: c/o Creative Artists Agy 3310 West End Ave 5th Fl Nashville TN 37203

HILL, FAY GISH, retired librarian; b. Rensselaer, Ind., Sept. 19, 1944; d. Roy Charles and Vergie (Powell) Gish; m. John Christian Hill, May 20, 1967; 1 child, Christina Gish. BA, Purdue U., 1967; MLS, U. Tex., 1971. Asst. libr. basic reference dept. Tex. A&M U., College Station, 1972, assoc. libr. sci. ref. dept., 1972-74, acting head libr. sci. reference dept., 1975; reference libr. Ctrl. Iowa Regional Libr., Des Moines, 1984—2003. Troop leader Girl Scouts U.S., Ames, Iowa, 1983—88; bd. dirs. Friends of Fgn. Wives, Ames, 1982—86, Iowa Questers, 2000—, state officer, 2001—. Mem.: ALA, Iowa Libr. Assn. Found. (bd. dirs. 1990—95), Iowa Libr. Assn. Presbyterian. Avocation: antiques. Home: 5604 Thunder Rd Ames IA 50014-9448

HILL, GRACE LUCILE GARRISON, education educator, consultant; b. Gastonia, NC, Sept. 26, 1930; d. William Moffatt and Lillian Tallulah (Tatum) Garrison; m. Leo Howard Hill, July 24, 1954; children: Lillian Lucile, Leo Howard Jr., David Garrison. BA, Erskine Coll., 1952; MA, Furman U., 1966; PhD, U. S.C., 1980. Lic. sch. psychologist, S.C. Tchr. Bible, Clinton (S.C.) Pub. Schs., 1952-53; tchr. English Parker High Sch., Greenville, SC, 1953-55; elem. tchr. Augusta Circle Sch., Greenville, 1955-57; tchr. homebound children Greenville County Sch. Dist., Greenville, 1961-64, psychologist, 1966-77; adj. prof. grad. studies in edn. Furman U., Greenville, 1977—, U. S.C., Columbia, 1982—; ednl. cons. Ednl. Diagnostic Svcs., Greenville, 1980—. Exec. dir. Camperdown Acad., Greenville, 1986-87; cons. learning disability program Erskine Coll., Due West, S.C., 1978—; Disting. lectr. Erskine Coll., 1999. Contbr. articles to profl. jours. Pres. Lake Forest PTA, Greenville, 1970-71; pres. of Women A.R. Presbyn. Ch., Greenville, 1973-75, adult Bible tchr., 1978—; sec. bd. trustees Erskine Coll., 1982-88; bd. dirs. Children's Bur. S.C., Columbia, 1981-87, YWCA, Greenville, 1984-88; bd.

advisors for adoption S.C. Dept. Social Svcs., Columbia, 1987-92. Recipient Order of the Jessamine, Greenville News award, 1994—95, Sullivan award, Erskine Coll., 2000, Chmns. award, 2005. Mem. Am. Edn. Rsch. Assn. (southeastern rep. 1982-84, editor newspaper for SIG group 1982-83), Jean Piaget Soc., Assn. for Supervision and Curriculum Devel., Orton Dyslexia Soc. (pres. Carolinas br. 1984-88), Ea. Ednl. Rsch. Assn., S.C. Psychol. Assn., Order of the Jessamine, 21st Century Learning Initiative, Delta Kappa Gamma. Democrat. Avocations: travel, writing. Home and Office: 28 Montrose Dr Greenville SC 29607-3034

HILL, HELEN MARGUERITE THACKER, academic administrator; b. Pike County, Ky., Feb. 16, 1923; d. Arvle and Ellen (Turner) Thacker; m. Wallace Charles Hill, Nov. 25, 1959 (dec. Oct. 18, 1968). BA, U. Ky., 1944, MA, 1953; student, U. Fla., 1956; EdD, Okla. State U., 1970; post doctoral, U. Ky., 1973, 76. Cert. secondary tchr., Ky. Instr. Pike County Schs., Pikeville, Ky., 1944-53; counselor U. Houston, 1956-59; dir. counseling, women's residence halls Purdue U., Lafayette, Ind., 1959-61; asst. dean of women Okla. State U., Stillwater, 1962-66; dean of women W.V. Inst. Tech., Montgomery, W.V., 1970-72, assoc. dean students, 1972-73; dir. commuter student affairs U. Mass., Amherst, 1973-75; prof., counselor Ea. Ky. U., Richmond, 1976; clin. psychologist Logan-Mingo Area Mental Health, Inc., Williamson, W.V., 1976-78; assoc. dean student Ga. Coll., Milledgeville, 1978-82, dir. student support svcs., 1982—. Bd. Ga. Rehab. Svcs., Atlanta, 1996—. Named to U. Ky. Coll. Edn. Hall of Fame, 1998. Mem. Nat. Rehab. Assn., Ga. Rehab. Assn., Ga. Assn. Women Deans, Counselors and Adminstrns. (treas. 1994-96), Order of Omega, Kappa Delta Phi, Phi Delta Kappa. Avocations: sewing, antique collecing. Home: 601 W Charlton St Milledgeville GA 31061-2302

HILL, JACQUELYN LOUISE HARRISON, secondary school educator; b. Summerville, S.C., July 26; d. Joe and Pearl Geneva (Tucker) Harrison; m. George Rutledge Hill, Jr., Sept. 28, 1969; children: George Rutledge III, Brian Desmond Harrison. BS in Biology, Benedict Coll., 1969; MEd in Elem. Edn., Coll. of Charleston, 1978; EdS in Adminstrn., The Citadel, 1989; postgrad., Nova U., 1993—. Tchr. biol. R.B. Stall High Sch., Charleston, SC, 1969-70; tchr. sci. and math. Givhans Elem. Sch., 1970—2003; tchr. sci. DuBose Mid. Sch., Summerville, 1985—. USDA summer food coord. Berkely, Dorchester and Colleton County Community Action Agy., summers 1977, 79; tchr. biology Morningside Mid. Sch., Charleston, summer 1986; tchr. adult edn. Garrett High Sch., 1991. Lay speaker Murray Meth. Ch., Summerville, pres. United Meth. Women, 1988-91, now v.p., mem. stewardess bd., 1989—; layman Bethel A.M.E. Ch., 1988-91. Music scholar Benedict Coll. 1965-68. Mem. NEA, S.C. Edn. Assn. (Outstanding Pres. award 1983), Summerville Edn. Assn. (pres. 1988-89), Zeta Phi Beta (pres. Lambda Nu Zeta chpt. 1985-91, coor.d S.C. Archotte 1991—). Avocations: assisting and volunteering with elderly, writing articles for community newspapers and newsletters, sewing, physical fitness. Home: 307 S Railroad Ave Ridgeville SC 29472-6306

HILL, JANE BOWERS, English language educator, editor; b. Seneca, S.C., Oct. 17, 1950; d. James Harrison and Mary Alberta (Ramey) Bowers; m. Lon Bolt Martin, Dec. 27, 1969 (div. 1977); 1 child, Elizabeth Bolt Martin; m. Robert White Hill, Aug. 16, 1980. BA in Sec. Edn., Clemson (S.C.) U., 1972, MA in English, 1978; PhD in English, U. Ill., 1985. Tchr. Beaufort (S.C.) High Sch., 1973-76; instr. Clemson U., 1978-79; tchr. Westminster (S.C.) High Sch., 1981-83; instr. U. Ga., Athens, 1983-85; asst. prof. Kennesaw State Coll., Marietta, Ga., 1985-86; asst. editor Peachtree Pubrs., Ltd., Atlanta, 1986-88; sr. editor Longstreet Press, Atlanta, 1988-91; prof. U. West Ga., Carrollton, 1992—, chmn. Dept. English and Philosophy, 2003—. Author: Gail Godwin, 1991, Cobb County At the Heart of Change, 1991; editor: (anthologies) You Haven't to Deserve: A Gift to the Homeless/Fiction by 21 Writers, 1991, Street Songs 1, New Voices in Fiction, 1990, Our Mutual Room: Modern Literary Portraits of the Opposite Sex (with Emily Ellison), 1987, An American Christmas: A Sampler of Contemporary Stories and Poems, 1986; editor: Heat Storm, 1991, Chaos Clear as Glass, 1991, Bang-Up Season, 1990, Crazy Ladies, 1990, many others; editor: Five Points, 2003—; contbr. numerous articles to profl. jours. Vol. Cobb YWCA Crisis Intervention, Marietta, Ga., 1985-91; bd. dirs. Cobb Marietta Winter Shelter, 1988-90. Democrat. Episcopalian. Home: 1419 Arden Dr SW Marietta GA 30008-3509 Office: Univ West Ga Dept English Carrollton GA 30118

HILL, JANE H., anthropologist, educator; Anthropology faculty Univ. Ariz., Tucson, 1983—, now regents prof., anthropology. Recipient Viking Fund Medal, Wenner-Gren Found. for Anthrop. Rsch., 2004. Mem.: AAAS, Soc. Study of Indigenous Languages of the Americas (pres.), Soc. Linguistic Anthropology (pres.), Am. Anthrop. Assn. (past pres.), Am. Assn. for Advancement of Sci. Office: Coll Social & Behavioral Sci 310 Haury Bldg PO Box 210028 Tucson AZ 85721-0028 Office Phone: 520-621-4735. Office Fax: 520-621-9424.

HILL, JANET ELIZABETH, lawyer; b. Morehead City, NC, Dec. 29, 1955; BS, NC State U., 1977; JD, U. Ga., 1982. Bar: Ga. 1982. Assoc. Nelson & Sweat, P.A., Athens, Ga., 1982-86, ptnr., 1986-88, Nelson & Hill, Athens, Ga., 1988, Nelson, Hill, Lord & Beasley LLP, Athens, Ga.; mng. ptnr. Hill & Beasley, Athens, Ga., 2002—. Fellow ABA Coll. Labor & Employment Lawyers; Mem. Ga. Trial Lawyers Assn. (Amicus Curiae chair Workers' Compensation Claimaints Lawyers sect. 1988—, exec. com. 1988—, v.p.), Nat. Employment Lawyers Assn. (pres. 2004-2005). Office: Hill & Beasley Ste 140 1160 S Milledge Ave PO Box 307 Athens GA 30603 Office Phone: 706-353-7272. Office Fax: 706-549-8446. Business E-Mail: hblaw@bellsouth.net.

HILL, JANINE, think-tank associate; m. J. Tomilson Hill, Feb. 2, 1980; 2 children. Assoc. Sullivan & Cromwell; v.p. corp. fin. dept. Salomon Bros.; asst. treas. Time, Inc.; dep. dir. studies adminstrn. Coun. Fgn. Rels., NYC. Bd. advs. Duke U. Nasher Mus. Art; mem. bd. Am. friends Louvre. Named one of Top 200 Collectors, ARTnews mag., 2003—06. Office: Coun Fgn Rels Harold Pratt House 58 E 68th St New York NY 10021 E-mail: jhill@cfr.org.*

HILL, JOAN ANN, retired university administrator; b. Cin., Sept. 11, 1934; d. George Leon and Theresa Delores (Krempa) H. BA, Mary Manse Coll., Toledo, Ohio, 1956; MA, U. Toledo, 1963, PhD, 1973. English tchr. Toledo Pub. Schs., 1956-59; tchr. Escuela Americana, San Salvador, El Salvador, 1959-60; instr. English Mary Manse Coll., Toledo, 1960-65, Dean of the Coll., assoc. prof. English, 1968-73; asst. prof. U. Toledo, 1965-67; instr. English Monroe (Mich.) County C.C., 1967-68; cons. in edn. St. Vincent's Hosp. and Med. Ctr., Toledo, 1973-75; acad. program coordinator Fla. Bd. Regents, Tallahassee, 1976-80; Dean of Gen. Studies Fla. C.C., Jacksonville, 1980-85, campus pres., 1985—98; ret. Bd. dirs. Mental Health Resource Ctr., Jacksonville. Mem. adv. coun. Alamanci Elem. Sch., 1990-98; friend Jacksonville Libraries, 1985-89. Named Outstanding Alumna Mary Manse Coll., 1973. Mem. Jacksonville Women's Network, Beaches C. of C. (bd. dirs. 1991-98), Delta Kappa Gamma. Home: Apt 504 1415 1st St N Jacksonville Beach FL 32250-7394

HILL, JOANNE MILLER, special education educator, consultant; b. Atlanta, Ill., Apr. 28, 1941; d. Euless D. and Edith L. Miller; divorced; children: Evan, Rachel, Scot Hill BS in Edn., Ill. State U., 1967; MA in Spl. Edn., U. Colo., Colorado Springs, 1992, MA in Gifted Edn., 1995. Cert. tchr., Tex., Colo. Tchr. Sch. Dist. 187, Springfield, Ill., 1967-68, Sch. Dist. 50 Queen Charlotte Island, B.C., Can., 1968-69, Sch. Dist. 51, Grand Junction, Colo., 1972-73; cons., tutor for learning disabled and gifted, 1973-81; dir., owner Ctr. for Individualized Edn., Anchorage, 1981-82; computer paraprofl. Sch. Dist. 20, Colorado Springs, 1990-91; tchr. spl. edn. Sch. Dist. 11, Colorado Springs, 1991-92, Dist. JE-T-23, Peyton, Colo., 1992-93, Falcon (Colo.) Sch. Dist., 1993-94; coord. supplemental svcs. U. Colo., Colorado Springs, 1995—2000; dir. disability and learning svcs. Willamette U., Salem, Oreg., 2000—. Cons. for spl. needs students, Colorado Springs, 1991—; adj. prof. U. Phoenix, Colorado Springs. Author: The Policy Book: Guidance for Disability Service Providers, 2000. Vol. Probation Ptnrs., Anchorage, 1969-70. Grantee Internat. chpt. P.E.O., 1991, State of Colo., 1991-92. Mem.: Disability Consortium, Assn. Higher Edn. and Disabilities. Avocations: reading, music, outdoor activities, volunteer public social work. Home: 777 Cottage St NE Salem OR 97301 Office: Willamette Univ 900 State St Salem OR 97301 Office Phone: 503-370-6471. Business E-Mail: jhill@willamette.edu.

HILL, JUANTONIA NEKESHIA, mathematics educator, consultant; b. Farmington Hills, Mich., July 30, 1975; d. Edward Jerome and Lavator Hill. BA in Human Resource Mgmt., Mich. State U., Lansing, 1997; MA in Math Edn., U. Detroit Mercy, 2001; grad., Perfecting Ch. Sch. Ministry, Mich., 2005. Cert. tchr. math. Mich., 2001. Prof. U. Detroit Mercy, 2002—03; educator Southfield Pub. Schs., Mich., 1999—. Mentor advisor Girls Empowered To Maintain Success, Southfield, Mich., 2004—. Recipient Tchr. of Yr., Southfield H.S., 2006, Founder's award, State of Mich., 2006. Mem.: Nat. Coun. Tchrs. Math., Phi Mu Epsilon. Mem. Holiness Ch. Avocations: travel, mentoring. Office: Southfield Pub Schs Thompson 16300 Lincoln Dr Southfield MI 48076 Office Phone: 248-746-7400. Office Fax: 248-746-7493.

HILL, JUDITH DEEGAN, retired lawyer; b. Chgo., Dec. 13, 1941; d. William James and Ida May (Scott) Deegan; children: Colette M., Cristina M. BA, Western Mich. U., 1960; cert., U. Paris, Sorbonne, 1962; JD, Marquette U., 1971; postgrad., Harvard U., 1984. Bar: Wis. 1971, Ill. 1973, Nev. 1976, D.C. 1979. Tchr. Kalamazoo (Mich.) Bd. Edn., 1960-62, Maple Heights (Ohio) Bd. Edn., 1963-64, Shorewood (Wis.) Bd. Edn., 1964-68; corp. atty. Fort Howard Paper Co., Green Bay, Wis., 1971-72; sr. trust adminstr. Continental Ill. Nat. Bank & Trust, Chgo., 1972-76; atty. Morse, Foley & Wadsworth Law Firm, Las Vegas, 1976-77; dep. dist. atty., criminal prosecutor Clark County Atty., Las Vegas, 1977-83; atty. civil and criminal law Edward S. Coleman Profl. Law Corp., Las Vegas, 1983-84; pvt. practice law, 1989-99; ret., 1999. Bd. dirs. YMCA, Highland Park, 1973-75, Planned Parenthood of So. Nev., 1977-78, Nev. Legal Svcs., Carson City, 1980-87, state chmn., 1984-87; bd. dirs. Clark County Legal Svcs., Las Vegas, 1980-87, St. Jude's Ranch for Children, 1999-2001; mem. Star Aux. for Handicapped Children, Las Vegas, 1986-96, Greater Las Vegas Women's League, 1987-88; jud. candidate Las Vegas Mcpl. Ct., 1987, New Symphony Guild, Variety Club Internat., 1992-93; mem. Nat. Conf. for Cmty. and Justice, So. Nev., 1998-2000; mentor in Clark County Sch., 1999-2005. Auto Splties. scholar, St. Joseph, Mich., 1957-60, St. Thomas More scholar Marquette U. Law Sch., Milw., 1968-69; juvenile law internship grantee Marquette U. Law Sch., 1970; named one of first 100 Women Attys. in the State of Nev., Oct. 1999. Children's Village Club (pres. 1980). Home: 4190 E Harmon Ave Las Vegas NV 89121-6138 Home Fax: 702-384-2244.

HILL, JUDY MARIE ZIMMERMONT, mayor, secondary school educator; b. Hillsboro, Kans., Jan. 16, 1949; d. Levi B. and Edna Martha Prieb; m. Robert E. Hill (dec.); m. Frederick W. Zimmerman (dec.); children: Jeffrey, Douglas, Darrell. BSE, Emporia State U., Kans., 1971; M in curriculum and instrn., Kans. State U., 1991. Tchr. USD 453, Cubu, Kans., 1971—74, USD 333, Concordia, Kans., 1978—. Office: Concordia Jr/Sr HS 436 W 10th St Concordia KS 66901-4122

HILL, KATHLEEN BLICKENSTAFF, lawyer, nursing educator, mental health nurse; b. Greenville, Ohio, Oct. 24, 1950; d. Donald Edward and Mary Ann (Subler) Berger; children: Benjamin Arin, Amanda Marie, Kathryn Megan; m. David M. Hill, Sr., Sept. 27, 2002. BS, Ohio State U., 1972, MS, 1973, sch. nurse cert., 1990; JD, Capital U. Law Sch., 1998. Cons. cmty. educator S.W. Cmty. Mental Health Ctr., Columbus, 1973-77; patient and cmty. educator Daniel E. Blickenstaff, DDS, Inc., Columbus, 1977-86; staff nurse Riverside Meth. Hosp., Columbus, 1987—90; clin. instr. Columbus (Ohio) State C.C., 1989; from asst. to assoc. prof. Capital U., Columbus, 1989-2000, prof., 2000—01; assoc. Porter, Wright, Morris & Arthur LLP, Columbus, 2000—06; ednl. cons. Ohio Bd. Nursing, Columbus, 2006—. Mem. cmty. svcs. com. Mid Ohio Dist. Nurses Assn., Columbus, 1990—2001, bd. dirs., 1991—94, mem. legis. com., 2002—; adj. prof. Capital U., Columbus, 2001—. Leader Girl Scouts, Grandview Heights, Ohio, 1989-93; bd. dirs. H.S. PTO, Grandview Heights (Ohio) City Schs., 1990-93, treas. H.S. PTO, 1990-92, co-chair oper. levy, 1991. Mem.: ANA, ABA, Columbus Bar Assn. (health law com.), Ohio State Bar Assn. (health and disability law com.), Ohio Nurses Assn., Am. Health Lawyers Assn., Sigma Theta Tau. Avocations: quilting, sewing, gardening. Home: 1415 Crest Rd Reynoldsburg OH 43068-2312 Office: State of Ohio Bd Nursing 17 S High St Ste 400 Columbus OH 43215 Office Phone: 614-227-2147. Personal E-mail: kathyhill@insight.rr.com. Business E-Mail: khill@porterwright.com.

HILL, LARKIN PAYNE, jewelry designer, manufacturer; b. Oct. 30, 1954; d. Max Lloyd and Jane Olivia (Evatt) H. Student, Coll. Charleston, S.C., 1972—73, U. N.C., Chapel Hill, 1973. Lic. real estate broker, N.C. Sec., property mgr. Max L. Hill Co., Inc., Charleston, S.C., 1973-75, sec., data processor, 1979-82, v.p. adminstrn., 1982—, Mt. Pleasant, SC, 2004—; ops. mgr. Shorline Internat. Real Estate, 2003—04; pres., jewelry designer and mfr. Pearl, LLC, 2004—. Resident mgr. Carolina Apts., Carrboro, N.C., 1975-77; sales assoc., Realtor, Southland Assocs., Chapel Hill, N.C., 1977-78; jewelry designer Pearl, LLC, pres.; cons. specifications com. Charleston Trident Multiple Listing Service, 1985. Bd. dirs. Charleston Area Arts Coun., 1992-93; co-chair Beaux Arts Ball, Sch. Arts. Mem. Royal Oak Found., Scottish Soc. Charleston (bd. dirs. 1989-91), Preservation Soc., Charleston Computer Users Group, N.C. Assn. Realtors, Spoleto Festival USA (chmn. auction catalog com. 1990-92). Republican. Methodist. Avocations: reading, crossword puzzles, American Staffordshire Terriers. Home: 7 Riverside Dr Charleston SC 29403-3217 Office: Max L Hill Co INc 824 Johnnie Dodds Blvd Mount Pleasant SC 29464 also: Pearl LLC PO Box 22813 Charleston SC 29413 Office Phone: 843-853-3947. Business E-Mail: info@pearlllc.com.

HILL, LAURA KERR, conductor, director, music educator; b. Morgantown, W.Va., Mar. 19, 1973; d. James Milton and Carolyn DeVault Kerr, adopted d. William Andrew and Elizabeth McMillin Kerr; m. John Emerson Hill, June 21, 1997. B in Music Edn. with honors, Butler U., 1995. Asst. dir. bands Met. Sch. Dist. Pike Twp., Indpls., 1996—99, Yorktown HS, 2002—03; edn. coord. Indpls. Symphony Orch., 2000—03; condr., music dir. orchs. Graves County Sch. Dist., Mayfield, Ky., 2003—. Cello instr. Indpls. Acad. Music, 1994—96; cellist Lafayette Symphony Orch., 1994—2002, Carmel Symphony Orch., 2002—03, Anderson Symphony Orch., 2002—03, Paducah Symphony Orch., 2003—; adj. faculty instr. Wabash Coll., Crawfordsville, 1995—98; adjudicator Ind. Bandmasters Assn. - All State Band, Indpls., 1995—99, Ind. State Sch. Music Assn., 2002—; clinician Archdiocese Indpls., Indpls., 1993—96, Ebony Essence String Orch., Indpls., 1994—96, Met. Sch. Dist. Warren Twp., Indpls., 1995—96, Murray State U., 2004—05, condr., 2004, 06, Western Ky. U., 2006; creative cons. Obion County HS, Troy, Tenn., 1999—; orch. chair-elect Ky. Music Educators Assn., 2005, mem. mentorship task force. Dance team dir. Our Time Has Come (Grand Champions Ind. State HS Dance Team Assn., 1998); prodr., dir.: (musical production) Curtain Call; author: (method book) The Best of Both Worlds: A Practical Blending of Suzuki and Traditional String Pedagogy. Vol. Humane Soc., Indpls., 1995; faculty advisor Tri-M Music Honor Soc., Mayfield, 2003. Named All-Star Tchr., City of Mayfield C. of C., 2005, Outstanding Am. H.S. Tchr., Nat. Honor Roll, 2006; recipient Top Ten Educator award, Met. Sch. Dist. Pike Twp., 1996—99, John R. Wooden Excellence in Edn. award, 2002; Music scholar, Butler U., 1993—95, Lincoln Ctr. Music grant, Indpls. Symphony Orch., 2002. Mem.: Nat. Sch. Orch. Conf., Music Educators Nat. Conf., Am. String Tchrs.' Assn. Independent. Methodist. Personal E-mail: lkhillartsed@aol.com.

HILL, LAURYN, vocalist, actress; b. South Orange, N.J., May 25, 1975; Student, Columbia U. Teamed with Prakazrel "Pras" Michel and Wyclef Jean as the Fugees while still in H.S.; trio produced 2 albums: Blunted on Reality, 1994, and The Score, 1996 (17 million copies sold). Solo albums: The Miseducation of Lauryn Hill, 1998, MTV Unplugged No. 2.0, 2002; wrote and produced On That Day for gospel artist CeCe Winans; wrote A Rose is Still a Rose for Aretha Franklin album, also directed song's accompanying video. Actress: (films) Sister Act 2: Back in the Habit, 1993, King of the Hill, 1993, Rhyme & Reason, 1997, Hav Plenty, 1997, Restaurant, 1998, Dave Chappelle's Block Party, 2006; television appearances As the World Turns, 1991, Daddy's Girl, 1997. Founder non-profit The Refugee Youth Camp Youth Project. With Fugees received 2 1996 Grammy awards--Best Rap Album for The Score and Best R&B Performance by a Duo or Group With Vocal (Killing Me Softly). Recipient 1999 Grammy awards for Album of Yr., Best New Artist, Best R&B Song, Best R&B Album, Best Female R&B Vocal Performance. Nominated for several awards at 13th Annual Soul Train Music Awards in L.A. Recipient 4 awards (Outstanding New Artist, Outstanding Female Artist, Outstanding Album and NAACP President's award) 30th Annual NAACP Image Awards, Pasadena, Calif., 1999. Other awards include Favorite New Soul/R&B Artist (26th Annual Am. Music Awards), Best New Artist (Danish Grammy Awards), Entertainer of Yr. (Entertainment Weekly), #1 Album of Yr. (Time mag., N.Y. Times), Best R&B Album of 1998 (USA Today), Artist of Yr. (Spin mag.), Artist of Yr. (Details mag.), 3 Rolling Stone Music Awards.*

HILL, LEDA KATHERINE, librarian; b. Bklyn., Feb. 16, 1952; d. David and Leda Louise (Jones) H. BA, Bklyn. Coll., 1974, MS in Edn., 1989; MLS, Queens (N.Y.) Coll., 1995. New bus. coord. INAC Corp., Cranford, N.J., 1974-80; paralegal Orgn. Women for Legal Awareness, Inc., East Orange, N.J., 1980-83; tchr. Roselle (N.J.) Bd. Edn., 1983-84; libr., tchr. N.Y.C. Bd. Edn., Bklyn., 1985—. Mem. ALA, Bklyn. Reading Coun., N.Y.C. Sch. Librs. Assn., N.Y. Libr. Assn., Am. Assn. Sch. Librs. Office: Middle School 2 655 Parkside Ave Brooklyn NY 11226-1505 Office Phone: 718-462-6992. E-mail: lhill4@nycboe.net.

HILL, LINDA MARIE PALERMO, elementary school educator; b. Newark; d. Peter and Florence (Desiderio) McCue; children: Michael, Christopher, Douglas. BA, Caldwell (N.J.) Coll., 1970; MA, Seton Hall U., 1973; postgrad., Salem (Mass.) State Coll., 1986. Cert. elem. tchr., reading specialist, project adventure instr. Tchr. Roxbury Bd. Edn., Succasunna, N.J., 1970-74; libr.-media specialist, tchr. Hopatcong (N.J.) Bd. Edn., 1983—. Founder, dir. Young Astronaut Coun. Hopatcong Borough Schs. Mem. NEA, N.J. Edn. Assn., Hopatcong Edn. Assn. Home: 14 Oklahoma Trail PO Box 905 Hopatcong NJ 07843-0905 Office: Durban Ave Sch Durban Ave Hopatcong NJ 07843-1504 E-mail: lhill@hopatcongschools.org.

HILL, LORIE ELIZABETH, psychotherapist; b. Buffalo, Oct. 21, 1946; d. Graham and Elizabeth Helen (Salm) H. Student, U. Manchester, Eng., 1966-67; BA, Grinnell Coll., 1968; MA, U. Wis., 1970, Calif. State U., Sonoma, 1974; PhD, Wright Inst., 1980. Instr. English U. Mo., 1970-71; adminstr., supr. Antioch-West and Ctr. for Ind. Living, San Francisco, Berkeley, 1975-77; dir. tng. Ctr. for Edn. and Mental Health, San Francisco, 1977-80, exec. dir., 1980-81; pvt. practice Berkeley and Oakland, Calif., 1976—; instr. master's program in psychology John F. Kennedy U., Orinda, Calif., 1985, 94—. Founder group of psychotherapists against racism; spkr. on cross-cultural psychology; creater Jump Start, a violence prevention and unlearning racism program for youth; trainer for trainers 3rd Internat. Conf. Conflict Resolution, St. Petersburg, Russia; sr. facilitator Color of Fear. Organizer against nuc. war; founding mem. Psychotherapists for Social Responsibility; psychologist Big Bros. and Big Sisters of the East Bay, 1986—88; vol. instr. City of Oakland Youth Skills Devel. Program; founder, dir. Providing Alternatives to Violence; creator JumpStart program; active Rainbow Coalition for Jesse Jackson's Presdl. Campaign, Ron Dellums Re-election Com.; campaigner for Clinton-Gore; co-founder Wellstone Progressive Dem. Club, 2003, East Bay Votes!. Mem. Calif. Psychol. Assn. (chair pub. interest divsn. 1997, Helen Margulies Mehr Pub. Svc. award 1996, chair social issues 1996—, Silver Psi award 1999), Wellstone Dem. Renewal Club (co-founder), East Bay Votes (co-founder). Democrat-Socialist. Avocations: sports, travel, music, reading. Office: 2955 Shattuck Ave Berkeley CA 94705-1808 Office Phone: 510-644-0922, 510-486-8088. E-mail: loriepav@aol.com.

HILL, LYNDA MCSEVENEY, mathematics educator; m. Bryan M. Hill, Dec. 19, 1992; 1 child, Maggie. EdB, Brigham Young U., Provo, Utah, 1997; MEd, Ga. So. U., Statesboro, 2002; cert. edn. specialist, Ga. So. U., 2003. H.s. math tchr. Effingham County, Springfield, Ga., 1999—. Relief soc. tchr. LDS Ch., Rincon, Ga. Mem.: Nat. Coun.Tchrs. of Math. Office: Effingham County HS 1589 Hwy 119 S Springfield GA 31329

HILL, MARALYN DENNIS, management consultant; d. Charles Leslie and Rose Ethel (Baer) Dennis; m. Edward Frank Brink, Jr. (div.); children: Lindsay Dennis Brink, Eric Charles Brink; m. Norman Ellison Hill, Mar. 28, 1990. Grad., Blackburn Coll., 1960; Masters, U. Mass., 1990. Pres. Brink Assocs., Simsbury, Conn., Noralyn Ltd., Charlotte, NC, 1990—, CEO Gilbert, Ariz., 2006—. Co-author 2 books, numerous articles; prodr.(host): (TV shows). Chef procurement chair March of Dimes-Star Chefs Charlotte, Charlotte, NC, 2003—04. Mem.: Internat. Food, Wine and Travel Assn., Orgnl. Devel. Network. Office: Noralyn Ltd 6322 S Sky Ct Gilbert AZ 85297 Office Phone: 480-840-3420. Business E-Mail: mdhill@noralyn.com.

HILL, MARGARET JANELL, elementary school educator; b. Gilmer, Tex., Dec. 28, 1950; d. Ruby Ida and Marvin Rudolph Denton; m. Michael Byrd Hill, Oct. 31, 1978; children: Jared Glen, Jennifer Jill Whitman, Heather Aileene, Grayson Michael, Ashlon David. BS with honors, East Tex. State U., Commerce, 1975; MEd, Stephen F. Austin, Nacogdoches, Tex., 1987. Cert. tchr. Tex., early childhood specialist Tex. Elem. tchr. Ore City (Tex.) Ind. Sch. Dist., 1988—. Sem. tchr. Ch. of Jesus Christ of LDS, Longview, Tex., 1977—78, young womens pres., 1980—81, nursery leader, 2001—04. Mem.: ATPE. Mem. Lds Ch. Home: 1817 Shenandoah Ct N Longview TX 75605 Office: Ore City Ind Sch Dist PO Box 100 Rebel Rd Ore City TX 75683 Office Phone: 903-968-3300. Personal E-mail: janellhill@gmail.com. Business E-Mail: hillj@ocisd.net.

HILL, MARION THELMA, elementary school educator; b. Chgo., Sept. 21, 1937; d. Herbert and Helen E. (Robinson) Hill. BEd, Chgo. Tchrs. Coll., 1963; MEd, Roosevelt U., 1971. Account clk. USDA, Chgo., 1957-58; ward clk. Cook County Hosp., Chgo., 1959-60; postal clk. U.S. P.O., Chgo., 1960-63; tchr. Chgo. Pub. Sch. System, 1963—98; real estate sales agt. Realty Assoc. Network, Inc., 1989—. Vol. tutor Salvation Army, Chgo., 1973; VBS tchr. Antioch-Bapt. Ch., Chgo., 1981-96, program coord. Roots Com. Orgn., Chgo. 1989. Mem.: African-Am. Hist. and Genealogical Soc., Morgan Pk. Golden Girls Assn., Internat. Sons and Daus. Slave Ancestry, Phi Delta. Democratic. Protestant. Avocations: travel, reading, writing, genealogy. Personal E-mail: marion.hill0360@sbcglobal.net.

HILL, MARJORIE JEAN, psychologist, association executive; b. Bklyn., Aug. 8, 1956; d. Walter James and Laura Beulah (Cherry) H. AA, The Coll. of Staten Island, 1975; BA, Adelphi U., 1977, MA, 1979, PhD, 1981. Asst. dir. child psychiatry Kings County Hosp., Bklyn., 1981-88; internship coord., psychiatric edn. Lincoln Med. and Mental Health Ctr., Bronx, NY, 1988-90; dir. NYC Mayor's Office for the Lesbian & Gay Community, NYC, 1990-93; asst. v.p. NYC Health and Hosps. Corp., 1993; interim exec. dir. Gay Men's Health Crisis, NYC, 2006—. Asst. prof. psychiatry NY Med. Coll., Valhalla, 1988-90; adj. faculty Coll. New Rochelle, 1988-91; adj. clin. assoc. Pace U., NYC, 1989—; adj. clin. prof. Yeshiva U., Bronx, NY, 1989—. Bd. dirs. NY Civil Liberties Union, NYC, 1990, AIDS Films, NYC, 1991-93, Columbia County Youth Project, 1989—; mem. Black Leadership Commn. on AIDS, NYC, 1991—; mem. NYC Fair Housing Task Force, 1990; bd. dirs., nat. chair Unity Fellowship Ch. of Christ, Inc., 1993—; mem. WNET-Channel 13 Community Adv. Bd., 1990—. Recipient Community Organizer award WBAI NYC Learning Alliance, 1988, Community Svc. award Nat. Lesbian and Gay Health Found., 1988, Hall of Fame award Staten Island Community Coll., 1989, Community Svc. award Nat. Lesbian Conf., 1991, Bayard Rustin award Nat. Black Lesbian and Gay Leadership Forum, 1991, Woman of Power award NOW, 1993, Polit. Svc. award Stonewall Dem. Com., 1992, Community Svc. award Empire Pride Agenda, 1992. Mem. APA, Coalition of 100 Black Women NYC, Assn. Women in Psychology (steering com. 1987), Assn. Black Psychologists (pres. 1988, treas. 1990, bd. dirs., Nelson Mandela Psychologist of Yr. 1991), Nat. Black Gay and Lesbian Leadership Forum (bd. govs.). Avocations: grassroots organizing, bike riding, aerobics. Office: Gay Men's Health Crisis The Tisch Bldg 119 West 24th St New York NY 10011 Office Phone: 212-367-1000.*

HILL, MARY C., hydrologist; b. Balt., Aug. 18, 1955; d. William E. and Ruth Jane Hill; m. J. Dungan Smith, Mar. 17, 1990; stepchildren: Wray C. Smith, Kirsten R. Smith, Martha H. Smith. AB, Hope Coll., 1976; MSE, Princeton U., 1979, PhD, 1985. Lectr. Rutgers U., New Brunswick, N.J., 1981; rsch. asst. Princeton U., 1977-81; hydrologist opers. profl. U.S. Geol. Survey, Trenton, N.J., 1981-87, rsch. hydrologist Lakewood, Colo., 1987-97, Boulder, Colo., 1997—. Adj. faculty Colo. Sch. of Mines, Golden, 1989—, U. Colo., Boulder, 1994—; coord./tchr. Internat. Groundwater Modeling Assn., U.S. Geol. Survey, 1983—. Author: (computer program) MODFLOWP, 1992, UCODE, 1998, 2005, MODFLOW-2000, 2000; contbr. articles to profl. jours. Grantee Yucca Mountain Project, U.S. Geol. Survey, DOE, 1995—. Mem. ASCE (Walter L. Huber rsch. prize 2000),, Am. Geophys. Union, Geol. Soc. Am., Nat. Ground Water Assn. (Darcy lectr. 2001, M. King Hubbert award, 2005). Achievements include rsch. in the use of numerical models and data in the simulation of groundwater systems. Office: US Geol Survey 3215 Marine St Boulder CO 80303-1066 Business E-Mail: mchill@usgs.gov.

HILL, PAMELA JEAN, middle school educator; b. Oxford Junction, Iowa, Jan. 6, 1964; d. Ronald Eugene and Marlene Joyce (Bright) Hansen; m. Bradley John Hill, July 25, 1987; children: Wade Alan, Ryan Thomas. BA, Luther Coll., 1986. Tchr. 5th and 6th grades Monroe (Iowa) Elem. Sch., 1986-87; tchr. 6th grade PCM Mid. Sch., Prairie City, Iowa, 1987—. Head dept. math., PCM Cmty. Schs., 1992-96, mem. instrnl. coun., 1992-96. Mem. NEA, Iowa Edn. Assn., Prairie City/Monroe Edn. Assn., PEO (chpt. BH), Delta Kappa Gamma. Democrat. Lutheran. Avocations: golf, cooking, walking, reading. Office: PCM Mid Sch PO Box 490 Prairie City IA 50228-0490

HILL, RUTH ELAINE, social studies educator, department chairman; d. Jack Joseph and Lois Virginia Bremigen; m. Larry Charles Hill, June 29, 1968; children: Jeffrey Wayne, Christopher Todd. BA, Houghton Coll., NY, 1968. Cert. tchr. elem. edn., history NY and Pa., tchr. social studies Pa., Hawaii and Mo. First grade tchr. Salford-Upper Salford Elem. Sch., Woxall, Pa., 1968—71; kindergarten tchr. DuBois (Pa.) Area Sch. Dist., 1971—76; social studies tchr. Lahainaluna H.S., Lahanina, Hawaii, 1989—. Social studies dept. chair Lahainaluna HS. Named We the People Hawaii State (Class) Winner, 1998; fellow, Nat. Coun. Social Studies/Keizai Koho Found., 2003. Mem.: NEA, Hawaii State Tchrs. Assn. Avocations: travel, sewing, reading. Home: PO Box 10111 Lahaina HI 96761 Office: Lahainaluna HS 980 Lahainaluna Rd Lahaina HI 96761 Office Phone: 808-662-4000 ext 258. E-mail: ruth_hill@notes.k12.hi.us.

HILL, RUTH FOELL, language consultant; b. Houston, Sept. 13, 1931; d. Ernest William and Florence Margaret (Kane) Foell; children: Linden Ruth, Andrea Grace. Student, Principia Coll., Elsah, Ill., 1950; BA, U. Calif., Berkeley, 1952; postgrad., San Diego State, 1955, Ctrl. Piedmont, 1981. Cert. tchr., Calif. Owner, dir. Art Gallery of Chapel Hill, NC, 1966-75; ecumenical bd. Campus Ministry, Charlotte; with referral svc. Charlotte Bed and Breakfast Registry, 1980-90; lang. cons. Berlitz Internat., Raleigh, N.C., 1988-91; ESL tchr. Albemarle Elem. Sch., 2000—. Est. cons. Performax Internat.; attendee UN Decade for Women Conf., NGO Forum, Nairobi, Kenya, 1985, Women and Global Security Conf., 1986, emerging issues forum N.C. State U., 1987-93; presenter Southeastern Women's Studies Conf. Author: (poetry) Noble House, 2003; contbr. poetry to Nat. Libr. of Poetry Internat. Hall of Fame. Bd. dirs., chmn. natural resources com. LWV; coord. USIA grant region 6, Internat. Exch. Network; mem. N.C. Leadership Forum, N.C. Citizens Assembly, 1989; chmn. Week of Edn. Pub. Forum on Energy, Union Concerned Scientists, 1990-93; bd. dirs. Nat. Women's Conf. Commn., 1994—; mem. edn. subcom. Mayor's Internat. Cabinet, 1995; mem. Congress House Spkr.'s Citizen Task Force, 1995—; mem. Rep. Platform Com. and Nat. Presdl. Task Force, 1999, Rep. Inner Cir., 1995; mem. edn. com. Charlotte/Mecklenberg Historic Properties, 1986-88; mem. groundwater subcom. Mecklenburg County Commrs., 1987. Named Outstanding Athlete Women's Athletic Assn., Internat. Poetry Hall of Fame, 1998; Hewlett Found. scholar, 1979-81. Mem. AAUW (v.p. membership com., bd. dirs.), Ams. for Legal Reform (nat. adv. bd.), Am. Farm Land Trust, UN Assn. U.S.A. (chpt. pres. 1991-93, co-chair UN Day Queens Coll. 1992, N.C. divsn. sec. 1993-94, UN50 chair 1995, So. Summit Queens Coll. 2002), Am. Biog. Inst. Rsch. Assn. (nominated to bd. govs.), Am. Biog. Inst. (apptd. adv. bd.), Carolina Coun. on World Affairs, Chapel Hill-Carrboro Sch. Art Guild (pres.), Midwest Acad., World Wide Women in Environment, N.Y. Acad. Sci. Republican. Christian Scientist. Avocations: travel, environmental issues, international exchange networking. Office: PO Box 220802 Charlotte NC 28222-0802 Personal E-mail: rhill37901@aol.com.

HILL, SUSAN BEASLEY, recreational therapist; b. Hattiesburg, Miss., June 16, 1944; d. William Lee Beasley, Jr. and Alice Odelle (Taylor) Beasley; 1 child, Susannah Odelle. BA in English, Speech and DRama, Greensboro Coll., 1966; MSW, U. N.C., 1982. Tchr., prin. John Umstead Hosp., Butner, NC, 1967—70; crisis counselor, co-founder Dial Help, Salisburg, NC, 1970—71; social worker Rowan County Dept. Social Svc., Salisburg, 1970—71; sales mgr./pub. rels. Beasley Lumber Co., Scotland Neck, NC, 1971—80; bus. owner, mgr. Repeat Performances, Raleigh, 1976—78; co-dir., counselor, tchr. Project Redirection Wake County Pub. Schs., Raleigh, 1978—79; clin. social worker, therapist Orange-Person-Chatham Mental Health Ctr., Chapel Hill, NC, 1980—81; clin. social worker, therapist Adult Outpatient Group Clinic N.C. Meml. Hosp., Chapel Hill, 1981—82; clin. social worker/family advisor Divsn. for Disorders of Devel. and Learning U. N.C., Chapel Hill, 1982; pvt. counselor, ednl. tchr. Harnett County, NC, 1982—; dir. Learning Ctr. Acads. Plus, Dunn, NC, 1993—95; activity profl. Dunn (N.C.) Rehab. and Nursing Ctr., 1998—. Shut-in and nursing home ministry Gospel Tabernacle Ch., Dunn, 1982—90. Author: (newspaper series) Aegism: A Six Party Study, 1981. Mem. women's bd. Gospel Tabernacle Ch., 1987, active, 1988—. Republican. Avocations: cooking, painting, politics, cats. Home: 106 Greenwich Ct Dunn NC 28334 Office: Dunn Nursing and Rehab Ctr 711 Susan Tart Rd Dunn NC 28334

HILL, SUSAN SLOAN, safety engineer; b. Quincy, Mass., June 1, 1952; d. Ralph Arnold and Grace Elenore (Sloan) Crosby; m. William Loyd Hill, Dec. 16, 1973 (div. July 1982); m. William Joseph Graham, Sept. 10, 1983 (div. Feb. 1985). AS in Gen. Engring., Motlow State C.C., Tullahoma, Tenn., 1976; BS in Indsl. Engring., Tenn. Technol. U., 1978. Intern, safety engr. Intern Tng. Ctr., U.S. Army, Red River Army Depot, Tex., 1978-79, Field Safety Activity, Charlestown, Ind., 1979, sys. safety engr. Comm.-Electronics Command Ft. Monmouth, N.J., 1979-84, gen. engr., 1984-85; chief sys. safety Arnold Air Force Sta., USAF, Tullahoma, 1984; sys. safety engr. U.S. Army Safety Ctr., Ft. Rucker, Ala., 1985-91; medically ret.; ind. cons. sys. safety, 1991—. Founder Fibromyalgia Support Group; leader Arthritis Found. Support Group; active Arthritis Found. Recipient 5 letters of appreciation, U.S. Army, letter of appreciation, Arthritis Found. Mem. NAFE, Assn. Fed. Safety and Health Profls. (regional v.p. 1980-84), Soc. Women Engrs., Nat. Safety Mgmt. Soc., Am. Soc. Safety Engrs., Sys. Safety Soc., Order Engr. Republican. Episcopalian. Avocations: reading, gardening, walking, cooking, golf. Home and Office: 1307 Bel-Aire Dr Tullahoma TN 37388

HILL, TERRI, diversified financial services company executive; BA in Orgnl. Comm., Ariz. State U.; cert. in human resources, Cornell U. With Am. Express, 1984—96, Nationwide Mutual Ins. Co., 1996—, sr. v.p. human resources and ops. Scottsdale Ins. Co., exec. v.p., chief adminstrv. officer, 2003—. Office: Nationwide Mutual Ins Co One Nationwide Plaza Columbus OH 43215-2220

HILL, TESSA, non profit environmental group executive; BA in Edn., Park Recreation Adminstrn., U. Minn., 1968. Tchr. elem. schs., 1970; founder Kids For Saving Earth Worldwide, Mpls., 1989—. Adv. com. U.S. Environ. Protection Agy., Dept. Health Human Svcs. Agy. Toxic Substances Disease Registry. Editor CHEC Report, Kids for Saving Earth News/Programs. Bd. dirs. Children's Health Environ. Coalition, Nat. Coalition Against Misuse Pesticides. Home and Office: Kids for Saving Earth Worldwide 5425 Pineview Ln N Minneapolis MN 55442-1704 Business E-Mail: KSEWW@aol.com.

HILL, VALERIE KOMKOV, dance educator, artist; b. Stockport, Eng., Apr. 25, 1950; arrived in U.S., 1957; d. Vadim Konstantine and Joyce Radford Komkov; m. Glenn Eugene Hill, Aug. 6, 1978; children: Ian Alexis, Naomi Elise. BFA in Art, Tex. Tech. U., Lubbock, 1973, BA in Dance, 1976, MA, 1987. Dance instr. Suzanne Aker Sch. Ballet, Lubbock, 1976—82; dance educator Lubbock Ind. Sch. Dist., 1983—. Com. mem. Tex. Tech. Mus. Exhibit Selection, Tex. Tech. U. Mus., 2005—. Named So. Dance Educator of Yr., SDAHPERD, 1996. Mem.: Tex. Assn. Health, Phys. Edn., Recreation and Dance (Tex. Dance Educator of Yr. 1995), Am. Fedn. Tchrs. Avocations: painting, quilting, gardening, reading, yoga.

HILL, VICTORIA RUTH, librarian; b. N.Y.C., Dec. 4, 1960; d. Arthur Burit and Patricia Smith Hill. BA, U. Pa., 1983; MS in Libr. Sci., Pratt Inst., Bklyn., 1989. Cert. profl. libr. N.Y. Mgr. of libr. svcs. Bklyn. Pub. Libr., 1984—, children's cluster specialist, 2001—. Recent grad. trustee Pratt Inst., 1990—92, mem. dean search com. Sch. Info. and Libr. Sci., 1991—92, 1999. Amb. People to People Amb. Tour, Rio de Janeiro and Manaus, Brazil, 2004; mem. vestry St. John's Episcopal Ch., Bklyn., 1984—97, past mem. spl. events com. Named one of Outstanding Young Women of Am., 1986; fellow Internat. Youth Libr., Munich, 1995, Libr.'s Study Tour of Germany, SUNY, Goethe Inst., 1992. Mem.: ALA, Assn. Libr. Svc. to Children (Robert F. Sibert Award com. 2002—03), N.Y. Black Libr.'s Caucus. Avocations: travel, public speaking. Home: 36 Saint John's Pl Aptt # 2 Brooklyn NY 11217-3206 Office: Bklyn Pub Libr Canarsie Br 1580 Rockaway Pky Brooklyn NY 11236 Office Phone: 917-309-6621. Home Fax: 718-257-6557; Office Fax: 718-257-6557. Personal E-mail: vickyhill@yahoo.com. E-mail: v.hill@brooklynpubliclibrary.org.

HILL-COOK, PATRICIA ANN, social services administrator; b. Cinn., Oct. 12, 1953; d. Clinton Hill, Willie Bell and Terrell Lewis (Stepfather); 1 child, Nathan G. Cook. A in Social Svc. Tech., U. Cinn., 1986, BS in Social Sci, 1997. Housing coord./case mgr. Welcome House Ky., Covington, 1993—95; outreach and recruitment specialist U. Cinn., 1995—97; workforce devel. specialist Work Resource Ctr., Cinn., 1997—. Spkr. in field. Author: Personally Speaking, 2001. Youth leader Golden Leaf Bapt. Ch., Cinn., 1997, pres. women's missionary group, 2001. Recipient Activist award, Voices in Action, Cinn., 2002; Martin Luther King Jr. scholar, U. Cinn., 1996. Democrat. Baptist. Office: Work Resource Ctr 2901 Gilbert Cincinnati OH 45207 Office Phone: 513-281-2316. Business E-Mail: pcook@workrc.org.

HILLENBRAND, LAURA, writer; b. Fairfax, Va., 1967; Student, Kenyon Coll. Contbg. writer editor: Equus Mag., 1989—; contbr. articles (Nat. Mag. award, 2003); author: Seabiscuit: An American Legend, 2001 (finalist Nat. Book Critics Cir. award, BookSense Nonfiction book award year, William Hill Sportsbook Year award Great Britain, 2001); cons.: (films) Seabiscuit. Spokesperson, advocate Chronic Fatigue Syndrome. Recipient Two time winner Eclipse award, Highest honor in thoroughbred racing journalism. Office: Ballantine Books Random House 1745 Broadway New York NY 10019*

HILLER, MARSHA KAY, physical therapist; b. Montevideo, Uruguay, Dec. 2, 1965; came to U.S, 1967; d. Larry Keith and Janet Arlene (Hutchinson) H. BS in Phys. Therapy, U. Puget Sound, Tacoma, Wash., 1988. Phys. therapist Tacoma Gen. Hosp., 1988-92, N.W. Therapy and Rehab, 1992-93, Allenmore Hosp.-Multicare, Tacoma, 1993—. Mem. Am. Phys. Therapy Assn., Wash. State Phys. Therapy Assn. Avocations: bowling, golf, camping, antiques, stamp collecting/philately. Home: 4811 161st St E Tacoma WA 98446-3805 Office: Allenmore Hosp-Multicare 19th & Union Sts Tacoma WA 98405

HILLERT, GLORIA BONNIN, anatomist, educator; b. Brownton, Minn., Jan. 25, 1930; d. Edward Henry and Lydia Magdalene (Luebker) Bonnin; m. Richard Hillert, Aug. 20, 1960; children: Kathryn, Virginia, Jonathan. BS, Valparaiso (Ind.) U., 1953; MA, U. Mich., 1958. Instr. Springfield (Ill.) Jr. Coll., 1953-57; teaching asst. U. Mich., Ann Arbor, 1957-58; instr., dept. head St. John's Coll., Winfield, Kans., 1958-59; asst. prof. Concordia Coll., River Forest, Ill., 1959-63; vis. instr. Wright Jr. Coll., Chgo., 1974-76, Ill. Benedictine Coll., Lisle, 1977-78, Rosary Coll., River Forest, 1976-81; prof. anatomy and physiology Triton Coll., River Grove, 1982-92, prof. emeritus, 1992—; vis. asst. prof. Concordia U., 1993—. Vis. instr. Wheaton (Ill.) Coll., 1988; advisor Springfield Jr. Coll. Sci. Club, 1953-57, Concordia Coll. Cultural Group, 1959-62; program dir. Triton Coll. Sci. Lectr. Series, 1983-87; participant Internat. Educators Workshop in Amazonia, 1993. Dem. campaign asst., Maywood, Ill., 1972, 88; vol. Mental Health Orgn., Chgo., 1969-73, Earthwatch, St. Croix, 1987, Costa Rica, 1989, Internat. Med. Care Team, Guatemala, 1995, Earthwatch End of Dinosaurs, 1997. Mem. AAUW, Ill. Assn. Community Coll. Biol. Tchrs., Nat. Assn. Biol. Tchrs. Lutheran. Avocation: travel. Home: 1620 Clay Ct Melrose Park IL 60160-2419 Office: Triton Coll 2000 N 5th Ave River Grove IL 60171-1907

HILLERY, MARY JANE LARATO, columnist, television personality, television producer, writer, military officer; b. Boston, Sept. 15, 1931; d. Donato and Porzia (Avellis) Larato; m. Thomas H. Hillery, Feb. 25, 1961; 1 son, Thomas H. Assoc. Sci. (scholar), Northea. U., 1950; BS, U. Mass. Harvard Extension, 1962; grad., Command and Gen. Staff Coll., 1982. Sales agt., linguist Pan Am. Airways, Boston, 1955-61; interpreter Internat. Conf. Fire Chiefs, Boston, 1966; tchr. Spanish YWCA, Natick, Mass., 1966-67; cmty. rels. cons., adv. bd. dirs., lectr. for migrant edn. project divsn., Mass. Dept. Cmty. Affairs, Boston, 1967-69; editor-in-chief Sudbury (Mass.) Citizen, 1967-76; assoc. editor The Beacon, 1976-79, contbg. editor, 1979-83; area editl. adviser Beacon Pub. Co., Acton, Mass., 1970-80, editor, 1976-80; columnist Town Crier, 1987—; contbg. editor Towne Talk, 1975-79, Citizens' Forum, 1975-81; editor Spl. Forces Ann. History, 1989-90; dir. pub. affairs Mass. Dept. Environ Quality Engring., 1981-83; prodr., host TV interview show For the Record, 1985—. Pub. affairs officer Fed. Emergency Mgmt. Agy., 1995-2003; women vets. spkr. State House Mass. ofcl. Vets. Day observances, ceremonies, 1999. Editor Hansconian, 1983-85. Mem. Bus. Adv. Com., 1972-77, Sudbury Sch. Com., 1976-77; mem. Meml. Day Celebration Com., 1972—, master of ceremonies, 1973—, parade marshal, 1997, 2003; chmn. Sudbury WWII Commemorativ e Cmty., 1992-96; chmn. Sudbury Korean War 50th Anniversary Commemorative Com., 2000—; mem. Sudbury Town Report, 1967-72, 85-88, chmn., 1969-72; chmn. Sudbury Vets. Adv. Com., 1986-92; panelist Internat. Women's Year Symposium, 1975, Women in Politics, 1987, Women in Mil., 1987; mem. congl. 5th dist. Mass. nomination bd. West Point, apptd. mil. aide-de-camp to Mass. Gov. Wm. Weld, 1992—; Veterans' agt. Town of Sudbury, 1992-2004. With USN, 1950-54, with USNR, 1954-56, lt. col. USAR; Persian Gulf, 1991-92; liaison officer U.S. Mil. Acad. West Point, 1976-89, 93-94; pub. affairs officer 94th USAR Command, 1982-83, Office of Sec. of Def., The Pentagon, Washington, 1989-93; dir. pub. rels. Mission One, Employer Support Guard and Res., Dept. of Def.; parade marshall Sudbury Meml. Day Parade, 1997, 2003; vet. svc. officer Town of Sudbury, 1992-2004. Decorated Meritorious Svc. medal, Joint Svc. Achievement medal, Nat. Def. medal with Bronze Star, Outstanding Svc. award Sec. Def. Pub. Affairs, Joint Meritorious unit award, Def. Superior Svc. medal, Employer Support Guard and Res. Mission One award; named Editor of Yr., Beacon Pub. Co., 1970; recipient medal of appreciation Internat. Order DeMolay, 1969, cert. of appreciation U.S. Def. Civil Preparedness Agy., 1975, Mass. Bicentennial Commn., 1976, Appreciation award U.S. Mil. Acad., 1976-86, citations Mass. State Senate, 1979, 82, Newswriting award Media Contest Air Force Sys. Command, 1984, Outstanding Svc. award Sec. Def. Pub. Affairs, 1991, Cmty. Citizen award Citizen of Yr., Sudbury Grange, 1999, Exec. Comm. Sudbury Grange, 2003-06, Cmty. Svc. award DAR, 2000, George Washington Honor medal Bay State chpt. Freedoms Found. at Valley Forge, 1998. Mem. LWV (dir. 1964-68), Nat. Editl. Assn., Nat. Newspaper Assn., Nat. Press Club, Rotary Internat. (mem. Sudbury chpt. scholarship chmn. 1993—, bd. dirs. 1994-95, 96-97, 97—, pub. rels. chmn. 1995-97, assoc. editor The Bull., 1996-97, Found. chmn. 1997-99, pres.-elect 2000-01, pres. 2001-02), New Eng. Press Assn., Internat. Platform Assn. (Silver Bowl award for poetry 1997), Bus. and Profl. Women's Club (Sudbury 1st v.p. 1973, pres. 1973-76, parliamentarian 1978-88, 90-92, legis. chair 1990-92, state bylaws com. 1977-78, 79-81, 86-88, state legis. chmn. 1979-81, 86-88, state polit. action com. chmn. 1988-89, Woman of Yr. 1979, Woman of Achievement 1982), Nat. League Am. Pen Women (exec. bd. Boston 1974-76, 78-88, pres. Boston br. 1976-78, 94-98, 2000—, state exec. bd. 1994-1998, publicity chmn. 1979-80, chmn. bylaws com. 1979-80, 86-88, parliamentarian 1978-80, 82-88, auditor 1980-82, 84-88, 1st v.p. 1988-92, nat. editor Achievements, The Pen Woman 1992-94, nat. protocol chair 1998, nat. scholarship chmn. 1998—, nat. 4th v.p. 2000-02, nat. 3d v.p. 2002-04), Res. Officers Assn. (life, dept. sec. 1978-79, dept. army v.p. 1992-95, pres. Boston chpt. 1986-88, dept. pres.-elect 1995-96, dept. pres. 1996-97, army v.p. 1995-96, army coun. rep. 1989-92, 1999—, budget com., 1990-91, dept. publicity chmn. 1988-92, editor Advisor 1991-95, Outstanding Svc. award 1978-79, co-chair Nat. Conv. 1995-98), Spl. Forces Assn. (Green Berets, asst. to chmn. nat. conv. 1999-2000), Am. Legion (post comdr. 2000-01, exec. bd. 1996—, chaplain 1996-2000, 02—), Korean War Vets. Mass. (life), Mil. Intelligence Assn. New Eng. (press officer 2004-06), Mil. ASsn. New Eng. (pres. 2006—), Omega Sigma. Home: 66 Willow Rd Sudbury MA 01776-2663

HILLERY, SUSIE MOORE, retired elementary school educator; b. Lunenburg County, VA, Feb. 25, 1928; d. William Edward and Sarah Anderson Moore; m. Herbert Vincent Hillery, June 17, 1956 (div. Jan. 1969); children: Vincent, Nathan. BA, Lynchburg Coll., 1950; MA, U. Ky., 1955; student, Lexington Sem., Ky.; student, U. Va., U. Tex. Youth min. Christian Ch. Disciples of Christ, Clarksville, Tenn., 1950—52; tchr. religious edn. Martinsville (Va.) Pub. Sch., 1952—53; elem. sch. tchr. Lynchburg (Va.) Pub. Schs., 1953—54, Austin (Tex.) Pub. Schs., 1956—58, 1964—69, Henrico County Pub. Schs., Richmond, Va., 1969—91; youth min. Colonial Christian Ch., Richmond, 1983—86; pastor/min. Christian Ch., Gordonsville, Va., 1993—98, Bella Grove Christian Ch., Louisa, Va., 1998—2000; vol. chaplain Henrico Drs. Hosp., Richmond, 1999—. Rep. Interfaith Coun., 1993—; with Ch. Women United, 1998—.

HILLEY, MARY KAY, music educator; b. Ft. Valley, Ga., Oct. 31, 1963; d. John Dunham and G. Joan (Baker) Warner; m. Harry Quinton Dunlap (div.); 1 child, John Quinton Dunlap; m. Daniel Grover Hilley, Sept. 15, 2001. AA in Music, Darton Coll., 1996; BS in Music Edn., Ga. Southwestern State U., 1999. Tchr. Wheeler Piano Studio, Americus, Ga., 1997—2000; pvt. piano tchr. Leesburg, Ga., 1999—. Organist 1st Presbyn. Ch., Albany, Ga., 1998—2000; pianist, choir dir. Northgate Presbyn. Ch., Albany, 2000—. Mem.: Nat. Guild Piano Tchrs. Avocations: reading, bicycling, sewing, camping. Home and Studio: 129 Lee Dr Leesburg GA 31763

HILLGREN, SONJA DOROTHY, journalist; b. Sioux Falls, S.D., May 17, 1948; d. Ralph Oliver and Priscilla Adaline (Mannes) Hillgren; m. Ralph Lee Hill (dec.). BJ, U. Mo., 1970, MA, 1972; postgrad., Harvard U., 1982—83. Washington corr. Ohio-Washington News Svc., 1972—73; reporter UPI, Annapolis, Md., 1974—76, reporter, editor Washington, 1976—78, farm editor, 1978—88; Washington corr. Knight-Ridder, Washington, 1988—90; Washington editor Farm Jour., 1990—95, editor, 1995—2004, sr. v.p., 2000—. Exec.-in-residence U. Mo., 1997; campaign steering com. U. Mo. Sch. Journalism, 2003—. Chair bd. dirs. Nat. Press Bldg. Corp., 1997; bd. dirs. Winrock Internat., Philabundance, 2000—05. Named Old Master, Purdue U., 1992, Agrl. Communicator of Yr., Nat. Agri-Mktg. Assn., 1996; recipient J.R. Russell award, Newspaper Farm Editors Am., 1985, Reuben Brigham award, Agrl. Comms. in Edn., 1988, Oscar in Agr. for Excellence in Agrl. Reporting, U. Ill., 1998, Recognition of Excellence in Print Media award, Ill. Soybean Assn., 2002, Prodr. Comms. award, United Soybean Bd., 2003; Nieman fellow, Harvard U., 1982—83, Woodrow Wilson vis. fellow, 1993—94. Mem.: Coun. on Fgn. Rels., Farm Found., Nat. Agri-Mktg. Assn., Am. Agrl. Editors' Assn., Am. Soc. Mag. Editors, N.Am. Agrl. Journalists (pres. 1987—88), Congl. Country Club, Nat. Press Club (bd. govs. 1991—96, chair 1993—94, v.p. 1995, pres. 1996), Alpha Zeta, Pi Beta Phi (Carolyn Helman Lichtenberg Crest award 1999). Lutheran. Avocations: sports, reading. Office: Farm Jour 1818 Market St Fl 31 Philadelphia PA 19103-3654 Business E-Mail: shillgren@farmjournal.com.

HILLIARD, CAROL, nurse, educator, consultant, researcher; d. Elias and Eula Mae (Holt) Hilliard. AAS, Bronx CC, 1971; BSN, Hunter-Bellevue Sch. Nursing, 1981, MSN, 1983. Staff nurse Fordham Hosp., NYC, 1971—73; per diem work in ER, ICU and post anesthesia care unit Columbia Presbyn. Hosp., 1973—90; per diem work in ER, ICU & PACU Lincoln Hosp., 1991—95, Bellevue Hosp., 1990, Lenox Hill Hosp., 1973—2003; from staff nurse to operating room instr. NY Med. Coll., NYC, 1974—78; from staff nurse to nurse edn. instr. ER, ICU, PACU Harlem Hosp., NYC, 1978—90; asst. prof. nursing Hostos CC, NYC, 1990—95; coord., nurse cons. The Exhale Nurse Cons., NYC, 1996—, The Exhale Nursing Review, 1998—. Tchr. state bd. review classes Megan Evers Coll., Bklyn., 1996—98. Instr. CPR & basic life support for health care profls. Am. Red Cross, 1980—. Mem.: NY Assn. Black Nurses, Critical Care Nurses Assn., NY State Nurses Assn., Emergency Dept. Nursing Assn., Am. Nursing Assn. Democrat. Baptist. Avocations: sewing, decorating, dance, jazz, computers. Home and Office: The Exhale Nurse Cons 1295 Grand Concourse Rm 3C Bronx NY 10452 Personal E-mail: budstallion@verizon.net.

HILLIARD, CELIA, cultural historian; b. Chgo., May 9, 1942; d. Carl Franz Schmid and Isabelle Grossman; m. David Craig Hilliard, Feb. 16, 1974. BA, Northwestern U., Evanston, Ill., 1964. Contbr. chapters to books, articles to profl. jours.; author: Providing a Home-A History of the Old People's Home of the City of Chicago, 1983, Then and Now-Thirty Years of the Newberry Library Associates, 1995, The Woman's Athletic Club of Chicago-A History, 1999. Trustee The Poetry Found., Chgo.; mem. Northwestern U. Women's Bd., Evanston, Ill., Chgo. Hist. Soc. Guild, Antiquarian Soc., Chgo., Textile Soc., Chgo. Mem.: The Casino, Woman's Athletic Club Chgo., The Caxton Club. Home: 1320 N State Pky Chicago IL 60610

HILLIARD, KATHLEEN J., costume designer; b. Glendale, Calif., Aug. 3, 1957; d. John Thomas and Jewel Kathrine Hickey; m. Robert Allen Hilliard, Feb. 4, 1978; children: Angela Celeste, Christel Jewell, Michelle Gabrielle, Robert John. BFA in Theatre Design, U. NC, 1995. Costume designer NJ Shakespeare Festival, Madison, 1999, 2000, The Great Am. Melodrama, Oceano, Calif., 2000—03, Shakespeare & Co., Lenox, Mass., 2005, 2003—06, Primary Stages, NYC, 2005, Juilliard, NYC, 2006. Costume designer The Peddie Sch., Heightstown, NJ, 2005—06. Designer (plays) In the Continumn, 2005. Leader Girl Scouts of Am., 1988—94. Home: P O Box 215 Middlesex NJ 08846

HILLIARD, LIL, sales executive; b. Montgomery, Ala, Sept. 30, 1955; d. Louis C. and Laura M. Brewington; (div. Feb. 1, 1992); 1 child, Jeremiah Brewington. AA, So. Jr. Coll., 1974; student, Ala. State U. Sales rep. Lucky Heart Cosmetics, Memphis, Vulcan Svc., Birmingham, Ala. Avon rep., 1998-2001. Sec. Gibbs Village Cmty. Ctr., Montgomery, 1996-97; pres. Levi Watkins Libr. Club Ala. State U., 1999-2000. Recipient Golden Poet award, Poetry Guild, Calif., 1990. Mem. Custom Clothier Assn., Xperte Profl. Orgn. Democrat.

HILLIARD-BRADLEY, YVONNE, library administrator; b. Jacksonville, Fla., Apr. 17, 1949; d. James Ernest and Dorothy Amy Hilliard; m. Gregory Earl Bradley, Feb. 26, 1983; 1 child, Amanda Loren Bradley. MLS, Rutgers

U., 1976. Cert. profl. libr. Va. From youth svcs. libr. to ext. svcs. mgr. Norfolk (Va.) Pub. Libr., 1976—99, asst. dir. for pub. svcs., 1999—, acting dir., 2002—03. Owner Earth Weaves, 2002—. Founding mem. Norfolk Healthy Families Coalition, 1997—2002, Regional Healthy Families Coalition, Norfolk, 1999—2002; asst. libr. dir. active Norfolk After-Sch. Initiative, 2004—; active British Isles Folk Dance Group; adv. bd. Politca Hist. Expn., 2002—; bd. dirs. Police Hist. Expn. Adv. Bd., Norfolk, 2002—05. Fellow, Va. State Libr., 1975—76; grantee, Norfolk Found., 1995, Tidewater Children's Found., 2000—01. Mem.: ALA, Pub. Libr. Assn., Va. Libr. Assn. (region chair 1977—78), Mu Phi Epsilon, Beta Phi Mu (life). Avocations: singing, canoeing, skiing. Home: 530 Washington Pk Norfolk VA 23517 Office: Norfolk Pub Libr 301 E City Hall Ave Norfolk VA 23510 Office Phone: 757-664-7382. Office Fax: 757-664-7320. Business E-Mail: yvonne.bradley@norfolk.gov.

HILLIS, CATHERINE H., artist; b. Miami, Oct. 20, 1953; d. John A. and Maxine Delores McQuaig; m. John David Hills, Nov. 23, 1975; children: Faith C., David E., Elizabeth N. BFA, U. Ga., 1975; student, U. Tex., 1979—80. Mgr. costumes Atlanta Costume Co., 1976—77; actress, costumer Am. Theater Co., Tulsa, 1977—78; instr. art The Palette Gallery, Cary, NC, 1979—80; pvt. practice artist and instr. Fairfax, Va., 1998—2004; studio artist, instr. Round Hills Arts Ctr., 2004—. Artist profl. mags., Party Animal, Washington, 2002, Panda Mania, 2003, Beach Birds, Ocean City, Md., 2003, Am. Artists Mag., 2006. Chaplaincy vol. Loudoun Hosp., 2005—; Stephen min. Burke (Va.) United Meth. Ch., 2000—04. Recipient North Light Books award, Balt. Watercolor Soc., 2004, Equal Merit award, The Art League, 2002, Honorable Mention award, 2000—02. Mem.: Balt. Watercolor Soc., So. Watercolor Soc., Va. Watercolor Soc., Potomac Valley Watercolor Soc. Avocations: gardening, reading, walking, writing. Office Phone: 703-431-6877. Personal E-mail: chhillis@aol.com.

HILLMAN, BARBARA HALL, retired elementary school educator; b. Summit, N.J., Dec. 5, 1947; d. Ralph Charles and Dorothy Jane (Young) Hall; m. Robert John Hillman, Dec. 21, 1969; children: Eric, Greg. BA in Elem. Edn., Kean Coll., 1974. Cert. elem. and early childhood tchr., N.J. Tchr. St. Rose of Lima Sch., Freehold, N.J., 1968-73, Wall Twp. Bd. Edn., Wall, NJ, 1974—2004, whole lang. tchr. trainer, 1989—. Whole lang. tchr. trainer Manalapan (N.J.)-Englishtown Bd. Edn., 1992, 93. Mem. Sea Girt (N.J.) Recreation Commn., 1991-96—; cub scout pack master Boy Scoutm., Sea Girt, 1984-91; treas. West Belmar PTA, Wall, 1982-92—; active Sea Girt Sh. PTO, 1982-94. Wall Found. for Ednl. Excellence grantee, 1993, 95; named Life Mem., PTA, 1991. Mem. NEA, Internat. Reading Assn., Monmouth County Reading Assn., N.J. Edn. Assn., Monmouth County Edn. Assn., Wall Twp. Edn. Assn. Avocations: children's literature, reading, travel. Home: 411 Chicago Blvd Sea Girt NJ 08750-2010

HILLMAN, CAROL BARBARA, communications executive, consultant; b. Sept. 6, 1940; d. Joseph Hoppenfeld and Elsa (Spiegel) Hoppenfeld Resika; m. Howard D. Hillman, May 25, 1969 BA with honors, U. Wis., 1961; postgrad., U. Lyon, France, 1961-62; MA, Cornell U., 1966. Asst. editor Holt Rinehart & Winston Pubs., 1965-66; staff assoc. pub. rels. Ea. Airlines, N.Y.C., 1966-74; pub. affairs mgr. Squibb Corp., N.Y.C., 1974-75; asst. dir. corp. pub. rels. Burlington Industries, N.Y.C., 1975-77, dir. corp. pub. rels., 1977-80, v.p. pub. rels., 1980-82; v.p. corp. comms. Norton Co., Worcester, Mass., 1982-89, sr. cons., 1989-90; nat. dir. pub. rels. and comms. Deloitte & Touche, Wilton, Conn., 1990-91; v.p. univ. rels. Boston U., 1991-95; prin. Hillman & Kersey Strategic Comms., 1995-2000, CB Hillman & Assocs., 2000—05; exec. com. Honoring Eleanor Roosevelt, Preserving her Val-Kill Home, Save Am.'s Treasures Nat. Trust Hist. Preservation, 2000—, chair, 2006—. Mem. pub. affairs coun. Machinery and Allied Products Inst., 1982-89; mem. dep. policy com., agenda com. Mass. Bus. Roundtable, 1982-89, vice-chair; trustee Mass. Econ. Stblzn. Trust, 1986-2003; bd. dirs. Commonwealth Corp., 1995—, vice chair, 2003—. Mem. Cornell Coun., Ithaca, 1981—85, pub. rels. com., 1981—88; mem. adv. coun. Coll. Human Ecology, Cornell U., Ithaca, 1982—84; mem. bd. visitors coll. letter sci. U. Wis., 1996—99; mem. adv. bd. Ct. Apptd. Spl. Advocates, Worcester, 1983—87; bd. dirs. Planned Parenthood League Mass., 1986—90, pub. affairs com., 1991—2002; trustee Quinsigamond C.C., Worcester, 1987—98; voting mem. Wis. Union Trustees, U. Wis., Madison, 1982—2005, trustee, 1990—; mem. Clark U. Assocs., Worcester, 1983—89. Fulbright scholar, U. Lyon, 1961—62, Cornell grad. fellow, 1962—63. Mem. Internat. Women's Forum, Mass. Women's Forum, The Wisemen, Phi Beta Kappa, Mortar Bd., Phi Kappa Phi. Home: 299 Belknap Rd Framingham MA 01701-4716 Office: Honoring Eleanor Roosevelt 299 Belknap Rd Framingham MA 01701-4716 Office Phone: 508-877-2916. Personal E-mail: chillman96@verizon.net.

HILLMAN, CHRISTINA JOY, mathematics educator; b. Peoria, Ill., May 10, 1979; d. James Bernard and Ronda Gay Hoffpauir; children: Magnolia Lynn, Veronica Lee. BS in Edn., La. State U., Baton Rouge, 2002. Lic. elem. edn. La. Dept. Edn., 2002. Math. and reading tchr. Glasgow Mid. Sch., Baton Rouge, 2002—04; math. tchr. Broadmoor Mid. Sch., Baton Rouge, 2004—. Leap summer remediation tutor and tchr. East Baton Rouge Parish Sch. Sys., 2002—. Grantee, Glasgow Mid. Parent and Tchr. Assn., 2003—04, Jordan Fundamentals Ednl., 2005—06, Title I, Broadmoor Mid. Sch., 2005—06. Mem.: La. Fedn.Tchrs., La. Assn. Tchrs. Math., La. Mid. Sch. Assn., Nat. Coun. Tchr. Math. D-Liberal. Roman Catholic. Avocations: painting, aerobics, scrapbooks. Home: 10791 Red Oak Dr Baton Rouge LA 70815 Office: Broadmoor Mid Sch 1225 Sharp Rd Baton Rouge LA 70815 Office Phone: 225-272-0540. Home Fax: 225-272-0195; Office Fax: 225-272-0195.

HILLMAN, JENNIFER ANNE, federal official; b. Toledo, Jan. 29, 1957; d. Charles Winchell and Anne Sylvia (Mossberg) H.; m. Mitchell Rand Berger, Oct. 20, 1990; children: Benjamin Stanley Berger, Daniel Charles Berger. BA, Duke U., 1978, MEd, 1979; JD, Harvard U., 1983. Bar: DC, US Ct. Internat., US Mil. Appeals. Asst. to chancellor Duke U., Durham, NC, 1979-80; freshman Proctor Harvard U., Cambridge, Mass., 1981-83; assoc. Patton, Boggs & Blow, Washington, 1983—; legis. asst. Senator Terry Sanford, Washington, 1987-88, legis. dir., 1988-92; dep. cluster coord. for fin. instns. US Presdl. and Vice Presdl. Transition Team, Washington, 1992-93; ambassador, chief textile negotiator Office of US Trade Rep., Exec. Office of Pres., Washington, 1993-95; gen. counsel Office of the US Trade Rep., 1995-97; commr. US Internat. Trade Commn., Washington, 1998—, vice-chmn., 2002—04. Trustee Duke U., 1977-80; adj. prof. Sch. Law Georgetown U., 2005—. Adviser Terry Sanford for Senate Campaign, 1986, 1992; Trinity Coll. bd. visitors Duke U., 1999—; commr. Stoddert Youth Soccer, 2000—; mem. Selection Panel on Truman Scholars, 2000—; pres. Trade Policy Forum, 2001—04; mem. N.C. Dems., Raleigh, 1986—, Georgetown Presbyn. Ch., 1988—; tchr. adult learning Sacred Heart, Washington, 1983—92. Mem. Coun. on Women's Studies Duke U., Phi Beta Kappa. Avocations: running, scuba diving, travel, reading. Office: Internat Trade Commn 500 E St NW Washington DC 20436-0003

HILLMAN, SANDRA SCHWARTZ, public relations executive, marketing professional; b. Chester, Pa., 1941; m. Robert S. Hillman, Apr. 1964; children: Pamela Hillman Loeb, Allison Buchalter. BA, Pa. State U., 1962. Assoc. editor McFadden-Bartell Pub., N.Y.C., 1963-64; pub. rels. account exec. Edward M. Meyers & Assocs., N.Y.C., 1964-66; info. officer Nat. Tchr. Corps, U.S. Office Edn., Washington, 1966-68, Balt. Dept. Housing and Cmty. Devel., 1968-71; prin., CEO Trahan, Burden & Charles, Inc., 1984—. Mktg., pub. rels. cons. to cities of Pitts., San Diego, Buffalo, Niagara Falls, N.Y., N.Y.C., Miami, Milw., Curacao, Netherlands Antilles, Charleston, Chattahooga, Edinburg; mem. bd. Gov.'s Tourism Task Force; presenter, lectr. in field. Bd. dirs. Balt. Symphony Orch., World Trade Ctr. Inst., Balt. City Found., Boy Scouts Am., Md. Film Commn., The Nat. Aquarium, Jr. League Cmty. Coun., Urban League; pres. Balt. Ctr. for Performing Arts, 1976-92. Recipient Lifetime Achievement award Balt. Pub. Rels. Soc., 1996. Fellow Pa. State U. (Disting. 1991); mem. Gov.'s World Trade Ctr. Inst. (mem. bd., coms.), Md. C. of C. (strategic planning com.), Children's Theater Assn.

HILLMER, MARGARET PATRICIA, library director; b. Cirencester, Gloucestershire, Eng., Mar. 17, 1936; came to U.S., 1960; naturalized, 1973; d. John Albert and Margaret Evelyn (Richardson) Hall; m. Max Lorraine Hillmer, Mar. 24, 1962; children: Felicity Margaret, Jennifer Anne. ALAM, London Acad. Music Dram. Art, London, 1955; AB magna cum laude, Heidelberg Coll., 1976; AM in Libr. Sci., U. Mich., 1977. Cert. libr. Ohio. Speech and ballet tchr., Cirencester, 1955-58; governess NSW, Australia, 1959—60; ballet instr., choreographer Heidelberg Coll., Tiffin, Ohio, 1969-73, adminstrv. asst. pub. rels. Water Quality Lab., 1978-79; head reference dept. Tiffin-Seneca Pub. Libr., 1979-80, libr. dir., 1980—. Contbr. articles to profl. publs. Chair Take Our Daughters to Work Day, 1993-2000; bd. dirs. Tiffin-Seneca Teen Ctr., 1992—; mem. Tiffin City Schs. Bd. Edn., 1991-2003, pres., 1995-96; mem. Seneca County Dept. Human Svcs. Bd., 1984-91, pres., 1987-89. Recipient Liberty Bell award Seneca County Bar Assn., 1990, People's Law Sch. award Ohio Acad. Trial Lawyers, 1993, Athena award Tiffin Area C. of C., 1999; named Ohio Libr. of Yr., 2004. Mem. ALA, AAUW, LWV (pres. Tiffin chpt. 1980-82, chair internat. rels. Ohio 1975-76), Ohio Libr. Assn. (legislation com. 1985-89, chair legis. network 1989-93, chair awards and honors com. 1995-96, seminar spkr. 1985—), Pub. Libr. Assn., Freedom to Read Assn., Tiffin Rotary Club (pres. 2001-02), Beta Phi Mu. Democrat. Episcopalian. Avocations: reading, theater, classical music. Home: 25 Southview Pl Tiffin OH 44883-3312 Office: Tiffin-Seneca Pub Libr 77 Jefferson St Tiffin OH 44883-2339 Office Phone: 419-447-3751. Business E-Mail: hillmepa@oplin.org.

HILL-ROSATO, JANE ELIZABETH, elementary school educator; b. Newton, NJ, Nov. 21, 1958; d. Howard Russell and Gloria Frances (Clark) Hill; m. Nicholas David Rosato, Oct. 14, 1989; 1 stepchild, Domenick Patrick; 1 child, Salvator John. BS, East Stroudsburg U., 1981. Cert. tchr. elem. and early childhood, N.J., Pa. Presch. tchr. Sunrise Learning Ctr., Branchville, N.J., 1981-82; tchr. Knowlton Twp. Elem. Sch., Delaware, N.J., 1982—. Recipient Tchr. Recognition award I N.J. Gov.'s Office, Dept. Edn., Princeton,1989; invitee: Commrs. Symposium for Outstanding N.J. Tchrs., Dept. Edn., Trenton State Coll., 1989, N.J. Rural Schs. Conf. Highlighting Exemplary Programs, Practices and Resources for Rural Educators, N.J. Rural Assistance Coun., 1990; Nat. Gardening Assn. Youth Garden grantee, 1998. Mem. NEA, N.J. Edn. Assn., Monarch Tchr. Network, Knowlton Twp. Edn. Assn. Republican. Methodist. Avocations: skiing, piano, walking, reading. Home: 510 S 5th St Bangor PA 18013 Office: Knowlton Twp Elem Sch Rt 46 PO Box 227 Delaware NJ 07833 E-mail: hill@epix.net.

HILLS, CARLA ANDERSON, lawyer, former secretary of housing and urban development; b. LA, Jan. 3, 1934; d. Carl H. and Edith (Hume) Anderson; m. Roderick Maltman Hills, Sept. 27, 1958; children: Laura Hume, Roderick Maltman, Megan Elizabeth, Alison Macbeth. AB cum laude, Stanford U., 1955; student, Oxford U., Eng., 1954; LLB (hon.), Yale U., 1958; degree (hon.), Pepperdine U., 1975, Washington U., 1977, Mills Coll., 1977, Lake Forest Coll., 1978, Williams Coll., 1981, Notre Dame U., 1993, Wabash Coll., 1997. Bar: Calif. 1959, DC 1974, US Supreme Ct. 1965. Asst. US atty. civil divsn. US Dept. Justice, LA, 1958-61; ptnr. Munger, Tolles, Hills & Rickershauser, LA, 1962-74; asst. atty. gen. civil divsn. US Dept. Justice, Washington, 1974-75; sec. US Dept. Housing & Urban Devel., Washington, 1975-77; ptnr. Latham, Watkins & Hills, Washington, 1978-86, Weil, Gotshal & Manges, Washington, 1986-88; US Trade Rep. Exec. Office of the Pres., Washington, 1989-93; chmn., CEO Hills & Co. Internat. Cons., 1993—. Chair Nat. Com. for US-China Rels.; bd. dir. Inst. for Internat. Econ.; bd. dirs. CSIS, Am. Internat. Group, Time Warner, 1993—2001, Time Warner Inc. (formerly AOL/Time Warner), 2001—, Lucent Tech., Inc., Chevron Corp., TCW Group, Inc.; mem. adv. bd. Calif. Coun. on Criminal Justice, 1969—71; adj. prof. Sch. Law UCLA, 1972; mem. corrections task force LA County Sub-Regional; mem. standing com. discipline US Dist. Ct. for Ctrl. Calif., 1970—73; mem. Adminstrv. Conf. US, 1972—74; bd. councillors U. So. Calif. Law Ctr., 1972—74; mem. at large exec. com. Yale Law Sch., 1973—78; mem. exec. com. law and free soc. State Bar Calif., 1973; trustee Pomona Coll., 1974—79; mem. com. on Law Sch. Yale U. Coun.; mem. Sloan Commn. on Govt. and Higher Edn., 1977—79, Internat. Found. for Cultural Cooperation and Devel., 1977—89, Am. Com. on East-West Accord, 1977—79, Trilateral Commn., 1977—82; mem. adv. com. Princeton U., Woodrow Wilson Sch. of Pub. and Internat. Affairs, 1977—80; mem. Fed. Acctg. Std. Adv. Coun., 1978—80; Gordon Grand fellow Yale U., 1978; trustee Brookings Instn., 1985, Am. Productivity and Quality Ctr., 1988; coun. mem. Calif. Gov. Coun. Econ. Policy Adv., 1993—98, Coun. Fgn. Rels., 1993—; mem. Trilateral Commn., 1993—; vice-chair bd. dir. Inter-Am. Dialogue, 1999—; vice chair Coun. Fgn. Rels., 2001—. Co-author: Federal Civil Practice, 1961; co-author, editor: Antitrust Adviser, 1971, 3d edit., 1985; contbg. editor: Legal Times, 1978-88; mem. editorial bd. Nat. Law Jour., 1978-88. Trustee U. So. Calif., 1977-79, Norton Simon Mus. Art, Pasadena, Calif., 1976-80; trustee Urban Inst., 1978-89, chmn., 1983-89; co-chmn. Alliance to Save Energy, 1977-89; vice chmn. adv. coun. on legal policy Am. Enterprise Inst., 1977-84; bd. visitors, exec. com. Stanford U. Law Sch., 1978-81; bd. dir. Am. Coun. for Capital Formation, 1978-82; mem. exec. com. Inst. for Internat. Econ., 1993—; mem. adv. com. MIT-Harvard U. Joint Ctr. for Urban Studies, 1978-82. Fellow Am. Bar Found.; mem. Am.'s Soc. (bd. dir.), LA Women Lawyers Assn. (pres. 1964), ABA (chair publ. com. antitrust sect. 1972-74, council 1974, 77-84, chair 1982-83), Fed. Bar Assn. (pres. LA chpt. 1963), LA County Bar Assn. (fed. rules and practice com. 1963-72, chair issues and survey 1963-72, chair sub-com. revision local rules for fed. cts. 1966-72, jud. qualifications com. 1971-72), Am. Law Inst., Am.-China Soc. (bd. dir. 1995-), Am. Soc. (bd. trustees 1996-2002), Asia Soc. (bd. trustees 1996-2002; Clubs: Yale of So. Calif. (dir. 1972-74); Yale (Washington). Office: Hills & Co 901 15th St NW Ste 400 Washington DC 20005 Office Phone: 202-822-4700.

HILLS, PATRICIA GORTON SCHULZE, curator, art historian; b. Baraboo, Wis., Jan. 31, 1936; d. Hartwin A. Schulze and Glennie Gorton Baker; m. Frederic W. Hills, Jan. 17, 1958 (div. Feb. 1974); children: Christina, Bradford; m. Guy Kevin Whitfield, Jan. 3, 1976; 1 child, Andrew. BA, Stanford U., 1957; MA, Hunter Coll., 1968; PhD, NYU, 1973. Curatorial asst. Mus. Modern Art, N.Y.C., 1960-62; guest curator Whitney Mus. Am. Art, 1971-72, assoc. curator 18th and 19th Century art, 1972-74; vis. asst. prof. art dept. Hunter Coll., 1973; adj. assoc. prof. fine arts Inst. Fine Arts NYU, 1973-74; assoc. prof. fine arts and performing arts York Coll. CUNY, 1974-78; assoc. prof. dept. art history Boston U., 1978-88, prof., 1988—, chmn. dept., 1995-97. Adj. assoc. prof. Grad. Sch. Arts and Scis., Columbia U., 1974—75; adj. curator Whitney Mus. Am. Art, 1974—87. Author: Eastman Johnson, 1972, The American Frontier: Images and Myths, 1973, The Painters' America: Rural and Urban Life, 1810-1910, 1974, Turn-of-Century America: Paintings, Graphics, Photographs, 1890-1910, 1977, Alice Neel, 1983, Social Concern and Urban Realism: American Painting of the 1930s, 1983, John Singer Sargent, 1986, Stuart Davis, 1996, Modern Art in the USA: Issues and Controversies of the 20th Century, 2001, May Stevens, 2005; co-author: The Figurative Tradition and the Whitney Mus. Am. Art, 1980, Jacob Lawrence: Thirty Years of Prints: 1963-1993, Eastman Johnson: Painting America, 1999, Syndicated Rhythms: 20th-Century African American Art from the George and Joyce Wein Collection. Danforth Found. grad. fellow for women, 1968-72, John Simon Guggenheim Meml. Found. fellow, 1982-83, Charles Warren Ctr. for Studies in Am. History fellow, 1982-83, W.E.B. DuBois Inst. for Afro-Am. Rsch. fellow, Harvard U., 1991-92, 2006—, NEH fellow, 1995, Gilder Lehrman Inst. of Am. History fellow, 2005, Smithsonian Am. Art Mus. fellow, 2005-06, Georgia O'Keeffe Mus. Rsch. Ctr. fellow, 2006. Mem. Coll. Art Assn., Women's Caucus for Arts, Am. Studies Assn., Am. Assn. Mus. Home: 238 Putnam Ave Cambridge MA 02139-3767 Office: Boston U Dept Art History Boston MA 02215 Office Phone: 617-353-2520. Business E-Mail: pathills@bu.edu.

HILLS, REGINA J., journalist; b. Sault Sainte Marie, Mich., Dec. 24, 1953; d. Marvin Dan and Ardithanne (Tilly) H.; m. Vincent C. Stricherz, Feb. 25, 1984. BA, U. Nebr., 1976. Reporter UPI, Lincoln, Nebr., 1976-80, state editor, bur. mgr., 1981-82, New Orleans, 1982-84, Indpls., 1985-87; asst. city editor Seattle Post-Intelligencer, 1987-99, online prodr., 1999—2001, mng. prodr., 2001—06; web editor U. Wash., Seattle, 2006—. Panelist TV interview show Face Nebr., 1978-81; vis. lectr. U. Nebr., Lincoln, 1978, 79, 80; columnist weekly feature Capitol News, Nebr. Press Assn., 1981-82. Mem.: U. Nebr. Alumni Assn., Zeta Tau Alpha. Office: Univ Wash Box 351210 Seattle WA 98195-1210 Office Phone: 206-543-2560.

HILLSMAN, JOAN RUCKER, music educator; b. Anderson, SC, Mar. 25, 1943; d. William Isaiah and Elizabeth Gilliard Rucker; m. Horace Jerome Hillsman (dec. Mar. 2002); 1 child, Quentin Jerome. B in Music Edn., Howard U., 1964, M in Music Edn., 1969; PhD in Musicology, Union Inst., 1978. Music tchr. St. Mary's County Pub. Schs., Leonardtown, Md., 1964—67, D.C. Pub. Schs., Washington, 1967—88, supr. music, 1988—96; ret.; prof. music Bowie (Md.) State U., 1996—. Owner, music cons., talent promoter Joan Hillsmans Music Network, Suitland, Md., 1996—; adj. music prof. Union Inst., Cin., Shenandoah Conservatory and Union Inst. Cmty. and Civic awards; organizer nation's Capitol 1st Gospel Homeless Choir. Author: Gospel: An African American Art Form, 1990, 1992, poetry. Vol. music for the elder various nursing homes, 2000—; vol. Prince George County Dems., 2002. Recipient Key to City of Detroit; Joan Hillsman's Day in the Nation's Capital named in her honor. Mem.: Gospel Music Workshop Am. (scholarship chair), Coll./Univ. Assn., Music Educators Nat. Conf. (D.C. pres. 1996—2000, Outstanding Educator award 1996), Nat. Coun. Univ. Women, Black Urban League, Top Ladies Orgn., Sigma Alpha Iota, Phi Delta Kappa, Alpha Kappa Alpha. Baptist. Avocations: music, poetry, bowling, research. Home: 3706 Stonecliff Rd Suitland MD 20746 Office: Bowie State Univ Fine and Performing Arts 14000 Jericho Park Rd Bowie MD Office Phone: 301-736-2838. Personal E-mail: joanhillsman@comcast.net.

HILLSMAN, SALLY T., sociologist; b. Teaneck, NJ, Aug. 28, 1941; d. Robert Bryan and Mary Andrew Hillsman. AB, Mt. Holyoke Coll., 1963; PhD, Columbia U., 1970. Asst. prof. sociology Queens Coll., CUNY, N.Y., 1971—76; project dir. Vera Inst. of Justice, N.Y., 1976—79, asst. dir., 1978—79, dir. rsch., 1979—91, assoc. dir., 1989—91; v.p. rsch. Nat. Ctr. for State Courts, Williamsburgh, Va., 1991—96; dep. dir. Nat. Inst. Justice USDOJ, Washington, 1996—2002; exec. officer Am. Sociol. Assn., Washington, 2002—. Trustee Vera Inst. of Justice, NYC, 2003—; mem. sec. adv. bd. Dept. U.S. Commerce, 2002—; exec. com. Consortium Social Scis. Assns., 2002—. Contbr. articles pub. to profl. jour. V.p. Soc. for the Study of Social Problems, 1982—83; com. of profl. ethics Am. Sociol. Assn., 2001—03. Fellow: Nat. Acad. of Pub. Adminstrn.; mem.: Am. Soc. of Criminologists, Am. Acad. for the Advancement of Sci., Phi Beta Kappa. Office: Am Sociol Assn 1307 NY Ave Ste 700 Washington DC 20005 Office Phone: 202-383-9005. Business E-Mail: hillsman@asanet.org.

HILLSMITH, FANNIE L., artist; b. Boston, Mar. 13, 1911; d. Clarence and Clara (Huston) H. Student, Sch. Boston Mus. Fine Arts, 1930-34, Art Students League, 1935-36, Alalier 17, 1946-50. Instr. Black Mountain Coll., N.C., 1945; vis. critic Cornell U., Ithaca, N.Y., 1963-64. One-woman exhbns. include Norlyst Gallery, N.Y., 1943, Egan Gallery, N.Y., 1949, 50, 54, Frameshop Gallery, Boston, 1949, Swetzoff Gallery, Boston, 1949-50, 52, 54, 57, 63, Santa Barbara (Calif.) Mus. Art, 1950, Milton (Mass.) Acad., 1952, Currier Gallery Art, Manchester, N.H., 1953, DeCordova and Dana Mus. and Park, Lincoln, Mass., 1953, 58, The Dayton (Ohio) Art Inst., 1954, Inst. Contemporary Art, Boston, 1954, Am. Acad. Arts and Letter, N.Y.C., 1957, Peridot Gallery, N.Y.C., 1957-58, 62, 65, Cornell U., 1963, Bristol (R.I.) Art Mus., 1972, So. Vt. Art Ctr., Manchester, 1978, Currier Gallery Art, N.H., 1987, Susan Teller Gallery, N.Y.C., 1994; group exhbns. include Art of this Century, N.Y.C., 1943-44, 45, Mus. Modern Art, N.Y.C., 1946-51, Riverside Mus., N.Y., 1946-58, Art Inst. Chgo., 1947-48, 54-55, Va. Mus. Fine Arts, Richmond, 1948, Whitney Mus. Am. Art, N.Y.C., 1949-51, 55, New Gallery, N.Y.C., 1951, Currier Gallery Art, 1952-58, 60, 78, 80, Walker Art Ctr., Mpls., 1953-54, Inst. Contemporary Art, Boston, 1954, Solomon R. Guggenheim Mus., N.Y.C., 1954, Springfield (Mass.) Mus. Fine Arts, 1954, Bklyn. Mus., 1955, Corcoran Gallery Art, Washington, 1955, 57, The Phillips Gallery, Washington, 1955, Phila. Print Club, 1955, Mus. Fine Arts, Boston, 1977, Washburn Gallery, N.Y.C., 1981, Graham Gallery, N.Y.C., 1987, Susan Teller Gallery, N.Y., 1993; permanent collections include Addison Gallery Am. Art, Andover, Mass., Currier Gallery Art, Fitchburg (Mass.) Art Mus., Fogg Art Mus., Cambridge, Mass., Met. Mus. Art, N.Y.C., Mus. Fine Arts, Boston, Mus. Modern Art, N.Y.C., N.J. State Mus., Trenton, N.Y. Pub. Libr., Newark Mus., Phila. Mus. Art. Alumni Travelling scholar Mus. Fine Arts, Boston, 1958; recipient The Currier Art Gallery award, 1952, 54, Pioneer Valley Art Exhbn. award Pioneer Valley Art Gallery, 1953, Boston and Maine Railroad First award The Berkshire Mus., 1956, Boston Arts Festival First award, 1957, 63, Second award, 1957. Portland Summer Festival award Portland (Oreg.) Art Mus., 1957.

HILL-STANFORD, HOLLY, language educator; m. Thomas Stanford. BA, Drury Coll., Springfield, Mo., 1978; MA, Iowa State U., Ames, 1980; PhD, U. Kans., Lawrence, 1989. Cert. lifetime secondary tchr. biology and English State of Mo. Lectr. English U. Kans., Lawrence, tchg. asst. English; adj. instr. English Johnson County C.C., Overland Park, Kansas; tchg. asst. English Iowa State U., Ames; assoc. prof. English SW Bapt. U., Bolivar, Mo., 1992—, bd. dirs. coll. liason. Rev. state competencies for 9-12 lang. arts State of Mo., Dept. Elem. and Secondary Edn., Jefferson City, Mo., 2004; textbook reviewer Pearson Merrill/Prentice Hall, 2006—. Contbr. articles story anthology. Ch. clk., pianist, sunday sch. tchr., vacation bible sch. tchr., by-laws com. First Bapt. Ch., Bolivar, 1992—; publicity chmn. Bolivar Cmty. Concert Assn., 1996—98; mem. Bolivar Band Parents Assn. Recipient Outstanding English Student award, Mo. Assn. Tchrs. of English; scholar Premium for Academic Excellence award, Iowa State U. Mem.: Nat. Coun.Tchrs. of English, Mo. Philol Assn., Midwest Writing Ctr. Dirs. Assn. Office: Southwest Baptist Univ 1600 University Ave Bolivar MO 65613 Office Phone: 417-328-1682.

HILL-WAGNER, AIMEE ELIZABETH, social studies educator; b. Dallas, Tex., Sept. 10, 1974; d. Wayne Roger and Ann Lehnhard Hill; married, Aug. 17, 2002. BA, Western Mich. U., Kalamazoo, 1999. Cert. prof. educator Va., 1999. Tchr. history Pk. View H.S., Sterling, Va., 1999—2003; tchr. advanced placement psychology Dominion H.S., Sterling, Va., 2003—. Sponsor Future Educators Am., Sterling, Va., 2003—05. Mem.: Am. Sociol. Assn. Office: Dominion HS 21326 Augusta Dr Sterling VA 20164 Office Phone: 703-444-8025. Office Fax: 703-444-8035.

HILSABECK, KRISTINE, social studies educator; m. Jon Hilsabeck, Nov. 7, 1981; children: Erich, Remy. MEd, No. Ariz. U., Flagstaff, 1988. Cert. tchr. grades 6-12 Ariz., 1976. Tchr. social studies Romeoville H.S., Ill., 1972—75, Shadow Mountain H.S., Phoenix, 1979—. Evangelical Lutheran Ch. Of America. Avocations: travel, weaving, knitting, entertaining.

HILTON, JEAN BULL, musician; b. Northampton County, Va., Sept. 29, 1926; d. Charles Russell and Margret Davis Bull; m. Ellis Baker Hilton Jr., July 3, 1948 (dec. Mar. 1988); children: Jeffery Allan, Ellis Baker, William Russell, Andrew Douglas. BA, Randolph-Macon Woman's Coll., 1947; MSc, Old Dominion U., 1974. Music tchr. Norfolk Pub. Schs., Norfolk, Va., 1947—48, Radford Pub. Sch., Radford, Va., 1948—49; minister of music First Luth. Ch., Portsmouth, 1951—91; tchr. Portsmouth Pub. Sch., Portsmouth, Va., 1961—68, music supr., 1969—91; minister of music First Luth. Ch., 1998—. Composer songs. Recipient 1st Place award, Va. Fedn. Music Clubs, 2000. Mem.: AAUW, Va. Gateway Ctr. for the Arts, Portsmouth Cmty. Concerts, Inc., Va. Fedn. Music Clubs, Nat. Fedn. Music Clubs, Va. Music Educators Conf., Music Educators Nat. Conf., Daughters of Am. Revolution, Jamestowne Soc., The Student Club, Delta Kappa Gamma (Gamma chpt.). Lutheran. Avocations: reading, genealogy, exercise.

HILTON, NICKY (NICHOLAI OLIVIA HILTON), apparel designer; b. Oct. 5, 1983; d. Rick and Kathy Hilton; m. Todd Andrew Meister, Aug. 15, 2004 (annulled Nov. 9, 2004). Designer Samantha Thavasa, Tokyo, 2001—. Actor: (films) Wishman, 1991. Contbr. Free Arts for Abused Children Found.

Achievements include appeared on cover of numerous mag. including Maxim, GQ, FHM, Vanity Fair, others; heiress and great-grand daughter of Conrad Hilton, founder of Hilton Hotel Chains; modeled for Anand Jon.

HILTON, PARIS, actress; b. NYC, Feb. 17, 1981; d. Rick and Kathy (Richards) Hilton. Student, U. Ariz. Designer Samantha Thavasa, Tokyo, 2001—. Founder Heiress Records, 2004—. Club Paris, Orlando, Fla., 2005—, Jacksonville, Fla., 2006—. Actor: (films) Wishman, 1991, Sweetie Pie, 2000, Zoolander, 2001, QIK2JDG, 2002, Nine Lives, 2002, Wonderland, 2003, The Cat in the Hat, 2003, L.A. Knights, 2003, Raising Helen, 2004, The Hillz, 2004, House of Wax, 2005; co-star: (TV series) The Simple Life, 2003; The Simple Life 2: Road Trip, 2004; The Simple Life 3: Interns, 2005; The Simple Life 4: 'Til Death Do Us Part, 2006; actor(guest appearances): Saturday Night Live, 2003, Las Vegas, 2003, The O.C., 2003, Veronica Mars, 2004, American Dreams, 2005; author: (novels) Confessions of an Heiress: A Tongue-in-Chic Peek Behind the Pose, 2004 (Publishers Weekly Bestseller list, 2004); singer: (albums) Paris, 2006, (songs) Stars Are Blind, 2006. Contbr. Toys for Tots. Achievements include appeared on cover of numerous mag. including Maxim, GQ, FHM, Vanity Fair, others; heiress and great-grand daughter of Conrad Hilton, founder of Hilton Hotel Chains; modeled for designers March Bouwer and Catherine Malandrino; worked on ad campaign for Italian label Iceberg.*

HILTS, RUTH, artist; b. Sparks, Nev., Dec. 4, 1923; d. William and Nellie Elisa (DeGoosh) Gonzales; m. Robert Norton Hilts, Sept. 28, 1942; children: Robert Norton Jr., Deirdre Lynne. BA, U. Nev., 1962. Grad. teaching asst. dept. English U. Nev., Reno, 1962-63, editor-interviewer dept. oral history, 1967-74; profl. artist Reno, 1975—. One-man shows include Gov.'s Mansion, Carson City, Nev., 1982, Sierra Nev. Mus. Art, 1987—88, Nev. Gallery, Reno, 1990, River Gallery, 1995, 1998, Red Mountain Gallery at Truckee Meadows C.C., 1995, Nev. Legis. Bldg., Carson City, 1997, Heritage Bank, Reno, 2001, Nev. State Libr. & Archives Gallery, Carson City, 2003, The Vision Place, Reno, 2005, exhibited in group shows at Watercolor West XIV, Riverside, Calif., 1982, Nev. Mus. Art Biennial, Reno and Las Vegas, 1990, 1996, Sierra Nev. Coll., Tahoe, 1992—93, Stremmel Gallery, Reno, 1992—94, River Gallery, 1993—94, Sierra Arts Found. Gallery, Reno, 1994, 1995, 1998, 1999, 2004, Nev. Hist. Soc.'s Centennial, Reno, 2004, Art Source Gallery, 2005, Represented in permanent collections Nev. Mus. Art, Tournament Players Club Summerlin, Las Vegas, Eureka (Nev.) Opera Ho.; contbr. articles art to publs. Mem. Nev. Mus. Art, Sierra Arts Found., Georgia O'Keeffe Mus.; charter mem. Nat. Mus. Women in Arts. Grantee for excellence, Sierra Arts Found., 1995. Mem.: Phi Kappa Phi. Avocation: reading. Home and Office: 1895 Wren St Reno NV 89509-2334

HILTZ, STARR ROXANNE, sociologist, educator, writer, consultant, computer scientist; b. Little Rock, Sept. 7, 1942; d. John Donald and Mildred V. Smyers; m. Murray Turoff, 1985; children: Jonathan David, Katherine Amanda. AB, Vassar Coll., 1963; MA, Columbia U., 1964, PhD, 1969. Prof. sociology Upsala Coll., 1969-85; info. sys. N.J. Inst. Tech., 1985-93, disting. prof. computer sci., 1993—. Cons. social impacts of computer systems. Author: Creating Community Services for Widows, 1976, (with M. Turoff) The Network Nation, 1978, 2d edit., 1993, (with E. Kerr) Computer-Mediated Communication, 1982, Online Communities, 1984, The Virtual Classroom, 1994, (with L. Harasim, L. Teles and M. Turoff) Learning Networks, 1995, (with Ricki Goldman) Learning Together Online, 2004. Recipient N.J. Woman of the Millennium for Ednl. Tech., 2000. Mem.: Assn. for Info. Sys., Assn. Computing Machinery. Unitarian Universalist. Home: 19 Meadowbrook Rd Randolph NJ 07869-3808 Office: NJ Inst Tech Info Systems Newark NJ 07102

HILTZ-SCERBO, LEIZA ANN, designer, photographer; b. Farmington, Maine, Nov. 20, 1955; d. Raymond George and Florence Catherine (MacLeod) Hiltz; m. Justin Robert Francis Scerbo, Apr. 1, 1980; 1 child, Christopher Justin. Student Haystack-Hinkley Sch. Art., 1971, Brigham Young U., 1974-75, U. Maine-Farmington, 1975-77, Maine Photographic Workshops, 1977; B.F.A. magna cum laude, L.I. U. Southampton Coll., 1980. Darkroom technician pub. relations alumni office U. Maine-Farmington, 1975-76; asst. photographer Lilienthal Studios, Wilton, Maine, 1975-77; darkroom technician Southampton Coll., N.Y., 1979-80; artist layout lettering Assocs. & Ferren, Easthampton, N.Y., 1979-81; apprentice designer East Hampton Leather, 1979-81, owner, designer Leiza's Leather to Lace, Farmington, 1981—, Marina Convenience Store, 1997-2002, Bob's Place, 1997-2002, The Chef, 2001-2002, ret. 2001; free-lance photographer, N.Y., Maine, 1976—; cons. design, Maine, 1981—; tchr. color perception Kis-Western Mt. Photolab, Wilton, Maine, 1984—; customer tng. mgr. KIS Corp. N.J. and Ga. HQ, 1985—87; substitute tchr., 1987-91; lectr. in field. Sec. Salvation Army, Maine, 1991-97; dir. Foodbank of the Mills, 1991-97, FEMA, Franklin County, Maine, 1993-99, Boy Scouts Am., 1991-97, dist. chmn., 1991-97; legal coord. True Mt. Alliance, 1991; vol. Republican Women's Com., Farmington, 1972—, Anti-Nuclear Power Orgn. of Maine, 1981—; donator Sweatt Winter Day Care, Farmington, 1984. Haystack-Hinkley Sch. Art scholar, 1970, Farmington Elks scholar, 1974, Maine Photographic Workshops scholar, 1979. Presbyterian. Avocations: cross country skiing; swimming; hiking; botany. Office: PO Box 291 Farmington ME 04938-9729 E-mail: leizahiltz@yahoo.com.

HIMMEL, LESLIE WOHLMAN, real estate manager; d. Robert Wohlman; m. Jeffrey Steven Himmel, July 14, 1984. Degree, U. Penn.; MBA, Harvard Bus. Sch., 1978. With Integrated Resources, Inc., 1979—84; mng. ptnr. Himmel and Meringoff Properties, N.Y.C., 1984—. Mem.: Young Presidents Org., Real Estate Bd. NY (bd. gov. 2000, exec. com. 2004). Office: Himmel and Meringoff Properties 30 W 26th St Fl 8 New York NY 10010

HIMMELFARB, GERTRUDE (MRS. IRVING KRISTOL), writer, educator; b. NYC, Aug. 8, 1922; d. Max and Bertha (Lerner) H.; m. Irving Kristol, Jan. 18, 1942; children— William, Elizabeth. BA, Bklyn. Coll., 1942; MA, U. Chgo., 1944, PhD, 1950; L.H.D. (hon.), R.I. Coll., 1976, Kenyon Coll., 1985, Adelphi U., 1989, Boston U., 1987, Yale U., 1990; Litt. D. (hon.), Smith Coll., 1977, Lafayette Coll., 1978, Jewish Theol. Sem., 1978, Williams Coll., 1989; LLD (hon.), Union Coll., 1989. Distinguished prof. history Grad. Sch., CUNY, 1965-88, prof. emeritus, 1988—. Author: Lord Acton: A Study in Conscience and Politics, 1952, Darwin and the Darwinian Revolution, 1959, Victorian Minds, 1968, On Liberty and Liberalism— The Case of John Stuart Mill, 1975, The Idea of Poverty, 1984, Marriage and Morals Among the Victorians, 1986, The New History and the Old, 1987, Poverty and Compassion: The Moral Imagination of the Late Victorians, 1991, Untimely Thoughts on Culture and Society, 1994, The De-Moralization of Society: From Victorian Virutes to Modern Values, 1995, One Nation, Two Cultures, 1999, The Road to Modernity: The British, French, and American Enlightenment, 2004, The Moral Imagination, 2006; editorial bd.: Am. Scholar, First Things. Trustee Nat. Humanities Ctr.; bd. Woodrow Wilson Internat. Ctr., Brit. Inst. of U.S., Inst. Contemporary Studies; mem. council scholars Library of Congress; mem. council acad. advisors Am. Enterprise Inst.; assoc. scholar Ethics and Pub. Policy Ctr. Recipient Rockefeller Found. award, 1962-63, 63-64, 80-81, Nat. Humanities Presdl. medal, 2004; Guggenheim fellow, 1955-56, 57-58; sr. fellow NEH, 1968-69; Am. Council Learned Socs. fellow, 1972-73; Phi Beta Kappa vis. scholar, 1972-73; Woodrow Wilson Ctr. fellow, 1976-77 Fellow British Acad., Am. Philos. Soc., Royal Hist. Soc., Am. Acad. Arts and Scis., Soc. Am. Historians; mem. Am. Hist. Assn., Conf. on Brit. Studies.

HINCKS, MARCIA LOCKWOOD, retired insurance company executive; b. NYC, July 3, 1935; d. John Salem and Dorothy Elinor (Tufts) Lockwood; m. John Winslow Hincks, June 14, 1958; children: Rebecca Towne, Jennifer Winslow, John Morris, Benjamin Lockwood. BA, Bryn Mawr Coll., 1956; LLB, Yale U., 1959. Bar: Conn. 1960. Atty. Aetna Life & Casualty, Hartford, Conn., 1961—64, 1967—70, counsel, 1970—81, v.p., ins. counsel, 1981—91, sr. counsel litigation, 1991—93. Chmn. United Way Capital Area, Hartford, 1984—85; trustee Hotchkiss Sch., Lakeville, Conn., 1973—78, Hartford Coll. Women, 1978—; bd. dirs. Hartford Hosp., 1983—, chmn., 1998—2002; bd. dirs. Conn. Water Co., Clinton, 1983—. Recipient Cmty. Svc. award United Way Capital Area, 1982, Alexis de Tocqueville award United Way of Am., 1987. Mem.: Assn. Life Ins. Counsel, Conn. Bar Assn., ABA, Hartford Golf. Democrat. Conglist.

HIND, ELISE CROMWELL, music educator; b. Aiken, S.C., Feb. 18, 1952; d. Chester W. and Virginia (Hall) Cromwell; m. John Charles Hind, Aug. 4, 1974; children: John Cromwell, Thomas Edwin. MusB Edn., U. S.C., Columbia, 1974, MusM Edn., 1978. Dir. band Olympia Mid. Sch., Columbia, 1974—77; tchr. music and band Anderson Sch. Dist. 5, SC, 1977—83; tchr. music Abbeville County Schs., 1992—. Named Tchr. of Yr., Abbeville County Sch. Dist., 2000, Den Leader of Yr. six and twenty dist., Boy Scouts Am., 1993. Mem.: Nat. Alliance for Mentally Ill, Anderson County Human Rels. Coun. (chmn. 1996), Palmetto Tchrs. Assn., Music Educators Nat. Conf., Honea Path Ladies League (sec.), Honea Path Recreation Bd. Baha'I. Home: 149 Tiny Greer Rd Honea Path SC 29654 Office: Cherokee Trail Elem Sch Donalds SC 29638

HINDLE, MARGUERITA CECELIA, textile chemist, consultant; b. Providence, Nov. 26, 1928; d. Joseph and Elsie Cecelia (Johnson) Lombardo; m. Robinson J. Hindle, June 17, 1950. BS in Chemistry, U. R.I., 1949, DSc, 1993. Textile chemist Kenyon (R.I.) Industries, 1950-88, lab. dir., 1960-88, R&D dir., 1968-88, v.p. R&D/tech., 1978-88; ind. textile cons., 1988—. Mem. textile adv. com. U. Mass., Dartmouth, 1979—; mem. textile adv. bd. U. R.I., Kingston, 1991—; environ. com. chair Am. Textile Mgrs. Inst., Washington. Mem. Am. Assn. Textile Chemists and Colorists (nat. pres. 1987-88). Home and Office: TCE Consulting Svcs 15 Belle Rose Dr Westerly RI 02891-3917

HINDLE, PAULA ALICE, nursing administrator; b. Cambridge, Mass., Feb. 26, 1952; d. Edward Adam and Geraldine Ann (Donahue) H. BSN, Fitchburg State Coll., 1974; MSN, Duke U., 1980; MBA, Simmons Coll., 1988. Staff nurse Mt. Auburn Hosp., Cambridge, Mass., 1974-75, U. Hosp., Boston, 1975-77, head nurse, 1977-79; staff nurse Duke U. Med. Ctr., Durham, N.C., 1979-80, clin. instr., 1980-81, area mgr., 1981; nurse leader, clin. dir. New Eng. Med. Ctr., Boston, 1981-87; cons. Ctr. for Nursing Case Mgmt., Boston, 1984-87; v.p. nursing Faulkner Hosp., Boston, 1987-94; v.p. nursing and support svcs. Alexandria (Va.) Hosp., 1994-97; v.p. for patient care, chief nurse exec. Loyola U. Med. Ctr., Maywood, Ill., 1997—. Mem. adv. com. Regis Coll. Nursing, 1993; mem. planning and resource com. Simmons Coll., 1993-94; mem. affiliate faculty George Mason U., 1994-95. Active Am. Heart Assn. Mem. Am. Orgn. Nurse Execs., Va. Orgn. Nurse Execs., Mass. Orgn. Nurse Execs. (treas. 1991-93), Humane Soc., Simmons Coll. Grad. Sch. Mgmt. Alumni Assn. (bd. dirs. 1991-93, pres. 1992-93), Sigma Theta Tau. Democrat. Roman Catholic. Avocations: ballroom dancing, reading, theater, music. Home: 1123 Mistwood Ln Downers Grove IL 60515-1284 Office: Loyola U Med Ctr 2160 S 1st Ave Maywood IL 60153-3304

HINDMAN, EMILY ELLEN, counselor, director; b. Torrington, Wyo., June 29, 1975; d. Robert D. and Linda R. Hindman. BA, Purdue U., West Lafayette, Ind., 1997; EdM, U. Okla., Norman, 1999. Lic. profl. counselor Tex. Psychology asst. So. Okla. Resource Ctr., Pauls Valley, 1997—99; assoc. clin. psychologist Tex. Youth Commn., Corsicana, 1999—2005; pvt. practice Emily Hindman, Lic. Counseling, 2001—; clin. dir. Mesa Family Svcs., 2005—. Expert witness Emily Hindman, Lic. Counseling, Corsicana, 2005—. Recipient Employee of Month, Tex. Youth Commn. Mem.: ACA. Avocations: reading, travel. Office: Emily Hindman Lic Counseling Ste 512C 100 N Main Corsicana TX 75110

HINDMAN, LESLIE SUSAN, auction company executive; b. Hinsdale, Ill., Dec. 1, 1954; d. Don J. and Patricia (de Forest) H. Student, Pine Manor Coll., 1972-74, U. Paris, 1974-75, Ind. U., 1975-76. Mgr. Sotheby Parke Bernet, Chgo., 1978—82; pres. Leslie Hindman Auctioneers, Chgo., 1982—97, Salvage One Archtl. Artifacts, Chgo., 1986—2002; former co-owner Chgo. Antiques Ctr.; pres. Sotheby's, Chgo., 1997—99; chmn. Leslie Hindman Enterprises, 1999—; founder, pres. Eppraisals.com, 1999—2001, Leslie Hindman Auctioneers, Chgo., 2003—, AntiquesChicago, 2003—. Bd. mem. MB Fin. Bank. Host HGTV's At the Auction and The Appraisal Fair, 1995—2003; author: Adventures at the Auction, 2001; columnist: What's It Worth?, 1999—2003. Bd. mem. Children's Meml. Hosp., The Goodman Theatre, Chgo. Pub. Libr. Found., The Arts Club Chgo. Mem. Com. of 200, Internat. Women's Forum, Young Pres's. Orgn., Arts Club Chgo. Clubs: Women's Athletic (Chgo.) (bd. dirs. 1988—). Office: 122 N Aberdeen Chicago IL 60607 Office Phone: 312-280-1212. Business E-Mail: leslie@lesliehindman.com.

HINDS, SALLIE ANN, retired township official; b. Saginaw, Mich., June 8, 1930; d. Alex W. and Elsie E. (Letourneau) Chriscaden; m. James F. Hinds; children: Amy Lynn Hinds-McLean, Jennifer L. Hinds-Wanner. Student, MacMurray Coll. for Women, Jacksonville, Ill., 1948-49. Rsch. sec. Lufkin Rule Co., Saginaw, Mich., 1949-51; traffic mgr. WKNX-TV, Saginaw, 1953-59; treas. Sims Twp., AuGres, Mich., 1980-92; clk. Sims Twp. Water Dept., AuGres, 1990-91; mem. East Tawas (Mich.) Planning Com., 1993—. Cons. Sims-Whitney Water Bd., AuGres, 1982-92; Mich. sr. poet laurate, 2004-05. Author: Bits and Pieces of Nature's Seasons, 1986, Simple Words.Quiet Thoughts, 1994, Halcyon Days, 1999, Daydreams and Memories, 2005, On The Edge of Woods and Water, 2002; participating author: Best Poems of the 90's (Editors Choice award 1996), Best Poems of 1996 (Editors Choice award 1996, 98), others. Instr. USCG Aux., AuGres, 1982-83; mem. Tawas St. Joseph Hosp., Aux. Vol., 1993—, East Tawas, 1980—; election insp. East Tawas Elections Bd., 1994—. Named Homemaker of Yr. award, Arenac County, Mich., Standish, Mich., 1980, Mrs. Mich. 60's, Beauties of Am., Orlando, Fla., 1990, Ms. Sr. Mich. rep. City of East Tawas, 1997; recipient Logo Winner, Vets. Meml. Honor Roll, VFW Post 8275, AuGres, Mich., 1987, Golden Poet award World of Poetry, Calif., 1987-92, Mrs. Scottish Am. Achievement 2001, Mrs. Universal Gem, 2002. Silver Cup and Poet of Merit Medallion award, Internat. Soc. of Poets, 2002-03, Editor's Choice award. Mem. Internat. Soc. Poets (life), Acad. Am. Poets, N.E. Mich. Arts Coun. (bd. dirs. 1984), Arenac County Hist. Soc. (pres. 1981-84), Ladies Lit. Club (treas. 1995-2002, Club Woman of Yr. 1997-98), Gen. Federated Women's Club (N.E. dist. treas. Mich. chpt. 2002-04, Woman of Achievement 2005). Avocations: writing, needlecrafts, artwork, nature and environmental study. E-mail: jim_sal@voyager.net.

HINE, BETTY DIXON, design consultant; b. San Francisco, May 9, 1920; d. Reginald Stanley and Sarah Elizabeth (Evey) Dixon; married; children: Charles Henri Hine III, Holly Elizabeth Hine Suich. BA, U. Pacific, 1941. Tchr. Calif. Pub. Schs., 1941-45; comm. svc. worker San Francisco Bay Area, 1950—; antiques and design cons., 1975—. Sec./treas. bd. dirs. Hine, Inc., San Francisco; mem. adv. bd. St. Mary's Coll. Art Mus.; bd. dirs. Achievement Rewards for Coll. Scientists. Bd. dirs. U. Calif. San Francisco Hosp., 1960—; trustee Calif. Coll. Arts and Crafts, Oakland, 1970—; life mem. Women's Bd. Oakland Mus., Calif., 1971—. Mem. Calif. Assn. of Mus. (founding mem.), The World Trade Club, The Villa Taverna/San Francisco. Office: Hine Inc 490 Bosphorous Ave Tampa FL 33606-3608

HINE, DARLENE CLARK, history educator, administrator; b. Morley, Mo., Feb. 7, 1947; d. Levester and Lottie Mae (Thompson) Clark; m. William C. Hine, Aug. 21, 1970 (div. 1975); m. Johnny Earl Brown, July 25, 1981 (div. Aug. 1986); 1 child, Robbie Davine. BA in Am. History, Roosevelt U., 1968; MA, Kent State U., 1970, PhD in Afro-Am. History, 1975, Hon. LHD, U. Mass, 1998, hon. LittD, Purdue U., 2002, SUNY hon. LHD, Buffalo State Coll., 2002. Teaching asst. Kent State U., Ohio, 1968-71; asst. prof. history, coordinator Black studies, SC State Coll., Orangeburg, 1972-74; asst. prof. Purdue U., West Lafayette, Ind., 1974-79, assoc. prof. history, 1979-85, interim dir. African Studies and Research Ctr., 1978-79, vice provost, 1981-86, prof. history, 1985-87; John A. Hannah Disting. prof. Am. History, Mich. State U., East Lansing, 1987-2004, adj. John A. Hannah Disting. prof. Am. History, 2004-; bd. trustee prof. of African Am. Studies, prof. history, Northwestern U., Evanston, Ill., 2004-; mem. Ind. Com. for Humanities, 1983-85; vis. disting. prof. history, Ariz. State U., 1985; vis. disting. prof. of women's studies, U. Delaware, 1989-90; Robert E. McNair vis. prof. So. Studies, U. SC, 1996; Harold Washington vis. prof., Roosevelt U, Chgo. Ill., 1996; Avalon Disting. vis. prof., Northwestern U., 1997; mem. adv. bd. ProQuest Women's History, 2001-02; inaugral dir. Ctr. for African Am. History, 2003-; mem. exec. com. Nat. Acad. for Critical Studies, 1996-; invited lectr. colls. and univs. including Harvard U., 1975, U. Ill., Chgo., 1981, Ind. U., 1982, U. Tex., Austin, 1983, So. Meth. U., 1983, Duke U., 1990, U. NC, Chapel Hill, 1992, Emory U., 1994; grant rev. panelist NEH, 1979-80, Ford Found., NRC, 1980, 81, 82. Fellow Ctr. for the Study of Behavioral Sciences, Stanford, CA, 2000-01; adv. bd. mem. Ctr. for New Deal Studies, Roosevelt U., 1997-, Jour. African American Men and Boys, The U. Kansas, Ctr. for Multicultural Leadership, 1999-, William J. Clinton Oral History Project, 2001 and several others; mem. adv. com. The Nat. Women's History Project, 1984-; mem. So. Historical Assn. Com. on Sexual Harassment, 2000-; bd. overseers, Wellesley Ctr. for Women, 2002-; mem. coun. scholars, Am. Slavery Meml. Mus., 2002-; mem. Bd. Scholars Consultants for the HistoryMakers, 2003-. Author: Black Victory: The Rise and Fall of the White Primary in Texas, 1979, new edit. 2003, When the Truth is Told: A History of Black Women's Culture and Community in Indiana, 1875-1950, 1981, Black Women in White: Racial Conflict and Cooperation in the Nursing Profession 1890-1950, 1989, Hine Sight: Black Women and the Re-Construction of American History, 1994, Speak Truth to Power: Black Professional Class in United States History, 1996; co-author A Shining Thread of Hope: The History of Balck Women in America, 1998, The African-American Odyssey, 2nd edit., 2002, African Americans: A Concise History, Combined Vol., 2003, The African-American Odyssey, 3rd edit., 2005, African-American History, 2006; edited books Black Women in the Nursing Profession: An Anthology of Historical Sources, 1985, The State of Afro-American History, Past, Present, and Future, 1986, Black Women in the United States 1619-1989, 1990, Black Women in America, 2nd edit., 2005; co-editor of several book; contbr. chpts. to books, articles to publs., book revs. to jours.; editl. adv. bd. Jour. Women's History, 1987-96, The Frederick Douglass Papers Project, 1988-, Martin Luther King Jr. Papers Project, 1987-, Black American and Diasporic Studies Series, 2001, African Am. Studies Ctr., 2005 and several others; mem. editl. bd. Dictionary of American Nurses, 1985, Jour. Negro History, 1979-87, Encyclopedia of the Harlem Renaissance, 2000, Encyclopedia of the Midwest, 2000 and several others; mem. editl. com. African American Research Library, 1996-; assoc. editor The Historian, 1995-; contbg. editor Souls: A Critical Journal of the Black Politics, Culture and Society, 1998-; NEH advisor, Remembering Jim Crow, American Radio Works, 1999-; mem adv. panel, Homer G. Philips Hosp. Project, 2000-; mem. adv. bd. Percy Julian Biography Project WGBH-NOVA, 2002-; guest appearance WGN-9 News, Black Women in America: An Historical Encyclopedia, Chgo., Ill., 2005, Power Point Radio, African American Historians and the History of Black Women in America, WCLK 91.9 FM, Atlanta, Ga., 2005. Alumni fellow Kent State U., 1971-72,Nat. Humanities Ctr. fellow, 1986, Am. Council Learned Socs. fellow, 1986; faculty devel. grantee Purdue U., 1978-79; research awardee Rockefeller Archive Ctr., 1978; Rockefeller Found. fellow for minority group scholars, 1980; research grantee Eleanor Roosevelt Inst., 1980-81; project grantee Fund for Improvement of Post-Secondary Edn., 1980-82; NEH grantee, 1982-83, Am. Coun. of Learned Societies Fellow, 1986-87, Nat. Humanities Ctr. Fellow, 1986-87, Emeline Bigelow Conland Fellow, Radcliffe Inst. for Advanced Study, Harvard U., 2003-04; recipient Women's Honors in Pub. Svc., Minority Fellowship programs and Cabinet on Human Rights, Am. Nurses Assn., 1988, Disting. Alumni award Roosevelt U., 1988, Lavina L. Dock Book award, Am. Assn. for the History of Nursing, 1990, Spl. Achievement award, Kent State U. Alumni Assn., 1991, Anna Julia Cooper award for Disting. Scholarship, Sage Women's Edl. Press, 1993, LeSteffin award, Steffin Found. Inc., 1994, Dartmouth award, ALA, 1994, Zora Neal Hurston-Paul Robeson award, Nat. Coun. for Black Studies, Inc., 1995, Avery Citizenship award, Avery Rsch.Ctr., Coll. Charleston, 1997, Disting. Black Women award, Black Women in Sisterhood for Action, Washington, DC, 1999, Carter G. Woodson medallion, ASALH, Washington, DC, 2001, Michiganian of Yr. award, Detroit News, Bingham Farms, Mich., 2002; Mem. Assn. for Study of Negro Life and History (exec. council 1979-84, 2nd v.p. 1985-88, program com. ann. mtg. 1982, 1997, 1999), Orgn. Am. Historians (mem. program com. 1981-87, co-chair 1998, nominating com. mem. 1983-85, pres. 2001-02), So. Hist. Assn. (mem. exec. coun., 1990-92, program com. mem. 1983, 1986, chair, 1989, nominating com. mem., 1995, pres-elect, v.p. 2001-02, pres. 2002-03), So. Assn. Women Historians (v.p. 1983-84, pres. 1984-85), Am. Hist. Assn.(mem. nominating com. 1987-88 chair 1988-89), Assn. Black Women Historians (v.p. 1981-82, Letitia Woods Brown Book award, 1990, Letitia Woods Brown Meml. Anthology prize, 1993,1995), Phi Alpha Theta. (hon.), Phi Beta Kappa (hon.), Delta Sigma Theta Sorority (hon.);Fellow Am. Acad. Arts & Sciences Democrat. Baptist. Home: 2357 Burcham Dr East Lansing MI 48823-7241 Address: African American Studies Dept 2-320 Kresge Hall 1880 S Campus Dr Evanston IL 60208-2209 Office Phone: 517-355-3418, 847-467-0269. Office Fax: 517-432-6268, 847-467-0271. Business E-Mail: hined@msu.edu, d-hine@northwestern.edu.*

HINEGARDNER, LAURA A., lawyer; BA, U. Ky., 1993; JD, U. Cin., 1996. Bar: Ky. 1996, Ohio 1997. Atty. Katz, Teller, Brant & Hild, Cin. Former mem. Class VIII, Cin. Acad. Leadership for Lawyers; bd. mem. Fort Thomas Edn. Found. Mem. Charities Guild of Northern Ky. Named one of Ohio's Rising Stars, Super Lawyers, 2006. Avocations: sports, pilates. Office: Katz Teller Brant & Hild 255 E 5th St Ste 2400 Cincinnati OH 45202-4724 Office Phone: 513-977-3484. Office Fax: 513-762-0084.*

HINERFELD, RUTH G., civic organization executive; b. Boston, Sept. 18, 1930; m. Norman Hinerfeld, children: Lee, Thomas, Joshua. AB, Vassar Coll., 1951; grad. Program in Bus. Adminstrn., Harvard-Radcliffe Coll., 1952. With LWV, 1954—, UN observer, 1969-72, chairperson internat. rels. com., 1972-76, 1st v.p. in charge legis. activities, 1976-78, pres., 1978-82. Dir. LWV Overseas Edn. Fund, 1975-76, trustee, 1975-86; chair LWV Edn. Fund, 1978-82; mem. White House Adv. Com. Trade Negotiations, 1975-82; sec. UN Assn. US, 1975-78, bd. govs., 1975—, vice-chmn., 1983—, mem. econ. policy coun., 1976-93; bd. dirs. Overseas Devel. Coun. 1974-00; trustee, vice chair Inst. of Internat. Edn., 1997—; mem. U.S. del. auspices of Nat. Com. on U.S.-China Rels. and Chinese People's Inst. Fgn. Affairs, 1978. Mem. coun. Nat. Mcpl. League, 1977-80, 83-86; del.-at-large Internat. Women's Yr. Conf., Houston, 1977; mem. exec. com. Leadership Conf. on Civil Rights, 1978-82; trustee Citizens Rsch. Found., 1978-2000; mem. Nat. Petroleum Coun., 1979-82; mem. U.S. del. to World Conf. on UN Decade for Women, 1980; mem. adv. com. Nat. Inst. for Citizen Edn. in the Law, 1981-91; mem. North South Roundtable, 1978-88; mem. nat. gov. bd. Common Cause, 1984-90; vice chmn. U.S. com. UNICEF, 1986-90, treas., 1990-91; mem. vis. com. Harvard U. Bus. Sch., 1984-90; bd. dirs. Com. for Modern Cts., 1993-96. Recipient Disting. Citizen award Nat. Mcpl. League, 1978; Outstanding Mother award Nat. Mother's Day Com., 1981; Aspen Inst. Presdl. fellow, 1981. Mem. Coun. on Fgn. Rels., Phi Beta Kappa. Office: 11 Oak Ln Larchmont NY 10538-3917

HINES, ALIDA N., marketing professional, researcher; d. Roosevelt Delano Hines and Verdell Lett Dawson. Student, Duke U., 1994—95; BA magna cum laude in Econs., Spelman Coll., 1998; MA with hons. in Mktg. Rsch., U. of Ga., 2000. Bus. rsch. intern Eastman Kodak Co., Atlanta, 2000, bus. rsch. analyst, 2001—03; market rsch. analyst The Home Depot, Atlanta, 2003—. Tutor Mt. Olivet Bapt. Ch., Rochester, NY, 2001—02; mentor Big Brothers Big Sisters, Atlanta, 2003—. Recipient, Nat. Merit Scholarship Corp., 1994; scholar, Armstrong World Industries, 1994, Motorola, 1997, UNCF scholarship, Quaker Oats Co., 1997, Coca-Cola Found., 1999—2000. Mem.: Nat. Assn. Female Execs. Office: The Home Depot 2455 Paces Ferry RD Atlanta GA 30329 E-mail: alida_hines@homedepot.com.

HINES, AMY CHRISTINE, business analyst; b. Omaha, Jan. 25, 1972; d. William Frank Hines and Jill Marie Goolsby. BA in History, U. Nebr., Omaha, 1998, MA in Secondary Edn., 2005. Cert. Tchr. - Social Scis., French, Spanish

Coll. St. Mary, 2004, Tchr.-ELL/ESL U. Nebr. Omaha, 2005. Programmer, analyst Sitel Corp., Omaha, 1994—98; tchr. English/ESL Funehiki English Sch., Funehiki, Tamura-gun, Japan, 1997—98; analyst bus. sys. CSG Sys., Inc, Omaha, 1998—2004; tchr. h.s. geography - ELL Millard South H.S., Omaha, 2004—06; bus. analyst II Blackbaud, Inc., 2006—. Vol. Heartland Refugee Resettlement, Omaha, 2005—06. Named Fast Track Tchr. of Yr., 2004. Mem.: TESOL (assoc.), Nat. Coun. Social Studies Tchrs. (assoc.). Personal E-mail: amigaogma@yahoo.com. E-mail: trvlfriend@yahoo.com.

HINES, CHERYL, actress; b. Miami Beach, Sept. 21, 1965; m. Paul Young, Dec. 30, 2002; 1 child, Catherine Rose. BA in radio and TV, U. Cent. Fla. Mem. The Groundlings Theater, star Cheryl Hines' One Woman Show; actor: (TV series) Curb Your Enthusiasm, 2000— (Emmy nomination best supporting actress, 2003), (voice) Father of the Pride, 2003,: (TV films) Double Bill, 2003; (films) Cheap Curry and Calculus, 1996, Along Came Polly, 2004, Our Very Own, 2005, Lucky 13, 2005, Herbie: Fully Loaded, 2005, RV, 2006, (guest appearances): (TV series) Unsolved Mysteries, 1997, Suddenly Susan, 1998, Wayans Brothers, 1998, Friends, 2000, Everybody Loves Raymond, 2002, Reno 911, 2003.*

HINES, COLLEEN M., clinical nurse specialist; d. David Walter Mullis and Jo Wilma Clary; m. Thomas E. Hines, Aug. 2, 1969. BS, Tex. Women's U., 1966, MS, 1979. RN Tex. Staff nurse Parkland Hosp., Dallas, 1966—67, head nurse, 1967—75, nursing care supr., 1975—80, clin. nurse specialist, 1980—2003; program coord. Region 10 Edn. Svc. Ctr., Richardson, Tex., 2004—. Past mem. breastfeeding task force State of Tex. Dept. Health, Austin. Contbr. articles to profl. jours. Named Employee of Yr., Parkland Hosp., 1989. Mem.: Am. Assn. Diabetes Educators (past pres. local chpt., diabetes in pregnancy interest group), Tex. Nurses. Assn. (bd. dirs. 2005—), Am. Nurses Assn. (bd. dirs. 2000—03, 2005—), Sigma Theta Tau (past pres. Tex. Women's U. chpt.). Baptist. Avocations: reading, travel. E-mail: cmhteh@sbcglobal.net.

HINES, DAISY MARIE, freelance/self-employed writer; b. Hanna City, Ill., Dec. 31, 1913; d. Frank W. and Edith Earl (Folger) Humphrey; m. Herbert Waldo Hines, Jr., Dec. 20, 1958; children: Grace Consuelo, Ruby Marie. Student, Western Ill. U., 1955-57, So. Ill. U., 1956. Mem. staff advt. dept. Macomb Daily Jour., Ill., 1943-47; writer, exec., dir., promoter McDonough County Tb Assn., 1949-58; sec. U.S. Dept. Agr., Macomb, 1955-58; rschr., writer 1st Nat. Bank, Springfield, 1963, adminstrv. asst. to state legislator, 1964-69; with Sentinel Printing Co., Illiopolis, Ill., 1965; newspaper columnist, free-lance writer, mem. survey staff Prairie Farmer Pub. Co., Decatur, Ill., 1965-79, Successful Farming, Des Moines, 1982; freelance corr. Automotive News divsn. Crain Comm., Inc. Active Altar Soc. Blessed Sacrament Cath. Ch., Springfield; freelance writer Springfield Cath. Times newspaper, 1991, Decatur (Ill.) Herald and Rev. newspaper, 1991; corr. Ill. State Jour.-Register, Springfield; chmn. Illiopolis unit Univ. Ill. Home Extension; pub. rels. dir. Springfield chpt. Am. Cancer Soc., 1961-68; 2d v.p. Ill. Conf. Tb Workers, 1952-53; mem. Sangamon County Farm Bur., women's com., chmn. health and safety, St. John's Hosp. Aux., Ill. Traffic Safety Leaders. Mem. Nat. League Am. Pen Women (pres. Springfield chpt. 1972-73, sec. Ill. br. 1974), Ill. Traffic Safety Leaders, Western Ill. U. Alumni Coun. (sec., Disting. Alumni award 1982, com. mem. Coll. Applied Scis. Agr. rep. Alumni Coun.), Illiopolis Am. Legion (aux. unit 521), Ill. Press Assn. USAF Air Def. Team (hon. life), Ill. Women for Agr., Civil War Round Table, Sangamon County Hist. Soc., Republican Women's Club. Address: PO Box 310 Canton IL 61520-0310

HINES, JACLYN LETTA, counseling administrator; b. Paris, Tex., Feb. 11, 1980; m. Gerry Don Hines, May 31, 2003; 1 child, Kate Morgan. BS Edn., Sam Houston State U., Huntsville, Tex., 2001; MS Counseling, U. Houston Clear Lake, 2005. Tchr. Barbers Hill Ind. Sch. Dist., Mont Belview, Tex.; sch. counselor Paris H.S. Coach Cheerleading Paris H.S. Office: Paris High School 2400 Jefferson Rd Paris TX 75460

HINES, LINDA TURNER, health services administrator, nurse; b. Feb. 10, 1958; BSN, Va. Commonwealth U., 1980, MSN, 1999. RN, nurse mgr. Med. Coll. Va. Hosp., Richmond, 1980-96; v.p. med. mgmt. Va. Premier Health Plan, Inc., Richmond, 1996—. Spokesperson for breastfeeding in managed care Nat. Breastfeeding Policy, Washington, 1998. Author: (prenatal program) Am. Assn. Health Plans (Best Practices award 1998). Office: Va Premier Health Plan Inc VP Med Mgmt 600 E Broad St Ste 400 Richmond VA 23219-1800

HINES, VONCILE, special education educator; b. Detroit, Dec. 1, 1945; d. Raymond and Cleo (Smith) H. AA, Highland Park Community Coll., 1967; BEd, Wayne State U., 1971, MEd, 1975; MA, U. Detroit, 1978. Tchr. primary unit Detroit Bd. Edn., 1971-79, spl. educator, 1979-94; self-employed ednl. rsch. edn. co-creations. Tchr. trainee Feuerstein's Instrumental Enrichment, 1988—; cons. Queen's Community Workers, Detroit, 1977—; evaluator Teen Profl. Parenting Project, New Detroit Inc., 1986-87; guest educator, critic "Express Yourself", Sta. WQBH 1400 AM, 1989; advisor to home sch. educators. Author: I Chose Planet Earth, 1988; inventor in field. Recipient cert. of merit State of Mich., 1978, 88, cert. of appreciation Queen's Cmty. Workers, 1980, Wayne County Bd. Commrs., 1988, award of recognition Detroit City Coun., 1984, 88. Mem. Assn. for Children and Adults with Learning Disabilities, Assn. Supervision and Curriculum Devel., Nat. Thinking Skills Network, NAFE, Nat. Council Negro Women (presenter 1987), Met. Detroit Alliance of Black Sch. Educators. Democrat. Avocation: travel.

HING, BARBARA LIM, elementary school educator, assistant principal, data processing executive; b. Jan. 06; arrived in U.S., 1973; d. Amado K. H. and Bee-chu Tan Lim; m. Y. Ray Hing, Oct. 11, 1975; children: Abigail Hing Wen, Byron Lim, Colleen Lim. BA, Maryknoll Coll., Quezon City, The Philippines, 1971; MA, Ea. Mich. U., 1975; prin. cert., Cleve. State U., 1994. Cert. tchr. Ohio, Ill., adminstr. Ohio, Ill. Instr. St. Claire Coll., Windsor, Ont., Canada, 1975; substitute tchr. Shawnee Local Schs., Lima, Ohio, 1980-84, Solon (Ohio) City Schs., 1984-86; tchr. Cleve. Pub. Schs., 1986-95, title I tchr., 1995—2000; asst. prin. Buhrer Elem. Sch., Cleve., 2000—02, data mgr., 2003—04. Contbr. strategic planning com. Solon Schs., 1989—91; chairperson Fundraising Com.; Cleve., 1995—98, Attendance Com., Cleve., 1995—. Author: (book) Joy the Spider, 1975; writer, editor, pub.: Harvey Rice Attendance Newsletter, 1996—99, Harvey Rice Newsletter, 1999—2000. Mem., supporter Heritage Found., Washington, 1991—, Cmty. Action Team, 1993—94, Concord Coalition, Washington, 1996; chairperson scholarship com. Solon Acad. Boosters Club, 1995—97; sustaining mem. Rep. Nat. Com., Washington, 1994—. Named Outstanding Leader, Health Den, Mentor, Ohio, 1999; recipient Outstanding award, Charities of Choice, Cleve., 1995—97. Mem.: Orgn. Chinese Ams. Greater Cleve. (supporter, v.p. 1998—2003, bd. dirs. 1999—, Outstanding Citizen award 1999, 2002), Chinese Women Assn. Cleve. (founder, treas. 1999—2001, pres. 2005—). Personal E-mail: chiuma@sbcglobal.net.

HINIKER, LUANN, management consultant, educator, researcher, grants consultant; b. Mankato, Minn., Sept. 30, 1956; d. Christopher Joseph Hiniker and Phyllis C. Krier; m. Donald George Olson, June 27, 1992. AS, Minn. State U., 1985, BS in Spanish summa cum laude, 1991, MS in Ednl. Adminstrn., 1995; PhD in Work Force Edn. and Devel., So. Ill. U., 2002. Admissions recruiter Minn. State U., Mankato, 1979-91, coord. Rsch. Enterprise, 1991-93, rsch. adminstr., 1991-96, dir. Info. Scis. Inst., 1997—; dist. dir. U. Minn. Ext. Svc. Heintz Ctr., Rochester, Minn., 2003—. Rsch. adminstr. Minn. State U., Mankato, 1991-96; mem. adv. coun. S. Ctrl. Minn. Tech. Coun., 1993-96, Region Nine Small Bus. Devel. Ctr., 1993-96; grants cons. Housing Authority Murray State U., 1998-99; instr. multimedia devel. Workforce Edn. and Devel. So. Ill. U., Carbondale, 1999-2000, rschr. videoconferencing technologies, 1999-2000; mem. bd. dirs. Minn. Tech., Inc., 1991-96. Presdl. scholar Minn. State U., 1994-95. Mem. AAUW, NAFE, Am. Ednl. Rsch. Assn., Phi Kappa Phi, Phi Delta Kappa, Omicron Tau Theta. Avocations: guitar, parrots, scuba diving, gardening. Office: U Minn Ext Svc Heintz Ctr Rochester MN 55904 Home: 39 Sunnydale Ln SE Rochester MN 55904-4965 Office Phone: 507-280-2865. Business E-Mail: luannh@umn.edu.

HINKEBEIN, KATHRYN ANN, retired education educator; b. St. Louis, June 4, 1945; d. John Joseph and Marian Ward (Harkins) Flavin; m. Richard Sylvester, Jan. 25, 1969; children: Matthew, Stephanie. BS in Edn., Semo U., 1967. Jr. high tchr. Parkway South, Ballwin, Mo., 1967-69, Cape Girardeau (Mo.) Schs., 1969-71, St. Pius X, Cedar Rapids, Iowa, 1982-93; tchr. English and algebra Rosary H.S., 1994—2004; ret. Pres. Ladies Soc., Marion, Iowa, 1977-79; troop leader Cub Scouts, Marion, Iowa, 1981; sec. St. Joseph Sch. Bd., Marion, Iowa, 1985-88. Roman Catholic. Avocations: reading, crafts, walking.

HINKELMAN, RUTH AMIDON, insurance company executive; b. Streator, Ill., June 4, 1949; d. Olin Arthur and Marjorie Annabeth (Wright) Amidon; m. Allen Joseph Hinkelman, Jr., Oct. 28, 1972; children: Anne Elizabeth, Allen Joseph III. AB in Econs., U. Ill., 1971. Underwriter Kemper Ins. Group, Chgo., 1971-75; acct. exec. Near North Ins. Agy., Chgo., 1975-76; underwriter Gen. Reinsurance Corp., Chgo., 1976-78, asst. sec., 1978-79, asst. v.p., 1979-83, 2nd v.p., 1983-87, v.p., 1987—. Home: 133 Linden Ave Wilmette IL 60091-2838 Office: Gen Reinsurance Corp 1 N Wacker Dr Ste 1700 Chicago IL 60606 Office Phone: 312-207-5332. Business E-Mail: rhinkelm@genre.com.

HINKLE, BETTY RUTH, retired academic administrator; b. Atchison, Kans., Mar. 18, 1930; d. Arch W. and Ruth (Baker) Hunt; m. Charles L. Hinkle, Dec. 25, 1950 (div.); children: Karl, Eric. BA, U. Corpus Christi, Tex., 1950; MS, Baylor U., Waco, Tex., 1956; MA, U. North Colo., Greeley, Colo., 1972, EdD, 1979. Cert. tchr., Tex., Mass., Colo.; cert. adminstr., Colo. Tchr. Alice (Tex.) Ind. Sch. Dist., 1950, Waco (Tex.) Ind. Sch. Dist., 1951-52, 53-58, Hawaii Pub. Schs., Oahu, 1952-53, Newton Pub. Schs., Newtonville, Mass., 1962-63, Colorado Springs (Colo.) Pub. Schs., 1966—75; cons., exec. dir. spl. project unit Colo. State Dept. Edn., Denver, 1975—95, asst. commr., 1995, ret., 1995, rep. fed. rels. Office Commr. Edn., 1995-96, ret., 1996. Pvt. cons., 1997-2001; pres. BH Cons., Colorado Springs, 1997-2001; mem. cabinet Colo. Dept. Edn., mem. Quality Coun., fed. liaison rep. to chief state sch. officers, Washington, chmn. 1996; alt. foreman Denver Grand Jury, 1983; mem. state exec. fellowship program Instn. Ednl. Leadership, Coun. Chief STate Sch. Officers and U.S. Dept. Edn., 1985. Vol. for Colo. Mountain Reclamation Projects, 2001—. Recipient Dept. Edn. Specialists award Colo. Assn. Sch. Execs., 1979, Employee Yr. award Colo. Dept. Edn., 1986, Fed. Ednl. Program Adminstrv. Coun. ann. award for Distinctive Svc. to Colo. Children, 1988; named an Outstanding Secondary Educator of Am., 1974. Mem. Am. Assn. Sch. Adminstrs., Colo. Assn. Sch. Execs. (coord. coun. 1976-79, v.p. dept. edn. specialists 1974-75, pres. 1975-76), Colo. Assn. Sch. Execs., Phi Delta Kappa. Home: 1011 N 18th St Colorado Springs CO 80904-2852 Personal E-mail: b3h@adelphia.net.

HINKLE, BONNIE, education educator; EdD, Tex. Woman's U., 1995. Lic. profl. counselor Tex. Dept. Health, 1989. Assoc. prof. Dallas (Tex.) Bapt. U., 1998—. Recipient Piper Outstanding Prof. award, Dallas (Tex.) Bapt. U., 2005. Mem.: Christian Counselor's Tex. (assoc.; state pres. 2000—01). Office: Dallas Baptist University 3000 Mountain Creek Parkway Dallas TX 75154 Office Phone: 214-333-6838. Office Fax: 214-333-5551. Business E-Mail: bonnie@dbu.edu.

HINKLE, ERICA, art educator; d. Rodney Millett and Verna Rose Terminello; m. Landon Lamont Hinkle, Apr. 25, 2004; children: Landon Junior Lamont, Xavier Millet. B in Art Edn., Ohio State U., 1998, M in Art Edn., 2002. Cert. visual arts K-12 Ohio. Art tchr. Westerville City Schs., Westerville, Ohio, 2000—. Exhibitions include Columbus Mus. Art, 1994, David Meyers Gallery, 2003—06. Mem. nat. peace rally, Washington, 2005. Grantee, Westerville Career Edn. Found., 2001. Mem.: Nat. Art Edn. Assn. D-Liberal.

HINKLE, JANET, psychologist; b. Groton, Conn., Mar. 26, 1958; d. David Randall and Muriel (Nelson) Hinkle; m. Richard Alden Wilcox, Oct. 1, 1983 (div. Mar. 1991); 1 child, Lillian Marie. AA in Fashion Design cum laude, Endicott Jr. Coll. Women, Beverly, Mass., 1978; BA in Psychology, Conn. Coll., 1981; MBA, Rensselaer Poly. Inst., 2004. Project leader Sonalysts, Inc., Waterford, Conn., 1983—. Coporator Lawrence and Meml. Hosp., New London, Conn., 1995—, mem. planned giving com., 1998—99; mem. gift com. adv. Cmty. Found., New London, 1998—; mem. curriculum com. planned sci. and tech. Magnet HS, 2003—; bd. dirs. United Way SECT. Named to Outstanding Young Women of Am., 1997. Mem.: Thames Club. Republican. Avocations: training horses, ballet, tennis, skiing, painting. Home: 221 Elm St Stonington CT 06378-1165 Office: Sonalysts Inc 215 Parkway N Waterford CT 06385-1209

HINKLE, MURIEL RUTH NELSON, naval warfare analysis company executive; b. Bayonne, N.J., Mar. 17, 1929; d. Andrew and Florence Martha Ida (Nuber) Nelson; m. David Randall Hinkle, June 5, 1954; children: Valerie Nelson, Janet Lee, Sally Ann. Student, Md. Coll. for Women, 1947-49; BA, U. Md., 1951. Mgr. Wildacres Thoroughbred Horse Farm, Waterford, Conn., 1960-70; illustrator naval warfare predictions/computer simulated naval engagements Analysis & Tech., Inc., North Stonington, Conn., 1970-73; pres. Sonalysts, Inc., Waterford, Conn., 1973-88, 94-98, CEO, 1973-2001, pres., CEO emerita, 2001—; also founder, past dir. Command Engring. & Tech. Svcs. Co.; pres., CEO, chmn. Stonington Farms Inc. (now Mystic Valley Hunt Club), 1983. Adv. bd. Conn. Nat. Bank, 1988-92; chmn., CEO Angiers Assocs., 1989-96, S.I. Devel. Corp., 1989-2001; cons. Def. Nuclear Agy. for Tactical Nuclear Effects in anti-submarine warfare, 1974-75; spl. edn. substitute tchr. Waterford Pub. Schs., 1968-74; bd. dirs. Sonalysts, Inc. Co-author: Scope of Acoustic Communications Systems in Naval Tactical Warfare, 1974, Non-Acoustic Anti Submarine Warfare, 1974, Nuclear Weapons Effects in Anti Submarine Warfare, 1974, Measures of Effectiveness, Naval Tactical Communications, 1975, Destroyer ASW Barrier, 1977. Bd. trustees Thames Sci. Ctr., 1979-82. Recipient commendation for svcs. to submarine force Comdr. Submarine Squadron Ten, 1973, SBA New Eng. Contractor of Yr. award, 1986, SBA Adminstr.'s award for excellence, 1985, 86, bus. assoc. of yr. award Naval Inst., 1999, Disting. Cmty. Svc. award Mitchell Coll., 2001, William Crawford Disting. Svc. award C. of C., 2002. Mem. Am. Horse Shows Assn., Nat. Audubon Soc., Submarine Devel. Group Two Wives Club (pres. 1968), Sigma Kappa (pres. Senesk chpt. 1987-89), Navy Wives Club. Republican. Baptist. Home: 9 Cove Rd Stonington CT 06378-2304 Office: Sonalysts Inc PO Box 280 215 Parkway N Waterford CT 06385-1209 Office Phone: 860-442-4355.

HINKLEY, NANCY EMILY ENGSTROM, foundation administrator, educator; b. St. Louis, Jan. 3, 1934; d. Sigfrid E. and Ida C. (Stenstrom) Engstrom; children: Karen Elizabeth, Christine Marie, Catherine Andrea. BA, Augustana Coll., 1955; MA, U. Fla., 1956; EdD, N.C. State U., 1975. Adult edn. specialist Nationwide Long Term Care Edn. Ctr., Raleigh, NC, 1975-77, dir., 1977-78; owner, pres. Aging and Long Term Care Ednl. and Cons. Svcs., Raleigh, 1978-82; dir. edn. Beverly Found., South Pasadena, Calif., 1983-84; dir. tng. and mgmt. devel. Care Enterprises, Anaheim, Calif., 1984-87; pres. The Hillhaven Found., Tacoma, 1987-93; dir. employment & tng. divsn. Kitsap Cmty. Resources, 1997-99; pres. AJM Assocs., 1993—. Bd. dirs. Tacoma Community Coll. Found.; mem. editorial bd. Nursing Homes, 1988—; mem. editorial bd. Aspen Rsch. Pub. Group, 1989-93. Author: (with others) A Time and Place for Sharing: A Practical Guide for Developing Intergenerational Programs, 1984; mem. editorial bd. Jour. Univ. Programs, 1988-93; contbr. articles to profl. jours. Vol. Big Bros./Big Sisters, Tacoma, 1989-90; bd. dirs. Jessie Dyslin Boy's Ranch, Tacoma, 1988-90. Mem. ASTD, Am. Med. Dirs. Assn. (assoc.), Am. Assn. Homes for the Aging (assoc.), Am. Coll. Health Care Adminstrs. (assoc.), Am. Soc. on Aging, Gerontol. Soc. Am., Phi Kappa Phi, Phi Alpha Theta, Alpha Kappa Delta, Alpha Psi Omega, Sigma Phi Omega.

HINMAN, EVE CAISON, retired academic administrator; b. Charleston, S.C., May 17, 1951; d. Robert Lee Jr. and Ella Louise (Cross) Caison; m. William DeLeon Thrasher, June 9, 1972 (div. 1997); 1 child, Beverly Ann Thrasher Varner; m. Charles Steven Hinman, Feb. 27, 1998. Student, Francis Marion Coll., 1974-78, Trident Tech. Coll., 1990-91. Adminstrv. asst. to dean, acad. v.p. Francis Marion Coll., Florence, S.C., 1973-78; bus. mgr. dept. neurology Med. U. S.C., Charleston, 1978—2001, part-time fiscal analyst, 2001—02; customer support rep. Universal Data Solutions, Charleston, SC, 2002—. Mem. Bluegrass Gospel band New Hope. Mem. Friendship United Meth. Ch., Cross, SC. Avocations: bluegrass guitar and bass, singing and performing. Office Phone: 843-556-5565. Business E-Mail: hinmane@universaldata.net.

HINNRICHS-DAHMS, HOLLY BETH, elementary school educator; b. Milw., Oct. 31, 1945; d. Helmut Ferdinand and Rae W. (Beebe) Hinnrichs; m. Raymond H. Dahms, June 11, 1983 (dec. Oct. 1983). Student, U. Wis., Milw., 1964, 66, 79—, Chapman Coll., 1965-67, Intenrat. Coll. Copenhagen, summer 1968, Temple U., summer 1970; BA, Alverno Coll., 1971; postgrad., Marylhurst Coll., 1972, Chapman Coll., World Campus Afloat, summer 1973, 74, Inst. Shipboard Edn., 1978—79, postgrad., postgrad., Inst. Shipboard Edn., 1994, postgrad., 2005. V.p. Hinnrichs Inc., Germantown, Wis., 1964-72; tchr. Germantown Recreation Dept., 1965; coach Milw. Recreation Dept., 1966-67; rep. for wis. Chapman Coll., Orange, Calif., 1967; clk. Stein Drug Co., Menomonee Falls, Wis., 1967-72; tchr. Milwa. Area Cath. Sch., 1967-72, 83, 90-91, 96—, Germantown Schs., St. Lawrence Sch., 1991-92; asst. mgr. Original Cookie Co. (Mother Hubbard's) Cookie Store, Northridge Mall, Milw., 1977-84, Sav-U Warehouse Deli, 1984-85, mgr. office, 1985-90; with Pilgrim Message Ctr., 1987—. Substitute tchr. Cath. schs. Milw. area, 1975-80, 83-89, 90, 92—, St. Rose Sch., 1989-90; tchr. Indian Cmty. Sch., Milw., 1971-72, 88, 94-2000, Martin Luther King Sch., 1973-74, Crossroads Acad., Milw., 1974-75, Harambee Cmty. Sch., 1980-83; tutor Brookfield (Wis.) Learning Ctr., 1986-87; Midwest rep. World Explorer Cruises, 1978-82; mem. replacement crew Hallmark Cards, 1997-98; with U.S. Census, 2000. Mem Wis. Math. Coun., Nat. Coun. Tchrs. Math., Internat. Inst. Milw. Friends of Mus., U.S. Lighthouse Soc., Great Lakes Lighthouse Soc., Miniss Kitigan Drum (Milw. chpt.), Golden Rule, Order Eastern Star, Hostelling Internat., Alpha Theta Epsilon. Christian Scientist. Home: N88w15041 Cleveland Ave # 3 Menomonee Falls WI 53051-2239 Office Phone: 262-253-2150. Personal E-mail: hhinnrichsdahms@yahoo.com.

HINOJOSA, SANDRA JOY, elementary special education educator; b. Laredo, Tex., Feb. 14, 1946; d. Jose D. and Grace Edith (Lockwood) Guerrero; m. Armando Hinojosa; children: Armando Roberto, David Andrew, Melissa Joy. BS in Elem. Edn., Texas A&I U., 1967, MS in Sch. Adminstrn., 1990. Cert. elem. tchr., bilingual edn., Tex. Tchr. Pearson Elem. Sch., Mission, Tex., 1967-68, Ryan Elem. Sch., Laredo, 1968-76, Pat-Ann's Nursery Sch., Laredo, 1977-88, United Day Sch., Laredo; oral lang. tchr. Honore Ligarde Elem. Sch., Laredo, 1988-94, Leo Cigarroa H. S., Laredo, 1994—. Cons. Modern Curriculum Press, 1993, World Book Internat., 1993, Creative Thinkers, Inc., 1992, Comm. Network Assoc., 1991; speaker, presenter in field; mem. com. Ctr. Profl. Devel. and Tech. Laredo State U., 1992. Field editor Learning Mag., 1991-92. Recipient Propessional Best Leadership award Oldsmobile, Mich. State U., Learning Mag., 1990; named Elem. Tchr. of Yr. Tex. Region 1 Edn. Svc. Ctr., Edinburg, 1991, Tchr. of Yr. 1991-92 Southwestern Bell Telephone Co., Outstanding Fgn. Lang./ESL Am. tchr. of Yr. Walt Disney Co., L.A., 1991, Hon. Citizen Walt Disney World, 1991; featured TV series Am. Tchr., 1992. Avocations: reading, writing. Home: 2702 Gustavus St Laredo TX 78043-2428

HINRICHS, S. JEAN, auditor; BS, MBA, San Francisco State Univ. Cert. internal auditor, fraud examiner. V.p., gen. auditor Fed. Reserve Bank, San Francisco, 1993—96; mng. dir., internal auditing Barclays Global Investors, San Francisco, 1997—99, mng. dir., risk, 1999—2004; chief audit exec. Fannie Mae, Washington, 2005—. Office: Fannie Mae 3900 Wisconsin Ave NW Washington DC 20016-2892

HINSCH, GERTRUDE WILMA, biology professor; b. Chgo., Oct. 20, 1932; d. Hans Rudolph and Gertrude Hinsch. BSEd, No. Ill. U., 1953; MS, Iowa State U., 1955, PhD, 1957. Instr. Mt. Holyoke Coll., South Hadley, Mass., 1957-60; asst. prof., then assoc. prof. Mt. Union Coll., Alliance, Ohio, 1960-67; assoc. prof. U. Miami (Fla.), 1966-74, U. South Fla., Tampa, 1974-80, prof., 1980—. Office: U S Fla Dept Biology Tampa FL 33620 E-mail: hinsch@chuma1.cas.usf.edu.

HINSDALE, STEPHANIE M., social worker; b. Reading, Pa., Sept. 11, 1975; d. Glenn William Krick, Joyce Krick; m. Lyle R. Hinsdale. BA, Coll. of William and Mary, 1997; MSW, Va. Commonwealth U., 1999. Cert. sch. social worker 1999. Intensive in-home counselor Interstate Corp. Ctr. Family Preservation Svcs.-Tidewater Region, 2004—. Office: Family Preservation Svcs Tidewater Region Interstate Corp Ctr #20 Ste 249 Norfolk VA 23502 Home: 173 Swanson Rd Norfolk VA 23503-4729

HINSHAW, ADA SUE, nursing educator, former dean; b. Arkansas City, Kans., May 20, 1939; d. Oscar A. and Georgia Ruth (Tucker) Cox; children: Cynthia Lynn, Scott Allen Lewis. BS, U. Kans., 1961; MSN, Yale U., 1963; MA, U. Ariz., 1973, PhD, 1975; DSc (hon.), U. Md., 1988, Med. Coll. of Ohio, 1988, Marquette U., 1990, U. Nebr., 1992, Mount Sinai Med. Ctr., NY, 1993, U. Medicine and Dentistry N.J., 1995, Grand Valley State U., 1995, U. Toronto, Can., 1996, St. Louis U., 1996, Georgetown U., 1998. Instr. Sch. Nursing U. Kans., 1963-66; asst. prof. U. Calif., San Francisco, 1966-71; prof. U. Ariz., Tucson, 1975-87; dir. nursing rsch. U. Med. Ctr., Tucson, 1975-87; dir. Nat. Inst. Nursing Rsch. Pub. Health Svc., Dept. Health and Human Svcs., NIH, Washington, 1987—94; prof. U. Mich. Sch. Nursing, Ann Arbor, 1994—, dean, 1994—2006, dean emeritus, 2006—. Contbd. articles to profl. jours. Recipient Kay Schilter award U. Kans., 1961, Lucille Petry Leone award Nat. League for Nursing, 1971, Wolanin Geriatric Nursing Rsch. award U. Ariz., 1978, Alumni of the Yr award Sch. Nursing U. Kans., 1981, Disting. Alumni award Sch. Nursing Yale U., 1981, Alumni Achievement award U. Ariz., 1990, Disting. citation Kans. Alumni Assn., 1992, Health Leader of the Yr. award Pub. Health Svc., 1993, Centennial award Columbia Sch. Nursing, 1993, Presdl. Meritorious Exec. Rank award, 1994. Mem. ANA (Nurse Scientist of Yr. Award 1985, Salute to Nurses award 1994), Coun. Nurse Rschrs. (Nurse Scientist of Yr. Award 1985), Md. Nurses Assn., Western Soc. for Rsch. in Nursing, Am. Acad. Nursing, Inst. Medicine (mem. 1989-, coun. mem. 1999-04, mem. com. 1995-99, Walsh McDermott medal, 2005), Sigma Xi, Sigma Theta Tau (Beta Mu Chpt. award of Excellence in Nursing Edn., 1980, Elizabeth McWilliams Miller Excellence in Rsch. Award, 1987), Alpha Chi Omega. Avocations: hiking, camping, bicycling. Office: U Mich Sch Nursing 400 N Ingalls St Rm 4221 Ann Arbor MI 48109-2003 E-mail: ahinshaw@umich.edu.*

HINSHAW, VIRGINIA, academic administrator; BA in Lab. Tech., Auburn U., 1967, MS in Microbiology, 1967, PhD in Microbiology, 1972. Clin. and rsch. microbiologist Med. Coll. Va., 1967—68; rsch. virologist U. Calif., Berkeley, 1974; rsch. assoc. divns. virology St. Jude Children's Rsch. Hosp.; assoc. prof. virology dept. patho-biol. scis. U. Wis., Madison, 1985—88, prof., 1988—92, interim assoc. dean for rsch. and grad. studies Sch. Vet. Medicine, 1992—93, assoc. vice-chancellor, 1994—95, vice chancellor for rsch., dean Grad. Sch., sr. rsch. officer, 1995—2001; provost, exec. vice chancellor U. Calif., Davis, 2001—. Office: Univ Calif Davis One Shields Ave Davis CA 95616

HINSON, CYNTHIA THOMAS, minister; b. Charlotte, N.C., Jan. 26, 1951; d. Frealon Ed Thomas and Frances Elizabeth Love; m. Yancy Gerald Hinson, Dec. 22, 1973; children: Y. Jerry Hinson, III, William Thomas, Elizabeth Anne. BA in English Linguistics, U. Houston, 1994; MDiv cum laude, So. Meth. U., 1998; Beeson Doctoral fellow in Ministry, Asbury Theol. Sem., 2001—. Lic. pastor The United Meth. Ch., Houston, Tex., 1996, ordained deacon The United Meth. Ch., Houston, Tex., 1997, ordained elder The United Meth. Ch., Houston, Tex., 2000, cert. pastoral care specialist Krist Samaritan Ctr. for Couseling and Edn., Clear Lake, Tex., 2000; lic. real estate broker Real Estate Licensing Bd., North Carolina, 1971. Guitar instr. YWCA, Charlotte, NC, 1966—72; lab. technician The ARC, Charlotte, 1972—74; mgr. Headen and Co., Charlotte, 1974—76, Jetero Properties, Houston, 1977—79; property mgr. Krupp Co., Houston, 1979—81; english tchr. Houston Ind. Sch. Dist., Bellaire, Tex., 1994—95; sr. pastor St. Paul United Meth. Ch., Conroe, Tex., 1995—. Registrar com. on ordained ministry Houston (Tex.) North Dist. United Meth. Ch., 2001—; divsn. of edn. Tex. Ann. Conf. United Meth. Ch., Houston, 2000—, mentor pastor Com. Rules and Structure, 2000—; bd. of trustees Montgomery County Interfaith Hospitality Network, Conroe, Tex., 2000—02; spiritual dir. Houston North Emmaus Cmty., Tex., 1999—; page Gen. Conf. 2000 of the UMC, Cleveland, Ohio, 2000—00; v.p. Friends of Bellaire (Tex.) Parks, 1985—92; faith-based initiative Montgomery Co. Dept. of Corrections and St. Paul United Meth. Ch., Conroe, 2001—; instr. Lay Spkr. Sch. United Meth. Ch., Houston, 1996—2002; spkr. in field. Russ Pitman Park Playground. Supervising pastor Clowns for Christ, Conroe, 1999—2003; trustee Mont. County Interfaith Hospitality Network, Conroe, 2000—02. Recipient Vision award, Friends of Bellaire (Tex.) Pks., 1996; fellow, Beeson Internat. Sch. for Bibl. Preaching, Asbury Theol. Sem., 2001—. Mem.: Renewal Network, Sam Houston State U. Parents' Assn. (bd. dirs.), Houston Emmaus Cmty. (spiritual dir. 1999—), The Confessing Movement United Meth. Ch., Ea. Star, Sigma Tau Delta. Republican. United Meth. Office: St Paul United Methodist Church 1100 W Semands / P O Box 506 Conroe TX 77305 Office Phone: 936-756-5442.

HINSON, JANE PARDEE HENDERSON, lactation consultant; b. Durham, N.C., Mar. 17, 1947; d. Harvey Constantine and Sarah Lodge (Pardee) Henderson; children: Jane Pardee, James Travis Jr., Sarah MacQueen. BA, U. N.C., 1969, MPH, 1992; postgrad., Clayton Coll. Natural Health, U. S.C., 1995. Cert. lactation cons.; cert. healing touch practitioner. Tchr. English Orleans Parish Sch., New Orleans, 1969-72, Charlotte(N.C.)-Mecklenburg Schs., 1972-76; pvt. lactation practice Charlotte, 1986-92; with Carolinas Lactation Ctr. Mercy Hosp. South, Charlotte, 1992—. Bd. dirs. Breastfeeding Peer Counselor Program, Charlotte, 1994-98; bd. dirs., Mecklenburg Coun. on Adolescent Pregnancy, Charlotte, 1989-94; mem. adv. bd. to county commrs. Mecklenburg County Human Svcs. Coun., Charlotte, 1992-98; mem. Jr. League, Charlotte. Mem. Internat. Lactation Cons. Assn. (treas. bd. dirs. 1993-95), Mid-South Lactation Cons. Assn. (treas. bd. dirs. 1990-92), PEO. Democrat. Avocations: reading novels, antiques, collecting antique infant feeders. Office: Carolinas Med Ctr-Pineville 10628 Park Rd Charlotte NC 28210-8407 Office Phone: 704-667-1400. E-mail: phinson@bellsouth.net.

HINSON, MARVIS THEDORIA, education educator; b. Amsterdam, Ga., Apr. 3, 1950; d. Lawyer and Edna Surlina (Smith) H. BS, Ft. Valley State U., 1972; MEd, U. Ga., 1981. Cert. food and beverage exec., culinary educator, chef of wine arts. Sec. Fayetteville (N.C.) State U., 1972-73; instr. R.W. Groves High Sch., Savannah, Ga., 1973-81; dept. head Savannah Tech. Inst., 1981—. Bd. dirs. Arthritis Found., Savannah, 1993—. Recipie contest winner Athens Phyllo Co., Cleve., 1990. Mem. Savannah Chef's Assn. (sec. 1993—), Am. Culinary Fedn. Avocations: tennis, bicycling, cooking. Office: Savannah Tech Inst 5717 White Bluff Rd Savannah GA 31405-5521

HINTHORN, MICKY TERZAGIAN, retired executive secretary, volunteer; b. Jersey City, July 5, 1924; d. Bedros H. and Aznive (Hynelian) Terzagian; m. Wayne L. Hinthorn, Aug. 11, 1957. BS in Occupational Therapy, U. So. Calif., 1953; MBA, Notre Dame de Namur U., Belmont, Calif., 1984. Gen. office worker Drake Secretarial Coll., Jersey City, 1941-42; sec., expediter Western Electric Co., Kearny, N.J., 1943-45; sec. div. edn. CBS, N.Y.C., 1945—46; sec. to v.p. sales Simon and Schuster, Inc., 1947—51; gen. office worker in Sch. of Edn. U. So. Calif., L.A., 1951—52; occupational therapist Palo Alto Clinic, 1954—55; chief occupational therapist Children's Health Coun., 1954—56; sec. to chief mil. engr. Lenkurt Electric Co., San Carlos, 1956—58; sr. sec. re-entry program Bank of Am., Redwood City, 1979—80; ret., 1980. Organizer occupational therapy dept. Children's Health Coun., Palo Alto, Calif., 1954, chief 1954-56; author and editor newsletters. Charter mem., membership chair U. So. Calif. Pres. Cir., San Francisco, 1978-80; treas. North Peninsula chpt. San Francisco Opera Guild, San Mateo, Calif., 1979; vol. pub. info. chair re-election San Mateo County Supr., Redwood City, Calif., 1978; founder, charter pres. Friends of Belmont (Calif.) Libr., 1974-75; mem. Coastside Fireworks Com., 1989-94, chair corp. sponsorship, 1992-93. Recipient Hon. Mem., Friends of San Francisco Pub. Libr., 1974, 1990-1995, Assoc. Mem. Half Moon Bay Coastside Chamber Comm. (chair Bus. Edn. scholarships 1992, 93), Recognition Award 1993. Mem. AAUW (hon. life, pres. San Mateo br. 1976-77, chair local scholarships Half Moon Bay br. 1992, historian 1992-94, corr. sec. 1995-97, scholarship com. 1999-2000, edn. found. com. 1999-2003, name grant honoree Edn. Found. Jodi Gordon Endowment 1991-92), U. So. Calif. Alumni Assn. (life), Notre Dame de Namur U. Alumni Assn., Friends of Filoli, Friends of Half Moon Bay Libr., Coastside Women's Club (scholarship com. 1999-2003, com. scholarships and charities 2003-06). Avocations: photography, walking, reading, writing, attending performing arts events. Home: PO Box 176 Half Moon Bay CA 94019-0176

HINTON, PAULA WEEMS, lawyer; b. Gadsden, Ala., Dec. 5, 1954; d. James Forrest and Juanita (Weems) H.; m. Steven D. Lawrence, Mar. 31, 1984; 1 child, David Hinton Lawrence. BA in Polit. Sci. magna cum laude, U. Ala., 1976, MPA, JD, U. Ala., 1979. Bar: Ala. 1979, U.S. Dist. Ct. (so. dist.) Ala. 1980, U.S. Dist. Ct. (so. dist.) Tex. 1981, U.S. Ct. Appeals (5th and 11th cirs.) 1981, Tex. 1982, U.S. Dist. Ct. (no. dist.) Tex. 1988, U.S. Dist. Ct. (ea. and we. dists.) Tex. 1989, U.S. Dist. Ct. (no. and mid. dists.) Ala. 1993, U.S. Supreme Ct. 1998. Law clk. to magistrate U.S. Dist. Ct. Ala., Mobile, 1979-80; assoc. Vinson & Elkins, LLP, Houston, 1981-88; ptnr. Akin Gump Strauss Hauer & Feld, L.L.P., Houston, 1989—2001, Vinson & Elkins, Houston, 2001—. Mem. Supreme Ct. Gender Bias Reform Implementation Com., 1998—, co-chair, 2000—, chair, 2002—; mem. faculty Tex. Coll. Judicial Studies, 2004; panel arbitrators Am. Arbitration Assn., 1989—97; spkr. in field. Contbr. articles to profl. jours. Mem. women's initiative cabinet United Way Tex. Gulf Coast; mem. adv. bd. Sch. Law Found. U. Houston; bd. dirs. Planned Parenthood Houston and S.E. Tex., Inc., 2000—03. Named a Tex. Super Lawyer, Tex. Monthly and Law and Politics, 2003, 2004; Rotary fellow, U. Sevilla, Spain, 1980—81. Fellow: Tex. Bar Found. (co-chmn. nominating com. 2002—03, chair new fellows com. 2003, liaison to bd. 2003—05), Houston Bar Found. (life; bd. dirs. 1994—96, chmn. 1996—97, bd. dirs. 2002—); mem.: ATLA, ABA (mem. litigation sect., internat. law and practice sect., women and the law sect., women's adv. com. on corp. counsel, bus. law sect., commn. on women's Margaret Brent League), Am. Bar Found., Surpeme Ct. Hist. Soc., Am. Law Inst., Am. Inns of Ct., Tex. Assn. Def. Counsel, Coll. State Bar Tex., Tex. Assn. Def. Counsel, Internat. Assn. Def. Counsel, Am. Law Inst., Tex. Ctr. for Legal Ethics and Professionalism, Tex. Exec. Women, London Ct. of Internat. Arbitration, Internat. Bar Assn. Section on Bus. Law (sect. bus. law, barristers & advocates forum), Houston Bar Assn. (minority opportunities in legal profession com. 1997, civil justice ctr. com. 1997—98), Greater Houston Partnerships, Exec. Women's Partnership (steering com. 2002—03), U. Houston Law Found. (adv. bd), State Bar Tex. (chair women in the profession com. 1996—98, ad hoc com. to select minority dirs. 1997, local grievance com. 1998, mem. disciplinary rules of profl. conduct com. 2000—01, bd. dirs. 2002—05, vice chair spl. pattern jury charge oversight com. 2003, exec. com. 2003—04, mem. disciplinary rules of profl. conduct com. 2004—05, coun. litig. sect. 2005, mem. litigation sect., women and law sect., internat. law sect., antitrust and bus. litigation sect., women and the sect. Ma'at Justice award 2003, Woman on Move award 2004), Alexis de Tocqueville Soc., Am. Inns of Ct., Supreme Ct. Hist. Soc., Phi Delta Phi, Omicron Delta Kappa, Pi Sigma Alpha. Office: Vinson and Elkins LLP First City Tower 1001 Fannin St Ste 2300 Houston TX 77002-6760 Business E-Mail: phinton@velaw.com.

HINTON, SUSAN FRAZIER, secondary school educator; b. Lebanon, Tenn., Dec. 13, 1951; d. Henry Edward and Frances (Fuston) Frazier; m. Jerry Lee Hinton, 1993; children: Troy E. Hinton, David L. Hinton, Rance Kelly Jr. BS, Belmont U., Nashville, 1972; Master's degree, Ala. A&M U., 1974, EdS, 1976. Cert. elem. tchr., Ala.; reading specialist, Ala.; cert. adminstrn. supr. schs. Dir. migrant edn. Morgan County Sch. Sys., Decatur, Ala., 1986-89, elem. tchr., 1972-86, 1989-98; lang. arts tchr. DeKalb Mid. Sch., Smithville, Tenn., 1998-2000; dir., tchr. Dekalb County H.S., 2000—. Cons., chmn. So. Assn. Colls. and Univs., 1993—. Vol. Hospice of Am., Huntsville, Ala., 1992—, 4-H Clubs of U.S., Morgan County, 1989-96; pianist Smithville (Tenn.) First Bapt. Ch., 1995-96, asst. choir dir., pianist Kingdom Kids; active DeKalb Art League, 1998—; mem. Southern Gospel Singing Group-The Harmoneers, 1998—; mem., pianist DeKalb Cmty. Chorus. Mem.: NEA (del. 1986, mem. pub. rels. com., pianist, Ala. Educator of Yr. 1986, Morgan County Tchr. of Yr. 1996), Morgan County Edn. Assn. (pres. 1972, 1976), Ala. Edn. Assn. (del., mem. various coms.), Nat. Coun. Tchrs. English, Red Hat Soc., Smithville Study Club (music chmn.), Smithville Bus. and Profl. Women's Club (pres. 2003—). Democrat. Home: PO Box 622 Smithville TN 37166-0622 Office Phone: 615-597-2254. E-mail: hinton@dtccom.net.

HINTZ, DAWN M., mathematics educator; b. Minot, ND, Mar. 21, 1970; d. Larry Melvin and Cheryl Diane Gerjets; m. Dave Hintz, Sept. 27, 1997; children: Amanda Marie, Cameron John. MEd in Math., Minot State U., 1988—92. Math tchr. Nedrose Sch. Dist., Minot, 1995—96, Bismarck Pub. Schs., Bismarck, ND, 1996—. Math team co-advisor Bismarck HS, 1996—2005. Mem.: Bismarck Edn. Assoc., ND Coun. Tchrs. Math. Independent. Lutheran. Avocations: yoga, reading, crafts.

HINTZKE, TERESA ANNA, illustrator; b. Bydgoscz, Poland, Aug. 1, 1934; arrived in U.S., 1953; d. Stanislaw Mikosz and Anna Reysowska; m. Edward Stanley Hintzke, Dec. 7, 1973; children from previous marriage: Richard A. Sobilo, Barbara M. Sobilo. PhB, Northwestern U., 1981. Tech. illustrator GM Corp., Detroit, 1969—73; chief tech. illustrator Apeco, Inc., Evanston, Ill., 1975—77, Telemedia, Inc., Chgo., 1977—79; pvt. practice Winnetka, Ill., 1979—. Author: (memoir) Six Years Til Spring, 2001. Docent Oriental Inst U. Chgo., 1975—, Field Mus., 1977, 2005—. Mem.: Pan Pacific and S.E. Asia Womens Assn. (nat. pres. 1997—2001, internat. rep. to UN CONGO Bd. 2005—), Internat. Women Assocs. Inc. Avocations: collecting antique maps, Mid.-East archaeology.

HINZ, DOROTHY ELIZABETH, writer, editor, corporate communications specialist; b. N.Y.C. AB, Hunter Coll.; student, Columbia U. Asst. to dir. devel. Columbia U., N.Y.C., 1953-55; mng. editor, econs. rschr.-analyst, writer speeches, position papers, mgr. pubs. W.R. Grace & Co., N.Y.C., 1955-64; staff writer Oil Progress, fgn. news media, speeches, films, internat. petroleum ops., pub. rels. dept. Caltex Petroleum Corp., N.Y.C., 1964-69; fin. editor Merrill Lynch, Pierce, Fenner & Smith, 1969-74; mgr. publs., mgr. speakers' bur., assoc. speech writer mktg. and corp. comm. dept. Mfrs. Hanover Corp., N.Y.C., 1974-88; mem. Internat. Seminars, Columbia U., N.Y.C., 1988—. Contbr. articles on multinat. corps., developing nations, trade and fin. to various publs.; researcher of policy proposals for J.P. Grace's book, It's Not Too Late in Latin America. Mem. The Ams. Found. Mem. N.Y. Press Club, Americas Soc., Bolivarian Soc. (sec., bd. dirs.), Fgn. Press Assn., Coun. of Ams. Home and Office: 600 W 115th St Apt 104 New York NY 10025-7720

HIRAI, MICHIYO, education educator; PhD, Va. Tech, 2002. Asst. prof. Wash. State U., Pullman, Wash., 2004—. Office Phone: 509-335-2802.

HIRANO, IRENE ANN YASUTAKE, museum director; b. LA, Oct. 7, 1948; d. Michael S. and Jean F. (Ogino) Yasutake; 1 child, Jennifer. BS in Pub. Adminstrn., U. So. Calif., 1970, MPA in Pub. Adminstrn., 1972. Project adminstr. U. So. Calif., 1970-72; assoc. dir. Asian Women's Ctr., 1972-73; nat. project coord., Japanese site supr. Nat. Asian Am. Field Study, L.A., 1973-75; cons. U.S. Dept. Health, Edn. and Welfare, Adminstn. on Aging, San Francisco, 1975; exec. dir. T.H.E. Clinic for Women, Inc., L.A., 1975-88; exec. dir., pres. Japanese Am. Nat. Mus., L.A., 1988—. Pres., CEO Nat. Ctr. for Preservation of Democracy, 2000-; lectr., spkr. in field. Mem. L.A. Ednl. Alliance for Restructuring Now, 1993—, Pres's. Com. on Arts & Humanities, 1994—, Commn. on Future of Smithsonian Inst., 1993—, L.A. Coalition, 1993—; trustee Malborough Sch., 1993—; co-founder Leadership Edn. for Asian Pacifics, 1983, pres. 1983-86, v.p. 1986-90; pres., bd. dirs. Asian Pacific Am. Support Group, U. So. Calif., 1984-88; bd. dirs. Liberty Hill Found., 1984-88, community funding bd., 1981-84; trustee, chair Kresge Found.; chairperson Calif. Commn. on the Status of Women, 1981-82, commn. mem., 1976-83, many others. Recipient Nat. Outstanding Asian/Pacific Islander award NEA, 1983, Outstanding Women of the '90's, Robinson's Corp., 1992, Outstanding Svc. award Nat. Women's Polit. Caucus, 1986, Nat. Inst. Women of Color, 1984, Outstanding Alumni award U. So. Calif., 1994, So. Calif. Hist. Soc. Cmty. award, 1995. Office: Japanese Am Nat Mus 369 E 1st St Los Angeles CA 90012-3901*

HIRATA, RHONDA GAY, advertising executive; b. Oxnard, Calif., Aug. 21, 1953; d. Willis Masato and Marlene Matsuye (Kozuki) Hirata. BA, U. Calif.-Berkeley, 1975; grad., Coro Found., 1985. Account exec. McCann-Erickson, Inc., San Francisco, 1976—79, D'Arcy, MacManus & Masius, Inc., San Francisco, 1979—81; account supr. Dancer Fitzgerald Sample, Inc., Corp. Advt. Group, San Francisco, 1981—87; account dir. Pallas Advt., 1987; chmn bd. dirs. Kimochi, Inc., San Francisco, 1987; dir., mktg., comms. Jack London Sq. Ptnrs., Oakland, Calif. Mem. Bay Area Vol. Mktg. Coun., Girl Scouts U.S.A., 1983; mem. (past bd. dir.) Japanese Cultural Cmty. Ctr. No. Calif.; bd. dirs. Chinatown YMCA, San Francisco, 1980, Asian Am. Theatre Co., 1989; Japanese Cultural and Cmty. Ctr. No. Calif., 1989; exec. com. Nihonmachi Polit. Assn., San Francisco, 1981, Asian-Am. Dance Collective, San Francisco, 1981. Democrat. Office: Pallas Advt 151 Union St Ste 500 San Francisco CA 94111-1223 also: Jack London Sq Ptnrs 481 Water St Oakland CA 94607 Office Phone: 510-645-9283. Office Fax: 510-645-9363. Business E-Mail: rhonda@jacklondonsquare.net.

HIRE, KATHRYN P. (KAY), astronaut, military officer; b. Mobile, Ala. BS in Engring. and Mgmt., USN Acad., Annapolis, 1981; MS in Space Tech., Fla. Inst. Tech., 1991. Commd. ensign USN, Annapolis, 1981; student pilot USN Flight Sch., 1981—82; pilot Oceanographic Devel. Squadron 8 USN, Patuxent River, Md., 1982—85; from navigation instr. to curriculum mgr. Naval air Tng. Unit, Mather AFB, Calif., 1986—89; pilot Naval Air Reserve, Naval Air Sta. Jacksonville, Fla., 1989—93; patrol plane navigator USN Atlantic Parrol, 1993—95; astronaut NASA Johnson Space Ctr., Houston, 1995—. Mem.: AIAA, Inst. Navigation, U.S. Sailing Assn., Soc. Women Engrs. (Disting. New Woman Engr. Space Coast chpt. 1993), Assn. Naval Aviation. Achievements include first U.S. female assigned to a combat air crew; 1 space flight. Avocations: fishing, sailing, scuba diving, skiing. Office: Astronaut Office/CB Johnson Space Ctr Houston TX 77058

HIRES, CHERYL LYNN, literature and language educator; b. Palm Beach Gardens, Fla., Nov. 13, 1976; d. Donald Richman and Cheryl Lynn Hires. BA, Fla. Atlantic U., Boca Raton, 2001. Cert. profl. educator Fla. Intensive reading tchr. Sch. Dist. of Palm Beach County, West Palm Beach, Fla., 2002—. Asst. softball coach Palm Beach Lakes HS, West Palm Beach, 2005—, asst. girls varsity soccer coach, 2002—05. Avocations: travel, camping, water sports. Home: 326 Country Club Dr Tequesta FL 33469 Personal E-mail: cheryh@juno.com.

HIRONO, MAZIE KEIKO, former lieutenant governor; b. Fukushima, Japan, Nov. 3, 1947; arrived in U.S., 1955, naturalized, 1959; d. Laura Chie (Sato) H. BA, U. Hawaii, 1970; JD, Georgetown U., 1978. Dep. atty. gen., Honolulu, 1978-80; Shim, Tam, Kirimitsu & Naito, 1984-88; mem. Hawaii Ho. of Reps., Honolulu, 1980-94; lt. gov. State of Hawaii, 1994—2002. Bd. dirs. Nat. Asian Pacific Am. Bar Assn.; chair Hawaii Policy Group, Nat. Commn. on Tchg. and Ams. Future, Govs. Task Force on Sci. and Tech. Dep. chair Dem. Nat. Com., 1997; bd. dirs. Nuuanu YMCA, Honolulu, 1982—2004, Moiliili Cmty. Ctr., Honolulu, 1984—, Blood Bank of Hawaii. Mem. U.S. Supreme Ct. Bar, Hawaii Bar Assn., Phi Beta Kappa. Democrat. E-mail: hirono@hawaii.rr.com.

HIRONS, JEAN LOUISE, librarian; b. Boston, Apr. 30, 1948; d. Kenneth Willis Hirons and Helen Marie (Roberts) Eldridge; m. Lawrence Allen Ott, Aug. 24, 1969 (div. Sept. 1985); m. John Adams Hansman, Sept. 23, 1995. BA in Art, Marietta (Ohio) Coll., 1970; MLS, U. R.I., 1973. Cataloger U. Mass., Dartmouth, 1970-76, Cath U., Washington, 1976; cataloger/supr. U.S. Govt. Printing Office, Washington, 1977-83, Libr. of Congress, Washington, 1983-97, CONSER coord., 1997—2003; pastel artist Creative Ptnrs. Gallery, Md., 2003—. Adj. prof. Montgomery Coll., Rockville, Md., 2005—. Editor: CONSER Editing Guide, 1986-2003; author/editor: CONSER Cataloging Manual, 1993-2003; editor CONSERline newsletter, 1994-2003; editl. bd. Serials Libr., 1996-2003. Recipient Bowker/Ulrich's Serials Librarianship award ALA, 1996. Democrat. Unitarian Universalist. Avocations: art, piano. Office: Library of Congress 101 Independence Ave SE Washington DC 20540-0002

HIRSCH, ANN ULLMAN, retired academic administrator; b. N.Y.C., Feb. 12, 1929; d. Julian S. and Louise (Levien) Ullman; m. James E. Galton, Aug. 22, 1948 (div. 1962); children: Beth, Jean; m. David I. Hirsch, Mar. 22, 1963; stepchildren: Peter, Amanda. BS, NYU, 1950; postgrad., Queens Coll., Flushing, N.Y., 1955-57. Music tchr. Herricks (N.Y.) Sch., 1950-52, East Meadow (N.Y.) Pub. Schs., 1952-53; exec. dir. Ea. Suffolk Sch. Music, Riverhead/Southampton, N.Y., 1977-88. Self-employed piano tchr., N.Y., 1950-95; dir. music edn. Unitarian Sunday Sch., Freeport, N.Y., 1956-63; singer Oratorio Socs., Levittown and Bridgehampton, N.Y., 1950-85, L.I. Philharm. Chorus, Westbury, N.Y., 1989—; violinist Sound Symphony, Shoreham, Wading River, N.Y., 1980—, orch. pianist, 1980—. Author: Basic Guide to the Teaching of Piano, 1974. Mem. Arts in Edn. Task Force, BOCES, Westhampton, NY, 1977—87; planning mem., panelist Nat. Guild Cmty. Schs. of the Arts, 1980—88; tchr. Literacy Vols. Am., Riverhead, Mastic, NY, 1988—91; bd. mem. LI Masterworks Chorus, Commack, NY, 1992—2000. Named East End Woman of Yr. in Edn., East End Mag., Suffolk County, N.Y., 1979. Mem.: LWV, Southampton Twp. Wildfowl Assn., Bay Area Friends of the Fine Arts, Westhampton Beach Hist. Soc., Peconic Land Trust. Avocations: reading, sewing, walking, golf, photography. Home: PO Box 304 Remsenburg NY 11960-0304

HIRSCH, BETTE G(ROSS), academic administrator, language educator; b. N.Y.C., May 5, 1942; d. Alfred E. and Gladys (Netburn) Gross; m. Edward Raden Silverblatt, Aug. 16, 1964 (div. Feb. 1975); children: Julia Nadine Silverblatt Young, Adam Edward Silverblatt; m. Joseph Ira Hirsch, Jan. 21, 1978; stepchildren: Hillary, Michelle, Michael. BA with honors, U. Rochester, 1964; MA, Case Western Res. U., 1967, PhD, 1971. Instr. and head French dept. Cabrillo Coll., Aptos, Calif., 1973-90, 2003—04, divsn. chair fgn. langs. and comms. divsn., 1990-95, interim dir. student devel., 1995-96, dean of instrn., transfer and distance edn., 1996—2003, emerita and adj. instr. French, 2004—. Mem. steering com. Santa Cruz County Fgn. Lang. Educators Assn., 1981-86; mem. liaison com. fgn. langs. Articulation Coun. Calif., 1982-84, sec., 1983-84, chmn., 1984-85; workshop presenter, 1982—; vis. prof. French Mills Coll., Oakland, Calif., 1983; mem. fgn. lang. model curriculum stds. adv. com. State Calif., 1984; instr. San Jose (Calif.) State U., summers 1984, 85; reader Ednl. Testing Svc. Advanced Placement French Examination, 1988, 89; peer reviewer for div. edn. programs, NEH, Washington, 1990, 91, 93; grant evaluator, NEH, 1995; mem. fgn. lang. adv. bd. The Coll. Bd., N.Y.C., 1986-91. Author: The Maxims in the Novels of Duclos, 1973; co-author (with Chantal Thompson) Ensuite, 1989, 93, 98, 2003, 05, Moments Litteraires, 1992, 2006, (with Chantal Thompson and Elaine Phillips) Mais Oui! workbook, lab. manual, video manual, 1996, 2000, 04; contbr. revs. and articles to profl. jours. Pres. Loma Vista Elem. Sch. PTA, Palo Alto, Calif., 1978-79; bd. dirs. United Way Stanford, Palo Alto, 1985-90, mem. allocations com., 1988, bd. dirs. Cabrillo Music Festival, 1996-2003, sec., 1998, v.p., 2000-2002; bd. dirs. Cmty. TV of Santa Cruz County, 1997-99, vice chair, 1997-98. Grantee NEH, 1980-81, USIA, 1992; Govt. of France scholar, 1982, 2003. Mem.: MLA (mem. adv. com. on fgn. langs. and lits. 1995—2000, chair 1999—2000, com. on info. tech. 2001—, chair 2003—, mem. com. on cmty. colls. 2004—), Am. Assn. Tchrs. of French, Assn. Depts. Fgn. Langs. (exec. com. 1985—88, pres. 1988), Assn. Calif. C.C. Adminstrs. Democrat. Jewish. Avocations: travel, reading, gourmet cooking, antiques. Home: 4149 Georgia Ave Palo Alto CA 94306-3813 Office: Cabrillo College 6500 Soquel Dr Aptos CA 95003-3194 Business E-Mail: behirsch@cabrillo.edu.

HIRSCH, ELISABETH SCHIFF, education educator emeritus; b. Szombathely, Hungary, June 14, 1918; d. Edmund and Hilda (Schlesinger) Schiff; m. Julius E. Hirsch, Dec. 4, 1939; children: Naomi, Susan BS, Columbia U., 1950; MA, New Sch. Social Rsch., 1954; PhD, NYU, 1967. Cert. early childhood edn. Tchr. Beth Hayeled Sch., N.Y.C., 1948—51, Sch. for Young Profls., N.Y.C., 1951—52; tchr., dir. Young Israel of Sunnyside, N.Y.C., 1952—53, Jackson Heights Coop Nursery, N.Y.C., 1953—57; dir. Montefiore Nursery Sch., N.Y.C., 1957—59; tchr. Little Red Sch. House, N.Y.C., 1959—68; asst. prof. H.H. Lehman Coll. CUNY, 1968—70, prof. City Coll., 1970—88, prof. emeritas City Coll., 1988—. Pres. Early Childhood Edn. Coun., N.Y.C., 1973-76; mem. Tchr. Edn. Conf. Bd., Albany, N.Y., 1973-75; participant Longitudinal In-Depth Study N.Y. Dept. Edn., Albany, 1976-81; dir. Comprehensive Day-Care Tng. Program, CCNY, 1977-81, part-time adj. prof., 1988-2001. Author, editor: The Block Book, 1974, 3d edit., 1996; author: Problems of Early Childhood, 1983, (pamphlet) Transition Periods, 1974; contbr. articles to profl. jours Bd. mem. Early Childhood Resource Ctr. N.Y. Pub. Libr., N.Y.C Mem. Nat. Assn. for Edn. Young Children, Assn. for Childhood Edn. Internat., Orgn. Mondiale pour l'Edn. Prescholaire Jewish. Avocations: classical music, opera, reading, crossword puzzles. Home: 235 Prospect Ave Hackensack NJ 07601-2510

HIRSCH, GILAH YELIN, artist, writer; b. Montreal, Que., Can., Aug. 24, 1944; came to U.S., 1963; d. Ezra and Shulamis (Borodensky) Y. BA, U. Calif., Berkeley, 1967; MFA, UCLA, 1970. Prof. art Calif. State U., Dominguez Hills, L.A., 1973—. Adj. prof. Internat. Coll., Guild Tutors, L.A., 1980-87, Union Grad. Sch., Cin., 1990 50 solo exhbns., mus. collections, 15 publs. Founding mem. Santa Monica Art Bank, Calif., 1983-85; bd. dir. Dorland Mountain Colony, Temecula, Calif., 1984-88 Named artist-in-residence, RIM Inst., Payson, Ariz., 1989—90, Tamarind Inst. Lithography, Albuquerque, 1973, Rockefeller Bellagio Ctr., Italy, 1992, Tyrone Guthrie Ctr. for Arts, Annamahkerrig, Ireland, 1993, Internat. Sympat., Slovakia, 2004, 2005; recipient Disting. Artist award, Calif. State U., 1985, Found. Rsch. award, 1988—89, 1997—98, Creative Rsch. award, Sally Canova Rsch. Scholarship and Creative Activities awards program, 1997—99, 2003; grantee, Nat. Endowment Arts, 1985, Class Found., 2003, Calif. State U., Dominguez Hills, 2005, Panavision grantee, Panavision Films, Inc., L.A., 2005; Dorland Mountain Colony fellow, 1981—84, 1983, 1984, 1992, 1995, 2003, fellow, Banff Ctr. for Arts Can., 1985, MacDowell Colony fellow, N.H., 1987. Office: Calif State Univ Dominguez Hills 1000 E Victoria St Carson CA 90747-0001 Personal E-mail: gilah@linkline.com.

HIRSCH, KERRI ANN, social studies educator; b. Orlando, Fla., Oct. 11, 1971; d. Walter Keith Huffman and Karen Elizabeth Gandy; m. James Scott Hirsch, May 7, 1994; children: Lanie Marie, Cody James. AA, Fla. CC, Jacksonville, 1990—92; BS, U. South Fla., Tampa, 1992—94. Social studies tchr. Daniell Mid. Sch., Marietta, Ga., 1996—. 6-1 team leader Daniell Mid. Sch., 2004—, social studies coord., 2005—. Sponsoring tchr. Jr. Achievement, Marietta, 2004—05. Recipient Staff Mem. of Month, Cobb County Schs., 2005; grantee Ednl. grant, Jr. League Cobb- Marietta, 1998. Mem.: PAGE (assoc.). Office: Daniell Mid Sch 2900 Scott Rd Marietta GA 30066 Office Phone: 678-594-8048. Business E-Mail: kerri.hirsch@cobbk12.org.

HIRSCH, MAXINE K., special education educator, councilman; b. Bklyn., July 31, 1932; d. Charles and Mary S. Kunitz; m. Stuart M. Hirsch, June 20, 1954 (dec. Nov. 2, 2000); children: Charles L., Robin F. Student, Bard Coll., 1950—51; BA, Bklyn. Coll., 1954; student, Rutgers U., 1956—58; MA, Kean Coll., 1982. Cert. tchr. N.J., supr. N.J., tchr. handicapped N.J. Tchr. Oak Tree Sch., Edison, NJ, 1955—56; realtor Stuart Hirsch Agy., Plainfield, NJ, 1966—68; tchr. Cook Sch., Plainfield, 1969—73; tutor Adolescent and Drug Abuse Unit Fair Oaks Hosp., Summit, NJ, 1974—78; tchr. Summit Jr. H.S., 1977—89; councilwoman Borough New Providence, NJ, 1984—2004. Mem. bd. trustees New Providence Cmty. Pool, 1980—83; trustee ch. coalition New Providence Affordable Housing, 1996—; mem. bd. trustees New Providence Sr. Citizens, 2005—, pres. bd. trustees, 2006; chmn. bd. New Providence Affordable Housing, 1989—; bd. dirs. New Providence Parent Tchr. Student Assn., 1972—76; mem. Union County Cmty. Devel. Bd., NJ, 1996—99, NJ, 2002—; mem. open space com. Borough New Providence, 2004—. Named to Hall Fame, N.J. League Municipalities, 2005. Mem.: N.J. Assn. Elected Women Ofcls. (bd. dirs., pres. 1990—91). Republican. Jewish. Avocations: reading, politics, investments, movies. Home: 11 Colonial Way New Providence NJ 07974 Personal E-mail: maxinehirsch@comcast.net.

HIRSCH, PHYLLIS SINMAN, biochemist, researcher; b. Seattle, Dec. 27; d. Hyman and Eleanor (Paster) Sinman; m. I. Don. Hirsch, July 4, 1967; children: H. Daniel, Moshe Y., Shoshana, Raquelle. BS in Chemistry, Suffolk U., 1965; MS in Biochemistry, U. N.H., 1967; MA in Endocrinology, U. Los Angeles, 1974. Cert. sci. tchr., Calif. Staff scientist Worcester Found. Exptl. Biology, Shrewsbury, Mass., 1967-69; supr. Tay Sachs Nat. Testing Lab., Torrance, Calif., 1975-79; instr. anatomy, physiology Southwest Coll., Inglewood, Calif., 1983—. Sci. dept. cons. Bais Yaakov Sch., Los Angeles, 1979. Editor: A Little Bit of This A Little Bit of That, 1975-76; contbr. articles to profl. jours. Base commdr. Fairfax Community Patrol, Los Angeles, 1984—; pres. PTA, Los Angeles, 1980-81. Trustee scholar Suffolk U., 1962-65; U. N.H. research fellowship, 1965-67. Mem. AAAS, Am. Assn. Univ. Profs., Sigma Xi. Avocations: cooking, playing accordion, camping, sewing.

HIRSCH, ROSEANN CONTE, publisher; b. N.Y.C., Feb. 5, 1941; d. Frank and Anna (Burzycki) Conte; m. Barry Jay Hirsch, Oct. 1, 1967; children: Brian Christopher, Nicholas Benjamin, Jonathan Alexander. Student, Boston U., 1958-61; BA, Columbia U., 2004. Editorial asst. Grolier, Inc., 1962-64; editor Ideal Pub. Corp., N.Y.C., 1968-74; editorial dir. Sterling's Mags., Inc., N.Y.C., 1975-78, Hearst Spl. Publs., Hearst Corp., N.Y.C., 1978-84; v.p. Ultra Communications, Inc., N.Y.C., 1984-89; pub., pres. Dream Guys, Inc., N.Y.C., 1986-93; pres. Lamppost Press, Inc., N.Y.C., 1989—. Author: Super Working Mom's Handbook, 1986; editor: Young & Married Mag., 1976-77, 100 Greatest American Women, Good Housekeeping's Moms Who Work; contbr. articles to various mags. Home and Office: Lamppost Press Inc 870 United Nations Plaza 10E New York NY 10017 Office Phone: 212-750-0706.

HIRSCHBERG, VERA HILDA, writer; b. N.Y.C., Sept. 19, 1929; d. Bernard and Minnie (Margolis) Lieberman; m. Peter Hirschberg, Aug. 21, 1949; children: Karen Hirschberg Reses, Paul. BA, Hunter Coll., 1950. Staff writer Pacific Stars and Stripes, Tokyo, 1956-64; corr. Newsweek, Guatemala, 1964-65; transp. staff writer N.Y. Jour. Commerce, Washington, 1969-70; transp. editor Nat. Jour. Mag., Washington, 1970-72; dir. women's programs, presdl. speechwriter The White House, Washington, 1972-74; dir. tech. transfer HUD, Washington, 1974-75; dep. spl. asst. to Sec. Pub. Affairs Dept. Treasury, Washington, 1975-77; press. sec. U.S. Sen. William Roth, Jr., Washington, Jan. to Dec. 1977; editorial cons. various govt. and non-govt. clients, 1977-78; pub. affairs dir. White House Conf. on Libr. and Info. Svcs., Washington, 1978-80; sr. writer, adminstr.'s speechwriter NASA, Washington, 1980-92; cons. in field., 1992—. Author numerous newspaper and mag. articles. Art info. vol. Nat. Gallery of Art. Recipient Outstanding Svc. citation The White House, 1973, Meritorious Svc. award Dept. Treasury, 1977, Exceptional Performance award NASA, 1982, Exceptional Svc. medal, 1988. Mem. Exec. Women in Govt. (founding mem. 1973), Zionist Orgn. Am., Wash. Concert Opera Soc. Mem. Wash. Hebrew Congregation. Avocations: gourmet cooking, foreign travel, reading, museums, art collecting. Office Phone: 202-333-0977.

HIRSCHFELD, ARLENE, civic worker, former secondary school educator; b. Denver, Apr. 6, 1944; d. Hyman and Gertrude (Schwartz) Friedman; m. A. Barry Hirschfeld, Dec. 17, 1966; 2 children. Student, U. Mich., 1962-64; BA, U. Denver, 1966. English tchr. Abraham Lincoln High Sch., Denver, 1966-70. Pres. Jr. League of Denver, 1986-87, v.p. ways and means, 1985-86, v.p. mktg., 1982-83, chmn. Colo. Cache cookbook mktg. com., 1978-79, chair holiday mart, 1981, 85-87, participant in Nat. Jr. League Mktg. Conf.; trustee Graland Country Day Sch., 1988-97, bd. sec., 1990-95, chmn. edn. com., 1989-95, pres. parent coun., 1982-83, auction chmn., 1980, 81; bd. dirs. Allied Jewish Fedn., 1988-96, 98—, women's campaign chair, 1993; bd. dirs. Allied Jewis Fedn. Colo., 1999-03, bd. chair 1999-2001; co-chmn. collector's choice event Denver Art Mus., 1989, 94, trustee, 1995—, chmn. mktg. com., co-chmn. capital campaign, mem. exec. com.; co-chair ann. dinner Inst. Internat. Edn., 1997; mem. awards for excellence selection commn. El Pomar Found.; co-chmn. benefit luncheon Pub. Edn. and Bus. Coalition, 1990, mini grants selection com., 1985-87; mem. bd. Minoru Yasui Comty. Vol. award, 1986-87; mem. Greater Denver C. of C. Leadership Denver, class of 1987-88; bd. dirs. Women's Found. Colo., 1992-97, hon. trustees coun., 1997—, annual event co-chair, 2001; bd. dirs. Anti-Defamation League, 1996-, Colo. Spl. Olympics Coun. Advisors, 1995-98, Mizel Ctr. for Art, Film and Culture, 1996-2003; bd. dirs. Mizel Mus., 2003—; trustee Rose Cmty. Found., 2000—, chmn. Jewish life com., chmn. found.; bd. dirs. Mile High coun. Girl Scouts U.S, 1998—; dean's coun. Harvard Div. Sch., 1992—, nat. leadership com. Harvard Women's Studies in Religion Program, 1994—; exec. com. Children's Diabetes Found., Denver, 1993—; mem. cmty. adv. bd. Wildlife Experience; appointee to exec. endemic bd. Gov. Roy Romer, 1989-99, residence bd. Gov. Bill Owens, 1999—; gov. appointee mem. Colo. Women's Econ. Devel. Coun., 1989-99. Named Humanitarian of Yr., Nat. Jewish Ctr., 1988, Sustainer of Yr., Jr. League, 1992, Collectors Choice honoree, Denver Art Mus., 2002, Outstanding Vol. Fundraiser, Nat. Philanthropy Day in Colo., 2003; named to Colo. Women's Hall of Fame, 2006; recipient Colo. Chpt. award, Nat. Women's Mus. of the Arts, 1991, Alumni Cmty. Svc. award, U. Denver Founder's Day, Colo. I Have A Dream Found. award, 1992, Woman of Distinction award, Rocky Mountain News and Hyatt Beaver Creek, 1993, Vol. award, Denver br. AAUW, Golda Meir award, Allied Jewish Fedn. Colo., 1999, Intermountain Jewish News Feature, 1999, Mizel Mus. Cmty. Cultural Enrichment award, 2001, Martin Luther King Bus. Social Responsibility award, 2002, Rex Morgan award, Sci. and Cultural Facilities Dist., 2002, Collectors Choice Honoree, Denver Art Mus., 2002, Outstanding Jewish Woman award, Rocky Mountain Jewish Hist. Soc., 2004, Heritage award, 2004, Ellis Is. Medal of Honor, 2004, Humanitarian award, Vols. Am., 2005. Mem. Colo. Women's Forum. Avocations: aerobics, snow and water skiing, golf. Address: 150 S Bellaire St Denver CO 80246

HIRSCHFELDER, ARLENE PHYLLIS, writer, educator; b. Chgo., Apr. 17, 1943; d. Louis David and Rhea (Amber) Boshes; m. Dennis Clark Hirschfelder, Aug. 21, 1966; children: Adam, Brooke. BA, Brandeis U., 1965; MAT in History and Edn., U. Chgo., 1967. Tchr. Horton Watkins H.S., Ladue, Mo., 1966—68; dir. scholarship Assn. Am. Indian Affairs, N.Y.C., 1969—91; mem. faculty New Sch. for Social Rsch., N.Y.C., 1984—96. Bd. advisors Ency. Native Ams. in Twentieth Century, N.Y.C., 1988—; bd. dirs. Native Am. Bibliography series Scarecrow Press, Metuchen, N.J.; mem. com. Native Am. Heritage, N.Y.C., 1987-91 Author: Guide to Research on North American Indians, 1983 (Choice Outstanding Acad. Book award 1984-85), Happily May I Walk, 1986 (Carter Woodson Book award 1987, Western Heritage Book award 1986), Rising Voices, 1992 (Boston Globe's Choices for 25 Best in Children's Nonfiction 1992), Encyclopedia of Native American Religions, 1992, 1999 (N.Y. Pub. Libr. Outstanding Reference Book 1992), Native American Almanac, 1993, American Indian Lives: Artists and Craftspeople, 1994, Native Heritage: Personal Accounts by American Indians 1790 to the present, 1995, American Indian Stereotypes in the World of Children, 1982, 1999, Encyclopedia of Smoking and Tobacco, 1999 (Libr. Jour. Best Reference Svcs. of 1999), Native Americans Today: Resources and Activities for Educators, Grades 4-8, 2000, Photo Odyssey: Solomon Carvalho's Remarkable Adventure, 1853-1854, 2000 (Assn. Jewish Librs. Notable Children's Book 2000, N.Y. Pub. Libr. Book for Teen Age 2002), Native Americans: A History in Pictures, 2000, Kick Butts: A Kid's Guide to a Tobacco-Free America, 2001, Children of Native America Today, 2003 (Notable Books for a Global Soc./IRA); series editor: It Happened to Me, 1990—; contbr. articles to profl. jours. Mem. task force intergroup rels. Anti-Defamation League of B'nai B'rith, N.Y.C., 1982— Recipient Native Am. Svc. award Colo. State U., 1989 Jewish. Avocations: drawing, gardening. Home and Office: 170 Copley Ave Teaneck NJ 07666-4100

HIRSCHHORN, ROCHELLE, genetics educator; b. Bklyn., Mar. 19, 1932; d. Hyman and Anna Reibman; m. Kurt Hirschhorn; children: Melanie D., Lisa R., Joel N. BA, Barnard Coll., 1953; MD, NYU, 1957. Intern NYU-Bellevue Med. Divsn., N.Y.C., 1958—59; rsch. fellow, tchg. asst. NYU Sch. Medicine, N.Y.C., 1963—65, assoc. rsch. scientist, 1965—66, instr. medicine, 1966—69, asst. prof. medicine, 1969—74, assoc. prof. medicine, 1974—79, prof. medicine, 1975—, head divsn. med. genetics, 1984—, prof. medicine and cell biology, 1996—. Hon. fellow Galton Lab. Human Genetics & Biometry Univ. Coll., London, 1971—72; assoc. attending physician in medicine Beffevue Hosp., N.Y.C., 1969—80, Univ. Hosp., NYU Sch. Medicine, 1974—81; attending physician Bellevue Hosp., 1980—, Univ. Hosp., 1981—; com. mem., study sect. NIH, 1973—; vis. prof. Harvard U., 1995, U. Calif., San Francisco, 1995. Trustee AIDS Med. Found./AMFAR; judge Westinghouse Nat. Sci. Talent Search; founding mem. Village Cmty. Sch.; senator NYU Senate, mem. pediatrics search com., 1987—89, human subjects instl. rev. bd., 1989—94, co-dir. second year med. genetics course, 1989—93, NYU appts. and promotions com., 1995—2002. Named Disting. Alumna, Barnard Coll. Master: Am. Coll. Rheumatology; fellow: AAAS, Hero Arthritis Found., Am. Coll. Med. Genetics (founder); mem.: Inst. of Medicine of NAS, Harvey Soc. (coun. 1989—92), Soc. for Inherited Metabolic Diseases, Peripatetic Soc., Interurban Clin. Club (pres. 1987—88), Am. Soc. Human Genetics (cert. 1987), Am. Assn. Immunologists, Assn. Am. Physicians, Am. Soc. for Clin. Investigation, Alpha Omega Alpha (councillor Delta of N.Y. 1982—2002). Achievements include elucidation of pathophysiologic mechanisms, delineation of molecular and biochemical defects of genetic disorders including adenosine deaminase and glycogen storage disease type II. Office: NYU Med Ctr 550 1st Ave CD612 New York NY 10016-6402 Office Phone: 212-263-6276. Business E-Mail: hirscr01@med.nyu.edu.

HIRSCHMAN, KAREN L., lawyer; b. York, Pa., Dec. 15, 1952; BA, U. Del., 1973; MA, U. Tex., 1980, JD with honors, 1983. Bar: Tex. 1983, DC 2002, NY 2003. Ptnr., co-head Litig. Sect. Vinson & Elkins LLP, Dallas. Fellow: Tex. Bar Found.; mem.: ABA, Am. Law Inst. Office: Vinson & Elkins LLP Trammell Crow Ctr 2001 Ross Ave, Ste 3700 Dallas TX 75201 Office Phone: 214-220-7795. Business E-Mail: khirschman@velaw.com.

HIRSCHMAN, SARAH, educator; b. Kaunas, Lithuania, Feb. 25, 1921; came to U.S., 1939; d. Nicholas and Fania (Waissman) Chapro; m. Albert O. Hirschman, June 22, 1941; children: Katia Salomon, Lisa. MA, U. Calif., Berkeley, 1942; postgrad., Columbia U., 1943. Instr. French, Russian Fgn. Svc. Inst. Dept. of State, Washington, 1948-50; research asst. Twentieth Century Fund, N.Y.C., 1960-63, Brookings Inst., Washington, 1964-66; research assoc. Ctr. Study on Edn. and Devel. Harvard U., Cambridge, Mass., 1967; instr. Dorchester Skill and Tng. Ctr., Boston, 1967-68; coord. field work Overseas Edn. Fund Inst., Boston, 1969; project dir. Latino Inst., Reston, Va., 1981-82, CEDES, Buenos Aires, 1983, N.J. Coun. for Humanities, New Brunswick, NJ, 1985—. Ind. scholar Princeton Research Forum, 1981—; founder People and Stories, N.J., 1973—. Author: Gente y Cuentos-Educación Popular y Literatura, 1984. Vol. various Latino community groups, Boston, and Trenton, N.J., 1972-80. Taussig Traveling fellow U. Calif., 1942-43; grantee Latino Inst., NEH, 1981-82, N.J. Coun. for Humanities, 1986—. Home and Office: 16 Newlin Rd Princeton NJ 08540-4916 Office Phone: 609-393-3230. E-mail: sh@ias.edu.

HIRSH, CRISTY J., principal; b. Dallas, Oct. 3, 1952; d. Bernard and Johanna (Cristol) Hirsh. BS in Early Childhood and Elem. Edn., Boston U., Mass., 1974; MS in Spl. Edn., U. Tex., Dallas, 1978; MEd in Counseling and Student Svcs., U. North Tex., Denton, 1991. Cert. counselor, sch. counselor; lic. profl. counselor, Tex.; cert. tchr., Tex., Mass.; cert. prin., Tex. Dir., learning specialist Specialized Learning, Dallas, 1981—93; counselor, mem. adj. faculty Eastfield Coll., Mesquite, Tex., 1992—95; counselor Grapevine-Colleyville Ind. Sch. Dist., Tex., 1995—2000, alternative sch. prin., 2000—. Mem. adj. faculty Richland Coll., Dallas, 1991—92. Mem. ACA, ASCD, Am. Sch. Counselor Assn., Coun. for Exceptional Children, Coun. for Children with Behavior Disorders, Tex. Assn. for Alternative Edn., Pi Lambda Theta, Phi Delta Kappa. Avocations: travel, theater, films, cooking, reading. Office: VISTA Alternative Campus 3051 Ira E Woods Ave Grapevine TX 76051-3817

HIRSH, SHARON LATCHAW, academic administrator, art history educator; b. Mt. Lebanon, Pa., Apr. 19, 1948; d. Raymond J. and Mary Cassel (Hudock) Latchaw; m. Neil Hirsh (dec.); 1 child, Michael. BA, Rosemont Coll., 1970; MA, U. Pitts., 1971, PhD, 1974. From asst. prof. to prof. Dickinson Coll., Carlisle, Pa., 1974—2005, Charles A. Dana prof. art history; acting pres. Rosemont Coll., Bryn Mawr, Pa., 2005—06, pres., 2006—. Vis. curator Montreal Mus. Fine Arts, 1989, Schweizerisch Institute für Kunstwissenschaft in Zurich; dir. Trout Gallery, Carlisle, Pa., 1992; vis. sr. fellow Ctr. for Advanced Studies in Visual Arts, Nat. Gallery, 1998; vis. scholar Art Inst. Chgo. Co-curator Ferdinand Hodler: Views and Visions exhibit, Cin. Mus. Art, Nat. Acad. Design, Ontario Art Gallery, Wadsworth Atheneum Mus.; author: Ferdinand Hodler, 1981, Hodler's Symbolist Themes, 1983, Fine Art of the Gesture, 1989, Symbolism and Modern Urban Soc., 2004; co-editor: Art, Culture, and National Identity in Fin-de-Siecle Europe, 2003; contbr. articles to profl. jours. Recipient Ganoe award for Inspiration Teaching, 1981, Lindback award for Disting. Teaching, 1991; Andrew Mellon grantee, 1972, 1973. Mem.: Interdisciplinary Nineteenth Century Studies Assn., Coll. Art Assn. Office: Rosemont Coll Office of Pres 1400 Montgomery Ave Bryn Mawr PA 19010 Office Phone: 610-527-0200.*

HIRSHBERG, JENNEFER, public affairs executive; BA, Cornell U., 1965; attended, Harvard U., UCLA; grad., Calif. State U., Los Angeles. Former dir., corp. comm. Bendix Automation; former dir., pub. affairs FTC; former press secretary First Lady Nancy Reagan; former asst. dir., office of mgmt. and budget for comm. and pub. liaison The White House; former sr. v.p., corp. strategic comm. Ogilvy & Mather Pub. Affairs; former exec. v.p. Kaufman Pub. Relations; with Capitoline Internat. Group, 1992—98, mng. dir. pub. relations then pres., CEO, 1999; pres. Capitoline Comm.; ptnr. Alcalde & Fay, 2000—, co-chair, edu. practice group. Bd. dirs. Multiple Sclerosis Soc., Girls Inc., Am. Woman's Economic Develop. Corp.; mem. President's Council of Cornell Women; mem. adv. com. Washington Race for the Cure. Office: Alcalde & Fay 400 N Capitol St NW Ste 475 Washington DC 20001

HIRSHTAL, EDITH, retired concert pianist, educator, chamber musician; b. Bregenz, Austria, May 31, 1950; d. Izak and Sabina (Silbershein) Hirschthal; 1 child, Jessica Elise. B of Music, Temple U., 1973, M of Music, 1975; artist diploma, Peabody Conservatory, 1983; studied with Leon Fleisher, studied with Adele Marcus, studied with Harvey Wedeen. Adj. faculty mem. Temple U., Phila., 1973-83, Bryn Mawr (Pa.) Conservatory, 1980-83; pianist, mem. faculty Downeast Summer Chamber Inst., 1983, Dobbs Ferry Chamber Inst., 1984; prof. piano emeritus Calif. State U., Long Beach, 1984—2001, ret., 2002. Collaborations with Phila. Opera Co., Sequoia Quartet, Joanne Faletta, Mostovoy Concerto Soloists, Stephanie Chase, Jonathan Mack, Antoinette Perry, Peter Marsh, Michael Carson, Dudley Moore. Musician: (compact discs) Impromptu, Despite the Odds; performed at Weill Recital Hall, N.Y.C., Carnegie Hall, Lincoln Ctr., Alice Tully Hall, co-prodr., co-artistic collaborator, music supr. (documentary) The Phoenix Effect, Nat. Holocaust Meml. Mus., Washington, D.C., 2003. Recipient Galica prize Paderewski Found., Phila., 1970. Democrat. Jewish. Personal E-mail: hirshtal@earthlink.net.

HIRST, KAREN L., theater educator; d. Louis Frederick and Betty Ann Hirst. BS in Theater Arts, MacMurray Coll., Jacksonville, Ill., 1973; student, Cir. in Sq., NYC, 1981. Cert. tchr. Ill., Maine. Mem. Second City, Chgo., 1974—76; artist in residence Oakland Mus., Calif., 1988—91; acting instr. Kathryn Delmar Burke Sch. for Girls, San Francisco, 1994—95; dir. fine arts dept. Harker Acad., Saratoga, Calif., 1995—96; instr. acting Acad. of Art U., San Francisco, 1996—. Tchr. trainer Creative Comedy in the Classroom, 1985—88; tchg. artist, program coord. Wolf trap Inst., 1983—88; tchr. trainer Kennedy Ctr., Washington, 1988. Writer, prodr.: (2 woman show) Digitally Yours, 1996—98; contbr.: Sing Your Sillies Out, 1990. Vol. Tenderloin Elder Friends, San Francisco, 1989—91; contbr. Network Ministries, San Francisco, 1995—. Mem.: Actors Equity, Theater Comms. Group, Theater Bay Area, Bay Area Cmty. of Women. Avocations: travel, improvisation, singing. Office: Acad of Art U 79 New Montgomery San Francisco CA 94105

HIRT, JANE, editor; B in Journalism, U. Nebr., Lincoln. With Chgo. Tribune, 1990—2002, sports copy editor, fgn. and nat. desk copy editor, fgn. and nat. news editor; founding co-editor RedEye, 2002—05, editor, 2005—. Named one of Top 40 Under 40, Crain's Chgo. Bus., 2006. Office: RedEye Tribune Tower 435 N Michigan Ave Chicago IL 60611 E-mail: jhirt@tribune.com.*

HIRT, JOAN B., education educator; b. Huntington, N.Y., Feb. 20, 1951; d. Warren G. and Ruth T. Hirt. BA in Russian Studies, Bucknell U., 1972; MAEd, U. Md., 1979; PhD, U. Ariz., 1992. Assoc. dir. housing and dining svcs. Humboldt State U., Arcata, Calif., 1979-88; assoc. dean students U. Ariz., Tucson, 1988-92; assoc. prof. higher edn. and student affairs Va. Tech. U., Blacksburg, 1994—. Cons. in edn.; corp. cons. Contbr. chpts. to books, articles to profl. jours. Mem. Am. Coll. Pers. Assn. (bd. dirs. CxII 1996-99), Assn. for Study of Higher Edn., Nat. Assn. Student Pers., Am. Coll. Pers. Assn. Office: ELPS 0302-Va Tech U 307 W Eggleston Hall Blacksburg VA 24061 Office Phone: 540-231-9700.

HISCAVICH, MICHELLE, music educator, consultant; b. Suffern, NY, July 14, 1962; d. Lawrence John and Rose Marie Hiscavich. MusB, U. Miami, Coral Gables, Fla., 1984; MEd, U. Mo.-Columbia, 1986; Sixth Yr. Degree in Ednl. Leadership, So. Conn. State U., New Haven, 1994. Cert. initial educator adminstr./supr. Conn., profl. educator music preK-12 Conn. Orch. dir. Ridgefield Pub. Sch., Conn., 1987—88, Newtown Pub. Sch., Conn., 1988—, dir. music, 1995—. Asst. condr. Ridgefield Youth Orch., Conn., 1988—91. Bd. dirs. Danbury Music Ctr., Conn. Mem.: ASCD, Music Educators Nat. Conf., Kappa Delta Pi. Avocations: music, outdoor activites. Office Phone: 203-426-7646. Business E-Mail: hiscavichm@newtown.k12.ct.us.

HISER, PAULA J., medical/surgical nurse; b. Marietta, Ohio, Oct. 9, 1953; d. Larry Richard and Beverly Jane (Wintersteen) Bartmess; m. Gary W. Hiser, June 29, 1973; children, Jeremy Wayne, Joshua Ryan. Diploma, Lakeview Med. Ctr., Danville, Ill., 1984. Med.-surg. nurse United Samaritans Med. Ctr., Danville, Ill., 1989, recovery rm. nurse, 2001—. Office: Ambulatory Surgery Ctr Danville Polyclinic 707 North Logan Ave Danville IL 61832

HISEY, BERNADETTE ANNE, music educator; b. Bay Village, Ohio, May 26, 1959; d. Noel Stephen and Frances Ilg; m. Ernest Lee Hisey, Dec. 28, 1986; children: Joseph, Susan. BS in Music Edn., Cleve. State U., 1982; MS in Music Edn., U. of Akron, Ohio, 1998. Cert. tchr. music K-12 Ohio, 1982. Music tchr. Lorain Cath. H.S., Lorain, Ohio, 1982—84, Bay Mid. Sch., Bay Village, Ohio, 1984—87; k-8 music tchr. St. Peter's Elem., Lorain, Ohio, 1989—93; k-5 music tchr. Harrison Elem. Sch., Lakewood, Ohio, 1993—; asst. music dir. Bay Presbyn. Ch., Bay Village, Ohio, 1980—89. Musical theater dir./actor Mighty Goliath Prodns., Avon Lake, Ohio, 1977—2006, bd. dirs. Avocations: reading, travel. Home: 160 Woodridge Dr Elyria OH 44035 Office: Harrison Elementary School 2080 Quail Ave Lakewood OH 44107 Office Phone: 216-529-4230.

HISLE, LINDA BETH See FRYE, LINDA BETH

HISLOP, KARE ELIZABETH, music director, educator; b. Calif., Aug. 20, 1948; m. Donald Lindsay Hislop, Sept. 9, 1967; children: Victoria, Laurel. BA, Chico State Coll., 1969; MA, Calif. State U., Chico, 1976. Cert. elem. and secondary tchr., Calif. Tchr. Red Bluff (Calif.) H.S., 1971-89, Evergreen Sch. Dist., Cottonwood, Calif., 1980, Elkins Sch., Paskenta, Calif., 1989-93; music dir. First United Meth. Ch., Red Bluff, 1980—; mem. extended edn. staff Shasta Coll., 1986—. Author: Recipies From the Adobe, 1993; co-author: Murder at the Grand Hotel, 1991, Murder in Paradise, 1992, Murder at Mugsy's, 1993, Death in the West, 1994, Death in the Caribbean, 1995, The Speakeasy Caper, 1996. Facilitator Tehama County Child Assault Prevention, Red Bluff, 1990-92; leader, trainer, cons. Sierra Cascade Girl Scout Coun., Red Bluff, 1971-02; dir. Christie Hill Ch. Camp, Red Bluff, 1979-95; bd. dirs., v.p. regional devel. Calif. League of Park Assns., 1998—. Mem. IDE Adobe Interpretive Assn. (pres. 1991-2000), Am. Lung Assn. (murder mystery chair 1990-94), Mystery Weavers (pres. 1994—), Kappa Delta Pi. United Methodist. Avocations: music, cake decorating, reading. E-mail: khislop@shastacollege.gov.

HISS, SHEILA MARY, librarian; b. Evanston, Ill., May 7, 1949; d. Bernard F. and Mary Cecelia (Schubert) H.; m. John D. Hales Jr., Oct. 16, 1976; children: Christina Marie, John D. III. BA in History, Mundelein Coll., 1971; MLS, Ind. U., 1973; postgrad., Florence (Italy) Study Ctr., 1986, Fla. State U. Libr. art and music dept. Jacksonville (Fla.) Pub. Libr., 1974-76; asst. libr. North Fla. Jr. Coll., Madison, 1977-91; dir. libr. svcs. North Fla. C.C., Madison, 1991—. Mem. adv. bd. Coll. Ctr. for Libr. Automation, Tallahassee, Fla., 1991—, mem. exec. com., 1994-96, 98-2004, chmn. exec. com. 2000-01, state joint selection com., 2001-02 Contbr. articles to profl. jours. Mem.: ALA, Beta Phi Mu. Roman Catholic. Avocations: weaving, basketry. Home: 13337 County Road 136 Live Oak FL 32060-6366 Office: North Fla Cmty Coll 325 NW Turner Davis Dr Madison FL 32340-1602

HITCH, MELANIE AUDREY, orthopaedic nurse; b. Chgo., Sept. 19, 1947; d. Alden Edwards and Frances (Gillette) Snell; m. David C. Hitch, Sept. 2, 1972; children: Charles Joseph, Kathryn Elizabeth Frances. AA, Va. Intermont, Bristol, Va., 1967; BSN, U. Va., 1969; MS, U. Okla., 1982. Head nurse U. Va. Hosp., Charlottesville, 1969-73; clin. nurse specialist Sunnybrook Med. Ctr., Toronto, Ont., Can., 1973-75; staff nurse Bapt. Hosp., Memphis, 1975; head nurse Porter Meml. Hosp., Denver, 1976-78; physician's asst. Kaiser Permanent, Denver, 1978; clin. nurse specialist Okla. Children's Meml. Hosp., Oklahoma City, 1978-82; instr. Cazonovia (N.Y.) Coll., 1983; clin. nurse specialist Onondaga County Health Dept. Long Term Health Care, Syracuse, NY, 1983-89; supr. Montgomery County Combined Health Dist., Dayton, Ohio, 1990—. Preceptor Syracuse U., 1986—89; adj. asst. prof. Sch. Nursing SUNY, Syracuse, 1988—89; mem. affiliate faculty Sch. Medicine Wright State U., Dayton, 1990—; reviewer Orthop. Nursing Jour., 1998—. Co-author: An Introduction to Orthopaedic Nursing: An Orientation Module, 1991; editor: (video) Total Hip Replacement-Patient Education (1st pl. Am. Jour. Nursing Patient Edn. Media award, 1994); reviewer: Orthopedic Nursing Jour., 2001—. Named Neonatal Intensive Home Care, Nat. Assn. Counties, 1987; recipient Otto Au Franc award, Hip Soc., New Orleans, 1982. Mem.: Dayton Area Orthop. Nurses (pres. 1992—93, 2004—05), Orthop. Nurses Assn. (bd. dir. 1974—75, mem. nat. nominating com. 1975—77, v.p. 1977—78, sec. 1978—80), Nat. Assn. Orthop. Nurses (edn. approval com. 1984—, com. chair 1991, mem. nominating com. 1998—2001, chair 2000—01). Episcopalian. Avocations: skiing, gardening, sailing. Home: 4962 Walther Rd Kettering OH 45429-1944 Office: 117 S Main St # 230 Dayton OH 45402-2005

HITCHCOCK, JANE STANTON, playwright, novelist; b. NYC, Nov. 24, 1946; d. Robert Tinkham Crowley and Joan (Alexander) Stanton; m. William Mellon Hitchcock, Oct. 10, 1975 (div. Jan. 1991); m. Jim Hoagland, July 14, 1995. BA, Sarah Lawrence Coll., Bronxville, 1964-68. Author: Grace, 1982, Trick of the Eye, 1992 (Edgar award nominee, Hammett prize nominee), The Witches' Hammer, 1994, Social Crimes, 2002, One Dangerous Lady, 2005; screenwriter Our Time, 1974, First Love, 1976; producer Stalking Immortality (documentary) 1978; playwright Grace, 1981, Bhutan or Black Tie in the Himalayas, 1983, The Custom of the Country, 1986, Vanilla, 1990. Mem. PEN, The Dramatists' Guild, The Writers' Guild. Avocations: weightlifter, medieval literature, book collecting.

HITCHCOCK, JOANNA, publisher; b. London; BA, Oxford (Eng.) U., 1960, MA in Modern History, 1965. Asst. publicity dept. Oxford U. Press, London, 1962-66; asst. promotion mgr. Princeton (N.J.) Univ. Press, 1966-68, advt. and exhibits mgr., 1968-69, staff editor, 1970-72, mng. editor, 1972-80, exec. editor, 1980-84, asst. dir., 1985-87, exec. editor for humanities, 1988-92; dir. U. of Tex. Press, Austin, 1992—. Mem. Princeton U. Libr. Coun., 1986-95; adv. com. Tex. Book Festival, 1996-. Mem. Am. Assn. Univ. Presses (bd. dirs. 1984-87, chair equal opportunities com. 1985-86, ann. program planning com. 1986-87, pres. 1997-98, past pres. 1998-99). Home: 1507 Preston Ave Austin TX 78703-1903 Office: Univ of Texas Press PO Box 7819 Austin TX 78713-7819

HITCHCOCK, KAREN RUTH, biology professor, dean, academic administrator; b. Feb. 10, 1943; d. Roy Clinton and Ruth (Wardell) H. BS in Biology, St. Lawrence U., 1964; PhD in Anatomy, U. Rochester, 1969. Postdoctoral fellow in pulmonary cell biology Webb-Waring Inst. Med. Rsch., 1968-70; asst. prof. dept. anatomy Tufts U. Sch. Medicine, Boston, 1970-75, assoc. prof. dept. anatomy, 1975-80, assoc. prof., acting chmn. dept. anatomy, 1978-80, prof., chmn. dept. anatomy and cellular biology, 1980-82, George A. Bates prof. histology, 1982-85, chmn. dept. anatomy and cellular biology, 1982-85; prof. dept. cell biology and anatomy Tex. Tech. U. Health Scis. Ctr.; assoc. dean Tex. Tech. U. Sch. Medicine, Lubbock, 1985-87; vice chancellor rsch., dean grad. coll. U. Ill., Chgo., 1987-91, prof. cell biology, anatomy and biol. scis., 1987-91; v.p. acad. affairs, prof. biol. scis. U. at Albany, SUNY, 1991-95, interim pres., 1995-96, pres., 1996—2004; prin. Queens Univ., ON, Canada, 2004—. Mem. nat. adv. rsch. resources coun. NIH, 1992-96, Nat. Bd. Med. Examiners, 1987-95; bd. dirs. N.Y. Capital Region Ctr. Econ. Growth, 1996—; mem. steering com. Assn. Colls. & Univs. State N.Y., 1995—; mem. N.Y. State Senate Higher Edn. com. adv. com., 1995—; pres., bd. dirs. Capital Region Info. Svc., N.Y., 1995—; bd. dirs. Charter One Bank F.S.B., 1999. Mem. exec. com. Gov.'s Sci. Adv. Com., Ill., 1991; pres. Albany-Colonie C. of C., 1999. Mem. Am. Assn. Anatomists (exec. com. 1981-85, v.p. 1986-88, pres. 1990-91), Nat. Assn. for Biomed. Rsch. (bd. dirs. 1990-92), Nat. Assn. State Univs. and Land-Grant Colls. (chair coun. acad. affairs com. 1994-95), Ill. Soc. Med. Rsch. (pres. 1988-91).

HITCHCOCK, SUSAN Y., principal; b. South Gate, Calif., Oct. 3, 1948; d. Ralph Wayne and Evelyn Angela Hitchcock; m. David Michael Akin, July 21, 1972 (div. 1989); 1 child, David Michael Akin Jr.; m. Jerry Lee Glenn, July 1, 1995. BS in Bus. Adminstrn., Calif. State U., Sacramento, 1979; MA in Edn., U. Pacific, 1997. Cert. tchr., adminstr. Calif., adminstrv. svcs. credential Calif. Loan officer Bank of Am. NT&SA, Mountain View, Calif., 1967-74; tchr. St. Anne Sch., Lodi, Calif., 1981-92, Lodi Mid. Sch., 1992-97, Morado Middle Sch., 1997—99, vice prin., 1999—2001; prin. Clairmont Elem. Sch., Stockton, 2001—. Spkr. on urban land use planning League Calif. Cities, Sacramento, 1985-95. Mem. City Coun., City of Lodi, 1998—, planning commr., 1981-95, Mayor, 2002—; grand juror San Joaquin County, Stockton, 1979-80. Mem. AAUW (pres.). Roman Catholic. Avocation: travel. Home: 2443 Macarthur Pkwy Lodi CA 95242-3252 Office: Clairmont Elem Sch 8282 LeMans Ave Stockton CA 95210

HITE, SHERE D., writer, historian; b. St. Joseph, Mo., Nov. 2, 1942; m. Friedrich Hoericke, 1985. BA cum laude, U. Fla., 1964, MA, 1968; postgrad., Columbia U., 1968-69. Dir. feminist sexuality project NOW, NYC, 1972-78; dir. Hite Rsch. Internat., NYC, 1978—; instr. female sexuality NYU, 1977—. Lectr. Harvard U., McGill U., Columbia U., Cambridge U. (Eng.), The Sorbonne, Paris, Oxford U., 1995-96, also numerous women's groups; internat. lectr., 1977-98; vis. prof. Nihon U., Japan, 1998—; mem. adv. bd. Am. Found. Gender and Genital Medicine, Johns Hopkins U. Author: Sexual Honesty: By Women for Women, 1974, The Hite Report: A Nationwide Study of Female Sexuality, 1976, The Hite Report on Male Sexuality, 1981, Women and Love: A Cultural Revolution in Progress, 1987, Fliegen mit Jupiter, 1993, The Hite Report on the Family: Icons of the Heart, 1994, Women as Revolutionary Agents of Change: The Hite Reports and Beyond, 1994, The Divine Comedy of Ariadne and Jupiter, 1994, The Hite Report on the Family: Growing Up Under Patriarchy, 1994, The Hite Report on Hite (on Herself): A Sexual & Political Autobiography, 1996, The Shere Hite Reader: Sex, Globalization, and Private Life, 2005; co-author: Good Guys, Bad Guys: The Hite Guide to Smart Choices, 1991, Sex and Business, 1999; cons. editor Jour. Sex Edn. and Therapy, Jour. Sexuality and Disability; columnist El Mundo, O Globo, America, Del Std. Recipient Nike Feminist award, 1997, 98, 99. Mem. NOW, AAAS, Am. Hist. Assn., Am. Sociol. Assn., Acad. Polit. Sci., Soc. for Women in Philosophy, Internat. Women Writer's Orgn. (v.p.). Office: 2 Soho Sq London W1V England Mailing: c/o Fifi Oscard Agy 16th fl 110 W 40th St New York NY 10018 Business E-Mail: info@hite-research.com.

HITSELBERGER, CAROL A., lawyer; b. Washington, Jan. 7, 1964; AB magna cum laude, Bryn Mawr Coll., 1986; JD cum laude, Univ. Pa., 1989. Bar: Ill. 1989. Assoc. Mayer Brown Rowe & Maw, Chgo., 1989—98, ptnr., fin. & securitization, 1998—. Author (contbg.): Securitization of Financial Assets, 2001. Mem.: ABA. Office: Mayer Brown Rowe Maw Llp 230 S La Salle St Ste 400 Chicago IL 60604-1407 Office Phone: 312-701-7740. Office Fax: 312-706-8151. Business E-Mail: chitselberger@mayerbrownrowe.com.

HIXSON, ALLIE CORBIN, retired adult education educator, advocate; b. Columbia, Ky., May 28, 1924; d. Alfred B. Corbin and Emma Triplett-Corbin; m. William Forrest Hixson, Aug. 16, 1945; children: Mary Emma, Clarence Hervey, Walter Lawrence. BA in English, Okla. A&M Coll., 1949; MA in Humanities, U. Louisville, 1961, PhD in English, 1969. Sec.-bookkeeper Ky. Farm Bur., Louisville, 1942-45; tchr. English Pub. H.S., Stillwater, Okla., 1949, various secondary schs., Louisville, 1957-64, Ind. U. S.E., Jeffersonville, 1965-69, Bellarmine Coll., Louisville, 1970; head English dept. Collegiate Prep. Girls Sch., Louisville, 1970-74; tchr. Began All-Vol. Feminist Advocacy, 1975-95; ret., 1995. Spkr. in field. Author: A Critical Study of Edwin Muir, 1977, (with Riane Eisler) ERA Facts and Action Guide, 1986 (Sally Bingham award, grant 1986), (with Martha Grise) Survey of Rural Displaced Homemakers, 1980 (nat. funding AAUW, 1979). Lobbyist women's issues Ky. Women Advs., Frankfort, 1975-78; co-organizer, chmn. Ky. Pro-ERA Alliance-Statewide, 1975-95; chmn. coordinating com. Ky. Internat. Women's Year, 1977; co-chmn. Internat. Women's Yr. continuing com. Houston Conf., 1985-89; state rep. Nat. Women's Polit. Caucus, Louisville, 1978; charter mem., State and Nat. Older Women's Leagues, Louisville, 1980; founder, chmn. Nat. ERA Summit, Washington, 1991-97. Recipient ERA Advocacy award Ky. Pro ERA Alliance, 1996, Women's Equity Action League, 1997, Celebration of Svc. Women of Distinction award, 2003; named Feminist of Yr. Ky. NOW, 1999, One of Most Prominent Feminist leaders in Ky., 2001; named to Ky. Women Remembered permanent exhibit. Mem. AAUW (pres. Ky. Divsn. 1980-84, Predoctoral U. Louisville Coll. Faculty award 1964-65), Campbellsville Bus. and Profl. Women (past pres., nat. ERA chmn. 1975-76; Ky. Woman of Distinction 1991, 2001, 2003), Kappa Delta Gamma (hon.). Democrat. Unitarian Universalist. Avocations: reading, writing memoir, caring for pets, bird watching, taking walks. Home: 3318 Hunsinger Ln Louisville KY 40220 Personal E-mail: alliec@iglou.com.

HIXSON, KATHRYN, art critic; Studio graduate, Sch. of the Art Inst. Chgo. Curator, contemporary art; tchr., contemporary art and conceptual art theory, dept. art criticism, history, and theory Sch. of the Art Inst. Chgo. Writer, art criticism, Chgo., 1985—, New Art Examiner, Arts Magazine, NY, Flash Art, Milan, Italy, writer (of catalogue essays for galleries and mus.), former editor New Art Examiner. Mem.: Chgo. Art Critics Assn. Address: 900 Grove St Evanston IL 60201 E-mail: kathrynhixson@earthlink.net.

HLAWATY, HEIDE, science educator, researcher; d. Rudolf and Elisabeth Hlawaty. BS in Biochem., SUNY, Stony Brook, 1987; MA in Biol. Sciences, Hunter Coll., NYC, 1992; PhD of Edn., St. John's U., Queens, NY, 2002. Rsch. asst. NY Blood Svcs., NYC, 1987—90; sci. tchr. John Adams HS, South Ozone Park, 1990—96, Hicksville HS, Hicksville, NY, 1996—2002; asst. prof. Ga. Coll. and State U., Macon, 2002—05, Met. Coll. NY, NYC, 2005—, chair-core curriculum, 2006—. Doctoral com. St. John's U., Queens, 2005—. Active Sacred Music Chorale of Richmond Hill. Grantee, Fulbright Assn., 1995—96. Mem.: AAUW, Am. Polit. Sci. Assn., Fulbright Assn., Nat. Sci. Tchr. Assn., Am. Ednl. Rsch. Assn., Amnesty Internat., Phi Delta Kappa. E-mail: hhlawaty@aol.com.

HLOZEK, CAROLE DIANE QUAST, finance company executive; b. Dallas, Apr. 17, 1959; d. Robert E. and Bonnie (Wootton) Quast. BS, BBA, Tex. A&M U., 1982. CPA Tex.; cert. prin. Nat. Assn. Securities Dealers. Internal auditor Brown & Root Inc., Houston, 1982-84; asst. contr. Wilson Supply Co., Houston, 1984-86; sr. acctg. supr. Hydro Conduit Corp., Houston, 1986-87; fin. analyst Am. Capital, Houston, 1989-94; dir. adminstrn. Am. Gen. Securities, Inc., Houston, 1994-98; CFO 1st Fin. Group Am., Houston, 1998-2000; contr. Clearworks, 2000-01; dir. Ornate Holdings Inc., Houston, 2001—02; full time cons. Robert Half Internat., 2002—03; contr., v.p. finance eLinear Technologics, 2003—04; dir. acctg., interim CAO Quantlab, 2004—. Chmn. bd. dirs. On Our Own, Inc., 1987-91; mentor CPA's Helping Schs.; treas. Sampson Elem. PTO, 2002-04. Mem. Mensa, Houston Livestock Show and Rodeo. Home: 13527 Greenwood Manor Cypress TX 77429-4840

HO, BETTY JUENYÜ YÜLIN, retired music educator, physiologist, educator; b. Nanking, China, Nov. 20, 1930; came to U.S., 1947; d. William Tien-Hu and Gwei-Hsin (Wang) Ho; m. Lajos Rudolf Elkan, Feb. 27, 1958 (div. Aug. 1967); children: Amanda, Anita, Julien (dec.), Raoul. Student, We. Coll., Oxford, Ohio, 1947—48; BS, Columbia U., 1952; postgrad., Lausanne U., Switzerland, 1955—56, piano studies with Maurice Perrin, Lausanne, 1956—58, CCNY, 1966—67, postgrad., 1972—74. Lab. technician Columbia U., N.Y.C., 1953—54; ct. report typist Palais de Justice, Lausanne, 1956—57; pianist, accompanist Ecole de Ballet Mara Dousse, Lausanne, 1958—60; tchr. English Montcalme Inst., Lausanne, 1960—61; tchr. piano Le Manoir Inst., Lausanne, 1960—61, N.Y.C., 1964—65. Rsch. dir. Juvenescent Rsch. Corp., N.Y.C., 1963— Author: The Living Function of Sleep, Life & Aging, 1967, The Origin of Variation of Races of Mankind & The Cause of Evolution, 1969, A Scientific Guide to Peaceful Living, 1972, A Chinese and Western Guide to Better Health and Longer Life, 1974, How to Stay Healthy A Lifetime Without Medicines, 1979, A Chinese & Western Daily Practical Health Guide, 1982, Immediate Hints to Health Problems, 1991, 101 Ways to Live 150 Years Young and Healthy, 1993, A Unique Health Guide for Young People, 1994, A Unique Guide for Health, Youth, and Longevity, 1993, How To Live a Long Life, 2004 Named Citizen of Yr. Principality Hutt River Province, Queensland, Australia, 1994, Royal Patronage Status for Life, 1995; recipient XXth Century Achievement award, I1997, nternat. Order Merit, 1993, World Medal Freedom, 2006. Achievements include patents for infant feeding method. Home and Office: Juvenescent Research Corp 807 Riverside Dr Apt 1F New York NY 10032-7352 Office Phone: 212-795-2292.

HO, YINHSIN, retired mathematician, artist; m. Chungwu Ho, June 20, 1964; children: Minnie, Ronald. BS, U. Wash., 1964; MS, Northeastern U., 1967; postgrad., St. Louis U., 1972—76. Lectr. U. Mo., St. Louis, 1974—76, So. Ill. U., Edwardsville, 1976—81; engr., sr. engr. McDonnell Douglas Inc., St. Louis, 1981—91; instr. Belleville (Ill.) Area Coll., 1991—97. One-woman shows include Chinese Cultural Ctr., St. Louis, 1999, exhibitions include East Meet West, 2000; actor: Chinese Arts Assn., 2002; painting included in, 20th Anniversary Art Book of Chinese Art Assn. Pres. St. Louis Chinese Painting Club, 1991; mem. South Bay Chinese Opera Group, San Jose, Calif., 2001. Recipient 3d place award, Gateway East Artist Guild, Belleville, 1997, award of excellence, Asian Pacific Art Inst., N.Y.C., 1999, medal, Asian Pacific Art Inst., 1999. Mem.: Chinese Art Assn. Avocations: Chinese opera singing, erhu, writing. Home: 3261 Falls Creek Dr San Jose CA 95135

HOAG, REBECCA EBNER, literature and language educator; b. Houston, July 31, 1949; d. Thomas and Corinne Hall Ebner; m. Richard A. Hoag (div.). BA, Trinity U., San Antonio, 1971, M in Edn., 1975. Lic. profl. counselor. English tchr. San Antonio Ind. Sch. Dist., San Antonio, 1971—79; counselor, English tchr. Boerne Ind. Sch. Dist., Tex., 1979—81; English tchr., film and creative writing tchr. Tom C. Clark HS, Northside Ind. Sch. Dist., San Antonio, 1981—. Home: 5150 De Zavala Rd San Antonio TX 78249-2096

HOAG, TAMI, writer; b. 1959; Author: McKnight in Shining Armor, 1988, The Trouble with J.J., 1988, Straight from the Heart, 1989, Mismatch, 1989, Man of Her Dreams, 1989, Rumor Has It, 1989, Magic, 1990, Tempestuous, 1990, The Rainbow Chasers: Heart of Gold, 1990, The Rainbow Chasers: Keeping Company, 1990, The Rainbow Chasers: Reilly's Return, 1990, Heart of Dixie, 1991, Sarah's Sin, 1991, Magic, 1991, The Restless Heart, 1991, The Last White Knight, 1992, Taken by Storm, 1992, Lucky's Lady, 1992, Still Waters, 1992, Cry Wolf, 1993, Dark Paradise, 1994, Night Sins, 1995, Guilty as Sin, 1996, A Thin Dark Line, 1997, Ashes to Ashes, 2000, Dust to Dust, 2002, Lucky's Lady, 2003, Dark Horse, 2004, Kill the Messenger, 2004. Office: Andrea Cirillo Jane Rotrosen Agency 318 East 51st St New York NY 10022

HOAGLAND, CAROLYN MARKHAM, retired secondary school educator; d. Henry Stuart and Mary Alice (Taylor) Markham; m. Richard Havis Hoagland Jr.; 1 child, Richard Havis III. BA in Christian Edn., James Madison U., Harrisburg, Va.; MA, Scarritt Coll., Nashville. Tchr. Patrick Copeland Sch., Hopewell, Va., Richard Bland Coll., Petersburg, Va., Carter Woodsen & Hopewell HS; tutoring coord. Hopewell HS. Home: 12704 Bay Hill Dr Chester VA 23836-2680

HOAGLAND, CHRISTINA GAIL, occupational therapist, industrial drafter; b. Long Beach, Calif., July 18, 1954; d. Joseph Richard and Dorothy Marian (Bell) H. BS in Occupl. Therapy, Loma Linda U., 1975; AS in Indsl. Drafting Tech., Mt. San Antonio Coll., 1985. Registered occupl. therapist; cert. brain injury specialist Am. Acad. for the Cert. Brain Injury Specialists. Occupl. therapist Yuka Mission Hosp., Zambia, Africa, 1976-77; staff occupl. therapist Glendale (Calif.) Adventist Med. Ctr., 1978-79; indsl. drafter Amerex Co., Riverside, Calif., 1985-88; re-entry occupl. therapist Rancho Los Amigos, Downey, Calif., 1989-90; staff occupl. therapist Corona (Calif.) Cmty. Hosp., 1990-92; occupl. therapist Linda R. Brown, Visalia, Calif., 1992; floating staff occupl. therapist Hilltop Rehab. Hosp., Grand Junction, Colo., 1992—95, St. Mary's Rehab. Ctr., Grand Junction, 1995—97; OTR, ind. living skills trainer supr. Interim Home Health Care, 1998—; floating staff occupl. therapist Grand Junction Cmty. Hosp., 2000—. Bd. mem. Brain Injury Trust Fund. Bd. dirs. LWV, Mesa County, Colo. Mem. Am. Occupl. Therapy Assn., Occupl. Therapy Assn. Colo. Nat. Mus. Women in Arts, Western Colo. Ctr. for the Arts. Democratic Socialist. Seventh-Day Adventist. Home: 578 N 26th St Grand Junction CO 81501-7961

HOARE, SISTER MARY GABRIEL, nun, educator; b. Denver, Mar. 28, 1929; d. Patrick Joseph Hoare and Mary Josephine Breen. BA in Speech and Drama, Loretto Heights Coll., Denver, 1951; MA in Art, Notre Dame U., South Bend, Ind., 1962; spl. student, Sch. Design and Arch. U. Calif., Berkeley, 1968; MA in Gerontology, Webster U., St. Louis, 1983. Cert. in gerontology U. Mich., 1972, mem. Sisters of Loretto. Tchr. Holy Family Elem. Sch., South Pasadena, Calif., 1954—56; tchr. art and drama Nerinx Hall H.S., St. Louis, 1956—63; chair art dept. Webster Coll. (now Webster U.), 1963—70, prof. art edn., 1974—89, asst. dean academic advising, 1974—84, prof. emeritus, 1989; svc. provider healthcare and aging Loretto Cmty., 1990—2000; coord. aesthetic edn. Nerinx Hall H.S., 1997—. Dir. Arts for the Elderly Mo. Office on Aging, St. Louis, 1978. Prin. works include Mary Meets Jesus, Road to Calvary (publ. in Mo. Arts, 1965). Bd. dir. The Learning Ctr., St. Louis, 1970, Webster U. Alumni, 1990—96. Recipient Faculty Recognition award, Nerinx Hall H.S., 2002. Mem.: Loretto Earth Network (bd. dir. Loretto cmty. 1990—). Avocation: environmental activist. Office: Nerinx Hall HS 530 E Lockwood Ave Saint Louis MO 63119-3217 Home: 2816 Manderly Dr Brentwood MO 63144

HOART, GLADYS GALLAGHER, language educator; b. N.Y.C., June 27, 1914; d. Martin and Edna (Parker) Gallagher; m. Francis Xavier Hoart, June 25, 1939; children: Robert, Helen, Andrew (dec.). AB cum laude, NYU, 1967, MA, 1970; MA in Liberal Studies, New Sch. for Social Rsch., 1975. Cert. mem. NYSE. Adj. prof. English Nassau C.C., Garden City, N.Y., 1970—. Dir. Career Seminars for Teenage Girls, Flushing, N.Y., 1963-64; tutor Black Studies Program, Manhasset, N.Y., 1968-69. Pres., co-founder Broadway Homeowners' Assn., Flushing, N.Y., 1964-65; committeewoman Dem. Party, Manhasset, N.Y., 1970; organizer Parkchester (N.Y.) Golden Age Club, 1953; trustee Dalcroze Sch. of Music, 1998-04, treas., 2001. Mem. AAUW, Alliance Floor Brokers, Musicians Club (bd. dirs. 1993—, v.p. 2001). Roman Catholic. Avocations: architecture, horseback riding, gardening, music.

HOBART, BILLIE, education educator, consultant; b. Pitts., Apr. 19, 1935; d. Harold James Billingsley and Rose Stephanie (Sladack) Green; m. W.C.H. Hobart, July 20, 1957 (div. 1967); 1 child, Rawson W. BA in English, U. Calif., Berkeley, 1967, EdD, 1992; MA in Psychology, Sonoma State U., Rohnert Park, Calif., 1972. Cert. tchr. Calif., Irlen screener 2003. Asst. prof. Coll. Marin, Kentfield, Calif., 1969-78; freelance cons., writer, 1969—; asst. prof. Contra Costa Coll., San Pablo, Calif., 1986-99, Santa Rosa Jr. Coll., Calif., 1999—. Author: (cookbook) Natural Sweet Tooth, 1974, (non-fiction) Expansion, 1972, Purposeful Self: Coherent Self, 1979, 2002, (non-fiction) Talking to Dead People, 1996, On the Subject of Prayer, 2000, SpaceFlight, 2006, (biography) Captain Granville Perry Swift, California Pioneer and Sonoma Bear, 1999, (fiction) Last Days of Gifted Light, 2000, Timethinner, 2001, Getting to Start, 2001, Clearing to Core, 2002, The Lori Stories, 2006; contbr. articles to profl. jours. Served with WAC, 1953-55. Mem. No. Calif. Coll. Reading Tchrs. Assn. (pres. 1996-98), Mensa, Commonwealth Club San Francisco, Phi Delta Kappa. Home and Office: PO Box 1542 Sonoma CA 95476-1542

HOBBS, ANN S., lawyer; b. Washington, Nov. 20, 1945; BS, U. Md., Coll. Park, 1968; PhD in Biophysics, U. Md., Balt., 1973; JD with honors, U. Md. Sch. Law, 1991. Bar: Md. 1991, US Ct. of Appeals, Federal Circuit 1992, DC 1993, US Patent and Trademark Office. Former rsch. scientist NIH, Md.; former faculty mem. U. Md. Sch. of Medicine; former patent advisor/atty. Office of Tech. Transfer, NIH; atty. priv. practice; ptnr., patent prosecution & intellectual property litigation Venable LLP, Washington, 2005—. Mem.: ABA, DC Bar Assn., Am. Soc. for Biochemistry and Molecular Biology, NY Acad. of Sci. Office: Venable LLP 575 7th St NW Washington DC 20004 Office Phone: 202-344-4651. Office Fax: 202-344-8300. Business E-Mail: ashobbs@venable.com.

HOBBS, BRITA SPENCE, science educator; b. Long Beach, Calif., Oct. 10, 1949; d. Eldon Merle and Dorothy Barber Spence; m. Floyd Mitchell Hobbs, Mar. 21, 1970; 1 child, Teresa Hobbs Manning. AA, Lake City C.C., Fla., 1969; BS, U. Fla., Gainesville, 1972. Cert. tchr. Fla., 1972. Tchr. 7th grade sci. Baker County Mid. Sch., Macclenny, Fla., 1972—. Acrylic paintings (portraits), Baker County historical figures. Sunday sch. tchr. First Bapt. Ch. Macclenny, Fla., 1973—95. Recipient Tchr. of Yr. award, Baker County Mid. Sch., 1984. Mem.: Baker County Edn. Assn. Avocations: painting, cake decorating, knitting. Office: Baker County Mid Sch 211 E Jonathan St Macclenny FL 32063 Office Phone: 904-259-2226. Office Fax: 904-259-0459. Personal E-mail: bhobbs@baker.k12.fl.us.

HOBBS, HELEN HASKELL, medical geneticist; BA, Stanford U., 1974; MD, Case Western Reserve U., 1979. Cert. Am. Bd. Internal Medicine, 1983, Endocrinology & Metabolism, 1986. Intern, internal medicine Columbia-Presbyn. Med. Ctr., NYC, 1979—80; resident, internal medicine Parkland Meml. Hosp., Dallas, 1980—82; chief resident, internal medicine U. Tex. Southwestern, 1982—83, postdoctoral fellow in endocrinology & molecular genetics, 1983—87, asst. prof., 1987—90, assoc. prof., 1991—94, prof. internal medicine & molecular genetics, 1995—; chief med. genetics divsn. U. Tex. Southwestern Med. Ctr., Dallas, 1995—, dir. McDermott Ctr. Human Growth & Devel., 2000—; investigator Howard Hughes Med. Inst., 2002—. Consulting editor Circulation, 2001—. Fellow: Am. Acad. Arts & Sciences; mem.: Am. Soc. Human Genetics, Am. Heart Assn. (est. investigator 1990—95), Am. Soc. Clin. Investigation (nat. coun. 1992—94, v.p. 1996—97), Assn. Am. Physicians, Inst. Medicine. Office: UT Southwestern Med Ctr at Dallas 6000 Harry Hines Blvd Dallas TX 75390-9046 Office Phone: 214-648-6724. Office Fax: 214-648-7539. E-mail: helen.hobbs@utsouthwestern.edu.*

HOBDY, JERRILYN, nurse midwife; b. Nashville, Apr. 24, 1952; BSN, U. Miss. Med. Ctr., Jackson, 1975; MS in Maternal-Child Nursing/Midwifery, Columbia U., 1978. Registered gen. nurse and midwife, U.K.; registered nurse-midwife, Pa. Educator Childbirth Edn. Assn., Jackson, 1974-75; staff nurse, charge nurse in obstetrics Roosevelt Hosp., N.Y.C., 1975-77; from instr. to asst. prof. maternal-newborn Yale U., New Haven, 1979-82; staff midwife Rosie Maternity Hosp., Cambridge (Eng.) Area Health Authority, 1984-85; pvt. practice clin. midwifery Buffalo, 1986-89; clin. midwife Woman Nurse-Midwifery Svcs. Inc., Pa. Hosp., Phila., 1989-94; mem. faculty, nurse-midwifery program U. Pa. Sch. Nursing, Phila., 1990-94; acad. adminstr. nurse midwifery program Frontier Sch. Nursing and Midwifery, Phila., 1994-96; assoc. dir. Inst. Midwifery, Women and Health, 1996-97, sec., 1996—, program dir., 1997—. Assoc. editor Jour. Nurse Midwifery, 1982, internat. editor, 1982-85; contbr. numerous articles to profl. jours.; presenter in field. Mem. Am. Coll. Nurse-Midwives. Office: Phila U Hayward Hall Inst Midwifery Women Health Schoolhouse Ln and Henry Av Philadelphia PA 19144

HOBERECHT, REYNOTTA JAHNKE, school system administrator, educator; b. Mattoon, Wis., Mar. 26, 1938; d. Laurence Herman and Magdalena Evelina (Waidelich) Jahnke; m. Hal G. Hoberecht, Sept. 19, 1970; 1 child, Marc. BS, U. Wis., 1961; MA, U. San Francisco, 1978, EDD, 1998. Tchr. Travis (Calif.) Unified Schs., 1971-99, adminstrv. asst., 1995—. Participant Unidad de Paleontologia Expdn., Las Hoyas, Spain, 1992. Ecosystems project award Travis Sch. Bd., 1993. Mem. Calif. Tchrs. Assn. (treas. 1994-99, sec. 1967-68).

HOBERMAN, MARY ANN, author; b. Stamford, Conn., Aug. 12, 1930; d. Milton and Dorothy (Miller) Freedman; m. Norman Hoberman, Feb. 4, 1951; children: Diane, Perry, Charles, Meg. BA, Smith Coll., 1951; MA, Yale U., 1984. With advt. dept. Gimbel's Dept. Store, N.Y.C., 1951-52; newspaper reporter Harrisburg, Pa., 1952; editor N.Y. Graphic Soc., Greenwich, Conn., 1963-64. Poetry cons.; lectr. in field; program coord. C.G. Jung Ctr., N.Y.C., 1981; adj. prof. Fairfield (Conn.) U., 1980-83; instr. Yale U., New Haven, 1989; founder, mem. The Pocket People, 1968-75; founder, performer Women's Voices, 1983-93. Author: All My Shoes Come in Two's, 1957, How Do I Go?, 1958, Hello and Good-by, 1959, What Jim Knew, 1963, Not Enough Beds for the Babies, 1965, A Little Book of Little Beasts, The Raucous Auk, 1973, The Looking Book, 1973, Nuts to You and Nuts to Me, 1974, I Like Old Clothes, 1976, Bugs, 1976, A House Is a House for Me, 1978, Yellow Butter, Purple Jelly, Red Jam, Black Bread, 1981, The Cozy Book, 1982, Mr. and Mrs. Muddle, 1988, A Fine Fat Pig and Other Animal Poems, 1991, Fathers, Mothers, Sisters, Brothers, 1991; editor: My Song is Beautiful, 1994, The Cozy Book, 1995, The Seven Silly Eaters, 1997, One of Each, 1997, Miss Mary Mack, 1998, The Llama Who Had No Pajama, 1998, And to Think that We Thought We Would Never Be Friends, 1999, The Cozy

Book, 1999, The Eensy Weensy Spider, 2000, the Two Sillies, 2000, Michael Finnegan, 2001, It's Simple, Said Simon, 2001, You Read to Me, 2001, The Looking Book, 2002, The Marvelous Mouse Man, 2002, Right Outside My Window, 2002, Bill Grogan's Goat, 2002, Mary Had a Little Lamb, 2003, You Read to Me, I'll Read to You II, 2003, Whose Garden Is It?, 2003, Yankee Doodle, 2003, You Read to Me, I'll Read to You III, 2005. Bd. dirs. Greenwich Libr., 1988-91, Literacy Vols., 1997-2003, Conn. Ctr. for the Book, 2003—. Recipient Nat. Book award, 1984, Poetry for Children award Nat. Coun. Tchrs. of English, 2003. Mem. Authors Guild. Avocations: dance, gardening, hiking, tennis. Home: 98 Hunting Ridge Rd Greenwich CT 06831-3134

HOBOR, NANCY ALLEN, communications executive; b. Chgo., Aug. 18, 1946; d. John Selden and Jane (Rinder) Coulson; m. Michael Joseph Hobor, Apr. 29, 1972; children: Aquinas Adam, Justinian Ram. BA, U. Chgo., 1968, MA, PhD, 1973; MBA, Northwestern U., Evanston, Ill., 1977. Pub. affairs analyst Standard Oil, Chgo., 1973-77; v.p. pub. affairs Am. Hosp. Supply Corp., Evanston, Ill., 1978-86;, 1986-88; dir. investor relations UAL Inc., Chgo., Ill., 1986-88; dir. communications and investor rels. Morton Internat., Ill., 1988--. Dir. AHSC Employee Credit Union, Evanston, Ill., 1984-86; mem. Chgo. Fin. Exchange, 1988—. Fellow: Ford Found., U. Chgo. 1972-73. Office: Morton Internat 100 N Riverside Plz Fl 34 Chicago IL 60606-1501

HOBSON, MELLODY, investment company executive; b. Chgo., Apr. 3, 1969; BA, Woodrow Wilson Sch. Internat. Rels., Princeton U., 1991. Joined mktg. team Ariel Capital Mgmt., Inc., 1991—94, sr. v.p., dir. mktg., 1994—2000, pres., 2000—. Bd. mem. Tellabs, Inc., 2002—; fin. corr. ABC's Good Morning Am. Bd. dir. Chgo. Pub. Edn. Fund, Chgo. Pub. Libr., Field Mus.; bd. trustees Princeton U. Named a Global Leader Tomorrow, World Econ. Forum, Davos, Switzerland, 2001; named one of 30 Leaders of Future, Ebony, 40 under 40, Crain's Chgo. Bus. Office: Ariel Capital Mgmt LLC 200 E Randolph Dr Ste 2900 Chicago IL 60601 Office Phone: 312-726-0140. Office Fax: 312-612-2702.*

HOBSON, SUELLEN ANN WEBER, retired elementary school educator; b. Houston, Apr. 25, 1947; d. Marvin Ernst Herman Weber and Anita Clair Perkins; children: Eric Austin Williamson, Jerod Michael Williamson. BS in Elem. Edn., N.Mex. State U., 1976. Tchr. Alamogordo Pub. Schools, N.Mex., 1977—2006. Educator mentor/workshop facilitator Alamogordo Pub. Sch., 1996—2004. Mem.: N. Mex.'s Classroom Tchr.'s Assn. (assoc.). Mem. Christian Ch. Avocation: reading, art design. Home: 2500 First St Alamogordo NM 88310 E-mail: suellen@barricklow.com.

HOCHBERG, FAITH S., US district court judge; BA summa cum laude, Tufts U., 1972; JD magna cum laude, Harvard U., 1975. Law clk. to Hon. Spottswood W. Robinson III U.S. Ct. Appeals (D.C. cir.), 1975-76; pvt. practice Washington, Boston, Roseland, N.J., 1977-83; asst. U.S. atty. Dist. N.J., Newark, 1983-87; ptnr. Cole, Schotz, Bernstein, Meisel & Forman, Hackensack, NJ, 1987-90; sr. dep. chief counsel Office Thrift Supervision, U.S. Treasury Dept., Jersey City; dep. asst. sec. law enforcement U.S. Treasury Dept., Washington; U.S. Atty. Dist. of N.J., 1994-99; judge U.S. Dist. Ct., 1999—. Office: US Courthouse and PO Bldg Newark NJ 07102

HOCHBERG, JENNIFER ANNE, counselor; b. Conn., May 4, 1974; d. David Keith and Carol Janice Hochberg. BS in Speech Pathology-Audiology, Ithaca Coll., NY, 1997. Residential counselor Kennedy Ctr. Inc., Trumbull, Conn., 1997—. Coord. V-Day Fairfield, 2004—06; com.mem. Fairfield Dem. Town, 2005—06. Vis. scholar Modern Music Masters inductee, Fairfield H.S. Tri-M Chpt., 1992. Democrat. Jewish. Avocations: writing, reading, music, cooking, dance. Home: 232 Church Hill Rd Fairfield CT 06825 Office: Kennedy Ctr Inc 2440 Reservoir Ave Trumbull CT 06611 Office Phone: 203-365-8522.

HOCHBERG, LOIS J., school psychologist; b. Bklyn., Dec. 22, 1942; d. Helen and George Robins; m. Martin N Hochberg, Mar. 5, 1967; children: Leigh Robert, Lauren Kim Benthien. EdM, Teachers Coll., Columbia U., 1974—77. School Psychologist State of NJ. Dept. of Edn., 1981, Learning Disabilities- Teacher Consultant NJ. Dept. of Edn., 1977, Teacher of the Handicapped NJ. Dept. of Edn., 1977, Kindergarten and Common Branch Teacher NY Dept. of Edn., 1964. Elem. sch. tchr. Lynbrook Pub. Schools, Hewlett, NY, 1964—68; ednl. coord. Young World Day Sch., Mahwah, NJ, 1971—75; sch. psychologist Valley Hosp., Ridgewood, NJ, 2001—. Sch. psychologst Woodcliff Lake and Maywood Schools, NJ, 1981—83; sch. psychologist St. Joseph's Hosp. and Med. Ctr., Paterson, NJ, 1982—2001. Mem. and pres. Bd. of Edn., Wyckoff, NJ, 1974—84; founding adv. bd. Wyckoff Cmty. Learning Ctr., NJ, 1976—86. Mem.: NJ. Assn. of Sch. Psychologists, Nat. Assn. Sch. Psychologists, Pi Lambda Theta. Achievements include research in developmental outcome of high-risk premature infants. Home: 344 West Shore Dr Wyckoff NJ 07481 Office: Valley Home Care 15 Essex Rd Ste 9 Paramus NJ 07652-1412 Office Phone: 201-447-8151. E-mail: lhochbe@valleyhealth.com.

HOCHBERG, MARCIA GAIL, psychologist; b. Bklyn., July 4, 1957; d. Bernard and Joan Zinderman; m. Jody Alan Hochberg, June 8, 1980; children: Robert, Shane BA, SUNY, Albany, 1978; PhD, SUNY, Stony Brook, 1985. Lic. psychologist, Pa., N.Y. Psychologist N.Y.C. Bd. Edn., 1982—85; postdoctoral fellow U. Wash., Seattle, 1986—87; psychologist Bryn Mawr Rehab. Hosp., Malvern, Pa., 1987—. Rschr. Stanley H. Kaplan Ednl. Ctr., N.Y.C., 1982-85 Mem. APA Office: Bryn Mawr Rehab Hosp 414 Paoli Pike Malvern PA 19355-3300

HOCHLERIN, DIANE, pediatrician, educator; b. NYC, Feb. 4, 1942; d. William J. and Bertha Hochlerin. BS, U. City of N.Y., 1958; MD, Med. Coll. Pa., 1966. Diplomate Am. Bd. Pediats. Intern Albert Einstein Hosp., Phila., 1966-67; resident Phila. Gen. Hosp., 1967-69; attending pediatrician St. Luke's Roosevelt Hosp., NYC, 1969—; now sr. attending physician St. Luke's Roosevelt Hosp, NYC; clin. assoc. prof. pediats. Columbia U., NYC, 1969—; asst. attending physician Cath. Med. Ctr., NYC, 1993-99. Faculty advisor Adelphi U., N.Y.C., 1994. Fellow Am. Acad. Pediats.; mem. N.Y. State Med. Soc., County Med. Soc. Home: 305 E 86th St New York NY 10028 Office: 241 Central Park West New York NY 10024

HOCHSCHILD, CARROLL SHEPHERD, computer company and medical equipment executive, educator; b. Whittier, Calif., Mar. 31, 1935; d. Vernon Vero and Effie Corinne (Hollingsworth) Shepherd; m. Richard Hochschild, July 25, 1959; children: Christopher Paul, Stephen Shepherd. BA in Internat. Rels., Pomona Coll., 1956; Teaching credential, U. Calif., Berkeley, 1957; MBA, Pepperdine U., 1985; cert. in fitness instrn., U. Calif., Irvine, 1988. Cert. elem. tchr., Calif. Elem. tchr. Oakland (Calif.) Pub. Schs., 1957-58, San Lorenzo (Calif.) Pub. Schs., 1958-59, Pasadena (Calif.) Pub. Schs., 1959-60, Huntington Beach (Calif.) Pub. Schs., 1961-63, 67-68; adminstrv. asst. Microwave Instruments, Corona del Mar, Calif., 1968-74; co-owner Hoch Co., Corona del Mar, 1978—. Rep. Calif. Tchrs. Assn., Huntington Beach, 1962-63. Mem. AAUW, P.E.O. (projects chmn. 1990-92, corr. sec. 1992-94, 98-2003, 05—, chpt. pres. 1994-95), NAFE, ASTD (Orange County chpt.), Internat. Dance-Exercise Assn., Assistance League Newport-Mesa, Orange County Philharm. Soc. (assoc., Alta Bahia chpt.), Toastmistress (corr. sec. 1983), Jr. Ebell Club (fine arts chmn. Newport Beach 1966-67), U. Calif. Town and Gown. Independent.

HOCHSTEDLER, LISA INEZ, educational association administrator; b. El Dorado Springs, Mo., Oct. 25, 1970; d. Gary Lee and Barbara Helene Messick; m. Bernard LeRoy Hochstedler, Aug. 16, 1989; children: Garren Machquade, Gunnar Levi. AS, Drury U., 2002; B of Psychology, Druru U., 2005. Child devel. assoc. Wash. Vol. West Ctrl. Mo. Cmty. Action Agy., Head Start, Stockton, Mo., 1996—98; substitute West Ctrl. Mo. Cmty. Action Agy., Head Start, Stockton, Mo., 1998—2000, co-tchr./driver, 2000—03; ctr. dir. Head Start West Ctrl. Mo. Cmty. Action Agy., El Dorado Springs, Mo., 2003—. Treas. Jerico Springs Picnic Com., Mo., 2003—; mem. Open Initiative Program. Christian. Avocations: cooking, sports, scrapbooks. Home: 307 East Logan Jerico Springs MO 64756 Office: El Dorado Springs Head Start 210 E Fields Blvd El Dorado Springs MO 64744 Office Phone: 417-876-5895. Personal E-mail: lategator647562000@yahoo.com.

HOCHSTETTER, SANDRA, state official; b. Shreveport, La. BA in Social Work, U. Ark., Fayetteville, 1982; JD, Wash. U., 1985. Asst. gen. counsel Reliant Energy ARKLA, 1986—98; regulatory liaison Gov.'s Office, Little Rock, 1999; exec. dir. Ark. Pub. Svc. Commn., Little Rock, 1999—2000, chmn., 2000—. Office: PSC Bldg 1000 Center St Little Rock AR 72203-0400

HOCKENBURY, SANDRA ELLEN, writer; b. Chgo., Sept. 22, 1952; d. Erwin Henry and Fern Hanson Schmidt; m. Don H. Hockenbury, July 28, 1989; 1 child, Laura Allison. BA in Humanities cum laude, Shimer Coll., Mt. Carroll, Ill., 1974; MA in English Lang. and Lit., U. Chgo., 1976. Rsch. assoc. Inst. Social & Behavioral Pathology, Chgo., 1978—83; sr. devel. editor William C. Brown Pubs., Madison, 1983—89; writer Worth Pubs., N.Y.C., 1990—. Cons. Coast Learning Sys., Fountain Valley, Calif., 1999—2000. Author (with Don H. Hockenbury): psychology textbooks, 1990—, Psychology, 4th edit., Discovering Psychology, 4th edit. Vol. clown asst. Gentle Jesters, vol. face painter. Mem.: AAAS, Assn. Psychol. Sci. Avocations: reading, wildlife, music, photography. Personal E-mail: sandyhockenburg@hotmail.com.

HOCKETT, SHIRLEY O., mathematics professor, writer; b. N.Y.C., Sept. 5, 1920; d. Morris and Rose Orlinoff; m. Charles Francis Hockett, Apr. 25, 1942 (dec. Nov. 4, 2000); children: Alpha Walker, Asher, Amy Robin Rose, Rachel Youngman, Carey Beth. BA in Math., Hunter Coll., 1941; MA in Math., U. Mich., 1942. Tchr. math. Seward Pk. H.S., N.Y.C., 1945—46; lectr. math. Cornell U., Ithaca, NY, 1946—65; prof. emerita math. Ithaca Coll., NY, 1965—91. Editor: N.Y.S. Math. Jour., 1969—74; co-author: How to Prepare for Advaned Placement Tests on Calculus, 1971, Applied Calculus, 1979, Finite Mathematics, 1983. Pres. Ithaca Coll. Faculty of Humanities and Sci., NY, 1977—80, Cayuga Chamber Orch., Ithaca, NY, 1979—84; mem. Ithaca Concert Band, Ithaca, NY, 1979—. Served with USN, 1942—43. Democrat. Avocation: listening to and making music. Home: 145 N Sunset Dr Ithaca NY 14850 Personal E-mail: shirleoh@twcny.rr.com.

HOCKFIELD, SUSAN, academic administrator, medical educator; d. Thomas and Elizabeth Byrne; m. Thomas Byrne; 1 child, Elizabeth Hockfield Byrne. BA in Biology, U Rochester, 1973; PhD in Anatomy & Neuroscience, Georgetown U, 1979; MA (hon.), Yale U, 1994. NIH Post-Doc Fellow Dept. of Anatomy and Neuroscience Program, U of Calif., San Francisco, 1979—80; jr. staff investigator Cold Spring Harbor Lab, Cold Spring Harbor, NY, 1980—82, sr. staff investigator, 1982—85; asst. prof. Sect. of Neurobiology Yale U Sch. of Med., New Haven, 1985—89, assoc. prof., 1989—91, 1991—94, prof. Dept. of Neurobiology, 1994—2004; dean, Grad. Sch. of Arts and Sci. Yale U., 1998—2002, provost, 2003—04; pres. MIT, Cambridge, 2004—. Mem. Nat. Adv. Neurological Disorders and Stroke Council (NIH), 2002—; mem. at large AAAS, Sect. on Neuroscience, 2000—04; bd. trustees Cold Spring Harbor Lab., Cold Spring Harbor, NY, 1998—; Brain Cancer Adv. Panel James S. McDonnell Found., 1997—2002; bd. dir. Haskins Lab., 1988—2002; U Adv. Council Yale-New Haven Tchrs. Inst., 1998—2002; elected mem. of the bd. Council of Grad. Sch., 2002; neuroscience adv. bd. Astra Pharmaceuticals, 1997—99; program dir. Summer Neurobiology Program Cold Spring Harbor Lab., Cold Harbor Springs, NY, 1985—97; councilor Soc. for Neuroscience, 1992—96; sci. adv. bd. Hereditary Disease Found., 1991—95, 1996—2000; mem. NIH Study Section (Visual Sci. B), 1988—92; chair Gordon Plasticity, 1997; participant, mem. of bd. several orgns., studies and soc.; mem. bd. WGBH Ednl. Found., Inc., 2004—. Contbr. articles,, in numerous profl. jours., chapters to books co-authored chapters in numerous books, book Molecular Probes of the Nervous System: Selected Methods for Antibodies and Nucleai Acid Probes Cold Spring Harbor Lab. Press, 1993. Recipient PHS Post-doctoral Rsch. Award, NIH, 1980, Grass Traveling Sci. Award, Soc. for Neuroscience, 1987, Charles Judson Herrick Award, Am. Assoc. of Anatomists, 1987, William Edward Gilbert Prof. of Neurobiology, Yale U., 2001; grantee Esther A. and Joseph Klingenstein Fellowship in the Neurosciences, NSF, NIH, 1985. Fellow: American Acad. Arts & Scis. (fell. 2004); mem.: FASEB, Soc. for Devel., Am Assn. for Advancement of Sci. (assoc.; mem.-at-large, Section on Neuroscience 2000—), Am. Assoc. of Anatomists (Charles Judson Herrick Award 1987), Soc. for Neuroscience (Grass Traveling Scientist 1987). Achievements include three patents in field of neuroscience. Office: Off of Pres Rm 3-208 MIT 77 Massachusetts Ave Cambridge MA 02139-4307 Office Phone: 617-253-0148. Office Fax: 617-253-3124.*

HOCKLESS, MARY FONTENOT, educational consultant; b. New Iberia, La., July 23, 1954; d. Gill B. and Thelma Fontenot; m. Jospeh W. Hockless; children: Kellie, Amie, Marcus. BA in Speech Pathology, U. La., 1978, EdM, 1984, postgrad., 2003—. Cert. speech pathology, early intervention guidance & counseling K-12, family svc. coord. Speech therapist Iberia Sch. Dist., New Iberia, La., 1977, presch. tchr., early interventionist; coord. La. Dept. Edn., 1992, regional coord., 1992—2000; rsch. U. Ark., Little Rock, 2000—03; pvt. practice First Steps Referral and Cons. LLC, New Iberia, 2003—. Contbr. articles to profl. jours.; author: (manual) Challenging Behavior Support, 2002, Perfect Rhythm, 2003. Named Tchr. of Yr., Jaycees, New Iberia, 1985, Outstanding Alumni, U. Southwestern La., 2003. Home: PO Box 12213 New Iberia LA 70562 Office: First Steps Refferal Consulting 134 E Main St Ste 4 New Iberia LA 70560-3798

HOCKMAN, LORI LYNN, biologist, educator; b. Point Pleasant, W.Va., Mar. 28, 1972; d. John Manley and Wanda Naomi Greenlee; m. Billy Bryan Hockman, June 8, 1990 (div. Oct. 17, 1999); children: Billi Bryanna, Jacob Nathaniel, Johnnie Ray. BS, U. Rio Grande, 2002. Lic. Tchg. Ohio Educators Assn. Earth sci., history tchr. Lexington (NC) City Sch., 2002—03; biology tchr. Wellston (Ohio) City Sch., 2003—. With USAF, 1991—93, AK. Decorated Stateside Asst. Desert Storm USAF, Letter of Commendation US Dept. of Army. Mem.: Wellston Tchrs. Assn. (assoc.), Ohio Educators Assn. (assoc.), Nat. Sci. Tchr. Assn. (assoc.). Bapt. Avocations: reading, travel. Office: Wellston City Schs 200 Golden Rocket Dr Wellston OH 45692 Office Phone: 740-384-2162.

HOCTOR, MICHANNE, dean; b. Boulder, Colo., June 15, 1966; d. Michael and Georganne Hoctor; life ptnr. Duane Thompson; 1 child, Francine Thompson. D, San Diego State U. and U. San Diego, 2006. Profl. clear tchg. credential Calif. Peer coach, staff developer San Diego City Schs., 2001—05, dean of students, 2005—. Reviewer ReadWriteThink.org, 2003—. Named Literacy Educator of Yr. Mem.: ISTE, Pi Lambda Theta. Democrat. Unitarian. Home: 1391 Blue Falls Dr Chula Vista CA 91910 Office: Mann Sch of Expression 4345 54th St San Diego CA 92115 Office Phone: 619-582-8990 ext 2503. Office Fax: 619-265-0583. Personal E-mail: mhoctor66@mac.com. E-mail: mhoctor@sandi.net.

HODAPP, HEIDI FRANCINE, middle school educator; b. Ventura, Calif., Dec. 12, 1975; d. Howard Leroy and Jo-Anne Frances Hodapp. BS in Interdisciplinary Studies, Old Dominion U., Norfolk, Va., 1998, MS in Edn., 1999. Tchr., chair sci. Bayside Mid. Sch., Virginia Beach, Va., 1999—. Mem. prins. adv. com. Bayside Mid. Sch., 2005—, mem. sch. planning coun., 2005—; mentor, 2004—. Mem.: Va. Edn. Assn., Nat. Sci. Tchrs. Assn., Va. Mid. Sch. Assn. Roman Catholic. Home: 604 Glengarry Ct Virginia Beach VA 23451 Office: Bayside Mid Sch 965 Newtown Rd Virginia Beach VA 23462 Business E-Mail: heidi.hodapp@vbschools.com.

HODARA, SUSAN MINA, writer; b. Washington, Nov. 7, 1953; d. Bernard and Selma Wenesky Rubin; m. Paul Sterling Hodara, Oct. 9, 1983; children: Sofie Elana, Ariel Marissa. BFA, Harvard U., 1975; MFA, Columbia U., 1979. Editor in chief Big Apple Parent, N.Y.C., 1991—2000; consulting editor Westchester Parent, No. White Plains, NY, 2000—; freelance writer. Tchr. Young Writers Workshop, Chappapua, NY, 1997—, Gilda's Club, White Plains, NY, 2002—03, No. Westchester Ctr. for the Arts, Mt. Kisco, NY, 2003—04; pub. reader Hudson Valley Writers Ctr., Sleepy Hollow, NY, 2001, Borders Books, N.Y.C., 2005. Author: Animation: The Art and The Industry, 1984; contbr. articles to profl. jours. and mags. Recipient Editl. Excellence award, Parenting Publs. Am., 1993. Home and Office: 204 Croton Ave Mount Kisco NY 10549 Office Phone: 914-666-6704. E-mail: susan.hodara@gmail.com.

HODES, MARTHA, history professor, writer; b. N.Y.C., June 12, 1958; d. Linda and Stuart Hodes; m. Bruce Dorsey, Nov. 28, 1996. BA, Bowdoin Coll., Brunswick, Maine, 1980; MA, PhD, Princeton U., N.J., 1991. Asst. prof. U. Calif., Santa Cruz, 1991—94, NYU, N.Y.C., 1994—99, assoc. prof., 2000—06, prof., 2007—. Workshop co-dir. Storytelling Across Disciplines N.Y. U. Humanities Coun., N.Y.C., 2003—04; presenter tchg. the Civil War N.Y. State Dept. Edn., 2004. Author: White Women, Black Men: Illicit Sex in the Nineteenth-Century South, 1997 (Soc. of Am. Historians Allan Nevins prize), The Sea Captain's Wife: A True Story of Love, Race, and War in the Nineteenth Century, 2006; editor: Sex, Love, Race: Crossing Boundaries in North American History, 1999; mem. expert adv. panel: (documentaries) American Lynchings: a Strange and Bitter Fruit, Bitter Fruit Prodns., 1999—; script cons.: (TV series) History Detectives, PBS, 2004—; contbr. chapters to books, articles to profl. jours. Exec. bd. Women's Faculty Caucus, N.Y. U., N.Y.C. Fellow, Whiting Found., 1989—90, Am. Coun. Learned Societies, 1994—95, NEH, 1994—95; grantee, Gilder Lehrman Inst. Am. History N.Y. Pub. Libr., 2003, Rockefeller Archive Ctr., 2003; Littleton-Griswold Legal History Rsch. grant, Am. Hist. Assn., 1990, Scholar-in-Residence fellow, Schomburg Ctr. Rsch. in Black Culture NY Pub. Libr., 1999, Andrew W. Mellon fellow, Libr. Co. Phila., 1999. Mem.: Am. Studies Assn., Berkshire Conf. History of Women (book prize, specialist reader in so. history 1997—99, Ann. Article award 2003), Orgn. Am. Historians (mem. Avery C. Craven book prize com. 2000—01), Orgn. of Am. Historians, Am. Hist. Assn. (mem. Merle Curti award book prize com. 2006—). Office: NY Univ Dept History 53 Washington Sq S New York NY 10012 Office Phone: 212-998-8612. E-mail: martha.hodes@nyu.edu.

HODGDON, PAULA DRAKE, retired physical education educator; b. Morristown, NJ, Aug. 2, 1928; d. Paul Woodhull and Madelon (Reeve) Drake; m. H. Sturgis Hodgdon, Nov. 29, 1967; stepchildren: Lileen Anderson, Janet, Matthew, Camela Parker. AA, Lasell Coll., Newton, Mass., 1948; BA in Sociology, Arcadia U., Glenside, Pa., 1950; MA in Phys. Edn., Columbia U., NYC, 1952; D in Phys. Edn., Springfield Coll., Mass., 1973. Instr. phys. edn. Bates Coll., Lewiston, Maine, 1954—58; instr. phys. edn., coach Cape Elizabeth HS, Maine, 1959—66; tchr. fellow phys. edn. Springfield Coll., 1966—67; prof. phys. edn. U. So. Maine, Gorham, 1967—93, field hockey coach, 1967—97, dir. athletics, 1990—93; ret., 1997. Home: 169 Darbick Terr Hollis Center ME 04042-3841

HODGE, DONNA LYNN, psychologist, educator; b. Perth Amby, N.J., July 7, 1956; d. Joseph and Evelyn Anita Hodge. BA in Psychology and Sociology cum laude, Conn. Coll., New London, 1978; MA in Guidance Counseling and Social and Cmty. Psychology, U. Mich., Ann Arbor, 1981, PhD in Social and Cmty. Psychology, 1984. Lic. social work Mich., Psychological Licensing Bd., Mich. Psychological intern Washtenow County Jail, Ann Arbor, 1983—84; clinical therapist Washtenaw County Sheriff's Dept., Ann Arbor, 1984—86; counselor East Stroudsburg U. Counseling Ctr., Pa., 1987—89; group facilitator Monroe County HIV/AIDS Support Group, East Stroudsburg, Pa., 1991—94; assoc. prof. East Stroudsburg U., Pa., 1986—93, prof. psychology, 1993—; clinical therapist pvt. practice, East Stroudsburg, Pa., 1989—. Psychological cons. Milan Correctional Inst., 1985—86; edn. cons., ind. contractor, East Stroudsburg, Pa., 1999—; corp. cons. East Stroudsburg U., Pa., 2001—. Presenter (numerous workshops). Mentor Summer Intensified Summer Program, East Stroudsburg, Pa.; advisor The Student Psychological Assn., East Stroudsburg, Pa.; bd. dirs., officer Saint Anthony's Ch., 2002—06. Grantee Grant, Pa. State Sys. of Higher Edn., 1993, ESU Found., 1998, 1999, 2000, Parent's Assn., 2001; Am. Psychological Assn. Fellowship, U. Mich., 1981, Nat. Sci. Found. Fellowship, 1984. Mem.: APA, NAACP, Assn. Black Psychologists, Am. Corrections Assn., Unity Coalition of Poconos, Rotary Club of Smithfields (spkr. 1999—2006). Office: East Stroudsburg Univ Psychology Dept 200 Prospect St East Stroudsburg PA 18301-2999 Personal E-mail: dhodge@po-boy.esu.edu.

HODGE, GAIL, dean, programming director, education educator; b. Iowa; BS, U. Dubuque, Iowa; MA, Clarke Coll. Asst. prof. U. Dubuque, 2001—06, assoc. dean profl. programs, dir. on-line programming, 2006—. Office: U Dubuque 2000 University Dubuque IA 52001 Office Phone: 563-589-3349.

HODGE, IDA LEE, retired physical therapist assistant; b. Ala., Aug. 6, 1940; d. John Louie and Rubye Lee (Williams) Hodge; m. Jimmie Arthur Beard, Mar. 12, 1959 (div. Aug. 1984); children: Tammie, Benita, Patti, Starr. AS, Wallace State C.C., Hanceville, Ala., 1982; AAS, U. Ala., Birmingham, 1984. Lic. phys. therapist asst., Tenn. Phys. therapist asst. Merihil Healthcare Ctr., Lewisburg, Tenn., 1984-86, Lincoln Skilled Care Ctr., Fayetteville, Tenn., 1986-89, Kennewick (Wash.) Gen. Hosp. Phys. Therapy Ctr., 1989-94, Lifecare Ctrs. of Am., 1996-98; on call/agy. work Phys. Therapy Ctr., Wallula, Wash., 1998—2004; ret., 2004. Author numerous poems. Recipient Cert. of Exceptional Artistry and Creativity, Nat. Libr. Poetry, 1988, 1st prize sandstone sculpture Benton-Franklin County Fair, 1990. Mem. Am. Phys. Therapy Assn. (mem. affiliate assembly, oncology group), Lifecare Ctrs. Am. (Whatever It Takes award 1997), Cullman (Ala.) Echotas Cherokee Tribe (sec./libr., demonstrator traditional pottery making). Avocations: sculpting, painting, poetry, writing, hiking, camping. Home: 509 Ohio Ave Hanceville AL 35077

HODGE, ISA ANN, elementary school educator; b. Marietta, Ohio, June 27, 1980; Music tchr. Palm Bay (Fla.) Elem., 2003—. Mem.: Fla. Music Educator's Assn.

HODGE, KATHERINE RHODES, retired school guidance counselor; b. Norfolk, Va., Oct. 17, 1928; d. E. Weldon and Mary (Eaton) Rhodes; m. Kenneth D. Hodge, June 13, 1949; children: Jeffrey M., Judith M. BA, Coll. William and Mary, Williamsburg, Va., 1948; MEd, SUNY, Buffalo, 1970. Cert. secondary tchr., Va.; cert. secondary tchr. guidance counselor, N.Y. Tchr. French and English, Norfolk County Schs., Norfolk, 1948-53; tchr. English Clarence (N.Y.) Sch. Sys., 1966-68, guidance counselor, 1969-86; ret., 1986. Co-writer Western N.Y. Vocat. Guidance Program, Buffalo, 1982-84; mem. first in Am. com. Moore County Schs., 2001-02. Vol. guardian ad litem Moore County, 1989—; clk. of session West End (N.C.) Presbyn. Ch., 1994-96; bd. dirs. Ruth Pauley Lecture Series, 1995-2001, Moore County Libr. Bd., 2003—; mem. Moore County Welfare Reform Com., 1997-2002, Pub. Edn. Found. Moore County, 2004-; bd. sec. Seven Lakes Civic Group, 2002—. Recipient Vol. Svc. award, N.C. Gov., 1998, Human Values award, Moore County Kiwanis, 1999, Citizen of Yr., Seven Lakes Landowners Assn., 2006. Mem. AAUW, LWV (edn. dir., observer chmn. 1988—, pres., 1991-93, budget chmn., 1994, v.p. 2003-2005), Moore County Hist. Assn., ADK, PEO, Phi Beta Kappa, Pi Beta Phi. Avocations: reading, gardening, bridge. Home: 1275 John Knox Dr Apt P002 Colfax NC 27235

HODGE, KATHLEEN O'CONNELL, academic administrator; b. Balt., Dec. 26, 1948; d. William Walsh and Loretto Marie (Wittek) O'Connell; m. Vern Milton Hodge, Apr. 8, 1972; children: Shea, Ryan. BS, Calif. State U., Fullerton, 1971, MS, 1975; EdD, U. So. Calif., 2002; postgrad., U. Calif., Irvine, 1977-84. Cert. marriage and family therapist. Counselor Saddleback Coll., Mission Viejo, Calif., 1975-87, prof. of psychology, speech, 1975—2002, dean of continuing edn., cmty. svcs., dean emeritus inst., 1987-95, vice chancellor, 1995—, acting chancellor, 1998-99. Accreditation liaison officer Saddleback Coll., 1986; mem. adv. bd. Nat. Issues Forum, Calif., 1985, 87, Saddleback Coll. Community Services, 1984, Access and Aspirations U. Calif., Irvine, 1979. Author: (workbook) Assessment of Life Learning, 1978; editor emeritus: Flavors in Time Anthology of Literature,

1992. Mem. Calif. Community Coll. Counselors Assn. (region coord. 1987), Calif. Tchrs. Assn., Am. Assn. Women Community and Jr. Colls., Assn. Marriage Family Therapists, C.C. Educators of Older Adults (pres. 1990-92). Democrat. Roman Catholic. Avocations: skiing, reading, political advocacy. Home: 4011 Calle Juno San Clemente CA 92673-2616 Office: South Orange County C C Dist 28000 Marguerite Pky Mission Viejo CA 92692-3635

HODGE, LINDA M., former educational association administrator; m. Bob Hodge; 3 children. Pres. Hawaii State PTA; chair Resource Develop., Bylaws, Tech./Safety, and Membership coms. Nat. PTA, region 7 dir. Alaska, Hawaii, Idaho, Mont., Oreg., Wash., Wyo., v.p. programs, 1999—2001, pres. elect, 2001—03, pres., 2003—05. Former mem. Exec., Budget, Elections, Leadership, and Nominating Coms., IOD Cultural Arts Subcommittee; com. mem. Nat. Rsch. Coun., NAS; nat. adv. bd. mem. Neag Sch. Edn., U. Conn. Recipient Hon. Svc. Award, Calif. PTA, Continuing Svc. Award, Vallejo Sch. Dist. Award. Office: Nat PTA Ste 1300 541 N Fairbanks Ct Chicago IL 60611-3396 also: 1090 Vermont Ave NW, Ste 1200 Washington DC 20005-4905 Office Phone: 312-670-6782, 202-289-6790. Office Fax: 312-670-6783, 202-289-6791.

HODGE, MARY GRETCHEN FARNAM, trade association administrator; b. DeFuniak Springs, Fla., Sept. 24, 1943; d. Thomas Dewey and Mary Catherine (Mixon) Farnam; m. Spessard L. Hodge, Apr. 28, 1962; children: Jennifer Robin, Monica Leigh Hodge Schulz, Stephanie Lea Hodge Glascock. Student, Orlando Coll.; grad., Citizens' Police Acad., Maitland, Fla., 1996. Adminstrv. asst. The Cameron and Barkley Co., Orlando, Fla., 1961-68, office mgr. machine tool divsn., 1975-76; mgr., corp. officer Frazer Machinery and Supply Co., Orlando, 1976-93, CFO, sec.-treas., 1988-93; CEO Frazer Machinery and Supply, Orlando, 1992—93; membership sales dir. Maitland Area C. of C., 2000—04, exec. dir., 2002, 2004—. Founder parent support group for gifted edn. Seminole County, 1979; sec. Parent of Gifted Edn., Seminole County, 1980—87; gov. apptd. mem. adv. bd. Exceptional Student Edn., Seminole County, Fla., 1980—87; chair Maitland (Fla.) Centennial Founders Bd., 1985; tour guide Orlando Opera Guild, Winter Park, Fla., 1985; celebrity waitress Leukemia Soc. Am., Orlando, 1986; co-chair Project Graduation Lyman H.S., Seminole County, 1986—87; chair Alzheimers Resource Auction Dinner, Winter Park, 1987—88; bd. dirs. Maitland Civic Ctr., 1983—86, sec., 1983—84, v.p., 1987—88, 1993—94, pres., 1988—89, 1994—96, ex-officio bd. dirs., 1989—90; v.p. Maitland Woman's Club, 1994—98, pres., 1997—99; mem. Cultural Corridor Com., City of Maitland, 1994—98, fin. com., mem. grant com., 1998—99; mem. Orlando Ave. Redevel. Subcom., City of Maitland, 1998—; bd. dirs. non-profit Showcase Group, 1994—95, chair, 1996; bd. dirs. Maitland Hist. Soc., 1996—99, vol. docent, 1996—; bd. dirs. Orlando Opera Guild, 1997—2000, v.p., 1999—2001, steering com. Designer's Showhouse, 1999, 2000, ho. mgr., 1998, 1999; bd. dirs. Maitland So. Sem. Chamber, 1998—99, chair Taste of Maitland, 1999; Am. Heart Assn. Lock-up Vol., 1995—96; vol. Golden Orch. and Chorus Aux., Over the Rainbow Auction, 1995—97; mem. Maitland Art Ctr.; ch. coun. College Park United Meth. Ch., 1999—2001; mem. steering com. Women's Lunch and Learn, 2005. Recipient Appreciation plaque Dividends, Seminole City, 1974-75, Cert. Appreciation Maitland Civic Ctr., 1986, 97, Alzheimer Resource Ctr., Winter Park, 1987, Pres.'s Gavel, 1989, 96, Northam award, 1995, Chamber Plaque, 1998, 1999, 2000, Designers' Showhouse Appreciation Cert., 1998-99, Presidents' award comty. svc., C. of C., 1999, 2002, 04. Mem. Am. Machine Tool Ditbrs., Soc. Mfg. Engrs., Maitland Woman's Club (several offices 1970—). Democrat. Methodist. Avocations: horticulture, bridge, reading. E-mail: mfhodge@cfl.rr.com.

HODGE, SHARON DENISE, mathematics educator; b. Milledgeville, Ga., Sept. 24, 1964; d. Moses Miller, Jr. and Eula B. Miller; m. David G. Hodge, Oct. 8, 1988; children: Derrell G., David G. Jr., DeJa S. BS Math., Paine Coll., Augusta, Ga., 1986. Cert. Tchr. Ga., 2006. Police officer Richmond County Sheriffs Dept., Augusta, 1987—88; tchr. math. Vidalia City Schs., Ga., 1996—2005; tchr. J.R. Trippe Mid. Sch., Vidalia, 2005—. Min. Jehovahs Witnesses, Vidalia, 1997—2006. Recipient Who's Who Among Am. Colls., Who's Who, 1986; Acad. Scholarship, Paine Coll., 1982, 1983. Home: 1303 N Grossman Dr Vidalia GA 30474 Office: JR Trippe Middle School 2200 McIntosh Street Vidalia GA 30474 E-mail: shodge@vidalia-city.k12.ga.us.

HODGE, SUSAN, oil industry executive; BS in Acctg., Iowa State U., 1979; MBA, U. Tex., 1993. CPA, Tex. From mem. staff to treas. Shell Oil Co., Houston, 1979-97, treas., 1997—; mem. staff Bankers Trust Co., N.Y.C., 1986-89; v.p. The First Nat. Bank Chgo., Houston, 1989-95; from asst. treas. to deputy treas. Enron Corp., Houston, 1995-97; leader global bus. line, 2000—; CFO Coral Energy (sub. of Shell Oil Co.), Houston; global head Fin. & Mgmt. Consultancy Shell Fin. Svcs., 2000—. Bd. dirs. Interfaith Ministries Greater Houston, Theater Under the Stars, Houston. Office: Royal Dutch Shell Group 30 Carel Van Bylandtlaan 2596 The Hague Netherlands also: Shell Oil Co One Shell Plaza 900 Louisiana St Houston TX 77002-4901

HODGES, ADELE E., military officer; b. Bridgeport, Conn., 1955; Grad., So. Conn. State Coll., 1977; MBA, M in Military Art and Sci.; M, Strategic Military Studies. Advanced through grades to col. U.S. Marine Corps, 1978—; with 3d supply battalion Support Activity Supply Sys. Mgmt. Unit, Okinawa, Japan, 1981—83, Marine Forces Pacific Hdqs., Hawaii, 1983—86; ground supply Marine Corps Property Purchasing and Contracting SASSY Mgmt. Officer 4th Marine Aircraft Wing, New Orleans, 1986—90; battalion supply officer Hdqs. Battalion 2d Marine Divisn, 1990; deployed with 2d marine divsn. Operation Dessert Storm, 1991—93; asst. base supply officer Marine Corps Air Ground Combat Ctr., 1993—97; project mgr. combined arms exercise program and enhanced equipment allowance pool Marine Corps Combat Devel. Command, Quantico, Va., 1997—2000; exec. officer brigade svc. support one, comdr. 1st maintenence batallion 1st Force Svce. Support Group, Camp Pendleton, Calif., 2000—02; stationed at NATO Joint Warfare Ctr., Stavanger, Norway, 2003—05; comdr. Camp Lejeune, NC, 2006—. Decorated Meritorious Svc. Medal, Navy Commendation Medal with 3 star, Navy Achievement Medal. Office: US Marine Corp Hdqs Code MMSB 10 Quantico VA 22134-5030*

HODGES, ANN, retired television editor, columnist; b. McCamey, Tex., Sept. 7, 1928; d. Ernest Cornelius and Margaret Isabel (Wood) Haynes; m. Cecil Ray Hodges, July 2, 1954 (div. Nov. 1974); children: Craig McNeley, Elizabeth Ann. BJ, U. Tex., 1948. Reporter Houston Chronicle, 1948-51; soc. editor The News, Mexico City, 1951-52, TV editor, columnist, TV critic, 1962—2003; ret., 2003. Mem. adv. bd. U. Miami TV Ctr. for Advancement of Modern Media, 1994—; U.S. juror Banff TV Festival, 1995. Mem.: Houston Press Club (pres. 1967), TV Critics Assn. (founder, exec. bd., v.p., pres.), Critics Consensus (dir. 1965—75). E-mail: ahodges@houston.rr.com.

HODGES, ANN, actress, singer, dancer; b. Elizabethtown, Ky., June 24; d. Henry Lavely and Margaret Rhodes (Lewis) H.; m. Richard Angleine; 1 child, Michael Christian Angeline; m. Barry C. Tuttle, Sept. 16, 1969 (div. 1972). Cert., registered yoga alliance tchr.; ordained min. Congl. Ch. Practical Theology. Yoga instr., Tampa, St. Petersburg, Safety Harbor, Clearwater, Fla., Under the Live Oak, Casa Bella Vista. Pvt. instr. Yoga, Fla. Appeared in (Broadway shows) No Strings, The Rothchilds, Heathen, (off-Broadway shows) The Boys From Syracuse, There Goes The Old Ballgame, Bella, (TV shows) The Jackie Gleason Show, The Steve Allen Show, The Ed Sullivan Show, Bell Telephone Hour, Ellery Queen, Omnibus, The Vic Damone Show, The Big Record, (TV spls.) Once Upon A Mattress, The G.M. Spectacular, The Esso Spectacular, (motion pictures) The Cardinal, The New Life Style, Oldsmobile, (plays) Applause, The Best Little Whorehouse in Texas, Gypsy,(leading roles in plays) Hello Dolly!, Sugar Babies, Chicago, Can Can, Sweet Charity, Mame, Damn Yankees, See How They Run, Catch Me If You Can., Legends!, I Ought to Be in Pictures, How the Other Half Loves, Pajama Tops, The Last of the Red Hot Lovers, Pal Joey, Cole Porter Reveiw, Gone with the Wind (role of Belle Watling in American Premiere Production), The Greenwich Village Scandals of 1923; also many commls., voice overs and indsls.; performer numerous charities including Am. Cancer Soc., Am. Heart Assn., Handicapped, Abused Wives and Children; star performer Gasparilla Coronation, 1991, guest performer Fla. Orch. at Clearwater Jazz Festival. Yoga instr. Safety Harbor Spa, Don CeSar, Harbour Island Athletic Club, Casa Bella Vista. Named the Queen of Mus. Theatre by the Press, one of Tampa Bay's top achievers. Mem.: Suncoast Yoga Tchrs. Assn. (past pres., bd. dirs.). Avocations: yoga, swimming, horse back riding, piano playing, embroidery.

HODGES, DEBORAH, investment company executive; BA, Princeton U.; MBA, Kellogg Grad. Sch. Mgmt. With Capital Mgmt. Group Bankers Trust; COO DB Capital Ptnrs., 2000; COO, ptnr. MidOcean Ptnrs. Office: MidOcean Ptnrs 320 Park Ave Ste 1700 New York NY 10022 Office Phone: 212-497-1400.

HODGES, EDNA (LEE) ELIZABETH, lawyer, educator; b. Neveda City, Calif., Apr. 29, 1938; d. Frank William Este and Ora Lee Burchette; m. Robert M. Derman (dec.); children: Lisa Marie Derman, James Arnold Derman; m. Clifton Doyle Hodges, Dec. 30, 1975 (dec.); 1 child, Michael Este. BA, Butler U., Indpls., 1963; JD, Washburn Law Sch., Topeka, 1973. Legal investigator Schroer, Rice, Bryan & Lykins, Topeka, 1983—86; assoc. prof. bus. law Washburn U., 1986. Kans. rep. ACLU, 1963—73, pres. NY chpt. NYC, 1973—76, lobbyist, 1963, 1973; v.p. United Meth. Ch., 1995—, Grantville United Meth. Women, 1995—98. With USCG, 1986—96, ret. USCG. Democrat. Avocations: hiking, gardening. Home: 4238 21st St Grantville KS 66429-9204

HODGES, ELIZABETH C., elementary school educator, principal; b. Newport News, Va. d. Rupert Ronald and Mary Belle Creech; m. Edward L. Jr. Hodges, May 29, 1977; children: Samuel David, Stephen Andrew, Sarah Elizabeth. BS in Bible and Elem. Edn., Free Will Bapt. Bible Coll., Nashville, 1976; MEd, Ga. So. Coll., Statesboro, 1980; postgrad., Tenn. State U., Nashville, 2004—. 1st grade tchr. Liberty Christian Sch., Durham, NC, 1976—77; 2d grade tchr. Fourth Dist. Elem. Sch., Surrency, Ga., 1977—81; 2d and 5th grade tchr. Satilla Elem. Sch., Douglas, Ga., 1981—83; 1st grade tchr. Coll. Hts. Christian Acad., Gallatin, Tenn., 1990—95, acad. coord., 1995—99, elem. prin., 1999—2006; 5th grade tchr. Watt Hardison Elem. Sch., Portland, Tenn., 2006—. Mem.: ASCD, Assn. Christian Schs. Internat. (accreditation commr. 1997—, chair vis. teams 1998—), Phi Kappa Phi. Baptist.

HODGES, ELIZABETH SWANSON, educational consultant, tutor; b. Anoka, Minn., Apr. 7, 1924; d. Henry Otto and Louise Isabel (Holiday) Swanson; m. Allen Hodges, June 27, 1944; children: Nancy Elizabeth, Susan Kathleen, Jane Ellen, Sara Louise. BA cum laude, Regis Coll., Denver, 1966; postgrad., U. No. Colo., 1966-79, Valdosta State U., 1979-81. Cert. secondary edn., hosp./homebound, learning disabilities, Colo., Ga., Ariz. Vol. emergency St. Anthony's Hosp., Denver, 1960-64; v.p., tutor St. Elizabeth's Adult Tutorial, Denver, 1964-69; hosp./homebound tchr. Liberty County Sch. System, Hinesville, Ga., 1979-87; edn1. tutor Colo. River Indian Tribes, Parker, Ariz., 1986-87; vol. Twin Cities Community Hosp., Templeton, Calif., 1987-89, Guardian Ad Litem Cir. Ct. 5th Dist. Fla., 1992—, Munroe Regional Med. Ctr., Ocala, Fla., 1991-92; cons., tutor Sylvan Learning Ctr., Ocala, 1990—. Vol. tutor Blessed Trinity Sch., Ocala, 1996—. Democrat. Roman Catholic. Avocations: swimming, reading, sewing, piano, gardening. Home and Office: 1661 SE 31st St Ocala FL 34471

HODGES, HEATHER M., ambassador; BA, Coll. St. Catherine; MA, NYU. Joined Fgn. Svc., US Dept. State, 1980; chief non-immigrant visa sect. US Embassy, Caracas, Venezuela, dep. chief of consular sect. Guatemala, 1983—85, Peru desk officer Washington, 1985—87, prin. officer US Consulate Bilbao, Spain, 1989—91, dep. dir. Office of Cuban Affairs Washington, 1991—93, dep. chief of mission Managua, Nicaragua, 1993—96, Lima, Peru, 1997—2000, Madrid, 2000—03; US amb. to Moldova US Dept. State, Chisinau, 2003—; counsel Senate Sub-com. on Immigration and Refugee Affairs US Congress, 1987—89. Office: US Embassy 7080 Chisinau Pl Washington DC 20521-7080

HODGES, JENNEFER RAE, sculptor; b. Bay City, Tex., Feb. 14, 1973; d. Bobby Owens and Ygerne Roxanne Michalec Hubbell; m.Craig Jefferson Hodges, May 17, 2003; children: Lexis DeVoe Beauford, Madison Nicole. Student, Richland Jr. Coll., 1991, 92; BFA with honors, U. Ctrl. Ark., 1998; MA, U. Ark. Little Rock, 2001. Intern, apprentice Richard Hunt Studios, Chgo., 1997; tech. asst. Chgo. Fine Art Foundry, 1997, Hunt Studios, Chgo., 1997; sculptor disability svcs. U. Ctrl. Ark., Conway, 1998; tchr. Assn. Retarded Citizens, Little Rock, 1999, U. Ala.-Little Rock Share Am. Cmty. Outreach Program, 2001—; tchr. sculpture Gallery B, 2002; prof. sculpture and Intro to Art U. Ark., Little Rick, 2003—05, prof. intro. to art, 2005—. Mem. com. Kramer Artist Coop., Little Rock, 1997; v.p. Kramer Sch. Artist Coop. Moon Meditation, 1997, Trinity, 2005, exhibited in group shows at U. Ctrl. Ark., Conway, 1997, 1998, Woman's City Club, 1999, Ctrs. Youth and Family, 1999, Art Found., Hot Springs, 1999, 2000, Youth Home Inc. Eggshibition, 2002, Hist. Ark. Mus., 2003, 2006. Scholar U. Ctrl. Ark., 1998. Mem. Art History Assn. (v.p. 1997). Democrat. Avocations: painting with oil, watercolors, acrylic, camping, canoeing, swimming, figure drawing. Home: 5809 Stonewall Rd Little Rock AR 72207-4325 Office Phone: 501-580-1460. Personal E-mail: jennefer@sbcglobal.net.

HODGES, KATHLEEN MCGILL, art educator; b. Mpls., Oct. 9, 1964; d. John Michael and Marilyn (Gore) McGill; m. Garry Allen Hodges, Dec. 28, 1991. BFA, U. North Tex., 1987; MEd, Tex. Woman's U., 1991. Elem. art specialist Garland (Tex.) Ind. Sch. Dist., 1988—. Illustrator Cooper Inst. Aerobics Rsch., Dallas, 1995—98, Garland ISD, 1988—, Med. Health Group Credit Union, 1988, Tex. Assn. Landscape Contractors, 1996; campus improvement team Walnut Glen Acad., Garland, 1991—2003, creator pet patrol, 1995—. Art and design com. Dallas Area Rapid Transit, 2000; creator ann. paper towel drive Rogers Wildlife Rehab. Ctr., Hutchins, Tex., 1996—; mem. PTA, Garland, 1988—, hon. life mem., 2003—. Named Tchr. of Yr., Wal-Mart, 2001; grantee, Garland Ind. Sch. Dist., 2001. Mem.: Tex. Art Edn. Assn., Nat. Art Edn. Assn., Pi Beta Phi. Avocations: skiing, antiques, travel. Office: Walnut Glen Acad Excellence 3101 Edgewood Dr Garland TX 75042

HODGES, MICHELE, chamber of commerce executive; b. 1967; 2 children. Pres. Troy Chamber of Commerce, Oakland Chamber Network, Mich. Named one of 40 Under 40, Crain's Detroit Bus., 2006. Office: Troy Chamber of Commerce 4555 Investment Dr 3rd Fl Ste 300 Troy MI 48098 Office Phone: 248-641-0197.*

HODGES, SHIRLEY MARIE, secondary school educator; d. Merle Marie Parenica; 1 child, Lance Wayne. AA, Victoria Jr. Coll., Tex., 1979; BS in Phys. Edn., Tex. A & M U., College Station, 1986. Provisional secondary tchg. cert. Tex., 1986. Bookkeeper Atzenhoffer Chevrolet Co., Victoria, 1980—84; tchr., coach Kenedy HS, Tex., 1986—88, El Campo HS, Tex., 1988—92; tchr. Tidehaven HS, El Maton, Tex., 1992—97, Bloomington (Tex.) H.S., 1997—. Mem.: Tex. Fedn. Tchrs. (assoc.). Republican. Avocations: swimming, hiking, basketball, softball.

HODGES MORGAN, ANNE, historian; b. 1940; BA, N. Tex. State U.; MA, Columbia U.; PhD in Am. History, U. Tex. Former legislative aide US Senate, Wash., DC; former staff mem. Senate Labor and Public Welfare Com., Wash., DC; former coord. of rsch. Congressional Rsch. Svc., Liberty of Congress, Wash., DC; former v.p. for programs Kerr Found., Oklahoma City, former pres., trustee. Pres., bd. chair Conf. of Southwest Found. Author: Prescription for Success: The Life and Values of Ewing Marion Kauffman, Robert S. Kerr, The Senate Years, Oklahoma: A History, Oklahoma Memories, Arizona Memories. Former chair Okla. State Regents for Higher Ed.; former mem. Okla. State Bd. of Elementary and Secondary Ed., Okla. State Bd. of Vocational and Tech. Ed., Okla. Historical Soc.; trustee Ewing Marion Kauffman Found., 1996—, Kirkpatrick Found., Kirkpatrick Family Fund, Community Found. Recipient Founder's Spirit award, Conf. of Southwest Found. Office: Ewing Marion Kauffman Found 4801 Rockhill Rd Kansas City MO 64110*

HODGES-ROBINSON, CHETTINA M., nursing administrator; b. Roosevelt, NY, Mar. 12, 1963; d. Clifford and Janice (Revis) Hodges-Jones; m. Darrell K. Robinson, Mar. 17, 1991. BSN, NYU, 1986; postgrad., C.W. Post U. Cert. med.-surg. nurse basic life support and advanced cardiac life support. Staff nurse NYU Med. ctr., NYC, 1986-87, Christ Hosp., Jersey City, 1986-87; cardiothoracic recovery rm. and post-anesthesia nurse, staff nurse Lenox Hill Hosp., NYC, 1987-94; asst. nurse mgr. critical care/intensive/coronary care unit Good Samaritan Hosp., West Islip, L.I., NY, 1994—; staff nurse cardiovasc. ICU U. Hosp. at Stony Brook, NY, 1995—; field nurse Staff Builders, Medford, NY, 1995—; asst. head nurse, sub-acute, rehab. unit Jewish Home and Hosp., Bronx, NY, 1996—2003; staff nurse neuroscience North Shore Univ. Hosp., Manhasset, Long Island, NY, 2003—. Mem. Luth. Ch. of the Good Shepherd, Roosevelt, N.Y. Mem. ANA, N.Y. State Nurses Assn., N.J. Nurses Assn., Black Nurses Assn. (L.I. chpt.), Zeta Alpha Beta (bd. election Suffolk County inspector). Home: 119 S 28th St Wyandanch NY 11798-2813 E-mail: Chettina@msn.com.

HODGSON, HARRIET W., health and wellness writer; b. Flushing, N.Y., Sept. 27, 1935; d. Alfred Earnst and Mabel Clifton Weil; m. C. John Hodgson, Aug. 10, 1957; children: Helen Anne, Amy Jeanne. BS in Early Childhood Edn., Wheelock Coll., 1957; MA in Art Edn., U. Minn., 1960. Former tchr. (12 yrs.). Author: Just for You, 1978, "I Made It Myself!", 1979, E is for Energy, M is for Me, 1980, Gameworks, 1986, Artworks, 1986, Toyworks, 1986, A Parent's Survival Guide: How to Cope When Your Kid is Using Drugs, 1986, Contraptions, 1987, My First Fourth of July Book, 1987, Parents Recover Too: When Your Child Comes Home from Treatment, 1988, Rochester: City of the Prairie, 1989, When You Love a Child, 1992, Powerplays Leader's Guide, 1993, Powerplays: How Teens Can Pull the Plug on Sexual Harassment, 1993, Heart Surgery and You: An Activity Book for Preschoolers, 1994, Heart Surgery and You: An Activity Book for Gradeschoolers, 1994, Heart Surgery and You: a Guide for Teens, 1994, Alzheimer's: Finding the Words, a Communication Guide for Those Who Care, 1995, 2002, The Alzheimer's Caregiver: Dealing with the Realities of Dementia, 1998, Smart Aging: Taking Charge of Your Physical and Emotional Health, 1999, Food Label Detective: An Activity Book, 2002, Catching the Exercise Thief: A Game Book for Kids, 2004, Cracking the Health Words Code: A Game Book for Kids, 2005; co-author (with Lois Krahn): Smiling Through Your Tears: Anticipating Grief, 2005; sr. editor: Scope newsletter of the Minn. Med. Assn.; contbr. articles to websites, reports, columns, and profl. jours. Vol. McGruff House; past mem. regional devel. bd. Minn. Pub. Radio; mem. Minn. Takes Action for Healthy Kids, Adolescent Health Com., Zumbro Valley Med. Soc., Minn. Med. Assn. Commn. Com.; past pres. Minn. Med. Assn. Alliance. Mem.: AAUW, Assn. for Death Edn. and Counseling, Assn. Health Care Journalists, Wing of the Aerospace Med. Assn. (past pres., chair mktg. com., past pres.), Zumbro Valley Med. Soc. Alliance (bd. dirs., past pres., v.p., sec., newsletter editor), Am. Med. Assn. Alliance, Minn. Manx Assn., N.Am. Manx Assn., The Study Club. Avocations: cooking, art projects. Home and Office: 1107 Foxcroft Ln SW Rochester MN 55902

HODGSON, HELEN, writer; AB in English, U. Mich.; MA in English, PhD in English, U. Denver; postgrad., Yale U., Oxford U., Eng. Freelance med. writer; prof. comm. Westminster Coll., New Wilmington, Pa., dir. Masters of Profl. Communication Program, dir. Communications and the Arts. Condr. seminars in field; tech. pubs. editor U.S. Geol. Survey; cons. in field; food editor Salt Lake Mag. Contbr. numerous articles to profl. jours. Mem.: Internat. Assn. of Bus. Communicators, Coun. for Programs in Tech. and Sci. Comm., Am. Med. Writers Assn. (pres. 2001—02), Assn. of Tchrs. in Tech. Writing (life), Soc. for Tech. Comms. (sr.). Office: Am Med Writers Assn 40 W Gude Dr Ste 101 Rockville MD 20850-1192 Address: Westminster College Dept Comm Market St New Wilmington PA 16172

HODISON, PATRICIA MARY KATHLEEN, science educator; b. Topeks, Kans., Jan. 1, 1979; d. Joann Walker and Starlyn Hodison. BSc in Edn., Emporia State U., Kans., 2001; B Music Edn., Emporia State U., 2001, MS, in Instrnl. Design and Tech., 2003. Sci. tchr. Topeka Pub. Schools, 2002—03, Kans. City Pub. Schools, 2003—. Curriculum writer Topeka Pub. Schools. Mem. Kans. City Kans. Cmty. Chorus; mem. polit. action com. KNEA; mem. Knights of St. Peter Claver Ladies' Aux., 2005—06. Recipient JC Penney Golden Rule award, JC Penney, 1999, Outstanding Sr. in Music and Chemistry, Rotary Club of Emporia, 2001. Mem.: NSTA, NEA (local exec. bd. mem.), Kans. Assn. of Teachers of Sci., Kappa Delta Pi, Alpha Kappa Alpha Sorority, Inc. Cath. Avocations: sewing, gardening, dance. Office: Kansas City Kans Pub Sch 2501 Minnesota Ave Kansas City KS 66102

HODNICAK, VICTORIA CHRISTINE, pediatrics nurse; b. Detroit, Dec. 29, 1960; d. Roderick Lewis and Beverly Caroline (Backus) Turner; m. Mark Michael Hodnicak, Sept. 20, 1986; children: (twins) Christopher Alan and Matthew Lewis (dec.). ADN, Henry Ford C.C., Dearborn, Mich., 1982. RN, Mich., Tenn. Charge nurse, surg. nurse Harper Grace Hosp., Detroit, 1982-86; neonatal nurse St. John Hosp., Detroit, 1986; home care nurse, coord. med. mgmt. Bloomfield Nursing Svcs., Clawson, Mich., 1986-88; coord. pediat. endocrine growth study So. Health Sys., Memphis, 1988-92; nurse specialist, growth study coord. U. Tenn. Med. Group/St. Jude Children's Rsch. Hosp., Memphis, 1992-98; care coord., educator Pediat. Svcs. Am., Memphis, 1998-99; edn. coord. nursing Meth. Alliance Healthcare, Memphis, 2001—05; supr. nurses Guardian Healthcare Cmty. Living Mentally Retarded, 2005—. Home care pediat. nurse Personal Pediat. Nursing Profls., Pontiac, Mich., 1987-88; staff nurse Nancy Kissick's Profl. Nursing Svc., Mt. Clemens, Mich., 1988; website cons. Family Pathfinder Resource Ctr. of Tenn.; parent advisor TIPS; mem. Project DOCC. Inventor Growth Hormone new dose form, 1991, Hydrocortisone dose and stress dosing card, 1990; contbr. articles to profl. jours.; inventor equipment cart for vent. patients. Mem. tng. com. Ctr. for Devel. Disabilities, 2000—. Mem. Pediat. Endocrinology Nursing Soc. (membership com. 1992), Endocrine Nursing Soc., Human Growth Found., Neurofibromatosis Found., Turner Syndrome Soc., MAGIC Found., Alexander Graham Bell Assn. for Deaf, Project DOCC. Lutheran. Avocations: crafts, doll collecting, travel. Office Phone: 901-682-1940. Personal E-mail: vnumber1survivor@aol.com.

HOEFER, GLADYS, lawyer; BBA, Wichita State U., 1991; JD, Washburn U., 1995. Bar: Kans. 1995. Of counsel Morris Laing Evans Brock & Kennedy, Chartered., Wichita, Kans., 2003—05; pvt. practice Wichita, 1995—2002, 2005—. Office: PO Box 3251 Wichita KS 67201-3251 Office Phone: 316-263-0987.

HOEFFER, BEVERLY, nursing educator, researcher; b. Spokane, Wash., June 14, 1944; BS, U. Wash., Seattle, 1966; MS, Rutgers U., New Brunswick, N.J., 1969; DSc in Nursing, U. Calif., San Francisco, 1979. Cert. clin. specialist adult psychiat./mental health nurse. Clin. nurse specialist Mission Community Mental Health Ctr., San Francisco, 1974-75; asst. clin. prof., dept. mental health/community nursing U. Calif., San Francisco, 1979-80; assoc. to prof., chmn. dept. mental health nursing Oreg. Health Scis. U., Portland, 1980—96, assoc. dean acad. affairs sch. of nursing, 1997—2003, prof. emerita, 2003—. Bd. govs. We. Inst. Nursing, 1999—2005; presenter in field. Contbr. articles to profl. jours. Recipient Geriatric Mental Health Acad. award NIMH, 1984-87, rsch. grants in field. Fellow Am. Acad. Nursing; mem. ANA (exec. com. psychiat./mental health nursing 1986-88, chmn. coun. of specialists), We. Acad. Nurses, Phi Beta Kappa.

HOELSCHER, MARGIE LYNN, nurse; b. Cameron, Tex., July 30, 1963; d. Henry C. and Katherine (Motl) Hubnik; m. Warren R. Hoelscher, Aug. 17, 1985; children: Andrew, John Henry, Jared, Darryl. BSN with honors, U. Tex., Austin, 1987. Cert. oncology nurse, chemotherapy nurse. Staff nurse IV Scott and White Hosp., Temple, Tex., 1991—. Mem. bone marrow transplant, hospice and pain mgmt. focus groups. Mem. Oncology Nursing Soc., Sigma Theta Tau. Home: 13700 Sugar Cane Ln Temple TX 76501-3461 Office: Scott and White Hosp S 31st St Temple TX 76508-0001 E-mail: marylynn63@aol.com.

HOENS, HELEN E., state supreme court justice; b. Elizabeth, NJ, July 31, 1954; m. Robert W. Schwaneberg; 1 child, Charles. BA with high honors, Coll. of William and Mary, 1976; JD cum laude, Georgetown U., 1979. Bar: NJ 1979, DC 1979, NY 1981, US Ct. Appeals (2nd cir.) 1985, US Ct. Appeals (3rd cir.) 1989, US Dist. Ct., NJ 1979, US Dist. Ct., DC 1979, US Dist. Ct., So. Dist. NY 1981. Law clk. to Hon. John Gibbons US Ct. Appeals (3rd cir.), 1979—80; assoc. Dewey Ballentine, NY, 1980—83, Law Offices of Russel H. Beatie, Jr., 1983—85, Pitney Hardin Kipp & Szuch, Morristown, NJ, 1985—88, Lum Hoens Conant Danzis & Kleinberg, Roseland, 1988, ptnr., 1989—94; judge NJ Superior Ct., Morristown, 1994—2002, appellate judge, 2002—06; assoc. justice NJ Supreme Ct., Trenton, 2006—. Contbr. articles to law jours. Recipient Spl. Recognition Award, Autism Soc. Am., 1993. Mem.: Essex County Bar Assn. (chair Rights and Persons with Disabilities). Office: NJ Supreme Ct PO Box 970 25 Market St Trenton NJ 08625*

HOERING, HELEN G., elementary school educator; b. Liberty, N.Y., Mar. 27, 1946; d. Lewis J. and Charlotte (Huggler) Gerow Sr.; m. Rudolf O. Hoering, Dec. 23, 1968; children: Otto, Katrina. BS, SUNY, Oneonta, 1968; MSEd, SUNY, 1971. Elem. tchr. Liberty Cen. Sch. at WSS, Liberty, N.Y. Mem. N.Y. State Reading Assn., Sullivan County Reading Coun., Alpha Delta Kappa (past pres.).

HOESLI, HANNA, dentist; BS in Biology, UCLA, 1978; DDS, U. So. Calif, 1982. Pvt. practive, LA, 1982—; clin. prof. U. So Calif Sch. Dentistry. Recipient Am. Assn. Dental Anesthesiology Sr. Recognition award. Mem.: Am. Dental Assn., Calif. Dental Soc., LA Dental Soc., U. So. Calif. Dental Sch. Alumni Assn., Acad. Gen. Dentistry, Phi Betta Kappa Alumni. Office: 7060 Hollywood Blvd #400 Hollywood CA 90028 also: U So Calif Sch Dentistry 925 W 34th St DEN 235 Los Angeles CA 90089 E-mail: drhanna@flash.net.

HOEY, LAURA GAFFNEY, lawyer; BA in History, summa cum laude, U. Notre Dame, 1998; JD, Yale U., 2001. Bar: Mass. 2002. Law clk. to Hon. George A. O'Toole Jr. US Dist. Ct. (Dist. Mass.); assoc. Litig. Dept. Ropes & Gray LLP, Boston, 2002—. Mem.: Boston Bar Assn., Mass. Bar Assn., ABA (founder & co-chair Boston Chpt. White Collar Crime Com.). Office: Ropes & Gray LLP One International Place Boston MA 02110-2624 Office Phone: 617-951-7228. Office Fax: 617-951-7050. E-mail: laura.hoey@ropesgray.com.*

HOFER, INGRID, artist, educator; b. N.Y.C., Aug. 25, 1926; d. William D. and Martha G. Kassul; m. Peter H. Hofer, Mar. 10, 1951; 1 child, Mark A. BFA, Meisterschule für Mode, Hamburg, Germany, 1949; postgrad., Traphagen Sch. Design, N.Y.C., 1949-51. Instr. Acad. Arts Trailside Mus., N.J., 1968-70, Grosse Pointe War Meml., Mich., 1974-78, Countryside Arts, Arlington Heights, Ill., 1981-93, Toledo Arts Club/Lourdes Coll., 1983-93, McCormick (S.C.) Arts Coun., 1994—2004. Represented in permanent collections Fairleigh Dickinson U., N.J., First Nat. Bank, Barrington, Ill., Good Shepherd Hosp., Ill., Lumus Co., N.J., Dana Corp., Ohio, Piedmont Tech. Coll., S.C., others; exhbns. include Nat. Juried Shows, 1972-99, Union League, Chgo., 1981, Winter Sojourn, Toledo, 1987, Women Alive Ohio, 1986, 87, 89, Women on Paper, Anderson, S.C., 1996, 2005, Am. Watercolor Soc., 2005, The Arnold Gallery, Aiken, S.C., 1997, 98, Aiken Ctr. Arts, 2001-02, USCA Etherredge Art Gallery, 2002-03. Vol. John De La Howe Sch., McCormick, 1993-2005, others. Fellow Am. Artist Profl. League; mem. Catharine Lorillard Wolfeart, N.J. Inst. Art, S.C. Inst. Art, Ga. Inst. Art, Ala. Inst. Art, Gertrude Herbert Inst. Art., Am. Watercolor Soc. Home: 209 Old Ferry Rd Mc Cormick SC 29835-3409

HOFF, MARGO, artist, printmaker, muralist; b. Tulsa, June 14, 1912; d. C.W. and Ada Almeda (Hayes) H.; m. George Buehr, 1940 (dec.); 1 child, Mia. Student, U. Tulsa, Art Inst. Chgo., Pratt Graphics; DFA (hon.), St. Mary's Coll., 1969, Drew U., 1987. Vis. lectr. N.E. U., Changchun, Jilin, Peoples Republic China Pub. collections Met. Mus. Art, Whitney Mus. Am. Art, Nat. Gallery Art, Washington, Victoria and Albert Mus., London, Smithsonian Instn., Washington, gallery exhbns. and one-man shows, Wildenstein Gallery, Paris, Betty Parson Gallery, N.Y.C., Fairweather Hardin Gallery, Chgo., Itau Gallery, San Paolo, Brazil, Art Inst., Chgo., Smart Gallery U. Chgo., 1987, Mt. Sinai Hosp., N.Y.C., 1989; commd. work Mural, Mayo Clinic, Rochester, Minn., Murals, Govt. Bldg., Plattsburgh, N.Y., Wall constrn., Home Fed. Bank, Chgo., Canvas collage, Peat-Marwick-Mitchell, Washington, George Ciscle Gallery, Balt.; artist-in-residence or vis. artist assignments Am. U. Beirut, R.I. Sch. Design, Art Sch. U. Denver, Goretti Sch., Ft. Portal, Uganda; tapestry designs for Ethiopian workshop, Addis Ababa; stage curtain and costumes, Murray Louis Dancer; illustrations 3 books; slide projections Carmina Burana, Notre Dame Theatre. Home: 114 W 14th St New York NY 10011-7304

HOFFER, ALMA JEANNE, nursing educator; b. Dalhart, Tex., Sept. 15, 1932; d. James A. and Mildred (Zimlich) Koehler; m. John L. Hoffer, Oct. 7, 1954; children: John Jr., James Leo, Joseph V., Jerome P. BS, Bradley U., 1970; MA, W. Va. Coll. Grad. Study Inst., 1975; EdD, Ball State U., 1981, MA, 1986. Reg. Nurse. Staff nurse St Joseph Hosp., South Bend, Ind., 1958-59, Holy Cross Cen. Sch., St Joseph Hosp., South Bend, 1959-63; sch. nurse South Bend Sch. Corp., 1970-72; faculty staff Morris Harvey Coll., Charleston, W.Va., W.Va. Inst. Tech., Montgomery, 1975-76; asst. prof. Ball State U., Ind., 1976-77, Ind. U.-Purdue U., Ft. Wayne, 1977-81; assoc. prof. U. Akron, Ohio, 1981-83, 91-95, asst. dean, grad. edn. Ohio, 1983-90, assoc. prof. Ohio, 1991-93; prof., chair Dept. of Nursing St. Francis Coll., Fort Wayne, Ind., 1993-95; prin. investigator rsch. project Well Begun is Well Done Children's Med. Ctr. Women's Bd. Akron, 1995-96; coord. parish nurse St. Hilary Ch., 2001—. Trustee Akron Child Guidance, 1983-88, 89-95, chair planning com., 1988; nursing Blick Clin., Akron, 1988; educator, coord. parish nurses Internat. Parish Nurse Resource Ctr., 2003—; rsch. cons. St. Joseph Hosp., Ohio, 1989; cons. Health Sense, 1996-98; online faculty U. Phoenix, 2005—; rschr., presenter in field. Contbg. author: Family Health Promotion Theories and Assessment, 1989, Nursing Connections, 1992. Task force mem. Gov. Celeste's Employee Assistance Program for State U. Campuses, Ohio, 1983-84, del. People to People Citizen Amb. Program to Europe, 1988; mem. health and wellness com., coord. St. Hilary Parish; parish nurse educator Internat. Parish Nurse Resource Ctr., St. Louis, 2004—. Mem. ANA, Nat. League for Nursing, Midwest Nursing Rsch. Soc., Transcultural Nursing Soc. (chair certification and recertification com. 2000—, Leininger Leadership award 2002, 05), Portage Country Club, Cleve. Country Club, Sigma Theta Tau. Republican. Roman Catholic. Avocations: tennis, golf, skiing. Office: PO Box 794 Bath OH 44210-0794 Personal E-mail: ajhoffer@earthlink.net. Business E-Mail: ajh1@uakron.edu.

HOFFHEIMER, MINETTE GOLDSMITH, community service volunteer; b. Cin., May 1, 1927; d. Philip Hess and Cecile (Crager) Goldsmith; m. Arthur Hoffheimer Jr., June 16, 1948; children: Craig R., Roger Steven, James Martin, Mark Todd. Student, Conn. Coll. for Women, New London, 1945-48. Editor, prodr. (book in braille) Lilias Yoga and You, 1974, (poems) Marjorie's Book, 1974; editor: Lilias Yoga and Your Life, 1981; contbr. short story: (anthology) Cincinnati Short Story Winners, 1985. Trustee, sec. Cin. chpt. Nat. Coun. Jewish Women, 1966-73, chmn. and developer Large Type Program of Aid to Visually Handicapped, 1964-75, chmn. Angel Ball, 1968, on Angel Ball com. 1964-69, treas. thrift shop, 1965-67, auditor, mem. budget, ways and means, survey and evaluation coms., 1971; trustee Clovernook Home and Sch. for Blind, Cin., 1980-87; founder, 1st pres. Clovernook Assocs., Cin., 1981-85; chmn. edn. com., Boca Raton Mus. Art, 1996-2006, bd. trustee, 1996-2006; program developer, tchr. of Yoga to Blind, Cin., 1973-87; initiated Artful Memories art program Memory and Wellness Ctr. Coll. Nursing, Fla. Atlantic U., Boca Raton, Fla., 2004—. Named Vol. of Yr. Clovernook Home and Sch. for Blind, 1976, Woman of Yr. Cin. Enquirer, 1983. Mem. Brandeis, Nat. Braille Assn. (After 4000 hours svc. award 1971, 35 yr. cert. 2006), Cin. Yoga Tchrs. Assn., Life Long Learning Soc. Fla. Atlantic U., Friends of Boca Raton Mus. Art., others. E-mail: mghno1@aol.com.

HOFFLEIT, ELLEN DORRIT, astronomer; b. Florence, Ala., Mar. 12, 1907; d. Fred and Kate (Sanio) H. AB, Radcliffe Coll., 1928, MA, 1932, PhD, 1938; DSc (hon.), Smith Coll., 1984, Ctrl. Conn. State U., 1998. From research asst. to astronomer Harvard Coll. Obs., 1929-56; mathematician Ballistic Research Labs., Aberdeen Proving Ground, Md., 1943-48; tech. expert, 1948-62; lectr. Wellesley Coll., 1955-56; mem. faculty Yale U., 1956—, sr. research astronomer, 1974—. Dir. Maria Mitchell Obs., Nantucket, Mass., 1957—78; mem. Hayden Planetarium Com., N.Y.C., 1975—90; editor Meteoritical Soc., 1958—68. Author: Some Firsts in Astronomical Photography, 1950, Yale Bright Star Catalogue, 4th edit., 1982, Astronomy at Yale, 1701-1968, 1992, (autobiography) Misfortunes as Blessings in Disguise, 2002; also rsch. papers. Recipient Caroline Wilby prize Radcliffe Coll., 1938, Grad. Soc. medal, 1964, cert. appreciation War Dept., 1946, alumnae recognition award Radcliffe Coll., 1983, George van Biesbroeck award U. Ariz., 1988, Glover award Dickinson U., 1995, Maria Mitchell Women in Sci. award, 1997; asteroid Dorrit named in her honor, 1987, Anni Mirabiles Symposium in hon. of 90th birthday Yale U., 1999; inducted into Conn. Women's Hall of Fame, 1998. Fellow AAAS, Meteoritical Soc.; mem. Internat. Astron. Union, Am. Astron. Soc. (Annenberg award 1993), Am. Geophys. Union, Astron. Soc. New Haven (hon.), Am. Assn. Variable Star Observers (hon., William Tyler Olcott Listing Svc. award 2002), Am. Def. Preparedness Assn., N.Y. Acad. Scis., Conn. Acad. Arts and Scis., Nantucket Maria Mitchell Assn. (hon.), Nantucket Hist. Soc., Yale Peabody Mus. Assocs., Astron. Soc. Pacific, Phi Beta Kappa, Sigma Xi, Harvard Club of So. Conn. Office Phone: 203-432-3032. Business E-Mail: hoffleit@astro.yale.edu.

HOFFMAN, ADRIA R., music educator; d. Carol Scholem and Ivan Bruce Hoffman. BS in Music Edn., U. Md., 2000; MEd in Social Founds. & Policy, U. Va., 2005. Cert. tchr. Va. Mid. sch. band dir. Arlington Pub. Schs., Va., 2001—05, Arlington County honors band dir., 2004—05; full grad. asst. dept. music edn. U. Md., College Park, 2005—. Music buddies mentor Am. Youth Philharm., Fairfax, Va., 2002—; marching and music instr. Yorktown H.S., Arlington, Va., 2002—. Vol. foster mother Beagle Rescue, Edn., and Welfare, Inc., Woodbridge, Va., 2002—06. Recipient Honors in Edn. award, Coll. of Edn., U. of Md., 2000; Pres.'s scholarship, U. of Md., 1996-2000, Naomi Hentz Edn. scholarship, Coll. of Edn., U. of Md., 1998-2000, Gifted Edn. grant, Arlington Pub. Schs., 2001, 2002, and 2003, Full Grad. assistantship, U. of Md., 2005-2006. Mem.: ASCD, Nat. Assn. for Music Edn.

HOFFMAN, ALICE, writer; b. NYC, Mar. 16, 1952; m. Tom Martin; children: Jake, Zack. BA, Adelphi U., 1973; MA, Stanford U., 1975. Author: Property of, 1977, The Drowning Season, 1979, Angel Landing, 1980, White Horses, 1982, Fortune's Daughter, 1985, Illumination Night, 1987, At Risk, 1988, Seventh Heaven, 1990, Turtle Moon, 1992, Second Nature, 1994, Practical Magic, 1995, Local Girls, 1999, Fireflies: A Winter Tale, 1999, Horsefly, 2000, The River King, 2000, Blue Diary, 2001, Aquamarine, 2001, Indigo, 2002, Green Angel, 2003, The Probable Future, 2003, Blackbird House, 2004, The Ice Queen, 2005, (screenplay) Independence Day, 1983. Mirelles fellow Stanford U., 1975, Breadloaf fellow, 1976. Office: c/o Putnam Berkley 200 Madison Ave New York NY 10016-3903

HOFFMAN, ALICIA CORO, retired federal executive; b. Havana, Cuba, Mar. 28, 1937; d. Daniel P. and Alicia G. (Mignagaray) Camacho; m. Carlos J. Coro, May 1958 (dec. 1983); children: Alicia Biciocchi, Carlos M. Coro, Christina Kunowsky; m. Kenneth M. Hoffman, Mar. 1997. Tchg. diploma, U. Havana, 1961; MEd, U. Md., 1972. Tchr., supr. Montgomery County Pub. Schs., Rockville, Md., 1966-71; edn. spcialist U.S. Dept. Edn., Washington, 1971-80, dir. Horace Mann Learning Ctr., 1980-85, dep. asst. sec., acting asst. sec., Office for Civil Rights, 1985-87, dir. bilingual edn., 1987-88, dir. sch. improvement, 1988-96, sr. advisor, 1996-97; ret., 1997. Bd. dirs. Montgomery Pub. TV, 1984-94, Md. Higher Edn. Commn., 2004-05; bd. regents U. Sys. Md., 2005-. Recipient Presdl. Meritorious Rank award, U.S. Sr. Exec. Svc., 1992, Hispanic Achievement award in Edn., Hispanic Orgns., 1992, named Hispanic Woman of Yr., 1986. Mem. Nat. Asns. Cuban Am. Educators (bd. dirs. 1992-98), Nat. Assn. Cuban Am. Women (advisor 1980-88). Roman Catholic. Home: 909 Parsons Dr Madison MD 21648-1103

HOFFMAN, AMY S., internist; d. David J. and Ilse Hoffman. BS, Yale U., New Haven, 1976; MD, Med. Coll. Pa., Phila., 1980. Resident St. Vincent's Hosp., NYC, 1980—84; physician Beth Israel Med. Ctr., 1984—91, Mt. Sinai Svcs.-Elmhurst Hosp. Ctr., 1991—. Fellow: Am. Psychiat. Assn., NJ Acad. Medicine.

HOFFMAN, ANN FLEISHER, labor union administrator, lawyer, consultant; b. Phila., June 1, 1942; d. Willis Jr. and Mary (Leffler) Fleisher; m. Charles Stuart Hoffman Jr., June 7, 1964 (div. 1979); m. Arnold Perry Rubin, Jan. 1, 1985 (div. 1993). BA, Barnard Coll., 1964; JD, U. Md., 1972. Bar: Md., 1972, N.Y., 1978. Reporter, producer Sta. WBAL-TV, Balt., 1965-68; assignment editor, producer Sta. WJZ-TV, Balt., 1968-69; assoc. Edelman Levy and Rubenstein, Balt., 1972-77; assoc. gen. counsel Internat. Ladies' Garment Workers Union, N.Y.C., 1977-79, dir. Profl. And Clerical Employees div., 1987-91, asst. dir. legis. dept. Washington, 1991-94, assoc. dir., 1994-95; exec. asst. to Atty Gen. U.S. Dept. Justice, Washington, 1979-81; counsel Dist. 1 Communications Workers Am., N.Y.C., 1981-85, adminstrv. asst. to v.p. N.Y.C. and Cranford, N.J., 1985-87; assoc. legis. dir. Union of Needletrades, Indsl. and Textile Employees, 1995-96, legis. dir., 1997—2001. Lectr. U. Md. Sch. of Law, Balt., 1972-77; adj. faculty Cornell U. Trade Union Women's Studies Program, N.Y.C., 1979-85; trustee Botto House Am. Labor Mus., Haledon, N.J., 1986-89; pub. mem. pub. employee rels. bd., D.C., 2004— Author: (with others) Legal Status of Homemakers in Maryland, 1978, Bargaining for Child Care, 1985, 2d edit., 1991. Founding mem. Women's Law Ctr., Balt., 1971-77; mem. Balt. City Charter Review Commn., 1973-76; bd. dirs. ACLU Md. Chpt., Balt., 1975-77, Campfire Girls Chesapeake Council, Balt., 1976-77; co-chair Sachs for Atty. Gen., Md., 1976-77; pub. mem. N.Y. State Banking Bd., N.Y.C., 1984-85. Mem. Coalition of Labor Union Women (treas. N.Y.C. chpt. 1981-83), Nat. Network of Women Union Lawyers (founder), Lawyers and Legal Workers for Working Women (founder), Cornell U. Adj. Faculty Fedn., Friends of Earth (bd. dirs. 1996—), Ams. for Democratic Action (bd. dirs. 2003-), Order of Coif. Home: 2810 Mckinley St NW Washington DC 20015-1216

HOFFMAN, BARBARA A., state legislator; b. Mar. 8, 1940; d. Sidney Wolf and Eve (Simonoff) Marks; m. Donald Edwin Hoffman, 1960; children: Alan Samuel, Michael Stuart, Carolyn Mara. BS, Towson State U., 1960; MLA, Johns Hopkins U., 1966; DHL (hon.), Towson U.; D of Pub. Svc. (hon.), U. Md. Baltimore County, U. Md., Balt., U. Md./Univ. Coll. Secondary sch. tchr., Balt., 1960-63; supr. student tchrs. Morgan U., Balt., 1968-73; exec. dir. Md. Dem. Com., 1979-84; mem. Dist. 42 Md. Senate, Annapolis, 1983—2002, chair budget and tax com.; dir. Internat. Programs and Special Projects Ctr. for Talented Youths, Johns Hopkins Univ., 2003—. Chmn. bd. Univ. Md. Medical Systems, 1997—2003. Mem. Edn. Commn. of the States; bd. dirs. U. Md. Med. Sys., Balt. Mus. Art, Living Classrooms Found. Recipient numerous awards and honors. Democrat. Jewish. Home: 2905 W Strathmore Ave Baltimore MD 21209-3810 E-mail: barbara_hoffman@senate.state.md.us.

HOFFMAN, BARBARA DIANNE, elementary school educator; b. N.Y.C., July 24, 1948; d. James Hamilton and Emily Ethel (Blazek) McGloin; m. Herbert Henry Hoffman, Dec. 27, 1969; children: Melissa Anne, Matthew Henry. BA in Elem. Edn., U. Cen. Fla., 1987. Tchr. Holly Hill (Fla.) Elem. Sch., 1987—. Republican. Roman Catholic. Avocations: tennis, crafts, sewing. Home: 257 Woodstock Ct Ormond Beach FL 32174-4863

HOFFMAN, DARLEANE CHRISTIAN, chemistry professor; b. Terril, Iowa, Nov. 8, 1926; d. Carl Benjamin and Elverna (Kuhlman) Christian; m. Marvin Morrison Hoffman, Dec. 26, 1951; children: Maureane R., Daryl K. BS in Chemistry, Iowa State U., 1948, PhD in Nuclear Chemistry, 1951; Doctorate (hon.), Clark U., 2000, U. Bern, Switzerland, 2001. Chemist Oak Ridge Nat. Lab., Tenn., 1952—53; staff radiochemistry group Los Alamos Sci. Lab., N.Mex., 1953—71, assoc. leader chemistry-nuclear group, 1971—79, leader chem.-nuclear divsn., 1979—82, leader isotope and nuclear chem. divsn., 1982-84; prof. chemistry U. Calif., Berkeley, 1984—91, prof. emeritus, 1991—93, prof. grad. sch., 1993—; faculty sr. scientist Lawrence Berkeley Nat. Lab., 1984—; dir.'s fellow Los Alamos Nat. Lab., 1990—; dir. G.T. Seaborg Inst. Transactinium Sci. Lawrence Livermore Nat. Lab., 1991—96. Subcom. on nuclear and radiochemistry NAS-NRC, 1978—81, chmn. subcom. on nuclear and radiochemistry, 1982—84, mem. bd. radioactive waste mgmt., 1994—98; titular mem. commn. on radiochem. and nuclear techniques Internat. Union of Pure and Applied Chem., 1983—87, sec., 1985—87, chmn., 1987—91, assoc., 1991—93; energy rsch. adv. bd. cold fusion panel Dept. Energy, 1989—90, nuclear energy rsch. adv. com, 2000—01; separations subpanel of separations tech. and transmutation systems panel NAS, 1992—94; mem. steering com. Accel. Transmutation Waste Roadmapping Study, 1999; mem. ANTT subcom. NERAC, 2002—06; Welch Found. Conf. lectr. Tex. Univs., 1991—97, Welch Found. lectr., 2000; mem. Commn. on Endpoints Spent Nuc. Fuel and Hi-level Radioactive Waste NAS-NRC Bd. Radioactive Waste Mgmt., 1994—99; active Commn. on Endpoints Spent Nuc. Fuel and Hi-level Radioactive Waste NAS-NRC BRWM Joint US/Russian Commn., 2001—02; mem. US-Russian Joint Commn. Collaboration to Prevent Radiol. Terrorism, 2004—06. Author: The Transuranium People, 2000; contbr. articles to profl. jours. Named Japan Soc. Promotion Sci. lectr., 1987, Disting. Lectr., Inst. Phys. Rsch. and Tech., Ames Lab., 1998; named to Women in Tech. Internat. Hall of Fame, 2000; recipient Alumni Citation of Merit, Coll. Scis. and Humanities, Iowa State U., 1978, Disting. Achievement award, Iowa State U., 1986, Berkeley Citation, U. Calif., 1996, US Nat. Medal Sci., 1997, Leonard A. Ford Lectureship, Mankato State U., 1998, Frontiers Sci. award, Soc. Cosmetic Chemists, 1998; Sr. Postdoc. fellow, NSF, 1964—65, fellowships, Guggenheim Found., 1978—79. Fellow: AAAS (coun. mem. 1995—97), Am. Acad. Arts and Scis., Am. Phys. Soc., Am. Inst. Chemists (pres. N.Mex. chpt. 1976—78); mem.: Radiochem. Soc. (Lifetime Achievement award 2003), Japan Soc. Nuc. and Radiochems. (hon.; internat. mem. 2004), Norwegian Acad. Sci. and Letters, Am. Chem. Soc. (John Dustin Clark award 1976, Nuc. Chemistry award 1983, Francis P. Garvan-John M. Olin medal 1990, Priestley medal 2000, Mosher award 2001), Sigma Xi (Procter prize for sci. achievement 2003), Alpha Chi Sigma (Hall of Fame 2002), Sigma Delta Epsilon, Pi Mu Epsilon, Iota Sigma Pi (nat. hon. mem. 1993), Phi Kappa Phi. Office: Lawrence Berkeley Nat Lab MS70R0319 NSD Berkeley CA 94720 Business E-Mail: dlhoffman@lbl.gov.

HOFFMAN, ELIZABETH, economics professor; b. Bryn Mawr, Pa. BA in History, Smith Coll., 1968; MA in History, U. Pa., 1969, PhD in History, 1972; PhD in Econs., Calif. Inst. Tech., 1979. Academic and adminstrv. positions U. Fla., Northwestern U., Purdue U., U. Wyo., U. Ariz., Iowa State U.; prof. econs., history, polit. sci., psychology U. Ill., Chgo., 1997—2000, prof. Inst. of Govt. and Pub. Affairs, 1997—2000, provost and vice chancellor, 1997—2000; pres. U. Colo. Sys., Boulder, Colo., 2000—05; prof. Grad. Sch. Pub. Affairs U. Colo., Denver, 2005—. Mem. bd. dir. Nat. Sci. Bd., 2002—. Author books; contbr. articles to profl. jours. Named one of 100 women making a difference, Today's Chgo. Woman, 1999, 25 Most Powerful People, Colo. Biz Mag., 2004; recipient Ronald H. Coase prize, Electronic Intelligence citation, ANBAR. Office: U Colo Grad Sch Pub Affairs PO Box 173364 - Campus Box 142 Denver CO 80217-3364 Office Phone: 303-315-2748. E-mail: elizabeth.hoffman@cu.edu.

HOFFMAN, EVA ALFREDA, author, editor, educator; b. Cracow, Poland, 1945; arrived in Canada, 1959; came to U.S. 1963; Student, Cracow Mus. Sch.; BA, Rice U., 1967; postgrad., Yale U., 1967-68; MA, PhD, Harvard U., 1976. Teaching fellow Eng., Harvard U., 1973-75; asst. prof. Eng. and Am. Lit., U. New Hampshire, 1975-76, Tufts U., 1976-77; guest lectr. univs., orgns.; resident Yaddo, summer 1991, MacDowell Colony, summer 1991; vis. prof. MIT, 1999-2005, Hunter Coll., 2006. Sr. editor Politics Today, 1979-80; editor Week in Review N.Y. Times, 1980-81, dep. editor Arts and Leisure, 1981-85, editor Book Review, 1987-90, book critic, 1989; author: Lost in Translation: A Life in a New Language, (Jean Stein award Am. Acad. Inst. Arts and Letters 1990), 1989, 90, Eng., 1989, France, 1992, Japan, 1992, Germany, Exit Into History, 1993, Shtetl, 1997, The Secret, 2001; contbr. articles book reviews to mags. Recipient Whiting award for writing, 1990; Woodrow Wilson fellow, 1967-68, Danforth graduate fellow, 1968-74, Carnegie-Mellon postdoctoral fellow, 1977-78, Am. Coun. Learned Socs. grantee, 1985-86, Guggenheim fellow, 1992-93, NY Inst. for Humanities fellow, NYU, Am. Assn. Polish-Jewish Studies fellow, vis. fellow Inst. Eastern European Studies, Columbia U. Mem. Am. PEN (exec. bd.).

HOFFMAN, FAITH LOUISE, social worker; b. Buffalo, June 7, 1944; d. William George Hoffman, Louise Caroline Hoffman; children: Donald Louis, Louis William, Christopher Robert. BS magna cum laude, Medaille Coll., 1983—87; MSW, SUNY, Buffalo, 1991—93. LCSW 1993. Case mgr. N.Y. Crime Victim's Assistance Program, Buffalo, 1987—88; dir. domestic violence program YWCA of Tonawanda's, 1988—90; dir. family support program Concerned Ecumenical Ministry, Buffalo, 1990—92; social worker Dept. Veteran's Affairs Med. Ctr., Buffalo, 1993—95, women veteran's program mgr., 1995—. Adj. prof. U. Buffalo Grad. Sch. Social Work, 2004—; dir., founder Hopegivers, Buffalo, 1991—; dir. VA Domestic Violence Program, Buffalo, 1995—; field faculty SUNY, Buffalo, 1996—; domestic violence cons. Erie County Dept. Health, Buffalo, 2000—02; spkr. in field. Named cmty. hero, torchbearer Western N.Y. Olympic Torch Relay, Atlanta Olympic Com., 1996—96; recipient Svc. to Mankind award, Sertoma Greater Buffalo, 1998—98, ann. leadership award, YWCA Western N.Y., 2001—01, Joan A. Levine award, Woman Focus, 2002, Fed. Woman of Yr. award, Buffalo (N.Y.) Fed. Exec. Bd., 2003, Person of Yr. award, Jewish War Vets. Am.-Buffalo Frontier Post 25, 2004. Office: VA Western NY Healthcare Sys 3495 Bailey Ave Buffalo NY 14215 Office Phone: 716-862-8675. Business E-Mail: faithhoffman@med.va.gov.

HOFFMAN, HELEN BACON, artist; b. San Antonio, Tex., July 14, 1930; d. Stanley and Helen Maverick Bacon; m. Richard Gurney Hoffman, Jan. 24, 1951; children: Katherine H. Thomason, Richard G. Jr., Cynthia Hoffman Hill. Represented in permanent collections Corcoran Gallery of Art, Washington, Smithsonian Instn., Nelson Art Gallery, Pa. Acad. Fine Art, Phila., Chgo. Art Inst., Inst. Norte Americano Mexicano de Relationes Culturales, Mexico City, one-woman shows include River Art Gallery, San Antonio, 1961, Wichita Art Assn., 1963, Veerhoff Galleries, Washington, 1965, 1967, 1972, 1977, 1981, 1987, 1997, Grand Cen. Art Galleries, N.Y.C., 1969, 1971, 1973, 1974, 1976, 1985, 1989, Pritchard Art Galleries, Houston and San Antonio, 1978, 1980, Musselman Gallery, San Antonio, 1982, 1986, Nanette Richardson Fine Art, San Antonio, 1996. Recipient awards, River Art Show, San Antonio, 1960—62, D.C. Outdoor Art Fair, Washington, 1965, Pa. Acad. Fine Arts, Phila., 1969, Salmagundi Club, N.Y.C., 1974, Pastel. Mem.: Pastel Soc. Am. (awards 1976, 1978, 1985). Avocation: growing orchids. Home: 8320 Woodgrove Rd Jacksonville FL 32256

HOFFMAN, JEAN LILLIAN, parochial school educator; d. Thomas Pompey and Edna Althea Priolo; children: Robert Thomas, Sharon Virginia. BS, U. Md., College Park, 1978. Cert. tchr. Md., ACSI. Math tchr. Pyle Jr. H.S., Bethesda, Md., 1979—81; math/sci. tchr. Tara-Reston Christian, Va., 1990—93; math/biology tchr. New Life Christian Sch., Frederick, Md., 1993—. Advisor student coun. New Life Christian Sch., Frederick, 2000—. Republican. Office: New Life Christian Sch 5909 Jefferson Pike Frederick MD 21703

HOFFMAN, JENNIFER ANNE, vascular technician, director; b. Bklyn., Aug. 29, 1971; d. Louis Frank Marchese and Carol Maryann Sclafani; m. Brian David Hoffman, Sept. 24, 2000. BS, SUNY, Bklyn., 1997. Registered vascular technologist, cert. EMT N.Y. Office mgr. Maimonides Med. Ctr., Bklyn., 1996—98, clin. vascular specialist, 1998—99; tech. coord. St. Luke's-Roosevelt Hosp. Ctr., N.Y.C., 1999—2001, tech. dir., 2001—03, Duke U. Med. Sch., Durham, NC, 2003—. Instr. SUNY Health Sci. Ctr., Bklyn., 1998—99; vascular ultrasound tng. dept. radiology St. Luke's-Roosevelt Hosp. Ctr., N.Y.C., 2001—03. Contbr. articles to profl. jours.; spkr. in field. Recipient Musical Achievement award, N.Y. State Bd. Edn., 1989, Am. Venous Found. Beiersdorf-Jobst Rsch. fellowship, 1999. Mem.: Soc. Vascular Tech., Am. Registry Diagnostic Med. Sonographers. Avocations: flute, saxophone, poetry, travel. Office: Duke U Med Ctr Box 2990 Durham NC 27710 Personal E-mail: vascsono@aol.com.

HOFFMAN, JETHA L., music educator, voice educator; b. New Orleans, Oct. 2, 1948; d. Jether Anthony and Dorothy Carmen (Adriani) Hübsch; m. James Tyre Dennis, Oct. 6, 1965 (div. Jan. 1972); 1 child, James Tyre Dennis; m. Gary William Hoffman, Oct. 2, 1988. Grad. h.s., New Orleans, 1966. Performer, soloist, entertainer, concert pianist, 1962—; prof. accompanist all opera and theatre, New Orleans; piano tchr., vocal tchr. New Orleans, Cathedral City, Calif., 1994—; performed in numerous bands, 1967—. Piano/vocals, entertainer Pete Fountain Enterprises, New Orleans, 1979-86, performed throughout U.S. Composer piano solos; arranger and editor for piano, vocals. Recipient numerous awards and trophies. Mem. Music Tchrs. Nat. Assn., Calif. Assn. Profl. Music Tchrs. Roman Catholic. Home: 68590 Tachevah Dr Cathedral City CA 92234-3879 Fax: 760-325-1220.

HOFFMAN, JOY YU, harpist, pianist; b. Nanjing, Jiangsu, People's Republic of China, Mar. 28, 1952; came to U.S., 1984; d. Zhong Hai and Xing Huang Yu; m. Paul Franklin Hoffman, July 16, 1988. Diploma in music, Shenyang Conservatory of Music, China, 1981; MusB, Roosevelt U., 1988; MusM, Northwestern U., 1991. Opera coach Harbin (China) Opera, 1970-83; piano, harp tchr. Morton Grove, 1989—; harpist Fox Valley Symphony, Aurora, Ill., 1993—, Ill. Chamber Symphony, St. Charles, Ill., 1996—. Adj. prof. harp Roosevelt U., Chgo., 1993-98; harpist Harbin Opera Co., 1980-83, concert pianist, 1970-83. Performer, composer (CD) Ballad, 1999; author: What is the Kong Hou Chinese Harp?, 1999, Chinese Folk Music and Kong Hou, 1995. Recipient 1st prize Young Artists Competition City Govt., 1982. Mem. Hist. Harp Soc., Great Lakes Harpers, Am. Harp Soc., Ill. Music Tchrs. Assn., Am. Fedn. Musicians. Avocations: photography, painting, garden design. Home: 8826 Menard Ave Morton Grove IL 60053-2461

HOFFMAN, JUDY GREENBLATT, preschool director; b. Chgo., June 12, 1932; d. Edward Abraham and Clara (Morrill) Greenblatt; m. Morton Hoffman, Mar. 16, 1950 (div. Jan. 1983); children: Michael, Alan, Clare. BA summa cum laude, Met. State Coll., Denver, 1972; MA, U. No. Colo., 1976, MA in Spl. Edn. Moderate Needs, 1996. Cert. tchr. Colo. Pre-sch. dir. B.M.H. Synagogue, Denver, 1968-70, Temple Emanuel, Denver, 1970-85, Congregation Rodef Shalom, Denver, 1985-88; tchr. Denver Pub. Schs., 1988—. Bilingual tchr. adults in amnesty edn. Denver Pub. Schs., 1989-90. Author: I Live in Israel, 1979, Joseph and Me, 1980 (Gamoran award), (with others) American Spectrum Single Volume Encyclopedia, 1991. Coord. Douglas Mountain Therapeutic Riding Ctr. for Handicapped, Golden, Colo., 1985—; dir. Mountain Ranch Summer Day Camp for Denver Pub. Schs., 1989-91. Mem. Nat. Assn. Temple Educators. Democrat. Avocations: riding, writing, music. Personal E-mail: jhoff3@earthlink.net.

HOFFMAN, KAREN A., foundation executive; b. L.A., Nov. 21, 1955; d. Robert Howard and Kathleen (Holser) Ahmanson; m. James Edward Hoffman, Sept. 6, 1980; children: Robert James, Kristina Marie. BS in Ednl. Devel., Occidental Coll., L.A., 1977. Asst. ednl. therapist Pacific Clinics, Pasadena, Calif., 1977-79; asst. sec. The Ahmanson Found., L.A., 1979-85, sec., sr. program officer Beverly Hills, Calif., 1986—. Trustee Childrens Hosp. of L.A., 1990-93, Marlborough Sch., L.A., 1985-93; judge bus. and industry awards L.A. Beautiful, 1983, 84, 85; sec. Ribet Acad. Ednl. Enrichment Found., L.A., 1997-2001. Mem. So. Calif. Assn. for Philanthropy, L.A. Tennis Club. Avocations: photography, hiking.

HOFFMAN, KARLA LEIGH, mathematician, educator; b. Paterson, NJ, Feb. 14, 1948; d. Abe and Bertha (Guthaim) Rakoff; m. Allan Stuart Hoffman, Dec. 26, 1971; 1 child, Matthew Douglas. BA, Rutgers U., 1969; MBA, George Washington U., 1971, DSc in Ops. Rsch., 1975. Ops. rsch. analyst IRS, Washington, 1970-72; rsch. asst. George Washington U., 1972-75, assoc. profl. lectr., 1978-85; NSF postdoctoral rsch. fellow NAS, Washington, 1975-76; assoc. prof. sys. engring. dept. George Mason U., Fairfax, Va., 1985-86, assoc. prof. ops. rsch. and applied stats., 1986-89, prof. ops. rsch., 1990—, disting. prof., 1989, interim dept. chmn., 1996-97, chmn., 1997-98, chmn. sys. engring. and ops. rsch., 1998—2000. Mathematician Nat. Bur. Stds., Washington, 1976—84; vis. assoc. prof. ops. rsch. U. Md., 1982; mng. ptnr. Optimization Software Assocs.; cons. Govt. Agys., Airline, Telecom. and Def. Industries; bd. dirs. Parkinsons Found. Nat. Capital Area, 2006. Assoc. editor Internat. abstracts of Ops. Rsch., 1991—96, The Math. Programming Jour., Series B, 1987—, The Ops. Rsch. Soc. Jour. on Computing, 1991—96, Jour. Computational Optimization and Applications, 1992—98, mem. editl. bd. Annals of Ops. Rsch., 2000—; contbr. articles to profl. jours. Bd. dirs. Nat. Capital Region Parkinsons Found., 2006. Recipient Applied Rsch. award, Nat. Inst. Stds. and Tech., 1984, Silver medal, U.S. Dept. Commerce, 1984, Disting. Prof. award, 1989, Kimball medal, Inst. Ops. Rsch. & Mgmt. Svc., 2005. Fellow: Inst. Ops. Rsch. and Mgmt. Sci. (treas. 1995—96, exec. com. 1995—99, pres. 1998, Kimball medal 2005); mem.: Math. Programming Soc. (editor newsletter 1979—82, chmn. com. algorithms 1982—85, coun. 1985—88, exec. com., chmn. membership com. 1988—89), Ops. Rsch. Soc. Am. (sec.-treas. Computer Sci. Tech. sect. 1979—80, vis. profl. lectr. 1980—, vice chmn. sect. 1981, chmn. sect. 1982, chmn. tech. sect. com. 1983—86, coun. 1985—88, chmn. Lanchester Prize com. 1989, treas. 1993—94). Home: 6921 Clifton Rd Clifton VA 20124-1525 Office Phone: 703-993-1679. Business E-Mail: khoffman@gmu.edu.

HOFFMAN, KATHALEEN MAY, biology educator; b. Gloversville, NY, May 18, 1952; d. William Edward Lafoe and Mary Patricia Williams; m. Keith E. Hoffman, Jan. 12, 1974; 1 child, Kelly May. BA in Biology/Chemistry, Coll. St. Rose, Albany, NY, 1974; MS in Ednl. Psychology, Coll. St. Rose, 1977. Cert. permanent tchg., gen. sci., biology, chemistry 7-12 NY. Sci. tchr. biology Keveny Meml. Acad., Cohoes, NY, 1974—79, sci. tchr. chemistry, 1982—83; pvt. tutor, 1979—83; biology tchr. Shaker HS, Latham, NY, 1983—. Adj. prof. Hudson Valley Cmty. Coll., Troy, NY, 2005—. Dir.: (handbell choir), 2002—. Vol. with therapy dog local nursing homes. Mem.: Nat. Sci. Tchrs. Assn., Biology & Life Scis. Assn., Sci. Tchrs. N.Y. State. Avocations: walking, church activites.

HOFFMAN, KATHERINE ANN, education educator; b. Queens, N.Y., Dec. 26, 1956; m. Robert Louis Hoffman, Aug. 29, 1981; 1 child, Ezra Jared. BS in Zoology, Tex. A&M U., College Station, 1978; MS in Biology, Calif. State U., Long Beach, 1981. Grad. tchg. asst. Calif. State U., Long Beach, 1980—81; instr. biology Long Beach City Coll., 1981—86; adj. faculty natural scis. Tarrant C.C., Hurst, Tex., 1987—91, instr. natural scis., 1991—97, asst. prof. natural scis., 1997—. Project dir. sci. enrichment program for children Tarrant C.C., 1999—, dental hygiene curriculum rev. com., 2003—. Judge Ft. Worth Regional Sci. Fair, Fort Worth, 1991; vol. Fed. Med. Ctr., Carswell, Fort Worth, 2002—04; mentor Covenant Christian Acad., Colleyville, Tex., 2004. Recipient Robert A. Welch Found. Undergraduate scholarship in Chemistry, Tex. A&M U., 1976—77, Disting. Student award, 1976—77, Transfer Achievement Awards Ceremony, Promoting Academic Excellence, U. Tex. Arlington, 2001, Chancellor's award for Exemplary Tchg., Tarrant C.C., 2004, Nat. Inst. for Staff and Orgnl. Devel. excellence award, U. Tex.,Austin, 2005; grantee Instrumentation and Lab. Improvement, NSF, 1995. Mem.: Delta Kappa Gamma Soc. Internat. Office: Tarrant CC 828 Harwood Rd Hurst TX 76054-3219 Office Phone: 817-515-6946. Business E-Mail: katherine.hoffman@tccd.edu.

HOFFMAN, LINDA M., chemist, educator; b. NYC, Dec. 18, 1939; d. Theodore and Esther Weiss; m. Robert G. Hoffman, Feb. 2, 1958; 1 child, Samuel A. BS in Chemistry, Queens Coll., 1959; MS, NYU, 1967, PhD in Organic Chemistry, 1970. Rsch. assoc. Kingsbrook Jewish Med. Ctr., N.Y.C., 1973-77; asst. prof. Baruch Coll., CUNY, N.Y.C., 1977-79, assoc. prof., 1979-82, prof., 1982—, chair dept. natural scis., 1995-98. Reviewer grant proposals NIH. Contbr. articles on Tay-Sachs disease and glycosphingolipids to profl. jours. Mem. edn. com. UN Internat. Sch., N.Y.C., 1981-84; bd. dirs. Forest Hills Gardens Corp., 1993-2000. Recipient Moore award Am. Soc. Neuropathologists, 1981, 84, Founders Day award NYU, 1971, 112th Precinct Cmty. Coun. award, 1993; postdoctoral fellow Sloan Kettering Inst. Cancer Rsch., N.Y.C., 1972-73. Mem. AAAS, Am. Chem. Soc., Sigma Xi. Office: Baruch Coll Dept Natural Scis One Bernard Baruch Way New York NY 10010-5518 E-mail: linda_hoffman@baruch.cuny.edu.

HOFFMAN, LINDA R., social services administrator; b. New Haven, July 23, 1940; d. Bernard Harry and Sylvia (Paul) Rosenfield; m. Peter A. Hoffman, Sept. 25, 1965; 1 child, Tracie Hoffman Cohen. BA, Russell Sage Coll., 1962; MSW, Columbia U., 1968. Cert. social worker NY. Case worker Conn. Dept. Welfare, New Haven, 1962-63, NYC Bur. Child Welfare, NYC, 1963-65, supr., 1965-66; asst. to commr. program planning NYC Dept. Social Svcs., NYC, 1968-70; spl. asst. to commr. NYC Spl. Svc. for Children, NYC, 1972-79; pres. NY Found. Sr. Citizens, NYC, 1979—. Cons. USIA, Teheran, Iran, 1975; adj. prof., dean's adv. coun. Columbia Sch. Social Work. Mem. Cmty. Bd. #8, NYC, 1982—; bd. dirs. Grosvenor Neighborhood House, 2002, West Side YMCA, 2004—. Recipient, Presdl. Recognition award for Cmty. Svc., 1983, East Manhattan C. of C., award for Disting. Civic Svc., 1990, The Mcpl. Art Soc. of NY award, 1997; named to Columbia U. Sch. Social Work Hall of Fame, 2000. Mem. NASW (cert.), Women's City Club of NY, YWCA NYC Acad. Women Achievers, Women's Forum. Avocations: boating, fishing, thoroughbred race horses. Office: NY Found Sr Citizens 11 Park Pl Ste 1416 New York NY 10007-2801

HOFFMAN, LINDA S., science educator, special education educator; BA, UCLA, 1964—66, Parent Edn. Credential, Spl. Edn. Credential, UCLA, 1987—88. Tchr. LA Bd. Edn., 1966—. Tchr. mentor LA Bd. Edn., 2004—. Recipient Making a difference in a Childs Life award, L.A. City Coun., 1987, Fedco award, 2003; Field Rsch. grant, Earthwatch, 1997 & 1999, Rsch./Mentoring grant, Armada Project, 2004—06, Alternative Energy grant, Brit. Petroleum, 2005—06. Mem.: Nat. Sci. Tchrs. Assn. (assoc.; spl. edn. adv. panel 2005—), Calif. League Mid. Schs. (assoc.; jr. Optimist Club advisor 1988—), United Tchrs. of L.A. (assoc.), Greater L.A. Tchrs. Sci. Assn. (assoc.; incoming pres. 2005—), Culver City Optimist Club (assoc.; first Calif. pswd woman lt. gov. 1995—96). Avocations: marine mammal research, youth service club. Office Phone: 310-837-5236.

HOFFMAN, M. KATHY, graphics designer, packaging designer; b. Sidney, Nebr., Aug. 30, 1956; d. Norman and Irline (Dillon) Barnica; m. Jeffrey W. Hoffman, Apr. 16, 1988. BA, U. Nebr., Kearney, 1978, BFA, 1984, MA, 1987. Product quality assurance Baldwin Filters, Kearney, Nebr., 1978-88, product technician, 1988-90, product devel. technician, 1990-92, product identification coord., 1992—93, packaging and graphics designer, 1993—. Mem. Inst. Packaging Profls., Assn. Corel Artists and Designers, Women in Packaging. Avocations: collect cat figures, reading, movies. Office: Baldwin Filters 4400 Highway 30 E Kearney NE 68847-0724

HOFFMAN, MARGARET ANN HOVLAND, artist, activist; b. Seattle, Feb. 20, 1930; d. Harold Kenneth and Gertrude Anne (Maxson) Hovland; m. Don Lee Hoffman, Apr. 2, 1955; children: Lori, Lee. Student, U. Wash., 1948-51; B Profl. Arts, Art Ctr. Coll. Design, 1955. Interior designer Bon Marché, Seattle, 1948-49; interior designer, coord. Paul Siegal, Seattle, 1949-51; asst. designer Seattle Design Ctr.; indsl. designer Olsen/Spencer, L.A., 1955-57; freelance artist L.A., 1957-61, 85—; designer, asst. Don Hoffman Jewelry, Beverly Hills, Calif., 1975-85; activist, creator, founder Oceanside Beach Restoration Assn., San Diego County, Calif., 1988—. Mem. grad. adv. bd. Art Ctr. Sch. Coll. Design, L.A. and Pasadena, Calif., 1956-80. Designer logos and pamphlets for Shell Oil, 1953, AEC, 1953-55, Owl/Rexall Drugs, 1954, Pegasus/Tidewater Oil, 1955-57, AEC; commd. Oceanside Beach Protection Com., 1996-98. Mem. Women in Arts (charter). Avocations: painting, interior decorating, horseback riding, swimming, travel. Home: 270 Tavistock Ave Los Angeles CA 90049-3229

HOFFMAN, MARGUERITE STEED, former art gallery director; m. Robert Kenneth Hoffman; 1 child, Katherine. Positions with Dallas Mus. Art; former dir. Gerald Peters Gallery. Bd. trustees Dallas Mus. Art, 1999—, chmn. bd.; bd. dirs. Tex. Freedom Network; mem. coun. Dallas Women's Found.; donated contemporary art collection and a $20 million endowment Dallas Mus. Art, 2005. Named one of Top 200 Collectors, ARTnews mag., 2003—06. Avocation: Collector postwar Am. and European art, Chinese monochromes. Office: Dallas Mus Art 1717 N Harwood Dallas TX 75201

HOFFMAN, MARIAN RUTH, singer, voice educator; m. Warren Marlyn Hoffman, Aug. 13, 1955; children: Mark Edward, Paul Stephen, Jeffrey Brian, Thomas Warren. MusB, U. Dubuque, Iowa, 1955; MFA, U. Minn., Mpls., 1973. Tchr. music Darlington Pub. Schools, Wis., 1955—58; instr. voice Inver Hills C.C., Minn., 1973—75, Home Studio, St. Paul, 1973—; profl. soloist Westminster Presbyn. Ch., Mpls., 1974—2004; instr. voice Normandale C.C., Bloomington, 1974—86, Bethel U., St. Paul, 1981—91. Pres.,, v.p., editor Thursday Musical, Mpls., 1974—; bd. mem. Schuessler Vocal Arts Ctr., 1990—; v.p. Young People's Symphony Concert Assn., 2005—. Singer: (recitals and concerts) 10-15 Appearances Yearly; singer: (various roles) (operas) Rape of Lucretia, Madame Butterfly, Savitri, Riders of the Sea, Tender Land, Wise Women; singer: (anna, mother superior, singer) (musical theater) King and I, Sound of Music, West Side Story, Oliver. Parish leader Westminster Presbyn. Ch., Mpls., 1990, elder, 2005—. Recipient Alumni Notable Achievement award, U. Minn., 2004. Mem.: Am. Guild Organists (sec. 1967—68), Nat. Assn. Tchrs. Singing (sec. 1978—80, emeritus 2002), Sigma Alpha Iota (life; v.p. 2000—05, Sword Honor, Alumni Distinction 2000, 2003). Avocations: travel, walking, knitting, gardening. Personal E-mail: marianhoffman@comcast.net.

HOFFMAN, MARY CATHERINE, retired nurse, anesthetist; b. Winamac, Ind., July 14, 1923; d. Harmon William Whitney and Dessie Maude (Neely) Hoffman. RN, Meth. Hosp., Indpls., 1945; cert. obstet. analgesia and anesthesia, Johns Hopkins Hosp., 1949; grad., Cleve. Sch. Anesthesia, 1952. Staff nurse Meth. Hosp., 1945-49; rsch. asst., then staff anesthetist Johns Hopkins Hosp., 1949-62; staff anesthetist Meth. Hosp., 1962-64, U. Chgo. Hosps., 1964-66; chief nurse anesthetist Paris (Ill.) Cmty. Hosp., 1966-80; staff anesthetist Hendricks County Hosp., Danville, Ind., Ball Meml. Hosp., Muncie, Ind., 1981-86; ret. Mem. Am. Assn. Nurse Anesthetists, Am. Heart Assn., Ind. Fedn. Bus. and Profl. Women's Clubs (Ill. dist. chmn. 1977-78, state found. chmn. 1978-79, Found. award 1979). Republican. Presbyterian. Home: 1700 N Maddox Dr Muncie IN 47304-2674

HOFFMAN, MARY HILLS, literature educator, publishing executive; MA in English, Sonoma State U., Rohnert Park, Calif., 1980. Assoc. prof. English Harrisburg Area CC, Pa., 1992—; pub. Plum Br. Press, Harrisburg, 2000—. Founder/pub. Sonoma Mandala Lit. Mag., Rohnert Park, Calif., 1973. Author. Mem.: MLA. Office: Harrisburg Area CC One HACC Dr Harrisburg PA 17110 Business E-Mail: mhhoffma@hacc.edu.

HOFFMAN, MERLE HOLLY, advocate, psychologist, writer; b. Phila., Mar. 6, 1946; d. Jack Rheins and Ruth (Dubow) H.; m. Martin Gold, June 30, 1979. BA magna cum laude in Psychology, Queens Coll., 1972; postgrad., CUNY, 1972-75. Founder, pres. Choices Women's Med. Ctr., Long Island City, N.Y., 1971—; family planning cons. Health Ins. Plan, N.Y.C., 1973-85; founder, pres. Ctr. for Comprehensive Breast Svcs., N.Y.C., 1979-82, Merle Hoffman Enterprises, N.Y.C., 1986—, Choices Mental Health Ctr., 1993—. Speaker, debator on women's rights and polit. issues; founder, pres. Nat. Liberty Com., 1981; active Choices East Project, Moscow, 1992—; provider of Project Liberty Svc., Sept. 11, 2001; bd. mem. Vet. Feminists Am. Cons. editor Female Health Topics and Diagnostic Reporter, 1979-81; editor, pub. On The Issues: The Progressive Woman's Quarterly; contbr. articles in field to various publs.; producer documentary film Abortion A Different Light; founder N.Y. Pro-Choice Coalition; host cable TV series MH: On the Issues, 1986. Recipient Women's Equality award, L.I. NOW, N.Y., 1995, Woman of Power and Influence award, N.Y. Chpt. NOW, 1998, Lifetime Svc. award, Vet. Feminists Am., 2000. Mem. APPA (bd. dirs.), Nat. Assn. Abortion Facilities (co-founder, pres. 1976-77), Nat. Abortion Fedn. (co-founder, sec. 1977-78), Vet. Feminists of Am., Nat. Adv. Bd., Phi Beta Kappa. Achievements include papers in Sallie Bingham Ctr. Women's History, Duke U. Office: Choices Women's Med Ctr Inc 29-28 41st Ave Long Island City NY 11101-3303 Office Phone: 718-349-9100 x 880. Personal E-mail: Mhoti@aol.com.

HOFFMAN, NANCY, art gallery director; b. NYC, 1944;, Wellesley Coll., 1964, Columbia U., 1966. Asst. registrar Asia House Gallery, N.Y.C., 1964-69; dir. Contemporary Gallery French & Co., N.Y.C., 1969-72; owner, pres. Nancy Hoffman Gallery, N.Y.C., 1972—. Lectr., jury exhibitor throughout U.S. Contbr. chpt. to text. Office: Nancy Hoffman Gallery 429 W Broadway New York NY 10012-3799 Office Phone: 212-966-6676. Business E-Mail: nancyhoffmangallery@hotmail.com.

HOFFMAN, PATRICIA PATRICK, retired psychologist; b. Paragon, Ind., Jan. 1, 1925; d. Bruce Tadd and Kathryn Jane (Moyer) Patrick; m. Paul G. Hoffman, Jan. 27, 1945; children: Jane, Mary Ann, Nancy, John, Peter. BA, Carleton Coll., 1945; MS, St. Cloud State U., Minn., 1964; PhD, Union Grad. Sch., Cin., 1982. Lic. cons. psychologist, Minn. Social worker Stearns Social Svcs., St. Cloud, Minn., 1964-66; instr. St. Cloud State U., 1966-76, from asst. to assoc. prof., 1976-86, prof. psychology, 1984-90, also past mem. faculty assoc. exec. coun., rsch. grant com., speakers bur., prof. emeritus, 1990—; pvt. practice in psychology/owner antique shops St. Cloud. Adj. faculty mem. Union Grad. Sch. St. Cloud State U., mem. com. women's study curriculum; cons. in field. Bd. dirs., mem. speakers bur. St. Cloud Area Women's Shelter, 1984—; bd. mem. Summit. Mem. Am. Psychol. Assn. (various divs.), Minn. Psychol. Assn., Cen. Minn. Psychol. Assn., DAR (past pres.). Mem. Democratic Farm Labor Party. Presbyterian. Avocations: antiques, sports. Home: 33 Highbanks Pl Saint Cloud MN 56301-4408

HOFFMAN, RUTH ELAINE, mathematics educator; b. Easton, Pa., Sept. 24, 1947; d. Ralph Edward and Jane Ella Playfoot; m. Harvey Edward Hoffman, Dec. 18, 1971. BA in Math., Houghton Coll., 1969; MEd, Kutztown U., 1972. Math. tchr. Easton Jr. H.S., 1969—71; teller, mgr. tng. coord. Valley Fed. Savings & Loan, Easton, 1972—88; dir. student ministry Toccoa Falls (Ga.) Coll., 1989—2000, asst. prof. math., 2000—. Bd. dirs. YMCA, Easton, 1980—; bd. dirs., pres. Inst. for Fin. Edn., Easton, 1973—88. Mem.: Math. Assn. Am., Optimist Club (v.p., pres., treas.,). Republican. Home: 7075 Whippoorwill Ln Toccoa GA 30577 Office: Toccoa Falls Coll PO Box 800884 Toccoa Falls GA 30598 Office Phone: 706-886-6831 ext 5466. Business E-Mail: rhoffman@tfc.edu.

HOFFMAN, SHARON LYNN, adult education educator; b. Chgo. d. David P. and Florence Seaman; m. Jerry Irwin Hoffman, Aug. 25, 1963; children: Steven Abram, Rachel Irene. BA, Ind. U., 1961; M Adult Edn., Nat.-Louis Univ., 1992. High sch. English tchr. Chgo. Pub. Schs., 1961-64; tchr. Dept. of Def. Schs., Braconne, France, 1964-66; tchr. ESL Russian Inst., Garmisch, Fed. Republic Germany, 1966, 67; tchr. adult edn. Monterey Peninsula Unified Schs., Ft. Ord, Calif., 1977-79; tchr. ESL MAECOM, Monmouth County, NJ, 1979-80; lectr., tchr. adult edn. Truman Coll./Temple Shalom, Chgo.; tchr. homebound Fairfax County Pub. Schs., Fairfax, Va., 1976; entry operator Standard Rate & Data, Wilmette, Ill., 1986-87; rsch. editor, spl. projects editor Marquis Who's Who, Wilmette, 1987-92; mem. adj. faculty Nat.-Louis U., Evanston and Wheeling, Ill., 1993-99, tutor coord., then coord. learning specialist, 1993-99; pres. Cultural Transitions, Pebble Beach, Calif., 1992—. Mem.: TESOL, ASTD, Nat. Coun. Tchrs. English. Personal E-mail: culturaltrans1@aol.com.

HOFFMAN, SUE ELLEN, retired elementary school educator; b. Dayton, Ohio, Aug. 23, 1945; d. Cyril Vernon and Sarah Ellen (Sherer) Stephan; m. Lawrence Wayne Hoffman, Oct. 28, 1967. BS in Edn., U. Dayton, 1967; postgrad., Loyola Coll., 1977, Ea. Mich. U., 1980; MEd, Wright State U., 1988. Cert. reading specialist and elem. tchr., Ohio. 5th grade tchr. St. Anthony Sch., Dayton, Ohio, 1967-68, West Huntsville (Ala.) Elem. Sch., 1968-71; 6th grade tchr. Ranchland Hills Pub. Sch., El Paso, Tex., 1973-74; 3rd grade tchr. Emerson Pub. Sch., Westerville, Ohio, 1976, St. Joan of Arc Sch., Aberdeen, Md., 1976-78, Our Lady of Good Counsel, Plymouth, Mich., 1979-80; 5th grade tchr. St. Helen Sch., Dayton, 1980—2002; ret., 2002. Selected for membership Kappa Delta Pi, 1988. Mem. Internat. Reading Assn., Ohio Internat. Reading Assn., Dayton Area Internat. Reading Assn., Nat. Cath. Edn. Assn. Roman Catholic. Home: 2174 Green Springs Dr Kettering OH 45440-1120 Personal E-mail: l-shoffman@msn.com.

HOFFMAN, SUSAN PATRICIA WARY, special education educator, elementary school educator; b. Newark, Mar. 3, 1946; d. Louis Stephen and Stella Elizabeth (Rucki) Wary; m. Charles Colin Hoffman, Dec. 23, 1967; children: Heather, Hope, Holly, Charles, Christopher. BS in Elem. Edn., Monmouth Coll., 1969; MA in Spl. Edn., U. Detroit, 1993. 5th grade tchr. St. Catherines, Spring Lake, N.J., 1967-68; 3rd grade tchr. Howell Township (N.J.) Pub. Schs., 1969-70, spl. edn. tchr., 1970-72; substitute tchr. Riverview (Mich.) Pub. Schs., 1973-81; pre-sch. tchr. Farmington (Mich.) Pub. Schs., 1985-93; substitute tchr. Southfield (Mich.) Schs., 1992-93, spl. edn. tchr., 1993—. Sec. Altar Soc., Riverview, 1974-76; trustee Riverview Forest Home Assn., 1977-79; leader Girl Scouts U.S., Mich., 1978-89 (Green Angle award 1988). Mem. Coun. for Exceptional Children, Univ. Women of Am., Smithsonian, Detroit Symphony Orch. (vol.), Kendall Club. Roman Catholic. Avocations: art, music, drama, skiing, boating. Home: 28633 Petersburg St Farmington Hills MI 48331-2448 Office: MacArthur Elem Sch 24501 Frederick Southfield MI 48331 E-mail: HoffmanS@southfield.k12.mi.us.

HOFFMAN, VALERIE JANE, lawyer; b. Lowville, NY, Oct. 27, 1953; d. Russell Francis and Jane Marie (Fowler) H. Student, U. Edinburgh, Scotland, 1973-74; BA summa cum laude, Union Coll., 1975; JD, Boston Coll., 1978. Bar: Ill. 1978, U.S. Dist. Ct. (no. dist.) Ill. 1978, U.S. Ct. Appeals (3rd cir.) 1981, U.S. Ct. Appeals (7th cir.) 1983. Assoc. Seyfarth Shaw LLP, Chgo., 1978—87, ptnr., 1987—. Adj. prof. Columbia Coll., 1985. Contbr. articles to legal publs. Dir. Remains Theatre, Chgo., 1981-95, pres., 1991-93, v.p., 1993-95; dir. The Nat. Conf. for Cmty. and Justice, Chgo. Region, 1993-2004, nat. trustee, 1995-2004; trustee bd. advisors Union Coll., 1996-99, trustee, 1999—, trustee and sec., Grad. Coll. Union U., 2003—; dir. AIDS Found. of Chgo., 1997-2004, exec. com., 1999-2003. Mem. ABA, Chgo. Bar Assn., Univ. Club Chgo. (bd. dirs. 1984-87), Phi Beta Kappa. Office: Seyfarth Shaw 55 E Monroe St Ste 4400 Chicago IL 60603-5713 Office Phone: 312-346-8000.

HOFFMANN, ELINOR R., lawyer; b. NYC, Apr. 18, 1954; BA magna cum laude, NYU, 1974, LLM in Antitrust and Trade Regulation, 1984; JD cum laude, Bklyn. Law Sch., 1977. Bar: N.Y. 1978, U.S. Dist. Ct. (so. and ea. dists.) N.Y. 1978, U.S. Supreme Ct. 1982, U.S. Ct. Appeals (2nd cir.) 1991, U.S. Ct. Appeals (5th cir.) 1994, U.S. Tax Ct. 1996. Ptnr. Coudert Bros. LLP, N.Y.C., 1986—; mediator U.S. Dist. Ct. (so. dist.) N.Y., 1994—. Mng. editor Bklyn. Law Rev., 1976-77; contbr. articles to profl. jours. Mem. ABA, Internat. Bar Assn., N.Y. State Bar Assn., Assn. Bar City NY, Phi Beta Kappa. Office: Coudert Bros LLP 1114 Avenue Of The Americas New York NY 10036-7710 E-mail: hoffmanne@coudert.com.

HOFFMANN, JOAN CAROL, retired academic dean; b. Cedarburg, Wis., Feb. 20, 1934; d. Frank Ernst and Althea Wilhelmina (Behm) H. Nursing diploma, Michael Reese Hosp., 1955; BS in Zoology, U. Wis., Madison,

1959; PhD in Physiology, U. Ill., Chgo., 1965. RN, Wis., Ariz. Sci. instr. Michael Reese Hosp., Chgo., 1959-62; USPHS trainee U. Ill., Chgo., 1962-64; NSF postdoctoral fellow Coll. de France, Paris, 1964-65; asst. prof. U. Rochester, NY, 1965-70; assoc. prof., prof. U. Hawaii, Honolulu, 1970-83; dean of students U. Mass. Med. Sch., Worcester, 1983-94; ret., 1994. Chmn. anatomy U. Hawaii, 1973-80. Contbr. articles to sci. jours. NIH rsch. grantee, 1966-75. Mem. Endocrine Soc., Soc. for Study of Reprodn., Am. Assn. Anatomists, Women in Endocrinology (sec. 1978-79, pres. 1987-88), Am. Coun. Edn. (bd. dirs., Mass. chpt., network identification program 1993-94), Phi Beta Kappa, Sigma Xi. Avocations: gardening, needlecrafts, wood turning, reading. Home: 3525 Cass Ct #416 Oak Brook IL 60523-3707 Personal E-mail: jchamc@comcast.net.

HOFFMASTER, NANCY JO CLEMENT, retired social services professional; b. Granite City, Ill., June 14, 1940; d. Cornelius Ellsworth and Ruth Virginia (Richardson) Townsend; m. David Eugene Clement, June 16, 1961 (div. Dec. 1984); children: Steve, Tom, Bret; m. B. H. Hoffmaster, Dec. 1, 1990. BS in Edn., U. Ill., 1962; student, Red Rocks Community Coll., Golden, Colo., 1979-88; postgrad., U. Colo., Denver, 1988. Cert. elem. tchr., Ill. Coord. homeless edn. program Jeffco Schs., 1998-2000, ret., 2001. Vol. Office of Jeffco Sch Dist., 1995-97. Pres. Jefferson County PTA, Golden, 1982-83; Jeffco chair Colo. Awards for Tchrs., Wheat Ridge, 1987-89, Jefferson Found., Golden, 1989-91, pres., 1989; chmn. enrichment program Jefferson County (Jeffco) Schs., Golden, 1982-91; chmn. Sch. Dist. Accountability, Jefferson County, 1983-85; bd. dirs. Interfaith Hosp. Network, 1996-2000; founder, chair Serving Kids, 1996—; hon. chair Jefferson Found. Crystal Ball, 1999. Named Citizen of Yr., Jefferson County Sch. Bd., 1984, Community Person of Yr. for Jefferson County, Phi Delta Kappa, 1990; recipient Kyffin award Jefferson County PTA, 1989, vol. award Nat. Assn. Ptnrs. in Edn., 1990, Good News Coalition award, 2000, Savvy award, 2000, Colo. Power of One, 2000. Home: 13902 E Marina Dr unit 307 Aurora CO 80014-3756

HOFFNER, MARILYN, university administrator; b. N.Y.C., Nov. 16, 1929; d. Daniel and Elsie (Schulz) H.; m. Albert Greenberg, May 29, 1949; children: Doren Roe, Peter Cooper. BFA, Cooper Union. Art dir. Printers' Ink mag., N.Y.C., 1953-63, Print Mag., N.Y.C., 1960-62; corp. art dir. Vision, Inc., L.Am., 1963-75, 92-95; dir. alumni rels. and devel. Cooper Union, 1974-96, exec. dir. instnl. advancement, 1996-99, cons., 1999-2001; pres. Alumni Assn., 1999-2001. Project dir. Nat. Graphic Design Archives, 1990-97; bd. dirs. Art Dirs. Club N.Y., 1973-75, 79-82, exec. sec., 1973-75, exec. treas., 1979-82. Contbg. editor Print mag., Art Direction, Graphis mag.; designer mags., advt., books and exhbns. Mem. Citizens Adv. Cultural Arts Com. Dutchess County, 1978-80. Recipient Gold medal Art Dirs. Club, 1979, N.Y. State Coun. of the Arts award, 1995; named Alumnus of the Yr., Cooper Union, 1968. Mem. Cooper Union Alumni Assn. (editor-in-chief 1971-74, 1st v.p. 1974-75), Coun. Advancement and Support of Edn., Type Dirs. Club (numerous awards), Nat. Arts Club (Exhbn. com.). Home: 51 5th Ave New York NY 10003-4320 E-mail: cu1948@aol.com.

HOFKIN, ANN GINSBURGH, photographer, poet; b. Holyoke, Mass., Dec. 20, 1943; d. Albert and Fruma (Winer) G.; m. Michael Gary Hofkin, June 30, 1966; children: Daniel, Benjamin. AB, Mt. Holyoke Coll., 1965; MSS, Bryn Mawr Coll., 1967. One-woman shows include Unicorn Galleries, Mpls., 1980, Warm Gallery, Mpls., 1982-85, 87-88, 90, 96, 98, St. Mary's Coll., Winona, Minn., 1986, U. Wis., Meml. Union, 1993, Bladin Found., 1990, Phipps Ctr. for the Arts, Wis., 1994, So. Light Gallery, Tex., 1994-95, MC Gallery, Mpls., 1986, 89, 91-92, 94, 97, Bethany Luth. Coll., Minn., 1999, Hoyt Inst. Fine Arts, 1999, Pietra di Luna Gallery, Fla., 2000, Coll. St. Benedict's, Minn., 2002, Bet Gabriel, Israel, 2003, Jerusalem Theatre, Israel, 2003, Alliance Francaise de Mpls./St.Paul, 2003, Mount Holyoke Coll, 2004, Tel Aviv Opera Ho., 2004; group shows include Gallery Triangle, Washington, 1996, Pindar Gallery, N.Y., 1987, Phinney Ctr., Seattle, 1987, Print Club, Phila., 1988, U. Minn., 1988, Plains Art Mus., 1988, U. Minn., 1989, Durango Arts Ctr., Colo., 1989, Northfield Arts Guild, Minn., 1982, 90, Mich. Friends of Photography, 1992, Jewish Cmty. Ctr., Houston, 1990, 92, Hennepin History Mus., 1992, LaGrange (Ga.) Coll., 1992, Chautauqua Art Assn., N.Y., 1992, Edn. Testing Svc., N.J., 1992, Slocumb Galleries, Tenn., 1993, Barrett House Galleries, N.Y., Erector Sq. Gallery, Conn., 1993, McPherson Coll., Ks., 1993, Middle (Tenn.) State U., 1993, Sioux City Art Ctr., Iowa, 1987, 89, 93, Mpls. Coll. Art and Design, 1987, 89, 94, Lubbock (Tex.) Fine Arts Ctr., 1995, Shoestring Gallery, N.Y., 1993, 94, 95, Phila. Art Alliance, 1995, Murray (Ky.) State U., 1996, Ctrl. Mo. State U., 1996, Stephen Austin State U. Tex., 1996, Houston Ctr. for Photography, 1995, 96, Perry House Galleries, Va., 1996, 97, U. S.D., Vermilion, 1994, 97, Nebr. Wesleyan U., 1997, U. No. Iowa, 1997, ekliktikos gallery, Washington, 1997, Chuck Levitan Gallery, N.Y., 1997-98; group exhibitions: Mpls. Inst. Arts, 85, 86, 2000, Minnesota State Fair, 1986-93, 95-97, 99-2000, U. Wisconsin, Green Bay, 1988, 94, 98, Coll. St. Catherine, MN, 1997, 99, Mpls., Jewish Community, Ctr., 1997, 99, Phipps Ctr. For the Arts, WI, 98, 99, Bausch & Lomb, Rochester, NY, 1998, Texas Nat., 1998, 2000, Savannah COll. of Art & Design, 1998, St. John's U., MN, 1999, Pentimenti Gallery, PA, 2000, Euro Galleries, MN, 2000, GOCAIA Gallery, AZ, 2000, San Diego Art Inst., CA, 2000, Wellington B Gray Gallery, NC, 2001, Rehab Inst. Chgo., 2003, Weisman Art Mus., U. Minn., 2003, Plains Art Mus., Fargo, 1988, 2001, 2003, Michael Lord Gallery, WI, 2003, FLATFILE, Chgo., 2001, 02, 03, Icebox Gallery, MN, 2004, Sande Webster Gallery, Phila., 2004; represented in permanent collections Dana Farber Cancer Inst., Fidelity Investments, Mass. Gen. Hosp., Hennepin History Mus., Savannah Coll. Art & Design, Minn. Ctr. Environ. Advocacy, Valley Hosp. Finalist Jerome Foundation, Erector Square Gallery, Warm Land Mark Print Project, Northfield Arts Guild; recipient Qualex award, Wellington B. Gray Gallery; fellow Rimon Cultural Arts. Home: 1422 Tamarack Dr Long Lake MN 55356 E-mail: aghofkin@aol.com.

HOFLER, KAY ROBERTSON, secondary school educator, department chairman, artist; b. Bluefield, W.Va., Apr. 26, 1947; d. Oscar Miles and Hazel Cleo Robertson; m. Arthur Richard Hofler, Dec. 15, 1945; children: Derek Van, Ian Thomas. BS, Longwood U., Farmville, Va., 1969; MA, Old Dominion U., Norfolk, Va., 1994. Postgrad. profl. lic. Va., 1994. Tchr., dept. chair Bayside Jr. H.S., Virginia Beach, 1965—82, Bayside H.S., Virginia Beach, 1982—85, Salem H.S., Virginia Beach, 1985—. Curriculum com. chair Virginia Beach City Pub. Schs., 2005—. One-woman shows include Artists' Gallery, Virginia Beach, 2000, exhibitions include Contemporary Art Ctr. Va., 2004, The Phillips Gallery, Cape Henry Collegiate Sch., Virginia Beach, 2005. Part-time Sunday sch. tchr. Thalia United Meth. Ch., Virginia Beach, 1985—2005. Named Bayside Jr. H.S. Tchr. of Yr., Virginia Beach City Schs., 1986, Tidewater Regional Tchr. of Yr., Va. Art Edn. Assn., 2002; recipient PTA Lifetime Membership, PTA, 1985, Sunlight award, Salem H.S., 1998. Mem.: Tidewater Art Edn. Assn., Va. Art Edn. Assn., Nat. Art Edn. Assn., Chrysler Mus., Artists' Gallery (exhibiting artist 1997—2006). Avocations: painting, travel, crafts, sewing. Home: 540 Rosalie Ct Virginia Beach VA 23462 Office: Salem High School 1993 Sundevil Dr Virginia Beach VA 23464 Office Phone: 757-474-8484. Office Fax: 757-474-8483. Personal E-mail: khofler@infionline.net. Business E-Mail: krhofler@vbschools.com.

HOFMAN, ELIZABETH ELVERETTA, retired mathematics educator, guidance counselor, dean; b. South Bend, Ind., Feb. 27, 1917; d. Curtis Hamilton and Ossie Marie (Meissner) Vernon; m. Raphael B. Hofman, June 10, 1942 (dec.). Diploma, Mich. County Normal Tng. Sch., Alpena, 1936—37; attended, Huntington Coll., Ind., 1941—42; BS, Western Res. U., Cleve., 1947, MA in Edn., 1948. Cert. HS math. tchr. Western Res. U., 1947, in pupil personnel svcs. Western Res. U., 1964. Tchr. grades K-8 Alpena County Schs., 1937—41; math. tchr. grades 4-8 Warrensville Heights Jr. HS, Ohio, 1945—63, math. tchr. jr. and sr. HS, advisor math., 1963—72, part time guidance counselor, 1960—64, 1963—72, tchr. math. grades 11 and 12, 1960—64, dean of girls, 1968—72, ret., 1972. Mem.: NEA, Ohio Ret. Tchrs. Assn., Nat. Ret. Tchrs. Assn. Home: 700 Brittany O Delray Beach FL 33446-1073

HOFMANN, CAROLE P., bank executive; b. Wilmington, Del., Feb. 22, 1951; d. Arthur Pavoni and Jean Ianni; children: Julie, Laurie, Jessie. BA, Coll. Notre Dame, 1972. Bank mgr., asst. v.p. Md. Nat. Bank, Balt., 1973—93; libr. assoc. Anne Arundel Pub. Libr., Annapolis, 1993—97; account mgr. Sun Trust Bank, Glen Burnie, Md., 1997—. Midshipmen sponsor program U.S. Naval Acad., Annapolis, Md., 1998—; active Big Bros. and Big Sisters, Balt., 1998—; pres., founder Anne Arundel Single Again, Millersville, Md., 1999—. Recipient Hist. Preservation award, Nat. Hist. Trust, 1996, 10 Yr. Vol. award, Anne Arundel County Pub. Schs., 2002. Mem.: PTA. Avocations: piano, reading, swimming. Office: Sun Trust Bank 1000 Stewart Ave Glen Burnie MD 21061

HOFMANN, IRENE E., art museum director; b. NY; B in Art Hist., Wash. U., St. Louis, 1991; M in Modern Art Hist., Sch. of the Art Inst., Chicago, 1993. Exhbn. curator Cranbrook Art Mus., Bloomfield Hills, Mich.; curator Orange County Mus. of Arts, Baltimore, 2001; exec. dir. Contemporary Mus., Baltimore, 2006—. Co-curator (exhibitions) Calif. Biennial, Orange County Mus. of Art, Baltimore, 2002, curator Poetic Engineering, 2005, co-curator Girls Night Out, 2005. Office: Contemporary Museum 100 W Centre St Baltimore MD 21201 Office Phone: 410-783-5720 ext. 102. E-mail: ihofmann@contemporary.org.*

HOFMANN, NOREEN, elementary school educator, music educator; b. LI, Feb. 29, 1960; d. Timothy and Sheila Lynch; m. Michael Hofmann, June 26, 1987; 1 child, Amy Elizabeth. AAS, Nassau C.C., Uniondale, NY, 1980; MusB, SUNY, Potsdam, 1982; MEd, U. NC, Charlotte, 1991. Tchr. gen. music Poughkeepsie City Schs., NY, 1982—87, Charlotte-Mecklenburg Schs., NC, 1987—. Recipient Dist. Music Tchr. Yr., Charlotte Mecklenburg Schs., 2000—01. Mem.: Piedmont N.C. Chpt. of the Am. Orff-Schulwerk Assn. (pres. 1999—2001). Home: 418 Catawba Cir N Matthews NC 28104 Office: Bain Elementary School 11524 Bain School Rd Charlotte NC 28227 Office Phone: 980-343-6915. Personal E-mail: noreen.hofmann@cms.k12.nc.us.

HOFSTETTER, JANE ROBINSON, artist, educator; b. Oakland, Calif., Feb. 23, 1936; d. Thomas O. and Fern (Worstell) Robinson; m. William R. Hofstetter, Aug. 3, 1958; children: David, Glen. Student, U. Calif., Berkeley, San Francisco Sch. of Design, Chouinard Art Inst., L.A. Lectr. in field. Represented in permanent collections Triton Mus. Art, Santa Clara, Calif., State of Calif. Collection, Asilomar, San Ramon and Santa Clara City Halls, Kayser Hosp., Calif., IBM Hdqs. and Gen. Facilities, Gould Inc., No. Calif. Savings and Loan, Systems Control Inc., Zerox Corp., Finance Am.; author Seven Keys To Great Paintings, 2005. Recipient Trinton Art Mus. award and numerous others. Mem. Nat. Watercolor Soc., Watercolor West Soc., Nat. Transparent Watercolor Soc. Am., Soc. Western Artists. Studio: 308 Dawson Dr Santa Clara CA 95051-5806

HOGABOOM, MAURINE HOLBERT, cultural organization administrator; b. Wichita Falls, Te., Feb. 3, 1912; d. Joseph Eggleston Holbert and Ada Viola Davis; m. Robert Edward Hogaboom, July 16, 1982 (dec. Nov. 1993). BA summa cum laude, Fordham U., 1976; MA, Goddard Coll., 1979; postgrad., U. of the South, 1992—95. Actor, dir., tchr., N.Y.C., 1955—57; founder Chrysalis Rsch. Ctr. for the Arts, N.Y.C., 1979—83; founder, co-dir. Synthesis Ctr. St. Mary's, 1990—. Founding mem., performer Arts Alliance, St. Mary's Coll., 1983—; active Trinity Episcopal Ch., St. Mary's City, Md., 2001—. Avocations: gardening, yoga.

HOGAN, BRIGID L.M., molecular biologist; b. England, Aug. 28, 1943; BA, U. Cambridge, 1964, PhD, 1968. NATO rsch. fellow dept. biology MIT, 1968-70; lectr. biochemistry U. Sussex, England, 1970-74; sci. staff Imperial Cancer Rsch. Fund, Mill Hill, England, 1974-84; head lab. molecular embryology Nat. Inst. Med. Rsch., Mill Hill, England, 1985-88; prof. cell biology Vanderbilt Med. Sch., Nashville, 1988—2002; prof. and chair dept. cell biology Duke U. Med. Ctr., 2002—. Hortense B. Ingram chair molecular oncology Howard Hughes Med. Inst., 1993-2002; vice chair Basement Membrane Gordon Conf., 1994, chair, 1996; co-chair sci. human embryo rsch. panel NIH, 1994; Jenkinson meml. lectr. U. Oxford, 1995; Margaret Pittman lectr. NIH, 1996. Mem. Br. Soc. Cell Biology (com. 1982-86), Br. Soc. Devel. Biology (com. 1984-88), NAS Inst. Medicine ((in conjunction with NRC) mem. adv. com. Human Embryonic Stem Cell Rsch., 2006-), European Molecular Biology Orgn. Office: Duke U Med Ctr 388 Nanaline Duke Bldg Box 3709 Durham NC 27710 Office Phone: 919-684-8085. Office Fax: 919-685-8592. E-mail: B.Hogan@cellbio.duke.edu.*

HOGAN, FELICITY, artist; b. England; m. Michael Clark, Dec. 1995. Co-dir. Mus. Contemporary Art, Washington, 1996—. Exhibitions include Clark & Hogan: Paintings & Collaborations, Barry Gallery, 2002—03, Mus. Contemporary Art, 1997—, Clark in Context: Day of the Revolutionary, 2003. Office: Mus Contemporary Art 1054 31st St Washington DC 20007 E-mail: felicityhogan@aol.com.

HOGAN, ILONA MODLY, lawyer; b. Erlangen, Fed. Republic of Germany, Nov. 23, 1947; arrived in U.S., 1951, naturalized, 1960; d. Stephen Bela and Gunda Pauline (Gastiger) Modly; m. Lawrence J. Hogan, Mar. 16, 1974; children: Matthew Lawrence, Michael Alexander, Patrick Nicholas, Timothy Stefan. Student, Marymount Coll., 1965-67; AB in Internat. Affairs, George Washington U., 1969; JD, Georgetown U., 1974. Bar: D.C. 1975, Md. 1975. Intern and clk. AID, 1965-69; adminstrv. and legis. asst. to mem. Ho. of Reps., 1969-72; editor Legis. Digest, Ho. of Reps., Washington, 1972-73; asso. and law clk. firm Trammell, Rand, Nathan and Lincoln, Washington, 1972-74; mng. ptnr. firm Hogan and Hogan, Washington and Md., 1974-93; of counsel Venable, Baetjer, Howard & Civiletti, Washington, 1989-91; pres. Amcom Inc., 1978—; of counsel Salisbury & McLister, Frederick, Md., 1993-2001; global mgr. Bechtel Telecom., 2001—. Mem. Prince George's Bd. Libr. Trustees, Md., 1976—78, Prince George's County Econ. Devel. Adv. Com., 1979—82; v.p. St. John's Sch. Bd., 1987—88, pres., 1989; treas. U. Md. Bd. Regents, 1988—95; trustee St. James Sch., 1989—90; mem. Lawyers Steering com. for Reagan-Bush, 1980; nat. vice-chmn. Assn. Execs. for Reagan-Bush, 1984; mem. bus. and industry adv. com. 50th Am. Presdl. Inaugural, 1985; mem. Md. steering com. Bush for Pres., 1988; mem. Presdl. Personnel Adv. Com., 1989, Gov.'s Higher Edn. Transition Team, 1988; elected mem. County Commrs. Frederick County, 1994—2001; Frederick County co-chair Bush-Cheney Campaign, 2000; bd. advisors Frostburg State U., 2001—03; trustee Frederick C.C. Found., 2001—03, Md. Higher Edn. Commn., 2003—. Mem.: ABA, D.C. Bar, Md. Bar Assn. Republican. Roman Catholic. Home: 5614 New Design Rd Frederick MD 21703-8306 Office: 5275 Westview Dr Frederick MD 21703-8306 E-mail: imhogan@bechtel.com.

HOGAN, JULIE A., lawyer; BS summa cum laude, Villanova U., 1997; JD cum laude, Harvard U., 2000. Bar: Mass. 2001. Assoc. State and Local Tax Group Wilmer, Cutler, Pickering, Hale and Dorr LLP, Boston, 2000—. Guest lectr. grad. tax program Boston U. Sch. Law. Mem.: Boston Bar Assn. (tax. sect.), ABA (tax. sect.). Office: Wilmer Cutler Pickering Hale and Dorr LLP 60 State St Boston MA 02109 Office Phone: 617-526-6543. Office Fax: 617-526-5000. E-mail: julie.hogan@wilmerhale.com.*

HOGAN, ROXANNE ARNOLD, nursing consultant, risk management consultant, educator; b. Connellsville, Pa. d. Tyree Franklin, Sr. and Reva Gayle (Thieler) Arnold; m. Patrick B. Hogan. AAS, Gloucester County Coll., 1983; BSN, Widener U., 1989. Lic. healthcare risk mgr. Fla.; RN Fla. Staff devel. instr., nursing supr., cardiac care nurse Meth. Hosp., Phila., 1982-89; emergency nurse Underwood Meml. Hosp., Woodbury, NJ, 1988-89; critical care nurse Jupiter Hosp., Fla., 1989—92; emergency clin. nurse III Indian River Meml. Hosp., Vero Beach, Fla., 1990-92; EMT/paramedic instr. Indian River CC, Ft. Pierce, Fla., 1990-92; emergency asst. nurse mgr. Holmes Regional Med. Ctr., Melbourne, Fla., 1992-94; post anesthesia clin. nurse III Indian River Meml. Hosp., Vero Beach, Fla., 1994-98; surg. dir. Rosato Plastic Surgery Ctr., Vero Beach, Fla., 1998-99; nurse mgr. pre-admissions, IV team, ambulatory infusion, spl. procedures GI lab. Ambulatory Surgery Ctr., Indian River Meml. Hosp., Vero Beach, Fla., 1999—2001; pres. Treasure Coast Cons., Inc., 2001—; risk mgmt. coord. HCA/St. Lucie Med. Ctr., Port St. Lucie, Fla., 2002—03; claims med. specialist S.E. Fla. Nationwide Ins., 2003—. Mem.: Am. Assn. Legal Nurse Cons., Sigma Theta Tau. Home: 5346 NW Rugby Dr Port Saint Lucie FL 34983-3384 Personal E-mail: roxannehogan@aol.com.

HOGANSON, MARY MARGARET, librarian; b. Corpus Christi, Tex., Feb. 1, 1919; d. Lawrence Stephen and Mary Virginia (Monroe) Dwyer; m. Willard Leroy Hoganson, June 9, 1943; children— Anne Hoganson Koehler, James, Stephen, Thomas. B.A., McMurry Coll., 1939. Tchr. English and Spanish, Dunn Pub. Schs., Tex., 1939-41, Moran Pub. Schs., Tex., 1941-42; tchr. 6th grade St. Bonaventure, Columbus, Nebr., 1961-62; tchr. English and French, Columbus High Sch., Nebr., 1962-74; library dir. Park County Library, Bailey, Colo., 1980—. Pres. Jane Jefferson Democratic Women, Bailey, Colo., 1976; mem. Platte Canyon Bd. Edn, 1995-1999; libr. dir. Park County Libr., Baily, Colo., 1980-1995. Mem. NEA, Colo. Library Assn., Columbus PTA (life), Platte Canyon Edn. Assn. Democrat. Lutheran. Home: PO Box 123 Bailey CO 80421-0123

HOGE, GERALDINE RAJACICH, elementary school educator; b. Eveleth, Minn., Apr. 8, 1937; d. Robert and Dora (Tassi) Rajacich; m. Gregg LeRoy Hoge, Sept. 15, 1963 (div. Feb. 1972); 1 child, Sheryl Maurine. BS, U. Minn., 1959; MA with honors, Pepperdine U. Cert. elem. tchr., Calif. Tchr. Chaska (Minn.) Pub. Schs., 1959-60, Minnetonka (Minn.) Pub. Schs., 1960-62, Norwalk (Calif.) La Mirada Pub. Schs., 1962-64, Culver City (Calif.) Unified Sch. Dist., 1966—. Fellow Culver City Guidance Clinic Guild, 1981-89; mem. Calif. State Rep. Ctrl. Com., Sacramento, 1986-90, 92-94, L.A. County Rep. Ctrl. Com., 1987—; vice chmn. 49th Assembly Dist. Ctrl. Rep. Com., Culver City, 1988—; bd. dirs. Selective Svc. Sys., Culver City, 1993—; mem. Santa Monica Rep. Women Federated, 2006—. Named Tchr. of the Yr. Elks Lodge, 1982; grantee, 1988-89, Fellow Am. Fedn. Tchrs.; mem. Internat. Platform Assn., Calif. Fedn. Tchrs., Culver City Fedn. Tchrs. (v.p. 1978-79), Alpha Delta Pi (historian 1956-59), Delta Kappa Gamma. Republican. Avocations: travel, gardening, race walking. Office: Culver City Unified Sch 4034 Irving Pl Culver City CA 90232-2810

HOGENSEN, MARGARET HINER, retired librarian, consultant; b. Ottawa, Kans., Oct. 11, 1920; d. Hebron Henry and Nellie Evelyn (Godard) Hiner; widowed. BA, U. Wichita, 1942; BS in Libr. Sci., U. Denver, 1945. Circulation librarian Boise Pub. Library, Idaho, 1945-49, Pomona Pub. Library, Calif., 1950-51; reference librarian WFIL-TV, Phila., 1963-69; rsch. dir. Concept Films, Washington, 1969-72; ind. researcher, cons. Greenbelt, Md., 1973-80; ret., 2000. Bd. dirs. Greenbelt Homes, Inc., 1977-93, 1998-2000, 2003-2004, pres., 1983-88, treas. 1998-2000; past bd. dirs. Greenbelt Consumer Coop., Nat. Coop. Bus. Assn.; pres. Ea. Coop. Housing Orgn., 1992-95. Mem.: Nat. Assn. Housing Coops (bd. dirs. 1986—87, 1990—94). Democrat. Christian Scientist.

HOGERHEIDEN, LAUREN MICHELLE VALENCIA, secondary school educator; b. Fullerton, Calif., Nov. 25, 1980; d. Paul F. and Sharon B. Valencia; children: Sima, Roscoe. BA in Psychology with honors, Biola U., La Mirada, Calif., 2001. Cert. tchr. Calif., 2004. Tchr. Temecula (Calif.) Valley Unified Sch. Dist., 2001—. Active Invisible Children, San Diego, 2005—06. Recipient Crystal Apple award, Temecula Valley Unified Sch. Dist. Students, 2006. Mem.: Torrey Honors Inst. (life). Avocations: backpacking, running. Office: Temecula Valley High School 31555 Rancho Vista Rd Temecula CA 92591 Office Phone: 951-695-7300 3133. Business E-Mail: lhogerheiden@tvusd.k12.ca.us.

HOGG, CINDA L.P., elementary school educator; married. MA in Curriculum and Tchg., Mich. State U., E. Lansing, 1995. Elem. tchr. Traverse City Area Pub. Schs., Mich., 1986—. Mem. TriCounty Med. Aux., Traverse City, 1978—97. Grantee for home learning bags, ACE, 2000. Mem.: NEA, Traverse City Edn. Assn. (sch. rep. 1989—), Traverse City Area Mich. State U. Alumni Assn. Office: Traverse City Area Public Schools PO Box 32 Traverse City MI 49685-0032 Office Phone: 231-933-74227. Office Fax: 231-933-7442. Business E-Mail: hoggci@oldmission.tcaps.net.

HOGG, VIRGINIA LEE, retired medical educator; b. Marblehead, Mass., July 30, 1938; d. Richard Caldwell and Leola Mary Jewett; m. Ronald James Hogg, July 13, 1964; children: Scott Jameson, Carol Lee. BS, Bridgewater State Coll., Mass., 1960, MEd, 1965; EdD, Boston U., Mass., 1980. Cert. health edn. specialist Nat. Commn. Health Edn. Credentialing, Inc., Pa., 1989. Tchr. Stoughton Pub. Schs., Stoughton, Mass., 1961—67; full prof. Bridgewater State Coll., 1968—97; ret., 1997. Cons. self-employed (Platinum Resources), Naples, Fla., 1999—2003. Legal advocacy chair AAUW, Naples, 2004—06. Recipient Honor award, Mass. Assn. Health, Phys. Edn. and Recreation, 1982, Profl. Merit award, Ea. Dist. Assn. Health, Phys. Edn. and Recreation, 1985, Franklin D. Roosevelt award, March of Dimes, 1992, Profl. Leadership award, Bridgewater State Coll., 1994; Fulbright scholar-Peoples Republic China, U.S. Govt., 1990. Mem.: Am. AAHPERD, Am. Coll. Health Assn., Am. Assn. U. Women (v.p. membership 2000—02). Avocations: tennis, mentoring, event planning, travel, cooking.

HOGG, YVONNE MARIE, special education educator; b. Adrian, Pa., Sept. 16, 1956; d. Finley Hamilton and Rose Ellen George; m. Ray Glenn Hogg, Dec. 1991; children: William Finley Brumbaugh, Dillon John. BS in Consumer Svcs., Indiana U. Pa., 1979; MEd in Spl. Edn., Slippery Rock U., Pa., 2001. Cert. elem. edn., spl. edn. Pa. Harvester, asst. crew leader, heavy equipment operator, disease control tech. Moonlight Mushrooms, Inc., Worthington, Pa., 1980—92; substitute Freeport Area Sch. Dist., Pa., 1994—95, Butler Area Sch. Dist., Pa., 1993—97, Armstrong Sch. Dist., Ford City, Pa., 1993—97; quality control supr. Freeport Brick-Kittanning Divsn., Adrian, Pa., 1997—99; quality control tech., customer svc. rep. CPG Nutrients-Agway Co., Adrian, Pa., 1999—2002; spl. edn. tchr. Adelphoi Village, Latrobe, Pa., 2002—. Transition coord. Adelphoi Village Armstrong Unit, Kittanning, Pa., 2004—. Mem.: Lions Internat. (bd. dirs. 2002—03, Student of Month coord. 2003—). Republican. Home: PO Box 413 Adrian PA 16210 Office Phone: 724-543-4238. Personal E-mail: yvonnehogg@peoplepc.com.

HOGGATT, CLELA ALLPHIN, language educator; b. Des Moines, Sept. 9, 1932; d. Addison Edgar and Frances (Buckallew) Phılleo; m. Charles Allphin; children: Beverly, Valerie, Clark, Arthur, Frances; m. John Hoggatt. AA, Grand View Jr. Coll., 1952; BA summa cum laude, U. No. Iowa, 1954; MA, Tex A&I U., 1961. Cert. life tchr. Iowa, Tex.; permanent life community coll. credential, Calif. Tchr. social studies Los Fresnos (Tex.) Jr. High Sch., 1954-55; tchr. English Cummings Jr. High Sch., Brownsville, Tex., 1956-59, Fickett Jr. High Sch., Tucson, 1963-66, Portola Jr. High Sch., L.A., 1956-59; instr. speech Tex. Southmost Jr. Coll., Brownsville, 1959; tchr. history and English Ysleta High Sch., El Paso, Tex., 1963-66; prof. English L.A. Trade-Tech. Coll., 1969-75, L.A. Mission Coll., 1975-95. Author: Women in the Plays of Henrik Ibsen, 1975, The Writing Cycle, 1986, Good News for Writers, 1990; contbr. to Words, Words, Words, 1981, Emily Dickinson: A Centennial Celebration, 1890-1990, In the West of Ireland, John Trumball: An Anthology in Memoriam. Grand View Jr. Coll. scholar, 1951-52, U. No. Iowa scholar, 1953-54. Mem. DAR, Am. Mensa, Pi Gamma Mu. Democrat. Avocations: travel, bridge, playing piano.

HOGLE, ANN MEILSTRUP, painter, art educator; b. San Francisco, Sept. 23, 1927; d. Carlton Fredrick Meilstrup and Lillian (Hackney) Meilstrup Willer; m. Richard Raymond (div.); children— Timothy, Megan, Catherine; m. George H. Hogle, Aug. 29, 1966. Student U. Oreg., 1945-47, Marylhurst Coll., 1949-50; B.F.A., Calif. Coll. of Arts and Crafts, 1976, M.F.A., 1978. One-person shows include Stanford U., Calif., 1966, Palo Alto Cultural Ctr., Calif., 1976, William Sawyer Gallery, San Francisco, Butters Gallery, Portland, 1993, Menlo Pk. Libr., Menlo Pk., Calif., 1994, Smith Andersen

Gallery, Palo Alto Calif., 1995, Bolinas Gallery, Bolinas, Calif., 1995, de Saisset Mus., Santa Clara, Calif., 1998, Fresno Art Mus., Fresno, Calif., 1998, Vorpal Gallery, San Francisco, 1999, Commonweal, Bolinas, Calif., 1999, John Natsoulas Gallery, Davis, Calif., 2001, guest artist Marin Agricultural Land Trust, Point Reyes Sta., Calif., 2003; exhibited in group shows at Portland Art Mus., Janus Gallery, Los Angeles, Richmond Art Ctr., William Sawyer Gallery, San Francisco, 84, Purdue U., Ind., Penninsula Mus., Monterey, Calif., 1993; represented in permanent collections Kemper Ins. Cos., St. Francis Meml. Hosp., Dysan Corp., First Interstate Bank. Portland Mus. Recipient Phelan awards exhibit Legion of Honor, 1965. Personal E-mail: ghogle711@earthlink.net. Business E-Mail: hogle@artistforum.com.

HOGLEN, JEWEL PAMELA, retired secondary school educator; b. Columbia, Miss., Sept. 22, 1919; d. Irvin Armstrong Blackburn and Inez Geraldine Dickens; m. Hubert J. Hoglen, Nov. 4, 1944; 1 child, Pamela J. BS, La. State Normal (now Northwestern State U. of La.), 1941; MA in Edn., Washington U., 1953. Cert. home economist, family & consumer scis. Home economist H.S., Kentwood, La., 1941—42; chmn. home economy Ward & Hanley Jr. H.S., U. City, Mo., 1947—69, Parkway N. H.S., Chesterfield, Mo., 1972—78; asst. prof. Meramec C.C., Kirkwood, Mo., 1972—75, ret., 1975. Vice chmn. profl. sect. Am. Home Econs. Assn., 1987—89; pres. Home Econs. Coun., St. Louis, 1964—65. Louis IX art mus. group Art Mus., St. Louis, 1978—. Recipient Disting. Svc. to the Profession award, Am. Home Econ. Assn., 1991—93, 50 Yrs. of Svc. award, Am. Home Econs. Assn., 1998. Mem.: AAUW, Mo. Home Econs. Assn. (pres. 1968—69, 1969—70, chmn. home economists in homemaking section, Cert. for Outstanding Contbn. & Svc. to the Profession 1985, 50 Years Dedication & Svc. to Home Econs. Profession award 1998), Am. Assn. Home (history & archives com., sec. to leader in leadership mtg.), Coll. Club of St. Louis (presider Centennial birthday celebration 2000, pres. 2001—03). Republican. Protestant. Avocations: tailoring, reading, horse back riding, travel. Home: 1009 Dougherty Ferry Rd Kirkwood MO 63122-2528

HOGUE, CAROL JANE ROWLAND, epidemiologist, educator; b. Springfield, Mo., Dec. 11, 1945; d. Perry Albright and Lois Virginia (Spencer) Rowland; m. L. Lynn Hogue, May 28, 1966; 1 child, Elizabeth Rowland. AB summa cum laude, William Jewell Coll., Liberty, Mo., 1966; MPH, U. N.C., 1971, PhD, 1973. From rsch. assoc. to asst. prof. U. N.C. Sch. Pub. Health, Chapel Hill, 1969-77; asst./assoc. prof., dir. epidemiology prog. divsn. biometry U. Ark. for Med. Scis., Little Rock, 1977-82; br. chief pregnancy epidemiology br. Ctrs. Disease Control, Atlanta, 1983-88, dir. divsn. reproductive health, 1988-92; Terry prof. maternal and child health, prof. epidemiology Rollins Sch. Pub. Health, Emory U., Atlanta, 1992—. Cons. FDA, Washington, 1978-80, EPA, Washington, 1980-81; vis. scientist Ctrs.,Disease Control, Atlanta, 1982-83; fellow Environ. Health Inst., Pittsfield, Mass., 1990-97; mem. com. on unintended pregnancy Inst. Medicine, 1994-96; mem. regional adv. panel human reprodn. program WHO, 1991-2000, chmn., 1997-2000, mem. sci. tech. adv. group, 1998-2000. Contbr. articles to profl. jours., chpts. to books. Mem. nat. perinatal health promotion com. March of Dimes, White Plains, N.Y., 1990-93; priority one adv. coun. Kiwanis Internat., 1990-91. Fellow Am. Coll. Epidemiology (pres., 2002-03); mem. Soc. Epidemiologic Rsch. (pres. 1988-89), Am. Epidemiological Soc., Am. Pub. Health Assn. (program devel. bd. 1976-78), Population Assn. Am., Internat. Epidemiol. Assn., Nat. Med. Com., Planned Parenthood Fedn. Am. Democrat. Episcopalian. Avocations: sailing, hiking, reading. Office: 1518 Clifton Rd NE Atlanta GA 30322-4201 Office Phone: 404-727-8095. E-mail: chogue@sph.emory.edu.

HOGUE, SHARON LEA, music educator; b. Houston, Sept. 10, 1956; d. William Guy and Ethel Marie (Van Namen) Hogue, Jr. B.Music Edn., Sam Houston State U., 1980. Tchr. music elem. sch. Spring Branch Ind. Sch. Dist., Houston, 1980-2005; choir dir., piano tchr; choral condr. Cornerstone, 1984, Potter's Clay, 1985. Pianist, soloist, dir. Candlelight Bible Ch., Houston, 1970-85; ch. musician Spring Branch Community Ch., 1984-91. Mem. Tex. Music Educators Assn., Kodaly Educators Tex., Assn. Tex. Profl. Educators (local com. chmn. 1984), Nat. Assn. Christian Educators, Sigma Alpha Iota (pres. Sam Houston State U. chpt. 1979, scholastic award 1980), Kappa Delta Pi, Phi Kappa Phi.

HOGUET, KAREN M., retail executive; m. David Hoguet; 2 children. Grad., Brown U.; MBA, Harvard U., 1980. With Boston Cons. Group, Chgo.; sr. cons. mktg. and long-range planning Federated Dept. Stores, Inc., Cin., 1982-85, dir. capital and bus. planning, 1985-87, operating v.p. planning and fin. analysis, 1987-88, corp. v.p., 1988-91, sr. v.p. planning, 1991—, treas., 1992—, sr. v.p., 1991, CFO, 1997—. Mem.: Phi Beta Kappa. Office: Federated Dept Stores Inc 7 W 7th St Cincinnati OH 45202-2424 Fax: 513-579-7555.*

HOHAUSER, MARILYN, artist; b. Bronxville, N.Y., May 7, 1934; d. Sterling Franklin Boos and Mildred Myntea Taylor; m. Sanford M. Hohauser, May 3, 1959; children: William Edward, Carol Miriam, Sanford Stephen. BA, Finch Coll., 1956. Pres. House Mart, N.Y.C., 1959-61, Hohauser Assocs., N.Y.C., 1959—, Rating The Svcs., Inc., N.Y.C., 1968—. Author: Architectural & Interior Models, 1969, 86, Rating the Services, 1968, The Score Never Changes, 2000, Hill City Designs, 2000. Avocations: making models, collecting miniatures, military history, medical research. Home: 248 E 31st St Apt 1B New York NY 10016-9711

HOHEB, CAMILLE E., healthcare executive; d. Albert Carlos Hoheb and Camille Aquino. BA in History, Hobart and William Smith, 1986; M in Healthcare Adminstrn., Calif. State U., Long Beach, 1996. Lic. Sales Calif. Dept. of Real Estate, 2005. Dir. bus. devel., physician relations, marketing Tenet Healthcare, LA, 1998—2001; dir. bus. devel. CORF Svcs., Phoenix, 2002—03, Healthwest Inc., Beverly Hills, Calif., 2003—04; v.p. ops. Radiance Medspa Franchise Group, Scottsdale, Ariz., 2004; v.p. devel. Solana Medspas, Irvine, Calif., 2004—. Katrina relief vol. Red Cross, San Antonio, 2005. Mem.: Women in Healthcare Adminstrn. Avocations: travel, food and wine, photography, writing. Office: Solana Medspas 1803 Von Karman Ave #550 Irvine CA 92612 Office Phone: 949 223 6444.

HOHENBERGER, PATRICIA JULIE, fine arts and antique appraiser, consultant; b. Holyoke, Mass. d. Ambrose Harrington and Irene Leo (Ducharme) Reynolds; m. John H. Hohenberger, June 27, 1953; children: Lisa Maria, Julie Suzanne, John Henry, James Reynolds, Patricia Antonia. BA in English, Coll. of New Rochelle, N.Y., 1950; MA in Folk Art Studies, NYU, 1983. Cert. elem. edn. tchr., Mass. Tchr. Hadley (Mass.) Pub. Schs., 1950-52, Springfield (Mass.) Pub. Schs., 1952-54; owner, dir. The Brown House Nursery Sch., Williamstown, Mass., 1962-64; tchr. Coindra Hall, Huntington, N.Y., 1970-71, St. Edward the Confessor, Syosset, N.Y., 1971-81; pres. Patricia Reynolds Hohenberger Appraisals, Northport, N.Y., 1983—. Cons. O'Toole-Edwald Art Assn., Inc., N.Y., 1984-91, Alexander-Benwood Co., Inc., Huntington, N.Y., 1991—; lectr. Symposium-Gen. Accident Ins., N.Y., 1994. Author: (monograph) Gentle Reminders of the Past, 1984. Recipient Recognition for Achievement award Alexander-Benwood Co., Inc., Huntington, N.Y., 1995. Mem. Nat. Trust for Historic Preservation, Nat. Mus. Women in the Arts (charter), New England Appraisers Assn. Roman Catholic. Avocations: collecting american decorative arts and antiques, photography. Home: 72 Burt Ave Northport NY 11768-2046 E-mail: prhohen@aol.com.

HOJAHMAT, MARHABA, research scientist; b. 1966; d. Hojahmat Yunus and Rehima Yusup; 1 child, Yifutehaer Nijiati. M in engring., Tokyo U. Sci., 1997, PhD, 2000. Post-doctoral rschr. U. Ky., Lexington, 2000—02, rsch. assoc., 2002; rsch. scientist Yaupon Therapeutics Inc., Lexington, 2002—. Contbr. articles to profl. jours. Japanese Govt. scholarship, Ministry of Edn., Sci. and Culture of Japan, 1996—2000, ITOCHU award, ITOCHU Co., Japan, 1995, STTR, NIH, 2002. Mem.: Soc. Silicon Chemistry, Japan, Chem. Soc. Japan, Am. Chem. Soc., Am. Assn. Pharm. Scientists. Home: 175 Malabu Dr Apt 33 Lexington KY 40503 Office: Yaupon Therapeutics Inc Univ Ky A169 ASTeCC Bldg Lexington KY 40506 Office Phone: 859-257-2300. Office Fax: 859-257-2489. E-mail: mhoja2@uky.edu.

HOJILLA-EVANGELISTA, MILAGROS PARKER, research chemist, research scientist; b. Quezon City, Philippines, Mar. 7, 1960; d. Hector Biaco and Carmen Felisa Parker Hojilla; m. Roque Lagman Evangelista, Apr. 20, 1985; children: Roderick Hojilla Evangelista, Mylene Hojilla Evangelista. BS Food Tech. cum laude, U. Philippines, Los Banos, 1980, MS in Food sci., 1984; PhD in Food Tech., Iowa State U., 1990. Instr. Inst. of Food Sci. and Tech., U. Philippines, Los Banos, Laguna, 1980—86; postdoctoral rsch. assoc. dept. food sci. and human nutrition Iowa State U., Ames, 1990—94, asst. scientist, 1994—97; rsch. chemist plant polymer rsch. USDA-ARS Nat. Ctr. Agrl. Utilization Rsch., Peoria, Ill., 1997—. Assoc. editor Jour. of the Am. Oil Chemists' Soc., Champaign, Ill. Contbr. articles to profl. jours. Pres. Filipino Assn. at Iowa State U., Ames, 1989—92; newsletter assoc./layout editor Filipino-Am. Soc. of Ctrl. Ill., Peoria, 2001—03. Recipient Outstanding Paper in Cereal Chemistry award, Am. Assn. of Cereal Chemists-Corn Refiners' Assn., 1990, Archer Daniels Midland-Protein Divsn. Best Paper award, Am. Oil Chemists Soc., 1993, 2003; scholarship, S.E. Asian Regional Ctr. for Grad. Study and Rsch. in Agr., 1982-1984. Mem.: Am. Chem. Soc., Am. Oil Chemists' Soc. (sec./treas. 2000—02, vice-chairperson protein divsn. 2002—04, chairperson protein divsn. 2004—), Gamma Sigma Delta, Phi Kappa Phi, Phi Beta Delta (v.p. 1991—92). Roman Catholic. Achievements include development of formulation for soybean flour-based foamed plywood adhesive (now used commercially); co-development of the Sequential Extraction Process for corn, an alternative corn milling process that uses ethanol for extracting oil and protein and generates novel value-added co-products; identifying the major protein fractions in the protein co-product from the Sequential Extraction Process, determined their functional properties and evaluated their potential applications. Avocations: travel, reading. Office: USDA ARS NCAUR 1815 N University St Peoria IL 61604 Office Phone: 309-681-6350. Office Fax: 309-681-6691. Business E-Mail: hojillmp@ncaur.usda.gov.

HOKANSON, CAROL, speech therapist, special education educator; b. Memphis, Oct. 21, 1954; d. William Thomas and Tommie Francis Sowell. BSE, Ark. State U., 1976, MSE, 1983. Speech and lang. pathologist. Speech therapist Evening Shade (Ark.) Sch., 1977-78; spl. edn. tchr. Sch. for Exceptional Children, Pocahontas, Ark., 1978-84, Eureka (Kans.) Pub. Schs., 1984-85; spl. edn. CBI tchr. Helena (Ark.) Pub. Sch., 1987-88; speech therapist Bearden (Ark.) Pub. Sch., 1988-91, Caddo Hills/Mt. Ida/Oden, Montgomery County schs., Norman, Ark., 1991—. Speech therapist Dawson Co-op, Arkadelphai, Ark., 1993—; psychol. examiner Psychol. Corps., Austin, Tex., 1997—. Participant chaperon Spl. Olympics, Pocahontas, Ark., 1978-84. Mem. NEA, Assn. Retarded Citizens. Presbyterian and Methodist. Home: PO Box 2112 Glenwood AR 71943-2112 Office: Caddo Hills Sch HC 65 Box 249 Norman AR 71957-9502

HOKE, SHEILA WILDER, retired librarian; b. Greensboro, N.C. d. Herbert Bruce Wilder and Virginia Dare (Caylor) Wilder-Dell; m. Robert Edward Hoke, Nov. 22, 1958 (dec.); children: Raymond Fellow, Philip Wilder. Student, Montclair Coll., 1948; BA in History, U. Kans., 1950, postgrad., 1951, BS in Edn., 1952; postgrad., John Hopkins U., 1955; MLS, U. Wis., 1955; MS in Edn., Southwestern Okla. State U., 1977; postgrad., Johns Hopkins U., Montclair State Coll. Tchr. history Fredonia (Kans.) High Sch., 1952-54; student asst. U. Wis., Madison, 1954-55; children's libr. BR Enoch Pratt Libr., Balt., 1955-58; libr. dir. U.S. Army Spl. Svcs., Bavaria, Fed. Republic Germany, 1958-59; libr. U.S. Army Dependent Schs., Straubing, Fed. Republic Germany, 1959-60; cataloger Southwestern Okla. State U. Libr., Weatherford, 1963-69, libr. dir., 1969-93; ret., 1993. Mem. spl. projects com. Okla. Dept. Edn., 1974, adv. com. Okla. State Regents Libr., 1975-77. Mem. Okla. State Regents for Higher Edn. Libr. Networking, 1989-93; mem. sr. citizens choir 1st Bapt. Ch., Weatherford; vol. with children Agape Med. Clinic; reading tutor to 1st grade student Weatherford Pub. Schs.; vol. helper for home-bound; active sr. citizens groups. Mem. AAUW (pres., state bd. dirs. 1980, Weatherford br. 1981-83), Nat. Assn. Ret. Fed. Employees, Okla. Libr. Assn. (chmn. tech. svcs. divsn. 1969-70, chmn. coll. and univ. divsn. 1972-73, chmn. adminstrs. workshop 1973, chmn. libr. edn. divsn. 1975-76, chmn. recruitment com. 1978, archives com. 1980), Okla. Ret. Tchrs. Assn., Weatherford C. of C. (edn. com. 1974-75, cert. meritorious achievement from Gov. Nigh 1985), Custer County Hist. Soc., western Okla. Hist. Soc., Higher Edn. Alumni Coun. Okla., Delta Kappa Gamma (pres. Lambda chpt. 1980-82), Phi Alpha theta, Kappa Kappa Iota (pres. Lambda chpt. 1984-85, 2005-06). Republican. Baptist. Avocation: travel. E-mail: shoke@itlnet.net.

HOKIN, JEANNE, education educator; b. NYC; d. Louis and Sophie (Gittleson) Winer; m. J. Robert Wills, June 15, 2002; children: Peggy Willoughby, Debra Linn, Jamie McQueen. BA summa cum laude, U. Calif., Santa Barbara, 1981, PhD, 1989. Prof., lectr. art history Ariz. State U., Tempe, Ariz., 1988—2003, prof. emeritus, 2003—. V.p. Friends of European Art, Phoenix Art Mus., 1998; vis. prof. in art history, Sch. of Art, Ariz. State U., Tempe, 1986; vis. lectr. ASU Main, 1989, others; lectr. in field. Author: (book) Pinnacles and Pyramids: The Art of Marsden Hartley, 1993; contbr. articles to profl. jours. Lectr. Phoenix Art Mus. Recipient Disting. Tchr. award Sch. of Art, Ariz. State U., 1993; grantee U. Calif., Santa Barbara, 1980-81, 81-82, 1987, Vidda Found., 1988-89; recipient Samuel H. Kress Found. fellowship, 1986, others. Mem. Coll. Art Assn. Home: 14002 E Coyote Rd Scottsdale AZ 85259-2225

HOLADAY, BARBARA (BOBBIE) HAYNE, writer; b. Pocantico Hills, N.Y., Aug. 5, 1922; d. Coe Smith Hayne and Ethel May Shandrew; m. George Robert Barfoot, Jan. 1944 (dec.); children: Bonnie Jean, Bettie Jane. BA, Denison U., 1944. Tech. writer GE, Phoenix, 1959—62; computer systems analyst Honeywell, Inc., 1963—86. Founder, exec. dir. Preserve Arizona's Wolves, Phoenix, 1988—98. Author: Return of the Mexican Gray Wolf: Back to the Blue, Wild Places. Sec. Internat. Soc. Writers & Pubs., 1968—70; apptd. by Gov. Ariz. Pub. Adv. Coun. Com. for Ariz. Comparative Environ. Risk Project, 1994. With USN, 1944—46, served WAVES USN, 1944—46. Recipient Svc. on Roosevelt Lake Task Force award, US Forest Svc., 1994, World of Outdoors, Cactus-Pine Girl Scout Coun., 1995, Environmentlist of Yr. award, Ariz. Game and Fish Commn., 1996, Wilderness Hero award, Campaign Am.'s Wilderness, 2004, Who Speaks for Wolf award, Internat. Wolf Ctr., 2005. Mem.: Ariz. Heritage Alliance (Vol. Svc. award), Internat. Wolf Ctr. (Who Speaks for Wolf award 2005), Ariz. Wilderness Coalition, Nat. Resources Defence Coun., Nat. Wildlife Fedn., Audubon Soc., Defenders of Wildlife (Conservation Award of Excellence 1998), Sierra Club (25 Yr. Mem. award 2005, Outstanding Achievement 2002). Democrat. Episcopalian. Achievements include helping return endangered Mexican wolf to the wild; sponsoring designation of two U.S. wilderness areas: Hellsgate, 1984, Eagletail Mountains, 1990. Avocations: hiking, camping, email correspondence, reading, canine companionship, writing. Home: 1413 East Dobbins Rd Phoenix AZ 85042 Personal E-mail: azwolflady1@cox.net.

HOLBERG, EVA MARIA, volunteer; b. Stralsund, Germany, Apr. 22, 1931; arrived in US, 1957, naturalized, 1962; d. Hans Herbert and Helene Wilhelmine (Engelhardt) Thieshen; m. Dieter E. Holberg, May 28, 1955; children: Marion (dec.), Astrid. Student, Free U. Berlin, 1952—55. Mgr. Pathways to Music Mt. St. Mary's Coll., L.A., 1972—74; pres., mgr. Palisades Symphony, Pacific Palisades, Calif., 1974—; pres. Theatre Palisades, 1979—81, 1982—83, 2006—, chmn. ways and means, 1981—, v.p., 1983—. bd. dir. Active mem. Westside Com. LA Philharm., 1971—, bd. dirs., 1972—85, pres., 1975—77, coord. affiliates for youth programs and season tickets, 1979—81; cultural rep. Palisades Cmty. Coun., 1976. Named Citizen of Yr. Pacific Palisades, 1981; recipient Cmty. Svc. award Pacific Palisades Cmty. Coun., 2005. Mem. Am. Symphony League. Home: 1081 Palisair Pl Pacific Palisades CA 90272-2459 Office: Box PO Box 214 Pacific Palisades CA 90272-0214

HOLBROOK, CONNIE C., lawyer; b. 1946; BA, Brigham Young U.; JD, U. Utah. Bar: 1974. Asst. sec. Mountain Fuel Supply Co., staff attty., v.p., sec.; sr. v.p. gen. counsel, corp. sec. Questar Corp., Salt Lake City, 1993—. Bd. dirs. United Way, Salt Lake City. Mem.: ABA, Am. Soc. Corp. Secs.

HOLBROOK, JENNIFER LYNN, elementary school educator; d. Thomas Stanley and Ardice Louise Holbrook. BS summa cum laude, Elizabethtown Coll., Pa., 2000; MS, McDaniel Coll., Westminster, Md., 2005. Cert. reading specialist Md., elem. tchr. Md. Pa. Tchr. grade 2 Taneytown Elem. Sch., Md., 2000—06; tchr. grade 4 lang. arts Spring Garden Elem. Sch., Hampstead, 2006—. Mentor tchr. for student intern McDaniel Coll., Westminster, 2002, 05, clin. supr. summer reading clinic, 2006—; new tchr. induction presenter Carroll County Pub. Schs., 2006; mentor tchr. for student intern Carroll CC, Westminster, Md., 2006—. Scholar, Md. Del. Carmen Amedori, 2001; Wilhelm scholar, Carroll County C. of C., 2001. Mem.: ASCD, Ctrl. Md. Assn. for the Edn. of Young Children, Nat. Assn. for the Edn. of Young Children, Md. ASCD, Carroll County Reading Coun., State of Md. Internat. Reading Assn. Coun., Internat. Reading Assn., Kappa Delta Pi, Psi Chi. Office: Spring Garden Elem Sch 700 Boxwood Dr Hampstead MD 21074 Office Phone: 410-751-3433.

HOLBROOK, KAREN ANN, academic administrator, biologist; b. Des Moines, Nov. 6, 1942; married, 1973; 1 child. BS, U. Wis., 1963, MS, 1966; PhD in Biol. Structure, U. Wash., 1972. From instr. to assoc. prof. U. Wash. Sch. of Medicine, Seattle, 1971-79, vice chmn. dept. biol. structure, 1981—93, prof., 1984—93, assoc. dean sci. affairs, 1985—93; sr. v.p. & prof. U. Ga., Athens, Ga., 1993—98; pres. Ohio State U., Columbus, Ohio, 2002—. Instr. biology Ripon Coll., 1966-69; NIH trainee, 1969-72, trainee, sr. fellow dermatology, 1976-78, mem. study sect. gen. medicine; adj. assoc. prof. med. dermatology, U. Wash., 1979-84; mem. spl. study sect. Nat. Inst. Arthritis & Metabollic Diseases, Nat. Inst. Arthritis, Diabetes & Digestive Kidney Diseases, 1985-88; adj. prof. med. dermatology, 1984-93. Named Disting. Woman Physician/Scientist, 1996; recipient Kung Sun Oh Mem prize, 34th Annual Mation Spencer Fay Nat. Bd. award, Disting. Contribn. to Rsch. Admin. award. Mem. AAAS, Am. Assn. Anatomists, Am. Soc. Cell Biology, Soc. Invest Dermatology, Soc. Pediat. Dermatology, Am. Assn. Of Univ., Nat. Assn of State Univ & Land Grant Coll., Assn of Am. Med. Coll. Commn on Higher Edn.; bd. dir. ACT, Am. Coun. On Edn., Nat. Merit Scholarship Corp, Nat. Coun. For Sci. and Environment, Huntington Bancshares, Reservoir Venture Ptnrs., Columbus Tech. Coun., Columbus Ptnrshp., Ctr. of Sci. & Industry, Columbus Downtown Dev. Corp., Ctrl. Ohio United Negro Coll. Fund, United Way of Ctrl. Ohio, Greater Columbus Area C. of C., CEOs for Cities, Columbus Sch. For Girls; Sigma Xi; trustee, Cap. So. Urban Redev. Corp. Achievements include research in fine structural & biochemical analysis of human skin including development of the human epidermis and dermis in vivo prenatal diagnosis of inherited skin diseases, structural abnormalities of the dermis in individuals with inherited disorders of connective tissue metabolism, epidermis in inherited disorders of keratinization. Office: Off of Pres 205 Bricker Hall 190 North Oval Mall Columbus OH 43210-1357 Office Phone: 614-292-2424. Office Fax: 614-292-1231. E-mail: holbrook.79@osu.edu.*

HOLBROOK, TARYL ANN, psychological consultant; b. Columbus, Ohio, Mar. 28, 1954; d. Argus and Mildred Arlene (Schiller) H. B.S. in Spanish, B.A. in Psychology, Ohio State U., 1976, M.A., 1978, Ph.D., 1983; Lic. psychologist, Ohio, Fla. Acad. advisor Univ. Coll., Columbus, 1977-81, 82-83; psychology intern Counseling Ctr. for Human Devel. U. South Fla., Tampa, 1981-82; counselor Counseling and Consultation Services, Ohio State U., Columbus, 1982-83; psychol. cons. Juvenile Ct. Pinellas County, Clearwater, Fla., 1983—1996; pvt. practice, Largo, Fla., 1990-1993; Adj. psychology instr. St. Petersburg Coll., 1997—, Pasco Hernando CC, 2000—. mem. Health and Rehab. Services, Case Rev. Com. for Severely Emotionally Disturbed Children and Adolescents, Clearwater, Fla., 1983. Mem. Am. Psychol. Assn., Fla. Psychol. Assn., Ohio Psychol. Assn. (mem.), Ohio State U. Alumni Assn., Phi Delta Kappa. Republican. Baptist. Home: 29200 Bay Hollow Dr Apt 3285 Wesley Chapel FL 33543-4365 Office: Pinellas County Juvenile Ct 14500 49th St N Clearwater FL 33762-2829

HOLBROOKS, FAYE GRIFFIN, elementary school educator; b. Anderson, SC, Nov. 14, 1946; d. Albert James and Alta Virginia (Griffin) Griffin; m. Truman Lee Holbrooks, June 15, 1974; children: E. Ashley, A. Lee, T. Ward. BA, Winthrop Coll., Rock Hill, S.C., 1969. Min. music and youth Waughtown Bapt. Ch., Winston-Salem, NC, 1969-71; tchr. 1st grade Oconee County Sch. Dist., Westminster, SC, 1972-73; resource tchr. spl. edn., 1973-74; tchr. 2d grade, 1974—2002; ret., 2002. Organist Richland Presbyn. Ch., 2003—. Bapt. Avocations: music, reading, cooking. Home: 201 Adams St Westminster SC 29693-1201 Office: Westminster Elem Sch Hall Rd Westminster SC 29693

HOLBROW, GWENDOLYN JANE, artist, writer; b. NYC, Aug. 22, 1957; d. Charles Howard and Mary Ross Holbrow; m. Mark Joseph Kacvinsky; children: Hilary, Charles, Giles, Felicity. BA with honors, U. Wis., 1980; BA, Framingham State Coll., 2001. Cert. fluency in German as fgn. lang. Goethe Inst. Freelance writer, 1997—; instr. Danforth Mus. Sch., Framingham, Mass., 2001—. Freelance editor, graphic designer, desk-top pub., Frankfurt am Main, Germany, 1990—98; contbg. author Main City, Frankfurter Allgemeine Zeitung, Frankfurt am Main, 1997—98, Middlesex Beat, Groton, 2001—04; lectr. Framingham State Coll., 2002—, AAUW, 2002; wedding officiant Commonwealth of Mass., 2005—; author, rev. artsMedia, Boston, 2002—04, Boston Glove, 2005, WBUR, 2006—. Mixed-media installation, The Throne Of The Queen Of The Universe and Her Handmaidens, 2000, mixed-media fountain with barbie doll, Keep It Clean, 2000 (First prize Concord Art Assn., 2000), acoustic copper sculpture, Gravity Chimes, 2001 (Juror's Choice award Cambridge Art Assn., 2001), poster, Universal Applicaton, 2002; author: (essay) Louse Bourgeois: Bridging the Chasm Between Self and Other, 2001 (Cheryl di Mento Art History Essay award Framingham State Coll., 2001); prin. works include Make Way for Calflings, Boston Cow Parade, 2006. Town meeting mem. Town Meeting, Framingham, 2001, 2006—. Recipient Silver medal, Mass. Hort. Soc., 2002, 2005, Gold medal, 2004, Best of Show for Queen Kong sculpture, Cambridge Art Assn., 2004; grantee winner, Artists' Valentine Grant Competition, 2003, 2006. Mem.: New Eng. Sculptors Assn. (bd. dirs.), Concord Art Assn., Cambridge Art Assn., Internat. Sculpture Ctr. Unitarian Universalist. Avocation: ballroom dancing. Business E-Mail: holbrow@hotmail.com.

HOLCOMB, ANNA LOUISE, physical science educator; b. Sherman, Tex., June 22, 1946; d. Louis Alvin and Louise Lorraine (Genthe) Franklin; m. Harold V. Holcomb, June 26, 1964; children: Cynthia Louise Holcomb-Wilson, John Harold. BA in Physics, U. Tex., Arlington, 1986. Cert. tchr. physics, phys. sci., English, Tex. Tchr. physics/phys. sci. Brewer H.S., Ft. Worth, 1986-91; tchr. physics, phys. sci., sci. discovery, environ. studies Ft. Worth Country Day Sch., 1991-96. Recipient Disting. Achievement award for sci. teaching DuPont Corp., Nat. Sci. Tchrs. Assn., Gen. Learning Corp., 1994, 95; 1st place winner nat. sci. competition DuPont Challenge Awards Program, 1995. Mem. Am. Assn. Physics Tchrs., Nat. Sci. Tchrs. Assn., Tex. Tchrs. Phys. Sci., Tex. Marine Edn. Assn., Associated Chemistry Tchrs. Tex. Office: Ft Worth Country Day Sch 4200 Country Day Ln Fort Worth TX 76109-4201 Home: 10409 Holly Grove Dr Fort Worth TX 76108 E-mail: outwest@sbcglobal.net.

HOLCOMB, CONSTANCE L., sales and marketing management executive; b. St. Paul, Oct. 28, 1942; d. John E. Holcomb and Lucille A. (Westerdahl) Hope; m. Walter D. Serwatka, May 1991. BS, U. Minn., 1965; MA in Intercultural Edn., U. of the Americas, Puebla, Mex., 1975. Rsch. analyst U.S. Dept. Def., Washington, 1965-66; br. gen. mgr. Berlitz Lang. Schs., Mexico City, 1966-68; pres., gen. mgr. Centro Lingüistico, Puebla, 1968-72; gen. mgr., prof. Lang. Ctr. Am. Sch. Found., Puebla, 1972-74; assoc. prof., dir. lang. programs U. of the Americas, Puebla, 1974-76; prof., dean faculty of langs. Nat. Autonomous U. Mex., Mexico City, 1976-78; dir. sales & mktg. Longman Pub. Co., N.Y.C., 1978-80, dir. internat. sales & mktg.,

1980-84; mng. dir. ESL Pub. Div. McGraw-Hill Book Co., N.Y.C., 1984-85; dir. mktg. mgmt. McGraw-Hill Tng. Systems and Book Co., N.Y.C., 1985-86; dir. mktg. electronic bus. McGraw-Hill Book Co., N.Y.C., 1986-87; info. industry mgmt. cons., career mgmt. cons., ind. contractor, N.Y.C., 1987-91; mktg. cons. Sarasota, Fla., 1991—. V.p. MexTESOL, Mexico City, 1977-78. Editor: English Teaching in Mexico, 1975; pub.: Rubens to Rhubarb, The Ringling Museum of Art, 1995, Baroque, Basil and Thyme, The Ringling Museum of Art, 1997, Ringling, the Art Museum, The Ringling Museum of Art, 2002; contbr. articles to profl. jours. Bd. trustees, devel. com. mem. John and Mable Ringling Mus., 1993-99; bd. dirs. Safe Place and Rape Crisis Ctr., Sarasota, 1995-2002; bd. dirs. Friends of Selby Pub. Libr., 1997-99. Recipient Outstanding Fundraiser of Yr. award, Assn. Fundraising Profls., 2001. Mem. Assn. Am. Pubs. (com. chmn. internat. div. 1980-84, exec. com. 1980-84), Info. Industry Assn., Nat. Assn. Women Cons., Am. Soc. Profl. and Exec. Women. Office: 340 S Palm Ave Apt 93 Sarasota FL 34236-6795

HOLCOMB, GENE ANN, federal loan officer; b. Munday, Tex., Jan. 11, 1937; d. L. C. Guinn, Jr. and Amerolis Magdalyn Hutcheson; m. Jerry Cobb (div.); children: Sheila Cobb, Simone Cobb. Grad. h.s., Knox City, Tex. County office clk. Farmer's Home Adminstrn. USDA, Haskell, Tex., 1970—74, county office asst. Farmer's Home Adminstrn. Knox City, 1975—92, program rev. asst. Farmer's Home Adminstrn. Tex., 1993—95, asst. loan officer Farm Security Administration Haskell, 1995—2000; ret., 2000. Asst. editor: Knox County News, 1968—70. Pres. Women's Club 1946 Study Club, Knox City, 1964—65; chmn. city-wide fund drs. Recipient Cert. Outstanding Accomplishment, USDA-Farmer's Home Adminstrn., 1976, 1987—88, Cert. Merit, 1992, Cert. Superior Performance, 1992. Mem.: Knox City Ex-Students Assn. Republican. Disciples Of Christ. Avocation: bus tours.

HOLCOMB, HELEN LEE, investor, interior designer; d. Edward Ancil Holcomb and Nellie Marshall. Grad., U. Montana, 1965. Art tchr. Lake Washington Sch. Dist., Kirkland, Wash.; chair art dept. Bellevue (Wash.) Sch. Dist., art tchr.; interior designer Bell Sq. Furniture, Bellevue; freelance interior designer Bellevue; gen. mng. ptnr. Holcomb Investments, LLP, Chandler, Ariz. Address: 747 Belmont Pl E Seattle WA 98102-4418

HOLCOMB, LINDA LAINE, elementary school educator, director; d. Raymond Marcel and Eda Brunk Laine; m. Steve Alan Holcomb, Sept. 10, 1972; children: Julie Holcomb Higdon, John David. BA in Edn., Stetson U., DeLand, Fla., 1973; MA in Edn., We. Carolina U., Cullowhee, N.C., 1999, EdS, 2004, student, 2002—. Lic. tchr. N.C., Nat. Bd. Profl. Tchg. Standards, 2000. Tchr. Murphy (N.C.) Elem. Sch., 1974—80; tchr. reading Andrews (N.C.) Elem. Sch., 1983—94, Cherokee County Schs., Murphy, 1994—, dir. staff devel., 2005—06. Instr. GED Tri-County C.C., Murphy, 1994—96; tchr. tnr., coord. reading Cherokee County Schs., 1998—2005; instr. Walden U., 2002—; presenter in field. Named Tchr. of Yr., Andrews Elem. Sch., 1996, Walmart, 1997; recipient Cmty. Svc. Vol. Recognition award, Cherokee County Literacy Coun., 1994. Mem.: NEA, ASCD, Nat. Staff Devel. Coun., Reading Recovery Coun. N.Am., N.C. Assn. Educators, Internat. Reading Assn. Independent. Episc. Avocations: writing, travel. Office: Cherokee County Title II Dir 911 Andrews Hwy Murphy NC 28906 Office Phone: 828-835-8483. Business E-Mail: lholcomb@waldenu.edu.

HOLCOMB, PAULA KAE, conductor, educator; d. Dillon Brydell Holcomb. MusB in Edn., Drake U., Des Moines, 1976, MusM in Edn., 1971; MusD, Northwestern U., Evanston, Ill., 1991. Dir. bands Ctrl. Coll., Pella, Iowa, 1979—98; dir. bands, prof. music SUNY, Fredonia, 1998—. Recipient Frank A Miller award, Kappa Kappa Psi, 2003; Individual Devel. grantee, SUNY, 2005, Carnahan Jackson grantee, 2005—06. Mem.: World Assn. Symphonic Bands and Ensembles (bd. 2002—04), Iowa Music Educators Assn. (pres. 1996—98), Coll. Band Dirs. Nat. Assn. (divsn. pres. elect 2005—06), Conductors Guild (bd. 2004—06). Office: State University of New York at Fredonia 1142 Mason Hall Fredonia NY 14063 Office Phone: 716-673-4637. Office Fax: 716-673-3154. Personal E-mail: holcomb@fredonia.edu.

HOLDCRAFT, JANET RULON, school system administrator; b. Bridgeton, NJ, Sept. 30, 1940; d. Mulford M. and Sarah Hansel (Dilks) Rulon; m. E. Larry Holdcraft, Feb. 21, 1964 (wid. Sept. 1979); children: Larry B., Jodi Holdcraft Coates. BA, Glassboro State, 1962, MA, 1968; EdD, Seton Hall U., 1994. Tchr. fourth grade Glassboro (N.J.) Bd. Edn., 1962-67, tchr. devel. reading grade 7, 1967-68, tchr. corrective reading, grades 6-8, 1968-75, coord. Right-to-Read, 1975-77, tchr. compensatory edn. reading, 1977-80, Title I reading tchr. grades 7-8, 1980-84, BSI/lang. arts tchr., grades 7-8, 1984-93, tchr. GED adult evening sch., 1988-89, head tchr., dir. student activities, 1988-93, asst. supt. curriculum and personnel, 1995—. Prin. BSI Spl. Edn. program Glassboro Bd. Edn., 1991-93; prin. alt. evening h.s. Supr. Adult Cmty. Sch., Glassboro, 1993-94; dir. curriculum and instrn. Pennsville Sch. Dist., NJ, 1994-95. Asst. leader Holly Shores chpt. Girl Scouts USA, Franklinville, NJ, 1979—82; mem. Mothers Football Club Delsea Regional High Sch., Franklinville, 1979—80; mem. Glassboro Mcpl. Alliance, 1995—, chair, 1995—97; mem. Gloucester County Curriculum Consortium, 1995—, treas., 1999—2002; mem. Ladies Rep. Club, Franklinville, 1980—83; mem. adminstrv. coun., budget com., pantry com., bd. dirs. Bright Promises Nursery Sch. Franklinville United Meth. Ch.; mem. adv. bd. so. region N.J. Statewide Systemic Initiative, 1999—2004. Co-dir. reading grant US Office Edn., 1978-80; named to Glassboro HS Hall of Disting. Alumni, 2005; recognized by Gov.'s Tchrs. Recognition Program, State of NJ, 1988; Elizabeth M. Bozarth scholar, NJ Alpha Zeta, 1990. Mem. ASCD, AASA, NJ Assn. Sch. Adminstrs., Reading Coun. So. NJ, NJ Assn. Supervision and Curriculum (So. region bd. dirs.), Rotary Club (Glassboro/Clayton/Elk Twp.), Delta Kappa Gamma (chpt. 1st v.p. 1990-92, rec. sec. 1988-90), NJ Coun. Edn., Kappa Delta Pi. Methodist. Avocations: golf, reading, collecting salt and pepper shakers. Home: 589 Judy Ave Franklinville NJ 08322-3913 Office: Glassboro Pub Schs Glassboro NJ 08028 Office Phone: 856-881-6366 322.

HOLDEN, BETSY D., former food products company executive; b. Lubbock, Tex., 1956; BA, Duke U.; MA in edn., Northwestern U., MBA, 1982. Asst. product mgr. desserts Gen. Foods Corp., 1982—84; brand mgr., venture div. Kraft Foods Inc., 1984—85, brand mgr., Miracle Whip Northfield, Ill., 1985—87, group brand mgr., confections & snacks, 1987—90, v.p. new product devel. and strategy Northfield, Ill., 1990—91, v.p., mktg., dinners, & enhancers, 1991—93, pres. Tombstone Pizza Northfield, Ill., 1993—95, exec. v.p., gen. mgr. cheese divsn., 1995—97, pres. cheese divsn., 1997—98, exec. v.p., ops., procurement, research & devel., consumer insights and E-commerce, 1998—2000; pres., CEO Kraft Foods North America, 2000—01; co-CEO Kraft Foods Inc., 2001—03, pres., global mktg. & category devel., 2004—05. Bd. dir. Kraft Foods, Tribune Co., Tupperware Corp., Western Union, 2006—. Pres. Chicago's Off the Street Club; mem., bd. Grocery Manufacturers of Amer., Evanston Northwestern Healthcare.*

HOLDEN, CAROL HELEN, county official; b. Boston, Nov. 6, 1942; m. Donald B. Holden; 4 children. BA, Trinity Coll., 1964; MAT, Boston Coll., 1965. Intern U.S. Senate, 1963-64; mem. N.H. Ho. of Reps., 1984-97, vice chair children, youth and juvenile justice com.; mem. state-fed. rels. com.; asst. majority leader, 1996. Vice chair Hillsborough County Bd. Commrs., 1997—; mem. Amherst Ways and Means Commn., 1983-86; tchr., vol. coord. Del. NH Constl. Conv., 1984; pres. Amherst Women's Rep. Club, 1986-88; v.p. NH Fed. Rep. Women's Club, 1989-94, pres., 1994-95; mem. Amherst Sch. Dist. Mod., 1990—; dir. N.H. Ptnrs. in Edn., 1987—, sec., 1989—, vice chair, 1990—, chair, 1992—; mem. Gov.'s Steering Com. Volunteerism, 1991-96; mem. NH Alliance for Effective Schs., 1991-96; v.p. NH Congress Parents and Tchrs., 1984-86, 90-92; trustee NH Childrens Trust Fund, 1997-98, Child and Family Svcs., 2005-; treas. Nat. Conf. County Rep. County Ofcls., 2004-; bd. dirs. Nashua Cmty. Coun., 2002; bd. dirs. Nat. Conf. Rep. Ofcls., 1999—, treas., 2004-05, sec., 2005—, Nashua Cmty. Coun., 2002-; mem., svcs. steering com. NACO, 2005—. Mem. Nat. Assn. of Counties (v.p.), Trinity Coll. Alumni Assn. (bd. dirs. 1980-87, sec. bd. dirs. 1994-97, 2d v.p. 1997-98), NH Assn. Counties (1st v.p. 1999-01, pres. elect, 2001-03, pres. 2003), Nat. Assn. Counties (steering com. labor and employment 1999—, bd. dirs. 2002—), Boston Coll. Club of N.H. (pres. 1999-01), Vesta Roy Series (v.p. 2002-05). Avocations: travel, sailing, tennis, skiing, reading. Home: PO Box 13 Amherst NH 03031-0013 Office: Bd Commrs 329 Mast Rd Ste120 Goffstown NH 03045 Personal E-mail: ccommish@bassriver.us. Business E-Mail: ccommish@rcn.com.

HOLDEN, LINDA KATHLEEN, medical educator; b. Rawlins, Wyo., May 31, 1949; d. Charles William Holden and Z. Ruth (Hart Holden) Parsons; m. John O. Itzen, Feb. 2, 2002; m. Jerry E. Hensley (div.); 1 child, Rebecca Suzanne Hensley. AAS in Radiography, Laramie County CC, Cheyenne, Wyo., 1991; BS in Med. Imaging Mgmt., Regis U., Denver, 1998, MS in Health Sci., Mgmt. and Adminstrn., 2000. Cert. radiologic technologist. Staff technologist Paracelsus Krankenhous, Ruit, Germany, 1971—73, Med. Ctr. Hosp., Tyler, Tex., 1973—75; staff technologist, supr. High Plains Bapt. Hosp., Amarillo, Tex., 1977—79; staff technologist Beth Israel Hosp., Denver, 1979—80; staff technologist, ultrasound technologist Wyo. Med. Ctr., Casper, 1980—85; ast. dir., ultrasound technologist Ivinson Meml. Hosp., Laramie, Wyo., 1985—89; adminstrv. dir. DePaul Hosp., Cheyenne, Wyo., 1989—92; clin. coord. radiography program Laramie County CC, Cheyenne, 1993—. Spkr. in field. Mem.: Assn. Educators in Radiologic Scis., Assn. Collegiate Educators in Radiologic Tech. (sec.-treas. 2001—03, Outstanding Educator of Yr. 2005), Utah Soc. Radiologic Technologists, Mo. Soc. Radiologic Technologists, Nebr. Soc. Radiologic Technologists, N.Mex. Soc. Radiologic Technologists, Am. Inst. Ultrasound in Medicine, Soc. Diagnostic Med. Sonographers, Am. Soc. Radiologic Technologists, Am. Cancer Soc., Wyo. Soc. Radiologic Technologists (life Escobedo award 1998—2000), Colo. Soc. Radiologic Technologists (life), Beta Sigma Phi. Democrat. Avocations: gardening, crocheting, painting, crafts, reading. Office: Laramie County Cmty Coll 1400 E College Dr Cheyenne WY 82007-3204

HOLDEN, SISTER MARGARET MARY, sister; d. Thomas Edward Holden and Florence Natalie Henaghan. BA in Social Studies and Psychology, Ladcliff Coll., Highland Falls, NY, 1971; MA in Spl. Edn., Cardinal Stritch U., Milw., 1976; MA in Religion and Religious Edn., Fordham U., Bronx, NY, 1989. Retreat dir., pub. rels. coord. Xavier Retreat Ctr., Convent Station, NJ, 1990—92; tchr. pre-sch. spl. edn. St. Dominic's Home, Bronx, 1992—97; dir. spiritual guidance St. Benedict Ctr., Madison, Wis., 1997—98; co-dir. ministry to persons with phys./mental disabilities Misericordia Home, Chgo., 1998—2003; min. pastoral care Franciscan Sisters of Peace, Haverstraw, NY, 2004—. Mem.: Franciscan Sisters of Peace. Home: 245 Bennett Ave Apt 4D New York NY 10040-2476 Personal E-mail: mholdenfsp@aol.com.

HOLDEN, REBECCA LYNN, artist; b. Monterey, Calif., Nov. 29, 1952; d. Derrel Wayne and Zella Fay (Reed) Holden; m. Mark Stuart Bales, June 3, 1971 (div. Nov. 1983); children: Shelly Dawn Bales(dec.), Matthew Gregory Bales. BA, U. Ark., 1995. Potter/owner Rebecca Holden Studio, Searcy, Ark., 1984-94; artist/owner Rebecca Holden's Red Lick Mountain Studio, Clarksville, Ark., 1994-00; owner Old Carriage House Gallery and Studio, Jasper, Ark., 2000—. Established Old Carriage House Gallery and Studio, Jasper, Ark., 2000. Potter, sculptor, artist specializing in natural art forms. Recipient Art scholarship Susan Jones Rand Foun., 1992, 93. E-mail: carriage@ritternet.com.

HOLDEN, SUSAN M., lawyer; BA magna cum laude, St. Cloud State Univ., 1984; JD cum laude, William Mitchell Coll. of Law, 1988. Cert.: civil trial specialist. Law clerk Sieben, Grose, Von Holtum & Carey, Mpls., 1985—88, atty., 1988—93, ptnr., bd. dir., 1993—. Fellow: Am. Bar Found.; mem.: ABA, Nat. Conf. of Bar Presidents, Assn. of Trial Lawyers of Am., Minn. Trial Lawyers Assn., Minn. Women Lawyers, Hennepin County Bar Assn. (pres. 1999—2000), Minn. State Bar Assn. (treas. 2003, pres.-elect 2004), Phi Alpha Delta. Office: Sieben Grose Von Holtum & Carey East Bldg 800 Marquette Ave Minneapolis MN 55402

HOLDENER, JUDY ANN, mathematics professor, researcher; b. Parma, OH, Sept. 14, 1965; d. Charles Dunn Newhauser and Joanne Laverne (Newhauser) Solgos; m. Eric James Holdener, June 26, 1993; children: Chase Alexander, Maxim Elias. BSc in Math., Kent State U., 1987; MSc in Math., U. Ill., 1989, PhD in Math., 1994. Tchg., rsch. asst. U. Ill., Urbana, 1987—94; asst. prof. US Air Force Acad., Colorado Springs, Colo., 1994—97, Kenyon Coll., Gambier, Ohio, 1997—2003, assoc. prof., 2003—. Cons. Wolfram Rsch. Inc., Urbana, 1989—90; vis. prof. U. Colo., Boulder, 2004—05. Contbr. math. papers to jours. in field. Recipient Tony M. Johnson Excellence Tchg. award, US Air Force Acad., 1995, Bd. Trustees Jr. Tchg. award, Kenyon Coll., 2003, Tomsich Sci. award, 2003. Mem.: Am. Math. Soc., Math. Assn. Am., Phi Beta Kappa. Avocations: painting, gardening, hiking, reading. Office: Kenyon Coll 307 Hayes Hall Gambier OH 43022 Office Phone: 740-427-5266. Business E-Mail: holdenerj@kenyon.edu.

HOLDER, ANGELA RODDEY, law educator; b. Rock Hill, S.C., Mar. 13, 1938; d. John T. and Angela M. (Fisher) Roddey; 1 child, John Thomas Roddey Holder. Student, Radcliffe Coll., 1955-56; BA, Newcomb Coll., 1958; postgrad., Faculty of Law-King's Coll., London, 1957-58; JD, Tulane U., 1960; LLM, Yale U., 1975. Bar: La. 1961, S.C. 1960, Conn. 1981. Counsel Roddey, Sumwalt & Carpenter, Rock Hill, SC, 1960-91; atty. criminal div. New Orleans Legal Aid Bur., 1961-62; counsel York County Family Ct., SC, 1962-64; asst. prof. polit. sci. Winthrop Coll., Rock Hill, 1964-74; research assoc. Yale U. Law Sch., 1975-77, exec. dir. program in law, sci. and medicine, 1976-77; lectr. dept. pediatrics Yale U. Sch. Medicine, 1975-77, asst. clin. prof. pediatrics and law, 1977-79, assoc. clin. prof., 1979-83, clin. prof., 1983-2001; prof. practice of med. ethics Duke U. Med. Ctr., Durham, NC, 2001—. Trustee Am. Bd. Pediatrics, 2003—; mem. com. on pediat. palliative care Inst. Medicine, 2001—02, mem. com. on clin. rsch. with children, 2002—04. Author: The Meaning of the Constitution, 1968, 3d edit., 1997, Medical Malpractice Law, 1975, 2d edit. 1978, Legal Issues in Pediatrics and Adolescent Medicine, 1977, 3d edit., 1997; contbg. editor: Prism mag.; contbg. editor., AMA; mem. editl. bd.: IRB, 1976-2000, Medicine and HealthCare, 1978-2000, Jour. Philosophy and Medicine; contbr. articles to profl. jours. Mem. Rock Hill Sch. Bd., 1967—68; chmn. bd. dirs. Family Planning Clinic, 1970—73; bd. trustees Ednl. Commn. for Fgn. Med. Grads., 1990—97, exec. com., 1997; bd. dir. Conn. Planned Parenthood, 1993—99, exec. com., 1996—99; mem. lawyers' rev. group Health Care Task Force, The White House, 1993; bd. trustees Cushing/Whitney Med. Libr. at Yale U., 1996—2001; ethics com. Leeway AIDS Hospice, New Haven, 1996—2001; alumnae bd. visitors Nat. Cathedral Sch., Washington, 2000—; cons. Artificial Reproductive Techs. Com., Ct. Ho. of Reps.; mem. adv. bd., grad. health programs Sarah Lawrence Coll., 2004—. Mem. Conn. Bar Assn., S.C. Bar Assn. (medico-legal com. 1973—), La. Bar Assn., New Haven County Bar Assn., Am. Soc. Law and Medicine (treas. 1981-83, sec. 1983-85, pres. 1986-88, bd. dirs. 1977-91). Democrat. Episcopalian. Home: 3408 Hope Valley Rd Durham NC 27707 Office: Ctr for Study of Med Ethics and Humanities Duke U Med Ctr Box 3040 108 Seeley G Mudd Bldg Durham NC 27710 Office Phone: 919-668-9010. Business E-Mail: angela.holder@duke.edu.

HOLDER, ELAINE EDITH, psychologist, educator; b. Boulder, Co., July 9, 1926; d. Joseph C. and Ethel M. (Woodhouse) Jones; m. Wayne B. Holder, Nov. 28, 1947 (div. 1981); children: Wayne B. Jr., Elaine J. Zieroth, Steven A., Linda LeCour. BA cum laude, U. Colo., 1948; MA, New Mexico State U., 1951; PhD, U. Mo., 1956. Lect. Calif. State Univ., Fresno, 1964-79, Calif. Poly State Univ., San Luis Obispo, 1979-83; assoc. prof. Calif. Poly. State Univ., San Luis Obispo, 1984-88, prof. San Luis, 1988-89; ret., 1989. Contbr. articles to profl. jours. Mem. Mothers for Peace, San Luis, 1981—; sec. bd. dirs. Hospice of San Luis Obispo County, 1987-93, Interfaith Coalition for the Homeless, 1994—; v.p. Mothers for Peace. Mem. Phi Beta Kappa, Pi Gamma Mu, Sigma Xi. Democrat. Avocations: gardening, sewing. Home: 274 Cuesta Dr San Luis Obispo CA 93405-1134

HOLDER, JANICE MARIE, state supreme court justice; b. Canonsburg, Pa., Aug. 29, 1949; d. Louis V. and Sylvia (Abraham) H.; m. George W. Loveland II, June 5, 1976 (div. Mar. 1987). Student, Allegheny Coll., 1967-68, Sorbonne, 1970; BS summa cum laude, U. Pitts., 1971; JD, Duquesne U., 1975. Bar: Pa. 1975, Tenn. 1979, D.C. 1988. Sr. law clk. to chief judge U.S. Dist. Ct. for Western Dist. Pa., Pitts., 1975-77; assoc. Catalano & Catalano, P.C., Pitts., 1977-79, Holt, Batchelor, Spicer & Ryan, Memphis, 1980-82; pvt. practice Memphis, 1982—87; assoc. James S. Cox & Assocs., Memphis, 1987-89; pvt. practice law Memphis, 1989-90; judge 30th Jud. Dist., Memphis, 1990-96; justice Tenn. Supreme Ct., 1996—. Solicitor Borough of McDonald (Pa.), 1978-79. Bd. dirs. Alliance for Blind and Visually Impaired, Memphis, 1985—94, Midtown Mental Health Ctr., 1995—97; trustee Memphis Bot. Garden Found., 1995—2002; mem. state coordinating coun. Tenn. Task Force Against Domestic Violence, 1994—96. Fellow: Tenn. Bar Found. (trustee 1995—99); mem.: ABA, Tenn. Trial Judges Assn. (exec. com. 1994—96), Tenn. Lawyers' Assn. for Women, Memphis Trial Lawyers Assn. (bd. dirs. 1988—90), Am. Inns Ct., Tenn. Jud. Conf. (treas. 1993—94, exec. com. 1993—96), Assn. for Women Attys. (treas. 1989, v.p. 1991, Marion Griffin-Frances Loring award 1999), Memphis Bar Assn. (bd. dirs. 1986—87, 1993—94, editor Memphis Bar Forum 1987—91, 1993—94, sec. 1993, treas. 1994, Sam A. Myar award 1990, Judge of Yr. divorce and family law sect. 1992, Chancellor Charles A. Rond award Outstanding Jurist 1992), Tenn. Bar Assn., Am. Bar Found. Office: Tenn Supreme Ct 119 S Main St Ste 310 Memphis TN 38103-3678

HOLDER, JULIE FASONE, chemicals executive; Grad. in Bus. Adminstrn., Mich. State U. Sales rep. Dow Chem. Co., San Francisco, 1975, mktg. mgr. polyurethanes bus., 1981, dist. sales mgr. Dow Latex, grp. mktg. mgr. formulation products, 1989—94, global bus. dir. performance chems. businesses, 1994, dir. sales and mktg. performance chems. bus. unit, 1997—2000, bus. v.p. indsl. chems., 2000—04, bus. v.p. specialty plastics and elastomers grp., 2004, corp. v.p. human resources, diversity & inclusion and pub. affairs, 2005—, mem. Office of the Chief Exec., 2005—. Co-founder Women Innovation Network Dow Chem. Co.; bd. dirs. Wolverine Bank, Dow Chem. Co. Found. Office: Dow Chem Co 2030 Dow Ctr Midland MI 48674*

HOLDER, MAXINE E., writer; b. Houghton, Mich., Apr. 24, 1939; d. Gordon R. and Elsie (Palosaari) Sincock; m. Marshall V. Holder, Dec. 23, 1957; children: Shelley, Laura. Student, San Jacinto Coll., Pasadena, Tex. Owner, pub. Holder Pub. Co., 1997—. CEO, founder, dir. Inspirational Writers Alive!, 1990—; lectr. in field. Contbr. articles to profl. jours. including The Christian Communicator, Secret Place, Reminisce mag., Down Memory Ln., Emu Today mag., Wattersound, World Mission mag., Chrysalis, Standard, Ariz. Author's Lit. Anthology, Our Write Mind, Writer's World, Streamline, Hungry Writer, Guidepost Mag., numerous Houston newspapers. Contest winner Ariz. Author's Assn., S.W. Writers, Inspirational Writers Alive Contest, ByLine Mag. Contest, Chrysalis Mag., Writers Club of Pasadena. Mem. Nat. Writers Assn., Houston Coun./Writers, Writers Club of Pasadena (pres., hon. life), Am. Christian Writers (faculty mem. 1995-96), South Tex. Conf. at Houston, Tex. Christian Writers Forum (coord. 1990—). Home and Office: Inspirational Writers Alive! RR 4 Box 81-h Rusk TX 75785-9410 Office Phone: 903-795-3986.

HOLDER, SALLIE LOU, training and meeting management consultant, coach; b. Cin., Jan. 25, 1939; d. David Clifford Austin and Ruth Margaret (Higby) Haver; m. Norman Horace Derwyn Holder, July 14, 1964 (div. Oct. 1975). Student, Duke U., 1957-59; BS in Home Econs. Edn., U. Md, 1962; MA in Human Resource Devel. and Edn., George Washington U., 1982.; completed Success Unltd. Network, Basic Coaching Program, 2000. Tchr. Prince Georges County Schs., Md., 1962-66; home econs. tchr. La Reine Sr. High Sch., Suitland, Md., 1966-68; adult edn. Home econs. tchr. Suitland Sr. High Sch, 1969-73; mgr./asst. area sales mgr. The Fabric Tree, Hyattsville, Md., 1972-75; trainer Woodward & Lothrop, Washington and Prince Georges County, Md., 1975-79; conf. coord., non-credit short course coord. Univ. Coll. U. Md., College Park, 1979-87; analyst SYSCON, Washington, 1987-88; meeting mgmt. and tng. cons. Holder & Assocs., College Park, Md., 1988—; tng. specialist Fed. Deposit Ins. Corp., Washington, 1990; instr. Marymount U., Arlington, Va., 1990, Goucher Coll., Balt., 1991-93. Facilitator New Beginnings, Takoma Park, Md., 1983-90, chmn. planning com., facilitator co-trainer, bd. dirs., 1983-84, chmn. facilitators, 1985-86. Mem. alumni bd. Coll. Human Ecology, U. Md., College Park, 1971-93, pres., 1973-74, 77-80, sec., 1985-86, v.p., 1988-90; bd. dirs., mem., cons. lay edn. com., cmty. edn. com. Pastoral Counseling and Consultation Ctrs., 1977-86; mem. seminarian com., search com., chmn. retreat com., vestry mem. Ch. of the Nativity, Camp Springs, Md., vestryman, 1990-93, 2002-2004; mem. Fisherfolk, 1993-98, region 5 rep., 1997-99, pledge sec., 1997-98; mem. congl. care com., 1993-2005, reader, greeter, 1996—, St. Andrews Episcopal Ch., College Park, Md.; vol. monitor Smithsonian Residents Assocs. Program, 1993—; vol. usher Arena State, 1989—; membership chair, bd. dirs. Columbian Women at George Washington U., 1999-2004; mem. adv. coun. dept. bus. and mgmt. Prince Georges CC, 1997-2004. Recipient Disting. Svc. award Alumni Bd. of Coll. Human Ecology, U. Md., 1981, Vol. award, 1991. Mem. AAUW (College Park chpt. 2003-, sec. 2005-), ASTD (Washington chpt. employer coord. 1984-85, co-chmn. program com. 1986, chmn. meeting arrangements 1987-88, treas. 1989, ASTD day chmn., nat. issues chair 1990, chair scholarship com. 1992, coord. spl. interest group 1993, Spl. Achievement award 1987, 88, 90, Pres.'s award 1993), Soc. Govt. Meeting Planners (program commn. 1987-88, communication com., ann. conf. com. 1988-89, chmn. nominating com. 1990, ann. conf. presenter 1990, 93, 94, 98, bd. dirs. 1991-92, 95-97, chmn. edn. com. for 1992 ann. conf. 1995-97, newsletter editor), U. Md. Coll. Park Alumni Assn. (bd. govs. 1989-93), Assn. Meeting Profls., Profl. Conv. Mgrs. Assn., Md. Prince Georges Alumni assn. (v.p. 1994-99, sec. 2004-), Delmarva Depression Glass Club, Washington Met. Glass Club, 1989-, Nat. Am. Glass Club, 1989-Prince Georges Hist. Soc, DAR (Toaping Castle chpt. historian 2004-, Episcopal Sr. Ministries (bd. dirs. 2001-), Art Gliner Humor Ctr. U. Md. (bd. dirs. 1999-), Nat. Interfaith Coun. On Aging (bd. dirs., 2005—). Episcopalian. Home and Office: 4102 Van Buren St University Park MD 20782-1185

HOLDREN, JAMIE LYNN, music educator; b. Cin. d. Dallas E. Harper and Marlene Kirby; m. William P. Holdren; children: Nicholas J., James D. MusB in Edn., Georgetown Coll., Ky., 1982; MEd in adminstrn. and supervision, Xavier U., 1989. Gen. music tchr. Oak Hills Sch. Dist., Cin., 1982—83; choral and gen. music tchr. Princeton Jr. H.S., Cin., 1983—89, Robert E. Lucas Intermediate Sch., Cin., 1989—95; choral dir. Princeton H.S., Cin., 1993. Asst. dist. music coord. Princeton City Schs., Cin., 1995—2000. Dir.: A Prayer, 2000, 13th Annual Intermountain Choral Festival, 2003 (2nd Pl. award, 2003), I Know A Song; contbr. articles to profl. jours. Musician Mt. Carmel Bapt. Ch., Cin., 1978—2003. Mem.: Ohio Choral Dir.'s Assn., Ohio Music Educators Assn., Music Educators Nat. Conf. (Young Composer award 2000), Am. Choral Dir.'s Assn. (assoc.), Delta Kappa Gamma. Avocations: genealogy, reading, travel, gardening. Office: Princeton High School 11080 Chester Road Cincinnati OH 45246 E-mail: jholdren@princeton.k12.oh.us.

HOLDRIDGE, BARBARA, book editor, writer, consultant; b. N.Y.C., July 26, 1929; d. Herbert L. and Bertha (Gold) Cohen; m. Lawrence B. Holdridge, Oct. 9, 1959; 2 children. AB, Hunter Coll., 1950. Asst. editor Liveright Pub. Corp., N.Y.C., 1950-52; co-founder Caedmon Records, Inc., N.Y.C., 1952, ptnr., 1952-60, pres., 1960-62, treas., 1962-70, pres., 1970-75; founder Stemmer House Pubs. Inc., Owings Mills, Md., 1975, pres., 1975—2003; founder Stemmer House, Inc., Owings Mills, 2003, pres., 2003—. Co-founder, v.p. Shakespeare Rec. So., Inc., N.Y.C., 1960-70, Theatre Rec. Soc., Inc., N.Y.C., 1964-70, BEDE Prodns., 1984, History Rec. Soc., Inc., N.Y.C., 1964, pres., 1964-70; lectr. on Ammi Phillips, 1959—; lectr. on book pub., 1992—; lectr. on Caedmon history, 1980-; adj. prof. writing media Loyola Coll., Balt., 1987-91. Author: Ammi Phillips, 1968, Aubrey Beardsley Designs from the Age of Chivalry, 1983, Chinese Cut-Out Designs of Costumes, 1989; articles on Am. paintings. Named to Hunter Coll. Hall of Fame, 1972, Nat. Women's Hall of Fame, 2001; recipient Am. Shakespeare

Festival award, 1962, N.Y.C. cert. of appreciation, 1972, Lifetime Achievement award, Audio Pubs. Assn., 2001, Peabody Instl. award, 1991. Mem. 14 West Hamilton Street Club, Phi Beta Kappa Alumni Assn. of Greater Balt. (bd. dirs.). Office: 2627 Caves Rd Owings Mills MD 21117-2919 Office Phone: 410-363-3690. Personal E-mail: stemmerhouse@comcast.net.

HOLDSCLAW, CHAMIQUE SHAUNTA, professional basketball player; b. Flushing, N.Y., Aug. 9, 1977; Grad., U. Tenn., 1999. Basketball player Washington Mystics, 1999—. Named Sports Illustrated and Sporting News Nat. Women's Player of Yr., 1999, Naismith finalist, AP Women's Basketball Player of Yr., 1997—98, 1998—99, N.Y.C. Player of Yr., Rawlings/WBCA Player of Yr., Player of Yr., Columbus, Ohio Touchdown Club, 1995, Rookie of the Yr., WNBA, 1999; named one of 12 female athletes selected as inspirational role models, Women's Sports and Fitness mag., 1998; named to Kodak 25th Anniversary Team, Women's Basketball Jour., Street & Smith All-Am., three-time, USA Today All-Am., WNBA All-Star Team, 1999, 2000, 2003, All-WNBA Team, 2000, 2001; recipient Sullivan award, Gold medal, 1998 World Championships, 1997 World Qualifying Tournament, 1995 Olympic Festival, USA Basketball Player of Yr. award, 1997, ESPY's for Female Athlete of Yr. award, second consecutive Women's Basketball Player of Yr. award, 1999, Naismith award, Atlanta's Tip-Off Club, 1995, Gold medal, U.S. Olympic Team, 2000. Office: Washington Mystics MCI Center 601 F St NW Washington DC 20004-1605

HOLDSWORTH, JANET NOTT, women's health nurse; b. Evanston, Ill., Dec. 25, 1941; d. William Alfred and Elizabeth Inez (Kelly) Nott; children: James William, Kelly Elizaveth, John David. BSN with high distinction, U. Iowa, 1963; M of Nursing, U. Wash., 1966. RN, Colo. Staff nurse U. Colo. Hosp., Denver, 1963-64, Presbyn. Hosp., Denver, 1964-65, Grand Canyon Hosp., Ariz., 1965; asst. prof. U. Colo. Sch. Nursing, Denver, 1966-71; counseling nurse Boulder PolyDrug Treatment Ctr., Boulder, 1971-77; pvt. duty nurse Nurses' Offcl. Registry, Denver, 1973-82; cons. nurse, tchr. parenting and child devel. Teenage Parent Program, Boulder Valley Schs., Boulder, 1980-88; bd. dirs., treas. Nott's Travel, Aurora, Colo., 1980—; nurse Rocky Mountain Surgery Ctr., 1996—. Instr., nursing coord. ARC, Boulder, 1979-90, instr., nursing tng. specialist, 1980-82. Mem. adv. bd. Boulder County Lamaze Inc., 1980-88; mem. adv. com. Child Find and Parent-Family, Boulder, 1981-89; del. Rep. County State Congl. Convs., 1972-96, sec. 17th Dist. Senatorial Com., Boulder, 1982-92; vol. Mile High ARC, 1980; vol. chmn. Mesa Sch. PTO, Boulder, 1982-92, bd. dirs., 1982-95, v.p., 1983-95; elder Presbyn. Ch. Mem. ANA, Colo. Nurses Assn. (bd. dirs. 1975-76, human rights com. 1981-83, dist. pres. 1974-76), Coun. Intracultural Nurses, Sigma Theta Tau, Alpha Lambda Delta. Republican. Home: 1550 Findlay Way Boulder CO 80305-6922 Office: Rocky Mountain Surgery Ctr 1630 30th St # 153 Boulder CO 80301-1014

HOLEC, ANITA KATHRYN VAN TASSEL, civic worker; b. Rahway, NJ, Nov. 11, 1947; d. Edward T. and Irene Eleanor (Barna) Van Tassel; m. Sidney W. Holec, Oct. 26, 1968. BS, U. Houston, 1969. Stockbroker Drexel Burnham Lambert, Inc., Miami, Fla., 1976-78, Merrill Lynch, Venice, Fla., 1979-80; fin. cons. Shearson Lehman Bros., Venice, 1981-87; owner, mgr. Closet Stretchers, Venice, 1987-89. Bd. dirs. Safe Place and Rape Crisis Ctr., Sarasota, 1987-99, Womens Resource Ctr., Sarasota, 1981-86, 90-94, Friends Venice Libr., 1992-94, New Coll. Libr., 1991-94, Planned Parenthood S.W. and Ctrl. Fla., 2001—; active Leadership Sarasota, 1991-95, Jr. League of Sarasota, 1982—, Argus Found., 1982— Mem.: Womens Resource Ctr. Sarasota County, Chautauqua Literary & Sci. Cir. Alumni Assn. (v.p. class of 2003), Chautauqua Women's Club. Avocations: reading, feminism. Mailing: PO Box 1049 Osprey FL 34229 Personal E-mail: ansloco@aol.com.

HOLEMAN, BETTY JEAN, counseling administrator; b. Timberlake, NC, Jan. 9, 1952; d. Stanley and Mallie Alice Holeman. BS in Profl. History cum laude, N.C. Agrl. and Tech. State U., Greensboro, 1974, MS in Edn. Guidance, 1978. Lic. sch. counselor NC, cert. continuing edn. Journ. Learning Internat. Youth counselor Barfield Recreation Ctr., 1968—69; nurse's aide ICU, VA Hosp., Durham, 1969; with PACE Program, page stacks Greensboro Pub. Libr., 1972; news editor A&T Register newspaper, 1973—74; inserter Circulation dept. Durham Herald Sun Newspaper, 1978—84; sub. tchr. Durham Pub. Schs., 1984—92. Program asst. Counseling Ctr. NC Agrl. and Tech. State U., Greensboro, intern; program adminstr. NC Agrl. and Tech. State U., Greensboro, 1974—76; hist. dept. rep. U. Senate, 1973—74. Author of poems; contbr. articles to profl. jours. Cmty. vol. Am. Diabetes Assn., Va., 2001—04. Recipient Outstanding Acad. Achievement, NC Agrl. and Tech. State U., 1973—74, Cub award, Journeyman award for continued svc., Editors award for dedicated svc.; scholar, Belk Found., 1970. Fellow: NC Sch. Counselor Assn.; mem.: ACA, N.C. Assn. for Counseling and Devel., Kappa Delta Pi (sec.), Phi Alpha Theta (charter mem.). Democrat. Baptist. Avocation: reading. Home: 2614 Red Valley Dr Rougemont NC 27572

HOLFORTY, PEARL MARTHA, accountant; b. Detroit, Oct. 31, 1928; d. Johannes and Martha Mary (Francoys) Kramer; m. Clifford W. Holforty, Mar. 27, 1948; children: Kathleen Diane, David Alan(dec.), Wendy Lauren, Michael Todd. Student, Mich. State U., 1945—47; BS, Wayne State U., 1970, MBA, 1973. Contr. Sta. WPON, Pontiac, Mich., 1958—60; bus. mgr. Holforty, Widrig & O'Neill Assocs., Inc., Troy, Mich., 1960—69; staff acct. Plante & Moran, CPA, Southfield, Mich., 1970—77, ptnr., 1977—91; founder, chair, pres., CEO Liberty BIDCO Investment Corp., 1988—2005; mgr. LBIC Liquidating, LLC, 2005—. Faculty Wayne State U., 1974-77; small bus. adv. coun. Fed. Res. Bank Chgo., 1985-87; del. White House Conf. on Small Bus., 1986. Past chair Met. Detroit YMCA; former mem. Gov.'s Entrepreneurial and Small Bus. Com.; former mem. employability skills task force State of Mich.; former trustee Mich. Accountancy Found.; former treas. Wayne County Intermediate Sch. Dist.-Found. for Excellence; past bd. dirs. United Way of S.E. Mich., United Am. Healthcare Corp.; bd. dirs. Auto Club Trust; past treas. Mich. Women's Found. Recipient Edward G. Erickson award, 1970, Elijah Watts Sells award, 1971, Headliners award Wayne State U., 1983, Corp. Leadership award Wayne State U., 1998; Phi Gamma Mu scholar, 1970; named Woman Advocate of Yr. SBA Mich., 1986. Mem. AICPA, Nat. Assn. Accts. (pres. chpt. 1979), Mich. Assn. CPAs, Nat. Assn. Women Bus. Owners (chpt. pres. 1986-87), Women's Econ. Club (pres. 1989-90), Beta Gamma. Presbyterian. Home and Office: # 316 41110 Fox Run Rd Novi MI 48377 E-mail: pholforty@lbico.com.

HOLGERS-AWANA, RITA MARIE, electrodiagnosis specialist; b. Chgo., Nov. 24, 1933; d. Joseph Theodore and Kathleen (Cooney) Konecny; m. Alan Miles Holgers, Aug. 8, 1960 (div. Sept. 1986); children: Dale, Ross; m. Benedict E.C. Awana, June 13, 1989 (dec. Feb. 1995). BS, N.Am. U., 1984, M of Nutripathic Sci., 1988, D of Nutripathy, 1988, PhD in Nutritional Philosophy, 1990. Nutritional cons. Vitality Testing, Phoenix, 1982-84, pres., CEO Glendale, Ariz., 1984-86, Zac Engrng. Inc., Lombard, Ill., 1986-2000; credentials coord. Prin. Health Care, Oakbrook Terrace, Ill., 1995-98; ptnr. Age-Less Group, Lombard, 2001—. Spkr. women's coffee break group Harvard Ave. Free Evangelical Ch., 1997-98; spkr. Dowser's Club, 1997-98, spkr. in field; cons.; presenter 3d Whole Life Expo, Chgo., 1999, Health, Beauty and Fitness Expo, Coll. of DuPage, Glen Ellyn, Ill., 2001; bd. dirs. Global Deactivation of Radiation. Author: Me and My Non-Disease, 1983, Radiation, The Hidden Enemy, 1995; invention electronic water filter unit. Pres., v.p. S.W. Herbal Edn. Assn., Phoenix, 1984-85; sec. Better Breathers Club, Chula Vista, Calif., 1992-93, Concerned Citizens, Biggsville, Ill., 1975; co-founder, charter mem. Exec. Women's Coun., Moline, Ill., 1974; cub scout den leader Boy Scouts Am., Eldridge, Iowa, 1973; treas. food coop., Asuncion, Paraguay, 1958; bd. dirs. Unity Ctr. Light Ch., 2004—. With U.S. Fgn. Svc., 1956-61. Recipient Internat. Championship Golf Trophy, U.S. Dept. of State, 1959, Championship Golf trophy Hend-Co-Hills, 1974, 75, 77, Tai Chi Black Belt, Shingumatsu Martial Arts, 1993; named Woman of the Year, Internat. Biog. Ctr., Cambridge, Eng., 1998. Mem.: AAUW (fin. officer 2004—06), Nat. Health Fedn., The Am. Dowsers Soc. (v.p. 1999), N.Am. Dowser's Club. Mem. Unity Ch. Avocations: golf, bowling, knitting, computers, martial arts. Home and Office: Apt E 239 S Westmore Ave Lombard IL 60148-3066 Office Phone: 630-627-8621. E-mail: docradrita@aol.com.

HOLIAN, KATHERINE STOVER, administrator; b. Modesto, Calif., Oct. 14, 1947; d. Lee and Della (Kopperud) Stover; m. Brad Lee Holian, Dec. 28, 1968 (div. May, 1984); children: Joshua, Matthew. Student, Whitter Coll., 1965-67, Pitzer Coll., 1967-68; BA, U. Calif., 1969; MBA, U. Nebr., Omaha, 1987. Research, adminstrv. asst. U. Calif. Physics Dept., Berkeley, 1969-72; adminstrv. sec. Los Alamos (N.Mex.) Nat. Lab., 1980-84; grad. rsch. asst. dept. mgmt. and econs. U. Nebr., Omaha, 1986-87; fin. analyst Majers Corp., Omaha, 1987; program coord. Met. Community Coll., Omaha, 1987-91; exec. dir. Met. Community Coll. Found., Omaha, 1991-97, project coord., exec. v.p. office, 1997—. Mem. Supt. Adv. Com. and Gifted Edn. Com., Los Alamos, 1981-84, Leadership Omaha, 1993-94; various ch. coms. at local and synod levels, Omaha, 1988—; mem. parent adv. com. of gifted edn. Millard Pub. Schs., 1989-91; vol. Planned Parenthood, 1991-93, Met. C.C. Day Care, 1990-93, U. of N.E. Med. Ctr., 1994-2000. Mem. AAUW, Beta Gamma Sigma. Democrat. Avocations: sailing, gardening, reading, music, dogs. Office: Met Community Coll PO Box 3777 Omaha NE 68103-0777

HOLIFIELD, MARILYN J., lawyer; b. Tallahassee, June 17, 1948; BA, Swarthmore Coll., 1969; JD, Harvard U., 1972. Bar: NY 1973, Fla. 1980. Law clerk, Hon. Paul H. Roney US Fifth Cir. Ct. of Appeals; gen. coun. NY State Divsn. for Youth; asst. counsel NAACP Legal Def. and Edn. Fund, NYC; ptnr., gen. litig. Holland & Knight, Miami, and co-leader, Caribbean Initiative. Bd. dirs. Harvard Alumni Assn.; pres. Harvard Law Sch. Assn. Fla., 1986—88; mem. Swarthmore Coll. Alumni Coun., 1987—89; mem. bd. mgrs. Swarthmore Coll., 1993—; mem. Fed. Magistrate selection panel So. Dist. Fla., 1989—90. Named one of America's Top Lawyers, Black Enterprise Mag., 2003. Fellow: Am. Bar Found.; mem.: ABA, Fla. Acad. Trial Lawyers, Am. Judicature Soc., Am. Law Inst., Nat. Bar Assn. Office: Holland & Knight 701 Bricknell Ave Ste 3000 Miami FL 33131 Office Phone: 305-788-7730. Office Fax: 305-789-7799. Business E-Mail: marilyn.holifield@hklaw.com.

HOLIFIELD, PATRICIA DIMICELI, educator; b. Chgo., June 19, 1945; d. Gus and Patricia Catherine (Cloutier) DiMiceli; m. James Allison Holifield Sr., Aug. 14, 1965; children: James Allison Jr., Suzanne Marie, Amanda Katherine. BS, U. So. Miss., 1967, MS, 1973, postgrad., 1973—. Cert. secondary edn. and English tchr., Miss. Tchr. South Jones High Sch., Ellisville, Miss., 1967-85; instr. Jones County Jr. Coll., Ellisville, 1985—. Tchr., cons. South Miss. Writing Project, Hattiesburg, 1989-93; mem. Southeastern Conf. on English in Two Yr. Coll. Mem. Miss. Coun. Tchr.'s of English, Nat. Coun. Tchr.'s of English, NEA, Miss. Edn. Assn., Assn. for Excellence in Edn., Faculty Assn., Delta Kappa Gamma (corr. sec. 1979). Methodist. Avocations: needlecrafts, reading, walking. Home: PO Box 23 Ellisville MS 39437-0023

HOLIFIELD, PEARL KAM (KAM HOLIFIELD, MOMI KAM HOLIFIELD), poet; b. Honolulu, Dec. 13, 1916; d. Albert Tin Kam and Helen Wo Soon Lyau; m. Harold Desmond Holifield, 1947; children: Wallace Grant, Harry. BA, U. Hawaii, 1944; MA, U. Calif., Berkeley, 1945; postgrad., U. Wash., 1946—47. Univ. libr. U. Hawaii, Honolulu, 1945—46; children's libr. N.Y. Pub. Library, N.Y.C., 1948—80; haiku poet N.Y.C., 1978—. Author: Workshop Poems, 1989. Mem.: Spring St. Haiku Workshop, Haiku Soc. Am. Avocations: gardening, singing, hula. Home: 85-190 Ala Hema St Apt E Waianae HI 96792-2426

HOLLACE, BARBARA JEAN, writer, property manager; b. Bellingham, Wash., June 8, 1959; m. William Francis Hollace, Apr. 17, 2002. BA in Bus. Adminstrn., Western Wash. U., 1981; JD, Gonzaga U., 1991. Bar: Wash. 1991; QPR- Suicide Prevention Gatekeeper Certificate QPR Inst., 2004. Office mgr. Donette Studio, Bellingham, Wash., 1981—88; owner Inner Peace Pub., Lynden, Wash., 1985—89; corp. counsel legal intern Gonzaga U., Spokane, 1989—91; real estate licensing instr. Inland Empire Sch. Real Estate, 1991—93; fundraising campaign mgr. Ogden Hall Women's Shelter, 1992—93; property mgr. Spokane Neighborhood Action Programs, 1995—; owner Hollace Writing Svcs., 2004—. Adv. bd. chmn., mem. Coalition Child Advocacy, Bellingham, 1987—88; pres. Single Parent Outreach Connection, Spokane, 1992—94; legal educator Ogden Hall Women's Shelter, 1992—94; spkr. in field. Author: (book) From Dust to Dust; co-author: Mistletoe Madness. Grant writer Dominican Outreach Services, Spokane, 1992—92; trainer Spokane C.O.P.S, 2001—; assist with fundraising events St. Luke's Rehab. Inst., 2003—06; trainer Intercollegiate Sch. Nursing, 2004—06. Mem.: Soc. Children's Book Writers and Illustrators, Nat. Health and Wellness Club. Personal E-mail: bjhollace@yahoo.com.

HOLLADAY, KELLY GAYLE, dean; b. Hobbs, N.Mex., Sept. 27, 1958; d. William Dallas Holladay and Robbie Geane (Barton) Eason. A in liberal arts, Tarrant County Jr. Coll., Ft. Worth, 1981; student, Tex. Tech. U., 1982-83; BS in geology, U. Tex., 1985; M in sci. edn., Tex. Women's U., 1990. Sales Zales Jewelers, Hobbs, 1976-77; clerical Ft. Worth Nat. Bank, Ft. Worth, 1978-79; sales Century 21 Loughty, Benbrook, Tex., 1980-81; technician Overland Exploration, Denver, 1985-86; tchr. Arlington (Tex.) Ind. Schs., 1987-89, Hobbs Pub. Sch., 1989-90; prof. New Mex. Jr. Coll, Hobbs, 1990—; conf. coord. New Mex. Adult Edn. Assn., Albuquerque, N.Mex., 1994—. Mem. N.Mex. Jr. Coll. faculty senate, 1991—; staff development Project 353, Albuquerque, 1993—. VIP vol. Nat. Pks., Carlsbad Cavers, N. Mex., 1994—; literacy tutor N.Mex. Literacy Vol., Hobbs, 1991-92, coord., 1991-92. Mem. N.Mex. Adult Edn. Assn. (bd. dirs. 1989—), Assn. Tex. Pub. Educators, Am. Assn. Petroleum Geologist, Ft. Worth Bd. Realtors, Gamma Sigma Sigma. Democrat. Baptist. Avocations: spelunking, photography, cooking, racquetball, scuba diving. Home: 2623 W Alabama St Hobbs NM 88242-9062

HOLLADAY, WILHELMINA COLE, interior designer, museum director; b. Elmira, NY, Oct. 10, 1922; d. Chauncy E. and Claire Elizabeth (Strong) Cole; m. Wallace Fitzhugh Holladay, Sept. 27, 1946; children: Wallace Fitzhugh, Scott Cole. BA, Elmira Coll., 1944; postgrad. art history, U. Paris, 1953—54, U. Va., 1960—61; PhD (hon.), Moore Coll. Art, 1988, Mt. Vernon Coll., 1988, Elmira Coll., 1994. Exec. sec. Howard Ludington, Rochester, N.Y., 1944-45, Chinese Embassy, Washington, 1945-48; staff Nat. Gallery of Art, Washington, 1957-59; dir. interior design div. Holladay Corp., Washington, 1970-95. Dir. Adams Nat. Bank, 1978-86, chmn., 1978-86; founder, chmn., bd. dirs., creator art collection by women (Renaissance through contemp.), Nat. Mus. Women in Arts, 1982—. Founder Archival Libr. of Periodicals, Books, Exhbn. Catalogs on Women's Art for Rsch. Purposes; bd. dirs. Am. Field Svc., 1964-80, Internat. Student House, 1973—, Leeds Castle Found.; mem. coun. Friends of Folger Shakespeare Libr., 1978-82; mem. world svc. coun. YWCA; trustee Corcoran Gallery of Art, 1980-90, The Fund for Endowment of Diplomatic Reception Rms.; mem. Mayor's Blue Ribbon Com., The Year of Visual Arts Com., Am. Acad. Rome; mem. adv. council The Girl Scouts of US; pres. Langley Sch. Decorated Order of Merit Norwegian Govt.; named laureate, Washington Bus. Hall of Fame, Washingtonian of Yr., Washingtonian Mag., 1987, Woman of Achievement, Washington Ednl. TV Assn., 1984, Woman of Distinction, Coun. Ind. Colls., 1987, Hon. Citizen, State of Tex., 1992, Hon. Athenian, Mayor of Athens, 2002; named one of 21 Leaders for 21st Century, Women's eNews, 2005; named to Women of Distinction, Birmingham So. Coll., 1991, Nat. Women's Hall of Fame, 1996; recipient Thomas Jefferson award, Am. Soc. Interior Designers, Horizon's Theatre award, 1986, Disting. Woman's award, Northwood Inst., 1987, award, Anti-Defamation League, 1987, Disting. Achievement award, Nat. League Am. Pen Women, 1991, Women Achievers award, Internat. Alliance, 1991, Key to City of Kansas City, 1991, Hon. Citizen award, State Tex., 1992, Women First award, YWCA, 1993, Women as Leaders award, The Wash. Ctr., Sears, 1994, Fellow award for disting. svc. to arts, New Orleans Mus. Art, 1997, Disting. Washingtonian award in lit. and the arts, Univ. Club Washington, 1998, Gold medal honor award, Nat. Inst. Social Scis., 2000, Honoree, Historic Georgetown Club, 2000, Leadership award, Pine Manor Coll., 2002, Nat. Women Arts award, Phoenix Art Mus. League, 2003, Visionary Woman award, Moore Coll. Art & Design, 2005. Mem. Am. Assn. Mus., Am. Fedn. Art, Women's Caucus for Arts, Mus. Modern Art, Art Librs. N.Am., Coll. Art Assn., Archives Am. Art, Art Table, Smithson Soc., Internat. Women's Forum, Nat. Women's Econ. Alliance (bd. dirs. 1984—, Soaring Eagle award 1988), Internat. Women's Forum (Woman That Makes a Difference award, 1991), Women's Caucus for Art (honors, 2001), The Smithsonian Soc., Golden Circle Kennedy Ctr., Am. News Women's Club., Capital Speakers Club. Episcopalian. Home: 3215 R St NW Washington DC 20007-2941 Office: Nat Mus Women Arts 1250 New York Ave NW Washington DC 20005

HOLLAND, AMY JEANETTE, psychiatrist; b. High Point, N.C., Jan. 25, 1964; d. Jefferson Dewey and Mary Esther (Marsh) H.; m. Dana Neal Martin, July 14, 1990; children: Bradley Neal Holland Martin, Zachary Tyler Holland Martin, Kyle Dylan Holland Martin. BS magna cum laude, Wake Forest U., 1986; MD, East Carolina U., 1991. Cert. med. technologist. Med. technologist Humana Hosps., Greensboro, N.C., 1986-87; intern U. N.C. Hosps., Chapel Hill, 1991-92, resident in psychiatry, 1992-94; fellow in child psychiatry Emory U. Hosps., Atlanta, 1994-96. Mem. AMA, Am. Psychiat. Assn. (author, presenter poster nat. mtg. 1991), Am. Assn. Psychiatry and the Law, Ga. Med. Soc., Ga. Psychiat. Assn., Ga. Coun. on Child and Adolescent Psychiatry, Am. Acad. Child and Adolescent Psychiatry. Avocations: antique collecting, doll collecting, roller skating. Office: Whitlock Park Ctr 707 Whitlock Ave SW Bldg H Marietta GA 30064-3033

HOLLAND, BETH, actress; b. N.Y.C. d. Samson and Florence (Liebman) Hollander; m. Louis L. Friedman, Aug. 28, 1953; children: Ellen Lynn, Cathy Jayne. Pvt. studies in acting, voice tng. Arts funding cons. N.Y. State Senate, 1974-89. Appeared in various roles on TV, film and theatre, also comedy video Your Favorite Jokes, 1988; cabaret debut, N.Y.C., 2004. Pres. Sonia Alden Found. Inc.; bd. dirs. Fla. Opera Soc., Symphony of Americas. Recipient Carbonell performance award, Theatre League of South Fla., 1996. Mem. AFTRA (pres. N.Y. chpt. 1989-91, bd. dirs., trustee Health and Retirement Funds, past treas.), SAG, English Speaking Union, N.Y. TV Acad. (past bd. dirs.), Actors Equity Assn., Twelfth Night Club, Episcopal Actors Guild (first women pres.), Players Club (libr. bd.), Lambs Club, Tower Club, Friars Club. Avocations: travel, politics, arts. E-mail: bethholland146@aol.com.

HOLLAND, BRANTI LATESSA, science educator; d. Jerry and Barbara Holland. B in Elem. Edn., Mich. U., Ypsilanti, 2001; M, Marygrove Coll., Detroit, 2006. Cert. tchr. Mich., 2001. Tchr. Detroit Pub. Schs., Detroit, Harcourt, Lansing, Mich. Adminstr. Edn. Sta., Detroit; curriculum writer mid. sch. scis. Detroit Pub. Schs. Sys., 2006, com. mem. textbook adoption, 06. Jr. girl scout leader Girl Scouts Am., Detroit, 2005—. Mem.: Mich. Sci. Tchrs. Assn., Metro Detroit Sci. Tchr. Assn. (assoc.). Christian. Avocations: reading, tutoring. Office Phone: 313-596-3800.

HOLLAND, CHRISTIE ANNA, biochemist, virologist; b. Newport News, Va., Aug. 25, 1950; d. Charles Everett and Helen (Bailey) Holland; 1 child, Helen. BS, U. Richmond, 1972; PhD, U. Tenn., 1977. Postdoctoral fellow Worcester Found. for Exptl. Biology, Shrewsbury, Mass., 1977-79, Ctr. for Cancer Rsch.-MIT, Cambridge, Mass., 1979-84; asst. prof. dept. radiation oncology U. Mass. Med. Ctr., Worcester, 1985-90, assoc. prof., 1990-91; dir. Ctr. for Virology, Immunology and Infectious Diseases Children's Nat. Med. Ctr., Washington, 1991—2003; assoc. prof. pediats., microbiology and biochemistry George Washington U. Med. Ctr., Washington, 1991-95, prof. pediats., assoc. prof. microbiology and biochemistry, 1995—2004. Mem.: AAAS, Am. Soc. Pediats., Am. Soc. Virology, Am. Soc. Cell Biology, Internat. Soc. Exptl. Hematology. Home: 9212 Gladys Farm Way Laytonsville MD 20882-1421 E-mail: toyzforus2@aol.com.

HOLLAND, ELLEN C., music educator; b. Washington, Nov. 6, 1960; d. Theodore R. and Frances W. Creel. BMus cum laude, East Carolina U., 1983; MMus, U. S.C., 1985. Candidate Nat. Bd. Profl. Tchg. Stds. Music tchr. Virginia Beach City Pub. Schs., Va., 1986—, coord. dept., 2002—03; accompanist First Bapt. Ch. Virginia Beach, 2004—06, dir. music, 2005—06. Music tchr. Holland Studio of Piano, 1986—95. Sec. Virginia Beach Chorale, 1988—92, audition com., 1988—98. Mem.: Virginia Beach Edn. Assn., Va. Music Educators Assn. (co-chair dist. chorus II 1999—2000, chair dist. chorus II 2000—01), Smart Stockers Investment Club (founder/treas. 1990—). E-mail: opy1dopy@cox.net.

HOLLAND, GENE GRIGSBY (SCOTTIE HOLLAND), artist; b. Hazard, Ky., June 30, 1928; d. Edward and Virginia Lee (Watson) Grigsby; m. George William Holland, Sept. 22, 1950; 3 children. BA, U. So. Fla., 1968; studied with, Ruth Allison, Talequah, Okla., 1947—48, Ralph Smith, Washington, 1977, Clint Carter, Atlanta, 1977, R. Jordan, Winter Park, Fla., 1979; student, Cedric Baldwin Egeli Workshop, Charleston, SC, 1984. Various clerical and secretarial positions, 1948-52; news reporter, photographer Bryan (Tex.) Daily News, 1952; clk. Fogarty Bros. Moving and Transfer, Tampa and Miami, Fla., 1954-57; tchr. elem. schs., Hillsborough County, Fla., 1968-72; salesperson, assoc. real estate, 1984-2000; owner, operator antique store, 1982-87. One-woman and group shows include Tampa Woman's Clubhouse, 1973, Cor Jesu, Tampa, 1973, Bank, Monks Corner, SC, 1977, Summerville Artists Guild, 1977-78, Apopka (Fla.) Art and Foilage Festival, 1980, 81, 82, Fla. Fedn. Women's Clubs, 1980, 81, 82; numerous group shows, latest being Island Gifts, Tampa, 1980-82, Brandon (Fla.) Sta., 1980-81, Holland Originals, Orlando, Fla.; represented in permanent and pvt. collections. Vol. ARC, Tampa, 1965-69, United Fund Campaign, 1975-76; pres. Mango (Fla.) Elem. Sch. PTA, 1966-67; pres. Tampa Civic Assn., 1974-75; vol. Easter Seal Fund Campaign, 1962-63; art chmn. Apopka Art & Foilage Festival, 1990; deaconness Ctrl. Christian Ch. Orlando, 1992-94, chmn. bible study, 1993-94; deaconness First Christian Ch. Tampa, 1996-99. Recipient numerous art awards, 1978-82. Mem. AARP (parlimentarian Apopka chpt.), DAR, Internat. Soc. Artists, Coun. Arts & Scis. for Ctrl. Fla., Fedn. Women's Clubs (pres. Tampa Civic 1974-75), Meth. Women's Soc. (sec. 1976-77), Nat. Trust Hist. PReservation, Nat. Hist. Soc., Fla. Geneal. and Hist. Soc., Am. Guild Flower Arrangers, The Nat. Grigsby Family Soc. (assoc. sec. 1991-92, corp. sect. 1992-96, dir. 1995-97, 99-2001, 06—, S.W. chpt. dir. 1997-2000, 06—), Internat. Inner Wheel Club (past chmn. dist. 696, pres. Tampa 1972-73), Friday Morning Musicale Club (1st v.p. bd. incorporators Tampa 1974-75, bd. dirs.), Gen. Fedn. of Fla. Clubs Apopka Woman's Club (pres. 1981-82, bd. dirs. 1983-85, Woman of Yr. 1991-92), Apopka Tennis Over 50's Group Club (pres. 1988-90), Federated Garden Club Plant City Fla. (conservation chmn.), South Bay Geneal. Soc., Tampa PC User Group, Computer Club Inc. of Sun City Ctrs., Lexington Geneal. Assn. Home: 231 Mooring Ln Lexington SC 29072-9106

HOLLAND, JEAN ELINOR, computer engineer, consultant; b. Detroit, May 16, 1950; d. Harold Ferguson and Anne (Kostrick) Holland; m. Le Verne Douglas Rizor, June 19, 1971 (div. Aug. 1977); 1 child, James Delbert; m. Sanford E. Walke, III, Aug. 23, 1980 (div. Aug. 1998). Student, U. Mich., 1968-71; BBA, Eastern Mich. U., 1980. Office mgr. Mich. Testing Engrs., Inc., Ann Arbor, 1972-75, Constrn., Testing & Inspection, Inc., Ann Arbor, 1977-78, pvt. practice word processor, 1978-81; systems analyst ADP Network Services, Dearborn and Ann Arbor, 1981-84; tech. mgr. ADP Dealer Services, Southfield, Mich., 1984-85; engring. supr. Applicon-Schlumberger, Ann Arbor, 1985-86; pvt. practice computer systems cons., 1986—. V.p., dir. Bay & Tool Rental, Inc., Ann Arbor, 1977-83; v.p., dir., cons. Am. Lender Services, Inc., Ann Arbor, 1984—1994; sr. mgr. U.S. product devel. Comshare, Inc., 1991—1992, dir. info. sys., Flat Rock Metal, Inc., 1994-2001, owner, Jean Holland Group, LLC, 2001-. Named Steward of the Meet, Criterium du Quebec, 1977; recipient award of appreciation City of Grayling, Mich., 1978; 6th Overall Nat. Championship for Co-Drivers, Sports Car Club Am., 1979; named tech. cons. of yr. Mich. region ADP Network Services, Ann Arbor, 1982. Mem. NAFE, Sports Car Club Ann Arbor (pres. 1973-74), Ralligators Club (treas. 1973-74). Republican. Presbyterian. Avocations: contract bridge, sports car rallying, billiards. Home and Office: 111 Golfview Ln Ann Arbor MI 48103-5819

HOLLAND, JIMMIE C., psychiatrist, educator; b. Forney, Tex., Apr. 9, 1928; m. James F. Holland; 5 children. BA, Baylor U., 1948, MD, 1952. Diplomate Am. Bd. Psychiatry, Am. Bd. Neurology. Instr. to prof. SUNY, Buffalo, 1956-73; assoc. prof., assoc. attending physician to asst. dir. cons.-liaison psychiatry Albert Einstein Coll. Medicine and Montefiore Med. Ctr., Bronx, 1973-77; chair dept. psychiatry and behavioral scis., Wayne E. Chapman chair in psychiat. oncology Meml. Sloan Kettering Cancer Ctr., NYC, 1997—2003. Prof. dept. psychiatry Weill Med. Coll., N.Y.C., 1977—; cons. NIMH-USSR joint schizophrenia study Psychiat. Rsch. Inst., Moscow, 1972-73, NIMH, Rockville, Md., 1973-75; chmn. psychiatry com. Cancer and Leukemia Group B Clin. Trials, Brookline, Mass., 1976-2001. Editor: Handbook of Psycho-oncology: Psychological Care of the Patient with Cancer, 1989, Psychooncology, 1998; co-editor Jour. Psycho-oncology; author, co-author: The Human Side of Cancer, 258 jour. articles, book chpts., monographs. Bd. dirs. Cancer Care, Inc., 1979-81. Recipient Disting. Alumna award Baylor U., Waco, Tex., 1982; Am. Cancer Soc. Medal of Honor, 1994 Fellow Inst. Medicine, Am. Coll. Psychiatrists, Am. Psychiat. Assn., Acad. Psychosomatic Medicine (founding pres.), Internat. Psycho-Oncology Soc. (founding pres.), Am. Psychosocial Oncology Soc., Am. Psychosomatic Soc., Am. Soc. Clin. Oncology. Office: Meml Sloan-Kettering Cancer Ctr 1275 York Ave New York NY 10021-6094 Office Phone: 646-888-0026. Business E-Mail: hollandj@mskcc.org.

HOLLAND, LAUREL LONG, sociologist, educator; b. Dunlap, Tenn., Apr. 30, 1962; d. Wanda Long. PhD, U. Tenn., Knoxville, 2000. Grad. tchg. asst. U. Tenn., 1995—2000; assoc. prof. U. West Ga., Carrollton, Ga., 2000—, dir. grad. studies dept. sociology, 2004—. Com. mem. Carroll County Environ. Projects Com., Carrollton, 2001—06. Faculty Rsch. grantee, U. West Ga., 2005. Mem.: Ga. Sociol. Assn. (v.p. 2006—). Office: U West Ga 1601 Maple St Carrollton GA 30118 Office Phone: 678-839-6331.

HOLLAND, LESLIE ANN, special education educator; b. Oak Lawn, Ill., Sept. 26, 1969; d. Ronald Leo and Rosemary Seymour; m. Brian Michael Holland, Dec. 31, 1999. AA, Moraine Valley C.C., Palos Hills, Ill., 1991; BS in Edn., Ea. Ill. U., 1995. Day camp site dir. Southwest Spl. Recreation Assn., Alsip, Ill., 1996—2000, spl. edn. dept. chair Momence, Ill., 1996—; tchr., spl. edn. dept. Sylvan Learning Ctr., Tinley Park, Ill., 2001—; chair, spl. edn. dept. Momence H.S., 1996—. Home: 14600 W Aston Way Lockport IL 60441 Office: Momence Unit Sch Dist # 1 101 N Franklin Momence IL 60954

HOLLAND, RUBY MAE, social welfare administrator; BA in Sociology, Shaw Coll., 1976, MA in Comparative Lit., 1978; D of Psychology, Western Mich. U., 1982; DD, Wayne Theol. Sem., 1992. Ordained min. Evangel Assn. Chs. and Ministries, 2004, ordained bishop Gospel Ministry, 2004. Adminstr. Terrell Day Care Ctr., 1980-83; instr. Reborn Acad., 1984-87; English instr. Ctrl. H.S., 1987-92; enabler Maplegrove children's program U. Mich., Dearborn, 1992—; adminstr., guidance counselor, tchr. Mothers Love, Oak Park, Mich., 1992—. Assoc. min. Unity Cathedral of Faith Ministries; mem. CEO Forums in Christ Ministries, Greater Haven of Rest; asst. pastor Lighthouse Ch. of Prayer. Mem.: Evangel Assn. Chs. and Ministries.

HOLLAND, SHERRY LYNN, elementary school educator; b. Orange, Tex., July 4, 1955; d. Jesse Lee and Jerry Dean Curry; m. Ronald Lowell Holland, Sept. 28, 1985; children: Lauren Leigh Eide, Andrea Michelle Christenson, Christina Marie Donovan, Angela Marie Borton, Scott Thomas. BS in Edn., SW Mo. State U., 1977; MA in Tchg., Webster U., 1994; postgrad., Truman State U. Cert. tchr. Mo. First/second grade looping tchr. Ritenour Sch. Dist., St. Louis, Mo., 1977—. Mem. Quality Curriculum Mgmt. Coun., St. Louis, 1992—. Pres. PTA, St. Louis. Recipient Diamond Cir. award for Tchr. of the Yr., Iveland Elem. Sch. Mem.: Am. Fedn. Teachers (assoc.). Republican. Roman Catholic. Avocations: travel, reading. Home: 3864 DePaul Meadows Ct Bridgeton MO 63044 Office: Iveland Elem Sch 1836 Dyer Ave Saint Louis MO 63114 Office Phone: 314-493-6330. Personal E-mail: rholl3864@aol.com. Business E-Mail: hollands@ritenour.k12.mo.us.

HOLLANDER, ANNE, writer; b. Cleve., Oct. 16, 1930; d. Arthur and Jean Hill (Bassett) Loesser; m. John Hollander, June 15, 1953 (div. 1977); children: Martha, Elizabeth; m. Thomas Nagel, June 26, 1979. BA, Barnard Coll., 1952. Author: Seeing Through Clothes, 1978, Moving Pictures, 1989, Sex and Suits, 1994, Feeding the Eye, 1999, Fabric of Vision, 2002. Guggenheim fellow, 1975. Fellow N.Y. Inst. for the Humanities (interim dir. 1995-96); mem. Costume Soc. Am., College Art Assn., PEN Am. Ctr. (pres. 1995-96), Century Assn.

HOLLANDER, ROSLYN, artist, educator; b. Bklyn., Aug. 22, 1935; d. Chaskel Turkin and Minnie Kimmel; m. Sanford Lloyd hollander, Feb. 16, 1958; children: Joseph, Andrew, David, Elizabeth. BFA, Parson's Sch. Design, N.Y.C., 1956. Fashion illustrator Simplicity Pattern Co., N.Y.C., 1956—59, Lit Brothers Dept. Store, Trenton, NJ, 1957—58; substitute art tchr. Sussex County Schs., NJ, 1980—95; pastellist The Artist mag., 1994, The Best of Pastel, 1996, Pastel Highlights, 1996. Represented in permanent collections Johnson & Johnson, N.J., Brinter Internat., Dallas, Standard and Poors, N.Y.C., McGraw-Hill Pub., N.J. Bergen Mus., Schering-Plough -N.J. Finalist Am. Artist; recipient 3d award, Pastel Jour., 1994—2000. Mem.: Pastel Soc. Am. (master pastellist). Home and Office: 5 Dogwood Dr Newton NJ 07860

HOLLANDSWORTH, PHYLLIS W., marriage and family therapist; b. Storm Lake, Iowa, Aug. 7, 1938; d. Lloyd Earl and Hildegarde Elaine (Uken) Williamson; m. James Richard Hollandsworth, Sept. 5, 1959; children: Michael, Mark. AA, Brewton-Parker Coll., 1984; BS, Valdosta State Coll., 1987, MS, 1988; cert. in marriage & family therapy, Voldosta State Coll., 1995; PhD in Human Sexuality, Maimonides U., 2004. Lic. marriage & family therapist Fla., 1996, cert. sex therapist Fla., 2002. Counselor Ga. Dept. Corrections, Albany, 1989—91; therapist, emergency screener North Fla. Mental Health, Lake City, Fla., 1992—96; therapist ACT Corp., Daytona Beach, Fla., 1996—2000; intake coord., therapist Children's Home Soc., Daytona Beach, Fla., 2000—02; therapist Fla. Health Care Plans, Daytona Beach, Fla., 2002—; pvt. practice Daytona Beach, Fla., 2000—. Mem.: Am. Acad. Clin. Sexologists (diplomate), Am. Psychotherapy Assn. (diplomate), Am. Assn. Marriage and Family Therapists (clin. mem.). Office: 1635 S Ridgewood Ave Rm 216 South Daytona FL 32119 Business E-Mail: hollyphyll@netzero.net.

HOLLAR, SUSAN STEFFENS, mathematics professor; d. Albert Raymond and Audrey Simmons Steffens; m. Dennis Ray Hollar, Oct. 11, 1980. BA, Western Mich. U., Kalamazoo, 1977, MA, 1980. Math. tchr. Three Rivers Cmty. Schs., Mich., 1979—82; math. prof. Kalamazoo Valley CC, 1982—. Recipient Robert C. Seber Meml.award, Western Mich. U. Math. Edn. Faculty, 1980. Mem.: AAUP, Am. Math. Assn. Two Yr. Colls., Mich. Math. Assn. Two Yr. Colls., Nat. Coun. Tchrs. Math., Mich. Coun. Tchrs. Math., Sweet Adelines Internat. Avocations: travel, golf, theater, volleyball. Office: Kalamazoo Valley CC 6767 West O Ave Kalamazoo MI 49003-4070 Office Phone: 269-488-4667. Business E-Mail: shollar@kvcc.edu.

HOLLEB, DORIS B., urban planner, economist; b. N.Y.C., Oct. 26, 1922; m. Marshall M. Holleb, Oct. 15, 1944; children: Alan, Gordon, Paul. BA magna cum laude, Hunter Coll., 1942; MA, Harvard U., 1947; postgrad., U. Chgo., 1959-60, 65-66. Economist Fed. Res. Bd., Washington, 1943—44; freelance journalist, 1945-63; econs. cons. Chgo. Dept. City Planning, 1963-64; rsch. assoc. Ctr. Urban Studies U. Chgo., 1966-78, sr. rsch. assoc., 1978-88; dir. Met. Inst., 1973-84, professorial lectr., 1979—2004, professorial lectr. emerita, 2004—. Chmn. edn. coun. Francis W. Parker Sch., 1963-80; cons., 1980-92; adv. coun. Ctr. for the Study Democratic Instns., 1975-79; nat. adv. com. White House Conf. on Balanced Nat. Growth and Econ. Devel., 1978; mem. Northea. Ill. Planning Commn., 1973-77; mem. Chgo. Met. Area Transp. Coun., 1980-84; adv. coun. to Nat. Ctr. Rsch. on Vocat. Edn., U.S. Dept. Edn., 1979-82, U.S. Dept. State adv. com. internat. investment, tech. and devel., 1979-81; mem. Chgo. Plan Commn., 1986—, Nat. Coun on Humanities, 1998-2003. Author: Social and Economic Information for Urban Planning, 1968, Colleges and the Urban Poor, 1972; mem. editl. bd. Ill. Issues, 1977—; contbr. articles to profl. jours Fellow: Nat. Phi Beta Kappa Soc. (bd. dirs.).

HOLLEBEKE, NORMA L., biologist, educator; b. El Paso, Tex., Mar. 29, 1964; d. L.W. Hollebeke and Norma Mae Dubuque; m. Warren J. Scoville, May 15, 1987; 1 child, Elisabeth L. Scoville. BS, U. Tex., El Paso, 1990, MS, 1994. Guest lectr., asst. instr. U. Tex., El Paso, 1997—2000, rsch. asst., 1998—2000; faculty El Paso C.C., 2000; faculty/sci. chair Radford Sch., El Paso, 2001—02; asst. prof. Sinclair C.C., Dayton, Ohio, 2004—. Biology coord. ECE/MCE Tchr. Edn. Com., Dayton, 2005—; mem. Sierra Club, Ohio, 1989—; exec. bd. Greene County Dem. Party, Ohio, 2005—; bd. dirs. Sun Country Regional Sci. Fair, El Paso, 2001—02. Fellow Open fellow, U. Toronto, Ont., 1994—95. Mem.: AAUW (life), Sigma Xi. Democrat. Office: Sinclair Community College 444 W Third St Dayton OH 45402

HOLLEMAN, MARIAN ISABEL, librarian, educator; b. Toronto, Ont., Can., July 23, 1923; came to U.S., 1961; d. Arnott Martin and Etta Margaret (Freeman) P.; m. Willard Roy Holleman (dec. 1969). BA, U. Toronto, 1945, MLS, 1946, MA, 1948. Libr. Acad. Medicine, Toronto, 1947-61, UCLA Biomed. Libr., 1962-63, Bishop's Sch., La Jolla, Calif., 1963-66, San Diego Coll. for Women, 1966-73, U. San Diego Copley Libr., 1973-88, libr. emeritus, 1988—; libr. James S. Copley Libr., La Jolla, 1989—. Pres. San Diego chpt. Spl. Librs. Assn., 1968, Toronto chpt., 1950's; conv. chmn. Med. Libr. Assn., Toronto, 1959. Editor Sci. Meetings jour., 1962; contbr. articles to profl. jours. Recipient Murray Gottlieb Essay prize Med. Libr. Assn., 1957, Twin award YWCA, San Diego, 1988. Avocations: gardening, needlepoint.

HOLLEMAN, SANDY LEE, religious organization administrator; d. Guy Lee and Gustine (Kirby-Sheets) Luna; m. Allen Craig Holleman. Cert., Eastfield Coll., 1979. With Annuity Bd. So. Bapt. Conv., Dallas, 1958—, mgr. personnel, 1983-85, dir. human resources, 1985-91, v.p. human resources, 1991-99; ret., 1999—. Mem.: Soc. Human Resource Mgmt., Dallas Soc. Human Resource Mgmt., Am. Mgmt. Soc. (dir. salary surveys local chpt. 1986—, v.p. chpt. svcs. 1987—), Am. Mus. Miniature Arts, Book End Rev. Club, Daus of Nile, Order of Ea. Star, Diversity Club Dallas (program chmn. 1976, v.p. 1977). Baptist. Avocations: needlepoint, genealogy, decorating, doll collecting, dollhouses and furniture.

HOLLENBECK, KAREN FERN, foundation administrator, consultant; b. Snover, Mich., Mar. 30, 1943; d. Glenn Lee and Ada Gertrude (Robinson) Roberts; m. Marvin Allen Hollenbeck, June 18, 1966. AA, Kellogg Community Coll., 1980; BSBA, Nazareth Coll., 1987. Dir. fellowships W.K. Kellogg Found., Battle Creek, Mich., 1979-85, asst. v.p. adminstrn., 1985-88, v.p. adminstrn., 1988—98; cons., 1999—. Bd. dirs. Cutting Edge Designs, Denver, 1993-96. Editor: Marco Messenger, 1999—2004. Bd. dirs. Arc Ministries, Allegan, Mich., 1982—, Vol. Bur., Battle Creek, 1984-86, ARC, Calhoun County, Mich., 1985-96, Emerging Young Leaders, 1996-2000; pres. com. Marco Presbyn. Ch., 2002—; trustee Ind. Wesleyan U., 2001—. Recipient Outstanding Young Women of Am. award. Mem. Am. Mgmt. Assn., Soc. Human Resources Mgmt. Avocations: knitting, music, drama activities. Home and Office: 1060 Borghese Ln #502 Naples FL 34114 Office Phone: 239-285-1230. E-mail: karenmi@earthlink.net.

HOLLENBERG, JULIA G., music educator; b. Balt., Nov. 8, 1959; BA in Music, Bridgewater Coll., Va., 1981; MusM, James Madison U., Harrisonburg, Va., 1988; cert. in Dalcroze/Orff/Kodaly, Towson U., Md., 1999. Vocal music tchr. Greene County Pub. Schs., Stanardsville, Va., 1981—84, Hampstead Elem. Sch., Md., 1990—. Youth and children's choir dir. Westminster Ch. of Brethren, Md., 1987—. Recipient Outstanding Tchr. award, Carroll County C. of C., 1999. Mem.: Music Educators Nat. Conf.

HOLLER, ANN K., music educator; b. Wytheville, Va., Sept. 22, 1946; d. Joseph C. and Alice (McKnight) Kelley; m. Peter D. Holler, Apr. 6, 1968; children: Elizabeth Ransom, Janet Bentley. BA in Math., King Coll., Bristol, Tenn., 1968; BA in Music, Va. Intermont Coll., Bristol, Va., 1983; MM in Music Theory, U. Tenn., 1993. Cert. tchr. music Tenn. Music Tchrs. Assn., 1992. Pvt. piano tchr. Holler Music Studio, Bristol, Tenn., 1973—2004; adj. instr. music King Coll., Bristol, Tenn., 2000—, East Tenn. State U., Johnson City, 1992—2002. Pres. Arts Alliance Mountain Empire, 2003—04. Chmn. editl. com. A! Magazine for the Arts, 2001—. Mem.: Am. Composers Forum, Am. Matthay Assn., Music Tchrs. Nat. Assn. Home: 112 Evergreen Pl Bristol TN 37620

HOLLERAN, KAREN ELAINE, literature and language professor; d. John Sayers and Marjorie Hughes Holleran. BA cum laude, Waynesburg Coll., Pa., 1979; MA magna cum laude, Duquesne U., Pitts., 1991. Instr. English Robert Morris U., Coraopolis, Pa., 1991—96, C.C. Allegheny County, Pitts., 1992—96; lectr. English C.C. Beager County, Monaca, 1993—94, U. Pitts., 1996; adminstrv. asst. Army Mgmt. Engring. Coll., Rock Island, Ill., 1997; asst. prof. Kaplan U., Davenport, Iowa, 2000—. Adj. instr. English Scott C.C., Bettendorf, Iowa, 1997—99. Mem. ACLU, Smithsonian Inst. Mem.: AAUW, Northeast Modern Lang. Assn. Home: 17631 290th St Long Grove IA 52756

HOLLERAN, PAULA RIZZO, psychology and counseling educator, researcher, consultant; b. N.Y.C.; d. A.M. and Jean T. Rizzo; m. Brian Patrick Holleran, Aug. 22, 1970; children: Tracy Lynn, Brett Daniel. BA, Bklyn. Coll., 1959; MA, U. Conn., 1963; PhD, U. Mass., 1969. Tchr. Shell Bank Jr. High Sch., Bklyn., 1960-62; instr. psychology SUNY, Oneonta, 1963-67, assoc. prof., 1969-70, prof. psychology and counseling, mem. grad. faculty, women's studies faculty, chair dept., 1970—, spl. asst. to assoc. commr. U.S. Office Edn., Washington, 1967-68; cons., specialist Headstart and Follow-through Projects, 1968-71; v.p. Rainbow Assocs./Cons., Oneonta, 1979—; presenter at nat. and regional confs.; developer several univ. level courses. Contbr. numerous articles to profl. jours.; reviewer ednl. rsch. jour.; co-author Nat. Assessment of Women's Studies Programs in Higher Edn.; co-developer Couples Communication Workshop and Gender Summit Game for Marriage Counselors. Officer Oneonta Taxpayers Assn. 1978-79; bd. dirs. Goodyear Lake Assn., Md., N.Y., 1984—; co-dir. Hillside Homeowner's Assn., 1987—. U.S. Office Edn. fellow HEW, 1967-68, rsch. grantee Commonwealth Mass. Bur. Rsch., 1969-70, Walter B. Ford Faculty grantee, 1988—, PDQ grantee SUNY, 1990, 94, UUP Classroom Scholarship grant, 1995. Mem. ACA, Am. Ednl. Rsch. Assn., Assn. for Women in Psychology, New Eng. Ednl. Rsch. Orgn (best paper award 1981, 87), N.E. Ednl. Rsch. Assn. Office: SUNY Dept Psychology and Counseling Oneonta NY 13820

HOLLEY, KATHLEEN, secondary school educator; b. Dallas, Mar. 3, 1958; d. William Morris and June Elizabeth McGee. BS in Biochemistry, U. Tex., Arlington, 1980; MA in Elem. Edn., Tex. Woman's U., Denton, 1991. Cert. tchr., Tex. Sch. health specialist Edn. Svc. Ctr. Region XI, Ft. Worth, 1986-91; sci. tchr. Lamar H.S., Arlington, Tex., 1990-91, Gunn Jr. H.S., Arlington, 1991; adj. instr. Tarrant County Coll., Ft. Worth, 1993-98; A.P. sci. tchr. Grand Prairie (Tex.) H.S., 1992-95, Crowley (Tex.) H.S., 1995-98, North Crowley H.S., Ft. Worth, 1998—2004, chair sci. dept., 2000—04; sci. tchr. Upper Sch., The Oakridge Sch., Arlington, Tex., 2004—. Sponsor, founder Masters of the Universe Sci. Demo Team, Arlington, 1993—, Active Sci. Unltd., Inc., Arlington, 1997—. Contbg. author Macmillan Ency. of Chemistry, 1996. Mem. Ft. Worth Civic Orch., 1985—, also past pres.; mem. Arlington Cmty. Band, 1989—, pres., 2000-02. Named Outstanding Sci. Tchr., Tex. Med. Assn., 1995, Tex. Chemistry Tchr. of Yr., 2003-2004; Tandy Tech. scholar, 1996. Mem. Am. Chem. Soc., Sci. Tchrs. Assn. Tex., Assn. Tex. Profl. Educators, Nat. Mole Day Found., Phi Delta Kappa. (rec. sec.). Avocations: playing flute, computers, electronics, pyrotechnics. Office: Oakridge Sch 5900 W Pioneer Pkwy Arlington TX 76013

HOLLEY, KAY MOFFITT, nutrition instructor, dietitian; b. Davenport, Iowa, Nov. 29, 1943; d. Glen and Cora (Vogler) Moffitt; m. Robert Coulter Holley, Feb. 14, 1970; 1 child, Robert Coulter II. BS, Western Ill. U., 1965; MS, U. Ky., 1967; postgrad., Ariz. State U., summer 1968, Okla. State U., summer 1969. Cert. dietitian, Ky.; cert. lifetime tchr., Ky. Adminstrv. asst. Supt. Schs., Taylor Ridge, Ill., summers 1961-65; grad. asst. U. Ky., Lexington, 1965-66; tchr. home econs. Rockridge High Sch., Taylor Ridge, 1966-67; chair dept. home econs. Midway (Ky.) Coll., 1967-70; cons. dietitian Mallory-Taylor Hosp. and other nursing homes, LaGrange, Ky., 1970-75; asst. prof. Morehead (Ky.) State U., 1972-73; tchr. adult edn. Fayette Co., Lexington, 1976-78; dietitian, adminstrv. planning VA Hosp., Lexington, 1974-82; instr. food svc. acctg. U. Ky., 1986; community dietitian VA Med. Ctr., Lexington, 1978-94; adj. instr. UK Lex Community Coll., 1995—. Fgn. student advisor Midway Coll., 1969, dietetics rep. Employees' Assn., Lexington, 1990-94. Dietetic chmn. Leestown and Cooper Dr. divs. VA Combined Fed. Campaign, Lexington, 1976; dietetic chmn. Leestown div. VA Bond Dr., Lexington, 1988; mem. communion com. Meth. Ch., Lexington, 1989-91; mem. Vol. Svc. POW-MIA Nat. Recognition Day Com., 1989-94, Salute to Vets. Week Com., 1990-94; asst. Head-Start program, Midway, Ky. Recipient Good Citizen award Am. Legion, Reynolds, Ill., 1961; named Outstanding Young Woman Am., Western Ill. U., 1970. Mem. Am. Dietetics Assn., Kappa Delta Pi, Kappa Omicron Phi. Avocations: attending theatre performances, college volleyball, horseracing, travel, collecting gourmet menus. Home: 2421 Wanda Way Lexington KY 40505-1919 Office: Lexington Community Coll Humanities and Bus Techs Academic Tech 101 Cooper Dr Lexington KY 40506-0001

HOLLEY, PAMELA SPENCER, retired librarian; b. Mpls., July 31, 1944; d. Boyd Edgar Gustafson, Jane Lenore Gustafson; m. Richard Howard Holley; m. Arthur Snow Spencer (dec. Oct. 24, 1996). BS Biology and Secondary Edn., Longwood Coll., Farmville, Va., 1965; MS, Coll. William and Mary, 1970; MLS, U. Md., 1973. Cert. libr. Va., 1973. Tchr. sci. Stephen Foster Intermediate/Fairfax County Pub. Schs., Alexandria, Va., 1965—72; libr. Lake Braddock Secondary Sch., Burke, 1973—75, Mount Vernon H.S., Alexandria, 1975—86; media specialist Area I Office, 1986—87; libr. Thomas Jefferson H.S. for Sci. and Tech., 1987—94; libr. program specialist Chapel Sq. Ctr., Annandale, 1994—96; coord. librs. FCPS, 1996—98; ret., 1998. Chair film series com. Virginia Beach Pub. Libr. Friends Bd., Va., 2000—02, v.p., 2002—03; mem. editl. adv. bd. Voice of Youth Advocates Mag., Lanham, 2000—; chair adv. com. Am. Econoclad Svcs., Topeka, 1988—95; host, co-host Cable 21 Ednl. Channel, Annandale, 1992—97; editl. adv. bd. Booklist Mag., Chgo., 1988—90; bd. dirs. Libr. Friends, v.p., 2002—03. Author: What Do Young Adults Read Next? (continuing series), 1993, Audiobooks, It Is!, 2002—, Column, VOYA, 2002—. Mem.: ALA (bd. dirs. divsn. young adult libr. svcs. assn. 1990—93, councilor 1995—99, v.p. 2004—05, pres. 2005—06, past pres. 2006—), Beta Phi Mu. Episcopalian. Avocations: kayaking, exercise, travel, reading, needlepoint. Home: PO Box 9 Assawoman VA 23302 Personal E-mail: pamsholley@aol.com.

HOLLEY, SUSAN L., psychologist; b. Coral Gables, Fla., 1951; d. Frank N. Holley III and Mary Lou Porlick, Robert A. Porlick (Stepfather) and Jean Holley (Stepmother); 1 child, H. Marie Warga. BA in Psychology, U. South Fla., 1973; MEd in Counseling, U. Miami, 1975; PhD in Clin. Psychology, Calif. Sch. Profl. Psychology, 1989. Licensed Clinical Psychologist, PSY 12646 Bd. of Psychology, 1992, Specialty Board Certification in Clinical Psychology #5770 Am. Bd. of Profl. Psychology, 2003, Health Service Provider in Psychology #46153 Coun. for the Nat. Register of Health Svc. Providers in Psych, 2001, Professional Alcoholism Specialist #137 Assn. of Profl. Alcoholism Specialists, Inc. (Fla.), 1979. Addiction counselor South Miami Hosp., South Miami, Fla., 1979—81; therapist New Beginnings Chem. Dependency Program, Century City, Calif., 1983—84; employee assistance adminstr. Aero Med. Advisors, Westchester, Calif., 1984—86; psychology practicum Switzer Ctr. of Ednl. Therapy, Torrance, Calif., 1986—87; employee assistance counselor Entertainment Industry Referral and Assistance Ctr., Burbank, Calif., 1986—88; psychology intern Vets. Adminstrn. Psychology Dept., Brentwood, Calif., 1988—89; postdoctoral fellow, rsch. asst. Family Project, Psychology Dept. U. of Calif., LA, 1990—91; clin. psychologist, pvt. practice Gelbart & Assocs., Redondo Beach, Calif., 1992—94, Susan Holley, PhD, Lancaster, Calif., 1993—. Clin. psychologist Out patient Mental Health Unit, Edwards Air Force Base, Calif., 1994—95; staff psychologist Palmdale Hosp., Calif., 1993—96; chem. dependency therapist Torrance Meml. Hosp. Chem. Dependency Ctr., Torrance, 1992—93. Mem. Lancaster West Rotary Club, Calif., 2000—. Postdoctoral scholar, NIMH, 1990. Mem.: APA, Sierra Club (bd. mem. Miami 1980), Calif. and LA Psychol. Assn., Lancaster West Rotary Club, Employee Assistance Program Assn. (assoc.; treas. 1985, newsletter editor 1991, Appreciation Plaque 1991). Methodist. Achievements include development of and presentation on the treatment of dual diagnosis patients with bipolar disorder and chemical dependency. Avocations: dressage horseback riding, photography, swimming, dance. Office: 43535 17th St W Ste 304 Lancaster CA 93534 Office Phone: 661-942-4079. Office Fax: 661-942-3887.

HOLLEY-ALLEN, LAUREN ALLANA, psychologist; b. Oct. 9, 1948; d. Winston Willouby and Mary Elizabeth (Hart) Holley. BS, Morgan State U., 1976; MA in Psychology, Antioch U., 1978. Lic. psychiatrist asst. Mental health and behavioral cons.; state tng. officer Md. Emergency Mgmt. Agy., Reisterstown, 1985—. Adj. faculty U. Md., Md. Fire and Rescue Inst., 2006—. Office: Md emergency Mgmt Agy 5401 Rue St Lo Dr Reisterstown MD 21136 Office Phone: 410-517-5114.

HOLLEY-GRAY, MARGARET N., minister; b. Marks, Miss., June 26, 1940; d. Mike Laverne Newsom and Jewel Elizabeth Reeves; m. Kenneth James Gray, Oct. 3, 2000; children: Elizabeth Carol Holley, Nila Candace Holley; m. Wesley Clint Holley (dec.). Degree in psychology, N.W. Jr. Coll., Senatobia, Miss.; diploma in ministry, RHEMA, Tulsa. Ordained min. Global Assn. Ministries, ordained Faith Christian Fellowship. Rec. artist Holley Prodns., Nashville; host, singer T.V.-Tri-State Christian TV, Marion, Ill.; pastor Christian Worship Ctr., West Frankfort, Ill. Composer songs. Mem.: West Frankfort C. of C., West Frankfort Ministerial Assn. Avocations: songwriting, reading, piano, sightseeing. Home: PO Box 452 West Frankfort IL 62896 Office: Christian Worship Ctr 2990 Ken Gray Blvd West Frankfort IL 62896

HOLLIDAY, BARBARA JOYCE, reference librarian, minister; b. Savannah, Ga. d. John Willie and Eula Mae Holliday. BSc, Savannah State Coll.; MSc in Libr. Sci., Clark Atlanta U. Cataloging libr. Tex. So. U. Law Libr., Houston, 1976—79; pharmacy libr. Tex. So. U. Pharmacy Libr., Houston, 1979—81; asst. ref. libr. Tex. So. U. Robert James Terry Libr., Houston, 1981—93; ref. libr. Tex. So. U., 1993—2005; ret. Recipient Nurse of the Yr., Miracle House of Prayer, Inc., 1984. Mem.: ALA, Nat. Women's Hist. Mus. Democrat. Avocations: reading, writing, poetry.

HOLLIE, GLADYS MIRIAM, nurse; b. Coupland, Tex., Nov. 2, 1932; d. John Charles and Cora Rebecca (Atkinson) H.; m. Simon Jackson Davis, Oct. 25, 1956 (div. 1961); 1 child, Harold Gene Holli Johnson. AD, McClennen Community Coll., Waco, Tex., 1980. Vocat. nurse St. Paul Hosp., Dallas, 1955-58, Tex. Children's Hosp., Dallas, 1958-60, Long Beach (Calif.) VA Med. Ctr., 1960-77, VA Med. Ctr., Waco, 1977-82, RN Fresno, Calif., 1982-95, ret., 1995. Vol. Am. Cancer Soc., Fresno, 1991, YWCA, Fresno, 1991, Ch. Women United. Mem. AARP, Order Ea. Star (asst. matron 1983—). Democrat. Mem. African Methodist Episcopal Ch. Avocations: reading, sewing, history, travel.

HOLLIEN, PATRICIA ANN, small business owner, researcher; b. N.Y.C., May 11, 1938; d. Leon and Sophia (Biernacki) Milanowski; m. Harry Hollien, Aug. 26, 1969; children: Brian, Stephanie, Christine. AA, Sante Fe Jr. Coll., 1969; ScD (hon), Marian Coll., 1983; student, U. Fla., 1977—. Rsch. asst. Marineland Rsch. Labs., 1965-69; co-owner, exec. v.p. Hollien Assocs., 1969—; owner, dir. Forensic Comm. Assocs., Gainesville, Fla., 1981—, The Eden Group, Gainesville, 1995-97. Vis. assoc. Royal Inst. Spl. Transmission Lab., Stockholm, 1970, Wroclaw Tech. U., Poland, 1974; asst. in research Inst. Advanced Study Communication Scis. U. Fla., 1977-83, assoc. in research, 1983—; adj. asst. prof. Communication Sci. Lab., N.Y., 1982—.

Co-author: Current Issues in the Phonetic Sciences, 1979; editor The Phonetician, 1991-98; contbr. articles to profl. jours. Treas. Soc. Son's of the Am. Revolution, 2001—; bd. dirs. Ann. Retirement Village, Waldo, Fla., 1981—93. Fellow Am. Acad. Forensic Scis., Internat. Soc. Phonetic Scis. (coun. reps. 1983—, Honors of the Assn. for 1995, 1997); mem. Am. Assn. Phonetic Scis., Acad. Forensic Application of the Comm. Sci., Internat. Assn. Forensic Phonetics (sec. gen. 7th ann. congress 1995), Ladies Aux. Fla. Soc. SAR (treas. 2003-05, pres. 2005—), Ladies Aux., Fla. Soc. Son's Am. Revolution (pres., 2005—, treas, 2002-2005). Home: 229 SW 43d Ter Gainesville FL 32607-2270 Office: Forensic Comm Assocs PO Box 12323 Gainesville FL 32604-0323 Office Phone: 352-377-8622. E-mail: fca@forcomm.com.

HOLLIES, LINDA HALL, pastor, pastoral counsel, educator, author, publisher; b. Gary, Ind., Mar. 29, 1943; d. James Donald and Doretha Robinson (Mosley) Adams; m. Charles H. Hollies, Oct. 14, 1972; children: Gregory Raymond, Grelon Renard, Grian Eunyke. BS in Adminstrn., Ind. U., 1975; M.Div., Garrett-Evang. Theol. Sem., 1986—; D of Ministry United Theol. Sem., Dayton, Ohio, 1996. Tchr. Hammond Public Schs., Ind., 1975-77; supr. Gen. Motors Corp., Willow Springs, Ill., 1977-79; gen. supr. Ford Motor Co., East Chicago Heights, Ill., 1979-82; coord. Women in Ministry, Evang. Theol. Sem., Evanston, Ill., 1984-86; clin. pastoral edn. intern supr., 1986-88; pastor Richards St. United Meth. Ch., 1988-92; pastor 1st Ch., Arlington Heights, Ill, 1992-94, Southlawn United Meth. Ch., 1994-96; assoc. coun. dir. W. Mich. ann. conf. United Meth. Ch., 1997—; founder, dir., cons. Woman Space, Inc., 2002, sr. pastor Mt. Hope United Meth. Ch., Lansing, Mich. Ford fellow, 1975, Benjamin E. Mays fellow, 1984; Crusade scholar United Meth. Ch., 1984; Lucy Ryder Myer scholar, 1985-86, Dr. Martin L. King scholar. Recipient Kilgore prize for creative ministry Claremont Sch. Theol., 1996. Mem. Zonta Profl. Women's Assn., Nat. Assn. Pastoral Educators, Internat. Toastmasters (pres. 1976-77). Author: Innner Healing for Broken Vessels, 1990, Womanist Rumblings, 1991, Womanistcare: Tending the Souls of Women, 1992, A Trumpet for Zion: Liturgical Resources for Year A, 1995, Taking Back My Yesterday, 1997, Jesus and Those Bodacious Women, 1997. Democrat. Avocations: reading, preaching, creative writing. Home: 2101 Okemos Dr SE Grand Rapids MI 49506-5356

HOLLIMON, ROBYN DELYN, music director; b. Humble, Tex., Oct. 30, 1967; d. Robert Edmund and Glenda LaVoris Wyatt; m. Thomas Scott Hollimon, Aug. 3, 1991. B in music edn., Baylor U., Tex., 1990. All level music dir. Grandview ISD, Tex., 1990—2000; choral dir. North Crowley HS, Ft. Worth, 2000—06; music dir. Genesis United Meth. Ch., Ft. Worth, 2006. Mem.: Am. Choral Dirs. Assn., Tex. Choral Dirs. Assn., Tex. Music Adjudicators Assn. (state judge for UIL competitions 2002—06), Tex. Music Educators Assn. (region VII vocal chair 2006—). Home: 678 Baldridge Rd Burleson TX 76028 Office: North Crowley HS Choirs 9100 South Hiven Fort Worth TX 76123 Business E-Mail: rhollimon@crowley.k12.tx.us.

HOLLINGER, PAULA COLODNY, state legislator; b. Washington, Dec. 30, 1940; d. Samuel and Ethel (Levy) Colodny; m. Paul Hollinger, Sept. 16, 1962; children: Ilene, Marcy, David. RN, Mt. Sinai Hosp. Sch. Nursing, N.Y.C., 1961. RN NY. Pub. health sch. nurse, resident camp nurse Balt. County Dept. Health; Myasthenia Gravis specialist Acute Stroke Unit U. Md. Hosp.; clin. instr. psychiat. nursing Tuskegee Inst.; head nurse surgery intensive care unit Mt. Sinai Hosp., NY, night charge nurse emergency rm. NY; Carter del., 1976; mem. Md. Ho. of Dels., Annapolis, 1978-86, Md. Senate, Annapolis, 1987—, majority whip, 2000—, vice chair senate edn. health and environ. affairs com., 1995—, senate chair joint com. on health care delivery and financing, 1995—, chair senate econ. and environ. affairs health sub-com., 1988—, chair edn., health and environ. affairs com., 2003—, majority whip, 2000—03. Chmn. adminstrv., exec., legis. rev. com., health subcom. Md. Senate, Annapolis, 1987, chmn. 1991-95, chmn. joint. com. health care delivery and financing, 1995, chmn. joint com. fed. rels., 1987-90, vice-chair econ. and environ. affairs com.,1995, mem. exec. nominations com., 1995—; vice-chair health com. Nat. Conf. State Legis., 1990-91, chair health com., 1991-92, chair sci. and resources tech. com., 1984, com. long term care, 1985, chmn. women's network, 1993, vice chmn. 1992, 96, chmn., 1992, rep. assembly fed. issues; mem. joint oversight com. on health care cost containment, Medicaid joint com.; chmn. joint protocol com. Md. Gen. Assembly, 1998—; alt. mem. So. Legis. Conf. Coun. State Govts. Human Svcs. And Pub. Safety Com.; mem. Gov.'s Task Forces to Study: Nursing Crisis, Uses of Methlphenidate, 1997—, Class Size Reduction Programs in Md., 1998—, Alternative Methods of Coll. Financing, Joint Legis. Task Force on Organ and Tissue Donation, 1997-98, Task Forces on Violence and Extremism, Quality of Care in Nurising Facilities, 1999, AIDS; mem. Gov.'s adv. coun. on AIDS; mem. Gov.'s com. nursing issues in Md.; mem. Gov.'s commns. black and minority health, black males, chmn. health subcom.; mem. interagy. Coordinating coun. for infants and toddlers; mem. exec. com. Nat. Assn. Jewish Legislators, 1997—; mem. state adv. com. Office for Children, Youth and Families; mem. state adv. coun. organ and tissue donation awareness, 1998—; pres. Women Legislators of Md., 1986-88, v.p., 1985; lectr., spkr., guest panelist in field. Bd. dirs. Nat. Coun. Jewish Women, Safety First, 1990, Jewish Family Svcs., 1995—, Progress Unlimited, Inc., Juvenile Diabetes Assn. (hon.); adv. to bd. dirs. United Way Cmty. Partnership Balt.; adv. bd. Second Step, Inc., Md. Organ procurement Ctr., Inc.; bd. trustees Transplant Resource Ctr. Md., Inc., 1997—, Group for Independent Learning Disabled; grad. adv. coun. Notre Dame Coll.; mem. com. adolescent drug and alcohol abuse Md. Bar Assn., Environ. Matters Com.; faculty assoc. U. Md. Sch. Nursing, 1998—. Recipient Murry Guggenheim award, 1961, Bramson award Women's American ORT, 1981, Legis. award Mental Health Assn., 1983, Legislator of Yr. award Md. Nurse's Assn., 1984, Human Svc. award Constant Care Med. Ctr. 1984, Outstanding Contbns. to Edn. award Tchr.'s Assn. Balt. County, 1984, Outstanding Commitment and Dedication to Treatment of Alcoholic award Pilot House, 1984, Dedication and Commitment to Health and Environ. award Ctrl. Md. Health Sys. Agy., Edith Rosen Strauss award, 1987, Outstanding Svc. award Md. Psych. Assn., 1987, Pres.' award Md. Assn. Non-Profit Homes for Aging, 1987, Humanitarian award, Liberty Rd. Cmty. Coun., 1987, Leadership Laurel award Safety 1st Club Md., 1987, Outstanding Legis. Leadership award On Our Own Md., 1988, Outstanding Support and Devel. Rehab. Programs award Johns Hopkins Dept. Rehab., Md. Health Care Found., 1988, Legis. Honor Roll award Md. Assn. Psychosocial Svcs., 1988, Spl. award leadership Pikesville revitalization Pikesville Cmty. Growth Corp., 1988, Pres.' award Md. Assn. Home Care, 1988, Verda Welcome award for outstanding polit. achievements and pub. svc., 1989, Cmty. Svc. award Balt. Hebrew U., 1990, Physician's Asst. Appreciation award, 1991, Leadership and Commitment award Walbrook H.S. Primary Health Care Ctr., 1991, Betty Tyler Pub. Affairs award Planned Parenthood, 1992, 93, Excellence in Social Work Legislation award Md. Social Work Coalition, 1993, award Chesapeake Bay Found. Environ. Leadership, 1994, Policy Maker Leadership award Adv. for Youth, 1995, Ann. Leadership award Md. State Sch. Health Coun., 1996, Legis. award Legis. and Pub. Info. Com. Balt. County Commn. Disabilities, 1997, Legis. award Md. Retired Tchrs., 1997, award Md./D.C. Soc. Respiratory Care, 1997, Dedication and Support award Nat. Kidney Found. Md., 1998, Legis. award Md. Assn. Counseling and Devel., 1998, Sch. Health Advocacy award Sch. Nurse Inst., 2000, Outstanding Svc. award Md. Psychol. Assn., 2000, Pres.'s award Md. Nat. Capitol Home Care Assn., 2000, Presdl. award of Recognition Md. Occupl. Therapy Assn., 2001, Legis. of Yr. award, Mental Health Assn. Md., 2001, Pacesetter award Nat. Women Legis.'s Lobby, 2001, Distin. Leadership award Abilities Network and Epilepsy Found. of Chesapeake Region, 2002; named Woman of Yr., Women Realtors Anne Arundel County, 1988, Pikesville C. of C., 1989, Sen. of Yr., Md. Assn. Psychiat. Support Svcs., 1993, Oustanding Legislator, Md. Speech, Lang., Hearing Assn., 1993, Most Disting. Alumnus, Mt. Sinai Hosp. Sch. Nursing Alumnae Assn., 1998, Md.'s Top 100 Women, Daily Record, 1999, 2001, 03, Legislator of Yr. AHA, 1999, Chesapeake Bay Bound., 2004. Mem. Am. Assn. Marriage and Family Therapy (Mid Atlantic Divsn., hon., hon. licensure), B'nai Brith Women, Hadassah, Na'Amat, Orgn. for Rehab. Tng. (Bramson award 1981), Chi Eta Phi (hon.). Office: Miller Senate Bldg Annapolis MD 21401-1991

HOLLINGER, PEGGY LOUISE, elementary school counselor; b. Mobile, Ala., July 17, 1956; d. Adam Lavaughn and Louise (Baggett) H. BS, Mobile Coll., 1979; MS in Edn., Troy (Ala.) State U., 1982; degree in Edn., U. South Ala., 1993. Cert. counselor U. South Ala., 1990. Tchr. Baldwin County Bd. Edn., Bay Minette, Ala., 1979-90, counselor, 1990—. Baptist. Avocations: singing, reading, travel. Home: PO Box 7208 719 Artillery Range St Spanish Fort AL 36527-7208 Personal E-mail: plh71756@bellsouth.net.

HOLLINGSHEAD, BONNE LOU, fine art artist; b. Mooreland, Okla., July 17, 1929; d. Floyd Nickolas and Opal Ellena (Lehman) Stoll; m. Gerald Eugene Hollingshead, Nov. 14, 1970. Student, Ft. Smith (Ark.) Jr. Coll., 1950s, Okla. A&M Coll., 1950s, Okla U., 1960s, Oklahoma City U., 1960s. Nurse N.W. Community Hosp., Mooreland, 1946-48; spl. nurse Sugg Clinic, Ada, Okla., 1948-50; acct. U.S. Army, Ft. Smith, Ark., 1951-57; nurse Enid (Okla.) Meml. Hosp., 1958-60; acct. Vance AFB, Enid, 1957-60, FAA, Oklahoma City, 1960-76; sec., office mgr. Senate Offices, Oklahoma City, 1979-90; real estate sales assoc. Abide Realtors, Inc., Oklahoma City, 1983-87; with consumer credit div. Atty. Gen., Oklahoma City, 1990. Atty. Gen. Oklahoma City, 1990; sec. to Senate Minority Leader, Okla. State Senate, 1980-82; sec. to Senate Caucus Chmn., 1983-84; co-owner Studio Gallery, Oklahoma City. Artist, editor: (craft book) Roses in Pink, 1994. Campaign mgr. office Senator John R. McCune, 1990. Recipient Internat. Fine Art Artist of Yr., 2004. Mem. Can. Valley Art Guild (sec. 1993-94), Edmond Art Guild, Okla. Art Guild (treas. 1989, 1st v.p. 1994, pres. 1994—, bd. dirs. 1991—), Okla. Watercolor Assn. (treas. 1994—), Ctrl. Arts Assn., Audubon Soc., Mid-Del. Art Guild, Women Artists of the West (100 Art awards). Avocations: music, reading, investments. Home: 12516 Deerwood Dr Oklahoma City OK 73142-5105

HOLLINGSWORTH, ALISON BERKELEY, ballet dancer, educator; d. Fred Clyde and Jacqueline Green Hollingsworth. Degree in commerce and bus. adminstrn., U. Ala., Tuscaloosa, 1990. Ballet dancer, tchr. Exclusivley Ballet, Birmingham, 1995—99; ballet tchr., ice coach Pelham Civic Complex Ice Skate Sch., Birmingham, 1997—99; ballet tchr., dancer Broadway Dance Ctr., NYC, 2001—05; ballet tchr. Keystone State Dance Festival, Wilkes Barre, Pa., 2002, Prog. Dance Summer Intensive, Englewood, NJ, 2004, Brant Lake Dance Camp, Brant Lake, NY, 2004—04, Gotta Dance, Redmond, Wash., 2005—, Ballet Arts, New York, NY, 2005, U. Wash. Exptl. Coll., Seattle, 2005—, Westlake Dance, Seattle, 2005—. Choreographer Exclusivley Ballet, Birmingham, 1996—99, Broadway Dance Ctr., NYC, 2001—05, Brant Lake Dance Camp, NY, 2004. Vol. Girls Inc., Birmingham, 1995—96.

HOLLINGSWORTH, BRENDA JACKSON, employment consultant; b. Roxboro, N.C., Aug. 12, 1958; d. John Vanstory and Effie Clayton Jackson; children: Brandy Effie, William (Denzel). BS, St. Augustine's Coll., Raleigh, N.C., 1981. Income maintenance caseworker Social Svcs., Durham, NC, 1987-89, fraud investigator Roxboro, 1990-92; youth counselor Job Tng. Partnership Act, Roxboro, 1992-94; employment cons. Employment Security Commn., Roxboro, 1997—. Avocations: volleyball, poetry, aerobics. Home: 95 Gatesworth Rd Roxboro NC 27573

HOLLINGSWORTH, DONEEN, state agency administrator; m. Rusty Hollingsworth; 2 children. BA, Univ. S.D. Staff mem. S.D. Bureau Fin. & Mgmt.; spl. asst. to S.D. Gov. Mickelson & Miller; adminstr. S.D. Dept. Edn. & Cultural Affairs; sec. S.D. Dept. Health, Pierre, 1995—. Office: Dept Health 600 E Capitol Ave Pierre SD 57501-2536*

HOLLINGSWORTH, HOLLY, newscaster; BA in Radio/Television Studies, Ashland U. Asst. prodr. Sta. WKYC-TV, Cleve., 1991; reporter, anchor, prodr. Sta. WEWS-TV; anchor Sta. WTVG-TV, Toledo, 1994—96; gen. assignment reporter Sta. WCMH-TV, Columbus, 1996—97, anchor, 1997—. Nominee Emmy award, 1999, 2000, 2001; recipient Media CrimeStopper of Yr. award, Ctrl. Ohio CrimeStoppers, 2001, Broadcast Media award, Ohio Pharmacists Assn., 2002, Media Vol. of Yr. award, March of Dimes, Ohio, 2002. Office: WCMH-TV 3165 Olentangy River Rd PO Box 4 Columbus OH 43202

HOLLINGSWORTH, LARA HUDGINS, lawyer; b. Houston, Dec. 28, 1970; m. Derek S. Hollingsworth; 2 children. BA in Hist., Baylor U., 1993, JD magna cum laude, 1996. Bar: Tex. 1996, US Supreme Ct., US Dist. Ct. (all dists. Tex.), US Ct. Appeals (5th and 10th cirs.). Law clk. Staff of Sam D. Johnson, US Ct. Appeals Fifth Cir., 1996—97; briefing atty. to James A. Baker Tex. Supreme Ct., 1997—98; atty. Carrington, Coleman, Sloman & Blumenthal, P.C., Hudgins, Hudgins, and Warrick, P.C., Houston, 2000—03; of counsel Rusty Hardin & Assocs., P.C., Houston, 2003—. Tex. Civil Procedure Symposium editor: Baylor Law Rev., 1995—96. Named a Rising Star, Tex. Super Lawyers mag., 2006. Mem.: Tex. Young Lawyers Assn. Office: Rusty Hardin & Assocs PC 1401 McKinney Ste 2250 Houston TX 77010 Office Phone: 713-652-9000. E-mail: larahollingsworth@rustyhardin.com.*

HOLLINGSWORTH, MARGIE ELLEN, counselor; b. Lubbock, Tex., Apr. 13, 1951; d. Ira Hancel and Mildred (Evans) H. BBA in Bus. and Psychology, Tex. Tech U., 1974, MEd in Ednl. Psychology, 1981, postgrad., 1978-81, 84-86, 91—. Lic. profl. counselor, substance abuse specialist, Tex. Sec. acad. dept. Tex. Tech U., Lubbock, 1971-76, acad. counselor, 1980, coord., counselor, 1985-88; med. sec. William F. Andrew, M.D., Lubbock, 1976-79; counselor Learn Ednl. Talent Search, Lubbock, 1981-85; pvt. practice Lubbock, 1988—. Paul Whitfield Horn fellow, 1980-81; Tex. Tech Dad's Assn. scholar, 1969-70, Tex. Tech U. scholar, 1970-74, Bernie J. Fallon scholar, 1985-86. Mem. AACD (treas., bd. dirs. Lubbock chpt. 1989-90), Internat. Assn. Addictions/Offenders Counselors, Tex. Assn. Counseling and Devel., West Tex. Assn. Counseling and Devel., Tex. Assn. Alcoholism and Drug Abuse Counselors, Student Substance Abuse Specialists. Avocations: sewing, swimming, exercising, pets, painting. Home and Office: 2607 35th St Lubbock TX 79413-2403

HOLLINGSWORTH, MARTHA LYNETTE, secondary school educator; b. Waco, Tex., Oct. 9, 1951; d. Willie Frederick and Georgia Cuddell (Bryant); m. Roy David Hollingsworth, Dec. 31, 1971; children: Richard Avery, Justin Brian. AA, McLennan C.C., 1972; BBA, Baylor U., 1974, MS in Ednl. Adminstrn., 1992. Tchr. Connally Ind. Sch. Dist., Waco, 1974—. With Adult Edn. Night Sch., 1974—78; chair Area III leadership conf. Vocat. Office Careers Clubs Tex., Waco, 1985—. Active Lakeview Little League Booster Club, 1985—; mem. PTA. Mem.: Assn. Tex. Profl. Educators (v.p. local chpt. 1988—90), Vocat. Office Edn. Tchrs. Assn. Tex., Tex. Future Farmers Am. (hon.), Future Homemakers Am. Area VIII (hon.), Delta Kappa Gamma (pres. Zeta chpt. 2005—). Baptist. Office: Connally Vocat Dept 200 Cadet Way Waco TX 76705 Office Phone: 254-296-6420. Business E-Mail: lhollingsworth@connally.org.

HOLLINGWORTH, BEVERLY A., former state legislator; b. Haverhill, Mass., Oct. 18, 1935; m. William P. Gilligan, 1978; children: David, Mary Beth. Therese, Kimberly. Student, U. N.H. Mem. N.H. Ho. of Reps., Concord, 1980-90; mem. Dist. 23 N.H. Senate, Concord, 1991—2002, pres., 1999-00; owner, mgr. Hollingworth Motor Ct., Hampton Beach, N.H. Chmn. appropriations com.; mem. ways and means com., mem. judiciary com., mem. fin. exec. com., mem. joint adminstrv. peals com. Active United Way, Heart Fund, ARC, Lane Meml. Friends Libr. Mem. Hampton Beach (N.H.) C. of C. Democrat. Roman Catholic.

HOLLINSHEAD, ARIEL CAHILL, oncologist, educator, researcher; b. Allentown, Pa., Aug. 24, 1929; d. Earl Darnell and Gertrude Loretta (Cahill) H.; m. Montgomery K. Hyun, June 12, 1957; children: William C., Christopher C. Student, Swarthmore Coll., 1947-48; AB, Ohio U., 1951, DSc (hon.), 1977; MA, George Washington U., 1955, PhD, 1957, MD, 1977. Asst. prof., fellow in virology Baylor U. Med. Ctr., 1958-59; asst. prof. pharmacology George Washington Med. Ctr., 1959-61, asst. prof. medicine, 1961-64, assoc. prof. medicine, head lab. virus and cancer rsch., 1964-73, prof., dir. lab. virus and cancer rsch., 1974-89; on sabbatical leave 1990, prof. medicine emeritus, 1991—; rschr. HI Virus and Cancer Rsch., 1991—2006. Mem. bd. Neogenix; clin. rschr. trials in oncology and virology; cons. to biotech. cos.; panelist FDA and NIH. Contbr. over 280 articles on active immunotherapy and immunochemotherapy of cancer and virus diseases to sci. jours. Bd. dirs. Nat. Women's Econ. Alliance, Ohio U., Med. Coll. Pa., 1980-2003, Women's Inst., 1995-97. Named Bicentennial Med. Woman of Yr., Joint Bd. Am. Med. Colls., 1976, one of Outstanding Woman of Am., 1987, Outstanding Alumnus of Yr., Ohio U., 1990; recipient Cert. Merit Med. Coll. Pa., 1975-76, Marion Spencer Fay Med. Woman of Year award Med. Coll. Pa.; decorated Star of Europe, 1980. Fellow AAAS (med. sci. com. 1993-96, 99—), Washington Acad. Sci. N.Y. Acad. Scis.; mem. Grad. Women in Sci. (nat. pres. 1985-86, bd. dirs. 1986-92, nat. liaison to Washington, 1992—), Internat. Soc. Preventive Oncology, Nat. Soc. Exptl. Biology and Medicine (Disting. Scientist award 1985, Disting. Scientist emeritus award for Outstanding Career in Tchg. and Rsch. in Medicine 1996, past pres. Greater Washington chpt.), Am. Soc. Microbiology, Am. Assn. Cancer Research, Am. Assn. Immunologists, Women in Cancer Rsch., Vet. Females Am., Clin. Immunology Soc., Internat. Soc. Antiviral Research, Am. Soc. Clin. Oncology, Internat. Assn. Study Lung Cancer, Internat. Union Against Cancer, Am. Med. Writers Assn., Soc. Profs. George Washington U. Emeriti, Blue Ridge Mountain Country Club, Twin Isles Country Club, Washington Forum (pres. 1987, 91), Phi Beta Kappa. Achievements include identification of antiviral drugs and vaccines; discovering resistance to antiviral drugs; being first to purify, develop and test cancer gene products, including peptides and to study activities; first to invent field called proteomics; peptides were studied and identified for the ability to induce long-lasting cell-mediated immunity; developed proteomics technology and pioneered clinical testing and monitoring epitope activity during seventeen clinical trials; patentee in field. Home: 23465 Harborview Rd #622 Punta Gorda FL 33980-2162

HOLLIS, DEBORAH D., systems analyst, application developer; d. Susan Tower and Allen Hollis. BS, Regis U., Denver, 1997; BA, St. John's Coll., Santa Fe, 1988; M in Computer Info. Sys., U. Denver, 1995; M in Libr. and Info. Sci., U. Wash., Seattle, 1989. Database analyst Ovid Technologies, Salt Lake City, 1998—2001; analyst Sandia Nat. Labs., Albuquerque, 2001—. Mem.: U.S. Equestrian Team, Padi Dive Soc., Arabian Horse Assn. Independent. Avocations: reading, horseback riding, scuba diving, Aikido, yoga. Office Phone: 505-845-9630.

HOLLIS, JULIA ANN ROSHTO, critical care, medical, and surgical nurse; b. Monroe, La., June 25, 1945; d. Joseph Edward Roshto and Eleanor Coverdale Larsen; m. William Davis Hollis, Mar. 2, 1964; children: David Terrel, Julia Allison. BSN, N.E. La. U., 1976. RN, La., Ala., Miss.; cert. critical care nurse practitioner, BCLS, ACLS. Staff nurse to head nurse E.A. Conway Hosp., Monroe, 1977-84; staff nurse, charge nurse ICU, critical care North Monroe Community Hosp., Monroe, 1984-87; staff nurse neurotrama surg. ICU U. South Ala. Med. Ctr., Mobile, 1988-89; staff nurse, charge nurse Norrell Health Care, Mobile, 1990—, Medforce Internat., New Orleans; owner Resource Mgmt., 1997; nurse practioner Sch. Medicine La. State U., New Orleans, 2004—. Mem. AACN, AAUW, Ala. Nurses Assn., Met. Writers Guild, Baldwin County Writers Assn. Home: 5073 Dawes Lane Ext Theodore AL 36582-9627

HOLLIS, JUNE D., secondary school educator; b. Jackson, Miss., June 11, 1943; d. David Eugene Davidson and Gladys Tate; m. L. Wendell Hollis, June 18, 1966; children: Scott, Mark, Drew. Degree, U. So. Miss., Hattiesburg, 1965, Miss. State U., Starkville, Miss., 1980. Thcr. Florence Jr. and Sr. H.S., Miss., 1965—68, Chastain Jr. H.S., Jackson, Miss., 1968—73, Pearl Jr. H.S., Miss., 1979—81, Brandon H.S., Miss., 1981—. Mem. adv. bd. Miss. Coun. Social Studies. Named Tchr. of Month, Brandon H.S.; fellow, Fulbright Found., 2003; grantee, Earthwatch, 1996, 1998, 2003. Mem.: Miss. Geographic Alliance (tchr. cons. 1989—, mem. adv. bd. 1989—, webmistress 2003—). Avocations: travel, reading, computers, photography. Office: Brandon High Sch 3090 Hwy 18 Brandon MS 39042

HOLLIS, KATHERINE MARY, information scientist, consultant; d. Albert George and Rosalyn Mary Duren; m. David Martin Hollis, Aug. 25, 1990; children: Kent David Miller, Jason Randolph Miller; children: Brittany Frances, David Christopher. MS in Nat. Security Strategy, Nat. War College, 1999; B in Polit. Sci., U. Minn., 1983. Dir. resource mgmt. installation support modules program Program Exec. Office - STD. Mgmt. Info. Sys., Ft. Belvoir, Va., 1989—93; program mgr. electronic commerce/electronic data interchange Def. Info. Sys. Agy., Falls Chruch, Va., 1993—96, spl. asst. to the dep., pub. key infrastructure program mgmt. office, 1999—2000; dep. dir. electronic processes initiatives coun. task force Office of the Deputy Sec. of Def., Rosslyn, Va., 1996—98; deputy dir. dept. def. Y2K office Office of the Sec. of Def., Crystal City, Va., 1998—99; exec. dir. security and privacy portfolio Electronic Data Sys., Herndon, Va., 2000—. Adv. com. Fed. Electronic Commerce Coalition, Falls Church, Va., 1999—; chair smart card integrated process team Def. Info. Sys. Agy., 1999—2000; spkr. in field. Vol. educator Prince William County Schools, Manassas, Va., 2001. Recipient Commanders award, Dept. of the Army, Dept. of Def., 1989, Federal 100 award, Federal Computer News, 1998. Avocations: archaeology, Egyptology, travel, writing. Office: Electronic Data Sys 13600 EDS Dr (A2S-D49) Herndon VA 20171

HOLLIS, MARY FRANCES, aerospace educator; b. Indpls., Sept. 18, 1931; d. Lucian Albert and Clara Frances Coleman; divorced; 1 child, Booker Albert Hollis. BS, Butler U., 1952, MS, 1962; postgrad., Stanford U., 1975, San Francisco State U., 1980-81. Cert. elem. tchr., Ind., Calif. Kindergarten tchr. Lockerbie Nursery Sch., Indpls., 1952, Indpls. Pub. Schs., 1952-69; tchr. K-6 San Mateo (Calif.) City Sch. Dist., 1969-91; summer sch. prin. San Mateo City Sch. dist., Foster City, Calif., 1983-91; aerospace educator, 1982—. Bd. dirs. Coun. of Math./Sci. Educators of San Mateo County, Belmont, Calif.; resident mgr. Lesley Found., Park Twrs., 1999—. Editor: San Mateo County Math./Sci. Coun. quarterly newsletter, 1988-90. Bd. dirs. Arts Coun. of San Mateo County, 1986-91, Mid-Peninsula chpt. ACLU, San Mateo, 1990—, Unitarian-Universalist Ch. San Mateo, 1996-98; bd. dirs. Peninsula Funeral and Meml. Planning Soc., 1996-2000, co-pres., 1998-99; office mgr. Roger Winston Campaign for San Mateo Union H.S. Dist. Bd. Trustees, 1993; mem. adv. com. USAF-Pacific Liaison Region-CAP, 1988-94; sr. peer counselor San Mateo County Mental Health, 1996-2004. Recipient Life Down to Earth award NASA, Moffet Field, Mt. View, Calif., 1985-86, Earl Sams Tchr. of Yr. award Calif. Assn. Aerospace Educators, 1989, award of merit Am. Legion, San Bruno, Calif., 1989, citation Air Force Assn., Mountain View, Calif., 1991, Aviation Summer Sch. cert. of appreciation Am. Legion Dept. Calif. Aerospace Commn., 1994. Mem. NEA (life), AAUW (bd. dirs. San Carlos chpt. 1993-95), NAACP (life), Am. Bus. Women's Assn. (rec. sec. Foster City chpt. 1985), World Aerospace Edn. Orgn. Democrat. Unitarian-Universalist. Avocations: reading, travel, music-jazz, rhythm and blues, swimming, aerospace/aviation. Office: PO Box 625 Belmont CA 94002-0625 E-mail: mfrances-pacbell@comcast.net.

HOLLIS, ROBBIE SMAGULA, marketing communications executive, advertising executive; b. Dover, Del., Oct. 15, 1957; d. Thomas David and Billie Jo (Talkington) Smagula; m. Mark Steven Dennis, May 26, 1979 (div. May 1982); 1 child, Gregory Steven; m. Stuart D. B. Hollis, Nov. 18, 1989; children: Hanna Joellen, Rachael Nicole. BS in Marine Biology, Tex. A&M U., 1978. Tech. writer Tex. Trans. Inst., College Station, Tex., 1978-80; documentation coord. Genentech, Inc., South San Francisco, Calif., 1980-82; sr. tech. writer Cen. & South West Svcs., Inc., Dallas, 1982-88; sales promotion mgr. Computer Assocs. (formerly UCCEL Corp.), Dallas, 1984-88; with corp. commn. J. Driscoll & Assocs., Dallas, 1988—89; mgr. mktg. comm. ANTRIM Corp., Plano, Tex., 1989—94; mgr. Hogan Corp. Commns., Dallas, 1994-96; comms. ministry First Presbyn. Ch., McKinney, Tex., 2000—02; instrnl. aide Anna (Tex.) Elem., 2002—03, tchr., 2003—. Mem. Soc. Tech. Communication (Best of Show and Excellence Achievement award 1985, 86), Internat. Assn. Bus. Communicators, NAFE.

HOLLIS, SHEILA SLOCUM, lawyer; b. Denver, July 15, 1948; d. Theodore Doremus and Emily M. (Caplis) Slocum (dec.); m. John Hollis; 1 child, Windsong Emily Hollis. BS in Journalism with honors, U. Colo., 1971, BS in Gen. Studies cum laude, 1971; JD, U. Denver, 1973. Bar: Colo. 1974, D.C. 1975, U.S. Supreme Ct. 1980. Trial atty. Fed. Power Commn., Washington, 1974-75; assoc. firm Wilner & Scheiner, Washington, 1975-77; dir. office enforcement Fed. Energy Regulatory Commn., Washington, 1977-80; pvt. practice, 1980—; ptnr. Vinson & Elkins, Washington, 1987-92; sr. ptnr. Metzger, Hollis, Gordon & Alprin, Washington, 1992-97; mng. ptnr. Washington office Duane Morris LLP, 1997—2004, chair Washington office, 2004—; exec. com., firm ptnrs. bd. Duane Morris LLP, 2003—. Professorial lectr. in energy law George Washington U., 1980—2000. Co-author: Energy Decision Making, 1983, Energy Law and Policy, 1989; mem. editl. bd. Oil and Gas Reporter, Pub. Utility Fortnightly; contbr. articles to profl. publs. Adv. bd. Pub. Utility Ctr. N.Mex. State U., 1986—94; adv. bd. N.Am. Energy Stds. Bd., 1998—; pres. Women's Coun. Energy and Environment, 1997—2003; bd. dirs. Am. Friends of Royal Soc.; chair Coun. of the Fund for Justice and Edn.; bd. dirs. U.S. Energy Assn., chair nominating com. U. Denver scholar, 1972-73; named Woman of Yr. Women's Coun. Energy and Environment, 2003, One of 50 Key Women in Energy-Global, Commodities Now Mag., 2004. Fellow: ABA (chair coord. group energy law 1989—92, ho. dels. 1992—, chair coord. group energy law 1995—97, chair standing com. environ. law 1997—2000, mem. bd. editors ABA Jour. 2000—, chair sect. environ., energy and resources 2001—02, standing com. fed. judiciary 2002—05, coun. chair fund for justice and edn.); mem.: Womens Fgn. Policy Group, Fed. Bar Assn., John Carroll Soc., Women's Bar Assn. D.C., D.C. Bar Assn., Colo. Bar Assn., Ctr. Am. and Internat. Law (trustee, v.p.), Oil and Gas Ednl. Inst. (v.p.), Energy Bar Assn. (pres. 1991—92), Am. Law Inst., Internat. Bar Assn., Comml. Bar of Eng. and Wales (hon.), Thomas More Soc. Am. (pres. 2003—05), Cosmos Club, Nat. Press Club, Dame of Malta of the Am. Assn. Roman Catholic. Office: Duane Morris LLP 1667 K St NW Ste 700 Washington DC 20006-1608 Office Phone: 202-776-7810. Business E-Mail: sshollis@duanemorris.com.

HOLLIS, SUSAN TOWER, history professor; b. Boston, Mar. 17, 1939; d. James Wilson and Dorothy Parsons (Moore) Tower; m. Allen Hollis, Nov. 10, 1962 (div. Feb. 1975); children: Deborah Durfee, Harrison. AB, Smith Coll., 1962; PhD, Harvard U., 1982. Cert. C.C. instr. history and humanities. Asst. prof. Scripps Coll., Claremont, Calif., 1988—91; prof. Coll. of Undergrad. Studies Union Inst., L.A., 1991—93; dean coll., prof. humanities Sierra Nev. Coll.-Lake Tahoe, Incline Village, Nev., 1993—95; ind. scholar, cons. Reno, 1995—96; ctr. dir., assoc. dean Ctrl. N.Y. Ctr. SUNY Empire State Coll., Syracuse, 1996—99, assoc. prof. Rochester, 1999—, coord. we. region MA in Liberal Studies program, 2000—. Convener hist. studies Empire State Coll. of SUNY, 2000—03; co-chair acad. policies and learning programs com. Empire State Coll. SUNY, 2003—04, mem. academic policies and learning program com., 2001—05. Author: The Ancient Egyptian "Tale of Two Brothers", 1990; editor: Hymns, Prayers and Songs: Anthology of Ancient Egyptian Lyrics & Poetry (by John L. Foster), 1996; asst. editor: Working With No Data, 1987; co-editor: Feminist Theory and the Study of Folklore, 1993; mem. adv. bd.: KMT, A Modern Jour. of Ancient Egypt, 1991—; contbr. articles to profl. jours, encys. Music vol. Open Readings, Belmont, Mass., 1982—88; vol. Sierra Club, 1988—; problem capt. Odyssey of the Mind, Nev., 1994—95, judge NY, 1997—98; crew chief Tahoe Rim trail, 1994—96; active Masterworks Chorale, NY, 1996—99. Recipient Susan H. Turben award for excellence in scholarship, Empire State Coll., 2006. Mem.: N.Y. State Network for Women Leaders in Higher Edn. (assoc. coord. 1999—2000, coord. 2000—03, bd. dirs. 1997—2006), N.Y. Acad. Scis., Egyptological Soc. N.Y., Soc. Bibl. Lit. (co-chair Egyptology and Ancient Israel group 1995—96, chair Egyptology and Ancient Israel group 1996—2005, convenor Ancient Near East Consortium 1998—, Outstanding Svc. in Mentoring award 2003), Soc. for Study Egyptian Antiquities, Internat. Assn. Egyptologists, Am. Rsch. Ctr. Egypt, Am. Oriental Soc., Am. Folklore Soc., Am. Assn. Higher Edn., Am. Acad. Religion, Am. Recorder Soc., Incline Village/Crystal Bay C. of C. (sec., bd. dirs. 1994—95), Ka-na-wa-ke Canoe Club (bd. dirs. 1998—2000), Adirondack Mountain Club, Appalachian Mountain Club (co-leader 1987—88). Democrat. Home: 7 New Wickham Dr Penfield NY 14526-2703 Office: Empire State Coll of SUNY 1475 Winton Rd N Rochester NY 14609-5803 Office Phone: 585-224-3246. Business E-Mail: susan.hollis@esc.edu.

HOLLIS-ALLBRITTON, CHERYL DAWN, retail paper supply store executive; b. Elgin, Ill., Feb. 15, 1959; d. L.T. and Florence (Elder) Saylors; stepparent Bobby D. Hollis; m. Thomas Allbritton, Aug. 10, 1985. BS in Phys. Edn., Brigham Young U., 1981; cosmetologist, 1981. Retail sales clk. Bee Discount, North Riverside, Ill., 1981-82, retail store mgr., Downers Grove, Ill., 1982, Oaklawn, Ill., 1982-83, St. Louis, 1983; retail tng. mgr. Arvey Paper & Office Products (divsn. Internat. Paper), Chgo., 1984, retail store mgr., Columbus, Ohio, 1984—. Republican. Mem. LDS Ch. Avocations: writing, reading, travel. Office: Arvey Paper & Office Products 431 E Livingston Ave Columbus OH 43215-5586 Office Phone: 614-221-0153.

HOLLMAN, K. HOLLYN, lawyer; b. Jackson, Miss. m. James McCall Smith. BA in Politics, Wake Forest U.; JD, U. Tenn. Coll. Law. Atty. McGuireWoods LLP, Washington, Waller Landsden Dortch & Davis, Nashville; gen. counsel (pub. affairs) Baptist Joint Com. Mem.: Tenn. Bar, DC Bar. Office: Baptist Joint Com Public Affairs 200 Maryland Ave NE Washington DC 20002

HOLLOMAN, MARILYN LEONA DAVIS, non profit administrator, new product developer; b. Bklyn., Oct. 6, 1952; d. Leon Courbourne and Gwendolyn Omega (Crichlow) Davis; m. Theodore Albert Holloman, July 30, 1971 (div. Apr. 1975); children: Tedette Ann (dec.), Amina Omega Suedi. AAS in Nursing, Queensboro C.C., Bayside, N.Y., 1973; FNP, U. Miami, 1980. Cert. family nurse practitioner. Founder, pres., CEO Women and Children First Inc., Miami, 1992—2004; v.p. Omega Health Network, inc., 2000—01. Allocations panel mem. United Way, Dade County, Fla., 1989-96; mem. at large Switchboard of Miami, 1992, treas., 1993-94, sec., 1994-95; fellow Common Ground Kellogg Found./U. Miami, 1993-95; primary cand. 1996 (Fla. House Rep., Dist 101). Author: Melody's of Life, 1982; editor Health Plan Baby Book, 1985; editor, pub. Legislative Update Women and Children 1st Inc., 1994—97. Former pres. Dem. Black Caucus-Dade County chpt., 1991-92; Dem. candidate Fla. Ho. Reps., 1996; mem. Planned Giving Coun. of Dade County, 1994-95; mem. Dade County Reapportionment Task Force, 1991-92. Mem.: ANA (cert. specialist family nurse practitioner), Miami Parliamentary Law Unit (pres. 1993—95, v.p. 1995—97), Nat. Assn. Parliamentarians, Fla. Nurses Assn. (legis. dist. coord. 1984—99). Democrat. Achievements include patents pending for 9-11 omega buddysack, injurvac vaccine and drawstring whizz. Avocations: drama, reading, dance, travel. Home and Office: 17 Anamosa Ct Derwood MD 20855

HOLLOWAY, BARBARA JEAN CHAMBERS, retired secondary school educator; b. Pensacola, Fla., June 23, 1938; d. Colon and Annie Bell (Mickles) Chambers; m. John Frederick Holloway Jr., May 11, 1962; Frederick Dwayne, Deloris Jeanette. BS, Bishop Coll., 1960; MEd, Cleve. State U., 1979; student, Kent State U., 1980-81. Sec. Horace Mann Jr. High Sch., Omaha, 1960-62; svc. rep. Northeastern Bell Tel. Co., Omaha, 1963-65; tchr. Pennsauken HS, NJ, 1969-72, Sawyer Bus. Coll., Cleve., 1972, John Adams HS, Cleve., 1972-73; tchr., coord. Bedford HS, 1973—89, chmn. bus. edn. dept., 1983—2000; ret., 2000; agt. Am. Gen. Life and Accident Ins. Co., Pensacola, Fla., 2006—. Part-time tchr. Cuyahoga Cmty. Coll., Warrensville, OH, 1975-85; spkr. Vocat. Edn. Div. OH Edn. Dept., 1978-79, Kent (OH) State Bus. Edn. Conf., 1979, AM Cleve. Talk Show, 1979, Bedford Rotary, 1979; bd. dirs. Saunder Office Computer Products, Inc., Solon, OH, Datalink Sys., Chagrin Falls, OH. Mem. Jay-cettes, Willingboro, NJ, 1971-72, Orange Bd. Edn. Task Force, Orange Village, OH, 1982-83; coord. Vocat. Bus. Edn. Drive-In Conf. Cleve. State U., 1974-75. Recipient Disting. Svc. award Cory United Meth. Ch., 1980. Mem. Northeastern OH Bus. Tchrs. Assn. (Tchr. of Yr. 1979, 86), Cleve. Area Bus. Tchrs. (bd. dirs., sec. 1978-80), OH Office Edn. Assn. (regional adviser 1975-78), Bus. Profls. Am., Am. Bus. Women's Assn., Pi Lambda Theta, Alpha Kappa Alpha, Phi Delta Kappa. Clubs: Couples, Funchasers Camping. Avocations: sewing, bowling, reading, golf, camping. Home: 7060 Rampart Way Pensacola FL 32505 Office: Am Gen Life and Accident Ins Co 7282Plantation Rd Ste 101 Pensacola FL 32504 Office Phone: 850-474-0023. Personal E-mail: bjch23@bellsouth.net.

HOLLOWAY, DIANE ELAINE, psychotherapist, consultant, writer; b. Tulsa, Oct. 19, 1937; d. Lawrence Lynn and Helen May (Six) Hatcher; m. 1961; children: Brian, Kathleen; m. 2d, Bob Cheney, 1980. BS, Tex. Woman's U., 1972, MA, 1974, PhD, 1979. Lic. psychotherapist, Tex. Brit. rep. Study Abroad, Inc., London, 1957-59; psychologist Presbyn. Hosp., Dallas, 1970-75, dir. psychol. svcs., assoc. dir. continuing edn. psychiatry, 1976-78; mental health/mental retardation cons. Drug Rehab. and Law Enforcement Offices, Dallas County, 1975-77; psychotherapist in pvt. practice Dallas, 1978-89; assoc. Pain Therapy Assn., Dallas, 1979-81; pres. Security & Mgmt. Sys., Dallas, 1979-81, Mental Health Profl. Group, Dallas, 1980-89; drug coord. Dallas Office of Mayor, 1989-92; vis. prof. various univs., 1993—. Author: Before You Say I Quit, 1990, The Mind of Oswald, 2000, Dallas and the Jack Ruby Trial, 2001, Analyzing Leaders, Presidents and Terrorists, 2002; contbr. newsletter, articles to profl. jours.;, editor internet sites. Hogg Found. grantee, Southwestern Med. Sch., 1972-73. Mem. APA, Am. Med. Writers Assn., Internat. Assn. Chiefs of Police, Archaeol. Inst. Am., Soc. Police and Criminal Psychology, Mensa. Office: 20402 N 150th Dr Sun City West AZ 85375-5765

HOLLOWAY, JACQUELINE, county commissioner; b. Knoxville, Tenn., Mar. 16, 1935; d. Clyde Herbert and Ernestine Cooper; m. George Rudolph Holloway, July 21, 1951; children: Lynda, George Jr., Michelle, Cheryl, Ingrid. AA in Bus., Cooper Inst., Knoxville, 1961; cert., U. Tenn. Ctr. Govt. Tng., 1990. Cert. pub. adminstr. U. Tenn. Biol. technician Oak Ridge Nat. Lab., Tenn., 1963—96; county commr. Anderson County, Clinton, Tenn., 1990—2002; with Tenn. Jud. Coun., 2004—. Chmn. Families First Coun., 1997—; vice chair Am.'s Promise, 1999—; bd. dirs. Anderson County Health Coun., 2000—, chmn., 2002, Quality Childcare Initiative, Tenn. Nutrition and Consumer Edn. Program; v.p. Coalition Oak Ridge Ret. Employees, 2000—03; v.p. cmty. problem solving United Way Anderson County; mem. Anderson County Headstart Policy Coun.; mem. exec. com. Anderson County Dems.; pres. Dem. Women, Tenn., 1996—98; v.p. Dem. Fedn., Tenn., 1996—2003; bd. dirs. Clinch River Home Health. Mem. Tenn. County Commn. Assn. (bd. dirs. 1991-2002), Tenn. County Svcs. Assn. Methodist. Home and Office: 102 Artesia Dr Oak Ridge TN 37830-7817 E-mail: G32284@aol.com.

HOLLOWAY, JENNIFER A., elementary school educator, assistant principal; b. Wichita Falls, Tex., July 28, 1978; d. Tony L. and Diane H. Walker; m. Troy G. Holloway, July 8, 2000; children: Jonas W., Troupe A. BSc in Interdisciplinary Studies, U. North Tex., Denton, 2000; M of Edn. Adminstrn., U. Tex., Arlington, Tex., 2003—04. Cert. Tchr. Tex. Bd. Edn., 2000, Prin. Tex. Bd. Edn., 2004. Asst. mgr. Winn Dixie, Denton, Tex., 1996—2000; 7th grade math tchr. Euless Jr. High, 2001—06, asst. prin., 2006—. Bd. mem. YMCA, Ft. Worth, 2006. Recipient Hugh O'Brien Youth Found. award, HS Tchrs., 1994, Prin. award, Prin. of Springtown HS, 1996; scholar, Springtown HS, 1996. Office Fax: 817-354-3345. Business E-Mail: hollowaj@hebisd.edu.

HOLLOWAY, JUDY MARIE, music educator, minister; m. Robert Wesley Holloway, June 6, 1970; children: Melinda Elizabeth, Wesley Ivan. MusB, Tex. Wesleyan U., Ft. Worth, 1970; MusM, So. Meth. U., Dallas, 1974; postgrad., Brite Div. Sch., Ft. Worth, 1996—2000. Cert. group spiritual director Shalem Inst. Spiritual Formation, dir. music Perkins Sch. Theology. Music tchr. Red Oak Ind. Sch. Dist., Tex., 1974—76, Winters Ind. Sch. Dist., Tex., 1981—84, Graham Ind. Sch. Dist., Tex., 2004—; dir. music ministries Acton United Meth. Ch., Granbury, Tex., 1984—96; worship dir. Upper Rm. Internat. Ministries, United Meth. Ch., Nashville, 1996—. Clinician for dirs. ch. music United Meth. Ch., Tex., 1984—2004; spiritual formation retreat leader various United Meth. and Disciple of Christ Chs., Tex., 1996—2003, worship cons., Tex., 1996—; coord. children's music United Meth. Ch., Graham, 2004—, mem. chamber vocal ensemble, 2005—. Soloist: various classical works. Troop leader Girl Scouts USA, Granbury; mem. arts team summer lunch program for children United Meth. Ch., Graham, 2005, deacon. Mem.: Tex. Orff-Schulwerk Assn. (assoc.), Tex. Music Educators Assn. (assoc.), Fellowship United Meth. Musicians and Worship Arts (assoc.), Chorister's Guild (assoc.), Sigma Alpha Iota (life; pres. coll. chpt. 1969—70, Deans Honor award 1970). Office Phone: 940-521-9592.

HOLLOWAY, SYBIL LYMORISE, psychologist, writer; b. NYC, Apr. 16, 1967; d. Thomas Carvin and Bannie Lymorise Holloway. BA, Smith Coll., Northampton, Mass., 1989; MA, Ind. Univ. of PA, Ind., Pa., 1991, D in Psychology, 1994. Lic. psychologist Pa. Coun. intern Univ. of Calif., Santa Barbara, Calif., 1993—94; psychol. coun., asst. prof. Bloomsburg Univ., Bloomsburg, Pa., 1999—. Bd. of dir. Smith club of Long Is., Long Is., NY, 1998—99. Recipient Fin. Aid Success Story, Nat. Assoc. of Student Fin. Aid Admin./Wash., D.C., 2000, Vol. Svc. Award, Alice Paul House/Ind., Pa., 1992, Alumnae Scholarship, Smith Coll./Northampton, Mass., 1989; fellow IUP Found. Fellowship, Ind. Univ. of Pa./Ind., Pa., 1989. Mem.: APA, AAUW, Pennwriters, Nat. Acad. Adv. Assoc., Assoc. for Women in Psychol., Pa. Psychol. Assoc. Avocations: writing, reading, tap, TV watching, stamp collecting/philately. Office: Bloomsburg Univ 400 E 2nd St (240 SSC) Bloomsburg PA 17815

HOLLOWAY, WANDA KAYE, psychotherapist, consultant; b. Mansfield, Mo., Sept. 10, 1960; d. Thomas McDonald and Patsy Jorene Smith; m. David Leigh Holloway, Sept. 7, 1996. BS, Coll. of the Ozarks, 1979—82; MEd, Univ. Ark., 1986—87; PsyD, Forest Inst. of Prof. Psychology, Springfield, Mo., 1995—2000. Vol. supr. of occupl. therapy Ozark Guidance Ctr., Springdale, Ark., 1983; outpatient counselor Decision Point, Springdale, Ark., 1983—88; therapist Charter Vista Hosp., Fayetteville, Ark., 1986—87; dir. substance abuse Burrell Behavioral Health, Springfield, Mo., 1988—99, intern, resident, 1999—2001, provisional lic. Psychologist, 2001—; therapist cons. Cox Med. Ctr., Springfield, Mo., 2003—. Mem.: Health Psychology Divsn., Am. Psychological Assn. Republican. Assembly Of God. Avocations: outdoor activities, bicycling, skeet shooting, target shooting, skiing, reading. Office: Burrell Behavioral Health 1300 Bradford Pky Springfield MO 65804 Office Phone: 417-269-5400.

HOLLY, ELLISTINE PERKINS, music educator; b. Grenada, Miss., Aug. 12, 1934; d. Addison Lampton and Anna Pearl (Powell) Perkins; m. Donald Beall, June 10, 1960 (div. June 1966); 1 child, Donna Camille; m. Kermit Wells Holly, Jr., Dec. 23, 1979. BA in Music and Piano, Fisk U., Nashville, 1955; M Music Edn., Ind. U., 1960; MusM, U. Mich., 1972, PhD, 1978. Tchr. Middleton Sr. High Sch., Tampa, 1955-58; instr. music Mary Holmes Jr. Coll., West Point, Miss., 1960-61; tchr. Jefferson Jr. High Sch., Pontiac, Mich., 1961-68; grad. asst. U. Mich., Ann Arbor, 1972-74; counselor Sch. Music, U. Mich., Ann Arbor, 1975-76; prof. music Jackson (Miss.) State U., 1976—. Vis. lectr. U. Paris, 1989, Institut du Monde Anglophone, Universite de Paris, 1989; reviewer travel grants Nat. Endowment for Humanities, 1986-87. Performing soloist Opera South Co., Jackson State U., 1983-85, U. Mich. Chamber Choir, U.S. Cultural Team to Russia, Germany, Spoleto, Italy, Opening Ceremonies Internat. Ballet Competition, Jackson, 1986, 90; editor, compiler: Biographies of Black Composers an Songwriters, 1989; contbr. articles to prol. jours.; creator, performer: (one woman show) Miss.'s African-Am. Divas. Mem. Jackson Arts Alliance, 1985—; bd. dirs. Miss. Musicians Hall of Fame, Miss. Inst. Arts and Letters, 1997-00, Miss. Opera Assn., 1998-00. Faculty rsch. scholar NEH, Harvard U., 1982, Chgo., 1985, Newberry Libr., Chgo., 1987, Ford Found., U. Miss., Oxford, 1987. Mem. Music Educators Nat. Conf., Nat. Assn. Tchrs. Singing (pres. Miss. chpt. 1984-87), Ctr. Black Music Rsch., Nat. Links, Inc., Miss. Hist. Soc., Sonneck Soc., Coll. Music Soc. (bd. dirs. so. region), Harmonica Music Club Inc. (pres. 1983-85), Delta Sigma Theta. Home: 261 Northgate Blvd Jackson MS 39206-2618

HOLLY, KRISZTINA J., entrepreneur, academic administrator; b. Mar. 1967; BS in Mech. Engring., MIT, 1989, M in Mech. Engring., 1992. V.p. Stylus (bought by Artisoft), 1993—96; with River Run Media, 1996—99, Direct Hit Technologies (acquired by Ask Jeeves in 2000), 1999—2002; founding exec. dir., Deshpande Ctr. for Tech. Innovation MIT, 2002—06; vice provost, exec. dir. U. So. Calif. Mark and Mary Stevens Inst. Tech. Entrepreneurship and Commercialization, 2006—. Judge MIT Ann. $50K Bus. Plan Competition; bd. dir. MIT Enterprise Forum. Co-author: Visual Basic Telephony; contbr. articles to profl. publs. Named to New England Mountain Bike Trail of Fame; recipient Shimano Action Figure award, Heidi Davis award. Mem.: Internat. Bicycling Assn. (bd. dir.), New England Mountain Biking Assn. (former pres.). Achievements include with MIT Media Lab team, developed the world's first computer-generated, full-color reflection hologram; co-designed and built head-eye vision robot and developed a robotic weld-seam-tracking program for the NASA space shuttle main engine; in 1991, co-wrote a business plan for MIT that won an Entrepreneurial Competition; with Michael Cassidy and John Barrus, invented and patented, "The Stylus", a system that enabled a user to scan bar codes to order items such as groceries in 1993; with Michael Cassidy and Chris Brookins, created Visual Voice, the first Windows based computer telephony development tool. Avocations: mountain biking, backcoutry skiing, recreational trail advocate. Office: U Park Campus Office of Provost University of Southern California Los Angeles CA 90089*

HOLM, CELESTE, actress; b. N.Y.C., Apr. 29, 1919; d. Theodor and Jean (Parke) H.; m. Wesley Addy, May 22, 1966 (dec. 1997); children: Theodor Holm Nelson, Daniel Schuyler Dunning; m. Frank Basile, April 29, 2004. Student, U. Sch. Girls, Chgo., Lycee Victor Durui, Paris, Francis W. Parker Sch., Chgo., Adelphi Acad., Bklyn.; DHL (hon.), Centenary Coll., 1980, Northwood U., 1981; AA (hon.), Middle Ga. Coll., 1982; ArtsD (hon.), Ea. Mich. U., 1984; DHL (hon.), Kean Coll. of N.J., 1984, Felician Coll., 1985, Jersey City State Coll., 1986; DFA (hon.), Monmouth Coll., 1987; D Liberal Arts (hon.), Fairleigh Dickinson U., 1988; D Pub. Svc. (hon.), Ea. Ill. U., 1989; DFA (hon.), Seton Hall U., 1990. Appeared in Broadway shows Gloriana, 1938, The Time of Your Life, 1939, Another Sun, 1940, Return of the Vagabond, 1940, Eight O'Clock Tuesday, 1941, My Fair Ladies, 1941, Papa Is All, 1941-42, All the Comforts of Home, 1942, The Damask Cheek, 1942-43, Oklahoma!, 1943-44, 48, Bloomer Girl, 1944-45, She Stoops to Conquer, 1949, Affairs of State, 1950-51, Anna Christie, 1952, The King and I, 1952, His and Hers, 1954, Interlock, 1958, Third Best Sport, 1958, Invitation to a March, 1960-61, Mame, 1967, Candida, 1970, Habeas Corpus, 1975-76, The Utter Glory of Morrissey Hall, 1979, I Hate Hamlet, 1991; appeared in films Three Little Girls in Blue, 1946, Gentleman's Agreement, 1947 (Acad. Award for Best Supporting Actress), Carnival in Costa Rica, 1947, The Snake Pit, 1948, Road House, 1948, Chicken Every Sunday, 1948, Come to the Stable, 1949 (Acad. Award nomination for Best Supporting Actress), Everybody Does It, 1949, Champagne for Caesar, 1950, All About Eve, 1950 (Acad. Award nomination for Best Supporting Actress), The Tender Trap, 1955, High Society, 1956, Bachelor Flat, 1961, Doctor, You've Got to be Kidding, 1966, Tom Sawyer, 1972, Three Men and a Baby, 1987, Still Breathing, 1996; other stage appearances include (tours) Hamlet, 1937, The Women, 1937-38, Back to Methuselah, 1957, Finishing Touches, 1974, Light Up the Sky, 1975, (one-woman show) Paris Was Yesterday, 1978, (other prodns.) A Month in the Country, 1963, Madly in Love, 1964, Night of the Iguana, 1964, Captain Brassbound's Conversion, 1966, Mame (nat. tour), 1967-68 (Sarah Siddons award), Hay Fever, 1979-83, Lady in the Dark (Eng.), 1981, The Trojan Women, 1985, The Road to Mecca, 1989, Love Letters, 1990, 94, The Cocktail Hour, 1990, 94, Allegro, 1994, 50th Anniversary of The Glass Menagerie, Chgo., 1994, Don Juan in Hell, Irish Rep., N.Y.C., 2000; numerous supper club appearances, N.Y.C., Chgo., San Francisco, Washington, L.A., 1943-59, (London cabaret debut) Pizza on the Park, 2003; U.S.O. entertainer, ETO, 1945; 21,000 mile tour of U.S. Army bases, 1949; TV appearances include (spls. & TV movies) Cinderella, 1965, The Shady Hill Kidnapping, 1979, Backstairs at the White House, 1979 (Emmy nomination), Nora's Christmas Gift, 1989, Polly, 1989, Polly, One Mo' Time, 1990; regular roles (series) Archie Bunker's Place, 1980-81, Falcon Crest, 1985, Loving, 1986 (Emmy nomination), 91-92, Christine Cromwell, 1989-90, Promised Land, CBS-TV, 1997-99, PBS Great Performances Talking With., 1994; guest starring roles on The Fugitive, Trapper John, M.D., The F.B.I., Disney's Wide World of Color, The Streets of San Francisco, Columbo, Medical Center, Captains and the Kings, Spencer For Hire, Magnum P.I., The Underground Man, Fantasy Island, The Love Boat, Third Watch, 2002, Whoopi, NBC-TV, 2004; radio interviewer People at the UN, 1963-65; toured with theatre-in-concert program Interplay, 1963-74; appeared in The Cole Porter 100th Birthday Celebration, Carnegie Hall, 1991. Past mem. gov. bd. U.S. Com. for UNICEF; mem. Nat. Mental Health Assn., 1965—, chmn., 1969-70; v.p. Arts and Bus. Coun.; mem. Nat. Arts Coun., 1982-88; chmn. bd. dirs. N.J. Film Commn., 1983—; bd. dirs. Mayor's Midtown Com., 1975—, Actor's Fund Am., 1988—; pres. bd. Creative Arts Rehab. Ctr., 1978—; mem. nat. vis. coun. for health scis. faculties Columbia U., N.Y.C., 1989—; mem. adv. bd. N.J. Sch. for the Arts, 1989—, adv. coun. UN Assn. of N.Y.C., 1992—; chmn. Stage South Supporting Players, S.C. State Theatre, 1977, Arts Horizons, 1995—. Decorated Dame King Olav of Norway; recipient Brotherhood award Nat. Conf. Christians & Jews, 1952, Disting. Svc. award United Jewish Appeal, 1953, Award of Merit, 1954, Achievement award Israel Bonds, 1958, Award of Appreciation March of Dimes, 1959, Hadassah, 1960, Nat. Assn. for Retarded Children award, 1961, Disting. Alumni award Francis W. Parker Sch., 1964, U.S. Com. for World Fedn. of Mental Health award, 1965, Performer of Yr. award Variety Clubs Am., 1966, Edward Strecker Meml. Medal for outstanding contbns. to mental health movement, rehab. of mentally disabled, 1971, Woman of Yr. award Anti-Defamation League, 1972, Golden Needle award Am. Home Sewing Coun., 1972, Woman of Yr. award N.Y. Variety Club, 1973, Woman of Yr. nomination Ladies Home Jour., 1975, Spirit of Am. award VFW, 1976, Woman of Yr. award Westchester Fedn. Women's Clubs, 1977, Woman of Yr. award Creative Arts Rehab. Ctr., 1977, Disting. Woman award Northwood Inst., 1977, Golden Scroll award Mayor's Midtown Citizens Com., 1979, Achievement in Arts award Northwood Inst./IASTA, 1979, Actor's Studio award, 1980, Mental Health Assn. Greater Chgo. award, 1982, Zonta Internat. Humanitarian award, 1984, Compostella award, 1984, Town Hall Friend of the Arts award, 1985, Humanitarian award Creative Arts Rehab. Ctr., 1988, Internat. Platform award, 1989, The Coalition of Arts Therapy Assn. Cert. Appreciation, 1990, Edwin Forrest award for Outstanding Contbn. to Theatre, Walnut St. Theatre, Phila., 1991, The Cardinal's Com of Laity Cardinal's award, 1991, The Ellis Island Medal of Honor, 1992, Gold medal Holland Soc. N.Y., 1994, Dorothea Dix award Mental Illness Found., 1995, Silver Circle award, 1999, The Gracie Allen award 2004; named to The Theatre Hall of Fame, 1992, Grandparent of Yr., 1997, Utah Shakespeare Festivals Imperial Order, 2000; rsch. scholar in semiotics, Claremont Grad. Sch., Calif., 1988-89.

HOLM, JOY ALICE, goldsmith, psychology professor, artist, art educator; b. Chgo., May 21, 1929; d. Alvin Herbert and Willette Eugenia (Miller) Holm. BFA, U. Ill., 1952; MS in Art Edn. Inst. Design, Ill. Inst. Tech., 1956; PhD in Edn., U. Minn., 1967. Tchr. art, Eng. West Chgo. H.S., 1952—54; instr., tchr. art J.S. Morton H.S. and Jr. Coll., Cicero, Ill., 1954—65; asst. prof. art & design Mankato (Minn.) State U., 1965—66; asst. prof. art Ill. State U., Normal, 1966—69; assoc. prof. art & design So. Ill. U., Edwardsville, 1969—71; assoc. prof. art, art edn. Winona (Minn.) State U., 1971—75; assoc. prof., chmn. dept. art St. Mary's Coll. of Notre Dame, Ind., 1975—76; assoc. prof. art & design, secondary, continuing edn. U. Wis., Eau Claire, 1976—78; assoc. prof. art & design Sch. Art & Design Kent (Ohio) State U., 1978—80; lectr. Jungian studies C.G. Jung Inst., Chgo., 1980—82; adj. assoc. prof. art edn. Sch. Art and Design, Sch. Edn. U. Ill., Chgo., 1981—82; lectr. U. Calif. Ext., Santa Cruz, 1983—; adj. prof. art edn., design San Jose (Calif.) State U., 1983—84; owner bus. designer-goldsmith Oak Park, Ill., 1980—82, Carmel, Calif., 1982—87, Atelier XII, Winona, 1988—. Curriculum cons. North Ctrl. Assn. Accreditation Team State of Ill., Edwardsville, 1970; regional cons. Supt. Pub. Instrn., Springfield, Ill., 1970; juror exhbns.; panelist, spkr., presenter confs., meetings. Contbr., cons. Alternative Medicine: A Definitive Guide, 1994; contbg. author: Living Science, 2003; contbr.

articles to profl. jours; one-woman shows at J. Sterling Morton HS & Jr. Coll., 1963, Russell Art Gallery, Bloomington, 1968, Owatonna (Minn.) Art Ctr., 1980, 86; exhbns. include La Grange (Ill.) Art League (Best of Show, 1st Place award prints), 1963-64, Minn. Mus. Art, 1974-75, Craft & Folk Art Mus., L.A., 1978, The Gallery Kent State U., 1978-79, Saenger Nat. Small Sculpture and Jewelry Exhibit, 1978, Diamonds Internat., NY, 1978, Inst. Design Alumni, 1988, Internat. Biographical Ctr. Congress Exhbn., Edinburgh, Scotland, 1994, others. Fellow World Lit. Acad.; mem. AAUP, Nat. Art Edn. Assn. (rep. Wis. Women's Caucus Houston Conf. 1978, higher edn. divsn. 1961—), Am. Assn. Higher Edn., Coll. Art Assn., Soc. N.Am. Goldsmiths, Gemological Inst. Am., C.G. Jung Inst. (Chgo.), Hon. Soc. Illustrators (hon.), Internat. Soc. Study of Subtle Energies and Energy Medicine, Inst. Noetic Scis., Order of Internat. Fellowship, Alpha Lambda Delta (hon.), Phi Kappa Phi (hon.). Methodist. Office: Atelier XII PO Box 183 Winona MN 55987-0183

HOLMAN, DEBORAH YOUNG, art educator; b. Knoxville, June 16, 1951; d. David Raymond and Dorothy Louise Young; m. Ernest Wayne Holman, Oct. 26, 1974; children: Cory Todd, Kelley Deanne. BA, Ea. Ky. U., 1973, MA, 1978. Radio operator Inter-County RECC, Danville, Ky., 1974—76; tchr. art Boyle County Bd. Edn., Danville, Ky., 1976—2006, tchr. phys. edn., 1977—2004. Ch. organist Bapt. Ch., Danville. Mem.: Boyle County Edn. Assn., Ky. Edn. Assn. Republican. Baptist. Avocations: painting, horseback riding, swimming, reading, playing the organ. Office: Boyle County Middle School 1651 Perryville Rd Danville KY 40422-9775 E-mail: n46385@kywimax.com.

HOLMAN, ILETTA MARCELLA, retired art educator; b. Wolseth, N.D., Jan. 12, 1904; d. George W. Holman and Julia Paulson. BS, U. Minn., 1939, postgrad., 1958; MS, Iowa State U., 1950. Instr. pub. sch., N.D., 1924-42, Des Moines, 1942-50, U. Moorhead, Minn., 1950-55; elem. art cons. Rochester, Minn., 1955-65; instr. Coll., Rochester, 1965-72; ret. Pres. Art Educators, Des Moines, 1947-49; asst., state dir. N.D. Ret. Tchrs., 1982-85. One-woman shows include Galerie internat. n.Y., 1970, Raymond Duncan Gallery, Paris, 1975, Washington, 1976, Chgo., 1978, Detroit, 1980, Boston, 1981. Vol. Commn. on Aging, Minot, N.D., 1980-87, Meals on Wheels, Minot, 1980-85. Mem. Nat. Mus. Women in Art (charter), Art Educators Minn. (com. chmn. 1994-97), Delta Kappa Gamma (com. chmn. 1995-97). Republican. Avocations: visual arts, painting. Home: 3456 Heritage Dr Edina MN 55435

HOLMAN, L. CHARLENE, elementary school educator; b. Broken Arrow, Okla., May 22, 1964; d. Charles Edward and Nora Mae Sutton; m. Randy Holman, Apr. 12, 1986. BS, Okla. State U., Stillwater, Okla., 1986. Lic. tchr. elem. edn. Ark., 2006. Tchr. Elmdale Elem. Sch., Springdale, Ark., 1995—, coord. title i, esl, migrant, 2000—04, coord. title i and migrant, 2004—05. Mem.: Ark. State Parent Tchr. Assn. (treas.). Home: 8501 White Oak Dr Rogers AR 72756 Office: Elmdale Elementary 420 N West End St Springdale AR 72764 Office Phone: 479-750-8859. Personal E-mail: cholman@sdale.org.

HOLMAN-RAO, MARIE, retail executive; b. 1949; Grad., Rutgers U. Pres. Perry Ellis Internat., 1986—89; v.p. creative devel. sport Adrienne Vittadini, 1989—92; sr. v.p., mgr. gen. merchandise Ann Taylor, 1992—93; v.p. product devel. Banana Republic, 1993—95, exec. v.p., 1995—97, pres., 1997; pres. design services Ltd. Brands Inc., 1997—2006, cons., 2006—. Bd. dirs. Crocs Inc., 2006—. Office: Limited Brands Inc Three Ltd Pkwy Columbus OH 43230*

HOLMBERG, LEONA ANN, oncologist; m. Drew T. Lambert, June 14, 1986. BA, Harvard Coll., Cambridge, Mass., 1973; PhD, Harvard U., Cambridge, Mass., 1984; MD, U. Miami, Miami, 1986. Assoc. mem. Fred Hutchinson Cancer Rsch. Ctr., Seattle, 2004—; assoc. prof. U. Wash., 2005—. Mem. adv. bd. Puget Sound Oncology Consort., Seattle, 2000—. Recipient Dr Ali AL-Johani award, Fred Hutchinson Cancer Rsch. Ctr., 2001. Mem.: Puget Sound Oncology Cons., SW Oncology, Am. Soc. Blood & Marrow Transplant, Am. Soc. Hematology, Am. Soc. Oncology. Office: Fred Hutchinson Cancer Research Center 1100 Fairview Ave N MS D5-390 PB19024 Seattle WA 98109-1024

HOLMBOE, SUSAN ANN, elementary school educator; b. Bremen, Ind., Sept. 17, 1949; d. John Chase and Marjorie Maxine (Sigler) Abbott; m. Lawrence Even Holmboe, Apr. 21, 1973; children: Even Jorgen, Erik Johan. Student, Chapman Coll., 1969; BA, Ariz. State U., 1971, MA, 1975. Tchr. San Pasqual Union Sch. Dist., Winterhaven, Calif., 1971-74; handicapped resource specialist Empire (Calif.) Unified Sch. Dist., 1976—. Mem. exec. com. Boy Scouts Am. troop 199, Modesto, Calif., 1986-91. Mem. Coun. Exceptional Children, Assn. Children and Adults with Learning Disabilities, Learning Disabilities Assn., Christian Women's Fellowship (pres. 1980). Democrat. Mem. Christian Ch. (Disciples Of Christ). Avocations: travel, gardening, cooking. Home: 3920 Midcrest Ct Modesto CA 95355-1128

HOLMES, ANDREA, chemistry professor, researcher; BA in Biology, minor Chemistry, U. North Fla., 1998; MS in Organic Chemistry, NYU, 2001, PhD in Organic Chemistry, 2004. Post-doctoral NIH fellowship Columbia U., 2004—05; asst. prof. chemistry Doane Coll., Crete, Nebr., 2005—. Contbr. articles to profl. jours. Achievements include working on the development of a tiny testing kit that women can carry in their purse and use to quickly detect date-rape drugs. Avocation: running. Office: Doane Coll Sci Math and Info Sci and Tech Divsn 1014 Boswell Ave Lied 229 Crete NE 68333 Office Phone: 402-826-6762. E-mail: andrea.holmes@doane.edu.*

HOLMES, ANN HITCHCOCK, journalist; b. El Paso, Apr. 25, 1922; d. Frederick E. and Joy (Crutchfield) H. Student, Whitworth Coll., 1940, So. Coll. Fine Arts, 1944. With Houston Chronicle, 1942—, fine arts editor, 1948-89, critic-at-large, 1989-98. Author: Presence, The Transco Tower, 1985, Joy Unconfined—Robert Joy in Houston: A Portrait of Fifty Years, 1986, Alley Theater: Four Decades in Three Stages, 1986. Mem. Houston Mcpl. Art Commn., 1965-74; mem. fine arts adv. coun. U. Tex., Austin, 1967—; bd. dirs. Rice Design Alliance, Houston, 1988-91, Alliance Francaise, Houston, 1989-93, Bus. Arts Fund, Houston, 1993-96. Recipient Ogden Reid Found. award for study of arts in Europe, 1953; Guggenheim fellow, 1960-61; recipient Ford Found. award, 1965, John G. Flowers award archtl. writing Tex. Soc. Architects, 1972, 74, 77, 80 Mem.: Am. Theater Critics Assn. (founding mem. 1974, exec. com. 1975—, co-chmn. 1987—88). Home and Office: 10807 Beinhorn Rd Houston TX 77024-3008 Personal E-mail: annhholmes@aol.com.

HOLMES, ANNA-MARIE, ballerina; b. Mission City, B.C., Can., Apr. 17, 1942; arrived in U.S., 1981; d. George Henry and Maxine Marie (Botterill) Ellerbeck; m. David Holmes; 1 child, Lian-Marie. Diploma, Royal Conservatory of Music. Tchr. Royal Ballet, London, 2005, Danish Ballet, Denmark, 2005, Toulous Ballet, 2005, Oslo Ballet, Norway, 2006, Royal Ballet Flanders, 2006, Atlanta Ballet, 2006, N.C. Sch. of Arts, 2006; artistic dir. Jacob's Pillow Ballet Program, 2002—06, Internat. Ballet Sch., Italy, 2006; lectr. in field. Dancer (ballets) Swan Lake, Cinderella, Romeo and Juliet, Sleeping Beauty, Bayadere, Laurencia, Paquita, Graduation Ball, Les Sylphides, Prince Igor, Giselle, Nutcracker, Firebird, Raymonda; guest appearances at numerous theatres Berlin Staarts Opera, Royal Albert Hall, London, Roy Alex, Toronto, Ont., Royal Festival Hall, London, Teatro Colon, Buenos Aires, Covent Garden, London; dancer Kirov Ballet, Leningrad, 1963, (films) Tour En L'Air, Ballet Adagio, Don Juan, Chinese Nightingale, numerous appearances on European N.Am. TV; artistic dir., prin. choreographer Tenn. Festival Ballet, Oak Ridge, 1981—, staged ballets Am. Ballet Theatre, —, Theatre of Harlem, —, Boston Ballet, 1984—, Ramonda, Am. Ballet Theatre, Met. Opera House, NYC, 2005, Corsaire, Am. Ballet Theatre, 2006, ballet mistress Ballet Theatre Francais, 1985—, tchr. Boston Ballet Co., 1985—, set Giselle Boston Ballet, 1987—; dancer Don Quixote, 1989—; mng. dir. Performing Arts/Dance Ctr., Oak Ridge, 1982—85; co-dir.: (ballets) Massimo Opera Theatre, 1993; asst. to artistic dir. Boston Ballet, 1989, dean, assoc. dir. Ctr. for Dance Edn., 1993, artistic dir., 1997—2001, guest tchr. Nervi Festival, Genoa, Italy; prodr.(film documentation): Kirov Vagonova Tchg. Sys.; artistic dir. Jackson Internat. Competition Sch., 1990, Internat. Ballet Competition Sch., 1994; choreographer Swan Lake, Tokyo, 1991, Norwegion Nat. Ballet, 1998, Sleeping Beauty Act III, Boston Ballet, 1991, Giselle, 1991, Sleeping Beauty, Boston Ballet, 1993, 1996, Tokyo, 1996, Le Corsaire, Boston Ballet, Am. Ballet Theatre, 1998, Great Performances, 1999, Met. Opera House, N.Y.C., 1999, Don Quixote, Boston Ballet, 2000; co-prodr.: Raymonda Finnish Nat. Ballet, 2003, Premier Am. Ball Theater, 2004; artistic dir. La Bayadere, Flanders-Antwerp Belgium, 2004; dir.: Jacob's Pillow Ballet Program, 2006, Ballet Adriatico, Italy, 2006. Recipient Emmy award, 2000. Office: Carnegie House 100 W 57th St Ste 11-O New York NY 10019 Office Phone: 917-365-5311. E-mail: Aellerbeck@aol.com.

HOLMES, BARBARAANN KRAJKOSKI, retired secondary school educator; b. Evansville, Ind., Mar. 21, 1946; d. Frank Joseph and Estella Marie (DeWeese) Krajkoski; m. David Leo Holmes, Aug. 21, 1971; 1 child, Susan Ann Sky. BS, Ind. State U., Terre Haute, 1968; MS, Ind. State U., 1969, specialist cert., 1976; postgrad., U. Nev., 1976—78. Acad. counselor Ind. State U., 1968-69, halls dir., 1969-73; dir. residence halls U. Utah, 1973-76; sales assoc. Fidelity Realty, Las Vegas, Nev., 1977-82; cert. analyst Nev. Dept. Edn., 1981-82; tchr. Clark County Sch. Dist., 1982-87, computer cons., adminstrv. specialist, instrnl. mgmt. sys., 1987-91, chair computer conf., 1990-92, adminstrv. specialist K-6, 1990-93; dean of student summer sch. site adminstr. Eldorado H.S., 1991-96; asst. prin. Garrett Mid. Sch., Boulder City, Nev., 1997-1999, So. Nev. Vocat. Tech. Ctr. Magnet H.S., 1999—2006; ret., 2006. Mem. leadership design team Clark County Sch. Dist., 1996—98, 2001—02, mem. dist. evaluation team, 2006—. Named Outstanding Sr. Class Woman, Ind. State U., 1969; recipient Dir.'s award U. Utah Residence Halls, 1973, Outstanding Tchr. award, 1984, Dist. Excellence in Edn. award, 1984, 86, 87, 88. Mem. AAUW, Am. Assn. Women Deans, Adminstrs. and Counselors, Am. Pers. and Guidance Assn., Nat. Assn. Sch. Adminstrs. (Clark County sch. adminstrv. sec., 2002-05), Clark County Assn. Secondary Sch. Prin. (sec. 2003-05, treas. 2005-06), Am. Coll. Pers. Assn., Alumnae Assn. Chi Omega (treas. Terre Haute chpt. 1971-73, pres., bd. officer Las Vegas 1977-81, state rush info. chair 1997-2006), Clark County Panhellenic Alumnae Assn. (pres. 1978-79), Computer Using Educators So. Nev. (sec. 1983-86, pres.-elect 1986-87, pres. 1987-88, state chmn. 1988-89, conf. chmn. 1989-92, sec. 1994-96, Hall of Fame 1995), Job's Daus. Club (guardian sec. 1995-99, dir. music 1999-2001, assisting Supreme Dep. 2001—, Bethel guardian 2005—, world youth v.p. 2004—), Order Eastern Star (worthy matron 2003-04, grand chaplin 2004-05), Phi Delta Kappa (Action award 1990-96, newspaper editor 1992-93). Achievements include developing personal awareness program U. Utah, 1973-76. Home: 1227 Kover Ct Henderson NV 89002-9017

HOLMES, CAROLYN COGGIN, museum director; b. Raleigh, N.C., Jan. 6, 1939; d. Robert Clifton and Nola (Henley) Coggin; m. David Lynn Holmes; children: Henley Madden, Catesby Coggin. BA, Wake Forest U., 1961; MAT, Duke U., 1962. Tchr. of French Needham Broughton Sr. High Sch., Raleigh, N.C., 1961-64, Washington-Lee R. High Sch., Arlington, Va., 1964-66; asst. prof. East Carolina U., Greenville, 1966-67, Campbell Coll., Buie's Creek, N.C., 1967-68; tchr. of French Tidewater Acad., Wakefield, Va., 1968-74; restoration contractor, cons. Smithfield, Va., 1972-75; exec. dir. Ash Lawn-Highland (home of James Monroe), Charlottesville, Va., 1975—. Cons. on restoration, Charlottesville, 1972—. Commr. Isle of Wight (Va.) Planning Com., 1973-77; mem. com. Shrinemont Art, Edith and Theodore Roosevelt Pine Knot Found. Mem. Am. Assn. Museums, Va. Assn. Museums (sec., coun. mem. 1985-89), Va. Assn. Presdl. Houses and Museums (sec., treas., pres. 1984—), Nat. Trust for Hist. Preservation, Assn. Presdl. Homes and Museums (pres.). Democrat. Episcopalian. Avocations: music, antiques, swimming, travel. Office: Ash Lawn-Highland 1000 James Monroe Pky Charlottesville VA 22902-8722

HOLMES, FONTAYNE, city librarian; Asst. dir. branches LA Pub. Libr., Calif., dir. ctrl. libr., dir. libr. facilities, asst. city libr., city libr., 2004—. Mem.: ALA. Office: LA Pub Libr Ctrl Libr 630 W 5th St Los Angeles CA 90071 Office Phone: 213-228-7515. Office Fax: 213-228-7519.*

HOLMES, JACQUELINE CHRISTOBEL WRIGHT, art educator; b. Chase City, Va., Aug. 17, 1947; d. James Christopher and Annie Smith Wright; m. Thomas E. Holmes, Aug. 12, 1978; children: Christal Shontre, Kimberly Monique. BS, N.C. Agrl. & Tech. State U., 1969; postgrad., Va. Commonwealth U. Art tchr. Mecklenburg County Pub. Schs., Boydton, Va., 1969—72, Richmond (Va.) City Pub. Schs., 1972—84, Fredericksburg (Va.) City Pub. Schs., 1984—. Recipient Outstanding Contbn. to Art Edn., Fredericksburg City Sch. Bd., 2006; Va. Commn. Arts grantee, 2005. Mem.: NEA, Va. Edn. Assn., Fredericksburg Edn. Assn. Democrat. Baptist. Avocation: painting. Home: 312 Durham Dr Fredericksburg VA 22407 Office: Hugh Mercer Elem Sch 2100 Cowin Blvd Fredericksburg VA 22401

HOLMES, JEAN LOUISE, real estate investor, humanities educator; b. Butler, Mo., Dec. 9, 1943; d. Victor Julius and Helen Emilia (Knapheide) Witte; m. Eugene Philmore Carter Jr., Aug. 21, 1965 (div. Aug. 1992); children: Kristin, Lance; m. Reed M. Holmes, Jan. 26, 1993. AA, Graceland Coll., Lamoni, Iowa, 1963; BA, Iowa State U., 1965; postgrad., U. Paris, 1965, Tufts U., 1973; MA in Judaic Studies magna cum laude, Hebrew Coll., Brookline, Mass., 1989; postgrad., Ratisbonne Ctr. of Judaic Studies, Jerusalem, 1993-95, Hebrew U./Yad Vashem, 1992, 95, Yad Vashem/Poland, 1998. Lic. bldg. constrn. supr. Mass. Tchr. French, Iowa, Mass., 1966-69; tchg. English lang. and lit. Iowa, 1966-67; real estate broker Carter Realty, Pepperell, Mass., 1975—; pres., mgr. Viewpax Mondiale, Independence, Mo., 1982—; pres. Keshet Hashalom, Jerusalem, 1989—. Clk. Ctrl. Middlesex Multiple Listing Svc., Concord, Mass., 1980-81, v.p., 1982, pres., 1983; lectr. Remembering for the Future II, Berlin, 1994, Internat. Holocaust Scholars Conf., Mpls., 1996; dir., adj. prof. student intercultural travel to Israel, Jordan, Egypt, Park U., Mo., Graceland U., 1982—. Co-author: The Forerunners, 2003. Adv. bd. Peace Ctr., Independence, 1989-91; interfaith rels. com. Cmty. of Christ, Independence, 2000—; dir. Maine Friendship House, 2003—; exec. com. Nat. Christian Leadership Conf. for Israel, 2001—. Recipient Friendship award Israel Ministry of Tourism, Jerusalem, 1992, Maine Preservation award, 1866 Maine Friendship House, Jaffa Am. Colony, 2004. Avocations: photography, archaeology, literature, travel. Home: PO Box 680 Pepperell MA 01463-0680 Personal E-mail: jaffacolony@mindspring.com.

HOLMES, JOAN, retired social welfare administrator; b. Jenkins Twp., Pa., Aug. 20, 1936; d. John and Eleanor Markowsky; m. Richard A. Holmes, June 14, 1958; children: Brian, Mark, Glenn, Colleen. BA, Montclair State U., 1958; gerontology cert., Rutgers U., 1994. Nursery sch. tchr. Christ Ch. Nursery Sch., Short Hills, NJ, 1971—78; tchr. Nature Discovery program Cora Hartshorn Arboretum, Short Hills, 1971—85, adult program dir., 1985—95; tchr. enrichment program Millburn-Short Hills Schs., Millburn Twp., 1980—85; asst. dir., Short Hills chpt. ARC, Millburn Twp., 1980—84; office mgr. Tanguay Assocs., Inc., Millburn, 1984—87; sr. citizen coord. Millburn Twp. Sr. Hotline Newsletter, 1988—95; dir. Sr. Ctr., Madison, NJ, 1995—2003; sr. citizen coord. Madison (N.J.) Borough, 1995—2003, ret. sr. ctr., 2003—. Editor: Sr. Prime Times, Madison Borough. Trustee New Eyes for the Needy, Short Hills, 1990-97; mem. adv. bd. Seton Hall U. Gerontology com., South Orange, N.J., 1988-95, St. Barnabas Hosp. Sr. Health, West Orange, 1988—, Essex County Coun. on Aging, East Orange, 1990-95; mem. gov.'s task force White House Conf. on Aging, Trenton, 1994; mem. Gov.'s Conf. on Aging, Trenton, 1994. Mem. Am. Soc. on Aging, Nat. Coun. on the Aging, Nat. Inst. of Sr. Ctrs., N.J. Assn. of Sr. Ctrs., N.J. Soc. on Aging. Republican. Roman Catholic. Avocations: book discussion, cooking, gardening, music.

HOLMES, KATIE (KATHERINE NOELLE HOLMES), actress; b. Toledo, Ohio, Dec. 18, 1978; d. Martin and Kathy H.; daughter with Tom Cruise, Suri. Actor: (films) The Ice Storm, 1997, Disturbing Behavior, 1998, Go!, 1999, Teaching Mrs. Tingle, 1999, Wonder Boys, 2000, The Gift, 2000, Phone Booth, 2002, Abandon, 2002, The Singing Detective, 2003, Pieces of April, 2003, First Daughter, 2004, Batman Begins, 2005, Thank You for Smoking, 2006; (TV series) Dawson's Creek, 1998—2003. Office: c/o BWR Pub Rels 9100 Wilshire Blvd West Tower 6th Fl Beverly Hills CA 90210*

HOLMES, KRISTEN JONES, academic administrator; b. Huntsville, Ala., Oct. 3, 1971; d. Donald Wayne and June Evelyn (Johnston) Jones; m. David Paul Holmes, Dec. 27, 1993. BA in Polit. Sci., Haverford Coll., Pa., 1993; MA in Journalism, U. Ala., Tuscaloosa, 1998; postgrad., Auburn U., Ala. Legal asst. St. John and St. John, Attys., Cullman, Ala., 1993—97; office mgr., editor Harold See Campaign for Ala. Supreme Ct., Tuscaloosa, 1996; rsch. asst. U. Ala., Tuscaloosa, 1998; publs. and proposals asst. PE LaMerdaux & Assocs., Environ. Cons., Tuscaloosa, 1997—99; editor Cullman.com, Cullman, 1999; exec. officer Cullman County Home Builders Assn., Cullman, 1999—2000; media rels. coord. Wallace State C.C., Hanceville, Ala., 2000—03, dir. comms. and mktg., 2004—. Adj. instr. Wallace State C.C., Hanceville, 1999—2000; pres. Cullman City Schs. Found., 2003—05; sec. Cultural Arts Com., Cullman, 2002—04; past pres. Cullman City Schs. Found., 2005—06; group leader ednl. trip to France and Spain, 2006. Coord. Adopt-a-Mile Cullman County People Against a Littered State, 2001—03; vol. caretaker family arrivals Our Lady of the Angels Monastary, Hanceville, 2003—; mem. legis. affairs com. Cullman Area C. of C., 2000. Named Media Person of Yr., Ala. C.C. Conf., 2004; named to 2006-2007 Class of Ala. C.C. Leadership Acad.; recipient Pyramid award, Ala. Coll. Sys. Pub. Rels. Assn., 2004, 2005, Medallion award, Nat. Comms., Mktg. and Publs. Assn. Dist. II, 2005. Mem.: Nat. Coll. Sect. Pub. Rels. Assn. (bd. dirs. 2004—06), Nat. Comms., Pub. Rels. and Mktg. Assn., Ala. Press Assn. Avocations: rowing, reading, running, travel, horseback riding. Home: 20424 Alabama Hwy 91 Hanceville AL 35077 Office: Wallace State C C 801 Main St NW Hanceville AL 35077

HOLMES, LEIGH ANN, web technician; b. Wilmington, Ohio, Oct. 14, 1969; Performance Diploma, Musician's Tech. Inst., Mpls., 1992; BA with honors, U. Wis., Milw., 2003. CPCU Inst. for Chartered Property Casualty Underwriters, 2000. Comml. lines underwriter Germantown (Wis.) Mut. Ins. Co., 1993—2005; web maintenance and acctg. M Roc Corp., New Berlin, Wis., 2005—. Recipient Disting. Grad. award, Inst. for Chartered Property Casualty Underwriters, 2001. Home: 10615 W Ridge Rd Apt 45 Hales Corners WI 53130 Personal E-mail: lah077@aol.com.

HOLMES, LOIS REHDER, composer, piano educator, voice educator; b. Canton, Ill., Jan. 8, 1927; d. John and Elizabeth Mary Grace (Staton) Kleinsteiber; div.; 1 child, Jessica Regina. BA in Sociology, Ill. Wesleyan U., Bloomington, 1949, MusB in Voice, Organ & Piano, 1950; MS in Reading, Western Ill. U., Macomb, 1981. Cert. tchr. Ill. Libr. worker Withers Pub. Libr., Bloomington, Ill., 1950-51; music tchr. Toledo (Ill.) Schs., 1951-52; music and art librarian Hutchinson (Kans) Pub. Libr., 1952-53; pvt. practice piano & voice tchr. various cities, Ill., 1955—. Tchr. 1st and 2d grades South Fulton Sch., Havana, Ill., 1972—81. Composer: Musical Notions, 1991, Seascape, 1993, Divertimento, 1995, Bittersweet, 1996, Buglers at Sunrise, 1997, Dream Catcher, 1998, Fourteen New Christmas Carols for the 21st Century, 1999, The Abandoned Lighthouse, 2001, Do Daisies Dream, 2003, Petals On the Pond, 2003, Dragon Mist, 2003, Giselle, The Gypsy, 2003, The Wisteria Arbor, 2005, Drifting Clouds, 2006, others. Organist/choir dir. Ctrl. Christian Ch., Havana, 1974-79; vol. March of Dimes, Chgo., 1997—, Amnesty Internat. USA, Chgo., 1993—. Mem. Nat. Guild Piano Tchrs. (adjudicator internat. piano composition contest 1996—), Phi Kappa Phi. Home: 321 Mary Alice Rd Rantoul IL 61866-2832

HOLMES, LORENE BARNES, academic administrator; b. Mineola, Tex., July 27, 1937; d. William Henry and Jessie Mae (Kelly) Barnes; m. Charles Murphy Holmes, Sr., Feb. 9, 1960 (dec.); children: Charles Murphy, Jr., James Henry, Jessyca Yvette. BS, Jarvis Christian Coll., 1959; M in Bus. Edn., U. North Tex., 1966, EdD, 1970. Dir. fin. aid Jarvis Christian Coll., Hawkins, Tex., 1966-68, asst. prof. bus., 1969-70, acting chair social and behavioral sci. divsn., 1970-71, chair social and behavioral sci. divsn., 1971-75, chair social sci. and bus. divsn., 1975-81, chair bus. adminstrn. divsn., 1981-96, exec. asst. to pres., 1996—98, exec. asst. to v.p., 1998—99, dir. Alumni Reclamation Program, 1999—2000, dir. career mgmt. svc., 2000—04, dir. student support svc., 2004—05, dir. Upward Bd. Program, 2005—06, dir. career planning and placement, 2006—. Nat. treas. Nat. Alumni Assn., Hawkins, 1960; exec. asst. to pres., 1996-98, 98-99; dir. alumni rec. profl., 1999-2000; dir. career mgmt., 2000-. Editorial reviewer Communication in Business, 1989; contbr. articles to profl. jours. Bd. dirs. Hawkins Helping Hands, 1987-93, Allen Meml. Pub. Libr., Hawkins, 1988-94; mem. Bethlehem United Methodist Church. Recipient Recognition plaque Nat. Urban League, N.Y.C., 1989, T.A. Abbott Teaching award Christian Ch., Indpls., 1988, Presdl. citation NAFEO; inductee Pioneer Hall of Fame, Jarvis Christian Coll., 1994, Tex. Bus. Educator Yr. award; honored by Nat. Alumni Assn. Dallas chpt. at Heritage Scholarship Banquet. Mem. AAUW, Nat. Bus. Educators Assn., Tex. Bus. Educators Assn. (Bus. Tchr. of Yr. award Dist. 8), Jarvis Christian Coll. Alumni and Ex-Students Assn. (life, Dist. Alumni Educator of Yr. award), Top Ladies of Distinction Inc. (Lady of Yr. award), Hawkins C. of C. (charter), Delta Sigma Theta (Golden life mem., S.W. Gen. Educator of Yr. award 1991), Delta Pi Epsilon (life). Democrat. Mem. United Methodist Ch. Avocations: reading, writing, sewing, Scrabble. Home: PO Box 858 Hawkins TX 75765-0858 Office: Jarvis Christian Coll PO Box 1470 Hawkins TX 75765-1470 Office Phone: 903-769-5795. Personal E-mail: lholmes@tyler.net.

HOLMES, MIRIAM H., publisher; b. Bavaria, Germany, June 2, 1951; came to U.S., 1952; d. Max J. and Mala (Rosenwasser) H.; m. Stephen H. Gelb, June 25, 1995. BA, Queens Coll., 1972; JD, Yeshiva U., 1987. Bar: N.Y. 1988. Pres. Holmes & Meier Pub., N.Y.C., 1990—. Mem. Assn. Jewish Book Coun. (bd. dirs.), Pubs. Mktg. Assn. Office: PO Box 943 Teaneck NJ 07666 Office Phone: 201-833-2270. Business E-mail: info@holmesandmeier.com.

HOLMES, NANCY ELIZABETH, pediatrician; b. St. Louis, Aug. 3, 1950; d. David Reed and Phyllis Anne (Hunger) Holmes; m. Arthur Erwin Kramer, May 15, 1976; children: Melanie Elizabeth Kramer, Carl Edward Kramer. BA in Psychology, U. Kans., 1972; MD, U. Mo., 1976. Diplomate Am. Acad. Pediatrics. Intern., resident in pediatrics St. Louis Children's Hosp., Washington U., St. Louis, 1976-81; pediatrician Ctrl. Pediatrics, St. Louis, 1981—. Sch. physician Sch. Dist. Clayton, Mo., 1985—92; asst. prof. clin. pediats. Washington U., St. Louis, 1993—2000, assoc. prof., 2000—; cons. 1st Congregational Preschool, Clayton, 1984—86, Jewish Hosp. Daycare Ctr., St. Louis, 1993—97, Flynn Park EArly Edn. Ctr., University City, Mo., 1994—; cmty. outpatient experience Preceptor Hosp., St. Louis Children's Hosp., 1991—93, 1994—; mem. med. exec. com. St. Louis Children's Hosp., 1992—94. Vol. reading tutor Flynn Park Sch., University City, 1992—98, cub scout leader, 1993—98; mem. com. Troop 493 Boy Scouts Am., 2000—; elder Trinity Presbyn. Ch., University City, 1989—92, 1996—2001, Webster Groves Presbyn. Ch., 2006—; bd. dirs. Children's Hosp. Care Group. Fellow Am. Acad. Pediatrics; mem. AMA, Mo. State Med. Assn., St. Louis Metro. Med. Soc, St. Louis Pediatric Soc. Presbyterian. Avocations: reading, gardening, photography, travel. Office: Ctrl Pediatrics Inc 8888 Ladue Rd Ste 130 Saint Louis MO 63124-2056 Office Phone: 314-862-4002.

HOLMES, PAULA ANN, elementary school educator; d. Victor Amundus and Ann Lynn Johnson; m. Thomas Louis Holmes, June 24, 1972 (div. Oct. 20, 1984); children: Brooke Ann, Bethany Christine. BA in Edn., Pacific Luth. U., Tacoma, 1971; MA in Edn., Lesley Coll., Cambridge, Mass., 1997. Cert. tchr. Wash. 1st grade tchr. Mt. Erie Elem. Sch., Anacortes, Wash., 1971—75; kindergarten tchr. Fidalgo Elem. Sch., Anacortes, 1975—76; 2d and 3d grade tchr. Island View Elem. Sch., Anacortes, 1981—2001, Title I reading specialist, 2002—; summer sch. coord. Anacortes Sch. Dist., 2003—04. Site supr, VISTA and reading corps vols. Wash. Svc. Corps, Olympia, 2004—. Mem. choir First Evang. Luth. Ch., Mt. Vernon, 1975—2006. Recipient Outstanding Educator award, Island View PTA, 2004. Mem.: NEA, Anacortes Edn. Assn. (bldg. rep. 2002—04), Wash. Edn. Assn. Avocations: attending cultural events, reading, needlework, music, exercise. Home: 1410 Mallard View Dr # 2 Mount Vernon WA 98274 Office: Island View Elem Sch 2501 J Ave Anacortes WA 98221 Office Phone: 360-293-3149. Business E-Mail: pholmes@asd103.org.

HOLMES, SANDRA, insurance underwriter; b. Boston, May 1, 1957; d. Edward and Ruth Ada (Hedman) H. Cert. ins. counselor Soc. Cert. Ins. Counselors, Profl. Ins. Woman. Workers comp. underwriter Indsl. Indemnity, Anchorage, 1976-77; acct. exec. asst. Alexander & Alexander, Anchorage, 1977-79; rating dept. supr. Providence Washington, Anchorage, 1979-81; acct. exec. asst. Erickson Ins., Anchorage, 1981-83; underwriting dept. supr. Alaska Nat. Ins., Anchorage, 1983-85; prodn. underwriter Cigna Ins. Co., Anchorage, 1985-92; sr. comml. underwriter Umialik Ins. Co., Anchorage, 1992—. Mem. Alaska Classification and Rating Com., Anchorage, 1994-96 Mem. edn. team Partnership Coun. on Safety, Anchorage, 1996-97; mem. Alaska Women's Resource Ctr., Amvets Aux., Anchorage; vol. Kids Voting, Anchorage, fire safety booth Alaska State Fair, 1997. Mem. Nat. Assn. Ins. Women (region IX Ins. Mem. of Yr. 1999, Communicate with Confidence 1st Runner Up 1999), Ins. Assn. Alaska, Soc. Cert. Ins. Counselors, Ins. Women Anchorage (Insurance Woman of Yr. 1998, past pres.). Avocations: advocate for women's rights, writing, reading, researching family history.

HOLMES, SERENA NICOLE, pre-school educator; b. Richmond, Va., June 24, 1980; d. George Elvis and Darlene Alexander Holmes. MS, U. Va., 2002; M Tchg., Va. Commonwealth U., 2005. Tchr. Pooh Corner Childcare, Ashland, Va., 2002—05. Mem.: Nat. Coun. Tchrs. Math., Va. Assn. Sci. Tchrs., Nat. Assn. Sci. Tchrs. Democrat. Avocations: reading, exercise.

HOLMES, SUZANNE MCRAE, nursing supervisor; b. Birmingham, Ala., June 23, 1952; d. Paul Bickman and Mabel E. (Tyler) McRae; m. Bryan Thomas Holmes, Jan. 14, 1989; 1 child, Meredith Rae. ADN, Jefferson State Coll., Birmingham, 1988. RN, Ala.; cert. BCLS instr.; cert. asthma educator, Am. Lung Assn. Staff nurse burn unit The Children's Hosp., Birmingham, 1988-89; staff nurse dept. medicine The Kirklin Clinic at U. Ala.-Birmingham, 1989-90, head nurse gen. medicine clinic, 1990-91, head nurse allergy clinic, 1991—2006, head nurse for pulmonary/allergy clinic, 2002—06, head nurse for pulmonary/allergy, PFT, Gastroenterology and Endoscopy Clinic, 2004; ret., 2006; head nurse Birmingham Allergy and Asthma Specialists, P.C., 2006—. Facilitator and spkr. on nursing at asthma workshops Aventis Pharms., Collegeville, Pa., 1994—; mem. faculty Genecom, N.Y.C., 1994—; operator 1-800 Allergy Info. Svc., 1991—92. Editor Allergy Update, 1991-92. Leader Girl Scouts Am., 1998—2004. Mem. Am. Coll. Allergy and Immunology, Am. Acad. Allergy, Asthma and Immunology,mem. Am. Lung Assn. (cert. asthma educator), Asthma and Allergy Found. Am. (charter bd. dirs. Ala. chpt.), Assn. Asthma Educators. Methodist. Avocations: baking, sewing, gardening. Office: Birmingham Allergy and Asthma Specialists PC 7191 Cahaba Valley Rd Ste 203 Birmingham AL 35242 Office Phone: 205-943-1197.

HOLMES, WILHELMINA KENT, community health nurse; b. Hamburg, N.J., Nov. 26, 1920; d. Harry Vanderhoof and Alison St. Clair (McDole) Kent; m. George Frederick Holmes Jr., Oct. 27, 1946 (dec. 1971); 1 child, Frederick Andrew. RN, Jersey City Med. Ctr., 1942; BSN, Seton Hall U., South Orange, N.J., 1953; cert., Bridgewater State Coll., 1961, Fitchburg State Coll., 1962; postgrad., Russell Sage Coll., Troy, N.Y., 1981-82. Sch. nurse, maternal child health nurse N.J. State Health Dept., Sussex County, N.J., 1947-53; acctg. asst. Bennington (Vt.) Coll., 1982-83; infirmary nurse Berkshire Farm Ctr. and Svcs. for Youth, Canaan, N.Y., 1982-86; emergency call nurse Blair Acad., Blairstown, N.J., 1989-94, clin. nurse, night nurse, 1994. Contbr. articles to profl. jours. Mem. Berkshire Farm Ctr. and Svcs. for Youth, Canaan. Mem. Jersey City Alumni Assn.

HOLMES, WILLA B., writer, former educator; b. Sterling, Colo., July 18, 1929; d. Arthur Bruce and Zelma DeForest Robbins; m. Thomas A. Holmes, June 26, 1948; children: Michael deForest, Steven T., Christina Holmes-Baker, David AA, Mt. Hood C.C., 1969; BS, Portland State U., 1971, MS Edn., 1975. Reporter, photographer Aurora Advocate, Colo., 1961—64; tchr. h.s. Portland Pub. Schs., Oreg., 1966—87. Author: She Who Watches, 1997; contbr. short stories to anthologies Foster parent Colo. Family and Children's Svcs., Denver, 1957-64, Oreg. Juvenile Justice, Portland, 1968-72; vol. East Multnomah County, Oreg., 1950-98, LWV Aurora Co., 1950-64, 65-98; bd. dirs. Friends Multnomah County Libr., Portland, 1994-99 Mem.: SCBWI, Willamette Writers. Avocations: photography, gardening, travel.

HOLMES-DAVIS, TINA, music educator; b. Colorado Springs, Colo., Feb. 1, 1978; d. Wally and Janet Holmes; m. Edward J. Davis, July 22, 2000; children: Emma Davis, Jonah Davis. MusB in Edn., Ga. Coll. and State U., Milledgeville, 2000; MEd, Auburn U., Ala., 2002. Band dir. Babb Mid. Sch., Forest Park, Ga., 2002—. Mem.: Music Educators Nat. Conf., Ga. Music Educators Assn., Pi Kappa Lambda, Phi Kappa Phi, Sigma Alpha Iota (Sword of Honor 2000). Office Phone: 404-608-2625. Personal E-mail: tinamarie1978@yahoo.com.

HOLMGREN, ANNA, psychiatrist; BS, U. S.C., Columbia, 1987; MD, Med. U. S.C., Charleston, 1992. Lic. M.D. Mass., Calif., N.Y., 1993. Pvt. practice, N.Y.C., 2002—06; attending psychiatrist Mt. Sinai Hosp., N.Y.C., 2002—. Mem.: APM, Am. Psychiat. Assn. Office: 30 East 60th St #1002 New York NY 10022 E-mail: aih2001@hotmail.com.

HOLOMAN, CONSTANCE CURRIER, academic administrator; d. Raymond Richard and Frances Harris Currier; m. Christopher Louis Holoman; children: Alair Currier, Frances Highsmith. AB, U. NC, 1976; MEd, Colo. State U., 1978. Dir. student housing U. Chgo., 1982—89; adminstr. Nat. Ctr. Geographic Info. & Analysis, Buffalo, 1990—93; asst. to pres. ops. sys. & accounts U. Buffalo, 1993—99, asst. to pres. univ. rels., 1999—2003, dep. to pres., 2003—06, asst. v.p. univ. rels., 2006—. Loaned exec. United Way Buffalo and Erie County, 1995, mem. cmty. investment team, 1996—2001, cmty. schs. task force, 2001—03; advisor United Way Emerging Leaders Soc., Buffalo, 2002—04; dir. Summit Ednl. Resources, Buffalo, 2002—; bd. dirs. United Way of NY State, 2005—; various leadership roles Asbury United Meth. Ch., Amherst, NY, 1990—. Democrat. Methodist. Avocations: acting, cooking, reading, winter sports, college basketball. Business E-Mail: cch@buffalo.edu.

HOLSCHER, CAROL ANN, retired secondary school educator; b. Denver, Aug. 23, 1935; d. Gerald John and Marcella Ann (Thillman) H. BS in Edn., U. Detroit, 1962; MEd, Bowling Green U., 1969. Cert. comprehensive bus. edn., cert. permanent high sch. standard. Tchr. Our Lady Queen of Heaven Elem. Sch., Detroit, 1955-64, Cardinal Stritch HS, Toledo, 1964-71, Tiffin Columbian HS, Ohio, 1971—; ret., 1996. Mem. faculty cons. team Tiffin Columbian High Sch., 1991-92. Co-author: (geneal. rsch.) Original Land Entries of Seneca County, Ohio, 1992. Former sec. Seneca County Geneal. Soc., Tiffin, cemetery rsch. com. mem., 1990-92, ch. records survey mem., 1990-92. Mem. Tiffin Edn. Assn. (former sec.). Democrat. Roman Catholic. Avocation: genealogy. Home: 169 Gibson Ct Tiffin OH 44883-3378

HOLSINGER, ADENA SEGUINE, music educator, community volunteer; b. Fostoria, Ohio, Aug. 8, 1926; d. Richard and Della Mable (Fry) Seguine; m. John Calvin Holsinger; 1 child, Coradella Elizabeth. BS in Edn., Ind. Wesleyan U., 1948. Cert. tchr., Ohio. Tchr. Canyonville (Oreg.) Christian Acad., 1948-50; music tchr. Ctrl. Bible Coll., Springfield, Mo., 1951—55, 1976—77; tchr. Bowling Green (Ohio) H.S., 1956-58; pvt. practice Costa Mesa, Calif., 1961—71, Springfield, Mo., 1971—. Pres., treas. Evangl. U. Aux., Springfield, 1984-2003. Mem.: DAR (vice regent 1994—96, regent 2001—02), Springfield Area Music Tchrs. Assn. (treas. 2000—, membership chmn. 2000—), Springfield Piano Tchrs. Forum (pres. 1989, sec. 1999), Nat. Fedn. Music Clubs (dist. coord. 1989—91), Springfield Federated Music Club (pres. 1979—81), Mo. Fedn. Music Clubs (state treas. 1980—87, state sec. 1987—89, regional v.p. 1991—99), Springfield Christian Women's Club (project advisor 1996—, treas.). Republican.

HOLT, AMANDA C., lawyer; AB magna cum laude, Harvard Coll., 1993; JD, Yale Law Sch., 1996. Bar: Mass. 1997. Law clk. to Hon. Miriam Goldman Cedarbaum US Dist. Ct. (So. Dist. NY); ptnr. Tax and Benefits Dept. Ropes & Gray LLP, Boston. Mem.: ABA, Boston Bar Assn. Office: Ropes & Gray LLP One International Place Boston MA 02110-2624 Office Phone: 617-951-7409. Office Fax: 617-951-7050. E-mail: amanda.holt@ropesgray.com.*

HOLT, BERTHA MERRILL, state legislator; b. Eufaula, Ala., Aug. 16, 1916; d. William Hoadley and Bertha Harden (Moore) Merrill; m. Winfield Clary Holt, Mar. 14, 1942; children: Harriet Wharton Holt Whitley, William Merrill, Winfield Jefferson. AB, Agnes Scott Coll., 1938; postgrad., U. N.C. Law Sch., 1939-40; LLB, U. Ala., 1941; grad., Sch. Creative Leadership, Greensboro, N.C., 1992. Bar: Ala. 1941. With Treasury Dept., Washington, 1941-42, Dept. Interior, Washington, 1942-43. Mem. N.C. Ho. of Reps. from 22d Dist., 1975-80, 25th Dist., 1980-94, chmn. select com. govtl. ethics, 1979-80, chmn. constl. amendments com., 1981, 83, mem. joint commn. govtl. ops., 1982-88, chmn. appropriation com. justice and pub. safety, 1985-88, co-chair House appropriation sub-com. transp., 1991-92, co-chair appropriation sub-com. Justice and Pub. Safety, 1993-94. Pres., Dem. Women of Alamance, 1962, chmn. hdqrs., 1964, 68; mem. N.C. Dem. Exec. Com., 1964-75, 95—; pres. Episcopal Ch. Women, 1968; mem. coun. N.C. Episcopal Diocese, 1972-74, 84-87, 95-98; chmn. budget com. 1987; chmn. fin. dept., 1973-75, parish grant com., 1973-80, mem. standing com., 1975-78; mem. Episcopal Diocese Eccles. Ct., 1998-2002; vestry mem. Ch. of Holy Comforter, 2005—, mem. bd. NC coun., 2005—; chmn. Alamance County Social Svcs. Bd., 1970; mem. N.C. Bd. Sci. and Tech., 1979-83; chair Legis. Women's Caucus, 1991-94; past bd. dirs. Hospice N.C.; bd. dirs. State Coun. Social Legis., pres. SCSL 1996-97, State Conf. Social Work, N.C. Epilepsy Assn., N.C. Pub. Sch. Forum, 1989, U. N.C. Sch. Pub. Health Adv. Bd., Salvation Army Alamance County, N.C., Nursing Found., 1989, Epilepsy Found., 1989; bd. Alternatives for Status Offenders Burlington, N.C., Sch. Pub. Health Adv. Bd.; bd. dirs. N.C. ACLU, Partnership For Children (N.C.), 1993-98; mem. Alamance County Home Health ADv. Bd., 2005-06; bd. dirs. Ctrl. Carolina Planned Parenthood. Recipient Outstanding Alumna award Agnes Scott Coll., 1978, Legis. award for svc. to elderly Non-Profit Rest Home Assn., 1985, health, 1986, ARC, 1987, Faith Active in Pub. Affairs award N.C. Coun. of Chs., 1987, Ellen B. Winston award State Coun. For Social Legis., 1989, N.C. Disting. Women's award in gov., 1991, Disting. Svc. award Alamance County, 1992, Chi Omega award Women in Leadership, 1st ann. Hallie Ruth Allen Dem. Women award Alamance County, 1992, Disting. Svc. award Chi Omega, 1996, Svc. award Triennial Conv., Episcopal Ch. Women of U.S., 1997, Outstanding Alumna award U. N.C.-Chapel Hill, 1998, Gwyneth B. Davis award N.C. Assn. Women Attys., 1998, Outstanding Svc. award N.C. Assn. Women Attys., 1998, Disting. Alumna award U. N.C.-Chapel Hill, 1999, AAUW award for Edn. and Equity for Women and Girls, 2004, Lifetime Achievement 200 award Alamance County Dem. Party, 2004, Award for Outstanding Svc., N.C. Sr. Dems., 2005; numerous others; named One of 5 Disting. Women of N.C. (Govt.), 1991; award established Bertha B. Holt award, NC Bar Juvenile Justice Sect., first recipient, 2004; honored as Legis. and Scholair award Jeannette Rankin Assn. N.C. Women, 2005. Mem. AAUW, NOW, N.C. Women's Forums, Law Alumni Assn. U. N.C. Chapel Hill (bd. dirs. 1978-81, 1994-99), N.C. Bar Assn. (bd. dirs. sr. lawyers sect., constnl. rights sect. 1998-04, 05, juvenile justice and children's rights 1999-, chair 2002-03), English Speaking Union, N.C. Hist. Soc., Soc. Wine Educators, Les Amis du Vin, Pi Beta Phi, Phi Kappa Gamma, Delta Kappa Gamma, Phi Theta Kappa, Century Club. Address: PO Box 1111 Burlington NC 27216-1111 Personal E-mail: bholt66@triad.rr.com.

HOLT, CHIFRA, dancer, educator, choreographer, artist; b. NYC, June 8, 1933; d. Harry Halebsky and Fannie Kaminsky; m. Maroin David Willis, May 19, 1984 (div.); 1 child, Eve Jaffe. BA, CCNY, 1963; MA, UCLA, 1972. Lifetime tchg. credential in cmty. coll. Calif., lic. real estate broker. Mem. dance faculty Smith Coll., Northampton, Mass., 1965—67; asst. prof., acting chair dance U. South Fla., Tampa, 1968—70; adj. prof. dance San Francisco State U., 1975—77; artistic dir., owner Chiefra-Leveque Dance Ctr., San Francisco, 1976—79; assoc. prof. dance, chair Wichita State U., Kans., 1979—82; mem. dance faculty De Anza Coll., Cupertino, Calif., 1983—92, Mira Costa Coll., Oceanside, Calif., 1993—98. Choreographer (solo) Tongue of Sulence, 1953, Dark Fiesta, 1965, Awakening Desert, 1972, Scenes of Men and Women, 1976, Night Mysteries, 1978, Holiday Celebration, 1979, Ripples of Joy, 1981, Beauty and the Beast, 1982, Welcome Spring, 1983, Celestial Vibrations, 1988, Seasons of My Life, 1996, Ragtime A La Carte, 1998, dancer Merry-Go-Rounders, NYC, 1955—57, Pearl Lang Dance Co., 1957—59; lead dancer, performer Paul Sanasaido Dance Co., NYC, 1958—63; stained glass exhibits. Helpline counselor U. Calif., LA, 1971—72; bd. dirs. Corona Hist. Preservation Soc., Calif., 2005—. Grantee San Francisco State U., 1976, Met. Arts Bd., Wichita, 1979, Kans. Arts Commn., 1981. Mem.: Mensa. Avocations: theater, dance, reading, gardening, gourmet dining. Studio: 3681 Alvarado Cir Corona CA 92882 Office Phone: 909-228-4043. Personal E-mail: chifra2000@sbcglobal.net.

HOLT, FRIEDA M., nursing educator, retired academic administrator; BSN with honors, U. Colo., Boulder, 1956; MS in Cmty. Health Nursing, Boston U., 1969, EdD, 1973. RN, Ariz., Calif., Colo., Mass., Md., Pa., Wash., Liberia, W. Africa. Instr., dir. of nursing Cuttington Coll., Liberia, Africa, 1964-67; teaching fellow sch. of nursing Boston U., 1969, asst. prof. sch. of nursing, 1969-74; assoc. prof., assoc. dean for grad. studies sch. of nursing U. Md., 1975-77, dean's dep. sch. of nursing, 1975-86, prof., assoc. dean for grad. studies sch. of nursing, 1977-86, acting dean sch. of nursing, 1978, acting asst. dean sch. of nursing, 1981-82, acting chmn. sch. of nursing, 1983-84, acting dean sch. of nursing, 1986-87, prof., assoc. dean for grad. studies, dean's dep. sch. of nursing, 1987-88, prof., exec. assoc. dean. sch of nursing, 1988-89, acting dean, prof. sch. of nursing, 1989-90, prof. sch. of nursing, 1990-91, prof., dir. sch. of nursing, 1992—94; dir. grad. programs Pa. State Sch. Nursing, 1994—2000; ret., 2000. Project dir. Primary Care Adult Nurse Practitioner Leadership grant, 1976-82, Preparation for Tchrs. in Maternal Child Nursing, judge U. Md. grad. sch. rsch. awards, 1979-84; author, project dir. Pa. State PhD Nursing Program Grant; NLN vis. for Accreditation of Baccalaureate and Masters Nursing Program, SREB/SCCEN Task Force on Grad. Edn., presenter seminars, confs., workshop; prof. emeritus U. Md. Sch. Nursing, 2006. Contbr. articles to profl. jours. Bd. dirs. Md. Nurses Found. (v.p., 1988—). Recipient VA Commendation award, 1990, Charter Trustee award Found. for Nursing of Md., 1990, Martin Luther King, Jr. Humanitarian award, 1990; named Pa. Nurse Educator of Yr., 1998. Mem. ANA, ANA (coun. nurse rschrs.), APHA, AAUP, Nat. League for Nursing, Am. Edn. Rsch. Assn., Am. Edn. Rsch. Assn., Md. Assn. for Higher Edn., Soc. for Rsch. in Nursing Edn., Sigma Theta Tau. Home: 151 Woodpecker Ln Port Matilda PA 16870 Personal E-mail: fmh16@hotmail.com.

HOLT, HELEN, librarian, consultant, former government official; b. Gridley, Ill., Aug. 16, 1913; d. William Edward and Edna (Gingerich) Froelich; m. Rush Dew Holt, June 19, 1941 (dec. Feb. 1955); children: Helen Jane Seale, Rush Dew Holt Jr. AA, Stephens Coll., Columbia, Mo., 1932; BA, Northwestern U., 1934, MS, 1938; postgrad., U. Mo., U. N.C., George Washington U., Marine Biol. Lab., Woods Hole, Mass. Sci. librarian, instrl. asst. Stephens Coll., 1934—37; instr. biology Nat. Park Coll., Forest Glen, Md., 1938—41; instr. sci. Greenbrier Coll., W.Va., 1955—58; mem. W.Va. Ho. of Dels., 1955—57; sec. of state W.Va., 1957—59, asst. commr. pub. instns., 1959—60; spl. asst. to commr., dir. mortgage ins. program for constrn. long term care facilities FHA, 1960—70; asst. to sec., dir. elderly programs Dept. Housing and Urban Devel., 1970—84; mem. adv. bd. Small Bus. Adminstrn., 1986—90. Cons. in field. Contbr. articles to profl. jours. Del.-at-large, vice chmn. platform com. State of W.Va. Rep. Nat. Conv., 1958; sr. citizen vol. Rep. Nat. Com., 1984; elder local Presbyn. Ch., 1975—, bd. trustees 1968-74, 80-86, bd. deacons, 1988-94; bd. dirs. Thompson Markward Hall, Nat. Alliance Sr. Citizens, Nat. Safety Council, exec. com. Women's div. 1975-87, chmn. 1987. NSF fellow, 1956; recipient Community Svc. Human Rights award, UN Assn., 1985, Stephens Coll. Alumnae award. Fellow Am. Coll. Health Care Adminstrs. (Community Svc. award 1978); mem. Am. Health Care Assn., Nat. League Am. PEN Women (br. pres., nat. chaplain), Washington Forum (pres.), Potomac Bus. and Profl. Women (pres. 1983, Woman of the Yr. 1978), Gen. Fedn. Women's Clubs (state v.p. 1989—, other offices), The Washington Club, Sigma Delta Epsilon, Sigma Xi, Delta Delta Delta (dist. pres.), Zeta Mu Epsilon (nat. pres.), Zonta (bd. dirs.). Republican. Presbyterian. Home and Office: 2500 Virginia Ave NW Apt 1107 Washington DC 20037-1901 Personal E-mail: hfholt@aol.com.

HOLT, ISABEL RAE, radio program producer; b. Vineland, N.J., Oct. 5, 1946; d. Frederick Rae and Isabella A. (Foley) Steinborn; m. Robert Eugene Darby, Aug. 13, 1977 (div. 1999); children: Rachel Elisabeth Darby, Nora Odette Darby. BA in Primary Edn., Rowan U (formerly Glassboro State Coll.), 1968; postgrad., Pierce Coll., 1991-93. Dir., coord. Washington Area Free U., 1972-74; prodr. music program Sta. WGTB Georgetown U., Washington, 1972-74; prodr. music program Sta. WMGM, Atlantic City, N.J., 1974, Sta. KJAZ, Alameda, Calif., 1974-76, Sta. KPFA, Berkeley, Calif., 1974-76, Sta. KCRW, Santa Monica, Calif., 1977-88, Sta. KPCC, Pasadena, Calif., 1989-93; program dir. Boise Cmty. Radio, Idaho, 2004—06. Concert prodr.; interviewer radio programs, 1980-95; prodr. tapes for dressage/equestrian free-style riders, 1994—, riding instr., trainer, 1999-2001; riding instr. Spl. Olympics, 1999. Mem. ACLU, Amnesty Internat., Childreach, Sierra Club. Independent. Office: 1519 N 23rd St Boise ID 83702-0409 Personal E-mail: irea4343@msn.com.

HOLT, LESLIE EDMONDS, librarian; b. Mpls. d. Peter Robert and Elizabeth Knox (Donovan) Edmonds; m. Glen Edward Holt, Jan. 29, 1994. BA, Cornell Coll., 1971; MA, U. Chgo., 1975; PhD, Loyola U., Chgo., 1984. Asst. children's libr. Indian Trails Libr. Dist., Wheeling, Ill., 1972-73; libr. Erikson Inst. for Early Edn., Chgo., 1973-75; youth svcs. libr. Rolling Meadows (Ill.) Libr., 1975-82; libr. multicultural head start resource ctr. Chgo. Pub. Libr., 1982-84; asst. prof. grad. sch. libr. and info. sci. U. Ill., Urbana, 1984-90, assoc. dean, 1988-89; dir. youth svcs. and family literacy St. Louis Pub. Libr., 1990—. Pre-sch. advisor Rolling Meadows (Ill.) Park Dist., 1978-85; cons. to reading program The Latin Sch., Chgo., 1980-82; vis. lectr. Loyola U. of Chgo., 1980-84, U. Ill. Extension, Belleville, 1992; product mgr. Mister Anderson's Co., McHenry, Ill., 1981-84; instr. Nat. Coll. Edn., Evanston, Ill., 1982-84, Webster U., Webster Groves, Mo., 1991; cons. for libr. devel. Ill. Math. and Sci. Acad., Aurora, Ill., 1986-90; peer reviewer, advisor U.S. Dept. Edn. Office Edn. Rsch. and Improvement, 1987-89; libr. cons. Reading Rainbow Resources Guide, Sta. WNET-TV, N.Y.C., 1987, 88; adj. instr. U. Mo., Columbia, 1991, 92, 93; literary advisor Grace Hill Neighborhood Svcs., 1991-95; cons. Paschen-Tishman-Jahn, 1988; presenter in field. Author: An Investigation of the Effectiveness of an On-Line Catalog in Providing Bibliographic Acccess to Children in a Public Library Setting, 1989, Family Literacy Programs in Public Libraries, 1990; contbr. articles to profl. jours. Mem. Success by Six Com., United Way of Met. St. Louis, 1993—. Grantee in field. Mem. ALA (mem. Carroll Preston Baber award jury 1992-94, World Book award 1986), Nat. Assn. Edn. Young Children, Internat. Reading Assn., Mo. Libr. Assn. (mem. summer reading program com. 1991, mem. Mark Twain award com. 1992), USA Toy Libr. Assn. (charter mem.), Assn. Libr. Svc. to Children (mem. toys, games and realia evaluation com. 1983-85, chair local arrangements 1984-85, chair rsch. com. 1985-88, mem. Randolph Caldecott com. 1987, mem. software evaluation 1988-89, mem. svc. to children with spl. needs 1989-91, chair Charlemae Rollins pres. program 1990-91, active, 1991, chair edn. com. 1991-93, 93—, bd. dirs. 1993-96, v.p., pres.-elect 1997-98, pres. 1998-99, past pres. 1999-2000), Children's Reading Round Table (mem. spl. award com. 1987-88). Office: St Louis Pub Lib 1301 Olive St Saint Louis MO 63103-2325

HOLT, MARJORIE SEWELL, lawyer, retired congresswoman; b. Birmingham, Ala., Sept. 17, 1920; d. Edward Rol and Juanita (Felts) Sewell; m. Duncan McKay Holt, Dec. 26, 1946; children: Rachel Holt Tschantre, Edward Sewell, Victoria. Grad., Jacksonville Jr. Coll., 1945; JD, U. Fla., 1949. Bar: Fla. 1949, Md. 1962. Pvt. practice, Annapolis, Md., 1962; clk. Anne Arundel County Circuit Ct., 1966-72; mem. 93d-99th Congresses from 4th Dist. of Md., 1973-86, mem. budget com., 1975—88, mem. joint econ. com., 1980; armed svcs. com., vice-chair Office Tech. Assessment, 1977; chair Rep. Study com., 1975-76; of counsel Smith, Somerville & Case, Balt., 1986-90. Supr. elections Anne Arundel County, 1963-65; del. Rep. Nat. Conv., 1968, 76, 80, 84, 88; mem. Pres.'s Commn. on Arms Control and Disarmament, Gov.'s Commn. on Carefirst, 2003; mem. ind. commn. USAR; bd. dirs. Annapolis Fed. Savs. Bank; adv. bd. Crestar; co-chair George W. Bush Presdl. campaign, Md., 2000. Co-author: Case Against The Reckless Congress, 1976, Can You Afford This House, 1978; mem. Fla. Law Rev., 1947. Bd. dirs. Md. Sch. for the Blind, Hist. Annapolis Found. Recipient Disting. Alumna award U. Fla., 1975, Trustees award U. Fla. Coll. Law, 1984, Alumnae Outstanding Achievement award, 1997. Mem. ABA, Md. Bar Assn., Anne Arundel Bar Assn., Phi Kappa Phi, Phi Delta Delta. Presbyterian (elder 1959). E-mail: Duncan_Holt@hotmail.com.

HOLT, MILDRED FRANCES, special education educator; b. Lorain, Ohio, July 30, 1932; d. William Henry and Rachel (Pierce) Daniels; B.S., U. Md., 1962, M.Ed., 1967, Ph.D., 1977; m. Maurice Lee Holt, Sept. 11, 1949 (dec.); children— Claudia, Frances, William, Rudi. Tchr. spl. edn. St. Mary's (Md.) County Public Schs., 1962-64, coordinator Felix Johnson Spl. Edn. Center, 1964-66; demonstration tchr. spl. edn. U. Md., College Park, summer 1970, instr. spl. edn. dept. Coll. Edn., 1969-73; supr. spl. edn. Calvert and St. Mary's (Md.) Counties, 1968-69; asso. prof. spl. edn. W. Liberty (W.Va.) State Coll., 1973-75; asst. prof. Eastern Ill. U., Charleston, 1975-77; supr. spl. edn. Warren County Public Schs., Front Royal, Va., 1977-85; spl. edn. tchr. Dallas Ind. Sch. Dist., 1985. Mem. NEA, Warren County Edn. Assn., Council Exceptional Children, Assn. for Gifted, Assn. Supervision and Curriculum Devel., Va. Edn. Assn., Va. Council Exceptional Children, Blue Ridge Orgn. Gifted and Talented, Assn. Children with Learning Disabilities, Nat. Assn. Gifted Children, Phi Theta Kappa, Kappa Delta Pi. Contbr. articles to profl. jours.; author: Reach Guidebook, 1979. Home: 2916 Sidney Dr Mesquite TX 75150-2253 E-mail: mholt@texas.net.

HOLT, PATRICIA ANNETTE, retired music educator; d. Macie Louise Holt. BM in organ, Youngstown State U., 1975; MA in tchg., Mary Grove Coll., 2000. Music specialist Warren City Sch., Ohio; ret. Avocations: reading, gardening. Home: 3170 Halsey Drive NE Warren OH 44483 Personal E-mail: pattiholt@aol.com.

HOLT, THELMA, theatrical producer; Doctorate (hon.), Middlesex U., UK, 1994; MA (hon.), Open U., UK, 1998; companion (hon.), Liverpool Inst. for Performing Arts, UK, 2002; DLitt (hon.), U. East Anglia, UK, 2003; emeritus fellow (hon.), St. Catherine's Coll., Oxford U., UK, 2003. Founder The Open Space Theatre, Eng.; dir. The Round House, Eng.; prodr. Royal Nat. Theatre, Eng., 1985-89; exec. prodr. The Peter Hall Co., Eng., 1989-90; founder, prodr., mng. dir. Thelma Holt Ltd., England, 1990—; assoc. prodr. Royal Shakespeare Co., England, 2004—. V.p. Citizens Theatre, Glasgow; dir. and chmn. Young Prodr. Bursary Panel Stage One; Cameron Mackintosh Prof. Contemporary Theatre Oxford U., 1998; dir. Almeida Theatre, 2001—; chmn. Yvonne Arnaud Theatre, 2002—05. Prodr. plays Orpheus Descending, The Merchant of Venice, Three Sisters, Hamlet, Electra, The Clandestine Marriage, The Glass Menagerie. Mem. ct. Middlesex U. Recipient Laurence Olivier/Observer award for Outstanding Achievement, Tyrone Guthrie Award for Best Prodn., Shakespeare Globe Classic Awards, 1993, Award for Excellence Intern. Theatre, British Intern. Theatre Inst., 1994, Tony Award for Best Revival (for A Doll's House), 1996, Order of the Rising Sun, Gold Rays and Rosette, Japanest govt., 2004. Mem. Arts Coun. of Eng., Drama Panel (chmn.). Office: Thelma Holt Ltd Waldorf Chambers 11 Aldwych London England WC2B 4D G E-mail: tholt@dircon.co.uk.

HOLT BALIS, CAROLYN M., secondary school educator; b. Cleve., Feb. 1, 1964; d. James R. and Regina S. Holt; m. Timothy G. Balis, June 27, 1987. BS in Secondary Edn., U. Akron, Ohio, 1987; MEd, Cleve. State U., 1992. Cert. master instr. Microsoft. Computer educator Cuyahoga Heights Bd. Edn., Ohio, 1988—; multimedia instnl. designer Cleve. Clinic, 2006—. Author: (online course) Intermediate Excel, 2006. Mem.: Ohio Bus. Tech. Assn., Cleve. Arts Bus. Tchr. Assn. Republican. Baptist. Home: 244 Kennedy Blvd Northfield Village OH 44067 Office: Cuyahoga Heights Bd Edn 4820 E 71st St Cuyahoga Heights OH 44125

HOLTE, DEBRA LEAH, investment company executive, financial analyst; b. Madison, Wis. BA, Concordia Coll., Moorhead, Minn., 1973. Chartered Fin. Analyst, Cert. Divorce Planner. Capital markets specialist 1st Bank Mpls., 1981-83; v.p. Allison-Williams Co., Mpls., 1983-86; exec. v.p. Hamil & Holte Inc., Denver, 1986-93; pres. Holte & Assocs., Denver, Taos, N.Mex., 1993—. Active Denver Jr. League, Western Pension Com., 1986—; bd. dirs. Denver Children's Home, 1987—, treas., 1987-91, chmn. fin. com., 1987-91, v.p., 1990—, chmn. nominating com., 1991—, pres.-elect, 1994-95, bd. pres., 1995—; adv. bd. Luth. Social Svcs., 1987; co-chair U.S. Ski Team Fundraiser; bd. dirs. Minn. Vocat. Edn. Fin., Mpls., 1984-86; bd. dirs. Colo. Ballet, 1988-93, chair nominating com., 1991-93, v.p., 1992-93, chmn. bd., 1993; mem. Fin. Analyst Nat. Task Force in Bondholder Rights, 1988-90; bd. dirs. Ctrl. City Opera Guild, 1994-95, Western Chamber Ballet, 1994-96, Taos Humane Soc., 1997—; social co-chmn. The Arapahoe Fox Hunt, 1993-94; bd. dirs., mem. steering com. Denver Dumb Friends League, 2001-, mem. exec. com., 2004-, mem. audit com., 2004-; mem. exec. com., chair devel. com. Dumb Friends League, 2005—. Mem. Fin. Analysts Fedn., Denver Soc. Security Analysts (bd. dirs. 1990-97, chair ethics and bylaws com. 1987—, chair edn. com. 1988, chair membership com. 1989, rec. sec. 1990, sec. 1991, treas. 1992, program chair 1993, pres. 1994-95, dir. 1995-96).

HOLTER, PATRA JO, artist, consultant; b. Ashland, Wis., Mar. 6, 1936; d. Cap and Sigrid (Gadda) H. BS, U. Wis., 1958; MA, U. Calif., Berkeley, 1962; student, Nat. Acad. Art and U. Oslo, 1963; cert. in adminstrn., Fairfield U., 1983; postgrad., New Sch. Social Rsch., UCLA, U. Colo., Pratt Inst. Cert. tchr., N.Y., Wis., adminstr., N.Y. Art tchr. Herricks Jr. H.S., New Hyde Park, N.Y., 1958-60; assoc. art U. Calif., Berkeley, 1961-62; adult art tchr. U. Calif. Alumni Camp, Pinecrest, summer 1961; elem. art tchr. Ctrl. Sch., Mamaroneck, N.Y., 1964, Edgewood Sch., Scarsdale, 1971-82; elem. and jr. H.S. art tchr. Quaker Ridge Sch., Scarsdale, N.Y., 1964-70; art tchr. Scarsdale Sr. H.S., 1982-84, chmn. art dept., 1984-93; dist. visual arts supr. Scarsdale Sch. Sys., 1989-93. Art tchr. workshops, curriculum developer, cons. in field, liaison Scarsdale; visual arts coord. Lincoln Ctr. Inst., N.Y.C., 1978-80; liaison art tchr. Westchester Coun. for Arts, Scarsdale, 1970's. Author, artist: Photography Without a Camera, 1972, reprinted 1980; contbr. articles, photographs to profl. publs.; group and solo exhbns. include Wis. Salon of Art, Madison, 1958, Worth Ryder Gallery, Berkeley, 1962, Am. Embassy, Oslo, 1963, Mount Mercy Coll. Gallery, Cedar Rapids, Iowa, 1988, Silvermine Galleries, 1994-2006, Waveny Carriage Barn, New Canaan, 1995-97, Washburn (Wis.) Arts and Cultural Ctr., 1995-2006, Northland Coll., Ashland, 1996-99, Meridian Internat. Ctr., Washington, 1997, Tweed Mus. Art, Duluth, Minn., 1997-99, Ct. Graphic Arts Ctr., Norwalk, 1997-98, Wis. Arts Bd. Internat., Madison, 1999, Manhattan Borough Pres.'s Gallery, N.Y.C., 2001, Madeline Island Art Guild, LaPointe, Wis., 2003, Riverfront Art Ctr., Stevens Point, Wis., 2003-06. Fulbright scholar, Norway, 1962-63, ext., summer 1963; recipient Exemplary Media award N.Y. Regents Adv. Coun., 1968; Scarsdale Sch. Sys. grantee, 1972. Mem., midwest rep. Fulbright Arts Task Force; mem. Fulbright Assn., Norwegian Fulbright Assn., Silvermine Guild of Art, N.Y. State United Tchrs. Assn., Am. Fedn. Tchrs., Nat. Mus. Women in Arts, N.Y. State Ret. Tchrs., Ashland Hist. Soc., Ashland Alliance for Sustainability, Chequamegon Bay Area Arts Coun., New Canaan Soc. for Arts, Wilton Garden Club, Nat. Coun. State Garden Clubs, Kappa Delta. Avocations: travel, horticulture, antiques. Home: 8 Grumman Ave Wilton CT 06897-4614

HOLTHAUSEN, MARTHA ANNE, interior designer; b. Columbus, Ohio, Oct. 28, 1934; d. Clyde Aloysius and Olive Letitia (Marlowe) Gloeckner; m. Don Trudeau Allensworth, Aug. 14, 1960 (div. 1976); 1 child, Karen Ayn; m. Ernest Arthur Holthausen, Dec. 9, 1989. BFA cum laude, Ohio State U., 1956; postgrad., Baldwin-Wallace Coll., Berea, Ohio, 1959, Mt. Vernon Coll., Washington, 1980, 81. Fashion illustrator The Marston Co., San Diego, 1956-57, The Higbee Co., Cleve., 1957-58; instr. art Lakewood (Ohio) Pub. Schs., 1958-60; tchr. Princes Georges County (Md.) Pub. Schs., 1960; account exec. Stansbury Design, Inc., Prince Georges County, Md., 1975-76; interior designer Berwin Interiors, Bethesda, Md., 1977-79, W. & J. Sloane, Inc., Washington, 1980-84; pres., interior designer Martha Allensworth Interior Design, Inc., Easton, Md., 1984—. Guest artist-in-residence Nat. Park Svc., Yosemite Nat. Park, Calif., summer 1988, 89, 91, 95; mem. Working Artists Forum, Easton, Md., 2003—; mem. Plein Air Painters of Ea. Shore, Md., 2005—. Watercolor and oil paintings in pvt. collections. Bd. dirs. C. of C. Herndon, Va., 1985-86; v.p. Montgomery County (Md.) Art Assn., 1962-63. Lutheran. Avocations: gardening, watercolor and oil painting.

HOLTKAMP, SUSAN CHARLOTTE, elementary school educator; b. Houston, Feb. 23, 1957; d. Clarence Jules and Karyl Irene (Roberts) H. BS in Early Childhood Edn., Brigham Young U., Provo, Utah, 1979, MEd, 1982. Cert. tchr. Utah, ESL endorsement U. Utah, 2002. 2d grade tchr. Nebo Sch. Dist., Spanish Fork, Utah, 1979-84, kindergarten tchr., 1984-85; tchr. 2d grade DODDS, Mannheim, Fed. Republic Germany, 1985-86; tchr. 3d grade Jordan Sch. Dist., Salt Lake City, 1987-92, tchr. 5th grade, 1992—2002, tchr. 6th grade, 2002—, dir. sch. choir, 1998—. Mem. NEA, JEA, ASCD, Utah Edn. Assn.

HOLTON, GRACE HOLLAND, accountant; b. Durham, N.C., Sept. 14, 1957; d. Samuel Melanchthon and B. Margaret (Umberger) Holton. BS in Math., U. N.C., Greensboro, 1978; MBA, U. N.C., Chapel Hill, 1984; M. Acctg., U. Ill., 1993. CPA NC, cert. mgmt. acct., internal auditor. Indsl. engr. Burlington Industries, Inc., Mayodan, NC, 1978—79, plant indsl. engr. Stoneville, NC, 1979—80; methods indsl. engr. Blue Cross and Blue Shield of N.C., Durham, 1980—82; fin. analyst R.J. Reynolds, Inc., Winston-Salem, NC, 1984—85; accounting cons. Ryder Truck Rental, Inc., Miami, Fla., 1985—88; contr. Ryder Jacobs (divsn. Ryder Distbn. Resources), Jessup, Md., 1988—90; grad. asst. in acctg. U. Ill., Urbana, 1990—93; contr. Salem NationaLease, Winston-Salem, 1993—94; fin. officer Chapel Hill-Carrboro City Schs., 1994—99; mgr. benefits and payroll Ryder Pub. Transp. Svcs., Cin., 1999—2000; exec. dir. budget and evaluation Charlotte-Mecklenburg Schs., 2000—02; instr. acctg. Alamance C.C., Graham, NC, 2003—. Scholar KPMG-Peat Marwick scholar, 1991—92. Mem.: AICPA, Inst. Internal Auditors, N.C. Assn. CPAs, Inst. Mgmt. Accts. Democrat. Methodist.

HOLTON, LESLI BELFLOWER, music educator; d. Charles Leon Belflower and Barbara Ann Rose; m. George Thomas Holton, July 9, 1988. AA in Music, Abraham Baldwin Coll., Tifton, Ga., 1992; MusB in Edn., Valdosta State U., Ga., 1994, MusM in Edn., 2002. Cert. tchr. music K-12 Ga., 1994. Flautist/performer Valdosta Symphony Orch., Ga., 1993—96; young musicians dir. First Bapt. Ch., Chula, Ga., 1994—; music appreciation tchr. Valwood Sch., Valdosta, Ga., 1994—95; flautist/performer Mannheim Musicians, Tifton, Ga., 1997—; choral music/gen. music tchr. Berrien County Mid. Sch., Nashville, Ga., 1997—2000; choral music tchr. Worth County Mid. Sch., Sylvester, Ga., 2000—; creative dir. Tifton Choral Soc., Ga., 2003—; flautist/performer Albany Symphony Orch., Ga., 2003—. Cons. Worth County Arts Alliance, Sylvester, 2006—. Dir.(Worth County Mid. Sch. treble choir): Festival of Gold (7th Pl. Nat. Title, 2006), Heritage Festival (1st Pl. Concert Choir Divsn., 2005), Southern Star Music Festival (Gold Rating, 2003). Mem.: Nat. Assn. Tchrs. Singing, Nat. Flute Assn., Ga. Music Educators Assn., Music Educators Nat. Conf., Sigma Alpha Iota. Office Phone: 229-776-8620.

HOLTON, LISA, writer, editor, researcher; BS in Journalism, Northwestern Univ., 1981; student med. editing, writing cert. program, Univ. Chgo., 2003. Reporter, editor Chgo. Sun-Times, 1981—96, bus. editor, 1992—93; founder Card Mktg., 1996—97; editor Business Journalist newsletter, 1998—99; founder The Lisa Co., Evanston, Ill., 1998—. Author: How to Be a Value Investor, 1999, Essential Dictionary of Real Estate, 2003. Mem.: Am. Med. Writers Assn., Am. Soc. Journalists & Authors, Internat Assn. Bus. Communicators. Office: The Lisa Co 2327 Brown Ave Evanston IL 60201 Office Phone: 847-869-7106. Business E-Mail: Lisa@TheLisaCo.com.

HOLTON, LISA, publishing executive; Graduate cum laude, Colgate Univ. Asst., spl. sales to mgr. sub rights, dir., prod. devel. Frederick Warne, dir. mktg., Puffin Books Viking Penguin, 1984—90; v.p., dir. mktg., merchandise devel. to v.p., assoc. pub., editor-in-chief HarperCollins Children's Books, 1990—96; v.p., pub. Hyperion Books for Children, Disney Press, 1996—99; group pub. Disney Children's Books, 1999—2001; sr. v.p., pub. Global Disney Books, 2001—05; pres. book fairs and trade, exec. v.p. Scholastic Inc., NYC, 2005—. Office: Exec VP Scholastic Inc 555 Broadway New York NY 10012 Office Phone: 212-343-6100.

HOLTZ, DIANE, retail executive; Divsnl. v.p. Bloomingdale's; v.p. career merchandise and tops Ann Taylor, mgr. gen. merchandise, sr. v.p.; v.p. spl. projects design svcs. Limited Brands, Inc., 2000—02; pres. Limited Stores, Limited Brands Inc., 2002—. Office: Limited Stores Three Ltd Pkwy Columbus OH 43230

HOLTZ, SARA, marketing consultant; b. LA, Aug. 7, 1951; BA, Yale U., 1972; JD, Harvard U., 1975. Bar: D.C. 1975, Calif. 1982. Assoc. Brownstein, Zeidman & Schomer, Washington, 1975-77; dep. asst. dir. FTC, Washington, 1977-82; divsn. counsel Clorox Co., Oakland, Calif., 1982-90; v.p., dep. gen. counsel Nestle U.S.A., Inc., San Francisco, 1990-94; prin. Client Focus, 1996—. Mem. Am. Corp. Counsel Assn. (bd. dirs. 1986-95, chmn. 1994-95). Office: 5320 Olive Tree Ct Granite Bay CA 95746-9484

HOLTZCLAW, DIANE SMITH, elementary education educator; b. Buffalo, May 26, 1936; d. John Nelson and Beatrice M. (Salisbury) Smith; m. John Victor Holtzclaw, June 27, 1959; children: Kathryn Diane, John Bryan. BS in Edn. magna cum laude, SUNY, Brockport, 1957, MS with honors, 1961; postgrad., SUNY, Buffalo, 1960-65, Canisus Coll., 1979, Nazareth Coll., 1981-82. Tchr. Greece Cen. Sch., Rochester, N.Y., 1957-60; supr. SUNY, Brockport, 1960-64, assoc. prof. edn., 1960-64; dir. Early Childhood Ctr., Fairport, N.Y., 1968-80; tchr. Fairport Cen. Schs., 1971—; ednl. cons. in field; specialist child devel. Ch. music dir., Rochester, N.Y., 1983—; pres. bd. dirs. Downtown Day Care Ctr., Rochester, 1974-83; mem. exec. bd. Rochester Theatre Organ Soc., 1988—. Mem. Fairport Edn. Assn. (exec. bd. 1982-83, del. 1983), N.Y. State United Tchrs., AAUW (exec. bd. 1973-74, 77-79, 83-84, pres. Fairport br. 1971-73), Internat. Platform Assn., Kappa Delta Pi. Home: 1455 Ayrault Rd Fairport NY 14450-9301 Office: Fairport Cen Schs 38 W Church St Fairport NY 14450-2130

HOLTZMAN, ELIZABETH, lawyer; b. Bklyn., Aug. 11, 1941; d. Sidney and Filia Holtzman. AB magna cum laude, Radcliffe Coll., 1962; JD, Harvard U., 1965; L.D.S., Regis Coll., 1975, Skidmore Coll., 1980, Simmons Coll., 1981, Smith Coll., 1982. Bar: N.Y. 1966. Assoc. Wachtell, Lipton, Rosen, Katz & Kern, N.Y.C., 1965-67; asst. to mayor N.Y.C., 1968-69; assoc. Paul, Weiss, Rifkind, Wharton & Garrison, 1970-72; mem. 93d-96th Congresses from 16th dist., N.Y.; vis. prof. Law Sch. and Grad. Sch. Pub. Adminstrn. NYU, 1981; dist. atty. Kings County, Bklyn., 1982-89; comptr. City of N.Y., 1990-93. Mem. Am. Jewish Commn. on the Holocaust, Nazi and Japanese War Criminal Records Interagency Working Group, 1999—; Dem. nominee U.S. Senate, 1980; N.Y. State Dem. committeewoman, 1970—72; mem. Pres.'s Nat. Commn. on U.S. Observance Internat. Women's Yr., Helsinki Watch Com., 1981—88, Select Com. on Immigration Policy, 1979—80; bd. overseers Harvard U., 1976—82; trustee Radcliffe Coll., 1999, Bklyn. Acad. Music Endowment Trust, 1999—; mem. Lawyers Com. Internat. Human Right, 1981—88. Recipient Nat. Coun. Jewish Women's Faith and Humanity award, YWCA Elizabeth Cutter Morrow award, Maccabean award N.Y. Bd. Rabbis, Alumni recognition award Radcliffe Coll. Alumnae Assn., 1973, N.J. and L.A. ACLU awards for contbns. to def. of Constn. and preservation of civil liberties, 1981, Athena award N.Y.C. Commn. on Status of Women, 1985, Woman of Yr. award N.Y. League Bus. and Profl. Women, 1985, Jan Korzak award 5th Ann. Kent State Holocaust Conf., 1986, Outstanding and Meritorious Svc. award Jewish War Vets. of U.S., 1986, Award of Remembrance Warsaw Ghetto Resistance Orgn., 1987, Gates of Freedom award State of Israel Bonds, 1987; Award of Honor United Jewish Appeal, 1988, Deed of Tzedakah award, 1991. Fellow N.Y. Inst. Humanities; mem. Assn. of Bar of City of N.Y., Nat. Women's Polit. Caucus (Outstanding Svc. award 1987), Phi Beta Kappa. Office: Herrick Feinstein LLP 2 Park Ave New York NY 10016-9302 Office Phone: 212-592-1400.

HOLTZMAN, MARY, engineering company executive; b. Sanford, Fla., Mar. 16, 1948; d. James Emory and Johnie Ruth (Hardy) McElhannon; m. Calvin Douglas Crenshaw, Sept. 1969 (div. July 1977); 1 child, Christa Ashlee Crenshaw; m. Dean Ward Hillegass, Sept. 1978 (div. July 1986); m. Joel Richard Holtzman, Jan. 12, 1990. BFA, U. Ga., 1972. Draftsman, designer Patterson & Dewar Engrs., Decatur, Ga., 1973-84; drafting supr. Mosler/Am. Standard, Norcross, Ga., 1984-86; GIS dept. mgr. Patterson & Dewar Engrs., Decatur, 1986—. Mem. DAR, Lake Jackson Homeowners Assn., Am. Assn. Ret. Persons, U. Ga. Alumni Assn., Peachtree Handspinners Guild, Red Hat Soc. Democrat. Avocations: photography, painting, internet design, reading, travel. Home: 3144 Caintal Ct Decatur GA 30033-1804 Office: Patterson & Dewar Engrs Inc 850 Center Way Norcross GA 30071 Office Phone: 770-453-1410. Business E-Mail: mholtzman@pd-engineers.com. E-mail: maryholtzman@mindspring.com.

HOLTZMAN, ROBERTA LEE, French and Spanish language educator; b. Detroit, Nov. 24, 1938; d. Paul John and Sophia (Marcus) H. AB cum laude, Wayne State U., 1959, MA, 1973, U. Mich., 1961. Fgn. lang. tchr. Birmingham (Mich.) Sch. Dist., 1959—60, Cass Tech. H.S., Detroit, 1961-64; from instr. to prof. French and Spanish, Schoolcraft Coll., Livonia, 1964—84, chmn. French and Spanish depts., 1984—2004, adj. prof. French, 2004—05, prof. emerita French and Spanish, 2005—. Trustee Cranbrook Music Guild, Ednl. Community, Bloomfield Hills, Mich., 1976-78. Fulbright-Hays fellow, Brazil, 1964. Mem. AAUW, NEA, MLA, Nat. Mus. Women in Arts (co-founder 1992), Am. Assn. Tchrs. of Spanish and Portuguese, Am. Assn. Tchrs. of French, Mich. Edn. Assn. Avocations: swimming, book collecting, photography, travel. Office: Schoolcraft Coll 18600 Haggerty Rd Livonia MI 45152-2696 Business E-Mail: rholtzma@schoolcraft.edu.

HOLWAY, SUSAN E., writer; b. Ilwaco, Wash., Dec. 26, 1944; d. Theodore Woodruff Holway and Ruth Virginia Tartar; m. Richard J. Pakener, 1984. BA, Wash. State U., Pullman, 1967; MA, Portland State U., Oreg., 1988. Tchr. Ocean Beach Sch. Dist., Ilwaco, 1967—74, part-time tchr., 1974—79; corr. Tribune, Ilwaco, 1974—82; editor Finn-Am. Lit. Heritage Found., Portland, 1983—84; grad. tchg. asst. theater dept. Portland State U., 1983—84; freelance writer, 1998—. Prof. Clatsop CC, Astoria, Oreg., 1988—94; ptnr. Holway Family Bus., Oysterville, Wash., 1998—; corr. Chinook Observer, Long Beach, Wash., 1998—. Founder, chmn., co-chmn. program com. Finnish-Am. Folkd Fest, Naselle, Wash., 1982—; mem. com. Ocean Park United Meth. Ch., Wash., 1995—; bd. dirs. Ocean Beach Sch. Dist., Ilwaco, 1992—2000, Finn Fest USA, Mpls., 2002—. Mem.: AAUW, Mentor Club (v.p., sec. 2001—). Democrat. Avocations: walking, birdwatching, gardening, reading, travel. Home: 33614 Territory Rd Oysterville WA 98641 E-mail: puhusch@willapabay.org.

HOLYER, ERNA MARIA, adult education educator, writer, artist; b. Weilheim, Bavaria, Germany, Mar. 15, 1925; d. Mathias and Anna Maria (Goldhofer) Schretter; m. Gene Wallace Holyer, Aug. 24, 1957 (dec. 1999). AA, San Jose Evening Coll., 1964; student, San Mateo Coll., 1965—67, San Jose State U., 1968—69, San Jose City Coll., 1980—81; DLitt, World U., 1984; DFA (hon.), The London Inst. Applied Rsch, 1992. Freelance writer under pseudonym Ernie Holyer, 1960—; tchr. creative writing San Jose (Calif.) Met. Adult Edn., 1968—. Exhibited in group shows at Crown Zellerbach Gallery, San Francisco, 1973-4, 76-77; I.B.C. Gallery, San Francisco, 1978 (medal of Congress, 1988, 89, 92, 94, Congress Challenge trophy, 1991), L.A., 1981, Cambridge, Eng., 1992, Cambridge, Mass., 1993, San Jose, Calif., 1993, Edinburgh, 1994, San Francisco, 1996; author: Rescue at Sunrise, 1965, Steve's Night of Silence, 1966, A Cow for Hansel, 1967, At the Forest's Edge, 1969, Song of Courage, 1970, Lone Brown Gull, 1971, Shoes for Daniel, 1974, The Southern Sea Otter, 1975, Sigi's Fire Helmet, 1975, Reservoir Road Adventure, 1982, Wilderness Journey, Golden Journey, California Journey, 1997, Self-Help for Writers: Winners Show You How, 2002, Dangerous Secrets: A Young Girl's Travails Under the Nazis, 2003, Survival: An Electrifying Tale, 2004; contbr. articles to mags. and newspapers Recipient Woman of Achievement Honor cert. San Jose Mercury-News, 1973, 74, 75, Lefoli award for excellence in adult edn. instr. Adult Edn. Senate, 1972, Women of Achievement awards League of Friends of Santa Clara County Commn., San Jose Mercury News, 1987, various art awards. Mem. N.L.A.P.W. Inc., World Univ Roundtable (doctoral). Home and Office: 1314 Rimrock Dr San Jose CA 95120-5611 Personal E-mail: holyerE@aol.com.

HOLYFIELD-VEGA, DORETTA JOYCE, religious studies educator; b. Birmingham, Ala., Feb. 9, 1960; d. Andrew Holyfield and Dora Lee Leonard; m. Jose Vega-Garcia, Jan. 26, 1980; children: Monretta Labrisa Vega, Jose Vega, III. AA, Ctrl. Tex. Coll., 1993; student, Ala. A&M U., 2006—. Cert. Sun. sch. tchr. Tchr. Messages For The Spirit Min., Huntsville, Ala., 1998—. Dir. Messages for The Spirit Tutoring, Huntsville, 2004—. Author: (book) Messages for the Spirit (from a sinner) Luke 18:13, 2000. Vol. Montview Elem. Sch., 1995—2002; mem. Wall of Tolerance, Montgomery, Ala., 2006, Nonprofit Resource Ctr. Ala., 2006. With U.S. Army, 1978—83. Decorated Army Svc. ribbon U.S. Army, Good Conduct medal, Overseas ribbon; recipient Cert. Achievement, Montview Elem. Sch., 1995—2002. Avocations: writing, singing, sewing, cooking, rollerskating. Office Phone: 256-651-6262.

HOLZER, JENNY, artist; b. Gallipolis, Ohio, July 29, 1950; d. Richard Vornholt and Virginia (Beasley) H.; m. Michael Andrew Glier, May 21, 1984; 1 child. Student, Duke U., 1968-70, U. Chgo., 1970-71; BFA, Ohio U., 1973, DA (hon.), 1994; MFA, RI Sch. Design, 1977; postgrad., Whitney Mus. Am. Art, 1977; DFA (hon.), RI Sch. Design, 2003, Williams Coll., 2000, New Sch. U., NYC, 2005. Resident artist Am. Acad., Rome, 2003. One-woman shows include Rüdiger Schöttle Gall, München, 1980, Barbara Gladstone Gallery, NYC, 1983, 86, 94, Kunsthalle, Basel, Switzerland, 1984, Des Moines Art Ctr., 1986, MIT, Cambridge, 1986, Mus. Contemporary Art, Chgo., 1987, Inst. Contemporary Art, London, 1988, Bklyn. Mus., NYC, 1988, DIA Art Found., NYC, 1989, Guggenheim Mus., NYC, 1989, Am. Pavilion, 44th Biennale, Venice, Italy, 1990, La. Mus., Humlebaek, Denmark, 1991, Albright-Knox Art Gallery, Buffalo, 1991, Walker Art Gallery, Mpls., 1991, Ydessa Hendeles Art Found., Toronto, 1992, Dallas Mus. Art, 1993, Haus der Kunst, Munich, 1993, Bergen Mus. Art, Norway, 1994, Art Tower Mito, Japan, 1994, Williams Coll. Mus. Art, Williamstown, Mass., 1995, Kunstmus. des Kantons Thurgau, Kartouse Ittingen, Warth, Switzerland, 1996, Contemporary Art Mus., Houston, 1997, Cheim & Read, NY, 1997, Yvon Lambert Gallery, Paris, 1998, 2004, Inst. Cultural Itau, São Paulo, Brazil, 1998, Centro Cultural Banco do Brasil, Rio de Janeiro, 1999, BALTIC Ctr. Contemporary Art, Gateshead, 2000, Neue Nat. Galeri, Berlin, 2001, Mus. Contemporary Art, Bordeaux, France, 2001, Monterrey, Mex., 2001, Mönchehaus Mus., Goslar, Germany, 2002, Monika Sprüth Philomene Magers, 2002, 04, Kunsthaus Bregenz, Austria, 2004, NYC, 2005, others; exhibited in group shows at Documenta 7, Kassel, Germany, 1982, Contemporary Arts Ctr., Cin., 1984, Mus. Art Carnegie Inst., Pitts., 1985, Israel Mus., Jerusalem, 1986, Frankfurter Kunstverein, Frankfurt, Germany, 1986, Europa/Amerika Mus. Ludwig, Koln, 1986, Sonsbeck, Arnhem, The Netherlands, 1986, Whitney Mus. Am. Art, NYC, 1989, Mus. Contemporary Art, LA, 1989, Mus. Modern Art, NYC, 1988, 90, 96, Documenta 8, Kassel, 1987, Ctrl. Mus., Utrecht, The Netherlands, 1991, Kunsthalle, Basel, 1992, Guggenheim Mus., Soho, NYC, 1993, 96, Lenbachhaus, Munich, 1994, SITE Santa Fe, 1995, Pompidou Ctr., Paris, 1996, Biennale di Florence, Italy, 1996, Joseph Helman Gallery, NY, 1997, Kunsthalle Wien, Vienna, Austria, 1998, Nat. Gallery Australia, Canberra, 1998, Rhona Hofman Gallery, 1998, Oslo Mus. Contemporary Art, 2000; represented in permanent collections Ujazdowski Castle, Warsaw, Poland, Black Garden, Nordhorn, Germany, Erlauf (Austria) Peace Monument, Guggenheim Mus., Bilbao, Bundestag, Berlin, U. So. Calif., LA, Ludwig Mus., Aachen, Germany, Neue Nat. Galerie, Berlin, Toyota Mclpl. Mus. Art, Hamburg Kunstalle, US Fed. Courthouse, Sacramento, Allentown, Pa., Telenor Hdqr., Norway, U. Pa., Phila., Paula Matersohn-Becker Mus., Bremen, Germany, Lawrence Conv. Ctr., Pitts., Stora Target, Karlstad, Sweden, others. Recipient Golden Lion award 44th Venice Biennale, 1990, Skowhegan medal for installation Skowhegan Sch. Painting and Sculpture, N.Y., 1994, Crystal award World Econ. Forum, Cologny-Geneva, Switzerland, 1996, BMW Art car, BMW, Munich, 1999, Kaiserring award City of Goslar, Germany, 2002. Fellow Am. Acad., Berlin, 2000, Am. Acad. Rome. Avocation: reading. E-mail: studio@jennyholzer.com, gallery@cheimread.com.

HOLZMER, SISTER ANITA, nun, theology studies educator; d. Nicholas Joseph Holzmer Jr. and Katherine Joan (Sutherlin) Holzmer. BS Edn., St. Francis Coll., Ft. Wayne, Ind., 1975; MS Edn., St. Francis Coll., 1982; diploma Franciscan Spirituality, Pontifical U. Antonianum, Rome, 2005. Sisters of St. Francis of Perpetual Adoration, 1970; lic. gen. elem. tchr. (life) Ind., 1982, La., 1982, elem. adminstrn. and Supervision Ind., 1999, cert. organist tng. program Diocese Ft. Wayne-South Bend, 1999. Tchr. grade 6 St. Agnes Sch., Chicago Heights, Ill., 1974—75; tchr. grade 5-8 Cath. schs. Ind., 1975—81; tchr. grade 5-6 St. Jude Sch., Diamond, La., 1981—83; tchr. grade 7-8 St. Therese and Our Lady of Grace Schs., Ft. Wayne and Highland, Ind., 1983—90; prin. St. Lawrence Sch., Lafayette, Ind., 1990—91; missionary, tchr. Inst. San Buenaventura, Comayaguela, Honduras, 1991—95; formation dir. Sisters in Temporary Vows Sisters of St. Francis of Perpetual Adoration, Mishawaka, Ind., 1996—98; prin. St. Mary Cath. Sch., Griffith, Ind., 1998—2002; instr. theology and Franciscan studies U. St. Francis, Ft. Wayne, 2005—. Spiritual asst. secular Franciscan order St. Michael the Archangel Fraternity, Hicksville, Ohio, 2005—; youth min., musician World Youth Day, Rome, 2000, Toronto, Ont., Canada, 02; youth min. Youth Retreat, St. John, Ind., 2000, 01. Recipient Salute to Women of Lake County in Religion, C. of C. Hammond, Ind., 2002. Avocations: music, crafts, baking, walking. Office: Univ Saint Francis 2701 Spring St Fort Wayne IN 46808

HOM, MEI LING, artist, educator; b. New Haven, Aug. 2, 1951; BA, Kirkland Coll., Clinton, N.Y., 1973; MFA, Alfred U., 1987. Asst. prof. art C.C. Phila., 1983—2002, assoc. prof. art, 2003—06. Mem. exhbn. com. Phila. Art Alliance, 1998—2003; interdisciplinary arts adv. panel Pa. Coun. Arts, Harrisburg, 1993—95; installed Offering for Balch Inst., 1998, Golden Mountain for Phila. Mus. Art, 1998, Silkworm Grind for Japanese Am. Nat. Mus., L.A., 2001, Neuberger Mus. Art, Purchase, NY, 2001, Waxed Memory, Meguro Mus. Art, Tokyo, 2001; commd. installation Chinawedge for Pa. Conv. Ctr., Phila., 1994, Moss Ghosts, 2000; bd. mem. Phila. Volunteer Lawyers for the Arts, 2003—; arts in edn. adv. panelist Pa. Coun. Arts, 1995, 2004; mem. exhbn. adv. bd. Moore Coll. Art and Design, Phila., 2006—. One-woman shows include Sculptfest '03, Vt., 2003, Fleisher Ollman Gallery, Phila., 2004, prin. works include Floating Mountains Singing Clouds, Sackler Gallery Smithsonian Inst., Washington, 2005. Visual artist fellow grantee Nat. Endowment for Arts, 1994, grantee Leeway Found., 1999, Joan Mitchell Found., 2005; fellow Independence Found., 2003, Pa. Coun. on Arts, 1991, 95, Creative Artist Exch. Nat. Endowment Arts and Japan Friendship Commn., 1996, Pew Found., 1998; Leeway Found. Window Opportunity grant, 2004; Asian Studies Devel. Program: Korean Culture NEH grant, 2002; fellow Djerassi Resident Artists Program Pritzker Found. Mem. Asian Am. Arts Alliance, Asian Arts Initiative, Ctr. Book Arts (artist mem.), Women's Studio Workshop (artist mem.), Internat. Sculpture Ctr. (artist mem.), Headlands Ctr. Arts (Marin County, Calif.).

HOM, TRUDY A., music educator; b. Orlando, Fla., Mar. 14, 1956; d. Herbert Leroy and Virginia Mae Gardner; m. Nelson Edward Hom, Nov. 10, 1984. BA, U. Ctrl. Fla., 1980. Presch. tchr. The Learning Ctr., Orlando, 1980-85; ch. musician Ocoee United Meth. Ch., Fla., 1981-91; piano instr. pvt. studio, Orlando, 1978—; ch. musician Faith Luth. Ch., Winter Garden, 1998—2000, Pine Castle United Meth. Ch., Orlando, 2002—04. Mem. Fla. Federation Music Clubs (dist. pres. 1997—), Music Tchrs. Nat. Assn., Nat. Guild Piano Tchrs.; life mem. Sigma Alpha Iota (sword of honor 1980). Republican. United Meth. Avocation: antique shopping. Home: 230 Enka Ave Orlando FL 32835-1920

HOMAN, PATRICIA ANN, counselor; b. Mineola, N.Y., Dec. 20, 1953; d. James Joseph and Barbara Ann (Hill) Breen; m. Gregory Bruce Homan, Dec. 28, 1975 (div.); children: Casey, Emily, James, Margaret. BA, Bethany Coll., 1975; MS, W.Va. U., 1977; PhD, Kennedy Western U., 2004. Cert. rehab. counselor, lic. profl. counselor Pa. Vocat. rehab. counselor Divsn. Vocat. Rehab., Fairmont, W.Va., 1977; rehab. counselor Eastern Maine Med. Ctr., Bangor, 1978-87, social worker, 1989-94; mgr. bereavement program Hospice of Lancaster, Pa., 1994—2004, program dir., Pathways Ctr. for Grief Loss, 2004—. Disaster mental health vol. ARC, 1992—; section chair Bereavement Profl. of the Nat. Coun. of Hospice & Palliative Care Profl., 2003—; exec. com. mem. Lancaster County CISM team, 1999—. Recipient Social Worker of Yr. award, Maine, 1992, Recognition of Achievement award Maine Hosp. Assn., 1993. Fellow: Assn. Death Edn. and Counseling; mem.: Nat. Coun. Hospice and Palliative Care Profls. United Ch. of Christ. Avocations: family, folk music, reading, skiing, horseback riding. Home: 148 Sunny Slope Ln Manheim PA 17545-2331

HOMAYSSI, RUBY LEE, small business owner; b. Jan. 14, 1945; d. Raymond and Elmira (Carter) K. BS in Food & Nutrition, So. U., Baton Rouge, 1967; MA, Pepperdine U., 1981; A.Hosp. Dietetics, Tuskegee Inst., Ala., 1969. Staff dietitian Nat. Naval Med. Ctr., Bethesda, Md., 1969-70; chief clin. nutrition and dietitian dept. Naval Hosp. Chelsea, Mass., 1970-74; chief dietitian, asst. food mgmt. officer Naval Submarine Med. Ctr., Groton, Conn., 1974-78; chief clin. nutrition Naval Hosp. Portsmouth, Va., 1978-83; chief clin. nutrition and dietetics Naval Hosp. Orlando, Fla., 1983-88; pres. Elmira's P.A.N.T.R.Y., Inc., Orlando, 1988—. Adv. bd. Fla. Hosp. Women; bd. dir. Bridgebuilders of Winter Pk.; cons. in field. Contbr. articles to profl. jours. Dir. Vol. Ctr. Seminole County, 1989-91; 3d v.p. Civic Theatre Bd. Ctrl. Fla., Orlando, 1989, 2d v.p., 1990—, pres., 1992-93; 1st v.p. Orlando Opera Co., 1987-88; bd. dirs. Maitland Arts Coun., New Hope For kids, gala chmn., 2002-03; pub. edn. chmn. Am. Cancer Soc., Orlando, 1987-90, bd. dirs.; prodn. chmn. March of Dimes, 1988—; bd. dirs. Hospice of Ctrl. Fla., Fla. Hosp. Diabetes Ctr. Found., Seminola County Arts Coun., 2003—, Holocaust Meml. Resource and Edn. Ctr.; cmty. advisors bd. TV-24; bd. dirs. Seminole Chamber-Cmty. Rels., 1990-93, Citrus Coun. Girl Scouts; cmty. advisors bd. Symphony Orch. Assocs., 1991-92 Symphony Ball; bd. dir., chmn. Festival of Orchs., Inc., 2001-03; trainer Jr. Achievement, 1993—; chmn. Bridgebuilders, 2000-01; chmn. bd. dirs. Festival of Orchs., 2001-03; devel. bd. Westside Winter Park Neighborhood, 2000—; 1st v.p. Seminole Cultural Arts Coun., Inc Named Woman of the Yr., Am. Bus. Women's Assn., 1987, Women of Achievement in Arts Downtown Exec. Women's Coun., 1989; recipient Angle award, 1989, Ruby Homayssi Day named in her honor City of Longwood, 199; Paul Harris fellow Rotary, 2000. Mem. AAUW, NAFE, Am. Dietetic Assn., Fla. Dietetic Assn., Am. Bus. Women's Assn. (pres. 1987), Pvt. Industry Coun. of Seminole County (bd. dirs.), Girl Friends Club, Torch Club, Leadership Seminole, Delta Sigma Theta, Orlando Coun. of Christian Bus. Women, Subuuran Rep. Woman (bd.), Femmes de Coeur (pr chair & underwriting chair), Rotary, Leadership Seminole Alumni Assn Republican. Baptist. Avocations: reading, travel, stock car racing, sewing. Home: General Delivery Altamonte Springs FL 32714-9999

HOMER, MELODIE ANTONETTE, oncological nurse, educator, consultant; b. Hamilton, Ont., Can., Aug. 29, 1966; arrived in U.S., 1989; d. Waldron Berrisford and Ena Gwendolyn Thorpe; children: Laurel, Alden. Nursing diploma, Mohawk Coll., Hamilton, 1987; BSN, Loma Linda U., 1991; MSN, Azusa Pacific U., 1995. RN Can., Calif., Pa., N.J. Staff nurse St. Josephs Hosp., Hamilton, 1988—89; pediat. staff nurse Loma Linda Children's Hosp., 1989—96, Children's Hosp. Phila., 1996—98; oncology nurse educator, cons. Marlton, NJ, 1997—2003. Nursing instr. various instns., 1994, 97. Author: (pediat. booklet) Sandoman Talks About ITP, 1996, Chemo Crusader and the Cancer Fighting Crew, 1999; contbr. chapters to books. Pres. LeRoy W. Homer Jr. Found., 2004—. Mem.: Sigma Theta Tau.

HOMESTEAD, SUSAN E. (SUSAN FREEDLENDER), psychotherapist; b. Bklyn., Sept. 20, 1937; d. Cy Simon and Katherine (Haas) Eichelbaum; m. Robert Bruce Randall, 1956 (div. 1960); 1 child, Bruce David; m. George Gilbert Zanetti, Dec. 13, 1962 (div. 1972); m. Ronald Eric Homestead, Jan. 16, 1973 (div. 1980); m. Arthur Elliot Freedlender, Apr. 1, 1995. BA, U. Miami-Fla., 1960; MSW, Tulane U., 1967. Diplomate Am. Bd. Clin. Social Work; Acad. Cert. Social Workers, 1971, LCSW, Va., Calif. Psychotherapist, cons., Richmond, Va., 1971—, Los Altos, Calif.; pvt. practice Homestead Counseling, Richmond, Piedmont Psychiatric Ctr., P.C. (formerly Psychol. Evaluation Rehab. Cons., Inc.), Lynchburg, Va., 1994-97; cons. Family and Children's Svcs., Richmond, 1981—, Richmond Pain Clinic, 1983-84, Health Internat. Va., P.C., Lynchburg, 1984-86, Franklin St. Psychotherapy & Edn. Ctr., Santa Clara, Calif., 1988-90; pvt. practice, 1971—, Santa Clara County Children's Svc., 1973-75, 86-88. Co-dir. asthma program Va. Lung Assn., Richmond, 1975-79, Loma Prieta Regional Ctr.; chief clin. social worker Med. Coll. Va., Va. Commonwealth U., 1974-79; field supr. 1980 Census, 1981-87. Contbr. articles to profl. jours. Active Peninsula Children's Ctr., Morgan Ctr., Coun. Cmty. Action Planning, Cmty. Assn. for Retarded, Comprehensive Health Planning Assn. Santa Clara, Mental Health Commn., Children and Adolscent Target Group Calif., Women's Com. Richmond Symphony, Va. Mus. theatre; mem. adv. com. Va. Lung Assn.; mem. steering com. Am. Cancer Soc.(Va. divsn.), Epilepsy Found., Am. Heart Assn. (Va. divsn.), Ctrl. Va. Guild for Infant Survival; mem. fin. com. Robb for Gov. Mem. NASW, Va. Soc. Clin. Social Work, Inc. (charter mem., sec. 1975-78), Internat. Soc. Communicative Psychoanalysis & Psychotherapy, Am. Acad. Psychotherapists, Internat. Soc. for the Study of Dissociation, Am. Assn. Psychiatric Svcs. for Children. Fax: 650-327-1330. E-mail: SueEF@aol.com.

HOMMICK, CAROL MARY, physical education educator; b. Buffalo, Feb. 18, 1946; AS in Phys. Edn., DeKalb Jr. Coll., Ga., 1970; BS in Phys. Edn., So. Conn. State U., New Haven, 1975, MS, 1977. Lic. phys. therapist. Home: 312 Providence Dr Dallas GA 30157-7465

HONAKER, STEVIE LEE, career counselor, consultant; b. Wewoka, Okla., Mar. 23, 1945; d. Joe Jack and Ruby Lee (Bowen) H.; 1 child, Charles Byron Howell. BA in Sociology, Colo. State U., 1994, BA in Social Sci., 1994, MEd, 1997, postgrad, 1997—. Lic. practicing counselor. Prin., owner Union Colony Shops, Greeley, Colo., 1970-79, Union Colony Interior Design, Greeley, Colo., 1980-83; career counselor Colo. State U. Career Ctr., Ft. Collins, Colo., 1996—. Trainer Colo. Sch. Counselors Assn., Denver, 1998; Myers-Briggs type indicato qualified, 1998; Strong interest inventory qualified, 1998; state rep. 1999. Co-author: Career Video Review, 1996-98. Active Commn. Status Women, Ft. Collins, 1993-95. Mem. Colo. Career Devel. Assn. (newsletter editor 1997-98, pres. 1998—, state rep. 1998), Alpha Kappa Delta. Avocations: scuba diving, mountain jeeping, gardening. Office: Colo State U Career Ctr 711 Oval Dr Fort Collins CO 80523-0001 Home: 10000 SW 52nd Ave Apt 134 Gainesville FL 32608-8305 Fax: (970) 491-1134. E-mail: shonaker@lamar.colostate.edu.

HONDA, SOCHIKO, apparel designer, educator; b. Akitashi, Japan, Oct. 21, 1946; d. Matsuo Kurokawa and Tama Honda. BS, Geulford Coll., 1973; MEd, U. N.C., 1975; MFA, Savannah Coll. Art and Design, 2004. Prof. fashion Savannah Coll. Art and Design, Ga., 1991—. Home: 114 W Hull St Savannah GA 31401 Office Phone: 912-525-6664. Business E-Mail: shondafe@scad.edu.

HONESTY, TARA MARIE, educational consultant, educator; b. Phila., Aug. 9, 1970; d. James Lee Honesty and Thelma Louise Dickens. BA, NC A&T State U., Greensboro, 1993; MPA, NC Ctrl. U., Durham, 2000. Minority admissions counselor/recruiter E. Carolina U., Greenville, NC, 2001—04, acad. advisor, 2004—. Coord.-multicultural day events E. Carolina U., Greenville, 2001—. Mem.: Delta Sigma Theta (life; v.p. 2003—05, chair social action 2005—06, Super Soror award 2005). Democrat. Baptist. Avocations: travel, teaching, reading, cooking. Home: PO Box 1679 Tarboro NC 27886 Office: E Carolina U 5th St Greenville NC 27858 Office Phone: 252-328-1084. Business E-Mail: honestyt@ecu.edu.

HONEYCUTT, BRENDA, secondary school educator; Tchr. sci. Fort Mill (S.C.) Middle Sch.; chmn. sci. dept. Rep. Nat. Mid. Sch. Conf. Recipient hon. mention Outstanding Earth Sci. Tchr. award Nat. Assn. of Geology Teachers, 1992, S.C. Earth Sci. Tchr. Yr., 1992. Office: Fort Mill Middle Sch 200 Highway 160 Byp Fort Mill SC 29715-8746 E-mail: honeycuttb@fort-mill.k12.sc.us.

HONEYCUTT, JANICE LOUISE, nurse; b. Plainfield Twp., Pa., Feb. 8, 1943; d. Mortimer Singer and Mary Irene (Chase) Purdy; m. Billie B. Honeycutt, Aug. 8, 1987; 1 child, Jason G. ThB, Penns Creek (Pa.) Bible Sch., 1972; ADN, Westark C.C., 1985. Bd. cert. in gerontology and gen. nursing practice. Clinic dir. Highlands, Papua, New Guinea, 1973-76; case mgr. Kimberly Quality Care, Amarillo, Tex., 1988-95; asst. dir. of nursing Olsen Manor Nursing Home, 1995; case mgr. Casha Resource, 1996, quality assurance rep. Amarillo, 1997—; dir. profl. improvement VIP Home Care, Amarillo, 1998-2000; charge nurse Country Club Manor, Amarillo, Tex., 2000—01, Plum Creek Specialty Hosp., Amarillo, 2001—. Author: The Lighthouse, 1975; contbr. articles to profl. jours. Local st. campaign leader Arthritis Found., Amarillo, 1996. Mem. NGNA. Avocations: water color painting, crafts, sewing. Office Phone: 806-351-1000.

HONG, ELLEE PAI, newscaster; b. Republic of Korea; B, EWHA Women's U., Seoul, Republic of Korea; M, Northwestern U. Former anchor WIFR-TV, Rockford, Ill., WAND-TV, Decatur, Ill.; weekday morning anchor WFSB-TV, Hartford, 2001—03; morning news anchor WMAQ-TV (NBC Chgo.), 2003—. Office: WMAQ-TV NBC Tower 454 N Columbus Dr Chicago IL 60611-5555 Business E-Mail: ellee.paihong@nbc.com.

HONG, MEI, chemistry professor; BA, Mt. Holyoke Coll., 1992; PhD, U. Calif. Berkeley, 1996. NIH postdoctoral fellow Mass. Inst. Tech., Cambridge; rsch. prof. U. Mass., Amherst; assoc. prof. chemistry Iowa State U., Ames, Iowa, 1999—. Mem. editl. bd.: Jour. Magnetic Resonance. Recipient Beckman Young Investigator award, 1999, Rsch. Corp. Innovation award, 2000, Career award, NSF, 2001, Pure Chemistry award, Am. Chem. Soc., 2003; Alfred P. Sloan Fellow, 2002. Achievements include development and application of solid-state NMR spectroscopy to investigate the structure and dynamics of membrane and insoluable fibrous proteins. Office: Dept Chemistry 1605 Gilman Hall Iowa State Univ Ames IA 50011-3111 Office Phone: 515-294-3521. E-mail: mhong@iastate.edu.

HONIG, ALICE STERLING, psychologist; b. Bklyn., Apr. 19, 1929; d. William and Ida (Bender) Sterling; divorced, 1975; children: Lawrence Sterling, Madeleine Honig Lenski, Jonathan David. BA magna cum laude, Barnard Coll., 1950; MA, Columbia U., 1952; PhD, Syracuse U., 1975. Lic. psychologist, N.Y. Rsch. assoc. Upstate Med. Ctr., Syracuse, N.Y., 1962-64; family devel. rsch. program dir. Syracuse U., 1964-77, instr. child devel., 1969-71, asst. prof., 1971-75, assoc. prof., 1975-81, prof., 1981—. Author: Discipline, Cooperation and Compliance: an Annotated Bibliography, 1987, Parent Involvement in Early Childhood Education, 1979, Playtime Learning Games for Young Children, 1982, (with J.R. Lally) Infant Caregiving: A Design for Training, 1981, (with Wittmer) Infant/Toddler Caregiving: An Annotated Bibliography, 1982, (with H. Brophy) Talking With Your Baby: Family as the First School, 1996, Secure Relationships, 2002; editor: Risk Factors in Infancy, 1986, Early Parenting and Later Child Achievement, 1990, Optimizing Early Child Care and Education, 1990, (with D. Wittmer) Prosocial Devel. in Children: Caring, Helping and Cooperating, 1992; N.Am. editor: ECDC, 1983—; rsch. rev. editor: Young Children, 1980-87, Early Childhood Ednl. Rsch. Quarterly, 1985-89. Bd. dirs. Pioneer Women. Recipient Woman Achievement in Child Devel. award State of N.Y., 1983, award Sparrowgrass Poetry Forum, 1991, Champions for Children, N.Y. State AEYC, 2005, Hero of Early Childhood award, 2005; U.S. Office of Edn. Nat. fellow, 1969-71. Fellow APA, Soc. for Rsch. in Child Devel.; mem. Nat. Assn. for Edn. Young Children, Internat. Soc. for Study Behavioral Devel.,Am. Orthopsychiat. Assn., Internat. Conf. on Infant Studies, Phi Beta Kappa. Jewish. Avocations: pottery, singing, poetry, collecting chinese snuff bottles. Office Phone: 315-443-4296.

HONIGBERG, CAROL CROSSMAN, lawyer; b. Salina, Kansas, Sept. 23, 1955; d. Robert Denfield and Barbara Jane (Eckberg) Crossman; m. Paul Mark Honigberg, Aug. 18, 1979; children: Michael, Margaret Ann. BA, Duke U., 1977; JD, Vanderbilt U., 1980. Bar: Va., 1980. Assoc. Hazel and Thomas, P.C., Alexandria, Va., 1980—86; propr. Hazel and Thomas, P.C., Falls Ch., Va., 1986—99; ptnr. Reed Smith LLP (formerly Reed, Smith, Hazel, and Thomas, LLP), Falls Ch., 1999—, mem. exec. com. Mem. ABA (mem. real property, probate and trust sect.), Va. State Bar (mem. real property sect.), CREW Network (pres. North Va. chpt. 1998-99, nat. del. 2000-01), Urban Land Inst. (mem. urban devel. and mixed use coun.). Office: Reed Smith LLP 3110 Fairview Park Dr Ste 1400 Falls Church VA 22042 Office Phone: 703-641-4220. Office Fax: 703-641-4340. Business E-Mail: chonigberg@reedsmith.com.

HONIGSFELD, ANDREA M., education educator; b. Debrecen, Hungary; arrived in US, 1993; d. Istvan Laboncz and Ilona Varga; m. Howard Honigsfeld; 1 child, Benjamin. BA, Kossuth U., 1988; M in edn., Queens Coll., 1997; EdD, St. John's U., 2001. Esl tchr. NYC Bd. Edn., 1994—97; instr. NY U., 1997—2000; doctoral rsch. fellow St. John's U., NYC, 1997—2000; instr. asst., assoc. prof. Molloy Coll., Rockville Ctr., NY, 2000—. Author: Hungaro Lingua Video Workbook, 1993; co-author: An Educator's Guide to the Learning Individual, 2002. Recipient Fulbright scholar, Fulbright Assn. Iceland, 2002, Outstanding Dissertation award, St. John's U., 2001. Mem.: TESOL, ASCD, Phi Delta Kappa. Home: 849 Virginia Ave North Bellmore NY 11710-1341 Office: Molloy Coll PO Box 5002 Rockville Centre NY 11571-5002

HONNER SUTHERLAND, B. JOAN, advertising executive; b. N.Y.C., Oct. 23, 1952; d. William John and Mary Patricia (Edwards) H.; m. Donald J. Sutherland, Oct. 3, 1987; children: Chelsea Lauren, Whitney Devon. Student, Endicott Coll., 1970-71. Art dir. Kerrigan Studio, Darien, Conn., 1971-73, Foote Cone and Belding, Phoenix, 1973-77, sr. art dir. Chgo., 1977-81; v.p., assoc. creative dir. J. Walter Thompson, Chgo., 1982-86; v.p., exec. art dir. BBDO Chgo., 1986-91; creative dir. Knautz & Co., Sarasota, Fla., 1992-93; co-owner X-L Advt., Sarasota, Fla., 1993-94, Beyond Design of Sarasota, Inc., 1994—; mktg. dir. Nelson Pub. Inc., Nokomis, Fla., 2001—. Cons. J. Walter Thompson, Toronto and San Francisco, 1983-84; owner Fla. Antiques, Geneva, Ill., 1986-90. Introduced Discover card, 1985. Tchr. elem. sch. art; mem. Southside Sch. PTA Bd., Sarasota, 1996-99; spl. projects Pine View Sch., Sarasota, 1999—2003. Recipient 1st pla. TV local campaign WGN, 6th dist. Addy, 1980, Kemp. Corp. Addy, 1990, Mktg. Flood awards FEMA/NFIP, 1997, 98, 99; Best Internat. TV campaign Pepsi Clio, 1985. Roman Catholic. Avocation: miniatures. Home: 4941 Commonwealth Dr Sarasota FL 34242-1421

HONNOLD, KATHRYN S., real estate agent; b. Pataskala, Ohio, Nov. 10, 1936; d. Harold S. and Stella E. (Slack) Williams; m. Robert I. Honnold, Aug. 18, 1956; children: Jayne, Robin. Student, Franklin U., N.Y. Sch. Modeling. Real estate sales cons. Villas at Four Farms, Ohio, 1978—; adminstrv. asst., office mgr., sec. Monsanto, Columbus, Ohio, 1983-87; coun. mem. Pataskala Village, 1987-98; adminstrv. asst. Bank One, 1988-99; asst. to exec. dir. United Svcs. for Effective Parenting Ohio, Inc., 2001—04; real estate profl. ReMax Achievers. Mem. Pataskala Village Coun., 1987-98, pres. 1990-92, 94, 96; mem. Pataskala Bd. Zoning Appeals Bd., 1997-2000; appointed mem. Licking County Sr. Citizen's Levy Adv. Bd., 1989-2005; adv. bd. Licking County Econ. Devel. Task Force, 1991-92; active Rep. Ctrl. Com. Licking County, 1998-2004; conf. coord. Nat. Assn. Women Hwy. Safety Leaders, 2001-04, exhibitor chmn. 2002, 03; model for fashion shows. Named Sec. of Yr., 1987. Mem.: Nat., State and County Real Estate Assoc., Internat. Assn. Adminstrv. Profls. Home: 325 Laurel Ln Pataskala OH 43062-8547 E-mail: bkhonnold@msn.com.

HONOUR, LYNDA CHARMAINE, research scientist, psychotherapist, educator; d. John Henry, Jr. and Evelyn Helena Roberta (Pietrowski) H. BA, Boston U.; MA, Calif. State U., Fullerton, UCLA; PhD, U. So. Calif. Lic. marriage, family and child psychotherapist and psychologist, Calif. Rschr. neuroendocrinology and behavioral neurosci., Calif., 1976—; pvt. practice psychotherapy Carlsbad Village, 1991—; mem. staff Sharp Healthcare, Sharp Mesa Vista Psychiat. Hosp., Sharp Meml. Hosp., San Diego, Mary Birch Hosp. for Women, San Diego. Vis. and clin. prof. Pepperdine U., 1989—, Malibu, Calif. Sch. Profl. Psychology, Calif. State U., Long Beach, Northridge; condr. rsch. Neuropsychiat. Inst., Brain Rsch. Inst., Mental Retardation Rsch. Ctr., UCLA, Tulane U. Med. Sch., V.A. Med. Ctr., New Orleans, Salk Inst. Biol. Studies; rsch. cons. U. Calif. Med. Ctr., Irvine; cons. in rsch. or psychotherapy, 1976—; guest expert on safety issues regarding magnetic imaging Premiere Radio Network, 2001; condr. rsch. Neuropsychiat. Inst., Brain Rsch. Inst., Mental Retardation Rsch. Ctr., UCLA, Tulane U. Med. Sch., V.A. Med. Ctr., New Orleans, Salk Inst. Biol. Studies; rsch. cons. U. Calif. Med. Ctr., Irvine, Salk Inst.; cons., ad hoc reviewer (textbooks) Wadsworth/Brooks-Cole, Thomson Internat. Pub., Pacific Grove, Calif.; cons., reviewer Allyn & Bacon Pub., Boston; hon. chmn., Bus. Adv. Coun. Nat. Rep. Congl. Com.; reviewer Pearson Pub. Group. Contbr. articles to profl. jours. Rsch. grantee Organon Internat. Rsch. Group, Netherlands, 1984-88. Mem. APA, Soc. for Neurosci., Internat. Behavioral Neurosci. Soc., Internat. Brain Rsch. Orgn., Calif. Assn. Marriage and Family Therapists, Sons and Daus. of Pearl Harbor Survivors, Psi Chi, Salk Inst. Alumni. Roman Catholic. Achievements include the discovery two peptides one which facilitates and one which inhibits learning and memory task performance permanently in a developmental paradigm in mice; research on the facilitation peptide reveal it can permanently reverse induced learning/memory deficit, with implications for mental retardation and other learning/memory deficit treatment; member of the research team which isolated and characterized the corticotropic hormone releasing factor, urocortin; the delineation of various effects of peptides on behavior including bipolar disorders, endogenous depression, mania and others; human research involving interface between cognition/mind and physiological processes/disease; research in the risks associated with MRI exposure; establishing new N.E. US swimming records in the 1960s; established developmental influences of peptides on cognition/learning processes; identified chemical moieties responsible for learning, memory, and cognition processing; investigating effect of cognitive process on physiological metabolisms. Avocations: art, quantum theory. Office Phone: 760-720-9665. Business E-Mail: DrLyndaHonour@cs.com.

HONSA, VLASTA, retired librarian; b. Žilina, Czechoslovakia, Sept. 1, 1924; came to U.S., 1951; d. František Petr and Marie (Širková) Petrova; m. Vladimir Honsa, June 26, 1948; children: Patricia, Eva Honsa-Hogg. BA, Charles U., Prague, 1947; MLS, Ind. U., 1968. Gifts libr. Ind. U. Libr., Bloomington, 1968-70; head reference dept. Clark County Libr., Las Vegas, Nev., 1970-80, asst. adminstr., 1980-94; ret., 1994. Coord. Found. Collection, part of the Found. Ctr.'s Cooperating Collections network, Clark County Libr., 1979-94. Author: Nevada Foundation Directory, 1984, 2d edit., 1989, 3rd edit., 1994. Bd. dirs. So. Nev. Musical Arts Soc., Las Vegas, 1989-92; organized and presented fundraising workshops for cmty. fund raisers sponsored by Las Vegas-Clark County Libr. Dist., 1979-94. Recipient Ind. U. grant-in-aid to conduct rsch. of publs. in cen. Am. univs. and nat. librs., 1970, Champion award Las Vegas-Clark County Libr. Dist., 1985. Mem. ALA, AAUW, Nev. Libr. Assn., Univ. Nevada Las Vegas Faculty Club. Roman Catholic. Avocations: reading, music, arts, travel. Home: 2680 Congress Ave Las Vegas NV 89121-1316 E-mail: honsa@worldnet.att.net.

HOOD, ANTOINETTE FOOTE, dermatologist; b. Honolulu, 1941; MD, Vanderbilt U., 1967. Cert. dermatology. Intern Vanderbilt Affiliated Hosps, 1967-68; fellow dermatology Harvard U., 1973-75, resident dermatology, 1975-76; resident dermatology-pathology Mass. Gen. Hosp., Boston, 1976-78; faculty Johns Hopkins School of Med., 1980—93; Dir. Dermatopathology Indiana Univ. School of Med., 1993—2002; exec. dir. American Board of Dermatology, Detroit, 2001—; Dir. Dermatopathology Ea. Va. School of Med, 2002—. Office: Pariser Dermatology Specialists Ltd 601 Medical Tower Norfolk VA 23507*

HOOD, GLENDA E., former state official, former mayor; b. Orlando, Fla., Mar. 10, 1950; m. Charles M. Hood III; 3 children. BA in Spanish, Rollins Coll.; postgrad., Harvard U., Ga. State U. Commr. City of Orlando, Fla., 1982-92, mayor Fla., 1992—2002; sec. of state State of Fla., Tallahassee, 2003—05. Pres. Glenda E. Hood & Assocs., Inc. Vice chmn. mcpl. planning bd. City of Orlando, mem. nominating bd., chmn. task force bd. and commn. restructure; past chmn., founding mem. bd. dirs. Found. Orange County Pub. Schs.; co-chmn. Orlando Fights Back-Coalition for a Drug-Free Cmty.; bd. dirs. U. Ctrl. Fla. Found., Met. Orlando Urban League; past pres. exec. bd. Ctrl. Fla. Coun. of Boy Scouts; bd. overseers Rollins Coll. Crummer Grad. Sch. of Bus.; mem. adv. bd. Valencia C.C., Fla.- Costa Rica Inst.; past co-chmn. United Negro Coll. Fund; pres. Jr. League Orlando-Winter Park, Vol. Svc. Bur.; mem. Orange County Commn. on Children. Named Mcpl. Leader of Yr., Am. City and County Mag., 1992, one of Ten Outstanding Young Americans, U.S. Jaycees, one of Seven Outstanding Youth Floridians, Fla. Jaycees, Woman of Yr., Downtown Orlando Inc., one of Ten People to Watch, Fla. Trend, one of 100 Young Women of Promise, Good Housekeeping; recipient Willie J. Bruton award for cmty. svc. Met. Orlando Urban League, Summit award Women's Resource Ctr., Svc. to Mankind award Leukemia Soc. Am. Ctrl. Fla. chpt. Mem. Nat. League of Cities (past pres.), Fla. League of Cities (past pres.), Fla. C. of C. (past pres.), Greater Orlando C. of C. (past v.p.). Republican. Episcopalian.*

HOOD, KATRINA, pediatrician; 3 children. BA in Linguistics, Northwestern U., 1987; MD, U. Louisville, 1994. Pediatric resident Naval Med. Ctr., San Diego, 1997; pediatrician US Navy, 1998—2001, Pediatrics & Adolescent Associates, Lexington, Ky., 2001—; chief pediatrics Ctrl. Baptist Hosp. With Girls Rock. Lt. comdr. USN. Recipient William J. Thomas Humanitarian award, Leadership award (Young Physician), AMA Found., 2005. Fellow: Am. Acad. Pediatrics.*

HOOD, LUANN SANDRA, special education educator; b. Bklyn., Jan. 10, 1955; d. Louie A. and Sylvia M. (Hall) Mayo; m. Stephen J. Hood. BA, St. Joseph's Coll., Bklyn., 1976; MS in Edn., Bklyn. Coll., 1979. Cert. tchr. N.K, 1-6, spl. edn., N.Y.C. lic. Edn. counselor adolescents Am. Indian Comty. House, Inc., N.Y.C., 1977-79; tchr. children with retarded mental devel. Pub. Sch. 273, Bklyn., 1979-83; tchr. early childhood Pub. Sch. 128, Bklyn., 1983-94; tchr. emotionally handicapped Pub. Sch.215, Bklyn., 1994-95; tchr. learning disabled Pub. Sch. 101, Bklyn., 1995-99, tchr. hard of hearing, 1999—2001, learning disabled tchr., 2001—. Mem. sch. leadership team, 1997—, recording sec., 2001—. Exec. sec. bd. trustees Am. Indian Cmty. House, Inc., N.Y.C., 1980-91. Regents scholar N.Y. State Edn. Dept., 1972; grantee Indian League of the Americas, Inc. 1972-75, Thunderbird Am. Indian Dancers, Inc., 1972-75, Internat. Order of King's Daughters and Sons, 1976. Mem. Coun. for Exceptional Children, N.Y. State Tchrs. of Handicapped. Democrat. Roman Catholic. Avocation: photography.

HOOD, MARY BRYAN, museum director, painter; b. Central City, Ky., July 5, 1938; d. Irving B. and Mary Louise (Anderson) Cayce; m. Ronnie L. Hood, Oct. 16, 1960. Student, Ky. Wesleyan Coll., 1956-59, 69-72. Exec. dir. Owensboro (Ky.) Arts Commn., 1974-76; founding dir. Owensboro Mus. Fine

Art, 1976—; pres. Owensboro Mus. Fine Art Found., Inc., 1996—. Curator exhbns. on Ky. and regional art. Author, editor: exhbn. catalogs. Chair Owensboro Mayor's Arts Com., 1970—75, Owensboro Sculpture Pk., Mayor's Sculpture Pk. Commn., 1998; mem. exec. com. Ky. Arts Coun., 1974—76, Ky. Citizens for Arts, 1980—86, Owensboro Arts Commn., 1996—97, chmn., 2003—; mem. Cmty. Appearance Planning Bd., 1988—90, Davies County Bicentennial Commn., 1990—92; mem. steering com. Yr. of the Am. Craft, Ky., 1991—93; mem. Mayor's Adv. Coun. Arts, 1996, Davies County Millennium, 1999; chmn. Owensboro Pub. Art Commn., Owensboro, 2003—; bd. dirs. Theatre Workshop Owensboro, 1968—70, Owensboro Area Mus., 1970—72, Owensboro Symphony, 1975—76, Japan-Am. Soc. Ky., 1987—89. Named Mary Bryan Hood Day in her honor, 1974. Mem.: Ky. Assn. Mus. (pres. 1980—82), Am. Assn. Mus., Southeastern Mus. Conf. Office: Owensboro Mus Fine Art 901 Frederica St Owensboro KY 42301-3052 Office Phone: 270-685-3181.

HOOD, PATRICIA R., music educator; d. Homer Livingston and Rosalyn Wingard Roof; m. Lester Homer Hood, Jr., June 19, 1976; children: Jennifer Renée, Michael Livingston, Daniel Tyler. MusB in Edn., U. S.C., 1979, MusM in Edn., 1988. Lic. tchr. Nat. Bd. Profl. Tchg. Standards, S.C., 2003. Compensatory aide Congaree Elem. Sch., West Columbia, SC, 1988—90; tchr. music Pelion (S.C.) Elem. Sch., 1990—99, Lexington (S.C.) Elem. Sch., 1999—. Pvt. music tchr., West Columbia, 1978—88; organist, choir dir. various chs., SC, 1978—95; keyboardist St. David Luth. Ch., West Columbia, 2002—. Grantee, Lexington (S.C.) Sch. Dist. One, 2001, 2004, S.C. State Dept. Edn., 1990, 1991—93. Mem.: S.C. Music Educators Assn., Pi Lambda Theta. Avocations: weightlifting, aerobics, reading, music.

HOOD, PHYLLIS ILENE, special education educator; d. James H Brown and Viola Mae Riggle, Brown, Jones; m. James Richard Morris, May 27, 1954 (div. Mar. 6, 1986); m. Charles Gary Hood, Feb. 18, 1988 (div. Nov. 8, 1993); children: Stacy Lynn Gebhardt, James Richard Morris, Teresa Rene Thompson, Vilas Lester Morris, Ruth Ilene Owens, Richard Hayden Morris. BS in edn., NW Mo. State U., 1985—89, MS in edn., 1989—96. Elem. Edn. NW Mo. State U., 1989, Learning Disabled NW Mo. State U., 1989, Mentally Handicapped NW Mo. State U., 1991, Reading NW Mo. State U., 1996, Mild/Moderate Behavior Disorder U. of Ctrl. Ark., 2000. Spl. edn. and reading tchr. North Andrew R-VI Elem. Sch., Bolkow, Mo., 1989—90; spl. edn. tchr. Nodaway-Holt R-VII H.S., Graham, Mo., 1990—92, Camdenton R-III Sch. Dist., Camdenton, Mo., 1992—98, Spl. Sch. Dist., Town and Country, Mo., 1998—. Cheerleader sponsor Nodaway-Holt R-VII Sch. Dist., Graham, Mo., 1991—92, Camdenton R-III Sch. Dist., Camdenton, Mo., 1992—94, Hazelwood Sch. Dist., St. Louis, 2000—01; sponsor Big Bros./Big Sisters, St. Louis, 2001—. Ladies aux. Mo. Army N.G., Maryville, Mo., 1989—96; club mem. Optimist Club of Camdenton, Mo., 1992—98, pres., 1997—98; club mem. Optimist Club of O'Fallon, O'Fallon, Mo., 1999—2003, pres., 2000—01. Named a Honor Pres., Optimist Internat. -East Mo. Dist., 2000—01; named Disting. Pres., Optimist Internat.-West Mo. Dist., 1997—98; recipient Cert. of Appreciation, Optimist Internat. -East Mo. Dist., 2001—02. Mem.: Coun. for Exceptional Children (corr.). D-Liberal. Christian. Avocations: dance, travel, swimming, walking, gardening. Office: Hazelwood East High School 11300 Dunn Rd Saint Louis MO 63138

HOOD, SANDRA DALE, librarian; b. Edmond, Okla., Nov. 28, 1949; d. Rufus Gustav and Hope Louvica (Hutton) Farber; m. Frank D. Hood Jr., May 17, 1971; 1 child, Charles Richard. BA, U. Okla., 1971, MLS, 1972; MA in Bicultural Bilingual Studies, U. Tex., San Antonio, 1996. Libr. South Oklahoma City Jr. Coll., 1973, Daus. of Republic of Tex. Libr. at the Alamo, San Antonio, 1980—88; acad. outreach prof., automation and libr. sys. libr. Palo Alto Coll. Learning Resources Ctr., San Antonio, 1988—. Pres. Palo Alto Coll. Faculty Sen., 2001—02, parliamentarian, 2004—06. Featured (TV game show) Jeopardy, 2004. Pres. tech. svcs. spl. interest group Coun. Rsch. and Acad. Librs., San Antonio, 1991-92, chmn. circulation and interlibr. loan spl. interest group, 1997—; sec., mem. exec. bd. Timberwood Park Property Owners Assn., San Antonio, 1991-94. Recipient NISOD award, 2003. Mem. ALA, Tex. Libr. Assn. (conf. planning com. 1992-93, 97-98, 2002-04, program com. 2005—), Tex. Accelerated Libr. Leader 1997, disaster relief com. 2002-05), Bexar Libr. Assn. (exec. bd., dir. editor 1988-90), Tex. Cmty. Coll. Tchrs. Assn. Democrat. Lutheran. Achievements include contestant on Jeopardy, Apr. 2004. Avocations: travel, reading, computers. Home: 27030 Foggy Meadows St San Antonio TX 78260-1822 Office: Palo Alto Coll Learning Resources Ctr 1400 W Villaret Blvd San Antonio TX 78224-2417 Office Phone: 210-921-5062.

HOOD-RYKER, JOAN CRANDELL, retired counselor; b. Spokane, Wash., Aug. 4, 1934; d. Millard Allerdice and Gertrude Lydia (Warren) Crandell; m. Wesley Dell Hood, Sept. 2, 1955 (div. Aug. 1971); 1 child, Wesley Dell Jr.; m. Michael E. Larkin, Sept. 29, 1984 (dec.); children: Michael, Karen, Christopher, Laurie; m. Brian D. Ryker, July 22, 1995; children: Eric Ryker, Michelle Batsford. BA in Psychology, Whitworth Coll., 1972; MA, Gonzaga U., 1974. Cert. mental health counselor, Wash.; cert. Nat. Bd. Cert. Counselors, Inc. Various bus. positions, Spokane, 1952-72; coord. N.E. Neighborhood Ctr., Spokane, 1973-75; dir. Spokane Neighborhood Ctrs., Spokane, 1975-76; pvt. practice Spokane, 1977-94; ret., 1994. Mem., tchr., Garland Ave. Alliance Ch., Spokane, 1972-99. Shiloh Hill fellow, 2001—. Mem. Am. Counseling Assn., Am. Mental Health Counselors Assn. Avocation: reading. Home: 702 E Bismark Ave Spokane WA 99208-3503

HOOGENBOOM, BARBARA JO, physical therapist, educator; b. Ann Arbor, Mich., Aug. 6, 1961; d. Francis Max and Carol Jean Rottman; m. David James Hoogenboom, Aug. 27, 1983; children: Lindsay Jo, Matthew David. BS, Calvin Coll., Grand Rapids, Mich., 1983; M of Health Sci., Grand Valley State U., Allendale, Mich., 1997; DEd, Ea. Mich. U., Ypsilanti, 2006. Cert. phys. therapist Cleve. State U., 1985, athletic trainer Nat. Athletic Trainers Assn., 1987, sports specialist in phys. therapy Am. Bd. of Phys. Therapy Specialities, 2003. Asst. prof. Grand Valley State U., Grand Rapids, Mich., 2000—05, assoc. prof., 2005—. Sports medicine clin. specialist St. Mary's Hosp./Mary Freebed Hosp., Grand Rapids, Mich., 1985—97; phys. therapist Rehab. Pros of West Mich., Grand Rapids, 1998—. Editor: (textbook) Musculoskeletal Rehabilitation. Recipient Outstanding Phys. Therapist award, Western Dist. of Mich. Phys. Therapy Assn., 1992. Mem.: ICCUS Soc. of Sports Phys. Therapists, Am. Orthop. Soc. for Sports Medicine, Nat. Athletic Trainers Assn., Sports Phys. Therapy Sect. (sec. 2000—06, Excellence in Acad. Edn. award 2006), Am. Phys. Therapy Assn. Office: Grand Valley State Univ 301 Michigan NE Rm 266 Grand Rapids MI 49503 Office Phone: 616-331-2695. Office Fax: 616-331-5999. E-mail: hoogenbb@gvsu.edu.

HOOGENBOOM, CAROL ANNETTE, clinical neuropsychologist; b. Grand Rapids, Mich., Jan. 31; d. Cornelius Adrian and Shirley Ann (Rassi) Hoogenboom. BS, Western Mich. U., Kalamazoo, 1985, MA, 1987; PsychD, Forest Inst., Wheeling, Ill., 1993. Lic. Clin. Psychologist Ill. Dept. Fin. & Profl. Regulation, 1995. Psychometrian Crawford Consulting Svc., Chgo., 1991—92, Behavioral Health Svcs., Chgo., 1993—94; intern, resident Cermak Hosp., Chgo., 1991—92; postdoctoral Psychealth Ltd., Evanston, Ill., 1993—95; pres., adminstr. Nat. Neuropsych. Svcs., Glenview, Ill., 1995—97, clin. psychologist, 1995—97; Neuropsychologist CAH Psychological Svcs., Chgo., 1998—. Personal injury cons. Area Personal Injury Attys., Chgo., 2003—05; domestic abuse cons. Sido's Shelter, Chgo., 2004; pro bono psychol. svcs. CAH Psychol. Svcs., Chgo., 2003—; mgr. Windsor Retirmeent Home, LaGrange, Ill., 2006—. Author: (manual) Starting a Domestic Abuse Shelter, 2004, Anti Social Personality Disorder Is Really a Delusional Disorder, 2006. AIDS speaker Area Hosps., Chgo., 2005; Provide free depression screening through local businesses, Chgo., 2003—; motivational speaker CAH Psycholog. Svcs., Chgo., 2005—; advisor Windsor Pl. Retirement Home, LaGrange, Ill., 2006. Fellow: APA; mem.: Am. Psychol Soc., Ill. Psychol. Assn., Behavior Book Club, Psi Chi. Achievements include Numerous awards in athletics: basketball, volleyball, track, softball and cycling, including All American honors; 1st female Native Am. to obtain doctoral degree in US. Avocations: coin collecting/numismatics, computers, sports, Equality and Civil Rights Issues, building trades. Office: CAH Psychol Svcs 28 E Jackson Bldg #10-H580 Chicago IL 60604 E-mail: carolhoogenboom@yahoo.com.

HOOKER, KAREN L., mathematics educator; m. Darrell Hooker. BA in Edn., Grove City Coll., Pa., 1983. Math tchr. Williamsburg/James City County Sch., Va., 1986—. Home: 158 Wellington Cir Williamsburg VA 23185

HOOLEY, DARLENE, congresswoman; b. Williston, ND, Apr. 4, 1939; d. Clarence Alvin and Alyce (Rogers) Olsen; m. John Hooley (div.); children: Chad, Erin. BS in Edn., Oreg. State U., Corvallis, 1961, postgraduate student, 1963-65, Portland State U., 1966-67. Tchr. Woodburn & Gervais Sch., Oreg., 1962-65, David Douglas Sch. Dist., Portland, Oreg., 1965-67, St. Mary's Acad., Portland, 1967-69; mem. City Coun., West Linn, Oreg., 1976-80, Oreg. State Ho. Reps., 1980-87; commr. Clackamas County Bd., Oreg., 1987-96; mem. US Congress from 5th Oreg. dist., 1996—, mem. fin. svcs. com., mem. vets. affairs com., mem. sci. com., ranking minority mem. rsch. subcommittee. Vice chair Oreg. Tourism Alliance, Portland, 1991; bd. dirs. Providence Med. Ctr., Portland, 1989, Cmty. Corrections Bd., Oregon City, 1990; acting chair Oreg. Trail Found. Bd., Oregon City, 1991; mem. Urban Growth Policy Adv. Com., Portland, 1991. Named Legislator of Yr. Oreg. Libr. Assn., 1985-86, Oreg. Solar Energy Assn., 1985; recipient Spl. Svc. award Clackamas City Coun. for Child Abuse Prevention, 1989. Mem. LWV, Oreg. Women's Polit. Caucus (Woman of Yr. 1988). Democrat. Office: US Ho Reps 2430 Rayburn Ho Office Bldg Washington DC 20515-3705 Office Phone: 202-225-5711.*

HOOPER, ANNE DODGE, pathologist, educator; b. Groton, Mass., July 16, 1926; d. Carroll William and Bertha Sanford (Wiener) Dodge; m. William Dale Hooper, June 17, 1952; children: Elizabeth Anne, Joan Elaine, Caroline Mae. AB, Washington U., St. Louis, 1947, MD, 1952. Diplomate Am. Bd. Pathology, Pathologic Anatomy, Clin. Pathology and Forensic Pathology. Rotating intern Virginia Mason Hosp., Seattle, 1952—53; resident in internal medicine St. Francis Hosp., Hartford, Conn., 1953—54; resident in pathologic anatomy and clin. pathology New Britain (Conn.) Gen. Hosp., 1954—57, Presbyn. Hosp., Phila., 1957—58; resident in forensic pathology Office Med. Examiner, Phila., 1958—60; from pathologist to acting chief lab svc. VA Hosp., Coatesville, Pa., 1960—66; dir. lab. St. Albans (Vt.) Hosp., 1966—69, Kerbs Hosp., St. Albans, 1966—71, Williamson Appalachian Regional Hosp., South Williamson, W.Va., 1971—73, Beckley (W.Va.) Appalachian Regional Hosp., 1974—76; asst. prof. pathology W.Va. Sch. Osteo. Medicine, Lewisburg, 1977, assoc. prof., 1978—97, cons. in pathology, 1997—. Lab. accreditation insp. CAP, 1992—, Am. Osteo. Assn., 1986—99; assoc. med. examiner State of W.Va., 1999—; med. missionary Kijabe Hosp., Kenya, 1998; med. missionary, pathologist Pathologists Overseas at SALFA Lab., Madagascar, 2000; med. missionary Glens Falls N.Y. Med. Missionary Found., Nueva Santa Rosa, Guatemala, 2001. Contbr. articles to profl. jours. Pres. local elem. sch. PTA, St. Albans, 1967—68; mem. profl. edn. com. W.Va. divsn. Am. Cancer Soc., Charleston, 1982—94, bd. dirs. W.Va. divsn., 1987—94, pres. Greenbrier unit Lewisburg, 1989—93; bd. dirs. ARC, Greenbrier County, W.Va., 2002—. Fellow: Am. Acad. Forensic Scis., Coll. Am. Pathologists; mem.: AMA, Am. Soc. Clin. Pathologists, Raleigh County Med. Soc., W.Va. Med. Soc. Avocations: violin, viola. Office: 63 Cedar Knoll Ronceverte WV 24970-9700 Personal E-mail: adhooper@mail.wnet.edu.

HOOPER, KAREN J., music educator; d. Kenneth J. and V. Elaine Hooper. AA in Music, Casper Coll., Wyo., 1995; MusB in Music Edn., U. Wyo., 1998. Elem. string tchr. Natrona County Sch. Dist., Casper, Wyo., 1998—99; orch. dir. Bryan (Tex.) Ind. Sch. Dist., 1999—2005, music tchr., 2004—05; orch. music tchr. Conroe Ind. Sch. Dist., 2005—. Violin, viola player Bryan (Tex.) County String Quartet, College Station, 2000—. Library asst. First Bapt. Ch., Bryan, Tex., 2003—05; vol. Second Chance Reserve Shelter, College Station, Tex., 2004—05. Nominee STAR award, Casper Star-Tribune, 1999. Mem.: Ams. String Tchrs. Assn., Tex. Orch. Dirs. Assn., Tex. Music Educator's Assn. Baptist.

HOOPER, KAY, writer; b. Merced, Calif., Oct. 30, 1957; d. James Henry and Martha Raye (Robbins) H. Author: Lady Thief, 1981, Mask of Passion, 1982, Return Engagement, 1982, Breathless Surrender, 1982, Taken by Storm, 1983, On Wings of Magic, 1983 (Best Ecstasy award Romantic Times Reviewers Choice 1984), Elusive Dawn, 1983, Kissed by Magic, 1983, CJ's Fate, 1984, Moonlight Rhapsody, 1984, Something Different, 1984, Pepper's Way, 1984, If There Be Dragons, 1984 (Bestselling Series Romance Waldenbooks 1985), Illegal Possession, 1985, Eye of the Beholder, 1985, Rebel Waltz, 1986, Belonging to Taylor, 1986, Larger than Life, Time After Time, 1986 (Best Loveswept award Romantic Times Reviewers Choice 1986), The Shamrock Trinity: Rafe, The Maverick, 1986 (Innovative Series award Waldenbooks 1987), On Her Doorstep, 1986, In Serena's Web, 1987, Raven on the Wing, 1987, The Delaneys of Killaroo: Adelaide the Enchantress, 1987, Rafferty's Wife, 1987, Zach's Law, 1987, the Fall of Lucas Kendrick, 1988, Unmasking Kelsey, 1988 (Silver Cert. Affaire de Coeur 1988), Summer of the Unicorn, 1988, Delaney Historicals: Golden Flames, 1988 (Spl. Acheivement award in Hist. Series Romantic Times Reviewers Choice 1988), Outlaw Derek, 1988, Shades of Grey, 1988, Delaney Historicals II: Velvet Lightning, 1988, Captain's Paradise, 1988, It Takes A Theif, 1989, Aces High, 1989, Enemy Mine, 1989, Golden Threads, 1989, The Glass Shoe, 1989, What Dreams May Come, 1990, Through the Looking Glass, 1990, The Lady and the Lion, 1990, Star-Crossed Lovers, 1990, Crime of Passion, 1991 (Contemporary Romantic Mystery award Romantic Times Reviewers Choice 1991), The Matchmaker, 1991, The Haviland Touch, 1991, House of Cards, 1991, Holiday Spirit, 1991, Christmas Future, 1992, The Touch of Max, 1993 (Bestselling Series Romance Paperback award Bookrack 1993), Maggie award Best Short Contemporary category Ga. Romance Writers 1993, Best Sales Performance award Barnes & Noble 1993), Hunting the Wolfe, 1993, The Trouble with Jared, 1993, The Wizard of Seattle, 1993 (Bestselling Fantasy award Waldenbooks 1993, Maggie award Best Mainstream catagory Ga. Romance Writers 1993, Best Futuristic award Romantic Times Viewers' Choice 1993), All For Quinn (Bestselling Loveswept award Waldenbooks 1993), Masquerade, 1994, The Haunting of Josie, 1994, Amanda, 1995, After Caroline, 1996, Finding Laura, 1997, Haunting Rachel, 2998, Hunting Fear, 2004, Chill of Fear, 2005, others. Recipient Love and Laughter award Romantic Times, 1984, Most Innovative Series award for Outstanding Contribution to Romance Genre, 1987, Lifetime Achievement award Innovative Series Romance, 1989, Lifetime Achievement award Series Romance, 1990, Career Achievement award Contemporary Romance, 1991. Office: PO Box 370 Bostic NC 28018-0370 Office Fax: 828-245-1805. E-mail: kay@kayhooper.com.

HOOPER, MARIE E., history professor; d. Charles R. and Freda H. Hooper. BA, Met. State Coll., Denver, 1986; MA, U. Calif., Davis, 1988; PhD, U. Pitts., 1999. Tchg. asst. U. Calif., Davis, 1986—88; lectr. U. Paris VII, X, 1989—91, MBAI, Paris, 1991—93, INSEEC, Paris, 1991—93, Am. U., Paris, 1991—93; tchg. fellow U. Pitts., 1995—99; asst. prof. history Oklahoma City U., 1999—2001, assoc. prof. history, 2001—. Fulbright program advisor Oklahoma City U., 2004—, academic dir. Office of Internat. Edn., 2004—. Bd. dirs. UN Assn., Oklahoma City, 2004—06, pres. local chpt., 2006—. Served with USAF, 1972—75. Recipient Outstanding Tchg. award, U. Pitts., 1999; fellow, Priddy Found., 2006. Avocations: dog sports, obedience. Office: Oklahoma City U 2501 N Blackwelder Oklahoma City OK 73106 Office Phone: 405-208-5453. Office Fax: 405-208-5200. E-mail: mhooper@okcu.edu.

HOOPES, MARGARET HOWARD, educator, psychologist, marriage and family therapist; b. Idaho Falls, Idaho, May 12, 1927; d. James Parley and Elizabeth Joyce (Humphrey) Howard; m. Ned Edward Hoopes, June 20, 1958 (div.) BS, Ricks Coll., Idaho, 1953; MS, Brigham Young U., 1962; PhD, U. Minn., 1969. Tchr. elem. and jr. high sch., Jerome, Idaho, 1948-52; tchr. jr. high sch. Ephrata, Wash., 1955-58; tchr. New Trier High Sch., Winnetka, Ill., 1958-66; instr. U. Minn., 1966-69, asst. prof., 1969-70; assoc. prof. Brigham Young U., Provo, Utah, 1973-81, prof., 1981—. Contbr. articles to profl. jours. Author: (with others) Readings in Ethical and Professional Issues for Marital and Family Therapists, 1980; Family Facilitation: Education, Enrichment and Treatment, 1984, Birth Order Roles and Sibling Positions in Individual and Family Therapy, 1987. Mem. Am. Assn. Marriage and Family Therapists, Am. Psychol. Assn., Nat. Council Family Relations Republican. Mem. Lds Ch.

HOORNBEEK, LYNDA RUTH COUCH, librarian, educator; b. Springfield, Ill., July 12, 1933; d. Willard Lee and Mabel Magdalene (Forberg) Couch; m. Louis Arthur Hoornbeek, Nov. 9, 1957; children— John Arthur, David William, Mark Benjamin. B.A. in Sociology, U. Ill., 1955; M.Ed., Cornell U., 1956; M.L.S., U. So. Calif., Los Angeles, 1973. Cert. tchr. Ill., N.Y. Tchr. elem. sch. North Haven (Conn.) Pub. Schs., 1956-57; library adminstr. Winfield (Ill.) Pub. Library, 1974-77; interim library adminstr. Bloomingdale (Ill.) Pub. Library, 1977-78; ref. librarian Franklin Park (Ill.) Pub. Library, 1978-83; state literacy dir. program Literacy Vols. of Ill., Chgo., 1983—84; research coordinator Ill. Literacy Council, Office of Sec. State, 1984—85; with office libr. outreach svcs. ALA, 1985-86; adult svcs. libr. Glen Ellyn (Ill.) Pub. Libr., 1986-94; ret., 1994. Bd. dirs. YWCA, Pitts., 1957—62; vol. archivist Glen Ellyn Hist. Soc., bd. dirs. 1994—. YWCA fellow 1954; Ford Found. fellow, 1955-56; U. Ill. scholar, 1951-55. Mem. Mortar Bd., Calif. Library Assn., Ill. Library Assn., ALA, AAUW, LWV, Beta Phi Mu, Pi Lambda Theta, Alpha Phi. Congregationalist. Home: 351 N Park Blvd Glen Ellyn IL 60137-5037

HOOVER, LINDA SUE, elementary school educator, coach; m. James Hoover, July 9, 1983. BA in Liberal Studies, Calif. State U., Northridge, 1985. Tchg. credential Calif., 1990. Tchr. Riverview Mid. Sch., Helendale, Calif., 1990—. Coach Riverview Mid. Sch., Helendale, Calif., 1990. Avocations: basketball, running, travel, national parks. Home: 17881 Link Rd Helendale CA 92342 Office: Riverview Mid Sch 15350 RIverview Rd Helendale CA 92342 Office Phone: 760-952-1266.

HOOVER, LYNN HORN, secondary school educator; b. Statesvillve, N.C., Feb. 9, 1961; d. James Price and Patricia Alice Horn; m. Dennis Gray Hoover, July 10, 1956; children: Sarah Elizabeth, Casey William, Callie Collins. BS, U. N.C., Greensboro, 1983. Tchr. math South Iredell H.S., Statesville, NC, 1997—. Recipient Tchr. of Yr. award, South Iredell H.S., 2005-2006. Home: 310 E Church Troutman NC 28166 Office: S Iredell HS 299 Old Mountain Rd Statesville NC 28677 Office Phone: 704-528-4536.

HOOVER, PEARL ROLLINGS, nurse; b. LeSueur, Minn., Aug. 24, 1924; d. William Earl and Louisa (Schickling) Rollings; m. Roy David Hoover, June 19, 1948 (dec. Mar. 1987); children: Helen Louise, William Robert (dec.). Grad. in nursing, U. Minn., 1945, BS in Nursing, 1947; MS in Health Sci., Calif. State U., Northridge, 1972. Dir. affiliate nursing sch. Mooselake State Hosp., Minn., 1948-49; nursing instr. Anchor Hosp., County Hosp., St. Paul, 1949-51; student nurse supr. and instr. Brentwood VA Hosp., LA, 1951-52; sch. nurse LA Unified City Schs., 1963-91, substitute sch. nurse, 1991-96. Camp nurse United First Meth. Ch., winter and summer past 40 yrs.; corr. sec. Reseda Women's Club, 1st v.p.; courtesy chmn. First United Meth. Women. Mem. LA Coun. Sch. Nurses, Calif. Sch. Nurses Orgn. Democrat. Methodist. Home: 17851 Lull St Reseda CA 91335-2237

HOPE, CAROL J., pharmacist, researcher, information technology manager; d. Inabelle Jean and John Finley Payne. BS chem. and petroleum-refining engring., Colo. Sch. of Mines, 1972—76, MS chem. and petroleum-refining engring., 1976—77; MS in biol. sci., U. of Colo. Health Sciences Ctr., 1991—96, BS in pharmacy, 1996—2000, PharmD, 2000—01; Pharmacy Fellowship, Purdue U./Regenstrief Inst., Specialties: Medical Informatics & Health Services Research, 2001—03. Lic. Pharmacist Colo., 2000, Ind., 2001, Miss., 2003. Asst. prof. schs. medicine and pharmacy U. Miss. Med. Ctr., Jackson, 2001—04; clin. staff pharmacist Baptist Meml. Hosp., Golden Triangle, Colo., 2004—05; info. sys. pharmacist John Hopkins Hosp., Balt., 2006—. Rsch. asst. U. Colo. Health Scis. Ctr., Denver, 1993—96, rsch. project mgr., 1997—98, rsch. asst., 1999; clin.rsch. asst. Rocky Mountain Soc. Multiple Sclerosis, 1996—97; rsch. pharmacy externship Kaiser HMO, 1999; rsch. pharmacy intern VA Coop. Studies Program Clin. Rsch. Pharmacy Coordinating Ctr., Albuquerque, 2000, U. Colo. Health Scis. Ctr. IRB, Denver, 2001; grant reviewer Office of Rsch. Integrity, Washington, 2005—. Contbr. articles to profl. jours. Recipient Suicide and Depression Anonymous Humanitarian award, 1995, Suicide and Depression Anonymous Outstanding Vol. award, 1992, On-the-Job Individual Performance award, Lowry AFB, 1990, Outstanding Young Women in Am. award, 1977, Hays award, Chem. Engring. Dept., 1976, AMAX Project Design award, 1976; grant, Drug Info. Assn., 2002—03, Sam and Mytrie Regenstrief Postdoctoral Grant, 2002—03, Colo. Undergraduate Merit scholarship, 1997—99. Mem.: Am. Pharm. Assn., Am. Soc. of Health-System Pharamacists (reveiwer), Am. Coll. of Clin. Pharmacology, Am. Med. Informatics Assn., Am. Soc. for Clin. Pharmacology and Therapeutics (edn. com., adverse drug event symposium steering com. 2003—05, reveiwer). Christian. Achievements include design of new method to detect adverse drug events using non-clinical personnel. Avocations: yoga, reading, needlecrafts. Business E-Mail: chope2@jhmc.edu.

HOPE, JUDITH H., former political organization administrator; b. Warren, Ark., Nov. 2, 1939; d. Carroll Charles and Mayme (Stevens) Hollensworth; m. Thomas A. Twomey, Jr.; children: Leif Erling, Nisse Elizabeth. Student, Gulf Park Coll. for Women, 1956-57, U. Ark., 1957-60, Tobe Coburn Sch., N.Y., 1960-61. Town supr., East Hampton, N.Y., 1974-76, 84-88; appointments officer to N.Y. Gov. Hugh L. Carey, 1976-79; spl. asst. to Gov. for L.I., 1979-81; mem. Dem. Nat. Com., 1989-92; 1st vice chairwoman N.Y. State Dem. Party, 1989-92; mem. exec. com. Dem. Nat. Com., 1997; chairwoman N.Y. State Dem. Party, 1995—2001. Mem. N.Y. Bldg. Codes Coun. Mem. N.Y. State Women's Dem. Leadership Coun., 1990-95; dir. Planned Parenthood of Suffolk County, 1988—; vice chmn. South Fork Nature Conservancy; founding mem. East End Women's Network; mem. N.Y. State Ctr. for Women in Govt., L.I. LWV; founder, chair Elenor Roosevelt Legacy Com., 2000—. Recipient Woman of Yr. award Suffolk County Human Rights Commn., 1986, Woman of Yr. award East Hampton Assn. Univ. Women, 1988, Pres.'s Pub. Svc. award Nature Conservancy, 1988, Environ. Roll of Honor, Group for the South Fork, 1990, Cmty. Svc. award Apple Inst., 1992. Mem. Pi Beta Phi. Home: #9 Two Holes of Water East Hampton NY 11937

HOPE, KATHRYN MARY, management consultant; b. Berkeley, Calif., Feb. 17, 1952; d. John Michael Reisert Hope and Mary Elizabeth McCarthy. BA, U. Calif. Irvine, 1974; MS Internat. Pub. Adminstrn., U. So. Calif., L.A., 1979. Vol. Peace Corps, Cameroon, 1974—76; asst. dir. USO Camp Hansen, Okinawa, Japan, 1980—81; mgr. chpt. ARC, Bremerton, Va., 1981—86, mgr. Armed Forces Emergency Svcs. Italy, Germany, Portugal, N.D., Saudi Arabia, P.R., Md., Nev., 1986—2002, asst. dir. Diaster Svcs. Santa Ana, Calif., 2002—. Recipient Civilian Svc. award Gulf War, Dept. Def., 1991. Mem.: Mensa. Avocations: travel, theater, cooking. Office: American Red Cross 601 N Golden Cir Santa Ana CA 92705

HOPE, MARGARET LAUTEN, retired civic worker; b. NYC; 1 son, Frederick H., III. Privately educated. Ball com. various charity fund raising events. Mem. Jr. League NYC; Everglades Club, Palm Beach, Fla.; Women's Nat. Rep. Club (NYC); St. James Club (London). Home and Office: 236 Dunbar Rd Palm Beach FL 33480

HOPKINS, BRENDA LUVENIA, social sciences educator, minister; b. Monroe, NC, Apr. 1, 1951; d. Willie and Marion Lomax Hopkins. BA, N.C. Ctrl. U., 1973; MA, Wingate U., 1989; ednl. specialist, Mich. State U., 2000; MDiv, No. Bapt. Theol. Sem., 2003; PhD in Ministry, Grad. Theol. Found., 2005, postgrad., 2005—; student, Hebrew U. Tchr. educator Johnson Jr. H.S., Washington, 1973—83, Coll. Moyen Gen. Enseignment, Benin, West Africa, 1983—87, Benin U., West Africa, 1983—87; tchr. educator, minister Union

County Pub. Sch., Monroe, NC, 1987—96; rschr., educator Mich. State U., East Lansing, 1996—2000; minister, counselor Theol. Sem., Lombard, Ill., 2000—03, Grad. Theol. Found., South Bend, Ind., 2003—. Chaplain, counselor Good Samaritan Hosp., Downers Grove, Ill., 2001—, Alexian Brothers Med. Ctr., Elk Grove, Ill., 2003—. Vol. Peace Corps, Contonon, West Africa, 1983—84; grant writer Partnership Grant, Washington, 1982—83; pastor, chaplain Elizabeth Bapt. Ch., Monroe, 1987—96. Mem.: Ministerial Alliance (sec. 1987—), Waynes Oates Inst. (scholar 2000—03), Writers' Soc. (life scholar 2003—). Avocations: walking, swimming, piano, reading and writing French and Spanish. E-mail: luveniahop60@hotmail.com, hopkinsb@msu.edu.

HOPKINS, CATHERINE LEE, music educator; d. John James and Eleanor May (Hubert) Sanderson; m. Stephen Ernest Hopkins, June 26, 1965; children: Cheryl Lynne Hopkins Naquette, Scott Eric. MusB Edn., New Eng. Conservatory, 1961. Tchr. Nagautuck Schs., Conn., 1961—62, Attleboro Schs., Mass., 1962—68, Smithfield Schs., RI, 1982—. Parent coun. Boy Scouts Am., Smithfield, 1992—; advocate Special Olympics, Trudeau Center, 1995—, No. ARC, Woonsocket, RI, 1997—. Mem.: Am. Choral Dirs. Conf., Music Educators Nat. Conf. Home: 8 Appleseed Dr Greenville RI 02828

HOPKINS, CYNTHIA, composer; Composer: A Simple Heart, Girl Gone, Hazard of Gravity (could you borrow me a hammer), Toast of Tears; actor: numerous film and theater projects; musician: (albums) Gloria Deluxe.

HOPKINS, DEBORAH C., diversified financial services company executive; b. Milw., Nov. 12, 1954; BS, Walsh Coll.; postgrad., U. Pa. With Ford Motor Co., Nat. Bank Detroit, Unisys Corp., v.p. corp. bus., 1991-93, v.p., corp. contr., chief acctg. officer, 1993-95, v.p., gen. mgr. worldwide info. svcs.; gen. auditor GM, 1995-97; v.p. fin., CFO GM Europe, Zürich, Switzerland; sr. v.p., CFO Boeing, Seattle, 1998—2000; CFO, exec. v.p. Lucent Tech., Murray Hill, NJ, 2000—01; sr. ptnr. Marakon Assocs.; chief ops. and tech. officer Citigroup, 2003—. Bd. dirs. E.I. DuPont De Nemours and Co. Bd. dirs. Seattle Symphony. Named one of 50 most powerful women in Am. bus. Fortune Mag., 1999, mgr. to watch in 2000 Bus. Week, 1999. Office: Citigroup 399 Park Ave New York NY 10043

HOPKINS, GINGER ALLEN, school system administrator; d. George Allen and Margo Malko Allen; m. Bob Hopkins, June 14, 1980; children: Carissa, Whitney, Thaddeus. BS in Math., Cedar Crest Coll., Allentown, Pa., 1980; M in Edn. Adminstrn., Wayne State U., Detroit, 2003. Cert. supt. S.C. Dept. Edn., 2006. Dir. elem. schs. Beaufort (S.C.) County Sch. Dist., 2003—05, asst. supt. academics and accountability, 2005—. Mem. S.C. h.s. redesign commn. S.C. Dept. Edn., Columbia, 2005—. Active mem. Winchester (Ind.) Congl. Ch., 2006—06. Home: 6 Purrysburg Dr Beaufort SC 29907 Office: Beaufort County School District 1300 King St Beaufort SC 29901 Office Phone: 843-322-8034. Personal E-mail: gingerhopkins@gmail.com. Business E-Mail: gh9008@beaufort.k12.sc.us.

HOPKINS, JAN, journalist, newscaster; b. Warren, Ohio, May 22, 1947; d. Walter Charles and Lois Avelene (Botroff) Reed; m. Walter Hopkins, June 14, 1969 (div. Nov. 1981); m. Richard Trachtman, Nov. 8, 1986. Dir. news Sta. WTCL, Warren, Ohio, 1973-75; reporter, anchor Sta. WERE, Cleve., 1975-77; reporter Sta. WKBN-TV, Youngstown, Ohio, 1977-80; reporter, anchor Sta. WLWT-TV, Cin., 1980-82; assignment editor CBS News, N.Y.C., 1983; reporter, prodr. ABC News, N.Y.C., 1983-84; anchor bus. news CNN, N.Y.C., 1984—. Author: (chapter) Knight Bagehot Guide to Business Journalism, 1990, 2d edit., 2000. Trustee Hiram Coll., 1988—94; adv. bd. Knight Bagehot program journalism Columbia U., N.Y.C., 1994; mem. nat. bd. Girl Scouts USA, 2001—. Recipient Peabody award U. Ga., 1988, Front Page award Newswomen Club N.Y., 1988, Lifetime Achievement award Women's Econ. Roundtable, 2002; Knight Bagehot fellow Columbia U. Sch. Journalism, 1982-83; named to Hall of Excellence Ohio Found. Ind. Colls., 1993, Warren, Ohio, H.S. Disting. Alumni Hall of Fame, 1995. Mem. Econ. Club N.Y. E-mail: jan.hopkins@turner.com.

HOPKINS, JEANNETTE ETHEL, book publisher, editor; b. Camden, N.J., Dec. 7, 1922; d. Carleton Roper and Gladys Eugenia (Hull) H. BA, Vassar Coll., 1944; MS, Columbia Sch. Journalism, 1945. Asst. to Sunday editor New Haven Register, 1945-46; reporter Providence Evening Bull., 1946-50, Oklahoma City Times, 1950-51; sr. editor Beacon Press, Boston, 1951-56, Harcourt Brace, N.Y.C., 1956-64, Harper & Row, N.Y.C., 1964-73; v.p. Met. Applied Res. Ctr., N.Y.C., 1970-72, cons. editor, 1973-80, 89—; dir. Wesleyan Univ. Press, Middletown, Conn., 1980-89. Adj. prof. English Wesleyan U., 1987-89, U. N.H., 1989; propr. Portsmouth Athenaeum, 1991—. Author: Books That Will Not Burn, 1952, 14 Journeys to Unitarianism, 1951, (with K.B. Clark) Relevant War Against Poverty, 1968, Legacy: A History of the South Church Endowment, 1995. Mem. coun. Inst. Religion in an Age of Sci., 1968-72, 80-82, 88-91, mem. adv. bd. 1962-72, 82-94; mem. bd. Unitarian UN Office, 1977-80; mem. Commn. on Appraisal, Unitarian Universalist Assn., 1976-78; bd. dirs. ACLU, 1970-79, mem. nat. adv. coun., 1986—; bd. govs. Comty. Ch. N.Y., 1960-66, Unitarian-Universalist Ch., Portsmouth, 1990-93, lay min., 1991-95; trustee South Ch. Endowment Fund, 1996-99; v.p. Unitarian Fellowship for Social Justice, 1958-62. Louise Hart Van Loon fellow, Vassar Coll., 1944; recipient Disting. Alumni award Columbia Sch. Journalism, 1981. Mem.: PEN, Authors Guild. Democrat. Unitarian. Home and Office: 39 Pray St Portsmouth NH 03801-5226

HOPKINS, KAREN BROOKS, performing arts executive; b. 1951; d. Howard and Paula Brooks; divorced; 1 child, Matthew. BA in Theater Arts with honors, U. Md., 1973; MFA, George Washington U., 1980. Mem. group sales staff Am. Theater, Washington, 1973; cmty. rels. dir. Qwindo's Windo Dance Trouing Co., Washington, 1975; theater mgr., asst. dir. Chelm Players Touring Co., 1975-76, prodr., 1975-78; theater dir. Jewish Cmty. Ctr. of Greater Washington, 1976-78; devel. dir. The New Playwright's Theatre, Washington, 1978-79; devel. officer Bklyn. Acad. of Music, 1979-81, v.p. planning and devel., 1981-88, exec. v.p., 1988-98, COO and exec. v.p., 1998-99, pres., 1999—. Adj. prof. program for arts adminstrn. Bklyn. Coll., 1980-84. Author: Successful Fundraising for Arts and Cultural Organizations, 1989, 2d edit., 1997. Fundraising cons. art instns., 1979—; chair Performing Arts Ctrs. Consortium, 1994-96, Cultural Instns. Group, 2002-04; mem. adv. com. Salzburg Seminar-Alberto Vilar Project of Critical Issues for the Classical Performing Arts; ex-officio mem. N.Y.C. Cultural Affairs Adv. Commn., 2003. Recipient King Olav medal Norwegian Nat. Ballet, 1982, Dramaten medal, 1995. Office: Brooklyn Acad Music 30 Lafayette Ave Brooklyn NY 11217-1430*

HOPKINS, MARTHA ANN, sculptor; b. Meridian, Miss., Feb. 4, 1940; d. Hugh Wallace Markline and Martha Lou Morton; m. Harry L. Hopkins, Aug. 19, 1961; children: Peter Ashley, Caroline Baker. BA in Spanish, U. So. Miss., 1961; BA in Visual Art, U. Montevallo, 1982; BFA in Sculpture, U. Ala., 2004. Exec. sec., engr. asst. Humble Oil & Refining Co., New Orleans, 1961—65; modern lang. tchr. Meridian HS, 1967—71. Arts camp tchr. Birmingham (Ala.) Mus. Art, 1999, sculpture tchr. hs students, 2000. Prodr.: (films, demonstration video for Pub. TV) Found Object Sculpture, 2000; exhibitions include Celebrating Women Artists of Ala., 2001, Nat. Small Sculpture Exhbn., 2000, Three Rivers Arts Festival, Pitts., 1999, Gadsden (Ala.) Cultural Arts Ctr., 1998, Meridian Mus. Art, 1995, Meridian (Miss.) Cmty. Coll., 2004, prin. works include Ala. Vets. Meml. sculpture, Red Tide sculpture, U. Ala., Birmingham, 1991, Wild Blue sculpture, Meridian Miss. Airport, 2003, (book) Carousels Abound, 2003. Bd. dirs. Planned Parenthood Ala., Birmingham, 1998—2001. Mem.: Ala. Designer/Craftsmen (pres. 1978—2001), Birmingham Doll Club. Avocation: antique dolls. Home and Studio: 1800 Woodcrest Rd Birmingham AL 35209

HOPKINS, MARTHA JANE, retired education educator; b. Astoria, Oreg., Mar. 21, 1938; d. Willie Lester and Della May (Solmon) H. BA, N.W. Nazarene Coll., 1959; MS, Ind. U., 1961; EdD, U. Idaho, 1971. Tchr. Lynch Elem. Sch., Portland, Oreg., 1959-60, Corvallis HS, Oreg., 1961-64, Bethany Nazarene Coll., Okla., 1964-66; athletic dir. N.W. Nazarene Coll., Nampa, Idaho, 1984-87, acad. dean, 1987-89, prof. health and phys. edn., 1966-2000, chair dept. bus., 1992-95, chair divsn. profl. studies, 1985-96, chair dept. kinesiology, 1997-98; ret., 2000. Bd. dirs. Coll. Ch. of Nazarene, Nampa, 1989. Named to Idaho New Agenda Hall of Fame, 1988, NAIA Coaches Hall of Fame, 1982, N.W. Nazarene Coll. Athletic Hall of Fame, 1990. Mem. AAHPERD, Am. Assn. for Higher Edn., Idaho Assn. Health Phys. Edn. and Dance (pres. 1971-72), DAR (chair nat. def. com. EEDAHHOW chpt. 1989-97, chptr. regent EEDAHHOW 2005—), Nat. Wellness Inst., IAHPER (disting. svc. award 1996). Avocations: genealogy, racquetball, skiing, crafts, reading. Home: 96 N Mirage St Nampa ID 83651-2284

HOPKINS, NANCY H., biology professor; BA, Radcliffe Coll., 1964; PhD, Harvard U., 1971. Asst. prof. MIT, Cambridge, 1973—76, assoc. prof., 1976—82, prof., 1982—, chmn. comm. on women faculty, Sch. Sci., co-chmn. council on faculty diversity, Amgen Inc. prof. molecular and devel. biology. Recipient Laya Wiesner Community Award, 2001, Women's History Month Honoree of NY Academy of Sciences; fellow Amer. Academy of Arts and Sciences. Fellow: Am. Acad. Arts and Scis.; mem.: NAS, Inst. Med. Office: MIT E17-341 77 Massachusetts Ave Cambridge MA 02139-4301 Office Phone: 617-253-6414. Business E-Mail: nhopkins@mit.edu.*

HOPKINSON, NICOLE JEAN, elementary school educator; d. Pamela Jean and Michael Wayne Larson; m. Kyle Edward Hopkinson, Nov. 25, 2005. BS in Psychology, Magna Cum Laude, U. Ctrl. Fla., Orlando, 2001—04. Cert. Tchr., Social Science Edn. Fla. Dept. Edn., 2004. With red lobster Darden Restaurants, Orlando, 2003—04; 6th grade geography tchr. Meadowbrook Mid. Sch., Orlando, 2004—. Soccer coach Meadowbrook Mid. Sch., Orlando, 2005—. Mem.: Kappa Delta Pi (life). Office Phone: 407-296-5130.

HOPKINSON, SHIRLEY LOIS, library and information scientist, educator; b. Boone, Iowa, Aug. 25, 1924; d. Arthur Perry and Zora (Smith) Hopkinson. Student, Coe Coll., 1942—43; AB cum laude, U. Colo., 1945; BLS, U. Calif., 1949; MA, Claremont Grad. Sch., 1951; EdM, U. Okla., 1952, EdD, 1957. Tchr. pub. sch., Stigler, Okla., 1946—47; tchr. Palo Verde HS., Jr. Coll., Blythe, Calif., 1947—48; asst. libr. Modesto Jr. Coll., Calif., 1949—51; tchr., libr. Fresno, Calif., 1951—52, La Mesa, Calif., 1953—55; asst. prof. librarianship, instrnl. materials dir. Chaffey Coll., Ontario, Calif., 1955—59; asst. prof. librarianship San Jose State Coll., Calif., 1959—64, assoc. prof., 1964—69, prof., 1969—. Bd. dirs. NDEA Inst. Sch. Librs., summer, 1966; mem. Santa Clara County Civil Svc. Bd. Examiners. Author: Descriptive Cataloging of Library Materials, Instructional Materials for Teaching the Use of the Library; editor: Calif. Sch. Libraries, 1963—64; asst. editor Sch. Libr. Assn. of Calif. Bull., 1961—63, book reviewer profl. jours.; contbr. articles to profl. jours. Honnold Honor scholar, Claremont Grad. Sch., 1945—46. Mem.: LWV (bd. dirs. 1950—51, publs. chmn.), AAUW (dir. 1957—58), NEA, ALA, AAUP, Kappa Delta Pi, Alpha Beta Alpha, Calif. Tchrs. Assn., San Diego County Sch. Librs. Assn. (sec. 1954—55), Sch. Librs. Assn. Calif. (treas. No. sect. 1951—52, com. mem.), Audio-Visual Assn. Calif., Calif. Library Assn., Bus. Profl. Women's Club, Alpha Lambda Delta, Phi Beta Kappa (scholar 1944), Delta Kappa Gamma (sec. 1994—96, legis. liaison 1996—2002, corr. sec. 2002—), Phi Kappa Phi (disting. acad. achievement award 1981). Office: 1340 Pomeroy Ave Apt 408 Santa Clara CA 95051-3658

HOPMAN, ELLEN EVERT, psychotherapist, author and herbalist; b. Salzburg, Austria, July 31, 1952; came to U.S., 1954; d. Abraham Nathan and Marcia Elizabeth Evert; m. Albert Novelli, Jr., Jan. 14, 1973 (div. 1980). BS in Art Edn., Temple U., Phila., 1978; MEd in Mental Health Counseling, U. Mass., Amherst, 1990. Teaching Cert. Art tchr. Upper Darby Sch. Dist., Upper Darby, Pa., 1978-80; teaching asst. Temple U. Art Hist. Dept., Phila., 1980-82; health educator, master herbalist pvt. practice, Amherst, Belchertown, Mass., 1983—, psychotherapist, 1990—. Environ. cons. Clean Water Action, Northampton, Mass., 1990-93. Author: Tree Medicine, Tree Magic, 1991, A Druid's Herbal for the Sacred Earth Year, 1994, Being a Pagan - The New Pagans Speak Out, 1995, Walking the World in Wonder - A Children's Herbal, 2006; author video: Gifts from the Healing Earth, Vol. 1, 1993, Gifts from the Healing Earth, Vol. II, Pagans; contbr. articles to profl. mags. Co-founder, co-chief Order of the White Oak (Ord na Darach Gile). Mem. Am. Herbalists Guild, Keltria (v.p., 1988-96). Democrat. Office: PO Box 219 Amherst MA 01004-0219

HOPPE, DOROTHE ANNA, chemistry professor; b. Mettingen, Westfalen, Germany, Sept. 11, 1958; d. Josef Franz and Gisela Aloisia Hoppe. MS, Freie Univ. Berlin, 1987; PhD, Ruprecht Karl Univ. Heidelberg, 1990. Cert. Tchg. Credential Chemistry, Biology State of Calif., 2000, Clad Credential State of Calif., 2000. Rschr. physiology and biophysics U. Calif., Irvine, 1990—92; sci. tchr. Santa Margarita HS, Rancho Santa Margarita, Calif., 1992—98; tchr. chemistry Calif. Acad. Math & Scis., Carson, 1998—2000; tchr. chemistry & biology Loara HS, Anaheim, Calif., 2000—01; tchr. Comenius Kolleg, Mettingen, NRW, Germany, 2001—02; tchr. sci. Santa Margarita HS, Rancho Santa Margarita, Calif., 2002—. Reader and writer for chemistry GSE, Calif., 2000—01; reader AP chemistry Ednl. Testing Svc. Clemson U., SC, 2005—; adj. instr. Irvine Valley Coll., Calif., 1993—97. Contbr. articles to profl. jours. Scholarship, Stiftung des deutschen Volkes, 1988—90. Mem.: NSTA (assoc.), Am. Chem. Assn. (assoc.), Alexander von Humboldt Found. (life Feodor Lynen Fellowship 1990). Office: Santa Margarita High School 22062 Antonio Parkway Rancho Santa Margarita CA 92688 Office Phone: 949-766-6000. E-mail: hopped@smhs.org.

HOPPE, ELIZABETH ANNE, philosopher, educator; b. Seattle, Oct. 14, 1963; d. Harley Henry and Mary Teresa Hoppe. BA in Philosophy, U. Notre Dame, South Bend, Ind., 1987; MA in Philosophy, Loyola U.-Chgo., 1990; PhD in Philosophy, DePaul U., Chgo., 2000. Assoc. prof., chair dept. philosophy Lewis U., Romeoville, Ill., 1999—, chair Title III taskforce, 2005—06, peace edn. com., 2000—. Author (and editor): Listening: A Jour. of Religion and Culture; contbr. articles to profl. jours. Collegium fellow, Collegium of Cath. Univs./Fairfield U., 2002. Mem.: Soc. for Phenomenology and Existential Philosophy, Am. Cath. Philos. Assn., Am. Philos. Assn., Delta Epsilon Sigma. Office: Lewis University One University Pkwy Romeoville IL 60446 Office Phone: 815-836-5312.

HOPPE, SHERRY LEE, academic administrator; b. Chickamauga, Ga. BS magna cum laude, U. Tenn., Chattanooga, 1969, MS, 1974; EdD, U. Tenn., Knoxville, 1981. Clk. new accounts Pioneer Bank, Chattanooga, 1965-66; asst. to dir. fin. aid, sec. U. Tenn., Chattanooga, 1966-69; counselor, tchr. Chattanooga Valley High Sch., 1969-77; from coord. vets. affairs to dean Chattanooga State Tech. Community Coll., 1977-87; interim pres. Nashville State Tech. Inst., 1987-88; pres. Roane State Community Coll., Harriman, Tenn., 1988; interim pres. Austin Peay State U., Tenn., 2000—01, pres. Tenn., 2001—. Contbr. articles to jours. in field. Bd. dirs. Meth. Med. Ctr., Community Devel. Coun., Roane County, Oak Ridge Community Found., Chattanooga Area Am. Heart Assn., Multiple Sclerosis Soc., Sentenga chptr., Jr. Achievement, Chattanooga Venture, Met. Coun., Cherokee Area Coun. Boy Scouts Am., Am. Lung Assn. Southeastern Region, Sovran Bank, Henry Devel. Ctr.; account exec., sect. leader United Way, 1882-84, strategic action com., 1987; Mem. Pub. Rels. Task Force Vision 2000, 1984-85, planning adv. com. Chattanooga-Hamilton County Regional Planning Commn., 1985; chmn. Homecoming '86 Enterprise Com. Greater Chattanooga Area, Made in Chattanooga Exhbn., 1986; participator Leadership Chattanooga, Leadership Roane County. Mem. NEA, Tenn. Edn. Assn., C. of C. (pub. rels. task force 1983), Nat. Coun. Instructional Adminstrs., Am. Assn. Women in Community and Jr. Colls. (participated in Leaders of the '80s 1981), Chattanooga Indsl. Pers. Club, Chattanooga Area Pers. Assn., Rotary. Office: Austin Peay State U Office of Pres BR 125 PO Box 4576 Clarksville TN 37044 Office Phone: 931-221-7567. E-mail: hoppes@apsu.edu.

HOPPER, ANITA KLEIN, molecular genetics educator; b. Chgo., Sept. 24, 1945; d. Irving and Rose (Warshawsky) Klein; m. James Ernest Hopper, Jan. 3, 1971; 1 child, Julie Victoria. BS, U. Ill., Chgo., 1967; PhD, U. Ill., 1972. Postdoctoral researcher genetics U. Wash., Seattle, 1971-75; asst. prof. microbiology U. Mass. Med. Sch., Worcester, 1975-78, assoc. prof. microbiology, 1978-79; assoc. prof. biochemistry Hershey Med. Sch., Pa. State U., Hershey, 1979-87, prof. biochemistry, molecular biology, 1987—. Genetic biol panel NSF, Washington, 1981—85; mem genetic study sect NIH, Bethesda, Md., 1985—89, mem CDFI study sect, 1997—2000, chair CDFI study sect, 2001—; chair symposia and meetings Pa. State U.; pres. RNA Soc., 2003—04. Editor: Molecular & Cellular Biology, 1989—2000; mem ed bd:, 1986—90, RNA, 1995—97. Named Distinguished Educator, Penn. State U., 2005; fellow Postdoctoral, NIH, 1971—73; grantee NIH, 1979—, Univ Louisville Med Sch, 1989, NSF, 1988—91. Fellow: Am. Acad. Microbiology; mem.: AAAS, RNA Soc. (pres. 2003—04), Genetics Soc. Am. (sec. 2004—), Am. Assn. Microbiology (chair Eli Lilly award com. 2000—), Am. Assn. Biochemists, Am. Soc. Microbiology (chair genetics and molecular biology divsn. 1988). Office: Pa State U Med Sch Dept Biochemistry & Molec Biol Hershey PA 17033

HOPPER, BETTE PATRICIA, retired elementary school educator; b. Holyoke, Colo., July 21, 1921; d. Frank Neville and Goldie Lora Sprague; m. Joseph Frederick Hopper, Dec. 29, 1955; children: Lori Jo, Charlotte Claire, Christopher Freedom, Frank;children from previous marriage: Jana Margaret Meyer, Cherie Joanne Meyer. BSc in Edn., Eas. Oreg. State Coll., 1956. Cert. tchr. Idaho, Oreg., Colo. Tchr. grade 5, Holyoke, 1941—42; tchr. grade 6, 1943—44; tchr. grade 2 Fruitland, Idaho, 1951—53; tchr. grade 4 Vale, Oreg., 1953—55; tchr. grade 3 Twin Falls, 1955—56; tchr. grade 2, 1956—57; tchr. grade 1 Ontario, 1961—62; tchr. grade 2, 1962—63, 1969—71; tchr. Head Start, 1972—73. Instr. violin Covenant of Sacred Heart, N.Y.C. Mem.: Delta Kappa Gamma (pres. music com. 1970—72). Democrat. Christian Scientist. Achievements include performing 200 concerts at assisted living organizations and church events in 2005.

HOPPER, CAROL, incentive program administrator, trade association administrator; b. Montreal, Que., Can., Apr. 23, 1952; m. Cedric Heimrath; stepchildren: Natasha, Erik. Student, McGill U., 1972; cert., Canadian Inst. Orgnl. Mgmt., 1991. Asst. Ben Fuller Assocs., 1973-89; show dir. Nat. Ski Industries Assn., Montreal, 1989-91, exec. dir., 1991-96, dir. show svcs., 1997-98; project mgr. Chateau Travel, Carlson Mktg. Group, 1998—2002; project leader Vision 2000 Travel Group, 2002—. Mem. adv. com. sporting goods bus. program Sir Sandford Fleming Coll., 1994-98. Mem. Jr. League Montreal (bd. dirs., chmn. coms. 1987-92). Avocations: skiing, golf, reading, travel, sports. Home: 302 Perrault Rosemere PQ Canada J7A 1B9

HOPPER, NANCY JANE, author; b. Lewistown, Pa., July 25, 1937; d. David Lewis and Joyce Evelyn (Beaver) Swartz; m. James Alvin Hopper, Aug. 20, 1960; children: Christopher James, Jennifer Anne. BA, Juniata Coll., 1959. Tchr. Tyrone (Pa.) High Sch., 1959-60, Freeport (N.Y.) High Sch., 1960-62. Author of over a dozen novels for young people. Vol. Alliance City Schs., Ohio, 1976-82, Marlington Schs. Alliance, 1987-2002, Alliance Area Domestic Violence Shelter. Avocations: reading, collecting and identifying shells, travel, birdwatching. Home: 1524 N Plaza De Lirios Tucson AZ 85745-1667

HOPPER, PEGGY F., education educator; b. Clarksdale, Miss., Nov. 19, 1955; d. John Hart and Peggy Sue (Foard) Fondren; m. George Martin Hopper, Nov. 23, 1976; children: Benjamin George Hopper, Summer LeMett Hopper. BS in Liberal Arts, Miss. State U., 1977; MS in Curriculum and Instrn., U. Memphis, 1986, EdS, 1991; PhD in Holistic Tchg./Learning, U. Tenn., 1996. Asst. to dir. U. of Memphis Grad. Ctr., Jackson, 1987; tchr. U. Sch. of Jackson, Tenn., 1987-89; coord. for young adult lit. Jackson/Madison County Libr., 1990; instr. Jackson State C.C., 1989-91; prof. Walters State C.C., Morristown, Tenn., 1992—2005; asst. prof. Miss. State U., 2005—. Adj. instr. U. Tenn., Knoxville, 1996—; adv. bd. Coll. of Edn. Admissions, U. Tenn., 1995-2005. Contbr. articles to profl. jours., articles to profl. newsletters. Pres. Gen. Fedn. of Women's Club - Jr. Chilhowee Club, Maryville, Tenn., 1998; bd. dirs. Blount County Jr. Playhouse, 1997-2001, Boys and Girls' Clubs of Blount County, 1998-99; promotion and tenure task force Tenn. Bd. Regents, 2001-03, acad. auditor, 2005 Grantee Nat. Assn. Developmental Edn., 1997, NEH, 2005; recipient Trailblazer award Tenn. Bd. Regents, 2002, Meritorious Leadership award Miss. State U., 2005. Mem. Tenn. Assn. Developmental Edn. (pres. 1996-97), Nat. Assn. Developmental Edn. (liaison 1996-97), Internat. Reading Assn., Phi Lambda Theta, Phi Kappa Phi, Kappa Delta Pi. Avocations: travel, reading. Home: 117 Tuxford Rd Starkville MS 39759 Office: Mississippi State U Box 9705 Mississippi State MS 39762 Office Phone: 423-585-6927.

HOPPER, RUBY LOU, clergy member; b. Harrison, Ark., May 21, 1950; d. George C. and Ethel M. (Bethany) Eddings; m. Alfred Hopper, Aug. 1, 1970. Diploma, Berean Bible Coll., Springfield, Mo., 1989. Cert. technician class III, Nat. Assn. Radio and Telecomm. Engrs., 1986; ordained minister Evangelistic Messengers, 1986. Youth leader Sycamore Log Ch., Branson, Mo., 1984—; adult Sunday sch. tchr. Branson Ch. of God. Ins. office sec. Mo. Farm Bur., Hollister, 1990-93; sec. Foxen Comm., Hollister, 1993; prodn. dept. Applied Digital, Inc., Branson, 1996; freelance writer, Hollister, 1996. Vol. ARC, Branson, 1986-87; emergency coord. Amateur Radio Emergency Svc., Branson, 1988; adult Sunday sch. tchr. Branson Ch. God, Mo., 2002—. Recipient Vol. Svc. award Pt. Lookout Health Care Ctr., 1991. Mem. Nat. Assn. Female Execs., Nat. Assn. Radio Telecomm. Engrs. (technician class III), Tri-Lakes Amateur Radio Club (v.p. 1984-88). Republican. Pentecostal. Avocations: sports, baseball cards, music, reading, travel. Home and Office: PO Box 332 Hollister MO 65673-0332 Office Phone: 417-335-6692.

HOPPES, LAURAL JEAN, elementary school educator; b. Alhambra, Calif., June 16, 1948; d. Raymond Eugene and Mercedese Earlene Winn; m. Raymond Charles Hoppes, June 21, 1971; children: Lynn Michele, Michael Raymond. BA, Calif. State U., Northridge, Calif., 1973. Cert. tchr. Colo. Tchr. Oxnard Elem. Sch. Dist., Calif., 1974—86, Boulder Valley Schs., Colo., 1988—94, Eagleview Mid. Sch., Colorado Springs, 1994—. Divsn. dir. Boys IV, Calif. Named Enterprising Tchr. Yr., Colo. Coun. Econs., 2001; recipient Outstanding Young Women Am. award, 1985. Mem.: Western Regional Mid. Level Consortium, Coun. Geographic Edn., Colorado Springs Quilt Guild.

HORAI, JOANN, psychologist; b. NYC; d. Charles J. and Stacia (Melnick) H. BA, U. Miami, Coral Gables, Fla., 1964, MS, 1968, PhD, 1970. Asst. prof. Hofstra U., Hempstead, NY, 1971-76; dir. APA, Washington, 1976-89; strategic planning and bus. process design cons. Washington, 1991—; pvt. practice quality mgmt., process improvement, innovation cons., 1992—. Mem. APA (officer 1988-89). Office Phone: 202-550-4956. Personal E-mail: jhoraj@aol.com.

HORAK, TRISH, city government worker; b. Grand Saline, Tex., Aug. 24, 1946; d. Clinton Lee and Jewell Ruth Collier; m. Larry G. Horak, June 1972; children: Clinton Hammonds, John W., Marie. Grad. h.s. Cert. legal asst. Acct. I City of Grand Prairie, Tex., 1966-72, acct. II Tex., 1973-81, sec. to city sec. Tex., 1981-82, sec. to city mgr. Tex., 1983-84, exec. asst. to mayor Tex., 1984-88, exec. sec. human resources Tex., 1989-91, exec. sec. City Mgrs. Office Tex., 1992—. Asst. sec. Lone Star Park at Grand Prairie, Tex. Bd. dirs. YMCA, Grand Prairie, 1985-88; sec. bd. dirs. United Charities, Grand Prairie, 1983-88, 92-98; ann. campaign cord. United Way, Grand Prairie, 1997; sr. rep. Parent, Tchrs., Student Assn. Grand Prairie, 2000. Mem. Profl. Secs. Internat., Grand Prairie C. of C. (sec.-treas. women's divsn. 1982, Woman of Yr. 1993). Baptist. Avocations: gardening, crafts, crocheting, reading, writing. Home: 1637 Brent St Grand Prairie TX 75051-4321 Office: City Mgrs Office 317 College St Grand Prairie TX 75050-5636 E-mail: phorak@gptx.org.

HORI, KEIKO, English literature educator; b. Himeji, Hyogo, Japan, Jan. 18, 1954; d. Takeshi Nishiyama and Fumiko Hori; 1 child, Grace. BA summa cum laude, Osaka (Japan) U., 1976, MA, 1978; postgrad., U. N.H., 1979—80, Osaka (Japan) U., 1978—82. Instr. Osaka Kyoiku U., 1981-82, tenured asst. prof., 1982-87, assoc. prof., 1987-2000, prof., 2000—; instr. Osaka U., Toyonaka, Japan, 1988-90, 92-95. Vis. prof. U. Wyo., Laramie, 1986—87; vis. scholar UCLA, 2001—02. Co-author: Imeji to shite no Toshi: Gakusaiteki Toshi Bunkaron, 1996; annotator: (textbook) American Businessman: Lessons from Life, 1994; co-annotator: (textbook) American and English Ideals, 1991. Recipient Kusumoto Shogakukai award, Osaka U., 1976. Mem. Modern Lang. Assn., English Literary Soc. Japan, Japan Assn. English Romanticism, Japan Assn. Coll. English Tchrs. Office: Osaka Kyoiku U 4-698-1 Asahigaoka Kashiwara Osaka 582-8582 Japan

HORISZNY, LAURENE HELEN, lawyer; b. Lansing, Mich., Oct. 14, 1955; d. Walter and Jennie Ann (Pellpshen) H.; m. Richard C. Stavoe Jr., June 25, 1983; children: Andrea Kristen, Charles Ross. BA, Mich. State U., 1977; JD, Ohio State U., 1980. Bar: Mich. 1980, U.S. Dist. Ct. (ea. and we. dists.) Mich. 1980. Lawyer Consumers Power Co., Jackson, Mich., 1980-85; corp. counsel Ex-Cell-O Corp., Troy, Mich., 1985-86; sr. lawyer, asst. sec. BorgWarner Automotive, Inc., Troy, 1986—. Exec. bd. Land 'O Lakes coun. Boy Scouts Am., 1984-85. Mem. ABA, Mich. Bar Assn., Nature Conservancy. Avocations: scuba diving, cross country skiing, down-hill skiing, tennis. Office: Borg Warner 3800 Automation Ave Ste 500 Auburn Hills MI 48326-1786

HORLER, NICHOLE, elementary school educator; b. Queens, NY, June 10, 1966; d. Paul Angelo and Marie Dolores Scagnelli; m. Mark Scagnelli, Feb. 14, 1997; children: Amanda Brianne Hilyard, Madeline Rose. BA in Secondary Edn., SUNY, New Paltz, 2000; MS in Instnl. Tech., NYIT, NYC, 2004. Permanant certification secondary edn. social studies NY State Dept. Edn., 2004. 7th grade social studies tchr. Monhagen Mid. Sch., Middletown, NY, 2000—, subject matter leader - social studies, 2005—06. Office: Monhagen Middle School 555 County Rt 78 Middletown NY 10941 Office Phone: 845-346-4800. Business E-Mail: nhorler@ecsdm.org.

HORLICK, RUTH, photographer; b. Frankfurt, Germany, July 17, 1921; came to U.S., 1937; d. Leo Don and Hanna Rosenstock; m. Max Horlick, 1942; children: Jeffrey, Jill, Robert. Student, Newark Sch. Fine & Indsl. Arts, U. Md., Latent Image Workshop; studied with, Lowell Anson Kenyon; student, Nikon Sch. Photography, Time Life Photography Workshop. One-woman shows include Prince George's County Arts Divsn. Gallery, 1991, Hyattsville Mcpl. Bldg., 1996, Jewish Cmty. Ctr. D.C., 1998, Colonial Theater, Annapolis, Md., 1999, U. Md. Sr. U., 1999, exhibited in group shows at Coun. Greater Md. Camera Clubs, Md. Soc. Photo Pictorialists, Prince George C.C., Internat. Artist's Support Group, New Delhi, 2000, 2001, Beijing, 2001, Cooper St. Gallery, Memphis, 2000, St. Petersburg, Russia, 2003, New Delhi, 2004, Open Studios-Passageways, East Pines, Md., 2005, Riderwood Celebration of the Arts, 2005, P.G. County Exec. Office, Upper Marlboro, Md., 2005, Learning and Sports Ctr. Gallery, Landover, Md., 2005, Cairo, Luxor, Aswan, 2005, Montpelier-Laurel, Md., 2006, Paint Br. Unitarian/Universalist, Adelphi, Md., 2006, Calvert House Inn, Riverdale, Md., 2006, Free State Press, Annapolis, 2006. Founding mem. Art Spin Gallery, West Hyattsville, Md. Recipient numerous awards Nikon Sch. Photography, Coun. Greater Washington Camera Clubs, Md. Soc. Photo Pictorialists, Prince George's C.C. Mem. Women in the Arts, Laurel Art Guild, Latent Image Workshop, Passageways Artists Studios, Wash. Project for the Arts Corcoran Art Gallery, Washington Ctr. for Photography, Hyattsville Cmty. Artists Alliance, Md.-Nat. Pk. and Planning Commn. Slide Bank, Rock Creek Gallery, Internat. Artist's Support Group. Avocations: foreign travel, symphonic music and opera, fine arts.

HORN, CINDY HARRELL, environmental advocate; b. Durham, NC; m. Alan F. Horn; 2 children. Model, actress, 1975—88. Mem. Nat. Edn. Adv. Coun., 1991; founding trustee Heal the Bay, Archer Sch. Girls; bd. mem. Coalition for Clean Air, Tree People, Natural Step, Bay Keeper, Ctr. Environ. Edn., UCLA Sch. Pub. Health; mem. painting conservatory coun. J. Paul Getty Mus. Named one of Top 200 Collectors, ARTnews mag., 2006; recipient Legis. Woman of Yr., State of Calif. Mem.: Environ. Media Assn. (co-founder, bd. mem.). Office: Environ Media Assn 10780 Santa Monica Blvd Ste 210 Los Angeles CA 90025*

HORN, FLORA LEOLA, retired administrative assistant; b. Putman, Tex., May 20, 1926; d. James Erasmos and Clara Maud (Davenport) Foller; m. Charles Edward Helm, Sr. (div.); children: Leola Florence Helm, Charles Edward, Jr. Helm, Barbara Ann Helm, Carol Elaine Helm, Beverly Sue Helm, Rodney Johnson Helm; m. Hoy Merie Duhon (dec.). Diploma in Writing, Long Ridge Writers Group, 2003. Contbr. poems in books. Active Bapt. Buckneer Home, Dallas. Named Silver leader, Comdrs. Club, 2001; recipient Golden award, World Poetry, 1986, award merit cert., 1987, cert. Appreciation, Marine Corps League, 1995, Good Work award, B.B.Q. Luncheon Fundraiser, 1997. Mem.: VFW Laides Aux. (life; chaplain 1991—2002, chmn. Nat. Children's Home 1999—2002, cert. Appreciation 1989—93), Nat. Children's Home (Rapid, Mich.) (life), Med. Ctr. Hosp. (Conroe, Tex.) (life), Women of the Moose (chaplain 1999—, Novice award 1977—99, Internat. Co-worker of Yr. award 2003). Avocations: writing, art, Bingo, shuffleboard, poetry. Home: 1720 Thomas St Titusville FL 32780-6259

HORN, JOYCE ELAINE, music educator; d. Alfred Irving Sette and Elma Louise Robertson; 1 child, Camilla Jeanne VandenBerg. MusB, Grand Rapids Bapt. Coll.; MusM, We. Mich. U, 1972. Assoc. prof. music Cornerstone U, Grand Rapids, Mich., 1962—. Republican. Baptist. Avocations: reading, studying Charles Dickens, music. Home: 7355 Casade Terrace Dr SE Grand Rapids MI 49546 Office Phone: 616-949-5300 1223. Personal E-mail: jhorn218@aol.com.

HORN, KAREN NICHOLSON, investment company executive, former bank executive; b. Los Angeles, Sept. 21, 1943; d. Aloys and Novella (Hartley) Nicholson; m. John T. Horn, June 5, 1965; 1 child. BA, Pomona Coll., 1965; PhD, Johns Hopkins U., 1971. Sr. economist, bd. govs. staff FRS, Washington, 1969-71; v.p., economist First Nat. Bank, Boston, 1971-78; treas. Bell of Pa., Phila., 1978-82; pres. Fed. Res. Bank, Cleve., 1982-87; chmn., CEO Banc One Cleveland NA, Cleve.; mng. dir., head internat. pvt. banking Bankers Trust, 1996—99; mng. dir., pres. Private Client Services Marsh, Inc. (divsn. Marsh & McLennan Companies, Inc), 1999—2003; ltd. ptnr. Brock Capital Group LLC, NYC, 2004—. Bd. dirs. TRW, Inc., Eli Lilly Co., 1987-, Rubbermaid, Brit. Petroleum, Coun. Fgn. Rels., Fannie Mae, 2006- Chmn., bd. trustees Case Western Res. U., Cleve., 1992-95; trustee Rockefeller Found., Cleve. Clinic Found., Cleve. Orch., Cleve. Tomorrow. Office: Brock Capital Group LLC 622 Third Ave Fl 12 New York NY 10017*

HORN, MARIAN BLANK, federal judge; b. NYC, June 24, 1943; d. Werner P. and Mady R. Blank; m. Robert Jack Horn; 3 children. AB, Barnard Coll., 1962; student, Columbia U., 1965, NYU, 1965-66; JD, Fordham U., 1969. Bar: N.Y. 1970, D.C. 1973, U.S. Supreme Ct. 1973. Asst. dist. atty. Bronx County, N.Y., 1969-72; assoc. Arent, Fox, Kintner, Plotkin & Kahn, 1972-73; project mgr. Am. U. Law Sch. study on alts. to conventional criminal adjudication U.S. Dept. Justice, 1973-75; litigation atty. Fed. Energy Adminstrn., 1975-76; sr. atty. office gen. counsel strategic petroleum res. br. US Dept. Energy, 1976-79, dep. asst. gen. counsel for procurement and fin. incentives, 1979-81; dep. assoc. solicitor div. surface mining US Dept. Interior, 1981-83, assoc. solicitor div. gen. law, 1983-85, prin. dep. solicitor, acting solicitor, 1985-86; judge U.S. Ct. of Federal Claims, 1986—. Adj. prof. law Washington Coll. Law, Am. U., 1973-76, George Washington U. Sch. Law, 1992—. Office: US Ct Fed Claims 717 Madison Pl NW Washington DC 20439-0002

HORN, RONI, artist; b. NYC, 1955; BFA, RI Sch. Design, 1975; MFA, Yale U., 1978. One-woman shows include Clocktower, Inst. Art & Urban Resources, NY, 1980, Glyptothek Mus., Munich, 1983, Galerie Heinz Herzer, Munich, 1983, Burnett Miller Gallery, LA, 1985, Neuberger Mus., SUNY, 1986, Galerie Maeght Lelong, NY, 1987, Unique Forms of Deviation in Space, Mario Diacono Gallery, Boston, 1988, Paula Cooper Gallery, NY, 1989, Surface Matters, Mus. Contemporary Art, LA, 1990, Mary Boone Gallery, NY, 1991, Jablonka Galerie, Cologne, 1992, 1993, Four Watercolors, Matthew Marks Gallery, NY, 1993, Inner Geography, Balt. Mus. Art, Md., 1994, Gurgles, Sucks, Echoes, Matthew Marks Gallery, NY, 1995, Earths Grow Thick, Wexner Ctr. Arts, Columbus, 1996, You Are the Weather, Fotomuseum Winterthur, Switzerland, 1997, Patrick Painter Gallery, LA, 1998, Pi, Matthew Marks Gallery, NY, 1999, Still Water (The River Thames, for Example), Whitney Mus. Am. Art, NY, 2000, Blah, blah, hair, Blah, blah, your eyes; Blah, blah care, Blah, blah skies, Dia Ctr. Arts, NY, 2001, Clowndoubt, Matthew Marks Gallery, NY, 2002, Galerie Xavier Hufkens, Brussels, 2003, Some Thames, Art Inst. Chgo., 2004, exhibited in group shows, Corning Mus. Glass, NY, 1976, Material Object, Hayden Gallery, MIT, Cambridge, Mass., 1980, Barbara Braatten Gallery, NY, 1984, Lorence-Monk Gallery, NY, 1985, Chris Middendorf Gallery, Washington DC, 1986, Lead, Hirschl & Adler Modern, NY, 1987, Inscribed Image, Lang-O'Hara Gallery, NY, 1988, Non-representation, Anne Plumb Gallery, NY, 1989, Sculptors' Drawings, Balt. Mus. Art, 1990, Whitney Biennial, Whitney Mus. Am. Art, 1991, 2004, Drawn in teh '90s, Ind. Curators Inc., NY, 1992, Drawing the Line Against AIDS, Peggy Guggenheim Collection, Venice, 1993, Photography, Margo Leavin Gallery, LA, 1994, Works on Paper, Matthew Marks Gallery, NY, 1995, Thinking Print: Books to Billboards, 1980-1995, Mus. Modern Art, NY, 1996, Sleight of Mind/Angle of Landscape, Ctr. Curatorial Studies Mus., Bard Coll., NY, 1997, Venice Biennial, 1997, Maverick, Matthew Marks Gallery, NY, 1998, 00, Barbara Gladstone Gallery, NY, 2000, Tenth Anniversary Exhbn., 100 Drawings & Photographs, Matthew Marks Gallery, NY, 2001, Some Chromes, Fogg Art Mus., Harvard U., 2002, Exhbns. of an Exhbn., Casey Kaplan Gallery, NY, 2003, I am the Walrus, Cheim & Read, NY, 2004, Fresh Works on Paper, 5th Anniversary Exhbn., James Kelly Contemporary, Sante Fe, NM, 2004. Recipient Awards Visual Arts, AVA 7, 1988, Moonhole Artists Assn., Bequia, 1996, Alpert Award Arts, 1998; Ford Found. Grant, 1978, Alice Kimball Traveling Fellowship, Yale U., 1978, Humanities Development Grant, Colgate U., 1983, Artist's Fellowship, Nat. Endowment Art, 1984, 1986, 1990, Guggenheim Fellowship, 1990. Mailing: c/o Mattthew Marks Gallery 523 West 24th St New York NY 10011*

HORN, SHARON K., government agency administrator; B in Bus. and Econs., U. Ga.; EdM, Tex. A&M U.; PhD in Higher Edn. and Curriculum, U. Tex. Legis. fellow labor and human resources com. US Senate; secondary sch. tchr. of bus., econs. and polit. sci. Tex., Ga.; tchr. U. Tex., Tyler, S.W. Tex. State U.; assoc. dir. Program on Ednl. Policy and Orgn. Nat. Inst. Edn., 1982; dir. info. svcs. Office Ednl. Rsch. and Improvement US Dept. Edn., Washington, program officer, dir. Nat. Awards Program for Model Profl. Devel., dir. evaluation and dissemination Office Innovation and Improvement. Office: US Dept Edn FOB-6 Rm 4W332 400 Maryland Ave SW Washington DC 20202

HORN, SUSAN DADAKIS, statistician, educator; b. Cleve., Aug. 30, 1943; d. James Sophocles and Demeter (Zessis) Dadakis; m. Roger Alan Horn, July 24, 1965; children: Ceres, Corinne, Howard. BA, Cornell U., 1964; MS, Stanford U., 1966, PhD, 1968. Asst. prof. Johns Hopkins U., Balt., 1968-76, assoc. prof., 1976-86, prof. stats. and health svcs. rsch. methods, 1986-92; sr. scientist Intermountain Health Care, Salt Lake City, 1992-95; prof. dept. med. informatics Sch. Medicine U. Utah, Salt Lake City, 1992—; rsch. prof. U. Tex.-Houston Sch. Nursing, 1999—2001. Sr. scientist Inst. for Clin. Outcomes Rsch., Salt Lake City; vis. prof. Vanderbilt U. Sch. Nursing, Nashville, 2004—05. Fellow Am. Statist. Assn., Assn. for Health Svcs. Rsch.; mem. Acad. Health, Sigma Xi, Phi Beta Kappa, Phi Kappa Phi. Presbyterian. Avocations: tennis, swimming. Home: 1793 Fort Douglas Cir Salt Lake City UT 84103-4451 Office: Inst Clin Outcomes 699 E South Temple Salt Lake City UT 84102-1282 Office Phone: 801-466-5595 125. Business E-Mail: shorn@isisicor.com.

HORNAK, ANNA FRANCES, library administrator; b. College Station, Tex., June 3, 1922; d. Josef and Anna (Drozd) Hornak. BA, U. Tex., Austin, 1944; B.L.S., U. Ill., Champaign-Urbana, 1945; Ed.M., U. Houston, 1956. Children's librarian Schenectady Pub. Library, N.Y., 1945-47; children's librarian Pasadena Pub. Library, Calif., 1947-49; supr. Juvenile Div. Houston Pub. Library, 1949-57, asst. dir., 1957-89, ret., 1989. Named Outstanding Woman, YWCA of Houston, 1977; Outstanding Houston Profl. Woman, Fed. Houston Profl. Women, 1982 Avocations: collecting miniature books, collecting Bohemian red glass, restoring antique furniture. Home: 2217 Woodhead St Houston TX 77019-6820

HORNAMAN, ELAINE VERNA, librarian; b. Ipswich, S.D., July 11, 1935; d. Gustave and Christian (Gugel) Job; m. Hornaman (div. July 1987); children: Linda, Dianna, Jill; m. JoeWayne Winkler, Mar. 2, 2003; adopted children: Mandy, Rudy(dec.). M, Northern State U., 1977. Cert. tchr. Tchr. Putny Schs., Brown County, 1961-63, Watertown, Aberdeen Sch., S.D., 1965-75; sec./bookkeeper Trucking Firm, Aberdeen, 1975-82; bookkeeper Oahe Rural Water, Aberdeen; sec. Area IV Sr. Nutrition, Aberdeen, 1983—; libr. Alexander Mitchell Libr., Aberdeen, 1983—98. Leader 4-H Clubs, Ipswich, 1952-53. Mem. AAUW, Daughters of Nile (officer), Phi Delta Kappa. Avocations: reading, gardening, fishing, skating, sewing. Office: Area IV Sr Nutrition Project Ste 600 202 S Main St Aberdeen SD 57401-4185 Home: 401 S Congress St Aberdeen SD 57401

HORNBAKER, ALICE JOY, writer; b. Cin., Feb. 3, 1927; children: Christopher Albert, Holly Jo, Joseph Bernard III. BA cum laude and honors in Journalism, San Jose State U., Calif., 1949. Asst. woman's editor San Jose Mercury-News, 1949-55; columnist Life After 50, Cin. Post newspaper, 1993—2002; freelance writer Cin., 1995—; writer, broadcaster The Alice Hornbaker Show www.wmkvfm.org and 89.3 FM Cin., 1996; freelance feature writer www.grandparentworld.com; broadcaster www.wmkvm.com. Owner, mgr. Frisch's Big Boy Restaurant, Cin., 1955—68; dir. pub. rels. Children's Home Soc. Calif., Santa Clara, 1968—71; asst. dir. pub. rels. United Fund Calif., Santa Clara, 1971—; editor Tristate Sunday Enquirer mag., 1986—89, columnist Generations, 1976—93; editl. dir. Writers Digest Sch., Cin., 1971—75; columnist, critic, mag. writer, reporter, copy editor Tempo sect. Cin. Enquirer, 1975—93, book editor, critic, columnist on aging, feature writer Tempo sect.; reporter news segments on aging Sta. WKRC-TV, 1983—86; commentator on aging Sta. WMLX-AM, 1991—93; broadcaster, writer Sta. WMKV-FM, 1995—; tchr. adult edn. Forest Hills Sch. Dist., Thomas More Coll., 1973—. Author: (Book) Preventive Care: Easy Exercise Against Aging, 1974; columnist: internet 3 times weekly Life After 50; contbr. articles to various publs. including: People, Modern Maturity, St. Anthony Messenger, N.Y. Times Sun mag., Ohio Heitage mag.others., fiction to Enquirer mag. Recipient Bronze award in Am. health journalism, Am. Chiropractic Assn., 1977, 1978, Golden Image award, Assn. Ohio Philanthropic Homes, 1989, 1st pl. for feature writing, Cin. Editors Assn., 1983, 1st and 3rd pl. feature writing awards, Ohio Profl. Writers, Inc., 1992, Journalist of Yr. award, Ohio chpt. Am. Coll. Health Care Adminstrs., 1993, Journalism award, Greater Cin. Joint Coun. on Geriat. Care, 1993, Bronze award, Nat. Mature Media, 2003, 2005. Mem. Blue Pencil of Ohio State U. (pres. 1981-82), Women in Comm., Ohio Newspaper Women's Assn. (v.p. 1981-83, 1st pl. human interest story 1977-85, 2d pl. column award 1979, Tops in Ohio award 1982, M.M. McMullen 2d pl. award, 1982, Recognition award 1985, 4th pl. on aging Nat. Legacies contest 1994), Soc. Profl. Journalists (treas. 1981-82), Ohio Press Women, Inc. (1st and 3d pl. awards for feature writing 1992). E-mail: ajhornbaker@yahoo.com.

HORNBLOW, DORIS H., retired nurse; b. Flushing, NY, May 4, 1935; d. William Frederick Hackenberger and Ella Graham; m. John Terry Hornblow (div.); children: Steven Crosby, Deborah Anne, Gwendolyn. Student, Columbia U., 1955—57, Trinity Coll., 1977—78, St. Luke's Sch. Nursing. Active West Hartford Health Adv. Bd., Conn., 1967—68; ways and means com., v.p., pres. PTO Noah Wallace Sch., Farmington, Conn., 1968—72; bd. dirs. sec., v.p., pres. Farmington Vis. Nurses', 1968—73; bd. dirs. Farmington Hist. Soc., 1969—74; pres. Farmington Preservation Soc., 1978—86; chmn. Farmington Bicentennial Com., 1975—77; docent Stanley-Whitman House, 1975—78; bd. dirs. Hill-Stead Mus., Farmington, 1977—81, chmn. aux. Hillsteaders, 1978—82, archtl. com., 1981—82. Recipient Pearl Trachtenroth award, Am. Cancer Soc. Greater Hartford Unit, 1994—95. Avocations: art, music, travel, antiques, reading. Home: 759 Farmington Ave #320 West Hartford CT 06119

HORNBY, SARA ANN, metallurgical engineer, marketing professional; b. Plymouth, Devon, Eng., Apr. 17, 1952; came to U.S., 1986; d. Foster John and Joanna May (Duncan) Hornby; m. John Victor Anderson, Sept. 2, 1978 (div. May 1987). BSc in Metallurgy with honors, Sheffield (Eng.) City Poly., 1973, PhD in Indsl. Metallurgy, 1980. Chartered engr. Metallurgist Joseph Lucas Rsch., Solihull, England, 1970, William Lee Malleable, Dronfield, 1972; tech. sales specialist Applied Rsch. Labs, Luton, Beds, 1973—74; quality assurance metallurgist Firth Brown Tools, Sheffield, 1974—75, rsch. metallurgist high speed steel, 1975; lectr. Sheffield City Poly., 1975—78; grad. metallurgist, strip devel. metallurgist British Steel Corp., Rotherham, 1978—80; program mgr. Can. Liquid Air, Montreal, Canada, 1980—85; group mktg. mgr. Liquid Air Corp., Countryside, Ill., 1986—90, tech. mgr. Walnut Creek, Calif., 1990—93; bus. devel. mgr.-metals and materials Can. Liquid Air, Toronto, Ont., 1993—97, N.Am. steel tech. mgr., 1995—97; dir. steelmaking tech. Goodfellow Techs. Inc., Mississauga, Ont., Canada, 1997, dir. ops., 1997—99; mgr. bus. devel. Stantec Global Techs. Ltd. (formerly Goodfellow Techs. Inc.), 1999; product mgr. steel making/ melting Midrex Techs., Inc., Charlotte, NC, 1999—2003; pres. Global Strategic Solutions, Inc., Charlotte, NC, 2003—06; process innovation specialist Linde Gas LLC, Cleve., 2006—. Bd. dirs., chmn. R & D com., mem. publs. com., chmn. promotions and mktg. com. Investment Casting Inst., Dallas; presenter to confs. in field. Contbr. articles to profl. jours.; patentee in field of metallurgy. Mem. AIME, Inst. Metals (young metallurgists com. 1974-80), Sheffield Metall. Soc. Inst. Metals (sec. 1978-80), Am. Foundry Soc., Iron and Steel Soc. (steering com. 1987-91, chmn. topics com. 1988-89, sec. 1992, vice chair 1993, chmn. process tech. divsn. 1994, bd. dirs., strategic planning com. 1995-98, internat. affairs com. 1998-2004, bd. dirs. ad hoc com. on internat. affairs 1998-99, univ. rels. com. 1998-2004), Assn. Iron and Steel Tech. (ironmaking com. 2004—). Avocations: scuba diving, horseback riding, swimming, siamese cats, gardening. Personal E-mail: shornbyanderson@carolina.rr.com.

HORNE, KATHRYN JENNIFER, elementary school educator; d. Richard M. and Judy P. Horne. BS, Wake Forest U., Winston-Salem, N.C., MA in Edn., 2001. Tchr. Marshfield Pub. Schs., Mass., 2001—. Head coach girls varsity volleyball Marshfield H.S., 2001—, class advisor, 2003—, head coach boys club volleyball, 2004—. Named Vol. of Yr., North and South River Watershed Assn., 2005, Person of Week, Marshfield Town Bd. of Selectmen, 2005—06; recipient Rick Pierce Sportsmanship award, Yankee Volleyball, 2003, Honor award, Plymouth County Edn. Assn., 2006. Mem.: NSTA. Liberal. Avocations: volleyball, sailing, reading.

HORNE, MARILYN BERNEICE, mezzo-soprano; b. Bradford, Pa., Jan. 16, 1934; d. Bentz and Berneice Horne; m. Henry Lewis, July 1, 1960 (div. 1974); 1 child. Student, U. So. Calif.; MusD (hon.), Rutgers U., 1970, Jersey City State Coll., 1973, Brown U., 1984, Juillard Sch. Music, 1994; DLitt (hon.), St. Peter's Coll.; LHD (hon.), Kean Coll., 1977. Vocal program dir. Music Acad. of the West, Santa Barbara, Calif., 1995—. Singer: (Operas) (debut) as Hata in The Bartered Bride, 1954, (La Scala debut) Oepidus Rex, 1969, (Met. Opera debut) as Adalgisa in Norma, 1970, (other roles) Rosina in Barber of Seville, Cleonte in The Siege of Corinth, Isabella in L'Italiana in Algieri, Carmen at Met. Opera, 1972—73, Laura in Harvest, Chgo. Lyric Opera, Marie in Wozzeck, San Francisco Opera, (appeared in) Phigenie en Tauride, Semiramide, Samson et Dalila at Met. Opera, 1987, The Ghost of Versailles, 1991, Pelléas et Mélisande, 1995, Venice Festival by invitation of Igor Stravinsky, Am. Opera Soc., N.Y.C., for several seasons, Vancouver Opera, Philharm. Hall, N.Y.C., Paris, Dallas, Houston, Covent Garden, London, roles at La Scala, Italy, Rossini Opera Festival, Pesaro, Italy, Met. Opera, 1987, (recital debuts) Madrid, Dresden, East Berlin, 1987; performer: (at inauguration) of U.S. President Clinton, 1993, ann. recital at Carnegie Hall, European tour with husband for Dept. State, 1963; rec. artist London, Columbia, Deutsche Grammaphon and RCA records, recs. include soundtrack Carmen Jones. Founder Marilyn Horne Found. Named Musician of Yr. Musical Am., 1995, Kennedy Ctr. honoree, 1995; named to Harold C. Schonberg's N.Y. Times' list of 9 All-Time, All-Star Singers in Met. Opera's 100 Years, 1984, Am. Classical Music Hall of Fame, Cin., 1999; recipient Grammy awards, 1964, 1981, 1983, 1994, Handel medallion, 1980, Premio d'Oro, Italian Govt., 1982, Commendatore al merito della Repubblica Italiana, 1983, Gold Merit medal Nat. Soc. Arts and Letters, 1987, Fidelio Gold medal, 1988, George Peabody award, 1989, Silver medal Covent Garden Royal Opera House, 1989, Disting. Dau. of Pa. Silver medal San Francisco Opera, 1990, Nat. Arts medal, 1992. Achievements include having the leading exponent florid vocal style, music of Rossini, Handel, Vivaldi. also: care Met Opera Assoc Attention: Artistic Dept Lincoln Ctr New York NY 10023 also: BMG Classics/RCA 1540 Broadway New York NY 10036-4039 Office: Music Academy of the West 1070 Fairway Rd Santa Barbara CA 93108-2899 also: Columbia Artists Management Llc 1790 Broadway # 6 New York NY 10019-1412

HORNE, MARJORIE, production stage manager, event consultant; b. Bklyn., Sept. 17, 1945; d. Clinton Davis and Pauline Sklar Horne. BA, Hunter Coll., NYC, 1990. Theater stage mgr., 1973—2004; event planner, 1999—; political and not-for-profit fundraiser, project cons. McEvoy and Assocs., NYC, 2002—. Actor: No Place to Be Somebody, over 25 other plays and musicals; stage mgr. (Broadway plays) Enchanted April, A Class Act, True West, Street Corner Symphony, Electra, St. Joan, prodn. stage mgr. over 100 prodns., including I'm Getting My Act Together and Taking It on the Road, 1978—81, Greater Tuna, 1982—85, prodns. for theater cos. including Lincoln Ctr. Theater, Nat. Actors' Theater, Manhattan Theater Club, Playwrights Horizons, 2d Stage, Cir. Repertory, NY Theater Workshop, 1973—2002, prodn. supr. Am. Theatre Wing TONY Awards, 2005, 2006, stage mgr., prodn. mgr. numerous corporate and pub. events. Vol. anthropology dept. Am. Mus. Natural History, NYC; fundraiser Ferraro for US Senate, 1992; mem. Cmty. Free Dems., NYC, 1992—; pres. Nat. Women's Polit. Caucus, NYC, 1994—96, treas., 1997—99; fundraiser Catherine Abate for Senate, 1994, Catherine Abate for Atty. Gen., 1997; dir. ops, vol. coord. Ferraro for Senate, NY, 1998; dir. nomination of Hillary Rodham Clinton for US Senate NY State Dem. Conv., 2000; campaign mgr. Joyce Johnson for Assembly, NYC, 2002; campaign cons. Joyce Johnson for City Coun., NYC, 2005; charter mem. Nat. Mus. Women in the Arts, Washington, Nat. Women's History Mus., Washington. Mem.: Stage Mgrs.' Assn. (chair 1991—93, bd. dirs. 1993—2002), Actors' Equity Assn. (councillor 1994—). Democrat. Avocations: archaeology, travel.

HORNER, CONSTANCE JOAN, federal agency administrator; b. Summit, NJ, Feb. 24, 1942; d. David Earl and Cecelia (Murphy) McNeely; m. Charles Edward Horner, May 7, 1965; children: David Bayer, Jonathan Purcell. BA in English Lit., U. Pa., 1964; MA in English Lit., U. Chgo., 1967. Dep. asst. dir. policy planning and evaluation ACTION Agy., Washington, 1981-82, acting assoc. dir. domestic & anti-poverty ops., 1982-83, dep. assoc. dir. for VISTA & service-learning, 1982-83; assoc. dir. for econs. & govt. Office of Mgmt. and Budget, Washington, 1983-85; dir. Office of Pers. Mgmt., Washington, 1985-89; deputy sec. HHS, 1989-91; asst. to pres. and dir. presdl. pers. The White House, Washington, 1991-93; mem. U.S. Commn. on Civil Rights, Washington, 1993-98. Commr. The White House Fellows Commn., Washington, 1985-89; guest scholar The Brookings Inst., Washington, 1993-05; vis. faculty Princeton (NJ) U., 1994; fellow, lectr. Johns Hopkins U., 1994-95; mem. adv. com. women in svcs. Dept. Def., 2003; bd. dirs. Pfizer, Inc.,

Prudential Fin., Inc., Ingersoll-Rand Co. Ltd. Bd. dirs. Annie E. Casey Found., Balt., 1994—. Fellow: Nat. Acad. Pub. Adminstrn.; mem.: Cosmos Club. Republican. Home: 3171 Porter St NW Washington DC 20008-3210

HORNER, JUDITH ANNE, music educator; b. Butler, Pa., Sept. 1, 1947; adopted d. Richard A. and Helen Rosalie Pierrel; m. Thomas E. Horner, Apr. 25, 1993; m. Dennis C. Dindinger, 1968 (div.); children: David Perry Dindinger, Amy Joy Dindinger. BA in Music Edn., Grove City Coll., Grove City, Pa., 1969; MA in Tchg., Marygrove Coll., Detroit, Mich., 1999. Teacher of Music K-12 NJ Dept. of Edn., 1969, Teacher of Elementary K-8 NJ Dept. of Edn., 1996. Tchr. of music Willingboro Pub. Schools, Willingboro, NJ, 1970—79, 6th grade tchr., 1997—2003, academic coach, 2003—04, instrnl. support tchr., 2004—. New tchr. mentor Willingboro Pub. Schools, 2000—, curriculum writer, 1999—. Mem. Blue Star Mothers of Am., 2005—06. Recipient Tchr. of Yr., NJ Dept. of Edn., 1998. Mem.: NEA, ASCD, Willingboro Edn. Assn. (Employee of Month 1996), NJ Edn. Assn. Office Phone: 609-835-3881. Personal E-mail: judyhorner@hotmail.com. E-mail: jhorner@wboe.net.

HORNER, MANDY SUE, athletic trainer; b. State College, Pa., May 5, 1979; d. Gary Marlin and Ginger Elizabeth Horner. BS in Biology, Susquehanna U., Selinsgrove, Pa., 2001; MEd, Lock Haven U. Pa., 2004. Cert. Nat. Athletic Trainers Assn. Intern athletic trainer Shippensburg U., Pa., 2001—02; pers. trainer, acct. mgr. East Coast Health and Fitness, State College, Pa., 2002—03; grad. asst. athletic trainer Lock Haven U., 2002—04; heat athletic trainer and program coord. Ctrl. Mountain Phys. Therapy, Lock Haven, 2004—. Mailing: PO Box 404 Millheim PA 16854

HORNER, MATINA SOURETIS, retired academic administrator, corporate financial executive; b. Boston, July 28, 1939; d. Demetre John and Christine (Antonopoulos) Souretis; m. Joseph L. Horner, June 25, 1961; children: Tia Andrea, John, Christopher. AB cum laude, Bryn Mawr Coll., 1961; MS, U. Mich., 1963, PhD, 1968; LLD (hon.), Dickinson Coll., 1973; LLD, Mt. Holyoke Coll., 1973; LLD (hon.), U. Pa., 1975, Smith Coll., 1979, Wheaton Coll., 1979, U. Mich., 1989; LHD (hon.), U. Mass., 1973, Tufts U., 1976, U. Hartford, 1980, U. New Eng., 1987, Bentley Coll., 1989, New Eng. Coll., 1989, Pine Manor Coll., 1989, Am. Coll. Greece, 1990; DLitt (hon.), Claremont U. Ctr. and Grad Sch., 1988, Hellenic Coll., 1990; LHD (hon.), Colby Sawyer Coll., 1991. Teaching fellow U. Mich., Ann Arbor, 1962-66, lectr. motivation personality, 1968-69; lectr. social relations Harvard U., Cambridge, Mass., 1969-70, asst. prof. clin. psychology, 1970-72, assoc. prof. psychology, 1972-89, cons. univ. health svcs., 1971-89; pres. Radcliffe Coll., Cambridge, 1972-89, pres. emerita, 1989—; exec. v.p. TIAA-CREF, NYC, 1989—2003; ret., 2003. Bd. dirs. Neiman Marcus Group, Boston Edison Co.-NSTAR, Black Rock Funds. Co-author: The Challenge of Change, 1983; contbr. psychol. articles on motivation to profl. jours. and chpts. to books. Mem. adv. coun. NSF, 1977-87, chair, 1980-86; bd. trustees Twentieth Century Fund, The Century Found., 1973—, Am. Coll. of Greece, 1983-90, Mass. Eye and Ear Infirmary, 1986-90, Com. for Econ. Devel., 1988—, vice-chmn., 1992-98; bd. trustees Mass. Gen. Hosp., Inst. Health Professions, 1988—, vice chmn., 1994, chair, 1995; bd. dirs. Coun. for Fin. Aid to Edn., 1985-89, Beth Israel Hosp., 1989-95; bd. dirs. Revson Found., 1986-92, chmn., 1992-97; bd. dirs. Women's Rsch. and Edn. Inst., 1979—, chair rsch. com., 1982—; mem. Coun. on Fgn. Rels., 1984—; exec. com. ACE Bus. Higher Edn. Forum, 1984-86; exec. com. New Eng. Colls. Fund, 1980—, 2d v.p., 1984-85, 1st v.p., 1985-88, pres., 1988-89; mem. nat. panel to study declining test scores Coll. Entrance Exam. Bd., 1976-77; exec. com., chair task force Pres.'s Commn. for Nat. Agenda for 1980s, 1979-80; adv. com. Women's Leadership Conf. on Nat. Security, 1982—; exec. com. Coun. on Competitiveness, 1986-89; chair task force on health care Challenge to Leadership Conf., 1987-89; bd. dirs. Greenwall Found., 1997, chair, 2004—; bd. dirs. Fund for City of N.Y., chair, 1997-2003. Recipient Roger Baldwin award Mass. Civil Liberties Union Found., 1982, citation of merit Northeast Region NCCJ, 1982, Career Contbn. award Mass. Psychol. Assn., 1987, Disting. Bostonian award, 1990, Ellis Island medal, 1990. Mem. NOW (nat. corp. adv. bd. of legal def. and edn. fund 1984—), Am. Laryngol. Voice Rsch. and Edn. Found. (pres.), Nat. Inst. Social Scis. (medal for outstanding svc. 1973), Phi Beta Kappa, Phi Delta Kappa, Phi Kappa Phi.

HORNER, SYLVIA ANN, minister, real estate broker; b. Indpls., June 22, 1940; d. Bonnie Lois and Kindeth Allen Kelley (Stepfather), C. W. Burton; m. Joseph Bruce Horner, Dec. 13, 1935; children: Joseph Bradley, Lisa Monique Stephens, Reginald Lee. BA, Ind. U., Indpls., 1998. Lic. Real Estate Broker Ind., 1967. Co-pastor Geist Apostolic Ch., McCordsville, Ind., 1994—. Dir. of music Geist Apostolic Ch., McCordsville, Ind., 1994—. Oil painting, Seascape (First Pl., Ind. State Fair, 1997); violinist Ind. Philharmonic Orchestra, Butler U. Orchestra. Prodr. Orchestration Praise Radio Program, 1994—98, host, 1994—98; pastor Geist Apostolic Ch., McCordsville, Ind., 1994—2005. Recipient Recognition Award, Pres. of Student Coun. Achievements include patents for carbon monoxide sensor for vehicles. Home: 509 Swan Ct Fortville IN 46040 Office Phone: 317-335-2454. Home Fax: 317-485-5522; Office Fax: 317-485-5522. Business E-Mail: shorner06@earthlink.net.

HORNER, WINIFRED BRYAN, humanities educator, researcher, consultant, writer; b. St. Louis, Aug. 31, 1922; d. Walter Edwin and Winifred (Kinealy) Bryan; m. David Alan Horner, June 15, 1943; children: Winifred, Richard, Elizabeth, David. AB, Washington U., St. Louis, 1943; MA, U. Mo., 1961; PhD, U. Mich., 1975. Instr. English U. Mo., Columbia, 1966-75, asst. prof. English, 1975-80, chair lower divorce studies, dir. composition program, 1974-80, assoc. prof., 1980-83, prof., 1984-85, prof. emerita, 1985—; prof. English, Radford chair rhetoric and composition Tex. Christian U., Ft. Worth, 1985-93, Cecil and Ida Green disting. prof. emerita, 1993-97. Disting. vis. prof. Tex. Woman's U. Editor: Historical Rhetoric: An Annotated Bibliography of Selected Sources in English, 1980, The Present State of Scholarship in Historical Rhetoric, 1983, Composition and Literature: Bridging the Gap, 1983, Rhetoric and Pedagogy: Its History, Philosophy and Practice, 1995; author: Rhetoric in a Classical Mode, 1987, Nineteenth-Century Scottish Rhetoric: The American Connection, 1993, Life Writing, 1996; co-author Harbrace Coll. Hancbook, 11th edit., 1990, 12th edit., 1994, 14th edit., 1998. Named Disting. prof. Tex. Woman's U., 1999, Disting. Alumna, Washington U.; Inst. for the Humanities fellow U. Edinburgh, 1987; NEH grantee, 1976, 87. Mem. Internat. Soc. for History Rhetoric (exec. coun. 1986), Rhetoric Soc. Am. (bd. dirs. 1981, pres. 1987), Nat. Coun. Writing Program Administrs. (v.p. 1977-85, pres. 1985-87), Coll. Conf. on Composition and Communication (exec. com.), Modern Lang. Assn. (mem. del. assembly 1981). Home and Office: 1904 Tremont Ct Columbia MO 65203-5467 Business E-Mail: hornerw@missouri.edu.

HORNICK, SUSAN FLORENCE STEGMULLER, secondary education educator, fine arts educator, curriculum specialist, artist; b. Aug. 29, 1947; d. August George and Florence Maybell (Meisinger) Stegmuller; m. Jesse Allan Hornick, July 20, 1974. BA, Queens Coll., 1969, MS in Art Edn., 1973; permanent N.Y. State reading cert., Hunter Coll., 1984, advanced cert. ednl. supervn./adminstrn. summa cum laude, 1996. Lic. tchr. fine arts, N.Y.C.; permanent cert. tchr. art, N.Y.; cert. in ednl. adminstrn. and supervision, N.Y.; permanent cert. sch. dist. adminstr., N.Y. Fine arts tchr. Hillcrest H.S., Jamaica, N.Y., 1973-74, Ea. Dist. H.S., Bklyn., 1974-75, Tottenville H.S., S.I., N.Y., 1975-76; fine arts tchr., title 1 reading tchr. Prospect Heights H.S., Bklyn., 1976-78; fine arts tchr. Grover Cleveland H.S., Ridgewood, NY, 1978—2003, dept. coord., 1986-98. Conceptual art tchr., conceptual facilitator, reading, writing and artistic skills with written and visual exemplification Grover Cleveland H.S., 1978—2003, yearbook advisor, 1979, tchr. reading. English and reading improvement through art, 1980—85, tchr. ecol. awareness, 1995—2003; cooperating tchr., trainer art tchrs. Queens Coll., Flushing, NY, 1991, 2000; tchr. "bridge" ESL and math. Newcomers Summer H.S., Long Island City, NY, 2000, ESL tchr., mem. Saturday lit. program, 2000—01. Exhbns. include U.S. Capitol, Washington, 1982, 86, 88, U.S. Capitol, Washington, Lever House Exhibit, 1984-97, City Hall, N.Y.C., 1984, Queensborough C.C. Art Gallery, Bayside, N.Y., 1984-94, N.Y.C. Transit Mus., 1987-99, Queens Borough Hall, Kew Gardens, N.Y., 1992, Sotheby's, N.Y., 1992, Internat. Arrivals bldg. JFK Kennedy Airport (award winning mural by Joanna Kadlubowska, 1992), Queens Theater in the Park, Flushing, N.Y., 1993, 97, Nat. Mus. Am. Indian, Smithsonian Inst., 1992, 93, Mus. of City of N.Y., 1998, Grover Cleveland H.S., Ridgewood, N.Y., 1998-2003, N.Y. Joint Bd. Unite, N.Y.C., 2000-01 Named Internat. Educator of Yr. award, Internat. Biographical Ctr. Cambridge, England, 2003; recipient Medal for Superior Performance, N.Y.C. Transit Authority, 1996, Cert. of Appreciation for Outstanding Performance as Art Educator in N.Y.C. Pub. Schs., N.Y.C. Bd. Edn., 1985, Cert. of Recognition for Accomplishments as Outstanding Tchr., Nat. Tchrs. Hall of Fame, 2000. Mem. ASCD, N.Y.C. Art Tchrs. Assn., United Fedn. Tchrs., Hunter Coll. Alumni Assn., Nat. Mus. Women in Arts (charter), Colonial Williamsburg Duke of Gloucester Soc., N.Am. Fishing Club (life), Downsville Women's Club. Home: 6602 Cherry Rd Ocala FL 34472

HORNIG, MADY, psychiatrist, educator; b. Bklyn., Feb. 6, 1957; d. Jerome and Judith (Savin) H.; m. James E. Rohan, Aug. 26, 1979 (div. Mar. 1997); children: Russell, Maxwell. AB, Cornell U., 1978; MA in Psychology, New Sch. Social Rsch., N.Y.C., 1983; postgrad., Northeastern U., 1981-82; MD, Med. Coll. Pa., 1988. Diplomate Am. Bd. Psychiatry and Neurology, Nat. Bd. Med. Examiners. Resident in psychiatry Med. Ctr. Hosp. Vt., Burlington, 1988-92; fellow in clin. and rsch. psychopharmacology U. Vt., Burlington, 1991-92; asst. instr. psychiatry U. Pa., 1992-93, asst. prof. psychiatry, 1994—; asst. adj. prof. lab. neurovirology, dept. neurology U. Calif., Irvine, 1997—. Lectr. in field. Editor Advances: Jour. Mind-Body Health, 1983—; mem. editl. adv. bd. Psychiat. Annals, 1995—; reviewer Biol. Psychiatry, 1992—, Jour. Neuropsychiatry and Clin. Neuroscis., 1994—, Jour. Affective Disorders, 1995—, Progress in Neuro-Psychopharmacology and Biol. Psychiatry, 1996—, Psychoneuroendocrinology, 1996—; co-editor: Mind and Immunity: Behavioral Immunology, 1983, Psychological and Behavioral Treatments for Disorders of the Heart and Blood Vessels, 1985, Treatment-Resistant Depression, Psychiatric Clinics of North America, 1996; contbr. articles to profl. jours. Recipient Soc. Women Engrs. and Mathematicians award, 1974; Hon. scholar Nat. Honor Soc., 1974; scholar Cornell U., 1974-78, N.Y. State Regents scholar, 1974-78; grantee NARSAD, 1993-95, Stanley Found., 1996-98, Organon, Inc., 1997-98, Pfizer, Inc., 1997-98. Mem. Am. Psychiat. Assn., Am. Soc. Clin. Psychopharmacology, Autism Soc. Am., Pa. Psychiat. Soc., Phila. Psychiat. Soc., Autism Soc. Am. (Greater Phila. chpt.). Office: U Calif 3107 Gillespie Bldg Irvine CA 92697-0001

HORNING, SHERI, dietician, educator; b. Wilkes-Barre, Pa., Sept. 24, 1975; d. Barnet and Joanne Weber; m. Thad Horning, Jan. 2, 1999; 1 child, Ethan. BS, Mansfield U., Pa., 1998; MS, Marywood U., Scranton, Pa. Registered dietitian Fla. Clin. dietitian Orlando (Fla.) Regional Med. Ctr., 2002—04, Fla. Hosp., Orlando. Tchr. Valencia C.C., Orlando. Achievements include research in difference in body image and eating attitudes between undergraduate nutrition majors and non-nutrition majors. Office: Florida Hospital Orlando FL

HORNSBY, JUDITH ELIZABETH, special education educator; b. Xenia, Ohio, Aug. 26, 1942; d. Harry Algeo and Mary Elizabeth (Graves) Bennett; m. Orson Hornsby, Dec. 21, 1963; children: Jeffery William, Mary Katherine Hornsby. BS Ohio U., 1964; MA Special Ed., Ohio State U., 1966. Tchr., visually impaired Cincinnati Public Schs., 1964—70, 1975—80, Hamilton City Schs., 1980—; reading tchr. Cincinnati County Day Sch., 1972—75. Organist Northern Hills United Methodist Church, Cincinnati, 1991—; chair, div. 13 Assn. for the Ed. and Rehab. of the Blind & Visually Impared, Alexandria, Va., 1994—96; pres. Assn. for the Ed. and Rehab. of the Blind & Visually Impaired in Ohio, 2000—. Cons. for visually impaired Hamilton YMCA, Camp Campbell, Ohio, 1983—2001; co-chmn. High Vision Games, Cincinnati, 1997, 1999, 2001. Recipient Outstanding Lay Person, Hamilton YMCA, 1992, Educator of the Year, AERO, 1992, Golden Apple award, Ashland Oil, 1995. Mem.: Nat. Braille Assn., DAR, Eastern Star (Organist 1988—). Republican. Methodist. Avocations: reading, investment club, golf. Office: Hamilton City Schs 1165 Eaton Ave Hamilton OH 45013

HORNY, KAREN LOUISE, library administrator; b. Highland Park, Ill., Apr. 22, 1943; d. Hugo O. and Margaret L. (Bailey) H. AB in French Lit. magna cum laude with honors, Brown U., 1965; MLS, U. Mich., 1966. Asst. core libr. Northwestern U., Evanston, Ill., 1966-68, head core collection, 1968-71, asst. univ. libr., 1971-95; dean libr. svcs., prof. libr. sci. Mo. State U., Springfield, 1995—. Bd. editors Jour. Acad. Librarianship, 1978-81, Advances in Librarianship, 1993-98; contbr. chpts. to books and articles to profl. jours. Pres. U. Mich. Libr. Sci. Alumni Soc., 1985-86; nat. chair U. Mich. Info. and Libr. Studies Fund, 1988-90, rep. Info. and Libr. Sci. U. Mich. Alumni Bd., 1991-94; mem. alumni scholarship coun. Sch. Info. U. Mich., 1996—; mem. adv. coun. U. Ill. Grad. Sch. Libr. Sci., 1975-77; chmn. NOTIS Network Adv. com. Northwestern U., 1988-95. Recipient Disting. Alumnus award U. Mich. 1983. Mem. ALA (coun. 1983-87, divsn. pres. 1980-81, chmn. divsn. 1973-74, 76-78, chmn. various com. 1981—, rep. White Ho. conf. com. 1990-97, exec. com. White Ho. conf. on libr. and info. svcs. task force 1997-2005), Mo. Libr. Assn. (pres.-elect 2006), Ill. Libr. Assn. (coms.), Freedom to Read Found., Brown U. Club, U. Mich. Club, Rotary Springfield Downtown, Phi Beta Kappa, Phi Kappa Phi (chpt. 170 pres., 2004-05), Beta Phi Mu. Episcopalian (subdeacon). Home: 1228 W Beekman St Springfield MO 65810-2292 Office: Mo State U 901 S National Ave Springfield MO 65897 Office Phone: 417-836-4525. Business E-Mail: karenhorny@missouristate.edu.

HOROWITZ, CAROLE SPIEGEL, landscape contractor; b. Pitts., Mar. 24, 1940; d. Alvin Duane and Leah (Greenstein) Spiegel; m. Don Roy Horowitz, Jan. 31, 1960 (dec. July 24, 2006); children: Cindy H. Urbach, Thomas Samuel. Student, Carnegie Mellon U., 1958-61. Cert. interior horticulturist, landscape profl. Owner Carole Horowitz Interior Design, Pitts., 1965-72; pres. Plantscape, Inc., Pitts., 1973—. Chmn. U. Pitts. Small Bus. Com., 1986-92; bd. dirs. United Way Allegheny County, Pitts., 1991-94, Jr. Achievment Allegheny County, Pitts., 1985-95, Vocat. Rehab. Ctr., Pitts., 1989-91. Recipient Nat. Landscape award White House and Am. Assn. Nurseryman, 1990, YWCA Entrepreneur Leadership award, 1990; named Entrepreneur of Yr. Ernst & Young & Inc. Mag., 1988, Pitts. Bus. Times Pa.'s Best 50 Women in Bus. award 1997. Mem. Interior Plantscape Assn. (sec., v.p., 1982-85), Associated Landscape Contractor of Am. (cert., chmn. Am. Bd. Govs. 1991-94), Internat. Facility Mgmt. Assn., Westmoreland Country Club, Longboat Key Club, Rotary (sec. Downtown Pitts. chpt.). Jewish. Avocations: travel, golf, painting. Office: Plantscape Inc 3101 Liberty Ave Pittsburgh PA 15201-1400 Office Phone: 412-281-6352. E-mail: ch@plantscape.com.

HOROWITZ, FRANCES DEGEN, academic administrator, psychology educator; b. Bronx, NY, May 5, 1932; d. Irving and Elaine Degen; m. Floyd Ross Horowitz, June 23, 1953; children: Jason Degen, Benjamin Meyer Levi. BA, Antioch Coll., 1954; EdM, Goucher Coll., 1954; PhD, U. Iowa, 1959. Tchr. elem. sch., Iowa City, 1954-56; grad. rsch. asst. Iowa Child Welfare Sta., U. Iowa, 1956-59; asst. prof. psychology So. Oreg. Coll., Ashland, 1959-61; asst. prof. home econs. U. Kans., Lawrence, 1961-62, USHPS rsch. fellow, 1962-63, assoc. prof. dept. human devel. and family life, 1964-69, prof. dept. human devel. and family life, psychology, 1969—91, chmn. dept., 1969-75, rsch. assoc., 1964-75, assoc. dean, 1975-78, vice chancellor rsch., grad. studies and pub. svc., also dean grad. sch., 1978-91, dir. Infant Rsch. Lab., 1964—91; pres. Grad. Sch. and Univ. Ctr. CUNY, 1991—2005, pres. emeritus, 2005—, univ. prof. Grad. Sch. and Univ. Ctr., 2005—. Bd. dirs. Feminist Press; guest rsch. assoc. Bur. Child Rsch. U. Kans., Parsons State Hosp. and Tng. Ctr., 1960; vis. prof. dept. psychology Tel Aviv U., 1973—74; vis. rschr. dept. pediat. Kaplan Hosp., Rehovot, Israel, 1973—74; vis. lectr. dept. psychology Hebrew U., Jerusalem, 1976, cons. rsch. programs in early edn., 1980—; pres. Ctr. for Rsch., Inc., Lawrence, 1978—91; adv. com. Carolina Inst. on Early Edn. of the Handicapped, 1978—83; reviewer NSF, 1978—91; mem. U. Kans. del. to Peoples Republic China, 1980; exch. scholar Chinese Acad. Scis., China, 1982; mem. Office Sci. Integrity Rev. Adv. Com. PHS, 1991—93; nominating com. Weizmann Women in Sci. award Am. Com. Weizmann Inst. Sci., 1994; mem. Nat. Task Force Grad. Edn., 1994—96; workforce devel. subcom. NYC Partnership, 1994—95; mem. US Nat. Com. for the Internat. Union of Psychol. Sci., 1995—97; mem. overseers' com. to visit dept. psychology Harvard U.; mem., founding adv. bd. Sackler Inst. for Human Brain Devel., 1998—; bd. dirs. Nat. Coun. for Rsch. on Women; adv. coun. Nat. Inst. Child Health and Human Devel., 1999—2004; chair nat. adv. bd. Office Child Devel., U. Pitts.; lectr. in field; cons. in field. Editor Memoir Essay, 2002—; co-editor science watch sect. Am. Psychologist, 1993-97; mem. editl. bd. Jour. Devel. Psychology, 1969-75, Early Childhood Edn. Quar., 1974, Devel. Rev., 1981-92, Infant Behaviour and Devel., 1984-90, Contemporary Psychology, 1986-1991; contbr. articles to profl. jours.; TV host Women to Women, 1994—. Trustee Antioch Coll., 1987-91, LI U., 1992-94; bd. dirs. Cmty. Children's Ctr., 1965-68, Douglas County Vis. Nurse Assn., 1968-69; mem. workforce devel. subcom., NYC Partnership; mem. coun. advisors, Nat. Ctr. for Children in Poverty; mem. commn. on women in higher edn. Am. Coun. on Edn. Ford Found. fellow, 1954, Ctr. Advanced Studies Behavioral Scis. fellow Stanford U., 1983-84, Alumni fellow U. Iowa Coll. Arts and Scis., 2005; recipient Trustees award medal Cherry Lawn Sch., Conn., 1971, Outstanding Educator of Am. award, 1973, Disting. Psychologist in Mgmt. award Soc. for Psychologists in Mgmt., 1993, Rebecca Rice Alumni award Antioch Coll., 1996, Sue Rosenberg Zalk award The Feminist Press, 2003; named to Women's Hall of Fame U. Kans., 1974; Spl. Commendation NYC comptroller's office, 1997, NY Women's Agenda Star award, 2002. Fellow APA (pres. divsn. devel. psychology 1977-78, mem. publs. bd. 1985-91, chief sci. adviser 1989-93, pres. 1991-94, Centennial award for Sustained Contbn. to Sci. Directorate, 1992), U. Iowa Coll. Arts and Scis. Alumni, NY Acad. Scis., Am. Acad. Arts and Scis.; mem. Soc. Rsch. in Child Devel. (editor monographs 1976-83, pres. 1997-02), Jewish Cmty. Rels. Coun. (mem. bd. 1999-2005), Hebrew Free Loan Soc. (mem. bd. 2000—), Am. Assn. on Mental Deficiency, North Ctrl. Accrediting Assn. (bd. commrs. 1977-80), Am. Psychol. Found. (pres. 1991-94), Coun. Rsch. Polic and Grad. Edn. (chair, mem. exec. com.), Assn. Grad. Schs. (mem. exec. com.), NY Women's Forum (bd. dirs. 1995-97), Nat. Assn. of State Univs. and Land-Grant Colls. (past chair commn. on human resources and social change, bd. dirs. 1999-02), Sigma Xi, Phi Beta Kappa (hon.). Home: 710 West End Ave #C/D New York NY 10025 Office: CUNY Grad Ctr 365 Fifth Ave New York NY 10016-4309 Office Phone: 212-817-7235. Business E-Mail: fdhorowitz@gc.cuny.edu.

HOROWITZ, MARY CURTIS See CURTIS, MARY

HOROWITZ, SARA, labor organizer; b. NYC, Jan. 13, 1963; BS, Cornell U., 1984; JD, SUNY, Buffalo, 1992; MPA, Harvard U., 1995. Labor atty. pvt. practice; pub. defender NYC; union organizer Nat. Health and Human Svc. Employees Union, 1199; founder, exec. dir. Working Today, 1995—. Arbitrator Am. Arbitration Assn., Task Force on Restructuring Am.'s Labor Market Institutions, MIT. Contbr. articles to profl. jours. Grantee, fellow Stern Family Fund, Rockefeller Found., Echoing Green. Office: Working Today Ste 710 45 Main St Brooklyn NY 11201 Office Phone: 718-532-1515. Office Fax: 718-222-4440. E-mail: info@workingtoday.org.

HORRELL, KAREN HOLLEY, insurance company executive, lawyer; b. Augusta, Ga., July 10, 1952; d. Dudley Cornelius and Eleanor (Shouppe) Holley; m. Jack E. Horrell, Aug. 14, 1976. BS, Berry Coll., 1974; JD, Emory U., 1976. Bar: Ohio 1977. Counsel Am. Fin. Corp., 1980-81; sec., asst. sec. numerous other fin. and ins. cos.; gen. counsel numerous subsidiaries Great Am. Ins. Co., corp. counsel Cin., 1977-80, v.p., gen. counsel, sec., 1981-85, sr. v.p., gen. counsel, sec., bd. dirs., 1985—; pres. corp. svcs. Great Am. Ins. Property & Casualty Group, 1999—. Bd. dirs. Tri-Health, Inc., Bethesda, Inc, spkr. in field, 2005. Trustee Cmty. Chest, 1987—91, Seven Hills Sch., 1991—2000, v.p., 1995—99; mem. cabinet United Appeal, 1984; bd. dirs. YWCA, 1984—90, v.p. fin., 1986—89; mem. Hamilton County Blue Ribbon Task Force on Child Abuse and Neglect Svcs., 1989—91; trustee Ohio Ins. Inst., 1994—2000, chair, 1996—99, Bethesda Hosp. Inc.; chair Ohio Joint Underwriting Assn., 1992—97; trustee Berry Coll., 1999—; mem. Hamilton County Hosp. Commn., 1999—, vice chair, 2002—; bd. dirs. Children's Home, 2001—. Mem. ABA, Cin. Bar Assn. (admissions com. 1978-91, nominating com. 1987-90). Democrat. Office: Great Am Ins Co 580 Walnut St Cincinnati OH 45202-3110 Home: 11817 Quarterhorse Ct Cincinnati OH 45249-1279

HORSCH, KATHLEEN JOANNE, social services administrator, educator, consultant; b. Mpls., June 27, 1936; d. Clement Nicholas and Delta Jesse (Steckman) Simmer; m. Lawrence Leonard Horsch, Aug. 25, 1956; children: Daniel L., Timothy J., Christopher G., Catherine J., Sarah E. Student, U. Minn., 1967-73. Various positions local, state and nat. levels Am. Cancer Soc., Mpls., 1965—, pres. Hennepin County bd. dirs., 1978, hon. life mem. Hennepin Unit bd., 1992—, chmn. bd. dirs. Minn. divsn., 1984-86, hon. life mem. Minn. divsn., 1993—; sec. nat. bd. N.Y.C., 1982-85, vice-chmn. nat. bd., 1985-87, chmn. nat. bd. Atlanta, 1987-89, past officer, dir. nat. bd., 1992-97, hon. life mem., 1997—, chair Lane W. Adams award com., 1993-98; pres. Dynamics of Vol. Effectiveness, Inc., Mpls., 1985-95. Mem. faculty Met. State U., St. Paul, 1982-94, U.S. Nat. Com./Internat. Union Against Cancer UICC, Washington, 1989-94. Mem. adv. bd. Look Good Feel Better, 1996-03, Drucker Found. Non-Profit Mgmt., 1992-03; mem. com. Joint Commn. Health, 1989; bd. govs. United Way Am., 1990-96, St. Croix area United Way, 1996-02, vice-chair, 1997; bd. govs. Youth for Understanding Internat. Exch., 1992-01, vice-chair, 1997, chair, 1998-00; bd. govs. Courage Ctr., 1993-04, vice-chair, 1996-00, chair, 2000-02; mem. coun. Internat. Cancer Union, 1990-94, chair Campaign orgn. Pub. Edn. and Svc. Program, 1990-94; bd. dirs. Josephson Inst. of Ethics, 1991-96; chmn. The Human Spirit Initiative, 2004—. Recipient Svc. to Mankind award, Disting. Svc. award, Am. Cancer Soc., 2006. Mem. Nat. Human Svcs. Assembly (bd. govs. 1995—), Minikahda Club. Avocations: boating, piano, swimming, hiking. Personal E-mail: klhorsch@earthlink.net.

HORSLEY, PAULA ROSALIE, accountant; b. Smithfield, Nebr., Sept. 7, 1924; Student, AIB Bus. Coll., Des Moines, 1942-44, YMCA Coll., Chgo., 1944-47, UCLA Extension, 1974. Acctg. mgr. Montgomery Ward & Co., Denver, 1959-62; acct. Harman & Co., CPAs, Arcadia, Calif., 1962-67; contr., officer G & H Transp., Montebello, Calif., 1967-78; comptroller Frederick Weisman Co., Century City, Calif., 1978-80; CFO, Luth. Shipping, Madang, Papua New Guinea, 1980-82; prin. village bookkeeper, acctg. cons. Moreno Valley, Calif., 1982-94; CFO, Insight Computer Products and Tech., Inc., San Gabriel, Calif., 1988—2003, Insight Video Net LLC, Rancho Cucamonga, Calif., 2003—. Vol. crisis counselor, supr. and instr. Melodyland Hotline, Anaheim, Calif., 1997-79. Home: 31130-100 S Gen Kearny Rd Temecula CA 92591 Office: Insight Video Net LLC 10400 Trademark St Rancho Cucamonga CA 91730 Personal E-mail: busterpava@aol.com.

HORSMAN, LENORE LYNDE (ELEANORA LYNDE), voice educator, soprano, actress; b. Saginaw, Mich., Apr. 21, 1931; d. George Clark and Gwendolyn (Steele) McNabb; m. Reginald Horsman, Sept. 3, 1955; children: John, Janine, Mara. BS in Music and Piano, Ind. U., 1956, MA in Theatre-Opera, 1958. profl. certs. in voice, Villa Schifanoia, Florence, Accademia Musicale Chigiana, Siena, Accademia Di Virgiliana, Mantua, Italy, Mozarteum, Salzburg. Tchrs: Tito Gobbi, Ettore Campogalliani. Dir. Mt. Clemens Studio of Music, Mich., 1950; tchr. voice, piano and acting for singers Milw. Conservatory of Music, 1964-65; dir., tchr. pvt. voice studio, 1965—; founder, dir., designer Milw. Opera Theater, 1966; vocal coach dept. opera U. Wis., Madison, 1969-70. Dir., performer Cameo Prodn., Milw., 1974, Opera for Two, Milw., 1975, Mu Phi Epsilon Sch. Music, Chgo., 1976-81; dir., tchr. pvt. voice studio, Chgo., 1976-92; voice coach Theatre X, Milw., 1977; tchr. of acting Northshore Theatre, Milw., 1978-80. More than 33 leading roles in opera, operetta, musicals and plays; performances and concerts in US and Italy. Pres. Wis. Women in the Arts, 1973-76; bd. dir. Internat. Women's Yr. Festival, Milw., 1975. Named Women of the Yr., Milw. Panhellenic Assn., 1975; recipient Career Achievement award, 1978, Singers medal of honor Amici della Lirica, Mantua, Italy, 1981, Palcoscenico Music Vocal Silver Stage award, Italy, 1981. Mem. AAUW (v.p. 1999-2000), Nat.

Assn. Tchr. Singing, Nat. Opera Assn., Wis. Music Tchr. Assn., Writers' Forum, Guild for Lifelong Learning, Mu Phi Epsilon, Theta Alpha Phi. Avocations: theater, opera, painting, poetry. Personal E-mail: rhorsman@wi.rr.com.

HORSNELL, MARGARET EILEEN, retired historian; b. St. Paul, Jan. 3, 1928; d. Kenneth George and Mary Elizabeth (Dowd) Horsnell. BA, U. Minn., 1961, MA, 1963, PhD, 1967. Instr. history U. Minn., 1966-67; mem. faculty Am. Internat. Coll., Springfield, Mass., 1967—, assoc. prof. history, 1976-84, prof., 1984-96, chmn. dept., 1987-96, emeritus prof. history, 2006—. Vis. sr. assoc. Mem. Sch. Classical Studies, Athens, 1997—99. Author: Spencer Roane: Judicial Advocate of Jeffersonian Principles, 1986; mem. editl. bd. This Constn., 1986—88; contbr. articles to publs. Mem. adv. panel 500 Yrs. Am. Clothing, 1989—92. Recipient Tozer Found. award, 1966, McKnight Found. award, 1967; Summer grantee, Am. Internat. Coll., 1970, Alt. fellow, AAUW, 1974—75. Mem.: Am. Legal Studies Assn., So. Hist. Assn., Inst. Early Am. History and Culture, Archeol. Inst. Am., Phi Alpha Theta. Home and Office: 15 Atwood Rd South Hadley MA 01075-1601 Office Phone: 413-533-6388. Personal E-mail: horsnell@aol.com.

HORST, BARBARA LYNN, primary school educator; b. Oakhill, W.Va., Sept. 9, 1951; d. Robert John and Margaret Leona Hamby; m. Eugene Alan Horst, June 13, 1975; children: Joshua Robert, Jeremy Lee, Jarad Alan, John Wesley. BS in Edn., Maranatha Bapt. Bible Coll., Watertown, Wis., 1978. Tchr. Calvary Bapt. Sch., Casper, Wyo., 1980—82, Liberty Bapt. Acad., Rapid City, SD, 1987—91, Am. Heritage Christian, Hayward, Calif., 1991—2004, Christian Cmty. Presch., Fremont, Calif., 2004—. Office: Christian Cmty Sch 39700 Mission Blvd Fremont CA 94539-3089

HORST, CAROL BERRY, art educator; b. St. Louis, Mar. 17, 1954; d. William Chapman Berry Jr. and Janet Nies Berry; m. Steven Lee Horst, Feb. 23, 1980; children: Jennifer Anne, Laura Horst-Jones. BA in Edn., Southeast Mo. State U., Cape Girardeau, Mo., 1976, MAT, 1980. Educator art Rockwood Sch. Dist., Eureka, Mo., 1976—80, Jackson Sch. Dist., 1983—. Mem. adv. bd. U. Mus., Jackson, 1994—98, Music Acad., Cape Girardeau, 1993—99. Scholar chair PEO, Jackson, 2000—06; juror Visual Art Coop., Cape Girardeau, 2004—. Named Tchr. Yr., Jackson C. of C., 2002; recipient Art Coun. award, 1996. Mem.: Jackson Tchrs. Assn. (pres. 2003—04), Southeast Mo. State Art Tchrs. Assn. (pres. 1996—98), Mo. State Tchrs. Assn., Optimists Club (chair 1999—). Avocations: reading, swimming, drawing. Office: JAckson R-2 Sch Dist 1701 S Hope St Jackson MO 63755

HORST, PAMELA SUE, medical educator, physician; b. Hershey, Pa., Jan. 23, 1951; d. Ralph H. and Helen (Fry) H.; m. Thomas H. Dennison, Feb. 6, 1982; 1 child, Elizabeth Dennison. BS, Pa. State U., 1972; MD, Pa. State U., Hershey, 1976. Diplomate Am. Bd. Family Practice, Am. Bd. Hospice & Palliative Medicine (cert). Resident in family practice Shadyside Hosp., Pitts., 1979; family physician North Jefferson Health Svcs., Clayton, N.Y., 1979-82; physician emergency rm. Geisinger Med. Ctr., Philipsburg, Pa., 1982-84; asst. prof. family medicine Albany (N.Y.) Med. Coll., 1984-88; assoc. prof. health sci. ctr. SUNY, Syracuse, 1988—. Med. dir. family practice ctr. St. Joseph's Hosp. Health Ctr., Syracuse, 1989—, assoc. residency dir. family practice residency, Syracuse, 1990—; physician Palliative Care Cons. Svc., 1999—, hospice physician, 2002—; chmn. St. Joseph's Health Alliance, 1995-97, SyraHealth, IPA, 1997-98. Author: (with others) Ambulatory Medicine, 1993, Manual of Family Practice, 1996. Mem. Am. Acad. Family Physicians, Soc. Tchrs. Family Medicine, Am. Assn. of Hospice and Palliative Medicine. Avocations: gardening, reading. Office: St Joseph's Health Ctr Family Practice Residency 301 Prospect Ave Syracuse NY 13203-1899

HORST, TERESA DALE, music educator; b. Loudon, Tenn., May 20, 1955; d. William Jefferson and Selma Elizabeth Hamilton; m. Thomas Dale Horst, June 6, 1976; children: Thomas Dale Jr., Tiffany DeAnn. BS in Music Edn., U. Tenn., Knoxville, 1977. Program devel and dissemination Bristol City Schs., Va., 1977—79; classroom music instr., dir. devel. Highland Hills Christian Acad., Lenoir City, Tenn., 1986—96; h.s. band camp instr. various schs., Tenn., 1999—2001; dir. music Joy of Music Youth Music Schs., Loudon, 2001—04; pvt. music instr. Tenn. Mem. Knoxville Symphony League, 2003—, East Tenn. Comty. Band, Knoxville, 1990—. Vol. Hist. Mus. Lenoir City, Lenoir City, 1996—2000; office vol. Lenoir City H.S., Lenoir City, 1996—2001. Recipient Award for Tchr. Recognition as Outstanding Tchr. in State, Tenn. Gov.'s Sch. for Performing Arts, 2005, John Philip Sousa award, John Philip Sousa Found., 1973. Mem.: Tenn. Sch. Band and Orch. Assn., East Tenn. Sch. Band and Orch. Assn., Internat. Horn Soc., Music Educators Nat. Conf., Sigma Alpha Iota. Church Of God. Avocations: horseback riding, travel, scrapbooks, gardening. Home: 15906 Hotchkiss Valley Rd E Loudon TN 37774

HORSTMAN, SUZANNE RUCKER, financial planner; b. Coral Gables, Fla., June 27, 1945; d. Thomas John Jr. and June Ethel Agusta (Stones) R.; m. James Winter Horstman, Dec. 28, 1989. BBA, Fla. Atlantic U., 1971, MBA, 1975. CFP; lic. real estate agt. Assoc. dir. Am. Soc. Cons. Pharmacists, 1971-73; assoc. dir. devel. Fairfax Hosp. Assn. Found., Springfield, Va., 1974-81; dir. devel. Arlington (Va.) Hosp. Found., 1982-86; prin. Suzanne June Rucker, CFP, Falls Church, Va., 1986-90; dir. devel. Phoenixville Healthcare Found., 1990-94, Tri-County TEC Found., 1994-96, philanthropy cons., 1996—; dir. devel. CARE, 1997—2002; exec. dir. Libr. Found. Martin County, 2002—. Instr. George Washington U., Washington; seminar spkr. in field. Mem. Treasure Coast Planned Giving Coun., Nat. Com. Planned Giving; co-chair Planet Philanthropy, 2004; bd. dirs. Ronald McDonald House, Wilmington, Washington, Salvation Army Aux., Washington, Rep. Working Women's Forum. Fellow: Assn. Health Care Philanthropy. Republican. Office Phone: 772-221-1409.

HORT, SUSAN, art collector; m. Michael Hort; children: Peter, Andrew, Shoshana, Rema Hort Mann(dec.). Founder Rema Hort Mann Found., NYC, 1995—. Named one of Top 200 Collectors, ARTnews mag., 2003—06. Avocation: Collector contemporary art. Office: Rema Hort Mann Found 135 Hudson St New York NY 10013

HORTON, DEBORAH JANE, performing arts educator; b. Bridgeport, Conn., Aug. 3, 1981; d. Gregory Munn and Janet VanHise Horton. BA in Arts Mgmt. and Dance magna cum laude, Am. U., Washington, 2003. Edn. assoc. Ballet Petite, Inc., Bethesda, Md., 2001—04; dance tchr. D'Valda & Sirico Dance Ctr., Fairfield, Conn., 2004—. Mem. Tappening Profl. Tap Co., Washington, 2000—, jazzdanz.dc Jazz Co., 2000—01. (tap performance) Stay Loose (Choreography Awards, Platinum Award, 2006), (lyrical dance performance) Cooling, (jazz dance performance) Ya Mama. Scholar, Am. U., 1999—2003. Mem.: Alpha Lambda Delta, Delta Gamma (v.p. panhellenic 2001, v.p. programming 2002). Personal E-mail: deborahjhorton@yahoo.com.

HORTON, JOANN, academic administrator; b. Lenoir, N.C., 1948; d. Jasper D. Horton and Laura Alice Patterson; m. Warren N. Moore (div.). BS in French, Appalachian State U., 1970, MA in French, 1971; PhD in Higher Edn. Adminstrn., Ohio State U., 1977. V.p. Olive Harvey Coll., City Coll. Chgo., 1982-86, provost, 1986-89; state adminstr. Iowa Divsn. C.C., Des Moines, 1989-93; pres. Tex. So. U., Houston, 1993-95; ind. cons., sr. fellow Am. Coun. on Edn., 1996-98; pres. Kennedy-King Coll., 1998-99; dep. chancellor for strategic planning City Colls. Chgo., 1998-99; pres. Team Masters, Inc., 2000—. Cons. evaluator, commr. at large North Cen. Assn. Commn. on Insts. for Higher Edn., Chgo., 1984-93; bd. dirs. Appalachian State U. Grad. Sch., Boone, N.C., 1995-99; ind. cons., Chgo., 1996-98. Bd. dirs. Greater Houston Partnership, 1993-95, chair workforce devel. task force, 1994-95; chair urban scouting com. Boy Scouts Am., Houston, 1995; strategic planning facilitator 7th Congl. Edn. Com., Chgo., 1999. Recipient Disting. Alumni award Appalachian State U., Boone, 1994, commendation 74th Tex. Legis., 1995, Image, Svc. and Achievement award Kizzy Found., Chgo., 1999; inductee Tex. Black Women Hall of Fame, 1994; fellow Leadership Greater Chgo. Mem. Am. Assn. Higher Edn., Am. Assn. State Colls. and Univs., Am. Assn. Women in C.C., Nat. Assn. Women Bus. Owners, Third World Conf. Found. (vice chair 1993—, Svc. award 1999), Assn. Colls. of Ill. Orgnl. Devel. Network. Avocations: tennis, reading, music, travel.

HORTON, LUCINDA, biology professor; b. Decatur, Ill., Jan. 30, 1954; d. Donald J. and Velma M. Messmore; children: Jesse L., Nathan A. BS in Botany, Ea. Ill. U., Charleston, 1984, MS in Botany, 1986. Instr. botany Ea. Ill. U., Charleston, 1989—94; instr. biology Lakeland Coll., Mattoon, 1994—. Mem.: Ill. State Acad. Scis., Ill. Assn. Coll. Biologists. Office: Lakeland Coll 5001 Lakeland Blvd Mattoon IL 61938

HORTON, PATRICIA MATHEWS, artist, violist and violinist; b. Bklyn., Mar. 6, 1932; d. Edward Joseph and Margaret (Briggs) Mathews; m. Ernest H. Horton Jr., Mar. 6, 1982; 1 stepchild, Carol Horton Tremblay. Student in viola, William Primrose Master Class, 1980; student, Glendale (Calif.) C.C., 1981—90, Glendale (Calif.) CC., 1993, Glendale (Calif.) C.C., 1999—2002, Art Ctr. Coll. Design, Pasadena, Calif., 1988-93; student in painting composition, Peter Liashkov, L.A., 1993-97. Profl. musician on violin and viola, 1951-86; musician on tour U.S., Can., Cuba, 1952-57. Played with New Orleans Philharm., 1959-61, U.S. Tour of San Francisco Ballet, 1965, L.A. Civic Light Opera, 1974-80, Bolshoi Ballet Co., LA, 1975, Am. Ballet Theatre, 1974-80, N.Y.C. Opera, 1974-80, Royal Ballet of London, 1978, Alicia Alonzo's Cuban Ballet, 1979, Harlem Ballet, 1984, Deutsche Oper Berlin, 1985, also motion picture and TV soundtrack recs.; one-woman shows include Claremont (Calif.) Sch. Theology, 1997, Pasadena First United Meth. Ch., 1997, 99, La Canada Flintridge Libr., 1999. Active Dem. Nat. Com., Women's Caucus for Art. Mem. Am. Fedn. Musicians (life). Avocations: hiking local mountains, desert and beaches, studying classical guitar.

HORTON, ROSALYN, underwriter; b. Nashville, July 13, 1946; d. W.D. and Irma Jean (Jackson) Donnell; m. Frederick Lee Horton, Aug. 6, 1965; children: Shane Scott, Sundai Horton Reeder, Shalako Lance. Broadcast Diploma, Elkins Inst., Nashville, 1973. Cert. ins. counselor; cert. profl. ins. woman. Office asst. Rich Printing Co., Nashville, 1973-76; office adminstr. Exhibit 4, Inc., Nashville, 1976-84; corp. sec. Horton Paper Svc., Nashville, 1984—; ocean/hull underwriter Fireman's Fund, Atlanta, 1992—2005, multi-line marine underwriter Nashville, 2005—. Mem. Mid. Tenn. Cath. Diocese Social Justice Conf., Nashville, 1997-2002; supporter Muscular Dystrophy Assn., Nashville, 1995—; strategy team leader Tying Nashville Together, 2000-02. Recipient T.J. Mims Achievement award, 1999, Achievement award Am. Assn. Mng. Gen. Agts., 1997, 2003; named Tenn. Coun. Ins. Woman of Yr., 2001 Mem.: Nat. Assn. Ins. Women (state dir. Tenn. coun. 1999—2000, co-chair nat. conv. 2003, diversified advanced edn. designation., region III Rookie of Yr. 1994, Tenn. State Ins. Woman of Yr. 2001), Nashville Ins. Profls. (pres. bd. dirs. 1995—99), Nashville Claims Assn. (parliamentarian 1998—2000, treas. 2000—01, asst. NAIW region III v.p. 2001—02, regional v.p. 2004—05). Democrat. Roman Catholic. Avocations: gardening, crafts, Harley Davidson motorcycle trips, reading. Office: Firemans Fund McGee Marine 341 Cool Springs Blvd Ste 130 Franklin TN 37067 Office Phone: 615-778-4800. Business E-mail: rhorton@ffic.com.

HORTON, STEPHANIE MCNEILL, psychologist; b. Golden Valley, Minn., Sept. 14, 1972; d. Richard William and Gloria Jean Mc Neill; m. Christopher Adam Horton, June 22, 2005. PhD, U. Minn., Mpls., 1996—2001. Nationally Certified School Psychologist NASP, 2002. Sch. psychologist Mpls. Pub. Schs., 2002—. Office: River Bend Edn Ctr 300 Industrial Blvd NE Minneapolis MN 55413 Office Phone: 612-668-1247.

HORTON, SUSAN PITTMAN, bank executive; m. Stan Horton; 1 child, Alexandria Rose. BA in Bus. Adminstrn., Wash. State U., 1984. CPA. Ptnr. McFarland & Alton PS, 1989—99; pres., CEO, chmn. Wheatland Bank, Spokane, Wash., 1999—; ptnr. Deloitte and Touche, Seattle. Mem.: Spokane Club. Avocations: barrel racing, quarter horses. Office: Wheatland Bank 222 North Wall St Spokane WA 99201

HORTON-WRIGHT, ALMA IRENE, retired elementary school educator; b. Austin, Tex., July 05; d. Ollon and Willie; m. Henry S. Wright, June 25; children: Sheila, Stanley, Gregory, Gerry. AA in Liberal Arts, San Bernardino Valley Coll., Calif., 1976; AA, Western Okla. State U., Altus, 1984; BA, Calif. State U., San Bernardino, 1979, postgrad.; MA in edn., Prairie View A&M U., 1993. Cert. tchr., Calif., life credential, Tex. Tchr. speed reading, edn. office Altus (Okla.) AFB; tchr. adult edn. Altus Sch. Dist.; elem. tchr. Rialto (Calif.) Unified Sch. Dist., Austin Ind. Sch. Dist. Mem. NEA, Tex. State Tchrs. Assn., Calif. State U. Almuni Assn., Edn. Austin, Phi Delta Kappa. Austin Ret. Tchrs. Assn., Tex. Ret. Tchrs. Assn. Avocations: travel, reading, art activities.

HORVAT, VASHTI, online marketing consultant; b. Rochester, Mar. 22; BS in Computer Info. Systems, DeVry Inst. Tech., Chgo. Cert. CISA. IT auditor BNSF Co., Ft. Worth, 1999—2001; mgr. email mktg. Travelocity.com, 2001—03; mgr. online mktg. Piidesign, LLC, 2003—; mng. prin. Orr Consulting LLC, 2003—. Patron Internat. Inst. Mem. Am. Mgmt. Assn., Info. Systems Audit Control Assn. (North Tex. chpt.), Alliance Francaise Home: 2105 Harwood Rd ste 215 PMB 149 Bedford TX 76021 Business E-Mail: info@orrconsulting.us.

HORVATH, ANNETTE, home care administrator; b. Bronx, N.Y., Mar. 12, 1963; d. Thomas and Roslyn DeGrazia; m. Leonard Horvath, Aug. 28, 1988; children: Jennifer, Rebecca. BSN, Lehman Coll., 1996; MS in Health Care Adminstrn., Iona Coll., 1999. RN. Case mgr. Montifiore Hosp., Bronx, 1993—98; project mgr. Jewish Home and Hosp., N.Y.C., 1998—99, dir. patient svcs. Bronx, 1999—2000; adminstr. Americare Inc., Bklyn., 2000—01, Village Care N.Y., N.Y.C., 2001—05, Revival Home Health, Bklyn., 2006. CEO Excellent Home Care, Bklyn., 2005—. Mem.: NAFE, N.Y. State Home Care Assn., Am. Coll. Health Care Execs., Women Health Mgmt., N.Y. State Health Care Providers, Women Arts Mus. Avocations: reading, cooking. Office: Revival Home Health Svcs 5350 Kings Hwy Brooklyn NY 11203 Office Phone: 718-387-5303, 718-629-1000 290. E-mail: ahorvath28@yahoo.com.

HORVATH, BETTY FERGUSON, writer; b. Jefferson City, Mo., May 20, 1927; d. Bransford Bolton and Augusta Kapell Ferguson; m. John Horvath, Mar. 11, 1954 (dec.); children: Sally, Polly, Jay. Student, Phillips U. Author: (children's book) Hooray for Jasper, 1966, Jasper Makes Music, Will The Real Tommy Wilson Stand Up, 1969, The Cheerful Quiet, 1969, Be Nice to Josephine, 1970, Not Enough Indians, 1971, Small Paul and the Bully of Morgan Court, 1971, Sir Galahad, Mr. Longfellow and Me, 1998. Mem.: Mensa, Soc. Children's Book Writers and Illustrators. Home: 1380 Marice Dr #451 Eagan MN 55120 Personal E-mail: bfhorvath@comcast.net.

HORVATH (SELAI), CYNTHIA M., secondary school educator; d. Robert R. and Elaine T. Selai; m. Scott A. Horvath, Nov. 25, 2005. B of Edn., Duquesne U., Pitts., 1996; MEd, Ind. U. Pa., 2002. Educator social studies West Mifflin Area Sch. Dist., Pa., 1997—. Faculty sponsor PASC Dist. 3, Pitts., 2005—06. Home: 270 Castle Dr West Mifflin PA 15122 Office: West Mifflin Area High School 91 Commonwealth Ave West Mifflin PA 15122 Office Phone: 412-466-7220. Personal E-mail: missselai@yahoo.com. E-mail: horvathc@wmasd.org.

HORVATH, DOLORES ANTIONETTE, nurse; b. Chgo., Sept. 29, 1947; d. Robert Clarence and Margaret Nancy Jackson; m. William John Goetzinger (dec. Oct. 1969); m. Raymond Herman Horvath, Aug. 30, 1980; 1 child, Stacy Anne Williamsen. BS, Lewis U., 1985; MS, LaSalle U., 1999. Cert. in healthcare quality Nat. Assn. Healthcare Quality. Assoc. exec. dir. Humana Hosp., Destin, Fla., 1989-91; regional dir. quality Humana Corp., Louisville, 1991-94; healthcare cons., 1994-96; regional dir. outcomes mgmt. Columbia Healthcare Corp., Chgo., 1996-97; assoc. v.p. Oak Park (Ill.) Hosp., 1997-99; healthcare cons. DGH Consulting, Inc., Rosa Beach, Fla., 1999—. Mem. Am. Heart Assn., Oak Park. Republican. Baptist. Avocations: sewing, needlecrafts, reading, walking.

HORVATH, POLLY, writer; b. Kalamazoo, Mich. married; 2 children. Co-author (with Gioia Fiammenghi): (book) An Occassional Cow, 1989; author: No More Cornflakes, 1990, The Happy Yellow Car, 1994, When the Circus Came to Town, 1996, The Trolls, 1999 (Nat. Book award finalist, 1999), Everything on a Waffle, 2001 (Newberry Honor Book), The Canning Season, 2003 (Nat. Book award, 2003), The Vacation, 2005. Office: Books for Young Readers Farrar, Straus & Giroux 19 Union Square West New York NY 10003

HORWITZ, BARBARA ANN, physiologist, educator, consultant; d. Martin Horwitz and Lillian Bloom; m. John M. Horowitz, Aug. 17, 1970. BS, U. Fla., 1961, MS, 1962; PhD, Emory U., 1966. Asst. rsch. physiologist U. Calif., Davis, 1968-72, asst. prof. physiology, 1972-75, assoc. prof., 1975-78, prof., 1978—, disting. prof., 2003—, chair animal physiology, 1991-93, chmn. neurobiology, physiology and behavior dept., 1993-98, vice provost acad. personnel, 2001—. Cons. Am. Inst. Behavioral Rsch., Palo Alto, Calif., 1980, Am. Inst. Rsch., Washington, 1993-99, NSF, Washington, 1981-84, NIH, Washington, 1995-99. Contbr. articles to profl. jours. Named postdoctoral fellow, USPHS, 1966—68, Arthur C. Guyton Physiology Tchr. of the Yr., 1996; recipient Disting. Tchg. award, 1982, U. Calif.-Davis prize for Tchg. and Scholarly Achievement, 1991, Pres.'s award for excellence in fostering undergrad. rsch., 1995. Fellow: AAAS; mem.: Phi Sigma (v.p. Davis chpt. 1983—, nat. v.p. 1989—), Phi Kappa Pi, Soc. Exptl. Biology and Medicine (exec. coun. 1990—94, pres.-elect 1999—2001, pres. 2001—03), N.Am. Assn. for Study of Obesity (exec. coun. 1988—92), N.Y. Acad. Scis., Am. Physiology Soc. (edn. and program coms. coun. 1993—96, pres.-elect 2001—02, pres. 2002—03), Sigma Xi (pres. Davis chpt. 1980—81), Phi Beta Kappa (pres. Davis chpt. 1991—92, 2000—02). Office: U Calif Dept Neurobiology Phys Davis CA 95616 E-mail: bahorwitz@ucdavis.edu.

HORWITZ, JOY A., foundation administrator; b. Apr. 18, 1958; BA in European History and English, Cornell U.; JD, U. Pa. Assoc. Pepper, Hamilton and Scheetz, Phila.; assoc. Environ. program Pew Charitable Trusts, Phila., 1992—98, dir. legal affairs, 1998—. Chair Environ. Commn., Haddonfield, NJ. Office: Pew Charitable Trusts 2005 Market St Ste 1700 Philadelphia PA 19103-7077

HORWITZ, KATHRYN BLOCH, molecular biologist, educator, breast cancer researcher; b. Sosua, Dominican Republic, Feb. 20, 1941; came to U.S., 1952; d. Werner Meyerstein and Olga (Schlesinger) Bloch; m. Lawrence David Horwitz, June 14, 1964; children: Phillip Andrew, Carolyn Anita. BA, Barnard Coll., 1962; MS, NYU, 1966; PhD, U. Tex. Southwestern Med. Sch., Dallas, 1975; postdoctoral, U. Tex. Sch. Medicine, San Antonio, 1978. Instr. U. Tex. Sch. Medicine, San Antonio, 1978-79; asst. prof. U. Colo. Med. Sch., Denver, 1979-84, assoc. prof., 1984-89, prof. of medicine, pathology and molecular biology, 1989—2004, disting. prof., 2004—. Cellular physiology panel NSF, 1985-88; biochem. endocrinology study sect. NIH, 1989-93; mem. Pres.'s Cancer Panel Spl. Commn. on Breast Cancer, 1992, Breast Cancer Task Force, NIH, 1981-84. Author over 150 breast cancer and steroid receptors research papers, books; assoc. editor, editl. bd. for several scientific jours. Chair, sci. adv. bd. Cancer League of Colo., 1987-91; organizer Keystone Symposia on Steroid Receptors, 1996, 98, 2000. Elected fellow AAAS, 2000; recipient Nat. Bd. award Med. Coll. Pa., 1986, Wilson Stone award M.D. Anderson Hosp. and Tumor Inst., 1976, Rsch. Career Devel. award Nat. Cancer Inst., 1981-86, MERIT award NIH, 1992, The U. Helsinki medal and Second Siltavouri lectr. Finland, 1993, William L. McGuire Meml. lectr., 1997, Bicenntenial lectr. U. Louisville, 1998, Disting. Sci. award Clin. Ligand Assay Soc., 2000; grantee NSF, Am. Cancer Soc., Nat. Found. Cancer Rsch. Dept. of the Army, NIH. Fellow AAAS; mem. Endocrine Soc. (program com. 1989-91, nominating com. 1989-91, chair 1991, coun. 1992-95, pres.-elect 1997-98, pres. 1998-99, immediate past pres. 1999-2000, mem. devel. com. 2000—), Fedn. Associated Socs. Exptl. Biology, Am. Fedn. Clin. Rsch., Am. Soc. Cell Biology, Am. Assn. Cancer Rsch. (program com. 1994-95, state legis. com. 1993—), Western Soc. Clin. Investigation, Am. Soc. Biochemistry and Molecular Biology, Fedn. Am. Socs. Exptl. Biology (bd. dirs. 2004). Democrat. Jewish. Avocations: skiing, reading, gardening, travel. Office: U Colo Dept Medicine Endocrinology MS 8106 PO Box 6151 Aurora CO 80045

HORWITZ, SUSAN BAND, pharmacologist; BA, Bryn Mawr Coll., 1958; PhD in Biochemistry, Brandeis U., 1963; PhD (hon.), Universite de la Mediterranee, 2002. Postdoctoral fellow dept. pharmacology, sch. medicine Tufts U., 1963-65, Emory U., 1965-67; rsch. assoc. dept. medicine Albert Einstein Coll. Medicine, N.Y.C., 1967-68, instr. dept. pharmacology, 1968-70, asst. prof. dept. medicine, 1970-75, asst. prof. dept. cell biology, 1973-75, assoc. prof. depts. molecular pharmacology and cell biology, 1980—, co-chair dept. molecular pharmacology, 1985—, Rose C. Falkenstein prof. cancer rsch., 1986—, assoc. dir. cancer rsch. ctr., 1991—. Mem. pharmacology-toxicology rsch. team Nat. Inst. Gen. Med. Sci., 1975-80; adv. com. Irma T. Hirschl Scientist award, 1979-85; bd. scientific counselors divsn. cancer treatment NCI, 1981-86, 87-90, mem. review com. Outstanding Investigators Grant award, 1984, ad hoc review com. in vitro and in vivo disease-oriented screening project, 1986; guest reviewer sci. adv. com. Damon Runyon/Walter Winchell Rsch. Fund, 1983, 88; vice chair Gordon Conf. Chemotherapy of Exptl. and Clin. Cancer, 1986, chair, 1987, mem. coun., 1990-93; Sterling Drug vis. prof. dept. pharmacology Boston U., 1987; mem. Charles F. Kettering selection com. Gen. Motors Cancer Rsch. Found., 1988-89, awards assembly, 1991. Contbr. articles to profl. jour., chapters to books. Recipient Rsch. Career Devel. award 1970-75, award Pharm. Mfrs. Assn., 1972, Irma T. Hirschl Career Scientists award, 1975-80, Warren Alpert Found. prize, 2005; grantee Merck, 1970, Nat. Cancer Inst., 1985-92, 92, Bristol-Myers, 1988-93; named Outstanding Woman Scientist metro N.Y.C. chpt. Assn. Women in Science, Barnard Medal of Distinction, 2003, PhRMA Found. award of Excellence, 2004. Mem. Am. Soc. Pharmacology and Exptl. Therapeutics (com. edn. and profl. affairs 1973-77), Am. Soc. Microbiology (vice chair antimicrobial chemotherapy), Am. Chem. Soc., Am. Assn. Cancer Rsch. (biochem. program com. 1983-84, Clowes award selection com. 1986-87, bd. dirs. 1987-90, spl. confs. com. 1989-92, chmn. Rhoads award selection com. 1990-91, co-chair conf. in cancer rsch. membrane transport in multidrug resistance, devel. and disease, 1991, Cain Meml. award 1992, pres., 2003-), Am. Soc. Cell Biology, Harvey Soc. (mem. coun. 1991—), Am. Acad. of Arts & Sciences, NAS. Office: A Einstein Coll Medicine Dept Molecular Pharmacology 1300 Morris Park Ave Bronx NY 10461-1926*

HOSANSKY, ANNE, writer; b. N.Y.C. d. Abraham and Ada Lichtman; children: Tamar, David. BA in Creative Writing, CUNY, Queen's Coll. In house editor Weight Watchers Internat., NY, 1973—85. Actor: (off Broadway regional theater); author: Widow's Walk, 1994, Turning Toward Tomorrow, 2002; contbr. articles to publs. Mem.: Am. Assn. Journalists and Authors, Writers Union, Authors Guild.

HOSEA, JULIA HILLER, psychotherapist, communications executive, paralegal; b. Cin., Oct. 19, 1952; d. Clifford John and Nancy Carol (Elberg) Hiller; m. Jon Michael Ausman, Nov. 3, 1973 (div. 1978); m. Robert Arthur Hosea, Mar. 22, 1987 (dec. Dec. 12, 1998). BA, Allegheny Coll., 1975; cert., Inst. Paralegal Tng., Phila., 1975; MA, Regis U., 2005. Gen. paralegal Pettigrew & Bailey, Miami, Fla., 1975-76, Joseph J. Weisenfeld Law Offices, Miami, 1976-81; corp. paralegal Wood & Lamping, Cin., 1981-85; pension specialist Katz, Teller Brant & Hild, Cin., 1985-89; owner, mgr. Chrysalis Communications, Cin., 1989-90, The Hosea Group, Grand Junction, 1990-95; owner Ruby Canyon Textiles, Grand Junction, 1996—2002; mgr. Action Potential, LLC, 2002—03. Grant adminstr. for advance med. directives program in Colo., 2000-04, Western Slope Counseling, 2005-; adj. instr. Coll.

Mt. St. Joseph, Cin., 1984-90. Contbr. articles to profl. publs. Mem. Cin. Paralegal Assn. (pres. 1984-85), Nat. Fedn. Paralegal Assn. (chmn. pension sect. 1986-87, editor Nat. Paralegal Reporter 1988-92). E-mail: jhosea@bresnan.net.

HOSKIE, LORRAINE, consumer products representative, poet; b. Nansemond County, Va., Aug. 26, 1953; m. Eddie Lewis Hoskie, July 7, 1972 (div. Oct. 1980); children: Jacqueline Marie, Quinton Lewis. BS, Va. Commonwealth U., 1977. Clk. Christian Children's Fund, Richmond, 1977—79, corr. rsch. clk., 1979—80; eligibility worker City of Richmond, 1982—83; substitute tchr. Sch. Bd., Richmond, 1983—86; telemarketer Energy Savs. Exterior, Richmond, 1995—96; CRT operator Snelling Pers. Svcs., Richmond, 1996; mail clk. Abacus, Richmond, 1997; office worker Kelly Svcs., Richmond, 1997; remittance processor Calipher, Inc., Richmond, 1997—2001; adminstrv. program specialist II VA Employment Commn., 2003—05; meat stocker Walmart Stores, Inc., Charlotte, NC, 2005—. Substitute tchr. Sch. Bd. of Franklin, Va., 1987; ch. sec. SDA-Ephesus, Richmond, 1981-82; vol. worker Bapt. Student Union Va. Commonwealth U., Richmond, 1971-72, math. tutor Spl. Svcs. Program, 1972. Sec. Ephesus Prison Ministry, 1996—; team sec. Ephesus Va. Dept. Correction, 1993-94; choir Ginter Park Meth. Ch., Richmond, Va., 2005— Named Golden Poet, World of Poetry, Sacramento, 1990, recipient award of merit cert., 1990; recipient Poet of Merit award Am. Poetry Assn., 1988, Appreciation award VA Dept. Corrections, 1994, Pres. award for literary excellence Nat. Authors Registry, 1994, Editor's Choice award Poetry website and Internat. Libr. Poetry, 2005 Democrat. 7th Day Adventist. Avocations: crocheting, creative writing, music, poetry writing. Home: 1412 B Murdock Rd Charlotte NC 28205 Personal E-mail: lorrainshoskie@yahoo.com.

HOSKINS, BARBARA R(UTH) WILLIAMS, retired elementary school educator, principal; b. Pineville, Ky., June 7, 1945; d. John and Patsy Ann (Buell) Williams; m. Teddy Michael Hoskins, Dec. 12, 1961; children: Susan Ann Hoskins Brown, Shelia Marie Hoskins Key. BS, Union Coll., 1977, MA, 1978, postgrad., 1980-89, U. Ky., 1990. Cert. elem. edn., elem./secondary principalship, elem./secondary supervision, dir. pupil pers., Ky. Tchr. Bell County Bd. Edn., Pineville, 1977—2004, prin., 1997—2000; ret., 2004. Edn. instr. S.E. C.C., Middlesboro, Ky., 1987—; BLS instr. Am. Heart Assn., Corbin, Ky., 1990—. Co-author: History of Bell County, 1994. Active Bell County Hist. Soc., 1992—, Laubach Literary Action Agy., Bell County, 1991—, Nat. Arbor Day Found., Nebr., 1995. Mem. NEA, AARP, Nat. Ret. Tchrs. Assn., Ky. Edn. Assn., Bell County Edn. Assn., Upper Cumberland Edn. Assn., Nat. Alliance Tchrs. Math. and Sci., Iota Sigma Nu. Republican. Baptist. Avocations: walking, jogging, science and math activities, local history research. Office: Bell Co Recovery Rte 1 Box 198E Pineville KY 40977-9712 Home: 69 Paula Dr Pineville KY 40977

HOSKINS, CHERISE LACHELLE, elementary school educator; d. Willie Edward Hoskins and Margaret Evelyn Madison; 1 child, Andre Justin Ward. BS in Biology, Azusa Pacific U., Calif., 1984; MEd, Pt. Loma Nazarene Coll., Arcadia, Calif., 2006. Plasma filtrator Traveral Labs., Hyland Divsn., L.A., 1984—86; exec. sec. Nelson-Brown Equities, Burbank, Calif., 1986—95; dir. vol. programs Union Sta. Found., Pasadena, Calif., 1995—98; sci. tchr. Pasadena Unified Sch. Dist., 1998—. Edn. cons. NASA, Pasadena, Calif. Recipient Tchr. of Excellence award, 2006; grantee, BP Am., Inc., 2005. Mem.: Nat. Sci. Tchrs. Assn. Office: Eliot Mid Sch 2184 N Lake Ave Altadena CA 91001 Office Phone: 626-794-7121. Business E-Mail: choskins@pucd.us.

HOSKINS, DEBBIE STEWART, librarian, artist; b. Bad Kreuznach, Germany, Sept. 24, 1962; d. Jesse Arthur and Rebecca Stewart; married, 2003; 1 child, Jesse. BA, Kent (Ohio) State U., 1984; MS in Libr. Sci., Drexel U., Phila., 1991. Cert. profl. librarian, Mich. Youth svcs. librarian Grand Rapids (Mich.) Pub. Library, 1994-99, youth svcs. specialist, 1999—. Lectr. in field. Reviewer: Sch. Library Jour., 2000—; Remembering Summer, 1999, one-woman shows include Franciscan Life Process Ctr., 2001, 2005. Active church choir Blessed Sacrament Ch., Grand Rapids, Mich., 1998—. Recipient juried art award Festival Regional Arts Exhbn., 2000, Franciscan Life Process Ctr., 1999, 2001, 03, 04, 05, First United Meth. Ch., 2000, 02, 05. Mem. Soc. Children's Book Writers & Illustrators (assoc., adv. com. Mich. 1998—, Mich. illustrator coord. 1999-2001), Am. Library Assn. (life). Roman Catholic. Avocations: music, gardening, balloon animals. Office: PO Box 230271 Grand Rapids MI 49523 Personal E-mail: debbiestudio@yahoo.com.

HOSKINS, LOU ANN, art educator; d. Stephen Daniel and Bernice Marie Brkljack; m. Thomas Michael Hoskins, June 18, 1983; children: Nathan Lee, Stephanie Marie. BS magna cum laude, U. Wis. Platteville, 1980; MA in Tchg. and Learning magna cum laude, Nova Southeastern U., Fla., 2004. Lic. Educator Iowa, 2004, Ill., 1980, Wis., 1980. Art tchr. K-12 Calamus/Lost Nation Sch. Dist., Calamus and Lost Nation, Iowa, 1980—81; elem. art tchr. Muscatine Cmty. Sch. Dist., Iowa, 1985—86, Bettendorf Cmty. Sch. Dist., Iowa, 1986—. Pencil drawing, Eagle Eye (Best of Show, 2002), Grosbeaks (Golden Key Award, 1976); contbr. articles to profl. jours. Vol. Bettendorf Cmty. Schools, Bettendorf, Iowa, 1986—. Scholar, State of Ill., 1976. Mem.: NEA, Bettendorf Edn. Assn., Iowa State Edn. Assn., Bettendorf PTA (pres.), Multiple Sclerosis Soc., Adopt a Hwy. Program (assoc.), Palisades Art League (assoc.), Kappa Delta Pi. Business E-Mail: lhoskins@bettendorf.k12.ia.us.

HOSKINSON, CAROL ROWE, middle school educator; b. Toledo, Mar. 10, 1947; d. Webster Russell and Alice Mae (Miller) Rowe; m. C. Richard Hoskinson, June 8, 1969; 1 child, Leah Nicole BS Edn., Ohio State U., 1968; MEd, Ga. State U., 1972. Tchr. Whitehall City Sch., Columbus, Ohio, 1968—69; tchr. DeKalb County Sch., Decatur, Ga., 1969—74, 1975—79, Mt. Olive Twp. Sch., NJ, 1974—75, Fulton County Sch., Atlanta, 1991—. Substitute tchr. DeKalb County Schs., Decatur, 1980-91, Fulton County Sch., Atlanta, 1989-91 Pres. Esther Jackson PTA, Roswell, Ga., 1988-89; treas. Women of Ch., Roswell, 1983-84; chairperson local sch. adv. Esther Jackson, Roswell, 1989-91; del. Women and Constn. Conv., Atlanta, 1988; mem. Supt.'s Adv. Com.; corr. sec. Chattahoochee H.S. PTSA, 1997-98; VIP dedicated hostess Olympic Games, Atlanta, 1996; treas. Chattahoochee Cotillion Club, 2000, 01; mem. leadership team Holcomb Bridge Mid. Sch., 1999— Named Vol. of Yr. Fulton County Schs., 1988-89 Mem. AAUW (v.p. Atlanta chpt. 1970-89, edn. scholarship honoree 1984, 86), Atlanta Lawn Tennis Assn., Roswell Hist. Soc., Roswell Hist. Preservation Com., Nat. Mid. Sch. Assn., Zoo Atlanta, High Mus. Art, Ga. PTA, Ohio State Alumni Assn., Ga. State Alumni Assn., Profl. Assn. Ga. Educators Democrat. Presbyterian. Avocations: tennis, reading, education-related activities, walking. Home: 8880 Willowbrae Ln Roswell GA 30076-3007

HOSLEY, MARGUERITE CYRIL, civic worker; b. Houston, July 29, 1946; d. Frederick Willard and Marguerite Estella (Arisman) Collister; m. Richard Allyn Hosley II, July 18, 1968; children: Richard A. III, Sean Frederick, Michelle Cyril. BS in Edn., U. Houston, 1968; postgrad., Tex. A&M U., 1970-71. Cert. tchr., Tex. Tchr. Sharpstown H.S., Houston, 1968-69, Bryan (Tex.) H.S., 1969-71; ins. asst. Farmers Ins., Stafford, Tex., 1981-83; adminstrv. asst., fin. asst. Christ United Meth. Ch., Sugarland, Tex., 1984-92; mem. planning and zoning commn. City of Sugarland, 1995-98; mem. Sugarland City Coun., 1998—; mayor pro tem City of Sugarland, 2000-2001, 2004—. Pres. bd. dirs. Ft. Bend Boys Choir, 1984-85; docent Bayou Bend Collection and Gardens, Houston Mus. Fine Arts, 1994—, day chair, 1997-98, spl. event chmn. 1999-2000, group tour chmn., 2001-2003, program chmn. 2004-05; mem. Ima Hogg Ceramic Cir., 1994—, social chmn., 1997-98; bd. dirs. Am. Cancer Soc., 1990-97; pres. Am. Cancer Soc. League, 1993-94; mem. Lone Star Stomp com. Ft. Bend Mus. Assn., 1991-97; parent vol. Ft. Bend Ind. Schs., 1980-94; raffle chmn. Ft. Bend Drug Alliance Gala, 1989; newsletter chmn. Am. Heart Assn. Guild, 1990-91, v.p., 1992-93; bd. dirs. Sugar Land Cultural Arts Found., 1999—, Battleship Tex. Found., 2001-02, Ctr. for Houston's Future, 2005-. Named Ft. Bend Outstanding Woman, Ft. Bend County, 1992. Mem. Houston Ladies' Tennis Assn. (team capt.), Ft. Bend Mus., Sweetwater Country Club (bd. govs. 1990-93), Sweetwater Women's Assn. (treas. 1985-87, pres. 1987-88), Friends of Casa (charter mem.), Aggie Moms Club, Chi Omega Alumnae. Republican. Methodist. Avocations: tennis, dance, reading, continuing education classes. Home: 427 W Alkire Lake Dr Sugar Land TX 77478-3527

HOSMAN, SHARON LEE, retired music educator; b. Bisbee, Ariz., Nov. 2, 1943; d. Roy Lee and Virginia Baldwin (Bandel) H. BA, Loretto Heights Coll., 1965; MA, U. No. Colo., 1979. Tchr. Livermore (Calif.) Sch. Dist., 1965-66, Jefferson County Pub. Schs., Golden, Colo., 1966-97; ret., 1997. Faculty rep. North Area Citizens Adv. Com., Arvada, Colo., 1979-81, S.I.P.C., Arvada, 1982-83, North Area Sch. Improvement Process Com., Arvada, 1984-91, North Area Accountability com., 1991-92. Piano accompanist for sch. groups, 1965-97. Mem. NEA, DAR, Jefferson County Edn. Assn., Colo. Edn. Assn., Music Tchrs. Nat. Assn., Colo. State Music Tchrs. Assn., Denver Area Music Tchrs. Assn., Musicians' Soc. Denver, Am. Guild Organists, Hereditary Order of First Families of Mass., Smithsonian, Denver Rescue Mission, Denver Dumb Friends League, St. Luke's Hosp. Aux. (life), The Regis U. Crest Club. Republican. Episcopalian. Avocations: art, music, drama, reading, gardening.

HOSPODKA, LENKA M., hotel and restaurant management educator; d. Jaroslav and Vera M Hospodka; m. Samuel Norris Powell, June 3, 1989. MBA, NYU, N.Y.C., 1979. Asst. prof. Widener U., Chester, Ariz., 1985—87; instr. No. Ariz. U. - Sch. of Hotel and Restaurant Mgmt., Flagstaff, 1987—. Contbr. text books. Mem. Big Bros./Big Sisters, Flagstaff, Ariz., 2000—06. Mem.: Cornell Soc. Of Hotelmen. R-Consevative. Roman Catholic Catholic. Avocations: reading, cooking, dogs. Home: 2334 S Highland Mesa Rd Flagstaff AZ 86001 Office: Northern arizona University PO Box 5638 Flagstaff AZ 86011-5638 Office Phone: 928-523-1704. Office Fax: 928-523-1711. Personal E-mail: lenka.hospodka@nau.edu.

HOSSLER, ELIZABETH, psychology professor, department chairman, institutional researcher, director; d. Horace and Edith Hossler. BS, Taylor U., Upland, Ind., 1976; MA, Wheaton Coll., Ill., 1982; MS, Ind. U., Bloomington, 1985; PhD, Andrews U., Berrien Springs, Mich., 1998. Women's athletic coach Bethel Coll., Mishawaka, Ind., 1976—90, psychology prof., 1982—, chair Dept. Phys. Edn., 1982—91, dir. instl. rsch., 1993—, self-study coord. reaccreditation (Higher Learning Commn. North Ctrl. Assn.), 1994—97, chair Divsn. Social Scis., 1999—2006. Dist. III volleyball chair Nat. Christian Coll. Assn., 1981—84, dist. IV volleyball chair, 1988—91; mem. Collaborative Rsch. Working Group Assessment Task Force Coun. Christian Colls. and Univs., 1993—2000. Named Dist. Volleyball Coach of Yr., Nat. Christian Coll. Athletic Assn., 1981, 1985, Outstanding Young Women of Am., 1985, Prof. of Yr., Bethel Coll., 1999; named to Athletic Hall of Fame, 1999; recipient Excellence In Tchg. award, Bethel Coll. Alumni Assn., 1999. Mem.: Phi Kappa Phi, Pi Lamda Theta, Phi Delta Kappa. Office: Bethel College 1001 W McKinley Ave Mishawaka IN 46545

HOSSMAN, REBECCA LYNN, special education educator; b. Bismarck, ND, Mar. 3, 1975; d. Ivan Lloyd and DyAnn Marie Ellwein; m. Christopher Michael Hoffman, Aug. 3, 1996; children: David Christopher Hoffman, Brett Anthony Hoffman. BSE in Mental Retardation Elm. Edn., Minot State U., 1997, MS in Spl. Edn. Early Childhood Spl. Edn., 2000. Cert. autism spectrum disorder U. ND. Early childhood spl. edn. tchr. Mandan (ND) Pub. Schs., 1997—. Assistive tech. mem. Mandan Pub. Schs., 2003—. Mem.: Nat. Edn. Assn., Delta Kappa Gamma. Office: Fort Lincoln Elem 2001 8th Ave SE Mandan ND 58554 Personal E-mail: cmhoffman4@juno.com.

HOSTER-BURANDT, NORMA J., musician, not-for-profit fundraiser; b. Phila., Sept. 29, 1956; d. Downey Delbert and Norma M. (Von Vital) H.; m. Timothy Lee Burandt; children: Jonathan Daniel Loudon, Jeremy Matthew Loudon BMus Piano Performance summa cum laude, Temple U., 1978, MMus Piano Pedagogy, 1980. Ordained deacon Presbyn. Ch. USA. Pvt. piano tchr., 1973—; devel. coord. Chesapeake Gen. Hosp., Va., 2001—. Piano tchr., accompanist Temple U. Music Prep., Phila., 1978-81; accompanist Choral Soc. Montgomery County, Blue Bell, Pa., 1991-93; founding accompanist Temple U. Children's Choir, 1992-99; organist Covenant Presbyn. Ch., Trenton, N.J., 1997-2001; accompanist Am. Choral Dirs. Assn. convs., 1996-98; accompanist in field; grants specialist Rec. for the Blind & Dyslexic Nat. Hdqrs., Princeton, N.J., 2000-01; guest organist Great Bridge Presbyn. Ch., Chesapeake, 2005-06 Performances on local/nat. radio broadcasts, 1995, 97, 98; rec. artist Temple U. Children's Choir, 2001 Mem. coun. Chesapeake Fine Arts Commn., 2006—; mem. Ignite Chesapeake leadership program Hampton Rds. C. of C., 2006. Mem.: Assn. Fundraising Profls., Crochet Guild Am. Avocations: choral singing, needlecraft. Home: 241 Bridgeview Cir Chesapeake VA 23322 Office Phone: 757-312-6556.

HOSTETLER, ELSIE J., musician, music educator; b. Sugarcreek, Ohio, Apr. 8, 1942; d. Jonas B. and Lovina Hostetler. Student, Akron (Ohio) U., 1969-70. Cert. tchr. choral approach to piano, New Sch. Am. Music. Receptionist to office mgr. Milk, Inc., Akron, 1964-78; adminstr. Christian Tng. Ctr., St. Louis, 1987-88, music dir., 1989-91; music sec. Gospel Assembly Conv. Ctr., Louisville, 1992—; piano tchr. Red Bud, Ill., 1997—. Workshop leader EZ-Creative Piano, Red Bud, 1999—. Band dir., choir dir. Gospel Assembly Ch., Akron, 1959-78; asst. pianist, organist, instrumental tchr. Gospel Assembly Ch., St. Louis, 1981-91; music dir., pianist-organist Christian Assembly Ch., Millstadt, Ill., 1992—. Mem. Music Tchrs. Nat. Assn., Ill. State Music Tchrs. Assn. Home: 98 Jennys Way Smithton IL 62285-1656 E-mail: ezpiano98@aol.com.

HOSTETLER, LISA (ELIZABETH) MARIE, nursing consultant; b. Sterling, Ill., Aug. 10, 1961; d. James Arthur Snyder; m. Daryl Arthur Hostetler, Aug. 6, 1983; children: Kenny Arthur, Erin Elizabeth, Madalyn Louise. BSN magna cum laude, Wichita State U., 1984. Cert. Lamaze childbirth educator, Lamaze Internat., 1988, legal nurse cons., Vickie Milazzo Inst., 2004. Cord blood educator Cord Blood Registry, San Bruno, Calif., 1997—2000; lamaze instr. The Childbearing Years, Austin, Tex., 1990—98; legal nurse cons. Austin Legal Nurse Cons., 2004—. Labor doula, Austin, 1988—. Youth leader Austin Mennonite Ch., Austin, Tex., 1989—92. Fellow: Am. Coll. Childbirth Educators with Lamaze Internat.; mem.: Assn. Women's Health, Obstetric and Neonatal Nurses (cert. in fetal monitoring 2002), Nat. Alliance Cert. Legal Nurse Cons. Office: Austin Legal Nurse Cons 409 N Tumbleweed Tr Austin TX 78733 Office Phone: 512-402-1660. Business E-Mail: info@AustinLegalRN.com.

HOSTETTER, MARGARET K., pediatrician, medical educator; MD, Baylor U. Diplomate Am. Bd. Pediatrics with subspecialty in pediat. infectious diseases. Resident Children's Hosp., Boston; fellow in pediat. infectious disease Harvard Med. Sch./Beth Israel Hosp., Boston; mem. faculty U. Minn., Mpls., 1982—98; prof. pediats., sect. chief pediat. immunology Yale U., New Haven, 1998, chmn. dept. pediatrs., Jean McLean Wallace prof. pediatrics, 2004—, founder Yale Internat. Adoption Clinic, 1998, dir. Yale Child Health Rsch. Ctr., 1998—2002; chair pediatrics, physician-in-chief Yale-New Haven Children's Hosp., 2002—. Recipient Am. Acad. Pediatrics award for Excellence in Rsch., Samuel Rosenthal award, E. Mead Johnson award, Soc. Pediat. Rsch. Mem.: Assn. Am. Physicians, Am. Soc. Clin. Investigation, Inst. of Medicine of NAS. Office: Yale Univ Sch Medicine 333 Cedar St LMP 4085 PO Box 208064 New Haven CT 06520-8064*

HOSTLER-VAUGHAN, REBECCA L., educational consultant; b. Fayetteville, N.C., Feb. 23, 1972; d. DeEtte E. and George E. Vaughan. BA in African Am. Studies, N.C. State U., Raleigh, 1995, BA in History, 1995; MA in History, Clark Atlanta U., 1997; EdS in Adult Edn., U. Ga., Athens, 2005. Cert. tchr. NBPTS, 2001, AFAA, 2002, endl. leadership U. Ga., 2003. Tchr. Fulton County Sch., Atlanta, 1997—. Ednl. cons. PBS, GA DOE, and others, Atlanta, 1999—; fitness instr. CDC & LWE-Toco Hills, Atlanta, 2003—. Vol. Rock the Vote, Atlanta, 2004. Scholar, Rotary, 2003; Fulbright-Hays fellow, Fulbright Found., 2004. Independent. Avocations: exercise, travel. Office Phone: 770-650-4230.

HOSTON, GERMAINE ANNETTE, political science professor; b. Trenton, NJ; d. Walter Lee and Veretta Louise H. AB in Politics summa cum laude, Princeton U., 1975; MA in Govt., Harvard U., 1978, PhD in Govt., 1981. Rsch. asst. Princeton U., NJ, 1973-75; tchg. asst. Harvard U., Cambridge, Mass., 1977-78; asst. prof. polit. sci. Johns Hopkins U., Balt., 1980-86, assoc. prof. polit. sci., 1986-92; prof. polit. sci. U. Calif., San Diego, 1992—, dir. Ctr. for Democratization and Econ. Devel., 1993-99; founder, pres. Inst. Trans Pacific Studies in Values, Culture and Politics, 1999—. Vis. prof. L'Ecole des Hautes Etudes en Sci. Sociales, Paris, 1986, Osaka City U., Japan, 1990, U. Tokyo, 1991; faculty advisor Chinese lang. program Johns Hopkins U., 1981-92, undergrad. ethics bd., 1980-83, pub. interest investment adv. com., 1982-85, undergrad. admissions com., 1983-84, 86-89, pres.'s human climate task force, 1987, dir. undergrad. program, 1987, 88-89, mem. com. undergrad. studies, 1987-91, organizer comparative politics colloquium, 1987-89, dept. colloquium, 1987-89, 91-92; Japanese studies program com. U. Calif., San Diego, 1992—, Chinese studies program, 1994—, field coord. comparative politics, 1994—95, dir. grad. studies comparative politics, 1997-98; bd. dir. Inst. East-West Security Studies, NYC, 1990-97; Am. adv. com. Japan Found., 1992—; edn. abroad program com. U. Calif., 1996—; adv. com. Calif. Ctr. Asia Soc.; mem. com. tech. comms. Inst. East West Security Studies, 1997—; participant numerous workshops and seminars; lectr. in field. Author: Marxism and the Crisis of Development in Prewar Japan: The Debate on Japanese Capitalism, 1986, The State, Identity, and the National Question in China and Japan, 1994, (with others) The Biographical Dictionary of Neo-Marxism, 1985, The Biographical Dictionary of Marxism, 1986, Culture and Identity: Japanese Intellectuals During the Interwar Years, 1990, The Routledge Dictionary of Twentieth-Century Political Thinkers, 1992; mem. editl. bd. Jour. Politics, 1997—2001; contbr. articles to profl. jours. Active Md. Food Com., 1983-92, program concepts subcom. CROSS ROADS Com., Diocese of Md., 1987-88, outreach com. St. David's Episcopal Ch., Balt., standing commn. human affairs Gen. Conv. of the Episcopal Ch., 1991-97; chair peace and justice commn. Episcopal Diocese Md., 1984-87, co-chair companion diocese com., 1987-92, chair CROSS ROADS program bd., 1988-92; exec. bd. dir. Balt. Clergy and Laity Concerned, 1985-86; alternate. regular lay del. 69th Gen. Conv. of The Episcopal Ch., Detroit, 1988; trustee Va. Theol. Sem., 1988-2000; lay del. 70th Gen. Conv. of The Episcopal Ch., Phoenix, Ariz., 1991; dep. Nat. Conv. Episcopal Ch., 1988-93. Am. Legion Aux. scholar, 1972, Am. Logistical Assn. scholar, 1972-76; fellow Harvard U., 1975-77, NSF, 1975-77; Lehman fellow Harvard U., 1978-79, Fgn. Lang. and Area Studies fellow, 1978-79; fellow Am. Assn. Univ. Women Ednl. Found., 1979-80; Fgn. Rsch. scholar U. Tokyo, 1979, 82, 84, 85, 86, 91; Travel grantee Assn. Asian Studies, Japan-U.S. Friendship Commn., 1981; Internat. fellow Internat. Fedn. Univ. Women, 1982, 83; Postdoctoral grantee Social Sci. Rsch. Coun., 1983; fellow NEH, 1983; Kenan Endowment grantee Johns Hopkins U., 1984-85; fellow Rockefeller Found. Internat. Rels., 1985-88; Travel grantee Assn. Asian Studies, 1991; grantee Japan-US Friendship Commn., 1997; rsch. grantee Acad. Senate Com. on Rsch., 1996. Mem. Asia Soc. (trustee 1994—2000), Am. Polit. Sci. Assn. (mem. coun. 1991-93, mem. com. on internat. polit. sci. 1997—2003, v.p. 1998—), Assn. Asian Studies (mem. N.E. Asia coun. 1992-95, vice-chair N.E. Asia coun. 1993—94, nominated editor Jour. Asian Studies 1994, mem. coun. on fgn. rels. 1990—), Internat. Platform Assn., Pacific Coun. on Internat. Policy, Women's Fgn. Policy Group. Democrat. Episcopalian. Avocations: reading, cooking, sailing, tennis, working out. Office: 9921 Carmel Mountain Rd Ste 323 San Diego CA 92129 Office Phone: 888-489-0882. Business E-Mail: ghoston@myesa.com.

HOTALING, CAREY, elementary school educator; d. Daniel Daley and Wilma Singer Hotaling; m. Peter Burden Milholland, June 20, 1987; children: Russell Taylor Milholland, Christopher Joseph Milholland. BS, Antioch New Eng.Coll., Keene, N.H., 1991. Cert. K-8 tchr. Maine, 1992. 6th grade tchr. Falmouth Mid. Sch., Falmouth, Maine, 1995—; mast landing sanctuary caretaker Maine Audubon Soc., Freeport, Maine, 1984—97, sch. sci. coord. Falmouth, Maine, 1986—90. Math and sci. acad. faculty U. of So. Maine, Gorham, Maine, 1994—95. Author: (k-6 curricula on estuaries:) DEPTHS. Mem.: Maine Environ. Edn. Assn. (assoc.; pres. 1990—92). Avocations: swimming, gardening, singing, writing, bookmaking. Office Phone: 207-781-9886.

HOTALING, DIANE ELIZABETH HICKEY, college administrator; b. Queens, N.Y., Jan. 2, 1961; d. Harold and Elizabeth Julia (Taggart) Hickey; m. Mark Hotaling, June 11, 1983; children: Matthew Christopher, Sara Rose. BS, Utica Coll., 1983. News bur. mgr. Utica Coll. of Syracuse U., NY, 1981-83; newswriter Randolph-Macon Woman's Coll., Lynchburg, Va., 1983-85; dir. pubs. Va. Wesleyan Coll., Norfolk, Va., 1985—97; dir. cmty. svc. The Virginia Wesleyan Mag., 1997—. Editor: The Virginia Wesleyan Mag., 1993-99; contbr. articles to profl. jours. Pres. Campus East Cmty. Assn., Va. Beach, 1991-92; chmn. 3d Police Precinct Citizens Adv. Bd., Va. Beach, 1991-92; pres. B.F. Williams Parent-Tchrs. Assn., 1992-93; bd. mem. Lee's Friends Helping People live with Cancer, 1999-2006, Southeastern Va. Foodbank, 2006—, Virginia Beach C.A.R.E., 2003—. Avocations: creative writing, photography, swimming. Office: Virginia Wesleyan Coll Wesleyan Dr Norfolk VA 23502

HOTCHKISS, HEATHER A., social worker, consultant; d. John L. and Patrecia W. Hotchkiss. MSW, U. Denver, 1996. Mental health clinician Colo. Mental Health Inst. at Ft. Logan, Denver, 1990—95; sr. cons. Colo. Dept. Edn., Denver, 1995—. Co-author: Making Standards Work: A Teachers Guide to Contextual Learning, 1999. Chair Colo. Sch. Social Work Com., Denver, 1998—2000. Named Colo. Sch. Psychologist Advocate of Yr., Colo. Soc. Sch. Psychologists, 2000—01; recipient Vision and Leadership award, Colo. Sch.-to-Career Partnership, 2001, All Means All School-to-Work award, 2000, Colo. Sch. Social Worker of Distinction award, Colo. Sch. Social Work Com., 2002. Mem.: NASW, Coun. for Exceptional Children (Donn Brolin award 2002). Office: Colo Dept Edn 201 E Colfax Ave Rm 300 Denver CO 80203

HOTCHKISS, JANET MCCANN, secondary school educator; b. White Plains, N.Y., July 11, 1950; d. Albino M. and and M. Catherine (Bodette) Grellet; m. Jonathan B. Hotchkiss, May 3, 1980; children: Craig, Kristina, Kevin, Marsha, Robert, Catherine. BS, Northeastern U., 1973; MS, Coll. New Rochelle, 1987. Cert. secondary English tchr., spl. edn. tchr., elem. tchr. Tchr. Greenburgh Eleven UFSD, Dobbs Ferry, NY, 1990—, White Plains (N.Y.) Pub. Schs., 1990—. Mem. Coun. Exceptional Children, 1995—, N.Y. State English Coun., 2003; mem. policy bd. Westchester Tchrs. Ctr., 1994—97; mem. N.Y. Adult and Continuing Cmty. Edn., 1995—. Co-author: Kosovo: Caught in the Middle, 2001. Named Tchr. of Yr. in N.Y. State, N.Y. Adult Continuing Cmty. Edn., 2001; grantee, Westchester Tchr.'s Ctr., 1996, 1999, 2002, Tech. and Literacy Challenge, 2000, The Living History Found., 2002. Mem.: Orton Guillingham Soc., White Plains (N.Y.) Coll. Club (scholarship com. 2003). Office: Greenburgh Eleven UFSD PO Box 501 Dobbs Ferry NY 10522

HOTCHNER, HOLLY, museum director, curator, conservator; BA in Art History and Studio Art, Trinity Coll., 1973; MA in Art History, diploma conservation, N.Y. Inst. Fine Arts, 1982. Exhbns. cataloguer, collections cataloguer Mus. Modern Art, N.Y.C., 1973-76; chief conservator N.Y. Hist. Soc., N.Y.C., 1984-88, dir. mus., 1984-95; dir. Am. Craft Mus. (now Museum of Arts and Design), N.Y.C., 1996—. Bd. dirs. Art Alliance for Contemporary Glass, 1999—, Friends of Fiber Art; chmn. bd. 235 E. 73rd Owners Corp., 1994-2000; mem. edn. com. Whitney Mus. Am. Art, 1994-98; mem. bd. trustees N.Y. Landmarks Conservancy, 1996—; mem. adv. bd. Friends of Contemporary Ceramics; lectr., panelist, juror in field. Fellow Am. Inst. Conservation, Internat. Inst. Conservation; mem. Am. Assn. Mus., Art Table, Phi Beta Kappa. Office: Museum of Arts and Design 40 W 53rd St New York NY 10019-6106 Office Phone: 212-956-3535.

HOTT, PEGGY A., mortgage banker; b. Flint, Mich., Dec. 15, 1952; d. Aaron Hilman and Alice E. (Fairs) Conger; m. Norman E. Baxter, Mar. 17, 1973 (div. 1986); children: Sarah, Stephanine, Alicia, Adam, Marcia; m.

Virgil G. Hott Jr., Aug. 27, 1988. Student, Charles Stewart Mott Coll., Flint, Mich., 1973. Pub. rels. rep. and receptionist Turner Elec. Wks., Jacksonville, Fla., 1984-89; personal banking rep. and data entry operator Fla. Nat. Bank and First Union, Jacksonville, 1989; compliance/arbitration rep. First Union Nat. Bank, Jacksonville, 1989-90; customer svc. rep./reconciliation Am. Express Centurion Svcs. Corp., Jacksonville, 1990-96; credit mortgage-mortgage resource specialist Merrill Lynch Credit Corp. Cendant Mortgage, Jacksonville, 1995—. Clio Lions Club scholar, 1971. Mem. NAFE, Am. Soc. Notaries, Nat. Notary Assn., Toastmasters (charter mem. Am. Express chpt.). Republican. Home: 10252 Pine Breeze Rd W Jacksonville FL 32257-7585

HOTTMAN, GENEVA RAE, elementary school educator; b. Elkhart, Ind., May 3, 1944; d. Homer A. and Geneva A. Merryfield; m. Lyle Wade (div.); m. Larry Alan Hottman, June 2, 1979; 1 child, Alan LeRoy. BSE, Emporia State U., 1966. Cert. tchr. art 7-9 Kans. State Bd. Edn., tchr. English 7-9 Kans. State Bd. Edn., tchr. elem. K-9 Kans. State Bd. Edn. Elem. tchr. Unified Sch. Dist. 487, Herington, Kans., 1967—68; elem. librn. Unified Sch. Dist. 475, Junction City, Kans., 1968—69; elem. tchr. Unified Sch. Dist. 481, Hope, Kans., 1969—79, elem. tchr. title I, 1991—. Dir., head tchr. Abilene (Kans.) Comty. Nursery Sch., 1986—90; tchr. liaison After Sch. Program, Hope, 2001—. Founding bd. mem. Parents as Tchrs., Abilene, 1986—87; mem. Dickinson County Hist. Soc., Abilene, 2002—05. Named Educator of Yr., Tri-County Area C. of C., 2004. Mem.: Eisenhower Area Reading Assn. (sec. 2000—01), Internat. Reading Assn., Assn. Am. Educators. Republican. Methodist. Avocations: oil painting, gardening, reading, travel. Office: Rural Vista Unified Sch Dist 481 200 Poplar Hope KS 67451

HOUCK, AMELIA ANN, elementary school educator; b. Douglas, Wyo., Oct. 3, 1949; d. James Harold and Amelia Amos Houck. AA, Ctrl. Piedmont CC, Charlotte, N.C., 1971—75; BS in Sociology & Anthropology, Western Carolina U., Cullowhee, N.C., 1973—75; BS in Edn., U. N.C., Asheville, 1986—87. Registered Radiologic Tech. Spartanburg Gen. Sch. Radiology, S.C., 1969. Eligibility specialist Dept. Social Svcs., Brevard, SC, 1975—76; owner, chef Golden Wheat Cafe, Brevard, 1976—78; nuc. medicine & radiology technologist Meml. Mission Hosp., Asheville, NC, 1979—81; office mgr./part-owner Chiropractic Clin., Hendersonville/Brevard, 1981—83; tchr. Brevard Mid. Sch., Transylvania Schs., 1986—97, Flat Rock Mid. Sch., Henderson County Schs., Hendersonville, NC, 2001—06. Office: Henderson County Schs 1333 Howard Gap Rd Hendersonville NC 28792-7286 Personal E-mail: aahouck49@bellsouth.net.

HOUDE, CARMEN MILAGRO, hotel executive; b. Trenton, NJ, May 5, 1969; d. Sixto Antonio and Luz Milagros Ruiz; m. Auguste James Houde, Nov. 4, 1991; children: Joseph James, Spencer Albert. Asst. supr. Lifetime Cutlery, Dayton, NJ, 1989—91; guest rep. Comfort Inn, Syracuse, NY, 1995—98; guest svc. rep. Extended Stay Am., East Syracuse, NY, 2001—. Contbr. poetry. Recipient Leadership Merit award, US Achievement Acad., 1987. Office: Extended Stay Am 6630 Old Collamer Rd East Syracuse NY 13057 Office Fax: 315-463-7966. Personal E-mail: choude@twcny.rr.com. Business E-Mail: syr@extendedstay.com.

HOUDE-WALTER, SUSAN, optics scientist, educator; b. NYC; BA, Sarah Lawrence Coll., 1976; MS, U. Rochester, 1983, PhD, 1987. Co-founder LaserMax, Inc., 1989, pres., 2000—02; prof. optics U. Rochester, 2002—. Presenter in field. Chair editl. adv. com. Optics & Photonics News, spl. editorship Jour. Non-Crystalline Solids, MRS Bulletin. Recipient 3M Faculty award for rsch. Fellow: Am. Ceramic Soc., Optical Soc. Am. (search com. 1997—98, nom. com. 1999, pres.-elect 2004, pres. 2005). Achievements include research in optical materials, especially optical glass and the molecular structure of multicomponent glasses. Office: Inst Optics Wilson Blvd Wilmont Bldg Rochester NY 14627-9000 Office Phone: 585-275-7629. Office Fax: 585-244-4936. Business E-Mail: shw@optics.rochester.edu.

HOUFF, BETHANY DIANNE, music educator, conductor; b. Lancaster, Pa., Nov. 13, 1978; d. Robert Arnold and Dawn Shonk Houff. MusB in Music Edn., James Madison U., Harrisonburg, Va., 2001; MusM in Choral Conducting, James Madison U., 2003. Choral music dir. Harrisonburg HS, 2003—. Mem.: Music Educators Nat. Conf. (choral rep. to Dist. V Va. 2005—), Am. Choral Dirs. Assn (chair h.s. mixed choir repertoire and stds. 2005—). Avocations: travel, reading, hiking, music. Office Phone: 540-433-2651.

HOUGH, BARBARA, library media specialist, educator; b. Peekskill, N.Y., July 24, 1950; d. Vincent Robert Hough and Sheila Josephine Nolan. BA in English Lit., Coll. of New Rochelle, 1972; MS in Libr. and Info. Sci., LI U., 1997. Lic. pub. sch. tchr. N.Y. State Edn. Dept., pub. libr. N.Y. State Edn. Dept. Sch. libr. media specialist Yonkers (N.Y.) Pub. Schs., 1996—. Mem. Yonkers Sch. Libr. Coun., 1996—, Dist. Instrnl. Tech. Com., Yonkers, 2002—; workshop presenter Annual Conf. of Internat. Sch. Libr. Assn., 2006. Sec., bd. dirs. Garrison (N.Y.) Art Ctr., 1980—82, mem., 1974—83. Recipient Honors-at-Entrance scholarship, Coll. of New Rochelle, 1968, New Student scholarship, L.I. U., 1994, Joseph F. Shubert Libr. of Excellence award, N.Y. State Regents Adv. Coun. on Librs., 2000. Mem.: ALA, N.Y. Libr. Assn., Westchester County Libr. Assn., Sch. Libr. Media Specialists of S.E. N.Y., Internat. Assn. of Sch. Librns., Appalachian Mountain Club, Sierra Club, Beta Phi Mu. Avocations: hiking, pottery, gardening, photography. Office: Yonkers Mid H S 150 Rockland Ave Yonkers NY 10705 Office Phone: 914-376-8197. Office Fax: 914-376-8197. E-mail: bhough@yonkers.ypschools.org.

HOUGHTALING, PAMELA ANN, communications professional, writer; b. Catskill, NY, July 8, 1949; d. Stanley Kenneth and Mildred Edythe (Fyfe) H. BA, Princeton U., 1971; M in Internat. Affairs, Russian Inst., Columbia U., 1974, cert., 1976. Internat. rels. analyst Libr. of Congress, Washington, 1974-75, US GAO, Washington, 1976-77; pub. affairs specialist IBM Corp., Washington, 1977-81; sr. external programs analyst IBM World Trade Americas/Far East Corp., North Tarrytown, NY, 1981-82; mgr. labor affairs/bus. practices US Coun. Internat. Bus., NYC, 1982-84; comms. specialist-advt. IBM Corp., Boca Raton, Fla., 1984-86, staff comms. specialist White Plains, NY, 1986-88, comms. cons., 1988-90; sr. mktg. specialist Wang Labs., Bethesda, Md., 1990-93; pub. rels. dir. STG Mktg. Comm., 1993-94; mgr. mktg. comm. Cable & Wireless, Inc., Vienna, Va., 1994-95; tech. comms. cons., journalist Falls Church, Va., 1995—98; contractor to Applied Physics Lab. Johns Hopkins U., 1998-99; mktg. mgr. Info. Tech. Lab. Nat. Inst. Stds. and Tech., Gaithersburg, Md., 2000—03, 2005—; fellow US Dept. Commerce Sci. and Tech., 2003—04; with Office Def. Rsch. and Engring. Dept. Def., 2003—04. Mem. AAAS, Armed Forces Comms. and Electronics Assn., Nat. Assn. Sci. Writers, Toastmasters Internat.

HOUGHTON, BARBARA JEAN, art educator, artist; b. Chgo., Nov. 2, 1947; d. Maurice Alden and Catherine Margaret (Dressel) Hemmingway; m. Keith Richard Farley, Oct. 19, 1995; m. James Blair Houghton (div.). BA, U. Ill., Chgo., 1971; MFA, Art Inst. Chgo., 1973. Asst. to full prof. art Met. State Coll., Denver, 1974—92, prof. and chair dept. art, 1985—99; chair dept. art No. Ky. U., Highland Heights, Ky., 1992—98, prof. art, photography and web design, 1992—. Author: Art and the Internet, 2000. Mem.: Coll. Art Assn., Soc. Photographic Edn. Avocation: travel. Office: Dept Art No Ky Univ 312 Fine Arts Nunn Rd Newport KY 41099

HOUGHTON, KATHARINE, actress; b. Hartford, Conn., Mar. 10, 1945; d. Ellsworth Strong and Marion Houghton (Hepburn) Grant. BA, Sarah Lawrence Coll., Bronxville, N.Y., 1965. Founding mem. Pilgrim Repertory Co. (Shakespeare touring co. sponsored by Ky. Arts Commn.), 1971-72, SC Arts Commn., 1972, Miss. Arts Commn., 1973, Conn. Arts Commn., St. Joseph Coll., 1974; lectr. in field. Debut on Broadway stage in A Very Rich Woman, 1965; appeared in stage plays Charley's Aunt, New Orleans Repertory, 1966, The Front Page, Broadway, 1968, Ten O'Clock Scholar, Royal Poinciana Playhouse, Fla., 1969, The Private Ear/The Public Eye, Sullivan, Ill., 1969, Sabrina Fair, Ivoryton Playhouse, 1968, The Miracle Worker, Sullivan, Ill., A Scent of Flowers (Theatre World award), Off Broadway, 1969, Misalliance, Hartford Stage Co., 1970, The Taming of the Shrew, Actors Theatre, Louisville, 1970, Poor Richard, Tartuffe, 1970, Ring Around the Moon, Hartford Stage Co., 1970, Major Barbara, The Glass Menagerie, Actors Theatre of Louisville, 1971, Play It Again Sam, Actors Theatre of Louisville, 1971, Suddenly Last Summer, Ivanhoe, Chgo., 1973, The Prodigal Daughter, Kennedy Ctr., Washington, 1973, Bell, Book and Candle, Pensacola, Fla., 1974, The Rainmaker, Ind. Repertory Co., 1975, Spiders Web, Atlanta, 1977, Hedda Gabler, Nashville, 1978, Dear Liar, Dayton, Ohio, 1978, 13 Rue de L'Amour, Ind. Repertory Co., 1978, Antigone, Nashville, 1979, Uncle Vanya, Acad. Festival Theatre, Lake Forest, 1979, Forty Carats, Radford U. Theatre, Va., 1979, A Doll's House, St. Edward's U. Theatre, Tex., 1979, The Sea Gull, Pitts. Pub. Theatre, 1979, The Glass Menagerie, Pa. Stage Co., 1980, Taming of the Shrew, Pa. State Festival, 1980, Terra Nova, Actors Theatre of Louisville, 1980, The Merchant of Venice, South Coast Repertory, Costa Mesa, Calif., 1981, A Touch of the Poet, Yale Repertory Theatre, 1983, To Heaven in a Swing, Am. Place Theatre, N.Y.C., tour various theaters, 1983-85, Sally's Gone She's Left Her Name, Am. Festival Theatre, NH, 1984-86, Vivat, Vivat Regina, Mad Woman of Chaillot, The Time of Your Life, Children of the Sun, Mirror Repertory Co., N.Y.C., 1985, A Bill of Divorcement, Westport Country Playhouse, Conn., 1985, One Slight Hitch, Charlotte Repertory Co., 1986, To Heaven in a Swing, Amherst Coll., Bowdoin Coll., 1986, and Bronson Alcott Centennial Celebration, 1988, The Hooded Eye, West Bank Downstairs Theatre Bar, 1987, Ivoryton Playhouse, 1987, Murder in the Cathedral, West Point Cadet Chapel, 1987, The Leaves of Vallombrosa, 1988, Our Town, Broadway, 1988-89, Love Letters, Ivoryton Playhouse, 1989, To Kill A Mockingbird, Paper Mill Playhouse, NJ, 1991, Best Kept Secret, A Dangerous Liaison in the Cold War, 1998, Berkshire Theatre Festival, 2000, NJ Repertory Theatre, 2001, Sch. House Theatre, Croton Falls, NY, 2001, Lettice & Lovage, Ivoryton Playhouse, 2002; motion pictures include Guess Who's Coming to Dinner, 1967, The Gardener, 1972, Eyes of the Amaryllis, 1981, Mr. North, 1987, Billy Bathgate, 1990, Ethan Frome, 1992, The Night We Never Met, 1992, Kalamazoo, 1993, Let It Be You, 1994, The Pursuit of Happiness, 2003, Kinsey, 2003; TV series The Adams Chronicles, 1975; TV mini-series I'll Take Manhattan, 1986; appeared on TV in Legacy of Fear, 1974, The Color of Friendship, 1981, (day-time serials) One Life to Live, 1989, All My Children, 1992; toured in Sabrina Fair, 1975, The Mousetrap, Arms and the Man, Dear Liar, 1976, The Streets of New York, Westport, Conn., Guildford, NH, Dennis, Mass., Denver, 1980; appeared in To True to Be Good, Acad. Festival Theatre, Lake Forest, Ill., 1977, Spingold Theatre, Waltham, Mass., 1977, Annenberg Ctr., Phila., 1977; author: (plays) To Heaven in a Swing, 1982, Merlin, 1984, Buddha, On The Shady Side, The Right Number, 1986, (book) The Marry Month of May, 1988; (stage prodns.) Phone Play, 1988, Good Grief, 1988, Mortal Friends, 1988 (stage prodn. premiere 1988), The Lick Penny Lover, 1988, Only Angels, 1997, Best Kept Secret, A Dangerous Liaison in the Cold War, 1998,(screenplays) The Heart of the Matter, 1989, Journey to Glasnost, 1990, Good Grief, 1991, Motherman, 1993, Acting in Concert, 1994, Spot, 1996; co-author: Two Beastly Tales, 1975; editor: MHG: A Biography, 1989; written, performed in lectr. engagements: The Secret Life of Louisa May Alcott, Small Press Ctr., NYC, 1998, Women of Achievement Series, The Mount, Lenox, Mass., 2002, My Grandmother's House Near the River, Conn. River Mus., 1999, The Wadsworth Atheneum, Conn., 1999, The Hope Club, Providence, 2000, The Cosmopolitan Club, NYC, 2002, Katharine Times Three, Conn. Hist. Soc., 1999, Wadsworth Atheneum, 2000, Denver Town Hall, 2001, Met. Mus. Art., NYC, 2001, How Katharine Hepburn Became A Political Activist Without Actually Being One (Conn. Womens Hall Fame 2003), Legacy Lite, Bryn Mawr Coll., 2006; appeared Larry King Live, 2003. Mem. Dramatists Guild.

HOUK, IRENE MILLER, dentist; b. Columbiana, Ohio, Aug. 1, 1921; d. Josiah Ellsworth and Ada Isophene (Rupert) Miller; m. George Albertus Houk, Mar. 23, 1949; children: Martha Helle, George. DDS, U. Pitts., 1944. Lic. dentist, Ohio. Gen. practice dentistry, Poland, Ohio. Sunday sch. tchr. 1st Presbyn. Ch., Columbiana, 1935-49, Emmanuel Luth. Ch., New Springfield, Ohio, 1951-2003; bd. dirs. Springfield Local Sch., New Middletown, Ohio, 1960-81, past v.p., past pres.; bd. dirs. Wittenberg U., 1962-70. Mem. ADA, Ohio Dental Assn., Corydon Palmer Dental Soc.

HOULD-WARD, ANN, theatrical costume designer; b. Glasgow, Mont., Apr. 8, 1955; children: Leah, John. Costume designer (Broadway plays) Sunday in the Park With George, 1984, Harrigan 'n' Hart, 1985, Into the Woods, 1987 (LA Drama Critics Cir. award), 1997, Falsettos, 1992, St. Joan, 1993, Three Men on a Horse, 1993, In the Summer House, 1993, Timon of Athens, 1993, Beauty & the Beast, 1994 (Ovation award, Tony award, best costume design, 1994, Am. Theatre Wing Design award, 1994), The Molière Comedies: The School for Husbands & The Imaginary Cuckold, 1995, On the Waterfront, 1995, Dream, 1997, More to Love, 1998, Little Me, 1998, Dance of the Vampires, 2002, Waiting for Godot, 2005, (off-Broadway) Hamlet, 1988, Surviving Grace, Lobster Alice, Cymbeline, On the Verge, Personals, (Am. Ballet Theatre) Othello, 1997, Meadow, 1999, The Pied Piper, 2001, Artemis, 2003, (plays) Indian Blood, 2006. Office: Palace Theatre Broadway at 47th St New York NY 10036*

HOULE, JEANNE LARSON, retired music educator; d. Robert Miles and Frances Elizabeth Larson; m. Thomas Delorn Houle, Dec. 20, 1959; children: Ronald James, Lawrence Robert, Laura Houle Stephens. MusB, U. Wis., 1959; MEd, Nat. Louis U., 1992. Cert. music tchr. K-12 Wis., Ill., elem. edn. tchr. Ill. Tchr. elem. gen. and string music Madison Pub. Schools, Wis., 1959—60; tchr. music, strings Waukegan Pub. Schools, Ill., 1971—74, tchr. elem. gen. music, 1974—2001. Music dir. First Bapt. Ch. Waukegan, 1980—2005; music cons. Jeanne Houle Music, 1994—; dir. jr. orch., grade sch. choruses, madrigal instruments, h.s. musicals' pit orchestras Waukegan Pub. Schools; judge, accompanist Ill. Grade Sch. Music Assn.; tchr. Christian Youth Theater, Gurnee. Author: (field research report (277 pages) Multicultural Awareness Through Elementary General Music in Waukegan Illinois Public Schools (Med, 1992), lesson plans. Facilitator bible study First Bapt. Ch., 2003—; pres. YWCA, Waukegan, 1969—71; violinist Waukegan Symphony Orch., 1965—; vocalist Bel Canto Chorus, Milw., 1997—; Waukegan ticket chmn. Ravinia Festival Assn., Highland Park, Ill., 2003—05. Recipient Cmty. Svc. award, Waukegan Pk. Dist., 2006. Mem.: Lake County Ret. Tchrs. Assn. (membership co-chair 2004—), Friends Waukegan Pub. Libr. (bd. 2003—05), Friends Jack Benny Ctr. Arts, Concert Call (orch. rep. 2005—), Lake County Cmty. Concert Assn. (subscription rep.), Nat. Alliance Mentally Ill Lake County (sec. 1999—), Am. Bus. Women's Assn. (sec. 2001—, Woman of Yr. 1990-91, Pres.'s award 2006), Fellowship Am. Bapt. Musicians, Nat. Assn. Music Edn. (25 Yr. cert.), Waukegan Hist. Soc. (life), Sigma Alpha Iota (life; pres. 1957—58, Sword of Honor 1959). Baptist. Avocation: collect and demonstrate world folk instruments. Home: 819 Keith Ave Waukegan IL 60085 Personal E-mail: houleteach@aol.com.

HOURANI, LAUREL LOCKWOOD, epidemiologist; b. Carmel, Calif., Sept. 10, 1950; d. Eugene Franklin and Katherine Ruth (Miller) Betz; m. Ghazi Fayez Hourani, Feb. 28, 1984; children: Nathan, Danna, Lisa. BA, Chico State U., 1977; MPH, Am. Univ. Beirut, 1983; PhD, U. Pitts., 1990. Prog. evaluator Community Hosp. Monterey Peninsula, Carmel, Calif., 1978-81; instr./researcher Am. Univ. Beirut, 1981-85; predoctoral fellow U. Pitts., 1985-89; researcher, cons. V.A. Med. Ctr., Pitts., 1988-90; dir., tumor registry Med. Ctr. U. Calif. Irvine, Orange, 1990-92; epidemiologist Naval Health Rsch. Ctr., San Diego, 1993-95, head divsn. health scis., 1995-2001; sr. epidemiologist Rsch. Triangle Inst., Research Triangle Park, N.C., 2001—. Cons. Nat. Devel. Commn. South Lebanon, 1981-83. Author: No Water, No Peace, 1985; contbr. articles to profl. jours. Bd. dirs. Am. for Justice in Middle East, Beirut, 1982-85, Nat. Devel. Com., South Lebanon, 1983-85. Recipient grant V.A., Pitts., 1989, rsch. grant U. Rsch. Bd., Beirut, 1985. Mem. Am. Psychol. Assn., Am. Pub. Health Assn., Soc. for Epidemiologic Rsch.

HOUSE, KAREN ELLIOTT, former publishing executive, editor, journalist; b. Matador, Tex., Dec. 7, 1947; d. Ted and Bailey Elliott; m. Arthur House, Apr. 5, 1975 (div. Sept. 1983); m. Peter Kann, June 4, 1984; children: Hillary, Petra, Jason, Jade. BJ, U. Tex., 1970; postgrad. Inst. Politics, Harvard U. Edn. reporter Dallas Morning News, 1970-71, with Washington bur., 1971-74; regulatory corr. Wall Street Jour., Washington, 1974-75, energy and agr. corr., 1975-78, diplomatic corr., 1978-84, fgn. editor NYC, 1984-89; v.p., Internat. Group Dow Jones & Co., 1989-95, pres. Internat. Group, 1995—, sr. v.p., pub. Wall St. Jour., 2002—05. Bd. dirs. Rand Corp.; mem. adv. bd. U. Tex. Austin Coll. Comm. Trustee Boston U. Recipient Edward Weintal award for Diplomatic Reporting, Georgetown U., 1980-81, Edwin Hood award for Diplomatic Reporting Nat. Press Club, 1982, Disting. Achievement award U. So. Calif., 1984, Pulitzer prize for Internat. Reporting, 1984, Overseas Press Club Bob Considine award, 1984, 88; Harvard fellow, 1982; named one of most powerful women, Forbes mag., 2005. Fellow Nat. Acad. Arts and Scis. Business E-Mail: karen.house@dowjones.com.

HOUSE, KAREN SUE, nursing consultant; b. San Francisco, July 16, 1958; d. Mathas Dean and Marilyn Frances (Weigand) House., Casa Loma Coll., 1985; AS in Nursing, SUNY at Albany, 1987. Psychiat. charge nurse Woodview Calabasas (Calif.) Hosp., 1985-87, Treatment Ctrs. Am., Van Nuys, Calif., 1987-88; cons., RN Valley Village Devel. Ctr., Reseda, Calif., 1988; plastic surg. nurse George Sanders, M.D., Encino, Calif., 1986—; nurse New Image Found., 1989—97, Mid Valley Youth Ctr., 1991—2000; dir. nursing Encino Surgicenter (Sanders), 1992—. Dir. nursing Devel. Tng. Svcs. for Devel. Disabled, 1988—95; nurse cons. New Horizons for Developmentally Disabled, 1993—2005, Exceptional Children's Found., 2001—05; nurse specialist, collagen and Botox trainer, 1998—. Instr., vol. ARC. Recipient Simi Valley Free Clinic Scholarship. Mem. Encino C. of C. Office: 16633 Ventura Blvd Ste 110 Encino CA 91436-1834 Office Phone: 818-981-3333. Business E-Mail: karen@drsanders.com. E-mail: khouse6783@aol.com.

HOUSE, RENEE S., theological librarian, minister; b. Grand Rapids, Mich., July 4, 1956; d. Phillip E. and Aletha M. (Boldt) Takken; m. Steven D. House. Student, Calvin Coll., 1974-77; BA in English Lit. and History, U. Ariz., 1979, MLS, 1981; MDiv, New Brunswick Theol. Sem., 1987. Ordained to ministry Reformed Ch. in Am., 1988. Libr. U. Ariz., St. Gregory's H.S., N.Y. Soc. Libr., 1981-84; student chaplain Columbia Presbyn. Hosp., N.Y.C., summer 1986; student asst. Washington Collegiate Ch., N.Y.C., 1985-87; English tchr. Presbyn. Women's Ctr., Taipei, Taiwan, 1987; libr. cons. Academia Sinica, Nanking, Taiwan, 1987; dir. libr. New Brunswick (N.J.) Theol. Sem., 1987—. Leader young people's group 2d Reformed Ch., New Brunswick; workshop leader Regional Synod of Mid-Atlantics, Crossroads Retreat, 1992, 93, Book Roundtable for Pastors, 1992, 93, 94, Gen. Synod, 1991, Freedom in Ministry Conf., 1993, Regional Synod of N.Y., 1993; preacher in more than 50 Reformed Chs. Author: Pre-exilic Prophets: A Five Unit Adult Study Course, 1992, The Inheritance That Heals: A Sermon, 1992, Homilies on Jonah, 1991; contbr. articles to profl. jours. Mem. task force on baptism, membership terminology Reformed Ch. in Am., 1993—, mem. commn. on theology, 1989—; mem. ethics com. for the treatment of human subjects in rsch. Rutgers U., 1989—; chair human support com. Classis of N.Y., 1988—; mem. planning bd. Elijah's Promise Hunger Ministry, New Brunswick, 1988-89. Recipient scholarship New Brunswick Theol. Sem., 1984-85, 85-86. Mem. Southeastern Pa. Theol. Libr. Assn. (planning bd. 1988—), Am. Theol. Libr. Assn. (continuing edn. com. chair 1993—), Beta Phi Mu. Avocations: poetry, cooking, sewing, volleyball, tennis. Office: New Brunswick Theol Sem 17 Seminary Pl New Brunswick NJ 08901-1107

HOUSE, ROBIN CHRISTINE, real estate agent, art consultant; b. Orlando, Fla., Mar. 4, 1967; d. Roy Wilson and Joan Teresa (Leslie) H. BA in Art History, Coll. of Charleston, S.C.; AA in Art History, Ctrl. Piedmont C.C., Charlotte, N.C. Lic. N.C. Real Estate. Art cons. Charlotte Pipe and Foundry Co., Charlotte, N.C., 1996; real estate agt. Helen Adams Realty, Charlotte, N.C., 1997-2000; gallery dir. Ctr. of Earth Gallery, Charlotte, NC, 2000—01. Cons. Claudia Heath Fine Arts, Charlotte, N.C.; chair Dealer Hospitality Mint Mus. of Art Aux. Antiques Show, Charlotte, N.C.; loan exhibit chair Mint Mus. ARt Antiques Show, 2000; owner HouseFrog.com, 2001. Author: (poem) Am I Like A Black Man?, 1994, The Art Collection of Charlotte Pipe and Foundry Company, 1997. Chair (CouSins) Christ Ch. Young Adult Group, Charlotte, N.C., 1997—; mem. Jr. League. Recipient Scholarship in Art History, 1993, Outstanding Student award, 1993, Coll. of Charleston; named Salesperson of Month, Helen Adams Realty, Charlotte, N.C., 1999. Independent. Episcopalian. Avocations: horseback riding, shotgun shooting. Address: 4217 Walker Rd Charlotte NC 28211-1519 E-mail: houser1234@hotmail, Robin@housefrog.com.

HOUSEKNECHT, KAREN L., research scientist, educator; b. Feb. 3, 1964; 1 adopted child, Aislinn 1 child, Aidan. PhD, Cornell U. Postdoctoral tng. Harvard Med. Sch.; asst. prof. endocrinology and metabolism Purdue U.; joined Pfizer, Inc., New London-Groton, Conn., 1998—, assoc. rsch. fellow, dept. cardiovascular, metabolic and endocrine disease, sr. rsch. fellow, dept. cardiovascular, metabolic and endocrine disease. Vis. prof. clin. medicine Karolinska Inst., Stockholm; past pres. Pfizer Women's Leadership Network; adj. faculty Purdue U., Salve Regina U. Author of several scientific publs. Recipient Power of Women award, 2005, Women of Innovation award for large bus. innovation and leadership, Conn. Tech. Coun., 2006.*

HOUSEL, NATALIE RAE NORMAN, physical therapist, educator; b. Syracuse, N.Y., July 25, 1959; d. Rudolf Anthony and Pauline Mary (Proia) Norman; m. Thomas Hugh Housel, June 25, 1988; children: Heather, Tommy and Tiffany (twins). BS in Phys. Therapy, Ithaca Coll., 1981; MA in Applied Psychology, Fairfield U., 1986; EdD in Curriculum and Instrn., U. Ctrl. Fla., 2002. Cert. geriatric clin. specialist Am. Bd. Phys. Therapy Specialties. Staff phys. therapist, NY, 1981-85; sr. phys. therapist Rome (N.Y.) Devel. Ctr., 1987-89; asst. dir. phys. therapy Tioga (N.Y.) Gen. Hosp. and Nursing Home, 1989-91, Corning (N.Y.) Hosp., 1991-92; asst. dir. rehab. svcs. Arnot Ogden Med. Ctr., Elmira, NY, 1992-93; sch. phys. therapist Collier County Pub. Schs., Naples, Fla., 1993-94; pvt. practice phys. therapist Ft. Myers, Fla., 1995-96; dir. phys. therapy Beverly Enterprises, Ft. Myers, Fla., 1995-96; therapy supr. Lee Meml. Health Sys. Health Park Care Ctr., Ft. Myers, Fla., 1996-97; rehab. mgr. occupl., speech and phys. therapy Lee Meml. Home Health, Fort Myers, Fla., 1997-98. Instr phys. therapy assts. Broome C.C., 1989, wound care nutrition for Hosp. Food Adminstrs., 1997; oral examiner for phys. therapy licensees N.Y. State, Albany, 1988-90; adj. faculty S.W. Fla. Coll., Ft. Myers, 2003-05, Edison C.C., 2003-05, Trevecca Nazarene U., 2004-2006; assoc. prof. Tenn. State U., 2006—; mem. praise team Cypress Lake Presbyn. Ch., 2004—. Adult group leader Family Faith Formation, St. Columbkill Ch., Ft. Myers, Fla., 1996-97. Mem.: APA. Avocations: flute, piano, swimming. Home: 7112 Legacy Dr Antioch TN 37013 E-mail: nhozzle@yahoo.com.

HOUSEMAN, ANN ELIZABETH LORD, educational administrator; b. New Orleans, Mar. 21, 1936; d. Noah Louis and Florence Marguerite (Coyle) Lord; m. Evan Kenny Houseman, June 25, 1960; children: Adrienne Ann, Jeannette Louise, Yvonne Elizabeth. BA, Barnard Coll., 1957; MA, Columbia U., 1962; PhD, U. Del., 1969. State supr. reading Dept. Pub. Instrn., Del., 1977-79; prin. M.L. King Jr. Elem. Sch., Wilmington, Del., 1979-80; adminstr., exec. dir. Del. State Arts Coun., Wilmington, 1980-84; acting dir. Divsn. Hist. and Cultural Affairs State of Del., Wilmington, 1983-84; prin. P.S. du Pont Intermediate Sch., Wilmington, 1984-91; dir. Mid.-Atlantic States Arts Consortium, Balt., 1980-84. Adv. bd. Rockwood Mus., Wilmington, 1981-94; bd. dirs. Opera Del., Inc., Wilmington, 1984-97, pres., 1991-93, dir. devel., 1994-95, coord. adv. bd., 1996; bd. dirs. Del. Theatre Co., Wilmington, 1984-90; bd. dirs. Aux. Alfred I. duPont Hosp. for Children, 1997-2004, pres., 2000-01. Republican. Presbyterian.

HOUSER, CONSTANCE W., writer, artist; b. Goshen, N.Y., Aug. 16; d. Charles A. and Josephine E. Woodward; m. James C. Houser, Sept. 21, 1972; children: J. Jackson, Katrina J. AA, Palm Beach C.C., Fla., 1970; BFA, Fla. Atlantic U., 1971. News, editl., features Palm Beach Post-Times, Miami Herald, Fla., 1954—62; columnist, book reviewer Palm Beach Times, Lake Worth News, Fla., 1962—69; art reviewer Art Mags., N.Y.C., 1960—70; art features, art profiles Art Voices South, Fla., 1960—70; artist profiles Art News, 1970—89; assoc. Gordon Rule program Palm Beach CC, 1989—92. Owner 4 Points Photo Ctr., West Palm Beach, Fla., 1958—69; art tchr. for srs., computer tutor, judge art and photo competitions. Over 10 one-woman shows, Exhibited in group shows at Gallery Camino, Real, Fla., Peter Rudolph Galleries, N.Y.; contbr. articles to profl. mags. and newspapers; exhibitions include Soc. Four Arts Contemporary Exhibits, Ft. Lauderdale Mus. Horit Competition. Mem. Hobe Sound Art League, Fla., 1996—2004, Hobe Sound Women's Club, Fla., 1996—2006; lifetime mem. Rep. Nat. Com.; v.p. Rep. Club, West Palm Beach, Fla., 1960—80. Recipient awards, Norton Gallery of Art, West Palm Beach, 1967, Soc. of the 4-Arts, 1970—74, Art Competition awards, Hortt Mus., 1974—79. Mem.: AAUW, Nat. Soc. Arts and Letters, Gallery Players (bd. dirs., pres., v.p.), 4-Points Photo Club (pres.). Republican. Episcopalian. Home: 8338 SE Coconut St Hobe Sound FL 33455

HOUSER, KYRA MARTIN, counselor; b. Norristown, Pa., Aug. 3, 1973; d. Robert David and Angela Marie Martin; m. Jeffrey Robert Houser, July 15, 1995; children: Noah Robert, Elijah, Leia. BA, U. NC, Greensboro, 1995, MS in Edn., 1997. Lic. Prof. Counselor NC, 1998. Case mgr. Family Svc. Greensboro, 1994—95; family therapist intern Family Svc. Highpoint, NC, 1996—97, Family Svc. Davidson County, Lexington, NC, 1997; clin. substance abuse counselor Randolph County Mental Health, Asheboro, NC, 1998—2001; marriage & family therapist Baptist Counseling Ctr., Greensboro, 2000—. Therapist Moses Cone Hosp., Greensboro, 2001. Contbr. chapters to books Personality Disorders in the DSM IV, 1999. Mem.: ACA (workshop presenter world conf. 2000), NC Counseling Assn. (divsn. pres. 2001—02, conf. workshop presenter 1997, 1998). Baptist. Avocations: crafts, gardening, reading, writing.

HOUSER, RUTH G., corporate financial executive, accountant, municipal official; b. Virginia Beach, Va., Feb. 25, 1953; BS in Acctg. cum laude, Wheeling Coll., 1975. CPA, Fla., Ga., W.Va. Sr. acct. Price Waterhouse, Pitts., 1975-79; mgr. Lockheed Space Opers. Co., Cape Canaveral, Fla., 1980-84; mgr. info. systems AT&T, Morristown, NJ, 1984—87, fin. dir. France and Italy Paris, 1987-89, mgr. acctg. policy Morristown, 1989-90, dir. billing svcs. Bridgewater, N.J., 1990-92; fin. billing team dir. WorldPartners/WorldSource AT&T, Bridgewater, N.J., 1993-95; dist. mgr. Lucent Technologies Intellectual Property, Coral Gables, Fla., 1995—98; CFO, mergers and acquisitions mgr. Lucent Technologies, Tierra Verde, Fla., 1999—2001; CFO intellectual property Agere Sys., Orlando, Fla., 2001—04; CEO Blue Horse Investment Group LLC, Orlando, 2005—. Vol. C. Dillon Libr., Bedminster, NJ, 1985, v.p. bd. trustees, 1988—92; sec., trustee Friends of C. Dillon Libr., 1992—95; committeewoman Bedminster Twp., 1995; trustee Ct. Against Spouse Abuse, St. Petersburg; treas. League to Aid Abused Children and Adults, St. Petersburg, 1999—2001, Cross of Lorraine Am. Lung Assn., 1999—2002, Disney 2002 Marathon, Orlando, Fla.; chmn. spring spectacular Ct. Against Spouse Abuse, St. Petersburg, 2001; active Heart of Fl. United Way Leadership Club, 2001, treas., Central Fla. Real Estate Investors, 2004—; active Col. Potter Cairn Terrier Rescue, 2002—; committeewoman Somerset County Reps. Dist. 5, Bedminster, 1993—95. Recipient Cmty. Vol. award, Queen's Ct., Inc., 2001, Myers Book award, Bustanus Myers Ctr., 2002. Mem. AICPA, Fla. Inst. CPAs, Ctrl. Fla. Realty Investors (treas. 2004—). Avocations: international travel, reading, real estate investing. Home: 14121 Snead Cir Orlando FL 32837 Office Phone: 407-857-4711, 479-925-3191. Business E-Mail: ruth@bluehorsenotes.com.

HOUSHIAR, BOBBIE KAY, retired language arts educator; b. Fort Smith, Ark., Nov. 28; d. Ernest and Virgil Straham. BA, Saginaw Valley State U., 1973; MA in Elem. Edn. Adminstrn., Cen. Mich. U., 1975, Cert. Gen. Edn. Adminstrn., 1978. Elem. tchr. Saginaw (Mich.) Pub. Schs., 1973-74, jr. high tchr., 1975-76, tchr. middle sch., 1983—2005; learning ctr. coord. Saginaw Valley State U., University Center, Mich., 1974-75, instr. reading, 1974-75; tchr. ESL Refugee Ctr. of Saginaw, 1982-83. Instr. ind. study Cen. Mich. U., Saginaw, 1988-90; tutor bilingual students Delta Coll., Saginaw, 1987-96; supr./student tchrs. Saginaw Pub. Schs., 1988—; oratorical/writing instr. Saginaw Pub. Schs., 1983—. Editor: Young Writers in Michigan, 1989. Vol. Saginaw County chpt. ARC, 1996-99; mem./vol. League of Cath. Women, Saginaw, 1976—. Recipient Recognition award Saginaw Infant Mortality Coalition award, Saginaw Cooperative Hosp., 1998, Educator of Yr. award, Saginaw Coop. Hosp., 1999, Excellence in Tchg. English Writing Skills award, Saginaw Bd. Edn., 2002, Accent on Achievement award, Saginaw Pub. Sch. Bd. of Edn., 2002, others. Mem. NEA, Saginaw Edn. Assn., Mich. Edn. Assn., Nat. Coun. Tchrs. of English, ASCD, Mich. Mid. Sch. Assn., Delta Sigma Theta. Democrat. Roman Catholic. Avocations: reading, student mentor, tennis, swimming, horses. Office Phone: 989-791-4145. Business E-Mail: bhoushiar@spsd.net.

HOUSMAN, B. JANE, secondary school educator; b. N.Y.C., Oct. 15, 1937; BS, Syracuse U., 1959, MA in Edn., 1961; postgrad., C.W. Post coll., 1985; EdD, Hofstra U., 1991. Cert. elem. edn. tchr., tchr. math., sch. dist. adminstr., sch. adminstr. and supr., N.Y. Tchr. math./computer Roosevelt Jr./Sr. H.S., 2000—01, staff devel. facilitator, presenter, 2000—01. Adj. Manhattanville Coll., purchase, N.Y., 2006—; grant writer, presenter in field. Mem. West Islip (N.Y.) Bd. Edn., 1978-81; mem. Family Svc. League, West Islip, 1990-93. Mem. ASCD, Internat. Soc. for Tech. in Edn., N.Y. State Assn. for Computers and Tech. in Edn., Nat. Coun. Tchrs. Math., Nassau-Suffolk Coun. Adminstrv. Women in Edn., Nassau Reading Coun., Phi Delta Kappa (v.p. membership 1992-2002). Home: 1785 215th St Apt 5H Bayside NY 11360-1708

HOUSTON, ALMA FAYE, psychiatrist; b. Chgo., Oct. 4, 1944; d. Harlan Eugene and Ruth Viola (Minster) H. BA, U. Ark., 1966; BS in medicine, MD, U. Ark., Little Rock, 1969, JD, 1980. Diplomate Am. Bd. Psychiatry and Neurology. Intern Baylor U. Med. Ctr., Dallas, 1969-70; resident in psychiatry U. Utah Univ. Hosp., Salt Lake City, 1970-72; with U. Ark. Med. Ctr., Little Rock, 1972-73; fellow child psychiatry Lafayette Clinic, Detroit, 1973-74; dir. Fullerton Adolescent Ctr. Ark. State Hosp., Little Rock, 1975-78; pvt. practice Little Rock, 1978-81; asst. prof. psychiatry Coll. Medicine Northeast Ohio U., Canton, 1981—2003, dir. psychiatry residency Coll. Medicine Akron, 1983-84; pvt. practice, cons., 1985-86; child psychiatrist Child Guidance and Family Solution, Akron, Ohio, 1983—, med. dir., 1989—93. Republican. Baptist. Avocation: percussionist in a folk music band. Office: Child Guidance and Family Solution 312 Locust St Akron OH 44302

HOUSTON, GAIL TURLEY, English language educator; b. Santa Cruz, Calif., Sept. 29, 1950; d. Eugene Tolton and Inez (Udall) T.; m. Douglas Lee Houston, Apr. 21, 1977 (dec. Apr. 1977); 1 child, Melissa Louise; m. Michael Thomas Amundsen, Feb. 14, 1986; 1 child, Katherine Margaret. BA, Brigham Young U., Provo, Utah, 1973, MA in English, 1981; MA in Humanities, Ariz. State U., Tempe, 1978; PhD in English, UCLA, 1990. Tchr. Carl Hayden H.S., Phoenix, 1974-75; tchg. asst. humanities and English Brigham Young U., Provo, Utah, 1979-81; tchg. asst., assoc. UCLA, 1984-88; asst. prof. Brigham Young U., Provo, 1990-96, U. N.Mex., Albuquerque, 1996—, dir. grad. studies, 1999—2001, dir. women studies, 2003—. Author: (book) Consuming Fictions, 1994, From Dickens to Dracula: Gothic Economics and Victorian Fiction, 2005, also book chpt.; contbr. articles to jours. including Comitatus, Philol. Quar., Studies in English Lit., Royalties; Queen Victoria and the Writer, 1999. Faculty adviser BYU VOICE, Brigham Young U., 1995-96, BYU Rhizobia, 1994-96. Mem. AAUP, MLA. Democrat. Office: U N Mex English Dept Humanities 353 Albuquerque NM 87131-0001

HOUSTON, GERRY ANN, oncologist; b. Baldwyn, Miss., July 16, 1953; d. Jeff Davis and Frances Holland (Agnew) Goodson; m. Terry L. Houston, Dec. 18, 1976 (dec. May 1987); 1 child, Claire Holland; m. Abe John Malouf, July 23, 1988. BA, U. Miss., 1974, MD, 1978. Diplomate Am. Bd. Internal Medicine, Am. Bd. Med. Oncology, Am. Bd. Hospice and Palliative Care. Intern U. Med. Ctr., Jackson, Miss., 1978-79; resident U. Med. Ctr., Jackson, Miss., 1979-81, fellow oncology, 1981-83; ptnr. Jackson (Miss.) Oncology Assocs., 1987—. Staff physician Miss. Bapt. Med. Ctr., Jackson, 1983—, Ctr. Miss. Med. Ctr., Jackson, 1983—, St. Dominic Hosp., Jackson, 1983—, River Oaks Hosp., Jackson, 1983—, Univ. Med. Ctr., Jackson, 1983—; med. dir. Hospice Ministries, Jackson, 1989—; mem. exec. com. Bapt. Med. Ctr., 1994, 1998—, credentials com., 2005—, pres. staff, 2003-04; med. dir. Bapt. Comprehensive Breast Ctr., 1997— Contbr. articles to profl. jours. Chmn. exec. com. Miss. divsn. Am. Cancer Soc., 1993-95, pres., bd. dirs., 1989-93,; exec. com. Bapt. Med. Ctr., 1994, 1999-; credentials com. Bapt. Med. Ctr., 2005-. Clin. rsch. fellow, Am. Cancer Soc. Fellow ACP; mem. AMA, Nat. Hospice Orgn., Acad. Hospice Physicians, So. Assn. Oncology, Am. Soc. Clin. Oncology, Alpha Omega Alpha. Episcopalian. Avocations: jogging, reading, skiing. Office: Jackson Oncology Assocs 1227 N State St Ste 101 Jackson MS 39202-2413 Office Phone: 601-355-2485. Business E-Mail: ghouston@mbmc.org.

HOUSTON, GLORIA, author, educator, consultant; b. Marion, NC, Nov. 24; d. James Myron and Ruth Houston; children: M. Diane Gainforth, Julie Ann Floen. BS, Appalachian State, Boone, N.C., 1963; MEd., U. S.Fla., 1983, PhD, 1989. Lit., writing cons. various orgns., 1979—; founding coord. Suncoast Young Authors Conf. Coll. Edn., U. So. Fla., Tampa, 1985-94, adj. instr., 1982—87. Cons. IBM/Goodhousekeeping Tell Me a Story Project, 1989; lectr. in field; presenter workshops nationwide. Author: The Year of the Perfect Christmas Tree, 1988 (Pubs. Weekly best seller list, other commendations), Littlejim, 1990, 2d edit., 2005, My Great Aunt Arizona, 1991, Littlejim's Gift, 1994, Mountain Valor, 1995, Littlejim's Dreams, 1997, Bright Freedom's Song, 1998, How Writing Works, 2003, Little Jim, 2006; contbr. articles to profl. jours. and mags. Fla. Endowment for the Humanities scholar, 1988-89; recipient Disting. Alumnae Rododendron Soc.award Appalachian State U., Excellence in Edn. award for Literacy from Partnerships in Edn., 1990. Mem. Authors Guild (Disting. Educator). Avocations: travel, reading, folklore. Office Phone: 704-542-6497. Personal E-mail: gloriahouston@bellsouth.net.

HOUSTON, VELINA HASU, education educator, writer; d. Lemo Houston and Setsuko Takechi; m. Peter Henry Jones; children: Kiyoshi, Kuniko Leilani. BA, Kans. State U., 1979; MFA, UCLA, 1981; PhD, U. So. Calif., 2000. Prof. theatre and dir. of dramatic writing U. So. Calif. Sch. Theatre, Los Angeles, 1990—, resident playwright, 1990—. Author: (plays) Tea, 1986, Kokoro, 1986, Calling Aphrodite, 2005. Recipient Silver medal, Pinter Rev. Prize for Drama, 2003; James Zumberge fellow, James Zumberge Found., 2000, Japan Found. fellow, 2000. Mem.: Writers Guild of America West, Dramatists Guild. Episc. Office: USC Sch Theatre 1029 Childs Way Los Angeles CA 90019

HOUSTON, WHITNEY, vocalist, recording artist; b. East Orange, N.J., Aug. 9, 1963; d. John R. and Cissy Houston; m. Bobby Brown, July 18, 1992 (separated Sept. 13, 2006); 1 child, Bobbi Kristina Houston Brown. LHD (hon.), Grambling U., 1988. Mem. New Hope Bapt. Jr. Choir, 1974, background vocalist Chaka Khan, Lou Rawls, Cissy Houston, 1978, appeared in Cissy Houston night club act, fashion model Glamour Mag., Seventeen mag., 1981, record debut (duet with Teddy Pendergrass) Hold Me, 1984; singer: (albums) Whitney Houston, 1985 (Grammy Award Best Pop Vocal Performance, 1985, Favorite Pop/Rock Album and Favorite Soul/R&B Album, Am. Music award, 1986), Whitney, 1987 (Grammy Award Best Pop Vocal Performance, 1987, Album of Yr., Soul Train Music Award, 1988, Best LP R&B/Dance and Best LP Rock/Pop, First Annual Garden State Music Award (NJ), 1988), I'm Your Baby Tonight, 1990 (Best R&B Album, Billboard Music Award, 1991), My Love Is Your Love, 1998 (Grammy Award Best Female R&B Vocal Performance, 2000), The Greatest Hits, 2000, Love, Whitney, 2001, Just Whitney, 2002; singer: (appears on) The Bodyguard soundtrack (song "I Will Always Love You"), 1992 (Grammy Awards: Record Of The Year, Album Of The Year, Best Pop Vocal Performance, 1993, Favorite Pop/Rock Single and Favorite Soul/R&B Single, Am. Music Award, 1994, Favorite Pop/Rock Album and Favorite Adult Contemporary Album, Am. Music Award, 1994, Best R&B Single, Soul Train Music Award, 1993, Best R&B Song of Yr., Soul Train Music Award, 1994, Album of Yr., Billboard Music Award, 1993, Soundtrack Album, Billboard Music Award, 1993, Album Most Weeks at #1, Billboard Music Award, 1993, World Single, Billboard Music Award, 1993, Hot 100 Single, Billboard Music Award, 1993, Single Most Weeks at #1, Billboard Music Award, 1993, R&B Single, Billboard Music Award, 1993, R&B Album, Billboard Music Award, 1993, Outstanding Album, NAACP Image Award, 1994, Outstanding Soundtrack Album, Film, or TV, NAACP Image Award, 1994, Favorite New Music Video, People's Choice Award, 1993, Best Song, MTV Movie Award, 1993), Waiting to Exhale soundtrack, 1995 (Favorite Soundtrack, Am. Music Award, 1997, Outstanding Album, NAACP Image Award, 1996, Outstanding Soundtrack, NAACP Image Award, 1996), The Preacher's Wife, 1996 (Outstanding Album, NAACP Image Award, 1997), Prince of Egypt soundtrack (song "When You Believe" with Mariah Carey), 1998; appeared in HBO TV spl. Welcome Home, Heroes, With Whitney Houston, 1991 (Performance in a Musical Special or Series, Cable Ace Award, 1991); actor: (films) The Bodyguard, 1992, Waiting To Exhale, 1995, The Preacher's Wife, 1996 (Image award Outstanding Lead Actress in a motion picture, 1997, Outstanding Gospel Artist, NAACP Image Award, 1997, Outstanding Actress in a Motion Picture, NAACP Image Award, 1997, Favorite Female-R&B, Blockbuster Entertainment Award, 1997), Scratch the Surface, 1997; (TV series) Being Bobby Brown, 2005; performer: Rainforest Benefit at Carnegie Hall, 1994; actor, exec. prodr.: (TV films) Cinderella, 1997, The Cheetah Girls, 2003; prodr.: (films) The Princess Diaries, 2001. Founder The Whitney Houston Found. for Children, Inc. Named Favorite Pop/Rock Female Vocalist, Am. Music Award, 1986, 1987, 1988, Favorite Soul/R&B Female Vocalist, 1986, 1988, Favorite Pop/Rock Female Artist, 1994, Favorite Soul/R&B Female Artist, 1994, Favorite Adult Contemporary Artist, 1997, Best R&B Singles Artist, Billboard Music Award, 1991, Best R&B Album Artist, 1991, Best R&B Artist, 1991, World Artist, 1993, Hot 100 Singles Artist, 1993, R&B Singles Artist, 1993, Entertainer of Yr., NAACP Image Award, 1994, Outstanding Female Artist, 1994, 2000, Favorite Female Musical Performer, People's Choice Award, 1987, 1988, 1989, 1993, 1998, Best Female Vocalist, Rock/Pop and Best Female Vocalist, R&B/Dance, First Annual Garden State Music Award (NJ), 1988, Best Female Singer, Nickelodeon Kids Choice Award, 1988, Favorite Female Vocalist, People Mag. Reader Poll, 1988, Best Selling Am. Recording Artist of Yr., World's Best Selling: Pop Artist, R&B Artist, Overall Recording Artist, Recording Artist of Era, World Music Award, 1994; named to Hall of Fame Inductee, Nickelodeon Kids Choice Award, 1996; recipient Favorite Soul/R&B Single for You Give Good Love, Am. Music Award, 1985, Favorite Soul/R&B Video Single for Saving All My Love, 1985, Favorite Pop/Rock Single for I Wanna Dance With Somebody, 1987, Outstanding Music Video for I'm Every Women, NAACP Image Award, 1994, Outstanding Song for OExhale (Shoop Shoop), 1996, Best Female Video of Yr. for How Will I Know, MTV Award, 1986, Best Music Video for I Wanna Dance With Somebody, First Annual Garden State Music Award, NJ, 1988, Best Single Rock/Pop and Best Single R&B/Dance for So Emotional, 1988, Best R&B/Soul Single, Female for O Exhale (Shoop Shoop), Soul Train Music Award, 1996, Emmy award, Outstanding Individual Performance in a Variety or Music Program, 1986, Emmy award, Outstanding Musical Performance in a Sports Program for One Moment In Time, Special Olympics, 1988, Disting. Artist/Humanitarian award, Nat. Urban Coalition, 1988, Outstanding Achievement in Humanitarian award, Govt. Switzerland, 1988, Light Contributing Leadership award, appointed by George Bush Points of Light, 1990, Frederick D. Patterson award, United Negro College Fund Founder award, 1990, Hitmakers award, Songwriters Hall of Fame, 1990, Essence award for Performing Arts, 1990, Am. Cinema Performer of Yr. award, 1991, Music award, Am. Black Achievement award, 1991, Brass Ring award, Children's Diabetes Found., 1992, Award of Merit, Am. Music Award, 1994, Sammy Davis Jr. Entertainer of Yr. award, Soul Train Music Award, 1994, VH-1 Honor for Whitney Houston Found. for Children, 1995, Disting. Achievement in Music and Fil/Video, Second Annual Internat. Achievement in Arts award, 1995, Soul Train 25th Anniversary Hall of Fame award, 1995, Triumphant Spirit award, Essence Mag., 1997, Top Contribution to Gospel by a Mainstream Artist, Gospel Music Assn., 1997, Pop Award for Count On Me, ASCAP, 1997, Quincy Jones Career Achievement award, Soul Train Music Award, 1998, Artist of the Decade, 2000, Internat. Album of Yr., NRJ Award, 2000, BET Lifetime Achievement award, 2002.

HOVAKIMYAN, NAIRA, mathematician, educator; b. Yerevan, Armenia, Sept. 21, 1966; arrived in U.S., 1998; d. Viktor Hovakimyan and Emma Tumanyan. BS, MS in Theoretical Mechanics and Applied Math., Yerevan State U., 1988; PhD in Physics and Math., Russian Acad. Scis., Moscow, 1992. Jr. rsch. scientist Inst. Mechanics, Armenian Acad. Scis., Yerevan, 1992—94, sr. rsch. scientist, 1995—97; postdoctoral scholar INRIA (French Nat. Inst. Computer Sci. and Control), Sophia Antipolis, France, 1997—97; vis. rsch. scientist Sch. Aerospace Engring., Ga. Inst. Tech., Atlanta, 1998—2000, rsch. scientist II, 2001—03; assoc. prof. Va. Poly. Inst. and State U., Blacksburg, 2003—. Presenter in field. Contbr. articles to profl. jours. Recipient Internat. Best Paper award, Soc Instrument and Control Engrs., 1996, Pride@Boeing award, Boeing Co., 2004, 2006; fellow, Va. Tech. Coll. Engring., 2006; grantee, Soros Found., 1993—94; German Acad. Exch. Svc. scholar, Stuttgart U., Inst. for Computer Applications, 1994—95. Fellow: AIAA (assoc.); mem.: AMS, IEEE Control Sys. Soc. (sr.), Internat. Soc. Dynamic Games. Orthodox Christian. Achievements include patents for adaptive control system having direct output feedback and related apparatuses and methods; patents pending for error observer for adaptive output feedback; adaptive state estimation for unknown nonlinear processes; an improved method for adding adaptation to an existing control system applicable to non-minimum phase nonlinear systems; adaptive control with input saturation; a low-pass adaptive control design with improved transient performance. Office: Va Poly Inst and State Univ Dept AOE 215 Randolph Hall Blacksburg VA 24061-0203 Office Phone: 540-231-7989. Business E-Mail: nhovakim@vt.edu.

HOVER, DAWN A., director; b. Endicott, NY, June 10, 1965; d. Gerald A. and Emily Adelaide Hover. BA in Biology and Chemistry, Keuka Coll., 1987; M in Art of Tchg., SUNY, Cortland, 1990, cert. advanced study/sch. dist. adminstr., 2005. Tchr. biology, chemistry, and earth sci. Seton Cath. Ctrl. H.S., Binghamton, NY, 1990—2000, asst. prin., 2000—02; dir. spl. programs Oxford (NY) Acad. and Ctrl. Schs., 2002—. Mem. com. United Ch. of Christ Sherburne (N.Y.), 2002—. Mem.: Coun. N.Y. Spl. Edn. Adminstrs., Coun. NY Spl. Edn. Adminstrs., NY State Assn. Women in Adminstrn., Sch. Adminstrs. Assn. N.Y. State, Chi Beta Phi (Key award). Home: 6362 Craine Lake Rd Hamilton NY 13446 Office: Oxford Acad and Central Sch 12 Fort Hill Pk Oxford NY 13830 Office Phone: 607-843-7185. Personal E-mail: dhover1965@yahoo.com. Business E-Mail: dhover@oxac.org.

HOVER, MELISSA KAYE, music educator; b. Des Moines, June 10, 1980; d. Dale Craig and Mary Elizabeth Hover. MusB in Edn., Wartburg Coll., Waverly, Iowa, 2002. Instr. h.s. band Columbus H.S., Waterloo, Iowa, 2002—04; instr. 5-12 band Jesup Cmty. Schs., 2004. Music dir. St. Patrick Ch., Circles Youth Group, Cedar Falls, Iowa, 2004—05. Recipient Govs. Favorite/Most Influential Tchr. award, Gov. Tom Vilsack, 2005. Mem.: Nat. Assn. Music Edn., Iowa Music Educators Assn., Iowa Alliance Arts Edn., North East Iowa Bandmasters Assn., Iowa Bandmasters Assn., Kappa Delta Pi. Roman Catholic. Office: Jesup Community Schools 531 Prospect Street Jesup IA 50648 Office Phone: (319) 827-1700, 1342. Office Fax: 319-827-3905. E-mail: mhover@jesup.k12.ia.us.

HOVLAND, GLADYS MYHRE, secondary school educator; Tchr. Pelican Rapids (Minn.) H.S.; prin., owner Hovland Music Studio, Pelican Rapids. Mem.: NEA, Am. Choral Dirs. Assn., Minn. Edn. Assn. Office: Pelican Rapids High Sch 310 So Broadway PO Box 642 Pelican Rapids MN 56572

HOWARD, BETTIE JEAN, surgical nurse; b. Balt., Sept. 26, 1926; d. Milton James and Elizabeth Maria (Morgan) Knight; m. Stanley Lewis Howard; children: Amanda J. Scott, Sarah L. Howard, Mary McK. Strobel, Elizabeth M. Shaner, Roderick S. Diploma, Ch. Home and Hosp., Balt., 1947. RN, Md.; cert. bd. gastroenterology nurse. Head nurse med.-surg. unit Ch. Home & Hosp., Balt., 1947-48; surg. pediat. staff nurse Johns Hopkins Hosp., Balt., 1948-51, surg. pediat. acting head nurse, 1951-52, otolaryngology endoscopy head nurse, 1952-56; pediat. emergency rm. triage nurse U. Md. Hosp., Balt., 1966-68; head nurse surg. endoscopy nurse U. Md. Med. Ctr., Balt., 1968—2002, endofiberscope team coord. perioperative/trauma, 2002—. Adv. bd. Astra Merck for Patient Self Mgmt. Programs; spkr. in field. Contbr.: (book chpt. sect.) Policy and Politics for Nurses, 1993; contbr. articles to profl. jours. Chmn. Digestive Disease Nat. Coalition, Washington, 1993-95; coord. exec. panel Nat. Digestive Disease Info. Clearinghouse, NIH, Bethesda, Md., 1992-2002; adminstrv. bd. Grace United Meth. Ch., Balt., 1993-95. Mem. Soc. Gastroenterology Nurses and Assocs., Inc. (pres. 1988-89, Gabriele Schindler award 1991), Soc. Internat. Gastroenterol. Nurses and Endoscopy Assocs. (charter, spkr. 1998), Chesapeake Soc. Gastroenterology Nurses and Assocs. (charter, pres. 1981-83), Certifying Bd. Gastroenterology Nurses and Assocs. Inc. (pres. 1992-93). Republican. Avocations: reading, interior decorating, sewing, native-american collection. Home: 905 Saxon Hill Dr Cockeysville MD 21030-2905 Office: U Md Med Ctr 22 S Greene St Baltimore MD 21201-1544 Business E-Mail: bhoward@umm.edu.

HOWARD, BONNIE, bank executive; BS, Univ. Mo. CPA, registered Fin. & Ops. Principal, NASD. Acct. KPMG, Ernst & Young; mng. dir. J.P. Morgan, 1988—2000; dep. auditor FleetBoston Fin. Corp., 2000—02; mng. dir. audit & risk review Citigroup Inc., NYC, 2003—04, chief auditor, mem. mgmt. com., 2004—. Mem. adv. council YWCA Acad. Women Leaders; mem. exec. steering com. Women's Health Symposium; co-chmn. Hunter Coll. High Sch. Annual Fund. Office: Citigroup 399 Park Ave New York NY 10043*

HOWARD, CAROLE MARGARET MUNROE, retired public relations executive; b. Halifax, NS, Can., Mar. 5, 1945; came to the U.S., 1965; d. Frederick Craig and Dorothy Margaret (Crimes) Munroe; m. Robert William Howard, May 15, 1965. BA, U. Calif., Berkeley, 1967; MS, Pace U., 1978. Reporter Vancouver (Can.) Sun, 1965; editl. assoc. Pacific N.W. Bell, Seattle, 1967-70, employee info. supr., 1970-72, advt. supr., 1972, project mgr. EEO, 1972-73, mktg. mgr., 1973, info. mgr., 1974-75; dist. mgr. media rels. AT&T, N.Y.C., 1975-77, dist. mgr. planning, 1977-78, dist. mgr. advt., 1978-80; media rels. mgr. Western Electric, N.Y.C., 1980-83; divsn. mgr. regional pub. rels. AT&T Info. Sys., Morristown, N.J., 1983-85; v.p., pub. rels. and comm. policy The Reader's Digest Assn., Inc., Pleasantville, N.Y., 1985-95; ret., 1995. Faculty profl. pub. course Stanford U., summer, 1993-95; bd. dirs. Andrew Corp. Author: On Deadline: Managing Media Relations, 1985, 2d edit., 1994, 3rd edit., 2000; contbg. author: Communicators' Guide to Marketing, 1987, Experts in Action: Inside Public Relations, 2d edit., 1988, Travel Industry Marketing, 1990, The Business Speakers Almanac, 1994, Majoring in the Rest of your Life, 2000, Marketing Communications, 2002; newsletter editor Wash. State Rep. Ctrl. Com., 1973-74; contbg. editor Pub. Rels. Quar.; pres. The Reader's Digest Found.; adv. bd. Pub. Rels. News, Pub. Rels. Rev., Jour. Employee Comm. Mgmt., Ragan Pub. Rels. Jour. Corp. adv. bd. Caramoor Ctr. for Music and the Arts; bd. dirs. The Hundred Club of Westchester, Inc., The Lila Acheson Wallace Fund for Met. Mus. of Art, Madison Square Boy's and Girl's Club of N.Y.C. Mem. Women in Comm. (bd. dirs. Wash. state 1973), Internat. Assn. Bus. Communicators, Pub. Rels. Soc. Am., Nat. Press Women, Wash. Press Women (bd. dirs. 1972), Issues Mgmt. Assn., Pub. Rels. Seminar, Am. Cancer Soc., Arthur Page Soc., Wisemen, The Aspen Club, La Paloma Country Club, Gray Wolf Ski Club, Sr. Golfers Am., San Juan Outdoor Club, Pagosa Springs Arts Coun., Pi Beta Phi. Anglican. Home and Office: PO Box 5499 Pagosa Springs CO 81147-5499

HOWARD, DONNA JEAN, retired counselor; b. Milw., Aug. 8, 1950; d. Charles E. and Charlena V. (Crandall) Disert. BS in Edn., Black Hills State Coll., 1972; MA in Guidance and Counseling, Adams State Coll., 1977. Cert. tchr., sch. counselor, Colo. Tchr. Pleasant View Mid. Sch., Pueblo, Colo., 1972-77; counselor Widefield HS, Security, Colo., 1977-80, Gunnison (Colo.) HS, 1980-86; instr. Western State Coll., Gunnison, 1985-86; counselor, Impact coord. Aurora (Colo.) Ctrl. and Hinkley HS, 1986-87, Hinkley HS, 1986-91; counselor, coord. student assistance program Overland HS, Aurora, 1991—2004. Ednl. cons., Aurora, 1987—; off-campus instr. Adams State Coll., 1987—. Contbr. articles to newsletters. Named Impact Counselor of Yr., Care Unit Colo., 1990. Mem. Nat. Orgn. Student Assistance Program and

Ptrs. (Outstanding Student Assistance Profl. 1991, 92), Colo. Sch. Counselor Assn. (newsletter editor 1987-89, Secondary Counselor of Yr. 1990). Avocation: breeding horses. Office: Overland High Sch 12400 E Jewell Ave Aurora CO 80012-5398

HOWARD, ELENA CALVILLO, retired elementary school educator; arrived in U.S., 1960; d. Jose Calvillo and Edith De Calvillo; children: Anna Williams, Andrés Capra. BA in English, The U. N.Mex., Albuquerque, 1967. Cert. tchr. secondary edn. N.Mex., tchr. elem. edn. Tex., in ESL Bilingual ESL Cert. Bd. Tchr. Spanish St. Vincent Acad., Albuquerque, 1967—68; tchr. Holy Ghost Sch., Albuquerque, 1968—70; tchr. ESL elem. sch. Escuela Antonio Caso, Guadalajara, Mexico, 1976—79; tchr. lang. elem. sch. Fredericksburg Ind. Sch. Dist., Tex., 1979—96, ret., 1996. Vol. Free Clinic, Fredericksburg, 1985—89; bd. dirs. Boys and Girls Club, Fredericksburg, 2002—06. Mem.: Delta Kappa Gamma. Avocations: reading, latch hooking, exercise, cooking.

HOWARD, JENNIFER LEE, not-for-profit fundraiser; b. Hazard, Ky., Feb. 22, 1974; d. James Edward and Glenna Howard. BA magna cum laude, Morehead State U., Ky., 1996; MA, Ea. Ky. U., Richmond, 1988. Health instr. Morehead State U., 1999—2006; change specialist, adv. Save The Children, Berea, Ky., 2006—. Adv. Am. Heart Assn., Ky., 2004; vol. CPR, first-aid instr. ARC, Morehead, 1999—. Mem.: KAHPERD (assoc.; v.p. health 2004—05), Am. Alliance for Health, Phys. Edn., Recreation & Dance, Ky. Assn. Health, Phys. Edn., Recreation & Dance (conv. mgr. 2005—06), Eta Sigma Gamma. Avocations: travel, photography. Home: 175 North Locust Hill Dr Apt 2910 Lexington KY 40509 Office: SaveThe Children 126 Main St Berea KY 40403 Office Fax: 859-986-1642. Business E-Mail: jhoward@savechildren.org.

HOWARD, JOAN ALICE, artist; b. N.Y.C., Apr. 28, 1929; d. John Volkman and Mary Alice Devlin; m. Robert Thornton Howard, June 26, 1949; children: Barbara Jo, Robert Thornton Jr., Gregory Lyon, Brian Devlin. Student, Hunter Coll., N.Y.C., 1947-48, UCLA, 1967-68, L.A. Valley Coll., 1970-71. Dir., choreographer Acad. Dance, Floral Park and Forest Hills, N.Y., 1947-57; dir. dance. Cath. Parochial schs., N.Y.C., Bklyn., and Floral Park, N.Y., 1948-55; chair dept. dance Molloy Coll., 1958-67; artist sta. KNBC-TV, L.A., 1967-74, NBC, N.Y.C., 1974-78, sta. WNBC-TV, N.Y.C., 1978-79; artistic dir. Brookville Sch., N.Y., 1980-85; tchr. adult continuing edn. Lewisboro Sch. Sys., N.Y., 1995-98; instr. Art Works, Litchfield, SC, 1998—, Coastal Carolina U., SC, 2003—04. Dir. dance N.Y.C. YMCA, 1948; founder, dir. Queens-Nassau Regional Dance Theatre, 1950-55; choreographer Molloy Coll. Dance Theatre, 1959-67; cons. pre-natal exercise, L.I., N.Y., 1980—; judge art show Westbury Mural Project, N.Y., 1979; art cons. Chase Manhattan Bank, 1994-96, curator Chase Manhattan Bank, Cross River, N.Y., 1993-94, art. cons. 1996-97; instr. continuing edn. Lewisboro Cross River, N.Y., 1996, 97, 98, Ridgefield, Conn., 1996, 97, 98; instr., speaker in field; instr. adult edn., Ridgefield and Lewisboro, N.Y., 1995-99; instr. all media Painted Fern Ct. Studio, 1998-2000, Brockgreen Gardens Murrells Inlet, S.C., 1999-2000; instr. painting Brookgreen Gardens and Art Works, Litchfield, S.C., 2001; instr. art Coastal Carolina U., Conway, S.C., 2003, 04, 05; demonstrator Sumi e painting Georgetown, 2005, Time Warter Cable S.C. Channel 17, Southern Style, 2005, CBS, Myrtle Beach, 2005; instr. Coastal Carolina U., 2006; art works instr. Litchfield, S.C., 2006. One-woman shows include Dime Savs. Bank, Manhasset, N.Y., 1986-87, Ridgefield (Conn.) Guild Gallery, 1989-90, 91, 92, 93, Nardin Gallery Fine Arts, 1990, Chase Manhattan Bank, 1990-97, Manhasset Libr. Gallery, 1990-91, Hutchinson Gallery L.I. U., 1991, Rose Gallery, Kent, Conn., 1991, 92, 93, 94, Chelsea House, N.Y., 1991, Plandone Gallery, L.I., 1991, Sacco's, Ridgefield, 1991, Great Neck (N.Y.) Libr. Gallery, 1991, N.Y. Inst. Tech., Greenvale, N.Y., 1992, 93, Chase Manhattan Bank, Cross River, N.Y., 1992-93, 95-96, 96-97, Hicksville (N.Y.) Gallery, 1993, Chase Manhattan Bank, N.Y., 1995-97, Burroughs Chapin Mus., Myrtle Beach, S.C., 2002, 03, Aldrich Mus., 1995, 96, Ridgefield Libr., 1997, Adam Broderick Image Group, mural project Logans, S.C., Januven Gallery, S.C., 2001-02, Great D Art Gallery, Murrells Inlet, S.C., 2006-, Coastal Carolina Bank, 2006-; exhibited in group shows at Valley Ctr. Arts Gallery, L.A., 1968-72, Home Savs. & Loan Art Exhibits, L.A., 1969-70, Westwood Art Gallery, L.A., 1972, Onion Gallery, L.A., 1972, North Ridge Women's Ctr. Gallery, L.A., 1972, Great Neck (N.Y.) Ctr. Gallery, 1976, A&S Gallery, Manhasset, 1976, Gloria Vanderbilt Designers Showcase, 1978, Ridgefield (Conn.) Guild Artists, 1983, Manhasset Libr. Gallery, 1985-89, Great Neck House Gallery, 1986-87, Hutchins Gallery C.W. Post Coll., L.I., 1986-90 (awards 1986, 87, 88, 89, 90), Dime Savs. Bank, Manhasset, N.Y., European Am. Bank, 1988, Nardin Fine Arts, Cross River, N.Y., 1989, Plandome Gallery, N.Y.C., 1990, Aldrich Mus., 1992-93, Hicksville (N.Y.) Gallery, 1993, Ridgefield (Conn.) Guild of Artists Gallery, 1993, Rose Gallery, Hicksville Gallery, 1993, Chase Manhattan Bank, N.Y.C., 1993-94, Tchr. Cont. Edn. Lernsboro Sch. Dist., N.Y., 1995-96, Adam Broderick Image Group, Ridgefield, Conn., 1995-96, Narden Gallery, N.Y., 1996, Masters Art Show, Litchfield, S.C., 2001, Sea Mist Resort, Myrtle Beach. S.C., 2003, Burroughs Chapin Mus., Myrtle Beach, S.C., 2004, Rice Mus., Georgetown, S.C., 2004-05, Time Warner Cable Southern Style, 2004-05, CBS Nightly News, 2005, Borouth Chopin Mus., S.C., 2005, others; exhibited in juried shows Nassau County Mus. Fine Arts, Roslyn, N.Y., 1985, Plandome Gallery, 1987-88, Great Neck House Gallery, 1986-89 (hon. mention), East Meadow Libr. Gallery, 1988, Freeport Gallery, 1988, Shelter Rock Gallery, 1989, Ridgefield Gallery Portrait Show, 1989-90, Ridgefield Artists' Guild, 1989, 93, Nardin Gallery, 1989, Hutchins Gallery L.I. U., 1991, Rose Gallery, Kent, Conn., 1991, 92, 94, Chelsea House Mus. Cultural Commn., 1991, Manhasset Gallery, 1990-91, Sacco, Ridgefield, 1991, Great Neck Libr. Gallery, 1991, Chase Manhattan Bank, Cross River, N.Y., 1992-94, 95, Tchrs. Art Yorktown Artists Club, 1994, Aldrich Mus., 1993-94, Ridgefield (Conn.) Art Guild Gallery, 1993, 95, 96, 97, Hicksville (N.Y.) Art Gallery, 1993, Chase Manhattan Bank, N.Y., 1993, 94, 95, 96, 97, 98, HBO, N.Y.C., 1995, Ridgefield Libr. Gallery, 1997, instr. Brookgreen Gardens, Lichtfield, SC, Rici Mus, Georgetown, SC, 2004, others; exhibitor (exhbn.) Art Works Gallery, Litchfield, 2000, Janssen Gallery, Pawley's Island, S.C., 2000; murals, Logan's Roadhouse, SC, Adam Broderick Image grp., CT, Art Works Litchfield, S.C., 2000-02; choreographer contemporary ballet Crucifixion, 1960, Persephone, 1961, Cubes of Truth, 1962, Somewhere, 1965; appeared on radio show Coast to Coast on a Bus, 1939-47; Broadway prodn. Lady in the Dark, 1940-42; performed ballet in TV show Stars of Tomorrow, 1942, Sleeping Beauty, 1942; creator 7 murals Logam Road House, North Myrtle Beach, S.C., 4 paintings Eastport (N.Y.) Animal Hosp.; executor commd. work at color workshops All Media, 1998-2000, numerous others. Dem. committeewoman, Glen Cove, N.Y., 1954-58. Recipient Del Rey Perpetual Race championship trophy, 1974, Little Sabot Perpetual Race trophy, 1972-74, So. Calif. Women's Sailing Conf. sabot championship, 1972-74, 1st Woman trophy Olympic Regatta, 1973. Mem. Dance Educators Am., Manhasset Art Assn., Women's Sailing Com. of U.S. Yacht Racing Union (fund raiser 1980-81), Am. Women's C. of C. L.A., Tri-County Artists Ridgefield Art Guild, Waccamaw Art & Crafts Guild, Georgetown Watercolor Soc. Avocation: racing sail boats and rally cars. Home and Studio: 4545 Painted Fern Ct Murrells Inlet SC 29576-6380

HOWARD, JOYCE ANNE, elementary school educator; b. N.Y.C., Oct. 24, 1940; d. Walter Theodore and Jessie Lillian Sattler; m. Philip Laurance Howard, Aug. 14, 1959; children: Robert, Douglas. BA Elem. Edn., Adelphi U., MA, 1976; AA, Nassau C.C. Cert. teacher k-6 N.Y.C. Tchr. North Bellmore; retirement rep. North Bellmore Dist., 1997—; exec. bd. North Bellmore Tchrs. Assn., 1997—. Cons. Nassau County Health Ctr., Nassau, NY, 1990—2000, Learn City, San Ronson, Calif., 1990—2000. Author: (Book) Windows, 2000. Recipient Lifetime award, North Bellmore Sch. PTA, N.Y., 2000. Mem.: North Bellmore Tchrs. Assn. (retirement rep. 1997—, bldg. rep. 2001—04, Recipient Lifetime award 2000, Disting. Svc. award 2005), North Bellmore Tchr. Ctr. Home: 14 Prade Ln Massapequa Park NY 11762 Office: Park Ave Sch 1599 Park Ave Merrick NY 11566 E-mail: jhow1024@aol.com.

HOWARD, KAREN S., retail executive; b. Little Rock, Feb. 21, 1965; d. James Neilly and Zeola Marie Howard; m. Frank Daniel Brown, Jan. 16, 1996 (div. Oct. 1998); 1 child, Frank Daniel II. BS, Western Carolina U., 1993. Store mgr. Lane Bryant, Atlanta, 1989-91; dist. mgr. One Price Clothing, Atlanta, 1991-93; area mgr. Mervyns Dept. Stores, Atlanta, 1993-95; regional visual merchandiser Pier 1 Imports, Atlanta, 1995-97, internat. visual tng. mgr. Ft. Worth, 1997-98, internat. merchandising mgr., 1997-2000, interactive merchandising mgr., 1999-2000; e-bus. mdse. dir. The Container Store, Dallas, 2000—04; dir. online store ops. and mdse. Benchmark Brands Inc., Atlanta, 2004—05; mgr. online user experience Home Depot, 2005—. Home: 3751 Monticello St Douglasville GA 30135 Office Phone: 770-630-5121. E-mail: Karenhoward221@cs.com.

HOWARD, KATHLEEN, computer company executive; b. Norman, Okla., Nov. 3, 1947; d. Robert Adrian and Jane Elizabeth (Morgens) H.; m. Lawrence W. Osgood, Aug. 10, 1968 (div. Sept. 1970); m. Norman Edlo Gibat, Oct. 15, 1971. Student, U. Okla., Norman, 1966—68. Typesetter Selenby Press, Norman, 1968—72; owner, pres. Noguska Industries, Fostoria, Ohio, 1973—; co-founder Home Wine Mchts., Chgo., 1976; cons. Bechtel Corp., Ann Arbor, Mich., 1980—, Gaithersburg, Md., 1980—; chairperson Am. Software Project, 1985; ptnr. Popular Topics Pubs., 1993—; cons. Xerox Corp., Rochester, NY, 1998—. Author: All You Need to Know About MSDOS, 1993; co-author, illustrator: Lore of Still Building, 1972; co-author: Making Wine, Beer and Merry, 1973, Computer Comix Mag., 1986; pres. Popular Topics Press, Inc., also jours. and bus. mgmt. software. Treas. United Way of Fostoria, 1986-88, 2d v.p. 1988-90; bd. dirs. Pvt. Industry Coun., 1988-90. Recipient Founders award Home Wine and Beer Trade Assn. Chgo., 1976. Mem. BBB, Nat. Fedn. Ind. Bus., C. of C. (bd. dirs. 1986-92), Employer's Assn. Toledo, Altrusa Internat. Club (sec. Fostoria chpt. 1984-85, pres. 1986-88, editor dist. #5 1988-90, pres. 2001-03, webmaster Dist. #5, 2004-). Avocations: painting, printing, travel, reading. Office: Noguska Industries 741 N Countyline St Fostoria OH 44830-1586 Office Phone: 419-435-0404. Personal E-mail: knoguska@yahoo.com. Business E-Mail: khoward@noguska.com.

HOWARD, KELLI MICHELLE, science educator; b. Ft. Walton Beach, Fla., June 14, 1969; d. Grover Hicks and Janice Faye Young; m. Ted R. Howard, July 20, 1991; 1 child, Madison Olivia. AA, Lurleen B. Wallace Coll., Andalusia, Ala., 1989; BA cum laude, U. West Fla., Pensacola, 1991. Cert. elem. edn. grades 1-6 Fla. State Dept. Edn., gen. sci. grades 5-9 Fla. State Dept. Edn. Tchr. Richburg Mid. Sch., Crestview, Fla., 1992—97, Davidson Mid. Sch., 1997—. Student coun. sponsor Davidson Mid. Sch., 1992—2002, tennis coach, 1997—99, yearbook sponsor, 1999—. Recipient Tchr. of Yr., Davidson Mid. Sch., 2003—04. Republican. Baptist. Avocations: reading, swimming, scrapbooks, basketball. Office: Davidson Mid Sch 6261 Old Bethel Rd Crestview FL 32536-5507 Home: 5818 Antler Way Crestview FL 32536 Office Phone: 850-683-7500 707.

HOWARD, LOU DEAN GRAHAM, elementary school educator; b. Conway, Ark., Aug. 11, 1935; d. Nathan Eldridge and Martha Regina (Sutherland) Graham; m. Robert Hunt Howard, June 4, 1961; 1 child, Kenneth Paul. BSE, U. Cen. Ark., 1957; MA, Vanderbilt U., 1960. Cert. sch. adminstr., prin./supr., curriculum specialist, mentor, grad. elem. Elem. tchr. Hughes (Ark.) Pub. Schs., 1957-59; supervisory tchr. Peabody Demonstration Sch., Nashville, 1959-61; elem. tchr. Orange County Pub. Schs., Orlando, Fla., 1965-68; elem. tchr., K-5 adminstr. Westchester Acad., High Point, N.C., 1968-77; tchr. alternative learning ctr.-mid. sch. Randolph County Pub. Schs., Archdale-Trinity, 1978; elem. tchr. Greensboro (N.C.) Pub. Schs., 1978-93, Guilford County Schs., High Point, N.C., 1993-97, ret., 1997. Contbr. articles to newspapers and AAUW Bull. Active Stephen Ministry, commnd. Stephen Leader, 2002; citizen ambassador program of People to People Internat. del. to U.S./China Joint Conf. on Women's Issues, Beijing, 1995; precinct chmn. county exec. com., state exec. com. of Dem. Party; mem. High Point (N.C.) Racial Justice Task Force. Mem.: AAUW (pres. N.C. state 1982—84, assn. nominating com. 1985—87, pres. High Point br. 1988—90, co-pres. 1998—2002, N.C. state parliamentarian 2002—04, Gift honoree Ednl. Found.), NEA (sch. rep., mem. instrnl. and profl. devel. com.), ASCD, Clan Graham Soc. (sec. 1982—2002, soc. archivist 2002—, Disting. Svc. award), N.C. Coun. of Women's Orgns., Peabody Coll. Elem. Coun. (sec.), Ind. Schs. Assn., Assn. Childhood Edn. Internat. (past pres.), Order of The Golden Thistle (charter), Phi Delta Kappa, Delta Kappa Gamma (rsch. chair 1998—2000, Beta XI chpt. newsletter editor 2004—, ETA State Exemplary award for newsletter 2004—05, 2005—06). Methodist. Home: 1228 Kensington Dr High Point NC 27262-7316

HOWARD, LYN JENNIFER, medical educator; b. Buxton, Eng., Jan. 19, 1938; came to U.S., 1965; naturalized, 1971; d. Peter and Bess (Donnelly) Marsh; m. Burtis Howard, Mar. 13, 1965 (div. 1988); children: Peter Howard, Thia Howard; m. Jack Alexander, Sept. 10, 1995. BA, Oxford U., 1960, MA, BM, BCh, 1964. Diplomate Am. Bd. Internal Medicine, Am. Bd. Nutrition. Intern London Hosp., 1964-65, Kans. City Med. Ctr., 1965-66, resident, 1966-70; fellow in clin. nutrition and gastroenterology Vanderbilt Hosp., 1971-73; dir. clin. nutrition program Albany (N.Y.) Med. Coll., 1973-80, asst. prof. medicine, pediat., 1973-76, assoc. prof. medicine, pediat., 1977-84, prof. medicine, 1984—, head divsn. clin. nutrition, 1986—. Asst. dir. Clin. Studies Ctr., Albany Med. Ctr., 1973-78; attending physician Albany Med. Ctr. Hosp., 1973—; attending physician, cons. clin. nutrition Albany VA Hosp., 1973—; cons. pediat. gastroenterology St. Peter's Hosp., Albany, 1974—; med. dir. Albany Home Health Resources, 1991-92; mem. working group Nat. Commn. Digestive Diseases, 1977; mem. NIH Consensus Devel. Conf., 1978, nutrition rsch. directions, 1979, spl. study sect. clin. nutrition rsch. units, 1980, nutrition study sect., 1989-93; cons. AMA Drug Evaluations, 1982, Medicare, Blue Cross/Blue Shield S.C., 1987—; keynote spkr. Australian Soc. Parenteral and Enteral Nutrition, Perth, 1993, 1st Clin. Nutrition Symposium, Kuala Lumpor, Malaysia, 1994. Contbg. editor Nutrition Reviews, 1981-87, 89; mem. editl. bd. Jour. Drug-Nutrient Interactions, 1984, Contemporary Issues in Clin. Nutrition, 1985, Jour. Am. Soc. Parenteral and Enteral Nutrition, 1987-90; contbr. articles, abstracts to profl. jours., chpts. to books. Exec. dir. Oley Found. for Home Parenteral and Enteral Nutrition, 1983-87, pres., 1987-91, med. dir., 1991; pres. Camphill Found., Pa., 1994. Recipient Clifton C. Thorne Cmty. Svc. award, 1990, Physician of Yr. award Albany chpt. Crohn's Colitis Found. Am., 1991; elected 1st woman mem. Great Lakes Interurban Club, 1990; Major County scholar, 1956; grantee Nutrition Found., 1973-79, U.S. Dept. Agriculture, 1978-81, William F. Donner Found., 1983, Oley Found. for Home Parenteral and Enteral Nutrition Patients, 1983—, Home Health Care of Am., 1983-88, Hosp. for Incurables Found., 1987-88, 91, Schaeffer Found. for Faculty Devel., 1988. Fellow Royal Coll. Physicians, Am. Coll. Physicians, Am. Coll. Nutrition (dir. 1985-88); mem. Am. Bd. Nutrition (dir. 1980, pres. 1982-84), Brit. Med. Assn., Am. Soc. Parenteral and Enteral Nutrition (abstract selection com. 1980, nutrition support standards com. 1984, future directions com. 1991, OASIS working group 1991-92, award 1992), Am. Soc. Clin. Nutrition (rsch. com. 1978, edn. com. 1979, councilor 1982-85, chair post grad. clin. nutrition tng. com. 1983-88, clin. practice in health and disease 1991), Am. Inst. Nutrition, Am. Gastroent. Assn. (co-organizer post grad. tng. course 1987, tng. and edn. com. 1988-91, abstract selection com. 1989), N.Am. Soc. Pediat. Gastroenterology, Am. Fedn. Clin. Rsch. (abstract selection com. 1986), Alpha Omega Alpha. Office: Albany Med Coll Albany NY 12208 Office Phone: 518-262-5299.

HOWARD, MARILYN, state school system administrator; BA in Edn., U. Idaho, 1960, MSc in Edn., 1965; EdD, Brigham Young U., 1986; postgrad., Idaho State U. adj. faculty Idaho State U., U. Idaho. Prin. Moscow West Park Elementary Sch., 1988—99; supervisor, devel. pre-school Moscow sch. dists., 1996—99; supt. pub. instrn. Idaho State Dept. Edn., Boise, Idaho, 1999—. Past state pres. Internat. Reading Assn., nat. rsch. and studies com; bd. dirs. State Bd. Edn., State Land Bd., Northwest Regional Edn. Lab. Office: Idaho State Dept Edn 650 W State St PO Box 83720 Boise ID 83720-0027 Office Phone: 208-332-6811.

HOWARD, SANDRA DIANNE, secondary school educator; b. Decatur, Ala., Dec. 26, 1961; d. David F. and Laura Ann Bittle; m. Stanley Gene Howard, Nov. 26, 1983; children: Elizabeth Dianne, Michael Stanley. BS in Chemistry, U. Ala., Huntsville, 1985, MS in Chemistry, 1987. Sci. tchr. Grace Bapt. Schs., Decatur, 1988—92; rsch. chemist U. Ala., Huntsville, 1991—93; sci. tchr. Decatur Heritage Christian Acad., 1995—96, HS sci. tchr., 2000—. Tchr. Southside Bapt. Ch., Decatur, 1996—2004. Rsch. grantee, Nat. Space Found., 1985—87, Nat. Merit scholar, 1980. Avocation: reading. Office: Decatur Heritage Christian Acad 2014 Sandlin Rd SW Decatur AL 35601 Office Phone: 256-351-4275.

HOWARD, SHERYL ANDREA, lawyer; BA in As. Studies, Smith Coll., 1997; JD, Cornell U., 2001. Bar: NY 2002, Mass. 2002. Mem.: Vol. Lawyers Arts, Women's Bar Assn. (elder law project), Boston Bar Assn. (vol. lawyers project). Office: Foley Hoag LLP Seaport World Trade Center West 155 Seaport Blvd Boston MA 02210 Office Phone: 617-832-3012. E-mail: showard@foleyhoag.com.*

HOWARD, TIFFANY, theater educator; d. Robert and Vicky Murphy; m. Geoffrey F. Howard, Aug. 15, 1998. BA in Theatre Arts, Tex. A&M U., 1996; MFA, Tex. Tech U., Lubbock, 2001. Grad. tchg. asst. Tex. Tech U., Lubbock, 1998—2001; asst. prof. theatre Mo. Valley Coll., Marshall, Mo., 2003. Mem.: ATHE, Alpha Psi Omega. Office: Mo Valley Coll Theatre Dept 500 E College St Marshall MO 65340 Office Phone: 660-831-4052.

HOWARD, WILMA PARKS, elementary school educator; m. V. Jack Howard, Dec. 5, 1964; children: Victor J., Christopher W. BA, Sam Houston State U., Huntsville, Tex., 1986—89. Elem. tchr. Anderson Elem. Sch., Spring, Tex., 1990—. Team leader Anderson Elem. Sch., 1994—. Recipient Tchr. of Yr., Anderson Elem. Sch., 2004. Mem.: Nat. Coun. Tchrs. of Math., Tex. State Tchrs. Assn., Kappa Delta Pi, Golden Key. Baptist. Avocation: travel. Office Phone: 832-249-2375.

HOWARD-PEEBLES, PATRICIA NELL, clinical cytogeneticist; b. Lawton, Okla., Nov. 24, 1941; d. J. Marion and R. Leona (prestige) Howard; m. Thomas M. Peebles, Aug. 16, 1975. BSEd, U. Ctrl. Okla., 1963; student, Randolph-Macon Coll. Women, 1964; PhD in Zoology (Genetics), U Tex. at Austin, 1969. Diplomate Am. Bd. Med. Genetics; cert. clin. cytogeneticist, med. geneticist. Sci. and history tchr. Piedmont (Okla.) Pub. Schs., 1963-64; biochem. technician biochemistry sect. biology divsn. Oak Ridge (Tenn.) Nat. Lab., 1964-66; instr. rsch. pediatrics dept. pediatrics, instr. cytotech. U. Okla. Health Scis. Ctr., Oklahoma City, 1971-72; asst. prof., dir. Cytogenetics Lab. U. So. Miss., Hattiesburg, 1973-77, assoc. prof., dir. Cytogenetics Lab., 1977-80; assoc. prof. dept. pub. health, staff Lab. Med. Genetics U. Ala., Birmingham, 1980-81; assoc. prof., dir. Cytogenetics Lab. dept. pathology U. Tex. Health Sci. Ctr., Dallas, 1981-85, prof., dir. Cytogenetics Lab., 1985-87; prof. dept. human genetics Med. Coll. Va., Richmond, 1987—; clin. cytogeneticist, dir. postnatal lab. Genetics & IVF Inst., Fairfax, Va., 1987-98, co-dir. cytogenetics lab., 1998-2000; genetic, cytogenetic cons., 2000—. Am. Cancer Soc. postdoctoral fellow dept. human genetics U. Mich. Med. Sch., Ann Arbor, 1969-70, dept. human genetics and devel. Coll. Physicians and Surgeons, Columbia U., N.Y.C., 1970-71; genetic cons. Ellisville (Miss.) State Sch., 1973-80; attending staff dept. pathology Parkland Meml. Hosp., Dallas County Hosp. Dist., 1981-87; mem. sci. adv. com. Fragile X Found., 1985-2002; mem. Internat. Standing Com. on Human Cytogenetic Nomenclature, 1991-96. Contbr. articles to profl. jours., chpts. to books; reviewer Am. Jour. Human Genetics, Am. Jour. Med. Genetics, Clin. Genetics, Human Genetics. Fellow Am. Coll. Med. Genetics (founding mem.); mem. Am. Soc. Human Genetics, Assn. Genetic Technologists, Tex. Genetics Soc. (chmn. planning com. ann. meeting 1984), Am. Cytogenetics Conf., Delta Kappa Gamma, Sigma Xi. Bapt. Office Phone: 214-893-8635. Personal E-mail: phpeebles@yahoo.com.

HOWARD-WYNE, JOSIE, elementary school educator; b. Columbus, Miss., Nov. 6, 1947; d. Frank Earl Howard and Annie Lee Nelson-Howard; m. William James Wyne, Jr.; 1 child, Lisa Shennet Stinson. BS, Western Mich. U., Kalamazoo, 1972, Masters, 1976. Tchr./instructional specialist Kalamazoo Pub. Schs., 1972—. Mem.: NEA, Kairos Dwelling (bd. dirs. 1998—99), Chain Lake Dist. Assn. (treas. 2002—), Kalamazoo Ednl. Assn., Northside Assn. for Ednl. Advancement (sec. 1986—), Dulcet Club (program chmn. 1975—), Delta Sigma Theta (Golden Life mem. 1975—), Alpha Delta Kappa. Baptist. Avocations: singing, travel, sewing, crossword puzzles, mentoring. Home: 4202 Kingsbrook Dr Kalamazoo MI 49006 Office: Kalamazoo Pub Sch 1220 Howard St Kalamazoo MI 49006

HOWATT, SISTER HELEN CLARE, human services administrator, director, retired school librarian; b. San Francisco, Apr. 5, 1927; d. Edward Bell and Helen Margaret (Kenney) H. BA, Holy Names Coll., 1949; MS in Libr. Sci., U. So. Calif., 1972; cert. advanced studies, Our Lady of Lake U., 1966. Joined Order Sisters of the Holy Names, Roman Cath. Ch., 1945. Life tchg. credential, life spl. svcs. credential, prin. St. Monica Sch., Santa Monica, Calif., 1957-60, St. Mary Sch., L.A., 1960-63; tchr. jr. high sch. St. Augustine Sch., Oakland, Calif., 1964-69; tchr. jr. high math St. Monica Sch., San Francisco, 1969-71, St. Cecilia Sch., San Francisco, 1971-77; libr. dir. Holy Names U., Oakland, Calif., 1977-94; Spanish instr. Collins Ctr. Sr. Svcs., 1994-99; acct. St. Monica Sch., San Francisco, 1999—2002; libr. St. Martin de Porres Sch., Oakland, 2003—04; tutor Aurora Sch., Oakland, Calif., 2004—. Contbr. math. curriculum San Francisco Unified Sch. Dist., Cum Notis Variorum, publ. Music Libr., U. Calif., Berkeley. Contbr. articles to profl. jours. Grantee, NSF, 1966, NDEA, 1966. Mem. Cath. Libr. Assn. (chmn. No. Calif. elem. schs. 1971-72). Home and Office: 4660 Harbord Dr Oakland CA 94618-2211

HOWE, ANNE MARIE, director, educator; d. Edward Frank and Anna Mae Uhlik; children: Jo Anne, Bryon Patrick, Deanna Marie. BSc, U. Mich., 1976; MEd, Ariz. State U., 1992. Tchr. Saewon (Ariz.) Pub. Schs., 1986—96, Coolidge (Ariz.) Pub. Sch., 1996—2001; dir. sci. engring. Math. Aerospace Acad., Coolidge, 2001—06. Mem. state standards rev. and devel. com. Ariz. State Dept. Edn., Phoenix, 2003—. Mem.: Nat. Sci. Tchrs. Assn., Ariz. Assn. Math. Tchrs. (regional v.p. 2000—), Delta Kappa Gamma (v.p. chpt. 2001—05, scholar 2005). Avocations: needlecrafts, rubber stamping, scrapbooks. Office: Sacaton Public Sch PO Box 98 Sacaton AZ 85247

HOWE, FLORENCE, literature educator, writer, publisher; b. NYC, Mar. 17, 1929; d. Samuel and Frances (Stilly) Rosenfeld. AB, Hunter Coll., 1950; AM, Smith Coll., 1951; postgrad., U. Wis., 1951—54; DHL (hon.), New Eng. Coll., 1977, Skidmore Coll., 1979, DePauw U., 1987, SUNY Coll., Old Westbury, 1992, Pace U., 2000, Chatham Coll., 2000, U. Wis., 2004. Tchg. asst. U. Wis., Madison, 1951-54; instr. Hofstra Coll., 1954-57; lectr. English Queens Coll., CUNY, 1956-57; asst. prof. English Goucher Coll., 1960-71; prof. humanities and Am. studies SUNY, Old Westbury, 1971-85; prof. English City. Coll. and Grad. Sch., CUNY, 1985-95, Grad. Sch./CUNY, 1995—2001; pres., dir. The Feminist Press at CUNY, 1970—2000, exec. dir., 2005—06, pub., 2006—. Vis. prof. U. Utah, 1973, 75, U. Wash., 1974, John F. Kennedy Inst. Am. Studies Free U. Berlin, 1978, Oberlin Coll., 1978, Denison U., 1979, MLA Summer Inst. U. Ala., 1979, Coll. of Wooster, 1980; found. edit. Women's Studies Quar., 1972-82. Author: The Conspiracy of the Young, 1970, Seven Years Later: Women's Studies Programs in 1976, 1977, Myths of Coeducation: Selected Essays, 1964-1984, 1984; editor: (with Ellen Bass) No More Masks! An Anthology of Poems by Women, 1973, Women and the Power to Change, 1975; (with Nancy Hoffman) Women Working: An Anthology of Stories and Poems, 1979; (with Suzanne Howard, Mary Jo Boehm Strauss) Everywoman's Guide to Colleges and Universities, 1982; (with Marsha Saxton) With Wings: An Anthology of Literature by and About Disabled Women, 1987; (with John Mack Faragher) Women and Higher Education in American History, 1988, Tradition and the Talents of Women, 1991, No More Masks, An Anthology of 20th Century American Women Poets, 1993, The Politics of Women's Studies: Testimony from 30 Founding Mothers, 2000, (with Jean Casella) Almost Touching the Skies: Women's Coming of Age Stories, 2000; mem. editl. bd. Women's Studies: An Interdisciplinary Jour., 1971—, SIGNS: Women in Culture and Society, 1974-80, Jour. Edn., 1976—, The Correspondence of Lydia Marie Child,

1977-81, Research in the Humanities, 1977—; contbr. articles to profl. jours. Recipient Mina Shaughnessy award, Fund for Improvement of Post-Secondary Edn., 1982—83, Rockefeller Found., Bellagio, 2001, 2002, 2003, 2004, 2005; grantee U.S. Dept. State, 1983, 1993; NEH fellow, 1971—73, Ford Found. fellow, 1974—75, Fulbright fellow, India, 1977, Mellon fellow, Wellesley Coll., 1979, Rockefeller Found. fellow, Bellagio, 1997. Office: The Feminist Press at CUNY 365 Fifth Ave New York NY 10016-4309 Office Phone: 212-817-7917. Business E-Mail: fhowe@gc.cuny.edu.

HOWE, JANICE W., lawyer; BA cum laude, Conn. Coll., 1973; JD cum laude, Suffolk U., 1981. Bar: Mass. 1981. Asst. dist. atty. Mass.; ptnr. Bingham McCutchen LLP, Boston, co-chairperson product liability practice group. Appointed by Governor Mass. to Judicial Nominating Com. Ea. Region, 1996—2002; appointed to Spl. Judicial Nominating Com. Juvenile Ct., 1993—95. Office: Bingham McCutchen LLP 150 Federal St Boston MA 02110-1726 Office Phone: 617-951-8504. Office Fax: 617-951-8736. Business E-Mail: janice.howe@bingham.com.

HOWE, LINDA ARLENE, nursing educator, writer; b. Pitts., Dec. 12, 1948; d. Alfred Robert and Zella Jane (Lintner) Somerhalder; m. John Joseph Howe, Dec. 7, 1968; 1 child, Thomas Patrick. Diploma in nursing, Columbia Hosp., 1969; Assoc. in English, Richland Coll., 1981; BSN, U. Tex., Arlington, 1982; MS in Nursing, Tex. Woman's U., 1988; MAE in English, The Citadel, 1992; PhD in Higher Edn. Adminstrn., U. S.C., 1997. RN, Pa., S.C.; cert. BCLS, ACLS. Staff nurse Columbia Hosp., Pitts., 1969-70; staff nurse ICU Brownsville (Pa.) Hosp., 1970-72; charge nurse ICU Kennestone Hosp., Marietta, Ga., 1972-73; staff devel. dir. Autumn Breeze N.H., Austell, Ga., 1973-74; dir. nursing Hideaway Hills N.H., Austell, 1974-76; mgmt. cons. Unicare Svcs., Dallas, 1976-79; supr. ICU Meml. Hosp. of Garland, Tex., 1979-84; dir. edn. Montgomery Gen. Hosp., Olney, Md., 1984-89; dir. Roper Hosp. Sch. Nursing, Charleston, S.C., 1989-95; nurse Richland Meml. Hosp. Columbia, S.C., 1995-96; dir. Olsten Home Health Svcs., Eugene, Oreg., 1996-98; dir. critical care Valley Hosp., Santa Maria, Calif., 1998; educator St. Francis Health System, Greenville, SC, 1998—99; assoc. prof. Clemson U. Sch. Nursing, 1999—. Instr. U. Md., College Park, 1985-89; instr. English Trident Tech. Coll., Charleston, 1992-95; speaker and presenter in field; legal nurse cons., 2004— Author: Passion and Persistance: A Biography of Mary Adelaide Nutting, 1997. Leader Girl Scouts USA, Marietta, 1974-76; cub scout den mother Boy Scouts Am., Dallas, 1977-80, counselor, Dallas and Olney, 1981-88; Sunday sch. tchr. Holy Comforter Luth. Ch., 1994-96, congregational coun. sec., 1994-96; bd. dirs. Pickens County ARC, 2003-05; parish nurse Jones Ave. Bapt. Ch., 2005—. Recipient Outstanding Advisor award Student Nurses Assn. S.C., 2002, Faculty Excellence award Clemson U. Bd. Trustees, 2003, 05, Excellence in Nursing Edn. award S.C. Nurses Assn., 2002; named Instr. of Yr. Nat. Fedn. LPNs, 1990, 92 Mem. ANA (chair Hall of Fame com.), Nat. League for Nursing, S.C. League Nurses (pres.), S.C. Nurse Educators (treas. 1991-93), Am. Assn. Nurse Historians, Am. Assn. Critical Care Nurses, Sigma Theta Tau, Phi Delta Kappa. Avocations: needlecraft, gardening, music, writing. Home: 103 Hollingsworth Dr Easley SC 29640-2612 Office Phone: 864-656-5480.

HOWE, MARTHA MORGAN, microbiologist, educator; b. NYC, Sept. 29, 1945; d. Charles Hermann and Miriam Hudson (Wagner) M.; m. Terrance Gary Cooper. AB, Bryn Mawr Coll., 1966; PhD, MIT, 1972. Postdoctoral fellow Cold Spring Harbor Lab, NY, 1972-74; asst. prof. bacteriology U. Wis., Madison, 1975-77, assoc. prof., 1977-81, prof., 1981-84, Vilas prof., 1984-86; Van Vleet prof. virology U. Tenn., Memphis, 1986—. Mem. genetic biology rev. panel NSF, 1980-82, adv. panel prokaryotic biology, 2004—; mem. gen. rsch. support rev. com. NIH, Bethesda, 1982-86, mem. microbial physiology and genetics 2 study sec., 1997-2001; mem. sci. adv. com. instnl. rsch. grants Am. Cancer Soc., 1991-94. Assoc. editor Virology, 1983-92, Genetics, 1994; mem. editorial bd. Jour. Bacteriology, 1985-90; contbr. articles to profl. jours. and books. Recipient Rsch. Career Devel. award NIH, 1978; H.I. Romnes Faculty fellow U. Wis., 1981; Amoco Teaching award U. Wis., 1981. Fellow Am. Acad. Microbiology (bd. govs. 1991-99); mem. Am. Soc. Microbiology (chmn. divsn. H 1983, councillor divsn. H 1989-91, chmn. com. on awards 1990-96, pres.-elect 1999-2000, pres. 2000-2001, past pres. 2001-2002, Eli Lilly award 1985, ASM Founders Disting. Svc. award 1999), Am. Soc. Biochemistry and Molecular Biology, Genetics Soc. Am. (bd. dirs. 1989-91, program com. 1989-90). Office: U Tenn Dept Molecular Scis 858 Madison Ave Memphis TN 38163-0001 Office Phone: 901-448-8215. Business E-Mail: mhowe@utmem.edu.

HOWE, NANCY, artist; b. Summit, N.J., Nov. 17, 1950; d. Herbert Benedict and Ruth Audrey (Guerard) H.; m. Richard Gray Kelley Jr., Jan. 7, 1973 (div. Dec. 1987); children: Ryan Travis Kelley, Tyler Gray Kelley; m. James Anthony Russell, May 20, 1989. AB in Art, Middlebury Coll., 1973. Federal duck stamp artist U.S. Dept. Interior, 1991-92; conservation stamp and print Nat. Fish and Wildlife Found., 1993. Exhibited in groups shows at Cin. Mus., 1996-99, Colo. History Mus./Denver Rotary Club, 1994-99, Soc. Animal Artists, 1993-99, Nat. Park Acad. of the Arts Nat. Tour, 1987, 90, 92, 94-95, 97, Leigh Yawkey Woodson Art Mus., 1990, 97, U.S. Embassy residence, 1990-92, Settlers West, 1998, Nat. Mus. Wild Life Art, 1997, 98, Fall Classics Show, 1996-98, Southeastern Wildlife Exposition, 1998, others; permanent collections include R.W. Norton Art Gallery, Leigh Yawkey Woodson Art Mus., John and Alice Woodson Forester Miniature Collection, Ella Carothers Dunnegan Gallery of Art; illustrtor Working With Your Woodland, 1983, Country Jour., Rod and Reel. Mem. Soc. of Animal Artists (Wildlife Art News award 1993, Actitives Press Printers award 1993, Award of Excellence, 1995-96), Am. Acad. Women Artists. Avocations: gardening, skiing, hiking. Home: 3916 Mad Tom Rd East Dorset VT 05253-9738

HOWE, TINA, playwright; b. NYC, Nov. 21, 1937; d. Quincy and Mary (Post) H.; m. Norman L. Levy, Aug. 31, 1961; children: Eben, Dara. BA, Sarah Lawrence Coll., Bronxville, N.Y., 1959; LittD (hon.), Bowdoin Coll., Brunswick, Maine, 1988, Whittier Coll., 1997. Adj. prof. playwriting NYU, 1983—; vis. prof. Hunter Coll., N.Y.C., 1990—. Author: (plays) The Nest, 1969, Museum, 1976, The Art of Dining, 1979, Appearances, 1982, Painting Churches, 1983, Coastal Disturbances, 1986 (Tony award nomination for best play 1987), Approaching Zanzibar, 1989, One Shoe Off, 1993, Pride's Crossing, 1997; Rembrandts Gift, 2002, publs. include Coastal Disturbances: Four Plays by Tina Howe, 1989, Approaching Zanzibar and other plays, 1995, Birth and After Birth, 1995, Prides Crossing, 1998. Nat. Endowment of Arts fellow, 1985, 95, Guggenheim fellow, 1990; Rockefeller grantee, 1984; recipient Obie award, 1983, Outer Critic's Circle award, 1983, Acad. award in Lit. Am. Acad. Arts and Letters, 1993, N.Y. Drama Critics Circle award, 1997-98, Sidney Kingsley award, 1998. Mem. Dramatists Guild (mem. coun. 1990—). Office: care Biff Liff William Morris Agy 1325 Ave of Americas New York NY 10019

HOWELL, ALLIE RHEA, retired educator; b. Ropesville, Tex., July 23, 1927; d. Alfred and Allie Olivia (Northam) Martin; m. Raymond Cecil Gordon, Aug. 26, 1945 (dec. Nov. 1955); m. Seale Cecil Edward, Dec. 31, 1959 (dec. Mar. 1967); m. Richard Elea Howell, Nov. 17, 1972 (dec. Sept. 1998); children: Kenneth Ray Gordon, Barbara Kay Gordon. Accredited med. records technician. Med. sec. Meth. Hosp., Lubbock, Tex., 1954-55; med. records dir. West Tex. Hosp., Lubbock, 1955-91; instr. med. records tech. South Plains Coll., Lubbock, 1992—. Mem. Am. Health Info. Mgmt. Assn., Tex. Health Info. Assn., Caprock Health Info. Assn. Home: PO Box 417 New Deal TX -2709

HOWELL, BERYL A., lawyer; b. 1956; m. Michael Rosenfeld; 3 children, Jared, Alina, Calla. BA with honors, Bryn Mawr Coll., 1978; JD, Columbia Univ. Law clk. to Hon. Dickinson A. Debevoise U.S. Dist. Ct. N.J.; assoc. Schulte Roth & Zabel, N.Y.; asst. U.S. atty. (ea. dist.) N.Y. US Dept. Justice, 1987—93; gen. counsel U.S. Senate Judiciary Com., 1993—2003; exec. v.p., mng. dir. & gen. counsel Stroz Friedberg LLC, Washington, 2003—. Commr. U.S. Sentencing Commn., 2004—. Recipient First Amendment award, Soc. Profl. Journalists, 2004; Harlan Fiske Stone scholar, Columbia Univ. Office: Stroz Friedberg LLC Suite 200 1150 Connecticut Ave NW Washington DC 20036

HOWELL, BRADLEY SUE, retired librarian; b. McKinney, Tex., July 15, 1933; d. Jessie Leonard and Carrie Pearl (Nickerson) LaFon; m. Richard Dunn Howell, May 18, 1957; children: Mark Richard, Celeste Ella, Jane Elizabeth. BS in Edn., So. Meth. U., Dallas, 1955; MS in Libr. Sci., East Tex. State U., 1968. Tchr. J.B. Hood Jr. High Sch., Dallas, 1955-56, Mineral Wells (Tex.) Jr. High Sch., 1957-58; libr. Ascher Silberstein Sch., Dallas, 1963, San Jacinto Sch., Dallas, 1960-62, 65-81, Woodrow Wilson High Sch., Dallas, 1981—. Pres. Tex. United Meth. Hist. Soc., 1980—84, v.p., 2000—04; sec. South Ctr. Jurisdiction Archives and history of United Meth. Ch., 1980—88; v.p. local ch. sect. The United Meth. Hist. Soc., 1989—95, chmn., 1995—99; pres. PTA Woodrow Wilson H.S., 1983—84; leader Camp Fire, Inc., 1970—. Recipient Wakan award Camp Fire, Inc., 1976, Hilteni award, 19782, Sawnequas award, 1988, Gulick Vol. award, 1998, Terrific Tchr. award Tex. PTA, 1984, Jim Collins Outstanding award, 1986, Honor award Nat. Sch. Pub. Relation Assn., 1986, Dallas Positive Parents award, 1987, Golden Flame award, 1990, excavator award Ptnrs. in Edn., 2005; elected Woodrow Wilson H.S. Hall of Fame, 1999. Mem.: Am. Libr. Svcs. to Children (Newbery com. 1980), Tex. Libr. Assn. (chmn. archives and history roundtable 1990—92), Tex. Assn. Sch. Librs., Dallas Assn. Sch. Librs. (pres. 1975—76), Freedoms Found. and Valley Forge (pres. Dallas chpt. 1997—99, v.p. edn. 2003—05), Pi Lambda Theta (pres. Alpha Sigma chpt. 1997—2002), Delta Psi Kappa, Phi Delta Kappa, Alpha Delta Pi, Delta Kappa Gamma (state achievement award 1988, Golden Gift Leadership Mgmt. award 1985). Democrat. Home: 722 Ridgeway St Dallas TX 75214-4453 Personal E-mail: bshowell@ont.com.

HOWELL, DEBORAH, editor; b. San Antonio, Jan. 15, 1941; m. C. Peter Magrath; 8 stepchildren. Editor St. Paul Pioneer Press; chief Washington bur., editor Newhouse News Svc.; ombudsman Washington Post, 2005—. Adv. bd. Univ. Tex. Coll. Comm. Office: Office of Ombudsman Washington Post 1150 15th S Washington DC 20071 E-mail: deborah.howell@newhouse.com.*

HOWELL, DEBRA LYNNE, information technology executive; b. Bowling Green, Ohio, Oct. 31, 1969; d. David Austin and Sheryl Anne Howell; life ptnr. Andri Goncarovs; 1 child, Kevin Austin. BA, Wells Coll., 1996; M in Indsl. and Labor Rels., Cornell U., 2006. Microsoft Cert. Systems Engr. Assoc. dir. info. tech. Cornell U.-Facilities Svcs., Ithaca, NY, 1999—; teambuilding facilitator Cornell Outdoor Edn., Ithaca, 2005—. Asst. coach Ithaca United Track Club, 2005—. Served with USAR, 1992—2000. Mem.: IEEE (assoc.), Am. Mgmt. Assn., Soc. Human Resource Mgmt. (cert. profl. in human resources), Mensa. Democrat. Office: Cornell U-Facilities Svcs B03 Humphreys Ithaca NY 14853 Office Phone: 607-255-4986. E-mail: dlh19@cornell.edu.

HOWELL, ELIZABETH F., psychiatrist, educator; BS, U. Ga., 1974, MS, 1976; MD, Med U. SC., 1980. Cert. Addictions Am. Soc. Addiction Medicine, Psychiatry Am. Bd. Psychiatry, Neurology, Addiction Psychiatry Am. Bd. Psychiatry, Neurology. Instr. psychiatry Med. U. SC., Charleston, 1984—87; asst. med. dir. Fenwick Hall Hosp., Johns Island, SC, 1986—87; asst. prof. psychiatry Emory U. Sch. Medicine, Atlanta, 1987—93, clin. asst. prof. psychiatry, 1993—2005; pvt. practice psychiatry Atlanta, 1993—2005; clin. dir. Atlanta West Intake & Treatment Ctr., Atlanta, 1993—96; spl. asst. Ga. Dept. Human Resources, Atlanta, 1996—97, state dir. substance abuse svcs., 1997—2000; med. dir. MARR, Inc., Atlanta, 2000—05; assoc. prof. psychiatry U. Utah Sch. Medicine, Salt Lake City, 2005—. Reviewer, resource allocation United Way Met., Atlanta, 1996; gubernatorial appointee, mem. Joint Legis. Study Com., Atlanta, 1997; mem. Mission New Hope, Atlanta, 1998—2000, Ga. Coun. Substance Abuse, Atlanta, 2000—04. Named one of Best Doctors Am., Best Doctors, Inc., 1995-1997; 1999-2005; recipient Psychiatrist of Yr., Ga. Psychiat. Physicians Assn., 1999; King's Fund fellowship, Duke Endowment, 1979. Fellow: Am. Soc. Addiction Medicine (treas. 1999—2003, pres. 2005—, Fellow 1998), Am. Psychiat. Assn. (ga. legis. rep. 1995—2000, dist. fellow 2003); mem.: AMA (rep. 2006—), Utah Psychiatric Assn., Utah Med. Assn., Ga. Psychiat. Physicians Assn. (pres. 2000—01), Nat. Assn. State Alcohol, Drug Abuse Dirs. (mem. joint work group 1997—2000), Med. Assn. Ga. (mem. legis. coun. 1996—2004), Ga. Soc. Addiction Medicine. Office: U Utah Neuropsychiatric Inst 501 Chipeta Way Salt Lake City UT 84108 Office Phone: 801-583-2500. Business E-Mail: elizabeth.howell@hsc.utah.edu.

HOWELL, EMBRY MARTIN, researcher; b. Bethesda, Md., Nov. 18, 1945; d. David Grier and Louise Martin; m. Joseph Toy Howell III, Dec. 28, 1965; children: Andrew Martin, Jessica Ramsey. AB, Barnard Coll., 1968; MSPH, U. N.C., 1972; PhD, George Washington U., 1991. Computer programmer Corp. Trust Co., N.Y.C., 1968; computer programmer dept. city and regional planning U. N.C., Chapel Hill, 1969-70; summer intern State Bd. Health, Raleigh, N.C., 1972; rsch. asst. dept. ob-gyn Georgetown U. Hosp., Washington, 1972-73; health planner, biostatistician Health Systems Agy. No. Va., Falls Church, 1973-75; biostatistician Nat. Capital Med. Found., Washington, 1975-79; dir. SysteMetrics, Inc., Washington, 1979-92; v.p. Mathematica Policy Rsch., Washington, 1992—2000; prin. rsch. assoc. The Urban Inst., Washington, 2001—. Dir. Nat. Evaluation Healthy Start Program; sprk. in field. Contbr. numerous articles to profl. jours. Vol. Children's Hosp. Hospice. USPHS trainee, 1971-72; recipient Agy. for Health Care Policy and Rsch. Dissertation Rsch. grant, 1990-91. Mem. Am. Pub. Health Assn., Acad. Health, Am. Evaluation Assn., Phi Beta Kappa. Avocations: singing, tennis, swimming.

HOWELL, EVA JANE WOOD, medical/surgical nurse; ADN magna cum laude, Albany (Ga.) Jr. Coll., 1986. Surg. floor staff nurse HCA Palmyra Med. Ctr., Albany, 1986-87, surg. ICU staff nurse, 1987-89; charge nurse surg. floor Tift Reg. Med. Ctr., Tifton, Ga., 1989-93, endoscopy charge nurse, 1993—97, med. oncology, 1998—2006, radiation oncology nurse, 2006—. Home: 136 Howells Hill Rd Ty Ty GA 31795-3419

HOWELL, HOLLY LYN, athletic trainer; d. Chuck T and Sue R Howell. BS, U. of Tex. at Arlington, 2003; MEd, U. of Tex. at Tyler, 2005. Cert. athletic trainer Nat. Athletic Trainers Assn. Bd. of Certification, 2003, lic. Adv. Bd. of Athletic Trainers/Tex. Dept. of Health, 2003, cert. tchr. State Bd. for Educator Certification/Tex., 2003. Grad. asst. athletic trainer Azalea Orthop. and Sports Medicine, Tyler, Tex., 2003—05; athletic trainer/tchr. Juan Seguin H.S., Arlington, Tex., 2005—. Mem.: Tex. State Athletic Trainers Assn., Nat. Athletic Trainers Assn., S.W. Athletic Trainers Assn. Baptist. Avocations: billiards, poker, basketball, collecting sports memorabilia, collecting vinyl records. Office: Juan Seguin High School 7001 Silo Rd Arlington TX 76002 Office Phone: 817-375-6829. E-mail: hhowell@aisd.net.

HOWELL, JEANETTE HELEN, retired cultural organization administrator; b. Portsmouth, Hampshire, Eng., June 2, 1925; arrived in U.S., 1976; d. Henry Augustus and Mary Scott (Randall) Butler-Frere; m. Reginald Robert Howell, Aug. 14, 1948; children: Josephine Thalia Howell, Robert Henry Adam Howell, Matthew Charles Howell. Student, High Wycombe Coll. Art, 1967-71, Sutton Sch. Art. Dir./owner Bourne End (pre-sch.), Bucks, Eng., 1965-69; adminstr. Historic Denver, Denver, 1980-83; mgr. II Bur. Conservation, State of Maine, Thomaston, 1987-90; dir. Lincoln County Hist. Assn., Wiscasset, Maine, 1990-93; ret., 1993. Founder Decorative and Fine Arts N.J., pres., 1977; co-founder Decorative and Fine Arts Soc. U.K., 1966, Decorative and Fine Arts Soc. N.J. ednl. lectrs. and seminars (pres. 1977); bazaar chmn. St. John's Cathedral, Denver, 1981; pres. Damariscotta (Maine) Arts Coun., 1984-86; sr. warden St. Andrew's Ch., Newcastle, Maine, 1992-96; co-founder Friends of Colonial Pemaquid (Maine), 1993, pres., 2004—; trustee Maine Archives and Mus., 1999-2000; bd. dirs. Lincoln Home Assisted Living. Nurse emergency med. hosp., Weymouth, Dorset, Eng., 1942-48. Recipient Americans-By-Choice Outstanding Svc. award Citizenship Day com., Denver, 1983, Appreciation award Maine Vols. in Parks, 1997, Jefferson award enrichment of arts Maine Today Portland Press Herald, 2004. Mem.: Friends Colonial Pemaquid (pres. 2004—), Maine Archives and Mus. (v.p. 2000, pres. 2002—04). Avocations: gardening, archaeology, history research, literature. Home: 534 Harrington Rd Pemaquid ME 04558-4214 E-mail: howell@lincoln.midcoast.com.

HOWELL, KAREN JANE, private school educator; b. Mpls., Apr. 24, 1946; d. John and Lorraine (Quale) Borgen; m. John Morris Howell; children: Laura, John. AS in Math. and Sci., Cottey Jr. Coll., Nevada, Mo., 1966; BS in Elem. Edn. Sci. and Math., U. No. Colo., Greeley, 1968; MS Science & Gifted Education, University Of Virginia, Alexandria, Va, 1980—83. Cert. 5/6th Grade Team Tchr. 1968, 6th Grade Gifted Tchr. 1971, K-6th Gifted Program Tchr. 1983. Team tchr. John Adams and Carver Elem. Schs., Colorado Springs, Colo., 1968—73; tchr. gifted 3-6th grade Math. and Sci. Washington Mill and Stratford Landing Elem. Schs., Alexandria, Va., 1973—83; tchr. gifted program Tokeneke Elem. Sch., Darien, Conn., 1983—85; 5-8th science, 1-8 art teacher Hillel Academy, Fairfield, Ct, 1985—. Art / science docent Smithsonian Instn. and Am. Mus. Nat. History, Washington, 1974—82; guide Discovery Mus., Bridgeport, Conn., 1985—. Author: (various workshops, teaching modules) Using Art Properties With Mus. Tours, 1980-1990, 1990, (teacher's guide) Motivational Techniques, Math Manipulatives, 1988,1992, 1994. Chairperson, bd. dirs. Fairfield (Conn.) Internat. Dance Co., 1990—2002; judge Conn. State Invention Conv., Hartford, 1983—87. Recipient Presdl. award for Excellence in Sci. Tchg., State of Conn., 1989, Presdl. award for Excellence in Math. Tchg., 1989, First Sci. Tchr. award, State Sci. Fair Conn., 1996, 1st Place, Middle Schs., Conn. State Sci. Fair, 1995, 1996, 1997, 1998, 1999. Mem.: NEA, Am. Chem. Soc., Nat. Math. Tchrs. Assn., Conn. Earth Tchrs. Assn., Conn. Sci. Tchrs. Assn. (Conn. Sci. Tchr. of Yr. award 2002), Nat. Sci. Tchrs. Assn., Audubon Soc., Am. Mensa, Am. Ballet Theater (assoc.). Methodist. Avocations: ballet, jazz, dance. Office: Hillel Academy 1571 Stratfield Rd Fairfield CT 06432 Personal E-mail: j.howell@comsoc.org.

HOWELL, KATHY AILEEN, advertising executive; b. Memphis, Tenn., Mar. 14, 1952; d. Avelino L. and Kathleen Jane Saquing; m. James Mack Howell, July 9, 1971; children: Karen Klemis, James Mack Jr., Kimberly Marie, Richard Mack. Office mgr. Winston Network, Inc., Memphis, 1984—85; ops., real estate mgr. Transp. Displays Inc., Memphis, 1985—96; owner, CEO Howell Advt. Svc., West Memphis, 1996—. Mem.: Ea. Star, Quota. Republican. Baptist. Avocations: travel, camping. Office: Howell Advt Svc PO Box 5360 West Memphis AR 72301 Office Phone: 870-735-3388. E-mail: chowell3@midsouth.rr.com.

HOWELL, KIMBERLY LYNNE, science educator; d. Wallace III and Vetis Kay Cathcart; m. Gary Richard Howell, June 15, 2001. B of Edn. Sci., U. Alaska, Anchorage, 2000, postgrad., 2004—. Tchr. 6th - 8th grade sci. Von Tobel and Schofield Mid. Sch., Las Vegas, 2000—02; tchr. 7th grade geography Teeland Mid. Sch., Palmer, Alaska, 2002—03, tchr. 8th grade sci., 2003—. Mem.: Phi Kappa Phi. Roman Catholic. Avocations: soccer, running, music.

HOWELL, LAURA CLARK, biologist, educator, small business owner; d. Louie Earl Clark and Laura Elizabeth Stewart; m. Charles Samuel Howell. BS in Biology, Jacksonville State U., 1968; MS in Biology, Samford U., 1970; EdS, Jacksonville State U., 1984; postgrad., U. Ala., Birmingham. Cert. profl. tchr. Ala., profl. guidance counselor Ala., registered psychometrist Ala., cert. profl. tchr. Ga. Microbiologist Ala. Dept. Pub. Health, Anniston, 1968; tchr. biology B.B. Comer Meml. Sch., Sylacauga, Ala., 1970—71; tchr. sci., anatomy, physiology, biology, chmn. sci. dept. Wellborn H.S., Anniston, 1971—94. Adj. instr. biology Jacksonville State U., Ala., 1975, supr. student tchrs., 96; adj. instr. biology, botany, zoology Gadsden State C.C., Anniston, 1983—91. Recipient Medal and Cert. Appreciation, SAR, 2003, Educator award, United Daus. Confederacy, 1980, Martha Washington medal, SAR, 2005. Mem.: DAR (Ala. Soc. scholarship chair 2003—, field genealogist), Order Descs. of Ancient Planters (charter) (Ala. br. historian), Nat. Assn. Biology Tchrs., The Plantagenet Soc., Colonial Dames XVII Century (state historian 2005—), Ala.-Benton Geneal. Soc., Anniston Mus. League, Ala. Geneal. Soc., U.S. Daus. War of 1812, Magna Charta Dames & Barons (herald, state v.p.), The Jamestowne Soc., Athena Study Club, Persephone Garden Club, Ams. Royal Descent, Colonial Order of Crown, Knights of Most Nobel Order Garter, Kappa Delta Pi, Alpha Delta Kappa, Delta Kappa Gamma. Methodist. Office: Anniston Coin Jewelry PO Box 2534 Anniston AL 36202-2534

HOWELL, MARIA DELANE, elementary school educator; b. Smithfield, N.C., Nov. 13, 1956; d. Pablo Vasquez Gonzales and Mary Gladys (Jordan) Gaynor; m. Dwight Thomas Howell, Nov. 12, 1988; 1 child, Hamilton Paul. AA, Peace Coll., 1977; BA in Edn., Atlantic Christian Coll., 1979. Interim elem. phys. edn. tchr. Wilson (N.C.) County Schs., 1979, elem. phys. edn. tchr., 1979—. Summer camp counselor YWCA, Raleigh, N.C., 1976, 77, Learning Tree, Raleigh, 1978, 79; girls tennis coach Beddingfield H.S., Wilson, 1979-90. Mem. AAHPERD, N.C. Assn. Health, Phys. Edn., Recreation and Dance (Ea. regional rep. Phys. Edn. Assn. 1989-91), Profl. Educators N.C., Wilson (N.C.) Area Shag Assn. Democrat. Methodist. Office: Rock Ridge Elem Sch 6605 Rock Ridge School Rd Wilson NC 27893-7756 Home: 3511 Astor Dr Nw Wilson NC 27896-1603

HOWELL, MARY JEAN, artist, administrative assistant; b. Cin., Aug. 15, 1944; d. Lenard Howell and Edna Unger, Frank Unger (Stepfather). BA, U. Cin., 1968. Cert. comml. floristry James W. White Sch. Floral Design. Decorative artist Soc. Decorative Painters, Cin., 1991—. Editor: Education Center Cookbook, Pioneer and Antique Hobby Association Cookbook, Cleves Ohio/Miami Senior Citizen Ctr. Cookbook. Artist, painter memory boxes www.memoryboxes.org, Cin., 2001—03. Fellow, U. Cin., U. Salamanca, Spain, 1968, 1969. Mem.: Cin. Art Club (assoc.; writer biog. sketches Dragonfly newsletter), Soc. Decorative Painters (life). Avocations: crafts, sewing, weaving, stained glass.

HOWELL, NELDA KAY, commissioner; b. Kinston, N.C., Apr. 30, 1938; d. John Franklin, Sr. and Reba Ellen (Davis) Howell. BS in Home Econs., East Carolina U., Greenville, 1960; MEd in Adult and CC Edn., N.C. State U., Raleigh, 1970. Home agt. agrl. ext. svc. N.C. State U., Hyde County, 1959-62, home econs. ext. agt. Craven County, 1965-71; vocat. home econs. tchr. Richlands (N.C.) HS Onslow County Sch. Sys., 1962-65; assoc. dist. leader Piedmont Clemson (S.C.) U. Coop. Ext. Svc., 1971-84, dist. ext. chmn. Savannah Valley, 1984-87, dist. ext. dir. Savannah Valley, 1987-91; commr. Onslow County Hosp. Authority, 2001—; chair Onslow Ambulatory Svcs., 2003—, mem. hospitalists commr., 2003, mem. adult resources com., 2003—06. Mem. land use and devel. com. Onslow County Comprehensive Plan, 2001—02; mem. policy com. Joint Land Use Study Onslow County, 2002. Bd. dirs. Onslow Women's Ctr., 2000—05, sec., 2003, asst. sec., 2004; mem. adv. com. Jacksonville H.S. Health Scis. Acad.; mem. staff com. 1st Bapt. Ch., Swansboro, NC, sec., 2000—01. Named Woman of the Yr., Swansboro Area C. of C., 1999; Kellogg fellow, Agrl. Policy Inst. N.C. State U., 1969. Mem.: AAUW (N.C. state membership v.p. 1996—98, parliamentarian 2001—02), N.C. Assn. Family and Consumer Scis. (southeastern region treas. 1996—97), Swansboro High Sch. Alumni (treas. 2003—05, scholarship com. 2004—), N.C. Women United (bd. dirs. 2003—04, fin. com. 2005—), Onslow County Coun. Women (sec. 1994—95, co-chair 1999—2000), Swansboro Toastmasters (pres. 1997), Women's Forum N.C. (sec. 2001—02, treas. 2003—05), E. Carolina U. Alumni Assn. (sec. Onslow County chpt. 1998), Gamma Sigma Delta. Democrat. Baptist. Avocations: volunteering, reading, travel, public policy. Home: 109 Howell Rd Hubert NC 28539-3911 E-mail: nhowell@ec.rr.com.

HOWELL, SANDRA STROUD, assistant principal; b. Grenada, Miss., Sept. 10, 1952; d. Charles Robert and Joy Gillon Stroud; m. Stephan Wayne Howell, May 12, 1951; children: Matthew Stephan, Nathan Wayne. BS in

Liberal Arts, U. Miss., 1973; AA in Curriculum and Instruction, Delta State U., Miss., 1991; AAA in Ednl. Leadership, U. Miss., 2005. Cert. Nat. Bd. Profl. Tchrs. Tchr. Grenada (Miss.) Upper Elem. Sch., 1986—, asst. prin., curriculum coord. grades 1-12, grant writer. Presenter Nat. Supr. Conf., San Francisco, 2002. Youth vol. Grenada Jr. Auxiliary, Miss. Extension Svc. 4-H; vol. AMA, March of Dimes. Recipient Public Edn. Forum award, Public Edn. Forum Miss., 2001; grantee, Miss. Dept. Edn., 2006. Mem.: Kappa Delta Phi, Delta Kappa Gamma. Episc. Avocations: tennis, reading. Home: 109 Gillon Rd Grenada MS 38901 Office: Grenada Upper Elem Sch 1875 Fairground Rd Grenada MS 38901 Office Phone: 662-226-8844. Personal E-mail: howells52@yahoo.com.

HOWELL, SARALEE FISHER, retired pilot; b. Stillwater, Okla., Dec. 10, 1930; d. Earl E. and Ruth Carr (Cleverdon) Fisher; m. Jack Howell, Sept. 3, 1973 (dec. Jan. 1978). BS in Bus. Adminstrn., Okla. State U., 1953. Cert. airline transport pilot. Asst. editor The Shell Roar Shell Oil Co., Tulsa, 1953-55; exec. sec., office mgr. Dyer Drilling Co., Casper, Wyo., 1956-59; corp. pilot Read Pipe & Supply, Farmington, N.Mex., 1961-65; flight instr., charter pilot adminstr. VA flight records Clinton Aviation Co., Denver, 1966-70; corp. pilot Colo. Constructors, Inc., Denver, 1970-72; photogrammetric pilot Kucera & Assocs., Inc., Denver, 1972-74; co-owner, instr. pilot Howell Flight Proficiency, Denver, 1975-78; owner, pilot Avi-Graphics Aerial Photography, Denver, 1975-78; real estate broker assoc. L.C. Fulenwider, Inc., Denver, 1982-86; broker assoc. Sanibel & Marco Island Properties, Inc., Sanibel, Fla., 1987—97, John Gee & Co., Sanibel, 1997—2001; ret., 2001. Treas. Barrier Island Group for the Arts, Sanibel, 1988; participant Pacific Air Race, 1969, All Women's Internat. Air Race, 1970, All Women's Transcontinental Air Race, 1972, Arapahoe Hunt, Littleton, Colo., 1980-86. Mem. Ninety-Nines, Inc. (sec. Colo. chpt. 1969, chmn. 1970), Sanibel Captiva Power Squadron (editor the Soundings 1992-93), Kappa Kappa Gamma (ad sales/asst. editor Denver Alumnae directory 1982-85). Avocations: air races, horses, computers.

HOWELL, SHARON L., counseling administrator; b. L.A., Dec. 22, 1956; d. Joe H. Lain and Catherine Lukemeyer; m. Robert D. Howell, Jan. 3, 1987; children: Laura Lanin, Peter Zachary. BA, UCLA, 1983, MA, 2001. Cert. PPSC, Elem. Edn. Early childhood educator Easter Seals, Robert Pk., Calif., 1999—2000; CC counselor Santa Rosa Jr. Coll., Santa Rosa, Calif., 2001—; HS counselor Capa Grande HS, Petalums, Calif., 2001—. Mem.: ACA, Assn. for Supervision and Counselor Devel., Am. Sch. Counselors Assn. Office: Casa Grande HS Petaluma CA 94954

HOWELL, TERESA CHRISTINE WALLIN, elementary school educator; b. Corinth, Miss., Jan. 14, 1952; d. Reece and Agness (Winfield) W.; m. Bobby Braxton Howell, July 3, 1976 (div. Oct. 30, 1996); children: Chad Braxton Howell, Brad Braxton Howell. BS in Health, Phys. Edu., Miss. State Coll. for Women, 1975; MEd in Curriculum and Instr., U. Miss., 1990. With Gibson Discount Store, Corinth, Miss., 1975—76; factory worker ITT Telecom., Corinth, 1976—87; tchr. Alcorn County Sch. Sys., Corinth, 1977—, bus driver, 1987—. Brownie leader Girl Scouts U.S., Corinth, 1977-78; cub scout leader Boy Scouts Am., Corinth, 1990-93. Mem. Ea. Star. Democrat. Baptist. Avocations: coin collecting/numismatics, stamp collecting/philately, antiques, pepsi memorabilia.

HOWELL, VICKY SUE, health data analyst; b. Beaver, Okla., June 16, 1948; d. Alvin Henry and Alice Odessa (Redemer) H.; m. Ramiro Martinez, Aug. 20, 1971 (div. June 1977); 1 child, Micaela Martinez; m. Timothy Arthur Pierson, June 5, 1982 (div. July 1995). BA, U. Okla., 1971, MA, 1973, PhD, 1979. Lectr. U. Tex., El Paso, 1973-74, 77-78; tchg. asst. U. Okla., Norman, 1979; asst. prof. U. Miss., Oxford, 1980-81, Wichita (Kans.) State U., 1981-82; rsch. analyst II Mo. Dept. Health, Jefferson City, 1984-88, rsch. analyst III, 1988—99; epidemiologist New Mex. Dept. Health, Santa Fe, 1999—2001, epidemiologist, mgr. natality stats., 2001—03, epidemiologist office policy and multicultural health, 2003—. Contbr. articles to profl. jours. Mem. Friends for Peace, Jefferson City, 1993-94; vol. House of Clara, Jefferson City, 1992-95. Democrat. Roman Catholic. Avocations: gardening, reading. Office: N Mex Dept Health 1190 S St Francis Dr PO Box 26110 Santa Fe NM 87502

HOWELLS, MARTHA LOUISE, secondary school educator; b. Hanover, Pa., June 24, 1951; d. G. Benjamin and Helen Young (Forney) H BA English, Wittenberg U., 1973; cert., York Coll., Pa., 1975; MLA, We. Md. Coll., 1982. Cert. lang. arts tchr., Pa., Md. Tchr. York Country Day Sch., 1975—76, Bryn Mawr Sch., Balt., 1976—78, Carroll County Bd. Edn., Westminster, Md., 1978—. Coord. talented and gifted North Carroll H.S., Hampstead, Md., 1980-85; instr. dramatics summer enrichment program Carroll County Bd. Edn., Westminster, 1989—. Mem. Hanover Area Hist. Soc., 1975— Fulbright scholar U.K., 1982-83 Mem. Alpha Xi Delta (chartered) Republican. Lutheran. Avocations: music, piano, acting. Home: 42 Amanda Ave Hanover PA 17331-9272 Office: North Carroll High Sch 3801 Hampstead Mexico Rd Hampstead MD 21074-1699 E-mail: mlhowel@k12.carr.org.

HOWERTON, CHERYL ALLEY, secondary school educator; d. Kenneth William and Carol Mills Alley; m. David Keith Howerton; 1 child, Jeremy Andrew. BA, Marshall U., Huntington, W.Va., 1979, MA, 1985. Permanent tchg. cert. W.Va. State Edn. Dept., 1985. Art tchr. Logan County Bd. of Edn., Logan, W.Va., 1979—80, Wayne County Bd. of Edn., Wayne, W.Va., 1980—. Quilt trainer AEL, Charleston, W.Va., 1996—; presenter/trainer Wayne County Bd. of Edn., Wayne, W.Va., 1995—. Mem. C-K High Local Sch. Improvement Coun., Kenova, W.Va., 1995—96. Mem.: Am. Fedn. Teachers. Democrat. Avocations: drawing, photography, dog training & competition showing, travel, devoted sports mom. Home: 7 Mahood Trace Huntington WV 25705 Office: Spring Valley High Sch 1 Timber Wolf Drive Huntington WV 25704 Business E-Mail: chowerto@access.k12.uv.us.

HOWERTON, HELEN F., artist; b. Tulsa, Okla., Apr. 5, 1944; d. Leo Francis and Helen Nester Murray; m. Ronald G. Howerton, Aug. 27, 1966; children: Jeff A., Greg L. BFA, U. Tulsa, 1966. Comml. artist Okla. State U., Stillwater, 1966—67; advt. sales rep. Brazosport Daily Newspaper, Freeport, Tex., 1967—73; art instr. Tulsa Parks Dept., 1979; full-time wildlife artist Tulsa, 1980—; co-owner Color Connection Art Gallery, 2004—. Founding mem. Signature 16 Artists Soc., National, 1997—; founder Arts Ltd. Gallery, Tulsa, Okla., 1991—95; canine artist registry Am. Kennel Club Mus. of the Dog, 1994—. Represented in permanent collections State of Okla., Fine Art Mus., Wichita Falls, Tex., Tulsa Pub. Schs. Mem. Nature Conservancy, Okla., 1999—2002. Recipient Commn. / Design Artist, Haldor-Topsoe, Inc., 1992—97, 2001—04, Commn. Artist, Sutton Avian Ctr., 2000, Okla. Artist of the Yr., Ducks Unlimited Conservation, 1991. Mem.: Okla. Visual Arts Coalition, Nat. Oil and Acrylic Painters Soc., Signature 16 Artists Soc., Women Artists of the West (bd. dirs. 2000—), Nature Conservancy, Am. Women Artists (assoc.), Oil Painters Am. (assoc.). Conservative. Avocations: travel, hunting, motorcycle riding. Office: Howerton Studio 6304 S 69th E Place Tulsa OK 74133 Office Phone: 918-494-5994. E-mail: howerton@howertonart.com.

HOWES, LORRAINE DE WET, fashion designer, educator; b. Port Elizabeth, South Africa, Dec. 24, 1933; arrived in U.S., 1957; d. Jacobus Egnatius and Johanna Elizabeth (Lowenburg) de W. Student, Sch. Fashion Design, Boston, 1957-58. Apprentice Jonathan Logan & Adam Leslie, Johannesburg, South Africa, 1953-55; apprentice, wookroom asst., model Norman Hartnell, designer to the Queen, London, 1955-57; model Peter Lumley Agy., London, 1955-57; designer, dept. mgr. Design Rsch. Inc., Cambridge, Mass., 1957-59; model Hart Agy., Boston, 1957-76; designer, mgr. Estabrook & Newell, Boston, 1959-62; designer, owner Lorraine de Wet, Boston, 1962-79; mem. adj. faculty dept. apparel design RISD, Providence, 1972-76, asst. prof., assoc. prof., 1976-82, acting head dept., 1976-79, head dept., 1979-99, prof., 1988-2000, prof. emeritus, 2000—, interim dean arch. and design, 2000-2001. Designer, cons. apparel industry and theatre, 1979—2000; dir. Hamilton Cornell Mass., 1986-2000; design and tech. edn. cons. apparel and textiles Hangzhou Econ. Commn., China, 1986-88; mem. individual grants panel Nat. Endowment for Arts, 1994. Named Faculty Mem. of Yr., RISD Alumni Assn., 1984-85; recipient John R. Frazier Excellence in Tchg. award RISD, 1993, Hon. Alumna award RISD, 1995, Helen Rowe Metcalf award 2003; named champion R.I. Pub. Links, 1983, 84. Mem.: Costume Soc. Am., Fashion Inst. Tech. Design Lab., Fashion Group. Avocation: golf. Office: RISD Dept Apparel Design 2 College St Providence RI 02903-2784

HOWES, SOPHIA DUBOSE, writer; b. Balt., Apr. 20, 1954; d. John Carleton and Marie Josephine (Meeth) Jones; m. Edward Phillip Howes, Jan. 26, 1996; 1 child, Michael Laurence. BFA with honors, NYU, 1982, MFA, 1994; JD, Fordham U., 2002. Legal asst. Skadden, Arps, Slate, Meagher & Flom, NYC, 1984-93; script reader Haft Nassiter Co., NYC, 1994; editl. assoc. Matthew Bender & Co. Inc., NYC, 1994-97. Extern Fordham U. Sch. Law, Surrogate's Ct., NYC, 1999; rsch. asst. Securities Arbitration Clinic, Fordham Law Sch., 2000, Writing Rsch., ECPAT, summer 2001. Playwright: Better Dresses, Rosetta's Eyes, 1988, 1988, Adamov, 1992, two-act play The Poisoned Kiss, 1994; mem. staff Fordham Environ. Law Jour., 1999-2000; sr. notes and comments editor, 2000-01; dir. Who's Afraid of Virginia Woolf, 2004, The Tempest, 2004. Recipient Grad. award in playwriting, NYU-Tisch Sch. Arts, 1994, Seidman award for talent, 1982. Mem. Dramatists Guild. Avocation: mountain climbing. E-mail: edwardhowes@juno.com.

HOWETH, LYNDA CAROL, small business owner; b. Okemah, Okla., Sept. 19, 1949; d. Clyde Leon and Hattie Arlene (Hymer) Williamson; children: Amanda B. Knowles, Harold W., Jennifer M. Student, Okla. State Tech. U., 1969, South Okla. City C.C., 1974. Mgr. five stores European Flower Markets, Oklahoma City, 1972-76; dist. sales rep. Profl. Office Systems, Inc., Oklahoma City, 1976-81; exec., owner Bus. Med. Systems, Inc., Oklahoma City, 1981—. V.p. dist. 41 Sch. Bd. Western Heights, Oklahoma City, 1991-94, pres., 1994-98; founding mem. steering com. Okla. Bus. Health Inst., 1994; chair Okal. County Tinker Bond Oversight Com., 2004—. Mem. Nat. Sch. Bd. Assn., Okla. State Sch. Bd. Assn., Vital Info. Profls. (v.p., treas. 1988-90), Med. Tips Club (v.p., treas. 1990-91). Democrat. Avocations: reading, walking. Home: 264 E Fox Ln Newcastle OK 73065-5422 also: 2840 S Utah Ave Oklahoma City OK 73108-1703

HOWITT-EASTON, DEBORAH, lawyer; b. Brookyn, NY, Mar. 12, 1969; BA, U. Mich., 1991; JD, Union U., 1994. Bar: NY 1995, Fla. 1995, Mass. 1998. Real estate atty., Albany, NY; of counsel Real Estate Dept. Sherin and Lodgen LLP, Boston. Mem.: Fla. Bar Assn., New England Women in Real Estate, Boston Bar Assn., Order of Barristers. Office: Sherin and Lodgen LLP 101 Federal St Boston MA 02110 Office Phone: 617-646-2235. E-mail: dhowitteaston@sherin.com.*

HOWL, JOANNE HEALEY, veterinarian, writer; b. Mariemont, Ohio, Mar. 16, 1957; d. Joseph Daniel and Claire Helen (Baillargeon) H.; m. Arthur Wesley Howl, May 12, 1990; children: Bryan Arthur, Martha Grace Claire DVM, U. Tenn., 1987. Sr. lab. animal technician Lab. Animal Facility, Knoxville, 1983-84; gnotobiology technician U. Tenn., Knoxville, 1984-86; assoc. vet. Mynatt Vet. Clinic, Knoxville, 1987-89; veterinary med. officer USDA Animal and Plant Health Inspection Svcs., Raleigh, N.C., 1989-90; owner Creature Comfort Vet. Relief Svc., Laurel, Md., 1991-95; assoc. veterinarian Muddy Creek Animal Hosp., West River, Md., 1996-97; freelance writer, West River, Md., 1995—. Author: Your Cat's Life, 1999; editor VMAT-2 News, 1996—; contbr. articles to profl. jours. Adminstrv. officer Vet. Med. Assistance Team-2. Mem. AVMA, Md. Vet. Med. Assn. (chmn. pub. rels. com. 1995-98, sec./treas. 1998-2002, pres. 1999-2000), Am. Acad. Vet. Disaster Medicine (sec./treas. 1998-2002). Episcopalian. Avocations: hiking, gardening, house remodeling. Home and Office: 4304 Tenthouse Ct West River MD 20778-9797 E-mail: jovet@aol.com.

HOWLAND, BETTE, writer; b. Chgo., Jan. 28, 1937; d. Sam and Jessie (Berger) Sotonoff; m. Howard C. Howland (div.); children— Frank, Jacob. BA, U. Chgo., 1955. Assoc. prof. com. social thought U. Chgo., 1993-97. Author: W-3, 1974, Blue in Chicago, 1978 (1st prize Friends of Am. Writers), Things to Come and Go, 1983, Trial, 1998, Calm Sea and Prosperous Voyage, 1999. Fellow Rockefeller Found., 1969, Marsden Found., 1971, Guggenheim Found., 1978, Nat. Endowment for the Arts, 1981, MacArthur Found., 1984. Jewish. Home: 4474 N County Rd 400 S Logansport IN 46947 Personal E-mail: bettehowland@yahoo.com.

HOWLAND, JOAN SIDNEY, law librarian, educator; b. Eureka, Calif., Apr. 9, 1951; d. Robert Sidney and Ruth Mary Howland. BA, U. Calif., Davis, 1971; MA, U. Tex., 1973; MLS, Calif. State U., San Jose, 1975; JD, Santa Clara (Calif.) U., 1983; MBA, U. Minn., 1997. Assoc. librarian for pub. svcs. Stanford (Calif.) U. Law Library, 1975-83, Harvard U. Law Library, Cambridge, Mass., 1983-86; dep. dir. U. Calif. Law Library, Berkeley, 1986-92; dir. law libr., Roger F. Noreen prof. law U. Minn. Sch. of Law, 1992—, assoc. dean info. tech., 2001—. Questions and answers column editor Law Libr. Jour., 1986-91; memt. column editor Trends in Law Libr. Mgmt. & Tech., 1987-94. Mem. ALA, ABA (com. on accreditation 2001—), Am. Assn. Law Librs., Am. Assn. Law Schs., Am. Indian Libr. Assn. (treas. 1992—), Am. Law Inst. Office: U Minn Law Sch 229 19th Ave S Minneapolis MN 55455-0400

HOWLAND, NINA DAVIS, historian; b. Wichita, Kans., June 2, 1939; d. Earle Rosco Davis and Kathrine Keene Laurie; m. Kenneth Eugene Howland, Sept. 27, 1959; children: Douglas Earle, Christopher Keene, Karen Laurie, Rebecca Kathrine. BA with high honors, U. Md., London Center, Eng., 1970; PhD, U. Md., College Park, 1983; MA with distinction, U. London, 1972. Instr. U. Coll., U. Md., College Park, 1978-79, 82, Hood Coll., Frederick, Md., 1981; archivist Nat. Archives, Washington, 1984-85; historian Office of Historian U.S. Dept. of State, Washington, 1985—. Editor: Foreign Relations of the United States, 1961-63, vol. XXI, Africa, 1995, Foreign Relations of the United States, 1964-68, vol. XVI, Africa, 1999, Foreign Relations of the United States, 1964-68, vol. XXII, Iran, 1999, vol. XXI Near East Region, Arabian Peninsula, 2000; divsn. chief Middle East, South Asia and African divsn., 2002—05. Rsch. grantee William Randolph Hearst Found., 1980. Mem. Soc. for Historians of Am. Fgn. Rels., Soc. for History in Fed. Govt., Peace History Soc., Phi Kappa Phi. Home: 9808 E Bexhill Dr Kensington MD 20895-3223 Office: Office of Historian US Dept of State 2401 E St NW Dept of State Washington DC 20522-0001 Personal E-mail: ninakenhowland@juno.com.

HOWLAND, REPEKA MOATA'A ISARA, retired government community services administrator; b. Moata'a, Western Samoa, Aug. 12, 1932; m. ERic Tuātagaloa Howland. Grad., Kaiser Found. Sch. Nursing, Oakland, Calif., 1957; BSN, UCLA, 1965; MPH, U. Hawaii, 1983. Dir. nursing svcs. dept. health svcs. LBJ Tropical Med. Ctr., Pago Pago, Am. Samoa; health care adminstr. Am. Samoa Territorial Adminstrn. on Aging Agy.; adminstr. Territory's Human Svcs. Info. & Referral Svcs. Ctr Am. Samoa Govt. Dept. of Human Resources, Pago Pago, asst. dir. community svcs. div.; spl. asst. for rsch. and analysis Am. Samoa Govt., Pago Pago, 1989—93, dep. dir. human resources and social svcs., 1993, ret., 1993. Mem. Am. Samoa Coordinating Health Coun., 1977-84; sec. Health Svcs. Regulatory Bd. of Am. Samoa, 1974-82; mem. adv. bd. Tafuna Family Health Ctr., 2002—, chmn. 2005—. Author: (with others) Culture, Child-Bearing, Health Professionals, 1978. Mem. ARC, past chair nursing and community svcs. com., past bd. chair, past disaster program chair Am. Samoa chpt.; hon. pres. Women's Hosp. Aux. Assn., 2002-; treas. Common Cause (Am. Samoa) Inc., 2005—. Recipient Award of Disting. Svcs., Pacific div. ARC, 1977, Merit award for outstanding vol. svcs. ANRCPD, 1977-78. Mem. ANA, Nat. League for Nursing, Am. Pacific Nursing Leaders' Conf. (past sec.), Am. Samoa RN's Assn., Am. Samoa Nurses Assn. (del. to 1995 White House conf., hon. mem. 2005), Common Cause Orgn. (bd. dirs. 1999-2000), Sigma Theta Tau. Home: PO Box 273 Pago Pago AS 96799-0273

HOWLETT, PHYLLIS LOU, retired athletics conference administrator; b. Indianola, Iowa, Oct. 23, 1932; d. James Clarence and Mabel L. (Fisher) Hickman; m. Jerry H. Howlett, Jan. 2, 1955 (dec. June 1972); children: Timothy A. (dec. Jan. 2005), Jane A. Field; m. Ronlin Royer, Dec. 30, 1977. BA, Simpson Coll., 1954. Tchr. phys. edn. Oskaloosa (Iowa) H.S., 1954-55; psychometrist Drake U., Des Moines, 1956-57, asst. to men's athletics dir., 1974-79; asst. dir. athletics U. Kans., Lawrence, 1979-82; asst. commr. Big Ten Conf., Inc., NCAA, Park Ridge, Ill., 1982-97. Mem. football TV com., NCAA, 1980-87, women's golf com., 1983-89, chmn. com. on women's athletics, 1987-94, spl. com. women's basketball TV, 1989-90, chair com. for women's corp. mktg., 1990-94, divsn. I championship com., 1990-95, first woman chair exec. com., 1990-97, chair task force on gender equity, 1992-94, exec. dir. search com., 1993, spl. com. divsn. I football playoff, adminstrv. com., 1995-97, joint policy bd., 1995-97, sec.-treas., 1995-97, coun., 1995-97, fin. com., chair, 1995-97, treas. found. bd., 1995-97 Editor: (yearbook) Simpson Coll., 1953—54. Chair Iowa Commn. Status of Women, 1976-79; pres. Vol. Bus. of Greater Des Moines, 1969-70; chair Arts and Recreation Coun. of Greater Des Moines, 1975; pres. Iowa Children's and Family Svcs., 1973; nat. pres. Assn. Vol. Bus. Am., Inc., 1972-73. Named to, Simpson Coll. Hall of Fame, 1985, Indianola H.S. Hall of Fame, 1997, NACDA Hall of Fame, 2000; recipient Alumni Achievement award, Simpson Coll., 1988, Adminstrv. Achievement award, NACDA, 1995, Honda award of Merit, 1997, Spl. award, All-Am. Football Found., 1998, Lifetime Achievement award, Ind. Sports Corp., 1997, Svc. award, Assn. Vol. Mem. Nat. Assn. Coll. Women's Athletics Adminstrs. (Lifetime Achievement award 2000), Pi Beta Phi (pres. Iowa Beta chpt. 1953-54). Home: PO Box 1117 Abiquiu NM 87510-1117

HOWSE, CATHY L., writer, researcher, entrepreneur; b. Murfreesboro, Tenn., Dec. 16, 1955; d. John Edd Sr. and Elmira Howse; children; Gregory Simpson Jr., Brandon J. BS, Met. State Coll., Denver, 1987. Author: Ultra Black Hair, 1990, 2000, Ultra Black Hair Growth II, 1994. Achievements include development of a method for hair growth and lengthening for black women. Office: UBH Publs Inc PO Box 22678 Denver CO 80222 E-mail: mail@ubhpublications.com.

HOWSE, JENNIFER LOUISE, foundation administrator; b. Glendale, Calif., Jan. 31, 1945; d. Benjamin McCausland and Patricia Louise (Naylor) H. BA, Fla. State U., 1966, MA, 1968, PhD in Child Lang. Devel., 1973; LHD (hon.), SUNY, Bklyn., 1990. Rsch. asst., instr. Inst. Human Devel. Coll. Edn., Fla. State U., Tallahassee, 1967-69; dir. planning and evaluation Wakulla County (Fla.) Sch. System, 1969-72; dir. NARC/HEW Liaison Project Nat. Assn. for Retarded Citizens, Govtl. Affairs Office, Washington, 1972-73; dir. Developmental Disabilities Bur., dir. Bur. Tech. Assistance and Regulation Fla. Dept. Health and Rehab. Svcs., Tallahassee, 1973-75; exec. dir. Willowbrook Rev. Panel, N.Y.C., 1975-78; assoc. commr. N.Y. State Office Mental Retardation and Developmental Disabilities, N.Y.C., 1978-80; state commr. for mental retardation Dept. Pub. Welfare, Harrisburg, Pa., 1980-85; exec. dir. Greater N.Y. chpt. March of Dimes Birth Defects Found., N.Y.C., 1985-89, pres. White Plains, NY, 1990—. Advisor Ctr. for Family Life in Sunset Park, Bklyn., 1992—. Bd. dirs. Salk Inst., La Jolla, Calif.; active Pew Environ. Health Commn. Office: March Dimes Birth Defects Found 1275 Mamaroneck Ave White Plains NY 10605-5298*

HOWSMON, DEBRA SUE, biology educator; b. Tipton, Ind., Feb. 17, 1961; d. David Lee and Violet Margaret Hardebeck; m. Gregg Johnston Howsmon, Dec. 18, 1988; children: Adam, Daniel, Matthew, Hanna. BA in Agrl. Edn., Purdue U., West Lafayette, Ind., 1979—83, MS in Ednl. Comp., 1985—90. Sci./agrl. tchr. Salem HS, Ind., 1983—84; sci. tchr. Bat Runnels Schs., Baton Rouge, La., 1997—2004, Humble 9th Grade, Tex., 2004—06. Mem.: NSTA, Nat. Biology Tchrs. Assn. Avocations: reading, watching children's sporting events. Office: Humble 9th Grade 1131 Wilson Rd Humble TX 77338

HOWSON, TAMAR D., pharmaceutical executive; Sr. v.p., dir. bus. devel., mgr. SR One Ltd. venture capital fund SmithKline Beecham, 2000—01; biotechnology cons. to CEO Bristol-Myers Squibb, 2000—01, sr. v.p. corp. devel., 2001—. Former ind. bus. cons., corp. advisor. Office: Bristol-Myers Squibb Co 345 Park Ave New York NY 10154-0037

HOWZE, KAREN AILEEN, newspaper editor, lawyer, multi-cultural communications consultant; b. Detroit, Dec. 8, 1950; d. Manuel and Dorothy June (Smith) H.; children: Charlene Marie-Aileen, Karie JoAnn, Lucinda Gloria Patrice. BA in Journalism, U. So. Calif., 1972; JD, Hastings Coll. Law, San Francisco, 1977. Bar: Md. 1989, D.C. 1990. Intern Detroit Free Press, 1971; reporter San Francisco Chronicle, 1972-78; asst. editor Newsday, L.I., 1978-79; asst. mng. editor Rochester Times Union, N.Y., 1979-80; Sunday features editor Rochester Democrat & Chronicle, N.Y., 1980-81; mng. editor sys. USA Today, Arlington, Va., 1981-86, mng. editor internat. edit., 1986-88; editor, dir. corp. news systems newspaper divsn. Gannett Co. Inc., Washington, 1988-90; prin. Howze & Assocs., Washington, 1990—, Law Office of Karen Aileen Howze, Washington, 1990—. Spl. master family divsn. Abuse & Neglect Remedial Project D.C. Superior Ct., 2000-2001; lectr. comm. Am. U., Washington, Howard U., Washington; presenter Am. Press Inst., Poynter Inst. Media Studies, Maynard Inst. Journalism Edn. Author: Making Differences Work: Cultural Context in Abuse and Neglect Practice for Attorneys and Judges, 1996; editor: People & Product, 1993-95. Bd. dirs. N.Am. Coun. Adoptable Children, 1990-97, Maat Inst., 1990-97, The Chelsea Sch., 1991-98; pres., founder Adoption Support Inst., Washington, 1990. Mem. ABA (mem. Ctr. on Children and the Law 2001—), Nat. Assn. Black Journalists (bd. dirs. 1975-81, sec., parliamentarian, ANPA vice chair minority opportunity com. 1986), Am. Soc. Newspaper Editors (chair press rm. convention, mem. pres. and bar com.). Clubs: Capital Press, Washington Press. Roman Catholic. Avocations: painting; piano; house renovations and real estate.

HOY, MARJORIE ANN, entomology educator; b. Kansas City, Kans., May 19, 1941; d. Dayton J. and Marjorie Jean (Acker) Wolf; m. James B. Hoy; 1 child, Benjamin Lee AB, U. Kans., 1963; MS, U. Calif., Berkeley, 1966, PhD, 1972. Asst. entomologist Conn. Agrl. Expt. Sta., New Haven, 1973-75; rsch. entomologist U.S. Forest Svc., Hamden, Conn., 1975-76; asst. prof. entomology U. Calif., Berkeley, 1976-80, assoc. prof. entomology, 1980-82, prof. entomology, 1982-92, prof. emeritus, 1992—; Fischer, Davies and Eckes prof., dept. entomology and nematology U. Fla., Gainesville, 1992—; chmn. Calif. Gypsy Moth Sci. Adv. Panel, 1982—; mem. genetics resources adv. com. USDA, 1992—, mem. adv. com. agrl. biotech., 2000—02; mem. com. on biol. threats to agrl. plants and animals NRC and NAS, 2001—02. Chmn. Calif. Gypsy Moth Sci. Adv. Panel, 1982—; mem. genetics resources adv. com. USDA, 1992—, mem. adv. com. agrl. biotech., 2000—01; F.E. Guyton disting. lectr. Auburn (Ala.) U., 1997; mem. com. on biol. threats to agrl. plants and animals NRC and NAS, 2001—02; sci. cons. transgenic insects Pew Initiative Food and Biotech. Editor, co-editor: Genetics in Relation to Insect Managment, 1979, Recent Advances in Knowledge of the Phytoseiidae, 1982, Biological Control of Pests by Mites, 1983, Biological Control in Agricultural IPM Systems, 1985, Insect Molecular Genetics, 1994, 2d edit., 2003, The Phytoseiidae as Biological Control Agents of Pest Mites and Insects: A Bibliography, 1996, Managing the Citrus Leafminer, 1996; mem. editl. bd. Internat. Jour. Pest Mgmt., Biol. Control, Biocontrol Sci. and Tech., Environ. Biosafety Rsch.; contbr. articles to profl. jours. Mem. Sec. Agr.'s adv. com. agrl. biotech.; cons. Pew Charitable Trust. Recipient citation for outstanding achievments in regulatory entomology Fla. Divsn. Plant Industry, 1995, USDA honor award Sec. of Agr., 1996, award for sci. Nat. Agri-Mktg. Assn., 1998, sr. faculty award U. Fla. chpt. Gamma Sigma Delta, 1998, Biol. Control Scientist of Yr., Internat. Orgn. Biol. Control, 2004. Fellow AAAS, Royal Entomol. Soc. London, Entomol. Soc. Am. (mem. Pacific br. governing bd. 1985, Bussart award 1986, Founder's Meml. award 1992), Coun. Agr. Sci. and Tech. (Charles Black award 2004); mem. Nat. Acad. Scis. (com. on biol. threats to agr. plants and animals), NY Acad. Scis., Am. Genetic Assn., Internat. Orgn. Biol. Control (v.p. 1984-85, Disting. Scientist award 2004), Am. Inst. Biol. Scis. (adv. coun. 1996-98, governing bd. 1999-2001),

Acarological Soc. Am. (governing bd. 1980-84, pres. 1992), Soc. for Study of Evolution, Fla. Entomological Soc. (Team Rsch. award 1997, Outstanding Tchg. award 1999), Phi Beta Kappa, Sigma Xi (chpt. sec. 1979-81, Sr. Faculty Rsch. award 1996). Avocations: hiking, gardening, snorkeling. Home: 4320 SW 83rd Way Gainesville FL 32608-4131 Office: U Fla Dept Entomology and Nematology PO Box 110620 Gainesville FL 32611-0620 Office Phone: 352-392-1901. Business E-Mail: mahoy@ifas.ufl.edu.

HOYE, GWYNNE SANDERS, retired mathematics educator; d. Samuel Nathaniel and Lurena Hunt Sanders; m. Lionel S. Hoye, June 5, 1965; children: Mashia Bashira, Atiya Nataki, Ayana Demali. BS, Cheyney U., Pa., 1964. Math. team coach Fitler Academic Plus Sch., Phila., 1992—97, advisor student coun., 1994—99, tchr. sci. resource, 1995—99, tchr. math. resource, 1990—99; tchr. Phila. Bd. Edn.; ret. Adj. prof. Phila. Edn. Fund, 2001—04; program officer Core Philly Scholarship Program, 2006—. Bd. dirs. Student Welfare, Phila., 1990—. Recipient Four Chaplains, Chapel of the Four Chaplains, Phila., 1982. Mem.: Phila. Assn. Retired Tchrs., Am. Bridge Assn., African Genesis Inst., Cheyney U. Alumni Assn., Phila. Pinochle Bugs Soc. & Civic Club, Inc. (treas. 2000—, founder Girls Night Out 2003), Alpha Kappa Alpha (co-chair scholarship com. Omega Omega chpt. 1999—). Avocations: mentoring, reading, bridge, travel, dance. Personal E-mail: hoyelove@aol.com.

HOYE, MARIA PILAR, lawyer; BS, Calif. State U., Northridge, 1988; JD, UCLA, 1991. Bar: Calif. 1991. With Latham & Watkins, L.A., 1991—, ptnr., 1998—. Former adj. prof. environ. law U. So. Calif. Mem.: Orange County Bar Assn. (mem. exec. com. environ. law sect.), Calif. State Bar. Office: Latham and Watkins LLP 633 W Fifth St Ste 4000 Los Angeles CA 90071

HOYER, MARY CATHERINE, elementary school educator, director; b. Lake Forest, Ill., Feb. 1, 1962; d. Allen G. and Mary Jane Tiegs; m. David J. Hoyer, June 15, 1996; children: Kaitlin Tiegs Larson, Sarah Jane. BS in Phys. Edn., Ea. Ill. U., 1984; MEd, Nat. Louis U., 1994. Nat. bd. cert. tchr. NBPTS, Ill., 2004. Phys. edn. tchr. Northwood Jr. H.S., Highland Park, Ill., 1987—. Athletic dir. Northwood Jr. H.S., 2004; varsity head softball coach Libertyville H.S., 2005—. Mem.: Ill. Assn. Health, Phys. Edn., Recreation and Dance. Home: 703 S Fourth Ave Libertyville IL 60048 Office Phone: 847-432-4770.

HOYER, MARY LOUISE, social worker, educator; b. Wausau, Wis., Dec. 4, 1925; d. Jacob and Julia (Anderson) Stuhlfauth; m. William Henriksen Hoyer, June 30, 1948; children: Mark Charles, Gail Maren. BS in Biochemistry, U. Minn., 1948; MSW, Cath. U., 1985, PhD, 1994. Lic. cert. clin. social worker, Md.; bd. cert. diplomate in clin. social work. Rsch. biochemist NIH, Bethesda, Md., 1948-50; dir. Teller Tng. Ctr. Internat. Telephone and Telegraph, Washington, 1967-69; specialist employee devel. Civil Svc. Commn., Washington, 1969-75, supr. sys. sect., 1975-78; mgr. agy. assistance divsn. Office Pers. Mgmt., Washington, 1978-82; vol. counselor Cmty. Crisis Ctr., Bethesda, 1980-82; classroom and field instr. Cath. U., Washington, 1986-91; clin. social worker St. Francis Ctr., Washington, 1985-88; pvt. practice as clin. social worker Bethesda, 1987—. Dep. exec. dir. task force on exec. devel. in sr. exec. svc.: Policy Initiatives for Reform of Civil Svc., Office of Pers. Mgmt., Washington, 1978-79. Contbr. rsch. articles to profl. jours. Precinct chairperson Dem. Action Group, Bethesda, 1962-66; fin. cons. Sch. Bd., Hamilton, Mont., 1950-54; cons. Internat. Visitors Info. Svc., Washington, 1962-66; vol. Md. Fair Housing, Bethesda, 1962-66. Legis. fellow U.S. Congress, Washington, 1980. Mem. NASW, Greater Washington Soc. Clin. Social Workers. Democrat. Lutheran. Home and Office: 5901 Lone Oak Dr Bethesda MD 20814-1845

HOYER, PHYLLIS SCARBOROUGH, retired elementary education educator; b. Salisbury, Md., Oct. 14, 1938; d. Paul Daniel and Norma (Luettinger) Scarborough; m. Lawrence Cogswell Hoyer, July 8, 1961; children: Brian Lawrence, Andrew Scarborough. BS, Hood Coll., 1960; MEd, Towson State U., 1986; postgrad., Hood Coll., U. Md. Cert. early childhood edn., home econs., Md. Tchr. Anne Arundel County Bd. Edn., Annapolis, Md., 1960-61, Washington County Bd. Edn., Hagerstown, Md., 1961-64, Frederick County Bd. Edn., Md., 1972-97; ret., 1997. Chair comm. com., 1984-85, tchr. adv. com., 1977-80, 87-89, team leader, 1989-92, rep. kindergarten class, 1989-92. Instr. frederick County YMCA, 1976-79; participating mem. Earthwatch, Orca Survey, 1989, Fiji Coral Cmtys., 1990, Canary Island Sea Life, 1992, Sierra Wildlife, 1993, Baja Island Predators, 1998; vol. ARC, 1993, Hospice, 2002-06; active Frederick County Sr. Recreation Coun.; mem. Frederick Meml Hosp. Aux., 2002—, Cornerstone Soc. Cmty. Found. Frederick County Recipient hon. mention photography contest Nat. Geog. Soc., 1991. Mem. NEA, Md. Tchrs. Assn., Frederick County Tchrs. Assn. (tchrs. rep. 1980-83, 94), Nature Conservancy., Mental Health Assn. Frederick County (mem. supervised visitation program 2002-05, ct. apptd. spl. adv. 2004—), Friends of Waterford Park (bd. mem. 2005-06). Republican. Avocations: gardening, travel, reading, dance. Home: Apt 10 1612 Rock Creek Dr Frederick MD 21702-3904

HOYLAND, JANET LOUISE, clergywoman; b. Kansas City, Mo., July 21, 1940; d. Robert J. and Dora Louise (Worley) H. BA, Carleton Coll., 1962; postgrad. in music, U. Mo. at Kansas City, 1964-67; M.L.A., So. Meth. U., 1979; MDiv, St. Paul Sch. Theology, 1986. Policy writer Lynn Ins. Co., Kansas City, 1963-64; music librarian U. Mo. at Kansas City, 1966-68; benefit authorizer Social Security Adminstrn., Kansas City, Mo., 1969-75, tech. specialist, 1976-79, claims authorizer, 1980-83; pastor Mercer United Meth. Ch., 1986-88, Adrian (Mo.) United Meth. Ch., 1988—. Piano tchr. Leta Wallace Piano Studio, Kansas City, 1963, 68; piano accompanist Barn Players, Overland Park, Kans., 1972-75, Off Broadway Dinner Playhouse, Inc., Kansas City, 1973. Co-chmn. Project Equality work area, 1971; work area chmn. on ecumenism Council on Ministries, 1969-70; sec. fair housing action com. Council on Religion and Race, Kansas City, 1968; chmn. adminstrv. bd. Kairos United Meth. Ch., 1982; active ward and precinct work Democratic Com. for County Progress, 1968. Mu Phi Epsilon scholar, 1966. Mem. Baton Soc. Kansas City Symphony, Friends of Art Kansas City, Fellowship House Assn. Kansas City, Internat. Platform Assn., Kansas City Mus. Club (chmn. composition dept. 1967-68), Lions Club (treas.), Mu Phi Epsilon (v.p. Kansas City 1968, sec. 1971, pres. 1975-76), Pi Kappa Lambda. Address: Adrian United Meth Ch 8800 Summiton St Kansas City MO 64114

HOYLE, KAREN NELSON, author, curator, educator; b. Boston, Jan. 8, 1937; d. Arthur and Ruth (Rasmussen) Nelson BA English, St. Olaf Coll., 1958; MLS, U. Calif., Berkeley, 1964; MA 1970Scandinavian Area Studies, U. Minn., 1970, PhD Libr. Sci., 1975; D (hon.), U. St. Thomas, 1992. Libr., civil svc. Univ. Librs., 1967—68, libr., instr. Mpls., 1968—75, curator, asst. prof., 1975—80, assoc. prof., 1980—87, curator, prof., 1987—. Adj. faculty Am. Studies, 1983—; grad. sch. faculty examining coms., 1984—; cons. Bloomington Pub. Schs., 1984-85, curriculum materials collection Moorhead State U. Libr., 1982, Five Owls, 1986— Author: Wanda Gag, 1994; contbr. articles to profl. jours Cons. Brown County Hist. Soc., 1993, Globe Exhibit, 1994 George C. Marshall fellowship, 1972; recipient Disting. Alumna award St. Olaf Coll., 1994, Kay Sexton award for Outstanding Contbr. to Minn.'s Book Cmty., 2003. Mem. ALA (chmn. Caldecott Award Com. 1985, Bechtel Fellowship com., Caldecott, Newbery, Batchelder, Wilder Award Coms.), Children's Lit. Assn. (scholarship 1981, pres. 1993-94), Internat. Rsch. Soc. for Children's Libr. (sec., bd. dirs. 1987-89), Internat. Bd. Books for Young People (U.S. Bd. 2002-04, Hans Christian Andersen award com. 1988-89, U.S. chmn. reading promotion award nomination com., 1989-92), Minn. Libr. Assn. (Disting. Achievement award 1992), Minn. Libr. Assn. Found. (bd. dirs. 2000-03) Office: Childrens Lit Rsch Collections U Minn 113 Andersen Libr 222 21st Ave S Minneapolis MN 55455 Office Phone: 612-624-4576.

HOYLE, SHETINA YEVETTE, librarian; b. Jackson, Tenn., Sept. 21, 1969; d. Alecia Yevette Brown; 1 child, Brandon. BFA, Lambuth U., 1991. Tchr. aide Lambuth Presch., Jackson, 1988—89; sales assoc. Goldsmith's, Jackson, 1988—89; customer svc. rep. Bancorp South, Jackson, 1991—97; libr. Jackson Madison County Libr., Jackson, 1997—. Ch. musician First Bapt. Ch., Jackson, 1989—. Mem.: Jaycees, Delta Sigma Theta. Baptist. Avocations: reading, crafts, piano, aerobics. Home: 1005 N Royal St Jackson TN 38301 Office: Jackson Madison County Libr 433 E Lafayette St Jackson TN 38301

HOYSETH, LUANN ROSE, secondary school educator; b. Hamilton, Ohio, Jan. 25, 1977; d. Glenn Norbert and Theresa Aline Lauer; m. Colin Dale Hoyseth, July 1, 2000; children: Victor Glenn, Eva Marie. BS, U.S. Mil. Acad., West Point. N.Y., 1999; MEd, Columbus State U., Ga., 2006. Cert. tchr. sci. and social sci. Ga. Program mgr. Lucent Technologies, Alpharetta, Ga., 2000—01; sci. tchr. Bradwell Inst., Hinesville, Ga., 2001—02; project mgr. Environ. and Natural Resources Divsn., Fort Stewart, Ga., 2002—03; social sci. tchr. Liberty County H.S., Hinesville, Ga., 2003—04; phys. sci. tchr. Pacelli H.S., Columbus, Ga., 2004—, sci. dept. head, 2005—. Track and field coach Pacelli H.S., Ga., 2004—, sci. bowl coach, 2004—, relay for life coord., 2004—05. Family readiness group leader U S Army 2/7 Inf., Fort Stewart, Ga., 2001—03. Cadet US Army, 1995—2000, West Point, NY. Recipient Hollis award for prism design, U.S. Army, 2000. Mem.: Nat. Honor Soc. (adviser 2004—06). Office: Pacelli High School 3556 Trinity Dr Columbus GA 31907 Office Phone: 706-561-8243. Personal E-mail: c_hoyseth@hotmail.com.

HOYT, KAY MARIE, elementary science specialist; b. Deer Lodge, Mont., May 30, 1944; d. Allen P. and Marian (Christoffersen) Johnson; m. Carl F. Hoyt, June 8, 1968; children: Grant A., Gretchen, Carl A. BA, Graceland Coll., 1966; MS, U. Iowa, 1977. Tchr. elem. grades Davenport (Iowa) Community Schs., 1966-67, 79—, Clarke Community Schs., Weldon, Iowa, 1967-69; tchr. Cedar Rapids (Iowa) Community Schs., 1969-79; elem. sci. specialist Davenport (Iowa) Comm. Schs., 1979-91, also K-3 at risk team facilitator Davenport, 1991—2002. Basic patroller Snowstar Ski Patrol; mem. Cmty. Ch. Christ. Named candidate of the year Snowstar Ski Patrol, 1986-87. Mem. NEA, Iowa Acad. Sci., Iowa State Edn. Assn., Davenport Edn. Assn. Reorganized Church of Jesus Christ of Latter Day Saints. Avocations: snow and water skiing, reading, travel. Home: 3 Cherokee Ct Eldridge IA 52748-9608

HOYT, MARY G(ENEVIEVE), artist, educator; b. Oct. 7, 1929; d. Alvin Chase and Genevive Therese (Cahill) H.; children: John Frederick, Mary Elizabeth, Diane Marie, Jill Marie, Patricia Anne. BA in Art, Coll. St. Francis, 1950. Art instr. Malta Pub. High Sch., Dekalb, Ill., 1958; tchr. Lock Port (Ill.) Pub. Grade Sch., 1959; art tchr. Yauapai Coll., Prescott, Ariz., 1974-77, Allan Hancock Coll., Santa Maria, Calif., 1977-95. Lectr. in field; rschr., tchr. metaphysics and spirit, 1983-95. Author: the Spirit Masters' Guide Book to Enlightenment, 1995. Avocations: camping, fishing, reading, travel. Home: 228 Varner Ct Santa Maria CA 93458-9038 E-mail: spirit8A@yahoo.com.

HOYT, ROSEMARY ELLEN, trust advisor; b. Iowa City, Iowa, Apr. 12, 1949; d. Joseph Asa Hoyt and Mary Jane (Brobst) Vandermark; m. Louis O. Scott, Oct. 16, 1965 (div. Nov. 1968); children: Wayne L. Lawson, Jo Anna Jane Kollasch; m. David K. Duckworth, July 23, 1983 (div. Dec. 1994); 1 child, Mary Rose Duckworth. Cert. in applied banking/consumer credit, Am. Inst. Banking, 1988; BBA, So. Calif. U., 1992, MBA, 1997. Cert. in trust adminstrn; cert. trust ops. specialist; cert. in trust tax. Teller Community Bank of Fla., St. Petersburg, 1973-75; bookkeeper Chevron Svc. Sta., St. Petersburg, 1975-77, Landmark Bank, St. Petersburg, 1977-80; teller First Nat. Bank of Ely, Nev., 1981, Nev. Bank and Trust, Ely, 1982; asst. v.p. and trust officer First Nat. Bank Farmington, N.Mex., 1983-96; asst. v.p., trust officer Bank One, Dallas, 1997—. Pres., founder Day Camp Southside, St. Petersburg, 1976-77. Planning chmn. terr. 5 ann. meeting ARC, Farmington, 1990-91, babysitting instr., 1990-96, basic aid tng. instr., 1992, Project Read instr., 1994; coord. United Way, 1997. Recipient Appreciation award ARC, 1991. Mem. Fin. Women Internat. (by-laws com. 1990-91, treas. 1993-94), Nat. Assn. Trust Ops. Specialists (bd. dirs. 1992), Am. Bus. Women's Assn. (v.p. 1991, pres. 1992, Appreciation award 1989, Woman of Yr. 1995). Republican. Avocations: crocheting, cooking, gardening. Office: 1717 Main St 11th Fl Dallas TX 75243 E-mail: rehoyt@sbcglobal.net.

HRANIOTIS, JUDITH BERINGER, artist; b. NYC, Jan. 11, 1944; d. Richard Frederick and Barbara Ann Beringer; children: Anthony J. Bellantoni, Robert John Bellantoni. Student, Sch. Visual Arts, N.Y.C., 1962, NYU, 1994; studied with, John Hamburger; grad. in graphics, Orange County C.C., 2003. Exhibited in group shows at Hudson Valley Art Assn., White Plains, NY, 1990—91, 1998—99, Milford (Conn.) Arts Ctr., 1991—95, Am. Artists Profl. League, NYC, 1991, 1995—96, 1998—99, Ridgewood (N.J.) Art Inst., 1992, 99, Mt. St. Mary Coll., Newburgh, N.Y., 1993, 96, Arts Coun., Orange County, Middletown, 1994, Mamaroneck Artist Guild at Westbeth Gallery, NYC, 1994, Green County Coun. on the Arts, NY, 1996, Salmagundi Club, 1997, 2001, Catharine Lorillard Wolfe Art Club, N.Y.C., 1991—92, 1995, 1996—99, 2001, Kent (Conn.) Art Assn., 1991—99, 2001, 2003, 2004, CLWAC-Broome St. Gallery, NYC, 1999, 2001—02. Recipient 1st Pl. Graphics award, Mt. St. Mary Coll., 1994, 1996, Newburgh, 1990, 1991, Grumbacher Silver medal, Mt. St. Mary Coll., 1993, 1st Pl. Graphics award, Ann. Open Art Exhibit, Arts Coun. of Orange County, 1994, Dutchess County Art Assn., 1995, 1997. Fellow Am. Artist Profl. League, Catherine Lorillard Wolfe Art Club (bd. dirs., asst. treas.); mem. Nat. Mus. of Women in the Arts, Kent Art Assn. (bd. dirs., rec. sec. 1993-95, 96, 97, 98, 99, Cert. of Merit, 1991, 96), Hudson Valley Art Assn. (elected), Woodstock Art Assn. (Prof. Active Artist), Scenic Hudson, Sierra Club, Salmagundi Club N.Y.C. Avocations: perennial gardening, local history, international cooking, amateur naturalist, travel. Home: 245 Browns Rd Walden NY 12586-3056 Personal E-mail: judithh@hvc.rr.com.

HRBEK, SUSAN W., school librarian; b. Painesville, Ohio, Jan. 22, 1947; d. James and Alice Waterman; m. David H. Hrbek, Aug. 10, 1968 (dec. July 29, 2004); children: Bret W., D. Chadwick, Carey A. BS in Elem. Edn., Kent State U., 1970; MS, James Madison U., 1982. Cert. tchr. Va. Tchr. Crestwood Schools, Mantua, Ohio, 1970—75, Rappahannock Schools, Sperryville, Va., 1975—78, Warren County Schools, Front Royal, Va., 1978—85, elem. sch. libr., 1985—2001, HS libr., 2002—. Chmn. ch. com. Front Royal United Meth., 1976—2006; bd. dirs. Front Royal (Va.) Oratorio Soc., 1976—2006, Front Royal/Warren County United Way, Front Royal, 1995—2001. Named Women of Yr., Warren County C. of C., 1985; recipient Svc. Candle award, Front Royal United Meth. Ch., 1998. Mem.: Beta Sigma Phi (pres. 2005—06). Home: 432 Locust Dale Rd Front Royal VA 22630 Office: Warren County HS 240 Luray Ave Front Royal VA 22630 Office Phone: 540-635-4144.

HRICAK, HEDVIG, radiologist; came to U.S., 1972; MD, U. Zagreb, 1970; DMS, Karolinska Inst., 1992; Dr. (hon.), Ludwig Maximilion U., 2005. Diplomate Am. Bd. Radiology 1978. Intern in radiology Hosp. M. Stojanovic, Zagreb, 1971—72; resident in radiology St. Joseph Mercy Hosp., Pontiac, Mich., 1974—77; fellow in diagnostic radiology Henry Ford Hosp., Detroit, sr. staff diagnostic radiology, 1978—81; asst. clin. prof. diagnostic radiology U. Mich., Ann Arbor, 1979—81; from asst. prof. to assoc. prof. U. Calif., San Francisco, 1982—86, prof. radiology, urology, radiation oncology, ob-gyn., 1986—99; chief abdominal sect. dept. radiology U. Calif. Med Ctr., San Francisco, 1982—2000; chmn. dept. radiology Meml. Sloan-Kettering Cancer Ctr., NY, 1999—; prof. radiology Weill Med. Coll. Cornell U., NY, 2000—. Hon. prof. U. Zagreb, 1997; vis. prof. ovr 30 instns. Author 20 books in field; assoc. editor, Jour. of Magnetic Resonance Imaging, 2001—, Radiology, 1998—, Jour. of Women's Imaging, 1996—, others; contbr. more than 280 articles to sci. and profl. jours. Recipient Marie Curie award, Soc. Women in Radiology, 2002, Beclere medal, 2005; grantee numerous grants in field, including NIH, Nat. Cancer Inst., Am. Cancer Soc., Dept. of Def.;, numerous hon. lectureships. Fellow Am. Coll. Radiology, Internat. Soc. Magnetic Resonance in Medicine (gold medal 2003), Soc. Uroradiology (corrs. mem., pres. 2001-03); mem. Acad. Radiology Rsch. (bd. dirs. 1997—), Radiol. Soc. N.Am. (chmn. pub. info. adv. bd. 1997-2002, bd. dirs. 2003—), Soc. for the Advancement of Women's Imaging (pres. 1997-99), Calif. Acad. Medicine (pres. 1999), Croation Acad. Sci. and Art (hon.), German, Radiol. Soc. (hon.), German Roentgen Soc. (hon.) Brit. Inst. Radiologists (hon.), Inst. of Medicine. Business E-Mail: hricakh@mskcc.org.

HRICIK, LORRAINE E., bank executive; m. Nicholas DeGuercio; 2 children. B in Math. and Computer Sci., Ind. U., Pa., 1973; MBA, Columbia U., 1991. With Securities Industry Automation Corp.; exec. v.p. Chase Manhattan Bank; exec. v.p., head Treasury Services J.P. Morgan Chase, 2004—. Mem. Chase Technology Governance Bd.; chair The Clearing House Interbank Payment Co. L.L.C. Adv. Bd.; mem Federal Reserve Bank of N.Y. Payments Risk Com., N.Y. Clearing House Steering Com.; bd. dirs. Internat. Ctr. N.Y. Inductee Academy of Women Achievers, YWCA, 1990. Office: Chase Manhattan Bank 270 Park Ave Fl 12 New York NY 10017-2089*

HRINAK, DONNA JEAN, lawyer, former ambassador; b. Sewickley, Pa., Mar. 28, 1951; d. John and Mary (Pukach) H.; m. Gabino (Lou) Flores, July 15, 1977; 1 child, Wyatt A. Flores. Student, George Washington U., 1971; BA, Mich. State U., 1972; Student, U. Notre Dame, 1973—74. Dep. prin. officer Am. Embassy, Mexico City, 1974—76, Warsaw, 1977-79, narcotics affairs officer Bogota, Colombia, 1979-81; regional affairs officer for C.Am. US Dept. State, Washington, 1982-84; dep. prin. officer U.S. Consultate Gen., Sao Paulo, Brazil, 1984-87; political counselor Am. Embassy, Caracas, Venezuela, 1987—89, dep. chief of mission Teguciagalpa, Honduras, 1989-91; dep. asst. sec. for inter-Am. affairs US Dept. State, Washington, 1991-93; coord. for policy Miami Summit of Ams., 1994; amb. to Dominican Republic US Dept. State, Santo Domingo, 1994—98, amb. to Bolivia La Paz, 1998—2000, amb. to Venezuela Caracas, 2000—02, amb. to Brazil Brasilia, 2002—04; sr. counselor, internat. trade & govt. affairs Steel Hector & Davis LLP, Miami, 2004—. Named one of Ams. Ten Outstanding Young Working Women, Glamour mag., 1985. Mem. Am. Fgn. Svc. Assn., Exec. Women in Govt., Inter-Am. Dialogue Fgn. Policy Assn. Avocations: reading mysteries, playing tennis, watching baseball. Office: Steel Hector & Davis LLP 200 S Biscayne Blvd Miami FL 33131-2398 E-mail: dhrinak@steelhector.com.

HRISAK, CAMI ANN, mental health therapist; b. Butler, Pa., Jan. 6, 1961; d. Donald Keith and Margaret Elaine Mullen; m. Robert Michael Hrisak, Sept. 26, 1981; children: Rachael Mae, Sarah Ann, Elizabeth Ranée. BA in Psychology, Clarion U., 2000; student, Case Western Res. U., 2005—. Cert. direct svc. worker Pa., 2004. Pastor United Meth. Ch., Emlenton, Pa., 1994—97; co-pastor Free Meth. Ch., Smock, Pa., 2000—02; therapeutic support staff Alliance Health Wraparound, Uniontown, Pa., 2002; mem. staff therapeutic support Regional Counseling Ctr., Oil City, Pa., 2002; case mgr., family therapist Family Links, Clarion, Pa., 2002—03; caseworker family svcs. Clarion (Pa.) County, 2003—. Adv. bd. Crisis Ctr., Oil City, Pa., 1994—97. Organizer parent vol. program Riverview Sch. Dist., Ohio. Mem.: Psi Chi. Republican. Avocation: stained glass work. Home: 10956 Rte 322 PO Box 63 Shippenville PA 16254 Office: Clarion Co Counseling Ctr 214 S 7th Ave Ste B Clarion PA 16214

HRNCIR, JENNIFER WELCH, elementary school educator; b. Columbus, Ga., Nov. 6, 1955; d. James and Betty Welch; m. Craig Hrncir, Mar. 6, 1981; children: Ally, Craig. Masters Degree, Columbus State U., 2004. Cert. tchr. Ga., 2006. Tchr. Muscogee County, Columbus, 1987—96, Harris County Bd. Edn., Hamilton, Ga., 1996—. Parent coord. Harris County, Hamilton, 1994—96. Educator Rosehill Ch. of Christ, Columbus, 1981—2006. Mem.: Phi Kappa Phi, Delta Kappa Phi (assoc.). Republican. Mem. Church Of Christ. Office: Harris County Board of Education Barnes Mill Rd Hamilton GA 31811 Office Phone: 706-628-4951.

HROMADA, LAUREN SPADA, athletic traniner; b. Medford, Mass., Feb. 19, 1975; d. Louis A. and Francine E. Spada; m. Eric M. Hromada, June 11, 2005. AS in physical therapy with honors, N.Shore CC, Danvers, Mass., 2000; BS Athletic Training, Salem State Coll., Mass., 1998. Cert. athletic trainer, lic. physical therapist asst., approved clinical instr., cert. CPR/First Aid 1995. Physical therapy aide Advance Physical Therapy & Sport Rehab., Lynn, Mass., 1999—2000, physical therapist asst., 2000—04; athletic trainer Danvers HS, Mass., 2000—03, Malden Cath. HS, Mass., 2003—; clinical instr. Salem State Coll., 2002—; physical therapist asst. Sports Aid Rehab./Hallmark Health, Malden, 2004—. Recipient Svc. Excellence award, Hallmark Health, 2006. Mem.: APTA, ATOM, NATA. Roman Catholic. Office: Sports Aid Rehab/Hallmark Health 18 Jackson St Malden MA 02148 Personal E-mail: spada1975@aol.com.

HRUBEC, JANE M., advertising executive; b. N.Y.C., Sept. 20, 1942; d. A. Andrew and Beatrice (Gaines) Hrubec. BA, Briarcliff Coll., 1963. Copywriter DeGarmo-McCaffery, Inc., 1966—69, Foote-Cone-Belding, Inc., 1969—71; copy supr. Ted Bates, Inc., 1971—73; assoc. creative dir. Ogilvy & Mather, N.Y.C., 1973—. Conf. speaker Woman Bus. Owners N.Y., Inc., N.Y.C., 1983—84. Contbr. articles to mags. Bd. dirs. Friends of Parks, Chgo., 1976—79. Recipient Gold Medal award Art Dirs. Club, 1980, Silver award Internat. Radio's TV Festival, 1981, Gold and bronze, 1984, Adweek All-Am. Creative Team award, 1983, Clio Best Regional Campaign, 1984, Big Apple Best Humor Radio, 1984, Big Apple Best Music Radio, 1984. Democrat. Presbyn. Office: Ogilvy & Mather 2 E 48th St New York NY 10017-1923

HRYNKOW, SHARON HEMOND, federal agency administrator, neuroscientist, researcher; BA in Biology, RI Coll., 1983; PhD in Neuroscience, U. Conn., 1990; postdoctoral studies, U. Oslo, Norway, 1990-92. Health/sci. officer Bur. Oceans and Internat. Environ. and Sci. Affairs US Dept. State, Washington, 1992-95; sci. policy analyst Fogarty Internat. Ctr., NIH, Bethesda, Md., 1995-97, spl. asst. office of dir., 1997-99, dep. dir., 2000—04, acting dir., 2004—. Mem. adv. bd. Nat. Coun. for Internat. Health, Washington, 1997. Contbr. articles to profl., peer-reviewed journals includng Jour. Neuroscience, Developmental Brain Rsch., and others; chief drafter on strategy and policy toward internat. HIV/AIDS, US Dept. State. Recipient Lette N. Sangstad award (rsch. stipend) Oslo, Norway, 1990-92, Order of Merit, King of Norway, 2005. Mem. AAAS (Sci., Engring. and Diplomacy fellowship 1992-94), APHA, Coun. Fgn. Rels., Am. Scandinavian Assn., Norwegian Soc. of Washington, Soc. Neuroscience, Women in Neuroscience. Office: Fogarty Internat Ctr Bldg 31 Rm B2C29 31 Center Dr MSC 2220 Bethesda MD 20892-2220 Office Phone: 301-496-1415. Office Fax: 301-402-2173. E-mail: hrynkows@mail.nih.gov.*

HSIA, IRENE YEE, electrical engineer; b. Chgo., June 10, 1963; d. Yu-ping and Ting-mei Hsia; m. George Ernest Antilla, Aug. 15, 1993; children: Katie An-yu, Sarah An-ning, Joshua An-hsia. BSEE summa cum laude, U. Calif., L.A., 1984, MSEE, 1986, PhD in Elec. Engring., 1991. Asst. U. Rsch. Libr. U. Calif., L.A., 1980—84, rsch. asst. Dept. Elec. Engring., 1984—91, tchg. asst. Dept. Elec. Engring., 1986—89; engr. Hughes Space and Comms., El Segundo, Calif., 1992—2000, Nanowave, Inc., El Segundo, 2000—02, Northrop Grumman Co., El Segundo, 2002—. Instr. Chinese Cultural Assn. So. Calif., Cerritos, Calif., 1982. Contbr. articles to profl. jours. Fellow, Dept. of Water and Power Sch., 1983—84, Grad. Opportunity fellowship, 1984—86; Mabel Wilson Richards scholar, 1981—83, Chancellor's scholar, 1980—81, Northrop fellowship, 1986—89. Mem.: Tau Beta Pi, Eta Kappa Nu, Phi Beta Kappa. Avocations: volleyball, basketball, dance, music, movies. Office: Northrop Grumman Co 1 Hornet Way El Segundo CA 90245

HSIA, SOPHIE S., language educator, researcher; b. Shanghai; came to U.S., 1973; d. Harvey J. and Helen (Tang) Hsia. MS, Georgetown U., 1976; EdD, Harvard U., 1989. Lectr., rschr. Free U. Brussels, 1978-83; lectr., instr., tchg. fellow Tufts U., Lesley Coll., Northeastern U., Harvard U., 1986-90; assoc. prof. City U. Hong Kong, 1991-97; sr. fellow, assoc. prof. Nanyang Tech. U., Republic of Singapore, 2000—01; online faculty doctoral program, mentor U. Phoenix Sch. Advanced Studies, 2002—, area chair rsch. EdD program, 2003—. Mem. acad. program coun. U. Phoenix, Ariz., 2002—. Rsch. grantee Hong Kong Govt., others. Home: 5555 N Sheridan Rd Apt 1816A Chicago IL 60640-1611 Personal E-mail: shsia376@aol.com. Business E-Mail: shsia@email.uophx.edu.

HSIEH, TSUI-HSIA, artist, educator; b. Chia-yi, Taiwan, 1946; arrived in US, 1986; d. Wan-jin and Moo-chin Hsieh. BA, Nat. Taiwan Normal U., Taipei, 1981. Founder Jay Yuan Tong Arts Sch., Flushing, NY, 1986—; prin., owner Jay Yuan Tong Art Gallery, Flushing, 2005—. One-woman shows include Taipei Provincial Mus., 1983, Nat. Mus. History, Taipei, 1984, Princeton U., 1995, St. John's U., 1999, Hsin-Chu Cultural Ctr., Taiwan, 2002; author: Tsui-Hsia Hsieh's Paintings, 1999. Named Disting. Art Educator, Ministry Edn., Taiwan, 1982. Office Phone: 718-591-5227.

HSU, APO (CHING HSIN HSU), conductor; b. Keelung, Taiwan, Republic of China, Oct. 7, 1956; came to U.S., 1981; d. Ying-Shyr and Yueh-Shur (Lin) H. BA, Nat. Taiwan Normal U., Taipei, 1980; MusM, Hartt Sch. of Music, 1984, artist diploma, 1985. Bassist Taipei Mcpl. Symphony Orch., 1979-80; piano instr. Kung-Jen Music Sch., Taipei, 1979-81; condr. Young People's Orch., Hartford, Conn., 1983-86; conductor Loomis Chaffee Sch., Windsor, Conn., 1985-86; asst. condr. Hartt Contemporary Players, Hartford, 1985-86; music dir. St. Cloud (Minn.) State U. Orch., 1986-91, Heartland Symphony Orch., Little Falls, Minn., 1988-91; condr., artistic dir. Women's Philharmonic, San Francisco, 2003—05; orchestra dir. Nat. Taiwan Normal Univ., 2004—; condr. in residence Bard Coll. Condrs. Inst., 2005. Music dir. Cen. Minn. Youth Orch., St. Cloud, 1989-91; condr. in residence Peter Britt Festivals, Jacksonville, Oreg., 1990-91; bassist St. Cloud Symphony Orch., 1987-90; Affiliate Artists/NEA condr. Oreg. Symphony, 1991-94; music dir. Oreg. Mozart Players, Eugene, 1991-97; artistic dir., condr. The Women's Philharm., 1997-2001; music dir., condr. Springfield (Mo.) Symphony, 1995; faculty Interlochen, summer 2002, Okla. Arts Inst., 2002. Named one of Outstanding Young Women of Am., Com. of Outstanding Young Women of Am., 1988; Chamber Orch. Series grantee, Central Minn. Arts Coun., St. Cloud, 1989, Faculty Improvement grantee, St. Cloud State U., 1987, 88, 89. Mem. Am. Symphony Orch. League, Condr.'s Guild, Am. String Tchrs. Assn., Pi Kappa Lambda. Avocations: movies, cooking, softball, travel, hiking.

HSU, CORNELIA WANG MEI-CHIH, education educator; arrived in U.S.A., 1969; m. Justin Chin-Chung Hsu, Dec. 29, 1973; 2 children. BS, Providence Coll., Taiwan, 1967; MS, W.Va. Univ., Morgantown, W. Va., 1971. High sch. math tchr. Tainan Girls Middle Sch., Tainan, Taiwan, 1967—69; instr. St. Pauls Coll., Lawrenceville, Va., 1972—73, Morgan State Univ., Balt., 1973—. Cons. Urban Inst., Washington, 1973; prin. Chinese Lang. Sch. of Balt., 1990—91. Dep. sec. Global Alliance for Democracy and Peace, Washington, 2002. Mem.: Math. Assn. Am. Avocations: ballroom dancing, gardening, singing. Office: Dept Math Morgan State Univ Cold Spring Ln Hillen Rd Baltimore MD 21251

HSU, GLORIA, piano educator; b. Taipei, Taiwan, Mar. 26, 1959; d. Robert and Anna Chieu (Lu) Hsu. Student, Juilliard Sch., 1970-75; BA, Hayward (Calif.) U., 1992. Cert. prof. music tchr. Profl. piano tchr. MTNA, Calif., 1992—. Fundraiser for Vietnamese refugees S.I. Orphanage, 1980. Appeared on World Jour. fundraiser for Vietnamese Refugees. Great Neck Symphony Soc. winner Tchrs. of Piano, 1972. Mem. Music Tchrs. Nat. Assn. Democrat. Christian. Avocations: listening to medieval music, reading culture and history books. Home: 3371 Isherwood Way Fremont CA 94536-3566

HSU, HELEN HUA, psychologist, consultant; b. Taipei, Taiwan, Feb. 12, 1974; d. Adam Chi Hsu and Linda Ker-ming Yang; m. Pruthipong A. Leelaluckanakul, May 3, 2003. AA, De Anza Coll., 1992; BA, U. Calif., 1995; MA in Psychology, Alliant U., 1998, PsyD in Psychology, 2001. Coord. sch.-based clin. programs Asian Cmty. Mental Health Svcs., Oakland, Calif., 2001—, clin. supr., 2002—; assoc. clin. psychologist Frugé Psychol. Assocs., Oakland, 2004—. Found. bd. mem. Chinese Am. Mental Health Network, Alamo, Calif., 2001—. Sec. Family Support Healthy Minds, Oakland, 2002—. Mem.: APA, Asian Am. Psychol. Assn. Office: Asian Cmty Mental Health Svcs 310 8th St Ste 201 Oakland CA 94607

HSU, KYLIE, language educator, researcher, linguist; BA, U. Mich., 1980; MA, Calif. State U., Northridge, 1994; PhD, UCLA, 1996. Lang. and math. instr. U. Mich., Ann Arbor, 1976-80; asst. to pres. Am. GNC Corp., Chatsworth, Calif., 1980-86, exec. v.p., 1986-93; instr. in Chinese UCLA, 1994-95; dir. Lang. Inst. Pacific States U., L.A., 1996-97; asst. prof. Calif. State U., L.A., 1997—2002, assoc. prof., 2002—, assoc. chair dept. modern lang. and lit., 2003, assoc. dir. Chinese Studies Ctr., 1999—, assoc. chair dept. modern lang. lit., 2003. Conf. chair Eng. Lang. Tchg. Conf., L.A., 1996; editor-in-chief Pacific States U. Newsletter, 1997; judge Chinese Poetry Recital Contest, L.A., 1997; manual evaluator Edwin Mellen Press, Lewiston, NY, 1998—; com. chair Chinese Studies Scholarships, 1999—. Author: (book) Discourse Analysis, 1998, Selected Issues in Mandarin Chinese Word Structure Analysis, 2002; assoc. editor: Multimedia Ednl. Resource Learning and Online Tchg., 2000—; contbr. articles to profl. jours. Named one of 2000 Outstanding Scholars of 20th Century, 2000; recipient Hon. Sci. award, Bausch & Lomb, 1976; fellow, State of Calif., 1996—97; Olive M. Roosenraad Meml. scholar, 1976—80, Vieta Vogt Woolfolk scholar, 1976—80, Lit., Sci. and Arts scholar, U. Mich., 1977—80, Alumnae Coun. scholar, 1976—80, Martin Luther King scholar, 1977—80, W. K. Kellog Found. scholar, 1977—78, James B. Angell scholar, 1979—80, Presdl. fellow/Rsch. grantee, U. Calif., Berkeley, 1996—97, Advanced Rsch. Lang. Acquisition grantee, U. Minn., Mpls., 2001, Regents-Alumni scholar, 1976—77. Mem.: IEEE (exhibits chair 1993), Assn. Linguistic Typology (scholar 1995), Am. Assn. Applied Linguistics (session chair 1995), Am. Coun. Tchg. Fgn. Langs. (panel chair 1997), Chinese Lang. Tchrs. Assn., Linguistic Assn. S.W. (organizer 31st ann. meeting), Phi Beta Kappa, Phi Kappa Phi. Office: Calif State U LA 5151 State University Dr Los Angeles CA 90032-8112 E-mail: kyliehsu@msn.com.

HSU-LI, MAGDALEN, singer, poet, painter; d. George Tze-Ching Li. BFA in Painting, Rhode Island Sch. of Design; attended, Cornish Coll. of Arts. Founder Chickpop Records, 1997—, Femme Vitale, Seattle Women's Music and Arts Coalition, 1997. Singer: (albums) Muscle and Bone, 1997, Evolution, 1998, Fire, 2001.

HTUN, MALA, political science professor; b. Honolulu, Aug. 23, 1969; d. Ko Moe Htun and Helen Juliette Muller; m. Douglas William Turner, Jan. 7, 2006. AB, Stanford U., Calif., 1991; PhD, Harvard U., Cambridge, Mass., 2000. Prof. polit. sci. New Sch. Social Rsch., NYC, 2000—. Bunting fellow Radcliffe Inst. Advanced Study, Cambridge, 2002—03; fellow Kellogg Inst. for Internat. Studies, Notre Dame, Ind., 2004, U. Tokyo, 2006—. Author: Sex and the State. Grad. fellow, NSF, 1994—99, internat. dissertation fellow, Social Sci. Rsch. Coun., 1997, dissertation fellow, Nat. Security Edn. Program, 1997. Mem.: Latin Am. Studies Assn., Am. Polit. Sci. Assn. (Heinz Eulau award 2005), Coun. Fgn. Rels. (internat. affairs fellow 2006—). Achievements include research in states and sex equality in 71 countries. Avocations: ashtanga yoga, alpine skiing. Office Phone: 212-229-5747.

HU, HUA-LING WANG, writer, historian; d. Kai-ting and Shui-yan Wang; m. Chia-lun John Hu; 1 child, Carl Chun-hui. BA, Tunghai U., Taichung, Taiwan, 1959; MA, U. Colo., 1962, PhD, 1971. Instr. U. Colo., Boulder, 1963—70; assoc. prof. Nat. Chiao Tung U., Hsin Chu, Taiwan, 1972—74, Nat. Chung Hsin U., Taichung, Taiwan, 1973—74, Tunghai U., Taichung, 1973—74; asst. prof. Denver U., 1977—78; editor Jour. of Studies of Japanese Aggression against China, 1990—95. Cons. Rsch. Ctr. Nanjing Massacre, Nanjing Normal U., 2004—. Author: (short stories and novelette) Destiny of Fate, 1992, Ginling Forever (Conventional Chinese characters), 1997, 2000, Ten Thousand days of Laughter and Tears, 1999, (rev. edit.) simplified Chinese characters, 2000, American Goddess at the Rape of Nanking: The Courage of Minnie Vautrin, 2000; contbr. articles to profl. jours.; appearance (documentary) Minnie Vautrin, 2003. Recipient medal of honor, Chinese Lit. and Arts, Taiwan, 1998. Mem.: So. Ill. Writers Guild, Assn. for Asian Studies. Personal E-mail: hualinghu@aol.com.

HU, YUINSIEN IRENE, obstetrician, gynecologist; b. Shanghai, May 28, 1918; arrived in U.S., 1947, naturalized, 1955; d. Zan Gaen Hu and Sing Yo Dien; m. Kuang Han Ronald Chang; 1 child, June Irene Chang. BS, St. John's U., Shanghai, 1940, MD, 1943; postgrad., NYU, 1958. Resident in ob-gyn. Gu Sye-Ming Hosp., Shanghai, 1944—47, State Infirmary, Providence, 1949—51, White Cross Hosp., Columbus, Ohio, 1951—52, Genesee Hosp., Rochester, NY, 1953—56, rotating intern, 1952—53; chief resident ob-gyn. dept. New England Hosp. for Women and Children, Boston; pvt. practice Tri County Meml. Hosp., Gowanda, NY, 1959—86; ret., 1986. Home: 211 S Grove St East Aurora NY 14052-2936

HUANG, ALICE SHIH-HOU, biologist, educator, virologist; b. Nanchang, Kiangsi, China, Mar. 22, 1939; came to U.S. 1949; d. Quentin K.Y. and Grace Betty (Soong) H.; m. David Baltimore, 1968. Student, Wellesley (Mass.) Coll., 1957-59; BA in Human Biology, Johns Hopkins U., 1961, MA in Microbiology, 1963, PhD in Microbiology, 1966; MA (hon.), Harvard U., 1980; DSc (hon.), Wheaton (Mass.) Coll., 1982, Mount Holyoke (Mass.) Coll., 1987, Med. Coll. Pa., Phila., 1991. Postdoctoral fellow The Salk Inst., San Diego, 1967; postdoctoral fellow dept. biology MIT, 1968-69, rsch. assoc., 1969-70; asst. prof. Harvard U. Medical Sch., 1971-73, assoc. prof., 1973-78, prof. microbiology and molecular genetics Boston, 1979-91, prof. microbiology in health scis. and tech., 1979-91; prof. microbiology and molecular genetics Harvard Med. Sch., 1979-91; dean sci., prof. biology NYU, N.Y.C., 1991—97; sr. councilor for external relations, faculty assoc. in bio. Calif. Inst. Tech., 1997—2006. Program dir. NIH-Nat. Cancer Inst. Instnl. Nat Rsch. Svc. award, 1957-90; mem. com. on Biol. Scis. Yale U., Conn., 1981-85; dir. Ctr. for Pediatric Viral Diseases as part of Program on Great Neglected Diseases, Rockefeller Found., 1984-87; mem. med. rsch. and devel. command adv. com. U.S. Army, Frederick,Md., 1989-92; mem. sci. adv. bd. Inst. Molecular Cell Biology, Nat. U. Singapore, 1985-2003; N.Y. Acad. Sci., 1993; 6th Hattie Alexander Meml. lectr. Columbia U., N.Y.C., 1981; Lee Kuan Yew disting. visitor Nat. U. Singapore, 1985; chair Found. for Microbiology, N.Y., 1993; acad. adv. com. Inst. Molecular Biology, Academia Sinica, Taiwan, 1994—. Mem. editl. bd. Intervirology, 1973-90, Archive of Virology, 1975-78, Jour. Virology, 1976-93, ASM News, 1982, Microbial Pathogenesis, 1985-90, Jour. Women's Health, 1992-96; assoc. editor Revs. of Infectious Diseases, 1978-89; contbr. articles to profl. jours. Trustee Waksman Found. Microbiology, N.Y., 1986—, Keystone (Colo.) Ctr., 1993-98, U. Mass., 1987-91, Johns Hopkins U., 1992—, Pub. Agenda, N.Y., 2001—, Rockefeller Found., 2004—; mem. bd. overseers Shady Hill Sch., Cambridge, 1987-89. Recipient Eli Lilly award in microbiology and immunology, 1977, Alumnae Citation award Nat. Cathedral Sch., Washington, 1978, Ann. award San Francisco Chinese Hosp., 1989, award for outstanding woman scientist N.Y.-AWIS, 1994; Burroughs Wellcome traveling fellow to Gt. Britain, 1979. Fellow Infectious Diseases Soc. Am., Assn. women in Sci. (Outstanding Woman Scientist award 1994); mem. AAAS, Am. Soc. Microbiology (pres. 1988-89), Am. Soc. Biochemistry and Molecular Biology, Am. Soc. Virology, Am. Acad. Microbiology, Soc. Chinese Bioscientists Am. (councilor 1997-98), Acad. Sinica, Phi Tau Phi. Office: Calif Inst of Tech Mail Code 1-9 Pasadena CA 91125 Office Phone: 626-395-3446.

HUANG, CHANG-YU, retired elementary school educator; b. Shanghai, China, May 23, 1943; arrived in U.S., 1985; d. Teh-Ling Huang and Yun-yi Xu; m. Yuan Han, Jan. 1, 1969; children: Joy Han, Liz Han. BA, Shanghai U., 1965; MA in Comparative Lit., Ohio State U., Columbus, 1984, MA in Math. Edn., 1986. Tchr. Kiang-Qing Mid. Sch., Shanghai, 1965—80; math. instr. Ohio State U., Columbus, 1984—86; math instr. Phillips Acad., Andover, Mass., 1986—2005; retired, 2005. Recipient award for Tchg., Frederick Beinecke Found., 2004; grantee Abbott grant, 1993, Kenan grant, 1995, 2003. Home: 39 Lane 168 Qing Tong Rd Pudnig Shanghai 201203 China

HUANG, LINDA CHEN, plastic surgeon; b. Ithaca, NY, July 24, 1952; MD, Stanford U., 1979. Office: 1601 E 19th Ave Ste 3150 Denver CO 80218-1220 Office Phone: 303-831-8400.

HUANG, WENDY WAN-JUOH, lawyer; b. Taipei, Taiwan, Aug. 3, 1966; came to the US, 1977; d. Tsung-Che and Sheree (Shen) H.; m. Kermit Marsh, July 6, 1996; children: Dermot, Connor, Morgan. BA, Cornell U., Ithaca, N.Y., 1988; JD, Boston U., 1992. Bar: Calif. 1993, DC 1994, NY 1994. Intern UN Com. on US-China Rels., NYC, 1986, Internat. Bus. Cons., Washington, 1987; asst. editor P.C. Mag., NYC, 1988-89; law clk. San Diego City Attys., Calif., 1990, US Atty.-So. Dist. NY, NYC, 1991, LA Dist. Attys., Calif., 1991; assoc. Law Firm of Kinkle, Rodiger & Spriggs, LA, 1992-94, Knapp, Marsh, Jones & Doran, LA, 1994-97, Burkley, Greenberg, Fields & Whitcombe, 1997—2000; chief gen. counsel Olen Cos., Newport Beach, Calif., 2000—05; exec. v.p., gen. counsel Crown Realty and Devel. Corp., Irvine, Calif., 2005—. Sec., chmn. Pacific Rim bd. govs. Calif. Chinese Bar Assn., LA, 1993—; judge pro tem, LA Superior Ct.; arbitrator LA County Bar Client Dispute Svcs.; legal cons. Sta. KPFK Radio, Voice of Am. Radio, Chinese Daily News. Writer, actress Words Across Cultures Theatre Co., LA, 1993; actress, dancer Bethune Theatre Danse, LA, 1993; editl. bd. LA Lawyer mag. Recipient Westinghouse Nat. Sci. Talent Search scholarship NSF, Washington, 1984; named a Superlawyer Rising Star, LA Mag., 2006. Mem. LA County Bar Inns of Ct., Orgn. Chinese Ams. (pres.), So. Calif. Chinese Lawyer Assn. (bd. mem.), Screen Actors Guild. Republican. Avocations: tennis, piano. Home: 8571 Edgemont Cir Westminster CA 92683-7216 Office: Crown Realty and Devel 18201 Von Karman Ave Ste 950 Irvine CA 92612 Office Phone: 949-567-5861. E-mail: whuang@crowndev.com.

HUBACZ, JOAN REBECCA, director, private school educator; d. Ernest Eugene and Alice Rose Waterman; m. Frank Hubacz Jr., Mar. 15, 1975; children: Jessica Rose, Daniel. BS in Math., U. Mass., Amherst, 1970, MS in Elec. and Computer Engring., 1983; MEd of Early Childhood Edn., Worcester State Coll., Mass., 1990. Computer operator Coughlin Elec. Co., Worcester, Mass., 1974—76; tchr. math. Mascenic Regional Jr.-Sr.High Sch., Greenville, NH, 1976—78; sr. tech. Sanders Corp., 1978—80; microwave design engr. Raytheon Co., Northboro, Mass., 1980—88; coach girl's basketball North Brookfield Jr. High Sch., 1995—96; owner, dir. Mad. Brook Acad., 1988—. Mem. North Brookfield CPC Coun., 1999—; treas. North Brookfield Soccer League, 1994—96; coach North Brookfield Youth Soccer, 1992—96, North Brookfield Youh Basketball, 1992—95; mem. Christian edn. com. North Brookfield Congrl. Ch., 1990—93, 2000—, tchr. Sunday sch., 1988—90. Avocations: kayaking, bicycling, rollerblading, skiing, reading.

HUBBARD, CARLA DAWN, secondary school educator; d. George Carl and Marjorie Joyce Ingalls; m. Mac Floyd Hubbard, June 24, 1978; children: Andrea, Jarred. EdB, Columbus State U., Ga., 1977, MEd, 1986. Tchr. Morgan County Sch., Madison, Ga., 1978—83, Harris County Mid. Sch., Hamilton, Ga., 1983—91, Harris County H.S., Hamilton, 1991—. Coord. Econ. Am. Alliance, Atlanta, 1985—; cons. Columbus State U., 2000—; review cons. Dept. of Edn., Atlanta, 2000—. Contbr. articles to newspapers. Chairperson Relay for Life Am. Cancer Soc., Harris County, 2005; chairperson Relay for Life, Harris County, 2006. Named Star Tchr., Ga. Dept. of Edn., 1992, 1996, 2006, Tchr. of Yr., 2006. Avocation: travel. Office: Harris County High Sch 8281 Hwy 116 Hamilton GA 31811 Office Phone: 706-628-4278. Fax: 706-628-4335. Business E-Mail: hubbard-c@harris.k12.ga.us.

HUBBARD, CONSTANCE E., language educator, piano teacher; b. Rapid City, S.D., Nov. 29, 1957; d. Charles Bruce and Helen Goodwin (Moorhouse) Crosswait; m. Todd Eugene Hubbard, June 1, 1991; children: Tobias Charles, Elizabeth Anne. BA in German, U. S.D., 1980; MA in German and English, U. Nebr., 1985. Tchr. German and English, Kimball (S.D.) H.S., 1980—81, Sundance (Wyo.) H.S., 1985—97; piano tchr. Hubbard Piano Studio, Sundance, 1990—2000; adj. instr. German and piano Black Hills State U., 2000—. Trustee Crook County (Wyo). Sch. Bd., 1998—2001; keyboardist Sundance Jazz Band, 1986—2001; accompanist h.s. choirs, 1985—; pianist, accompanist Spearfish UMC, 2001—; adj. German prof. Black Hills State U., 2000—; violinist Dakota Chamber Orch., 2001—. Actor: Sundance Cmty. Theater, 1987—97. Music dir., pianist United Meth. Ch., Sundance, 1988—2001. Mem. Am. Assn. Tchrs. German, Music Tchrs. Nat. Assn., Phi Beta Kappa, Alpha Lambda Delta. Democrat. Avocations: piano, reading, travel, music, violin. Home: 1407 Charles St Spearfish SD 57783

HUBBARD, ELIZABETH, actress; b. NYC; d. Benjamin Alldritt and Elizabeth (Wright) H.; divorced; 1 son, Jeremy Danby Bennett. AB cum laude, Radcliffe Coll.; postgrad., Royal Acad. Dramatic Art, London. Leading role: CBS daytime TV serial As the World Turns, 1984— (9 Emmy nominations for Best Leading Actress), NBC daytime TV serial The Doctors (Best Leading Actress Emmy), First Ladies' Diary (Best Leading Actress Emmy); appeared on Broadway in Present Laughter, Joe Egg, Time for Singing, Look Back in Anger, I Remember Mama (musical), The Physicists (Clarence Derwent award), others; appeared in off-Broadway prodn. Boys from Syracuse, Threepenny Opera (musicals); movie appearances include I Never Sang for My Father, The Bell Jar, Ordinary People, Center Stage; frequent guest TV talk shows. Former bd. dirs. Found. in Motion, U.S. Com. for Refugees, Women's Commission for Refugee Women and Children. Recipient Silver medal, Royal Acad. Dramatic Art. Mem.: NATAS (bd. govs.), AFTRA (former nat. bd. dirs.).

HUBBARD, ELIZABETH LOUISE, lawyer; b. Springfield, Ill., Mar. 10, 1949; d. Glenn Wellington and Elizabeth (Frederick) H.; m. A. Jeffrey Seidman, Oct. 27, 1974 (div. May 1982). BA, U. Ky., 1971; JD with honors, Ill. Inst. Tech.-Chgo. Kent Coll. Law, 1974. Bar: Ill. 1974, U.S. Dist. Ct. (no. dist.) Ill. 1974, U.S. Ct. Appeals (7th cir.) 1976, U.S. Supreme Ct. 1984. Atty. Wyatt Co., Chgo., 1974-75, Gertz & Giampietro, Chgo., 1975-81, Baum, Sigman, Gold, Chgo., 1981-98, Elizabeth Hubbard, Ltd., 1981-98, Hubbard & O'Connor, Ltd., Chgo., 1998—. Legal counsel NOW, Chgo., 1978-94, sec., 1977. Editor: Chgo. Kent Law Rev., 1970, Litigating Sexual Harassment and Sex Discrimination Cases, 1997—. Bd. dirs., mem. The Remains Theatre, 1985-94; com. mem. Dance for Life AIDS Found., 2006. Mem. Ill. State Bar Assn., Nat. Employment Lawyers Assn. (chair Ill. chpt. 1992-95, sec.-treas. 1997—). Home: 420 W Grand Ave Apt 4A Chicago IL 60610-4087 Office: Ste Six West 900 W Jackson Blvd Chicago IL 60607-3024 Fax: (312) 421-5310. Office Phone: 312-421-5960. Business E-Mail: ehubbard@hubbardoconnor.com.

HUBBARD, KIM, computer engineer; married; 2 children. BSEE. Computer engr. computational scis. divsn. NASA Ames Rsch. Ctr., 1994—. With USAF. Avocations: working out, hiking, cooking, jewelry making. Office: NASA Ames Rsch Ctr Bldg 269 Rm 190 Moffett Field CA 94035 Business E-Mail: khubbard@mail.arc.nasa.gov.

HUBBARD, MARGUERITE, retired elementary school educator; b. Elmhurst, Ill., Oct. 23, 1948; d. Edward C. and Mary Margaret Hinchley; m. Gary Lowell Hubbard, June 10, 1989; stepchildren: Audrey, Todd. BA, Elmhurst Coll., 1970; MS, U. Ill., 1975. Cert. tchr. music K-12 Ill., elem. tchr. Ill. Music tchr. Bellflower Sch. Dist., Ill., 1971—79, Belvidere Sch. Dist., Ill., 1979—, ret., 2003. Singer Rockford Cmty. Chorale, Ill., 1980—89, 1998—2000. Mem.: NEA, Belvidere Edn. Assn. (bldg. rep. 1996—), Music Educator's Nat. Conf. Avocations: reading, swimming, crafts, walking.

HUBBARD, NANCY, architecture educator; BA, U. Ill., 1968; PhD, Northwestern U., 1984. Lectr. Sch. of The Art Inst. Chgo., 1977—84; instr. Northeastern Ill. U., Chgo., 1986—87; vis. asst. prof. U. Wis., Milw., 1987—88, asst. prof., 1988—93, assoc. prof. dept. arch. Sch. Arch. and Urban Planning, 1993—. Prin. preservation projects Hubbard & Hubbard, Archs., Chgo., 1982—88; preservation cons., 1988—; mem. State Wis. Hist. Preservation Rev. Bd., 1988—91; bd. dirs. Frankl Lloyd Wright/State Wis. Heritage Tourism, 1991—93. Recipient Phalin/Field Enterprises prize for rsch., 1977, Fromkin Meml. grant and lectureship, U. Wis., Milw., 1990. Mem.: AIA Wis. (chair environ. edn. com. 1993—), Wis. Trust for Hist. Preservation (bd. dirs. 1992—), Assn. for Preservation Tech., Alliance for Hist. Landscape Preservation, Soc. Archtl. Historians. Office: Univ Wis Miw Sch Arch and Urban Planning PO Box 413 Milwaukee WI 53201

HUBBARD, RUTH, retired biology professor; b. Vienna, Mar. 3, 1924; arrived in US, 1938; d. Richard and Helene (Ehrlich) Hoffmann; m. Frank Twombly Hubbard, Dec. 26, 1942 (div. 1951); m. George Wald, June 11, 1958; children: Elijah, Deborah Hannah. AB, Radcliffe Coll., 1944, PhD, 1950; DSc (hon.), Macalester Coll., 1991, U. Toronto, Ont., Can., 1991, So. Meth. U., 1997, Clark U., 2003; LHD (hon.), So. Ill. U., Edwardsville, 1991. Lab. technician Tenn. Pub. Health Svc., Chattanooga, 1945-46; fellow U. Coll. Hosp. Med. Sch., London, 1948-49; Guggenheim fellow Carlsberg Lab., Copenhagen, 1952-53; rsch. fellow Harvard U., Cambridge, Mass., 1950-52, 54-58, rsch. assoc., lectr., 1958-74, prof., 1974-90, prof. emerita, 1990—. Vis. prof. MIT, Cambridge, 1972; cons. Boston Women's Healthbook Collective 1982—; Regents lectr. U. Calif, Berkeley, 2002. Author: (with Margaret Randall) The Shape of Red: Insider/Outsider Reflections, 1988; author: The Politics of Women's Biology, 1990, (with Elijah Wald) Exploding the Gene Myth, 1993, 97, 99, Profitable Promises: Essays on Women, Science and Health, 1995; editor: Women Look at Biology Looking at Women, 1979, Genes and Gender II, 1979, Biological Woman--The Convenient Myth, 1982, Woman's Nature: Rationalizations of Inequality, 1983, Reinventing Biology: Respect for Life and the Creation of Knowledge, 1995; contbr. more than 250 articles on sci. and women's issues to profl. and lay books and jours. Adv. coun. mem. Nat. Women's Health Network, Washington, 1980-85; bd. dirs. Coun. Responsible Genetics, Boston, 1982-2002, Boston Women's Health Book Collective, 1998-99; mem. adv. bd. Boston Women's Fund, 1983-85, 2000-02; mem. adv. bd. Civil Liberties Union of Mass., 1990-91, 95—, bd. dirs., 1991-95. Recipient Paul Karrer medal Swiss Chem. Soc., 1967, Peace and Freedom award Women's Internat. League for Peace and Freedom, 1985, Feminist Marathoner award Boston chpt. NOW, 1991, Disting. Svc. award Am. Inst. Biol. Sci., 1992, Luther Knight Macnair award, ACLU, 2005. Fellow AAAS; mem. Marine Biol. Lab. (trustee 1973-78, trustee emerita 1990—), Soc. Biol. Chemists, Nat. Women's Studies Assn., Phi Beta Kappa, Sigma Xi. Avocations: reading, music, yoga, swimming. Home: 21 Lakeview Ave Cambridge MA 02138-3325

HUBBS, VIOLET ELIZABETH SHAMBLIN, retired filmmaker, retired photographer; b. Charleston, W.Va., July 15, 1933; d. Charles Luke Shamblin and Lenora Edna Rust; m. Charles Taylor Hubbs, Nov. 21, 1953 (dec.); children: Elizabeth Romayne, Heather Hazlett, Holly Keith. Student, Case Western Res. U., 1951—52; AA, Mira Costa/Carlsbad Coll., 1957; Cert. in Motion Picture Arts, Brooks Inst., 1975; BA magna cum laude, UCLA, 1978, MFA, 1982. Singer, actress Camp Pendleton Marine Corps Band, Oceanside, Calif., 1952—53; tchr. drama Oceanside Parks & Recreation Commn., Oceanside, 1957; sec. The Jewish Hosp., Cin., 1960—63, US Atty. Gen., SW Ohio Dist., 1964—64; pub. rels. So. Calif. Mental Health Soc., L.A., 1979—80, Inst. Rational Emotive Behaviour, 1980—81; founder, pres. VS Hubbs Productions, Inc., 1978—. Singer: (performances) Camp Pendleton Marine Corps Band (First Woman Singer in any Marine Corps Band, 1952); singer: (actress) (ktla tv/kabc national radio performances) Marines in Review and At Ease; dir.(writer, producer, editor): (documentary) Lena - A Forgotten Minority. Vice pres. Nat. Assn. Gifted Children, Cin., 1964—67; chairwoman Jr. Women's Club Western Cin., 1966—68; chmn. Child Conservation League, Cin., 1967—69; docent William O. Douglass Outdoor Classroom/Santa Monica Mountain Conservancy, Beverly Hills, 1978—80; founding mem. WCET/PBS Action Auction, Cin., 1965—66; chmn. Cin. Summer Opera Gala, 1968—69; mem. PTA, 1960—70, Beverly Hills, 1975—83; woman's com. chmn. Cin. Symphony Orch., 1967—69; chmn. United Fine Arts Fund, 1967—69; hostess Nat. Governor's Conf., 1968. With USMC, 1952—53. Mem.: AAUW (assoc.), Women Marines Assn. (assoc.), Internat. Documentary Assn. (assoc.).

HUBER, SISTER ALBERTA, academic administrator; b. Rock Island, Ill., Feb. 12, 1917; d. Albert and Lydia (Hofer) H. BA, Coll. St. Catherine, St. Paul, 1939; MA, U. Minn., 1945; PhD, U. Notre Dame, 1954. Mem. faculty Coll. St. Catherine, 1940—, prof. English, 1953-97, prof. emerita, 1997, chmn. dept., 1960-63, acad. dean, 1962-64, pres., 1964-79, pres. emeritus, 2005. Trustee Avila Coll., Kansas City, Mo., 1986-97, St. Joseph's Hosp., St. Paul, 1971-80; pres. UN Assn. Minn., 1980-81; bd. dirs. St. Paul YMCA, 1986-92. Decorated Chevalier, Ordre des Palmes Acad.; recipient Outstanding Achievement award U. Minn. Alumni Assn., 1981. Mem. Phi Beta Kappa, Pi Gamma Mu. Office: Apt 111 1322 Alton St Saint Paul MN 55116 Personal E-mail: mthom17349@aol.com.

HUBER, ANNE MARRS, lawyer; BA magna cum laude, Marquette U., 1989; JD cum laude, U. Minn., Mpls., 1992. Bar: Minn. 1992, Ill. 1995. Atty. U.S. Trustee's Office, Mpls.; ptnr. Kirkland & Ellis, Chgo., 1994—. Recipient Transaction of the Year award, Turnaround Mgmt. Assn., 2004. Mem.: Chgo. Bar Assn., Ill. State Bar Assn., ABA, Phi Beta Kappa. Office: Kirkland & Ellis 200 E Randolph Dr Chicago IL 60601

HUBER, CHERYL S., music educator; b. Pa., Apr. 10, 1948; d. Gerald F. and Erma King Snyder; m. Carl W. Huber, Jr., Apr. 30, 1977; 1 child, Elysia Lord. BS, Susquehanna U., Selinsgrove, Pa., 1970. Tchr. music Johnson City Schs., NY, 1970—72, York City Schs., Pa., 1972—74; tchr. music, band and choral dir. Ea. York Sch. Dist., Wrightsville, Pa., 1977—. Musician (pipe organ recitals). Sec. NOW, York, Pa., 2001—06. Mem.: Am. Guild of Organists (bd. mem. 1981—83), Delta Kappa Gamma (local pres. 2002—04, state music com. 2003—05). Home: 2990 Lehigh Rd York PA 17402 Office: Ea York Sch Dist 300 Chestnut St Wrightsville PA 17368 Office Phone: 717-252-3676.

HUBER, JOAN ALTHAUS, sociology educator; b. Bluffton, Ohio, Oct. 17, 1925; d. Lawrence Lester and Hallie (Althaus) H.;; m. William Form, Feb. 5, 1971; children: Nancy Rytina, Steven Rytina. BA, Pa. State U., 1945; MA, Western Mich. U., 1963; PhD, Mich. State U., 1967. Asst. prof. sociology U. Notre Dame, Ind., 1967-71; asst. prof. sociology U. Ill., Urbana-Champaign, 1971-73, assoc. prof., 1973-78, prof., 1978-83, head dept., 1979-83; dean Coll. Social and Behavioral Sci., Ohio State U., Columbus, 1984-92; coordinating dean Coll. Arts and Sciences, Ohio State University, Columbus, 1987-92, provost, 1992-93; sr. v.p., provost emeritus prof. Sociology emeritus, 1994. Author: (with William Form) Income and Ideology, 1973, (with Glenna Spitze) Sex Stratification, 1983. Editor: Changing Women in a Changing Society, 1973, (with Paul Chalfant) The Sociology of Poverty, 1974, Macro-Micro Linkages in Sociology, 1991. NSF research awardee, 1978-81 Mem. Am. Sociol. Assn. (v.p. 1981-83, pres. 1987-90), Midwest Sociol. Soc. (pres. 1979-80). Office: Ohio State U Dept Sociology 300 Bricker Hall 190 N Oval Mall Columbus OH 43210-1321 Home: Apt 34 1864 Riverside Dr Columbus OH 43212 Office Phone: 614-292-8872. Business E-Mail: huber.3@osu.edu.

HUBER, MARIANNE JEANNE, art dealer, art appraiser; b. Amboy, Ill., June 9, 1936; d. John Francis and Jeannette Marie (Wurth) Faivre; m. Robert L. Huber, Oct. 3, 1959; children: Michael Robert, Stephan Louis, Edward Francis. BA, Cardinal Stritch Coll., Milw., 1958. 6th grade tchr. St. Andrew's Sch., Rock Falls, Ill., 1958-59; jr. high tchr. Garside Sch., Mexico City, 1959-61; art dealer, cons. Huber Primitive Art, N.Y.C. and Dixon, Ill., 1963—; founder, pres. New World Art Svcs., N.Y.C. and Dixon, Ill., 1993—. Lectr., cons. Primitive Art Soc., Chgo., 1987, Freeport (Ill.) Art Mus., 1993, Indpls. Mus. Art, 1994, Nprstk Mus., Prague, Czech Republic, 1995; participant Maya Meetings, Austin, Tex., 1985—. Author: Echoes of a Distant Flute, 1984; co-prodr., author (documentary films) The Cuna, 1980, Nebaj, Cotzal and Chajul, 1987, 2003 Maya Calendar, 2004 Maya Calendar, collector, organizer traveling exhbns. The Cuna, 1980—. Election judge Ogle County, Ill., 1993—; committeewoman Dem. Precinct, 2002—. Mem.: LWV, AAUW, Ethnographic Art Soc., Am. Appraisers Assn., Am. Soc. Appraisers, Am. Assn. Dealers in Ancient Oriental and Primitive Art, Phidian Soc., Ill. Dem. Women, Indpls. Met. Mus. Art, Internat. Platform Assn. (gov. 1993—2001), Delta Epsilon Sigma. Democrat. Avocations: hiking, wilderness camping, painting, piano, travel. Home and Office: 1012 Timber Trail Dr Dixon IL 61021-8934 Office Phone: 815-652-4196. E-mail: tellapple@yahoo.com.

HUBER, MARY SUSAN, music educator; b. Buffalo, Feb. 14, 1946; d. Floyd M. Zaepfel and Thelma Zaeptel; m. David Conrad Huber, Dec. 27, 1971; children: David Conrad Jr., Kevin Michael. BS in Music, Daemen Coll., 1969; MEd in Music, State U. Buffalo, 1971; M in Ednl. Leadership, U. North Fla., 1991. Elem. music tchr. Maryvale Sch. Sys., Buffalo, 1969—74, Lakeland Prep, Orlando, Fla., 1980—81, North Shore Elem., Jacksonville, Fla., 1981—85, Loretto Elem., Jacksonville, 1985—89, Mandarin Oaks Elem., Jacksonville, 1989—90; mid. sch. choral dir. Mandarin Mid. Sch., Jacksonville, 1990—. Contbr. articles to mags. and newsletters. Mem. citizens opinion rsch. forum County of Duval, Jacksonville, 1987; life mem. Duval County PTA, 1987—; mem. choir St. Joseph Cath. Ch., 1999—2002. Named Educator of Yr., Jaycee's, Jacksonville, 1987, Tchr. of Yr., Rotary, Mandarin, 1998. Mem.: Duval County Elem. Tchrs. Assn. (past elem. pres.). Republican. Roman Catholic. Home: 11068 Great Western Ln W Jacksonville FL 32257

HUBER, MELBA STEWART, dance educator, dance studio owner, historian, retailer; b. Tex., Oct. 1, 1927; d. Carl E. and Melba (Holt) Stewart; m. William C. Kinsolving Jr.; children: William Carey Kinsolving, Keith Brian Kinsolving; m. James M. Huber (dec.); 1 child, Melba Laurin. AA, Lamar Coll., 1946; student, U. Tex. Establisher, owner Melba's, Inc., McAllen, Tex., 1958—; founder McAllen (Tex.) Dance Theatre Co., 1970; tchr. Black Cmty. at Huston-Tillotson Coll., 1948—49. Columnist, tap amb. Internat. Tap Assn.; panelist St. Louis Tap Festival, NY Tradition in Tap, NY Tap Festivals. Columnist Tap Talk, NY Dance Pages, Dance and the Arts mag., 1988-97; columnist Tappin' In, Dancer mag., 1998—; prodr.: (broadway) Jelly's Last Jam. Recipient Plaudit award Nat. Dance Assn. Am. Alliance for Health, Physical Edn. and Recreation, 1970, Flo-Bert award N.Y. Com. to Celebrate Nat. Tap Dance Day, 1996, Savion Glover award St. Louis Tap Festival, 1998, Preservation of Our Heritage in American Dance award, Oklahoma City U., 1999, Women of Distinction award Detroit Tap Festival, 2000, Tradition in Tap Historian, Educator, Writer award 2005; named for Life Achievement in the Art of Dance and Gymnastics, presented Tex. Flag Tex. State Senate, 1997; honored by Savion Glover, 2006. Mem. Tex. Assn. Tchrs. Dancing (pres. 1973-74, honoree 1997), South Tex. Dance Masters Assn. (Mem. of Yr. 1989). Home: PO Box 3664 Mcallen TX 78502-3664 Office: Melbas Inc PO Box 3664 Mcallen TX 78502-3664 Office Phone: 956-686-1411. Personal E-mail: melhuber@swbell.net.

HUBERT, HELEN BETTY, epidemiologist; b. NYC, Jan. 22, 1950; d. Leo and Ruth (Rosenbaum) H.; m. Carlos Barbaro Arostegui, Sept. 11, 1976 (div. May 1987); 1 child, Joshua Daniel Hubert. BA magna cum laude, Barnard Coll., 1970; MPH, Yale U., 1973, MPhil, 1976, PhD, 1978. Rsch. assoc. Yale U., New Haven, 1977-78; rsch. epidemiologist Nat. Heart, Lung and Blood Inst., Bethesda, Md., 1978-84; rsch. dir. Gen. Health, Inc., Washington, 1984-87; sr. rsch. scientist Stanford (Calif.) U., 1988—. Peer rev. Am. Jour. Epidemiology, Am. Jour. Pub. Health, Chest, Jour. AMA (JAMA), Archives Internal Medicine; contbr. articles to profl. jours., chpts. to books. NIH grantee, 1997—. Mem. Am. Coll. Epidemiology, Soc. Epidemiol. Rsch., Assn. Rheumatology Health Profls., Phi Beta Kappa, Sigma Xi (grant-in-aid for rsch. 1978). Office: Stanford Univ Med Ctr 701 Welch Rd Ste 3305 Palo Alto CA 94304-1701 Business E-Mail: hhubert@stanford.edu.

HUBER WARREN, GRETCHEN, artist; b. Hartford, Conn. d. Donald Keith and Sally (Haley) Huber; m. Peter Aggaziz Warren, Apr. 7, 1994 BFA, Syracuse U., 1985. One-woman shows include Kennedy Studios Gallery, Brookline, Mass., 1990, Town and Country Club, Hartford, 1992, Davios, Boston, 1993, Smith-Klein Gallery, Boulder, Colo., 1996-, Copley Soc. Art, 2004, Gallery on Chase Hill, Kennebunkport, Maine, 2005, Wright Gallery, Cape Porpoise, Maine, 2006; exhibited in group shows at Lowe Art Gallery, Syracuse, 1985, Ellin Baker Gallery, Phila., 1985-87, Copley Soc., Boston, 1992—, Frame Dimensions Gallery, West Hartford, Conn., 1993, Cry of the Loon Gallery, Sebago Lake, Maine, 1993-94, Smith-Klein Gallery, Boulder, 1996—, Maine Art Gallery, Kennebunkport, 1997—, Wright Gallery, Cape Porpoise, 1986—, No. Colo. Artists Assn. Nat. Show, Ft. Collins, 1995, 96, Nat. Realists Exhbn., Springfield, Mass., 1997, Inst. Contemporary Art, Boston, 1997, Silvermine Art of the Northeast Ann. Show, New Canaan, Conn., 1997, Internat. Native Fine Arts Competition, Millbury, Mass., 1998 (purchase prize and second pl. award 1998), Powers Gallery, Acton, Mass., 2002, 2003, Ocean Edits., Kennebunk, 2002, 2003, Arts for Pks. Nat. Competition, 2000, 03, 04, 06; represented in permanent collections The Nature Arts Orgns. Mus., Millbury; featured artist Harvard Hist. Soc., 2004; contbr. illustrations to Readers Digest, 1986, 87, Soc. Illustrators Ann. Publ., 1986, 87, Best of Oil Painting, 1996; featured artist Artist's Mags. calender, 1998, Artist's Mag., 2002,; pub. by Leanin' Tree Greeting Cards, 1997—, Bloomin' Flower Cards, 1998—, Frontier Mag., 2003, Oil Painting Basics Mag., 2005, Arts For Pks., 2000, 03, 04, 06; featured in Carol Schwartz book Colorworks. Recipient Young Artists' award Temple Beth El, West Hartford, Conn., 1985, First Pl. Opaque Media award Longmont (Colo.) Artists Assn., 1995, 96, Best of Show award Louisville (Colo.) Art Assn. Nat. Show, 1996, Kent (Conn.) Art Assn., 1997; recipient Grumbacher award Wintonburg Art League, West Hartford, 1989 Mem. The Kennebunk River Club (Best of Show 1985), The Copley Soc. (head of art com.), The Boulder Art Assn. (Best of Show 1996) Avocations: collecting old gas station and grocery signs, collecting antique Christmas decorations, collecting E.T. movie parathernalia. Home: 209 Mount Vernon St Newton MA 02465-2516 Office Phone: 617-630-5667. Personal E-mail: ghwarren@rcn.com.

HUBLEY, ELIZABETH, Canadian senator; b. Howlan, Prince Edward Island, Can., Sept. 8, 1942; m. Richard B. Hubley; children: Brendan, Susan, Allan, Amos, Jennifer, Florence. Student, Prince of Wales Coll., Charlottetown, Nova Scotia Coll. Art and Design, Halifax. Dance tchr., Prince Edward Island; owner, artistic dir., choreographer Stepping Out, Prince Edward Island, 1980—; rep. old dist. of Fifth Prince Prince Edward Island Legis. Assembly, 1989—96; apptd. mem. Fed. Vets. Rev. and Appeal Bd., 1998—2001; senator The Senate of Can., Ottawa, 2001—. Mem. Prince Edward Island Coun. Arts; pres. Prince Edward Island Fiddlers Soc., Prince County Fiddlers; past pres. Kensington and Area Cultural Found.; founding mem. Kensington Step Dancing Festival. Liberal. Office: The Senate of Canada 351 East Block Ottawa ON Canada K1A 0A4

HUBLOU, ROSEMARIE See EDELSTEIN, ROSEMARIE

HUCAL, MICHELLE, editor; b. 1978; Degree in Journalism, Mich. State U., 2000. Assoc. editor Home Décor Buyer, Chgo.; editor Environ. Design + Constrn. mag., Troy, Mich., 2002—. Bd. dirs. US Green Bldg. Coun. Named one of 40 Under 40, Crain's Detroit Bus., 2006. Mem.: Am. Soc. Bus. Publ. Editors (Editorial Excellence award 2005). Office: Environmental Design + Contruction 2401 W Big Beaver RD Ste 700 Troy MI 48084 Office Phone: 248-244-1280. Office Fax: 248-362-5103. Business E-Mail: hucalm@bnpmedia.com.*

HUCKABEE, CAROL BROOKS, psychologist; b. Marion, Ohio, Aug. 2, 1945; d. William Richard and Marjorie (Beal) Brooks; m. Roy M. Huckabee, Dec. 22, 1967; 1 child, Lear Elizabeth BA, U. Colo., 1967; MS, NYU, 1982, PhD, 1985. Lic. psychologist, N.Y., Conn. Psychology intern Downstate Med. Ctr., Bklyn., 1982—84; staff psychologist Blythedale Children's Hosp., Valhalla, NY, 1984—86; dir. psychol. svcs. Arms Acres Hosp., Carmel, NY, 1986—88, cons., 1988—89; cons. psychologist Putnam Cmty. Hosp., Carmel, 1988—; pvt. practice Carmel, 1987—. Sch. psychologist N.Y.C. Bd. Edn., 1984— NIMH clin. tng. grantee, 1980-81, 81-82 Mem. APA, N.Y. State Psychol. Assn., Conn. State Psychol. Assn Democrat. Avocations: skiing, golf. Office: Carmel Psychol PC Stoneleigh Ave Carmel NY 10512

HUCKABEE, EBONY, counselor, director; d. Eddie and Rona Dawn Huckabee. BA, Emory U., Atlanta, 2002. Sr. counselor Atlanta Surgi-Ctr., 2003—05, dir. counseling, 2005—. Mem.: ACA (student mem.), Lic. Profl. Counseling Assn. Ga. (student mem.), Chi Sigma Iota. Avocations: reading, exercise. Office Phone: 404-892-9878.

HUCKEBA, EMILY CAUSEY, retired elementary school educator; b. Carrollton, Ga., Aug. 26, 1941; d. Edward Clark and Audie Farmer Causey; m. Dale Malloy Huckeba, Aug. 27, 1961; 1 child, Catherine Nan. BS Elem. Edn., West Ga. Coll., 1962, M Edn., 1977. 2nd grade tchr. Whitesburg (Ga.) Elem. Sch., 1962—63; 1st grade tchr. Ctrl. Elem. Sch., Carrollton, Ga., 1963—68; tchr. Roopville Elem. Sch., Ga., 1968—96, substitute tchr., 1998—. Mem. alumni coun. West Ga. Coll., Carrollton, 1991—93; pilot tchr. Whole Lang. Program Roopville (Ga.) Elem. Sch., 1993—95. Charter mem. Roopville Hist. Soc., 1984—; mem. The Ga. Trust for Historic Preservation, 2001—; organist, pianist Roopville Bapt. Ch., 1960—. Mem.: NEA, Ga. Ret. Educators Assn., Ga. Music Educators Assn., Carroll Heard Ret. Educators, Ga. Assn. Educators, Alpha Delta Kappa. Baptist. Home: 1135 S Hwy 27 Roopville GA 30170-2516

HUCKSTEAD, CHARLOTTE VAN HORN, retired home economist, artist; b. Garwin, Iowa, Jan. 13, 1920; d. George Loren and Esther Olive (Carver) Van Horn; m. Lowell Raine Huckstead (dec.); children: Karen C., Roger H. (dec.), Martha E., Paul R., Sarah S. BS, U. Wisc., 1942; BFA, Boise (Idaho) State U., 1989. Merchandising Montgomery Ward, Chgo. and Santa Monica, Calif., 1941-42; "Rosie the Riveter" WWII, Chgo. and Beloit, Wis., 1942-46; woman's editor Dairyland News, Milw., 1950-54; interior designer, cons., tchr. South Bend, Marshfield, Wis., Merced, Calif., 1952-69; extension home economist U. Minn., Rochester, 1973-78; dir. food svcs. Milton (Wisc.) Sch. Dist., 1978-85; artist, 1952—. Painting and sculpture. Vol. Idaho Genealogy Libr., 1994—99, Dakoto County Hist. Soc., 2000—05; treas. Wis. Food Svcs. Assn., 1980—85; leader/mem. Girl Scouts Am., 1934—78; bd. dirs. Rock County Hist. Soc., Janesville, Wis., 1979—84, Milton Hist. Soc., 1979—85. Mem. AAUW, Nature Conservancy, Idaho Hist. Soc. (vol. 1985-99), Idaho Centennial Art Group (sec. 1991, show chmn. 1992, historian 1993-95), Idaho Water Color Soc., Morrison Ctr. Aux. (vol. 1986-99, bd. dirs. 1992-93, 97-99, Auxilian of Yr. 1995), Boise State Alumni Assn., Audubon Soc., Ch. Women United (editor 1985-86), Sierra Club, Boise Art Mus., Wis. Alumni Assn., Friends of Hist. Mus. Boise, Dakota County Geneology Soc. Protestant. Avocations: reading, history, archaeology, theater, travel.

HUCLES, ANGELA KHALIA, professional soccer player; b. Va. Beach, Va., July 5, 1978; BA in anthropology, U. Va., 2000. Soccer player, midfielder U.S. Women's Nat. Team, 2001; mem. Boston Breakers, WUSA, 2001—03, San Diego Spirit, 2003—. Columnist women's sports Boston Metro, 2002. Named First Team All-ACC, 1996, 1997, 1998, 1999, Mid Atlantic All-Star, 1996, 1997, 1998, 1999. Office: US Soccer Fedn 1801 S Prairie Ave Chicago IL 60616

HUDACHEK-BUSWELL, MARY R., mathematics professor; b. Wurzburg, Germany; d. John W. and Anne H. Hudachek; m. Daniel F. Buswell, May 9, 2003; children: David A., Melissa M. BS in Math., Mary Washington U., Va., 1980; MS in Math., Auburn U., 1993. Instr. Okaloosa-Walton C.C., Okaloosa, Fla., 1987—91; tchg. asst. Auburn, Auburn, Ala., 1991—93; prof. Clayton State U., Morrow, Ga., 1993—. Author: (manual) Study World Guide to Interactive Math., 1998, Deluxe Skill Building Workbook, 1999. Grantee, Eisenhower Higher Edn. Mem.: Assn. Computing Machinery, Nat. Coun. Tchrs. Math., Am. Math. Assn. Two-Yr. Colls., Math. Assn. Am.

HUDAK, CHRISTINE ANGELA, nursing informatics educator, specialist; b. Cleve., Dec. 13, 1950; d. Ernest J. and Helen M. (Orovets) H. BSN, Case Western Res. U., 1974; MEd in Post-Secondary Edn., Cleve. State U., 1980, PhD, 1998. Cert. profl. health info. mgmt. sys. 2006. Pub. health nurse Vis. Nurse Assn. of Cleve., 1974-75; clin. preceptor physician's asst. program Cuyahoga Community Coll., Cleve., 1975-77; staff nurse MetroHealth Ctr. for Skilled Nursing Care, Cleve., 1977-78; staff devel. instr. The MetroHealth System, Cleve., 1978-82, instr. in continuing edn., 1982-85, health care analyst, info. specialist, 1985-87; coord. clin. info. systems tng. Metro Health System, Cleve., 1987-90, mgr. specialized instnl. progs., 1990-94; mgr. user support svcs. Metro Health Sys., Cleve., 1994-95; lectr., lead instr. nursing informatics Case Western Res. U., Cleve., 1995-98, asst. prof. nursing informatics and mgmt., 1998—, dir. Nurse Web, 2002—, assoc. prof., 2006—. Coord. MS in nursing informatics program Case-Western Res. U., 2002—; instr. in health care info. systems adult degree program Capital U., Cleve.; instr. div. continuing edn. Cleve. State U.; clin. instr. nursing info. systems Case Western Res. U., 1990, part-time instr. nursing info. systems, 1990-95. Mem. Am. Assn. Artificial Intelligence, Ctr. Profl. Ethics (charter), Ednl. Computer Consortium Ohio, Midwest Alliance for Nursing Informatics, Am. Nursing Informatics Assn., Hosp. Info. and Mgmt. Systems Soc., Nat. League for Nursing, Phi Delta Kappa, Pi Lambda Theta, Sigma Theta Tau. Office: Case Western Res U Frances Payne Bolton Sch Nursing 10900 Euclid Ave Cleveland OH 44106-4904 Office Phone: 216-368-6315. Business E-Mail: cah16@case.edu.

HUDALLA, KAREN, dean, director, court reporter; b. Chgo., June 11, 1951; d. Edward Mitchell Sr. and Stella Phyllis (Walenda) Kozak; m. Gregory A. Hudalla Sr., Dec. 23, 1972; children: Gregory A. II, Nicholas Mark. Cert. ct. reporter, Chgo. Coll. Commerce, 1980; cert. paralegal, Paralegal Inst., Phoenix, 1984; AS in Bus., Coll. DuPage, Glen Ellyn, Ill., 1994; BS, Ohio U., 1999. Cert. reporting instr. Tchr. Chgo. Coll. Commerce, 1980-82, South Suburban Coll., South Holland, Ill., 1999, Career Colls. Chgo./De Paul U., Chgo., acting dir. edn., acad. dean, 1980—; ofcl. ct. reporter Chgo., 1980—. Sec., owner K&G Svcs., Ltd., Downers Grove, 1975—. Cub scout leader Boy Scouts Am., Downers Grove, Ill., 1988-94; Resource Ctr. vol. Dist. 58, Downers Grove, 1988-92; tchr.'s aide vol. Burr Ridge (Ill.) Sch. Disst., 1986-88; bd. dirs. Burr Ridge Homeowners Assn., 1986-88, Near West Neighborhood Assn., Chgo., 1973-83. Mem. Nat. Shorthand Reporters Assn. (cert. ct. reporter). Avocations: reading, sewing, educational classes.

HUDDLESTON, BETH SIMPSON, middle school educator; b. Roanoke, Va., Oct. 13, 1950; d. Basil Poff and Alice Elizabeth (Falls) Simpson; divorced; children: Adam Ryan, Lucas Aaron. BS in Edn. with honors, Radford U., 1972. Cert. collegiate profl. tchr., Va.; nat. bd. cert. tchr. Tchg. asst. White Meml. Presch., Raleigh, N.C., 1973; tchr. Page County Schs., Luray, Va., 1973-78, 1984-86, 88-89, Winchester (Va.) City Schs., 1989—; pvt. music tchr. Luray, 1978-84; bus. mgr. A Veritable Wealth, Inc., Luray, 1986-88. Presenter in field; backstage coord. Queen's Command Performance-Apple Blossom Festival, 1993-2000, mem. coronation ball and ct. gifts com., 1993-2006; marketing agent Appalachian Artists; coord. pilot program Kennedy Ctr. and Satellite Ednl. Resources Consortium, History and Storytelling, 1998; chmn. English dept. Morgan Mid. Sch. Pub. VILTAS folk dance mag., 1993. Mem. Supt.'s Adv. Com., Winchester, 1995-97; mem. Va 4-H All Stars, 1968—; music steward United Meth. Ch., Luray, 1980-84; bd. dirs. AIDS Response Effort, Winchester, 1994-99; mem. Preservation of Hist. Winchester, 1990-2000; vol. Shenandoah Valley Music Festival, 1995—; asst. jr. dir. No. Va. Woman's Clubs, 1983-85. Named Outstanding Mem. Luray Jr. Women's Club, 1976, 78, Ednl. Programming award AIDS Response Effort, 1997, Stewart Bell award for excellence in edn., 2004. Mem. Va. Edn. Assn., Va. Mid. Sch. Assn., Apple Valley Reading Coun., Va. Poetry Soc., Assembly for Lit. and Culture of Appalachia, Winchester DAR (History tchr.), Phi Beta Kappa, Kappa Delta Pi. Republican. Avocations: writing, music, skiing, physical fitness, cooking. Office: Winchester City Schs 48 S Purcell Ave Winchester VA 22601-5557 Office Phone: 540-667-7171. E-mail: bethhud@shentel.net.

HUDDLESTON, VICKI JEAN, ambassador; b. San Diego, Dec. 13, 1942; d. Howard Stevens and Duane Louise (Dickinson) Latham; m. Robert Webb Huddleston, Jan. 31, 1970; children: Robert Stevens, Alexandra Duane. BA, U. Colo., 1964; MA, Johns Hopkins U., Balt., 1975. Chief econ. sect. Am. Embassy, Freetown, Sierra Leone, 1977-80, Bamako, Mali, 1983-86; internat. economist Dept. State, Washington, 1980-82, econ. officer Office of Mexican Affairs, 1982-83, country officer for Bolivia, 1986-89, dep. dir. Office Cuban Affairs, 1989-91, dir. Office Cuban Affairs, 1991-93; charge d'affaires Am. Embassy, Port au Prince, Haiti, 1993, dep. chief of mission, 1993-95; amb. Republic of Madagascar, 1995-97; dep. asst. sec. for Africa Dept. State, Washington, 1997—99; prin. officer US Interest Sect., Havana, Cuba, 1999—2002; US amb. to Mali, 2002—05; Charge d'affaires Am. Embassy, Addis Ababa, Ethiopia, 2006—. Dep. dir. Am. Inst. for Free Labor Devel., Rio de Janiero, Brazil, 1969-72, prog. officer, Lima, Peru, 1966-68. Vol. US Peace Corps, 1964-66. Am. Polit. Sci. Congl. fellow, 1988-89; fellow Kennedy Sch., Harvard U., 2005; recipient Disting. Honor award, Presdl. Meritorious Svc. award, several Superior Honor awards, Disting. Svc. award. Mem. Am. Fgn. Svc. Assn., Alumni Johns Hopkins. Presbyterian. Avocations: skiing, yoga. Office: Am Embassy Entoto Street PO Box 1014 Addis Ababa Ethiopia

HUDELSON, JUDITH GIANTOMASS, elementary school educator; b. Phila., May 11, 1954; d. Thomas Peter and Viola D. Giantomass; m. Bradley A. Hudelson, Jan. 30, 1993; 1 child, Joshua Bradley. BE, Millersville U., Pa., 1976, ME, 1979; EdD in Edn. Adminstrn., Widener U., Pa. Tchr. grade 3 Rothsville Elem., Lititz, Pa., 1976—77; tchr. grade 3 and 5 Beck Elem., Lititz, 1977—94; tchr. grade 5 Bonfield Elem., Lititz, 1994—. Com. mem. Pa. Dept. Edn., Harrisburg, Pa., 1992—2003. Author: (book) Metacognition and Journaling in Process Reading: Their Relationships to Comprehension and Motivation to Read, 1997. Mem.: ASCD, Warwick Edn. Assn., Pa. State Edn. Assn., Nat. Edn. Assn., Warwick Edn. Assn. for PACE (chairperson 2000—), Phi Delta Kappa. Democrat. Roman Catholic. Avocations: swimming, golf, skiing, aerobics, reading. Home: 5739 Pine St East Petersburg PA 17520 Office: Warick Sch Dist 101 N Oak St Lititz PA 17543 Office Phone: 717-626-3705.

HUDES, NANA BRENDA, marketing professional; b. NYC, Nov. 25; d. Harry and Anita Lorraine (Seiken) Richter; m. Barton Hudes, Sept. 2, 1958 (div. Sept. 1972); children: Layne A., Michael F., Meredith A. Student, Skidmore Coll.; BA magna cum laude, Pace U., 1974; MS with honors, Coll. of New Rochelle, 1976. Dir. mail mktg. mgr. Pergamon Press, Elmsford, N.Y., 1979-80, spl. sales mgr., 1980-81; mktg. mgr. Knowledge Industry Publs., White Plains, N.Y., 1981-82, Grolier Electronic Pub., Danbury, Conn., 1982-84, dir. mktg., 1984-86; mktg. mgr. R.R. Bowker, New Providence, N.J., 1986-88, mktg. dir., 1988-91, sr. dir. mktg., 1991-99. Tchr. social studies Rye Neck (N.Y.) Mid. Sch., 1978-79; pres. NH Assocs., Mktg. Cons., 2000-01; dir. libr. mktg. Columbia U. Press, 2001—. Dist. leader, county committeeperson Dem. Party, Matawan Twp., N.J., 1964. Home: 233 E 69th St New York NY 10021-5414 Personal E-mail: nhudes@mindspring.com.

HUDGENS, JEANNE ELLIS, advocate; b. Winston-Salem, Sept. 17, 1925; d. William J. and Cora N. Holland; m. Cornell Franklin Ellis, June 10, 1948 (dec. Oct. 1979); children: Cornell Jr. Ellis, Larry T. Ellis, Michael B. Ellis; m. Charles Edward Hudgens, July 18, 1981 (dec. Dec. 2000). BA, N.C. Ctrl. U., 1945; MA, Columbia U., 1969. Tchr. Mecklenburg County Pub. Schs., Charlotte, 1951—55, J.E. Wright H.S., Fredericksburg, Va., 1957—59; adminstr. Stamford (Conn.) Early Childhood, 1960—85; dir. Guilford County Head Star, Greensboro, NC, 1985—91; exec. dir. NAACP, Greensboro, 1991—. Mem. Child Care Study Commn., Norwalk, Conn., 1984—85. Recipient Edn. award, NAACP, 1996, Head Start award, Head Start, 1985, Presdl. Citation, Nat. Assn. for Equal Opportunity in Higher Edn., 1980, Letter of Recognition, Pres. Ronald Reagan, 1985, African-Am. Atelier Unsung Heroes award, 1995, State of Conn. Ofcl. citation, 1985; grantee No Puffing grantee, Moses Cone Long Cmty. Health Found., 2000. Mem.: Commn. on Status of Women (chair 1996—, Cert. 2000), Nat. Assn. Negro Bus. and Profl. Women (pres., Sojourner Truth award 1999), Lady Sertoma (pres., treas. 1987—, Sertoma of the Yr. 1990). Democrat. Baptist. Avocations: writing, music, travel, reading. Home: 3 Bent Oak Ct Greensboro NC 27455-3007 Office: NAACP 1200 E Market St Greensboro NC 27401

HUDGENS, SANDRA LAWLER, retired state official; b. New Orleans, Feb. 15, 1944; d. Avril Lawler and Peggy V. (Crager) Kelly; m. Adolfo DiGennaro, Oct. 20, 1967 (div. 1970); 1 child, Daniel Darryn DiGennaro; m.

Stanley Dalton Hudgens, Feb. 17, 1973; children: Stephanie Hudgens Cap, Richard Stanley, Michael Shane. Student, U. Nev., 1962-64, U. Grenoble, France, 1964-65, U. Aix-Marseille, Nice, France, 1965, U. Nev., Las Vegas, 1980-2000. Traffic ct. clk. III Clark County Juvenile Ct. Svcs., Las Vegas, 1965-71; planning commr. City of Las Vegas, 1988-92, chmn. planning commn., 1991-92; br. mgr. registration divsn. Dept. Motor Vehicles and Pub. Safety, State of Nev., Las Vegas, 1971-96. Rep. Weststar FCU, Las Vegas, 1988-96; advocate State of Nev. Employees Assn., Las Vegas, 1971-96; coord. State of Nev. team City of Las Vegas Corp. Challenge, 1987-90; dir. so. chpt. Am. Fedn. State, County and Mcpl. Employees/State Nev. Employees Assn. retirees AFL/CIO. Past treas., sec. Las Vegas Civic Ballet Assn., Las Vegas, 1987-93; treas. Women's Dem. Club Clark County, Las Vegas, 1996-97, pres., 1998; chmn., vice-chmn. United Blood Svcs. Adv. Coun., Las Vegas, 1993-96; chmn. 1st Ann. Flood Awareness Week, mem. adv. coun. Clark County Regional Flood Dist., Las Vegas, 1987-88; treas., sec., badge and advancement counselor Boy Scouts Am., Las Vegas, 1976-90; internat. living stones coord. Episcopal Diocese of Nev., 2002—. Mem.: Am. Bus. Women's Assn. (chmn. souvenir program Western Regional Conf. 1997), Commn. Ministries, Ret. Pub. Employees Nev. (v.p. 1999—2000, pres. 2000—01, 2002—04). Democrat. Episcopalian. Avocations: hunting, knitting, photography, rving, biking. Home: PO Box 2103 Dayton NV 89403-2103 Personal E-mail: hudgens@hotmail.com.

HUDSON, ANN ELIZABETH, music educator; d. Carl Louis Maxey and Gussie Lee Mobley; m. Dewitt H. Hudson Jr. (div.); children: Dewitt(dec.), Tony Dean, Eric Donald. BS, Fla. A&M U., Tallahassee, 1955; MA in Music Edn. magna cum laude, Tex. Woman's U., Denton, 1988. Music specialist post schs., Ft. Dix, NJ, 1957—58; choral dir. pub. schs., Ocala, Fla., 1968—69, music tchr., 1974—75, 1989—, Ft. Hood, Tex., 1969—72, post schs., Frankfurt, Germany, 1972—74, Killeen, Tex., 1975—76, pub. schs., Tallahassee, 1977—78, St. Petersburg, Fla., 1980—81; chmn. Elem. Music Tchrs., Killeen, 1980—82. Pvt. music tchr. Min. of music St. Augustine Episcopal Ch., St. Petersburg, 1989—92; dir. of drama Covenant Missionary Bapt. Ch., Ocala, 2005—. Grantee Stonecrest, Summerfield, Fla., 2004, Stonecrest Ladies Club, 2005, Stonecrest Women's Aux., 2006. Mem.: Marion County Music Assn. (pres. 1995—97, presenter 1998—2000), Music Educators Nat. Conf. Avocations: acting, reading, composing. Home: 45 Pecan Pass Ocala FL 34472 E-mail: sonataina1@cs.com.

HUDSON, BRENDA LOUISE, soprano, opera singer, vocal coach; b. Bronx, N.Y., Oct. 1, 1952; d. Jerry William and Doris Virginia Johnson; m. Winston Alexander Hudson, July 1, 1995; m. John Henry Pretlor (div.); 1 child, Raymond Aljon Pretlor. BS in Music cum laude, Adelphi U., Garden City, N.Y., 2001, BA in Social Sci. cum laude, 2001. Broadcasting tech. NBC-TV, N.Y., 1971—73, ABC-TV, N.Y., 1973—77, NBC-TV, N.Y., 1977—78, ABC-TV, N.Y., 1978—79, HBO, N.Y., 1979—2001; opera singer Palm Beach Opera Co., West Palm Beach, Fla., 2002—; dir. cmty. chorus City of Pembroke Pines, 2005. V.p. L.I. Singers Soc., Glen Cove, NY, 1989—93, Home Owners Assn. Bd., Pembroke Pines, Fla., 2001—02. Recipient scholarship, Chaperons Club, Bergen County, N.J., 1970, Choreography award, United Black Artists Cornell U., 1971, Social Svc., Meml. House Social Svc. Found., 1966, Fundraiser Com., Am. Diabetes Assn., 1993, Project Head Start Cert. award, Project Head Start, 1966, 1976. Mem.: Nat. Music Tchrs. Assn., Fla. Music Tchrs. Assn., Cornell Univ. Black Alumni Assn., Sickle-Cell Anemia Found. (vol.), Afro-Am. Hist. and Genealogy Soc., Spritualist Assn. of Great Brit. Episc. Avocation: genealogy. Home: 1881 NW 140th Ter Pembroke Pines FL 33028-2846 Office Phone: 954-450-4315. Personal E-mail: thbomjjg@aol.com.

HUDSON, CAROLYN BRAUER, application developer, educator; b. Durham, NC, Dec. 17, 1945; d. Alfred Theodor and Hildegard Franziska (Wolf) Brauer; children: Paul Benjamin, Joel Stephen. BS in Math., U. NC, 1967; MA in Forestry, Duke U., 1969; MS in Geology, U. SC, 1979, PhD in Geology, 1995. Assoc. dir. office rsch. and evaluation, asst. prof. NC Ctrl. U., Durham, 1970—72; rsch. assoc. Nat. Lab. for Higher Edn., Durham, 1971—72; tchg. assoc. U. SC, Columbia, 1973—74, tchg. asst., 1990—92, tchg. assoc., 1993—, applications analyst, 1999—; vis. scientist Geol. Survey of Can., Ottawa, Ontario, 1979—82; statistician SC State Govt., Columbia, 1997—98. Mem. SC Gov's Nuc. Adv. Coun., Columbia, 2001—; tech. coord. profl. women on campus U. S.C., Columbia, 2000—05. Contbr. articles to profl. jours., photos to books and juried exhibits. Vol. area pub. sch., 1978—93; leader Boy Scouts of Am./Scouts Can., 1979—95; vol. Congaree Nat. Pk., Hopkins, SC, 1999—. Named Scouting Family of Yr., Boy Scouts of Am., 1986, 1986; recipient Dist. Merit award, 1988, Silver Beaver award, 1991, Butterfield Svc. award, 1991, Shofar award, 1993, Profl. Devel. award, Profl. Women on Campus, 2000. Mem.: U. N.C. Alumni Assn. (life), Friends of Congaree Swamp (edn. com. 1996—2005, bd. dirs. 2005—), Women of Reform Judaism (v.p. 1975—76), Audubon, Sierra Club (nuc. affairs subcom. 2001—, computer chair 2003—05), Hadassah (life; bd. dirs. 1983—84, mem. Jewish cmty. rels. coun. 2006—), LWV. Democrat. Jewish. Avocations: hiking, music, travel, reading, photography. Home: 115 Arcadia Springs Cir Columbia SC 29206 Office: Univ SC Univ Tech Svcs 1244 Blossom St Columbia SC 29208 Office Phone: 803-777-2358. Business E-Mail: carolyn.hudson@sc.edu.

HUDSON, CHERYL L., communications executive; Pres. Intouch Comm. Group GlobalHue, Inc., Southfield, Mich. Recipient Outstanding Women in Mktg. and Comms. award, Ebony Mag., 2001. Office: GlobalHue Inc 26555 Evergreen Rd Ste 1700 Southfield MI 48076-4206

HUDSON, DAWN EMILY, food service company executive; b. Worcester, Mass., Nov. 27, 1957; d. Kenneth Dunlap and Nancy (Selin) Hudson; m. Bruce Kershaw Beach, Aug. 31, 1980. BA, Dartmouth Coll., 1979. Asst. acct. exec., acct. exec. Compton Advt., NYC, 1979-82; product mgr. Clairol, Divsn. Bristol Myers, NYC, 1982-83; acct. supr., mgmt. supr. ptnr. Tatham-Laird Kudner Inc., Chgo., 1983-86; mgmt. supr. grp. acct. dir. sr. v.p., mng. ptnr., exec. v.p. DDB Needham, Worldwide, Chgo., 1986-94; exec. v.p., dir. client svcs. DDB Needham Worldwide NY, NYC, 1994; mng. dir. D'Arcy Masius Benton & Bowles, NY; exec. v.p. sales and mktg. Frito-Lay (subs. of Pepsi), 1996—98; sr. v.p. strategy and mktg. Pepsi-Cola N.Am., 1998—2002, pres., 2002—. Mem. editorial bd. Dartmouth Coll. Alumni Mag., 1993—. Mem. Dartmouth Coll. Alumni Coun., 1993—, career counsel grads., 1979-88. Named one of 100 Most Powerful Women, Forbes mag., 2005, 2006, 50 Most Powerful Women in Bus., Fortune mag., 2006. Republican. Methodist. Avocations: avid tennis player, golf, skiing. Office: Pepsi Co North America 700 Anderson Hill Rd Purchase NY 10577*

HUDSON, KAREN ANN SAMPSON, music educator; b. Greenville, Mich., Nov. 1, 1946; d. Elton J. Sampson and Freda Sampson Grunwald; m. James Gary Hudson, May 23, 1970; children: Alexander E., Annemarie M., Elaine K., Veronica L. BA, U. Mich., 1968. Piano tchr. Karen Hudson's Piano Studio, Reno, 1994—. Lay Carmelite Little Flower Lay Carmelites, Reno, 1997—. Mem.: Nat. Music Tchrs. Assn., Autism Soc. Am. Democrat. Home: 2055 Severn Dr Reno NV 89503

HUDSON, KATE, actress; b. L.A., Calif., Apr. 19, 1979; d. Bill Hudson and Goldie Hawn; m. Chris Robinson, Dec. 31, 2000 (separated Aug. 2006); 1 child, Ryder. Co-head (with Kurt Russell, Goldie Hawn, Oliver Hudson) Cosmic Entertainment, 2003. Actor: (films) Desert Blue, 1998, Ricochet River, 1998, 200 Cigarettes, 1999, About Adam, 2000, Gossip, 2000, Almost Famous, 2000 (Golden Globe award for Best Supporting Actress, 2001), Dr. T and the Women, 2000, The Cutting Room, 2001, The Four Feathers, 2002, How to Lose a Guy in 10 Days, 2003, Alex and Emma, 2003, Le Divorce, 2003, Raising Helen, 2004, The Skeleton Key, 2005, You, Me and Dupree, 2006; (TV series) Party of Five, 1996, EZ Streets, 1997; exec. prodr.: (TV films) 14 Hours, 2005. Named one of Most Powerful People in Hollywood, Premiere mag., 2003.*

HUDSON, KATHERINE MARY, manufacturing executive; b. Rochester, N.Y., Jan. 19, 1947; d. Edward Klock and Helen Mary (Rubacha) Nellis; m. Robert Orneal Hudson, Sept. 13, 1980; 1 child, Robert Klock. Student, Oberlin coll., 1964-66; BS in Mgmt., Ind. U., 1968; postgrad., Cornell U., 1968-69. Various postitions in fin., investor rels., communications, gen. mgr. instant photography Eastman Kodak Co., Rochester, 1970-87, chief info. officer, 1988-91, v.p., gen. mgr. printing and pub. imaging, 1991-93; pres., CEO Brady Corp., Milw., 1994—2003, chmn. bd., 2003. Bd. dirs. CNH Global N.V., Charming Shoppes, Inc. Trustee Alverno Coll., 1994—; bd. dirs. Med. Coll. Wis., 1995—. Recipient Chief of the Yr. award Info. Week Mag., 1990, Athena award Rochester C. of C., 1992, WESG Breaking Glass Ceiling award, 1993, Sacajewea award, 1995; Lehman fellow N.Y. State, 1968; named Wis. Bus. Leader of Yr., 1995. Republican. Avocations: golf, fishing, creative writing. E-mail: knh53092@yahoo.com.

HUDSON, KELLY COLLEEN PATRICK, personal trainer, educator; b. Syracuse, NY, Jan. 26, 1970; d. Kevin E. and Joan B. Walsh; m. Brian Tyler Hudson, Dec. 29, 1998; children: Maggie Rose, Daniel Walsh, Nolan Mic Patrick. BS, Syracuse U., 1992; MS, Ohio U., Athens, 1996. Cert. athletic trainer Nat. Athletic Trainers Assn.; water safety instr. ARC. Head athletic trainer Flowing Wells HS, Tucson, 1996—99; orthop. asst., athletic trainer Orange Orthop., Calif., 1999—2002; athletic trainer St. Joseph Hosp., Orange, 2000—. Ct. apptd. spl. advocate CASA, Orange, 2001—05. Mem.: Nat. Athletic Trainers Assn., Toastmasters, Women's Book Club. Roman Catholic. Avocations: creating greeting cards, community and church activities. Office: St Joseph Hosp Stewart Ave Orange CA 92868 Office Phone: 714-781-3224. Personal E-mail: iceit@socal.rr.com.

HUDSON, KIMBERLY LYNN, music educator; b. Traverse City, Mich., May 23, 1970; d. Paul David and Linda Elaine Sayther; m. Jeffery Scott Hudson, May 7, 1994; children: Jaycie Kimberly, Jaelyn Kay. MusB, U. Minn., Mpls., 1992. Band dir. Wood River Hartford Sch. Dist. 15, Wood River, Ill., 1996—. Performer Edwardsville Mcpl. Band, Ill., 1998—2006. Recipient Excellence in Tchg. award, Emerson Electric, 2000. Mem.: Delta Kappa Gamma. Home: 531 West Lake Dr Edwardsville IL 62025 Office: Wood River Hartford School District 15 501 Lorena Ave Wood River IL 62025 Office Phone: 618-254-4355. Business E-Mail: khudson@madison.k12.il.us.

HUDSON, LINDA, health facility administrator; b. Tuscaloosa, Ala., Feb. 12, 1950; d. Elvin and Clara (Duke) Hudson; m. Charles Garrett Kimbrough, May 26, 1984. BS Edn., U. Ala., 1971; MS Psychology, U. So. Miss., 1984. Lic. profl. counselor. Recreational therapist West Ala. Rehab. Ctr., Tuscaloosa, 1971—72; flight attendant Delta Air Lines, Miami and New Orleans, 1972—80; pvt. practice psychotherapist Hattiesburg, Miss., 1984—, Atlanta, 1984—. Program dir. Eating Disorders Adventist Health Sys./Wedst, Atlanta, 1985-88, regional dir./cons., 1986-87, exec. dir. mental health svcs., 1988-89; owner Hudson Cons. Assocs., 1989—, nat. cons., 1986— Contbr. articles to profl. jours. Mem. Covington Jr. Svc. League, La., 1981-83; co-chmn. St. Tammany Rep. Polit. Action Com., 1980-81; coord. United Way of St. Tammany Parish, 1979-80. Mem. Am. Assn. Mental Health Counselors, Ga. Mental Health Counselors Assn., Soc. for Advancement of Sexual Health (advisor to bd.). Democrat. Avocations: interior design, antiques, swimming. Office: Bldg 29 Ste 300 1640 Powers Ferry Rd Marietta GA 30067 Office Phone: 770-426-5157. Personal E-mail: linh@mindspring.com.

HUDSON, PATRICIA ANN SIEGEL, psychologist; b. Louisville, Mar. 29, 1955; d. Roy John and Theresa (Preate) Siegel. BS in Human Svc., Pa. State U., Scranton, 1977, M in Psychosocial Sci., 1982. Field rep. Am. Cancer Soc., Bethlehem, Pa., 1978-80; teen dir. YWCA, Harrisburg, Pa., 1980-82; mgr. membership devel. AAUW, Washington, 1982-85; mgr. membership Boat Owners Assn., U.S. (BOAT/US), Alexandria, Va., 1985-88; asst. v.p. leadership and membership devel. Nat. Assn. Home Builders, Washington, 1988-95; prin. Siegel and Assoc. Internat., San Francisco, 1995—; founder and pres. Ctr. for Excellence in Assn. Leadership, San Francisco. Cons. in field. Contbg. author: The National Chpt. Partnership, 1993; co-author: Thriving on Change: Discovering the Power of Your Assn. to Affect Soc. Change, 1999; Beyond Membership Mktg.: Developing on Innovative Plan that Guarantees Results, 1999; Get Them Active! Using Icebreakers, Energizers and Summarizers to Enhance Group Productivity, 1999, Pathway to Leadership: Practical Approach to Cultivating Effective Leaders, 2004. Recipient Award for Disting. Svc. in Cmty. Psychology, Pa. State U. Harrisburg Campus, 2000. Mem. Am. Soc. Assn. Execs. (cert. trainer, presenter conf. and meetings 1990-95, bd. dirs. 1993-95, edn. com. 1995, charter chmn. chpt. rels. sect. 1993-95, award of membership excellence, 1992, cert. assn. exec. 1990). Avocations: reading, travel, walking. Office: 236 W Portal Ave # 782 San Francisco CA 94127-1423 Office Phone: 650-355-4094. Business E-Mail: info@cealweb.com.

HUDSON, RHONDA ANN, science educator; b. Cullman, Ala., Aug. 18, 1953; d. Mary W. Rodgers; children: Kimberly Lynn Melendez, David Bradley, Stephen Blake. BS in Edn., Athens State U., Ala., 1986; MA in Biology Edn., U. Ala., Birmingham, 1998. Cert. profl. educator Ala. Dept. Edn., 1986. Tchr. Decatur City Schs., Ala., 1988-89; sci. tchr. Morgan County Schs., Decatur, 1989—. Nat. field test pilot teacher-organisms Nat. Sci. Resource Ctr., Washington, 2000—03. Sunday sch. tchr. First Bapt. Ch., Decatur, 1976—82. Recipient Presdl. award For Excellence Among Sci. and Math Tchrs., Pres. Coun., 1995; grantee Nat. Sci. Tchrs. Conv., Amoco Chems., 1999, Ala. Dept. Edn., 2000; scholar, Athens State U., 1984—86; Sci. Edn. Tuition scholar, Ala. Dept. Edn., 1987, Tchg. scholar, Dupont/Monsanto Corps., 1994. Mem.: NEA, NSTA (assoc.), Ala. Aerospace Assn. (assoc.; leadership rep. 2004—05), Morgan County Edn. Assn. (assoc.; bldg. rep. 2001—04), Ala. Edn. Assn. (assoc.). Baptist. Avocations: scuba diving, gardening, reading, designing garden crafts. Office: Eva School 20 School Rd Eva AL 35621 Office Phone: 256-796-5141. Office Fax: 256-796-7108. Business E-Mail: rahudson@morgank12.org.

HUDSON, SHARON MARIE, communications executive; b. Chgo., Oct. 26, 1956; d. Lue James and Laura LaVerne (Mosby) H. AAS, Prairie State Coll., 1990; BA, Gov.'s State U., 1993, MA, 1995; EdD, No. Ill. U., 2001. Mental health specialist Elisabeth Ludeman Ctr., Park Forest, Ill., 1977-83; ins. agt. Met. Ins. Co., Chgo., 1983-84, Allstate Ins. Co., Park Forest, 1984-86; telemarketing rep. Progressive Mktg. Co., Hazel Crest, Ill., 1987-88; sales asst. AT&T, Chgo., 1988-89; customer sales rep. Ameritech, Chicago Heights, Ill., 1989-95, credit and collection specialist, 1995—2000, tng. mgr., 2000—; adj. prof. Gov.'s State U., University Park, Ill., 2001—. Participant PhD project, 1995; adj. prof. Lewis U., Romeoville, Ill., 2002—. Contbr. articles, mng. editor to univ. paper. Mem. Human Rels. Commn., Park Forest, 1992; mentor Project Choice, Country Club Hills, Ill., 1995; mem. Park Forest Youth Task Force, 1994-95; vol. Pub. Action to Deliver Shelter, Chicago Heights, 1993, 95. With Ill. N.G., 1976-79; co-chair Regional Action Project 2000, 1995. U.S. Academic Achievement All-Am. scholar Gov.'s State U., 1993. Mem.: NAFE, AAUW, ASTD. Baptist. Avocations: reading, walking, horseback riding, auto racing.

HUDSON, SUNCERRAY ANN, research and development company executive; b. San Francisco, Jan. 20, 1960; d. Charles Hudson and Nan Katherine (Coleman) Wagoner. BA, U. San Francisco, 1982; student, S.E. C.C., San Francisco, 1988; MA, U. Phoenix, 2005. Stock transfer clk. Bank Calif., San Francisco, 1983-85; prin. clk. U. Calif., San Francisco, 1985-87, adminstrv. asst. II, 1987-88, adminstrv. asst. III, 1988-95, adminstrv. analyst, 1995—; ind. dealer Nat. Safety Assocs., Inc., San Francisco, 1990-92. Art cons. Artistic Impressions, Inc., 1994—96; mem. Notary Pub. Commn., 1997—; shape rite distbr., 1997—99. Mem.: Nat. Coun. Negro Women, Acad. Bus. Officers' Group, Am. Soc. Notaries, Gamma Phi Delta. Avocations: donating to various orgns. and the homeless, rollerskating, reading. Office: U Calif Campus Box 0440 521 Parnassus Ave San Francisco CA 94122-2722 Business E-Mail: Suncerray.Hudson@ucsf.edu.

HUDSON-ZONN, ELIZA, nurse, psychologist; b. Monrovia, Liberia, Dec. 12, 1956; arrived in U.S., 1978; d. Hartzell Gleh and Joan Eliza (Roberts) Killen; m. Henry Clay Hudson, July 28, 1979 (div. Apr. 1985); 1 child, Kimberly Clayde; m. Mawuli Sonny Zonn, July 31, 1988; 1 child, Jewel Lorraine. BA in Psychology, BSC in Nursing, U. So. Miss., 1984. RN, N.J., Tex. Pvt. duty nurse Maxim Healthcare, Inc., South Orange, NJ, 1990—; critical care nurse Midpoint Profl. Agy., East Orange, NJ, 1988; supervising nurse Interim Healthcare, Inc., Morristown, NJ, 1990—; staff nurse Montclair Gen. Hosp., NJ, 1989—91; pvt. nurse Beth-Israel Med. Ctr., Newark, 1988—92; staff nurse United Children's Hosp., Newark, 1989—92; critical care nurse Nat. Staffing Assn. Inc., East Orange, 1988—2004; DON Med. Day Care Ctr., New Cmty. Extended Care, Newark, 2003—. Charge nurse Cmty. Psychiat. Ctr., Houston, 1993. Rural health vol. Red Cross Liberia, Monrovia, 1973—74; women's refugees health adv. Union Sierra Leone for Liberia, 1990—95; human rights adv. Movement for Justice in Africa, 1975—; coord., health svcs. dir. Liberian Cmty. Assn. N.J., 2001; membership recruiter Student Unification Party, Monrovia, 1975—76; counselor Providence Bapt. Ch., 1975, St. Elmo Bapt. Ch., 1982. Recipient Pub. Svc. award East Miss. Bapt. Women Conv., 1972; So. Bapt. Conv. scholar, 1978-84, Nat. Bapt. Conv. scholar, 1972-84. Mem.: Nat. Staffing Assn. Skilled Home Care Nursing, Suehn Acad. Alumni Assn. (founding mem. 1995). Democrat. Avocations: reading, writing, sports, decoration, antiques. Home: 64 Hillyer St Orange NJ 07050 Office: Nat Staffing Assocs Inc 134 Evergreen Pl East Orange NJ 07018 Office Phone: 973-675-1163.

HUDSPETH, ALMETRA KAVANAUGH, retired elementary school educator; b. San Antonio, Jan. 22, 1952; d. Wilbert L.D. Kavanaugh and Kathryn Kavanaugh Gray; m. Vernon Howard Hudspeth Jr., Aug. 17, 1974; children: Crystal LaShell, Almetra Joy. BA, St. Mary's U., San Antonio, 1974; M Edn., U. Incarnate Word, San Antonio, 1997. Cert. K-8 tchr. Tex. Tchr. Ave. D Elem. Sch. Killeen Ind. Sch. Dist., Tex., 1975—80; tchr. Graebner Elem. Sch. San Antonio Ind. Sch. Dist., 1980—2005; ret., 2005. Mem. various coms. Graebner Elem. Sch. San Antonio Ind. Sch. Dist., 1980—. Contbr. articles to profl. jours. Sunday sch. tchr. Rainbow Hills Bapt. Ch., 1988—, choir mem., 1988—. Scholar, St. Mary's U., 1970. Avocations: bowling, reading, gardening, computer games. Home: 2702 Oak Mill San Antonio TX 78251 Personal E-mail: almetra_h@yahoo.com.

HUEFNER, DIXIE SNOW, special education educator; b. Washington, Dec. 7, 1936; m. Robert Paul Huefner, July 30, 1960; children: Steven Frederick, Eric William. BA in Polit. Sci., Wellesley Coll., 1958; MS in Spl. Edn., U. Utah, 1977, JD, 1986. Clin. instr. dept. spl. edn. U. Utah, 1978-86; jud. clk. to hon. Stephen H. Anderson U.S. Ct. Appeals (10th cir.), 1986-90; vis. asst. prof. dept. spl. edn. U. Utah, Salt Lake City, 1989-90, asst. prof. dept. spl. edn., 1990—94, assoc. prof., 1994—99, prof., 1999—. Presenter in field. Contbr. articles prof. jours.; author: (book) Getting Comfortable with Spl. Edn.Law /Christopher-Gordon Pub., 2d edit., 2006; co-author: Edn. Law and the Pub. Sch./ Christopher-Gordon Pub., 1998. Apptd. to Utah State Bd. Edn. Adv. Com. on the Handicapped; bd. dirs., chair Utah Parent Ctr Mem. Utah Bar Assn., Coun. for Exceptional Children, Learning Disability Assn., Learning Disability Assn. Utah, Nat. Assn. for Retarded Citizens, Women Lawyers Utah, Edn. Law Assn. Office: U Utah Dept Spl Edn 1705 E Campus Ctr Dr Rm 221 Salt Lake City UT 84112-9253

HUEGEL, DONNA MARIE, historian, writer, artist, archivist; b. New Hampton, Iowa, Apr. 14, 1951; d. Herbert Henry and Marceile (Gilbert) Christoph; m. Leonard James Huegel, June 10, 1972; children: Eric Benjamin, Ryan Joseph. Student, Mount Mercy Coll., 1969—72, U. Iowa, 1974, Western Wis. Tech. Coll., LaCrosse, 1999. Writer Houston County News, LaCrescent, Minn., 1994—; mus. curator LaCrescent Area Hist. Soc., 1993—. Author: Many A Grove and Orchard--The Story of John S. Harris, 1994, (anthology) America's Heartland Remembers--Stories Before, During and After 9-11, 2001, 2002. Pres., chair PTA, Badger, Iowa, 1982—88; pres., chair art appreciation program Blanden Art Mus., Ft. Dodge, Iowa, 1982—88; sec. LaCrescent Area Hist. Soc., Minn., 1992—95. Named Edn. Vol. of Yr., Ft. Dodge Bd. Edn., 1988. Mem.: Writers' Group-LaCrosse, Wis., La Crescent Area Hist. Soc. Roman Catholic. Avocations: dance-skating, dance, singing, guitar, needlecrafts. Office Phone: 507-895-1857.

HUEHLS, FRANCES A., librarian; b. Biloxi, Miss., Feb. 26, 1951; d. Alfred A. and Stella F. Johns; m. Patrick N. Huehls, May 12, 1973; children: Ann C., Amelia M. BA in Biol. Sci., Ind. U., Bloomington, 1973, MLS, 1992, PhD in Higher Edn., 2001; MA in Philanthropic Studies, Ind. U., Indpls., 1998. Assoc. libr. Ind. U. Purdue U., Indpls., 2000—. Mem.: Assn. for Rsch. on Nonprofit Orgns. and Voluntary Action. Home: 668 E Brunswick Ave Indianapolis IN 46227 Office: University Library-2111 755 W Michigan St Indianapolis IN 46202 Office Phone: 317-278-2313. Business E-Mail: fhuehls@iupui.edu.

HUELSKAMP, WILLAMARIE ANN, artist; b. Covington, Ky., Sept. 16, 1959; d. Raymond Willabald and Elizabeth Louise Huelskamp; m. Ira Bennet Rubinfeld, Aug. 25, 1990; 1 child, Sonia Marie Rubinfeld. BS in Civil Engring., U. Utah, Salt Lake City, 1982, BFA, 1990. Artist Willamarie Inc., Salt Lake City, 1990—. Art tchr. Life Long Learning Program U. Utah, Salt Lake City, 1996—. 2-dimensional work on canvas, and paper, Today (Best of Show Utah Watercolor Soc., 2001), 2-dimensional mixed media, Thanksgiving (Ga. Watercolor Soc. Purchase award, 2001), 2-dimensional mixed media on canvas, Tulips/Home/ Pretty (Best of Show Utah Statewide Eccles Ctr., 2003), 2 dimensional painting on paper, Above City Creek Canyon (NW Watercolor Soc. award, 1993), 2-dimensional on paper, Circles, Spheres and Elipses (Watercolor West Juror's award, 1997), corporate and pvt. collections, Salt Lake Intenational Airport, Salt Lake C.C., The Entrada Country Club. Mem.: Utah Watercolor Soc. (assoc.). Avocations: yoga, ice skating, skiing. Office: Willamarie Inc 159 West Broadway #203 Salt Lake City UT 84101 Office Phone: 801-596-7026. E-mail: willa@aros.net.

HUERTA, DOLORES FERNANDEZ, labor union administrator; b. Dawson, N. Mex., Apr. 10, 1930; d. Juan and Alicia Fernandez; children: Celeste, Lori, Fidel, Emilio, Vincent, Alicia, Angela, Juanita, Maria, Elena, Ricky, Camilla. D. in Edn., U. of Pacific's Delta Community Coll.; PhD (hon.), New Coll. San Francisco, 1990, San Francisco State U., 1993, State U. of NY at New Paltz, 1999. Co-founder, first v.p. United Farm Workers of Am., Keene, Calif., 1962—. Co-founder, first v.p., bd. mem. Fund for the Feminist Majority. Recipient Martin Luther King award NAACP, Roger Baldwin award ACLU, 1993, Labor award Eugene V. Debs Found., 1993, Trumpeters award Consumers Union, Women First award YWCA, 1993, Ellis Island Medal of Freedom award; inductee Nat. Women's Hall of Fame, 1993; named one of three Women of the Year, Ms. Mag., 1998, 100 Most Important Women 20th Century, Ladies Home Journal. Office: PO Box 9189 Bakersfield CA 93389-9189*

HUERTA, MARY ZAPATA, English and foreign language educator; b. Monterrey, Nuevo Leon, Mex., Jan. 31, 1952; came to U.S., 1956; d. Encarnacio and Maria De Jesus (Diaz) Zapata; m. Rogelio Huerta, Dec. 8, 1974; children: Rogelio Gil, Gerardo, Angel De Jesus. BA, Our Lady of the Lake, San Antonio, 1974, MEd, 1980. Cert. provisional elem.-sociology, provisional elem.-gen., provisional bilingual, provisional kindergaten, Tex. Pre-sch. migrant tchr. South San Antonio Ind. Sch. Dist./Kindred Elem. Sch., 1975-77; kindergarten bilingual tchr. San Antonio Ind. Sch. Dist./J.T. Brackenridge Elem. Sch., 1977-92, grade level chair, 1982-84, acad. coord. tchr., 1989-91; first grade bilingual tchr. San Antonio Ind. Sch. Dist./Cotton Elem. Sch., 1992—. Mem. Kindergaten Ciirculum Com., San Antonio Ind. Sch. Dist, 1981, cooperating tchr. Alternative Cert. Program, 1986; cons. Intercultural Devel. Rsch. Assn., 1978, Pers. Evalution and Rsch. Systems, 1978, AVANCE Parent-Child Care Devel. Ctr., 1979, Harcourt Brace Jovanovich Pubs., 1985-86; panelist Conf. on Students at Risk, Tex. Edn. Agy, 1990; presenter workshops in field. Compiler anthology poetry, pub. Read-at-Home books Bright Start Publs., 1989. Active Leadership Edn., 1985. Recipient Outstanding Alumni award Our Lady of the Lake, 1990, Hall of Fame award Edgewood Ind. Sch. Dist., 1990. Mem. Nat. Assn. for Bilingual Edn.

(Bilingual Tchr. of Yr. award 1990, Nat. Bd. for Profl. Teaching Standards (vice chair 1992—), Tex. Assn. for Bilingual Edn. (panelist state conf. 1990, Bilingual Tchr. of Yr. award 1989), San Antonio Area Assn. for Bilingual Edn. (sec. 1993, Bilingual Tchr. of Yr. award 1988), San Antonio Fedn. Tchrs. (past del.). Avocation: embroidery.

HUETTEMAN, SUSAN BICE, writer; b. Crossville, Ill., Jan. 24, 1934; d. John Oren Fulkerson and Laverne Brown, adopted d. Francis Joseph Bice; m. Albert George Huetteman, June 12, 1956; children: Scott Christopher, Mark Bice. AA in Voice, Colby-Sawyer U., 1953; MusB in Voice, New Eng. Conservatory, 1956; MA in Comms., Goddard Grad. Sch., 1979. Owner Huetteman Studio, Iowa, Ohio, Nebr., Ill., and Mass., 1958—98, author, cons., 1966—; dir. arts, mgmt. cons. and tchr. voice Performing Arts Divsn. U. Mass., Amherst, Mass., 1977—98. Cons. mgmt. Nat. Guild Cmty. Sch. of the Arts, Englewood, N.J., 1995-98; Web site cons. Hallinan Consulting, Venice, Calif., 1998—. Am. Collection Masterpiece Theatre, Nat. Coun. Tchrs. English. Author: (poetry set to music) The Seasons, 1966 (Ohio State Archives 1973), (book and lyrics) The Hatch, Jeff Holmes composer, 1999; prodr. The Hatch, 1999; editor: Iowa Music Tchr., 1974-75; columnist: Valley Advocate, Amherst Bull., 1986-87; contbr. essays, articles, and poetry to anthologies and Web sites. Coord. Bike Safety U. Mass., Town of Amherst, 1977-79. Named Woman of Yr., Optimists, 1980s. Mem.: NAFE, Theatre Comm. Group, Soc. for Childrens Writers and Book Illustrators, Nat. Assn. Tchrs. Singing (pres. Western chpt. 1996). Avocations: water sports, walk races. Home and Office: 82 E Quail Run Charlestown RI 02813-2808 E-mail: shuett@cox.net.

HUEY, CONSTANCE ANNE BERNER, mental health counselor; b. Tacoma, Wash., Jan. 20, 1938; d. Julian Boyd Berner and Beatta Kathryn (Day-Berner) Schoel; m. Donn R. Huey, July 26, 1961 (dec. June 1990); 1 child, Jennifer Anne. BA, U. Wash., 1959, MEd, 1976; cert. alcohol studies, Seattle U., 1980. Cert., lic. mental health counselor, Wash. H.S. speech and Eng. tchr., Seattle, 1959—68; tchr., supr., adminstr. U. Wash., 1968—82; instr. in addiction studies program Seattle U., 1980—86; pvt. practice, 1980—. Cons. in field; guest speaker Bastyr U.; presenter and trainer in workshops and seminars; specialist in only children. Contbg. author: We Did the Best We Could, 1993; guest on radio talk shows. Mem. Am. Counseling Assn., Seattle Counseling Assn., Women's Mental Health Assn., Nat. Assn. Alcoholism and Drug Abuse Counselors, Washington Assn. Alcoholism and Drug Abuse Counselors. Avocations: gardening, walking, reading, travel, photography. E-mail: cbhuey59@msn.com.

HUEY, PEGGY J., communications educator, performing company executive; b. Lockbourne AFB, Ohio, Nov. 24, 1951; d. David Jonathon and Ann Eyman Knowlton. BA in Speech Comm./Theater, Miami U., Oxford, Ohio, 1973; AAS in Avionics Sys. Tech. and Aircrew Ops., C.C Air Force, Charleston, S.C., 1978; MA in English Edn., U. South Fla., Tampa, 1987, PhD in English Lit. and Drama, 1996, post doctoral in Speech Comm., 2004—05. E-4 USAF, 1974—78; airborne comm. tech. USAF Res., Charleston AFB, SC, 1978—81, aircraft load master, 1981—92, 1st sgt., 1994—2002; tchg. asst dept. English U. South Fla., Tampa, Fla., 1989—94; instr. dept. English U. Ala., Tuscaloosa, Ala., 1994—96; instr. and facilitator Command First Sgt.'s Acad. USAF Res., Warner-Robbins AFB, Ga., 1996—2000, Non-Commissioned Officer Leadership Devel. Program USAF Res., 1996—2002; lang. trainer Cendant Mobility, Chgo., 2004—05; adj. prof. speech U. Tampa, Tampa, Fla., 1998—2001, asst. prof. speech, 2002—. Program coord. Am. Heart Assn., Tampa, Fla., 1979—82, asst. exec. dir., 1982—85; mng. dir. Arts Fusion, 1985, Stageworks, 1996—; adj. instr. Hillsborough C.C., 1988—89, 2000—02; advisor English majors U. Ala., Tuscaloosa, 1994—96, trainer grad. tchg. assts. Norton Textra Connect, 1995, list mgr. and group leader Connect discussion group, 1995—96; instr. Am. Lang. Acad. U. Tampa, Fla., 2000; academic adv. com. U. Tampa, 2002—, chair academic adv. com., 2003—; presenter to profl. confs.; book reviewer in fields of medieval and Renaissance English lit. Contbr. chapters to books, articles to profl. jours. Mem. chmn. Grad. Student Union U. South Fla., Tampa, 1991—92. Named Joyce D. Keller Faculty/Staff Vol. of Yr., U. Tampa, 2006, commencement spkr., C.C. Air Force, Charleston AFB, 1997. Mem.: MLA, Voice and Trainers Assn., So. States Comm. Assn., Fla. Assn. Women in Edn., Assn. Theatre in Higher Edn., South Atlantic Modern Lang. Assn. (treas. women's caucus 1998—), Southeastern Renaissance Conf., Internat. Spenser Soc., Marlowe Soc. Am. Achievements include member of first all female crew USAF. Avocations: gardening, reading, jigsaw puzzles. Office: U Tampa 401 W Kennedy Blvd Tampa FL 33606-1490 Home: 1404 E Sligh Ave Tampa FL 33604 Office Phone: 813-253-3333.

HUFF, AMY M., art educator, artist; b. Augusta, Ga., Nov. 22, 1972; d. John Wynn and C. Kay Vintson Matlock; m. Matthew David Huff, June 19, 1993; children: David Alexander, Lauren Elizabeth. BA in Music Edn., Augusta State U., Ga., 1995. Cert. in music edn. pre-k-12, in art edn. pre-k-12 2005. Music tchr. Richmond County Bd. Edn., Augusta, Ga., McDuffie County Bd. Edn., Thomson, Richmond County Bd. Edn., Augusta, McDuffie County Bd. Edn., Thompson; art tchr. Columbia County Bd. Edn., Harlem, Ga., 2005—. Artist CSRA, 1990, piano instr., Ga., 91, muralist, 1997—. Musician: Harry Jacobs Chamber Soc., 1994. Relay for Life luminary chair Thomson Jr. Women's Club, 1999; corp. sponsor chair Am. Cancer Soc., 2001; chair McDuffy county Relay for Life Am. Cancer Soc., 2002; dir. vacation Bible sch. Ft. Creek Bapt. Ch., 2005. Grantee, McDuffie County Bd. Edn., 2002; Mary S. Byrd scholar, Augusta State U., 1990. Mem.: Music Educators Nat. Conf., Profl. Assn. Ga. Educators, Kilpatrick Bapt. Assn., Thomson Jr. Women's Club (3d v.p. 1999, regional Ga. dir. 2005—, Club Woman of Yr. 1999). Republican. Avocations: painting, piano, gardening, organ, French horn. Office: N Harlem Elem Sch 525 Fairview Dr Harlem GA 30814 Office Phone: 706-556-5995 330.

HUFF, HARRIET, art educator, artist; b. Tulsa, Dec. 24, 1949; d. Roy Robert and Barbara L. Huff; m. Addison A. Gooding, Sept. 30, 1982 (div. Dec. 16, 2005); 1 child, Vanessa Ann Gooding. BFA, Calif. Coll. Arts & Crafts, Oakland, 1972; MFA, Belford U., Humble, Texas, 1998. Profl. fine art master printmaker/artist Harriet Huff Fine Arts, Pukalani, Hawaii, 1972—; art instr. Philbrook Art Mus., Tulsa, 1972—73; owner-art gallery De La Grabadora, Santa Fe, 1973—75; art instr. Colo. Mountain Coll., Steamboat Springs, 1978—81; owner- art gallery The Intaglio, Steamboat Springs, 1978—82; art instr. Houston Watercolor Soc., 1988—89; art instr./continuing edn. Eanes Sch. Dist., Austin, Tex., 1994—98; art instr./interdisciplinary art chair Seabury Hall Secondary Sch., Makawao, Hawaii, 2000—. Bd. dirs., gallery dir. Houston Watercolor Soc., 1988—90; pvt. art workshops A Rm. with a View Art Gallery, Pukalani, Hawaii, 1987—; printmaking studio tech. Hui No'eau Visual Art Ctr., Makawao, Hawaii, 1998—; workshop presenter Hawaii Assn. Mid. Schs., Maui Ind. Sch. Tchrs., Maui, Hawaii, 2001—. Exhibitions include Okla. Ann./Philbrook Mus., Tulsa (hon. mention, 1975), one-woman shows include ColorKing, Upper Gallery, Wichita, exhibitions include Colo. Women Artist Invitational, Crested Butte, Northwest Colo. Artists, Steamboat Springs (winter show, 1st & 2nd Pl./ summer show, 1st Pl. graphics, 1980), Delta Prints, Drawing and Crafts, Ark. Art Ctr., Little Rock, Knickerbocker, NY, one-woman shows include 20 year retrospect, Steamboat Depot, Colo., exhibitions include Internat. Art Expo, Coliseum, NYC, Le Centre Internat. d'art contemporian, Paris, Four Clover Invitational, Houston, Northwest Colo., Steamboat (2d Pl. profl., 1986), AAUW, Auburn, Calif. (purchase prize, 1971), exhibited in group shows at 15year Profl. Retrospect, Williams Ctr., Tulsa, exhibitions include Houston Watercolor Art Soc. Ann., Women Caucus for Arts Membership, Houston, one-woman shows include Steamboat Strings, Colo., exhibitions include Urantia Internat. Conf., Snow, Mass., 1990, Flagstaff, Ariz., 1997, Estes Park, Colo., 2002, one-woman shows include Holy Land Series, Westlake Meth., Austin, exhibitions include Hui No'eau Visual Art Ctr., Maui, Maui CC, U. Hawaii Cmty. Traveling Show (Windward Artist Merit Choice for ceramics), Iowa Biennial Print, U. Iowa, Nat. Print and Drawing, Oklahoma City Art Ctr., Pratt, Venice, NY, Calif. Coll. Artist South Am. Traveling Exhibit, Catherine Lorillard Wolfe, NY (2d Pl., 1974, Bronze medal 1974, Ida Becker Award, 1979), AAUW, Evanston, Ill. (Hon. Mention, 1976), Crested Butte Arts and Crafts (Hon. Mention 1977/Best of Show 1978), exhibited in group shows at Field Contemporary, Santa Fe, exhibitions include 1st Telleride Blue Grass Music Festival, Colo. Co-chair bldg. fund Westlake Meth. Ch., Austin, 1997; bd. mem., gallery dir. Houston Watercolor Soc., 1988—89. Mem.: Catherine Lorillard Wolfe Art Club (assoc.), Hui No'eau Visual Art Ctr. (assoc.), Hawaii Watercolor Soc. (assoc.). Achievements include work selected for permanent collection, Philbrook Art Museum, 2003. Office: Seabury Hall School 480 Olinda Road Makawao HI 96768 Office Phone: 808-572-7235. Office Fax: 808-572-7196. Personal E-mail: harriethuff@yahoo.com. E-mail: hhuff@seaburyhall.org.

HUFF, MELINDA LOUISE, art educator; m. Dennis E. Huff, June 28, 1996; m. Thomas Allen Munson, Nov. 10, 1974 (div.); children: Miranda Lindsey Munson, Derek Thomas Munson. B in Art Edn., Northeastern State U., Tahlequah, Okla., 1970—74. Cert. Tchr. Okla. Dept. Edn., 1974. Elem. art tchr. Peters Elem., Union Pub. Schs., Broken Arrow, 1992—. Grantee, Northeastern State U., Broken Arrow, 2003; scholar, Northeastern State U., 1970. Mem.: NEA, Okla. Edn. Assn., Kappa Delta Pi, Sigma Tau Delta, Rho Theta, Alpha Chi, Delta Zeta. Office: Peters Elem 2900 West College Broken Arrow OK 74012-2100 Office Phone: 918-357-6759.

HUFF, REBECCA SUZETTE, psychologist; b. Rochester, N.Y., June 21, 1977; d. Roger Elwyn and Barbara Anne Huff. BA in Psychology and Comm. summa cum laude, Roberts Wesleyan Coll., Rochester, N.Y., 1999; MEd, Coll. William and Mary, Williamsburg, Va., 2000, EdS, 2002. Cert. sch. psychologist Nat. Sch. Psychology Cert. Bd., lic. pupil personel Va. Dept. Edn., cert. first aid and CPR Nat. Safety Cert. bd. Gymnastics coach Bright Raven Gymnastics, Rochester, NY, 1997—99, Williamsburg Gymnastics, Va., 1999—2002, Va. Internat. Gymnastics, Midlothian, 2002—06; sch. psychologist Colonial Heights Pub. Schs., 2002—. Supr. interns and practicum students, 2003—; presenter at profl. meetings. Editor: (newsletter) A Message from Your School Psychologist and Social Worker, 2004—06. Mem.: USA Gymnastics, Nat. Assn. Sch. Psychologists. Republican. Baptist. Avocations: running, soccer, dodgeball. Office: Colonial Heights Pub Schs 3451 Conduit Rd Colonial Heights VA 23834 Office Phone: 804-524-3445.

HUFF, SARA DAVIS, nursing manager; b. Moundville, Ala., May 16, 1935; d. George W. and Maggie A. (Callahan) Davis; m. Eugene H. Huff, May 21, 1956 (div. June 1992); children: John Davis Huff, Timothy Eugene Huff. RN, Druid City Hosp. Sch. Nursing, Tuscaloosa, Ala., 1956; BS, Oglethorpe U., 1980. CNOR. RN, oper. rm. Druid City Hosp., Tuscaloosa, 1956-58; asst. head nurse, thoracic cardiovascular St. Joseph's Hosp., Atlanta, 1958-60; charge nurse/open heart thoracic Emory U. Hosp., Atlanta, 1960-64, edn. coord. oper. room, 1974-75; oper. rm. supr. H. Egleston Hosp. for Children, Atlanta, 1964-73; nurse cons. Cons. Surg. Svcs., Atlanta, 1986-92; dir. surg. svcs. Northside Hosp., Atlanta, 1975-86; staff nurse oper. rm. Northlake Hosp., Atlanta, 1990-92; dir. surg. svcs. Atlanta Hosp., 1989-90, Newton Gen. Hosp., Covington, Ga., 1992—98; clin. resource mgr. Emory Dunwoody Med. Ctr., Atlanta, 2002—. Spkr. in field. Mem. AORN (nat. bd. dirs. 1980-84, gen. AORN nat. congress 1980, other coms.), ANA, Assn. of Oper. Rm. Nurses of Atlanta (Nurse of Yr. 1975), Atlanta Area Oper. Rm. Suprs. (chmn. 1973-75). Home: 2534 Warwick Cir NE Atlanta GA 30345-1632 E-mail: graceD8669@aol.com.

HUFFINES, MARION LOIS, academic administrator, language and linguistics educator; BA magna cum laude, Maryville Coll., 1963; MA, Ind. U., 1969, PhD in Germanic Linguistics, 1971; postgrad., U. Ill., 1969, postgrad., 1978, SUNY, Oswego, 1976, Georgetown U., 1985. Asst. prof. German Bucknell U., Lewisburg, Pa., 1971—77, assoc. prof. German and linguistics, 1977—88, prof. German and linguistics, 1988—, dir. linguistics program, 1975—84, dir. German program, 1982—84, chair dept. modern langs., lits. and linguistics, 1984—85, dir. writing program and writing ctr., 1987—98, dir. grad. studies, 1987—, dir. summer sch., 1990—98, affirmative action officer, 1993—2004, assoc. dean for spl. acad. programs, 1996—98, assoc. v.p. for acad. affairs, 1998—. Office: Assoc VP for Acad Affairs Bucknell Univ Lewisburg PA 17837

HUFFINGTON, ARIANNA (ARIANNA STASSINOPOULOS), writer; b. Athens, Greece, July 15, 1950; came to U.S., 1980; d. Constantine Stassinopoulos and Helen Georgiadis; m. Michael Huffington, Apr. 12, 1986 (div. 1997); children: Christina, Isabella. MA in Econ., Cambridge U., Eng., 1971. Syndicated columnist Tribune Media Svcs., 1995—; co-founder Detroit Project. Bd. mem. A Place Called Home, LA, Archer Sch. for Girls, Reform Inst.; adv. bd. Coun. on Am. Politics, George Washington Univ.; Independent party candidate for gov State of Calif., 2003. Author: The Female Woman, 1974, After Reason, 1978, Maria Callas: The Woman Behind the Legend, 1981, Picasso: Creator and Destroyer, 1988, The Gods of Greece, 1993, The Fourth Instinct, 1994, Greetings From the Lincoln Bedroom, 1998, How to Overthrow the Government, 2000, Pigs at the Trough: How Corporate Greed and Political Corruption are Undermining America, 2003, Fanatics and Fools: The Game Plan for Winning Back America, 2004, On Becoming Fearless:.in Love, Work, and Life, 2006; guest appearances on Larry King Live, Oprah, Nightline, Inside Politics, Charlie Rose, Crossfire, Hardball, Good Morning America, Today Show, McLaughlin Group, and the O'Reilly Factor, founder, writer a news and opinion web site including blogs written by more than 200 celebrities and leaders, including a feature called The Huffington Post, 2005— (Webby award and People's Voice award-Blog-Political, Internat. Acad. Digital Arts and Sciences, 2006), co-host (nationally syndicated pub. radio prog.) Left, Right & Center. Named one of 100 Most Influential People, Time Mag., 2006. First place, Funniest Celebrity in Washington standup comedy contest. Office: Arianna Online 1158 26th St PO Box 428 Santa Monica CA 90403 Business E-Mail: arianna@ariannaonline.com.*

HUFFMAN, AMIE MICHELLE BREAUD, science educator; b. Arlington, Tex., Mar. 24, 1974; d. Gary Paul and Susan Rae (Shook) Breaud; m. Timothy Huffman, June 10, 2000 (div. June 25, 2002). BS, U. North Tex., Denton, 1996. Cert. elem. tchr. grades 1-8 Tex., 1996, math. tchr. grades 1-8 Tex., 1996, sci. tchr. grades 4-8 Tex., 2003. Tchr. 1st grade Lewisville Ind. Sch. Dist., Tex., 1996—2002, tchr. sci. 8th grade, 2002—. Sci. adv. Southridge Elem. Sch., Lewisville, 1999—2002; chair sci. dept. Durham Mid. Sch., Lewisville, 2002—05, team leader 8th grade, 2003—05, Downing Mid. Sch., Lewisville, 2005—. Short-term missionary Yucatan The Village Ch. & Yucatan Evangelistic Assn. Recipient Faculty Mem. of Month, Durham Mid. Sch., 2004, Downing Mid. Sch., 2006; grantee, NASA, 2004. Christian. Office Phone: 972-350-1400. Personal E-mail: amiehuffman@yahoo.com.

HUFFMAN, CADY (CATHERINE ELIZABETH HUFFMAN), actress; b. Santa Barbara, Calif., Feb. 2, 1965; d. Clifford Roy and Lorayne Dolores (Rote) H.; m. William Healy, 1994. Pvt. studies with, Nathan Lam, L.A., 1983-85, Maria Gobetti, 1984-85, Bill Reed, N.Y.C., 1987-90, Fred Kareman, 1988. Actress Broadway plays La Cage Aux Folles, 1983-84, Big Deal, 1985, The Will Rogers Follies, 1991-93, Steel Pier, 1997, The Producers, 2001-03 (Tony award best actress in a musical, 2001, Drama Desk award outstanding featured actress in a musical, 2001); (off Broadway) Gemini, 1990, Italian American Reconciliation, 1990, As You Like It, 1989, The Baker's Wife, 1982, They're Playing Our Song, 1983, Jekyll and Hyde, 1989, Dame Edna: The Royal Tour, 1999-2000, Short Talks on the Universe, 2002, The Cartells, 2006, Plain & Fancy, 2006; solo show Cady Huffman: Live at Ars Nova, 2006; TV shows The Guiding Light, 1986, Another World, 1987, Pig Sty, 1995, Mad About You, 1995, Law & Order: Criminal Intent, 2001, Curb Your Enthusiasm, 2004; films Hero, 1992, Space Marines, 1996, Sunday on the Rocks, 2004 (also prodr.), Billy's Dad is a Fudge-Packer, 2004, Romance & Cigarettes, 2005, Twenty Dollar Drinks, 2006; appeared in Law & Order: Criminal Intent, 2003, Law & Order: Trial by Jury, 2005, Frasier, 2004; also appeared in more than 30 TV commls., 1985-90. Vol. recreational therapist The Lighthouse, N.Y.C., 1986-87 Recipient 3d Place award Pacific REgional Ballet Assn., 1980. Avocations: piano, swimming, dance, singing.*

HUFFMAN, CAROL CICOLANI, retired educational association administrator; b. Mansfield, Ohio, Apr. 12, 1950; d. John Joseph and Donna Mae Cicolani; m. Philip Dean Huffman, Aug. 29, 1970; 1 child, Nathan Curtiss. MusB in Edn., Ind. U., Bloomington, 1973; MA in Edn., Baldwin-Wallace Coll., Berea, OH, 1988; post grad., 2003—. Master of Orff Schulwerk Memphis State U. Dept. of Music/Tenn., 1981. Pres. greater Cleve. chapt. Am. Orff Schulwerk Assn., Cleve., 1980—81; regional rep. Am. Orff-Schulwerk Assn., 1983—85, nat. conf. chairperson Chgo., 1986—88, nat. interim treas., 1997—98, v.p., 1999—2001, pres., 2001—03, past pres., 2003—, chairperson of undergraduate music curriculum reform com., 2003—04, ret., 2004. Workshop clinician AOSA Local Chapters, 1973—; elem. music tchr. Parma (Ohio) City Schools, 1974—2006; adj. prof. Hofstra U., Hempstead, NY, 1990—; supr. of student teachers Baldwin-Wallace Coll., Berea, Ohio, 1998—; workshop cons. Kennedy Ctr. For the Performing Arts, Washington, 1999—; guest condr. Chorister's Guild; guest tchr., Dalian, China, 2004. Composer: Share The Music (Supt. Commendation for Outstanding Tchg., 1997); co-author: Spotlight on Music; contbr. chapters to books, articles to profl. jours. Lay vol. Vol. Optometric Svcs. to Humanity, Ukraine, 1995. Named Outstanding Tchr. of Dist., 1991; recipient Martha Holden Jennings Found. Distinctive Tchg. award, 1997; grantee, Ohio, 1976.

HUFFMAN, CAROL KOSTER, retired middle school educator; b. L.I., N.Y., Nov. 4, 1933; d. Harry C., Jr. and Mary M. (Wilchin) Koster; m. William Leslie Huffman; children: John Michael, Laura Huffman Tek; children: Eric Kjell Thompsen, Lauren Kristina Thompsen. BS, Hofstra U., 1954, MS, 1967. Cert. elem., art, nursery and spl. edn. tchr. N.Y., advanced Irlen screener I and area coord. Dir. Child's World Sch., New Orleans; in-svc. instr. Half Hollow Hills Schs., Dix Hills, NY, resource, self-contained program, art and learning strategies tchr.; instr. in spl. edn. Hofstra U., Hempstead, NY; cons. curriculum, spl. edn. and reading. Rschr. identification and ednl. accomodations students with visual disabilities affecting schoolwork. Editor: The Communicator, The Phoenix, Williamsburg Directory Sect., 2000—05. Former del. N.Y. State Retirement Sys.; former bd. dirs. Win-Gate Village Club, Orlando, Fla.; chair Neighborhood Beautification Grant Com., 2002—05. Recipient award, Orange County, Fla., 2001—02, 2002—04. Mem.: AFT, Half Hollow Hills Tchr. Assn., N.Y. State United Tchrs., Half Hollow Hills Active Ret. Tchrs. Assn., Am. Assn. Tchrs. Rschrs. Those with Augsberger Syndrome, Kappa Delta Pi, Kappa Pi.

HUFFMAN, CATHY LILLEY, gifted and talented educator, special education educator; b. Mt. Kisco, N.Y., June 22, 1962; d. Charles Francis and Christine Larkin Lilley; m. Arthur Mark Huffman, June 18, 1994; children: Austin, Larkin. BS, U. N.Y., Buffalo, 1984; M in Edn., U. Houston, 1990. Cert. spl. edn. K-3 tchr. N.Y., K-6 tchr. Conn., K-8 tchr. Tex. Tchr. for gifted Westport Pub. Schs., Conn., 1985—; adj. prof. U. Bridgeport, Conn., 2006; tchr. of gifted Kate Pub. Schs., Tex.; tchr. Spring Woods Mid. Sch., Houston; spl. edn. tchr. Meml. Mid. Sch., Houston, BOCES, North Collins, NY. Edn. cons. Mindchallenge Consulting, Newtown, Conn., 1995—; adj. prof. U. Bridgeport, Conn., 1995—; presentor Nat. Conf. for Gifted, 1995—. Mem.: Nat. Assn. for Gifted Conn., Conn. Assn. for Gifted. Avocations: reading, travel. Home: 751 Morningside Dr S Westport CT 06880

HUFFMAN, CINDY KAY, elementary school educator; b. Hammond, Ind., Sept. 18, 1955; d. Bernal and Nedra Story; m. Robert Gene Huffman, Aug. 17, 1979; 1 child, Alan Matthew. MEd, Ind. State U., Terre Haute, 0190. Tchr./coach Franklin Twp. Sch. Corp., Indpls., 1979—. Tchr. Sunday sch. Greenwood Christian Ch., Ind., 1997—. Grantee, Franklin Twp. Edn. Found., 2000—06. Mem.: IAHPERD (Ind. State Elem. PE Tchr. of Yr. 2005). Home: 1584 Olive Branch Lane Greenwood IN 46143 Office: Wanamaker Elem Sch 4150 Bazil Ave Indianapolis IN 46239 Office Phone: 317-862-4100. Personal E-mail: huffman732@aol.com. Business E-Mail: cindy.huffman@ftcsc.k12.in.us.

HUFFMAN, FELICITY (FLICKA HUFFMAN), actress; b. Bedford, NY, Dec. 9, 1962; m. H. William Macy, Sept. 6, 1997; children: Sofia Grace, Georgia Grace. BFA in Drama, NYU, Tisch Sch. Arts, 1988. Actress (TV films) A Home Run for Love, 1978, Lip Service, 1988, Golden Years, 1991, Quicksand:No Escape, 1992, The Water Engine, 1992, The Heart of Justice, 1993, Harrison: Cry of the City, 1996, The Underworld, 1997, A Slight Case of Murder, 1999, Snap Decision, 2001, The Heart Department, 2001, Path to War, 2002, Reversible Errors, 2004, (films) Things Change, Reversal of Fortune, 1990, Hackers, 1995, The Spanish Prisoner, 1997, Magnolia, 1999, House Hunting, 2003, Raising Helen, 2004, Christmas with the Kranks, 2004, Transamerica, 2005 (Best Actress, Nat. Bd. Review, 2005, Best Performance by an Actress in a Motion Picture-Drama, Hollywood Fgn. Press Assn. (Golden Globe award), 2006, Best Female Lead, Independent Spirit award, 2006), (TV series) Bedtime, 1996, Sports Night, 1998, Desperate Housewives, 2004— (co-recipient, Outstanding Performance by an Ensemble in a Comedy Series, Screen Actors Guild award, 2005, 2006, Outstanding Lead Actress in a Comedy Series, Emmy award, 2005, Outstanding Performance by a Female Actor in a Comedy Series, Screen Actors Guild award, 2006), (TV miniseries) Out of Order, 2003; performer: (plays) Speed-the-Plow, The Three Sisters, Boy's Life, Cryptogram (Off Broadway Theater award (OBIE), 1997); guest appearances The Human Factor, 1992, Raven, 1992, Law & Order, 1992, 1997, The X Files, 1993, Early Edition, 1996, Chicago Hope, 1997, The West Wing, 2001, Kim Possible, 2002, 2003, Frazier, 2003, The DA, 2004. Recipient Best Actress award, Nat. Bd. Rev., 2005. Office: Desperate Housewives Touchstone Televison 100 Universal City Plaza Bldg 2128 Ste G Universal City CA 91608*

HUFFMAN, JANET FAYE, secondary school educator; b. Liberal, Kans., Feb. 20, 1946; d. Kenneth D. and Ursula Idella Garten; divorced; children: Heidi Ann, Heather Sue. BA, U. Colo., 1968; MS, Ft. Hays (Kans.) State U., 1970. Cert. secondary English tchr., Mo. Tchr. Platte Community Coll., Columbus, Nebr., 1970-71, Arriba (Colo.) High Sch., 1980-82; English tchr. Limon (Colo.) High Sch., 1982—. Author: (poems) Inward Perspective, 1990. Mem. Limon Edn. Assn. (sec. 1990-91), Order of Eastern Star (worth matron 1989-90), First United Meth. Ch., Limon Heritage Soc. Avocations: reading, travel. Home: PO Box 846 Limon CO 80828 Office: Limon Sch PO Box 249 Limon CO 80828-0249

HUFFMAN, JOAN BREWER, history professor; b. Springfield, Ohio, Aug. 18, 1937; d. James Clarence and Berniece (Notter) Brewer; m. James Russell Huffman, Aug. 21, 1959; children: Jill Elizabeth, Jean Elaine. AB, Ohio U., 1959; MA, Ga. State U., 1968, PhD, 1980. Adj. prof. Wesleyan Coll., Macon, Ga., 1981-82; instr. history Macon State Coll., 1968-72, asst. prof., 1972-81, assoc. prof., 1981-86, prof., 1986-2000, prof. emerita, 2000—; owner The Printed Page, Macon, Ga., 1993-97, Picture Perfect, 1995—. Chmn. History adv. com. U. Sys. Ga., 1986—87. Contbr. articles to profl. jours. Mem., bd. dirs. Oklahatchee Pk., Perry, Ga., 1966-68, Macon State Coll. Found., 1985-90, Ga. Humanities Coun., Atlanta, 1983-87. Katharine C. Bleckley scholar English-Speaking Union, 1977; recipient Gov.'s award in the humanities, 1998. Mem. N.Am. Conf. on Brit. Studies, Am. Hist. Assn., Southern Hist. Assn. (membership com. 1988-89), Ga. Assn. Historians (pres. 1982-83), Phi Beta Kappa, Phi Alpha Theta (award 1978). Home: 135 Covington Pl Macon GA 31210-4445 Office Phone: 478-746-6365. E-mail: huffmanj@bellsouth.net.

HUFFMAN, LAURA CHRISTINE, computer programmer, educator; b. Celina, Ohio, Dec. 3, 1971; d. Richard Dean and Nancy Kay Huffman; 1 child, Kaitlan Danielle. BS in Bus. Adminstrn., Bowling Green State U., 1994. Computer instr. Lima (Ohio) Tech. Coll., 1996-98; programmer/analyst Ctrl. Mut. Ins., Van Wert, Ohio, 1997—. Mem. Nat. Assn. Ins. Women (cmty. svc. com.). Office: Ctrl Mut Ins 800 S Washington St Van Wert OH 45891-2357

HUFFMAN, LOUISE TOLLE, middle school educator; b. Tallahassee, Fla., July 24, 1951; d. Donald James and Mary Alice (McNeill) Tolle; m. Terry Lee Huffman, July 17, 1976; children: Cody McNeill, Hunter Tolle. BSED in Spl.

Edn./Elem. Edn., So. Ill. U., 1973; MSEd, No. Ill. U., 1979. Cert. elem. tchr., spl. edn. tchr. Ill. Tchr. Title I reading, Tonica, Ill., 1973—74; tchr. learning disabilities St. Charles, Ill., 1974—78; tchr. spl. edn. McWayne Elem. Sch., Batavia, Ill., 1978—80; tchr. grades 1, 3, 4, and 5 Steeple Run Elem. Sch., Naperville, Ill., 1980—98; tchr. Kennedy Jr. H.S., Naperville, 1998—. Com. to develop dual maj. in elem. edn. and sci. Benedictine U., Lisle, Ill., 1999—2000; curriculum developer Brookfield (Ill.) Zoo, 2001—02; facilitator of tchr. workshops Jurica Sci. Mus./ Benedictine U., Lisle, 1992—; facilitator sci. workshops Mus. Sci. and Industry, Chgo., 1991—96, Hamline U., St. Paul, 1990—93; Saturday Morning TV Sci. tchr. Dist. 203, Naperville, 1994; author Earth Rhythms Saturday Sch. program Benedictine U., 1996; tchr. summer sci. workshop Golden Apple Found., 1999—; mem. steering com. World Sch. Adventure Learning St. Thomas U., St. Paul, 1992—94; steering com. World Sch. Adventure Learning Hamline U., 1995, 2002; adj. faculty Benedictine U., Lisle, Ill., 2004—; convener, facilitator NSF Polar Sci. Workshop, 2005; U.S. rep. edn. outreach com. Internat. Polar Yr., 2005—. Co-author: Antarctica: A Living Classroom, 1991; contbg. author: Project Circles: The World School for Adventure Learning, 2002; contbr. articles to Cobblestone Mag., Good Apple Newspaper, Children's Digest; author of poetry. Covenor, facilitator, NSF Polar Sci. Workshop, 2003; convenor NSF Midwest Regional Sci. Workshop, 2005; confirmation class tchr. Cmty. United Meth. Ch., 1999-2001; US rep. Inernat. Polar Yr. Edn. Outreach Commn., 2005—. Recipient award of Excellence, Ill. Sci. Tchrs. Assn., 1992, 1996, Golden Apple award, 2002; grantee, Naperville Edn. Found., 1994, 2002, Jeanine Nicarico Lit. grant, 1999; NSF grantee, Antarctica, 2001—03. Methodist. Office: Kennedy Junior High Sch 2929 Green Trails Dr Lisle IL 60532-6262 E-mail: lhuffman@naperville203.org.

HUFFMAN, MELANIE DIANE, art educator; b. Kansas City, Kansas, Nov. 9, 1962; d. E. Melvin Bliss and R. Carolyn Elledge; m. Brian David Huffman, July 4, 1997; children: Louis Joshua Greaves, Laura Jessica Greaves. BE in French, Pittsburg State U., Kans., 1985; MSc in Art Edn., Wichita State U., Kans., 2000. Art, French tchr. Pittsburg Mid. Sch., Kans., 1985—88; dir. youth ministries First United Meth. Ch., Independence, Kans., 1989—92; art tchr. Independence HS, 1992, McKinley Mid. Sch., Coffeyville, Kans., 1992—97, Goddard HS, Kans., 1997—. Adj. faculty Independence CC, 1992—97. Sculpture Walk, 2000. Sponsor Nat. Art Honor Soc., Goddard, 1997—, Kans. Assn. Youth, Goddard, 1997—; co-chair family resource network Am. Diabetes Assn., Wichita, Kans., 2002—, co-dir. Diabetes day coms., 2004—, legis. adv. Kans. Washington, 2002, 2004, adv. bd. mem. Wichita, Kans., 2005. Art Edn. Scholastic grant, Prairie Quilt Guild, Wichita, 2000. Mem.: Nat. Art Edn. Assn., Kans. Art Educators Assn. Avocations: travel, reading, singing, quilting. Business E-Mail: mhuffman@goddardusd.com.

HUFFMAN, PATRICIA NELL, entrepreneur; b. Springfield, Mo., Sept. 25, 1947; d. Rex Eugene and Helen Marie (Appleby) Riggs; m. Frank Dale Huffman, June 18, 1966 (div. Apr. 2003); children: Chad, Heather, Tyler. Student, Joplin Jr. Coll., Mo., 1966. Saleswoman Sta. KTVJ-TV, Joplin, Mo., 1972—77; designer, mktg. ADI-Comml. Interiors, Tulsa, 1983—84; pres., designer Bittersweet, Inc., Joplin, 1984—89; founder, pres. By Invitation Only, 1986—89. Co-owner, bd. dirs., sec. J-Town Billiards, Sports Bar and Grill, 1999—; cons. in field. Designer country gift items, 1978—. Vol. Mental Health Ctr., Joplin, 1965, Am. Heart Assn., Joplin, 1980, Family Self Help Ctr., Joplin, 1981—, United Way, Joplin, 1982; pres. Women's Support Group, Joplin, 1983-85, Family Violence Coun., 1996-97, bd. dirs., pres. bd.; bd. dirs. Children's Ctr., 1997-2001; co-founder S.A.F.E. Coalition, 1989-97. Recipient Women Helping Women award, 1998, House Resolution No. 785 for volunteerism with children and women State of Mo., 1994. Mem. Exch. Club (Book of Golden Deeds award 1996). Avocations: bridge, creative writing, billiards, painting, illustrating and writing children's books. Office: PO Box 2159 2502 S Main St Joplin MO 64803-2159 Office Phone: 417-434-5957. Personal E-mail: jtownsportsbar@sbcglobal.net, paintinglibra@sbcglobal.net.

HUFFMAN, ROSEMARY ADAMS, lawyer, corporate executive; b. Orlando, Fla., Oct. 18, 1939; d. Elmer Victor and Esther (Weber) Adams; divorced; 1 child, Justin Adams Fruth. A.B. in Econs., Ind. U., 1959, J.D., 1962; LL.M., U. Chgo., 1967. Bar: Ind. 1962, Fla. 1963. Dep. prosecutor Marion County, Ind., 1963; ct. adminstr. Ind. Supreme Ct., 1967-68; pro-tem judge Marion County Mcpl. Ct., 1969-70; jud. coordinator Ind. Criminal Justice Planning Agy., 1969-70; dir. ctr. for Jud. Edn., Inc., 1970-73; pub. Jud. Xchange, 1972-73; instr. bus. law Purdue U., Indpls., 1962-63, Ind. U., Indpls., 1963-64; asst. Ind. Jud. Council, 1965; legis. intern Ford Found., 1965; sole practice, Indpls., 1962—; pres., owner Abacus, Inc., Indpls., 1980—. Mem. Ind. Bar Assn., Fla. Bar Assn. Home and Office: 6630 E 56th St Indianapolis IN 46226-1781

HUFNAGEL, LINDA ANN, biology professor, researcher; b. Teaneck, N.J., Nov. 7, 1939; d. Ernest Albert and Frances Marie (Hrbek) H.; m. Dov Jaron, 1969; children: Shulamit, Tamara; m. Robert Van Zackroff, June 1984. BA, U. Vt., 1961, MS, 1963; PhD, U. Pa., 1967. Lectr. U. Pa., Phila., summer 1967; NSF postdoctoral fellow Yale U., New Haven, 1967-69; rsch. assoc. Columbia U., N.Y.C., 1970; asst. prof. Oakland C.C., Farmington, Mich., 1970; rsch. assoc. Wayne State U., Detroit, 1971-73; lectr. biology U. R.I., Kingston, 1973-75, asst. prof., 1975-79, assoc. prof., 1979-86, prof., 1986—, dir. cen. electron microscope facility, 1973-96. NSF rsch. grantee, U. R.I., 1975, Am. Heart Assn. rsch. grantee, 1979, Steps fellow, Marine Biol. Lab., Woods Hole, Mass., 1978—79. Office: U RI Dept Cell Mol Biol Kingston RI 02881 Office Phone: 401-874-5914. Business E-Mail: lhufnagel@uri.edu.

HUFSTEDLER, SHIRLEY MOUNT, lawyer, former federal judge; b. Denver, Aug. 24, 1925; d. Earl Stanley and Eva (Von Behren) Mount; m. Seth Martin Hufstedler, Aug. 16, 1949; 1 son, Steven Mark. BBA, U. N.Mex., 1945, LLD (hon.), 1972; LLB, Stanford U., 1949; LLD (hon.), U. Wyo., 1970, Gonzaga U., 1970, Occidental Coll., 1971, Tufts U., 1974, U. So. Calif., 1976, Georgetown U., 1976, U. Pa., 1976, Columbia U., 1977, U. Mich., 1979, Yale U., 1981, Rutgers U., 1981, Claremont U. Ctr., 1981, Smith Coll., 1982, Syracuse U., 1983, Mt. Holyoke Coll., 1985; PHH (hon.), Hood Coll., 1981, Hebrew Union Coll., 1986, Tulane U., 1988. Bar: Calif. 1950. Mem. firm Beardsley, Hufstedler & Kemble, L.A., 1951-61; practiced in L.A., 1961; judge Superior Ct., County L.A., 1961-66; justice Ct. Appeals 2d dist., 1966-68; circuit judge U.S. Ct. Appeals 9th cir., 1968-79; sec. U.S. Dept. Edn., 1979-81; ptnr. Hufstedler & Kaus, L.A., 1981-95; sr. of counsel Morrison & Foerster LLP, L.A., 1995—. Emeritus dir. Hewlett Packard Co., US West, Inc.; bd. dirs. Harman Internat. Industries. Mem. staff Stanford Law Rev, 1947-49; articles and book rev. editor, 1948-49. Trustee Calif. Inst. Tech., Occidental Coll., 1972-89, Aspen Inst., Colonial Williamsburg Found., 1976-93, Constl. Rights Found., 1978-80, Nat. Resources Def. Coun., 1983-85, Carnegie Endowment for Internat. Peace, 1983-94; bd. dirs. John T. and Catherine MacArthur Found., 1983—2002; chair U.S. Commn. on Immigration Reform, 1996-97. Named Woman of Yr. Ladies Home Jour., 1976; recipient UCLA medal, 1981. Fellow Am. Acad. Arts and Scis.; mem. ABA (medal 1995), L.A. Bar Assn., Town Hall, Am. Law Inst. (coun. 1974-84), Am. Bar Found., Women Lawyers Assn. (pres. 1957-58), Am. Judicature Soc., Assn. of the Bar of City of N.Y., Coun. on Fgn. Rels. (emeritus), Order of Coif. Office: Morrison & Foerster LLP 555 W 5th St Ste 3500 Los Angeles CA 90013-1024 Office Phone: 213-892-5804. Business E-Mail: shirhufs@mofo.com.

HUGENBERG, PATRICIA ELLEN PETRIE, product designer; b. N.Y.C., Oct. 17, 1934; d. Milton John Petrie and Miriam Lois Lampke-Rubenstein-Petrie; m. George John Hugenberg, Jan. 18, 1958; 1 child, Kurt John James. Student, Briarcliff Jr. Coll., 1954, U. Calif., Berkeley, 1966. Guidette NBC, N.Y.C., 1956; designer, resch. developer Designs for Prodn., Sausalito, Calif.; inventor games, toys, med. items, Sigi Design, San Francisco; pres. PPH Designs. Mem. pending bd. Milton & Carroll Petrie Found. for New Millenium, N.Y.C. Photographer: (book cover jacket) Baltimore; prin. works include plexiglass knitting needles, plexiglass embedded light space age stardust galaxy hammocks, space age crutch, new saddle design for mobile riding easels, kitchen veg-garnisher punch; designer (plank easels) Navel Hist. Tours, Mare Island, Air-Boat Everglade, Health care walkers and "walking sticks" canes; patents pending in field. Mem. NRA. Avocations: music, painting, horseback riding, travel, gardening. Home and Office: 10 Leeward Rd Belvedere CA 94920-2321 Office Phone: 415-435-9689, 415-435-9155. Personal E-mail: botanigirl@comcast.net.

HUGGINS, AMY BRANUM, music educator; b. Memphis, Dec. 20, 1954; d. Leon and Scharlene Oney Branum; m. R. David Huggins, May 8, 1976; children: Alexander, Stephanie. MusM in Edn. with Kodaly emphasis, Holy Name Coll., Oakland, Calif., 1985; MusB in Edn., Peabody Conservatory of Music, 1976. Pvt. piano instr., Balt., 1973—; early music tng. faculty prep. divsn. Peabody Conservatory of Music, Balt., 1976—83, music theory faculty prep. divsn., 1976—83, curriculum designer prep. divsn., 1976; condr., founder The Pine Grove Madrigals, Balt., 1976—; vocal music specialist Pine Grove Elem. Sch., Balt., 1976—; master tchr., supr. of student tchrs. Peabody Conservatory of Music, Shenandoah Conservatory of Music, Towson State U., U. of Md., Loyola Coll., Balt., 1978—; organizer, dir. choral festivals Balt. County Pub. Schs., Balt., 1980—90; instr. Children's Chorus of Md., Balt., 1983—86; curriculum designer Balt. County Pub. Schs., 1991; pvt. voice instr. Balt., 1997—; cons. Children's Chorus of Md., Balt., 1998—99; dir., co-founder The Am. Kodaly Inst., Balt., 2000—; instr. grad. studies program Loyola Coll. in Md., Balt., 2001—. Kodaly clinician, cons. Orgn. of Am. Kodaly Educators, Moorhead, Minn., 1978—, Md. United Specialists in Kodaly, Balt., 1978—. Author: Elements: A Sight Singing and Rhythm Reading Book for Beginners, 1982, Kodaly, American Style, 2001, Folk Guitar for the Music Educator, 2002, 5-String Banjo for the Music Educator, 2003; columnist: The Kodaly Envoy, 2003—06; contbr. articles to profl. jours. Bd. dirs., sec. Children's Chorus of Md., 1981—83. Scholar, Mu Phi Epsilon Alumni Assn., 1975. Mem.: OAKE (overseer 1997—98, chair nat. conf. planning com. 1997—98, 1983—85, overseer tchr. tng. com. 1983—85, 1997—98), MENC, The VoiceCare Network, Soc. for Rsch. in Music Edn., Soc. for Music Tchr. Edn., Md. Music Educators Assn., Am. Choral Dirs. Assn., Orgn. of Am. Kodaly Educators (v.p. 1983—85, 1997—98), Md. United Specialists in Kodaly (pres. 1996—98, 1982—84, 1998—99, mem. at large 1995—96, sec. 1980—82), Mu Phi Epsilon. Home: 307 Southway Baltimore MD 21218 Office: Pine Grove Sch 2701 Summit Ave Baltimore MD 21234 Office Phone: 410-887-5267. Personal E-mail: amybhuggins@yahoo.com.

HUGGINS, CHARLOTTE SUSAN HARRISON, retired secondary school educator, writer, travel company executive; b. Rockford, Ill., May 13, 1933; d. Lyle Lux and Alta May (Bowers) Harrison; m. Rollin Charles Huggins Jr., Apr. 26, 1952; children: Cynthia Charlotte Peters, Shirley Ann Cooper, John Charles. Student, Knox Coll., 1951-52; AB magna cum laude, Harvard U., 1958; MA, Northwestern U., 1960, postgrad., 1971-73; cert. in conversation French, Berlitz Lang. Sch. Asst. editor Hollister Publs., Inc., Wilmette, Ill., 1959—65; tchr. advanced placement English New Trier H.S., Winnetka, Ill., 1965—97, master tchr., 1979, leader tchr., 1988. With Task Force Commn. on Grading, 1973—74; Sabbatical project 1 yr. world travel History-Lit. Prospectus; cons. Asian Studies New Trier, 1987—88; mem. New Trier Supts. Commn. on Censorship, 1991; critic tchr. Northwestern U.; cons. McDougall-Littel's Young Writer's Manual, 1985—88; asst. sponsor Echoes, 1981—Trevia, 1982, 83; sponsor New Trier News, 1988—; pres. Harrison Farms, Inc., Lovington, Ill., 1976—; spkr. North Suburban Geneal. Soc., 1990; instr., travel expert New Trier Adult Edn. Keys to the World's Last Mysteries, 1986—; presenter in field. Author: A Sequential Course in Composition Grades 9-12, 1979, A History of New Trier High School, 1982, Passage to Anaheim: An Historical Biography of Pioneer Families, 1984, Cambodia: A Place in Time, 1987; author: (video tapes) The Glory That was Greece, 1987; author: The World of Charles Dickens, 1987; editor: Pinnacles of the Years, 2001, The Cornog Years, 2002; asst. editor newsletter: New Trier Ret. Tchrs. Women's bd. St. Leonard's House, Chgo., 1965—75; active Ctrl. Sch. PTA Bd., Wilmette, Ill., 1960—64; assocs. bd. Northwestern U. Settlement, Chgo., 1965—, pres., 1999—, fundraising com., 1997—, ctrl. bd. com., 2003—; mem. Glenbard 50th Reunion Com. Recipient Citizenship award, DAR, 1953, award, Phi Beta Kappa, 1957, Am. Legion, 1959, Cert. of Merit Graphic Arts Competition, Printing Industries of Am., 1983, 1st pl. award, Am. Scholastic Press Assn., 1990, Cert. of Merit, Am. Newspaper Pubs. Assn., 1990. Mem.: DAR (historian 1999—2000, regent 2000—02, parliamentarian 2002—), ASCD, MLA, NEA, Ill. Ret. Tchrs. Assn., Ill. Journalism Edn. Assn. (sec. 1990—97, awards chmn., bd. dirs., Life Achievement award 2001), New Trier Edn. Assn. (sec. 1992, pres.-elect 1994, pres. 1995—96, parliamentarian 2003—), Ill. Assn. Tchrs. English, Ill. Edn. Assn., Nat. Scholastic Press Assn. (conv. del. 1991, spring conf. rep. 1991—92, 1992—93, 1993—94, presenter fall and spring conv. 1993—94, spring conf. rep. 1994—95, presenter fall and spring conv. 1994—95, 1994—95, spring conf. rep. 1995—96, presenter fall and spring conv. 1995—96, 1996—, newspaper judge, All-Am. Newspaper award 1990—91, Life Achievement award 2001), Nat. Coun. Tchrs. English, Silent Samaritan Assn. (bd. dirs. 2006), Alliance Français, Harvard U. Alumni Assn. (admissions candidate interviewer), Radcliffe Coll. Alunmae Assn., Lyric Opera (assoc.), New Trier Ret. Tchrs. Assn. (newsletter editor), Women Comm., Inc., Nat. Huguenot Soc., Quill and Scroll (bd. dirs. 1992—93, George Gallup award 1990), Ill. Huguenot Soc., Columbia Scholastic Press Assn. (del. 1990, newspaper judge), Jr. Aux. U. Chgo. Cancer Rsch. Bd., Northwestern U. Alumni Assn., Mary Crane League, Art Inst. Chgo. (life), Chgo. Farmers, Terra Mus. Chgo. (charter), Knox Coll. Alumni Assn. (class rep. 2005, 50 Yr. Club 2005, class donations rep.), Wilmette-Kenilworth Club, Univ. Club Chgo., Women's Club Wilmette, Mich. Shores Club, Pi Beta Phi (North Shore Chgo. alumnae bd., publicity chair, 50 Yr. Club 2002). Home: 700 Greenwood Ave Wilmette IL 60091-1748 Office: 385 Winnetka Ave Winnetka IL 60093-4238 Personal E-mail: chantezch@aol.com.

HUGGINS, ELAINE JACQUELINE, nurse, retired military officer; b. San Jose, Calif., Mar. 26, 1954; d. William Burt and Edith Gwendolyn (Schindler) Moreland; m. Bruce Carlton Allanach, Oct. 8, 1976 (div. Oct. 1989); stepchildren: Dawn Louise, Christopher Bruce, Jeffrey Scott, Sean Michael; m. Michael Henry Huggins, Dec. 8, 1991; children: Phoebe Marie, Chloe Anne, Michael Henry Jr.; stepchildren: Abbey Rose, Jamin Michael. BSN, U. Md., 1976; MSN, Med. Coll. Ga., 1988; postgrad., Calif. Inst. Integral Studies. RN Ga., Md., Calif.; cert. Myers-Briggs personality typing counselor. Commd. 1st lt. Nurse Corps U.S. Army, 1972, advanced through grades to maj., 1986; staff nurse gen. medicine-oncology Walter Reed Army Med. Ctr., Washington, 1976-78, team leader gen. medicine-oncology, 1978-79, head nurse med. splty. ward, 1979-80; asst. head nurse gynecol. oncology unit Tripler Army Med. Ctr., Honolulu, 1980-81, head nurse med. splty. clinic, 1981-83; staff nurse orthopedics Eisenhower Army Med. Ctr., Ft. Gordon, Ga., 1983-84, patient edn. coord., 1984-85, head nurse recovery rm., 1985-86; head nurse oncology/neurology unit Letterman Army Med. Ctr., Presidio of San Francisco, 1988-89, clin. nurse psychiat. unit, 1989-90, chief nursing adminstrn. E/N, 1990-92, ret., 1992; case mgr. Vis. Nurses Pomona, Claremont, Calif., 1993-94; nursing supr. Vis. Nurses Assn./Hospice of Pomona, San Bernandino, Calif., 1994-95, quality risk resource mgr., 1995-96; performance improvement mgr. Santa Barbara Vis. Nurses Assn., 2000—01; dir. edn. performance improvement and credentialising 30th Med. Group, Vandenburg AFB, Calif., 2001—03, dir. performance improvement, risk mgr. and patient safety officer, 2003—. Sabbatical to Australian outback with rsch. interests in cross-cultural health care and spirituality in health care, 1996—99; freelance writer, cons., 1999—2000; mem. adj. faculty Sch. Nursing U. Phoenix-So. Calif. Campus, 1995—96; owner Hugg 'Ems Telephone Peer Counseling, 2002—03; entrepeneur Huggins Health web based health and nutrition, 2004—; lectr. in field. Contbr. articles to nursing, mil., and med. publs. Mem. pub. edn. com. Am. Cancer Soc., Honolulu, 1982. Recipient Humanitarian Svc. medal, 1990. Mem. Am. Diabetes Assn., Am. Assn. Diabetic Educators, Grad. Student Nurses Assn. (sec. 1986-87), ANA, Mensa, Sigma Theta Tau. Avocations: reading, walking, beach combing. Office: 30th Med Group 338 South Dakota Ave Vandenberg Afb CA 93437 Home: 3763 Uranus Ave Lompoc CA 93436-1927 Office Phone: 805-606-0345. E-mail: elaine.huggins@vandenberg.af.mil.

HUGGINS, HOLLIE ANN, athletic trainer, reporter; d. Mickey Don and Phyllis Ann Huggins. BS, Tex. Womans U., Denton, 2000; A in Real Estate Fin., U. North Tex., Denton, 2003; MS, California U., Pa., 2005. Lic. athletic trainer Tex.; cert. Realtor Tex. Athletic trainer Presbyn. Sports Network, Dallas, 2000—; head athletic trainer Hockaday Sch., Dallas, 2002—; motorsports reporter ESPN radio, Dallas, 2006—. Mem.: Nat. Athletic Trainers Assn. (assoc.). Office: 11600 Welch Rd Dallas TX 75229 Office Phone: 214-363-6311.

HUGGINS, LOIS M., human resources specialist, consumer products company executive; BA, Franklin and Marshall Coll. Various positions Sara Lee Corp., Chgo., 1987—97; divisional v.p. human resources Sara Lee Intimate Apparel, 1997—2000; leader orgn. devel. and diversity initiative Sara Lee Corp., 2000—03, v.p. human resources, 2003—04, sr. v.p. global human resources, 2004—. Co-chair global human resources steering com. Sara Lee Corp., Chgo., bd. dirs. Office: Sara Lee Corp 3 First National Plz Chicago IL 60602-4260 Office Phone: 312-726-2600. Office Fax: 312-726-3712.

HUGHES, A. N., psychotherapist; b. Ft. Meade, Md. d. G.M. and G.T. Nolen; m. E.L. Hughes, Oct. 21, 1961; 1 child, Andrew G. BS in Psychology, Rollins Coll., 1985, MA in Counseling, 1986; student in pub. speaking and human rels., Dale Carnegie Inst., 1981; student, Duke U., 1950-52. Lic. mental health counselor Nat. Bd. Cert. Counselors, nat. cert. counselor, nat. cert. gerontol. counselor. Supr. top secret control, audio/visual and small parts supply U.S. Army, Continental U.S. and Tokyo; adminstrv. sec. Sys. Devel. Corp., Rand Corp., Santa Monica, Calif.; adminstrv. asst., editor, exec. sec., adminstrv. sec. Aerospace Corp., El Segundo, Calif.; staff therapist Circles of Care, Melbourne, Fla. Developer program for leading divorce support groups for Brevard Women's Ctr. Various leadership positions PTA, Pittsford, NY, Brookfield, Wis., 1968—81; mem. Brevard Cmty. Chorus, 1991—, adv. bd., 1997; mem. Citizen's Emergency Response Team (CERT), 1999—2001; various vol. positions in several organizations in Brevard County, 1991—. Mem. DAR, Fla. Coun. on Aging, Space Coast PC Users Group, Geneal. Soc. South Brevard, Suntree Country Club, Suntree Master Homeowners Assn. (Twin Lakes rep. 1997—), Brevard County Alumnae Assn. of Kappa Kappa Gamma, Kappa Kappa Gamma. Avocations: photoimaging, fitness, genealogy, choral singing, growing orchids. Office: PO Box 410162 Melbourne FL 32941-0162

HUGHES, ANN HIGHTOWER, retired economist, trade association administrator; b. Birmingham, Ala., Nov. 24, 1938; d. Brady Alexander and Juanita (Pope) H. BA, George Washington U., 1963, MA, 1969. Asst. U.S. trade rep. Exec. Office of Pres., Washington, 1978-81; dep. asst. sec. trade agreements Dept. Commerce, Washington, 1981-82, dep. asst. sec. Western Hemisphere, 1982-95; dir. C & M Internat., Washington, 1995-97; ret. Recipient meritorious exec. award Pres. of U.S., 1982, 88, disting. exec. award, 1993. Avocation: breeding champion miniature Schnauzers.

HUGHES, ANN M., medical/surgical nurse; b. Co. Mayo, Ireland, Jan. 4, 1955; d. Thomas and Catherine (Heneghan) Meenaghan; m. Michael Hughes, Aug. 30, 1980; children: John, Mary, Thomas. Diploma, Newham Sch. Nursing, 1976. RN, Eng., Ireland, N.Y. Staff nurse rehab. North Cen. Bronx (N.Y.) Hosp.; staff nurse med./surg. unit Doctor's Hosp., Manhattan, N.Y.; staff nurse per diem Physicians Hosp., Jackson Heights, N.Y.; agy. nurse CMC Registry, N.Y.C.; staff nurse St. Johns Queens Hosp., Elmhurst, NY, 2000—. Office: St Johns Queens Hosp Med Unit 90-02 Queens Blvd Elmhurst NY 11373

HUGHES, BARBARA ANN, dietician, public health administrator; b. McMinn County, Tenn., July 22, 1938; d. Cecil Earl and Hannah Ruth (Moss) Farmer; m. Carl Clifford Hughes, Oct. 13, 1962. BS in Home Econs. cum laude, Carson Newman Coll., Jefferson City, Tenn., 1960; MS in Instl. Mgmt., Ohio State U., Columbus, 1963; MA (Adonarium Judson scholar), So. Bapt. Theol. Sem., 1968; MPH, U. N.C., Chapel Hill, 1972; postgrad. in nutrition, U. Iowa, 1974, U. N.C., 1975-85, Case Western Res. U., 1979, Walden U.; PhD, 1988. Registered, lic. nutritionist, dietitian. Instr., clin. dietitian Riverside Meth. Hosp., Riverside Whitecross Sch. Nursing, Columbus, 1963-66; consulting dietitian Mount Holly Nursing Home, Ky. Dept. Mental Health, 1966-68, Eastern Region N.C. Bd. Health, Raleigh, 1968-73; dir. Nutrition and Dietary Svcs. br. Divsn. Health Svcs. N.C. Dept. Human Resources, Raleigh, 1973-89, also dir. Women-Infants-Children Program; pres. B.A. Hughes and Assocs., 1990—; dir. adult nutrition Inst. Lifestyle and Weight Mgmt., 2006—. Instr. Wake Tech. C.C., 1996—97; med. nutrition therapist CIGNA Health Care of N.C., Inc., United Behavioral Health, Blue Cross, Blue Shield N.C.; asst. to rep. Karen Gottovi 14th dist. N.C. Ho. of Reps., Gen. Assembly N.C., 1994; adj. instr. Case Western Res. U., Cleve., 1988—89; adj. asst. prof. dept. nutrition Sch. Public Health U. N.C., Chapel Hill, 1975—89; adv. bd. Hospitality Edn. program NC Dept. Cmty. Colls., 1974—80; adv. com. Ret. Senior Vol. Program, Raleigh and Wake County, NC, 1975—79, N.C. Network Coordinating Coun. for End-Stage Renal Disease, 1975, Nat. Adv. Coun. on Maternal, Infant and Fetal Nutrition, Spl. Supplemental Food Program for Women, Infants and Children, Dept. Agr., 1976—79; adv. com. Nutrition Edn. and Tng. program N.C. Dept. Pub. Instrn., 1978—80; chmn. adv. leadership coun. N.C. Cooperative Ext. Svc., 1997—99, advisor com. to Wake County, 1992—, chair adv. coun., 1994—96; coord. undergrad. program in gen. dietetics East Carolina U.; apptd. rep. Coll. of Agrl. and Life Scis. N.C. State U. to Nat. Coun. for Agrl. Rsch. Extension and Tchg., 1996—2000; apptd. mem. strategic planning and new directions com. Wake County Bd. Commrs. to Wake County Human Svcs. Bd., 1996—, new dirs. strategic planning com., children's com., bd. liaison, partnership com., 2001—, agy. performance com., 1998—2000; chmn. agy. svcs. com., exec. com. Wake County Human Svcs. Bd., 2004, cmty. health comm., 2005—; apptd. to adv. bd. Agromedicine Program East Carolina and N.C. State Univs., 1996—99; apptd. N.C. Dept. Human Resources Sec.'s Adv. Coun. Alternative/Contemporary Medicine Consortium Natural Medicine and Pub. Health, 2000; adv. coun. N.C. Gov.'s Office Citizen Affairs; cons. dietitian Augusta Victoria Hosp. and Jerusalem (Israel) Crippled Childrens Ctr., 1968; witness U.S. congressional and Senate hearings in field; mem. planning com. NC Summit on Natural Med. Products, 2002; dietitian, dir. food svcs. archaeol. expedition, Israel, 1968; mem. accreditation bd. Health Dept., 2006; mem. human rels. commn. Raleigh City Coun., 2005; dir. adult nutrition Inst. Lifestyle and Weight Mgmt., 2006—. Co-author: Diet and Kidney Disease, Assn. for N.C. Regional Med. program, 1969, Ohio State U., Alumni Assoc., sec. Triangle chpt.; contbr. numerous papers, articles to symposia, periodicals in field, vol. areas. Trustee Gardner-Webb Coll., Boiling Springs, NC, 1978—82, chmn. curriculum com., 1981—82; chmn. adv. bd. dept. home econ. Carson-Newman Coll., 1975—78; chmn. Edn. and Cmty. Com., 1992; pres. NC Coun. on Spl. Teens, 1993—94; appt. mem. accrediting bd. N.C. Local Pub. Health Accreditation Program, 2005—; appt. mem. Raleigh Human Rels., 2005; v.p. Wake County Literacy Coun., 1986—87, bd. dirs., 2004, mem. cmty. health com., 2005—; del. various Dem. Convs., 1981—84, precinct sec.-treas., 1981—83, 1st vice chmn., 1983—85, 2nd vice chmn., 1993—96, 1998—, chair, 1985—87, 1998—2000, 2005—; adv. bd., del. NC Dem. Party Exec. Com., 1998—2002, precinct chair; active edn. program Pullen Meml. Bapt. Ch., Raleigh, Raleigh, deacon, 1976—80, 1994, area ministry capt., 1977—78, personnel com., 1978—80; bd. dirs. Cmty. Outreach, 1989—92, futuring com., 1995—96, coordinating coun. vice-chair, 1996—97, chmn., 1997—98; bd. dirs. NC Literacy Assn., 1978—83, 1993, 1995, pres., 1981—83. Fellow Am. Dietetic Assn. Commn. Dietetic Registration, 1998—; named Woman of Yr., Wake County, 1975, N.C. Outstanding Dietitian of Yr., 1976, N.C. Outstanding Dietitian, Southeastern Hosp. Conf. for Dietitians, 1978; recipient Disting. Alumna award Carson-Newman Coll., 1983, Eleanor Roosevelt Humanitarian award Altrusa Internat., 1995, S.E. Trustee award Nat. Assn. Local Bd. Health, 2002, Women in Bus. award Triangle Bus. Jour., 2002. Fellow: Am. Dietetic Assn. (nat. chair coun. on practice 1982—83, bd. dirs.-at-large 1999—, chair elect 2003—04, chair nutrition edn. for the pub. 2004—05, Ann Gallagher award 2003, Medallion award 2004, Outstanding Nutr. Entrepreneur 2005, Excellence in Practice and in Consultation and Bus. Practice

2005), N.C. Inst. Polit. Leadership (pres. 2002, immediate past pres. 2004—05); mem.: APHA, APHA (mem. nutrition sect. 1969—, chair nom. com. 1975—77, chmn. nominating com. 1975—77, chair pub. policy com. 1977—79, mem. pub. policy com. 1977—79, mem. publs. com. 1979—80, chair award com. food and nutrition sect., other offices 1995—96, chair awards com. 1995—96, chmn. awards com., Catherine Cowell award 1994), AAUW (life; pres. Raleigh/Wake County br. 1971—75, pres. N.C. divsn. 1978—80, area rep. 1980—82, mem. Program Com. Legis./Pub. Policy Com. 1980—82, ednl. founder 1980—82, nat. bd. dirs. 1980—92, nat. edn. found. bd. dirs. 1987—91, mem. found. 1987—91, pres. Raleigh/Wake County br. 1991—93, ednl. equity roundtable 1992, coord. Wake Women Celebrate 1995, coord. ptnrs. for heart disease and stroke prevention 1995), Women's Forum N.C. (young leadership award com. 1989—90, 1992—, newsletter editor bd. dirs. 1992—, adminstr. 1995—2003), N.C. Acad. Pub. Health (pres.-elect 2001, pres. 2002), Nutrition Today Soc., Soc. Nutrition Edn., Am. Acad. Health Adminstrn., N.C. Coun. Women's Orgns. (Wellness in State Employees adv. bd. 1989—91, mem. at large bd. dirs. 1989—92, leadership com. 1991—, chair nutrition subcom.), N.C. Coun. Foods and Nutrition (chmn. membership 1975, dir. 1976—78, nominating com. 1979), N.C. Assn. Bds. of Health (dir. 1994—98, nominating com. 1998—2000, treas. 1999—2000, awards com. 1999—2006, mem. com. 1999—2005, pres. 2002—03, immediate past pres. 2004—06), Assn. State and Territorial Pub. Health Nutrition Dirs. (pres. 1977—79, dir. 1981—89, chair legis. and pub. policy com. 1984—89, liaison to Assn. Faculties Grad. Program in Pub. Health Nutrition, Commendation award 1989), So. Health Assn. (pres. 1982—83, chair nominating com. 1985—86, 1991—92, awards com. 1992—93, Spl. Meritorious award 1989), Greater Raleigh C. of C. (mem. west area bus. coun., chair legis. com. rep. leadership Raleigh Alumni Assn.), Altrusa Internat. Found. (1st v.p. 1985—87, chmn.-elect 1990—92, chmn. 1992—, bd. dirs. 1993—97, pres. Raleigh chpt. 2005—), U.N.C. Pub. Health Alumni Assn. (life), U.N.C. Gen. Alumni Assn. (life), Ohio State U. Alumni Assn. (life), Altrusa Internat. (pres. Raleigh club 1973—74, pres. Raleigh chpt. 1973—74, dir. 1976—78, Internat. vocat. svcs. chmn. 1977—79, 1st vice gov. 1978—79, chmn. nomination com. 1980—82, 1st v.p. 1985—87, pres.-elect 1987—89, pres. 1989—91, dir. 1990—, chmn. 1992—93, pres. Raleigh club 2005—, gov. dist. Three, 1979-80, Triangle Bus. Jour. Women in Bus. award 2002), Kappa Omicron Nu. Achievements include olympic torchbearer, 1996. Home and Office: 4208 Galax Dr Raleigh NC 27612-3714 Office Phone: 919-787-2949. Business E-Mail: barbara-ann@bahughes.com.

HUGHES, BARBARA BRADFORD, manufacturing executive, community health nurse; b. Bragg City, Mo., Jan. 21, 1941; d. Lawrence Hurl Bradford and Opal Jewel (Prater) Puttin; m. Robert Howard Hughes, Dec. 9, 1961; children: Kimberly Ann Hayden, Robert Howard II. ASN, St. Louis Community Coll., 1978; student, Webster U., 1980. RN, Mo. Med. surg. nurse Alexian Bros. Hosp., St. Louis, 1979-80; staff nurse Midwest Allergy Cons., St. Louis, 1980; nurse high altitude Aviation Nurse, Ltd., St. Louis, 1980-81; cardiac telemetry staff nurse Jefferson Meml. Hosp., Crystal City, Mo., 1992-94, 1998-2001; CEO Supreme Tool & Die, Fenton, Mo., 2001—. Chmn. bd. dirs., CEO, ptnr. Supreme Tool & Die Co., Fenton, Mo., 1988—; pvt. practice real estate mgmt., 1962—2004; mem. nursing adv. com. Jefferson Coll., Hillsboro, Mo., 1999, mem. adv. bd., 2000—01. Vol. Luth. Hosp., St. Louis, 1967—70; mem. Mo. Bot. Garden, St. Louis, 1976—, Mo. Hist. Soc., 1976, St. Louis Zoo Friends Assn., 1986—87, Nat. Trust for Hist. Preservation, 1990—2000, Channel 9-Ednl. TV, St. Louis; vol. health tchr. Spartan Aluminum Products, Sparta, Ill., 1984; mem. Rosie the Riveter women's pilot group project, readying a DC3 for FAA recert. through Wings of Hope, TWA and Remote Area Med. Knoxville, for use in med. relief in remote areas of U.S. and the world; mem. med. missions to nat. and internat. remote areas sponsored by Wings of Hope, 2000—; mem. field and med. support team Wings of Hope, St. Louis, vol. flight nurse in midwest, 2003—; mem. field and med. support team Remote Area Medical, Knoxville, Tenn.; triage nurse Seven Day Vol. Med. Mission, New Orleans, 2006. U. Mo. scholar, 1959. Mem.: AACN, Nat. Tool and Machining Assn., U.S. Pilots Assn., Mo. Pilots Assn., Wings of Hope (St. Louis), Women in Aviation Internat. (charter), Tyospaye Club. Republican. Achievements include Giving direct med. treatment to patients in remote areas of the U.S.A. and Central and South Am. Avocations: flying, reading. Office: Supreme Tool & Die 1536 Fenpark Dr Fenton MO 63026

HUGHES, BRIGID, former editor; d. Patrick and Patricia. BA in English, Northwestern U., 1994. Intern The Paris Rev., N.Y.C., 1995, editor, 1995—2000, mng. editor, 2000—04, exec. editor, 2004—05. Office: The Paris Review Foundation 62 White St New York NY 10013-3593

HUGHES, CAROL SCELONGE, retired secondary school educator; b. Chgo., June 11, 1947; d. Francis and Eunice Winifred (Olson) Scelonge; m. Thomas Kenney Hughes, June 8, 1968; 1 child, Carrie Anne. BS, So. Ill. U., 1972; MA, St. Xavier U., 1996. Cert. med. lab. technician. H.s. tchr. Winnebago (Ill.) Cmty. Unit District, 1973—2002; ret., 2002. Tutor Rockford Rescue Mission, Rockford, 2003. Cons. Boy Scouts Am., Winnebago, 1973-2002; vol., tchr. Edn. Ctr., Rockford Rescue Mission, 2003-. Mem. Ill. Sci. Tchrs. Assn., Winnebago Edn. Assn. (v.p. 1975-76, treas. 1996-99), Am. Med. Technologists (10 Yr. award 1996). Avocations: hiking, gardening, reading. Home: 2407 Devonshire Dr Rockford IL 61107-1500 Personal E-mail: thughes675@aol.com.

HUGHES, CAROLYN WRIGHT, elementary school educator, director; d. Gilbert Cornelius and Florida Bryant Wright; m. King David Hughes III, Apr. 12, 1978; children: Nicole A. Presley, King David IV. BS, Edward Waters Coll. Cert. Fla. A&M U., 1968, tchr. D.C., 1973, Fla., 1978, in ESOL Dept. Contg. Edn. Duval County, 1999. Tchr. Project Headstart, Atlanta, Washington, Lecki Elem. Sch., Washington, Greenfield Elem. Sch., Jacksonville, Fla. Asst. dir. Extended Day Greenfield Elem. Sch. Contbr. poetry to mags. Coord. United Way Greenfield Elem., 2001—05, coord. all campaign, 2002—05; mem. choir Philippian Cmty. Ch., Jacksonville, tchr. Sunday sch., asst. dist. leader. Nominee Tchr. of Yr. award, Vietnam Vets., 2005; recipient The Wall Reading Project award, V.P. Chaney, The White House, 2004. Mem.: Am. Fedn. Tchrs. Democrat. Avocations: gardening, singing, cooking, football. Home: 2510 Spring Park Rd Jacksonville FL 32207 Office: Greenfield Elementary Sch 6343 Knights Ln N Jacksonville FL 32216 Office Phone: 904-739-5249. Personal E-mail: kdh2510@comcast.com.

HUGHES, CATHERINE L. (CATHY HUGHES), radio personality, broadcast executive; b. Omaha, Apr. 22, 1947; 1 child. Student, Creighton U., HHD (hon.), 2006; student, U. Nebr. Lectr., asst. to dean comm. Howard U., Washington, 1971—73; gen. sales mgr. WHUR Radio, 1973—78; v.p., gen. mgr. WYCB Radio, 1978—80; owner, operator WOL-AM Radio, 1980—; now founder, chairperson Radio One. Trustee Lincoln U.; small bus. adv. com. Fed. Res. Bank. Bd. mem. Piney Woods Sch., Balt. Mus. Art. Named Bus. Person of the Yr., Nat. Black C. of C., 1998, Prudential Media Black Woman on Wall St., 1999; named one of 50 Most Powerful Women in Bus., Black Enterprise Mag., 2006, 100 Most Influential Black Americans, Ebony mag., 2006; recipient Mayor's Bus. award, 1995—99, Thomas A. Dorsey Leadership award, 1996, D.C. Cmty. Svc. award, 1995; scholar, Living Vision Scholarship Fund, 1995. Achievements include first to to be an African American woman to head a firm publicly traded on a stock exchange in the United States. Office: Radio One Inc 1705 Whitehead Rd Gwynn Oak MD 21207-4004*

HUGHES, CHERYL DEMPSEY, theology studies educator; b. Miami Beach, Fla. d. William E. and Vivian Humphrey Dempsey; m. William E. Hughes; children: Christine, Robert, Alexander. MA, Boston U., 1969; M Theology, U. Dallas, 1999; postgrad., U. Durham, England, 2001—06. Dir. humanities Arts and Humanities Coun. Tulsa, 1986—90; prof. humanities and religious studies Tulsa C.C., 1990—. Actor: (one person performance) Lucy Stone, 1995—99. Mem. exec. com. Jr. League Tulsa, 1989—90. Grantee, Okla. Humanities Coun., 1984—94. Mem.: Am. Acad. Religion. Office Phone: 918-595-7129.

HUGHES, CINDI BAKER, special education educator; b. Joliet, Ill., Apr. 18, 1957; d. Richard M and Evelyn M Baker; m. Forrest Rodrick Hughes; 1 child, Steven LeMond; m. Rick Tynes (dec. 1979). AA in applied sci., Waubonsee C.C., Sugar Grove, Ill., 1978; BSc, Ill. State U., Normal, 1983; M in elem. edn., Morehead State U., Ky., 1987. Tchrs. aid, deaf program Joliet Pub. Sch., 1978—80; summer counselor Lions Club of No. Ill., 1981—82, Trailways Girl Scouts, 1983; tchr. hearing impaired West Ctrl. Ill. Spl. Ed. Co-Op., Macomb, Ill., 1983—84; tchr. Jack and Jill Daycare, Joliet, Ill., 1984—85; tchr. of deaf Ky. Sch. for the Deaf, Danville, 1985—86; tchr. deaf and hearing impaired Floyd County Sch., Prestonsburg, Ky., 1986—96, tchr. hearing K-8, 1996—. Sign lang. tchg. asst. Ill. State U., 1982. Org. Deaf Awareness Night, Ill. State U. Deaf Edn. Dept., 1981; spring pow-wow planning com. Waubonsee Cmty. Coll.; mem./trustee Mountain Christian Acad., 1999—2001, pres., 1998—2000. Grantee, Very Spl. Art of Ky., 2005; Tchr. Initiated Project grant, Ky. Arts Coun., 2004. Mem.: Ky. Edn. Assn., Ill. Tchrs. Hearing Impaired, Humane Soc. of the U.S., Creative Home Arts Club, Phi Theta Kappa. Avocations: sewing, crafts. Office: Floyd County Sch JM Stumbo Elem 6945 Ky Rte 979 Grethel KY 41631 Office Phone: 606-587-2213. Business E-Mail: Cindi.Hughes@floyd.kyschools.us.

HUGHES, DEANNA ELMA, psychologist; b. Jacksonville, Fla., Nov. 28, 1971; d. Victor Alexander II and Charlene Boggs Hughes. BA Psychology, Furman U., Greenville, S.C., 1994; M Rehab. Counseling, Fla. State U., 1996; M Clin. Psychology, Fla. Inst. Tech., 2000, D Clin. Psychology, 2002. Lic. clin. psychologist Fla. Dept. Health. Doctoral residency Miami Vet. Med. Ctr., 2001—02; post-doctoral resident Coastal Behavioral Healthcare, Sarasota, Fla., 2002—03; clin. psychologist Tricare South, Jacksonville, 2004—; pvt. practice, nursing home cons. Jacksonville, 2004—. Com. mem. First Presbyn. Ch., Sarasota, 2003; cmty. missions, com. mem. Riverside Presbyn. Ch., Jacksonville, 2004; com. mem. Sarasota United for Responsibility, Justice and Equity. Contbr. articles to profl. jours. Mem.: APA, Fla. Psychol. Assn. Avocations: painting, music, bicycling. Office Phone: 904-504-5412.

HUGHES, DEBORAH BRAY, special education educator; b. Dallas, May 29, 1953; d. Von M. Bray and Francis Barton Harris; m. David M. Park; children: Delain Barton, Devon Bray Miller. BS Magna cum laude in interdisciplinary studies, U. No. Tex., 2001. Cert. tchr. Tex., 2002. Tchg. asst. autistic group Garland (Tex.) Coop. Behavioral Ctr., 1977—79; tchr. Lake Highlands Christ. Child Enrichment Ctr., Dallas, 1983—84, Rockwall (Tex.) Pvt. Sch., 1987—88; tchr., dir. ops., v.p. mktg. Mem. Sch. of the Oaks, Houston, 1988—91; legal asst. Brown & Brown, Wetzel, Herron, & Drucker, LLP, Houston, 1991—94; behavioral therapist Pvt. Practice, The Woodlands, 1995—98, U. Houston, Tex. Young Autism Project, 1995—98; spl. edn. tchr. Denton Ind. Sch. Dist., 2002—. Adv. bd. Mem. Sch. Oaks Found., 1988—91. Author: (poem) World of Poetry Anthology, 1988 (Golden Poet award, 1988). Vol. So. Poverty Law Ctr., ACLU, March of Dimes, Habitat for Humanity, The Carter Ctr. Mem.: Families Early Autism Treatment, No. Tex., Nat. Assn. Edn. of Young Children, Golden Key Nat., Kappa Delta Pi, Internat. Honor Soc. in Edn. Avocations: reading, writing, art, music. Office: Denton Ind Sch Dist 3300 Evers Pkwy Denton TX 76201

HUGHES, DEBRA, writer, educator; b. Alamogordo, N.Mex., Oct. 3, 1955; d. Clinton Don and JoEllyn Hughes; children: Austin Hughes-Blanks, Merritt Hughes-Blanks; m. Gary Paul Tyc. Diploma superior, U. Sorbonne, Paris, 1976; BA, U. Colo., 1977; MA, Ohio State U., 1986. Staff reporter The Albuquerque Tribune, 1978-80; freelance writer N.Mex. Mag., Bristol-Meyers-Squibb, USA Today, others, 1978—. Instr., creative writing workshop tchr. Ohio State U., Santa Fe C.C., Santa Fe Prep. Sch., Rio Grande Sch., 1983-96; v.p. bd. dirs. N.Mex. Lit. Arts, Santa Fe, 1995-97; lit. judge State Arts Couns. for Wyo., Colo., Utah, 1994-96. Author: (short stories) New Letters, 1995, Walking the Twilight, 1994, Tierra, 1989; contbr. articles to profl. jours. Vol. St. Elizabeth's Shelter, Santa Fe, 1996; vol. instr. Santa Fe Pub. Schs., 1994-99. Recipient Silver award, Internat. Regional Mag. Assn., 2001; fellow, Ohio State U., 1986; scholar, Bread Loaf Writer's Conf., 1992. Mem. PEN, PEN West, Assoc. Writing Programs.

HUGHES, DIANE L. HICKS, elementary school educator, secondary school educator; b. Auburn, N.Y., May 1, 1956; d. Wilbur Lewis Hicks and Eunice Clara Hicks Miller; m. Richard James Hughes, July 6, 1985; 1 child, Keenan James. BS in Edn., SUNY, Cortland, N.Y., 1978, MS, 1985. Dir. aquatics K-12 Lansing Ctrl. Schs., NY, 1980—, coach girls swimming and diving, 1981—. Instr. Am. Red Cross, Lansing, 1974—. Contbr. articles to profl. jours. Named Female Coach of Yr., Ithaca Jour., 1989, 2004, Robert Springer Coach of Yr., IAC League, 1994, Robert Splagal Coach of Yr., 1995; recipient Clare Bartal award, Am. Red Cross, 2006, Female Coach of Yr., Ithaca Jour., 1984. Mem.: AAPHERD, Nat. Fedn. Interscholastic Ofcls. Assn., Am. Swim Coaches Assn., Nat. Interscholastic Coaches Assn., Nat. Fedn. Ofcls. Assn., Am. Swim Coaches Assn., N.Y. State Coaches Assn. (Honor award 2003, 2004, named Coach of Yr. 2005, 2004, 1989, 1984), N.Y. State Athletics Assn. (coord. girls swim and diving, coord. girls swim and diving sect. IV), N.Y. State PHSAA (coach sect. 4 girls swim and diving 1988—, coach girls swim and diving 1999—), Nat. Fedn. State H.S. Assn. (mem. aquatic com. Indpls. chpt. 2002—, sect. rep. scuba and dive 2003—). Home: 119 Park Ln Ithaca NY 14850

HUGHES, ELIZABETH R. (BETH), lawyer; b. Easton, Md., Apr. 13, 1956; AB cum laude, Harvard Univ., 1978; JD with honors, Univ. Md., 1981. Bar: Md. 1981, DC 1999, Va. 2001. Joined Venable LLP, 1981, ptnr., chairwoman, corp. fin., mergers, acquisitions group Washington. Bd. dir. Open Door of Baltimore, Inc. Finalist Top Wash. Lawyers in corp. fin., Wash. Bus. Jour., 2004. Mem.: ABA, Va. Bar Assn., DC Bar Assn., Md. State Bar Assn. (chair, com. on corp. law 2000—01), Bar Assn. Baltimore City. Avocations: golf, fishing. Office: Venable LLP 575 7th St NW Washington DC 20004 Office Phone: 202-344-8049. Office Fax: 202-344-8300. Business E-Mail: erhughes@venable.com.

HUGHES, GRACE-FLORES, federal agency administrator; b. Taft, Tex., June 11, 1946; d. Adan Flores and Catalina San Miguel; m. Harley Arnold Hughes, May 25, 1980. BA, U. D.C., 1977; MPA, Harvard U., 1980. Sec. Dept. Air Force Kelly AFB, San Antonio, 1967-70, Pentagon-Office Sec. of Def., Washington, 1970-72; program asst., social sci. analyst HEW, Washington, 1972-78; social sci. analyst, acting dir. Office Hispanic Ams. HHS, Washington, 1978-81; vis. prof. Nebr. Wesleyan U., Lincoln, 1982-83, U. Nebr., Omaha, 1984; spl. asst. SBA, Washington, 1985-88, assoc. adminstr. for minority small bus., 1988; dir. community rels. Dept. Justice, Washington, 1988-92; pres. Grace, Inc., Alexandria, Va.; v.p. for intergovtl. affairs USTAK, LLCcs., Inc. Spl. asst. Reagan/Bush '84 Campaign, Nebr. and Washington, 1984, 50th Presdl. Inaugural, Washington, 1984-85, Office Pub. Liaison, The White House, 1985. Author: The Bureaucrat, Categorized Workforce, 1992; co-author: New Book of Knowledge, 1980; chair adv. bd. Harvard Jour. Hispanic Policy, 1989—; The Use and Abuse of Diversity Mag., 1994, Hispanic Mag., 1996. Adv. mem. U.S. Senate Rep. Task Force, Washington, 1988-91; alumni exec. bd. J.F. Kennedy Sch. Govt., Harvard U., Cambridge, Mass., 1989-93; mem. Rep. Hispanic Assembly, 1984—; apptd. by Gov. Allen of Va. to Bd. for Profl. and Occpl. Regulations, 1994—, Bd. for Agr. and Consumer Svcs., 1997—; bd. dirs. Hispanic Found. for Arts; apptd. by Pres. Bush Fed. Svc. Impasses Panel, 2000. Recipient Excellence award Nev. Econ. Devel. Corp., 1988, Leadership award Am. GI Forum, Omaha, 1989; named one of 100 Most Influential Hispanics in U.S. Hispanic Bus. Mag., 1988. Mem. Assn. Pub. Adminstrs. (Outstanding Pub. Svc. award 1990), Hispanic Bus. Roundtable, Coun. in Excellence in Govt. (prin.), Fedn. Rep. Women, Mex.-Am. Women's Nat. Assn., Univ. Club (Washington). Episcopalian. Avocations: tennis, jogging, aerobics, equestrian. Home and Office: 5208 Bedlington Ter Alexandria VA 22304-3551 Office Phone: 703-395-2863. E-mail: harley45@aol.com.

HUGHES, HELEN ELIZABETH, psychologist; b. Damariscotta, Maine, Apr. 23, 1922; d. Thomas Bennett and Sarah Barbara (Mayhew) H.; m. Richard Garland Purinton, Sept. 5, 1942 (div. 1952); children: Richard Jordan, Jonathan Mayhew. Student, Butler U., 1940-42; BA, Calif. State U., L.A., 1954; MA, Calif. State U., Long Beach, 1960; PhD, U. Chgo., 1970. Sch. psychologist Torrance (Calif.) Unified Sch. Dist., 1960-66; lab supr. U. Chgo., 1967-70; asst. prof. U. Ill., Chgo., 1970-74; pvt. practice Chicago Heights, Ill., 1974-86; prof. psychology Gov.'s State U., University Park, Ill., 1974-88, ret., 1988, adj. prof., 1988—92. Leader workshops neuropsychology Michael Reese Hosp., Chgo., 1977, Ill. Sch. Psychol. Assn., 1981, Cen. States Sch. Psychol. Conf., 1983. Editor: The Creative Woman, 1977-93; contbr. numerous articles to profl. jours. Hon. co-chmn. Ill. Theater Ctr. Fund Raising Com., Park Forest, Ill., 1990. Mem. Am. Psychol. Assn. Democrat. Unitarian-Universalist. Home: 7 Union St Belfast ME 04915-6800

HUGHES, JENNIFER, utilities executive, photographer; b. Chgo., June 28, 1963; d. Harold Henry and Mable (Lee) H. Student, U. Ill., 1982-83. Girls basketball coach, driver's edn. asst. Carver Area H.S., Chgo., 1981-83; drivers edn. tchr. Continental Driving Sch., Chgo., 1989-91; security guard Zayre Dept. Store, Chgo., 1985-89; utilities exec. Commonwealth Edison, Chgo., 1989-92, mem. maintenance crew, 1992-94, control ctr. operator, 1994—2001; utilities executive CPI, 1994—2001. Author: Inspired By It All, 2000, It's All About Her, 2000; author numerous poems. Cert. CPR instr., ARC. With USAR, 1983-89. Mem. Order Eastern Star. Avocations: creating abstract art, biking, tennis, movies, theater.

HUGHES, JOYCE ANNE, law educator; b. Feb. 7, 1940. BA, Carleton U., 1961; JD, U. Minn., 1965. Bar: Minn. 1965, Ill. 1976. Law clk. Earl R. Larson U.S. Dist. Judge Minn., 1965-67; assoc. Howard, LeFevere, Lefler, Mpls., 1967-71; assoc. prof. U. Minn., 1971-75; assoc. prof. Northwestern U., 1975-79, prof., 1979—; gen. counsel Chgo. Transit Authority, 1984-88; dir. Fed. Home Loan Bank of Chgo. 1980-84; mem. Ill. Sup. Ct. Com. on Evidence, 1971-77; mem. U.S. del. to Belgrade Conf. to Review Helsinki Accord, 1977-78. Mem. Chgo. Bd. Edn., 1980-82. Mem. Order of Coif, Phi Beta Kappa. Office: Northwestern U Sch Law 357 E Chicago Ave Chicago IL 60611-3059 Office Phone: 312-503-8373. E-mail: jahughes@law.northwestern.edu.

HUGHES, JULIE, casting director, owner; b. N.Y.C., Sept. 07; d. Delbert Charles and Julia (Johnston) H.; m. Norman E. Rothstein, Dec. 28, 1971; children: Jeffrey E., Elisa M. BA, St. Lawrence U., 1963. Asst. gen. mgr. Music Fair Enterprises, N.Y.C., 1964-69; assoc. producer Orin Lehman Prodns., N.Y.C., 1969-73; asst. to Mr. Cohen Alexander H. Cohen, N.Y.C., 1971-76; owner Hughes Moss Casting, N.Y.C., 1978—. Assoc. producer, casting dir. (plays) including Effects of Gamma Rays on Man in the Moon Marigolds, (TV movie) A Matter of Conscience, 1989 (Artios award); casting dir. for over 60 Broadway shows. Mem. Casting Soc. Am. (dir. 1988-91). Home: 180 W End Ave New York NY 10023-4902

HUGHES, KAREN PARFITT, federal agency administrator; b. Paris, Dec. 27, 1956; m. Jerry L. Hughes; 1 child, Robert. BA in English, So. Meth. U., 1977, BFA in journalism, 1977. Television reporter KXAS-TV, Dallas/Ft. Worth, Tex., 1977—84; Tex. media coord. Reagan/Bush Campaign, 1984; media cons. Rep. Party of Tex., 1985—91, exec. dir., 1991—94; dir. comm. to Gov. George W. Bush State of Tex., 1994—2001; dir. comm. Bush-Cheney campaign, 2000; counselor to Pres. The White House, Washington, 2001—02; advisor Bush-Cheney campaign, 2004; under sec. for pub. diplomacy & pub. affairs US Dept. State, Washington, 2005—. Author: Ten Minutes From Normal, 2004. Office: US Dept State 2201 C St NW Rm 7261 Washington DC 20520

HUGHES, KAYLENE, historian, educator; b. Modesto, Calif., Aug. 4, 1952; BA, Miami-Dade (Fla.) Jr. Coll., 1972, Fla. Internat. U., 1976; MA, Fla. State U., 1977, PhD, 1985. Intern Fla. State Dept. Archives Records Mgmt., Tallahassee, 1977; Claims Control Supr. Sys. Devel. Corp., Tallahassee, 1978-81; editl. asst. Fla. Hotel and Motel Jour., Tallahassee, 1983-85; dir. edn., rsch. mgr. Fla. Hotel and Motel Assn., Tallahassee, 1985-87; historian U.S. Army Aviation & Missile Command, Redstone Arsenal, Ala., 1987—. Grad. asst. Fla. State U., Tallahassee, 1976-77, tchg. asst., 1981-83; adj. instr. history John C. Calhoun C.C., Huntsville, Ala., 1990—. Author: Florida's Lodging Industry: The First 75 Years, 1987, The Missile's Red Glare, 1992, Redstone Army Airfield: A Tradition of Aviation Support, 1992, Redstone Arsenal's Role in Operation Desert Shield/Desert Storm, 1992; contbr. articles to jours. and newspapers. Grantee Fla. State U., 1983. Mem. Phi Alpha Theta (sec. 1982-85), Phi Theta Kappa. Home: 342 Pawnee Trl SE Huntsville AL 35803-2280 Business E-Mail: kaylene.hughes@redstone.army.mil.

HUGHES, LIBBY, writer; b. Pitts, Aug. 11, 1932; d. Lloyd Alfred and Vera Abby (Walker) Pockman; m. R. John Hughes, Aug. 20, 1955 (div. 1988); children: Wendy E., Mark E BA, U. Ala., 1954; MFA, Boston U., 1955. Profl. actress, Kenya, South Africa, 1955—59; drama critic and feature writer Cape Cod Newspapers, 1977—86, assoc. pub., 1977—81, pub., 1981—85. Pres. Desert Starfield Prodn., 1994 Author: Bali, 1969, Margaret Thatcher, 1989, Benazir Bhutto, 1990, Nelson Mandela, 1992, Good Manners for Children, 1992, H. Norman Schwarzkopf, 1992, West Point, 1992, Valley Forge, 1992, Colin Powell, 1996, School Manners Workbook, 1998, Christopher Reeve, 1997, Tiger Woods, 2000, Yitzhak Rabin, 2001, George W. Bush, 2003, John Grisham, 2004, Ronald Reagan, 2005; editor: Ginger Rogers Autobiography, 1989, 91; playwright: Sin in the Attic (Chatham Drama Guild award 1999-2000), Pasta and Curry (New Opera and Musical Theatre Initiative award 2000), Here Come the Bullies, 2004, 2nd edit, 2006, Weapon in Her Pocket, 2006, Tiger, Tiger Hits the Ball and That's not All!, 2006, 37 others; theater critic, reviewer www.capecodtoday.com Bd. dir. Wisdom Inst., 1984-86, Cape Cod Mus., 1984-86 Recipient Songwriting award, Eventide Arts Festival Cape Cod, 2001, 2003, 2005, 2006, Life Achievement award, Emma Willard Sch., 2005. Mem. ASCAP, Dramatists Guild, Authors Guild, Ala. Wildlife Rescue Svc. (pres. 1988-89), Nat. Soc. Arts and Letters (chpt. pres. 1984-86, protocol officer 1984-86), Nat. League Am. Pen Women Avocations: theater, news, wildlife, rhodesian ridgebacks. Home: September to May 993 Memorial Dr #301 Cambridge MA 02138 E-mail: libhughes@aol.com.

HUGHES, LINDA J., newspaper publisher; b. Princeton, BC, Can., Sept. 27, 1950; d. Edward Rees and Madge Preston (Bryan) H.; m. George Fredrick Ward, Dec. 16, 1978; children: Sean Ward, Kate Ward. BA, U. Victoria (B.C.), 1972; LittD (hon.), Athabasca U., 1997; diploma in journalism (hon.), Grant MacEwan C.C., Edmonton, Alta., Can., 1999; LLD (hon.), U. Alberta, 2003. With Edmonton Jour., Alta., Canada, 1976—, from reporter to asst. mng. editor Alta., 1984-87, editor Alta., 1987-92, pub. Alta., 1992—. Southam fellow U. Toronto, Ont., Can., 1977-78; recipient Disting. Citizen award Grant MacEwan C.C., 1999, Dist. Alumni award U. Victoria, 2000. Office: Edmonton Journal 10006 101st St PO Box 2421 Edmonton AB Canada T5J 2S6 E-mail: lhughes@thejournalcanwest.com.

HUGHES, MARIJA MATICH, law librarian; b. Belgrade, Yugoslavia; came to U.S., 1960, naturalized, 1971; d. Zarija and Antonija (Hudowsky) Matich. BA in Music, Mokranjac, Belgrade; BA in English, U. Belgrade and Calif. State U.; MLS, U. Md.; student, McGeorge Sch. Law; MHA in Health Care Adminstrn., George Washington U., 1985, M. in Adminstrv. Scis., 1989. Counselor, gen. mgr. Career Counseling Service, Sacramento, Calif., 1962-64; sec. to mgr. Sacramento State Coll., 1965-66; student librarian High John program U. Md., Fairmont Heights, 1967; reference librarian Calif. State Law Library, Sacramento, 1968; head reference library-faculty liasion librarian Hastings Coll. Law U. Calif., San Francisco, 1969-72; head law librarian AT&T, Washington, 1972-73; chief law librarian Nat. Clearinghouse Library, U.S. Commn. on Civil Rights, Washington, 1973-86; tech. info. specialist U.S. Dept. Labor, OSHA, Tech. Date Ctr., 1988—; owner, pub. Hughes Press. Author (compiler): The Sexual Barrier, Legal and Econ. Aspects of Employment, vols. 1 and 2, 1970—73, The Sexual Barriers: Legal, Medical, Economic and Social Aspects of Sex Discrimination, 1977, Computer Health Hazards, 1990, 1993, Computer Health Hazards, Eng. translation, 1996, Sick From Computers, 1994, Computers, Antennas, Cellular Telephones and Power Lines Health Hazards, 1996, Shadow at the Ball, 2001; contbr. articles to profl. jours. Mem. Am. Assn. Law Librs., Bioelectromagnetics Soc., Consumer Utilities Bd. Home: 2400 Virginia Ave NW Apt C501 Washington DC 20037-2644 Office Phone: 202-293-2686.

HUGHES, MARVALENE, academic administrator; Student, Tuskegee U., NYU, Columbia U.; PhD in Counseling and Adminstrn., Fla. State U.; postgrad., Harvard U., U. Calif., San Diego. Dir. counseling and career devel. Eckerd Coll., Fla.; dir. counseling svcs. and placement, prof. and adminstr. San Diego State U.; assoc. v.p. student affairs Ariz. State U.; v.p. student affairs, prof. counseling and human svcs. U. Toledo; v.p. student affairs, vice provost, prof. ednl. psychology U. Minn.; pres. Calif. State U., Stanislaus, 1994—2005, Dillard U., New Orleans, 2005—. Nat., internat. keynote spkr. Contbr. chpts. to books and articles to profl. jours. Keynoter Pres.-to-Pres. Address, Internat. Conf. Pres. and Chancellors, Puerto Rico, 1999; chmn. Women Pres. and Chancellors Am. Assn. State Colls. and Univs., 1999—, prof. devel. com.; adv. bd. 1st Nat. Women's Mus.; mem. divsn. II pres. coun. NCAA, mem. divsn. II budget and fin. com., liason pres. coun. divsn. II student athlete adv. com.; mem. evaluation com. Accrediting Commn. Sr. Colls. and Univs., We. Assn. Schs. and Colls.; mem. Lt. Gov.'s Commn One Calif., 1999. Mem. Leadership Calif. Office: Dillard Univ 2601 Gentilly Blvd New Orleans LA 70122

HUGHES, MARY KATHERINE, lawyer; b. July 16, 1949; d. John Chamberlain and Marjorie (Anstey) Hughes; m. Andrew H. Eker, July 7, 1982. BBA cum laude, U. Alaska, 1971; JD, Willamette U., 1974; postgrad., Heriot-Watt U., Edinburgh, Scotland, 1971. Bar: Alaska 1975. Ptnr. Hughes, Thorsness, Gantz, Powell & Brundin, Anchorage, 1974—95; mcpl. atty. Municipality of Anchorage, 1995—2000; of counsel Hughes, Thorsness, Powell, Huddleston & Bauman, 2001—05; Alaska state dir. Office US Senator Lisa Murkowski, 2005—. Talk show host AM 700 KBYR, 2002—. Trustee Willamette U., 1997—; bd. visitors WUCL, 1978—2001; bd. dirs. Alaska Repertory Theatre, 1986—88, pres., 1987—88; commr. Alaska Code Revision Commn., 1987—94; bd. visitors U. Alaska, Fairbanks, 1994—2002, bd. regents, 2002—, chair bd. regents, 2005—; bd. dirs. Anchorage Econ. Devel. Corp., 1989—, chmn., 1994; mem. Providence Anchorage Adv. Coun., 1993—2005, Providence Alaska Found., 1998—2005, chair, 2002—04; lawyer rep. 9th Cir. Jud. Conf., 1995—2000; pres. Alaska Bar Found., 1984—98, trustee, 2001—, Athena Soc., 2003—. Fellow: U. Alaska Found. (trustee 1990—), Am. Bar Found.; mem.: Internat. Mcpl. Lawyers Assn. (state chair 1995—96, regional v.p. 1997—2000), Anchorage Assn. Women Lawyers (pres. 1976—77), Alaska Bar Assn. (bd. govs. 1981—84, pres. 1983—84), Soroptimists (pres. 1986—87), Delta Theta Phi. Republican. Roman Catholic. Home: 1592 Coffey Ln Anchorage AK 99501-4977 Office Phone: 907-274-6290. E-mail: mkhughes@acsalaska.net.

HUGHES, MARY KATHERINE, nurse; b. Phila., Nov. 3, 1945; d. James Simon and Mary Katherine (MacLellan) Kiening; m. Robert William Hughes June 11, 1967; children: William, Jonathan, Sarah. BS, Tex. Woman's U., 1968, MS, 1988. Cert. grief therapist. Staff nurse Planned Parenthood, Houston, 1968-70, Staff Builder's, Houston, 1979-81, Meml. Southwest Hosp., Houston, 1981-90; nurse psychotherapist Woman's Christian Home, Houston, 1989-90; clin. nurse specialist U. Tex. MD Anderson Cancer Ctr., Houston, 1990—, clin. instr., 1995—. Mem. adj. faculty Tex. Woman's U., Houston, 1989-96; Mary Mazzwy lectr. Houston Oncology Nursing Soc., 1993. Facilitator Patient Group Am. Cancer Soc., 1993—, co-facilitator Grief Group, 1983—, Family Group, 1994—, bd. dirs., 1983-86, adv. bd., 1986-95. Recipient Sword of Hope award Am. Cancer Soc., 1986, Outstanding Nurse Oncologist Brown Found., 1993, Outstanding Vol. St. John's Presbyn. Ch., 1995; named 100 Gt. Nursing Alumni Tex. Woman's U., 2001. Presbyterian. Avocations: reading, music, opera, ballet, singing. Office: U Tex MD Anderson Cancer Ctr 1515 Holcombe Blvd # 431 Houston TX 77030-4009 Office Phone: 713-792-7546. E-mail: mhughes@mdanderson.org.

HUGHES, MARY SORROWS, artist; b. Washington, Oct. 28, 1945; d. Howard Earl and Martha Jane (Summerville) Sorrows; m. Frank Broox Hughes, May 22, 1967; 1 child, Broox Bradley. BA in Art, Centenary Coll., 1967, BA in Edn., 1978. Draftsman for civil engring. dept. Texaco, New Orleans, 1967-70; owner, freelance artist Shreveport, La., 1979—. Illustrator Total Tales, 1984; included in The Best of Watercolor, 1995, Best of Watercolor: Painting Color, 1997, Floral Inspirations, 1998, Splash 7: The Qualities of Light, 2002, The New Creative Artist by Nita Leland, 2006; represented in permanent collections Southwestern Electric Power Co., Shreveport, Burgess Corp. Collection, Calif.; featured artist Watercolor Mag., 2003; featured artist donor Phila. House Auction and Fund Raiser for AIDS, 2003. Bd. dirs. Child Care Svcs., Inc. of N.W. La., Shreveport, 1987-91, pres., 1991; Artport Airport Exhibit and Fundraiser for AIDS, Shreveport, 1991-2002; worker Habitat for Humanity, Shreveport, 1992, 94; trustee St. Luke's Meth. Ch., Shreveport, 1993-95, chair bldg. com., 1986; bd. dirs. Shreveport Art Guild, Friends of the Meadows Mus., 2000-03. Named one of 10 Artists for Highway Haiku, 2002; recipient Gary, Field, Landry & Bradford award, La. Women Artists, 1994. Mem.: La. Watercolor Soc. (signature mem., Pres. award Internat. Show 2005), Hoover Watercolor Soc. (pres. 1986, treas., publicity chair, others, Jurors Choice award 2001, Transparent Watercolor award 2003, Jurors Choice award 2006, Transparent Watercolor award 2006), La. Artists (pres. 1994, 1998), Watercolor West (Yarka St. Petersberg Mdse. award 1995, Signature Mem. award 1996, W. Burgess Purchase prize 1998), Southwestern Watercolor Soc. (Signature Mem. award 1991, Edgar A. Whitney award 1992, Ansel Merchandise award 1999, Canson-Talons Inc. award 2000), Med. Aux. Wives Club. Democrat. Avocations: exercise, gardening, travel, reading, flute. Home: 530 Atkins Ave Shreveport LA 71104-4448 Studio: 1700 Creswell Ave Shreveport LA 71101-4726 Office Phone: 318-222-2912. E-mail: maryhughes@marysorrowshughes.com.

HUGHES, MICHAELA KELLY, actress; b. Morristown, N.J., Mar. 31; d. Joseph Francis and Mary Elizabeth (Coughlin) H. Scholarship student, Houston Ballet Acad., 1970-73; part-time scholarship student, Sch. Am. Ballet, 1971. Founder, owner Classic Stocking Co., 1992—. Child actress with Alley Theatre, Houston, 1969, 71, mem. Houston Ballet, 1974, Eliot Feld Ballet, N.Y.C., 1975—, prin. dancer, 1974-79, mem. Am. Ballet Theatre, 1979-81; Broadway appearances include On Your Toes, 1982, as Gloria Upson in Mame, 1983, Raggedy Ann, 1986, as Cassie in A Chorus Line, 1987, Anything Goes, 1988, (films) Hellfighters, A Chorus Line, Alice, The Human Quality; appeared as Fiona in Another World (serial), Loving, Saturday Night Live, Veronica's Closet (sitcom), numerous television commls. Mem. AFTRA, SAG, AEA, Am. Guild Mus. Artists.

HUGHES, NANCY COPELAND, early childhood education educator; b. Plattsburgh, NY, Nov. 7, 1946; d. George Rogers and Ruth Foljambe Copeland; m. Robert Charles Hughes, Mar. 17, 1968; children: Bonnie, Christopher, Robert, Daniel. BA in Psychology, U. N.H., Durham, 1968; MS in Edn., SUNY, Plattsburgh, 1983. Cert. tchr. nursery, 6th grad, reading, K-12, phys. edn. K-12 N.Y. Phys. edn. tchr. Northeastern Clinton Sch., Champlain, NY, 1969—76, primary devel. tchr., 1976—85, 3d grade tchr., 1985—99, reading tchr., 1999—2005; early childhood edn. instr. SUNY, Plattsburgh, 2005—. Lectr. in field. Bd. dirs. Champlain Children's Learning Ctr., Rouses Point, NY, 2005—. Grantee Model Schs. Tch. Integration grantee, N.Y. State Model Schs., 1999. Mem.: Nat. Assn. for Edn. Young Children. Avocations: kayaking, antiques. Home: 3633 Rt 9 Peru NY 12972 Office: SUNY Ward Hall 112D 101 Broad St Plattsburgh NY 12901

HUGHES, RHONDA J., mathematics professor; children: Sarah, Jeremy. BS, MS, U. Ill., Chgo., PhD in Mathematics. Prof. Dept. Math. Bryn Mawr Coll., 1980—, Helen Herrmann prof. math. Co-founder & co-dir. (with Sylvia Bozeman) Spelman-Bryn Mawr Summer Math. Program, 1992, EDGE Enhancing Diversity in Grad. Edn.: A Transition Program for Women in Math. Sci., 1992. Mem.: AAAS (Lifetime Mentor award 2004), Assn. Women in Mathematics (former pres.). Office: Bryn Mawr Coll Park Science Bldg 332 Bryn Mawr PA 19010 also: The EDGE Program Bryn Mawr Coll 101 North Merion Ave Bryn Mawr PA 19010 Office Phone: 610-526-5351. E-mail: rhughes@brynmawr.edu.

HUGHES, ROSEMARY A., counselor, educator; b. Detroit, Dec. 30, 1950; d. John J. and Muriel Grace Hughes; 1 child, James E. Tompkins. BA, Wayne State U., Detroit, Michigan; post grad., U. Notre Dame, South Bend, Ind., 1971—73; MA, Wayne State U., Detroit, Mich., 1989—91; post grad., Nat. U. Ireland, Dublin, Ireland, 1999—2000, The Union Inst. and U., Cin. Lic. profl. counselor State of Mich., 1991. Welfare to work program for women Women's Survival Ctr., Pontiac, Mich., 1992—94; exec. dir. NOW Found., Birmingham, 1994—96, Sojourner Found., Detroit, 2000—01; program dir. women to work Jewish Vocat. Svcs., Southfield, 2001—03; prof. Oakland U., Rochester, 1994—; counselor and cons. Aishlinn Group, Inc., Grosse Pointe Park, Mich., 1991—, pres. and CEO. Cons. Women's Survival Ctr., Pontiac, 1995—96, Woman's Ctr. Oakland C.C., Auburn Hills, 1997—98, U. Mich., Dearborn, 2004—05; judge Mich. Women's Hall of Fame, Lansing, 1999—99; grant writer Resource Connections, Dearborn, 2000—02. Dir. YWCA, Pontiac, Mich., 1994—95; pres. and CEO Aishlinn Women's Ctr., Grosse Pointe Park, 1991. Recipient George E. Leonard Career Devel. Women award, Wayne State U., 1990, 1991, Tchr. Excellence award, Oakland U., 2005. Mem.: NOW (assoc.), AAUP (assoc.), Am. Assn. Counselors and Devel. (assoc.), Mich. Women's Studies Assn. (assoc.), Wayne State Alumni Assn. (assoc.), Women of Wayne (assoc.), Soroptomist Internat. (assoc.). Office: Oakland Univ Rochester MI 48309-4401 Home Fax: 313-885-9840. E-mail: rhughes@oakland.edu.

HUGHES, SARAH, figure skater; b. Great Neck, N.Y., May 2, 1985; Student, Yale U. Mem. U.S. Olympic Team, Salt Lake City, 2002. Competitive history includes: 1st place North Atlantic Novice, 1997, 1st place North Atlantic Novice, 1998, 1st place Eastern Jr., 1998, 1st place U.S. Championships Jr., 1998, 1998, 1st place World Jr. Team Selection Competition, 1st place Vienna Cup, 1999, 4th place Skate America, 1st place Keri Lotion vs. The World (Team USA-1st place), 1999, Gold Medal, Olympic Winter Games, 2002. recipient Sullivan award, 2002, ESPY award for best olympian; names USOC Sports Woman of the Yr., 2002, March of Dimes Sports Woman of the Yr., 2002 Avocations: reading, tennis, violin. Office: USFSA 20 1st St Colorado Springs CO 80906-3624

HUGHES, SUE MARGARET, retired librarian; b. Cleburne, Tex. d. Chastain Wesley and Sue Willis (Payne) H. BBA, U. Tex., Austin, 1949; MLS, Tex. Woman's U., Denton, 1960, PhD, 1987. Sec.-treas. pvt. corps., Waco, Tex., 1949-59; asst. in public svcs. Baylor U. Libr., Waco, 1960-64, acquisitions libr., 1964-79, acting univ. libr., summer 1979, dir. Moody Libr., 1980-89; interim univ. libr. Baylor U., Waco, 1989-91, spl. materials cons., 1991-92; ret., 1992. Mem. AAUP, ALA, Tex. Libr. Assn., AAUW, Brazor Forum, Hist. Waco Found., Delta Kappa Gamma, Beta Phi Mu, Beta Gamma Sigma. Clubs: Altrusa. Methodist.

HUGHES, SUSAN MICHELE, science educator, researcher; d. Joseph Patrick and Lucille Hughes. BS, SUNY, Binghamton, 1998; PhD, SUNY, Albany, 2004. Grad. lectr. SUNY, Albany, 2000—04; adj. instr. Albany Med. Coll., 2001, Hudson Valley C.C., Troy, NY, 2002—04, Schenectady County C.C., 2003, Union Coll., Schenectady, 2004; vis. asst. prof. Vassar Coll., Poughkeepsie, NY, 2004—06; asst. prof. Albright Coll., Reading, Pa., 2006—. Mem. selection panel for Excellence in Tchg. award SUNY, Albany, 2004; test item writer for GRE and CLEP Ednl. Testing Svc., Princeton, NJ, 2005. Contbr. articles to profl. jours.; reviewer Evolution and Human Behavior Jour., 2003, 2005. Sponsor Australian Koala Found., 2000—. Recipient Pres.'s award for excellence in tchg., SUNY, Albany, 2003, Outstanding achievement award as grad. lectr., Psi Chi, 2003. Mem.: Am. Psychol. Soc., Human Behavior and Evolution Soc. Office Phone: 610-929-6732. E-mail: shughes@alb.edu.

HUGHES, TERESA MEAD, psychologist; d. Jack Lee Mead and Christine Terese Jones; m. John Robert Hughes, June 30, 2001; 1 child, Jason Robert. BS, USAF Acad., Colorado Springs, 1998; MS, U. Health Scis., Bethesda, Md., 2002, PhD, 2004. Lic. clin. psychologist Ala., 2004. Commd. 2d lt. USAF, 1998, advanced through grades to capt., 2002; staff psychologist Wilford Hall Med. Ctr., USAF, San Antonio, 2003—05, chief outreach and testing, 2005; chief alcohol and drug abuse prevention & treatment program Peterson AFB, Colorado Springs, 2005—. Team chief Critical Incident Stress Mgmt. Team, Colorado Springs, 2005—. Mem.: APA.

HUGHES STANBACK, FRANCINE, elementary school educator, school system administrator; d. Willie Ceasar and Marie Letita Hughes; m. Willie James Stanback, Apr. 15, 1989; 1 child, Rhonda Francine. BS in Early Childhood Edn., Pa. State U., Univ. Pk., Pa., 1977; MS in Elem. Edn., Cheyney State U., Pa., 1997. Cert. tchr. Pa. Tchr. Archdiocese Phila., 1978—87; from tchr. to academic coach Sch. Dist. Phila., 1987—2003, academic coach, 2003—. Nominee Presdl. award, 1993, 1994, Sci. Tchr. of Yr. award, Chem. Mfg., 1995, Tchr. of Yr. award, Ruth Hayre Wright Found., 1996. Mem.: Phila. (Pa.) Fedn. Tchrs., Phila. (Pa.) Urban Systematic Program, Nat. Sci. Tchrs. Assn., Delta Sigma Theta. Office: Regional Sci Coach Sch Dist Phila 9438 Fairgreen Ln Fl 1 Philadelphia PA 19114

HUGHES-TEBO, JACQUELINE EMMA, regional coordinator; b. Baltimore, Md., Feb. 10, 1968; d. Hugh Price Hughes Jr. and Reta Theresa Hughes; m. Donald W. Tebo, Jr. BA in Psychology, Coll. Notre Dame Md., Balt., 1990; MBA, U. Phoenix, Columbia, Md., 2001; doctoral canidate, Capella U., 2005—. CPR, First Aid, and AED Instructor ARC, 2002. Armorer USMC Reserves, Savannah, Ga., 1988—99; counselor Mgmt. Tng. Corp., Washington, 1992—99; counseling mgr. Adams and Assocs., Laurel, Md., 1995—96; regional coord., info. systems specialist TCU Manpower Tng. Dept., Rockville, Md., 1999—. Innovation com. mem. Mgmt. Tng. Corp., Randallstown, Md., 1993; cultural diversity coord. Adams and Assocs., Laure, Md., 1995—96. Author: (poetry) Look, 1999. Chair, Relay for Life Am. Cancer Soc., 2002—03. Mem.: AAUW, NAFE. Avocations: travel, volunteer work. Personal E-mail: jetebo@comcast.net.

HUGHEY, BRENDA JOYCE, supervisor; b. Linton, Ind., Jan. 23, 1951; d. William L. and Mary Margaret Pritchard; m. David Nelson Hughey, July 23, 1977; children: Allison, Brock. BS, Ind. State U., 1973, MS, 1977. Cert. administr. and supr. Middle Tenn. State U., 1994, career ladder III. Tchr. Switz City (Ind.) Elem. Sch., 1973—77, Franklin (Tenn.) Jr. High, 1978—84, Franklin (Tenn.) Mid. Sch., 1984—89; asst. prin. Liberty Elem. Sch., Franklin, Tenn., 1990—96; spl. edn. supr. Franklin (Tenn.) Spl. Sch. Dist., 1996—. Bd. dirs. Ct. Apptd. Spl. Adv., Franklin, Tenn., 2003—. Mem.: Tenn. Assn. Spl. Edn. Suprs., Assn. of Supervision and Curriculum Devel., Coun. for Exceptional Children. Baptist. Avocations: reading, gardening. Office: Franklin Spl Sch Dist 507 New Hwy 96W Franklin TN 37069 Home: 1420 Lewisburg Pike Franklin TN 37064 Office Phone: 615-794-6624. E-mail: Brenda@fssd.org.

HUGILL, CHLOE, artist, foundation administrator; b. Fundao, Portugal, May 18, 1943; came to U.S, 1970; d. Herculano Rebordao and Guilhermina Carlota (Godinho) Ramos; m. John Varty Hugill, Jan. 14, 1967; children: John Rebordao Hugill, Claudia Rebordao Hugill. Grad., Pontifical U. Rio de Janeiro, 1961-62, 63-64, Montessori Coll., Rio de Janeiro, 1966. Cert. tchr. in Neo-Latin langs. and their lits. Tchr. Pontifical U. Rio de Janeiro, 1965-70; office mgr. John V. Hugill MD PA Plastic Surgery Office, Ft. Myers, Fla., 1970—. Judge art in pub. schs. Lee County (Fla.) Schs., 1999; spkr. in field. Fine artist working in watercolor, oils, acrylics. Hospital chmn. charity ball Lee County Med. Aux., Ft. Myers, 1979-81,; mem. fundaising coms., 1979-81; vol. Abuse Counseling and Treatment, 1981—. Recipient awards in oils and watercolor Charlotte County Visual Arts Ctr., 1995. Mem. Frizzel Artists Guild (pres. 1995, treas. 1996). Roman Catholic. Avocations: tennis, skiing, hiking, boating. Office: 8660 College Pkwy Ste 100 Fort Myers FL 33919-4873 Home: 250 Stable Gate Dr Campobello SC 29322-8037

HUGO, JESSICA LYN, physical education educator; d. Mike Joseph and Lori Lyn Hugo. BA, Saginaw Valley State U., Mich., 2003; postgrad., Cen. Mich. U. Fitness instr. Midland Comty. Ctr., Mich., 2001—02; tchr. phys. edn. Alcona Comty. Schs., Lincoln, Mich., 2003, Standish-Sterling HS, 2004, Ohio State U., Columbus, 2004—. Mem.: NASPSA, AAHPERD, Ohio Assn. Health, Phys. Edn., Recreation and Dance. Avocations: exercise, dance. Home: 4428 Carnegie Hall Blvd Dublin OH 43016

HUGO, MIRIAM JEANNE, counseling psychologist, educator; b. Pitts., Feb. 28, 1926; d. James Elmer and Gladys Marguerite (Bartlett) Hugo. BS, Miami U., Oxford, Ohio, 1948; MA, Ohio State U., 1953; PhD, Ohio U., 1969. Cert. counselor, Fla. Tchr. Lemon-Monroe Twp., Hamilton County, Ohio, 1948-49; head tchr. Ohio State Juvenile Diagnostic Ctr., Columbus, 1950-54, Columbus Children's Psychiat. Hosp., Columbus, 1954-59; tchr. Exptl. Class for Emotionally Disturbed Children, Miami, Fla., 1959-60; elem. sch. counselor Dade County (Fla.) Schs., Miami, 1960-66, sch. psychologist, 1969-70; counseling psychologist U. Wis., Eau Claire, 1970-76, assoc. dir. counseling svcs., 1976-84, assoc. dean of students, 1984-90, ret., 1990. Mem. adv. bd. County Coun. on Drug and Alcohol Abuse Prevention, Eau Claire, 1983, Planned Parenthood of Eau Claire, 1976-77. Mem. exec. bd. Friends of L.E. Phillips Meml. Pub. Libr., Eau Claire, 1993-96, v.p., 1993-94, pres., 1994-95. Mem. AAUW, Kiwanis Internat. (bd. dirs. Clear Water Club 1997-98), Phi Delta Kappa. Democrat. Episcopalian. Avocations: reading, travel, art and painting, volunteering. Home: 1450 Cummings Ave Eau Claire WI 54701-6569

HUGUENARD, JOAN, writer; b. South Bend, Ind., Apr. 30, 1931; d. Peter Albert and Clementine (Dominski) Gadomski; children: Cathie, Jim, John, Tom, Bob, Frank, Charlie, Andy. BA in Theology, Marquette U., 1983. Advt. cons., sales mgr. Penny Saver, South Bend, Ind., 1973-76; records mgmt. cons. TAB Products Co., Palo Alto, Calif., 1976-84; chaplain in residence Frost Valley YMCA Camp, Oliveria, N.Y., 1984; ESL tchr. Univs. at Shenyang, Nanjing, Tianjin, China, 1986-89; recruiter in China WorldTeach, Harvard U., Cambridge, Mass., 1988-89; exec. dir. Office of Haitian Ministries, Norwich, Conn., 1990-91; cons. in office efficiency and assoc. dir. Washington Office on Haiti, Washington, 1992; small bus. owner, mgr. Clutterfly Corner, various locations, 1983—; freelance writer, 1989—. Pub. lectr.; columnist just joan, www.sonomasun.com. Author: Embracing the Yes!: A Life Recycled, 1999; weekly columnist, freelance reporter Sonoma Sun, Calif., 2004—; contbr. articles to newspapers and mags. Founder, pres. S.T.A.R.T. Students Taking Action to Recycle Trash, South Bend, Ind., 1970-75; co-founder local chpt. Beginning Experience, South Bend, 1977-81; vol. tchr., study tours coord. Biblical Resources Pilgrim Ctr., Jerusalem, 1997—. Roman Catholic. Avocations: clowning, Scrabble, theater. Home: 735 Oregon St Sonoma CA 95476-6428 Personal E-mail: joan@firstcentrylive.com. E-mail: joan@justjoanonline.com.

HUHEEY, MARILYN JANE, ophthalmologist, educator; b. Cin., Aug. 31, 1935; d. George Mercer and Mary Jane (Weaver) H. BS in Math., Ohio U., Athens, 1958; MS in Physiology, U. Okla., 1966; MD, U. Ky., 1970. Diplomate Am. Bd. Ophthalmology. Tchr. math. James Ford Rhodes H.S., Cleve., 1956-58; biostatistician Nat. Jewish Hosp., Denver, 1958-60; life sci. engr. Stanley Aviation Corp., Denver, 1960-63, N.Am. Aviation Co., L.A., 1963-67; intern U. Ky. Hosp., 1970-71; emergency room physician Jewish Hosp., Mercy Hosp., Bethesda Hosp., Cin., 1971-72; ship's doctor, 1972; resident in ophthalmology Ohio State U. Hosp., Columbus, 1972-75; practice medicine specializing in ophthalmology Columbus, 1975—. Mem. staff Univ. Hosp., Grant Hosp., St. Anthony Hosp., 1975-79; clin. asst. prof. Ohio State U. Med. Sch., 1976—, dir. course ophthalmologic receptionist/aides, 1976; mem. Peer Rev. Sys. Bd., 1986-92, exec. com., 1988-92; mem. Ohio Optical Dispensers Bd., 1986-91; bd. dirs. Ctrl. Ohio Radio Reading Svc., 1997—2003; mem. Ohio Bd. Cosmetology, 1999—. Dem. candidate for Ohio Senate, 1982; mem. Wicked Investment Club, 1998—, pres. 1999-2004, treas., 2005—. Fellow Am. Acad. Ophthalmology; mem. AAUP, Am. Assn. Ophthalmologists, Ohio Ophthalmol. Soc. (bd. govs. 1984-89, del. to Ohio State Med. Assn. 1984-88), Franklin County Acad. Medicine (profl. rels. com. 1979-82, legis. com. 1981-89, edn. and program com. 1981-88, chmn. 1982-85, chmn. cmty. rels. com. 1987-90, chmn. resolution com. 1987-92, mem. fin. com. 1988-92), Ohio Soc. Prevent Blindness (chmn. med. adv. bd. 1978-80), Ohio State Med. Assn. (dr.-nurse liaison com. 1983-87), Columbus EENT Soc., Am. Coun. of the Blind (bd. dirs. 1995-96), Life Care Alliance (pres. sustaining bd. 1987-88), United Way (planning com. 1992-93), LWV, Columbus Coun. World Affairs, Columbus Bus. and Profl. Women's Club, Columbus C. of C., Grandview Area Bus. Assn., Federated Dem. Women Ohio, Columbus Area Women's Polit. Caucus, Columbus Met. Club (forum com. 1982-85, fundraising com. 1983-84, chmn. 10th anniversary com. 1986), Mercedes Benz Club (dir. 1981-83), Zonta (program com. 1984-86, chmn. internat. com. 1983), Herb Soc., Phi Mu. Home: 2396 Northwest Blvd Columbus OH 43221-3829 Office: 1335 Dublin Rd Ste 25A Columbus OH 43215-1000 Office Phone: 614-488-8836. E-mail: mhuheey.1@yahoo.com.

HUHTALA, MARIE THERESE, federal agency administrator, former ambassador; b. LA, Mar. 26, 1949; d. Joseph E. Sr. and Rosemary E. (Williamson) Mackey; m. Eino A. Huhtala Jr., July 10, 1971; children: Karen Rose, Jorma David. BA in French, Santa Clara U., 1971; diploma, Nat. War Coll., 1988; MA, Laval U., 1995. Joined Fgn. Svc., Dept. State, Washington, 1972; consular officer Am. Embassy, Paris, 1973-75; vice consul U.S. Consulate, Chiang Mai, Thailand, 1976-79; secretariat staff officer Fgn. Svc., Dept. State, Washington, 1979-80, congl. rels. officer, 1980-81, country officer for Chad, 1981-83, polit. officer U.S. Consulate Gen. Hong Kong, 1985-87, chief East Asian assignments, bur. pers. divsn. Washington, 1988-90, dep. dir. Vietnam, Laos and Cambodia affairs, 1990-92, consul gen. U.S. Consulate Gen. Que., Canada, 1992—95; dep. chief mission U.S. Embassy, Bangkok, 1998—2001; U.S. amb. to Malaysia US Dept. State, 2001—04, dep. asst. sec. E. Asian & Pacific affairs Washington, 2004—. Bd. dirs. Orchestre Symphonique de Que., 1992—. Recipient Superior Honor award, Dept. of State, Meritorious Honor award. Mem. Am. Fgn. Svc. Assn., Acad. Polit. Sci., Nat. War Coll. Alumni Assn., Rotary Club of Que. (hon.). Roman Catholic. Achievements include speaks fluent French and Thai. Avocation: choral singing. Office: US Dept State 2201 C St NW Washington DC 20520

HUIE, CAROL P., information science educator; b. Kingston, Jamaica; AAS, Hostos CC, NYC, 1986; BSc, Lehman Coll., NYC, 1988; MS, CCNY, 1994; postgrad., CUNY, 1994—99, Nova Southeastern U., 2001—. Patient acct.coord. New Rochelle Med. Ctr., New Rochelle, NY, 1988-91; coll. lab tech. Hostos Community Coll., Bronx, NY, 1991-98, instr., 1994—2000, asst. professor, 2000—. Mem.: IEEE, Assn. Computing Machinery, Schomburg Ctr. Rsch. Black Culture, Consortium for Computing in Small Colls., CUNY Acad. for Humanities and Scis., Delta Pi Epsilon. Office Phone: 718-518-6550. E-mail: chuie@hostos.cuny.edu.

HUKILL, MARGARET ANNE, physical therapist, rehabilitation services professional, educator; b. Columbus, Feb. 17, 1924; d. Ralph Wentworth and Laura Bebb Hukill; m. John Glenn Kinn (div.). BS, U. Wis., 1946; diploma in physical therapy and rehab. counseling, Va. Commonwealth U., 1949; MS, William and Mary Coll., Va., 1956. Lic. physical therapist Ohio, cert. rehab. counselor Va. Rehab. counselor Vets. Adminstrn., Dayton, 1948; physical therapist Butterworth Hosp., Grand Rapids, 1950—52; rsch. asst. U. Cin., Applied Sci. Rsch. Lab., 1953—54; physical therapist Nightengale Cottage, Columbus, 1954—55; program counselor Ohio TB and Health Assn., Columbus, 1956—62; asst. prof. Ohio State Univ., Columbus, 1962—76; coord. rehab. clin. edn. Mt. Carmel East Hosp., Columbus, 1979—94; ret., 1994. Sr. advisory bd. Mt. Carmel Health, Columbus, 1980—94; project grant evaluator Ohio Program with Humanities, Capitol U., 1976—77; editl. asst. Battelle Meml. Inst., Columbus, Ohio, 1978. Contbr. articles to jours. and mags. Bd. mem. Ctr. for New Directions, Columbus, 1980—85; sec. Ohio chpt. Gray Panthers of Am., Columbus, 1985—88; mem. Elder Hostel, Inc.: Worldwide, Boston, 1987—2003; mem., elder, trustee Broad St. Presbyn. Ch., 1962—2006. Avocations: golf, Welsh ancestory, singing, travel. Home: 72 Jessica Way Columbus OH 43230

HULBURT, LUCILLE HALL, artist, educator; b. Portland, Oreg., Oct. 31, 1924; d. Allen Bergen and Agnes Edna (Davis) Hall; m. Frank Theodore Hulburt, Nov. 28, 1943; children: Robert, Carol Davalos, Clarke. Grad. h.s., Whitefish, Mont. Asst. milliner, illustrator Hat Co., N.Y.C., 1944; cafe owner, operator San Diego, 1950—52; profl. artist Vancouver, Wash., 1978—; resident artist Artist's Gallery 21, Vancouver, 1988—. Tchr. children and adult art clases, schs. and home studio, Vancouver, 1978—; artist in residence Wash. State Arts Commn., 1987-88; co-founder, coop. Artists Gallery 21, Vancouver, 1988—; cons. nat. Western Art Show and Auction, Trails West, Vancouver; organizer, com. mem. ann. Summer Art at the Ctr., Vancouver, 1986; judge/jurist art exhibits. Founder, pres. Boundary Assn. Retarded Children, Bonners Ferry, Idaho, 1964-65; com. mem. 1st Bldg. Com., Columbia Arts Ctr., Vancouver, 1980-81; bd. mem. Local Arts Promotion, Vancouver, 1992, 93. Recipient Best of Show award Western Art Show and Auction, Chinook, Mont., 1983, 84, Cmty. Svc. award Arts Coun., Clark County, Wash., 1988, Windsor-Newton award Watercolor 91, 1991. Mem. S.W. Wash. Watercolor Soc. (co-founder, pres. 1979, 80, 84), Soc. Washington Artists (Grumbacher Silver medal 1990), Am. Artists Profl. League, Order Ea. Star (life), N.W. Watercolor Soc. Avocations: gardening, sewing, swimming. Office: Hulburt Studio 5515 NE 58th St Vancouver WA 98661-2146

HULET, MARJANNA M., literature educator; b. Malad, Idaho, Feb. 9, 1963; d. William Joseph and Anna Jean Davidson; m. Barry D. Hulet, Dec. 19, 1962; children: Cedar Steven, Colter Barry, Kestrel Anna. Bachelor's, Brigham Young U., Provo, Utah, 1987; Masters, Idaho State U., Pocatello, 1992. River guide Western Rivers, Moab, Utah, 1985—86; merchandiser JCPenneys, Bozeman, Mont., 1987—90; English tchr. Idaho State U., Pocatello, 1990—. Founder Pocatello Cmty. Charter Sch., Idaho Charter Sch. Network. Chair facility study com. Sch. Dist. #25, Pocatello, 2000—01; mem. planning and zoning City of Pocatello Cmty. Devel. Commn., 2002—06; founder Sagebrush Steppe Regional Land Trust, Pocatello, 2002—06; adult vol. Boy Scouts Am., Pocatello, 2003—06. Named Non-profit Bus. Person of Yr., Idaho State Jour., 2000. Progressive. Mormon. Avocations: camping, baking, writing. Home: 353 Washington Pocatello ID 83201 Office: Idaho State University Pocatello ID 83209 Office Phone: 208-282-5817. Business E-Mail: hulemarj@isu.edu.

HULICKA, IRENE M., psychologist, educator; d. George Andrew and Violet (Rose) Mackintosh; m. Karel Hulicka, May 27, 1957; 1 child, Charles Hulicka Mackintosh. BA Hons. MA, U. Saskatchewan, Saskatoon, 1949; BEd, U. Alberta, Edmonton, Can., 1952; PhD, U. Nebr., Lincoln, 1954. Various tchg. positions Canadian Schs., 1943—52; asst. prof. U. Okla., Norman, 1954—59; clin. psychologist VA Med. Ctr., Buffalo, 1959—67; prof. of psychology SUCB, Buffalo, 1967—91, SUNY Disting. prof., 1983—; rsch. prof. medicine SUNY, Buffalo, 1984—; clin. psychologist pvt. practice, Buffalo, 1988—. Sr. Fulbright scholar Moscow State U., Russia, 1981; lectr. (invited) in many countries US, Can., Potugal, Spain, Czechoslovakia, Thailand, etc. Author: (Book) Soviet Institutions, The Individual and Society, 1967, Studies in Caring; contbr. articles to profl. jours. Fellow: APA (pres. divsn.Adult Devel. and Aging 1981—82), Gerontol. Soc. Am. (pres. social scis. divsn. 1985—86). Office: Psychology Office 142 Niagara Falls Blvd Buffalo NY 14214 Office Phone: 716-836-9441. Fax: 716-836-9441.

HULL, CATHY, artist, illustrator; b. NYC, Nov. 4, 1946; d. Max H. and Magda M. (Stern) H.; m. Neil S. Janovic; 1 child, Julie. BA, Conn. Coll., 1968; cert., Sch. Visual Arts, N.Y.C., 1970. Instr. illustration and portfolio Sch. Visual Arts, N.Y.C., 1983-94, Parsons Sch. Design, N.Y.C., 1994—. Juror The 6th World Cartoon Gallery, Skopje, 1974, Soc. Pub. Designers, N.Y.C., 1982, Soc. Illustrators, N.Y.C., 1983, The Biennale of Humor, Fredrikstad, Norway, 1987, The 6th Internat. Simavi Cartoon Competition, Istanbul, Turkey, 1988 Contbr. to anthologies, books, mags. and newspapers including Time, Penthouse, Newsweek, Esquire, Playboy, MSNBC, Fortune, Wall Street Jour., Washington Post, Forbes, Chgo. Tribune, Ency. Brit., Disney, Sports Illustrated, N.Y. Times, Bus. Week, Travel and Leisure, Money, others; group shows include The 17th Nat. Print Exhbn., Bklyn., 1970, AIGA Show, N.Y.C., 1970-71, 74, Printing Industries Am., 1971, Soc. Illustrators, 1973, 80, 85, 94, 01, World Cartoon Gallery, Skopje, former Yugoslavia, 1972-75, Art Dir.'s Club, 1974, 82, Internat. Cartoon Exhbn., Istanbul, Turkey, 1974, Switzerland, 1974, 78, 80, 82, 90, Athens, Greece, 1975, Soc. Publ. Designers, 1974, 82, Musée de Beaubourg, Paris, 1977, Pacific Design Ctr., L.A., 1980, The Md. Inst., 1981, Scottsdale (Ariz.) Ctr. for Arts, 1981, Soc. Newspaper Design, 1984-85, Butler Inst. Am. Art, Youngstown, Ohio, 1983, Am. Peace Poster Exhibit, 1985, Quebec City Exhbn., Society of Illustrators, 2002; represented in permanent collections including Mus. Caricatures and Cartoons, Basel, Switzerland, Soc. Illustrators Advt. Ann. show, Smithtown Twp. Arts Coun.; designer and pub. playing cards sold at Cooper Hewitt Mus., N.Y., N.Y. Pub. Libr., L.A. County Mus. Art, St. Louis Art Mus., Chgo. Mus. Art, Nat. Mus. Scotland, Seibu, Japan, Contemporary Mus. of Honolulu, Contemporary Mus. San Diego, High Mus. Atlanta, Meml. Exhbn., Mus. Am. Illustration, 2002, Herbert F. Johnson Mus. of Art, 2002, Cornell U., Karikatur and Cartoon Mus., Basel, Switzerland, 2003, Mus. Am. Illustration, 2005, RSVP Portraits Show, N.Y. Times Show and The Ripple Effect, Mus. of Am. Illustration, 2006. Exec. bd. Friends of the H.S. Art and Design, 2002—. Office: 180 E 79th St New York NY 10021-0437 Business E-Mail: chull@nyc.rr.com.

HULL, ELAINE MANGELSDORF, psychology professor; b. Houston, Aug. 15, 1940; d. Paul August and Mary Eleanor (Stephens) Mangelsdorf; m. Richard Thompson Hull, May 30, 1962; 1 child, Geoffrey Alaric (dec.). BA, Austin Coll., Sherman, Tex., 1963; PhD, Ind. U., 1967. Asst. prof. psychology SUNY, Buffalo, 1967-73, assoc. prof., 1973-86, prof., 1986—2004, dir. biopsychology grad. program, 1996—2004; prof. psychology Fla. State U., Tallahassee, 2004—. Contbr., 75 articles to sci. jours. Recipient Chancellor's award for excellence in teaching SUNY, Buffalo, 1975, Tchg. award, SUNY Students Assn., 1986, N.Y. State Union Univ. Profls. Excellence award 1990, Disting. Alumna award Austin Coll., 2004; grantee NIMH. Mem. APA, AAAS, Am. Psycol. Soc., Internat. Acad. Sex Rsch., Soc. Neurosci., Internat. Soc. Psychoneuroendocrinology, N.Y. Acad. Scis Democrat. Avocations: jogging, classical music. Office: 3241 Heather Hill Ln Tallahassee FL 32309 Office Phone: 850-645-2389. Business E-Mail: hull@psy.fsu.edu.

HULL, FRANK MAYS, federal judge; b. Augusta, Ga., Dec. 9, 1948; d. James M. Hull Jr. and Frank (Mays) Pride; m. Antonin Aeck, Apr. 16, 1977; children: Richard Hull Aeck, Molly Hull Aeck. AB, Randolph-Macon Women's Coll., 1970; JD cum laude, Emory U., 1973. Bar: Ga. 1973, U.S. Ct. Appeals (5th cir.) 1973, U.S. Dist. Ct. (no. dist.) Ga. 1974, U.S. Ct. Appeals (11th cir.) 1982. Law clk. to Hon. Elbert P. Tuttle U.S. Ct. Appeals (5th cir.), Atlanta, 1973—74; assoc. Powell, Goldstein, Frazer & Murphy, Atlanta, 1974—80, ptnr., 1980—84; judge State Ct. Fulton County, Atlanta, 1984—90, Superior Ct. Fulton County, Atlanta, 1990—94, U.S. Dist. Ct. (no. dist.) Ga., 1994—97, U.S. Ct. Appeals (11th cir.), 1997—. Mem. commn. on family violence State of Ga., 1992—94, commn. on gender bias in jud. sys., 1988—90. Mem. Leadership Atlanta, 1986—, program co-chair criminal justice com., 1988—89; Sunday sch. tchr. Cathedral St. Philip, Atlanta, 1983—88, children's com., 1981—82, outreach com., 1989—91; bd. dirs. Met. Atlanta Mediation Ctr., Inc., 1976—79, Atlanta Vol. Lawyers Assn., 1988—91. Fellow, AAUW, 1973—. Mem.: ABA (fin. sec. long range planning com. tort and ins. practice sect. 1979—82, chmn. contract documents divsn., forum com. on constrn. industry 1983—85, editl. staff jour. 1981—85, vice chmn. fidelity and surety law com. 1978—85), Nat. Assn. Women Judges, Ga. Assn. Women Lawyers, Atlanta Bar Assn., Am. Judicature Soc. (bd. dirs. 1990—96), Ga. Bar Assn., Order of Coif. Office: US Ct of Appeals 56 Forsyth St NW Rm 300 Atlanta GA 30303-2289*

HULL, GLYNDA, language educator; BA, Miss. U. for Women; PhD, U. Pitts. Co-editor (with Katherine Schultz): (book) School's Out! Bridging Out-of-School Literacies with Classroom Practice, 2002; author: Changing Work, Changing Workers: Critical Perspectives on Language, Literacy, and Skills, 1997; co-author (with J. Gee et al): The New Work Order: Behind the Language of the New Capitalism, 1996. Recipient Richard Braddock Meml. award for best article of yr. (2), Coll. Composition and Comm., award for best article reporting qualitative or quantitative rsch. related to tech. or sci. comm., Nat. Coun. Tchrs. English, 2001. Office: U Calif Berkeley Dept Edn 5629 Tolman Berkeley CA 94720-1670

HULL, GRETCHEN GAEBELEIN, lay worker, writer, lecturer; b. Bklyn., Feb. 5, 1930; d. Frank Ely and Dorothy Laura (Medd) Gaebelein; m. Philip Glasgow Hull, Oct. 24, 1952; children: Jeffrey R., Sanford D., Meredyth Hull Smith. BA magna cum laude, Bryn Mawr Coll., 1950; postgrad., Columbia U., 1950-52; DLitt (hon.), Houghton Coll., 1995. Major presenter Internat. Coun. on Bibl. Inerrancy, Chgo., 1986; guest lectr. London Inst. on Contemporary Christianity, 1988; lectr. at large Christians for Bibl. Equality, St. Paul, 1988-2000; major presenter Presbyn. Ch. (U.S.A.) Nat. Abortion Dialogue, Kansas City, Mo., 1989; disting. scholar lectr. Thomas F. Staley Found., Stony Brook, N.Y., 1991. Elder Presbyn. Ch. (U.S.A.); mem. Madison Ave. Presbyn. Ch., N.Y.C.; vis. prof. Regent Coll., Vancouver, B.C., 1992. Author: Equal to Serve, 1987; (with others) Women, Authority and the Bible, 1986, Applying the Scriptures, 1987, Study Bible for Women (New Testament), 1996, The Global God, 1998, The Gospel with Extra Salt, 2000, The IVP Women's Bible Commentary, 2002; editor Priscilla Papers, 1989-99; contbg. editor Perspectives, 1992—; mem. editl. bd. Prism, 1994—; contbr. articles to religious mags. Trustee Cold Spring Harbor Village Improvement Soc., 1966-69, Soc. of St. Johnland, Kings Park, N.Y., 1972-75. Mem. Woman's Union Missionary Soc. Am. (bd. dirs. 1954-71), Presbyns. United for Bibl. Concerns (bd. dirs. 1973-75), L.I. Presbytery (gen. coun. 1981-83), Christians for Bibl. Equality (bd. dirs. 1987-94), Latin Am. Mission (trustee 1989-95), Evangelicals for Social Action (bd. dirs. 1991-99, 2001—), Network Presbyn. Women in Leadership (steering com. 1994-98), Presbyns. for Renewal (bd. dirs. 1994-2000). Home and Office: 63 Meadow Lakes Hightstown NJ 08520

HULL, JANE DEE, former governor, former state legislator; b. Kansas City, Mo., Aug. 8, 1935; d. Justin D. and Mildred (Swenson) Bowersock; m. Terrance Ward Hull, Feb. 12, 1954; children: Jeannette Shipley, Robin Hillebrand, Jeff, Mike. BS in elem. edn., U. Kans., 1957; postgrad. in polit. sci., Ariz. State U., postgrad. in econs., 1972-78; grad., Josephson Sch. of Ethics, 1993. Former state legislator Ariz. Ho. of Reps., Phoenix, 1979—93, spkr. pro tem, 1993, chmn. ethics com., chmn. econ. devel., 1993, mem. legis. coun., 1993, mem. gov.'s internat. trade and tourism adv. bd., 1993, mem. gov.'s strategic partnership for econ. devel., 1993, mem. gov.'s office of employement implementation task force, 1993, spkr. of house, 1989—93, house majority whip, 1987-88; former sec. of state State of Ariz., Phoenix, 1995—97, former gov., 1997—2003; pub. del. to the UN, 2004—05. Author (edited by Michael S. Josephson and Wes Hanson): The Power of Character; author: Character in Sec.: The Challenge of Pub. Svc.; contbr. opinion pieces to periodicals and newspapers. Mem. dean's coun. Ariz. State U., 1989—92; assoc. mem. Heard Mus. Guild; mem. Maricopa Med. Aux., Ariz. State Med. Aux., Valley Citizens League, Charter 100, Ariz. Women's Forum; hon. chmn. Race for the Cure; hon. bd. mem. Teach for Am.; assoc. mem. Cactus Wren Rep. Women; mem. Freedom Found., North Phoenix Rep. Women, 1970; Trunk 'N Tusk Legis. Liaison Ariz. Rep. Party, 1993; mem. Gov.'s Emergency Coun., Ariz. -Mex. Commn., Phoenix Commn. on Internat. Rels.; Ariz. chmn. George W. Bush for Pres., 2000; mem. Adv. Coun. Hist. Preservation; chmn. Western Gov.'s Assn., 2002, Border Gov.'s Assn., 2002; bd. dir. Morrison Inst. for Pub. Policy, Beatitudes D.O.A.R., 1992, Ariz. Town Hall, Ariz. Econs. Coun. Recipient Econ. Devel. award, Ariz. Innovation Network, 1993, Spl. Achievement award, Nat. Notary Assn., 1997, Appreciation award, No. Ariz. U. Sch. of Forestry students, 2000. Mem. Nat. Orgn. of Women Legislators, Am. Legis. Exch. Coun., Nat. Rep. Legislators Assn. (Nat. Legislator of Yr. award 1989), Soroptimists (hon.). Republican. Roman Catholic.

HULLETT, SANDRAL, hospital administrator, health facility administrator; b. Birmingham, Ala. BS in Biology, Ala. A&M U., 1967; MD, Med. Coll. of Pa., 1976; MPH, U. Ala., Birmingham, 1987, LHD (hon.), 1999. Lic. home nursing adminstr., Ala., 1988. Resident in family practice; physician, dir. Family HealthCare of Ala.; exec. dir. West Ala. Health Svcs., Inc., 1976—2001; interim dir. Cooper Green Hosp., Birmingham, 2001, CEO, med. dir., 2001—. Project dir., prin. investigator grants NCI, The Robert Wood Johnson Found., The Kellogg Found., Nat. Heart, Lung and Blood Inst., The Ford Found.; mem. practicing physicians adv. coun. U.S. Dept. HHS, Intercultural Cancer Coun.; mem. steering com. Ala. Partnership for Cancer Control in Underserved Populations; adv. com. Minority Med. Edn. Program; treasurer Nat. Assn. Public Hospitals & Health Sys., 2003—. Contbr. articles to profl. jours. Active numerous civic orgns. including Ala. Women's Hall of Fame, Leadership Am., Family Practice Rural Health Bd.; bd. trustees U. Ala., 1982—2001; trustee U. Ala. System, 1995—2001; bd. dirs. UAB Health System. Named Rural Practitioner of the Yr., Nat. Rural Health Assn.; named one of Top 100 Black Physicians in Am., Black Enterprise Mag., 2001; recipient Clin. Recongition award for edn. and tng., Nat. Assn. Cmty. Health Ctrs., 1993, Disting. Leadership award, Leadership Ala., 1996, Rural Leadership Image award, Nat. Black Chs. Family Coun., 1998, Women in Sci. award, Environmental & Occupational Health Sci. Inst., 2002. Mem.: Inst. of Medicine of NAS (com. on environ. justice, com. on changing mkt., managed care and the future viability of safety). Office: Cooper Green Hosp 1515 6th Ave S Birmingham AL 35462

HULLINGER, CHARLOTTE M., psychotherapist; b. Houston, Apr. 1, 1934; d. Anton A. and Ada A. (Baepler) Froehlich; m. Robert Neil Hullinger, Sept. 1, 1957; children: Lisa, Jennifer, Robert Jr. AA, St. John's Coll., Winfield, Kans., 1953; BA, Luther Coll., Decorah, Iowa, 1958; MA, U. Cin., 1988. Ordained Internat. Coun. Community Churches, 1988. Elem. sch. tchr., 1953-55; adminstrv. asst. various, Cin., 1970-75; pvt. practice therapist Cin., 1988—; therapist Employee Asst. Program City of Cin., 1989—2000; dir. Cin. Ctr. Soul Psychology, 1993—. Therapist counseling week Sancta Sophia Seminary, Tahlequah, Okla., 1990-2005; victim counselor Victim Svc. Ctr., 1988-89; founder, exec. dir. Parents of Murdered Children, Inc., 1978-86; legal asst. Richard H. Glazer, Cin., 1974—; instr. So. Ohio Coll., Cin., 1978-80; apptd. Pres. Reagan's task force on law enforcement, 1980-83, Ohio adv. bd. on victims, 1980-83, City/County task force on victims, 1980-83, Ad. Bd. Nat. Victims of Crime, 1980-83. Tech. asst. tng. cons. Nat. Orgn. Victim Assistance, Washington, 1986-90, cons. U.S. Dept. Justice, 1986-90. Recipient Edith Surgan award for outstanding leadership, Nat. Orgn. Victim Assistance, 1987; named one of ten top women of 1984, Cin. Enquirer. Home: 1739 Bella Vista St Cincinnati OH 45237-5705

HULME, JANET A., physical therapist, writer, small business owner; b. Seattle, July 2, 1946; d. John C. and Anna C. (Wick) Bower; children from previous marriage: Erika, Abigail. BS, U. Mont., Missoula, 1968; MA, Stanford U., Palo Alto, Calif., 1970. Owner Janet Hulme Rentals, Missoula, Mont., 1971—; dir., prof. phys. therapy U. Mont., 1979—88; pvt. practice Phoenix Phys. Therapy, 1987—97; owner Bagels on Broadway, 1993—96; owner, publ. Phoenix, Inc., 1994—; prin. Phoenix Seminars, 1994—. Author: Beyond Kegels, 2d edit., 1994, Fibromyalgia A Handbook for Self-Care and Treatment, 3d edit., 1994, Beyond Kegels Book II, 1996, Geriatric Incontinence, 1998, Bladder and Bowel Issues in Kids, 2002, Pelvic Rotator Cuff in Human Function, 2004. Mem.: Am. Assn. Biofeedback, Am. Phys. Therapy Assn., Kiwanis. Office: Phoenix Inc PO Box 8231 Missoula MT 59807-8231

HULSTEIN, MARY KATHLEEN, music educator; d. Charles Bruce and Bonnie Lou Holcomb; m. Brent Lee Hulstein, July 14, 2001; children: Hannah Christine, Amanda Danielle. BA in Music Edn., Ctrl. Coll., Pella, Iowa, 1992. Cert. tchr. Iowa. Instrumental music tchr. Beckman HS, Dyersville, Iowa, 1992—94, Interstate 35 Cmty. Schs., Truro, Iowa, 1994—98; assoc. instrumental music tchr. MOC-Floyd Valley Cmty. Sch., Orange City, Iowa, 1998—. Pvt. tchr. piano and brass, Orange City, 1989—; instr. Dubuque Colt Cadets, Dubuque, Iowa, 1993; horn instr. Iowa's Ambassadors of Music, Iowa City, 1994—2000; mem. horn sect. NW Iowa Symphony Orch., Sioux Center, Iowa, 1998—2002. Bd. dirs., sec. Orange City Arts Coun., 1998—2002; substitute praise team, pianist, orch. and kitchen coord. New Hope Evang. Free Ch., Orange City, 2001. Named to Nat. Tchr. Honor Roll, Outstanding Am. Tchrs., 2006. Mem.: Internat. Jazz Educators Assn. (assoc.), Profl. Educators Iowa (assoc.), NW Iowa Bandmasters Assn. (assoc.; pres. 2000—01), Iowa Bandmasters Assn. (assoc.). Republican. Avocations: antiques, scrapbooks, collecting Boyds bears, gardening. Office Phone: 712-737-4871.

HUMBACH, MIRIAM JANE, publishing executive; b. N.Y.C., May 18, 1965; d. William Walter and Mildred (Wender) Humbach. BA in Bus.-Econs./Psychology, SUNY, Oneonta, 1986; MBA, Adelphi U., 1996; MS in Acctg., Pace U., 2002. Fin./acctg. staff N.Y. Times Co., N.Y.C., 1987-92, media svcs. rsch. asst., 1992-93, circulation/staff asst., 1993-95, mktg. cons., rsch. analyst, 1995—. Mem. staff Office of the NY State Atty. Gen. Spl. Projects Divsn., 2004—. Editor: Rethinking Equity Trading at Nasdaq, 1998, The Electronic Call Auction: Market Mechanism and Trading Building a Better Stock Market, 2001. Mem.: NAFE, Beta Alpha Psi (dir. cmty. svc.). Personal E-mail: mjhumbach@yahoo.com.

HUMBURG, BARBARA ANN, elementary school educator; b. Kansas City, Mo., Jan. 20, 1952; d. George John and Norma Lucille (Bowen) Smith; m. James Rolla Humburg, Apr. 9, 1951; children: Jennifer Leigh Stevenson, Jaime Lynn. AA, Longview CC, Lee's Summit, Mo., 1972; EdB, U. Mo., Kansas City, 1974; post grad. Earth sci. tchr. Marshall Sch. Dist., Mo., 1976—78; gen. sci. tchr. Slater Sch. Dist., 1984—. Mem. adv. bd. A+ Com., Slater, 1999—; curriculum chair Slater Sch., 2000—; mem. grant writing com. Ctrl. Meth. U., Fayette, Mo., 2005—06. Nominee Math and Sci. Excellence in Tchg. Presdl. award, 1992; named Cmty. Tchr. of Yr., Slater Sch., 1989; named an Outstanding Am. Tchr., Nat. Honor Roll, 2006. Mem.: Cmty. Tchrs. Assn., Mo. State Tchrs. Assn., Nat. Sci. Tchrs. Assn., Sci. Tchrs. Mo. Avocations: gardening, travel. Home: Rt # 1 Box 47 Nelson MO 65347

HUME, ELLEN HUNSBERGER, media analyst, educator, journalist; b. Chevy Chase, Md., Apr. 24, 1947; d. Warren Seabury and Ruth (Pedersen) H.; m. John Shattuck, Feb. 14, 1991; 1 child, Susannah; stepchildren: Jessica, Rebecca, Peter. BA, Harvard U., 1968; PhD (hon.), Daniel Webster Coll., 1990, Kenyon Coll., 2001. Reporter Somerville (Mass.) Jour., 1968-69; feature writer Santa Barbara (Calif.) News Press, 1969-70; pub. service dir., copy writer KTMS Radio, Santa Barbara, 1970-72; edn. reporter Ypsilanti (Mich.) Press, 1972-73; bus. reporter Detroit Free Press, 1973-75; met. reporter L.A. Times, 1975-77, congl. reporter Washington, 1977-83; White House corr., polit. writer Wall St. Jour., Washington, 1983-88; exec. dir. Shorenstein Ctr. on Press and Politics Harvard U., Cambridge, Mass., 1988-93; moderator The Editors TV program, Montreal, Que., 1990-93; adj. lectr. Kennedy Sch. Govt., 1991-93, Medill Sch. Journalism, 1993-94; founding dir. Ctr. on Media and Soc., U. Mass., Boston. Commentator Washington Week in Rev. PBS-TV, 1973—88, CNN, 1993—97; exec. dir. The Democracy Project PBS, 1996—98; bd. dirs. Internews, Shorenstein Ctr., Domini Found. Fellow Kennedy Inst. Politics, Harvard U., 1981, Annenberg Washington Program, 1993—95. Mem.: Coun. on Fgn. Rels. Episcopalian. Address: 121 Hunnewell Ave Newton MA 02458 Business E-Mail: ellen.hume@umb.edu.

HUME, LINDA JEAN, music educator; b. Batavia, NY, Aug. 9, 1965; d. Frank A. Meier, Jr. and Virginia I. Meier; m. John W. Hume, Nov. 28, 1997; children: Lauren Ann, Nicole Marie. MusB in music edn., SUNY, 1987, MusM in music edn., 1992. Mid. sch. music tchr. Alden Ctrl. Sch. Dist., Alden, NY, 1987—88; hs music tchr. Perry Ctrl. Sch. Dist., Perry, NY, 1988—. Performer: Genesee Symphony, Alexander Fire Dept. Band. Mem.: Genesee Valley Sch. Music Assn., NY State Sch. Music Assn., Music Educators Nat. Conf. Avocations: snowmobiling, bicycling, fishing, reading. Home: 9561 Creek Rd Batavia NY 14020 Office: Perry Ctrl Sch 33 Watkins Ave Perry NY 14530 E-mail: lhume@perry.k12.ny.us.

HUME, SUSAN RACHEL, finance educator; b. Englewood, N.J., Aug. 25, 1952; d. Philip and Anna Ann (Petrowski) Nachtigal; m. John Elliott Hume, Dec. 27, 1975; children: Philip John, Scot Elliott. BA, Douglass Coll., 1974; MBA, Rutgers U., 1976; PhD, CUNY, 2003. Bank analyst N.Y. Fed. Res. Bank, 1976-77, sr. credit analyst, 1977-79; sr. comml. loan officer 1st Pa. Bank, Phila., 1979-81; asst. v.p. Mfrs. Hanover Trust Co., N.Y.C., 1982-83, v.p., 1983-84, dept. head, hedge funding and asset liability mgmt., 1984-88; adj. assoc. prof. fin. and econs. Rider Coll., 1988-90; asst. adj. prof. Fairleigh Dickinson, Madison, NJ, 1991-93; adj. prof. dept. fin. and econs. Baruch Coll., N.Y.C., 1993—. Mem. Douglass Alumnae Endowment Fund Fin. Com., 1985—; pres. Douglass Coll. Class of 1974, 1990-; mem. internat. seminar interest rate risk mgmt. N.Y. Inst. Fin., N.Y.C., 1990-92. Mem. choir, Sunday Sch. tchr. Presbyn. Ch., Glendale; mem. investment com. Glendale Presbyn. Ch.; active Boy Scouts Am., PTO Cedar Hill and Ridge H.S.; former chairperson McGinn Elem. Sch. PTA Reading Program. Recipient Heller alumni award Rutgers U., 1976. Mem.: Beta Gamma Sigma.

HUME, WENDELIN M., criminologist, educator; b. St. Louis Park, Minn., Feb. 4, 1961; d. William Davis and Donna Mae Mitchell; m. William Wayne Hume, Jr., Feb. 23, 1980; children: James Davis, Sherina Mae, William Lance. BS in Sociology and Psychology, Black Hills State U., 1987; MA in Criminal Justice and Criminology, Sam Houston State U., Huntsville, TX, 1991, PhD in Criminal Justice and Criminology, 2000. Tchg. asst. Sam Houston State U., Huntsville, Tex., 1987—88, rsch. asst., 1989—91; asst. prof. U. N.D., Grand Forks, ND, 1991—2001, assoc. prof., 2001—, chmn. Dept. Criminal Justice, dir. Women's Studies Program. Rschr. gen. edn. longitudinal study Bush Found., Grand Forks, 1999—; prin. investigator N.D. Supreme Ct., Bismarck, ND, 1996—98; analyst, rschr. Ctr. Legal Studies, Huntsville, Tex., 1990—91, coord. survey rsch. program, 1987—91; chmn. pres.'s adv. coun. women U. N.D., Grand Forks, ND. Contbr. chapters to books, articles to profl. jours. Sec. pine to prairie coun. Girl Scouts Am., Grand Forks, 2002—06. Named Outstanding Student Orgn. Advisor, U. N.D., 2000; recipient Oustanding Svc. award, Coll. Arts and Scis. U. N.D., 2005. Mem.: Feminist Majority Found., Midwestern Criminal Justice Assn. (constn. com. 2001—03), Nat. Women Studies Assn. (coord. mentoring project 2003—06, mem. governing coun. 2005—06, chmn. accessibility 2005—06), Native Americans into Criminal Justice Assn. (adv. 1999—2006). Avocations: ranching, gardening, trail riding, aquariam hobbiest. Home: 25539 422nd Ave SW East Grand Forks MN 56721 Office: University of North Dakota 303a O'Kelly Hall Grand Forks ND 58202-8050 Office Phone: 701-777-4001. Business E-Mail: wendelin.hume@und.edu.

HUMES, ELAINE, mathematics educator; b. Marion, Ohio, Jan. 12, 1960; m. Jeffery Humes, June 5, 1960; children: Garrett, Ross. BA, Ohio Wesleyan U., Delaware, 1995; MAT, Mary Grove Coll., Detroit, 1999. Choreographer, Delaware Hayes H.S., Delaware, Ohio, 1982—2002; tchr. math. Olentangy H.S., Lewis Center, Ohio, 1995—, chair dept. math., 2001—, mentor to new tchrs., 2001—. Named Tchr. of the Yr., Olentangy Local Schys., 2004, Outstanding Promising Educator, Ohio Wesleyan U., 1995. Mem.: ASCD, Math. Assn. Am., Ohio Coun. Tchrs. Math., Nat. Coun. Tchrs. Math. Methodist. Avocations: knitting, crocheting, reading, gardening, outdoor activities.

HUMISTON, MARILYN KOSLOV, music educator; b. Granite City, Ill., Jan. 2, 1948; d. Martin Siegfried and Terry Koslov; m. Ronald Squier Humiston, Feb. 6, 1971; children: Daniel Squier, Sara Alisa. BS in edn. and music, U. of Mo., 1966—70; MA in edn. and music, Lindenwood U., 1987—89. String music educator Sch. Dist. of Ladue, Ladue, Mo., 1970—75, Pky. Sch. Dist., Chesterfield, Mo., 1985—. Dir. string camp Pky. Sch. Dist., Chesterfield, Mo., 1995—. Pres. St. Louis Philharm. Orch., 1990—. Mem.: St. Louis Suburban Music Educators Assn., Manhasset Strings Quartet, Musician's Assn. of St. Louis, Mo. Am. String Teachers and Nat. Sch. Orch. Assn. (editor Soundpost Mag. 1990—, sec./treas. 2002—04, registration chairperson 2006—, Disting. Svc. award 1998), St. Louis Suburban Music Educators Assn. (elem. instrumental v.p. 1998—2001, recognition night chairperson 2001—, awards chairperson 2005—, Merit award 2001), Mo.

Music Educators Assn. (v.p. orch. 2004—06). Avocations: tennis, reading. Office: Parkway Sch Dist 555 South Weidman Rd Ballwin MO 63021 Office Phone: 314-415-4118. E-mail: mhumiston@pkwy.k12.mo.us.

HUMMEL, DANA D. MALLETT, librarian; BA in art history, Smith Coll., 1957; postgrad., Def. Lang. Inst., 1961, Instituto Mexicano-Norteameric, 1962; MA in libr. and info. sci., Denver U., 1968; postgrad., Cath. U. Am., 1974, Nat. War Coll., 1976, No. Va. Bus. Sch., 1978, Cath. U. Am., 1981; diploma, U. Italiana Stranieri, Perugia, Italy, 1997. Head libr., adminstrn. Howard AFB, Libr., Panama, 1969—70; asst. libr. Holmes Intermediate Sch., 1970-71; tchr. Spanish, substitute tchr. J.E.B. Stuart HS, 1972-77; sec., Office of Exec. Dir. Africa The World Bank, 1978-79; personal sec. rector Falls Church, Va., 1979—81; mgr. Info. Svcs. Ctr. BDM Internat., subs. Ford Aerospace Co. (now Northrop Grumman), McLean, Va., 1981-88. Mem. vestry Falls Church Epis. Ch., 1982; del. Rep. State Conv., 1981, 86; pres. Ravenwood Civic Assn., 1979-80, 80-81, 81-82; rep. Mason Dist., Fedn. Civic Assns.; mem. ann. plan rev. task force Mason Dist., 1981-82; gov. trustee Fairfax County Pub. Libr. Bd., 1982-88, chmn. bd. trustees; lead fund raiser Smith Coll., 1998-2002; active St. Boniface Epis. Ch.; v.p. bd. dirs. Carriagehouse II, 20060. Named Outstanding Woman of Yr., Fairfax County Bd. Suprs. and Com. of Women, 1982. Mem. AAUP, ALA, Am. Soc. for Info. Sci., Spl. Libr. Assn., Va. Libr. Assn., DC Libr. Assn., Women in Def., Villa D'Este Assn. (bd. dirs. 1995-98, pres. 1997-98), Jr. League Sarasota, Fla., Tournament Players Club Prestancia, Fla., The Field Club, Marie Selby Bot. Gardens, The Smith Club of Sarasota (v.p. 2005—), Sarasota PC Users Group. Home: 4933 Kestral Park Way N Sarasota FL 34231-2346

HUMMEL, GAYLE GILLETTE, artist, poet; b. Cin., Nov. 27, 1941; d. Arthur Davenport and Mary Gillette; m. David Edward Hummel, June 26, 1965; children: David Jr., Ellis. BA, U. Cin., 1964. Artist Cont Art Ctr., 1985—90, Clossons', Cin., 1990—. Pres. Mental Health Assn., 1981, bd. dirs., Cin. Contemporary Arts Ctr. One-woman shows include Decon Gallery, LA, John McEnroe Gallery, NYC, others, 1995—2005. Mem.: Jr. League Cin. Episcopalian. Achievements include ancestor of King Camp Gillette, founder of The Gillette Co. Avocation: photography. Home: 3435 Golden Ave 502 Cincinnati OH 45226 Office Phone: 513-871-2405. Personal E-mail: gaylemeridian@hotmail.com.

HUMMEL, MARGARET P., state representative; b. Binghamton, N.Y., Mar. 24, 1940; m. Manfred K. Hummel; four children. BA, Coll. New Rochelle, 1962; MA, Boston Coll., 1968, St. Michaels Coll., 1981. Mem. Vt. Ho. of Reps., 1996—2004. Mem. Underhill Selectboard, 1992—2001; chair Underhill Planning Commn.; mem. Burlington Sch. Gifted and Talented Task Force; trustee U. Vt., 1999—2005. Roman Catholic. Home: 262 Lake Ave # 1 Newton Highlands MA 02461-1210

HUMMEL, MARIAN, retired art educator, photographer; b. Bethlehem, Pa., May 12, 1943; d. Donald Clare and Helen Florence (Harman) Conner; m. Gerard G. Hummel, June 29, 1998. BA in Fine Arts, Fairleigh Dickinson U., 1966; MA in Visual Arts, William Paterson Coll., Wayne, N.J., 1971, postgrad., 1991. Cert. art tchr., supr., prin., N.J. Tchr. art Hopatcong Sch. Sys., Lake Hopatcong, N.J., 1966-67; art instr. Am. Acad. for Girls, Istanbul, Turkey, 1967-68; art. instr. Boonton Twp. (N.J.) Sch. Sys., 1968-99, gifted/talented coord., 1989-99. Photographer for greeting cards; exhibited photographs in shows at Kemerer Mus., Bethlehem, Pa., 1974, Jockey Hollow Gallery, Morristown, N.J., 1979, Bergen Cmty. Mus., 1981; photos in permanent collection Lehigh U., Bethlehem. Vol. for animal shelters. Recipient awards for tchg. and for photography. Mem ASCD, Art Educators N.J., Boonton Twp. Edn. Asn. (v.p. 1989-99, negotiations chair 1989-99), Order of the Eastern Star. Republican. Presbyterian. Avocations: landscape and travel photography, reading, walking.

HUMMEL, MARILYN MAE, retired elementary school educator; b. Cleve., June 20, 1931; d. John Winfield and Meta E. (Timm) H. BS, Ohio U., 1953. Cert. elem. educator. Elem. tchr. Lakewood (Ohio) Bd. of Edn., 1953-83. Mem. Centennial Planning Com., Lakewood, 1989; vol. United Way, Lakewood Hosp. Jennings scholar, 1969-70; named Tchr. of Yr., Franklin Sch., 1983. Mem.: Lakewood Hist. Soc., Kiwanis Club, Civil Club West, Delta Kappa Gamma. Republican. Presbyterian.

HUMMER-SHARPE, ELIZABETH ANASTASIA, writer, genealogist, researcher; b. Morristown, N.J., Dec. 15, 1931; d. Harold Arlington and Sophia Anastasia (Dombrowski) Hummer; divorced; children: Dean T., Dana E., Robert K., Jean F., Christopher K. Student, Santa Monica Coll., 1968-69. Cashier L. Bamberger Co., Morristown, 1949; telephone sales, asst. office mgr. L.A. Times, Santa Monica, 1968-69; unit sec. St. Johns Hosp., Santa Monica, 1969-75; telephone sales L.A. Times, Culver City, 1976-79; mktg. dir. Ramsgate Films, Santa Monica, 1976-78; sr. file clk. Crown Wholesale Co., L.A., 1979-80; telephone sales L.A. Times, Santa Monica, 1988-91. Bd. dirs. Desert Opera Theatre, Palmdale, Calif., 1994-99; vol. on call ARC, Palmdale. Mem. Internat. Platform Soc., Antelope Valley Geneal. Soc., Nat. Audubon Soc., Arbor Day Found., Planetary Soc. (charter mem.), UFO Soc., Bibl. Archaeology Soc., Smithsonian Inst., Wildlife Land Trust, Nat. Geographic Soc., Nature Conservancy N.J. Roman Catholic. Avocations: travel, walking, jewelry making, art, gardening.

HUMPHREY, CAMILLA MARIE, retired special education educator; b. Devils Lake, N.D., July 3, 1928; d. George O. and Annette Sophia (Monson) Loftness; m. Thomas Milton Humphrey, Dec. 26, 1950 (dec. Nov. 1992); children: Ana Oliva Johns, Marlena Marie Hensley. AA, Coll. Marin, 1948; student, U. Calif., Berkeley, 1948-49; BA in Edn., Pacific Luth. U., 1950; postgrad., U. Oreg., 1951-53, U. Nev., 1968. Cert. spl. edn. Oreg. Tchr. Albany Elem. Sch., Oreg., 1950-51; spl. edn. tchr. Children's Hosp. Sch., Eugene, Oreg., 1951-53, Eugene Jr. HS, 1953-54, Clark County Sch. Dist., Las Vegas, 1968-71; ret., 1971. Contbr. articles to profl. jours. Avoc. world concerns children's issues, preservation natural beauty; bd. dirs. Adult Day Health Care, McKinleyville, 1994—95; nurse's aid Red Cross, Tripoli, Libya, 1958; fgn. rels. chmn. LWV, Carson City, Nev., 1963; mem. adv. bd. Salvation Army, Las Vegas, 1983—86; vol. tutoring Mid. Sch., Olympia, Wash., 1999—2003; vol. English tchr. Luth. Mission, 1955—56; pres. Oil Wive's Club, Bogota, Colombia, 1956—57, Assistance League, Las Vegas, 1980—81; fin. sec. Gen. fedn. Women's Clubs, Las Vegas, 1983—84; vol. R.S.V.P., 1993—95, Thrift Store and Food Bank, McKinleyville, Calif., Patricks Point State Pk. Bookstore, Trinidad, Calif. Recipient 1st and 2d pl. photography award, Gen. Fedn. Women's Clubs, 1982, Nev. Short Story award, 1984, Vol. Svc. plaque, Help Ctr., Las Vegas, 1986, Silver Platter award, Evang. Luth. Ch. Am. Mission, Bogota, 1956. Mem.: DAV Aux., AAUW, Nat. Assitance League (at-large), Am. Polar Soc., Pacific Luth. U. Alumni Assn. Avocations: photography, reading, travel, art and sculpture, interior decorating. Home: 115 Maple Park Dr SE Olympia WA 98501-8701

HUMPHREY, DIANA YOUNG, fundraiser; b. Balt., Feb. 7, 1938; d. Edwin Parson and Elizabeth Miller (Hoskins) Young; m. David Henry Carls, July 27, 1963 (div. Dec. 17, 1997); children: Peter Van Patten Carls, Elizabeth Roy Carls, Susan Montanye Carls; m. George Lee Humphrey, May 22, 1999. AB, Smith Coll., Northampton, Mass., 1960. Lic. real estate broker, Mass., 1978. Fgn. rights sales Little, Brown & Co., Inc., Boston, 1960-63; speech writer DNA Rsch., N.Y.C., 1963-64; vol. fund raiser John V. Lindsay, N.Y.C., 1964-65, Smith Coll., Northampton, Mass., 1970-75, 90-95, Smith Coll. Club, Concord, Mass., 1976-89, Jr. League of Boston, 1967—; bd. mem. devel. Ctr. House, Inc., Boston, 1981-94; fund raiser events Boston Symphony Orch., 1975—; dir. edn. Hawthorne Ptnrs. Inc. Fund raising, events Mass. Soc. for Prevention of Cruelty to Children, Boston, 1997—. Editor: Huntington Hartford Gallery Modern Art, N.Y.C., 1963. Speechwriter, Nelson A. Rockefeller Presdl. campaign, NYC, 1963-64; active John V. Lindsay for Mayor, NYC, 1964-65; chmn. Wayland Planning Bd., Mass., 1976-81, Wayland Housing Partnership, 1987-2004; adv. com. REACH, Waltham, Mass., Bay Cove, Boston; active Patriots' Trail coun. Girl Scouts U.S. Mem. Jr. League of Boston, Weston Golf Club. Episcopalian. Avocations: golf, travel, gardening, singing, politics. Home: 42 Cutting Cross Way Wayland MA 01778-3845

HUMPHREY, JUDITH POOLE, retired elementary school educator; b. Winchendon, Mass., May 8, 1936; d. William Thomas Poole and Elizabeth Francis Poole Fish; m. Robert Stone Humphrey, Aug. 18, 1957; children: Tamara Elizabeth Humphrey Davis, Lindsey Stone. BA, BS, Salem Tchrs. Coll., Mass. Bus. tchr. Littleton HS, Mass., 1957—59, Masconomet HS, Boxford, Mass., 1972—73, substitute tchr., 1973—80; ret., 1980. Pres. women's group, deaconess, Sunday sch. tchr., adult Bible tchr. 1st Congl. Ch., Boxford; chmn. Christian Women's Club, Boston; adult Bible tchr. 1st Presbyn. Ch., Naples, Fla. Mem.: Philharm. League. Republican. Avocations: reading, knitting, crocheting, counted cross stitch, painting. Home (Summer): 7 Dana Pl Melvin Village NH 03852 Home (Winter): 2992 W Crown Pointe Blvd Naples FL 34112 E-mail: judithhumphrey9@aol.com.

HUMPHREY, LOUISE IRELAND, civic worker, equestrienne; b. Morehead City, N.C., Nov. 1, 1918; d. R. Livingston and Margaret (Allen) Ireland; m. Gilbert W. Humphrey, Dec. 27, 1939; children: Margaret (Mrs. K. Bindhart), George M. II, Gilbert Watts. Educated pvt. schs. Nurse's aide ARC, 1944-64. Past. dir. Nat. City Bank, Cleve., Nat. City Corp., Cleve. 1981-86. Trustee Mus. Arts Assn.; hon. trustee, past pres. Vis. Nurse Assn.; hon. trustee Lake Erie Coll.; life trustee United Way Cleve.; trustee Archbold Med. Ctr. and Hosp., Thomasville, Ga.; hon. trustee Case Western Res. U., Bus. Coun. Internat. Understanding Inc.; bd. dirs. Monticello (Fla.) Opera Ho.; mem., former trustee, 2d v.p. Jr. League Cleve.; past pres., hon. chmn. bd. dirs. Met. Opera Assn., NY; bd. dirs. Lincoln Ctr., NY, Thomas County Entertainment Found.; past pres. No. Ohio Opera Assn.; mem. adv. bd. Coll. Vet. Medicine U. Fla., Gainesville; mem. Ohio Arts Coun., 1975—85; treas., trustee Wildlife Conservation Fund Am.; former master Foxhounds Chagrin Valley Hunt, Gates Mills, Ohio; past dir., zone v.p. U.S. Equestrian Team Inc., now hon. life dir.; mem. Garden Club Cleve.; bd. dirs., past pres. Nat. Homecaring Coun.; treas., bd. dirs. Wildlife Legis. Fund Am. Conservation Fund; past pres. bd. dirs. Thomasville Cultural Ctr.; bd. dirs. Cmty. Found. North Fla.; commr. Fla. Game & Fresh Water Fish, 1984—99. Home: Box 91102 Woodfield Springs Plantation Tallahassee FL 32309

HUMPHREY, MITZI GREENE, artist; b. Johnson City, Tenn., Feb. 10, 1936; d. Sterling Augustus and Alta Marie (Ferguson) Greene; m. Thomas MacGillivray Humphrey, June 4, 1957; children: Sheryl Lynn, Thomas MacGillivray Jr. and Elizabeth Eleanor (twins). BS in Art Edn., Fine Arts, U. Tenn., 1957; MA in British and Am. Lit., Auburn U., 1970; BFA in Painting and Printmaking, Va. Commonwealth U., 1988, MFA in Painting and Printmaking, 1997. Tchr. art, English Knoxville City Schs., 1957-59; dir., co-founder Wofford Coll. Art Gallery, Spartanburg, S.C., 1960-61; sec. chemistry dept. Newcomb Coll., New Orleans, 1962-63; asst. to dir. Scott-McKennis Gallery, Richmond, Va., 1975-76; curator nat. xerographic exhibit 1708 East Main Gallery, Richmond, Va., 1988-89; curator nat. book art exhibit Artspace, Richmond, Va., 1993-94, pres., 1992-94. Adj. faculty English dept. J. Sargeant Reynolds C.C., Richmond, 1975-76, U. Richmond, 1982-84; instr. workshops Va. Mus. Fine Arts, 1990-91; instr. travel jour. workshop Valentine Mus., Richmond, 1992; lectr. women's resource ctr. U. Richmond, 1992; reps. women's caucus for art Nat. Book Art Conf., N.Y.C., 1989; founder, co-dir. Art6 Gallery, Richmond, Va., 2004—; chair, exec. bd., 2004—. Producer (ednl. videos) Art Ex Libris at Artspace, 1994, Clifford Edwards and Books as Icons in the Paintings of Van Gogh, 1994, Isota Epes and How Virginia Woolf Brought Me Up, 1994. Sec. Richmond Interfaith Coun., 1982-83; mem. Conservation Coun. Va., Richmond, 1989-94. Va. Commn. Arts grantee, 1989, 94. Mem. Internat. Soc. Copier Artists (Va. rep. 1980-91), Richmond Artists Assn. (pres. 1984-86) Women's Caucus Art (mem. exec. bd. 1991-93, grantee 1989, Richmond chpt. Va. visual artist of yr. award 1996), Briarwood Book Club, Richmond Roadunners Club, (Grandprix winner, 2003), Phi Kappa Phi, Pi Lambda Theta. Independent. Presbyterian. Avocations: travel, tennis, gardening, writing, pub. speaking. Home: 2201 Conte Dr Midlothian VA 23113-2363 Office: 300 N Lombardy St Richmond VA 23220-3532

HUMPHREY, PHYLLIS A., writer; b. Oak Park, Ill., July 22, 1929; d. Richard William and Antoinette (Chalupa) Ashworth; m. Herbert A. Pihl, Sept. 13, 1946 (div. 1957); children: Christine Pihl Gibson, Gary Fraizer Pihl; m. Curtis H. Humphrey, June 21, 1965; 1 child, Marc. AA, Coll. San Mateo, Calif., 1972; postgrad., Northwestern U., 1945-47. Ptnr. Criterion House, Palm Desert, Calif., 1972—. Author: Wall Street on $20 a Month, 1986, Golden Fire, 1986, Sweet Folly, 1990, Flying High, 1995, Once More With Feeling, 1998, Tropical Nights, 2000, Choices, 2001, North by Northeast, 2001, Charade, 2002, The Green Bough, 2005, Masquerade, 2006; author radio scripts Am. Radio Theatre, 1983-84; contbr. short stories and articles to popular mags. Mem. Mensa. Republican. Christian Sci. Ch. Avocations: reading, travel.

HUMPHREY-JEFFERSON, BEVERLY C., daycare administrator; b. Jamaica, West Indies; came to the U.S., 1974; d. Clifton Campbell and Linneth E. Ledgister; m. Edward Humphrey, July 19, 1972 (div. July 1982); children: Leonard, Lennox, FeAna; m. Michael L. Jefferson, Sept. 13, 1984. AS in Surg. Tech., Highland Park (Mich.) C.C., 1984; BS in Mental Health, Ga. State U., 1991; MA in Mgmt., Webster U., 1997. Lic. day care dir. Ednl. para-profl. Highland Park (Mich.) C.C., 1984-88; psychiat. unit clk. Mount Carmel Hosp., Detroit, 1988; supr., instr., outreach worker REACH, Atlanta, 1990-91, 94; group home supr. Edison Park Homes, Park Ridge, Ill., 1992; coord. Alzheimers program Parkside Sr. Svcs., Northfield, Ill., 1992-94; activities dir. Oakmont West Nursing Ctr., Greenville, S.C., 1995, Rolling Green Village, Greenville, S.C., 1996-98; sr. health svcs. technician Ga. Retardation Ctr.-State of Ga., Atlanta, 1998; owner, operator Granny B's Daycare, San Diego, 1999—. Vol. mem. adv. com. ARC, Greenville, S.C., 1996-99. Mem. Am. Counseling Assn., Nat. Cert. Coun. for Activities Profls., Webster U. Alumni Assn., Ga. State U. Alumni Assn., Golden Key Nat. Honor Soc. E-mail: beva51@hotmail.com.

HUMPHREYS, BETSY L., librarian; BA, Smith Coll., 1969; MLS, U. Md., 1972. Joined Nat. Libr. Medicine NIH, 1973, dep. asst. dir. libr. ops., 1984—99, asst. dir. health svcs. rsch. info, 1993—, assoc. dir. libr. ops., 1999—. Pub. and presenter in field including Eileen Roach Cunningham Lectr., Vanderbilt U., 1999, Priscilla Mayden Lectr., U. Utah, 1999, Janet Doe Lectr., Med Libr. Assn., 2001. Contbr. articles to profl. jours. Recipient Alumna of Year, Coll. Info. Studies Alumni Chpt., 2003. Fellow Am. Coll. Med. Informatics (1990-); mem. Inst. Medicine Nat. Acad. Sciences, Acad. Health Info. Profls. (disting. mem.), Am. Med. Informatics Assn., Med. Libr. Assn., Acad. Health Svcs. Rsch. and Health Policy. Office: Nat Libr Medicine NIH 8600 Rockville Pike Bldg 38 Bethesda MD 20894-0001

HUMPHREYS, JOSEPHINE, writer; b. Charleston, S.C., Feb. 2, 1945; d. William and Martha Humphreys. AB, Duke U., 1967; MA, Yale U., 1968. Author: Dreams of Sleep, 1984 (Ernest Hemingway Found. award 1985), Rich in Love, 1987, The Fireman's Fair, 1991, Nowhere Else on Earth, 2000 (So. Book award 2001). Recipient Lyndhurst Found. prize, 1985, Hillsdale prize, 1993; Guggenheim fellow, 1984; Woodrow Wilson Found. fellow, 1967, Danforth Found. fellow, 1967. Fellow So. Writers. Home and Office: care Harriet Wasserman Agy 137 E 36th St Ste 190 New York NY 10016-3528

HUMPHREYS, KAREN LYNNE, language educator; b. Philadelphia, Sept. 20, 1965; d. Richard Llewellyn Humphreys and Camilla Elise Schwieger; m. Bret R. Bowin, Dec. 24, 1997. BA, Bucknell U., 1987; MA, U. Pitts., 1990; PhD, Princeton U., 1995. Lectrice d'anglais Université de Caen, Caen, France, 1987—88; vis. asst. prof. Randolph-Macon Coll., Ashland, Va., 1996—98, Trinity Coll., Hartford, Conn. Adv. bd. Ctr. for U. Programs Abroad, Amherst, Mass., 2003—. Grantee Faculty Rsch. Grant, Trinity Coll., 2001-2002, Princeton U. Grad. Fellowship, 1991-1994, Armstrong Summer Rsch. Grant, Princeton U., 1993, Faculty Devel. Grant, Randolph Macon Coll., 1997; Faculty Rsch. grant, 1998. Mem.: Conseil Internat. d'Etudes Francophones, Am. Assn. of Teachers of French, MLA. Avocations: travel, paper marbling. Office: Trinity Coll Dept Modern Languages 300 Summit St Hartford CT 06106 Office Phone: 860-297-4237. Office Fax: 860-987-6261.

HUMPHREYS, LOIS H., retired realtor; b. Abingdon, Va., Sept. 25, 1931; d. Howard Barnett Hagy and Deltia Sylvia Caudill; m. Paul Everett Humphreys, Apr. 15, 1951; children: Richard Everett, Jill Hagy Humphreys Dalton. Student, Am. Floral Arts, 1969. Cert. floral designer. Dental asst. Drs. Loving and Buchanan, Bristol, Abingdon, Va., 1949-54; sales staff Maxine's, Abingdon, 1955-65; sec. Gentrys Furniture, Abingdon, 1966-68; audio visual coord. Washington County Schs., Abingdon, 1968-70; retail merchant Humphreys Flowers and Gifts, Abingdon, 1969-87; realtor Va. Realtors Assn., Abingdon, 1976-93; ret. Mem. Archtl. Rev. Bd., 1988—; chairperson Mount Rogers Planning Commn. Disabilities Bd., Marion, Va., 1988-98. Coun. mem. Town of Abingdon, 1988—, mayor, 1998—, mem. archtl. rev. bd., 1988-98, tree commn., 1998-2005; mem. Washington County Hist. Soc. Named Women of Yr., Abingdon Bus. and Profl. women, 1991-92. Mem.: DAR, C. of C., Abingdon United Meth. Women (pres. 1998—2002), Va. PTA (life), Johnston Meml. Ladies Aux., Creeper Trail Club. Avocations: doll collecting, travel. Home: 490 Court St #24 Abingdon VA 24210 also: PO Box 789 Abingdon VA 24212-0789

HUMPHREYS, LYNNE M., secondary school educator; d. Nancy Campbell and Robert Guy Morefield; m. Patrick Arnold Humphreys, May 3, 1980; children: Sarah Lynne, Ryan Patrick. BA, Emory and Henery Coll., Va., 1980. Cert. tchr. Va., 1980. Tchr. Richlands Mid. Sch., Va., 1980—84, Lord Botetourt H.S., Daleville, Va., 1984—. Office Phone: 540-992-1261.

HUMPHREYS-HECKLER, MAUREEN KELLY, nursing home administrator; b. N.Y.C. d. Henry James and Eileen Frances (Kelly) Humphreys; m. Robert P. Heckler, Sept. 12, 1992. BA, Villanova U., 1983; M in Mgmt., Pa. State U., 1998. Lic. nursing home adminstr., cert. Asst. adminstr. Pennsburg (Pa.) Manor, 1983-84, adminstr., 1984-85, Roslyn (Pa.) Nursing and Rehab. Ctr., 1985-88; exec. adminstr. Gracecare, Inc., Blue Bell, Pa., 1988-92; adminstr. St. Mary Manor, Lansdale, Pa., 1992-98; dir. resident svcs. The Fairfax, Ft. Bervoir, Va., 1998—2000; gen. mgr. Marriott Brighton Gardens, Bethesda, Md., 2000—01; cadre gen. mgr. no. region Marriott Sr. Living Svcs., 2001, area dir. of ops., 2002—. Fellow: Am. Coll. Health Care Adminstrs.; mem.: Am. Assn. Sovereign Mil. Order of Knights of Malta (Dame), Villanova U. Alumni Assn. Republican. Roman Catholic. Avocations: golf, travel, reading, wine collecting. Home: 23 Brittany Ln Glenmoore PA 19343

HUMPHREYS TROY, PATRICIA, communications executive; b. Birmingham, June 3, 1946; m. Stephen Richard Troy; 1 child, David. BS in Edn., Auburn U., 1968, MEd, 1969; cert. advanced study in edn., Loyola Coll., 1989; cert., Inst. Orgn. Mgmt., U.S. Chamber at U. Del., 1999; MBA, U. Kans., 2005. Cert. assn. exec. Grad. tchg. asst. Auburn U., 1968—69; asst. libr. McKendree Coll., 1969—71; adj. instr. Chapman Coll., 1972—75; libr. Wroxeter-on-Severn, 1978—80; adminstrv. dir., media dir. Chesapeake Acad.1, 1980—89; pres., CEO Bay Media Inc., 1989—, Next Wave Group LLC, 2001—; CEO, Facetswoman, Inc., 2004—. Past vice-chair bd. trustees, chair strategic planning com. Anne Arundel Health Sys. and Anne Arundel Med. Ctr.; exec. dir., adminstr. Assn. for Women in Comms., 1996—2005; exec. dir. Mid-Atlantic Carwash Assn., 2002—, Md./D.C. Soc. Clin. Oncology, 2006—. Unit pres. Am. Cancer Soc., 1986—92; pres. Panhellenic of Annapolis, 1976, Cultural Arts Found. Anne Arundel County, 1995—99, Greater Severna Park Coun., 1990—93; chair Small Area Plan for Severna Park, Anne Arundel County, 1997—2002, Anne Arundel County Cancer Control Task Force, 1994—96; bd. trustees, founding vice chair Chesapeake Acad., 1980—; grad. Leadership Anne Arundel; founding chair Assn. for Severna Park Improvement, Renewal and Enhancement, Inc., 1994—; bd. dirs. Stop the Silence, 2006. Named Independence Day Parade Grand Marshal, Greater Severna Park Chamber, 1993, Bus. Leader of Yr., Anne Arundel Trade Coun., 1996, Women in Bus. Advocate, Md. Small Bus. Assn., One of Md.'s Top 100 Women, Daily Record, 1997, 1999, 2001, Cmty. Activist of Yr., Taste of the Bay Mag., 2006, Entrepreneur of Yr., Annapolis and Anne Arundl County C. of C., 2006; recipient Exec. citation for cmty. svc., Anne Arundel County, 1999, Disting. Alumni award, Leadership Anne Arundel, 1997, TWIN award, Anne Arundel County YWCA, 1996, Anne Arundel County Cmty. Svc. award, YWCA, 2005, AA County Svc. award. Mem.: Am. Soc. Assn. Exec. (cert.), Anne Arundel Trade Coun./Annapolis and Anne Arundel County Chamber (edn. chmn. 1990—), Am. Bus. Women's Assn. (pres. Severn River/Md. Capital chpt. 1980—81, Woman of Yr. Severn River 1991, Bus. Assoc. of Yr., Severn River 1992, named among Top 10 Women in Bus. 2003), Women in Comms. (pres. Md. profl. chpt. 1991—92, Georgina Mac Dougall Davis award 2004). Office: 550M Ritchie Hwy 271 Severna Park MD 21146 Office Phone: 410-647-8402, 410-647-5002. E-mail: pat@facetswoman.com.

HUMPHRIES, CELENE, lawyer; b. Saint Petersburg, Fla., Sept. 24, 1966; d. Wayne and Linda Harrell; m. Sean Humphries, Nov. 11, 1994; children: Megan Nicole, Aidan Matthew. BA, Tulane U., 1987, JD, 1990. Bar: Fla. 1991, cert.: Fla. (specialist in appellate practice) 2005. With Swope, Rodante P.A., Tampa, Fla., 1990—. Named one of Florida's Legal Elite, Fla. Trend Mag., 2004, Florida's Super Lawyers, Fla. Super Lawyers Mag., 2006; recipient award, Philip C. Jessup Internat. Moot Ct. Appellate Competition, 1990. Mem.: Fla. Bar Assn. (vice chmn. grievance com. appellate sect. 2005—, chmn. programs com. appellate sect. 2005—, mem. continuing legal edn. com. 2005—, mem. steering com. appellate justice conf.), Hillsborough County Bar Assn. (licentiate; chmn., co-chmn. appellate sect. 2004—06), Tampa Bay Trial Lawyers Assn. (licentiate), Acad. Fla. Trial Lawyers (licentiate; mem. exec. coun. appellate sect. 2005—, mem. amicus curiae com. appellate sect. 2005—), Justice William Glenn Terrell Am. Inn Ct. (assoc.; barrister 2005—). Avocations: playing ice hockey, reading. Office: Swope Rodante PA 1234 East 5th Ave Tampa FL 33605 Office Fax: 813-223-3678.

HUMPHRIES, JOAN ROPES, psychologist, educator; b. Bklyn., Oct. 17, 1928; d. Lawrence Gardner and Adele Lydia (Zimmermann) Ropes; m. Charles C. Humphries, Apr. 4, 1957; children: Peggy Ann, Charlene Adele. BA, U. Miami, 1950; MS, Fla. State U., 1955; PhD, La. State U., 1963. Registered lobbyist State of Fla. Part-time instr. psychology dept. U. Miami, Coral Gables, Fla., 1964—66; prof. behavioral studies dept. Miami-Dade Coll., 1966—. Presenter, lectr. in field cruise ship Costa Romantica. Editl. staff, maj. author The Application of Scientific Behaviorism to Humanistic Phenomena, 1975, Rev. Edit., 1979, prodr. & host, Sigma Series video, cert. for TV Strategies in Global Modern Academia: Issues and Answers in Higher Education, 1993—94, Strategies in Global Modern Academia: Issues and Answers in Higher Education II, 1995; prodr.: (video series) Strategies in Global Modern Academia: Issues and Answers in Higher Education, III, 1996—97, Strategies in Global Modern Academia: Issues and Answers in Higher Education, IV, 2001—02, W2RN (cert.). Mem. Biofeedback Del., China, Hong Kong, 1995; mem. Citizen Amb. Program Psychic Arts Del. to Russia, 1997; mem. Citizen Amb. Program Am. Mus. Natural History; life mem. Pastorius Home Assn., Inc., 2001; mem. Citizen Amb. Program Vizcayans Mus., Alden Kindred of Am., Inc.; mem. Citizen Amb. Program Nat. Trust Hist. Preservation, The Charles F. Menninger Soc., People to People; mem. ladies aux. Fla. Soc. SAR; mem. Nat. Mus. Women in Arts; mem. women's history month com. Jr. Honor Women Recognition, women's leadership seminar. Recipient award in hon. of women recognition, Women's Hist. Month com. and Women's Leadership Seminar, 2003. Mem.: AAUP (past v.p. Fla. conf. 1986—88, pres. of chpt., Miami-Dade Coll. 1986—, mem. exec. bd. Fla. conf. 1989—90, former v.p., sec. Miami-Dade Coll.), AAAS, AAUW (life; former v.p. Tamiami br. 1983—88, Appreciation award 1977), APA (life), Dade-Monroe Psychol. Assn., Fla. Psychol. Assn., Biofeedback Soc. Am. (pres. 1990—), Noetic Scis., NY Acad. Scis. (life), Assn.

Applied Psychophysiology and Biofeedback, Inst. Evaluation, Diagnosis and Treatment (past v.p. 1975—87, pres. 1987—, former bd. dirs.), Internat. Soc. for Study Subtle Energies and Energy Medicine (charter), Physicians for Social Responsibility, Am. Psychol. Soc. (charter), Am. Inst. Parliamentarians, (Biltmore Hotel) Coral Gables, Pilgrim John Howland Soc., Hist. Homeowners Coral Gables, Heredity Order Descs. of Colonial Govs., Regines in Miami, North Campus Spkrs. Bur. (Cmty. Lecture Series award), Internat. Platform Assn. (bd. govs. 1979—, Silver Bowl award 1993), Mexico Beach C. of C. (bus. 1991—95), Colonial Dames 17th Century, Soc. Mayflower Descs. (elder William Brewster colony), Cellar Club, Coral Gables Country Club (life), Jockey Club (life), Phi Lambda Pi, Phi Lambda (Founder's Plaque 1976, Appreciation award 1987). Democrat. Achievements include research in biofeedback and human consciousness. Home: 1311 Alhambra Cir Coral Gables FL 33134-3521 Office Phone: 305-443-8433.

HUMPHRIES, SHERRY LYNN, special education educator; b. Waukegan, Ill., Feb. 25, 1967; d. O'Neal and Betty Humphries. BS in Edn., No. Ill. U., 1990, MS in Edn., 1994. Cert. Nat. Bd. Profl. Tchng. Standards Ill. Educator of deaf Dirksen Sch., Joliet, Ill., 1991—95, Ill. Sch. for Deaf, Jacksonville, Ill., 1995—. Actor: Journey of a Teen Survivor (Award of Distinction, 2002). Named Outstanding Woman Grad., No. Ill. U., 1990; recipient Golden Apple award, Lincoln Land Coll., Channel 20, 2003, All-USA Tchr. Team, USA Today, 2005, Shell Sci. Tchg. award Semi-finalist, NSTA, 2006; fellow Holocaust and Jewish Resistance, Jewish Labor Com., 1997, Ednl. Experience, Japan Fulbright Meml. Fund, 2001, Ednl. Workshop, NASA, 2002; Mandel fellowship, U.S. Holocaust Meml. Mus., 2001. Mem.: Nat. Mid. Sch. Sci. Tchrs. Assn. (assoc.), Sci. Tchrs. Students with Disabilities (assoc. Scadden Award, Sci. Tchr. of Yr. 2004), Ill. Teachers Hard-of-Hearing, Deaf Individuals (assoc. Hazel Bothwell grant 2006), Delta Kappa Gamma (assoc.). Avocations: baton twirling, travel. Office: Ill Sch for Deaf 125 Webster Ave Jacksonville IL 62650 Office Phone: 217-479-4250. Personal E-mail: slh9999@aol.com.

HUNDLEY, CAROL MARIE BECKQUIST, music educator; b. L.A., Oct. 19, 1936; d. Paul Albert and Virginia Mary (Noll) Beckquist; m. Norris Cecil Hundley, Jr., June 8, 1957; children: Wendy Michelle Hundley Harris, Jacqueline Marie Hundley Reid. Student, Mt. St. Mary's Coll., L.A., 1954-55; AA, Mt. San Antonio Coll., Tex., 1956; postgrad., Calif. State U., L.A., 1981-82, 85-86. Tchr. pvt. piano studio, Arcadia, Calif., 1955-58, Pacific Palisades, Calif., 1965-95; vocal coach Corpus Christi Sch., Pacific Palisades, Calif., 1980-95, dir. instrumental music, 1980-95. Vocal and instrumental accompanist Theater Palisades, Pacific Palisades, 1986-87, music arranger, 1970-95; accompanist in field. Author: (play) Bach to Broadway, 1986, The Spirit of America, 1987; arranger and choreographer in field. Piano recitals Tuesday Musicale Jrs., Pasadena, Calif., 1950-54; accompanist Arcadia (Calif.) Women's Club, 1953-54; choral music provider Optimist Club, Pacific Palisades, 1989-92. Recipient scholarship Tuesday Musical Srs., 1954, Mt. St. Mary's Coll., 1954. Mem.: Santa Barbara Symphony League. Democrat. Roman Catholic. Avocations: reading, composition and improvisation, dance, interior decorating. Business E-Mail: hundley@history.ucla.edu.

HUNING, DEVON GRAY, actress, audiologist, dancer, photographer; b. Evanston, Ill., Aug. 23, 1950; d. Hans Karl Otto and Angenette Dudley (Willard) H.; divorced; 1 child, Bree Alyeska. BS with honors, No. Ill. U., 1981, MA, 1983; AAS in Vet. Tech. with honors, Colo. Mountain Coll., 2000. Actress, soloist, dancer, dir. various univ. and community theater depts., Bklyn., Chgo. and Cranbrook, B.C., Can., 1967—; audiologist, ednl. programming cons. East Kootenay Ministry of Health, Cranbrook, 1985-89; contractor, cons., trainer ednl., clin. and indsl. audiology BC, Wash., Oreg., 1989—97; ind. video prodn./photographer, 1979—; owner Maxaroma Espresso and Incredible Edibles, 1993-95; vet. technician specializing in exotics and avianix, writing and edn. rsch., 2000—; vol. Dept. Homeland Security, 2001—. Master of ceremonies East Kootenay Talent Showcase, EXPO '86, Vancouver B.C., Can., 1986; creator, workshop leader: A Hearing Impaired Child in the Classroom, 1986. Producer, writer, dir., editor (video) Down With Decibels, 1992; author: Living Well With Hearing Loss: A Guide for the Hearing-Impaired and Their Families, 1992. Sec., treas. Women for Wildlife, Cranbrook, 1985-86; assoc. mem. adv. bd. Grand County Community Coll., Winter Park, Colo., 1975-77; assoc. mem. bd. dirs. Boys and Girls Club of Can., Cranbrook, 1985. Mem. Phi Theta Kappa. Avocations: snow and water skiing, scuba diving, dance, marine animals, studying animal behavior. Personal E-mail: d_huning@hotmail.com.

HUNNICUTT, VICTORIA ANNE WILSON, educational consultant; b. Tyler, Tex., July 23, 1944; d. Leroy G. and N. Joseline (Bobo) Wilson; m. John Walter Hubble, July 29, 1967 (div. Oct. 1972); m. Buford D. Hunnicutt, Aug. 1, 1982. BA, Emory and Henry Coll., 1966; MEd, Mercer U., 1970; Ed Specialist, U. Ga., 1993; EdD, Ga. So. U., 1998. Tchr. Spanish/English Marion (Va.) Sr. H.S., 1966-67; tchr. Spanish Ballard Hudson Middle Sch., Macon, 1967-68; reading specialist Robins AFB Sch. System, Warner Robins, Ga., 1973-74, Spanish tchr., 1968-70, classroom tchr., 1970-86, computer/sci. specialist, 1986-90, prin. Robins Elem. Sch., 1991, curriculum coord., 1990-99; asst. prof. Early Childhood Ga. Coll. and State U., 1999—2004. Adj. prof. Tift Coll., Forsyth, Ga., 1985-88, Ft. Valley State Coll., 1993-99. Treas. Bibb County Dem. Women, Macon, Ga., 1986-88, membership chair 1989-93. Mem.: NSTA, ASCD, Nat. Coun. Tchrs. English, Aerospace Edn. Found. (nat. bd. trustees 1998—, nat. sec. 2000—03, Tchr. of Yr. 1995, Jane Shirley McGee award 1990, Medal of Merit 1990, Exceptional Svc. award 1997, George C. Hardy award for excellence in aerospace edn. 1999, Pres.'s citation 2001), Air Force Assn. (treas. chpt. 296 1989—91, v.p. 1991—92, v.p. for aerospace edn. chpt. 296 1991—2004, v.p. for aerospace edn. Ga. State AFA 1992—, regional v.p. for aerospace edn. 1997—), Ocmulgee Audubon Soc. (edn. chair 1986—93), Nat. Audubon Soc., HOPE Coun. (pres. 1994—95), Internat. Reading Assn., Ga. Coun. of Internat. Reading Assn., Bus. and Profl. Womens Club (Woman of Achievement local, regional, and state levels 1999), Phi Delta Kappa (chpt. sec. 2002—04). Democrat. Methodist. Avocations: reading, gardening. Office Phone: 478-745-0495, 478-745-0495. E-mail: vhunnictt@direcway.com.

HUNSAKER, JILL ANN, public health official; b. Wheatridge, Colo., Oct. 28, 1968; d. William J. and Janet Lavon (Jeanneret) H. BA in Psychology and Sociology, U. Colo., 1991; MPH, U. No. Colo., 1998. Residentialtreatment counselor Alternative Homes for Youth, Lakewood, Colo., 1991-94, asst. dir. emacipation program, 1994-95; teen outreach specialist Jefferson County Dept. Pub. Health, Lakewood, Colo., 1995-97; adminstrv. program specialist Colo. Dept. Pub. Health & Environment, Denver, 1997-99, health planner, 1999—2004; pub. health mgr. Eagle County, Colo., 2004—. Head gymnastic coach Jefferson County Pub. Schs., Golden, Colo., 1992—96. Mem. Nat. Fedn. Interscholastic Ocfls. Assn., Colo. Pub. Health Assn. (com. mem. 1997). Democrat. Avocations: piano, water-skiing, skiing. Office: Eagle County Dept Health and Human Svcs PO Box 660 Eagle CO 81631 Office Phone: 970-328-8819. Business E-Mail: jill.hunsaker@eaglecounty.us.

HUNSTEIN, CAROL, state supreme court justice; b. Miami, Fla., Aug. 16, 1944; AA, Miami-Dade Jr. Coll., 1970; BS, Fla. Atlantic U., 1972; JD, Stetson U., 1976, LLD (hon.), 1993. Bar: Ga. 1976; U.S. Dist. Ct. 1978; U.S. Ct. Appeals 1978; U.S. Supreme Ct. 1989. Atty. Hunstein & Hunstein, Atlanta, 1976-84; judge Superior Ct. of Ga. (Stone Mt. cir.), 1984-92; justice Supreme Ct. of Ga., Atlanta, 1992—, presiding justice, 2005—. Chair Ga. Commn. on Gender Bias in the Judicial System 1988-1991; pres. Coun. of Superior Ct. Judges of Ga., 1990-91; adj. prof. Sch. Law Emory U., 1991—; former chair State Commn. on Child Support, 1992, 1993, 2000; former mem. Chief Justice's Commn. on Professionalism. Bd. dirs. Ga. Campaign Adolescent Pregnancy Prevention, 1992—. Recipient Clint Green Trial Advocacy award 1976, Women Who Made A Difference award Dekalb Women's Network 1986, Outstanding Svc. commendation Ga. Legislature, 1993, Cmty. Svc. award Emory U. Legal Assn. for Women Students., 1993, Gender Justice award Ga. Commn. Family Violence, 1999, Margaret Brent award ABA, 1999; inducted to Fla. Atlantic U. Hall of Fame, 1993. Mem. Ga. Assn. of Women Lawyers, Nat. Assn. of Women Judges (dir. 1988-90), Bleckley Inn of Ct., State Bar Ga. (mem. com. women and minorities in profession 2006, Commitment to Equality award). Office: Supreme Ct Ga 244 Washington Street Atlanta GA 30334-9007 Office Phone: 404-656-3475. Business E-Mail: hunsteic@gasupreme.us. E-mail: hunsteic@supreme.courts.state.ga.us.

HUNT, ANDREA WHEATON, nurse; b. Cin., Mar. 31, 1955; d. Harlan Richard Wheaton and Geraldine Meade Smithers; m. David Ralph Hunt, June 4, 1999; children: Kristopher W. Stafford, Laura Ann Elizabeth Bolling. Studied, Marshall U., Huntington, W.Va., 1973—76. LPN Roanoke Meml. Hosp., Va., 1981—92; paralegal Law Office of Marc James Small, Roanoke, Va., 1983—91; LPN Cmty. Hospice, Ashland, Ky., 1999—2001; adminstrv. dir. Med. Res. Corps., Ashland, Ky., 2003—. Health officer ABC Emergency Mag., Ashland, Ky., 2004—. Sec. Catlettsburg Cemetary Corp., Ky., 2002—; mass care coord. ARC, Ashland, Ky., 2002—04, disaster com. chmn., 2004—. 1st lt. Tenn. Def. Force, 1987—91. Republican. Methodist. Office: 100 Academic Pky PO Box 713 Grayson KY 41143-2205 Office Phone: 606-472-6201. Business E-Mail: ahunt@abcem.net.

HUNT, BONNIE, actress; b. Chgo., Sept. 22, 1961; m. John Murphy, July 8, 1988 (separated). Actor: (films) Rain Man, 1988, Beethoven, 1992, Dave, 1993, Beethoven's 2nd, 1993, Only You, 1994, Now and Then, 1995, Jumanji, 1995 (Saturn award for best actress), Getting Away with Murder, 1996, Jerry Maguire, 1996, Kissing a Fool, 1998, A Bug's Life (voice), 1998, Random Hearts, 1999, The Green Mile, 1999, Monsters, Inc. (voice), 2001, Stolen Summer, 2002, Cheaper By the Dozen, 2003, Loggerheads, 2005, Cheaper by the Dozen 2, 2005, (voice) Cars, 2006; (TV series) Davis Rules, 1992, The Building, 1993; actor, prodr. The Bonnie Hunt Show, 1995 (Founder's award Viewers for Quality TV awards 1996); actor, dir., writer (films) Return to Me, 1998 (TV series) Life With Bonnie, 2002-04. Office: Creative Artists Agy 9830 Wilshire Blvd Beverly Hills CA 90212-1825*

HUNT, CATHY STEVENSON, academic administrator; b. Scranton, Pa., Jan. 15, 1953; d. Chester J. and Helen R. Stevenson; m. Brian Bassett Hunt, June 9, 1979; children: Sarah, Whitney. BA, U. Ky., Lexington, 1975; MusM, U. Ky., 1978, MSLS, 1981. Music libr. U. Ky., Lexington, 1981—88, acad. advisor, 1991—2001, asst. dir. ctrl. advising, 2001—01, dir. student svcs. Coll. Comm. and Info. Studies, 2002—. Vol. United Way, Lexington, 2002—. Named Outstanding Acad. Advisor, U. Ky., 1998. Mem.: Nat. Acad. Advising Assn. (Outstanding Advisor 1999). Democrat. Avocations: reading, needle-crafts, church organist. Office: University of Kentucky 105 Grehan Bldg Lexington KY 40506-0042

HUNT, DENYSE, chemistry educator; b. Old Forge, Pa., June 24, 1958; d. Donald Hunt and Jean Ann Volpe. BS, Pa. State U., 1980. Cert. secondary tchr. Fla. Biology tchr. Ft. Pierce (Fla.) Ctrl. HS, 1985—95, chemistry tchr., 1989—; adj. instr. biology Indian River C.C., Ft. Pierce, 1989. Spkr., presenter in field. Named Tchr. of Yr., Ft. Pierce Ctrl. H.S.; recipient Edn. Lamp award, St. Lucie County Sch. Bd. Mem.: Fla. Educators of Tech., Nat. Assn. Biology Tchrs., Am. Chem. Soc., Fla. Assn. Sci. Tchrs., Nat. Sci. Tchr. Assn. Avocations: swimming, travel, reading, gardening. Home: 459 NE Lima Vias Jensen Beach FL 34957 Office: Treasure Coast HS 1000 SW Darwin Blvd Port Saint Lucie FL 34953 Office Phone: 772-468-5877.

HUNT, DIANNA, editor; With Corpus Christi (Tex.) Caller-Times, Houston Chronicle, 1983—96, Dallas Morning News, 1996—2001; investigative reporter Fort Worth Star-Telegram, 2001—03, asst. govt. affairs editor, 2003—. Bd. dirs. Investigative Reporters & Editors, 2002—, treas., 2006—. Co-recipient First Amendment award, Houston Trial Lawyers Found., 1995, spot news reporting award, Tex. AP Mng. Editors, 1997; recipient freedom of info. reporting award, 1996. Mem.: Native Am. Journalists Assn. (Phoenix award 1995). Office: Fort Worth Star-Telegram PO Box 1870 Fort Worth TX 76115 Office Phone: 817-390-7084. Office Fax: 817-390-7789. E-mail: dlhunt@star-telegram.com.*

HUNT, EFFIE NEVA, retired dean, literature educator; b. Waverly, Ill., June 19, 1922; d. Abraham Luther and Fannie Ethel (Ritter) H. AB, MacMurray Coll. for Women, 1944; MA, U. Ill., 1945, PhD, 1950; postgrad., Columbia U., 1953, Univ. Coll., U. London, 1949-50. Key-punch operator U.S. Treasury, 1945; spl. librarian Harvard U., 1947, U. Pa., 1948; Instr. English U. Ill., 1950-51; librarian Library of Congress, Washington, 1951-52; asst. prof. English Mankato State Coll., 1952-59; prof. Radford Coll., 1959-63, chmn. dept. English, 1961-63; prof. Ind. State U., 1963-86; dean Ind. State U. (Coll. Arts and Scis.), 1974-86, dean and prof. emerita, 1986—. Author articles in field. Fulbright grantee, 1949-50 Mem. AAUP, MLA, Nat. Council Tchrs. English, Am. Assn. Higher Edn., Audubon Soc. Home: 3365 Wabash Ave Apt 4 Terre Haute IN 47803-1655 Office: Ind State U Root Hall Eng Dept Terre Haute IN 47809-0001

HUNT, ELIZABETH HOPE, psychologist; b. Hattiesburg, Miss., Oct. 14, 1943; d. Emory Spear and I. Elizabeth (Burkett) Hunt; m. John Volney Allcott, III, Sept. 9, 1978; children: Hunt Allcott, Elizabeth Allcott. AB, Sweet Briar Coll., 1965; MSW, U. Pa., 1971; PhD, U. Oreg., 1980. Lic. psychologist Oreg. Peace Corps vol., Santiago, Chile, 1967—69; civil rights specialist Region III HEW, Phila., 1971—74; doctoral fellow Rehab. Rsch. and Tng. Ctr. in Mental Retardation, U. Oreg., Eugene, 1974—77; intern Phila. Child Guidance Ctr., U. Pa., 1977—78; psychologist in pvt. practice Oreg. Family Ctr., Eugene, 1980—. Rschr., civic activist, lectr. workshops in field. Contbr. articles to profl. jours. Bd. dirs. Lane County Relief Nursery for Abused and Neglected Children, 1981—; activist, bd. dirs. Eugene Edn. Found., 1993—2002; vol. psychologist Friend of Torture Survivors; oversight com. Eugene Friends Meeting, 2006—; steering com. clerk Quaker North Pacific Yearly Meeting Religious Soc. of Friends, 2003—05. Grantee, Nat. Inst. Handicapped Rsch., 1977—79. Mem.: Profl. Women's Network Oreg., Physicians for Social Responsibility (co-chmn. Eugene spkrs. bur. 1982—), Lane County Psychologists Assn. (pub. affairs com.), Oreg. Psychol. Assn., APA. Home: 2650 Cresta De Ruta St Eugene OR 97403-1849

HUNT, ELLEN, minister, evangelist; b. Ocala, Fla., Nov. 7, 1951; d. Roosevelt Sr. and Vera Hunt; m. Earmon Rucker, Jr. (div.); children: Angela Brown Jesaly, Ruby Earmon Rucker III. At, CFCC C.C., Ocala, Fla., PFGC Biblical Coll. Lic. pastor, evangelist. Pastor Salvation and Praise Ministry, Winston-Salem, NC, PFGC Ministry, Ocala, Fla., Ch. of Living God, United Holiness. Evangelist PFGC Ministry, 1980—; convalescent visitor Salvation and Praise Ministry, Winston-Salem, NC, 2001—; homeless ministry. Democrat. Pentacostal. Avocations: visiting sick and elderly, praying for sick and afflicted. Home: 1829 Pleasant St Winston Salem NC 27107

HUNT, GLADYS MAE, writer; b. Moline, Mich., Oct. 23, 1926; d. Wilbur J. and Clara Jeanette (DeWeerd) Schriemer; B.A. in Journalism, Mich. State U., 1948, postgrad., 1958-59; m. Keith L. Hunt, Oct. 9, 1948; 1 son, Mark Earl. Author books: Does Anyone Here Know God?, 1967, Honey for a Child's Heart, 1969, Listen to Me, 1969, Focus on Family Life, 1970, How-to Bible Study, 1971. Don't Be Afraid to Die, 1971, Ms Means Myself, 1972, Family Secrets, 1985; co-author: Not Alone: The Necessity of Relationships, 1985, also Bible study guides; contbr. numerous articles for periodicals; asso. dir. Cedar Campus, a univ. student tng. center, 1954-86; hist. researcher Inter-Varsity Christian Fellowship USA, 1986-91; editorial bd. Leadership Mag., 1979. Mem. AAUW, Authors Guild. Baptist. Home: 6348 Tahoe Ln SE Grand Rapids MI 49546-7167

HUNT, HAZEL ANALUE STANFIELD, retired accountant; b. Butler, Mo., Apr. 4, 1921; d. Vernon Arthur and Myrrl Millicent (Henderson) Stanfield; m. Marvie Avanell Hunt, July 25, 1942; 1 child, Roger LeRoy Grad., Sawyer Sch. Bus., L.A., 1939. Supr., bookkeeper, sec. Nethercutt Labs., Santa Monica, Calif., 1940—45; v.p., treas. Dwyer-Curlett, Inc., L.A., 1946—86; ret., 1986. Pres. Nat. Assn. Accts., West L.A., 1970-96, other offices Mem. DAR, Clan Henderson Soc. U.S., Beta Sigma Phi (pres. 1942, other offices) Presbyterian. Home: 1575 E Washington Blvd Apt 312 Pasadena CA 91104-2663 Personal E-mail: hash@mailstation.com.

HUNT, HOLLY, small business owner; b. San Angelo, Tex., Nov. 19, 1942; d. Cagle O. and Zelma (Richardson) H.; m. Rowland Tackbary, Dec. 14, 1974 (div. 1987); children: Hunt Tackbary, Jett Tackberry, Trent Tackberry. BA in Eng. Lit., Tex. Tech., Lubbock, 1965. Buyer Foley's Dept. Store, Houston, 1965-68; designer Tempo, N.Y.C., 1969-73; owner, designer Holly Hunt Inc., N.Y.C., 1973-83; owner, exec. v.p. Availco Equity Availco Syatems, Chgo.; owner, pres. Holly Hunt, Ltd., Chgo., 1983--, 1986. Mem., art collector, Mus. Contrary art Chgo., 1978--. Mem. ASN, ISID. Republican. Presbyterian. Avocations: tennis, skiing, reading, art. Office: Holly Hunt Ltd 1728 Merchandise Mart Chicago IL 60654

HUNT, JANE HELFRICH, volunteer; b. Buffalo, Jan. 3, 1925; d. Henry Jacob Helfrich and Julia Christina Swanson; m. Charles Stuart Hunt, Dec. 27, 1946; children: Stephen, John(dec.), Peter, Kathleen. BS Nursing, Skidmore Coll., Saratoga Springs, N.Y., 1945. RN NY State. RN Children's Hosp., Buffalo, 1946—48; lic. real estate agt. Hunt Real Estate Corp., Buffalo, 1963, lic. gen. ins. agt., 1966. Cons. Hunt Vanner Ins., Buffalo, 1991—; bd. dirs. Hunt Real Estate Corp., H.R.E. Comml. Corp. Mem. Ctrl. Pk. Meth. Ch., 1948—, choir; bd. dirs. Longview Niagara DayCare, Buffalo, Goodwill Industries, Buffalo. Recipient Dewitt Clinton Masonic award, Vol. Svc. to Cmty., 1998. Mem.: P.E.O. Sisterhood, Twentieth Century Club. Republican. Methodist. Avocations: golf, singing, bridge, painting, gardening. Home: 187 Koster Row Buffalo NY 14226

HUNT, KAY NORD, lawyer; b. Carver, Minn., June 26, 1955; d. Edward John and Carol Valentine (Lunde) Nord; m. Gary C. Hunt, June 25, 1977 (div. Dec. 1987). BA summa cum laude, Gustavus Adolphus Coll., 1977; JD, Marquette U., 1981. Bar: Wis. 1981, Minn. 1982, US Dist. Ct. (ea., we. dist. Wis. 1981, Minn. 1982), US Ct. Appeals (7th, 8th cir. 1982), US Supreme Ct. 2000. Law clk. Wis. Ct. Appeals, Milw., 1981-82; atty., appellate litig. Lommen Nelson Cole & Stageberg, Mpls., 1982—. Adj. prof. Univ. St. Thomas Sch. Law, 2003—. Bd. mem. Ramsy County Humane Soc., St. Paul, 1997—. Mem. ABA, Am. Acad. Appellate Lawyers, State Bar Wis., Minn. State Bar Assn., Minn. Def. Lawyers (amicus curia com.), Hennepin County Bar Assn., Amdahl Inn of Ct. Office: Lommen Nelson Cole & Stageberg 2000 IDS Ctr 80 S 8th St Minneapolis MN 55402-2100 Office Phone: 612-336-9341. Office Fax: 612-339-8064. Business E-Mail: kay@lommen.com.

HUNT, L. SUSAN, publishing executive; BA in Acctg., Stetson U., 1982; MBA, Rollins Coll., 1996. Auditor Peat Marwick Mitchell, Jacksonville, Fla., 1982—86, Price Waterhouse, Orlando, Fla.; asst. contr., ops. adminstrn. mgr., prodn. mgr. Orlando Sentinel, 1986—97; v.p. ops. South Fla. Sun-Sentinel, Ft. Lauderdale, 1997—99, v.p., gen. mgr., 1999—2001; pub., pres., CEO Morning Call, Allentown, Pa., 2001—05.

HUNT, LINDA, actress; b. Morristown, NJ, Apr. 2, 1945; Student, Interlochen Arts Acad., Mich., Goodman Theatre and Sch. of Drama, Chgo. Stage appearances include Hamlet, 1972, 74, The Soldier's Tale, 1974, The Knight of the Burning Pestle, 1974, Down by the River Where Waterlilies are disfigured Every Day (off-Broadway debut) 1975, Ah, Wilderness (Broadway debut) 1975, The Rose Tattoo, 1977, Five Finger Excuse, 1975, The Recruiting Officer, 1978, Elizabeth Dead, 1980, A Metamorphis in Miniature (Obie award), 1983, Mother Courage and Her Children 1983, Top Girls (Obie award) 1983, Little Victories, 1983, End of the World, 1983, (Tony nomination 1984), Aunt Dan and Lemon, 1985, The Cherry Orchard, 1988; films include Popeye, 1980, The Year of Living Dangerously, 1982 (Acad. award Best supporting actress 1983), Dune, 1984, The Bostonians, 1984, Eleni, 1985, Silverado, 1985, Waiting for the Moon, 1987, She-Devil, 1989, Kindergarten Cop, 1990, If Looks Could Kill, 1991, Rain Without Thunder, 1993, Twenty Bucks, 1993, Younger and Younger, 1993, Ready to Wear (Prét-a-Portér), 1994, Pocahontas, 1995 (voice), Eat Your Heart Out, 1997, Amazon (voice), 1997, The Relic, 1997, Dragonfly, 2002, A Lot Like Love, 2005, Yours, Mine and Ours, 2005; TV appearance in Ah, Wilderness, 1976, Fame (series) 1978, The Room, 1987, Chico Mendes: Voice of the Amazon, 1989, The Room Upstairs (T.V. movies) 1987, Distant Lives (host) 1989, Space Rangers (series), 1993, The Practice, 1997. Office: care William Morris Agy 151 S El Camino Dr Beverly Hills CA 90212-2704*

HUNT, LORRAINE T., lieutenant governor; b. Niagara Falls, NY, Mar. 11, 1939; Student, Westlake Coll. Music. Former pres., CEO Perri Inc.; founder, also bd. dirs. Continental Nat. Bank; lt. gov. State of Nev., 1998—; pres. Nev. State Senate, 1999—. Bd. dirs. First Security Bank Nev.; chmn. bd. trustees Las Vegas Convention and Visitors Authority; former commr. and vice chair Nev. Commn. on Tourism; dir. Nev. Hotel/Motel Assn.; vice chmn. Nev. Motion Picture Found., Nev. Motion Picture Commn. Commr. Clark county Commn., 1995-99; mem. cmty. bd. Wells Fargo Bank Named U.S. Small Bus. Adv. of the Yr., 1989, Nev. Restauranteur of Yr., 1992, Rep. Woman of Yr., 1996, Woman of Yr., Nev. Ballet Theater, 1998; recipient Govs. award for excellence in bus., 1987, Free Enterprise award, 1993, First Lifetime Achievement award, Govs. Conf. on Tourism, 1993. Republican. Office: 101 N Carson St Ste 2 Carson City NV 89701-4786 also: Office Lt Governor 555 E Washington Ave Ste 5500 Las Vegas NV 89101-1081*

HUNT, MARTHA, sales executive, researcher; b. NYC, May 17, 1924; d. Paul Andrew and Monika (Dobberstein) Pankau; children: Philip Brian Hunt, Susan Monica Hunt. Student, Syracuse U., N.Y., 1943—47. Asst. contr. Commonwealth Fund, NYC, 1947-50; sales tech. Caldwell & Bloor, Mansfield, Ohio, 1958-64; sales promotion mgr. Vita Craft Corp., Shawnee, Kans., 1964-91, cons., 1964—. Mem. Meeting Planners Internat., Kansas City, 1982—. Author and editor: cookbooks, 1965-91. Pres. LWV, Akron, Ohio, 1951-53; gov. Soroptimists, 1978-80, bd. dirs., Phila., 1978-80, coord. 1980-84, pres., Kansas City, 1973-74; bd. dirs. Kansas City chpt. Shepherd's Ctr., 1972—; nat. bd. dirs. Shepherd's Ctrs. Am., 1990—2004; bd. dirs. Rose Brooks Ctr., 1979-86, v.p., 1984-85; bd. dirs., founder Safehome, Inc., 1979—, hon. chmn. as founder for Celebration of Safehome 1980-2000, 2000; pres. Metro Citizens Crusade Against Crime, Kansas City., 1983. Recipient Meritorious Svc. award, Kans. City Police Dept., 1975, Disting. Govs. award, Soroptimist Internat. Am., Phila., 1978-79, 79-80, Woman of Distinction award Santa Fe Trail Girl Scouts, 1993, Soroptimist Internat. Am., 1995, Milan Hulbert Humanitarian award Sales Profls. Internat., 1996, Mother of Our Movement award Kans. Coalition Against Sexual and Domestic Violence, 1999, Kansas City Chiefs/NFL Cmty. Quarterback award, 2002, Victims of Domestic and Sexual Violence 25 Yrs of Svc. award, 2005. Mem. Kappa Kappa Gamma (pres. 1948-49), Alumnae Assn. (NYC). Republican. Presbyterian. Achievements include 25 years of service to victims of domestic and sexual violence, 2005. Avocations: travel, volunteering. E-mail: mhunt5607@aol.com.

HUNT, MARY ALICE, retired humanities educator; b. Lima, Ohio, Apr. 14, 1928; d. Blair T. and Grace (Henry) H. BA, Fla. State U., Tallahassee, 1950, MA, 1953; PhD, Ind. U., Bloomington, 1973. Instr., librarian Fla. State U., Tallahassee, 1955-61, asst. prof., 1961-74, assoc. prof., 1974-82, prof., 1982-95, assoc. dean, 1986-95, prof. emerita, 1995—. Author: Transitions: An Informal History of a School Celebrating its 50th Anniversary, 1997; co-author: Multimedia Indexes, Lists, etc., 1975; editor: Multimedia Approach To Children's Literature, 1983, (periodical) Fla. State U./SLIS Alumni Newsletter, 1966-95, Florida Libraries, 1961-67; assoc. editor: Folders of Ideas for Library Excellence, 1991. Mem. Sr. Ctr. Art Coun., 2004—. Recipient Art Vol. of Yr. award, Sr. Ctr. Art Coun., 2004. Mem. ALA (councilor at large 1986-94, 96-2000), Southeastern Libr. Assn., Fla. Assn. Media in Edn., Delta Kappa Gamma, Pi Lambda Theta, Pi Kappa Phi, Beta Phi Mu. Avocations: gardening, reading, photography, pastel drawing and watercolor painting. Home: 1603 Kolopakin Nene Tallahassee FL 32301-4733 Business E-Mail: mhunt@mailer.fsu.edu.

HUNT, MARY ELIZABETH, religious studies educator; b. June 1, 1951; BA magna cum laude, Marquette U., Milw., 1972; M of Theol. Studies, Harvard Div. Sch., 1974; MDiv, Jesuit Sch. Theology, Berkeley, Calif., 1979; PhD, Grad. Theol. Union, Berkeley, 1980. Vis. prof. theology ISEDET Frontier Internship in Mission, Buenos Aires, 1980-82; co-dir., co-founder Women's Alliance for Theology, Ethics and Ritual, Silver Spring, Md., 1983—; vis. asst. prof. religion Colgate U., Hamilton, NY, 1986-87; rsch. fellow Ctr. for Study of Values in Pub. Life, Harvard Div. Sch., 2000—01. Lectr., condr. workshops in field; adj. assoc. prof. women's studies program Georgetown U., 1995-99. Author: Fierce Tenderness: A Feminist Theology of Friendship, 1990; mem. editl. bd. Jour. Feminist Studies in Religion, Jour. Religion and Abuse, Theology and Sexuality Jour.; editor: Good Sex: Feminist Perspectives from the World's Religions, 2001, A Guide for Women in Religion: Making Your Way from A to Z, 2004; contbr. articles to profl. jours. Mem. Am. Acad. Religion, Alpha Sigma Nu. Office: Women's Alliance Theology 8121 Georgia Ave 310 Silver Spring MD 20910-4933 Office Phone: 301-589-2509. Office Fax: 301-589-3150. Personal E-mail: mhunt@hers.com.

HUNT, MARY REILLY, organization executive; b. N.Y.C., Apr. 17, 1921; d. Philip R. and Mary C. (Harten) Reilly; m. Robert R. Hunt, Apr. 10, 1943,; children: Marianne Schram, Philip R., Robert R., Elise Hannah. Student, CCNY, 1939; DHL (hon.), Thomas More Coll., 2005. Tax investigator Ind. Dept. Revenue, 1970-80; pres. Ind. Right to Life, 1973-77; treas. Nat. Right to Life Com., Washington, 1974, 77, 78, mem. exec. com., 1974, 76-81, vice chmn., 1976, exec. dir., 1978, dir. devel., 1979-94, v.p. devel., 1994-97, hon. bd. mem., 1983—; v.p. devel. Nat. Life Ctr., Woodbury, 1997—; pres. Mary Reilly Hunt & Assoc., Inc., South Bend, Ind., 1985—. Bd. dirs., v.p. YWCA, 1968-73, bd. dirs. Mental Health Assn. St. Joseph Co., 1972-78; candidate for state legis., 1988; mem. St. Joseph County Rep. Women precinct com., South Bend, 1964-79, alt. del. to Nat. Rep. Conv., 1976, 84, 88, 92; mem. Souht Bend Symphony Women's Assn.; mem. Coun. for Nat. Policy, 1988—, mem. exec. com., 2000-06. Recipient St. Patrick's medal St. Patrick's Coll. and Sem. (Ireland), 1996. Mem. NAFE, Women Bus. Owners, Am. Soc. Sovereign Mil. Order of Malta. Republican. Roman Catholic. Avocations: gardening, antiques. Office: Nat Life Ctr 1102 N Lafayette Blvd South Bend IN 46617-1136

HUNT, REBECCA R., elementary school educator; b. Salt Lake City, May 16, 1950; d. Rulon Moroni and Golda Larsen Richards; m. Hyde Barry Hunt, Apr. 22, 1971; children: Cloe, Clayton, Russell, Patrick, Heidi, AnneLouise. BS in Elem. Edn., U. Utah, 1972; postgrad. in Edn., Brigham Young U., 1995—. Tchr. grade 6 Kaysville (Utah) Elem., 1987-95; adminstrv. intern Windridge Elem., Kaysville, 1995—. Master tchr. Nat. Tchrs. Tng. Inst., Salt Lake City, 1993-95. Recipient Exemplary Use of Instrn. TV award Utah Edn. Network, 1994, Presdl. Math. award NSF, 1995. Mem. Nat. Coun. Tchrs. Math., Utah Coun. Tchrs. Math., Soc. Presdl. Awardees. Mem. Lds Ch. Avocation: distance learning. Office: Windridge Elem 700 E 1300 N Kaysville UT 84037-1285

HUNT, SWANEE G., public policy educator, former ambassador; b. Dallas, May 1, 1950; m. Charles Alexander Ansbacher; 3 children. BA, Tex. Christian U., 1972; MA, Ball State U., 1976; MA in Religion, Iliff Sch. of Theology, 1977, PhD (hon.), 1986, Webster U., 1994. Pres. Hunt Alternatives Fund, 1981—; co-founder Karis Community, 1980-83; min. pastoral care Capital Heights Presbyn. Ch., 1983; vice chair Denver Community Mental Health Commn., 1983-87; with Gov. Policy Acad. on Families and Children at Risk, 1989-90; chair Colo. Coord. Coun. Housing and the Homeless, 1989-92; U.S. amb. to Austria, 1993-97; dir. Women and Pub. Policy Program, Kennedy Sch. Govt. Harvard. Composer The Witness Cantata, 1985; author: This Was Not Our War: Bosnian Women Reclaiming the Peace, 2004; syndicated columnist Scripps Howard. Bd. dirs., co-founder Women's Found. Colo.; chair Mayor's Human Capital Agenda Coun., 1992-93; co-chair Denver Initiative Children and Families; mem. UN High Commn. on Refugees; mem. Internat. Crisis Group, Internat. Alert. Recipient Martin Luther King Humanitarian award U. Colo., 1992, NCCJ, 1992, Denver Urban Ministries, 1991, United Meth. Ch., 1989, Internat. Women's Forum, 1989, Sta. KUSA-TV, 1989, Caring Connection, 1989, Nat. Mental Health Assn., 1985, Mental Health Assn. Colo., 1984, 94, Mile High award United Way, 1993, Am. Heritage award Anti-Defamation League, 1995, Cordon Bleu du Saint Esprit Peace award, 1996, Humanitarian Lifetime Svc. award Denver Holocaust Awareness, 1997, Together for Peace award, 1997, 3 decorations Austrian Govt., 1997, Amb. award The Conflict Ctr., 1997, Inst. for Internat. Edn. award, 1998, PEN New Eng. award, 2005. Office: 168 Brattle St Cambridge MA 02138-3309 also: Harvard Univ Kennedy Sch Government 79 JFK St Cambridge MA 02138-5801 Office Phone: 617-547-8921. Business E-Mail: swanee_hunt@huntalternatives.org.

HUNT, VALERIE VIRGINIA, electrophysiologist, educator; b. Larwill, Ind., July 22, 1916; d. Homer Henry Hunt and Iva Velzora Ames. BS in Biology, Fla. State Coll., 1936; MA in Physiol. Psychology, Columbia U., 1941, EdD in Sci. Edn., 1946; DD, Phoenix Inst., San Diego, 1984. Sci. tchr. Anniston (Ala.) H.S., 1936-38; asst. anatomy nursing dept. Columbia U., N.Y.C., 1939-40; chmn. health edn. Boston YWCA, 1942-43; instr. Columbia U. Tchrs. Coll. and Coll. Physicians and Surgeons, N.Y.C., 1943-46; asst. prof. U. Iowa, Iowa City, 1946-47; assoc. prof., dir. divsn. phys. therapy UCLA, 1947-64, prof. physiology, dir. electromyographic lab., 1964-80, prof. emeritus, 1980—; dir. BioEnergy Fields Lab. BioEnergy Fields Found., Malibu, Calif., 1980—; CEO Malibu Pub. Co., 1995—. Cons. Nat. Bd. YWCA, 1943-46, Nat. Early Childhood Edn., 1948-50, UCLA Sch. Engring. Prosthetics Inst., 1949-51, Calif. Dept. Edn., 1950-60, Chrysler Motor Co. Space Divsn. Rsch., 1952, NASA Space Biology, 1958, Grand Kamalani Wellness Ctr., Maui, Hawaii; field reader U.S. Dept. HEW, 1958-65; reviewer sci. textbooks McMillan Pub., Prentice-Hall, McGraw-Hill, W.B. Saunders & Co., 1959-67; cons. Fetzer Found. Energy Field Rsch., 1989, Heart Math Found., 1992. Author: Recreation for the Handicapped, 1955, Corrective Physical Education, 1967, Movement Education for Preschool, 1972, Guidelines for Movement Behavior: Curricula for Early Childhood Education, 1974, Infinite Mind: Science of the Human Vibrations of Consciousness, 1996, Mind Mastery Meditations, 1997, Naibhu, 1998; contbr. articles to profl. jours. Pres. United Cerebral Palsy, L.A., 1947-51; mem. adv. com. Harlan Shoemaker Clinic for Neurol. Disabilities, 1948-53; bd. dirs. Found. for Jr. Blind, 1949-52, Crippled Children Soc., 1953-58, YWCA, L.A., 1955-65; adv. com., Internat. Congress for Exceptional Children, 1964-72, Rory Found., L.A., 1998—; vestry bd. mem. St. Matthew Episcopal Ch., L.A., 1965-69. Rsch. grantee USPHS, 1957-61, Adelphi Found., 1960-63, Rolf Found., 1965-71; recipient Heritage award Calif. Dance Educator Assn., 1987, N.B. Rudman award Found. Exceptional Leadership, 1995; Dame Order of St. John of the Ams., 1996. Mem. NSF, N.Y. Acad. Scis., Pi Lambda Theta, Kappa Delta Pi. Avocations: travel, gardening, music, art, lecturing. Office: BioEnergy Fields Found PO Box 6653 Malibu CA 90264-6653 Office Phone: 310-457-4694. Business E-Mail: admin@bioenergyfields.org.

HUNTE, BERYL ELEANOR, mathematics professor; b. N.Y.C. BA, CUNY-Hunter Coll., 1947; MA, Columbia U., 1948; PhD, NYU, 1965. Instr. math. So. U., Baton Rouge, 1948-51; tchr. math. Bloomfield (N.J.) H.S., 1951-57; tchr. maths. Friends Sem., N.Y.C., 1957-62; asst. prof. maths. Rockland C.C., Suffern, N.Y., 1962-63; instr. maths., supr. tchr. trainees NYU, N.Y.C., 1964; chmn. dept. math. Borough of Manhattan C.C., N.Y.C., 1964-67, 70-73, prof. maths., 1970-95, prof. maths. emerita, 1996, acting dean students, 1985-87, acting dean acad. affairs, 1987-88; dean for spl. projects CUNY, 1988-89. Assoc. U. Seminar on Higher Edn., Columbia U., N.Y.C., 1989-95. Author: (with others) (textbook) Mathematics Through Statistics, 1973. NSF fellow, summer 1960, 1963-64, Chancellor's Faculty fellow CUNY, 1980. Mem. N.Y. Acad. Scis., Am. Math. Soc., CUNY Acad. for Humanities and Scis. (bd. dirs. 1991—, first v.p. 1994—), UN Assn. N.Y.C. (bd. dirs., sec. 1980-86). Avocations: opera, concerts, ballet, bridge.

HUNTER, ANITA J., pediatric nurse practitioner, educator; b. Deland, Fla., Sept. 15, 1945; d. Harry Hunter and Marjorie J. Haymaker; children: Darren H. Krzynowek, Kerry A. Krzynowek. BSN, Elms Coll., Chicopee, Mass., 1984; MSN, U. Mass., Amherst, 1987; PhD, U. of Conn., Storrs, 1994. Pediat. nurse practitioner, Northeaster U., Boston, RN Wash. Nurse Baystate Med. Ctr., Springfield, Mass., 1967—75, pediat. nurse practitioner, 1975—87; assoc. prof. Elms Coll., Chicopee, Mass., 1987—94; asst. prof. U. Mass., Amherst, 1994—99, Clemson U., SC, 1999—2003; assoc. prof. U. of San Diego, 2003—. Dir. RN-BSN program Elms Coll., Chicopee, 1987—94; dir. pediat. nurse practitioner program U. of Mass., Amherst, 1988—99, co-coord. internat. med. missions, 1995—99; cons. Fitzgerald Health Edn. Assocs., Boston, 1997—; coord. internat. med. missions Clemson U., 1999—2003, U. of San Diego, 2003—, dir. accelerated programs, 2003—; nurse practitioner, educator for vulnerable populations Preparing Culturally Sensitive Health Providers. Contbr. articles to profl. jours. (Nursing Writing award, 2002). Recipient Instrument Devel. for Latino Populations grant, USD, 2003—06, Health Care for Migrant Farm Workers grant, Heath Resources & Svc. Adminstrn., 2001—03, Adolescent Resilience: An Internat. Study award, U. Mass., Sigma Theta Tau, Clemson Univ., 1998—2003, Life Time Achievement award, San Diego C. of C., 2006. Mem.: ANA, Nat. Ass. Pediat. Nurse Practitioners, Nat. Org. Nurse Practitioner Faculties (chair global advancement com. and intern. sig. 2000—05), Sigma Theta Tau (faculty counselor 1985—2006). Office: U San Diego 5998 Alcala Park San Diego CA 92110 Office Phone: 619-260-7609. Office Fax: 619-260-6814. Personal E-mail: hunter_a@sbcglobal.net. Business E-Mail: ahunter@sandiego.edu.

HUNTER, ANNE GRAVES, counselor; b. Albemarle County, Va., Feb. 4, 1934; d. Andrew Leslie and Ladys Marshall Graves; m. E. Sidney Hunter Jr., 1956 (div. 1976); children: E. Sidney III, James Andrew, Robert S., Bruce A., Mary Frances. RN, Grace Hosp. Sch. Nursing, 1954; BS magna cum laude, Old Dominion U., 1978, MS in Edn., 1985. Cert. Nat. Bd. Cert. Counselors; family therapy cert. Ea. Va. Med. Sch. RN DePaul Hosp., Norfolk, Va., 1978-79, clin. mgr. for mental health, chem. dependency, pain mgmt., 1979-90; clin. therapist Crossroads Clin. Svcs., Virginia Beach, Va., 1988-91, Pembroke Counselings Svcs., Virginia Beach, 1991-93, Anne G. Hunter, LPC, NCC, LMFT, Virginia Beach, 1993—. Bd. mem. Mental Health Assn. Tidewater; bd. mem., facilitator Amputee Support Group; facilitator SHARE, 1982—. Mem. ACA, Va. Counselors Assn., Lic. Profl. Counselors Hampton Roads, Mid-Atlantic Group Psychotherapy Soc., Phi Kappa Phi, Alpha Chi. Methodist. Office: Ste 217 1604 Hilltop West Exec Ctr Virginia Beach VA 23451

HUNTER, BARBARA WAY, public relations consultant; b. Westport, N.Y., July 14, 1927; d. Walter Denslow and Hilda (Greenawalt) Way; m. Austin F. Hunter, Jan. 24, 1953; children: Kimberley, Victoria. BA, Cornell U., 1949. Assoc. editor Topics Pub. Co., N.Y.C., 1949-51; publicist Nat. Dairy Product Corp., N.Y.C., 1951-53; account exec. Sally Dickson Assn., 1953-56; assoc. D-A-Y Pub. Relations (div. Ogilvy & Mather Co.), N.Y.C., 1964-70, exec. v.p., 1970-84, pres., 1984-89, Hunter & Assocs., Inc., 1989-97, chmn., 1997-2000. Bd. dirs. Mr. Steak Inc., Denver, Great River Arts Inst. Trustee Cornell U., Ithaca, N.Y., 1980-85; life mem. Cornell U. Coun.; bd. dirs. Point O'Woods Assn., Fire Island, N.Y., 1980-87, 2002—, pres., 2003—. Recipient Sparkplug award Internat. Foodservice Mfrs. Assn., 1970, Matrix award N.Y. Women in Communications Inc., 1980, Entreprenurial Woman award Women Bus. Owners, 1981, Nat. Headliner award Women in Communications Inc., 1984. Fellow Pub. Rels. Soc. Am. (pres. 1984, pres.-elect 1983, treas. 1982, pres. N.Y. chpt. 1980, Nat. Gold Anvil award 1993); mem. Found. Pub. Rels. Rsch. and Edn. (trustee 1982, 84), Walpole Hist. Soc. (bd. dirs. 2002-), Cornell Club of N.Y., The Club at Point O'Woods.

HUNTER, BEVERLY CLAIRE, research scientist, educator; b. Pitts., Apr. 19, 1941; d. Eldon Clare and Ethel Mae (Kamer) Roberts m. Harold G. Hunter, Jan. 7, 1966; children: Cynthia Claire, Gregory Shawn. BA cum laude (Nat. Merit scholar), U. Pitts., 1963. Cert. Geographic Info. Sys. George Mason Univ., 2003. Computer programmer U.S. Navy, 1964-65; systems engr. IBM Corp., 1965-66; dir. instructional programming Human Resources Rsch. Orgn., Alexandria, Va., 1966-68, sr. staff scientist, 1970-87; staff scientist Matrix Rsch., Alexandria, 1969; lead scientist BBN Corp., 1993-98, NSFf, program mgr. rsch. on tchg. and learning, 1989—93; scientist Boston Coll., 1998-99; pres. Piedmont Rsch. Inst., Amissville, Va., 1999—. Cons. U.S. Congress, U.S. Office Edn., Bell Labs., Telenet Comms.: pres. Targeted Learning Corp., 1983-89; adj. prof. U. San Francisco, 1985-86; v.p. Piedmont Rsch. Ctr., 1979-80; peer reviewer. Co-author: Learning Alternatives in U.S. Education: Where Student and Computer Meet, 1975, Computer Literacy, 1982; Author: My Students Use Computers, 1984 Guide to Learning Resources for Users of IBM Personal Computers, Scholastic U.S. History Data Bases, 1985, Scholastic U.S. Government Data Bases, 1985, Scholastic Life Science Data Bases, 1985, Scholastic Physical Sciences Data Bases, 1985, Scholastic World Geography Data Bases, 1986, Scholastic Poetry and Mythology Data Bases, 1986, Scholastic Literature Data Bases, 1986, Scholastic Constitution Then and Now Data Files, 1987, Scholastic Weather and Climate Data Files, 1987, Working with the U.S. Congress, 1988, Online Searching in the Curriculum, 1989; Scientists at Work hypermedia data base; editor Edn. and Computing Internat. Jour.; contbr. articles to publs. Grantee, N.S.F., 1979—2003. Mem.: Internat. Soc. Tech. in Edn., Rappanhannock League Environ. Protection (bd. dirs.), Nature Conservancy, Assn. Computing Machinery. Office: Piedmont Rsch Inst 130 Mossie Ln Amissville VA 20106-4152

HUNTER, BRENDA ANN, writer, psychologist; b. Statesville, NC, Feb. 2, 1941; d. Ray Cameron and Florence Maureen (Smith) Morrison; m. David Lynn Larson, June 23, 1963; children: Holly Larson, Kristen Blair; m. Don R. Hunter, Feb. 23, 1975. BA in English, Wheaton Coll., 1963; MA in English, SUNY, Buffalo, 1967; PhD in Psychology, Georgetown U., 1990. Psychologist Minirth, Meier and Byrd Clinic, Arlington, Va., 1991—97; pvt. practice, 1980—. Instr. U. NC, Asheville, Georgetown U.; conf., presenter, spkr. in field. Author: Beyond Divorce, 1978, Where Have All the Mothers Gone?, 1984, Home by Choice, 1991, In the Company of Women, 1994, What Every Mother Needs to Know About Babies, 1994, A Wedding is a Family Affair, 1995, In the Company of Friends, 1996, The Power of Mother Love, 1997, My God, Do You Love Me?, 1998, Staying Alive: Life Changing Strategies for Surviving Cancer, 2004; contbr. articles to profl. jours. Home: 95147 Vance Knoll Chapel Hill NC 27517 Personal E-mail: drbrendamhunter@bellsouth.net.

HUNTER, DEBORA ANN BROBECK, secondary school educator; b. Valparaiso, Ind., 1954; d. Donald Stanislaus and Nancy Louise Reason Brobeck; m. Caleb Keith Hunter, 1977; children: Brian Caleb, Michael Charles children: Elizabeth Kathleen. BS in English magna cum laude, Ball State U., Muncie, Ind., 1974; MA in English, Purdue U., Hammond, Ind., 1979. Lic. Tchr. Ind. Bd. Edn., 1979. Tchg. grad. asst. English dept. Ball State U., 1974—75; tchr. English Kouts H.S., Ind., 1975—77, LaPorte H.S., Ind., 1977—83, tchr. AP English, 1999—. Mem. LaPorte H.S. Parent Tchr. Student Assn.; vol. music dept. LaPorte H.S.; vol. LaPorte Show Choir, LaPorte Marching Band; advisor Nat. Honor Soc. LaPorte H.S., Ind., 2005—. Vol. Bldg. Blocks Nursery Sch., LaPorte, Indian Trail Elem. Sch., LaPorte, Singing Sand Girl Scout Coun., LaPorte, Cub Scouts Am., LaPorte. Mem.: Am. Fedn. Tchrs. (assoc.), LaPorte Fedn. Tchrs. (assoc.), Mythopoeic Soc., Pi Lambda Theta, Lambda Iota Tau. Office: LaPorte HS 602 F St La Porte IN 46350

HUNTER, DEBORAH H., elementary school educator; b. Binghamton, NY, Nov. 12, 1952; d. Joseph Herman and Daisy Moran. BS, Appalachian State U., 1975. Tchr. J. Sam Gentry Mid. Sch., Mt. Airy, NC, 1976—. Exec. dir. Walk/Run for Yr., 2003—06. Recipient Tchr. of Yr., Gentry County, 1991—92, 2005—06, Surry County, 2005—06, NC Health Educator of Yr., 2005—06. Home: 105 Blake Dr King NC 27021

HUNTER, DOROTHY EVELYN, mathematician, educator; b. Austin, Tex., May 25, 1941; d. Tom and Effie Carter; children: Duane T., Lewis E. BS in Edn., U. Tex., 1963, MS in Edn., 1976. Math. tchr. Ft. Worth Pub. Schs., Ft. Worth, Austin (Tex.) Ind. Schs.; computer programmer Pioneer Ins. Co., Ft. Worth; instr. Huston-Tillotson Coll., Austin. Mem. adv. com. HBCU Coll. Algebra Reform; mem. adv. bd. Tex. Higher Edn. Conf. pres., officer Women's Missionary Soc., African Methodist Episcopal Ch., 1993—97. Mem.: Math. Assn. Am., Phi Delta Kappa (officer 1995—2002). Avocations: writing, sewing, event planning. Office: Huston Tillotson U 900 Chicon St Austin TX 78702

HUNTER, FRANCES ELLEN CROFT, music educator; b. Greensboro, N.C., Jan. 25, 1941; d. John Wilkins Croft Sr. and Zara Louise Fisher Croft; m. C. Linwood Hunter, Jan. 25, 1964 (dec. Sept. 2, 1996); 1 child, Leticia Collette. BFA, Ohio U., Athens, 1962. Cert. tchr. music N.C., Ohio. Tchr. music Hoke County Schs., Raeford, NC, 1962—64, Harnett County Schs., Johnsonville, NC, 1964—65, Fayetteville City Schs., NC, 1965—70, Ft. Bragg Schs., NC, 1971—2001. Singer Cumberland Oratorio Singers, Fayetteville, 2003, bd. dirs., 2004—; singer and accompanist Stars and Stripes Singers, Fayetteville, 2003. Composer: Here's Looking At You Yr. 2000, 1987. Vol. Fayetteville Festival of Flight, 2003, Teen Involvement Projects, Inc.; vol. reader svc. for blind Southeastern NC Radio Reading Svc. Inc., 2004. Recipient Svc. award, Music Educators Nat. Conf./N.C. Music Educators Assn., 1999, Cert. of Retirement, Dept. Def. Edn. Activity, 2001. Mem.: Nat. Assn. Ret. Fed. Employees, NC Ret. Govt. Employees' Assn., Music Educators Nat. Conf. Lutheran. Avocations: reading, dance.

HUNTER, GEORGIA L., clergywoman; b. Wiergate, Tex., June 14, 1938; d. George Clavert and Leria (Thomas) Spikes; m. LeRoy Hunter, Feb. 2, 1967; children— Balenda M. Spikes, Maria A. Spikes. Student Bible Moody Bible Inst; MDiv Universal Life Ch. Sch., Modesto, Calif.; A in Theology Grace Theol. Seminary, Atlanta, 1998. Ordained to ministry Christian Meth. Episcopal Ch., 1983; cert. tour guide. Counselor Ill. Dept. children and Family Services, Freeport, 1970-74; food service dir. Retirement Inc., Freeport, 1978—; pastor Christian Meth. Episcopal Ch., Madison, Wis., 1983-91; asst. pastor Miles Meml. Christian Meml. Episcopal Ch., Rockford, Ill., 1993; pastor Christ Mission Christian Meth. Episcopal Ch., Milw., 1993; corr. Jour. Standard, Freeport, 1982-83; chairperson expansions and missions sect. Milw. dist. Christian Meth. Episcopal Ch.; mem. Com. Milw. Dist. Leadership Tng. Sch.; coord. Interdenominational Theol. Ctr. Ext. Program, Atlanta. V.p. Freeport Bd. Edn., 1977—; pres. Ch. Women United, Freeport, 1970-83; asst. dir. youth Rockford and Vicinity Dist. Assn., 1980-82; sec. Freeport Good Samaritan Refuge House; food pantry coord. Christian Meth. Episc. Ch., Milw.; supr. Rainbow Ridge Residential Home, 1996; mem. Freeport Mins. United For Change; site mgr. Ill. Linkchull House, Stephenson County, 1997. Recipient Human Relations award City Council Freeport, 1974, Spiritual Achievement award Martin Luther King Ctr., Freeport, 1983, Good Neighbor award Freeport Jour. Standard, 1983, Achievement award Ch. Women United, 1983. Mem. Fully Gospel Women Assn. (bd. dirs., coord.), Young Adult Christian Women (pres.). Democrat. Avocations: bowling; researcher; reading; sewing; writing poetry.

HUNTER, GLORIA ELEANORE, secondary school educator; b. Chgo., May 24, 1927; d. David Waldren and Eleanore Dorothy (Kline) H.; m. Thomas Alexander Hunter III; children: Thomas A. IV, William Craig, Eleanore Tracey. BA, U. Mich., 1949; MS, U. Bridgeport, 1972. Tchr. Fenger H.S., Chgo., 1949-50, U. Mich. H.S., 1950-55; reporter, columnist Westport News, 1965-68; program writer Action for Bridgeport Cmty. Devel., 1968-70; tchr. Fairfield Jr. H.S., 1970-72; tchr., dir. reading Weston Schs., 1972-91. Cons. in field. Author (cassette program) Speed, Learning and Retention for Managers, (book) Who Invited These Tackey People Anyway, 2005; columnist for local newspaper Westport Minuteman, 1993—; contbr. columns to newspapers; contbr. articles to mags. and newspapers. Mem. Westport Bd. Edn., 1991-95; candidate Conn. Ho. of Reps., 1994. Mem. NEA (life), LWV. Democrat. Avocations: gardening, travel, knitting, entertaining, theater. Home: 33 High Point Rd Westport CT 06880-3908 Personal E-mail: gloandtom@aol.com.

HUNTER, HOLLY, actress; b. Conyers, Ga., Mar. 20, 1958; d. Charles Edwin and Opal Marguerite (Catledge) Hunter; m. Janusz Kaminski, May 20, 1995 (div. Dec. 21, 2001); 2 children. BFA, Carnegie-Mellon U., 1980. Actress: (films) The Burning, 1981, Swing Shift, 1984, Broadcast News, 1987 (Acad. Award nomination for best actress, 1988), Raising Arizona, 1987, End of the Line, 1988, Always, 1989, Miss Firecracker, 1989, Animal Behavior, 1989, Once Around, 1991, The Piano, 1993 (Cannes Film Festival Award for best actress, 1993, Golden Globe for best actress, 1994, Acad. Award for best actress, 1994), The Firm, 1993 (Acad. Award nomination for best supporting actress, 1994), Home for the Holidays, 1995, Copycat, 1995, Crash, 1996, Hurly-burly, 1997, A Life Less Ordinary, 1997, Living Out Loud, 1998, Jesus' Son, 1999, Things You Can Tell Just By Looking at Her, 2000 (Emmy nomination for best supporting actress in a miniseries or movie, 2001), Woman Wanted, 2000, Timecode, 2000, O Brother, Where Art Thou, 2000, Moonlight Mile, 2002, Levity, 2003, Little Black Book, 2004, The Incredibles (voice), 2004, Nine Lives, 2005, The Big White, 2005; (TV) Svengali, 1983, An Uncommon Love, 1983, With Intent to Kill, 1984, A Gathering of Old Men, 1987, Roe vs. Wade, 1989 (Emmy for best actress in a miniseries or special, 1989), Crazy in Love, 1992, The Positively True Adventures of the Alleged Texas Cheerleader-Murdering Mom, 1993 (Emmy for best actress in a miniseries or special, 1993, CableACE award for best actress in a movie or miniseries, 1994), Harlan County War, 2000 (Emmy nomination for best actress in a miniseries or movie, 2000), When Billie Beat Bobby, 2001 (Emmy nomination for best actress in a miniseries or movie, 2001); (Broadway stage prodns.) Crimes of the Heart, 1982, The Wake of Jamey Foster, 1982, Impossible Marriage, 1998; (regional stage prodns.) Buried Child, A Doll's House, Artichoke; (other stage prodns.) include A Lie of the Mind, L.A., Battery, N.Y.C., Miss Firecracker Contest, 1984, The Person I Once Was, N.Y.C.; Actress, exec. prodr.: (films) Thirteen, 2003 (Acad. Award nomination for best supporing actress, 2004, Golden Globe nomination for best supporting actress, 2004, Screen Actors Guild Award nomination for best supporting actress, 2004). Bd. dirs. Calif. Abortion Rights Action League.*

HUNTER, JUANITA WALTERS, minister; d. Leon Percy Vick and Virginia Mildred Barnes; m. Tyrone Darryl Hunter, June 17, 1967; foster children: Bob Rogers, Patricia Barnes children: Jonita T., Darryl A., Rita C., Tonya M., Teresa M. AA, Pentecoastal Sch. Theology, 1988, BA, 1990; MA, Bethlehem Bible Coll., 2000, PhD, 2002; DHL (hon.), Epistle Bible Coll., Greensboro, 2005. Co-pastor St. Thomas Chapel Ch., Greensboro, NC, 1978—. Pres. women's fellowship St. Thomas Chapel, Greensboro, 1995—; instr. Living Epistle Bible Coll., Greensboro, 2004—. Vol. adminstr. Cmty. Crisis Ctr., Greensboro, 1999—, Epistle Bible Coll., Greensboro, 2000—. E-mail: ehecttadyin2005@yahoo.com.

HUNTER, KATHLEEN, writer, educator; b. Portland, Oreg., Apr. 11, 1944; d. Harold Wayne and Ruthann (Breitmayer) McKenzie; m. Duncan Bert (Lillywhite) Hunter, July 13, 1963; children: Mindy Lynn, Dana Brad. Student, La. State U., Baton Rouge, 1962, Portland State U., 1963; BA in Journalism, U. Alaska, Fairbanks, 1984. Bookkeeper Consol. Freightways Ltd., others, 1964-72; advt. sales, feature writer Kodiak (Alaska) Fishwrapper, others, 1975-85; freelance writer and editor Palmer, Alaska, 1984-88; English and life stories tchr. Mat-Su C.C., Palmer, 1989-93; life stories tchr., writer, storyteller Enterprise, Oreg., 1997—; prodr. Fishtrap Storytime, 2003—; pres., v.p. cmty. and bd. mem. Fishtrap, Enterprise, 1989—. Author, pub.: Tracking the "Bear," 1986, Alaska Nicknames, 1988; editor mag. Alaska Today, 1984. Bd. dirs., sec. Kids Are People, Palmer, 1993-97; sec., v.p. Valley Performing Arts, Palmer, 1991-97; mem., sec. Palmer Hist. Soc., 1985-88. Recipient Joe and Claire Fejes Book Writing award U. Alaska, 1982, James Gordon Bennett award, 1984, various awards Alaska Press Women, 1984, 86, 3d Pl. award nat. Fedn. Presswomen, 1986; Natural Resource grantee Alaska N.W. Pub. Co., 1982, Lola Tilly scholar, 1982. Mem. AAUW, Phi Kappa Phi. Avocations: stained glass art, genealogical research, gardening, acting, vocal music. Home: 68762 Allen Canyon Loop Wallowa OR 97885-8507

HUNTER, MATTIE SUE (MATTIE SUE MOORE), health facility administrator; b. Brownwood, Tex., Apr. 7, 1944; d. Robert and Florence Irene (Shaw) Moore; divorced; children: Roberta Sharlene, Hank William, Charlie Ervin. Student, Howard Payne Coll., 1963-64. Unit mgr., supr. Girling Health Care, Inc., Austin, Tex., 1976—. Chairperson Keep Brownwood Beautiful, 2001. Mem. Tex. Assn. Home Care, Brownwood Garden Culture Club (pres. 1996-97), Hist. Soc., Blvd. Beautification. Democrat. Mem. Church of Christ. Avocations: greenhouse, gardening, craft making, bowling, cooking.

HUNTER, MIRIAM EILEEN, artist, educator; b. Cin., June 6, 1929; d. James R. and Bertha (Oberlin) H BS, Ball State U., 1951, MA Art, 1957; MA Christian Edn., Wheaton Coll., 1958; EdD, Nova U., 1979. Tchr. art and English Madison-Marion Consol. Schs., 1951—52; tchr. art Wheaton Coll., Ill., 1952—84; dir. Sch. Edn. Calvin Simmons Coll., Lawrenceville, Ga., 1984—. Freelance art cons.; chair art dept. Wheaton Coll., Ill., 1969-70, 1975-79; asst. prof., assoc. prof. art Fine Arts Gallery, Chgo., 1971-84broker First Am. Nat. Securities Corp., 1982—; divsn. mgr. A.L. Williams Corp., Chgo. and Lilburn, Ga., 1982—; mgr. House of Frames, Frameland, Ltd. Edit. Galleries, 1985-99, night auditor Howard Johnson, Lithonia, Ga., Comfort Inn, Muncie Ind., 2002-03, Lee's Inn, Muncie, 2004-05 Vol. Cook County Hosp., Chgo., 1955-58; mem. Wheaton Human Rels. Orgn., 1965-67 Recipient Ingersol award for painting, 1946, 47, 2d pl. award DuPage Sesquicentennial, 1968, Outstanding Alumnus award Ball State U., 1975 Mem. Ill. Art Edn. Assn., Nat. Soc. Lit. and Arts, Art Inst. Chgo., Delta Phi Delta, Sigma Tau Delta, Kappa Delta Pi Home: 2800 N Timber Ln Muncie IN 47304-5430

HUNTER, PATRICIA O., psychologist; b. Wheeling, W.Va., Apr. 4, 1952; d. John Burton Hunter and Betty Lee O'Grady; m. William Louis Marcus, Oct. 7, 2000. BA, W.Va. U., 1974; MA, U. of the Pacific, 1977; D in Psychology, U. No. Colo., 1985. Cert. psychoanalysis, lic. psychology N.Y. Psychologist Albert Ellis Inst., N.Y.C., 1985—88, Northwestern Counseling Ctr., Mt. Kisco, NY, 1986—92; pvt. practice psychologist N.Y.C., 1988—. Psychologist Fortune Soc., N.Y.C., 1999—; faculty Suffolk (N.Y.) Inst. for Psychoanalysis and Psychotherapy, 2004—. Author: Why Am I Always Broke?, 1991; contbr. chapters to books. Fellow: Albert Ellis Inst.; mem.: APA. Democrat. Avocations: running, piano. Office: 425 W 23 St #1B New York NY 10011

HUNTER, PATRICIA RAE (TRICIA HUNTER), state official; b. Appleton, Minn., June 15, 1952; d. Harlan Ottowa and Clara Elizabeth (Tryhus) Hunter; m. Clark Waldon Crabbe, May 28, 1978 (dissolved July 1994); 1 child, Marcantonio Samantha. AS in Nursing, Good Samaritan Hosp., Phoenix, 1974; BSN, U. San Diego, 1981; MSN, UCLA, 1985. RN, cert. oper. rm. nurse. Surg. svcs. educator Stanford (Calif.) Hosp., 1983-85; oper. rm. supr. Alexian Bros., San Jose, Calif., 1985-86; dir. surg. svcs. Cmty. Hosp. Chula Vista, Calif., 1986-89; mem. Calif. State Assembly, San Diego, 1989-92; spl. asst. Gov. Wilson Office Statewide Health Planning and Devel., Sacramento, 1993-94; commr. Calif. Med. Assistance Commn., Sacramento, 1994—98, sr. v.p., mng. dir., 1998—2002, The Flannery Group, San Diego, 1997—2002; prin., owner Govt. Rels. Group, Inc., 2004—. Cons. hosp., Monterey, Calif., 1984—. Summit Schs., Ontario, Calif., 1992—93; bd. dirs. Premier Home & Health, Phoenix, 1994—95. Mem. adv. bd. Alzheimers Assn., San Diego, 1990—92, Arthritis Found., 1990—92; pres. Calif. Rep. League, 1995—97. Named Rookie Legislator of the Yr., Calif. Psychol. Assn., 1990, Legislator of the Yr., Calif. Nurse Practitioners Assn., 1992; recipient Alice Pauly award, Nat. Women Polit. Caucus San Diego, 1991. Mem.: NWPC, ANA (v.p. 1982—85), Bus. and Profl. Orgn., Assn. Oper. Rm. Nurses, Rotary (bd. dirs. 1993—94), Sigma Theta Tau (Leadership award 1991). Republican. Lutheran. Home: 3260 E Fox Run Way San Diego CA 92111-7723 Office: Govt Rels Group Inc 1121 L St Ste 409 Sacramento CA 95814 Office Phone: 916-447-7821. Personal E-mail: thunter930@aol.com. Business E-Mail: grg@saclobby.com.

HUNTER, SARAH ANN, community health nurse; b. Clarksdale, Miss. d. Albert Wiliam and Allean Hunter. Cert. in practical nursing, Miss. Delta Jr. Coll., Clarksdale, 1973; ADN, Alcorn State U., Natchez, Miss., 1979, BSN, 1986. Staff nurse N.W. Miss. Regional Med. Ctr., Clarksdale, 1974—79; head nurse Jefferson County Hosp., Fayette, Miss., 1979—86; supervising nurse Medgar Evers Home Health, Fayette, 1986—91; discharge planning nurse Quitman County Hosp., Marks, Miss., 1991—92; asst. DON DON Ruleville Health Care Ctr., 1992-93, operating, circulating nurse, 1993—94; orthopedic nurse NW Miss. Regional Med. Ctr., 1994—95; coord. quality improvement Delta Home Health, 2002—. Orientation inservice coord. Delta Cmty. Home Health, 1995.

HUNTER, TRUDY PEARL, surgical nurse; b. Beaver, Ky., Apr. 8, 1950; d. Charlie Hatler and Goldie Edith (Hall) Hamilton; m. James Norman Hunter; 1 child, James Randall. ADN, U. Ky., Prestonsburg, 1986. LPN 1979; RN, Ky.; cert. nurse oper. room Assn. Oper. Room Nurses; ACLS; Circulator Open Heart Surgery and Neurosurgery, 2005, cert. in laser tng., arthroscopy, mgmt. and care of anesthetized patient, advance EKG interpretation. Scrub nurse Meth. Hosp. Ky., Pikeville, Ky., 1979-82; scrub nurse/circulator Pikeville Surg. Ctr., Pikeville, Ky., 1982-88; circulator/scrub nurse Meth. Hosp. Ky., Pikeville, Ky., 1988-94, OR charge nurse, 1995-96, O.R. supr., 1996—. Avocations: reading, camping, travel, woodworking. Home: 104 Lower Hollow Rd Betsy Layne KY 41605-7020 Office: Pikerville Med Hosp 911 Bypass Rd Pikeville KY 41501-1689

HUNTER BLAIR, PAULINE CLARKE, author; b. Kirkby-in-Ashfield, Eng., May 19, 1921; d. Charles Leopold and Dorothy Kathleen (Milum) Clarke; m. Peter Hunter Blair, Feb., 1969. BA with honors, Somerville Coll., Oxford U., Eng., 1943. Free-lance writer, 1948—. Lectr. Author (writing as Pauline Clarke): (novels) The Pekinese Princess, 1948, The Great Can, 1952, The White Elephant, 1952, Smith's Hoard, 1955, The Boy with the Erpingham Hood, 1956, Sandy the Sailor, 1956, James, The Policeman, 1957, James and the Robbers, 1959, Torolv The Fatherless, 1959, 2d edit., 1973, The Lord of the Castle, 1960, The Robin Hooders, 1960, James and the Smugglers, 1961, Keep the Pot Boiling, 1961, The Twelve and the Genii, 1962 (Libr. Assn. Carnegie medal, 1962, Lewis Carrol Shelf award, 1963, Deutsche Jugend Buchpreis, 1968), Silver Bells and Cockle Shells, 1962, James and the Black Van, 1963, Crowds of Creatures, 1964, The Bonfire Party, 1966, The Two Faces of Silenus, 1972; author: (under pseudonym Helen Clare) Five Dolls in a House, 1953, Merlin's Magic, 1953, Bel The Giant and Other Stories, 1956, Five Dolls and the Monkey, 1956, Five Dolls in the Snow, 1957, Five Dolls and Their Friends, 1959, Seven White Pebbles, 1960, Five Dolls and the Duke, 1963, The Cat and the Fiddle and Other Stories from Bel, the Giant, 1968; author: (writing as Pauline Hunter Blair) The Nelson Boy, 1999, A Thorough Seaman, 2000, Warscape, 2001, Jacob's Ladder, 2003; book reviewer, contbr.: Times Lit. Supplement. Mem.: Brit. Soc. Authors. Home: Church Farm House Bottisham Cambridge CB5 9BA England Office: care Curtis Brown Ltd Haymarket House 28/29 Haymarket London SW1Y 4SP England also: care John Cushman Assocs Inc 24 E 38th St New York NY 10016-2502 Office Phone: 01223/811223.

HUNTER-GAULT, CHARLAYNE, journalist; b. Due West, S.C., Feb. 27, 1942; d. Charles S.H. Jr. and Althea Hunter; m. Walter Stovall (div.); 1 child, Suesan; m. Ronald Gault, 1971; 1 child, Chuma. Attended, Wayne State U., Detroit; BA in Journalism, U. Ga., 1963. With The New Yorker, 1963-67; editor Trans-Action Mag., 1967; investigative reporter, anchorwoman local evening news WRC-TV; also with N.Y. Times; with MacNeil/Lehrer Report PBS, 1978—99, became nat. correspondent, 1983, former chief nat. correspondent; Johannesburg bur. chief and correspondent CNN, 1999—. Author: In My Place, 1992; contbr. various publs. Recipient NYT Publisher's award, 2 Emmys for national news and documentaries, the Nat. Urban Coalition for Dist. Urban Reporting, George Foster Peabody award for Excellence in broadcast Journalism, Journalist of Yr. award Nat. Assn. Black Journalists, 1986, Sidney Hillman award, 1990, Good Housekeeping Broadcast Personality of Yr. award Am. Women in Radio and TV, Tom Paine award, Media Spotlight award Amnesty Internat., Chmns. award for excellence in media and for balanced reporting on Africa, African-Am. Inst., 2000. Achievements include first African American woman to graduate from the University of Georgia in 1962.

HUNTER HARRIS, PHYLLIS IRENE, retired secondary school educator; b. Poplar Bluff, Mo., Aug. 10, 1927; d. Golly and Beulah Ruth (Tompkins) Hunter; m. Paul William Harris, May 27, 1950 (iv. 1962); 1 son, Kevin Paul. BS, Loyola U., Chgo., 1958; MS, Chgo. State U., 1971, MS, 1980; PhD, U. So. Ill., 1983. Tchr. mentally challenged children Chgo. Pub. Schs., 1960—93; work/study coord. exceptional students Robeson H.S.; tchr., counselor mentally challenged adults Kennedy King Coll.; ret., 1993. Vol. Sr. Citizen Mental and Spiritual Health Counseling Group Therapy, 1995—2004. Mem. Am. Assn. Ret. Persons, NAACP, Am. Fedn. Tchrs., Coun. for Exceptional Children, Chgo. Assn. Retarded, Ret. Tchrs. Assn. (life). Mem. Bahai Faith. Home: 5201 S Cornell Ave Apt 4E Chicago IL 60615-4202 E-mail: pharris404@aol.com.

HUNTLEY, BARBARA NERINE, secondary school educator; b. Long Beach, Calif., Oct. 22, 1942; d. Edgar and Helen Nerine (King) Kinsey; m. John Wayne Huntley, Dec. 26, 1964; children: Heather Nerine Hitt, Wayne Marvin. BA in Math. Edn., Hardin-Simmons U., 1964; MEd in Curriculum and Instrn., Tex. A&M U., 1972. Tchr. math. Travis Jr. H.S., Temple, Tex., 1964-66, Gatesville (Tex.) State Sch. for Boys, 1966-68, Gatesville Ind. Sch. Dist., 1968—, Ctrl. Tex. Coll., Gatesville, 1985-86, Windam Sch., Gatesville, 1993—. Mem. NEA, Nat. Coun. Tchrs. Math., Tex. State Tchrs. Math. (pres. 1993-94), Assn. for Cmty. and Family Affairs, Tex. Math. Tchrs. Assn., Beta Sigma Phi, Delta Kappa Gamma. Baptist. Avocations: collecting postcards, sewing, cooking, crafts, outdoor activities. Office: Gatesville Ind Sch Dist 304 S Lovers Ln Gatesville TX 76528-1815

HUNTLEY-WRIGHT, JOAN AUGUSTA (JOAN AUGUSTA HUNTLEY), musician; b. Tulsa, Aug. 17, 1934; d. John Augustus and Edna Ruby (Van Brunt) Murphy; m. Robert Walter Huntley, Sept. 6, 1955 (div. Feb. 14, 1981); children: Robert John, Gene Bush, Dawn Elise, Ben Patrick; m. Wilfred Cleveland Wright, Sept. 13, 1992 (dec. Apr. 2001). Student, New Eng. Conservatory, 1952-53, U. Tulsa, 1953-54, Boston U. & N.E. Conservatory, 1954-55, Roosevelt U., Chgo., 1970-72, Thronton C.C., 1970-72; B in Violin Performance, New Eng. Conservatory Music, 1981; M in Violin Performance, U. Mass., Lowell, 1990. Violinist Tulsa Philharm. Symphony, 1949-52, 53-54; first violinist Tassan Quartet, Chgo., 1962-64, Hucasa Trio, Chgo., 1964-72; concert mistress, leader of various orchestras and chamber ensembles, 1964—; artist in residence Thornton C.C., Harvey, Ill., 1968-72; first violinist Bowforte Ensemble, Boston, 1973-81; assoc. prof. Berklee Coll. of Music, Boston, 1985-91. Designer, tchr. pre-sch. instrumental and ear tng. classes Raygor Day Sch., Matteson, Ill. 1963-65, Humpty-Dumpty and YMCA Nursery Schs., Beverly, Mass., 1976-78; organizer benefit concerts for tornado victims, Ill., 1968. Creator, performer radio program Music Personalities KAKC, Tulsa, 1953; mgr., music dir., founder LaFemme/LaFemme Women Composers Ensemble, 1990-95; soloist Tulsa Philharm., 1952, Park Forest (Ill.) Symphony, 1958, 60, 62, Salem (Mass.) Philharm., 1981, 89; performer with Phila. Piano Quartet, 1997-99, S.W. Fla. Symphony, 1993—, Charlotte (Fla.) Symphony Orch., 2001—. Mem. Ill. Constitutional Com.; active in Boy Scouts Am. and Girl Scouts; active in PTA. Recipient Profl. Devel. award Mass. Assn. Women in Edn., 1995. Mem. AAUW, S.W. Fla. Symphony. Avocations: avid reader, walking, working out. Office Phone: 978-973-1860. E-mail: wcompwill@cs.com.

HUNTRESS, BETTY ANN, retired small business owner, retired secondary school educator; d. Emmett Slater and Catherine V. Brundage; m. Arnold Ray Huntress, June 26, 1954; children: Catherine, Michael, Carol, Alan. BA, Cornell U., 1954. Tchr. h.s., Bordentown, N.J., 1954-55; tchr. Midland (Mich.) Pub. Schs., 1968—98; ret., 1998. Asst. to prof. Delta Coll., Northwood Inst., Midland; tchr. Midland Pub. Schs., 1998—2000; owner, mgr. The Music Stand, Midland, 1979—82. Bd. dirs. Midland Ctr. for Arts, 1978-86, v.p., 1980-84, Friends of the Ctr., 1985—; charter bd. mgrs. Matrix Midland Ann. Arts and Sci. Festival, 1977-80; cons. Girl Scouts U.S., 1964-76; bd. dirs. Literacy Coun. Midland County, 1986-94, sec., 1987-91; active Mich. Internat. Coun., 1975-76, Midland Hist. Soc., 1990—, Dow Chem. Centennial Com., 1996-98; mem. Presbyn. ch. choir, 1963—. Named Midland Musician of Yr., 1977. Mem. AAUW (dir. 1962-73, pres. 1971-73, mem. Mich. state divsn. 1983-85, bd. dirs. 1993-95, Outstanding Woman as Agt. of Change award 1977, fellowship grant named in her honor 1976), LWV (bd. dirs. 1986-90, com. charter schs. 1995-99), Music Soc. Midland Ctr. for arts (dir. 1971-86, chmn. 1976-79), Midland Symphony League Soc. (2d v.p. 1995-99), Cmty. Concert Soc., Woman's Study Club of Midland (pres. 1995-96), Friends of Libr., Kappa Delta Epsilon, Pi Lambda Theta, Alpha Xi Delta. Presbyterian.

HUOT, RACHEL IRENE, biomedical educator, research scientist, physician; b. Manchester, N.H., Oct. 16, 1950; d. Omer Joseph and Irene Alice (Girard) Huot. BA in Biology cum laude, Rivier Coll., 1972; MS in Biology, Cath. U. Am., 1976, PhD in Biology, 1980; MD, La. State U. Health Sci. Ctr., Shreveport, 2000. Sr. technician Microbiol. Assocs., Bethesda, Md., 1974-77; chemist Uniformed Svcs. Univ. of Health Scis., Bethesda, 1977-79; biologist Nat. Cancer Inst., Bethesda, 1979-82; postdoctoral fellow S.W. Found. for Biomed. Rsch., San Antonio, 1982-85, asst. scientist, 1985-87, staff scientist, 1987-88; instr. U. Tex. Health Sci. Ctr., San Antonio, 1988-89; asst. prof., dir. basic urologic rsch. La. State U., New Orleans, 1990-96; resident in family practice Aultman Hosp., Canton, Ohio, 2001—02; resident in family practice Mayo Clinic U. Minn., Waseca, 2002—05; resident in family practice Ea. Va. Med. Sch., 2005—. Judge sr. divsn. Alamo Regional Sci. Fair, San Antonio, 1989—90. Contbr. Vol. ARC, Christus Schumpert Hosp., Shreveport; patient educator vol. Martin Luther King Clinic, Shreveport, 1996—2000. Recipient Young Investigator award, Searle, 1994; grantee, NSF, 1972—74, NIH, 1983—86. Mem.: AMA, AAUW, LWV, AAAS, Am. Acad. Family Practice, Am. Soc. Experiment Biology, St. Vincent De Paul Soc., N.Y. Acad. Scis., Soc. In Vitro Biology, Fedn. Am. Scientists, Am. Soc. Cell Biology, Am. Assn. Cancer Rsch., Am. Soc. Microbiology, Sierra Club, Sigma Xi, Delta Epsilon Sigma, Iota Sigma Pi. Democrat. Roman Catholic. Avocations: drawing, painting, reading, cooking, stamp collecting/philately. Home: 330 W Brambleton Ave Apt 1104 Norfolk VA 23510 Personal E-mail: huotrachel@hotmail.com.

HUPE, PALLAS, announcer; b. Ankara, Turkey; married; 2 children. M in Politics, Philosophy and Econs., Oxford U., Eng. Host children's TV show, Saudi Arabia; from asst. prodr. to prodr., reporter, anchor various stas. in Tallahassee, Fla. and Wilmington, N.C.; main anchor WPBN/WTOM, Traverse City, Mich.; freelancer WJBK-TV, Detroit; co-anchor, med. reporter weekend 10 pm WKBD-TV, Detroit, 2002—03; co-anchor noon, weathercaster, spl. projects reporter WJBK-TV, Detroit, 2003—. Recipient Best Spot News coverage award in N.C., RTNDAC, Best Pub. Affairs coverage award in Fla., AP. Office: WJBK Fox 2 PO Box 2000 Southfield MI 48037-2000

HURD, DIANE FINORE, marketing executive, publisher; b. Abington, Pa., Aug. 11, 1950; d. Carmen George and Anna B. (Signore) F. AS, Tobe Coburn Sch., 1972; BA cum laude, Temple U., Phila., 1974; MA, NYU, 1984. Dir. spl. events Mus. Am. Folk Art (now Am. Mus. Folk Art), N.Y.C., 1982—85; pub. rep. Taxi Pub. Inc., N.Y.C., 1986-87; sales rep. CHILD Magazine, N.Y.C., 1986—87; dir. sales SALES, Inc., N.Y.C., 1987-88; pres. Finore Mktg. Svcs., Stone Harbor, N.J., 1989—. Founding pub./editor Seven Mile Times, Seven Mile Beach Party, Sea Isle Times. Office: Finore Mktg Svcs PO Box 71 Stone Harbor NJ 08247-0071 E-mail: fms.hurd@gmail.com.

HURD, ELIZABETH SHAKMAN, social studies educator; b. Boston, May 15, 1970; d. Stephen Arthur and Susan Curtis Shakman; m. Ian Hurd, Oct. 4, 1998; children: Alexandra Catherine, Sophie Emily. BA with hons., Wesleyan U., 1992; MA, Yale U., 1996; PhD, The Johns Hopkins U., 2002. Vis. asst. prof. Northwestern U., Evanston, Ill., 2002—04, asst. prof., 2004—. Fellow, U.S. Govt., 1995, European-American Young Scholars' Insts. Program, 2003—04, U. Va., 2004—05; grantee, Inst. Turkish Studies, 2001. Mem.: Coun. European Studies, Mid. East Studies Assn., Internat. Studies Assn. Democrat. Avocations: yoga, reading, baking, skiing, kayaking. Office: Northwestern Univ 601 University Pl Evanston IL 60208 Office Phone: 847-467-5412. Business E-Mail: eshurd@northwestern.edu.

HURD, GALE ANNE, film producer; b. LA, Oct. 25, 1955; d. Frank E. and Lolita (Espiau) Hurd; m. James Cameron, 1985 (div. 1989); m. Brian DePalma, July 20, 1991 (div.); 1 child; m. Jonathan Hensleigh, June 19, 1995. Degree in econs. and communications, Stanford U., 1977. Dir. mktg. and publicity, co-producer New World Pictures, L.A., 1977-82; pres., producer Pacific Western Prodns., L.A., 1982—. Producer: (films) The Terminator, 1984 (Grand Prix Avoiriaz Film Festival award), Aliens 1986 (nominated for 7 Acad. awards, recipient Best Sound Effects Editing award, Best Visual Effects award Acad. Picture Arts & Scis.), Alien Nation (Saturn award for best sci. fiction film), The Abyss, 1989 (nominated for 4 Acad. awards, Best Visual Effects award), The Waterdance, 1991 (2 TFP Spirit awards, 2 Sundance Film Festival awards), Cast a Deadly Spell, 1991 (Emmy award), Raising Cain, 1992, No Escape, 1994, Safe Passage (Beatrice Wood award for Creative Achievement), 1994, The Ghost and the Darkness,(Acad. award) 1996, The Relic, 1996, Going West in America, 1996, Dante's Peak, 1997, Virus, 1997, Dead Man on Campus, 1997, Armageddon, 1998, Dick, 1999, Clockstoppers 2002, The Hulk, 2003 (TV series) Adventure, Inc., 2002, Punisher, 2004, Aeon Flux, 2005, (TV pilot) Coven, 2004; exec. producer: (films) Switchback, 1997, Tremors, 1990, Downtown, 1990, Terminator 2, 1991 (winner 3 Acad. awards), Witch Hunt, 1994, Sugartime, 1995, Terminator 3, 2004, Punisher, 2004; creative cons. (TV program) Alien Nation, 1989-90. Juror Focus Student Film Awards, 1989, 90; chmn. Nicholl Fellowship Acad. Motion Picture Arts & Scis., 1989—; mem. Show Coalition, 1988—; mem. Hollywood (Calif.) Women's Polit. Com., 1987—; mem. U.S. Film Festival Juror; bd. dirs. IFP/West, Artists Rights Found.; trustee Am. Film Inst.; bd. dirs. L.A. Internat. Film Festival, Coral Reef Rsch. Found., Ams. for a Safe Future; mentor Peter Stark Motion Picture Producing Program, Sch. of Cinema-TV, U. of So. Calif., Women in Film Mentor Program. Recipient Spl. Merit award Nat. Assn. Theater Owners, 1986, Stanford-La Entrepreneur of Yr. award Bus. Sch. Alumni L.A., 1990, Fla. Film Festival award, 1994, Women in Film Crystal award, 1998, Ind. Vision award Temucala Film Festival, 2001, Nat. Bd. Rev. Prodr.'s award, 2004, Global Green Millennium award, 2004, Israel Film Festival Visionary award, 2004, Saturn awards, Donald Reed award, 2004; named Prodr. of Yr., Stunt Awards, 2003. Mem. AMPAS (prodr.'s br. exec. com. 1990—, chair festival grants com.), Am. Film Inst. (trustee 1989—), Americans for a Safe Future (bd. dirs. 1993—), Prodr.'s Guild Am. (bd. dirs.), Women in Film (bd. dirs. 1989-90, 2000—03), Inst. for Rsch. on Women and Gender (nat. adv. panel 1997-2000), Feminist Majority, The Ocean Consrvancy (bd. dirs. 2001—, Heal the Bay (adv. bd.), Reef Check Internat. (adv. bd.), Seakeepers Soc., Mulholland Tomorrow, The Trusteeship (bd. dirs. 2006-), Explorers Club (N.Y.C.), Jamestowne Soc., Nat. Soc. DAR, Phi Beta Kappa. Avocations: scuba diving, paso fino horses. Office: Valhalla Motion Pictures 8530 Wilshire Blvd Ste 400 Beverly Hills CA 90211 Office Phone: 310-360-8540.

HURD, HEIDI M., dean, humanities educator, law educator; b. Laramie, Wyo., Oct. 19, 1960; d. Carroll Parsons and Jeanne Marie H.; children: Gillian K.J. and Aidan A. (twins). BA with honors, Queen's U., Kingston, Ont., Can., 1982; MA, Dalhousie U., Halifax, N.S., Can., 1984; JD, U. So. Calif., L.A., 1988, PhD, 1992. Asst. prof. U. Pa. Law Sch., Phila., 1989-94, prof. law and philosophy, 1994—2002, assoc. dean, 1994-96, co-dir. Inst. Law and Philosophy, 1998—2000; Herzog rsch. prof. law U. San Diego, 2000—02; dean, prof. philosophy, David Baum prof. law U. of Ill. Coll. Law, 2002—. Vis. asst. prof. dept. philosophy U. Iowa, Iowa City, 1991-92; vis. prof. law U. Va. Law Sch., Charlottesville, 1997-98. Author: Moral Combat, 1999; contbr. articles to profl. jours. Office: U Illinois College Law Dean Office 504 E Pennsylvania Ave Champaign IL 61820-6909 Office Phone: 217-333-9857. E-mail: hhurd@law.uiuc.edu.

HURD, MARY K., civil engineer, writer; BSCE, Iowa State U., Ames; postgrad. U. Chgo., U. Mich., U. Ill. Assoc. editor spl. tech. publs. Am. Concrete Inst., 1966-67, staff engr. Detroit, 1967-76; engr.-writer, cons., 1976-80, 90—; engring. editor Concrete Constrn. Mag., Addison, Ill., 1983-90, editor, 1981-83; pres. Engr. Publs., Farmington Hills, Mich. Past chmn. bd. dirs. Concrete Improvement Bd. Author: Formwork for Concrete, 1963, 7th edit., 2005; contbr. articles in field to profl. jours. including Constrn. Specifier, Concrete Internat., Jour. Am. Concrete Inst., Internat. Jour. of Ferrocement, Revista IMCYC Mexico, Pub. Works, Concrete Constrn., Concrete Prodr., PCI Jour., presenter and organizer in field. Recipient Profl. Achievement in Engring. Citation award Iowa State U., 1982, Outstanding Achievement award Concrete Improvement Bd. Detroit, 1990, Anson Marston medal Iowa State U. Coll. Engring., 2004; named one of 125 Top People of Past 125 Years in Constrn. Industry. Mem. ASCE (life), Am. Concrete Inst. (hon. mem., past mem. bd. dirs., organizing chmn. com. 124 concrete aesthetics, com. 347 formwork for concrete, past pres. Mich. chpt., Constrn. Practice award 1982, 88, Delmar L. Bloem Disting. Svc. award 1990, 2006, Arthur Y. Moy award Mich. chpt. 1994, Henry C. Turner medal 1995), Am. Soc. Concrete Contractors, Precast/Prestressed Concrete Inst. (profl.), The Concrete Soc. (U.K.), Constrn. Writers Assn., Tau Beta Pi, Phi Kappa Phi. Address: 33742 Lyncroft Rd Farmington Hills MI 48331-3647 Office Phone: 248-474-1369.

HURD, NICOLE FARMER, director; d. Lawrence William and Susan Farmer; m. William Lewis Hurd, May 31, 1997; children: Monica Katharine, Matthew Lawrence. BA, U. Notre Dame, Ind., 1992; MA, Georgetown U., Washington, 1996; PhD, U. Va., Charlottesville, 2002. Adminstrv. officer Georgetown U., Washington, 1995—96; asst. dean for rsch. U. Va., Charlottesville, 2002—05, founding dir. Ctr. for Undergrad. Excellence, 2002—; dir. Coll. Guide Program, Charlottesville, Va., 2005—. Coll. Access grantee for Va., Jack Kent Cooke Found., 2004—, Dupont fellow, U. Va., 2001—02, Marchant fellow, 2001—02. Mem.: Am. Hist. Assn., Am. Acad. Religion, Nat. Assn. Fellowship Advisors, Nat. Coll. Access Network, Omicron Delta Kappa. Home: 1011 Wildmere Pl Charlottesville VA 22901 Office: U Va PO Box 400874 Charlottesville VA 22904 Office Phone: 434-924-6058. Office Fax: 434-924-3832. E-mail: nhurd@virginia.edu.

HURFORD, CAROL, retired lawyer; b. Friedensburg, Pa., Sept. 30, 1940; d. Harvey Sydney and Ada Aldine (Lengle) Zerbe; m. John Boyce Hurford, Sept. 16, 1961 (div. 1975); m. Thomas W. McEnerney, Dec. 28, 1984. BA, UCLA, 1963; JD, Rutgers U., 1975. Bar: N.Y. 1976. Assoc. Breed, Abbott & Morgan, N.Y.C., 1975-78, Reavis & McGrath, N.Y.C., 1978-84; ptnr. Munves, Tannenhaus & Storch, N.Y.C., 1984-90. Editor Rutgers U. Law Rev. Pres. West Brooklyn Ind. Dems., 1970; bd. dirs. Ballet Tech. Found., Inc., N.Y.C., 1994—. Mem. LWV (chair voter svc. New Castle chpt. 1993-96, v.p. 1994-96, pres. 1996-98, bd. dirs. 1999—, bd. dirs. Chappaqua summer scholarship program 1991—). Democrat. Avocations: travel, reading, skiing, bicycling. Home: 49 Marcourt Dr Chappaqua NY 10514-2506

HURLEY, ALLISON RUTH, mentor coach specialist; b. Escanaba, Mich., Nov. 2, 1961; d. Paula Ann and Donald Faye Marvic (Stepfather). BS in Edn., Marian Coll. of Fond du Lac, Wis., 1986. Site dir. YMCA of Greater Sacramento, 1988—91; practicum/placement coord. Calif. Nanny Coll., Sacramento, 1991—92; resource and referral counselor Child Action, Inc., Sacramento, 1997; early head start program mgr. Calif. Human Devel. Corp. Head Start/Early Head Start for Yolo County, Woodland, 1999—2003; mentor coach specialist Devel. Assocs., Inc., Walnut Creek, Calif., 2003—; exec. dir. First Bapt. Head Start, Pittsburg, Calif., 2003—05; family childcare mgr. E Ctr. Migrant and Seasonal Head Start, Marysville, La., 2005—. Edn.

specialist Calif. Human Devel. Corp. Head Start for Yolo County, Woodland, Calif., 1997—99. Mem.: NAFE, AAUW (treas. 1986—87), Calif. Head Start Assn., Infant Devel. Assn. (bd. dirs. 2001), Nat. Head Start (assoc.). Office: Nat Migrant and Seasonal Head Start 1128 Yuba St Marysville CA 95901

HURLEY, CHERYL JOYCE, book publishing executive; b. Pitts., Oct. 30, 1947; d. John and Violet der Norsek; m. Kevin Hurley, July 27, 1974. Lang. and lit. cert., Université de Lyon, France, 1968; AB, Ohio U., 1969; MA, U. Mich., 1971. Research assoc. MLA, N.Y.C., 1972-74, dir. spl. programs, 1974-79; pub. The Library of America, N.Y.C., 1979—88, pres., 1988—. Cons. in field. Contbr. articles to profl. jours. Trustee French Inst./Alliance Francaise, 1992—, v.p., exec. com., 1994—, chmn. libr. com., 1996—, Samuel H. Kress Found., 1999—; adv. com. N.Y. 100 Centennial, 1997-98; mem. humanities adv. coun. N.Y. Pub. Libr., 1996—; mem. dean's adv. bd. Rackham Grad. Sch. U. Mich., 2000-; mem. vis. com. printed books Pierpont Morgan Libr., 2005-. Rackham fellow, 1969—70. Mem.: Assn. Internationale de Bibliophilie, Am. Antiquarian Soc. (councillor 1999—), Bridgehampton Club, Colony Club, Grolier Club, Century Assn., Phi Beta Kappa. Home: 1172 Park Ave New York NY 10128-1213 Office: Libr of Am 14 E 60th St New York NY 10022-1006

HURLEY, ELIZABETH, actress, model, film producer; b. Hampshire, Eng., June 10, 1965; Student, London Studio Ctr. Head devel. Simian Films, London and L.A., 1994—; model, cosmetic rep. Estee Lauder. Actress appearing in TV programs and movies including (films) Die Tote Stadt, 1987, Rowing with the Wind, 1988, Bloody Atlantic, 1991, The Orchid House, 1991, Passenger 57, 1992, El Largo Invierno, 1992, Beyond Bedlam, 1993, Goldeneye, 1995, Mad Dogs and Englishmen, Austin Powers: International Man of Mystery, 1997, (TV movies) The Shamrock Conspiracy, 1995, Samson and Delilah, 1996, Permanent Midnight, 1998, Edtv, 1999, My Favorite Martian, 1999, Austin Powers: The Spy Who Shagged Me, 1999, The Weight of Water, 2000, Bedazzled, 2000, Serving Sarah, 2002, Method, 2004, (TV series) Cristabel, 1989, Rumpole and the Barrow Boy, 1989, Sharpe II, 1995; host (TV spl.) The World of James Bond, 1995; prodr. Mickey Blue Eyes, 1999. Office: Creative Artists Agy 9830 Wilshire Blvd Beverly Hills CA 90212-1804

HURLEY, KATHY LEE, mental health services professional, director; d. Essie B. and Dent R. Hurley, J.C. Crowson (Stepfather); m. Edmond J. Moloney, Dec. 13, 2002; 1 child, Breckin M. Moloney. BA, U. Ctrl. Fla., 1985; AA, MS, Nova U., 1988; PhD, Maimonides U., Ft. Lauderdale, Fla., 2003. Diplomate Am. Bd. of Sexologists; cert. social work counselor Fla. Sr. counselor Ctr. for Drug-Free Living, Kissimmee, Fla., 1991—94; program mgr. Grove Counseling Ctr., Sanford, 1994—95; sr. counselor Stewart-Marchman Ctr., Daytona, Fla., 1995—99; clinician Children's Home Soc., Daytona, 1999—2000, Three Springs, Daytona, 2000—03; clin. dir. Devereux of Fla. Found., Orlando, 2003—. Cons. Sch. Bd., Daytona, 2000—03. Exec. com./vol. Dem. Party, Daytona, 2000—02; choirister, musician Grace Episcopal Ch., Port Orange, Fla., 2000—02; tchr., counselor First Bapt. Ch., Daytona, 1997—2001; musician, vocalist Rima Ridge Bapt. Ch., Ormond Beach, Fla., 1995—97, Ch. of Christ, Longwood, Fla., 1992—95. Recipient High Scholastic Achievement award, Nova U., 1986—88; grantee, Daytona Beach C.C., 1982. Mem.: Nat. Assn. of Forensic Counselors (assoc.; cert.), Assn. for the Treatment of Sexual Abusers (assoc.), Am. Assn. of Christian Counselors (assoc.), Am. Counselor's Assn. (assoc.), Am. Mental Health Counselor's Assn. (assoc.; voting mem. 2000—05). Democrat. Avocations: piano, singing, acting, travel, swimming. Office Phone: 407-296-5300.

HURLEY, KRISTIE DELYNN, primary school educator; b. Lubbock, Tex., Dec. 6, 1978; d. Thresa Elaine and Ronnie Henry Rieff; m. Shaun Michael Hurley, Mar. 15, 2003. BS in Early Childhood, Tex. Tech U., Lubbock, 1997—2002. Classroom Tchr., Generalist EC-4 Tex. Bd. Edn., 2002. Dir. Oakwood Family Life Ctr., Lubbock, 1998—2001; lab tchr. Tex. Tech U. CDRC, Lubbock, 2002—04; kindergarten tchr. Lubbock Ind. Sch. Dist., 2004—. Dir., founder Dress to be the Best, Lubbock, 1999—2001. Recipient FISH Award, Lubbock Ind. Sch. Dist., 2005, Tchr. of the Yr. Nominee, Wolffarth Elem./ Lubbock Ind. Sch. Dist., 2004-2005 & 2005-2006. Mem.: NSTA, Nat. Assn. Edn. Young Children, High Scope Ednl. Rsch. Found., Assn. Tex. Profl. Edn. Baptist. Avocations: reading, travel. Home: 5010 Hanover St Lubbock TX 79416 Office: Lubbock Independent Sch Dist 3202 Erskine Lubbock TX 79415 Office Phone: 806-766-1899. Personal E-mail: kristiehurley@xanadoo.com.

HURLOCK, JOAN EMMA, physician; d. Edward Lang Rosenbaum; m. David Thomas Hurlock, June 25, 1955 (dec.); 1 child, David Thomas Jr. RN, Temple U., Phila., 1953; BA in Chemistry, Beaver Coll., Glenside, Pa., 1965; MD, Women's Med. Coll. Pa., Phila., 1970. Cert. family medicine 1978. Family physician pvt. practice, Phila., 1971—93; staff physician Gary Baiocchi & Assocs., Phila., 1993—96, Temple Physicians Inc., Phila., 1996—2005; family physician pvt. practice, Phila., 2006—. Med. dir. Roxborough Home for Women, Phila., 1972—, Samaritan Hospice, Phila., 2001—04; mem. exec. com. Roxborough Meml. Hosp., 1984—, pres. med. staff, 1984—86, chief family practice, 1986—, chmn. liaison com., 1986—. Mem. bd. Cathedral Village, Phila., 1972—; pres. Garden Club St. Matthias Cath. Ch., Bala Cynwyd, 2005—. Recipient Babcock award, Temple U. Sch. Nursing, 1953, Dr. of Yr., Under the Wing Clinic, New Delhi, India, 1985, Physician of Yr., Phila. County Med. Soc., 1987, Dr. of Yr., Samaritan Hospice, 2002. Fellow: Am. Acad. Family Practice; mem.: Pa. Acad. Family Practice (del.), AMA. Roman Catholic. Avocation: gardening. Office: 5735 Ridge Ave Philadelphia PA 19128

HURST, ANITA ROSE, social worker, counselor; b. Covington, Ky., Oct. 28, 1979; d. James and Nancy Hurst. BS in Psychology, No. Ky. U., MA in Pub. Adminstrn. Cert. in non-profit mgmt. Ky. Advisor Kenton County Family Resource Youth Svc. Ctr., Independence, Ky., 2003—04; social worker, counselor Kenton County Schs., Independence, 2003—. Chmn. Asset Bldg. Com., Cin., 2003—. Sec. Champions for a Drug Free No. Ky., Florence, 2003—. Mem.: Hampton Investment Club (pres. 2002—05).

HURST, ANNETTE L., lawyer; b. July 19, 1965; BA, BS magna cum laude, Miami U., 1987; JD, NYU, 1990. Bar: Calif. 1990. Ptnr., dir. litigation dept. Howard, Rice, Nemerovski, Canady, Falk & Rabkin, San Francisco; shareholder, intellectual property litig. Heller Ehrman LLP, San Francisco, 2005—. Named one of Top 20 Lawyers Under 40, Daily Jour., No. Calif. Top 100 Super Lawyers, No. Calif. Super Lawyers mag., Top 50 Female Super Lawyers, Top 40 Lawyers Under 40, Nat. Law Jour., 2005. Mem.: ABA, Bar Assn. San Francsico, Barristers Club San Francisco, Am. Intellectual Property Law Assn., No. Calif. Intellectual Property Inns of Ct. (barrister), Assn. Bus. Trial Lawyers (No. Calif. Chpt.) (bd. govs.), Legal Aid Soc. Employment Law Ctr. (bd. dirs.), Bar Assn. San Francisco (bd. dirs.), State Bar Calif. Office: Heller Ehrman LLP 333 Bush St San Francisco CA 94104-2878 Office Phone: 415-434-1600, 415-772-6840. Business E-Mail: annette.hurst@hellerehrman.com. E-mail: ahurst@howardrice.com.

HURST, DEBORAH, pediatric hematologist; b. Washington, May 9, 1946; d. Willard and Frances (Wilson) H.; m. Stephen Mershon Senter, June 14, 1970; children: Carlin, Daniel. BA, Harvard U., 1968; MD, Med. Coll. Pa., 1974. Diplomate Nat. Bd. Med. Examiners, Am. Bd. Pediatrics, Am. Bd. Pediatric Hematology-Oncology. Intern Bellevue Hosp., NYU Hosp., N.Y.C., 1974-75, resident in pediatrics, 1975-76; ambulatory pediatric fellow Bellevue Hosp., N.Y.C., 1976-77; hematology, oncology fellow Bellevue Hosp., Columbia U., N.Y.C., 1977-80; assoc. hematologist Childrens Hosp. Oakland, Calif., 1980-92; asst. clin. prof. U. Calif. San Francisco Med. Ctr., 1992—; med. dir. Bayer Corp., Berkeley, Calif., 1992-98; sr. dir. clin. devel. Chiron Corp., Emeryville, Calif., 1998—. Hematology cons. Assn. Asian/Pacific Community Health Orgns., Oakland; dir. Satellite Hematology Clinic/Valley Childrens Hosp., Fresno, Calif., 1984-92; cons. state dept. epidemiology Calif. State Dept. Health, Berkeley, 1992; chelation cons. lead poisoning program Childrens Hosp., Oakland, 1986-92. Contbr. articles to profl. jours. Vol. cons. lead poisoning State Dept. Epidemiology and Toxicology, Berkeley, 1986-92. Fellow Am. Acad. Pediatrics; mem. Am. Soc. Hematology, Am. Soc. Gene Therapy, Am. Soc. Clin. Oncology, Am. Soc. Pediat. Hematology/Oncology, Nat. Hemophilia Found., Internat. Soc. Thrombosis and Hemostasis. Office: Chiron Corp 4560 Horton St MS120 Emeryville CA 94608-2900

HURST, FRANCES See MAYHAR, ARDATH

HURST, HEATHER, illustrator; b. Aug. 14, 1975; BA, Skidmore Coll., 1997. Archeological artist and illustrator focusing on creating representations of Mesoamerican structures. Exhibitions include Nat. Gallery Art, Washington, Peabody Mus. Nat. History, illustrations published in National Geographic and Arqueologia Mexicana. Named MacArthur Fellow, John D. and Catherine T. MacArthur Found., 2004. Achievements include the reproduction of the Maya murals of Bonampak.

HURST, MARY JANE, language educator; b. Hamilton, Ohio, Sept. 21, 1952; d. Nimrod and Leckie Gaines; m. Daniel L. Hurst, June 5, 1974; 1 child, Katherine Jane. BA summa cum laude, Miami U., 1974; MA, U. Md., 1980, PhD, 1986. Tchr. Groveport (Ohio) H.S., 1974-77; tchg. asst. U. Md., College Park, 1978-79, master tchr., 1979-82; asst. prof. English, Tex. Tech U., Lubbock, 1986-92, assoc. prof., 1992-99, prof., 1999—, assoc. dean Coll. Arts and Scis., 2000—05, faculty asst. to pres., 2006—. Vis. scholar Stanford U., summer 1987; steering com. Nat. Cowboy Symposium, Lubbock, 1988-89. Author: The Voice of the Child in American Literature, 1990; tech. editor: HTLV-I and the Nervous System, 1989; book rev. editor S.W. Jour. Linguistics, 1995-98; contbr. articles to profl. jours. Active Lubbock Cultural Affairs Coun., 1986-92, Lubbock Symphony Guild, 1992—; vol. Meals on Wheel, Lubbock, 1986-97, Habitat for Humanity, Lubbock, 1986-97, Interfaith Hospitality Network, 1998—. Mem.: MLA, AAUP (regional v.p. 1990—94), AAUW (alt. fellowships panel in linguistics 1988—90), South Ctrl. MLA, Coll. Tchrs. English Tex., Linguistic Assn. S.W. (pres. 1996—97, exec. dir. 1998—2001), Linguistic Soc. Am., Phi Beta Kappa, Alpha Lambda Delta, Sigma Tau Delta, Phi Kappa Phi. Avocations: genealogy, travel, west highland white terriers. Office: Tex Tech U Dept English Lubbock TX 79409

HURST, MICHELE LYNN, elementary school educator; b. Pitts., Apr. 10, 1971; d. Thomas Michael and Joyce Carol Andolina; m. Michael Christopher Hurst, July 10, 1999; children: Michael Thomas, Madison Alexis. BS in Edn., Duquesne U., Pitts., 1993, MS in Edn. Sci. tchr. Seneca Valley Sch. Dist., Harmony, Pa., 1995—98; math., sci. tchr. Upper St. Clair (Pa.) Sch. Dist., 1998—99; sci. tchr. Hampton Twp. Sch. Dist., Allison Park, Pa., 1999—, leadership team sponsor. Literacy coach We. Pa. Writing Project, Allison Park, 2000—. Grantee, Pa. Dept. Edn., 2002; Mid. Sch. Sci. grant, Soc. for Analytical Chemists, 2002, Edn. grant, Hampton Alliance for Edn. Excellence, 2002—03. Mem.: Nat. Sci. Tchrs. Assn. Office: Hampton Twp Sch Dist 4589 Sch Dr Allison Park PA 15101

HURST, PATRICIA ANN, professional golfer; b. San Leandro, Calif., May 23, 1969; m. Jeff Heitt, Oct. 14, 1995; children: Jackson, Reilly. Student, San Jose U. Tchg. pro golfer La Quinta Country Club; golfer Players West mini-tour, winner 5 titles; winner USGA Jr., 1986, USGA Amateur, 1990, Oldsmobile Classic, 1997, Nabisco Dinah Shore, 1998, Electrolux USA, 2000; mem. US Solheim Cup, 1998, 2000, Captain's pick, 2002; mem. U.S. World Amateur team. Avocation: music. Office: care LPGA 100 International Golf Dr Daytona Beach FL 32124-1082

HURST, REBECCA MCNABB, language educator; b. Lynchburg, Va., July 17, 1951; d. Eugene Randolph and Lucy Margurite McNabb; m. Larry Lee Hurst, June 26, 1971; children: Monica Hurst Ferrebee, Meredith Hurst Mabe. MEd Ednl. Adminstrn., William and Mary U., Williamsburg, Va, 1988. Cert. post grad. profl. Va., 1988, nat. bd. cert. tchr., cert. in adolescent/young adult English/lang. arts. Tchr. Menchville H.S., Newport News, Va., 1986—99; lead tchr. H.S. Enterprise Acad., Newport News, 1999—. Coord. devel. assets Enterprise Acad., Newport News, Va., 2001—, mem. sch. improvement team, 2000—, founder and sponsor sch. newspaper, 2000—. Founding mem. Nat. Campaign For Tolerance, Montgomery, Ala., 2000—03. Recipient Outstanding Youth Adv. award, Greater Peninsula Workplace Devel. Consortium, 2002. Mem.: NEA, ASCD, Va. Assn. Tchrs. English, Nat. Coun. Tchrs. English, Newport News Edn. Assn., Va. Edn. Assn. Office: Enterprise Acad Ste 110 813 Diligence Dr Newport News VA 23606 Office Phone: 757-591-4971. Business E-Mail: becky.hurst@nn.k12.va.us.

HURST, TACY MARCELLA, literature and language educator; d. Tim Allen and Kristan Iva Bell; m. Richard James Hurst, July 24, 1993; children: Hillary Nicole, Kaylee Michelle. B in English Edn., Southwestern Okla. State U., 1993. Nat. Bd. Cert. for Tchrs. Nat. Bd. Orgn., 2004. English instr. Woodward HS, Okla., 1993—. Mem.: Okla. Edn. Assn., Woodward Edn. Assn. (Classroom Grant 2003, Bright Idea award 2006). Office: Woodward HS 13th and Downs Woodward OK 73801

HURST, WENDY R(OBIN), obstetrician; b. Elmira, N.Y., Aug. 29, 1960; MD, Tufts U., 1986. Diplomate Am. Bd. Ob-Gyn. Resident Pa. Hosp., Phila., 1986—90; mem. staff Englewood (N.J.) Hosp. & Med. Ctr., 1990—96, obstetrician, 1996—; mem. staff Hackensack (N.J.) Med. Ctr., 1994—96. Named one of Top. Drs. in N.Y. Metro Area, Castle Connolly, 2001, 2002, 2003, 2004, Top Doctors, N.J. Monthly Mag., 2003. Fellow: Am. Coll. Obstetrics and Gynecology. Office: Englewood Hosp and Med Ctr 370 Grand Ave Englewood NJ 07631-4109 Office Phone: 201-894-9599.

HURT, MARY BETH, actress; b. Marshalltown, Iowa, Sept. 26, 1948; d. Forrest Clayton and Delores Lenore (Andre) Supinger; m. William Hurt, 1971 (div. 1981); m. Paul Schrader, Aug. 6, 1983; 1 child, Molly. Student, U. Iowa, NYU. Actress: (stage prodns.) New Girl in Town, 1963, On the Town, The Drunkard, Three Wishes for Jamie, As You Like it, 1973, More Than You Deserve, 1974, Pericles, 1974, Love for Love, 1974 (Clarence Derwent award 1974), Member of the Wedding, 1975, The Cherry Orchard, 1977; Dusa, Fish, Stas and Vi, 1978, All-Shakespeare Concert, 1978, Father's Day, 1979, The Rainmaker, 1981, Crimes of the Heart, 1981, 82, 83 (Obie award 1981), The Misanthrope, 1983, The Nest of the Woodgrouse, 1984, Benefactors, 1985, (feature films) Interiors, 1978, Head over Heels, 1979 (re-released as Chilly Scenes of Winter 1982), A Change of Seasons, 1980, The World According to Garp, 1982, D.A.R.Y.L., 1985, Compromising Positions, 1985, Six Degrees of Separation, 1993, The Age of Innocence, 1993, Affliction, 1997, Bringing Out the Dead, 1999, Autumn in New York, 2000, The Family Man, 2000, Perception, 2005, The Exorcism of Emily Rose, 2005, Lady in the Water, 2006, (TV films) Secret Service, 1977, The Five Forty Eight, 1979, Baby Girl Scott, 1987, After Amy, 2001, (TV series) Tattingers, 1988-89, Working it Out, 1990. Mem. Actors' Equity Assn., Screen Actors Guild. also: Screen Actors Guild 5757 Wilshire Blvd Los Angeles CA 90036-3635*

HURT, SHANNA L., secondary school educator; d. Howard D. and Marjorie Hudgeons; m. Tony Hurt, July 6, 2000; children: Dustin Lee Lippiatt, Patrick Vincent Lippiatt. BS, U. Tex., Austin, 1987; MS, East Tex. State U., Commerce, 1993. Lic. Profl. Tchr. Colo. Dept. Edn., 1993. Social studies tchr. Littleton Pub. Schs., Colo., 2001—. Home: 5884 S Oak St Littleton CO 80127 Office: Arapahoe HS 2201 E Dry Creek Littleton CO 80122 Office Phone: 303-347-6000. Business E-Mail: shurt@lps.k12.co.us.

HURTADO-ORTIZ, MARIA T., psychology professor; d. Narciso and Maria E. Hurtado; m. Sergio Ortiz, Dec. 26, 1998; children: Daniel S., Emanuel S. BA in Psychology, U. Calif., Riverside, Calif., 1992, MA in Developmental Psychology, 1994, PhD in Developmental Psychology, 1997. Tchg. asst. U. Calif., Riverside, 1995—97, lectr. psychology, 1998, 1999; sr. rsch. assoc. Thomas Rivera Policy Inst., Claremont, Calif., 1998—99; asst. prof. Calif. State U., Carson, Calif., 1999—2003, assoc. prof., 2003—. Adv. bd. Latino Scholastic Achievement Corp., L.A., 1999—. Contbr. articles to profl. jours. Mem.: APA, Am. Psychol. Soc., Latino Faculty and Staff Assn., Sigma Xi. Democrat. Roman Catholic. Avocations: reading, travel. Office: Calif State Univ Dominguez Hills 1000 E Victoria St Carson CA 90747 Office Phone: 310-243-3508. Business E-Mail: mhortiz@csudh.edu.

HURTWITZ, ANN, lawyer; b. 1953; BA, U. SC, 1977; JD, U. NC, Chapel Hill, 1980. Bar: NC 1980, DC 1981, Tex. 1983. Ptnr. DLA Piper Rudnick Gray Cary, Dallas. Editor-in-chief Franchise Law Jour. ABA, 1993—97. Mem.: State Bar Tex. (chair Franchise and Distbn. Com. 1994—95, 1995—96), Dallas Bar Assn., DC Bar Assn., NC State Bar Assn., Tex. State Bar Assn., ABA (mem. Forum on Franchising 1987—, Com. on Franchising Antitrust Law Sect. 1987—, Forum Franchising Governing Com. 1997—2000). Office: DLA Piper Rudnick Gray Cary 1717 Main St Suite 4600 Dallas TX 75201-4605 Office Phone: 214-743-4521. Office Fax: 214-743-4545. E-mail: ann.hurwitz@dlapiper.com.

HURWITZ, ANN, lawyer; b. Portsmouth, Va., Aug. 19, 1953; d. Frederick Dean and Mildred (Wood) Hardy; m. Mitchell Seth Hurwitz, May 30, 1981. BA, U. S.C., 1977; JD, U. N.C., 1980. Bar: Tex. 1983, D.C. 1981, N.C. 1980. Assoc. Thompson, Pikrallidas & Schott, Alexandria, Va., 1980-82, Smith, Underwood, Carmichael & Floyd, Dallas, 1982-84, Evans, Fernandez, Forgerson & Hurwitz, Dallas, 1984-86, Smith, Underwood & Hunter, Dallas, 1987-88; ptnr. Smith & Underwood, Dallas, 1988; mng. ptnr. Dallas off. DLA Piper Rudnick Gray Cary, Dallas. Contbr. articles to profl. jours. Named a Texas Super Lawyer, 2003—04. Mem. ABA (franchising subcom of the small bus. com. of bus. law sect. of corp., banking and bus. law), Tex. State Bar Assn. (franchising com. of intellectual property law sect.), Dallas Bar Assn., N.C. Bar Assn., D.C. Bar Assn. Democrat. Baptist. Office: DLA Piper Rudnick Gray Cary 1717 Main St Dallas TX 75201-4605 Office Phone: 214-743-4521. Office Fax: 214-743-4545. Business E-Mail: ann.hurwitz@dlapiper.com.

HURWITZ, DEENA R., law educator; b. Washington; BA, U. Calif., Santa Cruz, 1980; JD, Northeastern U., 1996. Bar: Mass. 1999. Mem. staff Resource Ctr. for Nonviolence, Calif.; project exec. adminstr. Ctr. Internat. Human Rights Enforcement, Ramallah, 1997; legal counselor UN High Commr. Refugees, Washington, 1997—99; Orgn. for Security and Co-operation in Europe liaison officer to Human Rights Coordination Ctr. of Office High Rep., Bosnia-Herzegovina; dir. Bosnia program Internat. Human Rights Law Group; Robert M. Cover/Allard K. Lowenstein Fellow in Internat. Human Rights Yale Law Sch., 2000—03; dir. human rights program and Internat. Human Rights Law Clinic U. Va. Sch. Law, 2003—. Editor: Walking the Red Line, Israelis in Search of Justice for Palestine, 1992. Office: U Va Sch Law 580 Massie Rd Charlottesville VA 22903-1789 Office Phone: 434-924-4776. E-mail: deena@virginia.edu.

HURWITZ, ELLEN STISKIN, college president, historian; b. Stamford, Conn., May 4, 1942; d. D.O. Bernard and Marjorie (Kanter) Stiskin; children: Jason, Sarah. BA, Smith Coll., 1964; MA, Columbia U., 1965, PhD, 1972. Vis. asst. prof. Wesleyan U., Middletown, Conn., 1972-73; asst. prof. Lafayette Coll., Easton, Pa., 1974-80, assoc. prof., assoc. dean, 1980-88; dean acad. affairs Ill. Wesleyan U., Bloomington, 1988-89, provost, dean of faculty, 1989-92; pres. Albright Coll., Reading, Pa., 1992—99, New England Coll., Henniker, NH, 1999—2004. Cons. Nat. Faculty Arts and Scis., Inst. for Ednl. Mgmt., Harvard U., 1990. Author: Andrej Bogoljubskij: Man and Myth, 1972. NEH fellow, 1973-74. Mem. AAAS, Am. Assn. Higher Edn., Phi Beta Kappa. Avocations: tennis, art and book collecting, gardening.

HURWITZ, JOHANNA (JOHANNA FRANK), writer; b. N.Y.C., Oct. 9, 1937; d. Nelson and Tillie (Miller) Frank; m. Uri Hurwitz, Feb. 19, 1962; children: Nomi, Beni. BA, Queens Coll., 1958; MLS, Columbia U., 1959. Libr. children's sect. N.Y. Pub. Libr., 1959-64; lectr. in children's lit. Queen's Coll., N.Y.C., 1965-69; libr. Calhoun Sch., N.Y.C., 1968-75, New Hyde Park (N.Y.) Sch. Dist., 1975-77; libr. children's sect. Great Neck (N.Y.) Pub. Libr., 1978-92. Author: Busybody Nora, 1976, Nora and Mrs. Mind-Your-Own-Business, 1977, The Law of Gravity, 1978, Much Ado About Aldo, 1978, Aldo Applesauce, 1979, New Neighbours for Nora, 1979, Once I Was a Plum Tree, 1980, Superduper Teddy, 1980, Aldo Ice Cream, 1981, Baseball Fever, 1981, The Rabbi's Girls, 1982, Tough-Luck Karen, 1982, Rip-Roaring Russell, 1983, DeDe Takes Charge!, 1984, The Hot and Cold Summer, 1984, The Adventures of Ali Baba Bernstein, 1985, Russell Rides Again, 1985, Hurricane Elaine, 1986, Yellow Blue Jay, 1986, Class Clown, 1987, Russell Sprouts, 1987, The Cold and Hot Winter, 1988, Teacher's Pet, 1988, Anne Frank: Life in Hiding, 1988, Hurray for Ali Baba Bernstein, 1989, Russell and Elisa, 1989, Astrid Lindgren: Storyteller to the World, 1989, Class President, 1990, Aldo Peanut Butter, 1990, School's Out, 1991, E Is for Elisa, 1991, Roz and Ozzie, 1992, Ali Baba Bernstein, Lost and Found, 1992, The Up and Down Spring, 1993, Make Room for Elisa, 1993, Leonard Bernstein: A Passion for Music, 1993, New Shoes for Silvia, 1993, A Word to the Wise, 1994, School Spirit, 1994, A Llama in the Family, 1994, Ozzie on His Own, 1995, Birthday Surprises, 1995, Elisa in the Middle, 1995, Even Stephen, 1996, Down and Up Fall, 1996, Spring Break, 1997, Ever-Clever Elisa, 1997, Helen Keller: Courage in the Dark, 1997, Faraway Summer, 1998, Starting School, 1998, A Dream Come True, 1998, Llama in the Library, 1999, Just Desserts Club, 1999, Summer with Elisa, 2000, Peewee's Tale, 2000, One Small Dog, 2000, Lexi's Tale, 2001, Russell's Secret, 2001, Oh No, Noah!, 2002, PeeWee & Plush, 2002, Dear Emma, 2002, Ethan, Out & About, 2002, Ethan at Home, 2003, Elisa Michaels, Bigger and Better, 2003, Fourth Grade Fuss, 2004, The Unsigned Valentine, 2006. Recipient Bluebonnet award Tex. Libr. Assn., 1987, Wyoming Indian Paintbrush award 1987, W.Va. Children's Book award 1989, Sunshine State award Fla. Libr. Assn., 1990, Miss. Children's Book award Miss. Libr. Assn., 1990, S.C. Children's Book award, 1990, Garden State award N.J. Sch. Libr. Assn., 1991, 94, Weekly Reader Book Club award, 1993, Land of Enchantment award N.Mex., 2004. Mem. PEN, Author's Guild, Soc. Children's Book Writers, Amnesty Internat. Address: 10 Spruce Pl Great Neck NY 11021-1904

HUSAR, LINDA S., lawyer; b. Chgo., Sept. 12, 1955; BS summa cum laude, Boston U., 1977; JD magna cum laude, Loyola Law Sch., 1980. Bar: Calif. 1980, US Dist. Ct. (No. Dist.) Calif. 1981, US Dist. Ct. (Ea. Dist.) Calif. 1981, US Dist. Ct. (So. Dist.) Calif. 1981, US Dist. Ct. (Ctrl. Dist.) Calif. 1981, US Ct. Appeals (9th Cir.) 1981. Ptnr., labor & employment dept. Thelen Reid & Priest LLP, LA. Mem.: LA County Bar Assn. (Labor Law Sect.), ABA (Labor Law Sect.), Calif. State Bar. Office: Thelen Reid & Priest LLP 333 S Hope St Ste 2900 Los Angeles CA 90071-3048 Office Phone: 213-576-8017. Office Fax: 213-687-1817. Business E-Mail: lshusar@thelenreid.com.

HUSE, HEIDI ANNE, language educator; PhD in English, Miami U., Oxford, Ohio, 1997—2001. Tchg. asst. Miami U., 1997—2001; asst. prof. U. Tenn., Martin, 2001—. Office: Univ Tenn Dept English Martin TN 38237

HUSE, REGINA MARIE, biologist, educator; b. Corpus Christi, Tex., Oct. 10, 1959; d. Darlene Feuerborn; m. George V. Huse, Jr., June 3, 1983; 1 child, Travis Austin. BS, MS, U. Tex., Arlington, Tex., 1997. Instr. biology Tarrant County Coll., Arlington, Tex., 1999—. Author: General College Biology 1408 and 1409 Lab Manual. Recipient Second Pl., Poster Divsn. award, U. Tex. Grad. Rsch. Symposium, 1996, Chancellor's Exemplary Tchg. award, Tarrant County Coll., 2005, Excellence award, Nat. Inst. Staff and Orgnl. Devel., 2006. Republican. Roman Cath. Avocations: gardening, pets, travel. Office: Tarrant County College 2100 Southeast Parkway Arlington TX 76018 Office Phone: 817-515-3338. Business E-Mail: regina.huse@tccd.edu.

HUSEN, S. AINO MARIA, retired elementary school educator; b. Laurium, Mich., Nov. 15, 1929; d. Antti and Sigrid Matilda (Hakola) Lepisto; m. Harold Lester Husen, June 15, 1952 (div. June 1965); children: Paavo Hans, Maria Elizabeth. BS, U. Minn., 1951, MA, 1968; cert., Boston U., 1968. Lic. elem. classroom tchr. Minn. Dept. Edn., cert. elem. remedial reading tchr. Minn. Dept. Edn., reading cons. K-12 Minn. Dept. Edn., ESL Hamline U., 1994. Tchr. grade 4 Lakefield (Minn.) Pub. Sch., 1951—55; tchr. grades 4 and 5 Windom (Minn.) Pub. Sch., 1955—56; remedial reading tchr. Minnetonka

(Minn.) Pub. Sch., 1961—68, reading cons., 1968—93; ret., 1993. English tchr. Evang. Luth. Ch., Ondangwa, Namibia, 1995—2005; translator of texts and rsch. from Finnish to English, 2000—. Chair Jackson County Libr. Assn., Minn., 1958—59; co-facilitator WE CARE, Mpls., 1974—79. Mem.: Minn. Acad. Reading. (pres. 1974, 1984), Internat. Reading Assn., NEA, Minn. Reading Assn. (historian 1986—, Cert. for Svc. 1975, 2000). Avocations: reading, gardening, hiking, travel, music. Home: 2625 Boone Ave S Saint Louis Park MN 55426

HUSER, GERI D., state official; b. Des Moines, Iowa, July 14, 1963; m. Dan Huser. BA, Briar Cliff Coll., 1985; MBA, Drake U., 2003, JD, 2004. Social worker Polk County Gen. Relief, 1986—90; program mgr. Polk County Family Enrichment Ctr., 1990—96; mem. Met. Planning Orgn., 1990—, Altoona City Coun., 1991—; planning specialist Polk County Social Svcs., 1996—; state rep. Iowa, 1997—. Mem. adminstrv. and rules com.; mem. local govt. com.; mem. transp. com.; mem. ways and means com. Mem. Child Abuse Prevention Coun., 1993—95, Greater Des Moines Housing Partnership, 1995—97; chmn. Met. Planning Orgn., 1996—. Mem.: East Polk Interagy. Assn., Mitchellville C. of C., Pleasant Hill C. of C., S.E. Polk Booster Club. Democrat. Office: State Capitol E 12th and Grand Des Moines IA 50319

HUSKY, ANREA DALENE, elementary school educator, director; d. Glover Andrew and Anna Ruth Husky; AA with honors, Jacksonville Coll., Tex., 1982; BFA with honors, U. Tex., Tyler, 1984; M in Mus. Edn., Tex. Tech. U., Lubbock, 1987. Elem. music tchr. Mt. Pleasant Ind. Sch. Dist., Ind., 1984—85; elem. music tchr., choir dir. Lubbock Ind. Sch. Dist., 1985—99; edn. dir. Lubbock Symphony Orch., 1999—2000; elem. music tchr., choir dir. Deer Valley Unified Sch. Dist., Phoenix, 2001—04; prep choir dir. Phoenix Children's Chorus, 2003—04; jr. high choir dir. Big Spring Ind. Sch. Dist., Tex., 2004—05. Sec. U. Civic Chorale, Lubbock, 1988—90; creator elem. music curriculum Lubbock Ind. Sch. Dist., 1996. Alto sect. leader Ariz. Arts Chorale, Scottsdale, 2002; dir. Lubbock Boys and Girls Choirs, 1994—95; Chancel chair First United Meth. Ch., Lubbock, 1992—2001, 2005—; bd. dirs. Wheelock Elem. PTA, Lubbock, 1998—99. Recipient Ensemble award, Jacksonville Coll., 1982, Way to Go award, Lubbock Ind. Sch. Dist., 1987; scholar, Tex. Tech. U., 1985—87. Mem.: Am. Choral Dirs. Assn., Tex. Choral Dirs. Assn., Tex. Music Educators Assn. (chair elem. divsn. region XVI), Tex. PTA (hon.). Avocation: singing.

HUSMAN, CATHERINE BIGOT, retired insurance company executive, consultant; b. Des Moines, Feb. 10, 1943; d. Edward George and Ruth Margaret (Cumming) Bigot; m. Charles Erwin Husman, Aug. 5, 1967; 1 child, Matthew Edward. BA with highest distinction, U. Iowa, 1965; MA, Ball State U., 1970. Actuarial asst. Am. United Life Ins. Co., Indpls., 1965—68, assoc. actuary, 1971—74, group actuary, 1974—84, v.p., corp. actuary, 1984—97, v.p., chief actuary, 1997—2002; cons., 2002—04. Mem. group tech. com. Mut. Life Ins. Co., 1986-98; mem. profitability studies com. Life Office Mgmt. Assn. Inc., 1991-99. Mem. women's adv. com. United Way Ctrl. Ind., 1991—93; mem. Exec. Svc. Corps, 2002—, asst. treas., 2005—; docent Pres. Benjamin Harrison Home, 2002—; vol. Indpls. Mus. Art, 2002—05, Clowes Meml. Hall, 2002—, Indpls. Civic Theater, 2002—, Ronald McDonald House, 2004—; bd. dirs., mem. fin. com. St. Elizabeth's Home, 1991—99, sec., 1994, mem. exec. com., treas., 1995; bd. dirs., mem. adminstrv. svcs., mem. exec. com. Heritage Place, 1993—99, treas., 1995—99. Fellow Soc. Actuaries; mem. Am. Acad. Actuaries, Actuaries Club Ind., Ky. and Ohio, Actuarial Club Indpls. (pres. 1979-80), Phi Beta Kappa. Republican. Roman Catholic. Avocations: reading, tennis. Home: 13530 Belford Ct Carmel IN 46032-8209 Personal E-mail: cbhusman@earthlink.net.

HUSS, BETTY JO, education educator; b. Louisville, Ill., July 3, 1932; d. Orison Edwin and Mary Mildred (Cutter) N.; m. John Calvin Wasson Jan 26, 1952 (div. Apr. 1977), children: David John, Susan Kay, Carol Ellen.; m. William Anthony Huss, Dec. 10, 1983. AS, Thorton Comm. Coll., 1970-73; BA, Purdue U., 1974-76, MA, 1976-80. Tchr. Cert. in Ill. and Ind. Reading cons. Memorial Jr. High, Lansing, Ill., 1976-77; tchr. asst. Purdue U. Calumet, Hammond, Ind., 1977-78, tchr. mentor, 1977-78; eng. indtr. Thorton Fractional N., Calumet City, Ill.; reading instr. Parker Jr. High, Flossmoor, Ill., 1988—; English instr. S. Suburban Coll., Ill., 1988-89, Acad. Our Lady, Chgo., 1989-90; ESL tchr. Cypress Fairbanks Ind. Sch. Dist., Houston, 1990—. Mem. Nat. Coll. of Tchrs Eng., Ind. Coll. Tchrs. of Eng., Mid Am. Assn. of Educational Opportunity, NEA, Purdue Womens Club, Beta Gamma Upsilon. Democrat. Avocations: research, reading, flowers. Home: 18306 Kitzman Rd Cypress TX 77429-1290

HUSS, BONNIE JEAN, intensive cardiac care nurse; b. Nashville, Kans., May 11, 1962; d. Eugene Edward and Betty Marie (Venard) Hauser; 1 child, Jamie Marie Huss; m. Harold Gene Huss, Jul. 3, 1989; 1 child, Skyler Matthew. LPN, Pratt Cmty. Coll., Pratt, Kans., 1983, AS, 1984, A of nursing, 1988; BSN, Newman U., Kans., 1998; MS in Nursing, Ft. Hays State U., 2000. Cert. ACLS. Charge nurse LPN Hilltop Manor, Cunningham, Kans., 1983-88; charge nurse medical surgy Medicine Lodge (Kans.) Meml. Hosp., 1988-91; charge nurse SCU Pratt Regional Medical Ctr., 1991-94. Instr. BLS Red Cross, Pratt, 1993—; ACLS cert. St. Joe, 1993. Mem. Am. Acad. Nurse Practitioners, Ft. Hays Grad. Nursing Assn., Kans. State Nurses Assn., Critical Care Nurses. Democrat. Roman Catholic. Avocations: reading, walking, family, religion. Home: 292 W Broadway Ave Nashville KS 67112-8302

HUSS, CAROL BERRYHILL, mathematics educator; d. Wilma Y. and James C. Berryhill; m. Malcolm L. Huss Jr., Nov. 24, 1985; children: Justin Collins, Kelsey Elizabeth. BA, U. N.C., Chapel Hill, 1982. Nat. bd. cert. tchr. adolescent/young adult math. 2000. Tchr. math. J.T. Williams Jr. H.S., Charlotte, NC, 1982—86, Independence H.S., 1986—. Candidate support provider CMS Nat. Bd. Profl. Tchg. Stds., Charlotte, NC, 2002—. Mem.: N. C. Coun. Tchrs. Math., Nat. Coun. Tchrs. Math. Office: Independence HS 1967 Patriot Dr Charlotte NC 28227

HUSSEY, SHELLEY, graphic design company owner; b. Akron, Ohio, June 7, 1951; d. Sheldon Rex and Juanita Fay Harper; m. Frederick James Hussey, Jr., July 28, 1978; children: James, Mary, Beth. Student, U. Guam, Agana, 1969—70; BA, Cleve. State U., 1973. Copywriter, announcer Sta. WPVL Radio, Painesville, Ohio, 1973—76, Sta. WHK Radio, Cleve., 1976—78; owner Gifted Greetings, Columbia, SC, 1985—87, Greetings Inc., Acworth, Ga., 1987—2005, Greetings Inc. DBA Harper Ink., Acworth, 2005—. Leader Women's Profl. Networking, Kennesaw, Ga., 1994—95; spkr. in fields of entrepreneurship, business relationships. Author: Divine Secrets of the Boa, 2004, I'm Not OK You're Not OK, 2005; columnist: Shameless Husseys, 2002—. Recipient Chmn.'s award, Lakewood Jaycee Women, 1982. Mem.: Christian Author's Guild. Republican. Mem. Ch. Of God. Avocations: hiking, reading, writing. Home: 4980 Thornwood Cove Acworth GA 30102 Office: Harper Ink 4980 Thornwood Cove Acworth GA 30102 Office Phone: 770-928-0389. E-mail: shelleyhussey@bellsouth.net.

HUSTED, CHARLENE E., library media specialist, educator; b. Knowles, Okla., Sept. 10, 1930; d. Merle Lester and Bertha Mary Paasch Bond; m. Glenn Ray Husted, Oct. 5, 1947; children: Lester Glenn, Anita Faye Husted Whiteley. BA in Elem. Edn. summa cum laude, Okla. Panhandle State U., 1968; BS in Edn. summa cum laude, Pittsburg (Kans.) State U., 1975, libr. media cert., 1975; postgrad. with honors, Cen. State U., Edmond, Okla., 1989, U. Okla., 1989; postgrad., U. Guadalajara, Jalisco, Mex., 1989. Cert. in elem. edn.; cert. libr. media specialist; cert. in Spanish. Tchr. Washington Elem. Sch., Liberal, Kans., 1968-71; libr. media specialist Garrett Elem., Elmwood, Okla., 1971-77; tchr. Southlawn Elem. Sch., Liberal, 1977-80, Buffalo (Okla.) Jr./Sr. H.S., 1981-90; tchr. ESL and citizenship edn. Guymon, Okla., 1991-97; libr. media specialist, tchr. elem. Spanish Forgn (Okla.) H.S., 1995—. Workshop leader, Liberal schs., 1971, Ednl. Dist. Meeting, Woodward, Okla., 1988. Coord. local Heartland Share from Topeka; bd. dirs. Gate Mus. Libr.; sec.-treas. Zelma Cemetery; pianist Nazarene Ch., Knowles; mem. Beaver County Nursing Home Aux. Mem. AAUW, NAFE, NEA (v.p., program chair Kans. chpt. 1970-71), Okla. Edn. Assn., Okla. Libr. Media Specialists (pres. 1981-90), Beaver County Edn. Assn., Panhandle State Assn., Knowles Alumni Assn. (com. mem.), Smithsonian Instn., Libr. of Congress Assocs., Nat. Mus. of Women in the Arts. Republican. Avocations: showing horses, reading, travel. Home: RR 1 Box 165 Gate OK 73844-9617 Office: Forgan Pub Schs PO Box 406 Forgan OK 73938-0406

HUSTON, ANGELA C., lawyer; b. Tulsa, Jan. 23, 1973; BS cum laude, Tex. Woman's U., 1995; JD, Baylor U. Sch. Law, 2001. Bar: Tex. 2001, US Dist. Ct. (no. dist. Tex.) 2001. Assoc. Holmes Firm, P.C., Dallas. Mem. Assoc. Leadership Coun., 2005—06. Named a Rising Star, Tex. Super Lawyers mag., 2006. Mem.: Internat. Coun. Shopping Ctrs., Real Estate Coun., Tex. Young Lawyers Assn., Dallas Bar Assn. Office: Holmes Firm PC 14911 Quorum Dr Ste 340 Dallas TX 75254 Office Phone: 469-916-7700. E-mail: angela@theholmesfirm.com.*

HUSTON, ANJELICA, actress; b. Santa Monica, Calif., July 8, 1951; d. John and Enrica Huston; m. Robert Graham, May 23, 1992. Student, Loft Studio. Actress appearing in Hamlet, Roundhouse Theatre, London, Tamara, Il Vittorale Theatre, L.A.; appeared in films including A Walk with Love and Death, 1969, Hamlet, 1969, Sinful Davey, 1969, Swashbuckler, 1976, The Last Tycoon, 1976, The Postman Always Rings Twice, 1981, Rose for Emily, 1982, This is Spinal Tap, 1984, The Ice Pirates, 1984, Prizzi's Honor, 1985 (Academy award for best supporting actress 1985, N.Y.Film Critics award 1985, L.A. Film Critics award 1985), Captain Eo, 1986, Gardens of Stone, 1987, The Dead, 1987 (Best Actress award Ind. Filmakers 1987), Mr. North, 1988, A Handfull of Dust, 1988, Witches, 1989, Crimes and Misdemeanors, 1989, Enemies, A Love Story, 1989 (Acad. award nomination 1990), The Grifters, 1990 (Acad. award nomination 1991), The Addams Family, 1991, The Player, 1992, Addams Family Values, 1993, Manhattan Murder Mystery, 1993, The Crossing Guard, 1995, The Perez Family, 1995, Buffalo '66, 1997, Phoenix, 1998, Ever After, 1998, The Golden Bowl, 2000, The Man From Elysian Fields, 2000, The Royal Tenenbaums, 2001, Blood Work, 2002, Barbie as Rapunzel, (voice only), 2002, Daddy Day Care, 2003, Kaena: The Prophecy (voice only), The Life Aquatic with Steve Zissou, 2004, These Foolish Things, 2006, Art School Confidential, 2006, Material Girls, 2006; TV films include The Cowboy and the Ballerina, 1984, Family Pictures, 1993, And The Band Played On, 1993, Buffalo Girls, 1995, The Kentucky Derby, 2002, Iron Jawed Angels, 2004 (Golden Globe award for best supporting actress series, miniseries or TV movie, 2005), Covert One: The Hades Factor, 2006; dir. (films) Bastard Out of Carolina, 1996, (TV films) Riding the Bus with My Sister, 2005; dir, prodr., actor (films) Agnes Browne, 1999; TV mini-series include Lonesome Dove, 1989, The Mists of Aalon, 2001; TV guest appearances Laverne & Shirley, 1976, Inside the Actors Studio, 1994. Office: Internat Creative Mgmt c/o Toni Howard 8942 Wilshire Blvd Beverly Hills CA 90211-1934*

HUSTON, JOYCE A., web site design company executive; d. Herman and Loyce (Pickens) Huston; m. Z. Lipsky, July 21, 2001. BSBA, U. Redlands, 1988; postgrad., Rockhurst Coll. Continuing Edn. Ctr., 2000—. Trumpeter, vocalist, arranger Albert King Blues Band, St. Louis, 1980—82; word processing specialist TRW, Los Angeles, Calif., 1986—88; pres. UniSun Prodns., Las Vegas, Nev., 1993—; website adminstr., sys. analyst U.S. DOE (Bechtel SAIC, TRW, SAIC Contractors), Las Vegas, Nev., 1989—. Webmaster, spokesperson Las Vegas Fibromyalgia/Chronic Fatigue Syndrome Support Group; presenter in field. Prodr.(composer, singer, trumpeter, synthesizers): (CD) Soul Stir Fry; composer: Songs Forever; musician (front trumpeter): The Music Man with Tony Randall, 1978; musician: (trumpeter) (albums) Howard University Jazz Ensemble; performer: Bill Pinkney and the Original Drifters, 1992, Shower of Stars, 2000; performer: (one woman show) Fitzgerald's Hotel & Casino, 1997; author: The Black O'Kelleys in America, 1998. Recruiter asst. Rainbow Coalition, Washington, 1982; Census 2000 program asst. African Am. Cmty. Coalition of So. Nev., Las Vegas, 2000; mem. P.U.S.H Coalition, St. Louis, 1978—79. Recipient Dr. Barbara O'Rourke award, Las Vegas Fibromyalgia/Chronic Fatigue Syndrome Support Group, 2006. Mem.: Las Vegas Blues Soc., Clark County Geneal. Soc., Las Vegas Songwriters Assn. (assoc.), Nat. Spiritualist Assn. of Chs. (assoc.). Democrat. Avocations: genealogy, computers, music, reading, swimming. Office: UniSun Prodns 2375 E Tropicana Ave Ste 353 Las Vegas NV 89119 Office Phone: 702-391-3040. Personal E-mail: thelady@msjoyce.com.

HUSTON, KATHLEEN MARIE, library administrator; b. Sparta, Wis., Jan. 7, 1944; BA, Edgewood Coll., 1966; MLS, U. Wis., Madison, 1969. Libr. Milw. Pub. Libr., 1969-90; city libr. Milw. Pub. Libr. System, 1991—. Office: Milwaukee Pub Libr 814 W Wisconsin Ave Milwaukee WI 53233-2309

HUSTON, MARGO, journalist; b. Waukesha, Wis., Feb. 12, 1943; d. James and Cecile (Timlin) Bremner; m. James Huston, Dec. 9, 1967 (div.); 1 son, Sean Patrick. AB in Journalism, Marquette U., 1965. Editl. asst. Marquette U., Milw., 1965—66; feature editor, reporter Waukesha Freeman, Wis., 1966—67; feature reporter Milw. Jour., 1967—70, reporter Spectrum, women's and food sects., 1972—79, editl. writer, 1979—84, polit. reporter, 1984—, asst. picture editor, 1985—91, copy editor, 1992—95; reporter Milw. Jour Sentinel (merger Milw. Jour. and The Sentinel), 1995—99; mem. working bd. Cath. Herald, 2000—01; freelance journalist Milw., 2001—. Instr. mass comm. U. Wis., Milw. Mem. Milw. Restorative Justice Task Force, 2004. Recipient Penney-Mo. award for consumer abortion series, 1977, Pulitzer Prize for investigation into plight of elderly, 1977, Clarion award, 1977, Knight of Golden Quill award, Milw. Press club, 1977, Wis. AP writing award, 1977, Spl. award Milw. Soc. Profl. Journalists, 1977, Penney-Mo. Paul Myhre award for excellence, 1978, By-Line award Marquette U. Coll. Journalism, 1980, Wis. UPI Best Editl. award, 1982, Wis. Women's Network award for journalist achievement for women's issues, 1983, Dick Goldensohn Fund award, 1991, 1st place award for investigative reporting Inland Press Assn., 1997, 98, 2d award Enterprise interpretive reporting Wis. Newspaper Assn., 1998; Wis. Arts Bd. Lit. Arts grantee, 1992. Mem. European Project for Interreligious Learning (founder, cert. in Muslim-Christian Dialogue 2004), Milw. Press Club (Hall of Fame 2000). E-mail: margo.huston@gmail.com.

HUSTON, NANCY ELIZABETH, civic worker, educator; b. NYC, July 13, 1947; d. Cord Henry and Catherine Frances (Nahrwold) Sump; m. Rea Askew Huston, June 22, 1974; 1 child, Mary Catherine. AB with honors in Spanish, U. Chattanooga, 1969; MA, U. Ga., 1971. Cert. tchr. NC, Tenn. Chmn. fgn. lang. dept. Hixson Jr. High Sch., Tenn., 1970—74, tchr. Spanish, French and music Tenn., 1975—78; tchr. Spanish, Charlotte Mecklenburg Schs., NC, 1975; substitute tchr. Hamilton County Schs., Snow Hill Elem. Sch., Chattanooga, 1983—, chmn. living curriculum conf. fgn. lang. sect., 1971—72; interim tchr. Coltewah Middle Sch; tchr. French and Spanish Chattanooga Sch. Liberal Arts, 1992—. Pub. chmn. Chattanooga Girls Choir, 1991, pres.-elect, 1991—92, pres., 1992—93; singer Chattanooga Opera Chorus, 1966—67; chmn. pub. rels. and fund drive Cystic Fibrosis Assn., Harrison, Tenn., 1981—82; scrapbook chmn. Hickory Valley Garden Club, Chattanooga, 1986—87; docent Chattanooga Regional History Mus., 1986—87; leader Girl Scouts US, 1986—87; 3d v.p. PTO, 1987, sec., 1991—92; deacon Brainerd Presbyn. Ch., 1992; mem. vestry St. Francis of Assisi Epis. Ch., 2000—03. Ford Found. fellow, U. Ga., 1969—71. Mem.: Nat. Assn. Supervision and Curriculum Devel., Tenn. Assn. Supr. and Curriculum Devel., Phi Delta Kappa, Sigma Delta Pi, Chi Omega. Avocations: counted cross stitch, piano, hiking, sewing, teaching young peoples' choir. Home: 7637 Morgan Estate Rd Ooltewah TN 37363-9138 Office Phone: 423-855-2614. Personal E-mail: nehuston@lycos.com.

HUSTON, SUSAN KAY MYERS, elementary school educator; b. Lancaster, Ohio, Feb. 25, 1952; d. Frederick Martin and Fern Venetta (Flood) Myers; m. Roger Loy Huston, Oct. 15, 1974; children: Audrey Melissa Huston Meixner, Ethan Roger. BS cum laude, Ohio U., 1990; MEd with honors, Ashland U., 1998. Accts. receivable supr. Winchester Farm, Inc., Canal Winchester, Ohio, 1984—87; elem. educator grades 4-5 Tallmadge Elem., Lancaster, Ohio, 1990—. Mentor Ohio U.-Lancaster Campus and Lancaster City Schs. Partnership, 1995—. Fellow Project Discovery Initiative, State of Ohio Dept. Edn., Muskingham Coll., 1994. Mem.: Sigma Phi Gamma (Mu Beta chpt. and Gamma province, past pres., treas., editor). Avocations: swimming, jogging, reading, quilting, volunteering at homeless soup kitchen. Office: Tallmadge Elem Sch 611 Lewis Ave Lancaster OH 43130-4599

HUSZAI, KRISTEN RENEE, insurance agent; b. Pensacola, Fla., May 19, 1974; d. Stephen Edward and Mary Ellen Huszai. Grad. H.S., Gaithersburg, Md. Lic. ins. agt. Md. Sales asst. Paul Revere Ins., Rockville, Md., 1993—97; sec. CompDesign, Bethesda, Md., 1997—98; sr. account asst. Mut. Omaha, Washington, 1997—2004; new bus. coord. Assurance Employee Benefits, Landover, Md., 2004—05; account exec. Lifetime Benefits LLC, Gaithersburg, Md., 2005—. Republican. Roman Catholic. Avocations: reading, travel, sports. Office Phone: 301-840-9669.

HUSZAR, ANGELIA, lawyer; b. Hammond, La., May 21, 1974; d. Urban Robert and Brenda McKinney Fontenot; m. Daniel William Huszar, Jr., Aug. 12, 1995; 1 child, Madison Michelle. BA, Southeastern La. U., Hammond, 2000; JD, Loyola U., New Orleans, 2004. Atty. Anderson & Boutwell, Hammond, 2004—06; solo practice Hammond, La., 2006—. Mem.: La. Trial Lawyers Assn., La. State Bar Assn. Roman Catholic. Home: PO Box 1146 Albany LA 70711 Office: 107 S Cherry St Hammond LA 70403 Office Phone: 985-902-8755. Business E-Mail: angelia@huszarlaw.com.

HUTCHENS, GAIL R., chemist; b. Bentonville, Ark., Aug. 22, 1938; d. Sidney Baxter and Mary Dena Maurine (Harral) Rakes; m. Charles Verlin Hutchens, Mar. 4, 1967 (dec. 2002); children: David Charles, Kimberly Gail. Student, Ark. State Tchrs. Coll., 1955—58; grad., U. Tenn., 1961. Exec. v.p. Galbraith Labs., Inc., Knoxville, Tenn., 1959—93; supr. analytical svcs. Materials Engring. & Testing, Oak Ridge, Tenn., 1993—96, Techmer PM, LLC, Clinton, Tenn., 1996—. Emergency first responder instr. Video editor Democrates, Knoxville, TN, 1998. Mem.: ASTM, Small Chem. Bus. (sec. 1974—75), Am. Chem. Soc., Soc. Plastic Engrs. (local sect. sec. 2002—06, treas. 2004—06), Assn. Ofcl. Analytical Chemists, Crestwood Hills Garden Club (pres. 1968—69), Beta Club, Alpha Chi. Avocation: diving instruction. Office: Techmer PM LLC 1 Quality Cir Clinton TN 37716-4017 Office Phone: 865-457-6700. Business E-Mail: ghutchens@techmerpm.com.

HUTCHEON, LINDA ANN, English language educator; b. Toronto, Aug. 24, 1947; d. Vincent Roy and Elisa (Rossi) Bulfon Bortolotti; m. Michael Alexander Hutcheon, May 30, 1970. BA, U. Toronto, 1969, PhD, 1975; MA, Cornell U., 1971. Prof. McMaster U., Hamilton, Ont., Canada, 1976-88, U. Toronto, 1988—95, 1995—. Vis. prof. U. Toronto, 1980-81, 81-82, 84-85, U. Wis., Madison, 1995, U. Ga., 1998, U. Queensland, Australia, 2001, U. Mich. Inst. for the Humanities, 2003. Author: Narcisstic Narrative, 1980 (choice award, 1980), Formalism and the Freudian Aesthetic, 1984, A Theory of Parody, 1985, 2000, A Poetics of Postmodernism, 1988, The Canadian Postmodern, 1988, The Politics of Postmodernism, 1989, 2002, Splitting Images, 1991, Irony's Edge, 1995, A Theory of Adaptation, 2006; author: (with M. Hutcheon) Opera: Desire, Disease, Death, 1996, Bodily Charm: Living Opera, 2000, Opera: The Art of Dying, 2004; assoc. editor: RS/SI, 1982—84, U. Toronto Quar., 1993—; mem. (editl. bd.) Texte, Toronto, 1983—, English Studies in Can., 1984—94, Italian Canadiana, 1984—, Textual Practice, 1987—2003, Can. Rev. Comparative Lit., 1987—, Can. Poetry, 1987—93, PMLA, 1990—92, Essays on Can. Writing, 1992—, Contemporary Lit., 1992—, Modern Fiction Studies, 1993—, CLIO, 1994—, Parallax (U.K.), 1994—. Recipient Killam prize Hunanities, 2005; Woodrow Wilson Found. fellow, 1969, Social Scis. and Humanities Rsch. Coun. Can. fellow, 1983, 93-95, 96-99, 2000-03, 04—, co-fellow maj. collaborative rsch. initiatives, 1996-2000; Can. Coun. fellow, 1972-75, Killam Found. fellow, 1978-80, 86-88, Connaught fellow, 1991-92, Guggenheim fellow, 1992-93. Fellow Am. Acad. Arts and Scis. (Killiam prize in humanities 2005); mem. MLA (del. assembly 1985-88, exec. coun. 1992-96, 2d v.p. 1998, 1st v.p. 1999, pres. 2000), AAAS (elected), Assn. Can. Coll. and Univ. Tchrs. English (exec. mem. 1978-81), Can. Comparative Lit. Assn. (sec.-treas. 1981-83), Internat. Comparative Lit. Assn. (coord. com. lit. history 1992-97) Office Phone: 416-978-6616.

HUTCHERSON, DONNA DEAN, retired music educator; b. Dallas, July 10, 1937; d. Lamar Shaffer and Lenora Fay (Newbern) Clark; m. George Henry Hutcherson, Jan. 31, 1959; children: Lamar, Michael, Mark Lee, Holly (dec.), Shela. B. Music Edn., Sam Houston State U., Huntsville, Tex., 1959; MA in Music, Stephen F. Austin State U., Nacogdoches, Tex., 1974; postgrad., Memphis State U., 1986-89. Cert. tchr. music K-12, Orff levels 1, 2, 3, Master, cert. computer literacy, Tex. Tchr. music 4th and 5th grades Carthage (Tex.) Ind. Sch. Dist., 1958-59; tchr. music grades 1-5 and H.S. choir Hallsville (Tex.) Ind. Sch. Dist., 1969-75, tchr. music K-4, 1975-78, tchr. music grades 3-4, 1978-86, tchr. music 4th grade, 1986-97; ret., 1997. Contbr. Jour. of Music Edn. Delegation to Vietnam Citizen Ambassador Program, 1993; chmn. Tex. Ann. Conf. United Meth. Ch. Commn. on Archives/History. Contbr. articles to profl. jours. Fellow United Meth. Musicians in Worship and Other Arts; mem. Music Educators Nat. Conf. (registered music educator), Tex. Music Educators Conf. (state Tri-M chmn. 1993-98), Tex. Music Educators Assn. (region IV chmn. 1975-93), Am. Orff Schulewerk Assn., Tri M Internat. Music Honor Soc. (local chpt. sponsor 1992—, hon. mem.). Methodist. Avocations: square dancing, sewing, travel, church work, summer mission trips. Home: 119 Mcpherson Rd Hallsville TX 75650-7707 E-mail: ddhutch@juno.com.

HUTCHERSON, RENE RIDENS, medical social services administrator; b. Memphis, Feb. 26, 1944; d. Samuel Haskins Sr. and Arahwana (Hendren) Ridens; 1 child, John Ridens. BA, Vanderbilt U., 1965; MSW, U. Tenn., 1967. Lic. social worker, Colo. Clin. social worker U. Colo. Med. Ctr., 1967-83; dir. med. social svc. dept. U. Colo. Health Scis. Ctr., 1983-90, clin. social worker Denver, 1990—. Contbr. articles to profl. jours. Mem. NASW, Nat. Soc. Hosp. Social Work Dirs., Am. Assn. Continuity of Care, Acad. Cert. Social Workers (cert.), Colo. Soc. Clin. Social Worker (cert., diplomate).

HUTCHINS, CARLEEN MALEY, acoustical engineer, consultant; b. Springfield, Mass., May 24, 1911; d. Thomas W. and Grace (Fletcher) Maley; m. Morton A. Hutchins, June 6, 1943; children: William Aldrich, Caroline. AB, Cornell U., 1933; MA, NYU, 1942; DEng (hon.), Stevens Inst. Tech., 1977; DFA (hon.), Hamilton Coll., 1984; DSc (hon.), St. Andrews Presbyn. Coll., 1988; LLD (hon.), Concordia U., Montreal, Que., Can., 1992. Tchr. sci. Woodward Sch., Bklyn., 1934—38, Brearley Sch., NYC, 1938—49; asst. dir., asst. prin. All Day Neighborhood Schs., NYC, 1943—45. Sci. cons. Coward McCann, Inc., 1956-65, Girl Scouts Am., 1967-65, Nat. Recreation Assn., 1957-65; permanent sec. Catgut Acoustical Soc., Montclair, NJ, 1962-2000; exec. dir. New Violin Family Assn. Inc., 2000—; hon. cons. Catgut Acoustical Soc., Inc., 2000-04; maker violins. Author: Life's Key, DNA, 1961, Moon Moth, 1965, Who Will Drown the Sound, 1972; author (with others): Science Through Recreation, 1964; contbr. violin acoustics sect. Grove's Dictionary of Music and Musicians, 1964, 96; editor: (2 vols.) Musical Acoustics, Part I, Violin Family Components, 1975, Musical Acoustics, Part II, Violin Family Functions, 1976, The Physics of Music, 1978, Research Papers in Violin Acoustics, 1973-94, 96; contbr. articles to profl. jours. in Sci. Am. Jour. Acoustical Soc. Am., Jour. Audio Engring. Soc., Physics Today, Am. Viola Soc., Catgut Acoustical Soc. Martha Baird Rockefeller Fund for Music grantee, 1966, 68, 74, NSF grantee, 1971, 74; Guggenheim fellow, 1959, 61; recipient spl. citations in music, Carleen Maley Hutchins medal (1st recipient) Catgut Acoustical Soc., Hon. Fellowship award Acoustical Soc. Am., 1998. Fellow AAAS (electorate nominating com. 1974-76, Outstanding Performance in the Scis. award 1994), Audio Engring. Soc. (life), Acoustical Soc. Am. (emeritus, membership com. 1980-86, exec. coun. 1984-87, medal and awards com. 1987-89, nominating com. 1987-88, Silver Acoustics Medal 1981, tech. com. music acoustics 1964—, chmn. pres.'s ad hoc com. 1987-88, archives com. 1988—, mem. com. on women 1989-97); mem. So. Calif. Violin Makers Assn. (hon.), Viola da Gambda Soc. Am. (hon.), Scandinavian Violin Makers Assn. (hon.), NY Viola Soc., Guild Am. Luthiers, Am. Viola

Soc., Violoncello Soc., Amateur Chamber Music Players Assn., Am. Philos. Soc. (award violin acoustics 1968, 81), Mich. Violin Makers Assn., New Violin Family Assn. Inc. (exec. dir. 1999—), Materials Rsch. Soc., Three O'Clock Club, Dot and Circle, others, Sigma Xi, Pi Lambda Theta, Alpha Xi Delta. Home and Office: 42 Taylor Dr Wolfeboro NH 03894

HUTCHINS, DIANE ELIZABETH RIDER, librarian; b. Kearny, NJ, June 25, 1951; d. Thomas Lindsay and Dorothy Jane (Sommer) Rider; m. Clifford James Hutchins, Feb. 14, 2002. MusB magna cum laude, Westminster Choir Coll., 1973; MLS, Fla. State U., 1993. Intern preservation dept. U. Fla., Gainesville, 1993; intern free-net libr. Tallahassee Free-Net, 1993; reference libr. Broward County Main Libr., Ft. Lauderdale, Fla., 1994-95; libr., instr. Art Inst. Ft. Lauderdale, 1995-96, dir. Learning Resource Ctr., 1996-98; dean Nevin C. Meinhardt Meml. Libr., 1998-99; collection devel. coord. Washington State Libr., Olympia, 1999—2002, program mgr. collection mgmt., 2002—06, program mgr. for preservation and access svcs., 2006—. Vice chair, assoc. mem. com. S.E. Fla. Libr. Info. Network, 1996-97, chair assoc. mem. com., 1997-98, ex officio mem. bd. dirs. S.E. Fla. Libr. Info. Network, 1996-99; spl. librs. rep. Fla. Libr. Network Coun., 1998-99. Soloist St. Paul's Chapel, Columbia U., N.Y.C., 1973, Ch. of St. Mary the Virgin, N.Y.C., 1974. Recipient Outstanding Leadership award Wash. State Libr., 2000; Fla. State U. fellow, 1993-94, Coll. Tchg. fellow, 1992-93; Louis Shores scholar, 1992-93. Mem. Spl. Librs. Assn. (dir. Fla. and Caribbean chpt. 1997-99, Fla. rep., steering com. South Atlantic Regional conf. 1997-99), New Eng. Hist. Geneal. Soc., Geneal. Soc. Southwestern Pa., Geneal. Soc. of N.J., Phi Kappa Phi, Beta Phi Mu. Avocations: cooking, genealogy, gardening, reading. Office: The Wash State Libr Office of Sec of State PO Box 42460 Olympia WA 98504-2460 Office Phone: 360-704-7137. Business E-Mail: dhutchins@secstate.wa.gov.

HUTCHINS, KAREN LESLIE, psychotherapist; b. Denver, Sept. 9, 1943; d. Kimball Frederick and Bonnie Illa (Small) H.; divorced; 1 child, Alec Klinghoffer. BA, U. Denver, 1965; MA, George Washington U., 1972. Lic. profl. counselor, Reiki master, shamanic practitioner, spiritual regressist, cert. Nat. Bd. Clin. Hypnotherapists. Tchr. Washington Schs., 1966-70; asst. housing adminstr. George Washington U., Washington, 1970-72; counselor/instr. No. Va. C.C., Annandale, 1972-77, Austin (Tex.) C.C., 1977-80; co-owner Hearts Day Care, Austin, 1980-81; supr./therapist MaryLee Resdl. Treatment, Austin, 1981-82; child protective svc. worker Dept. Human Resources, Austin, 1982-84; probation officer Adult Probation Travis County, Austin, 1984-90; lead therapist Cottonwood Treatment Ctrs., Bastrop, Tex., 1990-91; psychotherapist Austin, 1991—. Presenter in field. Vol. trainer Hotline, Austin, 1993—. Mem.: ACA, Internat. Soc. for Study of Dissociation, Internat. Soc. Trauma and Stress Studies, Soc. for Shamanic Practitions, Soc. Spiritual Regression. Democrat. Jewish. Avocations: sewing, birdwatching, custom jewelry. Office: Cicada Recovery Svcs 3004 S 1st St Austin TX 78704-6388 Office Phone: 512-440-9082. Personal E-mail: karencicada@sbcglobal.net.

HUTCHINSON, ANN, management consultant; b. East Stroudsburg, Pa., May 15, 1950; d. David Ellis and Susie (Ingalls) Hutchinson; m. Paul Harrison McAllister, Jan. 2, 1986. BS in Vocat. Edn., Fla. Internat. U., 1985; MBA, Pepperdine U., 1990. Cert. advanced vocat. tchr. Fla., cmty. coll. educator Ariz., pub. mgr., quality award examiner Ariz., 1997, Ariz. Tech. Integrity Coun., 2002. Motorcycle technician, Ft. Lauderdale, Fla., 1973-78; machinist, 1978-79; instr., motorcycle tech. Sheridan Vocat. Tech. Sch., Hollywood, Fla., 1979-85; adminstr., tng. program Am. Honda Motorcycle Divsn., Torrance, Calif., 1985-86, curriculum developer motorcycles svc. tech., 1986-90, coll. program coord., 1990-92; edni. devel. dir. Clinton Tech. Inst., Phoenix, 1994-96; dep. mgr. tng. unit Ariz. State Dept. Econ. Security, Phoenix, 1996-99, mgmt. cons. office of total quality, 1999-2001; instrnl. sys. specialist Bur. Land Mgmt. Nat. Tng. Ctr., 2001—. Adj. faculty Ariz. State U., 2001—; chmn. high tech. acad. steering com. Pasadena (Calif.) United Sch. Dist., 1991—94; mem. cert. pub. mgr. program adv. bd. Ariz. State U., 1998—2001; cons. in field. Examiner Gov.'s Award for Excellence, 1997—99; mem. Ams. With Disabilities Act com. Ariz. Dept. Econ. Security, 1995—2001; mem. Desert Hill Improvement Assn., 1996—, bd. dirs., editor, 1998—99, v.p., 1999—2001, pres., 2001—04, comm. dir., 2004—; exec. v.p., sec. North County Conservancy, 2003—. Recipient State of Ky. Col. award, 1990, Ariz. State Quality award, Tech. Integrity Coun., 2003—. Mem.: ASTD, Am. Vocat. Assn., Vocat. Indsl. Clubs Am. (co-chmn. motorcycle tech. com. 1988—90, 1994—95, automotive nat. tech. com. 1990—94, adv. Hollywood, Fla. 1979—85), Cert. Pub. Mgr. Assn., Am. Motorcycle Assn., Toastmasters Internat. (Zenge Miller cert. 1996—). Avocation: Avocations: hiking, camping, st. motorcycle riding. Office: Bur Land Mgmt Nat Tng Ctr Renewable Resources 9828 N 31 Ave Phoenix AZ 85051 Office Phone: 602-906-5640. Personal E-mail: behomes@attglobal.net.

HUTCHINSON, EDNA M., home care nurse; b. Phoenix, Mar. 13, 1940; d. William Henry and Mary L. Hutchinson; children: Wendell, Antoinette, Lynette, Mary Maxine. Cert., San Diego C.C., 1981, Grossmont C.C., El Cajon, Calif., 1988. Cert. electrocardiographic technologist, Calif.; sec. sci. lab. Calif. Nurse asst., Phoenix, 1965—66, San Diego, 1966—69; med. asst. Med. Clinic, San Diego, 1980—85; electrocardiogram tech. Maricopa County Hosp., Phoenix, 1989—91; home care nurse Home Health Care, San Diego, 1991—. Songwriter Hill Top Records, Hollywood, Calif., 2000—. Author: (book) Inspiration Songs and Poems, 2000; songwriter In the Beginning, 2000, Jesus in the Inside, 2000; author: Etches in Time, 1997, (songs) God Creation, 2000; co-author: Best Poems and Poets, 2000, Poetry's Elite's Best Poets of 2001, 2001; contbr. over 400 poems to pubs. Daycare provider County of Riverside, Calif., 2001. Finalist Top Model, San Diego, Calif., 1976; named Ten Best Dressed, 1983; recipient Editor's Choice award for Outstanding Achievement in Poetry, State of Md., 1997, Poet of Merit award, Internat. Soc. Poets, 1997, Achievement award, Creative Writing Skills, 1999, Cert., Wall of Tolerance Nat. Campaign, 2001. Avocations: reading, music, songwriting.

HUTCHINSON, FRANCINE NELSON, biology educator, consultant; b. Sarasota, Fla., Aug. 15, 1949; d. Franklin and Evelyn Jewell Nelson; m. Bruce Hutchinson, June 16, 1989; children: Mary East, Jacob Kohute, Ruth Kohute Kimberly. MS in Biology, Jacksonville State U., Ala., 1998. Cert. tchr. Nat. Bd. for Profl. Tchg. Standards, 2005. Sci. tchr. Ranburne H.S., Ala., 1998—2005; biology tchr. Jacksonville H.S., 2005—. Environ. edn. cons., 1991—. Wilderness chairperson Ala. Environ. Coun., Birmingham, 1991—2000. Named Water Quality Monitor of the Yr., Ala. Water Watch Assn., 1997; recipient Malcom Stewart award, Ala. Environ. Coun.; grantee, Southtrust Bank of Ala., 1996, Nat. Bd. Cert. Classroom grantee, Ala. Dept. of Edn., 2006. Mem.: Alpha Delta Kappa (assoc.; mem.). Democrat-Npl. Avocations: kayaking, hiking, gardening, music, sewing. Home: 105 Shamrock Rd Anniston AL 36207 Office: Jacksonville High School 1000 George Douthit Dr SW Jacksonville AL 36265 Office Phone: 256-435-4177.

HUTCHINSON, GLENDA DAGUE, elementary school educator, small business owner; b. Connellsville, Pa., Dec. 17, 1971; d. Glenn Reed and Dina Rae Dague; m. Jason Devan Hutchinson, Dec. 22, 2001; 1 child, Noah Reed. BS in Elem. Edn., Pa. State U., University Park, 1993. Cert. elem. tchr. Pa., 1993, mid-Level Math tchr. Pa., 2003. Tchr. Lafayette Sch., Uniontown, Pa., 1999—; co-owner Tribal Sisters Jewelry, Hopwood, Pa., 2003—. Nominee Am. Tchr. award, Disney, 2002, 2006; recipient Tchr. of Yr. award, Wal-Mart, 2005. Mem.: Uniontown Area Edn. Assn., Penn. State Edn. Assn. Republican. Methodist.

HUTCHINSON, JANET LEE CLARK, elementary school educator; b. Belle Fourche, S.D., July 18, 1955; d. Straitor and Elaine Clark; m. Michael Hutchinson, May 28, 1977; children: Cody Ryan, Josie Renee. AA, Sheridan Coll., Sheridan, Wyo., 1975; ME, U.Wyo., Laramie, Wyo., 2001; BS in Elem. Edn., Black Hills State Univ., Spearfish, S.D., 1977. Cert. Elem. Edn. Wyo. Profl. Tchg. Standards Bd., 1977. Kindergarten tchr. Moorcroft Elem. Sch., Moorcroft, Wyo., 1977—79; homebound tutor Crook County Sch. Dist. # 1, Moorcroft, Wyo., 1979—85; rural sch. tchr. Kitty Moats Sch., Osage, Wyo., 1989—. Adult edn. instr. Ea. Wyo. Coll., Torrington, Wyo., 1983—91; substitute tchr. Weston County Sch. Dist. #1, Newcastle, Wyo., 1985—89; adult edn. instr. Ea. Wyo. Coll., Torrington, Wyo., 2001—04. Presenter (edn.) Meeting Educational Standards through Play. Mem. Moorcroft Recreation Bd., Moorcroft, Wyo., 1983—85; sec. Newcastle Centennial Com., Newcastle, Wyo., 1987—92; ch. sch. tchr. Christ Episcopal Ch., Newcastle, Wyo., 1985—99; sec./treas./mem. Weston County Fair Bd., Newcastle, Wyo. Recipient Wyo. Educator of the Week, Wyo. Student Loan Corp., 1996. Mem.: NEA, Nat. Sci. Tchrs. of Am., Nat. Assn. for the Edn. of Young Children, Internat. Soc. for Tech. in Edn., 4-H (leader, Outstanding 4H Leader 1993, Oustanding 4H Alumni), Order of the Ea. Star (grand electa 2004—05, 25 yr. mem. 1999, Grand Electa 2004—05), Delta Kappa Gamma (sec. 2002—04). Episcopalian. Achievements include Significant Contbn. to Edn; Outstanding Female Student, Sheridan Coll., 1977. Avocations: life long learner, antiques, cooking, sewing, outdoors. Home: 200 Third Ave Newcastle WY 82701-2431

HUTCHISON, BARBARA BAILEY, singer, songwriter; Recipient Grammy award for Best Musical Album for Children "Sleepy Time Lullabyes", 1996. E-mail: barbara@bbhsings.com.

HUTCHISON, DORRIS JEANNETTE, retired microbiologist, educator; b. Carrsville, Ky., Oct. 31, 1918; d. John W. and Maud (Short) H. BS, Western Ky. U., 1940; MS, U. Ky., 1943; PhD, Rutgers U., 1949. Instr. Russell Sage Coll., 1942-44, Vassar Coll., 1944-46; research asst. Rutgers U., 1946-48, research assoc., 1948-49; instr. Wellesley Coll., 1949-51; asst. Sloan-Kettering Inst., N.Y.C., 1951-56, assoc., 1956-60, assoc. mem., 1960-69, mem., 1969-90, mem. emeritus, 1990—, sect. head, 1956-90, acting chief div. exptl. chemotherapy, 1965-66, div. chief drug resistance, 1967-72, co-head lab. exptl. tumor therapy, 1973-74, lab. head drug resistance and cyto-regulation, 1973-84, coordinator field edn., 1975-81. Instr. Sloan-Kettering div. Cornell U. Grad. Sch. Med. Sci., N.Y.C., 1952-53, rsch. assoc., 1953-54, asst. prof., 1954-58, assoc. prof., 1958-70, prof. microbiology, 1970-90, prof. emeritus, 1990—, chmn. biology unit, 1968-74, assoc. dir., 1974-87; assoc. dean Cornell U. Grad. Sch. Med. Sci., 1978-87, asst. dean Cornell U., Ithaca, 1978-87; mem. Meml. Sloan-Kettering Cancer Ctr., 1984-90, mem. emeritus, 1990—; del. dir. Am. Cancer Soc., Inc., 1986-90. Bd. dirs. Westchester div. Am. Cancer Soc., 1976-90, exec. com., 1976-91; project chmn. Target 5, 1977-80, v.p., 1979-81, pres., 1981-83, sec., 1983-87, charter mem. So. Westchester Unit, 1984, pres., 1984-86. Named to Order of Ky. Cols., 1988; recipient Disting. Alumna, Western Ky. U., 2003; faculty fellow, Vassar Coll., 1946, USPHS fellow, 1951—53, Phillippe Found. fellow, Paris, 1959, Dorris J. Hutchison fellowship established in her honor, 1999. Fellow N.Y. Acad. Sci., Am. Acad. Microbiology (charter), N.Y. Acad. Medicine (assoc.); mem. AAAS, Am. Assn. for Cancer Edn., Am. Assn. Cancer Research (emeritus), Harvey Soc., Genetics Soc. Am., Am. Inst. Nutrition, Am. Soc. for Microbiology (hon., councilor N.Y.C. br. 1954-58, pres. N.Y.C. br. 1958-60, nat. councilor 1961-63, chmn. nat. meeting 1967, mem. pres.'s fellowship com. 1973-76, chmn. 1975-76), Soc. for Cryobiology (hon. mem.), Am. Genetic Assn., Internat. Soc. Biochem. Pharmacology, N.Y. Soc. Ky. Women (pres. 1988—), N.Y. Found. Ky. Women (pres. 1990-2000), Bronxville Field Club, Elizabeth Hamilton Cullem Svc. Club, 2000—. Achievements include numerous publs. antibiotics and chems. effective in treatment of Tb and leukemia, reports on mechanisms explaining how leukemic cells become resistant to treatment; searches for more effective antileukemia drugs. Home: Stoneridge Unit 4504 186 Jerry Browne Rd Mystic CT 06355

HUTCHISON, EDNA RUTH, artist; b. Paoli, Ind., Mar. 7, 1920; d. Charles Floyd and Ora May (Agan) Wright; m. William Ira Hutchison, Mar. 24, 1940; 1 child, Carol Ann Hutchison Wyatt. Student, Ind. U., 1940—46, student, 1957—60. Exhibitions include Brown County Art Gallery, 1960—61, Indiana U., 1961, Morton West Coll., Chgo., 1965, Port St. Lucie Libr., Fla., 1994, others. Teddy Bear lady Treasure Coast Cmty. AIDS Network, Ft. Pierce, Fla., 1997, Christmas Kids St. Lucie County, Ft. Pierce, Fla., 1997—. Recipient 1st pl. oil painting, Nat. League/Am. Penwomen, 1990, 1992, 2nd pl. oil painting, 1991, 1994, 1995, 2nd pl. needlepoint classic, Scripps Aux., 1986. Mem.: Nat. League Am. Pen Women. Avocations: writing, jewelry making, travel, decorating, crafts.

HUTCHISON, HEATHER NICOLE, secondary school educator; b. Jonesboro, Ark., Sept. 1, 1981; d. Eric Lavern and Phyllis Anne Kieffner; m. Daniel Curtis Hutchison, May 8, 2004. BS in Biology, Ark. State U., Jonesboro, 2004. Cert. sci. tchr. grades 7-12 Ark. Dept. Edn., 2004. Earth sci. tchr. Nettleton Pub. Schs., Jonesboro, 2004—05; biology and physics tchr. Valley View H.S., Jonesboro, 2005—. Republican. Baptist. Avocations: travel, cooking, outdoor activities. Office Phone: 870-932-3737.

HUTCHISON, KAY BAILEY, senator; b. Galveston, Tex., July 22, 1943; d. Allan and Kathryn Bailey; m. Ray Hutchison; four children. BA, U. Tex., 1992, LLB, 1967. Bar: Tex. 1967, US Supreme Ct., 1977. TV news reporter, Houston, 1969-71; pvt. practice law, 1969-74; press sec. to Anne Armstrong Rep. Nat. Com., 1971; vice-chair Nat. Transp. Safety Bd., 1976-78; asst. prof. U. Tex., Dallas, 1978-79; sr. v.p., gen. counsel Republic Bank Corp., Dallas, 1979-81; pntr. Boyd-Levinson, Ltd., Houston and Dallas, 1981-91; mem. Tex. Ho. of Reps., 1972-76; elected treas. State of Tex., 1990; US Senator from Tex. Washington, 1993—. Chmn., bd. visitors, US Military Acad. at West Point, US Delegate to Commn. on Security and Cooperation in Europe (The Helsinki Commn.); owner McCraw Candies; co-founder Fidelity Nat. Bank; mem. com. appropriations, US Senate, com. commerce, sci., and transp., com.rules and adminstrn., com. veterans affairs. Author: (books) American Heroines: The Spirited Women Who Shaped Our Country, 2004. Recipient Eagle award valued commitment to our nation's Hispanic Cmty., 1993, Silver Ingot Ward Coastal Conservation Assn, 1997, CLEAT award, 2000, Nat. Family Mil. Assn. award, 2001, Nat. Leadership award Hispanic Assn. Coll. and U., 2002, Congl. Leadership award Women's Fgn. Policy Grp., 2004, Disting. Pub. Svc. award Alliance for Aging Rsch., 2004, Adam Smith Fed. Elected Official medal Bus. Industry Polit. Action Com., 2004, Wetland Sponser of Yr. award Ducks Unlimited, 2005, Disting. Pub. Svc. award Am. Legion Nat. Comdr., 2006; named Rep. Woman of Yr. Nat. Fedn. Rep. Women, 1995, Outstanding U. Tex. Alumnus, 1995, Texan of Yr. Tex. Legis. Conf., 1997, Mr. South Tex. Washington's Birthday Celebration Assn.,2005, Legislator of Yr. Deep East Tex. Coun. of Govt., 2005; named to Tex. Women's Hall of Fame, 1997, named one of 100 Most Influential Texas Women of the Century Tex. Women's Chamber of Commerce, 1999, 100 Most Powerful Women in World, Forbes mag., 2005. Fellow, U. Tex. Law Alumni Assn. (pres. 1985-86). Republican. Episcopalian. Office: US Senate 284 Russell Senate Bldg Washington DC 20510-4304 also: District Office Ste 1160 Lock Box 606 10440 North Central Expressway Dallas TX 75231-2223 Office Phone: 202-224-5922, 214-361-3500. Office Fax: 202-224-0776, 214-361-3502.*

HUTCHISON, MONICA LEIGH, music educator; b. Lubbock, Tex., Sept. 15, 1971; d. G. Q. Nell and Glenda Helfrich; m. Mike V. Hutchison, Dec. 19, 1998; children: Hannah Leigh, Maggie Kay. B in Vocal Performance, Tex. Tech U., Lubbock, 1994, M in Vocal Performance, 1999. All-Level Teacher's Cert. in Music Tex., 1998. Choir dir. Lubbock ISD, Tex., 1996—98; music tchr. Allen ISD, Tex., 1998—2000, McKinney ISD, Tex., 2000—. Author: (music curriculum) MISD Elementary Music Curriculum; singer: (soloist) Lord Nelson Mass, Elijah, Messiah; actor: (role of the queen) Once Upon a Mattress. Youth sponsor First United Meth. Ch., Lubbock, Tex., 1995—97; youth choir dir. Stonebridge United Meth. Ch., McKinney, Tex., 2001—03, nursery helper, 2004—06. Mem.: TMEA (life), OAKE (life), Mu Phi Epsilon (life; chaplain 1992—93), Kappa Alpha Theta (life). Liberal. Methodist. Avocations: singing, travel, interior decorating. Home: 504 Clover Leaf Ln Mc Kinney TX 75070 Office: Wolford Elem 6951 Berkshire Ave Mc Kinney TX 75070 Office Phone: 469-742-4700. Office Fax: 469-742-4701. Personal E-mail: monica.hutchison@comcast.net. Business E-Mail: mhutchison@mckinneyisd.net.

HUTSELL, JANICE, nurse midwife; d. Charles Gummerson and Bettie Fortson; m. Anselm Davis; children: Shawn Davis, Stephen Davis. Diploma in nursing-midwifery, Meharry Med. Coll., Nashville, Tenn., 1976; BS in Edn., SUNY, Albany, 1986; MA in Human Behavior, Nat. U., San Diego, Calif., 1989; PhD in Psychology, Kennedy-Western U., Cheyenne, Wyo., 2004. RN Calif., Wis., Tex. Co-owner Best Start Birth Ctr., San Diego, 1979—89; faculty U. Calif., 1989—91, Baylor Coll. Medicine, Houston, 1993—96, U. Tex., Galveston, 1996—98; dir. midwifery svcs. Sis. Charity, St. John Hosp., Nassau Bay, 1998—2000; nurse midwide, sex counselor pvt. practice, Pearland, 2000—; lectr. sexual sci. Sexual Sems. Scholars, 2002—. Mem.: Am. Assn. Sex Educators, Counselors and Therapists, Am. Coll. Nurse Midwives, Mensa. Office: Sexual Sems Scholars 8325 Broadway Ste 202-1 Pearland TX 77584

HUTSON, BETTY SWITZER, art educator, artist; b. Brunswick, Mo., Aug. 14, 1930; d. Henry William and Pearl Evelyn (Sayler) Switzer; m. Don L. Hutson, Sept. 7, 1952; children: Eric, Sheila Hutson, Robin Hutson-Montoya, Heather Hutson. BFA, Ctrl. Meth. U., 1952; postgrad., U. Mo., 1953-54, Kansas City Art Inst., 1958-60, Avila Coll., 1981; MA in Art Edn., U. Mo., Kansas City, 1986. Cert. tchr. grades K-12, Mo. Elem. art cons. Md. Pub. Schs., Rockville, 1954-58; art instr. Ruskin High Sch., Hickman Mills, Mo., 1958-60, East High Sch., Kansas City, Mo., 1961-62, N.E. Sr. High Sch., Kansas City, 1964-65; dir. edn. All Souls Unitarian Ch., Kansas City, 1975-77; art instr. Westport Jr. High Sch., Kansas City, 1977-87; art instr., cons. De LaSalle Edn. Ctr., Kansas City, 1987-88; art instr. Nelson Mus. Art, Kansas City, 1987-88; visual arts resource tchr. Kansas City Middle Sch. Arts, 1988—99; ret., 1999. Art instr. U. Md., College Park, summer, 1956; resource cons. U. Mo., Kansas City, 1984-86; arts ptnrs. devel. Kansas City Sch. Dist. Learning Exch., 1985-86; curriculum author, task force mem. Kansas City Middle Sch. the Arts, 1988-90, Paseo Acad. Fine & Performing Arts, Kansas City, 1988-90; supervising tchr. student and practicum tchrs. Rockhurst Coll., Kansas City, 1976-92, Avila Coll., Kansas City, 1976-92, U. Mo., Kansas City, 1976-92, 94, Truman U., 1996-97, Park U., 1997-98. Author: Sampling the Basics, 1985; one-woman shows include Unitarian Gallery, 1987, 2001, Lebanon Gallery, 1988, Tchrs. Credit Union Gallery, 1989—90, Open Studios, 2000, 2002, 2004, Le Fou Frog, 2002—03, Ashby Hodge Gallery Am. Art, Fayette, Mo., 2005, Bistro 303, 2006, Makiato's Espresso Cafe, 2006, exhibited in group shows at Unitarian Gallery, Kansas City, 1985, 1987, 1989, 1991, 1993, 1995, 1997, 1999, 2001, 2003, 2004, Nelson Mus. Art, 1989, Fed. Res. Bank, 1990, Kaw Valley Gallery, 1990, Blue Springs (Mo.) Art Exhbn., 1990, 1991, Heartland Art Festival, St. Joseph, Mo., 1990—93, Allied Arts Coun., St. Joseph, 1990—93, Bruce Watkins Cultural Ctr., Kansas City, 1993—95, Muse Gallery, 1995, Kansas City Artists Coalition, 2000, 2002, 2004, 2005, 2006, Ashby-Hodge Art Gallery, 2001, Cultures w/o Borders Exhbn., 2001, Open Studios, 2001—02, others; illustrator Children's History of CME Church, 1997. Den mother, art leader Boy Scouts Am., Raytown, Mo., 1967—69, Girl Scouts Am., Raytown, 1969—75; vol. AIDSWalk, 1998, 1999, 2000, 2001, 2002, 2003, 2004, 2006, Habitat for Humanity, 1992, 1993, 1994, 1996, 2002—06, soup kitchen Ward Chapel AME, 1999—, World Federalists, Kansas City, 1989—, Scholastic Arts Regional Com.; vol., fundraiser Peaceworks, Kansas City, 1986—; vol., leader, officer PTA, Kansas City, 1965—76, Jr. Gt. Books, Picture Lady, Headstart, Planned Parenthood, Friends of the Zoo; trustee All Souls Unitarian-Universalist, 1976—79, 1996—99; vol. usher various orgns.; bd. dirs. Unitarian Gallery, 1989—, chairperson, 2004—, curator Elizabeth Layton exhibit, 1992. Recipient Disting. Svc. award All Souls Unitarian Ch., Kansas City, 1977, Outstanding Tchr. award Westport Jr. High Sch., Kansas City, 1987, Excellence in Tchtg. Art award, 1995. Mem.: AAUW (v.p. 2002—06, art study club 2002—), Mo. Mid. Sch. Assn., Friends of Art-Nelson Mus. Art, Mo. Art Edn. Assn. (Outstanding Art Tchr. 1992), Art Edn. Connection (Svc. award 1991—92), Nat. Art Edn. Assn., Kansas City Artists Coalition, Demeters (v.p. 1965—68, pres. 1978—80, v.p. 1979, 1989, pres. 1990—91, co-pres. 2001—03, Svc. award 1987). Democrat. Unitarian Universalist. Avocations: travel, swimming, gardening, drawing, painting. Home: 7625 Baltimore Ave Kansas City MO 64114-1813

HUTSON-COMEAUX, SARAH LOUISE, psychology professor, department chairman; b. Dover, Ohio, June 19, 1969; d. Lawrence Raymond and Carol Diane Hutson; m. James Francis Comeaux, Aug. 12, 1995; children: Abigail Marie, Isabella Dyann, Malcolm Xavier. BS, Denison U., Granville, Ohio, 1991; MS, Purdue U., West Lafayette, Ind., 1993, PhD, 1997. Vis. prof. psychology Denison U., Granville, 1997—2001, asst. prof. psychology, 2001—04, assoc. prof. psychology, 2004—, chairperson dept. psychology, 2006—. Mem.: Assn. Psychol. Sci., APA. Office: Denison Univ Dept Psychology PO Box M Granville OH 43023 Office Phone: 740-587-6675. Office Fax: 740-587-5675. Business E-Mail: hutson@denison.edu.

HUTSON COUNCELL, JANET KERN, retired secondary school educator; b. Denton, Md., Nov. 27, 1924; d. Clarence J. and Mildred R. (Ramsdell) Kern; m. Wallace Edward Hutson, Mar. 14, 1945 (dec. Mar. 1992); children: Wallace Edward Hutson, Janet Kaye Hutson Magaha; m. William S. Councell, Oct. 6, 1996 (dec. Feb. 2000). Student in cosmetology, Georgia Maude Beauty Sch., Balt., 1941—42; cert. in Vocat. Cosmetology Tchg., U. Md., Coll. Park, 1967, cert. in Vocat. Cosmetology with M equivalency, 1977. Lic. cosmetology tchr. Md. Owner, operator Janet's Beauty Shoppe Salons, Denton and Goldsboro, Md., 1942—74. Tchr. cosmetology Caroline Vocat. Ctr., Ridgely, Md., 1966—87; adv. Vocat. Indsl. Clubs Am.; mfr. Kura Kreme Cosmetic Cream. Chmn. Keep Md. Beautiful Com. of Caroline County; mayor Town of Denton, 1984; treas. Caroline County Dem. State Ctrl. Com., 1986—90; bd. dirs. St. Luke's Meth. Ch., Denton, 1964; pres. United Meth. Women, 1965—67, fin. chmn., 1979—82, trustee, 1987—. Named Woman of Yr., Gov. Md., 1980. Mem.: NEA, Md. Cosmetologists Assn. (3d v.p. 1967—68, 2d v.p. 1968—69), Ea. Shore Cosmetologists Assn. (pres. 1955—57), Caroline County Bus. and Profl. Women's Club, Inc. (pres. 1974—76, state chaplain 1976—77), Md. Fedn. Bus. and Profl. Women (1st v.p. 1979—80, pres. 1980—81), Md. Bus. and Profl. Women's Club, Inc. (2d v.p. 1978—79), Caroline County Tchrs. Assn. (1st v.p. 1976—77, pres. 1977—78, chmn. polit. action 1980—83), Md. State Tchrs. Assn. (dir.), Md. Assn. Tech. Trade Indsl. Educators (past pres.), Md. Vocat. Assn. (pres.), Am. Vocat. Assn., Denton C. of C. (treas. 1979—81), Caroline County Commn. Aging (chmn. 1972—74), Ea. Shore Ladies (pres. Oriental Shrine 1990—91), Order Ea. Star, Bethany House Aux. (charter pres. 1964—65), Ladies of Elks, Ladies Shriners, Iota Lambda Sigma. Home: PO Box 125 Goldsboro MD 21636-0125

HUTTER, TERESA ANN, art educator; b. Great Bend, Kans., Jan. 25, 1952; d. Harry and Wilma Witterstaetter; children: Trina, Troy. BA in Art Edn., U. Ctrl. Okla., 1987. Nat. bd. cert. tchr. Tchr. art Mustang Pub. Schs., Okla., 1988—; tchr. art camp So. Nazarene U., Bethany, Okla., 1996—2000; host Internat. Children's Art Exhbn., 1995, 2001; tchr. art Jr. Tng. Pks. Assn. Edn. program Okla. C.C., 1994—95. Okla. state judge state reflections program PTA, Oklahoma City, 1996—97. Mem.: NEA, Mustang Area Reading Coun., Nat. Art Edn. Assn., Okla. Edn. Assn., Okla. Art Edn. Assn. (sec. 1992—94, treas. 1994—98, chmn. young talent in Okla. 1998—2000, chmn. we. region div. 1998—2000, chmn. Okla. elem. div. 2000—04, pres. 2006—, newsletter editor 2004—, Okla. Elem. Art Educator of Yr. 1995, Okla. Art Educator of Yr. 2000, Youth Arts Month Svc. award 1996, 2000), Delta Kappa Gamma (music chmn. 2000—01). Republican. Methodist. Avocations: reading, pottery, flute, hand bells. Office: Mustang Pub Schs 906 S Heights Dr Mustang OK 73064 Office Phone: 405-376-2409. E-mail: huttert@mustangps.org.

HUTTNER, CONSTANCE S., lawyer; b. Youngstown, Ohio, 1958; BS in Cellular Immunology, Ohio State U., 1977; JD magna cum laude, Boston Coll., 1980. Bar: NY 1981. Ptnr., patent litigation Skadden, Arps, Slate, Meagher & Flom, LLP, NYC. Co-chmn., Patent Litigation Seminar Practising Law Institute, 2001. Author: Unfit for Jury Determination: Complex Civil Litigation and the Seventh Amendment Right of Trial By Jury, Boston Coll. Law Review, Vol. XX, No. 3, 1979, Markman Practice, Procedures and Tactics, Patent Litigation, Practising Law Inst., 1999, 2000, Markman Practice, Procedures and Tactics, Patent Litigation Strategies Handbook, ABA

Sect. of Intellectual Property Law, 2000. Order of the Coif. Mem.: Am. Intellectual Property Law Assn., NY Intellectual Property Law Assn., Phi Beta Kappa. Office: Skadden Arps Slate Meagher & Flom LLP 4 Times Sq New York NY 10036 Office Phone: 212-735-2038. Office Fax: 917-777-2038. Business E-Mail: chutter@skadden.com.

HUTTON, CAROLE LEIGH, newspaper editor; b. Framingham, Mass., Aug. 23, 1956; d. James and Norma Inez (Vitali) Hamilton; m. Tom Huff. B Journalism, Mich. State U., 1978. Editor Natick (Mass.) Sun, 1978—79; reporter, city editor, mng. editor Hammond (Ind.) Times, 1979—87; dir. publs. CNA Ins. Cos., Chgo., 1987—88; day city editor, accent editor Detroit News, 1988—90; city editor Detroit Free Press, 1992—95, dep. mng. editor for news, 1995—96, mng. editor, 1996—2002, exec. editor, 2002—03, pub. and editor, 2004—05; with Knight Ridder Co., 2005—. Tutor Detroit Pub. HS, 1994—94. Named one of 100 Most Influential Women in S.W. Mich., Crain's Detroit Bus.; recipient Local News Coverage award, Hoosier State Press Assn., 1982. Mem.: AP Mng. Editors, Mich. AP Editors Assn. (pres., bd. dirs. 2000—), Am. Soc. Newspaper Editors, IAP Mng. Editors.

HUTTON, LAUREN (MARY LAURENCE HUTTON), model, actress; b. Charleston, S.C., Nov. 17, 1943; d. Laurence Hutton. Student, U. Fla., Sophia Newcombe Coll. Fashion model, 1960—. Actress: (feature films) Paper Lion, 1968, Little Fauss and Big Halsey, 1970, Pieces of Dreams, 1970, The Gambler, 1974, Gator, 1976, Welcome to L.A., 1977, Viva Knievel!, 1977, A Wedding, 1978, American Gigolo, 1980, Zorro, the Gay Blade, 1981, Paternity, 1981, Lassiter, 1984, Once Bitten, 1985, A Certain Desire, 1986, Malone, 1987, Guilty As Charged, 1991, My Father, The Hero, 1994; (TV movies) Someone's Watching Me, 1978, Institute for Revenge, 1979, The Cradle Will Rock, 1983, Starflight: The Plane that Couldn't Land, 1983, Scandal Sheet, 1985, Timestalkers, 1987, Perfect People, 1988, Fear, 1990, 54, 1998; (TV series) The Rhinemann Exchange, 1977, Central Park West, 1995-96, (stage prodn.) Extremities.

HUXLEY, MARY ATSUKO, artist; b. Stockton, Calif., Mar. 5, 1930; d. Henry K. and Kiku H. (Kisanuki) Taniguchi; m. Harold Daniels Huxley, 1957. Student, Armstrong Coll., Berkeley, Calif., 1950, San Francisco Art Inst., 1968; pvt. studies with, Thomas C. Leighton, 1970—75. Art show judge regional art clubs, corps., pvt. orgns., and county fairs, 1972-2005. Solo shows include Artists' Coop., San Francisco, 1973, 75, 76, The Univ. Club Invitational, San Francisco, 1976, I. Magnin, San Mateo, 1976, Palo Alto Med. Found., 1992, Galerie Genese, San Mateo, 1993; exhibited in juried group shows at Catharine Lorillard Wolf Art Club, N.Y.C., 1979, Knickerbocker Artists of Am., N.Y.C., 1979, Salmagundi Club Ann., N.Y.C., 1981, Butler Inst. Am. Art, Youngstown, Ohio, 1982, Am. Artists Profl. League, N.Y.C., 1982, 83, 86, 87, 88, Oil Painters of Am. Ann. Nat. Juried Shows, Gallery at Long Grove, Ill., 1993, 94, Taos, N.Mex., 1997, Oil Painters of Am. Ann. Pacific Coast Regional Juried Show, Jones & Terwilliger Gallery, Carmel, Calif., 1997, San Francisco Ann. Art Festival, 1970-74, Renaissance Gallery, Santa Rosa, Calif., 1973, Paramount Theater, Oakland, Calif., 1974, Met. Club Invitational, San Francisco, Marin Soc. Artists Ann., Ross, Calif., 1976, 79, Soc. Western Artists Ann., San Francisco, 1976, 78, 80, Peninsula Art Assn. Ann., Belmont, Calif., 1980, Fresno (Calif.) Fashion Fair Ann., 1981, 84, De Saisset Gallery, U. Santa Clara, Calif., 1979, Lodi (Calif.) Ann. Grape and Art Festival, 1970, 71, 72, 73, 74, 75, 76, 77, 78, 79, 81, San Mateo County Ann. Floral Fiesta, 1975, 76, 77, 78, 79, 81, Charles & Emma Frye Mus. Gallery, Seattle, 1975, Redwood City Women's Club Ann. Flower Show, 1978, Fremont Art Assn. Anns., 1987, 88, 89, John Muir Med. Ctr. invitational, 1999-2000, 3 Com-Synopsis Invitational Traveling Exhibit, 2000-01; numerous others; represented in numerous pvt. and corp. collections in U.S., Europe and Asia. Recipient Marjorie Walter Spl. award San Mateo County Exhbn., 1975, Gold medallion and 1st award San Mateo County Fair Fine Arts Exhbn., 1976, Best of Show award Cultural Arts of Palo Alto and Palo Alto Art Club, 1979, Best of Show and 1st award U. Art Ctr. and Palo Alto Art Club Ann., 1981, Spl. Merit award Oakland Art Assn., John Muir Med. Ctr. Ann., 1989, 1st award Burlingame Art Soc. Anns., 1976, 77, 1st award Redwood City Women's Club Ann. Flower Show, 1978, 1st award Soc. Western Artists Palo Alto Med. Ctr. Ann., 1983, 1st award Soc. Western Artists John Muir Med. Ctr. Ann., 1986, 1st award Fremont Art Assn. Ann., 1989, numerous others. Fellow Am. Artists Profl. League; mem. Soc. Western Artists (signature, trustee 1986-97, bd. dirs. 1972-75, 98, chmn. juried exhbns. 1972-81), Oil Painters Am. (signature), Allied Artists Am., Marin Soc. Artists (signature). Studio: PO Box 5467 San Mateo CA 94402-0467

HUXTABLE, ADA LOUISE, architecture critic; b. N.Y.C. d. Michael Louis and Leah (Rosenthal) Landman; m. L. Garth Huxtable. AB magna cum laude, Hunter Coll.; postgrad., Inst. Fine Arts, NYU; degree (hon.), Harvard U., Yale U., NYU, Washington U., U. Mass., Oberlin Coll., Miami U., RI Sch. Design, U. Pa., Radcliffe Coll., Oberlin Coll., Smith Coll., Skidmore Coll., Md. Inst., Mt. Holyoke Coll., Trinity Coll., LaSalle U., Pace Coll., Pratt Inst., Colgate U., Hamilton U., Williams Coll., Rutgers U., Finch Coll., Emerson Coll., LI U., Cleve. State U., Bard Coll., Fordham U., Parsons Sch. Design, Mass. Coll. Art, Nottingham U. Asst. curator architecture and design The Museum of Modern Art, N.Y.C., 1946-50; Fulbright fellow for advanced study in architecture and design Italy, 1950, 52; free-lance writer, contbg. editor to Progressive Architecture and Art in America, 1950-63; architecture critic N.Y. Times, N.Y.C., 1963-82, mem. editorial bd., 1973-82; Cook lectr. in Am. instns. U. Mich., 1977; Hitchcock lect. U. Calif.-Berkeley, 1982. Corp. vis. com. Harvard U. Grad. Sch. Design, Sch. Visual and Environ. Arts; mem. adv. bd. Am. Trust Brit. Libr.; archtl. cons. Nat. Gallery, London, J. Paul Getty Trust, L.A., San Francisco Pub. Libr., Mus. Contemporary Art, Chgo., Kansas City Art Mus.; archtl. critic The Wall Street Jour., 1996—. Author: Pier Luigi Nervi, 1960, Classic New York, 1964, Will They Ever Finish Bruckner Boulevard?, 1970, Kicked a Building Lately?, 1976, The Tall Building Artistically Reconsidered: The Search for a Skyscraper Style, 1985, Goodbye History, Hello Hamburger 1986, Architecture Anyone? 1986, The Unreal America: Architecture and Illusion, 1997, Frank Lloyd Wright, 2004. Recipient 1st Pulitzer prize for disting. criticism, 1970, Spl. award Nat. Trust for Historic Preservation, 1971, Archtl. Criticism medal AIA, 1969, medal for lit. Nat. Arts Club, 1971, Diamond Jubilee medallion City N.Y., 1973, Mayor's Cultural award, 1984, Woman of Yr. award AAUW, 1974, Sec.'s award for conservation U.S. Dept. Interior, 1976, Thomas Jefferson medal U. Va., 1977, Archtl. Criticism medal Acad. d' Architecture Française, 1988; Guggenheim fellow for studies in Am. architecture, 1958, MacArthur fellow, 1981-86, fellow Ctr. for Scholars and Writers, N.Y. Pub. Libr., 1999-00; Henry Allen Moe prize Humanities Am. Philosophical Soc., 1992. Fellow Am. Acad. Arts and Scis., Royal Inst. Brit. Architects (hon.), AAAL; mem. AIA (hon.), Am. Acad. Arts and Letters, Soc. Archtl. Historians. Home: 969 Park Ave New York NY 10028-0322

HUYSMAN, ARLENE WEISS, psychologist, educator, writer; b. Phila., 1929; d. Max and Anna (Pearlene) Weiss; m. Pedro Camacho; children: Pamela Claire, James David. BA, Shaw U., 1973; MA, Goddard Coll., 1974; PhD, Union Inst. Grad., 1980. Diplomate Am. Bd. Psychol. Specialties, Med. Psychology, 1997. Actress, dir. Dramatic Workshop, N.Y.C., 1956—68; music and drama critic and columnist Orlando (Fla.) Sentinel Star, 1966—68; psychodramatist Volusia County Guidance Ctr., Daytona Beach, Fla., 1966—68; free-lance journalist, 1968—70; psychodramatist Psychiat. Inst. Jackson Meml. Hosp., Miami, 1972—77; dir. Adult Day Treatment Ctr., 1974—77, Lithium Clinic, 1976—77; psychodramatist South Fla. State Hosp., Hollywood, 1971—72; psychotherapy supr., Neurosci. program coord. Miami Heart Inst., 1984—; clin. dir. Family Workshop, 1985—, Adult Day Treatment Ctrs., 1987—; founder, dir. Geriatric Adult Day Treatment Ctrs. Adj. asst. prof. Med. Sch. U. Miami, 1976—; adj. prof. Union Inst., 1992—, Antioch U., 1995—; specialist in Bi Polar Disorders, U. Wis., 1980—. Author: A Mother's Tears, 1998, 2002, The Postpartum Effect: Deadly Depression in Mothers, 2003. Mem. adv. panel Fine Arts Coun. Fla., 1976—77. Recipient Best Dirs. award and Best Actress award, Fla. Theatre Festival, 1967. Mem.: APA, Fla. Assn. Practicing Psychologists (bd. dirs., pres.), World Fedn. Mental Health, Am. Assn. Group Psychotherapy and Psychodrama, Am. Soc. Aging, Internat. Assn. Group Psychotherapy, Mental Health Assn. Dade County, Dade County Psychol. Assn. (bd. dirs.), Fla. Psychol. Assn., Am. Coll. Forensic Examiners, Fedn. Partial Hospitalization Study Groups, Moreno Acad., Union Inst. Grad. Alumni Assn. (bd. dirs., southeastern rep., pres.-elect). Office: Ptnrs in Health 3050 Biscayne Blvd Miami FL 33137-4143 Office Phone: 305-571-9996. Personal E-mail: drhuysman@yahoo.com.

HUZAR, ELEANOR GOLTZ, historian, educator; b. St. Paul, June 15, 1922; d. Edward Victor and Clare (O'Neill) Goltz; m. Elias Huzar, June 21, 1950 (dec. Dec. 1950); m. Bruce I. Granger, Oct. 11, 1991. BA, U. Minn., 1943; MA, Cornell U., 1945, PhD, 1948. Instr. history Stanford U., Palo Alto, Calif., 1948-50; asst. prof. classics U. Ill., Urbana, 1951-55; assoc. prof. history S.E. Mo. Coll., Cape Girardeau, 1955-59; assoc. prof. classics Carleton Coll., Northfield, Minn., 1959-60; prof. history Mich. State U., East Lansing, 1960-90, chmn. program in classical studies, 1965-90. Mem. selection com. Nat. Endowment for Humanities, Washington, 1979-84, Coun. for Internat. Exchg. Scholars, Washington, 1979-81, Mich. Rhodes Scholars, Ann Arbor, 1981-84, Prix de Rome, Am. Acad., NYC, 1978-80. Author: Mark Antony: A Biography, 1978; contbr. articles and revs. to profl. jours. George Boldt fellow, Cornell U., 1947—48. Mem. Classical Assn. of Mid. West and South (pres. 1984-85), Am. Hist. Assn., Am. Philol. Assn., Archael. Inst. Am. (local pres. 1979-80), Mich. Classical Conf. (pres. 1984-85), Am. Acad. in Rome (adv. coun. 1963-92, exec. com. 1970-73, 88-92), Am. Sch. in Athens (mng. com. 1964-92), Phi Beta Kappa, Phi Kappa Phi. Democrat. Roman Catholic. Avocations: hiking, skiing, travel. Home: 2945 Lincoln Dr Apt 132 Saint Paul MN 55113-1341

HYATT, ANNA DALE, music educator; b. Waco, Tex., Nov. 14, 1950; d. George and Anna Dale Gibbs; m. Johnathon Gilbert Hyatt, Aug. 7, 1997; children: Julie Anna Neal, Casey Gibbs-Hood Pittman. BS, Tarleton State U., Stephenville, Tex., 1980. Cert. elem. tchr. Tex., 1980. Fifth grade tchr. St. Mary's Sch., West, Tex., 1984—85; elem. music tchr. China Spring ISD, Tex., 1985—. Dir.: (musical play) Annie, Tom Sawyer, (seasonal plays). Office: China Spring ISD PO Box 250 Bob Johnson China Spring TX 76633

HYDE, ALICE BACH, artist; b. Montgomery, Ala., Jan. 7, 1939; d. Orville Euing and Margaret Pinkney (Knowlton) Bach. BA, Auburn (Ala.) U., 1961. Intake officer foster home finder Atlanta Children's Home, 1962-65; fashion illustrator Gayfers Dept. Store, Montgomery, 1970-72; artist illustrator Ala. Dept. Pub. Health, Montgomery, 1972-86; self employed artist Longwood, Fla., 1986—, Orlando, Fla., 1986—. Artist: (posters) Winter Park sidewalk Art Festival, 1988, Lake Mary/Heathrow Arts Festival, 1988, Beach Break, 1989, Boats at Monterey, 1989; invited by Walt Disney World to paint in Epcot World Showcase Ctr. as part of first "Art in the Gardens" promotion, 1994; exhibited Nat. Arts Club, Pastel Soc. Show, N.Y.C., 1994. Recipient Purchase awards Pastel Soc. of Am., N.Y., 1988, Walt Disney World, 1990, Excellence awards Beaux Arts Festival of Arts, Miami, Fla., 1990, Mainsail Arts Festival, St. Petersburg, Fla., 1991, First Place in Category awards Plantation Art in the Pk., Fla., 1989, 90. Mem. Pastel Soc. Am. (Columbus Club for Excellence, 1989). Republican. Avocations: music, travel, gardening, tennis, antique collecting.

HYDE, DIANA CAROLINE, retired real estate agent; b. Bermuda, Oct. 22, 1924; arrived in U.S., 1948; d. Allan Chalmers and Elsie Joyce Smith; m. Bryden Bordley Hyde, Aug. 10, 1948 (dec.); children: Elizabeth Bordley Gamble, Stephen Bordley, Anne Blackburn, Jonathan Hinson. Diploma, Gloucestershire Tng. Coll. for Domestic Sci., 1946. Lic. real estate agt. Chef's asst. Thurlestone Hotel, Cheltenham, England, 1946; asst. to mgr. Horizons guest haven, Bermuda, 1946—47; real estate agt., assoc. broker Russell T. Baker/Coldwell Banker, Anne Arundel County, Md., 1980—92; ret., 1992. Presenter on history. Vol. Md. Hist. Soc., Balt., 1952—92, mem. coun., 1960—75, co-chmn. antiques show, 1977; mem. cmty. sch. com. Balt. City Pub. Schs., 1960; vol. cook harvest camp London County Coun. Schs., Farnsworth Village, England, 1945; vol. child life program Johns Hopkins Hosp., Balt.; mem. Friends of Balt. Mus. Art; chief Rep. election judge Pasadena, Md., 1980—; bd. dirs. women's guild St. Christopher by the Sea Ch., Gibson Island, Md., 1980—. Mem.: Nat. Bd. Realtors, Women in Arts, Walter Art Gallery, Winterthur Mus. Avocations: sewing, gardening, writing, watercolors, cooking. Home: PO Box 123 Gibson Island MD 21056 also: The Brae 4 Southcote Rd Paget 8604 Bermuda

HYDE, GERALDINE VEOLA, retired secondary school educator; b. Berkeley, Calif., Nov. 26, 1926; d. William Benjamin and Veola (Walker) H.; m. Paul Hyde Graves, Jr., Nov. 12, 1949 (div. Dec. 1960); children: Christine M. Graves Klykken, Catherine A. Graves Okerlund, Geraldine J. Graves Hansen. BA in English, U. Wash., 1948; BA in Edn., Ea. Wash. U., 1960, MA in Edn., 1962. Cert. tchr. K-16, Wash.; life cert. specialist in secondary edn., Calif. English educator Sprague (Wash.) Consol. Schs., 1960-62, Bremerton (Wash.) Sch. Dist., 1962-63, Federal Way (Wash.) Sch. Dist., 1963-66; English, journalism and Polynesian humanities educator Hayward (Calif.) Unified Sch. Dist., 1966-86; ret., 1986. Charter mem. Hist. Hawaii Found., Honolulu, 1977-; founding mem. The Cousteau Soc., Inc., Norfolk, Va., 1973-; life mem. Hawaiian Hist. Soc., Honolulu, 1978-; mem. Molokai Mus. and Cultural Ctr., Kaunakakai, 1986-, Bishop Mus. Assn., Honolulu, 1973-, Mission House Mus., Honolulu, 1994, Bklyn. Hist. Assn., N.Y., 1994, Berkshire Family History Assn., Pittsfield, Mass., 1994-, Richville (N.Y.) Hist. Assn., 1994-, Swanton (Vt.) Hist. Soc., 1998-, N.Y. Geneal. and Biog. Soc., 1999-, New Eng. Hist. Genealogic Soc., 1998-, Gouverneur Hist. Assn., NY, 1998-, New Wing Luke Asian Mus., Seattle, 1994, Upham Family Soc., Inc., Melrose, Mass., 2001-, Calif. Ret. Tchrs Assoc. 2003, RHS Golden Grads, 2006—. Mem. Libr. Congress Assocs. (charter), Nature Conservancy of Hawai'i, Smithsonian Inst. (contbg.), Nat. Geog. Soc., Nat. Trust Historic Preservation, U. Wash. Alumni Assn. (life), Ea. Wash. U. Alumni Assn. (life). Episcopalian. Avocations: historic and ecologic preservation, genealogy, shell collecting, needlecrafts, crafts. Home: 2050 Springfield Drive 470 Chico CA 95928

HYDE, M. DEBORAH, neurosurgeon; b. Laurel, Miss., Jan. 18, 1949; d. Sellus Hyde and Ann (Huff) McDonald; m. James Joseph Jackson, June 28, 1986. BS in Biology, Tougaloo Coll, Miss., 1970; MS in Biology, Cleve. State U., 1973; MD, Case Western Reserve U., Cleve., 1977. Diplomate Am. Bd. Neurol. Surgery. Resident Univ. Hosps., Cleve., 1978-82; neurosurgeon Guthrie Med. Ctr., Sayre, Pa., 1982-87; pvt. practice Canoga Pk., Calif., 1987—. Contbg. author: The Courage of Conviction, 1985. Mem. AMA, Congress Neurol. Surgeons, Nat. Med. Assn., Alpha Omega Alpha. Democrat.

HYDE, PAMELA SUZON, housing and human services administrator; b. Thayer, Mo., Nov. 7, 1950; d. Gaston Clark Hyde and Leta Vineta (Crass) Sponsler. Student, S.W. Bapt. U., 1968-70; BA, S.W. Mo. State U., 1972; JD, U. Mich., 1976. Law clk. Vedder, Price, Kaufman, Kammholz, Chgo., 1975; audio-visual media specialist law sch. U. Mich., Ann Arbor, 1974-76; VISTA atty. Ohio State Legal Svcs. Assn., Columbus, 1976-77; atty. Ohio Legal Rights Svc., Columbus, 1977-78, chief mental health unit, 1978-80, dir., 1980-83, Ohio Dept. Mental Health, Columbus, 1983-90, Ohio Dept. Human Svcs., Columbus, 1990-91, Seattle Dept. Human Svcs., 1991, Seattle Dept. Housing and Human Svcs., 1992—93; pres., CEO ComCare, 1994—96; sr. cons. Tech. Asst. Coll., 1996—2003; sec. N.Mex. Human Svcs. Dept., 2003—. Del. leader Mental Health Leader's People-to-People tour of USSR and China, 1987; mem. adv. com. Ctr. Cmty. Change, Burlington, Vt., 1989—. Reviewer: (jour.) Psychiatric Svcs., 1985—, Jour. Mental Health Policy Adminstrn., 1988—. Active Ohio Commodores, Columbus, 1983-90. Recipient Disting. Svc. to State Govt. award Nat. Govs.' Assn., 1987, Excellence in Case Mgmt. award Nat. Case Mgmt. Conf., Cin., 1990; named Young Woman of Achievement in Govt., Nat. Coun. Women, N.Y.C., 1984. Mem. Nat. Assn. State Mental Health Program Dirs. (pres. 1989-90), Mac Arthur Found. Networks on Mental Health Policy Rsch. and Mandated Cmty. Treatment, Women Execs. in State Govt. (founding mem.). Democrat. Avocations: hiking, golden retrievers, music. Home: 60 Balsa Rd Santa Fe NM 87508-8736 Office Phone: 505-827-7750.

HYDE, REBECCA MEDWIN, financial consultant; b. Frederick, Md., Aug. 30, 1947; d. William Herbert and Clella Evelyn Hyde. BA, Cath. U. Am., 1969; tchr. edn. cert., Towson State Coll., 1971; M Liberal Arts, Johns Hopkins U., 1973. Cert. fin. planner. Sr. jumbo underwriter, asst. v.p. Chase Home Mortgage Corp., Woodland Hills, Calif., 1988—95; fin. advisor Am. Express Fin. Advisors (now known as Ameriprise Finl.), Columbia, Md., 1995—. Guest lectr. U. Balt. Sch. Law, 2000—01. Mem.: Fin. Planning Assn. Home: 5764 Stevens Forest Rd # 421 Columbia MD 21045 Office: Ameriprise Fin 5764 Stevens Forest Rd Ste 421 Columbia MD 21045 Office Phone: 410-772-2397. E-mail: rebeccamhyde@yahoo.com.

HYDEN, DOROTHY LOUISE, consulting company owner; b. Fort Collins, Colo., July 19, 1948; d. Douglas Stewart and Elizabeth Lenore (Stewart) Neilson; m. Michael J. Daley, Dec. 27, 1969 (div.); 1 child, Shannon; m. Howard E. Hyden, July 17, 1976; children: Kent Stewart, Tiffany Nicole. BA, U. Calif., Santa Barbara, 1970; MBA, Pepperdine U., 1980. Head tchr. Sawyer Bus. Coll., Anaheim, Calif., 1974-75, admissions rep., 1975-76; mktg. specialist Anthony Schs., Orinda, Calif., 1976-77; adminstrv. dir. Escrow Tng. Ctr., Orinda, Calif., 1977-78; pvt. practice consulting Mpls., 1979-88; exec. v.p., owner Hyden & Hyden, Mpls., 1988—95; exec. v.p. Ctr. For Customer Focus, Colo. Springs, Colo., 1995—. Mem. ASTD, NAFE, PEN, NEHGS, Soc. Preservation New Eng. Antiquities, Wayland (Mass.) Hist. Soc., Pepperdine U. Alumni Assn., Internat. Platform Assn., Edmond Rice (1638) Assn., Clan MacKay Soc., Littleton Family Assn., Watertown Geneal. Soc., Milwaukee County Geneal. Soc., Wis. State Geneal. Soc. Republican. Episcopalian. Avocations: bridge, horseback riding, travel, languages. Home: 549 Vista Grande Dr Colorado Springs CO 80906-5825

HYDER, DEBORAH JEAN, elementary school educator; b. Crossville, Tenn., Jan. 20, 1958; d. John Dawson and Wilma Jean (Roberts) H. BMusEdn, George Peabody Coll. Tchrs., of Vanderbilt, 1980; MA, Mid. Tenn. State U., 1986. Cert. music educator K-12, Tenn. Mem. NEA, Tenn. Edn. Assn., Music Educators Nat. Con., Music Tchrs. Nat. Assn., North Cumberland PTO. Home: 70 Shadowmont Ct Crossville TN 38572 Business E-Mail: dhyder10@charter.net.

HYLAND, CHERYL C., health services administrator; b. Tulsa, Okla., Mar. 27, 1960; d. Clifford E. and Sue E. Foley; m. Thomas Patrick Hyland, June 1, 1985 (div. Sept. 1994); children: Kelli Sue, Sean Thomas. BS, Okla. State U., 1982; MEd, U. Okla., 1985. Lic. marriage and family therapist; cert. mediator. Primary clinician Heritage Treatment Ctr., Provo, UT, 1985-91, Shadow Mt. Hosp., Tulsa, Okla., 1991-92, dir. clin. outpatient svc. Bartlesville and Pawhuska, Okla., 1992-98; dir. therapeutic foster care Children's Med. Ctr., Tulsa, Okla., 1998—; asst. divsn. chair Tulsa Cmty. Coll., Okla., 1999—. Pres. Profl. Staff Orgn., Provo, Utah, 1987-88; instr., faculty liberal arts, Tulsa Cmty. Coll. Author: Essential Guide for Graduate Students, 1999. Mem. Habitat for Humanity, Tulsa, Okla., 1999. Recipient award of Appreciation for Crisis Intervention, Okla. City bombing, Gov. Okla. Clin. mem. Am. Assn. Marriage and Family Therapists. Methodist. Avocations: reading, collecting antiques. Office: Tulsa Comm Coll 3727 E Apache St Tulsa OK 74115-3150

HYLAND, VIRGINIA LING, small business owner; b. North Plainfield, N.J., Sept. 20, 1947; d. James C. and Juliet (Tchou) Ling.; m. Dale J. Hyland, June 7, 1967,(dec.); children: Devin K., Christopher. Cert. in Ct. Reporting, Tampa Coll., 1975. Dep. ofcl. Conley & Swain, St. Petersburg, Fla., 1975-76; reporter Jud. Reporters, St. Petersburg, 1976-77; reporter, owner Suncoast Reporting Svcs., St. Petersburg, 1977—. Mem. Fla. Ct. Reporters Assn. (bd. dirs. 1983-85, 87-89, chief examiner 1986-89, mem. coms., v.p. 1994-95, pres.-elect 1995-96, pres. 1996-97), Nat. Ct. Reporters (chief examiner 1986-89). Republican. Office Phone: 727-823-1876. Business E-Mail: vlhyland@suncoastreportingonline.com.

HYLE-WORBETS, MARY ELIZABETH, nurse; b. Pauls Valley, Okla., Feb. 27, 1973; d. Charlotte A. Gregory; m. Jon R. Worbets, Feb. 16, 1999; 1 child, Ava Rose Worbets. BSN, Thompson Rivers U., Kamloops, BC, Can., 2002; postgrad., U. Ala., Tuscaloosa, 2006. RN Tex. RN Corpus Christi Med. Ctr., Tex., 2002—04. Author: Quality Practice Environments. Vol. South Tex. Women's Shelter, Corpus Christi, 2004—05; mem. Planned Parenthood Action Network, NYC, 2003—. Recipient recognition for contbn. to health and wellness of families, Coastal Bend Family Counseling Ctr., 2006. Mem.: Tex. Ready Nurses, Am. Assn. Health Edn., US-Mex. Border Health Assn.

HYLLA, LINDA KAY, sister, social worker; b. Granite City, Ill., Mar. 1, 1961; d. Leonard Albert and Loretta Ann Hylla. BA, Fontbonne U., 1987; MSW, Wash. U., St. Louis, 1992. Entrance into Sisters of Divine Providence, 1980; LCSW 1995. Coord. youth and human svc., Granite City, Ill., 1992—95; child care worker St. Elizabeth Med. Ctr., Granite City, 1986—95, outpatient therapist, 1995—2000; vocations dir. Sisters of Divine Providence, Bridgeton, Mo., 2000—. Clin. supr. pvt. practice, Madison, Ill., 1998—; founder Quest Ho., Madison, Ill. Contbr. poetry poetry.com. Bd. dirs. New Opportunities, Madison, 1989—91; chmn. bd. Rm. at the Inn Homeless Shelter, St. Louis County, 2002—03. Named an Internat. Poet of Merit, Internat. Soc. of Poets, 2002; named to, Internat. Soc. Conf., 1999, TREND Hall of Fame, Nat. TREND Conf., St. Louis, 2000; Vocation grant, KC, 2003. Office: Sisters of Divine Providence 3415 Bridgeland Bridgeton MO 63044 Office Phone: 618-660-9736. Personal E-mail: srlindahylla@hotmail.com.

HYLLAND, SUE, sports association executive; Team capt., edn. 1998 & 2000 Olympic games Can. Olympic Assn.; exec. dir. Can. Assn. for Advancement of Women & Sport & Phys. Activity, 2000—; pres., CEO Canada Games Coun., Ottawa, Canada, 2002—. Office: Can Assn Adv Women & Sport & Phys Activ N 202-801 King Edward Ave Ottawa ON K1N 6n5 Canada

HYMAN, BETTY HARPOLE, technology executive; b. Jasper, Tex., Nov. 20, 1938; d. Russell Charles and John Francis (Hilton) Harpole; m. Arthur Siegmar Hyman (dec.); children: Norma Sullivan, Eric, Jonathan, Lee Ann BA Psychology, U. Tex., San Antonio, 1979. Coord. spl. project Tex. Stores, San Antonio, 1975—79; cons. comm. Southwestern Bell Tel., Midland, Tex. and San Antonio, 1980—82; tech. cons. AT&T/Lucent Technologies, San Antonio, 1983—85; cons. IMS Group, San Antonio, 1985—87; tech. cons. Intelliserve Corp., Dallas, 1987—88; ret., 2000; comm. specialist W/IG Comm., 2001—05; comm. specialist, comm. svcs. IG Comm., 2005—. Singer: Sweet Adelines, 2002—. Vol., mem. devel. com. San Antonio Spl. Olympics, 1985—; mem. devel. com. San Antonio Conservation Soc., 1975—, San Antonio World Affairs Coun., 1985—92, 1994—; mentor Coaching for Success, 2000—01; mem. Alamo Metro Chorus, 2002—; sec. bd. trustees Unity Ch., 2001—06; bd. trustees, 2001—06; bd. dirs. South Tex. Children's Habilitation Ctr., San Antonio, 1985—87, bd. trustees, 2003—; mem. Riverfront Task Force in Asheville; bd. dirs. Elf Louise Christmas Project, 2006—. Mem. Am. Bus. Women's Assn. (program com. 1987-88), Tex. Tennis Assn. (ranked player 1976-90), Prime Time Tennis Club (v.p. 1985-86), Blue Ridge Dance Club (pres. 1993-94) Republican. Avocations: tennis, gardening, dance, aerobics. Home: 14223 Savannah Pass San Antonio TX 78216

HYMAN, GAYLE M., lawyer; d. Maurice M. and Carol B. Hyman. AB, Stanford U., Calif.; MBA, U. Chgo.; JD, NY Law Sch. Bar: NY 1993, Calif. 1995, Hong Kong 1999, Pa. 2004, Nev. 2006. Atty. Sullivan & Cromwell LLP, NYC, 1992—96, Paul, Weiss, Rifkind, Wharton & Garrison LLP, NYC, 1996—98, 2000—03, Hong Kong, 1998—2000; dep. gen. counsel Allegheny Energy, Inc., Greensburg, Pa., 2003—05; asst. gen. counsel Las Vegas Sands Corp., Nev., 2005—. Pro bono legal work for small bus. incubators in distressed urban areas. Mem.: Assn. Corp. Counsel, Audubon Soc. (assoc.). Avocations: hiking, cello, travel. Office Phone: 702-733-5322. Personal E-mail: ghyman@stanfordalumni.org.

HYMAN, MARY BLOOM, science education programs coordinator; m. Sigmund M. Hyman, 1947 (dec.); children: Carol Hyman Piccinini, Nancy Louise. BA, Goucher Coll., 1971; MS, Johns Hopkins U., 1977. Asst. dir. Edn. Md. Sci. Ctr., Balt., 1976-81, dir. edn., 1981-90; coord. sci. edn. programs Loyola Coll., Balt., 1990—, coord. Inst. for Child Care Edn., 1992—. Trustee Goucher Coll., Balt. Mus. Art; bd. dir. Balt. Sch.-Age Child Care Alliance, Johns Hopkins U. Ctr. Talented Youth; mem. bd. visitors Franklin and Marshall Coll., 2006-; mem. Gov.'s Task Force on Compensation of Child Care Providers, 1995-96. Recipient Disting. Women award Gov.'s Office, Annapolis, Md., 1981; Meritorious Svc. award Johns Hopkins U., 1983; Outstanding Svc. to Sci. Edn. award. Assn. Sci. Dept. Chairmen Balt. County Pub. Schs., 1989. Mem. Md. Assn. Sci. Tchrs. (bd. dir.), Phi Beta Kappa, Phi Delta Kappa. Home: 10815 Longacre Ln Stevenson MD 21153-0665 E-mail: mhyman@loyola.edu.

HYMAN, PAMELA DRONETTE, science educator; d. Barbara Jean Copeland; 1 child, Marshall LaVernon Hyman-Grant. BS in Interdisciplinary Studies, Norfolk State U., Va., 1987, MA in Secondary Sch. Leadership, 2002. Educator Virginia Beach City Pub. Sch., Va., 1991—2006. Tchr. Upward Bound, Norfolk, Va., 1995—. Mem.: NSTA, NEA, Va. Beach Edn. Assn., Va. Edn. Assn., Pi Lambda Theta, Alpha Kappa Alpha (rec. sec. 2002—04). Pentecostal. Avocation: reading. Office: Bayside High Sch 4960 Haygood Rd Virginia Beach VA 23455 Office Phone: 757-473-5050.

HYMAN, PAULA E(LLEN), history professor; b. Boston; d. Sydney Max and Ida Frances (Tatelman) H.; m. Stanley Harvey Rosenbaum, June 7, 1969; children: Judith Hyman Rosenbaum, Adina Hyman Rosenbaum. BJED, Hebrew Coll., Brookline, Mass., 1966; BA, Radcliffe Coll., 1968; MA, Columbia U., 1970, PhD, 1975; degree (hon.), Jewish Theol. Sem., 2002. Asst. prof. Columbia U., N.Y.C., 1974-81; assoc. prof. history Jewish Theol. Sem., N.Y.C., 1981-86; dean. Sem., Coll. Jewish Studies, 1981-86; Lady Davis vis. assoc. prof. Hebrew U., Jerusalem, 1986; Lucy Moses prof. history Yale U., New Haven, 1986—. Author: From Dreyfus to Vichy, 1979, The Emancipation of the Jews of Alsace, 1991, Gender and Assimilation in Modern Jewish History, 1995, The Jews of Modern France, 1998; co-author: The Jewish Woman in America, 1976; co-editor: The Jewish Family: Myths and Reality, 1986, Jewish Women in America: An Historical Encyclopedia, 2 vols., 1997; editor: My Life as a Radical Jewish Woman, 2002; series editor Ind. U. Press, Bloomington, 1982—; contbg. editor Sh'ma Mag., N.Y.C., 1977—; contbr. articles to publs. Vice chmn. Zionist Acad. Coun., N.Y.C., 1982-83. NEH summer grantee, 1977; Am. Coun. Learned Socs. fellow, 1978; grantee N.Y. Coun. for Humanities, 1980; NEH fellow, 1986-87. Fellow Am. Acad. Jewish Rsch. (treas. 1995—, v.p. 1999-); mem. Am. Hist. Assn. (com. 1983), Assn. for Jewish Studies (bd. dirs. 1978-81, 83-85, 86—, v.p. for membership 1995-97), Nat. Found. Jewish Culture (chair acad. adv. com. 1996—), Leo Baeck Inst. (bd. dirs. 1979—), Yivo Inst. for Jewish Rsch., Phi Beta Kappa. Jewish. Office: Yale U Dept History New Haven CT 06520

HYMAN, SYLVIA GERTRUDE, artist, designer, craftsman, educator; b. Buffalo, Sept. 9, 1917; d. Norman Nathan and Ida (Diamond) Risman; m. Maurice Hyman, Oct. 25, 1944 (dec. Dec. 1979); children: Paul Maurice, Jackie Diamond Hyman Wilson; m. Arthur Gunzberg, Sept. 8, 1985. Diploma in fine arts, Albright Art Sch., Buffalo, 1937; BS in Art Edn., State Tchrs. Coll., Buffalo, 1938; MA in Art, Peabody Coll.(Vanderbilt U.), 1963. Tchr. art Buffalo Pub. Schs., 1937-43, Jefferson County Schs., Middletown, Ky., 1957-60; asst. prof. art George Peabody Coll., 1964-71; chmn. planning bd. Internat. Ceramic Symposium, Memphis, 1973; cons. in field. solo exhibns: Cheekwood Fine Arts Ctr., Nashville, Tenn., 1983, 1995, Cumberland Gallery, Nashville, Tenn., 1989, 97, 2001, 03, Tenn. State Mus., 1995, OK Harris Gallery, N.Y.C., 2003, Mid. Tenn. State U., 2004, Tenn. Arts Commn. Gallery, 2004, Nashville Pub. Libr. Art Gallery, 2006, Nashville Pub. Libr. Art Gallery, 2006; group shows include: Mus. Contemporary Crafts, N.Y.C., 1964, 65, Mint Mus. Art, Charlotte, N.C., 1964, 71, 73, Speed Mus., Louisville, 1968, 72, Brooks Gallery, Memphis, 1969, 77, Met. Mus. and Art Ctr., Miami, Fla., 1976, SEECA, Winston-Salem, N.C., 1979, Smithsonian Instn., Washington, 1980, Can. Clay and Glass Gallery, Waterloo, Can., Saga (Japan) Prefecture Mus., Tenn. State Mus., Nashville, Tenn., Birchfield-Penney Mus., Buffalo, 2004, Acad. Art Mus., Easton, Md., 2005, George Broderick Gallery, Portland, Oreg., 2006; numerous pub. and pvt. collections including Smithsonian Am. Art Mus., Renwick Gallery, Washington, Choson Royal Kiln Mus., Kwangju, Korea, Saga Prefecture Mus., Japan, Tenn. State Mus., Ariana Mus., Geneva, Ogden Mus. So. Art, New Orleans, Tenn. State Mus., Ft. Wayne Art Mus., Ind.; exhibitor 1st World Triennial, Muzejski Prostor, Zagreb, Yugoslavia, 1984, Frist Ctr. Visual Arts, Nashville, Tenn., 2001, 02, 03, Finer Things Gallery, Sofa, N.Y., 2002, SOFA, NY & SOFA, Chgo., 2002, 03, 04; contbr. articles to profl. jours. Chmn. adv. com. Tenn. Arts Commn., Nashville, 1968-72; mem. Century III Commn., Nashville, 1977-79; mem. Mayor's Task Force for Community Excellence, Nashville, 1981-82; Chmn. Internat. Ceramic Symposium, Appalachian Ctr. Crafts, 1985. Recipient Commendation Outstanding Service award ARC & U.S. Army, 1944; Best in Clay award Arts Festival Arts Ctr, Oak Ridge, Tenn., 1979, Lifetime Achievement award Tenn. Gov., 1994, Lifetime Achievement in The Craft Arts award Nat. Mus. Women in Arts, Washington, 1993, Creative Excellence award Lipscomb U., 2004; numerous other awards. Mem. Tenn. Artist-Craftsmen's Assn. (co-founder), Tenn. Ann. Crafts Fair (bd. chmn. 1971-74), Am. Craft Coun. N.Y., Internat. Acad. Ceramics (hon.), Nat. Coun. on Edn. in Ceramic Art, Nashville Artist Guild (pres. 1964-66), Tri-Arts (pres. 1972-74). Democrat. Jewish. Personal E-mail: sylviart@comcast.net.

HYMAN, URSULA H., lawyer; BA, Immaculate Heart Coll., 1973; MEd, Loyola Marymount Coll., 1977; JD, U. So. Calif., 1983. Bar: Calif. 1983. With Latham & Watkins, L.A., 1983—, ptnr., 1990—. Founding mem. ad hoc com. Chpt. 9 Reform. Bd. dirs. Calif. Philharmonic. Named LA Super Lawyers, LA Mag., 2004, 2005, 2006. Mem.: ABA, L.A. Women's Lawyers Assns., Nat. Assn. Bond Lawyers, L.A. County Bar Assn., State Bar Calif., Order of the Coif. Office: Latham & Watkins LLP 633 W Fifth St Ste 4000 Los Angeles CA 90071 Office Phone: 213-485-1234. Business E-Mail: ursula.hyman@lw.com.

HYMES, NORMA, internist; b. N.Y.C., July 20, 1949; d. Richard and Ellen (Posner) H.; m. Vincent M. Esposito, Nov. 1978 (div.); 1 child, Richard Hymes-Esposito. BS, Oberlin Coll., 1971; MD, Mt. Sinai, 1975. Diplomate Bd. of Internal Medicine. Intern, resident Maimonides Med. Ctr., Bklyn., 1975-78; internist Manhattan Health Plan, N.Y.C., 1978-81, Manhattan Med Group, P.C., N.Y.C., 1981-92, N.Y. Med. Group, P.C., 1992-2000, Continuum Health, 2000—01; pvt. practice, 2001—. Mgr. The Colonnade Condominium, N.Y.C., 1982-85; trustee N.Y. Soc. For Ethical Culture, N.Y.C., 1989-93, 96-2001. Mem. ACP, Am. Med. Women's Assn. Office Phone: 212-595-1234.

HYNDE, CHRISSIE, musician; b. Akron, Ohio, Sept. 7, 1951; m. Jim Kerr, 1984 (div. 1990); 1 child, Yasmin Kerr; m. Lucho Brieva, 1997. Student, Kent State U., 1970. Lead singer, songwriter, guitarist Pretenders, 1978. Recordings include The Pretenders, 1980 (Brass in Pocket top-selling single), Prentenders II, 1981, Learning to Crawl, 1984 (songwriter Middle of the Road, Show Me, Back in the Chain Gang), Get Close, 1986 (songwriter Don't Get Me Wrong), The Prentenders Live, 1988, Packed!, 1990, Last of the Independents, 1994 (songwriter I'll Stand By You), The Isle of View (live), 1995, Viva el Amor, 1999, Loose Screw, 2002; two songs featured in film G.I. Jane; song "Brass in Pocket" (I'm Special), featured in film Lost in Translation, 2003. Mem.: PETA (People Ethical Treatment Animals). Mailing: Artemis Records 130 5th Ave 7th Fl New York NY 10011

HYNDMAN, ROBERTA, education educator; m. Chris Hyndman, Mar. 22, 1980. BBA, West Tex. A&M U., Canyon, Tex., MBA, 1999. Instr. West Tex. A&M U., Canyon, Tex., 1998—2001; tchr. Amarillo Coll., Tex., 2001—. Cons. Boy Scouts Am., Amarillo, 1998—99. Contbr.: text Exploring Microsoft Visual Basic.NET Brief, XML, Web Warrior Series, Information Technology Associates. Vol. Amarillo Food Bank, 2005—06; tchr., youth advisor Polk St. United Meth. Ch., Amarillo, 1998—2006. Recipient Online Class Devel. award, Amarillo Coll., 2003. Mem.: Tex. Cmty. Teachers Assn., Alpha Kappa Psi (life). Office Phone: 806-371-5217.

HYNES, AEDHMAR, public relations executive; b. Galway, Ireland; married; 4 children. Degree in econs., Univ. Coll., Galway; postgrad. diploma in mktg. Account mgr. Text 100, 1990—96, regional dir. N.Am. San Francisco, 1996—2000, CEO, 2000—. Bd. dir., in charge of client svc. Text 100, 1996. Office: Text 100 26 W 17th 2nd Fl New York NY 10011 Office Phone: 212-529-4600. Home Fax: 415-593-8401; Office Fax: 212-989-7149.

HYNES, PATRICIA M., lawyer; b. NYC, Jan. 26, 1942; BA, CUNY, 1963; LLB, Fordham U., 1966. Bar: N.Y. 1966, U.S. Dist. Ct. (so. and ea. dists.) N.Y. 1969, U.S. Ct. Appeals (2d cir.) 1982. Law clk. to Hon. Joseph C. Zavatt U.S. Dist. Ct. (ea. dist.) N.Y., 1966-67; mem. civil divsn. U.S. Dist. Ct. (so. dist.) N.Y., 1967-71; asst. U.S. atty. (so. dist.) NY US Dept. Justice, 1967-82, chief consumer fraud unit, 1971-78, chief ofcl. corruption and spl. pros. unit, 1978-80, exec. asst. U.S. atty., 1980-82; ptnr. Milberg Weiss Bershad Hynes & Lerach LLP, NYC, 1983-99; of counsel Milberg Weiss Bershad & Schulman LLP, NYC, 2000—06, Allen & Overy LLP, NYC, 2006—. Adj. prof. law Fordham U., 1978—83; lectr. trial advocacy Harvard U. Law Sch., 1983; lectr. Practising Law Inst.; chmn. merit selection panel for N.Y. magistrate judges U.S. Dist. Ct. (so. dist.) N.Y., 2002—; mem. dept. disciplinary com. of appellate divsn. supreme ct. First Jud. Dept., 2005—. Mem. editl. bd. NY Law Jour., 1994—. Mem. NYC Charter Revision Commn., 2002, Gov.'s Exec. Adv. Com. on Adminstrn. Criminal Justice, 1981—82, N.Y. Gov.'s Commn. on Govt. Integrity, 1987—90, Mayor's Adv. Com. on Jud., 1994—2001; chairperson N.Y. Regional Consumer Protection Coun., 1971—72. Named one of 50 Top Women Lawyers, Nat. Law Jour., 1998, 2001. Fellow: Am. Coll. Trial Lawyers; mem.: ABA (chair govt. litig. com. litig. sect. 1984—87, chair securities litig. com. 1987—89, coun. litig. sect. 1989—92, chair pre-trial practice and discovery com. 1992—94, standing com. on fed. jud. 1995—2000, chair 2000—01, criminal justice sect.), Legal Aid Soc. (bd. dirs. 1998—2003, chair bd. dirs. 2004—), Fed. Bar Coun. (trustee 1983—91, treas. 1987—90, v.p. 1990, 1996—), Assn. Bar City N.Y. (consumer affairs com. 1974—78, criminal law com. 1980—84, police law and policy com. 1981—83, sec. 1982—84, ho. dels. 1983—84, exec. com. 1984—88, second century com. 1988—92, del. to ABA, ho. dels. 1990—94, chair fed. cts. com. 1992—95, del.), Am. Law Inst. (spl. advisor 1995—2001), Fordham Law Alumni Assn. Office: Allen & Overy LLP 1221 Ave Americas New York NY 10020 Business E-Mail: patricia.hynes@allenovery.com.

HYNES-LASEK, NANCY ELLEN, secondary school educator; b. Jersey City, N.J., June 13, 1956; d. Timothy Joseph and Alice Mae (Menig) H. BA, N.J. City U., 1978, MA, 1979. Cert. nursery tchr., N.J., elem. tchr., N.J., prin., supr., N.J., reading tchr., N.J. Tchr. St. Bridget's Sch., North Bergen, N.J., 1978; tchr. reading, writing Bd. Edn. East Orange (N.J.), 1979-86; unit coord. HSPT program Bd. Edn. City of East Orange (N.J.), 1985; dir. Nancy's Sch. Dance, West N.Y., 1981-85; tchr. computer Bd. Edn. City of Elizabeth (N.J.), 1986-95; tchr. Huntington Learning Ctr., Woodbridge, N.J., 1987—; reading tchr. Bd. Edn. City of Elizabeth (N.J.), 1992-95, Plainfield (N.J.) Bd. Edn., 1995—, 1995-96, Passaic (N.J.) Bd. Edn., 1997—2001; tchr. elem. sch. City of Linden (N.J.) Bd. Edn., 1999; dir. Sylvan Learning Ctr., Wayne, NJ, 2000—01; prof. reading Middlesex County Coll., Edison, NJ, 1996—; reading specialist, coord. Create Charter H.S., Jersey City, 2005—. Mem. com. Computer Curriculum Guide, 1989, Language Arts Curriculum Guide, 1989; tchr. dance N.J. Workshop Arts, Westfield, 1990; prof. reading Middlesex County Coll., Edison, N.J., 1996—; CEO Nancy's Shoppers Svc., 1997—, cons. Discovery Toys, 2004—. Chmn. Dance for Heart, 1985; mem. com. Jingle Bells Run for Arthritis, 1994-95; capt. Profl. Dance and Exercise Group, 1993—. Grantee Bd. Edn. City of Elizabeth, 1989. Mem. ASCD, Phi Delta Kappa (historian 1989-91), Secondary Sch. Women's Club (Elizabeth). Roman Catholic. Avocations: skiing, dance, reading, tennis. Home: 1702 Forest View Dr Avenel NJ 07001-2172 E-mail: lasekavenel@aol.com.

HYNSON, JAN I., federal ombudsman, artist; b. Balt., Feb. 1, 1948; d. Nelson F Einwaechter and Mariette F Fryns; children: Jahnis K. Pironis, Jessica A. Pironis; m. Richard Hynson, Jr., Nov. 17, 1984; stepchildren: Corey, Anne R. Acken. BFA, L'Academie Royale des Beaux Arts, 1966—69. Uniform securities cert. State of Md., 1983. Asst. v.p. T. Rowe Price Mut. Funds, Balt., 1970—86, MNC Fin./Goldleaf Banking, Balt., 1986—89; program dir. Helix Health Systems, Balt., 1989—91; br. chief Fed. Bur. Prisons, Washington, 1991—94, fed. ombudsman, 1994—. Mem. Acad. Art Mus., Easton, Md., 2000, Chesapeake Bay Maritime Mus., Easton, Md., 2000; part-time vol. Friends of Talbot Hospice, Easton, Md., 2004; part time vol. Talbot County Humane Soc., Easton, Md., 2000. Recipient Premier Prix, L'Academie Royale des Beaux-Arts, 1969. Avocations: art, gourmet cooking, gardening. Office: Fed Bureau of Prisons/FPI 320 First St NW 400 First St Bldg Washington DC 20534 Office Phone: 202-305-3515. Office Fax: 202-305-7340. Personal E-mail: jhynson@goeaston.net. Business E-Mail: jhynson@central.unicor.gov.

HYTIER, ADRIENNE DORIS, French language educator; d. Jean and Katharine (Hytier) Matson. BA summa cum laude, Barnard Coll., 1952; MA, Columbia U., 1953, PhD, 1958. Instr. French Vassar Coll., Poukeepsie, NY, 1959—61, asst. prof., 1961—66, assoc. prof., 1966—70, prof. French, 1970—96, Lichtenstein Dale prof. French, 1974—96. Vis. assoc. prof. Columbia U., 1966, U. Calif., 1968—69. Editor for French lit.: The 18th Century: A Current Bibliography Since 1970, 25 vols., Two Years of French Foreign Policy: Vichy 1940-42, 1958, 2d edit., 1974, Les Dépêches diplomatiques du Comte de Gobineau en Perse, 1959, La Guerre, 1975, 4th edit., 1991; contbr. articles to profl. jours. Decorated chevalier des Palmes Académiques; fellow, Guggenheim Found., 1967—68. Mem. MLA, Am. Soc. 18th Century Studies, Internat. Soc. 18th Century Studies, Phi Beta Kappa. Home: 71 Raymond Ave Poughkeepsie NY 12603-0372 Office: Vassar Coll Box 372 Poughkeepsie NY 12604-0001

HYTTINEN, NICOLE MARIE, elementary school educator; b. Ishpeming, Mich., Dec. 16, 1973; d. James Robert and Karen Ann Paquette; m. Terry Edward Hyttinen, May 18, 1996; children: Allison Marie, Adam James. MA in Secondary Edn., No. Mich. U., Marquette, 2002. Tchr. Aspen Ridge Mid. Sch., Ishpeming, 1997—. Named Tchr. of Yr., NICE Cmty. Sch., 2002. Mem.: Mich. Sci. Tchrs. Assn., Mich. Coun. Tchrs. Math. Lutheran. Home: 2300 Woodland Dr Ishpeming MI 49849 Office: Aspen Ridge Middle School 350 Aspen Ridge School Road Ishpeming MI 49849 Office Phone: 906-485-3176.

IANNOTTA, PATRICIA N., physician; b. New Brunswick, N.J., May 24, 1953; d. Pasquale Thomas and Carmella Marion (Certo) I.; 1 child, Kelsey Rose. BA, U. Pa., 1975; MSW, Cath. U. Am., Washington, 1979; MD, Thomas Jefferson Med. Coll., 1989. Diplomate Am. Bd. Dermatology. Dermatologist Ctrl. Bucks Dermatology and Dermatol. Assocs., Fountainville, Pa., 1993-94, Ctrl. Bklyn. Med. Group, P.C., 1994-96, N.Y. Med. Group, P.C., Bronx, 1997—. Mem. Soc. Pediat. Dermatology. Office: NY Med Group PC 2532 Grand Concourse Bronx NY 10458-4902

IANNUCCI, MARILYN BUTLER, music educator; d. William Frank and Jane Estelle Butler; m. John Iannucci; children: Elaine Lisa, John William. MusB in Oboe, Manhattan Sch. Music, N.Y.C., 1966, MusM in Edn., 1967; cert. in Biblical Studies, Berean Sch. Bible, Springfield, Mo., 1984. Cert. tchr. music (permanent) N.Y. Tchr. music ed. Blecker Jr. H.S. 185Q, Whitestone, NY, 1966—73, Valley Stream Dist. 13, 1988—91, Uniondale Schs., 1991—. Pres. Music Tchrs. Assn. Dist. 250, Queens, NY, 1970—73. Author: (lesson books) Quick Start for Flute, 2000, Quick Start for Flute Upper Register, 2001. Nominee N.Y. State Tchr. of Yr., 2003; named Cmty. Day honoree, No. Pky. Sch., 2002. Mem.: Nassau Music Educators Assn., Music Educators Nat. Coun., N.Y. State Sch. Music Assn. (chmn. woodwinds 1971—74).

IAPAOLO, CATERINA A., psychiatrist; d. Felice M. and Anna Maria Iapaolo; m. Dan Deac, June 19, 1999. MD, U. Padua, Italy, 1990. Intern in internal medicine U. Minn., Mpls., 1994—95; resident in psychiatry U. Ill., Chgo., 1995—98; psychiatrist Carrier Clinic, Belle Mead, NJ, 2000—02; psychiatrist, cons. Family & Cmty. Svcs., Bound Brook, 2002; psychiatrist Oakwood Ctr. Palm Beaches, West Palm Beach, Fla., 2003—, Hanley Ctr. - Drug Rehab. Inst., 2004—. Recipient Dr. Henry P. & M. Page Durkee Merit award, U. Ill., 1998. Mem.: AMA, Assn. Women Psychiatrists, Am. Psychiat. Assn. Avocations: bicycling, piano, yoga, travel. Office: Cmty Mental Health Ctr Oakwood Ctr Palm Beaches 1041 45th St West Palm Beach FL 33407 also: Hanley Ctr 5200 East Ave West Palm Beach FL 33407

IAROVICI, DORIS M, psychiatrist, writer; b. Romania; BS, Yale U., 1987; MD, Yale U. Sch. Medicine, 1992. American Board Psychiatry and Neurology ABPN, 1997. Psychiatrist Duke U., Durham, NC, 2000—. Author: (short stories) American Dreaming and Other Stories, Facts. Sec. Duke Sch., Durham, NC, 2002—05. Recipient Laughlin fellowship, Am. Coll. of Psychiatrists, 1996; fellow APA/Burroughs-Wellcome fellowship, Am. Psychiat. Assn., 1994—96; Emerging Artist grant, Durham Arts Coun., 2003—04, Borchardt Fiction scholarship, Sewanee Writers' Conf., 2002. Fellow: Am. Psychiat. Assn. (disting.). Office: Duke Univ Counseling and Psych Svc Box 90955 Durham NC 27708 Office Phone: 919-660-1000.

IBA, SHIRLEY, artist; d. Arthur Roy and Idell Carolina Riba. BFA, Calif. Coll. of Arts & Crafts, Oakland, 1977. Sales/dept. display Gumps Oriental Antique Dept., San Francisco, 1979—90; owner ARTRIBA, Laporte, Colo., 1995—. Exhibitions include Corcoran Sch. Art, Washington, D.C., 1977—78, Calif. Coll. of Arts & Crafts, San Francisco, 1977, E.B. Crocker Kingsley, Sacramento, 1979, Gump's Gallery, San Francisco, 1979—90, 1981, 1986, Represented in permanent collections Bohemian Found., Calif., prin. works include Mural After Parrish, 2002, represented in pvt. collections. Home: PO Box 800 Laporte CO 80535 Office Phone: 970-221-2023.

IBARRA, AVELINA C., music educator; b. Manila, Nov. 10, 1934; came to the U.S., 1963; d. Benjamin Jamias and Anita Quevedo Dela Cuesta; m. Rufino Paras Ibarra, Apr. 6, 1963; children: Pearl Marie C., Kenneth Joseph C., Gina Ann I. Coss, Alan Anthony C. A in Music, cert. tchr., Concordia Sch. Music, Manila, 1957; BS in Pharmacy, U. Santo Thomas, Manila, 1959. Music tchr. Am. Coll. Musicians, Austin, 1976—; adjudicator, faculty mem. Nat. Guild Piano Tchrs., Austin, 1990—. Mem. entertainment com. Filipino Womens Club Tidewater, Norfolk, Va., 1967-72, United Iloco Assn. Tidewater, Norfolk, 1972-77. Named to Hall of Fame, Piano Guild, 1985. Mem. Music Tchr. Nat. Assn. (profl. cert.), Nat. Fedn. Music Clubs (award of merit 1996, 97), Va. Music Tchrs. Assn. (profl., provisional and std. certs.), Tidewater Music Tchrs. Forum (historian 1995—), Scherzo Music Club (photographer 1998—, mem. hostess com. 1989—)

IBARRA, IRENE M., foundation administrator; JD, U. Wash.; MPA, U. Denver, MS in Social Work in Community Svcs. & Social Planning; sr. exec. program, Harvard U. Dep. mgr. Dept. of Social Services City of Denver, 1984—87; former exec. dir. Dept. Health & Human Services State of Colo., 1987—91; atty., corp. & bus. law Hillis, Clark, Martin and Peterson, Seattle; COO Alameda Alliance of Health, 1996—98; CEO Alameda Alliance for Health, 1998—2003; dir. LA Health Action, 2003—05; exec. v.p. Calif. Endowment, 2005—. Mem. Calif. Performance Review Commn. Trustee Blue Shield of Calif. Found., Casey Family Programs, 2003—. Office: Calif Endowment 1000 N Alameda St Los Angeles CA 90012*

IBENDAHL, JEAN AYRES, retired elementary and secondary educator; b. Bement, Ill., June 10, 1918; d. Charles Edward and Minnie Nora (Burns) Ayres; m. Calvin Frederick Ibendahl, Dec. 31, 1958. BS, U. Ill., Urbana-Champaign, 1952, MEd, 1957. Cert. elem. and secondary edn. educator, Ill. Tchr. Union Grove Sch. Hillsboro Pub. Schs., Ill., 1938—39, 1940—41, tchr. Burbank Sch., 1939—40; secondary educator Wilmington Unit Dist., Ill., 1952—53, elem. educator, 1942—52; tchr. social studies Lakeview Jr.-Sr. H.S., Decatur, Ill., 1953—57; tchr. biology DuQuoin H.S., Ill., 1966—67; substitute tchr., 1967—80; ret., 1980. A founder Ag in the Classroom Program, 1984. Author: Pork Primer, 1977. Dir. Nat. Livestock and Meat Bd. Chgo., 1966-72, Perry County Health Dept., Pinckneyville, 1992; pres. Ill. Porkettes, 1974-76, Ill. Agri-women, 1978-80, 1988-89; sec. Perry County Pub. Bldg. Com., Pinckneyville, Ill., 1984—; bd. mem. Rend Lake Coll. Found., 1988-94; candidate state rep., 115th Dist., Ill., 1992; coord. Perry County Bush/Quayle Campaign, 1992; founder Perry County Jail Mus., 1994, chmn., 1993-97; v.p. Perry County Hist. Soc., 1995-; 4H leader, 1984-88; founder, dir. Ill. Ag Leadership Found., 1986. Inducted into Ill. Hall of Fame, 1996, Silver Haired Congresswoman, 12th dist., 1996. Mem. Am. Agri-Women (awards com. 1992), Ill. Agri-Women (regional dir. 1990—), Perry County Home Ext. (first vice chmn. 1989-91, 1994-95, cultural arts chmn. 1992—), Perry County Hist. Soc. (v.p. 1992—), LWV, P.E.O., Order of Eastern Star. Republican. Methodist. Avocations: reading, travel, sewing, antiques. Home: Apt 6 912 N Washington St Du Quoin IL 62832-1232

IBI, KEIKO, film director; b. Tokyo; came to U.S., 1991; m. Greg Pak. Student in lit., Japan Women's U.; student, Syracuse (N.Y.) U.; degree, NYU, 1996, MFA in Film, 1998. Motion picture dir., writer, 1999—. Films include The Personals: Improvisations on Romance in the Golden Years, 1998 (Oscar award for documentary 1999). Office: Keiko Films 561 Hudson St Ste 115 New York NY 10014-2463 E-mail: keikofilms@aol.com.

ICEMAN, SHARON LORRAINE, retired elementary school educator; b. Canton, Ohio, Nov. 2, 1953; d. Robert H. and Jean Young; m. Rodney Alan Iceman, Aug. 5, 1978; children: Lisa Lorraine, Julie Alane. BS, Malone Coll., Canton, 1975; MS, U. Akron, 1980. Cert. elem. tchr., Ohio. Tchr. grades 1-2 Plain Local Schs., Canton, 1975—2005. Jennings scholar, 1978-79.

ICHINO, YOKO, ballerina; b. Los Angeles, Cali. m. David Nixon. Studied with Mia Slavenska, L.A. Mem. Joffrey II, N.Y.C., Joffrey Ballet, N.Y.C., Stuttgart Ballet, Fed. Republic Germany; tchr. ballet, 1976; soloist Am. Ballet Theatre, 1977-81; guest appearances, 1981-82; prin. Nat. Ballet Can., Toronto, Ont., 1982-90. Various guest appearances including World Ballet Festival, Tokyo, 1979, 85, Tokyo Ballet, 1980, with Alexander Godunov and Stars, summer, 1982, Sydney Ballet, Australia, N.Z. Ballet, summer 1984, Ballet de Marseille, 1985-87, Deutsche Opera Ballet Berlin, 1985-90, Munich Opera Ballet, 1987-90, Australian Ballet, 1987, 89, Staatsoper Berlin, 1989, 90, Komische Opera, Berlin, 1991-93, David Nixon's Dance Theater, Berlin, 1990, 91, Birmingham Royal Ballet, 1990-93, Deutsche Opera Ballet, Berlin, 1994-95; tchr. Australian Ballet, 1989, Birmingham Royal Ballet, 1991, 93, Nat. Ballet of Can., 1993, Cullberg Ballet, Sweden, 1994, Nat. Ballet Sch., 1994, 95, Ballet de Monte-Carlo, 1994, Geneva Ballet, 1995-98, Nederlands Dance Theater, 1995, Rambert Dance, 1995, Royal Winnipeg Ballet, 1999; tchr. numerous ballet workshops; dir. profl. program Ballet Met, 1995-2003; guest master tchr., coach No. Ballet Theatre, 2002—. First Am. trained woman recipient medal Third Internat. Ballet Competition, Moscow, 1977. Office: No Ballet Theatre West Park Centre Spen Ln Leeds LS16 5BE England

IDDINGS, KATHLEEN, poet, editor, publisher, consultant; b. Ohio, June 25, 1945; d. Ralph Myers and Ruth Amelia Wolfe. BS in Edn., Miami U., Oxford, Ohio, 1968. Tchr. various Ohio schs., 1962-74; freelance photojournalist La Jolla, Calif., 1976-80; freelance pub. rels. mgr. San Diego, 1980-81; cons., 1981—; editor, pub. La Jolla Poet's Press, 1981—. Poetry cons. San Diego City Schs., 1990; resident Djerassi Artists' Colony, 1990. Author: (poetry) Sticks, Friction & Fire, 2001, 5 other books of poetry. Named Poet of Millenium, Internat. Poets Acad., 2000; fellow, NEA, 1989; grantee, PEN, 1988, 1990, Calif. Arts Coun., 1994, Carnegie Authors; scholar, Napa Poetry Conf. Mem.: PEN, San Diego Ind. Scholars, Associated Writers Program, Acad. Am. Poets, Univ. Club, Calif. San Diego Faculty Club (Chancellor's

Assoc. 1999—2004). Democrat. Avocations: poetry readings, photography, college lectures, poetry contest judge. Office: La Jolla Poets Press PO Box 8638 La Jolla CA 92038-8638 E-mail: KathleenIddings@aol.com.

IDOL, ANNA CATHERINE, magazine editor; b. Chgo., July 8, 1941; d. Melvin Oliver and Louise Hildegard (Bullington) Lokensgard; m. William Ross Idol, Oct. 25, 1959 (div. Mar. 1962); 1 child, Laura Jeanne; m. Michael Wataru Sugano, Jan. 28, 1990. BS, Lake Forest (Ill.) Coll., 1980; MBA, Northwestern U., Evanston, Ill., 1982. treas. Chgo. Women in Pub., Chgo., 1970-71. Editor Rand McNally Co., Chgo., 1968-78, product mgr. adult reference, 1983-84; founder, pres. Bullington Laird, Inc., Chgo., 1986—; mng. editor Elks Mag., Chgo., 1997—. Pub.: Center Within, 1988 (award Heartsong Rev. 1989); writer, concept advt. alert, 1990 (Harvey Comm. award). Pres. Am. Buddhist Assn., 1985-93; mem. bd. Buddhist Temple Chgo., 1985-93; v.p. Buddhist Coun. Midwest, 1985-89. Democrat. Buddhist. Avocations: wilderness adventure, travel, reading. Office: Elks Mag 425 W Diversey Pkwy Chicago IL 60614-6196 Office Phone: 773-755-4894. Business E-Mail: annai@elks.org.

IDOL, LORNA, education educator, writer; b. Glenwood Springs, Colo., Mar. 7, 1947; d. Loren Ellis and Lana (Gregory) Idol; 1 child, Paz Timoteo. Student, U. Denver, 1965—67; BS Edn., U. Nev., 1969, MEd, 1974; PhD Edn., U. N.Mex., 1979. Cert. spl. edn. and elem. edn. tchr. Nev., literacy specialist, lic. mediator. Tchr. Vets. Meml. Elem. Sch. Washoe County Sch. Dist., Reno, 1970—74; tchr., lang. acquisition Albuquerque Pub. Schs., 1976; grad. asst. spl. edn. U. N.Mex., Albuquerque, 1975, instr., 1976—78; asst., assoc. prof., coord. Resource/Cons. Tchr. Program Dept. Spl. Edn. U. Ill., Champaign-Urbana, 1978—86; instr. grad. courses, vis. scholar U. Tex., Austin, 1986—87, 2001—02; prof. literacy edn. Concordia U., Austin, 2002—. Supervising tchr. Student Tchg. Program Dept. Spl. Edn. U. Nev., Reno, 1970—74; field supr. Spl. Edn. U. N.Mex., Albuquerque, 1977—78; grad. intern Lovelace-Bataan Clinic, Albuquerque, 1976; dir. reading improvement lab. Reading Study Ctr. U. Ill., 1985—86; cons. pub. sch. in-svc. tchr. edn., 1975—; dir. Reading Improvement Ctr., Austin, 1986—95. Author: Special Educator's Consultation Handbook, 1993, Collaborative Consultation, 2006, Models of Curriculum-Based Assessment, 2006, Collaboration in the Schools: Communicating, Interacting, and Problem-Solving, 1989; editor: Jour. Remed. and Spl. Edn., 1986—96, Grace Fernald's Remedial Techniques in Basic Short Subjects, 1987, Creating Collaborative and Inclusive Schools, 2001, Reading Success: A Specialized Literary Program, 1997; editor-in-chief Remedial and Spl. Edn. Jour., 1987—; co-editor: Dimensions of Thinking and Cognitive Instruction, 1990, Educational Values and Cognitive Instruction: Implications for Reform, 1990; mem. editl. bd. Jour. Tech. Edn. and Spl. Edn., 1984—87, Jour. Spl. Edn., 1987—, Jour. Ednl. and Psychol. Cons., 1990—; contbr. articles to profl. jours. Recipient Outstanding Presentation award, Internat. Coun. Exceptional Children, 1981; fellow, U. Nev., 1974, U. N.Mex., 1975—78; scholar, U. Denver, 1965—67, U. Nev., 1968—69. Democrat. Methodist.

IDOS, ROSALINA VEJERANO, secondary school educator; b. Ligao, Philippines, Mar. 18, 1944; arrived in U.S., 1987; m. Salvador Salcedo Idos, Dec. 21, 1969; children: Nathaniel, Rey, Lady Lou. BSc in Edn., U. of the East, Philippines, 1965; MSc in Edn., Nat. U., 2000. Cert. single subject tchg. in English, social studies, Filipino Calif., 1989. Tchr. Mayon H.S., Ligao City, Philippines, 1965—67; master tchr. in charge of student tchrs. U. of the East, Manila, Philippines, 1967—69, prof., 1969—87; tchr. San Diego Unified Sch. Dist. Morse H.S., San Diego, 1988—. Workshop presenter in field; curriculum writer Project Inclusion San Diego City Schs., San Diego, 1993—95. Recipient Outstanding Tchr. award, U. Calif., 1995—96, Educator of the Decade award, Filipino-Am. Educators Assn. San Diego, 1999, Svc. award, Fgn. Lang. Coun. San Diego, 1999, Recognition award, Filipino-Am. Educators of Calif., 2000. Fellow: Calif. Fgn. Lang. Project; mem.: San Diego Internat. Lang. Network (leadership team), Filipino-Am. Parents Assn. (adv. 1993—), Kaisahan Club (adv. 1990—). Roman Catholic. Avocations: reading, writing. Home: 6333 Viewpoint Ct San Diego CA 92139 Office: Morse High School 6905 Skyline Drive San Diego CA 92114

IEZZA, ANITA KAY, physician assistant; b. Austin, Tex., Oct. 11, 1956; d. Bobby Ray and Elizabeth Frances (McDowell) Hazen; m. Joseph Thomas Iezza, Jan. 5, 1982 (div. Sept. 1993); children: Joseph Thomas, Jr. (dec.), Anita Elizabeth. BS, Trevecca Nazarene Coll., Nashville, 1979, Physician Assoc., 1979; MS, L.I. U., 1998. Physician asst. Montefiore Med. Ctr., Bronx, N.Y., 1979—, sr. physician asst., 1992—, HIV primary care trainer, 1991-92. Programs and edn. region v.p. Chpt. 21 Parents Without Ptnrs., Westchester County, N.Y., 1995-96. V.p. Parents Club, St. Catharine Acad., 2001-2002, pres., 2002-03. Mem.: NY State Physician Asst. Assn., Am. Acad. Physician Assts. Roman Catholic. Avocations: art, music, jazz, sports, reading. Office: Montefiore Med Ctr 111 E 210th St Bronx NY 10467-2401 Business E-Mail: aiezza@montefiore.org.

IEZZONI, LISA I., medical educator, healthcare educator, researcher; MSc, Harvard U., 1978; MD, Harvard U., Boston, 1984. Sr. rschr. health care rsch. unit Boston U., 1984—85, asst. rsch. prof. dept. medicine, 1985—90, dir. health svcs. rsch. Health Policy Inst., 1988—90, asst. prof. health svcs., 1989—90; asst. prof. medicine Harvard Med. Sch., Boston, 1990—93, prof. medicine, 1993—; co-dir. rsch. divsn. gen. medicine and primary care Beth Israel Deaconess Med. Ctr., Boston. Mem. Nat. Com. on Vital and Health Stats.; bd. dirs. Nat. Forum for Health Care Quality Measurement and Reporting. Contbr. articles to profl. jours.; mem. editl. bds of maj. med. and health svcs. rsch. jours.; author (and editor): Risk Adjustment for Measuring Healthcare Outcomes; author: When Walking Fails: Mobility Problems of Adults with Chronic Conditions, 2003. Recipient Investigator Award in Health Policy Rsch., The Robert Wood Johnson Found., 1996, Founder's award for Outstanding Contbns. to Field, Am. Coll. Med. Quality. Mem.: Inst. of Medicine of NAS. Avocations: gardening, painting, reading. Office: Beth Israel Deaconess Med Ctr Divsn Gen Medicine Libby 326 330 Brookline Ave Boston MA 02215*

IFANDIS, ANASTASIA, lawyer; d. Vasilios Demetrios and Eleni Ifandis. BA, York U., Toronto, 1998; LLB, U. Wales, Aberystwyth, 2000; LLM, SUNY, Buffalo, 2002. Bar: NY 2004. Of counsel Law office Anthony M. Miranda, Buffalo; atty. Erie County Aid for Indigent Persons. Avocations: sports, traditional Greek dancing. Office: PO Box 1245 Amherst NY 14226 Office Phone: 716-816-8679. Office Fax: 716-837-4549.

IFILL, GWEN, moderator, political reporter; b. Queens, NY, Sept. 29, 1955; d. O. Urcille Ifill, Sr. and Eleanor Ifill. BA in Comm., Simmons Coll., Boston, 1977; recipient of 15 hon. degrees. Food columnist Boston Herald American, 1977—80; covered nat. and local affairs for Baltimore Evening Sun, 1981—84, Washington Post, 1984—91; White House corr., journalist NY Times, 1991—94; chief congl., polit. corr. NBC News, 1994—99; panelist Washington Week; moderator, mng. editor Washington Week with Gwen Ifill, Pub. Broadcasting Svc. (PBS) and WETA-TV, 1999—; sr. corr., back-up anchor The NewsHour with Jim Lehrer, Pub. Broadcasting Svc. (PBS), 1999—. Bd. dir. Harvard U. Inst. Politics, Com. to Protect Journalists, Mus. TV and Radio, U. Md. Philip Merrill Coll. Journalism; spkr. in field. Covered Bill Clinton's rise from So. gov. to Pres. US, 1992—93, moderator first v.p. debate, 2004. Fellow: Am. Acad. Arts & Sciences. Methodist. Office: Washington Week Pub Broadcasting Svc 2775 S Quincy St Arlington VA 22206 Address: The NewsHour with Jim Lehrer Pub Broadcasting Svc 3620 27th St S Arlington VA 22206 Office Phone: 703-998-2600, 703-998-2137.*

IGLESIAS, LISA G., lawyer; b. 1965; BS in Acctg., MS in Acctg., U. So. Fla.; JD, U. Miami, 1994. CPA Fla.; bar: Fla. 1994. Sr. tax specialist KPMG Peat Marwick; atty. Greenberg Traurig; assoc. counsel Spherion Corp., 1998—2003, sr. v.p., gen. counsel, sec., 2003—. Bd. dirs. Am. Staffing Assn., Am. Arbitration Assn.; mem. bd. dirs. Spherion Corp., 2003—. Mem.: ABA, Am. Soc. of Corp. Secretaries, Am. Corp. Counsel Assn. Office: Spherion Corp 2050 Spectrum Blvd Fort Lauderdale FL 33309

IGNAGNI, KAREN, healthcare association executive; Degree, Providence Coll.; MBA, Loyola U. Formerly with Com. for Nat. Health Ins., HHS; former profl. staff mem. U.S. Senate Labor and Human Resources Com.; dir. Dept. Employee Benefits AFL-CIO, 1990—93; pres., CEO Group Health Assn. Am., 1993—95, Am. Assn. Health Plans, 1995—.

IGNATIUS, NANCY WEISER, foundation administrator; b. Holyoke, Mass., Sept. 10, 1925; d. Richard Mather Weiser and Louise Gilbert Reynolds; m. Paul Robert Ignatius, Dec. 20, 1947; children: David, Sarah, Amy, Adi. BA, Wellesley Coll., 1947; MA, Am. Univ., 1969. With Dept. of Energy, Washington, 1977-79, cons., 1975-76, EPA, Washington, 1980-81. Contbr. articles to Cathedral Age mag. Trustee, bd. dirs. Washington Chorus, 1996-2004, chmn., 2000—; pres. Nat. Cathedral Assn., 1986-90, trustee, 1993—; pres. Com. for Nat. Security, 1998—; active chpt. Washington Nat. Cathedral. Mem. Chevy Chase Club, Sulgrave Club. E-mail: nanig3650@aol.com.

IGNAZITO, MADELINE DOROTHY, music educator, composer; b. Long Branch, N.J., Mar. 12; d. Henry George Jr. and Katherine (Manuel) Pigage; m. Martin Donald Ignazito, Feb. 15, 1969; children: Karen Ignazito-Cripps, Susan Ignazito-Wilhelm. BMus, Westminster Coll., 1962; MMus, U. Hartford, 1966. Nat. cert. tchr. music in piano, compostion and theory. Tutor Hartt Coll., West Hartford, Conn., 1964-66; music tchr. Hazlet (N.J.) Twp., 1966-69, Champaign, Ill., 1970-81, Charleston, Ill., 1981—; keyboard, aural theory instr. Lakeland Coll., Mattoon, Ill., 1985-88, music tchr., 1992-95. Composer Variations and Fugue, 1979 (Mu Phi Epsilon nat. 1st place), duet for violins and flute, 1987, Alchemies, 1999. Recipient Achievement award Mu Phi Epsilon, 1962, Composer's award Hartt Coll. Alumnae, 1965. Mem. Ill. State Music Tchrs. Assn. (state theory syllabus chair 1988-94), Coles County Art Coun. (pres., music dir. 1986-89), Charles Area Music Tchrs. Assn. (pres., co-founder 1986-99, treas., 2006-), Champaign Urbana Music Tchrs. Assn. (pres., co-chair 1998-2000), Zonta (fin. v.p. 1996-97, pres.-elect 1999-2000 pres 2001-2003, treas. 2003-2005, One award 1999), Tues. Morning Club (pres. 1997-98), Mu Phi Epsilon Avocations: math puzzles, gardening, emboidery, swimming, walking. Home: 13961 E County Road 620N Charleston IL 61920-7831 E-mail: madii@consolidated.net.

IHM, DANA ELIZABETH, music educator; b. Dallas, Mar. 7, 1961; d. Edgar Maurice and Gloria (Vonnabeth) Glover; m. C. Harley Ihm. MusB, Pitts. State U., Kans., 1984; MusM, Pitts. State U., 1985; PhD in Music Edn., U. SC, Columbia, 1994. Pvt. voice tchr., 1984—2006; piano, voice, music theory instr. Ozark Christian Coll., Joplin, Mo., 1986—87; choral dir. Brodhead (Mo.) Pub. Schs., 1988—90; music dir. Ctrl. Christian Ch., Savannah, Ga., 1990—93; gen. music tchr. Westminster Sch., Savannah, 1990—91; music dept. chair, dir. choral activities Dallas Christian Coll., Dallas, 1993—2003; dir. choral activities Colo. State U., Pueblo, 2003—. Choral dir. New Glarus (Wis.) Manner Choir, 1987—90, Monroe (Wis.) Cmty. Chorus, 1987—89, Fremont Civic Choir, Canon City, Colo., 2005—; assoc. dir. Pueblo Chorale Soc., 2006—. Participant Carnegie Hall Profl. Choral Workshop, 2000, 2002. Recipient Winner Aria Competition, Pitts. State U., 1985. Mem.: Music Educators Nat. Conf., Am. Choral Dirs. Assn., Kapa Lambda Nat. Music. Republican. Achievements include Black Belt in Tae Kwon Do, 1999. Avocations: reading, mountain climbing. Office: Colo State U 2200 Bonforte Blvd Pueblo CO 81001 Office Phone: 719-549-2125. Business E-Mail: dana.ihm@colostate-pueblo.edu.

IKAWA-SMITH, FUMIKO, anthropologist, educator; arrived in Canada, 1960; d. Jokei and Sachi Ikawa; m. Takao Sofue, Jan. 1955 (div. 1958); m. Philip Edward Lake Smith, Nov. 1959; 1 child, Douglas Philip Edward. BA, Tsuda Coll., Tokyo, 1953; student Tokyo Met. U., 1954-55; AM in Anthropology, Radcliffe Coll., 1958; PhD in Anthropology, Harvard U., 1974. Asst. prof. McGill U., Montreal, 1968—74, assoc. prof., 1974—79, chmn. dept. anthropology, 1975—80, prof., 1979—2003, dir. Ctr. East Asian Studies, 1983—88, chmn. dept. East Asian langs. and lits., 1983—88, assoc. acad. vice prin., 1991—96. Vis. prof. Canadian studies Kwansei Gakuin U., Japan, 1996-97. Editor: Early Palaeolithic in South and East Asia, 1978, Proc. of First Meeting of The Social Scis. Assn. Can., 1989; mem. editl. bd. Anthrop. Sci., 1998-2002. Decorated Order Sacred Treasure, Gold Rays with Rosette Japan. Fellow Am. Anthrop. Assn. (exec. at-large archeology divsn. 1988-90), Current Anthropology (assoc.); mem. Pacific Sci. Assn. (life), Soc. Am. Archeology, Soc. for East Asian Archaeology (pres. 2004—), Japan Studies Assn. Can. (acting pres. 1988-90, pres. elect 1998-99, pres. 1999-2000, 04—), Indo-Pacific Prehistory Assn. (exec. com. 1990-98), Can. Asian Studies Assn. (chair Japan com. 1991-94), Quebec-Japan Bus. Forum (bd. 1998-2000). Avocations: horticulture, piano. Home: 3955 Ramezay Ave Montreal PQ Canada H3Y 3K3 Office: McGill U Dept Anthropology 855 Sherbrooke St W Montreal PQ Canada H3A 2T7 Office Phone: 514-398-4300. E-mail: fumiko.ikawa-smith@mcgill.ca.

IKEDA, NANCY, mathematician, educator; d. Akihisa George and Nobuko Ikeda. BA in Applied Math., U. Calif., Irvine, 1993; MA in Math., Calif. State U., Fullerton, 1996, MS in Geology, 2004. Cert. tchr. Calif. Math tchr. Tustin HS, Calif., 1995—2000; math instr. Irvine Valley Coll., Calif., 1998, Fullerton Coll., Calif., 2000—. Office: Fullerton Coll 321 E Chapman Ave Fullerton CA 92832 Office Phone: 714-992-7787. Business E-Mail: nikeda@fullcoll.edu.

IKUTA, SANDRA SEGAL, federal judge; b. LA, June 24, 1954; m. Ed Ikuta; 1 child. Student, Stanford U., 1972—74; AB, U. Calif. Berkeley, 1976; MS, Columbia U., 1978; JD, UCLA, 1988. Law clk. to Hon. Alex Kozinski US Ct. Appeals (9th Cir.), 1988—89; law clk. to Justice Sandra Day O'Connor US Supreme Ct., Washington, 1989—90; assoc. O'Melveny & Myers LLP, 1990—97, ptnr., 1997—2004; dep. sec., gen. counsel Calif. Resources Agy., 2004—06; judge US Ct. Appeals (9th. Cir.), 2006—. Office: US Ct Appeals 95 Seventh St San Francisco CA 94103*

ILANGOVAN, SAROJA, retired pathologist; b. Trichy, Tamil Nadu, India, June 2, 1948; arrived in U.S., 1974; d. Ondimuthu Neelamegam and Thangaponnu Sangilimuthu; m. Somasundaram Ilangovan, Feb. 11, 1974; children: Kani, Chandru, Kumar. MB, BChir, Thanjavur Med. Coll., Tamil Nadu, 1973; MD, U. Ill., 1980. Diplomate Am. Coll. Pathologists, Am. Assn. Neuropathologists. Pathologist Oak Forest Hosp., Ill., 1981—91; neuropathologist Cook County Hosp., Chgo., 1991—2001. Contbr. articles to mags. Mem.: Tamil Nadu Found. (life), Fedn. Tamil Sangams N.Am. (life). Avocations: travel, snorkeling. Home: 12913 Cedar Ln Palos Heights IL 60463

ILEY, JENNY REBECCA, elementary school educator; b. Corbin, Ky., July 15, 1971; d. Clemon R. and Lois E. Mitchell; m. H. Matt Iley, Apr. 11, 1998; 1 child, Zoe Paris. BS Edn., Ea. Ky. U., Richmond, 1994; M Edn., Cumberland Coll., Williamsburg, Ky., 2000. Tchr. West Knox Elem. Sch., Corbin, 1994—2003, tchr. sci. K-6, 2003—. Mem. sch. coun. West Knox Elem. Sch., 2003—, coord. yearbook, 2003—, sponsor PRIDE Club, 2004—, sponsor Sci. Club, 2004—. Mem.: NSTA, Ky. Assn. Sch. Couns. Baptist. Avocations: reading, scrapbooks. Office: West Knox Elem Sch 366 N Ky 830 Corbin KY 40701

ILEY, MARTHA STRAWN, music educator; b. Marshville, NC, June 1, 1925; d. Stephen Hasty and Lila Faircloth Strawn; m. Bryce Baxter Iley, Aug. 7, 1948; children: Deborah Iley Hodde, Sheila Iley McLean, Cheryl Iley Lindstrom, Stephanie Iley Salb. BA, East Carolina Tchrs. Coll., 1946; MA, Western Ky. State Coll., 1947; MusM, Winthrop Coll., 1973; EdM, U. NC, Charlotte, 1974; EdD, Nova U., 1979; M Theol. Studies, Gordon-Conwell Theol. Sem., 1998. Cert. Music Tchrs. Nat. Assn. Music tchr. Lincolnton City Sch., 1947—48, Alexander Graham Jr. HS, Charlotte, NC, 1948—52, Charlotte Country Day Sch., 1955—59; min. music Providence Bapt. Ch., Charlotte, 1954—57, Carmel Bapt. Ch., Charlotte, 1968—70, 1975—76; project dir. music edn. Ctrl. Piedmont C.C., Charlotte, 1974—83; founder, chmn. bd. dirs. Met. Music Ministries, Charlotte, 1984—. Editor: (newsletter) ARTY-FACTS, 1983. Bd. dirs., sec. Charlotte Cmty. Concert Assn., 1980—93; dir. recital series Shepherd Ctr., Charlotte, 1980—83; adjudicator piano and voice various orgns., NC, 1980—. Recipient Disting. Music Alumni award, East Carolina U., 2002. Mem.: Charlotte Piano Tchrs. Forum (bd. dirs., pres. 1979—81), Charlotte Clergy Assn., NC Music Tchrs. Assn. (cert. chmn., v.p. 1981—83), Charlotte Music Club (bd. dirs.). Republican. Baptist. Avocations: writing, painting. Home: 10151 Robinson Church Rd Harrisburg NC 28075-6607 Office: Met Music Ministries Inc 1311 Paddock Cir Charlotte NC 28209-2443

ILITCH, MARIAN, professional hockey team executive, food service executive; m. Michael Ilitch; children: Denise Ilitch Lites, Ron, Mike Jr., Lisa Ilitch Murray, Atanas, Christopher, Carole. Co-owner, sec.-treas. Little Caesar Internat., 1959—, Detroit Red Wings, 1982—; sec.-treas. Olympia Arenas, Inc. (Olympia Entertainment Inc.), 1982—; co-owner, sec.-treas. Fox Theatre, 1987—, Detroit Tigers, 1992—, Little Foxes Fine Gifts, 1992—, The Second City, 1993—, Olympia Devel. LLC, 1996—, Hockeytown Cafe, 1999—, Blue Line Distributing, Uptown Entertainment, Champion Foods; co-founder, vice-chmn. Ilitch Holdings, Inc., 1999—. Recipient Pacesetter Award, Roundtable for Women in Foodservice, 1988, Nat. Preservation Honor Award, 1990. Office: Ilitch Holdings Inc Fox Office Ctr 2211 Woodward Ave Detroit MI 48201-3400

ILLNER-CANIZARO, HANA, physician, researcher, oral surgeon; b. Prague, Czechoslovakia, Nov. 2, 1939; came to U.S., 1968; d. Evzen Pospisil and Emilie (Chrastna) Pospisilova; m. Pavel Illner, June 14, 1963 (div. 1981); children: Martin Illner, Anna Illner; m. Peter Corte Canizaro, Nov. 1, 1982. MD, Charles U., Prague, 1961. Diplomate Am. Bd. Oral Surgery. Resident in oral surgery Inst. of Health, Pribram, Czechoslovakia, 1961-63; attending physician Oral Surgery Clinic, Prague, 1963-68; rsch. assoc. dept. surgery U. Tex. Southwestern Med. Sch., Dallas, 1969-72, instr. surgery, 1972-74, U. Wash. Sch. Medicine, Seattle, 1974-77; asst. prof. surgery Cornell U. Med. Coll., N.Y.C., 1977-81, assoc. prof. surgery, 1981-83, Tex. Tech U. Health Scis. Ctr., Lubbock, 1984-88, prof. surgery, 1988—. Site visitor NIGMS Postdoctoral Tng. Grant, Bethesda, Md., 1987. Mem. editorial bd. Circulatory Shock, N.Y.C., 1981—; manuscript reviewer Surgery, Gynecology and Obstetrics, Chgo., 1985—; contbr. chpts. to books, articles to profl. jours. Grantee NIH, 1979-83, 87-92, Tex. Tech U. Health Scis. Ctr., 1985-86, U.S. dept. Army, 1988-90; Fogarty Sr. Internat. fellow, 1991-92. Mem. Shock Soc. Avocations: remodeling of historical homes, gardening, skiing, pottery. Home: 4622 8th St Lubbock TX 79416-4722 Office: Tex Tech U Health Scis Ctr 3601 4th St Lubbock TX 79430-0001

ILSE-NEUMAN, URSULA, curator; d. Hermann Ilse and Charlotte Troeltsch; m. Lawrence Donald Neuman; 1 child, Andreas Neuman. BA, Hunter College (CUNY), 1977; MA, The New Sch., N.Y.C., 1992; postgrad., Bard Graduate Ctr. Studies Decorative Arts, N.Y.C., 1998—2002. Curator Mus. Arts and Design, N.Y.C., 1992—. Exhbn. juror various nat. and internat. orgns.; curator Corporal Identity - Body Lang., 2003, essayist, 03. Curator, essayist, editor (book) Made in Oakland: The Furniture of Garry Knox Bennett, 2001, (exhbn. catalog) None That Glitters: Perspectives on Jewelry in the Donna Schneier Collection, 2002, Radiant Geometries: Fifteen International Jewelers, 2001; author: (exhbn. catalog) Cabinets of Curiosities: Cabinets of Wonder and Delight; curator, essayist, editor (exhbn. catalog) Corporal Identity-Body Language, 9th Triennial for Form and Content, USA and Germany, 2003; author: (exhbn. catalog) Treasures from the Vault: Contemporary Jewelry, Schmuck, 2006, Glass Wear, 2007, (Essay) Worthy of the Muses: The Furniture of John Eric Byers, 2001; contbr. essays and articles to publs., selections to exhbn. catalogs; curator, essayist, editor Six Continents of Quilts: The Museum of Arts & Design Collection, 2003; mem. editl. adv. bd.: Metalsmith Mag. Fellow, Bard Grad. Ctr., 1999—2002, 20th Century Visual Arts fellow, Grad. Ctr., CUNY, 1992. Mem.: Glass Art Soc., Coll. Art Assn., Am. Mus.Assn., Internat. Curators Assn., Art Table, Furniture Soc. (mem. adv. bd. 1999—2002), Phi Beta Kappa. Office: Mus Arts and Design 40 W 53d St New York NY 10019 Office Phone: 212-956-3535 x 119. Personal E-mail: ursula.neuman@madmuseum.org. Business E-Mail: uneuman@nyc.rr.com.

IM, HYEPIN CHRISTINE, not-for-profit developer; BS, U. Calif., Berkeley; MBA, U. So. Calif.; MDiv, Wesley Theological Seminary. Sponsorship mgr. Calif. Sci. Ctr., community gifts mgr.; venture capitalist Renaissance Capital Partners; founder & pres. Korean Churches for Community Develop., 2001—. Lecturer & speaker Christian Community Develop. Assn., Nat. Council of Korean So. Baptist Churches, US Dept. of Housing and Urban Develop., Asian Am. for Equality, So. Calif. Conference of AME Churches; Am. Memorial Marshall fellow German Marshall Fund, 2001. Pres. Korean Am. Coalition, 1995—96; mem. Pacific Council, 2001—; state commr. Calif. Svc. Corps. Office: Korean Churches for Community Develop PO Box 76146 Los Angeles CA 90076-0146 Office Phone: 213-216-3676. Personal E-mail: hyepin@yahoo.com.

IMAI, DOROTHY KUNIYE, psychotherapist; b. Seattle; d. Kunizo and Masaye (Kaita) Mayeno; 1 child, W. Brent. BA in Human Svcs., UCLA, 1976; MA in Art Therapy, Goddard Coll., 1978; MA in Psychology, Internat. Coll., 1983; PhD in Psychology, Summit U., 1995. Art therapist Jeffrey Found., L.A., 1978-80; program dir., art therapist, mem. founding staff Adult Day Ctr., Older Persons Info. and Counseling Assocs, L.A., 1979—83; art therapist Artsreach program UCLA, 1980-81; pvt. practice L.A., 1984—; instr. stress mgmt. Cardiac Therapy Group, YMCA, L.A., 1985-86; art therapist Wise Care Ctr., Santa Monica, Calif., 1990-93. Exhibited art in various group shows, 1965-74. Chmn. commn. on edn. West L.A. Community Meth. Ch., 1965-66; officer Mar Vista PTA, L.A., 1965-67; rep. United Way Welfare Planning Coun., L.A., 1967-68; bd. dirs. Westwood Ctr. of the Arts, L.A., 1976-78. UCLA/U. So. Calif. Long Term Care Gerontology Ctr. fellow, 1983; United Way Art Therapy grantee, 1990. Mem. Am. Art Therapy Assn. (registered), Calif. Assn. Mariage and Family Therapists (lic.), UCLA Alumni Assn. Democrat. Avocations: travel, reading, holistic health, art, music.

IMAN, (IMAN ABUDULMAJID), model; b. Somalia, July 25, 1955; m. Spencer Haywood (div. 1987); 1 child, Zulekha; m. David Bowie, Apr. 24, 1992. Student, U. Nairobi, Kenya. Joined Wilhelmina Model Inc., 1975; introduced to U.S. Iman's Kikois. Appearences include (films) The Human Factor, 1979, Out of Africa, 1985, Star Trek VI, 1986, No Way Out, 1987, Surrender, 1987, House Party II, 1991, Exit to Eden, 1994, The Deli, 1997, Omikron: The Nomad Soul, 1999, (TV) Heart of Darkness, 1994; (TV series) Miami Vice, The Cosby Show, In the Heat of the Night; author: (with Tia Williams) The Beauty of Color: The Ultimate Beauty Guide for Skin of Color, 2005.

IMBACH, JANICE SPRUNGER, marriage and family therapist, education educator; b. Ft. Wayne, Ind., Aug. 23, 1924; d. Elam Elver and Alma Laura Sprunger; m. Albert Dean Imbach, May 1, 1948; children: Patrick, Michael, Gregory. BA, U. Calif., Los Angeles, 1946; MA, Calif. State U., 1967. English tchr. Los Angeles Bd. Edn., 1958—60, h.s. counselor, 1960—83; marriage, family, child counselor State of Calif., Sacramento, 1984—86. Author: (novels) Dancing in the Fields of God, 2001. Avocations: violin, reading, piano, painting, ceramics. Home: 1508 Pear Tree Lane Napa CA 94558

IMBER, ANNABELLE CLINTON, state supreme court justice; b. Heber Springs, Ark., July 15, 1950; m. Ariel Barak Imber (dec. 2001); 1 child, William Pierce Clinton. BA magna cum laude, Smith Coll., Northampton, Mass., 1971; postgrad., Inst. for Paralegal Tng., 1971, U. Houston, Tex., 1973-75; JD, U. Ark., 1977. Atty. Wright, Lindsey & Jennings Law Firm, Little Rock, Ark., 1977-88; apptd. cir. judge (5th divsn.) Pulaski and Perry Counties, Ark., 1984, elected chancery and probate judge (6th divsn.) Ark., 1989-96; elected assoc. justice Ark. Supreme Ct., 1997—. Bd. dirs. Ark. Advs. for Children and Families, 1985-90, pres. 1986-88; bd. dirs Pulaski County Hist. Soc., 1992-95, Congregation B'Nai Israel, 1988-92, 2001-05, Kiwanis Club 1995-98, YMCA of Greater Little Rock and Pulaski County,

Our House-A Shelter for Homeless, 1992—, St. Vincent Devel. Found., 1989-93, UAMS Med. Ctr. Dept. Pastoral Care and Edn., 1996-2005. Mem. ABA, AAUW, Nat. Assn. Women Judges, Ark. Bar Assn., Ark. Women Exec., Assn. of Ark. Women Lawyers (pres. 1980-81, Judge of the Year award 1994), Pulaski County Bar Assn. (bd. dirs. 1982-84). Office: Ark Supreme Ct Justice Bldg 625 Marshall St Little Rock AR 72201-1054 Office Phone: 501-682-6867. Business E-Mail: annabelle.clinton-imber@arkansas.gov.

IMBRESCIA, MARCIA, landscape company executive; BA in Mktg. and Journalism, grad. cert. in landscape design. Media dir. Drumbeater; owner Peartree Designs, Wellesley Hills, Mass., 2003—. Mem. com. on Guidelines for Human Embryonic Stem Cell Rsch. NAS, 2005—; mem. adv. com., Human Embryonic Stem Cell Rsch. NRC and Inst. Medicine., 2006—. Mem. Am. Juvenile Arthritis Orgn., 1996—98, 2001, chairperson, 2002—03; bd. trustee, nat. and chpt. vol. Arthritis Found. Recipient Vol. of Yr., Mass. Chpt. Arthritis Found., 1992. Office: Peartree Designs 51 River St Wellesley Hills MA 02481*

IMBROGNO, CYNTHIA, judge; b. 1948; BA, Indiana U. Pa., 1970; JD cum laude, Gonzaga U., 1979. Law clk. to Hon. Justin L. Quackenbush U.S. Dist. Ct. (Wash. ea. dist.), 9th circuit, 1980-83; law clk. Wash. State Ct. of Appeals, 1984; civil rights staff atty. Ea. Dist. of Wash., 1984-85, complex litigation staff atty., 1986-88; with Preston, Thorgrimson, Shidler, Gates & Ellis, 1988-90, Perkins Coie, 1990-91; magistrate judge U.S. Dist. Ct. (Wash. ea. dist.), 9th circuit, Spokane, 1991—. Office: 740 US Courthouse 920 W Riverside Ave Spokane WA 99201-1010

IMBUS, SHARON HAUGHEY, neuroscience nurse; b. Norfolk, Va., Jan. 7, 1947; d., Everett Wayne and Bettie Louise Haughey; m. Charles Eugene Imbus, June 14, 1969; children: Edward Allen, Andrew Haughey. BSN, Ohio State U., 1969, MSN, 1971. RN, NP, Calif.; BLS instr. Charge nurse Children's Hosp., Columbus, Ohio, 1969-71; staff nurse L.A. County-U. So. Calif. Burn Ctr., 1971-72; biostatistician U. So. Calif., L.A., 1973-78; dir., spl. studies L.A. County-U. So. Calif. Burn Ctr., 1978-86; clin. specialist, nurse practitioner Imbus Fortanasce Neurology Ctr., Arcadia, Calif., 1989—2001; dir. neurol. rsch., clin. specialist, nurse practitioner Charles E. Imbus, MD, Inc., Arcadia, 1997—. Legal nursing cons., 1992; cert. ACE aerobis cinstr./rehab. staff Meth. Hosp., Arcadia, 1990; mem. ethics com. Meth. Hosp. of So. Calif., Arcadia, 1986—; speaker Internat. Ethics Conf., San Francisco, 1979. Contbr. articles to profl. jours. Mem.: Am. Assn. Neurosci. Nurses, Am. Burn Assn., Calif. Nurses Assn. Roman Catholic. Avocations: aerobic dancing, exercise, reading. Office: Charles E Imbus MD Inc 665 W Naomi Ave Ste 202 Arcadia CA 91007-7563 Office Phone: 626-445-6275. Personal E-mail: simbus@earthlink.net, drimbus@sbcglobal.net.

IMEL, ELIZABETH CARMEN, retired physical education educator; b. Galesburg, Ill., Oct. 21, 1936; d. Leo Henry and Anna Imel. BS in Edn., Ill. State U., Normal, 1957; MA, U. Iowa, Iowa City, 1964, PhD, 1966. With U. Iowa, Iowa City, 1962—64; prof. Ill. State U., Normal, 1964—95; ret., 1995. Pres. Ill. Dance Assn., 1978—80. Editor: AAHPERED Periodical, 1968—70, Focus on Dance VIII Dance Heritage, 1977. Active Ill. Arts Commn., 1981—82, Citizen's Rev. Commn., San Marcos, 2000—02; chmn. San Marcos Arts Commn., 2003—05; fundraising adv. bd. Tex. State U., 2005—06; sec., bd. mem. Lyndon B. Johnson Mus., San Marcos; pres.-elect Friends of the Cemetery, San Marcos; regent DAR. Mem.: Heritage Assn. San Marcos (bd. dirs. 2000—06). Lutheran. Home: PO Box 1248 San Marcos TX 78667

IMMANUEL, LAURA AMELIA, dentist; b. Jakarta, Java, Indonesia, May 11, 1971; d. Gamaliel and Dewi Immanuel. BS, Union Coll., Schenectady, N.Y., 1993; postgrad., Columbia U., N.Y.C., 1993—94; DMD, Tufts U., 1999. Resident in AEGD program SUNY-Stony Brook Dental Sch., 1999—2000; assoc. dentist Total Dental Care, Middle Island, NY, 2000, Dr. Norman Rich, Wantagh, NY, 2000—02, Gentle Dental, Arlington, Mass., 2002—. Recipient award, Internat. Congress of Oral Implantologists, 1999. Mem.: ADA, Mass. Dental Soc., Sigma Xi. Presbyterian. Avocations: photography, painting, music, travel. Office: Gentle Dental 725 Massachusetts Ave Arlington MA 02476

IMMEL, CYNTHIA LUANNE, medical sales specialist; b. Spokane, Wash., Oct. 21, 1958; d. Robert Leon and Barbara Ann (Milholland) I. Student, U. Minn., 1977-79, 81, 92. Asst. prof. photographer U. Minn., 1977, sr. pub. events attendant, 1978; flight attendant Pan Am, N.Y.C., 1979-91; with Fairview Southdale Hosp., 1993—99; key acct. mgr. trauma specialist Smith & Nephews Orthops., 1999—. Swim coach and instr. Carleton Coll., Northfield, Minn.; judge, attendant Spl. Olympics, Baton Rouge, 1982; pub. event rels. Pan Am. N.Y., 1981-85. Artist: Mural, 1973. Named Outstanding Athlete Coaches award, Northfield, 1977, Am. Legion Outstanding Citizen award, Northfield, 1977. Mem. Ind. Union Flight Attendants, World Wings Internat., Northfield Golf Club (exec. bd. mem., v.p., pres.), Pi Beta Phi. Republican. Meth. Avocation: sports. Home: 1220 Washington St Northfield MN 55057-2824

IMMERGUT, KARIN J., prosecutor; b. Bklyn. BA, Amherst Coll., 1982; JD, U. Calif., Berkeley, 1987. Bar: Calif. 1987, Vt. 1995, Oreg. 1996. Asst. US atty. Central. Dist., Calif., 1988—94; atty. Gravel & Shea, Burlington, Vt., 1994—96, Covington & Burling, Washington, 1987—89; assoc. independent counsel Office Independent Counsel, Washington, 1998; dep. dist. atty. Portland, Oreg., 1996—98; asst. US atty. dist. Oreg. US Dept. Justice, 1998—2001, US atty. Oreg., 2003—. Office: US Attys Office Mark O Hatfield US Courthouse 1000 SW Third Ave Ste 600 Portland OR 97204-2902 Office Phone: 503-727-1000.*

IMPELLIZZERI, ANNE ELMENDORF, insurance company executive, non-profit executive; b. Chgo., Jan. 26, 1933; d. Armin and Laura (Gundlach) Elmendorf; m. Julius Simon Impellizzeri, Oct. 12, 1961 (dec.); children: Laura, Theodore (dec.). BA, Smith Coll., 1955; MA, Yale U., 1957. CLU; ChFC. With Met. Life Ins. Co., NYC, 1959—79, from asst. v.p., corp. social responsibility to v.p. group ins., 1979—88; v.p. N.Y.C. Partnership, NYC, 1988-90; pres., CEO Blanton-Peale Inst., NYC, 1990-98; exec. dir. Russel Wright's Manitoga, Garrison, NY, 1998—2001. Bus. urban issues coun. The Conf. Bd., 1981—85; bd. dirs. Bard Music Festival, 1990—; trustee Smith Coll., 1991—96; bd. dirs. Scenic Hudson, 1997—, treas., 1999—2002, sec., 2004—; trustee Nuveen Mut. Funds, 1994—2004. Trustee Lakeland Bd. Edn., Westchester County, NY, 1967-71, pres., 1970-71; bd. dirs. Nat. Safety Coun., 1974-80; pres. Am. Assn. Gifted Children, 1975-85, chair, 1985-90. Named to Acad. of Women Achievers, YWCA NY, 1978; Fulbright grantee, 1955-56. Mem. Yale Club NYC, Smith Coll. Club N.Y., Women's City Club N.Y. (bd. mem. 2002-06, v.p. 2004-06), Yale Alumni Assn. (bd. govs. 1985-88), Phi Beta Kappa.

IMRAN, AYESHA, internist; b. Karachi, Pakistan, Feb. 13, 1967; came to U.S., 1993; d. Muhammed Iqbal Ali Khan and Rasheed Fatima Iqbal; m. Muhammed Imran, Mar. 18, 1993; children: Samar, Saba, Ahmed Ismail, Ishaq. BA, U. Karachi, 1986, MBBS, 1992. Cert. Am. Bd. Internal Medicine. House officer in surgery and medicine Dow Med. Coll. Civil Hosp., Karachi, 1992-93; rsch. asst. Rush Presbyn. St. Lukes Med. Ctr., Chgo., 1994—95; resident in internal medicine Chgo. Med. Sch., 1996—99; practice primary care internal medicine Chgo., 1999—2002; fellow in geriat. Loyola U., Maywood, Ill., 2002—. Social worker Patients Welfare Assn., Pakistan, 1985, Pediats. Dept., Pakistan, 1990. Mem. ACP. Avocations: current news, travel, cooking. Home: 204 Bridle Path Cir Oak Brook IL 60523-2615 E-mail: geriatrics2@yahoo.com.

INA, KYOKO, professional figure skater; b. Tokyo, Oct. 11, 1972; Competitive history includes placing 1st, U.S. Championships, 1997-98, 2000-02; 3rd, World Championships, 2002; 4th, Winter Olympics, 1998; 5th, Winter Olympics, 2002; among others with ptnrs. Jason Dungjen, 1991-98, John Zimmerman, 1998-. Canadian Stars on Ice Tour, 2003; Stars on Ice Tour, 2004-. Avocations: jet skiing, horseback riding, Broadway shows, tennis.

INAN, ZABRIN, psychiatrist; d. Sabit and Czatdana Inan; children: Eden Inan-Lynch, Gabriel Inan-Lynch(dec.). BS magna cum laude, Loyola U., 1989; MD, U. Ill., 1994. Am. Bd. Psychiatry and Neurology. Child, adolescent and adult psychiatrist Linden Oaks Hosp., Naperville, Ill., 2001—02; child and adolescent psychiatrist Helen Ross McNabb Ctr., Knoxville, Tenn., 2002; pvt. practice Chicago, 2002—, Northbrook, Ill., 2002—. Contbr. med. jours. including Psychiatry & Psychopharmacology. Inst. Juvenile Rsch., Child and Adolescent Psychiatry fellow, U. Ill., Chgo., 2001. Mem.: Ill. State Psychiat. Inst., Ill. Med. Soc. (licentiate), Am. Psychiatry Assn. (licentiate), Am. Acad. Child & Adolescent Psychiatry (licentiate). Avocations: tennis, ballet. Office: 680 N Lake Shore Dr Ste 917B Chicago IL 60611 Office Phone: 312-286-1785.

INCE, LAUREL T., music educator; b. Gonzales, Tex. m. Joe C. Ince; children: Joe C. Ince, Jr.(dec.), Mark A., Susan I. Burns, William C. BMus, Trinity U., 1950. Piano tchr. Ince Piano Studio, Gonzales, 1950—. Performer various internat. workshops, Austria, Can., Switzerland, Scotland, France; south ctrl. coord. music Link Found., 1990—; mem. founders coun. Internat. Festival Inst. at Round Top. Contbr. articles to profl. jours. Advisor City Coun., Gonzales; accompanist First Bapt. Ch., Gonzales; pres. Sesame Club, Gonzales. Recipient Tchr. of Yr. award, Austin Music Tchrs. Assn., 1995, Pillar of the Point award, Inspiration Point Fine Arts Colony. Mem.: Music Tchrs. Nat. Assn. Found. Fund (Tex. chair), Nat. Guild Piano Tchrs., Tex. Music Tchrs. Assn. (state pres., Tchr. of Yr. award 1995), Nat. Fedn. Music Clubs (life; chmn. FAMA 1991, co-chmn. nat. conv. 2005, recording sec., lectr., performer, Tex. rep. to bd. dirs.), Tex. Fedn. Music Clubs (founder jr. state festival 1975, state pres.), Sigma Alpha Iota (life). Avocations: entertaining, travel. Home: 723 St Francis Str Gonzales TX 78629 Home Fax: 830-672-5808. Personal E-mail: ljince@gvec.net.

INCO, ELIZABETH MARY, nurse, consultant; b. Troy, N.Y., Jan. 23, 1960; d. Theresa Mary and Andrew Albert Inco. AS in Med. Asst., Becker Jr. Coll., Worcester, Mass., 1978—80; BSN, Russell Sage Coll., Troy, N.Y., 1980—83; Cert. for Legal Nurse Cons., Northeastern U., Boston, 2000—01. RN Mass., 1984, N.H., 1995. Primary nurse Faulkner Hosp., Boston, 1983—84, Lahey Clinic, Burlington, Mass., 1984—85; mktg. mgr., liaison nurse and cmty. health nurse VNA of Middlesex East, Stoneham, Mass., 1985—95; case mgr. Tufts Health Plan, Waltham, Mass., 1995—96; hosp. liaison nurse Sommerville Hosp. Home Care, Mass., 1996—2000; cmty. liaison mgr. VNA of Greater Lowell, Mass., 2000—. Past pres., pres., bd. mem. and v.p. N. Reading Cmty. Chorale, Mass., 1985—; bd. mem. The Cmty. Family, Mass., 2002—. Mem.: Am. Assn. of Legal Nurse Consultants (hon.; legal nurse cons. 2001), Sigma Theta Tau Internat. (hon.; pub. rels. 2001). Office: VNA of Greater Lowell 336 Central St Lowell MA 01853 Office Phone: 978-459-9343. Personal E-mail: bettyinco@earthlink.net.

INDENBAUM, DOROTHY, musician, researcher; b. N.Y.C., Nov. 24; d. Abraham and Celia (Pine) Shapiro; m. Eli Indenbaum; children: Arthur, Esther. BA, Bklyn. Coll., 1942; MS, Queens Coll., 1962; PhD, NYU, 1993. Prof. Dalcroze Sch. Music, N.Y.C., 1957-93, chmn., 1995—; prof. Hunter Coll., N.Y.C., 1970-77. Assoc. dir. Aviva Players, N.Y.C., 1977—. Performed piano with chamber music ensembles. Chmn. Am. Jewish Congress, 1958-60, YIVO, 1980—, Bohemian Club, 1980—, 92nd St YMHA, 1985—. Mem. Am. Women Composers (bd. dirs. 1988-93), Internat. Alliance for Women in Music (bd. dirs. 1993—), Sonneck Soc., League for Yiddish, Musicians Club (bd. dirs. 1983—), Sigma Alpha Iota (program chmn.).

INES, AMY, elementary school educator; b. Wichita, Kans., Sept. 24, 1969; d. Stanley Daniel Baldwin and Karen Lee Swisher; m. David Teofilo Ines, June 26, 1993; children: Daved-Mychal, Jordan Daniel, Estevan Teofilo, Kaylie Hope. BEd, Wichita State U., 1993, M in Curriculum and Instrn., 1997. ESOL endorsement; cert. K-9 tchr. Tchr. grade 7 Pleasant Valley Middle Sch., Wichita, 1993-96, ESOL tchr., 1996—. Coord. Youth to Youth, Pleasant Valley; recycling coord., Pleasant Valley; sponsor student coun. qpa writing chair principal's leadership team. Democrat. Avocations: family activities, reading, walking. Office: Pleasant Valley Middle Sch 2220 W 29th St N Wichita KS 67204-4835

INFANTE, BEATRIZ V., information technology executive; b. Cuba; BS, Princeton Univ., 1976; MS, Calif. Inst. Tech. With Hewlett Packard Corp.; co-founder, dir. software develop. Momenta, 1992; with Taligent; sr. v.p. application server div. Oracle Corp., 1997—98; exec. v.p. Aspect Communications, 1998—2000, chmn., pres., CEO, 2000—03; interim CEO Synchron, 2005; CEO, dir. VoiceObjects Inc., San Mateo, Calif., 2006—. Bd. dir. Netli; bd. mem. Joint Venture Silicon Valley Network. Mem. adv. bd. Princeton Univ. Sch. Engring. Office: VoiceObjects Inc Ste 720 1875 S Grant St San Mateo CA 94402*

INFANTE, ISA MARIA, political scientist, educator, lawyer, writer; b. Santo Domingo, Dominican Republic, Sept. 8, 1942; d. Rafael Infante and Dolores Nieves; 1 child, Nina Maria. BA, U. Calif., Santa Cruz, 1973; MA in Comparative Polit. Sys., Yale U., 1975; PhD in Polit. sci., U. Calif., Riverside, 1977; JD, Northeastern U., 2005. Mgmt. trainee Calif. Savs. and Loan Assn., L.A., 1960—61; asst. fgn. corr. L.A. Times, Mexico City, 1961—62; bus. enterprise officer L.A., 1962—64; regional mgr. Strout Realty, Pasadena, Calif., 1964—66; entrepreneur retail stores L.A., Lake Elsinore, Anaheim, Calif., 1966—70; exec. dir. coll. adult rehab. program U. Calif., Riverside, 1970—71; dir. nat. immigration bd. Nat. Lawyers Guild, L.A., 1977; acad. adv. to provost Antioch Coll. West, Antioch U., San Francisco, 1977—78; sr. devel. officer U.S. Human Resources Corp., San Francisco, 1978; spl. asst. to Sarah Weddington, Esq. Interdepartmental Task Force on Women, White House, Washington, 1978—79; policy fellow and program officer Inst. for Ednl. Leadership/Fund for Improvement of Postsecondary Edn., HEW, Washington, 1978—79; assoc. dean Labor Coll. Empire State Coll., SUNY, N.Y.C., 1979—81; pres. Iml Assocs, internat. cons., 1980—. Prof. polit. sci., dir. L.Am. studies dept. Jersey City State Coll., Jersey City, 1983—86; pres. Nat. Hispanic Coalition, Washington, 1978—80; notary pub., 1980—82; mem. Am. Coun. on Edn., 1980—82, Cmty. Bd. 12, Borough of Manhattan, NY, 1980—82; pres. Free, Inc., 2005—. Author (with others): Field Preparation Manual, 1973; contbg. author: Voices From the Ghetto, 1968, The Politics of Teaching Political Science, 1978, Labor Studies Jour., 1981, Political Affairs, 1984. Bd. dirs. Nagle House Co-op, N.Y.C., 1980—82, Solidaridad Humana, Inc., N.Y.C., 1980—82; trustee Ctr. for Integrative Devel., N.Y.C., 1979—82. Pease Barker scholar, 1972—73, Marius de Brabant scholar, 1970—71, Rsch. scholar, NEH, Washington, 1984. Fellow: Am. Polit. Sci. Assn.; mem.: ATLA, NAFE, ABA, Knoxville Bar Assn., Women's Bar Found. of Mass., Nat. Women's Health Networn, Nat. Women's Polit. Caucus, Univ. and Coll. Labor Assn., L.Am. Studies Assn., Am. Ednl. Rsch. Assn., Internat. Polit. Sci. Assn., Soc.Internat. Devel., Yale Club of Boston, Yale Club of N.Y.C. Home: 601 Gill Ave Knoxville TN 37917-7233 Office Phone: 865-637-4074. Personal E-mail: isainfante@bellsouth.net. Business E-Mail: isa@aya.yale.edu.

INFANTE-OGBAC, DAISY INOCENTES, sales executive, real estate agent, marketing professional; b. Marbel, The Philippines, Aug. 3, 1946; came to U.S., 1968; d. Jesus and Josefina (Inocentes) I.; children: Desiree Josephine, Dante Fernancio, Darrell Enerico; m. Rosben Reyes Ogbac, Jan. 30, 1987. AA with highest honors, Notre Dame of Marbel, Philippines, 1963; AB in English magna cum laude, U. Santo Tomas, Manila, 1965, BS in Psychology, 1966; MA in Comms., Fairfield U., 1971. Real estate broker, Fla. Columnist, writer Pinoy News mag., Chgo., 1975-76, Philippine News, Chgo., 1977-80; cons. EDP Cemco Systems, Inc., Oak Brook, Ill., 1980-81; pres. Daisener, Inc., Downers Grove, Ill., 1980-82; cons. EDP Robert J. Irmen Assocs., Hinsdale, Ill., 1981-82; pres. Data Info. Systems Corp., Downers Grove, Ill., 1982-84; broker, co. mgr. Gen. Devel. Corp., Chgo., 1984-86; columnist, writer Via Times, Chgo., 1984-86; owner, pres. Marbel Realty, Chgo., 1984-88; exec. v.p. Dior Enterprises, Inc., Chgo., 1986-88; real estate sales mgr. M.J. Cumber Co., Grand Cayman, Cayman Islands, 1988-89, Vet. Real Estate, Orlando, Fla., 1989-90; sales mgr. All Star Real Estate, Inc., Orlando, 1990-92; ruby network mktg. exec. Melaleuca, Inc., 1991—; pres. Dior Enterprises, Inc., Orlando, 1992—; prin., owner All Travel, Inc., 2002—. Team leader, sr. team leader The Winners Circle, 1998-99. Author: Songs of Love, Prayer, and Worship to the Lord, 1998, Poems of My Youth, 1982; (lyrics and music) My First Twenty Songs, 1981, The Lord is My Rock; song contbrn. CD Songs of Priase 2000; featured contbr. poems; American Poetry Anthology, vol. VIII, no. 4, Best New Poets of 1987, Journey of the Mind, 1995; composer lyrics and melody The Lord in My Rock, 2001; inventor fryer-steamer. Sec. Movement for a Free Philippines, 1984; active OO Pinoy Orgn., 2003. Mem. NAFE, Am. Soc. Profl. Exec. Women, Philippine C. of C. (sec. Chgo. chpt. 1985), Bayanihan Internat. Ladies Assn., Lions (twister Fil-Am. club 1978-79). Roman Catholic. Avocations: bowling, swimming, racquetball, tennis. E-mail: diorentintl@yahoo.com.

INGALLS, MARIE CECELIE, former state legislator, retail executive; b. Faith, S.D., Mar. 31, 1936; d. Jens P. and Ida B. (Hegre) Jensen; m. Dale D. Ingalls, June 20, 1955; children: Duane (dec.), Delane. BS, Black Hills State Coll., 1973, MS, 1978. Elem. tchr. Meade County Schs., Sturgis, SD, 1957-72, Faith Sch. Dist. 46-2, 1973-76; elem. prin. Meade Sch. Dist. 46-1, Sturgis, 1976-81; owner, operator Ingalls, Sturgis, 1978-99; mem., asst. majority whip S.D. House Reps., Pierre, 1986-92; lobbyist S.D. Legislature. Bd. dirs. S.D. Retailers Assn., 1990—98, treas., 1992—93. Former sec. S.D. Rep. Orgn; Rep. nominee S.D. Commr. Sch. and Pub. Lands, 1998. Recipient Woman of Achievement award City of Sturgis, 1986, Retail Bus. of Yr. 1998. Mem. S.D. Cattlewomen, S.D. Stockgrowers (edn. chair), S.D. Farm Bur. (bd. dirs. dist. V 1993-2001, 03—, dist. dir. women's com. 2003-05 women's chair 2005—), Meade County Farm Bur., Faith C. of C. (pres. 1989), Sturgis C. of C. (past bd. dirs.), Key City Investment Club. Republican. Lutheran. Avocations: knitting, crocheting, piano, reading, golf. Home: 17054 Opal Rd Mud Butte SD 57758 Personal E-mail: mcingalls@gwtc.net.

INGANO, KATHRYN MARITA, secondary school educator; d. John and Janice M. Donahue; m. Adam Michael Ingano, Jan. 1, 2005. BA, Framingham State Coll., Mass., 1999; MEd, Worcester State Coll., Mass., 2002; student in Pub. Adminstrn., Framingham State Coll., Mass., 2004—. Coord. commuter svcs. Worcester State Coll., 1999—2001; tchr. social studies Canton HS, Mass., 2001—03, Hudson Cath. HS, Mass., 2003—. Mem.: APA, Am. Hist. Assn., Nat. Coun. Social Studies, Tower Hill Botanic Gardens, Mus. Fine Arts. Office: Hudson Cath High Sch 198 Main St Hudson MA 01749

INGBERMAN, SIMA, real estate company officer; b. Berlin, Nov. 10, 1947; arrived in U.S., 1956; children: Nina Ingberman Genauer, Abraham, Efram. BA, Bklyn. Coll., 1970, MA in Art History, 1978; PhD in Art History, CUNY, 1987. Ptnr. Brumenfelt Partnership, 1998—2003; gen. ptnr. Ingberman Assocs., 2003—. Author: ABC - International Constructivist Architecture, English, German and Japanese edits., 1994. Avocation: collecting architecture and design posters.

INGEBO, MARILYN KAY, human services manager, rehabilitation services professional; b. Le Mars, Iowa, June 11, 1941; d. Robert James Deegan and Margaret Florence Deegan-Lathrum; m. Phillip Stewart Ingebo, July 13, 1963; children: Leonard F. Julie K. BSN, Ariz. State U., 1964; MSN in Nursing Health Svcs. Adminstrn., U. Mich., 1982. RN; cert. case mgr., Office of Workers Compensation; cert. pub. health nurse; cert. life care planner; corp. trainer Total Quality Mgmt. Asst. dir. nursing Beyer Hosp., Ypsilanti, Mich., 1982-83; nursing supr. Kelly Health Care, Ann Arbor, Mich., 1983-84; v.p. sales Sabre Sys. Corp., San Jose, Calif., 1985-88; nursing supr. Vis. Nurses Assn., San Jose, Calif., 1988; dir. nursing, home care supr. Nursefinders, San Jose, Calif., 1988-91; contract nurse OWCP U.S. Dept. Labor, San Francisco, 1992—; from med. case mgr. to dist. mgr. Corvel Corp., San Jose, 1991-95, regional life care planner, 1998—. Sec., treas. Sabre Sys. Corp., San Jose, 1985-88; adv. bd. Santa Clara Valley Med. Ctr., San Jose, 1998-99. Art docent San Jose Mus. Art, 1992-99. Kellogg scholar U. Mich.; Rackham fellow U. Mich. Mem. Case Mgmt. Soc. Am. (bd. dirs., legis. chair 1998—), Rehab. Ins. Nurses Group (bd. dirs., legis. chair 1998—), Sigma Theta Tau (nursing hon.). Republican. Roman Catholic. Avocations: swimming, hiking, reading. E-mail: mingebo@aol.com.

INGERSOLL, CAROLINE YEE, director; d. Paul Yee and Violet Kau; m. Richard King Ingersoll, Aug. 31, 1968; children: Kristin Paula Juk Yee, Karin Eleanor Juk Ling. BA, Occidental Coll., 1966; tchg. credential, U. Calif., Berkeley, 1967; MA, U. Ill., 1970; MBA, U. Hawaii, 1982. Tchr. Willard Intermediate Sch., Berkeley, 1967—69, Maine Twp. HS, Park Ridge, Ill., 1970—73; mktg. and bus. planner GTE Hawaiian Tel. Co., Honolulu, 1984—97; dir. internat. advancement and prin. gifts U. Hawaii Found., Honolulu, 1997—. Bd. dirs., sec. LWV, Honolulu, 1995—98; bd. dirs. Hawaii Symphony Orch., Honolulu, 1998, YWCA, 1997—2003. Home: 944 Waiholo St Honolulu HI 96821 Office: Univ Hawaii Found 2444 Dole St Bachman Hall 101 Honolulu HI 96822

INGERSON, NANCY NINA MOORE, special education educator; b. Springfield, Ill., Sept. 10, 1940; d. Irvin Lysle and Dorothe Nina (Spencer) Moore; m. Paul Gates Ingerson, Aug. 13, 1966 (divorced); children: Paul G., Gregory M. BA in English Lit., U. Ill., 1963. Cert. secondary edn. educator, cert. spl. edn. educator. Sec., adminstrv. asst. Elec. Engring. Rsch. Lab. U. Ill., Urbana, 1958-66; adminstrv. asst. Hughes Aircraft Space and Comm., El Segundo, Calif., 1988-92; tchr. spl. edn. Narbonne H.S. L.A. Unified Sch. Dist., Harbor City, Calif., 1994—, social club chmn., 1996, 1997, 1999—2002, social club co-chmn., 2000—03, mem. leadership coun., 1999—2004, chmn. dept. spl. edn., 2001—03. Independent. Lutheran. Avocations: porcelain doll making, tile painting, print making, drawing. Home: 765 W 26th St 503 San Pedro CA 90731-6351

INGLE, BETTYE See HARRISON (INGLE), BETTYE

INGLE, BEVERLY DAWN, elementary school educator; d. Elmer and Laura Mae Ingle. BS in Elem. Edn., U. Wis., 1978; MA in Diverse Learning, U. Phoenix, 1997. Tchr. Thompson R2J, Loveland, Colo., 1979—82, Cherry Creek Schs., Englewood, Colo., 1982—. Chmn. Front Range UniServ Unit, Aurora, Colo., 1988—94; del. Edn. Internat., 2001. Mem.: NEA (bd. dirs. 1999—2005), Colo. Edn. Assn. (Hazel Petrocco Women's Leadership award 1998), Cherry Creek Edn. Assn. (pres. 1988—92, mem. exec. com. 1999—).

INGLE, MARTI ANNETTE, protective services official, educator, chef; b. Waynesville, N.C., Apr. 3, 1972; d. William Carroll Ingle, Shirley Grooms Ingle. Student, East Coast Bible Coll., 1987—89; EMT-paramedic cert., Haywood C.C., Clyde, NC, 1993, tech. rescue and fire fighting, 1996; degree culinary arts and scis., Alaska Vocat. Tech. Coll., Seward, AK, 2000—01. Cert. emergency rescue technician 1996; tech. rescue instr., swiftwater rescue technician II 1997, haz mat ops. 1994, sr. fire investigations 1999, emergency boat ops. 1999, personal watercraft rescue 1999, PALS 1991, ACLS 1992, advanced trauma life support 1991, pediat. emergencies for prehospital providers 2001, tchr. Alaska, 2001. EMT-paramedic Haywood County Emergency Med. Svcs., Waynesville, NC, 1991—2002; EMS/tech. rescue instr. Haywood C.C., Clyde, NC, 1994—2002; EMS evaluator State of N.C., Raleigh, 1994—2002; EMS/tech. rescue instr. Blue Ridge C.C., Hendersonville, NC, 1995—2002, Tri-County C.C., Murphy, NC, 1996—2002, Southwestern C.C., Sylva, NC, 1998—2002; EMS/fire/rescue instr. Alaska Vocat. Tech. Coll., Seward, Alaska, 2001—03; chef Maritime Ent., Homer, Alaska, 2003—. Mem.: N.C. Assn. Paramedics, N.C. EMS and Rescue Assn., N.C. Assn. Fire Svc. Instrs., Haywood County Rescue Squad (life; 1st lt. and sgt. 1994—99). Avocations: travel, white-water rafting, cooking, reading, mountain biking. Home: 151 Children St Waynesville NC 28786 Personal E-mail: rafty981@yahoo.com.

INGLESI, NOREEN MARY, music educator, poet, composer; b. Providence, June 14, 1952; d. Anthony John and Mary (Marsella) Inglesi. A of Fine Arts/Music, C.C. of R.I., 1990; MusB, U. R.I., 1994, M in Music Edn., 1997. Cert. music tchr. grades PreK-12 pub. sch. Pvt. tchr. Robert's Music, Warwick, RI, 1994-95; tchr. music and chorus Warwick Sch. Dept., 1995, Scituate Pub. Sch., RI, 1995—; grad. asst. U. R.I., 1995-97; tchr. music N. Providence Sch. Dept., 1997—; instr. music C.C. R.I., 1997—2000. Composer, arranger Andreau Marc Pub. Co., NY; composer, singer for performance group Double Helix; composer music for fall events Habitat for Humanity, 2003; composer original music Shakespeare's Comedy of Errors, Merchant of Venice Colonial Theatre, 2002—03. Author: (poetry) Stockpiled Passions, 1993; composer: Somalia, 1994, Children's Song Cycle, 1996, Symphony #2: Wonders of Nature, 1999, (poetry CD) Somalia, 1995, Digital Mystery Tour, Dance of the Firefly, 1998; contbr. concert revs. to jours. and newspapers; performer: (CD) Where the Rivers Bend, 2001, CD, duet for flute and harp. Singer C.C. R.I. Chorus, Warwick, 1990—95, peer tutor; singer Feminist Chorus, Providence, 1990—94; orchestral piece performed by Culver Chamber Music Series, 1998, 1999; avante-garde arrangement of nursery rhymes performed by Insight Quartet, Italy, 1999. Recipient award, Am. Tuberculosis Soc., 1968, recognition, Billboard Nat. Songcontest, 1994—95, Composers Guild, 1994—96, honorable mention, Providence Jour. Bul. Poetry Contest, 1995; grantee, NEA, 2001, R.I. State Coun. Arts Nature Conservancy, 2005, Rhode State Coun. on the Arts, 2000, 2005; scholar All Am., 1995. Mem.: Music Educators Nat. Conf. (Excellence award 2004), R.I. Songwriters Assn., R.I. Music Educators Assn. (pub. rels. mgr. 1995—96), R.I. Poetry Soc., Assn. Author/Composers, Nat. Educators Assn., Nat. Choral Soc., Phi Kappa Lambda, Phi Kappa Phi. Avocations: writing short stories, painting. Personal E-mail: noreeninglesi@cox.net.

INGOLD, CATHERINE WHITE, academic administrator; b. Columbia, S.C., Mar. 15, 1949; d. Hiram Hutchison and Annelle (Stover) White; m. Wesley Thomas Ingold, June 13, 1970; 1 child, Thomas Bradford Hutchison. Student, U. Paris-Sorbonne, 1969; BS in French with honors, Hollins Coll., 1970; MA in Romance Langs., U. Va., 1972, PhD in French, 1979; DHum honoris causa, Francis Marion U., Florence, S.C., 1992. Assoc. prof. romance langs. Gallaudet U., Washington, 1973-88, dir. hons. program, 1980-85, dean arts and scis., 1985-86, provost, v.p. acad. affairs, 1986-88; pres. Am. U. of Paris, 1988-92, Curry Coll., Milton, Mass., 1992-96. Dir. Nat. Fgn. Lang. Ctr. Johns Hopkins U.; bd. dir. U. Md. Recipient Prix Morot-Sir de Langue et Littérature françaises (Hollins). Mem. MLA, Nat. Collegiate Honors Coun., Lychnos Soc. (U.Va.), Phi Beta Kappa. Episcopalian. Home: 2015 N Brandywine St Arlington VA 22207-2200 Office: Nat Fgn Lang Ctr Patapsco Bldg Ste 2132 5201 Paint Branch Pkwy College Park MD 20742 Office Phone: 301-405-9828. Business E-Mail: cwingold@nflc.org.

INGOLD, JENNIFER CARRIE, educator; b. Greensboro, NC, June 12, 1976; d. Susan Boatner Morris; m. James Brian Ingold, Sept. 27, 1977; 1 child, Maxton Thomas. BS, U. NC, Chapel Hill, 1998. Clin. assoc. Moses Cone Meml. Hosp., Greensboro, NC, 1998—99; tchr. Guilford County Schs., 1999—. Advisor SE Guilford Jr. Civitan, Greensboro, 2001—06; bd. dirs. SE Guilford Civitan, 2004—06. Mem.: NC Tchrs. Assn. (sch. rep. 1999—2001). Southern Baptist. Avocations: swimming, travel, singing. Office: Southeast Guilford High School 4530 Southeast School Road Greensboro NC 27406 Office Phone: 336-674-4300. Home Fax: 336-674-4290; Office Fax: 336-674-4290. Personal E-mail: ingoldj@gcsnc.com.

INGOLFSSON-FASSBIND, URSULA G., music educator; b. Zurich, Switzerland, Dec. 22, 1943; arrived in U.S., 1980; d. Franz Bernardin Fassbind and Gertrud M. Schmucki; m. Ketill Ingolfsson; children: Katla Soffia, Judith, Mirjam, Bera Bjorg. Nat. tchrs. diploma, Conservatory Zurich, 1965, soloist diploma, 1968; postgrad., U. Ariz., 1969—70. Tchg. asst. Conservatory Zurich, 1966—68; with Reykjavik (Iceland) Music Coll., 1970—79, Settlement Music Sch., Phila., 1987—2000; founder, dir., tchr., performer Leopold Mozart Acad. and Franz Fassbind Found., Phila., 2001—. Founder, dir. Leopold Mozart Chamber Music Concerts, 2002—. Grantee Excellency in Tchg. grant, Wilmington (Del.) Piano Co., 2003. Mem.: Am. Composers Guild, Music Tchr. Nat. Assn. Democrat. Avocations: painting, gardening. Home and Office: Leopold Mozart Academy 4833 Pulaski Ave Philadelphia PA 19144 Office Phone: 215-848-1370. Personal E-mail: lmozartacademy@aol.com.

INGRAHAM, LAURA, lawyer, political commentator; b. Glastonbury, Conn., June 19, 1964; BA in Russian and English lit., Dartmouth Coll.; JD, U. Va. Sch. of Law, 1991. Speechwriter White House and Dept. Edn. and Transp., 1986—88; law clerk to Supreme Ct. Justice Clarence Thomas and Ralph K. Winter, US Ct. Appeals Second Cir., 1992—93; criminal def. lawyer Skadden, Arps, Slate, Meagher & Flom, Wash., DC, 1993—96; host Watch It! with Laura Ingraham, MSNBC, 1996—2000, nat. syndicated radio program, The Laura Ingraham Show, 2001—. Co-founder The Dark Ages Weekend. Author: The Hillary Trap: Looking for Power in All the Wrong Places, 2000, Shut Up & Sing: How the Elites in Hollywood, Politics.and the UN are Subverting America, 2003; contbr. NY Times, Wash. Post, LA Times, San Francisco Chronicle. Office: Talk Radio Network PO Box 3755 Central Point OR 97502

INGRAM, BARBARA AVERETT, minister; b. Decatur, Ga., May 8, 1960; d. Charles Cole and Avarilla Gleen (Caldwell) Averett; m. George Conley Ingram IV, Nov. 7, 1987; children: Martha-Conley Elizabeth, Rebekah-Ann Elizabeth. AS, Montreat-Anderson Coll., 1981; BA, Pfeiffer Coll., 1983; MDiv, Emory U., 1986; D of Ministry, Columbia Theol. Sem., 2003. Ordained to ministry United Meth. Ch. as deacon, 1986, as elder, 1988. Assoc. min. 1st United Meth. Ch., Lenoir, NC, 1986-87, Cen. United Meth. Ch., Mt. Airy, NC, 1987-88; sr. min. Ogburn Meml. United Meth. Ch., Winston-Salem, NC, 1988—91, Ann St.-Bogers Chapel UMC, Concord, NC, 1991—, Shiloh UMC, Concord, 1997, Lebanon-Fairfield United Meth. Ch., Denver, NC, 2000—05; assoc. pastor Midway United Meth. Ch., Alpharetta, Ga., 2004—05; sr. pastor Woodstock (Ga.) United Meth. Ch., Big Springs, Ga., 2005. Del. conf. Rule Ch. Ministry, 2004. Republican. E-mail: circleofprayers@comcast.net.

INGRAM, HELEN MOYER, political science professor; b. Denver, July 12, 1937; d. Oliver Weldon and Hazel Margaret (Wickard) Hill; m. W. David Laird; children from by previous marriage: Mrill, Maia, Seth. BA, Oberlin Coll., 1959; PhD, Columbia U., 1967. Lectr., asst. prof. polit. sci. U. N.Mex., 1962-69; with Nat. Water Commn., Washington, 1969-72; assoc. prof. polit. sci. U. Ariz., Tucson, 1972-77, prof. polit. sci., 1979-96; dir. Udall Ctr. Studies Pub. Policy, 1988-96; Warmington chair Sch. Social Ecology U. Calif., Irvine, 1995—. Author: (with Dean Mann) Why Policies Succeed of Fail, 1980, (with Nancy Laney and John McCain) A Policy Approach to Representation: Lessons from the Four Corners States, 1980, (with Martin, Laney and Griffin) Saving Water in a Desert City, 1984, (with Brown) Water and Poverty in the Southwest, 1987, Water Politics: Continuity and Change, 1990, (with Nancy Laney and David Gillilan) Divided Waters: Divided Waters: Bridging the U.S.-Mexico Border, 1995, (with Ann Schneider) Policy Design for Democracy, 1997; editor: (with Rathgeb Smith) Public Policy for Democracy, 1993, (with Joachim Blatter) Reflections on Water, 2001 (with Anne Schneider) Deserving and Entitled: Social Constructions and Public Policy, 2005, (with David S. Meyer and Valerie Jenness) Routing the Opposition: Social Movements, Public Policy and Democracy, 2005; book rev. editor Am. Polit. Sci. Rev., 1987-92. Mem. ind. sci. bd. Calif. Bay Delta Authority, 2002—05. Sr. fellow, Resources for Future, Washington, 1977—79. Mem. Policy Studies Orgn. (pres. 1985), Am. Polit. Sci. Assn. (coun., treas. 1985-87), Western Polit. Sci. Assn. (past pres., v.p.). Home: 4749 E San Francisco Blvd Tucson AZ 85712-1238 E-mail: hingram@uci.edu.

INGRAM, JUDITH ELIZABETH, writer; b. Alameda, Calif., May 6, 1951; d. William Ralph and Elizabeth (Lelis) Madler; m. Frank David Ingram, Sept. 4, 1971; 1 child, Melanie Anne. AA, Chabot Coll., Hayward, Calif., 1972; BS in Biology summa cum laude, Calif. State U., Hayward, 1978; MA in Counseling, St. Mary's Coll. of Calif., Moraga, 1996. Tech. writer Tech. Writing Svcs., Dublin, Calif., 1990-93; counselor trainee Valley Christian Counseling, Dublin, 1995-96, counselor, dir. devel., 1996-97. Mem.: ACA, Assn. for Spiritual, Ethical and Religious Values in Counseling, Am. Assn. Christian Counselors, We. Assn. Counselor Edn. and Supervision. Presbyterian. Avocations: writing, desktop publishing and computer graphic designing, reading psychology, philosophy and women's issues. Home: 8724 Augusta Ct Dublin CA 94568-1063 E-mail: jingramtws@aol.com.

INGRAM, MARTHA RIVERS, publishing executive; b. Charleston, SC, Aug. 20, 1935; m. E. Bronson Ingram (dec. 1995), Oct. 4, 1958; children: Orrin Henry III, John Rivers, David Bronson, Robin. BA in History, Vassar Coll., 1957. V.p., pub. affairs Ingram Industries Inc., Nashville, 1979—95, mem., bd. directors, 1981—, chmn. bd. dirs., 1995—. Bd. dirs. Baxter Internat., Weyerhaeuser Co., Ashley Hall, Vassar Coll., Harpeth Hall Sch., Ingram Micro Inc.; mem. adv. bd. Kennedy Ctr. for Performing Arts, Washington. Chmn. Tenn. Bicentennial Commn., 1996; bd. dirs. Tenn. Performing Arts Ctr., Nashville Ballet, Nashville Opera, Nashville Inst. for Arts, Nashville Symphony, Nashville Cmty. Found.; past chmn. United Way's Alexis de Tocqueville Soc.; founder, bd. dirs. Tenn. Repertory Theater; chmn. bd. trustees Vanderbilt U., 1999-; co-founder Ingram Charitable Fund, 1995. Named one of Richest Americans, Forbes, 2001—, World's Richest People, 2001—; named to Jr. Achievement Nat. Bus. Hall of Fame, 1999, SC Bus. Hall of Fame, 1999; recipient Mary Harriman Cmty. Leadership award, Jr. League Internat., Inc., Joe Kraft Humanitarian award, Cmty. Found., 2006. Mem. Nashville Area C. of C. Office: Ingram Industries Inc One Belle Mead Pl 4400 Harding Rd Nashville TN 37205-2244

INGRAM, SHIRLEY JEAN, social worker; b. Louisville, Oct. 22, 1946; BA in Social Sci., U. Hawaii, Pearl City, 1979; MSW, Fla. State U., 1982. Diplomate Am. Bd. Social Work; lic. social worker, Ala.; qualified clin. social worker, Md. Case mgr. Geriatric Residential Treatment Ctr., Crestview, Fla., 1982-84; case mgmt. supr. Okaloosa Guidance Ctr., Fort Walton Beach, Fla., 1984-86; family counselor Harbor Oaks Hosp., Fort Walton Beach, 1986-87; pvt. practice Fort Walton Beach, 1987-95; social worker USAF Family Advocacy Office, Hurlburt Field, Fla., 1995—2001; exec. dir. ct.-apptd. juvenile advocates program Madison County Courthouse, Huntsville, Ala., 2001—. Quality assurance bd. dirs. State Dept. Human Svcs., Madison County, Ala. Mem. Mental Health Assn. Okaloosa County (sec. bd. dirs. 1988—, mem. adv. bd. dirs. Area Agy. on Aging, chmn. adv. bd. dirs., Okaloosa County Area Agy. on Aging, pres.), NASW, Long Term Care Ombudsman Coun., AAUW, Sertoma. Home: 312 Mossy Oak Dr Huntsville AL 35806 Office: Madison County Courthouse 100 Northside Sq Huntsville AL 35801 Office Phone: 256-532-6988. Business E-Mail: cajaoir@co.madison.al.us.

INGRAM, TRESSIA M., mechanical engineer; d. Phillip C. Burnett and Josephine Ingram. BS in Mech. Engring., Wayne State U., 1998. From intern to project engr. Fed. Mogul Corp., Southfield, Mich., 1995; dynamometer support engr., intern GM, Ypsilanti, Mich., 1996; mfg. process engr. Ford Motor Corp., Dearborn, Mich., 1997; indsl. engr., intern Unisys Corp., Plymouth, Mich., 1998; performance engr. GM, Warren, Mich., 1998—. Employment recruiter asst. GM, Detroit, 2003—. Mentor Big Bros. Big Sisters, Detroit, 1996—2005; spkr. radio broadcast campaign Big Bros. Big Sisters, WWJ News Radio, 2004; pres. Crary St. Mary's Cmty. Coun., Detroit, 2005, sec., 2005; mem. Third New Hope Bapt. Ch. Recipient Newspaper Article Recognition, Mich. Chronicle Newspaper, 2004, Employee Spotlight Article Recognition, GM, 2004, Cmty. Svc. Letter Recognition, Charles H. Wright Mus. African Am. History, 2004, award for radio broadcast campaign for Big Bros. Big Sisters, WWJ News Radio, 2004; scholar, Coleman A. Young Found., 1989—93; Student Life Endowment scholar, Oakland U., 1989—90. Mem.: Women Econs. Club. Baptist. Avocations: reading, travel, bicycling. Office Phone: 586-492-4672.

INKSTER, JULI, professional golfer; b. Santa Cruz, Calif., June 24, 1960; m. Brian Inkster, July, 1980; 2 daughters. Student, San Jose State U. Professional golfer LPGA, 1983—. Mem. U.S. Solheim Cup teams, 1992, 98, 2000, 2002, 2003; mem. U.S. World Cup Team, 1980, 82. Named a Collegiate All-American, 1979, 1981—82; recipient Rookie of the Year, Golf Digest, 1983, Espy, Outstanding Woman Golfer, ESPN, 2000. Achievements include winning 30 career LPGA victories including the Du Maurier Classic in 1984, and the Kraft Nabisco Championships in 1984 and 1989; winning the the McDonald's LPGA Championship in 1999 and 2000, and the U.S. Women's Open in 1999 and 2002; won U.S. Women's Amateur Title from 1980-1982. Office: care LPGA 100 International Golf Dr Daytona Beach FL 32124-1082

INMAN, JANICE ELAINE, special education educator; b. Indpls., Oct. 31, 1944; d. William Thomas and Rosemary (Zeph) Stader; m. Kenneth Albert Inman, June 17, 1967; children: Therese Marie, Kenneth Alexander, Eric William, Nancy Jane. BA, Our Lady Of Lake U., 1966; postgrad., Ft. Hays State U., 1988-91. Cert. speech and lang. tchr., Tex., Mo., Ind., early childhood spl. edn. tech., Mo., Ind. Speech therapist Indpls. Speech and Hearing Ctr., 1967-69, Greenfield (Ind.) Community Schs., 1969-70, Warren Achievement Sch., Monmouth, Ill., 1970-74; coord. religious edn. St. Robert Parish, Flushing, Mich., 1977-83; speech therapist Cerebral Palsy Tri-County, Joplin, Mo., 1984-88, tchr. early childhood spl. edn., 1989-90, Russell Child Devel. Ctr., Garden City, Kans., 1988-89; tchr. vocat. resources edn. Perry County Sch. Dist. # 32, Perryville, Mo., 1990—93; early childhood spl. edn. tchr. Spl. Sch. Dist. St. Louis County, St. Louis, 1993—2001; learning cons. Our Lady of Providence Sch., St. Louis, 2001—. Spl. edn. trainer Boy Scouts Am., Galesburg, Ill., 1970-74; handicapped advocate Cath. Diocese Lansing, Mich., Flint, Mich., 1980-83; para-profl. trainer Cerebral Palsy Tri-County, Joplin, 1986-88, 90. Cub scout leader, Oshkosh, Wis., 1974—75, Flushing, Mich., 1977—83; vol. in edn. Wheaton, Ill., 1975—77; boy scout leader Neosho, Mo., 1985—88; brownie leader, 1985—88; leader Explorer Scouts, Garden City, Kans., 1988—89; religeous vol., 1988—89; religeous edn. vol. Perryville, Mo., 1991—92. Named Mother of Yr. Flushing Observer, 1983. Mem. Coun. Exceptional Children, Vocat.-Indsl. Clubs Am. (jr. dist. advisor 1991). Roman Catholic. Avocations: youth group work, walking, crocheting. Home: 2903 Chevron Dr Saint Louis MO 63125-3044 E-mail: jan_inman@hotmail.com.

INMAN, MARIANNE ELIZABETH, academic administrator; b. Berwyn, Ill., Jan. 9, 1943; d. Miles V. and Bessee M. (Hejtmanek), Plzak; m. David P. Inman; Aug 1, 1964. BA, Purdue U., 1964; AM, Ind. U., 1967; PhD, U. Tex., 1978. Dir. Comml. Div. World Instruction and Translation, Inc., Arlington, Va., 1969-71; program staff mem. Ctr. for Applied Linguistics, Arlington, 1972-73; lectr. in French No. Va. Community Coll., Bailey's Crossroads, 1973; faculty mem., linguistic researcher Tehran (Iran) U., 1973-75; intern mgmt. edn. rsch. & devel. S.W Ednl. Devel. Lab., Austin, Tex., 1977-78; asst. prof., program dir. Southwestern U., Georgetown, Tex., 1978; dir. English lang. inst. Alaska Pacific U., Anchorage, 1980-87, chairperson all-U. requirements, 1984-88, assoc. dean acad. affairs, 1988-90; v.p. dean of coll. Northland Coll., Ashland, Wis., 1990-95; pres. Ctrl. Meth. Univ., Fayette, Mo., 1995—. Contbr. Pres. Commn. Foreign Lang. and Internat. Studies, Washington, 1978-79; manuscript evaluator The Modern Lang. Jour., Columbus, Ohio, 1979-84; cons. Anchorage Sch. Dist., 1984-90; cons., evaluator The Higher Learning Commn. of N. Cen. Assn. Colls. and Schs., Chgo., 1990—; mem. dean's task force Coun. on Ind. Colls., 1993-95; pres. Ind. Colls. and Univs. Mo., 1996-00. Co-author: English for Medical Students, 1976; co-author and editor: English for Science and Engineering Students, 1977; contbr. articles to profl. jours. Treas. Alaska Humanities Forum, Anchorage, 1982-87; mem. Anchorage Matanuska-Susitna Borough Pvt. Industry Coun., 1983-86; mem. Sister Cities Commn., Anchorage, 1984-90; mem. Multicultural Edn. Adv. Bd., Anchorage, 1987-90; with speakers bur. Wis. Humanities Com., 1992-95, Mcpl. Libr. Bd., 1993-95; active Mo. Humanities Coun., 1997-03, 04—, vice chmn., 2005—; bd. dirs. Mo. Colls. Fund, Ind. Colls. and Univs. of Mo., Nat. Assn. of Ind. Colleges and Universities, 2005-; mem. bd. Great Rivers Coun. Boy Scouts Am., 1996—; mem. presdl. adv. com. Mo. Coordinating Bd. for Higher Edn. Named Fellow of Grad. Sch., U. Tex. Austin, 1977-78, Nat. Teaching Fellow, Alaska Pacific U., Anchorage, 1980-81; recipient Pub. Svc. award Sister Cities Commn., Anchorage, 1987, Kellogg Found. Nat. fellowship, Battle Creek, Mich., 1988-91. Mem. LWV, Nat. Assn. Women Edn., Nat. Assn. Ind. Colls. and Univs. (bd. dirs.), Am. Assn. Higher Edn., Am. Coun Tchg. Fgn. Langs., Nat. Assn. Schs. and Colls. of United Meth. Ch. (bd. dirs.), Tchrs. English to Speakers Other Langs., Nat. Coun. Tchrs. English, Gold Peppers, Mortar Board, Alpha Chi, Alpha Lambda Delta, Delta Rho Kappa, Kappa Delta Pi, Omicron Delta Kappa, Phi Kappa Phi, Pi Delta Phi, Pi Lambda Theta, Sigma Delta Pi, Sigma Epsilon Pi, Sigma Kappa. Avocations: community theater, hiking, camping, fishing. Office: Central Methodist Univ 411 Central Methodist Sq Fayette MO 65248-1198 Business E-Mail: minman@centralmethodist.edu.

INNES, DEBBIE, bank executive; V.p., treasury mgmt. Amegy Bank of Texas (subsidiary of Southwest Bancorporation of Texas, Inc.), Houston, 1992—94, exec. v.p., treasury mgmt., 1994—. exec. v.p., retail banking, 2005—. Bd. secy. and chair of volunteer services I Have a Dream, Houston; bd. mem. ESCAPE Family Resource Ctr., Juvenile Diabetes Rsch. Found., Houston. Named one of 25 Women to Watch, US Banker mag., 2005. Office: Amegy Bank of Texas 4400 Post Oak Pkwy Houston TX 77027-7459*

INNES, LAURA, actress; b. Pontiac, Mich., Aug. 16, 1959; BA in Theater, Northwestern U. Appeared in local and nat. plays, including A Streetcar Named Desire, Edmund, Two Shakespearean Actors, Our Town, Three Sisters; appeared in TV series, including Wings, My So-Called Life, Party of Five, Brooklyn Bridge, Louis, ER, 1995— (also dir. episodes); dir. episodes of The West Wing, Presidio Med; TV films include And the Band Played On, 1993, See Jane Run, 1995, Just Like Dad, 1995, The Price of a Broken Heart, 1999, Taking Back Our Town, 2001; appeared in feature film Deep Impact, 1998, Can't Stop Dancing, 1999.

INNES-BROWN, GEORGETTE MEYER, real estate broker, insurance broker; b. Wilmington, Del., Mar. 20, 1918; d. George and Flora Sue (Saunders) Meyer; m. Andrew T. Innes, Jr., Nov. 26, 1947 (dec.); m. Roy Glen Brown, Jr., Mar. 6, 1991. Grad. Real Estate Law, theory, Conveyancing and Practice, Phila. Bd. Realtors Sch., 1945; grad. Fire, Marine, Casualty Ins., North Phila. Realty Bd. Sch., 1946; cert. appraiser, Villanova Coll., 1974. Lic. realtor, Pa., ins. broker and appraiser, Phila. Ins. broker, realtor, Phila., 1945—; ins. broker, 1946—; also appraiser. Residential and single family home builder, Bucks County, Pa., Princeton, N.J., 1955-61. Mem., spkr. Juniata Pk. Civic Assn., Phila., 1984. Recipient Knights Legion award Italian-Am. Press, 1971. Mem. Nat. Assn. Realtors (sec.-treas. and v.p. chpt. 1975-80), Am. Bus. Women's Assn. (chpt. v.p. 1971, Businesswoman of Yr. 1971), Phila. Women's Realty Assn. (pres. bd. govs. 1949-85, pres. 1949-51, Woman of Yr. 1972-73), Phila. Bd. Realtors (v.p. residential divsn. 1975), North Phila. Realty Bd. (v.p. 1975, 76, pres. 1977, Gustav A. Wick award 1979), Del. Coun. Realty Bds. (sec. 1974), Real Estate Multiple Listing Burs. (treas. 1972-76), Sigma Lambda Soc. (chpt. pres. 1948). Avocations: golf, dance, gardening, cooking, embroidery. Home: 1162 SW Walnut Ter Boca Raton FL 33486-5565

INNIS, PAULINE, writer, publishing company executive; b. Devon, England; came to U.S., 1954; m. Walter Deane Innis, Aug. 1, 1959. Attended, U. Manchester, U. London. Author: Hurricane Fighters, 1962, Ernestine or the Pig in the Potting Shed, 1963 (paperback 1992), The Wild Swans Fly, 1964, The Ice Bird, 1965, Wind of the Pampas, 1967, Fire from the Fountains, 1968, Astronumerology, 1971, Gold in the Blue Ridge, 1973, 2d edit., 1980, reprinted 1995, My Trails (transl. from French), 1975, Prayer and Power in the Capital, 1982, The Secret Gardens of Watergate, 1987, Attention: A Quick Guide to Armed Services, 1988, Desert Storm Dairy, 1991, The Nursing Home Companion, 1993, Bridge Across the Seas, 1995, The Gospel of Joseph, 1998, I've Smashed the Devil's Window, 1999; co-author: Protocol, 1977. Bd. dirs. Washington Goodwill Industries Guild, 1962-66; membership chmn. Welcome to Washington Club, 1961-64; co-chmn. Internat. Workshop Capital Spkr.'s Club, 1961-64; pres. Children's Book Guild, 1967-68; dir. Ednl. Commn., bd. dirs. Internat. Conf. Women Writers and Journalists, Nat. Arboretum, 1992-96; criminal justice com. D.C. Commn. on Status of Women; founder vol. program D.C. Women's Detention Ctr.; chmn. women's com. Washington Opera, 1977-79; mem. Liaison Com. Med. Edn., 1979-85; nat. trustee Med. Coll. Pa., 1980—; mem. Edn. Commn. for Fgn. Med. Grads., 1986-97. Named Hoosier Woman of Yr., 1966. Mem. Soc. Women Geographers, Authors League, Smithsonian Assocs. (women's bd.), English-Speaking Union, Spanish-Portuguese Group D.C. (pres. 1965-66), Br. Inst. U.S., Am. Newspaper Women's Club (pres. 1971-73), Internat. Soc. Poets (disting.), Sulgrave Club, Internat. Clubs (co-chair 1997), Venerable Order St. John Jerusalem (comdr.), Internat. Neighbors Club. Home: 2700 Virginia Ave NW Washington DC 20037-1908

INNMON, ARLENE KATHERINE (TARA INNMON), artist, writer, entertainer; b. Mpls., Oct. 28, 1950; d. Morris Jentof and Hulda Cecilia (Levine) Bangsund; children: Carl David, Erica Arlene. BS in Occupl. Therapy, U. Minn., 1973; student in Writing, Hamline U., 2000—. Activities dir. Mother of Perpetual Health Home, Brownsville, Tex., 1973-74; occupl. therapist Corpus Christi Meml. Med. Ctr., Corpus Christi, Tex., 1975—76, Mpls. Soc. for Blind, 1976-81, Grand Ave. Rest Home, Mpls., 1985-87, Tara's Healing Arts, 2000—. One-woman shows include Gus Lucky's Gallery, Mpls., 1987, Paul Whitney Larsen Gallery, St. Paul, 1998, Mayday Cafe, 1999, Anodyne Coffeehouse, 1999, Faribault, 2001, Betseys Back Porch, Mpls., 2002; group exhbns. include Art of Eye I, 1985—, II (multi-yr. traveling exhibits), 1998—, Katherine Nash Gallery, Mpls., 1994, Art and Soul Festival, San Francisco, 1999, Rose Resnick Lighthouse Show-Insights (Outstanding Artist award), San Francisco, 2002, Waterfall Gallery, Mpls., 2002; represented in permanent collections St. Paul Company, Sister Kenney Inst., pvt. collectors.n, Minn. Mem. Minn. Chpt. Abortion Rights, Mpls., 1981. Recipient 1st pl. award drawing, Sister Kenny Internat. Show, Mpls., 1988, People's Choice award bronze, 1990, Artist Appreciation award, Very Spl. Arts, Mpls., 1997, Jaehny award, 1998, 1st pl. award, Artists Beyond Disabilities, Long Beach, Calif., 1997, Docent award, Pa. Acad. Fine Arts, 1999, Sister Kenny Encouragement award, 1999, 2000, 2002, 2003, Best of Show award, Schenectady, N.Y., 2000, Outstanding Artist Insights, San Francisco, 2002, 2d pl. award, Art First, Princeton, N.J., 2003, Hon. Mention award, Insights, Louisville, 2003, award, Guild for the Blind, Phila., 2004, hon. mention, Art First, Princeton, 2005, Jurors award, Art Ability, Malvern, Pa., 2005, Outstanding Artist, Insights, San Francisco, 2005. Mem. SASE, The Loft. Avocations: dance, reading. Home: 2016 27th Ave S Minneapolis MN 55406-1108

INOS, RITA HOCOG, school system administrator; MA in Sch. Adminstrn. and Supervision, San Jose State U., 1983; EdD in Ednl. Planning, Policy and Adminstrn, USC, 1993. Commr. No. Mariana Islands Pub. Sch. System, Saipan, 2002—. Office: No Mariana Islands Pub Sch System 3rd Fl Retirement Fund Bldg Capitol Hill Saipan MP 96950

INSALACO, LISA A., reading specialist; m. Joseph Insalaco, Aug. 22, 1992; children: Nicholas Mical, Emily Rose. BS, Buffalo State U., N.Y., 1987, MS, 1991. Reading specialist Buffalo Schs., 1989—93, North Tonawanda City Schs., North Tonawanda, 1993—. Coord. reading is fundamental Buffalo Schs., 1989—, North Tonawanda Sch. Dist., 1989—, parent leader, 2004—. Recipient Vol. of Yr. award, Reading is Fundamental, 2004. Mem.: Niagra Frontier Reading Counsel, Internat. Reading Assn. Avocations: travel, photography, birdwatching. Home: 5538 Irish Rd North Tonawanda NY 14120

INSALACO-DE NIGRIS, ANNA MARIA THERESA, middle school educator; b. NYC, Oct. 18, 1947; d. Salvatore and Rosaria (Colletti) Insalaco; m. Michael Peter De Nigris, July 12, 1969; children: Jenniffer Ann, Tamara Alicia. BA in English and Langs., CCNY, 1969; MA in English Linguistics, George Mason U., 1988; postgrad., U. Va. Cert. endorsement in Adminstrn. and Supervision U. Va., 2002, English secondary tchr. Va. Tchr. Spanish and core subjects St. John's, Rubidoux, Calif., 1969—70; ESL specialist Sunset Hills Elem. Sch., San Diego, 1980; tchr. Sunrise Acres Elem. Sch., Las Vegas, Nev., 1984—85; tchr. 1st grade Talent House Pvt. Elem. Sch., Fairfax, Va., 1987—88; tchr. ESL Hammond Jr. H.S., Alexandria, Va., 1988—90; tchr. Fairfax County Pub. Mid. Schs., 1995—; summer mid. sch. vol. asst. prin. Longfellow Mid. Sch., 2002. Tchr. adult ESL George Mason H.S., Falls Church, Va., 1988—89; chmn. for multicultural forum Coun. for Applied R&D George Mason U., 1990—94; mem. steering com., faculty adv. com. Herndon Mid. Sch., 1995—, program sponsor Reach for Tomorrow, 1998—2004, sch.-based lead mentor, 1998—, mentor tchr. for new tchrs., 1999—; coach for Krasnow Inst. George Mason U., 2000—, mem. curriculum adv. com. for social studies with county; mem. sch. adoption com. Va. Dept. Transp., 1991, human rels. com., 1990—96, ESL Portfolio Assessment com., 1993—98; sch.-based mem. for minority achievement in prin.'s cabinet F.C. Hammond Jr. H.S., Alexandria, 1989—90; mem. Continuing Edn. Bd. Fairfax County, 1998—; co-chair WATESOL Secondary Interest Group, 1998—99, chair, 1999—2001; presenter in field; mem. World English Spkrs. Team, 2002—05. Vol. Family Svcs., Wright Patterson AFB, Ohio, 1971-72, ARC, Ohio and SC, 1971-73; leader Girl Scouts U.S., 1980-87; scholarship chair Fairfax Edn. Assn. Mem. Va. Edn. Assn. (del. 1990—), Nat. Assn. Bilingual Edn., ESL Multi-Cultural Conv. (presenter, facilitator 1989-2004, socio-polit. concerns immigrant rights advocate 1995—), Tchrs. ESL, Washington Tchrs. ESL, Calif. Tchrs. ESL, Va. Assn. Tchrs. English, Fairfax Edn. Assn. (sch. rep., scholarship chmn., del. Va. Edn. Assn. and NEA), Italian-Am. Caucus (v.p. 1997-2000, pres. 2000-2004). Roman Catholic. Avocations: writing, reading, politics, helping others. Office Phone: 703-904-4800. Personal E-mail: annamaria1@verizon.net. Business E-Mail: annamaria.denigris@fcps.edu.

INSCHO, JEAN ANDERSON, retired social worker, landscape artist; b. Camden, NJ, Oct. 31, 1936; d. George Myrick and Alfrida Elizabeth (Anderson) Hewitt; m. James Ronald Inscho, June 4, 1955 (div. Mar. 1982); children: James Ronald Jr., Cynthia Ann, Michael Merrick. BA, Fla. Atlantic U., 1971; MA in Coll. Teaching, Auburn U., 1974, postgrad., 1998-99. Instr. So. Union State Jr. Coll., Wadley, Ala., 1973-75; social worker Jefferson County Dept. Human Resources, Birmingham, Ala., 1976-77, Shelby County Dept. Human Resources, Columbiana, Ala., 1977-78, Houston County Dept. Human Resources, Dothan, Ala., 1978-98. Adj. instr. Troy State U., Dothan, 1984-97. Bd. dir., v.p. Adolescent Resource Ctr., 1992-93, sec., 1993-95; mem. Alzheimer's Assn. EPDA fellow Auburn U., 1973, 74. Mem.: Am. Horticultural Therapy Assn. (Ga.-Ala. chpt.), Wiregrass Master Gardeners (pres. 1994—95), Ala. Master Gardeners Assn. (bd. dir., sec. 2003—, sec. 2003, recipient award 2004, Outstanding Svc. and Dedication award 2004), Dist. 7 State Employees Assn. (polit. action com. rep. 1994—98), Ala. State Employees Assn. (bd. dir.), Am. Daffodil Soc. Episcopalian. Avocations: gardening, needlecrafts, church activities.

INSELMAN, LAURA SUE, pediatrician, educator; b. Bklyn., Nov. 2, 1944; d. Alexander M. and Rae (Bloom) Inselman. BA, Barnard Coll., 1966; MD, Med. Coll. Pa., 1970. Diplomate Am. Bd. Pediatrics, Am. Bd. Pediatric Pulmonology. Intern and resident St. Lukes Hosp. Ctr., N.Y.C., 1970-73; fellow in pediatric pulmonary disease Babies Hosp., N.Y.C., 1973-76; chief pediatric pulmonary divsn. Interfaith Med. Ctr., Bklyn., 1976-81, Newington Con. Children's Hosp., 1987-92; pulmunologist, med. dir. dept. respiratory care duPont Hosp. for Children, Wilmington, Del., 1992-99, med. dir. pulmonary function lab., 1992—. Asst. prof. pediatrics Cornell U. Med. Coll., N.Y.C., 1981-86; asst. clin. prof. pediatrics, Yale U. Sch. Medicine, New Haven, 1987-92; asst. prof. pediatrics, U. Conn. Health Ctr., Farmington, 1987-92; assoc. prof. pediatrics, Jefferson Med. Coll. Thomas Jefferson U. Hosp., Phila., 1992—; mem. staff Good Samaritan Hosp., West Islip, N.Y., 1982-87. Bd. dirs. Am. Lung Assn. Nassau-Suffolk, East Meadow, N.Y., 1983-86, Del., 1992—. Fellow Am. Acad. Pediatrics, Am. Coll. Chest Physicians; mem. Am. Thoracic Soc., Am. Fedn. Med. Rsch., N.Y. Acad. Medicine, Harvey Soc., Soc. Pediatric Rsch. Office: DuPont Hospital for Children 1600 Rockland Rd Wilmington DE 19803-3607 Office Phone: 302-651-6400.

INSENGA, ANGELA SUZANNE, literature educator; b. Toledo, Sept. 17, 1971; d. Dolores Ann Insenga-Jennings. BA, U. West Ga., Carrollton, 1994; Master's, Clemson U., SC, 1997; PhD, Auburn U., Ala., 2004. Vis. asst. prof. U. West Ga., Carrollton, 2003—. Recipient Martha Saunders Excellence in Tchg. First-Year Writing award, U. West Ga. English Dept., 2005—06; fellow Presdl. Fellowship, Auburn U., 2001—03. Democrat. Roman Catholic. Home: 101-C Danny Dr Carrollton GA 30117 Office: University of West Georgia 1601 Maple St Carrollton GA 30118 Office Phone: 678-839-4864. Business E-Mail: ainsenga@westga.edu.

INTILLI, SHARON MARIE, television director, small business owner; b. Amsterdam, N.Y., Aug. 11, 1950; d. Francisco Joseph Intilli and Virginia Eleanor (Tallman) Monaco. Cert., Paralegal Inst., 1973; BA in Psychology, Fordham U., 1995. Group assoc. editor Matthew Bender & Co., N.Y.C., 1974-77; prodn. sec. 20/20 program, ABC, N.Y.C., 1977-78, prodn. assoc., 1979-80, program prodn. asst., 1980-82; legal contract adminstr. ABC Sports, N.Y.C., 1978-79, dir., assoc. dir. for freelance projects, 1984-87; staff assoc. dir. ABC Television Network, N.Y.C., 1982-98; freelance assoc. dir., 1998—. Owner GreenBeing, Inc. Contbg. editor Bender's Forms of Discovery, Vols. 15 & 16, 1975. Active Bd. Health, Hillsdale, N.J., 1989-95. Recipient Outstanding Individual Achievement cert. Nat. Acad. TV Arts & Scis., 1980-81. Mem. Dirs. Guild of Am. Avocations: writing, photography, cooking, singing. Personal E-mail: greenbe8@warwick.net.

INTRATER, CHERYL WATSON WAYLOR, career management consultant; b. Montreal, Que., Can., Sept. 8, 1943; naturalized, 1978; d. Alan Douglas and Jean Mary (Hughes) Watson; m. Donald L. Intrater, Nov. 11, 1990. BBA, Ga. State U., 1980. CPCU. Instr. ins. DeKalb Coll., Clarkston, Ga., 1978-79; mgr. divsn. Kemper Group, 1979-85; owner Ins. Support Svcs., Inc., Overland Park, Kans., 1986-91; v.p. Fortune and Co. Risk Mgrs., Inc., Overland Park, 1987—94. Owner Career Trend, Overland Park, 1994-97; v.p. orgnl. devel. and outplacement, ptnr., prin., career mgmt. cons. Alexander, Hoyt & Assocs., Overland Park, 1997-2001; owner Career Sys., Overland Park, Kans., 2001—; sr. cons. CSG Ptnrs. Inc., Overland Park, 2001-04; dir. Career Mgmt. Svcs., Jewish Vocat. Svc., Overland Park, Kans., 2002—; adv. coun. Johnson County C.C. Ins. Inst., Overland Park, 1990—; lectr. in field. Mem. Ctrl. Exch., 1998—; mem. fin. resources com. Temple B'nai Jehudah, 2003—, mem. nominating com., 2005—; selected mem. Helzberg Leadership Inst. Helzberg Leadership Fellows, 2006, Program of the Yr. award, Jewish Fedn. Kansas City, 2005. Mem.Assn. of Career Profls. Internat. of Kansas City (charter mem. 2001, pres. 2002), CPCU Soc. (Kansas City chpt.). Avocations: fitness training, reading, travel.

INTRILIGATOR, DEVRIE SHAPIRO, physicist; b. NYC; d. Carl and Lillian Shapiro; m. Michael Intriligator; children: Kenneth, James, William, Robert. BS in Physics, MIT, 1962, MS, 1964; PhD in Planetary and Space Physics, UCLA, 1967. NRC-NASA rsch. assoc. NASA, Ames, Calif., 1967—69; rsch. fellow in physics Calif. Inst. Tech., Pasadena, 1969—72, vis. assoc., 1972—73; asst. prof. U. So. Calif., 1972—80; mem. Space Scis. Ctr., 1978—83; sr. rsch. physicist Carmel Rsch. Ctr., Santa Monica, Calif., 1979—; dir. Space Plasma Lab., 1980—. Cons. NASA, NOAA, Jet Propulsion Lab.; chmn. NAS-NRC com. on solar-terrestrial rsch., 1983-86, exec. com. bd. atmospheric sci. and climate, 1983-86, geophysics study com., 1983-86; U.S. nat. rep. Sci. Com. on Solar-Terrestrial Physics, 1983-86; mem. adv. com. NSF Divsn. Atmospheric Sci. Co-editor: Exploration of the Outer Solar System, 1976; contbr. articles to profl. jours. Recipient 3 Achievement awards NASA, Calif. Resolution of Commendation, 1982. Mem. AAAS, Am. Phys. Soc., Am. Geophys. Union, Cosmos Club. Achievements include being a participant Pioneer 10/11 missions to outer planets; Pioneer Venus Orbiter, Pioneers 6, 7, 8 and 9 heliocentric missions. Home: 140 Foxtail Dr Santa Monica CA 90402-2048 Office: Carmel Rsch Ctr PO Box 1732 Santa Monica CA 90406-1732

INZANA, BARBARA ANN, musician, educator; b. Milw., Mar. 21, 1939; d. Joseph Lindsley and Marie Julia (Haerter) Raynor; m. John Thomas Inzana, June 19, 1965; children: Carolyn Marie, JoAnn Marian. BMus in Edn., Violin, Ind. U., 1961, MMus in Theory, 1969. Music tchr. Deerfield (Ill.) Pub. Schs., 1961—63; grad. teaching asst. theory dept. Ind. U. Music Sch., Bloomington, 1963—65; tchr. music St. James Elem. Sch., Falls Church, Va., 1975—82, St. Mary's Elem. Sch., Alexandria, Va., 1982—83; master tchr. music George Washington U., Washington, 1983—91; choir dir., soloist Nativity Ch., Burke, Va., 1986—91; music dir. Burke Presbyn. Ch., 1992—2002; substitute tchr. Fairfax County (Va.) Schs., 2002—. Pvt. instr. voice, violin, viola, piano, composition and theory, Falls Church, Va.; vocal cons. St. Phillips Ch., Falls Church, 1990—91; poster presenter Nat. Voice Found., 2001. Pub. Washerwoman's Holiday for intermediate string orch., 1997, He Is Born, the Holy One, soprano/alto, flute and piano. Mem. AFTRA, SAG, Am. Guild Mus. Artists, Am. String Tchrs. Assn., N.Am. Bluebird Assn. (founder), Ind. U. Alumni Assn. (life). Home: 403 W Rosemary Ln Falls Church VA 22046-3847

INZINGA, JACQUELINE MARIE, counselor; b. Rochester, N.Y., Feb. 26, 1967; d. Bradley Richard and Connie Marie (Casciani) Gisel; m. Christopher R. Inzinga, Oct. 5, 1991; children: Bradley, Mary Kate, John. BS in Criminology & Criminal Justice, Niagara U., 1989, MS in Sch. Counseling, 1991. Residence counselor Women's Place, Rochester, 1990-93; employment cons. Rochester Rehab. Ctr., Webster, N.Y., 1992-93, placement specialist, 1993-97; vocat. rehab. counselor N.Y. State Vocat. & Ednl. Svcs. for Indiv. with Disabilities, 1998—2004; vocational transitional specialist Monroe 2-Orleans Boles, 2004—. Democrat. Roman Catholic. Avocations: softball, reading, creative writing. Home: 582 Pineglen Dr Webster NY 14580-1135 E-mail: jackie36@rochester.rr.com.

IOLANA, PATRICIA ELVIRA, foundation administrator, consultant; b. Kenosha, Wis., June 15, 1965; d. Richard Schenkel and Maria Johanna Van Dijk; m. Howard Clark (div. Jan. 2005); children: Konane Sage, Kaipo'i Chace. Student, Grand Valley State U., 1988—90; AA with honors, U. Hawaii, 1993; BA magna cum laude, U. No. Colo., 1995; grad., Calif. State U., 2005—. Owner Performance Initiatives, Kailua-Kona, 1995—. Program creator Aloha Performing Arts Ctr., Kealakekua, Hawaii, 1997—98; advisor, funds adminstr. West Hawaii Tobacco Free Coalition, Kailua-Kona, 2001—; advisor County Hawaii Mayor's Office, Hilo, 2002; playwright-in-residence The Artists' Gym, 1998—2000; presenter in field. Author: (plays) A Matter of Opinion, 1995, The Gatehouse, 1998; dir.: (plays) A Matter of Opinion, 1995, 1997, 1998, 2000, 2004, MacBeth, 2004, Bang Bang You're Dead, 2006; prodr.(creator): Banned, 1995, Love Letters, 1998, Gypsy, 1998; dramaturge: The Rose Tattoo, 1995; Hamlet, 1997; Othello, 2005; Romeo and Juliet, 2006; author: The Graffiti Subculture: A Social and Linguistic Community, 1995, The Women of Greek Drama: Social Casting of Gender Roles in Ancient Greek Society, 1995, False Witnesses: The Morality of Arthur Miller's The Crucible, 1996, (publ.) TPAG Publs., 2006, (mag. publ.) Sacred History Mag., 2006. Bd. pres. Aloha Performing Arts Ctr., Kealakekua, 1996—98; founder, bd. chair The Poliokekoa Advocacy Group, Kailua-Kona, 2004—; sr. advisor The Aloha Teen Theatre, Kealakekua, 2004—. Scholar, U. No. Colo. English Dept., 1994—95. Mem.: Internat. Soc. for Religion, Lit. and Culture, Am. Acad. Religion, Sacred History Soc., Sigma Tau Delta (Zeta Psi pres. 1994—95). Avocations: theater, reading, gardening, interior decorating. Office: Performance Initiatives 73-4327 Malu Pl Kailua Kona HI 96740 Office Phone: 808-987-2470.

IONE, AMY, artist, researcher; b. Phila., Sept. 3, 1949; d. Martin Kessler and Barbara Angert. BA, Pa. State U., 1967; MA, John F. Kennedy U., Orinda, Calif., 1995. Instr. John F. Kennedy U., Orinda, Calif., 1995. Bd. dirs. Diatrope Inst.; presenter in field. Exhibited in group shows at U. Sch. Edn., Ann Arbor, Mich., 1974, ASUC Studio Gallery U. Calif., Berkeley, 1979, Haggin Mus., Stockton, Calif., 1985, Nat. Artists Equity Assn., Washington, 1986, Walnut Creek (Calif.) Civic Arts Gallery, 1985, 88; pvt. and permanent collections include Mills Coll. Art Gallery; creator for logo Visual Art Access, 1995; illustrator (with J. Bass) Tjokjok, 1989, 2d edit., 2002; (poster) San Francisco Arts Commn. Festival, 1986, Campanus Houses, 1976; author: Nature Exposed to our Method of Questioning, 2002, Innovation and Visualization, 2005 Home: 1312 Curtin St State College PA 16803 Office Phone: 814-238-2003. Personal E-mail: ione@diatrope.com.

IORIO, PAM, county official; b. Waterville, Maine, Apr. 27, 1959; d. John J. and Dorothy (Lockett) I.; m. Mark S. Woodard, May 30, 1987; children: Caitlin, Graham. BS in Polit. Sci., The Am. U., 1981; MA in History, U. South Fla., 2001. County commr. Hillsborough County, Tampa, Fla., 1985—92, supr. elections, 1993—2003; mayor Tampa, 2003—. Recipient Disting. Alumnus award, Leadership Fla., 2002. Mem.: Fla. State Assn. Suprs. Elections (pres. 2000). Office: City of Tampa Mayor's Office 306 East Jackson St Tampa FL 33602

IOVINO, PAMELA M., federal agency administrator; B in Polit. Sci., Gettysburg Coll. Advanced through grades to capt. USN, 1980—2003, manpower tng. officer Naval Reserve Readiness Command Region Six, 1987, commdg. officer Naval and Marine Corps Reserve Ctr., head legis. liaison br., commdr. Naval and Marine Corps Reserve centers Pitts., Ebensburg, Pa., Moundsville, W.Va., 1998—2001; ret., 2003; acting asst. sec. congl. & legis. affairs US Dept. Veterans Affairs, Washington, 2004, asst. sec. congl. & legis. affairs, 2004—. Decorated Legion of Merit Medal, Meritorious Svc. Medal (two gold stars), Navy Commendation Medal, Navy Achievement Medal, Nat. Def. Medal (two awards), Armed Forces Reserve Medal.

IQBAL, SYMA U., information technology executive; b. Karachi, Sind, Pakistan, Dec. 24, 1967; d. Hafeezuddin and Feroze Munshi; m. Umair Iqbal, Nov. 29, 1995; 1 child, Hamza. BComm, U. Karachi, Pakistan, 1989. Assoc. Chartered Acct., Inst. Chartered Accountants of Pakistan, 1995; cert. profl. Oracle U., 2001. Audit supr. Ernst & Young Pakistan, Karachi, Sind, Pakistan, 1989—93; Oracle applications functional cons. Softech Microsystems, Karachi, Sind, Pakistan, 1999—2000; mgr. accounts Security Leasing Corp. Ltd. - A Merrill Lynch, USA and CDC, UK Co., Karachi, Sind, Pakistan, 1994—99; Oracle financials cons. Amtex Systems Inc, N.Y.C., NY, 2001—. Bus. cons., ERP fin. applications Bi-State Devel. Agy. of St Louis, Mo., 2003; Oracle financials specialist Ingersoll Rand - Air Solutions Group, Davidson, NC, 2003, Ingersoll Rand - Constrn. and Mining Group, Annandale, NJ, 2002—03; Oracle financials cons. GE Power Systems, Milpitas, Calif., 2002; Oracle fin. applications - functional specialist Human Resource Adminstrn., N.Y.C., NY, 2001—02. Achievements include design of Business Process re-engineering architecture for financial applications at Ingersoll Rand - ASG; Business Process re-engineering architecture - NY City Human Resource Administration; Business process re-engineering documentation at GE Power Systems. Office: Amtex Systems Inc 50 Broadway Suite 801 New York NY 10004 Home: 382 Marywood Ct Ballwin MO 63021-6323 Office Phone: 314-982-1400. Personal E-mail: syma_iqbal@hotmail.com.

IRATENE, MARY SUSAN, elementary school educator; d. Russell Harry and Nancy Sue Osborn; m. Mary Susan Osborn, Apr. 31, 2001; 1 child, Kaden Ryan. AA in Gen. Edn. magna cum laude, Santa Rosa Jr. Coll., Calif., 1990; BA in Psychology magna cum laude, Calif. State U., Sacramento, 1993; Tchg. Credential summa cum laude, Chapman U., Sacramento, 1995; MS in Instrnl. Tech., Nat. U., 2006. Multiple subject tchg. credential with social studies authorization Calif., 1995. E.L.L. and mainstream social studies and lang. arts tchr. San Juan Unified Sch. Dist. Jonas Salk, Sacramento, 1995—2000; social studies tchr. San Juan Unified Sch. Dist. Will Rogers Mid. Sch., Fair Oaks, Calif., 2000—. Curriculum trainer for Visions textbook Thomson and Heinle pub., Sacramento, 2004—. Advisor initial steering com. Collins Teen Ctr., West Sacramento, Calif., 1996—98. Mem.: NEA (assoc.), Calif. State Edn. Assn. (assoc.). Democrat. Avocations: travel, technology, camping, hiking, swimming. Office Phone: 916-971-7889. Business E-Mail: siratene@sanjuan.edu.

IRBY, JOCELYN ADKINS, language educator, consultant; d. Joseph and Lillie (Merriweather) Adkins; m. William Harold Hardy; children: Jayme Hardy, William Hardy, Robert Hardy; children: Anthony Jerome-Adkins, Malcom Adkins. BA, Bennett Coll., Greensboro, N.C.; MA English, Tenn. State U., Nashville; MS guidance, counseling, Ft. Valley State Coll., Georgia; PhD English, So. Ill. U., Carbondale, 1995. Advisor Project Thrust U. South Fla., Tampa; career edn. specialist Nashville State Tech. Inst., dir., spl. svcs.; instr. Mid. Tenn. State U., Murfreesboro; prof. Tenn. State U., Nashville. AP reader Ednl. Testing Svc., Daytona Beach, Fla.; adj. prof. Fisk U., Nashville; instr. Smart Acad. Vanderbilt U., Nashville. Mem. Daughters of the King, Nashville, 1990—2006, St. Luke's Episcopal Ch., Nashville, 1982—2006. Recipient Roby Honoree for Academics, So. Ill. U., 1993; fellow ICEOP, State of Ill., 1992—94; Fullbright-Hays grant, Dept. Edn., 1998. Mem.: Alpha Kappa Alpha. Achievements include research in Double-voiced Discourse: Composing Processes of African American Students; Jounrnal of Commonwealth and PostColonial Studies; Journal of African Studies. Home: 7139 Birch Bark Drive Nashville TN 37221 Office: Tennessee State University 3500 John Merritt Blvd Nashville TN 37209-1561 Office Fax: 615-963-5725. E-mail: jirby@tnstate.edu.

IREDALE, NANCY LOUISE, lawyer; BSFS summa cum laude, Georgetown U., 1969; JD, Yale U., 1972. Bar: D.C. 1973, Calif. 1977. Tax counsel to Senator William Brock Senate Finance Committee, 1976; ptnr. Paul Hastings, Janofsky & Walker, LA, with. Named one of Top 100 LA County Super Lawyers, Law & Politics Media, 2004, Top 50 Female Super Lawyers, Super Lawyers Tax, 2006. Fellow: Am. Coll. Tax Counsel; mem. Yale Law Sch. Assn. (exec. com. 1982-85), Phi Beta Kappa, Phi Beta Kappa Alumni (councilor alpha assoc.). Achievements include graduating first in class from Sch. Fgn. Svc., Georgetown U; elected first woman pres. 100-years Jonathan Club. Office: Paul Hastings Janofsky & Walker LLP 515 S Flower St Fl 25 Los Angeles CA 90071-2228 Office Phone: 213-683-6232. Office Fax: 213-627-0705. Business E-Mail: nancyiredale@paulhastings.com.

IRELAND, BETTY, state official; b. Charleston, W. Va. m. Sam Haddad; children: Chuck, Andy, Alex, Janie. Former teacher W. Va. Pub. Sch. Sys.; former owner Retirement Sys. & Svc.; former v.p. & head pension div. Trust Dept. Nat. Bank of Commerce, Charleston; pres. & CEO Jackson & Kelly Solutions LLC, 2002—; sec. of state State of W. Va., Charleston, 2005—. Mem. City of Charleston Bd. of Zoning Appeals, W.Va., 1985—86; rep.-at-large Charleston City Coun., W.Va., 1987—91; citizen expert Pub. Safety Retirement Task Force of Joint Legis. Com. on Pensions & Retirement, W.Va., 1991—92; exec. dir. W. Va. Consolidated Pub. Retirement Bd., 1998—2001. Republican. Office: Office of Sec of State Bldg 1 Suite 157 K 1900 Kanawha Blvd East Charleston WV 25303-0770 Office Phone: 304-558-6000. Office Fax: 304-558-0900. Business E-Mail: wvsos@wvsos.com.*

IRELAND, BETTY JEAN, retired principal, music educator; b. Hale, Mo., Apr. 14, 1940; d. Howard Allan and Ruby A. Kirker; m. Donald L. Ireland, Sr., Jan. 18, 1957; children: Donna Forrest, Joyce Bell, Donald Lee Jr. BS in Edn., Mo. Valley, 1968, State Certification in Vocal & Instrumental Music, 1974; MSE in Elem. Sch. Adminstrn. & Supervision, Ctrl. Mo. State U., 1979. Cert. pub. sch. tchr. Mo., 1968, elem. sch. adminstrn. and supervision Mo., 1979. Pub. sch. tchr. Tina-Avalon Sch., Tina, Mo., 1967—74; vocal & instrumental music tchr. K-12 Wheeling R-V Sch., Mo., 1975—93, elem. prin. and asst. HS prin., 1979—92; prin. Crest Ridge R-7 Elem. Sch., Centerview, Mo., 1993—96. Celebrity auctioneer Kans. City Pub. TV, Mo., 1990, coun. pres., 1990—93, bd. mem., 1990—93. 4-H leader Bosworth Fireballs, Mo., 1967—89; pianist Bosworth Bapt. Ch., 1959—2005, sec./treas., 1990—2005; ch. camp co-dir. Grand Oaks Bapt. Assembly, Chillicothe, Mo.; sec. Carroll Bapt. Assn., 2004—; bd. dirs., treas. Baptist Joint Mission, Carroll-Saline Bapt. Assn. Recipient Tchr. of Yr., Mo. State Tchrs. Assn., 1990. Mem.: DAR, Carroll County Ret. Tchrs. Assn., Mo. Profl. Women's Assn., Mo. Ret. Tchrs. Assn. (corr.), Mo. State Tchrs. Assn. (life), Carrell County Daus. Am. Revolution, Daus. Am. Revolution (mem. vets. com.), Rural Adult Assn., Order Ea. Star (corr.). Conservative. Southern Baptist. Avocations: crocheting, travel, gardening, music. Home: 17877 Cr 321 Bosworth MO 64623 Personal E-mail: direland@cvalley.net.

IRELAND, KATHY, actress, apparel designer; b. Glendale, Calif., 1962; d. John and Barbara Ireland; m. Greg Olsen, 1988; children: Erik, Lily, Chloe. CEO, chief designer Kathy Ireland Worldwide. Designer Kathy Ireland Brand began 2000, appearances in Sports Illustrated's Ann. Swimsuit Issues, 25th Anniversary Show Swimsuit Edit., Kathy Ireland LPGA Championship, ESPN, 2001; films include: Alien from L.A., 1988, Necessary Roughness, 1991, Mom and Dad Save the World, 1992, National Lampoon's Loaded Weapon I, 1993, The Player, Mr. Destiny, Amore, Backfire; TV films include Beauty and the Bandit, 1994, Danger Island, 1994, Miami Hustle, 1995, Gridlock, 1996, Once Upon A Christmas, 2000, Twice Upon A Christmas, 2001; TV appearances include: Down the Shore, The Edge, Tales from the Crypt, Without a Clue, Grand, Charles in Charge, Perry Mason, Boy Meets World, Melrose Place, The Watcher, Deadly Games, Sabrina the Teenage Witch, Suddenly Susan, Gun, Cosby, Touched by an Angel, Pensacola, For Your Love, Strong Medicine. Recipient Entrepreneur of Yr., 2001, Mother of Yr., 2004, Received Good Housekeeping Seal, 2004, Bus. Owner of Yr., 2004, Entrepreneural Champian award, 2005. Office: Kathy Ireland Worldwide 15th Fl 10900 Wilshire Blvd Los Angeles CA 90024-4341 Office Phone: 310-557-2700.

IRELAND, PATRICIA, lawyer; b. Oak Park, Ill., Oct. 19, 1945; d. James Ireland and Joan Filipek; m. James Humble, 1968. BA, U. Tennessee, 1966; JD, U. Miami Law Sch., 1975; degree (hon.), U. R.I., U. Mass. Coll. Law, U. Ind., Sweetbriar Coll. Flight attendant Pan Am. World Airlines, 1967-75; ptnr. Stearns, Weaver, Miller, Weissler, Alhadeff & Sitterson, Miami; nat. pres. NOW, 1991—2001; of counsel Katz, Kutter, Alderman, Bryant & Yon, 2001—03; campaign mgr. Carol Moseley Braun for pres., 2004; of counsel Phillips, Richard & Rind, 2005—. Author: What Women Want, 1996; contbr. law rev. Miami Law Sch. Mailing: PO Box 1569 Homestead FL 33090-1569 Office Phone: 305-412-8322. Personal E-mail: pireland@phillipsrichard.com. Business E-Mail: patriciaireland2@aol.com.

IREY, ROBIN ELIZABETH, performing company executive, performing arts educator; b. Arlington Heights, Ill., Dec. 29, 1971; d. James Delloyd and Jacquelyn Myers Irey. BA in Orgnl. Comm., No. Ill. U., DeKalb, 1995, BFA in Dance Performance, 1995; cert. of completion, Ballet Intensive of Moscow, Chgo., 2003, cert. of completion, 2004. Cert. dance educator Chgo. Nat. Assn. Dance Masters. Dance capt. Busch Gardens, Tampa Bay, Fla., 1995—96; claim rep. Allstate Ins. Co., Northbrook, 1996—99; soloist Northwest Ballet Ensemble, Schaumburg, 1996—98; owner and artistic dir. Cary-Grove Performing Arts Ctr., Cary, 1999—. Benefactor Joe Irey Meml. Scholarship, Cary, Ill., 1990—, Cary Grove Performing Arts Ctr. Dance Scholarships, 1999—; participant Chgo. Marathon, 2005, Chgo. Distance Classic, Indpls. Mini-Marathon, 2006; founder and com. mem. Disaster Aid Needs Cmty. Effort, Cary, Ill., 2005; com. mem. and benefit performer Dana Floor Legacy Fund, 2005, Invisable Children Crisis in Uganda, 2006. Mem.: Chgo. Area Runners Assn., Dance Masters of Wis., Chgo. Nat. Assn. Dance Masters. Democrat. Unitarian Universalist. Avocation: running. Home: 574 Cary Woods Cir Cary IL 60013

IRISH, CAROLYN TANNER, bishop; d. Obert Clark and Grace Adams Tanner; m. Lee Irish (div. 1988); children: Stephen, Jessica, Thomas, Emily; m. Frederick Quinn, 2001. Student, Stanford U.; B in Philosophy with high honors, U. Mich., 1962; MLitt in Moral Philosophy, Oxford U., 1968; MDiv cum laude, Va. Theol. Sem., 1983, doctoral degree (hon.), Westminster Coll., Salt Lake City, U. Utah, Ch. Div. Sch. of the Pacific, Berkeley, Calif., Salt Lake Cmty. Coll., Utah State U. Taught ethics, history, lit. Edmund Burke Sch., Washington; ordained deacon, 1983, priest, 1984; served congregations in Washington, DC, Va, and Mich.; named archdeacon Episcopal Diocese of Mich., 1986; mem. staff Shalem Inst. Spiritual Found., Washington Nat. Cathedral; bishop Episcopal Diocese of Utah, 1996—. Chmn. bd. O.C.

Tanner Co., Salt Lake City. Mem. adv. bd. Shalem Inst. Spiritual Formation. Episcopalian. Office: Episcopal Diocese of Utah PO Box 3090 Salt Lake City UT 84110-3090 Office Phone: 801-322-4131.

IRISH, DIANA MARIA, wildlife rehabilitation agent; b. Grand Rapids, Mich., May 24, 1950; d. Robert Leroy and June Lorraine (Centilli) Newman; m. Harvey Alan Irish, Nov. 22, 1968; children: Timothy, Jamy, Corey, Windy, Robert, Wayne, Shellie. Grad. h.s., Grand Rapids, Mich. Author: My Talking Heart, 1992, Pictures of My Mind, 1994, Wings of Thought; recordings include A Rose for My Daddy and Forest Lane in (tape) Hilltop Country, 1998, Hight Country, Light of the World, Roll Gordon Roll, 1999, Freedom in the Meadow and Prayer of Our Ancesters in (CD) High Country, 1998, Rainbows End, Little Windy and Please Don't Worry in (CD) Light of the World, 1998. Bd. dirs. Coalition Rep. for Govt., Grand Rapids, 1997-99. Recipient Golden Poet award World of Poetry, 1988-99, Homer Honor Soc., 1990, Poet of Merit Internat. Soc. of Poets; named to Internat. Poets Hall of Fame, 1997-99. Mem. Weaving Ethnisity (sec. 1992-2002), C.R.G. (bd. dirs. 1998-2002), Grand Valley Am. Indian Lodge (bd. dirs., sec. 1992-2002), Inter Tribal (mem.-at-large). Avocations: writing, fishing, hunting, native american dancing, doll designer. Home: 5909 Ramsdell Dr NE Rockford MI 49341-9067

IRIZARRY, DORA L., federal judge; b. San Sebastian, Puerto Rico, Jan. 26, 1955; 1 child. BA, Yale U., 1976; JD, Columbia U., 1979. Bar: NY 1981. Asst. D.A., Appeals Bureau Office of the Bronx, 1979—87; with Bronx County Office Special Narcotics Prosecutor, 1981—87; with NY County Office Special Narcotics Prosecutor, 1987—95; asst. D.A. NY County, 1987—95; judge Criminal Ct. NYC, 1995—97, NY State Ct. Claims, 1997—2002; of counsel Hoguet Newman & Regal LLP, 2002—04; judge US Dist. Ct. (Eastern Dist. NY), 2004—. Mem.: Bar Puerto Rican Bar Assn., Com. on the Bench, Assn. Judges Hispanic Heritage (pres. 1997—2002), Fed. Bar Eastern Dist. NY, Fed. Bar Southern Dist. NY, NY State Bar. Office: 225 Cadman Plaza E Brooklyn NY 11201 Business E-Mail: Dora_L_Irizarry@nyed.uscourts.gov.

IRMAS, AUDREY MENEIN, not-for-profit developer; m. Sydney Milton Irmas Jr., June 26, 1949 (dec.); children: Deborah, Robert, Matthew. Co-founding trustee Audrey & Sydney Irmas Charitable Found., 1983—, projects include Audrey & Sydney Irmas Campus of the Wilshire Blvd. Temple, Audrey & Sydney Irmas LA Youth Ctr., many others; bd. trustees Mus. Contemporary Art, LA, 1992—, past pres., chmn.; trustee Hirshhorn Mus. and Sculpture Garden, Washington; bd. govs. ctr curator studies Bard Coll., NY. Named one of Top 200 Collectors, ARTnews mag., 2004. Avocation: Collector contemporary art, photography. Office: Audrey & Sydney Irmas Charitable Found Ste 364 16830 Ventura Blvd Encino CA 91436-2797 Office Phone: 818-382-3313. Office Fax: 818-382-3315.*

IRONBITER, SUZANNE, writer, educator; b. Milw., June 4, 1941; d. John Spoden and Willena Kalmbach; m. John Matthew Potter, Feb. 5, 1966 (wid. Apr. 1992); children: Sarah Curry, Anna Potter. BA, U. Mich., 1963; MA, Columbia U., 1966, PhD, 1972. Lectr. E. Mich. U., Ypsilanti, 1966-77; adj. asst. prof. NYU, 1968-80, Hunter Coll., N.Y.C., 1986—92, SUNY, Purchase, 1992—. Author: Devi, 1987, Devil Mother of My Mind, 2006. Recipient Summer Seminar grant NEH, 1995. Mem. Am. Acad. Religion, Poets House, Poetry Soc. Am.

IRONS, ELLEN JANE, educational leadership educator; b. Lewiston, Idaho; m. Ernest M. Irons Jr.; children: Jo Ann Ponder, Teresa Carmack, Elaine Irons, Dan Pavlica. BS in Edn., U. Fla., 1971; MEd, Trinity U., 1975; EdD, Northeastern U., 1984. Tchr. math. San Antonio Ind. Sch. Dist., 1971—74; edn. diagnostician Ft. Sam Houston Ind. Sch. dist., San Antonio, 1975—78; ednl. rschr. Behavior Rsch. Lab., Aberdeen Proving Ground, Md., 1978; sch. psychologist Cecil County Ind. Sch. Dist., Rising Sun, Md., 1978—80; lectr. math. Northeastern U., Boston, 1981—83; spl. edn. specialist Tex. Edn. Agy., Austin, 1984; dir. instrn. Am. Prep. Inst., Killeen, Tex., 1985; elem. prin. La Pryor (Tex.) Ind. Sch. Dist., 1986; ednl. program dir. Tex. Edn. Agy., Austin, 1987—90; dir. curriculum and instrn. Tex. Youth Commn., Austin, 1990—2003; prof. tchr. edn. Tex. Woman's U., Denton, 1993—2004; prof. ednl. leadership Lamar U., Beaumont, Tex., 2004—. Contbr. articles to profl. jours. Mem.: NASP, Assn. Tchr. Educators, Nat. Coun. Profs. Ednl. Adminstrn., Tex. Coun. Adminstrs. Spl. Edn., Phi Delta Kappa, Kappa Delta Pi. Office: Lamar Univ Dept Edn Leadership and Counseling PO Box 10034 Beaumont TX 77710 Office Phone: 409-880-7954. E-mail: jane.irons@lamar.edu.

IRONS, PAULETTE RILEY, state legislator, lawyer; b. New Orleans, May 19, 1953; d. Florida Wilson; m. Alvin L. Irons; children: Marseah Irons Delatte, Paul-Alvin. BBA, Loyola U., New Orleans, 1975; JD, Tulane U., 1991. Bar: La. 1991. Sr. cons. Small Bus. Devel. and Mgmt. Inst., New Orleans, 1992-93; mem. La. Ho. of Reps., Baton Rouge, 1992-94, La. Senate, Baton Rouge, 1994—. Vice-chmn. transp., hwys. and pub. works com., mem. health and welfare com., formr mem. fin. com., pres. women's caucus,1998, sgt.-at-arms legis. black caucus, 1993-95; sr. cons. Small Bus. Devel. and Mgmt. Inst., New Orleans, 1992-93; adj. prof. Tulane U. Law Clinic, New Orleans, fall 1995; atty. 1st City Ct., New Orleans, 1996-98; atty. Recorder of Mortgages Office, New Orleans, 1997—; adv. bd. women's network Nat. Conf. State Legislators, Denver, 1996—. Pres. bd. dirs. La. Initiative on Teen Pregnancy Prevention, 1995-2001; bd. dirs. New Orleans Area Literacy Coalition. Recipient Woman of Excellence award 2d Bapt. Ch., 1994, Outstanding African Am. Woman, Tulane Black Law Students, 1996, Good Housekeeping award, 2001; named Legislator of Yr., New Orleans Alliance for Good Govt., 1995. Fellow Japan Soc.; mem. LWV, AAUW, Nat. Order Women Legislators, Nat. Order Black Elected Legislators, Women for a Better La., Ind. Women's Orgn., La. League Good Govt. Democrat. Avocations: reading, travel. Address: La Senate Ofc PO Box 94183 Baton Rouge LA 70804-9183 Office: Jud Civil Dist Ct 421 Loyola Ave Room 200B New Orleans LA 70112 Office Phone: 504-592-9250.

IRONS, SHARON LYNN ERICKSON, elementary school educator, client relationship director; d. Eleanor Virginia and James Ozzro Erickson; m. Robert Irons, June 15, 1974; children: Heidi Lee Thompson, Lindsey Michelle Hooper. BS in Music Edn., Heidelberg Coll., 1972; MusM, Bowling Green State U., 1978; trained arts in edn. workshops, Kennedy Ctr., 2004—. Tchr. Findlay City Schs., 1972—; client relationship mgr. Right Thing Inc., Findlay, 2003—. Ice show dir. Silver Blades Skating Club, Findlay, 1994—98; founder Mallets and Movers Group; founder elem. show choir Kids In Action, 1996. Martha Holding Jennings grantee, 1990. Mem.: Ohio Music Educators Assn. Home: 451 Scarlet Oak Dr Findlay OH 45840 Office: Findlay City Schs Southwest St Findlay OH 45840 Office Phone: 419-425-8332.

IRVAN, ASHLEE DEANN, elementary school educator; b. Memphis, Aug. 29, 1981; d. Pat Lynn and Dale Dosier Irvan. BSE, U. Ctrl. Ark., 2004. 7th and 8th grade sci. tchr. East Jr. High, West Memphis, Ark., 2004—. Vol. leader YoungLife Conway, Ark., 2002—04. Missionary, Kenya, 2005. Mem.: Nat. Sci. Tchr. Assn., Kappa Delta Pi. Avocation: travel. Office Phone: 870-735-2081.

IRVIN, LORETTA REGAN, elementary school educator; d. Robert William and Doris Lee Regan; m. Warren D. Irvin (dec.); children: Christopher Ronald, Patricia Anne Alford, Kelli Elaine. Master's degree, Ga. State U., 2002. Lic. T-5 Ga. Profl. Stds. Commn. Tchr. Cobb County Sch. Sys., Marietta, Ga., 1974—. Sunday sch. tchr. United Meth. Ch., Dallas and Marietta. Grantee, Women's Jr. League of Cobb County, 1990. Mem.: CEC, Ga. Assn. of Educators. Democrat. Methodist. Avocation: gardening. Office Phone: 678-594-8252. Personal E-mail: lorirvin@hotmail.com.

IRVINE, CAROL STONE, elementary school educator; b. Phila., Jan. 6, 1949; d. Gene C. and Viola Kirchner Stone; m. James Brinckerhoff Irvine, June 5, 1971; children: Scott, Molly. BA, Westminster Coll., 1971. 4th-6th grade tchr. West End Sch., North Plainfield, NJ, 1971—. Leader Girl Scouts U.S.A., Warren, NJ, 1984—89; vol. Union County Coalition for Homeless, NJ, 1990—, Friends of Long Lake Libr., 1995—; active West End PTA, 1971—. Named NJ Gov. Tchr. of Yr., North Plainfield Bd. Edn., 1997. Mem.: AAUW, NEA, Somerset County Edn. Assn., N.J. Edn. Assn., N.J. Reading Assn. Avocations: reading, walking, furniture refinishing. Office: West End Sch 447 Greenbrook Rd North Plainfield NJ 07063 Business E-Mail: carol_irvine@nplainfield.org.

IRVINE, ROSE LORETTA ABERNETHY, retired communications educator, consultant; b. Kingston, N.Y., Nov. 14, 1924; d. William Francis and Julia A.; m. Robert Tate Irvine Jr., Dec. 18, 1965 (dec. June 1968). BA, Coll. St. Rose, 1945; MA, Columbia U., 1946; PhD, Northwestern U., 1964. Tchr. English, Kingston H.S., 1946-47; tchr. English and speech Croton-Harmon H.S., Croton-on-Hudson, NY, 1947-49; instr. speech SUNY, New Paltz, 1949-53, asst. prof. New Paltz, 1953-57, assoc. prof., 1957-64, prof. speech communication, 1964-85, prof. emeritus, 1985—. Guest prof. Yon Sei U., Seoul, 1970; U.S. del. U.S. Bi-Nat. Conf., Manila, 1976; adv. bd. Rondout Nat. Bank Norstar (now Bank Am.), 1973-85; U. Chancellor's adv. bd. SUNY Senate, Albany, 1974-80; guest prof. Celtic lore Princess Grace Libr., Monaco, 1987; mem. faculty sr. rsch. partnership program SUNY, Albany, 1999—; cons., rschr., writer, 1985—; presenter in field. Contbr. articles to profl. jours.; hist. rsch. John Vanderlyn Letters from Paris, 2000, A Tale of Three Lives: Aaron Burr, his Daughter Theodosia, and John Vanderlyn, 2001; writer, performer hist. scripts. Active Nat. Jr. League, Kingston, 1958-90; dir. Puppet Theater for Srs., N.Y., 1982-83; bd. trustees Friends of the Senate House State Hist. Site, Kingston, 1996-99, pres. 1999; bd. Ulster County adv. coun. to Office for Aging, 1998—2004, v.p., 2000—, pres. 2001-04; mem. Gov. Pataki's Adv. Coun. Aging Svcs., 2000-04; allocations com. United Way, Ulster County, 1998-2000; mem. Cornell Coop. Extension Program Com., 2003—. Honor Tuition scholar Coll. St. Rose, Albany, N.Y., 1941; named Outstanding Educator of Am., 1971, Internat. Educator of Yr., 2004, N.Y. State Sr. Citizen of Yr., 2004. Mem. AAUW (liaison SUNY New Paltz 1966-85), Speech Comm. Assn. (mem. legis assembly 1967-68, emeritus), N.Y. State Speech Assn. (emeritus), Zeta Phi Eta, Delta Kappa Gamma, Kappa Delta Pi, Pi Lambda Theta. Roman Catholic. Avocations: historic preservation, golf, swimming, travel, local history. Home: 105 Lounsbury Pl Kingston NY 12401-5231

IRVING, AMY, actress; b. Palo Alto, Calif., Sept. 10, 1953; d. Jules Irving and Priscilla Pointer; m. Steven Spielberg, Nov. 27, 1985 (div. Feb. 2, 1989); 1 child, Max Samuel; m. Bruno Barreto, 1990 (div. 2005); 1 child, Gabriel Davis Barreto Student, Am. Conservatory Theatre, London Acad. Dramatic Art. Films include Carrie, 1976, The Fury, 1978, Voices, 1979, Honeysuckle Rose, 1980, The Competition, 1980, Yentl, 1983, Mickey and Maude, 1984, Rumpelstiltskin, 1987, Crossing Delancey, 1988, (voice) Who Framed Roger Rabbit, 1988, A Show of Force, 1990, (voice) An American Tail: Fievel Goes West, 1991, Benefit of the Doubt, 1993, Kleptomania, 1995, Carried Away, 1996, I'm Not Rappaport, 1996, Deconstructing Harry, 1997, One Tough Cop, 1998, The Confession, 1999, Teh Rage: Carrie 2, 1999, Blue Ridge Fall, 1999, Bossa Nova, 2000, Traffic, 2000, Thirteen Conversations About One Thing, 2001, Tuck Everlasting, 2002, Hide and Seek, 2005; TV appearances include: The Rookies, Policewoman, Happy Days; TV movies I'm a Fool, 1975, James Dean, 1975, James A. Michener's Dynasty, 1976, Panache, 1976, Anastasia: The Mystery of Anna, 1986, Nightmare Classics, 1989, Heartbreak House, 1986, The Turn of the Screw, 1989; miniseries Once an Eagle, 1976-77, The Far Pavilions, 1984, Twilight Zone, 1994; appeared as Juliet in Romeo and Juliet, Seattle Repertory Theatre, 1982-83; appeared on Broadway in Amadeus, 1981-82, Heartbreak House, 1983-84, Broken Glass, 1994, Three Sisters, 1997, Coast of Utopia, 2006; off Broadway The Road to Mecca, 1988, The Heidi Chronicles, 1990-91.*

IRVING, GITTE NIELSEN, secondary school educator; b. Copenhagen, Nov. 5, 1954; came to U.S., 1976; d. Sven Aage and Aase (Espersen) Nielsen; m. Richard Frederick Irving, June 5, 1976; children: Erik Christian, Emilie Jessica. BA, U. Iceland, Reykjavik, 1976; MEd, Lesley Coll., 1977. Cert. elem. tchr., spl. edn. tchr., Mass.; cert. by Mass. Gen. Hosp. in use of Orton-Gillingham strategies for remediation of dyslexia, 1989. Spl. edn. aide Brookline (Mass.) Pub. Schs., 1977-78; spl. edn. tchr. Ashland (Mass.) Pub. Schs., 1978-81, Greater Lawrence Ednl. Collaborative, Andover, Mass., 1981-82; owner, dir. Comprehensive Academics, Inc., Winchester, Mass., 1983—. Tutor The Rivers Sch., Weston, Mass., 1998—; mem. com. early edn. planning Winchester Pub. Schs., 1986; com. missions and social concerns United Meth. Ch., Winchester, 1987, co-chair, 1988-91; adv. coun. Spl. Edn. Parents, Winchester, 1985-2001; mem. com. on sch. configurations, subcom. to Sch. Com., Winchester, 1991-92; spkr. European League of Mid. Level Edn. Ann. Conf., Amsterdam, The Netherlands, 1996. Editor spl. edn. presch. newsletter, 1985-86; guest columnist Winchester Star, 1986. V.p. Neighborhood Coop. Nursery Sch., Winchester, 1988-90; mem. sch. improvement coun. Muraco Elem. Sch., Winchester, 1993-95; parents' coun. exec. com. mem., Simmons Coll., Boston, 2006-. Avocations: reading, furniture refinishing, knitting and needlework, gardening. Home: 12 Stone Ave Winchester MA 01890-1332 Office: Comprehensive Acads 573 Main St Winchester MA 01890-2900 Office Phone: 781-729-3686. Personal E-mail: Gitte@dkirvings.com.

IRVING, SARA, art educator; b. Exeter, N.H., Feb. 15, 1954; d. Colin F. N. and Frances Winslow Irving. BFA, Mass. Coll. Art, Boston, 1976; MFA, N.Mex.State U., Las Cruces, 1996. Forestry tech./fire lookout Gila Nat. Forest, Silver City, N.Mex., 1982—; grad. asst. N.Mex. State U., 1993—96, adj. instr., 1996—99, instr. art Alamagordo, 1999—2003, asst. prof. art, 2003—. Grantee Wendover Residency grant, Ctr. for Landscape Use & Interpretation, Utah, 1989, Nat. Grad. Seminar fellowship, Am. Photography Inst., 1996. Mem.: Nat. Assn. Photoshop Profls., Soc. Photog. Edn. Achievements include paticipating in 2006 Ironman World Championship. Avocations: hiking, backpacking, birdwatching, travel. Office: N Mex State Univ 2400 N Scenic Dr Alamogordo NM 88310

IRVING, SUSAN JEAN, government executive; b. Washington, Apr. 25, 1949; d. Frederick and Dorothy Jean Irving; m. Joseph Alexander Rieser Jr., Feb. 28, 1976; 1 child, Alexander Hoon Irving Rieser. BA, Wellesley Coll., 1971; MAT, Harvard Grad. Sch. Edn., 1972; M in Pub. Policy, Harvard U., 1974, PhD, 1976. Cert. Govt. Fin. Mgr., Assn. Govt. Accts. Legis. asst. to U.S. Sen. Abe Ribicoff, Washington, 1976-79; staff dir. Exec. Office of the Pres. Pres.'s Coun. of Econ. Advisers, Washington, 1979-81; external rels. officer Internat. Monetary Fund, Washington, 1981-82; v.p. Com. for a Responsible Fed. Budget, Washington, 1982-84; sr. econ. advisor Mondale for Pres., 1984; legis. dir. for U.S. Sen. Max Baucus Washington, 1985; lectr. pub. policy John F. Kennedy Sch. Govt. Harvard U., Cambridge, Mass., 1986-89; faculty Tng. Inst. U.S. Govt. Accountability Office, Washington, 1989—92, assoc. dir. for fed. budget issues, 1992-2000, dir. fed. budget analysis, 2000—; fellow Inst. Politics Harvard U., 1986. Bd. dirs. Am. Assn. Budget and Program Analysis. Co-pres. Stoddert PTA, Washington, 1997-98. Recipient Cert. of Appreciation Am. Assn. for Budget and Program Analysis, 1997, Outstanding Svc. award, 1993. Fellow Nat. Assn. for Pub. Adminstrn.; mem. Assn. Pub. Policy and Mgmt. Avocations: walking, needlepoint on plastic. Office: US GAO 441 G St NW Washington DC 20548-0001 Office Phone: 202-512-9142. Business E-Mail: irvings@gao.gov.

IRVIN-MAYS, VERNITA, medical educator; b. Oct. 7, 1941; Cert. radiologic tech., Cook Co. Grad. Sch. Medicine, 1963; BS, Roosevelt U., Chgo., 1971; MA, N.E. Ill. U., Chgo., 1975; EdD, Nova U., Ft. Lauderdale, 1979. Nuclear medicine tech. U. Ill. Med. Ctr., Chgo., Ill., 1963-71; radiography prof. Malcolm X Coll., Chgo., Ill., 1971—. Bd. dirs. Midsouth Planning & Devel. Commn., Chgo., 1999, dep. dir. cmty. devel. Chgo. Better Housing Assn., Chgo., 1999. Office: Health Scis Dept Malcolm X Coll 1900 W Van Buren St Chicago IL 60612-3145

IRWIN, FRANCES DARLENE, nurse; b. Merrill, Oreg., Apr. 16, 1941; d. Harold Eugene and Hazel Irene (Lyman) Herrett; m. James Robert Irwin, June 12, 1964; children: Paul Eugene, Timothy Robert. Diploma, Deaconess Sch. Nursing, Spokane, Wash., 1963; BSN, Whitworth Coll., 1964. RN, Wash. Nurse Student Health Ctr., Whitworth Coll., Spokane, 1964; sch. nurse Sch. Dist. Kansas City, Mo., 1964-67; nurse cons., rschr. Planned Parenthood Iowa, Des Moines, 1968-70; staff nurse surg. and obstetrics unit Deaconess Hosp., Spokane, 1967; mission co-worker, tchr. United Presbyn. Ch. USA, Ganta, Liberia, 1974-75; office mgr., nurse James R. Irwin, M.D., Colville, Wash., 1975-78; staff nurse Mt. Carmel Hosp., Colville, 1979-86; office mgr., nurse Irwin Surg. Group, Inc., Moses Lake, Wash., 1988—2006. Facilitator interpersonal skills seminar PPR, Moses Lake, 1984-88; mem. com. to develop immunization policy State of Mo., 1966. EMT Stevens County Emergency Svcs., Colville, 1977—87; mem., presenter Women in Bus. Conf., Moses Lake, 1989—98; adv. bd. Kargel and Bardeke Sch., St. Petersburg, Russia, 2005—; coun. Gen. Assembly, 2006; Ctrl. Wash. rep. Wash. State Med. Soc. Pol. Action Com., Olympia, 1995—2000; elder Presbyn. Ch. U.S.A.; moderator Ctrl. Wash. Presbytery, 1995—96; mem. Gen. Assembly Coun. Presbyn. Ch. U.S.A., 2001—06; mem. Worldwide Ministries Divsn. Presbyn. Ch. USA, 2001—; mem. missionary and ch. to ch. Russian Network Taskforce, 2005—. Mem. Am. Med. Alliance, Wash. State Med. Alliance (past state sec. and pres.), Am. Endurance Ride Assn. Avocation: raising arabian horses. Home: 5582 Road J SE Moses Lake WA 98837-9023 Business E-Mail: irwingr@atnet.net.

IRWIN, MARY JANE, engineering educator; b. Cairo, Ill., July 14, 1949; BS in Math., Memphis State U., 1971; MS in Computer sci., U. Ill., 1975, PhD in Computer sci., 1977; Doctorate (hon.), Chalmers U., Sweden, 1997. Grad. rsch. and grad. tchg. asst. computer sci. U. Ill., Champaign-Urbana, 1972—77; asst. prof. computer sci. Pa. State U., University Park, 1977—83; rsch. staff Supercomputing Rsch. Ctr. Inst. for Def. Analysis, Bowie, Md., 1986; assoc. prof. computer sci. Pa. State U., University Park, Pa., 1983—89, dept. head computer sci., 1991—93, prof. computer sci. and engring., 1989—99, disting. prof. computer sci. and engring., 1999—. Fellow: IEEE (Cert. of Appreciation 1993—95), Assn. Computing Machinery (Leadership award 1993); mem.: Nat. Acad. Engring. Office: Pa State Univ Dept Computer Sci and Engring 227 Pond Lab University Park PA 16802 Home: 108 Yost Dr Spring Mills PA 16875

IRWIN, MIRIAM DIANNE OWEN, publishing executive, writer; b. Columbus, Ohio, June 14, 1930; d. John Milton and Miriam Faith (Studebaker) Owen; m. Kenneth John Irwin, June 5, 1960; 1 child, Christopher Owen. BS Home Econs., Ohio State U., 1952, postgrad., 1961—62. Editl. asst. Am. Home Mag., N.Y.C., 1953—56; salesman Owen Realty, Dayton, Ohio, 1957—58, Clevenger Realty, Phoenix, 1958—59; home economist Columbus and So. Ohio Electric Co., 1959—60; pub. Mosaic Press, Cin., 1977—. Owner Bibelot Bindery, 1987—; ptnr. Owen & Irwin, 1978—. Author: Lute and Lyre, 1977, Forty is Fine, 1977, Miriam Mouse's Survival Manual, 1977, Miriam Mouse's Costume Collection, 1977, Miriam Mouse's Marriage Contract, 1977, Miriam Mouse, Rock Hound, 1977, Silver Bindings, 1983; editor: Tribute to the Arts, 1984, Chunging, 1996; contbg. author: Publisher's Favorite, 1988; Corals of Pennekamp, 1979. Daytime crew chief Wyoming Life Squad, Ohio, 1966—71. Recipient Norman Forgue award, 2000. Mem.: Miniature Book Soc. (chair 1987—89, past bd. dirs., Glasgow cup 2003), Studebaker Family Nat. Assn. (archivist 2000—, bd. dirs.). Presbyterian. Avocation: book collecting. Home and Office: 358 Oliver Rd Cincinnati OH 45215-2615 Personal E-mail: mirwin@cinci.rr.com.

ISAAC, SUSAN VICTORIA, literature and language professor, department chairman; b. Sevierville, Tenn., Aug. 27, 1970; d. Robert Carl Wells and Elaine Joann Tallman, Dolores Wells (Stepmother); m. Walter Lon Isaac, Aug. 18, 1993. MA, East Tenn. State U., Johnson City, 1997. Asst. prof. English Ga. Mil. Coll., Milledgeville, Ga., chair of humanities, 2000—. Author fiction. Mem. St. Stephen's Episcopal Ch., Milledgeville, Ga., 2000—06. Recipient Moore Family Fund award, Ga. Mil. Coll., 2004. Mem.: Sigma Tau Delta (life), Phi Kappa Phi (life). Avocations: writing, reading, stained glass, gardening. Office Phone: 478-445-1469.

ISAAC, TERESA ANN, mayor, lawyer; b. Lynch, Ky., July 3, 1955; d. Samuel Thomas Sr. and Barbara Ann (Thomas) I.; children: Jacob, Alicyn. BA, Transylvania U., 1976; JD, U. Ky., 1979. Bar: Ky. 1979, U.S. Dist. Ct. (ea. dist.) Ky. 1979, U.S. Ct. Appeals (6th cir.) 1980, U.S. Supreme Ct. 1981, U.S. Ct. Appeals (D.C. cir.) 1984. Pvt. practice, Lexington, Ky., 1979—; vice mayor City of Lexington, 1993-99, mayor, 2002—. Asst. atty. Fayette County Prosecutors Office, Lexington, 1986-88; judge U. Ky. Trial Adv. Competition, Lexington, 1981; assoc. prof. dept. govt. and law Eastern Ky. U., 1983-88; acting dir. Eastern Ky. U. Paralegal Program, Richmond, 1985; legal counsel Ky. Women's Heritage Mus., Inc., 1986, v.p., 1987; selected as one of six Arab-Am. elected ofcls. to monitor the first Palestinian elections, 1996; econs. and govt. prof. Lexington C.C., 1996-97; mem. bldg. com. Fayette County Justice Ctr., 1997. Editor newsletter At Issue, Lexington Forum, 1983-85; pub. The Full Ct. Press, 1986—; author: Sex Equity in Sports Leadership: Implementing the Game Plan in Your Community, 1987. Mem. Lexington Human Resources Adv. Bd., 1982-85, Ky. Displaced Homemaker Adv. Bd., Lexington, 1982-84, NCAA Final Four Host Com., Lexington, 1985; chmn. Ky. Women's Suffrage Day Celebration, 1986—; project dir. Sports Equity Program-Model for South, Ky., 1986—; mem. Philmarm. Guild, 1986—; chmn. Ky. Nat. Women in Sports Day Celebration, 1988; mem.-at-large Lexington-Fayette Urban County Coun., 1990—; bd. dirs. Ky. World Trade Ctr., 1993-97, Housing Found., 1993-97; bd. control Ky. H.S. Athletic Assn., 1993-97; mem. adv. bd. LPGA Jr. Girls Golf Club, 1993-97; mem. Criminal Justice Commn., 1993-97; mem. nat. adv. bd. Dems. 2000, 1993-97; mem. Mil. Support Com., 1997; exec. dir. Lexington Fair Housing Coun., 1999—. Recipient Outstanding Svc. award Lexington Forum, 1985, Woman of Achievement award Miss Ky. Pageant, 1996, Pub. Advocacy award Nat. Assn. Women Bus. Owners, 1998, Sports Equity Leadership award, 1999; named Top 16 Women in Bus., 1995, Best Elected Ofcl. in the Bluegrass, 1994, 50 Most Powerful People in Sports, 1992. Mem. ABA (exec. com. delivery of legal svcs. to women, chair 1987-88, spl. com. on housing and urban devel. law, recipient Silver Key award 1979), AAUW (sec. 1986, state bd. dirs. 1987-88) Fed. Bar Assn., Ky. Bar Assn. (bd. of editors 1983-85, mem. Task Force on Gender Bias in Cts. 1987—), Ky. Acad. Trial Lawyers Assn., Am. Soc. for Pub. Adminstrn., Am. Assn. for Paralegal Edn., Nat. Assn. Women Lawyers (brief bank coord. 1985—), ACLU (chairperson legal panel 1983—), League of Women Voters (voter svc. com. 1985—), Ky. Women Advs. (treas. 1987—, v.p. 1988), Leadership Am., Ky. Women's Polit. Caucus (pres. 1992-93), Lexington C. of C., Phi Mi (legal advisor 1985—). Democrat. Roman Catholic. Avocation: running marathons. Office: Lexington-Fayette Govt Ctr 200 E Main St Lexington KY 40507 Office Phone: 859-258-3100. E-mail: mayor@lfucg.com.

ISAAC, YVONNE RENEE, construction executive; b. Cleve., Apr. 13, 1948; d. Leon Warren and Vernice Leona (Hallom) I.; m. Harold E. Rhynie, Dec. 30, 1984. BA, Sarah Lawrence Coll., 1970; MS, Rensselaer Poly. Inst., 1973, Bklyn. Poly. Inst., 1976. Market rschr. GE Co., Phila., 1971-72; cons., planner SPA/Redco (subs. Perkins & Will), Chgo., 1972-75; sr. assoc. Perkins & Will, N.Y.C., 1975-76, project mgr., 1978-81; supply assoc. Mobil Oil Corp., N.Y.C., 1976-78; project mgr. Ehrenkrantz Group, P.C., N.Y.C., 1981-84; asst. dir. Met. Transp. Authority, N.Y.C., 1984-86; group dir. N.Y.C. Health & Hosps. Corp., N.Y.C., 1986-92; v.p. McDevitt Street Bovis, Atlanta, 1992-96; v.p., dir. profl. svcs. Bovis Constrn. Corp., Atlanta, 1996-98, sr. v.p., 1998—. Vis. assoc. prof. Pratt Inst., Bklyn., 1977; asst. prof. Columbia U. Grad. Sch. Architecture and Planning, N.Y.C., 1977-78. Mem. games adv. team Atlanta Paralympic Orgn. Com., 1995-96; bd. dirs. Girl Scout Coun. NW Ga., 1999—, exec. com., 2000—. Mem. Nat. Assn. for Equal Opportunity in Edn. (corp. advisory com.). Democrat. Home: 2333 Scarlett Walk Stone Mountain GA 30087-1106 Office: Bovis Lend Lease Inc 5909 Peachtree Dunwoody Rd NE Ste 500 Atlanta GA 30328-8103

ISAAC-EMMONS, MERLYN HULDA, academic administrator, educator; b. Mt. St. George, Trinidad and Tobago, July 13, 1954; arrived in U.S., 1991, naturalized; d. Vonley and Carona Abigail Isaac; m. Kelvin Strickland Emmons, Nov. 24, 1994; children: Kezreel Emmons, Uzziel Emmons, Kemuel Emmons. AA, Caribbean Union Coll., Maracas, Trinidad, 1977; BS in Edn., Lang. Arts, Andrews Univ., Berrien Springs, Mich., 1989; MEd in Spl. Edn., Atlantic Union Coll., South Lancaster, Mass., 1996; PhD in Ednl. Adminstrn. and Supervision, Trinity Internat. Univ., Springfield, Mo., 1999. Cert. reading U. West Indies, Trinidad, 1984. Clk. I Ministry for Tobago Affairs, Tobago, Trinidad and Tobago, 1972—73; tchr. South Caribbean Conf. Seventh Day Adventists, Trinidad, Trinidad and Tobago, 1973—84, prin., 1984—91; tchr. Northeastern Conf. Seventh Day Adventist, Jamaica, NY, 1993—2004; instr. Medgar Evers Coll., Bklyn., 2001—; v.p., prof. Jehova Jireh Non-Denominational Biblical Inst. Trinity Internat. U., Bklyn., 2002—; instr. Ctr. for Career Pathways Initiatives, 2005—. Instr. GED CUNY, 2003—. Author: Brighten Your Corner: Stories Are Fun, 2001, He Will Not Depart from It, 2003; contbr. articles. Foster parent Jewish Childcare Agy., Miracle Makers Agy., 1996—, Mercy First Guardian Angel Foster Boarding Home, Bklyn., 2005—. Democrat. Seventh Day Adventist. Avocations: reading, travel, writing children's stories, soap operas, storytelling. Home: 573 Van Siclen Ave Brooklyn NY 11207 Office: Young Adult Borough Ctr Thomas Jefferson HS 400 Pennsylvania Ave Brooklyn NY 11208 Personal E-mail: merlynemmons@juno.com. Business E-Mail: memmons@mec.cuny.edu.

ISAACMAN, CARRIE EDEL, actress, educator; d. Max David Isaacman and Joyce Glick (Stepmother), Joanne Isaacman; m. Roger Dale Stude, Mar. 7, 2004. BA, San Francisco State U., 1993; MA, Antioch U., Yellow Springs, Ohio, 2000. Cert. substitute tchr. N.Y. Bd. Edn., 1999. Substitute tchr. N.Y. Bd. Edn., N.Y.C., 1999—2001; contract fin. adminstr. Bear Sterns, N.Y.C., 2001—. Tchg. artist Black Moon Theatre Co., Bklyn., San Francisco Shakespeare Festival, 1996—97. Actor: Calif. Shakespeare Co., N.J. Shakespeare Co., Workshop Theater Co., Kings County Shakespear Co. Recipient Critic's Choice award, Off-Off Broadway Reveiw, 2000. Home: 2 Adrian Avenue #6A Bronx NY 10463 Office Phone: 917-202-1135. Personal E-mail: carrieedel@earthlink.net.

ISAAC NASH, EVA MAE, secondary school educator; b. Natchitoches Parish, La., July 24, 1936; d. Earfus Will Nash and Dollie Mae (Edward) Johnson; m. Will Isaac Jr., July 1, 1961 (dec. May 1970). BA, San Francisco State U., 1974, MS in Edn., 1979, MS in Counseling, 1979; PhD, Walden U., 1985; diploma (hon.), St. Labre Indian Sch., 1990. Nurse's aide Protestant Episcopal Home, San Francisco, 1957-61; desk clk. Fort Ord (Calif.) Post Exchange, 1961-63; practical nurse Monterey (Calif.) Hosp., 1963-64; tchr. San Francisco Unified Schs., 1974; counselor, instr. City Coll. San Francisco, 1978-79; tchr. Oakland (Calif.) Unified Sch. Dist., 1974—. Pres. sch. adv. coun., Oakland, 1977-78, faculty adv. coun., 1992-93; advt. writer City Coll., San Francisco, 1978; instr. vocat. skill tng., Garfield Sch., Oakland, 1980-81; pub. speaker various ednl. insts. and chs., Oakland, San Francisco, 1982—; lectr. San Jose State U., 1993; creator Language Arts-Step By Step program E. Morris Cox Elem. Sch., Oakland, 1995, 96; author, presenter material in field. Author video tape Hunger: An Assassin in the Classroom, 1993-94. Recipient Community Svc. award Black Caucus of Calif. Assn. Counseling and Devel., 1988, Cert. of Recognition, 1990; named Citizen of the Day, Sta. KABL, 1988. Mem. ASCD, Internat. Reading Assn., Nat. Assn. Female Execs., Am. Personnel and Guidance Assn., Calif. Personnel and Guidance Assn., Internat. Platform Assn. (Hall Fame 1989, Profl. Speaking cert. 1993), Phi Delta Kappa. Democrat. Avocations: travel, hiking, tennis, music, dance. Office: Oakland Unified Sch Dist 1025 2nd Ave Oakland CA 94606-2296

ISAACS, DIANE SCHARFELD, English educator; b. Washington, Nov. 11, 1939; d. Arthur William Sharfeld and Lucille Speer Smith; m. Stephen D. Isaacs, June 8, 1963 (dissolved 2000); children: Deborah, David, Sharon; m. Jay L. Halio, May 26, 2002. BA with honors, Smith Coll., 1961; MA, Stanford U., 1972; EdD, Columbia U., 1982. Cert. tchr. English K-12, Social Studies, 7-12, prin., N.Y., N.J. Tchr. English, George Mason H.S., Falls Church, Va., 1963-65, Woodrow Wilson H.S., Washington, 1966-71; tchr. English and social studies Fieldston Sch., Riverdale, N.Y., 1971-74; tchr. English, Sidwell Friends Sch., Washington, 1974-78; asst. prof. Afro-Am. studies U. Minn., Mpls., 1978-83; vice prin. humanities Tenafly Bd. Edn., Tenafly, N.J., 1985-87; assoc. prof. Fordham U., Bronx, 1983-99; chmn. English dept. Nyack (N.Y.) Pub. Schs., 1987-93; coord. English grades 6-12 Manhasset (N.Y.) Pub. Schs., 1993-95; English dept. chair Wayne Hills, N.J., 1997-99; ret. Reader U. Del.; tchr. U. Md., George WashingtonU., Am. U., 2000—. Sec., treas. adminstrv. unit dist. dept. chairs, 1998—, class meml. chair Smith Coll., 1991-2001; class sec. Nat. Cathedral Sch., 1957—; mem. Westchester Holocaust Commn. Recipient Yavner award N.Y. State Bd. of Regents, 1991. Mem. MLA, ASCD, Nat. Coun Tchrs. English (exec. com.), Conf on English Leadership, Am. Studies Assn., Toni Morrison Soc., F. Scott Fitzgerald Soc. Avocations: theater, black memorabilia, travel, folk art. Home: 8 Country Hills Dr Newark DE 19711 E-mail: dsipst@yahoo.com.

ISAACS, SUSAN, writer, scriptwriter; b. Bklyn., Dec. 7, 1943; d. Morton and Helen (Asher) I.; m. Elkan Abramowitz, Aug. 11, 1968; children: Andrew, Elizabeth. Student, Queens Coll., 1965, DHL (hon.), 1996; LittD (hon.), Dowling Coll., 1988. From editorial asst. to sr. editor Seventeen mag., N.Y.C., 1965-70; freelance writer, 1970-76. Author: Compromising Positions, 1978, Close Relations, 1980, Almost Paradise, 1984, Shining Through, 1988, Magic Hour, 1991, After All These Years, 1993, Lily White, 1996, Red, White and Blue, 1998, Brave Dames and Wimpettes: What Women Are Really Doing on Page and Screen, 1999, Long Time No See, 2001, Any Place I Hang My Hat, 2004; screenwriter Compromising Positions, 1985; screenwriter, co-producer Hello Again, 1987. Trustee Queens Coll. Found.; bd. dirs. North Shore Child and Family Guidance Assn; adv. bd. Nassau County Coalition Against Domestic Violence; bd. trustees Walt Whitman Birthplace Assn. Recipient Writers for Writers award Poets and Writers, 1996, The John Steinbeck award, 1999. Mem. PEN, Mystery Writers Am. (pres. 2001-02), Nat. Book Critic Circle, Poets and Writers (bd. dirs. 1994—, chmn. 1998—), Authors Guild, Internat. Assn. Crime Writers, Feminists for Free Expression, Creative Coalition, Am. Soc. Journalists and Authors. Jewish.

ISAACSON, BARBARA DOROTHY, retired elementary school educator, retired secondary school educator; d. Ernest Louis Shapiro and Rose Pearl Silbert; children: Cheryl, Mark, Bruce, Jonathan, Gregg Ernest. BSc, U. Mass., Amherst. Diet supr. Lynn Hosp., Mass., 1952; tchr. Saugus Schs., Mass., 1953—56; travelling educator Boston Schs., 1975—81, tchr., 1981—85, ednl. specialist, 1985—90; ret., 1990. Motivational spkr. Author: Saving Your Time, Money, Steps, Energy, Your Life, 1995; contbr. articles to numerous pubs. Founder Internat. Movement Human Rights, North Boston. Recipient Student award, East Boston Schs., 1970, Hyde Pk. H.S., 1980. Mem.: AARP (legis. chmn.), Boston Tchrs. Union (bldg. rep.), Mensa (exec. com. Boston chpt.). Independent. Jewish. Home: 65 Clifton Ave Marblehead MA 01945

ISAACSON, EDITH L., civic leader; b. N.Y.C., Jan. 18, 1920; d. I.A. and Bertha (Evans) Lipsig; m. Selian Hebald; children: Anne Mandelbaum, Selian Jr.; m. William J. Isaacson. Student, Radcliffe Coll., 1936-39, 41; LLB, St. Lawrence U., 1943. Pres. Forest Knolls Corp., N.Y.C., 1960-95, Norman Homes Corp., N.Y.C., 1968-95. Bd. govs. Medford Leas Residents Assn., 1990-92, v.p., 1991-92. Author biographies Am. artists; writer club handbooks. Fellow Pierpont Morgan Libr., N.Y.C.; mem. Carnegie Coun. Ethics Internat. Affairs, founders com. Am. Symphony Orch., N.Y., 1962; nat. sec. Women's Am. Orgn. Rehab. through Tng., 1950; trustee Allergy Found. Am.; bd. govs. Medford Leas Residents Assn., 1991; mem. Res. Fund Com., 1992-2000. Mem. Radcliffe Coll. Alumnae Assn. (chmn. clubs 1966), Harvard Clyb (N.Y.C.), Cosmopolitan Club (N.Y.C.) (bd. govs. 1987-2000), Radcliffe Club (pres. Washington 1969, N.Y.C. 1959, 63, bd. sponsors 1974-2000). Home and Office: 499 Medford Leas Medford NJ 08055-2215

ISAACSON, ELAINE MARIE, insurance agent; b. Jersey City, N.J., Aug. 16, 1963; d. George Agamemnon and Pauline (Skokos) Poulo; Student, Rutgers U., 1981—82, George Mason U., 1992, No. Va. C.C., Sterling, 1992—93. Legal sec. various law firms, Jersey City and Washington, 1979—91; exec. sec. Ritz-Carlton, Tysons Corner, Va., 1992; internal help desk Am. Online, Tysons Corner, Va., 1994; regional sales mgr. Pulsecom, Herndon, Va., 1995—2002; enroller NASE, 2002—; UGA sr. ins. agt. Mega Life and Health Ins., 2003—. Pres. and owner Isaac's Pearl poetry and short stories, Herndon, Va. and Germantown, Md., 1992—. Author (book of poetry): I Wander Lonely as a Cloud, 1991, The Dark Side of Yesterday A Brighter Tomorrow, 1995, One Sun One Moon and a Star, 2000. Chorus leader Pulsecom, Herndon, 1996—99; commencement spkr. St. Basil Acad., 2001; mem. missions team Reston (Va.) Presbyn. Ch., 1995; steward St. George Greek Orthodox Ch., 1998—. Greek Orthodox. Avocations: poetry, reading, power walking, weightlifting, volunteer work. Home: 12114 Flag Harbor Dr Germantown MD 20874 Office Phone: 301-972-5655. Business E-Mail: elainenase16@yahoo.com.

ISABELLE, BEATRICE MARGARET, artist; b. Phila., Dec. 8, 1930; d. Renaud Joseph Isabelle, Carmela Didio; m. Sven Fritz Carstens, Jan. 1953 (div. Jan. 1977); children: Jana C. Young, Kai Bruce Carstens, Dane Fritz Carstens; m. Robert Dean Graves, Sept. 6, 1984. AA L.A. City Coll., 1973; BA, Calif. State U., L.A., 1975, MA, 1979. Cert. tchr. K-9 Calif., bilingual/cross cultural specialist pre-K-12, adult, cmty. coll. ethnic studies. Tchr. Hobart St. Elem. Sch., L.A., 1971—73, McDonnell Ave. Sch., L.A., 1973—76, Albion St. Elem. Sch., L.A., Calif., 1976—85, Dolores St. Elem. Sch., L.A., Calif., 1985—91; ret., 1991. Exhibitions include Huntington Beach Art Ctr., 1995, 1999, 2000, 2001, 2001, 2002, Golden West Coll. Art Gallery, 1997, 1998, 1999, 2000, 2001, 2002, Guggenheim Gallery, Chapman U., 2001. Vol. mental health svcs., Amigas Program L.A. Unified Sch. Dist., 1967—69; vol. Chicano field work EPIC, 1978; vol. youth facility MacLaren Hall, 1978. Recipient Award for Marine Edn. Program, Sch. Edn., U. So. Calif., 1981, award for theatre, Herald Examiner, 1982, Children's Theatre, 1983, Sculpture award, Orange County Artists, 2000, Orange Art Assn., 2001; scholar Scholarship award, Orange County Fine Arts, 2001. Mem.: Kappa Delta Pi, Psi Chi. Avocations: travel, reading, painting, sculpting, flying. Home: 6941 Cumberland Dr Huntington Beach CA 92647

ISAJIW, SOPHIA O., artist, educator, curator, writer; d. Wsevolod W. Isajiw and Christina Solhan. BFA (hon.), U. Toronto, 1988; MFA (hon.), Calif. Inst. Arts, 1992. Gallery asst. Wynick/Tuck Gallery, Toronto, Ont., Canada, 1987—89; dir. Sophia Isajiw Fine Art Svcs., Toronto, 1989—93; adminstrv. coord., Robert F. Harney professorship, program in ethnic, immigration and pluralism studies U. Toronto, 1990—92; adminstr. spl. events dir. Toronto Sch. Art, 1992—93; dir., print and paper media Banff Centre Arts, Alta., Canada, 1993—97, founder, Velvet Antler Studio for print media, 1994—2005; vis. lectr. and dir. art gallery Calif. State U., Turlock, 1999—2003; arts commr. City Turlock Arts Commn., 2000—03; asst. prof. U. Windsor, Ont., Canada, 2004—. Curator A Space, Toronto, Ontario, Canada, 1988—93; dir., u. art gallery Calif. State U., Stanislaus, Turlock, Calif., 1999—2003. Exhibitions include But, what does feminism mean to us now? (Ahmanson Found. Award, 1991), Art and Ethnicity (Purchase Award, 1992), Scenic Sites (installation Purchase Award, Alta. Biennial of Contemporary Art, 1998), Skoki Stories (Artist Residency and Exhbn.: The Trail to Skoki, 1999), Release (The Glenbow Mus. and Gallery, 1999), Myth of Modern Times 2000 (Santiago, Chile, Can. Coun. Travel Grant, 2000), artist bookwork/printmaking exhbn., Objects In Mirror Are Closer Than They Appear (Vis. Guest Artist Award, Open Studio, Toronto, 1990); author: (curatorial catalog essay) Postmodern Daughter, We don't need another hero: you made me, now you have to deal with me. (I won't become what I mean to you), (anthology) The Velvet Antler Studio Print Theory Reader; interdisciplinary installations, Take this longing from my tongue. (Bemis Ctr. for Contemporary Arts, Artist Residency, 2004), printmaking/exhibitions, CAMP/ing, from series: Scenic Sites: Gulags for Tourism in Canada's Mountain Parks (Award for Excellence in the Arts, Commemorating 50th Anniv. of Universal Declaration of Human Rights, Honourable Mention, Govt. of Can., 1998), conference presenter, The Artist's Role in Social Transformation (Nat. Conf. Peace Reconciliation Scholarship Award, 1999). Pub. arts commr. City Turlock, Turlock, Calif., 2000—04; juror Pittsburg State U., Art Gallery, Pittsburg, Kans., 1997—97, Lathrop City Arts Commn., Lathrop, Calif., 2000—00, Pub. Art Selection Com., Stockton, Calif., 2004—04. Recipient Award Excellence in Arts, Commemorating 50th Anniversary of Universal Declaration of Human Rights, Can. Artists and Prodrs. Profl. Rels. Tribunal, Govt. Can., 1998, Arts Project Award, Ahmanson Found., Calif., 1991, Vis. Guest Artist, Open Studio, Toronto, 1990, Gallery Award, Justina M. Barnicke Gallery, 1986; grantee, Can. Coun. Arts, 2000; scholar, Nat. Art Assn., 1990, Anna and Alex Beverly Meml., Faculty Arts and Sci., U. Toronto, 1987, C. L. Burton Meml., 1984, Archibald MacMurchy Meml., 1983; Faculty Scholar, U. Toronto, 1984—88, B Grant, Can. Coun. Arts, 1999, Exhbns. Grant, Ont. Arts Coun., 1993, Exhbn. Grant, 1990, Scholarship Award, Ahmanson Found., 1991. Achievements include first to Founded the first student-run gallery at the University of Toronto's downtown St. George campus, A Collective Stroke Gallery, ran juried exhibitions, exchange shows with other universities; Founder, Velvet Antler Studio for Print Media, Banff Centre for the Arts and Velvet Antler Editions, an innovative print program; research in Art research into little known period of Canadian history, the internment of Canadian citizens during WW1, became a new installation/exhibition which brought media and tourist attention to this issue. Office: SchoolofVisualArts Univ Windsor 401 Sunset Blvd Ontario Windsor Canada N9B 3P4 Office Phone: 519-253-3000 x 2846. E-mail: sisajiw@uwindsor.ca.

ISAKI, LUCY POWER SLYNGSTAD, lawyer; b. Jersey City, Oct. 21, 1945; d. Charles Edward and Ann Mary (Power) Slyngstad; m. Paul S. Isaki, Aug. 26, 1967. BA summa cum laude, Seattle U., 1973; JD cum laude, U. Puget Sound, 1977. Bar: Wash. 1977. Case worker San Joaquin County Welfare, Stockton, Calif., 1968-70, Alameda County Welfare, Oakland, Calif., 1971-73; legal intern King County Prosecutor's Office, 1976-77; law clk. to hon. Justice Hamilton Wash. Supreme Ct., 1977-78; ptnr. Bogle & Gates, Seattle, 1978—99; sr. asst. atty. gen. State of Wash., 1999—2006; mem. exec. team for Atty. Gen. Gregoire, Seattle, 2001—04; sr. asst. dir., legal counsel, risk mgmt. contracts divsn. Office Fin. Mgmt., State of Wash., 2006—. Cons. Region X, HHS, 1975; chair task force on alternative dispute resolution Atty. Gen. Gregoire, 1993-94; mem. sentencing guidelines commn. State of Wash., 2006—. Bd. dirs. King County Family Svcs., Seattle, 1982-84, Wash. State Coun. Crime and Delinquency, 1981, Northwest Kidney Ctr., 2001—, vice chair, 2003-05, chair, 2005—; treas. Mother's Against Violence in Am., 1994; trustee emeritus U. Puget Sound, 1985—, Seattle Youth Symphony, 1995, Ea. Wash. U., 1998-99; chmn. law sch. bd. visitors Seattle U., 1984-96; trustee Legal Found., Wash., 1992-95, sec. bd. dirs. 1993, v.p. bd. dirs. 1994, pres. 1995; pres. Kinnear Vistas Homeowners' Assn., 2003-05. Dean's scholar U. Puget Sound, 1976-77; recipient Disting. Law Grad. award U. Puget Sound, 1984, Majis award Seattle U., 1997. Mem. Wash. Women Lawyers (pres. Seattle-King County chpt. 1982, v.p. 1984), ABA (ho. of dels. 1995-97), Wash. State Bar Assn. (bd. govs. 2000-03), King County Bar Assn. (sec. 1986-87, trustee 1987-90, treas. 1995-97, 1st v.p. 1998, pres. 1999-2000, chair govt. lawyers sect. 2004—), U. Puget Sound Law Alumni Soc. (pres. 1979). Democrat. Office: Office of Fin Mgmt PO Box 41027 Olympia WA 98504-1027 Office Phone: 360-902-3058. E-mail: lucy.isaki@ofm.wa.gov.

ISBELL, RITA ANETTE, special education educator; d. Bill Newton and Eva Pearl (White) Smith; m. Robert James Isbell; 1 child, James Robert. BA, Wayland Bapt. U., 1973; MEd, Midwestern State U., 1995. Cert. profl. recognized spl. educator Coun. for Exceptional Children, profl. ednl. diagnostician Tex. Tchr. Alvord (Tex.) Ind. Sch. Dist., 1985—88; spl. edn. tchr. Lakeworth Ind. Sch. Dist., Ft. Worth, 1990—94, Goldburg Ind. Sch. Dist., Stoneburg, Tex., 1994—96; ednl. diagnostician Matagorda County Spl. Edn., Bay City, Tex., 1996—98, Castleberry Ind. Sch. Dist., Ft. Worth, 1998—2000, Wise County Spl. Edn., Bridgeport, Tex., 2000—02; tchr. English Internat. Sch. Que., Queretaro, Mexico, 2002. Contbr. articles to spl. edn. jours. Mem.: Tex. Profl. Ednl. Diagnosticians, Tex. Ednl. Diagnostician Assn., Coun. for Exceptional Children, Delta Kappa Gamma.

ISBIN, SHARON, classical guitarist, guitar educator; b. Mpls., Aug. 7, 1956; d. Herbert Stanford and Katherine (Brudnoy) I. BA, Yale U., 1978, MusM, 1979. Prof. of guitar Manhattan Sch. Music, N.Y.C., 1979-89, Mannes Coll. Music, N.Y.C., 1984-89; prof., dept. head The Juilliard Sch. Music, N.Y.C., 1989—. Artistic dir. Guitarstream Internat. Festival Carnegie Hall, N.Y.C., 1985, Guitarfest Ordway Music Theatre, St. Paul, 1985-87, Guitarjam series Am. Pub. Radio, 1988-89. Recordings include Dances for Guitar, 1984, 3 Guitars 3, 1985, Brazil with Love, 1987, Rhapsody in Blue/West Side Story, 1988, J.S. Bach: Complete Lute Suites, 1988 (named Critic's Choice Recording of Yr. Gramaphone mag. 1989, Editor's Choice Best Recording CD Rev. 1989), Road to the Sun: Latin Romances, 1989 (named Favorite Selection CD Rev. 1990), Rodrigo & Vivaldi Concerti, 1991, Lullabies & Love Songs, 1991. NEA solo recitalist grantee; recipient 1st Prize Toronto Internat. Guitar Competition, 1975, Top Prize Munich Internat. Competition, 1976, 2nd Prize Queen Sofia Internat. Competition, 1979. Avocations: cross country skiing, hiking, backpacking, languages.

ISBURGH, ANNE MARIE, engineering manager; b. Ft. Dix, N.J., July 29, 1957; d. Ernest Francis and Virginia Marion Condina; m. Robert Karl Isburgh, Oct. 17, 1981; 1 child, Dane Karl. BSME, Rensselaer Poly. Inst., 1979, MSME, 1980. Registered profl. engr., Ohio. Engr. Buckeye Cellulose, Memphis and Perry, Tenn./Fla., 1980-84; engr. turbine aero & cooling design GE Aircraft Engines, Cin., 1984-88, lead engr. turbine aero & cooling design, 1988-94, staff engr. Turbine Airfoils Ctr. of Excellence, 1994-97, engring. black belt, 1997-99, subsect. mgr. Turbine Airfoils Ctr. of Excellence, 1999—2005, mgr. onpoint growth tech., customer tech. programs, 2005—. Patentee in field. Recipient Clarence E. Davies award ASME, 1980. Mem. Elfuns. Home: 11637 Windy Hill Ct Loveland OH 45140-1969 Office: GE Aircraft Engines MD A406 1 Neumann Way Cincinnati OH 45215-1915 Fax: 513-243-3621. Office Phone: 513-243-3697. E-mail: anne.isburgh@ae.ge.com.

ISENBERG, ANN MARIE, psychologist; b. Bellefonte, Pa., Sept. 30, 1949; d. Melvin William and Edna Saby Isenberg. BA in Psychology, Pa. State U., 1982; PhD in Clin. Psychology, Mich. State U., 1991. Lic. psychologist Del., 1998, Pa., 2005. Rehab. counseling specialist VA-Vet Ctr., St. Paul, 1989—90; tech. asst., rschr. Louise Guerney, PhD, University Park, Pa., 1991—93; psychologist-in-tng. L.T. Clayton & Counseling Assocs., State College, Pa., 1993—98; outpatient therapist Altoona Regional Health Sys., Pa., 1999—2005; psychologist Susquehanna Valley Profl. Assn., 2005—. In-plant rep., Corning-Asahi EAP Design, State College, 1993—96; agy. rep. to Centre County Coun. Human Svcs. L.T. Clayton & Counseling Assocs., State College, 1995—98; bd. mem. Ctrl. Pa. Drug & Alcohol Tng. Consortium, State College, Pa., 1995—98; behavioral health svc. rep. to hosp. safety com. Altoona Regional Health Sys., 2002—05. Contbr. Vol. AAUW, State College, 1994—, Centre County Dem. Party, 1992—. Mem.: APA, Pa. Psychol. Assn., Ctrl. Pa. Civil War Round Table, Psi Chi, Phi Kappa Phi, Phi Beta Kappa, Alpha Delta Pi. Democrat. Episcopalian. Avocations: reading, antiques, walking, music, films. Home: 721 S Sparks St State College PA 16801 Office Phone: 814-867-0670. Personal E-mail: amifriend2@msn.com.

ISENBERG, JANE FRANCES, writer, retired language educator; b. Paterson, N.J., Aug. 27, 1940; d. Hymen and Marian Alma (Spitz) Siegendorf; m. Donald Windham Isenberg, Aug. 19, 1962 (dec. June 1985); children: Rachel, Daniel; m. Philip J. Tompkins, Dec. 20, 1997. BA in English, Vassar Coll., Poughkeepsie, N.Y., 1962; MA in English, Southern Conn. State Coll., 1971; PhD in Applied Linguistics, N.Y.U., 1993. English tchr. Richard C. Lee, James Hillhouse H.S., New Haven, Conn., 1962-69; tchr. South Central C.C., New Haven, Conn., 1969-77; dir. Outreach Program Human Resources Adminstrn., New Haven, Conn., 1976-77; tchr. Goddard Coll., Plainfield, Vt., 1975-77; prof. English Hudson County C.C., Jersey City, N.J., 1979—. Tchr. Yale U., New Haven, summers 1977-78, Stevens Inst. Tech., Hoboken, NJ, summer 1982; bd. trustees Jewish Family and Counseling Svcs., Bayonne, NJ, 1994—, The Hudson Sch., Hoboken, NJ, 1979-89, Stevens Coop. Sch., Hoboken, 1978-84; presenter in field. Author: Going by the Book: The Role of Popular Classroom Chronicles in the Professional Development of Teachers, 1994 (James N. Britton award Nat. Coun. Tchrs. English 1994); (novels) The 'M' Word, 1999, Death in a Hot Flash, 2000, Mood Swings to Murder, 2000, Midlife Can Be Murder, 2001, Out of Hormone's Way, 2002, The Proof is in The Patch, 2003, Hot and Bothered, 2003, Hot on the Trail, 2004, Hot Wired, 2005; co-editor Award Winning Papers, 1993—. Grantee Am. Studies, Yale U., New Haven, Conn., 1965, NDEA, Wesleyan U., Middleton, Conn., 1966; recipient Mid-Career fellowship Princeton (NJ) U., 1991-92. Mem. MLA, Hudson County Country Club Profl. Assn., Hudson Reading Coun., Lang. Educators Appying Reflection Now, Nat. Coun. Tchrs. English, NJ Edn. Assn., NJ Reading Assn., NY Metro. Assn. for Developmental Edn., NY State TESOL. E-mail: janeisenberg@aol.com.

ISENHOUR, KATHLEEN CHANEY, special education educator, consultant; b. Lexington, Ky., Aug. 26, 1960; d. John Kenneth and Tommye Joe Chaney; m. Mark S. Isenhour, June 21, 1996; children: Drew, John-Richard, Sammy. BA, U. Ky., 1983. Cert. tchr., spl. edn. Tchr. Fayette County Pub. Schs., Lexington, 1991—; cons. Academic & Behavioral Cons., Lexington, 2002—. Coord. Children and Adults with Attention Deficit Disorder, Lexington, 2001—06; area coord. Behavior Disorder Divsn. Coun. Exceptional Child, Lexington, 2002—; presenter in field. Pres. women's group Tates Creek Ch., Lexington, 1988—2006. Mem.: Ctrl. Ky. Edn. Assn. Avocations: scrapbooks, stamping. Home: 3036 Old Field Way Lexington KY 40513

ISERBYT, CHARLOTTE THOMSON, researcher, writer, educational consultant; b. Bklyn., Oct. 26, 1930; d. Clifton Samuel and Charlotte Deyer Thomson; m. Johan Louis Iserbyt, Sept. 26, 1964; children: Robert Louis, Samuel Thomson. Diploma in Secretarial, Exec., Academic Studies with honors, Katharine Gibbs Sch., 1949. Social worker ARC, Anderson ARB, 1953—55; sec. to amb. US Dept. State, Pretoria, South Africa, 1959—60, Brussels, 1961—63; co-founder Guardians Edn. Maine, Camden, 1978—2000; sr. policy advisor US Dept. Edn., Washington, 1980—82; pres. 3D Rsch. Co., Bath, Maine, 1999—. Freelance writer, 1973—2005; host, guest radio talk shows, 1999—2005. Author: (books) Back to Basics Reform or.OBE.Skinnerian International Curriculum, 1985, 2d edit., 1993, the deliberate dumbing down of america.A Chronological Paper Trail, 1999, 3d edit., 2003; contbr. articles various profl. jours. and newspapers. Elected sch. bd. mem. Camden-Rockport Sch. Dist., 1976—79. Mem.: DAR. Independent. Roman Catholic. Avocations: languages, collecting old books, history. Home: 519 River Rd Dresden ME 04342 Office Phone: 207-442-0543. Office Fax: 207-442-0551.

ISHIKAWA-FULLMER, JANET SATOMI, psychologist, educator; b. Hilo, Hawaii, Oct. 17, 1925; d. Shinichi and Onao (Kurisu) Saito; m. Calvin Y. Ishikawa, Aug. 15, 1950; 1 child, James A.; m. David W. Fullmer, June 11, 1980. B of Edn., U. Hawaii, 1950, MEd, 1967, MEd, 1969, PhD, 1976; postgrad., Queen's Med. Ctr., 1980—82. Diplomate Am. Acad. Pain Mgmt. Postdoctoral trainee Queen's Med. Ctr., intern pain diagnosis tng., biofeedback/self-hypnosis tng.; prof. Honolulu Bus. Coll., 1953-59; prof., counselor Kapiolani C.C., Honolulu, 1959-73; prof., dir. counseling Honolulu C.C., 1973-74, dean of students, 1974-77; psychologist, pres., treas. Human Resources Devel. Ctr., Inc., Honolulu, 1977—. Cons. United Specialties Co., Tokyo, 1979, Grambling (La.) State U., 1980, 81, Filipino Immigrants in Kalihi, Honolulu, 1979-84, Legis. Ref. Bur., Honolulu, 1984-85, Honolulu Police Dept., 1985; co-founder Waianae (Hawaii) Child and Family Ctr., 1979-92. Co-author: Family Therapy Dictionary, 1991, Manabu: The Diagnosis and Treatment of a Japanese Boy with a Visual Anomaly, 1991; contbr. articles to profl. jours. Commr. Bd. Psychology, Honolulu, 1979-85; co-founder Kilohana United Meth. Ch. and Family Ctr., 1993—. Recipient Outstanding Educator award, Grambling State U., 1977, Pres.'s award, 1984, Disting. Benefactor award, U. Hawaii Coll. Edn., 2004, Disting. Alumna award, 2005. Mem. APA, ACA, Hawaii Psychol. Assn., Pi Lambda Theta (sec. 1967-68, v.p. 1968-69, pres. 1969-70, 96-98), Delta Kappa Gamma (sec., v.p. scholarship 1975, Outstanding Educator award 1975, Thomas Jefferson award 1993, Francis E. Clark award 1993, Donor Recognition award 2004). Avocations: jogging, tennis, dance. Home: 154 Maono Pl Honolulu HI 96821-2529 Office: Human Resources Devel Ctr 1750 Kalakaua Ave Apt 809 Honolulu HI 96826-3725 Office Phone: 808-942-2072.

ISIDRO, ROSE MARIE, physician; b. Philippines; d. Genaro Alvarez and Mercedes Montilla; children: Gil, Marie, Hernando, Rose. MD, U. Santo Tomas, 1964. Diplomate Am. Bd. Forensic Medicine. Pvt. practice, Manila, 1964-68; resident in psychiatry Crownsville (Md.) Hosp. Ctr., 1969-72, staff psychiatrist, 1972-79, staff psychiatrist forensic unit, 1972-75; med. dir. Anne Arundel County, 1975; physician-in-charge Tricounty Unit, Md., 1977-79; psychiat. cons. Family Svcs. of Prince Georges County, 1979-81, Mt. Vernon Ctr. for Cmty. Mental Health, 1979—; pvt. practice Manassas, Va., 1979—. Mem. Am. Psychiat. Assn., Washington Psychiat. Soc., Prince William County Med. Soc.

ISKENDERIAN, MARY ELLEN, bank executive; b. 1958; d. Ara Iskenderian; m. Gregory Owen Lipscomb, Oct. 26, 1991. BS in internat. econ., Georgetown U. Sch. Fgn. Svc.; MBA, Yale Sch. Orgn. With World Bank Group, Washington, 1989—2006; mgr. fin. markets, Europe II dept. Internat. Fin. Corp. (IFC), regional head fin. markets, Latin Am. & Caribbean dept., dir. South Asia regional dept., dir. global fin. markets portfolio, dir. partnership devel.; pres. & CEO Women's World Banking, NYC, 2006—. Bd. dirs. Nat. Bank Commerce, Tanzania, ShoreCap Internat. Office: Womens World Banking Lbby 8 W 40th St New York NY 10018*

ISMAIL-BEIGI, JUDITH KAYE, social worker; d. John Raymond and Ruby Rebecca (Balding) Baker; m. Farhad Ismail-Beigi (div.); children: Reza David, Pari Kaye, Richard Hassan. Diploma in Nursing, St. Thomas Sch. Nursing, Nashville, 1962; BA, Chatham Coll., Pitts., 1980; MSW, U. Pitts., 1989. RN Pa. Staff nurse various hosps. and agencies, 1962—2002; social worker, counselor St. Francis Hosp., Pitts., Women's Ctr. and Shelter, Pitts. Mem.: AAUW (bd. dirs., mem. hospitality com. 2004—06). Democrat. Un Itarian-Universalist. Avocations: reading, hiking, ballroom dancing. Home: 2128 Teal Tree Pittsburgh PA 15237-3858

ISOM, KAWANYA KENYETTA, assistant principal; d. Tyrome and Renee Elizabeth Himes; m. Terrance Bernard Isom, May 17, 1996; 1 child, Alexis. BS, Ala. State U., Montgomery, 1996; M, Ft. Valley State U., Ga., 2001; EdS, Columbus State U., Ga., 2002. Cert. Tech. Mil. Comm. USAF, 1990, Gifted Edn. Mid. Ga. RESA, 2002, Reading Endorsement Ft. Valley State U., 2001. Tchr. Perry H.S., Ga., 1996—2004; asst. prin. Northside H.S., Warner Robins, Ga., 2004—. Named Tchr. of Yr., Perry H.S.

ISRAEL, JOAN, social worker; b. Bklyn., July 19, 1943; d. Joseph Israel and Irene (Solon) Kansey; 1 child, Ariel Naomi Janesh. BA, Bklyn. Coll., 1965; MSW, U. Mich., 1974. Lic. clin. social worker, Nev. Social worker Alameda County Welfare Dept., Oakland, Calif., 1965-72; group therapist Pacific Ctr. for Human Growth, Berkeley, Calif., 1975-77; individual and group therapist, bd. dir. Bi-Ctr., San Francisco, 1976-78; clin. social worker, supr. Audrey L. Smith Devel. Ctr., San Francisco, 1977-78; psychiat. social worker South Nev. Adult Mental Health Dept., Las Vegas, 1978-84, part-time clin. social worker, 1988—; pvt. practice clin. social worker Las Vegas, 1984—. Contbr. articles to profl. jours. Organizer Drug/Alcohol Abuse Task Force, Las Vegas, 1983-84, Task Force on AIDS, Las Vegas, 1985-86. Mem. NASW (chair nominating com. 1978-80, 82-84, sec. 1984-86, chair com. on inquiry 1988—, legis. chair 1982-84, diplomate clin. social work), Sierra Club. Democrat. Jewish. Avocations: hiking, singing, opera, dance. Office: Ste 120 7200 Cathedral Rock Dr Las Vegas NV 89128 Office Phone: 702-804-6686. Personal E-mail: joanofisrael@aol.com. E-mail: israeljoan@wgbtv.com.

ISRAEL, LESLEY LOWE, retired political scientist; b. Phila., July 21, 1938; d. Herman Albert and Florence (Segal) Lowe; m. Fred Israel, Dec. 18, 1960; children: Herman Allen, Sanford Lawrence. BA, Smith Coll., 1959. Dir. media advance Humphrey for Pres., Washington, 1967-68, dir. polit. intelligence, 1972; dir. scheduling Bayh for Pres., Washington, 1971; spl. asst. Jackson for Pres., Washington, 1975-76; coord. nat. labor Kennedy for Pres., Washington, 1979-80; sr. v.p. Kamber Group, Washington, 1981-87; pres., CEO Politics, Inc., Washington, 1987-95. Mem. nat. commn. ADL, 1991—, mem. nat. exec. commn., 1994—; v.p. Nat. Conf. Soviet Jewry, 1990—; dir. Internat. Found. Election Sys., 1997—, treas., 2006—; pres. Jewish Cmty. Ctr. Greater Washington, Rockville, Md., 1981—83, internat. election monitor and coord., 1995—; chmn. Washington regional bd. ADL, 1991—94; sr. election officer Orgn. Security and Coop. Europe, Bosnia-Herzegovina, 1996; internat. election expert U.S. Dept. State, 1997—; mem. Dem. Charter Commn., 1982—83, Dem. Del. Selection Commn., 1983—84, Dem. Site Selection Com., 1989—90, 1990—; bd. mgrs. Adas Israel Synagogue, 1981—83; former chmn. Washington bd. Friends Tel Aviv U. Named one of 100 Most Powerful Women, Washington mag., 1990; recipient Spl. Svc. award, Jewish Cmty. Ctr., 1984. Jewish. Home: PO Box 69 Royal Oak MD 21662-0069

ISRAEL, MARGIE OLANOFF, psychotherapist; b. Atlantic City, Apr. 30, 1927; d. Herman and Mary (Salter) Olanoff; m. Allan Edward Israel, Sept. 20, 1953; 1 child, Janet. Student U. Miami, 1945-46, 50, Am. Acad. Dramatic Arts, 1946-47; BA in Psychology cum laude, Hunter Coll., 1970; MSW with honors in fieldwork, Hunter Sch. Social Work, 1972; psychoanalytic tng. N.Y. Soc. Freudian Psychologists, 1965-70, Manhattan Ctr. for Advanced Psychoanalytic Studies, 1972-74, 76. Bd. cert. diplomate in clin. social work Am. Bd. Examiners of Clin. Social Workers. Celebrity interviewer Lunchin' with Marge radio show Sta. WFPG, Atlantic City, 1947-48; co-host Steel Pier Midnight radio show, 1949; publicity writer Hy Gardner Astor Hotel, N.Y.C., 1948; writer theatrical interviews Miami (Fla.) Daily News, 1950-51; sec. to exec. dir. Hebrew Old Age Ctr., Atlantic City, 1951-55; sec. to dir. TV-films and radio Nat. Office, Am. Cancer Soc., N.Y.C., 1959-66, asst. to dir. TV-films and radio,1966-70; social worker Bellevue Hosp., N.Y.C., 1972-76; field instr. socialworkN.Y. U., 1975-76; pvt. practice psychotherapy, N.Y.C., 1973—, Providence, 1991—, Wilmington, N.C., 1996—. Mental health disaster vol. Cape Fear N.C. chpt. Red Cross, 1997—. Fellow N.Y. State Soc. Clin. Social Work, Am. Orthopsychiat. Assn.; mem. NASW (diplomate), Nat. Fedn. Socs. Clin. Social Work (com. on psychoanalysis), Acad. Cert. Social Workers, N.Y. Acad. Scis. AAAS, Psi Chi. Home and Office: 5711 Andover Rd Wilmington NC 28403-3409

ISRAELOV, RHODA, financial planner, entrepreneur; b. Pitts., May 20, 1940; d. Joseph and Fannie (Friedman) Kreinen; divorced; children: Jerome, Arthur, Russ. BS in Hebrew Edn., Herzlia Hebrew Tchrs. Coll., N.Y.C., 1961; BA in English Lang. and Lit., U. Mo., Kansas City, 1965; MS, Coll. Fin. Planning, 1991. CFP, CLU. Hebrew tchr. various schs., 1961-79; ins. agt. Conn. Mut. Life, Indpls., 1979-81; fin. planner, 1st v.p. investments Smith Barney, Inc., Indpls., 1981—. Instr. for mut. fund licensing exams. Pathfinder Securities Sch., Indpls., 1983-87; cons. channel 6 News, 1984-85; guest Radio Sta. WTUX Contbr. columns in newspapers Indpls. Bus. Jour., 1982, Jewish Post & Opinion, 1982—86, Beacon, 1985, Indianapolis Star. Named Bus. Woman of Yr., Network of Women in Bus., 1986; recipient Gold Medal award, Personal Selling Power, 1987. Mem. Fin. Planning Assn., Nat. Assn. Life Underwriters, Women's Life Underwriters Conf. (founder), Soc. Fin. Svc. Profls., Nat. Coun. Jewish Women, Nat. Assn. Profl. Saleswomen, Nat. Spkrs. Assn. (pres. Ind. chpt. 1986-87, treas. 1984), Registry Fin. Planning Practitioners, Toastmasters (chpt. ednl. v.p. 1985-86), Soroptimists (bd. dirs.), Ctrl. Ind. Mensa. Avocations: piano, folk, square, folk and ballroom dancing, theater. Office: Smith Barney Bank One Center Tower 111 Monument Cir Ste 3100 Indianapolis IN 46204-5193 Personal E-mail: israelov@yahoo.com. Business E-Mail: rhoda.israelov@smithbarney.com.

ISSAPOUR, MARJANEH, engineering educator, consultant; d. Reza and Badri Moghaddasi; m. Ira Issapour, Feb. 1, 1986; children: Ashely, Victoria, Kevin. BSEE summa cum laude, SUNY, Stony Brook, 1985; MSEE, Columbia U., NYC, 1986. Cert. NetWare adminstr., Cisco cert. network assoc., Cisco cert. acad. instr. Design engr. AT&T Info. Sys., Homdel, NJ, 1985—87; sr. design engr. Siemens SPS, Hauppage, NY, 1987—88; sr. software engr. NEC Am., Hauppage, 1988—90; asst. prof. SUNY, Farmingdale, 1990—2000, assoc. prof., 2000—. Ind. elec./software engring. cons., Syosset, NY, 1990—; mem. various coms. SUNY, Farmingdale. Contbr. articles to profl. jours. Grantee, NSF, 2000—01, 2001—02, Coca Cola Found., 2001—02, LI Power Authority, 2002—04, US Dept. Edn., 2004—05, NYSERDA, 2004—05, EPA, 2004—05. Home: 46 Jumena Blvd Woodbury NY 11797 Office: SUNY Rt 110 Farmingdale NY 11735

ISSELBACHER, RHODA SOLIN, lawyer; b. Springfield, Mass., June 12, 1932; d. Jay Zachary and Theo L. (Michelman) S.; m. Kurt J. Isselbacher, June 22, 1955; children: Lisa Isselbacher-Ramirez (dec.), Karen Isselbacher-Epstein, Jody Isselbacher-Coukos, Eric M. BA, Cornell U., 1954; JD, Harvard U., 1959. Bar: Mass. 1960, U.S. Dist. Ct. Mass. 1984. Assoc. firm Melvin Dangel, Boston, 1960-67, Sherin & Lodgen, Boston, 1965-67, Pollock & Katz, Boston, 1967-70; ptnr. firm Epstein, King & Isselbacher, Boston, 1971-91; gen. counsel Dana-Farber Cancer Inst., Boston, 1979-89; pvt. practice law Newton Centre, Mass., 1989-91; of counsel Edwards and Angell, Boston, 1991-92; legal counsel Mass. Gen. Hosp. Svc. League, 1969-85; legal cons. Children's Sch. of Sci., Woods Hole, Mass., 1969—. Cons. med. programming WGBH-TV, 1972-73. Alderman, Woods Hole, Mass., 1968; chmn. Newton United Fund, Mass., 1961; trustee Beaver Country Day Sch., 1975-77. Mem. Mass. Bar Assn., Boston Bar Assn., Mass. Health Lawyers Assn. Home and Office: 20 Nobscot Rd Newton MA 02459-1323 Office Phone: 617-332-7549. Business E-Mail: isselbacher@helix.mgh.harvard.edu.

ISTAFANOUS, AFIFA W., physician; b. Cairo, Apr. 3, 1941; d. Ibrahim Fanous and Refka Yacob; m. Wageeh Sorial Istafanous, July 20, 1967; children: Nabil, Jean. MS, Cairo U. Intern, resident Kings County Hosp., NYC, 1970—74; physician in charge Drug/Alcohol Program, Jersey City, 1975—76; dir. occupational health Ft. Monmouth Mil. Base, Eaton Town, 1977—2001; ret., 2001. Republican. Home: 11 Bloomfield Ct Dayton NJ 08810

ISTOMIN, MARTA CASALS, retired school president, performing company executive; b. PR, Nov. 2, 1936; d. Aquiles and Angelica M. (Martinez) Montanez; m. Pablo Casals, Aug. 3, 1957 (dec. 1973); m. Eugene Istomin, Feb. 15, 1975. Student, Mannes Coll. Music, N.Y.C., 1950-54; Mus.D. (hon.), World U., P.R., 1972; L.H.D. (hon.), Marymount Coll., 1975; Doctorate (hon.), U. P.R., 1984, Dickinson Coll., Carlisle, Pa., 1986; D (hon.), Shenandoah Coll., 1986, Interam. U., P.R., 1989. Prof. cello Conservatory Music, San Juan, P.R., 1961-64; vis. prof. cello Curtis Inst., Phila., 1974-75; co-chmn. bd., music dir. Casals Festival, 1974-77; artistic dir. John F. Kennedy Center for Performing Arts, Washington, 1980-90; dir. gen. Evian Music Festival, France, 1990—; pres. Manhattan Sch. Music, NYC, 1992—2005, ret., 2005. Mem. Nat. Coun. on Arts, 1990; cons. Latin Am. ednl. projects. Trustee Marlboro Sch. Music and Festival; trustee Marymount Sch., NYC, World U. Recipient Puerto Rican Fedn. Women's Clubs award, 1967; award for cultural achievements City of San Juan, 1975; Nat. Conf. Puerto Rican Women award, 1975; Casita Maria medal for outstanding contbns. to culture N.Y.C., 1978; Outstanding Contbns. Performing Arts in Nation's Capitol award, 1983; Family Place Outstanding Community Service award, 1986; Mayor's Excellence in Service Arts award, Washington, 1986; Nat. Fedn. Music Clubs citation, 1987; named Outstanding Woman of Yr. P.R., 1975; Woman of Achievement Sta. WETA-TV, Washington, 1981; Order of Isabella the Cath. govt. Spain, 1986; Officer, Order Arts and Letters govt. France, 1986; Officer's Cross Order Merit govt. Fed. Republic Germany, 1987. Mem. Nat. Coun. on the Arts. Roman Catholic. Office: Manhattan School Music 120 Claremont Ave New York NY 10027-4698

ITTS, ELIZABETH ANN DUNHAM, retired psychotherapist, consultant; b. Columbus, Ohio, May 11, 1928; d. Dalton Dee and Elizabeth Farrell (Beck) Dunham; m. Frank Joseph Itts, June 23, 1951; children: Cynthia Ann Robbins, Mark Dunham, Deirdre Elizabeth Jones, Andrea Lee Schoenfeld. Student, St. Mary of the Springs, Columbus, Ohio, 1946-47; BFA in Archtl. Design, Ohio State U., 1950; MS in Edn. Guidance, Youngstown State U., Ohio, 1979. Lic., cert. counselor Nat. Bd. Cert. Counselors. Dir. activity ctr. pilot program Mahoning County Health Dept., Youngstown, 1974-76; dir. Career Devel. Ctr. for Women, Youngstown, 1978-79; asst. to dir. Youngstown State U. Alumni Assn., 1979-81; pvt. practice psychotherapist, cons., 1981-85, 87-92; dir. career planning, placement and spl. programs Kent State U., Salem, Ohio, 1985-87. Writer grants funding for workshops, 1978-79; established career planning and placement office Kent State U., Salem, 1985, initiated and developed human svcs. tech. degree, 1986-87; writer acad. challenge grants; chmn. curriculum devel. Inst. Learning Retirement Youngstown State U., 1994-2000. Mem. Planning and Zoning Commn., Canfield, Ohio, 1980-90, Ohio Speakers Forum, 1990, Friends of Art (Butler Art Gallery), Youngstown, 1965—, Ohio Hist. Soc., Columbus, 1984—; chmn. nominating com. United Way Scholarship Commn., Youngstown, 1978-82; mem. Youngstown 2010 Revitalization, Northea. Ohio Regional Consortium. Mem. Ea. Ohio Counselor's Assn., Jr. Women's League, Youngstown State U. Alumni (life), Ohio State U. Alumni (life). Roman Catholic. Avocations: painting, sculpture, poetry. Home: 1323 Red Tail Hawk Ct Unit 1 Youngstown OH 44512-8026

IVANCHENKO, LAUREN MARGARET DOWD, pharmaceutical executive; b. West Orange, NJ, Mar. 20, 1958; d. Bernard Peter and Virginia (Morsell) Dowd; m. John Ivanchenko, Aug. 12, 1990; 1 child, Liana Katherine. BS in Psycho.-Biology, Albright Coll., 1980; postgrad., Rutger's U., 1991—92; MBA, St. Joseph's U., 2002. Sales Bourroughs Wellcome Co., Rsch. Triangle Pk., NC, 1981—84, acct. mgr. med. ctr., 1984—96; therapeutic area specialist Glaxo Wellcome, Inc., 1996—2000; sr. exec. clin. specialist Glaxo Smith Kline, Inc., 2000—. Mem.: Am. Epilepsy Soc., N.J. Epilepsy Soc. (mem. profl. adv. bd. 2001—), Nat. Exch. Club, Beta Gamma Sigma, Phi Delta Sigma. Avocations: piano, reading. Business E-Mail: lauren.ivanchenko@gsk.com.

IVANCIC, MONIKA, director, research scientist; d. Marko and Susan Imelda Ivancic; m. George Christian Sliter, Aug. 27, 1999. BS, Sonoma State U., Rohnert Park, Calif., 1993; PhD, Oreg. State U., Corvallis, 2001. Postdoctoral assoc. U. Vt., Burlington, 2001—03; asst. NMR dir. U. Wis., Madison, 2003—. Green Party. Achievements include research in DNA structures by NMR, protein structure and dynamics by NMR. Avocations: travel, hiking. Office: U Wis 1101 University Ave Madison WI 53706 Office Phone: 608-262-7536.

IVANICK, CAROL W. TRENCHER, lawyer; b. Springfield, Mass., Mar. 6, 1939; d. Joseph George and Daisy Wolf; m. Michael Ira Trencher, July 30, 1960 (div. Feb. 1984); children: Christopher, Daniel, Deborah; m. Peter Alan Ivanick (div. 1998). BA, Wellesley Coll., 1959; JD, Yale U., 1962. Bar: N.Y. 1963. Assoc. Cleary, Gottlieb et al, N.Y.C., 1962-67; ptnr. Dewey, Ballantine LLP, N.Y.C., 1976—2004, of counsel, 2004—. Chmn. adv. com. Pension Benefit Guaranty Corp., Washington, 1978-80; visiting lectr. Yale Law Sch., New Haven, Conn., 1978-79, 82-83. Avocations: ceramics, bowling, tennis. Home: 110 Riverside Dr New York NY 10024-3715 Office: Dewey Ballantine 1301 Avenue Of The Americas New York NY 10019-6022 Office Phone: 212-259-7800. E-mail: civanick@dbllp.com.

IVEN, MARJORIE L., assistant principal; m. Max A. Iven, Dec. 28, 1973; children: Amy D. W., Makala M. B., Andrew P., Alex C. BS in Art Edn., SUNY at New Paltz, 1973; MS in Edn., Elmira Coll., N.Y., 1974. Cert. prin./tchr. Okla., 1974. Tchr. art grades K-12 Savona Ctrl. Sch., NY, 1973—74; art tchr. Western Heights Jr. H.S., Oklahoma City, 1974—76; freelance math, English, and sci. tutor Oklahoma City, 1976—90; tchr. of the gifted Western Oaks Mid. Sch., Oklahoma City, 1990—2006; asst. prin. Putnam City Schs., Oklahoma City, 2006—. Seminar presenter Putnam City Schs., 1995—. Pres. Okla. Assn. of Gifted, Creative, and Talented, Inc., Oklahoma City, 2006. Named Tchr. of Yr., Okla. Media & Libr. Specialists, 1999; recipient Tchrs. Tchg. Tchrs., Okla. Educators Assn., 2000; Belfer scholar, U.S. Holocaust Meml. Mus., 1997, 1999. Republican. Roman Catholic. Avocations: travel, reading, quilting, painting, antiques. Office: Putnam City Central Elem Sch 5728 NW 40th St Oklahoma City OK 73122 Office Phone: 405-789-5696.

IVENS, MARY SUE, microbiologist, medical mycologist; b. Maryville, Tenn., Aug. 23, 1929; d. McPherson Joseph and Sarah Lillie (Hensley) Ivens. BS, East Tenn. State U., Johnson City, 1949; MS NIH rsch. trainee, Tulane U. Sch. Medicine, New Orleans, 1963; PhD, La. State U. Sch. Medicine, New Orleans, 1966; postgrad., Emory U. Sch. Medicine, Atlanta, 1960. Diplomate Am. Bd. Microbiology. Dir. microbiol. and mycol. labs. Lewis-Gate Hosp., Roanoke, Va., 1953—56; rsch. mycologist Ctrs. Disease Control, Atlanta, 1957—60; rsch. assoc. La. State U. Sch. Medicine, New Orleans, 1963—66; instr. medicine La. State U., 1966—72, instr. microbiology, 1966—72, clin. prof., 1972—. Dir. micology lab. La. State U. Sch. Medicine, 1963—72, lectr. sch. dentistry, 1968—70; assoc. prof. natural scis. Dillard U., New Orleans, 1972—; assoc. Marine Biol. Lab., Woods Hole, Mass., 1978—; cons. in field; mem. exec. bd. Trinity Dental Assn., 2006. Contbr. articles to profl. jours. Commr. conf. on ctr. Mycotic sera WHO, 1969; mem. La. assn. def. counsel expert witness bank, 1985—; bd. dirs. La. coun. Girl Scouts US, Cmty Relationships Greater New Orleans, Zoning Bd. River Ridge, La.; mem. exec. bd. River Ridge Civic Assn., 1982—98, sec., 1982—84; chmn. pers. bd. Riverside Bapt. Ch., River Ridge; dir. outreach First Bapt. Ch., New Orleans, 1989—97; chmn. gold medal award com. Sigma Xi, 1978. Recipient Rosicrucian Humanitarian award, 1981; fellow Macy, MBL, 1978—79; grantee NSF, NIH. Mem.: Nat. Inst. Sci., AAAS, Am. Soc. Microbiology (Nat. com. on membership 1983—87), Med. Mycological Soc. Am., Internat. Soc. Human and Animal Mycology, Sigma Xi. Office: Dillard U Div Natural Sci New Orleans LA 70122 Home: 809 Prestwick Dr Maryville TN 37803-6757

IVERSON, CAROL JEAN, retired library media specialist; b. Villisca, Iowa, July 2, 1937; d. Paul Gerald and Garnet Blanche (Dunn) Smith; m. Merlin Gerald Iverson, June 11, 1961; children: Robert Mark, Jean Marie Iverson Howe. BA, U. No. Iowa, 1960. Elem. tchr. Manning (Iowa) Community Schs., 1957-58, Mason City (Iowa) Sch. Dist., 1960-61, Manson (Iowa) Community Schs., 1961-63, Blooming Prairie (Minn.) Community Schs., 1963-64, 65-66; elem. tchr., K-12 librarian Rockwell (Iowa) Swaledale Community Schs., 1973-80; libr. media specialist Mason City Sch. Dist., 1980-96. County co-chair Cerro Gordo County Reps., Howard Baker campaign, 1979; campaign worker Dukakis for Pres., 1987. Mem. AAUW (v.p. 1989-91, pres. 1993-95), NEA (del. rep. assembly), Iowa State Edn. Assn. (del., resolutions com. 1975-78), Iowa Ednl. Media Assn. (legis. chair 1987-89), Delta Kappa Gamma Soc. Internat. (pres. chpt. 1986-88, Upsilon state pres. 1999-2001), U.S. Forum (N.W. rep.), Iowa Ednl. Equity Coun., Phi Delta Kappa. Democrat. Lutheran. Avocations: travel, gardening, reading, children's literature. Home: 1505 Limestone Ct Mason City IA 50401-6976

IVERSON, KRISTINE ANN, federal agency administrator; b. Elgin, Ill, Aug. 15, 1953; d. Theodore and Vivian (Schumaker) I. BA, DePauw U., Greencastle, Ind., 1975; MA, George Mason U., 1985; postgrad., Va. Poly. Inst. and State U., 1978. Legis. aide Rep. John B. Conlan, Washington, 1975-76; legis. asst. Sen. Orrin G. Hatch, Washington, 1977-81, sr. policy advisor, 1993-94, legis. dir., 1995—2001; employment policy dir. Senate Labor and Human Resources Com., Washington, 1981-88, minority staff dir., 1988-92; asst. sec. congl. intergovernmental affairs US Dept. Labor, Washington, 2001—. Cons. Reagan-Bush Transition, 1980 Pres. The Ron Freeman Chorale, Arlington, Va., 1987-2000; steering com. George Mason U. Tech. Forum, 1983; del. 11th Dist. Rep. Conv., Fairfax, Va., 1992; mem. DePauw U. Alumni Bd., Greencastle, Ind., 1993-99; mem. Bd. of Visitors 2000-03. Recipient Young Alumni award DePauw U., Greencastle, 1993, John C. Stennis Congrl. fellow, 1999-2000. Mem. Alpha Omicron Pi;mem. The Falls Ch. (Episcopal). Avocations: music, sports. Office: US Dept Labor Congressional Intergovt Affairs 200 Constitution Ave NW Washington DC 20210

IVERSON, ONA LEE, retired elementary school educator; b. Kiester, Minn., Jan. 31, 1930; d. George Conrad and Elsie Esther (Bartz) Wittman; m. Roger Duane Iverson, Feb. 10, 1951; children: Joan, Richard, Neal. Student, Gustavus Adolphus Coll., 1948-51; BA, Briar Cliff Coll., 1971. Tchr. Sioux City Community Schs., Iowa, 1971-90. Author plays for upper elem. students. Activist Dem. Party, 1986—; supts. adv. bd. Sioux City Community Schs., 1987-90. Mem. AAUW, NEA (conv. del. 1977, 1986), Iowa State Edn. Assn. (conv. del. 1986, 1987, Sioux City League Women Voters (bd. dirs. 1983-86), Sioux City Edn. Assn. (pres. 1986-87), Interprofl. Inst. Sioux City (pres.), Sierra Club. Lutheran. Avocations: camping, hiking, travel, reading, playing piano. Home: 33354 Grouse Ave Sioux City IA 51108-9780

IVERSON, SUSAN VAN DEVENTER, education educator; d. George V. and Arlene Van Deventer; m. Yale H. Iverson, Jr.; 1 child, Mia. MA, Boston Coll., 1992; MEd, Bridgewater State Coll., Mass., 1992; EdD, U. Maine, Orono, 2005. Resident dir. Bridgewater State Coll., 1989—92; student affairs adminstr. Dean Coll., Franklin, Mass., 1992—96, Sweet Briar Coll., Va., 1996—99; asst. dir. housing U. Maine, 1999—2002; assoc. dir. Safe Campus Project, Orono, 2003—06; asst. prof. Kent State U., Ohio, 2006—. Mem.: Am. Coll. Pers. Assn. Office: Kent State Un 404 White Hall TLCS Dept Kent OH 44242

IVES, COLTA FELLER, museum curator, educator; b. San Diego, Apr. 5, 1943; m. E. Garrison Ives, June 14, 1966; 1 child, Lucy Barrett. BA, Mills Coll., 1964; MA, Columbia U., 1966. Staff Met. Mus. Art, N.Y.C., 1966—, curator in charge prints and photographs, 1975-93, curator dept. drawings and prints, 1993—; guest scholar J. Paul Getty Mus., 2002. Adj. prof. Columbia U., 1970-87, NYU Inst. Fine Arts, 2001—. Author: The Great Wave, 1974, Art Libraries Assn. award, 1975, The Flight Into Egypt, 1972, R. Rauschenberg Photos In and Out City Limits: New York, 1981, French Prints in the Era of Impressionism and Symbolism, 1988, Toulouse-Lautrec in the Metropolitan Museum of Art, 1996; co-author: The Painterly Print, 1980, Pierre Bonnard: The Graphic Art, 1989, Daumier Drawings, 1992, Goya in the Metropolitan Museum of Art, 1995, The Private Collection of Edgar Degas, 1997 (Best Show of 1997-98 N.Y.C. Mus. Internat. Assn. Art Critics), Romanticism and the School of Nature, 2000, The Lure of the Exotic: Gauguin in New York Collections, 2002, A Private Passion: Winthrop Collection, Harvard University, 2003 (Best Mus. Catalog of 2003 Assn. Art Mus. Curators), Wrightsman Pictures, 2005, Vincent van Gogh: The Drawings, 2005. Chmn. grants com. Met. Mus. Art, 1986-87; bd. dirs. Bidwell House Mus., Mass. Mem. Print Coun. Am. (exec. bd. 1975-77, 84-87, v.p. 1989-93), Assn. Art Mus. Curators (exec. bd. 2002-04, bd. dirs. 2003-04), Grolier Club.

IVEY, ANDI, special education educator; d. Costas and Antoinette Zacharoudis; m. R. Mike Ivey, Sept. 29, 1973; children: Tonya Michelle, Brett Jason. BS in Elem. and Spl. Edn., No. Ariz. U., 1973. Ednl. profl. developer. cons. Ivey League, Kailua, Hawaii, 1996—; spl. educator Scottsdale Unified Schs., Ariz., 1983—99. Acad. dean, dept. chairperson Desert Mountain H.S., Scottsdale, 1995—99; dist. profl. developer Scottsdale Unified Schs., 1996—99; team leader, spl. edn. rep. Mohave Mid. Sch., Scottsdale, 1990—95; trainer of trainers - Project Adapt Dept. Edn. State of Ariz., Phoenix, 1994—98, mem. creating equity and access com. Dept. Edn., 1995—95. Named Tchr. of the Yr., Phi Delta Kappa Scottsdale Chpt., 1997, Tchr. of the Yr. - State of Ariz., Learning Disabilities Assn. of Ariz., 1993. Mem.: ASCD, Coun. for Exceptional Children, Phi Delta Kappa (Scottsdale Chpt. Tchr. of the Yr. 1997). Avocations: scuba diving, walking on the beach, swimming, golf, travel. Home and Office: 41 Palione Pl Kailua HI 96734 Personal E-mail: iveyleague@hawaii.rr.com.

IVEY, DANA ROBINS, actress; b. Atlanta, Aug. 12, 1941; d. Hugh Daugherty and Mary Nell (McKoin) I. BA, Rollins Coll., 1963. Appeared in Off-Broadway plays MacBeth, 1981, A Call From the East, 1981, Vivien, 1982, Baby With the Bathwater, 1983, Quartermaine's Terms (Drama Desk nomination, OBIE award 1983), Driving Miss Daisy (Drama Desk nomination, Outer Critics Circle award 1988, OBIE award 1987), Wenceslas Square, 1988 (Outer Critics Circle award 1988), Mrs. Warren's Profession, 2005 (OBIE award 2006); Broadway plays Present Laughter, 1982, Heartbreak House (Tony nomination 1984), Sunday in the Park with George (Tony nomination 1984), Pack of Lies, 1985, The Marriage of Figaro, 1985, Indiscretions, 1995, Sex and Longing, 1996, The Last Night of Ballyhoo, 1997, Waiting in the Wings, 1999, Major Barbara, 2001, A Day in the Death of Joe Egg, 2003, Henry IV, 2003, The Rivals, 2004; in films including Explorers, 1984, The Color Purple, 1985, Dirty Rotten Scoundrels, 1988, Sabrina, 1995, Legally Blonde II, 2003, Two Weeks NOtice, 2003; in TV shows including Easy Street, Heartbreak House, Sunday in the Park. Recipient Drama League award Calif. Shakespeare Festival, 1979; Fulbright grantee London Acad. Dramatic Art, 1964. Mem. Actors Equity Assn., SAG, AFTRA, Can. Actorws Equity Assn., Assn. Can. TV and Radio Actors.

IVEY, ELIZABETH REEVES, school system administrator; d. Charles Lester and Louise Bailey Reeves; m. Robert A. Ivey, June 2, 1956; children: Timothy Reeves, John Brent, Mary Beth Ivey Sprouse. Student, Lander Coll., 1956; BA in Elem. Edn., Furman U., 1958; M in Reading Specialist, Winthrop U., 1977; M, U. SC, Spartanburg, 1991; cert. program in strategic planning, SC. Sch. Bd. Assn. and Nat. Strategic Planning Ctr. for Edn., 1994. Tchr. 6th grade Northside Elem., Woodruff, SC, 1958—59; tchr. 4th grade Freemont Elem., Spartanburg, 1959—66; tchr. 2nd grade South Hill (Va.) Primary, 1968—74; tchr. 5th grade Grassy Pond Elem., Gaffney, SC, 1974—75; tchr. 2nd grade J.Paul Beam Elem., Gaffney, 1975—78; chpt. 1 coord. tchr. Cherokee County Sch. Dist. Office, Gaffney, 1978—84, coord. gifted talented and compensatory, remedial, 1984—91, dir. staff devel., 1991—94, coord. secondary edn., 1994—2006; ret., 2006. Bd. dirs. SC Consortium Gifted Edn., Columbia. Den mother Boy Scouts Am.; chaplain Market Pl. Ministries; min. music Draytonville Bapt. Ch.; bd. dirs. Cherokee County Arts Coun., Gaffney, 1995—2002; bd. regents C. of C., Gaffney, 1998. Named to Hon. Kitty Hawk Air Soc., ROTC, 2003; recipient Outstanding Young Educator award, Jaycees South Hill, Va., 1969. Mem.: NEA, Assn. Supervision and Curriculum Devel., Cherokee County Reading Assn., SC Edn. Assn., Cherokee County Edn. Assn., Friends of Libr., Delta Kappa Gamma, Phi Delta Kappa. Home: 118 Crestview Dr Gaffney SC 29340 Office Phone: 864-902-3546. Office Fax: 864-902-3554. E-mail: elizabeth.ivey@gw.cherokee1.k12.sc.us.

IVEY, ELIZABETH SPENCER, retired physicist, educator; b. Schenectady, NY, Apr. 21, 1935; married, 1957 (div.), remarried, 1982; 5 children. BS in Physics, Simmons Coll., 1957; MA in Tchg., Harvard U., 1959; PhD in Mech. Engring. Acoustics, U. Mass., 1976. Prof. physics Simmons Coll., 1958-59, Bucknell U., 1960-63, Colo. State U., Ft. Collins, 1964-68, assoc. dean faculty, 1982-85, Louise Wolff Kahn prof., from 1985; prof. physics Smith Coll., 1969-90, chmn. dept. physics, 1983-90; provost Macalester Coll., St. Paul, 1990-95, U. Hartford, West Hartford, Conn., 1995-2000, provost emerita, 2000—. Vis. prof. Yale U., 1982. Bd. dirs. Minn. Inst. Talented Youth, 1990-95, World Press Inst., 1990-93, St. Paul Area United Way, 1990-95, Women's Edn. and Leadership Fund, Hartford, 2005—; trustee Hartford Coll. Women, 1995-2005, Mitchell Coll. 2003-; corporator Simmons Coll., 2000-05. Recipient Woman Engr. award Soc. Women Engrs., 1988. Fellow AAAS; mem. Acoustical Soc. Am., Am. Assn. Physics Tchrs., Assn. Women in Sci. (bd. dirs. 2001—, pres.-elect 2003-04, pres. 2004-06). Personal E-mail: ivey@hartford.edu.

IVEY, JUDITH, actress; b. El Paso, Tex., Sept. 4, 1951; d. Nathan Aldean and Dorothy Lee (Lewis) I.; m. Tim Braine, 1989; children: Maggie, Thomas Carter. BS, Ill. State U., 1973. Actress in stage plays: The Sea, 1974, The Philanthropist, Hay Fever, Romeo and Juliet, Two Gentlemen of Verona, Mourning Becomes Electra, 1975, Don Juan, Cactus Flower, As You Like It, Design for Living, 1976, The Goodbye People, The Moundbuilders, Oh, Coward, Much Ado About Nothing, 1977-78, Bedroom Farce, 1979, Dusa, Fish, Stas and VI, 1980, Piaf, 1980-81, The Dumping Ground, 1981, The Rimers of Eldritch, 1981, Pastorale, 1982, Two Small Bodies, 1982, Steaming, 1982-83 (Tony award 1983, Drama Desk award 1983), Second Lady, 1983, Hurlyburly, 1984 (Tony award 1985, Drama Desk award 1985), Precious Sons, 1986, Blithe Spirit, 1987, Mrs. Dally Has a Lover, 1988, Park Your Car in Harvard Yard, 1991, The Moonshot Tape, 1994 (Obie award 1994), A Fair Country, 1996, A Madhouse in Goa, 1997, The Subject Was Roses, 2006; (films) Harry and Son, 1984, The Lonely Guy, 1984, The Woman in Red, 1984, Compromising Positions, 1985, Brighton Beach Memoirs, 1986, Hello Again, 1987, Sister Sister, 1987, Miles from Home, 1988, In Country, 1989, Everybody Wins, 1990, Love Hurts, 1991, There Goes the Neighborhood, 1992, Washington Square, 1996, A Life Less Ordinary, 1997, Devil's Advocate, 1997, Without Limits, 1998, The Stand-In, 1999, Mystery, Alaska, 1999, What Alice Found, 2003; (TV films) The Shady Hill Kidnapping, 1980, Dixie Changing Habits, 1982, Piaf, 1984, We Are The Children, 1986, The Long, Hot Summer, 1985, Jesse and the Bandit Queen, 1986, Decoration Day, 1990, Frogs!, 1991, Her Final Fury: Betty Broderick, the Last Chapter, 1992, Other Mothers, 1993, On Promised Land, 1994, Almost Golden: The Jessica Savitch Story, 1995, The Summer of Ben Tyler, 1996, What the Deaf Man Heard, 1997, Texarkana, 1998, Half a Dozen Babies, 1999; (TV series) Down Home, 1990-91, Designing Women, 1992-93, The Five Mrs. Buchanans, 1994; (TV miniseries) Rose Red, 2002; guest appearances Cagney & Lacey, 1982, Buddies, 1995, Will & Grace, 2002, Law & Order:Special Victims Unit, 2005, Related, 2005.*

IVEY, KAY ELLEN, state official; b. Repton, Ala., Oct. 15, 1944; d. Boardman Nettles and Barbara Elizabeth Ivey. BS, Auburn U., 1967; cert. in mktg., U. Colo., 1975; cert. in banking, U. South Ala.; cert. in Strategic Leadership for State Execs., Duke U., 1989. Tchr., coach forensics Rio Linda (Calif.) High Sch., 1968-69; asst. v.p. Mchts. Nat. Bank, Mobile, Ala., 1970-79; cabinet officer Office of the Gov., State of Ala., Montgomery, 1979-81; reading clk. Ala. Ho. Reps., 1981-82; exec. v.p. St. Margaret's Hosp. Found., 1982-85; dir. govt. affairs Ala. Commn. Higher Edn., 1985—98; treas. State of Ala., 2003—. Owner, cons. Ivey Enterprises, Montgomery, 1982—; speaker in field. Editor (audio-visual presentation) What Price Freedom (award of Excellence), 1976, St. Margaret's Hosp. Heart tabloid, 1983. Mem. adv. bd. Sch. Bus. Auburn U., 1980-83; candidate Ala. State Auditor, 1982; sec. Ala. div. Am. Cancer Soc., 1985—; bd. dirs. Ala. Girl's State Sch., 1983-85, Stetson Hoedown Rodeo Queen's Pageant, Montgomery, 1986—; bd. trustees Sheriff's Boys and Girls Ranches. Mem. Indsl. Developers Ala., Young Men's Bus. Orgn., Pub. Relations Council Ala. (bd. dirs. 1976-82), DAR (state chmn. 1985-86), Alpha Gamma Delta (disting. citizen award 1986). Republican. Presbyterian. Avocations: horseback riding, public speaking. Office: State Treasurers Office Rm S-106 State Capitol Bldg Montgomery AL 36130

IVEY, MARY BRADFORD, counselor; b. Bemidji, Minn., May 27, 1941; d. Rupert William and Florence V. (Jenson) Bradford; m. Thomas William Bohn, June 20, 1941 (div.); children: Elizabeth Ann, Kathryn Marie; m. Allen Eugene Ivey, Aug. 2, 1982. BA, Gustavus Adolphus, 1963; MS, U. Wis., Madison, 1969; EdD, U. Mass., 1978. Cert. Nat. Cert. Counselor (NCC), lic. Mental Health Counselor (LMHC). Counselor Amherst Pub. Schs., Mass., 1976—98. Vis. prof. Flinders U., Adelaide, Australia, 1982, 1998, Keene (N.H.) State Coll., 1988, U. Mass., Amherst, 1991, U. Hawaii, 1996; lectr. and workshop presenter in field. Co-author seven books; contbr. articles to profl. jours. Named Exemplary Guidance Program Top Ten in Country Christi McAuliff Conf., Va. Tech. U., 1988; recipient O'Hann award for multicultural contbns. Am. Counseling Assn. Fellow: Am. Counseling Assn.; mem.: AACD. Democrat. Episcoplian. Avocations: swimming, walking, tennis.

IVEY, SHARON DEE, secondary school educator; b. Norfolk, Va., June 19, 1961; d. Gerald Thomas and Beverly Ann Everton; m. Edward Eugene Ivey, Nov. 22; children: Edward LeRay, Scott Christopher, Sharrin Nichole. BS in Phys. Edn. Health, Old Dominion U., Norfolk, Va., 1985. ATC. Athletic trainer, tchr. secondary edn. Great Bridge H.S., Chesapeake, Va., 1986—.

IVEY, SUSAN LEE, health services researcher, emergency physician; b. Newport News, Va., Jan. 2, 1955; d. Henry Sr. and Margaret (Farmer) I.; m. Peter Berl Bernhard, May 18, 1985; children: Rachel, Lauren, Daniel. BA in Psychology, U. So. Calif., 1975; BS in Biol. Sci., BA in Chemistry, U. Calif., Irvine, 1977; MD, St. George U., Grenada, 1981; M in Health Svcs. Adminstrn., George Washington U., Washington, 1995. Diplomate Am. Bd. Family Practice, Am. Bd. Emergency Medicine. Intern in internal medicine Mt. Sinai Hosp., Hartford, Conn., 1981—82; resident dept. family practice U. Conn., Farmington, 1982—84; physician Manchester (Conn.) Meml. Hosp., 1984—85, LDS Hosp., Salt Lake City, 1985-88, 95-97, Jordan Valley Hosp., West Jordan, Utah, 1985—89, Potomac Hosp., Woodbridge, Va., 1990—94, Urgent Med. Care, Lakeridge, Va., 1990—94, Calif. Emergency Physicians/Delta Meml. Hosp., Antioch, 1996—98; rsch. fellowship NIMH U. Calif., Berkeley, 1995—97; physician pvt. practice, 1998-99; asst. clin. prof. joint med. program U. Calif. Berkeley Sch. Pub. Health, Calif., 2000—03, assoc. adj. prof., 2003—. Assoc. adj. prof. Sch. Nursing, U. Calif., San Francisco. Contbr. articles to profl. jours.; book editor: Immigrant Women's Health, 1999. Mem. Teen Pregnancy Prevention Better Beginnings Coalition, Woodbridge, Va., 1993-94, Calif. Cardiovascular Disease Prevention Coalition, 1998—, chair resources & devel. com., 1999-2000; physician Prince William Free Clinic, Manassas, Va., 1994. Fellow: Am. Acad. Family Practice, Am. Coll. Emergency Physicians; mem.: Am. Med. Women's Assn. (state dir. Calif. chpt. 1995—99, chmn. govt. affairs 1996—98, publs. com. 1998, program chair 1999, v.p. program 2002—04, v.p. comms. 2004, pres.-elect 2005, pres. 2006). Democrat. Unitarian Universalist. Avocations: walking, dance, reading, movies, skiing. Home: 131 Emerald Dr Danville CA 94526-2426 Office: Sch Pub Health U Calif Ctr Family and Cmty Health 140 Warren Hall Berkeley CA 94720-7360 E-mail: sliveymd@socrates.berkeley.edu.*

IVEY, SUSAN M., tobacco company executive; b. Schenectady, NY, Oct. 31, 1958; m. Trevor Ivey, 1997. BS, U. Fla., Gainesville, 1980; MBA, Bellarmine U., 1987. Trade mktg. repr. Brown & Williamson Tobacco Corp., 1981—83, dist. sales mgr., 1983, dir. mktg. Far East, head internat. brands U.K. London, 1990—94, dir. mktg. British Am. Tobacco Hong Kong, 1994—96, mgr. internat. brands London, 1996—99, sr. v.p. mktg. Louisville, 1999—2000, pres., CEO, 2001—04; chmn., CEO, dir. RJ Reynolds Tobacco, 2004—; pres., CEO Reynolds American Inc., Winston-Salem, NC, 2004—, chmn., 2006—. Bd. mem. Bellarmine Univ.; mem. Committee of 200. Named one of 100 Most Powerful Women in Bus., Fortune mag., 2005—06, 50 Most Powerful Women in Bus., 2006. Office: Reynolds American Inc 401 N Main St Winston Salem NC 27101*

IVINS, MARCIA S., astronaut; b. Balt., Apr. 15, 1951; d. Joseph L. Ivins. BS in Aerospace Engring., U. Colo., 1973. Lic. pilot. Engr. NASA Johnson Space Ctr., Houston, 1974—80; flight engr. Shuttle Tng. Aircraft, Aircraft Ops., Houston, 1980—; co-pilot NASA Adminstrv. Aircraft, Houston, 1980—. Mem. Exptl. Aircraft Assn., 99's, Internat. Aerobatic Club. Achievements include over 6000 flight hours in civilian and NASA aaircraft, 5 space missions, 1, 318 hours in space. Avocations: flying, reading, baking. Office: Astronauts Office NASA Johnson Space Ctr Houston TX 77058

IVINS, MOLLY (MARY TYLER IVINS), columnist, writer; b. Monterey, Calif., Aug. 30, 1944; d. Jim and Margo I. BA, Smith Coll., 1966; postgrad., Inst. Polit. Sci., 1966; MA in Journalism, Columbia U., NYC, 1967. Former reporter The Houston Chronicle, The Mpls. Star Tribune, 1964-1976; reporter The Texas Observer, Austin, 1970-76, The New York Times, 1976-82, Rocky Mountain bur. chief Denver, 1976-82; former columnist The Dallas Times Herald, 1982-91; columnist Fort Worth Star-Telegram, 1992—2001; syndicated columnist Creators Syndicate, LA, 2001—. Author: Molly Ivins Can't Say That, Can She?, 1991, Nothin' But Good Times Ahead, 1993, You Got to Dance with Them What Brung You, 1998, Shrub, 2000, Bushwhacked, 2003, Who Let the Dogs In?, 2004; contbr. to periodicals including The Nation, N.Y. Times Book Rev., Mother Jones, Ms., Progressive, others. Co-recipient Damon Runyon award, Denver Press Club, 1996; finalist Pulitzer prize (3 times); named Outstanding Alumna, Columbia Sch. Journalism, 1976; recipient Headliner's award for best Tex. column, 1991, William Allen White award, Univ. Kans., 2001, Smith medal, Smith Coll., 2001, Ivan Allen Jr. prize for Progress and Svc., 2003, Pringle prize for Washington Journalism, Columbia Univ., 2003, Eugene V. Debs award, 2003, David Brower award, Sierra Club, 2004, Otis Social Justice award, Wheaton Coll., 2004. Mem.: Nat. Acad. Arts and Scis., ACLU. Speaks French, Spanish. Office: Creators Syndicate 5777 W Century Blvd Los Angeles CA 90045 Home: Austin TX*

IVORY, GOLDIE LEE, retired social worker, educator; b. Apr. 19, 1926; d. Percey Carr and Edna M. (Scott) Carr Williams; m. Sam Ivory, Aug. 7, 1947; children: Kenneth L., Kevin D. BS, Ind. U., 1949; MA, U. Notre Dame, 1956; MSW, Ind. U.-Purdue U., Indpls., 1977. Registered cert. clin. social worker, Ind. Juvenile probation officer St. Joseph County Juvenile Probation Dept., South Bend, Ind., 1949-56, intake supr., 1956-59; chief probation officer South Bend City Ct., 1959; psychiat. social worker Beatty Meml. Hosp., Westville, Ind., 1960; instr. sociology Ind. U., South Bend, 1960-67; relocation rep. Urban Redevel. Commn., South Bend, 1960-62; social worker Elkhart (Ind.) Cmty. Schs., 1962-66, supr. social svcs., 1966-69, dir. human rels., 1970-87; mem. faculty Goshen (Ind.) Coll., 1971—, asst. prof. social work, 1981-91, assoc. prof. social work emerita, 1993—. Pvt. practice social work Ivory Caring Corner, 1981-87; family therapist Family Learning Ctr., South Bend, 1987-94, clinician emerita, 1994—; workshop cons. human social svcs.; instr. sociology and social work St. Mary's Coll., 1967-69, dir. Upward Bound program, 1970; guest lectr. dept. sociology U. Swaziland, South Africa, 1983. Author articles in field. Recipient Human Svc. award Acad. Human Svcs., 1974-75, Merit award Indpls. Pub. Schs. Dept. Social Work, 1977, Designation BCD award Am. Bd. Examiners in Clin. Soc., 1985, plaque for cmty. svcs. Mayor of Elkhart, 1981, Black Achiever award in edn. Ind. Black Expo, 1983; state chpt. Delta Kappa Gamma scholar, 1969-70. Mem. NASW, AAUW, Nat. Black Child Devel. Inst., Nat. Assn. Black Social Workers, Acad. Cert. Social Workers, The Links, Delta Kappa Gamma, Delta Sigma Theta, Alpha Delta Mu. Mem. Church of God in Christ. Home: 1309 Bissell St South Bend IN 46617-2108

IVY, BERRYNELL BAKER, critical care nurse; b. Shreveport, La., June 24, 1954; d. Berry William and Zilphia Margaret (Nix) Baker; m. Kenneth James Ivy, Sr.,Apr. 17, 1988. ADN, Northwestern State U., 1981. RN, La., Tex., Nev.; cert. BLS, ACLS; cert. neurosci. RN; cert. CCRN. Charge nurse Doctors Hosp., Shreveport, La., 1982-85; staff nurse ICU Schumpert Med. Ctr., Shreveport, La., 1985-88, Bayshore Med. Ctr., Pasadena, Tex., 1988-89, asst. head nurse ICU, 1989-92; staff nurse/charge nurse ICU Bossier Med. Ctr., Bossier City, La., 1993-99, U. Tex. Med. Ctr., Galveston, 1999—2001; staff nurse neuro-ICU, relief charge nurse Sunrise Med. Ctr., Las Vegas, 2001—. Mem. AACN, Nat. League Nurses, Am. Assn. Neurosci. Nurses, Soc. Critical Care Medicine. Avocations: raising boxers, sports, travel. Home: 3055 S Nellis Blvd Apt 1039 Las Vegas NV 89121 Personal E-mail: ken-berrynell-ivy@msn.com.

IVY, MARILYN ATKINSON, artist, educator, art director; m. Larry Don Ivy; children: Lauren Ivy Chiong, Travis Wade. BFA, Tex. Christian U., 1970; M, Tex. Woman's U., 2000. Cert. tchr. Tex., Nat. Bd. Profl. Tchg. Stds. Artist Smith Stained Glass Studios, Ft. Worth, 1968—74, Ft. Worth, 1970—; art tchr. Hurst-Euless-Bedford Ind. Sch. Dist., Tex., 1980—2005; coord. art edn. Tex. Christian U., Ft. Worth, 2003—. Liaison, cons. State Farm Ptnrs. in Learning Cmty./Nat. Bd. Profl. Tchg. Stds., Dallas, 1998—2004, El Paso, Tex.; mem. of renewal devel. team Nat. Bd. for Profl. Tchg. Standards, Edn. Testing Svc., Philadelphia, Pa., 2003—04; presenter Nat. Bd. Profl. Tchg. Stds., Washington, 1998—. Exhibited in group shows at 500X Gallery Open Show, 20th Ann. Nat. Juried Exhbn., Navarro County, Tex., 2003 (3d pl., 2003), TCU Faculty Insights Show, 2003, 2005—06. Grantee, Fulbright Meml. Fund. Mem.: Tex. Art Edn. Assn. (assoc.), Nat. Art Edn. Assn. (assoc.), Tex. State Tchr. Assn. (assoc.). Mem. Disciples Of Christ. Avocations: reading, remodeling houses, travel. Home: 2608 S University Dr Fort Worth TX 76109 Office: Art Edn Coord Tex Christian U PO Box 298000 Fort Worth TX 76129 Personal E-mail: m.ivy@tcu.edu.

IZAWA, CHIZUKO, psychologist, researcher; b. Tokushima, Japan; came to U.S., 1961; m. Robert G. Hayden, July 15, 1973; 1 child, Althea J.E.K. Izawa-Hayden. BA in Psychology, U. Tokyo, 1960; MA in Psychology, Stanford U., 1962, PhD in Psychology, 1965. Asst. prof. psychology San Diego State U., Calif., 1965-67; postdoctoral fellow Inst. Human Learning U. Calif., Berkeley, 1967-68; asst. prof. psychology SUNY, Buffalo, 1968-72; assoc. prof. psychology Tulane U., 1972-80, prof. psychology, 1980—. Cons., question constructor Am. Assn. State Psychology Bds.; examiner, interviewer selection com. JET program Consulate Gen. Japan, 1983—; invited vis. fgn. scientist U. Tsukuba, Japan, 2001; co-organizer, chair 4th Tsukuba Internat. Conf. on Memory, 2003-; visiting scholar, Univ. Tsukuba, 2001. Author: Current Issues in Cognitive Processes, 1989, Cognitive Psychology Applied, 1993, On Human Memory, 1999; reviewer numerous jours. including Am. Psychologist, Am. Jour. Psychology, Jour. Exptl. Psychology: Gen. Jour. Exptl. Psychology: Learning, Memory, and Cognition, Memory & Cognition, Jour. Math. Psychology, Jour. Appl. Psychology, Japanese Jour. Psychonomic Sci., Cognitive Psychology, others; cons. reviewer NSF, NIMH, Oxford U. Press, Cambridge U. Press, Stanford U. Press, Harcourt, Sage, others; review panelist Directorate Sci. Edn., Div. Sci. Manpower Improvement, NSF; contbr. numerous articles to profl. jours.; presenter in field. NIMH grantee; Flowerree Found. grantee; Japanese Edn. Rsch. Publ. grantee; Japanese Edn. Min. grantee; Aron Found. grantee; Japanese Monbusho, educ. ministry grantee. Fellow APA, WPA, Am. Psychol. Soc. (charter), WPA; mem. AAUP, Asian Am. Psychol. Assn., Japanese Psychol. Assn., Southeastern Psychol. Assn. (co-chair annual meeting local arrangements subcom. 1972-73, co-chair commn. for status women student rsch. awards 1975-78, chair com. on equality profl. opportunity rsch. awards 1978-80, various program coms. 1975-90, program com. learning, memory, cognition 1995—, chair com. equality profl. opportunity minority interest group 1996-98, exec. com. mem.-at-large 1998-2001, chair spl. grad. rsch. awards 1998-2000), Regional Psychol. Assn., Psychonomic Soc., Psychometric Soc., Soc. Math. Psychology, Soc. Cross-Cultural Psychology, Soc. Cross-Cultural Rsch., Internat. Coun. Psychologists (co-chair annual meeting local arrangements 1973-74), Southeastern Workers in Memory (chmn. 1974-75), Japan Prize World-Wide Nomination Com., Sigma Xi.

IZZO, LUCILLE ANNE, sales representative; b. Rochester, NY, Apr. 1, 1954; d. Peter George and Dorothy June Izzo. B of Gen. Studies, U. Conn., 1995. Regional sales mgr. T.R. Miller Co., Inc., New Milford, Conn., 1986-87; program mgr. Jr. Achievement SW Conn., Stamford, 1987-88, adviser, cons., 1986-93; sec. Eastman Kodak Co., Rochester, 1972-84, consumer products sales rep. Oklahoma City, 1984-86, copy products sales rep. Stamford, 1988-91, office imaging sales rep. Hartford, Conn., 1992-94, major account rep., 1994-96; nat. acct. exec. Lexis-Nexis, Danbury, Conn., 1996-98; sr. account mgr. Gartner Group, Stamford, Conn., 1998—2002; major acct. exec. Ikon Office Solutions, Milford, Conn., 2003—04; relationship exec. Tower Group, 2004—05; dir. corp. accounts Prime Pay, 2005—. Grad. asst. Dale Carnegie Human Rels. Course, 1987, 88, 96. Bus. cons. Region One Jr. Achievement Conf., 1988, 90; guest speaker West Conn. Jr. Achievement Conf., 1990; adviser, recruiter Greater Rochester Jr. Achievement, 1980-83, Small Bus. Owner, Accessorize, 1994—. Mem. NAFE, Am. Mgmt. Assn. Avocations: travel, reading, music. Home: 2006 Eaton Ct Danbury CT 06811 Office: Primepay 5 Commerce Dr Cromwell CT 06416

JABLONSKY, ATARAH, retired music educator; b. Jerusalem, Nov. 25, 1927; came to U.S., 1929; d. Abraham Itzak and Sarah (Haack) Wishengrad; m. Marvin Jablonsky, Nov. 30, 1947; children: Karen, Andrew, Eugene, Elliott, Benjamin. MusB, Manhattan Sch. Music, 1948; MS in Edn., Xavier U., 1969. Tchr. piano Neighborhood Music Sch., N.Y.C., 1947-52, U. Cin., 1958-70; lectr. Edgecliff Coll., Cin., 1972-74; tchr. piano Teodtman Sch. Music, Cin., 1986—2002; ret., 2002. Adj. asst. prof. music Coll. Mt. St. Joseph, Cin., 1970—; adjudicator U. Cin., 1970—2001. Contbr. articles to profl. jours. Named Nat. Cert. Tchr. of Yr., Ohio Music Tchrs. Assn., 2000; recipient Found. Fellow, Music Tchrs. Nat. Assn., 2005. Mem. Nat. Guild Piano Tchrs., Ohio Tchrs. Music Assn. (4th v.p.; Tchr. of Yr. award 2000), Tri-County Piano Tchrs. Assn., Keyboard Club Cin. (pres. 1990—). Avocations: reading, swimming, travel. Home: 21 W Charlotte Ave Wyoming OH 45215-2063

JABS, AURA LEE, minister, educator; b. Lewistown, Mont., Apr. 21, 1932; d. Stephen Ellias and Mabel Harriet Sande; m. Edward Henry Jabs, June 20, 1954; children: Mark Allan, Mary Kay, David Stephen. BS, Mont. State U., 1954; MDiv, Iliff Sch. Theology, 1982, MA in Religion, 1983. Ordained to ministry United Presbyn. Ch., 1984. Tchr. Spanish Gallatin County H.S., Bozeman, Mont., 1953—54; tchr. English Box Elder H.S., 1954—55; tchr. English, French Williams Bay H.S., Wis., 1957—58; tchr. English Am. Dependent Sch., Molesworth AFB, England, 1959—60; pastor Vale (Oreg.) United Meth. Ch., Oreg., 1984—90, Southside Blvd. United Meth. Ch., Nampa, 1990—93, Sutherlin/Wilbur United Meth. Churches, Sutherlin, Oreg., 1993—2002. Bd. trustees Oregon-Idaho Conf., Portland, 1988—90; chair Ctrl. Dist. Com. Superintendency, Bend, 1989—90; mem. So. Dist. Leadership Team, Eugene, 2002—04, Conf. Bd. of Elders Task Force, Portland, 2004—. Vol. driver Silver Key, Colorado Springs, 1976—78; sr. deaconess United Ch. Christ, Colorado Springs, 1976—79; bd. mem. Sutherlin/Oakland Emergency Food Pantry, Oreg., 1993—2002; vol. Suicide Crisis Hotline, 1983—84. Recipient Iliff Preaching prize, Iliff Sch. Theology, 1982. Methodist. Avocations: reading, travel, photography, computers.

JACARUSO, DIANA, biology professor; d. Robert and Margaret Landesman; m. Stephen Lee Jacaruso, Oct. 14, 1978. BS in Biology, U. Tex., Arlington, 1989, MS in Biology, 1999. Clin. rsch. assoc. III Children's Med. Ctr., Dallas, 1989—95; adj. faculty biology labs. Mountain View Coll., Dallas, 1995—99; lectr. mycology lab. U. Tex., Arlington, 2001; adj. faculty biology Tarrant County Coll., Hurst, Tex., 2002—. Adj. faculty adv. com. Tarrant County Coll., 2005. Contbr. to adj. faculty handbooks. Counselor Camp Jubilee, Meridian, Tex., 1994—95; lectr. North Lake Coll., Twenty First Century Coll. for Young People, Irving, Tex., 1996; chaperone Diocesan Cath. Youth Conf., Dallas, 2003—04. Recipient award, Outstanding Coll. Students Am., 1989—90. Catholic. Avocation: reading. Office: Tarrant County Coll 828 Harwood Rd Hurst TX 76054 Office Phone: 817-515-6842. Business E-Mail: diana.jacaruso@tccd.edu.

JACHINO, DANEEN L., legal administrator; b. Chgo., Feb. 16, 1947; d. James and Lee Jachino. BA, DePaul U., 1985; MBA, Ill. Inst. Tech., 1995. Asst. buyer Chas A. Stevens, Chgo., 1967—70; sec. Lord, Bissell and Brook, Chgo., 1970—78; adminstrv. asst. to Judge David Linn Ill. Appellate Ct., Chgo., 1978—85; legal sec., sr. legal asst. Kirkland and Ellis, Chgo., 1986—95; mgr. mergers/acquisitions clearance Kirkland and Ellis LLP, Chgo., 1995—2005, dir. mergers/acquisitions clearance, 2006—. Presenter Fed. Trade Commn., Washington, 2002. Contbr. chapters to books. Vol. underprivileged children Shama Ministries; mem. Art Inst. Chgo., 1995—, Friends of Park, Chgo., 2002—, Lincoln Park Zoo, Chgo., 2004—. Mem.: Alzheimer's Assn. (support group facilitator 2001—, steering com. memory walk 2003, 2005, co-chair 2006). Roman Catholic. Avocations: running, sailing, skiing, bicycling. Office: Kirkland & Ellis LLP 200 E Randolph Dr Chicago IL 60601 Office Phone: 312-861-2137. Business E-Mail: djachino@kirkland.com.

JACIR, EMILY, photographer, conceptual artist; b. Palestine, 1970; BA in Art, U. Dallas, 1992; MFA, Memphis Coll. Art, 1994; attended, Whitney Ind. Study Program, NYC, 1998—99. One-woman shows include, Anderson Ranch Arts Ctr., Snowmass Village, Colo., 1997, Eastfield Coll. Gallery,

Mesquite, Tex., 1997, Everywhere/Nowhere, SPACES, Cleve., 1999, From Paris to Riyadh (Drawings for my mother), U. Gallery, U South, Sewanee, Tenn., 2000, New Photographs: Bethlehem to Ramallah, Debs & Co. Project Room, NY, 2002, Where We Come From, 2003, Belongings, O-K Ctr. Contemporary Art, Linz, Austria, 2003, Mus. Modern Art, Arnhem, The Netherlands, 2003, LA Internat. Art Biennial, Frumkin Duval Gallery, Santa Monica, Calif., 2003, Artspace Annex II, New Haven, CT, 2003, Woher wir kommen, Künstlerhaus, Bremen, 2004, Den I: a på Moderna: Emily Jacir: Where We Come From, Moderna Museet, Stockholm, 2004, The Khalil Sakakini Cultural Ctr., Ramallah, 2004, Nuova Icona, Venice, 2004, Kunstraum Innsbruck, Innsbruck, 2004, Accumulations, Alexander & Bonin, NY, 2005, exhibited in group shows at 7th Ann. McNeese Nat. Works on Paper, McNeese State, Lake Charles, La., 1994, Women in Art: 12 Tex. Women, Contemporary Art Ctr., Houston, 1997, Xmas, Kent Gallery, NY, 1999, Free for All, Temporary Art Svcs., Chgo., 2000, Carnival in the Eye of the Storm: War/Art/New Technologies, Pacific Northwest Coll. Art, Portland, Oreg., 2000, Greater New York, PS I Contemporary Art Ctr., LI City, 2000, Strangers/Estrangers, PS I Clocktower Gallery, NY, 2001, Lecture Lounge, 2001, Uncommon Threads, Herbert F. Johnson Mus., Cornell U., NY, 2001, Made in Transit, Vacancy Gallery, NY, 2001, Unjustified, Apex Art, NY, 2002, Submerged, Nuremberg, 2002, Right2Fight, Sarah Lawrence Coll., Bronxville, NY, 2002, Queens Internat., Queens Mus. Art, 2002, Settlement, Gallery 400, Chgo., 2002, Global Priority, Hester Art Gallery, U. Mass., 2003, Shatat, Colo. U. Art Galleries, Boulder, 2003, Made in Palestine, Art Car Mus., Houston, 2003, VEIL, Inst. Internat. Arts, London, 2003, 8th Istanbul Biennial, 2003, 100 Cuts, Gallery 312, Chgo., 2004, Empire: Videos for a New World, Md. Inst. Coll. Art, Balt., 2004, Whitney Biennial, Whitney Mus. Am. Art, 2004, Cover Girl: the Female Body & Islam in Contemporary Art, Ise Cultural Found., NY, 2004, Neither Here Nor There: Video Artists Navigate Cultural Displacement, Cheekwood Mus. Art, Nashville, 2004, Election, Am. Fine Arts, NY, 2004, Sometime: Six Works for Film & Video, Anthony Reynolds Gallery, London, 2004, Desenhos: A-Z, Porta 33, Funchal, Ilha da Madeira, 2005.

JACK, JANIS GRAHAM, judge; b. 1946; RN, St. Thomas Sch. Nursing, 1969; BA, U. Balt., 1974; JD summa cum laude, South Tex. Coll., 1981. Pvt. practice, Corpus Christi, Tex., 1981-94; judge U.S. Dist. Ct. (so. dist.) Tex., Corpus Christi, 1994—. Jud. mem. The Maritime Law Assn. U.S. Mem. ABA, Fed. Judges Assn., Fifth Cir. Dist. Judges Assn., Nat. Assn. Women Judges (jud. conf. com. info. tech.), Tex. Bar Found., State Bar Tex., The Philos. Soc. Tex., Order of Lytae, Phi Alpha Delta. Office: US Dist Ct 1133 N Shoreline Blvd Corpus Christi TX 78401

JACK, MORGANN TAYLOR, writer, artist; d. William H. and Emma Lee (Williams) Blanks; m. Charles D. Jack, July 21, 1957 (dec. Sept. 20, 1979). AA in Fine Arts, Allan Hancock Coll., 1975. Editl. asst. The Cycler Champlin Oil Co. house organ, Ft. Worth, 1957; columnist, reporter, corr. Santa Barbara News-Press, Lompoc, Calif., 1961—64; freelance journalist AP, Springfield (Mass.) Rep., 1966—68; staff reporter features, 1st editor weekend entertainment supplement, Lompoc Record, 1968—71; feature writer Lompoc Valley News, 1980—84; feature writer, cover artist Cen. Coast Mag., Santa Maria, Calif., 1989—90. Guest artist Binnenheide Art Exhbn., Kevelaer, Germany, 1994. Creator, editor, artist (monthly mag.) Space 'n Lace, VAFB, Calif., 1961—63, (weekly newsletter) Reeflector, Recife, Brazil, 1964—65; commd. garden sculpture, for Lompoc Mayor (reception benefitting Lompoc Mus.), 1978; illustrator (book) A Word About Birds in Rhyme Time, 1984; commd. art, Office Idaho State Treas., 1988—93. Mem. Santa Barbara County Commn. for Women, 1999—2000. Recipient regional awards, juried art shows and competitions, 1951—86, Plaque in Appreciation of Outstanding Cmty. Svcs., City of Lompoc, 1968—71. Mem.: Santa Barbara Mus. Art, Nat. Mus. Women in the Arts (charter mem.). Avocations: travel, reading. Home: PO Box 598 Lompoc CA 93438

JACK, NANCY RAYFORD, retired supplemental resource company executive, consultant; b. Hughes Springs, Tex., June 23, 1939; d. Vernon Lacy and Virginia Ernestine (Turner) Rayford; m. Kermit E. Hundley, Dec. 19, 1979; 1 child by previous marriage, James Bradford Jack, III. Cert. in bus. adminstrn., Keller Grad. Sch. Mgmt., 1980; cert. in acctg., Harper Coll., 1972, cert. in corp. law and tax law, paralegal, 1973. Sr. sec. Gould, Inc., Rolling Meadows, Ill., 1971-73, staff asst., 1973-74, asst. sec., 1974-77, corp. sec., 1977-89, v.p., 1985-89; pres. The Corp. Ofcl. Sec., Wheaton, Ill., 1989-92, Corp. Minutes and More, Wheaton, 1992-99; assoc. dir. The Bus. Owners' Trustee, The Woodlands, Tex., 1999—2005, ret., 2005. Recipient cert. of leadership YWCA Met. Chgo., 1975 Mem.: Kingwood Country Club, Beta Sigma Phi.

JACKER, CORINNE LITVIN, playwright, writer; b. Chgo., June 29, 1933; d. Thomas Henry and Theresa (Bellak) Litvin. Student, Stanford U., 1950-52; BS, Northwestern U., 1954, MA, 1955, postgrad., 1955-56. Editor Liberal Arts Press, 1959-60, Macmillan Co., 1960-63, Scribner's, 1963-65; story editor Sta. WNET-TV, N.Y.C., 1969-71, CBS-TV, N.Y.C., 1972-74; instr. playwrighting NYU, 1976-78; vis. prof. playwriting Yale U., 1979-81. Adj. prof. Princeton U., 1986, 88, Columbia U., 1988-99, Breadloaf Sch. of English, 1988, NYU, 1990-91, U. Ga., 1995—2003; sci. cons. Benton Project for Broadcasting, U. Chgo., 1988-90. Exec. story editor, head writer (TV series) Best of Families, PBS, N.Y.C., 1975-77; head writer (TV series) Another World, 1981-82; author: Man, Memory, and Machines, 1964 (N.Y. Pub. Library 50 Best Books of Yr. 1964), Window on the Unknown, 1966 (AAAS 50 Best Books of Yr. 1966), A Little History of Cocoa, 1966, The Black Flag of Anarchy, 1968 (Pubs. Weekly 25 Best Books of Yr. 1968), The Biological Revolution, 1971, The Chocolate Bar Bust, 1994; playwright: The Scientific Method, 1970, Seditious Acts, 1970, Travellers, 1973, Breakfast, Lunch, & Dinner, 1975, Bits and Pieces, 1975 (Obie award 1975), Harry Outside, 1975 (Obie award 1975), Night Thoughts & Terminal, 1976, Other People's Tables, 1976, My Life, 1977, After the Season, 1978, Later, 1979, Domestic Issues, 1981, In Place, 1982, Songs from Distant Lands, 1985, (adaptation) Hedda Gabbler, 1989, The Island, 1991, (adaptation) Three Sisters, 1992, In the Dark, 1993, Light, 1993, Getting Home, 1994, A New Life, 1995, The Promised Land, 1995, The Machine Age, 1996, Parties, 2000; TV writer, including: 3 episodes Actors' Choice, NET, 1970 (Emmy citation 1970), Virginia Woolf: The Moment Whole, NET, 1972 (CINE Golden Eagle award 1972); story editor: 4 episode series Benjamin Franklin, CBS, 1974 (Emmy citation 1974); The Adams Chronicles, 1975 (Peabody award 1975); Bicentennial Minutes, 1975, Loose Change, 1978, 3 episode series, NBC, 1978, 3 episodes of Best of Families, NET, 1978, The Jilting of Granny Weatherall, NET, 1980, Night Thoughts and Terminal BBC, 1978, Overdrawn at the Memory Bank, NET, 1983 (Rotterdam Film Festival, Am. Film Inst. Video Feature Film Festival). Rockefeller Found. grantee, 1979-80; residency Villa Serbelloni, Bellagio, Italy, 1987. Mem. Dramatists Guild, Writers Guild Am. East, PEN Home and Office: 110 W 86th St New York NY 10024-4049 Office Phone: 212-496-9698. E-mail: jacaranda@verizon.net.

JACKMAN DABB, HOLLY PIEPER, publisher; b. Scottsbluff, Nebr., Jan. 12, 1965; d. John Matthew and Mardell B. Pieper; m. Lynn Richard Jackman, Dec. 28, 1985 (div. Nov. 17, 1993); children: Matthew, Jace, Lance; m. Randy Dabb, Sept. 27, 2003. AS, Western Wyo. Cmty. Coll., Rock Springs, 1985; BS, U. Wyo., 1986. Reporter Rock Springs Newspaper, Wyo., 1987-90; bus. mngr. Jackman Construction, Rock Springs, 1990-93; special editions editor Rock Springs Newspaper, 1993-98, publisher, 1998—. Squadron comdr. CAP, Wyo., 1991-1995; mem. Local Emergency Planning Commn., 1994—; Wyo. rep. USA West Policy Bd. for squaredance policy, 2002—; mem. Sr. Citizen Found. Bd., 2004-, Downtown Bus. Authority Bd., 2005. Brewer award Civil Air Patrol, 1993, Bus. and Profl. Woman of the Year award BPW, 1993, 98. Mem. Soc. Profl. Journalists (bd. dirs. 2002—), C. of C. (bd.dirs., 2001-02), Sashay Pardners (v.p. 1999, treas. 1997, pres. 1999-2001), Kiwanis, Rock Springs (Wyo.) Soccer Assn. (bd. mem. 1999-2002, chmn. econ. environ. com.), Wyo. Press Assn. (bd. dir. 2003—, chmn. leg. com.), Downtown Bus. Assn. Democrat. Avocations: reading, gardening, water sports, square dancing, skiing. Home: 3 Wardell Ct Rock Springs WY 82901-7248 Office: Rock Springs Newspaper 215 D St Rock Springs WY 82901-6234

JACKOBOICE, SANDRA KAY, artist; b. Detroit, July 22, 1936; d. Virgil Ellsworth and Lucille Elizabeth LeSeur; m. Edward James Jackoboice, Jan. 11, 1958; children: E. Michael, Timothy Jon. BA, Aquinas Coll., Grand Rapids, Mich., 1989. Co-owner Fashion Plate, Grand Rapids, 1975-79; wardrobe cons. Steketees, Grand Rapids, 1980-82; owner Color Plus, Grand Rapids, 1983—. Instr. pastel Von Liebig Ctr. Arts, Naples, Fla., 2001—, Art League, Marco Island, 2003, 05, Art League Ft. Myers, 2003—05, Frederik Meijer Gardens, Grand Rapids, 2006. One-woman shows include FMB, Lowell, 1993, 1995, City Hall, Bielsko-Biala, Poland, 1995, Terryberry Gallery, Grand Rapids, 1997, Frederick Meijer Gardens, 1998, Betten Imports Gallery, 2005—06, Collier County Libr., Naples, Fla., 2006, exhibited in group shows at Bot. Images Exhbn., Lansing, Mich., Artist Alliance Group Shows, represented by, Grand Gallery, Grand Rapids and Ada, Treeline Gallery, Suttons Bay, Mich.; featured in Artists' Photo Reference Book, Pastel Artist Internat. mag., Pastel Jour., The Ultimate Guide to Painting from Photographs, 2005, others. Mem. Jr. League, Grand Rapids, 1962—96, Downtown Mgmt. Bd., Grand Rapids, 1993—96, Grand Rapids Parking Commn., 1993—96; bd. dirs. Arts Coun. Greater Grand Rapids, 1997—2000, United Arts Coun. Collier County, 2006—. Recipient awards for art work. Mem.: Naples Fla. League Club, Internat. Assn. Pastel Socs. (publicity chair and membership chair 2001—, bd. dirs. 2003—, v.p. 2005—), Grand Valley Artists, Artists Alliance, Great Lakes Pastel Soc. (pres. 1997—2001, advisor bd. dirs. 2001, co-founder), Pastel Soc. Am. (assoc.; sig. 2004—), S.W. Fla. Pastel Soc. (life; founder and advisor bd. dirs. 2002—). Republican. Avocations: travel, art, tennis, golf. Office: Color Plus PO Box 6775 Grand Rapids MI 49516-6775 Home (Winter): 81 11 Bay Colony Dr Naples FL 34108 Office Phone: 616-956-6000. Personal E-mail: skjartist@aol.com.

JACKOWITZ, ENID DUCHIN, psychotherapist; b. Phila., Feb. 4, 1943; d. Herman and Betty (Cohen) Duchin; m. Sydney Lawrence Jackowitz, Aug. 24, 1963; children: Michael, Howard. AA, Valencia C.C., Orlando, Fla., 1980; BA, U. Ctrl. Fla., 1991. Nat. cert. counselor. Psychotherapist Ctr. for Counseling and Consulting, Winter Park, Fla., 1996—. Mem. LMHC, Phi Kappa Phi, Golden Key Soc., Psi Chi, Chi Sigma Iota. Democrat. Jewish. Avocations: movies, writing, pottery, meditation, storytelling. Home: 2502 Chanute Trl Maitland FL 32751-4011 Office: Ctr for Counseling and Consulting 661 Seminola Blvd Casselberry FL 32707 E-mail: eniddj@aol.com.

JACKSON, ANITA LOUISE, otolaryngologist, editor-in-chief; b. Augusta, Ga., Apr. 24, 1963; d. Lawrence Joseph and Louise Madelynne (Tarver) J. AB in Biochemistry, Princeton U., 1984; MS in Biology and Neurobiology, Stanford U., 1986; MD in Medicine and Surgery, U. Ill., Chgo., 1990; MPH, Harvard U., 1993. Biochemist Biogen, Geneva, 1983; neurobiologist Vets. Hosp., Palo Alto, Calif., 1984-86; health educator, rschr. Stanford Hosp., Palo Alto, 1985-86; health policy rschr. U. Ill., Chgo., 1986-88; otolaryngology rschr. Johns Hopkins, Balt., 1989; resident gen. surgery Howard U. Hosp., Washington, 1990-92; resident otolaryngology U. Tenn., Memphis, 1993-97; chief otolaryngologist Greater Carolina Ear, Nose and Throat, Lumberton, N.C., 1997—; med. staff FirstHealth Richmond Memorial Hospital, Rockingham, NC, 2004—. Chair resident sect. D.C. Med. Soc., Washington, 1992-93; alumni coun. rep. Harvard Sch. Pub. Health, Boston, 1993-96; health cons. and presenter in field. Editor: Health Homecookin' Cookbook, 1992; founder, editor-in-chief Harvard Jour. Minority Pub. Health, 1993—; contbr. articles to profl. jours. Recipient Schweitzer award Albert Schweitzer Found., Boston, 1993, U.S. Surgeon Gen.'s award USPHS, 1997; named one of Top 100 Black Physicians in Am., Black Enterprise Mag., 2001. Mem. AMA, Am. Acad. Otolaryngology, Nat. Med. Assn. (chair resident sect. 1995-97). Methodist. Avocations: writing, jogging, skiing. Office: FirstHealth Richmond Memorial Hospital 925 S Long Dr Rockingham NC 28379 also: Greater Carolina Ear Nosethroat Pa PO Box 1046 Lumberton NC 28359-1046

JACKSON, ANNE (ANNE JACKSON WALLACH), actress; b. Allegheny, Pa., Sept. 3, 1926; d. John Ivan and Stella Germaine (Murray) J.; m. Eli Wallach, Mar. 5, 1948; children: Peter, Roberta, Katherine. Studied with Sanford Meisner and Herbert Berghof at Neighborhood Playhouse, with Lee Strassberg at Actor's Studio; DFA, South Hampton Coll. Tchr. Herbert Berghoff Sch. Profl. debut: Cherry Orchard; mem. Am. Repertory Co.; Broadway plays include: Summer and Smoke, Oh, Men! Oh, Women!, Middle of the Night, Major Barbara, Rhinoceros, Luv, Waltz of the Toreadors, Diary of Anne Frank, 1978, Twice Around the Park, 1982-83, Nest of the Woodgrouse, 1984, Café Crown, 1989, Love Letters, 1991-92, Lost in Yonkers, 1992, In Person, 1993, The Flowering Peach, 1994, off-Broadway plays: Tennessee Williams Remembered, 1999, Mr. Peter's Connection, 1998, Down the Garden Path; London stage performances of The Typists, The Tiger, 1966; film appearances include: So Young, So Bad, 1950, Secret Life of an American Wife, 1968, Dirty Dingus McGee, 1970, Lovers and Other Strangers, 1970, The Shining, 1980, Sam's Son, 1985, Funny About Love, 1992, Folks, 1992, Johnnie Twenties, 1998, Something Sweet, 2000; TV appearances include: 84 Charing Cross Road, Private Battle, Everything's Relative, 1987, Law & Order, 1997, Education of Max Bickford, 2002; TV films: Family Man, Golda I and II, Out on a Limb, Baby M, 1988, The Rescuers: The Lady on the Bicycle, 1997; author: (autobiography) Early Stages, 1979. Recipient Obie award. Mem.: Actor's Studio (life). Office: care Paradigm 200 W 57th St Ste 900 New York NY 10019-3211

JACKSON, B. ELLEN HURSEY, music educator; d. Floyd Curtis and Barbara Louise (Moore) Hursey; m. James Eugene Jackson; children: James Eugene Jr., Joseph Dewey. BS in Music Edn., U. NC, Pembroke, 1986. Cert. choral dir. U. N.C.-Pembroke, 1986. Tchr. music edn. Pub. Schs. Robeson County, Lumberton, NC, 1986—. Min. music Robeson Bapt. Area Chs., Lumberton, 1989—. Musician (vocalist): ch. and wedding music performances. Mem.: Music Educators N.C. (assoc.). Home: 322 W McLean St Saint Pauls NC 28384 Office: Purnell Swett HS PO Box 1210 Pembroke NC 28272 Office Phone: 910-521-3253.

JACKSON, BETTY EILEEN, music and elementary school educator; b. Denver, Oct. 9, 1925; d. James Bowen and Fannie (Shelton) J. MusB, U. Colo., 1948, MusM, 1949, MusB in Edn., 1963; postgrad., Ind. U., 1952-55, Hochschule fur Musik, Munich, 1955-56. Cert. educator Colo., Calif. Tchr., accompanist, tchr. H.L. Davis Vocal Studios, Denver, 1949-52; tchg. assoc. Ind. U., Bloomington, 1952-53, U. Colo., Boulder, 1961-63, vis. lectr., summers 1963-69; tchr. Fontana (Calif.) Unified Sch. Dist., 1963—2002; pvt. studio, 1966—. Lectr. in music Calif. State U., San Bernardino, 1967-76; performer, accompanist, music dir. numerous musical cos. including performer, music dir. Fontana Mummers, 1980—, Riverside Cmty. Players, Calif., 1984—; performer Rialto Cmty. Theatre, Calif., 1983—; head visual and performing arts com. Cypress Elem. Sch., 1988-92. Performances include numerous operas, musical comedies and oratorios, Cen. City Opera, Denver Grand Opera, Univ. Colo., Ind. Univ. Opera Theater (leading mezzo), 3 tours of Fed. Rep. Germany, 1956-58; oratorio soloist in Ind., Ky., Colo., and Calif., West End Opera (lead roles), Riverside Opera (lead roles). Judge Inland Theatre League, Riverside, 1983-92; mem. San Bernardino Cultural Task Force, 1981-83; bd. dirs. Riverside-San Bernardino Counties Met. Auditions, 1988—; mem. adv. bd. Riverside Concert Opera, 1990-95. Fulbright grantee, Munich, 1955-56; named outstanding performer Inland Theatre League, 1982-84; recipient Outstanding Reading Tchr. award, 1990, Tchr. of Yr. nominations, 1990, 91, hon. svc. award, 1992. Mem. AAUW (bd. dirs., cultural chair 1983-86), NEA, Nat. Assn. Tchrs. Singing (exec. bd. 1985-89), Internat. Reading Assn., Music Educators Nat. Conf., Calif. Tchrs. Assn., Calif. Elem. Educators Assn., Fontana Tchrs. Assn., Music Tchrs. Assn., Arrowhead Reading Coun., San Bernardino Valley Concert Assn. (bd. dirs. 1977-83), Internat. Platform Assn., Nat. Assn. Preservation and Perpetuation of Storytelling, Order Eastern Star, Kappa Kappa Iota (v.p. 1982-83), Sigma Alpha Iota (life), Chi Omega. Avocations: community theater and opera, travel, collecting hummels and plates. Home: PO Box 885 Rialto CA 92377-0885

JACKSON, BETTY L. DEASON, real estate developer; b. Wichita, Kans., Mar. 31, 1927; d. Orville John and Ida Mabel (Wolfe) Deason; m. James L. Jackson, July 2, 1966 (dec. Feb. 1983); children: Rebecca Lou, Jennifer Mae. AA, SW Baptist U., Bolivar, Mo., 1946; BA, Cen. Mo. State U., 1963; MA, U. Mo., 1964. Lic. realtor, Kans. Salesperson Sears, Kansas City, Mo., 1943-44; bookkeeping clk. Hallmark Cards, Kansas City, Mo., 1945-46; civil service Camp Pendleton, Oceanside, Calif., 1947; sec. Ford Motor Co., Kansas City, Mo., Jim Taylor Olds Co., Independence, Mo., 1952-54; tchr. Consol. Sch. Dist. #2, Mo., 1954-55, tchr. adminstr. Raytown, Mo., 1963-78; owner mgr. B.J.'s Florist Car Wash Laundramat, Stockton, Mo., 1979-82; owner, ptnr. J and S Realty, Stockton, Mo., 1983—. Officer J-S Corp., Stockton, 1986-94. Mem. Nat. Assn. Realtors, Mo. C. of C., AARP, Greater Ozark Bd. Realtors. Democrat. Baptist. Avocations: piano, church clubs, organ. Office: Coldwell Banker J-S Realty PO Box 159 Stockton MO 65785-0159 Home: 1600 Garfield St Apt 10 Enumclaw WA 98022-2278

JACKSON, CAROL E., federal judge; BA, Wellesley Coll., 1973; JD, U. Mich., 1976. With Thompson & Mitchell, St. Louis, 1976-83; counsel Mallinckrodt, Inc., St. Louis, 1983-85; magistrate US Dist. Ct., Ea. Dist. Mo., 1986-92, dist. judge, 1992—, now chief judge. Adj. prof. law Washington U., St. Louis, 1989-92. Trustee St. Louis Art Mus., 1987-91; dir. bi-state chpt. ARC, 1989-91, Mo. Bot. Garden. Mem. Nat. Assn. Women Judges, Fed. Magistrate Judges Assn., Mo. Bar, St. Louis County Bar Assn., Bar Assn. Metro. St. Louis, Mound City Bar Assn., Lawyers Assn. St. Louis. Office: US Dist Ct Eagleton US Courthous Ste 14-148 111 S 10th St Saint Louis MO 63102

JACKSON, CHERYL ANN, music educator, director; b. Appleton City, Mo., Mar. 3, 1947; d. Woodrow Clifton and Orpha Mae Bray. BA in Music Edn., Ctrl. Mo. State U., Warrensburg, Mo., 1984, MA in Music Edn., 1989; PhD Music Edn., Mich. State U., East Lansing, 1996. Cert. instrumental and vocal music (K-12) Mo., music composite (K-12) S.D. Dir. music Deepwater (Mo.) Sch. Dist., 1970; dir. music Davis R-12 Sch. Dist., Clinton, Mo., 1979—81, Miami R-1 Sch. Dist., Amoret, Mo., 1984—87, Smithton R-6 Sch. Dist., Smithton, Mo., 1989—90; dir. bands Avon Sch. Dist4-1, Avon, SD, 1990—93; assoc. prof. music edn. Ea. Ky. U., Richmond, Ky., 1996—. Asst. music dir. First United Meth. Ch., Richmond, Ky., 1997—; private music instr., Richmond, 1963—. Contbr. articles to profl. jours. Member Ctrl. Ky. Concert Band, Lexington, 1998—. Grantee Collaborative Rsch. Grant, Ky. Music Educators Assn., 2000—01. Mem.: Coll. Music Soc., Music Educators Nat. Conf., Phi Delta Kappa Internat. (Ea. Ky. U. chpt.) (rep. Ednl. Found. 2000—02). Methodist. Avocations: sewing, travel. Office: Eastern Kentucky Univ 521 Lancaster Ave Richmond KY 40475

JACKSON, CLORA ELLIS, counseling administrator, psychologist, educator; d. Scott and Ethel J. (Peeler) Ellis; m. Harold Coyage Jackson, Jr.; children: Sheriel, Lauren (dec.), Adrienne, Duaine. AA in Secretarial Sci., L.A. S.W. Coll., L.A., 1971; BS in Psychology, U. So. Calif., 1975, MS in Higher Edn., 1977; MS in Counseling, Calif. State U., Long Beach, 1979. Cert. psychologist Calif., 1981. Bus. edn. instr. Orange Coast Coll., Costa Mesa, Calif., 1979-80; tchr., counselor L.A. Unified Sch. Dist., 1977-81, sch. psychologist, 1981-83; tchr. bus. edn./math. Long Beach Unified Sch. Dist., 1983-90, counselor, 1990—99. Vol. Habitat for Humanity, 1990—. Mem. AAUW, Women in Arts, Pi Lambda Theta. Mem. Baha'i Faith.

JACKSON, CYNTHIA WILLIFORD, special education educator; b. Mobile, Ala., Oct. 30, 1949; d. Gerald Dee and Mary Evelyn (Johnson) W.; m. Alan P. Jackson, Aug. 18, 1973; 1 child, Julie Lynette. BS in Elem. Edn., John Brown U., 1971; MS in Spl. Edn., U. Ctrl. Ark., 1972; EdD, U. Ala., 1998. Cert. tchr., Ala. Resource tchr. Decatur (Ark.) Elem. Sch., 1972-73, Montgomery (Ala.) County Sch. System, 1973-75, Birmingham (Ala.) City Schs., 1976-80; instr. Horizons Program-UAB, Birmingham, 1992-94; rsch. asst., adj. U. Ala., Tuscaloosa, 1995-98, asst. prof., 1998-99, State U. West Ga., Carrollton, 1999—2002; ednl. evaluator Douglas County Sch. Sys., 2002—. Pvt. cons. Auburn (Ala.) City Schs., 1989-91; psychometrist, Montgomery, 1975-76. Author: (with others) Profile of Commitment, 1995; contbr. chpt. to Mental Retardation, 5th edit.; contbr. articles to profl. jours. Mem. Coun. for Exceptional Children, Kappa Delta Pi, Phi Delta Kappa. Baptist. Avocations: reading, needlepoint, walking. Home: 2520 Gold Hill Ct Villa Rica GA 30180-8458 Office: Fairplay Middle Sch 8309 Hwy 166 Douglasville GA 30135 Office Phone: 770-651-5340. Personal E-mail: drcindy@yahoo.com.

JACKSON, DANA LEE, science educator; d. Jerry Wayne and Margaret Jewel Barnett; m. William Rodney Jackson, Dec. 9, 1995; children: Margaret Elizabeth, Reagan Leigh. BS in Elem. Edn., Athens State U., Ala., 1998. 911 emergency dispatcher Athens-Limestone Hosp., 1995—97, data entry clk., 1997; sci. educator Clements HS, Athens, 1998—. Active Sheriff's Ladies Aux., Athens, 1995—. Mem.: NEA, Limestone County Edn. Assn. (sec. 2004—05), Ala. Edn. Assn.

JACKSON, DAVIDA JANAE, science educator; b. Birmingham, Ala., Jan. 25, 1979; d. David Carl and Loda Jackson; children: David Carl, Carey Antonius. BS in Biology, Grambling State U., La., 2001. Educator Birmingham City Schs., Ala., 2004—. Sponsor AH Parker H.S. Sci. Club, Birmingham, 2002—, AH Parker H.S. Flag Team, Birmingham. Home: PO Box 13271 Birmingham AL 35202 Office: Birmingham Bd Edn 900 4th St N Birmingham AL 35202

JACKSON, DIONNE BROXTON, chemist; d. Leon and Joan Broxton; m. Brian Jackson, 1998. BS in Chemistry, Spelman Coll., 1991; MA in Indsl. Engring., U. Ctrl. Fla., 1994. Chemist materials sci. lab. NASA Kennedy Space Ctr., 1991—. Mem. environ. monitoring lab. Bionetics Corp., 1988—89, mem. microchem. analysis lab., 1990. Scholar, Spelman Coll. Avocations: reading, singing, travel.

JACKSON, FRANCES I., music educator; d. Edgar Earl and Mary Belle Wickliff; children: Justin A., Simon M., Sharon V. BS, U. Indpls., 1975; M in Music Edn., Ind. U./Purdue U., Indpls., 1979. Life lic. tchr. music K-12 Ind. Music tchr. Shelbyville Ctrl. Schs., 1971—. Leader 4-H, Shelbyville; mem. Waldron HS Band Boosters, Ind., Waldron HS Athletic Boosters; sec. Ind. State Racquetball Bd., 1998—2002; choir dir. 1st Christian Ch., Shelbyville, 1971—79; mem. choir Mt. Pisgah Ch., Shelbyville, 1985—, chorister, 1995—. Recipient cooking awards, Shelby County Fair, 1979—99, Ind. State Fair, 1990—91. Mem.: Ind. Orff Soc., Mu Phi Epsilon. Office: Loper Elem Sch 901 Loper Dr Shelbyville IN 46176 Office Phone: 317-398-9725. E-mail: frances389@hotmail.com.

JACKSON, GERALDINE, entrepreneur; b. Barnesville, Ga., Oct. 30, 1934; d. Charles Brown and Christine (Maddox) Jackson; 1 child, Prentiss Andrew. Nurses aide Grady Hosp., Atlanta, 1953—54; mail handler U.S. Post Office, Cicero, Ill., 1966-70; sec., tour guide Walgreens Lab., Chgo., 1970-74; credit clk. Sterling Jewelers, Atlanta, 1974-2000; receptionist Willie A. Watkins Funeral Home, Atlanta, 2000—. Mem. Nat. Law Enforcement Officer Meml. Fund; assoc. mem. presdl. task force Rep. Nat. Com.; active Sacred Heart League. Mem. AARP, DAV, NAACP, Nat. Assn. Police Orgn., Internat. Assn. Chief Police, Ga. Sheriff's Assn., Nat. Right to Life. Democrat. Home: 1890 Myrtle Dr SW Apt 422 Atlanta GA 30311-4954 Office Phone: 404-758-1731.

JACKSON, GERALDINE, literature and language educator; d. Arizona and Elizabeth Smith Jackson. BA, Stillman Coll., Tuscaloosa, Ala., 1964; Spanish endorsement, Rice U., Houston, 1965; Master's degree, U. Ill., Chgo., 1984; humanities endorsement, Northwestern U., Evanston, Ill., 1988. Sponsor Sophisticated Scholars Lake View H.S., Chgo., 1981—87, sponsor Black Students Assn., 1985—87; sponsor sr. class Jones H.S., Chgo., 1988—98; tutor U. Ill., Chgo., 2005—06. Founder, CEO Fashion Trendsetters of Chgo. Vol. Ill. Reading Assn., 2003, Internat. Reading Assn., 2006; mem. Sta. WTTW Pub. Radio. Recipient Appreciation/Recognition award, United

Negro Coll. Fund, 1985—99; grantee, Chgo. Pub. Sch., 1994. Mem.: Univ. Women, Haute Couture Club of Chgo., Alpha Kappa Alpha (treas. 1964). Presbyterian. Avocations: crafts, singing, travel. Home: Unit 1804 910 S Michigan Ave Chicago IL 60605

JACKSON, GUIDA MYRL, writer, editor, literature educator; b. Clarendon, Tex., Aug. 30; d. James Hurley and Ina (Benson) Miller; m. Prentice Lamar Jackson (div. Jan. 1986); children: Jeffrey Allen, William Andrew, James Tucker, Annabeth Broomall Davis; m. William Hervey Laufer, Feb. 14, 1986. BA, Tex. Tech U.; MA, Calif. State U., 1986; PhD, Greenwich U., 1990. Tchr. secondary sch. English, Houston Ind. Sch. Dist., 1951—53, Ft. Worth Ind. Sch. Dist., 1953—54; pvt. tchr. music, freelance writer, Houston, 1956—71; editor newsletter Tex. Soc. Anesthesiologists, Austin, 1972—80; editor-in-chief Tex. Country Mag., Houston, 1976—78; mng. editor lit. mag. Touchstone, Houston, 1976—. Contbg. editor Houston Town and Country mag., 1975—76; book editor Arte Publico, 1987—88; editor, pub. Panther Creek Press, 1999—; lectr. English U. Houston, 1986—95; instr. Montgomery Coll., 1996—; freelance writer, Houston, The Woodlands, Tex., 1978—. Author: (novels) Passing Through, 1979, A Common Valor, 1980; (play) The Lamentable Affair of the Vicar's Wife, 1989, Showdown at Nosegay Cottage, 1997, The Man From Tegucigalpa, 1998, Julia is Peculiar; (biog. reference) Women Who Ruled, 1990 (best reference lists award Libr. Jour. and Sch. Libr. Jour. 1990), (nonfiction) Virginia Diaspora, 1992, Virginia Diaspora CD-ROM, 2001, (lit. reference) Encyclopedia of Traditional Epic, 1994 (best reference list award ALA), (lit. reference) Traditional Epics: A Literary Companion, 1995, Encyclopedia of Literary Epics, 1996; (reference) Women Rulers Throughout the Ages, 1999; (fiction) The Other Texas, 2005; editor: Heart to Hearth, 1989, African Women Write, 1990, Fall From Innocence, Memoirs of the Great Depression, 1998; (nonfiction) Legacy of the Texas Plains, 1994, Through the Cumberland Gap, 1995, The Patchwork Mind, 2006. Mem.: Houston Writers Consortium, Writers' Forum, Montgomery Lit. Arts Coun., Dramatists Guild, Woodland Writers Guild, Houston Writers Guild, PEN Ctr. West, Women in Comm. Avocations: music, gardening, poetry. Office: Panther Creek Press PO Box 130233 Spring TX 77393-0233 Personal E-mail: panthercreek3@hotmail.com.

JACKSON, HERMOINE PRESTINE, psychologist; b. Wilmington, Del., Mar. 11, 1945; d. Herman Preston Sr. and Ella Brooks Jackson. BA, Elizabethtown (Pa.) Coll., 1967; MA, Ohio State U., 1979, PhD, 1991. Tchr. Wilmington (Del.) pub. sch. sys., 1967-68, Phila. Pub. Sch. Sys., 1968-74; psychologist Midland (Mich.) Hosp., 1979-81, Cen. Mich. U., Mt. Pleasant, 1979-81, West Seneca (N.Y.) Devel. Ctr., 1981-90, N.Y. State Div. for Youth Buffalo Residential Ctr., 1990-94, Tryon Girls Ctr., 1994, Va. Dept. Juvenile Justice, Beaumont, 1994-97, Bon Air, 1997—2002, Bermuda Dept. Corrections, St. George, 2002—. Mem. admissions/discharge com. St. Augustine Ctr., Buffalo, 1983-90. Co-author test manual: Manual of Assessment Instruments for the MR/DD Population, 1978. Mem. Planning Coun., Buffalo, 1989-94. Named Outstanding Instr., Ctrl. Mich. U., 1981. Mem. APA, Am. Assn. on Mental Retardation, Psychol. Assn. Western N.Y., Coalition of 100 Black Women (corr. sec. 1988-91). Office: Bermuda Dept Corrections 31 Ferry Rd Saint Georges GE 01 Bermuda Office Phone: 441-297-1280.

JACKSON, JACQUELINE DOUGAN, literature educator, writer; b. Beloit, Wis., May 3, 1928; d. Ronald Arthur and Vera Arlouine (Wardner) Dougan; m. Robert Sumner Jackson, June 17, 1950 (div. 1973); children—Damaris Lee, Megan Trever, Gillian Patricia, Jacqueline Elspeth. BA, Beloit Coll., 1950, H.H.D., 1977; MA, U. Mich., 1951; D.Litt., MacMurray Coll., 1976. Instr. English Kent (Ohio) State U., 1964-68; prof. lit. U. Ill. (formerly Sangamon State U.), Springfield, 1970—. Writer, presenter: radio shows The Author is You, U. Wis. WHA Sch. of Air, 1969-78, Reading and Writing and Radio, WSSU, Springfield, Ill., 1975-94; author: Julie's Secret Sloth, 1953, The Taste of Spruce Gum (Notable Book award 1966), 1966 (Dorothy Canfield Fisher award 1967), Missing Melinda, 1967, Chicken Ten Thousand, 1968, Spring Song, 1969, The Orchestra Mice, 1970, The Endless Pavement, (with William Perlmutter), 1973, Turn Not Pale, Beloved Snail, 1974, Stories from the Round Barn, 1997, More Stories from the Round Barn, 2002; author-illustrator: The Paleface Redskins, 1958, The Ghost Boat, 1969; illustrator: (Chad Walsh) Knock and Enter, 1953. Mem. Phi Beta Kappa. Episcopalian. Home: 816 N 5th St Springfield IL 62702-5215 Business E-Mail: jackson.jacqueline@uis.edu.

JACKSON, JANE, filmmaker, educator; BA in Theatre Arts and Film, Humboldt State U., Arcata, Calif., 1972, MA in Theatre Arts and Film, 1974. C.C. tchg. credential in theatre arts and film Calif., 1979. Instr. Coll. Redwoods, Eureka, Calif., 1974—79; prodr. and dir. Harcourt, Brace, Jovanovich Films, 1979—81, Photo and Sound Co., 1981—91; post prodn. supr. and facility mgr. Am. Zeotrpe, 1991—93; lectr. Humbolt State U., Arcata, 1995—97; prodr. and dir. Idaho Pub. Television, 1997—2000; prodr. and instr. U. Idaho, Moscow, Idaho, 1997—2000; asst. Prof. SUNY, Freedonia, 2000—, asst. chair comm. dept., 2002—05. Juror Redwoods Film Festival, 1974, Calif. State U. Media Arts Festival, 1997; instr. arts enrichment summer program Oishei Found., 2001—02; freelance prodr. and dir. KVIQ-TV, KEET-TV, Corporate Prdns.; mem. academic coms.; spkr. and panelist profl. confs. Post supr.: (films) Bram Stoker's Dracula (Acad. award sound design); Secret Garden; Wind; post cons. Bugsy; Joy Luck Club; Hearts of Darkness; Toys; Godfather Part 3; Godfather Trilogy; Fried Green Tomatoes; Invasion of the Body Snatchers 2; Stork Club; asst. editor Cannonball Express; cinematographer and editor: (documentaries) Fish On!; prodr. and dir. Look Back Into the Future; (music special) An Evening of Coutry Music; An Evening with Jason; (ednl. films) 20th Century Series (nat. awards (2); cinematographer: (documentaries) Pyramid of Giza; dir.: (educational film) Rape Evidence Collection; editor: (educational film) Trial Preparation; prodr., dir. and editor: (documentaries) Visions on the Poulouse; Old Traditions New Visions (Internat. Videographer award of distinction); prodr. and editor Girls Make TV; (video prodn.) Six Characters in Search of an Author; videographer: (documentaries) Creating a Balance - Idaho Women and the Land; The Farmer's Daughter (IdahoPress Club award); prodr. and dir.: (films) Idaho Repertory Theater; prodr., dir. and editor Dream Prints (First Pl. Internat. Film Festiva; Broadcast Edn. Assn., 2000); Portrait of an Artist - Pat Boyer; The Quiet Sound (nat. awards (2); Triangle. Mem. media and the courts com. Idaho State Supreme Ct., 1998—99. Mem.: Univ. Film and Video Assn., Assn. Ind. Video and Film Makers, Broadcast Educators Assn. Home: 145 Baghdad Rd Collins NY 14034

JACKSON, JANET (JANET DAMITA JO JACKSON), vocalist, dancer; b. Gary, Ind., May 16, 1966; d. Joseph and Katherine J.; m. James DeBarge, Sept. 7, 1984 (annulled Nov. 18, 1985), m. René Elizondo, March 31, 1991 (div. March 13, 2000). Albums include Janet Jackson, 1982, Dream Street, 1984, Control, 1986, Rhythm Nation 1814, 1991, janet, 1993, Design of a Decade: 1986-1996, 1995, The Velvet Rope, 1997, All For You, 2001 (Grammy award, Best Dance Recording, 2002), Damita Jo, 2004, 20 Y.O., 2006; actress (TV series) Good Times, 1977-1979, A New Kind of Family, 1979, Diff'rent Strokes, 1981-1982, 1984, Fame, 1984-1985; (films) Poetic Justice, 1993 (Academy award nomination Best Original Song 1993), Nutty Professor II: The Klumps, 2000. Recipient 6 Am. Music awards, 1987, 1988, 1991, 5 Grammy nominations, MTV Video Vanguard award, 1990, Grammy award, Best R&B song 1994 for "That's the Way Love Goes" with Terry Lewis and James Harris III; MTV Best Female Video for "If", named one of 50 Most Influential African-Americans, Ebony Mag. 2004. Office: Creative Artists Agency 9830 Wilshire Blvd Beverly Hills CA 90212-1825

JACKSON, JEANINE E., ambassador; BS, Hastings Coll.; MS, Fla. Tech. Consular officer Jeddah Consulate Gen., Saudi Arabia; pers. officer Hong Kong and Consulate Gen.; gen. services. officer Kenya; mgmt. counselor Afghanistan; coord. for Iraq transition US Dept. State, amb. to Burkina Faso, 2006—. Office: US Dept State 2440 Ouagadougou Pl Washington DC 20521-2440

JACKSON, JEWEL, retired state agency administrator; b. June 3, 1942; d. Willie Burghardt and Bernice Jewel (Mayberry) Norton; children: Steven, June Kelly, Michael, Anthony. With Calif. Youth Authority, 1965-91, group supr. San Andreas & Santa Rosa, 1965-67, youth counselor Ventura, 1967-78, sr. youth counselor Stockton, 1978-81, parole agt., 1986, treatment team supr., program mgr. Whittier & Ione, 1981-91; ret., 1991. Owner Access Legal Document Assistance; v.p., mem. bd. nonprofit orgn. New Toyz Assn. Past bd. dirs. Samuel Hancock Christian Sch.; past pres. San Joaquin Valley Girls Horsewomen's Assn.; bd. dirs., regional dir. New Toyz Assn. Mem. Internat. Egg Art Guild. Avocations: reading, decorative egg art, decoupage. Home and Office: PO Box 8267 Stockton CA 95208-0267 Office Phone: 209-466-3570. Personal E-mail: accesslda@sbcglobal.net.

JACKSON, JUDY FAYE, academic administrator; b. Robersonville, N.C. d. S. T. and Estella Jackson. BA in French Lang. and Lit., U. N.C., Greensboro; M in Francophone African Lit., Geography and Fgn. Policy, Bucknell U.; PhD in Adminstn., Planning and Social Policy, Harvard U. Mem. faculty English dept. Susquehanna U., 1981—85; various positions Cornell U. Coll. Engring., 1985—89, asst. dir. for advising and counseling, asst. dean for minority programs, asst. dean for advising counseling and minority programs; various positions MIT, 1989—2000, assoc. dean undergrad. edn. and student affairs, dir. minority edn., ombudsman Pres. Office, staff mem. Provost Office, spl. adviser to provost on faculty diversity; exec. asst. to pres., clk. of the corp. Babson Coll., Babson Park, Mass.; assoc. provost for instnl. engagement NYU, NY, 2002—04; dean Vassar Coll., Poughkeepsie, NY, 2004—. Office: Vassar Coll 124 Raymond Ave Poughkeepsie NY 12604

JACKSON, JULIE ANN, mathematics professor; b. New Orleans, La., May 25, 1972; d. Alfred and Ella P. Jackson. BS, Xavier U. of La., 1995; MA, Auburn U., 1997. Analyst Entergy Svcs., Inc., The Woodlands, Tex., 1997—99; instr. Remington Coll., Ft. Worth, 1999—2001, Xavier U. La., New Orleans, 2001—05, Keiser Coll., Ft. Lauderdale, Fla., 2005—, Kaplan U., Ft. Lauderdale, 2005—, Emory U., Atlanta, 2005—06. Cons. JRL Enterprises, New Orleans, 2002—05. GAANN fellow, Auburn U., 1997, jr. GAANN fellow, 1998. Mem.: Assn. Women in Math., Delta Sigma Theta, Young Leadership Coun. Avocations: travel, reading, swimming, painting, candy making. Home: 102 Crest Ridge Dr East Point GA 30344

JACKSON, KAREN, elementary school educator; m. Ronald Jackson, Aug. 29, 1984. AA, Temple (Tex.) Jr. Coll., 1984; BS, U. Tex., 1993. Tchr. Temple Ind. Sch. Dist., 1993—. Tchr. trainer in reading success insvc. Tex. Edn. Agy., Killeen, 1994. Author: (poetry) Collage, 1983. Mem. Tex. Edn. Exes. Republican. Avocations: gardening, auto tours, reading. Home: PO Box 1496 Temple TX 76503-1496

JACKSON, KATE, actress; b. Birmingham, Ala., Oct. 29, 1949; d. Hogan and Ruth Jackson; m. Andrew Stevens, Aug. 23, 1978 (div. 1981); m. David Greenwald, 1982 (div. 1984). Student, U. Miss.; student, Birmingham U.; grad., Am. Acad. Dramatic Arts, 1971. Worked as model. Appeared in TV series Dark Shadows, 1966-71, The Rookies, 1972-76, Charlie's Angels, 1976-79, The Scarecrow and Mrs. King, 1983-87, Baby Boom, 1988-89; TV appearances include Movin' On, The Jimmy Stewart Show; TV movies include: Satan's School for Girls, 1973, Death Cruise, 1974, Killer Bees, 1974, Death Scream, 1975, Charlie's Angels, 1976, Death at Love House, 1976, James at 15, 1977, Topper, 1979, Inmates: A Love Story, 1981, Thin Ice, 1981, Listen to Your Heart, 1983, The Stranger Within, 1990, Quiet Killer, 1992, Homewrecker, 1992, Adrift, 1993, Empty Cradle, 1993, The Shrine of Lorna Love, 1993, Arly Hanks, 1993, Armed and Innocent, 1994, Justice in a Small Town, 1994, The Silence of Adultery, 1995, The Cold Heart of a Killer, 1996, A Kidnapping in a Family, 1996, New Passages, 1996, Panic In the Skies, 1996, What Happened to Bobby Earl, 1997, Sweet Deceptions, 1998, Satan's School for Girls, 2000, A Mother's Testimony, 2001, Miracle Dogs, 2003, Larceny, 2004, No Regrets, 2004; motion picture appearances include: Dirty Tricks, 1981, Making Love, 1982, Loverboy, 1989, Error in Judgement, 1998, Larceny, 2004; dir. numerous episodes The Scarecrow and Mrs. King. Recipient 3 Emmy award nominations Nat. Acad. TV Arts and Scis. Mem. AFTRA, Screen Actors Guild, Actors Equity Assn., Dirs. Guild Am.

JACKSON, KATIE J., dancer, educator; d. Gary and Debbie Jackson. BA, Tex. Tech U., Lubbock, 2002. Cert. tchr. Tex. Tchr. MacArthur H.S., Aldine, Tex., 2002—03, Willis H.S., Tex., 2003—06. Dance team dir. Willis Sweethearts, Tex., 2003—. Dance dir. (univ. works, contest pieces) Masquerade (Grand Champion Team, 2006). Cmty. svc. events Willis Sweethearts, Tex., 2003—06. Recipient numerous choreography and profl. awards, ShowTime Internat., Am. Dance/Drill Team Sch., Tex. Dance Educators Assn., 2002-2006. Mem.: Tex. Dance Educators Assn. (assoc.). Office Phone: 936-856-1325.

JACKSON, KELLY SUE, social studies educator; b. Oskaloosa, Iowa, Jan. 5, 1959; d. Nancy Darlene and Larry Mark Doonan; m. Craig Stephen Jackson, Feb. 26, 1977; 1 child, Ryan Patrick. BA Edn., Ariz. State U. West, Glendale, 2000. Cert. Tchr. State of Ariz., 2000. Tchr. social studies Cartwright Elem. Sch. Dist., Phoenix, 2000—. Mentor tchr. Cartwright Elem. Sch. Dist., Phoenix, 2004—06.

JACKSON, LENORE, computer technician; Grad., Morgan State U.; postgrad., U. Md. User cons., info. specialist NASA Sci. Internet, 1989—. Office: NASA Ames Rsch Ctr Bldg 204 Moffett Field CA 94035

JACKSON, LINDA B., social worker; b. N.Y.C., Feb. 16, 1956; d. Willie Chester Jackson, Fannie Mae Jackson; children: Athena Johnson, Alethea, Althea, Walter. BSW, Mercy Coll., 1986; FDC tng., Cornell U., 2002. Social worker Peekskill City Sch. Dist., Peekskill, NY, 1987—. Author: Poetry From the Soul; author: (poetry) Titanic, 2001 (Pres.'s award). Recipient Famous Poets award, 2002, Shakespeare trophy of excellence, Poet of Yr. medalliion, 2002. Mem.: Poetry Soc. Am. Avocation: writing. Home: 218 N James St Peekskill NY 10566-2848 Office Phone: 914-788-3662 12. Personal E-mail: athena10566@yahoo.com.

JACKSON, LINDA SHORTER, nutritionist, educator; b. Birmingham, Ala., Feb. 10, 1955; d. Wiley and Mary Russell Shorter; 1 child, Ramikiel L. Jackson-Macon. BS, Jacksonville State U., Ala., 1976; Assoc., U. Md., Baumholder, West Germany, 1991; M in Tchg., Wayne State U., Detroit, Mich., 2005. Cert. tchr. Mich. Food mgr. U. South Ala. Med. Ctr., Mobile, 1976—77, Springhill Meml. Hosp., Mobile, 1980—83; food and nutrition mgr. Colo. Coll., Colorado Springs, Colo., 1983—86; supr. U.S. Army, Baumholden, Germany, 1986—89; food mgr. Detroit Med. Ctr., 1990—2000; tchr. Detroit Pub. Schs., 2000—; direct care worker Metro Staff, Southfield, Mich., 2000—. Coord. singles ministry Seventh Day Adventist, 1992—2000, coord. childrens ministries, 1994—2002. Recipient Plaque for Faithful Svc., Women's Ministries of Seventh Day Adventist, 2002, scholarship, Detroit Fedn. Tchrs., 2004. Mem.: Mich. Coun. Social Studies, Nat. Coun. Tchrs. of English, Delta Sigma Theta. Seventh Day Adventist. Avocations: travel, community work, walking. Home: 20111 Regent Dr Detroit MI 48205 Office Phone: 313-866-2072. Office Fax: 313-866-2074. E-mail: Linderf7@aol.com.

JACKSON, LOIS ANN, mental disabilities educator; b. Clinton, Iowa, Aug. 23, 1948; d. Alvin E. and Vera Miranda (Barnes) Roberts; m. Darrell John Jackson, Jan. 1, 1972; children: Vanessa Ann, Brian Nicholas, Valerie Rose. B.A., U. No. Iowa, 1970. Cert. tchr. mental retardation, elem., Iowa. Tchr. trainable mentally retarded Pottawattamie County Schs., Council Bluffs, Iowa, 1970-72; head tchr. Skyline Ctr., Inc., Clinton, Iowa, 1972-76, program mgr., 1976-87. mental disabilities, self-contained with integration tchr, Bellevue Community Schs., Bellevue, Iowa, 1987-2001; tchr. learning disabilities Ctrl. Clinton High Sch., 2001—. Mem. Antique Automobile Club Am. Lutheran. Avocations: reading, antique and auto shows. Home: 740 12th Ave N Clinton IA 52732-5130 Office: Ctrl Clinton High Sch PO Box 110 De Witt IA 52742-0110 Office Phone: 563-659-0720.

JACKSON, MARGARET ELIZABETH, science educator; b. Richmond, Va., Mar. 15, 1930; d. Joseph and Bertha Annette Jackson. BS, Va. Union U.; MA in Sci. Edn., Trinity Coll.; postgrad., Oxford U., 1976—78, George Washington U., 1981, Roehampton Inst. Higher Learning, England, 1985. Resource tchr. sci. Garrison Elem. Sch., Washington, 1968—. Tchr. Howard U., Washington, 1984; devel. sci. materials U.S. Dept. Agr., 1970; tchr. English Elem. Schs., Campo De Criptana, Spain, 1987; writer curriculum Elem. Pub. Schs., Washington, 1980—93; mentor Carnegie Acad. Sci. Edn. Carnegie Instn., Washington, 1995—96. Co-author: Addison Wesley Science Textbook for Elementary School, 1987. Named Internat. Educator of Yr., 2003. Mem.: ASCD, Smithsonian Instn., N.Y. Acad. Scis., D.C. Sci. Tchrs. Assn., Nat. Sci. Tchrs. Assn. Home: 2505 -13th St NW Apt 501 Washington DC 20009 Office Phone: 202-673-7263.

JACKSON, MARION ELIZABETH, art educator; b. Saginaw, Mich. d. Wendall Cleves and Virginia Wagner Jackson. BA, U. Mich., Ann Arbor, 1963, PhD, 1985. Assoc. prof., assoc. dean U. Mich., Ann Arbor, 1968—91; prof. Carleton U., Ottawa, Canada, 1991—95, Wayne State U., Detroit, 1995—. Co-founder, co-dir. Con/Vida: Popular Arts of Americas, Detroit, 2000—; curator exhibitions. Co-editor: Contemporary Inuit Drawings, 1987, Pudlo: 30 Years of Drawing, 1990, Inuit Women Artists, 1994. Grantee, Fulbright Found., 1986—. Office: Wayne State Univ 150 Community Art Bldg Detroit MI 48202 Office Phone: 313-577-1801, 313-577-2980. Business E-Mail: mjackson@wayne.edu.

JACKSON, MARY ALICE, retired elementary school educator, retired realtor; d. Morris Cleland and Alice Elinor Humes; m. Charles Wayne Jackson, July 18, 1965; 1 child, Jill Alice; 1 child, Charles Wayne III. BS in Elem. Edn., Kans. State U., Manhattan, 1962. Lic. real estate salesperson Tex. State Real Estate Commn., 1996. Tchr. Jefferson County Pub. Schs., Arvada, Colo., 1962—65, Topeka Pub. Schs., 1966—66; lectr./facilitator U.S. Army Command and Gen. Staff Coll., Ft. Leavenworth, Kans., 1982—84; tchr. Duncanville Ind. Sch. Dist., Tex., 1984—96; realtor - residential Henry S. Miller, Realtors, Duncanville, 1996—2001, Coldwell Banker Residential Brokerage, DeSato, 2001—02. Bd. mem. Southwest Ctr. Arts and Culture, Duncanville, 2004—05; pres./mem. Duncanville Regional Arts Assn., 1986—2003, Duncanville Women's League, 1987—95, Duncanville Bd. Adjustments, 1991—95. Recipient Lifetime PTA Mem., Hastings Elem. PTA, 1990. Mem.: Duncanville Rotary Club (pres. 2004—05, Rotarian of Yr. 2002—03), Epsilon Sigma Alpha (pres./treas./race chmn. 1993—2005), Delta Kappa Gamma. Methodist. Avocations: golf, tennis, jogging, swimming, skiing. Personal E-mail: cmajack@earthlink.net.

JACKSON, MARY L., health services executive; b. Phila., June 25, 1938; d. John Francis and Helen Catherine (Peranteau) Martin; m. Howard Clark Jackson III, Dec. 17, 1954; children: Michael, Mark, Brian, Bert. Student, Bucks County C.C., 1977-83. Asst. mgr. retail divsn. Sears Roebuck & Co., Bensalem, Pa., 1972-77; educator, adminstr., dir. Trevos Behavior Modification Program, Pa., 1975—, leadership tng. workshops, 1979—. Participant rsch. studies in field; salesman Makefield Real Estate, Morrisville, Pa., 1977-78; mortgage fin. cons. Tom Dunphy Real Estate, Feasterville, Pa., 1978-81; weight loss cons., Hulmeville, Pa., 1984—, also TV and radio appearances on behavior modification for weight loss and maintenance. Co-author: The Official Calorie Book; pub., columnist monthly newsletter The Modifier, 1977—; pub. several studies in weight loss field; pub. co-author multi-studies in field. Recipient Chapel of Four Chaplain award, 1977. Mem. Assn. Advancement Behavior Therapy, Bucks County Bd. Realtors, Hulmeville Hist. Soc. (founder, charter mem.). Democrat. Presbyterian. Avocations: reading, classical music, speed walking, knitting, fishing. Home: 218 Main St Hulmeville PA 19047-5635

JACKSON, NANCY ELLEN, retired internist; b. Detroit, Jan. 11, 1941; d. Laurence James and Hazel Katherine Jackson; m. Robert Edward Goll, Sept. 25, 1970; 1 child, Amy Ellen Lang. BS in Chemistry, Wayne State U., Detroit, Mich., 1962, MD, 1966. Diplomate Am. Bd. Internal Medicine. Physician Freedom Med. Clinic, Livonia, Mich., 1970—94; physician adviser St. Mary Mercy Hosp., Livonia, Mich., 1982—99; ret., 1999. Mem.: AMA, Wayne County Med. Soc., Mich. State Med. Soc. Roman Catholic. Avocations: reading, fishing. Home: 9784 S Shore Dr Pigeon MI 48755

JACKSON, PAMELA HALL, school system administrator; d. Leroy and Bonita Hall; m. Larry Jackson; children: Melanie Scott, Megan. BA in Humanities, LeMoyne Owen Coll., 1974; MA in Guidance and Counseling, Memphis State U., 1981. HS English tchr. Memphis City Schs., 1974—81, HS guidance counselor, sch. prin., 1976—. Mem.: Delta Sigma Theta (life). Office: Memphis City Schs/Rozelle Elem 993 Roland Memphis TN Personal E-mail: jacksonph@bellsouth.net. Business E-Mail: jacksjonp@mcsk12.net.

JACKSON, PATRICIA ANNE, primary school educator, consultant; b. Jersey City, Sept. 29, 1940; d. John Patrick and Helen Harriet (Jarvis) Gallagher; m. Peter Robert Jackson, Oct. 3, 1970; children: Julie Anne, Andrew Iain, Jennifer Mary. BA in Elem. Edn., Caldwell Coll., 1965; AA magna cum laude, Columbus State C.C., 1997. Cert. tchr., N.J. Elem. tchr. St. Elizabeth of Hungary, Linden, N.J., 1961-66, Mt. St. Dominic Acad., Caldwell, N.J., 1966-67, Pub. Sch. # 24, Jersey City, 1967-68, Leelands Sch., Walmer, Kent, Eng., 1968-77; presch. tchr. Ridgeview Hills Christian Pre-Sch., Littleton, Colo., 1983-84, Canyon Pre-Sch., Colorado Springs, Colo., 1985-87, Ruth Washburn Co-op. Nursery Sch., Colorado Springs, Colo., 1987-95, Holy Trinity Child Devel. Program, Columbus, Ohio, 1996-97, First Step Presch., Littleton, Colo., 1997-98. Children's tchr. Child Advocacy Resource and Edn., 1998-2001; presch. tchr. First Christian Ch. Presch., 2000-01; presenter Colo. Assn. for the Edn. of Young Children, Denver, 1993-95, 2000, Imagination Celebration, Colorado Springs, 1994; jr. Gt. Book presenter Eugene Field Sch., Littleton, 1984, Broadmoor Elem. Sch., Colorado Springs, 1985; coord., presenter Art in a Suitcase, Dist. 12, Colorado Springs, 1986-88. Author, illustrator: Free to be Creative, 1994. Bd. dirs., vol. PTO Eugene Field Sch., Littleton, 1983. Avocations: drawing, painting, interior decorating, needlecrafts. Home: 33120 County Rd 29 Greeley CO 80631-9382

JACKSON, REBECCA LEE, history educator, social studies educator; b. Fitchburg, Mass., Dec. 15, 1981; d. Stephen Robert and Barbara Jean Jackson. BA in History, Westfield State Coll., Mass., 2003; postgrad., Salem State Coll., Mass. Lic. tchr. Mass., 2003. History/social studies tchr. North Middlesex Regional Sch. Dist., Townsend, Mass., 2003—. Mem.: Nat. Coun. for the Social Studies, Mass. Tchrs. Assn., Rep. Nat. Com. Republican. Avocations: politics, exercise, travel, historical biographies, sports. Home: 28 Victoria Ave Worcester MA 01607 Office: Nissitissit Middle School 33 Chase Ave Pepperell MA 01463 Office Phone: 978-433-0114. Personal E-mail: beckswsc@yahoo.com.

JACKSON, REBECCA M., elementary education educator, English as a second language educator; b. Franklin, Tenn., Oct. 29, 1962; d. Ralph Newton and Dewey Fay Miller. AA, Western Tex. Coll., Snyder, 1984; BS cum laude, All-Am. Tex. Tech U., 1987. Cert. tchr., tex. Tchr. Klondike Ind. Sch. Dist., Ackerly, Tex., 1988—89, Highland Bapt. Sch., Lubbock, Tex., 1991—92, Union Ind. Sch. Dist., Brownfield, Tex., 1993—96, Coahoma (Tex.) Ind. Sch. Dist., 1997—98, Grandfalls (Tex.)-Royalty Ind. Sch. Dist., 1998—99; ESL instr. Odessa (Tex.) Coll., 1998—99; ESL instr., ESL coord. Dalby Correctional Facility, Post, Tex., 1999—2003, Northeast Elem. Sch., Tex., 2003—04. Recipient Outstanding Achievement award Adult Basic Edn. Program, Internat. Educator of Yr., 2004; Honoree Wall of Tolerance Nat. Campaign for Tolerance, 2003. Mem. Tex. Classroom Tchrs. Assn., Delta Psi Kappa (v.p.), Golden Key, Phi Epsilon Kappa (Outstanding scholar 1986-87). Baptist. Home: 1203 R Miller Rd Fluvanna TX 79517-3027

JACKSON, RHONDA GAIL, secondary teacher; b. Albuquerque, Oct. 12, 1954; d. Jack Harold and Glenna Janelle (Welborn) Furr; m. Robert Evans Jackson, June 20, 1975; children: Richard Paul, Lindsey Beth. B in Social

Work, Tex. Woman's U., 1977. English secondary edn. Adminstrv. asst. Tex. Women's U., 1977-84; secondary tchr. English and sociology Frisco H.S., Tex., 1990—, English dept. chair, 1998—. Mem. Nat. Coun. Tchrs. English. Home: 11507 Prestige Dr PO Box 2231 Frisco TX 75034-8231 Office: 6401 Parkwood Dr Frisco TX 75034-7239 E-mail: jacksonr@friscoisd.org.

JACKSON, ROBBI JO, agricultural products executive, lawyer; b. Nampa, Idaho, Apr. 12, 1959; d. William R. Jackson and Marilyn K. Samp Jackson Nunez. BS in Fin., U. Colo., Boulder and Denver, 1981; JD, U. Denver, 1987, LLM in Taxation, 1990. Bar: Colo. 1988. Asst. office mgr. Jerome Karsh & Co., Denver, 1982; office mgr. Almirall & Assocs., Englewood, Colo., 1983-84; assoc. Moye, Giles, O'Keefe, Vermeire & Gorrell, Denver, 1989-90, Holme Roberts & Owen, Denver, 1990-92; in-house gen. counsel Cmty. Corrections Svcs., Denver, 1992-96; CEO Enviro Cons. Svc., LLC, Lakewood, Colo., 1996—; of counsel Grund & Nelson, P.C., 2004—. Presenter in field. Mem. staff Adminstrv. Law Rev., Denver, 1985, editor, 1985, mng. editor, 1986-87; co-author course of study materials. Fin. com. Mile-High chpt. ARC, Denver, 1990-92; food delivery person Vols. of Am., Meals-on-Wheels, Denver, 1990-92. Recipient scholarships. Mem.: ABA, Colo. Bar Assn. (chmn. ethics com. 2003—04). Republican. Avocations: running marathons and other races, biking, hiking, swimming, piano and organ playing.

JACKSON, ROSA M., retired elementary school educator; b. Columbia, S.C., Dec. 8, 1943; d. Alvin Jr. and Rosa Lee (Reese) Oree; m. Olin D. Jackson, June 14, 1969; children: Zandra Lalita, Delin Jawaski. BA, Benedict Coll., 1966; MEd, S.C. State U., Orangeburg, 1981. Cert. tchr. Tchr. 1st grade Richmond County Bd. Edn., Augusta, Ga.; tchr. 2nd grade McDuffie County Bd. Edn., Thomson, Ga.; tchr. 5th grade Lancaster County Bd. Edn., Kershaw; tchr. 2nd grade Richmond County Bd. Edn., Augusta, Ga. Mem. Richmond County Schs. Leadership Team. Sci. tchr. in residence; pres. Reese Meml. Singers, pulpit aide, sr. musical choir mem., mem. nurses guild, chairperson kitchen com., art tchr. vacation bible sch. Antioch Bapt. Ch. Mem. GAE, RCAE, NEA, Nat. Sci. Tchrs Assn., Ga. Sci. Tchrs. Assn., Ga. Staff Devel. Coun., Assn. for Multicultural Sci. Edn. Home: 3003 Bramble Wood Trl Augusta GA 30909-4105

JACKSON, RUTH MOORE, academic administrator; b. Potecasi, N.C., Sept. 27, 1938; d. Jesse Thomas and Ruth Estelle (Futrell) Moore; m. Roderick Earle Jackson, Aug. 14, 1965; 1 child, Eric Roderick. BS in Bus., Hampton Inst., 1960; MSLS, Atlanta U., 1965; PhD, Ind. U., 1976. Asst. edn. libr. Va. State U., Petersburg, Va., 1965-66, head reference dept., 1966-67, asst. prof., 1976-77, assoc. prof., program coord., 1977-84, interim dept. chair, 1978-79; teaching fellow Ind. U., Bloomington, Ind., 1968, vis. lectr., 1971-72; asst. dir. librs. U. N. Fla., Jacksonville, 1984-88; dean univ. librs. W.Va. U., Morgantown, W.Va., 1988—, asst. to provost libr. outreach programs. Pers. cons. Va. State U., 1980; archival cons. N.C. Ctrl. U., Durham, N.C., 1984-85; automation cons. W.Va. Acad. Libr. Consortium, 1991—; co-prin. investigator State-Wide Electronic Libr. Network (Project Infomine), 1994-98. Editor: W.Va. U. Press, 1990—; contbr. to books. Active Big Brother/Big Sister of Am., Jacksonville, Fla., 1985-88; den leader Boy Scouts of Am., Petersburg, Va., 1976-78. U.S. Office Edn. fellow, 1968-71, Rsch. fellow So. Fellowships Found., 1973-74; recipient Outstanding Alumni award Hampton Inst., 1980, Non-Italian Woman of Yr. award, 1992, Disting. West Virginian award Gov. W.Va., 1992. Mem. NAFE, ALA, Southeastern Libr. Assn. (mem. standing com.), Assn. Coll. and Rsch. Librs. (mem. standing com., mem. Fla. chpt.), W.Va. Libr. Assn., Libr. Info. Tech. Assn., Coalition for Networked Info., Coun. of State Univ. Librs. (founding mem.), Addison-Wesley Higher Edn. Tech. Bd., Alpha Kappa Alpha. Democrat. Roman Catholic. Avocations: walking, sightseeing, collecting rare coins and artifacts. Office: WVa Univ Main Libr PO Box 6069 Morgantown WV 26506-6069 Home: 5535 Via San Jacinto Riverside CA 92506-3652

JACKSON, RUTHA MAE, pastor, military reserve officer, secondary school educator; d. Willie James Porter Sr. and Mattie Ruth Smith; m. Clarence Jackson, Nov. 22, 1971; children: Nikesha Monique, Michelle Shenique, Kimbria None. B, Ft. Valley State U., Ga., 1993; MDiv, Interdenomination Theol. Sem., Atlanta, 2006. Pastor Christian M.E.Ch., Atlanta, 1980—; supt. Air Force Res., Warner Robins, Ga., 1980—; tchr. Houston County Bd. of Edn., Perry, 1993—. Coord. activities NAACP, Warner Robins, 1991—2000. Sr. master sgt. USAR, 1980—. Mem.: Ga. Assn. Educators (assoc.). Home: 302 Athens St Warner Robins GA 31088 Office: Houston County Bd Edn 110 Main St Perry GA 31069 Office Phone: 478-929-7832.

JACKSON, SANDRA LEE, health facility administrator; b. Tulsa, July 15, 1955; d. Marvin Cecil and Helen Lee (Wright) J. BSN, U. Tulsa, 1979. From staff nurse CCU to adminstrv. dir. clin. data svcs. Hillcrest Med. Ctr., Tulsa, 1979-90; v.p. patient svcs. Cancer Treatment Ctr., Tulsa, 1990-91, v.p. ops., 1991-95, pres./CEO, 1995—. Mem. NAFE, Am. Burn Assn., Rsch. Inst. Am. Coll. Osteopathic Health CAre Execs., Okla. Nursing Assn., Am. Coll. Healthcare Execs., Assn. of Cancer Execs. Home: PO Box 702317 Tulsa OK 74170-2317 Office: Cancer Treatment Centers Of America 10109 E 79th St Tulsa OK 74133-4564

JACKSON, SHEILA BENSON, counselor; b. Pocatello, Idaho, Apr. 4, 1956; d. Vincent Roy and Ilene (Morris) Benson; m. Jerry LaMar Jackson, June 21, 1987; 1 child, Chad Aric. BA in Criminology, Boise State U., 1980. Cert. rehab. counselor. Presentence investigator Dist. Ct., Boise, Idaho, 1977-82; placement counselor Job Svc., Blackfoot, Idaho, 1982-83; vocat. rehab. counselor Idaho Div. Vocat. Rehab., Blackfoot, 1983—. Bd. mem. Idaho State Univ. Vo-tec., 1986-87. Mem. Social Svcs. com., Blackfoot, 1983—; sec., Webelo leader Cub Scouts, Pingree, Idaho, 1987—; bd. mem. Road to Recovery, 1990, Sho-Ban Rehab., 1985-90; sec., bd. mem. Foster Grand Parent Program, 1984-90; chmn., mem. Mayors Com., 1984-86. Mem. Blackfoot C. of C., Soroptimist (pres., bd. mem. 1984-90). Mem. Ch. Latter Day Saints. Avocations: gardening, camping, water-skiing, skiing. Home: 464 S 1300 W Pingree ID 83262-1318

JACKSON, SHIRLEY ANN, academic administrator, physicist; b. Washington, Aug. 5, 1946; d. George Hiter and Beatrice (Cosby) Jackson; m. Morris A. Washington; 1 child, Alan. BS in Physics, MIT, 1968, PhD in Theoretical Elementary Particle Physics, 1973; DSc (hon.), Bloomfield Coll., 1991, Fairleigh Dickinson U., 1993; LLD (hon.), Villanova, 1996. Rsch. assoc. Fermi Nat. Accelerator Lab, Batavia, Ill., 1973—76; mem. tech. staff AT&T Bell Labs, Murray Hill, NJ, 1976—91; prof. physics Rutgers U., Piscataway, NJ, 1991—95; chairperson Nuclear Reg. Commn., 1995—99; U.S. Rep. to Gen. Conf. Internat. Atomic Energy Agy., 1995—99; pres. Rensselaer Poly. Inst., Troy, NY, 1999—. Vis. scientist European Orgn. Nuclear Rsch., Geneva, 1974—75; visitor Stanford Linear Accelerator Ctr., 1976, Aspen Ctr. Physics, 1976—77; mem. com. edn. and employment women in sci. and engring. Nat. Rsch. Coun., 1980—95, cons., 1977—91, NSF, 1977; mem. ednl. coun. MIT, 1976—80; chmn. Internat. Nuclear Regulators Assn., 1997—99; bd. trustees Lincoln U., Pa., 1980—92, exec. com., 1985—92; mem. advisory coun. Inst. Nuclear Power Ops.; bd. trustees Rutgers U., 1986—91, bd. gov., mem. ednl. planning and policy com., 1990; bd. trustees Associated U., Inc., 1993, Brookings Instn., 2000—; trustee Georgetown U., Rockefeller U., Emma Willard Sch., Troy, NY; bd. dirs. NY Stock Exch., NYC, 2003—06, NYSE Group, Inc., 2006—, IBM, FedEx Corp., AT&T Corp., Marathon Oil Corp., U.S. Steel Corp., Medtronic, Inc.; mem. Coun. Fgn. Rels.; mem. exec. com. Coun. Competitveness; coun. mem. Govt.-U.-Industry Rsch. Roundtable; life mem. bd. trustees MIT Corp.; mem. Nat. Adv. Coun. Biomedical Imaging and Bioengineering, Nat. Inst. Health (NIH); US Comptroller-Gen. adv. com. Govt. Acctg. Office (GAO). Editl. adv. bd. (jour.) Jour. Sci. Tech. and Human Values, 1982; contbr. articles to physics jours. Mem. NJ Commn. Sci. and Tech., Com. Status Women in Physics, 1986—88. Named one of 50 Most Important Women in Sci., Discover mag., 2002, 50 Most Inspiring African Am., pub. book, ESSENCE, 2002, 50 R&D Stars to Watch, Industry Week mag., 2002; named to Nat. Women's Hall Fame, 1998, Women Tech. Internat. Found. Hall Fame (WITI), 2000; recipient Candace award, Nat. Coalition 100 Black Women, Salute to Policy Makers award, Exec. Women NJ, 1986, Black Achievers in Industry award, Harlem YMCA, 1986, Thomas Alva Edison award (NJ Gov.'s award), 1993, 100 Women Excellence award, Albany-Colonie Regional C. of C. and Women's Bus. Coun., 2000, eLeadership award, Ctrl. NY Tech. Devel. Orgn. and CASE Ctr., Syracuse U., 2000, Golden Torch award for Lifetime Acheivement in Academia, Nat. Soc. Black Engrs., 2000, Richtmyer Meml. Lecture award, Am. Assn. Physics Tchrs., 2001, Immortal award, 15th Annual Black History Makers award, Associated Black Charities, 2001, Black Engr. Yr. award, US Black Engr. and Info. Tech. mag., 2001; fellow, Ford Found., 1971—73; grantee, 1974—75; trainee, NSF, 1968—71. Fellow: Am. Acad. Arts and Scis., Am. Phys. Soc. (mem. com. status of women in physics 1986); mem.: AAAS Am. Assn. Advancement Sci. (com. sci., freedom and responsibility, pres. 2004), Nat. Acad. Engring., Nat. Soc. Black Physicists (pres. 1980—82), Nat. Inst. Sci., NY Acad. Scis., MIT Alumni Assn. (v.p. 1986), Delta Sigma Theta, Sigma Xi. Office: Rensselaer Polytechnic, Pres Office 3031 Troy Bldg, 3rd Fl 110 8th St Troy NY 12180-3590 also: NYSE Group Inc c/o Corp Sec 11 Wall St New York NY 10005*

JACKSON, SONDI ELIZABETH, language educator; b. New Haven, Conn., Jan. 19, 1961; d. LaMotte and Thelma Jackson. BA, Tufts U., 1982; MS, So. Conn. State U., 1993, diploma in Ednl. Leadership, 2004. Cert. clin. competence Am. Speech and Hearing Assn., 1994, tchr. State Bd. Edn. Conn., 1994, speech pathologist Conn. Dept. Health, 1994. Speech lang. pathologist New Haven Pub. Schs., 1993—; adj. clin. supr. So. Conn. State U., New Haven, 1996—. Pres. Conn. Affiliate Nat. Black Assn. for Speech, Lang. and Hearing, New Haven, 1994—2005; fin. sec. Elm City Adult Club of Nat. Assn. Negro Bus. & Profl. Women's Clubs, Inc, New Haven, 2004—. Recipient Presdl. award, Elm City Club of Nat. Assn. Negro Bus. and Profl. Woman's Clubs, Inc., 1999, Appreciation award, 2000, Woman of Substance, Conn. Post, 2005. Mem.: Theta Epsilon Omega (membership chairperson 2005—). Episcopal. Avocation: reading. Office: New Haven Bd Education 54 Meadow St New Haven CT 06510 Office Phone: 203-946-7099 1228.

JACKSON, TAMRA LYNN, literature and language educator; m. Jeffrey Jon Jackson, June 21, 1997. BA English, Ea. Wash. U., Cheney, 1986—86, minor French, minor psychology, Ea. Wash. U., Cheney, 1986, MA English, 1990. Cert. Emergency Medical Technician Wash. State Dept. Health-EMS & Trauma Sys., 2003; Secondary Continuing Tchr. OSPI, Wash. State, 1982. Tchr. English H.S. Bridgeport Sch. Dist., Wash., 1986—. Instr. CPR and first aid Bridgeport Vol. Fire and Ambulance, Bridgeport, 2005—, EMT, 2000—; mem. writing assessment leadership team Wash. State Supt. Pub. Instrn., Olympia, 2006—, mem. 10th grade writing assessment rangefinding team, 2006—; chairperson self-study Bridgeport H.S., 2005—, 1997—98; asst. dir. camp, dir. waterfront, instr. swimming Camp Dart-Lo Camp Fire Girls, Spokane, 1985—86, counselor Camp Sweyolakan, 1982—85; instr. lifeguard and swimming YWCA, Spokane, 1984—86; dir. co-crisis line Ea. Wash. U., Cheney, 1984—86. Sec. Bridgeport Vol. Fire and Ambulance, 2003—06; leadership coun., ch. bd. Cornerstone Christian Fellowship Free Meth. Ch., Omak, Wash., 2003—06, chairperson women's stewards, 2003—06. Avocations: cooking, gardening, hiking, travel.

JACKSON, TERESA ROBERTS, principal, consultant; b. Grenada, Miss., June 2, 1971; d. Bobby and Linda Roberts; m. Michael Lloyd Jackson, July 7, 1990; children: Corey Michaela, Tanner Lloyd. AA, Holmes CC, Grenada, 1992; BS in Elem. Edn., Delta State U., 1994; MS in Ednl. Leadership, Miss. State U., 2003; postgrad., U. Miss., 2005—. Cert. tchr. early adolescent/generalist Nat. Bd. Profl. Tchg. Stds. Tchr. Grenada Mid. Sch., 1994—2004; asst. prin. Grenada Upper Elem., 2004—06, prin., 2006. Cons. Ednl. Resources, LLC, Nettleton, Miss., 2006—. Mem. Jr. Aux. of Grenada, 2005—06. Recipient Educator of Yr., Grenada Mid. Sch., 2001. Mem.: ASCD, Phi Kappa Phi, Kappa Delta Pi, Alpha Theta Chi. Office: Grenada Upper Elem Sch 500 Pender Dr Grenada MS 38901 Office Phone: 662-226-2818. Office Fax: 662-227-6107. Business E-Mail: tjackson@gsd.k12.ms.us.

JACKSON, TRACHETTE L., biologist, educator; b. Monroe, La., July 24, 1972; d. Isaiah and Ernestine Jackson; m. Patrick Nelson, Aug. 8, 1998; children: Joshua Patrick Nelson, Noah Aaron Nelson. BS in Math. summa cum laude, univ. honors, honors in major, Ariz. State U., 1994; MS in Applied Math., U. Washington, 1996; PhD of Applied Math., U. Wash. Seattle, 1998. NIH MARC trainee, dept. math. and zoology Ariz. State U., 1993—94; rsch. asst., dept. math. Ohio State U., 1994; rsch. asst., dept. applied math. U. Washington, 1995—96, NSF math. biology trainee, dept. zoology, 1995—96, NSF grad. fellow, dept. applied math., 1995—98; postdoctoral assoc., Inst. Math and Applications U. Minn., Mpls., 1998—99; John Hope Franklin postdoctoral fellow, Ctr. for Math. and Computation in the Life Sciences and Medicine, dept. math. Duke U., Durham, NC, 1999—2000; asst. prof., dept. meth. U. Mich., Ann Arbor, 2000—03, assoc. prof. dept. math., 2003—. Grad. tchg. asst. U. Washington, 1997; instructor Ariz. State U., 1997, 98, Duke U., 2000, U. Mich, 2000, course developer, instructor, 01, 02; vis. scientist, Nat. Health and Environ. Effects Rsch. Lab. EPA, Durham, 1999—2000; invited presenter. Contbr. articles to profl. jours. Recipient Elizabeth Caroline Crosby Rsch. Award, ADVANCE Project, 2003; Rsch. Fellow, Alfred P. Sloan Found., 2003—, Career Enhancement Fellowship for Jr. Facutly, Woodrow Wilson Nat. Fellowship Found., 2003, Grant to study tumor encapsulation, NSF, 2001—. Mem.: Assn. for Women in Math., Soc. for Indsl. and Applied Math., Soc. for Math. Biology. Office: Dept Math 3856 East Hall Univ Mich 525 E University Ann Arbor MI 48109-1109 Office Phone: 734-764-8537. Office Fax: 734-763-0937. Business E-Mail: tjacks@math.lsa.umich.edu. E-mail: tjacks@umich.edu.*

JACKSON, VALERIE LYNNETTE, social worker; b. Vicksburg, Miss., June 7, 1959; d. Eugene and Joyce (Flood) J. BS in Social Work, Jackson State U., 1980; MSW, U. So. Miss., 1983. Lic. social worker. Social work teaching asst. Miss. Adoption Tng. Project, Jackson, 1979; collection correspondent Sears Dept. Store, Jackson, 1977-81; resident mgr. Univ. So. Miss., Hattiesburg, 1981-82; relief program specialist Cath. Charities, Jackson, 1983-85; sr. med. social worker Miss. Meth. Rehab. Ctr., Jackson, 1983—. Chmn. housing com. Handicapped Svc. Coalition, Jackson, 1985; chmn. nominations Living Independence for Everyone, Jackson, 1986; chmn. ctrl. Miss. chpt. Nat. Spinal Injury Assn., 1995-98. Named Outstanding Young Women Am., 1988. Mem. NASW (chmn. merit award com. 1984-88, chmn. hospitality com. 1995—), Support Group for Families Individuals with Disabilities, Am. Assn. Spinal Cord Injury Psychologists and Social Workers, State Wide Edn. Enforcement Prevention System. Baptist. Avocations: travel, shopping.

JACKSON, VALERIE PASCUZZI, radiologist, educator; b. Oakland, Calif., Aug. 25, 1952; d. Chris A. Pascuzzi and Janice (Mayne) Pacuzzi; 1 child, Price Arthur III. AB, Ind. U., 1974, MD, 1978. Diplomate Am. Bd. Radiology. Intern, resident in diagnostic radiology Ind. U. Med. Ctr., 1978-82; from asst. prof. radiology to prof. radiology Ind. U. Sch. Medicine, Indpls., 1982-94, John A. Campbell prof. radiology, 1994—. Dir. residency program in radiology Ind. U. Sch. Medicine, 1994—2003, chair dept. radiology, 2004—; trustee Am. Bd. Radiology. Contbr. over 80 articles to profl. jours., chapters to books. Fellow: Soc. Breast Imaging (pres. 1990—92), Am. Coll. Radiology (bd. chancellors, chair 3 coms., pres. 2002—03); mem.: AMA, Radiol. Soc. N.Am., Am. Roentgen Ray Soc., Am. Inst. Ultrasound in Medicine, Alpha Omega Alpha. Office: Indiana U Sch Med Dept Rad 550 N Univ Blvd Rm 0663 Indianapolis IN 46202-2859

JACKSON, VELMA LOUISE, lawyer; b. Sewickley, Pa., Aug. 2, 1945; d. Matthew Edward and Sarah Frances (Carter) J. BS, Duquesne U., 1968; MEd, U. Pitts., 1977; JD, U. Cin., 1982. Bar: W.Va. 1985, Pa. 1986. Chemist Calgon Corp., Pitts., 1969-70; mgr. lab. svcs. Polytech Inc., Cleve., 1970-76; engr. Procter & Gamble Co., Cin., 1976-79; v.p. F.U.T.U.R.E. Assocs., Sewickley, 1982—; law clk., jud. asst. Orphans Ct. div. Ct. Common Pleas, Pitts., 1985-89; pvt. practice Pitts., 1989—. Environ. cons. Creative Mgmt. Systems, Detroit, 1979-81; tech. writer O.H. Materials Inc., Findlay, Ohio, 1980-81; instr. bus. law Carlow Coll., Pitts., 1986-91; bd. dirs. Sentinel Fin. Svcs. Inc. Writer poetry; contbr. articles to profl. jours.; developed cut plant preservative, 1975. Bd. dirs. Sewickley Cmty. Ctr., 1983-89, 91—, Group Against Smog and Pollution, Pitts., 1987-1995, Aliquippa Hosp., 2003-2004; treas. Quaker Valley Dist. Dems., 1984-92, commr. Police Civil Svcs. Commn., Sewickley, 1986—; invitee Citizen Amb. Project to India, Republic of China and USSR Internat. Amb. Programs Inc., Spokane, Wash., 1987-88; trustee Sewickley Valley Hosp., 1996-99, Pitts. Tech. Inst., 1997—, Meade Educultural Cons., 1997—. Mem. ABA, AAUW, Nat. Assn. Colored Women's Club (local pres. 1985-87, state 1st v.p. 1988-92), Nat. Assn. Negro Bus. and Profl. Women, Pa. Bar Assn., W.Va. Bar Assn., African Ams. for Self-Determination (co-founder), Am. Biographical Inst. Rsch. Assn. (mem. adv. coun.), Internat. Biographical Ctr., Delta Sigma Theta. Baptist. Avocation: fiction and poetry writing. Home: 339 Little St Sewickley PA 15143-1468 Personal E-mail: vljesq@yahoo.com.

JACKSON, VICKI ANNETTE, elementary school educator; b. Harriman, Tenn., Feb. 26, 1957; d. Garnet Vaughn and Ramona Anne Justice; m. John Alfred Jackson, June 21, 1975 (dec. July 12, 1998); children: Jada Leigh Jackson-Chamblee, Jada Leigh Jackson Chamblee. B, Tenn. Tech. U., Cookeville, 1990—93. Elem. Edn. Profl. Tenn. Dept. Edn., 1997. Jr. high reading tchr. Coalfield Sch., Tenn., 1997—2003, mid. sch. sci. tchr., 2003—06. CEO John Jackson Meml. Scholarship, Inc., Coalfield, Tenn., 2004—06; bd. dirs. Pleasant Grove Bapt. Ch., Coalfield, 2004—06, ch. coun., 2004—06. Mem.: NSTA (assoc.), Delta Kappa Gamma Soc. Internat. (assoc.; pres. 2002—04, parlimentarian 2004—06, state literacy com., state comm. com.), TSTA (assoc.). Democrat. Baptist. Avocations: singing, jewelry making, flower gardening, local missions, interior decorating. Home: 126 Sierra Ln Harriman TN 37748 Office: Coalfield Sch 1720 Coal Hill Rd Coalfield TN 37719 Office Phone: 865-435-7332. Home Fax: 865-435-2646; Office Fax: 865-435-2646. Business E-Mail: jacksonv@mcsmail.net.

JACKSON, VICTORIA LYNN, actress, comedienne; b. Miami, Fla., Aug. 2, 1959; d. James McCaslin and Marlene Esther (Blackstad) J.; m. Nisan Mark Eventoff, Aug. 5, 1984; 1 child, Scarlet Elizabeth. Student, Fla. Bible Coll., 1976-77, Furman U., 1977-79, Auburn U., 1979-80. Actress Summerfest/Town & Gown, Birmingham, Ala., 1980; stand-up comedienne Variety Arts Ctr., LA, 1982-83, Tonight Show with Jonny Carson, NBC, LA, 1983; actress-comedienne The Half Hour Comedy Hour, Dick Clark, LA, 1983; comedienne Bizarre/John Beiner, Toronto, Can., 1983; actress comms. LA, 1983—; comedienne Bob Munkhouse Show, London, 1983; actress-comedienne Saturday Night Live, NBC, NYC, 1986—. Actress series Half Nelson, NBC, L.A., pilot Walter Fox, L.A. Actress (films) Stoogemania, Double Exposure, The Pick Up Artist, 1986, Baby Boom, 1987, Couch Trip, 1987, Dream a Lil Dream, 1988, Casual Sex, 1988, UHF with Weird Al, 1989, Family Business, 1990, I Love You to Death, 1990. Mem. ASCAP, SAF, AFTRA. Baptist. Avocations: motherhood, photography, gymnastics.

JACKSON, WYNELLE REDDING, educational association administrator, accountant, tax specialist; b. Atlanta, Sept. 3, 1947; d. Edwin Turner and Eva Josephine (Davis) Redding; m. Ronald Van Watson, Aug. 10, 1974 (div. Aug. 1978); m. Toney Jackson, Sept. 16, 1995. BA in Elem. Edn., CUNY, 1968; MEd in Supervision and Adminstrn., U. N.H., 1982. Lic. notary pub., N.Y. Tchr. Pub. Sch. 129 N.Y.C. Bd. Edn., Bklyn., 1969-74, coord. career edn. dist. 16, 1974-75, tchr. Pub. Sch. 243, 1975-80, tchr. Pub. Sch. 85 Queens, 1980-82; dir. ednl. svcs. The Salvation Army Social Svcs. for Children, N.Y.C., 1982—. Treas. Black Am. Heritage Found., Jamaica, N.Y., 1982—; mem. Wayanda Civic Assn., Queens Village, N.Y., 1994—. Recipient Josephine H. Pettie Humanitarian award Black Am. Heritage Found., 1993. Mem. ASCD, Nat. Notary Assn., N.Y. State Assn. Supervision and Curriculum Devel., Phi Delta Kappa, The Nat. Sorority of Phi Delta Kappa, Inc. (fin. sec. Beta Omicron chpt. 1980-81, treas., 1983-87, fin. sec. eastern region 1991-95). Episcopalian. Avocation: bowling. Home: 99-10 211th St Queens Village NY 11429 Office: The Salvation Army Social Svcs for Children 132 W 14th St New York NY 10011-7389

JACKSON, YVONNE RUTH, former pharmaceutical executive; b. L.A., June 30, 1949; d. Giles B. Jackson and Gwendolyn (Battle); m. Frederic Jackson, Jr., Mar. 24, 1989; children: Cortney, Douglass. BA, Spelman Coll., 1970; MA, Harvard U., 1985. Asst. dept. mgr. to dept. mgr. Sears, Roebuck & Co., Torrance, Calif., 1970—71, asst. buyer, asst. retail sales mgr. NYC, 1972—77, pers. mgr., 1977—79; exec. recruiter employee rels. mgr., dir human resources Avon Products, Inc., 1979—85, dir. mfr., redeployment, fir human resources internat., 1985—87, v.p. internat., v.p. human resources, 1987—93; sr. v.p. worldwide human resources Burger King Corp., 1993—99; sr. v.p. human resources Compaq Computer Corp., Houston, 1999—2002, Pfizer, Inc., NYC, 2003—05; founder, pres. BeecherJackson, Coral Gables, Fla., 2005—. Apptd. Pfizer Leadership Team; bd. trustees Spelman Coll., 1996—, chmn., 2004—; bd. dirs. Inst. Women's Policy Rsch., Girls, Inc., Winn-Dixie Stores, Inc., 2006—; mem. adv. bd. Catalyst, 1993—. Named a Black Achiever, YMCA, 1986, Woman Achiever, YMCA of Greater NY, 1992; recipient Bus. Achievement award, Spelman Coll. Alumnae Assn., 1993. Office: BeecherJackson 13633 Deering Bay Dr Ste 235 Coral Gables FL 33158 Office Phone: 212-733-2323.*

JACKSON-CALLANDRET, SHIRLEY LORRAINE, music educator; b. New York city, NY, Aug. 4, 1964; d. Grover and Bert Jackson; m. Shirley Lorraine Jackson, Feb. 24, 1990. BA, Bennett Coll., 1982—86; MA, Fla. Atlantic U., 2000—02. Music tchr. Broward County Pub. Schools, Fort Lauderdale, Fla., 1988—. Adjudicator Broward County NAACP ACTSO Talent Competition, Ft. Lauderdale, Fla., 1991—93; treas. Broward County Music Educator Conf., Ft. Lauderdale, Fla., 1994—95; coord. Broward County Area Music In Our Schools Month, Ft. Lauderdale, Fla., 1995; adjudicator Omega Psi Pfi Frat. Talent Hunt, Ft. Lauderdale, Fla., 1995—2000; coord. Broward County Elem. Honor Choir, Ft. Lauderdale, Fla., 1995, Broward County North Area Music In our Sch. Month Concert, Ft. Lauderdale, Fla., 1995—96; adjudicator South Fla. Regional Showtime At The Apollo Auditions, Ft. Lauderdale, 1995; membership Music Educators Nat. Conf., Ft. Lauderdale, Fla., 1988—; grade chairperson N. Andrews Gardens Elem. Sch. Performing Arts Dept., Ft. Lauderdale, Fla., 2000—01, magnet coord., 2001—. Music director: performance Fla. Citrus Bowl, Disney Magic Music Days; music teacher (performance) Miami Heat Halftime Show, Music Usa Festival (first pl. in elem. show choir category, 2000), Annie Jr; Fiddler On The Roof, Jr; Oklahoma; Into The Woods, Jr. Music dir. Rising Stars Summer Theatre Camp, Ft. Lauderdale, Fla., 1999—2001. Mem.: Nat. Aspiring Educators Sch. Pers., Fed. Educators Assn., Broward County Teachers Union, Fla. Music Educator Assn. (corr.), Nat. Dance Alliance (assoc.). Avocations: singing, dance, travel. Home: 11440 NW 41 St Sunrise FL 33323 Office: Broward County Schools/ North Andrews Ga 345 NE 56 St Fort Lauderdale FL 33334 E-mail: shirlnotes@aol.com.

JACKSON LEE, SHEILA, congresswoman; b. Queens, NY, Jan. 12, 1950; d. Erica Shelwyn and Jason Cornelius Bennett; m. Elwyn C. Lee; 2 children. BA with honors in Polit. Sci., Yale U., New Haven, 1972; JD, U. Va. Sch. Law, Charlottesville, 1975. Bar: Tex. Sr. counsel select com. on assassinations US Congress, 1977—78; trial atty. Fulbright and Jaworski, 1978-80; sr. atty. United Energy Resources, Inc., 1980; assoc. judge Mcpl. Ct., Houston, 1987-89; mem. City Coun., Houston, 1990-94, US Congress from 18th Tex. dist., 1995—, mem. judiciary com., ranking mem. immigration, border security and claims subcommittee, mem. sci. com., mem. homeland security com., founder Congl. Children's Caucus. Named one of 100 Most Influential Black Americans, Ebony mag., 2006; recipient Top Women in the Sciences Award, Nat. Tech. Assn. of Scientists and Engrs., 1998, Policy award, Phillip Burton Immigration & Civil Rights Awards, 2006. Mem.: Tex. Mcpl. Judges Assn., State Bar Assn. Justice Com. Democrat. Office: US Ho Reps 2435 Rayburn Ho Office Bldg Washington DC 20515-4318 Office Phone: 202-225-3816.*

JACKSON MCCABE, JEWELL, not-for-profit developer; b. Wash., DC, Aug. 2, 1945; d. Hal Jackson; m. Frederick Ward (div.); m. Eugene L. McCabe, Jr. (div.). Attended, Bard Coll., 1963—66; doctorates (hon.), Iona,

Tugaloo Coll. Dir. pub. affairs NY Urban Coalition, 1970—73; pub. rels. officer Special Svc. Children NYC, 1973—75; assoc. dir. pub. info. Women's Divsn. Office Gov., NY State, 1975—77; dir. gov. comm. affairs WNET-TV/Thirteen, 1977—82; pres. Nat. Coalition 100 Black Women, 1977—91, chair, 1981—; pres. Jewell Jackson McCabe Assoc. Bd. mem. Reliance Group Holdings, Inc., Alight.com, NYC Investment Fund, Wharton Sch. Bus., Bard Coll., Nat. Alliance Bus., NYC Partnership, Rsch. Am., NYC Commn. Status Women, Children's Advocacy Ctr. Manhattan; chair NY State Job Training Partnership Coun. Mem. US Holocaust Meml. Coun., NY State Coun. on Fiscal and Econ. Priorities. Recipient Guild award, Urban League, 1979, Civic award, Seagrams, 1980, 1980, Cmty. Leadership award, Malcolm/King Coll., 1980. Office: National Coalition Of 100 Black Women 1925 Adam Clayton Powell Jr Blvd Apt 1I New York NY 10026-2227 Office Phone: 212-947-2196.

JACKSON-VANIER, LINDA M., art educator; b. Murfresborrow, Tenn., Sept. 21, 1953; d. George Alfred and Elizabeth (Rousseau) Vanier; children: Lakee, Ezekiel, Zebadiah. AAS in Early Childhood Edn., Hudson Valley CC, Troy, NY, 1977; BS in Elem. Edn. and English, Coll. St. Rose, Albany, NY, 1986. Head tchr. Seton Day Care Ctr., Watervliet, NY, 1978—81; counselor Rennselaer County Sexual Assault and Crime Victims Ctr., Troy, NY, 1998—2006. Mem.: Colonie Art League, Capital Dist. Ctr. Arts, Portrait Soc. Am. Avocations: crafts, reading, writing, drawing, painting.

JACKSON WRIGHT, ADRIENNE A., educational consultant; b. L.A., 1960; d. Harold and Clora (Ellis) J.; m. Kenneth E. Wright, Nov. 2005. BA, Chapman U., Orange, Calif., 1982, MA, 1988; EdD, U. So. Calif., 1997. Teaching and Adminstrv. Svcs. Cert., Calif. Dance instr. Centinela Valley Union High Sch. Dist., Lawndale, Calif., 1987-90; dir. of activities Tustin (Calif.) Unified Sch. Dist., 1990-93; vice prin. Grossmont (Calif.) Union High Sch. Dist., 1993—97; prin. Inglewood Unified Sch. Dist., 1997—2000, Montgomery County Pub. Schs., 2000—05; ednl. cons. Coastline C.C., 2006—. Mem. ASCD, Coalition of One Hundred Black Women (charter mem. San Diego chpt.), Phi Delpa Kappa, Delta Gamma. Avocations: choreography, travel, cooking, reading. Office Phone: 949-355-6078. Personal E-mail: jacksal2@sbcglobal.net.

JACOB, DEIRDRE ANN BRADBURY, manufacturing executive, finance educator, consultant; b. Providence, Mar. 7, 1952; d. John Joseph and Marion Damon (Shute) Bradbury; m. Thomas Keenan, Nov. 15, 1975 (div. Dec. 1980); 1 child: Victoria Irene; m. Robert A. Jacob, June 22, 1996; 1 child, Meggin Rosemary. BA in Govt. and Law, Lafayette Coll., 1973. Supr. Procter & Gamble Mfg. Co., S.I., N.Y., 1973-76, mgr. warehouse dept., 1976-79, mgr. shortening and oils, 1979-81, fin. mgr. food plant, 1981-82, mgr. personnel, 1982-86, mgr. total quality and pub. affairs, 1986-91; ptnr. Avraham Y. Goldratt Inst., New Haven, 1991—2005, exec. v.p., 2005—06, mng. ptnr., 2006—; pres. AYG, Inc., 2006—. Cons. Procter & Gamble, S.I., 1987—89, Cin., 1989—91. Trustee Lafayette Coll., 1985-90. Mem. Lafayette Coll. Alumni Assn. (pres. 1992-94, Clifton P. Mayfield award), Maroon Club (Easton, Pa., pres. 1987-89). Roman Catholic. Avocation: singing. Office: Avraham Y Goldratt Inst 442 Orange St New Haven CT 06511-6201 E-mail: dee.jacob@goldratt.com.

JACOB, DIANNE, county official; m. Paul, 1961; 1 son, Tom. Tchr. East County; mem. Jamul/Dulzura Sch. Bd.; supr. dist. 2 San Diego County Bd. Suprs., 1992—. Co-chmn. Criminal Justice Coun.; mem. San Diego (Calif.) Planning Commn., chmn.; pres. Calif. State Sch. Bds.; adv. bd. Mothers Against Drunk Driving; bd. dir. East County Econ. Devel. Coun. Recipient Alumna of Yr. award San Diego State U. Coll. Edn., 1993, Women Who Mean Bus. award San Diego Bus. Jour., 1995, Legislator of Yr. award Indsl. Environ. Assn., 1995, Most Accessible Politician award Forum Publs., award of excellence Endangered Habitats League, 1999, Legislator of Yr. award Calif. Narcotics Assn., 1998, Legislator of Yr. award Border Solution Task Force, 1998, Legislator of Yr. award San Diego Mchts. Assn., 2000, Ofcl. of Yr., San Diego Domestic Violence Coun., 2000, Legis. of Yr. award Indsl. Environ. Assn., 2000, Legis. of Yr. award Bldg. Owners and Mgrs. Assn., 2001, Headliner of Yr. award San Diego Press Club, 2002. Avocation: golf. Office: Office County Supr County Adminstrn Ctr 1600 Pacific Hwy Ste 335 San Diego CA 92101-2470

JACOB, JULIE ANN, special education educator; b. St. Louis, Apr. 14, 1957; d. Albert Carl and Rita Dorothy (Creamer) Clemens; m. Terry Francis Jacob, Oct. 9, 1982; children: Nicholas, Christina. BS cum laude, U. Mo., St. Louis, 1979, MEd, 1983. Cert. elem. edn., spl. edn., learning disabled, behavior disordered, sch. psychol. examiner. Tchr. asst. Spl. Sch. Dist., St. Louis, 1979; tchr. Judevinne Ctr., St. Louis, 1979-80; head tchr. Childhaven, St. Louis, 1980-86; tchr. Spl. Sch. Dist., St. Louis, 1986—. Vol. supr. Childhaven, St. Louis, 1980—86; com. mem. Sch. Improvement Team, 2000—, Profl. Devel., 2000—05, Mo. Achievement Program Test Devel., 2005—06, Assistive Tech. Team, 1999, Literacy Team, 2003—. Recipient Tchr. of the Month, 1996, Excellence in Tchg. award, 1997, Soar award, 1999. Mem. Coun. for Exceptional Children, Learning Disability Assn. Office: Gotsch Sch 8348 S Laclede Station Rd Saint Louis MO 63123-2199 Personal E-mail: juliejacob@peoplepc.com.

JACOB, ROSAMOND TRYON, librarian; b. Mpls., May 20, 1928; d. Philip Dorn and Rachel Chase (Denison) Tryon; m. Bernard Michel Jacob, Feb. 17, 1951; children: Clara, Paul. BA summa cum laude, Smith Coll., 1949; MA in Libr. Sci., U. Minn., 1974. Sec. Thames & Hudson Pubs., N.Y.C., 1950-51, Columbia Law Sch., N.Y.C., 1952-54, U. Minn., Mpls., 1955-59; libr. St. Paul Pub. Libr., 1976—98, ret. Coun. mem. Depository Libr. Coun. to Pub. Printer, Washington, 1985-88. Co-author: Minnesota State Documents: A Guide for Depository Libraries, 1984; author: (newsletter) Documents/Classified, 1980-96; editor: (newsletter) DOCSOUP, 1980-90. Mem. St. Paul LWV, 1965—. Mem. ALA (Bernadine Abbott Hoduski Founder award govt. documents roundtable divsn. 1994), Minn. Libr. Assn. (Disting. Achievement award 1990).

JACOB, SUSAN MARIE, nurse; b. New Brunswick, N.J., Dec. 30, 1961; BSN, U. Del., 1984; M Nursing Adminstrn., La. State U. Health Sci. Ctr., 2001. RN, La.; cert. coding specialist, cert. profl. coder. Staff/charge nurse Tex. Children's Hosp., Houston, 1984—90; coord. patient care Lakeview Home Health, Covington, La., 1994—96; dir. nursing Trinity Home Health, New Orleans, 1996—98; coder Children's Hosp., New Orleans, 1998—99; auditor Ochsner Clinic, New Orleans, 1999—. Mem. Am. Acad. Profl. Coders, Inst. Internal Auditors, Sigma Theta Tau. Home: 525 Rue de la Parc Slidell LA 70461 Office Phone: 504-842-6926. Business E-Mail: sjacob@ochsner.org.

JACOB, VALERIE FORD, lawyer; b. Orange, NJ, Dec. 29, 1952; BS, Boston U., 1975; JD, Cornell U., 1978. Bar: NY 1979. Joined Fried, Frank, Harris, Shriver & Jacobson LLP, NYC, 1978, ptnr., 1986—, co-mng. ptnr. Governance Com. Contbr. articles to profl. jours. Mem.: NY State Bar Assn., Assn. Bar City NY, ABA. Office: Fried Frank Harris Shriver & Jacobson LLP One New York Plz New York NY 10004-4000 Office Phone: 212-859-8158. Office Fax: 212-859-4000. Business E-Mail: valerie.jacob@friedfrank.com.

JACOB, WENDY, artist, art educator; BA, Williams Coll., 1980; MFA, Sch. of Art Inst. Chgo., 1989. Instr. performance dept. The Sch. of the Art Inst. of Chgo., 1993; asst. prof. dept. sculpture Coll. Fine Arts Ill. State U.; asst. prof. visual arts MIT, Cambridge, 1999—. Mem. HaHa artists collaborative, 1989—. Work has appeared at, Whitney Mus. Art, NYC, Galerie Walcheturm, Zurich, The Sch. of the Art Inst. of Chgo., Emmanuel Perrotin, Paris, Galerie Karin Schorm, Vienna, Milw. Inst. Art & Design, Schipper and Krome, Cologne, Germany, Centre Nat. d'Art Contemporain, Grenoble, France, Temple Gallery, Tyler Sch. Art, Phila., Krannert Art Mus., U. Ill., Champaign, Cranbrook Art Mus., Cranbrook Acad. Art, Bloomfield Hills, Mich., MIT List Visual Arts Ctr., Cambridge, Chgo. Project Rm., Kemper Mus. Contemporary Art, Kansas City, Madison Art Ctr., Wis., Centre Georges-Pompidou, Paris, Forum for Contemporary Art, St. Louis, Mass. Mus. Contemporary Art, Kunsthaus Graz, Austria. Recipient Bicentennial Medal for disting. achievement, Williams Coll., 1996; New Forms Regional Initiative Grant (with HaHa), Nat. Endowment for the Arts/Rockefeller Found., 1988, Ill. Arts Coun. Artist's Fellowship Award, 1989, Cmty. Arts Assistance Program Grant (with HaHa), City of Chgo., 1990, Louis Comfort Tiffany Found. Artist Fellowship (with HaHa), 1993, Arts Internat. Travel Grant (with HaHa), 1993, U. Rsch. Grant, Ill. State U., 1996, 1998, Creative Capital Found. Grant, 1999, Ill. Arts Coun. Artist's Fellowship Award, 1999, HASS Rsch. Award, MIT, 2001, Class of 1947 Career Devel. Professorship, 2001—04, Mary I. Bunting Inst. Fellow, Radcliffe Inst. Advanced Study, Harvard U., 2004—05. Office: MIT Visual Arts Program 265 Massachusetts Ave N51-317 Cambridge MA 02139

JACOBER, AMY ELIZABETH, theology studies educator; b. Burbank, Calif., Dec. 01; d. John Arthur and Betty Jean Jacober; m. Cory Ke Michael Peacock, Nov. 21, 2006. MDiv, MA, Southwestern Theol. Sem., Ft. Worth, Tex., 1995; MSW, Ariz. State U., Tempe, Ariz., 2000; PhD, Fuller Theol. Sem., Pasadena, Calif., 2003. Asst. prof. Seattle Pacific U., 2003—04, Azusa Pacific U., Calif., 2004—. Youth pastor Agape Christian Ch., Pasadena, Calif., 2005—. Author: Come Together; A Practical Theology of Youth Ministry, A Pastor's Guide to Youth Ministry, 2006; author: (editor) Annual Youth Minsitry Sourcebook; contbr. articles to profl. jours. Coord., leader mission trip Markas Al Bishara, Tamale, Northern Region, Ghana, 2005—06; leader mission trip Malachi/Cadence Ministries, Cescenatico, Italy, 2005—06; mem. capernaum nat. com. Young Life, San Jose, Calif., 2004—; mem. adv. bd. Jour. Student Ministries, Nashville, 2006—; mem. Agape Life Change, Pasadena, Calif., 2006—. Recipient Last Lecture Series award, Azusa Pacific U., 2005; grantee, Lilly Found., 2001. Mem.: Nat. Assn. Christians in Social Work, Internat. Assn. Study Youth Ministry, Assn. Youth Ministry Educators (conf. moderator 2006—, Rsch. award 2004). Achievements include research in youth ministry with special needs teens and their families. Avocations: cooking, gardening, eating. Office Phone: 626-815-6000 ext. 5625. Personal E-mail: amy.jacober@gmail.com.

JACOBI, KERRY LEE, information systems specialist; b. Smithtown, N.Y., Jan. 19, 1970; d. Patrick R. and Karen A. (Koch) J. BS in Acctg., Marymount Coll., 1991; MPA, Marist Coll., 1993; student, SUNY, New Paltz, 1998; student in biodynamic massage therapy, instr. Arthur Giacolone, Walnut Creek, Calif., 1999—. Cert. in Reiki II. Asst. adminstr. Dutchess Radiology Assoc. P.C., Poughkeepsie, N.Y., 1992-94; planning, mktg. exec. Vassar Bros. Hosp., Poughkeepsie, N.Y., 1994-97; billing ops. mgr. Dutchess Radiology Assocs., Poughkeepsie, N.Y., 1997-98; dir. mktg. DRA Imaging, Poughkeepsie, 1998-99, info. tech. specialist, 1999—. Mem. Marist Coll. MPA Adv. Coun., Marist Coll. Mentoring Program; campaign fin. mgr. Citizens to Elect Judy Green, 96th Assembly Dist., N.Y. State Assembly, City of Poughkeepsie mayoral race, 1999. Mem. NOW (past pres. mid-Hudson chpt. 1995-97). Democrat. Avocations: competitive weight lifting, fencing, scuba diving. Office: DRA Imaging PC Westage Med Office Bldg Reade Pl Poughkeepsie NY 12601-1749 E-mail: KLJACOBIZ@aol.com.

JACOBOWITZ, ELLEN SUE, curator, museum administrator; b. Detroit, Feb. 21, 1948; d. Theodore Mark and Lois Clairesse (Levy) Jacobowitz. BA, U. Mich., 1969, MA, 1970; postgrad. in art history, Bryn Mawr Coll., 1976-83; postgrad., Wharton Sch., 1997. Curator Phila. Mus. Art, 1972-90; adminstr. Cranbrook Inst. Sci., Bloomfield Hills, Mich., 1991-94; adminstr. Temple Emanu-El, Oak Park, Mich., 1995-96. Cons. ArtServe Mich., 1997; primary caregiver, 1998—2004. Author: The Prints of Lucas Van Leyden, 1983, American Graphics, 1860-1940, 1982. Treas. Sat. Luncheon Club, 1995—96, pres., 1999—2000; active Leadership Oakland, Detroit Inst. Arts; bd. dirs. Nat. Coun. Jewish Women, Detroit, 1990—91; mem. Franklin Archives Temple Beth El; bd. dirs. Print Coun. Am., Balt., Netherlands Am. Amity Trust, Washington, 1982—84, Mich. Mus. Assn., 1993—94. Mem.: Detroit Inst. Arts, U. Mich. Alumni Assn., Am. Jewish Com. Avocations: cooking, gardening, reading, the arts, sports.

JACOBS, ALICIA MELVINA, account executive; b. Newark, June 24, 1955; d. Alvin and Melvina (McKinney) J. BA, Oberlin Coll., 1977. Caseworker Essex County Welfare Bd., Newark, 1977-78; sr. audit analyst N.J. Blue Cross, Newark, 1978-80; fin. analyst N.Y. State Office of the Spl. Cont., N.Y.C., 1980-81; account exec. Fortune Temporary Personnel, N.Y.C., 1981-84; sales mgr. Wall St. Temporary, N.Y.C., 1984-85; account exec. Prentice Hall, N.Y.C., 1985-90, Rsch. Inst. Am., Newark, 1990-91, Westfield, 1992-93, Century City, Calif., 1993-96; regional acct. mgr. Interactive Search, Calif., 1997-98, Giga Info. Group, Calif., 1998-99, v.p., dir. bus. devel. Calif., 1999—; v.p. client svcs. Right Mgmt. Cons., 2001—. Fund-raising chmn. The Africa Project, N.Y.C., 1989-91; sec. We Are Family, Newark, 1989—; mentor, tutor Welcome Bapt. Ch., Newark, 1991—; vol. Scott-Krueger Cultural Ctr., Newark, 1991—; vol. mentor Jr. Achievement, Sisters Having Our Say, SOS Group, Faithful Central Employment Vol., The Restaurant Club, Women Who Cook 1994; chairperson Oberlin Coll. AA Cluster Reunion, Ohio, 1997; mem. alumni com. to select bd. trustee mems. Oberlin Coll., 2001-02; bd. dirs. People Coordinated Svcs., 2002. Recipient Heroine award Montclair (N.J.) High Sch., 1990, Participant award Madison Ave. Sch., Newark. Mem. NAACP, N.J. Law Librs. Assn., Coalition of 100 Black Women. Avocations: teaching children, aerobics, reading. Home: 6922 Knowlton Pl Apt 305 Los Angeles CA 90045-2099

JACOBS, ANNETTE M., music educator; MusB in Music Edn., Miami U., Oxford, Ohio, 1999, BA in History, 1999; MusM in Music Edn., Miami U, Oxford, OH, 2006. Orch. dir. Troy City Schs., Ohio, 1999—2000; band dir. Lynchburg-Clay Local Schs., 2000—01; elem. music tchr. Twin Valley Cmty. Local Schs., West Alexandria, Ohio, 2001—. Mem., asst. band dir. Oxford Cmty. Band, Ohio, 2001—; mem. Fayette County Cmty. Band, 2000—01. Mem.: NEA, Ohio Edn. Assn., Ohio Music Edn. Assn., Music Educators Nat. Conf. (vol. book reviewer, Music Educators Jour. 2003—), Nat. Flute Assn., Girl Scouts of Am. (life). Avocations: historical research, quilting, flute, computer.

JACOBS, BETTY JANE LAZAROFF, communications educator; d. Saul and Rae (deceased) Lazaroff; m. Rabbi Sidney J. Jacobs, July 1, 1971 (dec. 2001). BSc in Comm., U. Ill., Champaign, 1966; MA in Mass. Comm., Calif. State U., Northridge, 1978. Prodn. assoc. Broadcasting Comm., Chgo., 1965—67; dir. broadcasting Chgo. Bd. of Rabbis, 1967—2001; prof, comm. West L.A. Coll., Culver City, Calif., 1972—, chair, lang. arts divsn., 2003—. Media cons. C.C. Consortium, L.A., 1973—75. Co-author (non-fiction books) Clues About Jews For People Who Aren't, (book) 122 Clues For Jews Whose Children Intermarry, Jewish Clues to Your Health and Happiness. Bd. dirs. Zero Pet Population Growth, L.A., 1979—81. Recipient NISOD Tchg. Excellence award, U. of Tex. at Austin, 1993, Emmy Nomination, Chgo. Acad. of TV Arts and Sci., 1968, Excellence in TV Writing and Prodn. award, Tikvah Inst., 1971, Creative TV Writing award, Hadassah, 1970. Mem.: Alpha Gamma Sigma (Tchg. Excellence award 2000, 2002, Tchg. Excellence award 2000, 2001, 2003). Jewish. Avocations: running, tennis, vegan lifestyle, dogs, reading. Office: West Los Angeles College 9000 Overland Ave Culver City CA 90230 Office Phone: 310-287-4207. Business E-Mail: jacobsbl@wlac.edu.

JACOBS, BONITA CHERYL, educational administrator; b. Lufkin, Tex., Apr. 1, 1949; d. George Bowden and Dorothy Lee (Jones) Simpson; m. Glenn Curtis Jacobs, Dec. 26, 1970; children: Craig, Ashlee, Scott. BA in Spanish and History, Stephen F. Austin State U., 1971, MEd in Counseling, 1973; PhD in Ednl. Adminstrn., Tex. A & M U., 1985. Tchr., counselor pub. schs., Lufkin, 1971-74, Nederland, Tex., 1974-77; univ. counselor Stephen F. Austin State U., Nacogdoches, Tex., 1978-80, coord. residence life, 1980-83, instr., 1980—86, dir. residence life, 1983-86; dean for student devel. Western Carolina U., Cullowhee, NC, 1986-91, staff devel. coord., 1986—, instr., 1989—, asst. vice chancellor, 1991—, interim v.p. student devel.; assoc. prof. higher edn. U. North Tex., 1998—, v.p. student devel., 1998—. Founder Inst. Study of Transfer Students; past pres. Tex. Assn. Coll. and Univ. Student Pers. Adminstrs.; mem. grant adv. bd. Acad. One; faculty mem. Donna M. Bourassa Mid-Level Mgmt. Inst. Author: (textbook) Starting From Scratch: Strategies for the Successful College Experience, 1993, The College Transfer Student in America: The Forgotten Student; former editor Jour. of Coll. Orientation and Transition; contbr. chpts. to books, articles to profl. jours. Recipient Ted K. Miller Achievement of Excellence award Coun. for Advancement of Stds., John Jones award Nat. Assn. Student Pers. Adminstrs., 2005; named Notable Woman of Tex. Awards and Honor Soc. Am., 1984. Mem. Am. Coll. Pers. Assn. (chair commn. II directorate 1992-94), Tex. Residence Hall Assn. (state advisor 1986), Nat. Orientation Dirs. Assn. (bd. dirs. 1991-94, Outstanding Contbs. to Orientation Profession award, Pres.'s award), N.C. Teaching Fellows (campus adv. bd. 1988—), S.W. Coll. and Univ. Housing Officers (treas. 1984-86, Instl. Excellence in Programming award 1985), S.W. Affiliate Coll. and Univ. Residence Halls (Mita Musick award 1981, regional conf. advisor 1984), So. Assn. for Coll. Student Affairs (chair associational liaison 1990-91). Methodist. Home: 3101 Forrestridge Dr Denton TX 76205-8511 Office: PO Box 305358 Denton TX 76203-5358 Business E-Mail: BJacobs@unt.edu.

JACOBS, CAROLYN DIANNE CROUCH, science educator; b. Casper; d. William and Marge Crouch; m. Marvin Jacobs; children: Kevin, Keiffer, Josef. AS Biololgy, Casper Coll., Wyo., 1985; BS Edn., U. Wyo., 1987; M Natural Sci., U. Wyo., Laramie, 2003. Cert. Secondary Tchr. Profl. Tchg. Stds. Bd. Wyo. Tchr. sci. h.s. North Bend Sch. Dist., Oreg., 1988—89; tchr. sci. jr. high sch. Natrona County Sch. Dist. #1, Casper, 1990—. Prof. U. Wyo., Casper Coll., 2003—. Mem. bd. edn. Wyo. Audubon, Casper, 2000—03. Recipient Presdl. Award for Excellence in Math. and Sci. Tchg., NSF, 2002, Medallion of Excellence in Tchg., Natrona County Sch. Dist. #1, 2001. Mem.: NSTA. Office: Natrona County Sch Dist #1 Dean Morgan Jr High Sch 1440 S Elm Casper WY 82601

JACOBS, CARYN LESLIE, lawyer, former prosecutor; b. Chgo., Mar. 3, 1958; d. Edward Jesse and Ann Marie (Paun) J.; m. Daniel Goldman Cedarbaum, Sept. 6, 1987; children: Jacob Jesse, Samuel Goldman. AB with distinction, Stanford U., 1980; JD cum laude, Harvard U., 1983. Bar: Ill., U.S. Dist. Ct. (no. dist.) Ill. 1984, U.S. Ct. Appeals (8th cir.) 1986, U.S. Ct. Appeals (7th cir.) 1987. Law clk. U.S. Dist. Ct. (no. dist.) Ill., Chgo., 1983-85; assoc. Mayer Brown & Platt, Chgo., 1985-88; asst. U.S. atty. Chgo., 1988-93; ptnr. Mayer Brown Rowe & Maw, Chgo., 1993—. Mem. ABA. Mem. Phi Beta Kappa. Office: Mayer Brown Rowe Maw Llp 230 S La Salle St Ste 400 Chicago IL 60604-1407 Office Fax: 312-701-7621, 312-706-8645.

JACOBS, CHARLOTTE DE CROES, medical educator, oncologist; b. Oak Ridge, Tenn., Jan. 27, 1946; BA, U. Rochester, 1968; MD, Washington U., St. Louis, 1972. Diplomate Am. Bd. Internal Medicine, Am. Bd. Med. Oncology, Nat. Bd. Med. Examiners. Intern, jr. resident dept. medicine Washington U. Sch. Medicine, St. Louis, 1972—74; sr. resident dept. medicine U. Calif., San Francisco, 1974—75; postdoctoral fellow divsn. oncology Stanford (Calif.) U. Med. Sch., 1975—77, acting asst. prof. oncology, 1977-80, asst. prof. medicine and oncology, 1980-86, assoc. prof. clin. medicine, 1986-92, assoc. prof. medicine and oncology, 1992-96, prof., 1996—, sr. assoc. dean. edn. and student affairs, 1990-97, acting dir. Clin. Cancer Ctr., 1994-97; dir. Oncology Day Care Ctr. Stanford Med. Ctr., 1977-90, dir. Clin. Cancer Ctr., 1997—2001. Bd. dirs. Nat. Comprehensive Cancer Network, Rockledge, Pa., 1994-2001. Recipient presdl. citation Am. Soc. for Head and Neck Surgery, 1990, Aphrodite Hofsomner award Washington U., 1993. Mem. AMA, Am. Soc. Clin. Oncology (bd. dirs. 1992-95), Am. Assn. for Cancer Rsch. Office: Clin Cancer Ctr Rm 2241 875 Blake Wilbur Dr Stanford CA 94305-5826 Office Phone: 650-725-8738. Business E-Mail: cjacobs@stanford.edu.

JACOBS, DIANE MARGARET, academic administrator; b. Port-of-Spain, Trinidad, Tobago, Mar. 24, 1940; came to U.S., 1940; d. Saul and Eleanor (Rosenberger) J.; m. Michael K. Shelley, June 15, 1985. AB, Radcliffe Coll., 1961; PhD, Harvard U., 1966. Instr., lectr. Hebrew U. - Hadassah Med. Sch., Jerusalem, 1967-71; rsch. assoc. Salk Inst. Biol. Studies, La Jolla, Calif., 1974-76; assoc. prof. microbiology SUNY, Buffalo, 1976-80, prof. microbiology, 1980-89; assoc. vice chancellor rsch., dean grad. sch., prof. biology East Carolina U., Greenville, N.C., 1989-94; prof. molecular biology and microbiology U. Ctrl. Fla., Orlando, 1994—, v.p. for rsch. and grad. studies, 1994-98, chair dept. health professions, 2002—. Reviewer NIH, Bethesda, Md., 1977—, NSF, Washington, 1989—; bd. dirs. Ctrl. Fla. Innovation Corp. Contbr. articles to Jour. Immunology, Jour. Exp. Medicine, Recent Devel. Mucosal Immunity. Mem. Am. Assn. Immunologists (mem. com.), Am. Soc. Microbiology, N.Y. Acad. Scis., Assn. Women Sci., Oak Ridge Assn. Univs. (councilor 1993—), Coun. Grad. Schs. (bd. dirs. 1993-96, chair 1996), Conf. So. Ga. Grad. Schs. (exec. com. 1993-96, pres. 1995-96). Office: U Ctrl Fla 4000 Fla Blvd HPAII Ste 210 Orlando FL 32816-2205

JACOBS, ELEANOR, art consultant, retired art administrator; b. N.Y.C., July 25, 1929; d. Samuel and Mary (Praw) Cohen; m. Raymond Jacobs, Dec. 29, 1955; children: Susan, Laura. BA, NYU, 1979. Co-founder, v.p. The Earth Shoe Co., N.Y.C., 1969-79; art adminstr. Print Dept., Sotheby's, N.Y.C., 1980-81; exec. asst. Care, N.Y.C., 1982-84; exec. adminstr. Hirschl & Adler Galleries, N.Y.C., 1984-93. Art cons. Recipient Founders Day award NYU, N.Y.C., 1978; Artists fellow, 1985—. Mem. Nat. Arts Club (gov. 1989-97, exhbns. com. 1984—, curatorial com. 1990—, founder, editor exhibiting artists newsletter 1987—, admissions com. 1995—), Nat. Trust for Hist. Preservation, Artists Fellowship, 1985, Dutch Treat Club. Avocations: tennis, travel.

JACOBS, GENEVIEVE M., psychology professor, communications educator; d. Michael Collins and Janet G. Jacobs; m. Claude F. DesJardins (div.); 1 child, Ivan M. Student, St. John's Coll., Annapolis, Md., 1982; BA, Burlington Coll., Vt., 1991; MA in Counseling Psychology, Norwich U., Montpelier, Vt., 1993. Freelance writer, 1983—; counselor Pathways to Wellbeing, Burlington, 1998—; prof. Burlington Coll., 1991—, CCV, Vt., 1997—, Champlain Coll., Burlington, 1997—, St. Michaels Coll., Colchester, Vt., 2000—. Author: Bay of the Orphan, 1992. Founder, organizer Front St. Neighborhood, Burlington, 1992—2002; founder, spokesperson Dinner Key Anchorage Assn., Miami, Fla., 1980—83. Recipient Jane Glassman Meml. award, Burlington Coll., 1989. Progressive. Avocations: sailing, writing, gardening, painting, dance. Office: Pathways to Wellbeing 168 Battery St Burlington VT 05401

JACOBS, GERA M., early childhood educator; b. Cin., Jan. 18, 1952; d. Charles R. and Charlotte Hirt; m. Gerard A. Jacobs, Jan. 18, 1974; children: Meriah Hope Jacobs-Frost, Kate M., Bridget C. BS in Elem. Edn.; EdD, U. SD, 1993. Tchr. St Francis Elem. Sch., Cin.; presch. dir., tchr. Athens (Ohio) Recreation Dept., 1984—88; preschool and kindergarten tchr. St. Agnes Sch., Vermillion, SD, 1988—93; early childhood specialist Ctr. for Disabilities, Vermillion, SD, 1993—95; prof. U. SD, Vermillion, SD, 1995—. Coord. com. writing presch.l stds. for SD, SD, 2003—. Author: (6 eric document articles) The ERIC System, (manual) South Dakota Early Childhood Inclusion Support Manual; prodr., prodr.: Inclusion: Celebrating Children's Successes; author: (on line book revs.) Project CLAS website; contbr. articles to profl. jours. V.p. Ctr. for Children and Families, Vermillion, SD, 1995; pres. SD Assn. for Edn. of Young Children, 1999—2004; chairperson Head Start Grantee Bd., Vermillion, SD, 2003—. Named SD Prof. of Yr., Carnegie Found. and CASE, 2002; recipient Svc. Award, SD Assn. for Edn. of Young Children, 2002; grantee, SD Dept. Spl. Edn., 1995—99. Mem.: SD Coalition for Children, Divsn. Early Childhood in Coun. for Exceptional Children, Nat. Assn. Early Childhood Tchr. Educators, Nat. Assn. for Edn. of Young Children (affiliate coun. rep. 2001—04, SD rep. to nat. affiliate coun. 2001—04), Phi Delta Kappa (del. 1998—2004). Office: Univ SD Dept C&I 414 E Clark St Vermillion SD 57069 Office Phone: 605-677-5822. Business E-Mail: gera.jacobs@usd.edu.

JACOBS, GRETCHEN HUNTLEY, psychiatrist; b. NYC, July 20, 1941; d. L. Gordon and Gertrude Mary (Eberz) La Pointe; m. Michael Edward Jacobs, Dec. 26, 1965 (div.); children: Dylan Huntley, Danielle La Pointe. BS, Fordham U., N.Y.C., 1963; MD, SUNY, Bklyn., 1968. Diplomate Am. Bd. Psychiatry and Neurology, Am. Bd. Child and Adolescent Psychiatry. Pediatric intern St. Luke's Hosp., N.Y.C., 1968—69; psychiatry resident George Washington U. Hosp., Washington, 1969—71; child psychiatry resident Beth Israel Hosp., Boston, 1972—73, McLean Hosp. Children's Ctr., Waltham, 1973—74; coord. health and human devel. Martha's Vineyard Sch. Sys., 1974—80; pvt. practice adult and adolescent/child psychiatry, 1974—; asst. clin. prof. child psychiatry Tufts U. Med. Sch., Boston, 1974—. Contbr. articles to profl. jours. Cons. Mass. Dept. Pub. Health Svcs. to Multi-Handicapped Children, 1974-75; bd. dirs. Mass. Dept. Social Svcs., 1979-83; founding mem., clin. dir. Vineyard Child Assault Prevention Project, 1986, Com. on Rural Child Psychiatry, 1988-92; mem. Coun. for Young Children. Mem. AMA, NAACP, LWV, Am. Psychiat. Assn., Am. Acad. Child and Adolescent Psychiatry, Mass. Med. Soc. Avocations: music, dance, travel, sailing, theater, basketball. Home and Office: Tashmoo Farm RR 1 Box 600 Vineyard Haven MA 02568-9733

JACOBS, JANICE LEE, ambassador; b. Dearborn, Mich., Dec. 5, 1946; d. Robert and Oma Lee (Corgan) J.; m. Royce J. Fichte, June 16, 1968 (div. Dec. 1982); children: Eric A. Fichte, Kurt M. Fichte; m. Kenneth B. Friedman, Mar. 21, 1985. BA in French, So. Ill. U., Carbondale, 1968; postgrad., Fla. Internat. U., Miami, 1986; MS in Nat. Security Strategy, Nat. War Coll., 1995. Cert. tchr., Ill. Consular officer, econ. officer Am. Embassy, Lagos, Nigeria, 1980-81, consular chief Addis Ababa, Ethiopia, 1982-83, consular officer Paris, 1983-85; geog. case officer coordination divsn. visa office US Dept. State, Washington, 1987-88, chief coordination divsn., 1988-90, dep. dir. Office of Cuban Affairs, Inter-Am. Affairs Bur., 1995-98, sr. watch officer Ops. Ctr., 1990-91; prin. officer Am. Consulate, Matamoras, Mexico, 1991-94; dep. chief of mission Am. Embassy US Dept. State, Santo Domingo, Dominican Republic, dep. asst. sec. visa services Bur. Consular Affairs Washington, 2002—05, US amb. to Senegal Dakar, 2006—. Mem. Phi Kappa Phi. Methodist. Avocations: running, hiking, civil war history. Office: Am Embassy 2130 Dakar Pl Dulles VA 20189*

JACOBS, JUDITH, county legislator; b. N.Y.C., Jan. 13, 1939; d. George and Dorothy Bodkin; m. Sidney N. Jacobs, June 7, 1959; children: Jacqueline, Leonard, Linda. BA, Hunter Coll., 1960. Cert. in early childhood edn., N.Y. Mem. Nassau County Legislature, Mineola, N.Y., 1996—, minority leader, 1999—, presiding officer, majority leader, 2000—. Committeeperson, zone leader, asst. dist. leader, Town of Oyster Bay leader Dem. Party Nassau County, 1970—. Democrat. Jewish. Avocation: reading.

JACOBS, KAREN LOUISE, musician, educator, medical technician; b. Kingston, NY, May 7, 1943; d. William Charles and Vera Elizabeth (Kelly) J. BS in Applied Tech., Empire State Coll., 1976; MS in Pub. Svc. Adminstrn., Russell Sage Coll., 1982. Sr. lab. tech., hosp. lab. supr. City of Kingston Labs., 1962-68; sr. rsch. asst. Dudley Obs., Albany, NY, 1972-75; lab. adminstr. Albany Med. Coll., 1976-99, faculty, 1982-97; office asst. accounts and bookkeeping Dievendorf & Co., 2003—05; freelance musician Singerlands, NY, 2003—; pvt. piano tchr., 2003—. Tchr. environ. edn. Five Rivers Environ. Edn. Ctr., Delmar, N.Y., 1999-; tchr. natural sci. Heideberg Workshop, 2002-05; guest lectr. Sage Coll.; coord. complex labs. JCAHO regulations, 1997; infection control com. and subcoms. on AIDS mgmt. and human immunodeficiency virus universal precautions Albany Med. Ctr. Infection Control, 1987-97, accreditation regulatory oversight com.; pvt. piano tchr. Albany Acad. for Boys, 1999—; accompanist Siena Coll./Cmty. Chorale; accompanist Colonie Sr. Citizens, 2002-03; tchr. Heldeberg Workship. Bd. dirs. chpt. Leukemia Soc. Am., 1983-87; judge sci. and tech. summer issue on excellence in Am. U.S. News and World Report; vol. asst. naturalist Five Rivers Environ. Ctr. Mem. Clin. Lab. Mgmt. Assn. (del. citizen amb. program to China 1989), Am. Soc. Clin. Pathologists, Earthwatch, Nat. Speleological Soc., Hudsonia (bd. dirs. 1995). Home: 50 Meadowbrook Dr Apt 149 Slingerlands NY 12159-2146 Office Phone: 518-489-4257.

JACOBS, LIBBY SWANSON, state official; b. Lincoln, Nebr., Oct. 1, 1956; m. Steven G. Jacobs. BA, U. Nebr.; MPA, Drake U. Dir. pub. rels. Am. Lung Assn., 1983—86; dir. comms. IA Bankers Assn., 1986—88; mgr., ops. mgr. disability income svcs. Prin. Fin. Group, 1989—96, asst dir., 1996—2002, dir. cmty. rels., 2002—; mem. Iowa Ho. of Reps., Iowa, 1994—, majority whip. Mem. adminstrn. and rules com.; mem. appropriations com.; mem. commerce and regulation com.; mem. state govt. com. Bd. mem. Drake Univ., Blank Children's Hosp.; co-chair Downtown Cmty. Alliance; past chair Midwestern Legis. Conf. Mem.: PEO, LWV, Jr. League Des Moines, Variety Club Iowa. Republican. Office: State Capitol E 12th and Grand Des Moines IA 50319

JACOBS, LINDA ROTROFF, elementary school educator; b. Peebles, Ohio, June 10, 1942; d. Joseph Harold Rotroff and Mary Lucille (Peterson) Rotroff Nixon; m. Donald Eugene Jacobs, Nov. 29, 1968; 1 child, Donald Brett. BS in Edn., Ohio State U., 1963; MA in Edn., U. Cin., 1968; postgrad., U. Cin., Miami U., Xavier U., 1968—. Coll. Mt. St. Joseph, 1968—. Cert. tchr., Ohio. Tchr. K-8 Forest Hills Bd. Edn., Cin., 1963-74, 77—; tchr. kindergarten Chillicothe (Ohio) Bd. Edn., 1974-77; tchr. reading adult edn. Cin., 1975; tchr. kindergarten Mercer Elem. Forest Hills, Cin., 1977—, tchr. pupil enrichment program, 1997—. Cooperating tchr. student tchrs. Ohio U., U. Cin., No. Ky. U., 1965—; tchr. summer sch. 4th-7th grades math./lang. arts, Cin., 1964-68, kindergarten and 1st grade Forest Hills, Cin., 1978-82; tchr. rep. Head Start, Chillicothe, 1975-77; kindergarten coord. Forest Hills and Hamilton County, Cin., 1965-70, 83-85; mem. supt.'s coun. Forest Hills, Cin., 1979, 82, 88; tchr. rep. PTA, Cin., 1967, 73, 82, 89; facilitator Forest Hills Summer Sch., 1993-96, 97-99; master tchr./advisor entry tchrs. Forest Hills, 1993—; career mentor Ashford-McCarthy Resources, Inc., 1993-94; coord. early entrance screening Hamilton County, 1994, 95, faculty mem. Intervention Based Multifactored Evaluation Com., 1994, 95, mem. Collaboration Team for Inclusion of Spl. Children, 1994, 95; mem. responsive classroom team, 1996-97; mem. steering com. accelerated schs., 1997-98, mem. diversity cadre Accelerated Schs., Great Aspirations pilot program Mercer Elem. Sch., mem. profl. devel. cadre, 1999-2000. Author: Getting Ready for Kindergarten, 1978, Parenting Tips, 1982, Intervention Assistance Team Handbook, 1992 Cons. Women Helping Women, Cin., 1989. Recipient Ohio State U. Scarlet and Gray award, 1995; named Hamilton County Tchr. of Yr., 1965, Educator of Yr., Anderson Hills C. of C., 2000. Mem. NEA, Nat. PTA (rep.) Tchrs. Applying Whole Lang., Ohio Edn. Assn. (del. 1965), Southwestern Ohio Edn. Assn., Forest Hills Educators Assn. (sec. 1964-68, Martha Holden Jennings scholar 1976-77), DAR, Ohio State U. Alumni Club of Clermont County (sec. 1995—), Anderson Hills Hist. Soc., Forest Hills Ret. Staff Assn., Hamilton County Ret. Tchrs. Assn., Police Officers Hall of Fame (hon.), Clermont County Herb Soc., Alpha Kappa Delta (sec. 1975—). Mem. Ch. of Christ. Avocations: interior decorating, writing stories/poems, music, landscaping, reading.

JACOBS, M. LOUISE, secondary school educator; b. Macon, Miss., Jan. 1, 1947; d. James Wallace and Mary Elizabeth Cade, Virginia Cade (Stepmother); m. Steven Paul Jacobs, May 25, 1969 (div. June 13, 1991); children: Steven Paul Jr., Rachael Mary Jacobs-Geiser, Cade Jourdan, Faith Elizabeth. BS in Edn., U. Memphis, 1979. Cert. tchr. Tenn., 1990. Tchr. Memphis City Schs., 1983—. Sgt. USAF, Vietnam. Recipient Econs. Tchr. of Yr. award, Jr. Achievement, 2000. Mem.: NEA, Tchrs. Edn. Assn., Phi Kappa Phi, Kappa Delta Pi. Republican. Roman Catholic. Avocations: travel, nature, reading. Home: 1090 Cambrain Dr Memphis TN 38134 Office: Memphis City Schs - Cordova HS 1800 Berryhill Dr Cordova TN 38016 Office Phone: 901-416-4540. Personal E-mail: louisecadejacobs@midsouth.rr.com.

JACOBS, MADELEINE, professional society administrator, writer; b. Washington; m. Joseph Jacobs; 1 stepchild. BS in Chem., George Washington U., 1968, DSc (hon.), 2003; M course work in Organic Chem. completed, U. Md. Writer, editor Nat. Inst. Allergy and Infectious Disease, 1972—74; with Nat. Bur. of Standards (now Nat. Inst. of Standards & Tech.), 1974—79; head, Smithsonian News Svc. and publications mgr. Smithsonian Inst., 1979—86, dir., public affairs, 1986—93; reporter Chem. and Engring. News, 1969—72, mng. editor, 1993—95, editor-in-chief, 1995—2003; exec. dir., CEO Am. Chem. Soc., 2004—; also bd. dirs. Spkr. in field. Freelanced Physics Today, Smithsonian mag., asst. editor and writer Chemical & Engineering News, Am. Chem. Soc., 1969—72, mng. editor, 1993, editor-in-chief (first women), 1995. Recipient Smithsonian Inst. Secretary's Gold medal, 1993, Exec. Director's award, Am. Chem. Soc., 1999, award for Encouraging Women into Careers in Chemical Sciences, 2003, George Braude Meeml. award (Md. sect.), 2004, award for Exec. Excellence, Comml. Develop. and Mktg. Assn., 2004. Fellow: AAAS; mem.: NY Acad. Scis. (bd. trustee, Women's History Month award 2001), Coun. Advancement Sci. Writing (bd. dirs.), Nat. Assn. Sci. Writers, Phi Beta Kappa. Avocations: cooking, photography, swimming, gardening, writing, weight training. Office: Am Chem Soc 1155 16th St NW Washington DC 20036

JACOBS, MARIAN, advertising executive; b. Stockton, Calif., Sept. 11, 1927; d. Paul and Rose (Sallah) J. AA, Stockton Coll. With Bottarini Advt., Stockton, 1948-50; pvt. practice Stockton, 1950-64; with Olympius Advt., Stockton, 1964-78; pvt. practice Stockton, 1978—. Pres. Stockton Advt. Club, 1954, Venture Club, Stockton, 1955; founder Stockton Advt. and Mktg. Club, 1981. Founder Stockton Arts Comms., 1976; co-founder Sunflower Entertainment for Institutionalized, 1976, Women Execs., Stockton, 1978; founding dir. Pixie Woods, Stockton; bd. dir. Goodwill Industries, St. Mary's Dining Room, Alan Short Gallery; mem. Calif. Coun. for the Humanities, 1994-95. Named Stocktonian of Yr., Stockton Bd. Realtors, 1978, Outstanding Citizen, Calif. State Senate and Assembly, 1978, Woman of Yr., State of Calif. Assembly, 2002, Woman of Achievement, Kaiser-Permanente Women's Wellness Conf., 2002, Disting. Alumni Vol., U. of the Pacific, 2003, Marian Jacobs Lit. Forum Stockton Arts Commn. established in her honor; recipient Woman of Achievement award, San Joaquin County Women's Coun., Stockton, 1976, Achievement award, San Joaquin Delta Coll., Stockton, 1978, Friend of Edn. award, Calif. Tchrs. Assn., Stockton, 1988, Stanley McCaffrey Disting. Svc. award, U. of the Pacific, Stockton, 1988, Athena award for businesswoman of Yr., Greater Stockton C. of C., 1989, Role Model award, Tierra del Oro Girl Scouts U.S., 1989, Heart of Gold award, Dameron Hosp. Found., 2000, Bravo award, Stockton Civic Theater; Paul Harris fellow, Rotary Club, 1994. Republican. Roman Catholic. Avocations: art, photography. Home and Office: 4350 Mallard Creek Cir Stockton CA 95207-5205

JACOBS, MARIANNE, anthropologist, educator, medical/surgical nurse; m. John Michael Jacobs, Nov. 20, 1971; children: Matthew Christopher, Amy Rebecca. Grad., St. Joseph Hosp. Sch. Nursing, Tacoma, 1969; BA, U. Wash., Seattle, 1980, PhD, 1990. RN Wash., 1969. Civilian nurse practitioner US Army, Tacoma, 1972—76; anthropology instr. Green River Cmty., Auburn, Wash., 1992—, chair social sci. divsn., 2006—. Cons., guest lectr., presenter in field, 1988—; adj. faculty U. Wash., Tacoma, 1995—. Trustee Pierce County Libr., Wash., 1990—2000. 1st lt. U.S. Army, 1968—71, Vietnam. Doctoral Opportunity fellow, US Veterans Adminstrn., 1988—90. Mem.: Soc. for Anthropology in Cmty. Colls., Soc. for Med. Anthropology, St. Joseph Hosp. Sch. Nursing Alumni Assn. (bd. mem. 2003—), Am. Anthrop. Assn., Phi Beta Kappa. Avocations: reading, Native American art, travel. Office Phone: 253-833-9111 4625. Business E-Mail: mjacobs@greenriver.edu.

JACOBS, MARION KRAMER, psychologist; b. Bklyn., Jan. 11, 1938; d. Milton Julius and Edith (Rosenel) Kramer. BA, Brooklyn Coll., 1959; PhD in Clin. Psychology, U. South Calif., 1969. Assoc. prof. of bio med. and psychology W.Va. U., 1969-73; dir., counseling ctr. U. Calif., Irvine, 1973-77; adj. prof. and coordinator psychology clinic UCLA, 1977-95, co-dir., co-founder Calif. Self-Help Ctr., 1984-91; sr. cons. Calif. Self-Help Ctr., 1991-95, Neighborhood Youth Assn. L.A., 1978—. Adj. prof. emeritus UCLA Psychology dept., 1995—. Contbr. rsch. articles to profl. jours. Mem. APA, Nat. Register Health Care Providers in Psychology, Western Psychol. Assn., Assn. Psychol. Sci. Democratic. Jewish. Avocations: sailing, writing.

JACOBS, NANCY CAROLYN BAKER, writer; b. Milw., Dec. 9, 1944; d. Alvin Donald and Wilma Carolyn (Robertson) Moll; m. James Ross Baker, Aug. 28, 1965 (div. 1979); 1 child, Bradley; m. Jerome Martin Jacobs, June 20, 1981. BA, U. Minn., 1965, MA, 1973; MFA, U. So. Calif., 1977. Reporter St. Paul Dispatch, 1965-66; pub. rels. writer U. Minn., Mpls., 1966-67, Northwest Airlines, St. Paul, 1967-69; TV scriptwriter Control Data Corp., Mpls., 1971-73; dir. news and pub. Met. State U., St. Paul, 1973-75; author, free lance journalist, 1975—; pvt. investigator Spl. Reports, L.A., 1986-90; journalism lectr. Calif. State U., Northridge, 1977-92. Author: Deadly Companion, 1986, The Turquoise Tattoo, 1991, A Slash of Scarlet, 1992, See Mommy Run, 1992, The Silver Scalpel, 1993, Cradle and All, 1995, Daddy's Gone A-Hunting, 1995, Rocking the Cradle, 1996, Double or Nothing, 2001, Star Struck, 2002, Flash Point, 2002, Ricochet, 2003 (nominated Mary Higgins Clark award Mystery Writers Am.), Desperate Journeys, 2004; (as Nancy C. Baker) Babyselling: The Scandal of Black Market Adoption, 1978, Act II: The Mid-Career Job Change and How to Make It, 1980, New Lives for Former Wives: Displaced Homemakers, 1980, Cashing in on Cooking, 1982, The Beauty Trap: Exploring Woman's Greatest Obsession, 1984, Relative Risk: Living with a Family History of Breast Cancer, 1991 (Am. Med. Writers Assn. Rose Kushner award). Mem. Mystery Writers Am., Pvt. Eye Writers Am., Authors Guild, Sisters in Crime, Internat. Thriller Writers, Nat. Writers Union. Personal E-mail: Nancy@NancyBakerJacobs.com.

JACOBS, PATRICIA H., social welfare organization executive; b. Chgo., Dec. 24, 1941; d. Clarence Joseph and Frances Irene Hayden; m. E. Lowell Jacobs, Aug. 21, 1941; children: Andrew, Thomas, John. BS, Loyola U., Chgo., 1963; MSW, U. Ill., 1972. Day care licensing rep. Ill. Dept. Children and Family Svcs., Champaign, 1963-64, instn. and pvt. agy. licensing rep. Springfield, 1968-70; child welfare supr. Cecil County Social Svcs., Elkton, Md., 1978-79; social worker Children's Bur. of Del., Wilmington, 1980-85; program dir. CHILD, Inc., Newark, Del., 1985-2001, ret., 2001. Contbr. articles to profl. jours. Election judge Bd. of Elections, New Castle County, Del., 1995—; bd. dirs. S.O.A.R., Inc., Wilmington, 1998-2000; vol. capt. Riverfront Art Ctr., Wilmington, 1998-99; mem. planning com. Charity and Justice Conf., Wilmington, 1997-99. Mem. NASW, Foster Family Based Treatment Assn. (editl. com. 1986—). Democrat. Roman Catholic. Avocations: crafts, beach home vacations.

JACOBS, RHODA S., state legislator; b. Bklyn. 3 children. BA, Bklyn. Coll. Co-founder, formerly co-dir. Bklyn. Coll. Day Care Ctr.; mem. N.Y. State Assembly, 1978—, asst. spkr., mem. task force New Americans, mem. banks com., higher edn. com., ins. com., health com., women's caucus. Mem. Nat. Assn. Jewish Legislators. Office: NY State Assembly LOB Rm 736 Albany NY 12248-0001 Office Phone: 718-434-0446. Business E-Mail: jacobsr@assembly.state.ny.us.

JACOBS, RUTH HARRIET, poet, playwright, sociologist, gerontologist; b. Boston, Nov. 15, 1924; d. Samuel J. Miller and Jane G. (Miller); m. Neal Jacobs, Aug. 1948 (div.); children: Eli, Edith. BS, Boston U, 1964; PhD, Brandeis U., 1969. Reporter, feature writer Herald-Traveler, Boston, 1943-49; tchr. Mass. Bay C.C., Northeastern U., 1961-69; prof. sociology Boston U., 1969-82; prof., chmn. dept. sociology Clark U., Worcester, Mass., 1982-87; rsch. scholar women's ctr. Wellesley Coll., Mass., 1985—; prof. human svcs. Springfield Coll., Manchester, N.H., 1988—; lectr. Regis Coll., Weston, Mass., 1989—2002, tchr. lifetime learning, 2005; tchr. Brandeis U. Lifetime Learning, 2000—. Vis. prof. Coll. William and Mary, 1990; vis. rsch. scholar Five Colls. Women's Rsch. Ctr., Mount Holyoke Coll., 1992; spkr. in field. Author: Life After Youth: Female, Forty, What Next, 1979, Button, Button, Who Has the Button, 1983, rev. edit., 1996, (manual) Older Women Surviving and Thriving, 1987, Out of Their Mouths, 1988, Be an Outrageous Older Woman: A.R.A.S.P., 1991, rev. edit., 1993, 2d rev. edit., 1997, We Speak for Peace: An Anthology, 1993, Women Who Touched My Life: A Memoir, 1996, The ABC's of Aging: Mother Ruth Rhymes for Ageing, Sageing and Rageing, 2000, rev. edit., 2005, ABC's for Seniors: Advice from an Outrageous Gerontologist, 2006; co-author: Re-Engagement in Late Life: Re-Employment and Re-Marriage, 1979, (play) Happy Birthday, 2003; contbr. articles to profl. jours., chpts. to books, poetry to anthologies and mags. NIMH grantee, 1972-75; Faculty fellow NSF, 1977-78; recipient Dewing Peace award, Pendle Hill, Walingford, Pa., 1993 Mem.: New Eng. Sociol. Assn. (v.p. 1976, Pioneer award 1993, Athena award for mentoring 1998). Mem. Soc. Of Friends. Home and Office: 75 High Ledge Ave Wellesley MA 02482-1042 Office Phone: 781-237-1793.

JACOBS, SUSAN S., ambassador; b. Detroit, Jan. 1945; m. Barry Jacobs; 3 children. BA in Polit. Sci., U. Mich.; postgrad., George Washington Univ. Various former positions in Caracas, Tel Aviv, New Delhi and San Salvador U.S. Dept. of State; former dep. asst. sec. for global affairs Bur. of Legis. Affairs, Washington; U.S. amb. to Papua New Guinea, 2000—.

JACOBS, TONYA A., lawyer; b. Yoakum, Tex. BA with honors in Hist., U. Tex., Austin, 1991; JD cum laude, U. Houston, 1994. Bar: Tex. 1994, US Dist. Ct. (so. dist. Tex.) 1995, US Dist. Ct. (ea. dist. Tex.) 1996, US Dist. Ct. (no. dist. Tex.) 1999. Ptnr. labor and employment grp. Baker Hostetler, Houston. Mng. editor: Houston Law Rev. Named a Rising Star, Tex. Super Lawyers mag., 2006. Mem.: Tex. Bar Assn., Houston Young Lawyers Assn., Houston Mgmt. Lawyer's Forum, ABA, Houston Bar Assn. Office: Baker Hostetler 1000 Louisiana St Ste 2000 Houston TX 77002 Office Phone: 717-646-1358. E-mail: tjacobs@bakerlaw.com.*

JACOBS, WENDY, editor, realtor; b. Conn. d. Gerald and Eileen Jacobs. BA with hons., U. Conn., 1974; postgrad., The Russian Sch., Northfield, Vt., 1974, Ind. U., 1975, U. Toronto, 1978—79, Three Schs. Art, Toronto, Ont. Coll. Art. With Jours. divsn. Plenum Pub., N.Y.C., 1974—76, 1976—77; with HIAS, Vienna, 1976, Yorkville Press, Toronto, 1977, Macmillan Can., 1977—78, U. Toronto, 1979—80, Harlequin Books/Torstar Enterprises, 1980—81; cons. and editor, 1981—; realtor Prudential Fla. WCI Realty, Boynton Beach. Recipient Svc. award, Internat. Assn. Bus. Communicators, 1992, Hist. Mus. So. Fla., 2004; fellow, U. Toronto, 1978—79. Mem.: Nat. Assn. Realtors, Hist. Mus. So. Fla., Hadassah. Office: 5645 Lakeview Mews Dr Boynton Beach FL 33437 Office Phone: 561-317-3878. Personal E-mail: wjacobs1@aol.com.

JACOBSEN, BARBARA ANN, biology educator; b. Kewanee, Ill., Apr. 7, 1956; d. Allan Duncan and Ruth Caroline Mather; m. Mark Allen Jacobsen, May 30, 1982; children: Joel Allen, Jeremy Mark, Jess Duncan. BA, Augustana Coll., Rock Island, Ill., 1978; M, Truman State U., Kirksville, Mo., 1985, MA, 1984. Tchr. biology Bettendorf Cmty. Sch. Dist., Iowa, 1979—. Curriculum leader Bettendorf Cmty. Sch. Dist., 1991—; team leader Bettendorf H.S., 2000—03. Commn. mem. Bettendorf Recycling Commn., 1979; com. chair Cub Scout Pack 81, 1999—; tchr. Sunday sch. Praise Fellowship, 1997—. Recipient Outstanding Biology Tchr. Iowa, Nat. Biology Tchrs. Assn., 1998. Mem.: Iowa Sci. Tchrs. Assn. (exhibitor coord. 2003—), Bettendorf Edn. Assn. Office: Bettendorf High School 3333 18th Street Bettendorf IA 52722 Office Phone: 563-332-7001.

JACOBSEN, BONNIE LEE, artist, educational consultant; b. Kingston, N.Y., Dec. 15, 1946; d. Ralph Hiram and Olive May Stewart; m. Richard T. Jacobsen, Oct. 19, 1973; m. Kenneth William Lustig, Sept. 7, 1967 (div. Mar. 2, 1973); stepchildren: Richard T Jr., Eric Ernest, Pamela Sue Moats children: Erik David Lustig, Jay Michael. BS, U.Idaho, Moscow, 1983. Employment asst., temp. employment program mgr. Human Resource Svcs., U. Idaho, Moscow, 1988—90; ednl. outreach program mgr. & mgmt. asst. Aquaculture Rsch. Inst., U. Idaho, Moscow, 1990—2002; projects coord. Inland NW Rsch. Alliance, Idaho Falls, 1999—2002; ednl. outreach program cons. Mus. Idaho, Idaho Falls, 2004—05; program mgr., adminstr. profl. and sci. pers. program Wash. State U. & Idaho Nat. Lab., Idaho Falls, 2004—. Various office and project support positions U. Idaho, Moscow, 1968—87. Coach City of Moscow Little League, 1974—75; mem. parents' fund raising com. Found. for Inspiration and Recognition of Sci. and Tech., Moscow, 1995—97; den mother Cub Scout Den Boy Scouts Am., Moscow, 1979—79; vol. ann. blood drive ARC, Moscow, 1990—96; com. mem., & merit badge counselor Boy Scouts Am., local troop, Moscow, 1992—94; mem. parent fund-raising com. Correlli Ensemble Select String Orch., Moscow, 1986—90; mem. McDonald Elem. Sch. PTO, Moscow, 1987—89; com. mem. & chair Cub Scout Pack Boy Scouts Am., Moscow, 1987—88; mem. ednl. program cons., docent Mus. Idaho, Idaho Falls, 2003—05; mem. Art Guild, Idaho Falls, 2000—; U Idaho coll. of engring. vol. project facilitator Found. for Inspiration and Recognition of Sci. and Tech., Moscow, 1996—97; mem. Eagle Rock Art Mus., Idaho Falls, 2001—, Tautphaus Park Zool. Soc., Idaho Falls, 2003—04, BBWI Spouses Orgn., Idaho Falls, 2000—02; various tchg. and leadership roles in women's aux. Ch. of Jesus Christ of Latter-day Saints, Moscow and Idaho Falls, 1978—, pres., children's aux. Idaho Falls, 2001—04. Aquaculture Workshop for Educators, Idaho Dept. of Edn., Sci. and Math Divsn., 2001, Aquaculture: Birth to Release Workshop, Idaho State Bd. of Edn./Eisenhower Found., 1999, Consumer Perceptions of Trout as a Commercial Food Item, (co-author), Idaho Dept. of Agr., 1996-1997. Avocations: art, jewelry design, photography. Home: 2626 Birdie Thompson Dr Pocatello ID 83201 Personal E-mail: bonniejacobsen@msn.com.

JACOBSEN, KAREN LEE, educator, researcher, veterinarian; b. N.Y.C., Feb. 9, 1951; d. Donald James Jacobsen and Dolores Winifred (Sefchik) Bocher: m. Michael Edmund Mispagel, Oct. 3, 1981; children: Heather Michelle, Benjamin Lee BS, Antioch Coll., 1973; DVM, U. Ga., 1978; MS, Mich. State U., East Lansing, 1982. Rsch. assoc. Kettering Labs., Yellow Springs, Ohio, 1973—74; postdoctoral fellow Mich. State U., 1981—82, resident iarge animal medicine, 1979—81, asst. prof., 1982—89, assoc. prof., 1989—. Chmn. rsch. com. U. Ga., Athens, 1986-87 Contbr. articles to profl. jours. and pubs Recipient Norden Disting. Tchr. award U. Ga. Coll. Vet. Medicine, 1987, Outstanding Tchr. awards, 1988, 90 Mem. AVMA (Reviewer 1985—), Am. Assn. Vet. Immunologists, Internat. Soc. Interferon Rsch., Assn. Women Vets. (Spl. award 1978), Am. Assn. Bovine Practitioners, Am. Assn. Vet. Clinicians, Ga. Vet. Med. Assn., Phi Zeta, Omega Tau Sigma, U. Ga. Alumni Assn. (award 1976, 77) Home: 1120 Cherokee Cir Athens GA 30606-5206 Office: U Ga Coll Vet Medicine Dept Large Animal Medi Athens GA 30602

JACOBS GIBSON, ROSE, alderman, not-for-profit developer; b. Fisher, La., Mar. 18, 1947; d. Henry Lee and Clara Lee (Williams) Jacobs; 1 child, Andre Lynard Gibson. Student, San Francisco City Coll., 1965-66, Canada Coll., Redwood City, Calif., 1987, Foothil Coll., 1988-91. Lic. ins. agt., Calif. Ops. officer Bank of Am., Palo Alto, Calif., 1969-72; pers. asst. SRI Internat., Menlo Park, Calif., 1972-75; ins. saleswoman John Hancock Mut. Life, San Jose, Calif., 1975-77; banking office mgr. Security Pacific Bank, San Carlos, Calif., 1978-87; office mgr. YMCA, Palo Alto, 1988-90; founder, pres., CEO Hagar Svcs. Coalition, Inc., East Palo Alto, Calif., 1994—. Co-founder Comty. Network, E. Palo Alto, 1993—; pres. Reign Women's Orgn., E. Palo Alto, 1989-91, E. Bayshore divsn. Am. Heart Assn., E. Palo Alto, 1993-95; mem. Internat. Bible Study Fellowship, Los Altos, 1987-94, Svc. League of San Mateo County, Redwood City, 1993-98; bd. dirs. Am. Heart Assn., Silicon Valley Civic Action; pers. commr. City of E. Palo Alto, 1990-92, city coun. mem., 1992-99, mayor, 1995, 96; mem. San Mateo County Success Adv. Com., Redwood City, 1995—; appointed San Mateo County Bd. Supervisors for the 4th dist. (Redwood City, Menlo Park, E. Palo Alto, N. Fair Oaks), 1999—. Recipient Govt. Svc. award Santa Clara County Mcpl. African Am. Employees Assn., San Jose, 1996, Golden Mic award Frederick Gilbert Assn., Inc., Redwood City, 1996. Mem. Nat. League of Cities, League of Calif. Cities, Calif. Elected Women Assn. Edn. Rsch. Democrat. Baptist. Avocations: creative crafts (gift baskets), bookstore ministry, walking, event planning.

JACOBSON, ANNETTE MOFF, chemical engineer; b. Latrobe, Pa., May 6, 1957; d. Charles James Jr. and Mary Agnes (Antinori) Moff; m. Donald Bruce Jacobson, Aug. 22, 1981; children: Jennifer Lynn, Amanda Rose.

BSChE, Carnegie Mellon U., 1979, PhD in Chem. Engring., 1988. Chem. engr. PPG Inds., Inc., Pitts., 1979-81, sr. rsch. engr., 1981-85; assoc. dir. colloids, polymers & surface program Carnegie Mellon U., Pitts., 1988-89, dir. colloids, polymers and surfaces program, 1989—, lectr. in chem. engring., 1988-95, sr. lectr. chem. engring., 1996-2001, outreach dir. data storage systems ctr., 1999-2001, prin. lectr. chem. engring., 2001—04, prof. chem. engring., 2004—. Workshop lectr. in field. Inventor in field. Recipient G.D. Parfitt award Chem. Engring. Student Group, 1987, Acad. Adv. award Carnegie Mellon U., 2003; Amoco Found. fellow, 1986-88, Carnegie Mellon U. Women's Clan scholar, 1978-79, Babcock & Wilcox scholar Carnegie Mellon U., 1977-79. Mem. AIChE, Am. Chem. Soc., Internat. Assn. Colloid and Interface Scientists, Sigma Xi (corr. sec. 1994-99, v.p. 1996-98). Avocations: gardening, reading, hiking.

JACOBSON, BARBARA DINGER, music educator; d. Norman Bennetch and Ethel Hickernell Dinger; m. Howard Newman Jacobson, Aug. 20, 1961. MusB, New Eng. Conservatory of Music, 1957—62, MusM, 1972—76. Permanent Professional Certification Music Teacher's Nat. Assn., 2001. Music tchr. various Boston schools, 1961—65; mem. New England Chamber Trio, 1972—74; flutist Basking Ridge Symphony Orch., NJ, 1974—78; adj. flute tchr. U. NC, Chapel Hill, NC, 1979—81; flutist Greensboro Symphony Orch., NC, 1979—83; music tchr. Elon Coll., NC, 1983—86; 1st flute Space Coast Symphony Orch., Brevard County, Fla., 1987—91; adj. faculty-flute Fla. So. Coll., Lakeland, 1988—, dir. summer flute workshop, 1993—2005; performer New Eng. Conservatory Orch. Flutist Quintessence Woodwind Quintet, Boston, 1972—74, Radley Woodwind Quintet, Scotch Plains, NJ, 1974—78; sec., v.p., pres., chair of bd. Fla. Flute Assn., 1987—98. Musician: (holiday concerts) Colorado Flute Orchestra, (exchange concerts) American Flute Orchestra; performer: (master classes) Accademia Chigiana, Ramsgate, Royal Coll. of Music. Mem.: Music Teacher's Nat. Assn., Fla. Bandmaster's Assn., Nat. Flute Assn., Fla. Flute Assn. Avocations: photography, travel, reading, stamp collecting/philately. Office: Florida Southern Coll 111 Lake Hollingsworth Dr Lakeland FL 33801-5698 Office Phone: 863-680-4575. E-mail: barbaradjacobson@mac.com.

JACOBSON, BONNIE BROWN, writer, energy executive, statistician, researcher; b. Annapolis, Md., Feb. 15, 1952; d. Albert Robert and Ruth Marie (Puhak) Brown. BS cum laude, LaRoche Coll., Pitts., 1974; MS, U. Pitts., Pa., 1976. Rsch. assoc. Squibb Inst. Med. Rsch., Princeton, NJ, 1976-78; assoc. statistician N.E. Utilities Svc. Co., Hartford, Conn., 1978-80, statistician, 1980-82, sr. statistician, 1982-83, mgr. consumer rsch., 1983-87, corp. statistician, 1987-89; project mgr. energy div. ICF Kaiser Engrs., Fairfax, Va., 1989-91, v.p., 1991-92, AUS Conss., Phila., 1992-94; owner/cons. Energy Access, Maple Glen, Pa., 1995—. Cons. stats., Hartford, 1976—89; adviser Electric Power Rsch. Inst., Palo Alto, Calif., 1978—89; rsch. plan developer Conn. Energy Assistance Study Project, Hartford, 1983—84; evaluation prin. investigator Conn. Low Income Weatherization Conservation Program, 1988—92; microgravity rschr. KC-135 Mission 89-2 NASA, 1989; chmn. Space Access, Inc., 1989—90; mkt. transformation policy devel. MA, 1998—2001; mkt. assessment conservation New England, NJ, Midwest and Southern States, 2001—05; website design and devel. various, 2000—06. Rsch. scholar, U. Pitts., 1974—76. Mem.: Electric Utility Market Rsch. coun., Am. Mktg. Assn., Am. Statis. Assn., Amelia Earhart Soc. Avocations: golf, skiing, tennis, racquetball, reading. Home and Office: Energy Access 1804 Hood Ln Maple Glen PA 19002-6104 Office Phone: 215-542-8659. E-mail: energybbj@aol.com.

JACOBSON, CARRIE ISABELLE, lawyer; BA with distinction, U. Wis., Madison, 1995; JD magna cum laude, Hamline U. Sch. Law, 2000. Bar: Minn. 2000, US Dist. Ct. (dist. Minn.) 2001. Atty. adult prosecution divsn. Hennepin County Atty.'s Office, 1998—2000; assoc. atty. workers' compensation def., underinsured and uninsured motorist def., no-fault arbitrations and personal injury def. litig. Hansen, Dordell, Bradt, Odlaug & Bradt, 2000—02; assoc. atty. workers' compensation def., no-fault arbitrations and personal injury def. litig. Brown & Carlson, P.A., Mpls., 2002—. Primary editor, assoc.: Hamline Jour. Pub. Law and Policy. Named a Rising Star, Minn. Super Lawyers mag., 2006. Mem.: Minn. Women Lawyers, ABA, Minn. State Bar Assn., Minn. Def. Lawyers Assn. Office: Brown & Carlson PA 5411 Circle Down Ave Ste 100 Minneapolis MN 55416 Office Phone: 763-591-9950.*

JACOBSON, ELAINE ZEPORAH, clinical psychologist; b. Bklyn., Feb. 10, 1942; d. Julius Y. and Eleanor (Lebowitz) Finkelstein; m. Howard Jacobson, June 10, 1965; children: Michael, Daniel, Joel, David. AB summa cum laude, Bklyn. Coll., 1963; PhD, Adelphi U., 1968. Lic. psychologist, Ill. Staff psychologist Staten Island (N.Y.) Mental Health Soc., 1967-68, Adler Zone Ctr., Champaign, Ill., 1968-71, chief psychologist mentally ill children's program, 1981-82; rsch. cons. Eric Clearinghouse, Urbana, Ill., 1976-77, Mediax, Urbana, 1977-78; assoc. psychotherapist Family Svc. Champaign County, Champaign, 1977-81, 84-85; staff psychologist Wizo Found., Jerusalem, 1979-80; clin. supr. dept. psychology and psychol. clinic U. Ill., Champaign, 1986-88, 2001—05; pvt. practice Champaign, 1977-81, 84—. Founding chair Patient Adv. Bd. dept. ob-gyn., Carle Hosp., Urbana, 1972-74. Active Hillel Found., U. Ill., 1975—; Zionist affairs chair Hadassah, Champaign, 1980-83. USPHS fellow Adelphi U., 1963-67. Mem. APA, Ill. Psychol. Assn., Champaign Area Psychol. Soc. (officer 1993-94), Phi Beta Kappa. Democrat. Jewish. Avocations: baking, reading, walking, gardening. Office: 1 Greencroft Dr Champaign IL 61821-5118

JACOBSON, FRANCES M., history professor; b. Norfolk, Va., June 23, 1942; d. Joseph Alexander Morris Jr. and Ann Beatrice Ball; m. John Albin Jacobson, June 13, 1967 (deceased); 1 child. BA in Polit. Sci., Old Dominion U., 1983, MA in History, 1990. Figure skating instr. Haygood Skating Ctr., Virginia Beach, Va., 1983-90; adj. prof. history Tidewater C.C., Virginia Beach, 1990-97, asst. prof., 1997—. Adj. prof. history Old Dominion U., Norfolk, Va., 1990-99; dir. internat. studies honors program Tidewater C.C., Virginia Beach, 1998—. Editor: The American Story as Told by Participants, 1999, Voices From History, 2005. Historiographer Episcopal Diocese So. Va.; former vestry mem. St. Andrew's Ch. Avocations: tai chi, skating. Office: Tidewater CC 1700 College Cres Virginia Beach VA 23456-1918 Office Phone: 757-822-7449. Business E-Mail: fjacobson@tcc.vccs.edu.

JACOBSON, JEANNE MCKEE, humanities educator, writer; b. New Brunswick, NJ, Oct. 26, 1931; d. Edward Price and Jean Sheppard McKee; m. John H. Jacobson; children: John E., Jean K. Pokrzywka, Jennie, James G. BA, Swarthmore Coll., 1953; MS, SUNY, Brockport, 1973; PhD, SUNY, Albany, 1981. Gen. studies prin. Hebrew Acad. Capital Dist., Albany, N.Y., 1980-87; adj. faculty SUNY-Albany, Coll. St. Rose, 1983-87; from asst. to assoc. prof. Western Mich. U., Kalamazoo, 1987-95, interim dept. chair, 1993-95; adj. prof. Hope Coll., Holland, Mich., 1995-99; rsch. fellow A.C. Van Raalte Inst., Holland, 1995—2003, rsch. fellow emeritus, 2003—. Author (with others): Albertus C. Van Raalte: Dutch Leader & American Patriot, 1996, A Dream Fulfilled, 1997; author: (textbook) Content Area Reading: Integration with the Language Arts, 1998, Detecta-Crostics: Puzzles of Mystery, 2003; editor: Reading Horizons, 1988—95; assoc. editor: Drood Rev. of Mystery, 1989—. Active majority coun. EMILY's List. Democrat. Presbyterian. Avocations: reading, creating puzzles. Home and Office: 1521 S Lakeshore Dr Sarasota FL 34231-3405 E-mail: jacobsonj@hope.edu.

JACOBSON, JOAN LEIMAN, writer; b. NYC, Apr. 17, 1928; d. Jacob and Sally Grossman Leiman; m. Wilbur Arnold Cowett (div. Nov. 1, 1973); children: Frederick D. Cowett, Anne F. Cowett; m. Julius H. Jacobson II, MD, Nov. 2, 1973. BA, Smith Coll., 1947. Editor bull. Parents League NY, 1965—68; pres. YM-YWHA of NY, N.Y.C., 1978—83, also bd. dirs. Mem. planning and allocations cabinet United Jewish Appeal/Fedn. Jewish Philanthropies, N.Y.C., 1983—; mem. adv. coun. and leadership coun. Harvard Sch. Pub. Health, Boston, 1997—; conservator NY Pub. Libr., N.Y.C., 1995—; bd. dirs. Hudson Rev., N.Y.C., 1999—; leadership coun. & internat. leadership coun. Harvard AIDS Inst., 2005—. Founder Jacobson Ctr. for Writing, Teaching and Learning Smith Coll., Northampton, Mass., 1997; trustee Hebrew Imgrant Aid Soc., 1990—98, mem. scholarship com., 1997—; mem. Harvd AIDS Inst. Leadership Coun., 2005—; bd. overseers Ctr. for Jewish History, 2004—. Mem.: Smith Coll. Club NY (bd. dirs. 1965—68), Poetry Soc. Am. (bd. govs. 1999—), Cosmo. Club.

JACOBSON, KAREN, retired elementary school educator; b. N.Y.C. d. Lawrence and Doris (Case) J. BA in Elem. Edn., SUNY, Potsdam, 1966; MS in Elem. Edn., SUNY, Cortland, 1975; AAS in Advt. Design and Prodn., Mohawk Valley C.C., 1997. Cert. tchr., N.Y. Kindergarten tchr. Mohawk (N.Y.) Sch., summers 1966-72; primary grades tchr. Oriskany (N.Y.) Ctrl. Sch., 1966—96; curator Oriskany Mus., 1998—. Mem. Oriskany PTA; bd. trustees Oriskany Pub. Libr., 1995-2000; mem. Battle of Oriskany Hist. Soc., Friends of Oriskany Battlefield. Mem. Oriskany Tchrs. Assn., N.Y. State United Tchrs. Avocations: church, golf, watercolor painting. Home: 310 Ridge Rd Oriskany NY 13424-4723 Personal E-mail: kjake152@aol.com.

JACOBSON, KATHERINE LOUISE, musician, music educator; b. Mpls., Feb. 16, 1948; d. Donald Robert Jacobson and Clarice Adeline Graff; m. Leon Fleisher, Oct. 6, 1982. MusB, St. Olaf Coll., 1970; MusM, Cleve. Inst. Music, 1974. Piano instr. Cleve. Inst. Music, 1970—76, Peabody Inst. Preparatory, Balt., 1976—86; asst. prof. Goucher Coll., Towson, Md., 1980—2005. Piano ensemble coach Peabody Conservatory Music, Balt., 2000—; performer NPR Performance Today, Aspen Summer Music Festival, 2001, 02, 03, Santa Fe Chamber Music Festical, 2005, Fountainebleau Chamber Music Festival, 2005. Performer: Chgo. Symphony, Balt. Symphony, Balt. Chamber Symphony, Gulbenkian Orch. Portugal, Royal Conservatory Orch., Carnegie Hall, Phila. Orch. Pres. Fleisher-Jacobson Internat. Children's Edn. Found., Balt., 1990—2001; bd. mem. Young Audiences Md., Balt., 1988—90. Recipient 1st prize, Nat. Piano Ensemble Competition, 1977; grantee, Mayor's Adv. Com. on Art and Culture, Balt., 1990. Mem.: Daus. of Norway. Democrat. Avocations: ballet, yoga, swimming. Office: Peabody Conservatory Music I E Mt Vernon Pl Baltimore MD 21202 Office Phone: 410-659-8100 1135.

JACOBSON, LESLIE SARI, biologist, educator; b. NYC, May 22, 1933; d. William and Gussie (Mintz) Goldberg; m. Homer Jacobson, Aug. 18, 1957 (div. Dec. 1995); children: Guy Joseph, Ethan Samuel. BS, Bklyn. Coll., 1954, MA, 1955; postgrad., Columbia U., 1956, Calif. Inst. Tech., 1960; PhD, NYU, 1962. Instr. dept. biology Bklyn. Coll., 1954-57; prof. biology L.I. Coll. Nursing, Bklyn., 1963-74, dean Grad. Sch., 1973-74; asst. prof. biology L.I. U., Bklyn., 1963; fellow dept. chemistry Bklyn. Coll., 1961-63, prof. health sci., 1974—, dean Sch. Gen. Studies and Continuing Higher Edn., 1974-80, dean grad. studies and continuing higher edn., 1980-82, dean grad. studies, 1980-88, dean grad. studies and rsch., 1988-89, prof. dept. health and nutritions scis., 1989—, chair dept. health and nutrition sci., 2003—, exec. dir. Applied Scis. Inst., 1994-95, Koppelman prof., 1995-97; acting v.p. Rsch. Found. CUNY, N.Y.C., 1998—2000. Nat. program chmn. Assn. Continuing Higher Edn., 1978, nat. bd. dirs., 1978-81, pres.-elect, 1980-81, pres., 1981-82; bd. dirs. Ctr. for Labor and Mgmt., N.Y.; dir. N.Y. Regional Cabinet Adult Continuing Edn., 1982—; mem. adv. com. on minorities Coun. Grad. Schs., 1987-90, svcs. com. Grad. Record Exam. Bd., 1990-93; exec. com. univ. com. rsch. awards, CUNY, 1994, vice chmn. com. rsch. awards, 1995-97, co-chair univ. com. rsch. awards, 1996-97; bd. dirs. Hyperion Capital Mgt.; invited spkr. at nat. meetings Issues in Higher Edn.; founder Inst. Ret. Profls. and Execs., Bklyn. Coll., 1976. V.p. Alpha Sigma Lambda Found., 1983-88, Mapleton Midwood Cmty. Health Bd. Inc., 1990-2000, B'nai B'rith Hillel JACY Assn., 1986-93; exec. mem. Hillel of N.Y., 1986-97; bd. dirs. Meth. Hosp., 1989—; trustee St. Francis Coll., Bklyn., 1999— NIH fellow, 1960; recipient Founders Day award NYU, 1961, N.Y. Outstanding Adult Educator award, N.Y.C., 1978, Nat. Merit award, Assn. Continuing Higher Edn., 1984, Leadership award, 1986, Citation for svc. to cmty. N.Y.C. Coun., 1987, Citation for excellence in edn. Bklyn. Boro Pres., 1987, Citation for outstanding svc. to cmty. N.Y. State Assembly, 1987, N.Y. State Senate, 1987, Disting. Preventive Health Leadership award Am. Lung Assn. Bklyn., 1999, Trustee of Yr. award NY Meth. Hosp., 2006. Mem. Am. Lung Assn. (mem. exec. bd. N.Y.C. 2000—, v.p. Bklyn. chpt., pres.-elect 2002—), Sigma Xi, Alpha Sigma Lambda (nat. pres. 1978-80). Achievements include research and publications in bacterial virology and endocrine physiology, and on issues in higher education. Office: Bklyn Coll CUNY Dept Health Nutritional Sci Bedford Ave & Ave H Brooklyn NY 11210 Office Phone: 718-951-5000 Ext. 1234. Business E-Mail: jacobson@brooklyn.cuny.edu.

JACOBSON, MARIAN SLUTZ, lawyer; b. Cin., Nov. 10, 1945; d. Leonard Doering and Emily Dana (Wells) Slutz; m. Fruman Jacobson, Sept. 21, 1975; 1 child, Lisa Wells. BA cum laude, Ohio Wesleyan U., 1967; JD, U. Chgo., 1972. Bar: Ill. 1972, U.S. Dist. Ct. (no. dist.) Ill. 1972, U.S. Ct. Appeals (7th cir.) 1973. Assoc. Sonnenschein Nath & Rosenthal, Chgo., 1972-79, ptnr., 1979—. Mem. vis. com. U. Chgo. Law Sch., 1992-94, 05-. Mem. ABA, Chgo. Coun. Lawyers, Met. Club Chgo. (bd. govs. 1998—), Hyde Park Neighborhood Club (bd. dirs. 2003-). Office: Sonnenschein Nath & Rosenthal 7800 Sears Tower Chicago IL 60606-6491 Office Phone: 312-876-8167. Business E-Mail: mjacobson@sonnenschein.com.

JACOBSON, NINA R., former film company executive; b. 1965; life ptnr.; 2 children. Grad., Brown Univ., 1987. Doc. rschr. Arnold Shapiro Prodns.; story analyst Disney Sunday Movie, 1987; dir. develop. Silver Pictures; head develop. McDonald/Parkes Prodn.; sr. v.p. prodn. Universal Pictures, 1994—95; sr. film exec. DreamWorks SKG, 1995—98; exec. v.p. prodn. Walt Disney Pictures/Hollywood Pictures, 1998; co-pres. Buena Vista Motion Pictures Group (divsn. The Walt Disney Co.), Burbank, Calif., 1999—2000, pres., 2000—06. Named one of 100 Most Powerful Women in Entertainment, Hollywood Reporter, 2004, 2005, 100 Most Powerful Women in World, Forbes mag., 2005, 50 Most Powerful People in Hollywood, Premiere mag., 2004—06; recipient Crystal award, Women in Film, 2003.*

JACOBSON, SABINA, library administrator; b. Bronx, N.Y., Aug. 8, 1929; d. Benjamin and Lena Zeidner; m. Robert I. Jacobson, July 30, 1950; children— Beth, Alice, Marion. BS cum laude in Edn., CCNY, 1950; M.L.S., C.W. Post Coll., Westbury, N.Y., 1968. Head tech. services SUNY-Farmingdale, 1968-72; chief reference librarian George Washington U., Washington, 1972-74; head cataloging U.S. Bur. Census, Suitland, Md., 1974-80; head tech. processes U.S. Dept. Labor, Washington, 1980-83, library dir., 1983—. Mem. Spl. Libraries Assn. Home: 7505 Shadywood Rd Bethesda MD 20817-2065 Office: US Dept Labor Libr 200 Constitution Ave NW Washington DC 20210-0001

JACOBSON, SANDRA W., lawyer; b. Bklyn., Feb. 1, 1930; d. Elias and Anna (Goldstein) Weinstein; m. Irving Jacobson, July 31, 1955; 1 child, Bonnie Nancy. BA, Vassar Coll., 1951; LLB, Yale U., 1954. Bar: N.Y. 1955, U.S. Supreme Ct. 1960, U.S. Dist. Ct. (so., ea. dists.) N.Y. 1972, U.S. Ct. Appeals (2nd cir.) 1975. Ptnr. Mulligan, Jacobson & Langenus, N.Y.C., 1964-88, Hall, McNicol, Hamilton & Clark, N.Y.C., 1988-92; sole practitioner N.Y.C., 1992—2003; atty. NY Sisters Place Legal Counsel Ctr., 2003—. Lectr. in family law. Contbr. articles to profl. jours. and chpts. to books. Mem.: ABA (family law sect.), Internat. Acad. Matrimonial Lawyers, Westchester Women's Bar Assn., Ind. Jud. Screening Panel, Com. to Improve Availability of Legal Svcs., Am. Acad. Matrimonial Lawyers (bd. mgrs. N.Y. chpt. 1987—89, 1991—93, chair lawyer specialization com. 1999—2000, bd. mgrs. N.Y. chpt., 1995-98, 2000-2002, v.p., 1998-2000, 2002-), Westchester County Bar Assn., Assn. of Bar of City of N.Y. (com. women in the cts. 1986—96, sec. 1987—90, state cts. of superior juridiction 1987—90, women in the profession 1989—92, chair 1990—93, chmn. 1990—93, judiciary 1995—99, family law 1999—2000, com. matrimonial law, 1984-87, 2001-, chmn. 1990-98), Women's Bar Assn. of State of N.Y. (chair cts. com. 1987—88, CLE com. 1998—99, by-laws 1999—2001, co-chair amicus com. 2002—, matrimonial com., co-chmn. 1987-89, co-chair task force on ct. reogrn.), N.Y. Women's Bar Assn. (matrimonial and family law com. 1984—2000, chmn. 1986—88, jud. screening com. 1987—88, pres. 1989—90, ethics commn. 1990—), N.Y. State Bar Assn. (co-chair lawyer specialization 1999—, family law sect., legis. and exec. com.), Phi Beta Kappa. Office: NY Sisters Place 2 Lyon Pl Ste 300 White Plains NY 10601

JACOBSON, SIBYL C., insurance company executive; b. Waukon, IA, Sept. 30, 1942; Student, U. Vienna, 1963; BA cum laude, St. Olaf Coll., 1964; MAT, Northwestern U., 1965; PhD, U. Wisc., 1972; certificate Bus. Program, N.Y.U. Grad. Sch. Bus. Adminstrn. Instr. in English Iowa Wesleyan Coll., Mt. Pleasant, 1965-66, Quinsigamond C.C., Worcester, MA, 1966-68; admin. asst. U. Wisc., Madison, 1968-70, instr. Whitewater, 1970-71, asst. prof. English, 1972; Fullbright-Hays sr. lectr. U. Jyvaskyla, U. Turku, Åbo Akademi, Finland, 1973-74; joined Met. Life Found., N.Y.C., 1978; asst. v.p. corp. contributions dept. Met. Life Ins. Co., N.Y.C., 1982—; pres., CEO Met. Life Found., N.Y.C., 1982—; sr. v.p. Met. Life Ins. Co., N.Y.C., 1997—. Cons. arts and bus. coun. N.Y.U.; adj. faculty Grad. Sch. Mgmt. and Urban Professions, Program of Fund Raising Mgmt., New Sch. Social Rsch., N.Y.U. Contbr. articles, reviews to lit. jours. Recipient Outstanding Young Women of Am. award, 1974, Robert E. Kingsley Meml. award Arts and Business Coun., 1981; named among The Acad. of Women Achievers of YWCA, N.Y.C., 1982. Bd. dirs. Nat. Assn. Drug Abuse Problems; Phi Kappa Delta, Phi Beta Kappa. Office: Met Life 27-01 Queens Plaza North Long Island City NY 11101

JACOBSON, SIG-LINDA, obstetrician, educator; b. Klamath Falls, Oreg., Aug. 16, 1951; d. Clarence Holt Jacobson and Sarah Elizabeth Moore; m. John Eric Holmes, June 27, 1979; children: Marie Elizabeth Holmes, Tristan Douglas Holmes. BS, U. Calif., Davis, 1973; MPH, U. Calif., Berkeley, 1974; MD, U. So. Calif. Sch. Medicine, L.A., 1978. Lic. MD 1980, cert. ob/gyn 1980, maternal-fetal medicine. Staff physician Shiprock PMS Indian Hosp., N.Mex., 1982—86; sr. registrar John Radcliffe Maternity Hosp., Oxford, England, 1986—88; asst. prof. ob/gyn Oreg. Health & Scis. U., Portland, 1988—96, assoc. prof. ob/gyn, 1996—. Internat. sci. editor: Brit. Jour. Ob/Gyn, 2005—. Bd. dirs. NARAL Pro-Choice, Portland, 1995, Ctr. for Women's Health, OHSH, Portland, 2003—, Planned Parenthood of Columbia-Willamette, Oreg., 2004—. Fellow: Am. Coll. Obstretricians and Gynecologists; mem.: Internat. Soc. Study of Hypertension in Pregnancy, Soc. Maternal-Fetal Medicine. Democrat. United Methodist. Avocations: gardening, bicycling, piano, reading. Office: Dept Ob-Gyn 3181 SW Sam Jackson Park Rd Portland OR 97239 Business E-Mail: jacobs@ohsu.edu.

JACOBSON, SUSAN BOGEN, psychotherapist; b. Far Rockaway, N.Y., June 19, 1957; d. Paul and Blanche (Itzkowitz) Bogen; m. Adam Hartley Jacobson. BS in Bus. Adminstrn., SUNY, Albany, 1977; MS in Mental Health Counseling, Nova U., Ft. Lauderdale, Fla., 1992. Nat. cert. counselor; lic. mental health counselor, Fla. Pvt. pactice psychotherapist, Boca Raton, Fla., 1992—; instr. CCM Partnerships, Inc., Delray Beach, Fla., 1995—. Officer Coun. for Marriage Preservation and Divorce Resolution, Boca Raton, 1995; mem. 15th Judicial Cir. Ctl Arbitration Com. for Fla. Bar, 1999-2000. Bd. dirs. Aid for Victims of Domestic Assault, 1998. Mem.: ACA. Avocations: golf, boating, gourmet cooking. Office: Ste 104 4710 NW Boca Raton Blvd Boca Raton FL 33431 Office Phone: 561-912-0190. E-mail: sueshrink1@aol.com.

JACOBSON, TRACEY ANN, ambassador; m. Lars Anders Johansson; 1 stepchild, Emmelie Johansson. BA, MA, John Hopkins U. Dep. exec. sec. Nat. Security Coun., Washington; dep. chief of mission US Embassy, Riga, Latvia, 2000—03; US amb. to Turkmenistan US Dept. State, Ashgabat, 2003—06, US amb. to Tajikistan Dushanbe, 2006—. Recipient Superior Honor award, US Dept. State, Meritorious Honor award. Office: US Embassy 7090 Dushanbe Pl Washington DC 20521*

JACOBSON, VERA LEE, secondary school educator; b. San Francisco, Jan. 14, 1952; d. Leo David and Doris Bush (Mulford) Jacobson; m. Paul Vasiliy Kopeikin, Nov. 27, 1975 (div. Feb. 1990); 1 child, Katie Elizabeth Kopeikin; m. Leonard Flores, Jr., Dec. 29, 1993 (div. Feb. 1999). BA in Theatre Arts, Calif. State U., Hayward, 1992; M in Arts Edn., San Francisco State U., 1998. Cert. tchr. English/drama Calif. Realtor Trotter Realty, Burlingame, Calif., 1977-79; tchr. Visitacion Valley Sch., San Francisco, 1994-96, Potrero Hill Mid. Sch. of the Arts, San Francisco, 1996-98, Carlmont HS, Belmont, Calif., 1998—, chair Dept. Bus. Tech. Acad., 2001—. Mem. leadership team Visitacion Valley Sch., 1995—96; judge Shakespeare Festival Calif. State U., Hayward, 1994—95. Dir.: (musical) The Wiz, 1995, Little Shop of Horrors, 1996, 2000, Around the World, 1998, Murder for Rent, 1998, Kiss Me Kate, 1999, Harvey, 1999; actor: Internat. Greek Theatre Festival, 2001, Edinburgh (Scotland) Fringe Festival, 2002. Mem.: Calif. Arts Project (tchr.), Nat. Urban Alliance, Women in Arts, Epilepsy Soc. Am., Calif. Ednl. Theatre Assn. (bd. dirs., New Tchr. of the Yr. 1998), Autism Soc. Am., Performing Arts Libr. Mus., San Francisco Mus. Modern Art. Democrat. Epsicopalian. Avocations: running, performing, sailing, painting, travel. Office: Carlmont H S 1400 Alameda de las Pulgas Belmont CA 94002 Office Phone: 650-595-0210 x8618. Business E-Mail: vjacobso@seg.org.

JACOBS-QUAM, VIVIEN MARIE, retired music educator; b. Dover, N.J., Apr. 8, 1943; d. Charles Jacobs and Elizabeth Toth; m. Leonard Egil Quam, Jan. 6, 1964; 1 child, Leonard Charles Quam. B in Music Edn., Westminster Choir Coll., 1965; MA, Montclair State U., 1972. Cert. music tchr. K-12 NJ. State Dept. Edn., 1965, elem. sch. tchr. NJ. State Dept. Edn., 1986. Tchr. vocal music Sparta Alpine Sch., 1965—66; catering mgr., owner Viking House Delicatessen, Denville, 1972—91; tchr. vocal music Frelinghuysen Twp. Sch., Newton, 1981—85; organist, choir dir. Union Hill Prebyterian Ch., Denville, NJ, 1982—85; tchr. vocal music Lafayette Twp. Sch., Augusta, NJ, 1982—85, Morris Hills Regional Bd. Edn., Rockaway, NJ, 1986—2002; organist, choir dir. Sparta United Meth. Ch., Sparta, 1989—2001. Cons. tchr. fine and performing arts Morris Hills Regional Bd. Edn., Rockaway, NJ, 1997—2002; coach debate and forensics Morris Hills H.S., N.J. Debate League, N.J. Forensics League. Singer (soprano soloist): (high holy days) Northwestern U. Orch, Lakeland Youth Symphony, Westminster Choir Coll. Alumni; dir.(Morris Hills H.S. vocal students): (performance of music with orchestra) Carnegie, Avery Fisher, and Alice Tully Halls (included 25th Ann. Bklyn. Philharm., 1990). Tennis coach Morris Hills Regional Bd. Edn., Rockaway, NJ, forensics coach, 0988—2000, debate coach, 1888—2002, dir. music, 1986—2000; chair choral procedures NJ Music Edn. Assn., 1998—2002; chair region I choral performance Region I Sch. Music Assn., 1988—91. Recipient Honor award, Morris Hills Bd. Edn., 1992, Superior Ratings, Madrigal Choir, Music Performance Festivals, 1998—2002, Northwestern N.J. Music Tchr. of Yr., William Paterson U., 2001; fellow, Northwestern U. Sch. Music, 1986. Mem.: N.J. Ret. Educators Assn. Achievements include original design and a refit for new hardware and software used in the teaching of music theory ear/training and graphic arts in computer labs at Morris Hills Regional District schools; development of general music course in the curriculum at Morris Hills Regional District schools for the non-performance student; an accepted (model) proposal for NJ All- State Women's Chorus which allows many additional talented young NJ women to perform in an honor's choir. Avocations: piano, cross stitch, beading. Home: 41 Rogers Ln Sparta NJ 07871 Office Phone: 973-729-6587. Personal E-mail: vmjq53le@earthlink.net.

JACOBS-SMITH, RUBY EUDORA, retired medical/surgical nurse, retired public health service officer; b. Georgetown, Guyana, Aug. 13, 1921; arrived in U.S., 1963; d. Eustace LeRoy and Emily Alene (Edey) Skeete; m. Randolph C.F. Jacobs (dec.); 1 child, Seth Noel Jacobs; m. William Spencer Smith (dec.). Degree in nursing, midwifery and pub. health, Georgetown Hosp. U., 1944; degree in pub. health adminstrn., Seton Hall U., 1964; degree in psychology and sociology, Upsala Coll., 1968. Cert. pub. health officer NJ; RN NJ. Pub. health officer, nurse NJU State Dept. Health, Trenton, 1964—; health fisitor Newark Health Dept., 1964—75; nurse in charge Univ. Hosp., Newark, 1975—92; ret., 1998. Contbr. articles to profl. jours. Mem. So. Poverty Law Ctr., Montgomery, Ala., 2004; counselor Caribbean Youth Assn., East Orange, NJ, 1971, NJ Fellowship Units Inc., East Orange, 1971. Named Woman of Yr., NJ Fellowship Forum, 1972, East Orange Record, 1972; recipient award for pub. health nursing, NJ State Dept. Health, 1992, award, Union Twp. City Hall, 1992. Mem.: AAUW, Guyanese Cultural Assn.

(founder, fin. sec. 1963, Cmty. Svc. award 1992). Democrat. Episcopalian. Avocations: travel, sports. Home: 213 Hilton Ave Vauxhall NJ 07088 Office: NJ Fellowship Units Inc 213 HIlton Ave Vauxhall NJ 07088 Office Phone: 708-687-7113.

JACOBUS, ELIZABETH LOOMIS, volunteer; b. Chgo., Apr. 18, 1922; d. Eustis Holcomb and Elsie Violet (Cole) Loomis; student public schs., Bothell, Wash.; m. Elbert Ross Jacobus, July 3, 1995, div. Samuel Walker Griffin,; children: James Loomis Ferguson, Thomas Eustis Wells. Bookkeeper, Bekins Moving Co., 1940-42, Keener's Meat Market, 1957-67. Mem. Northshore Bicentennial Com., Bothell, 1974-76; vol. Northshore Senior Ctr.; pres. Colonial Dames XVII Century, 1974-76; dist. pres. Vets. World War I Aux., 1977-78; state regent DAR, Wash., 1978-80. Recipient Americanism award VFW, 1978; medal of appreciation SAR, 1978. Mem. New Eng. Women, Am. Legion Aux., Daus. Brit. Empire, Bothell Hist. Soc., Wash. Gens., Freedom Found., Daus. Am. Colonists. Republican. Baptist. Clubs: Navy Mother's, Rebekahs. Home: 23632 N Lake Cir Bothell WA 98021-8574

JACOBUS, MARY, publishing executive; b. 1957; m. Dean Jacobus; 3 children. BA in English, Le Moyne Coll., Syracuse, NY, 1979. With Buffalo News, NY, Buffalo Courier Express, NY, Long Beach Press-Telegram, NY, 1981—89; dir. sales & mktg. Escondido Times Adv., Calif., 1989—95; v.p. sales & mktg. Colorado Springs Gazette, 1995—98; pres., pub. News Tribune, Duluth, Minn., 1998—2001; pub. News-Sentinel, Ft. Wayne, Ind., 2001—05; CEO Ft. Wayne Newspapers, Inc., Ft. Wayne, Ind., 2001—05; pres., gen. mgr. Boston Globe, 2006; pres., COO Regional Media Group NY Times Co., 2006—. Office: NY Times Regional Media Group 2202 N Westshore Blvd Ste 370 Tampa FL 33607*

JACOBY, BEVERLY SCHREIBER, art consultant; b. Cin., Mar. 25, 1950; d. Ben and Sylvia Schreiber; m. John Eric Jacoby, Aug. 3, 1975; children: Elizabeth, Charles. BA magna cum laude, Barnard Coll., 1972; PhD in Fine Arts, Harvard U., 1983. Expert dept. old master drawings Sotheby's, N.Y.C., 1979-82; fine art cons. Nordstern Ins. Co. Am., N.Y.C., 1985-87; from head dept. old master drawings to sr. tech. expert Christie's, N.Y.C., 1989-92; founder and pres. specializing in appraisals, art adv. svcs. and collections mgmt. Beverly Schreiber Jacoby Fine Arts & Appraisal Svcs., Ltd., N.Y.C., 1992—. Art adv. Weininger Found., Inc., 1999-; cons. Naval War Coll. Ctr. Naval Wargaming Studies (CNWS), Newport, R.I., 2000-01; adj. faculty N.Y.U., Programs in Art Adminstrn., Sch. Continuing and Profl. Studies, 2002-; conf. co-dir., Art in an Age of Uncertainty, 2002; lectr. in field of old master drawings, 18th century French art and the life and career of Francois Boucher. Contbg. author, N.Y. Law Jour.; contbr. articles to profl. jours and mus. exhbn. catalogs. Chair arts & culture adv. com. 14th Congl. Dist., N.Y.C., 1992—; active Sec. Navy's Adv. Subcom. on Naval History, Washington, 1995-2004; juror 14th Congl. Dist. N.Y. Congl. Arts Caucus Art Competition, 2003-. Guest scholar J. Paul Getty Art Mus., Malibu, 1986; Smithsonian fellow, 1978-79, Agnes Mongan Travelling fellow Harvard U., 1977. Fellow The Pierpont Morgan Libr.; mem. Am. Assn. Mus., Appraisers Assn. Am., N.Y. Hist. Soc. (collections com. 1994-2003, juror scholastic art & writing awards 1995), Soc. History Art Francais, Harvard Club N.Y.; mem. ArtTable, Inc.

JACOBY, ERIKA, social worker; b. Miskolc, Hungary, May 1, 1928; came to U.S. 1949; d. Jeno and Malvina (Salamonovits) Engel; m. Emil Jacoby, Sept. 24, 1950; children: Jonathan D., Benjamin M., Michael D. BA, Calif. State U., Northridge, 1971; MSW, U. So. Calif., L.A., 1975. Tchr. Adat Ari El Religious Sch., North Hollywood, Calif., 1961-73; tchr./counselor Camp Ramah, Ojai, Calif., summers 1961-72; clin. social worker Family Svc. of L.A., Van Nuys, 1975-80; psychiatric social worker Kaiser Psychiatry, Van Nuys, 1980—97; ret., 1997; clin. social worker in pvt. practice Valley Village, Calif., 1975—. Lectr. in field; conductor workshops in field. Author: I Held the Sun In My Hands, 2004; contbr. articles to profl. jours. Mem. Nat. Assn. Social Workers, Common Cause, Hadassah, Amnesty Internat., Adat Ari El. Democrat. Jewish. Avocations: reading, biking, music, arts. Office Phone: 818-505-1658.

JACOBY, TERESA MICHELLE, zoologist, consultant, small business owner, entrepreneur; b. El Dorado, Ark., Feb. 12, 1956; d. Ray Ralph and Billie Jean (Burns) Phillips; m. Robert Gregory Oshel Jr., June 23, 1973 (div. Sept. 1975); m. Max Mason Jacoby, Aug. 30, 1976; children: Misty Marie, Melany Michelle. BS in Animal Psychology, Pa. State U., 1980. Nat. spokesperson, show judge Am. Dog Breeders Assn., Salt Lake City, 1984—; owner Rocking J Ranch, Emory, Tex.; First Choice Contractors; co-owner Totalease Concepts Corp. Owner MDM Interior Painting and Design. Author: Innervisions. Mem. S.W. Pit Bull Assn. (charter, founding, past pres.), Lone Star State Pit Bull Club (past sec.), Endangered Breed Assn. (nat. rep.), Responsible Dog Owners of Tex. (founding), North Tex. Pit Bull Club, Am. Quarter Horse Assn., World Wildlife Fedn., Greenpeace. Baptist. Home: 2704 White Oak Dr Plano TX 75074-2931

JACOBY HURD, JENNIFER, foundation administrator; b. 1972; m. Timothy Marc Hurd, July 2002. B in Polit. Sci., Princeton U.; M in Pub. Policy, Harvard U. Strategy cons. Bain & Co., Wilkerson Grp.; exec. dir. Arie and Ida Crown Meml., Chgo. Office: Arie and Ida Crown Memorial 222 N LaSalle St Ste 2000 Chicago IL 60601-1109 Office Phone: 312-750-6671. Office Fax: 312-984-1499.*

JACOFF, RACHEL, Italian language and literature educator; b. N.Y.C., Apr. 5, 1938; d. Richard and Natalie (Wiener) J. BA, Cornell U., 1959; MA, Harvard U., 1960, MPhil, 1963; PhD, Yale U., 1977. Acting asst. prof. U. Va., Charlottesville, 1974-78; asst. prof. Italian, Wellesley (Mass.) U., 1978-83, assoc. prof., 1983-85, prof., 1985—, Carlson prof. comparative lit., 2001—. Vis. prof. Cornell U., Ithaca, N.Y., 1984; vis. prof. Stanford (Calif.) U., 1989, dir. NEH Stanford Dante Inst., 1988. Co-author: Inferno II: Lectura Dantis Americana, 1989; editor: (essays) Dante: The Poetics of Conversion, 1986 (hon. mention Marraro prize 1987), The Poetry of Allusion, 1991, The Cambridge Companion to Dante, 1993, The Poets' Dante, 2001. Fellow NEH, 1981-82, 91-92, Bunting Inst., 1981, Villa I Tatti, 1982, Stanford Humanities Ctr., 1986-87, Rockefeller Found. Bellagio, 1993, 99, Bogliasco Found., 1999. Mem. MLA, Dante Soc. Am. (coun. 1989-92), Medieval Acad. (asst. editor Speculum 1986-99), Save Venice Charter. Office: Wellesley Coll Dept Italian 106 Central St Wellesley MA 02481-8268

JACOX, MARILYN ESTHER, chemist; b. Utica, NY, Apr. 26, 1929; d. Grant Burlingame and Mary Elizabeth (Dunn) J. BA, Syracuse U., 1951; PhD, Cornell U., 1956; ScD (hon.), Syracuse U., 1993, U. Waterloo, 2006. Postdoctoral rsch. assoc. U. NC, Chapel Hill, NC, 1956-58; fellow in fundamental rsch. Mellon Inst., Pitts., 1958-62; rsch. chemist Nat. Bur. Std., Washington, 1962—; fellow Nat. Bur. Std. (now Nat. Inst. Std. and Tech.), Gaithersburg, Md., 1986-95, sci. emeritus, 1996—. Mem. editl. bd. Revs. Chem. Intermediates, 1984-89, Jour. Chem. Physics, 1989-91; contbr. numerous articles to profl. jours. Recipient gold medal U.S. Dept. Commerce, 1970, Fed. Women's award, 1973, Lippincott award, 1989, Hillebrand prize Chem. Soc. Washington, 1990, WISE lifetime achievement award, 1991, E. Bright Wilson award in Spectroscopy, Am. Chem. Soc., 2003, George C. Pimentel award advances in matrix isolation spectroscopy, 2005. Fellow AAAS, Am. Phys. Soc., Washington Acad. Scis. (Phys. Sci. award 1968); mem. Am. Chem. Soc. (bd. mgrs. Chem. Soc. Wash. Sect. 2005-), Exec. Women in Govt. (sec. 1981, vice-chmn. 1982), Inter-Am. Photochem. Soc. (exec. com. 1978-79), Sigma Xi (pres. NBS chpt. 1988-89). Office: Nat Inst Standards & Tech Optical Technology Division Gaithersburg MD 20899-8441 Office Phone: 301-975-2547. E-mail: marilyn.jacox@nist.gov.

JACQUES, PAULA G., literature and language educator; d. Sandra L. Humphrey and Carl J. Gigee; m. Patrick N. Jacques, Dec. 19, 1992; children: Cameron Renee, Hunter Matthew. M in English Edn., E. Carolina U., Greenville, N.C., 2006. English tchr. Havelock (N.C.) H.S., Havelock, 1993—. Mem.: N.C. English Tchrs. Assn. Home: 131 Stonebridge Tr Havelock NC 28532 Office: Havelock High Sch 101 Webb Blvd Havelock NC 28532 Office Phone: 252-444-5112. Personal E-mail: pjacques@ec.rr.com.

JACQUETTE, KATHLEEN MARIE, literature educator; d. George Lawrence and Felicia Penncavage; m. James Hubert Jacquette, Dec. 20, 1969; children: Cynthia, Matthew. BA in English, Bklyn. Coll., 1966, MA in English, 1972; PhD in English, CUNY, 1996. Adj. instr. English dept. Hofstra U., Hempstead, NY, 1983—86; instr. English dept. Farmingdale State U., NY, 1986—88, asst. prof. English, 1988—2000, assoc. prof. English, 2000—06, prof. English, 2006—. Spkr. in field. Recipient NY State Chancellor's award for Excellence in Faculty Svc., 2005. Mem.: MLA, Coordinating Conf. on Coll. Composition, Internat. Assn. for the Study Irish Lit. Avocations: travel, skiing, theater, reading, hiking. Office: Farmingdale State Univ English Dept Knapp Hall Farmingdale NY 11735 Office Phone: 631-420-2258.

JACQUETTE, YVONNE HELENE, artist; b. Pitts., Dec. 15, 1934; Student, R.I. Sch. Design, 1952-56; studies with John Frazier, Robert Hamilton, Herman Cherry, Robert Roche. Instr. Moore Coll. Art, Phila., 1972; instr. painting, vis. artist U. Pa., 1972-76, 79-82, instr. Grad. Sch. Fine Arts, 1979-84; instr. Parsons Sch. Design, 1975-78; instr. painting Pa. Acad. Fine Arts Grad. Sch., 1991—. Vis. artist Nova Scotia Coll. Art, 1974; artist in residence Harvard U., 1995; represented by DC Moore Gallery, N.Y.C., Mary Ryan Gallery (Prints) N.Y.C.; instr. in field. One-woman shows include St. Louis Art Mus., 1983-84, Berggruen Gallery, San Francisco, 1984, Yuracho Seibu-Takanawa Art, Tokyo, 1985, Brooke Alexander Inc., 10 shows 1974-88, 90, 92, 95, NY Mus. Art, Bowdoin Coll. Mus. Art, Maine, 1986, D.C. Moore Gallery, 1997, 00, 03, 06, Mary Ryan Gallery, 1997, Huntington (W.Va.) Mus., 1997, Mention: Retrospective, Cantor Arts Ctr., Stanford (Calif.) U., 2002, Colby Coll. Mus., Waterville, Maine, 2002, Utah Mus., Salt Lake City, 2002, Hudson River Mus., Yonkers, NY, 2003, Arrivals and Departures; 2-person show Mary Ryan Gallery, 1997; exhibited at Rutgers U. Art Gallery, 1972, Whitney Mus. Art, 1972, NY Cultural Ctr. and U.S. Travelling Show, 1972-73, Internat. Biennial, Tokyo, 1974, Art Inst. Chgo., 1975, Mus. Modern Art, NY, 1981-82, Weatherspoon Gallery, NC, Met. Mus. Art, Mus. Modern Art, Whitney Mus. Am. Art, NY, Colby Coll. Mus., Libr. Congress, Washington, Staatliche Mus., Berlin, Carnegie Inst. Mus. Art, Pitts., Am. Acad. Inst. Arts and Letters, NY; represented in permanent collections at North Cen. Bronx Hosp., Horace Mann Sch., Riverdale, NY, Fed. Bldg. and Post Office, Bangor Maine; prints commissioned by Provincetown Fine Arts Workcenter, 1992, Zimmerli Mus. Rutgers, 1993, Bus. Com. for the Arts, 1994, Cleve. Print Club, 1999; illustrator Country Rush, Adventures in Poetry, 1982, Aerial, Eyelight Press, 1981, Fast Lanes, 1984, (with Maureen Owen) Erosion's Pull, 2004; film (with Rudy Burckhardt) Night Fantasies, 1992; set designer Sch. Hardknocks, Dance Theatre Workshop, NYC and nat. tour, 1989 Recipient Nat. Acad. Painters award, 1998; Guggenheim Meml. Found. grantee, 1997-98. Mem.: Am. Acad. Arts and Letters (Painting award 1990), Artists Equity Assn., Nat. Acad. (Painting award 1998, Print award 1999). Office: 50 W 29th St New York NY 10001-4227 Personal E-mail: yvonnejb@mymailstation.com.

JACUS, ANN MARGARET, secondary school educator; b. Allegan, Mich., Aug. 6, 1968; m. Steven Michael Jacus, Aug. 5, 1991; children: Victoria Avalon, Isabelle Grace. MA, Western Mich. U., Kalamazoo, 1999. Cert. tchr. Mich. Math. tchr. Plainwell (Mich.) Mid. Sch., 1996—97, Gobles (Mich.) HS, 1997—. Office: Gobles Pub Schs 409 N State St Gobles MI 49055 Office Phone: 269-628-2113. Office Fax: 269-628-2748. Business E-Mail: ajacus@gobles.org.

JAEGER, ELLEN LOUISE, small business owner; b. Spokane, Wash., Nov. 11, 1949; d. L. Walter and Patricia E. (Kelly) Matson; m. Jerald J. Jaeger, Mar. 24, 1948; children: Jennifer Ann, Jason Joseph. BS in Bus. Mgmt., Lewis-Clark State Coll., 1993; MA in Counseling and Human Svcs., U. Idaho, 1993, M specialist degree in sch. psychology, 1999, D in Counseling and Human Svcs., 2002. Lic. profl. counselor, Idaho. Owner, operator, buyer Reflections Gift Shop, Coeur d'Alene, Idaho, 1986-96; cons. Eagle Springs Gift Shop, Bonners Ferry, Idaho, 1987-90; sch. counselor Sorensen Elem. Sch., 1996—2001; clin. psychologist, 2004—. Appointee N.W. Retail Adv. Bd., Seattle, 1991-95; lic. clin. psychologist, 2004. Vol. office support staff Coeur d'Alene H.S., 1985—86; fundraiser United Way Kootenai County, 1988; mem. Gov.'s Task Force on Immunization and Sch. Safety Panel, 1999—2000, Gov.'s Transition Team, 1999, Gov.'s Task Force on Child Care, 1999; bd. dirs., fundraiser Cancer Cmty. Charities, 1971—91, hon. bd. dirs., 1991—; bd. dirs. PTA-Lakes Jr. H.S., 1980—84, rpes. bd. dirs., 1983—85; bd. dirs., sec. bd. dirs. Kootenai Med. Ctr. Found.; bd. dirs. Coeur d'Alene Pub. Libr. Found. Mem. Rotary Internat. (chmn. group study exch. com. 1992-95, bd. dirs.), Coeur d'Alene C. of C. (bd. mem.).

JAEGER, PATSY ELAINE, retired secondary school educator, artist; b. Douglas, Ariz., Mar. 18, 1936; d. Thomas Conrad and Cora Maxine Forbes; m. John Walter Jaeger, Aug. 26, 1956 (div. Feb. 1984); children: Sherilee Jaeger Zigan, John Everett. BA in Fine Arts, Chapman U., 1961; MA in Art History, Calif. State U., L.A., 1970; MA in Edn. Adminstrn., San Francisco State U., 1988. Life gen. secondary credential life gen. jr. h.s. spl. secondry credential, spl. secondary art credential, preliminary adminstrv. credential, Calif. Tchr. adult edn. oil painting Novato Unified Sch. Dis., 1973—78; tchr. art, chmn. fine arts dept. Torrance (Calif.) H.S., 1962-71; tchr. art and math., chmn. art dept. San Jose Jr. H.S., Novato, Calif., 1974—79; tchr. art and English, chmn. site coun. Hill Jr. H.S., Novato, 1979-83; tchr. English, San Marin H.S., Novato, 1983-95, leadership tchr., 1995-96, tchr. art, 1996-98; semi-ret., 1998; specialist tobacco use edn. Marin County Office Edn., 2000—03, ret., 2003—. Chmn. site rev. team Novato Unified Sch. Dist., 1981; specialist tobacco use edn. Marin County Office Edn., 2000-03. Set designer Cavalleria Rusticana, 1981; cover designer Dimensions III, 1987, NOvato United Meth. Ch. Register, 2005; contbr. articles to profl. jours. Coord. cmty. vol. program Hill Jr. H.S., 1981-83; chair worship Novato United Meth. Ch., 2005—; co-v.p. Novato United Meth. Women, 2005—; co-chair Lydia Cir. United Meth. Women, 2005—. Recipient Pub. Svc. award U.S. Postal Svc., Torrance, 1968, Tchr. of Yr. award Parent-Tchr.-Student Assn. Hill Jr. H.S., 1983, Extra Step award Marin Spl. Edn. Adv. Com., 1996. Mem. Nat. Mus. Women in Arts (charter), Fine Arts Mus. San Francisco, Novato United Meth. Women (co-v.p. 2005—). Republican. Avocations: book illustration, painting, gardening, singing. Home: 40 Brown Dr Novato CA 94947-7404

JAFFE, ELAINE SARKIN, pathologist; b. N.Y.C., Aug. 27, 1943; d. David and Mona (Shane) Sarkin; m. Michael Evan Jaffe, July 22, 1967; children: Gregory, Caleb. AB, Cornell U., 1965; MD, U. Pa., 1969. Cert. Am. Bd. Pathology. Intern in pathology Georgetown U. Hosp., 1969; resident anatomic pathology Clin. Ctr. NIH, Bethesda, Md., 1970-72; sr. investigator lab. pathology Nat. Cancer Inst., NIH, Bethesda, Md., 1974-80, chief hematopathology sect. lab. pathology, 1980—, dep. chief lab. pathology, 1982—2005; acting chief lab of pathology Nat. Cancer Inst. NIH, Bethesda, Md., 2005—. Med. dir. USPHS, 1970—2000; exec. coun. assembly scientists NIH, 2005—; lectr. in field. Assoc. editor: Cancer Rsch.; mem. editl. bd. Am. Jour. Pathology, Blood; mem. editl. bd.: Clin. Lymphoma; mem. editl. bd. Am. Jour. Surg. Pathology; editor: Surgical Pathology of the Lymph Nodes and Related Organs, 1984, 2d edit., 1996, WHO Classification of Hematopoietic and Lymphoid Neoplasms, 2001; contbr. articles to New Eng. Jour. Medicine, Blood. Recipient Fred W. Stewart award, Meml. Sloan Kettering Cancer Ctr., 2002, Walter Putscher Lectureship, Harvard U., 2003, Dir.'s award, NIH, 2005. Fellow AAAS (chair med. scis. sect. 2004-2005); mem. Am. Soc. Hematology (exec. coun. 1988-91), U.S.-Can. Acad. Pathology (pres. 1998-99), Am. Soc. Investigative Pathology (Meritorious awards), Soc. for Hematopathology (pres. 1994-96). Office: NCI NIH Lab of Pathology 10 Center Dr MSC-1500 Bethesda MD 20892-1500 Office Phone: 301-496-0183. Business E-Mail: ejaffe@mail.nih.gov.

JAFFE, GWEN DANER, museum program director, educator; b. NYC, July 8, 1937; d. Izzy and Selma (Hess) Daner; m. Anthony R. Jaffe; children: Thomas, Elizabeth. BA in Art History, Skidmore Coll., 1957; cert. in elem. tchg., Hofstra U., 1960; postgrad., N.Y. Sch. Interior Design, 1964, Columbia U., 1973. Spl. edn. tchr. Payne Whitney Hosp., 1958-65, Bd. Coop. Ednl. Svcs., Westchester, N.Y., 1958-65; designer Jaffe-Halperin Design Firm, N.Y.C., 1965-86; tour guide Walker Art Ctr., Mpls., 1987-89; tchr. Art Express Sch. mus. program Carnegie Mus. of Art, Pitts., 1989—; mem. staff Peace Arts Exch. program Pitts. Children's Mus., 1992-93; interior designer pvt. practice, 1998—. Designer briefcases and handbags Gwynne Collection, 1993-95, fabric design, 2003; art therapist Western Psychiat. Hosp., U. Pitts. Med. Ctr. and Transition Svcs. for Mental Health, 2004—. Mem. Fiber Arts Guild. Home: 1056 Lyndhurst Dr Pittsburgh PA 15206

JAFFE, HELENE D., lawyer; BA magna cum laude, Barnard Coll., 1976; JD, Columbia U. Sch. Law, 1976; Harlan Fiske Stone Scholar. Bar: NY 1977, US Dist. Ct. (So. and Ea. Districts, NY) 1980, US Ct. Appeals (2nd, 3rd, and 8th Districts) 1982, US Supreme Ct. 1982, US Ct. Internat. Trade 1982. Co-head antitrust/competition practice, trade practices and regualtory law dept. Weil, Gotshal & Manges LLP, NYC. Assoc. asst. prof. to adj. assoc. prof. NY U. Sch. Law, 1983—; faculty mem. Ohio Legal Ctr., 1980—; chair Consumer Protection Com.; lectr. in field. Contbr. articles on antitrust, merger, advertising, and marketing issues to profl. publs. Mem.: Assn. Bar City NY (mem. trade regulation com.), NY County Lawyer Assn. (chair, com. on trade regulation), ABA (mem. council antitrust sect., vice-chair Clayton Act Com., antitrust sect.). Office: Weil Gotshal & Manges LLP 767 Fifth Ave New York NY 10153 Office Phone: 212-310-8572. Office Fax: 212-310-8007. Business E-Mail: helene.jaffe@weil.com.

JAFFE, IRMA BLUMENTHAL, art educator; b. New Orleans; d. Harry and Estelle (Blumenthal) Levy; m. Donald Korshak, July 15, 1935 (div. 1941); 1 child, Yvonne; m. Samuel B. Jaffe, June 12, 1941. BS, Columbia U., 1958, MA, 1960, PhD, 1966. Rschr., curator Whitney Mus. Am. Art, N.Y.C., 1963-66; asst. prof. art Fordham U., Bronx, N.Y., 1966-68, assoc. prof., 1968-70, prof., 1970—; cons. Md. Ctr. Public Broadcasting, 1984-85; cultural cons. Italian Encyclopeida Inst., 1986—. Author: Joseph Stella, 1970, John Trumbull: Patriot of the American Revolution, 1975, John Trumbull's Declaration of Independence, 1976, The Sculpture of Leonard Baskin, 1980, Joseph Stella, The Tropics, 1988, Joseph Stella's Madonnas, 1993, Richard Vaux, 1993, Joseph Stella's Symbolism, 1994, Shining Eyes, Cruel Fortune The Lives and Loves of Italian Renaissance Women Poets, 2002, Guiseppe Betussi and Eleonora Falletti: Polygraph and Poet at the Dawn of Popular Literature, 2006; co-author: Selections from the Permanent Collection of the Arkansas Art Center, 1983; contbg. author: Genius of American Painting, 1973, The American Revolution and Eighteenth Century Culture, 1986, Art of the Western World, 1989; editor: (with R. Wittkower) Baroque Art The Jesuit Contribution, 1972, The Italian Presence in American Art 1st vol. 1760-1860, 1989, 2d vol. 1860-1920, 1992; mem. editorial bd. Am. Art Jour., 1981—; contbg. editor Art News jour., 1983—; contbr. articles to profl. jours. Recipient Owl award Columbia U., Virgilliana medal Instituto della Enciclopedia Italiana, Cavaliere Order of Merit Italian Republic, 1995, Cornaro award Ausonian Soc., 2003; NEH fellow, 1973-74; grantee in field. Mem. Am. Studies Assn., Coll. Art Assn., Am. Soc. Italian Legion Merit, Phi Beta Kappa. Avocation: tennis. Home: 880 5th Ave New York NY 10021-4951 Personal E-mail: lbjaffe100@aol.com.

JAFFE, KATHARINE WEISMAN, retired librarian; b. Cambridge, Mass., Apr. 27, 1927; d. Maurice and Esther (Feinberg) W.; m. Myron I. Jaffe, Dec. 18, 1949; children: Stephen Philip, Jane Elizabeth J. Martin, Samuel Morris. AB in Am. Civilization, Colby Coll., 1948; MS in Libr. Sci., Simmons Coll., 1952. Asst. children's libr. Boston Pub. Libr., 1948-51; libr. Mishkan Tefila Synagogue, Newton, Mass., 1955-58, Temple Emmanuel, Newton, 1958-59; reserve libr. Brandeis U., Waltham, Mass., 1960-62; reference libr., archives libr., rare books libr. Boston Coll., 1963-75; vol. libr. and archives libr. Berkshire Hist. Soc., Pittsfield, Mass., 1994-96; chairperson Friends of Libr., New Marlborough, Mass., 1978-94. Libr. rep. to design referenc and Atrium New Libr. Boston Coll., 1973-75; founding chair bookstore Brandeis Women's Com., Noami Lodge, 1950-75; book group leader, organizer, 1955-75; voter edn. chair South and Ctrl. Berkshire chpt. LWV, 1994-96, 97-2001, pres. 1996-97, mem. governing bd.; docent Edith Wharton Home, Mount Lenox, 1988-92; class sec. Colby '48, 1993-98, class agt., 2000—; assoc. editor New Marlborough Hist. Soc. Pictorial Hist. New Marlborough, 2001, sec. New Marlborough Hist. Soc., 2002—; vol. Fairview Hosp., 2006—. Jewish. Avocations: reading, travel. Home: PO Box 113 Mill River MA 01244

JAFFE, LOUISE, literature and language professor, writer; b. Bronx, NY, May 17, 1936; d. Joseph and Anna (Movitz) Neuwirth; m. Steven Jaffe, Aug. 26, 1962 (div. 1975); 1 child, Aaron Lawrence; m. Leo Gerber, 1993. BA, Queens Coll., 1956; MA, Hunter Coll., 1959; PhD, U. Nebr., 1965; MFA, Bklyn. Coll., 1991. From instr. to prof. English Kingsborough C.C., Bklyn., 1965-95, prof. emerita, 1995—. Author: Hyacinths and Biscuits, 1985, Wisdom Revisited, 1987, Light Breaks, 1995, The Great Horned Owl's Proclamation and Other Hoots, 1997, Feminine Prerogative: Three Tales of Empowerment, 2006; author numerous poems and fiction stories; mem. editl. bd. Cmty. Review CUNY, 1984—. Recipient First prize N.Y. Poetry Forum, 1980, First prize, First honorable mention Shelley Soc. N.Y., 1983-84, others. Mem.: Am. Mensa. Democrat. Jewish. Avocations: writing, poetry. Office: Kingsborough Cmty Coll Oriental Blvd Brooklyn NY 11235-4906 E-mail: athena9x@aol.com.

JAFFE, MARCIA WEISSMAN, elementary school educator; b. Bklyn., June 23, 1934; d. Adolph and Marigold (Bush) Weissman; m. Stanley Jaffe, Nov. 23, 1957; children: David, Andrew, Steven. BA, Bklyn. Coll., 1956; MA, John Carroll U., 1977. Tchr. 3d grade E. Meadow (N.Y.) Sch. Dist.; 6th grade tchr., race rels. advisor, pupil pers., learning disabled instr. orgn. Shaker Heights (Ohio) Bd. Edn., 1996—. Founder, adviser student group race rels. S.G.O.R.R, 1983—. Recipient Gov.'s award, Nat. Sch. Bd., Martin Luther King award City of Shaker Heights. Address: 2729 Rochester Rd Cleveland OH 44122-2166 Office Phone: 216-295-4271.

JAFFE, SUSAN, ballerina; b. Washington, 1962; Student, Md. Sch. Ballet; student, Sch. Am. Ballet, Am. Ballet Theatre Sch. With Am. Ballet Theatre II, 1978-80; with Am. Ballet Theatre, 1980—, soloist, 1981-83, prin., 1983—2002, tchr., advisor. Repertoire includes: Le Corsaire, The Merry Widow (by Ronald Hynd), Apollo, Eugene Onegin (by John Cranko), La Bayadere, Bouree Fantastique, Carmen, Cinderella, Concerto, Duets, Giselle, The Guards of Amager, Push Comes to Shove, Symphonie Concertante, Ballet Imperial, Coppelia, Etudes, Giselle, Jardin auxLilas, Romeo and Juliet, The Sleeping Beauty, Other Dances, Theme and Variations, Swan Lake, La Sylphide, Undertow, Voluntaries, Dim Lustre, Manon, Gala Performance, Don Quioxte, Cruel World, Sextet, The Snow Maiden, Fall River Legend, Grande Pas Classic, Stepping Stones, Without Words (by Nacho Duato), Anastasia, others; created role Lynne Taylor-Corbett's Great Galloping Gottschalk, Bruch Violin Concerto No. 1, Serious Pleasures; appeared Spoleto in An Evening of Jerome Robbins Ballets, 1982, Known by Heart (Twyla Tharp); appeared with Kirov Ballet, 1988; guest appearances with The Royal Swedish Ballet, The Royal Danish Ballet, The English Nat. Ballet, La Scala Ballet, Milan, 1997, 98, The Royal Ballet, 1998, 2000, Stuttgart Ballet, 1998, 2000, The Munich Opera Ballet, The Vienna State Opera Ballet; dir. (movie) Angie, by Martha Koolidge. Recipient N.Y. Woman-Lancome Paris Woman of Yr. award, 1989, Dance Mag. award, 2003 Office: Am Ballet Theatre 890 Broadway 3d Fl New York NY 10003-1211

JAFRI, AYESHA, family physician; b. Washington, Dec. 26, 1966; d. Mohammad Haris and Salma Jafri. AB in Chemistry with honors, Bryn Mawr (Pa.) Coll., 1988; MD, Med. Coll. Pa., Phila., 1993. Diplomate Am. Bd. Family Practice. Rsch. asst. NIH, Bethesda, Md., 1987, rsch. scientist, 1988-89; resident in family medicine Lancaster (Pa.) Gen. Hosp., 1993-96; family physician Twin Rose Primary Healthcare, Columbia, Pa., 1996—. Rsch asst. NHBLI, Bethesda, 1987, rsch. scientist, 1988-89; family medicine preceptor Lancastor Family Medicine Residency, 1996—. Vol. physician Water Street Rescue Mission Med. Clin., Lancaster, 1994—; tutor lancaster Literacy Coun., 1993-95. Mem. Am. Acad. Family Physicians, Pa. Med. Soc. Avocations: hiking, bicycling, soccer. Office: Twin Rose Primary Healthcare Box 926 306 N 7th St Columbia PA 17512-2137

JAGACINSKI, CAROLYN MARY, psychology professor; b. Orange, N.J., Apr. 12, 1949; d. Theodore Edward and Eleanor Constance (Thys) Jagacinski; m. Richard Justus Schweickert, Dec. 27, 1980; children: Patrick, Kenneth. AB with honors in psychology, Bucknell U., 1971; MA in Psychology, U. Mich., 1975, PhD in Psychology and Edn., 1978. Rsch. assoc. U. Mich., Ann Arbor, 1978-79, Purdue U., West Lafayette, Ind., 1979-80, vis. asst. prof., 1980-83, rsch. psychologist, 1983-86, vis. lectr., 1986-88, asst. dean, 1988-89, asst. prof. psychology, 1988-94, assoc. prof., 1994—. Contbr. articles to profl. jours. U. Mich. predoctoral fellow, 1977-78, dissertation grantee, 1977-78; Exxon Edn. Found. grantee, 1983-84. Mem. APA, Midwestern Psychol. Assn., Soc. for Judgment and Decision Making, Am. Ednl. Rsch. Assn., Psychonomic Soc., Sigma Xi, Psi Chi. Avocations: tennis, reading. Office: Purdue Univ Dept Psychol Scis West Lafayette IN 47907

JAGDFELD, JUDY A., coach, secondary school educator; b. Elcho, Wis., Oct. 30, 1942; d. Larry Elvis Harteau and Martha Sylvia Boomer; m. James A. Jagdfeld, June 18, 1966; children: Geoffrey A., John C. BS, Wis. State U., Oshkosh, 1964; MEd, Ea. Mich. U., Yipsilanti, 1976. Tchr. and coach Hartland Consolidated Schs., Mich., 1964—, dept. chairperson health and phys. edn., 1974—99. Varsity club sponsor Hartland Consolidated Schs., 1979—99. Pks. and recreation commr. City of Howell, Mich., 1991—2001. Named Tchr. of Yr., Hartland Consolidated Schs., 1999, Boys Regioanl Coach of Yr., 2002, State Coach of Yr. for Mich., 2002, Girls Regional Coach of Yr., 2003. Mem.: USTA (award 2006). Democrat. Avocations: tennis, travel, gardening, golf. Home: 708 W Grand River Howell MI 48843

JAGDMANN, JUDITH WILLIAMS, former state attorney general; b. 1958; d. Glen and Jane Williams; m. Joseph V. Jagdmann; children: Emily, Daniel. Grad., U. Va; JD, U. Richmond. Staff atty. Va State Corp. Commn., 1985—91, asst. gen. counsel, 1991—95, assoc. gen. counsel, 1995—98; dep. atty. gen. State of Va., Richmond, 1998—2005, atty. gen., 2005—06.

JAGERMAN, ADRIENNE, retired elementary school educator, nurse; d. Herman and Margaret (Roth) Israel; m. David Lewis Jagerman; children: Diane, Barbara, Laurie. Student, CCNY; BS, Newark State Coll., 1972. Tchr. 4th grade Cranford Bd. Edn., Cranford, NJ, 1972—94; orthop. nurse Overlook Hosp., Summit, NJ, 1984—94; ret. Tutor, Cranford, NJ, 1976—89; tchr. ednl. workshops, Cranford, NJ; pvt. duty nurse, 1984—90. Mem.: Alpha Sigma Lambda.

JAGGARD, VICKY LYNN, literature and language educator; d. Roger Keith and Nancy Mae Folger; children: Joshua Ryan, Steven Thomas. BS, Hyles-Anderson Coll., Crown Point, Ind., 1982. From sec. to pres. Hyles-Anderson Coll., Crown Point, 1982—84, part-time faculty mem., 1984; part-time tchr. English Chestertown Christian Acad., Ohio, 1992—96; tchr. English and speech Heritage Christian Sch., Brooklyn, Ohio, 1992—. Office: Heritage Christian Sch 4403 Tiederman Rd Brooklyn OH 44144-2329

JAGODZINSKI, CECILE MARIE, librarian; b. Buffalo, Oct. 15, 1951; d. Edwin and Dorothy Evelyn (Majchrowicz) J. BA in English, Canisius Coll., 1978; MLS, SUNY, Buffalo, 1979; CAS in Libr. Sci., U. Chgo., 1985; MA in English, Northwestern U., 1988; PhD, U. Ill., 1996. Cert. tchr. English 7th-12th grade, N.Y., cert. pub. libr., N.Y. Tchr. English various schs., Buffalo, 1972-78; libr. I Buffalo and Erie County Pub. Libr., Buffalo, 1979-80; asst. libr. Quincy (Ill.) Coll., 1980-83; cataloger Northwestern U. Law Libr., Chgo., 1983-84, head retrospective conversion project, 1984-86; mgr. tech. svcs. AMA Libr., Chgo., 1986-88; cataloger Ill. State U., Normal, 1988-89, head catalog dept., 1989-93, coord. collection mgmt., 1993—2002; asst. dir. Ind. U., 2002—03, dir. collection devel., 2003—. Contbr. book revs. and articles to acad. jours. Scholar Canisius Coll., 1969, N.Y. State Bd. Regents, 1969, U. Chgo. Grad. Libr. Sch., 1983. Mem. ALA, MLA, Assn. Coll. and Rsch. Librs., Soc. for History of Authorship, Reading, and Publishing, Renaissance English Text Soc., Renaissance Soc. Am., Beta Phi Mu. Office: Ind U Librs 1320 E Tenth St Bloomington IN 47405

JAGOE, TONYA BURR, elementary school educator; b. Springfield, Tenn., Sept. 12, 1966; d. Aaron Douglas and Lynda Ellis Burr; m. Chuck Jagoe, Apr. 4, 1966; children: Cameron E., Elizabeth C. B in Indsl. Mgmt., Ga. Inst. Tech., Atlanta; M in Tchg., U. N.C., Charlotte. Cert. Nat. Bd. Profl. Tchg. Stds., 2005. Project engr. McKenneys, Inc., Chattanooga, Tenn., 1995—99; 7th grade math tchr. Lincolnton Mid. Sch., NC, 2000—01; 8th grade math tchr. Bradley Mid. Sch., Huntersville, 2001—. Mentor Bradley Mid. Sch. Office: Bradley Mid Sch 13345 Beatties Ford Rd Huntersville NC 28078 Office Phone: 980-343-5750. Personal E-mail: tonya.jagoe@cms.k12.nc.us.

JAGOW, SHELLEY, music educator, musician; BA in Music Edn., U. Sask., Can., 1989; MA in Music Edn., U. Mo., Columbia, 1995; PhD, The Union Inst. and U., Cin. Band dir. Sask. Sch. Sys., Regina and Elrose, 1989—94; assoc. prof. music Wright State U., Dayton, Ohio, 1996—. Vis. scholar Queen's U., Kingston, Ont., Canada, 2000. Conf. co-chair Ohio Music Educators Assn., Columbus. Grantee, New Music Cultivation Fund, 2002; Artist fellow, Culture Works, Montgomery County, Ohio, 2006—. Mem.: N.Am. Saxophone Alliance, Coll. Band Dirs. Assn., Music Educators Nat. Assn., Nat. Assn. Coll. Wind and Percussion Instrs., Coll. Music Soc. Office: Wright State U 3640 Col Glenn Hwy Dayton OH 45435 Office Phone: 937-775-2178.

JAHNKE, CHRISTIANE LYNN, mathematics educator; b. Wis., July 11, 1979; d. Bliss and Maureen Crane; m. Joshua Jahnke, May 4, 2002. BS Math. Edn., U. Wis. Stevens Point, 2001; M Edn., St. Mary's U. Minn., Mpls., 2005. Math tutor Tutoring and Learning Ctr. U. Wis. Stevens Point, 1998—2000, tchg. asst. Math. dept., 2000; tchr. summer sch. Wautoma H.S., Wautoma, Wis., 2001; tchr. H.S. math. Waupaca Sch. Dist., Waupaca, 2001—. Intern coop. Ctr. Small Cities U. Wis. Stevens Point, 2000—01. Mem. choir Zion Evang. Luth. Ch., Neshkoro, Wis., 2001—06. Recipient Chancellor Leadership Award, U. Wis. Stevens Point, 2001, Disting. Achievement in Math. award, 2000; scholar Joseph V. Collins award, 2001; Orville Rice Scholarship, 2000, Kenneth W. Boylan Scholarship, 1999. Mem.: Wis. Math. Coun., Phi Kappa Phi, Phi Eta Sigma, Kappa Delta Pi. Office: Waupaca High School E2325 King Road Waupaca WI 54981 Office Fax: 715-258-4135. E-mail: cjahnke@wsd.waupaca.k12.wi.us.

JAHNKE, LISA JO, secondary school educator; b. La Crosse, Wis., Nov. 3, 1959; d. Richard George and Barbara Jean Caulum; children: Amanda Jo, Mitchel Joe. BS in English Edn., U. Wis., Platteville, 1982; MA in English, Loras Coll., Dubuque, Iowa, 2002. English educator Fennimore (Wis.) Cmty. Schs., 1983—. Drama dir. Fennimore H.S., Wis., 1983—89, cheerleading coach, 1984—99, forensics coach, 2005—. V.p. Fennimore Athletic Booster Club, 2001—06; v.p. ch. coun. St. Peter Luth. Ch., Fennimore, 2002—06; bd. mem. Fennimore Cmty. Theatre Group, 1982—2006. Mem.: Wis. Edn. Assn. Coun., Wis. Coun. Tchrs. English Langauge Arts, Nat. Coun. Tchrs. English, Alpha Omicron Pi. Democrat. Lutheran. Avocations: reading, travel, gardening, golf. Office: Fennimore High School 510 7th St Fennimore WI 53809 Office Phone: 608-822-3245. Business E-Mail: jahnkel@fennimore.k12.wis.us.

JAIN, ASTRID GENDA, obstetrician, gynecologist; b. NYC, Feb. 9, 1967; d. Nirmal Singh and Ute Jain; 1 child, Alexa Kate. BS in Neuroscience, Brown U., Providence, RI, 1989; MD, Vanderbilt U., Nashville, Tenn., 1993. Resident ob-gyn Carolinas Med. Ctr., Charlotte, NC, 1993—97; ob-gyn Eastover Ob-Gyn Assoc., Charlotte, 1997—. Vice chief Cardinas Med. Ctr., Charlotte, 2005—, chmn., quality assessment com., 2005—. Mem.: ACOG, NC Ob-Gyn Assoc. Avocations: exercise, travel, home improvements. Home: 716 Templeton Ave Charlotte NC 28203 Office: Eastover ObGyn Assoc 7810 Providence Rd Ste 105 Charlotte NC 28226

JAITE, GAIL ANN, retired music educator; b. Painesville, Ohio, Mar. 11, 1953; d. Gail Clarence King and Barbara Mary Safick; m. Charles E. Jaite, Jr., Mar. 22, 2003. BA, Hiram Coll., 1975. Music tchr. Jordak Elem. Sch., Middlefield, Ohio, 1975—2005; ret., 2005; prin., owner, trainer in obedience and agility Tall Pines Dog Tng., 2002—. Instr. dog agility Kenston Cmty. Edn., Auburn, Ohio, 2000—02; dir. tri-sch. honors band Cardinal Schs., Middlefield, 1984—2002. Active in cmty. theatre; soloist Geauga County hunger task force. Mem.: Therapy Dog Internat., Music Educators Nat. Conf., Northeastern Ohio Edn. Assn. (leader workshops), Ohio Music Edn. Assn. (American pet dog trainer), Delta Pet Ptnr., Lake Erie Labrador Retriever Club, Buckeye Retriever Club, Northeastern Ohio Dog Club, Delta Kappa Gamma. Home: 13769 Old State Rd Middlefield OH 44062 E-mail: tallpinesk9@hotmail.com.

JAKAB, IRENE, psychiatrist; b. Oradea, Rumania; came to U.S., 1961, naturalized, 1966; d. Odon and Rosa A. (Riedl) J. MD, Ferencz József U., Kolozsvar, Hungary, 1944; lic. in psychology, pedagogy, philosophy cum laude, Hungarian U., Cluj, Rumania, 1947; PhD summa cum laude, Pazmany Peter U., Budapest, 1948; Dr honoris causa, U. Besançon, France, 1982, U. Pécs, Hungary, 1999. Diplomate Am. Bd. Psychiatry, Am. Bd. Pediatric Neuropsychology. Rotating intern Ferencz József U., 1943-44; resident in psychiatry Univ. Hosp., Kolozsvar, 1944-47, resident in neurology, 1947-50; resident internal medicine Univ. Hosp. for Internal Medicine, Pécs, Hungary, 1950-51; chief physician Univ. Hosp. for Neurology and Psychiatry, Pécs, 1951-59; staff neuropathol. rsch. lab. Neurol. Univ. Clinic, Zurich, 1959-61; sect. chief Kans. Neurol. Inst., Topeka, 1961-63; dir. rsch. and edn., 1966; resident psychiatry Topeka State Hosp., 1963-66; asst. psychiatrist McLean Hosp., Belmont, Mass., 1966-67, assoc. psychiatrist, 1967-74; prof. psychiatry U. Pitts. Med. Sch., 1974-89, prof. emerita, 1989—, co-dir. med. student edn. in psychiatry, 1981-89. Dir. John Merck Program, 1974-81; faculty dept. psychiatry Med. Sch., Pecs, 1951-59; asst. Univ. Hosp. Neurology, Zurich, 1959-61; assoc. psychiatry Harvard U., Boston, 1966-69, asst. prof. psychiatry, 1969-74, program dir. grad course mental retardation, 1970-87; lectr. psychiatry, 1974—; editor in chief newsletter Am. Bd. Pediatric Neuropsychiatry. Author: Dessins et Peintures des Aliénés, 1956, Zeichnungen und Gemälde der Geisteskranken, 1956, Pictorial Expression in Psychiatry, 1998; editor: Psychiatry and Art, 1968, Art Interpretation and Art Therapy, 1969, Conscious and Unconscious Expressive Art, 1971, Transcultural Aspects of Psychiatric Art, 1975; co-editor: Dynamische Psychiatrie, 1974; mem. editl. bd. Confinia Psychiatrica, 1975-99; contbr. articles to profl. jours. Recipient 1st prize Benjamin Rush Gold medal award for sci. exhibit, 1980, Bronze Chris plaque Columbus Film Festival, 1980, Leadership award Am. Assn. on Mental Deficiency, 1980; Menninger Sch. Psychiatry fellow, Topeka, 1963-66. Mem. AMA, Am. Psychol. Assn., Am. Psychiat. Assn., Société Medico Psychologique de Paris, Internat. Rorschach Soc., N.Y. Acad. Scis., Internat. Soc. Psychopathology of Expression (v.p. 1959—), Am. Soc. Psychopathology of Expression (chmn. 1965—, Ernst Kris Gold Medal award 1988), Royal Soc. of Medicine (overseas fellow), Internat. Soc. Child Psychiatry and Allied Professions, Internat. Assn. Knowledge Engrs. (v.p. for medicine 1988-95), Deutschsprachige Gesellschaft für Psychopathologie des Ausdruckes (hon. Prinzhorn prize 1967), Hungarian Psychiat. Assn. (hon. 1992), World Psychiat. Assn. (co-chmn. sect. on mass and media and mental health, co-chmn. sect. on psychopathology of expression). Home and Office: 74 Lawton St Brookline MA 02446-5801

JAKIMOWICZ, JOAN MARIE, elementary school educator; b. Passaic, N.J., June 21, 1964; d. John Michael, Sr. and Lillian Alice (Abel) Wojtowicz; m. Philippe Claude Jakimowicz, July 14, 1990. BS in Elem. Edn., Seton Hall U., South Orange, NJ, 1986. Cert. elem. edn. tchr. N.J. Dept. Edn., 1986, social studies tchr. N.J. Dept. Edn., 1986, nursery sch. tchr. N.J. Dept. Edn., 1986. Tchr. 6th grade Passaic Bd. Edn., NJ, 1986—87, tchr. 3d grade, 1987—96, tchr. 4th grade, 1996—. Mem. & former co-chairperson # 3 Sch. Leadership Coun., Passaic, 1995—; mem. sch. adv. bd. #3 Sch. Instrnl. Leadership Team, Passaic, 2003—; mem. Sch. Focus on Results Com., Passaic, 2003—. Current soloist and former lead soprano in defunct ch. choir Holy Rosary R.C. Ch., Passaic, 1980—. Mem.: Assn. for Curriculum Devel., NEA, N.J. Edn. Assn. Home: 59 Elm Hill Rd Clifton NJ 07013 Office: Mario J Drago Sch # 3 155 Van Houten Ave Passaic NJ 07055 Office Phone: 973-470-5503.

JAKUB, KATHLEEN ANN, medical/surgical nurse; b. Pitts., June 9, 1947; d. Michael E. and Mary Ellen (Kirchner) J. Diploma, St. Francis Med. Ctr., 1968; BA in Sociology, BA Adminstrn. Justice, U. Pitts., 1979, BSN, 1992; MS in Profl. Leadership, Carlow Coll., 1996. Cert. intermediate care nurse, trauma nurse, otorhinolaryngology and head-neck nurse. Staff nurse phys. rehab. St. Francis Med. Ctr., Pitts., 1968—70; staff nurse-orthopedics-plastics U. Pitts. Med. Ctr., 1970-75; staff nurse head/neck and ophthalmology, 1975—88; patient care mgr. med. and surg. unit U. Pitts. Med. Ctr., 1988—96, case mgr. neurosurgery dept., 1996—99, case mgr. performance improvement dept. Pitts., 1999—2001; mgr. quality improvement U. Pitts. Cancer Ctrs., 2001—03; triage nurse, outpatient dept. Hillman Cancer Ctr., 2003—. Nursing rep. radiation safety com. U. Pitts. Med. Ctr. Mem. Soc. Head and Neck Nurses, Am. Trauma Soc. Home: 4372 Winterburn Ave Pittsburgh PA 15207-1185 E-mail: jakubk@msx.upmc.edu.

JAKUBS, DEBORAH, university librarian; BA, U. Wis. Madison; MLIS, U. Calif. Berkeley; PhD in Latin Am. history, Stanford U., 1986. With Duke U., Durham, NC, 1983—, previously libr. for Latin Am. & Iberia, head Internat. and Area Studies Dept., dir. Collections Svc., now Rita DiGiallonardo Holloway U. Libr. and Vice Provost for Libr. Affairs, 2005—. Assoc. dir. U. NC-Duke U. Consortium in Latin Am. Studies, 1995—97, 2000—02, dir., 1997—99; chair Area Studies Coun. of Ctr. for Rsch. Libr.; mem. steering com. Program for Latin Am. Libr. & Archival Collections Harvard U.; adj. prof. history Duke U. Mem.: Assn. Rsch. Libraries (vis. program officer 1996—2002). Office: 220 Perkins Libr Duke U Durham NC 27708 Office Phone: 919-660-5800. E-mail: deborah.jakubs@duke.edu.*

JALALI, BEHNAZ, psychiatrist, educator; b. Mashad, Iran, Jan. 26, 1944; came to U.S., 1968; d. Badiolah and Bahieh (Shahidi) Samimy; m. Mehrdad Jalali, Sept. 18, 1968. MD, Tehran U., Iran, 1968. Rotating intern Burlington County Meml. Hosp., Mt. Holly, NJ, 1968—69; resident in psychiatry U. Md. Hosp., Balt., 1970—73; asst. prof. psychiatry dept. psychiatry Sch. Medicine Rutgers U., Piscataway, NJ, 1973—76, Yale U., New Haven, 1976—81, assoc. clin. prof. psychiatry, 1981—85; assoc. clin. prof. psychiatry dept. psychiatry UCLA, 1985—94, clin. prof. psychiatry dept. psychiatry Sch. Medicine, 1994—. Dir. psychotherapy Sch. Medicine Rutgers U., Piscataway, 1973-76; dir. family therapy unit dept. psychiatry Yale U., New Haven, 1976-85; chief clin. med. svcs. Mental Health Clinic, 1987-96; coord. med. student edn. in psychiatry West LA VA Hosp., 1985—2000; dir. family therapy clinic W.Va. VA Hosp., 1991—, co-leader Schozophrenia Clinic, Mental Health Clinic, West LA VA Med. Ctr., 1996—; med. dir. Mental Health Clinic, West LA VA Med. Ctr., 2004-. Author: (with others) Ethnicity and Family Therapy, 1982, Clinical Guidlines in Cross-Cultural Mental Health, 1988; contbr. articles to profl. jours. Fellow Am. Psychiatric Assn., Am. Orthopsychiatry Assn., Am. Assn. Social Psychiatry; mem. Am. Family Therapy Assn., So. Calif. Psychiatric Assn. (chair com. for women 1992), World Fedn. Mental Health. Avocations: photography, hiking, cinema, painting. Home: 1203 Roberto Ln Los Angeles CA 90077-2304 Office: UCLA Dept Psychiatry West LA VA Med Ctr B116aa Los Angeles CA 90073-1003 Office Phone: 310-268-4651. Business E-Mail: behnaz.jalali@med.va.gov.

JALBERT, AMY, science educator; b. Farmington, Maine, Dec. 11, 1974; d. Michael and Sue Jalbert. BS in Biochemistry, U. Maine, 1998, M in Edn., 1993. Gifted & talented tchr. Londonderry (NH) Mid. Sch., 1998—2000; life sci. tchr. McKelvie Mid. Sch., Bedford, NH, 2001—. Soccer coach McKelvie Mid. Sch., 2002—. Office Phone: 603-472-3951.

JALBERT, JANELLE JENNIFER, executive recruiter, secondary school educator; d. Gerald Edward and Linda S. Jalbert. AA, Pasadena City Coll., 1995; BA cum laude, Calif. State U. Northridge, 1998; MEd, Nat. U., 2004, MA in Cross Cultural Tchg., 2006. Character edn. cert. U. San Diego Ext., 2004, cert. tchr. AP English lit., composition UCLA, 2005. Tchr. Sun Valley Mid. Sch., Calif., 1999—2000, New Ave. Ednl. Ctr., Monterey Park, Calif., 2000—02; owner, educator Solteria Acad., Monrovia, Calif., 2001—; prin., owner Jalbert-Thomason Photography, Arcadia, Calif., 2003—04; tchr. English, activities dir. Monrovia H.S., 2004—05; tchr. English Bonita H.S., La Verne, Calif., 2005—. Bd. dirs., pres., assoc. Delta Dimensions, 2003—; cons. Hondiat Inc., Arcadia, Calif., 1994—; co-founder, cons. YouCanDo-Travel.com, 2004—; presenter in field. Author: Success Skills, 2001, Get Gatsby and Other Greats in Five Minutes a Day, 2006. Fundraiser, mem. crew Calif. AIDS Ride 4 &5, LA, 1997—98; founder Nat. U. Sigma Tau Delta, 2006—; ptnr. Life in the Word, Fenton, Mo., 2001—, World Changers Ministries, College Park, Ga., 2001—, Jesse Duplants Ministries, New Orleans, 2002—; ptnr. Aaron's Army TD Jakes Ministries, Dallas, 2003—04. Grantee Ednl. award, Sunshine Brooks Found., 1994, Sushine Brooks Found., 1995, John Glyes Ednl. Fund, 1997; scholar Collegiate Honor scholar, Nat. U., 2002. Mem.: Jr. C. of C. (com. Kasukabe, Japan Visitation 1999), Soroptimist Internat. (mem.Arcadia/Monrovia chpt. 2003—04, Youth Citizenship award 1991), Pi Lambda Theta (presenter internat. convention 2005), Blue Key (bd. dirs. 1996—98, Cmty. Svc. award 1996), Foothill Panhellenic, Omicron Delta Kappa (pres. 1997—98), Alpha Gamma Sigma (chair fundraising 1994—95), Sigma Kappa Alumnae (1st v.p. membership 2003—05). Avocations: travel, languages, wine, marine activities, photography. Office: Bonita High Sch 3201 D Street La Verne CA 91750 E-mail: booksnmore4u@hotmail.com.

JALENAK, PEGGY EICHENBAUM, volunteer; b. Little Rock, Oct. 14, 1935; d. E. Charles and Helen Lockwood Eichenbaum; m. Leo Richard Jalenak, Jr., Aug. 28, 1955; children: Laurie J. Williamson, Terri J. Mendelson, Jan J. Ordway, E. Charles. Commr., vice chair Tenn. Art Commn., Nashville, 1975—80; bd. dirs., exec. com. Tennesseans for Arts, Nashville, 1981—85; bd. dirs. Tenn. State Mus. Found., Nashville, 1994—2003. Bd. dirs. Nat. Found. Jewish Culture, N.Y.C., 1999—; former bd. dirs. Ballet Memphis, Theatre Memphis, Memphis Arts Coun., Memphis Jewish Fedn., 1997—, Bornblum Solomon Schechter Sch., 2002—; former bd. dirs., sec., treas. Opera Memphis; bd. dirs., past pres., sec. Memphis Jewish Hist. Soc. Memphis & Mid-South, 1998—; bd. dirs. Temple Israel Mus., 2001—; adv. bd. Judaic studies program U. Memphis, 2000—. Named Tenn. Arts Amb., Tenn. Arts Commn., 1985. Home: 6025 River Oaks Rd Memphis TN 38120

JALONEN, NANCY LEE, academic administrator, educator; b. Hollywood, Calif., Oct. 28, 1927; d. Earle Reynolds and Hazel Lee (Griffin) MacNaught; m. John William Jalonen, June 26, 1955; children: Wendy Anne Fawthrop, Christopher Lee. BA, Stanford U., 1948, MA, 1950. Instr. drama Pasadena City Coll., Calif., 1950—55; instr. Coll. San Mateo, Calif., 1956—78; exec. dir. San Mateo County Arts Coun., 1978—84; chair dept. comm. Notre Dame de Namur U., Belmont, Calif., 1985—95. Prodr., moderator ednl. TV Sta. KCSM-TV, San Mateo, 1965—78; comm. cons., 1977—79. Trustee Theatreworks, Palo Alto, Hillbarn Theatre, Foster City, 2000—06, San Mateo Pub. Libr., 2001—. Named to San Mateo County Women's Hall of Fame, 1989; recipient BRAVO! award, 2002. Mem.: Am. Arts Coun., AAUW. Democrat.

JALONGO, MARY RENCK, educator; b. Pitts., Jan. 30, 1950; d. Herbert Hanson and Felicia Ann (Gemmellaro) Renck; m. Frank Severio Jalongo, Aug. 13, 1977. BA in English, U. Detroit Mercy, 1971; MAT, Oakland U., 1972; PhD, U. Toledo, 1978. Tchr. Capac (Mich.) Local Sch., 1971-72, Cloverleaf Local Sch. Dist., 1972-75; grad. asst. U. Toledo, 1975-78, instr., 1977-78; asst. prof. Ind. U. of Pa., 1978-82, assoc. prof., 1982-85, prof. profl. studies in edn., 1985—. Lectr. in field; conductor seminars in field; cons. in field. Author: Young Children and Picture Books, 1988, 2d edit., 2004, Early Childhood Language Arts, 3d edit., 2007, Thinking Creative and Arts-Based Learning, 4th edit., 2006, The World's Children and Their Companion Animals, 2004, Exploring Your Role: A Practitioner's Introduction to Early Childhood Education, 2007; contbr. articles to profl. jours., chapters to books. Recipient nat. award Am. Assn. Higher Edn., 1985, Ednl. Press Assn. Am., 1988, 91, 2004, Pa. Outstanding Young Woman award, 1983, others; named Disting. Prof. Ind. U. Pa., 1991-92. Home: 654 College Lodge Rd Indiana PA 15701-4015 Office: Ind U Pa 122 Davis Hl Indiana PA 15705-0001 Office Phone: 724-357-2417. E-mail: mjalongo@iup.edu.

JAMELLI, MIRIAM H., music educator, counseling administrator; b. Hazleton, Pa., Oct. 3, 1941; d. William Francis and Grace Gertrude Howells; m. Robert Louis Jamelli, Mar. 9, 1974; children: Roseann, Max Brian. MusB, Coll. Misericordia, 1963; MS, U. Scranton, 1965. Tchr. Hazleton Area Sch. Dist., 1963—75; tchr., counselor Diocese of Scranton, Hazleton, 1996—. Dir. music Holy Rosary Ch., Hazleton, 1966—, Choralairs, Hazleton, 1966—. Recipient Fine Arts Achievement, Hazleton C. of C., 1976. Mem.: Nat. Pastoral Musicians, Music Edn. Nat. Assn. Republican. Roman Catholic.

JAMERSON, SANDRA MARIEA, music educator; b. El Dorado, Ark., June 5, 1961; d. Willie and Mary Helen Davis; m. William Napoleon Jamerson, June 8, 1985; 1 child, LaNora Nichelle. BA, Lane Coll., Jackson, Tenn., 1983; MEd, S.W. Kansas U., Magnolia, Ariz., 2001. Min. of music Russell Temple CMEC, 1978—98, FBC-Cordell, El Dorado, 1987—2006; choral dir. gen. music Southside Elem., El Dorado, 1983—86, Watson & Fairview, El Dorado, 1983—86, Retta Brown, El Dorado, 1993—2005; choral dir. Barton J. H.S., El Dorado, 2005—. Pvt. piano instr., El Dorado, 1983—; mem. adv. bd. edn. El Dorado Schs., 2002—04; music instr. Upward Bound Magnolia So. Ark. U., 2001—04. Composer: (gospel songs) Jesus the Light of the World, 1985, I Want the Word to Know about Your Love, 1986. Recipient African-Am. Tchr. award, 2003, Achievement award, 1st Bapt. Ch. Mem.: Ark. Choral Dirs., Music Educators Nat. Conf. Baptist. Avocations: reading, movies, HG-TV. Office: Barton Jr H S 400 W Faulkner El Dorado AR 71730

JAMES, ANN, physical therapist; b. LA, Aug. 10, 1970; d. Dennis Alton and Kathleen Ann Shanelec; m. Frank Anthony James, 2006. BA in Bus. Econs., U. Calif., Santa Barbara, 1993; MS in Phys. Therapy, Columbia U., NYC, 1997. Lic. phys. therapist Calif. Phys. therapist King/Drew Med. Ctr., LA, 2000—03, Cedars Sinai Med. Ctr., LA, 2000—; case mgr. OrthoNet, Long Beach, Calif., 2003—; sales rep. USANA, Long Beach, 2006—. Tutor, mentor Covenant Presbyn. Ch., Long Beach, 2004—. Presbyterian. Avocations: yoga, tennis, hiking. Home: 2621 E 20th St # 17 Signal Hill CA 90755 Personal E-mail: tas2107@columbia.edu.

JAMES, BETTY M., secondary school educator; b. Cleve., Aug. 23, 1923; d. Frank E. Jankovsky and Libbie Kopecky; m. Bart M. James Jr., June 20, 1952 (div.); children: Bart, Tom(dec.), Leslie. BS, Miami U., Oxford, Ohio, 1945; MS, NYU, NYC, 1951. Tchr. North Royalton HS, Ohio, 1945—51, Bedford HS, Ohio, 1951—52, Lansing Jr. HS, Mich., 1952—53, South HS, Lansing, 1953—54. Named Vol. of Month, 1987, Vol. of Yr., 1999; recipient Phoenix 100 award, 1989. Home: 3028 W Morrow Dr Phoenix AZ 85027-4920

JAMES, CLARITY (CAROLYNE FAYE JAMES), mezzo soprano; b. Wheatland, Wyo., Apr. 27, 1945; d. Ralph Everett and Gladys Charlotte (Johnson) J. Mus.B., U. Wyo., 1964; Mus.M., Ind. U., 1967. Cert. instr. Radiance Technique. Prof. voice Radford (Va.) U., 1990—. Asst. prof. voice U. Iowa, Iowa City, 1968-72 Debut in opera as Madame Flora in: The Medium, St. Paul Opera, 1971; also sang role with Houston Grand Opera,

1972, Opera Theatre St. Louis, 1976, Augusta (Ga.) Opera Co., 1976; N.Y.C. Opera debut as Baroness in: The Young Lord, 1973; N.Y.C. Opera debut as Widow Begbick in Mahogonny, Opera Co. of Boston, 1973; created role Mother Rainey in: The Sweet Bye and Bye, 1973; Mrs. G. in: Captain Jinks, 1976; Mrs. Cratchit in A Christmas Carol (Musgrave), 1979; created Mrs. Doc in world premiere of A Quiet Place (Leonard Bernstein), Houston, 1983; debut Chgo. Lyric Opera, 1983, Vienna Staatsoper, 1986, National Symphony, 1986, Phila. Orch., 1986; numerous appearances with opera cos. throughout U.S. and fgn. countries including, Dallas Civic Opera, Cin. Opera Co., Netherlands Opera, Amsterdam, Florentine Opera. Rec. artist. Martha Baird Rockefeller grantee, Corbett Found. grantee, 1968; Met. Opera Assn. grantee; recipient Lillian Garabedian award Santa Fe Opera, 1967, Exemplary Alumni award U. Wyo., 1994; named Young Artist Nat. Fedn. Music Clubs, 1972. Office: Radford U Dept Music Radford VA 24142 Office Phone: 540-831-5296. Business E-Mail: cjames@radford.edu.

JAMES, CLAUDIA ANN, public speaker, corporate trainer, writer; b. Kansas City, Mo., July 23, 1948; d. Claude Jr. and Edna Mae (Henderson) Hinton; m. Wavy L. James, Oct. 21, 1967 (dec. Apr. 1991); children: Edward Allan, Sheryl Evonne. AA cum laude, Maple Woods CC, Kansas City, Mo., 1987; BSE cum laude, Mo. Western State Coll., St. Joseph, 1989. Cert. Myers/Briggs type indicator. Fin. sec. EBC, Kansas City, 1977-87; instr. Capital City Bus. Coll., Kansas City, 1989-90, Career Point Bus. Sch., Kansas City, 1990-91; owner James Ednl. Mtgs./Seminars (JEMS), Kansas City, 1992—; nat. spkr. Nat. Seminars Group, 1997—. Instr. Mo. Western State Coll., St. Joseph, 1993—, Independence Sch. Dist., Mo., Park Hill Sch. Dist., Kansas City, Mo., North Kansas City Sch. Dist., 1993—, Maple Woods CC, Kansas City, 1990—; guest spkr. on radio and TV; regularly featured in local newspapers and mags.; presenter more than 900 workshops; nat. and internat. trainer. Mentor WNET-SBA and WISE-UP-DOL, Kansas City, 1992—. Higgs Art scholar, 1987. Mem. ASTD, Nat. Spkrs. Assn., Kansas City C. of C., Mo. We. State Coll. Alumni Assn., Kappa Delta Phi. Democrat. Baptist. Avocations: art, music, poetry, travel, theater. Office: James Ednl Meetings/Seminar 2501 NW 79th Terr Ste 203 Kansas City MO 64151 Office Phone: 816-420-8686. E-mail: jemscaj@aol.com.

JAMES, DIANNE, mathematics educator; b. Asheville, N.C., June 16, 1962; d. Billy C. and Dell W. Hawkins; m. William C. James, Mar. 17, 1989. BSBA, Appalachian State U., Boone, N.C., 1984; MEd, Ga. Southwestern U., Americus, 2001. Purchasing mgr. Kellwood Co., Perry, Ga., 1992—97; planner Hollingsworth & Vose, Hawkinsville, Ga., 1997—98; tchr. 8th math Crisp County Mid. Sch., Cordele, Ga., 2000—02, Bonaire Mid. Sch., Bonaire, Ga., 2002—. Office: Bonaire Mid Sch 125 Hwy 96 E Bonaire GA 31005 Office Phone: 478-929-6235.

JAMES, DONNA A., diversified financial services company executive; m. Larry James; children: Christopher, Justin. B in Acctg., NC Agrl. & Tech. State U. CPA. Auditor Coopers and Lybrand; with Nationwide Mutual Ins. Co., 1981—, v.p., asst. to chmn. and CEO, 1996, v.p. human resources, 1996—97, sr. v.p. human resources, 1997—99, sr. v.p., chief human resources officer, 1999—2000, exec. v.p., chief adminstrv. officer, 2000—03, dir. life ins. and life and annuity ins., 2001—02, pres. strategic investments, 2003—. Bd. dirs. Ltd. Brands, Inc. Bd. govs. United Way; bd. advisors sch. bus. NC Agrl. Tech. Sate U.; trusususutee Bennett Coll. Recipient Spirit of Advocacy award, 2001, Outstanding African-Am. Woman in Fin. Svcs. award, Mark D. Philmore Urban Bankers, Ohio Women of Courage award. Office: Nationwide Mutual Ins Co One Nationwide Plaza Columbus OH 43215-2220

JAMES, DOROTHY LOUISE KING, special education educator; b. Columbus, Miss., Jan. 1, 1952; d. T.B. and Dorothy (Lee) King; m. Willie Earl James, July 7, 1979, children: Ebun, Shantana, Leah, Trinita, Caleb. BS magna cum laude, Harris Stowe Coll., 1979; M in Spl. Edn., U. Mo., 1988; EdD in Guidance Counseling, Lael Coll. and Grad. Sch., 1998. Itinerant resource instr. Northwest High Sch., St. Louis, 1978-80; instr. learning disabilities Cleveland High Sch., St. Louis, 1980-84, Clinton Mid. Sch., St. Louis, 1984-91; resource tchr., unit leader A-team for alternative edn. Stevens Mid. Sch., St. Louis, 1992—2002; resource tchr. Vashon H.S., 2003—. Team leader, resource tchr., The New Vashon HS, 2003—; "A" team unit leader alternative edn. Stevens Mid. Sch. 1988-2000, Drug Free Schs. and Communities Program, 1993; counselor King-James Enterprises, St. Louis, 1988—; team leader, resource tchr., founder Student Response Team, St. Louis, 1988—. Editor (speech) Internat. Yr. of the Child, 1979 (Bravo award Youth Adv. Comsn. St. Louis County Youth Programs), Clinton Middle School Student Handbook, 1989, team leader Drug Free Schools Community Program. Youth adv. mem. Conflict Mediation, 1992-96; mem. support coun. Stevens Mid. Sch., 1992-96; active New Ebenezer Bapt. Ch. Recipient Excellence in Drug Prevention award U.S. Dept. Edn., 1994, cert. of commendatio, 1994; granteee Power X, The Positive Peer Coalition; winner KPLR-TV Promoting Pers. and Comty Health, 1997. Mem. Coun. for Exceptional Children, Alpha Kappa Alpha. Avocations: reading, walking, stamp collecting/philately, cooking. Home and Office: 2431 Strawberry Fields Ct Florissant MO 63033-1765

JAMES, ELIZABETH JEANETTE THOMPSON, science educator; b. Auburn, Ala., Nov. 6, 1950; d. Robert Ingram and Bettye Weaver Thompson; m. Dwight Moody James Jr., June 23, 1972; children: Ashley, Kristin. BA, West Tex. A&M U., Canyon, 1972; MS, U. N.C., Greensboro, 1980. Cert. secondary edn. Tex. Tchr. Copperas Covo Ind. Sch. Dist., Tex., 1973—75, Buncomo County Schs., Ashville, NC, 1975—77; supr. DNA lab. Gene Proof Tech., Nashville, 1989—99; tchr. Williamson County Schs., Franklin, 2001—. Expert witness State of Tenn.; elder Hillsboro Presbyn. Ch., Nashville, 1989—. Named Tchr. of Yr., Ravenswood H.S. Faculty, 2006. Mem.: NEA, Tenn. Edn. Assn., Williamson County Edn. Assn., Book Club. Democrat. Achievements include development of Gene Proof Technologies' DNA laboratory. Avocations: reading, gardening, travel. Office: Ravenwood HS 1724 Wilson Pl Brentwood TN 37027

JAMES, ELIZABETH JOAN PLOGSTED, pediatrician, educator; b. Jefferson City, Mo., Jan. 15, 1939; d. Joseph Matthew Plogsted and Maxie Pearl (Manford) Plogsted Acuff; m. Ronald Carney James, Aug. 25, 1962; children: Susan Elizabeth, Jason Michael. BS in Chemistry, Lincoln U., 1960; MD, U. Mo., 1965. Diplomate Am. Bd. Pediat., Am. Bd. Neonatal-Perinatal Medicine. Resident in pediat. U. Mo. Hosps. & Clinics, Columbia, 1965-68, fellow in neonatology, 1968-69, dir. neonatal-perinatal medicine Children's Hosp., 1971—; fellow in neonatal-perinatal medicine U. Colo. Hosps., Denver, 1969-71; from asst. to assoc. prof. pediatrics and obstetrics sch. medicine U. Mo., 1971-83, prof. child health and obstetrics, 1983—. Dir. pediatric edn. program dept. child health sch. medicine U. Mo., Columbia, 1989-98. Mem. editl. bd. Mo. Medicine, 1983—; contbr. chpts. to books and articles to profl. jours. Fellow Am. Acad. Pediat. (sect. neonatal-perinatal medicine); mem. Mo. State Med. Assn., Boone County Med. Soc., Alpha Omega Alpha. Roman Catholic. Avocations: classical music, bicycling, gardening. Office: U Mo Hosps & Clinics Childrens Hosp 1 Hospital Dr Columbia MO 65201-5276 Office Phone: 573-882-7919. Business E-Mail: jamese@health.missouri.edu.

JAMES, ELIZABETH R. (LEE LEE JAMES), bank executive; b. Columbus, Ga., June 11, 1961; m. David M. (Sandy) James Jr.; children: David, Parker. BA in polit. sci., Auburn U., 1983; grad., Cannon Fin. Inst. Trust Sch., 1988; grad, Duke U. Exec. Edn., 1990. Mem. staff Trust Dept. Columbus Bank and Trust Co. Synovus Fin. Corp., Columbus, Ga., 1986—89, dir. training TSYS, 1989—90, v.p., human resources dir. TSYS, 1990—94, sr. v.p., human resources dir. TSYS, 1994—95, sr. v.p., human resources divsn. officer Synovus Svc. Corp., 1995—96, pres. Synovus Svc. Corp., 1996—2000, chief people officer, 1996—, vice chmn., chief info. officer, 2000—, dir., 2001—. Mem. tech. secretariat adv. group Banking Industry. Chmn. staff parish St. Paul United Meth. Ch., mem. adminstrv. bd.; chmn. The Alexis de Tocqueville Soc. of United Way; bd. dir. Columbus (Ga.) Symphony, Ronald McDonald House; mem. YMCA Task Force Com.; chmn. Leadership Devel. Task Force Gov.'s Comm. for a New Ga. Named Woman of Yr. in Tech., Tech. Assn. of Ga., 2002; named one of The 25 Most Powerful Women in Banking, US Banker mag., 2003, 2004. Mem.: Alexis deTocqueville Soc. United Way (past chmn.), Library Found., Fin. Svcs. Roundtable. Office: Synovus Financial Corp PO Box 120 Columbus GA 31902*

JAMES, ESTELLE, economist, educator; b. Bronx, NY, Dec. 1, 1935; d. Abraham and Lee (Zeichner) Dinerstein; m. Ralph James (div. 1971); children: Deborah, David; m. Harry Lazer, June 27, 1971 (dec. 1994). BS, Cornell U., 1956; PhD, MIT, 1961. Lectr., econs. dept. U. Calif., Berkeley, 1964—65; acting asst. prof. Stanford U., 1965—67; assoc. prof. SUNY, Stony Brook, 1967—72, prof., 1972—94, provost, div. Social and Behavioral Sci., 1975—79, chmn. dept., 1982—86. Vis. scholar Yale U., Australian Nat. U., Tel Aviv U., Brookings Inst., others; cons. World Bank, Washington, 1986—91, sr. economist, 1991—94, lead economist, 1994—2000, cons., 2000—; vis. fellow Urban Inst., Washington, 2002—04; mem. governing bd. Kosovo Pension Saving Trust, 2001—. Author: (book) Hoffa and the Teamsters, 1964, The Nonprofit Sector in Market Economies, 1986, Pub. Policy and Pvt. Ed. in Japan, 1988, The Nonprofit Sector in Internat. Perspective, 1989, Averting the Old Age Crisis, 1994; contbr. articles to profl. jour. Fellow, Woodrow Wilson Internat. Ctr., Washington, 1981—82, Netherlands Inst. Advanced Study, 1986—87, U.S. Dept. Edn., 1988, Sec. of Navy, 1990, AAUW, Soc. Sci. Rsch. Coun.; grantee, Spencer Found., USAID, NEH, Exxon Edn. Found., Mich. Retirement Rsch. Consortium, Smith Richardson Found.; Fulbright awardee, 1979. Mem.: Am. Econs. Assn. Office Phone: 202-338-7108. Business E-Mail: ejames@estellejames.com.

JAMES, ETTA (JAMESETTA HAWKINS), recording artist; b. LA, Jan. 25, 1938; d. Dorothy Leatherwood Hawkins; m. Artis Dee Mills, May 20, 1969; children: Donto, Sametto. Blues singer Johnny Otis, L.A., 1954, Bihari Bros. Record Co., L.A., 1954, Leonard Chess Record Co., L.A., 1960, Warner Bros., L.A., 1978, Fantasy Record, L.A., 1985, Island Record, L.A., 1988. Record Albums include Respect Yourself, 1997, Love's Been Rough on Me, 1997, Come A Little Closer. The Essential Etta, 1993, Etta James Rocks the House, Etta, Red Hot'n Live, Her Greatest Sides, Vol. 1, Live, 1994, Mystery Lady: Songs of Billie Holliday, 1994 (Grammy award 1994), R&B Dynamite, 1987, reissue, 1991, The Right Time, 1992, Rocks the House, 1992, The Second Time Around, 1989, Seven Year Itch, 1988, Sticking to My Guns, 1990, The Sweetest Peaches, 1989, The Sweetest Peaches: Part One, 1989, The Sweetest Peaches: Part Two, 1989, Tell Mama, 1988, These Foolish Things: The Classic Balladry of Etta James, 1995, Time After Time, (with Eddie Cleanhead Vinson) Blues in the Night, Lane Supper Club, 1986, Blues in the Night, Vol. 2, 1987, Twelve Songs of X-mas, 1988, Life, Love & the Blues, 1988, Heart of a Woman, 1999, 20th Century Master: The Best of Etta James, 1999, Platinum Series, 2000, The Chess Box, 2000, Matriarch of the Blues, 2000, Etta James, 2001, Love Songs, 2001, Blue Gardenia, 2001, Blowin' in the Wind, 2002, Live and Ready, 2002, Burnin' Down the House, 2002, Let's Roll, 2003, Rock Me Baby, 2004, Live in New York, 2005. Recipient Lifetime Achievement award Rigby & Blues Assn., 1989, Living Legends award KJLH, 1989, Image award NAACP, 1990 W.C. Handy award, 1989, Blue Soc. Hall of Fame award, 1991; 5th Handy Blues award, 1993, 94, Soul of Am. Music award, 1992; 8 Grammy nominations, Beyond War award, Best Song, 1984; inducted into Rock & Roll Hall of Fame, 1993; sang opening ceremony of 1984 Olympics. Office: Etta James Enterprises 16409 Sally Ln Riverside CA 92504-5629

JAMES, JEANNETTE ADELINE, state legislator, accountant, small business owner; b. Maquoketa, Iowa, Nov. 19, 1929; d. Forest Claude and Winona Adeline (Meyers) Nims; m. James Arthur James, Feb. 16, 1948; children: James Arthur Jr., Jeannette, Alice Marie. Student, Merritt Davis Sch. Commerce, Salem, Oreg., 1956-57, U. Alaska, 1976—77. Payroll supr. Gen. Foods Corp., Woodburn, Oreg., 1956-66; cost acctg., inventory control clk. Pacific Fence & Wire Co., Portland, Oreg., 1966-67, office mgr., 1968-69; substitute rural carrier U.S. Post Office, Woodburn, 1967-68; owner, mgr., acct. and tax preparer James Bus. Svc., Goldendale, Wash., 1969-75, Anchorage, 1975-77, Fairbanks, Alaska, 1977—83, North Pole, Alaska, 1983—; co-owner, mgr. Jolly Acres Motel, North Pole, 1987—; mem. Alaska Ho. of Reps., Juneau, 1993—2003; chmn. House State Affairs, 1995-2000, Ho. of Reps., 1998—2002; vice chmn. Legis. Coun., 1995-96; chmn. joint com. jud. com., 1998—2002; vice chmn. Legis. Coun., 1995-96; chmn. joint com. Adminstrv. Regulation Rev., 1997-98, ho. majority leader, 2001—02. Instr. workshop Comm. Dynamics, 1988; railroad advisor to Gov. Murkowski, 2003-. Vice chmn. Klickitat County Dems., Goldendale, 1970-74; bd. dirs. Mus. and Art Inst., Anchorage, 1976-80; pres. Anchorage Internat. Art Inst., 1976-78; chmn. platting bd. Fairbanks North Star Borough, 1980-84, mem. Planning Commn., 1984-87; treas., vice chmn. 18th Dist. Reps., North Pole, Alaska, 1984-92; mem. City of North Pole Econ. Devel. Com., 1992-93; mem. Rep. State Ctrl. Com., 2004—. Named Legislator of Yr., Alaska Farm Bur., 1994, Alaska Outdoor Coun., 2000, Juneau Empire, 2002, Guardian of Small Bus., Nat. Fedn. Ind. Bus., 1998, Friend of Psycology, 2001; recipient Defender of Freedom award, NRA, 1994, Friend of Municipalities award, Alaska Mcpl. League, 1996, Courage in Preserving Equal Access award, Alaska chpt. Safari Club Internat., 2000, Cmty. Svc. award, Arctic Alliance for People, 2001. Mem. Internat. Tng. in Comm. (Alaska State winner speech contest 1981, 86), North Pole C. of C., Emblem Club, Rotary (treas. North Pole 1990, v.p. membership 2004-05, pres.-elect 2005-), Eagles, Women of Moose Presbyterian. Avocations: bowling, dolls, children. Home: 3068 Badger Rd North Pole AK 99705-6117 Office Phone: 907-488-9339. Personal E-mail: jamesjeannette@gci.net, usually@acsalaska.net.

JAMES, JENNIFER DUFAULT, lawyer; BA summa cum laude, Rutgers U., 1988; JD cum laude, Harvard U., 1991. Bar: Supreme Ct. of US, US Ct. Appeals (1st. & 3rd. cir.), US Dist. Ct. (ea. dist.) Pa. Ptnr., vice chair Litig. Svcs. Dept. Schnader Harrison Segal & Lewis LLP, Phila. Named one of 40 Under 40, Phila. Bus. Jour., 2006. Mem.: ABA, Phila. Bar Assn., Pa. Bar Assn., Phi Beta Kappa. Office: Schnader Harrison Segal & Lewis LLP 1600 Market St, Ste 3600 Philadelphia PA 19103-7286 Office Phone: 215-751-2446. E-mail: jdjames@schnader.com.*

JAMES, KATHLEEN MARIA, music educator; b. Evergreen Park, Ill., Apr. 8, 1949; d. Rozalyn Gaddis and Thomas White; m. Richard Ellery James, Apr. 3, 1982; children: Patricia Carol, Teresa Maureen. MusB in Edn. (hon.), U. Fla., Gainesville, 1971, MEd, 1972. Cert. tchr. music edn. k-12 Fla. Elem. specialist and choral dir. Summers Elem. Sch., Lake City, Fla., 1972—73; music educator, band and chorus dir. Ft. Clarke Mid. Sch., Gainesville, 1973—75; music specialist K-8, band dir. 4-8 St. Mary Magdalen Sch., Altamonte Springs, Fla., 1977—96; choral dir., piano lab instr. Milwee Mid. Sch., Longwood, Fla., 1997—. Dir. St. Mary Magdalen Handbell Choir, Altamonte Springs, Fla., 1984—2006; mem. St. Mary Magdalen Handbell Choir, Altamonte Springs, 1984—2006. Named Tchr. of Yr., Milwee Mid. Sch., 2005; recipient Crystal Apple Nat. award, Time Warner, 1998—99, 2002, Star Tchr. Nat. award, Bright House Networks, 2003—04, 2006, Teacherrific award, Disney, 2001; grantee, Found. for Seminole County Sch., 1997—98. Mem.: Fla. Music Educators Assn. (assoc.), Music Educator Nat. Conf. (assoc. 25 yr. svc. award 2002), Optimist Club (assoc.). Avocations: golf, dog training. Home: 524 Ridgeline Run Longwood FL 32750 Office: Milwee Mid Sch 1341 S Ronald Reagan Blvd Longwood FL 32750 Office Phone: 407-320-3846. Office Fax: 407-320-3899. Personal E-mail: kathyj0407@aol.com. E-mail: kathleen_james@scps.k12.fl.us.

JAMES, KATHRYN A., secondary school educator; b. Springfield, Mo., Aug. 1, 1925; d. Joseph Fred and Sybil Mae (Rogers) Giboney; m. Charles Elwyn James, Jan. 24, 1948 (wid. May 1999); children: Kathryne Janette, Jacquelyn Annette, Charles Roger. BSEd, S.W. Mo. State Tchrs. Coll., Springfield, 1945; MA, U. Mo., 1955; postgrad., U. Va., 1968. Cert. tchr. Calif., Kans., Ky., Ind., Mo., Va. Art supr. Mountain Grove (Mo.) Pub. Schs., 1945-47; art instr. Moberly (Mo.) Jr. Coll., 1947-49, Exptl. Sch., Springfield, Mo., 1949-54; art and home econs. instr. Ashland (Ky.) Pub. Schs., 1954-59; intinerant art tchr. Boyd County (Ky.) Pub. Schs., 1960-63; tchr. U. Ky., Lexington, 1963-65; art inst. Fairfax Pub. Schs., Va., 1965-68; art tchr. Terre Haute (Ind.) Pub. Schs., 1968-73, Springfield (Mo.) Pub. Schs., 1973-87. Judge sewing contests Singer Sewing Machine Co., Ashland, 1957-59, tchr. sewing classes pub. schs., adult evening and pub. sch. art classes, Ashland, 1956-58, Springfield, 1982-83. Author curriculum/art dept. Ashland and Terre Haute schs., 1955, 67-68; designer/banner constructor: Richard Ghephardt, Springfield, 1987. Campaigner Mo. State Legislators, Springfield, 1980-81, others. Recipient Gov.'s award Hon. Order of Ky. Cols., Lexington, 1965. Mem. Ky. Cols., Nat. DAR (flag chmn. 1991—2004, art awards 1995-97). Methodist. Avocations: china painting, interior decorating, freelance art work. Home: 1019 Joanne Dr Webb City MO 64870-1778 Personal E-mail: jameswood@joplin.com.

JAMES, KAY COLES, former federal agency administrator; b. Portsmouth, Va., June 1, 1949; d. Susie Armistead Coles; m. Charles Everett James; children: Charles Jr., Elizabeth, Robert III. BS, Hampton (Va.) Inst., 1971. Traffic svc. advisor C&P Telephone, Roanoke, Va., 1971-72, group supr., 1973, force mgr., 1974; conf. coord. devel. disabilities project State of Va., Richmond, 1978-79; asst. to housing coord. Housing Opportunities Made Equal, Richmond, 1980-81, dir. community edn. and devel., 1981-83; personnel dir. Cir. City Stores, Beltsville, Md., 1983-85; dir. pub. affairs Nat. Right to Life Com., Washington, 1985-88; asst. sec. pub. affairs US Dept. Health & Human Services, Washington, 1989—90; assoc. dir. Office of Nat. Drug Control Policy, 1991—93; sr. v.p. Family Rsch. Coun., 1993—94; sec. Va. Dept. Health & Human Resources, Richmond, 1994—96; dean Sch. of Govt. Regent U., 1996—99; sr. fellow of the Citizenship Project Heritage Found., 1999—2001; dir. US Office of Pers. Mgmt., Washington, 2001—05. Pres. Black Ams. for Life, Washington, D.C., 1985-88; asst. sec. pub. affairs HHS Office of the Sec., Washington, D.C., 1989—; mem. White House Com. on Children, Washington, D.C., 1988, White House Task Force on Blacks, Washington, D.C., 1988, Nat. Coalition on Pro-Family Issues, Washington, D.C., 1988; co-founder Nat. Family Inst., Washington, D.C., 1987; chair, Nat. Gambling Impact Study Com., 1999-2001. Contbr. numerous articles to jours. and newspapers. Recipient Disting. Fed Svc. award, Nat Assn. Hispanic Fed. Executives, 2004. Republican. Presbyterian. Avocations: reading, walking, cooking.

JAMES, LINDA COATES, elementary school educator; b. Reno, Nev., Jan. 20, 1954; d. David Allison and Ethel Bluemel Coates; m. Donald Lyle James, Nov. 3, 1977; children: Camille James Bradshaw, Spencer, Laurel, Craig, Janelle. BS in Elem. Edn., Brigham Young U., Provo, Utah, BS in Early Childhood, 1977, diploma in ESL, 2000; postgrad., So. Utah. U., Cedar City. Tchr. Uintah County Sch. Dist., Lyman, Wyo., 1976—77, Provo Sch. Dist., 1977—78, Alpina Sch. Dist., American Fork, Utah, 1978—80; kindergarten tchr. Jordan Sch. Dist., Sandy, Utah, 1980—83, 5th grade tchr., 1994—. ESL specialist Columbia Elem., West Jordan, Utah, 1995—97, Jordan Hills Elem., West Jordan, 1997—2003; team leader Jordan Hills 5th Grade, West Jordan, 2004—. Mem. Women's Relief Soc., 1972—, pres., 1989—2001; Rep. county del. Salt Lake City, 1986—94; Rep. state del., 1994—98. Grantee, Jordan History Acad., 2005—06. Mem. Lds Ch. Avocations: scrapbooks, gardening, sewing, basketball. Office: Jordan Hills Elem 8892 S 4800 W West Jordan UT 84088 Office Phone: 801-565-7163.

JAMES, LINDA DIANE, media specialist; b. Dalhart, Tex., June 21, 1957; d. Lewis Daniel Wilcox and Claudene (Isaacs) Mayhan; m. Russell Dean James, Nov. 22, 1974; children: Steffanie, Ryan. BS, West Tex. A&M U., 1989, postgrad., 1991—; MS in Info. Sci., U. N. Tex., 2002; cert. in libr. media specialist. Cert. generic spl. edn. tchr., Tex.; cert. elem. sch. tchr., Tex. Tchr. spl. edn. reading and lang. Willow Vista Elem. Sch., River Road Ind. Sch. Dist., Amarillo, Tex., 1989-92, content mastery coord., 1993—95, at-risk coord., 1994—98; with Rolling Hills Elem., 1999—2004; libr. media specialist River Rd. Mid. Sch., 2004—. Mem. strategic planning com. River Road Ind. Sch. Dist., 1992-93, 2001-03, mem. dist.-wide ednl. improvement coun., 1995-96; mem. Children's Emergency Home Com., 1995-96. Author pilot program Mastering Acad. Curriculum, Willow Vista Elem. Sch., 1993-95. Mem. com. mid. high youth group Lawndale Ch. of Christ, Amarillo, 1994-96; mem. com. Hi Plains Children's Home, Amarillo, 1995-96; mem. com. Boy Scouts Am., 1990-94, Explorer advisor, 1993-94; active Bonham Mid. Sch. PTA, 1993—; content mastery facilitator Region XVI, 1996; com. mem., treas. Boy Scouts Am., 1994-2006 Named one of Outstanding Young Women of Am., 1988. Mem. Am. Tchrs. and Profl. Educators, Coun. for Exceptional Children (mem. divsn. for learning disabilities), Assn. Tex. Profl. Educators (pres. 2005-06, resolutions com. chair, 2005-06 region dir. 2006—) Mem. Ch. of Christ. Avocations: painting, reading, boating, scrapbooks. Office: Willow Vista Elem Sch 5703 W 48th Ave Amarillo TX 79109-5701 Office Phone: 806-383-8721. Business E-Mail: linda@mac2.net.

JAMES, LULA BONDS, science educator, small business owner, apparel designer; b. Meadville, Miss., Mar. 16, 1948; d. Luther and Clara P. Bonds; m. Lawrence Earl James, Dec. 18, 1971; children: Valliery, Sandra, Lawrence Jr. Student, Alcorn A&M Coll., 1971; MS, Alcorn State U., 1978; BS in Biology, Alcorn State U, 1988. Phys. edn. tchr. Franklin H.S., Meadville, Miss., 1972—83, Franklyn Elem., 1983—88; health tchr. Co-Lin Jr. Coll., Natchez, Miss., 1983—84, Ruthwood Elem. Sch., Newellington, La., 1988—89; sci. tchr. Higgins Middle Sch., McComb, Miss., 1989—91, Natcliez Mid. Sch., 1991—. Treas. supr. Neighborhood Youth Corp., Chgo., 1967; owner Lorenata's Wedding Boutique, Natchez, 2001—05. Mem. Natchez Recreation Bd., 1990—92, Natchez Bus. Civic League, 2005; mem. Chair Ptnr. Edn., 2004—. Recipient Tchr. of Year, Natchez Adams Sch Dist., 2003—04. Mem.: NAACP (Medgar Evers award 1993), Miss. Assn. Educators, Nat. Sci. Tchr. Assn., Delta Sigma Theta. Democrat. Methodist. Avocation: flower arranging. Home: 106 Meadowlane Dr Natchez MS 39120 Office Phone: 601-442-5926. Personal E-mail: luladst@bellsouth.net.

JAMES, MARIE MOODY, clergywoman, musician, vocal music educator; b. Chgo., Jan. 23, 1928; d. Frank and Mary (Portis) Moody; m. Johnnie James, May 25, 1968. B Music Edn., Chgo. Music Coll., 1949; postgrad., U. Ill., Champaign-Urbana, 1952, 72, Moody Bible Inst., Chgo., 1963-64; MusM, Roosevelt U., 1969, MA, 1976; DD, Internat. Bible Inst. and Sem., Plymouth, Fla., 1985; postgrad., Trinity Evang. Div. Sch., Deerfield, Ill., 1995; DRE, Logos Grad. Sch., 1995. Key punch operator Dept. Treasury, Chgo., 1950-52; tchr. Posen-Robbins Bd. Edn., Robbins, Ill., 1952-59; tchr. vocal music Englewood High Sch., Chgo., 1964-84; music counselor Head Start, Chgo., 1965-66. Exec. dir. House of Love DayCare, 1983, 88, Mary P. Moody Christian Acad., 1989, supt., 1989; dir. Handbell Choir for Srs. Maple Park United Meth. Ch., 1988-92; bd. dirs. Van Moody Sch. Music, Chgo. Composer, arranger choral music: Hide Me, 1963, Christmas Time, 1980, Come With Us, Our God Will Do Thee Good, 1986, The Indiana House, 1987, Behold, I Will Do a New Thing, 1989, Mary P. Moody Christian Academy School Song 1989, Glory and Honor, 1992. Organist Allen Temple A.M.E. Ch., 1941-45; asst. organist Choppin A.M.E. Ch., 1945-49; organist-dir. Progressive Ch. of God in Christ, Maywood, Ill., 1950-60; missionary Child Evangelism Fellowship, Chgo., 1955-63; unit leader YWCA, New Buffalo, Mich., 1956-58; min. of music God's House of All Nations, Chgo., 1960-80; pastor God's House of Love, Prayer and Deliverance, Robbins, 1982—; chmn. Frank and Mary Moody Scholarship Com., 1984—; dir. music Christian Women's Outreach Ministry, 1984-88; mem. Robbins Community Coun., 1987-88; camp counselor Abraham Lincoln Ctr., 1951-53. Coppin A.M.E. Ch. scholar, 1946; recipient Humanitarian award God's House of Love, Prayer and Deliverance, 1992, Disting. Leadership award God First Ministries, 2002. Mem. Music Educators Nat. Conf., Good News Club (tchr. 1987-90, Robbins, Ill.). Home: 8154 S Indiana Ave Chicago IL 60619-4712

JAMES, MELISSA MARIE, religious studies educator; b. Minneapolis, Minn., July 24, 1980; d. Bruce and Kathy James. BA, Wartburg Coll., 2002; MA, Luth. Sch. Theology, 2004. Rostered diaconal minister Evang. Luth. Ch. Am., 2004. Assoc. discernment and mentoring Wartburg Coll., Waverly, Iowa, 2004—, lectr. in religion, 2005—. Mem. HIV/AIDS task force mem. Northeastern Iowa Synod Evang. Luth. Ch. Am., Waverly, 2005—06. Mem.: Nat. Academic Advising Assn., Am. Acad. Religion. Christian: Evangelical Lutheran Church Of America. Office Phone: 319-352-8651. Personal E-mail: melmjames@yahoo.com.

JAMES, MURIEL MARSHALL, writer, educator, psychotherapist; b. Berkeley, Calif., Feb. 14, 1917; d. John Albert and Hazel (Knowles) Marshall; m. Paul Wesley James (div.); children: Ann, Duncan, John. BA with honors, U. Calif., Berkeley, 1956; MDiv, Ch. Divinity Sch. Pacific, 1957; EdD, U. Calif., 1964; DMin, U. Calif., Berkeley, 2000. Lic. family psycho therapist, Calif. Instr., coord. ARC, San Francisco, 1941-43; safety inspector Kaiser Shipyards, Richmond, Calif., 1943-44; tchr. Oakland (Calif.) Pub. Schs., 1948-52; min. Orinda (Calif.) Cmty. Ch., 1957-59; dean Laymen's Sch. Religion, Berkeley, Calif., 1959-68; instr. U. Calif. Ext., Berkeley, 1966-69; dir., therapist Oasis Edn. & Treatment Ctr., Lafayette, Calif., 1968-73; psychotherapist pvt. practice, Lafayette, Calif., 1969—. Lectr. James Inst., Lafayette, 1969—. Author, co-author: Born to Win: Transactional Analysis with Gestalt Experiments, 1971, Winning with People: Group Exercises in Transactional Analysis, 1973, Born to Love: Transactional Analysis in the Church, 1973, Transactional Analysis for Moms and Dads: What Do You Do With Them Now That You've Got Them?, 1974, The Power at the Bottom of the Well, 1974, The OK Boss, 1975, The People Book: Transcational Analysis for Students, 1975, The Heart of Friendship, 1976, Techniques for Psychotherapists and Counselors, 1977, A New Self: Self Therapy with Transactional Analysis, 1977, Marriage is for Loving, 1979, Breaking Free: Self-Reparenting for a New Self, 1981, Winning Ways in Health Care, 1981, It's Never Too Late to Be Happy, 1985, expanded edit. 2002, The Better Boss in Multicultural Organizations, 1991, Hearts on Fire: Romance and Achievement in the Lives of Great Women, 1991, Passion for Life: Psychology and the Human Spirit, 1991, Religious Liberty on Trial: Hanserd Knollys, Early Baptist Hero, 1997, Perspectives in Transactional Analysis, 1998, It's Never Too Late to Be Happy: Reparenting Yourself for Happiness, 2002; contbr. chpts. to books, articles to profl. jours. Named to Internat. Educators Hall of Fame, 2000. Mem. Interat. Transactional Analysis Assn. (pres. 1980-82). Avocations: travel, teaching, creating new books.

JAMES, ROSE VICTORIA, sculptor, poet; b. East Amherst, N.Y., Feb. 11, 1922; d. Joseph and Mary (Plewniak) Glichowska; m. Clarence William James, Aug. 28, 1943 (dec. Dec. 1995); children: Robert, Sandra Lee, David, Mary, Kevin. Attended, Atlanta Coll. Art, 1960-64; B in Visual Arts in Sculpture, Ga. State U., 1973, postgrad., 1977-78. Legal sec. Law Office, Buffalo, 1941-42; sec. to comdr. Air Stas. Navy Dept., Washington, 1942-43; with pers. dept. Naval Air Station, Alameda, Calif., 1943-44; radio programmer, announcer ARC, Vets. Hosp., Buffalo, 1950-54, Atlanta, 1956-62; tchr., owner Studio 7 North Art Gallery, Roswell, Ga., 1974-76. Freelance artist, studio art instr. regional adult programs, 1960-72; competitive exhibiting artist, 1976-2003; chairperson 1st profl. women artist show Cushman Corp. Colony Sq., Atlanta, 1976; chairperson Atlanta Women in Arts Coop. Gallery, 1979-83; spkr. in field. Exhibited in group shows including Galleria Complex, Marietta, Ga., Colony Sq., Atlanta, Atlanta Hilton Ctr., Peachtree Ctr. Complex, Atlanta, Peachtree Summit, Atlanta, Atlanta Coll. Art Gallery, Woodruff Art Ctr., Atlanta, Bklyn. Coll. Student Ctr., N.Y.C., Alt. Space, N.Y.C., La Grange Coll., Ga., Ga. State U., Atlanta, Southeastern Colls. and Univs. 1-Yr. Traveling Exhibit, Auburn U., Ga. Inst. of Tech., Atlanta, DeKalb Coll., Atlanta, Hanson Gallery, New Orleans, AWIA Gallery, Atlanta, M. Baird Gallery, Atlanta, Handshake Gallery, Atlanta, Marietta Fine Arts Ctr., Ga., High Mus. of Art Regional Juried Art Shows, others. Visual arts panel Fulton County Commrs., Atlanta, 1980-81; panel moderator Ga. State U. So. Scholars on Women, 1981, Atlanta-Fulton County Libr., 1984. Grantee Bur. Cultural Affairs and Atlanta Arts Festival, 1978, Corp. Funding, 1980-81; recipient Mortar Bd. Honor Soc. Outstanding Leadership award, 1973. Mem. Internat. Sculpture Ctr. Republican. Roman Catholic. Avocations: golf, travel, reading, poetry, photography. Home: 6240 Weatherly Dr NW Atlanta GA 30328-3630

JAMES, RUBY MAY, retired librarian; b. Tucson, Ariz., Nov. 13, 1924; d. Theophil Frederic and Etelka Eva (Blumberg) Buehrer; m. Hubert R. James, Apr. 7, 1945; 1 child, Judith M. Victor. BA, U. Ariz., 1946, MEd, 1976; student, U. Iowa. Cert. elem. libr. Tchr. Tucson Unified Sch. Dist., 1947-48, elem. libr., 1974-89; ret. Recipient YMCA Svc. to Children award; Edn. Enrichment grantee. Mem. Pi Lambda Theta, Alpha Delta Kappa, Delta Kappa Gamma. Home: 1550 E River Rd #314 Tucson AZ 85718-5897

JAMES, SHARON ANN, elementary school educator; b. Bayshore, N.Y., Sept. 29, 1948; d. John Joseph Melton and Pauline Rita Tranovich; m. Robert Taylor James, July 22, 1978; children: Kelly Ann, Robert John, Kathleen Megan. BA, SUNY, Oneonta, 1970; MS in Edn., SUNY, New Paltz, 1971. Elem. tchr. C.I. Pub. Schs., Central Islip, NY, 1971—. Mem.: Ctrl. Islip Tchrs. Assn. (bldg. com. rep. 2004, math task force mem. 2005, mem. math curriculum writing team 2005, PTA programmer 1975), Alpha Delta. Home: 40 Offenbach St Centereach NY 11720 Office: CI Pub Schs 299 Sycamore Ave Central Islip NY 11722

JAMES, VIRGINIA LYNN, contracts executive; b. March AFB, Calif., Feb. 6, 1952; d. John Edward and Azella Virginia (Morrill) Anderson; children: Raymond Edward, Jerry Glenn James Jr. Student, Sinclair C.C., 1981-83, U. Tex., San Antonio, 1980, Redlands U., 1986, San Diego State U., 1994. With specialized contracting USAF, Wright-Patterson AFB, Ohio, 1973-77, with logistics contracting Kelly AFB, Tex., 1977-81, contract specialist Wright-Patterson AFB, Ohio, 1981-84; spl. asst. Peace Log, Tehran, Iran, 1977; acting chief of contracts cruise missile program Gen. Dynamics/Convair, San Diego, 1984-86; contracts mgr. VERAC, Inc., San Diego, 1986-90, Gen. Dynamics, San Diego, 1990-92; mgr. contracts Scientific-Atlanta, San Diego, 1992-93; dir. contracts GreyStone, San Diego, 1993-95; dist. constn. mgr. OHM, San Diego, 1995-98; v.p. contract and procurement MWH Ams., Inc., Louisville, 1998—2004; v.p. bus. compliance Quanta Services, 2004—. Cons. Gen. Dynamics, San Diego, 1985, Efratrom, 1986. Mem.: NAFE, Nat. Contract Mgmt. Assn., Nat. Mgmt. Assn. Republican. Office: Quanta Svcs 1360 Post Oak Blvd Ste 2100 Houston TX 77041 Office Phone: 713-985-6490.

JAMES, VIRGINIA STOWELL, retired elementary school educator, retired secondary school educator; d. Austin Leavitt and Doris Carolyn Stowell; m. William Hall James, June 24, 1950; 1 child, Hillery. BA, Middlebury Coll., 1947; MA, Yale U., 1955; PhD, U. Conn., 1988. Cert. tchr. cert. art tchr. Tchr. elem. Bd. Edn., Westport, Conn., 1950—58; tchr, art grades 6-9 Wallingford Bd. Edn., Conn., tchr. gifted/talented grades 4-5, kindergarten, 1958—91; ret., 1991. Contbr. articles to profl. jours. Mem. NEA, AAUW, DAR, Soc. Children's Book Writers and Illustrators, Nat. Assn. for Gifted Children, Conn. Assn. for Gifted, Conn. Edn. Assn., Nat. Mus. Women in Arts, Nat. Women's History Mus., Nature Conservatory, Conn. Women's Edn. and Legal Fund, Phi Delta Kappa, Pi Lambda Theta, Delta Kappa Gamma. Address: PO Box 234 Northford CT 06472-0234 Home: 373 Reeds Gap Rd Northford CT 06472-1106 E-mail: jinnyjamvsj@att.net.

JAMESON, JENNIFER A., lawyer; BA, U. Minn., 1996, JD cum laude, 1999. Bar: Minn. 1999. Law clk. to Hon. Gary Larson Hennepin County Dist. Ct., 2000; assoc. McGrann, Shea, Anderson, Carnival, Straughn & Lamb, Chartered, Mpls. Vol. Chrysalis Legal Progs., 2001—. Named a Rising Star, Minn. Super Lawyers mag., 2006. Mem.: Minn. Women Lawyers, Minn. State Bar Assn., Collaborative Law Inst. Office: McGrann Shea Anderson Carnival Straughn & Lamb Chartered 2600 US Bancorp Ctr 800 Nicollet Mall Minneapolis MN 55402 Office Phone: 612-338-2525. E-mail: jaj@mcgrannshea.com.*

JAMESON, MARGARET JOHNSON, retired elementary school educator; b. Covington, Va., Feb. 8, 1939; d. Murrell Edward and Frieda Doris (Martin) Johnson; m. Robert B. Jameson, 1959; children: David, Linda, Donnie(dec.). BA, Erskine Coll., 1959. Cert. English tchr. S.C. Tchr. Iva (S.C.) Elem. Sch., 1964-65, Greenville St. Elem. Sch., Abbeville, SC, 1965-71, Wright Mid. Sch., Abbeville, 1971—98; ret., 1998. Docent Burt-Stark House, Abbeville, 1993—; bd. dirs., treas. Heritage House, Abbeville, 1999—. Mem.: NEA, Abbeville County Edn. Assn., S.C. Edn. Assn., Delta Kappa Gamma. Baptist.

JAMESON, PATRICIA MADOLINE, science librarian; b. Rhinelander, Wis., Mar. 17, 1939; d. Errol Donald and Mary Maxine (Shields) J. BS, Carroll Coll., 1961; PhD, Ind. U., 1965; MLIS, U. Wis., Milw., 1988. Microbiologist U.S. Dept. Def., Frederick, Md., 1965-69; instr. Med. Coll. Wis., Milw., 1969-70, asst. prof., 1970-80, assoc. prof., 1980-88; asst. prof. Eastern Ill. U., Charleston, 1989-91; reference libr. U. Wis., Milw., 1991—2000. Cons. P-L Biochems., Milw., 1969, Wadley Inst. Medicine, Dallas, 1978, World Book-Childcraft Internat., Chgo., 1979. Contbr. articles to profl. jours. Mem. Am. Guild Organists, Am. Theatre Organ Soc., Dairyland Theatre Organ Soc., Kimball Theatre Organ Soc., Order of Eastern Star (Wauwatosa chpt., officer 1971-88, 1995-2005, grand chpt. Wis. treas., 2001-04), Order of Amaranth (Milw. court officer, 1992—, trustee 1998-99, grand ct. Wis. officer, 2001-02, 2003-04, Order of True Kindred (officer Aloha Conclave 1992—, presiding officer 1998, 2004, grand conclave of Ill./Wis. officer, 2002-06, presiding officer, 2004-05, supreme conclave officer, 2001-02), Daus. of the Nile (officer Shelomoth Temple 1993-2004, presiding officer, 2002-03), Sigma Xi.

JAMESON, PAULA ANN, retired lawyer; b. New Orleans, Feb. 19, 1945; d. Paul Henry and Virginia Lee (Powell) Bailey; children: Paul Andrew, Peter Carver. BA, La. State U., 1966; JD, U. Tex., 1969. Bar: Tex. 1969, D.C. 1970, U.S. Dist. Ct. D.C. 1970, U.S. Ct. Appeals (D.C. cir.) 1972, Va. 1973, U.S. Supreme Ct. 1973, U.S. Dist. Ct. (ea. dist.) Va. 1976, U.S. Ct. Appeals (4th cir.) 1976, N.Y. 1978, U.S. Ct. Appeals (5th cir.) 1978, U.S. Ct. Appeals (2d cir.) 1985. Asst. corp. counsel D.C. Corp. Counsel's Office, 1970-73; sr. asst. county atty. Fairfax County Atty.'s Office, Fairfax, Va., 1973-77; atty. Dow Jones & Co., Inc., N.Y.C., 1977-79, ho. counsel, 1979-81, asst. to chmn. bd., 1981-83, ho. counsel, dir. legal dept., 1983-86; sr. v.p., gen. counsel, corp. sec. PBS, Alexandria, Va., 1986-98; ptnr. Arter & Hadden, Washington, 1998-2000; v.p., gen. counsel Gibson Guitar Corp., Nashville, 2000-01; pres. Jameson Legal & Cons. Svcs., McLean, Va., 2000—03; exec. v.p., COO Children's Def. Fund., Washington, 2003—04; ret., 2004. Mem.: D.C. Bar Assn., Fed. Comms. Bar Assn. Democrat. Roman Catholic. Personal E-mail: paulajameson@att.net.

JAMIESON, LEAH H., engineering educator; BS in Math., MIT, 1972; MA in Elec. Engring. and Computer Sci., MSE in Elec. Engring. and Computer Sci., Princeton U., 1974, PhD in Elec. Engring. and Computer Sci., 1977. Asst. prof., sch. elec. engring. Purdue U., West Lafayette, Ind., 1976—82, assoc. prof., sch. elec. engring., 1982—86, prof., sch. elec. engring./sch. elec. and computer engring., 1986—2002, grad. coord., sch. elec. engring., 1990—94, dir. grad. admissions, sch. elec. engring./sch. elec. engring. and computer engring., 1994—96, co-founder, Ctr. for Engring. Projects in Cmty. Svc. (EPICS), sch. engring., 1995, co-director, Ctr. for Engring. Projects in Cmty. Svc. (EPICS), sch. engring., 1996—2002, Ransburg prof. elec. and comp. engring., 2002—, interim head, sch. elec. and computer engring., 2002, mem., Dean's advisory com., 2002—, dir., EPICS: Engring. Projects in Cmty. Svc., 2003—, assoc. dean for undergraduate edn., coll. engring., 2004—; co-founder, co-director, Nat. EPICS, 1999—; vis. scientist, Computer Sci. lab. SRI Internat., Menlo Park, Calif., 1985, 1986. Chair. elec. engring. grad. com. Purdue U., 1986—89, mem. senate, 1987—90, 1992—95, chair, computer engring. area com., 1991—92, chair, senate steering com., 1992—95, mem., Task Force on Women's Issues, 1995—97, vice-convener, Coun. on the Status of Women, 1999—2000, mem., Neil Armstrong Hall of Engring. Planning Com., 1999—, founding chair, Women Faculty in Engring. Com., 1999—, co-convener, Coun. on the Status of Women, 2000—01, mem. engring. leadership team, 2004—, co-chair, Engring. Curriculum Reform Task Force; workshop organizer for workshops with Girl Scouts, jr. high, and HS girls, part of Expanding Your Horizons in Math and Sci. Program Soc. of Women Engr. and Purdue U. Women in Engring. Career Day; chair Policy Com. on World Wide Web Publishing, 1996—97, Rsch. Computing and Communications Advisory Com., 1997—2001; spkr. in field. Contbr. articles to profl. jours. Co-recipient Chester F. Carlson award for Innovation in Engring. Edn., Am. Soc. for Engring. Edn., 1997, Class of 1922 award for outstanding innovation in helping students learn, Purdue U., 1997; finalist with Edward J. Coyle, Boeing Outstanding Educator award, 1998, with Edward J. Coyle, Thomas Ehrlich Faculty award for Svc. Learning, 2000; named Ind. Prof. Yr., Carnegie Found. and Coun. for the Advancement and Support of Edn., 2002. Fellow: IEEE (assoc. editor, Transactions on Acoustics, Speech and Signal Processing 1986—87, assoc. editor, Transactions on Parallel and Distributed Sys. 1991—94, chair, Jack S. Kilby Signal Processing medal com. 1996—99, pres., Signal Processing Soc. 1998—99, mem. editl. bd., Proceedings of the IEEE 1999—2001, v.p. tech. activities 2003, IEEE bd. dir. and Excom 2003, chair, tech. activities bd. new tech. directions com. 2004—06, v.p. for publ. svcs. and products 2005, IEEE bd. dir. and Excom 2005, chair, Publ. Svcs. and Products Bd. 2005, pres.-elect 2006, pres. 2007, founder, organizer, Women in Signal Processing Lunch 1993—, IEEE Edn. Soc., Harriet B. Rigas, Outstanding Women Engring. Educator award 2000, Third Millennium medal 2000, IEEE Signal Processing Soc., Meritorious Svc. award 2004); mem.: NAE (co-recipient, Bernard M. Gordon prize 2005), NSF (mem. advisory com. for NSF directorate, computer & info. sci. engring. 1997—2000, Director's award for Disting. Teaching Scholars 2001), Computing Rsch. Assn. (editor, Expanding the Pipeline, Computing Research News 1993—96, co-chair, com. on the status of women and computing rsch. 1996—99, bd. dir. 1998—2000, sec. 1999—2000, bd. dir. 2001—07, co-chair, Snowbird Conf. 2002). Office: Sch Elec and Computer Engring Purdue U 465 Northwestern Ave West Lafayette IN 47907-2035 Address: Purdue U 400 Centennial Mall Dr West Lafayette IN 47907-2016 Office Phone: 765-494-4966. Office Fax: 765-496-1180. Business E-Mail: lhj@purdue.edu.*

JAMISON, ELIZABETH ALEASE, drafting and design business owner; b. Rockwood, Tenn., July 8, 1954; d. Ross Leslie and Alice Elizabeth (Collier) J.; life ptnr. Virginia Eddy. Student, Roane State C.C., Harriman, Tenn., 1974-75, Tenn. Tech. U., 1980-83. Cert. Autocad Level I. Drafter ETE Consulting Engrs., Inc., Oak Ridge, Tenn., 1983-84, Edge Group, Nashville, 1984-88; sr. drafter Woodard & Curran, Inc., Portland, Maine, 1988-91; owner Casco Bay Drafting & Design, Portland, Maine, 1991—; tech. program coord. Portland Adult Edn., 1994—; exec. dir. Women Unltd., Augusta, Maine, 2004—. Adj. faculty mem. So. Maine Tech. Coll., South Portland, 1990—; instr. Women Unltd., Augusta, Maine, 1993—; archtl. drafting & design instr. Portland Arts & Tech. H.S., 1997-2003; exec. dir. Women Unltd., Augusta, Maine, 2004—. Featured in film Women Working, 1994. Bd. officer Portland YWCA, 1992-94; exec. bd. mem. Coalition Women in Trades & Tech., 1996—; mem. Maine Fire Svc. Tech. Women's Task Force, 1998-2000, Main Reentry Network, 2005—; mem. adv. bd. Brownfields Initiative for Local Devel., Lewiston, Maine, 2004—; mem. women's subcom. Maine Jobs Coun., 2005—. Mem. NOW (1st v.p. Tenn. chpt. 1986-88, Tenn. state pres. 1988). Avocations: cooking, travel, reading, motivational speaking. Home and Office: 122 Middle Rd Cumberland ME 04021 Office Phone: 207-623-7576, 207-623-7576. Personal E-mail: ejamison@womenunlimited.org, ejamison@womaneunlimited.org.

JAMISON, JAYNE, publishing executive; m. Jan Philip Browne, 1986 (div.); 2 children; m. Edward J. Bisno, June 11, 2006. Grad., Penn. St. U., 1978. With Elkman Advt., Phila.; acct. mgr., advt. Family Circle mag.; advt. dir. American Health, pub.; group pub., parenthood group Gruner & Jahr USA Pub., N.Y.C., 1994—97; pub. v.p. Redbook, 1997—2003; pub., v.p. Seventeen, 2003—. Office: Seventeen Mag 1440 Broadway 13th Fl New York NY 10018 Office Phone: 212-204-4300, 917-934-6601. Office Fax: 917-934-6650.*

JAMISON, JOI NICHOLE, media specialist, performing company executive, educator; b. Portsmouth, Va., Feb. 26, 1981; d. Bruce and Veronica W. Jamison. BS in Mass Comm. cum laude, Norfolk State U., Va., 2003. Promotions coord. Sta. KISS-FM, Clear Channel Radio, Norfolk, 2004—. Artistic co-founder Rythmic Creacion, Va., 2004—; mem. alumni rels. bd. Norfolk State U. Choreographer Virginia Thunder, dancer Norfolk Nighthawks Hawtime Dance Girl (Most Attitude on the Dance Field, 2003). Active mem. Salvation Army, Va., 2004; pub. rels. chair Womens Aux. Salvation Army, Norfolk, 2005—; cardio dance and aerobics trainer YMCA; young adult advisor scholarship com. St. Paul AME Ch., Va. Named Celebrity Reader Day, Pk. View Elem. Sch., 2005. Mem.: Coalition Young Black Profls. (membership chair 2005—), Hampton Rds. Black Media Profls., Delta Sigma Theta. Democrat. Avocations: travel, reading, mentoring to youth, shopping, performing. Home: 4212 Queenswood Dr Apt A Portsmouth VA 23703 Office: Clear Channel Radio Norfolk 1003 Norfolk Sq Norfolk VA 23502 Office Phone: 757-466-0009. Personal E-mail: joij99@yahoo.com. Business E-Mail: joijamison@clearchannel.com.

JAMISON, JUDITH, dancer; b. Phila., May 10, 1943; d. John Jamison. Student, Fisk U., Phila., Phila. Dance Acad. (now U. of Arts); studied with, Anthony Tudor, John Hines, Delores Brown, John Jones, Joan Kerr, Madame Swaboda. Dancer Alvin Ailey Am. Dance Theatre, N.Y.C., 1965-80, artistic dir., 1990—; dancer, choreographer touring U.S., Europe, Asia, S.Am., Africa, 1980—; formerly with Maurice Hines Dance Sch., N.Y.C.; founder Jamison Project, 1988-91. Vis. disting. prof. U. Arts; guest assoc. artistic dir. 30th ann. tour Alvin Ailey's Am. Dance Theatre, 1990—; guest appearances Harkness Ballet, Am. Ballet Theatre, San Francisco Ballet, Dallas Ballet. Dancer debut Agnes DeMille's The Four Marys, 1965, (Broadway plays) Joseph's Legend, Vienna Opera, Le Spectre de la Rose, Brussels, Paris, N.Y.C., Maskela Language, 1969, Cry, 1971, Choral Dance, 1971, Mary Lou's Mass, 1971, The Lark Ascending, 1972, The Mooche, 1975, Passage, 1978, (Broadway plays) Sophisticated Ladies, 1980, choreographer Divining Hymn for Alvin Ailey Am. Dance Theatre, works for Maurice Bejart, Dancers Unltd., Dallas, Washington Ballet, Jennifer Muller/The Works, Alvin Ailey Repertory Ensemble, Ballet Nuevo Mundo de Caracas, Riverside for Alvin Ailey Am. Dance Theatre, (Operas) Boito's Mefistofele, Opera Co. Phila.; author: Dancing Spirit, 1993. Recipient Dance Mag. award, 1972, Key to City, N.Y.C., 1976, Spirit of Achievement award Nat. Women's Divsn., Yeshiva U. Albert Einstein Coll. Medicine, 1992, Golden Plate award, Am. Acad. Achievement, 1993. Office: Alvin Ailey Dance Theatre 405 W 55th St New York NY 10019-4402

JAMISON, PEGGY LOUISE, elementary school educator; b. Hamilton, Ohio, May 13, 1951; d. Thomas Patrick and Rita Frances (Kelly) Glynn; m. Steven Charles Jamison, Dec. 29, 1979; children: Christopher, Kevin. BA in Speech Comm., Marquette U., 1973; elem. cert., Miami U., Oxford, Ohio, 1976; MEd in Reading, Xavier U., 1980. Cert. tchr., Ohio. Elem. tchr. St. Richard's Sch., Cin., 1976-77; reading tchr., tutor Princeton Jr. High Sch., Cin., 1978-79; elem. tchr., reading dept. coord. Fairfield (Ohio) Mid. Sch., 1979-1984, Eng. tchr. Mem. NEA, Ohio Edn. Assn., Fairfield Classroom Tchrs. Assn. Avocations: music, photography, sailing, quilting. Home: 16 Carrie Cir Oxford OH 45056-9203 Office: Fairfield City Schs 1111 Nilles Rd Fairfield OH 45014-3006

JANCE, J.A. (JUDITH ANN JANCE), writer; b. Watertown, SD, Oct. 27, 1944; married. BA in English, Secondary Edn., Univ. Ariz., 1966, MEd in Libr. Sci., 1970. English tchr. Pueblo High Sch., Tucson; libr. Indian Oasis Sch. Dist., Sells, Ariz.; life ins. sales. Author: (J.P. Beaumont Series) Until Proven Guilty, 1985, Injustice for All, 1986, Trial by Fury, 1986, Taking the Fifth, 1987, Improbable Cause, 1987, A More Perfect Union, 1988, Dismissed with Prejudice, 1989, Minor in Possession, 1990, Payment in Kind, 1991, Without Due Process, 1993, Failure to Appear, 1994, Lying in Wait, 1995, Name Withheld, 1997, Breach of Duty, 2000, Birds of Prey, 2002, Partner in Crime, 2003, Sentenced to Die, 2005, Long Time Gone, 2005, Edge of Evil, 2006, (Joanna Brady Series) Desert Heat, 1993, Tombstone Courage, 1995, Shoot/Don't Shoot, 1996, Dead to Rights, 1997, Skeleton Canyon, 1998, Rattlesnake Crossing, 1998, Outlaw Mountain, 2000, Devil's Claw, 2001, Paradise Lost, 2002, Partner in Crime 2003, Exit Wounds, 2003 (thrillers) Hour of the Hunter, 1990, Kiss of the Bees, 2001, Day of the Dead, 2004, (poetry) After the Fire, 2004. Recipient Am. Mystery award, 1991. Mailing: Author Mail Harper Collins Pub Wm Morrow Avon Books 10 E 53rd St New York NY 10022 Home: Bellevue WA Business E-Mail: jajance@jajance.com.*

JANDREY, BECKY LEE, psychologist; b. Appleton, Wis., Apr. 20, 1951; d. Elton and Eleanor Jandrey; life ptnr. Dean Nelson; stepchildren: Jeremy Nelson, Joshua Nelson. BS, Ariz. State U., Tempe, Ariz., 1974; MA, Fielding U., Santa Barbara, Calif., 1994, PhD, 1998. Licensed Psychologist Calif. Bd. of Psychology, 2000. Corp. real estate broker Dempsey Constrn. Corp., Mammoth Lakes, Calif., 1978—84; regional pers. mgr. Staffing Svcs., L.A., Calif., 1984—91; psychol. asst. La Vie Counselling Ctr., Pasadena, Calif., 1992—96; fellow Kaiser-Permanente Outpatient Psychiatry, Santa Rosa, Calif., 1998—99; psychologist Pvt. Practice, Santa Rosa, Calif., 1997—. Tchr. Kaiser Permanent Health Edn., Santa Rosa, Calif., 1999—2000; presenter Kaiser Permanent Women's Health Week, Santa Rosa, Calif., 2000—02. Contbr. scientific papers (Dissertation Recognition Award - Fielding U., 1997). Vol. - counselling, crisis hotline Pasadena Mental Health Ctr., Pasadena, Calif., 1992—93; fin. organizer/contbr. Valley of the Moon Children's Found., Santa Rosa, Calif., 2004, Heifer Internat., Little Rock, 2003; vol. counselor/mentor for amputees Nova-Care Prosthetics, L.A., Calif., 1981—96; vol. Veterans Adminstrn. - Geriatric neuropsychiatry, Sepulveda, Calif., 1996. Recipient Frieda Fromm Reichmann Award, Fielding U., 1998; scholar DAR Leadership Scholarship, DAR, 1969, 4-yr. Coll. Leadership Scholarship, Rotary Club, 1969-1973. Mem.: APA (assoc.), Calif. Psychol. Assn. (assoc.). Achievements include First amputee to learn downhill skiing at Mammoth Mountain, Calif. (ski sch. instr. - Jim Northrup). Avocations: writing, amputee skiing, reading, swimming, yoga. Office: Becky L Jandrey PhD 825 College Ave Santa Rosa CA 95404

JANECZEK, MARY, secondary school educator, mathematician, department chairman; b. New Haven, Apr. 11, 1955; d. Walter Joseph and Sophie Frances (Ludwe) J. AB, Boston Coll., 1977; MEd, So. Conn. State U., 1981; C.A.S., Fairfield U., 1989. Tchr. Dr. Carl C. Giannotti Jr. High Sch., West Haven, Conn., 1977-83, West Haven HS, 1983—. Assoc. faculty Albertus Magnus Coll. Mem. Assn. Tchrs. Math. in Conn., Assn. Tchrs. Math. in New England, Delta Kappa Gamma. Home: 725 Racebrook Rd Orange CT 06477-1915 Office: West Haven High Sch 1 McDonough Plz West Haven CT 06516-5299

JANECZEK, TERRY ANN, director, science educator; b. Long Branch, N.J., Nov. 30, 1950; d. Frank and AnnaMarie Torchia; m. Walter Janeczek, June 29, 1974; children: Kristen, Eric. BS in Biology, U. Bridgeport, Conn., 1968; MS in Entomolgy and Economic Zoology, Rutgers U., New Brunswick, N.J., 1981; MA in Ednl. Adminstrn., Monmouth U., N.J., 2000. Cert. tchr. comprehensive sci. K-12 State of N.J., 1972, prin. State of N.J., 2000. Facilitator sci. and social studies Long Br. Pub. Schs., NJ, 2001—. Math., sci. and tech. network coord. (Long Br.) Brookdale C.C., Lincroft, NJ, 2000; dist. parent involvement coord. Long Br. Pub. Schs., 2001—, no child left behind coord. student activities, 2004—; adv. bd. ESTEEMS Program Rutgers U., New Brunswick, 2005—. Chmn. City of Long Br. Zoning Bd. Adjustment, NJ, 1992—. Recipient Tchr. of Yr., Long Br. Pub. Schs., 1995. Mem.: ASCD. Avocations: swimming, gardening, landscaping, reading, running. Home: 97 Franklin Ave Long Branch NJ 07740 Office: Long Branch Pub Schs 540 Broadway Long Branch NJ Office Phone: 732-571-2868. E-mail: taj4@aol.com.

JANES, RAENA, private school educator; b. 1973; m. Craig Janes; children: Chloe, Cole. Founder, superintendent La Paloma Acad., 2002—. Founder Grace Chapel Early Edn. Ctr. Named one of 40 Under 40, Tucson Bus. Edge, 2006; recipient Excellence in Special Edn. Cmty. award, Ariz. Dept. Edn. Mem.: Nat. Assn. Edn. Young Children, Jr. League of Tucson. Office: La Paloma Academy 225 N Country Club Rd Tucson AZ 85716 Office Phone: 520-733-7373.*

JANG, JEONG, professional golfer; b. Taejeon, Korea, June 11, 1980; Attended, JoongBoo U. Winner Korea Women's Open, 1997, Korea Women's Amateur, 1998, Women's British Open, 2005, Wegmans LPGA, 2006. Mem.

Korea Women's Nat. Team, 1997—98, World Amateur Championship Team, 1998. Achievements include five top-ten finishes, 2002; six top-ten finishes, 2003; seven top-ten finishes, 2004. Avocations: skiing, nintendo. Office: c/o LPGA 100 International Golf Dr Daytona Beach FL 32124-1092*

JANI, SUSHMA NIRANJAN, pediatric psychiatrist; b. Gwalior, Madhya, Pradesh, India, Sept. 26, 1959; arrived in U.S., 1983; d. Kirty Ambalal and Purnima Kirty (Bhatt) Dave; m. Niranjan Natwerial Jani, Mar. 30, 1983; children: Suni Jani, Raja Jani, Roma Jani. Intern Sci., Mithibai Coll., Bombay, India; MB, BS, B.J. Med. Coll., Ahmedabad, India; MD in Adult Psychiatry, Ind. U., 1984; MD in Child Psychiatry, Johns Hopkins U., 1987. Diplomate Am. Bd. Psychiatry and Neurology, sub-bd. Child Psychiatry, Am. Bd. Pediat., Am. Bd. Forensic Examiners; cert. in addiction medicine Am. Soc. Addiction Medicine; cert. med. review officer Med. Rev. Officer Cert. Courell. Pediat. emergency physician Mercey Hosp., Balt., 1997—99; child psychiatrist Johns Hopkins Univ. Hosp., Balt.; asst. clin. prof., mem. faculty dept. pediats. and psychiatry Georgetown U. Med. Ctr., Balt., assoc. prof. pediat. and psychiatry; assoc. prof. psychiatry Georgetown U.; med. dir. Chesapeake network Devereux Found., Md., Va., W.Va., Washington and Del., 1998-99; med. dir. Riverside Hosp., Washington, 1999—2005; pediat. emergency physician Howard County Hosp., 1999—; chief med. officer Maple Shade Youth and Family Svcs., Mardela Springs, Md., 2005—. Chief cons. psychiatrist Balt. Detention Ctr., 1988-89, cons. psychiatrist Vets. Hosp., Indpls., 1986-87. Vol. Radha-Krishna Leporsy Camp, Bombay, 1981—83. Mem. AMA, Am. Acad. Child & Adolescent Psychiatry, Am. Psychiatry Assn., Md. Psychiat. Soc., Columbia Assn., India Assn., Am. Acad. Podiatrics, Am. Soc. Addiction Medicine (cert.). Hindu. Avocations: reading, knitting, sewing, letter-writing. Home: 10485 Owen Brown Rd Columbia MD 21044-3835 Office: 9650 Santiago Rd Ste # 10 Columbia MD 21045 Office Phone: 410-997-5500.

JANIGA, MARY ANN, art educator; b. Lackawanna, NY, June 14, 1950; d. Jacob and Julia Mazurchuk; m. William B. Janiga, Nov. 23, 1972; children: Nicholas, Matthew. BS, State U. Coll., Buffalo, 1972, MS, 1974. Cert. in sch. adminstrn. and supervision, in gifted and talented edn., advanced study State U. Coll., Buffalo, 1996. Tchr. art Buffalo Pub. Schs., 1972—2005; art supr. State U. Coll. Buffalo, 2006—. Art facilitator Olmsted Sch., Buffalo, 1985-2005, World Connect Multi-cultural Program, 2003, 04; supervising tchr. State U. Coll., Buffalo, PT3 mentor, 2004-06, student supr., 06; liaison Albright-Knox Art Gallery, 1994—; art presenter fed. pre-kindergarten program, 1998; wrote art curriculum Buffalo Pub. Sch., 2002. Carnegie Hall, NYC, 2002; co-ordinated with Fisher-Price Designers, Buffalo Pub. Sch. Art Program, 2003; del. Buffalo Tchrs. Fedn., 2004-05, N.Y. State Tchrs. Retirement Conv., 2003-04, NEA of N.Y., 2001-05. Exhibited in group shows at Cheektowaga (N.Y.) Art Guild, 1979, Erie County Parks Art Festival, 1979, Lockport Art Festival, 1980, Allentown Art Exhibit, Kennan Ctr. Recipient various awards for art; grantee Buffalo Tchr. Ctr., 1986-90, Olmstead Home Sch. Assn., 1991-97, Allentown Village Soc., 1994; grantee Fisher Price, 2003. Mem. NEA, PAT (life), Olmsted Home Sch. Assn., SUNY-Buffalo Alumni Assn., Buffalo Tchrs. Fedn., Buffalo Fine Arts Acad., Buffalo Soc. Natural Scis., Zool. Soc. of Buffalo, Lancaster HS Home Sch. Assn. (rec. sec. 1998-99, co-pres. 1999-2001), NEA Retired, Buffalo Retired Tchrs. Assn. Avocations: reading, concerts, theater, art exhibits. Office: State Univ Coll Buffalo Art Education Dept Bishop Hall 1300 Elmwood Ave Buffalo NY 14222-1095

JANIK, MELINDA A., real estate company executive; With PricewaterhouseCoopers LLP, Washington; v.p., ntreas. NCR Corp., Dayton, Ohio, 1997—2002; sr. v.p., CFO Glimcher Realty Trust, Columbus, Ohio, 2002—. Office: Glimcher Realty Trust 150 E Gay St Columbus OH 43215

JANIK, NICOLE ELIZABETH, secondary school educator; b. Pitts., July 14, 1979; d. Richard Allen Janik and Sharon Louise Dompa, Carl Charles Dompa (Stepfather). BS in Edn., Pa. State U., State College, 2001. Cert. tchr. Pa., Va. Tchr. 7th grade math. Pocono Mountain Sch. Dist., Tobyhanna, Pa., 2001—04; tchr. h.s. math. Prince William County Schs., Woodbridge, Va., 2004—. Sponsor Mu Alpha Theta; mem. nat. nominating com. Nat. Youth Leadership Coun. Mem.: Prince William Edn. Assn. Office: Freedom HS 15201 Neabsco Mills Rd Woodbridge VA 22191 Office Phone: 703-583-1405. E-mail: janikne@pwcs.edu.

JANIS, ELINOR RAIDEN, artist, educator; b. N.Y.C., Dec. 8, 1934; d. Edward and Lea Raiden; m. Leon Janis, July 14, 1957 (div. Jan. 5, 1970); children: Madeline, Richard, Cheryl. BA in Elem. Edn., UCLA, 1957; MFA, Instituto Allende, 1975. Instr. elem. schs., 1957—66, Woman's Workshop, Granada Hills, Calif., 1971—73; painting instr. Instituto Allende, 1974, 1976—77, Santa Monica Pks. and Recreation, Calif., 1977; instr. L.A. City Schs., 1978—86; profl. artist, 1986—. One-woman shows include Galeria Conde, San Miguel de Allende, Mex., 1974, Beyond Baroque Gallery, Venice, Calif., 1977, Canyon Cafe, Glendale, Calif., 2000—01, exhibited in group shows at Barnsdall Pk., L.A., 1972, Emerson Gallery, 1972, Brentwood (Calif.) Art Ctr., 1973, McCaffery Galleries, L.A., 1973, Ryder Gallery, 1973, Galeria Pintora de Jovenes, Mexico City, 1974, Powerhouse Gallery, Montreal, Can., 1975, Woman's Bldg., L.A., 1975, Woman's Ctr., Ridgefield, Con., 1975, Assn. Humanist Artists, San Francisco, 1975, Museo de Arte Contemporaneo, San Miguel de Allende, 1977, Viva Gallery, Sherman Oaks, Calif., 2000—05, others. Mem. Amnesty Internat., L.A., 1995—2001, NOW, 1985—2001, Handgun Control, 1990—2001. Recipient scholarship, Instituto Allende, 1974, 2d prize, Burbank Creative Arts Ctr. Show, 2001. Mem.: Valley Artists Guild, L.A. County Mus. Art. Democrat. Jewish. Avocations: pottery, stone carving, etching. Office: Elinor Janis Studio 14417 Chase St # 298 Panorama City CA 91402 Personal E-mail: erjanis@aol.com.

JANNEY, ALLISON, actress; b. Dayton, Ohio, Nov. 19, 1960; BA, Kenyon Coll.; pvt. studies in acting, Neighborhood Playhouse, N.Y.C. Appeared in feature films: Big Night, 1996, Private Parts, 1997, Primary Colors, 1998, Six Days, Seven Nights, 1998, The Ice Storm, 1997, Celebrity, 1998, 10 Things I Hate About You, 1999, Drop Dead Gorgeous, 1999, Nurse Betty, 2000, American Beauty, 1999, Leaving Drew, 2000, Finding Nemo (voiceover), 2003, How to Deal, 2003, Over the Hedge (voice), 2006; plays (on Broadway) A View From The Bridge (Tony award nominee 1998, Outer Critics Circle award,Drama Desk award); appearances on TV: The West Wing (role C.J. Gregg), 1999-2006, (Emmy award Outstanding Lead Actress in a Drama Series, 2004), A Girl Thing (TV mini), 2000 Recipient Outstanding Featured Actress in a Play for "A View From the Bridge", Drama Desk Award, 1998, Outstanding Supporting Actress in a Drama Series for "The West Wing", Emmy Award, 1999, 2000, Best Actress in a Television Series Drama for "The West Wing", Golden Satellite, 2000, Best Ensemble Cast Performance for "The West Wing", 2000, Outstanding Female Actor in a Drama Series for "The West Wing", The Actor Awards, 2000, Outstanding Ensemble in a Drama Series for "The West Wing", 2000, Outstanding Supporting Actress in a Drama Series for "The West Wing", Emmy Awards, 2001, Outstanding Female Actor in a Drama Series for "The West Wing", The Actor Awards, 2001, Outstanding Ensemble in a Drama Series for "The West Wing", 2001, Outstanding Female Actress in a Drama Series for "The West Wing", Emmy Awards, 2002.*

JANNEY, KAY PRINT, retired performing arts educator, theater director; b. Cleve., June 22, 1938; d. Walter James and Zenza Mae (Williams) Print; m. Frederick George Janney, Feb. 6, 1960; children: Brooke Hopkins, Eric Matthew, Catherine Marie. BA cum laude, Case We. Res. U., Cleve., 1959, MA, 1962. Copywriter Howard Marks Advt., Cleve., 1958—59; tchr. Speech, drama and English South-Euclid Lyndhurst Pub. Schs., Ohio, 1960—61, Lakewood Pub. Schs., Ohio, 1961—62; tchr. speech and drama, dept. head Berea H.S., Ohio, 1962—65; instr. comm. scis. U. Conn., Storrs, 1966—70, instr. comm. and dramatic arts Avery Point and Groton, 1971—74, asst. prof. comm. and dramatic arts, 1975—80, assoc. prof. comm. and dramatic arts, 1981—89, prof. dramatic arts, 1990—97, prof. emeritus, 1997—. Author: (monographs) A Bibliography on the Mask, 1989, Masks: The Power of Transformation-Put a New Face on Your Curriculum, 1989, Scriptsearch, 1988; book reviewer Speech Communication Teacher, 1990, Black Like My Soul Is Black (Michael Bradford), 1994-95; dir. (theatre prodns.) Mother Hicks, 1992, The Hide 'N Seek Odyssey of Madeline Gimple, 1991, The Angel With The Broken Wing, 1990, In A Room Somewhere, 1990, others; contbr. articles to profl. jours. Adjudicator Cmty. Theatre Coun., New London County, Conn., 1977, 93-97, chair of judges, 1987-89; various appts. P.E.O., 1980-; adjudicator Mass. Drama Guild, 1986-93, Conn. Drama Assn., 1989; state bd. govs. Ballard State Mus. and Inst., 2005—, Mus. Puppetry, 2005—; ch. moderator Mystic Congl. Ch., 2005-. Named to Parma City (Ohio) Schs. Hall of Fame. Mem. AAUW, Am. Alliance for Theatre and Edn. (co-chair, founder mid./jr. H.S. program com. 1972—, chair membership com. 1989, bd. dirs. 1988-91, chair conv. 1993), New Eng. Theatre Conf. (chair children's theatre divsn. 1986-89, judge John Gassner Meml. Playwriting Contest 1989-95, v.p. nat. conf. 1993, coll. fellows 1993—), Conn. Alliance for Arts, Ballard Inst., Mus. of Puppetry (chair 1995-2003, adv. 2003—). Republican. Avocations: music, needlecrafts, travel.

JANOO, JABIN, obstetrician, gynecologist; b. Nairobi, Kenya, Aug. 26, 1969; arrived in U.S., 1997; d. Tajdin Kassam and Jenab Ismail Janoo; m. Farrukh Mamfuz Jalisi; children: Inara Farrukh Jalisi, Alina Sanniya Jalisi. MB, BChir, Aga Khan U., Karachi, Pakistan, 1994; MD, U.S. Med. Licensing Examination, 1997. Lic. physician W.Va., cert. Am. Bd. Ob-gyn. Ho. officer Aga Khan U. Hosp., Karachi, 1995—96, rsch. officer, 1996—97; resident in internal medicine W.Va. U. Hosp., Morgantown, 1997—98, resident in ob-gyn., 1999—2002, chief resident, 2002—. Organizer, designer health survey Aga Khan Found./UNICEF, Tajikistan, 1995—96; facilitator, advisor Aga Khan U., 1995. Contbr. articles to profl. jours. Scholar Aga Khan Found., 1989. Fellow: Am. Coll. Ob-Gyn.; mem.: ACP (Best Rschr. award 1999). Avocations: swimming, reading, writing, walking. Office: WVa Univ Hosp Dept ObGyn Stadium Dr Morgantown WV 26506 Office Phone: 304-293-5632. Office Fax: 304-293-2131. E-mail: jajezfj@hotmail.com.

JANOS, ELLEN L., lawyer; b. 1951; BA with honors, Simmons Coll., 1973; JD magna cum laude, New Eng. Sch. Law, 1977. Bar: Mass. 1977, US Supreme Ct. 1984, US Ct. Appeals (1st Cir.). Adminstrv. counsel Mass. Atty. Gen. Office; asst. atty. gen. Commonwealth of Mass.; ptnr., Health Care Sect. Mintz Levin Cohn Ferris Glovsky & Popeo PC, Boston, coord., Fraud & Abuse & Corp. Compliance Practice Group. Contbr. editor Health Care Fraud & Abuse Newsletter, NY Law Pub. Co., spkr. in field. Mem. Mass. Bd. Medicine Task Force, 1992. Office: Mintz Levin Cohn Ferris Glovsky & Popeo PC One Financial Ctr Boston MA 02111 Office Phone: 617-348-1662. Office Fax: 202-542-2241. Business E-Mail: ejanos@mintz.com.

JANOVEC, MADELINE MEZA, artist, educator; b. L.A., Feb. 14, 1935; d. Joachim Joseph and Martha (Meza) J.; m. Morton Kaplan, 1964 (div. 1973); 1 child, Pietra Anna Kaplan. BS, Portland (Oreg.) State U., 1971; postgrad., Pacific Northwest Coll. of Art, 1980-82. Instr. art Clark C.C., Vancouver, Wash., 1978—2001, Mt. Hood C.C., Gresham, Oreg., 1989—91; faculty cmty. edn. Portland C.C., 1988—. Vis. art faculty Exploration of Visual Lang., The Evergreen State Coll., Olympia, Wash., 1987-88; co-leader Contemporary Art Tours to Western Europe, 1986—; co-coord. UN 4th Women Conf., Beijing, 1995. Exhibited in 30 one-woman shows and 35 group shows; group exhibn. Daegu S. Korea, 2001, 2006. Mem. Women's Caucus for Art (founding pres. Portland, 1987-2006, Oreg. chpt.). Studio: 4504 SE Milwaukie Ave 5 Portland OR 97202-4726 Home: 4504 SE Milw Ave Portland OR 97202 Office Phone: 503-231-8646. Personal E-mail: madolano@aol.com.

JANOWITZ, PHYLLIS, poet, educator; b. N.Y.C.; d. Morris and Lillian (Reiner) Winer; m. Julian Janowitz (div. 1968); children— Tama, David. B.A., Queens Coll.; M.F.A., U. Mass., 1970. Vis. asst. prof. Saint Cloud State U., Minn., spring 1978; vis. asst. prof. Cornell U., Ithaca, N.Y., 1980-82, poet-in-residence, 1982-83, asst. prof. English, 1983-90, prof., 1990—; writer-in-residence Ind. Central U., Indpls., spring 1979; vis. lectr. Princeton U., N.J., spring 1980. Author (poems): Rites of Strangers, 1978 (Assoc. Writing Program first selection award); Visiting Rites, 1982 (Nat. Book Critics Circle award nominee), Temporary Dwellings, 1988. Recipient Poetry Prize Stroud Internat. Poetry Festival, 1983; Alfred Hodder fellow Princeton U., 1979; N.E.A. grantee, 1974-75, 88-89. Mem. Assoc. Writing Program (anniversary award 1984), P.E.N., Poetry Soc. Am. (Emily Dickinson award 1983). Home: One Lodge Way Ithaca NY 14850 Office: Cornell U Goldwin Smith Hall Ithaca NY 14853 E-mail: pj26@cornell.edu.

JANSEEN, FAMKE, actress; b. Amsterdam, Noord-Holland, Netherlands, Nov. 5, 1965; m. Tod Williams, 1995 (div. 2000). Actor: (films) Fathers and Sons, 1992, Relentless IV: Ashes to Ashes, 1994, Lord of Illusions, 1995, GoldenEye, 1995, Dead Girl, 1996, City of Industry, 1997, Snitch, 1998, The Gingerbread Man, 1998, Deep Rising, 1998, RPM, 1998, Celebrity, 1998, Rounders, 1998, The Adventures of Sebastian Cole, 1998, The Faculty, 1998, House on Haunted Hill, 1999, Love and Sex, 2000, Circus, 2000, X-Men, 2000, Made, 2001, Don't Say a Word, 2001, I Spy, 2002, X2: X-Men United, 2003, Eulogy, 2004, Family of the Year, 2004, Hide and Seek, 2005; (TV films) Model by Day, 1994; TV appearances include: Star Trek: The Next Generation, 1992; Melrose Place, 1994; The Untouchables, 1994; Ally McBeal, 2000, 2001; Dinner for Five, 2002, 2003; Nip/Tuck, 2004. Office: Creative Artist Agency 9830 Wilshire Blvd Beverly Hills CA 90212-1825

JANSEN, ANGELA BING, artist, educator; b. N.Y.C., Aug. 17, 1929; d. Lester and Jean Bing; m. Gunther Jansen, Mar. 8, 1956; children— Edmund, Douglas. BA, Bklyn. Coll., 1951; MA, NYU, 1953; student, Bklyn. Mus. Art Sch., 1947-50, Atelier 17, N.Y.C., 1950-52. Tchr. art, public schs., N.Y.C., 1954-60. One-man shows: Madison (Wis.) Art Center, 1977, Gimpel & Weitzenhoffer, N.Y.C., 1974, 78, group shows: Bklyn. Mus., 1950, 70, 76, Library of Congress, Washington, 1969, 71, Ljubljana Internat. Print Biennale, Yugoslavia, 1971, 73, 75, 77, Venice Biennale, 1972, Internat. Exhbn. Drawing, Rejeka, Yugoslavia, 1972 (award), Internat. Print Biennale, Cracow, Poland, 1978; represented in permanent collections: Mus. Modern Art, N.Y.C., Met. Mus. Art, N.Y.C., N.Y. Pub. Library, Art Inst. Chgo., Tate Gallery, London, Victoria and Abert Mus., London, Bibliotheque Nationale, Paris, Bklyn. Mus., Phila. Mus. Art, Fonds d'Art Contemporain, Centre de Recherche et d'Etude de la Sculpture Contemporaine, Mauberge, France, Musée du Petit Format, Couvin, Belgium, Bklyn. Mus., Francine Tyler Art Forum, summer, 1979. Nat. Endowment for Arts grantee, 1974—75.

JANSON HEINTZ, MAUREEN, dancer, educator, choreographer; b. Chgo., May 8, 1961; d. Gene and Peg Janson; m. Heintz Claude Richard, July 22, 2005. BS in Ballet with distinction, Ind. U., Bloomington, 1983; MFA in Modern Dance with honors, U. Mich., Ann Arbor, 1993. Tchr. Sigurdson Sch. Ballet, Chgo., 1987—89, Meml. HS, Madison, Wis., 1996—99; artistic dir. Smartdance, Madison, 1993—; tchr., lectr. U. Wis., Madison, 1994—, coord. dance, fitness and movement, 2002—. Choreographer Am. Players Theatre, Spring Green, Wis., 2000—, Madison Repertory Theatre, 2003—05, Gt. River Shakespeare Fest, Winona, Minn., 2004—; presenter in field; tchr. Victory Gardens Theatre, Chgo., 2001—02; dance divsn. coord. U. Alaska, Fairbanks, 1992—94; coord. Arts Talkback performance series, Madison, 1994; tchr. master classes, resident various univs., art and dance orgns. Freelance writer: arts, travel, features pieces; solo dancer numerous nat. venues, 1990—, dancer numerous group programs. Grants panelist Dane County Cultural Affairs Commn., 1998—2003; mem. bd., grants panel Madison Arts Commn., 2004—; sec. bd. dirs. Wis. Dance Coun., 1996—2000; mem. arts focus group Chgo. Cmty. Arts Project, 1992; bd. dirs. Friends of Dance, U. Mich., 1991—92. Fellow, Dance Critics Assn., 2004; grantee, Dance County Cultural Affairs Commn., 1994, Innovative Prodn. Fund, 1995, fellowship, Wis. Arts Bd., 1995, Dade County Cultural Affairs Commn., 1995—, Madison Citiarts, 1999, 2004, 2006, Madison Civic Ctr. Found., 1999, 2002, Wis. Arts Bd., 2001, Chgo. Dance Tchg. Initiative, 2003; Rackham Dissertation grantee, U. Mich., 1992—93. Mem.: Nat. Dance Edn. Assn., Chgo. Dance and Music Alliance. Address: 113 Lansing St Madison WI 53714-2232

JANSSEN, CARRON JOYCE, music educator; b. Chgo., Aug. 28, 1955; d. Howard Armstrong and Shirley Lois Turpin; m. Uwe Detlof Janssen, June 18, 1983; children: Noel Uwe, Rachel Frances, Erica Heather. AA, William Rainey Harper Coll., 1980; MusB, Elmhurst Coll., 1997; MA in Tchg., Aurora U., 2002. Cert. tchr. State of Ill., 1997. Elem. music specialist Sch. Dist. U-46, Elgin, Ill., 1997—, mem. music/art/spl. edn. task force, 2005—. Music dept. com. Sch. Dist. U-46, Elgin, 1999—, Sunnydale bldg. com., 2004—, dist. stds. and reporting com., 2000—04. Clk. course Hanover Pk. Pk. Dist. Swim Team, Ill., 1998—. Mem.: NEA, Nat. Campaign for Tolerance, Elgin Tchrs. Assn., Ill. Edn. Assn., Ill. Music Educators Assn., Nat. Assn. Music Edn., Omicron Delta Kappa, Lambda Sigma Psi, Kappa Delta Pi, Phi Kappa Phi. Mem. United Church Christ. Avocations: various musical instruments, singing, reading, swimming. Home: 216 Carver Ln Schaumburg IL 60193-1219 Office Phone: 630-213-5610. Personal E-mail: carronuwe6183@sbcglobal.net. E-mail: carronjanssen@u-46.org.

JANSSEN, JANICE BEATY, writer, educator; b. Elmira, N.Y., Jan. 31, 1930; d. Henry A. and Marjorie Finch Janowski; m. James B. Beaty (dec.); children: William Beaty, Bruce Beaty, David Beaty; m. Dale H. Janssen (dec.). BS, Geneseo State U., 1952; MS, Elmira Coll., 1969; PhD, Cornell U., 1975. Tchr. Kenmore Pub. Schs., NY, 1952—53; office mgr. Manpower, Inc., Buffalo, 1953—54; tchr. Elmira Pub. Schs., 1954—56, Guam Pub. Schs., 1956—58; ednl. coord. Head Start, Elmira, 1969—70; prof. human svcs. Elmira Coll., 1977—91, prof. emerita, 1991—. Cons. U. Rsch. Corp., Washington, 1977—78. Author (with H. Tucker): (textbook) The Computer as a Paintbrush, 1987; author: Picture Book Storytelling, 1994, Converting Conflicts in Preschool, 1995, Building Bridges with Multicultural Picture Books, 1997; author: (with L. Pratt) Transcultural Children's Literature, 1999; author: Prosocial Guidance for the Preschool Child, 1999; author: (with L. Pratt) Early Literacy in Preschool and Kindergarten, 2007; author: Safety in Preschool Programs, 2004, Skills for Preschool Teachers, 2004, Fifty Early Childhood Literacy Strategies, 2005, Observing Development of the Young Child, 2006, 50 Early Childhood Guidance Strategies, 2006, (adult nonfiction) Discovering Guam, 1967; author: (with D. Janssen) Mark Twain Walking America Again, 1987, Storytelling Mark Twain Style, 1988, Traveling West Mark Twain Style, 1989; author: (children's books) Plants in His Pack, 1964, Seeker of Seaways, 1966, Guam Today and Yesterday, 1968, Nufu and the Turkeyfish, 1969. Participant People-to-People Early Childhood Conf., Beijing, 1992, Moscow, 1992, Warsaw, 1992—93, 1994—95. Mem.: Mark Twain Soc., Nat. Assn. for Edn. of Young Children, Kappa Delta Pi. Avocations: birdwatching, photography, petroglyphs, travel. Home: Unit 4 3913 SE 11th Pl Cape Coral FL 33904

JANUSKI, LAURIE A., secondary school educator; b. Kankakee, Ill., Feb. 24, 1965; d. Gene E. and Sandra Ann Donley; m. Kevin Januski; children: Matthew, Mallory. BS, Ea. Ill. U., Charleston, 1988; MA in Edn., Olivet Nazarene U., Bourbonnais, Ill., 2005. Tchr. Blue Mound Sch. Dist., Ill., 1992—94, BBCHS, Bradley, Ill., 1996—. Office: BBCHS 700 W North St Bradley IL 60915 Office Phone: 815-937-3707. Business E-Mail: ljanuski@bbchs.k12.il.us.

JANZEN, NORINE MADELYN QUINLAN, clinical laboratory scientist; b. Fond du Lac, Wis., Feb. 9, 1943; d. Joseph Wesley and Norma Edith (Gustin) Quinlan; m. Douglas Mac Arthur Janzen, July 18, 1970; 1 son, Justin James. BS, Marian Coll., 1965; med. technologist, St. Agnes Sch. Med. Tech., Fond du Lac, 1966; MA, Ctrl. Mich. U., 1980. Med. technologist Mayfair Med. Lab., Wauwatosa, Wis., 1966—69; supr. med. technologist Drs. Mason, Chamberlain, Franke, Klink & Kamper, Milw., 1969—76, Hartford-Parkview Clinic, Ltd., 1976—94; supr. patient svc. ctrs. Med. Sci. Labs., Wauwatosa, 1994—97; supr. patient svc. ctrs. Poole Med. Tech. Med. Sci. Labs, 1997—98; clin. mgr. Planned Parenthood Wis., 1997—99; coord. health in bus. Hartford Parkview Clinic, 1990—91, coord. drug program, 1991—94; lab. outreach coord. Cmty. Meml. Hosp., Menomonee Falls, Wis., 2000—. Co-chair joint mtg. Clin. Lab. Mgrs. Assn. and Wis. Assn. for Clin. Lab. Scientists, 1993-94. Mem. Dem. Nat. Com., 1973—; substitute poll worker Fond du Lac Dem. Com., 1964—65; recognition coord Cmty. League Youth Coll., 2000—; focus team leader Coll. Youth Ministries, Meth. Ch., 2000—; mem., coord. Post Card Ministry Bd., 1998—2001; lay del. to ann. conf. United Meth. Ch., Menomonee Falls, 2004—, bd. dirs. Teen Ctr., 2000—; bd. dirs. Menomonee Falls Teen Ctr., 2000—, Iowa State Parents Assn., 2001—04. Mem.: AAUW (corr. sec. 1994—96, rec. sec. 1996—98, pub. policy chair 1998—2001, chair Evening of Literary Excellence 2001—02, pres. 2001—03, treas. 2003—06, state, dist. 2 coord. 2003—, co-chair ann. meeting 2004—05), Southea. Suprs. Group (co-chmn. 1976—77), Milw. Soc. Clin. Lab. Scientists (pres. 1971—72, bd. dirs. 1972—73, exec. sec. 1999—), Clin. Lab. Mgmt. Assn. (co-chair joint meeting 1993—94), Wis. Assn. Clin. Lab. Scientists (chmn. awards com. 1976—77, treas. 1977—81, dir. 1977—84, pres.-elect 1981—82, pres. 1982—83, chmn. awards com. 1984—85, dir. 1985—87, chmn. awards com. 1986—87, chair ann. meeting 1987—88, exec. sec. 1991—, Mem. of Yr. award 1982, 1995, Svc. award), Nat. Soc. Clin. Lab. Scientists (awards com. chair 1984—87, 1988—91, nominations com. 1989—92), Am. Soc. Clin. Lab. Scientists (people to people clin. lab. scientist del. to People's Rep. China 1989, Mem. of Yr. award 1997), Warhawk Band Boosters (uniform fundraiser chair 1996—98, chair Trysting Place tent party fundraiser 1997—2000), Comm. Wis. (chmn. 1977—79, originator), LWV, Cmty. League, Alpha Mu Tau, Alpha Delta Theta (nat. dist. chmn. 1967—69, nat. alumnae dir. 1969—71). Home: N101 W17383 Tanglewood Dr Germantown WI 53022 Office: Cmty Meml Hosp W180 N 8085 Town Hall Rd Menomonee Falls WI 53051 Office Phone: 262-257-3453. Personal E-mail: nmjanzen@aol.com.

JAPPINEN, AMY JO, middle school educator; b. Lancaster, Wis., Sept. 5, 1968; d. Ronald Wesley and Edith Ann Hunter; m. Erik David Jappinen, July 20, 1996; children: Tessa Josephine, Alyssa Marie. BS, U. Wis., Platteville, 1991; M in Curriculum and Instrn., U. Wis., Whitewater, 1997. Long term substitute tchr. Chippewa Falls Sch. Dist., Wis., 1992—92; mid. sch. tchr. Oconomowoc Area Sch. Dist., Wis., 1992—. Mid. sch. musical dir. Oconomowoc Area Sch. Dist., Wis., 1992—. Sec. bd. dirs. Little Lambs, Oconomowoc, 2006—. Recipient Outstanding Alumni award, U. Wis. Platteville Alumni Assn., 1991. Mem.: Oconomowoc Edn. Assn. (assoc.). Methodist. Avocations: walking, piano, needlecrafts, dance, scrapbooks. Office Phone: 262-560-4305 ext. 4380.

JARAMILLO, ALBA, community educator; b. Mex., 1980; Rschr., cmty. educator Southern Ariz. Ctr. Against Sexual Assault, Tucson. Mem. Tucson Youth Take Back the Night; dir., coordinator cmty. com., V-Day Tucson: The Vagina Monologues; bd. dirs. Borderlands Theatre Co. Named one of 40 Under 40, Tucson Bus. Edge, 2006. Office: Southern Arizona Center Against Sexual Assault 1600 N Country Club Tucson AZ 85716 Office Phone: 520-327-1171. Office Fax: 520-327-2992.*

JARAMILLO, JUANA SEGARRA, chancellor; b. San Sebastian, P.R., Mar. 24, 1937; d. Joaquin M. and Carmen M. (Gerena) Segarra; m. Edgar J. Jaramillo, Apr. 13, 1957; children: Jeanette, Yila, Yvonne, Melissa, Edgar Jr. BA, Poly. Inst. P.R., San German, 1956; postgrad., U. Fla., 1956-57; MS, La. State U., 1963. Libr. dir. Inter-Am. U., Aguadilla (P.R.) Regional Coll., 1975-76, cons. libr. and accreditation, 1983—; libr. U.P.R.-Aguadilla Regional Coll., 1976-77, libr. dir., 1983-86, libr., 1986-89, chair steering com. for accreditation, mem. directive coun. honors program, 1989—, dir. instl. planning and rsch., 1989-90, libr. dir., 1990-94, acting assoc. acad. dean, 1994—, dean, dir., 1994-99; libr. dir. EDP Coll. P.R., San Sebastian, 1979-83; acting assoc. acad. dean U. P.R., Aguadilla, 1994, dean, dir., 1994—; chancellor U. P.R. at Aguadilla, 1999—. Mem. steering com. nat. edn. program Am. Coun. Edn., P.R., 1982-86, adv. bd. Coun. Higher Edn., P.R., 1982—; external evaluator Middle States Assn. Colls. and Schs., 1997—. Author: Manual bibliografico Electronica, 1987; co-author: El Desarrollo del Pensamiento Critico en Futuros Maestros, 1989; contbr. articles to profl. jours. Mem. Club Civico de Damas, Aguadilla, 1989—. With U.S. Army, 1963-66. Mem. ALA, Am. Assn. Higher Edn., Assn. Caribbean Univs., Rsch. and Instl. Librs., Sociedad de Bibliotecarios de P.R. (pres. continuing edn.

1984-90), Mid. States Assn. Colls. and Schs. (evaluating team mem. 1998—), Rotary-Anns (pres. 1974), Internat. Altrusan, Alpha Delta Kappa. Avocations: cooking, water sports, travel. Office: UPR Aguadilla PO Box 160 Ramey Aguadilla PR 00604-0160 E-mail: losjara@prtc.net, j_segarra@cora.upr.du.edu.

JARAMILLO, MARI-LUCI, retired federal agency administrator; b. Las Vegas, N.Mex., June 19, 1928; BA magna cum laude, N.Mex. Highland U., 1955, MA with honors, 1959; PhD, U. N.Mex., 1970. Tchr., Albuquerque and Las Vegas, N.Mex., 1955-65; asst. prof. U. N.Mex., 1965-72, assoc. prof., chmn. dept. elem. edn., 1972-75, assoc. prof. edn., 1976-77, prof., 1977, spl. asst. to pres., 1981-82, assoc. dean Coll. Edn., 1982-85, v.p. for student affairs, 1985-87; amb. to Republic of Honduras U.S. Dept. State, 1977-80, dep. asst. sec. for Inter-Am. affairs Washington, 1980-81; asst. v.p., dir. Ednl. Testing Service, Emeryville, Calif., 1987-93; dep. asst. sec. for Inter-Am. affairs Dept. Def., Washington, 1993-95. Bd. trustees Tomas Rivera Nat. Policy Ctr., Claremont (Calif.) Coll. Grad. Sch., 1985-93; minority recruiter Dept. State, Washington, 1990-2000; commr. Calif. Commn. of Post-Secondary Edn., Sacramento, 1990-93; active Coun. Am. Ambs., Washington, 1983-; bd. dirs. Latin Am. Scholarship Program for Am. Univs., Boston, Children's TV Workshop, N.Y.C.; cons. for curriculum, tchr. tng. and sch. reform, 1960-; vice chair, bd. regents, N.Mex. Highlands U., 2001—. Author: Madame Ambassador; The Shoe Maker's Daughter, 2002; contbr. articles to jours., chpts. to books. Bd. dirs. Internat. House, U. Calif., Berkeley, 1989-93; scholar panelist Nat. Latino Comm. Ctr., L.A., 1990—; active Bay area Network L.Am. Women, San Francisco, 1987-93; regent N.Mex. Highlands U., 2003—, vice chair, 2000—. Decorated Order Francisco Morazan (Honduras), Order of Great Silver Cross (Honduras); recipient Cubberly award Stanford U., 1975, N.Mex. Disting. Svc. award, 1977, Anne Roe award Harvard U. Grad. Sch. Edn., 1986, PRIMERA award Mex. Am. Women's Nat. Assn., 1990; named Outstanding Chicana, 1975, Hon. Honduran Citizen, Govt. of Honduras, 1980, Disting. Woman of Yr., U. N.Mex. Alumni Assn., 1985, Disting. Hispanic lectr. Calif. State U. at Fullerton, 1988, Outstanding Hispanic Educator, 1988, Outstanding Leader in Edn. to Hispanic Cmty., 1991. Mem. Nat. Assn. Bilingual Edn., Latin Am. Assn., Am. Assn. Colls. for Tchr. Edn., Nat. Council La Raza. Home: 10501 Lagrima de Oro NE Apt 342 Albuquerque NM 87111

JARANILLA, SARAH J., critical care nurse, consultant; arrived in U.S., 1976; d. Angelo C. and Leonor J. Jaranilla; children: Christine Joy Reynoso, Jerome Jay Laguilles, Sarah Joy Laguilles. BSN, Philippine Union Coll., Manila, 1973. RN Tex. Head nurse med./surg. unit Bacolod (The Philippines) Sanitarium & Hosp., 1973—75; charge nurse med./surg. unit Hansford Hosp., Spearman, Tex., 1976—77; critical care RN Monterey Park (Calif.) Hosp., 1978—80; DON, owner Sarnel Nurse Registry, West Covina, Calif., 1980—85; DON CJS Nursing Svcs., West Covina, 1985—93; adminstr., dir. patient svcs. Alpha Omega Home Health Svcs., Inc., Glendora, Calif., 1994—96; adminstr., owner Alternative Staffing, Inc., Torrance, Calif., 1997—2002; adminstr., dir. patient svcs. Gen. Home Health Care, Glendale, Calif., 2003—. Recipient Virgo Nurse of the Yr. award, Virgo Prodn., 2000. Mem.: Philippine Nurses Assn. So. Calif. (assoc.). Office Phone: 323-578-8533. Personal E-mail: sjaranilla@aol.com.

JARCHO, JUDITH LYNN, artist; b. Mpls., Mar. 24, 1944; d. Paul and Lillian (Garetz) Brazman; m. Michael Jarcho, Nov. 24, 1968; children: Jason M., Johanna Molly. BFA, Mpls. Coll. Art & Design, 1968; tchg. credential elem. and art edn., Coll. St. Rose, Albany, N.Y., 1975. Grades K-6 art tchr. Albany Sch. Dist., 1971-74; art tchr. Portrait Soc., La Jolla, Calif., 1996, San Digeto Art Assn., Del Mar, Calif., 1996, El Cajon (Calif.) Art Assn., 1997. Juror Del Mar Art Fair/Art Exhbn., 1995, El Cajon Art Assn. Annual Exhbn., 1996, San Diego Art Inst., 1998. Works exhibited San Diego Mus. Art, 1994, Rose-Hulman Inst. Tech., Terre Haute, Ind., 1994, Nat. Arts Club, N.Y.C., 1994, Poudre Valley Artist League, Denver, 1995, Tijuana (Mexico) Cultural Ctr., 1995, Hampton Classic, Bridgehampton, N.Y., 1995, Perry House Galleries, Old Town Alexandria, Va., 1995, Linda Joslin Gallery, La Jolla, Calif., 1995, Mpls. Found., 1996, Robert Mondavi Food & Wine Ctr., Orange County, Calif., 1996, The Parrish Art Mus., South Hampton, N.Y., 1996, San Diego Mus. Art, 1995-99, Univ. Club, San Diego, 1998, Brenda Taylor Gallery, NYC. Philantropist Helen Woodward Animal Ctr., Rancho Santa Fe, Calif., 1996-98; past pres. San Diego Mus. of Art Artist Guild. Named Entrepreneur of Yr., Vishe Corp., San Diego, 1998, Best Canine Artist, Manhattan Guest mag., 2001, Overall Gold award ann. report competition League Am. Comm. Profls., 2001. Office Phone: 888-518-2424. E-mail: jjarcho@msn.com.

JARDINE, CINDY M., music educator; b. Tucson, Ariz., May 26, 1953; d. Lawrence Ralph Crouch, Arlene Ione (Fish) Crouch; m. Herald J. Jardine, Aug. 7, 1971; 1 adopted child, Brian P. Lima children: Robbi Ann, Tony, Nanette, Miken, Barbara, Janni. Cert. baton/dance tchr., Sharonlee's Sch. Dance, Elko, Nev., 1971. Tchr. choir and drill team Buhl Sch. Dist., Buhl, Idaho, 1981—84; tchr. choir, string, drill team Butte County Sch. Dist., Arco, Idaho, 1993—. Owner, operator Cindy's Majorettes, Arco, Castleford, Mustaugh, Idaho, 1971—; pvt. music tchr., Arco, 1971—; music cons. State of Idaho, 1993—. Author: (plays) What Goes Beyond "Z". Dir. Murtaugh Little Theatre, 1986—90; pres. Lost Rivers Cmty. Arts, Arco, 1998—; bd. dirs. Lost Rivers Cmty. Choir and Theater, Arco. Mem.: Music Tchr. Assn. (6th dist. Idaho, Music Tchr. of Yr. 1996, 1998), Music Educators Nat. Conf. Mem. Lds Ch. Home: RR 1 Box 480 Arco ID 83213-9753

JARDINE, KATHY JO, science educator; b. Comfrey, Minn., July 23, 1979; d. Elmer James and Jane Ann Evers; m. James William Jardine, Jr., July 16, 2005. BS in Biology Edn., Winona State U., Minn., 2001, MS in Edn., 2004. Sci. tchr. grades 7-10 Swanville (Minn.) H.S., 2001—03; sci. tchr. grades 10-12 Maccray H.S., Clara City, Minn., 2003—. Home: PO Box 353 Clara City MN 56222

JARLES, RUTH SEWELL, education educator; d. Nashville Clyde Sewell and Zetta Marie Hurt; m. Terry Waters Milligan, June 16, 1990; m. Marion Evert Jarles, Dec. 19, 1957 (div. Mar. 1980); children: Leslie Marie Murphy, Eva Colleen Wakeley, Brian Keith. AA, Western Okla. State Coll., 1976; BA magna cum laude, U. Colo., Colorado Springs, 1982; MDiv, Iliff Sch. Theology, 1985; PhD, U. Denver, 1993. Dir. Christian edn. Patrick Henry Village Army Chapel, Heidelberg, Germany, 1973—74; dir. curriculum Grace Child Devel. Ctr., Altus, Okla., 1976—77; dir. Christian edn. First Congl. Ch., Colorado Springs, Colo., 1980—84; asst. to the dir. joint PhD program U. Denver, Iliff Sch. Theology, 1991—92; adj. faculty, tchg. or rsch. asst. U. Denver, Iliff Sch. Theology, Front Range and Auraria C.C., 1983—98; asst. materials sci. br. Nat. Renewable Energy Lab., Golden, Colo., 1994—95; exec. dir. Colo. Libr. Assn., Denver, 1995—98; gen. edn. faculty Art Inst. Colo., Denver, 1998—. Seminar leader Gender Differences in Comm. in the Workplace; session convenor, panel mem. Women in Religion; lectr. in field. Contbr. articles to profl. jours. Student senate Iliff Sch. Theology, Denver, 1984—86; mentor students cmty. svc. projects Art Inst. Colo., Denver, 1997—; chair/mem. South Africa task force, race and religion com., women's com. Iliff Sch.Theology, Denver, 1984—92; mem. publs. com. Colo. Women's Agenda, Denver, 1993—95, 2005; chair/mem. edn., fin., adminstrv. bd., music and fine arts, peace with justice coms. Trinity United Meth. Ch., Denver, 1984—92; mem. exec. com. Nat. Renewable Energy Lab. Women's Network, Golden, 1994—95; active Art Inst. Colo. Christmas project Denver Safe Ho., 2001—. Recipient E. Craig Brandenburg award, United Meth. Ch.; scholar Ea. Star Tng. awards for Religious Leadership, The Grand Chpt. Colo., Order Ea. Star, 1984—86; Oliver Read Whitley scholar, Iliff Sch. Theology, Seminarian scholar, Ctr. for Biblic Studies, Jerusalem, Israel, Ga. Harkness scholar, United Meth. Ch. Mem.: AAUW, Nat. Mus. Women in the Arts. Office: Art Inst Colo 1200 Lincoln St Denver CO 80203 Home: 6240 W 24th Ave Edgewater CO 80214-1034 Office Phone: 303-824-2151. Personal E-mail: jarlesr@earthlink.com.

JARMANN, JANET, systems administrator, systems analyst; Computer sys. analyst human resources divsn. NASA, Moffett Field, Calif. Avocations: cooking, gardening, movies, travel, museums. Office: NASA Ames Rsch Ctr Bldg 241 Rm 152 Moffett Field CA 94035

JARMON, JEANETTE, artist, educator; b. Vicksburg, Miss., Feb. 21, 1954; d. Henry McLean and Ola Mae Jarmon; children: Sarah Grace Ford, Benjamin Carl Carver, Jesse McLean Carver, Aaron Grayson Carver. BS of Edn. and Art, Miss. Coll., Clinton, 1976, M of Edn. and Art, 1991. Nat. Bd. Cert., Miss. Artist Art by JNET, Clinton, 1991; art tchr. Terry (Miss.) H.S., 1999; art instr. Miss. State Hosp., Whitfield, 2001—. Chosen artist Jackson (Miss.) Zoo, 1995, Neshoba County Fair, Philadelphia, Miss., 1997; artist-in-residence Bapt. Healthplex, Clinton, 2004—; spkr. in field. Video series, The Creative Child, 1991 (Hon. Mention, Internat. Film and Video Festival, 1992), mural, The Owl Cafe, 1998. Mem. Leadership Clinton, 1995, Right to Life, Jackson, 1990; art tchr. Vet. Ctr., Jackson. Recipient artist-in-residence grant, NEA, 2000. Mem.: Clinton C. of C., Nat. Assn. Women in Arts. Home: 509 Oakwood Dr Clinton MS 39056 Office: Art by JNET 509 Oakwood Clinton MS 39056 Office Phone: 601-906-3458. Business E-Mail: jarmoje@msh.state.ms.us.

JAROSH, COLLEEN MARIE, nursing educator, consultant; b. Cresco, Iowa, July 4, 1951; d. Raymond James and Marjorie Ester (Burr) McGee; m. Kenneth Charles Jarosh, July 21, 1979; children: Michael, Rebecca. ADN, N.E. Iowa Tech. Inst., Calmar, 1974; BSN, Upper Iowa U., Fayette, 1980; MAE in Edn., U. No. Iowa, Cedar Falls, 1984. RN, Iowa. Nurse Schoitz Meml. Hosp., Waterloo, Iowa, 1974-76, USPHS, Tuba City, Ariz., 1976-77, Phoenix Indian Med. Ctr., 1977-78, Palmar Meml. Hosp., West Union, Iowa, 1978-79; instr. N.E. Iowa Tech. Inst., 1979; sch. nurse Upper Iowa U., 1979, adj. instr., 1979-83; writer, co-editor newsletter Dept. Human Svcs., Waterloo, 1994-98; ednl. cons. Janesville, Iowa, 1980—. Mediator Child Welfare, 1998—. Vol. St. Mary's ch., Waverly, Iowa, 1994—; support group leader Luth. Social Svcs., Waterloo, 1994. Mem. Rosary Soc., Iowa Foster Adoptive Parents Assn (bd. dirs.), Acad. Family Mediators. Avocations: special needs adoption, prairie restoration, tree planting, reading. Home: 1774 County Road W14 Calmar IA 52132-7517 Office Phone: 563-534-7675.

JAROSZEWSKI, LISA ELAINE, literature and language educator; b. Houston; d. Warren and Waldine Winter; m. Richard Jaroszewski, Dec. 16, 1989; children: Hannah, Michael. BJ, BA in English, U. Tex., Austin, 1987. Cert. secondary English tchr. Tex., 1990. Tchr. English, Sam Houston H.S., 1987—92, New Braunfels H.S., Tex., 1993—. Office: New Braunfels HS 2551 Loop 337 North New Braunfels TX 87130 Office Phone: 830-627-6202. Personal E-mail: ljaroszewski@newbraunfels.txed.net.

JARQUIN, THERESA BINNING, gifted and talented educator; d. Joe and Maxine Binning; m. Janio Jarquin, Dec. 18, 1982; children: Joe, Katie. B in Bus., U. La., Monroe, 1982; MEd, Northwestern State U., Natchitoches, La., 1992. Gifted edn. tchr. North Desoto H.S., Stonewall, La., 2003—. Dir. religious edn. St. Joseph's Cath. Ch., Mansfield, 1992—94. Office: North Desoto HS 2571 Highway 171 Stonewall LA 71078 Office Phone: 318-925-6917.

JARRELL, BRENDA HERSCHBACH, lawyer; b. 1967; AB magna cum laude, Harvard U., 1988, MA, 1988, JD, 1998; PhD, U. Calif., 1993. Bar: Mass. 1998. Ptnr., chmn. life sciences group Choate, Hall & Stewart, LLP, Boston. Named one of Top 40 Lawyers Under 40, Nat. Law Jour., 2005. Office: Choate Hall & Stewart 2 International Pl Boston MA 02110 Office Phone: 617-248-5175. Office Fax: 617-248-4000. E-mail: bjarrell@choate.com.

JARRELL, IRIS BONDS, elementary school educator, retired small business owner; b. Winston-Salem, N.C., May 25, 1942; d. Ira and Annie Gertrude (Vandiver) Bonds; m. Tommy Dorsey Martin, Feb. 13, 1965; 1 child, Carlos Miguel; m. 2d, Clyde Rickey Jarrell, June 25, 1983; stepchildren: Tamara, Cris, Kimberly. Student, U. N.C., Greensboro, 1960-61, 68-69, student, 1974-75, Salem Coll., 1976; BS in Edn., Winston-Salem State U., 1983; M in Elem. Edn., Gardner-Webb Coll., 1992. Cert. tchr., N.C. Tchr. Rutledge Coll., Winston-Salem, 1982-84; owner, mgr. Rainbow's End Consignment Shop, Winston-Salem, 1983-85; tchr. elem. edn. Winston-Salem/Forsyth County Sch. Svcs., 1985-96; dir. Knollwood Bapt. Pre-Sch., 1996-97; tchr. gifted/talented students Winston-Salem/Forsyth County Schs., 1998; tchr. Clemmons Elem. Sch., 1998—. Author: numerous poems. Mem. Assn. of Couples for Marriage Enrichment, Winston-Salem, 1985-86; mem. Winston-Salem Symphony Chorale; mem. Planned Parenthood. Mem. NOW, AAUW, ACLU, Internat. Reading Assn., N.C. Assn. Adult Edn., Forsyth Assn. Classroom Tchrs., World Wildlife Fund, Greenpeace, KlanWatch, Humane Soc. Democrat. Baptist. Avocations: singing, writing, sewing, gardening, reading. Home: 101 Cheswyck Ln Winston Salem NC 27104-2905 Personal E-mail: ijarrell@triad.rr.com.

JARRETT, ALEXIS, insurance agent, lawyer; b. Independence, Kans., July 2, 1948; d. Robert Patterson and Betty June (Johnson) Jarrett. BS, U. Minn., Duluth, 1970; postgrad., U. Mo., 1974—77; JD, John Marshall Law Sch., 2001. Lic. property and casualty ins. Ind., life and health ins. Ind., cert. Life Underwriting Tng. Coun.; coach Minn. Tchr. Esko (Minn.) Pub. Schs., 1970—74; asst. dir. athletics, head coach basketball, softball, track U. Mo., Columbia, 1974—77; pvt. practice Schererville, Ind., 1984—; pres., CEO INFINITE Sports and Entertainment, Inc., 2002—. Women's basketball and softball color analyst Regional Radio Sports, N.W. Ind., 1992—94; with Moot Ct. Coun., 1999; jud. extern Cir. Ct. Cook County, Chgo., 1999; coord. women's sports info. dept. U. Mo., 1974—77; v.p. legal affairs Nat. Assn. State Farm Agts., Inc., 1997—2000; contract advisor NFL Players Assn., 2002—, Women's Nat. Basketball Players Assn., 2002—, CFL Players Assn., 2003—. Contbr. articles on sports to newspapers. Sponsor Lake County HS Girls Basketball Banquet, Ind., 1989—99; bd. dirs. Samaritan Counseling Ctr. N.W. Ind., pres., 1994; bd. dirs. VNA Found., sec.-treas., 1994; celebrity Am. Heart Assn. Celebrity Dinner; v.p. S.W. Lake divsn. Am. Heart Assn., 1992—94; mem. bd. advisors Basketball Hall of Fame, 1999—; bd. dirs. Boys and Girls Club N.W. Ind.; mem. adv. bd. indsl. rsch. liaison program Ind. U., Bloomington, 1990—96. Recipient Individual with Vision award, Ind. HS Athletic Assn., 1996. Mem.: ABA (entertainment and sports law forum, labor and law com., ins. law com., sports law subcom.), Sports Lawyers Assn., Chgo. Bar Assn. (labor and employment law com., ins. law com., immigration law com., health law com.), Ind. State Med. Assn. Alliance (chair media rels. 1990—91, treas. 1992—93, chair media rels. 1993—94), Am. Bus. Women's Assn. (pres. New Image chpt. 1983, Woman of the Yr. 1983), Lake County Med. Soc. Alliance (pres. 1992—94), Nat. Life Underwriters (bd. dirs. N.W. Ind. chpt. 1995, 1996, 1997). Address: 2330 Wicker Blvd Schererville IN 46375-2810

JARRETT, BENITA V., medical/surgical nurse, minister; b. Chgo., Jan. 16, 1950; d. Curtis and Ella Louise Lewis; m. James Jarrett Jr., Sept. 21, 1990; children: Kathleen Head, John Jr., Kimberly Glynn. BSN, DePaul U., 1972; MDiv, McCormick Theol. Seminary, 1986, PhD, 1996. RN Ill., Ga., cert. pub. health nurse Ill.; ordained minister Am. Bapt. Ch., 1986. Nurse Jackson Pk. Hosp., 1983—93; home health nurse Evang. Home Care, 1993—94; sch. nurse, 1994—98; case mgr. Intracorp, 2000; sch. nurse Decatur Bd. Edn., Ill., 2001—. Home health nurse Rush Home Care, 1990—95; dir. Calvary Bapt. Ch.; dir. christian edn. Fellowship United Meth. Ch.; pastor Agape Bapt., Chgo. Contbr. articles to profl. jours. Voter registration NAACP, Atlanta, 2000; mem. Coalition Against Police Brutality, Chgo., 1998; vol. chaplain Dekalb Women's Prison, Ga., 2000; christian educator Holy Cross Episcopal Ch., Ga., 1999; initiated outreach children's ministry St. Thomas Episcopal Ch., Chgo.; exec. dir. Agape-Koinonia Ministries, Chgo. Avocations: gardening, music, painting, interior decorating. Home: 3207 Watson Meadow Ln Loganville GA 30052-8298 E-mail: jarrettbyj@aol.com.

JARRETT, POLLY HAWKINS, retired secondary school educator; b. Columbia, S.C., May 6, 1929; d. William Harold and Ann Beatrice (Carson) Hawkins; m. Nov. 21, 1953 (dec. Aug. 1984); children: William Guy Jr., Henry Carson. Student, Montreat Coll., 1947-49; BS in Secondary Edn., Longwood Coll., 1951. Tchr. 7th grade McDowell County Schs., Marion, N.C., 1951-52; tchr. 8th grade Marion City Schs., 1952-53, Burke County Schs., Morganton, N.C., 1954-56; tchr. 7th grade Wake County Schs., Raleigh, N.C., 1956-58, Durham (N.C.) County Schs., 1958-59; tchr. 7th and 8th grade Raleigh City and Wake County Schs., Raleigh, 1959-79; tchr. social studies Wake County Pub. Schs., Raleigh, 1979-90, ret., 1990. Adv. bd. State Employees Credit Union, Raleigh, 1988—92, Raleigh, 1994—2000. Mem. United Daus. of the Confederacy (chpt. pres. 1978-81, 91-96, divsn. historian 1981-83, dist. VI dir. 1983-85, divsn. chaplain 1986-90, divns. parliamentarian 1994-96, chmn. bd. trustees 1990-91), Delta Kappa Gamma (chpt. pres. 1988-90, regional dir. 1990-92, state 2d v.p. 1997-99, chmn. N.C. divsn. State Conv. 2001, mem. S.E. regional steering com. 2003), Kappa Delta Pi, Pi Delta Epsilon, Pi Gamma Mu. Democrat. Methodist. Avocations: travel, growing roses, reading, pets. Home: 3405 White Oak Rd Raleigh NC 27609-7620

JARRETT, VALERIE BOWMAN, real estate company executive, stock exchange executive; b. Shiraz, Iran, Nov. 14, 1956; d. James Edward and Barbara (Taylor) B.; 1 child, Laura Allison. BA, Stanford U., 1978; JD, U. Mich., 1981. Bar: Ill. 1981, U.S. Dist. Ct. (no. dist.) Ill. 1981. Assoc. Pope, Ballard, Shepard & Fowle Ltd., Chgo., 1981-84, Sonnenschein, Carlin, Nath & Rosenthal, Chgo., 1984; dep. corp. counsel for fin. and devel. City of Chgo., dep. chief of staff for Mayor Richard Daley, commr., dept. planning and devel.; exec. v.p., mng. dir. The Habitat Co., Chgo. Dir. USG Corp., 1998—, Joyce Found., Met. Planning Coun.; chmn. The Chgo. Stock Exch., 2003—, Local Initiative Support Corp.; exec. counsel Chgo. Metropolis 2020. Dir. RREEF Am. II, Navigant Cons., Inc.; pres. Southeast Chgo. Commn., Chicago-land C. of C.; trustee Mus. Sci. and Industry, Windows to the World Comm., U. Chgo.; vice chmn. U. Chgo. Hosps. Leadership Greater Chgo. fellow, 1985-86. Mem. Econ. Club, Comml. Club. Democrat. Avocation: travel. Office: The Habitat Co 350 West Hubbard St Chicago IL 60610 Office Phone: 312-527-5400.*

JARVIS, CHARLENE DREW, academic administrator, former scientist; b. Washington, July 31, 1941; 2 children. BA, Oberlin Coll., Ohio, 1962; MS in Psychology, Howard U., 1964; PhD in Neuropsychology, U. Md., 1971; DSc (hon.), Amherst Coll., 1994, George Washington U., 2001. Supr. statis. lab. Howard U., 1965-66, prof. psychol. Washington, 1970-71; rsch. psychologist NIMH, 1971-78; coun. mem. Coun. of the D.C., 1979-2000; chair com. on housing and econ. devel. coun. of the D.C., 1981-2000; chair pro temp Coun. of the D.C., 1994-2000; pres. Southeastern Univ., Washington, 1996—. Chair bd. dirs. Met. Washington Coun. of Govts.; bd. dirs. Pa. Ave. Devel. Corp., Nat. Health Mus., Fed. City Coun., BB&T Regional Bank, Washington office; mem. steering com. Greater Washington Mktg. Partnership of the Greater Washington Bd. of Trade, 1993—; mem. coms. NIMH, adv. coun., 1993—; mem. breast cancer task force, 1993—; mem. Ronald Reagan Ctr. for Emergency Medicine, George Washington U. Hosp., 1993—. Bd. dirs. Girl Scouts Am., Pvt. Industry Coun., 1986—; mem. Leadership Washington, 1991-92; chair transp. subcom. D.C. chpt. ARC; del. Nat. Dem. Conv., 1980, 84, 88, 92; nat. co-chair Mondale for Pres., 1984, Clinton/Gore campaign, 1992; candidate for mayor, D.C., 1982, 90; chair pro tempore Coun. D.C., 1997—; chair cmty. bus. partnership com. Greater Washington Bd. of Trade; chair, bd. dirs. Washington D.C. Conv. and Tourism Corp., 2001—. Recipient Howard U. Alumni award, 1993, over 100 others; Named one of 50 Most Powerful Women in the Washington Area Washington Bus. Jour., 1985, 100 Most Powerful Women in the Washington Area, Washingtonian Mag., 1989, 94, Washingtonian of Yr. Washingtonian Mag., 1999. Mem. Nat. Assn. Ind. Colls. and Univs. (bd. dirs.), D.C. C. of C. (pres.-elect). Home: 1789 Sycamore St NW Washington DC 20012-1030 Office: Southeastern Univ 501 I St SW Washington DC 20024-2715 E-mail: president@admin.seu.edu.

JARVIS, DAPHNE ELOISE, laboratory administrator; b. Lithia, Fla., Feb. 18, 1945; d. Grady Edwin and Vera Eloise (Smith) Smith; m. Hubert E. Jarvis, Aug. 1, 1964; 1 child, Jessica Ellen. BS, Blue Mountain Coll., 1966; MA, Spalding U., 1972. Cert. med. technologist with specialist in blood bank. Med. technologist St. Anthony's Hosp., Louisville, 1968-69, Clark County Meml. Hosp., Jeffersonville, Ind., 1969-73; asst. to edn. coord. ARC, Washington, 1973-75; dir. Grace Bapt. Ch. Sch., Bryans Rd., Md., 1978-83; sect. chief blood bank Physicians Meml. Hosp., LaPlata, Md., 1975-76, 83-84; supr. donor blood labs. Southwest Fla. Blood Bank, Tampa, 1984-87, dir., 1987-89; asst. dir. tech. svcs. Ark. Region ARC, Little Rock, 1989-93, dir. tech. svcs./hosp. svcs. Ark. Regional Blood Svcs., 1993-95; mfg. team leader Lifeblood-Midsouth Regional Blood Ctr., Memphis, 1995-2000, tech. mgr., 2000—. Lectr. UAMS Sch. Med. Tech., Little Rock, 1989-95. Children's leader Ingram Blvd Bapt. Ch., West Memphis, Ark., 1995—. Mem. Am. Assn. Blood Banks, Am. Soc. Quality, South Ctr. Assn. Blood Banks (membership com. 1989-95). Office: Lifeblood Midsouth Reg Blood Ctr 1040 Madison Ave Memphis TN 38104-2198

JARVIS, REBECCA, financial reporter; b. Mpls., 1981; Grad., U. Chgo., 2003. Interest rate trader fgn. exchange desk Citigroup, London; investment banking analyst Banc of Am. Securities, Chgo.; fin. journalist Chgo.; assoc. reporter CNBC, 2006—. Pro bono cons. Pivot Consulting. Participant (TV series) The Apprentice 4, 2005. Founder Minn. Alliance with Youth; bd. dirs. Youthrive. Named one of 20 Teens Who Will Change the World, Teen People mag., 2000.

JARVIS, SUE KAY, science educator; b. Cherokee, Iowa, Feb. 9, 1959; d. Virgil Harry Schlinz; m. Stephen Lee Jarvis (div.); children: Stephanie Cady, Jason Lindsay. BA in Edn., Wayne State Coll., Nebr., 1986; post grad., Marycrest Coll., Davenport, Iowa, 1986—89, U. No. Iowa, Cedar Falls, 1990—96, post grad., 2003, post grad., 2002, Morningside Coll., Sioux City, 1996—98, Iowa State U., Ames, 1997, Iowa Ctrl. Cmty. Coll., Fort Dodge, 1999. Cert. tchr. Iowa, endorsements in biology, anatomy, physiology, gen. sci., chemistry, physics, phys. edn. and coaching Iowa. Tchr. jr. high biology St. John's Cath. Sch., Bancroft, Iowa, 1987—89, Holy Family Schs., Sioux City, 1989—95; tchr. phys. sci., biology, chemistry and physics Albert City-Truesdale Combined Sch. Dist., 1995—99; substitute tchr. Pocahontas Area Combined Sch. Dist., 2000; tchr. biology, chemistry and TAG Schaller-Crestland Combined Sch. Dist., Early, 2000—03; tchr. biology, anatomy and physiology, health Pocahontas Area Combined Sch. Dist., 2003—. Advisor Nat. Honor Soc.; asst. H.S. softball and basketball; head softball and volleyball; jr. high softball and volleyball; jr. high athletic dir.; advisor dist. and state sci. fairs; faculty sponsor Iowa State Bar Assn. Mock Trial State Tournament. Named AEA 12 Demonstration Sci. Classroom. Mem.: NEA, Ia. State Edn. Assn., Nat. Sci. Tchrs. Assn., Iowa Girls H.S. Athletic Union (volleyball official). Republican. Roman Catholic. Avocations: kayaking, gardening, house remodeling. Office: Pocahontas Area CDS Pocahontas IA 50574 Office Phone: 712-335-4848.

JARY, MARY CANALES, business owner; b. Premont, Tex., Nov. 22, 1936; d. Gus and Ruth (Shively) Canales; m. Lloyd Walker Jary, Apr. 18, 1958; children: Lloyd Walker III, Elisa Jary, Bettina Mathis, Pamela Rosser. Student, Rollins Coll., 1955-56, U. Tex., 1956-58, Incarnate Word Coll., 1959-60, Trinity U., 1966—. Prin., owner Restoration Assocs., San Antonio, 1985—. Pres. San Antonio PTA, 1971; vice chmn. Night in Old San Antonio, 1989—; bd. dirs. San Antonio Conservation Soc., 1972-90, 2d v.p. 1997—. Mem.: AIA (aux. pres. San Antonio chpt. 1970), Assn. of Preservation Tech. (v.p. 2005), Am. Inst. Conservation (assoc.). Republican. Roman Catholic. Avocations: tennis, hunting. Office: Restoration Assn Ltd 3617 Broadway St Ste 302 San Antonio TX 78209-6509 Fax: 210-820-3447. Office Phone: 210-820-3432. E-mail: cisi@prestorationassociates.com.

JASINSKI-CALDWELL, MARY L., insurance company executive; b. Chester, Pa., May 8, 1959; d. A. Robert and Helen M. Jasinski; m. William A. Caldwell, Aug. 4, 1990; children: Helaina M., Anna L. Student, student, Loyola Coll., Balt., 1980; AS, Goldey Beacom Coll., Wilmington, Del., 1982,

BS, 1983. Registered orthotic fitter; cert. sr. pharmacy technician. Gen. mgr. pension plan City Pharmacy of Elkton (Md.), Inc., 1975-96, treas., 1987-96, jr. ptnr., 1994, v.p., 1996—; founder, pres. City Home Health Care, Inc., Elkton, 1997—. Disc jockey, promoter Garfield's Restaurant, Elkton; editl. writer local newspapers; pro-life columnist KC newsletter; nat. bd. advisors McKesson Drug Co., 2001—. Creator ednl. program PARTICIP.A.A.T.E. For Life. Advisor Cecil County Pregnancy Ctr., Cecil County Bd. Edn. Textbook Adoption Policy Com., 1995; pro-life educator City of Elkton, Inc.; varsity I coach Christian Youth Orgn., 2004—06, coach youth volleyball, 2002—; asst. volleyball coach Mason Dixon Volleyball Club, 2005—; chmn. arts and environment com. Immaculate Conception Parish, 2004—; bd. dirs. Cecil County chpt. ARC, 1996—2001, fin. devel. chmn. Cecil County chpt., 2000—01; bd. dirs. Mission Am., Inc., Md. Right to Life, 1993—94, co-chair Cecil County chpt., 1993—94. Alpha Chi scholar, Lindback scholar; recipient J.W. Miller award, Outstanding Achievement in Excellence award K.C., 1994, Ralph and Eleanor Hicks Outstanding Vol. svc. award ARC, Cecil County, Md., 1999-2000; named Family of Yr., 1995; named to Honor Roll of Best 250 Independents in U.S., Drug Topics, 1992, Cecil County Md.'s "Favorite Pharmacy" Cecil Whig's Reader's Poll, 2002, 03, 04, 05, 06. Mem. NAFE, NRA, Am. Pharmacists Assn. (assoc.), Am. Mgmt. Assn., Nat. Fedn. Ind. Bus., Bd. Orthotic Cert., Am. Assn. Pharm. Technicians, Nat. Right to Life Com., Am. Life League, Internat. Platform Assn., Pro-Life Md., Christian Coalition, Cath. Alliance, Cecil County C. of C., Stopp Internat., Human Life Internat., Concerned Women for Am., Pharmacists for Life, Goldey Beacom Coll. Alumni Assn., Movement for a Better Am., Cath. League, Liberty Alliance, Epic Pharmacies, Inc., Susan B. Anthony List, Alpha Chi. Republican. Roman Catholic. Avocations: gardening, pro-life education, reading. Office: City Pharmacy Inc 723 N Bridge St Elkton MD 21921-5398 Office Phone: 410-398-4383 ext 413. Personal E-mail: williamandmarycaldwell@msn.com. Business E-Mail: citypharmacy@dol.net.

JASKA, SUSAN PARK, retired radar systems engineer; b. Seoul, Aug. 20, 1961; d. Benjamin N. and Ann C. Park; m. Esko A. Jaska, Dec. 21, 1990; children: Arlan, Ender. BSEE, Ga. Inst. of Tech., 1984, MSEE, 1987. Aircraft engr. Lockheed-Ga. Co., Marietta, Ga., 1984-85; rsch. engr. Ga. Tech. Rsch. Inst., Atlanta, 1985-90; program mgr. SM&A Corp., Arlington, Va., 1993-99; dept. mgr. Solers, Inc., Arlington, 1999—2003. Contbr. articles to profl. jours. With U.S. Peace Corps., Koforidua, West Africa, 1991-92. E-mail: sjaska@cox.net.

JASON, J. JULIE, portfolio manager, writer, lawyer; b. Owensboro, Ky. d. Richard and Grazina Pauliukonis; m. Marius J. Jason, Dec. 19, 1970; children: Ilona, Leila. BA, Baldwin-Wallace Coll., 1971; JD, Cleve. State U., 1974; LLM, Columbia U., 1975. Bar: Ohio 1974, N.Y. 1976, U.S. Dist. Ct. (so. dist.) N.Y. 1976, U.S. Ct. Appeals (2d cir.) 1976, U.S. Supreme Ct. 1978. Pvt. practice, N.Y.C., 1974—78; asst. gen. counsel Paine Webber, N.Y.C., 1978—83; pres. P.W. Trust and Paine Webber Futures Mgmt. Co., N.Y.C., 1983—88; sr. fin. svcs. atty. Donovan, Leisure, Newton & Irvine, N.Y.C., 1988—89; co-founder, pres. Jackson, Grant & Co., Stamford, Conn., 1989—. Arbitrator N.Y. Stock Exch.; mediator U.S. Bankruptcy Ct., 1997. Author: You and Your 401(K), 1996, The 401(K) Plan Handbook, 1997, Strategic Investing, 2001, Julie Jason's Guide to Connecticut Probate, 2006; columnist: 401-OK, Road to Security. Mem.: AAUW (chair scholarship com. 1992—93), ABA, Investment Co. Inst. (sec. regulation com. 1978—83), Am. Soc. Journalists and Authors, Nat. Assn. Securities Dealers (arbitrator, mediator), Wesfaca, Columbia U. Alumni Club Fairfield County (pres. 1993—94, chair pres.'s coun. 1994—96). Office: Jackson Grant 2 High Ridge Pk Stamford CT 06905-1203 Office Phone: 203-322-1198. Business E-Mail: julie@jacksongrant.us.

JASON, SONYA, writer; b. Jefferson, Pa. d. Michael and Sophia (Kovac) Negra; m. John J. Jason; children: John Jr., Gary. BA in Journalism, Calif. State U.-Northridge, L.A., 1963. Social worker Dept. Pub. Social Svcs., LA, 1964-66; probation officer LA Probation, 1966-76; West Coast editor Ethnic Am. News, LA, 1977-78; freelance writer, 1978—. Spkr. in field. Author: Concomitant Soldier, 1974, Icon of Spring, 1993, Helper, 1994, Professional Angel: A P.O's Story; contbr. articles to profl. jours. Pres. Am. Citizens Together, LA, 1986-90. Recipient award Freedom Found. Valley Forge, Pa., 1987; named to Greenwood Ency. of Multi Ethnic Am. Lit., 2006. Avocations: travel, historical research, golf, bridge. Home: 21165 Escondido St Woodland Hills CA 91364-5904 Office Phone: 818-347-2553.

JASPER, DORIS J. BERRY, nurse; b. Banner, Miss., Sept. 12, 1933; d. William Richard and Lena Martha (Gambill) Berry; m. Lyman W. Jasper, Jan. 8, 1949; children: Richard L., Lynn William. Student, Blytheville (Ark.) Sch. Nursing, 1949, Purdue U., Westville, Ind., 1979-80, Lake Mich. Coll., Benton Harbor, 1980—83. Staff nurse St. Anthony's Hosp., Michigan City, Ind., 1951-66; pvt. duty nurse Michigan City, 1962-68; emergency rm. nurse St. Anthony's Hosp., 1968-74; charge nurse, emergency rm. nurse Meml. Hosp., Michigan City, 1974-75; pvt. duty nurse Three Oaks, Mich., 1972-84, Michigan City, 1981-88; staff nurse Alpha Christiansan Registry, New Buffalo, Mich., 1988—; pvt. practice Three Oaks, 1989-90; owner, practitioner Jaspers Health Care, Three Oaks, 1991—; owner, mgr. D.J.'s Frolick Kennel. Pvt. practice No. Ind., So. Mich.; co-owner, mgr. grain farm. Med. missionary Chiadoc, El Paso, Tex., 2002. Mem. Bus. and Profl. Women's Club, Inc. (legis. chair dist. 2 1987-88, rec. sec. dist. 2, exec. bd. mem.), Mich. Fedn. Bus. Profl. Women USA (legis. chair dist. 9), New Buffalo Area Bus. Profl. Women (legis. chair), Tenn. Walking Horse Assn., Smithsonian Inst. Republican. Baptist. Avocations: reading, horseback riding, travel. Home and Office: 1883 Bethel Church Rd Camden TN 38320 Personal E-mail: jasperdoris@yahoo.com.

JASPERSON, JILL O., law educator; d. Burt Hiatt Oliphant and Adelia Nadene Peggy Smith; m. Louis Vincent Jasperson, Jan. 5, 1981; children: Conner Smith, Bryant Louis, Kelvin O., Chase Christian. BA, Brigham Young U., Provo, Utah, 1976; JD, J. Reuben Clark Law Sch., Provo, 1993. Bar: Utah 1994. Prosecutor, Sandy City, Utah, 1995—96; instr. Utah Valley State U., Orem, 1997—2000, asst. prof., 2000—04, assoc. prof., 2004—, chmn. faculty excellence com. Exec. bd. mem. Peace and Justice Studies, Orem, 2005—; vis. prof. law Beijing Inst. Machinery, 2002; rschr., London, 04. Broadcaster (internet radio broadcasts) Jill o'Justice, various titles in consumer issues; contbr. articles to profl. jours. Mem. Womens Forum, Orem; truancy mediator 4th Dist. Ct., Provo; mem.-at-large Women in Leadership, Provo; mem. alumni exec. bd. J.Reuben Clark Law Sch. Recipient Faculty in Industry and Bus. Internship award, Utah Valley State Coll., 2005, 2006, Woodbury Faculty Scholar Fund award, Sch. Bus., Utah Valley State Coll., 2005, Faculty Excellence award, 2005, Champion of the Yr. Utah Region and 7 State Western Region, SBA, 2005; Ctr. for Study of Ethics fellow, Utah Valley State Coll., 2001—02. Mem.: Am. Assn. Paralegal Educators, Utah Bar. Office: Utah Valley State Coll 800 West University Parkway Orem UT 84058-5999 Office Phone: 801-863-8856.

JASSEN, ALISON P., chemistry professor, biology professor; b. N.Y.C., Oct. 3, 1951; d. John C. and Penelope R. Putnam; m. Kerry R. Jassen; children: Amy K., Karl A. MS, Ctrl. Conn. State U., New Britain, Conn., 1993. Lab. technician, lectr. Northwestern Conn. C.C., Winsted, Conn., 1990—93, faculty Dept. Chemistry and Biology, 1993—. Coord. Pre-Nursing Program Northwestern Conn. C.C., 2000. Facilitator breast cancer support group Charlotte Hungerford Hosp., Torrington, Conn., 1993—2006. Named Outstanding C.C. Faculty Mem. of the 90's, State Conn., 2000; recipient Outstanding Grad. Student award, Ctrl. Conn. State U., 1993, Cmty. Svc. award, Legis. State of Conn., 2000. Mem.: Human Anatomy and Physiology Soc. (assoc.). Avocations: reading, bicycling, gardening. Office: Northwestern Connecticut Community Colle Park Place Winsted CT 06098 Office Phone: 860-738-6391. Business E-Mail: ajassen@nwcc.commnet.edu.

JASSO, GUILLERMINA, sociologist, educator; b. Laredo, Tex., July 22, 1942; d. José Jasso-Rodríguez and Guillermina de los Santos-Lozano. BA, Our Lady of the Lake Coll., 1962; MA, U. Notre Dame, 1970; PhD, Johns Hopkins U., 1974. Asst. prof. Barnard Coll. and Columbia U., N.Y.C., 1974-77; spl. asst. to commr. U.S. Immigration and Naturalization Svc., Washington, 1977-79; dir. rsch. U.S. Select Commn. on Immigration and Refugee Policy, Washington, 1979-80; asst. prof. U. Mich., Ann Arbor, 1980-82; assoc. prof. U. Minn., Mpls., 1982-86, prof., 1986-87; prof., dir. theory workshop U. Iowa, Iowa City, 1987-91; prof. NYU, N.Y.C., 1991—, dir. methods workshop, 1991-97. Mem. study sect. on social sci. and population NIH, 1991-95; mem. U.S. Com. for Internat. Inst. for Applied Sys. Analysis, 1993-2001; mem. various programs NSF, 1987-96, 98-99; panel on demographic and econ. impacts of immigration NAS, 1995-97; population rsch. subcom. Nat. Inst. Child Health and Human Devel., NIH, 1998-2002, adv. com. SBE Directorate, NSF, 2003—; mem. com. on redesign of U.S. naturalization test NAS, 2004-05; vis. prof. Zentrum Umfragen, Methoden, und Analysen, Mannheim, Germany, 1995, U. Leipzig, Germany, 1996; core rsch. team bination study on migration between Mex. and US, U.S. Commn. on Immigration Reform, 1995-97; disting. alumni lectr. U. Notre Dame, 1987; pub. lectr. Our Lady of Lake U., 1989; disting. lectr. NSF, 2003; spkr. in field. Author: The New Chosen People, 1990; mem. editl. bd. Social Justice Rsch., 1985—, Jour. Math. Sociology, 1985—, Rationality and Society, 1999—, European Sociological Review, 2000—, Internat. Jour. Comparatine Sociology, 2001-; dep. editor Am. Sociol. Rev., 1996-99, Social Forces, 2004-2007, Contemporary Sociology, 2006-2007; contbr. articles to profl. jours. Grantee Russell Sage Found., 1983-85, Rockefeller Found., 1985-86, NSF, 1994-97, 2000-02, NIH, 1995-99, 2000-, PEW, 2001-; fellow Ctr. for Advanced Study in Behavioral Scis., Stanford, Calif., 1999-2000; rsch. fellow Inst. for the Study of Labor (IZA), Bonn, Germany. Fellow Johns Hopkins Soc. Scholars; mem. Am. Sociol. Assn. (chair internat. migration sect. 1996-99, chair theory sect. 1996-99, chair rational choice sect. 2000-03, chair soc. psychol. sect. 2002-04), Sociol. Rsch. Assn. Office: NYU Dept Sociology 295 Lafayette St New York NY 10012-9605 Office Phone: 212-998-8368. E-mail: gj1@nyu.edu.

JATTAN, LYNETTE S., pediatrician; b. Trinidad, West Indies, Oct. 7, 1951; d. David Gildharry and Dolly Agnes (Ramserran) J. MBBS, U. Coll. West Indies, Kingston, 1982; diploma in dermatology, U. London, 1987. Diplomate Am. Bd. Pediats. Intern Port of Spain Gen. Hosp., Trinidad, West Indies, 1983; resident in pediats. Carolinas Med. Ctr., Charlotte, N.C., 1993-95; with Conyers (Ga.) Pediats. Fellow Am. Acad. Pediats. Baptist. Office: Conyers Pediats 1388B Wellbrook Cir NE Conyers GA 30012-3872

JAUDON, VALERIE, artist; b. Greenville, Miss., Aug. 6, 1945; d. Baize R. and Gladys E. (Hill) J.; m. Richard Kalina, Oct. 23, 1979. Student, Miss. State Coll. for Women, 1963—65, Memphis Acad. Art, 1965, U. of Americas, Mexico, 1966—67, St. Martins Sch. Art, London, 1968—69. One-woman shows of paintings include Holly Solomon Gallery, N.Y.C., 1977-79, 81, Pa. Acad. Fine Arts, Phila., 1977, Galerie Bishofberger, Zurich, Switzerland, 1979, Galerie Hans Strelow, Dusseldorf, Fed. Republic Germany, 1980, Corcoran Gallery, L.A., 1981, Sidney Janis Gallery, N.Y.C., 1983, 85, 86, 88, 90, 93, 96, Quadrat Mus., Bottrop, Fed. Republic Germany, 1983, Amerika Haus, Berlin, 1983, Dart Gallery, Chgo., 1983, Fay Gold Gallery, Atlanta, 1985, Macintosh/Drysdale Gallery, Washington, 1985, Barbara Scott Gallery, Bay Harbor Islands, Fla., 1994, Miss. Mus. Art, Jackson, 1996, Betsy Senior Gallery, N.Y.C., 1998, Stadel Mus., Frankfurt, Germany, 1999-2000, Von Lintel Gallery, N.Y.C., 2003, 05; numerous group shows including, Mayor Gallery, London, 1979, Galerie Habermann, Cologne, Germany, 1979, Galerie Hans Strelow, Dusseldorf, 1979, Galerie Modern Art, Vienna, Austria, 1980, Mus. Modern Art, Oxford, Eng., 1980, Greenberg, Gallery, St. Louis, 1980, Sidney Janis Gallery, N.Y.C., 1980, San Francisco Art Inst., 1980, Mus. Modern Art, N.Y.C., 1980, Leo Castelli Gallery, N.Y.C., 1980, Thomas Segal Gallery, Boston, 1980, Venice (Italy) Biennale, 1980, Nat. Gallery of Art, Washington, 1980, Chgo. Art Inst., 1981, Mus. Fine Arts, Boston, 1982, Neuberger Mus., Purchase, N.Y., 1982, Hudson River Mus., Yonkers, N.Y., 1983, Berkshire Mus., Pittsfield, Mass., 1983, La Jolla Mus., Calif., 1983, Margo Leavin Gallery, L.A., 1984, Bronx Mus., 1985, Am. Ctr., Paris, 1986, Dayton Art Inst., 1987, Cin. Art Mus., 1989, Tel Aviv Mus. Art, 1992, Robert McClain Gallery, Houston, 1996, Turner/Runyon Gallery, Dallas, 1997, Kunsthallen Brandts Kaledefabrik, Odense, Denmark, 2001, Angel Row Gallery, Nottingham, England, 2001, Porin Taidemuseo, Eteläranta, Finland, 2002; executed ceramic mural Equitable Bldg., N.Y.C., 1988, brick and granite plaza Police Plaza, N.Y.C., 1989; Blue Pools Courtyard Birmingham (Ala.) Mus. Art, 1993; mosaic floor Washington Nat. Airport, 1997, grass garden Thomas Eagleton Courthouse, St. Louis, 2004; represented in permanent collections including Hirshhorn Mus., Washington, Mus. Modern Art, N.Y.C., Albright-Knox Art Gallery, Buffalo, N.Y., Fogg Art Mus., Cambridge, Mass.,Sammlung-Lugwig Mus., Aachen, Fed. Republic Germany, Dayton (Ohio) Art Inst., Nat. Museum of Women in the Arts, Washington, St. Louis Art Mus., Ludwig Mus., Budapest, Hungary, Miss. Mus. Art, Jackson. Recipient 1st prize award So. Contemporary Arts Festival, 1967, Art award Miss. Inst. Arts and Letters, 1981, 97, Excellence in Design award N.Y.C. Art Commn., 1988, civic Spirit award Women's City Club of N.Y., Merit award Am. Soc. Landscape Architects Ala. chpt., 1994; named Honored Artist from State of Miss. Nat. Mus. Women in Arts, Washington; N.Y. State CAPS grantee for graphics, 1980; Visual Arts Fellowship grant Nat. Endowment Arts, 1988; N.Y. Found. for Arts grantee in painting, 1992. Address: 795A Accabonac Rd East Hampton NY 11937-1807 E-mail: vjaudon@earthlink.net.

JAUQUET-KALINOSKI, BARBARA, library director; b. Crystal Falls, Mich., Mar. 12, 1948; d. Herbert Francis and Lenore Mary (Roell) Jauquet; m. Gregory Clem Kalinoski, Nov. 12, 1983; children: Stacia Amee, Sara Amee, Michael Thomas and Thomas Michael (twins.). BS, No. Mich. U., 1970; MLS, Western Mich. U., 1974. Adminstrv. asst. Mid-Peninsula Libr. System, Iron Mountain, Mich., 1970-74, asst. dir., 1975-79; periodical libr. U. Wis., Superior, 1980; dir. N.W. Regional Libr., Thief River Falls, Minn., 1981—. Chmn. planning, evaluation and reporting curriculum com. for sch. dist., also mem. other sch. dist. coms. Named Woman of Honor, AAUW, 1990. Mem. ALA, Minn. Libr. Assn. (past pres., mem. continuing edn. com.), Thief River Falls C. of C., Rotary (past pres.). Roman Catholic. Avocations: children's activities, community issues, architecture and interior decoration, travel, sports. Office: NW Regional Libr 101 1st St E Thief River Falls MN 56701-2041

JAVERNICK, AMY SUE, special education educator; b. Canon City, Colo., July 19, 1969; d. James Joseph Javernick and Linda Ruth (Dilley) Thrush; 1 child, Nathan Monte. BA History, Western State Coll., Gunnison, Colo., 1991; MA Spl. Edn., U.Colo., Colo. Springs, 1994. Cert. elem. tchr. Colo., 1991, spl.edn. tchr. Colo., 1994. Rsch. asst. U. Colo., Colo. Springs, 1993—96; spl. edn. tchr Mitchell HS, Colo. Springs, 1994—95, Florence Elem. Sch., Colo., 1994—96, Gunnison HS, Colo., 1996—2006; spl. edn. tchr. Grand Junction HS, Colo., 2006—. Resource mem. Colo. State Autism Task Force, Denver, 2000—04; online instr. U. Phoenix, Ariz., 2003—. Mem.: Coun. for Exceptional Children. Republican. Avocations: bicycling, cross stitch, hiking, quilting, reading.

JAVIER-DEJNEKA, AMELIA LUISA, accountant; arrived in U.S., 1964; d. Ladislao Walter Dejneka and Elena Angelica Gomba; m. Washington Javier, July 14, 1973 (dec. June 1985); children: Walter Daniel, Maria Elena. BBA, Fla. Internat. U., 1976; degree in Computer Programming, Miami Tech. Coll., 1986. Investor Atlantic Acct. & Investment, Miami, Fla., 1984—; acct., owner A&M Acct. & Mgmt., Miami, 1999—; designer, owner A&M Designer Gallery, Miami, 1999—; prin., owner A&M Profl. Svc., Miami, 2002—. Recipient Blue Ribbon award, Argentina Consulate & Com., 1995. Avocations: swimming, dance, walking, travel. Home: 9449 Byron Ave Miami FL 33154

JAVITCH, ANKI WOLF (ANN LOUISE WOLF JAVITCH), psychologist; b. Newton, Mass., Oct. 30, 1949; d. Leo E. and Natalie (Wasserman) Wolf; children: Matthew Ethan, Jacob Micah. BA, Russell Sage Coll., 1971; MEd, Boston Coll., 1972; PhD, Ohio State U., 1980. Learning disabilities specialist Concord (Mass.) Pub. Schs., 1972-74; learning disabilities specialist supr. Hudson (N.H.) Pub. Schs., 1975-77; sr. clin. supr. Valley Adult Counseling Ctr., Milford, Mass., 1980-81; pvt. practice Newton, Mass., 1981-90; clin. therapist Coping with Pregnancy/Parenting Experiences (C.O.P.E.), Boston, 1984-90; cons. Javitch Assoc., Newton, 1990—2000; neuropsychologist McLean Hosp., Belmont, 1990—2001; clin. instr. Harvard Med. Sch., Boston, 1990—. Bd. dirs. Cambridge Sch. of Weston, Mass., 1986-93, Newton Symphony Orch., 1991—. Mem. APA. Avocations: skiing, tennis, cooking, reading. Office: 133 Waban Ave Waban MA 02468-2101

JAVITS, JOAN (ZEEMAN), writer, inventor; b. N.Y.C., Aug. 17, 1928; d. Benjamin Abraham and Lily (Braxton) Javits; m. John Huibert Zeeman III, Mar. 20, 1954; children: Jonathan Huibert, Andrea Zeeman Deane, Eloise Zeeman Scharff, Phoebe Zeemon Fitch, Merrily Margaret Zeeman Bodell. BA, Vassar Coll., Poughkeepsie, N.Y., 1949; MEd, U. Vt., Burlington, 1976. Pub. rels. exec. Benjamin Sonnenberg, N.Y.C., 1949-51; freelance writer, 1952—; pres. Javitz Zeeman Music Assocs., JJZ Realty. Author: The Compleat Child, 1964, lyricist mus. plays Young Abe Lincoln, 1961, Quality St., 1964, Hotel Passionato, 1965; author, lyricist Young Columbus, 1992; song lyricist Santa Baby, 1953; patentee Alphocube. Trustee Theatreworks (formerly Performing Arts Repertory Theatre), N.Y.C., 1953-83, Profl. Childrens Sch., N.Y.C., 1980-89, Palm Beach Sch. Arts Found., 1993-2000, 2006—, Fla. Theatrical Assn., 1994—; bd. dirs. Baroque Srings Quartet, 1996-2000. Mem. ASCAP, Dramatists Guild, Gilbert and Sullivan Soc., Vassar Club (Westchester, N.Y. and Palm Beach, Fla.) (sec. 1978-84, v.p. 1984-86(. Home: 230 Palmo Way Palm Beach FL 33480-3135 Home (Summer): 4331 E Warren Rd Warren VT 05674 Personal E-mail: joanjav@aol.com.

JAWORSKA, TAMARA, artist; b. Archangel, Russia; arrived in Can., 1969; d. Antoni Jankowski; m. Tadeusz Jaworski, 1957; children: Ewa, Piotr. BFA in Painting, State Acad. Fine Arts, Lodz, Poland, 1950, MFA in Design and Weaving Art, 1952; M of Painting (hon.), Accademia Italia, 1982. From asst. prof. to sr. asst. prof., lectr. State Acad. Fine Arts, Poland, 1952-58. One-woman shows include State Gallery of Textiles, Lodz, 1965, State Gallery of Fine Arts, Warsaw, 1965, Pushkin Nat. Mus., Moscow, 1966, Fine Arts Mus., Plymouth, U.K., 1968, Scottish Woolen Gallery, Galashields, 1968, Richard Demarco Gallery, Edinburgh, Scotland, 1968, Rothman's Art Gallery, Stratford, 1970, Merton Gallery, Toronto, 1970, London Art Gallery, 1971, Glendon Art Gallery, Toronto, 1972, Nienkamper Art Gallery, Toronto, 1979, Art Gallery of Hamilton, 1980, Nat. Museums and Art Galleries in Spain, 1980-81, Can. Cultural Ctr., Paris, 1981, Galerie Inard, Paris, 1981, Munich Art Gallery, Germany, 1982, Galerie Inard, Toulouse, France, 1982, 91, Galerie Inard, Paris, 1984, 91, Leo Kamen Gallery, Toronto, 1987, 89, John B. Aird State Gallery, Toronto, 1992, Peak Gallery, Toronto, 1997, Solo Gallery, Toronto, 2003, 04, 05, Toronto Weavers Art Gallery, 2005, Designers Walk Gallery, Toronto, 2006, Weavers Art Gallery, Toronto, also in France, Germany, Belgium, Switzerland, Luxembourg, U.K., Spain, Austria, Poland, Russia, Hungary, U.S., Mex., Can., Paris, Eng., Scotland, Holland, Austria, Spain, Moscow, Poland, Hungary, Can., U.S., others; group exhbns. include Warsaw and Lodz art galleries, Pushkin Mus., European Art Gallery, Moscow, Richard Demarco Gallery, Edinburgh, Fine Art Mus., Plymouth, Eng., Merton Gallery, Toronto, Hermitage Leningrad Mus., USSR, Nat. Art Gallery, Teheran, Mus. Modern Art, Mexico City, Art Gallery of Ont., RCA-Art 2000, Toronto and Stratford, 2000, Weavers Art, Toronto, 2006; exhibited tapestries at New Coll., Galerie Inard, Ctr. Nat. de la Tapisserie d'Abusson, Paris, later in Madrid, Barcelona, Valencia, San Sebastian, Paris, Munich, Zurich, others; works in permanent collections of Pushkin Nat. Mus., European Art Gallery, Moskau, Russia, Nat. Mus., Warsaw, Nat. Mus. of Textile Arts, Lodz, Poland, Nat. Mus. of Home Army, King City, Krakow, Poland, Galashields Art Inst., Scotland, Bank of Montreal, Toronto, Bell Can., Ottawa, Molson Canadian, Toronto, Mut. Ins. of Can., Toronto, First Can. Pl. Main Lobby, Gulf Can. Sq. Main Lobby, and many corp. and pvt. collections in Europe, Am., Mid. East, Centre Nat. de la Tapisserie D'Aubusson Galerie Inard, Paris; subject of articles in art books and mags. Decorated Order of Can.; recipient Gold medal-Triennial di Milano, Interior Design and Architecture, Milan, 1957, award for excellence Wool Gathering, Montreal, 1974, Gold medal Academia Italia delle Arti, 1980, Gold Centaur, Academia Italia delle Arti, 1982, Gold medal and 1st prize Internat. Art Competition, N.Y.C., 1985, Commemorative medal Gov. Gen. Can., 1993, Highest Civilian Recognition for Achievements in Field of Creative Visual Arts, 1994, Golden Jubilee medal Her Majesty Elizabeth II, 2002. Fellow York Univ.; mem. Royal Can. Acad. Arts, Academia Italia delle Arti, Ontario Soc. Artists. Home: 49 Don River Blvd Toronto ON Canada M2N2M8 Office Phone: 416-222-8491. Personal E-mail: weaversartgalleryinfo@weaversart.com. E-mail: tamtad@rogers.com.

JAWORSKI, LISA, information technology executive; Prin. security engr. Sci. Applications Internat. Corp., San Diego. Named a Heroine in Tech., Women in Tech., March of Dimes, 2005. Office: SAIC 10260 Campus Point Dr San Diego CA 92121*

JAY, DANIELLE MARY, dancer, educator; b. Detroit, Oct. 3, 1947; d. Roman Login and Harriet Alice Jay. BS in Dance, Ea. Mich. U., 1969; MA in Ballet, U. Cin., 1971; student, Ea. N.Mex. U., 1972—77, U. Wis., 1976, Wash. U., 1977; student in Biomechics, No. Ill. U., 1979—80; PhD in Dance and Related Art, Tex. Women's U., 1987; studied with, numerous ballet and modern companies and people, 1963—2003. From instr. to asst. prof. dance Ea. N.Mex. U., Portales, N.Mex., 1971—75, asst. prof., 1975—78; from instr. to prof. dance No. Ill. U., De Kalb, Ill., 1978—99, prof. dance, 1999—. Guest tchr. dance Wright Elem. Sch., Malta, Ill., 2003; coord. dance SPEC, De Kalb, 1980—89; tchr. spl. children St. Louis Sch. Dist., De Kalb, 1999—2003; tchr. Pedagogy Dance and Ballet, 1999; cons. in field; presenter in field; numerous coms. in univs. where worked. Choreographer Stage Coach Players, DeKalb, Ill., 1992—2002; co-prodr.: Dance Movement Resource Manual for Curriculum Planning, 1991; co-author: Teaching Beginning Ballet Techniques, 1998, DanceTeaching Methods for Curriculum Planning, 2003; dancer Transition 'n Dance, PBS, 1982, De Kalb (Ill.) Cmty. Children Theater, 1992; co-author: (CD) DanceTeaching Method and Curriculum Design, 2003; author: Dictionary of Ballet Terms, 2002, Ballet I Center Work, 2002; dir.: (films) The Wall Within, 1987, Japanese Dance, 1988; dancer (films) Hawaiian Dance, 1988, Korean Dance, 1988, Vision Quest, 1989, Belgium Folk Dance, 1990, Dance is for Everyone, 1991, Folk Dance, 2001, African and Carribean Dance, 2002, Multi cultural Dances, 2003, Meditation in Motion, 2003, choreographer The Fairy Thorn, Northwest Ballet Ensemble, Chgo., Ill., 1994, Diversity in Unity, Am. Alliance Health, Recreation, Phys. Edn. and Dance Conv., Cin., Ohi, 2000, Rising, Borders, Sycamore, Ill., 2003, numerous others; contbr. articles to profl. jours. Recipient Disting. Alumni award, Ea. Mich. U., 1987, Recognition award, No. Ill. U., 1989, 1996, N.Mex. Arts Coun. and N.Mex. U., 1975—77; grantee, No. Ill. U., 1990, 1994. Mem.: Am. Alliance Health Physical Edn., Nat. Dance Edn. Org., Nat. Dance Assn. (chmn. performance midwest chpt. 1994—97), Delta Kappa Gamma. Home: 1531 Timberwood Ct Sycamore IL 60178 Office: Northern Ill Univ Anderson Dekalb IL 60178 Office Phone: 815-753-3903.

JAY, NORMA JOYCE, artist; b. Wichita, Kans., Nov. 11, 1925; d. Albert Hugh and Thelma Ree (Boyd) Braly; m. Laurence Eugene Jay, Sept. 2, 1949; children: Dana Denise, Allison Eden. Student, Wichita State U., 1946-49, Art Inst. Chgo., 1955-56, Calif. State Coll., 1963. Illustrator Boeing Aircraft, Wichita, 1949-51; co-owner Back Door Gallery, Laguna Beach, Calif., 1973-88. Guest artist Coos Art Mus., 2003. One-woman shows include Milcir Gallery, Tiburon, Calif., 1978, Newport Beach City Gallery, 1981, exhibited in group shows at Am. Soc. Marine Artists ann. exhbns., 1978—2004, Peabody Mus., Salem, Mass., 1981, Mystic Seaport Mus. Gallery, Conn., 1992—95, Grand Ctrl. Gallery, N.Y., 1979—84, The Back Door Gallery, Laguna Beach, 1973—88, Mariners' Mus., Newport News, Va., 1985—86, Nat. Heritage Gallery of Fine Art, Beverly Hills, Calif., 1988—, Md. Hist. Mus., 1989, Kirsten Gallery, Seattle, 1991—97, R.J. Schaefer Gallery Mystic (Conn.) Seaport Mus., 1992, Vallejo Gallery, Newport Beach, 1992, Caswell Gallery, Troutdale, Oreg., 1994—95, Columbia River Maritime Mus., Astoria, Oreg., 1994, Arnold Art Gallery, Newport, Conn., 1994, Mystic Internat. Exhbn., 1995, Lu Martin Galleries, Laguna Beach, 1996—, Frye Art Mus.,

Seattle, 1997, Cummer Mus. Art & Gardens, Jacksonville, Fla., 1997—98, Cape Mus. Fine Arts Inc., Dennis, Mass., 2001, Coos Art Mus., Coos Bay, Oreg., 2003, Newport (R.I.) Art Mus., 2003, Maine Maritime Mus., Bath, 2003, Connecticut River Mus., Essex, 2004, Vero Bearch Mus. of Art, Fla., 2004, Represented in permanent collections James Irvine Found., Newport Beach, Niguel Art Assn., Laguna Niguel, Calif., Deloitte, Haskins & Sells, Costa Mesa, Calif., M.J. Brock & Sons Inc., North Hollywood, Calif., others. Recipient Best of Show award Fort Mason Nat. Competition, 1961, First Pl. award Traditional Artists Exhbn., San Bernadino County Mus., 1976, artist award Chriswood Gallery Invitational Exhbn., Rancho California, Calif., 1973, Dirs. Choice award, People's Choice award Coos Art Mus. Marine Exhbn., 1996, featured guest artist, 1998, Coos Art Mus., 2003, 1st Pl. award Maritime Art Exhibit, Newport Harbor Nautical Mus., Newport Beach, 1998-99. Fellow Am. Soc. Marine Artists (charter); mem. Niguel Art Assn. (first pres. 1968, hon. life mem. 1978), Artists Equity, Am. Artists Profl. League. Democrat.

JAYE, KAREN A., human resources specialist; b. New Hyde Park, N.Y., May 15, 1964; d. Rubin and Moira Chernow; m. Douglas P. Jaye, Jan. 14, 1989; 1 child, Amanda Lee. Assocs. Degree, SUNY, Farmingdale, 1984; BS in Fin., SUNY, Old Westbury, 1989. Cert. internal auditor, govt. fin. mgr. From internal auditor to sr. internal auditor internal audit dept. Lee County Clk. Cts., Ft. Myers, Fla., 1991—2002, human resources dir., 2002—. Mem.: Assn. Govt. Accts., Inst. Internal Auditors (bd. govs., pres. 1996—97, Gold award Chpt. Achievement Program 1997). Avocations: rollerblading, photography. Office: Lee County Clk Cts 2115 Second St Fort Myers FL 33902

JAYSON, MELINDA GAYLE, lawyer; b. Dallas, Sept. 29, 1956; d. Robert and Louise Adelle (Jacobs) J. BA, U. Tex., 1977, JD, 1980. Bar: Tex. 1980, U.S. Dist. Ct. (no. dist.) Tex. 1980, U.S. Ct. Appeals (5th and 11th cirs.) 1981, U.S. Dist. Ct. (so. dist.) Tex. 1989, U.S. Ct. Appeals (8th cir.) 1990, U.S. Supreme Ct. 1991. Assoc. Akin, Gump, Strauss, Hauer & Feld, Dallas, 1980-86, ptnr., 1987-96, Melinda G. Jayson, P.C., 1996—; gen. counsel Hall Fin. Group, Dallas, 1999—. Comml. arbitrator, mem. regional adv. coun. Am. Arbitration Assn.; arbitrator, mediator N.Y. Stock Exch., NASD Regulation, Inc., Nat. Arbitration Forum, CPR Inst. Dispute Resolution; mediator U.S. EEO Commn., 1999-2000; arbitrator Nat. Arbitration Forum, 2000—. Named one of Outstanding Young Women Am., 1983. Mem.: Am. Health Lawyers Assn. (arbitrator, mediator), Tex. Bar Assn., Dallas Bar Assn., State Bar of Tex. (mem. dist. 6A grievance com. 1997-99, mem. professionalism enhancement com. 1997-99). (mem. dist. 6A grievance com. 1997—99, mem. professionalism enhancement com. 1997—99). Office: Ste 2015 5445 Caruth Haven Ln Dallas TX 75225-8166 Office Phone: 972-377-1145. Business E-Mail: mjayson@hallfinancial.com.

J.C., Mrs. See COTHREN, EVANGELINE

JEAN, CLAUDETTE R., retired elementary school educator; b. Nashua, NH, Sept. 26, 1930; d. Thomas Noel and Elise Marie (Archambault) J. BA, Rivier Coll., 1952; MA, Fitchburg (Mass.) Coll., 1956. Cert. tchr. Elem. tchr. Donald St. Sch., Beford, NH, 1952-53, Arlington St. Sch., Nashua, NH, 1953-56, J.B. Crowley Sch., Nashua, NH, 1956-65, Sunset Heights Sch., Nashua, NH, 1965-91, Nashua; ret. Rep. N.H. Gen. Ctr., Concord, 1992—. Negotiating team Nashua Tchrs. Union, 1969—; state Dem. com. N.H. Dems., Concord, 1992; Hillsborough County com. County Delegation, Manchester, N.H., 1992. Recipient Toland award AFL-CIO, 1991. Mem. Nashua Tchrs. Union (cons. 1991-94), Sr. Citizens Club, Retired Tchrs. Assn., Nashau Coll. Club. Roman Catholic. Avocations: golf, travel, reading.

JEAN-BAPTISTE, TRICIA, public relations executive; married; 1 child, Nicholas. Pub. rels. positions Le Parker Meridien Hotel, NY, Doral Hotels and Resorts; mgr. corp. comm. Days Inn Am., Parsippany, NJ, 1998; founder Tricia Jean-Baptiste Comm., 1998—. Recipient Golden Bell Bronze award, Hotel Sales and Mktg. Assn. Mem.: NY Women in Comm. (past bd. mem.). Office: Tricia Jean-Baptiste Comm 375 Greenwich St Ste 804 New York NY 10013 Office Phone: 212-941-3988. Office Fax: 212-941-3989. Business E-Mail: trica@tricapr.com.

JEANBART-LORENZOTTI, EVA, retail executive; b. Geneva; m. Lorenzo Lorenzotti; children: Allegra, Amedeo. BA, Columbia U. Investment banker mergers and acquisitions dept. Lazard Freres; founder, CEO Vivre, 1996—. Guest spkr. Harvard Bus. Sch. Entrepreneurship Conf., Internat. Herald Tribune Luxury Conf., Am. Express Luxury Conf., CNN, CNBC, Fine Living Channel. Mem. Guggenheim Mus. Young Collector's Club, Robin Hood Found., Save Venice Inc., Henry Street Settlement, Kips Bay Decorator Showcase. Named one of 10 most stylish women in fashion, Vogue mag., 40 Under 40, Crain's NY Bus., 2006. Mem.: Young Presidents Orgn. Internat. Achievements include fluent in five languages. Office: Vivre 15th Floor 11 East 26th St New York NY 10010 E-mail: ejl@vivre.com, eva@vivre.com.*

JEANS, MARY MILLICENT, educational association administrator; d. Robert Frederick and Katherine Fay Jeans; children: William Edward, Jennnifer Lynn. AA, Triton Coll., River Grove, Ill., 1991; BA, Concordia U., RiverForest, Ill., 2001; MA, Northeastern Ill. U., Chgo. Ill., 2003. Dir. Adult Basic edn. Triton Coll., Rivergrove, Ill., 1995—2001, dir. Hillside, Ill., 2001—05, dir. human resources and equal opportunity programs, 2005—, ethics advisor, 2006—. Pres. Hillside C. of C., Hillside, Ill., 2005, Triton Coll. Mid Mgmt. Assn., Rivergrove, Ill., 1999—2005; delegate Am. Fedn. Tchrs. Ill. Fedn. Tchrs., 1999—2005; exec. bd. mem. Cook County C. Tchrs. Union Local 1600, House of Reps., 1999—2005. Office: Triton Coll 2000 5th Ave Rm D105A River Grove IL 60171 Office Phone: 708-456-0300 3075. Business E-Mail: mjeans@triton.edu.

JECKLIN, LOIS UNDERWOOD, art corporation executive, consultant; b. Manning, Iowa, Oct. 5, 1934; d. J.R. and Ruth O. (Austin) Underwood; m. Dirk C. Jecklin, June 24, 1955; children: Jennifer Anne, Ivan Peter. BA, U. Iowa, 1992. Residency coord. Quad City Arts Coun., Rock Island, Ill., 1973-78; field rep. Affiliate Artists Inc., N.Y.C., 1975-77; mgr., artist in residence Deere & Co., Moline, Ill., 1977-80; dir. Vis. Artist Series, Davenport, Iowa, 1978-81; pres. Vis. Artists Inc., Davenport, 1981-88; pres., owner Jecklin Assocs., Davenport, 1988—2004; personal mgr. to composer Bright Sheng, 2005—. Asst. to exec. dir. Walter W. Naumburg Found., N.Y.C., 1990-2004; personal mgr., composer Bright Sheng, 2005—; cons. writer's program St. Ambrose Coll., Davenport, 1981, 83, 85; mem. com. Iowa Arts Coun., Des Moines, 1983-84; panelist Chamber Music Am., N.Y.C., 1984, Pub. Art Conf., Cedar Rapids, Iowa, 1984; panelist, mem. com. Lt. Gov.'s Conf. on Iowa's Future, Des Moines, 1984. Trustee Davenport Mus. Art, 1975-98, hon. trustee, 1998-2003; mem. nat. adv. coun. Figge Art Mus., Davenport, 2005; trustee Nature Conservancy Iowa, 1987-88; steering com. Iowa Citizens for Arts, Des Moines, 1970-71; bd. dirs. Tri-City Symphony Orch. Assn., Davenport, 1968-83; founding mem. Urban Design Coun., HOME, City of Davenport Beautification Com., 1970-72; bd. dirs. Mus. Arts and Design, NYC, 1995—; devel. coun. U. Iowa Mus. Art, 1996-2002; mem. Washington chpt. Arttable, 2005—. Recipient numerous awards Izaak Walton League, Davenport Art Gallery, Assn. for Retarded Citizens, Am. Heart Assn., Ill. Bur. Corrections, many others; LaVernes Noyes scholar, 1953-55. Republican. Episcopalian. Home and Office: 1232-27th St NW Washington DC 20007

JEETAH, USHA, Mauritius ambassador to the United States; married; 4 children. PhD, Delhi U., India. Secondary sch. tchr., 1971—91; full-time social worker and politician Mauritius, 1991—2001; ambassador of Mauritius to the U.S. Washington, 2001—. Lectr. philosophy and culture various univs.; pres. women's wing Movement Socialiste Militant. Creator radio, TV and Mauritius Coll. of Air programs, 1971—. Organizer seminars on HIV/AIDS, sports and women's entrepreneurship, women's legal rights, Mauritius.

JEEVARAJAN, JUDITH A., chemist; b. Madras, India, June 6, 1964; arrived in U.S., 1988; d. Susei Kulandai and Mary Jaya Raja; m. Antony Susiah Jeevarajan, May 18, 1988; children: Jessie, Jerome, John. BS, Stella Maris Coll., 1984; MS, Loyola Coll., Madras, 1986, U. Notre Dame, 1991; PhD, U. Ala., 1996. Scientist Lynntech, Inc., College Station, Tex., 1996-97; postdoctoral rschr. Tex. A&M U., College Station, 1997; scientist Lockheed Martin Space Ops., Houston, 1998—2003; sr. scientist NASA-Johnson Space Ctr., Houston, 2003—. Contbr. articles to profl. jours. Recipient award, Dept. Def., USAF. Mem.: Internat. Assn. Advancement Space Safety, Electrochem. Soc. Roman Catholic. Avocations: reading, gardening, travel. Home: 15407 Pinenut Bay Ct Houston TX 77059 Office: NASA-JSC MSEP5 2101 NASA Pky Houston TX 77058 Office Phone: 281-483-4528. Business E-Mail: judith.a.jeevarajan@nasa.gov.

JEFF, GLORIA JEAN, city official; b. Detroit, Apr. 8, 1952; d. D. Lee and Harriette Virginia (Davis) J. BSE in Civil Engring., U. Mich., 1974, MSE, 1976, M in Urban Planning, 1976; cert. program in Urban Transp., Carnegie Mellon U., 1979; cert. program sr. mgrs. in govt., Harvard U., 1994. Prin. planner, program analyst, equipment engr. Southeastern Mich. Transp. Authority, 1976-81; divsn. adminstr., multi-regional planning divsn. Mich. Dept. Transp., 1981-83, divsn. adminstr., urban transp. planning divsn., 1983-85, asst. dep. dir. Bur. of Transp. Planning, 1985-90, dep. dir. Bur. Transp. Planning, 1990-93; assoc. adminstr. for policy Fed. Hwy. Adminstrn., U.S. Dept. Transp., Washington, 1993-97, acting adminstr., 1997—2000, dep. adminstr., 1997—2000; transp. programs mgr. Atlantic Dist. Parsons, Brinckerhoff, Quade & Douglas, 2000—03; dir. Mich. Dept. Transp., 2003—06; gen. mgr. Transp. Dept. City of LA, 2006—. Adj. prof. Coll. Architecture and Urban Planing U. Mich., Ann Arbor, 1988—; chair standing com. on planning Mississippi Valley Conf. State Hwys. and Transp. Ofcls., 1987-89, vice chair strategic issues com., 1990-94; mem. Transp. Rsch. Bd., 1989—; adv. bd. U. Mich. Coll. Engring., 1995—, U. Calif., Davis, 1995—. Bd. dirs. Capitol chpt. Child and Family Svcs. of Mich. Inc., 1990-93, chair long-range planning com., 1991-93, sec. bd. dirs., 1993. Recipient Young Engr. of Yr. award Detroit chpt. Soc. Women Engrs., 1979, Young Engr. of Yr. award Detroit chpt. NSPE, 1979, Disting. Alumni award U. Mich., 1991, 92, Regional Amb. award S.E. Mich. Assn. Govts., 1993, Adminstrs. award for superior achievement FHWA, 1996, Trailblazer award Garrett A. Morgan Soc., A.D. Gaither Leadership award FHWA 2004. Mem. Am. Assn. Hwy. and Transp. Ofcls. (mem. modal adv. tech. com. 1988-91, mem. econ. expansion and devel. com. 1990-91, vice chair intermodal issues com. 1990-93), Am. Planning Assn. (v.p. for programs Planning and the Black Cmty. divsn. 1990-92, mem. nat. membership com. 1990-92, chair transp. planning divsn. 1994—, pres. Mich. chpt. 1990-91), Am. Inst. Cert. Planners, U. Mich. Alumni Assn. (bd. dirs. 1985-90, v.p. 1995—), U. Mich. Coll. Architecture Alumni Soc., Delta Sigma Theta, others. Office: LA Dept Transp 100 S Main St 10th Fl Los Angeles CA 90012*

JEFFCOTT, JANET BRUHN, statistician, consultant; b. Madison, Wis., Dec. 5, 1939; d. Hjalmar Diehl and Janet H. (Weber) Bruhn; m. Robert Gordon Jeffcott, Apr. 20, 1963. BA, U. Wis., 1962, MA, 1968. Asst. librarian Madison Area Tech. Coll., 1968-83, dist. librarian, 1983—91, adminstr. instructional media, telecommunications, 1988—91, media tech. adminstr., 1989—91. Pres. and treas. Fidelity & Assocs., Madison, 1982—; prin. J.B. Jeffcott & Assocs., Madison, 1989—, Edumetrics, Manistique, Mich., 2003-; sec.-treas. Manistique (Mich.) Mfg. & Tech., Inc., 1990-99, pres., treas., 1999-2002. Home and Office: Edumetrics 711 Oak St Manistique MI 49854 E-mail: jbjeff@chartermi.net.

JEFFERIS, BERNICE K., education educator; b. Cleve., Oct. 5, 1931; BS in Edn., Cleve. State U., 1970, M of Edn., 1975. Cert. elem. tchr. Tchr. Cleveland Heights, University Heights (Ohio) Bd. Edn. Vis. prof. Miami U. Mythology Inst. Mem. Cleve. Heights Univ. Heights Bd. Edn., 2002—06. Fellow NEH; Martha Holden Jennings scholar. Mem. Greater Cleve. Tchr. Ctr. Adv. Coun. (chmn. bd.), Tchr. Resource Ctr., Cleve. Mus. Art, Elem. Tchrs. Classics (pres.), Phi Delta Kappa. Presbyn. E-mail: bjefferis@adelphia.net.

JEFFERS, BEVERLY MAYNARD, volunteer; b. NYC, Sept. 2, 1923; d. Richard Field and Lorraine Huling Maynard; children: Alexander, Fiona, Alisandra, Ian, James, Sharon. Student, Radcliffe Coll., 1941—44; BA, Bryn Mawr Coll., 1946. Exhibited in group shows at Cookham Arts Club, 1976—80, Maidenhead Libr., 1976—80, Guidhall, London, 1980, Salmagundi Club, N.Y.C., 1990, Mercer County Libr., 1990—2003, West Windsor Town Hall, 2003, Princeton Hyatt, 1990—2003. Com. mem. Art and Cmty. Ctr., Maidenhead, England, 1977—87; initiator, leader play reading group West Windsor (N.J.) Sr. Ctr., 1997—, initiator choral and poetry groups, 2002—03; founding mem. Conn. Playmakers, 1946—47. Recipient 1st prize oil paintiing, Mercer County, 2004, 3d prize oil painting, N.J., 2006. Mem.: Art Students League N.Y.C. (life), Maidenhead Painting Club (life; founding mem., exec. sec. 1976—87). Democrat. Unitarian. Avocations: art, writing, drama, entertaining, photography, family. Home: 37 Wiggins St #2 Princeton NJ 08540 Office Phone: 609-430-1343. Personal E-mail: b.jeffers@worldnet.att.net.

JEFFERS, EVE JIHAN See EVE

JEFFERS, LYNETTE A., anesthetist; b. Cleve., Oct. 21, 1952; m. Jerry L. Jeffers, Oct. 1, 1950; children: Mark, Michael, Matthew. BA, BSN, Ursuline Coll., 1990; MSN, Case Western Reserve U., 1992, postgrad. RN; cert. registered nurse anesthetist. Anesthetist Mt. Sinai Med. Ctr., Cleve., 1985—, Medina (Ohio) Cmty. Hosp., 1993—; clin. instr. Sch. Nurse Anesthesia, Case Western Reserve U., Cleve., 1996—; pres. Sports Trauma Network, Medina, 1996—. Contbr. articles to profl. jours. Fellow Am. Acad. Pain Mgmt. (bd. cert.); mem Am. Assn. Nurse Anesthetists, Internat. Trauma Anesthesia and Critical Care Soc. Home: 4744 Sleepy Hollow Rd Medina OH 44256-8336

JEFFERS, SUSAN JANE, publishing executive, writer; b. N.Y.C. d. Leon and Jeanne Gildenberg; m. Larry Gershman (div. 1972); children: Gerald Gershman, Leslie Gershman; m. Mark E. A. Shelmerdine; stepchildren: Alice Shelmerdine, Guy Shelmerdine. BA summa cum laude, Hunter Coll., 1960; MA, Columbia U., 1966, PhD, 1970. Exec. dir. The Floating Hosp., N.Y.C., 1971-82; assoc. producer The Global Report Series BBC TV, London, 1983. Author: Feel the Fear and Do It Anyway, 1987, softcover edit., 1988, Opening Our Hearts to Men, 1989, softcover edit., 1990, Dare to Connect: Reaching Out in Romance, Friendship and the Workplace, 1992, The Journey from Lost to Found, 1992, Thoughts of Power & Love, 1995, End the Struggle & Dance with Life, 1996, softcover edit., 1997, I"m Okay.You're a Brat, softcover edit, 1999, Embracing Uncertainty softcover edit, 2004, Life is Hugel, 2004, The Little Book of Confidence, 2004, The Little Book of Peace of Mind, 2004, The Feel the Fear Guide to Lasting Love, 2005; contbr. articles to publs.; author audiotapes. Named to Hall of Fame, Alumni Assn. of Hunter Coll.; recipient award for significant contbns. to the well-being of Blacks within the area of met. N.Y., Spirit of Discovery award Assocs. Breast Cancer Studies. Mem. Phi Beta Kappa. Avocations: reading, dance, learning, travel. Home: PO Box 5338 Santa Monica CA 90409-5338

JEFFERS, VICTORIA WILKINSON, psychologist; b. Orange, NJ, Feb. 20, 1939; d. John Whitmore and Marian Lorene (Vaughan) Wilkinson; m. Richard S. Smith, div. June 1965; children: Lisa Bonsall, Richard S. Jr.; m. Albert Brown Jeffers, Aug. 10, 1968; children: Albert III, James Wilkinson. AAS, Briarcliff Coll., 1959; AB, Rutgers U., 1970, MS, 1974, PhD, 1976. Cert. sch. psychologist, N.J. Adj. asst. prof. psychology County Coll. Morris, Randolph, N.J., 1976-77, Coll. of St. Elizabeth, Convent Station, N.J., 1976-83, Rutgers U., Newark and New Brunswick, N.J., 1976-80; sch. psychologist Morris County Edn. Svc. Commn., N.J., 1980-84; pvt. practice Morristown, N.J., 1980—. Cons. Cheshire Home, Florham Park, N.J., 1990-92; faculty Psychoanalytic Ctr. No. N.J., 1997-2003; chair N.J. Bd. Psycol. Examiners, 2002-. Mem.: APA. Avocation: guitar. Home and Office: 670 Winding Brook Rd Califon NJ 07830 Personal E-mail: vj4467@earthlink.net.

JEFFERSON, DENISE, dance school director; b. Chgo. Studied ballet with, Edna L. McRae; BA, Wheaton Coll.; MA, NYU; Ph.D. (hon.), Wheaton College, 2000. Co-founder, co-dir. Chgo. Dance Ctr.; tchr. dance U. Ill., Chgo.; with Pearl Lang Dance Co.; mem. dance faculty Sch. Arts NYU, Alvin Ailey Dance Ctr., 1975—80; dir. Alvin Ailey Am. Dance Ctr. Scholarship program, 1980-84, Alvin Ailey Dance Sch., 1984—; v.p. Nat. Assoc. of Schools of Dance. Remedial writing tchr. Seek program Hunter Coll.; developed modern dance program Benedict Coll.; guest tchr. U.S., internat.; mem. internat. team dance profls. Dutch govt. to evaluate Dance acads. in Holland, 1990; adjudicator Arts Recognition, Talent Search Confederation Nat. de Danse, Fedn. Interprofl. de la danse, 1992. Mem. adv. bd. Profl. Children's Sch.; mem. adv. com. dance dept. U. Okla.; trustee Elisa Monte Dance Co. Grantee Nat. Endowment Arts and Humanities; scholar Martha Graham Sch. Contemporary Dance. Mem. Nat. Assn. Schs. Dance (bd. dirs. 1989-91, program evaluator, mem. commn. accredation), N.Y. State Coun. Arts (dance panel, appeal panel). Office: Alvin Ailey Dance Theatre 405 W 55th St New York NY 10019-4402

JEFFERSON, HELEN BUTLER, public health service officer; b. Edgefield, SC, Aug. 4, 1954; d. W.D. and Martha H. Butler; m. John H. Jefferson, July 2, 1977; children: Sheldon H., Brandon D. Assoc. Computer Prgramming, Kerr Bus. Coll., Augusta, Ga., 1984; BS in Orgnl. Mgmt. with honors, Voorhees Coll., Denmark, SC, 2006. IBM keypunch operator Piedmont Tech. Coll., Greenwood, SC, 1976; health protection inspector WSRC, Aiken, SC, 1985—. Mem., leader AB Miles Voices of Praise Choir, Aiken; cmty. leader Edgefield County Assn., SC, 2005; Sunday sch. tchr. Friendship Bapt. Ch., Aiken, 2003—. Mem.: Health Physics Soc., Alpha Kappa Mu. Democrat. Baptist. Avocations: reading, cooking, writing, walking. Home: 721 Teague St NW Aiken SC 29801 Office: WSRC PO Box 616 Aiken SC 29801

JEFFERSON, KATHLEEN HENDERSON, retired secondary school educator; b. Pine Bluff, Ark., Sept. 20, 1928; d. Horace and Fannie Henderson; children: Ellen, Regina. BS in Chemistry, U. Ark., 1951; MEd in Maths. Edn., Tuskegee (Ala.) Inst., 1973. Cert. tchr., D.C., Ark. Tchr. Ark. Pub. Schs., Pine Bluff, 1952-78, U. Ark., Monticello, 1978-79, D.C. Pub. Schs., Washington, 1979—; chairperson maths. dept., tchr. Dunbar Sr. High Sch., Washington, 1982-96; ret., 1996. Adj. prof. U. D.C., 1997—. Mem. LWV, Pine Bluff, 1973-77, St. Francis De Sales Ch., Washington; vol. mathematics tutor, St. Francis De Sales Sch., 2000—. NSF fellow, 1960, Internat. Paper Co. fellow, 1970-73. Mem. ASCD, D.C. Coun. Tchrs. of Maths., D.C. Tchrs. Union Local, Delta Sigma Theta. Roman Catholic. Avocations: reading, swimming, chess.

JEFFERSON, KRISTIN MARIE, art dealer, consultant, film producer, writer; b. Tacoma, Jan. 15, 1947; d. Edward Harold and Helen Marie (Chandler) J BA, Bard Coll., 1968; MFA, Hunter Coll., 1974; MPS Tisch Sch. Arts, NYU, 1999. Facilities adminstr. Sterling Inst., Washington, 1969—71; prof. art CUNY, 1971—79; art dealer N.Y.C., 1979—. Founding pres., exec. dir. Mus. of World Art, 1989— Author: She-Images of Woman in Art, 1983, Magic in the Mind's Eye-Alchemy of Collecting, 1987; curator mus. quality art exhibits, 1982—; prodr. The Nanzetta Legacy, Choreography of Memory, When the Spirit Moves Shared Visions Prodn. Studio, 1997-99; assoc. prodr. Free to Dance, PBS-TV Series/Am. Masters; line prodr. AMC-TV documentary Hattie McDaniel; prodr., creative dir. Shared Visions Prodn. Studio, 1997—; coordinating prodr. Martha Graham Legacy Project, 2002 Mem. pub. rels. staff Sotheby's benefit for Cath. Relief Svcs. to Benefit the Famine Victims of Ethiopia, 1985 Episcopalian. Home: 330 W 56th St New York NY 10019-4248

JEFFERSON, LETITIA GIBSON, rehabilitation counselor; b. Providence, Dec. 5, 1937; d. Walter J. Vreeland (stepfather) Jr. and Mary Ledore Halton; m. Carl F. Jefferson, Jr., Sept. 13, 1961 (div. 1968); children: Halton Matthew, Nancy, Robert. BA, Wells Coll., 1959; postgrad., Syracuse (N.Y.) U., 1966. Sr. employment counselor N.Y. State Dept. Labor, Albany, 1963-67; labor specialist Suffolk County Dept. Labor, Hauppauge, NY, 1967—99, asst. dir.; ret., 1999. Mem. St. Marks Choir, Hampton Coun. of Chs. Ecumenical Choir, Westhampton Beach, N.Y., mem. prayer group, St. Phillip Ch.; lay leader, chalice adminstr., eucharistic min. St. Marks Ch.; performer Hampton Theatre Co., Quogue, N.Y.; co-founder Eleventh Step Meditation Workshop, St. Marks Ch. Mem. Nat. Rehab. Assn. (co-founder Suffolk chpt.), Suffolk County Rehab. Coun. (past pres.), Southampton Town Rep. Club. Republican. Episcopalian. Avocations: sailing, poetry, theater, art, singing. Home: 8 Majestic Trce Hendersonville NC 28739-8466 Personal E-mail: mamajeff@webtv.net.

JEFFERSON, MARLENE ROCHELLE, municipal official, director, minister; b. Washington, Mar. 22, 1967; d. Manuel Joseph and Marilyn Elizabeth Morris; 1 child, Morgan Rochelle. BS, Towson State U., Balt., 1989; MDiv, Howard U., Washington, 1999. Sr. fin. analyst Student Loan Mktg. Assn., Reston, Va., 1990—98; sr. fin. cons. PriceWaterhouse Coopers, LLC, Rosslyn, Va., 1998—2001; dir. ops. Exec. Office of the Mayor, Washington, 2001—04; dep. dir. DC Office Partnerships and Grants Devel., Washington, 2004—. Sr. adv. religious affairs Exec. Office of the Mayor, Washington, 2003—04. Assoc. pastor Allen Chapel AME Ch., Washington, 1998—2004; asst. pastor First AME Ch., Alexandria, Va., 2004—06, Lee Meml. AME Ch., Kensington, Md., 2006. Recipient Cmty. Enrichment and Empowerment Program award, Towson State U., 1986—89. Mem.: Delta Sigma Theta (assoc.; local chair program planning and devel. 1993—94). Democrat. Methodist. Avocations: reading, travel, cooking. Office Phone: 202-727-6518.

JEFFERSON, MYRA LAVERNE TULL, sales executive; b. Chester, Pa. d. Clarence Ernest and Mary Marie (Gaines) Tull; m. Bernard Carr Jefferson III, Mar. 11, 1983. BS in Computer Sci., Roosevelt U., 1987; postgrad., Chaminade U., 1986-87. Computer programmer Integrated Computer Techs., Phila., 1979-83; cons. Honolulu, 1983-88; data base mgr. E.S.R.D. Network Coordinating Council, Honolulu, 1984-88; comptr. Static Control Products, Phoenix, 1989-93; pres. Lion-S Sales & Svc., Mesa, Ariz., 1991—. Cons. NCC #1 Med. Rev. Bd., Honolulu, 1985, Thrifty Constrn. Co., Honolulu, 1986-87, Computer Support, 1985. Apptd. by mayor to the city of Mesa Economic Devel. adv. bd.; apptd. to Industrial Devel. Authority Commn. of Maricopa County; apptd. by gov. Econ. Security Adv. Bd.; treas. bd. Mesa Cmty. Action Network, 1992-95, 2d vice chair, 1995-96; bd. dirs. WOW Project; alumnae Mesa Leadership Tng. Program, Valley Leadership Program, black bd. dirs. project; bd. dirs., co-chair Black Women's Task Force, 1994-95, bd. dirs. the Family Svc. Agy.; treas. Pol. Dist. 29. Recipient award for Outstanding Contbns. to Data Processing, Am. Inst., 1987, Profl. and Scholastic Achievement award Am. Inst., 1986, Outstanding Achievement in Data Processing Profession, Am. Inst., 1986; fellow Ariz. Edn. Policy Fellowship Program. Mem. AAUW, Math. Assn. Am., Am. Math. Soc., Women in Computing, Am. Assn. Ind. Investors, Am. Express Com. Diversity Bd., Coalition for Tomorrow, U.S. Congressman Matt Salmon's Small Bus. Adv. Group, captain Precinct 54 Committeemen. Avocations: reading, crosswords, chess, computers. Home and Office: PO Box 3149 Tempe AZ 85280-3149

JEFFERSON, NANETTE HAWKINS, special education educator; b. Little Rock, Mar. 4, 1969; d. Edwin Luther Hawkins and Lana Rachelle Mitchell; m. Authur Allen Jefferson, July 13, 2002; children: Attrice Onee, Emily. BS in Edn., U. Ctrl. Ark., 1995. Spl. edn. tchr. Little Rock Sch. Dist., 1999—. Mem.: Alpha Delta Kappa. Democrat. Methodist. Avocations: reading, gardening.

JEFFERSON, ZANOBIA BRACY, art educator, artist; b. Chgo., Sept. 3, 1926; d. Francis Wright and Hattie Ocie (Robinson) Bracy; m. Robert L. Jefferson, June 4, 1950 (dec. Dec. 23, 1983); children: Heidi V. Long, Robyn F. Sims, Ionis M. Swoope, Robert L. Jr., Gisele Z. Mestre. BA, Fisk Univ., Nashville, Tenn., 1948; MEd, Nova Univ., Ft. Lauderdale, Fla., 1987. Tchr. Fla. A & M Univ., Tallahassee, 1948—50; adult educator Ft. Pierce, Fla. Sch., Ft. Pierce, Fla., 1950—70; art tchr. St. Lucie Co. Pub. Sch., Ft. Pierce, Fla.,

1960—93; tchr. art edn. Nova Univ., Ft. Pierce, Fla., 1980. Sculpture, 3-4ft. children, St. Anatasia Cath. Ch., 1988, Felix Elem. Sch., 1986. Bd. dirs. Backus Art Gallery; manpower com. Gov. Graham, Tallahassee; bd. Sunrise Theater, St. Pierce, Fla. Recipient 1st Lifetime Arts Achievement award, St. Lucie County Cult. Affairs Coun., 2005. Mem.: Opera Soc., African Am. Exo. for the Arts, Ret. Educators of Fla., Links Inc., Alpha Kappa Alpha. Christian. Achievements include mentor to highwaymen artists group, tchr. of original group, Afred Hair, James Gibson, Rodney Demps, etc. Avocations: art, crafts, travel, gardening, coin collecting/numismatics. Home: 2300 Valencia Ave Fort Pierce FL 34946 Office Phone: 772-461-4109.

JEFFERY, SUZANNE, retired elementary school educator; b. Cin., Jan. 24, 1943; d. Walter Dare and Inez Evelyn McGilliard; m. Allen Huntley Nixon (div.); children: James Nixon, Michael Nixon, Brian Nixon; m. Ned Kenneth Jeffery, Nov. 28, 1997. BS, Bowling Green State Univ., Bowling Green, Ohio, 1965; MA, Ashland Univ., Ashland, Ohio, 1985. Tchr. 4th grade Sandusky Pub. Sch., Ohio, 1965—66; tchr. Remedial Reading Norwalk (Ohio) Pub. Sch., 1971—72; tchr. reading tutor Monroeville (Ohio) Pub. Sch., 1978—79; tchr. special edn. South Ctrl. Pub. Sch., Greenwich, Ohio, 1979—2005; ret., 2005. Pres. North Ctrl. Ohio Edn. Assn., Mansfield, Ohio, 1999—2001; treas. dist. leaders Ohio Edn. Assn., Columbus, Ohio, 2001—03. Mentor Zion Luth. Ch., Sandusky, Ohio, tchr., 2002—05. Scholar Jennings Scholar, Martha Holden Jennings Found., 1991—92. Mem.: Delta Kappa Gamma. Avocations: reading, travel, gardening. Home: 12508 US Hwy 250N Milan OH 44846 Personal E-mail: jsuzanne890@aol.com.

JEFFERY, VALERIE, secondary school educator; m. Paul Roberts Jeffery, June 9, 2001; 1 child, Taylor Rae. BA, Coll. of St. Benedict, St. Joseph, Minn., 1994—97. Tchr. Dassel Cokato HS, Minn., 2001—. Office Phone: 320-286-4100.

JEFFORDS, MARY MARGARET, community activist; b. Huntington Station, N.Y., Mar. 20, 1956; d. Harry McClean and Margaret Marion (Gill) J. AA, Briarcliff Coll., 1977. Case worker County Govt., L.I., N.Y., 1980-89; journalist Metro Comm. News, Buffalo, 1989-91; freelance writer N.Y., 1989—; pub. rels. person-in-charge Injured Workers of N.Y., Syracuse, 1990—, statewide pres. Sanborn, N.Y., 1991—. Cons. med. malpractice Alliance for Mentally Ill, Buffalo, 1991—. Author: Panic and Anxiety Disorders, 1992. Labor organizer Injured Workers of N.Y., Buffalo, 1991-93; organizer Reach to the Stars C. of C., Niagara Falls, 1990-94; coord. Niagara Falls Anxiety Group, 1990-96; exhibitor T-shirt project, Niagara Falls, 1992-96. Mem. N.Y. State Workers' Compensation Bd. (mem. practices and procedures com. 1995—), Soc. Profl. Journalists, Niagara Falls Assn. Profl. Women Writers, Coalition of Econ. Justice, Coalition on Safety and Health, Anxiety Disorders Assn. of Am. Methodist. Home: PO Box 252 Sanborn NY 14132-0252

JEFFREY, JUDY, school system administrator; BA, U. of No. Iowa, 1963; MA, Creighton U., 1981. With Council Bluffs Cmty. Sch. Dist.; adminstr. Early Childhood, Elementary and Secondary Edn. div. Iowa Dept. Edn., 1996—, dir. edn., 2004—. Tchr. Cedar Falls and Goldfield dists., Iowa; instr. Creighton U.; pres. Coun. of Chief State Sch. Officers Dep. Commn., 2001—03, bd. dirs. Office: Iowa Dept Edn Grimes State Office Bldg Des Moines IA 50319-0146 Office Phone: 515-281-5294. Office Fax: 515-242-5988.

JEFFREY, SHERI, lawyer; BS cum laude, Loyola Marymount U., 1982, JD, 1985; LLM, NYU, 1986. Bar: Calif. 1985. Ptnr. Corp. & Fin. Dept., mem. Entertainment Group Kaye Scholer LLP, LA. Mem.: State Bar Calif. Office: Kaye Scholer LLP Ste 1700 1999 Ave of the Stars Los Angeles CA 90067 Office Phone: 310-788-1270. E-mail: sjeffrey@kayescholer.com.

JEGEN, SISTER CAROL FRANCES, religious studies educator; b. Chgo., Oct. 11, 1925; d. Julian Aloysius and Evelyn W. (Bostelmann) J. BS in History, St. Louis U., 1951; MA in Theology, Marquette U., 1958, PhD in Religious Studies, 1968; degree (hon.), St. Mary of the Woods, Terra Haute, Ind., 1977. Elem. tchr. St. Francis Xavier Sch., St. Louis, 1947-51; secondary tchr. Holy Angels Sch., Milw., 1951-57; coll. tchr. Mundelein Coll., Chgo., 1957-91; prof. pastoral studies Loyola U., Chgo., 1991—. Adv. coun. U.S. Cath. Bishops, Washington, 1969-74; trustees Cath. Theol. Union, Chgo., 1974-84. Author: Jesus the Peace Maker, 1986, Restoring Our Friendship with God, 1989; co-author: (with Byron Sherwin) Thank God, 1989; editor: Mary According to Women, 1985. Participant Nat. Farm Worker Ministry, Fresno, Calif., 1977—; mem. Pax Christi, U.S.A., 1979—, Jane Addams Conf., Chgo., 1989. Recipient Loyola Civic award Loyola U., Chgo., 1981, Chgo. medallion for Excellence in Catechesis, 1996, Sor Juana award Hispanic Ministry, 2000; named one of 100 Women to Watch Today's Chgo. Woman, 1989. Mem. Cath. Theol. Soc. Am., Coll. Theology Soc., Cath.-Jewish Scholars Dialog, Liturgical Conf. Democrat. Roman Catholic. Avocations: music, gardening. Home: Wright Hall 6364 N Sheridan Rd Chicago IL 60660-1700

JEHLEN, PATRICIA D., state legislator; b. Austin, Tex., Oct. 14, 1943; d. Paul Kindred Jr. and Ruth Miller (Zumbrunnen) Deats; m. Alain Peter Jehlen, Aug. 29, 1969; children: Nicholas, Wendy, Peter. BA, Swarthmore Coll., 1965; MA in Teaching, Harvard U., 1969. Rschr. Harvard Sch. Edn., Cambridge, Mass., 1966-67; tchr. history Brookline (Mass.) H.S., 1968-71; mem. Somerville (Mass.) Sch. Com., 1976-91, Mass. Ho. of Reps., Somerville, 1991—. VISTA vol. Cook County Migrant Coun., Chicago Heights, Ill., 1965-66. Democrat. Home: 67 Dane St Somerville MA 02143-3730 Office: Mass Ho of Reps Rm 275 Boston MA 02133 Office Phone: 617-722-2676. Business E-Mail: rep.patricia.jehlen@hon.state.ma.us.

JELALIAN, CHRISTINE, elementary school educator, secondary school educator; d. Anthony and Isabel Gargiulo; m. Peter Jelalian, Dec. 19, 1992; 1 child, Theresa. BS in Phys. Edn., Bklyn. Coll., 1977, MS in Secondary Edn., 1990. Mgr. fitness Bally's Health Spa, Bklyn., 1977—84; coach N.Y.C. (N.Y.) Bd. Edn., 1984—. Instr. Am. Red Cross, N.Y.C., 1984—; trainer personal health Aerobic and Fitness Assn. Am., N.Y.C., 1995—. Home: 4 Vincent St Nanuet NY 10954 Office Phone: 718-892-5270. E-mail: jellybean@icu.com.

JELINEK, POLLY MADISON, retired elementary school educator; b. Austin, Minn., Jan. 12, 1933; d. Edwin Maurice and Irene Elizabeth (Crandall) Madison; m. Eugene Richard Jelinek, May 1, 1965; 1 child, Anne Elizabeth. BS, Winona State Coll., 1961; MEd in Elem. Edn., U. Minn., 1990, MEd. Classroom tchr. Austin Pub. Schs.; tchr. kindergarten, 4th grade Elkton Pub. Sch., Minn.; tchr. rural sch. Mower County Dists. 57, 98, Mower, Mo.; tchr. 3d grade Austin Pub. Schs.; ret. Mem. NEA, Minn. Edn. Assn., Am. Edn. Assn., Internat. Reading Assn., Minn. Reading Assn., Parent-Tchr. Coun., Delta Kappa Gamma (past pres.). Home: 1604 12th St SW Austin MN 55912-2623

JELINEK, VERA, dean; b. Kosice, Czechoslovakia, Dec. 16, 1935; came to U.S., 1947; d. Joseph and Margit (Lefkovits) Schnitzer; m. Josef E. Jelinek, June 19, 1960; children: David, Paul. BA in History, CUNY, 1956; MA, Johns Hopkins U., 1958; PhD in Modern European History, NYU, 1977; diploma, Sch. Advanced Internat. Study, Bologna, Italy. Translator Rockefeller Bros. Fund, NYC, 1958-59; exec. dir. US Youth Coun., 1959-63; dir. internat. programs, social and natural scis. NYU, 1985—; dir. NYU Lillian Vernon Ctr. Internat. Affairs, 2000—04, NYU Energy Forum, 2000—05; asst. dean, dir. NYU Ctr. Global Affairs, 2004—. Mem. adv. com. N.Y.C.-Budapest Sister City Program, 1991-94; prin. dir. pilot tng. program for new UN diplomats NYU, 1996-97. Author audio cassette: Before You Go-Italy, 1985. Mem. edn. com. Mus. Am. Folk Art, N.Y.C.; edn. co-chair The Am. Antiques Show, 2002—03. Recipient fellowship Ford Found., 1960, grant NYU Curriculum Challenge Fund, 1989, 90, 99, Phillip E. Frandson award Nat. Univ. Continuing Edn. Assn., 1991. Mem. Am. Folk Art Soc., Carnegie Coun. on Ethics and Internat. Affairs, Women's Fgn. Policy Group, Phi Beta Kappa. Democrat. Avocations: tennis, jogging, folk art, cooking, travel. Office: Woolworth Bldg 15 Barclay St New York NY 10007 Office Phone: 212-992-8380.

JELKS, MARY LARSON, retired pediatrician; b. Galva, Ill., 1929; MD, U. Nebr., 1955. Diplomate Am. Bd. Pediats., Am. Bd. Allergy and Immunology. Intern Johns Hopkins Hosp., Balt., 1955-56, resident, 1956-57, 58-60, Grace-New Haven Hosp., 1957; fellow U. Fla. Tchg. Hosp., 1960-61; clin. asst. prof. U. South Fla.; ret.; active aerobiology, 1985—. Fellow Am. Acad. Allery and Immunology, Am. Acad. Pediats.; mem. AMA. Achievements include active research in aerobiology. Home: 1930 Clematis St Sarasota FL 34239-3813 E-mail: mjelks99@cs.com.

JELLISON, BEVERLY IRENE, literature and language educator; d. Edward Robert and Julia Etta Dornoff; m. Walter Thomas Jellison, Mar. 24, 1972 (div.); children: Janet Irene Tait Waugh, Nancy Elizabeth Tait Carrillo. BS in Speech English, U. Ill., 1952—57; MA in Theater Arts, CA State U., 1959—61. English drama tchr. Stephen Decatur H.S., 1957—58, Arcadia H.S., 1958—61; English tchr. Helix Adult Sch., 1968—71; English, AP English, creative writing, Shakespeare, tchr. Santana H.S., 1971—2001, Grossmont Union High Sch. Dist. (GUHSD), 1993—2003. Support provider CA tchr. evaluation program GUHSD, 2001—03, support provider, 2003—, GATE Liaison, 2003—; tng. future tchrs. various, 1975—2002. Profl. adv. comm. GUHSD, 1974—, superintendent's adv. comm., 1983—85, mem. purchasing rev. cmty., 1993, chair, 1993—2001, mem. curriculum master plan steering cmty., 1994—2001, mem., 75th anniversary task force, 1996; literary book adv. Santana H.S., 1975—87, mem. WASC leadership team, 1996—97, coord. adv.; edn. bd. J. Paul Getty Mus., 1983—85; secondary lang. arts adv. cmty. San Diego County, 1993—2001. Recipient Key to the City, City of San Diego, 1969, Tchr. of Year, GUHSD, Golden G award, 1999, 2003. Mem.: Greater San Diego Coun. Tchr. English (presenter conf. 1974—, speaker 1995), Am. Assoc. U. Women, Nat. Coun. Tchr. English (presenter nat. conv. 1988), Calif. Assoc. for the Gifted (presenter state conv. 1985—), Calif. Assoc. Tchr. English (presenter state conv. 1972—), Nat. Edn. Assoc., Calif. Tchrs. Assoc., Grossmont Edn Assoc., Kappa Delta. Avocations: travel, bridge, art history, classical music. Home: 6912 Maury Dr San Diego CA 92119 Personal E-mail: bevejell@cox.net.

JELLISON, JENNY LYNNE, psychology professor; d. Lewis and Cathy Robbins; m. Chad Jellison, July 8, 2000. PhD, U. Toledo, 2003. Prof. psychology Waynesburg Coll., Pa., 2004—. Office Phone: 724-852-3242.

JELSMA, ELIZABETH BARBARA, music educator; b. Newark, Aug. 24, 1934; d. Joseph Augsdorfer and Clara Stiehl; m. Lawrence Franklin Jelsma, June 15, 1967 (div. Sept. 30, 1976); children: Deborah Lynn, Lawrence Frank, Elizabeth Louise, Mark Andrew. Degree in music edn., Northwestern U., 1959, MusM, 1961. Tchr. 1st grade Jenner Sch., Chgo.; tchr. music grades K-8, Yavapai Sch., Scottsdale, Ariz., 1969—95; pvt. piano tchr. NJ, Ill., Ariz. Judge piano Ariz. State U., Tempe, 1962—63; accompanist Bach Madrigal Soc., Phoenix, 1964—66. Singer (soloist): Northwestern Symphony Orch., 1960. Recipient various awards for solo performances. Mem.: Sigma Alpha Iota. Republican. Roman Catholic. Avocations: reading, travel, swimming.

JELUS, SUSAN CRUM, writer, editor; b. Cin., Sept. 14, 1952; d. Robert Malcolm and Jean Moses Crum; m. Raymond Jelus, Aug. 1, 1975 (div. Dec. 1989). BA, Miami U., Oxford, Ohio, 1974. Continuity mgr. Sta. WLWT TV, Cin., 1975-77; traffic mgr. Sta. WCKY-WWEZ, Cin., 1977-79; advt. coord. Cintas Corp., Cin., 1979-80; audio-visual writer-prodr. Dayton, 1981-84; tech. writer Sinclair C.C., Dayton, 1984-86; sr. instrnl. developer The Reynolds & Reynolds Co., Dayton, 1986-95; publs./on-line help author, editor Rsch. Computer Svcs. divsn. NCR Corp., Dayton, 1995—; editor, pub. New Song Press, Dayton, 1995—2003. Editor: (lit. jour.) A New Song, 1996-2003; contbr. poetry to anthologies and lit. mags. Bd. dirs. Hist. Dist. Archtl. Rev. Bd., Germantown, Ohio, 1990-93; campaign tng. chairperson United Way, Dayton, 1987; dir. Jr. Handbell Choir, South Park United Meth. Ch., Dayton, 1995; dir. youth choir Centerville (Ohio) United Meth. Ch., 2000-01; dir. handchime choir Huffman Pl., 2002-05; publicity chair Dayton Mandolin Orch., 2005-06, pres., 2006. Recipient Commendation award for poetry Chester H. Jones Found., 1995, Award of Merit, Soc. for Tech. Comm., 1989. Mem. AAUW, Nat. Mus. for Women in the Arts, Soc. Tech. Comm. Democrat. Avocations: painting, guitar, mandolin. Home: 122 La Belle St Dayton OH 45403-2326 E-mail: susanjelus@sbcglobal.net.

JEMISON, MAE CAROL, physician, engineer, entrepreneur, philanthropist, educator, former astronaut; b. Decatur, Ala., Oct. 17, 1956; d. Charlie and Dorothy (Green) J. BS in ChemE, BA in African-Am. Studies, Stanford U., 1977; MD, Cornell U., 1981. Physician Peace Corps, Sierra Leone, Western Africa, 1983—85; pvt. practice L.A.; mission specialist NASA, Houston, 1987—93, astronaut on space shuttle Endeavor, 1992; prof. Dartmouth Coll., 1995—2002; mem. bd. dirs. Scholastic Inc.; national sci. literary advocate Bayer Corp., 1995—. Founder, pres. BioSentient Corp., The Jemison Group, Inc., 1993—, The Earth We Share Internat. Sci. Camp; A.D. White prof.-at-large Cornell U.; founder, pres. The Dorothy Jemison Foundation for Excellence, 1994—; mem., bd. dirs. Scholastic, Inc.; national sci. literary advocate Bayer Corp., 1995—; bd. dirs. Valspar Corp., Kimberly-Clark Corp. Author: Find Where The Wind Goes, 2001; TV host Discovery Channel, World of Wonder, 1994—95. Named one of World's 50 Most Beautiful People, People Mag., 1993. Mem.: NAS Inst. Medicine. Achievements include being first woman of color to fly in space. Office: Jemison Group Inc PO Box 591455 Houston TX 77259

JEMISON, SANDRA J., educational association administrator; d. James and Virginia Johnson; m. Walter Jemison, Mar. 16, 1974; children: Stephen, Lance. MA, U. Ala., 1975, EdS, 1988, PhD, 2002. Cert. sch. psychologist Ala., instructional leadership Ala., tchr. Spl. edn. tchr. Hale County Bd. Edn., Greensboro, Ala., 1973—74, Tuscaloosa City Schs., Ala., 1974—79, sch. psychometrist, 1979—88, sch. psychologist, 1988—92, chpt. I supr., 1992—96, elem. dir., 1996—2000, fed. programs adminstr., 2000—04; dir. Thumbs Up Svc. Agy., Tuscaloosa, 2005—. Contbr. articles to profl. jours. Bd. mem. Tombigbee Girl Scouts, Tuscaloosa, 2004—, Skyland SDA Sch., Tuscaloosa, 2004—; personal ministries leader Skyland SDA Ch., 2004. Recipient Breakthrough Literacy award, Nat. Alliance Black Sch. Educators, 2000; grantee Patricia Roberts Harris fellowship, U. Ala., 1994—95, Even Start Family Literacy grant, Ala. State Dept. Edn., 2000—, Appalachian grant, Office Sch. Readiness, 2002—, Comprehensive Sch. Reform grant, Ala. State Dept. Edn., 2003—. Mem.: NEA, Ala. Assn. Supr. & Curriculum Devel., Nat. Assn. Sch. Psychologists. Home: 9908 Fieldstone Ln Tuscaloosa AL 35405

JEMMOTT, LORETTA SWEET, HIV/AIDS researcher, nursing educator; m. John B. Jemmott III. BSN, Hampton Inst., 1978; MSN in Psychiatric Mental Health, U. Pa., 1982, PhD in Human Sexuality Edn., 1987. Asst. prof. nursing Rutgers U. Coll. of Nursing, Newark, 1987-93, assoc. prof. nursing, 1993-94; dir. Ctr. for AIDS Rsch. Columbia U. Sch. Nursing, NYC, 1994-95; assoc. HIV Ctr. for Clin. & Behaviors Studies Columbia U. and NY State Psychiatric Inst., NYC, 1994; vis. rsch. scholar dept. psychology Princeton U., NJ, 1995—; rsch. assoc. Population Studies Ctr. U. Pa., Phila., 1995—, assoc. prof. grad. sch. edn., 1995—, assoc. prof. nursing Ctr. for Urban Health Rsch., 1995—, dir. Ctr. for Urban Health Rsch. Sch. Nursing, 1996—, asst. provost, gender and minority equity issues, 2004—, prof. Sch. Nursing, van Ameringen chair psychiatric mental health nursing Sch. Nursing, dir. Ctr. Health Disparities Rsch., Sch. Nursing. Contbr. articles to profl. publ., chapters to books. Ednl. bd. Nursing Outlook. Recipient Outstanding Nursing Achievement and Rsch. award, Concerned Black Nurses, 1989, Outstanding Svc. award, Rutgers Coll. Nursing, 1990, Nurse Merit award advanced nursing practice, Gov. NJ, 1992, Outstanding Rsch. award, Northern NJ Black Nurses Assn., 1992, Congressional Merit Recognition award, 1995, Red Ribbon award outstanding svc. in field of HIV/AIDS, HIV Prevention Curriculum award, Ctr. Disease Control and Prevention and Divsn. Adolescent & Sch. Health, 2001, Exemplary Substance Abuse Prevention award, Ctr. Substance Abuse Prevention, 2001, Women Making a Difference award, Phila. City Coun., 2002, Cmty. Health Promotion Svc. award, Health Ministry Program, Eli Lilly and Keystone Mercy Health Plan, 2002, Gloria Twine Chisum Faculty Leadership award, U. Pa., 2002. Fellow: Am. Acad. Nursing; mem.: Inst. Medicine. Office: U Pa Sch Nursing Rm 239 NEB 420 Gaurdian Dr Philadelphia PA 19104-6096 Office Phone: 215-898-8287. E-mail: jemmott@nursing.upenn.edu.*

JENAI, MARILYN, psychotherapist; children: Michael Stover, Dianne Stover. BA in Psychology and Comm., Oakland U., 1973, MA in Counseling Psychology, 1974; MA in Culture and Spirituality, Holy Names Coll., 1990, DMin in Integral Psychology and Spirituality, 2000. Lic. marriage and family therapist Fla., massage therapist Fla., cert. social worker Mich., Nat. Bd. Cert. Clin. Hynosis, compassion fatigue specialist. Group leader, workshop cons. Contiuum Ctr., A First Women's Ctr., Oakland U., Rochester, Mich., 1967—75; psychotherapist, coord. Threshold Ctr. for Drug Studies and Cmty. Mental Health, Hazel Park, Mich., 1970—74; psychotherapist, instr. St. Mary's Hosp., Redford, Mich., 1974—76; psychotherapist Sarasota Guidance Clinic, 1976—78; instr. Manatee C.C., Bradenton, Fla., 1978—81; dir. counseling Safe Place and Rape Crisis Ctr., Sarasota, 1986—88; pvt. practice psychotherapy Ctr. Integrative Psychotherapy, Sarasota, Fla., 1979—, Berkeley, Calif., Portland, Oreg. Trainer in field; workshop leader in field. Democrat. E-mail: jenaipsy@comcast.net.

JENCKS, PENELOPE, sculptor; b. Balt., Mar. 23, 1936; d. Gardner Platt and Ruth DeWitt (Pearl) J.; m. Sidney Jack Hurwitz, Dec. 20, 1958; children: Edwin David, Adam Gardner, Erica Ruth. Student, Swarthmore Coll., 1954-56, Hans Hoffmann Sch., 1955, Skowhegan Art Sch., 1956, 57, Stuttgart (Germany) Kunstakademie, 1959; BFA, Boston U., 1958. Instr. Braintree (Mass.) Art Assn., 1971-72, Art Inst. Boston, 1975-79, Boston Coll., Newton, Mass., 1978; prof., Saltzman vis. artist Brandeis U., Waltham, Mass., 1981-83. Resident MacDowell Colony, 1975, 76, 78, 87; guest lectr. in field. One-woman shows include Fitchburg (Mass.) Art Mus., 1976, Landmark Gallery, N.Y.C., 1977, 81, Art Inst. Boston, 1978, Helen Shlein Gallery, Boston, 1981, 85; exhibited in group shows at U.S.I.S. Amerika Haus, Freiburg, Germany, 1960, Nat. Inst. Arts & Letters, N.Y.C., 1966, Mass. Coun. Arts & Humanities, Boston, 1966, Thayer Acad., Braintree, 1971, Boston Visual Artists Union, 1974, Pa. State Univ. Mus. Art, 1974, Kennedy Galleries, N.Y.C., 1977, GVW Smith Art Mus., Springfield, Mass., 1977, Clark Univ. Mus., Worcester, Mass., 1978, Mass. Artists Found. Fed. Res. Bank, Boston, 1980, Danforth Mus., Framingham, Mass., 1980, 84, Rose Art Mus. Brandeis U., 1982, MacDowell Colony Benefit, Cambridge, Mass., 1983, Brockton (Mass.) Art Mus., 1983, Currier Gallery Art, Manchester, N.H., 1984, Fitchburg Art Mus., 1984, Newton Arts Ctr., 1985, Boston U., 1986, Alchemy Gallery, Boston, 1987, Helen Bumpus Gallery, Duxbury, Mass., 1989, Rising Tide Gallery, Provincetown, Mass., 1989, Contemporary Sculpture, Chesterwood, Stockbridge, Mass., 1989. Recipient Mass. Artists Found. award, 1977, Commendation for Design Excellence, NEA, 1981, Henry Hering Meml. medal Nat. Sculpture Soc., 1988; winner numerous competitions and commns.; grantee Brandeis U., 1983. Office: 175 Parker St Newton MA 02459-2549 Mailing: c/o National Academy Design 1083 Fifth Ave New York NY 10128

JENERETTE, JOYCE WILLIAMS, elementary school educator, educational consultant; b. Oct. 29, 1948; d. George Milford Williams and Esther L. Morris-Williams; children: David Duane Williams, Deninne Brittanie Pritchett, DaShanda Nichole Pritchett; m. James E. Jenerette, June 25, 1988. A in Personnel Mgmt., Salem CC, 1982; BS in Bus. Mgmt. & Supervision, Wilmington Coll., 1985; MS, Wilmington Grad. Ctr., 1989; M in Ednl. Adminstrn., Grand Canyon U., 2005. Tchr. Salem Bd. of Edn., NJ, 1990—93; cons. ETS Nat. Bd. Profl. Tchg., Princeton, 1998—2001; tchr., tutor Trenton Bd. Edn., 1993—. Assessor, validator Nat. Bd. for Profl. Tchg. Stds., Tex., 1999—; next generation test team developer Ednl. Testing Svc., Princeton, 2000—; literacy curriculum team mem. Trenton Bd. Edn., 2003—04. Contbg. author Blessed Assurance: Stories of the Heart, 2004. Mem.: Handy-Simmons Scholarship Com. (chair), NJ AME Ministers Spouses (pres. 2002—04), Women's Missionary Soc. (3rd v.p. Phila conf.), NJ Ednl. Assn. Fast Coord. (sch. coord. 2003—). Avocations: reading, public speaking, missionary activities. Home: 18 Mayfair Cir Willingboro NJ 08046

JENICEK, ALICIA JOANNE, nursing consultant; d. John Andrew and Alice Jeanette Jenicek; children: James Josef Wong, John Daniel Wong. BS in Biology, Tex. A&M U., 1982; BSN, U. Tex. Med. Br., 1984. Cert. legal nurse cons., Med.-Legal Consulting Inst., Inc., RN Tex.; cert. massage therapist Dept. Health, Tex., massage therapy instr. Dept. of Health, Tex. Staff nurse U. Tex. Med. Br., Galveston, 1984—85, La. State U. Med. Ctr., Shreveport, 1986, Hosp. Corps. Am. Highland Hosp., Shreveport, 1986—87, Highland Clinic, Shreveport, 1987, Schumpert Med. Ctr., Shreveport, 1987—92; tchr. San Jacinto Med. Ctr., Baytown, Tex., 1992—2001; massage therapist Healing With Feeling, Taylor Lake Village, 1997—, massage therapy instr., 1998—; legal nurse cons. Med.-Legal Consulting, Taylor Lake Village, 2001—; paramed. technician Exam One, Houston, 2004—. Instr. European Massage Therapy Inst., Houston, 1999—2001; cons. James M. Andersen, Esquire, Houston, 2002—, Sanes, Matthews and Forester, Houston, 2004—; admission nurse Compassionate Care Hospice, 2006—. Editor: (newsletter) Medical-Legal Consulting. Mem. St. Paul Cath. Cmty., Houston, 1992. Mem.: U. Tex. Med. Br. Aux., Internat. Massage Assn., Healing Arts Network, Am. Specialty Health Networks, Am. Assn. Legal Nurse Cons., Nat. Alliance Cert. Legal Nurse Cons., Bay Area Aggies Former Student Assn. (scholarship reviewer 2003—04), Massage and Bodywork Educators Alliance. Roman Catholic. Avocations: art, crafts, reading. Home and Office: Med-Legal Consulting 1126 Live Oak Ln Taylor Lake Village TX 77586 Office Phone: 281-460-8239. Personal E-mail: ajajenicek@cs.com. Business E-Mail: ajenicekwongclnc@cs.com.

JENKINS, ADRIENNE, women's health nurse; b. Valentine, Nebr., June 17, 1949; d. William Jay Spelts, Jr. and Sarah Agnes (Digneo) Spelts; children: Angela Marie, Francesca Christine. BSN, U. Colo., 1972, degree in Women's Health Care Nurse Practioner Program, 1981. RN Colo., Nat. Cert. Corp., 1985. Nurse psychiat. divsn. Fort Logan Mental Health Ctr., Denver, 1973—73; nurse Newborn Nursery U. Colo. Med. Ctr., Denver, 1973—74; nurse ob.-gyn. Rose Med. Ctr., Denver, 1977—82; nurse Eating Disorders Unit Harbor View Med. Ctr., San Diego, 1987; nurse practioner U. Calif., San Diego, 1988—89, San Diego (Calif.) State U., 1988—89; nurse practioner ob. Perinatal Program U. Colo., San Diego, 1988—89; nurse practioner womens health Beach Area Cmty. Clinic, San Diego, 1988—89, Reproductive Med. Group, San Diego, 1989—94, Naval Med. Ctr., San Diego, 1994—2002; nurse practioner student health Miramar C.C., San Diego, 2003—. Scholar, Rose Med. Ctr., 1980. Mem.: Calif. Assn. Nurse Practitioners. Democrat. Avocation: writing. Home: 10653 Caminito Memosac San Diego CA 92131 Office: San Diego Community Coll Miramar Coll 10440 Black Mtn Rd San Diego CA 92126

JENKINS, ALICE MARIE, secondary school educator; b. Adair, Iowa, June 7, 1922; d. Charles Erwin Hall and Elizabeth Catherine Clarke Hall; m. Doyce Gwendon Pitts, June 27, 1943 (dec. Mar. 27, 1977); 1 child, Beverly Lou; m. Richard Jenkins, June 24, 1978. BA, Drake U., 1963. Tchr. rural and county schs., 1940—54, Linden (Iowa) Pub. Sch., 1954—55, Woodward (Iowa) State, 1955—60, 1971—93, Boone (Iowa) Pub. Sch., 1960—71, Woodward Cmty., 1993—. Mem.: VFW, Am. Legion Aux. (past pres.), Alpha Delta Kappa (past pres.). Democrat. Methodist. Avocations: cooking, reading, music. Office: Woodward-Granger HS 306 W 3rd St Woodward IA 50276-1033

JENKINS, BARBARA ALEXANDER, pastor, overseer; b. Ft. Bragg, N.C., Oct. 13, 1942; d. Archie Herman Alexander and Hattie Elizabeth (Thigpen) Truitt; m. Warren Keith Jenkins, Aug. 22, 1964 (div. Sept. 1980); children: Pamela, Eric, Jason. BS, Ea. Mich. U., 1964, postgrad., 1964-66, Duke U.,

1978; DD (hon.), Ch. of Christ Bible Coll., Madras, India, 1988. Ordained to ministry, World Faith Clinic Inc., 1983, A.M.E. Zion Ch., 1982. Min. World Faith Clinic Inc., Fayetteville, N.C., 1981-83, A.M.E. Zion Ch., Fayetteville, 1982-84; pastor Noah's Ark Ministry, Fayetteville, 1985-86; founder, pastor Rainbow Tabernacle of Faith Ministries, Inc., Winston-Salem, N.C., 1984—; founder Rainbow Raleigh (N.C.) Outreach Ministries, 1986—, Rainbow Tabernacle of Faith, Charlotte, N.C., 1987—. Dir. Spotlight on Truth Internat. Radio Ministries, Winston-Salem, 1985—, overseer hdqrs. Ogun State, Nigeria, 1992, others; founder Rainbow Internat. Crusade Ministry, Winston-Salem, 1986—; pres. Rainbow Bible Coll., Winston-Salem; dean Rainbow Inst. Commensurate Studies, Winston-Salem, 1985—; mem. Internat. Conv. Faith Ministries, Tulsa, 1989—. Author: Guidelines for Ministers, 1994; contbr. articles to religious jours. Concert vocalist N.C. Black Repertory Co., Winston-Salem, 1987, 88; youth coord. Jerry Lewis Muscular Dystrophy Telethon, Raleigh, 1987, 88; guest speaker Wake Forest U., Winston-Salem, 1991. Recipient Outstanding Svc. award Rainbow Tabernacle Faith, Inc., 1987; scholar March of Dimes-Easter Seals, 1960-64. Mem. NAFE, N.C. Women in Ministry (bd. dirs.), Am. Assn. Christian Counselors, Nat. Assn. Religious Profls., Delta Theta (project coord. 1979-80). Democrat. Office: Rainbow Tabernacle Faith Ministries Inc 4091 New Walkertown Rd Winston Salem NC 27105-9734 Home: 5490 Woodcliff Dr Winston Salem NC 27106-1922 E-mail: elect.lady@excite.com.

JENKINS, BILLIE BEASLEY, film company executive; b. Topeka, June 27, 1943; d. Arthur and Etta Mae Capelton; m. Rudolph Alan Jenkins, Nov. 1, 1935; 1 child, Tina Caprice. Student, Santa Monica City Coll., 1965-69. Exec. sec. to v.p. prodn. Screen Gems, L.A., 1969-72; exec. asst. Spelling/Goldberg Prodns., 1972-82; dir. adminstrn. The Leonard Co./Mandy Films, 1982-85, v.p., 1985-87; exec. asst. to pres. and chief oper. officer 20th Century Fox Film Corp., L.A., 1986-87, dir. adminstrn., 1987-90, dir. prodn. svcs. & resources Fox Motion Pictures div., 1990-92. Program coord. Am. Film Inst. Gary Hendler Minority Filmmakers Program, 1990-93; pres., CEO Masala Prodns., Inc., 1991—. Asst. to exec. producer: (films) War Games, 1984, Spacecamp, 1986; (movies for TV) Something about Amelia, 1984, Alex, The Life of a Child, 1985; (series) Paper Dolls, 1985, Cavanaughs, 1987, Charlie's Angels, Rookies, others; exec. prodn. cons. (documentary) The Good, The Bad, The Beautiful, 1995-96. Commr. L.A. City Cultural Heritage Commn., 1992-93. Named 1991 Woman of Excellence, Boy Scouts Am.; honored First African-Am. Women Pioneers of So. Calif. Top Ladies of Distinction City of Angels chpt. L.A., 1999. Mem.: Motivating Our Students Through Experience (mem. exec. bd.), Ind. FeatureProdns./West, Am. Film Inst., Black Women's Network, Women in Film Assn. (pres. 1991, 1992, advisor to exec. bd. 1993—95), Top Ladies of Distinctions. Avocations: photography, gardening, writing. E-mail: masalainc@aol.com.

JENKINS, BRENDA GWENETTA, pre-school administrator, special education educator; b. Durham, N.C., Aug. 11, 1949; d. Brinton Alfred and Ophelia Arden (Eaton) Jenkins. BS, Howard U., 1971, MEd, 1972, cert. advanced grad. studies, 1975; postgrad., Trinity Coll., Am. U., U. DC, Marymount Coll., 1976—. Cert. tchr., Washington; cert. Advanced Grad. Studies Spl. Edn., aerobics instr., Nat. Dance Exercise Instr.'s Tng. Assn. Cheerleading coach Howard U., Washington, 1971—86; tchr. DC Pub. Schs., Washington, 1972—, aerobics instr., 1982—97, Goals 2000 English, lang. arts, history writer, 1995—96; v.p. Nerdlihc Corp., Washington, 1985—; ptnr. Jenkins, Trapp-Dukes and Yates Partnership, Washington, 1984; co-owner Fantasia Early Learning Acad., Washington, 1985—98; instr. aerobics Washington Dept. Recreation, Washington, 1988—93; instr. You Fit, Inc. Nat. Children's Ctr. Washington, 1991—93, Anthony Bowen YMCA, Washington, 1992—93; instr. health, nutrition support Rockville, Md., 1992; instr., coach Maryvale PomPom/cheerleaders, Montgomery County, Md., 1992—94, asst. chmn. tchr. collaborative program, 1992—94, co-chair program com. tchr. collaborative, 1995—96; fitness instr. Oxedine Performing Arts Acad., Prince George's County, 1995—96. Aerobic instr. Coun. Exceptional Children, Washington, 1982, recreation svcs., City of Rockville, 1986—; developer My Spl. Friend program, 1984, BJ's Thinking Cap, 1991, Learning Creations, 1994, Girlfriends; bldg. rep. Washington Tchrs. Union AFT, AFL-CIO, 1987-89, 91-94, 96-04, asst. bldg. rep., 1990-91, 94-95, 04-05; supr. Foster Grandparent program Sharpe Health Sch., 1988—; trainer AIDS in Workplace, 1990, Early Childhood Substance Abuse Project Tng., 1992-93, Substance Abuse Prevention Edn., 1995, Metro Foster Grandparent Program Adv. Bd., Washington, 1992; mem. preschool adv. bd. DC Pub. Schs., 1992-93, coord. curriculum coun., 1994-96; master tchr. Coop. Tchr. Corp., 1993; curriculum writer, 1993; v.p. spl. edn. Washington Tchrs. Union Local 6, 1994-04; stds. specialist, 1997—; conv. del. Am. Fed. Tchrs., 1998, 04; adv. bd. Supt.'s Tchr. Affairs, 1999-; mem. Spl. Edn. State Adv. Panel, Washington, 1998-00, D.C. Parent Tng. and Info. Ctr., ARC, Inc. Adv. Panel; exec. bd. dirs. Assembly of Petworth, 1998—; DC Pub. Schs. recruiter Nat. Alliance Black Sch. Educators, Nashville, 1999, resident mentor tchr., 1999-04; mem. Disting. Educators Roundtable, 1998-04; supt. search com. D.C. Pub. Schs., 2004; pre-test participant Corp. for Nat. and Cmty. Svc., 2004; presenter, spkr. in field. Singer: 2000 Voices Lincoln Meml., 2000. Active DC Spl. Edn. State Adv., 1998, Internat. Space Camp, Huntsville, Ala., 1998; mem. Martin Luther King Tribute Choir, 2005-06; leadership/anchor stds. team DC Pub. Schs., 2005—. Recipient Outstanding Svc. award Kappa Delta Pi, 1978-79, 81-82, 84, citation Washington Tchr. Union, 1985, State winner Elem. Level Nat. Citizenship Edn. Tchr.'s award Ladies Aux. VFW, Washington, 2002, 03, Educator Excellence award Masonic Scottish Rite, 2001; named DC Tchr. of Yr., Coun. Chief State Sch. Officers, 1998, U. DC Cooperating Tchr., 2004, Tchr. of Month, DC Pub. Schs., 2006; grantee DC Pub. Sch. State Office, 1993, Citibank, 1994, Washington Post, 1999-04; named to Hall of Fame Bison Found. Inc., Howard U., 1995. Mem.: ASCD, Am. Fedn. Tchrs. (presiding officer WTU Spl. Educator and Svc. Provider Forums 1998—2005, sch. to careers tchr. extern 2001, DC Pub. Schs. new tchr. orientation trainer 2001—04, new tchr. coord. 2001—04, WTU Positive Tchr. ad campaign 2004, DCPS stds. facilitator 2005, WTU new tchr. coord. 2001—04), Coun. Exceptional Children, Howard Alumni Cheerleaders Assn. (co-founder 1977, pres. 1990—94, v.p. 1998—, Outstanding Recognition award 1984, Recognition award named Brenda G. Jenkins Outstanding Cheerleader award 1987), DC Parents and Friends of Children with Spl. Needs (critical ptnrs. group/supts. task force 2003, DCPS leadership/anchor stds. team mem. math specialist 2005—, bd. dirs.), Pi Lambda Theta, Kappa Delta Pi (exec. com. Theta Alpha chpt.). Democrat. Avocations: alumni cheerleading, fashion design, cooking, dance, poetry. Office Phone: 202-576-6161.

JENKINS, DAWN PAULA, special education educator, dancer; b. Harrisburg, Pa., Sept. 12, 1955; d. Reese Walls and Catherine Verbos Jenkins. EdB magna cum laude, U. Miami, Fla., 1977, EdM, 1978. Cert. profl. educator Fla., cert. assoc. master tchr. Fla. Tchr. of mentally challenged Holmes Elem. Sch., Miami, 1978—79; tchr. of deaf and hard of hearing Auburndale Elem. Sch., Miami, 1979—80; tchr. elem. deaf and hard of hearing Arcola Lake Elem., Miami, 1980—93; tchr. of deaf and hard of hearing Palm Springs Mid. Sch., Hialeah, Fla., 1993—. Applicant tchr. in space, 1986; choreographer and tchr. South Fla. Theatre of the Deaf, Miami, 1990—96; presenter Very Spl. Arts movement workshop, incorporating dance into curriculum Mid. Sch. Conv., Ft. Lauderdale, Fla., 1997; conf. presenter What's Up in Deaf Education; choreographer, dance tchr. for deaf students Very Spl. Arts program VSA Internat., Brussels; adj. prof. Interpreters Deaf program Miami Dade Coll., 1998—2000; developer deaf dance program MDCPS, 1991. Mem. Homeowners' Assn., Miami Lakes, Fla., 1995—98; founding mem. local club for the deaf Optimist Internat., Miami Lakes, 1996—97; fund raising sponsor Am. Cancer Soc., Miami, 1995—2003. Recipient Outstanding ESE tchr., Miami-Dade County, 1996; grantee, Impact II Com. of Miami Dade Schs., 2000; scholar, U. Miami Marching Band, 1973—77. Mem.: Nat. Dance Edn. Orgn., Fla. Educators of Hearing Impaired, Fla. Registry Interpreters, Nat. Dance Edn. Orgn., Nat. Assn. of the Deaf, Coun. Exceptional Children, Conv. Am. Instrs. Deaf. Presbyterian. Achievements include students performing The Wind That Blew at Internat. Very Spl. Arts Festival, representing Fla., Belgium, 1994. Avocations: dance, exercise, travel, reading, yoga. Office: Palm Springs Mid Sch 1025 W 56th St Hialeah FL 33012 Office Phone: 305-821-2460. Personal E-mail: dancindawn@bellsouth.net. Business E-Mail: dpjenkins@dadeschools.net.

JENKINS, ELAINE, middle school educator; d. Adam and Anne Kolasa; children: Allison, Laura. BA, William Paterson Coll., Wayne, NJ, 1973; MEd, William Paterson Coll., 1977. Cert. elem. sch. tchr. K-8 NJ, reading specialist NJ, tchr. of handicapped NJ. Substitute tchr. Elmwood Pk. Bd. Edn., NJ, 1973—76, compensatory edn. tchr., 1976—82; mid. sch. lang. arts tchr. Hawthorne Bd. Edn., NJ, 1988—89; mid. sch. basic skills lang. arts and math tchr. Paramus Bd. Edn., NJ, 1989—. Office: West Brook Mid Sch 550 Roosevelt Blvd Paramus NJ 07652 E-mail: ejenkins@paramus.k12.nj.us.

JENKINS, ELIZABETH ANN, federal judge; b. 1949; BA, Vanderbilt U., 1971; JD, U. Fla. Coll. Law, 1976. Bars: Fla. 1977, D.C. 1978. Atty. advisor U.S. Dept. of Justice, 1976-78; asst. U.S. atty. Middle Dist. of Fla., Orlando, Fla., 1978-82, Southern Dist. of Fla., West Palm Beach, Fla., 1983-85; magistrate judge U.S. Dist. Ct. (mid. dist.) Fla., 1985—. Office: US Courthouse 801 N Florida Ave Ste 32 Tampa FL 33602-3849 Office Phone: 813-301-5774.

JENKINS, FRANCES OWENS, retired small business owner; b. Leonard, Tex., Nov. 12, 1924; d. R. Melrose and Maureen (Durrett) Owens; m. William O. Jenkins (div. 1961); children: Steven O., Tamara. Student theatre arts, East Tex. State U., 1939-42, Ind. U., 1945-48, U. Tenn., 1954-56. Fashion model Rogers Modeling Agy., Boston, 1950-52, Rich's, Knoxville, Tenn., 1955-60; owner, instr. Arts Sch. Self-Improvement and Modeling, Knoxville, 1959-69; onwer, pres. Fran Jenkins Boutique, Knoxville, 1964-95; ret., 1995. Cons. Miss Am. Pageant, Knoxville, 1958-66. Actress Carousel Theatre, Knoxville, 1955-58. also: 71 Pelican Cir Panama City Beach FL 32413-7018

JENKINS, GAYE RANCK, adult education educator, consultant; d. Arthur Harry and Faith Newbury Ranck; m. Thomas Eugene Jenkins, Sept. 14, 1974; children: Gregory A. West, Timothy E. AAS, Pa. Coll. Tech., Williamsport, 1996, BHS, 1997; MEd in Adult Edn., Pa. State U., University Park, 2001, postgrad., 2001—. Vol. coord. Wise Options/YWCA, Williamsport, Pa., 1986—92; field aide, adult recruiter Hemlock Girl Scout Coun., Montoursville, Pa., 1993—94; dir. Women's Resource Ctr., Williamsport, 1994—96; adj. faculty Pa. Coll. Tech., Williamsport, 2002—04, Pa. State Continuing Edn., University Park, 2004—; cons. grassroots orgn. Intern Pa. Coalition Against Domestic Violence, Harrisburg, Pa., 1997; intern adult edn. program world campus Pa. State U., University Park, 2001—02, practicum tchr. world campus, 2000—01; proposal com. Pa. Adult Edn. Rsch. Conf., 2003; presenter in field, 1998—. Editor: (newsletters) Wise Options Quar., 1991—94, Women's Resource Center Quar., 1994—96, Pa. State U. Adult Edn. Program, 1999—2001; contbr. articles to profl. jours. Founding mem. com. for cmty. directed rsch. and edn. Pa. State U., University Park, 1999—2005; program coord. 2d Ea. Regional Adult Edn. Rsch. Conf., University Park, 2000. Recipient Vol. of Yr., AIDS Resource Alliance, 1994, Monk Profl. Devel. Endowment, Coll. of Edn., Pa. State U., 2002, The Chancellor's List, 2005. Mem.: Pa. NOW, AAUW, Am. Assn. Adult and Continuing Edn., Pa. Assn. Adult and Continuing Edn., Pi Lambda Theta, Phi Delta Kappa. Avocations: card playing, dance, crossword puzzles, reading, jazz. Home: 1020 Back Rd Allenwood PA 17810 Office: Pa Coll Tech One College Ave Williamsport PA 17701

JENKINS, JILL M., gifted-talented education educator; b. Indpls., May 12, 1963; d. Gerald C. and Patricia S. (Bland) J. BA magna cum laude, Ball State U., 1985; postgrad., Ind. U., 1986-87, Butler U., 1987—. Cert. English and history tchr., Ind. Tchr. English Kankakee Valley Schs., Wheatfield, Ind., Greenfield (Ind.) Cen. Schs. Mem. NEA, Nat. Coun. Tchrs. of English, ISTA, CTA.

JENKINS, LAWANDA W., publishing executive; b. Balt., Mar. 18, 1963; m. Bryant Jenkins; children: Morgan, Miles. BS, Towson State U., 1983; M of Adminstrv. Sci., Johns Hopkins U., 1990. Pub. rels. officer Provident Bank Md., 1984—88; mktg. mgr. Office Tourism Md. Dept. Econs. and Devel., 1988—94; dir. Gov.'s Office of Minority Affairs State of Md. Exec. Dept., 1994—97; dir. cmty. affairs The Balt. Sun, 1997—. Vol., bd. dirs. Associated Black Charities, 1996—; mem. cmty. rels. com. Nat. Aquarium, 1997—; grad. GBC Leadership, 1999; Bd. dirs. Women Entrepreneurs of Balt., 1998—99; bd. dirs. Jr. Achievement of Cen. Md., 2000. Named one of Md.'s Top 100 Women, Daily Record, 1996, Disting. Black Marylanders, 1999; recipient Top 20 Under 40 award, Newspaper Assn. Am., 2000. Mem.: Coalition of 100 Black Women, Assn. Balt. Area Grant Makers. Office: 501 N Calvert St Baltimore MD 21278

JENKINS, LAWANNA, elementary school educator; d. Duffie E. and Ree F. Jenkins. MEd, Lamar U., 1989; BS in Elem. Edn., Delta State U., Cleve., 1975. Cert. tchr. Tex. Tchr. Beaumont (Ind.) Ind. Sch. Dist., 1986—90, Dallas Pub. Schools, 1990—98, Pflugerville (Tex.) Ind. Sch. Dist., 1998—2003, Ft. Bend Ind. Sch. Dist., Sugarland, Tex., 2003—. Cons. Coll. Bd., Austin, 1999—. Contbr. curriculum materials to ednl. publs. Tchr. Bapt. chs., Okahoma City, 1884—1986. Named Tchr. of Yr., Beaumont PTA, 1991; recipient Governor's Recognition award, Office of Gov., Tex., 1994, proclamation, Senate of State of Tex., 1997; grantee, Ft. Bend Edn. Found., 2005—06. Mem.: Sci. Teachers Assn. Tex. (assoc.). Office Phone: 281-634-3850.

JENKINS, LOUISE SHERMAN, nursing researcher, educator; b. Normal, Ill., Jan. 19, 1943; d. Fred and Zylpha Louise (Garrett) Sherman; m. Gary L. Jenkins, Oct. 30, 1965 (div. July 1976). Diploma, Evanston Hosp. Sch. Nursing, 1963; BS, No. Ill. U., 1979; MS, U. Md., Balt., 1982, PhD, 1985. Asst. head nurse intensive care Cmty. Meml. Hosp., LaGrange, Ill., 1963—65; head nurse coronary care Luth. Gen. Hosp., Park Ridge, Ill., 1965—69; nurse clinician hemodialysis unit Evanston (Ill.) Hosp., 1969—74; head nurse Skokie (Ill.) Valley Cmty. Hosp., 1974—75; faculty dept. continuing edn. N.W. Cmty. Hosp., Arlington Heights, Ill., 1975—80; Walter Schoeder chair nursing rsch. U. Wis. Milw. Sch. Nursing and St. Luke's Med. Ctr., Milw., 1987—96; faculty Sch. Nursing U. Md., Balt., 1996—, acting dir. grad. studies, 1997—98, dir. grad. studies, 1998—2003, co-dir. clin. edn. and evaluation lab., 2000—, coord. tchg. in nursing and health professions postgrad. cert. program, 2004—; interim co-dir. Inst. for Nurse Educators, 2004—05; co-dir. Inst. for Educators in Nursing and Health Professions, 2005—. Mem. editl. bd. Jour. Cardiopulmonary Rehab., Jour. Hispanic Health Care, mem. rev. panel Am. Jour. Health Behavior, Nursing Rsch., Heart & Lung. Bd. dirs. Am. Heart Assn., Milw., 1988—95, exec. bd. dirs. Wis. affiliate, 1995—96, fellow, 2001, chair coun. cardiovasc. nursing Dallas, 1995—97, fellow coun. cardiovasc. nursing. Fellow, Am. Heart Assn., 2001; fellow, Clin. Nurse scholar, Robert Wood Johnson Found., U. Calif., San Francisco, 1985—87. Mem.: Heart Rhythm Soc., N.Am. Soc. Pacing and Electrophysiology, Coun. Nursing Rsch., Midwest Nursing Rsch. Soc. (gov. bd. 1993—95), Wis. Nurses Assn. (bd. dirs. 1988—90, Excellence in Nursing Rsch. award 1995), Am. Assn. Cardiovasc. and Pulmonary Rehab. (bd. dirs.-at-large 1993—95), Sigma Xi, Sigma Theta Tau (immediate past pres. Pi chpt.). Office: Sch Nursing U Md 655 W Lombard St Ste 311 Baltimore MD 21201-1512 Office Phone: 410-706-4296. E-mail: jenkins@son.umaryland.edu.

JENKINS, LYNN M., state official, former state legislator; b. Topeka, June 10, 1963; m. Scott M. Jenkins; children: Hayley, Hayden. AA, Kans. State U., 1984; BS, Weber State Coll., 1985. CPA. CPA, 1985—; rep. Kans. State Ho. Reps., 1998—2000; mem. Kans. State Senate, 2000—03, mem. gen. govt. budget com., ins. com., post audit com., govt. orgn. and elections com., taxation com.; treas. State of Kans., 2003—. Mem. adv. bd. Ct. Apptd. Spl. Advocate; bd. dirs. YMCA Metro, Family Svc. and Guidance Ctr.; treas., bd. dirs. Prince of Peace Presch.; active Jay Snideler PTO, Susanna Wesley United Meth. Ch. Mem. Kans. Soc. CPAs. Republican. Methodist. Office: 900 SW Jackson St Ste 201 Topeka KS 66612-1235

JENKINS, MARGARET BUNTING, human resources executive; b. Warsaw, Va., Aug. 3, 1935; d. John and Irma (Cookman) Bunting; children: Sydney, Jr., Terry L. Student, Coll. William and Mary, 1952, AA in Bus. Adminstrn., 1973; BA in Human Resource Devel., St. Leo Coll., 1979; M in Adminstrn., George Washington U., 1982; PhD in Human Rsch. Mgmt., Columbia Pacific U., 1986. Rehab. counselor, tchr. York County Schs., Yorktown, Va.; mgr. Waterfront Constrn. Co., Seafood Corp., Seaford, Va., 1960—72; labor rels. specialist Naval Weapons Sta., Yorktown, 1974—77, staffing specialist, 1977—78, position classification specialist, supr. shipbuilding, conversion and repair Newport News, Va., 1978-81, supr. pers. mgmt. specialist, supr. shipbuilding, conversion and repair, 1981—90, pers. mgmt. specialist Yorktown and Cheatham, Va., 1990—94. Bd. dirs. various health orgns.; owner Jenkins Consulting. Author: Organizational Impact on Human Behavior, 1996; (poetry) Heron Haven Reflections, 1996; poetry published in Mists of Enchantment, 1995, Treasured Poems of America, 1996, Poets of the 90's, A Celebration of Poets, Showcase Edit., 1998, 99, The Best Poems of Poets award 2001; featured in: Cancer Has Its Privileges, Stories of Hope and Laughter (Christine K. Clifford), 2002 (Best Poets award 2002, 03, 04, 05, Internat. Poetry award 2003, 04, 05). Decorated Meritorious Civilian Svc. award USN Supvr. Shipbuilding, Converstion and Repair, 3 Navy commendations; recipient award Newport News, 1990, Alumni medallion Coll. William and Mary, 1994-2000 Mem.: Chesapeake Writers Assn., Classification and Compensation Soc. (pres. 1984), Soc. for Human Resource Mgmt., Long Ridge Writers Group, Toastmasters Internat. (pres. 1985—87, various offices, award), Nature Conservancy, Audubon Soc., 4-Alumni Assn., Internat. Soc. of Poets (Disting. mem. 1996, 2005), Sierra Club, Fedn. Women's Clubs. Methodist. Avocations: art, writing, crafts. Home: PO Box 203 Seaford VA 23696-0203

JENKINS, PAMELA LYNN, music educator; b. Flint, Mich., Dec. 16, 1950; d. Thressabelle O'Dell -Jenkins and Edgar Raymond Jenkins; life ptnr. Patti-Jean Cousens, Sept. 23, 1987. MM, Ctrl. Mich. Univ., 1994—97. Cert. Piano Technician 1981. Asst. prof. U. of Maine at Augusta, 1997—; piano technician Acoustic Piano tuning, Gardiner, Maine, 1974—; musician Boogie2Shooz, East Tawas, Mich. Mem.: North Am. Saxophone Alliance, Piano Technicians Guild (assoc.). Democrat. Siddha Yoga. Avocations: hiking, camping, boating, skiing. Office: University of Maine at Augusta 46 University Dr Augusta ME 04330 Personal E-mail: pam@boogie2shooz.com. E-mail: pjenkins@maine.edu, pj@boogie2shooz.com.

JENKINS, PATTY, film director, scriptwriter; Student in Painting, Cooper Union; degree in Dir.'s Program, Am. Film Inst. Dir.: (films) Just Drive, 2001; author: (films) Just Drive, 2001; dir.: (films) Velocity Rules, 2001 (Short Film award Telluride Indiefest, 2001); author: (films) Velocity Rules, 2001; dir.: (films) Monster, 2003 (nominated Golden Bear award Berlin Internat. Film Fest, 2004, nominated Ind. Spirit award, 2004); author: (films) Monster, 2003. Office: Creative Artists Agency 9830 Wilshire Blvd Beverly Hills CA 90212-1825

JENKINS, PEARL G., retired elementary school educator, realtor; b. Charleston, SC, June 22, 1940; d. Francis and Estelle Jenkins; adopted children: Kimberly, Robert. BA, SC State U., Orangeburg, 1963. Tchr. Charleston County Schs., Chareston, SC, 1963—93; realtor Agt. Owned Realty Charleston Group, 1993—. Advisor sr. class Burke HS, Charleston, 1992—93. Advisor Y-Teens, Charleston, 1963—91; docent Hist. Charleston, 1987—; chair rev. bd. 9A Children's Foster Care, Charleston, 1990—2000; tour guide Middleton Pl. Gardens, Charleston, 1993—2001; usher Charleston Symphony Orch. League, 1990—. Recipient Excellence in Tchg., NCNW, 1993, Dan C. Joyner Cmty. Svc. award, 2003. Mem.: Charleston Trident Assn. Realtors (honor bd. chair 1986—). Avocations: singing, writing, bicycling, gardening, travel. Home: 1820 Meadowlawn Dr Charleston SC 29407 Office: Agt Owned Realty Charleston Group 902 Savannah Hwy Charleston SC 29407

JENKINS, RENEE R., medical educator, pediatrician; b. Phila., Jan. 16, 1947; m. Charles Jenkins; 1 child, Kristinza. MD, Wayne State U. Diplomate Am. Bd. Pediatrics. Intern Jacobi/Albert Einstein Hosp., Bronx, 1971—72, resident in pediats., 1972—74; fellow in adolescent medicine Montefiore Hosp. Ctr., Bronx, 1974—75; prof., chmn. dept. pediats. Howard U., Washington; staff pediatrician Howard U. Hosp., Washington. Adj. prof. George Washington U. Mem.: SAM, NMA, APS, Am. Acad. Pediats. (pres.-elect 2006), Inst. Medicine of NAS. Office: Howard Univ Hosp 2041 Georgia Ave NW Washington DC 20060*

JENKINS, SHARON LEIGH, special education educator; b. Boynton Beach, Fla., Sept. 10, 1975; d. Allan Lee and Candace Esther Barnett; m. Tony Hayes Jenkins. BSc in Edn., Baylor U., 1998; M in Edn., Tex. Christian U., 2004. Spl. edn. tchr. Arlington Ind. Sch. Dist., Tex., 1999, 1999—2001, Mansfield Ind. Sch. Dist., Tex., 2001—. Mentor Mansfield Ind. Sch. Dist., 2003—04. Mem.: United Educators Assn., Coun. for Exceptional Children. Republican. So. Bapt. Avocations: reading, scrapbooks, walking. Home: 4311 Foster Ln Killeen TX 76549 E-mail: tsjenkins@earthlin.net.

JENKINS, VIRGINIA, artist, educator; b. Bay City, Mich., Nov. 6, 1951; d. James George and Florence Virginia (Schultz) Jenkins; m. David T. Morrison, Aug. 31, 1974 (div. Aug. 1986). BFA, Mich. State U., 1973; MFA, U. Utah, 1975. Instr. Loretto Hts. Coll., Denver, 1982-85, Red Rocks C.C., Lakewood, Colo., 1987-88, U. No. Colo., Greeley, 1986-88, asst. prof. painting, 1988-92, assoc. prof. painting, 1992-96, prof. painting, 1996—2005, chair visual arts dept.; prof., head dept. art and design U. Minn., Duluth, 2005—06. Exhibitor paintings at Tointon Gallery, Greeley, 1998, Edge Gallery, Denver, 1999. Mem.: Colo. Art Edn. Assn., Nat. Art Edn. Assn., Colo. Artists Registry, Coll. Art Assn. Home: 2801 E 2d St Duluth MN 55812 Office: U Minn Duluth Dept Art and Design Duluth MN 55812

JENKINS-ANDERSON, BARBARA JEANNE, pathologist, educator; b. Chgo. d. Carlyle Fielding and Alyce Louise (Walker) Stewart; m. Sidney Bernard Jenkins, Sept. 22, 1951 (div. June 1970); children: Kevin Jenkins, Judy Kelly, Sharolyn Sanders, Marc Jenkins, Kayla French; m. Arthur Eugene Anderson, Sept. 30, 1972. BS, U. Mich., 1950; MD, Wayne State U., 1957. Diplomate Am. Bd. Pathology. Intern Providence Hosp., Detroit, 1958-59, resident in psychiatry, 1959-60; resident in pathology Henry Ford Hosp., 1961-62, U. Mich. Affiliated Program, 1962-65; staff pathologist Wayne County Hosp., 1966-70, Detroit Receiving Hosp., 1970-72; asst. prof. pathology Wayne State U. Med. Sch., Detroit, 1970—72, assoc. prof. pathology, 1973—; adminstrv. med. dir. Detroit Med. Ctr. Univ. Labs., Detroit, 1988—; chief pathology Detroit Receiving Hosp./Univ. Health Clinic, Detroit, 1990—. Instr. U. Mich., 1966-70. Recipient Leonard Sain award U. Mich., 1980. Mem. Alpha Omega Alpha. Avocations: golf, interior design. Office: DMC Univ Labs 4201 Saint Antoine St Detroit MI 48201-2153 Office Phone: 313-993-0539. Business E-mail: banderso@dmc.org.

JENKINS-BRADY, TERRI LYNN, publishing executive, journalist; b. Albuquerque, Sept. 19, 1952; d. Hubert Arnold Jenkins and Helen Hope Zumwalt; m. Timothy Daniel Brady, July 4, 2000; stepchildren: Cori Danielle Brady, Colt Mitchell Brady. Student, U. Albuquerque, N.Mex., 1971—75, U. N.Mex., Albuquerque, 1976. Pub. rels./fund-raiser March of Dimes, 1980; asst. to editor Prime Time, Albuquerque, 1995—2000, columnist, 2000—02; editor Al Bowl Querque Times, Albuquerque, 2000; editor in chief, ptnr. Write Up The Road Pub., Kenton, Tenn., 2002—; retail sales rep., freelance writer, 1974—79. Co-author: Romancing the Road, 2002, You Know You're Married To A Trucker When., 2003, Three Wise Cats, 2005, Twilight's Last Gleaming, 2006; editor: Driven 4 Profits Fin. Newsletter, 2003, Oh, Pegasus: A Work of Love Thoughts, 2003, Driven 4 Profits, 2002, Plonk Goes the Weasel, 2004, Gearing Up 4 Profits, 2004, Death Had A Yellow Thumb, 2005,

Simpatico Patio!, 2005, Billy Beaver's Traveler, 2001—04, Reflections Thru My Windshield, 2005, Me and You and a Truck Named Blue, 2005, With Powder on My Nose, 2005, Three Arm Truckin' and Other Tales of the Highway, 2006. Mem. adv. bd. Hiland Sr. Ctr., Albuquerque, 1996—97; co-founder Further Up the Road scholarship Rotary Club, Union City, Tenn., 2002. Recipient Bronze and Silver medals, Imperial Soc. Tchrs. Ballroom Dance, 1981. Mem.: Small Pubs. Assn. N.Am., Writer's Ink. Avocations: travel, writing, designing wearable art, ballroom dancing. Office: Write Up The Road Pub PO Box 69 Kenton TN 38233-0069 Office Phone: 731-749-8567. Business E-Mail: terrijenkins-brady@writeuptheroad.com.

JENKINS-RUSS, THERESA ELIZABETH, music educator; b. N.Y., Aug. 15, 1963; d. Warren B. and Rita V. Jenkins; m. Leon Russ. BA, Wheaton Coll., Mass.; studied Violin with Nancy Cirillo, New Eng. Conservatory Music, Boston; MS Edn., L.I. U.; postgrad., Hofstra U., N.Y., Converse U. Tchr. music L.I. Pub. Sch., NY, 1987—94; tchr. orch. Arlington Pub. Schs., Va., 1994—2004; tchr. music Spartanburg Dist. 7, SC, 2004—. Dir. Arlington Youth Orch.; condr. Carolina Cool Jazz Orch. Mem.: Music Educator's Nat. Conf., Am. Symphony Orch. League, S.C. Music Educator's Assn., Internat. Assn. Jazz Edn., Am. String Tchrs. Assn. (bd. dirs. S.C. chpt., presenter conf. 2006). Home: 294 Heathwood Dr Spartanburg SC 29307

JENKS, ABIGAIL, social worker, educator; b. Natick, Mass., Mar. 24, 1949; d. Edwin Hamilton jenks and Nancy Arnold; m. Jeremiah Mew, Aug. 25, 1984 (div. Mar. 2000); children: Colin Jedediah Mew, Benjamin Joseph Mew. BA in English Lit., U. Mass., Amherst, 1972; EdM, Antioch U., Silver Springs, Ohio, 1980; MSW, Smith Coll. Sch. Social Work, Northampton, Mass., 1984. LCSW Mass., diplomate NASW, cert. sch. adjustment counselor, nat. bd. cert. diplomate clin. social work. Coord. Title XX daycare tng. program, head tchr. Title XX day care ctr., residential mgr., foster parent Dept. Youth Svcs., 1975—80; case mgr. Dept. Social Svcs., Springfield, Northampton, Greenfield, 1980—84, clin. supr., 1984—87; sch. adjustment counselor South Hadley Sch. Dept., Mass., 1986—89; ind. therapist Specialized Geriatric Svcs., Ipswich, Mass., 1989—92; pvt. practice ind. therapist Amherst, 1989—; prof. peace and social justice studies, psychology and human svcs. Greenfield C.C., Mass., 1998—. Pvt. cons. local elem. sch. systems, 1988—91; cons. New Medico Nursing and Head Injury Facility, Northampton, 1990—94; OBRA cons. River Valley Counseling, Holyoke, Mass., 1991—98; adj. faculty social work dept. Elms Coll., Chicopee, 1996—98; program coord. human svc. program Greenfield C.C., 1998—, mem. domestic violence awareness com., 1998—2000, advisor to Human Svcs. Club, 1999—; presenter in field. Mem. steering com. SAGE, Amherst, Mass., 2000—; active Coalition for a Safe Cmty., Greenfield, 2001—, Greenfield C.C. Response Initiative, 2001—, Kanagasaki Sister City Com., Amherst, 1998—2003. Mem.: APA, New England Orgn. Human Svc. Educators (v.p. 2003—05, membership chair 1998—2000), New England Peace Studies Assn., Peace and Justice Studies Assn., Mass. Arts Coun. Avocations: mountain climbing, hiking, gardening, running. Office: Greenfield Cmty Coll 1 College Dr Greenfield MA 01301

JENKS, EILEEN A., academic administrator, real estate agent; b. N.Y.C., Oct. 8, 1951; d. Robert K. and Katherine M. Petrausch; 1 child, Eileen K. Straiton. AB, Grace Inst., N.Y.C., 1982; BA, Mercy Coll., Yonkers, 1984, Coll. New Rochelle, N.Y., 1986. Lic. real estate Conn. Adminstrv. asst. Mobil Oil Corp., N.Y.C., 1983—85; bus. mgr. dept. pediatrics Albert Einstein Coll. Medicine, Bronx, 1985—87; bus. mgr./adminstr. N.Y. Med. Coll., Valhalla, 1987—. Mem.: Academic Assn. Univ. Women. Home: 40 Big Trail Sherman CT 06784 Office: NY Med Coll Valhalla NY Office Phone: 914-594-4117. Personal E-mail: Eikedia@aol.com. Business E-Mail: eileen_jenks@nymeikdeic.edu.

JENNE, CAROLE SEEGERT, minister, marriage and family therapist; b. Ypsilanti, Mich., Nov. 22, 1942; d. Ellsworth Noah and Ruby Loretta (Stetter) S.; m. Eugene Ervin Jenne, Feb. 25, 1961; children: Jeanne-Marie Segler, Philip John. AS, Monroe Co. Community Coll., 1972; BS, Eastern Mich. U., 1974; MSW, U. of Mich., 1979; PhD, Intl. Sem., 1986. Lic. marriage counselor, cert. social worker, ordained elder/pastor. Pastor, tchr. Rapha Christian Ctr., Erie, Mich., 1997—. Family therapist, 1980—, retreat/conf. speaker Author: The Power-Filled Life, 2002. Mem. Internat. Coalition Apostles. Mem.: Resurrection Apostolic Internat. Network. Interdenominational. Office: Rapha Christian Ctr 11166 S Dixie Hwy Erie MI 48133-9712

JENNE, SUE OAK, secondary school educator; b. Alexandria, Va., Oct. 7, 1959; d. Jesse Calvin and Betty Ann Oak; 1 child, Jordan Michael. BS, Va. Commonwealth U., 1982; MA, Georgetown Coll., 1985; postgrad., Ind. Wesleyan U., 2002—03. Tchr. Franklin County Pub. Schs., Frankfort, Ky., 1984—98; tchr. spl. edn. Owen County Schs., Owenton, 1982—84; instrnl. coach Jefferson County Pub. Schs., Louisville, 1998—. Mem.: NEA, LWV, Ky. Tchrs. Assn., Jefferson County Tchrs. Assn., Phi Sigma Sigma Sorority (pres. 1981—82). Democrat. Avocations: reading, travel. Home: 9517 Palladio Ct Louisville KY 40299 Office: Jefferson County Pub Schs 3526 W Muhammad Ali Blvd Louisville KY 40212 Office Phone: 502-485-8354. Personal E-mail: soj1007@aol.com. E-mail: sue.jenne@jefferson.kyschools.us.

JENNESS, REBECCA ESTELLA, artist, educator; b. L.A., Aug. 16, 1946; d. Russell Albert and Estella Virginia (Guzman) J. Student, Cape Sch. Art, Provincetown, Mass., 1971; diploma, Vesper George Sch. of Art, 1972; BFA, Southeastern Mass. U., 1981. Mem. panel R.I. State Coun. on the Arts, 1989-93; mem. adv. bd. Warwick Art Mus., R.I., 1990-94, New Eng. Found. on the Arts, Boston, 1990-94, Sarah Doyle Gallery, Brown U., 1991-95; mem. multicultural art literacy coun. State Coun. on the Arts, R.I., 1991-94. Exhibited in group shows at Soviet Hall of Art, Moscow, 1988, U. N.H., 1989, Fitchburg Art Mus., 1990, R.I. Sch. Design Mus. of Art, 1992-93, Lyman Allen Mus., Conn., 1994, Artists for Shelter, Providence, 1995, Mus. of Art, 1995, 97, Woods Gallery, RI, 2001-2006, Providence Art Club, RI, 2004-2006; One Woman Show: Ctrl. Congrl. Gallery, Providence, 2004. Art advocate New England Artists Trust, 1990-95, Perishable Theater, Providence, 1993, New Eng. Conf., Providence, 1993-94, Studio and Living Spaces for Artists, Providence, 1995-96; artists for food Amos House, Providence, 1993. Democrat. Avocations: mexican indian art and design studies, poetry, gardening, urban puppet design. Home: PO Box 41395 Providence RI 02940-1395 Studio: 428 Branch Ave #2 Providence RI 02904

JENNETT, SHIRLEY SHIMMICK, health facility administrator; b. Jennings, Kans., May 1, 1937; d. William and Mabel C. (Mowry) Shimmick; m. Nelson K. Jennett, Aug. 20, 1960 (div. 1972); children: Jon W., Cheryl L.; m. Albert J. Kukral, Apr. 16, 1977 (div. 1990) Diploma, Rsch. Hosp. Sch. Nursing, Kansas City, Mo., 1958. RN, Mo., Colo., Tex., Ill. Staff nurse, head nurse Rsch. Hosp., 1958-60; head nurse Penrose Hosp., Colorado Springs, Colo., 1960-62, Hotel Dieu Hosp., El Paso, Tex., 1962-63; staff nurse Oak Park (Ill.) Hosp., 1963-64, NcNeal Hosp., Berwyn, Ill., 1964-65, St. Anthony Hosp., Denver, 1968-69; staff nurse, head nurse, nurse recruiter Luth. Hosp., Wheat Ridge, Colo., 1969-79; owner, mgr. Med. Placement Svcs., Lakewood, Colo., 1980-84; vol., primary care nurse, admissions coord., team mgr. Hospice of Metro Denver, 1984-88, dir. patient and family svcs., 1988, exec. dir., 1988-94; pres., profl. geriatric care mgr. Care Mgmt. & Resources, Inc., Denver, 1996—. Mem. NAFE, Nat. Women Bus. Owners Assn., Nat. Hospice Orgn. (bd. dirs. 1992-95, coun. former bd. mems. 1995—), Nat. Orgn. Profl. Geriatric Care Mgrs., Denver Bus. Women's Network. Mem. Ch. of Religious Sci. Avocations: reading, walking, golf. Office: Care Mgmt & Resources Inc 2055 S Oneida St Ste 150 Denver CO 80224-2435 Office Phone: 303-639-5455. Business E-Mail: shirleyj@denvercmr.com.

JENNINGS, DEBORAH E., lawyer; b. Washington, Feb. 8, 1949; BA with honors, U. Md., 1970; JD, Georgetown U., 1974. Bar: Md. 1974, D.C. 1984. Asst. state's atty. Montgomery County, Md., 1975-77; asst. atty. gen. Md., 1977-80; chief Criminal Investigations Divsn., 1978-80; ptnr. Piper & Marbury, Balt., 1983—99, Piper Marbury Rudnick & Wolfe, 1999—2004; ptnr., chmn. Environ. practice group DLA Piper Rudnick Gray Cary, Washington, 1995—. Co-author: Md. Handbook on Environ. Law. Mem. & past pres. Network 2000. Fellow Am. Bar Found. Office: DLA Piper Rudnick Gray Cary 1200 19th St NW Washington DC 20036-2412 Office Phone: 202-861-3842. Office Fax: 202-223-2085. Business E-Mail: deborah.jennings@dlapiper.com.

JENNINGS, DENISE ELAINE, art educator; b. Dalton, Ga., July 8, 1951; d. Arthur and Dorothy J.; m. Donald E. Montgomery. BS magna cum laude, U. Ga., 1974; MEd in Visual Arts summa cum laude, Ga. State U., 1983. Cert. tchr. art, Ga.; nat. bd. cert. tchr., 2001. Secondary art tchr. Campell H.S., Atlanta, 1974, Milton H.S., Atlanta, 1975-77; tchr., chair dept. art Fulton County Schs., Atlanta, 1977—2001, curriculum coord. art and drama edn., 2001—. Cons. Ga. Dept. Edn., 1988-89, 91-93, mem. quality core curriculum writing team-visual arts, 1997; mem. Fulton County Bd. Edn., 1986—; mid. and high schs. accreditation coms. So. Assn. Colls. and Schs., 1985; nat. bd. dirs., secondary dir. Nat. Art Edn. Assn., 1995-97; cons. ednl. testing svc. Nat. Assessment on Ednl. Progress, 1997; mem. Nat. Bd. for Profl. Tchg. Stds. Eary Adolescent Through Young Adulthood, Art Com., 2000; cons. Ga. Dept. Edn., 1999-2000; mem. leadership team Milton H.S. Pay for Performance Grants, 1997, 98; mem. supt. adv. coun. Fulton County Bd. Edn., 1998-2000. Author: (with others) Fulton County Middle School Art Curriculum Guide, 1985, School Arts, 1985, Arts and Activities, 1985, Fulton County High Sch. Art Curriculum Guide, 1990, 99, Art Heritage and Criticism Resource Guide, 1991, Visual Arts Comprehensive II Resource Guide, 1992; originator, editor Articulation: A Forum for the Exchange of Ideas, 1983-85; mem. editl. bd. Art Edn.: The Jour. of the Nat. Art Edn. Assn., 1998-2000. Scholar Nat. Gallery of Art, 1991, grantee 1993; Getty fellow Coun. for Basic Edn., 1993, Ga. Christa McCaliffe fellow, 1998; named Secondary Art Educator of Yr., Nat. Art Edn. Assn., 2000. Mem. Ga. Art Edn. Assn. (bd. dirs. West Metro dist., pres. 1977-79, ad hoc coms. 1976—, Ga. Art Educator of Yr. 2000). Avocations: reading, hiking, camping, gardening. Office: Fulton County Schools 786 Cleveland Ave SW Atlanta GA 30315 Office Phone: 404-763-6767. E-mail: jennings@fultonschools.org.

JENNINGS, JAN NOREUS, public relations executive, writer; b. Chgo., Apr. 4, 1943; d. Stanley B. and Evelyn D. Noreus. BS in Journalism, Northwestern U., 1965; postgrad., U. Mo., 1965—66. Cert. desktop publishing Advt. Arts Coll., Calif., 1992. Writer San Diego Tribune, 1966—88; asst. to dir. Mingei Internat. Mus., San Diego, 1990—91; writer, publicist univ. comms. U. Calif.-San Diego, La Jolla, 1994—; art dir./writer The Frederic Whitaker and Eileen Monaghan Whitaker Found., San Diego, 2001—. Freelance writer SW Art, Art of Calif., Am. Artist, Ranch & Coast, Art of San Diego, 1988—. Author: Contrasts That Complement: Eileen Monaghan Whitaker - Frederic Whitaker, 2005. Mem.: Mingei Internat. Mus., Mus. Contemporary Art San Diego, San Diego Mus. of Art. Avocations: travel, art collecting, swimming. Office: Univ Calif San Diego 9500 Gilman Dr - Dept 0938 La Jolla CA 92093-0938 Office Phone: 858-822-1684. Personal E-mail: jnorjenn@inetworld.net. Business E-Mail: jnjennings@ucsd.edu.

JENNINGS, KAREN, human resources specialist, telecommunications industry executive; b. Mich. BA, U. Ark., Fayetteville. Various positions Southwestern Bell, Ark., 1972—95; chmn. SBC Asset Mgmt, Inc., 1995—96; assoc. v.p. chmn.'s office SBC Comm., Inc., 1995—96; pres. Southwestern Bell, Mo., 1996—97; v.p., gen. mgr. operator svcs. SBC Telecom., Inc., 1997—98; sr. v.p. human resources SBC Comm. Inc., 1998—99, sr. exec. v.p. human resources, 1999—2002, sr. exec. v.p. human resources and comm., 2002—05; sr. exec. v.p. human resources & comm. AT&T Inc., San Antonio, 2005—. Bd. mem. Cullen/Frost Bankers, San Antonio Spurs. Bd. dirs. Elizabeth Glaser Pediatric AIDS Found.; bd. mem. AT&T Found., Marion Koogler McNay Art Mus., United Way San Antonio. Mem.: Leaders Forum. Office: AT&T Inc 175 E Houston St PO Box 2933 San Antonio TX 78205 Office Phone: 210-821-4105. Office Fax: 210-351-2071.*

JENNINGS, MARCELLA GRADY, rancher, investor; b. Springfield, Ill., Mar. 4, 1920; d. William Francis and Magdalene Mary (Spies) Grady; student pub. schs.; m. Leo J. Jennings, Dec. 16, 1950 (dec.). Pub. relations Econolite Corp., Los Angeles, 1958-61; v.p., asst. mgr. LJ Quarter Circle Ranch, Inc., Polson, Mont., 1961-73, pres., gen. mgr., owner, 1973—; dir. Giselle's Travel Inc., Sacramento; fin. advisor to Allentown, Inc., Charlo, Mont.; sales cons. to Amie's Jumpin' Jacks and Jills, Garland, Tex. Investor. Mem. Internat. Charolais Assn., Los Angeles County Apt. Assn. Republican. Roman Catholic. Home and Office: 509 Mount Holyoke Ave Pacific Palisades CA 90272-4328

JENNINGS, REBA MAXINE, retired critical care nurse; b. Gainesville, Mo., Oct. 28, 1936; d. William Claude and Osa Marie (Whillock) Loftis; m. Robert Wayne Jennings, Nov. 10, 1953; children: Sherry Anita, Robert Allen, Lalia Marie. Diploma, Burge Sch. Nursing, Springfield, Mo., 1983. ACLS, RN Mo. Med-surg. staff nurse AMI-Springfield Community Hosp., 1983-84; pvt. duty nurse Western Med. Svcs., Springfield, 1984; staff nurse in CCU, ICU, emergency dept. Tri-County Sisters of Mercy Hosp., Mansfield, Mo., 1984-85; cardiac telemetry staff nurse St. John's Regional Health Ctr., Springfield, 1985-93; nurse obs. unit Valley Hosp., Palmer, Alaska, 1993-94; nurse PCU Alaska Regional Hosp., Anchorage, 1994; PCU nurse Providence Alaska Med. Ctr., Anchorage, 1995-98; ret., 1998.

JENNINGS, TONI, lieutenant governor; b. Orlando, Fla., May 17, 1949; d. Jack C. and Margaret (Murphy) J. BA, Wesleyan Coll., Macon, Ga., 1971; postgrad., Rollins Coll., 1972-73. Pres. Jack Jennings and Sons, Inc., Gen. Contractors, Orlando, 1973—; mem. Fla. Ho. of Reps., 1976-80, Fla. Senate, 1980—2000, pres., 1996—2000; lt. gov. State of Fla., Tallahassee, 2003—. Republican leader pro tempore, 1982-83, 85, 86, Rep. leader, 1984, 86-88. legis. del. Orange County, 1980-82, 86-88. Bd. dirs. Salvation Army; active Rep. Women's Federated Club of Winter Park, Orlando Women's Rep. Club Federated. Recipient Spl. Commendation award Fla. Restaurant Assn., 1979, Meritorious Svc. award Fla. Fedn. Humane Socs., 1979, Disting. Alumni awrd Wesleyan Coll., 1981, Freedom award Women for Responsible Legislation, 1982, Support of Law Enforcement award Fla. Sheriffs Assn., Outstanding Efforts award Tampa Missing Children Help Ctr., 1983, Outstanding Svc. award Grocers' Assn. Fla., 1983, Legis. award Fla., 1983, Legis. award Fla. Chiropractic Assn., 1983, 86, Appreciation award Fla. Med. Assn. and Physicians of Fla., 1983, 2d Ann. Frank J. Fahrenkopf, Jr. Outstanding State Minority Leader award, 1988, Ann. Legis. award for Leadership in Econ. Devel. Legislation award Fla. C. of C., 1987; named Legislator of Yr., Orange County Young Rep. Club, 1980-81. Mem. Orlando Area Bd. Realtors (Friend of Realtors award 1989), Builders and Contractors, Ctrl. Fla. Builders Exch., Delta Kappa Gamma, Phi Kappa Phi, Kappa Delta Epsilon. Republican. Office: Office Lt Governor The Capitol 400 S Monroe St Tallahassee FL 32399 Office Phone: 850-488-4711. Office Fax: 850-921-6114. E-mail: Toni.Jennings@MyFlorida.com.*

JENNINGS, SISTER VIVIEN, literature and language professor; b. Jersey City; d. Eugene O. and Alice (Smith) J. BA, Caldwell Coll.; MA in English, Cath. U. Am.; MS in Telecommunications, Syracuse U.; PhD in English, Fordham U.; postgrad., Oxford U., Eng., 1994; EdD (hon.), Providence Coll.; LittD (hon.), Caldwell Coll.; DHL (hon.), St. Peter's Coll. Prof. English Caldwell Coll., 1960-69; major supr. Dominican Sisters-Caldwell, 1969-79; instr. broadcasting writing Syracuse U., 1979-80; with community affairs dept. Sta. WIXT TV, Syracuse, NY, 1980; dir. telecommunications Barry U., 1982-83; dir. pub. affairs Cath. Telecommunications Network Am., 1983-84; pres. Caldwell Coll., 1984-94, prof. English, 1995-99; prin. St. Dominic Acad., Jersey City, 1999—. Originator, designer campus TV studios Caldwell Coll., Barry U.; curriculum planner, coord. new grad.-level curriculum in telecommunications Barry U.; lectr. on ednl. and media issues. Producer: Centenary Journey, 1981, Advent Vesper Chorale, 1981, American Immigrant Church, 1982, Las Casas: Ministry of Presence, 1987; co-producer: The Boat People, 1980. Founder, dir. Children's TV Experience; founder Project Link Ednl. Ctr., Newark. Recipient Gov.'s Pride N.J. Albert Einstein award for edn., 1989. Office: St Dominic Acad 2572 Kennedy Blvd Jersey City NJ 07304-2107

JENSEN, ANNETTE M., mental health nurse, administrator; b. Albert Lea, Minn., Jan. 16, 1952; d. Oliver H. and Ardis R. (Nelson) J. BSN, Winona (Minn.) State U., 1974. Cert. psychiatric-mental health nurse; lic. sch. nurse; registered pub. health nurse. Staff nurse in adolescent mental health U. Minn. Hosp., Mpls., 1974-75; staff nurse in adolescent psychiatry C.B. Wilson Ctr., Faribault, Minn., 1975-76, 79-80; staff nurse in adolescent mental health Abbott Northwestern Hosp., Mpls., 1981-82; charge nurse in child psychiatry Med. Coll. Ga., Augusta, 1983-87; adminstr. child psychiat. program Charter Hosp. of Augusta, 1987-91; staff educator/quality mgmt. in psychiatry Ga. Regional Hosp. at Augusta, Augusta, 1990-92; team leader child psychiatry Charter Peachford Hosp., Atlanta, 1992-97; child and adolescent psychiat. nurse supr. Wilson Ctr., Faribault, Minn., 1997-2001; sch. nurse EBD program Intermediate Sch. Dist. 917, South St. Paul, Minn., 2000—. Mem. Girl Scouts of Am. Mem. ANA, Internat. Soc. Psychiat. Nurses, Assn. Child/Adolescent Psychiat. Nurses, Nat. Assn. Sch. Nurses, Am. Camping Assn., Ga. Nurses Assn., Sch. Nurse Assn. Minn. Presbyterian. Home: 2311 Cornell Dr Faribault MN 55021-3420 E-mail: amjensen@clear.lakes.com.

JENSEN, BARBARA WOOD, interior design business owner; b. Salt Lake City, Apr. 30, 1927; d. John Howard and Loretta (Sparks) Wood; m. Lowell N. Jensen, June 26, 1947 (dec. Aug. 2000); children: Brent Lowell, Robyn Lynn, Todd Wood; m. Thomas A. Mackey, Feb. 24, 2001. Interior decorator paint and wall paper co., 1947-49; cons., interior designer, 1950-60; pres., treas. Barbara Jensen Interiors, Inc., Salt Lake City, 1960-79; interior designer, 1979—; owner Barbara Jensen Designs, St. George, Utah and Las Vegas; lectr. in field. Lectr. in field; dir. 1st Women's Bancorp, Utah. Chmn. Utah Legis. Rep. Ball, 1970, Utah Symphony Ball, 1979. Fellow Inst. Profl. Designers (London); mem. Assistance League, Com. Fgn. Affairs, Interior Design Soc. (assoc.), Ft. Douglas Country Club, Knife and Fork Club, Hi-Steppers Dance Club, Ladies Lit. Club, Pres.'s Club of Utah, Bloomington Country Club, Elks. Mem. Lds Ch. Home: 2575 Kuhio # 1504 Honolulu HI 96815

JENSEN, DANA G., literature educator; b. Frostburg, Md., Mar. 11, 1948; d. Robert Clinton and Anna Virginia (Skidmore) Harden; m. Richard Walter Jensen, Dec. 31, 1969; children: Richar, Matthew (Kelly), James, Andrew. BA, Frostburg U., Md., 1973. Tchr. Raymond Elem. Sch., Franksville, Md., 1992—. Republican. Baptist. Avocations: antiques, boating, snowmobiling, golf. Home: 6500 W 6 Mi Rd Caledonia WI 53108 Office: Raymond Elem Sch Franksville WI 53126 E-mail: rwjensen@core.com.

JENSEN, EVA MARIE, medical/surgical nurse; b. Santa Maria, Calif., Sept. 2, 1956; d. Paul Cabello and Dolores Margaret Gutierrez; m. Royal George Jensen, Mar. 22, 1986 (div. Mar. 15, 1993). AA, Cuesta Coll., Calif., 1977; lic. vocation nurse, Hartnell Coll., 1980. RN Calif., 1982, cert. psychiat. and mental health nurse, Calif., 1995. Nurse Atascadero (Calif.) State Hosp., Atascadero, 1986—2003, Twin Cities Hosp., Templeton, 1982—86, 2003—. Participant nurses' health study Harvard Med. Sch., Boston, 1992—. Democrat. Roman Catholic.

JENSEN, GLORIA VERONICA, adult nurse practitioner; b. Montreal, Que., Can., Aug. 29, 1931; arrived in U.S., 1955; d. William Russell Boyd and Veronica Elizabeth Clarke; m. Joseph Edgar Jensen Jr., May 26, 1955 (div. June 11, 1989); children: William, Joanne, Neil, Christina, Karen. RN Calif.; lic. real estate agt. Calif. Nurse emer. rm. Royal Victoria Hosp., Montreal, 1953—55; postpartum nurse Good Samaritan Hosp., L.A., 1955—56; pvt. duty nurse Laguna Hills, Calif., 1988—91; relief work nurse Allergy and Asthma Assn., Mission Viego, Calif., 1992—99; nurse Saddleback Med. Group, Laguna Hills, 1998—. Vol. ARC, Subic Bay, Philippines, 1965—67, chmn. vols., 1965—67; mem. Valiant Women Mission Hosp., Mission Viejo, Calif. Mem.: Kiwanis. Republican. Roman Catholic. Avocations: opera, sewing, music, sailing. Home: 30922 Lucia Ln Laguna Beach CA 92677

JENSEN, HANNE MARGRETE, pathologist, educator; b. Copenhagen, Dec. 9, 1935; came to US, 1957; d. Niels Peter Evald and Else Signe Agnete (Rasmussen) Damgaard; m. July 21, 1957 (div. Apr. 1987); children: Peter Albert, Dorte Marie, Gordon Kristian, Sabrina Elisabeth. Student, U. Copenhagen, 1954—57; MD, U. Wash., 1961. Resident and fellow in pathology U. Wash., Seattle, 1963-68; asst. prof. dept. pathology U. Calif. Sch. Medicine, Davis, 1969-79, assoc. prof., 1979—2001, dir. transfusion svc., 1973—, prof., 2001—. McFarlane prof. exptl. medicine U. Glasgow, Scotland, 1983. Mem. No. Calif. Soc. for Electron Microscopy, U.S. and Can. Acad. of Pathology, Am. Cancer Soc., Am. Soc. Clin. Pathologists, AAAS, Am. Assn. of Blood Banks, Calif. Blood Bank Sys., People to People Internat., Internat. Platform Assn; fellow Pacific Coast Obstetrician and Gynecol. Soc., Coll. of Am. Pathologists. Office: U Calif Sch Medicine Dept Pathology Davis CA 95616 Office Phone: 530-752-7229. Business E-Mail: hmjensen@ucdavis.edu.

JENSEN, JILL SUSAN, music educator; b. Milw., Aug. 14, 1956; d. Joan and James Jensen. BS Music Edn., U. Wis. Madison, 1979. Cert. Tchr. K-12 Music Edn. Wis., 1980. Music educator Appleton Sch. Dist., Wis., 1980—87, Cudahy Mid. Sch., Wis., 1990—96, Inter-Am. Acad., Guayaquil, Ecuador, 1996—98, Nichols Sch., Monona, Wis., 2003—. Named Tchr. of Yr., Cudahy Sch. Dist., 1995. Office: Nichols School 100 Nichols Road Monona WI 53713 E-mail: jill_jensen@monongrove.org.

JENSEN, JUDY DIANNE, psychotherapist, consultant; b. Portland, Oreg., Apr. 8, 1948; d. Clarence Melvin and Charlene Augusta (Young) J.; m. Frank George Cooper, Sept 4, 1983; stepchildren: Pamela Cooper, Brian Cooper. BA in Sociology and Anthropology with honors, Oberlin Coll., 1970; MSW, U. Pitts., 1972; postgrad., U. Wis., 1977. Lic. clin. social worker, marriage and family therapist, Oreg. Social worker Day Hosp. Western Psychiat. Inst. and Clinic, Pitts., 1972-73, South Hills Child Guidance Ctr., Pitts., 1973-74; mem. drug treatment program Umatilla County Mental Health Clinic, Pendleton, Oreg., 1975-77; social worker Children's Services Div. State of Oreg., Pendleton, 1978-80, therapist intensive family services project, 1980—2001, dir. intensive family services project, 1986—2001; pvt. practice Pendleton, 1980—2004, Sandy, Oreg., 2004—; founder Cherryville Heartsongs LLC, 2004—. NIMH grantee, 1970-72; NDEA fellow 1977; Gen. Motors scholar Oberlin Coll., 1966-70 Mem. Am. Assn. Marriage and Family Therapists (clin.), Nat. Assn. Social Workers. Avocations: photography, personal jour. and poetry writing, hiking, dog and miniature horse training. Home: 53755 E Terra Fern Dr Sandy OR 97055 Office: 57355 E Terra Fern Dr Sandy OR 97055 E-mail: aeriejjj@aol.com.

JENSEN, JULIE MAE, educator; b. Hutchinson, Minn., Dec. 6, 1943; d. Axel M. and Mae A. Jensen. BS, U. Minn., 1965, MA, 1968, PhD, 1970. Tchr. Mpls. Pub. Schs., 1965-67; instr. U. Minn., 1967-70; prof. U. Tex., Austin, 1970—. Author: (with Fagan and Cooper) Measures for Research and Evaluation in the English Language Arts, vols. 1, 1975, vol. 2, 1985, (with Petty) Developing Children's Language, 1980, Composing and Comprehending, 1984, Stories To Grow On, 1989; editor: Language Arts, 1976-83; contbr. revs., articles, chpts to books. Recipient Excellence in Profl. Journalism award Ednl. Press Assn. Am.; NDEA fellow, Nat. Conf. Research in English fellow. Mem. Nat. Council Tchrs. of English (pres. 1987-88, award for promising research in teaching of English). Office: U Tex Austin 406 Education Bldg Austin TX 78712

JENSEN, KATHRYN PATRICIA (KIT), broadcast executive; b. Fairbanks, Alaska, June 20, 1950; d. Edward Leroy and Doris Patricia (Fee) Bigelow; 1 child, Alexander Morgan. BA, U. Alaska, 1974. Sta. mgr., program dir. Sta. KUAC-FM, U. Alaska, Fairbanks, 1976-82; gen. mgr. Sta. KUAC-FM-TV, U. Alaska, Fairbanks, 1982-87; pres., gen. mgr. Sta. WCPN-FM, 1987—2001; COO Stas. WVIZ/PBS and 90.3 WCPN Ideastream, Cleve., 2001—. Founding mem. Alaska Pub. Radio Network, 1978-85; bd. dirs. Nat. Pub. Radio, 1983-89, Pub. Radio Internat., 1997—. Bd. dirs. United Way, Cleve., 2001—04. Recipient Elaine B. Mitchell award Alaska Pub. Radio Network, 1988, Oebie award, 1992, 95, William H. Kling Innovation and Entrepreneurship award Pub. Radio Internat., 1995, Leadership in Non-profit Mgmt. award Case We. Res. U., Mandel Ctr. Non-Profit Orgns., 1999; named Pub. Radio Gen. Mgr. of Yr., DEI/PRADO, 1999. Episcopalian. Avocations: reading, gardening. Office: Stas WVIZ & WCPN Ideastream 1375 Euclid Ave Cleveland OH 44115

JENSEN, MARGARET, real estate broker; b. Payson, Utah, Aug. 12, 1948; d. Basil D. Broadbent and V. Merlene Ellsworth; m. Don E. Jensen, Sept. 27, 1997; children: Chad, Troy, Kristin, Dean, Debbie, Sean, Julie. AS, Casper Coll., Wyo., 1968; BS with distinction, Colo. State U., Ft. Collins, 1989, postgrad., 1990. Grad. Realtor Inst., CRB, CRS, EMT. Clk. Colo. 8th Jud. Dept., Loveland; owner, CEO Lil Rascals, Ft. Collins, 1980-96; real estate salesperson Hometown Advantage, Loveland, 1996, Century 21, Ft. Collins, 1996; pres. Home Sweet Home Realty, Inc., Ft. Collins, 1997—; owner Home Sweet Home Bakery, Inc., Home Sweet Home Knitted Creations, Inc. Rental cons. Ft. Collins, 1985-99; tax cons., Ft. Collins, 1975-90; family cons. Ft. Collins, 1990-97. Instr. ARC, Ft. Collins, 1975-85; tax preparer for VITA IRS, Ft. Collins, 1975-90; supr. trip to Russia People to People, 1990. Finalist Miss Am. Pageant, 1968; named Grand Champion Baking Divsn., Larimer County Fair, 2005. Mem. Lions Club Internat., Mortar Bd., Golden Key Nat. Honor Soc., Colo. Assn. of Realtors, Nat. Assn. of Realtors, Omicron Nu, Alpha Gamma Delta, Phi Kappa Phi. Avocations: piano, baking. Home and Office: 2205 Stonecrest Dr Fort Collins CO 80521-1318 Office Phone: 970-482-2320. Personal E-mail: buycolorado@aol.com.

JENSEN, MARION PAULINE, singer; b. Glendale, Calif., June 29, 1931; d. Paul Morton and Marion (Grus) Bellows; m. Maynard I. Jensen, Aug. 15, 1959; children: Clare, Steven, Jeannetta, Lauretta, Paul, Tony, Phil. Studied voice with, Barbara Burk Prosper, San Francisco Opera, Christina Carlson, Edward Schick, Robert Kyber, Gibner King, David Jimerson; currently studies voice with, Christine Meadows. Pvt. tchr. music. Profl. performer of stage, concert, radio and TV; piano bar entertainer; author: So You Want To Sing, 1983; opera/stage roles include mother in Amahl and the Night Visitors, Kate in Brigadoon, Olga Navakovich in Merry Widow, Tuptim in The King and I, Mable in Pirates of Penzance, Bride in trial by Jury, Josephine in H.M.S. Pinafore, Sherry in Paint Your Wagon, Dolly in Rio Rita, others; opera cos. performed with include Oregon Light Opera, Pacific Theatre Arts, Oreg. Opera Ensemble, Vancouver Civic Theatre, Portland Opera; numerous concerts and recitals in L.A., San Francisco, various cities in Wash., Oreg.; strolling entertainer Nendels Inn, Sylvia's Downtown Restaurant; singer/hostess Frontier Room; singer Portland Hilton, others. Tchr. English Laubach (Oreg.) Literacy, 1972—. Mem. Internat. Assn. Musicians, Nat. Assn. Tchrs. Singing, Music Tchrs. Nat. Assn., Oreg. Music Tchrs. Assn., Nat. Fedn. Music Clubs of Am. (state chmn. student auditions). Democrat. Roman Catholic. Avocations: raising birds, designing and sewing, writing and illustrating children's books. Home: 10230 N Tyler Ave Portland OR 97203-1251

JENSEN, NANCY DAGGETT, music educator; b. LA, Sept. 10, 1942; d. Daniel Thomas and Louise Helen (Kuljian) Daggett; m. Sven Oxfeldt Jensen, Nov. 19, 1978; children: Lori, Brian. BA, San Jose State U., Calif., 1964, MA, 1967. Cert. master tchr. in music. Pvt. piano tchr., Los Altos, Calif., 1967—. Mem. Music Tchrs. Assn. of Calif. (pres. 1972-74, 82-83, 85-86, 93-94, state chmn. cert. of merit 1974-79), Calif. Assn. of Profl. Music Tchrs., Steinway Soc. (bd. dirs.). Personal E-mail: nanchopin@sbcglobal.net.

JENSEN, SUSAN, design educator, multi-media specialist; b. Salt Lake City, Dec. 13, 1961; d. Ronald Ray and Carolyn Jensen. BA in Comms., Brigham Young U., 1985. Intern Pt. Authority of N.Y. and N.J., N.Y.C., 1985; designer, prodr. The Ch. of Jesus Christ of LDS, Salt Lake City, 1985-87, Help-U-Sell, Inc., Salt Lake City, 1987-88; tech. writer, editor Unysis Inc., Salt Lake City, 1989-90; designer, prodr. Allen Comm., Salt Lake City, 1990-95; multimedia dir. Infobases Inc., Provo, Utah, 1995, v.p. of devel., 1995-96; pres., cons. The Ditigal Ranch, Salt Lake City, 1996—. Cons. in multimedia, Salt Lake City, 1985—. Designer, prodr.: (children's multimedia) The Adventures of Andrea and Alexander "Sunday.That One Day," 1995. Tchr. children's orgn., Bountiful, Utah, 1993-95, teenager's orgn., 1995-98, Sunday sch., Salt Lake City, 1990-92; pres. Young Women's Orgn., Bountiful, 1998-99, sec. regional presidency, 1999—. Mem. Acad. Interactive Arts and Scis. (bd. govs. 1994-96). Avocations: travel, theater, films, skiing, tennis. Office: The Digital Ranch 1354 E 3300 S Ste 300 Salt Lake City UT 84106-3082

JENSON, PAULINE ALVINO, retired speech and hearing educator; b. Orange, N.J. m. Bernard A. Jenson; 1 child, Mark J. BS, Trenton State Coll., 1948; MA, Columbia U., 1950, PhD, 1969. Tchr. English and history Bordentown (N.J.) H.S., 1948-49; tchr. Lexington Sch. for Deaf, N.Y.C., 1950-51, with rsch. dept., 1969-70; tchr. N.J. Sch. for Deaf, West Trenton, 1951-56, 58-61, St. Mary's Sch. for Deaf, Buffalo, 1956-58; speech pathologist Hunterdon Med. Ctr., Flemington, N.J., 1959-60, dir. speech and hearing, 1960-62; asst. prof. Trenton (N.J.) State Coll., 1962-65; instr., lectr. Teacher's Coll., Columbia U., N.Y.C., 1966-69; prof. dept. speech pathology and audiology Trenton (N.J.) State Coll., 1970-95; Yrbk Dedica, 1978; prof. dept. lang. and comm. sci. Coll. N.J. (formerly Trenton State Coll.), 1995-98, chmn. dept., 1991-94, prof. emerita, 1998. Cons. Universal Films & Visual Arts, N.Y.C., 1968-70, State Agys. and Schs. for Handicapped, N.J., N.Y., 1976-98; evaluator Coun. on Edn. of Deaf, Washington, 1979-83. Author: (with others) Speech for the Deaf Child, 1971; inventor cueing system for deaf speakers, 1976; editor: (info. booklets) Topics, Princeton, N.J., 1980-86 Help line vol. N.J. Assn. for Children with Hearing Impairments, Princeton, 1973-95; co-author, cons. Senate Bills on Deafness, Trenton, 1979-98; commr. Legislative Commn. to Study Svcs. for Hearing Impaired Children, Trenton, 1988-90. Post Master's scholar U.S. Office Edn., Tchrs. Coll., Columbia, U., 1965-66; grantee N.J. Dept. Edn., 1973, N.J. Dept. Human Svcs., 1992-96. Mem. N.J. Assn. for Children with Hearing Impairment (founder, exec. dir. 1973-95, Pauline Jenson award at The Coll. of N.J. named in her honor, 1996), N.J. Speech, Lang. and Hearing Assn. (life, Disting. Svc. award 1985, disting. clin. svc. award 1998), Am. Speech, Lang. and Hearing Assn. (cert., life). Avocation: bibliophily. Office: PO Box 1336 Princeton NJ 08542-1336 Office Phone: 609-924-8689.

JENSVOLD, MARY LEE ABSHIRE, research scientist; b. Washington, Mar. 19, 1962; d. David Manker and Carolyn Sample Abshire; m. Steven Douglas Jensvold, Mar. 28, 1993; 1 child, Hannah Mae. BA, U. Oreg., Eugene, 1985; MS, Ctrl. Wash. U., Ellensburg, Wash., 1989; PhD, U. Nev., Reno, 1996. Asst. dir. Chimpanzee and Human Comm. Inst., Ellensburg, Wash., 2000—. Adj. faculty Ctrl. Wash. U., Ellensburg, 1993—, adj. rsch. assoc., 2005—; bd. dirs. Friends of Washoe, Ellensburg, N.W. Chimpanzee Retirment Sanctuary, Seattle; adb. bd. mem. Fauna Found., Quebec, Canada. Contbr. articles to profl. jours. Bd. dirs. Friends of Roslyn (Wash.) Libr., Roslyn Hist. and Preservation Commn., 2003—05. Recipient Refinement award, Animal Welfare Inst., Washington, 2006; Rsch. grant, Earthwatch, 1998—. Mem.: Internat. Soc. Anthrozoology, Rocky Mt. Psychol. Assn., Nat. Soc. of Colonial Dames Am., Phi Kappa Phi. Avocations: bicycling, cross country skiing. Office Phone: 509-963-2215. Office Fax: 509-963-2234. Business E-Mail: jensvold@cwu.edu.

JERDEE, SYLVIA ANN, minister; b. Alpine, Tex., Apr. 18, 1941; d. Rolf Walter and Marjorie O. Kaasa; m. Joseph C. Jerdee, June 15, 1963; children: Jonathan, Peter, Theodore. BA, Luther Coll., 1963; EdM, Boston U., 1978; MDiv, Luther Seminary, 1995. Ordained min. Evang. Luth. Ch. Am., 1995. Tchr. Washington H.S., Sioux Falls, SD, 1963—64, Army Edn. Ctr., Dept. of Def., Germany, 1974—78, Frankfurt (Germany) Am. H.S., 1978—85, guidance counselor, 1985—91; pastor Calvary LUth. Ch., Orr, Minn., 1995—99, Faith Little Norway Luth. Parish, Mentor, Minn., 1999—. Pastor Calvary Luth. Ch. Avocations: travel, reading. Office: Faith Little Norway Luth Parish Box 186 Mentor MN 56736

JERDEN, ALISON D., human resources consultant; d. Michael W. Duncan and Linda H. Marcum; m. Eddie Jerden, July 15, 2000. B, Stamford U., 1997; M, Middle Tenn. State U., 1999. Cons. Assessment Plus, Stone Mountain, Ga., 1999—2000, Towers Perrin, Atlanta, 2000—05; sr. human resources Coca-Cola Co, Atlanta, 2005—. Mem.: APA (assoc.), Soc. Indsl. Orgnl. Psychology (assoc.). Home: 1843 Flagler Ave Atlanta GA 30309 Office: Coca Cola Co PO Box 1734 Atlanta GA 30301 Office Phone: 404-676-9453. Personal E-mail: alijerden@hotmail.com.

JEREMIJENKO, NATALIE H.M., design engineer, educator, artist; b. Mackay, Australia, 1966; m. Dalton Conley; 3 children. Student in Physics and Phys. Chemistry, Monash U., Australia, 1987; BS in Neuroscience and Biochemistry, Griffith U., Australia, 1988; student, U. Melbourne and Royal Melbourne Inst. Tech., 1991—93; BFA with honors, Royal Melbourne Inst. Tech., Australia, 1992; student, Stanford U., 1994—97; PhD in Info. Tech. and Elec. Engring., U. Queensland, 2002. Tchg. asst. Deakin U., Australia, 1991—93; tchg. asst., lectr. dept. hist. and philos. of sci. U. Melbourne, 1991—93; rschr. Exploratorium, 1993—94; cons. rsch. scientist computer sci. lab. Xerox Palo Alto Rsch. Ctr., Calif., 1994—96; grad. rsch. asst. Stanford U. Ctr. Design Rsch., 1995—97; mech. engr. Ove Arup and Associates, San Francisco, 1996; vis. faculty digital imaging ctr. San Francisco Art Inst., 1996; adj. prof. Sch. Visual Arts, NYC, 1998; acting dir. engring. design studio, lectr. faculty engring. Yale U., 1998—99, design cons. engring. design studio faculty engring., 2000, lectr. convertible dept. mech. engring., 2001—02, dir. exptl. product design initiative dept. mech. engring.; postdoctoral asst. rsch. scientist NYU Advanced Computer Graphics Ctr. and Media Rsch. Lab., 2000; cons. dept. computer sci. NYU Ctr. for Advanced Tech. and Media Rsch. Lab., 2001—02; vis. rsch. fellow Santa Fe Inst., 2001; disting. vis. critic dept. art Va. Commonwealth U., 2001—02; co-founder, engr. Bur. Inverse Tech., Melbourne, Australia, 1991—; asst. prof. visual arts U. Calif., San Diego. Exhibitions include, Ars Electronic prix, 1996, Documenta, 1997, Tree Logic, Mass. Mus. Contemporary Art, 1999, OneTrees, 2003, Activist Robots, Eyebeam, NYC, 2003, Ooz: Goosing, De Veerbeelding, 2003, MoMA, Rotterdam Film Festival, Tate Gallery, Guggenheim Mus., Mus. Moderne Kunst; mng. editor: Biotech Hobbyist mag. Named one of Top 100 Young Innovators, MIT Tech. Rev., 1999, 40 Most Influential People in Design, International Design mag., 2005; grantee Rockefeller fellowship, 1999. Office: Lavin Agy 222 Third St Ste 1130 Cambridge MA 02142*

JERG, KAREN LESLIE, elementary school educator; b. Milw., Dec. 20, 1948; d. Ralph C. and Irene M. Tersen; m. Phil Jerg, Aug. 12, 1978. BS in Phys. Edn., U. Wis., LaCross, Wis., 1971; MS in Sch. Counseling, Ea. Ill. U., Charleston, Ill., 1977. Lic. tchr. K-12, in phys. edn. and sch. counseling. Tchr. phys. edn. Stevens Point Area Sch. Dist., Wis., 1972—78; guidance counselor Princeton Pub. Sch. Dist., Wis., 1978—81; tchr. phys. edn. Berlin Cath. Schs., Wis., 1981—86; guidance counselor West Elem. Sch. Jefferson Sch. Dist., Wis., 1987—88; guidance counselor Waterloo Elem. Sch., Waterloo, 1988—, tchr. phys. edn. Elem. Sch., 1988—. Home: 1178 Atcheson Ave Sun Prairie WI 53590-3812

JERGE, MARIE CHARLOTTE, minister; b. Mineola, NY, Dec. 26, 1952; d. Charles Louis and Helen Marie (Scheld) Scharfe; m. James Nelson Jerge, Aug. 27, 1977. AB, Smith Coll., 1974; MDiv, Luth. Theol. Sem. of Phila., 1978. Pastor St. Mark Evang. Luth. Ch., Mayville, NY, 1978-88; co-pastor Zion Evang. Luth. Ch., Silver Creek, 1983-88; asst. to the bishop Upstate NY Synod, Buffalo, 1988—2002; dir., bd. dirs. Acad. of Preachers, Phila., 1995-99; bishop Upstate NY Synod, ELCA, Syracuse, 2002—; v.p. NY State Coun. of Chs., 2003—. Bd. dirs. Acad. Preachers, Phila., 1982-99. Chairperson Chautauqua County Commn. of Family Violence and Neglect, Mayville, 1981-82, bd. dirs., 1978-88. Named one of outstanding Young Women in Am., 1980. Avocations: needlecrafts, aerobics, golf, cross country skiing. Office: Upstate NY Synod 890 E Brighton Ave Syracuse NY 13205

JERGENS, MARIBETH JOIE, school counselor; b. Cleve., May 3, 1945; d. Raymond Wenceslaus and Elsie Koryta J.; children: Annemarie Gurchik, Keith Robert Gurchik. Student, St. Joseph Acad., Cleve., 1959—63, U. Vienna, Austria, 1965; BS in Elem. Edn., Coll. Mt. St. Joseph on-the-Ohio, 1967; MEd in Ednl. Counseling, Cleve. State U., 1984; cert. in Ednl. Adminstrn., Akron U., 1988; postgrad. in edn. and clin. psychology, Kent State U., 1989—. Cert. elem., spl. edn. and adult edn. tchr., counselor. Coord. info. svcs. Halle Bros., Cleve., 1961—67; tchr. North Olmstead (Ohio) City Schs., 1967-75; tchr. adult basic edn. Polaris Vocat. Sch., Berea, Ohio, 1977-78; tchr. adult edn., ESL Lakewood (Ohio) City Schs., 1978-79; tchr. 2d grade St. Rose Sch., Lakewood, 1979-80; tchr. learning disabled students, tutor Cleve. Pub. Schs. Watterson-Lake Elem. Sch., 1980-85; tutor handicapped Cleve. Christian Home, 1982-84; elem. sch. counselor, tchr. learning disabilities Cleve. Pub. Schs., A.B. Hart Mid. Sch., 1995-97; tchr. human devel. and learning Kent (Ohio) State U., 1997-98; sch. psychologist asst. PSI Assocs., Inc., 1998-99; tchr. Wade Park Sch. Cleve. Mcpl. Sch. Dist., 1999-2000; pvt. practice Rocky River Psychol. Svcs., Ohio, 1999—2003; intervention specialist Cleve. Pub. Schs., 2000—. Counselor West Side Cmty. Mental Health Ctr., Cleve., 1983-84; sales mgr. Field Enterprises Inc., Cleve., 1975-77; fund raising spkr., vol. Cerebral Palsy Camp Rosemary Home for Children United Torch, Cleve., 1961-65; coordinated vol. svcs. area colls. Allen Halfway Ho., Cin., 1965-67; rschr. interventions children with guns and violence in Am. schs., 1998-99; elem. counselor Cleve. Pub. Schs. Adams-Rhodes Cluster, 1985-94; spkr. in field. Contbr. articles to newspapers. Vol. Fairview Gen. Hosp., Cleve., 1959-63, Cerebral Palsy Camp, 1959-63, Allen Halfway House for Children, Cin., 1963-67; co-founder Westshore Separated, Div. and Remarried Caths., Cleve., 1975-85; chair North Olmsted Jr. Women's Club; parish coun. St. Brendan Ch., North Olmstead, 1975-87, founder cath. separated and div. ministry, 1976-85, counselor; mem. com. Cleve. Symphony, Cleve. Art Mus.; summer civil rights activist to implement Fed. Ct. Order Desegregation, Ctrl. H.S., Little Rock, 1957, New Orleans, 1958, Mobile, Ala., 1959; active Am. Aeobics and Fitness Assn., Audobon Soc., Cleve. Natural History Mus., Cleve. Mus. Art, Dem. Party, Edgewater Yacht Club (NCSS), English-Speaking Union, Holden Arboretum, St. Malachi Cath. Ch., Cath. Ch. Spl. Commn. on Priests Sexual Abuse, 2002-03; mem. rev. bd. Cleve. Cath. Diocese, 2003-. Recipient Speaker's United Torch award United Way, Cleve., 1st Pl. prize in clothing design Stretch & Sew, 1975, 1st Pl. prize in needlepoint Framemakers Art, 1983, 1st Pl. in three interstate art contests, musical rec., singing with the Cleve. Symphony Orch., NCSS regatta. Mem. Am. Assn. Counseling and Devel., AAUW, Am. Assn. Marriage and Family Therapists, Am. Psychol. Assn., Assn. for Curriculum and Supervision, Am. Sch. Counselor Assn., N.E. Ohio Counselors Assn., Ohio Counselors Assn., Ohio Assn. Counseling and Devel., Coun. for Exceptional Children, Am. Sch. Counselor Assn., ASCD, Gestalt Inst., Audubon Soc., Cleve. Psychol. Assn., Cleve. Mus. Art, Cleve. Natural History Mus., Cleve. Tchrs. Union, Gestalt Inst., Am. Aerobics and Fitness Assn., Edgewater Yacht Club, English Speaking Union, Holden Arboretum, Pi Lambda Theta. Democrat. Avocations: aerobics, art, bicycling, dance, gardening. Home: 727 Tollis Pky Broadview Heights OH 44147 Office Phone: 216-408-6727. E-mail: maribethjergens@aol.com, counselingdetr@aol.com.

JERGER, HOLLY ANNE, museum staff member, artist; d. Earl J. and Margie M. Jerger; m. Matthew D. Wittmer, Aug. 8, 2004. BFA, Ball State U., Muncie, Ind., 1997; MFA, U. Nebr., Lincoln, 2000. Mus. educator Fullerton Mus. Ctr., Calif., 2001—02; recreation coord. LA City Dept. Recreation and Parks, 2002—05; edn. and cmty. outreach dir. Craft and Folk Art Mus., LA, 2005—. One-woman shows include Ojala Gallery, LA, 2002; contbr. articles to profl. jours. Grantee Undergrad. Creative Arts grant, Ball State U., 1995; Regents fellow, U. Nebr., Lincoln, 1999. Mem.: Coll. Art Assn., Mus. Educators So. Calif., LA Printmaking Soc.

JERGESEN, ARVELLA G., elementary school educator; b. Bozeman, Mont., June 7, 1970; d. Dick Ernest and Hermina Visser; m. Doug Kuper Jergesen, Sept. 13, 1997; children: Madison Jacoba, Tanner Richard. BA, Dordt Coll., Sioux Center, Iowa, 1992; MEd, Mont. State U., Bozeman, 2001. 4th grade tchr. Kaufman Christian Sch., Tex., 1993—95; 4th-7th grade tchr. Conrad Christian Sch., Mont., 1995—96; 6th grade math. and sci. tchr. Chief Joseph Mid. Sch., Bozeman, 2001—02, Fernley Intermediate Sch., Nev., 2002—. Mem.: Nat. Coun. Tchrs. Math., Internat. Reading Assn. Office: Fernley Intermediate Sch 320 Hwy 95A Fernley NV 89408 Office Phone: 775-575-3390. Business E-Mail: ajergesen@lyon.k12.nv.us.

JERN, DONNA L., social studies educator; b. Blue Island, Ill., June 9, 1981; BA in History, Ill. Coll., Jacksonville, 2003. Cert. secondary edn. in social studies Ill. Tchr. Bloom Twp. H.S., Chicago Heights, Ill., 2004—. Conservative. Office Phone: 705-755-1122.

JERNIGAN, HILARY DAWN, art educator, artist; b. Albany, Ga., Jan. 25, 1972; d. Virgil Weaver and Hilda Morgan Jernigan. BS in Art Edn., Bob Jones U., 1995. Cert. art & Spanish tchr. S.C. Tchr. art & Spanish League Acad., Greenville, SC, 1995—97, Greenville HS, 1997—, fine arts dept. chair, 2004—; lead tchr. H.S. art tchrs. Greenville (S.C.) County Schs., 2005—. Galleries & exhibitions, Llyn Strong Gallery, Greenville, 1995—2001, Gallery at 291, 1996, Sea Island Art Gallery, 2002—, juried exhibit, Anderson County Arts Ctr., SC, 2004. Bd. mem. Carolina Ballet Theater, 2006. Recipient 5th Place award, Belton Stand Pipe Festival, 2003, PTSA Tchr. of Yr. award, Greeville H.S., 2005. Mem.: Upstate Visual Arts (2nd Pl. award 2003, Best of Show, Art in the Pk. 2005, 3rd Pl. award 2006, 3rd Pl. award, Art in the Pk. 2006), Metropolitian Arts Coun., SC Art Edn. Assn. Republican. Nondenominational Protestant. Avocations: painting, bicycling, travel. Office Phone: 864-241-3220.

JERNIGAN, MELISSA MCGLAUN, secondary school educator; b. Americus, Ga., June 23, 1978; d. Michael A. and Sandra S. McGlaun; m. Luke D. Jernigan, June 1, 2002. BS in Edn., Valdosta State U., Ga., 2000; MS in Counseling and Psychology, Troy State U., Phenix City, Ala., 2003, postgrad., 2005—. English tchr. Marion County H.S. (Formerly Tri-County High), Buena Vista, Ga., 2000—, guidance counselor, 2003—. Sec. Marion County H.S. Coun., Buena Vista, 2005—. Vol. Ga. 4-H Club, Richland/Buena Vista, 2002; cmty. svc. chairperson Enterprise Bapt. Ch., Richland, Ga., 2006. Recipient STAR Tchr. award, Tri-County H.S./Profl. Assn. Ga. Educators, 2004. Mem.: Pprofl. Assn. Ga. Educators, Ga. Master 4-H Club (life), Chi Omega Alumna (life; new mem. educator 1999—2000). Republican. Baptist. Avocations: travel, writing. Home: 75 Enterprise Church Rd Richland GA 31825 Office: Marion County High School (formerly Tri) 656 Ga Hwy 30 W Buena Vista GA 31825 Office Phone: 229-649-7520.

JERNIGAN, VICKI LOUISE MACKECHNEY, clinical nurse specialist; b. Joliet, Ill., Aug. 2, 1953; d. Arthur Frank and Edna Eloise (Baker) Mackechney; m. George Norman Jernigan, Dec. 11, 1981 (div.); children: Nicole Dyan, Lani Michelle, Lindsey Lauryn. Diploma, Galveston County Meml. Hosp., LaMarque, Tex., 1976; RN assoc. degree, Galveston Coll., 1986; BS in nursing, MS in nursing, U. Conn., 2000. RN. Staff ward clerk, LUN & RN Galveston Memorial Hosp. (med. surg., ICU, CCU, ER, constant care units, skilled nursing units, post partum, nursery, surg., out patient, home health, La Marque, TX; indsl. nurse Gulf Coast Marine Works, Galveston, TX; nurse Staff Relief Inc., Houston; same day surg. recovery room nurse Surgi-Med. Inc., Dickinson, TX. Recruited as a Nurse Warrant Ofcr., Desert Storm/Desert Shield, United States Nurse Corps., 1991, A/D Lt., Nurse Corps., USN. Recipient, Navy Achievement Medal, 2 Navy Meritorious Unit Commendation Medals, Nat. Defense Svc. Medal, Outstanding Vol. Svc. Medal, Navy & Marine Corps Svc. Ribbon (3. yrs.), expert Pistol Merkmenship Ribbon. Home: PO Box 498 Santa Fe TX 77510-0498

JEROME, DOLORES, retired electronics executive; d. Otley Otis and Hariet (Redella) Rice; m. Byron Max Jerome, Aug. 2, 1941; children: Jeffrey Max, Joyce Jerome Gressner. BA in Polit. Sci., Wright State U., Dayton, Ohio, 1987; AAS in Bus. Mgmt., Sinclair CC, Dayton, 1984, AAS in Procurement and Def. Contract, 1984, AAS in Legal Assisting, 1988. Asst. clk. Wright Patterson AFB, Dayton, 1942, mgmt. analyst, 1950—53, dir. procurement and prodn., 1954—57; mail, file and record clk. Rome Air Svc. Command, NY, 1943—44; sys. designer Def. Electronics, Kettering, Ohio, 1960—66, procurement agt., contract termination specialist, 1968—81; ret., 1981. V.p. programs Dayton LWV; observer Ct. Awareness Program, 1984; chpt. legis. chmn. Federally Employed Women; 3d v.p. Dayton Bus. and Profl. Women's Club. Home: 4080 Woodman Dr Dayton OH 45440-1610

JEROME, KATHLEEN A., writer, retired publishing executive; b. Biloxi, Miss., May 14, 1955; d. Clarence and Marianne M. Boehm; children: Lindsay, Eric. BS in Biology Edn., Miami U., Oxford, Ohio, 1977. High sch. biology tchr., Ill., 1978-79; home tutor Fed. Homebound Program, Ill., 1980; from sci. editor to pres. Scott Foresman & Co., Glenview, Ill., 1981—95; pvt. practice Daniel Island, SC, 1996—. Mem. Nat. Sci. Tchrs. Assn., Internat. Reading Assn., Trident Literacy Assn. (bd. dirs. 2003—). Office Phone: 843-856-3532. E-mail: kjerome@verticalconnectpress.com.

JEROME, MARLENE S., nurse; b. Van Wert, Ohio, Feb. 27, 1949; d. Donald Eugene and Phyllis Arlene Turner; m. J. David Jerome, Dec. 18, 1971; children: Emmalyn Joy, Matthew David, Benjamin Andrew. RN, Lima (Ohio) Meml. Hosp. Neurointensive care nurse Lima Meml. Hosp., 1970-71, Doctors Hosp., Columbus, Ohio, 1971-73; intensive care surg. nurse Dr. Ly Soo, Lima, 1973-74, Nazarene Med. Missionary, Swaziland, 1975-79, 85-89; endoscopy nurse Mt. Carmel Med. Ctr., Columbus, Ohio, 1993—. Mem. Meadow Park Ch. God. Mem. Nat. Assn. Pro-Life Nurses. Avocations: reading, politics, collecting quotes, computers.

JEROME, NORGE WINIFRED, nutritionist, anthropologist, educator; b. Grenada, Nov. 3, 1930; arrived in U.S.A., 1956, naturalized, 1973; d. McManus Israel and Evelyn Mary (Grant) Jerome. BS magna cum laude (hon.), Howard U., 1960; MS, U. Wis., 1962, PhD, 1967. Cert. nutrition splty.; fellow Am. Coll. Nutrition. Asst. prof. U. Kans. Med. Sch., Kans. City, 1967—72, assoc. prof., 1972—78, prof., 1978—95, dir. cmty. nutrition divsn., 1981—95; dir. Office of Nutrition, AID, Washington, 1988—91; sr. rsch. fellow Univ. Ctr., AID, Washington, 1991—92; interim assoc. dean minority affairs U. Kans. Med. Sch., Kans. City, 1996—98, prof. emerita, 1996—. Tech. adv. group The Nat. Ctr. for Minority Health; dir. ednl. resource centers U. Kans. Med. Center, 1974-77, head cmty. nutrition lab., 1978-95; cons. Children's TV Workshop, 1974-77; chair adv. bd. Teenage Parents Ctr., 1971-75; planning and budget coun., children and family svc. United Cmty. Svc., 1971-80; panel on nutrition edn. White House Conf. on Food, Nutrition and Health, 1969; bd. dir., health care com. Prime Health, 1976-79; bd. dir. Coun. on Children, Media and Merchandising; consumer edn. task force Mid Am. Health Systems Agy., 1977-79; commr. N. Am. working group Commn. Anthropology Food and Food Habits, Internat. Union Anthrop. and Ethnol. Sci., 1979-80; chmn. com. nutritional anthropology Internat. Union Nutritional Sci., 1979-80; lipid metabolism adv. com. NIH, 1978-80; nat. adv. panel multi-media campaign to improve children's diet U.S. Dept. Agrl., 1979-81; bd. advisers Am. Coun. on Sci. and Health, 1985-88; cons. in field. Sr. author: Nutritional Anthropology, 1980; asso. editor: Jour. Nutrition Edn., 1971-77; adv. council, 1977-80; editor: Nutritional Anthropology Communicator, 1974-77; mem. editl. bd.: Med. Anthropology: Cross Cultural Studies in Health and Illness, 1976-88, Internat. Jour. Nutrition Planning, 1977-88, Nutrition and Cancer: An Internat. Jour. 1978-2000, Jour. Nutrition and Behavior, 1981-86; contbr. articles to profl. journals. Mem. com. man food sys. NRC, 1980-83; bd. dirs. Kans. City Urban League, 1969-77, Crittenton Ctr., Kans. City, Mo., 1979-80, Johnson County Kans. Libr. Found., 2004—, exec. com., 2005—; mem. awards com. in nutrition edn. Met. Life Found., 1983-85; pres. Assn. for Women in Devel., 1991-93; trustee U. Bridgeport, Conn., 1992—; trustee Child Health Found., 1992-2000, chmn. bd. dirs., 1996-98; v.p., bd. trustees U. Bridgeport, Conn., 1997—; bd. dirs. Black Health Care Coalition of Kansas City, 1993-2002, Sun Cookers Internat., 1992-2000, pres., 1998-2000, Johnson County, Kans. Found. on Aging, 2001-04, Health Care Found. Greater Kansas City, 2004—; mem. Commn. on Aging, Johnson County, Kans., 1997—; bd. dirs., vice chair cmty. adv. com. Kansas City Health Care Found., 2004. Decorated Dau. Brit.

Empire; recipient First Higuchi Irvin Youngberg Rsch. Achievement award U. Kans., 1982, Excellence in Academia award Inst. Caribbean Studies, 2002, Disting. Svc. award NAACP, 2005, Johnson County Trailblazer award, 2006. Fellow Am. Soc. for Nutritional Sci., Am. Anthrop. Assn. (chair com. nutritional anthropology 1974-77, founder com. nutritional anthropology 1974), Soc. Applied Anthropology, Am. Coll. Nutrition, Soc. Med. Anthropology, Am. Soc. Nutritional Sci., 1998; mem. Am. Public Health Assn. (food and nutrition coun. 1975-78, governing coun. 1982-85), Am. Inst. Nutrition (program com. 1983-86), Am. Soc. Clin. Nutrition, Am. Men and Women of Sci., Nat. Acad. Sci. (world food and nutrition study panel), N.Y. Acad. Sci., Inst. Food Technologists, Am. Dietetic Assn., Assn. for Women in Devel. (pres. 1991-93), Soc. Behavioral Medicine, Club of Rome (U.S. assoc.). Office: U Kans Med Ctr 3901 Rainbow Blvd Mail Stop 1008 Kansas City KS 66160 Office Phone: 913-588-2770. Business E-Mail: njerome@kumc.edu.

JERVIS, JANE LISE, academic administrator, historian; b. Newark, June 14, 1938; d. Ernest Robert and Helen Jenny (Roland) J.; m. Kenneth Albert Pruett, June 20, 1959 (div. 1974); children: Holly Jane Pruett, Cynthia Lorraine Pruett; m. Norman Joseph Chonacky, Dec. 26, 1981; children: Philip Joseph Chonacky, Joseph Norman Chonacky. AB, Radcliffe Coll., 1959; MA, Yale U., 1974, MPhil, 1975, PhD in History of Sci., 1978. Freelance sci. editor and writer, 1962-72; lectr. in history Rensselaer Poly. Inst., 1977-78; dean Davenport Coll., lectr. in history of sci. Yale U., 1978-82; dean students., assoc. prof. history Hamilton Coll., 1982-87; dean coll., lectr. in history Bowdoin Coll., 1988-92; pres. Evergreen State Coll., Olympia, Wash., 1992-2000; acad. dean Goddard Coll., 2004—. Cons. in field. Author: Cometary Theory in 15th Century Europe; contbr. articles to profl. jours.; book reviewer; presenter in field. Trustee Maine Hist. Assn., 1991-92, Stonehill Coll., 1996-02, Providence St. Peter's Hosp., 1997-2000; chair Maine selection com. Rhodes Scholarship Trust, 1990-92, chair N.W. selection com., 1992-93; commr. N.W. Assn. Schs. and Colls. Commn. on Colls., 1994-99. Office: Goddard College 123 Pitkin Road Plainfield VT 05667 Business E-Mail: jane.jervis@aya.yale.edu. E-mail: jjervis99@comcast.net.

JERVIS-HERBERT, GWENDOLYN THERESA, mental health services professional; b. N.Y.C., July 15, 1950; d. Nehemiah (Stepfather) and Margaret Rose Campbell; m. Samuel A. Herbert, Sept. 13, 1970 (div. May 1984). BS in Edn., SUNY, Buffalo, 1976, MS, 1989. Coord. case mgr., counselor Geneva B. Scruggs HEalth Care Ctr., Buffalo, 1983—87; counselor mental health Kaleida Health, 1987—2001, med. social worker, 2001—02, sr. counselor, 2002—. Clin. liaison Women Human Rights & Dignity, Buffalo, 1993—2001; clins. cons., conf. planner Mental Health Assn., 1997. Multicultural diversity com. Kalieda Health, Buffalo, 1995—99; cons., presenter Strive for Women, Inc., 2002. Scholar, Neighborhood Youth Corp., Bronx, 1968. Democrat. Avocations: reading, jazz, travel, mentoring. Home: 347 Florida St Buffalo NY 14208 Office Phone: 716-859-2886.

JERVISS, JOY J. (JOANNE JACKSON JERVISS), artist, educator, small business owner; b. Palmerton, Pa., Feb. 14, 1941; AA, SUNY, Old Westbury, 1989, BS, 1990. Pres. Joy J. Industries, Inc., Northport, N.Y. Instr. Northport Continuing Edn., Northport Art League, North Shore Cmty. Art Ctr., N.Y. Assn. for Brain Injured Children, Bd. Coop. Edn. Represented in permanent collections Bibliotheque Nationale, Miami Mus. Modern Art, Princeton U., Syracuse U., Ariz. State U., others. Mem. Northport Art League (pres., founder). Personal E-mail: jerviss@juno.com.

JESCHKE, CAROL T., arts/theater consultant, real estate investor; b. Cazenovia, N.Y., May 22, 1938; d. Howard Edward Trivelpiece and Pearl Ada Chapman Trivelpiece-Duva; m. Edmund H. Jeschke, Feb. 11, 1961 (dec. July 1990); children: Edaina E., Eric B. Student, Vt. Coll. for Women, 1956; BA in English, Syracuse U., 1960, postgrad., 1966, Purdue U., 1973, Harvard U., 1976. Cert. womens bus. enterprise; cert. facility exec. Acting exec. dir., dep. dir., dir. programming & pub. rels. Cultural Resources Coun., John H. Mulroy Civic Ctr., Syracuse, N.Y., 1966-91; exec. dir. Stone Quarry Hill Art Park, Cazenovia, 1991-94; pres. CME Real Estate Assocs., Ltd., 1996—; arts/theater cons. Carol T. Jeschke & Assocs. Founder Nat. Showcase of Performing Arts for Young People, 1979; U.S. rep. to Conf. on Arts and Culture, Austria, 1983, Arts Dialogue/Australia, 1987; founding trustee Assn. Internat. Performing Arts Festivals for Children, 1990-92. Editor: On the Dotted Line: The Anatomy of a Contract, 1979, Help! A Guide to Selecting and Surviving an Arts Consultant, 1983. Mem. Internat. Assn. Auditorium Mgrs. (hon., founding trustee, Mid Grood Perry award for creativity 1981). Avocations: art, writing. Home and Office: 433 West Lake Rd De Ruyter NY 13052

JESPERSEN, WYN CHERIE, music educator; b. Berea, Ohio, Sept. 27, 0956; d. Columbo Franklin and Shirley Beth Meyo; m. Robert William Jespersen, July 15, 1980; children: Courtney Elise, Eric William. MFA, U. Nebr., Omaha, 1979. Cert. profl. Conn. Dept. Edn. Music tchr. Omaha Pub. Schs., 1979—87, Suffield Pub. Schs., Conn., 1996—. Instr. Warehouse Point Jr. Fifes and Drums, Conn., 2001—; pvt. music instr. and performer. Musical dir., worship leader Village Ch. Bartlett, Ill., 1989—93, music dir., svc. planner, 1989—93; musical dir., svc. planner, worship leader Agawam Ch. of the Bible, Mass., 1995—2002. Mem.: Conn. Edn. Assn. Republican. Baptist. Avocations: crafts, gardening, cooking, interior decorating. Home: 51 Quail Run Rd Suffield CT 06078 Office: Spaulding Elementary School 945 Mountain Rd West Suffield CT 06093 Office Phone: 860-668-3826. Personal E-mail: wjespersen@sps.suffield.org.

JESSEN, JOEL ANNE, not-for-profit executive, art educator; b. Seattle, Sept. 7, 1940; d. John Paagard and Anne Vilma Jessen. BA, U. Wash., 1962, MFA, 1964. Instr. Cornish Coll. Arts, Seattle, 1965—76; pres., CEO Kappeler Inst., Inc., Seattle, 1975—. Instr. U. Wash., Seattle, 1970—71, Highline Coll., Seattle, 1970—71. Author: The Imperative Step, 1972, The Physical, The Mental, and The Spiritual, 1978. Recipient Patrick Gavin Meml. prize, Boston Printmakers, 1965. Mem.: U. Wash. Alumni. Avocation: art. Office: Kappeler Inst Inc PO Box 99735 Seattle WA 98139-0735 Business E-Mail: joel@kappelerinstitute.org.

JESSEN, SHIRLEY AGNES, artist; b. Bklyn., Jan. 23, 1921; d. Arnold Peter and Agnes Veronica (Maguire) Hemmersbach; m. Albert Vern Jessen, Nov. 23, 1944; 1 child, Gregory Vern (dec.). Student, NY Sch. Applied Design (now Pratt Inst.), 1939-42, Fashion Inst., NYC, 1942-43, Garden City Cmty. Club Art Studio, NY, 1961—2000. Tchr. art Cmty. Club Garden and Hempstead, 2004—, Nassau U. Med. Ctr., 2000—05, Club of Hempstead and Garden City. One-woman shows include N.Y. State Coun. Arts, 1972, 7-12 Assn., 1972, Wantagh (N.Y.) Libr., 1972, Security Nat. Bank, 1972-73, Bank N.Am., 1972-73, Expo Fine Arts Instructional Movie, 1973-74, Instructional TV, 1996-2005, Cmty. Arts Program, Cinema Theatre, 1973, Nat. Bank N.Am., 1973, S.E. Nassau (N.Y.) Guidance Clinic, 1973, Nassau County Office Performing and Fine Arts, 1973, N.Y State Coun. Arts, 1974, Garden City Libr., 1975, 97, Merrick (N.Y.) Mall Theatre, 1976, Galleries D'Art, 1976, Reynold Securities, Inc. Art Gallery, N.Y.C., 1977, Nassau County Mus. Fine Arts, 1979, Adelphi U. Alumni House, 1980, Town of Oyster Bay (N.Y.) Hall and Dept. Cmty. Svcs., 1981, Cent. Savs. Bank Syosset, N.Y., 1981, GEICO Art Gallery, Woodbury, N.Y., 1981, Oyster Bay Libr., 1981, Cathedral of Incarnation Mercer Libr., 1981, Molloy Coll. Kellenberg Art Gallery, 1984, Expo Art Gallery, 1987, Art League of LI, 1989—2003, Huntington Art League, 1998, Nassau U. Med. Ctr., 2000-03, Syosset Woodbury Cmty. Ctr., 2003, Jones Manor Bayville, 2003, State of LI Bank, 2003, Oyster Bay Libr., 2003, Plainview Libr. Massapequa, 2003, Oyster Bay Pub. Info., 2003, Freeport Art League, 2003, Saks Fifth Ave., 2004, Freeport Art League, 1950-2004, Garden CIty Libr., 2005, others; group shows at St. Frances de Chantal Art Show, 1974, North Shore U. Show, 1974, Union Carbide Art Gallery, 1977, Nat. Soc. Painters in Casein and Acrylic, 1978, Long Beach Mus. Juried Competition, 1979, Rosyln Mus. Fine Arts, 1979, 80, 81, 82, 83, 84, 85, PBS Channel 21 Art and Antique Benefit Auction, 1979-85, Les Etoiles Galerie D'Art, France, 1980 (Internat. award), Nat. Art Ctr., N.Y., 1980, South Shore Art League, 1981 (1st prize), Citibank Gallery, Merrick, 1981, Wilbur Arts Ctr. Molloy Coll., 1981, 82, Xavier Art Gallery, N.Y., 1981-82, Cork Gallery Lincoln Ctr., N.Y.C, 1982 (finalist prize 1981-82), PBS Channel 13 Benefit Art Auction, 1979-85, Chase Manhattan Bank, 1988—, Chase Salutes Artists, 1989-90, Shelter Rock Libr., 1988-89, Chelsea Art Ctr. Shows, 1991—, de Seversky Art Ctr., N.Y. Inst. Tech., Old Westbury, 2004, L.I. Mus. Am. Art, 2005, others. Illustrator Wantagh PTA, 1950-65, Mercy Hosp., Hempstead, N.Y., 1980-82, 2003, Georgia O'Keeffe lectures, Garden City-Hempstead Community Club, 1987, 89; founder, bd dirs. United Cerebral Palsy, Wantagh, 1955-78, pres. 1959-61, del. to AMA conventions, illustrator 1959; bd. dirs. Nassau County Med. Soc. Aux., 1955-91, pres. 1961-62, pres.-elect 1988-89; bd. dirs. PRO Arté Symphony Orch., Hofstra U., N.Y., 1955—, Nassau County Med. Soc. Alliance (hon. life. mem.), 1955—, Mercy Hosp., 1996-98; active Rosary Soc. St. Francis de Chantal, Salvation Army, Winthrop U. Hosp., St. Joseph's Roman Cath. Ch., 1971—; bd. dirs. Mercy Hosp., 1996-98; organizer benefits various local hosps., charitable orgns., 1976—; organizer benefit fashion shows, 1955—; vol. tours of art studio, house and gardens Mercy Hosp., 1976, Salvation Army, 1981, Winthrop U. Hosp., 1982, Garden City Hist. Soc., 1983—; vol. benefit garden parties Mercy Hosp., 1977, Nassau Hosp., 1985; bd. dirs. Nassau County Med. Soc. Aux., 1955-2006, Mercy Hosp., 1996-98, com. mem., 1992-2005. Recipient Grumbacher award Am. Artist mag., 1978, Suburban Art League prize, Long Beach Mus., 1981, award Excellence in Oil, Township of Oyster Bay, 2004; Queens Borough scholar N.Y. Sch. Applied Design, 1939-42, Red Cross awards, 1974-2005, award of Excellence in Oil Town of Oyster Bay, 2004, Cert. of Honor Mus. Am. Art, 2005 Mem. Internat. Soc. Artists (finalist Foothills Mus. Colo.), South Shore Art League (bd. dirs. 1975-85, publicity chmn. 1982, 1st prize 1981), Artists Equity N.Y., Audubon Artists Assn., Ind.'s Art League, Art League L.I., L.I. Artists Alliance, Freeport Arts Coun., Garden City Hist. Soc. (life), L.I. Arts Coun. Clubs: Garden City Community Club Suburban Art League, LI Arts coun. of Freeport Village Art Club, Vaali-Visual Alliance of LI., Cherry Valley Golf Club. Roman Catholic. Avocations: flying, dance, reading. Office Phone: 516-741-6332.

JESSIE, SARAH ELROD, educational consultant; b. Murfreesboro, Tenn., Apr. 29, 1957; d. Granville Perry and Betty Jo Bradley Elrod; m. Michael Ray Jessie, Mar. 29, 2003; children: Marcus James Jackson, Ryan Cole. EdS, Mid. Tenn. State U., 2002. Instrnl. specialist for sci. Rutherford County Schools, Murfreesboro, Tenn., 1992—; ednl. cons. Self-employed, Murfreesboro, Tenn., 1998—; sci. cons. Abrams & Co. Publishers., Waterbury, Conn., 2003—. Pres. Beta Epsilon Chpt. of Delta Kappa Gamma, Murfreesboro, Tenn., 2002—04. Sec. Murfreesboro Soccer Club, Tenn., 1994—2004. Recipient Tchr. of Excellence, Tenn. State U., 1996, 1997, Grad. Student of the Yr., Mid. Tenn. State U., 2002. Mem.: NSTA, Delta Kappa Gamma (pres. 2002—04). Independent. Presbyn. Avocations: reading, gardening, sewing. Home: 1623 SE Broad Street Murfreesboro TN 37130 Office: Rutherford County Schools 6309 Lebanon Pike Murfreesboro TN 37129 Office Phone: 615-849-1634. Home Fax: 615-849-1634; Office Fax: 615-849-1634. Personal E-mail: jessies@rcs.k12.tn.us.

JESSUP, CATHARINE P., retired medical/surgical nurse; b. Reading, Pa., Nov. 20, 1935; d. H. Edward and Anna (Fick) Phillipson; m. Richard R. Jessup, Aug. 15, 1959; children: Elizabeth A. Nemeth, Rosalind M. Ebert, Joanne M. Moretz. Student, St. Peter's Hosp., New Brunswick, N.J.; BA, Rutger's U., 1977. Staff nurse King James Nursing Home, Somerset, N.J., 1973-80, St. Anne Villa, Convent Station, N.J., 1980-88; med.-surg. staff nurse Muhlenberg Regional Med. Ctr., Plainfield, N.J., 1988-91; with VA Hosp., Lebanon, Pa., 1992—96, ret., 1996. Instr. ARC; med.- surg. cons. in field, 1995—. Vol. Hurricane Andrew relief efforts W. Lawn United Meth. Women, 1993—94; vol. mission trips Okla. Cherokee Nation. Recipient Ambassador award Muhlenberg Regional Med. Ctr., 1989, Florence Nightingale award Lebanon VA Hosp., 1993, Special Recognition for Leadership in Cmty. Svcs. award Am. Businesswomen's Assn., 1996.

JESSUP, CONSTANCE M., music educator; b. Niagara Falls, N.Y., Nov. 22, 1925; BM, Oberlin Conservatory, 1948; postgrad., Tanglewood Inst., Mass., 1965, Westminster Choir Coll., Princeton, N.J., N.Y. State U. Pvt. studio for piano and voice, Poughkeepsie, N.Y., 1952-82; music educator adult edn., Poughkeepsie, 1955-57, Regina Coeli Sch., Hyde Park, N.Y., 1960-63; choir dir. Holy Trinity Ch., Poughkeepsie, N.Y.; pvt. studio Royal Palm Beach, Fla., 1982-98, Raleigh, 1998-99. Asst. condr., soloist Cmty. Mixed Chorus, Poughkeepsie, 1955-65; soloist, bd. dirs. Hudson Valley Opera, Poughkeepsie, 1962-70; workshop clinician Fla. State Music Tchrs. Conv., 1988. Historian, editor: Reserch Music Transformations, 1983; performer compositions of Charles Gilbert Spross. Mem. Music Tchrs. Nat. Assn. (cert.), Nat. Assn. Tchrs. Singing (founder, pres. Intracoastal chpt. 1996-98, mem. N.C. chpt.), Sonneck Soc. Am. Music, Raleigh Piano Tchrs. Assn.

JESSUP, JAN AMIS, arts volunteer, writer; b. Chgo., Aug. 10, 1927; d. Herman Harvey and Anita (Lincoln) Sinako; m. Everett Orme Amis, Dec. 20, 1970 (dec. Nov. 1981); m. Joe Lee Jessup, Apr. 16, 1989. BA, U. Minn., 1948; postgrad., Rutgers U., 1969-70. Bd. dirs., mem. exec. com. Broward Ctr. Performing Arts Pacers, Ft. Lauderdale, Fla., 1985—88, pres., 1987—88; spkr. U. Internat. Bus., Beijing, 1985; v.p. sec. treas. Leading Edge Design Assoc., LLC. Mem. beautification com. Lighthouse Point, Fla., 1978—89, sec. beautification com., 1988—91; bd. govs. Fla. Philharm. Orch., 1981—98, v.p. representing all affiliates, 1985—87, 1992, 1994—96, exec. com., 1989—93, v.p. individual giving, 1991—92, Boca Raton bd. dirs., 1994—2002, chmn. affiliate com., 1994—95; rep. Fla. Art Orgns., 1987—88; bd. dirs. Archways, Ft. Lauderdale, 1987—91, Fla. Grand Opera, 1993—, Symphony of the Ams., 2004—, Master Chorale South Fla., 2004—; trustee Miami City Ballet, 1991—94, Harid Conservatory, 1997—; adv. bd. Guild of the Palm Beaches, Fla., 1994—95; founding pres. Harid Guild, 1997—99; program com. Boca Raton Ctr. for Arts, 2002—05; founding pres. symphony soc. Symphony of the America's Soc., 2004—; bd. advs. Youth Automotive Tng. Corps, 2004—; leadership coun. Boca Raton Philharmonic Symphonia; v.p. Leading Edge Design Assocs., 2006—. Mem.: Symphony Am. Soc. (pres. 2004—06), Univ. Club of Washington, Royal Dames Cancer Rsch. (trustee 1995—97), Opera Soc. (sec. 1986—87, bd. dirs. 1986—, v.p. pub. rels. 1987—88), Ft. Lauderdale Philharm. (bd. dirs. 1986—2003), Royal Palm Dinner Theatre (bd. dirs. 1998—2000), Gold Coast Jazz Soc. (bd. dirs. 1992—98, v.p. 1994—98), The Opus Soc. (chmn. 1981—85, bd. dirs., mem. exec. com. 1981—96, pres. 1989—93), Am. Symphony Orch. League (bd. dirs. 1998—, liaison and com. mem. Nat. Youth Orch. Festival 2000 Com. 2000—01), Internat. Game Fish Assn. (adv. coun. 2001—), Nat. Soc. Arts and Letters, Am. Symphony Orch. League Vol. Coun. (sec. 1986—87, bd. dirs. 1986—92, v.p. 1987—88, vice chmn. 1989—90, pres. 1989—90, advisor 1990—91, assoc. Resource Devel. Inst. 1996—98), Harvard Club NY, Centre For The Arts (program com. 2002—04), Ocean Reef Club, Sea Grape Garden Club (past pres.), Royal Palm Yacht and Country Club Women's Club, Boca Raton Resort and Club. Republican. Avocations: music, boating, fishing, writing, bridge. Home: 133 Coconut Palm Rd Boca Raton FL 33432-7975 Office Phone: 561-338-6572. Personal E-mail: janjessup@aol.com, amisj@bellsouth.net.

JESTER, NADINE ANDERSON, music educator, elementary school educator; d. James Edward and Corinne Echols Anderson; m. Dennis Lyle Jester, Dec. 29, 1973. AA in Music Edn., Palm Beach Jr. Coll., Lake Worth, Fla., 1971; BA in Music Edn., Barry U., Miami Shores, Fla., 1973. Music tchr. Mirror Lake Elem. Sch., Plantation, Fla., 1974—78, Dillard Traditional Sch., Fort Lauderdale, Fla., 1978—80, Nova Blanche Forman Elem., Davie, Fla., 1980—96, Indian Trace Elem. Sch., Weston, Fla., 1996—97, Watkins Elem. Magnet Sch., Pembroke Park, Fla., 1997—. Choir mem. Plantation United Meth. Ch., 1990—2006. Scholar, Barry Coll./U., 1971—73. Mem.: Family Motor Coach Assn. Avocations: singing, RV travel, swimming. Office Phone: 754-323-7800.

JETT, JOAN (JOAN LARKIN), musician; b. Phila., Sept. 22, 1960; Guitarist, vocalist The Runaways, 1975—79, Joan Jett & the Blackhearts, 1981—; signed with Mercury Records, 1976. Musician (with The Runaways): (albums) The Runaways, 1976, Queens of Noise, 1977, Live in Japan, 1977, Waitin' For The Night, 1977, Little Lost Girls, 1981, I Love Playing With Fire, 1982, And Now.The Runaways, 1978, Flaming Schoolgirls, 1980, Best Of The Runaways, 1987, Born To Be Bad, 1993, Neon Angels, 1991, The Runaways featuring Joan Jett and Lita Ford, 1998; musician: Joan Jett, 1981, Bad Reputation, 1981, I Love Rock 'n' Roll, 1981, Album, 1983, Glorious Results Of A Misspent Youth, 1984, I Need Someone, 1984, Good Music, 1986, Up Your Alley, 1988, Hit List, 1990, Notorious, 1991, Flashback, 1993, Do You Wanna Touch Me, 1993, Pure & Simple, 1994, Fit To Be Tied: Great Hits, 1997, Fetish, 1999, Naked, 2004; prodr.(by The Germs): (album) G.I.; co-author: (songs) House of Fire performed by Alice Cooper on album Trash, 1989; actor: (films) Light of Day, 1987, Talking About the Weather, 1994, Boogie Boy, 1997, By Crook or By Hook, 2001, The Sweet Life, 2003, (guest appearances): (TV series) Highlander, 1992, Walker, Texas Ranger, 2000,: (Broadway plays) The Rocky Horror Picture Show, 2001. Nominee Grammy award for best rock performance by a group for single I Hate Myself for Loving You, 1989. Office: Blackheart Records 636 Broadway New York NY 10012

JEVICKY, MARGO K., secondary school educator; b. Tuscola, Ill. d. Roland and Ann Smith; m. Ed Jevicky; children: Eddie, Matthew, Michael. BA, Valparaiso U., Ind., 1978; MEd, U. Ark., Monticello, 1999. Cert. tchr. NJ, 2005. Tchr. Scotland Sch., Ark., 1995—2006, Clinton Schs., Ark., 2005—. Class sponsor Scotland Sch., Ark., 1995—2005, dir. of sch. play, 1995—2005, sponsor of Christian student orgn., 1995—, chairperson of literacy com., 2000—, advisor for sch. newspaper, 2001—03; sponsor for ann. Washintong D.C. trip Faulkner County Schs./Am. Student Travel, Greenbrier, Ark., 1997—99; sponsor of knitting club Clinton Sch., Ark., 2005—. Servant's team Christian Motorcyclists Assn., Hatfield, Ark., 2004—06. Grant for grad. studies on the Holocaust, Israel, and the Arab States, Ark. Humanities Coun., 1997, grant for Ark. History Summer Inst., 2000, grant for Ea. European studies, Fulbright Hays Group Projects Abroad, 1998, grant for grad. studies on Islam in West Africa, NEH, 1999. Mem.: NEA, Ark. Edn. Assn., Ark. Reading Assn., Internat. Reading Assn., Pi Lambda Theta. Avocations: writing poetry, travel, knitting, reading. Home: 307 Banister Rd Greenbrier AR 72058 Office: Clinton HS 849 Edd St Clinton AR 72031 Office Phone: 501-745-2450. Personal E-mail: jevicky@cyberback.com.

JEWEL, (JEWEL KILCHER), folk singer, songwriter; b. Payson, Utah, May 23, 1974; d. Lenedra Carroll and Atz Kilcher. Grad., Interlochen Arts Acad., Mich., 1992. Co-founder/owner Magic Lantern Entertainment, 2002—. Musician: (albums) Pieces of You, 1995, Spirit, 1998, Joy: A Holiday Collection, 1999, This Way, 2001, 0304, 2003, Goodbye Alice in Wonderland, 2006, (singles) Woman to Woman, 1994, For the Last Time, 1995, Who Will Save Your Soul, 1996, (performs on soundtracks) I Shot Andy Warhol, 1996, The Craft, 1996, Phenomenon, 1996, Wizard of Oz in Concert: Dreams Come True, 1996, Batman & Robin, 1997, Ride with the Devil, 1999, Life or Something Like It, 2002, Sweet Home Alabama, 2002; actor: (films) Ride With the Devil, 1999; author: (book of poetry) A Night Without Armor, 1998, (memoir) Chasing Down the Dawn, 2000. Co-founder Higher Ground for Humanity, 1998—. Recipient Am. Music Award for Favorite Pop/Rock New Artist, 1997.

JEWELL, LINDA L., ambassador; b. Little Rock; married; 2 children. B, Yale U.; MA in Internat. Pub. Policy, Johns Hopkins U. Sch. Adv. Internat. Studies. With Prentice-Hall, Inc.; joined Fgn. Svc. US Dept. State, 1976, ednl. exchanges officer Jakarta, Indonesia, economics program officer Mexico City, press attaché New Delhi, Warsaw, dep. dir., Office We. Hemisphere Affairs, US Info. Agy. Washington, 1996—97, dir., Office We. Hemisphere Affairs, US Info. Agy., 1997—99, dep. chief of mission, US Embassy San Jose, Costa Rica, 1999—2002, dir. Office Policy Planning and Coordination Washington, dep. asst. sec. of state, Bur. Western Hemisphere Affairs, Amb. to Ecuador Quito, 2005—. Mailing: US Dept State 3420 Quito Pl Washington DC 20521-3420

JEWELL, VANESSA YODER, surgical physician's assistant; b. June 19, 1956; BMS, Alderson Broaddus Coll., Phillipi, W.Va., 1978; MHA, Ctrl. Mich. U., 1986. Physician asst. thoracic surgery Bay Pines VAMC, Fla., 1987—; asst. clin. prof. of health care svc. George Washington P.A. program, Washington, 1996—; surgical preceptor U. Fla. P.A. program, Gainesville, 1990—; asst. clin. prof. physician asst. program South U., Savannah, Ga., 1999—. Instr. water safety ARC, 1972-90; bd. dirs. (event planner) Gifted Assn. Pinellas Co., 1995-98; various dist. level. positions West. Ctrl. Fla. coun. Boy Scouts Am., 1989-98. Office: 10000 Bay Pines Blvd Surg Svc-112 Bay Pines FL 33744 Office Phone: 727-398-6661 ext. 5203. E-mail: Vanessa.Jewell@Med.Va.gov.

JEWELL-SHERMAN, DEBORAH, school system administrator; m. Cornelius Sherman; 2 stepchildren. EdB, NYU, 1976; EdM, Kean U., 1981, Harvard U., 1992, EdD, 1995. Former tchr., N.Y.C., Newark, Fairfax County, Va., former guidance counselor, asst. prin., prin.; prin. Hampton, Va., 1989—92; asst. supt. Virginia Beach, Va., 1992—95; assoc. supt. Richmond, Va., 1995—2002; supt., 2002—. Office: Richmond Pub Schs 301 N 9th St Richmond VA 23219

JEWETT, MARY (BETSY) ELIZABETH, artist, conservationist; b. Spokane, Wash., Aug. 13, 1954; d. George Frederick and Lucille Winifred (McIntyre) Jewett; m. David Kemp Coombs, Dec. 8, 1984 (div. Mar. 2003); children: Sarah Elizabeth, David Frederick; m. Richard T, Gill, Jan. 02, 2006. AB in Biology, Dartmouth Coll., 1976; MES, MPPM, Yale U., 1982; postgrad., Corcoran Sch. Art, 1982-83. Devel. field coord. Nature Conservancy, Arlington, Va., 1977-79; intern U.S. Nat. Pk. Svc., Rocky Mountain Nat. Pk., 1980; bus. analyst Weyerhauser Co., Tacoma, 1981; program dir. Am. Farmland Trust, Washington, 1982-83; cons. Calif. Acad. Scis., San Francisco, 1984; project coord. EPA, San Francisco, 1985-86; bd. v.p. Coombs Mfg. Co., 1996—2003. Bd. dirs. World Wildlife Fund, Washington, 1983-89, No. Lights Inst., Missoula, Mont., 1983-93; bd. dirs. Mobius, 2003—, chmn. design com.; bd. dirs. Inland Northwest Land Trust, Spokane, 1991-2004, treas., 1991-97, chmn. land protection com., 1998-2004. Mem. Spokane Club. Avocations: gardening, photography, skiing, hiking.

JEYNES, MARY KAY, college dean; b. Miami, Fla., Oct. 31, 1941; d. Nasrallah and Martha Demetry; m. Paul Jeynes, Sept. 30, 1978. BS, Fla. State U., 1963. Program dir. Orange County YMCA, Orlando, Fla., 1964-69, Ea. Queens YMCA, Belrose, N.Y., 1970-73; regional coord. N.Y. State Park and Recreation Commn., N.Y.C., 1974-77; dir. health, fitness and recreation YWCA of N.Y.C., 1978-79; dean continuing edn., dir. spl. events Marymount Manhattan Coll., N.Y.C., 1980—2005, dir. spl. events, 2005—. Mem.: Manhattan (N.Y.) C. of C. (hon.; pres. 1996—97, chmn. bd. dirs. 1998—2002). Office: Marymount Manhattan Coll 221 E 71st St New York NY 10021-4532

JHABVALA, RUTH PRAWER, writer; b. Cologne, Germany, May 7, 1927; lived in India, 1951-75; came to U.S., 1975; d. Marcus and Eleonora (Cohn) Prawer; m. Cyrus S. H. Jhabvala, 1951; 3 children. MA, London U., 1951, DLitt (hon.), 1986, LHD (hon.), 1995, D Arts (hon.), 1996. Author: To Whom She Will, 1955, The Nature of Passion, 1956, Esmond in India, 1957, The Householder, 1960, Get Ready for Battle, 1962, A Backward Place, 1965, A New Dominion, 1972, Heat and Dust, 1975 (Booker award for fiction Nat. Book League 1975), In Search of Love and Beauty, 1983, Three Continents, 1987, Poet and Dancer, 1993, Shards of Memory, 1995; (short story collections) Like Birds, Like Fishes and Other Stories, 1964, A Stronger Climate: Nine Stories, 1968, An Experience of India, 1971, How I Became a Holy Mother and Other Stories, 1976, Out of India: Selected Stories, 1986, East Into Upper East, 1998, My Nine Lives, 2004; (film scripts) The

Householder, 1963; (with James Ivory), Shakespeare Wallah, 1965, The Guru, 1968, Bombay Talkie, 1970, Autobiography of a Princess, 1975, Roseland, 1977, Hullabaloo over Georgie and Bonnie's Pictures, 1978, The Europeans, 1979, Jane Austen in Manhattan, 1980, Quartet, 1981, Heat and Dust, 1983, The Bostonians, 1984, A Room With a View, 1986 (Writers Guild of Am. award for best adapted screeplay 1986, Acad. award for best adapted screenplay 1986); (with John Schlesinger) Madame Sousatzka, 1988, Mr. and Mrs. Bridge, 1990, Howards End, 1992 (Acad. award for best adapted screenplay 1992), Remains of the Day, 1993 (Acad. award nomination for best adapted screenplay 1993), Jefferson in Paris, 1995, Surviving Picasso, 1996; (with James Ivory) A Soldier's Daughter Never Cries, 1998, The Golden Bowl, 2000. Decorated comdr. Brit. Empire; Guggenheim fellow, 1976; Neil Gunn. Internat. fellow, 1979; MacArthur Found. fellow, 1984-89. Home: 400 E 52d St New York NY 10022-6404

JIBBEN, LAURA ANN, state agency administrator; b. Peoria, Ill., Oct. 1, 1949; d. Charles Otto and Dorothy Lee (Skaggs) Becker; m. Michael Eugene Hagan, July 7, 1967 (div. Apr. 1972); m. Louis C. Jibben, July 14, 1972. BA in Criminal Justice, Sangamon State U., 1984; MBA, Northwestern U., 1990. Asst. to chief of adminstrn. Ill. Dept. Corrections, Springfield, 1974-77, exec. asst. to dir., 1977-80, dep. dir., 1980-81; mgr. toll services Ill. Tollway Dept., Oak Brook, 1981-86; chief adminstrv. officer Regional Transp. Authority, Chgo., 1986-90, fund mgr. loss financing plan, 1987-90, also, chmn. pension trust, exec. dir., 1990-96; v.p., gen. mgr. MTA, Inc., Chgo., 1996-99; ptnr. Hanson Engrs., Inc., Oak Brook, Ill., 1999-2000; sr. project mgr., cons. mgmt. Alfred Benesch & Co., 2000—02, v.p., 2002—. Cons. labor studies Sangamon State U., Springfield, 1981; bd. dirs. Chgo. Found. for Women. Mem. surface tranps. adv. panel U. Ill., 1997—2000; apptd. mem. transp. adv. bd. City of Naperville, 1988—90; bd. dirs. Family Shelter Svcs., 1990—91; bd. dirs., chair devel. com. Govt. Assistance Program, 1997—2000, sec. bd., 1999; mem. nat. adv. bd. Women's Transp. Seminar, 1996—2004; mem. Peoria Women's Fund Grants Com., 2003—; mem. Midwest Traffic Conf. program com. Bradley U., 2002—; acting pres. Ctrl. Ill. chpt. WTS, 2004—, pres., 2004—05. Recipient Appreciation award VFW, Chgo., 1983, award Ill. State Toll Hwy. Authority, 1986; named Woman of Yr., Nat. Women's Transp. Seminar, 1991, AAUW, 1991. Mem. NAFE, Women's Transp. Seminar (Woman of Yr. award Chgo. chpt. 1991, Nat. Woman of Yr. 1991), Beta Sigma Phi (treas., v.p., corr. sec. Naperville and Easton, Ill. chpts.), Lambda Alpha. Avocations: reading, jogging, gardening, golf. Office: Alfred Benesch & Co 205 N Michigan Ave Ste 2400 Chicago IL 60601 Office Phone: 312-565-0450. Business E-Mail: ljibben@benesch.com.

JIMENEZ, BETTIE EILEEN, retired small business owner; b. LaCygne, Kans., June 8, 1932; d. William Albert and Ruby Faye (Cline) Montee; m. William R. Bradley, Aug. 21, 1947 (div. Sept. 1950); 1 child, Shirley; m. J.P. Jimenez, Feb. 20, 1951 (div. Nov. 1978); children: Pamela, Joe Jr., Robin Michelle. Student, Ft. Scott Jr. Coll., Paola, Kans., 1979-81. Reporter LaCygne Jour., 1943-45; union recorder I.L.G.W.U., Paola, 1956-57; mgr. Estes Metalcraft, Osawatomie, Kans., 1977-82; owner El Rey Tavern, Osawatomie, 1980-95; ret., 1995; with Estes Metalcraft, 2002—05. Home: 4902 Raytown Rd Sp 175 Kansas City MO 64133

JIMENEZ, JOSEPHINE SANTOS, portfolio manager; b. Lucena, Quezon, Philippines, June 6, 1954; came to U.S., 1972; d. Jose Hirang and Virginia Villapando (Santos) J. BS, NYU, 1979; MS, MIT, 1981. Securities analyst Mass. Mut. Life Ins. Co., Springfield, 1982-83; investment officer One Fed. Asset Mgmt., Boston, 1984-87; sr. analyst, portfolio mgr. Emerging Markets Investors Corp., Washington, 1988-91; mng. dir., sr. portfolio mgr. Montgomery Asset Mgmt., San Francisco, 1991—2003, Wells Capital Mgmt., San Francisco, 2003—. Trustee M.I.T. Corp., 1996—2001. Mem. Inst. Chartered Fin. Analysts. Office: Wells Capital Mgmt 525 Market St 10/F San Francisco CA 94105 Office Phone: 415-396-5679. E-mail: jimenezj@wellscap.com.

JIMENEZ, KATHRYN FISHER, nurse, educator; b. Indiana, Pa., Nov. 23, 1948; d. Homer Leonard Fisher and Ruth Maxine (Foltz) Barclay; m. Adalberto Beltran Jimenez, Apr. 24, 1971; 1 child, Adalberto Jr. AAS in Nursing, Borough Manhattan C.C., 1982. RN, N.Y.; cert. BCLS Am. Heart Assn. Dietary cons. Indiana Hosp., 1966-68; LPN Brookdale Hosp. Med. Ctr., Bklyn., 1970-79, staff nurse, 1982—, asst. head nurse diabetes edn., 1990—. Presenter workshops on diabetes mgmt.; presenter at profl. confs. Mem. Am. Assn. Diabetes Educators (cert.), Am. Diabetes Assn. Office: Brookdale Hosp Med Ctr 1 Brookdale Plz Brooklyn NY 11212-3139

JIMENEZ, MERCY, corporate financial executive; BA, Northwestern U.; MBA, Harvard Grad. Sch. Bus. Mgr. fin. product lines Citigroup-Global Payments Products; v.p. corp. devel. Chase Manhattan Mortgage Corp., Tampa, Fla., 1994—96; joined Fannie Mae, 1996, v.p. corp. devel. Wash., DC, 1996, v.p. sr. products, 1998, v.p. mktg. Southwestern region Dallas, 2000, sr. v.p. Southwestern region, 2000—02, sr. v.p. bus. and product devel., 2002—. Bd. dirs. Nat. Assn. Hispanic Real Estate Profl., Tex. Mortgage Bankers Assn., Atlantic Coun. Office: Two Galleria Tower 13455 Noel Rd Ste 600 Dallas TX 75240-5003 Office Phone: 972-773-7444.

JIMMAR, D'ANN, elementary school educator, educational consultant; b. Leighton, Ala., Dec. 10, 1942; d. Harry D. Qualls and Lillian Jimmar. BS in Elem. Edn., Ala. A&M U., Normal, 1965, MS in Urban Studies, 1973; PhD in Higher Edn., Iowa State U., Ames, 1986. Elem. tchr. Limestone County Bd. Edn., Athens, Ala., 1966-68, Huntsville City Bd. Edn., Ala., 1968-71; instr. dept. cmty. planning and urban studies Ala. A&M U., Huntsville, Ala., 1973-78; rsch. asst. dept. sociology and anthropology Iowa State U., Ames, Iowa, 1978-79, rsch. aide, 1980-81, 82-83; ednl. aide, substitute tchr. Ames Cmty. Sch. Dist., Iowa, 1983-86; coord. practicums Nova U., Ft. Lauderdale, Fla., 1986-87; tchr. Downtown Adult Edn. Ctr., Ft. Lauderdale, Fla., 1987-88, Apollo Mid. Sch., Hollywood, Fla., 1988-89, Greenview Elem. Sch., Columbia, SC, 1989-91; dir. rsch. edn. NuWAE Ent., Houston, 1991-92; cosmetic cons., counter mgr. Elizabeth Arden Foley's/May Co., 1992-99; resource cons. RCI, Inc., Tex. So. U., 1999-2000; ednl. cons. Houston, 2000—. Mem. editl. bd., cons. editor Rsch. Inst. for Integrative Brain Studies, Omaha and N.Y.C., 2003—. Mem. editl. bd, cons. editor Rsch. Inst. for Integrative Brain Studies, 2003—. Sec.-treas. Ames Tenant Landlord Svcs., 1982-83, bd. dirs. 1982-, 83, 84-85, chmn., 1984-85. Recipient svc. award Local Govt. Study Commn., Huntsville, 1972, Ms. Alumni award Ala. A&M U., 1978. Mem. ASCD, Ala. A&M U. Alumni Assn. (chaplain 1977-78), Phi Delta Kappa, Delta Sigma Theta. Home: 2056 Antoine Dr # 413 Houston TX 77055-1850 Office Phone: 713-812-7196.

JINDRA, CHRISTINE, editor; b. Cleve., Sept. 18, 1947; d. Lad Joseph and Ann Frances (Makar) J.; m. Peter J. Junkin, Aug. 1, 1970 (div. Dec. 1987); children: William Patrick, Michael Lad. BS in Journalsim, Ohio State U., 1969. City reporter Buffalo News, 1969-70; metro reporter Plain Dealer, Cleve., 1970-82, assignment editor, nat. reporter, 1982-84, state editor, 1984-86, metro editor, 1986-88, feature editor, 1988-92, asst. mng. editor, 1992-2001, Sunday editor, 2001—. Mem.: Women's Cmty. Found., Women's City Club. Avocations: skiing, gardening, travel, cooking. Office: Plain Dealer 1801 Superior Ave E Cleveland OH 44114-2198 Office Phone: 216-999-4839. E-mail: cjindra@plaind.com.

JIRAVA, CARRIE, music educator; d. Curtis and Ardis Christianson; m. Matt Jirava, Aug. 2, 2002; children: Toby Bjerklie, Karli, Evan. BA in Music Edn., U. Mary, Bismarck, ND, 1999. K-12 music tchr. Gackle (ND)-Streeter Pub. Sch., 2000—02; half time music tchr. Dilworth (Minn.)-Glyndon-Felton Pub. Sch., 2002—03; vocal music tchr., sch. to work coord. Waubun (Minn.)-Ogema-White Earth Pub. Sch., 2002—. Student coun. advisor Waubun HS, 2003—, musical co-dir., bldg. leadership team mem., 2005—. Dir.: cmty. choir. Blood dr. co-coord. Waubun HS Student Coun., 2003—06. Named MTNA State Vocal winner, 1997; fellow, Fla. State U., 1999. Mem.: NEA, Edn. Minn., WOWE Local Edn. Assn. Avocations: bicycling, accompanyist, reading. Office Phone: 218-473-6119.

JIROVEC, MARY ANN, music educator; b. Milw., Sept. 6, 1952; d. John Frank and Irene Doris (Spychalski) J. BFA, U. Wis., Milw., 1974, MS in Mus. Edn., 1978. Music tchr. grades 5-12 Harlem (Mont.) Pub. Schs., 1974-76; music tchr. grades 5-9 West Allis (Wis.) Sch. Dist., 1976-89, 91-93; O.M. summer ministry team Ukraine and Poland, 1992; music tchr. West Allis (Wis.) Sch. Dist., 1995—; overseas refugee worker Operation Mobilisation, Austria, Poland, Romania, Czech Republic, 1989-90; secondary English tchr. Szczecinek (Poland) Schs., 1994-95. Participant tchr. exch., Novosibirsk, Russia, 1996, Wales/Poland cultural exch. program, 1998; English tchr. Beijing Chaoyang Edn. Coll., China, summer 2004, 05, 06; clarinet instr. Cardinal Stritch U., 2005—. Music and drama teams, English workshops, Int. Messengers, Operation Mobilization local Polish chs., Ukraine, Czech Republic, 1989—, Poland summer campaign coord., 1990; spl. ministry team leader, Yucatan, Mex., 1999, 2001; vacation bible sch. leader, 2001-03; coord., praise leader Milw. March for Jesus, 1992-94, 1996-2001; musician Bay Players, Whitefish Bay, Patio Players, Menomonee Falls. U. Wis. Grad. Music grantee, 1976-77. Mem.: Wis. Contemporary Music Forum (sec. 1977), Knighwind Ensemble, Delta Omicron (pres. Wis. chpt. 1973—74), Phi Kappa Phi. Avocations: international travel, cultural events, reading, community theater musicals. Home: 6183 W Howard Ave #14 Greenfield WI 53220

JITOMIRSKAYA, SVETLANA, mathematics professor; b. Kharkov, Ukraine, June 4, 1966; US citizen; married; 3 children. BS, MS in Math., summa cum laude, Moscow State U., 1987, PhD in Math., 1991. Researcher Internat. Inst. of Earthquake Prediction Theory and Math. Geophysics, Moscow, 1990—; lectr. U. Calif., Irvine, 1991—92, vis. asst. prof., 1992—94, asst. prof., 1994—97, assoc. prof., 1997—2000, prof., dept. math., 2000—; vis. asst. prof. Caltech, 1996. Invited prof. CPT, CNRS, Marseille, 1998; rsch. prof. Math. Sciences Rsch. Inst., 2003; lectr. in field. Contbr. articles in profl. jours.; reviewer (for several profl. jours.). Alfred P. Sloan Rsch. Fellowship, 1996—2000. Mem.: Am. Math. Soc. (editl. bd. com. 2002—05, Ruth Lyttle Satter prize in Math. 2005). Office: U Calif Dept Math 243 Multipurpose Science and Technology Irvine CA 92697-3221 Office Phone: 949-824-3221. Office Fax: 949-824-7993. Business E-Mail: szhitomi@math.uci.edu.*

JOACHIM, PEGGY L., secondary school educator; b. Berwyn, Ill., Jan. 16, 1942; d. Roy Lee and Helen Lucille (Davis) Wilborn; m. James A. Olson, Aug. 31, 1963 (div. 1995); children: Douglas, Geoffrey A.; m. Peter Joachim, Nov. 24, 1996. BS Math., No. Ill. U., 1965, MS Edn., 1988. Tchr. math. Stillman Valley HS, Ill., 1979-88, Byron Schs., Ill., 1965—69, 1988—2000; dir. edn. Ombudsman Alternative Sch., 2000—01; math tchr. Rockford Luth. HS, 2001—04; tchr. Sylvan Learning Ctr., 2000—. City clk. Stillman Valley, 1974-78. New Mast Hons. Tchr. NSF, NASA, NSTA, UT, Cleve., 1985. Mem. Nat. Coun. Tchrs. Math., Ill. Coun. Tchrs. Math., No. Ill. Assn. Tchrs. Math. (bd. dirs., pres. 1991-92), Math. Assn. Am. Avocations: reading, golf, exercise. Home: 4401 Centerville Rd Rockford IL 61102-4411

JOBE, KIMBERLY R., art educator; b. Waynesville, Mo., July 21, 1967; d. Jack W. Smith and Loretta K. Simily; m. Douglas E. Jobe, July 22, 2000; children: Allie Marie, Steven E., Amanda K., Krista L. BS in Elem. and Early Childhood Edn., Ctrl. Mo. State U., Warrensburg, 1991, MS in Reading, 1998. Title i communication arts tchr. St. Clair (Mo.) R-13 Sch. Dist., 1994—. Sponsor St. Clair Jr. High Builders Club, 1997—. Mem.: Internat. Reading Assn., Kiwanis (pres. St. Clair 2005—06, 2006—), Kappa Gama Rho. Lutheran. Avocations: reading, gardening. Office: Edgar L Murray Elem 1044 High School Dr Saint Clair MO 63077 Office Phone: 636-629-1121. Business E-Mail: kjobe@stclair.k12.mo.us.

JOBES, JANET SUE, elementary school educator; b. Scottsbluff, Nebr. m. Stewart Keith Jobes; children: Maggie, Brook. AA, Nebr. Western Coll., Scottsbluff, 1976; BS, U. Nebr., Lincoln, 1978; MEd, Chadron State Coll., Nebr., 1980; MS in Reading, U. Nebr., Kearney, 2001. Cert. elem. tchr. K-8, K-12 phys. edn. Health, phys. edn. tchr. Bayard Pub. Schs., Nebr., 1978—79; grad. asst. Chadron State Coll., 1979—80; tchr. elem. phys. edn. Hastings Pub. Schs., 1980, tchr. phys. edn., 1980—82; tchr. aide Kearney Pub. Schs., Nebr., 1982—83; substitute tchr. Polk County Schs., Stromsburg, Nebr., 1983—90; substitute/aide Gering/Scottsbluff Schs., 1990—94; elem. reading specialist Grand Island Schs., Grand Island, Nebr., 1994—. Com. chmn. Sch. Improvement Team, Grand Island, 1996—2005, reading chmn., 2005—. Mem., treas. Sr. High Athletic Booster Bd., Grand Island, 2003—06; mem. Sr. High Fine Arts Booster Bd., Grand Island, 2002—; co-chair Sr. High Post Prom, Grand Island, 2006. Mem.: Internat. Reading Assn., Alpha Delta Kappa. Methodist. Avocations: reading, sewing, bicycling, swimming. Office: Grand Island Public Schools 2013 N Oak St Grand Island NE 68803

JOCHUM, PAM, state representative; b. Dubuque, Iowa, Sept. 26, 1954; AA, BA, Loras Coll. Pub. info. and mktg. dir. Loras Coll.; instr. N.E. Iowa C.C.; mem. Iowa Ho. Reps., Des Moines, 1993—, mem. various coms. including judiciary, mem. state govt. ways and means com. Chair Alzheimer Memory Walk, CROP Walk; del. Dem. Nat. Conv., 1980, floor whip, 1984; chair Dubuque County Dem. Ctrl. Com., 1982; statewide co-chair U.S. Senator Tom Harkin's Re-Election Com.; former bd. dirs. Dubuque County Assn. for Retarded Citizens, Dubuque County Compensation Bd., Loras Coll. Arts and Lectr. Series, Nat. Cath. Basketball Tournament, Sacred Heart Cath. Ch., Women's Recreation Assn., Mississippi Valley Promise, LWV. Democrat. Office: State Capitol East 12th and Grand Des Moines IA 50319 also: 2368 Jackson St Dubuque IA 52001 E-mail: pam.jochum@legis.state.ia.us.

JOCHUM, VERONICA, pianist; b. Berlin; d. Eugen and Maria (Montz) J.; m. Wilhelm V. von Moltke, Nov. 15, 1961. MusM, Staatliche Musikhochschule, Munich, 1955, Concert Diploma, 1957; pvt. study with, Edwin Fischer, Josef Benvenuti, 1958—59, Rudolf Serkin, Phila., 1959—61. Faculty Settlement Sch. Music, Phila., 1959-61, New Eng. Conservatory Music, Boston, 1965—, Berkshire Music Center, Tanglewood, 1974, Radcliffe Inst., Cambridge, Mass. Recs. with Laurel, Deutsche Grammophon, Philips, Golden Crest, Pro Arte, GM Recs., CRJ, Tahra recs., Tudor; Numerous tours, throughout N. and S. Am., Asia, Europe and, Africa; as soloist with world renowned orchs., including Boston Symphony, Balt. Symphony, London Philharmonic, Los Angeles Chamber Orch., London Symphony, Mpls. Symphony, Berlin, Hamburg and Munich Philharmonics, Bavarian and Bamberg Symphonies, Munich Chamber Orch., radio orchs. of Hamburg, Munich, and Frankfurt, Orch. Maggio Musicale, Florence, La Fenice Orch., Venice, RAI-Orch., Naples, Mozarteum Orch., Salzburg, Concertgebouw Orch., Amsterdam, The Hague Philharmonic, Venezuelan Symphony, Caracas, Jerusalem Symphony, others; appearances on radio, TV, and films, recitals in more than 50 countries on 4 continents; participant, Marlboro Music Festival, Montreux Festival, Bregenz Festival, Mecklenburg Festival, Festival de Vallonie (Belgium), Tanglewood, N.W. Bach Festival, Spokane, Ea. Music Festival, Chambermusic East. Bd. mem. Berkshire Inst. Theology and the Arts. Recipient cross Order of Merit (Germany); Bunting fellow Harvard U., 1996-97. Office: New Eng Conservatory Music 290 Huntington Ave Boston MA 02115-5018 Personal E-mail: veromusica@aol.com.

JOEL, KATIE (KATIE LEE JOEL, KATHERINE LEE), television personality; b. Huntington, W. Va., Sept. 1981; m. Billy Lee, Oct. 2, 2004. B in English and Journalism, Miami U., Ohio; studied a wide range culinary classes including a semester in Florence, Italy. Helped open Jeff and Eddy's Restaurant, Hamptons, 2003. Critic (TV series) George Hirsch: Living It UP! (PBS); contbr. "East End Girl", Hamptons Mag.; co-creater (culinary website) www.oliveandpeach.com, 2005, host (TV series) Top Chef (Bravo), 2006—.*

JOERSZ, FRAN WOODMANSEE, secondary school educator; b. Bismarck, N.D., Apr. 29, 1954; d. Joe G. and Winnie (McGillic) Woodmansee; m. Jon D. Joersz; children: Brett, Ben, Courtney. Student, Bismarck State Coll., 1972; BA in Edn., U. Wyo., 1975. Tchr. 3rd grade Deer Trail (Colo.) Pub. Sch., 1975-76; tchr. 8th grade remedial reading Mandan (N.D.) Jr. High Sch., 1976-78; tchr. title I reading Saxvik St. Mary's Grade Sch., Bismarck, 1979; tchr. 8th grade devel. reading Wachter Jr. High Sch., Bismarck, 1979-81; tchr. 7th grade devel. reading written and oral communications Hughes Jr. High Sch., Bismarck, 1981—. Bd. dirs. Rape Victim Adv. Program; founding bd. dirs. Our Kids Need to Know; state bd. dirs. Make A Wish Found. Recipient Milken award, 1994; named Edn. alumna of Yr., U. Wyo., 2003. Mem. PEO, N.D. Edn. Assn. (Tchr. of Yr. 1991, Profl. Courage award 1994), Internat. Reading Assn., Nat. Assn. Student Activity Advisers. Avocations: walking, reading, volleyball, writing, travel. Home: 520 N Mandan St Bismarck ND 58501-3748 Office: Horizon Mid Sch 500 Ash Coulee Dr Bismarck ND 58503 Office Phone: 701-221-3555. Business E-Mail: fran_joersz@educ8.org.

JOFEN, JEAN, foreign language educator; BA, Bklyn. Coll., 1943; MA, Brown U., 1945; PhD, Columbia U., 1960; MS, Yeshiva U., 1961. Cert. sch. psychologist, N.Y. Teaching fellow Brown U., 1943-44; lectr. adult edn. Bklyn. Coll., 1951-61; assoc. prof. Yeshiva U., N.Y.C., 1955-62; assoc. prof., chmn. dept. Germanic and Slavic langs. Bernard M. Baruch Coll., N.Y.C., 1962-77, prof., 1977—, chmn. dept. modern langs., 1977-83, chmn. dept. Germanic, Hebraic and Oriental langs., 1983—, bd. govs., 1973—. Mem. adv. bd. Jewish Studies CUNY, 1986; lectr., speaker various sci., civic and religious orgns. and socs. in U.S. and Europe; scholar abroad, Vienna, Austria, 1991. Author: A Linguistic Atlas of Eastern European Yiddish, 1964, rev. edit., 1967, Das letzte Geheimnis (in German), 1972, The Jewish Mystic in Kafka, 1987, (textbooks) Yiddish for Beginners, 1963, Yiddish Literature for Beginners, 1972, (with Y. Kerstein) Hebrew for Beginners, 1975, (with E. Mok) Chinese for Beginners, 1980; editor Elizabethan Concordance series: The Concordance of The Works of Christopher Marlowe, 1979, A Concordance to The Shakespeare Apocrypha, 3 Vols., 1987; Nat. Endowment for Humanities; assoc. editor Jour. Evolutionary Psychology; contbr. numerous articles to profl. jours. Recipient Nat. Jewish Culture Found. award, 1963, Kohut Found. award, 1966, Bernard M. Baruch Coll. medal for 35 yrs. svc., AAUW award, 1968, 69, others; fellow Inst. for Yiddish Lexicological Rsch. CUNY, 1963—; grantee Ford Found., 1970, Population Coun. Rockefeller Inst., 1970-71, Rsch. Found. CUNY, 1985, Lucius N. Littauer Found., 1986, Austrian Fed. Ministry for Sci. and Rsch., 1991. Fellow Jewish Acad. Arts and Scis.; mem. Am. Assn. Tchrs. German, MLA, AAUP, Am. Assn. Profs. Yiddish (pres.), Am. Psychol. Assn., Marlowe Soc. Am. (founder 1975, pres. 1975-84, organizer 1st. Internat. Congress in Eng. 1983), Mich. Acad. Arts and Scis., Acad. Scis. and Humanities CUNY, Sigma Alpha. Address: 409 Avenue I Brooklyn NY 11230-2619

JOFFE, BARBARA LYNNE, business transformation architect; b. Bklyn., Apr. 12, 1951; d. Lester L. and Julia (Schuelke) J.; 1 child, Nichole. BA, U. Oreg., 1975; MFA, U. Mont., 1982. Cert. project mgr. IBM; cert. project mgmt. profl. Project Mgmt. Inst. Applications engr., software developer So. Pacific Transp., San Francisco, 1986-93; computer fine artist Barbara Joffe Assocs., San Francisco, Englewood, Colo., 1988—; instr. computer graphics Ohlone Coll., Fremont, Calif., 1990-91; adv. programmer, project mgr.-client/server Integrated Sys. Solutions Corp./IBM Global Svcs. So. Pacific/Union Pacific Railroads, Denver, 1994-97; applications sys. mgr. IBM Global Svcs./CoBank, Greenwood Village, Colo., 1997-99; exec. project mgr. IBM/GM Web Hosting, 2000—01, IBM/Cendant, 2001—. Artwork included in exhibits at Calif. Crafts XIII, Crocker Art Mus., Sacramento, 1983, Rara Avis Gallery, Sacramento, 1984, Redding (Calif.) Mus. and Art Ctr., 1985, Euphrat Gallery, Cupertino, Calif., 1988, Computer Mus., Boston, 1989, Siggraph Traveling Art Shown, Europe and Australia, 1990, 91, 4th and 7th Nat. Computer Art Invitational, Cheney, Wash., 1991, 94, Visual Arts Mus., N.Y.C., 1994, 96, IBM Golden Circle, 1996. Recipient IBM Project Mgmt. Excellence award, 1998. Mem. Project Mgmt. Inst. (cert.), Assn. Computing Machinery. Avocations: art, gardening, hiking. Personal E-mail: joffeb@aol.com.

JOHANANOFF, PAMELA, jewelry designer, gemologist; b. Edinburg, Scotland, Oct. 17, 1964; came to the U.S., 1965; d. Samuel Cohen and Ann Merriman Johananoff. BA in Internat. Rels., Emory U., 1986; grad. gemologist, Gemol. Inst. am., 1993; MFA, Royal Soc. Art, Paris, 1997. Broker Shearson Lehman Hutton, Paris, 1986-89; market developer Comptoir Africain du Batiment, Paris, Tunis, Tunisia, 1989-92; ptnr. Ann Cline Art Objects, Little Rock, 1993-97; jewelry dir. Christie's Edn., Paris, 1997; owner PMJ Designs, Little Rock, Paris, 1997—. Mem. adv. bd. Piranese, N.Y.C., 1994—, French Friends Israeli Mus., Paris, 1998—. Bd. dirs. Jr. Guild, Paris, 1994—, G&P Found., N.Y.C., 1997—, Reps. Abroad, Paris, 1997—. Fellow Aspen Inst.; mem. Delta Delta Delta. Episcopalian. Avocations: art, tennis, horses, travel, gardening. Office: 4817 Country Club Blvd Little Rock AR 72207-4719

JOHANSEN, IRIS, writer; 2 children. Author: (novels) The Forever Dream, 1985, The Wind Dancer, 1991 (Rita award winner), Storm Winds, 1991, Reap the Wind, 1991, Golden Barbarian, 1992, Last Bridge Home, 1992, Tiger Prince, 1993, Magnificent Rogue, 1993, Beloved Scoundrel, 1994, Midnight Warrior, 1994, Dark Rider, 1995, Lion's Bride, 1996, Ugly Duckling, 1996, Long After Midnight, 1997, The Face of Deception, 1998, And Then You Die, 1998, Killing Game, 1999, The Search, 2000, Final Target, 2001, Body of Lies, 2002, No One to Trust, 2002, Dead Aim, 2003, Fatal Tide, 2003, Firestorm, 2004, Blind Alley, 2004 (NY Times and USA Today Bestseller lists), Countdown, 2005 (Publishers Weekly Hardover Bestseller list), On the Run, 2005, Delaney series, Killer Dreams, 2006, Stalemate, 2006, (novels) 34 books in Bantam Loveswept series. Recipient Career Achievement award, Romantic Times. Mailing: c/o Author Mail Bantam Dell Publ 1745 Broadway New York NY 10019 E-mail: mail@irisjohansen.com.

JOHANSEN, KAREN LEE, retired sales executive; b. Sheldon, Iowa, Dec. 5, 1945; d. Alvin Anthony and Marjory Gertrude (Kuiper) Eich; m. Pete Brunsting, May 15, 1964 (div. Dec. 1983); children: Jeffrey Brunsting, Keri Wallenstein; m. Alan Brockberg, Oct. 30, 1988 (div. Apr. 1991); m. Alan Johansen, Aug. 21, 1993. Student, Sioux Valley Hosp. Sch. Nsg., 1963-65; grad., S.D. Police Acad., 1978; postgrad., Phoenix Paralegal Inst., 1981-82. Owner Redwood Steak House and Lounge, White, S.D., 1975-76; dep. sheriff Brookings (S.D.) County Sheriff's Office, 1978-79; clk. of ct. City of Gillette, Wyo., 1980-82; child support enforcement officer Campbell County, Gillette, 1982-84; jud. asst. Wyo. Dist. Ct., Sheridan, 1984-85; office mgr. Felt & Martin Law Firm, Billings, Mont., 1985-87; owner paralegal svcs. office, Pipestone, Minn., 1987-89; dist. agt. Prudential Ins. Co. Am., Pipestone, 1989-91, sales mgr. Austin, Minn., 1991-93; mgr. S.W. Minn. Prudential Ins. Co., Worthington, Minn., 1993-94; cons. Aanenson Agy., Inc., Fulda, Slayton, Minn., 1994-95; estate planner, agt. Farm Bur. Ins. Co., Slayton, Minn., 1994-96, Prudential Ins., Slayton, Minn., 1996-97; ret. Asst. Campaign to Re-Elect Andy Steensma, Pipestone, 1990; mem. Ihlen (Minn.) City Coun., 1990; chair Brookings Summer Art Festival, 1976-79, chair, 1977-79, chair entertainment, 1976. Mem. Nat. Assn. Life Underwriters, Nat. Assn. Security Dealers. Democrat. Avocations: reading, travel, animals. Office Phone: 507-395-2131. E-mail: haneyho@iw.net.

JOHANSEN, RUTHANN KNECHEL, education educator, writer; d. Robert Wadsworth and Martha Anna (Jacoby) Knechel; m. Robert Charles Johansen; children: Erik Christopher, Sonia Lisbeth. BS, Manchester Coll., N. Manchester, Ind., 1964; MA, Columbia U. Tchrs. Coll., N.Y.C., 1966; PhD, Drew U., Madison, N.J., 1983. Vis. lectr. Rutgers U., New Brunswick, NJ, 1981—85; asst. prof. Stockton State Coll., Pomona, NJ, 1985—87; adj. faculty U. Notre Dame, Ind., 1987—91, profl. spl. faculty Ind., 1991—2001, assoc. prof. Ind., 2001—04, vis. assoc. prof. Ind., 2004—. Com. chair Behtany Seminary Bd., 1985—90; faculty fellow Kroc Inst. U. Notre Dame, 1991—; adj. faculty Bethany Theol. Seminary, Oak Brook, Ill., 1992. Author: (book) Coming Together, 1977, The Narrative Secret of Flannery O'Connor, 1994, Listening, in the Silence, Seeing the Dark, 2002. Mem. bd., vice chair Samaritan Ctr. Bd., South Bend, Ind.; vice chair Timbercrest Bd., N. Manchester, 2003—. Named Disting. Notre Dame Woman, Woman's Resource Ctr., U. Notre Dame, 2004; recipient Elizabeth Argee Prize, U. Notre Dame, 1992, Kaneb Tchg. award, 1999. Mem.: Soc. for Study of Narratives, Modern Lang. Assn., Am. Weil Soc. Achievements include co-founding

Global Woman's Project, designed to assist and support women and children in developing countries and in the U.S. Avocations: walking, gardening, music. Office: Univ Notre Dame 208 Decio Faculty Hall Notre Dame IN

JOHANSON, PATRICIA MAUREEN, artist, architect; b. NYC, Sept. 8, 1940; d. Alvar Einar and Elizabeth (Deane) J.; m. E.C. Goossen (dec.); children: Alvar Deane, Gerrit Hull, Nathaniel James. Student, Bklyn. Mus. Art Sch., 1958, Art Students League, 1961; AB, Bennington Coll., 1962; MA, Hunter Coll., 1964; BS, BArch, City Coll. Sch. Architecture, 1977; DFA (hon.), Mass. Coll. of Art, 1995. Vis. prof. art SUNY-Albany, 1969; vis. artist MIT, 1974, Oberlin Coll., Ohio, 1974, Alfred U., NY 1974, West Tex. State U., 1988, Yale U., 1989, Mass. Coll. Art, Boston, 1994, Calif. State U., Monterey Bay, 1997, 99, 2006; Southworth lectr. Colby Coll., Waterville, Maine, 1981; cons. Mitchell-Giurgola Assocs., architects, NYC, Phila., 1972—, Oikos, Seoul, South Korea, 1996, Yukong Ltd., Ulsan, South Korea, 1996, Seoul Devel. Inst., Seoul, 1999, Millenium Park, Seoul, 1999, Nat. Endowment for Arts, Washington, 1988, City of Petaluma, Calif., 1999, Carollo Engrs., 2001, The Murie Ctr., Moose, Wyo., 2001—; bd. dirs. Islands Inst. Salt Spring Island B.C.; bd. advisors Hall Farm Ctr. Arts and Edn., Townshend, Vt., 2006; artist-in-residence NY Found. for Arts, 1987—; del. Survival and the Arts, Sundance Inst., Utah, 1991; del. Global Forum Gen. Assembly, Kyoto, Japan, 1993, Art & Environ., Ankara, 1997, Year 2000 Symposium, Dumbarton Oaks, Washington, keynote spkr. Internat. Fedn. of Landscape Architects, Belem, Brazil, 2002, Wuhan U., China, 2004, Art in Embassies program US Dept. State; mem. grants selection com. NEA, 2000. Solo shows Tibor de Nagy Gallery, NYC, 1967, SUNY at Albany, 1969, Montclair State Coll., NJ, 1974, Rosa Esman Gallery, NYC, 1978, 79, 81, 83, Dallas Mus. Art, 1982, Philippe Bonnafont Gallery, San Francisco, 1984, New Arts Program, Kutztown, Pa., 1987, Albany Acad., 1987, Painted Bride Art Ctr., Phila., 1991; National Museum of Kenya, Nairobi, 1996—, Salina Art Ctr., Kans., 2001, Allegheny Coll., Pa., 2006; retrospectives, Bennington Coll., 1973, 91, Twining Gallery, NYC, 1987, Berkshire Mus., Pittsfield, Mass, 1987, Coll. St. Rose, Albany, NY, 2004; numerous group shows including most recently Gallery Route One, Point Reyes, Calif., 1999, The Presidio, San Francisco, 1999, Villa Medici, Rome, 2000, Mass. Coll. Art, 2000, French Cultural Svcs. Gallery, NYC, 2000, Institut Francais D' Architecture, Paris, 2000, Contemporary Arts Ctr., Cin., 2002, Mus. of Contemporary Art, LA, 2004, Armory Ctr. Arts, Pasadena, Calif., 2004, The Natural World Mus., San Francisco, 2004, Antioch Coll., Ohio, 2006; represented in permanent collections, Detroit Inst. Arts, Dallas Mus. Art, Mus. Modern Art, Met. Mus. Art, NYC, Nat. Mus. Women in Arts, Washington, Herbert F. Johnson Mus., Cornell U., Berkshire Mus., NY State Coun. on Arts Film Collection, Syracuse, Storm King Art Ctr., Mountainville, NY, Crawford and Chester Sts. Park, Cleve., Oberlin Coll., Bennington Coll., Brandeis U., U. Mass., Amherst, Dumbarton Oaks Contemporary Landscape Design Collection, Washington, pvt. collections; films The Art of the Real, USIA, 1968, Stephen Long, CBS-TV, 1968, Patricia Johanson: Cyrus Field, 1974, The City Project: Cleveland, 1977, A Conversation with Patricia Johanson, Heritage Cablevision, 1985, Patricia Johanson, Berks (Pa.) Community TV, 1990, Patricia Johanson: The Leonhardt Lagoon, 1992, Patricia Johanson: A Sense of Place, 1992, Patricia Johanson: Multilevel Designs, Aesthetic, Ecological, Functional, Cedar Arts Forum, Iowa, 1994, Q&A with Patricia Johanson, PBS, 1998, Chicken Scratch with Patricia Johanson, Petaluma, California Cmty. TV, 1999, Johanson interview The Environment Show Nat. Pub. Radio, 2000, Patricia Johanson: Zhang Jia Jie National Forest Park, Wulingyuan-TV, China, 2004; author: Art and Survival: Creative Solutions to Environmental Problems, 1992; co-author: (with Caffyn Kelley) Art and Survival: Patricia Johanson's Environmental Projects, 2006; works include park design, sculpture, ecol. landscapes, street furniture, pavement designs, site planning for Consol. Edison Co., Yale U., Columbus East HS, Ind., House and Garden mag., Internat. Yr. of Child Commn., Fair Park Lagoon, Dallas, Corning Preserve, Albany, Cathedral Sq., Sacramento, Pelham Bay Pk., NYC, Candlestick Pt. State Park, San Francisco, Omame Project, Brasilia, Brazil, Park for the Amazon Rainforest, Brazil, Nairobi River Park, Kenya, Ulsan Dragon Park, Ulsan, Korea, The Rocky Marciano Trail, Brockton, Mass., Millenium Park, Seoul, French Cultural Svcs. Garden, NY, South Ninth St. Corridor, Salina, Kans., Ellis Creek Water Recycling Facility and Tidal Wetlands Park, Petaluma, Calif., Pub. Art Master Plan, Rockland County, NY, 1990, Ecol. Master Plan Greater Boston Met. Region, 1994—, Sugarhouse Pedestrian Crossing, Salt Lake City, Bayfront Stormwater Garden, Duluth, Minn. Bd. dirs. New Arts Program, Pa., 1988—, Islands Inst. Interdisciplinary Studies, Can., 2005; bd. advisors Artists Representing Environ. Arts, Inc., NYC, 1991—. Guggenheim fellow, 1970, 80, NEA fellow, 1975, Olesen fellow Bennington Coll., 1991; Adolph & Esther Gottlieb Found. grantee, 1998; recipient 1st prize Environ. Design Competition, Montclair State Coll., 1974, Internat. Womens Yr. award, 1976, Gold medal Acad. Italia delle Arti, Parma, 1979, Townsend Harris medal CCNY, 1994, Arts and Healing Network award, 2003, Gov.'s Quality Growth Grand Achievement award Envision Utah, 2004; named to Hunter Coll. Hall of Fame, 1987; named to Mepham HS Hall of Fame, 1998. Mem. Global Forum Arts Group. Home: 179 Nickmush Rd Buskirk NY 12028-3202 Personal E-mail: johansonsite@aol.com.

JOHANSON, WANDA L., medical association administrator, critical care nurse; married. Grad., Holy Cross Sch. Nursing; BS in Nursing, M in Nursing, Univ. Wash. Registered prof. nurse, Wash., Calif., NC. Dir., profl. devel./ethics AACN, 1993—97; v.p. ops. InnoVision Group (AACN subs.), 1998; assoc. operating officer, med./surg./critical care svcs. Duke Univ. Health Sys., Durham, NC, 1998—99; now CEO AACN, Aliso Viejo, Calif. Office: AACN 101 Columbia Aliso Viejo CA 92656-4109 Office Phone: 949-362-2020.*

JOHANSSON, ALICIA BARBARA, musician; b. Warsaw, May 21, 1941; d. Boleslaw Bielik and Halina Helena Napiorkowska; m. Evert Johansson, May 13, 1972 (div. 1978); m. Kjell Johansson, Jan. 2, 1980 (div. 1986); 1 child, Sandra; m. James McClung, Nov. 29, 1986 (div. 1995). BA Piano Solo, Conservatory Warsaw, 1961, MA Musical Sci., 1968; cert. organist, U. Stockholm, 1984. Radio anchor Polish Radio and TV, Warsaw, 1959—63; piano accompanist Royal Opera, Stockholm, 1973—78, Cramer and Cullberg Ballet, Stockholm, 1974—80, Opera Ballet Sch., Stockholm, 1973—86, various concerts, Stockholm, 1978—86, Cleve. Ballet, 1986—90, Colo. Ballet, Denver, 1990—2000; organist various chs., Cleve. and Denver, 1987—; pvt. accompanist; tchr. piano and organ Denver, 1990—; organist, choir dir. Jefferson Ave. United Meth. Ch., Denver, 2003—. Performer: numerous organ and piano concerts; composer ch. music, 1973—. Organizer Royal Opera and Ballet Club, Stockholm, 1975—86. Mem.: Music Tchrs. Assn., Am. Guild Organists, Musicians Union. Democrat. Avocations: investing, hiking, travel, nature. Home and Studio: 7165 S Gaylord St E-6 Littleton CO 80122 Personal E-mail: aliciajohansson@ricochet.com.

JOHANSSON, SCARLETT, actress; b. N.Y.C., Nov. 22, 1984; d. Karsten and Melanie Johansson. Student, The Lee Strasberg Theatre Inst., N.Y.C.; Grad., Profl. Children's School, 2002. Actor: (films) North, 1994, Just Cause, 1995, If Lucy Fell, 1996, Manny & Lo, 1996, Fall, 1997, Home Alone 3, 1997, The Horse Whisperer, 1998, My Brother the Pig, 1999, Ghost World, 2000 (best actress award Toronto Film Critics Assn., 2001), The Man Who Wasn't There, 2001, An American Rhapsody, 2001, Eight Legged Freaks, 2002, Lost in Translation, 2003 (award for best actress Boston Soc. Film Critics, 2003, Upstream prize for best actress Venice Film Festival, 2003), Girl with a Pearl Earring, 2003, The Perfect Score, 2004, A Love Song for Bobby Long, 2004, A Good Woman, 2004, (voice only) The SpongeBob Squarepants Movie, 2004, In Good Company, 2004, Match Point, 2005, The Island, 2005, Scoop, 2006, The Black Dahlia, 2006; (TV series) Entourage, 2004. Office: Artists Mgmt Group 9465 Wilshire Blvd #519 Beverly Hills CA 90212-2604*

JOHANYAK, DEBRA L., literature educator, consultant; d. John and Leone Holodnak; m. Michael F. Johanyak, Mar. 22, 1986 (div. 2006); children: Jason Nathaniel Kamalie, Mathew Borzu Kamalie, Stephen Michael, Bethany Elizabeth. BA in English, U. Akron, Ohio, 1977, MA in English, 1982; PhD, Kent State U., Ohio, 1988. Adj. instr. U. Akron, 1988—91, Kent State U., Ohio, 1988—91, vis. prof. English, 1991—92; prof. English The U. Akron Wayne Coll., Orrville, Ohio, 1992—. Author: Shakespeare's World, 2004, Behind the Veil, 2006; contbr. articles to profl. publs., stories to lit. publs. Grantee, Ohio Bd. Regents, 2001—02. Mem.: Ohio Assn.Two-Yr. Colls. (pres. 1999—2000). Independent. Avocations: reading, travel, hiking, writing. Office Phone: 330-972-8752. Business E-Mail: dljohan@uakron.edu.

JOHMANN, NANCY, librarian; b. N.Y.C., Apr. 18, 1948; d. Robert Richard and Mary Stewart (Heath) J. BA, SUNY, Cortland, 1970; MLS, SUNY, Geneseo, 1971. Reference libr. Yonkers (N.Y.) Pub. Libr., 1971-76; cons., coord. Mass. Bd. Libr. Commrs., Boston, 1976-78; head info. and reference dept. Bridgeport (Conn.) Pub. Libr., 1979-84, asst. city libr., 1984-91, city libr., 1992—. Pres. bd. trustees Greater Bridgeport Symphony Orchestra, 1987-94. Treas. bd. trustees Greater Bridgeport Symphony Orchestra, 1987. Mem. ALA, Conn. Libr. Assn. Avocations: swimming, singing, classic cars, music. Office: Bridgeport Pub Libr 925 Broad St Bridgeport CT 06604-4871

JOHN, DOLORES, architect, consultant; b. Morgantown, W.Va., June 20, 1959; d. Thomas and Anna (Marrara) John; m. Joseph Ambrusico; children: Gabriella Ambrusico, Thomas Ambrusico. MArch, Cath. U. Am., 1986; BS, W.Va. U., 1981. Registered arch., N.Y., N.J. Assoc. SBLM Archs., N.Y.C., 1986—93; archtl. constrn. mgr. Pathmark Stores, Inc., Woodbridge, NJ, 1993—96; pres. Dolores John Arch., P.C., Blairstown, NJ, 1996—2003; dir. archtl. svcs. Pathmark Stores, Inc., Carteret, NJ, 2003—. Big Sister Catholic Big Sisters, New York, NY, 1991—2001; Member H.O.P.E. Historic Preservation, Hope, NJ, 2001—01. Roman Catholic. Avocations: gardening, cooking. Office: Pathmark Stores Inc 200 Milik St Carteret NJ 07008

JOHN, LYVIE PAIGE, music educator; b. Concord, N.H., Jan. 25, 1982; d. James P. and Mary Lou K. John. MusB in Music Edn., U. N.H., Durham, 2000—04. Dir., instrumental music Lebanon Jr. HS, NH, 2004—05, Gilford Mid. HS, 2005—. Counselor Summer Youth Music Sch., U. N.H., 2001—04. Recipient Coolest Sch. Website, N.H. Mag., 1999, John Philip Sousa Band award, 2000; grantee Gilford Music Boosters scholarship, 2000, Marching Band scholarship, U. N.H., 2002—03. Mem.: MENC (corr.; sec. 2002—03), Kappa Kappa Psi (assoc.; festival chair 2001—02). Office: Gilford HS 88 Alvah Wilson Rd Gilford NH 03249 Office Phone: 603-524-7146. Business E-Mail: ljohn@gilford.k12.nh.us.

JOHN, SUSAN V., state representative; b. Nov. 20, 1957; BA, George Washington U.; JD, Syracuse U. Bar: N.Y. Assoc. Phillips, Lytle, Hitchcock, Huber and Blaine, 1983—; mem. N.Y. State Assembly, mem. jud. com., edn. com., also mem. energy com., librs. and edn. tech. com., chair labor com. Chair Legis. Commn. on Solid Waste Mgmt., 1995—97, Alcholism and Drug Abuse Com., 1997—99, Govtl. Ops. Com., 1999—2000; served on First Legis. Joint Budget Conf. Com. on Mental Health, 1998, Joint Budget Conf. Com. on Edn., 1999—2000. Chair Majority Steering Com.; serves on Judiciary, Edn., Energy, Libraries and Tech. and Social Svcs. Coms. Mem. Greater Rochester Assn. Women Attys. Office: 840 University Ave Rochester NY 14607 also: NY State Assembly LOB Rm 522 Albany NY 12248-0001 Office Phone: 518-455-4527. Business E-Mail: johns@assembly.state.ny.us.

JOHNS, BEVERLEY ANNE HOLDEN, special education administrator; b. New Albany, Ind., Nov. 6, 1946; d. James Edward and Martha Edna (Scharf) Holden; m. Lonnie J. Johns, July 28, 1973. BS, Catherine Spalding Coll., 1968; MS, So. Ill. U., 1970; postgrad., Western Ill. U., 1973—74, postgrad., 1979—80, postgrad., 1982, U. Ill., 1984—85. Cert. adminstr., tchr. Ill. Demonstration tchr. So. Ill. U., Carbondale, 1970-72; instr. MacMurray Coll., Jacksonville, Ill., 1977—79, 1990—93, 2002—; intern Ill. State Bd. Edn., Springfield, 1981; program supr. Four Rivers Spl. Edn. Dist., Jacksonville, 1972—2003; learning and behavior cons., 2003—. Chair Ill. Spl. Edn.; conf. coord. Ill. Alliance, Champaign, 1982-94; lectr., cons. in field. Author: Report on Behavior Analysis in Education, 1972; author: (with V. Carr) Techniques for Managing Verbally and Physically Aggressive Students, 2002, Reduction of School Violence: Alternatives to Suspension, 2005; author: (with B. Johns, E. Crowley & E. Guetzloe) Effective Curriculum for Students with Behavioral Disorders, 2002; author: (with J. Keenan) Techniques for Managing a Safe School, 1997; author: (with E. Paula Crowley) Students with Disabilities & General Education: A Desktop Reference for School Personnel, 2003; author: Getting Behavioral Interventions Right, 2005, Preparing Test-Resistant Students for Assessments: A Staff Training Guide, 2005; author: (with M. McGrath) The Teacher's Reflective Calendar & Planning Journal, 2006; author: (with M. McGrath and S. Mathur) Surviving Internal Politics Within the School, 2006; editor: Position Papers of Ill. Council for Exceptional Children, 1981; contbr. articles to profl. jours. Bd. dirs. Jacksonville Area Assn. Retarded Citizens, v.p., 1993-94, sec. 1996-99; govt. rels. chair Internat. Coun. Exceptional Children, 1984-87; fed. liason Ill. Adminstrs. Spl. Edn., 1985-86. So. Ill. U. fellow, 1968; resolution honoring Beverly H. Johns Internat. Coun. for Exceptional Children Conv., 1982; recipient Recognition cert. Ill. Atty. Gen., 1985, Outstanding Leadership award Internat. Coun. Exceptional Children, 2000; named Jacksonville Woman of Yr., Bus. and Profl. Women, 1988, Unsung Hero Jacksonville Jour.-Courier, 1993. Mem. ASCD, Assn. Retarded Citizens (com. 1982-85), Ill. Coun. for Children with Behavioral Disorders (founder, past pres., pres. Ill. divsn. for learning disabilities 1991-92, Presdl. award 1985), Ill. Alliance for Exceptional Children (v.p. 1982-94), Learning Disabilities Assn. (bd. dirs., pres. 2000-03), Ill. Coun. Exceptional Children (past pres., chair govt. rels. com. 1982-95, 97-98, 2002—, governing bd. 1984-95, Presdl. award 1983, Lifetime Achievement award 1989, First Lady 1993), Internat. Coun. for Citizens with Behavioral Disorders (pres. 1997), West Ctrl. Assn. for Citizens with Learning Disabilities (founder, com. chair 1997), Internat. Assn. Spl. Edn. (pres.-elect), Internat. Pioneer Press (editor CEC pioneer divsn., pres. internat. pioneers divsn.), Internat. Divsn. Learning Disabilities (exec. bd.), Delta Kappa Gamma (chpt. pres. 1988-90, state exec. bd. 1991—), Internat. Assn. Spl. Edn. (pres. 2006—), Phi Delta Kappa. Roman Catholic. Avocation: world travel. Home: PO Box 340 Jacksonville IL 62651-0340 Office Phone: 217-245-5781. Personal E-mail: bevjohns@juno.com.

JOHNS, KAREN JORDAN, music educator, small business owner; b. Bridgeport, Conn., Apr. 18, 1949; d. Samuel Clifford and Kathleene (Bible) Jordan; m. Stephen David Johns; children: Alina Dawn, Crystal Brook, Byron Jordan. MusB, Fla. State U., 1971. Cert. K-12 music tchr., Fla. Coord. music therapy Sunland Ctr., Tallahassee, 1973-75, unit dir., 1975-77, supr. resident life facility, 1977-79; unit dir. Fla. State Hosp., Chattahoochee, 1980-81; presch. tchr. St. Mark's Sch., Venice, Fla., 1982-90; tchr. music Sarasota County Sch. Bd., Sarasota, Fla., 1990—. Owner, operator Custom Sawing & Ornamentals, plant nursery, Marianna, Fla., 1979-82, Johns Music Studio, Venice, 1984-90, wellness bus., Nokomis, Fla., 1996—; cons. Recipient Arts Educator Leadership award, Sarasota County Arts Coun., 1994. Mem. Music Educators Nat. Conf., Fla. Music Educators Assn. (cons. 1990—), Sarasota Assn. for Music Edn. (pres. 1997-99). Avocations: nutrition, botany, women's issues, choral and orchestral music. Home and Office: PO Box 1242 Nokomis FL 34274-1242

JOHNS, LAURIE MARIE, dentist, hypnotherapist; b. Almeria, Spain, Dec. 2, 1944; came to U.S., 1968; d. Raphael and Laura I. (Galindo) Gonzalez; m. Richard E. Johns, Feb. 24, 1968 (div. Mar. 1987); children: Laurie C. Johns-Stoutemire, Richard Michael. BA in Scis., U. New Orleans, 1979; DDS, La. State U., 1984; BA in Langs. summa cum laude, U. North Fla., Jacksonville, 1989. Lic. profl. hypnotherapist. Pvt. practice dentistry, Orange Park, Fla., 1985—; gen. dentistry resident U. Fla. Sch. Dentistry, Gainesville, 1989; profl. hypnotherapist Orange Park, 1986—. Vol. dentist for elderly Moosehaven, Orange Park, 1980-88, underpriviledged children various schs. and Charles C. Bennett Sch. and pub. health dept., 1986-88. Bd. mem. Clay County Edn. Found., Orange Park, 1985-89. Mem. ADA, Acad. Gen. Dentistry, Am. Assn. Profl. Hypnotherapists, Nat. Guild Hypnotists, Acad. One Hundred, North Fla. Dental Assn., Clay Dental Soc. Roman Catholic. Avocation: flower arrangements. Address: 2326 Foxwood Dr Orange Park FL 32073-5134

JOHNSEN, BARBARA PARRISH, writer, educator; b. Fort Madison, Iowa, Feb. 21, 1933; d. Lloyd Lynn and Genevieve Agnes (Peter) P.; m. James Cotten Johnsen (dec.); 1 child, Holly Ann. BA, Fla. So. Coll., 1959; MEd, Boston U., 1964. Cert. tchr. Calif. Account exec. Ledger Pub. Co., Lakeland, Fla., 1954-62; tchr., counselor Long Beach (Calif.) Unified Sch. Dist., 1965-74; owner Ednl. Counseling and Cons., Cazenovia, N.Y., 1990-2000. Mem. Madison County Coun. on Alcohol and Substance Abuse, 1986-92. Chair Madison County Cmty. Svcs. Bd., 1987-95; v.p. LWV N.Y. State, Albany, 1993-97. Avocations: writing, poetry, travel. Personal E-mail: BarbJJohnsen@aol.com.

JOHNSEN, KAREN KENNEDY, marketing professional; b. Easton, Pa., June 28, 1939; d. Charles Edward and Gladys Swensen Kennedy; m. Henry Lehmann Johnsen, May 26, 1962; children: Erik Lehmann, Elisa Beth Johnsen Peters. BS in Bus. cum laude, Russell Sage Coll., Troy, N.Y., 1961; MS in Bus. Edn., SUNY, Albany, 1970. Cert. bus. tchr. N.Y., 1970. With account svc. divsn. McCann-Erickson, Inc., N.Y.C., 1961—62; exec. asst. pub. rels. Johnson & Johnson, New Brunswick, NJ, 1962—65; staff writer investment divsn. Glens Falls Ins. Co., NY, 1965—66; exec. sec. to pres., sec.-treas. Glens Falls Portland Cement Co., 1966—69; dir. devel. (funding and audience) Lake George Opera Festival, Glens Falls, 1970—73; publicity dir. fund raising campaign Glens Falls YMCA; freelance writer, adminstrn./media/mktg. cons., 1974—; exec. asst., media dir., staff writer Kimberly Comm., Inc., Chatham, NJ, 1974—82; sales mgr. Lifelines Gifts & Cards, N.Y.C., 1982—84; entrepreneur mktg., sales and mgmt. KJ Assocs., 1985—; ind. Mary Kay beauty cons., 1994—. Charter sec. pub. relations Scotch Plains Assn. Concerning Environment, 1999—; former bd. dirs. Plainfield Symphony Soc.; charter sec. Lake George Opera Guild, 1970—73; charter sec. adv. bd. Project 2000, Norwegian Immigration Assn. Mem.: AAUW (chpt. treas., comm. chmn.), Vesterheim Norwegian-Am. Mus., Russell Sage Coll. Alumnae Assn. (class agt., alumnae admissions liaison 1995—, class reunion chair 2001, 2006), Am. Scandinavian Found., Vasa Order of Am. (past NJ dist. sec., cultural leader, supr. children's clubs, past local lodge chmn., sec., supr. children's club, past chmn., cultural leader, supr. children's clubs local lodge), Order Ea. Star, Delta Pi Epsilon. Presbyterian. Avocations: skiing, singing, writing, folk-art painting. Home and Office: 109 Glenside Ave Scotch Plains NJ 07076 Office Phone: 908-928-9061. E-mail: kkjohnsen@comcast.net.

JOHNSEN, LISA L., lawyer; b. Bremerton, Wash., June 21, 1964; BA with distinction, Whitman Coll., 1986; JD magna cum laude, Seattle U., 1991; LLM in taxation, NYU, 1996. Bar: Wash. 1991. Ptnr., mem. exec. com. Preston Gates & Ellis LLP, Seattle. Mem.: ABA, Wash. State Bar Assn. Office: Preston Gates & Ellis LLP Ste 2900 925 Fourth Ave Seattle WA 98104-1158 Office Phone: 206-370-6614. Office Fax: 206-370-6093. E-mail: lisaj@prestongates.com.

JOHNSEN, MAY ANN, artist, sculptor; b. Port Chester, N.Y., May 12; d. Michael Colangelo and Mary Agnes (Visconti) Visconti; m. David Stanley May Johnsen, Nov. 6, 1940; 1 child, David Mark. Artist Silver Point Gallery, Brainard, N.Y. Exhibited national and internationally including: Hamilton Miniature Nat. Exhibit, Ohio (miniature marine award), World Miniature Art Exhbn., Tasmania, Australia, Silvermine Guild Artists Nat. Exhibition of New Canaan, Conn. (marine award), Nat. Marine Painter Internat. show Breverd Mus. Florid, Internat. Soc. Marine Painters show Heritage Plantation Mus., Sandwich, Mass., Miniature Soc. Painter Sculptors Internat. show, Fla., Miniature Soc. Painters Sculptors Gravers Internat. show, Ga., Miniature Soc. Painter Graders Scuptor N.C. Internat. show, Miniature Internat. show Painters Gravers Sculptors Ark., Harness Racing Art Exhibit, Lexington, Ky., Allegheny Internat. Miniature Painters show, Bluefield, W.Va., Nat. Miniature Show, South Port, N.C., Albany Inst. History and Art, Albuquerque Nat. exhibit, Bertrand Russel Peace Found., Gold Medal Competition for Distinguished Marine Art, Franklin Mint Gallery, Pa., Internat. Exhibit, Smithsonian Inst., Washington, Drawings Internat., Barcelona, Spain, Nat. Exhibit, Catherine Lorillard Wolf, N.Y.C., Mural Exhibit, Schuyler Sch., Albany, N.Y., others. Recipient Spl. Mariner award, Nassau, N.Y., two first prizes Columbia County Fair, Chatham, N.Y. Recipient 1st and 2d Pl. Watercolor awards, 2nd Pl. Graphic Silver Point award, Calvatone, Italy. Mem. Am. Soc. Miniature Painters of N.J., Soc. Marine Painters, Marine Painters Am., Miniature Painters, Sculptors and Gravers of Washington, D.C. (assoc.), N.J. Soc. Miniature, Graver, Sculptors, Painters, Washington D.C. Miniature Soc., Ohio Miniature Soc., Soc. Internat. Marine Painters, Wolfd Fedn. Miniaturists. Roman Catholic. Home: Silver Point Gallery Box 5 Route 20 Brainard NY 12024 Office: Silver Point Gallery Rt 20 Box 5 Brainard NY 12024

JOHNSEN, SHERYL B., secondary education educator, consultant; b. Salt Lake City, June 6, 1933; d. Harry A. and Bessie (Cook) Baer; m. Woodrow M. Johnsen, June 6, 1952; children: Michael W. and Susan S. BA in History and Anthropology summa cum laude, Calif. State U., Hayward, 1971; MA in History, Holy Names Coll., 1987. Lifetime cert. secondary tchr., Calif. Tchr. Bishop O'Dowd High Sch., Oakland, Calif., 1972-86; advanced placement tchr. San Jose (Calif.) State U., 1985-89. Sponsor Jr. Statesmen Found., Palo Alto, Calif., 1972-86, trustee, 1980-83; cons. Nat. Coll. Bd., San Jose, 1978-89, advanced placement U.S. History Test Devel. Com., 1983-89; advanced placement essay reader Ednl. Testing Svc., 1981-89. Recipient Taft fellowship U. Pacific, Freedoms Found. award, East Asian Regional Coun. grant, 1985. Mem. ASCD, LWV, Nat. Coun. Social Studies, Orgn. Am. Historians, Calif. Coun. Social Studies, East Bay Coun. Social Studies, Pi Gamma Mu. Avocations: music, travel, reading. Home: 6946 Hollow Ridge Rd Salt Lake City UT 84121-3466

JOHNSEY-ROBERTSON, ANITA COLLEEN, special education educator; b. Birmingham, Ala., June 14, 1966; d. Judith Colleen (Bradberry) Steger. BS in Spl. Edn./Mental Retardation, Livingston U., Ala., 1988, MEd in Spl. Edn./Mental Retardation, 1990; EdS in Spl. Edn./Mental Retardation, U. Ala., Tuscaloosa, 1994; EdD, U. So. Miss., 1997—2000. Lic. tchr. spl. edn, area mental retardation. Tchr. multihandicapped Linden (Ala.) Elem. Sch., 1988-90; tchr. mentally retarded Jefferson County Schs., Hillview Elem. Sch., Birmingham, Ala., 1990-94, Jefferson County Schs., Pittman Mid. Sch., Birmingham, Ala., 1994-98, Jefferson County Schs., Lipscomb Elem., 1999—2000, Oak Grove H.S., 2000—. Del. Citizens Ambassador Program, 1995. Named Outstanding Spl. Educator, Ala. CEC, 2006. Mem. AFCEC (pres. 2006-), Coun. Exceptional Children (presenter Ala. conf. 1996, 2000, 03, 05, 06, nat. conf. 1996), Ala. Edn. Assn., Phi Delta Kappa. Avocations: reading, special olympics. Home: 1510 Lilly Ln Bessemer AL 35023-4377 E-mail: acjohnsey@bham.rr.com.

JOHNSON, ABBIE MAE, language educator; b. Ft. Worth, Aug. 29, 1953; d. ELijah and Eddie Mae Johnson. A in Early Childhood Edn., Lamar U., Beaumont, Tex.; B in English, Tex. Wesleyan U., Ft. Worth. Tchr. English Ft. Worth Ind. Sch. Dist., 1975—91; tchr. Head Start Program, 1991—93; tchr. English & Spanish Ambassadors of Christ, 1993—2005, Theresa B. Lee Acad., 2005—. Dir. daycare Magic Magnets, Ft. Worth, 1993. Mem.: NEA, Nat. Assn. Children With Learning Disabilities. Avocations: creative writing, poetry. Home: 5525 Capers Ave Fort Worth TX 76112

JOHNSON, ABIGAIL PIERREPONT, investment company executive; b. Boston, Dec. 19, 1961; d. Edward C. Johnson; m. Christopher J. McKown; 2 children. BA in Art History, Hobart and William Smith Coll., 1984; MBA, Harvard U., 1988. Rsch. assoc. Booz, Allen and Hamilton; portfolio mgr. Fidelity Investments, Boston, 1988—, assoc. dir., 1994—, sr. v.p., 1998—, pres. Fidelity Mgmt. & Rsch., 2001—05, pres., Fidelity Employers Services, 2005—. Bd. dirs. FMR Corp. Named one of Most Powerful Women, Forbes mag., 2005, Top 50 Women to Watch, Wall St. Jour., 2005, Forbes Richest Americans, 2006, 50 Most Powerful Women in Bus., Fortune mag., 2006. Office: Fidelity Investments 82 Devonshire St Boston MA 02109-3605*

JOHNSON, ABIGAIL RIDLEY, tour/travel and performing arts executive; b. Vancouver, B.C., Can., Jan. 28, 1945; d. Frederic Neville and Cara Lee (Smith) Ridley; m. Ralph Maxwell Johnson, Sept. 17, 1971 (div.). BA Music, Colo. Women's Coll., 1967; postgrad. study summer, San Jose State U., Calif., 1967. Cert. Co. rep. Manhattan Festival Ballet, San Francisco, 1967—68; asst. booking mgr. Western Opera Theatre, San Francisco, 1968—69; asst. to consul and trade commr. Can. Consulate Gen., San Francisco, 1969—71; office mgr. Whitney Properties, San Francisco, 1971—72; sales mgr. Sutter Travel Service, San Francisco, 1973—80; dir., owner Tour Arts, San Francisco, 1980—. Bd. dirs. Chanticleer, Inc., San Francisco. Active mem. Opera, Symphony, Ballet (Support Groups), San Francisco. Mem.: Inst. Cert. Travel Agts. (cert.), Jr. League San Francisco. Episcopalian. Office: Tour Arts 231 Franklin St San Francisco CA 94102-5113

JOHNSON, ADDIE COLLINS, secondary school educator, retired dietician; b. Evansville, Ind., Feb. 28; d. Stewart and Willa (Shamell) Collins; m. John Q. Johnson, Sept. 6, 1958 (dec. Aug. 1991); 1 child, Parker. BS, Howard U., 1956; MEd, Framingham State Coll., Mass., 1967. Registered dietitian, Mass. Dietitian Boston Lying-In Hosp., 1957-61; dietitian Diet Heart Study, Harvard U. Sch. Pub. Health, Boston, 1962-63; tchr. Foxboro (Mass.) Pub. Sch., 1968-2000; dietitian Sch. Medicine Boston U., 1975-77, Westinghouse Health Systems, Boston; faculty Dept. Nursing Boston State Coll., 1979-82; real estate sales assoc. Century 21, Sharon, Mass., 2001—. Nutrition cons. Head Start program Westinghouse Sch., Boston, 1979-82; instr. dept. nursing U. Mass., 1981-89, Bridgewater (Mass.) State Coll., 1982-97; mem. state adv. coun. Dept. Edn Bur. Nutrition Edn., 1981-83; participant NSF Project Seed, 1992; chmn. edn. com., bd. dirs. Consumer Credit Counseling Svcs. of Mass., Inc., 1996-99; scorer licensure tests Mass., 2000—; nat. evaluatins sys. scorer U. Mass. Health & Sci., 2001—. Bd. dirs. Norfolk-Bristol County Home Health Assn., Walpole, Mass., 1975-78; presenter Nat. Social Studies Assn., Boston, 1984-85; instr./trainer health svcs. edn. ARC, 1987-90. Nominated for Mass. Tchr. of Yr., 1999. Mem.: AAUW, NAACP (life), Consumer Credit Counseling Svc. (bd. chair edn. com. 1998—99), Mass. State Dept. Edn. (adv. bd. 1995—98), Soc. Nutrition Edn., Mass. Tchrs. Assn. (higher edn. com. 1984—87), Ea. Mass. Home Econs. Assn. (bd. dirs. 1978), Am. Home Econs. Assn., Am. Dietitic Assn., Delta Kappa Gamma (journalist Iota chpt. 1986—88, membership com. 1988—92, v.p. 1994, pres. Iota chpt. 1996—98, state world fellowship chairperson, Internat. Area Achievement award 2001). Avocations: travel, bicycling. Home: 92 Morse St Sharon MA 02067-2719 Office Phone: 781-784-6771. E-mail: johnsoa1@rcn.com.

JOHNSON, ADELE CUNNINGHAM, small business owner; b. Vineland, N.J., May 14, 1934; d. Charles and Lorraine (Durand) Cunningham; m. Carl H. Johnson Jr., May 14, 1955; children: C. Howard III, Lorraine Johnson Bonifield, Charles Victor. BS, Syracuse U., 1955. Owner, mgr. Avalon (N.J.) Anchorage Marina, 1984—. Mem. U.S. Power Squadron, 1968—; capt. lic., USCG, 1985; adv. bd. Bank of N.J., Vineland, 1970-75. Organizer, dir. Millville (N.J.) Youth Week, 1956; organizer Millville Hosp. Vol. Svcs., 1966, dir., 1966-70; bd. dirs. United Way Millville, Millville YMCA Swim Team, 1969-77; v.p. Millville YMCA, 1970-75; mem. Newcomb Hosp. Found., Vineland, 1981-88; pres. Cumberland County Coll. Found., Vineland, 1986—. Mem. N.J. Marine Trades Assn., Millville Womens Club, State Fedn. Womens Clubs (2d dist. v.p. 1982-84), Avalon C. of C., Cape May County C. of C., Zonta. Republican. Methodist. Home: 403 20th St Avalon NJ 08202-2103 Office: Avalon Anchorage Marina 885 21st St Avalon NJ 08202-2116

JOHNSON, ADRIA ELAINE, financial analyst, accountant; b. Louisville, Ky., Apr. 13, 1971; d. William Phillip and Brenda Carole Swafford; children: Brenlie Elaine Rhodes, Kenneth Lafranzo Rhodes; m. John Edward Johnson, June 29, 2002. BS, Ball State U., 1994. Accountant Humana, Louisville, 1994—97, LG&E Energy Corp., Louisville, 1997—99; fin./mktg. analyst Brown & Williamson Tobacco Corp., Louisville, 1999—. Contbr. poems to various publs. Pres. Sanctuary Choir-5th Street Baptist Ch., Louisville, 1999—2001. Mem.: Nat. Black MBA Assn. Democrat. Baptist. Home: 12511 Bridgetown Pl Louisville KY 40245 Office: Brown and Williamson Tobacco Corp 401 South 4th St Ste 200 Louisville KY 40202

JOHNSON, ALISA B., lawyer, energy company executive; b. NYC, Jan. 14, 1958; BA, Rice U., 1980; JD cum laude, U. Houston, 1985. Bar: Tex. 1985. Assoc. Brodsky & Ketchand, 1985—88; v.p., sec. North American Mortgage Co., 1988—89; assoc. Webster & Sheffield, 1989—90; sr. v.p., gen. counsel Dynegy Generation Div.; sr. v.p., gen. counsel, corp. sec. Helix Energy Solutions, Houston, 2006—. Contbr. articles to profl. jours. Mem.: ABA, State Bar Tex., Phi Delta Phi. Office: Helix Energy Solutions 400 N Sam Houston Pkwy E, Ste 400 Houston TX 77060-3500*

JOHNSON, ALLISON, corporate communications specialist, marketing executive; b. Pa. B.J, U. Fla. With Chem. Banking Corp., Wells Fargo Bank, Apple Computer Co.; dir. corp. comm. Netscape, IBM; v.p. global brand and comm. Hewlett-Packard Co., Palo Alto, Calif., sr. v.p. global brand and comm., 2001—05; v.p. global mktg. comm. Apple Computer Inc., Cupertino, Calif., 2005—. Office: Apple Computer Inc 1 Infinite Loop Cupertino CA 95014

JOHNSON, ALLYCE A., musician; b. Little Rock, Feb. 22, 1974; d. Danny Ray and Carolyn Ann Plummer; m. Scottie Lamar Johnson, Dec. 17, 1994; 1 child, Henry Owen. B.Mus.Edn., Ouachita Bapt. U., Arkadelphia, Ark., 1997. Adminstrv. asst. Stephens Inc., Little Rock, 1998—99; music tchr. K-6 England Pub. Schs., Ark., 1999—2000, McGehee Sch. Dist., Ark., 2000—03; choral dir. Rogers Pub. Schs., Rogers, Ark., 2003—. Mem. Western Ark. Chamber Choir, 2006—. Mem.: Music Educators Nat. Conf., Am. Choral Dirs. Assn. Republican. Baptist. Avocations: singing, reading, piano.

JOHNSON, ANITA (MARY ANITA JOHNSON), physician, medical association administrator; b. Clarksburg, W.Va., Oct. 18, 1926; d. Paul F. and Mary Elizabeth (Harris) Johnson; m. Lawrence J. Ciessau, Aug. 22, 1959 (div. 1974); children: Matthew A., Susan E., Sharon L., Mark A.; m. Ralph Allen Fretwell, Dec. 18, 1976 (dec. Aug. 18, 2001). BS, North Tex. U., 1946; MD, Woman's Med. Coll. Pa., 1950. Intern Baylor U. Hosp., Dallas, 1950-51, resident, 1951-54; practice medicine specializing in internal medicine Dallas, 1954-58, Chgo., 1958—; instr. internal medicine Southwestern Med. Coll., U. Tex., Dallas, 1954-58; med. dir. YWCA, Dallas, 1955-58; physician for infant welfare Chgo. Bd. Health, 1960-63; house physician, emergency physician St. Mary of Nazareth Hosp. Ctr., Chgo., 1963-81, instr. nurses ICU, 1963-80, asst. cardiologist, 1963-86, sec. med. staff, 1974-75, treas. med. staff, 1980, pres. med. staff, 1982, 84; med. dir. Family Care Ctr., 1973-74, chief med. clinics, 1977-78, chmn. credentials com., 1982-92, chief internal medicine, 1983-92; clin. instr. medicine U. Health Scis., Chgo. Med. Sch., North Chicago, Ill., 1982-95; nat. med. dir. Nat. Cath. Soc. Foresters Ins. Co., Chgo., 1975-77. Chmn. ann. benefit com. St. Mary of Nazareth Hosp. Ctr., 1992; cons. internal medicine Lisbon VA Hosp., Dallas, 1955-56; lectr. to cmty. elem. sch. students on opportunities in health field, 1967—; gov. bd. St. Mary Nazareth Hosp. Ctr., 1991-94, life trustee, 1994—. Named Med. Woman of Yr., St. Mary of Nazareth Hosp. Ctr., 1973. Mem. ACP, AMA (del. hosp. med. staff sect. 1980-92), Ill. Soc. Internal Medicine (councillor 1990-93), Am. Soc. Internal Medicine, Am. Coll. Angiology, Am. Med. Women's Assn. (S.W. regional dir. 1955-58, nat. chmn. publicity and pub. rels. 1991-93, pres.-elect br. 2, 1981, 82, 89, 90, pres. 1983-85, 91-94, regional gov. Midwest sect. 1985-91, bd. dirs. 1985-91, 92-98, v.p. fin. 1997-98, cmty. svc. award 1991, nat. chmn. retirement issues com. 1993-2000, nat. pres.-elect 1998-99, Pres.'s Recognition award 1998, Bertha Van Hoosen Nat. award 1999, found. bd. dirs. 1999-05), Ill. State Med. Soc. (trustee 1987-90, com. on CME accreditation 1987-96, coun. on pub. rels. on membership svcs 1992, govt. affairs com. 1991-05, jud. panel mem. 2003—, site accreditation surveyor), Chgo. Med. Soc. (councillor 1980—, chmn. malpractice ins. com., del. to Ill. Med. Soc. 1981—, pres. Northside br. 1985-87, chmn. practice mgmt. com. 1990-93, nominating com., Midwest Clin. Conf. 1991—, Cook County jud. panel 1995-2000, chmn. sr. physicians com. 1997-99, chmn. subcom. continuing med. edn. 1997-98, chmn. presdl. ad hoc com. sr. physicians 1997-99, chmn. continuing med. edn. com. 1998-2004, chmn. election com. 2002—, created M. Anita Johnson award 1999—), Zeta Phi. Home and Office: 6226 Edgebrook Ln W Indianhead Park IL 60525-6983 Personal E-mail: ajohnsonmd@sbcglobal.net.

JOHNSON, ANN RUTH, musician; b. Mt. Carmel, Ill., Dec. 23, 1963; d. Karl Frederick and Nancy Jane Kirkman; 1 child, Karli Ann. MB in Music Therapy, U. Evansville, Ind.; Tchg. Cert., U. Wis., Stevens Point. Music therapist, activity dir. Genesis Health Venture, Seaford, Del.; music therapist North Ctrl. Health Care, Wausau, Wis.; instrumental music-orch. D.C. Everest Area Schs., Schofield, Wis. Cellist Wausau Conservatory of Music, Ind., 1993—. Mem.: Susuki Assn. Musicians, Music Educators Nat. Conf. Avocations: jogging, swimming, gardening, home decorating, houseplants. Office: Everest Sr HS 6500 Alderson St Rudolph WI 54475 Home: 916 River St Schofield WI 54476-1805 Office Phone: 713-559-6561 ext. 4114.

JOHNSON, ANNE ELISABETH, medical assistant; b. Springfield, Mass., Nov. 3, 1955; d. Michael Francis Xavier and Miriam Rose (Coombs) Gigliotti. Grad., NSCC, Beverly, Mass., 1976. Cert. med. transcriptionist; cert. med. asst.; Nat. Marine Fisheries permit as operator of all comml. vessels and fishing vessels, state and fed. waters; lic. capt. USCG 100GT; permit as Marine Radio Operator. Lab technician, EKG technician, phlebotomist Addison Gilbert Hosp., Gloucester, Mass., 1976—81; exec. asst. MGA Inc., Gloucester, Mass., 1980—99; med. asst. Cape Ann Med. Ctr., Gloucester, 1983—98; lic. capt. Marine/Passenger Yacht Svcs., 2001—06; exec. asst. exec. offices Marine Tng. Sch. and Capt. Svcs., Gloucester, 2006—. Dance instr., 1973-85. Active, People for the Ethical Treatment of Animals. Home: 127 Eastern Ave PMB # 135 Gloucester MA 01930 Office: Marine Trng Sch and Cpt Svcs Gloucester MA 01930 Office Phone: 978-281-4897.

JOHNSON, ANNE STUCKLY, retired lawyer; b. Axtell, Tex., Jan. 8, 1921; d. Arnold Joseph and Angeline (Morris) Stuckly; m. Edward James Johnson, Oct. 9, 1943 (dec. 1967); children: Edward M., Ronald J., Dennis L., Shawn T., Rozlynn Jan, Anne J'lynn, Kevin J, Karal Ian, Donna Lynn. BA, Baylor U., 1940; MA in Econs., St. Mary's U., 1974, JD, 1980. Bar: Tex. 1980. Claims clk. Social Security Adminstrn., Amarillo, Tex., 1940-42; asst. chief divsn. pers. Pantex Ordnance Plant, Amarillo, Tex., 1942-43; chief divsn. pers. Cactus Ordnance Works, Dumas, Tex., 1943-44; citations unit supr. Gen. Hdqrs. Far East Command, Tokyo, 1950-51; v.p., treas. Drive-Safe Corp., San Antonio, 1967-69; counseling psychologist ARC, San Antonio, 1968-69, Divsn. Pers. Office, Ft. Sam Houston, 1969, pers. mgmt. specialist, 1969-77; pvt. practice Oliver B. Chamberlin Offices, San Antonio, 1981-86, San Antonio, 1987-93; ret., 1994. Active Am. Heart Assn., 1983—. Mem. ABA, San Antonio Bar Assn., Tex. Bar Assn., Am. Trial Lawyers Assn., Assn. Social Econs., Tex. Trial Lawyers Assn., Phi Alpha Delta, Pi Gamma Mu, Omicron Delta Epsilon. Home: 11406 Woodwaters Way San Antonio TX 78249-1918

JOHNSON, ARICA RENEÉ, elementary school educator; d. Heulet and Virginia Arnold; m. Calvin Johnson, Jr., Dec. 24, 1980; children: Erica, Calvin Jr., Wali, Elan. BA, Clark Coll., Atlanta; MA, Clarka Atlanta U., 1997; EdD, Clark Atlanta U., 2006. Cert. Tchr. Mid. Grades, Math. & Lang. Arts Ga. Dept. Edn., Tchr., Early Childhood Edn. Ga. Dept. Edn., Ga. Dept. Edn. Rsch. grad. asst. W. Ga. U., Carrollton, 1992—94; tchr., chairperson Fulton County Schs., East Point, Ga., 1992—98, Atlanta Pub. Schs., 1998—99, model tchr. leader/facilitator, 1999—. Presenter in field. Contbr. papers to profl. jours. and pubs. Grantee Academic scholarship, NAACP, DeWitt Wallace Academic scholarship. Mem.: NSTA, Ga. Sci. Tchrs. Assn., Ga. Coun. Tchrs. Math., Nat. Coun. Tchrs. Math., Assn. Supervision and Curriculum Devel., Nat. Assn. Elem. Sch. Principals: Aspiring Principals, Kappa Delta Pi, Phi Tau Omega (edn. chairperson), Alpha Kappa Alpha. Avocations: the arts, writing, painting, reading, exercise.

JOHNSON, BADRI NAHVI, social studies educator, real estate company officer; b. Tehran, Iran, Dec. 1, 1934; came to U.S., 1957; d. Ali Akbar and Monir Khazraii Nahvi; m. Floyd Milton Johnson, July 2, 1960; children: Rebecca, Nancy, Robert. BS, U. Minn., 1967, MA, 1969, PhD, 2001. Stenographer Curtis 1000, Inc., St. Paul, 1958-62; lab. instr. U. Minn., Mpls., 1966-69, teaching asst., 1969-72; chief exec. officer Real Estate Investment and Mgmt. Enterprise, St. Paul, 1969—; prof. emeritus sociology Anoka-Ramsey C.C., Coon Rapids, Minn., 1973—2003. Pub. speaker, bd. dirs., sponsor pub. radio KFAI, Mpls., 1989-93; established an endowed scholarship for women Anoka Ramsey C.C., 1991. Radio talk show host KCW, Brookline Parks, Minn., 1993. Organizer Iranian earthquake disaster relief, 1990; bd. dirs. dist. 7 Cmty. Coun., 1996-98. Recipient Earthquake Relief Orgn. citation Iranian Royal Household, 1968, Islamic Republic of Iran citation for organizing earthquake disaster relief, 1990. Mem.: NEA, Sociologists of Minn., Minn. Edn. Assn., Women's Leadership Forum, Nat. Social Scis. Assn., U. Minn. Alumni Assn. Avocations: world travel, classical and historical novels, exotic food, gardening. Home: 1726 Iowa Ave E Saint Paul MN 55106-1334 Office Phone: 651-771-8000. Business E-Mail: john1800@tc.umn.edu.

JOHNSON, BARBARA E., adult education educator; b. Butte, Mont., Jan. 27, 1924; d. Warner Alexander and Ellen Onerva (Hermanson) Newman; m. Harold Arvid Johnson, Dec. 13, 1941; children: Carol Johnson Evans, Beth Johnson Egner, Adele Johnson Osborne, Divra Johnson Perkins, Eden. Adult edn. credential, Yuba Coll., 1980; clear life credential, Sacramento State Coll. Nurse's asst. Kaiser Hosp., Walnut Creek, Calif., 1970-75; dental nurse U.S. Army, Camp Abbot, Oreg., 1940-42; dental nurse, San Francisco, 1940-41; tchr. adult edn. Marysville (Calif.) Sch. Dist., 1975-79; instr. adult edn. Umpqua C.C., Roseburg, Oreg., 1996—. Bd. dirs. Yuba County Resource Conservation Dist., Yuba City, Calif., 1976-80. Mem. Epsilon Sigma Alpha (pres. 1974). Democrat. Lutheran. Avocations: gardening, painting, sculpting, dance. Home: 180 Emerald St Sutherlin OR 97479-7604

JOHNSON, BARBARA ELIZABETH, lawyer; b. Des Moines, Aug. 2, 1957; d. William Frederick and Dorothy Jane (Colvin) Spotz; m. Richard Gordon Johnson, Mar. 4, 1984. BS, Grove City (Pa.) Coll., 1979; JD, Coll. of William and Mary, 1984. Bar: Pa. 1984, U.S. Dist. Ct. (we. dist.) Pa. 1984, U.S. Ct. Appeals (3d and Fed. cirs.) 1984. Patent agt. NASA-Langley Rsch. Ctr., Hampton, Va., 1982-84; assoc. atty. The Webb Law Firm, Pitts., 1984-92, shareholder, dir., 1992—. Mng. dir. The Webb Law Firm, 2001-04; bd. dirs. Precision Staffing Svcs., Inc., Metro Family Practice. Recipient Alumni Achievement award, Grove City Coll., 2004. Mem.: Pitts. Intellectual Property Law Assn. (pres. 2000—01), Am. Chem. Soc. (chmn. Pitts. sect. 1995), Pitts. Chemists Club. Republican. Avocations: piano, writing, figure skating, auto repairing. E-mail: bjohnson@webblaw.com.

JOHNSON, BARBARA ELLA JACKSON, city official; b. Lexington, Ky., Aug. 4, 1934; d. William Atress and Nancy Lee (Thomas) Jackson; widowed; children: Elizabeth Y., William C., Antojean. Food activities mgr. Army and Air Force Exch., Ft. Campbell, Ky., 1973-90; vol. various orgns., Clarksville, Tenn., 1990—; mem. City Coun., Clarksville, 1999—. Mem. adv. bd. Tenn. Vocat. Tng. Ctr., Clarksville, 1999—; mem. bus. adv. coun. Goldwill Industries, Clarksville, 1999—. Mem. Montgomery County Millennium, 1999—; mem. Leadership Clarksville, 1999—. Mem. NAACP (prs. 1997—), Clarksville C. of C., Tenn. Mcpl. League Women in Govt., Internat. Tng. in Comm. (prs. 1982-90), Order Eastern Star. Democrat. Baptist. Avocations: working with people with disabilities, voter registration, teaching Sunday school. Home: 2218 Robin Dr Clarksville TN 37042-5696

JOHNSON, BARBARA L., retired municipal official; b. Birmingham, Ala., Nov. 20, 1927; d. Robert F. Nichols and Lula Henderson; m. Sam Johnson Jr., Apr. 9, 1949; children: William Mark, Karen Ann, Pamela Denise. Inventory acct. Birmingham Bd. Edn., 1970—94. 4 time pres., mem. com. PTA, Birmingham, 1960—70; vol. Birmingham Mus. Art, 2001; mem. Blount County Edn. Found.; host, 8 foreign students; active in mission work Smoke Rise Bapt. Ch. Recipient Citizen of Yr. award, Blount County, 2000. Mem.: Smoke Rise Homeowners Assn. (past pres.), Smithsonian Instn., Smoke Rise Garden Club, Blount County C. of C. Home: 1556 Grandview Trl Warrior AL 35180

JOHNSON, BARBARA PIASECKA, volunteer, art historian, investor; b. Staniewicze, Poland; d. Pelagia and Wojciech Piasecki; m. J. Seward Johnson 1971 (dec.1983). Grad., U. Wroclaw. Chair., dir. trustee Barbara Piasecka Johnson Found., 1974—. Owner extensive art collection, Barbara Piasecka Johnson Collection; mem. bd. mgrs. Wistar Inst., Phila., 1989-91; mem. chmn.'s coun. Met. Mus. Art, N.Y.C., 1986; mem. adv. com. Nat. Gallery Art, Washington, 1980-91; bd. dirs. Inst. for Polish-Jewish Studies, Oxford, Eng.; mem. fine arts com. U.S. Dept. State, 1978-85; mem. strategic adv. com. dept. molecular genetics and microbiology Robert Wood Johnson Med. Sch., U. Medicine and Dentistry N.J. Trustee, bd. dirs. Atlantic Found., 1972-85, Harbor Br. Found., 1972-85; trustee, chair Paderewski Ctr.; mem. coun. Found. for U. Wroclaw, 1991-92. Recipient Heritage award Polish Am. Congress, 1989, Nat. Citizen of Yr. award Am-Pol Eagle, 1989, Disting. Svc. award Am. Coun. for Polish Culture, 1990, Award St. Brother Albert Chmielowski, 1990, Hon. Citizen award State of Calif., 1990, Appreciation diploma Min. Fgn. Affairs Republic Poland, 1991, Gold medal U. Wroclaw, 1991, Sci. Devel. award Acad. Agriculture Wroclaw, 1991, Crystal Heart award Found. for Devel. Cardiac Surgery Zabrze, 1992, Merit cert. Pres. Coun. N.Y.C., 1993, Champion of Democracy award Coll. Democracy Washington, 1993, Waclaw Nizynski medal Polish Artists Agy, 1994, Living Legacy award Women's Internat. Ctr., 1994, The Order of Saint Charles Officer decoration conferred by H.S.H. Prince Rainier III in recognition of svcs. rendered to the Principality of Monaco, 1995; named one of Forbes' Richest Americans, 2006. Mem. Am. Assn. for Polish-Jewish Studies (hon. chmn.), Rotary Internat. (Paul Harris fellow 1988). Office: BPJ Holding Corp 4519 Province Line Rd Princeton NJ 08540-2211*

JOHNSON, BERIT BAILEY, psychologist, consultant; b. Houston, Nov. 1, 1974; d. Weldon D. and Paula McIlvain Bailey; m. Jeffrey Shane Johnson, Apr. 13, 2002. BA with honors, U. Texas, Austin, 1993—97; PhD, U. of Tex. Southwestern Med. Ctr., Dallas, 2001. Licensed Psychologist Tex. State Bd. Examiners of Psychologists, 2003. Tchg. asst. U. of Tex. Southwestern Med. Ctr., Dallas, 1998—2001, clin. intern and rschr., 1998—2001; psychology resident Tex. Pain Medicine Clinic, Dallas, 2001—03; pvt. practice clin. psychologist Dallas Mind/Body Medicine, Dallas, 2003—. Psychotherapy supr. U. of Tex. Southwestern Med. Ctr., Dallas, 2003—, blind evaluator depression rsch., 2003—. Contbr. articles to profl. jours. Recipient Phi Beta Kappa, Alpha Chpt. of Tex., 1997; scholar Undergraduate Rsch. Scholarship, U. of Tex. at Austin, 1997. Mem.: APA, Tex. Psychol. Assn., Phi Beta Kappa. Achievements include research in effects of physical and sexual abuse on treatment outcomes of chronic pain patients. Office: Berit Johnson PhD PC Ste 106 3100 Carlisle St Dallas TX 75204 E-mail: beritjohnsonphd@flash.net.

JOHNSON, BERNETTE JOSHUA, state supreme court justice; b. Ascension Parish, La. d. Frank Joshua Jr. and Olivia W. Johnson. BA, Spelman Coll., Atlanta, 1964; JD, La. State U., 1969; LLD (hon.), Spelman Coll., 2001. Bar: La. Law intern Civil Rights divsn. U.S. Dept. Justice; judge La. Civil Dist. Ct., 1984-94, chief judge, 1994; assoc. justice La. Supreme Ct., New Orleans, 1994—. Legal svc. atty. New Orleans Legal Assistance Corp.; community organizer NAACP Legal Defense & Educational Fund, NYC; chair New Orleans Chapter So. Christian Leadership Conference. Bd. dirs. YMCA, New Orleans; chmn. bd. Learning Ctr., Greater St. Stephen Full Gospel Bapt. Ch.; bd. dirs. NOLAC, 1992-99. Named Woman of Yr., LaBelle chpt. Am. Bus. Women's Assn., 1994; Named one of Outstanding Women on Bench New Orleans Assn. Black Women Attorneys; recipient Ernest N. Morial award NOLAC, Daniel Byrd award NAACP, A.P. Tureaud Citizenship award NAACP, Margaret A. Brent Women Lawyers of Achievement award ABA. Office: La Supreme Ct 400 Royal St New Orleans LA 70130*

JOHNSON, BETSEY LEE, fashion designer; b. Hartford, Conn., Aug. 10, 1942; d. John Herman and Lena Virginia J.; m. John Cale, Apr. 4, 1966; 1 child, Lulu; m. Jeffrey Olivier, Feb. 7, 1981. Student, Pratt Inst., N.Y.C., 1960-61; BA, U. Syracuse, 1964. Editorial asst. Mademoiselle mag., 1964-65; prin. designer Paraphernalia (owned by Puritan Fashions, Inc.), 1965—69; ptnr., co-owner Betsey, Bunky & Nini, N.Y.C., 1969; designer Alvin Duskin Co., San Francisco, 1970; head designer Alley Cat by Betsey Johnson (div. LeDamor, Inc.), 1970—74; freelance designer jr. women's div. Butterick Pattern Co., 1971—75; designer Betsey Johnson's Kids Children Wear, Shutterbug, Inc., 1974—77, Jeanette Maternities, Inc., 1974-75, 1974—75; designer first line womens clothing Gant Shirtmakers, Inc., 1974—75; designer Tric-Trac by Betsey Johnson, Womens Knitwear, 1974—76; head designer jr. sportswear Star Ferry by Betsey Johnson and Michael Milea, 1975—77; owner, head designer B.J., Inc., N.Y.C., 1978—; owner retail stores N.Y.C, L.A., San Francisco, Coconut Grove, Fla., Venice, Calif., Boston, Chgo., Seattle, London, Eng., Vancouver, B.C. Hon. chair. Fashion Targets Breast Cancer initiative, CFDA, 2004. Named to Fashion Walk of Fame, 2002; recipient Coty award, 1972, Timeless Talent award, CFDA, 1999. Mem. Coun. Fashion Designers Am., Women's Forum. Office: Betsey Johnson Co 251 E 60th St New York NY 10022*

JOHNSON, BETSIE RUTH, pre-school educator; b. Phila., Pa., Sept. 14, 1943; d. George Edmond and Gertrude Marjorie (Davis) Johnson; 1 child from previous marriage, Bettina Joneé Miller. AA, St. Mary's Seminary, St. Mary City, Md., 1963; BS magna cum laude, U. Md., Coll. Pk., 1965; MEd, Towson State Coll., Towson, 1975. Tchr. 1st grade Balto County, Md., 1965—77, Kindergarten, pre-K tchr. Md., 1985—; reading specialist Tampa, Jacksonville, Fla., 1977—79. Supervising tchr. Towson State Students, Balto, 1976—. Usher, greeter Towson United Meth. Ch., 1989—. Mem.: AAUW, Paint & Powder Club, Inc. (sec. 2005—), Phi Beta Kappa, Beta Sigma Phi (pres. 2003—05), Pi Beta Phi (pres. 1965—). Republican. Methodist. Avocations: bear collector, crafts, gardening. Office Phone: 410-887-0761. Personal E-mail: betsiebear@verizon.net.

JOHNSON, BEVERLY J., lawyer, congressman; b. Alameda, Calif., Oct. 2, 1958; d. Robert Harold and Jean Ann Follrath; m. Michael Francis Johnson, Feb. 21, 1982; children: Geoffrey Michael, Katherine Ann. MusB, Calif. State U., Hayward, 1980; JD, U. Pacific, 1986. Bar: Calif. 1986, U.S. Dist., 1986, U.S. Cir. Ct. (9th Cir.), 1986, U.S. Supreme Ct., 1996. Law clerk U.S. Atty.'s Office, Sacramento, Calif., 1984-85; atty. Law Offices of Wilance Russum, Alameda, 1986-93, Dist. Atty.'s Office, Alameda, 1994-95; prin. Law Offices Beverly J. Johnson, Alameda, 1997—; mem. city coun. City of Alameda, 1999—. Commr. Alameda Reuse and Redevel. Authority, 1998—, Alameda Housing Authority, 1998—. Trustee Alameda Hosp. Found., 1991—, Children's Learning Ctr., Alameda, 1993—; trustee, bd. dirs. Alameda Edn. Found., 1999—; bd. dirs. Alameda Planning Bd., 1995-98. Mem. U.S. Supreme Ct. Hist. Soc., State Bar Calif., Kiwanis Club Alameda. Avocations: sports, music, art. Office: City of Alameda 2263 Santa Clara Ave Alameda CA 94501-4400 also: 512 Westline Dr Ste 300 Alameda CA 94501-5870 Fax: 510-865-1882. E-mail: Bkillybegs@aol.com.

JOHNSON, BONNIE, art educator; b. Keyser, W.Va., Jan. 8, 1947; BA, Berea Coll., Ky., 1968; MA Tchg., Wesleyan U., Middletown, Conn., 1970; MA Liberal Studies, Wesleyan U., 1981; cert. supr., Ctrl. Conn. State U., New Britain, 1989. Cert. tchr. K-12, Conn., Mass. Instr. art Valley Regional H.S., Deep River, Conn., 1969—79; studio artist Farmington Valley Arts Ctr., Avon, Conn., 1980—88; instr. art Conn. pub./pvt. schs., 1987—91; adj. asst. prof. Iowa State U., Ames, 1991—95. Chmn. art dept. Valley Regional H.S., Deep River, 1972—78; dir. program Farmington Valley Arts Ctr., Avon, 1981—83. Artist abstract murals Recipient Best in Show award 57th Ann. Art Exhbn., New Haven, 1986, Commd. Artwork John Dempsey Hosp., Farmington, Conn., 1988 Avocations: hiking, writing, 2-D, 3-D, travel, toy design. Home: 42 Graham Rd Hartford CT 06118-2128

JOHNSON, BRENDA L., university librarian; MLS, Rutgers U. Reference libr. Rutgers U., 1979, head interlibrary loan svcs. and NJ reference svcs.; libr. U. Mich., Ann Arbor, 1985—, assoc. univ. libr., 1997—, interim co-univ. libr., 2006—. Office: Libr Adminstrn U Mich 818 Hatcher S Ann Arbor MI 48109-1205 Office Phone: 734-764-9356. Office Fax: 734-764-5080. E-mail: bljohn@umich.edu.*

JOHNSON, BRENDA LAGRANGE, ambassador; BA, Duke U.; MA, Columbia U. Ptnr. BrenMer Industries, 1977—2005; tchr. Operation Head Start, Adminstrn. for Children and Families US Dept. Health & Human Svcs., supr., mem. nat. cancer advisory bd., nat. inst. health, 1989—94; mem. Nat. Fin. Com. Bush-Cheney Presdl. Campaign, 2004; U.S. amb. to Jamaica US Dept. State, Kingston, 2005—. Trustee President's advisory coun. on the arts John F. Kennedy Ctr. for Performing Arts Smithsonian Inst., 2002—. Office: 3030 K St NW Washington DC 20007-5107*

JOHNSON, BROOKE BAILEY, broadcast executive; b. LA, May 12, 1951; d. Edwin Beauvais and Jeanne (Foote) Bailey; m. Peter Michael Johnson, Sept. 18, 1982; children: Bailey Peter, Lee Keating. BA, Northwestern U., 1973, MS in Journalism, 1974. Promotion dir. Sta. KGUN-TV, Tucson, 1975-77; asst. programming dir. Sta. WLS-TV, Chgo., 1977-82; dir. programming Sta. WABC-TV, NYC, 1982-89; became v.p. programming Arts & Entertainment Network, NYC, 1989, sr. v.p. programming and production, 1989—2000; cons. A&E; sr. v.p. and gen. mgr. The Food Network, NYC, 2003—04, pres., 2004—. Mem. NOW. Mem. Nat. Cable Acad., Cable TV Assn., NATAS, Nat. Assn. TV Program Execs. (Iris award), Kappa Alpha Theta. Office: The Food Network 1180 Avenue of the Americas New York NY 10036

JOHNSON, CAMILLE, media executive; BA in Journalism, U. Oreg. With Chiat/Day Advt., San Francisco, 1980-90; sr. v.p., media dir. GMO/Hill Holliday, San Francisco, 1990—.

JOHNSON, CANDICE ELAINE BROWN, pediatrician, educator; b. Cin., Mar. 21, 1946; d. Paul Preston and Naomi Elizabeth Brown; m. Thomas Raymond Johnson, June 30, 1973; children: Andrea Eleanor, Erik Albert. BS, U. Mich., 1968; PhD Microbiology, Case Western Reserve U., 1973, MD, 1976. Diplomate Am. Bd. Pediat., 1981. Intern, resident in pediat. Rainbow Babies and Children's Hosp./Met. Gen. Hosp., Cleve., 1976-78; fellow in ambulatory pediatrics Met. Gen. Hosp., 1978-79; asst. prof. pediat. Case Western Res. U., Cleve., 1980-90, assoc. prof., 1990-97; prof. pediat. U. Colo., Denver, 1997—; pediatrician Children's Hosp., Denver, 1997—. Mem. rev. panel NIH, Washington, 1993; faculty sen. Case Western Res. U., 1988-91; mem. spkrs. bur. Merck, GlaxoSmithKline, Abbott Labs. Contbr. articles profl. jours. Mem. Am. Acad. Pediat., Pediat. Infectious Disease Soc., Infectious Diseases Soc. Am., Soc. for Pediatric Rsch., So. Utah Wilderness Alliance, Sierra Club. Home: 2290 Locust St Denver CO 80207-3943 Office Phone: 303-861-6007.

JOHNSON, CARLA CONRAD, library dean; b. Cleve., June 10, 1948; d. James Procop and Joanne Graham Conrad; m. Roger Jeffrey Freeman, Mar. 23, 1979 (div. 1995); children: Jason Hale Freeman, Johanna Erica Freeman; m. Jeffery Harry Johnson, 1997. BA, U. Pa., 1969; MLS, SUNY, 1982; MS in Art Edn., Alfred U., 1988. Visual resources asst. Scholes Libr. Ceramics, NYS Coll. Ceramics Alfred U., NY, 1979—85, asst. libr., visual resources & art ref., Scholes Libr. Ceramics, NYS Coll. Ceramics, 1985—90, assoc. libr., visual resources & art ref., Scholes Libr. Ceramics, NYS Coll. Ceramics, 1990—95, dir., Scholes Libr. Ceramics, NYS Coll. Ceramics, 1993—, libr., 1995—, dean librs., 2005—. Cons. Vassar Coll., Art Libr., Poughkeepsie, NY, 1994; evaluator NSF Industry U. Ctr. Glass Rsch., Pa., 1995—2005; evaluator Internat. Mats. Inst. New Functionality in Glasses NSF, 1995—. Editor: (reference book) The Visual Resources Directory: Art Slide and Photograph Collections in the United States and Canada, 1995 (Worldwide Books Publ. award, Art Libraries Soc. N.Am., 1997); contbg. editor: (book) Fusion: A Centennial History of the New York State College of Ceramics, 2003. Recipient Chancellor's award for Excellence in Librarianship, SUNY, 1993; grantee Rsch. and Publ. grant, The Visual Resources Directory, Samuel H. Kress Found., 1992. Mem.: Visual Resources Assn. (pres. 1990—92), Am. Ceramic Soc. (design divsn. chair 1998—99), SUNY Librarians Assn., SUNY Coun. Libr. Directors (sec. 2002—04, chair elect, program chair 2005—06, chair 2006—), Phi Kappa Phi (chpt. pres. 1992—93). D-Liberal. Avocations: book collecting, photography, drawing, painting. Office: Alfred U Scholes Libr 2 Pine St Alfred NY 14802-1297

JOHNSON, CAROL R., school system administrator; BA in Elem. Edn., Fisk U., 1969; MA in Curriculum and Instrn., U. Minn., 1980, D in Edn. Policy and Adminstrn., 1997. Elem. tchr. Washington Pub. Schs., 1969; elem. tchr., coord. career opportunities Mpls. Pub. Schs., 1970-76; coord. R&D, project dir. tng. urban educators U. Minn., Mpls., 1976-86; prin., asst. prin. elem. schs. Mpls. Pub. Schs., 1986-89, asst. to assoc. supt. elem. edn., assoc. supt., 1989-95; supt. St. Louis Park (Minn.) Schs., 1995-97, Mpls. Pub. Schs., 1997—2004, Memphis Pub. Schs., 2004—. Spkr. in field. Bd. dirs. The Found., Health Sys. Minn., Boy Scouts Am. Viking Coun., adv. com. Learning for Life; commn. mem. Golden Valley Police, Civil Svc., 1990—, chair, 1994-95, U. Minn. Alumni Assn., comm. and fin. com. Bush Leadership fellow, 1993-94; recipient Apple for Teacher award Iota Phi Lambda, 1992-93, Leadership award Omega Psi Phi, 1996. Mem. ASCD (Minn. chpt.), NAS/Nat. Rsch. Coun. (strategic edn. rsch. program feasibility study 1996—), Am. Assn. Sch. Adminstrs., Minn. Assn. Sch. Adminstrs. (edn. policy com. 1996-97), LWV Golden Valley, Mpls. Links, Inc. (St. Paul chpt.), Jack and Jill, Inc. (Mpls. chpt.), Children First Exec. Com. and Vision Team St. Louis Park, Delta Sigma Theta. Office: Memphis Public Schools RM 215 2597 Avery Memphis TN 38112 Office Phone: 901-416-5300. Office Fax: 901-416-5578.

JOHNSON, CAROLE JEAN, investment company executive; b. Temple, Tex., June 5, 1959; d. Lloyd Melvin Johnson and Shirley Faye (Bruss) Druley; 1 child, James Adam. AA, NE Wis. Tech. Coll., Green Bay, 1988. Bookkeeper, sec. White House Music, Waukesha, Wis., 1976-77; acct. Lamplight Farms, Brookfield, Wis., 1979; prodn. clk. W.A. Krueger, Brookfield, 1979-80; data processing asst. Video Images, West Allis, Wis., 1980-85; adminstrn. asst. Jones Intercable, Brookfield, 1985; computer programmer Anamax Corp., Green Bay, Wis., 1988-89; quality assurance analyst Nielsen Mktg. Rsch., Green Bay, 1989; applications programmer N.E. Wis. Tech. Coll., Green Bay, 1990—95; programmer, analyst Fabry Glove & Mitten Co., Green Bay, 1995-96; tech. svcs. mgr. Technology Cons. Corp., Green Bay, Wis., 1996—2001; pres. Strategic Property Investments, Thornton, Colo., 2001—; CFO & v.p. Tool Belt Enterprises, LLC, Thornton, 2003—. Roman Catholic. Office: 12301 Grant St Ste 160 Thornton CO 80241 Office Phone: 303-545-6460. Personal E-mail: ladytchboss@hotmail.com.

JOHNSON, CAROLYN ELIZABETH, librarian; b. Oakland, Calif., May 29, 1921; d. Ferdinand Orin and Clara Wells (Humphrey) Hassler; m. Benjamin Alfred Johnson, Feb. 12, 1943; children: Robin Rebecca, Anne Elizabeth, Delia Mary. BA, U. Calif.-Berkeley, 1946; cert. libr., Calif. State U. Fullerton, 1960; MLS, Immaculate Heart Coll., 1968. Cert. libr. Calif. Asst. children's libr. Fullerton Pub. Libr., 1951—59, coord. children's svcs., 1959—81, city libr., 1981—90, ret., 1990, apptd. curator Mary Campbell collection hist. children's lit., 1990. Part-time instr. Rio Hondo City Coll., Whittier, Calif., 1970—72, Calif. State U.-Fullerton, 1972—77; vice chmn. 3d Pacific Rim Conf. Coun., 1983—86; mem. Korczak award com. U.S. Bd. Books for Young People, 1988. Author: (book) The Art of Walter Crane, 1988. Founding bd. dirs. Youth Sci. Ctr., Fullerton, 1958; mem. Libr. Tech. Tng. Adv. Com., Fullerton Coll., 1970; chmn. adv. bd. YWCA Child Devel. Ctr., 1992—; bd. dirs. Fullerton Pub. Libr. Found., mem. endowment fund, 1994, sec., 1995; bd. dirs. Friends of the Fullerton Pub. Libr. Named Profl. Woman of Yr., North Orange County YWCA, 1986, Woman of Yr., Fullerton C. of C., 1990, North Orange County YWCA, 2003. Mem.: LWV, AAUW, ALA, PTA (life), So. Calif. Coun. on Lit. for Children and Young People (pres. 1979—81, Dorothy C. McKenzie award 1987), Orange County Libr. Assn. (v.p.), Calif. Libr. Assn. (chmn. children's service div.), Theta Sigma Phi, Phi Beta Kappa. Methodist. Home: 644 Princeton Cir E Fullerton CA 92831-2728

JOHNSON, CAROLYN M., librarian, writer; b. Bklyn., Apr. 3, 1949; AA in Liberal Arts, Queensborough C.C., Bayside, N.Y., 1970; BA in English and Am. Lit., Hunter Coll., 1973; M Libr. and Info. Sci., St. John's U., Jamaica, NY, 1975, MA in English and Am. Lit., 1980. Cataloging libr. Pace U. Libr., N.Y.C., 1978—79, N.Y. Bot. Garden Libr., Bronx Park, NY, 1979—81; libr., web rschr., writer Greenwood Press, Westport, Conn., 1980—2002, Librs. Unltd. mem. Greenwood Pub. Group, Westport, 2002—. Online libr., ednl. writer THE BOOK BAG on Am. Online, N.Y.C., 1996—2001; web site rschr., evaluator, site summary writer studyweb.com, San Diego, 1999—2000; web site evaluator Ctr. for Montessori Tchr. Edn., White Plains, NY, 1997—99. Author: Discovering Nature with Young People: An Annotated Bibliography and Selection Guide, 1987, Using Internet Primary Sources to Teach Critical Thinking Skills in the Sciences, 2003; contbr. articles to profl. jours., articles to lit. mags., children's ednl. mags. and to ednl. websites; primary host AOL Children's Writers Online Chat/Workshop, 2005—. Mem.: Soc. Children's Book Writers and Illustrators. Avocations: photography, reading, genealogy, classical music. E-mail: WriterLibr@aol.com.

JOHNSON, CARRIE CLEMENTS, pharmaceutical executive; b. Atlanta, Sept. 2, 1931; d. Emanuel G. and Lucile Clements; 1 child, Alfia Katherine. BA, Morris Brown Coll., Atlanta, 1951; MA, Columbia U., N.Y.C., 1954; DEd, SUNY Buffalo, 1978. Tchr. Fulton County Schs., Atlanta, 1951—54, 1955; dir. Career Planning Morris Brown Coll., Atlanta, 1961—67; assoc. prof., asst. prof. Buffalo State Coll., 1967—86; dir. affirmative action, staff devel. Fulton County Schs., Atlanta, 1986—95; CEO Johnson & Johnson, Atlanta, 1996—. Author: Career Opportunities for the Minorities, 1974. Bd. dirs. Atlanta br. NAACP; mem. pers. bd. Fulton County Cathechist, Atlanta, 2003—. Named Atlanta's Woman of Yr., Health Bus. League Atlanta, 2005; named to Who's Who Black Humanists, 1978, Who's Who Black Women, 2000; recipient Edn. award, Alpha Kappa Alpha, 1984. Mem.: LWV, Zeta Phi Beta. Avocations: piano, attending plays and concerts. Home: 3965 Old Fairburn Rd SW Atlanta GA 30331

JOHNSON, CARYN ELAINE See GOLDBERG, WHOOPI

JOHNSON, CECILE RYDEN (MRS. PHILIP JOHNSON), artist; b. Jamestown, N.Y. d. Ernest Edwin and Agnes E. (Johnson) Ryden; children: Pamela Cecile, Stevan Philip. AB, Augustana Coll.; postgrad., Am. Acad. Fine Arts, Art Inst. Chgo., U. Wis., U. Colo., Pa. Acad. Fine Art, Scripps Coll. One-woman shows include Grand Cen. Gallery, N.Y.C., 1965, 67, 69, 71, 73, 75, TWA Paris, 1973, Greenville Mus. Art, Remington Mus., 1980; exhibited with Am. Watercolor Soc., Washington Watercolor Soc., Artist Guild of Chgo., Art Dirs. Annual, Nat. Acad., N.Y.C., Soc. of Illustrators; designed and executed stained glass windows for Nursery Chapel, Augustana, Chgo., 12 paintings on Bermuda for collection Bank of Bermuda, 1964, mural for Bermuda Airport, 1966, 32 paintings for U.S. Naval Art Collection on women in naval service, ofcl. lithographs, nat. fine art com. Lake Placid Olympic Organizing Com., 1980; traveling solo exhibit Am. Univs., 1964-66; designed covers Ford Times, Chgo. Tribune Sunday Mag., others; designed Am. UNICEF Christmas card for 1968; illustration in Motor Boating, Ford Times, Lincoln Mercury Times; designed and executed Memorable Mountains series for Skiing Mag., 1965-74, folios of ski prints for Aspen, Vail, Snowbird, Lake Tahoe, series of 16 prints for TWA on Paris, London, Rome, 1973, series of paintings and folio prints for Napa Valley Vinters, 1975, Broadmoor Hotel, Colorado Springs, 10 originals and 450 signed prints for Broadmoor West, 1976, mural for 1st Fed. Savings and Loan, St. Paul, Bicentennial painting of St. Paul's Fed. Courts Bldg., silk screen for U.S. Hockey Team, 1976 Olympics; represented in permanent collections Augustana Coll., Gen. Mills, Minn. Mining, Ford Motor Co., Nat. Safety Council, Henderson Coll., Wagner Coll., Skiing Mag., Davenport Mcpl. Art Gallery, Windjammer Gallery, Bermuda, Driscol Gallery, Beaver Creek, Colo., Scoble Gallery, Keystone, Colo., Kimball Art Ctr., Park City, Utah, others; affiliation Grand Cen. Galleries, N.Y.C., others; featured in film Creating in Watercolor, on ABC Wide World of Sports, 1977, 79, in Am. Artists Mag., Jan. 1983, 87. Recipient awards All Ill. Watercolor, 1953, Ill. Fedn. Music Clubs, 1955, Outstanding Achievement award Alumni Assn. Augustana Coll., 1962, Woman of Achievement award in Art Nat. League Pen Women, 1962, Catherine Lorillard Wolffe gold medal for watercolor, 1965, Disting. Citizen citation Macalester Coll., 1979; named 1st Woman Artist by USN and NACAL Com. Salmagana Club. Mem. Am. Watercolor Soc., Soc. Illustrators, Allied Artists, Knickerbocker Soc., Audubon Art Soc., Nat. Arts Club. Lutheran. Studio: One W 67th St New York NY 10023

JOHNSON, CHARLENE ELIZABETH, adult education educator, language educator, consultant; b. Aurora, Ill., June 7, 1933; d. Floyd Clark and Marion Priscilla Smith; m. Bennett F. Johnson, July 25, 1955 (div. 1961); children: Roderick Julian, Marshall Floyd. BSE, Butler U., Indpls., 1960, MSE, 1968, EdS, 1982; EdD in Leadership Early & Mid Childhood, Nova U., Villanova, Pa., 1992. Classroom tchr. Indpls. Pub. Schs., 1960-68, reading tchr., 1968-71, lang. arts cons., 1972-82, reading tchr., 1982-90. Condr. parent workshops in reading Flanner House, 1980, 4 parent workshops, N.E. orgns., 1988; conducted workshops for Even Start Parents, 1990-92; adult edn. tchr. Even Start Family Literacy Program, 1990-99, ret., 1999. Author: Parent Primer, 1979. Instrumentalist Butler U. Orch., 1971-92, Christian Ch. String Ensemble, Indpls. Philharm. Orch., bd. dirs. 1995; trainer reading tutors Pub. Housing Authority; vol. Ptnrs. in Edn., Harshman Jr. H.S. Mem. NEA, NAACP, Nat. Assn. Edn. Young Children, Internat. Reading Assn., Indpls. Reading Assn., Ind. Reading Assn., Nat. Coun. Negro Women, Indpls. Edn. Assn., Ind. State Tchrs. Assn., Indpls. Assn. for Edn. Young Children, Midwest Assn. Edn. of Young Children, Nat. Assn. for Edn. of Young Children, Delta Sigma Theta, Sigma Alpha Iota, Phi Delta Kappa.

JOHNSON, CHARLENE ROSE, writer; b. Sharon, Pa., Oct. 15, 1950; d. Charles Ralph Wilson and Lena Belle (Wilson) Moore. Student, Drew U., U. Fla., Thomas Edison U., 2002. Staff writer Horseman's Jour., Rockville, Md., 1980-82; editor Fla. Horse Mag., Ocala, 1982-84; free-lance writer. Author: Florida Thoroughbred, 1993, Animal Angels, 2003. Chmh. Marion County Hist. commn., Ocala, 1990-96, Marion Sesquicentennial Commn., Ocala, 1995—; profl. esoteric astrologer, pk. svcs. specialist, Fla. Pk. Svc. Recipient writing award Fla. Thoroughbred Breeders Assn., 1982, 85, 86. Mem. Fla. Outdoor Writers Assn. Democrat. Avocations: sailing, diving, horses, Native Am. crafts. Home: 14971 SE 107th Ave Summerfield FL 34491-3779 Office Phone: 352-465-8539. Personal E-mail: ospreyrose@earthlink.net.

JOHNSON, CHARLOTTE LEE, librarian; b. Ladysmith, Wis., Dec. 22, 1951; d. Wesley Carl and Ethel Margaret (Lowers) J. BA in Art Edn. and Integrated Liberal Studies, U. Wis., 1974, MLS, 1975. Tchr., librarian Victorian Edn. Dept., Victoria, Australia, 1976-80; freelance artist, photographer Asia, Europe, Can., 1980; asst. phys. scis. librarian Okla. State U., Stillwater, 1981-83, So. Ill. U., Edwardsville, 1983, dir. user svcs., 1983—. Artist (multi-media) Harmony is in the Green, 1986 (Grand prize Artists at the Sta., St. Louis); contbr. articles to profl. jour. Library senator So. Ill. U. Senate, Edwardsville, 1983-86; pres. So. Ill. Network of Women, 1987; mem. Friends of St. Louis Art Mus.; bd. dirs. Friends of Lovejoy Library, Edwardsville, 1986—. So. Ill. U. grantee, 1986. Mem. ALA, AAUP (treas. So. Ill. U. chpt. 1985-88, treas. Ill. chpt. 1986-88), Ill. Library Assn., Assn. of Coll. and Research Libraries, Am. Entrepreneurs Soc., Popular Culture Assn. (presenter ann. conf. 1988), Friends of Bard Hunter Paper Mus. Office: Lovejoy Library Southern Illinois Univ Edwardsville IL 62026-0001

JOHNSON, CHERYL L., nursing administrator; 1 child. BSN, U. Mich., 1972. Critical care nurse U. Mich. Health Systems, Ann Arbor; pres., chair United Am. Nurses, 1999—. Mem. AFL-CIO Exec. Coun. Named one of 100 Most Powerful People in Health CAre, Modern Healthcare mag., 2003; recipient, 2004. Mem.: U. Mich. Profl. Nurse Coun. (chair, vice-chair), Mich. Nurses Assn. (pres. 2003—, former v.p., pres. Washtenaw-Livingston-Monroe chpt.). Office: United Am Nurses 8515 Georgia Ave Silver Spring MD 20910 Office Phone: 301-628-5118. Business E-Mail: UANinfo@uannurse.org.

JOHNSON, CHERYL LYNN HALL, secondary education educator, website designer; b. Elmhurst, Ill., Aug. 7, 1951; d. Leslie Eugene Gutzmer and Betty Ann (Rink) Denson; m. A. Burton Hall, Jr., Sept. 9, 1972; children: Jason, Casey; m. Everett Alan Johnson, July 3, 1999 BA, We. Ill. U., 1975; MEd, DePaul U., 1981. Cert. Webmaster, 1997. Tchr. English St. Charles H.S., Ill., 1975—79, Glenbard West H.S., Glen Ellyn, Ill., 1979—2006; ret., 2006. Collaborator Compu-Write Glenbard West H.S., 1988; conv. participant Read Ill. Sch. Dist. 87 rsch. grantee We. Ill. U., 1989, 90, Eng., 1990. Mem. NEA, Nat. Coun. Tchrs. English, Ill. Assn. Tchrs. English (presenter at conv. 1991), Glenbard Edn. Assn., Multi-Ethnic Lit. U.S., N.Am. Torquay Pottery Soc. (nat. sec. 1992-94, editor/pub. 1994-96), Torquay Pottery Collectors Soc. Avocations: stained glass art, travel, bicycling, antiques. Home: 11881 Covey Ln Huntley IL 60142-6222

JOHNSON, CHRISTINE TOY, actress, writer; d. Tom You and Mary Huie Toy; m. Bruce Alan Johnson, Aug. 22, 1996. BA, Sarah Lawrence Coll., Bronxville, N.Y. Voter Am. Theatre Wing Tony Awards, N.Y.C., 1992—; bd. dir. Non-Traditional Casting Project, 2001—; lectr. in field. Prodr.(and writer): All American Eyes, 2004; author: (screenplays) Old, Fat & Ugly, 2005, Jumping the Third Rail, 2005, (plays) The New Deal, 2005, The Perfect Wife, 2006; actor: (films) Marci X, Conspiracy Theory, Jungle 2 Jungle, All American Eyes, L.I.E., Private Parts, Sliver; (TV series) Law and Order: Criminal Intent, Crossing Jordan, Grounded for Life, Blind Justice pilot, Paul Reiser pilot, The Chevy Chase pilot, One Life to Live; (Broadway plays) The Music Man, Flower Drum Song, Grease, Chu Chem, Cats, Bombay Dreams; (plays) Cinderella, Heading East, Falsettoland, Merrily We Roll Along, Stay Carl Stay, Genesis, Balancing Act, The Little Hours, Pacific Overtures. Councillor Actors' Equity Assn., N.Y.C., 1992—, co-chair EEOC, 1998—; bd. dir. and treas. Non-Traditional Casting Project, N.Y.C., NY, 2001—. Nominee Best Television Actress, aMedia Awards L.A., 2000—01. Mem.: Dramatists Guild, Am. Fedn. TV and Radio Artists, Screen Actors Guild, Diversity Coalition, Actors Equity Assn. (councillor 1992—, co-chair EEOC 1998—). Avocation: painting. Office: Reimagined World Entertainment 160 Cabrini Blvd #23 New York NY 10033 Office Phone: 212-543-9416. E-mail: ctj@christinetoyjohnson.com.

JOHNSON, CORNELIA, city sheriff, small business owner; b. Charlottesville, Va., Sept. 14, 1943; d. Murry McKinnley and Ellen Marie (Williams) Dowell; m. Willie Davis Johnson, Nov. 22, 1970 (div. June 1984); 1 chlid, Carmelita Annette Johnson Fields; m. James Parham Robinson III, Dec. 10, 1985. Cert., Blue Ridge Coll., Wyers Cave, Va., 1976, Jefferson Nat. Bank Sch., Charlottesville, 1995. Law enforcement officer Charlottesville Police Dept., 1976-98; mgr., owner Dynasty Gift Shop, Charlottesville, 1985-99; sheriff Charlottesville City Sheriffs Office, 1998—. Bd. dirs. Charlottesville Hist. Soc., 1994—, Oratorio Soc., Charlottesville, 1995—, PVCC C.C., Charlottesville, 1993—; mem. Regional Jail Bd., 1998—; pres. Charlottesville Minority Bus., 1993-95. Recipient Women First award City of Charlottesville, 1999. Mem. Exch. Club, Bus. and Profl. Women. Democrat. Baptist. Avocations: tennis, entertaining, travel, visiting historical sites. Home: 1100 Hilltop Rd Charlottesville VA 22903-1221 Office: Charlottesville Sheriff Office 315 E High St Charlottesville VA 22902-5118

JOHNSON, CRYSTAL DUANE, psychologist; b. Houston, Mar. 2, 1954; d. Alton Floyd and Duane (Mullican) J. BA, U. Tex., 1983, MS, 1985. Lic. profl. counselor, psychol. assoc., marriage and family therapist, specialist in sch. psychology, cert. chem. dependency specialist. Student devel. specialist U. Tex., Tyler, 1985-86, intake counselor, 1986-88; staff psychologist Sabine Valley Ctr., Longview, Tex., 1987-88, Mental Health/Mental Retardation Ctr. of East Tex., Tyler, 1988-89; pvt. practice psychologist Tyler, 1989—. Counselor Juvenile and Adult Probation Depts., 1988—, ICF/MR Resdl. Homes, 1991—, Children's Advocacy Ctr., 2000—; spl. edn. counselor, 1990—. Mem. Smith County Humane Soc., Tyler, 1985—, Humane Soc. of the U.S., Washington, 1987—, Am. Soc. Prevention Cruelty to Animals, 1987—, Nat. Wildlife Fedn., 1986—, World Wildlife Fedn., 1986—. Avocations: horticulture, oil and watercolor painting, travel.

JOHNSON, CYNDA ANN, physician, educator; b. Girard, Kans., July 16, 1951; BA in Biology and German with honors, Stanford U., 1973; MD, UCLA, 1977; MBA, U. Mo., Kansas City, 1999. Diplomate Am. Bd. Family Medicine (bd. dirs., pres. 1999-2000). Tchg. fellow U. N.C., Chapel Hill, 1980-81; intern U. Kans. Med. Ctr., Kansas City, 1977-78, 1978-80, prof., acting chair dept. family medicine, 1998—99; prof., head dept. family medicine U. Iowa Coll. Medicine, Iowa City, 1999—2003; dean Brody Sch. Medicine East Carolina U., Greenville, NC, 2003—. Mem. Am. Acad. Family Physicians, Soc. Tchrs. Family Medicine, N.C. Acad. of Family Physicians, N.C. Med. Soc. Office: E Carolina U Brody Sch Medicine Brody AD52 600 Moye Blvd Greenville NC 27834 Office Phone: 252-744-2201. E-mail: johnsoncyn@ecu.edu.

JOHNSON, D'ELAINE ANN HERARD, artist, consultant; b. Puyallup, Wash., Mar. 19, 1932; d. Thomas N. Herard and Rose-ella Berry; m. John Lafayette Johnson, Dec. 22, 1956. BA in Art Edn., Ctrl. Wash. U., Ellensburg, 1954; MFA in Painting, U. Wash., Seattle, 1958, postgrad., 1975, U. London, 1975. Instr. art Seattle Pub. Schs., 1954—78, instr. art workshops, 1960—70; instr. Mus. History and Industry, Seattle, 1954—56; art dir., instr. Martha Washington Sch. Girls, Seattle, 1955—58; dir. Mt. Olympus Estate, Edmonds, Wash., 1971. Cons. art groups, Wash., 1954—; lectr. Ctrl. Wash. State U., Seattle PTA, Creative Arts Assn., Everett, Everett CC, Women's Caucus Art, Seattle, Llubs Art Gallery d'Elaine, Edmonds, Wash., 1957—62, others; pvt. art instr., Seattle, 1960—68; art juror numerous shows; TV art instr. Sta. TV-9 U. Wash., 1968; lectr. in field. Exhibited in group shows at Seligman Gallery, Seattle, 1956, Woessner Gallery, 1957, 1958, Henry Art Gallery, 1958, 1962, 1964, 1965, 1969, 1972, 1973, Seattle Art Mus., 1959, 1965, 1975, Mus. History and Industry, Seattle, 1959, 1960, 1963, 1964, Wash. State Art Exhbns., Wenatchee, 1959, 1960, 1962, 1967, Pacific N.W. Arts and Crafts Fair, Bellevue, 1959, 1960, 1972—78, Nova Scotia Art Mus., Halifax, 1960, 1971, Seattle U., 1965, Nat. Art Gallery, Seattle, 1966—, Art Gallery Hawaii, Oahu, The Gallery, Maui, 1966—68, Park's Gallery, San Jose, Calif., San Francisco, Santa Barbara, Calif., Carmel, Calif., Newport Beach, Calif., 1967, 1968, State Capitol Mus., Olympia, Wash., 1968—70, 1974, 1980, Diamond Head Gallery, Honolulu, 1968, 1969, Gallery Lahaina, Hawaii, 1969, Centennial Art Gallery, Halifax, 1970, Dartmouth Heritage Mus., 1970, 1971, Mt. St. Vincent U. Art Gallery, 1970, Zwicker's Gallery, 1970—73, Gallery 1667, 1970—71, Avelles' Gallery, Creative Fine Arts Gallery, Vancouver, Creative Eye Gallery, Friday Harbor, Wash., 1970, 134th St. Gallery, Halifax, 1971, Panaca Gallery, Bellevue, 1971, 1973, Anacortes Arts and Crafts Fair, Wash., 1972, 1976—78, Seattle Art Mus., 1973—75, Meml. U., St. John's, Nfld., 1974, Whatcom Mus., Bellingham, Wash., 1974, 1975, 1980, 1982, Grand Gallery, Seattle, 1975, Mus. No. B.C., Maritime Mus., Vancouver, Frye Art Mus., Seattle, 1975, 1976, 1988, 1989, 1991, 1992, Shoreline Mus. History, Wash., 1976—80, Wash. State Cousteau Soc., Seattle, 1980, U. Oreg., 1981, Edmonds Art Mus., Wash., 1984, 1994, Missoula Art Mus., Mont., 1984, Gallery II, Phoenix, 1985, Newport Mus., Oreg., 1986, New Space Gallery, Seattle, 1987, Viking Gallery, Chrysalis Gallery, Bellingham, Art 54 Gallery, N.Y., Emory U., Atlanta, 1988, Prince George Art Gallery, B.C., 1989, Nordic Heritage Mus., Seattle, Rosicrucian Egyptian Mus., San Jose, 1990, King County Arts Commn. Gallery, St. Mark's Cathedral, Seattle, 1991, Kinsey Gallery, 1992, Karshner Mus., Puyallup, Wash., 1994, 1995, Ilwaco Heritage Mus., Wash., 1994, Northlight Gallery, Everett, Wash., Newmark Gallery, Seattle, 1995, Columbia River Maritime Mus., Astoria, Oreg., 1997, Bon Marché Gallery, Seattle, 1998. Founder Mt. Olympus Preserve Arts, Edmonds, 1971, sponsor art events, 1971—; active Wash. Coalition Citizens with Disabilities. Named to Wash.

State Art Commn. Registry, Olympia, 1982; recipient numerous awards. Mem.: Nat. Pen Women, Internat. Platform Assn., Nat. Women's Studies Assn., Am. Coun. Arts, Creative Arts Assn., Internat. Soc. Artists, Nat. Artist Equity, Retired Tchr.'s Assn., Assn. Am. Culture, Women's Caucus Art, Nat. Mus. Women Arts, Costeau Soc., Kappa Pi, Kappa Delta Pi. Avocations: scuba diving, camping, travel, violin, writing. Home and Office: 16122 72nd Ave W Edmonds WA 98026-4517 Office Phone: 425-743-2902.

JOHNSON, DARYL DIANE, painter; b. N.Y.C., Aug. 28, 1953; d. Wilbur Henry and Dorothy (Hinton) J.; m. C. Roth Benson, May 8, 1982; children: Sven Hardy Benson, Astrid Posey Benson. BFA, Hope Coll., 1975; postgrad., U. Cin., 1976, Art Student's League, N.Y.C., 1978, Vt. Studio Sch., Johnson, 1988. Paintings in permanent collections of: Aetna Ins. Co., Hartford, Conn., Delta Airlines, Boston, Gen. Electric, Greenwich (Conn.) Hosp., Mariott Hotels, N.Y.C. and St. Louis, Pepsico, Purchase, N.Y., WMUR-TV, Manchester, N.H. One-man shows: Bell Gallery, Stamford, Conn., 1983, Cityarts Gallery, New Haven, 1987, Hatfield Gallery, Manchester, 1989, McGowan Gallery, Concord, N.H., 1990. Author commd. works Mary Immaculate Hosp., 1983, mural "New Hampshire Triptych" WMUR-TV, 1992. Recipient painting award Conn. Painters and Sculptors Show, Stamford Mus., 1981. Mem. N.H. Art Assn. (in juried shows recipient 1st prize 1989, 90, Miriam Sawyer award 1989, Connor award 1990), N.H. Creative Club. Avocation: motorcycling. Home and Office: 31 Storybrook Ln Amherst NH 03031-2604 Office Phone: 603-672-4422.

JOHNSON, DAWN SUNDENE, chemistry educator; d. John W. Sundene and Marilyn R. Jordan; m. Tracy L. Wahl (div.); children: Christopher J. Wahl, Jeri Lynne Wahl; m. Matthew L. Johnson, July 18, 1992. BS in Sci. Edn., East Carolina U., Greenville, 1995; MA in Ednl. Leadership, Aurora U., Ill., 2003. Cert. sci. tchr. Ill., adminstr. Ill., sci. tchr. NC. Biology tutor Craven County Schs., New Bern, NC, 1991—94; chemistryand physics tchr. New Bern HS, NC, 1995—99; chemistry tchr. Oswego HS, Ill., 1999—2006, chmn. sci. divsn., 2004—. Lab and tchg. asst. Craven CC, New Bern, 1991—94, sci. tutor, 1991—94; guest lectr. Newport Elem. Sch., NC, 1991—94. Contbr. poetry to lit. publs. HS-univ. sci. and math liaison Sci./Math Edn. Ctr., Greenville, NC, 1999. Recipient WGKTC Tech. award, Regional Office Edn., Will, Grundy, Kendall counties, 2005; grantee, Oswego Found. for Excellence, 2005; Prospective Tchr. scholar, NC Dept. Edn., 1992—95, Daryl Thompson scholar, Daryl Thompson Found., 2005. Mem.: ASCD (assoc.), AAAS (assoc.), Gold Key (assoc.), Phi Theta Kappa (assoc.), Phi Kappa Phi (life). Republican. Lutheran. Avocations: Norwegian American genealogy, literature, writing poetry. Office: Oswego HS 4250 Rt 71 Oswego IL 60543 Office Phone: 630-636-2025. Personal E-mail: djohnson_308@yahoo.com.

JOHNSON, DEBORAH VALERIE GERMAINE, parish administrator; b. Bakersfield, Ca., Jan. 16, 1957; d. Joseph Harvey and Fern (Stoker) J.; m. Robert Arthur Richmond, Jr., Oct. 2, 1982; children: Abelard, Neville, Bane. BA, U. Calif., Davis, 1979; MA, Sch. for Internat. Tng., Brattleboro, Vt., 1981; PhD, Loyola U., L.A., 1988. Life cert. Master Catechist, Calif. Conf. Cath. Bishops; life credential Adult Edn. Philos. and Theology, Calif. Legis. analyst 94th Congress, Washington, 1976-78; adult edn. analyst Orgn. Am. States, Washington, 1979-80; adult edn. dir. Diocese of Fresno, Bakersfield, Calif., 1988-91; lit. and philos. prof. Cerro Coso Coll., Kern Valley, Calif., 1989-98; philos. prof. Porterville (Calif.) Coll., 1997-98; parish adminstr. St. Joseph's Ch., Bakersfield, Calif., 1997—; master prof. U. Phoenix, Bakersfield, Calif., 1996—. Reconnaissance adv. Buziman Acad., Bakersfield, Calif., 1992—; fibonacci forcaster Furman, Jameson & Rumpole, Dover, 1993—; devel. analyst Naylor and Naylor, Mt. Eldora, Calif., 1997—; sr. assoc. Tigrone Excursions, Bakersfield, Calif., 1998—. Author: Volcan, 1989, Freirean Andragogy, 1991, Wittgenstein, 1993, General Systems Theory, 1994. Mem. Audubon Soc., Bakersfield, Calif., 1994—, Sequoia Forest Alliance, Kernville, Calif., 1994—, Internat. Human Rights Campaign, N.Y.C., 1995—; lay assoc. Sisters of Mercy, Burlingame, Calif., 1988—. Named Tchr. of Yr. Cerro Coso Coll., Kern Valley, Calif., 1990, Kern C.C., Bakersfield, Calif., 1992; recipient Prof. Achievement award Hoyden Found. Mt. Eldora, Calif., 1995, Innovation in Andragogy award Synesthetic Soc., Bakersfield, Calif., 1998. Mem. AAUP, APA, Asakawa Assn. Calif., Johnson Garry Partnership Ltd., Internat. Herge Ecolier, Mt. Eldora Decartes Excursions. Roman Catholic. Avocations: cricket, arboreal architectonics, fractal synergy, hagiography, gastronomy. Office: 2225 Eldora Pl Bakersfield CA 93306-3329

JOHNSON, DELORES GRESHAM, retired counselor; b. Memphis, Jan. 11, 1934; m. Earl Redmond Johnson Sr., Mar. 29, 1952 (dec.); children: Jacqueline, Regina, Earl Jr., Patricia, William. Tchr. asst. El Paso City Schs., Tex., 1966—70; counselor State of Tenn., Memphis, 1970—95; ret, 1995. Head GED Com. Greater South Memphis, 1997—99. Vol. care-giver; organizer home-based food program; election judge Shelby County Election Commn., Memphis, 1999—. Recipient City of Memphis Disting. Svc. award, Mayor W.W. Herenton, 1995, cert. Merit State of Tenn., State Rep. Rufus Jones, 1995, proclamation, U.S. Rep. Harold Ford, 1995, cert. Appreciation, Mayor Jim Roat Shelby County, Tenn., 1995. Home: 541 Moline Rd Memphis TN 38109-3129

JOHNSON, DENISE REINKA, state supreme court justice; b. Wyandotte, Mich., July 13, 1947; Student, Mich. State U., 1965-67; BA, Wayne State U., 1969; postgrad., Cath. U. of Am., 1971-72; JD with honors, U. Conn., 1974; LLM, U. Va., 1995. Bar: Conn. 1974, U.S. Dist. Ct. Conn. 1974, Vt. 1980, U.S. Ct. Appeals (2d cir.) 1983, U.S. Dist. Ct. Vt. 1986. Atty. New Haven (Conn.) Legal Assistance Assn., 1974-78; instr. legal writing Vt. Law Sch., South Royalton, 1978-79; clerk Blodgett & McCarren, Burlington, Vt., 1979-80; chief civil rights divsn. Atty. Gen.'s Office, State of Vt., 1980-82; chief pub. protection divsn. Atty. Gen.'s Office, Montpelier, Vt., 1982-88; pvt. practice Shrewsbury, Vt., 1988-90; assoc. justice Vt. Supreme Ct., Montpelier, 1990—. Chair Vt. Human Rights Commn., 1988-90. Mem. Am. Law Inst., Am. Judicature Soc. Office: Vt Supreme Ct 109 State St Montpelier VT 05609-0001*

JOHNSON, DIANA ATWOOD, business owner, innkeeper; b. Rochester, N.Y., Nov. 3, 1946; d. Edwin Havens and Barbara (Field) A.; m. Kenneth Durant Milne, June 10, 1967 (div. Apr. 1982); m. Howard Samuel Tooker, May 5, 1985 (div. Aug. 1994); m. John Samuel Johnson, June 2, 1996. BA, Skidmore Coll., 1968. Owner, innkeeper Old Lyme (Conn.) Inn, 1976-2001; dir. Bank of Southern Conn., 2006—. Vice chmn. Maritime Bank, 1995-99, dir. 1989-99; incorporator Lawrence Meml. Hosp., New London, Conn., 1990-95. Trustee Conn. River Mus., Essex, 1976-98, pres., 1989-94, chmn., 1994-96; trustee Lyme Hist. Soc., Old Lyme, 1985-87; bd. dirs. Lyme Acad. Fine Arts, Old Lyme, 1980—, chmn. 1996-2003, chmn. emeritus, 2003—, treas., 1992-96; trustee Mystic Coast Travel and Leisure Coun., 1992-2005, chmn. 1994-96; bd. dirs. Lyme/Old Lyme Ednl. Found., 2005—; bd. dirs. Conn. chpt. Nature Conservancy, 1994-2004, sec., 2001, chair govt. rels. com. 2001-04; chmn. open space com. Town of Old Lyme, 1998-2000, 06—, mem. com., 1998—; mem. natural heritage, open space and watershed land acquisition rev. bd., Conn., 1998—; mem. adv. bd. Norwich Navigators, 1995-99, Tidewater Inst., 2004-; dir. Southeastern Conn. Enterprise Region, 1995-2001; del. rep. nat. conv., San Diego, 1996; chmn. rep. town com., Conn., 2000-02, vice chmn., 1998-99, mem. rep. fin. com., 1997-2003; mem. fin. com. Congressman Simmons, 1999—; state ctrl. committeewoman 20th Dist. Conn. Rep. Party, 2001-03. Recipient Disting. Adv. for the Arts award Conn. Commn. on the Arts, 1999. Mem. Nat. Restaurant Assn., Conn. Restaurant Assn. (bd. dirs. 1991-93, 99-2001), Prof. Assn. Innkeepers. Republican. Presbyterian. Avocations: american antiques, antique house restoration, croquet. Home: 12 Tantummaheag Rd Old Lyme CT 06371-1137 Office: 75 Crystal Ave New London CT 06320 E-mail: dianaajohnson@aol.com.

JOHNSON, DIANE LAIN, writer, critic; b. Moline, Ill., Apr. 28, 1934; d. Dolph Lain and Frances Eloise (Elder) Lain; m. John Frederic Murray, Nov. 9, 1969; children: Kevin, Darcy, Amanda, Simon Johnson. AA, Stephens Coll., 1953; BA, U. Utah, 1957; MA, PhD, UCLA, 1968. Mem. faculty dept. English U. Calif., Davis, 1968-87. Author: Fair Game, 1965, Loving Hands at Home, 1968, Burning, 1970, The Shadow Knows, 1975, Lying Low, 1978, Lesser Lives, 1972, Terrorists and Novelists, 1982, Dashiell Hammett, 1983, Persian Nights, 1987, Health and Happiness, 1990, Natural Opium, 1993, Le Divorce, 1997, Le Mariage, 2000, L'Affaire, 2003. Woodrow Wilson grantee, 1967; AAUW fellow, 1968; Guggenheim Found. fellow, 1977-78; Nominee Nat. Book Awards, 1973, 79; recipient Rosenthal award Am. Acad. Arts and Letters, 1979, Mildred and Harold Strauss Living, Am. Acad. & Inst. Arts and Letters, 1988. Mem. MLA, PEN.

JOHNSON, DOLORES ESTELLE, retired small business owner; b. Phila., Dec. 2, 1932; d. William Johnson Bellamy and Sadie Louise (Waddell) Messado; m. Edward Harding Johnson Jr., Aug. 29, 1953 (dec. Feb. 1981); children: Louise P., Edward A., Marie E., Michael G. Parking enforcement officer City of Phila. Police Dept., 1957—59; jeweler, owner LuBelle Jewelers, Phila., 1963—83; originator, owner, baker Pizzarama, Phila., 1965—67; armed guard Globe Security Corp., Phila., 1977—79; artist, jeweler, owner Piercing Eyes Indian Crafts, Phila., 1982—97; ret., 1997. Recipient Outstanding Cmty. Svc. award, Pepsi Cola Co., 1966, award, Chapel of the Four Chaplains for humanitarian works. Mem. United Am. Indians of Delaware Valley, Amerindian Soc. (v.p.), Atlantic City's Garden Ctr. Mus. Art (life). Episcopalian. Avocations: poetry, art, music, camping.

JOHNSON, DONNA MARIE, elementary school educator; d. Donald and Betty Kinner; m. Chris Johnson, Nov. 26, 1972. AA, Shasta Jr. Coll., Redding, Calif., 1978; BA, Chico State U., Calif., 1980. Cert. elem. tchr. Calif. Commn. Credentialing, 1980, Sdaie Calif. Commn. Credentialing, 2004. Tchr. Flournoy Elem., Calif., 1980—84; elem. tchr. Alturas Elem., Calif., 1984—. Bd. mem. PTO, Alturas, 1990—; active mem. Alturas Elem. Sch. Site Coun., 2004—. Vol. libr. Modoc County Libr., Alturas, 2003—06; mem. High Plateau Humane Soc., 2004—06. Recipient Edn. Achievement award, Modoc County SELPH Cmty. Adv. Com., 2003, Cmty. Advisory Com. Achievement award. Mem.: PTA (bd. mem. 1990—2006), Modoc Tchrs. Assn. (sec. 1992—95, v.p. 2002—04). Avocations: paleontology, camping, golf. Office: Alturas Elem Sch 809 West 8th St Alturas CA 96101 Personal E-mail: djohnson@hdo.net.

JOHNSON, DORIS JEAN, social worker; b. Raymond, Miss., July 16, 1946; AA, Wayne County C.C., Detroit, 1986; BSW, U. Detroit, 1989; MSW, Wayne State U., 1993. Supr. Ren, Detroit, 1993—94; psychiat. social worker Aurora Healthcare, Inc., Detroit, 1994—2001, Detroit Cmty. Health Connection, 2002—; clin. social worker Psychiat. and Behavioral Medicine Profls., 2003—. Author: (novel) A Reflection of Memories, 2003. Pres. Slum Lord Fighters, Detroit, 1981, Human Svcs. Orgn./Wayne County C.C., 1984; v.p. social work orgn./Univ. Detroit, 1988. Named to Wall of Tolerance, Civil Rights Meml. Ctr., 2005; recipient cert. Appreciation, Detroit Police Athletic League, 1989, award of Recognition, Detroit City Coun., 1989, cert. appreciation, 36th Dist. Ct., Detroit, 1997. Mem.: Black Expression Club. E-mail: doris0716@aol.com.

JOHNSON, DOROTHY CURFMAN, elementary school educator; b. Smithsburg, Md., Nov. 21, 1930; d. Paul Frank and Rhoda Pearl (Witmer) Curfman; m. Robert Nelson Johnson, Jan. 24, 1953 (div. Dec. 1965); children: Gregory Nelson, Eric Paul. Student, Gettysburg Coll., 1948-50, Waynesboro Bus. Coll., 1950, Broward C.C., Ft. Lauderdale, Fla., 1967; BS in Edn., Fla. Atlantic U., 1969, postgrad., 1975-76. Cert. tchr., Fla. Sec. to prodn. mgr. Westinghouse Elec. Corp., Sunbury, Pa., 1951-53; sec. to v.p., sales Metal Carbides Corp., Youngstown, Ohio, 1966; tchr. Sch. Bd. of Broward County, Ft. Lauderdale, Ohio, 1969-93, curriculum specialist, 1993-96. Masters in Edn. Prog., 1973-74, team coord. Sanders Park Elem., Pompano Beach, Fla., 1985-96; mem. North Area Adv. Bd., Pompano Beach, 1990-96; sec. Sanders Park PTA, Pompano Beach, 1994-96. Sec.-treas. Georgen Arms Bd. of Dirs., Pompano Beach, 1997—; dir. Georgen Arms Condo, Inc., Pompano Beach, 1974—; active Jr. League, Youngstown. Recipient Master Tchr. award State of Fla., 1981-82. Mem. Alpha Xi Delta. Lutheran. Home: 280 S Cypress Rd Apt 5 Pompano Beach FL 33060-7038

JOHNSON, EDDIE BERNICE, congresswoman; b. Waco, Tex., Dec. 3, 1935; d. Lee Edward and Lillie Mae (White) Johnson; m. Lacy Kirk Johnson, July 5, 1956 (div. Oct. 1970); 1 child, Dawrence Kirk. Diploma in Nursing, U. Notre Dame St. Mary's Coll., South Bend, Ind., 1955; BSN, Tex. Christian U., 1967; MPA, So. Meth. U., 1976; LLD (hon.), Bishop Coll., 1979, Jarvis Coll., 1979, Tex. Coll., 1989, Houston-Tillotson Coll., 1993, Paul Quinn Coll., 1993. Chief psychiat. nurse psychotherapist Vets. Adminstrn. Hosp., Dallas, 1956-72; mem. Tex. State Ho. Reps. from Dist. 33-0, Dallas, 1972-77; regional dir. Dept. Health, Edn. and Welfare, Dallas, 1977-79, exec. asst. to adminstr. for primary health care policy Washington, 1979-81; v.p. Vis. Nurse Assn. Tex., Dallas, 1981-87; mem. Tex. State Senate from Dist. 23, 1986-93, US Congress from 30th Tex. dist., 1993—, mem. transp. and infrastructure com., ranking minority mem. water resources and environment subcommittee, mem. sci. com. Cons. divsn. urban affairs Zales Corpn., Dallas, 1976-77; exec. asst. pers. divsn. Neiman-Marcus, Dallas, 1972-75; pres. Eddie Bernice Johnson & Assocs., Inc., Metroplex News, Dallas-Ft. Worth Airport. Bd. dirs. ARC. Recipient Citizenship award Nat. Conf. Christians and Jews, 1985, Tex. NAACP Heroes award, 2000, Pres.'s award Nat. Conf. Black Mayors, Visonary award Nat. Orgn. Black Elected Legis. Women, 2001, Woman of Yr. award 100 Black Men of Am., Inc., 2001, 25th Anniversary Outstanding Achievement award Nat. Black Caucus State Legislators; named an Outstanding Alumnus St. Mary's Coll. of Nursing, 1986; named one of Most Influential Black Americans, Ebony mag., 2006 Mem. Alpha Kappa Alpha. Democrat. Office: US Ho Reps 1511 Longworth Ho Office Bldg Washington DC 20515-4330 Office Phone: 202-225-8885.*

JOHNSON, EDNA RUTH, editor; b. Sturgeon Bay, Wis., Dec. 23, 1918; d. Charles Frederick and Georgina (Knutson) Johnson; m. Al Larson, 1955. BA, U. So. Fla., 1971. With The Churchman, 1950-89; editor The Human Quest (formerly The Churchman), St. Petersburg, Fla., 1958—98. Tchr. ballroom dancing to Eckerd Coll. Students, St. Petersburg, Fla., 1995-96. Co-author (with Antoni Gronowicz): Sergei Rachmaninoff, 1946; editor: Friendship News (USA-USSR), 1975—88; mem. editl. bd. The Humanist, Amherst, N.Y., 1980—. Bd. dirs. ACLU, Nat. Emergency Civil Liberties Com., N.Y.C. Named Fla. Humanist of Yr. Am. Humanist Assn. Fla., 1975, Pres. Soc. of Fine Arts Arts, Pinellas Park, Fla., 1970-90. Mem. Acad. Sr. Profls. at Eckerd Coll. Avocations: ballroom dancing, ballet, painting. Home and Office: 411 First Ave N Princess Martha Apt 901 Saint Petersburg FL 33701 Office Phone: 727-894-0097.

JOHNSON, ELAINE FRANCES, mathematics educator; d. Sam Morris and Margaret Christina Childers; m. Carl Mark Johnson, June 2, 1984; children: Emily Anne, Margaret Sydney, Katherine Imogene. M in Math. Edn., La. Tech, Ruston, 2002; BS, La. Tech. U., Ruston, 1982. Math tchr. Gibsland-Coleman HS, La., 1982—85, Ruston HS, La., 1985—. Sunday sch. tchr. St. Thomas, Ruston, 1996—2005. Named Lincoln Parish Tchr. of Yr., 2002. Home: 900 Pennington Ln Ruston LA 71270 Office: 900 Bearcat Dr Ruston LA 71270 Office Phone: 318-255-0807. Personal E-mail: cejohnson@cox-internet.com. E-mail: ejohns01@lincolnschools.org.

JOHNSON, ELEANOR MAE, education educator; b. St. Paul, Mar. 22, 1925; d. Emil H. and Leona W. (Warner) Busse; m. Edward Charles Johnson, May 13, 1950; 1 child, Mary Jo Johnson Tuckwell. BS, U. Wis., Stout, 1946, MS, 1959, edn. specialist, 1981. Cert. home economist, tchr., Wis. Instr. home econs. various pub. schs., Wis., 1946-48, 56-64; home economist U. Wis. Extension, various locations, 1948-51, 52-56; tchr. educator U. Wis.-Stout, Menomonie, 1965-87; ret., 1987. Summer session guest prof. U. Man., Winnipeg, Can., 1970, 71, S.D. State U., Brookings, 1978; dir. Native Am. curriculum for home econs. Fed. Vocat. Project, U. Wis.-Stout, 1978-80; cons. vocat. evaluation team U. Wis.-Stout, 1982-90; presenter at profl. confs.; team mem. interdisciplinary consumer edn. teaching materials Joint Coun. Econ. Edn., 1980-82. Editor teaching materials for Native Ams., 1978-80. Sr. statesman Wis. Coalition on Aging, 1990-2006; adv., vol. Office of Aging, 1992-2006. Mem. Am. Home Econs. Assn. (del. nat. and internat. confs., Inner City fellow 1970), Life mem. with - Am. Vocat. Assn., Wis. Edn. Assn., U. Wis.-Stout Alumni, Assn. Tchr. Educators and Am. Assn. Ret. Persons, Barron County Hist. Soc. Avocations: national and international travel, collecting historical canning jars, stamps, antique dolls, genealogy. Home: S6851 County Road B Eau Claire WI 54701-8695

JOHNSON, ELISSA SARAH, speech pathology/audiology services professional, writer; b. Bklyn., Nov. 3, 1932; d. Frank Wilford and Doris Antonia (Licorish) Ward; m. Edward Paul Johnson, Dec. 31, 1957 (div. July 1962); 1 child, Paul. BA in Edn. Speech, Bklyn. Coll., 1954, MA in Speech Pathology, 1955; postgard, Howard U., 1968-70. Speech tchr. therapist N.Y.C. Sch. Sys., Bklyn., 1954-67; speech pathologist Bklyn. Coll. Speech Clinic, 1955-57; instr. speech dept. Howard U., Washington, 1968-70; cons. Health Edn. Welfare, Washington, 1969-70; diagnostician speech pathology Tucson Unifed Sch. Dist., 1977-79, speech clinician spl. edn., 1979-86; writer poet Columbia, Md., 1970-77; freelance writer Tucson, 1986—. Mem. Harlem Writer's Guild, Bklyn., 1962-68. Author: (book of poetry) Soul of Wit, 1978; contbr. poetry and articles to profl. publs. and mags. Pres. Bunche House, Bklyn. Coll., 1954; mem. steering com. Dem. Nat. Com., 1995—. Recipient Fire Prevention Theme medal Mayor's Office, 1942; scholar Bklyn. Coll., 1950-54. Mem. AAUW, NOW, NEA. Avocations: playing organ, movies, plays, painting. Home: 500 S Placita Quince Tucson AZ 85748-6834

JOHNSON, ELIZABETH ERICSON, retired educator; b. Rockford, Ill., Oct. 5, 1927; d. Gunnar Lawrence and Victoria Amelia (Carlson) Ericson; m. Barent Olaf Johnson, June 2, 1951; children: Ann E. Arellano, Susan M. Taber. BA, U. Ill., Champaign-Urbana, 1949; MSEd, No. Ill. U., Dekalb, 1969. Tchr. Sch. Dist. 205, Rockford, Ill., 1949-53, 65-92. Mem. Ct. Appointed Spl. Advocate, Rockford, 1992—. Mem. AAUW, LWV (bd. dirs. 1994-96, local bd.), Ill. Ret. Tchrs. Assn., Winnebago Ret. Tchrs. Assn. (various bds.), Phi Delta Kappa emeritus. Avocations: music, viola, musician, violist. Home: 1902 Valencia Dr Rockford IL 61108-6818 Personal E-mail: evebridge@insightbb.com.

JOHNSON, ELIZABETH JEAN, psychology professor; m. Rick A. Johnson, June 27, 1981; 1 child, Daniel A. PhD, Loyola U., Chgo., 2002. Behavior specialist Child Devel. Centers, Park Forest, Ill., 1981—83; prof. Governors State U., University Park, Ill., 1983—. Recipient Faculty Excellence award, Governors State U., 2005. Mem.: APA, Am. Ednl. Rsch. Assn. Office: Governors State U 1 University Parkway University Park IL 60466

JOHNSON, ELIZABETH MISNER, health services executive; b. Lewiston, Idaho, May 16, 1939; d. Gervase Arthur and Blenda N. (Westerlund) Misner; m. Dohn Robert Johnson, Oct. 13, 1962; children: Dohn Robert Jr., Kevin Arthur. BS in Acctg., U. Idaho, 1961. CPA, Calif., Wash. Audit staff Randall, Emery, Campbell & Parker (now Pricewaterhouse Coopers), Spokane, Wash., 1961—62; audit staff, sr. Price Waterhouse, LA, 1962-65; CPA LA, 1966-73; CFO KLP, Inc. dba Call-America, Mesa, Ariz., 1995-98; gen. mgr. Life Line Screening, Phoenix, 2001—02; contr. MPR Homeowners Assn., Phoenix, 2002—. Treas., pres., hon. life mem. Arts Coun. Calif. State U., Northridge, 1975—; internat. dir. alumnae devel. Alpha Gamma Delta (recipient unusually outstanding svc. award, 1993), U.S. and Can., 1988-98; chmn. bd. trustees Alpha Gamma Delta Found., 1998-2001, trustee, 1998—2004. Pres. Soroptimist Internat., Coeur d'Alene, Idaho, 1991-92, regional nominating com., 1993-94. Mem. Ariz. Soc. of CPAs. Home: 14839 S 47th Way Phoenix AZ 85044-6881 Office: MPR Home Owners Assn 15425 S 40th St Ste 4 Phoenix AZ 85044 Office Phone: 480-704-5000. Personal E-mail: liz@mtparkranch.org.

JOHNSON, ELVIRA Q., dietician; Dir. clin. nutrition svcs. Cambridge Health Alliance. Mem.: Am. Dietetic Assn. (Medallion award 2001). Office: Cambridge Health Alliance Dept Nutrition 1493 Cambridge St Cambridge MA 02139

JOHNSON, ERMA JEAN, human services administrator; b. Little Rock, Dec. 20, 1951; d. Odessa Johnson; m. Willie R. Johnson, June 19, 1977 (div. Apr. 6, 1985); 1 child, Preya D. AA, Lamar Coll., Colo., 1970; BA, Chgo. State U., 1973; MS, Almeda Coll. and Univ., Boise, Idaho, 2002. Social worker, coord. East Ctr. Cmty. Mental Health, Toledo, 1977—78; social worker Toledo Mental Health Ctr., 1979—80, social program coord., 1980—84, mental health adminstr., 1984—85; supt. Ohio Dept. Youth Svcs., Warrensville, 1985—87, regional adminstr. Toledo, 1987—2002; pres., CEO New Hope Recovery Ctr., Holland, Ohio, 2002—. Mem. adv. bd. Children and Family First, Toledo, 1985—2002, Lourde Coll., Sylvania, Ohio, 1999—2001; v.p. Am. Bus. Women Am., Toledo, 1995—97. Recipient Humanitarian award, Youth Svc. Cmty. Svcs., 1999, recognition for vol. counseling ex-offenders, Lucas County Adult Probation Dept., Toledo, Operation DARE, Chgo.; grantee, Target Stores, 1999—2000. Mem.: NAFE. Baptist. Avocations: walking, bowling, flower arranging, creating community programs. Office Phone: 419-356-3320.

JOHNSON, ESTELLE TAYLOR, elementary school educator; b. St Augustine, Fla., Sept. 16, 1941; d. Clarence Taylor; 1 child, Frank E. Johnson III. BS in Elem. Music Edn., Fla. Meml. Coll., 1964; MEd, U. Cen. Fla., 1974. Tchr. music and English Screven County Bd. Pub. Instrn., Sylvania, Ga., 1965-67; tchr. music Lake County Bd. Pub. Instrn., Tavares, Fla., 1967-69; tchr. Orange County Bd. Pub. Instrn., Orlando, 1969—. Cons. Reading Coun., Orlando, 1990—. Pres. Tangelo Park Civic Assn., Orlando, 1977-79; bd. dirs. Pinecastle Community Svc. Ctr., Orlando, 1979—. Mem. Orange County Classroom Assn., Zeta Phi Beta. Democrat. Baptist. Avocations: reading, playing piano, tennis, volleyball, basketball. Home: 7124 Udine Ave Orlando FL 32819-8447 Office: Howard Middle Sch 800 E Robinson St Orlando FL 32801-2080

JOHNSON, EVA JO, educational consultant; b. Chattanooga, Aug. 9, 1941; d. Joseph Saddler and Wilma (Logue) Scruggs; m. Richard Louis Spence, Apr. 4, 1959 (div. Mar. 1967); children: Gail, Richard, Donald Lamarion, Stephani. BS, So. Conn. State U., 1975, MS, 1978; postgrad., Fairfield U., 1983. Cert. in spl. edn. and adminstrn. and supervision. Tchr. spl. edn. Hamden (Conn.) Pub. Schs., 1975-87, supr. alternative program, 1987-91; instr. psychology South Ctrl. C.C., New Haven, 1988-89; educator spl. edn. resources Hamden Pub. Schs., 1991—. Chairperson Profl. Devel., Hamden, 1984-85; cons. Hamden Pub. Schs., 1976-87, coord. ann. ethnic celebration, 1978-89 Devel. curriculum project Celebration of Excellence, 1990 (Edn. award 1990). Chairperson membership com. N.H. Urban League, New Haven, 1985-88; mem. League Women Voters, Hamden, 1988-91; v.p. Conn. Afro Am. Hist. Soc., New Haven, 1992—; vol. in missions. Recipient Prudence Crandall award Conn. Edn. Assn., 1987, John Rogers Meml. award Conn. Edn. Assn., 1989, Woman in Leadership award YWCA, 1989, Cmty. Svc. award Bus. and Profl. Women, 1992, So. Conn. State U. Alumni Citation award, 2001. Mem. Phi Delta Kappa, Alpha Kappa Alpha (pub. rels. chair 1992—, Svc. award). Mem. United Methodist Ch. Avocations: travel, writing, walking, cooking, interior decorating. Home and Office: 3 Fern Ln Branford CT 06405-3352 E-mail: evajo7@yahoo.com.

JOHNSON, EVA MARIA, retired translator; b. Ludwigshafen, Rhine, Germany, Jan. 19, 1920; came to U.S., 1951; naturalized 1955; d. George and Maria Regina (Wurzel) Lenz; m. Martin L. Johnson, June 8, 1952 (dec. Jan. 1994); 1 child, Michael Andrew. Student, Ludwigshafen, 1938, Vorbeck Lang. Sch., 1940-43. Interpreter, translator German, English and French, Police, Lampertheim, Germany, 1945-46; reporter Deutsche Presse Dienst, Wiesbaden, Germany, 1946-48; editl. specialist U.S. Mil. Govt., Wiesbaden, Germany, 1948-51; bilingual sec. Embassy of Austria, Washington, 1951-53; translator Internat. Affairs Dept. CIO, Washington, 1953—55; translator Combat Ops. Rsch. Group, CDC, Fort Belvoir, Va., 1965-70; freelance translator top secret clearance Dept. Def., Washington, 1970-72; sr. sect., translator Holman & Stern, Patent Law Office, Washington, 1972-85; ret.,

1985. Key-note spkr. Surviving POWs VA Hosp., Martinsburg, W.Va., 1996. Anti-Nazi activist, 1943-45. Mem.: The Ret. Mil. Officer Assn. (life). Avocations: photography, writing, eggeury, gardening, reading. Home: 352 Monastery Ridge Rd Stephenson VA 22656

JOHNSON, EVELYN BRYAN, airport terminal executive; b. Corbin, Ky., Nov. 4, 1909; d. Edward William and Myme Estelle (Fox) Stone; m. Wyatt J. Bryan, Mar. 21, 1931 (dec. 1963); m. Morgan N. Johnson, Feb. 25, 1965 (dec. Mar. 1977). Grad., Tenn Wesleyan Jr. Coll., 1929; student, U. Tenn., 1930—32. With Morristown (Tenn.) Flying Svc., Inc., 1947-97, designated pilot examiner, 1952—2005, sec.-treas., 1949-62, pres., 1962-82; mgr. Moore Murrell Airport, 1962—. Gov.'s appointee Tenn. Aero. Commn., 1983—2001, vice-chmn., 1987—89, chmn., 1989—91, 1994—96. Lt. col. CAP, 1949—. Recipient Carnegie Hero medal, 1958, Svc. to Mankind award Morristown Sertoma Club, 1981, Kitty Hawk award, FAA, 1991, Friends of Aviation award Tenn. Aviation Assn., 1992, Stewart G. Potter Aviation Edn. award Aviation Distbrs. and Mfrs. Assn., 1992, Elder Statesman of Aviation award Nat. Aeronautics Assn., 1993, Katherine Wright Meml. award Nat. Aeronautics Assn. and the Ninety Nines, 2002; named Flight Instr. of Yr., Nashville Dist. 1973, 79, So. region 1979, Nat., 1979 (all FAA), Outstanding Alumnus Tenn. Wesleyan Coll., 1981, Tenn. Divsn. Aviation Airport Mgr. of Yr., 2004; named to Women in Aviation Pioneers Hall of Fame, 1994, Hamblen Women Hall of Fame, 1997, Flight Instr. Hall of Fame, EAA Air Venture Mus., Oshkosh, 1997, Ky. Aviation Hall of Fame, 2000, Tenn. Aviation Hall of Fame, 2002, Kathryn Wright Meml. award Nat. Aeronautics Assn., 2002; holder of record most flying time for women pilots Guiness Book of Records 1995— Mem. CAP, Morristown Area C. of C., Nat. Assn. Flight Instrs. (bd. dirs., treas 1987-88, award 1992), Ninety-Nines (Award of Merit 1994), Whirly Girls (plaque 1992, Livingston award 2004, Airport Mgr. of the Yr. 2004, Wright Bros. Master Pilot award 2004), Aircraft Owners and Pilots Assn., Silver Wings (bd. dirs. 1987-2002, Woman of Yr. 1981, Carl Fromhagen award 1992), United Flying Octogenarians. Republican. Baptist. Home: 775 Commanche Dr Jefferson City TN 37760 Office: PO Box 1013 Morristown TN 37816-1013 Office Phone: 423-586-2483.

JOHNSON, EVELYN PORTERFIELD, journalist, educator; b. Kansas City, Mo., Jan. 7, 1937; d. Roy LaVerne and Lorraine (Lardie) Porterfield; m. Robert Luck Johnson, June 30, 1962 (div. 1972); children: Jennifer, Lara, Tracey, Virginia. BA, Ea. Bapt. Coll., St. Davids, Pa., 1958. Tchr. Lower Merion Sch. Dist., Ardmore, Pa., 1958—60, Prince Georges County, Md., 1961—62, Loudoun County Sch., Leesburg, Va., 1977—92; freelance journalist local newspapers and mags. Chmn. Regional English Tchrs. Conf., Leesburg, 1991. Author: book, 2003. Founder Bluemont (Va.) Fair, 1970—, Friends of Bluemont, 2002—; mem. Keep Loudoun Beautiful; mem. Blue Ridge Dist. Loudoun's Women Commn.; Blue Ridge rep. Loudoun County Archtl. Rev. Com., 1992. Mem.: Preservation Soc. Loudoun County (founder, pres. 1974—). Democrat. Baptist. Avocations: reading, collecting local history, antiques, old house tours. Home: PO Box 247 Bluemont VA 20135

JOHNSON, EVERLENE, materials engineer; d. DeWitt and Bernice Johnson; 1 child, Eggleston Clinton Jeter III. BS in Chemistry, Tuskegee Inst., 1975. Staff chemist Proctor and Gamble, Cinn., 1976—77; analytical and process phemist Naval Air Depot, Jacksonville, Fla., 1977—84, materials engrs., 1984—. Author poetry, (cookbook) A Twist of Soul Food, 2001. Named Black Engr. of Yr., 1998. Mem.: Internat. Soc. Poets (Outstanding Achievement award 2005, Silver Bowl, Bronze medal). Baptist. Avocations: singing, crossword puzzles, walking.

JOHNSON, FLORA MAE, retired elementary school educator; b. Troup, Tex., Nov. 16, 1932; d. Ector Smith and Allie Mae (Dickson) Walls; m. Earl B. Johnson, Mar. 2, 1956. Student, Kilgore Jr. Coll., 1951-53; BS, East Tex. State U., 1953-55. Elem. tchr. Big Sandy (Tex.) Ind. Sch. Dist., 1955-56, Kilgore (Tex.) Ind. Sch. Dist., 1956—95; ret., 1995. Sub. tchr., 1956—2005. Sunday sch. tchr. Ch. of Christ, Kilgore. Mem. NEA, PTA, Tex. State Tchrs. Assn., Classroom Tchrs. Assn. Mem. Ch. of Christ. Avocations: crocheting, knitting, needlecrafts. Office: Kilgore Ind Sch Dist 711 N Longview St Kilgore TX 75662-5413

JOHNSON, FLORENCE LESTER, retired elementary school educator; b. Chgo., Nov. 11, 1935; d. William Alexander Lester and Elizabeth Frances Clark; m. Justin Morris Johnson, June 25, 1960; children: William Oliver, Justin Llewellyn(dec.), Elizabeth Irene. BEd, Chgo. State Tchrs. Coll., 1957; MEd in Reading, U. Pitts., 1973. Elem. tchr. Chgo. Bd. Edn., 1957—60; clk. office adminstrn. U. Chgo., 1960—61; elem. tchr. Pitts. Bd. Edn., 1973—93, model tchr. open ct. reading program, 1975—77; ret., 1993. Contbr.: book From Pittsburgh to Beijing and Back, 1997. Cochmn. capital campaign YWCA, Pitts., 1994—96; mem. 4th UN Conf. on Women, Beijing, 1995; trustee Pitts. Phipps Conservancy and Bot. Gardens, Inc., 1999; co-chmn., CEO search com. Greater Pitts. Young Women's Christian Assn., 2000; vice-moderator Pittsburgh Presbytery, 1991; moderator Presbyn. Synod of Trinity, 1997. Named Outstanding Tchr., Martin Luther King Sch., 1985; recipient Thanks to Tchrs. award, U. Pitts., 1990, Gift of Time tribute, Am. Family Inst., Pitts., 1990, award writing contest on racism, Peacemaking Com., 1998. Mem.: Assn. Theol. Schs. US. and Can (mem. exec. com. 2006—). Democrat. Avocations: reading, gardening. Home: 4911 Ellsworth Ave Pittsburgh PA 15213

JOHNSON, FREDA S., financial analyst, consultant; b. NYC, Mar. 17, 1947; m. J. Chester Johnson, May 7, 1989. BA in Polit. Sci., CUNY, 1968; grad. Advanced Mgmt. Program, Harvard U., 1986. Analyst mcpl. div. Dun & Bradstreet Corp., N.Y.C., 1968-71; sr. analyst Moody's Investor Svc., Inc. (subs. Dun & Bradstreet), N.Y.C., 1972, v.p., assoc. dir. mcpl. dept., 1973-79, sr. v.p., dir. mcpl. dept., 1979-81, exec. v.p., 1981-90; pres. Govt. Fin. Assocs., Inc. pub. fin. adv. co., 1992—. Mem. Anthony Commn. for Pub. Fin.; former sr. credit advisor Ecolink, joint Soviet-Am. pub. fin. project; Congl. testifier U.S. Senate Com. on Banking, Housing and Urban Affairs, subcom. fiscal affairs and health U.S. Ho. of Reps., U.S. Senate Com. Govtl. Affairs, Joing Econ. Com. Congress; Nat. Assn. Ind. Pub. Fin. Advisors, 1993-95, Queens Coll. Corp. Adv. Bd., 1994-99; bd. govs. Coun. Mcpl. Performance, 1984-86; instr. New Sch. for Social Rsch., 1982-83; mem. adv. bd. City Almanac, 1982-84; trustee Citizens Budget Com.; spkr. numerous profl. orgns., univs.; adj. prof. Grad. Sch. Bus. Adminstrn. Columbia U., spring 1991. Avocations: theater, museums.

JOHNSON, GAYLE ANN, cardiology nurse; b. Chgo., Sept. 4, 1946; d. Russell Arthur and Helen Elizabeth (Lawrence) J.; children: Todd Osinski, Jennifer Johnson. ADN with honors, Elgin CC, Ill., 1986; student, Grossmont Coll., 1988. RN, Calif.; bd. cert. med. surg. RN, ANCC, 1998, 03; cert. ACLS, Am. Heart Assn., 2006. Office nurse Dr. Edward J. Kinn, Barrington, Ill.; staff nurse No. Ill. Med. Ctr., McHenry; asst. unit supr. cardiac unit telemetry, staff nurse Scripps Meml. Hosp., La Jolla, Calif., staff nurse, mem. Nursing Futures Task Force, 1987-88; owner, operator State Lic. Assisted Living (Colony Ct.), San Diego, 1993—96; staff RN UCSD, La Jolla, 2002—. Clin. advisor Va. Mason Med. Ctr., Seattle, 1998—2000; staff RN cardiac unit Swedish Med. Ctr., Seattle, 2000; shift mgr. Alvarado Med. Ctr., San Diego, 2000—02; mem. RN Ednl. Competency Com. USCO, LaJolla, Calif., 2002—. William Rainey Harper Coll., Palatine, Ill., McHenry County Coll., Crystal Lake, Ill., McHenry County Coll. Women's Re-entry scholar, 1982-83, Sherman Hosp. Women's Aux. Nursing scholar, 1984-85. Mem.: Calif. Nurses Assn. (staff Internat. Med. U.). Republican. Evangelical Free. Home: 9418 Stargaze Ave San Diego CA 92129-3801 Office: 9300 Campus Point La Jolla CA 92037 Business E-Mail: gjohnson3@san.rr.com.

JOHNSON, GERALDINE ESCH, language specialist; b. Steger, Ill., Jan. 5, 1921; d. William John Rutkowski and Estella Anna (Mannel) Pietz; m. Richard William Esch, Oct. 12, 1940 (dec. 1971); children: Janet L. Sohngen, Daryl R., Gary Michael; m. Henry Bernard Johnson, Aug. 23, 1978 (dec. 1988). BSBA, U. Denver, 1955, MA in Edn., 1958, MA in Speech Pathology, 1963; vocat. credential, U. No. Colo., 1978, postgrad., Metropolitan State Coll., U. Colo., Colo. State U., Colo. Sch. of Mines, U. Hawaii. Cert. speech therapist, Colo.; cert. tchr., class A counselor, tchr. educationally handicapped, Colo. Tchr. music Judith St. John Sch. Music, Denver, 1946—52; tchr. West High Sch., Denver, 1955—61, chmn. bus. edn. dept., 1958—61, reading specialist, 1977—78; speech therapist, founder South Denver Speech Clinic, 1965—71; tchr. Educationally Handicapped Resource Rm., Denver, 1971—74; tchr. Diagnostic Ctr. Belmont Sch., Denver, 1974—77; speech-lang. specialist elem. and jr. high schs., Denver, 1978—86; itinerant speech-lang. specialist various elem. and jr. high schs., Denver, 1978—; ret., 1986. Home lang tchr. Early Childhood Edn., Denver, 1975; mem. Ednl. TV Adv. com., Colo.; sec. Cen. Bus. Edn. Com., Colo; tchr. letter writing clinics, local bus., Denver, 1960—. Former judge Colo. State Speech Festivals; demonstrator, lectr. Speech-Lang. and Learning Disabilities area Colo. Edn. Assn., 1971-73; vol. comm. and prereading skills tchr. YMCA Recipient Spl. Edn. award, Denver Pub. Schs., 1986, 20 Yrs. Svc. award, YMCA, 2001. Mem. Speech-Lang.-Hearing Assn. (cert.), U. Denver Sch. Bus. Alumni Bd., Beta Gamma Sigma, Kappa Delta Pi, Delta Pi Epsilon. Home: 1950 S Dayton St Apt 301 Denver CO 80247-3455

JOHNSON, GERTRUDE COOGAN, educational consultant, elementary school educator; b. Pitts., Mar. 7, 1938; d. John Patrick and Gertrude Quinn Coogan. BS in Edn., Duquesne U., Pitts., 1960; MEd, U. Ill., Urbana, 1971. Tchr. Pitts. Pub. Schs., 1960—63, Dept. Def. Europe, Washington, 1963—65, Dept. Def. Japan, Washington, 1965—66; coord., tchr., gifted students Oak Park Sch. Dist. 97, Ill., 1966—94; cons. West 40 Intermediate Svc. Ctr., La Grange Park, Ill., 1994—. Coord. Reading First Program West Cook County. Mem.: ASCD, Nat. Staff Devel. Coun., Phi Delta Kappa. Home: 203 N Kenilworth 3J Oak Park IL 60302 Office: West 40 Intermediate Svc Ctr 928 Barnsdale Rd La Grange Park IL 60526 Office Phone: 708-482-4350. Business E-Mail: gjohnson@west40.k12.il.us.

JOHNSON, GLORIA JEAN, counseling professional; b. St. Louis, Jan. 30, 1945; d. Willie Jr. and Ruby Bernice (Haynes) Stevens; m. Louis W. Johnson, Dec. 2, 1963; children: Anthony Kenneth, Marvin Louis, Andre Darnell. MS in Counseling, Evang. Sem., PhD in Marriage and Family Counseling, 1993. Dir. counseling dept. EC Bible Coll., St. Louis, 1987-88; cons. in field St. Louis, 1987-94; founder, exec. dir. Life Source Cons., Inc., St. Louis, 1994—. Vol. counselor CMC C-Star Program, St. Louis, 1992-93; bd. dirs. Mo. Coalition Against Domestic Violence, Jefferson City, 1995-99, Mo. Coalition Against Sexual Assault, 1998-2005; chair Women of Color Task Force Against Domestic Violence State of Mo., 1996-97; mem. St. Louis County Domestic and Family Violence Coun., 1996-99, St. Louis City Family Violence Coun., 1998-, Family Support Task Force, 1998-99; mem. adv. coun. Sexual Assault Ctr., 1996—; founder Christian Women Against Abuse, 1998. Office: Life Source Cons Inc Ste 219 119 Church St Saint Louis MO 63135 Office Phone: 314-524-4130. E-mail: drjohnson@lifesourceconsultants.org.

JOHNSON, HOLLY L., elementary school educator; d. Larry Cummings and Sandra Oliver, Homer Oliver, Sr. (Stepfather); 1 child, Jaycee Haleh Johnson-Evans. BS, Jarvis Christian Coll., Hawkins, Tex., 2002. Cert. tchr. LeTourneau U., 2004. Tchr. Gilmer ISD, Tex., 2004—. Office Phone: 903-841-7538.

JOHNSON, IMOGENE POWERS, foundation administrator; BA in Math., Cornell U.; LHD (hon.), Carroll Coll.; PhD (hon.), Carthage Coll. Founding dir., chmn. bd. The Prairie Sch., Racine, Wis.; dir., Lab. Ornithology Cornell U. Bd. dir. Johnson Found., Racine, Wis., 2004—, bd. trustee. Named Women of Distinction in Edn., YWCA of Racine; named one of Forbes' Richest Americans, 2006. Office: Johnson Found 33 E Four Mile Rd Racine WI 53402 Address: The Prairie Sch 4050 Lighthouse Dr Racine WI 53402*

JOHNSON, JACQUELYN MARIE, elementary school educator; b. Elgin, Ill., Oct. 1, 1974; d. R. David and Judith Cummens; m. Corey Cummens, July 29, 2000; children: Aliyah, Sydney. BA, Ea. Ill. U., Charleston, 1996; M in Curriculum and Instrn., postgrad. in Ednl. Leadership, Nat. Louis U. Tchr. Sch. Dist. U-46, Elgin, Ill., 1997—. Theater dir. Abbott Mid. Sch., Elgin, Ill., 1997—2003. Office: Abbott Mid Sch 949 Van St Elgin IL 60123 Office Phone: 847-888-5160. E-mail: jackiejohnson@u-46.org.

JOHNSON, JANE, school psychologist; d. Robert W. and Edith (Wagner) Lewis; m. William B. Johnson, May 19, 1974; children: William, Elizabeth. BS, Valparaiso U., Ind., 1971; MA, Ball State U., Muncie, Ind., 1974, EdD, 1977. Sch. psychologist Bartholomew Consol. Sch. Cor, Columbus, Ind., 1979—. Mem.: NASP (nom. Nat. Exemplary Practice award 1999), NEA, Ind. Assn. Sch. Psychologists (Exemplary Practice award 1998), Phi Delta Kappa, Delta Kappa Gamma. Office: Bartholomew Consol Sch Cor 1200 Central Ave Columbus IN 47232 Home: 959 W 750N Elizabethtown IN 47232

JOHNSON, JANE PENELOPE, freelance/self-employed writer; b. Danville, Ky., July 1, 1940; d. Buford Lee Carr and Emma Irene (Coldiron) Sebastian; m. William Evan Johnson, July 15, 1958; children: William Evan Jr., Robert Anthony. Grad., Famous Writer's Sch. Fiction, Westport, Conn., 1967; grad. writer's divsn., Newspaper Inst. Am., NYC, 1969; grad., Am. Assn. Christian Counselors, 2001, student; LittD (hon.), The London Inst. Applied Rsch., 1993; student, World Harvest Bible Coll., 2006—. Lay counselor Caring for People God's Way. Author (poetry book) A Penny For Your Thoughts, numerous poems; author song lyrics: Everlasting Freedom, Answered Prayer, Glory Bound, Americans Standing Tall; recs. include America, 1997-98, The Light of the World, 1998-99, (poem) Interospection, 1996; contbr. Hilltop Gospel Songbook; contbr. songs to Sing Hosanna, CD sent to USA troops in Iraq, 2005. Patron Menninger; pres. Dwight D. Eisenhower Commn. signed by Pres. Ford, Reagan, George H. Bush, George W. Bush for lifetime contbns. Nat. Rep. Party; charter mem. Pres. George Bush & V.P. Dick Cheney Victory Team. Ennobled by Prince John, The Duke of Avram, Tasmania, Australia; semifinalist Internat. Libr. Poetry, N.Am. Poetry Open; recipient 28 Editor's Choice awards for poetry Nat. Libr. of Poetry, 1994, Editor's Choice award Internat. Libr. Poetry, 2000, Coat of Arms, Coll. of Heraldry; named to Internat. Poetry Hall of Fame, 1996, Pres. award, 2002; named World Laureate, Internat. Writer of Yr. Cambridge Gold Medal, Poet of Merit trophy Internat. Soc. Poets, Nobel Laureate Order Internat. Diplomats. Fellow The World Lit. Acad. Eng.; mem. NAFE, Smithsonian Assocs., Peale Ctr. for Christian Living, Sweet Adelines, Internat. Soc. Poets (laureate founder, life, advisor), Internat. Platform Assn., Charles Menniger Soc. (life), Internat. Order of Merit, Nat. Writer's Club, Nat. Authors' Registry, Poetry Guild NY, Norman Vincent Peale Fellowship (founder). Republican. Avocations: swimming, skating, dance, piano. Office: Gardenside Br PO Box 8013 Lexington KY 40504-8013 Personal E-mail: pennyspoems@yahoo.com.

JOHNSON, JANET HELEN, literature educator; b. Everett, Wash., Dec. 24, 1944; d. Robert A. and Jane N. (Osborn) J.; m. Donald S. Whitcomb, Sept. 2, 1978; children: J.J., Felicia. BA, U. Chgo., 1967, PhD, 1972. Instr. Egyptology U. Chgo., 1971-72, asst. prof., 1972-79, assoc. prof., 1979-81, prof., 1981—; dir. Oriental Inst., 1983-89; research assoc. dept. anthropology Field Mus. of Natural History, 1980-84, 94-99, 2003—; Morton D. Hull disting. svc. prof. U. Chgo., 2003—. Author: Demotic Verbal System, 1977, Thus Wrote Onchsheshonqy, 1986, 3d revised edit., 2000, (with Donald Whitcomb) Quseir al-Qadim, 1978, 80; editor: (with E.F. Wente) Studies in Honor of G.R. Hughes, 1977, Life in a Multi-Cultural Society, 1992. Recipient Morton D. Hall disting. svc., 2003; grantee, Smithsonian Instn., 1977—83, NEH, 1978—81, 1981—85, Nat. Geog. Soc., 1978, 1980, 1982. Mem. Am. Rsch. Ctr. in Egypt (bd. govs. 1979—, exec. com. 1984-87, 90-96, v.p. 1990-93, pres. 1993-96). Office: U Chgo Oriental Inst 1155 E 58th St Chicago IL 60637-1540 Office Phone: 773-702-9530. Business E-Mail: j-johnson@uchicago.edu.

JOHNSON, JANET LOU, real estate company executive, writer; b. Boston, Aug. 22, 1939; d. Donald Murdoch and Helen Margaret (Slauenwhite) Campbell; m. Walter R. Johnson, Mar. 31, 1962; children: Meryl Ann, Leah Kathryn, Christa Helen. Student, Gordon Coll., 1962—64. Adminstr., account exec. Fuller/Smith & Ross, Boston, 1958—63; adminstr. Walter R. Johnson, P.E., Gloucester and Rockport, Mass., 1970—; broker Realty World, Gloucester, 1976—77, Hunneman & Co., Gloucester, 1977—79; pres., owner Janet L. Johnson Real Estate, Gloucester, 1979—. Author, illustrator, pub: The Ritz Carlton Cat, 1999. Mem. Nat. Assn. Realtors, Mass. Assn. Realtors (bd. dirs. 1985-87), Cape Ann C. of C., Cape Ann Bd. Realtors (pres. 1984-85, state dir. 1985-86), North Shore Assn. Bd. Realtors. Office: Janet L Johnson Real Estate 160 Main St Rockport MA 01966 Home: 160 Main St Rockport MA 01966-2017 Office Phone: 978-546-6431. Business E-Mail: jjrealest@aol.com.

JOHNSON, J(ANET) SUSAN, psychologist; b. Ramey AFB, P.R., Mar. 24, 1948; d. Wesley Roger and Marie Dolores (Stecher) J.; m. Darrel Edwards, June 9, 1991. BA in Psychology, San Diego State U., 1970, Ma in Psychology, 1974. Coord. nat. exec. lab. Navy Nat. Elec. Lab., San Diego, 1970—72; assoc. dir. clin. decisions Navy Health Rsch. Ctr., San Diego, 1972—78; pvt. practice San Diego, 1972—; exec. dir. Edwards Assocs., San Diego, 1978—; clin. intern in clin. psychology TRI Cmty. Svcs. Outpatient Clinic, San Diego, 1978—80; pres. Strategic Vision, San Diego, 1983—. Co-founder Ctr. for Value Centered Life, 1999; key spkr., program coord. for nat. presidencies, prime mins., Fortune 100 CEO's, 1978—; mem. undergraduate mgmt. adv. bd. Marriott Sch. Bus. Brigham Young U., 2006—; guest rschr. in field; cons. in field. Contbr. articles to profl. publs. Undergraduate adv. bd. mem. BYU Marriott Bus. Sch., 2006. Avocations: skiing, boating, scuba diving, gardening. Office Phone: 858-576-7141. Business E-Mail: susan.johnson@strategicvision.com.

JOHNSON, JANICE E., education educator, writer; b. Portsmouth, Ohio, Sept. 15, 1956; d. James Elmer and Gwendolin Audrey Johnson. AD, Shawnee State U., 1988, B in Bus. Adminstrn., 1990; MBA, Morehead State U., 1992. Cert. Computer Professional Inst. for Certification of Computing Professionals, 1996, Bus. Info. Systems Inst. for Certification of Computing Professionals, 1996, Office Info. Systems Inst. for Certification of Computing Professionals, 1996; Med. Lab. Tech. Am. Soc. of Clin. Pathologists, 1977. Br. mgr. Roche Biomedical Laboratories, Livonia, Mich., 1985—86; bus. faculty Shawnee State U., Portsmouth, Ohio, 1990—. Author: (short stories) Fido, The Leading Edge, Crossroad, Planes of Reality, (novels) Heroes on Ice, Voice of Truth. Web leader Shawnee State U., Portsmouth, Ohio, 1996—2003; advisor Fantanime Club, Portsmouth, Ohio, 2001—, Shawnee State Computer Soc., Portsmouth, Ohio, 1990—2003. Recipient Wall St. Jour. Student Achievement award, Wall St. Jour., 1989, Presdl. scholarship, 1988—89, D.P.M.A. Student award, Data Processing Mgmt. Assn., 1987. Mem.: HTML Writers Guild, Internat. Webmasters Assn., Am. Soc. of Clin. Pathologists (assoc.). Christian. Avocations: writing, web design, reading, bird watching, gardening. Office: Shawnee State University 940 2nd St Portsmouth OH 45662 Home: PO Box 1048 Portsmouth OH 45662-1048 Office Phone: 740-351-3358. Personal E-mail: ravencatt@earthlink.net. Business E-Mail: jjohnson@shawnee.edu.

JOHNSON, JANIS G., Canadian senator; b. Winnipeg, MB, Can., Apr. 27, 1946; 1 child, Stefan. BA in Polit. Sci., U. Manitoba, 1968. Senator The Senate of Can., Ottawa, 1990—. Conservative. Avocation: Avocations: jogging, flyfishing, golf, theatre, literature. Office: 335 East Block The Senate of Canada Ottawa ON Canada K1A 0A4 Office Phone: 613-943-1430. E-mail: johnsj@sen.parl.gc.ca.

JOHNSON, JEAN ELAINE, nursing educator; b. Wilsey, Kans., Mar. 11, 1925; d. William H. and Rosa L. (Welty) Irwin. BS, Kans. State U., 1948; MS in Nursing, Yale U., 1965; MS, U. Wis., 1969, PhD, 1971; DS (hon.), Univ. Wis., 1998. Instr. nursing, Iowa, 1948—58; staff nurse Swedish Hosp., Englewood, Colo., 1958—60; in-svc. edn. coord. Gen. Rose Hosp., Denver, 1960—63; rsch. asst. Yale U., New Haven, 1965—67; assoc. prof. nursing Wayne State U., Detroit, 1971—74, prof., 1974—79; dir. Ctr. for Health Rsch., 1974—79; assoc. dir. oncology nursing Cancer Ctr. U. Rochester, NY, 1979—93, prof. nursing, 1979—95, prof. emerita, 1995—. Rosenstadt prof. health rsch. Faculty Nursing, U. Toronto, 1985; vis. prof. U. Utah Coll. Nursing, 1996—97, U. Wis., Madison, 1998. Author: Self-Regulation Theory: Applying Theory to Your Practice, 1997; contbg. author Handbook of Psychology and Health, vol. 5, 1984; contbr. articles to profl. jours. Recipient Bd. Govs. Faculty Recognition award, Wayne State U., 1975, award for disting. contbn. to nursing sci., Am. Nurses Found. and ANA Coun. for Nurse Rschrs., 1983, Grad. Tchg. award, U. Rochester, 1991, Disting. Rschr. award, Oncology Nursing Soc., 1992, Outstanding Contbns. to Nursing and Psychology award, divsn. of health psychology APA, 1993, recognized as a Living Legend, Am. Acad. Nursing, 2005; grantee, NIH, 1972—95. Fellow: AAAS, Am. Psychol. Soc., Acad. for Behavioral Medicine Rsch.; mem.: ANA (chmn. coun. for nurse rschrs. 1976—78, commn. for rsch. 1978—82), Inst. Medicine of NAS (com. on patient injury compensation 1976—77, membership com. 1981—86, gov. coun. 1987—89), Phi Kappa Phi, Omicron Nu, Sigma Xi. Home: 4924 Whitecomb Dr Apt 15 Madison WI 53711-2661 Personal E-mail: jean_joh@msn.com.

JOHNSON, JENNIFER J., federal official; Dep. sec., bd. mems. office Fed. Res. Sys., Washington. Office: Fed Res Sys Bd Mems Office 20th And C Sts NW Ofc Washington DC 20551-0001

JOHNSON, JENNIFER TOBY, military officer; b. Syracuse, N.Y., May 23, 1976; d. Norman Edward and Barbara Catherine Johnson. BS, U.S. Mil. Acad., 1998; attended, U.S. Army Flight Sch., 1998—2000, U.S. Army Capt. Career course, 2003—04; student, Harvard U., 2005—. Commd. 2d lt. U.S. Army 1st Battalion (Attack), 3d Aviation Regiment, 3d Inf. Divsn. (Mechanized), Ft. Hood, Tex., 2000—01, advanced through grades to capt., 2001—, served at Hunter Army Airfield, Ga., 2000—03, served Iraq, 2003—, Kuwait, 2003—. Decorated Presdl. Unit Citation Pres. George W. Bush. Republican. Lutheran. Avocations: golf, skiing, violin. Home: 38 Ellery St Cambridge MA 02138-4205 Office Phone: 912-596-3228.

JOHNSON, JERRILYN JENKINS, academic administrator; b. Winston-Salem, N.C. d. Frizzell James and Thessalonia Mae Jenkins; 1 child, Tessa Leigh. BS in Edn., Winston-Salem State U., NC; MEd in Edn. and Counseling, Wayne State u., 1978; MEd in Adminstrn., NC A&T State U., 1994. Tchr. Winston-Salem (N.C.) Forsyth County Schs., counselor, coord. homeless liaison; tchr. Detroit Pub. Schs.; prin., owner Land of Learning Tutorial Acad., Southfield, Mich.; tchr. Chapel Hill (N.C.) Carrboro Schs.; guidance counselor Asheboro (N.C.) Pub. Schs.; prin, owner Southland Consultants, Winston-Salem, 2003—. Author: Mommy, Are We Homeless?, 2004. Vice-chmn., chmn. adv. bd. Goodwill Industries Cmty., Winston-Salem, NC, 2002—04. Named Educator of Yr., Phi Beta Sigma, 2001; recipient Blue Ribbon award, Mayor, 1997, Outstanding Cmty. Impact award, N.C. Interagency Coun. Coordinating Homeless Programs, 1998. Mem.: Nat. Assn. Edn. Homeless Children and Youth (bd. dirs. 2000—02), 100 Women of Faith (pres. 2003—05), Advocates for the Poor. Democrat. Baptist. Avocations: reading, writing, travel.

JOHNSON, JOAN BRAY, insurance company consultant; b. Kennett, Mo., Nov. 19, 1926; d. Pleas Green and Mary Scott (Williams) Bray; m. Frank Johnson Jr., Nov. 6, 1955; 1 child, Victor Kent. Student, Drury Coll., Springfield, Mo., 1949-51, Cen. Bible Inst. and Coll., 1946-49. Staff writer Gospel Pub. Co., Springfield, Mo., 1949-51; sec. Kennett Sch. Dist. Bd. Edn., 1951-58; spl. features corr. Memphis Press-Scimitar, 1959-60; sec. to v.p. Cotton Exchange Bank, Kennett, Mo., 1959-60; proposal analyst Aetna Life Ins. Co., El Paso, Tex., 1960-64, pension adminstr., 1964-71, office mgr. Brokerage div. Denver, 1971-78, office adminstr. Life Consol. div. Oakland, Calif., 1979-82, office adminstr. PFSD div. Walnut Creek, Calif., 1983-86, office adminstr. PFSD-Health Mktg. div. Sacramento, 1986-89, regional adminstr. Hartford, Conn., 1989-91, cons. Santa Ana, Calif., 1991—, Met-Life Ins. Co., Dallas, 1998—, Transamerica Life, LA, 1999—, Reliar Star Ins., 1999—. Officer local PTA, 1964-71; pres. Wesley Svc. Guild, 1968-71; den mother Boy Scouts Am.; fin. sec. Green Valley United Meth. Ch., 1992—. Recipient Tex. Life Svc. award PTA, 1970. Fellow Life Office Mgmt. Assn. (instr. classes); mem. DAR (regent Silver State Nev. chpt. 1994-96, Nev. state treas. 1998—01, bd. dirs. Nev. 1996—, Nev. state chaplain 2003-2004, Nev. vice regent 2004-06, Nev. corr. sect. 2006—), Assn. Bus. and Profl. Women, Life Underwriters Assn., Clark County Heritage Mus., Last Monday Club, Opti-Mrs., Allied Arts Club. Democrat. Home: 2415 La Estrella St Henderson NV 89014-3608 E-mail: ojbjohnson1@juno.com.

JOHNSON, JOAN (JAN) HOPE VOSS, communications executive, photojournalist, public relations executive; b. Exira, Iowa, Nov. 18, 1922; d. George Carl Alfred Voss and Evelyn Hope Rendleman; m. Conrad Loren Johnson, Jan. 5, 1955 (div. Mar. 29, 1982); children: Scott Conrad, Dawn Ann Bissell, Lisa Ann Lewis; m. James Francis Pressnall, Nov. 23, 1941 (div. Nov. 15, 1952). Traffic/continuity dir., broadcaster KJAN Radio, Atlantic, Iowa, 1952—53; dir. of women's programming KVTV-TV, Sioux City, Iowa, 1953—57; prodr., dir., broadcaster, women's programming tv WMT-TV/WMT Radio, Cedar Rapids, Iowa, 1957—70; consumer cons. a.k.a. Bette Schaper, 1st lady of games industry Schaper Mfg. Co., Minneapolis, Minn., 1966—67; dir. publ. and cmty. rels. Grant Wood Area Edn. Agy., Cedar Rapids, Iowa, 1970—76; mktg./ins. coord. Perpetual Savs. and Loan, Cedar Rapids, Iowa, 1977—82; audio-visual cons., dir. of fund raising Muree Christian Sch., Jhika Gali, Pakistan, 1982—84; dir. pub. rels./devel. McKean Leprosy Inst., Chiang Mai, Thailand, 1984—85; dir. of devel./ Murree Christian Sch., Jhika Gali, Pakistan, 1986—88; profl. spkr. Jan Voss Johnson Enterprises, Atlantic, Iowa, 1988—. Nat. v.p. Am. Women in Radio and TV, Cedar Rapids, Iowa, 1966—67. Contbr. articles; author: (family history, paternal) Quo Fata Vocant; editor: (illustrated poetic anthology) Poems My Mother Taught Me. Dem. candidate for pub. office Iowa State Legislature, Cedar Rapids, Iowa, 1969—70. Seaman, second class S 2/C WAVES USN, 1942—43, N.Y. Mem.: Iowana Coun. (exec. bd.), Camp Fire Girls (bd. mem. 1966—67). D-Liberal. United Ch.Of Christ. Avocations: photography, cooking, travel, history of eastern cultures. Home: 1200 Brookridge Cir 401 Atlantic IA 50022-2304

JOHNSON, JO-ANN HUNTER, psychologist; b. Brackenridge, Pa., Apr. 29, 1936; d. Francis Lytle and Dorothy (Colin) Hunter; m. William R. Hughes (div.); children: Cynthia Jo O'Hara, William Hunter, Christopher Eric, Michael Patrick, Amy Elizabeth; m. John E. Farr (div.); 1 child, John Herschel. BS in Psychology and Physiology, Pa. State U., 1970, MS in Psychology, 1971, PhD in Psychology, 1974. Diplomate Am. Bd. Sexology, Am. Acad. Clin. Sexologists (founding clin. fellow 1991); cert. sex therapist, supv. sex therapy, sex educator; cert. clin. hypnosis; cert. con. in clin. hypnosis. Dir., therapist Devel. Vision Ctr., State College, Pa., 1969-71; cons. Park Forest Nursery Sch., State College, Pa., 1970-71; in-take supr. psychol. clin. Pa. State U., University Park, 1972-73; cons. Centre County Youth Svc. Bur., State College, 1972-78, Juniata Tri-County Mental Health/Mental Retardation Adminstrn., Lewistown, Pa., 1974-76; asst. prof. psychology Pa. State U., 1975-77; pvt. practice, State College, 1977—; sr. rsch. assoc. Inst. for Cellular and Molecular Biology, Austin, 1998; pvt practice Austin, 1998. Sponsored NIMH guest lectr. Kinsey Inst., Bloomington, Ind. Contbr. articles to profl. jours. Mem. Govs. Counsel for Sexual Minorities, Pa.; bd. dirs. Pa. Assoc. of Families, State Coll., Parents Without Ptnrs., State Coll. John W. White fellow Pa. State U., 1970-71, U.S. Pub. Health Svc. fellow Pa. State U., 1970-74; nominated Outstanding Pennsylvanian State Dept. of Health adn Welfare, 1986. Fellow Am. Acad. Clin. Sexologists (clin.); mem. APA, Sex Info. and Edn. coun. U.S. (assoc.), Assn. for Advancement of Behavior Therapy, Soc. for Sci. Study of Sex, Am. Soc. Sex Educators, Counselors and Therapists, Assn. Behavior Analysts, Pa. Psychol. Assn., Nat. Register Health Svc. Providers, Mental Health Profls. of Cen. Pa., Am. Soc. Clin. Hypnosis (cert. in clin. hypnosis, approved cons. in clin. hypnosis). Avocations: flying, needlecrafts, gardening, gourmet cooking. Office: U Tex Inst for Cellular and Molecular Biology 3 122 BA 2500 Speedway Austin TX 78712-1065 Office Phone: 512-471-0414. E-mail: jhjohnson@mail.utexas.edu.

JOHNSON, JOANN MARDELLE, federal agency administrator; b. Massena, Iowa, Feb. 24, 1949; BA in Edn., U. No. Iowa, 1971. Former tchr.; grain and livestock prodr.; mem. Iowa Senate from 39th dist., Des Moines, 1994—2000; mem. appropriations com., mem. commerce com.; chair ways and means com.; chair commerce com.; mem. Nat. Credit Union Admin., Alexandria, Va., 2002—, vice chair, 2003—. Mem. 4-H, Local Devel. Bd.; vol. various cmty. orgns.; campaign mgr. Rep. Dwight Dinkla, 1992, Congressman Jim Lightfoot, 1990, orgn. dir., 1986-88. Mem. Am. Legis. Exch. Coun., Farm Bur., Cattleman's Assn. Republican. Office: Nat Credit Union Adm Off of the Bd 1775 Duke St Alexandria VA 22314-3428 E-mail: boardmember.johnson@ncua.gov.

JOHNSON, JOSEPHINE POWELL, power and light company district manager; b. Goldsboro, N.C., Apr. 23, 1941; d. William Howard and Vennie Ann (Johnson) Powell; m. William Gene Stephenson, Dec. 24, 1959 (dec. Feb. 1979); 1 child, Teresa Lynn (dec.); m. 2d, Amos James Johnson Jr., Aug. 15, 1981; stepchildren: Amos James III, Edward Spencer, Brian Keith. Student Fayetteville Tech. Inst., 1975-79, Mt. Olive Coll., N.C., 1980-83. With Carolina Power & Light Co., 1961—, adminstrv. asst. to dist. mgr., Goldsboro, N.C., 1979-80, area mgr., Mt. Olive, 1980-86, area bus. mgr., Goldsboro, 1986-87, dist. mgr., 1989—; pres. Mt. Olive Bus. Devel. Corp., 1987-96, ret.; pres. Bus. Industry Assn. for Duplin, Samson and Wayne County, 1987—. Bd. dirs. United Way, Wayne County, N.C., 1983—, Am. Heart Assn. Wayne County, 1987, Wayne County Indsl. Coun., 1992, Wayne County Econ. Devel. Commn., Home Health & Hospice, 1992; com. mem. Wayne County Legis. Affairs Com., 1992, bd. dirs., 1992—; bd. dirs. Goldsboro Edn. Found., 1987, chmn., 1991; bd. dirs., pres. Mt. Olive Indsl. Com. of 100, 1984; bd. dirs. Com. of 100 Wayne County, 1987; precinct vice chmn. Cumberland County, Manchester Twp., N.C., precinct chief judge, 1999-2002; chmn. bd. Mt. Olive Family Medicine, 1997—. Mem. Am. Bus. Womens Assn. (v.p. 1983), N.C. Bus. and Profl. Women U.S.A. (v.p. 1982), C. of C. (v.p., bd. dirs. 1980—), Ea. N.C. C. of C. (vice chmn. 1992). Democrat. Home: 714 Club Knolls Rd Mount Olive NC 28365-9401

JOHNSON, JOY ANN, diagnostic radiologist; b. New Richmond, Wis., Aug. 16, 1952; d. Howard James and Shirley Maxine (Eidem) J.que BA in Chemistry summa cum laude, U. No. Colo., 1974; D of Medicine, U. Colo., 1978. Diplomate Am. Bd. Radiology, Nat. Bd. Med. Examiners; cert. added qualification pediatric radiology. Resident in radiology U. Colo., 1978-81, fellow in pediat. radiology, 1981-82; asst. prof. diagnostic radiology and pediatrics, chief sect. pediatric radiology Clin. Radiology Found. U. Kans. Med. Ctr., Kansas City, 1982-87; radiologist Radiology Assocs. Ltd., Kansas City, Mo., 1987-92; mem. staff Bapt. Med. Ctr., Kansas City, Mo., 1987-92; radiologist Children's Mercy Hosp., Kansas City, 1992-95, Leavenworth-Kansas City Imaging, 1996—; assoc. prof. U. Mo., Kansas City, 1992—; chief of staff Cushing Mem. Hosp., 2002—04. Speaker Radiol. Soc. Republic of China, 1985, RSNA 2000 panel mem. Contbr. articles to med. jours. Nat. Cancer Inst. fellow, 1982. Mem. AMA, Am. Coll. Radiology, Radiol. Soc. N.Am., Am. Inst. Ultrasound in Medicine (mem. program com. Kansas City 1984), Soc. Pediatric Radiology (mem. com. for cmty. bsed pediat. radiologists 1998-2003), Am. Assn. Women in Radiology, Lambda Sigma Tau. Avocations: horseback riding, physical fitness, sports, reading. Office: Leavenworth-Kansas City Imaging 9201 Parallel Pkwy Kansas City KS 66112-1528

JOHNSON, JOYCE, retired military officer; m. Jim Calderwood; 1 child, James. DO, Mich. State U., 1980; DSc (hon.), Des Moines U., 2002. Commd. into US Pub. Health Svc.; various positions US Food and Drug Adminstrn., Nat. Inst. Mental Health, Substance Abuse and Mental Health Svcs. Adminstrn.; chief med. officer, surgeon gen. US Coast Guard, 1997—2003, dir. health and safety, 1997—2003, ret., 2003; v.p. health scis. Battelle Meml. Inst., Arlington, Va., 2004—. Bd. trustees US Coast Guard Acad. Named Physician Exec. Yr.; recipient Dr. Nathan Davis award for outstanding govt. svc., Am. Med. Assn. Achievements include among the first to do AIDS rsch. with Ctr. Disease Control, Atlanta; first female flag officer with USCG; first woman to serve on bd. trustees Coast Guard Acad. Avocations: cooking, travel.

JOHNSON, JOYCE MARIE, psychiatrist, epidemiologist, public health officer; b. Baton Rouge, Jan. 30, 1952; d. Gene Addison and Helen Marie (Kalcik) J.; m. James Albert Calderwood, Mar. 28, 1987; 1 child, James. BA, Luther Coll., Decorah, Iowa, 1972; MA, U. Iowa, 1974; DO, Mich. State U., 1980; DFA (hon.), NY Inst. Tech., 2001. Cert. in psychiatry, pub. health and preventive medicine, and clin. pharmacology. Cooking instr. Kirkwood C.C., Iowa City, Iowa, 1974-76; health planner Iowa Regional Med. Program, Iowa City, 1974-76; commd. USPHS, advanced through grades to rear adm./asst. surgeon gen.; intern USPHS Hosp., Balt., 1980-81; med. epidemiologist Hepatitis Labs., Ctrs. Disease Control, Phoenix, 1981-83, AIDS, Ctrs. Disease Control, Atlanta, 1983-84; resident in psychiatry NIMH, 1984-87, staff psychiatrist, 1987-88; epidemiologist, divsn. dir. FDA, 1995—2003; dir. divsn. nat. treatment demonstrations, Substance Abuse and Mental Health Svcs. Adminstrn., 1993-97; chief med. officer USCG, 1997-2003; v.p. health scis. Battelle Meml. Inst., 2004—. Med. Perspectives fellow, New Guinea and Thailand, 1978-79; mem. clin. faculty Mich. State U., 1983-93, Georgetown U. Med. Ctr., 1988—, Uniformed Svcs. U. of the Health Scis. Recipient Dr. Nathan Davis award for Outstanding Work in Govt. Svc., 2001. Mem. Explorers Club, Mensa, Cosmos Club. Office: 5518 Western Ave Bethesda MD 20815-7122

JOHNSON, JUDY M., artist, writer; b. Marquette, Mich., Aug. 11, 1946; d. Lowell Kenneth and Helen C. (Heath) Johnson; children: Jenny R. Taliadoros, Kenneth R. Taylor. Student, Mich. State U., 1964-66. Cert. EFT energy practitioner, hypnotherapist and past-life regressions. Artist B. Shackman Pub., N.Y.C., 1984-90, Dover Publs., N.Y.C., 1986—; writer miscellaneous nat. publs., 1984—; lead artist Magicloth Toys, Concord, Mass., 1995—2000; owner Judy's Place Online Mail Order, Skandia, Mich., 1978—; artist Schilling Toys, Rowley, Mass., 2001—. Writer of verse Marion Heath Greeting Cards, Wareham, Mass., 1994-95; chmn. Art on the Rocks, Marquette, 1994, 2001; mng. editor Original Paper Doll Artists Guild "OPDAG Paper Doll Studio", Kingfield, Maine, 1984—. Author: (book and CD) Tapping into Joy, 2006; author, artist paper dolls; author, editor 2 Twp. Centennial History Books, 1992, 95, pictorial archives; author, pub. herb books, humor books; pub. Lake Superior Art Assn. newsletter KIOSK,1993-2001, self publish, paper doll art mail order and website. Lay spkr. United Meth. Ch., Alma and ctrl. Mich., 1983-88. Mem. Ancient Am. Artifact Preservation Found. (bd. dirs. 2004—, v.p. 2004—, editor, pub. newsletter 2005—), Lake Superior Art Assn. (chair arts show 1994-2001). Avocations: herbs, creative cooking, reading. Home: PO Box 216 Skandia MI 49885-0216 Office Phone: 906-942-7865. Personal E-mail: judyspapergoods@charter.net.

JOHNSON, JUDY VAN, minister, educator; b. Whiteville, NC; d. Henry Byrd and Maebell Bellamy Johnson. BS, Fayetteville State U., 1978, MA, 1987; DivM, Moriah Inst. Christian Studies, 2001, D of Ministry, 2003. Pastor Mt. Horeb, 1996—2002, McCormick Chapel AME, Lumberton, NC, 2002—, Evergreen; tchr. Robeson, Lumberton, NC, Bladen Co., Elizabethtown, NC, New Hanover Co., Wilmington, NC, Jefferson Co., Louisville, Ga. Bd. mem. NC Conf. Assn., 2000—; bd. examiners The North Conf., 2000—; dir. Christian edn., so. dist. N.C. Conf. Recipient Black Heritage award, McCormick Chapel, 2004—05, Advisor's award, Sci. Club, Star Tchr. award, Time Warner, 1997—98, Tchr. of the Yr., Bladen Co., 1993—94, Faith Initial grants, 2004—05. Avocations: reading, sports, travel. Home: 86 Edwards Lane Whiteville NC 28472 Office: McCormick Chapel AME Ch 215 Main St Lumberton NC 28358 Office Phone: 910-739-0461. Personal E-mail: belljvj@yahoo.com.

JOHNSON, JULIE MARIE, lawyer, lobbyist, judge; b. Aberdeen, S.D., Aug. 7, 1953; d. Howard B. and Jerauldine (Dilly) J.; m. Bryan L. Hisel. BA in Govt., Comm., U. S.D., 1974, MA in Polit. Sci., 1976, JD, 1976. Bar: S.D. 1977, U.S. Dist. Ct. S.D. 1977. Assoc. Siegel, Barnett Law Firm, Aberdeen, 1977; law clk. Fifth Judicial Circuit Ct., Aberdeen, 1977-78; ptnr. Maloney, Kolker, Fritz, Hogan & Johnson, Aberdeen, 1978-84; dep. sec. S.D. Dept. Labor, Aberdeen, Pierre, 1983-84, sec. Gov.'s Cabinet, 1985-87; pres. Industry and Commerce Assn. of S.D., Pierre, 1987-95; sec., Gov.'s Cabinet S.D. Dept. Revenue, Pierre, 1995; exec. dir. S.D. Rural Devel. Coun., Pierre, 1995—2003; acting exec. dir. S.D. Math., Sci. and Tech. Coun., 2002—03; adminstrv. law judge State of S.D., 2003—; chair Govs. Red Tape Task Force, 2004—. Adj. faculty S.D. State U., 1996—. Treas. S.D. Cmty. Found., Pierre, 1987-95; mem. Pvt. Industry Coun., 1985-87, S.D. Coun. on Vocat. Edn., 1985-87; bd. dirs. Mo. Shores Women's Resource Ctr., Pierre, 1988-89; chmn. S.D. Main St. Adv. Coun., 1987-91; bd. dirs. United Way, 1988-96, chmn., 1991; mem. Shortgrass Arts Coun., 1987—, South Dakotans for the Arts, 1981—, Solid Waste Mgmt. Plan Task Force, 1990, S.D. Citizens Adv. Coun. on Hazardous Waste, 1991-92, gov.'s adv. coun. on health care reform, 1992-93, gov.'s Homestate Underground Lab adv. coun., 2002-04; bd. dirs. Hist. S.D. Found., 1996-99; founding mem., legal counsel Outdoor Women of S.D., Inc., 1995—; bd. trustees USD Found., 1992—; trustee, mem. bus. affairs com., 1996—, com. on trustees, Kelley Ctr. for Entrepreneurship adv. bd., presdl. search com. Dakota Wesleyan U., 1999-2000; founding mem., treas. S.D. Discovery Ctr. and Aquarium, Inc., bd. dirs., 1988-92; mem. S.D. Water Congress, 1990-97, bd. dirs., 1987-95; bd. dirs. Nyoda Girl Scout Coun., 1997-99; mem. adv. bd. W.O. Farber Ctr. for Excellence in Civic Leadership, 1998—; bd. dirs. Farber Fund, 1987—; founding mem. S.D. Chambers and Econ. Devel. Coun., 1989—; mem. Network Mgmt. Team Nat. Rural Devel. Partnership, 1998-2001; course leader Leadership Ctrl. S.D., 1996—; mem. Children's Care Hosp. and Sch. Found. Bd., 1997—, vice chair, 2005—, investment com., 1999—, joint exec. com., 2003—, devel. com., 2004—, chair governance com., 2005—; mem. Nat. Rural Devel. Partnership Presdl. Transition Team, 2000-01, Agr. and Econ. Devel. Task Force, 2001, S.D. Habitat for Humanity Bd., 2001—, vice chair, 2005—; bd. dirs. Historic S.D. Found., 1995-98, Genesis of Innovation, 2000-03; acting exec. dir. S.D. Math., Sci. and Tech. Coun., 2000-03; vol. chmn. S.D. WWII Meml. Dedication, 2001; vol. chair S.D. Korean War Meml. Dedication Com., 2003-04, seating/decorating co-chair, 2003-04; chmn. Govs. Red Tape Task Force, 2004—, vice chiar, 2005—; bd. dirs. S.D. Habitat for Humanity, 2001—, vice chair, 2005—; founder, treas. Friends of Discovery Ctr., S.D.; trustee, mem. coms. Dakota Wesleyan U., Children's Care Hosp. Found., U. S.D. Found.; active S.D. Vietnam War Meml., 2005-06, chair dignitaries, 2005-06, legal counsel dedication com., 2005-06, mem. fundraising com., 2005-06. RJR Nabisco fellow Women Execs. in State Govt., Harvard, 1986; named Outstanding Young Citizen Jaycees, Aberdeen, 1982, S.D. Jaycees, 1983. Mem. S.D. Bar Assn. (chmn. adminstrv. law com. 2001-04, chair adminstrv. law sect., 2004—, mem. CLE com., Worker's compensation com., chmn. ad law sect. 2004—), Industry and Commerce Assn. S.D. (bd. dirs. 1985-87), U. S.D. Alumni Assn. (exec. com. 1987-96, pres. 1990-92), AAUW, Bus. and Profl. Women U.S.A. (nat. legis. chmn. 1987-88, 92-94, nat. chmn. issues mgmt. 1991-93, pres. S.D. 1984-85, Woman of Yr. award Aberdeen chpt. 1982), Women Execs. in State Govt. (bd. didrs. 1985-87), Coun. State Mfrs. Assn., S.D. Mining Assn. (bd. dirs. 1991-95, Gold PAC, 1995-), Nat. Indsl. Coun., Coun. State C.'s of C., Ducks Unltd., Rotary, WIG Investment Club, Rocky Mountain Elk Found. Republican. Lutheran. Address: 1100 E Church St Apt 352 Pierre SD 57501-2354 Office: 210 E 4th St Pierre SD 57501 Home: 1414 Sharpstone Dr Mitchell SD 57301-6250 Business E-Mail: juliem.johnson@state.sd.us.

JOHNSON, JUNE ALEXIS, counselor, social worker; b. Cleve., Dec. 8, 1945; d. Alexander Branshaw and Mary Annette Mangrum; divorced; children: Troy DeShon McQueen, Tara Elaine Johnson, Carrie Jean Johnson. AA, Cuyahoga C.C., 1992; BA, Notre Dame Coll. Ohio, 1995; MA, John Carroll U., 1997. Lic. profl. counselor, Ohio. Med. sec. Cuyahoga County, Cleve., 1970-80, social worker, dept. sr. and adult protective svcs., 1995—. Contbr. poetry to anthologies. Ch. usher Zion Chapel Bapt. Ch., Cleve. Recipient Golden Poet award The World of Poetry, 1989, 91, Editor's Choice award Nat. Libr. Poetry, 1994, 97. Avocation: poetry. Office Phone: 216-420-6731.

JOHNSON, JUNE MARILYN, music educator; b. Humbolt, S.D., June 2, 1937; d. Herman William and Mildred Ida (Carls) Meves; m. Alfred James Johnson, Feb. 19, 1955; children: Kathleen, Kenneth, Kevin. Pvt. music tchr., Humboldt, SD, 1955—; sec. & bookkeeper West Ctrl. Sch., Hartford, SD, 1975—80; computer data entry Sen. Larry Pressler, Sioux Falls, SD, 1981—86; tchr. aide Montrose Sch., Montrose, SD, 1988—2001. Treas. Parent Tchr. Assn., Humboldt, 1965—66; leader Brownie Scouts, Humboldt, 1968—69. Recipient Cmty. Fine Arts award, West Ctrl. Sch., 1991. Republican. Lutheran. Avocations: travel, piano playing. Home: 108 North Ford Street Humboldt SD 57035

JOHNSON, KAREN, professional society administrator; b. Jersey City; BS, Loretto Heights Coll., 1977; MS, Yale U., 1984. Cert. mental health clin. nurse specialist. Commd. nurse officer USAF, advanced through grades to lt. col., ret., 1992; from mem. staff to v.p. NOW, Washington, 1975—90, co-chair, nat. com. on racial diversity, 1990—93, v.p. Washington, 1993—2001, exec. v.p., 2001—. Mem., nat. bd. dirs, NOW, 1986-90; adv. bd. Cornell U. Peace Studies Program's Women in the Military Project. Contbr. articles to mags. Vol. soup kitchens, New Haven, Conn., Dayton, Ohio, San Antonio Free Clin., San Antonio Battered Women's Shelter; sr. ptnr. Partners Program, Denver; bd. mem. Am. Cancer Soc., Greene County, Ohio. Recipient Keeper of the Flame award State of Ohio, 1990; decorated Air Force Commendation medal 1992. Mem. Kappa Gamma Pi, Sigma Theta Tau.

JOHNSON, KAREN A., legal association administrator; b. Grand Island, Nebr., Aug. 27, 1954; d. Edward C. and Betty M. Johnson. Degree, Grand Island Sch. Bus., Prince George's C.C. Applicant coord. Dept. of Justice, Washington, 1976—77, rsch. analyst, 1977—98, supervisory legal adminstrn. specialist, 1998—. Recipient Incentive award, Dept. of Justice, 2002, 2004, 2006.

JOHNSON, KAREN ELAINE, secondary school educator, tax preparer; b. San Diego, Feb. 7, 1957; d. Alan Jerome and Clarex Irene Johnson. AA, Mesa Coll., San Diego, 1978; BA, San Diego State U., 1981; MA, Calif. State U, San Bernardino, 1985; MS, Nat. U., Vista, Calif., 1993. Cert. tchr., reading specialist, adminstrv. svcs. Calif. Tchr. William S. Hart Union H.S. Dist., Newhall, Calif., 1982, San Jacinto (Calif.) Unified Sch. Dist., 1982—85, Grossmont Union H.S. Dist., La Mesa, Calif., 1985—86, Oceanside Unified Sch. Dist., 1986—; tax preparer H & R Block, Encinitas, Calif., 1996—2001. Mem. Oceanside Unified Sch. Dist. Strategic Plan Com., 1996—; chair-8th grade lang. arts/social studies Oceanside Unified Sch. Dist., 1989—99. Mem.: AAUW (Carlsbad bd. dirs. 1992—2004, legal advocacy v.p. 2000—04, Carlsbad bd. dirs. 2002—05, named Gift Honoree 1993, 1996, 1999), Delta Kappa Gamma (Carlsbad chpt. rec. sec. 1993—95, 1997—99, corr. sec. 2000—04, chpt. pres. 2004—). Avocations: crocheting, knitting, music, reading. Home: 2651 Regent Rd Carlsbad CA 92010-6413 Office: Oceanside Unified Sch Dist 2111 Mission Ave Oceanside CA 92054 Personal E-mail: bigbodaciousbabe@yahoo.com.

JOHNSON, KARLA ANN, county official; b. Heber City, Utah, July 27, 1957; d. Henry Edward and Twila Faun (Jacobson) Kohler; m. Arthur Que Johnson, Sept. 22, 1977; children: Russell, Kohler Scott, Marc. Cattle rancher, Kanab, Utah, 1981—. Bd. dirs. S.W. Utah Dept. Health, St. George; bd. dirs., pres. Kanab C. of C.; charter mem. Nat. Coun. Women's Adv. to Congress, Washington; ambassador Mountain Am. Credit Union, St. George; sec. County Rep. Party, Kanab, Utah; pres. PTA, Kanab. Mem. Internat. Assn. Clks., Recorders, Election Ofcls., Treas., Friendship and Cultural Exch. Soc., Coalition of Resources and Economies, Utah Assn. Counties (bd. dirs.).

JOHNSON, KATHIE CARWILE, education educator; b. Lynchburg, Va., May 18, 1951; d. Walter DeWitt and Kathryn Mae (Wingfield) Carwile; children: Heather Alicia Johnson Ouintero, Rachael Kathryn. BS, Liberty U., 1976; MEd, U. Va., D of Edn., 1991. Tchr. Bedford (Va.) County Public Schs., 1976-80, Timberlake Christian Schs., Lynchburg, Va., 1980-82; tutor Bedford, 1983-91; instr. Roanoke Coll., Salem, Va., 1991-93; assoc. prof., reading and gifted edn. Liberty U., Lynchburg, 1993—. Bd. dirs. New Covenant Schs. of Bedford, 1996-97, Historic Avenel, Bedford, 1993-95, Brockhill Christian Sch., 2004—; regent NSDAR, Bedford, 1995-98. Mem. Internat. Reading Coun., Va. State Reading Assn., Piedmont Area Reading Coun. (treas. 1996-97, pres. 1998—), Kappa Delta Pi, Phi Delta Kappa. Republican. Baptist. Home: 20 Riverview Pl Lynchburg VA 24503-4114 Business E-Mail: kcjohnso@liberty.edu.

JOHNSON, KATHY VIRGINIA LOCKHART, art educator; b. Aberdeen, Miss., May 5, 1951; d. Clovis Clinton and Marium Kathleen (Bowen) Lockhart; m. Gary Wayne Johnson, Aug. 5, 1973; 1 child, Daniel Clinton. BFA, Miss. U. Women, 1973; postgrad., U. Ala., 1973—92. Cert. tchr. Ala. Inventory clk. Johnson Showroom, Columbus, Miss., 1970—73; student tchr. Amory Mid. Sch., Amory, 1973; tchr. art Huntsville Art League, Huntsville, 1974, 1983—84, Evangel Sch., 1974—75, 1st Christian Early Childhood, 1984—88, Huntsville Mus. Art, 1990, Huntsville City Schs., 1989—. One-woman shows include, 1974, Tchr. Show Youth Art Month, 1994, Ann. NASA Picnic, 1998. Mem.: Huntsville Edn. Assn., Ala. Edn. Assn., Nat. Art Edn. Assn., Alpha Delta Kappa (bd. dirs. 1999—, pres. 1996—, sec. 1999—2002). Mem. Christian Ch. (Disciples Of Christ). Avocations: painting, gardening, football. Home: 122 Regent Ctr Madison AL 35758

JOHNSON, KAY DURBAHN, real estate manager, consultant; b. Crookston, Minn., Apr. 4, 1937; d. Wilbert John and Frieda (Johnson) Durbahn; m. Ray Arvin Johnson, May 14, 1960; children: Sherry Kay Johnson Johnston, Diane Rosalind Johnson Peterson, Laura Faye Johnson Gill. BA, U. Minn., 1959. Reference analyst Indsl. Rels. Ctr. U. Minn., Mpls., 1959-61; real estate mgr. Minnetonka, Minn., 1976—; ptnr. Broadmoor Plantation Investors, Fargo, ND, 1976—2005; v.p. D&T Property, Inc., Minnetonka, 1990—, also bd. dirs.; v.p. Comreco, LLC, 2002—, bd. dirs. Tax reduction cons. R.A. Johnson & Assocs., Minnetonka, 1985—; bd. dirs. Empire Aggregate, Inc., 2001—. City of Minnetonka Planning Commn., 1972-74, vice chair, 1973-74; mem. Land Use Task Force, 1972-74; liaison Ridgedale Devel.; mem. choir, various coun. positions Minnetonka Luth. Ch. Mem. Mpls. Inst. Arts. Republican. Avocations: art, music, travel.

JOHNSON, KELLY A., federal agency administrator; BS in Environ. Mgmt., with high honors, Rutgers U.; MPA in Environ. Mgmt., Ind. U. Sch. Pub. and Environ. Affairs; JD magna cum laude, Ind. U. Sch. Law. Assoc. Holland & Hart, 1990—95; mem. Bush-Cheney transition team, US Dept. Interior; sr. counsel Senate Energy and Natural Resources Com.; primary adv. to asst. atty. gen., Environ. & Natural Resources divsn. US Dept. Justice, Washington, 2001—05, acting asst. atty. gen., Environment & Natural Resources divsn., 2005—. Office: US Dept Justice Environl and Natural Resources Divsn 950 Pennsylvania Ave Washington DC 20530

JOHNSON, KELLY OVERSTREET, lawyer; b. Tallahassee, Fla., May 3, 1958; m. Hal Johnson; 2 children. BS in Real Estate and pre-Law, Fla. State Univ., 1979, JD with honors, 1982. Civil litigator Fla. Dept. of Legal Affairs, 1983—85; atty. Ervin, Varn, Jacobs, Odom & Kitchen, 1985—88; pvt. practice, 1988—90; ptnr. Broad and Cassel, Tallahassee, 1990—. Mem.: Am. Bar Assn. (Ho. of Del. 1992—94, 2003—06), Tallahassee Women Lawyers (pres.), Tallahassee Bar Assn. (pres. 1990—91), Fla. Bar (young lawyers divsn. bd. gov. 1986—90, bd. govs. 1997—2004, pres. 2004—05), Leadership Fla. Class XXIV, Guardian Ad Litem Program, Legal Aid Found., Jr. League of Tallahassee. Office: Broad & Cassel 215 S Monroe St Ste 400 PO Box 11300 Tallahassee FL 32302-1300 Office Phone: 850-681-6810. Business E-Mail: kjohnson@broadandcassel.com.

JOHNSON, KIM G., medical/surgical nurse, consultant; b. LaCrosse, Wis., July 18, 1956; d. Richard E. and Lois A. (Temp) Graff; m. Robert A. Johnson, June 26, 1976; children: Erik, Erin, Ryan, Richie. BSN, U. Md., Balt., 1978; MSN, U. Tex. Health Scis. Ctr., San Antonio, 1988. RN, Wis. Parish nursing, Wis. Maj. U.S. Army; ret. Home: 2505 Glendale Ave La Crosse WI 54601-6810

JOHNSON, KIRSTEN DENISE, elementary school educator; b. L.A., Sept. 21, 1968; d. Daniel Webster Johnson and Marinella Venesia (Ishem) Johnson Miller; 1 child, Khari Malik Manning-Johnson BBA Ins., Howard U., 1990; student, Southwestern Sch. Law, L.A., 1991—92, Calif. State U., Dominguez Hills, 1994—97. Intern Travelers Cos., 1987—; asst. Ctr. for Ins. Edn. Howard U., Washington, 1988—89; intern Cigna Ins. Co., L.A., 1989; agt. asst. McLaughlin Co., Washington, 1989—90; legal sec. Harris & Baird, L.A., 1990—92; legal asst. Hamrick & Garrotto, L.A., 1992—94; tchr. 5th grade L.A. Unified Sch. Dist., 1993—, lead sci. tchr., 2003—, HEP coord., 2004—. Freelance writer Calif. Mus. Sci., L.A., 1994—; adv. team Ruby Bridges Program, 2004—; real estate investor, 2005—; presenter in field Participant UCLA/CSP Sci. Project; tutor Delinquent Teenage Group Home Residents, 1998— All Am. scholar, 1989, John Schumacher scholar, 1991, Martin Luther King Jr. scholar, 1996; Fedco grant, 2004 Mem. NEA (RA del.), UTLA (ho. of reps. 2005-06), CTA, Internat. Soc. Poets, Real Estate Investors Democrat. Avocations: reading, travel, movies, weightlifting.

JOHNSON, LADY BIRD (MRS. CLAUDIA ALTA TAYLOR JOHNSON), former First Lady of the United States; b. Karnack, Tex., Dec. 22, 1912; d. Thomas Jefferson and Minnie (Pattillo) Taylor; m. Lyndon Baines Johnson (36th Pres. US), Nov. 17, 1934 (dec. Jan. 22, 1973); children: Lynda Bird, Luci Baines. BA in History, U. Tex., 1933, BJ, 1934, LittD (hon.), 1964; LLD (hon.), Tex. Women's U., 1964; LittD (hon.), Middlebury Coll., 1967; LHD (hon.), Williams Coll., 1967, U. Ala., 1975; HHD (hon.), Southwestern U., 1967; LHD (hon.), Southwest Tex. State U., 1983, Washington Coll., Md., 1983; D Pub. Svc. (hon.), George Washington U., 1986; LHD (hon.), Johns Hopkins U., 1990, SUNY, 1990, Southern Meth. U., 1996, St. Edwards U., 1998, Boston U., 1998. Mgr., husband's Congl. office US Ho. of Reps., Washington, 1941—42; owner, operator KTBC radio-TV sta., Austin, Tex., 1942—63; owner, cattle ranches Tex., 1943—; First Lady of the US, 1963—68. Author: A White House Diary, 1970; co-author (with Carlton Lees): Wildflowers Across America, 1988. Trustee Am. Conservation Assn.; trustee emeritus Nat. Geog. Soc.; founder Nat. Wildflower Rsch. Ctr., Austin, Tex., 1982; trustee Jackson Hole Preserve; hon. mem. LBJ Meml. Grove on the Potomac, Washington; hon. chair Nat. Headstart Program, 1963—68, Town Lake Beautification Project; bd. regents U. Tex., 1971—77, mem. internat. conference steering com., 1969. Recipient Togetherness award, Marge Champion, 1958, Humanitarian award, B'nai B'rith, 1961, Businesswoman's award, Bus. and Profl. Women's Club, 1961, Theta Sigma Phi citation, 1962, Disting. Achievement award, Washington Heart Assn., 1962, Industry citation, Am. Women in Radio and TV, 1963, Humanitarian citation, Vols. of Am., 1963, Peabody award for Whit House TV visit, 1966, Eleanor Roosevelt Golden Candlestick award, Women's Nat. Press Club, 1968, Damon Woods Meml. award, Indsl. Designers Soc. Am., 1972, Conservation Svc. award, Dept. Interior, 1974, Disting. award, Am. Legion, 1975, Woman of Yr. award, Ladies Home Jour., 1975, Medal of Freedom, 1977, Nat. Achievement award, Am. Hort. Soc., 1984, Texan of Yr., State of Tex., 1985, Congl. Gold Medal, 1988, Gold Seal award, disting. svc. & achievement, Nat. Coun. State Garden Clubs, 1990, Charles Leonard Weddle Meml. award, Native Plant Soc., 1994, Lifetime Achievement award, Nature Conservancy of Tex., 1994, Motorola Earth Day award, 1995, Golden Plate award, Am. Acad. of Achievement, 1995, Laurance Spelman Rockefeller Conservation award, disting. svc., 1996, Lifetime Achievement award, Native Plant Conservation Initiative, 1999, Cornerstone award, Tex. Soc. Architects, 2000, Theodore Roosevelt Nat. Park Medal of Honor, Nat. Park Found., 2000, Medal of Honor, DAR, 2003, Edwin P. Hubble award, Edwin P. Hubble Soc., 2004, History Making Texan, The Tex. State History Mus. Found., 2005, Nat. Conservation Achievement award, conservationist of Yr., Nat. Wildlife Fedn., 2005, Lindy Boggs award, Stennis Ctr. for Pub. Svc., 2005. Fellow: Weizmann Inst. Sci. (hon.); mem.: Ex-Student Assn. U. Tex. (life). Democrat. Episcopalian. Address: LBJ Libr and Mus 2313 Red River St Austin TX 78705-5702*

JOHNSON, LATONYA, secondary school educator; d. Mary Ann Kinchen and Ernest Dexter Davis. Degree in Elec. Engring., U. La., Lafayette, 1999. Tchr. Grand Prarrie (Tex.) Ind. Sch. Dist., 2002—.

JOHNSON, LAURA STARK, secondary school educator, administrator; b. Unityville, S.D., Jan. 9, 1913; d. Fred Hartman and Catherine (Culver) Stark; m. Falk Simmons Johnson, June 11, 1940; children: Mark, Bruce, Martha, Craig (dec.). BA, Dakota Wesleyan U., 1937; MA, Northwestern U., 1966; MS in Edn., No. Ill. U., 1982. Tchr. pub. schs., Unityville, 1932-36, McIntosh (S.D.) H.S., 1937-38, Washington Sch., Wauwatosa, Wis., 1938-40, Mark Twain Sch., Des Plaines, Ill., 1964-65, Maine S. H.S., 1965-69, Evanston (Ill.) H.S., 1969-96. Tchr., reading cons., 1969-76; tchr. Adult Continuing Edn., 1972-85; adult edn. dept. coord. ABE/GED/Literacy, 1985-96; adj. faculty mem. Northeastern Ill., 1974-76, Loyola U., Chgo., 1974-75, Oakton C.C., 1977-79, Triton C.C., 1981-86; spkr. World Congress Reading, Singapore, 1976, Gold Coast, Australia, 1988, Stockholm, 1990; literacy Oakton C.C., 1998-2000. Chost writer Ency. Britannica Films, Sci. Rsch. Assn., 1958-60; author, cons. Coronet Instrnl. Media, 1974-79; editor Reading and Adult Learner, 1980, Internat. Reading Assn., Alaska Jour. Collection, 1981, Curriculum Guide for ABE Language Arts, 1988, Curriculum Pub. Clearing House, Reading in the Content Areas, New Readers Press, 1990-92; cons. Barron's Ednl. Series, 1994-2003; mem. adv. bd. Jour. Reading, 1972-76; contbr. articles to profl. jours. Mem. Internat. Reading Assn. (pub. com. 1976-79), Internat. Reading Assn., Ill. Reading Assn. (officer 1969-72), Suburban Reading League, Ill. Adult Continuing Edn. Assn. Home: 7624 Maple St Morton Grove IL 60053-1641

JOHNSON, LEONA MELISSA, psychology professor, researcher; b. Natchez, Miss., Oct. 15, 1950; d. Leon Matthews and Leona Stevenson Bradley; m. Arthur Johnson, Aug. 8, 1969; children: Sharika Danice, Amira Celeste. BA, Jackson State U., Miss., 1972; MBA, Strayer U., 1995; diploma in program mgmt., Def. Systems Mgmt. Coll., 1995; MEd, Howard U., 1998, PhD, 2003. With IBM Corp., Owego, N.Y. and Manassas, Va, 1973—95; project mgr. Loral Corp., Manassas, 1995—98, Lockheed Martin Corp., Manassas, 1998—2004. Rschr. United Negro Coll. Fund, Arlington, Va., 2001—02, Ednl. Rsch. Svcs., Arlington, 2001—02; adj. prof. Howard U., Washington, 2004. Pres. Circles of First Bapt. Ch., Manassas, 1993—2003; v.p. Howard U. Alumni, Woodbridge, 2001—03; pres. Tea Rose Investment Club, Woodbridge, 1999—2000. Recipient cert., Fairfax Pub. Sch. Sys., 1998, Nat. Women of Color award, Career Group Comm., 2003, Letter of Appreciation, Jr. Achievement of Am., 2004. Mem.: AAUW, APA (assoc.), Nat. Assn. African Am. Studies, Am. Evaluation Assn., Assn. Black Psychologists (assoc.), Alpha Kappa Alpha (assoc.; chpt. pres. 2000—04, Ednl. Advancement Found. Merit scholar 2002). Office: Hampton U Hampton VA 23668 Home: 1401 Marsh Wren Cir Portsmouth VA 23703 Office Phone: 757-727-5370. Home Fax: 703-257-4015. Personal E-mail: johnsonleonam@aol.com. Business E-Mail: leona.johnson@hamptonu.edu.

JOHNSON, LINDA ARLENE, transportation executive; b. Sparta, Wis., Mar. 6, 1946; d. Clarence Julius and Arlene Mae (Yahnke) Jessie; children: Darrick, Larissa. With Union Nat. Bank & Trust Co., Sparta, 1964-69, Hill, Christensen & Co., CPA's, Tomah, Wis., 1969-75; owner Johnson of Wis. Oil Co., Inc., Tomah, 1969-95; with Larry's Express, Inc., Tomah, 1975-78; owner Johnson Rentals, 1979—, Johnson of Wis. Transport Co., Inc., Tomah, 1982—. Mem. Forward Tomah Devel., Inc., 1999—; active St. Paul's Luth Ch., Tomah. Mem.: Wis. Motor Carriers Assn., Petroleum Marketers Assn. Wis., Tomah Area Credit Union (bd. dirs. 1993—, sec. 1993—94), Tomah Area C. of C., Rotary (bd. dirs. 1997—99), Beta Sigma Phi (Larueate Phi chpt.).

JOHNSON, LINDA SUE, academic administrator, state agency administrator, retired state legislator; b. Ft. Worth, Dec. 4, 1950; d. William Jr. and Helen Adelene (Loya) McCormick; m. Jerry Eugene Johnson, May 24, 1974 (div. 1984); children: Jeremy Scott, Nicholas Adam, Jennifer Leigh. BA in Biology, U. Tex., 1972; ADN, Shoreline C.C., Seattle, 1986; M in Healthcare Adminstrn., U. Wash., 1988. RN, Washington. Physician's asst. Children's Med. Ctr., Austin, Tex., 1973; collections corr. Sears Roebuck & Co., Seattle, 1973-77; nurse Northwest Hosp., Seattle, 1985-88; intern Univ. Hosp., Seattle, 1987-88; clin. mgr. ops. Evergreen Urgent Care Ctr., Woodinville, Wash., 1988-90; dir. med. staff Evergreen Hosp. Med. Ctr., Kirkland, Wash., 1990-94; mem. Wash. Ho. Reps., Olympia, 1993-95; immunization program mgr. Wash. Dept. Health, Olympia, 1995—98; dir. prof. svs. Ctrl. Oreg. Dist. Hosp., 1998—2000; assoc. provost Cascades campus Oreg. State U., 2000—03. Trustee, pres. Trustees Assn. Tech. and Community Colls., Olympia, 1990-92; trustee Shoreline C.C., 1987-92; active PTA. Mem. Am. Coll. Healthcare Execs., Wash. State Nurses Assn. (legis. com. 1991-93). Democrat.

JOHNSON, LOIS BROOKS, retired elementary guidance counselor; b. Richmond, Va., July 9, 1933; d. David Lee, Sr. and Lyda (Murray) Brooks; children from previous marriage: TuWaunda J. Barham, Michel L. BA in Elem. Edn., Va. Union U., 1955; MEd in Counselor Edn., Va. Commonwealth U., 1974. Elem. tchr. Surry County Pub. Schs., Surry, Va., 1955—56, Chesterfield (Va.) Pub. Schs., 1956—63, Richmond (Va.) Pub. Schs., 1963—69, elem. guidance counselor, 1973—91; ret., 1991. Author: Somebody is Knocking at My Door, 2001, We Must Be Held Accountable, 2002, It's Later Than You Think, 2004 (Life and Time Awareness Book), (poems) Life's Picture, 1999, (short stories) Sleepy Town, 2000. Recipient Golden Poet award, World Poetry Press, 1987, Silver Poet award, 1989, Cmty. Leadership plaque, 3200/3300 Lamb Ave Block Club, 1994, Ch. Historian Svc. plaque, Mt. Olive Bapt. Ch., 2004. Mem.: Richmond Edn. Assn. (Ret)., Va. Multi-Cultural Counseling and Devel. Assn., Richmond Area Counselors Assn., Va. Counselors Assn., Richmond-Henrico Ret. Tchrs. Assn., Eastern Star, Delta Sigma Theta (Richmond Alumnae Chpt.). Avocations: writing, singing, sewing, reading.

JOHNSON, LOLA NORINE, retired advertising and public relations executive, educator; b. Austin, Minn., Dec. 28, 1942; d. Alton E. and Evelyn M. (Quast) Milbrath; m. Dennis D. Johnson, June 15, 1963 (div. July 1973); children: Brenda J., Erik B. Attended, Coll. of St. Thomas. Pub. rels. account rep. Kerker & Assocs. Advt. and Pub. Rels., Bloomington, Minn., 1973-78; comm. mgr. Norwest Bank Mpls., 1978-83; dir. media rels., account supr. Edwin Neuger & Assocs. Pub. Rels., Mpls., 1983-85; v.p., mng. dir. The Richards Group, Mpls., 1985-86; owner, pres. PR Plus, Edina, Minn., 1986-2000; ret., 2000. Mem. cmty. faculty, instr., counselor Met. State U., Mpls., St. Paul, 1980-93. Cons. comm. United Way, Mpls., 1982. Recipient Gold award United Way Mpls., 1982. Home: 7151 York Ave S Apt 807 Minneapolis MN 55435-4435

JOHNSON, LORI HIGINBOTHAM, elementary school educator; b. Ottumwa, Iowa, Sept. 18, 1970; d. Norman Harold and Linda Kay Higinbotham; m. Scott Alan Johnson, Apr. 11, 1992; 1 child, Emily Margaret. BA Edn., Buena Vista U., Ottumwa, 1992. Cert. Elem. Tchr. Iowa, 1992. Tchr. title I k - 6 Cardinal Sch. Dist., Eldon, Iowa, 1992—. Head tchr. title I Cardinal Schs., Eldon, 2004—. Tchr. Sun. sch. Ch., Ottumwa, Iowa, 2003—05. Named to Who's Who Among Am. Tchrs. Avocation: drag racing. Home: 132 Shaul Ave Ottumwa IA 52501 Office: Cardinal Community Schools R R 1 Eldon IA 52554 Personal E-mail: dragladylj@yahoo.com.

JOHNSON, LUAN K., disaster management consultant; d. Jack R. and Colleen (Kesler) J. BA, Brigham Young U., 1981, MA, 1984; PhD, U. Wash., 1994. Dir. Tchg. Resource Ctr., Provo, 1980-84; tchg. asst. comms. dept. Brigham Young U., Provo, 1982-83; counselor Master Acad., Salt Lake City, 1985; ednl. designer, program mgr. City of Sunnyvale, 1986-90; tchg. asst., rsch. asst., speech comm. dept. U. Wash., Seattle, 1991-93; program mgr. City of Seattle, 1993—2005; program mgr. state of Wash. emergency mgmt. dir. SPAN disaster, svcs. a non-profit disaster preparedness & response orgn., 2004—; program mgr. Washington State Emergency Mgmt., 2005—. Recipient Best Ednl. Campaign award Internat. Assn. Emergency Mgrs., 1998, Nat. Coord. Coun. of Emergency Mgmt. Best Newsletter award, 1996, 98, 2002, 1st pl.-best ednl. campaign Internat. Assn. Emergency Mgrs., 1998, Outstanding Pub. Svc. award Seattle Police Dept., 1999, 1st pl.-best ednl. video Internat. Assn. Emergency Mgrs., 1999. Mem.: Phi Kappa Phi. Mem. Lds Ch. Avocation: collecting and flying kites. Home: 10018 Nineteenth Ave Ct S Parkland WA 98444

JOHNSON, LUCIE JENKINS, retired social worker, educator; b. Elizabethtown, Ky., Feb. 10, 1927; d. Alex Heady and Mary Lee (Igleheart) Jenkins; BA magna cum laude, Wake Forest U., 1949; MSW, Tulane U., 1953; postgrad. Va. Poly. Inst. and State U., 1974-80; m. Glenn E. Johnson, Oct. 24, 1952; children: Alexander, Rebecca, Catherine, Elizabeth. Psychiat. social worker with families in public/pvt. svc., 1952-67; chief psychiat. social worker Youth Services, Va. Dept. Welfare and Instns., Richmond, 1967-69; asst. prof. Va. Commonwealth U., 1969-74; asst. prof., coordinator continuing edn. in social work Wayne State U., Detroit, 1977-81; supr. oncology social work Harper Hosp./Wayne State U., Detroit, 1981-84; supr. med. social work Sinai Hosp. Detroit, 1984-88, med. social worker, 1988-93, ret., 1993. Mem. AAUW, AAUP, Nat. Assn. Social Workers, Acad. Cert. Social Workers (emeritus). Democrat. Presbyterian (elder and deacon). Home: 323 Carolina Meadows Villa Chapel Hill NC 27517-7520 E-mail: glennlucie@aol.com.

JOHNSON, LYNN MARIE THORNBURG, parochial school educator; d. Jason Dale and Jean Watkins Thornburg; m. Merrill Lee Johnson, Aug. 14, 1982; children: Erin Elizabeth, Alyssa Lynn. AB, Hope Coll., Holland, Mich., 1979; MEd, U. Ga., Athens, 1982. 7th/8th grade reading/English tchr. Coffee County Schs., Douglas, Ga., 1979—81; 6th/7th grade reading tchr. St. Tammany Parish Schs., Covington, La., 1982—84, kindergarten/1st grade tchr., 1984—91, K-2 title I tchr., 1995—2004, resource helping tchr., 2004—. Elder Northminster Presbyn. Ch., Pearl River, La., 1994—98, 2000—05. Named Walmart Tchr. of Yr., Slidell Walmart, 2003. Mem.: La. Reading Assn.-North Shore Reading Coun., Internat. Reading Assn. Avocations: cello, violin, reading, cross stitch. Office: Abney Elem Sch 825 Kostrayer Slidell LA 70458

JOHNSON, MADELINE MITCHELL, retired administrative assistant; b. Cleve., Oct. 24, 1930; d. Maidlon and Katherine (Reynolds) Mitchell; m. Elvyn Frank Johnson, Dec. 4, 1954. BS, Case Western Res. U., 1976. Adminstrv. asst. Fed. Res. Bank Cleve., 1950-92, tng. coord. data svcs., 1988-92, ombudsman rep., 1989-92; ret., 1992. Mem. tng. task force bd. govs. FRS, Washington, 1987-92; advisor Top Teens of Am., 1998-2005. Chair bd. trustees Affinity Bapt. Ch., 1990-93. Mem. Am. Bus. Women's Assn. (pres. 1986-88, Women of Yr. Cleve. chpt. 1987), Nat. Coun. Negro Women, Top Ladies of Distinction (Woman of Yr. Cleve. chpt. 1993-94, pres. 1995-97), chmn. status of women 2003-05), Am. Bapt. Women (treas. 1998-2001). Avocations: golf, swimming, reading. Home: 33705 Wellingford Ct Solon OH 44139-6600

JOHNSON, MADGE RICHARDS, business owner, fundraiser, consultant; b. Washington, Oct. 4, 1952; d. Benjamin Ellsworth and Virginia (Oliver) Richards; m. Jeffrey Leonard Johnson, June 25, 1977; children: Jared Benjamin, Jessica Lauren. B.S. in Bus. Mgmt., Strayer Coll., 1973; MBA Columbia Union Coll. 2004, Nat. govt. sales rep. G.F.C. Mfg. Co., Bklyn., 1972-75; ter. sales rep. John H. Breck, Am. Cyanamid, Wayne, N.J.; ter. sales mgr. Drackett Products Co., Cin., 1977-81, E.J. Brach & Sons., Chgo., Annapolis, Md., 1981-87, owner, pres. Madge Johnson Ltd., 1987—; sec.-treas. Recreation Environments Co., Annapolis, Md., 1988-90, asst. dir. Columbia Union Coll. Takoma Park, MD, 1999—; Treas. Martin Barr Sch., 1989-90 Mem. NAFE, Grocery Mfrs. Reps., Women in Consumer Product Sales. Home and Office: 17205 Magruders Ferry Rd Brandywine MD 20613-8358

JOHNSON, MARGARET ANN (PEGGY), library administrator; b. Atlanta, Aug. 11, 1948; d. Odell H. and Virginia (Mathiasen) Johnson; m. Lee J. English, Mar. 4, 1978; children: Carson J., Amelia J. BA, St. Olaf Coll., 1970; MA, U. Chgo., 1972; MBA, Met. State U., 1990. Music cataloger U. Iowa Librs., Iowa City, 1972-73; analyst Control Data Corp., Bloomington, Minn., 1973-75; br. libr. St. Paul Pub. Librs., 1975-77; head tech. svcs. St. Paul Campus Librs., U. Minn., 1977-86; collection devel. officer Univ. Librs., U. Minn., Mpls., 1987-90; asst. dir. St. Paul Campus Librs., U. Minn., 1987-95; planning officer U. Librs. U. Minn., Mpls., 1993-97, asst. univ. libr., 1997—2003, interim univ. libr., 2002, assoc. univ. libr., 2003—. Libr. cons. Mekerere U., Kampala, Uganda, 1990, U. Nat. Rwanda, 1990, Inst. Agr. and Vet. Hassan II, Rabat, Morocco, 1992—2000, Ecole Nat. Agr., Meknes, Morocco, 2000, China Agrl. U., Beijing, 2001—, Xi'an Eurasia U., Xi'an, China, 2005. Author: Automation and Organizational Change in Libraries, 1991, The Searchable Internet, 1996, Fundamentals of Collection Development and Management, 2004; editor: New Directions in Technical Services, 1997; editor Technicalities Jour., 2000—, Libr. Resources and Tech. Svcs., 2003—; editor Guide to Tech. Svcs. Resources, 1994, Recruiting, Educating and Tng. Librarians for Collection Devel., 1994, Collection Mgmt. and Devel., 1994, Virtually Yours, 1998; contbr. articles to profl. jours. Recipient Samuel Lazerow Rsch. fellowship Assn. Coll. and Rsch. Librs., Inst. for Sci. Info., 1987; Blackwell scholar Assn. for Libr. Collections and Tech. Svcs., 2005. Mem. ALA, Internat. Assn. Agrl. Librs. and Documentalists, U.S. Agrl. Info. Network, Assn. for Libr. Collections and Tech. Svcs. (pres. 1999-2000). Office: U of Minn Librs 499 Wilson Libr 309 19th Ave S Minneapolis MN 55455-0438 Office Phone: 612-624-2312. Business E-Mail: m-john@umn.edu.

JOHNSON, MARGARET H., welding company executive; b. Chgo., June 3, 1933; d. Harold W. and clara J. (Pape) Glavin; m. Odean Jack Johnson, Nov. 18, 1950; children: Karen Ann, Dean Harold. Student, Moody Bible Inst., 1976-78. V.p., sec. Seamline Welding, Inc., Grayslake, Ill., 1956-96, also bd. dirs. Author: Living Faith, 1973, 80, Lord's Ladder of Love, 1976, God's Rainbow, 1982; contbr. articles to religious mags. Trustee SWCEPS, Grayslake, 1963-99; life mem. Rep. presdl. Task Force, 1982—; trustee, 1986-88; charter founder Ronald Reagan Rep. Ctr., 1987; mem. lake View Neighborhood Group, Chgo., Small Group Ch. Cmty.; active Mary, Seat of Wisdom Cath. prayer groups, 1970-90, renew facilitator, 1986-88, co-chairperson, 1986-88; Sunday sch. tchr.; mem. parish coun. St. Gilbert parish, 1995-2000, evangelization chair, 1995-99, hospitality chair, 1995-99, welcome home program, 1998-99; mem. St. Raymond Cath. Ch., Mt. Prospect, 2000—; mem. spiritual life The Moorings of Arlington Heights, 2001, spiritual life chairperson, 2005. Recipient Internat. Peace Prize, United Cultural Convention of Am. Biog. Inst., 2005. Mem. AARP, ASCAP, Fedn. Ind. Small Bus., Internat. Platform Assn., Women's Aglow Fellowship, Grayslake c. of C., Exch. Club of Grayslake, Grayslake Devel. Corp. Home: Apt 415 811 E Central Rd Arlington Heights IL 60005-3279

JOHNSON, MARGARET HELLER, artist, educator; d. Henry and Elsie Heller; children: Kimberly Lauder, Adrienne. BA in Edn., U. Del., Newark, 1965. Cert. tchr. Del. Tchr. Wesley Presch., Dover, Del., 1979—85; art educator Capital Sch. Dist., Dover, 1985—. Contbr. art to profl. publs.; exhibitions include Del. Mus. Contemporary Art, Briggs Mus. Am. Art, Rehobeth Art League, Del. Women's Conf. Handmade paper demonstrator Winterthur Mus., Wilmington, Del., 2005, mem. tchr.'s adv. bd., 1997—; handmade paper demonstrator Lewes Hist. Soc., Del.; pres. Littleton Hosp. Aux., NH, 1974—76; mem. Del. Art Mus., Dover, 1991—2006. Excellence In Edn. grantee, MBNA, 2003. Mem.: Capital Educators Assn. (mem. exec. bd. 2001—).

JOHNSON, MARGO FAYE, elementary school educator, nurse; b. Hope, Ark., Sept. 15, 1953; d. Thomas Terrell and Annie Louise Ross; 1 child from previous marriage, Terrence Terrell. Cert. in mortuary adminstrn. and embalming, Dallas Inst. Mortuary Sci., 1974; cert. in nursing, Red River C.C., Hope, Ark., 1976; BS in Elem. Edn., East Carolina State U., Greenville, 2001. Cert. in nursing, Ark.; tchr. N.C., Ark. Mortician Sims Mortuary, Eldorado, Ark., 1976—77; nurse Nevada County Hosp., Prescott, Ark., 1977—81, U.S. Army, El Paso, Tex., 1981—92, Mountain View Pl., 1992—94, Britthaven, Smithfield, NC, 1994—2005; tchr. Norwayne Mid. Sch. Wayne County Pub. Schs., Goldsboro and Fremont, 2001—05; nurse Woodland Hills, Jacksonville, Ark., 2006—; tchr. Harris Elem. Sch., North Little Rock, Ark., 2006—. Sgt. U.S. Army, 1981—92. Mem.: Nat. Sci. Tchrs. Assn., Pinnacle Nat. Honor Soc., Golden Key, Delta Sigma Theta, Phi Kappa Phi. Democrat. Baptist. Home: 813 N James St Jacksonville AR 72076-4047

JOHNSON, MARGUERITE ANNIE See ANGELOU, MAYA

JOHNSON, MARIA ELIZABETH, psychiatrist, researcher; b. Decatur, Ga., Oct. 15, 1974; d. John Alfred and Gloria Tidmore Johnson; m. Jeffrey Lynn Rausch, May 4, 2005; 1 child, John Dylan Rausch. MD, Med. Coll. of Ga., Augusta, 2002. Psychiatry resident U. Ariz., Tucson, 2002—04; psychopharmacology rsch. fellow Med. Coll. of Ga., Augusta, Ga., 2005—. Recipient Janssen Scholar award, 2006. Mem.: Am. Psychiat. Assn. Office: Med Coll of Georgia 1515 Pope Ave Augusta GA 30912 Office Phone: 706-721-7793.

JOHNSON, MARIAN ILENE, education educator; b. Hawarden, Iowa, Oct. 3, 1929; d. Henry Richard and Wilhelmina Anna (Schmidt) Stoltenberg; m. Paul Irving Jones, June 14, 1958 (dec. Feb. 1985); m. William Andrew Johnson, Oct. 3, 1991. BA, U. La Verne, 1959; MA, Claremont Grad. Sch., 1962; PhD, Ariz. State U., 1971. Cert. tchr., Iowa, Calif. Elem. tchr. Cherokee (Iowa) Sch. Dist., 1949-52, Sioux City (Iowa) Sch. Dist., 1952-56, Ontario (Calif.) Pub. Schs., 1956-61, Reed Union Sch. Dist., Belvedere-Tiburon, Calif., 1962-65, Columbia (Calif.) Union Sch. Dist., 1965-68; prof. edn. Calif. State U., Chico, 1972-91. Avocation: travel. Home: 26437 S Lakewood Dr Sun Lakes AZ 85248-7246

JOHNSON, MARIE-LOUISE TULLY, dermatologist, educator; b. NYC, July 26, 1927; d. James Henry and Mary Frances (Dobbins) Tully; m. Kenneth Gerald Johnson, June 10, 1950. AB, Manhattanville Coll., 1948; PhD, Yale U., 1954, MD, 1956. Intern, then resident Yale-New Haven Med. Ctr., 1956-59; asst. prof. medicine, dermatology Yale U., 1961-67, clin. prof. dermatology, 1980—; chief dermatologist med. svc. Atomic Bomb Casualty Commn., Hiroshima, Japan, 1964-67; assoc. prof. dermatology NYU, 1967-70, 74-76, prof. dermatology, 1976-80; assoc. prof. dermatology, coord. continuing med. edn. Dartmouth Coll., Hanover, NH, 1971-74; chief dermatology Bellevue Hosp., N.Y.C., 1974-80; dir. med. edn. Benedictine Hosp., Kingston, NY, 1980-93. Cons. Health and Nutrition Exam. Survey I, II, Health Stats., Washington, 1967-84. Contbg. author: Cecil's Textbook of Medicine, 15th edit., 1979, 16th edit., 1982, 17th edit., 1985, Dermatology in General Medicine, 2d edit., 1979. Mem. Cardinal Cooke Pro-Life Commn., Albany, N.Y., 1986-87; bd. dirs. Maternity and Early Childhood Found., Albany, 1984-2001, pres., 1987-2001; bd. dirs. Sulzberger Inst. for Dermatologic Edn., 1986-93; pres. Mid-Hudson Consortium for the Advancement of Edn. for Health Professions, 1989-92; bd. govs. Yale U. Alumni Assn., 1991-94; v.p. Assn. Yale U. Alumni in Medicine, 1991-93, pres., 1993-95. Named Disting. Alumna, Manhattanville Coll., 1977, Rose Hirschler award Women's Dermatologic Soc., 1993, Papal Cross Pro Ecclesia et Pontifice Pope John Paul II, 1994, Clark W. Finnerud award Dermatology Found., 1997. Fellow Am. Acad. Dermatology (master 1995, bd. dirs. 1976-80, Presdl. citation 1999); mem. Am. Dermatol. Assn. (bd. dirs. 1986-92, v.p. 1991-92, pres. 2000-01), Inst. Medicine of NAS, Internat. Physicians for

Prevention of Nuc. War (del. 1982, 83, 87, 88, 89). Roman Catholic. Home: 15 Strawberry Bank Rd High Falls NY 12440-5128 Office: Kingston Hosp Med Arts Bldg Ste 202 368 Broadway Kingston NY 12401-5159 Office Phone: 845-338-7472.

JOHNSON, MARILYN, retired obstetrician, retired gynecologist; b. Houston, May 7, 1925; d. William Walton and Marilyn (Henderson) J. BA, Rice Inst., 1945; MD, Baylor U., 1950. Intern New Eng. Hosp. Women and Children, Boston, 1950—51; resident Meth. Hosp., Houston, 1951—53; fellow in gynecol. pathology Harvard Med. Sch., 1952—53; resident in gynecology M.D. Anderson Tumor Inst., Houston, 1954, fellow, 1955; practice medicine specializing in ob-gyn. Houston, 1954—81, Fredericksburg, Tex., 1981—97; ret., 1997. Mem. staffs St. Joseph's, Meml., Meth., Park Plaza, Hill Country Meml. Rosewood, South Austin Cmty., Comfort (Tex.) Cmty. hosps.; clin. instr. ob-gyn Coll. Medicine, Baylor U., 1954—, Postgrad. Sch. Medicine, U. Tex., 1954—; gynecologist De Pelchin Faith Home, Houston, 1954—, also Rice U., Richmond State Sch.; med. dirs. Birthright, Inc., Houston, 1973—; chief med. staff Hill Country Meml. Hosp., Fredericksburg, Tex., 1990-92; cons. Tex. bd. Blue Cross Blue Shield; pro-life public spkr. Bd. dirs. Right to Life, Houston, Found. for Life. Grantee Sandoz Labs., 1973, 75, Delbay Pharm. Co., 1977. Fellow Am. Coll. Obstetricians and Gynecologists; mem. AMA, Am. Soc. Colposcopic Pathologists, Tex. Med. Assn., Am. Med. Women's Assn., Internat. Infertility Assn., Harris County Med. Soc., Postgrad. Med. Assembly South Tex., Houston Ob-Gyn. Soc., Tex. Folklore Soc., Zonta, Fredericksburg Rockhounds. Republican. Baptist. Home: 10022 Briar Forest Houston TX 77042

JOHNSON, MARJORIE R., special education educator; b. Boston, Jan. 3, 1929; d. Irving Benjamin and Florence Emma (Alling) Akerson; m. Richard Johnson, May 19, 1951; children: William Benjamin, Gerald Dennis, Peter Charles. BS in Occupational Therapy, Columbia U., N.Y.C., 1951. Cert. tchr. spl. edn., primary edn. and occupational therapy, Pa. Occupational therapist ABC Children's Clinic, Reading, Pa., 1951-52; clerk Kaiser Metal Co., Bristol, Pa., 1952-54; spl. edn. tchr. Chester Co. Intermediate Unit, Coatesville, Pa., 1964-91; ret., 1991. Union v.p. CCIU branch PSEA, 1964, pres. 1965. Active in establishing group homes ARC, Chester County, 1973. Mem. Soc. Pa. Archaeology (sec. 1984-86, v.p. 1996-99). Avocations: archaeology, thread arts. Home: 40 Forrest Rd Honey Brook PA 19344-1731

JOHNSON, MARLENE M., nonprofit executive; b. Braham, Minn., Jan. 11, 1946; d. Beauford and Helen (Nelson) J.; m. Peter Frankel. BA, Macalester Coll., 1968. Founder, pres. Split Infinitive, Inc., St. Paul, 1970-82; pres., bd. dirs. Face to Face Health and Counseling Clinic, 1977-78; with Working Opportunities for Women, 1977-82; lt. gov. State of Minn., St. Paul, 1983-91; sr. fellow Family Support Project, Ctr. for Policy Alternative, 1991-93; assoc. adminstr. for adminstrn. GSA, Washington, 1994-95; v.p. for people and strategy Rowe Furniture Corp., McLean, Va., 1995-97; exec. dir., CEO NAFSA: Assn. Internat. Educators, 1998—. Founder, past chmn. Nat. Leadership Conf. Women Execs. in State Govt.; mem. exec. com., midwestern chair Nat. Conf. Lt. Govs.; bd. dirs. AFS-USA, Inc., 1992-98, Nat. Capitol Region coun. Girl Scouts U.S., 1997-2004, bd. trustees AFS Internat. programs, 1998-2002; mem. adv. bd. Comm. Consortium Media Ctr., 2000-, Ctr. for Children in Poverty, Columbia U., 2002. Chmn. Minn. Women's Polit. Caucus, 1973-76, Dem.-Farmer-Labor Small Bus. Task Force, 1978, Child Care Task Force, 1987; dir. membership sect. Nat. Women's Polit. Caucus, 1975-77; vice chmn. Minn. Del. to White House Conf. on Small Bus., 1980; co-founder Minn. Women's Campaign Fund, 1982; bd. dirs. Nat. Child Care Action Campaign; chair Children's 2000 Commn., 1990; candidate for Mayor St. Paul, 1993. Recipient Outstanding Achievement award St. Paul YWCA, 1980, Disting. Svc. award St. Paul Jaycees, 1980, Disting. Citizen citation Macalester Coll., 1982, Disting. Contbns. to Families award Minn. Coun. on Family Rels., 1986, Minn. Sportfishing Congress award, 1986, Royal Order of Polar Star Govt. Sweden, 1988, Children's Champion award Def. Fund, 1989, Jane Preston award Minn. State Coun. on Vocat. Tech. Edn., 1989, Legis. Leadership award Am. Fedn. Tchrs., 1991; named One of Ten Outstanding Young Minnesotans, Minn. Jaycees, 1980; Swedish Bicentennial Commn. grantee, 1987. Mem. Nat. Assn. Women Bus. Owners (past pres.). Office Phone: 202-737-3699 x 209. E-mail: marlenej@nafsa.org.

JOHNSON, MARLYS MARLENE, elementary school educator; b. Omak, Wash., Mar. 13, 1946; d. Beverly Wayne and Mary Etta (Greene) McGrath; m. Gary Vaughn Johnson, Aug. 13, 1967 (div. June 3, 2001); children: Chad, Shane, Aubrey. BS in Edn., Wash. State U., 1967, MEd, 1991. Cert. profl. educator Wash., tchr. Va. Substitute tchr. Pullman (Wash.) Sch. Dist., 1970—80, home hosp. tutor, 1973—77, tchr. 2d grade, 1980—2001; tchr. 5th grade Alexandria (Va.) City Pub. Schs., 2001—02, tchr. 1st grade, 2002—03, tchr. 3d grade, 2003—; coord. Millbrook Resident Svcs., 2002—. Pres. Profl. Edn. Adv. Bd. Office Supt. Pub. Instrn. and Wash. State U., Olympia and Pullman, 2000; tchr. leader Curriculum Instrn. Leadership Coun., Pullman, 1996—2001; presenter in field. Contbr. articles to profl. jours. Host family chair Wash. State Jr. Miss, Pullman, 1998—2001; awards chairperson Pullman Swim Club; mother advisor Rainbow for Girls; mem. scholarship com. 4-H. Recipient Christa McAuliffe Excellence in Edn. award, State of Wash./Office of Supt. Pub. Instrn., 1990; grantee Contextual Tchg. grantee, U.S. Dept. Edn., 1999—2001, Rsch. Tech. grantee, RMC Rsch. Corp., Pullman, 1999—2000. Mem.: Wash. Edn. Assn. (rep. assembly del.), Pullman Edn. Assn. (exec. sec.), Phi Kappa Phi, Pi Lambda Theta (pres.). Methodist. Home: 1501 N Highview Ln #110 Alexandria VA 22311 Office Phone: 703-461-4170. E-mail: marlysmmj@aol.com, mmmjohnson_2000@yahoo.com.

JOHNSON, MARTHA (MARTY) JUNK (MARTY JOHNSON), psychology professor; b. Dayton, Ohio, May 10, 1951; d. William Martin and Frances Smith Junk; m. John Morgan Gerhold, Feb. 14, 2001; m. John Charles Nemeth, Nov. 24, 1973 (div. Mar. 1, 1984); children: John Christian Nemeth, Megan Jeannette Nemeth, Ashley Jane Nemeth. BA in Sociology, Denison U., Granville, Ohio, 1973; MS in Counselor Edn., U. Dayton, Ohio, 1993; PhD in Ednl. Psychology, Capella U., Mpls., 2005. Cert. profl. counselor Counselor, Social Worker, Marriage & Family Therapist Bd. Ohio, 2003. Counselor trainee Dublin Counseling Ctr., Ohio, 1993; psychometrist Thelma White & Assocs., Worthington, Ohio, 1997—98; psychology asst. Xavier U., Cin., 1997—98, Cmty. Diagnostic and Treatment Ctr., Cin., 1998—99; adj. prof. psychology Columbus Coll. Art and Design, 2001—. Mem.: ACA. Avocations: running, travel, cooking, reading. Home: 8686 Caldwell Dr Westerville OH 43082 Office: Columbus Coll Art & Design 107 N Ninth St Columbus OH 43215 Office Phone: 614-437-2380. E-mail: johnsonmrgn@aol.com.

JOHNSON, MARY ALICE, magazine editor; b. Rochester, Ind., Apr. 16, 1942; d. Nolan Lee and Alice Lavida (Ruede) Lewis; m. Manford Warren Johnson, May 28, 1960 (dec. Oct. 1998); children: Nola (dec.), John Jay, June Jeannette. Grad. high sch., Hillsboro, Oreg., 1960. Owner, baker, decorator Mary's Custom Cakes and Cake Parts, St. Helens, Oreg., 1980-87; creator Sweet Tooth Confections Candy, 1981—; founder, mng. editor Sugar Art Sharing Confectionary Ideas mag., 1986-88; chmn. Sugar Art Ltd. Partnership, McMinnville, Oreg., 1986-93; owner Double Rainbow Enterprises (now Double Rainbow Ministries), Christmas Valley, 1993—. Tchr. cake decorating, candy and gingerbread houses, 1981—99; owner Peace Acres Bible Retreat, 2003—. Author: ABC Bible, 1967, I See God In Everything, 1975, The Wedding Book, 1983, Friends Feasts & Fellowship, 1992, God and Money, 1992, Looseleaf Pattern Library, 1992, Mary's Cook Book, 1993, It's Time to Oil the Lamps, 1994, (videotape) Gingerbread Mansions, 1996; mng. editor, founder Manna Food for Body and Soul mag., 2005—. Leader, Country Kids and Friends 4-H, St. Helens, 1979-85; organizer rural fire dept., Rainier, Oreg.; Sunday sch. tchr. Luth. Ch., 1956-74, officer women's groups, 1960-77; sec. Tualitan Vallye Rabbit Breeders Assn., 1964-67, fair dinner booth chmn., 1965-66; ballot clk. Columbia County Election Bd., 1972-80; decorated cake supt. Columbia County Fair, 1983-85; decorations chmn. Christian Women's Club, McMinnville, 1989-90; founder youth hobby club Pettis Fours Club, 1989. Winner awards for entries in numerous county and state fairs, cake shows. Republican. Lutheran. Avocations: crafts, painting, reading. Office: Double Rainbow Ministries 58486 Carrico Rd PO Box 196 Christmas Valley OR 97641

JOHNSON, MARY ELAINE, interior designer, writer, counselor; b. Atlanta, June 5, 1964; d. Joseph Donald and Elaine Ryals. AS in Applied Art, Art Inst., Dallas; BA in Psychology, Webster U. Asst. art dir. James Gang, San Diego, 1997; crisis counselor San Diego, 1997; creative dir. Inner Warrior Found., Den Haagi, Netherlands, 1997—98; spl. edn. tchr. Am. Sch. of Hague, Wassenaar, Netherlands, 1999—2002, pvt. counselor, 1999—2004; owner Nest Design, 2002—04, Santa Barbara, Calif., 2004—.

JOHNSON, MARY ELIZABETH, music educator, musician; b. Tyler, Tex., Mar. 29, 1933; d. Robert Edward and Mamie Oberia (Walters) Spaulding; m. George Devereaux Johnson, Mar. 31, 1955; children: Bradford D., Robin Elizabeth. BFA, So. Meth. U., 1955; pvt. studies with Bomar Cramer, Dallas, 1964—69. Music tchr. Dallas Country Day Sch., 1955; tchr. Dayton Pub. Schs., Ohio, 1956—57; pvt. tchr. piano Dallas, 1962—; profl. accompanist, 1985—; duo-pianist, 1965—; sponsor, tchr. creative and performing arts program Dallas Ind. Sch. Dist., 1981—82, 1983, 1984. Sponsor Jr. Melodie and Jr. Harmonie. Named to Hall of Fame, Am. Coll. Musicians, 1981. Mem. Nat. Guild Piano Tchrs. (cert., named to honor roll 1971, chmn. auditions Dallas chpt.), Tex. Fedn. Music Clubs (historian 1974-76, state chmn. music svc. in cmty. 1971-73, dist. jr. counselor 1971-78, dist. chmn. music svc. in cmty. 1971-78, rec. sec. 5th dist. 1975-76, 1st v.p. 1977-78, jr. festival chmn. 1977-80, dist chmn. Jr. Gold Cup awards 1980, 84, 85, 86, 87, 88, asst. chmn. North Dallas divsn. 5th dist. jr. festival 1981-82), Music Tchrs. Nat. Assn., Jr. Pianists Guild Dallas (chmn. jr. recitals 1983, chmn. sr. recitals 1984, treas. 2003-2005), Tex. Music Tchrs. Assn., Dallas Music Tchrs. Assn., Music Study Club Dallas (chmn. piano program 1981-82), Dallas Fedn. Music Clubs (del. 1969-78, 1st v.p. 1977), Daus. Republic Tex. (1st v.p. Bonham chpt. 1975-76), Alpha Delta Pi, Melodie Club (pres. 1969-71, 2d v.p. 1977—, 1st v.p. 2003-04, 2006-06, choral accompanist, counselor jr. club, historian, press sec. 1981-82, 1st v.p. 2003-2004, 2004—), Kalista Club (yearbook chmn. 1983-2000, v.p. 1984-85, pres. 1986-87), Park Cities Club, Tower Club, Kermis Club, Rondo-Carrousel Club, Trippers Club, Steinway Hall's Ptnrs. in Performance, Mu Phi Epsilon (patron). Methodist. Home: 3848 Cedarbrush Dr Dallas TX 75229-2701

JOHNSON, MARY ELIZABETH, retired elementary education educator; b. St. Louis, Sept. 17, 1943; d. Richard William Blayney and Alice Bonjean (Taylor) Blayney Needham; m. Clyde Robert Johnson, Aug. 31, 1963; children: Brian (dec. 1991), Elizabeth Johnson Meyer, David. BS cum laude, U. Ill., 1966; MA, Maryville U., 1990; postgrad., So. Ill. U., 1990. Cert. elem. tchr., Ill., Mo. Tchr. Hazelwood Sch. Dist., Florissant, Mo., 1971-93, positive intervention tchr., 1989-91. Author play: Say No to Drugs, 1991. Author: Secret Study Skills for Third Graders, 1990. Mem. Hazelwood Schs. Music Boosters, 1980-88; mem. coms. Townsend PTA, Florissant, 1976—; contbr. Schlarship Run-Walk, 1982—; mem. Children's United Rsch. Effort in Cancer, 1986—; vol. Spl. Love, Inc., camp for children with cancer, 1986—; active The Children's Inn, Bethesda, Md., 1990—, Bailey Scholarship Fund, U. Ill., 1994—; mem. scholarship com. Clark County Sch. Dist., Las Vegas, Nev., 2001-. Fred S. Bailey scholar, 1962-66, Edmund J. James scholar, 1964-65; named Townsend Tchr. of Yr., 1989-90. Mem. NEA, Internat. Platform Assn., Kappa Delta Pi, Alpha Lambda Delta, Phi Kappa Phi. Baptist. Avocations: travel, reading, crafts, writing, music. Home: 2016 Bay Tree Sun City Las Vegas NV 89134-5235

JOHNSON, MARY LOU, lay worker, educator; b. Moline, Ill., July 15, 1923; d. Percy and Hope (Aulgur) Sipes; m. Blaine Eugene Johnson, May 30, 1941 (dec.); children: Vivian Johnson Sweedy Maday, Michael D. (dec.), Amelia Johnson Harms Thomas, James Michael (dec.). From chmn. Christian edn. to dir. 1st Christian Ch., Moline, 1971—88, dir. Christian edn., 1988—93, ret., 1993, chmn. Christian edn., 2001—03. Sunday sch. tchr. 1st Christian Ch., Moline, 1958-84; cluster del. Christian Chs. Ill. and Wisc., Moline, 1988-89. Author: (poem) What Is A Mother?, 1965. Officer various positions PTA, Moline, 1972-75, hon. life mem. State of Ill., 1972; leader, dist. chair Girl Scouts U.S., Moline, 1955-65; skywatcher USAF Ground Observer Corps, Moline, 1955-57; vol. telethon coord. Muscular Dystrophy Assn., Moline, 1971-94; del. lt. gov.'s Commn. on Aging, Springfield, Ill., 1990; historian 1st Christian Ch., Moline, 1996—, libr., 2000—; vol. C.A.R.E. Ministry, 1999-2005, Ring for Care Ministry, 1999-2005, We. Ill. Area Agy. on Aging, 1998-2003; bd. dirs. Wee Care Day Care Ctr., 2003—06; chmn. 100th Birthday Celebration, First Christian Ch., Moline, 2004-06. Recipient Appreciation award Muscular Dystrophy Assn., 1964-94. Republican. Home: 2014 9th St Moline IL 61265-4779 Personal E-mail: grmalou624@aol.com.

JOHNSON, MARY MARGARET DICKENS, governmental and commercial researcher, consultant; b. Ottumwa, Iowa, July 10, 1955; d. Donald Milton and Maxine Margaret Dickens; m. Donald Hampton Johnson, July 30, 1944; children: Laurie Anne Davidson, Donald, Jr. Hampton. M, U. Hawaii, 1979; B, Iowa State U., 1976; M, Johns Hopkins Sch. Advanced Internat. Studies, 1986; postgrad. in pub. admin., Fla. Atlantic U., 2003—. Cert. purchasing mgr., cert. profl. contracts mgr., scuba diver 1974. Lab. asst. dept. entomolgy Iowa State U., Ames, 1973—74, rsch. asst. dept. sociology & anthropology, 1974—76; rsch. grantee East West Ctr., Honolulu, 1976—78; fgn. affairs specialist U.S. Dept. of State/AID, Washington, 1980—81; fed. summer intern U.S. Dept. of Commerce/Nat. Telecom. and Info. Adminstrn., Washington, 1980—80; export adminstrn. specialist U.S. Dept. of Commerce, Washington, 1982—85; English lang. tchr. INTERAC, Tokyo, 1985; tchr., pub. rels. officer Overseas Devel. Co., Kowloon, Hong Kong, 1986—87; English lang. tchr. Phillips Lang. Learning Systems, Tokyo, 1986; sr. contracts mgr. Systems Flow, Inc., Rockville, Md., 1997—98; with HSI Geotrans, Sterling, Va., 1992; contract specialist U.S. GSA, Washington, 1987—94, Wash. Suburban San. Commn., Laurel, Md., 1996—97; grad. asst. Fla. Atlantic U., Ft. Lauderdale, 2003—04; rsch. fellow Broward Sheriff's Offrice, 2005—06. Leader workshops and seminars; presenter in field. Contbr. articles and book revs. to profl. jours. Mem. CARE Women's Group; active St. Paul's by the Sea Episc. Ch., Ocean City, Md., 1988—; mem. altar guild St. Albans Anglican Ch., Tokyo, 1985; mem. edn. for ministry St. Patrick's Episcopal Ch., Falls Church, Va., 1995—96. Home Fellowship, Truro Episcopal Ch., 2003—. Fellow: Nat. Contract Mgmt. Assn. (cert. profl. contracts mgr. 2002, cert. assoc. contracts mgr. 2002, pres. 2003, grant to participate in World Congress 2002); mem.: Nat. Assn. Purchasing Mgmt. (workshop leader 2002), Tau Kappa Epsilon, Alpha Chi Omega. Avocations: bicycling, walking, needlepoint, cooking, gardening. Home: 1926 NE 2nd St Deerfield Beach FL 33441 Office: Florida Atlantic U 111 East Las Olas Blvd Fort Lauderdale FL 33301 Office Phone: 954-429-9019. Personal E-mail: conchcontracts@aol.com. Business E-Mail: mjohn110@fau.edu.

JOHNSON, MARY P., freelance writer; b. Balt., Sept. 23, 1927; d. Frederick and Marie Rosina (Walter) Manke; m. Alvin H. Walker, June 21, 1947 (div. Mar. 1955); m. Maurice P. Johnson, July 1, 1955; 1 child, Carol Joy. Student, Johns Hopkins U., 1959-63. Assoc. dir. Centennial planning and programs Johns Hopkins U., Balt., 1973-77; arts reviewer Balt. Sun-Arundel, 1997—; reviewer concerts and theater, reporter Severna Park (Md.) Voice, 1998—. Mem. Journalism and Women Symposium, 2002—. Bd. dir. Performing Arts Assn., Linthicum, Md., 1995—. Mem.: AAUW, Journalism and Women, Am. Theatre Critics Assn. Inc., Balt. Symphony, Balt. Opera, Met. Opera Guild. Democrat. Lutheran. Personal E-mail: marybud@toad.net.

JOHNSON, MARY PAULINE (POLLY JOHNSON), nursing administrator; b. Ohio, May 23, 1940; BSN summa cum laude, Ohio State U., 1962; MSN, Duke U., 1980. RN NC. Staff nurse psychiatry unit Univ. Hosps., Ohio, 1963-64; pediatric office nurse Gaithersburg, Md., 1971-73; clin. nurse coord. N.C. Meml. Hosp., Chapel Hill, 1973-86; grant coord. N.C. Assn. Home Care, 1988; practice cons. N.C. Bd. Nursing, Raleigh, 1988-96, assoc. dir. practice, 1996-97, exec. dir., 1997—. Mem. bd. trustees N.C. Ctr. for Hosp. quality and Patient Safety. Adv. com. PREP Project Citizens Advocacy Ctr. Fellow: Am. Acad. Nursing; mem.: ANA, NC Inst. Medicine (bd. dirs.), Nat. Coun. State Bds. Nursing (bd. dirs., v.p. 2002—06), NC Nurses Assn., N.C. Orgn. Nurse Leaders, Sigma Theta Tau. Office: NC Bd of Nursing 3724 National Dr Raleigh NC 27612-4070 Office Phone: 919-782-3211 ext. 250. E-mail: polly@ncbon.com.

JOHNSON, MARYANN ELAINE, educational administrator; b. Franklin Twp., Pa., Nov. 1, 1943; d. Mary I. Sollick; married. BS in Elem. Edn., Mansfield State U., Pa., 1964; MS in Elem. Edn., U. Alaska, College, 1973; EdD, Wash. State U., Pullman, 1981. Tchr. Nayatt Sch., Barrington, R.I., 1964-66, North Sch., North Chicago, Ill., 1966-67, Kodiak (Alaska) On-Base Sch., 1967-71, Eastmont Sch. Dist., 1971-74, reading coord. East Wanatchee, Wash., 1974-77, adminstrv. asst., 1977-82; asst. supt. Sec. Parent Advisory Com., 1982-93, South Kitsap Sch. Dist., Port Orchard, Wash., 1993-95, Clarkston Sch. Dist., Wash., 1995-97; chair Wash. State Discover Card Scholarship, 1993-97; pvt. cons. Reach for the Future, Inc., 1997—, Learning Workshop, 1999—. Shoebox ministry coord., 2001—05. Active Ctrl. Wash. Hosp. Bd., 1991-93, Ctrl. Wash. Hosp. Found. Bd., 1992-93. Named Eastmont Tchr. of the Year, 1973-74. Mem. ASCD (review coun. 1993-99), Wash. State ASCD (bd. dirs. 1986-89, pres. elect 1989-90, pres. 1990-91, Educator of Yr. 1981), NEA, Wash. Assn. Sch. Adminstrs. (bd. dirs., chmn. curriculum and instrn. Job-Alike, profl. devel. com., Project Leadership, pres. elect 1986-87, pres. 1987-88, leadership award, 1986, award of merit 1992, Exec. Educator 100 1988, 93, chmn. WASA 21st century scholarship com. 1988-96, leadership acad. 1993), Am. Assn. Sch. Adminstrs. (resolutions com. 1988-89, com. for advancement of sch. adminstrs. 1989-92), East Wenatchee C. of C. (bd. dirs. 1990-93, chair edn. com. 1990-91), Delta Kappa Gamma (pres. 1982-83), Phi Delta Kappa, Phi Kappa Phi E-mail: mjohnson@i70west.com.

JOHNSON, MARYL RAE, cardiologist; b. Fort Dodge, Iowa, Apr. 15, 1951; d. Marvin George and Beryl Evelyn (White) Johnson. BS, Iowa State U., 1973; MD, U. Iowa, 1977. Diplomate Am. Bd. Internal Medicine, Am. Bd. Cardiovasc. Diseases. Intern U. Iowa Hosps., Iowa City, 1977-78, resident, 1978-81, fellow, 1979-82; assoc. in cardiology U. Iowa Hosps. and Clins., Iowa City, 1982-86, asst. prof. medicine cardiovasc. divsn., 1986-88; asst. prof. medicine Med. Ctr. Loyola U., 1988-92, assoc. prof., 1992-94, Rush. U., 1994-97, Northwestern U. Med. Sch., 1998—2002; prof. medicine U. Wis. Med. Sch., Madison, 2002—. Med. dir. cardiac transplantation U. Iowa Hosp., 1986—88; assoc. med. dir. cardiac transplantation Loyola U., 1988—94, assoc. med. dir. Rush Heart Failure and Cardiac Transplant Program, 1994—97; dir. heart failure cardiac transplant program Northwestern U. Med. Sch., 1998—2001, dir. heart failure program, 2001—02; med. dir. heart failure and transplantation U. Wis. Hosp. and Clinics, 2002—. Editor (assoc. editor): Jour. Heart and Lung Transplantation, 1995—99; mem. editl. bd.:, 2000—. Mem. Nat. Heart Lung and Blood Adv. Coun., Bethesda, Md., 1979—83; mem. biomed. rsch. tech. rev. com. NIH, 1990—93, chairperson, 1992—93, chair biomed. rsch. tech. spl. emphasis panel, 1999—2002. Recipient Jane Leinfelder Meml. award, U. Iowa Coll. Medicine, 1977, Clin. Investigator award, NIH, 1981, New Investigator Rsch. award, 1981, 1986; Barry Freeman scholar, 1974. Mem.: ACP, AAAS, AMA, United Network Organ Sharing (thoracic organ com. 2005—, vice chair 2006—), Am. Soc. Transplantation (chair membership com. 2003—04, bd. dirs. 2004—06, sec.-treas. 2006—), Am. Coll. Cardiology (heart failure and cardiac transplant com. 2002—, chair 2004—), Am. Heart Assn., Ctrl. Soc. Clin. Rsch., Internat. Soc. Heart and Lung Transplantation (mem. program com. 2005), Order of Rose, Alpha Omega Alpha, Iota Sigma Pi, Phi Kappa Phi, Alpha Lambda Delta. Office: U Wis Madison E5/582D CSC 5710 600 Highland Ave Madison WI 53792 Office Phone: 608-263-0080. Business E-Mail: mrj@medicine.wisc.edu.

JOHNSON, MEGGAN D., school intervention specialist; B, U. Dayton, Ohio, 1999; M, Ind. Wesleyan U., Marion, 2006. Intervention specialist Dayton Pub. Schs., 1999—2001, Cin. Pub. Schs., 2001—.

JOHNSON, MELISSA ANN, special education educator; b. Austell, Ga., Nov. 1, 1976; d. Michael Daryl and Eileen De Luca Johnson. BS in Collaborative Tchg., U. Ala., 2000; M in Ednl. Leadership, Kennesaw State U., 2005. Intellectual disabled tchr. Kennesaw (Ga.) Elem. Sch., 2000—02; interrelated spl. edn. tchr. Frey Elem. Sch., Acworth, Ga., 2002—. Mem. Cobb Habitat for Humanity, Marietta, Ga., 2002—05. Presdl. fellow, Kennesaw State U., 2003, Catherine Turner Meml. scholar, Cobb County Ret. Tchrs. Assn., 2004. Mem.: NEA, Ga. Educators aSsn., Coun. Exceptional Children. Republican. Roman Catholic. Avocations: sports, gardening, shopping, travel. Office: Frey Elem Sch 2865 Mars Hill Rd Acworth GA 30101 E-mail: johns075@hotmail.com.

JOHNSON, MELISSA RAMIREZ, psychologist; b. N.Y.C., July 18, 1953; d. Fausto Arturo and Joan Phyllis (Schwartz) Ramirez; m. Robert Bruce Johnson, June 15, 1974; children: Laura Rebecca, David Colin. BA, Duke U., 1974; PhD, U. N.C., 1980. Psychologist Franklin (Pa.) Regional Med. Ctr., 1982-85; rsch. assoc., clin. asst. prof. U. N.C. Sch. Medicine, Chapel Hill, 1980-82; psychologist, clin. assoc. prof. pediatrics Wake Area Health Edn. Ctr., U. N.C. Sch. Medicine, 1986—. Contbr. articles to profl. jours. Fellow Am. Orthopsychiat. Assn.; mem. Am. Psychol. Assn., N.C. Psychol. Assn., Soc. for Pediatric Psychology. Democrat. Office: Wake Med Ctr Peds AHEC 3000 New Bern Ave Raleigh NC 27610-1247 Office Phone: 919-350-8527.

JOHNSON, MELODY JEAN, special education educator; b. Okmulgee, Okla., July 21, 1962; d. James Paul and Melinda Jean Madden; m. Kenneth Lee Johnson, Nov. 9, 1955; children: Kenneth Lee Jr., Randle Eugene, Jacob Daniel, Timothy Dakota; children: Kirk Edward Schwanke, Jr., Mary Ann Audliet, Christopher Carl Schwanke, Justin Michael Schwanke. BS Human Svcs., SUNY, Plattsurgh, 1990; MEd, Hardin-Simmons U., Abiiene, Tex., 1991. Lic. Profl. Counselor Tex. State Bd. Profl. Counselors, 1994, cert. Sch. Counselor Tex. State Bd. Educator Certification, 2002, Spl. Edn. Tchr. Tex. State Bd. Educator Certification, 2000. Profl. counselor Resources for Living, Austin, Tex., 1993—98; tchr. spl. edn. Smithville H.S., Tex., 1998—. Treas. Bluebonnet Counseling Assn., Bastrop, Tex., 2004—06. Office: Smithville High School PO Box 479 Smithville TX 78957

JOHNSON, MICHELLE L., lawyer; BSBA, U. Calif. Berkeley, 1975; JD, U. Denver, 1985. Bar: Calif. 1986. Ptnr., exec. dir. Thelen Reid & Priest LLP, San Francisco, mng. ptnr. adminstr. Spkr. in field. Mem.: Bar Assn. San Francisco (Bus. Law Sect.), State Bar Calif. (Bus. Law Sect.), ABA (Corp., Banking & Bus. Law Sect.), Order of St. Ives. Office: Thelen Reid & Priest LLP 101 Second St Ste 1800 San Francisco CA 94105-3601 Office Phone: 415-369-7101. Office Fax: 415-371-1211. Business E-Mail: mljohnson@thelenreid.com.

JOHNSON, MILDRED GRACE MASH, investment company executive; b. Castle Rock, Wash., Mar. 3, 1922; d. Percival and Hilda C. (Nyberg) M.; widowed, 1988; children: John, Joy, Judy, Chris, Steven. Student, U. Wash. Pres. Johnson Investment Co., Seattle, 1988—; gen. ptnr. Port Washington Marina, Bremerton, Wash., 2004—. Deacon U. Presbyn. Ch., Seattle, 1981—. Mem. Am. Bus. Women's Assn. (v.p. 1979-89, Woman of Yr. 1981), Apt. Opt. Assn. (hon. 25 Yr. Mem.), Master Builders, Daus. Nile, Order of Ea. Star. Republican. Avocations: entertaining, skiing, writing, reading, travel. Home: 730 N 85th St # 401 Seattle WA 98103-3836 Address: 805 Thompson Dr Bremerton WA 98337

JOHNSON, MORGAN LEA, artist, museum educator; b. Orlando, Fla., Nov. 1, 1975; d. Alvin Guy and Jeannette Beatty Johnson; m. Robert Norwood, Nov. 25, 2006. BFA in Art Edn., U. Ga., 1999; MAT in Mus. Edn., George Washington U., Washington, DC, 2004. Educator Learning Ctr., Marietta, Ga., 1995—97; coord. Ga. Mus. of Art, Athens, Ga., 1997—99; program asst. High Mus. Art, Atlanta, 2000; dir. edn. Von Liebig Art Ctr., Naples, Fla., 2000—03; fellow Hirshhorn Mus. Sculpture Garden, Washington, 2004—05; educator U.S. Botanic Gardens, 2004—. Cons. Sewall-Belmont House, Washington, 2004—05. Illustrator Tranquil Space Yoga, Washington, DC, 2004—, Fit Yoga Mag., NY, 2004—, Hip Tranquil Chick: A Guide for Life on and off the Yoga Mat; oil on canvas, The Guitar, 1996, Memory Dean, 1999. Activist Planned Parenthood, Washington, Va., 2004—; vol. Kennestone Hosp., Marietta, Ga., 1990—99. Grantee, United Arts Foun., Naples Fla., 2003; Edward P. Lawson fellow, Hirshhorn Mus., 2004. Independent. Avocations: painting, photography, running, hiking, botany.

JOHNSON, MYRTLE ALICE HARRIS, elementary and secondary school educator; b. Phila., Aug. 10, 1947; d. James and Margaret (Robinson) Harris; m. Ronald Walter Johnson, May 24, 1975; 1 child, Craig Noel. BS in Edn., Temple U., 1977; MDiv, New Brunswick Theol. Sem., 2000; D Bibl. Studies, DTh, Andersonville Theol. Sem., 2005. Cert. tchr., Pa., N.J. Tchr. Pine Hill Bd. Edn., NJ, 1977—84; lang. tchr. Passaic Bd. Edn., NJ, 1986—88. Creative bible instr. preachers kids Internat. Assn. of Min. Wives and Min. Widows, Inc., 1986—92, chair preachers kids, 1993—2002, coord. Nat. Stand Against Violence, 2001. Author: Teaching Tools/Materials: Bringing God's Word to Children, 2005. Sunday sch. tchr. Jones Meml. Bapt. Ch., Phila., dir., tchr. Vacation Bible Sch.; Sunday sch. tchr. Union Bapt. Ch., Passaic, N.J., organizer, dir. Vacation Bible Sch., coord., dir. summer program Recipient Outstanding Leadership award Vacation Bible Sch., Jones Meml. Bapt. Ch., Phila., Muriel Lemon Johnson Internat. award, 2001; crowned Queen Women's Convention, Nat. Bapt. Convention, 2002-03. Mem. Internat. Interdenominational Min.'s Wives and Min.'s Widows, Inc., N.J. Dist. Missionary Bapt. Assn., Inc. (1st v.p. women's aux. N.J. dist. 2001-05, pres. 2005—). Achievements include development of and coordination of six-week summer camp program Union Bapt. Ch. Home: 219 Myrtle Ave Passaic NJ 07055-3212 Office Phone: 973-851-9125.

JOHNSON, MYSTIE L., obstetrician, gynecologist, department chairman; b. Casper, Wyo., Nov. 16, 1968; m. James M. Johnson, Apr. 28, 2001; 1 child, Tyler R. MD, U. Ariz., Tucson, 1998. Ob-gyn. chair Banner Estrella Med. Ctr., Phoenix; pres. West Valley Women's Care, Phoenix, 2002—. Fellow: ACOG. Office: West Valley Women's Care 9305 W Thomas Rd Ste 155 Phoenix AZ 85037 Office Phone: 623-936-1780.

JOHNSON, NANCY LEE, congresswoman; b. Chgo., Jan. 5, 1935; d. Noble Wishard and Gertrude Reid (Smith) Lee; m. Theodore H. Johnson, June 27, 1932; children: Lindsey Lee, Althea Anne, Caroline Reid. BA, Radcliffe Coll., 1957; postgrad., U. London, 1957-58. Vice chmn. Charter Commn. New Britain, Conn., 1976-77; mem. Conn. Senate from 6th dist., 1977-82, US Congress from 5th Conn. dist., Washington, 1983—, mem. ways and means com., chmn. health subcom., com. on taxation. Pres. Friends of Libr., New Britain Pub. Libr., 1973-76, Radcliffe Club Northern Conn., 1973-75; bd. dirs., pres. Sheldon Cmty. Guidance Clinic, 1974-75; dir. religious edn. Unitarian Universalist Soc. New Britain, 1967-72; bd. dirs. United Way New Britain, 1976.79. Recipient Outstanding Vol. award United Way, 1976; English Speaking Union grantee, 1958-59 Republican. Home: 141 S Mountain St New Britain CT 06052-1511 Office: US Ho Reps 2409 Rayburn Bldg Washington DC 20515-0705 Office Phone: 202-225-4476.

JOHNSON, NICHOLE SHARESE, school nurse practitioner, basketball coach; b. NYC, Nov. 13, 1975; d. Lorelei Davis. BSN, Coll. New Rochelle, 1997; MSN, U. Phoenix, 2005. RN. Staff nurse NYU Med. Ctr., NYC, 1997—98; contract nurse Theracare, 1998—99; contract nursing Allcare Nursing, Hicksville, 1999—2000; sch. nursing NYC Dept. Edn., 1999—; homecare nursing Visting Nurse Svc. NY, Bronx, 2002—03. Jr. h.s. head basketball coach Rainbow Basketball Assn., Bronx, 2002—05. Named Coach of Yr., Rainbow Basketball Assn., 2004—05. Mem.: ANA (licentiate), NY State Sch. Nurse Assn. (licentiate), Nat. Assn. Sch. Nurses (licentiate), NY State Nurse Assn. (licentiate), Sigma Theta Tau.

JOHNSON, PAM CLARENE, radiographer, bone densitometrist, consultant; d. Clarence and Palma Johnson. Degree, St. Barnabas Sch. Radiologic Tech., 1971; BS in Med. Tech., U. Minn., 1976. Part-time radiographer St. Barnabas Hosp., Mpls., 1972—83, Hennepin County Med. Ctr., Mpls., 1973—74; radiographer U. Minn., Mpls., 1976—2000; radiographer, clin. supr. Health East Osteoporosis Care, St. Paul, 2002—; rsch. assoc. St. Luke's Body Composition Lab., NYC. Radiography instr. Curran Hosp., Zorzor, Liberia, 1982; bone densitometry cons., 2000—; cert. course instr. Internat. Soc. Clin. Densitometry, 2001; spkr. in field. Contbr. articles to profl. jours.; book & book proposal reviewer for major med. book publishers. Mem.: Internat. Soc. Radiographers & Radiologic Technologists, Am. Registry Radiologic Technologists (bone densitometry cert. com. 1999—2002), Am. Soc. Radiologic Technoloigsts (radiography del. 1995—99, nomination com. 1996, chair 1998—99, task force 1999, profl. standards adv. com. 2004—, publ. contrbr., practice stds. com. 2004—), Internat. Soc. Clin. Densitometry (pub. policy com. 1999—, tech. edn. subcom. 2000, liaison ARRT & ASRT 2000—03, bd. trustees 2001—03, interspecialty com. 2001—04, midwest reg. rep. 2001—, cert. exam. com. 2004—05, pub. contrbr., Oscar Gluck Humanitarian award 2005), Minn. Soc. Radiologic Technologists (life; pres., chair 1988—90, state del. to ASRT 1989—90, state jour. edit. 1991—98), Am. Soc. Clin. Lab. Specialists, Minn. Soc. Radiol. Tech. (life). Avocations: music, writing.

JOHNSON, PAM MCALLISTER, newspaper publisher, consultant; b. McAlester, Okla., Apr. 14, 1945; d. Elmer Reuben and Esther Queen (Crump) McAllister; m. Donald Nathanial Johnson, June 8, 1968; children: Jason, Dawn. BS, U. Wis., 1967, MS, 1971, PhD, 1977. Assoc. prof. journalism U. Wis., Madison, 1971—78; assoc. prof. Norfolk State U., Va., 1979—81; gen. exec. Gannett Co., Inc., Bridgewater, NJ, 1981—; asst. to pub. The Ithaca Jour., N.Y., 1981, pres., pub., 1981. Dir. First Bank Ithaca; bd. dirs. St. Bonaventure U., Olean, NY, Sta. WCNY-TV, Syracuse, NY; mem. adv. bd. Nat. Youth Communication, Syracuse, 1983. Mem.: Ithaca Bus. and Profl. Women, N.Y. Assn. Black Journalists, m. Newspaper Pubs. Assn., N.Y. State Pubs. Assn., Nat. Assn. Edn. in Journalism, Nat. Assn. Black Journalists, Zonta. Office: Ithaca Jour 123 W State St Ithaca NY 14850-5427

JOHNSON, PATRICIA ANN, music educator; b. Monroe, La., Nov. 6, 1951; d. William Asher and Eva Marie Agin; m. Michael Charles Johnson, Aug. 4, 1964; m. Rodney Allen Payne, Dec. 28, 1972 (div. Apr. 23, 1983); children: Michael Charles, Christopher Allen Payne, Jennifer Lynn. M, NLU, Monroe, La., 1973. Elem. music tchr. Richardson Ind. Sch. Dist., Tex., 1999—. Mem.: OAKE, TMEA. Office: RISD Brentfield Dr Dallas TX 75081 Office Phone: 469-593-5652. Business E-Mail: patricia.johnson@risd.org.

JOHNSON, PATRICIA DIANE, nurse anesthetist; b. Bklyn., Mar. 27, 1956; d. Evelyn Smith Walker; m. Gregory Leroy Johnson, Sept. 17, 1983; children: Ebony, Aisha, Clinton, Garrett, Gerald. BS in Biology, St. John's U., Queens, N.Y., 1977; BS in Nursing, Downstate Med. Sch. Nursin, Bklyn., 1979; anesthesia cert., Kings County Sch. Anesthesia, Bklyn., 1985; M Cmty. Health, Bklyn. Coll., 1994. Cert. anesthesia for nurses. Nurse cardiac ICU, neurology, oncology Mt. Sinai Hosp., N.Y.C., 1979-83; nurse anesthetist, instr. Kings County Hosp., Bklyn., 1985-88; nurse anesthetist Queens (N.Y.) Hosp. Ctr., 1988. Pres. First Jerusalem Bapt. Ch. Ednl. Club, Bklyn., 1994-95, pres. pastor's aide, 1994-99, Sunday Sch. tchr., 1993-99, choir mem., 1994—; v.p. PTA-St. Mark Day Sch., Bklyn., 1994—. Mem. Am. Assn. Nurse Anesthetists. Avocations: reading, volleyball, singing, computers, children's programs.

JOHNSON, PATRICIA JOSEPH, librarian; b. Kenton, Ohio, Dec. 29, 1949; d. Richard and Betty Lee Joseph; m. John H. Johnson, June 27, 1970; 1 child, John Richard Joseph. BS, Ohio State U., 1970; MS, Bowling Green State U., 1976. Cert. tchr., Ohio. English tchr. Wapakoneta (Ohio) City Schs., 1971—79, libr. and media specialist, 1979—2002. Mem. AAUW, Ohio Edn. Assn. (Columbus action team 1978—, Doris L. Allen minority award 1980), Wapakoneta Edn. Assn. (pres. 1982-89, 1995-2002), Internat. Reading Assn., Auglaize County Internat. Reading Assn. (pres. 1990—), Ohio Ednl. Libr. Media Assn., Bus. and Profl. Women (treas.), Ohio State U. Alumni Assn., Alpha Delta Kappa (pres. 1990-92). Democrat. Home: 160 Squire Ln Lima OH 45805-3667 E-mail: buckize@hotmail.com.

JOHNSON, PATRICIA MARY, writer; b. Evanston, Ill., Mar. 14, 1937; d. Harold W. and Florence M. (Miller) J.; children: William, Nancy, Richard. Student, Art Inst. Chgo., 1970-73; Degree in Interior Design, LaSalle U., 1972. Interior design communicator, prodr., host weekly syndicated cable tv program on interior design, 1980-86; owner Design Comms., R&D Splsts., Rosenhayn, NJ, 1976—2002; exec. dir., founder Corp. for Disabled/Handicapped, 1985—96, A Positive Approach. Author: Creation of the Barrier Free Interior, 1988, Guide to Securing Housing for People with Developmental Disabilities, 1993, numerous children's books, 1996—; pub. (mags.) A Positive Approach, 1985-96, An Approach to Barrier Free Design, 1992; prodr.: A Guide to Securing Independent Housing for Individuals with Disabilities, 1994; syndicated columnist Aging by Design, 2000—; nationally syndicated columnist on housing and design for seniors, 2004—; monthly columnist for numerous sr., consumer and children's mags. Recipient award N.J. Gov., 1985, Practitioner of Yr. award N.J. Rehab. Assn., 1987, Humanitarian Svc. award United Cerebral Palsy, 1987, Jefferson award, NBC, 1988, Healing Cmty. UN Pub. award, 1989, Cmty. Svc. award Pres. George Bush, 1991. E-mail: decorseven@aol.com.

JOHNSON, PENELOPE B., librarian; b. Lewiston, Maine, Nov. 26, 1946; d. Wesley I and Bertha (Leavitt) J.; m. Milton F. Bornstein, July 12, 1969. BA, U. Maine, 1969; MS, Simmons Coll., 1970; CAGS, Boston U., 1978. Cert. profl. librarian. Children's libr. Wilmington Mem'l Libr., Wilmington, Mass., 1970-71, Worcester Pub. Libr., Worcester, Mass., 1971-79; children's cons. Ctrl. Mass. Regional Libr. System, Worcester, Mass., 1979-80; divsn. head Worcester Pub. Libr., Worcester, Mass., 1980-87, assoc. libr., 1987-91, head libr., 1991-97. Pres. YMCA of Ctrl. Mass., 1989-91, bd. dirs., 1979-96; mem. exec. com. City Adminstrv. Officers Assn., 1993-97. Mem. ALA, New England Libr. Assn., Mass. Libr. Assn., Simmons Coll. Alumni Assn. (pres. grad. sch. libr. and info. 1990-91). Office: Worcester Pub Libr 3 Salem Sq Worcester MA 01608-2015

JOHNSON, PHYLLIS ELAINE, chemist, researcher; b. Grafton, ND, Feb. 19, 1949; d. Donald Gordon and Evelyn Lorraine (Svaren) Lanes; m. Robert S.T. Johnson (dec. Mar. 2001), Sept. 12, 1969; children: Erik, Sara. BS, U. N.D., 1971; PhD, 1976. Instr. chemistry Mary Coll., Bismarck, N.D., 1971-72; postdoctoral rsch. fellow U. N.D., Grand Forks, 1975-79, chemist, 1977-79; rsch. chemist USDA Human Nutrition Rsch. Ctr., 1979-87, rsch. leader for nutrition, biochemistry and metabolism, 1987-91; assoc. dir. Pacific West Area USDA-ARS, 1996-97; dir. Beltsville Area USDA, ARS, 1997—; Disting. Chemistry Alumni lectr. U. N.D., 1998. Editor: Stable Isotopes in Nutrition, 1984; mem. editl. bd.: Jour. Micronutrient Analysis, 1988—91, Jour. Nutrition, 1998—2004; contbr. articles to profl. jours. Chmn. Parents of Gifted and Talented, 1984—86. Recipient Arthur S. Flemming award Outstanding Sci. Achievement, 1989, Women in Sci. and Engring. award, 1993, Sioux award N.D. Alumni Found., 1998, Fed. Energy and Water Mgmt. award, 1998, Presdl. Rank award of Meritorious Exec., Pres. of U.S., 1999, White House Closing the Circle award for Environ. Mgmt. from Pres. Bush, 2002, for Biobased Products Program, 2003, Outstanding Achievement award United Soybean Assn., 2005. Mem. Am. Soc. Clin. Nutrition, Am. Chem. Soc., Am. Inst. Nutrition, Sr. Exec. Assn., Rotary, Sons of Norway (dist. v.p. 1984-86, dist. pres. 1986-88, internat. bd. dirs. 1988-92), Phi Beta Kappa, Sigma Xi, Gamma Sigma Delta. Lutheran. Avocations: cooking, skiing, needlecrafts, camping. Home: 7868 Manet Way Severn MD 21144-1649 Office: BARC-WestBldg 003 Rm 223 10300 Baltimore Ave Beltsville MD 20705-2350 Office Phone: 301-504-6078. Office Fax: 301-504-5863. Business E-Mail: johnsonp@ba.ars.usda.gov.*

JOHNSON, PING HU, nursing educator; d. Tinghong Hu and Bao Dan Lu; m. Roy D. Johnson, Mar. 6, 1999; 1 child, Joyce. MD, Bengbu Med. Coll., 1982; PhD, So. Ill. U., Carbondale, 1997. Cert. health edn. specialist. Instr. nursing sch. Anhui Provincial Hosp., Anhui Med. U., Hefei, China, 1984—86, resident and clin. instr., 1984—87, attending physician, clin. instr., 1987—92; grad. rsch. asst. Western Ill. U., Macomb, 1992—94; grad. tchg. and rsch. asst. So. Ill. U., 1994—97; asst. prof. Fla. Atlantic U., Davie, 1997—2000; rsch. fellow CDC, Atlanta, 2000—02; asst. prof. Kennesaw State U., Ga., 2000—05, assoc. prof., 2005—. Coun. mem., sec. Montgomery Elem. Sch., Atlanta, 2003. Recipient Donald N. Boydston Excellent Grad. Student award, So. Ill. U., 1997, Meritorious Performance award, Super Meritorious Performance award, Fla. Atlantic U., 1998, 1999, Found. prize, Kennesaw State U., 2004, Cmty. Based Learning award, Coll. Undergrad. Studies, Kennesaw State U., 2004, Disting. Scholarship award, Wellstar Coll. Health and Human Svcs., Kennesaw State U., 2005; rsch. fellow, CDC, 2000, 2001, 2002. Mem.: AAHPERD, APHA (program chair Alternative/Complementary Spl. Primary Interest Group 2002—05, Outstanding Svc. Contbn. to Pub. Health, Alternative and Complementary Health Practice Spl. Interest Group 2004), Am. Sch. Health Assn., Am. Assn. Health Edn. (com. 2000, bd. dirs. 2005—), Phi Kappa Phi, Eta Sigma Gamma (life), Phi Delta Kappa. Achievements include research in alternative and complementary health practice, health behaviors, health education and health promotion. Office Phone: 770-499-3149.

JOHNSON, RAYMONDA THEODORA GREENE, retired humanities educator; b. Chgo., Jan. 12, 1939; d. Theodore T. and Eileen (Atherley) Greene; m. Hulon Johnson, June 27, 1964; children: David Atherley, Theodore Cassell, Alexander Ward. BA in English, DePaul U., 1960; MA in English, Loyola U., Chgo., 1965. Cert. high sch. English tchr., Ill. Tchr. high sch. English, Chgo. Pub. Schs., 1960-65; instr. English, Harold Washington Coll. (formerly Loop Coll.), City Coll., Chgo., 1965-66, asst. prof., 1966-91, assoc. prof., 1991-96, faculty advisor coll. newspaper, 1989-92, 96-98, pres. faculty coun., 1990-92, mem. faculty coun., 1990-94, chair English and speech dept., 1992—2004, coord. coll. assessment plan com., 1995-99, prof., 1996—2004, prof. emeritus, 2004—. Mem. Brit. Partnership Articulation team, 1997—; EdD cohort U. Ill., Urbana-Champaign, 2003. Middle sch. v.p. parents coun. Latin Sch., Chgo., 1974-76, trustee, 1987-93; adv. bd. high jump program Latin Sch. Chgo., 1989-98; cubmaster, leader Boys Scouts Am., Chgo., 1974-81; black creativity adv. com. Mus. Sci. and Industry, Chgo., 1984-96; steering com. St. Thomas the Apostle Anti-Racism Ethnic Sensitivity, 1999-2003; chair St. Thomas the Apostle Parish Diversity Dinners, 1999-2003. Recipient Svc. award St. Thomas the Apostle Ch., Chgo., 1984. Mem. Twigs Mothers Club (pres. 1982-84), Alpha Kappa Alpha. Democrat. Roman Catholic. Avocations: reading, sewing, modern dance, theater, music. Home: 6747 S Bennett Ave Chicago IL 60649-1031 E-mail: rajohnson@ccc.edu.

JOHNSON, REBECCA GROOMS, music educator; b. Columbus, Ohio, Dec. 9, 1952; d. Fred Paul and Hazel (Burr) Grooms; m. Stephen Allen Johnson, Feb. 1, 1975. MusB, Capital U., Columbus, Ohio, 1975; MA in Piano Pedagogy, Ohio State U., 1977, PhD in Piano Pedagogy, 1982. Asst. prof. Circleville Bible Coll., Ohio, 1978-81; adj. asst. prof. Mercy Coll., Detroit, 1982-84; mem. faculty Cmty. Music Sch./Capital U., Columbus, 1988-95; lectr. Ohio State U., Columbus, 1995-98; dir. Cmty. Music Sch., adj. assoc. prof. Capital U., 1998—, dir. keyboard pedogogy program. Founder, dir. piano pedagogy conf. Capital U. Conservatory of Music, 1988-95; learning theories com. Nat. Conf. on Piano Pedagogy, 1988-94; presenter in field. Composer: (piano) O Come, O Come Emmanuel, 1993; mem. editl. bd.: Keyboard Companion Mag., 2005—; contbr. articles to profl. jours. Mem. MTNA (nat. chair pedagogy com. 2000-03), Ohio Music Tchrs. Assn. (state pres. 1996-98, 4th v.p. state bd. 1992-96, chmn. cen.-ea. dist. 1990-92, active adjudicator dist. and state competitions, lectr. workshop clinician state conv. 1986, 90, 96, nat. conv. 1994, 98, dist. confs.), Phi Kappa Phi, Pi Kappa Lambda. Mem. Church of God. Avocations: hiking, skiing, reading. Office: Cmty Music Sch Capital Univ Columbus OH 43209

JOHNSON, ROSEMARY WRUCKE, personnel management specialist; b. Leith, N.D., Sept. 21, 1924; d. Rudolph Aaron and Metta Tomina (Andersen) Wrucke; m. Robert Johnson Jr., Sept. 28, 1945 (div. 1964). Student, George Washington U., 1944-45, 47, Nat. Art Sch., Washington, 1943-45. Supr. Displaced Persons Commn., Frankfurt, Germany, 1950-52, FBI, Washington, 1942—49, 1952—81; cons. position mgmt. orgn. design Arlington, Va., 1981—. Mem. NAFE, Classification and Compensation Soc., Soc. FBI Alumni (membership chmn. 1985-91), Internat. Platform Assn. Lutheran. Avocations: painting, sketching. Home and Office: 3710 Lee Hwy Arlington VA 22207-3721

JOHNSON, RUBY DIANE, nursing educator, department chairman, nurse; b. Harrison, Ark. d. Lloyd Elmer Smith and Ruby Helen Carter; m. Joe Edward Johnson, July 17, 1975; children: Elizabeth, Bobbie Joe, Jeffrey, Samanthia, Emerald, Nicholas. ADN, Ark. State U., Jonesboro, 1994, B of Nursing, 2000. LPN, Ozarka Coll., Melbourne, Ark., 1991; cert. Clerical Sec. Black River Tech. Coll., Pocahontas, Ark., 1977. Outpatient, emergency room clk. Ea. Ozarks Hosp., Cherokee Village, Ark., 1986—91, LPN, fl. nurse, med. surg., 1991—94, RN, day shift supr., 1994—97, dir. of nurses, 1997—2000; LPN dir., instr. Ozarka Coll., 2000—, allied health divsn. chair, 2001—; RN coord. Ark. Rural Nurse Edn. Consortium, Melbourne, 2004—. Inventory/shipping clk. Okla. Furniture Factory, Guthrie, 1980—82; data processing asst. supr. Logan County Hosp., Guthrie, Okla., 1982—86. Author: (poetry) A Surrender to the Moon, 2005. Recipient Outstanding Alumni award, Ozarka Coll., Melbourne, Ark., 1997. Mem.: Ark. Assn. LPN (faculty), Ark. Assn. Two Yr. Colleges (faculty), Ark. Nurses Assn., Spring River Profl. Women's. Avocations: charcoal drawing, gardening, fishing, hunting, poetry. Office: Ozarka Coll PO Box 10 218 College Dr Melbourne AR 72556

JOHNSON, RUTH, small business owner; b. Kane, Pa., Apr. 1, 1937; d. Emil T. and Alice Mary (Mitchell) J. BS, Pa. State U., 1959; postgrad., Northwestern U., 1962, Stanford U., 1964. Speech pathologist McKean County Pub. Schs., Smethport, Pa., 1959-62, San Francisco Pub. Schs., 1963, Palo Alto (Calif.) Unified Sch. Dist., 1964-66; founder Phonic Ear Inc., Petaluma, Calif., 1964-74, Phonic Ear Ltd., Can., Phonic Ear Internat. A/S, Denmark, Phonic Ear GmbH, Fed. Republic Germany; navigator Ketch Phonic Ear, 1974-84; pres., owner, communications cons. Protocol Internat. Ltd., State College, Pa., 1984—. Patentee speech therapy tools and auditory tng. systems for hearing-speech-lang. impaired. Founder scholarship funds Kane (Pa.) High Sch., Pa. State U. Soc. Disting. Alumni and Scholarships. R. Mae Shultz coll. edn. scholar Pa. State U. Mem. Assn. Image Cons. Internat., Kappa Kappa Gamma (Peg Riley Loyalty award). Home and Office: Protocol Internat Ltd 301 Rolling Ridge Dr Apt 713 State College PA 16801-7659

JOHNSON, RUTH ANN, literature and language educator; d. Thomas Andrew Reibling and Naomi Ruth Oswald; m. Jack Jerrell Johnson, Apr. 3, 1981; 1 child, Jeff. BA, Easter Ky. U., Richmond, 1968; MA, Xavier U., Cin., 1978. Cert. banking I Xavier U., Cin., 1980. History tchr. Walnut Hills HS, Cin., 1970—72; homebound tchr. Salem Ind. Schs., Ill., 1973—77; English tchr. Boone County HS, Florence, Ky., 1978—83, Holmes HS, Covington, Ky., 1983—2003, Brentwood HS, El Mitchell, Ky., 2003—. Future problem solving coach, evaluation, state trainer, 1986—; asst. examiner Internabond Baccalaureate Orgn., Cardiff, Wales, 1991—. Recipient Tchr. award, Ashland Oil Co., 1993, Presdl. Scholar Tchr. of Distinction, U.S. Dept. of Edn., 2001, James B. Whitehead Tchr. award, Coca-Cola Co., 2002. Mem.: KCTE (writing contest chair), NCTE, Phi Delta Kappa. Avocation: dance. Business E-Mail: rjohnson@beechwood.kyschools.us.

JOHNSON, RUTH ANN, music educator; b. Duluth, Minn., Oct. 25, 1947; d. Roy and Dorothy Johnson. BS in Music Edn., U. Minn., Mpls., 1969. Cert. tchr. Minn., early childhood music Greensboro, NC, 2003, Godly play tchr. Ctr. Theology Children, Houston, 2003. Clk. Billy Graham Evangelistic Assn., Mpls., 1965—68; elem. music tchr. Atkin Pub. Schs., Minn., 1969—72; adminstrv. asst., children's choir dir. Calvary Temple-Soul's Harbor, Mpls., 1972—79, Zion Christian Ctr., St. Paul, 1982—94; tchr., dir. New Horizon Childcare, Mpls., 1979—82; music specialist pre-kindergarten and elem. Maranatha Christian Acad., Mpls., 1991—; adminstrv. asst., tchr., children's choir dir. North Heights Luth. Ch., St. Paul, 1995—. Curriculum cons. Vol. Met. Med. Ctr., Mpls., 1979—81, Animal Humane Soc., Hennepin County, Minn., 1983—86, iVillage.com, NYC, 2000—. Mem.: Choristers Guild, Music Educators Nat. Conf. Republican. Avocations: gardening, writing, photography, sewing, counted cross stitch.

JOHNSON, RUTH ANN CRAIG GOSWICK, psychology educator; b. Kansas City, Mo., Nov. 21, 1946; d. James Richard and Ruth (Dennis) Craig; children: Jeffrey Alan Goswick, David Michael Goswick. AA, Tulsa (Okla.) Jr. Coll., 1973; BS, U. Tulsa, 1976; MS, Okla. State U., 1980, PhD, 1984. Psychol. asst. Connor Correctional Ctr., Hominy, Okla., 1980-81; predoctoral intern VA Med. Ctr., Knoxville, Iowa, 1981-82; clin. psychologist Southeastern Iowa Mental Health Ctr., Burlington, 1982-86; assoc. prof., dept. of psychology Augustana Coll., Rock Island, Ill., 1986—. Contbr. chpt. to book and articles to profl. jours. Mem. founding bd. Iowa Psychol. Found., 1992—. Mem. APA (teaching of psychology divsn.), Soc. for Personality and Social Psychology, Soc. Sci. Study Sexuality, Assn. Sex Educators, Couns. and Therapists, Quad Citians Affirming Diversity (bd. mem. sec.), Sigma Xi (assoc.), Psi Chi. Avocations: antiques, bird watching, reading, genealogy. Office: Augustana College Dept Psychology Rock Island IL 61201

JOHNSON, RUTH ANNE, medical/surgical nurse; b. Mpls., May 18, 1940; d. Oscar Bruce and Leona Anne Gochnauer; m. Robert Milton Johnson (dec.); children: Rodney Milton, Rachel Anne. RN, Luth. Deaconess Hosp., Mpls., 1963. Nurse Chiayi Christian Hosp., Taiwan, 1964—67, Boston Lying-In Hosp., 1968—69, Newton Wesley Hosp., Mass., 1969—71, Weston Manor, Mass., 1972—80, Allston Manor, Mass., 1980—89; ret., 1990. Mem.: Red Hat Soc. Lutheran. Avocations: knitting, reading, puzzles, sewing. Home: 2706 W Ashen Ave #147 Fresno CA 93705

JOHNSON, RUTH FLOYD, educational consultant; b. Plateau, Ala., Apr. 19, 1935; d. Nathan Daniel and Ora Anna (Ellis) Floyd; children: Anthony, Walter, Camille, Quinitta, Annette. Student, Tuskegee Inst., 1951-53; BS in History, Bowie (Md.) State U., 1970; MEd in Counseling, U. Md., 1977; PhD in Human Svcs. Adminstrn., Univ. for Humanistic Studies, San Diego, 1982. Cert. tchr., counselor. Radio personality Sta. WMOZ, 1953-56; owner, dir. Azalea Sch. Dance, 1954-56; numerous posts for fed. govt., 1957-69; tchr., adminstr. Pub. Schs. of Prince George's County, Md., 1970-78; tchr.-counselor Dunbar S.T.A.Y. Sch., Washington, 1974-75; instr. child and youth study divsn. U. Md., 1977-78; CEO Diametron Corp., 1979-81; tchr. L.A. Unified Sch. Dist., 1980-82, Pasadena (Calif.) Unified Sch. Dist., 1982-83, Rialto (Calif.) Unified Sch. Dist., 1984—; profl. devel. coord. Calif. State Polytech. U., 1995—. Author: Remediating Mass Poverty: Development of a Model Program, 1982, Pep Squad handbook, 1991, (with others: Government/Contemporary Issues: A Curriculum Guide, 1976. Active PTAs; mem. organizing com. Peppermill Village Civic Assn., 1966; vol. Boy Scouts Am., 1968-72, Sr. Citizens of Prince George's County, 1974-76; bd. dirs.Mill Point Improvement Assn., 1975-78, Combined Communities in Action, 1976-78; mem. Prince George's County Hosp. Commn., 1978; mem. Altadena Town Coun., 1983; founder Rialto Freedom and Cultural Soc., 1988; mem. Calif. 36th Dist. Bicentennial Adv. Com., 1989; mem. exec. com. Rialto Police/Community Rels. Team, 1993. Recipient Outstanding Svc. to Children and Yourh award Md. Congress PTA, 1969, Services to Boy Scouts Am. award, 1969, Svcs. to Sr. Citizens award, 1975, Community Svc. award Rialto Freedom and Cultural Soc., 1993, others. Mem. NEA, NAACP, Nat. Assn. Univ. Women, Nat. Coun. Negro Women, Zeta Phi Beta, Gamma Phi Delta. Avocations: world travel, theater, tennis, spectator sports, outdoor activities. Home: PO Box 5184 Capitol Heights MD 20791-5184 Fax: 909-820-6001.

JOHNSON, SAKINAH, paralegal; b. Passaic, N.J., Nov. 10, 1971; d. Hosea P. Sr. and Claudette E. Johnson. B in Polit. Sci. magna cum laude, Norfolk State U., 1993. Paralegal Law Offices of Sellinger & Sellinger P.A., Clifton, N.J., 1993-98, Law Offices of Rosemarie Arnold, Ft. Lee, N.J., 1998—. Active Mt. Pilgrim Missionary Bapt. Ch., 1991—. Mem. NAACP, Norfolk State U. Alumni (N.J. chpt.), Spartan Alpha Tau. Avocations: exercise, reading, dance, travel, time with family and friends. Home: 164 Sherman St Passaic NJ 07055-8408

JOHNSON, SALLY A., nurse, educator; b. Rockford, Ill., Apr. 24, 1923; d. Herbert A. and Aileen (Peyton) Johnson; m. Bert Klackle; children: Ann Elizabeth Scannell, Stacey Aileen Lerager. RN Good Samaritan Hosp., 1945; nurse obstetrics delivery Women's Hosp., N.Y.C., 1947-49, St. Francis Hosp., Evanston, Ill., 1953; charge, head nurse Broward Gen. Hosp., Ft. Lauderdale, Fla., 1968; night supr. Ashbrook Convalescent and Nursing Hosp., Scotch Plains, NJ, 1968—. Owner Thomas A. Edison Brick Co., Sally Johnson Enterprises. Coun. chmn. Betty Merit Tchrs. Scholarship, 1962; area nat. organizer Girl Scouts U.S.A., 1962-65; Westfield (N.J.) Round-Up and Health chmn., 1962-63; pres. Tamaques Sch., 1965, adviser Parent Tchr. Orgn., 1966, fgn. relationship chmn., 1967-68; exec. bd. chmn. Westfield HS PTA Newsletter, 1968-70; chmn. Nat. Space Edn., Westfield, 1964; Westfield chmn. fgn. nurses Overlook Hosp., Summit, N.J., 1964-69. Recipient scholarship to Harvard U. Coll. Bus. Mem. Nat. Assn. Investors Corp., Nat. Dist. Nurses Assn., NOW (N.J. coord. 1967-68), Am. Contract Bridge League, Bridge Tchrs. Assn., Naples Investment Club (sec. 1995-96). Republican. Achievements include patent for marking devices. E-mail: sallyjohnson@comcast.net.

JOHNSON, SAMIRA EL-CHEHABI, marketing professional; b. Niagara Falls, NY, Mar. 2, 1958; d. Munzir and Ismat (Zakaria) El-Chehabi; m. Kenneth M. Johnson, Sept. 21, 1991; 1 child, Davis B. BS in Med. Tech. magna cum laude, SUNY, Buffalo, 1980. Component lab. supr. ARC, Detroit, 1982-85; sr. med. technologist Rush Presbyn. St Lukes Med. Ctr., Chgo., 1985-86; tech. cons. Baxter Internat., Deerfield, Ill., 1986-88, ednl. svcs. mgr., 1988-89, market mgr., 1989-93, sr. market mgr., 1993-99; dir. mktg. Cerus Corp., Concord, Calif., 1999—2003; freelance cons., 2003—. Assoc. editor Continuous Flow, 1988-90, Component Therapy Digest, 1988-90; patentee in field. Mem. Nat. Blood Data Resource Ctr., 1996—. Mem. ANA (program adminstr. 1988-98), Am. Soc. Clin. Pathologists, Am. Soc. Med. Technologists (program adminstr. 1988-98), Am. Assn. Blood Banks, Internat. Soc. Blood Transfusion. Avocations: sailing, scuba diving, theater, horseback riding, rollerblading. Home and Office: 159 Chestnut Cir Northport NY 11768 Office Phone: 847-812-4081. Personal E-mail: samira_johnson13@yahoo.com.

JOHNSON, SANDRA ANN, counselor, educator; b. Houston, Apr. 27, 1958; d. Johnnie and Area (Bradford) Johnson. AA, Houston C.C., 1991; BBA, Tex. So. U., 1994; MA, Prairie View A&M U., 1998; PhD, Tex. So. U., 2000; PhD in Psychology, Berne U. Lic. profl. counselor. Tchr. computers Houston Sch. Dist., 1981—. Instr. North Harris Coll., Houston, 1996—, Houston C.C.; counselor Houston C.C. Sys.; rsch. resident, Saint Kitts and Nevis. Vol. Herman Hosp., Houston, 1987—88, U. Tex. Health Sci. Ctr.; intern, vol. DePelchin Children Ctr., 1997—98; counselor Vision of Hope Women, Houston, 1996—97, Cmty. Devel. Corp.; contact person Houston Mayor's Camp, 1997; pres., bd. dirs. Vision of Hope; pres. CAP Cmty. Devel.; pro bono counselor Black Ams. in low income areas; summer resident St. Kitts, West Indies. Named Disting. Role Model of Houston, North Main Ch. of God in Christ, 1998; recipient Outstanding Counselor, Houston C.C. Sys. Mem. Chi Sigma Iota. Democrat. Pentecost. Avocations: tennis, golf, jogging, reading, racquetball. Office: Houston Cmty Coll System Southeast Campus Houston TX 77088-7102 Personal E-mail: sondra_johnson@yahoo.co.uk.

JOHNSON, SANDRA BARTLETT, city official; b. Phoenix; d. Hartley Williams and Alice C. (Johnson) Bartlett; divorced, 1994; 1 child, Nicole Elizabeth. Student, Fla. State U., 1958-61, Ga. State U., 1970-72. Chem. lab. tech. Agrl. Ext. Sta., U. Fla., Bradenton, 1963-65, The Coca-Cola Co., Atlanta, 1965-72, lab. supr., 1972-79, purchasing agt., tech. divsn., 1979-84; mem. city council City of Alpharetta, Ga., 1960—. Mgr. constitutent svcs. Fulton County Commn. Dist. # 2, Atlanta, 1995; bd. dirs. YMCA, Alpha Convention and Visitors Bd. Sr. Svcs. No. Fulton, Ga. Mcpl. Assn., vice chmn. Alpharetta Planning Bd., 1958-60, sec., treas., v.p., state pres., Ga. Assn. Zoning Adminstrs., 1976—. Named for Resolution of Commendation Ga. House Rep., 1997; recipient Diamond Clover 4H award St. Kitts, W.I., 1993, Achievement certs. U. Ga., 1996, 2000. Mem. AAUW (cmty. leader Roswell 1997), Nat. Assn. Purchasing Mgmt. (local and dist. mem. chmn.), Purchasing Mgmt. Ga., Ga. Mcpl. Assn., Am. Planning Assn., North Fulton Coun. Local Govts., Lions Club (bd. dirs., program chair 1994—), Alpharetta Rotary Club (various coms, 1991—, Paul Harris fellow 1996). Republican. Episcopalian. Home: 240 Pebble Trl Alpharetta GA 30004-1227 Office: City of Alpharetta 2 S Main St Alpharetta GA 30004-1936 E-mail: sandrajohnson@juno.com.

JOHNSON, SANDRA HANNEKEN, law educator; b. St. Louis, Jan. 20, 1952; d. Clarence F. and Mary Rose (Uykosky) Hanneken; m. Robert G. Johnson, 1973; children: Emily, Kathleen. AB summa cum laude, St. Louis U., 1973; JD, NYU, 1976; LLM, Yale U., 1977. Bar: N.Y. 1978. Asst. prof. law N.Y. Law Sch., 1977-78, St. Louis U., 1978-81, assoc. prof. law, 1981-84, prof. of law, 1984—, Tenet prof. health care law & ethics, 2000—, assoc. dean, 1979—81, 1985—88, interim dean, 1991—92, provost, 1998—2002; vis. prof. Univ. Houston Law Ctr., 1991, Washington U. Sch. Law, 1995. Dir. Ctr. for Health Law Studies, St. Louis, 1982-85, 88-91; cons. Inst. of Medicine Project on Nursing Homes, N.Y., 1985; mem. Hastings Ctr. Project on Ethics in Nursing Homes, N.Y., 1988-91. Co-author: Nursing Homes and the Law, 1985, Health Law, 1987, 2nd edit., 1991, Health Law Cases Materials & Problems, 4th edit.; mem. bd. editors Law, Medicine and Health Care, 1985—; contbr. articles to profl. jours. Participant St. Louis Leadership Devel. Program, 1980-81; bd. mem. Inst. for Peace & Justice, St. Louis, 1988-90; mem. Instl. Rev. Bd., St. Louis U., 1989-90. Grantee Nat. Inst. of Dispute Resolution, 1985, AARP, 1988; Edmund Pellegrino medal, 2003, HEAL Inst.; Woman of the Year 2002, St. Louis Daily Record; fellow, Hastings Ctr. Mem. ABA, Am. Soc. Law Medicine & Ethics (dir. Mayday Project on Legal & Regulatory Issues in Pain Relief, Disting. Health Law Tchr. award, William J. Curran award), Midwest Bioethics Roundtable, St. Louis Health Lawyers Assn. (chmn.), Phi Beta Kappa, Alpha Sigma Nu. Office: St Louis U Sch of Law 3700 Lindell Blvd Saint Louis MO 63108-3412

JOHNSON, SANDRA K., electrical engineer; b. Fukuoka, Japan, Sept. 19, 1960; arrived in U.S., 1961; d. George Garland and Gloria Dean (Hagger) Johnson. BSEE summa cum laude, So. U., Baton Rouge, La., 1982; MSEE, Stanford U., 1984; PhD, Rice U., 1988. Rsch. staff mem. T.J. Watson Rsch. Ctr. IBM, Yorktown Heights, NY, 1988—2000; mgr. Websphere database devel. IBM Silicon Valley Lab., San Jose, 2000—02; mgr. Linux Performance IBM, Austin, Tex., 2002—03, sr. tech. staff, 2003—; chief tech. officer global small and med. bus. IBM Sys. and Tech. Group, 2004—. Fellow: IEEE; mem.: Computing Rsch. Assn. (com. on status of women in computing sci. 1990—96), Assn. Computing Machinery, IEEE Computer Soc. Office: IBM 11501 Burnett Rd Austin TX 78758 Office Phone: 512-838-4983. Business E-Mail: sandrakj@sbcglobal.net.

JOHNSON, SANDRA KAY, music educator; b. Hampton, Va., Aug. 21, 1952; d. Charles Coburn and Anne Bevins Wilson; m. Jimmy Royce Johnson, Mar. 27, 1993; children: Suzanne Kate Oden, Brandy Brooke. Degree in elem. edn., Sam Houston State U., Huntsville, Tex., 1973. Data processor Tex.; kindergarten endorsement Tex., alphphonics Tex. Tchr. remedial math. Hearne Ind. Sch. Dist., Tex., 1973—74; tchr. kindergarten Pickwickian Schs., League City, Tex., 1978—79, Riyadh Internat. Cmty. Sch., Saudi Arabia, 1980—82, Fredericksburg Ind. Sch. Dist., Tex., 1982—83; tchr. gifted and talented math edn. Comfort Ind. Sch. Dist., Tex., 1983—84, tchr. kindergarten, 1984—85; tchr. kindergarten, 1st and 2d grade music Pearland Ind. Sch. Dist., Tex., 1985—. Compiler, presenter gifted and talented math. curriculum Comfort Ind. Sch. Dist., 1983—84; tchr. alphaphonic curriculum Pearland Ind. Sch. Dist., 1987, tchr. adult English as 2d lang., 86, tchr. adult edn. and citizenship, 86; contbr., bd. sec. to various children's singing and dancing prodns. Author: (children's book) The Baby Elephant. Mem.: Tex. Classroom Tchrs. Assn. (assoc.), Order Ea. Star (Worthy Matron). Methodist. Avocations: crafts, scrapbooks, artistry, community work, travel. Office Phone: 281-412-1412.

JOHNSON, SARAH N., music educator; b. Norway, Maine, May 16, 1978; d. Eric J. and Nancy R. Hanson; m. Sven O. Johnson. MusB, Houghton Coll., 2001. Cert. music tchr. grades K-12 Maine. Dir. music and drama Wasatch Acad., Mt. Pleasant, Utah, 2000—01; vocal music instr. Oxford Hills Sch. Dist., South Paris, Maine, 2002—. Pvt. voice tchr., South Paris, 2004—. Mem.: NEA, Am. Choral Dirs. Assn., Music Educators Nat. Conf., Choral Art Soc. (singer). Republican. Avocations: baseball, church, pets. Home: 42 Tiger Hill Rd Oxford ME 04270 Office: Oxford Hills Comprehensive HS 256 Main St South Paris ME 04281

JOHNSON, SHANNON, professional basketball player; b. Aug. 18, 1974; Grad., U.S.C., 1996. Mem. 2 ABL Champion Columbus Quest; profl. basketball player Valencia, Spain, Orlando Miracle (now Conn. Sun), 1999—2002, Conn. Sun, 2003, San Antonio Silver Stars, 2004—. Named All-WNBA 2nd Team, 1999, 2000, Inaugural WNBA All-Star Team, 1999, WNBA All-Star Team, 2000, 2002, 2003. Achievements include mem. US Women's Basketball Team, Athens Olympics, 2004. Office: c/o San Antonio Silver Stars 1 SBC Center San Antonio TX 78219

JOHNSON, SHARON ELAINE, elementary school educator; b. Grant County, Wis., Dec. 31, 1936; d. Ralph Philip and E. Blanche (Fry) Long; m. Edward Dean Johnson, Apr. 15, 1961; 1 child, Perry Edward; 1 stepchild, David Dwight. B Music Edn., Coe Coll., Cedar Rapids, Iowa, 1959; M Elem. Edn., Murray (Ky.) State U., 1965; M Spl. Edn., U. Mo., Kansas City, 1980. Cert. elem. and music tchr., Kans., Iowa, Ky.; cert. elem., music and spl. edn. tchr., Mo. Elem. tchr. Kans. City (Kans.) Bd. Edn., 1959-63, 65-66; tchr. vocal music Marshall County Bd. Edn., Benton, Ky., 1963-65; elem. tchr. Consol. Sch. Dist. 1, Hickman Mills Bd. Edn., Kansas City, Mo., 1966-79, tchr. kindergarten, 1980—93; sub. tchr. Sunshine Ctr. for Handicapped Pre-Sch., 1993—. Mem. NEA, ASCD, Internat. Reading Assn. (historian 1985-86), Mo. Edn. Assn. (bldg. rep. 1976—). Avocations: needlepoint, reading education journals, word puzzles, helping children learn, spectator sports. Home: 1022 S Park Ave Independence MO 64050-4225 E-mail: jsharon1231@sbcglobal.net.

JOHNSON, SHEILA CRUMP, entrepreneur; b. Pa. m. Robert L. Johnson (div. 2002); children: Paige, Brett; m. William T. Newman, 2005. Music tchr. Sidwell Friends Sch., Washington, 1973—89; former cultural liaison to Middle East U.S. Info. Agency; co-founder Black Entertainment TV; owner Salamander Farms, Middleberg, Va.; developer Salamander Inn and Spa, Middleberg, Va.; co-owner Lincoln Holdings, LLC; team pres. Washington Mystics WNBA; designer of luxury linens. Bd. dirs. Parsons Sch. Design; pres. Washington Internat. Horse Show; established first Nat. Music Conservatory, Amman, Jordan. Achievements include first Black female to be certified as billionaire. Avocations: horseback riding, music, violin. Office: c/o Lincoln Holdings LLC 401 9th St NW Washington DC 20004

JOHNSON, SHEILA LYNN, mathematician, educator; d. Vernon Henry and Geraldine Johnson; 1 child, Gerard A. Malveaux. BA, U. Ill., 1978; MSc, Prairie View A&M U., 1982. Cert. tchr. Calif. Grad. tchr. and rschr. Prairie View (Tex.) A&M U., 1979—82; supr. tchg. James Christian Academy, Compton, Calif., 1983—96; recreation asst. L.A. (Calif.) Pks. and Recreation, 1996—; prof. math. L.A. (Calif.) S.W. Coll., 1996—. Tutor Learning Tree Coll., L.A., 2004—; with health and nutrition Genesis Bldg. Restoration and Tng. Ctr., L.A., 1990—95. Recipient Appreciation cert., VA, 1979, Biology and Math. award, Nat. Inst. Sci., 1981. Mem.: Prairie View (Tex.) A&M U. Alumni Assn., U. Ill. Alumni Assn., Beta Beta. Avocations: bowling, swimming, hiking, tennis, fishing.

JOHNSON, SHERI, state agency administrator, psychologist; BA, Brown Univ.; MA, Boston Univ., PhD in clinical psychology. Clinical fellowship Harvard Med. Sch.; dir. Behavioral Health Svcs. Ctr. Isaac Coggs Health Connection; core scientist Ctr. for AIDS Intervention Rsch., Med. Coll. Wis.; adminstr., state health officer, Divsn. Pub. Health State of Wis., Madison, 2005—. Office: Wis Divsn Pub Health PO Box 2659 Madison WI 53701-2659*

JOHNSON, SHIRLEY ELAINE, management consultant; b. Terre Haute, Ind., Sept. 15, 1946; d. Mervil Ray and Sarah Kathryn (Tucker) W.; children: Richard Alan, Gary Michael. BA, DePaul U., 1991. Sec. to v.p. fin. Cenco Inc., Oak Brook, Ill., 1972-74, exec. asst. to group pres., 1974-75, asst. to chmn., 1975-77, corp. personnel/office mgr., 1977-80; corp. sec. Acadia Petroleum Corp., Denver, 1980-82; mgr. office Chapman, Klein & Weinberg, PC, Denver, 1982-84; asst. to chmn. The Heidrick Ptnrs., Inc., Chgo., 1984-92, v.p., 1992-98; assoc. Heidrick & Struggles Inc., Chgo., 1998-99; cons. Ray & Berndtson, Chgo., 1999—2003, Davis-Burns Group, Roswell, Ga., 2003—04; sr. assoc. Kensington Internat., Oak Brook, Ill., 2004—. Mem. NAFE, Am. Mgmt. Assn., Exec. Women Internat., Rsch. Roundtable. Home: 5674 Walnut Ave 2B Downers Grove IL 60516 Office: 1415 W 22d St Ste 500 Oak Brook IL 60523 Office Phone: 630-571-0123 ext 239. E-mail: sejchicago@sbcglobal.net.

JOHNSON, SIGRID, elementary school educator; MEd, George Mason U., Fairfax, VA, 1997. Tchr. sci. Fairfax County Pub. Schs., Springfield, Va., 1990—. Mem.: NSTA. Baptist.

JOHNSON, STEPHANIE L. B., small business owner, office manager; b. Colorado Springs, Colo., Sept. 29, 1945; d. George Edgar and Anne Eastwood Bates; m. Johnny B. Johnson, Dec. 26, 1964; 1 child, Jennifer L. B. Johnson-Bahr. A, Blair Coll., 1964. Office mgr., girl Friday W. E. Nash, Arch., Bryan, Tex., 1965—69; owner, mgr. Bates Enterprises, Colorado Springs, Colo., 1991—; office mgr. Becker-Johnson, Inc., 1991—. Chair Platte Ave. Improvement Dist. Maintenance Adv. Bd., Colorado Springs, 2000—; chairperson The RIDER Com. NSA Oversight Com., 2002—. Editor (creator): (newsletter) The Gold Std. (Sertoma Dist. Newsletter of the Yr., 2003), Knob Hill Neighbor. Pres. Platte Ave. Bus. & Neighborhood Assn., Colorado Springs, 1999—2003; v.p. Police Adv. Com., 2002—03. Mem.: History Day Scholars, Inc. (assoc.; sec.-treas. 1985—2003), Cheyenne Mountain Sertoma Club (assoc.; bd. mem. 1999—2003, Ben Franklin award 1996, Sertoman of Yr. award 2002), Rocky Mountain Youth Leadership Found., Inc. (assoc.; pres. 1989—99, Stephanie L. B. Johnson award 1995), Mil. Order of World Wars (life; treas. 1997—99, Patrick Henry Silver medal 1990). Conservative. Methodist. Avocations: historical preservation, travel, antique toy collecting, old english sheepdogs, classic & special interest cars. Home: 116 E Columbia St Colorado Springs CO 80907 Office: Becker-Johnson Inc 2601 Platte Pl Colorado Springs CO 80909 Office Phone: 719-473-5653. E-mail: oneblonde1@prodigy.net.

JOHNSON, SUSAN F., elementary school educator; d. Gregory Peter and Helen Anna (Dingel) Fettes; m. James R. Johnson, Aug. 26, 1966 (dec. Sept. 2005); 1 child, Christopher Russell. BS in Elem. Edn., Drake U., 1962; postgrad., Mankato State U., 1962—66; MS in English, Nova U., 1989. Cert. tchr. Fla. 6th grade tchr. Royal (Iowa) Cmty. Sch., 1954—56; 4th grade tchr. Carroll (Iowa) Pub. Sch., 1956—58; 6th grade tchr. Ames (Iowa) Pub. Schs., Ames, 1959—62, Mankato (Minn.) Pub. Schs., 1962—66; 7th - 8th grade tchr. Eau Claire (Wis.) Pub. Schs., 1966—69; 5-7th grade tchr. Rockbridge County Schs., Lexington, Va., 1969—72; 7-8 grade tchr. St. Francis (S.D.) Indian Sch., 1977—78; 1st grade tchr. Valentine (Nebr.) Pub. Sch., 1978—80; 4-6th grade tchr. Volusia County Schs., Daytona Beach, Fla., 1980—2004, substitute tchr. grades 2-8, 2004—. Adj. instr. Sinte Gleska Coll., 1978—80; adj. instr. English II Daytona Beach C.C., 1990—94; pres. Volusia County Reading Coun., Daytona Beach, 1995. Named Tchr. of Yr., Spruce Creek Elem., 1987—88, Tchr. of Month, 1987, 1990, Reading Tchr. of Yr., Volusia County Reading Coun., 2001. Mem.: LWV (sec. 2004—), Fla. Reading Assn. (bd. mem., dist. 12 rep. 2002—05), Internat. Reading Assn., Daytona Beach Choral Soc. (2nd v.p. 2002—05). Democrat. Roman Catholic. Avocations: reading, singing, piano, writing, cooking. Home: 929 Mill Road Ln Port Orange FL 32127

JOHNSON, SUZANNE BENNETT, psychologist; b. Johnson City, N.Y., Feb. 8, 1948; d. Carl Emil and Marion Sisson (Bennett) J.; m. Bruce Henry Taffel, June 14, 1970 (div. June 1977); m. Nathan Warren Perry, July 22, 1978; children: Erika Marion Perry, Marissa Clara Perry. BA, Cornell U., 1970; PhD, SUNY, Stony Brook, 1974. Lic. psychologist, Fla.; diplomate in health psychology. Postdoctoral fellow in clin. child psychology U. Fla. Health Sci. Ctr., Gainesville, 1974-75, asst. prof. clin. psychology, 1975-81, assoc. prof., 1981-87, prof., 1987—; dir. Ctr. for Pediatric Psychology Rsch., 1994—2004; prof. chair, dept. med. humanties and social svcs. Fla. State U. Coll. of Medicine, 2002—. Contbr. over 100 articles to profl. jours. and books. Rsch. grantee in behavioral childhood diabetes NIH, 1980—; recipient Rsch. Career Devel. award NIH, 1985-90; Health policy fellow, robert Wood Johnson, 2001-02. Fellow APA (pres. of Health Psychology divsn. 1994); mem. Fla. Psychol. Assn., Soc. Pediatric Psychology (pres. 1993, Significant Contbn. in Pediatric Psychology Rsch. award 1996), Am. Diabetes Assn. Democrat. Avocations: photography, hiking, tennis. Office: Fla State U Coll Medicine 1115 West Call St Tallahassee FL 32306-4300

JOHNSON, SUZANNE M. NORA, diversified financial services company executive, lawyer; b. Chgo., May 14, 1957; married. BA magna cum laude, U. So. Calif., 1979; JD, Harvard U. Bar: Calif. 1983. Law clk. to Hon. Francis Murnaghan US Ct. Appeals (4th Cir.), Balt.; atty. Simpson Thacher & Bartlett, 1980—84; with Goldman Sachs Group, NYC, 1985—, ptnr., 1992—, head global healthcare, investment banking div., 1994—2002, head global investment rsch. div., 2002—, mem. mgmt. com., 2002—, chmn. Global Markets Inst., 2004—, vice chmn., 2004—. Henry Crown Fellow Aspen Inst. Trustee Brookings Institution, Carnegie Institution, RAND Health, TechnoServe, Univ. So. Calif.; bd. dirs. Children Now, Markle Found., 2006—; mem. adv. bd. of councilors Harvard Med. Sch. Mem.: Council Fgn. Rels. Avocations: diving, kayaking, swimming, water-skiing. Office: Goldman Sachs Group 85 Broad St New York NY 10004*

JOHNSON, SYLVIA SUE, university administrator, educator; b. Abiline, Tex., Aug. 10, 1940; d. SE Boyd and Margaret MacGillivray (Withington) Smith; m. William Ruel Johnson; children: Margaret Ruth, Laura Jane, Catherine Withington. BA, U. Calif., Riverside, 1962; postgrad., U. Hawaii, 1963. Elem. edn. credential, 1962. Chmn. bd. regents U. Calif., 2000—. Mem. bd. regents U. Calif.; mem. steering com. Citizens Univ. Com., chmn., 1978-79; bd. dirs., charter mem. U. Calif.-Riverside Found., chmn. nominating com., 1983—; pres., bd. dirs. Friends of the Mission Inn, 1969-72, 73-76, Mission Inn Found., 1977—. Calif. Bapt. Coll. Citizens Com., 1980—; bd. dirs. Riverside Comty. Hosp., 1980—, Riverside Jr. League, 1976-77, Nat. Charity League, 1984-85; mem. chancellors blue ribbon com., devel. com. Calif. Mus. Photography; state bd. dirs. C. of C., 2003. Named Woman of Yr., State of Calif. Legislature, 1989, 91, Citizen of Yr., C. of C., 1989; recipient Golden Key award Soroptimist Internat., 2000, Outstanding Woman honoree U. Redlands Town and Gown, 2001, Chancellor's medal U. Calif. Riverside, 2002, Trustees award for extraordinary svc. U. Calif. Riverside, 2004, Silver Raincross medal Jr. League Riverside, 1993, Spirit of Excellence award Calif. Bapt. Coll., 2004, Annual Frank Miller Civic Achievement award, Mission Inn Found., 2005. Mem. U. Calif.-Riverside Alumni Assn. (bd. dirs. 1966-68, v.p. 1968-70), Calif. C. of C. (bd. dirs. 2003—). Business E-Mail: ssj@johnson-machinery.com.

JOHNSON, THELMA JEAN, secondary school educator; b. San Augustine, Tex., Mar. 17, 1952; d. Willie F. and Iola V. (Polk) Harp; m. Ronald J. Johnson, Oct. 31, 1975; 1 child, Tiffany Michelle. BA, North Tex. State U., 1974; MA, Tex. So. U., 1989. Cert. secondary tchr., Tex. Tchr. Jesse H. Jones H.S., Houston, 1977-81, B.F. Terry H.S., Rosenberg, Tex., 1981-82, Jack Yates H.S., Houston, 1982-90, James Madison H.S., Houston, 1990-94, William S. Holland Middle Sch., Houston, 1994—. Youth dir. Our Mother of Mercy Catholic Ch., Houston, 1992—. Mem. NAACP, Soc. of Profl. Journalists, Journalism Edn. Assn., Nat. Scholastic Press Assn., Interscholastic League Press Conf. (Edith Fox King Disting. Educator in Tex. award 1996), Houston Assn. of Black Journalists. Democrat. Home: 12222 Crystalwood Dr Houston TX 77013-4920

JOHNSON, THERESA M., retired special education educator; d. Otis and Sarah J. BS in Home Econs., N.C. Cen. U., 1972, MEd in Mental Retardation, 1974; PhD in Spl. Edn. Adminstrn., So. Ill. U., 1982; cert., People's Law Sch., 1990. Cert. spl. edn. tchr., supt., prin., supr., pre-sch. handicapped, project specialist, N.C. Tchr. educable mentally handicapped D.N. Hix Sch., Oxford, 1973-74; resource tchr. educable mentally handicapped John W. Neal Jr. HS, Durham, NC, 1974-76; tchr. educable mentally handicapped, learning disabled Lowe's Grove Jr. HS, Durham, 1976-78; instnl. resource specialist div. for exceptional children N.C. Dept. Pub. Instrn., Greensboro, NC, 1978-80; coord. continuing edn. Winston-Salem (NC) State U., 1982-84, asst. prof. spl. edn., 1982-89, assoc. prof. spl. edn., 1989-92, coord. spl. edn. program, 1989-92; ret., 2004. Mem. policy bd. Winston-Salem/Forsyth County Consortium, 1982-92; population coord. Chapel Hill-Carrboro Schs., 1992—. Contbr. to book: Career-Vocational Education for Handicapped Youths, 1982. Grantee Am. Assn. Col. for T.E., 1983-84; So. Ill. U. fellow, 1981-82. Mem. AAUP, Coun. for Exceptional Children, Black Caucus of Spl. Educators, Am. Assn. Mental Deficiency, Phi Delta Kappa. Democrat. Methodist. Avocations: reading, aerobics, travel, backgammon, movies. Home: PO Box 305 Pfafftown NC 27040-0305

JOHNSON, TRINA LYNN, special education educator; b. Hot Springs, Ark., Apr. 22, 1964; d. Mildred Maridean and William Kiney Couch. BSE, Henderson State U., Arkadelphia, Ark., 1992; MSE, Henderson State U., 2002. Cert. Nursing Asst., Petra Allied Health; TESOL Ark., 2005. Tchr. Malvern Schools, Ark., 2004—; cert. nursing asst. Alliance Home Health, Arkadelphia. Scholar, Fred's Dept. Stores. Mem. Assembly Of God Ch. Avocations: swimming, canoeing, dog breeding, hunting / fishing, concerts. Office Phone: 501-332-6452. Personal E-mail: trina@ezclick.net. E-mail: tjohnson@wilson1.dsc.k12.ar.us.

JOHNSON, URSULA ANNE, artist; b. St. Louis, Oct. 11, 1927; d. Lorenzo Bates and Ursula Agnes Lea; m. Herbert Crittenden Johnson, June 10, 1951; children: Amelia Anne Bosque, Raymond Brian. Student, Denison U., 1946—48, Ohio State U., 1951. Artist The Columbus Citizen, Ohio, 1951—52; fashion illustrator F & R Lazarus and Co., Columbus, Ohio, 1952—55. Artist's adv. coun. Marin Soc. of Artists, Ross, Calif., 1965—67, v.p., 1970—71, bd. dirs., 1970—72. Printmaking, Lost Words Found, 1980, Twice-told Tales, 1980, The Waiting Game, 1980, Aeon's Ago, 1980, Omen, 1980, Corrosion, 1981, Primitif, 1981, Symbol, 1981, Forgotten Image, 1981, Kehoe, 1983, Represented in permanent collections Bank Am. Corp., Bank San Francisco. Mem. Art Coun. of Placer County, Auburn, Calif., 1992—2003, Smith Gallery, Sacramento, 2003—05. Avocations: gardening, swimming, hiking, travel. Home and Office: 1203 Overland Ln Lincoln CA 95648 Office Phone: 916-543-9654. Personal E-mail: ursart@sbcglobal.net.

JOHNSON, VERA LLOYD, school system administrator; m. Stanley L. Johnson, Nov. 24, 1983 (dec. May 9, 1994); children: David, John. BS and MS in Elem. Edn., SUNY, Buffalo, 1971. Cert. sch. dist. adminstr. NY State Bd. Edn., sch. adminstr./supr. NY State Bd. Edn. Tchr. grades pre-K - 6 pub. schs., Buffalo, N.Y., Springfield, Mass., Roosevelt, N.Y., 1966—97; exec. dir. Day Care Coord. Coun., Newark, 1970—72; tng. coord. Econ. Opportunity Commn., Hempstead, NY, 1979—82; curriculum specialist Washington Rose Elem. Sch., Roosevelt, NY, 1998—. Dir. programs pub. schs., Buffalo,

Springfield, Roosevelt, 1970; adj. prof. Bloomfield Coll., NJ, 1977—78; part-time coord. adult edn. program Roosevelt Schs., 2003—06. Contbr. mag. Tchr., mentor Leadership Tng. Inst., Hempstead, 1995—2000. Recipient monetary grant, Pub. Broadcasting Network C, 1996. Mem.: N.Y. State Tchrs. Assn. Personal E-mail: vera_johnson@verizon.net.

JOHNSON, VERDIA E., marketing professional; B in Mktg., Howard U.; MBA in Mktg., NYU. With Colgate Palmolive Co., Standard Brands, Nabisco Brands; dir. advt. Black Enterprise Mag.; v.p. bus. devel. and sales Gannett Outdoor; v.p., gen. mgr. Stedman Graham & Ptnrs.; pres., founding ptnr. Footsteps, LLC, NYU, NY, 2000—. Named 25 Most Black Influential Women in Bus., Network Mag.; recipient Outstanding Women in Mktg. and Comm. award, Ebony Mag., 2001, Urban Wheels award, 2002. Office: Footsteps LLC 200 Varick St Rm 610 New York NY 10014-7487 Office Phone: 212-924-6432.

JOHNSON, VICKIE, professional basketball player; b. Apr. 15, 1972; B of Sociology & Psychology, La. Tech. Inst., 1996. Guard-forward Tarbes, France, 1996—97, WMBA - N.Y. Liberty, N.Y.C., 1997—. Named NCAA Tournament All-Final Four, 1994, Sun Belt Conf. Player of Yr., MVP, Kodak All-Am., 1995, Street & Smith All-Am., 1996; recipient La. Player of Yr., 1996. Avocations: movies, shopping, friends, tennis. Office: NY Liberty 2 Penn Plz New York NY 10121-0101

JOHNSON, VIKI, sociology professor; BA, Dickinson State U., ND, 1988; MS, ND State U., Fargo, 1997; PhD, U. ND, Grand Forks, 2003. Archive and rsch. asst. ND State U., 1995—97; rsch. and tchg. asst. U. ND, 2000—03; adj. instr. U. Minn., Crookston, 2002; asst. prof. Westminster Coll., Salt Lake City, 2004—06, Dakota State U., Madison, SD, 2006—. Author biographical summaries for archives. Vol., tour guide Utah Heritage Found., Salt Lake City, 2005—06; vol. svc. learning U. Minn., Crookston, 2002. Recipient Vol. award for Flood Recovery Work, Red Cross, 1997; Thomas Paul & Belle scholar, U. ND, 2002—03, Academic scholar, Dickinson State U., 1986—88. Mem.: AAUW, Mid-West Sociol. Soc., Gt. Plains Sociol. Soc. Office: Dakota State U 820 N Washington Ave Beadle Hall 331 Madison SD 57042 Office Phone: 605-256-5662.

JOHNSON, VIRGINIA BRISTOL, costume designer, educator, small business owner; d. Warren Lee and Gloria B. Johnson; m. Noah Dubreuil, Feb. 18, 2001. BA in Theater and English, Drake U., Des Moines, 1996; MFA in Costume Design, W.Va. U., Morgantown, 2000. Guest lectr. Drake U., 1997; instr. W.Va. U., Morgantown, 1998—2000; costume designer Williamstown Theatre Festival, Medford, Mass., 2000; head of design and tech. Tufts U., Medford, 2000—. Advisor Ex-Coll., Medford, 2001—; panelist NCSS Conf., Kansas City, 2005; costume historian Heinz History Ctr., Pitts., 2005. Costume designer: (films) Black Irish, 2005; Stifts, 2006; Normal Adolescent Behavior, 2006; (TV films) Gold Rush, 2005; Nova-Percy Julian, 2004; The American Experience-John & Abigail Adams, 2006; (TV miniseries) The War that Made America, 2006. Sustaining mem. Planned Parenthood, 2004—; prodn. mgr. Magic Cir. Children's Theatre, Medford, 2001—04. Arnott Fund grantee, Tufts Dept. Drama, 2001, 2003, Summer Scholars grantee, Tufts U. AS&E, 2004. Mem.: United Scenic Artists. Democrat. Avocations: knitting, kayaking, gardening, home improvement. Home: 599 High St Medford MA 02155 Office Phone: 617-627-3728. Office Fax: 617-627-3803. E-mail: virginia.johnson@tufts.edu.

JOHNSON, VIRGINIA MACPHERSON, secondary school educator, consultant; b. Washington, Feb. 23, 1923; d. Alfred Bradford and Margaret Edna (Breed) Macpherson; m. Robert Allen Johnson, Sept. 11, 1948; children: Ann Elizabeth, Constance Ellen. BS, Oreg. State, 1945. Tchr. secondary schs. Parkrose High Sch., Portland, Oreg., 1945-47, Redwood High Sch., San Mateo, Calif., 1947-48. Vol. food svcs., Kerr Children's Ctr., Portland, 1987-89; chmn., bd. dirs. Camp Fire Inc., Portland, 1967-70, Camp Fire (nat.), Kansas City, Mo., 1969-75; pres. Highland Games (Scottish), Portland, 1978-79; sec. St. Andrews Soc. Oreg., 1980-88, chmn. coll. scholarship selection com. 1986-91. Mem. Alpha Chi Omega Alumnae (pres. 1971-72). Clubs: Multnomah Athletic (Portland). Lodges: PEO. Republican. Presbyterian. Avocations: golf, free-lance promotion, travel. Home and Office: 8855 SW Birchwood Rd Portland OR 97225-2715 E-mail: johnsraj@aol.com.

JOHNSON, YVONNE AMALIA, elementary school educator, consultant; b. DeKalb, Ill., July 1, 1930; d. Albert O. and Virginia O. (Nelson) J. *Albert and Virginia spent their lifetimes farming. Albert's father returned to DeKalb after the Gold Rush. He homesteaded land which later became the family farm. Albert's mother was charter member of 1st Lutheran Church in DeKalb in 1858. Virginia's father was a blacksmith and made one of the first firewagons for DeKalb. Albert was a charter member of the DeKalb County Farm Bureau when it was established in 1912. Virginia did missionary work for Lutheran Church. Elaine, sister, was teacher and worked in the poultry division of DeKalb Agricultural Association, with Kenneth, brother. Elaine's husband, Leo, was the communications director for DeKalb Agricultural Association and developed the company logo.* BS in Edn., No. Ill. State Tchrs. Coll., 1951; MS in Edn., No. Ill. U., 1960. Tchr. Love Rural Sch., DeKalb, 1951-53, West Elem. Sch., Sycamore, Ill., 1953—2002; coord. Media Ctr. West Sch. Ill. honors sci. tchr., ISU, 1985-87. Contbr. articles to profl. publs. Bd. dirs. Sycamore Pub. Libr., 1974-98, pres. bd. dirs., 1984-98, chmn. maj. fund drive for addition to libr., 1994-98; founder Dekalb County Excellence in Edn. award, 1999; bd. trustees Midwest Mus. Natural History, 2001—, pres., 2006. Named DeKalb County Conservation Tchr., 1971, Gov.'s Master Tchr., State of Ill., 1984, Outstanding Agrl. Tchr. in the Classroom Dekalb County Farm Bur., 1993; grantee NSF, 1961, 62, 85, 86, 87, NASA, 1988; Sci. Lit. grantee State of Ill., 1992-94. Mem. NEA, NSTA (cert. in elem. sci.), Ill. Sci. Tchrs. Assn., Ill. Edn. Assn., Sycamore Edn. Assn., Coun. for Elem. Sci. Internat. Office: West Elem Sch 240 Fair St Sycamore IL 60178-1641

JOHNSON, YVONNE THOMAS, elementary school educator; b. Kingston, Jamaica, June 5, 1948; arrived in US, 1956; d. George Diaz Thomas and Lucille Adelle (McCurdy) Thomas-McPherson; m. Glenn Jacobs, Nov. 22, 1986 (div.); 1 stepchild, Brian Jacobs; m. Rick Frederick C. Johnson (div.); children: Lance Cabral, Amaris Kai. BA, Simmons Coll., Boston, 1971; EdM, Harvard Grad. Sch. Edn., Cambridge, Mass., 1982; CAGS, Wheelock Coll. and Harvard Edn. Sch., 1992. Tchr. John Marshall Sch., Boston, 1971—73; Chpt. 1 reading tchr. Lucy Stone Sch., 1974—77, first grad tchr., 1978—79; cluster support tchr. ESAA Schs. Without Failure, 1979—81; lang. arts, soc. studies tchr. Graham and Parks Alternative Schs., Cambridge, Mass., 1982—86; kindergarten tchr. Daniel A. Haggerty Sch., 1986—2002; ret. Mem. Meeting House Hill Neighborhood Assn., 2003—, Friends of Ronan Park, 2004—. Conant fellow, Harvard Edn. Sch. for CAGS Studies. Mem.: Cambridge Tchrs. Assn., Mass. Tchrs. Assn., Dorchester YMCA. Democrat. Baptist. Avocations: art, swimming, singing, reading, cooking.

JOHNSON ALDRICH, LESLIE DEBORAH, lawyer; d. Leslie William and Gail Edith Johnson; m. Kenneth Lloyd Aldrich, Feb. 17, 1996 (div.); children: Chad, Nicholas, Dieter Soetebier. BA, St. Cloud State U., Minn., 1979; JD with distinction, U. ND, Grand Fork, 1983. Bar: ND, Minn., Fed. Dist. Ct., State and US Ct., ND, Fed. Dist. Ct., State and US Ct., Minn. Placement officer U. ND, 1981—83; law clk. Minn. Seventh Jud. Dist., 1983, 1983—84; lawyer Legal Assistance of ND, Fargo, ND, 1984—89, Johnson Law Office PC, Fargo, 1989—. Treas. Cross Country Bar Assn., Fargo, ND, 1984—2006; past bd. mem. Fargo Heritage Soc., ND, Fargo Women's Golf, ND. Mem.: Am. Trial Lawyers, Nat. Assn. Criminal Def. Lawyers (life), Century Club. Conservative. Avocations: gardening, golf, antiques. Office: Johnson Law Office PC 1018 1st Ave N Fargo ND 58103

JOHNSON-BROWN, LINDA LEE, music educator; b. Anchorage, Alaska, Dec. 19, 1952; d. Charles Arthur Johnson and Marion Lorraine Bancroft-Johnson; m. Raymond Lee Brown, July 5, 1980; children: Michelle, Lorri, Joshua, Jennifer, Jacqui, Daniel; m. Robert Michael Arnold, Dec. 22, 1976 (div. Jan. 15, 1979); 1 child, Lorraine Marie. MusB, Ill. State U., 1976; MEd, Marygrove Coll., 2000. Tchr. Joliet (Ill.) Pub. Schs., 1976—79, Herscher (Ill.) Cmty. Schs., 1979—80, Watseka (Ill.) Cmty. Schs., 1980—81, St. Anne (Ill.) Pub. Schs., 1981—82, Donovan (Ill.) Cmty. Schs., 1985—90, Shelby County Pub. Schs., Memphis, 1990—94; tchr. Dillon Elem. Carman-Ainsworth Cmty. Schs., Flint, Mich., 1994—. Mem. curriculum devel. fine arts com. State of Ill., Watseka, 1989; mem. task force Gov. Jennifer Grandhilms, Flint, 2003. Pres. Kid's for Am. America's Fund Afghan Orphans, Flint, 2001—02; min. music Assemblies of God, 1995—2003. Mem.: DAR, Music Educators Nat. Conf., Music Educators Assn. Republican. Avocations: reading, history, writing, music, singing. Home: 13490 Lakebrook Drive Fenton MI 48430 Office: Carman Ainsworth Community Schs Dillon Elem 1197 E Schumacher Ave Burton MI 48529

JOHNSON-COHEN, YEVONNE B., minister, counselor; b. Flint, Mich., July 22, 1951; d. Andrew L. and Barbara Elizabeth Johnson; m. Benton Kline Cohen, May 31, 2004; 1 child, Nevlynn L. Johnson. BA, MA, Mich. State U., 1982; MDiv, Louisville Presbyn. Sem., 1997. LCSW Mich. Bd. Social Work, 2002; lic. profl. counselor Mich. Dept. Cmty. Health, 2002. Min. addictions counselor God's Ho. Mission, Owings Mills, Md., 2000—. Author: A Miracle in the House; co-prodr.: (films) Women and Addiction. Urban counselor God's Ho. Mission, Owings Mills, Md., 2000—04. Grantee, Profl. Bus. Women Flint, Mich., 1979. Mem.: NCADD (assoc.), Counselors Networking Assn. (assoc.), Sarasota Acad. Christian Counseling (assoc.). Achievements include development of female specific clinical addictions program; spiritual enrichment program for addictions program; clinical library for female addictions program. Avocations: travel, cooking, reading, community outreach. Office: Gods House Mission 8705 Groffs Mill Drive Owings Mills MD 21117 Office Phone: 410-654-5442. Personal E-mail: ybcohen@comcast.net. E-mail: ghmission@comcast.net.

JOHNSON HOLMES, SABRINA, music educator; d. Katie Johnson; m. Stephen Holmes, July 12, 1996; children: Keisha Mitchell, Latoya Jones, Stephen Holmes, Jr., Stacie Holmes. B of Music Edn., Miss. Valley State U., Itta Bena, 1982; M of Music Edn., Delta State U., Cleveland, Miss., 1984; DEd, Nova Southeastern U., Fort Lauderdale, Fla., 2006. Cert. band, instrumental music tchr. Miss., 1990, Level I instr. Orff Schulwerk, 1998. Choral dir., music specialist Nugent Ctr. Sch., Benoit, Miss., 1982—88; choral and band dir. Greenville Pub. Schs., Miss., 1988—90; tchr., music specialist Wilson Elem.-Seminole County Schs., Sanford, Fla., 1990—. Adminstr., dir. of music Carter Tabernacle CME Ch., Orlando, Fla., 1995—. Recipient Tchr. of Yr. award, Wilson Elem.-Seminole County, 1999; grantee, Musik Garden. Mem.: MENC, FEMEA, CFOC, SEA. Achievements include development of Seminole County Elementary Music Festival; adjudicator All County Marching Festival, Washington County. Office Phone: 407-320-6984. E-mail: same.

JOHNSON-HOUSTON, DEBBIE, librarian, educator; d. Calvin and Mary Jane (Johnson) Delafoisse; m. Fred Dorsey Houston, Sr., Apr. 13, 1992; children: Tariq, Danielle. BA in Speech/Pub. Rels., McNeese State U., 1979; MA in Libr. and Info. Sci., U. So. Fla., 1992. Br. libr., head interlibr. loan dept. Allen Parish Librs., Oberlin, La., 1985-88; br. libr. I NW Br., Pompano Beach, Fla., 1988-92; br. libr. II Tyrone Bryant Br., Ft. Lauderdale, Fla., 1992; br. libr. III Hallandale (Fla.) Br. Libr., 1992—. Adj. prof. grad. program U. So. Fla., 1993—. Campaign coord. United Way, 1993; coord. Outreach, 1993—; liaison Friends of Hallandale Libr. Recipient Hon. award for cmty. svc. through libr. programs and activigies Bus. and Profl. Women of Pompano Beach, 1992; ALA Libr. fellow, 1994—; Pompano Beach Friends of the Libr. scholar, 1989-92. Mem. ALA (exec. bd. Black Caucus 1993-94, career devel. and placement com. Black Caucus 1993-94), Broward County Libr. Assn. (v.p. 1993-94, pres.-elect 1994—), Beta Phi Mu. Office: Firefly Books Ltd 1739 E Carson St #358 Pittsburgh PA 15203

JOHNSONIUS, JENNY ROSS, nursing administrator; d. Billy and Nell Ross; m. J.B. Johnsonius, Sept. 21, 1974; children: Jennifer Jill Johnsonius Krebill, Natalie Jen. BSN, U. Tenn., Memphis, 1974; MSN, Murray State U., Ky., 1985; PhD in Nursing, U. Tenn., Memphis, 1997. Cert. FNP. Pub. health nurse II Tenn. Dept. Health and Environment, 1974—81, pub. health nurse IV, 1985—91; asst. prof. nursing U. Tenn., Martin, 1991—98; assoc. prof. nursing Austin Peay State U., Clarksville, Tenn., 1998—2002, nurse practitioner student health svcs., 1999—2002; PRN, emergency rm. nurse Henry County Med. Ctr., Paris, Tenn., 1993—; primary instr. LPN program Tenn. Tech. Ctr., McKenzie, 2003—05; dir. baccalaureate nursing program Bethel Coll., McKenzie, 2005—. Lectr. in field. Contbr. articles to profl. jours. Grantee Rsch. grantee, Austin Peay State U., 1999. Baptist. Office: Bethel College 325 Cherry Ave Mc Kenzie TN 38201-1735

JOHNSON-LEESON, CHARLEEN ANN, retired elementary school educator, insurance agent, consultant, executive secretary; b. Battle Creek, Mich., June 10, 1949; d. Kenneth Andrews Leeson and Ila Mae (Weed/Lesson) McCutcheon; m. Lynn Boyd Johnson, Aug. 8, 1970; children: Eric Andrew, Andrea Johnson McGrath. BA, Spring Arbor Coll., 1971; MS, Reading Specialist, Western Ill. U., 1990. Cert. elem. and secondary tchr., Mich., elem. tchr., Ill., reading K-9, Ill.; lic. series6,63. Tchr. Hanover (Mich.) Horton Schs., 1972-73, Virden (Ill.) Elem. Sch., 1984-90; ins. agt. State Farm Ins., Virden, Ill., 1991-95, cons. Springfield, Ill., 1995-97, regional exec. asst. Bloomington, Ill., 1997-99, agt. Myrtle Beach, S.C., 1999—. Collegiate and jr. high sch. cheerleading advisor in field; course leader Agt. Schs. 1, 2, and 3; agent Bronze Tablet Music dir., pianist Zion Luth. Ch., Farmersville, Ill., 1979-88, organist, pianist Olive St. Friends, Battle Creek, 1961-67. Recipient Honor the Educator award World Book, 1988, 89, Soaring Eagle award Millionair/Amb. Club, 1991-98, Amb. Club, 2001-02; Wilson Stone scholar, 1990, Mich. State scholar, 1967; select agt. Bronze Tablet Honor Agt. Mem. AUA, Internat. Reading Assn., S.C. Assn. Life Underwriters, Nat. Assn. Ins. and Fin. Advisors, Gideon Aux., Alpha Upsilon Alpha. Avocations: piano, music, writing, painting. Home: 8500 Margate Cir #1601 Myrtle Beach SC 29572-5217 Office: 119 Waccamaw Med Park Conway SC 29526-8902 Office Phone: 843-347-2824. Personal E-mail: beachjohn@earthlink.net. Business E-Mail: charleen.johnson.cyxd@statefarm.com.

JOHNSON-LEIPOLD, HELEN P., outdoor recreation company executive; b. 1957; V.p. consumer mktg. svcs. worldwide SCJ, 1992-95, exec. v.p. N.Am. businesses, 1995-97, v.p. personal and home care products, 1997-98, v.p. worldwide consumer products-mktg., 1999; chmn., CEO Johnson Outdoors (formerly Johnson Worldwide Assocs. Inc.), Miami Beach, Fla., 1999—. Named one of Forbes' Richest Americans, 2006. Office: 555 Main St Racine WI 53403 Office Fax: 262-631-6601.*

JOHNSON-MARQUART, WINNIE, consumer products company executive; married; 4 children. Attended, Vassar Coll., Cornell U. Project coord. corp. pub. affairs SC Johnson, 1986—. Pres. Johnson Family Found.; mem. bd. dirs. Johnson Fin. Group. Bd. trustees Norfolk Acad. Named one of Forbes' Richest Americans, 2006. Office: SC Johnson 1525 Howe St Racine WI 53403-5011*

JOHNSON-MILLER, CHARLEEN V., educational coordinator; b. Cleve., Ohio, Jan. 17, 1948; d. Leroy and Alice Vivian Carter; m. Sammy Richard Miller, Dec. 24, 1980; 1 child, Patrice. BS in Edn., Ctrl. State U., 1970; MS in Edn., Cleve. State U., 1979; postgrad., Clevel. State U., 1985, John Carrol U., 1983. Permanent tchg. cert. Ohio, 1985. Cleve. Tchrs. Union rep. Cleve. Pub. Schs., 1982—86, cons. tchr., mentor, 1988—93, guidance/drug liaison, 1992—95; lead tchr. Cleve. Mcpl. Schs., 1995—99, grade level chairperson, 1996—2000, safety patrol dir., 1998—, Helping One Student to Succeed/tutor vol. coord., 1999—. Cons. tchr., facilitator human devel. Kent (Ohio) State U., 1983—90; program developer, curriculum planner guidance program Cleve. Pub. Schs., 1985—91, dist. prof. developer, 1993—99. Mem. Present Day Bapt. Ch. Scholar Martha Holden Jenning scholar, Martha Holden Jennings Found., Cleve., 1990. Mem.: Cabinettes, Scrabblers (past pres., v.p., sec.), Alpha Kappa Alpha, Phi Delta Kappa, Inc. (life). Avocations: tennis, bowling, aerobics, kickboxing, line dancing.

JOHNSON-POTOK, FRIEDA T., elementary school educator, consultant; b. Danbury, Conn., Jan. 6, 1950; d. George Louis and Angela Eleanor Sacrider; m. Kenneth Andrew Potok, June 29, 1991; children: Michelle Lynn Witko, Aaron Raul Johnson. BS, Western Conn. State U., Danbury, 1971, MS in Edn., 1975; grad. credits, Fairfield U., Conn., 1984—89. 6th grade English tchr. Ridgefield Bd. Edn., Conn., 1971—85; 7th grade English tchr. E. Ridge Mid. Sch., Conn., 1985—90, 6th grade environ. sci. tchr., 1997—; 5th grade sci. tchr. Ridgebury E. Sch., Conn., 1990—97. Adj. prof. Fairfield U., Conn., 1982—86; prodn. staff mem. Ridgefield Now We're Talking, Conn., 1988—; cons. Beginning Educator Support Tng. Program, Hartford, Conn., 1991—, evaluator, portfolios of beginning tchrs., 1992—, seminar leader, 1992—; cons. Conn. State Dept. Edn., Hartford, Conn., 1991—. Recipient Celebration of Excellence in Sci. award, Conn., 2000. Mem.: NEA (ABCD award 1998), Conn. Edn. Assn. (profl. devel. com. 2000). Lutheran. Avocations: reading, poetry, gardening, golf, swimming. Office: E Ridge Mid Sch 10 E Ridge Rd Ridgefield CT 06877

JOHNSON-SHOCKLEY, WILLIE MAE, retired academic administrator; b. Little Rock, Dec. 5, 1912; d. Wade Hampton and Nancy Jane Johnson. BS, Philander Smith Coll., Little Rock, 1945, DHL (hon.), 1998; MS, Kans. State Coll., Manhattan, 1949. Assoc. registrar Philander Smith Coll., 1945—64, assoc. prof., 1964—79, dir. alumni affairs, 1970—77, dir. alumni affairs emeritus, 2003—. Recipient Disting. Alumni award, Philander Smith Coll., 1974, Svc. award, Nat. Alumni Assn. Philander Smith Coll., 2006, Fin. Com. Chair award, Wesley Chapel United Meth. Ch., 1973, Meritorious Svc. cert., Ark. Dept. Edn., 1974, Dedicated Svc. award, Philander Smith Coll. Alumni Student Govt., 1979. Mem.: AARP, Ark. Gerontol. Soc. (life), Alpha Kappa Mu (life; undergrad. adviser). Methodist. Home: 1200 Commerce St Little Rock AR 72202

JOHNSTON, APRIL M., elementary school educator; b. Hickory, NC, Jan. 7, 1976; d. Michael Avery and Pamela Wakefield Johnston. BS in Elem. Edn., Appalachian State U., Boone, NC, 1998. Tchr. 4th grade math. & sci., 7th grade math Holbrook Mid. Sch., Lowell, NC, 1999—2000; tchr. 8th grade math. West Jr. H.S., Taylorsville, 2000—01; tchr. 6th, 7th and 8th grades math. & sci. Weddington Mid. Sch., 2001—02; tch. 4th grade Bethlehem Elem. Sch., Taylorsville, 2002—. Creator, facilitator Discover Math. and Sci. Camp, Taylorsville, 1999—; chari arts and scis. Bethlehem Sch. Enrichment, 2002—05. Mem.: Nat. Sci. Tchrs. Assn., NC Sci. Tchrs. Assn., Kappa Delta. Avocations: hiking, camping, running. Home: 631 College Ave Lenoir NC 28645 Office: Bethlehem Elem Sch 7900 Hwy 127 Taylorsville NC 28681

JOHNSTON, BETTY PARKER, retired social service worker; b. Wilkes County, N.C., Mar. 1, 1932; d. Leslie Spurgeon and Sarah Beatrice Parker; m. Robert George Johnston, Jan. 6, 1962 (dec.); 1 adopted child, Korrin stepchildren: Gail, Gary, Robert III; m. Delmar Burdell Ronk (dec.). BA, Berea Coll., 1955; MA, Rosary Coll., 1958. Libr. Oak Park (Ill.) Pub. Libr., 1955—58, Riverside (Calif.) Pub. Libr., 1958—61; social svc. worker Riverside County, 1964—66, 1973—95; social worker Santa Barbara (Calif.) County, 1966—73; ret., 1995. Mem. families for kids project Iredell County, Statesville, NC, 1996—99, mem. candle light vigil com., 1998—. Recipient Gold and Bronze medals, Sr. Games, 2003, 2004, Silver medal, 2005. Mem.: Statesville Orotorio Soc., Mitchell C.C. Chorus, Sr. Serenaders (treas., soloist 1995—). Democrat. Avocations: reading, singing, crocheting, cross stitch, cooking. Home: 503 Randa Dr Statesville NC 28625

JOHNSTON, CAROLYN JUDITH, construction engineer; b. Atlanta, Nov. 24, 1961; d. Lynn H. and Doris S. (Lacy) J.; m. Paul William Miller, July 20, 1996; 1 child, Savannah Lee. BS in Constrn. Mgmt., So. Tech. U., 1990; MS in Constrn. Mgmt., Clemson U., 1997. Cert. profl. constructor. Journeyman plumber Quality Mech., Norfolk, Va., 1984-86; asst. supt. R.G.Moore Bldg., Virginia Beach, Va., 1986-87; asst. field engr. Holder Constrn., Atlanta, 1987-89; clk. of works Sharondale Constrn., Atlanta, 1989-90; constrn. engr. Bechtel, Aiken, S.C., 1990-95; project engr. R.W. Allen & Assocs., Augusta, Ga., 1995-97; project mgr. York Internat., Aiken, S.C., 1997-99; sr. project mgr. ACTS, Inc., New Ellenton, S.C., 2000; Bell Co. project engr. U.S. Dept. Energy Project/Tritium Extraction Facility, Aiken, SC, 2001—02; planner, scheduler Handscomb, Faithful & Guild Honda Mfg. Plant, 2002—05; spl. projects mgr. Atlanta airport multiple projects Limbach, Inc., 2005—. Nat. Assn. Women Constrn. scholar, Atlanta, 1990. Mem. Am. Inst. Constructors, Profl. Constrn. Estimators (sec. 1996-98, newsletter editor 1996-98), Nat. Mgmt. Assn., Constrn. Specification Inst. Office: Limbach Inc 600 Bohannon Rd Fairburn GA 30213-2898 Home: 1415 Brawley Cir NE Atlanta GA 30319 Office Phone: 678-479-1000. Personal E-mail: carolyn.johnston@limbachinc.com.

JOHNSTON, CATHERINE VISCARDI, former magazine publisher; Grad., Manhattanville Coll., 1975. With House & Garden mag., 1977; acct. exec. GQ mag., 1980; former pub. Mirabella mag., N.Y.C.; pub. Mademoiselle mag., N.Y.C., 1995-96; sr. v.p. sales & mktg. Conde Nast Publs., 1996—97, exec. v.p. sales & mktg. N.Y.C., 1997—99. Recipient Disting. Alumni award, Manhattanville Coll., 2000.

JOHNSTON, GWINAVERE ADAMS, public relations consultant; b. Casper, Wyo., Jan. 6, 1943; d. Donald Milton Adams and Gwinavere Marie (Newell) Quillen; m. H.R. Johnston, Sept. 26, 1963 (div. 1973); children: Gwinavere G., Gabrielle Suzanne; m. Donald Charles Cannalte, Apr. 4, 1981. BS in Journalism, U. Wyo., 1966; postgrad., Denver U., 1968-69. Editor, reporter Laramie (Wyo.) Daily Boomerang, 1965-66; account exec. William Kostka Assocs., Denver, 1966-71, v.p., 1969-71; exec. v.p. Slottow, McKinlay & Johnston, Denver, 1971-74; pres. The Johnston Group, Denver, 1974-92; chair, CEO JohnstonWells Pub. Rels., Denver, 1992—. Adj. faculty U. Colo. Sch. Journalism, 1988-90. Bd. dirs. Leadership Denver Assn., 1975-77, 83-86, Mile High United Way, 1985-90, Colo. Jud. Inst., 1991-2000, Denver's 2% Club, chair, 1996—, Spring Inst., 1997-2000, Lower Downtown Denver, Inc., Inst. for Internat. Edn., 1998-99, U. Wyo. Found., 2000—, Wyo. Bus. Coun., 2001—, Denver Athletic Club, 2005—. Recipient Athena award Colo. Women's C. of C., 1999. Fellow Am. Pub. Rels. Soc. (pres. Colo. chpt. 1978-79, bd. dirs. 1975-80, 83-86, nat. exec. com. Counselor's Acad. 1988-93, sec.-treas. 1994, pres.-elect 1995, pres. 1996, profl. award Disting. Svc. award 1992); mem. IPREX (pres. N.Am. 2005—), Colo. Women's Forum, Denver Athletic Club (bd. dirs.), Denver Press Club. Republican. Home: 717 Monaco Pky Denver CO 80220-6040 Office: JohnstonWells Pub Rels 1512 Larimer St Ste 720 Denver CO 80202-1610 Business E-Mail: gwin@johnstonwells.com.

JOHNSTON, JANIS CLARK, psychologist, consultant; b. South Bend, Ind., Jan. 5, 1947; d. Robert Dale and Lois Treasure (Whitacre) Clark; m. Mark Emmett Johnston, June 14, 1969; children: Ryan Clark, Megan Gale BA with distinction, Manchester Coll., 1969; MEd, Boston U., 1970, EdD, 1974. Lic. psychologist; cert. sch. psychologist. Psychol. examiner Harvard Pre-Sch. Project, Cambridge, Mass., 1973—74; sch. psychologist Lexington Pub. Schs., Mass., 1972—78; therapist and trainer Acorn Employee Assistance Program, Phila., 1979—81; sch. psychologist Oak Park-River Forest H.S., River Forest, Ill., 1981—89; pvt. practice family therapy and sys. consultation Oak Park, Ill., 1984—. Instr. Boston U., 1974-75; clin. asst. prof. and supr. psychologist Hahnemann Med. Coll. and Hosp., Phila., 1978-81; cons. Acorn, Chgo., 1984-88 Mem. bd. dirs. Oak Park Edn. Found., 1991-94, Parenthesis, 1991-94, DePaul Family Law Bd., 2003—. NDEA Title IV fellow, 1969-72 Mem. APA, Nat. Assn. Sch. Psychologists, Ill. Sch. Psychologists Assn. (region 1 Sch. Psychology Practitioner of Yr. 1984), Psychologists for Social Responsibility, LWV, NOW Avocations: yoga, tai chi, reading, gardening, writing. Office Phone: 708-848-0250.

JOHNSTON, JOSEPHINE ROSE, chemist; b. Cranston, R.I., Aug. 9, 1926; d. Robert and Rose (Varca) Forte; m. Howard Robert Johnston, Mar. 7, 1949 (dec.); 1 child, Kevin Howard. Student, Carnegie Inst., Pitts., 1945—47; BS, Mich. State U., East Lansing, 1972; MA, Mich. State U., 1973; postgrad., MIT, Cambridge, Mass., 1973. Med. technologist South Nassau Cmty. Hosp.,

Rockville Centre, NY, 1947—50, Mich. State U., East Lansing, 1950—53, faculty specialist, 1966—76; dept. pathology Albany Med. Ctr., NY, 1953—54; supr. med. lab. Bulova Watch Co., Jackson Heights, NY, 1954—57; sr. chemistry technologist Mid Island Hosp., Bethpage, NY, 1958—66; sr. rsch. assoc. Uniformed Svcs. Univ., Bethesda, Md., 1976—78, asst. to chmn. dept. physiology, 1978—82, assoc. to chmn., 1982—96; sr. scientist NASA-Spaceline/Archive, Bethesda, 1997—99; owner, operator Slipstream II, 1997—. Author: Patriarch: The Life of T.J. Haddy, 1994; contbr. articles to profl. jours. With Danzinger Found., Lauderdale, Fla., 1990-91; vol. tech. com. fundraising Twinridge Elem. Sch., 1997-98. Mem. Analytical Chem. Soc., Data and Electronic Soc., Internat. Platform Assn., Kiwanis (bd. dirs.). Lutheran. Office: Slipstream II 6813 Woodville Rd Mount Airy MD 21771-7611 Office Phone: 301-829-3509. Business E-Mail: zzman@msn.com.

JOHNSTON, KIMBERLY ANNE, social studies educator; b. West Islip, N.Y., Dec. 31, 1971; d. Judy Ruth (Marion) and Gerald James Skillen; m. Michael James Johnston, July 18, 1999; 1 child, Mackenzie Ruth. MS, L.I. U. C.W. Post Coll., Brookville, N.Y., 1999. Cert. Sch. Dist. Adminstr. N.Y. State Bd. Regents, 2005. Tchr. H.S. Social Studies Baldwin Union Free Sch. Dist., NY, 1997—, chairperson H.S. social studies dept., 2005—. Mem.: L.I. Coun. Social Studies. Avocations: travel, reading. Office: Baldwin Union Free Sch Dist 841 Ethel T Kloberg Dr Baldwin NY 11510 Personal E-mail: johnstonk@baldwin.k12.ny.us.

JOHNSTON, LYNN BEVERLEY, animator; b. Collingwood, Ont., Can., May 28, 1947; d. Mervyn and Ursula (Bainbridge) Ridgway; m. Rod Johnston; children: Aaron, Katherine. Student, Vancouver Sch. Art, 1964-67. Med. illustrator McMaster U. Cartoonist, For Better or For Worse, 1979—; author: David We're Pregnant 1974, Hi, Mom, Hi, Dad, 1975, Do They Ever Grow Up?, 1977, Growing Like a Weed, 1997; 18 collections of comic strips including Middle Age Spread, 1998. Recipient Reuben award Nat. Cartoonist's Soc., 1985; named to disting. Order of Can., 1992; nominated Pulitzer prize for editl. cartooning, 1994. Mem. Nat. Cartoonists Soc. (pres. 1988). Office: Universal Press Syndicate 4520 Main St Kansas City MO 64111 Business E-Mail: businessinfo@fborfw.com.

JOHNSTON, MARGUERITE, retired journalist; b. Birmingham, Ala., Aug. 7, 1917; d. Robert C. and Marguerite (Spradling) J.; m. Charles Wynn Barnes, Aug. 31, 1946; children: Susan, Patricia, Steven, Polly. AB, Birmingham-So. Coll., 1938. Reporter Birmingham News, 1939-44; Washington corr. Birmingham News, Birmingham Age-Herald, London Daily Mirror, 1945-46; columnist Houston Post, 1947-69, fgn. news editor, mem. editorial bd., 1969-85, assoc. editor editorial page, 1972-77, asst. editor editorial page, 1977-85; ret., 1985. Lectr. in field, 1947—; instr. creative writing U. Houston, 1946-47, lectr. feature writing, 1965-66; lectr. Baker Coll., Rice U., 1977-78; del. Asian Am. Women Journalists Conf., Honolulu, 1965, 1st World Conf. Women Journalists, Mexico City, 1969 Author: Public Manners, 1957, A Happy Worldly Abode, 1964, Houston: The Unknown City, 1836-1946, (Winedale Historical Ctr. Ima Hogg award, Otis Lock award East Tex. Historical Assn.), 1991. Mem. Mcpl. Art Commn., 1971—76, Houston Com. Fgn. Rels.; bd. dirs. Tex. Bill of Rights Found., 1962—64, Planned Parenthood, 1953—55, Population Inst., 1985—91. Recipient Theta Sigma Phi Headliner award, 1954, 1st ann. award of merit Houston Com. Alcoholism, 1956, cert. of merit Gulf Coast chpt. Am. Soc. Safety Engrs., 1960, Agnese Carter Nelms award Planned Parenthood, 1968, Sch. Bell award Tex. State Tchrs. Assn., 1974, 75, Gold Key award Nat. Council Alcoholism, 1975, Global award Population Inst., 1981. Mem. Tex. Soc. Architects (hon.), Philos. Soc. Tex., Phi Beta Kappa, Pi Beta Phi

JOHNSTON, MARILYN FRANCES-MEYERS, physician, educator; b. Buffalo, Mar. 30, 1937; BS, Dameon Coll., 1966; PhD, St. Louis U., 1970, MD, 1975. Diplomate Am. Bd. Pathology, Diplomate Nat. Bd. Med. Examiners. Fellow in immunology Washington U., St. Louis, 1970-72; resident in pathology Washington U. Hosp., St. Louis, 1975-77, St. John's Mercy Med. Ctr., St. Louis, 1977-79; research fellow hematology St. Louis U. Sch. Medicine, 1979-80; instr. biochemistry St. Louis U., 1972-75, asst. prof. pathology, 1980-87, assoc. prof., 1987-92, prof., 1992-99, prof. emeritus, 1999—, dir. transfusion svcs., 1980-99; staff pathologist Christian Hosp. Barnes Jewish Christian Hosps., St. Louis, 1999—. Med. dir. Mo./Ill. Regional Red Cross, 1983-88; area chmn. for inspection and accreditation Am. Assn. Blood Banks, Arlington, Va., 1984; med. dir. transfusion svc. Christian Hosps., Barnes-Jewish-Christian Hosp. Sys., St. Louis, 1999—. Author: Transfusion Therapy, 1985. Named Goldberger fellow, AMA, 1979; recipient Transfusion Medicine Acad. award, Nat. Heart, Blood and Lung Inst., 1984—. Mem. Am. Assn. Blood Banks, Am. Assn. Immunologists, Internat. Soc. Blood Transfusion, Am. Soc. Clin. Pathologists, Sigma Xi.

JOHNSTON, MARY HOLLIS, clinical psychologist; b. Woodward, Okla., Oct. 19, 1946; d. James Quincy and Mary Alda (Neighbors) J.; m. Randall R. Rowlett, Mar. 20, 1976 (div. 1982); 1 child, Nathan Rowlett. AB, Carleton Coll., 1968; MA, U. Chgo., 1971, PhD, 1975. Registered psychologist, Ill. Psychologist U. Ill. Med. Sch., Chgo., 1975-81; faculty Erikson Inst., Chgo., 1977-81; pvt. practice psychology Chgo., 1975—; faculty Ctr. for Psychoanalytic Studies, Chgo., 1983-93; lectr. U. Chgo. Med. Ctr., 1993—2003; adj. faculty Ill. Sch. Profl. Psychology, Chgo., 1993—2002. Cons. Virginia Frank Child Devel. Ctr., Chgo., 1975—. Author: Assessing Thought Disorder, 1976. Mem. APA, Soc. for Personality Assessment, World Assn. for Infant Mental Health, Am. Psychoanalytic Assn., Phi Beta Kappa, Sigma Xi.

JOHNSTON, NICKLETT ROSE, research nurse, clinical perfusionist; d. Robert Nick Moriana and Melba Grohe, Roger E. Grohe (Stepfather); m. Roy Edwin Johnston, Aug. 5, 1995; m. Michael Minnella, 1979 (div. 1992); children: Michael Paul Minnella, Anita Marie Minnella. ADN, Cochise Coll., Douglas, AZ, 1979; BSN, U. Phoenix, 2002; MSN, Graceland U., 2005. Cert. clin. perfusionist Tex., 1989, ACLS, Tex., 2002. RN Tucson Med. Ctr., 1982—87; clin. perfusionist, RN, Cardiovasc. Support Svcs., Dallas, 1988—89; clin. perfusionist, RN dept. cardiovascular and thoracic surgery U. Tex. Southwestern Med. Ctr., Dallas, 1989—2003, sr. rsch. nurse dept. cardiovascular and thoracic surgery, 2003—. Mem. ANA, Washington, 1979—90, Am. Soc. for Extra Corporeal Tech., Hattiesburg, Miss., 1989—, knowledge base com., 1999—2000; instr. Am. Heart Assn., Dallas, 1994—95. Author: The Emergency use of Recombinant Hirudin in Cardiopulmonary Bypass (Am. Soc. for Extra Corporeal Tech. Case Report award, 2000), Argatroban in Adult Extracorporeal Membrane Oxygenation, Simplified Solution to Eliminating Electrical Noise During Cardiac Surgery. Mem.: Am. Bd. Perfusionists, Am. Bd. Nursing (licentiate), Theta Tau. Home: 324 Harbor Landing Dr Rockwall TX 75032 Office Phone: 214-645-7728. Personal E-mail: johnstonr@sbcglobal.net.

JOHNSTON, RUTH DARROUGH, retired elementary school educator, counselor; d. Paul Gladstone and Margaret Archdeacon Darrough; m. O. B. Johnston, III, Feb. 27, 1971; children: Eric, David. BS, U. Okla., 1964; MEd, Ctrl. State U., 1969. Tchr. Albuquerque Pub. Schs., 1964—65, Dallas Pub. Schs., 1965—66, Highland Pk. Schs., Dallas, 1966—67, Dept. Defense, Okinawa, 1967—68; counselor WIN program Okla. Employment Security Dept., Okla. City, 1968—71. Pres. Craig County Cancer Bd., Vinita, Okla., 1976—78, Friends of Libr., Vinita, 1982—83; den mother Cub Scouts, Vinita, Okla., 1979—81, 1984—86; pres., re-organized bd. mem. Vinita Pub. Schs. Edn. Found., 2003—; mem. Bd. Higher Edn. & Campus Min. Okla. Annual Conf. Meth. Ch., 1995—99; sec. bd. trustees First Meth. Ch., Vinita, 2006; pres. bd. Vinita Pub. Libr., 2000—02; trustee Okla. Found. Excellence, 1997—2004. Mem.: PEO (pres.), PTA (pres.). Republican. Methodist. Avocations: hiking, reading, exercise, cooking, genealogy. Home: 116 Westwood Ave Vinita OK 74301

JOHNSTON, SUSAN A., lawyer; b. Dec. 16, 1953; BA, Wellesley Coll., 1975; JD, Harvard Univ., 1978. Bar: Mass. 1978. Assoc. Ropes & Gray, Boston, 1978—87, ptnr., 1987—, immediate past head tax & benefits dept. Co-author: Taxation of Regulated Investment Companies and Their Shareholders, 1999; contbr. articles to profl. jours. Mem. Tax Adv. Bd. Investment Co. Inst., 1988—. Mem.: ABA (chmn. Com. Regulated Investment Cos. 1987—89), Boston Bar Assn. (chmn. tax sect. 1985—87, chmn. Internat. Tax Com. 1985—87, chmn. State Tax Com. 1987—89). Office: Ropes & Gray 1 International Pl Boston MA 02110-2624 Office Phone: 617-951-7301. Office Fax: 617-951-7050. Business E-Mail: susan.johnston@ropesgray.com.

JOHNSTON, VIRGINIA EVELYN, retired editor; b. Spokane, Wash., Apr. 26, 1933; d. Edwin and Emma Lucile (Munroe) Rowe; m. Alan Paul Beckley, Dec. 26, 1974; children: Chris, Denise, Rex. Student, Portland C.C., 1964, Portland State U., 1966, 78-79. Proofreader the Oregonian, Portland, 1960—62, teletypesetter operator, 1962—66, operator Photon 200, 1966—68, copy editor, asst. women's editor, 1968—80, spl. sects. editor, 1981—83, editor FOOD day, 1982—2001; ret., 2002. Pres. Matrix Assocs., Inc., Portland, 1975—, chmn. bd., 1979—; past pres. Bones & Brew, Inc. Editor Principles of Computer Systems for Newspaper Mgmt., 1975-76. Cons. Portland Sch. Dist. No. 1, 1978, Dem. Party Oreg., 1969. Democrat. Home: 4140 NE 137th Ave Portland OR 97230-2624 E-mail: ginger1933@comcast.net.

JOHNSTON, YNEZ, artist, educator; b. Berkeley, Calif., May 12, 1920; BFA, U. Calif., Berkeley, 1941, MFA, 1946. Lectr. art U. Calif., Berkeley, 1950—51, Colorado Springs Fine Arts Ctr., 1954—55, Chouinard Art Inst., 1956, Calif. State U., LA, 1966—67, U. Judaism Sch. Fine Arts, LA, 1967, Otis Art Inst., LA, 1978—81; artist-in-residence Fullerton Coll., Calif., 1982. One-man exhbns. include: San Francisco Mus. Art, 1943, Redlands U., 1947, Santa Barbara (Calif.) Mus. Art, 1952, 57, Pasadena (Calif.) Mus. Art, 1955, 62, Colorado Springs (Colo.) Fine Arts Center, 1955, Calif. Palace Legion of Honor, 1956, The O'Hana Gallery, London, 1958, Paul Kantor Gallery, Los Angeles, 1952, 53, 55, 57, 58, 61-62, 63, Beloit (Wis.) Coll., 1961, Barbara Cecil Gallery, New Orleans, 1963, Mex., 1959, Occidental Coll., L.A., 1955, Esther Bear Gallery, 1967, Ball State U., 1967, Stewart-Verde Galleries, San Francisco, 1966, San Francisco Mus. Art, 1967, Mekler Gallery, L.A., 1970-82, 84, 89, Tokyo Shoten Gallery, N.Y.C., 1976, Mitsukoshi Gallery, Tokyo, 1977, Wiener Gallery, N.Y.C., 1977, Worthington Gallery, Chgo., 1982, 85, 88, Mekler Gallery, 1987, 89, Tomlyn Gallery, Fla., 1990-99, 2003, Fresno Mus. Art, 1992, Tortue Gallery, Santa Monica, 1994-96, Tobey Moss Gallery, L.A., 1994, 2003, 05, Kennedy Mus., Athens, Ohio, 1997, Lyman Allyn Mus., New London, Conn., 1998, Schmidt-Bingham Gallery, N.Y.C., 1998, 99, 2001, Santa Cruz Mus., Calif. 1998, Norton-Simon Mus., Pasadena, Calif., 2004, 05; also exhibited numerous group shows including: Whitney Mus. Am. Art, 1953-56, Mus. Modern Art, 1952, 54, Carnegie Inst., 1951, 55, I.F.A. Gallery, Washington, 1963, 100 Prints of the Year, N.Y.C., 1963, Bklyn. Mus., 1966, Vancouver (B.C., Can.) Print Internat., World Print Competition, San Francisco, 1977, Met. Mus., 1978, L.A. County Mus., 1980-81, Drawings from Their Collection, Nat. Gallery Smithsonian, Washington, Wight Gallery UCLA, 1988, Nat. Gallery Modern Art, New Delhi, 1988, Memory Gallery, Nagoya, Japan, 1990, Gallery IV, L.A., 1990, Worcester Art Mus., 1991, Amon Carter Mus., 1991, Women's Art Mus., Washington, 1994, Met. Mus. Fresno, Calif., 1994, Brigitie Haasner Gallery, Wiesbaden, Germany, Norton-Simon Mus., 1999, Traveling Show in China, Macao, Municipal Gallery, Rio Honda Coll., L.A., Taiwan, 2001, Norton Simon Johnston Collection, 2005, Metrospective Show, Worthington Gallery, Chgo., 2005, others; represented in permanent collections numerous museums including, Santa Barbara Mus. Art, Mus. Modern Art, Philbrook Art Center, Los Angeles County Mus., City Art Mus. St. Louis, Whitney Mus. Am. Art, Phila. Mus. Art, San Diego Mus. Art, U. Ill., Met. Mus. Art, Hirshhorn Collection, Herbert F. Johnson Collection (Cornell U.), San Francisco Mus. Art, Otis Art Inst., Milw. Art Center, Worcester Art Mus. (travelling print exhbn. to Terra Mus., Chgo., Amon Carter Mus., Ft. Worth, 1990), Santa Fe Mus. of Fine Art, The Nat. Mus. Israel, Jerusalem, Gift Gardens Bot./Sculpture Pk., Fla., Norton-Simon Mus., numerous schs. and colls., other museums, also pvt. collections. Recipient San Francisco Mus. Art award oil painting, 1946; awards Calif. State Fair, 1951, 61, 62; award etching Los Angeles County Mus., 1950; exhbn. first award Met. Mus. Art, 1952; purchase award Exhbn. Fgn. Artists, Rome, Italy, 1952; purchase award Otis Art Inst., 1963; purchase award Los Angeles Municipal Art Dept., 1967; also commns.; John Simon Guggenheim Found. grantee, 1952; Louis Comfort Tiffany grantee, 1955, 56; Huntington Hartford grantee, 1957; James Phelan grantee, 1958; MacDowell Colony grantee, 1959; Tamarind workshop fellow, 1966; Nat. Endowment Arts painting grantee, 1976, 85 Home and Studio: 579 Crane Blvd Los Angeles CA 90065-5019

JOHNSTONE, JOYCE VISINTINE, education educator; b. Columbus, Ohio, Nov. 12, 1943; d. James Joseph and Virginia (Vogel) Visintine; m. James S. Luckett, Nov. 27, 1965 (dec. May 1969); children: Anne, Robert; m. William E. Kuhn, Sept. 1, 1995. BA, Cath. U. Am., 1965; MA, Butler U., 1974; PhD, Ind. U., 1994. Tchr. Columbus Pub. Schs., 1965-68, Hawaii Pub. Schs., Wahiawa, 1968-69, Montgomery County (Md.), Wheaton, 1969-70; chair edn. dept. Marian Coll., Indpls., 1975-98; Ryan dir. ednl. Outreach U. Notre Dame, South Bend, 1998—, fellow Inst. for Ednl Initiative, 1998—. Dir. Ind. Cath. Prins. Inst., 1989-94. Cath. Prins. Inst. grantee Lilly Endowment, Indpls., 1990, Project Enhance grantee Ind. Bell, Indpls., 1991, 95; Parent Partnership grant Danforth Found., 1995-97. Mem. ASCD, Assn. Tchr. Educators (pres. 1990-91, Turkey Run Outstanding Educator 1990), Ind. Assn. Colls. for Tchr. Edn. (pres., 1990-92, Outstanding Svc. award 1995). Roman Catholic. Office: Inst Ednl Initiative Univ Notre Dame Notre Dame IN 46556

JOHNSTONE, KATHRYN I., lawyer; BS cum laude, Walla Walla Coll., 1979; MBA cum laude, Golden Gate U., 1983; JD cum laude, Harvard U., 1986. CPA Calif., 1981; bar: Calif. 1986. CPA KPMG Peat, Marwick's L.A. tax dept.; ptnr. Morrison & Foerster LLP, co-chmn. fin. group. Mem.: Fin. Lawyers Conf., State Bar Calif. (bus. law sect.), ABA (bus. law sect.), State Bar Calif. (Uniform Comml. Code Com. 1994—97). Office: Morrison Foerster LLP 555 W 5th St Ste 3500 Los Angeles CA 90013 Office Phone: 213-892-5200. Office Fax: 213-892-5454. Business E-Mail: kjohnstone@mofo.com.

JOHNSTONE, MARVA JEAN (JEANIE JOHNSTONE), insurance agency executive; b. Macon, Ga., Aug. 20, 1957; d. Preston Lester and Mable Marie Greenlee; m. Neil Scott Johnstone, June 17, 1978; children: Jeremy S., Aimee M. Grad. high sch., Rutledge, Tenn. Customer svc. rep. Fred S. James Ins., Wichita, Kans., 1979-80; comml. lines rep. Mannings Ins., Wichita, Kans., 1980-84; customer svc. rep. Marsh & McLennan, Wichita, Kans., 1984-85; small bus. mgr. Dorth Coombs Ins., Wichita, Kans., 1985-87; v.p. Fin. Guardian, Wichita, Kans., 1987-90; CEO Asset Builders Ins., El Dorado, Kans., 1990-91; mktg. mgr. Dulaney, Johnston & Priest, Wichita, 1991-2001; sr. mktg. specialist IMA of KS, Inc., Wichita, 2001—. Mem. Ins. Women Wichita (legis. officer 1987-89). Avocation: scuba diving. Office: IMA of KS Inc 250 W Water Wichita KS 67201 Office Phone: 316-266-6257. Personal E-mail: scubajeanie@hotmail.com. Business E-Mail: jeanie.johnstone@imacorp.com.

JOINER, JAMIE A., lawyer; BA, Westminster Coll., 1996; JD, La. State U. Law Ctr., 2000. Bar: Tex. 2000, US Dist. Ct. (so. dist. Tex.) 2001, US Supreme Ct. 2002, US Ct. Internat. Trade 2003, US Dist. Ct. (we. dist. Tex.) 2006. Assoc. Baker Hostetler, Houston. Local coord. Export Legal Assistance Network; mem. Dist. Export Coun. Named a Rising Star, Tex. Super Lawyers mag., 2006. Office: Baker Hostetler 1000 Louisiana St Ste 2000 Houston TX 77002 Office Phone: 713-646-1359. E-mail: jjoiner@bakerlaw.com.*

JOLEY, LISA ANNETTE, lawyer; b. Centralia, Ill., Mar. 30, 1958; BS magna cum laude, Murray State U., 1980; JD magna cum laude, So. Ill. U., 1983. Bar: Ill. 1983, Mo. 1984. Sr. assoc. gen. counsel litig. Anheuser-Busch Companies Inc., St. Louis, v.p., dep. gen. counsel litig., 2000—02, v.p., dep. gen. counsel, 2002—04, v.p., gen. counsel, 2004—. Mem.: Mo. Bar Assn., Ill. State Bar Assn., St. Clair County Bar Assn., Bar Assn. Met. St. Louis, ABA, Pi Sigma Alpha. Office: Anheuser-Busch Companies Inc One Busch Pl Saint Louis MO 63118

JOLIE, ANGELINA, actress; b. LA, June 4, 1975; d. Jon Voight and Marcheline Bertrand; m. Jonny Lee Miller Mar. 3, 1996 (div. Feb. 3, 1999); m. Billy Bob Thorton May 5, 2000 (div. May 27, 2003); children (adopted) Maddox Jolie-Pitt, Zahara Marley Jolie-Pitt; (one child with Brad Pitt) Shiloh Nouvel Jolie-Pitt Student, Strasberg Theatre Inst.; Grad. in Film, NYU. Actress. Former profl. model, London, NYC, LA; good will amb. UN High Commr. for Refugees, Geneva, 2001—. Actor: (films) Lookin' to Get Out, 1982, Cyborg 2, 1993, Angela & Viril, 1993, Hackers, 1995, Without Evidence, 1995, Foxfire, 1996, Mojave Moon, 1996, Love Is All There Is, 1996, True Women, 1997, George Wallace, 1997 (Goldon Globe award for best supporting actress, 1998, nominated Emmy award outstanding supporting actress, 1998), Playing God, 1997, Gia, 1998 (Grand Jury Award for best actress, 1998, Outfest award for outstanding actress, 1998, nominated Emmy award outstanding lead actress, 1998, SAG award for best actress, 1999, Golden Globe for best actress, 1999, Golden Satellite award for best actress, 1999), Hell's Kitchen, 1998, Playing by Heart, 1998 (Nat. Bd. of Rev. award for breakthrough performance, 1998), Pushing Tin, 1999, The Bone Collector, 1999, Girl, Interrupted, 1999 (Academy Award for best supporting actress, 2000, Golden Globe award for best supporting actress, 2000, SAG Award for best supporting actress, 2000, Broadcast Film Critics award for best supporting actress, 2000), Dancing in the Dark, 2000, Gone in Sixty Seconds, 2000, Original Sin, 2001, Life or Something Like It, 2002, Lara Croft Tomb Raider: The Cradle of Life, 2003, Beyond Borders, 2003, Taking Lives, 2004, Shark Tale (voice), 2004, Sky Captain and the World of Tomorrow, 2004, Alexander, 2004, Mr. and Mrs. Smith, 2005, (music videos) Meat Loaf, Lenny Kravits, Antonello Venditti, The Lemonheads. Named one of 50 Most Powerful People in Hollywood, Premiere mag., 2006, 100 Most Influential People, Time Mag., 2006; recipient ShoWest Award for supporting actress of yr., 2000, Cambodian citizenship for conservation work, King Norodom Sihamoni, 2005, Global Humanitarian award, UN Assn. USA, 2005. Office: Creative Artists Agy 9830 Wilshire Blvd Beverly Hills CA 90212*

JOLIS, ANNE, journalist; b. NYC, Feb. 9, 1983; d. John Francis and Carla (Berg) Jolis. B Philosophy and Writing, Carnegie Mellon U., 2004. Vis. scholar Columbia U., NYC, 2001; reporter Gloucester County Times, Woodbury, NJ, 2004—. Freelance book critic Pitts. Post-Gazette, 2003—. Vol. Cross-Cultural Solutions, Sloan, India, 2001, Habitat for Humanity, Pitts., 2003, Salvation Army, Pitts., 2003. Mem.: Phi Beta Kappa, Phi Kappa Phi. Avocations: Middle Eastern dance, banjo, languages. Home: 121 N Broad St Woodbury NJ 08097

JOLIVET, ANNA MARY, retired school system administrator, association executive; b. Tucson, Nov. 24, 1928; d. Joe Turner and Sadie Osborne; m. Clarence Warner Jolivet, June 7, 1952; children: Clarence Michael, Leslie Cecilia. BA in Elem. Edn., U. Ariz., 1950, MEd in Elem. Edn., 1965, EdS in Ednl. Adminstrn., 1972, EdD, 1976. Cer. tchr., prin., supt., Ariz. Tchr. Spring/Dunbar Elem.-Jr. High Sch. Tucson Pub. Schs. Dist. # 1, 1950-59, helping tchr. music dept., tchr. Booth Elem. Sch., 1961-67, prin. Richey Elem. Sch., 1967-70, prin. Cragin Elem. Sch., 1970-75; lectr. Coll. Edn. U. Ariz., Tucson, 1976; adminstrv. asst. learning and staff devel. Tucson Unified Sch. Dist. # 1, 1976-80, dir. planning svcs., 1980-89, asst. supt. high sch. region, 1989; cons. ednl. adminstrn., curriculum devel., 1989—. Organizing dir. Tucson Assn. for Child Care, 1970; mem. adv. bd. U. Ariz. Cultural Affairs; speaker AAUW, Nat. Assn. Sch. Pers., Rocky Mountain Ednl. Rsch. Assn. Conf., Nat. Coun. Adminstrv. Women Edn., Ariz. Black Town Hall, Baha'i Faith/ UN Assn. So. Ariz. Pres. Camp Fire Tucson, Inc., 1969-71, adv. bd.; pres. Downtown Devel. Corp., Tucson, 1988-90, Tucson Partnership, Inc., 1990-92, pres., 1998—; allocations divsn. chmn. United Way Tucson, 1982-84, exec. bd., bd. dirs.; v.p. Am.-Israel Friendship League, Tucson, 1989-98, coord. high sch. youth exch., 1990-96, pres., 1998-2000; exec. com. Tucson Community Found., 1990-96, chair discretionary grants, 1993, pres. bd. dirs., 1996-98; vice chmn. Tucson Pima County Community Profile, 1991-93; chair Sahuaro Coun. Girl Scouts, nominating com.; chair Older Adults Svc. and Info. Sys., 1992-94, Tucson Fund Raising Rev. Bd.; chmn. bd. dirs. Tucson Urban League, 1988-89, guild pres., 1983-84; exec. bd. Tucson Tomorrow; active Ariz. Adv. Health Coun., Tucson Bicentennial Com., Health Systems Agy. Screening com., Goals for Tucson; block grant com. Ariz. Dept. Health, chair proposal revs. 1981, 82; chmn. subcom. Crippled Children's Svc.; trustee Mt. Calvary Bapt. Ch., Tucson Mus. Art, 1988-92, 94—, supt. Sunday Sch., 1994—; bd. dirs. Ariz. Acad. Phoenix, 1983-86, 96—, YWCA, N.Y.C., 1982-94; active Tucson/Pima Libr.; nat. bd. dirs. YWCA of U.S.A., N.Y.C., 1982-94, past mem. nat. nominating com.; past bd. dirs. YWCA Tucson, past chmn. pers.; v.p. Pima Coun. on Aging, 1999—, pres.; mem. Coun. on Aging Found.; chair fundraising & exec. com. UA Womens Plaza of Honor, bd. mem. Ariz. Town Hall, 1995, mem.exec. com. 1998-2004, vice chair, Ariz.Town Hall, 2005. Recipient Women on Move award, YWCA Tucson, 1982, Tucson Met. C. of C., 1996, Woman of Yr., Alumni Achievement award U. Ariz., 1983, Phenomenal Woman award U. Ariz. Black Alumni, 1990, Ptnrs. Democracy award Am.-Israel Friendship League, 1997, U. Ariz. Alumni Centennial award, 1998, Outstanding Educator award Coll. Edn., U. Ariz., 2001. Mem. NEA, ASTD, ASCD (state sec. 1981-82, state pres. 1982-83, nat. bd. dirs. 1982-83, exec. coun. 1984-87), Coun. Ednl. Facility Planners Internat. (interface project), Nat. Assn. Elem. Sch. Prins., Nat. Coun. Adminstrv. Women in Edn., Am. Ednl. Rsch. Assn., Am. Assn. Sch. Adminstrs., Ariz. Edn. Assn., Ariz. Sch. Adminstrs., Inc. (region 5 legis. rep.), NAACP (life), Exec. Women's Coun. (v.p. 1992-93), Pi Lambda Theta (past v.p. Alpha Alpha chpt.), Delta Kappa Gamma, Phi Delta Kappa, Alpha Delta Kappa, Alpha Kappa Alpha (past mem. nat. constn. com., past far western region parliamentarian, chair far west regional conf. com. 1986, past pres. Tucson chpt., past treas., undergrad. acad. scholarship). Democrat. Avocations: travel, reading, walking, cooking. Home: 8818 E Harborage Dr Tucson AZ 85710-6225

JOLLES, JANET K. PILLING, lawyer; b. Akron, Ohio, Sept. 5, 1951; d. Paul and Marjorie (Logue) Kavanaugh; m. Martin Jolles, Mar. 6, 1987; children: Madeleine Sloan Langdon Jolles, Jameson Samuel Rhys Jolles. BA, Ohio Wesleyan U., 1973; JD, U. Mo., 1976; LLM, Villanova U., 1985. Bar: Pa. 1976, U.S. Tax Ct. 1976, U.S. Dist. Ct. (ea. dist.) Pa. 1976, Ohio 1996. Atty. Schnader, Harrison, Segal & Lewis, Phila., 1976-83; gen. counsel Kistler-Tiffany Cos., Wayne, Pa., 1983-95; lawyer Janet Kavanaugh Pilling Jolles & Assocs., Berea, Ohio, 1996-99; v.p. First Union Trust Co., Wilmington, Del., 1999—2002, Wachovia Trust Co., Wilmington, 2002—. Mem. Estate Planning Coun. Del., Wilmington Tax Group, Phila. Estate Planning Coun., Estate Planning Coun. Cleve., De Bankers Assn., Estate Planning Coun. Del. Mem.: ABA, Wilmington Women in Bus., Pa. Bar Assn., Phila. Bar Assn. (probate sect., tax sect.), Cuyahoga County Bar Assn., Cleve. Bar Assn., Ohio State Bar Assn., Berea Women's League, Phi Beta Kappa, Phi Delta Phi. Office: 505 Carr Rd 2d Fl Wilmington DE 19809 Business E-Mail: janet.jolles@wachovia.com.

JOLLOFF, NILDA ELIZABETH, art educator, artist; b. Bronx, Sept. 2, 1952; d. Frank Martinez, Jr. and Carmen (Del Arroyo) Martinez; m. William F. Jolloff, Jr., Aug. 30, 1969; children: Sandra Buckland, William F. III, Katherine Wagoner. A in Arts & Scis. cum laude, Blue Ridge CC, 2001; BA with distinction, Mary Baldwin Coll., 2003. Owner Frame It Yourself/You're the Framer, Matawan, NJ, 1979—92; art instr. Staunton/Augusta Fine Art Ctr., Va., 1995—2001, Blue Ridge CC, Weyers Cave, 1998—; art tchr. Shelburne Mid. Sch., Staunton, 2003—; after sch. site dir. Augusta County Parks & Recreation, Verona, 1995—2002; tchr. asst. Mary Baldwin Coll., Staunton, 2003. Art cons. L&S Framing & Stained Glass, Staunton, 1992—. Solo exhibition, Magical Realism, Augusty County Library, Fishersville, 2001, Blue Ridge CC, Weyers Cave, 2001, Works on Paper/Cultural Absorption, Hunt Gallery, Staunton, 2003, exhibited in group shows at The Virtual Art Gallery, Blue Ridge C.C., Weyers Cave, Va., 2000, The Anthem Project: Remembrance of 9/11, U. Va., 2002, Print Making Art Exch., U. Va./Mary

Baldwin Coll., 2003, Art in the Park, Staunton, 2005, Transitions: Seeds of Change, 2005, juried show, Hunt Gallery, Staunton, 2002, 2003. Sec. Student Fine Art Assn. Mary Baldwin Coll., Staunton, 2002—03; advisor Talented & Gifted Programs Staunton City Schs., Staunton, 2003—, found. Art For Humanity, 2004—. Recipient Honors Scholar award, Phi Theta Kappa, Cath. U. Am., 1999, Best Show Mixed Media, Augusta County, Fishersville, 2003, Best Show Oils, 2004, 1st Place Mixed Media, 2004. Mem.: Nat. Mus. Women Arts, Nat. Mus. Am. Indian, Nat. Edn. Assn., Staunton Augusta Art Ctr., Phi Theta Kappa Internat. Honor Soc. (Three Star Chpt. award 2000). Avocations: painting, drawing, printmaking, reading, writing. Home: 301 Thompon St Staunton VA 24401

JOLLS, CHRISTINE MARGARET, law educator; b. White Plains, NY, Oct. 1, 1967; d. Robert Talcott and Cecelia (Thurmaier) Jolls; m. Ranier Gavlilk; 2 children. BA in English & Quantitative Economics, Stanford U., 1989; JD, Harvard U., 1993; PhD in Economics, MIT, 1995. Bar: Mass. 1997. Jud. clk. to Judge Stephen F. Williams U.S. Ct. Appeals DC Cir., 1995—96; jud. clk. to Justice Antonin Scalia US Supreme Ct., 1996—97; asst prof. law Harvard Law Sch., Cambridge, Mass., 1994—95, 1997—2001, prof., 2001—, named vice dean scholarship & intellectual life, 2003; prof. of law Yale Law Sch., New Haven, 2006. Contbr. articles to univ. law reviews Stanford U., Harvard U., U. Chicago, 1998—2001; mem. editl. bd. Am. Law and Economics Rev., New Haven, 1999—; reporter Restatement of Employment Law, Phila., 2001—; fellow Mind/Brain/Behavior Interfaculty Initiative Harvard U.; vice dean Harvard Law Sch's for Scholarship and Intellectual Life, 2003—04. Dir. Prog. in Law and Economics Nat. Bureau of Economic Rsch. 2006-, (co-dir. 2003-2006). Dean's teaching award 2003, John M. Olin Prize in Law and Economics. Fellow: Nat. Bur. Econ. Rsch.; mem.: Phi Beta Kappa. Office: Yale Law Sch 127 Wall St New Haven CT 06520 Office Phone: 617-496-4643, 203-432-1958. Office Fax: 617-495-4299. Business E-Mail: christine.jolls@yale.edu.*

JOLLY, BARBARA LEE, home healthcare professional; b. Central City, Nebr., Dec. 23, 1952; d. Louis Carl and Elizabeth (Mesner) Lindahl; m. William C. Zimmerman, June 2, 1973 (div. Aug. 1986); m. Daniel Ehs Jolly,May 7, 1988 (div. Mar. 1996). BS in Pharmacy, U. Mo., Kansas City, 1976, MPA, 1984. Registered pharmacist. Pharmacy supr. Truman Med. Ctr., Kansas City, Mo., 1976-87; dispensing dept. mgr. Nursing Ctr. Svcs., Hilliard, Ohio, 1988-90; v.p. Pharmacy Systems, Inc., Dublin, Ohio, 1990-96; chief pharmacist Integrity Healthcare Svcs., Inc., Columbus, Ohio, 1996—2000, clin. pharmacist cardiology, 2000—03, dir. clin. svcs., 2004—. Trustee Ohio Cancer Pain Initiative, Columbus, 1987-2002. Bd. dir. Open Ch., Inc., Columbus, 1991-2000; mem. social svcs. bd. Salvation Army, Kansas City, 1986-88; co-dir. Siouxland Hotline, Inc., Sioux City, Iowa, 1972-73; med. missionary, Honduras, 1992-96; del. to state conv. Easter Seals of Ohio, Columbus, 1989-91. Recipient Outstanding Vol. award Salvation Army, Kansas City, 1987. Mem. Am. Soc. Hosp. Pharmacists, Ohio Soc. Hosp. Pharmacists, Ohio Pharmacists Assn., Ky. Soc. Hosp. Pharmacists, Midwest Pain Soc., Pi Alpha Alpha (pres. 1983-84). Mem. Cmty. Bible Ch. Mem. Christian Ch. Avocations: international travel, reading, international business development, real estate development. Home: 507 Grand Vista Pl Louisville KY 40243-1832 E-mail: joll653@bellsouth.net.

JOLLY, MEENAKSHI, rheumatologist; arrived in U.S., 1994; m. Neeraj Jolly. MBBS, Med. Coun. of India, India, 1991; MS in clin. profl., U. Chgo., 2004. Cert. Am. Bd. Internal Medicine (cert. in rheumatology), Clin. rsch. trng. program U. Chgo., 2003. Sect. chief, rheumatology Christ Med. Ctr., Chgo., 2003—06; asst. prof. clin. medicine U. Ill., Chgo.; asst. prof. Rush U. Med. Ctr., Chgo., 2006—. Cons., tchg., clin. rsch., mentoring Christ Med. Ctr., Oaklawn, Ill., 2003—. Mem.: Arthritis Found., Lupus Found., Am. Coll. of Rheumatology. Achievements include research in rheumatic issues; quality of life in lupus. Office Phone: 312-563-2924. Personal E-mail: meenakshijolly_1@hotmail.com. E-mail: meenaksh_jolly@rush.com.

JONAS, AMY JOY, music company executive; b. LI, Oct. 24, 1964; d. Peter Stephen and Gloria Jonas. BSBA, Calif. State U., LA, 1988; MBA, Pepperdine U., LA, 2003; postgrad., Glendale U., LA, 2003—. Copyright mgr. Chrycalis Music Group, LA, 1989—91; owner, program mgr. AJ Jonas Mgmt., 1991—95; copyright mgr. Warner Chappell Music, Inc., 1995—2003, Universal Music Group, 2003—. Vol. Make a Wish Found., LA, 2003, Rec. for Blind and Dyslexic, 2003. Jewish.

JONAS, CYNTHIA, social studies educator; d. Coit Eugene and Ann Broome Auten; m. Marion Gadsden Jonas, Oct. 17, 1968; children: Christopher Brent, Meredith Jonas Clinton, Stephanie Anne. BA, Winthrop U., Rock Hill, SC, 1971. Cert. tchr. SC Dept. Edn., 1971. Pianist Ctrl. Bapt. Ch., York, SC, 1965—; tchr. York Jr. H.S., 1971—, social studies dept. chairperson, 1975—. Named Tchr. of Yr., York Sch. Dist. #1. Mem.: SC Geography Alliance, SC Coun. for the Social Studies, Yorkville Hist. Soc. (bd. mem. 2001—05). Baptist. Avocations: crocheting, knitting, travel. Office: York Junior High 1280 Johnson Rd York SC 29745 Office Phone: 803-684-5008. Business E-Mail: cjonas@york.k12.sc.us.

JONAS, JEANIE LYNN, elementary school educator; b. Memphis, Tenn., Jan. 10, 1943; d. Bob Lynn Smith, Mary Jeanette Smith; m. Larry Alden Jonas. BS in Phys. Edn., Blue Mountain Coll., 1965; MS in Phys. Edn., Ark. State U., 1968. Phys. edn. specialist Kennett Pub. Schs., Mo., 1965—67; grad. asst. Ark. State U., Jonesboro, 1967—68; elem. phys. edn. specialist Marked Tree Schs., Ark., 1968—69, Dept. Def. Overseas Dependent Schs., Guantanamo Bay, Cuba, 1970—71; co-recreational intermural dir. La. State U., Baton Rouge, 1973—77; camp/field dir. Girl Scouts of Am., Baton Rouge, 1977—78; adapted phys. edn. specialist East Baton Rouge Parish Schs., 1978—84; elem. phys. edn. specialist Dept. of Def. Overseas Dependent Schs., Stuttgart, Germany, 1984—95; adapted phys. edn. Specialist East Baton Rouge Parish Schs., 1995—97; phys. edn. specialist Silverside Acad., Baton Rouge, 1997—99; adapted phys. edn. specialist East Baton Rouge Parish Schs., 2000—pres. Cons., presenter phys. edn. programs for children P.E. is More Than Duck, Duck, Goose, Baton Rouge, 1995—2002; personal fitness trainer Womne's Hosp. Fitness Ctr., Baton Rouge, 1995—. Adult activities dir. Unitarian Ch., Baton Rouge, 1997—2000; chair overpass cleanup South Side Civic Assn., Baton Rouge, 2001—02; track and field official La. State U. Track Assn., Baton Rouge, 1995—2001. Mem.: Am. Assn. Health Phys. Edn., Recreation and Dance (La. State phys. best coord. 1999—2002), La. Assn. Health, Phys. Edn., Recreation and Dance (chairperson presch. and adapted phys. edn. 1998—2000), La. Assn. Health, Physical Edn., Recreation and Dance (exhibit mgt. state conf. 2001—, La. Adapted Phys. Edn. Tchr. of Yr. 2000, fitness program for handicapped students grant 1997, study grant 1999). Unitarian Universalist. Avocations: running, weightlifting, travel, cooking, gardening. Home: 1630 Carl Ave Baton Rouge LA 70808 Office: 9765 Cuyhanga Pkwy Baton Rouge LA 70815-1308 Office Phone: 225-241-4921. Personal E-mail: Jonas1134@cox.net.

JONAS, JOAN (JOAN AMERMAN EDWARDS), artist; b. NYC, July 13, 1936; m. Gerald Jonas, 1959. BA in art history, Mt. Holyoke Coll., 1958; studied sculpture, Boston Mus. Fine Arts, 1958—61; MFA in sculpture, Columbia U., 1965. Joined faculty MIT, Cambridge, Mass., 2000, prof. dept. architecture, prof., acting dir. visual arts program. Exhibitions include Aspects de l'art actuel presentes par la Galerie Sonnabend, Musee Galliera, Paris, 1973, Stage Sets, Inst. Contemporary Art, U. Pa., Phila., 1976, Three Tales, Documenta 6, Kassel, Germany, 1977, Joan Jonas: The Juniper Tree, Stedelijk Mus., Amsterdam, 1979, Whitechapel Art Gallery, London, 1979, Music, Sound, Language Theater, Stedelijk Mus., Amsterdam, 1981, Double Lunar Dogs, Contemporary Arts Mus., Houston, 1981, Other Realities - Installations for Performance, 1981, Upside Down and Backwards, Documenta 7, Kassel, Germany, 1982, He Saw Her Burning, DAAD Galerie, Berlin, 1984, Revolted by the thought of known places.Sweeney Astray, Kunst-Werke, Berlin, 1992, Joan Jonas: Works 1968-1994, Stedelijk Mus., Amsterdam, 1994, Props: Works 1994-1997, Pat Hearn Gallery, NYC, 1997, In the Shadow a Shadow, 1999, Drawings, Reinhard Hauff Gallery, Stuttgart, Germany, 2000, Joan Jonas: Film and Video Work, 1968-76, Dia Ctr. for Arts, NYC, 2000, Joan Jonas: Performance, Video, Installation, 1968-2000, Galerie der Stadt, Stuttgart, Germany, 2000—01, Neue Galerie fur Bilden Kunst, Berlin, 2003, Joan Jonas: Video Retrospective, Mus. Carillo Gil, Mex. City, 2003, Joan Jonas: Five Works, Queens Mus. Art, NYC, 2003 (Award for Best Exhbn. of Time Based Art, Internat. Assn. Art Critics/USA, 2005), Lines in the Sand, Rosamund Felsen Gallery, Santa Monica, 2003, The Renaissance Soc., Chgo., 2004, The Shape, the Scent, the Feel of Things, 2004, film and videography, Wind, 1968, Paul Revere, 1971, Mirror Check, 1971, Vertical Roll, 1972, Organic Honey's Visual Telepathy, 1972, Duet, 1972, Left Side Right Side, 1972, Songdelay, 1973, Three Returns, 1973, Barking, 1973, Two Women, 1973, Disturbances, 1974, Merlo, 1974, Glass Puzzle, 1974, May Windows, 1976, Good Night, Good Morning, 1976, I Want to Live in the Country (And Other Romances), 1977, Upside Down and Backwards, 1981, Double Lunar Dogs, 1983, He Saw Her Burning, 1983, Big Market, 1984, Brooklyn Bridge, 1988, Volcano Saga, 1989. Recipient Polaroid Award for Video, 1987, Maya Deren Award for Video, Am. Film Inst., 1988, Hyogo Prefecture Mus. Modern Art Prize, Japan Internat. Video Art Festival, Anonymous Was a Woman Award, 1998. Office: MIT Visual Arts Program 265 Massachusetts Ave N51-315 Cambridge MA 02139

JONAS, MARY, mental health counselor; b. Waterbury, Conn., May 23, 1961; d. Joseph Peter and Barbara Anne (Stolfi) Szczepanski; m. Marc Charles Jonas, Feb. 6, 1988. BA, U. Miami, 1982; MS, St. Thomas U., 1990. lic. mental health counselor. Dir., counselor YMCA, Miami, Fla., 1983-84; domestic violence, lead victim, witness counselor Office of the State's Atty., Miami, 1984-89; pvt. practioner Inst. for Family Therapy, 1992—. Mem., cons. Adult Protection Team Spl. Task Force, 1987-90, Dade/Monroe Coalition on Aging, 1987-90, Developmentally Disabled Adults Task Force, 1988-89, Domestic Violence Task Force, 1987-89. Facilitator Parents of Murdered Children, 1986—. Recipient Polish Nat. Alliance scholarship, 1979, Cert. of Appreciation MADD, 1986. Mem.: ARC, FMHCA, APA, AACD, ACA, AAMFT.

JONAS, RUTH HABER, psychologist; b. Tel Aviv, Aug. 24, 1935; d. Fred S. and Dorothy Judith (Bernstein) Haber; m. Saran Jonas, Sept. 16, 1956; children: Elizabeth, Frederick. AB, Barnard Coll., 1957; MA, New Sch. for Social Rsch., 1977, PhD, 1987; grad. psychotherapy and psychoanalysis, NYU, 1996. Lic. psychologist, N.Y. 1st and 2d yr. intern clin. psychology NYU Med. Ctr.-Bellevue Hosp., N.Y.C., 1985-87; postdoctoral rsch. fellow NYU Med. Ctr., N.Y.C., 1987-88; clin. instr. psychiatry NYU Sch. Medicine, N.Y.C., 1987, clin. asst. prof. psychiatry, 1991; sr. psychologist forensic svc. Bellevue Hosp., N.Y.C., 1988—; pvt. practice psychotherapy N.Y.C., 1988—. Fellow Am. Orthopsychiat. Assn.; mem. APA, N.Y. State Psychol. Soc., Manhattan Psychol. Assn., Am. Heart Assn. (fellow stroke coun.). Office: 200 E 33d St Ste 2J New York NY 10016-4827 Office Phone: 212-684-2721.

JONAS, TINA WESTBY, federal agency administrator; BA, Ariz. State U.; MA, Georgetown U. Sr. budget examiner, intelligence br. nat. security divisn. U.S. Dept. Def., Washington, 1991—95, dep. under sec. fin. mgmt., 2001—02; mem. appropriations com., def. subcom. U.S. Ho. Reps., Washington, 1995—2001; asst. dir. fin., CFO FBI, Washington, 2002—04; under sec. (comptr), CFO U.S. Dept. Def., Washington, 2004—. Recipient Disting. Pub. Service medal, US Dept. Def. Office: US Dept Def 1100 Defense Pentagon Washington DC 20301

JONDAHL, TERRI ELISE, importing and distribution company executive; b. Ukiah, Calif., May 6, 1959; d. Thomas William and Rebecca (Stewart) J. AA in Bus. Adminstrn., Mendocino Coll., 1981; BA in Adminstrn. and Mgmt., Columbia Pacific U., 1993. Office systems analyst County of Mendocino, Ukiah, 1980-83; micro systems analyst Computerland of Annapolis, Md., 1983-84; controller Continental Mfg. Inc., Nacogdoches, Tex., 1984-87, mktg. mgr., 1987-89, dir. sales and mktg., 1989-95; exec. v.p., chief oper. officer CAB Inc., Oakwood, Ga., 1995—2002; CEO Cab Inc., 2002—. Co-author: National Federation of Business & Professional Women Local Organization Revitalization Plan, 1989. Mem. adv. bd. Gwinnett County Tax Commn. Mem.: NAFE, Am. Bus. Women's Assn., Ukiah Bus. and Profl. Women (pres. 1981—82), Nacogdoches Bus. and Profl. Women (pres. 1987—88), Tex. Fedn. Bus. and Profl. Women (state pres. 1994—95), Com. of 200 Orgns., Gwinnett Chamber Chmn.'s Club (bd. dirs.), Leadership Gwinnett, Hall County C. of C., Nacogdoches County C. of C. Home: 6009 Lanier Heights Cir Buford GA 30518 Office: CAB Inc 4161 Chamblee Rd Oakwood GA 30566-3518

JONES, A. ELIZABETH, corporate communications specialist, former federal agency administrator; b. Munich, May 6, 1948; d. William Charles Jones and Sara Demarest (Ferris); m. Thomas Anthony Homan, 1977 (div.); m. Donald Andrew Ruschman, 2000; 2 children. BA in history, Swarthmore Coll., 1970; studied Arabic, in Beirut, Tunis and Cairo, 1975—77; in Internat. Rels., Boston U., 1986. Joined Fgn. Svc., 1970; fgn. svc. post Kabul, Afghanistan, 1971—72; pub. affairs officer Near East and South Asia Bur., 1972—73; polit. officer Cairo, 1973—75, Amman, Jordan, 1977—79; dep. prin. officer U.S. Interests Sect., Baghdad, Iraq, 1979—80; dep. chief mission Islamabad, Pakistan, 1988—92; Lebanon desk officer, 1981—83; dep. dir. for Lebanon, Jordan, Syria, and Iraq, 1983—84; head econ./comml. sect. US Mission, West Berlin, 1985—88; dep. chief mission US Embassy, Bonn, Germany, 1992—93; exec. asst. to sec. US Dept. State, Washington, 1993—94, US amb. to Rep. of Kazakhstan, 1995—98, prin. dep. asst. sec. Bur. Near Eastern Affairs Washington, 1998—2000; sr. advisor Caspian Basin Energy Diplomacy, 2000—01; asst. sec. for European & Eurasian affairs US Dept. State, Washington, 2001—05; exec. v.p. APCO Worldwide, Washington, 2005—. Bd. dirs. AE Jones LLC, 2005—. Office: APCO Worldwide 700 12th St NW Ste 800 Washington DC 20005 Office Phone: 202-478-3559. Business E-Mail: bjones@apcoworldwide.com.

JONES, AMANDA BLAKEY, actor; b. Topsfield, Mass., Jan. 24, 1975; d. Robert Bruce and Jane Katherine Jones. BA, Dartmouth Coll., Hanover, N.H., 1997. Actor / co. mem. Jean Cocteau Repertory, N.Y.C., 2001—. Actor(Elsie Dorfman): (play) Walking Down Broadway - Mint Theater, (Elaine) Arsenic and Old Lace - Depot Theatre, (Dona Rosita) Dona Rosita the Spinster - Jean Cocteau Repertory, (woman) (short film) The Fisherboy, (Suzanne) (play) The Marriage of Figaro - Jean Cocteau Repertory, (boy and others) Henry V - Jean Cocteau Repertory, (Myrrhine) Lysistrata - Jean Cocteau Repertory, (Candida) Candida - Jean Cocteau Repertory, (Gillian) Bell Book and Candle - Sierra Repertory, (Solange) The Maids - Jean Cocteau Repertory, (Sonya) Uncle Vanya - Jean Cocteau Repertory, (Cecily) The Importance of Being Earnest - Jean Cocteau Repertory, (Raina) Arms and the Man - Jean Cocteau Repertory, (Minnie) Engaged - Depot Theatre, (Madge) Picnic - Sierra Repertory Theatre. Mem.: Actors Equity. Personal E-mail: missamandajones@gmail.com.

JONES, ANGELA M., secondary school educator, elementary school educator; b. Gary, Ind., Nov. 19, 1954; d. William Henry Jones and Marie Louise (Reed) Jones-Stacker. BS, Tuskegee U., 1977. Tutor, mgr. computer lab. Gary Cmty. Sch. Dist., 1980—, bldg. tech. asst., 2002—04, preschool tchg. asst., 2004—06. Mem.: NAFE, Gary Tchrs. Union (bldg. rep. 1995—2002), Tuskegee Alumni Club. Avocations: penpal writing, sewing, reading, window shopping, contests. Home: 5721 Hemlock Ave Apt 11 Gary IN 46403-1017

JONES, ANITA KATHERINE, computer scientist, educator; b. Ft. Worth, Mar. 10, 1942; d. Park Joel and Helene Louise (Voigt) J.; m. William A. Wulf, July 1, 1977; children: Karin, Ellen. AB in Math., Rice U., 1964; MA in English, U. Tex., 1966; PhD in Computer Sci., Carnegie Mellon U., 1973, PhD in Sci. and Tech. (hon.), 2000. Programmer IBM, Boston, Washington, 1966-69; assoc. prof. computer sci. Carnegie-Mellon U., Pitts., 1973-81; founder, v.p. Tartan Labs. Inc., Pitts., 1981-87; free-lance cons. Pitts., 1987-88; prof., head computer sci. dept. U. Va., Charlottesville, 1988-93, prof., 1997—, univ. prof., 1998—, Lawrence A. Quarles prof. engring. and applied sci., 1999; dir. def. rsch. and engring. Dept. Def., Washington, 1993-97. Mem. Def. Sci. Bd., Dept. Def., 1985-93, 98—; mem. sci. adv. bd. USAF, 1980-85; governing bd. Nat. Sci. Found.; vice-chair governing bd. NSF, 1998-2004; bd. dirs. Sci. Applications Internat. Corp., InQTel; trustee Mitre Corp., 1989-93, chair Va. Rsch. and Technology Adv. Commn., 1999-2002, Commonwealth of Va. Advs. Commn.; mem. corp. Charles Stark Draper Labs., 1999—; bd. dirs. BBN Techs. Editor: Perspectives on Computer Science, 1977, Foundations of Secure Computation, 1971. Recipient Air Force Meritorious Civilian Svc. award, 1985, Medal for Disting. Pub. Svc. Dept. of Def., 1996, Disting. Svc. award Computing Rsch. Assn., 1997, Augusta Ada Lovelace award, Assn. Women in Computing, 2004. Fellow IEEE, AAAS, Assn. Computing Machinery (editor-in-chief Transactions on Computer Sys. 1983-91), Am. Acad. Arts and Scis.; mem. Nat. Acad. Engring., MIT Corp., Sci. Found. of Ireland (bd. dirs. 2000-2003), Sigma Xi. Avocation: gardening. Office Phone: 434-982-2224. Business E-Mail: jones@virginia.edu.

JONES, ANN, writer, photographer; b. Eau Claire, Wis., Sept. 3, 1937; d. Oscar Trygve and Miriam Berenice (Rufsvold) Slagsvol. BS, U. Wis., 1960, PhD, 1970; MA, U. Mich., 1961. Tchr. writing and womens studies CCNY, N.Y.C., 1970-73, U. Mass., Amherst, 1973-75, Mt. Holyoke Coll., South Hadley, Mass., 1986-97. Author: Uncle Tom's Campus, 1973, Women Who Kill, 1980, Everyday Death, 1985, Next Time, She'll Be Dead, 1994, 2d edit., 2000, Looking for Lovedu, 2001, Kabul in Winter, 2006; co-author: When Love Goes Wrong, 1992 (Literary Guild). Mem. Authors Guild, PEN Am. Ctr., Nat. Writers Union.

JONES, ANNA, elementary school educator; b. Midland, Tex., July 30, 1980; d. Bryan Hunter and Cynthia Kim Wimberly; married, Oct. 6, 2001; 1 child, Jocelyne Marie. BS in Interdisciplinary Studies, U. North Tex., 2002. Cert. tchr. Tex. Mid. sch. sci. tchr. St. Ann's Sch., Midland, 2003—. Grantee, KC, 2005—06. Mem.: NSTA. Roman Catholic. Avocations: reading, writing, travel, piano. Office Phone: 432-684-4563. Personal E-mail: acj730@hotmail.com.

JONES, BARBARA CHRISTINE, linguist, educator, creative arts designer; came to U.S., 1964, naturalized, 1971; d. Martin and Margarete (Roth-Rommel) Schulz von Hammer-Parstein; m. Robert Dickey, 1967 (div. 1980); m. Raymond Lee Jones, 1981. Student, U. Munich, 1961, Philomatique de Bordeaux, France, 1962; BA in German, French, and Speech, Calif. State U., Chico, 1969, MA in Comparative Internat. Edn., 1974. Cert. secondary tchr., C.C. instr., Calif. Fgn. lang. tchr. Gridley Union H.S., Calif., 1970-80, home econs., decorative arts instr., cons. Calif., 1970-80, English study skills instr. Calif., 1974-80, ESL coord., instr. Punjabi, Mex. Ams. Calif., 1970-72, curriculum com. chmn. Calif., 1970-80; program devel. adv. Program Devel. Ctr. Supt. Schs., Butte County, Oroville, Calif., 1975-77; opportunity tchr. Esperanza H.S., Gridley, Calif., 1980-81, Liberty H.S., Lodi, Calif., 1981-82, resource specialist coord., 1981-82; Title I coord. Bear Creek Ranch Sch., Lodi, Calif., 1981-82, instr., counselor, 1982-83; sub. tchr. Elk Grove (Calif.) Unified, 1982-84. Freelance decorative arts and textiles designer, 1982-95; internat. heritage and foods adv. AAUW, Chico, Calif, 1973-75; lectr. German, Schreiner Coll., Kerrville, Tex., 1993; workshop dir. Creative Arts Ctr., Chico, 1972-73; workshop dir., adv. Bus. Profl. Women's Club of Gridley, 1972-74; mem. Cowboy Artists Mus., Kerrville, 1996-99; v.p. Golden State Mobile Home League, Sacramento, 1980-82; mem. publicity Habitat for Humanity, Kerrville br., 1992-94. Weavings-wall hangings (1st pl. 10 categories, Silver Dollar Fair, Chico, Calif., 1970). Removal vol. Supreme Ct. Ariz. Foster Care Rev. Bd., 2003—06. Mem.: AAUW (publicity dir. cultural activities Kerrville br. 1991—92), Am. Assn. German Tchrs., German Texan Heritage Soc., Turtle Creek Social Cir. (pioneer 1992—99), USAR Non-Commd. Officer's Assn. (ednl. adv. 1984—86), Am. Cancer Soc. (Tex. publicity 1992—95), Kingman Social Club (membership chair 2001—), United European Am. Club, Kappa Delta Pi. Avocations: textile design, swimming, travel, real estate, mosaics. Home: 3350 Pasadena Ave Kingman AZ 86401-5046

JONES, BARBARA ELLEN, neurologist, educator; b. Phila., Dec. 19, 1944; d. Charles and Ella (Yeager) J.; m. John Gordon Galaty, Aug. 12, 1972; 1 child, James Gordon. BA, U. Del., 1966, MA, 1969, PhD, 1971. Rsch. assoc., asst. prof. U. Chgo., 1972-77; asst. prof. dept. neurology and neurosurgery McGill U., Montreal, 1977-82, assoc. prof., 1982-88, prof., 1989—. Vis. lectr. U. Nairobi, Kenya, 1974-75; vis. scientist Oxford U., Eng., 1984-85; vis. prof. U. Geneva, 1991-92, 98-99. Contbr. articles to profl. jours. Postdoctoral fellow Coll. de France, Paris, 1970-72. Mem.: Am. Neurosci. Soc., Sleep Rsch. Soc. Avocations: horseback riding, skiing. Home: 97 Arlington Ave Westmount PQ Canada H3Y 2W5 Office: McGill Univ 3801 Univ St Montreal PQ Canada H3A 2B4 Office Phone: 514-398-1913. Business E-Mail: barbara.jones@mcgill.ca.

JONES, BARBARA PENDLETON, psychologist, educator; b. Atlanta, Apr. 2, 1947; d. Eugene Banks Jr. and Barbara Lee (Murlin) P.; m. Boisfeuillet Jones Jr., Sept. 13, 1969; children: Lindsay Pendleton, Theodore Boisfeuillet. BA, Wellesley Coll., 1968; MA, Boston U., 1974, PhD, 1977; grad., Balt.-Washington Inst. of Psychoanalysis, 1992. Diplomate Am. Bd. Profl. Psychology, Am. Bd. Clin. Neuropsychology. Staff psychologist dept. psychology and neurology McLean Hosp., Belmont, Mass., 1976-80; instr. psychology dept. psychiatry McLean Hosp. Harvard Med. Sch., Boston, 1977-88; asst. clin. prof. dept. psychiatry, behavioral scis. George Washington U., Washington, 1980-93; assoc. clin. prof., 1993—; pvt. practice psychologist Washington, 1981—; neuropsychologist NIMH, Bethesda, Md., 1985—96; asst. clin. prof. psychiatry Georgetown U., Washington, 1989-94, assoc. clin. prof., 1994—2003, clin. prof., 2003—; tng., supervising analyst Balt.-Washington Inst. Psychoanalysis, 1999—. Bd. dirs. Jenny Waelder-Wall Ctr. for Children. Contbr. articles to profl. jours. Recipient Lewis B. Hill award Balt. Washington Inst., Laurel, 1989. Mem. APA, Internat. Neuropsychol. Soc. (Phillip M. Rennick award 1977), Am. Psychoanalytic Assn., Phi Beta Kappa. Home and Office: 4331 Forest Ln NW Washington DC 20007-1137 Office Phone: 202-364-9367. E-mail: barbarapjones@gmail.com.

JONES, BARBARA S., federal judge; b. 1947; BA, Mount St. Mary's, 1968; JD, Temple, 1973. Special atty. honors prog. Manhattan Strike Force Against Organized Crime and Racketeering US Dept. Justice, 1973—77, asst. US atty. Office US Atty. (So. Dist. NY), 1977—83, asst. US atty. chief gen. crimes unit (So. Dist. NY), 1983—84, asst. US atty. chief organized crime unit (So. Dist. NY), 1984—87; chief asst. DA County of NY, NYC, 1987—96; judge US Dist. Ct. (So. Dist. NY), 1996—. Adj. prof. trial advocacy Fordham U. Sch. Law. Trustee Vera Inst. Justice, 2000—. Mem.: NY County Lawyers Assn., Assn. Bar City NY, American Coll. Trial Lawyers. Office: US Courthouse 40 Foley Sq Room 2103 New York NY 10007

JONES, BETTY ANN, elementary school educator; b. Harlingen, Tex., Nov. 30, 1943; d. Billy Martel and Charlotte Josephine Jones. B Music Edn., Tex. Christian U., Ft. Worth, 1965. Cert. tchr. Tex., Calif. Tchr. Comanche Schs., Tex., 1965—66, Mineral Wells Schs., Tex., 1966—68, Lancaster Schs., Calif., 1968—2004. Home: 43746 Claire Ct Lancaster CA 93535-5732

JONES, BEVERLY ANN MILLER, nursing administrator, retired patient services administrator; b. Bklyn., July 14, 1927; d. Hayman Edward and Eleanor Virginia (Doyle) Miller; m. Kenneth Lonzo Jones, Sept 5, 1953 (dec.); children: Steven Kenneth, Lonnie Cord. BSN, Adelphi U., 1949. Chief nurse regional blood program ARC, NYC, 1951-54; asst. dir., acting DON M.D. Anderson Hosp. and Tumor Inst., Houston, 1954-55; asst. DON Sibley Meml. Hosp., Washington, 1959-61; assoc. dir. nursing svc. Anne Arundel Gen. Hosp., Annapolis, Md., 1966-70; asst. adminstr. nursing Alexandria Hosp., Va., 1972-73; v.p. patient care svc. Longmont United Hosp., Colo., 1977-93; pvt. cons., 1993-99; ret. Instr. ARC, 1953-57, chmn. nurse enrollment com. D.C. chpt., 1959-61; mem. adv. bd. Boulder Valley Vo.-Tech. Health Occupations Program, 1977-80; del. nursing adminstrs. good will trip to Poland, Hungary, Sweden and Eng., 1980. Contbr. articles to profl. jours.

Mem.-at-large exec. com. nursing svc. adminstrs. sect. Md. Nurses' Assn., 1966-69; bd. dir. Meals on Wheels, Longmont, 1978-80, Longmont Coalition for Women in Crisis, Applewood Living Ctr., Longmont; mem. utilization com. Boulder (Colo.) Hospice, 1979-83; mem. task force on nat. commn. on nursing Colo. Hosp. Assn., 1982, mem. coun. labor rels., 1982-87; mem. U. Colo. Task Force on Nursing, 1990; vol. Champs program St. Vrain Valley Sch. Dist., 1986—, Prestige Plus program Longmont United Hosp., 1999—. Named Outstanding Vol. of Yr., St. Vrain Valley Sch. Dist., 1986—2004. Mem. Am. Orgn. Nurse Exec. (chmn. com. membership svc. and promotions, nominee recognition of excellence in nursing adminstrn.), Colo. Soc. Nurse Exec. (dir. 1978-80, 84-86, pres. 1980-81, mem. com. on nominations 1985-86, Outstanding Vol. of Yr. 2002). Home: 853 Wade Rd Longmont CO 80503-7017

JONES, BLANCHE, nursing administrator; b. Edgecombe, N.C., Nov. 11, 1935; d. Cosevelt Ewuell and Evelyn (Jones) Harrison. Diploma, CUNY Hunter Coll., 1971; AAS, CUNY Medgar Evers Coll., 1986; BS in Cmty. Health, Gerontology and Med. Surg. Sci., St. Joseph's Coll., 1990. RN, N.Y.; RN in med.-surg., ANCC. From nurse aide to head nurse Bellevue Hosp., N.Y.C., 1958-77; head nurse Coney Island Hosp., Bklyn., 1978-90, clin. supr., 1990—. Contbr. articles to profl. jours. Bd. dirs. Baisley Park Neighbors Inc., Jamaica, N.Y., 1968—. Mem. Orthopaedic Nurses Assn., N.Y. Nurses Assn. (del. 1972), Bowling League, Fishing Club, Target Pistol Club. Democrat. Baptist. Office: Coney Island Hosp 2601 Ocean Pkwy Brooklyn NY 11235-7791 Home: 1741 Oakville Pl Lady Lake FL 32162-7681

JONES, BONNIE QUANTRELL, automobile dealer; b. Detroit, Apr. 13, 1944; d. Arthur Everett and Eleanor Marie (Zander) Quantrell; m. Billy Gatton Jones. BA, U. Minn., 1966. Writer, producer Pillsbury Co., Mpls., 1966-68; writer, prodn. mgr. Creative Ctr., Inc., Mpls., 1968-71; freelance writer, producer Mpls., 1971-75; owner, pres. Cameron & Co., Mpls., 1975-79; sales mgr. Quantrell Cadillac, Lexington, Ky., 1979-81; pres., owner Quantrell Cadillac and Quantrell Porsche-Audi, Lexington, 1982—. Adv. bd. Cen. Bank, Lexington, 1987—. Pres. Jr. Achievement Bluegrass, Lexington, 1986-87, Better Bus. Bur. Lexington, 1987; mem. Lexington Philharm. Guild, 1986—. Mem. Nat. Automobile Dealers Assn., Ky. Automobile Dealers Assn., Internat. Automobile Dealers Assn., Cadillac Nat. Dealer Council (nat. rep. 1986-87), Volvo Nat. Dealer Council (nat. rep. 1985—, parts chmn. 1987-88), Phi Beta Kappa. Clubs: Lexington, Lexington Country. Avocation: tennis. Office: Quantrell Cadillac Inc 1490 E New Circle Rd Lexington KY 40509-1098

JONES, BRENDA KAYE, public relations executive; b. Oklahoma City, Jan. 4, 1958; d. Bobby Lee and Betty Ruth (Hillburn) J. Student, Okla. Bapt. U., 1976-77; BA in Journalism, U. Okla., 1980. Reporter The Okla. Daily, Norman, 1978-80; field dir. of Coll. Reps. Rep. Nat. Com., Washington, 1979; office mgr. "Reagan for Pres. in 80" Fundraising Com., Washington, 1980; pers. rsch. asst. The White House and Office of Pres.-Elect, Washington, 1980-81; pub. liaison officer U.S. Info. Agy., Washington, 1982-85; office of presdl. pers. sr. writer The White House, Washington, 1985-88; sr. asst. to ambassador Am. Embassy, Bern, Switzerland, 1988-89; spl. asst. to chmn. The Pres.'s Commn. on Mgmt. of AID, Washington, 1992-93; dir. pub. rels Feed The Children, Oklahoma City, 1993-95; v.p. pub. rels. Ackerman McQueen Agy., Oklahoma City, 1995—2001; pres. Jones Pub. Rels. Group, Oklahoma City, 2001—. Selected as one of Outstanding Young Women in Am., 1979. Mem. Women in Comm. Inc., Pub. Rels. Soc. Am., Greater Oklahoma City Chamber (vice chair membership), Jr. League, Reagan Alumni Assn. Republican. Avocations: hiking in europe, scuba diving. Office: Jones Pub Rels Group 228 Robert S Kerr #300 Oklahoma City OK 73102 Office Phone: 405-516-9686.

JONES, CAROL A., nutritionist, artist; d. John H. and Emma C. Jones. BS in Dietetics, U. So. Miss., Hattiesburg, 1975; MA in Nutrition Edn., U. Miss., Oxford, 1989; postgrad., Miss. State U., Statesville, 2000—. Registered dietitian ADA, lic. dietition Miss. Dietary dept. supr. Miss. Valley Food Scv., Kuscinsku; nutritionist supr. Miss. Dept. Health, Jackson; cons. Ellisville State Sch., Columbus, Miss.; part-owner Abigail's, Columbus. Exhibitions include Market Ctrl. Gallery, Memphis, Mid-Town Galleries, exhibitions include various local galleries. Deacon First Presbyn. Ch. Columbus; bd. dirs. Pilot Club of Columbus, 2004—06. Democrat. Presbyterian. Home: 616 N Browder St Columbus MS 39702 Office: Mississippi Dept Health 400A Wilkins Rd Columbus MS

JONES, CAROLE A., elementary school educator; b. Warren, Ohio, Feb. 19, 1949; d. Dale A. and Ann A. Huey; m. Kevin H. Jones, Nov. 21, 1992; children: Chad Ronyetz, Connie Ronyetz Swartzentruber. BS, Asland Coll., Ashland, 1971; MEd, Kent State Univ., Kent, Ohio, 1997. Grade 4-6 tchr. Strongsville City Sch., Strongsville, Ohio, 1971—80, enrichment tchr., 1989—94, mid. sch. tchr., 1994—99, grade 4 tchr., 1999—. Com. works Strongsville City Sch., Strongsville, Ohio, 1971—80, Strongsville, 1989—2005. Coord. Koinonia, Brook Pk., Ohio, 2004, chairperson, 2005. Recipient Women of the Yr., Brunswick United Meth. Ch., 1989; scholar Jenning Scholar, Martha Holdings Jennings Found., 1976, 2003. Meth. Avocations: reading, crafts, camping.

JONES, CAROLYN, dean, law educator; 1 child, Alison. BA, U. Iowa, 1976, JD, 1979; LLM, Yale U., 1982. Bar: Iowa. Asst. city atty. Sioux City, 1979—80; assoc. Klass, Whicher and Mishne, 1981—82; prof. St. Louis U. Sch. Law, 1982—90, U. Conn. Law Sch., 1990—2004, assoc. dean academic affairs; dean U. Iowa Coll Law, 2004—. Vis. prof. law U. Exeter, Washington U., U. Iowa, 1986—87, 1989, Moritz Coll. Law, Ohio State U., 2004. Recipient Sanxay Prize, Order of Coif. Office: U Iowa Coll Law 276 Boyd Law Building Iowa City IA 52242 E-mail: carolyn-jones@uiowa.edu.

JONES, CAROLYN ELLIS, retired employment agency owner; b. Marigold, Miss., Feb. 21, 1928; d. Joseph Lawrence and Willie Decelle (Forrest) Peeples; m. David Wright Ellis, May 30, 1945 (div. 1966); children: David, Lyn, Debbie, Dawn; m. Frank Willis Jones, Jan. 1, 1980. Student, La. State U., 1949. Owner, mgr. Personnel and Bus. Svc., Inc., Greenwood, Miss., 1962-88; owner Honor Pub. Co., 1988—2005; ret. ESL tchr. at a Spanish Mission, nr. Sunflower, Miss., 2004—. Author: The Lottie Moon Storybook, 1985, The John Wesley Storybook, 2003; editor: An Old Soldier's Career, 1974; contbr. articles to religious and gen. interest publs. Mem. adv. bd. career edn. Greenwood Pub. Schs., 1975-76, mem. adv. bd. vocat.-tech. dept., 1975-88; conf. leader Miss. Bapt. Convention Singles Retreat, 1980; Mission Svc. Corps del. Home Mission Bd., So. Bapt. Conv., Hawaii, 1979; team mem. United Meth. Vols. in Mission, Estonia/Russia, 1996 Mem. Greenwood C. of C. (edn. com. 1980—, guest spkr. career day program local high sch.), Mothers Against Drunk Drivers, Altrusa Internat., Nat. Fedn. Ind. Bus., Miss Delta Rose Soc., Miss. Native Plant Soc., Gideon Aux. (pres. 1986-88). Avocations: writing, rose exhibitions, wildflowers. Office: 802 W President Ave Greenwood MS 38930-3326

JONES, CAROLYN EVANS, writer; b. Middleboro, Mass., Sept. 5, 1931; d. King Israel and Kleo Estelle (Hodges) Evans; m. John Homer Jones, Sept. 9, 1956 (dec. July 1986); 1 child, David Everett. BA in English, Tift Coll., 1952; M Religious Edn., Carver Sch. Missions and Social Work, 1958; BA in Art, Mercer U., 1982. Cert. secondary tchr., Ga. Tchr. McDuffie County Bd. Edn., Thomson, Ga., 1952-53, Colquitt County Bd. Edn., Norman Park, Ga., 1953-55; missionary Home Mission Bd. SBC, New Orleans and Macon, 1958-66; spl. edn. tchr. Bibb County Bd. Edn., Macon, 1968-70, 75-79; owner, operator Laney Co. Imprinted Specialties, Macon, 1986-97; writer, 1998—. Author: Texts and Contexts: A Bible Study Handbook, 2005, numerous poems; contbr. articles to profl. jours. Bible tchr. YWCA, Macon, 1980-85; deacon 1st Bapt. Ch., Macon. Mem.: Inst. Noetic Scis., Bapt. Women in Ministry of Ga., Southeastern Writers Assn., Ga. Writers Inc. Democrat. Avocations: reading, travel, attending conferences.

JONES, CATHERINE CLARISSA, secondary school educator; b. Iowa City, Iowa, May 10, 1949; d. Dale E. and Clarissa T. Watt; m. Lawrence Lee Jones, Dec. 7, 1968; children: Christopher Ruppert, Katherine Anna. BA, U. of Iowa, Iowa City, 1971, MA, 1980. HS English tchr., dept. chair Coll. Cmty. Schs., Cedar Rapids, Iowa, 1971—. Tchg. asst. U. of Iowa, Iowa City, 1981—82; instr. Kirkwood Coll., Cedar Rapids, Iowa. Tutor Right to Read. Named Prairie H.S. Tchr. of the Yr., Coll. Cmty. Schs., 2005; recipient Paul C. Packer award for Outstanding Grad. Student Coll. of Edn., U. of Iowa, 1981, Tchr. of the Yr. award, Cedar Rapids Rotary, 2003, 2006. Mem.: Pi Lambda Theta, Phi Delta Kappa. Home: 3197 Dubuque St NE Iowa City IA 52240 Office Phone: 319-848-5330.

JONES, CHARLOTT ANN, retired museum director, art educator; b. Jonesboro, Ark., May 27, 1927; d. Arthur Philip and Mary Lillian (Falk) J. BA, St. Scholastica Coll., Duluth, Minn., 1962; MS in Edn., N. Tex. State U., 1970; PhD, Pa. State U., 1978. Tchr. St. Andrews Sch., Little Rock, 1947, Holy Souls Sch., Little Rock, 1951—55, Sacred Heart Sch., Muenster, Tex., 1955—56; prin. Holy Souls Sch., 1956—61, Sacred Heart High Sch., 1962—69; instr. art Ark. State U., Jonesboro, 1972—84, assoc. prof., 1974—90, mus., 1983—; mus. dir. Ark. State U. Mus., Jonesboro, 1983—2002; ret., 2002. Cons., writer art standard com. State of Ark., 1984; curator Ark. Women Artists Exhibit, Nat. Mus. Women in Arts, 1990-92. Contbr. articles to profl. jours. Grantee Inst. Mus. Svcs., Washington, 1986, 1995-97, Ark. Endowment Humanities, 1986, 88, 89, Ark. Historic Resources/Mus. Svcs., 1994. Mem. am. Assn. Mus., Nat. Art Edn. Assn. (Outstanding 18-state Region educator 1983), Ark. Mus. Assn. (pres. 1994-95, Outstanding Ark. Art Educator award 1983), Delta Kappa Gamma Internat. (arts com. chmn. 1982—), Phi Kappa Phi (pres. 1993-94). Democrat. Avocations: watercolor painting, canoeing.

JONES, CHARLOTTE, foundation administrator; b. Elk City, Okla., Dec. 21, 1949; d. S.G. and Mary Kathryn (Hartman) McLaury; m. Ray Loyd Jones, Apr. 3, 1969; children: Kathryn Denise, Ryan MacRay, Joshua Kyle. BS in Edn., U. Okla., 1976; MEd, Southwestern Okla. State U., 1991. Cert. tchr. math., counseling, social studies, lang. arts. Prin. Madison Elem. Sch., Norman, Okla., 1994—2004. Dir. Local Edn. Found. Outreach/Okla. Found. for Excellence. Paul Harris fellow, Rotary. Mem.: ASCD, Nat. Assn. Elem. Sch. Prins., Okla. Assn. Elem. Sch. Prins., Rotary, Phi Delta Kappa. Home: 4409 Oxford Way Norman OK 73072-3160 Office Phone: 405-325-1995. Business E-Mail: cjones@ofe.org. E-mail: jonesc@ou.edu.

JONES, CHERRY, actress; b. Paris, TN, Nov. 21, 1956; Founder Amer. Rep. Theatre, Cambridge, Mass., 1980—; guest artist Arena Stage, Washington, 1983-84. Stage appearances include: (with Amer. Rep. Theatre) King Lear, Twelfth Night, Major Barbara, Caucasian Chalk Circle, The Serpent Woman, Platonov, Life Is a Dream, The School for Scandal, The Three Sisters, As You Like It, Baby with the Bathwater, A Midsummer Night's Dream, Journey of the Fifth Horse, (Off Broadway) Desdemona, Goodnight Desdemona, Baltimore Waltz (Obie award), And Baby Makes Seven, Light Shining in Buckinghamshire, Big Time, Ballad of Soapy Smith, I Am a Camera, The Philanthropist, The Importance of Being Earnest, (Broadway) Angels in America, Our Country's Good, Macbeth, Stepping Out, The Heiress (Tony award Best Actress 1995), The Night of the Iguana, 1996, Doubt, 2005 (Outer Critics Cir. award, outstanding actress in a play, 2005, Lucille Lortel award, outstanding lead actress, 2005, Tony award, best performance by a leading actress in a play, 2005, Drama Desk award, outstanding actress in a play, 2005, Obie award, The Village Voice, 2005), Faith Healer, 2006; television appearances include: (movies) Alex: The Life of a Child, 1986; film appearances include: The Big Town, 1987, Light of Day, 1987, Housesitter, 1992, The Tears of Julian Po, 1997, (voice) Out of the Past, 1998, The Horse Whisperer, 1998, Murder in a Small Town, 1999, Cradle Will Rock, 1999, The Perfect Storm, 2000, Erin Brockovich, 2000, Signs, 2002. Office: The William Morris Agy 151 S El Camino Dr Beverly Hills CA 90212-2775*

JONES, CHERYL E., secondary school educator; d. Harvey A. and Uvah H. Ellington; m. Thomas O. Jones, July 14, 1990; 1 child, Justin T. BS, Mercer U., Macon, Ga., 1977; MEd, Valdosta State U., Ga., 1983. Cert. tchr. Ga., 1977. Tchr. Thomasville H.S., Ga., 1977—86, Rockdale County H.S., Conyers, Ga., 1986—2001, Rockdale Magnet Sch. for Sci. and Tech., Conyers, Ga., 2001—. Sec. Newton Hayriders Sqaure Dance Club, Covington, Ga., 2002—05. Recipient Impactor award, PACT Parents and Children Together, 2005—06; grantee, Rockdale Schools Found., 1999—2006. Mem.: Nat. Assoc. of Biology Tchrs., Profl. Assoc. of GA. Educators (bldg. contact 1998—2006). Office: Rockdale Magnet School for Science & Tec 1174 Bulldog Cir Conyers GA 30012 Office Phone: 770-483-8754. E-mail: cjones@rockdale.k12.ga.us.

JONES, CHRISTA M., secondary school educator; b. Wilmington, Del., May 6, 1972; BA in Theatre Arts and Grad. Studies, Old Dominion U., Norfolk, Va., 1997. Theatre tchr. and dir. Ocean Lakes H.S., Virginia Beach, Va., 1997—. Actor, dir.: (plays) Various. Bd. dirs. Generic Theater, Norfolk, Va. Recipient Dist. Tchr. award, Ocean Lakes HS, 2005—06; grantee, Bldg. Futures Grant, 2004.

JONES, CHRISTA WALKER, special education educator; d. William Kenneth and Edith Walker; m. Gary Jones, Apr. 10, 1993; children: Ansley Renee, Elise Clara. BS in Early Childhood Handicapped, Auburn U., 1991; MEd in Behavior Disorders, West Ga. Coll., 1995. Cert. tchr. Ga. Preschool spl. needs tchr. Calhoun (Ga.) City Schs., 1991—2000; preschool diagnostician Floyd County Schs., Rome, Ga., 2000—. Sunday sch. tchr. Belmont Bapt. Ch., Calhoun, Ga., 2000—06, R-Consevative. Bapt. Avocation: scrapbooking. Office: Floyd County Schs 600 Riverside Pkwy NE Rome GA 30161 Office Phone: 706-234-1031 7198. Business E-Mail: chjones@floydboe.net.

JONES, CHRISTINE, language arts educator; b. Hayti, Mo., Oct. 16, 1962; d. Jessie and Gracie (Amelena) Jones. BS in Elem. Edn., S.E. Mo. State U., Cape Girardeau, 1985, MA in English, 1997. Cert. Elem. Edn. 1985, Secondary Edn. 1997. Tchr. Mathis Elem. Sch., Hayti, Mo., 1986—92; tchr. computer tech. Hayti Jr. HS, 1992—94, tchr. language arts, 1994—. Tchr./tutor Boys and Girls Club of Bootheel, Caruthersville, Mo., 1990. Mem.: Mo. State Tchrs. Assn., Nat. Coun. Tchrs. of English. Avocations: reading, poetry, movies, travel. Home: 308 N Walnut St Hayti MO 63851 Office: Hayti Jr HS 400 N Fourth St Hayti MO 63851

JONES, CHRISTINE MASSEY, retired furniture company executive; b. Columbus, Ga., Nov. 7, 1929; d. Louis Everett and Donia (Spivey) Massey; divorced; children— James Raymond, Jr., James David. Student, Ga. Southwestern Coll., 1947-48. With Muscogee Mfg. Co., Columbus, Ga., 1948-56, Haverty Furniture Cos., Atlanta, 1956—97, v.p., corp. sec., 1978—97; ret., 1997. Deacon First Presbyn. Ch., Columbus, Ga., 2004—. Mem. Am. Soc. Corp. Secs. (securities industry com.)

JONES, CHRISTY D., lawyer; b. Memphis, Feb. 13, 1952; d. Blanton J. and Jean Ann (Kight) J. BA in Political Sci., U. Ark, 1974, JD, 1977. Ptnr. Butler, Snow, O'Mara, Stevens & Cannada PLLC, Jackson, Miss., 1977—, chair litig. dept., mem. health litig. group. Deacon Covenant Presbyn. Ch.; dir. Big Brothers Big Sisters of Miss. Fellow Am. Coll. Trial Lawyers, Miss. Bar Found., Am. Bar Found.; mem. ABA, Bar Assn. 5th Fed. Cir., Miss. Def. Lawyers Assn., Trial Attys. of Am., Am. Bd. Trial Advocates, Internat. Assn. Def. Counsel (mem. exec. com. 1994-97), Def. Rsch. Inst. (chair drug and device com. 2001-03, corp counsel subcom. 2005). Office: Butler Snow O'Mara Stevens & Cannada PLLC AmSouth Plz 17th Fl 210 E Capitol St PO Box 22567 Jackson MS 39225 Office Phone: 601-985-4523. E-mail: christy.jones@butlersnow.com.

JONES, COLETTA L., senior pastor; d. Raymond Jones, Sr. and Burnetta T. Jones; m. Ronald P. Jones, June 27, 1964; children: Phillip A., Catrina M., Michael R., David P. Attended, Morgan State U., 1992—96, Columbia Union Coll., 1998—99. Equal employment specialist US Dept. oEnergy, DC, 1970—82; sch. adminstr. Sunshine Christian Acad., Colmar Manor, Md., 1982—92; bus. adminstr., asst. pastor New Mt. Carmel Holiness Ch. Christ, DC, 1993—96; sr. pastor Mt. Carmel Christian Faith Ctr., DC, 1997—. Bd. mem. Collective Banking Group, Riverdale, Md., 2000—; mem. Jobs Coalition, DC, 2002—; sec., bd. dirs. Faith Based Cmty. Action Partnership, Inc., 2003—; instr. Jobs Partnership Inc., 2004—. Mem.: NW Clergy Assn. Non-Denomination. Avocations: traveling, reading, cooking. Office: Mount Carme Christian Faith Ctr 4100 Illinois Ave NW Washington DC 20011 Office Phone: 202-545-0230. Office Fax: 202-545-0230. Personal E-mail: ronaldandcoletta@aol.com.

JONES, CONSTANCE CORALIE, retired music educator; b. Bowling Green, Ky., July 5, 1921; d. Loton Brodie Jones and Constance Coralie Barrington; m. Harold E. Runyon, June 23, 1943 (dec.); children: Randolph Runyon, Constance Ford; m. Earle D. Jones, Dec. 26, 1979 (dec.). AB, Western Ky. State Coll., 1941, MA, 1944. Music tchr. Orangeburg HS, Mason County, Ky., 1941—42, Maysville City Schs., Maysville, Ky., 1942—46, Ripley Sch. Dist., Ohio, 1955—60, Mason County Schs., Ohio, 1960—82, Maysville CC, 1968—92. Mem. Lexington Symphony Orch.; guest condr., vis. tchr. Dana Hall Sch., Wellesley, Mass. Founder, conductor Maysville Civic Chorus; musical dir. Maysville Players Prodns.; conductor Limestone Chorale & Limestone Chamber Orchestra; dir. music Maysville Christian Ch., 1942—82. Named a Ky. Col., 1974, 1979; recipient Outstanding Woman Ky., U. Ky. Women's Assn., 1971, Lady of Yr., Maysville, 1979, Ky. Tchr. of Yr., 1982. Mem.: Am. String Tchrs. Assn., Am. Choral Dirs. Assn. (past pres., past. pres.). Achievements include conducting concerts in northern England, Vienna, Innsbruck, Neustadt, Neuremberg, Germany, Monaco and Brussels, Belgium; choir students have had records of superior ratings at the state contest-festival competitions for 32 years; establishing The Coralie Runyon-Jones Music Libr. wing of Maysville Pub. Libr., 2005. Personal E-mail: coralie@maysvilleky.net.

JONES, CORDIA CORTEZ, minister; b. Bottom Creek, W.Va., Dec. 8, 1941; d. Jose and Annitta Balderas; m. Billie Jean Jones, Jan. 30, 1960; children: Billie Jean Jr., Kimberly, Gloria, Clifford, Ambrue. Assembler, precision inspector Borg Warner Automotive, Bellwood, Ill., 1977—91; min. Emmanuel Deliverance Temple, Chgo., 1986—91; pastor Apostolic Ho. of Prayer, Chgo., 2000—; host, pastor The Children's Hour, Chgo., 2002—05. Home: 743 E 104th Pl Chicago IL 60628

JONES, CYNTHIA R., social studies educator; d. Helene C. and Thomas Stringas; m. Kenneth P. Jones, Oct. 19, 1996. BS Social Studies Edn., Elizabethtown Coll., Pa., 1990; MA Edn., Villanova U., Pa., 1995; Supervisory Certification, Millersville U., Pa., 2005. Cert. Instrnl. II Tchr. Pa., 1990, Supr.Curriculum and Instrn. Pa., 2006. Tchr. H.S. social studies Ephrata Area Sch. Dist., Pa., 1992—. Spkr. mid. states conf. Cooperative Learning. Named to Who's Who Among Am. Tchrs., 2005. Mem.: Nat. Coun. Social Studies, Ephrata Area Edn. Assn. (corr. sec. 2001—03), Pa. Coun. Social Studies, Phi Kappa Phi, Kappa Delta Pi. Greek Orthodox. Avocations: travel, exercise, sports, reading of professional journals, basket collecting.

JONES, CYNTHIA TERESA CLARKE, artist; b. Bklyn., Aug. 12, 1938; d. Arthur Ottio and Emma (Gibbs) Clarke; m. Robert H. Jones. Apr. 21, 1968 (div. Sept. 1977); 1 child, Kim Marie. Student, Bklyn. Mus., 1954-57, Art Career Sch., 1958, Hunter Coll., N.Y.C., 1963-65. One woman shows include Queens Borough Pub. Libr., Jamaica, N.Y., 1986, Baruch Coll., 1972; exhibited in group shows Queens Coun. on Arts Exhibit at Gertz Dept. Store, 1972, Queens Coll. Arts Festival, 1972, Dist. Coun. 37, First Art Exhbn., 1972, Artist Equity Group Shows Union Carbide, 1975, 77, Queensborough Community Coll. Invitational Show at Holocaust Resource Ctr., 1985, Pen and Brush, 1990, AQA Gallery, 1990, AQA at Chung Cheng Gallery at St. Johns U., 1987-90, Lowenstein Libr. Gallery Fordham U., 1989, Arlington Arts Ctr., 1991, Pursuit of Peace Ceres Gallery, 1991; designer cover Rsch. Papers Stats. Dept. Bernard M. Baruch Coll., 1973; works reprinted in Locally Speaking Local 384 newsletter. Donator work to MUSE Gallery, 1990, to Hale House Ctr., Inc.; active Women's Caucus for Art. Recipient Joseph Grumbacher Co. award, 1958, Scholastic Art award and key, 1957, Fine Arts award Queensboro Soc., 1973, Outstanding Painting award, 1973, France Lieber Meml. award Nat. Assn. Women Artists, Inc., 1992, two certs. of merit Latham Found., 1956-58; scholar Latham Found., 1958. Mem. Artists Equity Assn., Inc. N.Y., Alliance of Queens Artists, Coll. Art Assn., Queens Coun. on Arts, Ind. Arts Assn., Arlington Arts Ctr. Va., Queensboro Coll. Art Gallery (assoc.), Nat. Assn. Women Artists (The Kreindler Meml. award 1995), Print Club, Guild Am. Papercutters. Office: 11332 Mayville St Jamaica NY 11412-2410

JONES, DALE CHERNER, marketing executive, consultant; b. Chgo., Apr. 22, 1948; d. Morrie and Rose (Fidelman) Cherner; m. Jerome J. Jones, Dec. 16, 1973 (div. Feb. 1985); m. Edward Louis Kathrein, Oct. 24,1987; stepchildren: Janet Gaston, Brian Kathrein. BA, Northwestern U., 1968, M in Mgmt., 1986. Manuscripts librarian Chgo. Hist. Soc., 1968-69; mktg. coord. Perkins & Will Architects & Engrs., Chgo., 1969-73; owner Mktg. & Mgmt. Cons., Evanston, Ill., 1974-77; mktg. adminstr. Grumman-Butkus (formerly Enercon Ltd.), Evanston, 1977-79; assoc., mktg. dir. H.W. Lochner, Inc., Chgo., 1979-82; prin., owner JCS, Inc., Evanston, 1982-83; prin., dir. mktg. Schirmer Engring. Corp., Deerfield, Ill., 1983-88; pres., COO, ptnr. R.E. Timm & Assocs., Hinsdale, Ill., 1990-95; owner Jones Consulting, 1995—; v.p. AMKA/DLM Archs., Ltd., 1997—2000; prin. Jones Cons., 2001—. Mktg. advisor Chgo. chpt. Ill. Soc. Profl. Engrs., 1980—. Contbr. articles to profl. jours. Fellow Soc. for Mktg. Profl. Svcs. (founder Chgo. chpt., nat. bd. dirs. 1984-86, pres. 1979-82, Cert. of Achievement 1982); mem. AIA (affiliate; mem. adv. coun. 1984-86, Cert. 1985), Assn. Bus. Women Am. (founder Chgo. chpt., treas. 1973-74, pres. 1974-75, Bus. Woman of Yr. 1974), Kellogg Alumnae Club. Avocations: travel, books, public speaking.

JONES, DEBBIE JO, finance educator; d. Johnny Albert and Ruby Jones. Assoc. degree, Massey Bus. Coll., Atlanta, 1982. Tchr. Debbie Jones Ministries, Decatur, Ga., 2003—. Dir., tchr. Ruby Jones Leadership Acad. Editor: (monthly letters) LOV Ministries. Office: Debbie Jones Ministries PO Box 2106 Decatur GA 30031-2106 Office Phone: 404-376-1709. Business E-Mail: djjkmr02@yahoo.com.

JONES, DIANA WYNNE, writer; b. London, Aug. 16, 1934; d. Richard Aneurin Jones and Marjorie (Jackson) Hughes; m. John Anthony Burrow, Dec. 22, 1956; children: Richard, Michael, Colin. BA, St. Anne's Coll. U. Oxford, Eng., 1956; DLitt (hon.), Bristol U., Eng., 2006. Free-lance writer part-time, Essex, Oxford, Eng., 1944-70; full-time writer Oxford, Bristol, Eng., 1970—. Panel judge Guardian Award for Children's Books, London, 1979-83, Whitbread Prize for Lit., Children's Sect., London, 1988; judge World Fantasy Awards, 2001. Author: Wilkins' Tooth (in U.S. Witch's Business), 1973, The Ogre Downstairs, 1974, Eight Days of Luke, 1975, Cart and Cwidder, 1975, Dogsbody, 1975, Power the Three, 1976, Drowned Ammet, 1977, Charmed Life, 1977 (Guardian award 1978), Who Got Rid of Angus Flint, 1978, The Spellcoats, 1979, The Magicians of Caprona, 1980, The Homeward Bounders, 1981, The Time of the Ghost, 1981, Witch Week, 1982, Warlock at the Wheel, 1984, Archer's Goon, 1984 (Boston Globe/Horn Book award), Fire and Hemlock, 1985 (Phoenix award, 2005), Howl's Moving Castle, 1986 (Boston Globe/Horn Book award), A Tale of Time City, 1987, The Lives of Christopher Chant, 1988, Chair Person, 1989, Wild Robert, 1989, Hidden Turnings, 1989, Castle in the Air, 1990, Black Maria, 1991, A Sudden Wild Magic, 1992, The Crown of Dalemark, 1993, Stopping for a Spell, 1993, Hexwood, 1993, Fantasy Stories, 1994, Everard's Ride, 1995, The Tough Guide to Fantasyland, 1996, Minor Arcana, 1996, Deep Secret, 1997, Dark Lord of Derkholm, 1998, (retelling of) Puss n' Boots, 1999, Mixed Magics, Year of the Griffin, 2000, The Merlin Conspiracy, 2003, Unexpected Magic, 2004, Changeover, 2004, Conrad's Fate, 2005, The Pinhoe Egg, 2006; animated film: Howl's Moving Castle, 2004. Recipient, Mythopoaic Soc. award, 1995, 99, Joseph Wagner award Brit. Fantasy Soc.,

1999. Mem. Soc. of Authors, Brit. Fantasy Soc. Avocations: cooking, owning a cat. Home: 9 The Polygon Bristol BS8 4PW England Office: care Greenwillow Books 105 Madison Ave New York NY 10016-7418

JONES, DONNA LEE, lawyer; b. Phila., June 30, 1968; BA with honors, JD with honors, Rutgers U., 1997; LLM in Trial Advocacy, Temple U., 2005. Bar: Pa. 1997, US Dist. Ct. (ea. dist.) Pa. 2002. Ptnr. Saltz, Mongeluzzi, Barrett & Bendesky, P.C., Phila. Adj. prof. law Temple U. LLM Trial Program; lectr. in field. Mem.: Lawyers' Club of Phila. (bd. mem.), Assn. Trial Lawyers of Am., Phila. Trial Lawyers Assn., Pa. Trial Lawyers Assn., Pa. Bar Assn. Office: Saltz, Mongeluzzi, Barrett & Bendesky, PC One Liberty Place 1650 Market St, 52nd Fl Philadelphia PA 19103 Office Phone: 215-496-8282. Office Fax: 215-493-0999. E-mail: dljones@smbb.com.*

JONES, DONNA MARILYN, state agency administrator, former legislator; b. Brush, Colo., Jan. 14, 1939; d. Virgil Dale and Margaret Elizabeth (McDaniel) Wolfe; m. Donald Eugene Jones, June 9, 1956; children: Dawn Richter, Lisa Shira, Stuart. Student, Treasure Valley Community Coll., 1981-82; grad., Realtors Inst. Cert. residential specialist. Co-owner Parts, Inc., Payette, Idaho, 1967-79; dept. mgr., buyer Lloyd's Dept. Store, Payette, Idaho, 1979-80; sales assoc. Idaho-Oreg. Realty, Payette, Idaho, 1981-82; mem. dist. 13 Idaho Ho. of Reps., Boise, 1987-90, mem. dist. 10, 1990-94, mem. dist. 9, 1995-98; assoc. broker Classic Properties Inc., Payette, 1983-91; owner, broker ERA Preferred Properities Inc., 1991-98; mem. dist. 9 Idaho Ho. of Reps., 1992-98. Co-chmn. Apple Blossom Parade, 1982; mem. Payette Civic League, 1968-84, pres. 1972; mem. Payette County Planning and Zoning Commn., 1985-88, vice-chmn. 1987; field coordinator Idaho Rep. Party Second Congl. Dist., 1986; mem. Payette County Rep. Cen. Com. 1978—; precinct II com. person, 1978-79, state committeewoman, 1980-84, chmn. 1984-87; outstanding county chmn. region III Idaho Rep. Party Regional Hall of Fame, 1985-86; mem. Payette County Rep. Women's Fedn., 1988—, bd. dirs., 1990-92; mem. Idaho Hispanic Commn., 1989-92, Idaho State Permanent Bldg. Adv. Coun., 1990-98; bd. dirs. Payette Edn. Found., 1993-96, Western Treasure Valley Cultural Ctr., 1993-96; nat. bd. dirs. Am. Legis. Exchange Coun., 1993-98; mem. legis. adv. coun. Idaho Housing Agy., 1992-97; committeperson Payette County Cen.; chmn. Ways and Means Idaho House of Reps., 1993-97, House Revenue & Taxation Com., 1997-98; mem. Multi-State Tax Compact, 1997-98; Idaho chmn. Am. Legis. Exchange Coun., 1991-95; exec. dir. Idaho Real Estate Commn., 1998—. Recipient White Rose award Idaho March of Dimes, 1988; named Payette/Washington County Realtor of Yr., 1987. Mem. Idaho Assn. Realtors (legis. com. 1984-87, chmn. 1986, realtors active in politics com. 1982-98, polit. action com. 1986, polit. affairs com. 1986-88, chmn. 1987, bd. dirs. 1984-88), Payette/Washington County Bd. Realtors (v.p. 1981, state dir. 1984-88, bd. dirs 1983-88, sec. 1983), Bus. and Profl. Women (Woman of Progress award 1988, 90, treas. 1988), Payette C. of C., Fruitland C. of C., Wiesr C. of C. Republican. Avocations: reading, interior decorating. Home: 1911 1st Ave S Payette ID 83661-3003 Office: Idaho Real Estate Commn 633 N 4th St Boise ID 83720-0001

JONES, DONNA RUTH, librarian; b. Denver, June 23, 1948; d. Don and Ruth Virginia (Hampton) Lusk; 1 child, Matthew Trevor. BA, Ft. Hays State U., 1969; MLS, Emporia State U., 1972. Librarian, instr. Colby (Kans.) Community Coll., 1969-76; dir. library services Pioneer Meml. Library, Colby, 1976-85; dir. Ark. Valley Regional Library Service System, Pueblo, Colo., 1985—. Adj. prof. library sci. Ft. Hays State U., 1972-73, 78-80; cons. N.W. Kans. Library System, 1970-71, 74, humanities cons., 1979—. Researcher: (movie and brochure) Country School Legacy: Humanities on the Frontier, 1980-82. Mem., chmn. Kans. Com. for Humanities, Topeka, 1979-85; pres. Thomas County Day Care, Colby, 1983-85; chmn. state steering com. Humanities in Pub. Librs., 1980-85; chmn. Colo. Endowment for the Humanities, Denver, 1986—. Recipient Jr. Mems. Round Table award 3-M, 1975, Young Alumni award Ft. Hays State U., 1979. Mem. ALA, Mountain Plains Libr. Assn. (pres. 1984-85), Colo. Libr. Assn. (pres. 1989), P.E.O., Order Ea. Star, Beta Sigma Phi (Sister of Yr. award). Democrat. Presbyterian. Home: 4 Encino Pl Pueblo CO 81005-2948 Office: Arkansas Valley Regional Libr Svc System 635 W Corona Ave Ste 113 Pueblo CO 81004-1248

JONES, DORIS (ANNA DORIS VOGEL), retail buyer; b. Woodstock, Mich., Oct. 31, 1917; d. Lowren Orville and Lela Irene (Gallatin) Vogel; m. Verl Richard Huntley, April 13, 1946 (dec. 1966); 1 child, Karyl Lynn Huntley; m. Donald R. Jones, April 28, 1957 (dec. 1989). BA in Psychology, U. Mich., 1939. Salesperson J.L. Hudson Dept. Store, Detroit, 1939-40, Bullocks, L.A., 1940; asst. store mgr. Elaine Shop, Jackson, Mich., 1940-48; store mgr. Joseph Magnin, Sacramento, 1949-52; women's sportswear buyer Steinfelds Dept Store, Tucson, 1952-57; pvt. practice spiritual counselor Tucson, 1977—87; religious sci. practitioner, tchr. Golden Gate Ch. of Religious Sci., Corte Madera, Calif., 1982—2004, Santa Rosa (Calif.) Ch. of Religious Sci., 1992—98. Adv. bd. United Ch. of Religious Sci., L.A., 1994-98, practitioner emeritus religious sci., 1997. Recipient Meritorious Practitioner award United Ch. of Religious Sci., 1997, Profl. Practitioner award, 2005. Home and Office: 2375 Range Ave C225 Santa Rosa CA 95403 Personal E-mail: djones1917@aol.com.

JONES, DORIS LOGAN, portrait painter, art educator; b. Billings, Mont, May 5, 1926; d. William Ernest and Florence Mabel (Snow) Logan; m. Edward Evans Jones, Aug. 23, 1947; children: Mark, Kent, Stanton, Clifton, Konni; 7 foster children. Student, Denver U., 1944-45, Washburn U., Topeka, Kans., 1946-47; BA, Brigham Young U., Provo, Utah, 1949; postgrad., Ea. Mont. State Coll., 1954-55. One-woman shows include, Mont., Wyo., Colo., Ga., Calif., Tex., Pa., Paris. Mem. Billings Arts Assn., Cody Country Art League, Billings Book Club, West Extension Club (pres. 1992-93), Machine Knitting Club. Avocations: genealogy, organ music, sewing, knitting, architecture. Home: 1032 N 29th St Billings MT 59101-0730

JONES, DORIS MORELAND, minister, author; b. Mt. Vernon, Ill., Mar. 25, 1927; d. Gail O. Rutherford and Theo Mareta (Eater) Moreland; m. Harry Wilmont Jones, Mar. 22, 1945 (widowed Sept., 1991); children: Margaret M.J. Hostetter, James Michael. BA, Ky. Wesleyan Col., 1966; MDivinity, Methodist Theological Sch., Delaware, Ohio, 1969; M in Sacred Theology, Christian Theological Seminary, 1971; DDiv (honorary), Ky. Wesleyan Col., 1981. Diplomate Am. Assn. Pastoral Counselors. Pastor various U. Methodist chs. in Ky. and Ohio, 1961-69; dir. Buchanan Counseling Ctr. Methodist Hosp., Indpls., 1969-76; dir. Ordained Ministry U. Methodist Bd. Higher Edn., Nashville, Tenn., 1976-80; dir. counseling ctr. Methodist Evangelist Hosp., Louisville, Ky., 1980-92, Middletown (Ky.) U. Methodist Ch., 1992—. Bd. govs. Am. Assn. Pastoral Counselors, Washington; Nat. Bd. Col. Chaplains, Schomburg, Ill., 1975; adj. faculty Garrett Evangelical Theological Seminary, Evanston, Ill., 1981-91, Louisville (Ky.) Presbyn. Seminary. Author: And Not One Bird Stopped Singing, 1997, (with others) New Witnesses: United Clergywomen, 1980, Clergy Women: Problems and Satisfactions, 1984, God's Gift of Anger, 2005; editor: (book) Guidebook: Interviewing Pastoral Evaluation, 1979. Fellow Coll. Chaplains; mem. Am. Assn. Marriage and Family Therapy, Assn. Clin. Pastoral Edn., Theta Phi Beta. Avocations: walking, gourmet cooking, reading, writing. Office: Middletown U Methodist Counseling Ctr 11902 Old Shelbyville Rd Middletown KY 40243-1434 Office Phone: 502-245-5878.

JONES, EDITH HOLLAN, federal judge; b. Phila., Apr. 7, 1949; m. Sherwood (Woody) Jones; 2 children. BA Cornell U., 1971; JD with honors, U. Tex., 1974. Bar: Tex. 1974, U.S. Supreme Ct. 1979, U.S. Ct. Appeals (5th and 11th cirs.), U.S. Dist. (so. and no. dists.) Tex. Assoc. Andrews & Kurth, Houston, 1974—82, ptnr., 1982—85; judge US Ct. Appeals (5th Cir.), Houston, 1985—, chief judge, 2006—. Gen. counsel Rep. Party of Tex., 1981—83. Mem. bd. dir. Boy Scouts of Am. Master: ABA; mem.: Garland Walker Am. Inns of Ct., Houston Bar Assn., State Bar Tex. Presbyterian. Office: 12505 US Courthouse 1515 Rusk Ave Houston TX 77002-2655*

JONES, EDITH IRBY, internist; b. Conway, Ark., Dec. 23, 1927; d. Robert and Mattie (Buice) Irby; m. James Beauregard Jones, Apr. 16, 1950 (dec. Oct. 1989); children: Gary Ivan, Myra Vonceil Jones Romain, Keith Irby. BS, Knoxville Coll., 1948; MD, U. Ark., 1952; Doctorate (hon.), Mo. Valley Coll., Mary Holmes Coll., Knoxville Coll. Intern Univ. Hosp., Little Rock, 1952-53; gen. practice medicine Hot Springs, Ark., 1953-59; resident in internal medicine Baylor Coll. Medicine, Houston, 1959-62; pvt. practice medicine specializing in internal medicine Houston, 1962—; mem. staff Meth. Hosp., Houston, Hermann Hosp., Houston, St. Elizabeth Hosp., Houston, St. Anthony Ctr., Houston, St. Joseph Hosp., Houston, Thomas Care Ctr., Houston, Town Pk., Houston, chief of staff; chief med. staff Riverside Gen. Hosp., Houston, 2006—. Clin. asst. prof. medicine Baylor Coll. Medicine, U. Tex. Sch. Medicine, Houston; dir. Prospect Med. Lab.; bd. dirs., sec. Mercy Hosp. Comprehensive Health Care Group; ptnr. Jones, Coleman and Whitfield; grad. med. examiner Ct. Calanthe Jurisdiction, Tex.; cons. Social Security Agy., Tex. Pub. Welfare Dept., Vocat. Rehab. Assn., Tex. Rehab. Commn.; bd. dirs. Std. Savs. Assn., others. Contbr. articles to profl. jours. Bd. dirs. Drug Addiction Rehab. Enterprise, March of Dimes, Houston, Odessey House, Houston; adv. bd. Houston Coun. Alcoholism; mem. com. revising justice code Harris County, Tex.; impartial hearing officer Houston Ind. Sch. Dist.; mem. Cmty. Welfare Planning Assn., Friends of Youth, Human Svcs. Adv. Coun., Houston, PTA, YMCA; founder Edith Irby Jones Found.; bd. dirs. Houston Internat. U.; chmn. bd. trustees Knoxville Coll.; trustee Must. Assn. Profl. Svc.; bd. visitors U. Houston, others. Named Dr. Edith Irby Jones Day in her honor, State of Ark., 1985, NYC, 1986, Disting. Alumna, J. William Fulbright Coll. Arts and Scis., 2005, a clinic in her honor, Veracruz, Mex., Most Influential People of 1986, Ebony mag.; named one of 30 Most Influential Black Women Houston, 1984, 100 Leading Black Physicians, Black Enterprise mag., 2001; named to Tex. Black Women's Hall of Fame, 1986, Hall of Fame, U. Ark. Sch. Med. Scis., 2004; recipient proclamation, Houston City Coun., 1985, Mayor of Houston, 1986, cert. of citation, Tex. Ho. of Reps., 1986, commendation, Calif. Senate, 1989, Volunteerism and Cmty. Svc. award, Tex. Acad. internal Medicine, 2000, Scroll of Merit award, Nat. Med. Assn., 2001, Silas Hunt Legacy award, U. Ark., Fayetteville, 2006. Fellow: ACP, Am. Soc. Internal Medicine (Oscar E. Edward award 2001), Am. Coll. Medicine; mem.: NAACP, AMA, Physicians for Human Rights, Bus. and Profl. Women, Tex. Assn. Disability Examiners, Houston Med. Forum, Harris County Med. Assn., Lone Star Med. Assn., Nat. Med. Assn. (first female past pres., Scroll of Merit 2001, Living Legend), Am. Med. Women's Assn. (v.p. Houston chpt.), Nat. Coun. Negro Women (v.p. Dorothy Height chpt.), Women of Achievement (Hall of Fame 1985), Girl Friends, Tops Ladies of Distinction, Links, Order Eastern Star, Eta Phi Beta, Delta Sigma Theta, Alpha Kappa Mu. Democrat. Achievements include African American to graduate from the University of Arkansas School for Medicine Sciences; first African American woman resident at an all white school, the Baylor College of Medicine Affiliated Hospitals. Avocations: travel, walking, swimming. Home: 3402 S Parkwood Houston TX 77021 Office: 2601 Prospect St Houston TX 77004-7737 Office Phone: 713-529-3145. Business E-Mail: eijones@advmed.com.

JONES, ELAINE F., psychologist, educator; b. Phila., Aug. 10, 1961; d. Percy Edward and Frances Louise Jones. BS, U. Pitts., 1983, MS, 1988, PhD, 1991. Asst. prof. U. N.C., Chapel Hill, 1990—95, St. Louis U., 1995—2002; rsch. analyst Parents as Tchrs., Inc., St. Louis, 2002—03; asst. prof. Arcadia U., Glenside, Pa., 2003—05. Cons. editor Jour. Psychology, Washington, 1999—; advisor Naked Eye Prodns., N.Y.C., 1997; project rschr. Dateline NBC/Discovery Channel, N.Y.C., 2000. Panel mem. Youth Aid Panel, Montgomery County, Pa., 2004—. Fellow Minority Program fellow, APA, 1988—99, Tchg. fellow, Eli Lilly Endowment and U. N.C., 1992—93; grantee Lindback Found. Jr. Faculty grantee, Christian R. and Mary F. Lindback Found., 2004—05. Mem.: APA, Soc. for Rsch. in Child Devel., Delta Sigma Theta. Democrat. Avocations: travel, reading, films, music. Office: Arcadia Univ Dept Psychology 450 S Easton Rd Glenside PA 19038

JONES, ELAINE HANCOCK, humanities educator; b. Niagara Falls, N.Y., Feb. 17, 1946; d. Roy Elmer and June Edna (Clark) Hancock; m. Ralph Jones III, Oct. 9, 1971 (div. June 1981). AAS in Comml. Design, U. Buffalo, 1962; BFA, SUNY, Buffalo, 1971, MFA in Painting, 1975; postgrad., Fla. State U., 1993—. Med. illustrator Roswell Park Meml. Inst., Buffalo, 1967—70; designer, animator Acad. McLarty Film Prodns., Buffalo, 1970—73; publs. designer Buffalo/Erie County Hist. Soc., 1974—78; dir. publs. Daemen Coll., Amherst, NY, 1978—80; owner, art dir. Plop Art Prodns., Melbourne, Fla., 1981—86; instr. humanities Brevard C.C., Melbourne, 1986—; prof. humanities Brevard campus Rollins Coll., Melbourne, 1995—2004. One-woman shows include SUNY, Buffalo, 1974, Upton Gallery, N.Y., 1975, Gallery Wilde, Buffalo, 1978; exhibited in group shows at Fredonia Coll., N.Y., 1975, Upton Gallery, 1975, Brevard Art Mus., Melbourne, Fla., 1987. Mem. docent program Art Mus./Sci. Ctr., Melbourne, 1983-84, mem. edn. com., 1995—; officer Platinum Coast chpt. Sweet Adelines Internat., 1984-90. Nat. Merit scholar, 1971-75; recipient cert. of merit Curtis Paper Co., 1977; N.Y. State Coun. on Arts grantee, 1975. Republican. Home: 2240 Sea Ave Indialantic FL 32903-2524 Office: Brevard CC Liberal Arts Dept 3865 N Wickham Rd Melbourne FL 32935-2310 Office Phone: 321-632-1111 x5744.

JONES, ELAINE R., former legal association administrator, civil rights advocate; b. Norfolk, Va., Mar. 2, 1944; AB, Howard U., 1965; LLB, U. Va., 1970. Spl. asst. to sec. William T. Coleman Jr. US Dept. Trans., Washington, 1975—77; pres., dir.-counsel, atty. NAACP Legal Def. and Ednl. Fund, Washington, 1993—2004. Mem. panel arbitration Am. Stock Exch. Recipient Recognition award Black Am. Law Student Assn, 1974, Spl. Achievement award Nat. Assn. Black Women Attys., 1975, Olender Found. Peacemaker award, 2000, Lamplighter Award for Equity and Justice, Black Leadership Forum, 2003, Lifetime Achievement award, Am. Law mag., 2005 Mem. Nat. Bar Assn., Internat. Fedn. Women Lawyers, Old Dominion Bar Assn., Va. trial Lawyers Assn., Delta Sigma Theta.

JONES, ELIZABETH FLANIGAN, literature and language educator; b. Conyers, Ga., Aug. 17, 1957; d. James Flanigan and Annie Lee Hamm-Flanigan; 1 child, Carl Elvis Jr. BS, Clark Coll., Atlanta, 1979. Cert. ESOL Tchr. Ga., 2005, TSS Specialist Ga., 1988. Tchr. h.s. English Social Circle City Schs., Ga., 1979—81; tchr. mid. sch. English Dekalb County Schs., Lithonia, Ga., 1981—86, tchr. support specialist Decatur, Ga., 1988—, Tesol, 2005—. Dir. Christian edn. Israel Missionary Bapt. Ch., Atlanta, 2000—, dir. vacation Bible sch., 2000—. Instr. Fri. Night Women's Bible Study. Recipient Who's Who Among Am.'s Tchrs., Who's Who, 1995—2006. D-Conservative. Avocation: speaking. Home: 4632 Tara Woods Dr Ellenwood GA 30294 Office: Dekalb County Schools 5333 Salem Road Lithonia GA 30038 Personal E-mail: elizabeth_jones99@yahoo.com.

JONES, ELIZABETH HARDING, elementary school educator; b. Oahu, Hawaii, Feb. 8, 1954; d. Robert Trumbull and Joan Carol (Jenkins) Harding; divorced; children: Colin James Fisher-Jones, Ryan Matthew BA Art Edn., Georgian Ct. Coll., Lakewood, N.J., 1980; cert. elem. edn., Georgian Ct. Coll., 1983, MA Severely Multiple Handicapped, 1999. Cert. K-12 art tchr., tchr. of the handicapped, N.J., 1996. Secondary tchr. art Freehold Regional H.S. Dist., Englishtown, NJ, 1980—81; mid. sch. tchr. art Neptune Bd. Edn., NJ, 1984; elem. tchr. art Howell Twp. Bd. Edn., NJ, 1980, 1982—83, 1984. Adj. instr. Brookdale C.C., Lincroft, NJ; agt. real estate Welcome Home Realty, Manasquan, NJ. Instr. lifeguard tng., water safety instr. trainer, adapted water safety, water safety, stds. first aid, CPR, AED instr., 1988 Mem. Nat. Art Edn. Assn., Art Educators N.J., N.J. Edn. Assn. (women in edn. com. 1991), Monmouth County Edn. Assn. (rep. 1990), Howell Twp. Edn. Assn. (rep. 1989—) Roman Catholic. Avocations: swimming, reading, sewing. Home: 37 N Farragut Ave Manasquan NJ 08736-3127 Office: Grielding Elem Sch 130 Havens Bridge Rd Farmingdale NJ 07727 Address: Welcome Home Realty 20 Abe Voorhees Dr Manasquan NJ 08736

JONES, ELIZABETH JORDAN, literature and language educator, art historian; d. Milton Harold and Elizabeth Louise Jordan; m. George Gregory Jones, Aug. 14, 1974; children: Gregory, Alexandra, Caitlin. BA, Fordham U., N.Y.C., 1972; MA, Columbia U., N.Y.C., 1973, postgrad., 1974, City U. and Manhattanville Coll. Permanent cert. English 7-12 N.Y. State, lic. English 7-12 Va., ESOL K-12 Va. Tchr. English grades 7-8 St. Bartholomew Sch., Yonkers, 1972—73; tchr. Learning Ctr. Scarsdale Mid. Sch., NY, 1989—90; substitute tchr. ESOL Scarsdale Mid. Sch. and H.S., 1989—90; asst. dir. edn. Scarsdale Hist. Soc. and Cudner-Hyatt Mus., 1995—99; specialist reading and lang. arts St. Luke Sch., McLean, Va., 2001—. Part-time instr. Sch. Continuing Edn. Sarah Lawrence Coll., 1997—; v.p. bd. Friends of Hoff Barthelson Music Sch., Scarsdale, 1983—85; mem. exec. bd. Scarsdale Elem. Sch., 1982—87; co-creator mus. program Life in Westchester 100 Years Ago, 1998. Mem. social ministry IHM Ch., Scarsdale; mem. SHARE Social Ministry, McLean, 1999—. Recipient Seton Ctr. Outstanding Tchr. award, Diocese of Arlington, 2005. Mem.: Reading Tchrs. Assn. Avocations: reading, hiking, art collecting. E-mail: ejj767@aol.com.

JONES, ELLEN, elementary school educator; b. Lithonia, Ga., Apr. 16, 1954; d. Bobby and Margaret (Harper) Jackson; children: Gretchen Nichole, Mindy Tissie Antonia. AS in Edn., DeKalb C.C., Decatur, Ga., 1974; BS in Edn., Ga. State U., 1976; MEd, Clark U., 1987; Math. and Sci. specialist degree, Wynbrooke Theme Sch., Minn., 1995. Cert. K-8 tchr., Ga. Tchr. math. DeKalb County Bd. Edn., Decatur, 1980—. Spkr. Rock Eagle Math. Conf., Eaton, Ga., 1991—, Columbus (Ga.) Math. Conf., 1993, NCTM Conf., St. Paul, 2004; radio announcer WY2E. Tutor reading and math. God Life and Living Holiness Ch. of Jesus Christ, Ellenwood, Ga., 1991—, rep. N.Am. Russian Math. Conf., St. Petersburg, Russia, 1998; assoc. min. Big Miller Grove Missionary Bapt. Ch., Lithonia, Ga. Named Tchr. of Yr., Sky Haven Sch., 1990, 91. Mem. Nat. Coun. Tchrs. Math. Home: 1036 Chapman Cir Stone Mountain GA 30088-2558

JONES, ERIKA ZIEBARTH, lawyer; b. Washington, June 10, 1955; d. Thomas Arthur and Ruth (Helm) Ziebarth; m. Gregory Monroe Jones, June 2, 1978; 1 child, Katherine Anne. BA magna cum laude, Georgetown U., 1976, JD, 1980. Bar: D.C. 1980, U.S. Ct. Appeals (D.C. cir.) 1987, U.S. Supreme Ct. 1987. Staff mem. FCC, Washington, 1976—80; atty./regulatory policy analyst Office of Mgmt. Budget, Washington, 1980—81; spl. counsel to adminstr. Nat. Hwy. Traffic Safety Adminstrn., US Dept Transp., Washington, 1981—85, chief counsel, 1985—89; ptnr. Mayer, Brown, Rowe & Maw LLP, Washington, 1989—. Bd. dirs. Immaculata Coll. High Sch., 1985-88. Mem. ABA, D.C. Bar Assn., Phi Beta Kappa. Republican. Roman Catholic. Office: Mayer Brown Rowe & Maw LLP 1909 K St NW Washington DC 20006-1101 Office Phone: 202-263-3232. Office Fax: 202-263-5232. E-mail: ejones@mayerbrownrowe.com.

JONES, EVELYN GLORIA, medical technologist, educator; b. Roanoke, Va., Aug. 13, 1940; d. William Darnell and Elizabeth (Harris) Powell; m. Theodore Joseph Jones, Aug. 21, 1965. BS in Biology, Tenn. State U., 1973; cert. in med. tech., Vanderbilt U., 1974; MEd in Adminstrn. and Supervision, Tenn. State U., 1993. Cert. clin. lab. scientist Nat. Cert. Agy. Med. Lab Pers. Med. technologist Metro Gen. Hosp., Nashville, 1974-78, Vanderbilt Med. Ctr., Nashville, 1978-97; microbiologist Tenn. Dept. Health Lab. Svcs., Nashville, 1997—. Tech. cons. Vanderbilt Point of Care Program, 1993-96; lectr. St. Thomas Program Med. Tech., Nashville, 1991-94; mem. adv. bd. Tenn. State U./Meharry Med. Tech. Program, Nashville; instr. tchg. faculty Pub. Health Lab. Svcs., State Tenn., Nashville. Nashville bd. dirs. Tenn. Valley Region ARC Blood Svcs., 1996-2002; asst. sec. Henderville area chpt. The Links, Inc., 1997-2002; docent Frist Mus.; info. guide Fisk U. Mem.: AAAS, So. Assn. Clin. Microbiology, Am. Soc. Clin. Pathologist (assoc.; cert. med. technologist), Alpha Kappa Alpha, Phi Delta Kappa. Roman Catholic. Home: 1003 Cross Bow Dr Hendersonville TN 37075-9403 Office: Tenn Dept Health Lab Svcs Dept Microbiology Nashville TN 37202 Business E-Mail: Evelyn.Jones@state.tn.us.

JONES, FELICIA M., director; b. N.Y.C., June 20, 1961; d. Michael W. Toreno, Myrna L. Toreno. BS, Butler U., 1984; MS in Edn., Old Dominion U., 1997, student. Registered diagnostic med. sonographer, vascular technologist, diagnostic cardiac sonographer Am. Registry Diagnostic Med. Sonographers. Instr. Hillsborough C.C., Tampa, Fla., 1988—90; sect. leader sonography Mary Washington Hosp., Fredericksburg, Va., 1990—92; program dir. Tidewater C.C., Virginia Beach, Va., 1992—; chief sonographer Preferred Diagnostic Svcs., Inc., Largo, Fla., 1985—88. Coord. distance learning Tidewater C.C., Virginia Beach, 1998—2000; site visitor Joint Rev. Com. on Edn. in Diagnostic Med. Sonography, Bedford, 2000—. Co-author: Ultrasonography: An Introduction to Normal Structure and Function, 1995, Ultrasound Scanning: Principles and Protocols, 1999, Ultrasonography, 2004. Grantee, Va. C.C. Sys. Profl. Devel. Com., 1997, Tidewater C.C., 1998. Mem.: N.C. Ultrasound Soc., Am. Inst. Ultrasound in Medicine, Soc. Diagnostic Med. Sonographers. Office: Tidewater CC 1700 College Crescent Virginia Beach VA 23453 Office Phone: 757-822-7271. Home Fax: 757-427-1338; Office Fax: 757-427-1338. Business E-Mail: fjones@tcc.edu.

JONES, FLORENCE M., music educator; b. West Columbia, Tex., Apr. 11, 1939; d. Isaiah and Lu Ethel (Baldridge) McNeil; m. Waldo D. Jones, May 29, 1965; children: Ricky, Wanda, Erna. BS, Prairie View A&M U., 1961, MEd, 1968; postgrad., U. Houston, 1980, Rice U., 1988. Cert. in elem. edn., math. Tchr. English and typing Lincoln H.S., Port Arthur, Tex., 1961-62; tchr. grades three and four Houston Ind. Sch. Dist., 1963-90, tchr. gifted and talented, 1990-94; tchr. piano Windsor Village Liberal Arts Acad., Houston, 1994—. Dist. tchr. trainer Houston Ind. Sch. Dist., 1985-90; shared decision mem. Sch. decision Making Team, 1993-94; coord. gifted/talented program, Petersen Elem. Sch., Houston, 1990-94; participant piano Recital Hartzog Studio, 1985-88; film previewer Houston Media Ctr. Curriculum writer Modules to Improve Science Teaching, 1985; author sci. pop-up book, 1980, gifted/talented program, 1994; contbr. poems to lit. jours. Youth camp counselor numerous non-denominational ch. camps, US, 1961-89; active restoration of Statue of Liberty, Ellis Island Found., NYC, 1983-85; lay min. Ch. of God, 1961-94; charter founder The Am. Family History Immigration Ctr., Ellis Island, N.Y.C.; charter mem. Wall of Tolerance, honoree, 2005; co-chair Rosa Parks Commn.; founding sponsor Martin Luther King Jr. Nat. Meml. Project Found. Inc., 2006 Recipient Letter of Recognition Outstanding Progress in Edn., Pres. Bill Clinton, 1994, Congresswoman Sheilia Jackson Lee, Tex. Gov. George Bush, State Rep. Harold V. Sutton Jr., Houston Mayor Bob Lanier, Tex. Gov. Ann Richards; Gold Cup/Highest Music award Hartzog Music Studio, 1987, Diamond Key award Nat. Women of Achievement, 1995, Editors Choice award Nat. Libr. Poetry, 1995, cert. recognition Quaker Oats Co., 1999, Youth Advisors trophy and New Millennium Leader plaque Nat. Women Achievement, 2001, Humanitarian trophy, 2005; named Grandparent of Yr. Nat. Women of Achievement Youth Divsn., 2003; named to The Internat. Poetry Hall of Fame. Mem. NEA, Houston Assn. Childhood Edn. (v.p. 1985-88), Assn. for Childhood Edn. (bd. dir. 1979-91), Houston Zool. Soc., World Wildlife Fund, Nat. Storytelling Assn., Tejas Storytelling Assn. (life), Soc. Children's Book Writers and Illustrators, Nat. Audubon Soc., Am. Mus. Natural History, Tex. Ret. Tchrs. Assn. (life), Internat. Soc. Poets (life, Silver Cup award for outstanding poetry achievement 2003), Smithsonian Instn., Nat. Mus. Am. Indian, Nat. Mus. Women in Arts, Nat. Women's History Mus.(charter mem.) Democrat. Avocations: writing, reading, storytelling, collecting sea shells, crafts. Home: 3310 Dalmatian Dr Houston TX 77045-6520

JONES, GAIL PETERS, music educator; b. Bellefonte, Pa., Feb. 22, 1954; d. Ralph Edgar and Jane Shaffer Peters; m. John William Jones, June 16, 1979; children: Sarah Marie, R. Trevor. BS in Music Edn., Lebanon Valley Coll., Annville, Pa., 1976; MS in Edn., Temple U., Phila., 1983. Cert. in ch. music Episcopal Luth. Chs.; tchr. Orff-Schulwerk, 1986. Tchr. band Ctrl. Dauphin Sch. Dist., Hrrisburg, Pa., 1977—81, 1987—90; adminstr. student activities Gettysburg (Pa.) Coll., 1990—92; tchr. music Frederick (Md.) County Pub. Schs., 1992—97; tchr. band Gettysburg (Pa.) Area Sch. Dist., 1997—. Dir. choir Trinity United Ch. Christ, Gettysburg, 1996—2005; freelance musician, Pa., 1976—; pvt. instr. horn, Pa., 1976—; presenter in field. Vol. Local Soup Kitchen, Gettysburg, 2000—; mem. transp. adv. com. Cumberland Township, Adams County, Pa., 2005; mem. citizen's adv. bd.

WITF-FM and TV, Harrisburg, 1995—97. Mem.: Music Educators Nat. Conf., Pa. State Educators Assn., Pa. Music Educators Assn. (Citation of Excellence award 2004). Avocations: exercise, reading, gardening. Home: 70 Windbriar Lane Gettysburg PA 17325 Office: Gettysburg Area School Dist Lincoln Elem Sch 98 Lefever St Gettysburg PA 17325

JONES, GENIA KAY, critical care nurse, consultant; b. Dallas, Dec. 21, 1954; d. Joe and Juanita Sue (White) Self; m. Paul L. Jones, June 1, 1986. ADN, Tarrant County Jr. Coll., 1976; mgmt. cert., Cedar Valley Coll., 1980; postgrad., Mountain View Coll., Dallas, 1984—85; BSN, Regent's U., 2001. RN; cert. emergency nurse; cert. BLS, ACLS, pediat. advanced life support, trauma nurse core curriculum, ACLS instr. Instr. Steven's Pk. Hosp., Dallas, 1972-77; asst. dir. nursing svcs. Four Season's Conv. Ctr., Dallas, 1977-78; nurse surgery dept. Dallas/Ft. Worth Med. Ctr., 1978-80; dir. nursing Med. Staffing Svcs., Dallas, 1980, Reproductive Svcs., Inc., Dallas, 1981; adminstrv. supr. Dallas Family Hosp., 1982-85; patient care coord., emergency dept. Dallas S.W. Med. Ctr., 1985-90, staff nurse, emergency dept., 1990-99; medical consultant Needham, Johnson, Lovelace, and Johnson, 1992—2002; emergency nurse dir. Rockwall Minor Emergency Ctr., 1999—2001; emergency nurse Virtual Healthcare Svcs. Meth. Med. Ctrs. Dallas, 2001—03; emergency nurse Virtual Healthcare Svcs. emergency dept. Med. Ctr. Arlington, 2002—. Internat. flight nurse Air Ambulance Network, Inc., Dallas, 1987—92; instr. intravenous therapy, 1980—; cons., adv., 1980—; medicolegal cons., 1990—; clin. instr. Edn. Am., 1999—2001. Recipient Citizens award, Certs. Apprecition, HOSA Nat. Leadership Conf., Silver medal of Honor; Internat. Biog. Assn. fellow, 1990. Mem. NAFE, Am. Heart Assnb., Nurses' Svc. Orgn., Tex. Nurses' Assn., Emergency Nurses' Assn. Home: 108 Burkett Ln Red Oak TX 75154-7602 Office Phone: 214-803-4903. Personal E-mail: jgeniak@aol.com. E-mail: genia.jones@worldnet.att.net.

JONES, GEORGIA ANN, publisher; b. Ogden, Utah, July 6, 1946; d. Sam Oliveto and Edythe June Murphy; m. Lowell David Jones; children: Lowell Scott, Curtis Todd. Sculptor, 1964-78; journalist, 1968-80; appraiser real property Profl. Real Estate Appraisal, San Carlos, Calif., 1980-95; online columnist, 1995-97; prin., owner Ladybug Press, Sonora, 1996—, IA Connections Network, 2001—05; pres. NewVoices, Inc., Sonora, 2005—, CEO, 2005—. Leader workshops for writers, 1994—; founder, prodr. internat radio stas. Ladybughive, 1998—, Teen Talk Network, 1999—, Moose Meals, 2001— Author: A Garden of Weedin', 1997, Write What You Know: A Writer's Adventure, 1998, In Line at the Lost and Found, 2000, The Real Dirt on the American Dream: Home Ownership and Democracy, 2000; patentee Scruples-tag, 1980; editor, pub. Women on a Wire, 1996, vol. 2, 2001; author, playwright, The Porters, 1979, A Stitch in Time, 1995, The Usual Suspects, 1995. Spkr. Jubillenium Interfaith Conf. for World Peace, 1999. Mem. Internat. Forum of Lit. and Culture (bd. dirs., U.S. chpt., Pave Peace keynote spkr. internat. congress 1999). Avocations: drawing, designing and building homes, landscape gardening. Office: 16964 Columbia River Dr Sonora CA 95370 Office Phone: 209-694-8340. Personal E-mail: GeorgiaJ@ia-connections.com. Business E-Mail: georgia@ladybugbooks.com.

JONES, GERALDINE ANN JOHNSON, secondary school educator; b. Seaford, Del., July 30, 1939; d. Thomas E. and Marion Frances (Walker) Johnson; 1 child, Monica. BA, Del. State Coll., 1961; MBA, Cen. Mich. U., 1978; postgrad., Temple U., 1986—; PhD in Edn., Capella U., 1999; MDiv, Ea. Bapt. Theol. Seminary, 2005. Caseworker Div. Social Services, Dover, Del., 1962-64; tchr. English William C. Jason Sch., Georgetown, Del., 1966-67; vis. tchr. Capital Sch. Dist., Dover, 1967—. Home and sch. coord. migrant edn. program, Dover, 1967; paraprofl. Title I, Dover, 1964, 65; supr. Head Start Program, Camden, Del., 1970; speaker in field Active local polit. coms.; lay leader; pres. United Meth. Women, Whatcoat, pres. Peninsula conf., gen. bd. global minstries Peninsula-Del. conf., bd. laity, Dover dist. nominating com., com. on episcopacy/superintendency, coun. on ministries., del. to gen. conf. and jurisdictional conf., 1992; mem. nominating com. Upper Atlantic regional sch., dir. summer day camp, asst. dean; mem. Yesterdays Youth Choir, Seaford; min. Outreach Ministries United Meth. Ch.; pastor Union Wesley Unites Meth. Ch., Claresville, Del., 2005; pastor Union Wesley United Meth. Ch., Clarksville, Del., 2005— Named Woman of Yr., Whatcoat Ch., 1986; recipient Young award 2003. Mem. NEA, Internat. Assn. Pupil Pers. Workers, Del. Assn. Cert. Vis. Tchrs. (sec.-treas. 1984), Capital Educators Assn., Del. State Coll. Alumni Assn. (pres. Kent County chpt., Alumni of Yr. 1985, Ms. Alumni 1986-87), Nat. Alumni Assn. (pres.), William C. Jason Alumni Club (treas.), Delta Sigma Theta, Sigma Iota Epsilon. Democrat. Avocations: singing, writing, sewing, cooking, piano. Office: Capital Sch Dist 945 Forest St Dover DE 19904-3498 E-mail: gerryej@aol.com, gjones@capital.k12.de.us.

JONES, GWENYTH ELLEN, information technology executive; b. Omaha, Sept. 21, 1952; d. Robert Lester and Mary Ellen (Ouren) J.; m. William F. Knoff Jr. BA, U. Va., 1974, MA in English, 1982. Mktg. dir. John Wiley & Sons, N.Y.C., 1986-89, pub., 1989-90, dir. info. systems and tech., 1990-97, exec. dir. pub. info. systems and techs., 1997—2001; v.p. Pub. Info. Sys. and Techs., 2001—. Mem. Assn. Am. Pubs. Avocations: dance, tennis. Office Phone: 748-850-6109.

JONES, DAME GWYNETH, soprano; b. Pontnewynydd, Wales, Nov. 7, 1936; d. Edward George and Violet (Webster) J.; 1 dau. Student, Royal Coll. Music, London, Accademia Chigiana, Siena, Italy, Internat. Opera Ctr., Zurich, Switzerland; Dr. h.c. musica, U. Wales and Glamorgan. Mem. Royal Opera, Covent Garden, England, 1963—, Vienna State Opera, 1966—, Deutsche Opera Berlin, 1966, Munich Bavarian State Opera, 1967—. Guest performances in numerous opera houses including Hamburg, Bayreuth, Dresden, Paris, Zurich, Rome, Chgo., San Francisco, L.A., Tokyo, Buenos Aires, Munich, La Scala, Milan, Met. Opera, N.Y.C., Peking, Seoul, Bayreuth Festival, Hong Kong, Salzburg Festival, Verona; appeared in 50 leading roles including Tosca, Minnie, Turandot, Leonora in Il Trovatore, Desdemona in Otello, Lady MacBeth, Fidelio, Aida, Senta, Sieglinde, Marschallin, Isolde, Ortrud, Salome, Brunnhilde, Medea, Kundry, Madame Butterfly, Elizabeth/Venus in Tannhauser, Ariadne, Farberin, Elektra, Helena in Aegyptische Helena, Poppea, Santuzza, Donna Anna in Don Giovanni, Begbick in Mahagonny, Hannah Glawari, Erwartung, La Voix Humaine, Kostelnicka, Jenufa, Kabanicha, Katia Kabanowa Janacek; court singer, Bavaria, Austria; rec. artist for Decca, Deutsche Grammophon, Philips, EMI, CBS; dir., prodr.: Der Fliegende Hollander, Weimar Nat. Theatre, 2003; films, TV and concert appearances. Decorated dame comdr. Order Brit. Empire, 1986, Commandeur Des Arts Et Lettres, 1992, Ehren-Krenz I. Klasse, Austria Bundes Ver, 1998, others; recipient Shakespeare prize Hamburg, 1987, Verdienst Kreuz I Klasse Fed. Republic Germany, 1988, Golden Medal Honour, Vienna, 1991, Oesterreiche Ehren Kreuz Wissenschaft und Kunst Klasse, 1998, Premio Pucci award Torre Del Lago, 2003, Cymry for the World honor Wales Millennium Ctr., 2004, Kammersängerin, Austria, Bavaria. Fellow: Royal Welsh Coll. Music and Drama, Royal Coll. Music; mem.: Royal Acad. Music London (hon.), Rah (hon.). Address: Box 2000 CH-8700 Kusnacht Switzerland

JONES, HEDY JULIE, retired secondary school educator; b. New Haven, May 12, 1935; d. Geroge P. Rosensteel and Irma R. (Walter) Hegel; m. Richard Kish, June 23, 1955 (div. 1976); children: Kevin, Jennifer, Gretchen, Leonard; m. Robert Huhn Jones, July 17, 1982; children: Robert, Judy. BFA, Kent State U., Ohio, 1957; BS in Edn., U. Akron, Ohio, 1975, MS in Edn., 1978, PhD, 1992. Cert. sch. counselor, visual art tchr., Ohio. Artist Akron Pub. Libr., 1956-71; tchr. St. Paul's Nursery Sch., Akron, 1970-73, Revere Local Schs., Richfield, Ohio, 1973—96; ret., 1996. Instr. Coll. of Edn. U. Akron, 1993—; presenter papers in field. Author, illustrator: Let Us Pray Together, 1969; artist mural Ayres Br. Libr., 1970. Crisis line vol. Support, Inc., Akron, 1978-82; cultural arts coord Cuyahoga Valley nat. Recreation Area, Akron, 1982. Mem. NEA, Nat. Art Edn. Assn., Midwestern Ednl. Rsch. Assn., Ohio Edn. Assn., Ohio Art Educator's Assn., Pi Lambda Theta, Chi Sigma Iota. Episcopalian. Avocations: painting, crafts, swimming, sailing, hiking. Home: 1870 Oakridge Dr Akron OH 44313-5412 Personal E-mail: jhedy@aol.com.

JONES, HENDREE EVELYN, research scientist, psychologist; b. Richmond, Mar. 11, 1972; d. Clinton Edward Jones and Hendree Fitzgerald Mason; m. Erik Matthew Lensch, June 28, 1997; 1 child, Ashley Carter Lensch. BA, Randolph-Macon Coll., 1992; MA, U. Richmond, 1994; PhD, Va. Commonwealth U., 1997. From postdoctoral fellow to assoc. prof. Johns Hopkins U., Behavioral Pharm. Rsch. Unit, Balt., 1997—2004; assoc. prof. behavioral biology Dept. Psychiat. Johns Hopkins U., 2004—, dir. Ctr. Addiction and Pregnancy, 1998—, program dir. cornerstone, 2000—. Rsch. panel mem. Ctr. for Substance Abuse Treatment, Chevy Chase, Va., 2000; grant reviewer Nat. Inst. Drug Abuse, Washington, 2002, standing reviewer, 2004—; reviewer Nat. Registry for Effective Treatment Programs, Washington, 2003—. Contbr. articles various profl. jours. Vol. Hopkins House, Alexandria, Va., 2000—. Recipient Young Psychopharmacologist award, 1999. Fellow: APA (Early Career Contbn. to Applied Psychology award), Md. Psychol. Assn. (Career Contbn. to Sci. 2005); mem.: Coll. on Problems of Drug Dependence, Phi Beta Kappa. Achievements include development of animal model of abused inhalants during pregnancy; behavioral therapy for treating drug abusing partners of pregnant drug dependent women; research in pharmacotherapies for pregnant women. Avocations: reading, scuba diving, exercising, scrapbooks. Office: Johns Hopkins Bayview Med Ctr 4940 Eastern Ave D 3 E Baltimore MD 21224 Home: 318 Woodlawn Rd Baltimore MD 21210 Office Phone: 410-550-7684. Business E-Mail: hejones@jhmi.edu.

JONES, HETTIE COHEN, writer, educator; b. Bklyn. d. Oscar and Lottie (Lewis) Cohen; m. LeRoi Jones, Oct. 13, 1958 (div. 1965). BA in Drama cum laude, U. Va., 1955; postgrad., Columbia U., 1956. Freelance editl. svcs., N.Y.C., 1965—. Adj. prof. Parsons Sch. Liberal Studies, 1992-2004, Eugene Lang Coll., 2006—, L.I. U., 2006—; grad. writing program New Sch. U., 2003—; faculty writing 92nd St Y, N.Y.C., 1992—, New Sch., 1991, SUNY Purchase, NYU, CUNY, Mercy Coll., U. Wyo, 1993-94, Pa. State U., 1997; asst. to the editors Partisan Rev., 1957-61; staff writer Mobilization for Youth, 1966-68; editl. cons. Curriculum Concepts, Inc., 1984, Visual Edn. Corp., 1983, lectr. in field. Contbr. numerous articles to profl. jours.; contbr. poetry and fiction to publs.; author: All Told, 2003, How I Became Hettie Jones, 1990, paperbacks, 1991, 97, Drive, 1998 (Norma Farber award Poetry Soc. Am., 1999), The Trees Stand Shining, 1971, 2d edit. 1993, Big Star Fallin' Mama, 1974, 2d edit. 1995 (selected as one of 20 best new books for young adults N.Y. Pub. Libr.); co-author: (with Rita Marley) No Woman No Cry, 2004; co-editor: Yugen mag., 1958-61; bd. dirs. Cave Canem (African Am. Poetry). Chmn. bd. dir. Ch. of All Nations, 1972-76; cons. Grace Ch. Opportunity Project, Day Care Coun. of Greater N.Y., 1968-72, 85; chair PEN Prison Writing Com., 1999-2002; condr. writing workshop N.Y. State Correctional Facility Women, Bedford Hills, 1989-2002; grant recommender Lower Manhattan Cultural Coun., 1994—; mem. lit. panel N.Y. State Coun. on the Arts, 1994-97. E-mail: hettiej@msn.com.

JONES, INGRID SAUNDERS, food products executive; b. Detroit; EdB, Mich. State U.; EdM, Ea. Mich. U., 1973; HHD (hon.), Mich. State U., Atlanta Coll. Art, Morris Brown Coll. Tchr. pub. sch. sys., Detroit, Atlanta; exec. dir. Detroit/Wayne County Child Care Coordinating Coun.; legis. analyst to the pres. Atlanta City Coun.; exec. asst. to Mayor Maynard Jackson; asst. to v.p. for urban and govtl. affairs The Coca-Cola Co., 1982—86, mgr. urban projects, 1986—87, dir. urban affairs, 1987—88, asst. v.p., 1988—91, v.p., mgr. corp. external affairs, 1991, sr. v.p. corp. external affairs Atlanta, 2000—. Chair The Coca-Cola Found.; bd. dirs. Girls, Inc., Mich. State U. Found., Andrew Young Sch. Policy Studies, Ga. State U., Desmond Tutu Peace Found., Coca-Cola Scholars Found., Cmty. Found. Greater Atlanta, 1994—, Nat. Black Arts Festival, Coun. on Founds., Woodruff Arts Ctr., United Way Met. Atlanta, chair. Named to Hall of Fame, Ga. State U. Sch. Bus., 1998; recipient Pres. award, Morehouse Coll., 1988, Nat. Equal Justice award, NAACP Legal and Edn. Fund, 1997, Jondelle Johnson Legacy award, NAACP-Atlanta Chpt., 1998, Woman of Achievement award, YWCA Greater Atlanta, 1998, John B. Gerlach Devel. award, Ohio State U. Found., 1998, Nat. Action Networker's Keepers of the Dream award, 2001. Mem.: Soc. Internat. Bus. Fellows, Atlanta Rotary Club. Office: The Coca-Cola Co PO Box 1734 Atlanta GA 30301

JONES, JANE, artist; b. Denver, Apr. 3, 1953; d. Leslie Richard and Dorothy Mae (Hays) J.; m. John Q. Gaddis, Apr. 2, 1983. BS, Met. State Coll., 1976; MA, Regis U., 2005. Tchr. Red Rocks Cmty. Coll., Lakewood, Colo., 1990—, Met. State Coll., Denver, 2005—. One person shows include Le KAE Gallery, Scottsdale, Az., 1996, 98-99, 2003, 2005, Turner Art Gallery, Denver, 1998, Akontempo Gallery, Delray Beach, Fla., 1996-97, Horizon Fine Art, Jackson, Wyo., 2001; invitational exhbns.: Am. Art in Miniature, Gilcrease Mus., 2001-02, 04, 06, Nat. Mus. Wildlife Art, 2001-06, van de Griff/Marr Gallery, Santa Fe, N.Mex., 2001-02, West Valley Art Mus., Phoenix, 2003, Salon d'Arts, 2004, Colo. History Mus., Art Students League, Denver, 2004—, Metro. State Coll., Denver, 2005-06, Nat. Arts Club, NYC, 2005, 2006; group exhbns. include Aspen Art Mus., 1989, Oil Painters of Am. Prince Gallery, Chgo., 1992, Nabisco Art Gallery, E. Hanover, NJ, 1993, Denver Art Mus., 1994, Port Royal Mus. Galleries, Naples, Fla., 1994, Am. Artists Profl. League, NY, 1997, Women Artists of the West Show, San Juan Capistrano, Calif., 1998; author: Classic Still Life Painting, 2004; contbr. articles to profl. jours. Recipient Juror's Choice award, Colo. History Mus., Denver, 1997, Floral award, Am. Artists Profl. League, N.Y., 1992, 94, 99, First Place Purchase award, 30th Annual Fall Art Festival, Glenwood Springs, Colo., 1992, Juror's award, Arvada Ctr. for Arts/Humanities, Colo., 1991, Florence & Ernst Thorne Thompson Meml. award Allied Artists of Am. Mem.: Allied Artists of Am. (Florence and Ernst Thorne Thompson Meml. award 2002), Am. Artists Profl. League (Vera C. Rosenhaft award). Methodist. E-mail: jane@janejonesartist.com.

JONES, JANET DULIN, scriptwriter, film producer; b. Hollywood, Calif., Sept. 6, 1957; d. John Dulin and Helen Mae (Weaver) J. BA, Calif. State U., Long Beach, 1980. Developer mini-series and TV series Embassy Comm., LA, 1981-84; assoc. to producer Hotel Aaron Spelling Prodns., LA, 1984-85; writing intern Sundance Film Inst., LA, 1985; freelance screenplay and play writer, LA and NYC, 1986—. Author: (screenplays) Fad Away, 1986, Alone in the Crowd, 1987, Story of the Century, 1988, The Long Way Home, 1989, Cousin Judy, 1989, The Set-up, 1990, Roommates, 1991, Local Girl, 1991, Dickens and Crime, 1992, Little Bear Books, Vols. 1-5; actor: A Weighty, Waity Matter-My Adventures with India, 1992; author: (screenplays) Coming and Going, 1993, Watching the Detectives, 1994, The Ambassadors, 1994, Words of Love, 1995, Map of the World, 1995, Katherine, 1996, Vanity Fair, 1996, Sarah's Mark, 1998; dir.: Words of Love, 1998, Custom of the Country, 1999, Nevermore, 2002, The Romantics, 2001; author: (non-fiction) Cook & Tell, 2002, (plays) A Tale of Charles Dickens, 2003, (films) What If God Were The Sun, 2004, The Collapsible World, 2005. Bd. dirs. Sterling Cir. of Aviva Ctr. for Girls, 1990; bd. dirs., rec. sec., steering com. The Creative Coalition, 1991-92; mem. Canine Hosp. Vols., Santa Monica Hosp., Bd. dirs. Young Filmmakers Acad., 2004 Mem. ACLU, Women in Film, Earth Communication Office (TV and film coms.), Writers Guild Am., Ind. Feature Project, Am. Film Inst., Sundance Film Inst. (pre-selection com. 1985-87), The Antaeus Theatre Co., People for Am. Way, Habitat for Humanity, Anmesty Internat., Delta Gamma. Address: 1518 Franklin St # 4 Santa Monica CA 90404 Office Phone: 310-433-2227.

JONES, JANICE COX, elementary school educator, writer; b. Jackson, Miss., Nov. 4, 1937; d. Eugene Debs and Thelma Corelli (Beard) Cox; m. June 20, 1959 (div. June 1985); children: Allison Jones Griffiths, Tamara Jones McKee. BS with highest distinction, Miss. Coll., 1959; MEd magna cum laude, U. Miami, 1968. Cert. elem. edn. Tchr. Jackson Pub. Sch., 1959-60, Arlington (Tex.) Pub. Schs., 1960-63, Houston Pub. Schs., 1963-64, Miami-Dade County Pub. Schs., 1967-1980, 1988—97; pres. Palm Tree Prodns., Ltd., 1980-88. Tchr. English ESOL Say Sch., Tokyo, 1985; tutor, child welfare worker CBS, Twentieth Century Fox, N.Y.C., Miami, 1981-; pvt. tutor, owner Think, Ink!, Miami, 1983-; piano tchr. MDCPS Cmty. Sch., Miami, 1991-; participant Miss. Gov.'s Edn./Econ. Task Force, 1990-91; workshop presenter Children's Cultural Coalition & Arts for Learning; speaker/poet in field; usher Coconut Grove Playhouse, Actor's Playhouse, Gablestage, Biltmore. Author several books of poetry, Geography Fun Facts: A Trip Across the U.S.A. in Poetry, Numbered & Named: A Preventive for Math Anxiety in Children and Adults. Dist. exec. adv. com. to sch. bd. for gifted edn. Miami-Dade County Pub. Schs., 1987-91; adv. bd. Metro-Dade Rapid Transit, 1974-77; parent sponsor Olympics of the Mind Team, 1984; parent sponsor Queen's Ct., Jr. Orange Bowl, Coral Gables, Fla., 1983; vol. pianist, organist, music dir. Village Green Baptist Mission, Miami, 1973; vol. Habitat for Humanity, 1991-. Recipient nat. poetry award, Byline Mag., 2002, ann. conf. scholarship, World Future Soc.; grantee, NEA, 1973. Mem. Am. Fedn. Tchrs., Dade Heritage Trust (edn. com., writer), Miami Writer's Club, Fla. Freelance Writers Assn., Nat. Writers Assn. South Fla. chapt. (bd., exec. sec. 1997-, nat. writing contest chair, 1998-2001), United Tchrs. Dade (bldg. steward 1976-78), Tropical Audubon Soc., Coun. for Internat. Visitors, Internat. Platform Assn. (red carpet com.), Soc. Children's Book Writers and Illustrators, Miami Arts Exch., Nature Conservancy, Sierra Club. Avocations: Broadway plays and musicals, museums, fishing, photography, travel, accordion. Home: 6301 SW 93rd Ct Miami FL 33173-2317

JONES, JEANNE PITTS, pre-school administrator; b. Richmond, Va., Oct. 19, 1938; d. Howard Talliaferro and Anne Elizabeth Pitts; children: Jack Hunter Jr., Judith Anne, James Howard, Jon Martain. BA, Marshall U., 1961, postgrad., 1962, Presbyn. Sch. Christian Edn., Richmond, 1974, 94; MEd in Early Childhood Edn., Va. Commonwealth U., 2000. Cert. tchr. Va. Tchr. Richmond Pub. Schs., 1961-65; founder Bon View Sch. Early Childhood Edn., Richmond, 1971, tchr., 1971-91, dir., 1971—. Acad. affairs chmn. Good Shepherd Episcopal Sch. Bd., Ricmond, 1985—88; mentor Ecumenical Child Care Network Nat. Coun. Chs., Washington, 1990—92; validator Nat. Assn. Edn. Young Children, 1993—, mentor, 1994—98; ednl. cons., mentor Success By Six, 2002. Chmn. rm. parents Crestwood Sch. PTA Bd., Richmond, 1974—80; children's coord. Bon Air United Meth. Ch., Richmond, 1985—93; v.p. Bon Air United Meth. Ch. Women, Richmond, 1991—94; dir. Camp Friendship Bon Air United Meth. Ch., Richmond, 1992—; rep. Va. Conf. United Meth. Ch., 1993—95, weekday com., 1992—94; publicity chmn. Va. Swimming, Richmond, 1978—88; rep. Va. Children's Action Network. Recipient Spl. Mission recognition, Bon Air United Meth. Women, 1987. Mem.: Nat. Assn. Edn. for Young Children (validator 1993—, mentor 1994—98), Va. Assn. for Early Childhood Edn. (affiliate pres. 2002—04, 3d v.p. liaisons 2004—05, affiliate accreditation chair 2005—06), Chesterfield Coalition Early Childhood Educators (bd. dirs. 1993—97), Presch. Assn. Ch. Ednl. Dirs. (pres. 1993—95), Richmond Early Childhood Assn. (mem.-at-large 1994—96, rec. sec. 1996—98, 1998—2000, v.p. membership 2000—02, pres.-elect 2001—02, pres. 2002—04, past pres. 2004—06, affiliate accreditation chair 2006—, Richmond Early Childhood Adv. of the Yr. 2002). Republican. Avocations: aerobics, reading. Home: 9103 Whitaker Cir Richmond VA 23235-4053 Office: Bon View Sch Early Childhood Edn 1645 Buford Rd Richmond VA 23235-4274 Office Phone: 804-320-7043.

JONES, JERRY LOU HOLBERT, elementary school educator, rancher; b. Albemarle, N.C., Sept. 5, 1942; d. Edward Daniel and Ellen Geraldine (Gaddy) Holbert; m. James Vogler Jones, Dec. 5, 1975 (div. Aug. 2004). BA, Meredith Coll., 1964; postgrad., Pfeiffer Coll., 1967-68. Med. technician Stanly County Hosp., Albemarle, N.C., 1964-65, Office Dr. George E. Eddins, MD, Albemarle, 1965-67; tchr. Albemarle City Schs., 1969-72, Davie County Schs., Mocksville, NC, 1972—97; ret. Cons. N.C. Advancement Sch., Winston-Salem, N.C., 1971. Vice chmn. Davie County Rep. Exec. Com., Mocksville, N.C., 1982-86. Mem. NEA, N.C. Assn. Educators. Methodist. Avocations: hiking, bicycling, sewing, crafts, skiing. Home: 153 Riverview Townhouse Dr Advance NC 27006

JONES, JEWEL, social services administrator; b. Oklahoma City, Dec. 7, 1941; d. Joseph Samuel and Jewell (Hathyel) Fisher; m. Maurice Jones, July 17, 1976; children: Anthony, Carmen. BA in Sociology, Langston (Okla.) U., 1962; MA in Pub. Adminstrn., U. Alaska, Anchorage, 1974. Tchr. Seidman Sch., L.A., 1962; correctional ofifcer State of Calif. Dept. Corrections, Corona, 1963-65; probation officer County of San Bernardino, Calif., 1965-67; dep. exec. dir. Cmty. Action Agy., Anchorage, 1967-70; social svcs. dir. City of Anchorage, 1970-87; social svcs. mgr. Municipality of Anchorage, 1987-2000, dir. health & human svcs., 2000—. Chmn. bd. Alaska Housing Fin. Corp., Anchorage, 1995—; pres. Anchorage KidsPlace Project, 1994-95; chair Alaskan of the Yr. Scholarship Com., 1985—; chmn. bd. Janet Helen Tolan Gamble and Toby Gamble Ednl. Trust, 1998—. Mem. adv. bd. Salvation Army, Anchorage, 1982-87, Alaska R.R., Anchorage, 1990—; trustee United Way of Anchorage, 1990-97; bd. dirs Alaska Ctr. for Performing Arts, 1987-97. Recipient Pres.'s award Alaska Black Caucus, 1984, Employment of Handicapped award Mayor of Anchorage, 1979, Execs. in Profile award Region X Blacks in Govt. award, 1998. Mem. NAACP (Harambe award 1973), Alaska Black Leadership Conf. (Cmty. Svc. award 1979-80), Links Inc., Quota Club Intenrat., Valli Vue Homeowners Assn. (v.p.), Zeta Phi Beta. Democrat. Avocations: cooking, reading, gardening. Office: Municipality Anchorage PO Box 196650 Anchorage AK 99519-6650

JONES, JO ANN, retired elementary school educator; d. Harry Franklin and Evelyn Elizabeth Rittberger; m. James Richard Jones, June 25, 1960 (div. 1982); children: Douglas Richard, Michael Lee(dec.). BS in Edn., Muskingum Coll., New Concord, Ohio, 1960. Lic. elem. sch. tchr. Ohio. Tchr. 1st grade Philo Elem., Ohio, 1960—69, tchr. 6th grade tchr., 1969—70; tchr. 3d grade tchr. South Zanesville Elem., Ohio, 1970—95; substitute tchr. grades K-8 Maysville and Franklin Sch. Dist., Zanesville and Philo, Ohio, 1995—98; tchr. math and reading tchr. Maysville Elem., Zanesville, 1998—2005; tchr. reading support Maysville Elem. Sch., Zanesville, 2005—. Tchr. Sunday sch. Trinity Luth. Ch., Zanesville; vol. Bethesda Hosp., Zanesville; treas. South Zanesville PTO, Zanesville; tchr. leader intervention assistance team, grade level rep. Maysville Elem., Zanesville. Mem.: Ohio Ret. Tchrs. Assn. (life). Trinity Lutheran Church. Avocations: travel, playing cards, computers, photography. Home: 79 Halley Dr Zanesville OH 43701 Office: Maysville Elem Sch 3850 Panther Dr Zanesville OH 43701 Office Phone: 740-454-4490. Business E-Mail: jajones@laca.org.

JONES, JO CAROL, pilot, educator; b. Arkadelphia, Ark., Dec. 12, 1942; d. Joseph Edmund Hubbard and Marjorie Ruth David; m. Carroll Doyle Jones (dec. Apr. 14, 1984); children: Doyle Matthew, Christopher Joseph, Anthony Douglas. EdBS, U. Ark., 1964; MSEd, U. Ctrl. Ark., 1986; EdD, Tex. A&M U., 1995. Instrument rating, multi-engine rating, cert. comml. pilot, advanced and instrument ground instr., flight instr., instrument flight instr, multi-engine flight instr. Tchr. Little Rock Pub. Schs., 1964—67; pilot, flight instr. Favis Air, N. Little Rock, 1979—81; pilot Ctrl. Flying Svc., Little Rock, 1981—84, Pilot Svcs., Little Rock, 1984—88; head aviation dept. Navarro Coll., Corsicana, Tex., 1988; chair aerospace sci. dept. Met. State Coll., Denver, 1994—2000; cons. Ind. Aviation Cons., Little Rock, 2000—. Author: (textbook) Multi-engine Simulator Flight Training Manual, 1997, Airline Planning Textbook, 1999; contbr. articles to profl. jours., chapters to books. Vol. Vols. in Pub. Schs., Little Rock, 1978—88; presentor Air Bear, Denver, 1994—2000, Fantasy of Flight, Denver, 1996—2000; dir. Summer Aviation Camp, Corsicana, 1989—91; mem. exihibits com. Wings Over the Rockies, Denver, 1995—97; team leader Make A Difference Day, Aurora, Colo., 1995—2000; active Habitat for Humanity. Named Star, Vols. in Pub. Schs., 1984—86; grantee, Met. State Coll., 1998. Mem.: Women in Aviation, Aircraft Owners and Pilots Assn., Univ. Aviation Com. (chair aviation edn. com. 1998—2000), Audubon Soc., Nat. Wildlife Fedn., 99's, Civil Air Patrol (aerospace edn. officer 2000—01), Planetary Soc., Kappa Delta Pi, Alpha Eta Rho (life; sponsor 1988—94, Educator of the Year 1992). Avocations: hiking, reading, bridge, camping. Office: Ind Aviation Mgmt Cons 37 Kensington Drive Bella Vista AR 72714 E-mail: jonesjnd@yahoo.com.

JONES, JOAN MEGAN, anthropologist; b. Laramie, Wyo., Sept. 7, 1933; d. Thomas Owen and Lucille Lenoir (Magill) J. BA, U. Wash., 1956, MA, 1968, PhD, 1976. Mus. educator Burke Mus. U. Wash., Seattle, 1969-72; anthropologist Quinault Indian Nation, Taholah, Wash., 1976-77; researcher, corp. officer Profl. Anthropology Consulting Team/Social Analysts, Seattle, 1977-79; research assoc. dept. anthropology U. Wash., Seattle, 1982-91. Research investigator Dept. Social and Health Services State of Wash., Seattle, 1977; vis. lectr. Dept. Anthropology U. B.C., Vancouver, 1978; research specialist Artsplan Arts Alliance Wash. State, Seattle, 1978; vis. instr. Dept. Anthropology Western Wash. U., Bellingham, 1981; rsch. and archives dir. Samish Indian Nation, Anacortes, Wash., 2001-; cons. in field. Author: Northwest Coast Basketry and Culture Change, 1968, Basketry of Quinault, 1977, Native Basketry of Western North America, 1978, Art and Style of Western Indian Basketry, 1982, Northwest Coast Indian Basketry Styles. Wenner-Gren Found. Anthrop. Research fellow, 1967-68; Ford Found. fellow, 1972-73; Nat. Mus.'s. Can. grantee, 1973-74. Fellow Am. Anthrop. Assn., Soc. Applied Anthropology; mem. Nat. Assn. Practicing Anthropologists, Assn. Women in Sci., Skagit Valley Weavers Guild (v.p. Skagit County chpt. 1985-86, 89-90, corr. sec. 1988-89), Whidbey Weavers. Avocations: handweaving, hand spinning, knitting.

JONES, JUDITH MILLER, director; BA, George Washington U., 1965; student, Georgetown U., 1965—67; MA in Edn. Tech., Cath. U., 1969. With IBM, 1965—69; legis. asst. Sen. Winston L. Prouty Vt., 1969—71; spl. asst. Office Dep. Asst. Sec. Legis. Dept. Health, Edn. and Welfare, Washington, 1971—72; dir. Nat. Health Policy Forum The George Washington U., Washington, 1972—. Mem. Nat. Com. Vital and Health Stats., 1988—91, chmn., 1991—96; profl. lectr. health policy The George Washington U.; chmn. Ctr. for Advancement of Health. Office: National Health Policy Forum 2131 K Street NW Ste 500 Washington DC 20037 Office Phone: 202-872-1390. Business E-Mail: jmjones@gwu.edu.

JONES, JULIE ANN, elementary school educator, choreographer; b. New Brunswick, NJ, May 1, 1974; d. Timothy Paul and Ann Nealon Farrell; m. Brian Jones, July 10, 2004. BS magna cum laude, Univ. Scranton, Pa., 1996. Cert. K-6 Tchr. Pa., registered artist Keystone Coll., 2005. 2nd grade tchr. Scranton Sch. Dist., Pa., 1996—97, 5th grade tchr., 1997—; dance instr. ballet mistress Ballet Theatre of Scranton, 1996—2003; choregrapher Regional HS plays, Scranton, 1996—; registered artist Keystone Coll., La Plume, Pa., 2005—. Dist. coord. elem. Spanish instrn. Bancroft Sch., Scranton, 1998—, cheerleading coach, 2005—; registered artist Keystone Coll., LaPlume, Pa., 2005—. Contbg. author (ednl. curriculum guides). Mem. Ballet Theatre of Scranton, Pa., 1982—2003. Recipient Blue Ribbon award, Nat. Dept. of Edn., Washington, 2004. Mem.: Nat. Coun. of Pa. Tchrs. of Math., Scranton Fedn. of Tchrs., Am. Fedn. of Tchrs., Alpha Mu Gamma, Kappa Delta Pi. Democrat. Roman Catholic. Avocations: writing, art, piano, dance.

JONES, KAREN ANNETTE, civic volunteer; b. Breckenridge, Tex., Feb. 16, 1941; d. Ballard Dorsie and Iris Alvern (Hampton) Hutchison; m. Jerry Raymond Jones, Mar. 16, 1963; children: Lisa Rene Jones Story, Karen DeAnn Jones. BS, McMurry U., Abilene, Tex., 1963. Sec. McMurry Coll., Abilene, 1959-63, Continental Oil Co., Abilene, 1963; substitute tchr. Abilene Pub. Schs., 1967-68; tchr. continuing edn. Mountainview Community Coll., Dallas, 1974; floral designer/sec. Christopher Design, Dallas, 1978-80. Bd. dirs., sec. Wesley Rankin Community Ctr., Dallas, 1989-97; adminstrv. bd. Inglewood United Meth. Ch., Grand Prairie, Tex., 1986—, Breckenridge (Tex.) United Meth. Ch., 2001—; bd. dirs., Brighter Tomorrows Abused Women's Shelter, Grand Prairie, 1994-97; mentor, Breckenridge Jr. H.S., 2001—; regional dir., liaison Guillain-Barre Syndrome Found. Internat., 1999-. Mem. AAUW (sec. 1988—), Grand Prairie Women's Club (bd. dirs. 1986-88). Democrat. Methodist. Address: 10101 County Road 197 Breckenridge TX 76424-7005 E-mail: jerann@bitstreet.com.

JONES, KAREN FAULKNER, art educator; b. Rock Hill, S.C., Mar. 7, 1958; d. Hugh Grier and Hayes Mitchell Faulkner; m. Bruno Maximillian Jones, Sept. 1, 1979; children: Lydia Hayes, Grier Maximillian, Mitchell Faulkner. BA in Art, Winthrop U., Rock Hill, S.C., 1979, M in Secondary Edn. emphasis on art edn., 1993. Cert. art educator SC. Dept. Edn., 1980. Tchr. Long Valley Elem. Sch., Lassen County, Calif., 1980; art tchr. Cherokee H.S., Gaffney, SC, 1985, Draytonville Elem. Sch., Gaffney, 1985—89, Daniel Morgan Elem. Sch., Gaffney, 1985—89, Goucher Elem. Sch., Gaffney, 1985—89, Blacksburg Elem. Sch., Blacksburg, 1989—. Arts standards and grant writing presenter Cherokee County Sch. Dist., Gaffney, 1991, arts strategic planning com. mem., 2003—, arts curriculum constrn. presenter, 2005; summer instr. for visual art tchrs. participant Winthrop U., Rock Hill, 1989; grant writer art edn. Cherokee County Sch. Dist., 1989—, visual arts curriculum com. mem., 1997—98; staff devel. conf. evaluator Winthrop U., 1991; curriculum leadership instr. in the arts participant Arts in Basic Curriculum Project, S.C. State Dept. Edn., 2004, curriculum leadership instr. in the arts selected participant, 05, curriculum leadership instr. in the arts coach, 2006—. Author: (elementary visual art curriculum) Beyond the Basics: A Discipline-Based Visual Arts Curriculum for Cherokee County Sch. Dist. K-6, (revision of elem. art curriculum) Beyond the Basics; author: (co-author) Cherokee County Sch. Dist. Elem. Visual Art Curriculum. Mem.: S.C. Alliance for Arts Edn., Nat. Art Edn. Assn., S.C. Art Edn. Assn. Avocation: painting. Home: 178 Faulkner Rd Kings Creek SC 29702 Office: Blacksburg Elem Sch 402 Hardin St Blacksburg SC 29702 Office Phone: 864-839-2363.

JONES, KATHERINE R., nursing educator; BSN, U. Mich., MS in Med.-Surgical Nursing; PhD in Adminstrn. & Policy Analysis, Stanford U., 1983; post-doctoral studies in Healthcare Fin. & Quality, Johns Hopkins U. Asst./assoc. prof. Coll. Health Related Professions U. Fla., 1983—88, UCLA Sch. Nursing, 1988—91; assoc. prof. U. Mich. Sch. Nursing, 1991—98, dir. divsn. nursing & health care adminstrn.; prof. nursing U. Colo. Health Sciences Ctr., Denver, 1999—2003, sch. nursing faculty chair; prof. Yale Sch. Nursing, New Haven, 2003—, acting dean, 2004—, dir. Yale Program for the Advancement of Chronic Wound Care. Office: Yale U Sch Nursing PO Box 9740 100 Church St S New Haven CT 06536 Office Phone: 203-737-1791. Office Fax: 203-737-5034. Business E-Mail: katherine.jones@yale.edu.

JONES, KATHRYN CHERIE, pastor; b. Breckenridge, Tex., Nov. 26, 1955; d. Austin Thomas and Margaret May (Mohr) J. BA, U. Calif., San Diego, 1977; MDiv, Fuller Theol. Sem., 1982. Assoc. pastor La Jolla (Calif.) United Meth. Ch., 1982-84; pastor in charge Dominguez United Meth. Ch., Long Beach, Calif., 1984-88, San Marcos (Calif.) United Meth. Ch., 1988-90, Atascadero United Methodist Church, 2003—; dir. The Walk to Emmaus, Upper Rm. Ministries, Nashville, 1990-98, Resource Initiatives & Interpretation, Upper Rm. Ministries, Nashville, 1998—. Coord. chaplains Pacific Hosp., Long Beach, 1986-88. Bd. dirs. So. Calif. Walk to Emmaus Cmty., L.A., 1987-88, San Diego chpt., 1988-90; vol. victim advicacy groups, including You Have the Power, Forever Group. Mem. Christian Assn. Psychol. Studies, Evangs. for Social Action. Democrat. Office: Atascadero UMC PO Box 2037 11605 El Camino Real Atascadero CA 93423-2037 Office Phone: 805-466-2566. Office Fax: 805-466-2563.

JONES, KATHY W., research scientist, educator; b. Alexander City, Ala., June 27, 1955; d. Kenneth W. and Carol. A. Wall; m. George W. Jones, May 31, 1997; children: Megan N. Young, Michael C. Young. MSc, Troy U., Montgomery, Ala., 2004. Cert. med. technologist Am. Soc. Clin. Pathologists, 1980. Dept. supr. hematology St. Margaret's Hosp., Montgomery, 1984—90; edn. coord. St. Margaret's Hosp. Sch. Med. Tech., Montgomery, 1990—91; program dir. Ala. Reference Labs. Inc. Sch. Med. Tech., Montgomery, 1991—2004; instr. Auburn U. Montgomery Clin. Lab. Sci. Program, Montgomery, 2005—. Cons. Auburn U. Montgomery, 2005. Sec./treas. The Robert B. Adams Found., Montgomery, 1996. Mem.: Am. Soc. Clin. Lab. Scientists. Achievements include development of Medical Technology Program. Office: Auburn Univ Montgomery PO Box 244023 Montgomery AL 36124-4023 Office Phone: 334-244-3254. Office Fax: 334-244-3146. Business E-Mail: kjones31@mail.aum.edu.

JONES, KAYLIE ANN, writing educator, writer; b. Paris; came to U.S., 1974; d. James R. and Gloria J.; m. Kevin Michael Heisler, Aug. 12, 1995; 1 child, Eyrna Holland Heisler. BA, Wesleyan U., 1981; MFA, Columbia U., 1983; degree in Russian Lang. (hon.), Pushkin Inst., Moscow, 1987. Grants coord. Poets and Writers, N.Y.C., 1983-84, asst. to dir. devel., 1984-87; instr. writing The Writer's Voice, N.Y.C., 1988-95; prof. Southampton campus L.I. U., 1995—; writers in residence N.Y.C. pub. schs. Tchrs. and Writers, 1991—. Author: As Soon As It Rains, 1985, Quite the Other Way, 1989, A Soldier's Daughter Never Cries, 1990, Celeste Ascending, 2000; cons., writer (film) A Soldier's Daughter Never Cries, 1998, Speak Now, 2003. Mem. James Jones Lit. Soc. (bd. dirs., chmn. 1st novel, Fellowship award), Phi Beta Kappa. Avocations: scuba diving, yoga, weightlifting. Office: Humanities Southampton Coll Montauk Hwy Southampton NY 11968 E-mail: knones4@nyc.rr.com.

JONES, KIA TANETTA, daycare administrator; b. Phila., Pa., Feb. 25, 1971; d. Kevin Andrews and Acquanetta Dixon; m. Shawn Jones, Feb. 21, 1994; children: Shawn Jr., Siani. AA, CCP of Phila. Daycare dir., owner Past Your Bedtime Childcare, Phila.; headstart learning family Headstart Learning Tree, Phila.; adv. Caring People Alliance, Phila.; tchr. Head Start Learning Tree, Phila. Author: (book) Shamya and Friends, 2006. Office: Past Your Bedtime Childcare Ctr 2009 N 63d St Philadelphia PA 19151

JONES, KIM, computer company executive; BA with honors, U. Calif., San Diego. Sales, mktg. and mgmt. positions Wang Laboratories, Xerox Corp.; joined Sun Microsystems Inc., 1987, dir. internat. sales devel., v.p. global edn. and rsch., v.p Global Edn., Govt. and Health Sciences, 2006—, mem. diversity coun. Bd. trustees Western Governors U.; bd. dirs. Global Edn. Learning Cmty., Sun Found., John Wiley & Sons Inc.; adv. coun. World Bank Inst.; mem. Bus. Higher Edn. Forum. Named to WITI Hall of Fame, Women in Tech. Internat., 2006; recipient YWCA award women in bus. Office: Sun Microsystems Inc 4150 Network Circle Santa Clara CA 95054*

JONES, KRISTA MARIE, elementary school educator; b. Pottstown, Pa., Dec. 27, 1965; d. Curtis O'Dell and Sonja Virginia Behrmann; m. Larry Lee Jones, June 19, 1992; 1 child, Liam Lamont. AA, Olympic Coll., Bremerton, Wash., 1986; BA, Cen. Wash. U., Ellensburg, 1988. Edn. Wash., Idaho. Presch. tchr. Wee Wolf Presch., Port Orchard, Wash., 1981—83; retail salesperson Pay N Save, Seattle, 1981—88; tchr. 1st grade Bellevue Elem. Sch., Idaho, 1988—97, instr. tech. edn., 1989—. Math. tutor Bruhe & Assocs., Hailey, 1990—92; new tchr. trainer Blaine County Sch. Dist., Hailey, Idaho, 1995—97; curriculum cons. NASA/Internat. Tech. Edn. Assn., Reston, Va., 2005—. Contbr. articles to profl. jours. Mem. City Parks Com., Bellevue, 2004—06. Recipient Featured in Am.'s 21st Century's Best Practices in Tech. Edn., Tech. Found. of Am., 2006, Presdl. Award for Excellence in Math. and Sci. Tchg.-State Finalist, NSF, 2004, Robotics Grant, Idaho Nat. Lab., 2005—07. Mem.: NEA (assoc.; local regional rep. 1993—95), Idaho Sci. Tchrs. Assn. (assoc. Regional Sci. Tchr. of Yr. 2000), Idaho Tech. Edn. Assn. (assoc. Tech. Edn. Tchr. of Yr. 2005), Internat. Tech. Edn. Assn. (assoc. Tech. Edn. Program of Yr. award 2004), Tech. and Children Editl. Bd. (assoc.; bd. mem. 2004—06). Avocations: music, art, gardening. Office: Bellevue Elementary School 305 North 5th Street Bellevue ID 83313 Office Phone: 208-788-4012. Office Fax: 208-788-5156. Business E-Mail: kjones@blaineschools.org.

JONES, LASHAUNTA' LYNN, athletic trainer, academic advisor; b. Springfield, Ohio, Dec. 16, 1978; d. Charles Edward Barnes and Lou Esther Darlene Jones, Lawrence W. Wilkerson (Stepfather). BA in Mid. Childhood Edn. and Athletic Tng., Wright State U., Dayton, Ohio, 2003. Atc Nat. Athletic Trainer's Assn./, 2005. Mem. staff Extended Stay Hotels, Fairborn, Ohio, 2000—04; athletic trainer, academic advisor Ctrl. State U., Wilberforce, Ohio, 2004—. Youth advisor Mt. Carmel Missionary Bapt. Ch., Springfield, 1997—2006; dir. drug-free sports Ctrl. State U., Wilberforce, Ohio, 2005—. Named to Student Athletic Trainer Hall of Fame, Springfield North H.S., 1997. Mem.: GLATA, GDATA, Ohio Athletic Trainers Assn., Nat. Athletic Trainers Assn. (cert.), Order of Ea. Stars (life; youth matron, ednl. scholarship com. 1999—, yoth advisor 1997—). Baptist. Avocations: reading, travel, bicycling, gardening, board games. Home: 1412 N Broad St Apt 28 Fairborn OH 45324 Office: Ctrl State U 1400 Brush Row Rd PO Box 1004 Wilberforce OH 45384 Office Phone: 937-376-6617. Home Fax: 937-376-6291; Office Fax: 937-376-6040. Personal E-mail: lashauntaj@excite.com. Business E-Mail: ljones@centralstate.edu.

JONES, LAURETTA MARIE, artist, designer, computer science researcher; b. Cleve., Mar. 13, 1953; d. Richard Llewellyn and Loretta (Jares) J. BFA, Cleve. Inst. Art, 1975; postgrad., N.Y. Inst. Tech., 1981, 87. Instr. Sch. Visual Arts, N.Y.C., 1984-94, dir. undergrad. computer studies, 1988-90. Adj. prof. art Manhattanville Coll., Purchase, NY, 1985—86; instr. N.Y. Bot. Gardens, 2000—. Western Conn. State U., 2001—; cons. Trintex/Prodigy, White Plains, NY, 1986—87, IBM Gallery Sci. and Art, N.Y.C., 1987—88; cons. graphic design IBM T.J. Watson Rsch Ctr., Yorktown Heights, NY, 1988—90, adv. graphic designer, 1990—95, devel. engr., 1995—; rsch. staff mem. Network Transaction Systems, 1997—99, mgr., 1997—99; mgr. Cognitive Human-Computer Interaction, 1999—2000, Next Web HCI Components, 2001—. Exhibited paintings, drawings in shows worldwide, 1983—; represented in permanent collection Franklin Inst., Phila., Mus. Sci. and Industry, Chgo. Mem. ACLU, Assn. for Computing Machinery-Spl. Interest Group on Computer Human Interactions, Nat. Computer Graphics Assn. (speaker 1987), Guild of Nat. Sci. Illustrators (rec. sec. N.Y. chpt.), Am. Soc. of Bot. Artists (edn. adv. com.), Small Computers Arts Network (speaker 1984-89), Computer Arts Discipline Graphic Artists Guild (founding, steering com. 1984-88), ACM-SIGGRAPH (N.Y.C. chpt. editor newsletter, bd. dirs. 1986-92, speaker 1991, nat. courses com. 1991-92, design show jury 1993), Am. Inst. Graphic Arts, Amnesty Internat., NOW, Nature Conservancy, Nat. Resources Def. Coun. Avocations: tandem biking, hiking, ballroom dancing, gardening, botanical art. Office: IBM TJ Watson Rsch Ctr PO Box 704 Yorktown Heights NY 10598-0704

JONES, LAURIE LYNN, magazine editor; b. Kerrville, Tex., Sept. 2, 1947; d. Charles Clinton and Jean Laurie (Davidson) J.; m. C. Frederick Childs, June 26, 1976; children: Charles Newell (Clancy), Cyrus Trevor; 1 stepchild, Ariel Childs. BA, U. Tex., 1969. Asst. to dir. coll. admissions Columbia U., NYC, 1969-70; asst. to dir. Office Alumni-Columbia U., NYC, 1970-71; asst. advt. mgr. Book World, 1971-72, Washington Post-Chgo. Tribune, 1971-72; editl. asst. N.Y. Mag., NYC, 1972-74, asst. editor, 1974, sr. editor, 1974-76, mng. editor, 1976-92, Vogue Mag., 1992—. Mem. Am. Soc. Mag. Editors, Women in Coummunication, Advt. Women N.Y. Republican. Methodist. Home: 40 Great Jones St New York NY 10012-1109 Also: 62 Giles Hill Rd Redding Ridge CT 06876 Office: Vogue Magazine 4 Times Sq New York NY 10036-6561 Office Phone: 212-286-6910. Business E-Mail: Laurie_Jones@condenast.com.

JONES, LEONADE DIANE, media publishing company executive; b. Bethesda, Md., Nov. 27, 1947; d. Leon Adger and Landonia Randolph Jones. BA with distinction, Simmons Coll., 1969; JD, MBA, Stanford U., 1973. Bar: Calif. 1973, DC 1979. Summer assoc. Davis Polk & Wardwell, NYC, 1972; securities analyst Capital Rsch. Co., LA, 1973-75; asst. treas. Washington Post Co., 1975-79, 86-87, treas., 1987-96; dir. fin. svcs. Post-Newsweek Stas., Inc., Washington, 1979-84, v.p. bus. affairs, 1984-86; ind. mgmt. cons., pvt. equity investor, 1997-99, 2001—; CFO, sec. VentureThink, LLC, 1999-2001; exec. v.p., CFO Versura, Inc., 2000-01. Bd. ind. chmn. Am. Balanced Fund, Inc., Income Fund Am., Inc.; bd. dirs. Fundamental Investors, Growth Fund Am., Inc., The New Economy Fund, Smallcap World Fund, Inc.; mem. investment mgmt. subcom. of benefit plans com. Am. Stores Co., 1992—99; mem. investment adv. com. NY State Tchrs. Retirement Sys., 1999—; mem. investment mgmt. subcom. Albertson's Inc., 1999—. Bd. dirs. The Women's Found., 2000—03, Access Group, Inc., 2005—. Named to D.C. Women's Hall of Fame, 1992; recipient Candace award for bus., 1992, Serwa award, 1993. Mem.: DC Bar Assn., Calif. Bar Assn., Nat. Bar Assn., Stanford U. Bus. Sch. Alumni Assn. (bd. dirs. 1986—88, pres. Washington-Balt. chpts. 1984—85). Personal E-mail: leonade@att.net.

JONES, LIAL A., museum director; BA, U. Del., 1979; attended, Mus. Mgmt. Inst., U. Calif., Berkeley, 1996. Asst. dir. Del. Art Mus., Wilmington, 1979, dep. dir., CEO; dir. Crocker Art Mus., Sacramento, 1999—. Recipient Art Educator of Yr., Art Educators of Del., 1993, Paul Getty Trust Scholarship, 1996. Office: Crocker Art Mus 216 O St Sacramento CA 95814 E-mail: ljones@cityofsacramento.org.

JONES, LINDA, communications educator; BA in English, U. Mich., 1972; MS in Journalism with distinction, Northwestern U., 1985. Reporter The Chelsea (Mich.) Standard, 1973-75; county govt., police reporter The Marshall (Mich.) Evening Chronicle, 1975-77; edn. reporter The Bay City (Mich.) Times, 1977--79, asst. met. editor, 1979-81, met. editor, 1981-86; vis. asst. prof. dept. journalism Roosevelt U., 1986-88; asst. prof. Medill Sch. Journalism Northwestern U., 1988-92, dir. tchg. newspaper program, 1992—; assoc. prof. journalism Roosevelt U., Chgo., 1992—, dir. Sch. Comm., 1995—. Acting dir. Multicultural Journalism Ctr., Urban Journalism Ctr.; tchr. workshop sessions Journalism Edn. Assn./Nat. Scholastic Press Assn. convs., 1992-96, chair Multicultural Scholarship Com., 1996. Contbr. articles to profl. jours.; judge and lectr. in field. Office: Roosevelt Univ 505 E Ctr for Profl Advancement 430 S Michigan Ave Chicago IL 60605-1394 E-mail: ljones@roosevelt.edu.

JONES, LINDA L., literature and language educator, department chairman; b. Lynn, Mass., May 10, 1947; d. John P. and Beulah M. Fountain; m. Walter B. Jones, May 26, 1998; children: Sean M. Harrington, Laura L. Harrington. AA with highest honors, Mesa C.C., Ariz., 1992; BA summa cum laude, Ariz. State U., 1994, MEd in Curriculum and Instrn., 2002. Cert. secondary edn. tchr. Ariz. English tchr. Mesa (Ariz.) Pub. Schs., 1997—. English dept. chairperson Skyline HS, Mesa, 2001—. Recipient Disting. Educator award, Flinn Found., 2004. Mem.: Ariz. English Tchrs. Assn. (regional dir. 2002—), Nat. Coun. Tchrs. of English. Avocations: reading, camping, travel. Home: 1504 E Jensen St Mesa AZ 85203-3340 Office: Skyline HS 845 S Crismon Rd Mesa AZ 85208 Office Phone: 480-472-9485. E-mail: lljones@mpsaz.org.

JONES, LINDA MAY, tour guide, writer; b. El Dorado, Kans., Nov. 9, 1937; d. Forrest Edward and Edith May Carlson; m. William Stanley Conard, Sept. 1, 1957 (div. Nov. 1970); children: Chris Dale Conard, Carin Dene Lockhart, Curtis Dean Conard; m. Verl Ray Jones, Nov. 6, 1982. Student, U. Kans., 1955-57, U. Colo., 1970-71. Tour guide Queen City Tours, Denver, 1976-84, tour guide coord., 1977-84, Am. Travel Brokers, Denver, 1977-84; owner Columbine Tours, Denver, 1984-92; tour dir. Backyard Tours, Englewood, Colo., 1993—2002, Mountains and More Tour Co., Golden, Colo., 1993—, Colo. Conv. Assocs., 1998—. Tourism adv. com. Metro Denver Conv. and Visitors Bur., 1990; staff writer Colo. Gambler, 1994-, Gilpin County News; presenter in field. Co-author: Mile High Denver, A Guide to the Queen City, 1981, Up the Gulch-Historic Walking Tours of Black Hawk, Central City and Nevadaville, 2005; contbr. hist. articles to mags. V.p. Rep. Ctrl. Com., Gilpin County, Colo., 1983-93; v.p. Gilpin County Hist. Soc., Central City, Colo., v.p. 1988-90, pres., 1990—; commr. Gilpin County Hist. Adv. Commn., 2006. Mem. Mt. Lookout DAR, Rotary (pres. 2006—), Intertel, Alpha Phi. Methodist. Avocations: hiking, horseback riding, snowshoeing. Home: PO Box 615 Black Hawk CO 80422 Office Phone: 303-582-3858. Personal E-mail: linda@fairburnmountain.com.

JONES, LINDA R. WOLF, consulting company executive; b. Jersey City, Sept. 4, 1943; d. Eugene Leon and Lottie (Pinkowitz) Rubin; m. Frank Paul Jones, Oct. 21, 1973 (div. Nov. 1987); 1 child, Elisabeth Noel. AB, Bryn Mawr Coll., 1964; MA, Yale U., 1968; DSW, Yeshiva U., N.Y.C., 1985. Dir. planning and tng. N.Y.C. Dept. Employment, 1971-77; dir. legislation N.Y.C. Community Devel. Agy., 1977-78; supervisory legis. analyst N.Y.C. Human Resources Adminstrn., 1978; sr. policy analyst Community Svc. Soc. N.Y., 1978-85; dir. pub. policy YMCA Greater N.Y., 1985-89; dir. spl. projects Phoenix House, N.Y.C., 1990-92; dir. income security policy Community Svc. Soc., N.Y.C., 1992-94; exec. dir. Therapeutic Communities Am., Washington, 1994—2002; dir. internat. ops. Conwal divsn. Axiom Resource Mgmt., Falls Church, Va., 2002—. Adj. extension faculty Cornell U./NY State Sch. Indsl. and Labor Rels., NYC, 1975-80; dir. Nonprofit Coord. Com. NY, NYC, 1986-94, Govt. Affairs Profls., NYC, 1989-94. Author: Eveline M. Burns and the American Social Security System 1935-60, 1991; mem. editl. bd. New Eng. Jour. Human Svcs., 1981—; contbr. articles to profl. jours. Active Civic Affairs Forum, NYC, 1985-94; legis. task force NY State Gov.'s Office Vol. Svc., NYC, 1987-90. Mem. Women in Govt. Rels., Am. Pub. Welfare Assn. (dir. 1982), Bryn Mawr Club Westchester (bd. dirs., past pres. 1974-94), Bryn Mawr Club Washington. Home: 6621 7th Pl NW Washington DC 20012 Office: Conwal Divsn Axiom Resource Mgmt Inc Ste 703 5111 Leesburg Pike Falls Church VA 22041

JONES, LISA MARIA DRAPER, counselor; b. San Francisco, Nov. 7, 1966; d. Ponce DeLeon and Cosima (Zanzarelli) Draper; m. Reginald Joseph Jones, Dec. 29, 1990; children: Lauren Elizabeth, Ryan Joseph. BA, UCLA, 1989; MA Clin. Psychology, Antioch U., 2004; post grad., Alliant U., Calif. Trainee children's social worker Dept Children and Family Svcs., L.A., 1990; primary counselor Sasha Bruce Youthwork, Inc, Washington, 1991—92; family therapist The Family Connection, Landover Hills, Md., 1992—94; counselor in-home outreach Youth Intervention Program, L.A., 1994—2000, co- program mgr., 2000—02; sch. counselor Outreach Concern, Santa Ana, Calif., 2003—04. Democrat. Roman Catholic. Avocations: travel, reading, fundraising. Office Phone: 323-804-3768. Personal E-mail: rllj3@aol.com.

JONES, LOUISE CONLEY, drama and literature educator, academic administrator; b. Buffalo, Dec. 17, 1945; d. Donald Lee and Pauline Hoelle Conley; m. William O. Jones, May 28, 1966 (div. Nov. 1984); children: Jeffery, Joy. BA, St. Francis Coll., 1968, MS, 1972; PhD, Ball State U., 1991. Various English, speech and drama positions various high schs., 1968-83; with Ball State U., 1983-86, 90, U. Ctrl. Fla., 1986-88, Ind. U., Ft. Wayne, 1991, St. Francis Coll., 1992-94; asst. prof. William Penn Coll., 1991-93; vis. prof. Ind. U./Purdue U., Ft. Wayne, 1993; liberal arts modules Concordia U., Ft. Wayne, 1994-96; interpersonal comm. IVY tech. Coll., 1996—; tchr. drama Ft. Wayne Magnet Schs., 1996—; dir. Concordia U., Ft. Wayne, 1997—; dir. acad. assessment and devel. U. St. Francis, Ft. Wayne. Presenter in field. Author: Stage Action as Metaphor, 1996 (plays) The Ladies Room: Women as Artists, A Fine Madness: The Death of Christopher Marlowe; contbr.: Oxford Companion to Crime and Mystery Writing; contbr. articles to profl. jours.; dir numerous plays at local theatres. Mem. Ft. Wayne Police Merit Commn.; bd. dirs. Gra-light Theatre, Muncie, Ind.; co-founder Women in Theatre, Ft. Wayne; vol. CASA. Mem.: MLA, AAUW, Jane Austen Soc., Marlowe Soc. Avocations: antiques, gardening, travel, detective fiction. Office: U St Francis 2701 Spring St Fort Wayne IN 46808 Office Phone: 260-434-7688. Business E-Mail: ljones@sf.edu.

JONES, MALLORY See DANAHER, MALLORY

JONES, MARIAN C., music educator; d. Kenneth E. and Barbara M. Jones; children: Shayla, Brooke, Amber, Tia, Vida. BS in Music Edn., W. Chester State U., Pa., 1976. Cert. tchr., music edn. K-12 Pa. Dept. Edn., N.J. Dept. Edn. Music tchr. Willingboro Bd. Edn., NJ, 1976—78, Lawnside Bd. Edn., 1978—79; music tchr./mentor Downingtown I & A Sch., Pa., 1980—83; admin. asst. USN, Phila., 1983—89; music tchr. Ewing Twp. Bd. Edn., NJ, 1989—90, Mt. Laurel Twp. Bd. Edn., 1990—. Coop. tchr. for sr. music students U. Fine Arts, Phila., 2004, Rowan U., Glassboro, NJ, 2002; dir., various youth choruses in cmty., N.J. & Pa., 1980—. Mem.: NEA, Mt. Laurel Edn. Assn., N.J. Edn. Assn. Mem. Christian Ch. Avocations: reading, cooking, swimming, travel. Home: 4730 Hawthorne St Philadelphia PA 19124 Office: Larchmont Sch 301 Larchmont Blvd Mount Laurel NJ 08054 Business E-Mail: mcjones@mountlaurel.k12.nj.us.

JONES, MARILYN SCHLICHER, conductor, retired music educator; b. Highland Park, Mich., Oct. 23, 1933; d. Lee Roy and Dorothy Uphouse Schlicher; m. David V. Jones, Aug. 20, 1954 (dec.). BS, Wayne State U.,

Detroit, 1954, MA, 1969; PhD, U. Mich., Ann Arbor, 1979. Music tchr. Brighton Area Schs., Mich., 1954—57, Detroit Pub. Schs., 1958—87, Schoolcroft Coll., Livonia, Mich., 1977—78. Dir. choir Birmingham Unitarian Ch., Mich., 1967—74, Schoolcroft Coll., Livonia, Mich., 1977—84; v.p. Livingston Arts Coun., Howell, Mich., 1994—96; founding artistic dir. The Livingston Co. Chorale, 1991. Named Music Educator Emeritus, Mich. Sch. Vocal Music Assn., 1957. Mem.: Am. Choral Dirs. Assn. (bd. mem. 1983—97, Maynard Klein Award 1996). Home: 6036 Briggs Lake Dr Brighton MI 48116 Office: Livingston County Chorale Box 151 Brighton MI 48116

JONES, MARION, track and field athlete; b. LA, Oct. 12, 1975; d. George and Marion Jones; m. C.J. Hunter, 1998 (div. 2001); 1 child, Timothy Montgomery. Graduate, U. NC. Named Women's Athlete of Yr., Track and Field News, 1997, 1998, 2000, Athlete of Yr., ESPN, Reuters, and the IAAF, 2000, Female Athlete of Yr., AP, 2000; recipient AP and USOC Female Athlete of Yr. award, 2000, Jesse Owens award, U.S.A. Track & Field, 1997, 1998, 2002. Achievements include winning 100m gold, World Championships, 1997, 99; world 4x100m champion, 1997, 2001; ranked #1 in the world at 100m & 200m by Track and Field News, 1997-2002; won 100m, 200m, World Cup, 1998; USA Outdoor 200m champ US title in the event, 1998-2001, 100m and long jump, 1997; USA Outdoor 100m champion, 2006; undefeated in every competition until her last one of the year, 35 of 36 total, 1998; won Goodwill Games 100m, 1998, 2001, 200m, 1998; ran anchor on 4x200m USA team that set the world record (1:27.46) at USA vs. THE WORLD at the Penn Relays, 2000; ran anchor in gold medal winning 4x100m relay at Worlds, 2001; World 200m champion, 2001; 100m, 200m champion, USA, 2002; won World Cup 100m, which completed the first undefeated season of her career, 2002; won 3 gold medals for 100m, 200m, 4x400m, Sydney Games, 2000; won 100m at Reebok Grand Prix, 2006, Meeting Gaz de France Paris Saint-Denis, 2006, Athletissima, 2006. Office: c/o USA Track & Field 1 Rca Dome Ste 140 Indianapolis IN 46225-1023*

JONES, MARJORIE EVELYN, retired special education educator; b. Arlington, Mass., July 11, 1923; d. Frederick Clifton Fitch and Edith Rice Olds Washburn; m. Robert Payzant Jones, Sept. 4, 1947 (div. May 1961). Diploma, New Eng. Sch. Art, 1945; BS in Edn., Boston U., 1949, MEd, 1964. Office staff Boston & Maine Railroad, 1943-46; spl. edn. educator Newton (Mass.) Pub. Schs., 1949-64; spl. edn. supr. Norwalk (Conn.) Bd. Edn., 1964-66; learning disabilities specialist New Canaan (Conn.) Bd. Edn., 1966-86. Cons State Curriculum Devel. Com., Boston, 1956-58; demonstration tchr. U. Maine, Orono, 1956; free-lance comml. artist. Com. chair South End Planning Coun., Boston, 1955-60; fin. com., lector St. Davids Episcopal Ch., South Yarmouth, Mass., 1990—; active Cape Cod Womens Orgn., 1996—, vol. Cmty. Access TV Camera, 1995—. Recipient Coll. Chair award Boston U. Alumni Assn. Cape Cod, 1997. Mem. AAUW (bd. dirs. Cape Cod br., membership v.p., pub. rels. chair 1987—91, legal advocacy chair 2002—, scholarship com. 1996—), Hist. Soc. Old Yarmouth (trustee, bd. dirs., docent, lectr., edn. com. 1990—), Boston U. Alumni Club Cape Cod and Islands (bd. dirs., corr. sec., rec. sec. 1986—), Cape Cod Scrabble Club (treas. 1996-2004, pres. 2004—), Cape Cod Bird Club (sec. 1987-93). Episcopalian. Home: 26 Musket Ln Yarmouth Port MA 02675-2127

JONES, MARLENE ANN, retired education supervisor; b. Bluffton, Ohio, Nov. 22, 1936; d. Waldo J. and Blanche M. (Criblez) Wilkins; m. Marvin O. Jones, July 3, 1965; children: John O., Dianne M. BS, Bowling Green State U., 1958, EdS, 1978; MA, Ohio State U., 1962. Cert. family and consumer scis. Vocat. home econs. tchr. 7-12 Liberty Ctr. (Ohio) Bd. Edn., 1958-61; asst. state supr. Ohio Dept. Edn., Columbus, 1962-65; chair home econs. techs. Owens C.C. (formerly Penta Tech. Coll.), Toledo, 1965-71; supr. Penta County Vocat. Sch., Perrysburg, Ohio, 1965—2001. Pres. United Meth. Women, Colton, Ohio, 1967—. Named 1 of 10 Outstanding Women in Toledo Jaycees, 1971-72; recipient Disting. Centennial Svc. award Ohio Agrl. and Home Econs. Rsch. and Devel. Ctr., 1982, Home Econs. Grad. fellowship award Am. Vocat. Assn., 1990; named Alum of Yr. Coll. of Edn., Bowling Green State U., 1990. Mem. ASCD, Am. Ohio Vocat. Assn., Am. Family and Consumer Svcs. Assn. (past state pres.), Ohio Vocat. Family and Consumer Svcs. Suprs. Assn. (treas.), N.W. Ohio FHA/HERO Alumni Assn. (sec.), Phi Delta Kappa, Phi Upsilon Omicron (past pres. Alumni chpt. 1965—). Methodist. Home: 5-212 US Hwy 24 Liberty Center OH 43532 Personal E-mail: mo.majones@bright.net.

JONES, MARTHA LEE, social worker, consultant; b. Bklyn., Dec. 6, 1945; d. Harold L. and Janet R. (Holcomb) Utts; m. Steve R. Jones; 1 child, Erin R. BS, Juniata Coll., 1967; postgrad., Columbia U., 1967-68; MSW, U. Md., 1972; PhD, Fielding Inst., 1990. Lic. social worker, Pa. Dir. Child Welfare Svcs., Huntingdon, Pa., 1968-70, supr. Carlisle, Pa., 1970-75; dir. child care Meth. Children's Home, Mechanicsburg, Pa., 1975-76; pvt. practice Camp Hill, Pa., 1976-78; pres. Common Sense Assoc., Mechanicsburg, 1979-96, Common Sense Adoption Svcs., Mechanicsburg, 1993—; adminstr. Pa. Statewide Adoption Network, Mechanicsburg, 1995—2000. Contbr. articles to profl. jours. Office Phone: 717-766-6449. E-mail: martyjones900@msn.com.

JONES, MARY CATHERINE, medical/surgical nurse; d. Charles and Mary Catherine Daly; m. Leo E. Jones (dec.); 1 child, Mary Catherine Russell. AD, C.S. Mott CC, Flint, Mich. Nurse McLaren Hosp., Flint. Vol. St. Andrew Cath. Ch., Portland, Oreg., 1995—. Roman Cath. Avocation: travel.

JONES, MARY D., court clerk; b. Danbury, Wis., Aug. 12, 1951; d. Eugene F. and Darlene M. Burlingame; m. Larry James Truitt, Nov. 5, 1966 (div. June 1971); children: Jeanne Lynn Truitt Justice, Colleen Regina Truitt Elder; m. Cecil L. Jones, Mar. 5, 1972; children: James A., Andy D.; stepchildren: Gary Wayne Jones, Terri A. Jones. Cert., Muscatine (Iowa) Jr. Coll. With Plastic Factory, Muscatine, 1969-71; sec. Dr. Shoemaker, Kahoka, Mo., 1972-73; rschr. Clark County Abstract, Kahoka, 1973-74; dep. clk., recorder Clark County Cir. Clk. and Recorder's Office, Kahoka, 1974-94; elected officio Cir. Clk. and Recorder, Kahoka, 1995—. Mem. Clark County Dem. Com., Kahoka, 1988, State Dem. Com., Mo., 1995—, Clark County Crime Victim Program, Kahoka, 1997—; mem., past pres. Blackhawk PTO, Kahoka, 1995—; mem., past leader Boy Scouts Am., Kahoka, 1973—. Mem. Mo. Recorder's Assn., Mo. Cir. Clk.'s Assn., Kahoka Hist. Soc. Baptist. Avocations: reading, fishing, listening to radio. Home: 475 E Maple St Kahoka MO 63445-1274

JONES, MARY ELLEN SNOUFFER, language educator; b. West Chester, Pa., Sept. 13, 1972; d. Robert Craig and Sara Marie Snouffer; m. Kevin Dale Jones, May 21, 1994; children: Emily Kathleen, Quinn Kevin. AA, Harrisburg Area C.C., Pa., 1992; BS, Calif. U. Pa., 1994; MA, W.Va. U., Morgantown, 1999. Cert. Instr. II Dept. Edn., Pa., 2000, Instr. I Dept. Edn., Pa., 1994. Tchr. English Albert Gallatin Area Sch. Dist., Uniontown, Pa., 1995—. Reader advanced placement English lang. Ednl. Testing Svc., NJ, 2003—. Named Tchr. of Yr. for Albert Gallatin Area Sch. Dist., Fayette County C. of C., 2003. Mem.: AAUW, NEA, Nat. Coun. Tchrs. English. Democrat-Npl. Methodist. Avocation: reading.

JONES, MARY EMMA B., psychologist; b. Izmir, Turkey, Nov. 10, 1944; came to U.S., 1946; d. Lawrence Hartwell Brown and Erma Marie (Carl) Macfie; m. Robin Dee Jones, Sept. 11, 1966; children: Darcy Marie, Samuel Evan. BA in English, Campbell U., 1967; MEd in Mid. Grades, North Ga. Coll., 1984; EdS in Sch. Counseling, U. Ga., 1990, PhD in Counseling Psychology, 1997. lic. psychologist, Ga. Tchr. high sch. Harnett County Schs., Lillington and Buies Creek, N.C., 1967-69; craftsperson (weaver) Jugtown Pottery, Seagrove, N.C., 1969-70; designer, weaver Wolf Pen Crafts, Young Harris, Ga., 1970-78; instr. weaving Campbell Folk Sch., Brasstown, N.C., 1977-78; tchr. Union County Mid. Sch., Blairsville, Ga., 1978-90; sch. counselor St. Joseph Sch., Athens, Ga., 1990-94; intern in counseling psychology Park Ctr., Ft. Wayne, Ind., 1994-95; therapist Laurelwood Mental Health/Substance Abuse divsn. Northeast Ga. Med. Ctr., Gainesville, 1995-97; dir. Laurelwood Partial Hospitalization Program, Blairsville, Ga., 1997-98; pvt. practice lic. psychologist Blairsville, 1998—. Active PTA, Harnett County, N.C., 1967-69, Union County, 1978-90; active St. Joseph Sch. PTA, Athens, 1990-94. Named STAR Tchr., Union County Schs., C. of C. and Bus. Coun. Ga., 1984. Mem. APA, Ga. Psychol. Assn. Avocations: camping, swimming, hiking, sketching, tennis. Home: PO Box 141 Young Harris GA 30582-0141 Office: PO Box 881 Blairsville GA 30514-0881 Business E-Mail: mebjones@alltel.net.

JONES, MARY GARDINER, lawyer, educator, consumer products company executive; b. NYC, Dec. 10, 1920; d. Charles Herbert and Anna Livingston (Short) Jones. BA, Wellesley Coll., 1943; JD, Yale U., 1948. Bar: N.Y. 1949. Intern tchr. George Sch., Newtown, Pa., 1943—44; rsch. analyst, rsch. and analysis br. Internat. Law sect. OSS, Washington, 1944—46; assoc. Donovan, Leisure, Newton and Irvine, N.Y.C., 1948—53, Webster, Sheffield, Fleischmann, Hitchcock & Chrystie, N.Y.C., 1961—64; trial atty. antitrust divsn. Dept. Justice, N.Y.C., 1953—61; commr. FTC, Washington, 1964—73; prof. Coll. Commerce and Bus. Adminstrn. and Coll. Law U. Ill., Urbana, 1973—75; v.p. for consumer affairs Western Union Telegraph Co., Washington, 1975—82; founder, pres. Consumer Interest Rsch. Inst., Washington, 1983—2001; dir. MCA, Inc., Universal City, Calif. Mem. com. on sci. and tech. Fed. Coun. Sci. and Tech., non-trustee mem. rsch. and policy com.; mem. bd. Coun. Econ. Priorities, 1976—84, Inst. Future, 1977—; dir. Coun. Better Bus. Burs., 1982—; mem. Pres.'s Panel on Antitrust Laws, 1977—78. Bd. editors Jour. Consumer Affairs, editl. rev. bd. Jour. Consumer Interest; contbr. articles to profl. jours. Pres. Mental Health Assn., Washington, 1998—2004, mem. bd., 1982—2004, 2005—; trustee Colgate U., 1966—80, Wellesley Coll., 1971—89; nat. adv. coun. Hampshire Coll. Mem.: AAUW (2d v.p. Washington br. 1968—69, adv. coun.), Nat. Inst. Dental Health (institutional review bd. 2003—05), Yale Law Sch. Assn. (v.p. D.C. 1969—70, exec. com. 1971—76), Am. Arbitration Assn., Assn. Bar City of N.Y., Internat. Law Assn., Fed. Bar Assn. E-mail: mgjones@cgi.com.

JONES, MARY LAURA, not-for-profit developer; b. Mpls., 1946; d. William Ray and Emily H. Jones; children: Donald Aaron, Justin David, Mark Joseph Bushman. BA in English, U. S.C., 1968; MA in History, Northwestern U., 2004. Vol. U.S. Peace Corps, 1968—71; assoc. dir. funding and devel. The Inst. of Cultural Affairs, Chgo., 1971-75, dir. Cleve. region, 1975-79, dir. Pacific and Oceania region Apia, Western Samoa, 1979-83, co-creator Cmty. Devel. Tng. Curriculum Chgo., 1984—85, dir. Uptown Cmty. Resource Ctr., 1987—. Bd. dirs. Ebenezer Luth. Ch. Mem. Uptown C. of C. (bd. dirs.). Home and Office: Inst Cultural Affairs 4750 N Sheridan Rd Chicago IL 60640-5042 Office Phone: 773-769-6363 x 222. Business E-Mail: mljones@ica-usa.org.

JONES, MARY LOU, real estate broker, real estate company executive; b. Palermo, W.Va., Sept. 3, 1932; d. Robert R. and Elwa F. Lovejoy; m. Jerald E. Jones, Dec. 22, 1954; children: Jeffrey Todd, Perry Brooks, Suzanne Paige. Student, Marshall U., 1954. Sec. W.Va. U., Morgantown, 1956-59; real estate agt. Kaufman Real Estate, Bridgeport, W.Va., 1988-93; real estate broker/owner Homefinders Plus Real Estate, Inc., Bridgeport, 1993—. Pres. Friends of the W.Va. State Bar, 1997. Mem. Nat. Assn. Realtors, W.Va. Assn. Realtors, Harrison County Assn. Realtors, Clarksburg, W.Va., 1998-99. Republican. Avocations: reading, bridge, painting, poetry. Office: Homefinders Plus Real Estate 104 State St Bridgeport WV 26330-1376

JONES, MARY TRENT, endowment fund trustee; b. Durham, N.C., July 15, 1940; d. Josiah Charles Trent and Mary Duke (Biddle) Semans; m. James Parker Jones, June 27, 1964; children: James Trent, Benjamin Parker, Jonathan Edmund. AB, Duke U., 1963. Trustee The Duke Endowment, Charlotte, N.C., 1988—. Chmn. Josiah Charles Trent Found., Durham, 1978-83; bd. dirs. Mary Duke Biddle Found., Durham, 1983—, chmn. 2004, Concert Artists Guild, N.Y.C., 1996-00. Mem. Va. Perinatal Svcs. Adv. Bd., Richmond, 1986-91; sec. Va. Arts Commn., Richmond, 1989-92, bd. dirs., 1984-92; trustee Va. Intermont Coll., Bristol, Va., 1986-91, 98-2001; mem. State Coun. Higher Edn. Va., Richmond, 1991-95; trustee Va. Mu. of Fine Arts, Richmond, 1992-97; mem. bd. Washington County Pub. Libr. Found., 1997—; trustee William King Regional Arts Ctr., 1998-2004, Emory and Henry Coll., 1999-, Va. Hist. Soc., 2005-; bd. dirs. Blue Ridge Pub. TV, 2004-06. Recipient outstanding alumni award Durham Acad., 1991. Mem. Va. Highlands Festival Bd., 1997-2001 Episcopalian. Avocations: reading, walking, hiking. Home: 107 Hillside Dr NE Abingdon VA 24210-2013 E-mail: jjones107@earthlink.net.

JONES, MAUREEN GAIL, elementary school educator; b. Missoula, Mont., Sept. 27, 1950; d. Rudolph Ross Collins and Erna Mae (Adler) Blewett; m. David John Froehlich, Jan. 20, 1995; children: Devin Collins Jones, Corey Andrew Jones. BA, U. Mont., 1980. Cert. elem. tchr. Tchr. chpt. I Florence (Mont.) Schs., 1980-81; tchr. elem. Evergreen Sch. Dist., Kalispell, Mont., 1981-83, Alberton (Mont.) Sch. Dist., 1983—. Recipient Presdl. award NSTA, 1994. Mem. Nat. Coun. Tchrs. Math., Coun. Presdl. Awardees in Math., Soc. Elem. Presdl. Awardees in Math., Mont. Coun. Tchrs. Math. (bd. dirs., jour. editor 1993-95). Avocations: fishing, gardening, softball. Home: 1843 Frey Ln Missoula MT 59808-1249 Office: Alberton High School PO Box 330 Alberton MT 59820-0330

JONES, MELBA KATHRYN, elementary school educator, librarian; b. Marshall, Ark., Mar. 13, 1924; d. Willie Claud and Bessie Kathryn (Mason) Holder; m. Rex Gene Jones, Aug. 9, 1947; children: Mickey Gene, Terry John, Cathryn Jayne. BA, Coll. Ozarks, 1972. Tchr. Everton (Ark.) Pub. Schs., 1942-47; libr. Valley Springs (Ark.) Pub. Schs., 1966-85. Mayor City of Everton, 1979-87, council woman, 1988-91; bd. govs. North Ark. Regional Med. Ctr., 1993—; mem. bd. Ark. Cattlemen's Assn., 1993; mem. city coun., Everton, Ark., 1996—; dir. Cmty. Ctr., 2004; chmn. adminstrn. bd. Meth. Ch., 1980-2003. Grantee, Ark. Indsl. Devel. Commn., 1985, Ark. Dept. Econ. Devel., 1999, 2000, 2003. Democrat. Methodist. Avocations: painting, reading, sewing, crafts, cooking. Home: PO Box 12 Everton AR 72633-0012

JONES, MELISSA VINCENT, secondary school educator; d. Dale and Lynn Jones. BS, N. Tex. State U., Denton, 1991; MA, U. Ctrl. Okla., Edmond, 2002. Tchr. The Colony (Tex.) H.S., 1991—. Choreographer Showtime Internat., Lago Vista, Tex., 1999—; exec. dir. The DaVinci Inst., Oklahoma City, 2002—04. Mem.: Tex. Dance Educators Am. (assoc.), Drill Team Dirs. Am. (assoc.; 2nd v.p., pres.-elect 2005—, master adjudicator 1994). Office Phone: 972-625-9000.

JONES, NORAH, vocalist, musician; b. N.Y.C., Mar. 30, 1979; d. Ravi Shankar and Sue Jones. Student, U. North Tex. With Blue Note Records, 2001—. Musician: (albums) First Sessions, 2001, Come Away With Me, 2002 (Grammy awards: Album of Yr., 2002, Record of the Yr., 2002, Best New Artist, 2002, Best Female Pop Vocal Performance, 2002, Best Pop Vocal Album, 2002), Feels Like Home, 2004 (Best Female Pop Vocal Performance for Sunrise song, 2005); musician: (with Ray Charles) Genius Loves Company, 2004 (Grammy award: Record of Yr. for Here We Go Again song with Ray Charles, 2005, Best Pop Collaboration with Vocal for Here We Go Again song with Ray Charles, 2005); musician: (recording) A Very Special Acoustic Christmas, Where We Live: Stand For What You Stand On, Remembering Patsy Cline, Just Because I'm a Woman (tribute to Dolly Parton), (soundtrack for film) Love Actually, 2003. Named Best Young Female Singer, VH1, 2002. Office: Macklam Feldman Mgmt Ste 200 1505 W 2d Ave Vancouver BC V6H 3Y4 Canada

JONES, ORA MCCONNER, retired foundation administrator; b. Augusta, Ga., Jan. 2, 1929; d. Landirs and Mamie (Elderidge) Williams; m. Walter R. McConner, June 27, 1953 (div.); 1 child, Susan L.; m. Courtney P. Jones, Feb. 14, 1991. BA, Paine Coll., Augusta, 1949; MA, Boston U., 1951; EdD, Nova U., Ft. Lauderdale, Fla., 1982. Instr. Paine Coll., Augusta, 1951-55; tchr. Chgo. Pub. Schs., 1956-66, adminstr., 1966-79, asst. supt., 1979-89, supt. dist. 6, 1989-91; exec. dir. Branch County Comty. Found., Coldwater, Mich., 1991—. Pres., bd. trustees Paine Coll., 1996; mem. Profl. Women's Aux. Provident Hosp.; bd. dirs. Ryerson Libr. Found., Aquinas Emeritus Coll., YWCA, Clark Retirement Found. Danforth study grantee, 1955; recipient Image award League of Black Women, 1974, Silver Beaver award Boy Scouts Am., 1985; named Educator of Yr. Chgo. Black Sch. Educators, 1984; recipient Outstanding Educator's award Beatrice Coffee's, 1989. Mem. Am. Assn. Sch. Adminstrs., Nat. Alliance of Black Sch. Educators, Coun. for Exceptional Children, Altrusa Club, Beta Sigma Phi, Delta Kappa, Alpha Gamma Psi. Episcopalian. Home: 4956 N Quail Crest Dr SE Grand Rapids MI 49546-7539 E-mail: JonesOraB@aol.com.

JONES, PAMELA WALSH, science educator; b. Frankfurt, Germany, July 1, 1957; d. William Walker and Trudy Liebhilde Walsh; m. Malcolm Stuart Jones, June 2, 1984; children: Adam Stuart, Corey Austin, Erin Leah Clara. BS, Va. Tech, Blacksburg, 1979; degree in edn., Tex. Woman's U., 1993. Geologist Core Lab., Dallas, 1979—87; owner Jones Lawn & Landscaping, Lewisville, Tex., 1990—99; 8th grade sci. tchr. Huffines Mid. Sch., Lewisville, 1999—. Vol. Keep Lewisville Beautiful, 1996—2006. Recipient Miniyard Teacher of Week. Office: Huffines MId Sch 1440 N Valley Pky Lewisville TX 75077 Office Phone: 469-713-5990.

JONES, PATRICIA A., science educator; b. Denver, Mar. 14, 1955; d. Donald Charles and Margaret L. Alexander; children: Christopher E., Scott E., Audrey N. BS in Microbiology, Colo. State U., Ft. Collins, 1977; MA in Edn., U. N.Mex., Albuquerque, 1984; MS in Chemistry, Wright State U., Fairborn, Ohio, 1999. Cert. tchr. Ohio, N.Mex. Sci. tchr. Huber Hts. City Schs., Huber Hts., Ohio, 1995—99, ISUS Trade and Tech. Prep., Dayton, Ohio, 1999—2001, Jefferson Twp. Schs., Dayton, 2001—05, Ruidoso Mcpl. Schs., Ruidoso, N.Mex., 2005—; chemistry tchr. Sandia Prep. Sch., Albuquerque, 2006—. Chemistry adj. Clark State CC, Springfield, Ohio, 1997—2006, Ea. N.Mex. U., Ruidoso, 2006. Office: Sandia Prep Sch 532 Osuna Rd NE Albuquerque NM 87113 Office Phone: 505-338-3013.

JONES, PATRICIA BENGTSON, sculptor; b. Janesville, Wis., Aug. 5, 1932; d. Clarence Edward and Phyllis Ann (Eau Clair) Bengtson; m. Robert S. Jones, July 3, 1953 (div. Aug. 1986); children: Pamela Ann Eau Clair, Diane Marie. AA, DeAnza Jr. Coll., Cupertino, Calif., 1974; BA in Painting, San Jose State U., 1977, MA in Sculpture, 1983. Cmty. colls. instr. credential, Calif. Exhibit curator Yucca Gallery, Albuquerque, 1964-67. Curator N.Mex. Art League, Albuquerque, 1966-67, Peninsula Art Assn., San Mateo, Calif., 1969; co-chmn. fine arts San Mateo Fair, 1969; chmn. fine arts San Mateo County Fair, 1970; asst. installor De Young Mus., San Francisco, 1976; restorer Santa Clara Artist's Foundry, 1981-84; marble cons. Leitch & Co., San Francisco, 1984-86; instr. Studio Carlos Nicoli, Carrara, Italy, 1995; cutlery cons. R.H. Macy's, San Leandro, Calif., 1986-97; restoration cons., subcontractor, workshops; sculpture, 2005; mentor John F. Kennedy U., Berkeley, Calif., 2005. Exhibited in group shows at N.Mex. Art Mus., Santa Fe, 1965—66, Triton Mus. Art, Santa Clara, Calif., 1967—94, The Foothill Art Ctr., Colden, Colo., 1985—91, 1994, 2004, Frye Art Mus., Seattle, 1987, Downey Mus. Art, Calif., 1990—92, Bedford Gallery, Walnut Creek, Calif., 1991, Sho-en Sculpture and Gallery, Ramona, 1992—94, Contract Design Ctr, San Francisco, 1993, One Bush Gallery, 1994, Oakland Mus., 1994, Heritage Mus., Seattle, 1998, The Art Foundry Gallery, 1999, Contract Design Ctr., San Francisco, 2004, Claudia Chapline Gallery, Stinton Beach, Calif., 2004, New Leaf Garden Gallery, 2005, exhibitions include 600 Townsand, San Francisco, 2006, Internat. Sculpture Assn., Washington, 2006. Bd. dirs. YWCA, Beloit, Wis., 1956-60; various positions Gen. Fedn. Women's Clubs, Wis., 1956-60; vol. fund drives Mental Health Drive Wis., Beloit, 1956-60; room mother Campfire Girls, Albuquerque, 1961-62. Recipient John Cavanaugh Meml. award N.Am. Sculpture Exhbn., Golden, Colo., 1985. Mem. Internat. Sculptors Assn., Pacific Rim Sculpture Group (co-founder), Nordic Fine Arts Group (chmn. and curator, 2003), Fine Arts Mus. San Francisco, Sculptors Guild San Jose, Pacific Rim Sculpture Group (chmn. 2006), World Affairs Coun., San Francisco Mus. Modern Art, Sierra Club, Commonwealth Club Calif. Democrat. Studio: 2019 2d St Berkeley CA 94710

JONES, PATRICIA LOUISE, elementary counselor; b. Moorhead, Minn., Aug. 20, 1942; d. Harry Wilfred and Myrtle Louise Rosenfeldt; m. Edward L. Marks (div.); m. Curtis C. Jones, July 16, 1973; children: Michon, Andrea, Nathan, Kirsten, Leah. BS, Moorhead State U., Minn., 1965; MS, Mankato State U., Minn., 1990. Cert. K-12 sch. counselor, Minn. Tchr. Anoka Hennepin Schs., Minn., 1966-68; pvt. practice Youth Ctr., Truman, Minn., 1969-72; bookkeeper Fairmont Glass & Sign, Minn., 1973, Truman Farmers Elevator, 1973-87; libr. Martin County Libr., Truman, 1988-89; sch. counselor St. James Schs., Minn., 1989—2005; ret., 2005. Coord. Internat. Fun Fest, St. James, 1992, 96; originator, advisor Armstrong After Sch. Hispanic Club, St. James, 1991-2001. Coord. Truman Days Parade, 1991, 92, 94-2000; mem. adv. bd. Watonwan County Big Buddy Program, 1993—; mem. Watonwan County Corrections Adv. Bd., 1998-2002; foster parent, 1999. Mem. ACA, Am. Sch. Counselors Assn., Minn. Sch. Counselors Assn. (bd. dirs. 1997-99), S.W. Minn. Counselors Assn. (Elem. Counselor of Yr. 1993, pres. 1997-99). Avocations: genealogy, walking, photography. Home: PO Box 215 Truman MN 56088-0215

JONES, PHYLLIS DUYSER, physical education educator; b. Torrington, Conn., Mar. 26, 1957; d. Cornelius Anthony and Virginia Eleanor Duyser; m. Duane Ryan Jones, Dec. 7, 1984; 1 child, Ryan Cornel. BS in Phys. Edn., So. Conn. State U., New Haven, 1979; MS in Phys. Edn., Cen. Conn. State U., New Britain, 1993. Tchr. phys. edn. and health Devereux Glenholme, Washington, Conn., 1981—90; Burlington Sch. Dist. 10, Burlington, Conn., 1991—, chairperson K-12 phys. edn./health dept., 2003—. Chairperson Rural Sch. Dist. 10 Coordinated Sch. Health Team, 2004—. Named Tchr. of Yr., Rural Sch. Dist. 10, 2001; named to Lewis Mills Athletic Hall of Fame, 2005; recipient Jump Rope for Heart grant, Am. Heart Assn., 2005, Activity Policy grant, Conn. Dept. Edn., 2004. Mem.: Conn. Assn. Adminstrators of Health and Physical Aedn., AAHPERD, Conn. Alliance of Health, Phys. Edn., Recreation, and Dance. Avocations: hiking, home decoration and renovation. Office: Lewis Mills H S 26 Lynn Rd Burlington CT 06013

JONES, PHYLLIS EDITH, nursing educator; b. Barrie, Ont., Can., Sept. 16, 1924; d. Colston Graham and Edith Luella (Shand) J. BScN, U. Toronto, 1950, MSc, 1969; DNSc (hon.), U. Turku, Finland, 1993. With Victorian Order Nurses, Toronto, 1950-53, asst. dir., 1959-63; supr. Vancouver Dept. Health, 1953-58; prof. nursing U. Toronto, 1963-89, dean Faculty Nursing, 1979-88, prof. emeritus, 1989—. Cons. WHO, 1985—86. Contbr. articles to profl. jours. Can. Nurses Found. fellow, 1967-69; grantee Nat. Health R&D, Ont. Ministry Health. Fellow Am. Public Health Assn.; mem. Coll. Nurses Ont., Registered Nurses Assn. Ont., Can. Public Health Assn., Can. Soc. Study Higher Edn., N.Am. Nursing Diagnosis Assn. (charter), ProNursing Finland (hon.). Home: RR 2 Owen Sound ON Canada N4K 5N4

JONES, PHYLLIS GENE, judge; b. Fargo, ND, May 29, 1923; d. Joseph C. and Rosina Belle (Pinkham) Bambusch; m. Dwight Bangs Jones, May 29, 1945 (dec.); children: Stephanie Martineau, Jacqueline Ridge, Kent Carroll; m. David D. Norman, Oct. 9, 1970 (dec.). BA, Macalester Coll., 1944; JD, William Mitchell Coll. Law, 1960. Bar: Minn. 1960. Wirephoto operator AP, St. Paul, 1943-45; reporter St. Paul Pioneer Press, 1945-46; asst. county atty. Ramsey County, St. Paul, 1960-71; gen. counsel Minn. Urban County Attys. Bd./Minn. County Attys. Coun., St. Paul, 1971-75; pvt. practice St. Paul, Cottage Grove, Minn., 1975-84; judge Minn. Dist Ct. 10th Jud. Dist., Anoka, 1984-93. Mem. Minn. Adv. Coun. to State Investment Bd., 1983-84; mem. Washington County Pers. Com., Stillwater, Minn., 1982-84. Supr. Grey Cloud Town Bd., Minn., 1971—75. Mem. ABA, Minn. State Bar Assn. (chmn. victimless crimes com. 1974-75, co-chair sr. lawyers com. 1997-99), Ramsey County Bar Assn. (exec. com. 1982-83), Washington County Hist. Soc. (dir. 2000—).

JONES, REBA (BECKI) PESTUN, elementary school educator, music educator; b. Logan, W.Va., Apr. 30, 1949; d. John Rohac and Carolyn Kelly Pestun; m. Edgar Roger Jones, Aug. 22, 1968; 1 child, Karaleah Sabina Reichart. MusB in Edn., W.Va. U., 1970; EdM in Music Edn., U. Md., 1986; DMA, Shenandoah U., 2003. Cert. postgrad. prof. in music edn. grades K-12 Va., 1986, tchr. Am. Orff Schulwerk Assn., 1986. Choir dir. Asbury United Meth. Ch., Charles Town, W.Va., 1976—86; music tchr. grades K-5 Columbia Elem. Sch. - Fairfax County Pub. Schs., Annandale, Va., 1986—2002; music tchr. grades K-6 Herndon (Va.) Elem. - Fairfax County Pub. Schs., 2002—. Musician (composer/educator): (creative musical unit) A Musical Physical Fitness Workout (Semi-Finalist for the Nat. Music Found., 2000), (creative music units for grades k-3) Rabbit on My Mind (Winner of Impact II Nat. Grant and Va. Commn. for the Arts Grant for Outstanding Achievement, 1999), (original musical for grades k-6) Coal Mining Musical (Impact II Nat. Award Winner, 2001), (original musical unit for grades k-3) Sea Turtle Rhapsody (Impact II Nat. Award Winner, 2002), (original music unit for grades k-6) A True Whale Story (Winner Outstanding Achievement from the Va. Commn. for the Arts, 1998), (original musical with appalachian songs) Journey From the Mountain to the Sky (Hon. Mention from Nat. Music Found., 1999), (original music teaching unit) Musical Manatees (Impact II Nat. Grant Award Winner, 2003), (musical teaching unit and performance) Forever Free (Wash. Post Grant in Edn. Winner, 1998); musician: The Bully Butterfly, 2004 (winner Va. Commn. of Arts Grant, 2004). Mem.: Music Educator's Nat. Conf., Appalachian Studies Assn., Am. Orff Schulwerk Assn., Fairfax Gen. Music Educators Assn., Fairfax Edn. Assn. Office: Herndon Elem Sch 630 Dranesville Rd Herndon VA 20170 Office Phone: 703-326-3162. Business E-Mail: becki.jones@fcps.edu.

JONES, RENEE KAUERAUF, health facility administrator; b. Duncan, Okla., Nov. 3, 1949; d. Delbert Owen and Betty Jean (Marsh) Kauerauf; m. Dan Elkins Jones, Aug. 3, 1972. BS, Okla. State U., 1972, MS, 1975; PhD, Okla. U., 1989. Diplomate Am. Bd. Sleep Medicine. Statis. analyst Okla. State Dept. Mental Health, Okla. City, 1978-80, divisional chief, 1980-83, adminstr., 1983-84; assoc. dir. HCA Presbyn. Hosp., Oklahoma City, 1984-2000; mng. ptnr. Sleep Assocs., LLC, Oklahoma City, 2000—, Sleep REMedies, LLC, Okalhoma City, 2003—. Adj. instr. Okla. U. Health Sci. Ctr., 1979—; assoc. staff scientist Okla. Ctr. for Alcohol and Drug-Related Studies, Okla. City, 1979—; cons. in field. Assoc. editor Alcohol Tech. Reports jour., 1979-84; contbr. articles to profl. jours. Mem. assoc. bd. Hist. Preservation, Inc., treas. 1994. Mem. Am. Acad. Sleep Medicine, Assn. Health Svcs. Rsch., Alcohol and Drug Problems Assn. N.Am., Am. Sleep Disorders Assn., N.Y. Acad. Scis., So. Sleep Soc. (sec.-treas. 1989-91), Phi Kappa Phi. Democrat. Methodist. Avocations: skiing, scuba diving, racewalking, bicycling, painting. Home: 810 NW 15th St Oklahoma City OK 73106 Office: The Sleep Clinic 5530 N Francis Ave Oklahoma City OK 73118 Office Phone: 405-767-6970. Personal E-mail: sleepdr1@cox.net. Business E-Mail: sleepdr1@thesleepclinic.net.

JONES, RONNELL ANDERSEN, lawyer, educator; m. K. C. Jones; 1 child, Max. BA, Utah State Univ., 1995; JD, Ohio State Univ., 2000. Assoc. Jones Day, Columbus, Ohio, 2000—02, San Francisco, 2002—03; law clk. U.S. Ct. Appeals (9th cir.), San Francisco, 2002; law clk. to Hon. Sandra Day O'Connor U.S. Supreme Ct., 2003—04; vis. faculty fellow Univ. Ariz. Coll. Law, 2004—. Mem.: Ohio State Univ. Alumni Assn. (Thomson award 2003), Order of the Coif. Office: University of Arizona Rogers College of Law PO Box 210176 Tucson AZ 85721-0176

JONES, SALLY DAVIESS PICKRELL, writer; b. St. Louis, June 4, 1923; d. Claude Dildine Pickrell and Marie Daviess (Pittman) Pickrell; m. Charles William Jones, Sept. 2, 1943 (dec.); 1 child, Matthew Charles (dec.). Student, Mills Coll., Oakland, Calif., 1941-43, U. Calif.-Berkeley, 1945, Columbia U., 1955-58. Author: (novels) Lights Burn Blue, 1947. Mem. Met. Mus. Art, Nat. Coun. Women, Asia Soc., Fgn. Policy Assn., UN Assn. Episcopalian. Address: 1525 Pelican Point Dr Apt HA101 Sarasota FL 34231-6774

JONES, SANDRA LEE, retired dean; b. Chgo., May 21, 1950; d. Clifford Robert and Dorothy Lucille (Rutzen) Harry; m. Martin Dexter Jones, Sept. 5, 1970; 1 child, Matthew Shawn Jones. BA in English, Columbus Coll., 1972, MEd in English Edn., 1977; EdD in Vocat. and Adult Edn., Auburn U., 1991. Classroom English tchr. Don C. Faith Jr. H.S., Ft. Benning, Ga., 1972-73, McIntosh Jr. H.S., Albany, Ga., 1977-80; lang. arts supr. Dougherty County Schs., Albany, 1980-82; classroom English tchr. Carroll H.S., Ozark, Ala., 1982-83; adj. instr. English Troy State U. at Dothan, Ala., 1983-84, instr. of English Ala., 1984-93, asst. prof. edn. Ala., 1993—98, assoc. prof. edn., 1998—2002, dean, 2002—05, dir. profl. internship program Ala., 1994—99, certification officer, 1994—2001, prof. edn., 2002—05; ret.; edn. cons., 2005—. Profl. edn. pers. evaluation trainer of evaluators Ala. State Dept. Edn., 1997—; advisor Troy State U. chpt. Student Ala. Edn. Assn., 1995-2000, state advisor, 1998-2000. Mem. NEA, Ala. Edn. Retirees Assn., Nat. Coun. Tchrs. English, Internat. Soc. for Tech. in Edn., Mensa, Sigma Tau Delta (advisor 1996-2002), Kappa Delta Pi (advisor 2000-05), Delta Kappa Gamma. Avocations: reading, antiques, music, travel. Office: P O Box 8123 Dothan AL 36304 Office Phone: 334-798-0700. Personal E-mail: eddoc1991@sw.rr.com. Business E-Mail: sjones@troy.edu.

JONES, SANDY (SANDRA F. JONES), writer, speaker, parenting expert; b. Atlanta, Aug. 16, 1943; d. James L. and Virginia (McWhorter) Freeman; m. Paul Eugene Jones, Aug. 23, 1968 (div. 1983); 1 child, Marcie Virginia. BA, Furman U., 1965; MA in Psychology, Appalachian State U., 1972; postgrad., U. Va., 1973-74, U. Md., 1979-80. Author: Good Things for Babies, 1976, Learning for Little Kids, 1979, To Love a Baby, 1982, The Baby Equipment Buying Guide, 1986, The Consumer Reports Guide to Baby Products, 6 edits., 1988-99, Crying Baby, Sleepless Nights, 1983, Parent Support, A Step-by-Step Corporate Guide, 1989co-author (with Marcie Jones) Great Expectations: Your All-in-One Resource for Pregnancy and Childbirth, 2004, Great Expectations Pregnancy Journal and Planner, 2005; contbr. articles to Family Circle, Redbook, Am. Baby, Working Mother, Parents, Woman's World; featured guest Today Show, Good Morning America, CNN, CBS This Morning, others. Recipient Disting. Contbr. citation Nat. Media awards APA, 1982, others. Mem. Soc. Of Friends. Home: 150 W Southwood Dr Brevard NC 28712-8634

JONES, SARA SUE FISHER, librarian; b. Rupert, Idaho, May 2, 1962; d. Richard Sherman and Dana Louise Fisher; m. Martin R. Jones, Jan. 7, 1984; children: Russel, Elaine. BA in Comms., Boise State U., 1983; MLS, Syracuse U., 1999; postgrad., U. North Tex. Libr. dir. Stanley (Idaho) Cmty. Libr., 1984-86; English tchr. Minidoka County Schs., Rupert, Idaho, 1986-88; children's librarian Elko (Nev.) County Libr., 1988-95, libr. dir., 1995-2000; state libr., divsn. adminstr. Nev. State Libr. and Archives, 2000—. Commr. State Nev. Commn. on Ednl. Tech. Elko County Libr. Bd. scholar, 1997-99; IMLS scholar Mem. Nev. Libr. Assn. (pres. 2000—, pub. trustee, chair, Dorothy McAlindin award 1995, scholar 1997-98), Nev. Libr. Orgn. (chair N.E. dist.), Philanthropic Edn. Orgn., Soroptimist Internat. (pres. 1995-96). Avocations: reading, camping, golf. Office: 100 N Stewart St Carson City NV 89701

JONES, SARAH, actress, playwright, poet; Attended, UN Internat. Sch., Bryn Mawr Coll. Writer, performer (plays) Waking the American Dream, Women Can't Wait, Surface Transit, actress (films) Bamboozled, (plays) Vagina Monologues, poet Def Poetry Jam, HBO, writer, performer (solo show Broadway plays) Bridge and Tunnel, 2006— (Spl. Tony award, 2006). Recipient Helen Hayes award, Best One Person Show award, HBO's Aspen Comedy Arts Festival, Obie award, Village Voice. Mailing: 302 A West 12th St #121 New York NY 10014 Office Phone: 212-633-2433. Office Fax: 212-627-6659.*

JONES, SARAH ANN, science educator; b. Tamaqua, Pa., Sept. 17, 1980; d. William D. and Ann M. Jones. BS in Marine Sci., U. SC, 2003; M.T. Secondary Sci. Edn., U. of SC., Columbia, South Carolina, 2003—04; M Secondary Sci. Edn., U. SC, 2004. Intern Sea World Adventure Pk., Orlando, Fla., 2001—02; sci. tchr. Robert Smalls Mid. Sch., Beaufort, SC. Gateway to Tech. grantee, PLTW, 2006. Mem.: Nat. Sci. Tchr. Assn. Office: Robert Smalls Miod Sch 43 W K Alston Rd Beaufort SC 29906 Office Phone: 843-322-2500.

JONES, SARAH LUCILLE, principal, consultant; b. Pinewood, SC, Aug. 12, 1947; d. Aaron Mack and Sarah Jane Green; m. Flynn Raymond Jones, June 5, 1976; 1 child, Flynn Raymond Jones Jr. BS, S.C. State U., 1970; MS, Drexel U., 1974; Cert. in Supervision and Adminstrn., Georgian Ct. Coll., 1993. Cert. tchr. N.J., N.Y., Pa., Ind., S.C. Head tchr. Head Start, Phila., 1970—76; tchr. Rochester (N.Y.) City Schs., 1977—79; dir. ACEOC Head Start, Ft. Wayne, Ind., 1979—82; tchr., supr. Freehold Regional H.S., Englishtown, NJ, 1982—2000; edn. specialist Brookdale C.C., Lincroft, NJ, 1989—95; dept. supr. Manalapan (N.J.) H.S., 2000—; principal Mercer County Tech., Trenton, NJ, 2004—. Nutrition cons. MCEOC Head Start, New Brunswick, NJ, 1985—; state trainer AHEA/NJHEA, NJ, 1987—88; daycare cons. Espic Diocese, Keyport, NJ, 1987—88; mem. numerous curriculum coms., faculty rep., faculty advisor Freehold Regional H.S. Dist. Trustee Brookdale C.C. Mem.: NJPSA, Assn. for Supr. and Curriculum Devel., N.J. Assn. Family and Cons. Sci. (treas. 1992—93, corr. sec. 1993—94), Mon-Ocean Assn. Family and Cons. Sci. (pres. 1989—90, councilor 1994—, v.p. program 1999—2002). Avocations: reading, gardening. Office: Mercer County Tech Schs Assunpink Ctr 1085 Old Trenton Rd Trenton NJ 08690 Office Phone: 609-586-5144. Business E-Mail: ljones@mctec.net.

JONES, SHIRLEY, actress, singer; b. Smithtown, Pa., Mar. 31, 1934; d. Paul and Marjorie (Williams) J.; m. Jack Cassidy, Aug. 5, 1956 (div. 1975); children: Shaun, Patrick, Ryan; m. Marty Ingels, 1977. Grad. high sch., 1952; student, Pitts. Playhouse. Appeared with chorus South Pacific, 1953, in Broadway prodn. Me and Juliet, 1954; other state appearences include The Beggar's Opera, 1957, The Red Mill, 1958, Maggie Flynn, 1968, On a Clear Day, 1975, Show Boat, 1976, Bitter Suite, 1983; films include role of Laurey in Oklahoma, 1954, later stage tour Paris and Rome, sponsorship U.S. Dept. State, Carousel, 1956, April Love, 1957, Never Steal Anything Small, 1959, Bobbikins, 1959, Elmer Gantry, 1960 (Acad. Best Supporting Actress award 1961), Pepe, 1960, The Two Rode Together, 1961, The Music Man, 1962, The Courtship of Eddie's Father, 1963, A Ticklish Affair, 1963, Bedtime Story, 1964, The Secret of My Success, 1965, Fluffy, 1965, The Happy Ending, 1969, The Cheyenne Social Club, 1970, Beyond the Poseidon Adventure, 1979, Tank, 1984, There Were Times, Dear, 1985; night club tour with husband, 1958, later TV and summer stock; star TV series The Partridge Family, 1970-74, Shirley, 1979; guest star: TV series McMillan, 1976; starred with Patrick Cassidy (Broadway): 42nd Street; Silent Night, Lonely Night, 1969, But I Don't Want To Get Married!, 1970, The Girls of Huntington House, 1973, The Family Nobody Wanted, 1975, The Lives of Jenny Dolan, 1975, Winner Take All, 1975, Yesterday's Child, 1977, Evening in Byzantium, 1978, Who'll Save Our Children, 1978, A Last Cry for Help, 1979, The Children Of An Lac, 1980, Inmates: A Love Story, 1981, There Were Times Dear, 1987, Carousel, 2005; one-woman concert: TV series Shirley Jones' America 1981; author: Shirley and Marty: An Unlikely Love Story, 1990. Nat. chairwoman Leukemia Found. Named Mother of Yr. by Women's Found., 1978. Office Phone: 818-728-9505. Business E-Mail: martyingels@msn.com.

JONES, SHIRLEY ELLEN, hearing impaired educator; b. Ft. Lauderdale, Fla., Aug. 3, 1958; BS, Freed Hardeman Coll., 1982; Masters, Nova Southeastern U., 2004. Cert. in elem. edn. Rollins Coll., 1988, in early childhood edn. U. Ctrl. Fla., 1984, tchr. deaf & mentally handicapped U. N. Fla. Hearing dog trainer Fla. Dog Guides for the Deaf, Bradenton, Fla., 1994—. Mem. Ch. of Christ. Avocations: entering sweepstakes, reading, swimming, travel, helping others. Home: 359 Boynton Bay Cir Boynton Beach FL 33435-2571

JONES, SHIRLEY JOYCE, small business owner, fashion designer; b. Chgo., Aug. 13; d. Roman C. Carpen and Mary A. Mleczko; m. William T. Jones, May 2, 1959; children: Debra Ann, Lisa Courtney. Student, Wright Coll., 1955-56, Triton Coll., 1963-64; grad., Ippolito Beauty Sch., 1973. Lic. cosmetologist, Ill. Pres. St. Vincent Ferrer, River Forest, Ill., 1973-74; owner Shirley Jones Beauty Studio, Chgo., 1979-93, Flare Schaumburg, 1983-87, Surprise Boutique, Oakbrook, Ill., 1988-96, Shirley Jones Boutique, Chgo., 1993-96; founder, chmn. gala cancer charity September Surprise, Oak Brook, Burr Ridge, Ill., 1990—. V.p. Oak Brook Republican Womens Club, 1999; active Dupage Fedn. Republican Women, Nat. Fedn. Republican Women, Ill. Fed. Repub. Women (chief of protocol, vice chmn., chaplain). Grantee Ippolito Beauty Sch., 1973. Mem. Fashion Group Internat., Chgo. Fashion Group, Nat. Arts and Letters Soc., Oakbrook, Ill. Roman Catholic. Avocations: golf, dance, travel, antiques, gourmet cooking. Home and Office: 6812 Fieldstone Dr Burr Ridge IL 60527-6967

JONES, SONIA JOSEPHINE, advertising executive; b. Belize, Brit., Honduras, Nov. 9, 1945; arrived in U.S., 1962, naturalized, 1986; d. Frederick Francis and Elsie Adelia (Gomez) Alcoser; m. John Marvin Jones, Mar. 21, 1970; children: Christopher William Edward, Joshua Joseph Paul. Student, Lamar U., 1964-66. With Foley's Federated Dept. Store, Houston, 1965-67; media buyer Vance Advt., Houston, 1967-68; media buyer, planner O'Neill & Assocs., Houston, 1968-75; media supr. Ketchum Houston, 1975-76; v.p., media dir. Rives Smith Bladwin Carlberg/Y&R, Houston, 1976-86; sr. v.p. media dir. Black Gillock & Langberg, Houston, 1986—89; pres. JMM Group, Inc., Houston, 1989—. Lectr. U. Houston, 1983—. Vol. Women in Yellow, Houston, 1966; mem. Tom's Moms St. Thomas HS, 1992—, mem. sch. bd. spl. projects, fundraising vol. women's club, 1992—; vol. translator St. Cecilia Clinic, 1993—; mem. sch. bd. spl. projects St. Cecilia Cath. Sch.; bd. dirs. Santana Doston Found., 1998—; head sacristan St. Cecilia Cath. Ch., 1995—. Mem.: Houston Advt. Fedn. Republican. Office: JMM Group Inc 2902 W 12th Houston TX 77008

JONES, SOPHIA LASHAWN, architect; b. Mt. Holly, N.J., Apr. 24, 1979; d. Stanley Roosevelt and Cynthia Ann Jones. BA in Architecture, U. Miami, 2003; MS in Hist. Preservation, U. Pa., 2005. Draftsman Teletronics Tech. Corp., Bristol, 2000, Clear Choice Windows and Doors, Miami, 2002—03; preservation intern Eastern State Penitentiary, Phila., 2003—04; program asst. N.J. Hist. Preservation Office, Trenton, NJ, 2004—05. Bd. dirs. N.J. Hist. Sites Coun. Recipient scholarship, Nat. Trust Hist. Preservation, 2004; grantee Illona English Travel fellowship, U. Pa., 2004. Mem.: AIA (assoc.), Black Grad. Profl. Student Assn. (recording sec. 2004—05), Pa. Student Preservation Assn. (v.p. 2004—05), Nat. Trust for Hist. Preservation. Avocations: travel, cooking. Home: 3001 Rt 130 Apt 88K Delran NJ 08075 Office: Hist Bldg Arch 312 W State St Trenton NJ 08618 Office Phone: 609-393-3999. E-mail: sj@hba-llc.com.

JONES, STACIE ANN, elementary school educator; b. Hereford, Tex., Mar. 11, 1977; d. Larry Stephen and Dolores Ann Jones. BS, West Tex. A&M U., Canyon. Substitute tchr. Amarillo Ind. Sch. Dist., Amarillo, Tex., 2001—02; tchr. Highland Park Elementary Sch., Amarillo, 2002—. Com. chair Am. Cancer Soc. Relay for Life, Amarillo, 2004—06. Office Phone: 806-335-1334.

JONES, STELLA MARIE, retired school cousnelor; b. Osceola, Wis., Sept. 26, 1947; d. Bernard John and Stella Mary (Shimota) Minnichsoffer; m. Conrad Nagel Jones, Aug. 7, 1976; 1 child, Natasha Marie; stepchildren: Jason (dec.), Heidi. BA, St. Cloud State U., 1969, MS, 1970. Nat. cert. counselor. Sr. employment counselor Minn. Dept. Jobs and Tng., Mpls., 1971—93, summer office supr., 1987—93; coord. North HS Careet Ctr. Project, 1992—93; sch. counselor Mpls. Pub. Sch., 1993—2005, pres. Mpls. Sch. Counselors Forum, 1999—2000; sch. counselor North Cmty. HS, 1993—2005, Wallin scholarship coord., 2005—; ret. Chair adv. bd. Mpls. Career Edn. Project, 1976-77; vice-chair Youth Trust-Job Connection, Mpls., 1990-92. Leader 4-H Group, Mpls., 1990-96. Recipient Gov.'s Pub. Svc. award State of Minn., 1988, Counselors Forum Disting. Svc. award, 2005. Mem. ACA, Nat. Employment Counselors Assn. (pres. 1987-88, Profl. Devel. award 1993, Past Pres.'s award 1989), Minn. Assn. Counseling and Devel. (pres. 1977-78, Disting. Svc. award 1980), Minn. Employment Counselors Assn. (pres. 1975-76, 91-92), Am. Sch. Counselors Assn., Friends of North H.S. Found. (pres. 2003—). Democrat. Roman Catholic. Avocations: walking, skiing, golf, gardening. Office: Job Svc North High Sch 1500 James Ave N Minneapolis MN 55411-3161 Business E-Mail: sjones@mpls.k12.mn.us.

JONES, STEPHANIE TUBBS, congresswoman, lawyer, prosecutor; b. Cleve., Sept. 10, 1949; m. Mervyn L. Jones, Sr. (dec.); 1 child. BA in Sociology, Case Western Res. U. Flora Mather Coll., 1971; JD, Case Western Res. U. Sch. Law, 1974; D (hon.), Myers U., Notre Dame Coll., Ctrl. State U. Bar: Ohio 1974, US Dist. Ct. (no. dist.) Ohio 1975, US Ct. Appeals (6th cir.) 1981, US Supreme Ct. 1981. Asst. gen. counsel, EEO adminstr. N.E. Ohio Regional Sewer Dist., 1974-76; asst. prosecutor Cuyahoga County Prosecutor's Office, 1976-79; trial atty. Cleve. dist. office EEO, 1979-81; judge Cleve. Mcpl. Ct., 1982-83, Cuyahoga County Ct. of Common Pleas, 1983-91; prosecutor Cuyahoga County, Cleve., 1991-98; mem. US Congress from 11th Ohio dist., 1999—, mem. small bus. com., 1999—2002, mem. banking and fin. svcs. com., 1999—2002, mem. ways and means com., 2003—, mem. standards of official conduct com. Vis. com. bd. overseers Franklin Thomas Backus Sch. Law, Case Western Res. U. Bd. trustees Cmty. Re-entry Prog.; bd. trustees class of 1984 Leadership Cleve. Alumnae; mem. Task Force on Violent Crime, Substance Abuse Initiative; trustee Cleve. Police Hist. Soc.; bd. trustees Bethany Bapt. Ch. Recipient Outstanding Vol. Svcs. in Law and Justice award Urban League Greater Cleve., 1986, Women of Yr. award Cleve. chpt. Nat. Assn. Negro Bus. and Profl. Women's Clubs, Inc., 1987, award in recognition of outstanding svc. to judiciary and black cmty. Midwest region Nat. Black Am. Law Student Assn., 1988, Career Women of Achievement award YWCA, 1991, Disting. Svc. award Cleve. chpt. NAACP, 1997; named Black Profl. of Yr., Black Profl. Assn. Cleve., 1995, 1994; named one of Most Influential Black Americans, Ebony mag., 2006; Ohio Dem. of Yr., Ohio Dem. Party, 1995; inductee Collinwood HS Hall of Fame, 1994, Soc. Benchers of Case Western Res. U. Sch. Law, 1996. Mem. ABA, Nat. Black Prosecutor's Assn., Nat. Dist. Atty.'s Assn. (met. prosecutor's com.), Nat. Coun. Negro Women, Nat. Coll. Dist. Attys. (bd. regents), Ohio State Bar Assn. (Nettie Cronise Lutes award 1997), Ohio Prosecuting Attys. Assn. (exec. com.), Cleve. Bar Assn. (trustee), Norman S. Miner Bar Assn. (past treas.), Cuyahoga Women's Polit. Caucus, Delta Sigma Theta (Greater Cleve. Alumnae chpt., Althea Simmons award 1993). Democrat. Baptist. Office: US Ho Reps 1009 Longworth Ho Office Bldg Washington DC 20515-3511 Office Phone: 202-225-7032.*

JONES, SUSAN CHAFIN, management consultant; b. Bryan, Tex., July 14, 1951; d. Othel Viron and Norma Beatrice (Bartley) Chafin; m. Robert Lewis Jones, Apr. 9, 1973 (dec.); 1 child, Kelli Sanness. BS in Edn., Stephen F. Austin State U., 1973; MA, U. Tex., Austin, 1976. Cert. rehab. counselor; lic. marriage and family therapist. Tng. coord. Behavioral Systems Scis. Assoc., Austin, 1973-76; pres., CEO Jones Counseling & Cons., Inc. (formerly Jones, Bright Internat.), The Woodlands, Tex., 1976—; CEO Jones, Ragain Internat., Inc., The Woodlands, 1997-99; team leader Guatemala Med. Mission, 1999-2000; interim exec. dir. Interfaith of the Woodlands, Tex., 1999—2001. Author: Feelings Beneath Words and Messages in Action, 1974, Supervisor's Notes: Guidelines on Employee Counseling, 1977, Youth Ministry: A Manual for Youth Counselors, Leaders and Workers, 1991, 360o Intermetrics, Assessment for Individuals and Organizations, 1993, Therapeutic Approaches to Women's Health: A Program of Exercise and Education, 1995. Active McCullough High Sch. PTA, The Woodlands, 1992-95; v.p. McCullough Highsteppers Parent Club, 1993-95; dir. Stephen Ministry The Woodlands United Meth. Ch., 1992-96, mem. adminstrv. bd., 1993-96; bd. mem. Montgomery County Young Life, 1991-92. Mem. Montgomery County C. of C., Am. Assn. Marriage and Family Therapy (clin.), Am. Assn. Christian Counselors (profl., charter), Christian Counselors Tex., Rotary Internat., Women's Energy Network. Republican. Avocations: playing piano, skiing, writing. Office: Jones Counseling & Cons Inc 10655 Six Pines Dr #160 The Woodlands TX 77380-0655

JONES, SUSAN DELANTY, lawyer; b. Aberdeen, Wash., Jan. 5, 1943; BA cum laude, U. Wash., 1965; MA, U. Chgo., 1969; JD cum laude, U. Puget Sound, 1979. Bar: Wash. 1979. Law clk. to Justice William H. Williams Wash. State Supreme Ct., 1979—81; ptnr. Preston Gates & Ellis LLP, Seattle. Bd. dirs. Plymouth Housing Group, 1996—; bd. trustees Horizon House, 2000—. Mem.: Seattle-King County Bar Assn., King County Bar Assn. (mem. Judicial Conferencing Com. 1999—). Office: Preston Gates & Ellis LLP Ste 2900 925 Fourth Ave Seattle WA 98104-1158 Office Phone: 206-370-7654. Office Fax: 206-307-6096. E-mail: susanj@prestongates.com.

JONES, SUSAN DORFMAN, real estate broker, writer; b. NYC, Oct. 4, 1939; d. Joseph and Sarah (Sorrin) Dorfman; m. William Harry Jones, Sept. 18, 1960; children: Jeffrey Scott, Eric David, Timothy Mark BA, Syracuse U., 1961. Pres., owner Antiques Corp. Am., 1972—77, Susan & Sons Antiques, 1977—; comm. officer Riggs Bank, Washington, 1978—81; mgr. publs. Potomac Electric Power Co., Washington, 1981—82; sr. mgr. corp. comm. MCI Corp., Washington, 1982—83; dir. corp. comm. Sears World Trade, Washington, 1983—85; dir. corp. comm. and govt. rels. Oxford Devel. Corp., Bethesda, Md., 1985—87; comm. expert pub. health svc./health and human svcs. U.S. Alcohol, Drug Abuse, Mental Health Adminstrn., Rockville, Md., 1989—91; real estate broker Weichert Realtors, Washington, 1991—. Vol. staff Cleve. Clinics, Cleve. H.S. of Arts, 2003—; free-lance writer, cons., Washington, 1975-92; radio personality Sta. 4KQ, Brisbane, Australia, 1962; adj. prof. comms. Am. U., Washington, 1978-82. Author, editor, project mgr. corp. ann. reports. Recipient 1st pl. award for columns N.Y. Press Assn., 1961, Gold Quill award Internat. Assn. Bus. Communicators, 1980. Mem.: Greater Capital Area Assn. Realtors, Nat. Assn. Realtors, Pub. Rels. Soc. Am., Women in Telecommunications, Nat. Assn. Bank Women, Internat. Assn. Bus. Communicators, Jewish Cmty. Ctr. Cleve., Nat. Press Club. Democrat. Jewish. Home and Office: 30650 Jackson Rd Chagrin Falls OH 44022-1731 Office: 5035 Wisconsin Ave NW Washington DC 20016-4113 E-mail: suebillj@yahoo.com.

JONES, SUSAN EMILY, fashion educator, administrator, educator emeritus; b. N.Y.C., Sept. 9, 1948; d. David and Emily Helen (Welke) J.; m. Henry J. Titone, Jr., Oct. 21, 1974 (div. 1980); m. Douglas S. Robbins, Aug. 21, 1985. BFA, Pratt Inst., Bklyn., 1970. Designer Sue Brett, N.Y.C., 1970-74, St. Tropez, 1975; prof. fashion Pratt Inst., Bklyn., 1972-2000, chairperson fashion dept., 1981-2000, chairperson merchandising and design programs fashion dept., 1983-2000; computer software cons., 1988-89; owner, designer Sej Wearable Artworks, 1992—. Internat. observer Jeunes Createurs de Mode, Paris, 1987, judge, 1988; U.S. rep. SAGA Internat. Design Ctr., Copenhagen, 1992, serdesigns, Hawaii, 2001—. Tech. book reviewer, 1994—. Recipient Young Am. Designer award Internat. Ladies Garment Workers Union, 1970, Ptnr. in Edn. award N.Y.C. Pub. Sch. Sys. Chancellor, 1992-93. Mem. Fashion Group (regional com. 1983-87, mem. com. 1990-93, ednl. com. 1995-96, co-chair ednl. com. 1996-98), Nat. Retail Fedn., Under Fashion Assn. Office: Pratt Inst Dept of Fashion Design 200 Willoughby Ave Brooklyn NY 11205-3899 Personal E-mail: sejpratt@aol.com. Business E-Mail: sjones@pratt.edu, serdesigns@aol.com.

JONES, SUZANNE P., public relations executive; b. Niagara Falls, N.Y., Sept. 4, 1946; d. Morris G. and Betty (Connolly) J. BA in English, Niagara U., 1969; MA in Theater, U. Conn., 1971. Editor Niagara Observer, Niagara Falls, 1971-74, Niagara Free Press, Niagara Falls, 1974-75; pub. info. dir. City of Niagara Falls, 1975-76; advt. dir. Orion Enterprises, Lewiston, N.Y., 1976-79; v.p. Bozell and Jacobs Pub. Rels., N.Y.C., 1980-86, Porter/Novelli, N.Y.C., 1987-90, Geltzer & Co., 1991-93; dir. in-house pub. rels. Black & Decker Household Products, Shelton, Conn., 1993—. Mem. Theatre Hist. Soc., Larchmont Manor Soc., Larchmont Hist. Soc., Friends Niagara U. Theatre, Niagara U. Coun. Democrat. Roman Catholic. Home: 2221 Willow Ave Niagara Falls NY 14305-3051

JONES, SYLVIA CALPURNIA, investment company executive; b. Race Course Clarendon, Jamaica, Aug. 16, 1936; d. Aldron Benjamin and Vera Gwendolyn Taylor; m. Walter Gerald Jones, Feb. 7, 1959; children: Gerald, Ashford, Sean, Chester Rhoan, Desiree. BSc, Agrl. State U., Greensboro, NC, 1967; MA, Montclair State U., NJ, 1969; postgrad., U. Mass., Amherst. Tchr. Ministry of Edn., Kingston, Jamaica, 1958—64; tchr. home econs. Newark Bd. Edn., 1967—92; owner S&J Investment, Montclair, 1979—. Examiner Mid. States Accreditation Com., Trenton Ctrl. HS, NJ, West Babylon HS, NY. Recipient Key to City of Montclair, 1988. Mem.: NAACP, Am. Inst. Cancer Rsch., Am. Cancer Soc., Am. Diabetic Assn., So. Poverty Law Ctr. Home: 257 Orange Rd Montclair NJ 07042

JONES, TAMERA DAWN, elementary school educator; b. Lafayette, Ind., Mar. 9, 1961; d. Charles Thomas and Audrey Ann Felkner; m. Stephen Jay Jones, Dec. 19, 1992; children: Ara, Mike, Megan, Molly. BS, Ind. State U., 1984, MS, 1995. Tchr. Rockville Cmty. Schools, Ind., 1986—. Chair NCA Steering Com., Rockville, Md., 2003—06; mentor, tchr. I Team, Ind., 2004—06. Avocations: camping, hiking, travel, reading. Home: 164 N Nyesville Rd Rockville IN 47872 Office: Rockville Elem 406 Elm St Rockville IN 47872

JONES, THERESE MARGARET, language educator, editor; b. Evergreen Park, Ill., Mar. 17, 1964; d. John William and M. Eileen Gustafson; m. John Joseph Jones, May 5, 1989; children: Lara Anastasia, Andrew Sean, Christopher Gerard. MA, St. Xavier U., Chgo., 1996. Asst. prof. English Lewis U., Romeoville, Ill., 1994—, dir. writing placement, 2001—, summer soar writing prof., 2001—06. Editor (coord. and designer): Windows Fine Arts Mag., 2002—; editor: (scholarly compilation) Dimensions of Curiosity:Learning in the 21st Century. Grantee, Dean Coll. of Arts and Scis., 2005, Title III Funding, 2005. Right To Life Party. Roman Catholic. Avocations: painting, bowling, writing poetry, Chinese literature. Office: Lewis Univ One University Pkwy Romeoville IL 60446 Office Phone: 815-836-5321. Business E-Mail: jonesth@lewisu.edu.

JONES, TINA MOREAU, psychology educator; b. N.Y.C., Oct. 24, 1936; d. Alberto and Jennie (Kreinin) Moreau; m. Walter T. Jones, Jan. 20, 1968; 1 child, Deidre A. BA, CCNY, 1961, MA, 1963; PhD, CUNY, 1968. Rsch. asst. Albert Einstein Coll. Medicine, N.Y.C., 1964-66, rsch. assoc., 1966-68, instr., 1968-74; asst. prof. Queens Coll. CUNY, 1969-77, assoc. prof., 1977—. Contbr. articles to sci. jours. Mem. AAAS, Am. Psychol. Soc., Sigma Xi, Phi Beta Kappa. Office: CUNY Queens Coll 65-30 Kissena Blvd Flushing NY 11367-1575 Office Phone: 718-997-3237. Personal E-mail: tinamorjones@earthlink.net.

JONES, VIRGINIA MCCLURKIN, retired social worker; b. Anniston, Ala., Mar. 13, 1935; d. Louie Walter and Virginia Keith (Beaver) McClurkin; m. Charles Miller Jones, Jr., Mar. 16, 1957; children: Charles Miller III, V. Grace. BA, Agnes Scott Coll., 1957; MA, U. Tenn., 1965, MSSW, 1979. English instr. U. Tenn., Knoxville, 1967-71; religious edn. dir. Oak Ridge Unitarian Ch., 1972-73, 76-78; co-owner, mgr. The Bookstore, 1973-76; English instr. Roane State C.C., 1975-80; pvt. practice clin. social work Oak Ridge, 1980-98. Cons. Mountain Cmty. Health Ctr., Coalfield, Tenn., 1980-83, Valley Ridge Hospice, 1987-89. Contbr. articles to newspapers. Mem.: NASW, Concord Yacht Club, Rotary. Democrat. Episcopalian. Office: 969 Oak Ridge Turnpike Oak Ridge TN 37830-6554

JONES, VIVIAN BOOKER, speech pathology/audiology services professional; b. Spartanburg, SC, Apr. 2, 1945; d. Claude Cornelius and Tallulah Jane Booker; m. Thornell Tobias Jones; 1 child, Sean Liam. BA in Speech Corrections, SC State U., Orangeburg, SC, 1966; MA in Speech Lang. Pathologist, U. Conn., Storrs, Conn., 1973. Cert. Clin. Competence Speech Am. Speech and Hearing Assn. Speech pathologist Killington Pub. Schs., Danielson, Conn., 1969—73, Cherokee County Schs., Gaffney, SC, 1973—74, Spartanburg Sch. Dist. 3, Spartanburg, SC, 1974—75; asst. prof. SC State U., Orangeburg, SC, 1975—87; speech pathologist Spartanburg Sch. Dist. Six, Spartanburg, SC, 1987—99, Spartanburg Sch. Dist. seven, Spartenburg, SC, 1999—2003. Dir. Sat. Sch., Duncan, SC, 2003—05. U.S. Cons. EDA Agy. for Toxic Substances & Disease Recruiting, 2001—03; mem., mentor GHBC Missionary. Recipient Olympic Gold medal, United Way Piedmont, 1996. Avocations: crafts, cross stitch, needlepoint.

JONES, VIVIAN EILENE, music educator; b. Tulsa, Okla., Oct. 13, 1948; d. Lucius and Vivian Dotson Jones. BS in Music Edn., Morgan State U., Balt., 1970; EdM in Spl. Edn., Coppin State Coll., Balt., 1974. Cert. educator S.C., tchr. Mo. Tchr. Balt. City Pub. Schs., 1970—74, St. Louis Pub. Schs., 1974—84, Oakland (Calif.) Unified Sch. Dist., 1984—90, Kirkwood (Mo.) R-7 Sch. Dist., 1990—94, Charleston (S.C.) County Sch. Dist., 1994—2000, 2004—, Dorchester Dist. 2, Summerville, SC, 2000—04. Dir. Charleston Symphony Orch. Gospel Choir, 2000—; music coord. Charleston Devel. Acad. Charter Sch., 2004—; choral clinician B.E.A.C.H. Gifted and Talented Program, Georgetown, SC, 1999—. Composer: (radio comml.) It's Cajun Delight, (program theme song) If You Gear Up; arranger (Negro spirituals). Scholarship grantor Coastal Cmty. Found., Charleston, 2001—05. Recipient Key to the City, Jefferson City, Mo., 1989, Outstanding Contbn. in the Arts award, Moja Arts Festival Com., 2002. Mem.: Music Educators Nat. Conf., Am. Choral Dirs. Assn., Alpha Kappa Alpha (Neophyte of Yr. 1968). Avocations: travel, puzzles, swimming. Home: 8093 Shadow Oak Dr Charleston SC 29406 Office: Burke HS 244 President St Charleston SC 29403 Office Phone: 843-724-7757. Office Fax: 843-720-2359. E-mail: vivian_jones@charleston.k12.sc.us.

JONES, WINONA NIGELS, retired media specialist; b. Feb. 24, 1928; d. Eugene Arthur and Bertha Lillian (Dixon) Nigels; m. Charles Albert Jones, Nov. 26, 1994; children: Charles Eugene, Sharon Ann Jones Allworth, Caroline Winona Jones Pandorf. AA, St. Petersburg Jr. Coll., 1965; BS, U. So. Fla., 1967, MS, 1968; advanced MS, Fla. State U., 1980. Libr. media specialist Dunedin Comprehensive H.S., Fla., 1967-76; libr. media specialist, chmn. dept. Fitzgerald Mid. Sch., Largo, 1976—87; dir. media svcs. East Lake H.S., Tarpon Springs, 1987—93; ret., 1993. Author: Around Palm Harbor, 2005. Dir. and vol. North Pinellas Hist. Mus.; active Palm Harbor Hist. Soc., Pinellas County Hist. Soc.; del. White Ho. Conf. Libr. and Info. Svcs. Named Educator Yr. Pinellas County Sch. Bd. and Suncoast C. of C., 1983, 88, Palm Harbor Woman Yr. Palm Harbor Jr. Women's club, 1989, Palm Harbor Citizen Yr., Palm Harbor C. of C., 2002. Mem. ALA (coun. 1988-92), NEA, AAUW, ASCD, Assn. Ednl. Comm. and Tech. (divsn. sch. media specialist, coms.), Am. Assn. Sch. Librs. (com., pres.-elect 1989, pres. 1990-91, mem. exec. bd. 1991-92), Southeastern Libr. Assn., Fla. Libr. Assn., Fla. Assn. Media Edn. (pres.), U. So. Fla. Alumni Assn., Fla. State Libr. Sci. Alumni Assn., U. So. Fla. Libr. Sci. Alumni Assn. (pres. 1991-92, 92-93), Phi Theta Kappa, Phi Rho Pi, Beta Phi Mu, Kappa Delta Pi, Delta Kappa Gamma (parliamentarian 1989-90, legis. chmn. 1990, sec. 1994-96), Inner Wheel Club, Pilot Club, Civic Club, Order Ea. Star (Palm Harbor, past worthy matron). Democrat. Home: 911 Manning Rd Palm Harbor FL 34683-6344 Office Phone: 727-724-3054.

JONES COMPTON, CAROL ANN, science educator; b. Bypro, Ky., Dec. 19, 1946; d. Tilden Howard and Caroline Elizabeth (Sperry) Jones; m. Joe Wayne Compton, Dec. 31, 1970; children: Joe W. Compton II, Elizabeth Louise Compton, Phillip Ross Compton. BA in Chemistry, Pikeville Coll., Ky., 1967. Cert. 5th yr. Elem. Edn. Morehead State U., Ky., 1980, Physics Ea. Ky. U., Richmond, 1986. Sci. tchr. Lawrence County HS, Louisa, Ky., 1967—71, 1979—. Sunday sch. tchr. First Bapt. Ch., Louisa; aux. mem. Gideons Internat., Louisa chpt. Mem.: NSTA, NEA. Bapt. Avocations: gardening, reading, sewing, swimming. Home: 123 2nd St Louisa KY 41230 Office: Lawrence County HS 100 Bulldog Ln Louisa KY 41230 Business E-Mail: ccompton@lawrence.k12.ky.

JONES-EDDY, JULIE MARGARET, retired librarian; b. Hayden, Colo., Feb. 20, 1942; d. Hugh A. and Margaret E. (Tagert) J.; m. John H. Eddy Jr., June 3, 1965; 1 child, Mark. BA, U. Colo., 1964; MLS, U. Okla., 1976. Cert. libr. Art tchr. Fort Collins (Colo.) Pub. Schs., 1964-65, Gunnison (Colo.) Pub. Schs., 1965-66; govt. documents libr. Tutt Libr., Colo. Coll., Colorado Springs, 1977—2002; ret. Presenter in field of oral history project on women, 1984—. Author: (videotape) Women of Northwestern Colorado, 1890-1940: Glimpses of Our Lives, 1984; author: Homesteading Women: An Oral History of Colorado, 1890-1950, 1992. Grantee Colo. Endowment for the Humanities, 1984, 89. Mem. ALA, Colo. Libr. Assn., Oral History Assn.

JONES-KELNER, BARBARA TERYL, music educator; b. Buffalo, N.Y., Aug. 2, 1955; d. Paul Frederick Teryl and Dorothy Madeline Keller; m. Alan Lee Kelner, July 11, 2004; 1 child, Jessica Nicole Jones. MusB in Edn., Baldwin Wallce Conservatory Music, Cleve., Ohio, 1977; MEd, Ga. State U., Atlanta, Ga., 1986; degree in Curriculum, Lincoln Meml. U., Nashville, Tenn., 1999. Tchr. instrumental music Cherokee County Schs., Canto, Ga., 1980—. Mem.: Ga. Music Educators Assn. (assoc.). Office: Dean Rusk Middle School 4695 Hickory Rd Canton GA 30115 Office Phone: 770-345-2832. Office Fax: 770-345-5013. Personal E-mail: musicteacher78@aol.com. Business E-Mail: barbara.jones@cherokk.k12.ga.us.

JONES-KETNER, ELIZABETH BROWN, writer; b. Kansas City, Mo., Sept. 27, 1907; d. James Riley and Agnes Julia (Gammage) Brown; m. Clare Hartley Jones, June 4, 1929 (dec. July 3, 1981), m. Francis D. Ketner, Dec. 27, 1982 (dec. Nov. 2, 1990); children— Elizabeth Ann, Sara Denise, David Hartley, Phyllis Elaine. Student U. Mo., Kansas City, 1946, Mid-Am. Nazarene Coll., 1981. Free-lance writer, 1940-62, 78—; author numerous books, including: Teaching Primaries Today, 1974; Because God Made Me, 1975; Stories of Jesus, 1977; When We Share the Bible with Children, 1977; Let the Children Come, 1978; contbr. numerous stories, poems to children's publs.; author song lyrics; editor, curriculum planner, writer Nazarene Pub. House, Kansas City, Mo., 1962-78; workshop leader; speaker at writers' confs.; mem. nat. com. for planning Sunday sch. curriculum; book reviewer; speaker at parent's groups. Mem. Ch. of the Nazarene.

JONES-KOCH, FRANCENA, school counselor, educator; b. Bunnell, Fla., Dec. 3, 1948; d. Roosevelt Jones and Naomi Stafford; m. William H. Koch, July 1976 (div. Aug. 1980); 1 child, Ahmad Yussef Shaw. BS, Fla. Meml. Coll., 1972; M in Elem. Edn., Nova Southeastern U., 1984, specialist degree, 1994. Intermediate tchr. Miami (Fla.) Dade County Pub. Schs., 1973—88, guidance counselor, 1988—. Adj. prof. Fla. Meml. Coll., Miami, 1984—87; juvenile GED instr. Women's Detention Ctr., Miami, 1994—96; planner summer 2000 Inmate to Inmate Tutoring Program Dept. Corrections, Miami, 2000; mem. region 5 steering com. Dade County Pub. Schs., Miami, mem. dist.'s student svcs. adv. coun., 2002—; amb. United Way-Dade County Pub. Schs., Miami; pres. Dade Counseling Assn., Miami, 2002—; dir. comms. Herstory Inc., 1975—2000. Vol. United Way Dade County, Miami, 1999—. Mem.: Am. Sch. Counselor Assn., AAUW (Miami br. chair Gwen Cherry awards 2000—, designer 21st Century Women's Wisdom Project 2001, prodr. 21st Century Women's Wisdom Project 2001), Fla. Counseling Assn., United Tchrs. Dade County, United Way of Dade County, Zeta Phi Beta Sorority, Inc. (pres. Beta Zeta chpt. 1997—99). Avocations: reading, community service, creative writing, travel, visiting book stores. Home: 10850 SW 164th St Miami FL 33157

JONES-LUKÁCS, ELIZABETH LUCILLE, physician; b. Norfolk, Va. d. Oliver C. and Gertrude (Layden) Jones; m. Michel J. Lukacs (dec.); children: Amanda, Laurel, Angelique, Klara. BS, Oglethorpe U., 1955; MD, Ownstate Med. Ctr., 1964. Diplomate Am. Bd. Family Practice. Intern Beth Israel Hosp., N.Y.C., 1964-65; family practice medicine Goshen, NY, 1965-73, Buckingham, Va., 1973-78; commd. maj. U.S. Air Force, 1978; flight surgeon Andrews AFB, Md., 1978-85, chief exec. med. program Md., 1991-2000; med. dir. Armed Forces Benefit Assn., Alexandria, Va., 2000—04. Unit charge physician Student Health Ctr., U. Md., College Park, 1985—91; bd. dirs. Falcon's Landing Mil. Officers Retirement Home. Author: The Curies Radium & Radioactivity, 1962, The Golden Stamp Book of Flying Animals, 1963. Col. USAFR, commd. 459th USAF Clinic. Mem. Am. Med. Womens Assn. (pres. Br. I), Md. Connemara Breeders. Episcopalian. Home: 15430 Mount Calvert Rd Upper Marlboro MD 20772-9616 Personal E-mail: ejlukacs@juno.com.

JONES REYNOLDS, STAR (STARLET MARIE JONES), television host, lawyer, former prosecutor; b. Badin, NC, Mar. 24, 1962; m. Al Reynolds, Nov. 13, 2004. BA, Am. U.; JD, U. Houston. Bar: NY. Lawyer; sr. asst. dist. atty. Bklyn. Dist. Atty.'s Office, 1991; studio commentator Court TV, 1991; legal corrs. NBC's Today, Nightly News; host syndicated tv show Jones and Jury, 1994; former sr. corr., chief legal analyst Inside Edition, 1995; co-host ABC Daytime's The View, 1997—2006; nat. spokesperson Payless ShoeSource; host Live from the Red Carpet!, 2004. Notable guest appearances The Tonight Show with Jay Leno, Bravo's Celebrity Poker, Celebrity Jeopardy, The Daily Show with Jon Stewart, and The Late Show with David Letterman.; honored as a subject of Lifetime TV: Intimate Portrait, 2000, hosted It's All About You With Star Jones on ShopNBC, developer of own website, featured personality for Kohl's Target, and Salon Z of Saks Fifth Avenue, featured on numerous mags. such as: Newsweek, TV Guide, Essence, Black Enterprise, and New York, host E! Entertainment Television's Live Red Carpet Arrivals of the Primetime Emmy Awards, 2004; author: You Have to Stand for Something, or You'll Fall for Anything, 1998; guest appearance (TV series) Strong Medicine, 2001, Soul Food, 2002, Less Than Perfect, 2005; actor: Relative Strangers, 2006; author: Shine: A Physical, Emotional, and Spiritual Journey to Finding Love, 2006. Bd. dir. East Harlem Sch. at Exodus House, Dress for Success, God's Love We Deliver, Girls, Inc.; launched The Starlet Fund, 2002—. Named Chief of Consumer Style, 2002; honored for work in improving the educational opportunities for low income children in East Harlem, East Harlem Sch. at Exodus House; co-recipient with co-host from "The View", Safe Horizon Champion award, 2001. Achievements include launching signature line of shoes, Starlet by Star Jones, sold exclusively at Payless ShoeSource. Office: 320 W 66th St New York NY 10023-6304*

JONES TERGEOGLOU, BEVERLY GLORIA, special education services professional; d. Robert George and Gloria Sarafina (Castelvetere) Jones; children: Timothy Jon Tergeoglou, Nicolas Patrick Tergeoglou, Marc Tergeoglou, Paulina Klein. Attended, U. Conn., Langston Bible Coll., Catherdal Bible Coll. Cert. hospice, infection control, body mechanics & lupus erythematosus Timmonsville Area Vocat. Ctr., hospice McLeod Regional Med. Ctr., children & family svcs. Dist. 7, adminstrn., supervision adminstrn. medication, Fla. Children & Family Svcs. People Choice, in-house trng. van safety ARC, 1999, individual edn. plan ARC, 2004, Ctr. Disease Control HIV/AIDS, 1999, body mechanics & transfer trng. Easter Seals, 2001, devel. disabilities 2002, analysis trng. 2002, adminstrn. medications Fla. Devel. Disabilities Program, 2002, full life ahead trng. Brevard Sch. Dist., 2004, lic. devel. disabilities foster home Dist. 7, Fla., 2005. Instr. Indian River CC, Vero Beach, Fla., 1998—2000; assoc. dir. vocat. svcs., consumer svcs. mgr. Easter Seals, Fla., 2000—02; foster parent Devereux Therapeutic Foster Care Group Home, Devereux, Fla., 2002—; instr. Brevard Sch. Dist., Learner Empowerment Through Agency Partnerships Trng. Program, Melbourne, Fla., 2002—. Apptd. mem. Tree Adv., Sebastian; vol. Hospice, Florence, Red Cross, St. John, US Virgin Islands, Town's First Festival, Pamplico, Nat. Pks. and Forest, St. John, US Virgin Islands, Hosanna Book and Gift Shop, St. Croix, US Virgin Islands, Spl. Olympics, Vero Beach, Fla., 1998, soccer vol. Palm Bay, 2005; substitute tchr. Am. Sch. Mallorca, Spain, libr. vol.; mem. Woman's Coalition of Spouse Abuse, St. Croix, US Virgin Islands; stringer TV sta. Florence; reading instr. 2nd and 3rd grades Julius Sprave Sch., St. John, US Virgin Islands; vol. spl. and challenged needs kids, 2005; softball vol. spl. and challenged needs kids, 2005; spl. and challenged needs vol. Spotlight Theater, 2005; vol. children's ch. Zion's Ch., Palm Bay, 2002—05; mem. Our Lady of Grace Ch., Palm Bay, 2005; tchg. asst. St. Ann's RC, Florence, SC; bazaar vol. Our Lady of Mt. Carmel Ch., St. John, US Virgin Islands; mem. PTA, Pamplico, SC. Recipient Fla. Appreciation award, Tree and Landscape Adv. Bd., City of Sebastian, 2002, Learner Empowerment through Agency Partnerships Tng. award, Brevard County Offices of Exceptional Student Edn. and Adult Cmty. Edn., 2003, Cert. of Recognition, Devereux, 2003, Cert. Continued Dedication and Commitment to Helping Children That You Serve, 2003, Cert. Vol. Svc., PTA, Pamplico. Mem.: Coun. Exceptional Children, Newcomer's Club, Elks Lodge Palm Bay. Avocations: swimming, walking, bicycling, reading, history. Personal E-mail: inletjetty@aol.com.

JONES-THURMAN, ROSANNA MARIE, psychologist; d. Paul Edward Jones and Rosemary Butler Hopkins; m. Daniel Wayne Thurman, Dec. 30, 1995; children: Johnathan, Derek, Nichollis. PhD, Calif. Sch. Profl. Psychology, 1995; BA in Psychology, Whittier Coll., 1990. Lic. clin. psychologist, Iowa. Clin. psychologist Prairie Rose Mental Health Ctr., Harlan, Iowa, 1995—2000, Psychol. Svcs., Omaha, 2000—. Cons. Prairie Rose Mental Health Ctr., Harlan, Iowa, 2000—. Mem. APA (Jeffrey S. Tanaka PhD Meml. Dissertation award Com. on Ethnic Minority Affairs 1996), Psi Chi. Avocations: cultural events, hiking. Office: Psychological Services 10506 Burt Circle Omaha NE 68114 E-mail: drthurman@psychserv.net.

JONES-WILSON, FAUSTINE CLARISSE, retired education educator; b. Little Rock, Dec. 3, 1927; d. James Edward and Perrine Marie (Childress) Thomas; m. James T. Jones, June 20, 1948 (div. 1977); children: Yvonne Dianne, Brian Vincent; m. Edwin L. Wilson, July 10, 1981. AB, Ark. A.M.&N. Coll., 1948; AM, U. Ill., 1951, EdD, 1967; LLD, U. Ark., Pine Bluff, 2003. Tchr., sch. libr. Gary (Ind.) Pub. Schs., 1955-62, 1964-67; asst. prof. Coll. Edn., U. Ill., Chgo., 1967-69; assoc. prof. adult edn. Fed. City Coll., Washington, 1970-71; prof. edn., grad. prof. Howard U., Washington, 1969-70, 71-93, acting dean Sch. Edn., 1991-92, prof. emeritus, 1993—. Author: The Changing Mood in America; Eroding Commitment, 1977, A Traditional Model of Educational Excellence: Dunbar High School of Little Rock, Arkansas, 1981; co-author: Paul Laurence Dunbar High School of Little Rock, Arkansas: Take From Our Lips a Song, Dunbar to Thee, 2003; editor Jour. Negro Edn., 1978-91, 92-93; co-editor: Encyclopedia of African-American Education, 1996; assoc. editor Jour. of Edn. for Students Placed at Risk, 1996-2000. Chmn. East Coast steering com. Nat. Coun. on Educating Black Children, 1986—88, 1990—92, 3d v.p., 1992—94, bd. dirs., 1994—98. Recipient Frederick Douglass award Nat. Assn. Black Journalists, 1979, Disting. Scholar-Tchr. award Howard U., 1985, Exemplary Leadership award Am. Assn. Higher Edn. Black Caucus, 1988, Gertrude E. Rush award Nat. Bar Assn., 1990, Disting. Career award V.P. for Acad. Affairs, Howard U., 1993, Disting. Alumni award Coll. Edn. U. Ill., 1997; Phelps Stokes Fund sr. fellow, 1993-2000. Mem.: Soc. Profs. of Edn. (Mary Anne Raywid award 2002), Am. Ednl. Studies Assn. (pres. 1984—85), John Dewey Soc., Phi Delta Kappa (pres. Howard U. chpt. 1986—87, Svc. key 1990). Democrat. Methodist. Home: 6605 Allview Dr Columbia MD 21046-1005

JONG, ERICA MANN, writer; b. NYC, Mar. 26, 1942; d. Seymour and Eda (Mirsky) Mann; m. Michael Werthman, 1963 (div. 1965); m. Allan Jong (div. Sept. 1975); m. Jonathan Fast, Dec. 1977 (div. Jan. 1983); 1 child, Molly; m. Kenneth David Burrows, Aug. 5, 1989. BA, Barnard Coll., 1963; MA, Columbia U., 1965; PhD honoris causa, CUNY, 2005. Faculty, English dept. CUNY, 1964-65, 69-70, overseas div. U. Md., 1967-69; mem. lit. panel N.Y. State Council on Arts, 1972-74; faculty Breadloaf Writers Conf. Middlebury, Vt., 1982; mem. faculty Saltzburg Seminar, Saltzburg, Austria, 1993, 98. Author: (poems) Fruits and Vegetables, 1971, reissued edit., 1997, Half Lives, 1973, Loveroot, 1975, At the Edge of the Body, 1979, Ordinary Miracles, 1983, Becoming Light: Poems New and Selected, 1992; (novels) Fear of Flying, 1973, How to Save Your Own Life, 1977, Fanny: Being the True History of the Adventures of Fanny Hackabout-Jones, 1980, Parachutes and Kisses, 1984, Serenissima, 1987 (reissued as Shylock's Daughter, 1995), Any Woman's Blues, 1990, Inventing Memory, 1998, Sappho's Leap, 2003, (poetry and non-fiction) Witches, 1981, reissued edit., 1997, (juvenile) Megan's Book of Divorce, 1984 (reissued as Megan's Two Houses, 1995), (memoir) The Devil at Large, 1993, What Do Women Want?, 1998, Seducing the Demon: Writing for My Life, 2006; (autobiography) Fear of Fifty, 1994; composer lyrics: Zipless: Songs of Abandon from the Erotic Poetry of Erica Jong, 1995, (fiction) Inventing Memory, 1997. Recipient Bess Hokin prize Poetry mag., 1971, Prix Literaire, Deauville Film Festival, 1997; named Mother of Yr., 1982; Woodrow Wilson fellow; Nat. Endowment Arts grantee, 1973. Mem. PEN, Authors Guild U.S.A. (coun. 1975—, pres. 1991-93), Poets and Writers Bd., Writers Guild Am.-West, Poetry Soc. Am. (Alice Faye di Castagnola award 1972), Phi Beta Kappa. Office: Erica Jong Prodns c/o Kenneth David Burrows 451 Park Ave S FL 8 New York NY 10016-7390 Office Phone: 212-517-2907.

JONKER, PAMELA LYNN, artist; b. Denver, Apr. 25, 1947; d. William Espy and Geraldine Marie (Plumb) Ingram; m. L. Anton Jonker, Mar. 17, 1968 (div. Feb. 1994); children: Stephanie Lynn, Stacey Marie. BA in Polit. Sci., The Colo. Coll., 1969; postgrad., Calif. State U., Fresno, 1989-92. Artist-sculptor, painter, ceramist, fiber arts, Fresno, Calif. and, Espanola, N.Mex., 1979—; devel. coord. Fresno Arts Coun., 1992-93. Fiber artist/quilt hangings, 1980—; wheel-thrown manipulated ceramic bowls, 1992—; author: (exhibit catalog) Calif. State U. Fresno/Phebe Conley Gallery, 1992. Mem. Am. Quilter's Soc., Am. Craft Coun., Fresno Arts Coun., Kappa Alpha Theta. Avocations: gourmet cooking, gardening, interior design. Office: RR 3 Box 1333-9 Espanola NM 87532-9803 E-mail: pljart@netscape.net.

JONKOUSKI, JILL ELLEN, materials scientist, ceramics engineer, educator; b. Chgo. d. Joseph and Ruth Jonkouski. BS in Ceramic Engring., MS in Ceramic Engring., U. Ill. Former rschr. Battelle Meml. Inst., Columbus, Ohio; former ceramic engr. Austenal Dental, Inc., Chgo.; former rsch. scientist BIRL Indsl. Rsch. Lab. Northwestern U., Evanston, Ill.; ceramics mfg. engr., fed. project dir. Office of Sci., Office of Safety, Tech. and Infrastructure Svcs. divsn. U.S. Dept. Energy, Argonne, Ill., 1991—. Past adj. faculty Triton Coll., River Grove, Ill.; chair Internat. Gas Turbine Inst. ASME Turbo Expo, 2002, 03; presenter, spkr. in field. Mem. Am. Ceramic Soc. (chair Chgo.-Milw. sect. 1993-94), U. Ill. Alumni Assn. Avocations: ice skating, hiking, flying, tennis. Office: US Dept Energy Office of Safety Tech and Infrastructu 9800 S Cass Ave Argonne IL 60439-4899 Business E-Mail: jill.jonkouski@ch.doe.gov.

JONQUIÈRES, LYNNE, travel agent; b. Albany, N.Y., Dec. 12, 1946; d. Edward Livingston Trudeau and Margaret Wing Gray; m. Jean-Louis Jonguieres, July 20, 1969 (dec. Apr. 1974); 1 child, Alexandra Jonquieres Oakley. Owner, photographer Image 2, Albany, 1975-82; registered rep. Prudential, Albany, 1983—2002; travel agt., owner Lineage Travel, Albany, 1999—2001; coord. The Greater Loudonville Assn., NY, 2002—. Bd. dirs. Downtown Day Care Ctr., Albany, 1989-2002. Mem. Schyler Meadows Club. Republican. Episcopalian. Home: 3 Princess Green Albany NY 12211-1613

JONTZ, POLLY, retired college official, museum director; b. Akron, Ohio, Oct. 26, 1928; d. Clinton C. and Lora E. (Hunter) Prather; m. Leland D. Jontz, June 25, 1950; children: James P., Mary Lee Jontz Turk. AB in Journalism and Polit. Sci., Indiana U., 1949. Copy editor The Indpls. News, 1949-50; pub. rels. and devel. dir. The Children's Mus. of Indpls., 1963-82; v.p. Earlham Coll., Richmond, Ind., 1982-96; pres. Conner Prairie, Indpls., 1982-96, pres. emerita, 1996—; coord. seminar for hist. adminstrn. Colonial Williamsburg. Lectr. Lilly Endowment seminars, 1979, 80, 81, Pub. Rels. Soc. Am., Nat. Fedn. Press Women, Internat. Assn. of Bus. Comm., Assn. Sci. and Tech. Ctrs., Am. Assn. Mus., Am. Assn. State and Local Hist., Earlham Coll., Butler U., Ind. U., Ball State U., Ind. State U., Anderson Coll.; tchr. Ind. U.-Purdue U. divsn. continuing edn., 1979, 80; devel. and pub. rels. cons., tchr., lectr. Ind. Com. for Humanities, 1977-80, Ind. U.-Purdue U. divsn. continuing edn., 1980, Muncie Ballet, 1981, E. Ctrl. Ind. Community Singers, 1981. Past bd. dirs. Indpls. Speech and Hearing Ctr., Inc., Jr. League of Indpls. Community Adv. Coun., Ind. Dept. Pub. Instruction, Alliance for Arts in Edn. Com.; bd. visitors Def. Info. Sch. Ft. Benjamin Harrison; founding mem., first pres. Travel Ind., Inc., Inter Mus. Promotional Action Team.; past pres. The Children's Mus. Guild; bd. dirs. Friends of Holliday Park, Indpls. Day

Nursery, Ind. Rotary Found., Exec. Svc. Corps. Recipient Silver Anvil award Pub. Rels. Soc. Am, 1977, Sagamore of the Wabash, 1988, 95; named Communicator of Yr. by Ind. Bus. Communicators, 1974, Women of Achievement by Ind. Women's Press Club, 1976. Mem. Am. Assn. Mus. (cons. mus. assessment program, sr. accreditation examiner, grant reviewer Inst. Mus. Svcs.), Am. Assn. State and Local History (past bd. dirs.), Internat. Coun. Mus., Ind. Hist. Soc. (bd. dirs.), Assn. Ind. Mus., Indpls. Consortium Art Adminstrs. (past pres.), Women in Comm. (past pres. Indpls. profl. chpt., Clarion award 1977, Frances Wright award 1982, Matrix award 1988), Ind. Advs. for Arts, Midwest Mus. Conf. (chmn. ann. conf. 1990, Disting. Svc. award 1994), Morris-Butler House (adv. com.), Rotary (past bd. dirs.), Contemporary Club (bd. dirs.), Kappa Kappa Gamma (past pres. Indpls. alumnae).

JOOSTEN, KATHRYN (KATHRYN JOOSTYN), actress; b. Dec. 20, 1939; Actor: (films) Grandview, U.S.A., 1984, The Package, 1989, Best Man, 1997, Phoenix, 1998, Kiss Toledo Goodbye, 1999, Lehi's Wife, 2002, Cojones, 2002, Halfway Decent, 2003, Red Rose and Petrol, 2003, Breaking Dawn, 2004, Win a Date with Tad Hamilton, 2004, Fathers and Sons, 2005, Hostage, 2005, Taking Your Life, 2005, Wedding Crashers, 2005; (TV films) Lady Blue, 1985, The Stranger Beside Me, 1995, The Making of a Hollywood Madam, 1996, Combustion (Silent Killer), 2004, McBride: It's Murder, Madam, 2005; (TV series) Secret Santa, 2003, Highway to Oblivion, 2003; performer: (stage) Ladies of the Corridor; actor: (video) Hellraiser:Inferno, 2000; guest appearences include General Hospital, Grace Under Fire, 1995, Roseanne, 1996, Third Rock from the Sun, 1996, ER, 1996, The West Wing (several episodes), 1996—2001, Murphy Brown, 1996, Boston Common, 1996, Frasier, 1997, Men Behaving Badly, 1997, NYPD Blue, 1997, Brooklyn South, 1997, Dharma & Greg, 1998, Dharma & Greg (several episodes), 2000—01, Just Shoot Me!, 1998, The Nanny, 1998, The Drew Carey Show, 1998, 2003, Providence, 1999, 2001, Home Improvement, 1999, Tracey Takes On, 1999, Buffy the Vampire Slayer, 2000, Becker, 2000, Ally McBeal, 2001, Scrubs, 2001, Spin City, 2001, The X Files, 2002, Judging Amy, 2003, Monk, 2003, Hope & Faith, 2003, Joan of Arcadia (several episodes), 2003—05, Charmed, 2003, Less Than Perfect, 2003, Strong Medicine, 2003, The King of Queens, 2003, A.U.S.A., 2003, Curb Your Enthusiasm, 2004, Will & Grace, 2004, Yes, Dear, 2004, Life with Bonnie, 2004, Everwood, 2004, Gilmore Girls, 2004, Desperate Housewives, 2005 (Creative Arts Primetime Emmy award for guest actress in a comedy series, 2005), Grey's Anatomy, 2005. Mem.: SAG, AFTRA, AEA.

JOOSTYN, KATHRYN See JOOSTEN, KATHRYN

JORDAHL, KATHLEEN PATRICIA (KATE JORDAHL), photographer, educator; b. Summit, N.J., Aug. 23, 1959; d. Martin Patrick and Marie Pauline (Quinn) O'Grady; m. Geir Arild Jordahl, Sept. 24, 1983. BA in Art & Art History magna cum laude with distinction, U. Del., 1980; MFA in Photography, Ohio U., 1982. Lifetime credential in art and design, Calif. Teaching assoc. Sch. Art Ohio U., Athens, 1980-82; adminstrv. asst. A.D. Coleman, S.I., N.Y., 1981; placement asst. career planning & placement U. Calif., Berkeley, 1983; instr. Coll. for Kids, Hayward, Calif., 1987-88; supr. student/alumni employment office Chabot Coll., Hayward, 1983-87, tchr. photography, 1987-97; prof. photography and digital imaging Foothill Coll., Los Altos Hills, Calif., 1997—. Workshop coord. Friends of Photography, San Francisco, 1990; instr. PhotoCen. Photography Programs, Hayward, 1983—, co-dir., 1983—; mem., co-coord., publ. evaluation accreditation com. Chabot Coll., Hayward, 1984, instrnl. skills workshop facilitator, 1994, speaker opening day, 1986, coord. ann. classified staff devel. workshop, 1985; workshop leader Ansel Adams Gallery, Yosemite, Calif., 1991, 92, artist-in-residence Yosemite Nat. Park Mus., 1993; ind. curator numerous exhbns., 1984—; coord., curator Ann. Women's Photo Workshop & Exhbn., 1993-2003; spkr. Let Me Learn, Rowen U., N.J., 2000. Exhibited in group shows Parts Gallery, Minn., 1992, The Alameda Arts Commn. Gallery, Oakland, 1992, Panoramic Invitational, Tampere, Finland, 1992, Photo Forum, Pitts., 1992, Photo Metro Gallery, San Francisco, 1993, Ansel Adams Gallery, Yosemite, 1994, Yosemite Mus., 1994, 96, Vision Gallery, San Francisco, 1994, 95 (now San Francisco Mus. of Modern Art Artist's Gallery), San Francisco Mus. Modern Art Rental Gallery, 1994, Photographer's Gallery, Palo Alto, 1997, Hayward Art Coun. Members Show, 1997, Hayward City Hall Gallaria, 1998, Ansel Adams Gallery, Mona Lake, 1999, Yogenji Temple, Tokyo, 1999, Himawarmosato Gallery, Yokahama, Japan, 1999, Mumm Winery, 2000, 2004, Euphrat Mus., Cupertino, Calif., 2001, 2005, Modern Book Gallery, Palo Alto, 2005; represented in permanent collections Muse Gallery, Phila., 1982, Ohio U. Libr. Rare Books Collection, Athens, 1982, Yosemite Mus., 1994, Bibliotheque Nationale de France, Paris, 1996; contbr. photos and articles to photography mags. and publs. Recipient Innovative New Program award Calif. Parks and Recreation Soc., 1990, Congl. Cert. Recognition for Leadership and Svc. to Comty., 2004; Sons of Norway scholar U. Oslo, summer 1996. Mem.: Phi Beta Kappa. Democrat. Avocations: travel, reading. Office: PO Box 3998 Hayward CA 94540-3998 Office Phone: 650-949-7318. E-mail: kate@jordahlphoto.com.

JORDAHL, PATRICIA ANN, music educator, theater director; b. Clarkfield, Minn., June 1, 1951; d. Robert Stanley and Norma Burnette Shefveland; m. Owen Warren Jordahl, June 11, 1977; children: Melody Ann, Matthew Owen. BA, Luther Coll., Decorah, Iowa, 1969—73; MA, Western N.Mex U., Silver City, N. Mex, 1987—90. Cert. Cmty. Coll. Lifetime Tchr. Ariz., 1993. K-12 music tchr. Hubbard Cmty. Schools, Hubbard, Iowa, 1973—77; pvt. music tchr. Self-employed, Iowa Falls, Iowa, 1977—85; k-12 music tchr. Thatcher Cmty. Schools, Thatcher, Ariz., 1986—93; music/music theatre prof. Ea. Ariz. Coll., Thatcher, Ariz., 1993—. Music tech. chair/bd. of directors Ariz. Music Educator's Assn., Phoenix, 1995—99; music dept. chair Ea. Ariz. Coll., Thatcher, Ariz., 2001—. Recipient Kennedy Ctr. award for excellence in theater edn., Am. Coll. Theater Festival, 2005. Mem.: Am. Choral Dir. Assn. (assoc.), Music Educator Nat. Conf. (assoc.), Ariz. Music Educator Assn. (assoc.; sec. 1999—2001, O.M. Hartsell Excellence in Tchg. award 1998). Conservative. Meth. Avocations: travel, music, swimming, reading, theater. Office: Eastern Arizona Coll 615 North Stadium Ave Thatcher AZ 85552 Office Phone: 928-428-8467. E-mail: trish.jordahl@eac.edu.

JORDAN, ANNE E. DOLLERSCHELL, journalist; b. Mpls., Mar. 30, 1964; d. Allen L. and Marcia G. (Landeen) Dollerschell; m. James Lawrence Jordan, Aug. 16, 1986; children: Davyd, Scott. BA, U. Wis., 1986. From editl. asst. to mng. editor Governing Mag., Washington, 1987—. Mem. Phi Beta Kappa, Phi Kappa Phi, Phi Theta Kappa. Office: Governing Mag Ste 1300 1100 Connecticut Ave NW Washington DC 20036-4109

JORDAN, BRENDA MOORE, artist; b. Roanoke Rapids, NC, Feb. 4, 1946; d. John Leroy and Sarah (Williams) Moore; m. John Richard Jordan, Jr., June 26, 1982; m. James Edwin Harlow, Nov. 27, 1966 (div.); 1 child, Edwin Scott Harlow. BS cum laude in Art Edn. and Painting, Barton Coll., Wilson, NC, 1980; student, U. NC, Greensboro. One-woman shows include Chowan College, Murfreesboro, N.C., 2001, Wake County Mcpl. Bldg., Raleigh, N.C., 2001, Barton Coll., Wilson, N.C., Alumni Art Exhbn. Barton Coll., 1991, 2001, exhibited in group shows at Wilson (N.C.) Art Coun., 2001. Bd. dirs. (3 gubernatorial appointments) Murfreesboro Hist. Commn.; bd. dirs. U. N.C. Thurston Arthritis Rsch. Ctr., Chapel Hill, 1998—99, N.C. divsn. Am. Cancer Soc., Raleigh, 1982—92, N.C. Tri-Agy. Health Bd., Raleigh, 1990—92, Sch. Pub. Health, Chapel Hill, NC, N.C. Lit. and Hist. Assn., Raleigh, Wake County Hist. Assn., Raleigh, 1984—88, Friends Libr. D.H. Hill Libr. NC State U., 1992—98. Democrat. Baptist. Home: 809 Westwood Dr Raleigh NC 27607

JORDAN, CAROL MORGAN, music educator; d. Colby Shannon and Elizabeth Robertson Morgan; m. Michael Reed Taylor, July 1, 2006; children: J. Andrew Plunkett, Shelley Renee Taylor, T. Aaron. MusB, U. Ga., Athens, 1975, D Mus Arts, 2003; MusM, Ga. State U., Atlanta, 1979. Cert. tchr. Ga., 2003. Music specialist Clayton County Schs., Ga., 1975—78; choral dir. Riverdale Sr. H.S., Riverdale, Ga., 1978—82, Duluth Mid. Sch., Ga., 1982—90, Houston Mid. Sch., Germantown, Tenn., 1990—92, Meadowcreek H.S., Norcross, Ga., 1998—2004, Mill Creek H.S., Hoschton, Ga., 2004—; choral grad. asst. U. Ga., 1995—98. Choral clinician. Named Tchr. of Yr., Duluth, Miss., 1986. Mem.: Music Educators Nat. Conf., Am. Choral Dirs. Assn., Ga. Music Educators Assn. (officer 1973—, choral adjudicator 1993—). Home: 714 Beacon Cove Lawrenceville GA 30042 Office: Mill Creek HS 4400 Braselton Hwy 124 Hoschton GA 30548 Office Phone: 678-714-5918. Personal E-mail: jordancaem@aol.com.

JORDAN, CARRIE GRAYSON (CARRIE GRAYSON-JORDAN), writer, poet, drama designer; b. Laurel, Miss. children: Rickson Vancouver, Corichey Robert. AA in Liberal Arts with honors, Kennedy-King Coll., 1990. With Girl Scouts USA, Chgo., 1966—70, Operation lsh, 1970—71; admissions fgn. student specialist Kennedy-King Coll.; modeling group mgmt. Noir Fashions, 1976—78. Author: (book) Dear Butterflies; (plays) Grandpa's Stocking, Mr. Big Egg, Joy, Cassie, Curtains, Sky, Plays of Faith, Fun and Family, Black Barber Shop; columnist KKC Press; poet World of Poetry, 1991, Sparrowgrass forum, 1991, Crysopoets, 1997. Bd. dirs. S.E. Little League, Chgo., 1986-89; judge Act-SO Contest, NAACP, Chgo., 1996—, annually. Recipient Golden Poet award, World of Poetry, 1990. Mem. Chrysopoets, Renowned Poetry Club, Lyric Opera. Avocations: composing songs, writing, designing clothes, clown collecting, producing and directing own plays.

JORDAN, CRYSTAL L., music educator; MusB (hon.), Temple U., Phila., 2004. Tchr. music Ctrl. Bucks Sch. Dist., Doylestown, Pa., 2004—05, Oley Valley Sch. Dist., Oley, 2005—. Mem.: Pa. Edn. Assn. Office Phone: 610-987-4100.

JORDAN, DEOVINA NASIS, nursing administrator; b. Bangued, Abra, Philippines, May 7, 1960; d. Demetrio Villamor Nacis and Francisca Bicarme Baptista; m. James Lowell Jordan, July 25, 1992. BS in Nursing, U. Perpetual Help, Rizal, Philippines, 1980; MD in Surgery, U. Santo Tomas, Philippines, 1985; M in Pub. Health, Loma Linda U., 2001; MS in Nursing, UCLA, 2004. Cert. Ednl. Comm. for Foreign Med. Grads. Phila., Pa.; Ped. Nursing, Am. Nursing Credentialing Ctr., Wash. DC. Clin. nurse Hosp. for Joint Dis. Ortho. Inst., NYC, 1987—88; clin. nurse III Mattel Children's Hosp, UCLA, L.A., 1988—; admin. nurse IV UCLA Med. Ctr., L.A., 2002—; v.p., founder Jordan Rsch. Inst., Murietta, Calif., 1994—; pres Fil-Am Assoc., Murietta, 1994—. Rsch. adv. bd. Am. Biographical Inst., 2002—. Contbr. articles various prof. jours. Recipient Outstanding Profl. Woman award, Am. Biographical Inst., 2001. Mem.: Philippine Nurses Assn. So. Calif., Assn. Calif. Nurse Leaders, Am. Assn. Critical Care Nurses, Calif. Nurses Asn., Am. Coll. Healthcare Execs., Alpha Tau Delta, Sigma Theta Tau. Office Phone: 310-612-4898. Personal E-mail: djjord@verizon.net.

JORDAN, GRACE CAROL, music educator; b. Fernandina Beach, Fla., June 15, 1956; d. Benson Henry and Annie Dee Riggin; m. David Howell Jordan, July 2, 1983; children: David Benson, Rebecca Grace. B Music Edn., La. State U., MusM, 1984. Cert. tchr. Fla. Music tchr. Azalea Pk. Elem. Sch., Orlando, Fla., 1983—89, Arbor Ridge Sch., Orlando, 1989—. Sect. leader, soloist All Saints Episcopal Ch., Winter Park, Fla., 1983—; dir. various honor choirs, Fla. Named Tchr. of Yr., Azalea Pk. Elem. Sch., 1986, Arbor Ridge Sch., 2001. Mem.: Orff Assn. (pres. Fla. chpt. 1990—92, Disney Teacherrific Award 1993). Democrat. Episcopalian. Avocations: singing, travel. Home: 825 Hickory Hill Ct Orlando FL 32828 Office: Arbor Ridge Sch 2900 Logandale Dr Orlando FL 32817 Office Phone: 407-672-3110. Office Fax: 407-672-1310.

JORDAN, JUDITH VICTORIA, clinical psychologist, educator; b. Milw., July 28, 1943; d. Claus and Charlotte (Backus) J.; m. William M. Redpath, Aug. 11, 1973. AB, Brown U., 1965; MA, Harvard U., 1968, PhD, 1973; DHL (hon.) (hon.), New Eng. Coll., 2001. Diplomate Am. Bd. Profl. Psychology. Psychologist Human Relations Service, Wellesley, Mass., 1971-73; assoc. psychologist McLean Hosp., Belmont, Mass., 1978-93, psychologist, 1993—, dir. women's studies program, 1988—, dir. tng. in psychology, 1991, dir. Women's Treatment Network, 1992—. Vis. scholar Stone Ctr. Wellesley Coll., 1985—; asst. prof. psychiatry Harvard Med. Sch., 1988—; co-dir. Jean Baker Miller Tng. Inst., dir., 2006, Wellesley Coll. 1998; adv. bd Fox TV Network, Women First healthcare., 1998; disting. prof. Menninger Clinic, 1999; dir. Jean Baker Miller Tng. Inst., 2006. Author: Empathy and Self Boundries, 1984, Women's Growth in Connection, 1991, (with others) The Self in Relation, 1986; editor, author: Relational Self in Women; editor: Women's Growth in Diversity, 1997; editor: The Complexity of Connection, 2004. Recipient Outstanding Contbn. award, Feminist Therapy Inst., 2002. Fellow Am. Psychol. Assn.; mem. Mass. Psychol. Assn. (bd. dirs. 1983-85, Career Achievement award for outstanding contbns. to advancement of psychology as a sci. and a profession), Phi Beta Kappa. Office: McLean Hosp 114 Waltham St Lexington MA 02421-5415

JORDAN, KARLA SALGE, retired primary school educator; b. Berlin, July 4, 1943; came to U.S. 1965; d. Hubert Ernst Richard and Irmgard Klara Salge; m. William Jackson Jordan, May 28, 1963 (div. 1980); 1 child, Michael Bond. BA, Berlin Tchrs. Coll., 1964, Meth. Coll., Fayetteville, N.C., 1974; MA, Fayetteville State U., 1986. Cert. tchr., N.C., ednl. supr., 1995, cert. early childhood generalist Nat. Bd. Edn., 2000. Tchr. Eastover Elem. Sch., Fayetteville, 1974-75, Montclair Elem. Sch., Fayetteville, 1975—2005; ret., 2005. Workshop presenter Cumberland County Sch., Fayetteville, spring 1983, 92-95; mem. bldg. leadership team Montclair Elem. Sch., 1992-93, chair, 1994-95, grade chair, 1980-90, 1999-2001, 2002-2003, 2003-2004, sch. improvement team chair, 1995-98, 2001-03. Treas. Montclair PTA, 1987-88, sec., 1988-90, pres. 1985, 86; youth choir dir. Eureka Bapt. Ch., Fayetteville, 1990—, min. of music, 1995—; mem., bible study leader for German fellowship Walstone Bapt. Ch., Fayetteville, German fellowship coord., 1999—. Fayetteville Jr. League mini grantee, 1991; named Tchr. of the Yr. Montclair Elem. Sch., 1987-88; recipient Fayetteville Tchr. of the Week Jr. League and the Huntington Learning Ctr., 1997. Mem. Cross Creek Reading Coun. (rec. sec. 1990), Fayetteville Assn. for Edn. of Young Children, N.C. Assn. of Edn. (bldg. rep. 1981-83), Pi Lambda Theta. Republican. Baptist. Avocations: sewing, crafts, gardening, travel, reading. Home: 845 Mary Jordan Ln Fayetteville NC 28311-7075 Personal E-mail: karla-sjs@msn.com.

JORDAN, KATE See JORDAN, KATHERINE

JORDAN, KATHERINE D. (KATE JORDAN), lawyer; BA with honors, Emory U.; JD, Vanderbilt U. Law clk. to Judge Ewing Werlein Jr. US Dist Ct., Tex.; atty. Vinson & Elkins LLP, Tex., Powell, Goldstein, Frazer and Murphy, Atlanta, 2001—03; law clk. to Chief US Magistrate Judge Gerrilyn Brill No. Dist. Ga., 2003—05; sr. counsel Southeastern Legal Found., Atlanta, 2005—. Rsch. editor Vanderbilt Jour. Transnational Law. Republican. Office: Southeastern Legal Found 6100 Lake Forrest Dr Ste 520 Atlanta GA 30328

JORDAN, LILLIAN B., judge; b. Asheboro, N.C., May 19, 1939; d. Obert Charles and Lilly Irene Burrow; m. Thomas Andrew Jordan, Apr. 24, 1999; m. Thomas Lorenzo O'Briant, Sept. 5, 1959 (dec. May 31, 1995); children: Thomas Lorenzo O'Briant, Jr., Patrick Marvin O'Briant, Michael Heilig O'Briant, John Curt O'Briant. BA, Guilford Coll., Greensboro, N.C., 1961; JD, Wake Forest U., Winston Salem, 1979. Bar: N.C. 1979, U.S. Dist. Ct. (mid. dist.) N.C. 1979, U.S. Supreme Ct. 2001, cert.: (specialist in family law) 1995, Adminstrv. Office of the Courts, NC (juvenile ct. judge) 1998, (family law mediator) 2003. Ptnr. O'Briant, O'Briant, Bunch and Robins, Asheboro, NC, 1979—97; dist. ct. judge State of N.C., Asheboro, Troy, Carthage, NC, 1997—2002, emergency dist. ct. judge, 2002—. Bd. of trustees IOLTA N.C. State Bar, Raleigh, 1985—92, bd. of law examiners, 1992—97, bd. of law examiners, emeritus mem. Pres. Guilford Coll. Nat. Alumni Assn., Greensboro, NC, 1982—83; mem., bd. of dirs. Merce Clinic, Asheboro, NC, 2000—; mem., bd. dirs. Randolph County Day Reporting Ctr., Asheboro, NC, 1999—; mem., bd. of dirs. United Way of Randolph County, Asheboro, NC, 1981—93, Asheboro/Randolph C. of C., Asheboro, NC, 1986—89, Women's Aid, Inc., Asheboro, NC, 1980—83; chairperson Randolph County Coun. on the Status of Women, Asheboro, NC, 1975—76; mem. N.C. Cts. Commn., Raleigh, NC, 1987—91, Revenue Laws Study Commn. of the N.C. Legis., Raleigh, NC, 1991—95; mem., bd. of dirs. Randolph Hosp. Cmty. Health Found., Asheboro, NC, 1996—2002; bd. trustees Randolph Cmty. Coll., Asheboro, NC, 2004—08; del. Dem. Nat. Conv., N.Y.C., 1980—80. Recipient Athena award, Asheboro/Randolph C. of C., 1994, Paul Harris fellow, Asheboro Rotary Club, 1997, Alumni Excellence award, Guilford Coll., 1998. Mem.: N.C. Ctr. for Justice and Cmty. Devel. (mem. of directors 1997—2005), 19B Jud. Bar Assn. (former pres.), Randolph Bar Assn. (former pres.), N.C. Bar Assn. (bd. of governors 1985—88), N.C. Assn. of Women Attys. (pres. 1995—96), N.C. State Bar (licentiate). Democrat-Npl. Episcopal. Avocations: travel, reading, gardening. Home: 645 Holly Grove Dr Randleman NC 27317 Personal E-mail: lilliob@yahoo.com.

JORDAN, LISA ANNE, dancer, educator; d. Clement Joseph Zumpella and Nancy Lou DeForest-Mancino; m. John Samuel Jordan, Jan. 4, 1999. Grad., Liberty H.S., Youngstown, Ohio, 1986. Dancer, tchr. Cleve. Ballet, 1993—97; dancer, singer Busch Gardens, Williamsburg, Va., 1987—88; prin. dancer Ballet Mich., Flint. Tchr. Akron U. and Inst., Ohio, 1997—99; guest ballerina Cleve. Orch., 2002; profesional dancer Pointe Of Departure, 2003; children's dir. Moscow Ballet, Youngstown, Ohio, 2004; dir. fine arts program Windham Pub. Sch. Sys., Ohio, 1995—2005; tchr./coach/choreographer numerous pvt. schs., Youngstown and Cleve.

JORDAN, LOIS EVELYN, retired educator; b. Henry County, Ind., July 17, 1929; d. Clyde Cornelius and Frances Rebecca (White) Harned; m. Carl Eugene Jordan, June 13, 1954; children: Karen, Janet, Phillip. BA, Earlham Coll., 1951; MA, Ball State U., 1967. Cert. elem. tchr., Ind. Elem. tchr., Richmond, Ind., 1952, Lewisville, Ind., 1952-56; reading tchr. Dudley and Franklin Twp., Ind., 1961-66; elem. tchr. South Henry (Ind.) Sch. Corp., 1969-90, mem. sci. curriculum, young author's and earthday coms. Author: Ramallah Teacher, 1995, Journey by Faith, 2002. Trustee Earlham Coll., 1990-99, bd. advisors Sch. Religion, 1998-2006. Mem.: United Soc. of Friends Women (bd. dir. 1995—, editor The Advocate United Soc. Friends Internat. 2001—), Henry County Ret. Tchrs. Assn. (co-pres. 1997—2001). Democrat. Mem. Soc. Of Friends. Avocations: gardening, birds, wildflowers, writing, reading. Home: 6877 S County Road 250 E Straughn IN 47387-9724 Personal E-mail: locarl@nltc.net.

JORDAN, LOIS WENGER, foundation official; b. Madison, Wis., Dec. 28, 1943; d. Alfred and Phyllis Mae (Shaffer) Wenger; m. William Malcolm Jordan, Dec. 28, 1963; children: William Andre, Christopher Allan Wenger. BS, Millersville (Pa.) U., 1969. Tchr. Hempfield Sch. Dist., Lancaster, Pa., 1969-70, Lancaster Sch. Dist., 1975-80; dir. Upward Bound, Millersville U., 1980-82; dir. devel. St. Joseph Hosp., Lancaster, 1982-87; assoc. dir. devel. Pa. State U. Coll. Medicine, Hershey, 1987-97; dir. devel. Pa. State U., Capital Coll., 1997-2000; nat. dir. revenue devel. Am. Coll. Physicians/Am. Soc. Internal Medicine, 2000—02; pres. Jordan Assocs., Lancaster, Pa., 2002—. Author: (children's book) What's a Hospital Like?, 1972. Mem. Lancaster Jr. League, 1975—; trustee St. Joseph Hosp., 1979—82, James Buchanan Found., Lancaster, 1982—94; bd. trustees Penn Manor Found., 1998—2000; trustee Highland Presbyn. Ch., Lancaster, 1982—85. Recipient Cheston M. Berlin Svc. award Pa. State U. Alumni Assn., 1995, Outstanding Cmty. Svc. award Jr. League Assn., 1995. Mem. Assn. Healthcare Philanthropy (bd. dirs. 1990-92). Republican. Avocations: travel, hiking, international cooking. Home: 1734 Colonial Manor Dr Lancaster PA 17603-6034

JORDAN, LOUISE HERRON, art educator; b. Shanghai, Dec. 25, 1938; d. Edwin Warren Herron and Marie Standley; m. Michael Dean Salmon, June 21, 1958 (div. Jan. 21, 1976); m. John Patrick Jordan, June 24, 1995; children: Catherine Louise Boggess, Michael Dean Salmon, Richard Dean Salmon, Marianne Gabriel Fisher. Student, Smith Coll., 1956—58. Parish sec. St. Lawrence Cath. Ch., Alexandria, Va., 1977—80; dir. meetings and mem. Am. Inst. Biological Sci., Wash., DC, 1985—93; exec. asst. to pres. Lawrence Tech. U., Southfield, Mich., 1993—95; tchr. art Jewish Cmty. Ctr., New Orleans, 2002—. One-woman shows include The Long Gallery, Oschner Hosp., New Orleans, La., 2000, 2002, St. Tammany Art Assn., Holiday Inn, Covington, La., 2001, The Upstairs Gallery, 2001, Café Degas, New Orleans, La., 2002, exhibited in group shows at Masur Mus. Juried Show, 1997, Fest for All, Baton Rouge, La., 1997, New Orleans Art Assn. Nat. Exhibit, 1997, River Road Juried Exhibit, Baton Rouge, La., 2002, Dominican Inst. Arts Group Show, Sparkill, NY, 2003. Bd. dirs. Bancroft Pk. Civic Assn., New Orleans, 1997—; professed lay mem. Dominican Order, New Orleans, 1997—; mem. Dominican Inst. of the Arts, Adrian, Mich., 2001—. Mem.: St. Tammany Art Assn. (assoc.), New Orleans Art Assn. (assoc.), La. Watercolor Soc. (life; pres. 1998—2000, signature mem., pres. 1998—2000, chmn. internat. exhbn. 1997—99, workshop dir. 1999—), Xavier U. Alumni Assn. (hon.), Smith Coll. Alumni Assn. (assoc.). Roman Catholic. Office: St Anthony Studio 6218 St Anthony St New Orleans LA 70122 Personal E-mail: bayoulou222@aol.com.

JORDAN, MARTHA B., lawyer; m. David Lee; children: Stacy, Kristen. BS, Pa. State U., 1976; MBA, U. Cin., 1978; JD, U. Calif., Berkeley, 1983. Bar: Calif. 1983. With Latham & Watkins, LLP, L.A., 1983—90, ptnr., 1990—98, mng. ptnr., 1998—2004. Named one of Calif.'s Top 100 Most Influential Lawyers, Calif. Law Bus., 1999. Office: Latham and Watkins LLP Ste 4000 633 W Fifth St Los Angeles CA 90071 Office Phone: 213-485-1234.

JORDAN, MARY LUCILLE, commissioner; m. Ben C. Elliott, Aug. 23, 1980; children: Elizabeth Elliott, Armando Elliott, C. Daniel Elliott. Student, Hull U., 1969-70; BA cum laude, Bonaventure U., 1971; JD, Antioch Law Sch., 1976. Bar: N.Y., 1977, D.C., 1978. Atty. Office of Fed. Register Nat. Archives & Records Adminstrn., Washington, 1976-77; sr. staff atty. United Mine Workers Am., Washington, 1977-94; chmn. Fed. Mine Safety and Health Rev. Commn., Washington, 1994—2001, commissioner, 2001—.

JORDAN, MICHELLE DENISE, judge; b. Chgo., Oct. 29, 1954; d. John A. and Margaret (O'Dood) J. BA in Polit. Sci., Loyola U. Chgo., 1974; JD, U. Mich., 1977. Bar. Ill. 1977, U.S. Dist. Ct. (no. dist.) Ill. 1978. Asst. state's atty. State's Attys. Office, Chgo., 1977-82; pvt. practice Chgo., 1983-84; with Ill. Atty. Gen.'s Office, Chgo., 1984-90, chief environ. control div., 1988-90; ptnr. Hopkins & Sutter, Chgo., 1991-93; apptd. dep. regional adminstr. region 5 U.S. EPA, Chgo., 1994—. Active Operation Push, Chgo., 1971—. Recipient Kizzy Image Achievement and Svc. award, 1990, Suzanne E. Olive Nat. EEO award 1996, Rainbow-PUSH Seed Sower award, 2004; named in Am.'s Top 100 Bus. and Profl. Women, Dollars and SenseMag., Chgo., 1988. Mem. Ill. Bar Assn., Chgo. Bar Assn. (bd. mgrs., chmn. criminal law com. 1987-88, mem. hearing divsn., jud. evaluation com. 1987-88, exec. coun. 1987-88), Cook County Bar Assn., Nat. Bar Assn., Alpha Sigma Nu. Democrat. Baptist.

JORDAN, MILDRED RICE LORETTA, education educator; b. Chgo. d. Walter Henry Rice and Winnie Beatrice Smith; m. John Richard Medley, July 26, 1997; 1 child, Allison Monique Jordan. BS, Temple U., 1966, DEd, 1989; MEd, Arcadia U., 1977; DHL (hon.), Ea. N.C. Theol. Inst., 2001. Cert. elem. tchr./reading specilist, Pa. Tchr. Phila. Sch. Dist., 1966-72, Abington (Pa.) Sch. Dist., 1972—91; assoc. prof. Rider U., Lawrenceville, NJ, 1991—2006, prof. emerita, 2006—. Dir. Rider U., 1992—; founder, advisor scholarship fund, 1999—; presenter in field Contbr. articles to profl. jours. Amb. People to People Internat., 1997, 2003, 04; adv. bd. minding our bus. mentoring program Rider U., St. Mary Med. Ctr. Found., Langhorne, Pa. Named Ziegler Gee Woman of Yr., Rider U., 2002; recipient Dr. Selma H. Burke Positive Image award, NAACP, 2002. Mem. ASCD (assoc.), NAACP (Dr. Selma H. Burke Svc. award 2000), Phi Delta Kappa Avocation: travel. Office: Rider U 2083 Lawrenceville Rd Lawrenceville NJ 08648 Home: 12 Captiva Ct Hamilton NJ 08691 E-mail: ricejordan@rider.edu.

JORDAN, NORA MARGARET, lawyer; b. Cleve., July 24, 1958; d. Thomas and Nora (Campbell) J.; m. Walter Allen Reiser, Nov. 8, 1986; children: Julia, Mary, Martha. BA, U. Notre Dame, 1980; JD, Duke U., 1983. Bar: N.Y. 1984. Ptnr. Davis Polk and Wardwell, N.Y.C., 1983—. Office: Davis Polk & Wardwell 450 Lexington Ave Fl 31 New York NY 10017-3982 Business E-Mail: njordan@dpw.com.

JORDAN, PATRICIA COLGAN, physical education educator; b. Stamford, Conn., Oct. 18, 1932; d. Thomas Leo Colgan and Alice Peters Hershfelt; m. Michael Alexander Jordan, May 15, 1981; m. John Elwood Losinger (div. Jan. 18, 1978); children: Thomas John Losinger, Patti Losinger Clark. BPE, Pa. State U., 1954; MEd, U. Ctrl. Fla., Orlando, 1973. Tchr. Laurelton State Village, Pa., 1954—55, Bellefonte Area Sch., Bellefonte, Pa., 1955—58, Mt. Vernon Sch., Fortville, Ind., 1965—66; tchr., coach, adminstr. Brevard County Sch., Titusville, Fla., 1966—80; adj. instr. Brevard Cmty. Coll., 1979—80; tchr., coach Irving Ind. Sch., Tex., 1981—94; ret., 1994. Pres. Brevard County PE Edn. Assn., 1970—72; co-chmn. Sch. Health Adv. Coun., 1971—72; chmn., task force com. PE Curriculum Guide, 1970, Adapted PE, 1971, Health Edn. Curriculum, 1972, 74, 75; spkr. in field. Author: The Community and School Health, 1972, Title IX and Physical Education, 1976; editor: Fla. Coaches Manual. Troop leader Girl Scouts, Greenfield, Wis., 1959—65; mem. aquatic bd., water safety instr. Red Cross; CPR instr. Am. Heart Assn.; bd. dirs., program com., coach swim team YMCA, Titusville, Fla., 1966—80; 1st v.p. Palm Harbor Newcomers Club, 1995—96, pres. elect, 1996—97, pres., 1997—98, adv., 1988—99. Recipient Citizen of Yr., Greenfield C. of C., 1965. Mem.: Nat. Soc. of Arts and Letters, Dunedin Fine Arts Soc., Leading Ladies of PAC Found., Inc. (rec. sec. 1997—99, pres.-elect 1999—2003, pres. 2002—04, advisor 2004—06, parliamentarian exec.com. 2006), Fla. Athletic Coaches Assn. (coord. girls sports clin. 1975, vice chmn., athletic dir. 1975—77), Fla. Assn. for Health, PE, Recreation and Dance, Abilities Found., Palm Harbor Garden Club. Avocations: gardening, bridge. Home: 3817 Muirfield Ct Palm Harbor FL 34685

JORDAN, PHYLLIS C. VACCARO, special education educator; b. Cambridge, Mass., Jan. 1, 1948; d. Orazio E. Vaccaro and Margaret Grosso; m. Lewis G. Jordan, Apr. 18, 1970; children: Eric L., Karen M., James J. BS in Edn., Framingham State Coll., Mass., 1969; MEd, U. Mass., 1991, cert. advanced grad. studies, 2002. Cert. tchr. elem./young children with spl. needs Mass. Dept. Edn. Integrated presch. tchr. Gill-Montague (Mass.) Pub. Schs., 1990—91; spl. edn. tchr. Sunderland (Mass.) Elem. Sch., 1991—. Intern supr. Sunderland Elem. Sch., 1994—2002, tchr. rep. sch. coun.; mem. curriculum devel. and assessment coms. Sch. Union 38, Deerfield, Mass., workshop presenter; edn. cons. St. Brigid's Ch. CCD, Amherst, Mass., 2002; tchr., coord. St. Brigid's Ch. Elem. CCD. Author: (educational resource book) Fifty Nifty Games to Make and Play, 1996, (plays) The Reluctant Prophet, 2001, The Love Tree, 1983. Leader, key leader, town com. mem. 4-H Clubs of Hampshire County, Amherst, 1980—91; bd. dirs., costumer Valley Light Opera, Amherst, 1994—2006; stage dir., prodr., playwright St. Brigid's Players, Amherst, 1985—2005; children's choir dir. St. Brigid's Ch., Amherst, 1990—2006, lector; parish coun. rep. and commn. mem. St. Brigid'sChurch, Amherst, Mass.; founding mem., pres. St. Brigid's Ch. Social Club. Recipient Marion award, Archdiocese of Boston, 1961, St. Pius X award, Diocese of Springfield, Mass., 1998. Mem.: Western Mass. Assn. for Edn. of Young Children (co-pres. 1996—98), Mass. Tchrs. Assn., Coun. for Exceptional Children, Nat. Assn. for Edn. of Young Children. Roman Catholic. Avocations: theater, music. Business E-Mail: pjordan@educ.umass.edu.

JORDAN, SAMANTHA KRISTINE, communications director; Student, Tex. Christian U., 1989-92; BA in History, Tex. A&M U., 1994. Intern U.S. Rep. Joe L. Barton, Washington, 1995, dist. asst., 1995, dist. asst., caseworker, dist. sys. mgr., 1996, dist. liaison, dep. press sec., 1996-97, dep. press sec., sys. mgr., legis. corr., 1997-98, press sec., 1998, comm. dir., 1998—. Mem. Leadership Press Sec. Working Group. Mem. adv. bd., alumnae club Alpha Omega Sorority; vol. Kimbell Art Mus. Mem. Rep. Commn. Assn., Tex. A&M Assn. Former Students, Tex. State Soc., 12th Man Found., Smithsonian Assocs., Libr. Congress Assocs. Office: Congressman Joe Barton 2264 Rayburn Ho Office Bldg Washington DC 20515-0001 Home: 100 Luna Park Dr Apt 339 Alexandria VA 22305-3160 Fax: 202-225-3052.

JORDAN, SANDRA, public relations professional; b. Pasadena, Tex., Oct. 10, 1952; d. Royal Wilson and Kathryn Ann (Speck) J.; m. William Anderson Mintz, Aug. 10, 1974 (div. 1980). B of Journalism, U. Tex., 1974. Reporter Austin (Tex.) American Statesman, 1974-76; news dir. KTAE Radio, Taylor, Tex., 1974-76; dir. of news and info. Inst. of Texan Cultures, San Antonio, 1976-82; pub. rels. dir. San Antonio Mus. Assn., 1982-83; dir. news/info. Univ. Tex., San Antonio, 1983-86; sr. publicist Rogers & Cowan, Inc., Washington, 1986-87; communications dir. NARAL, Washington, 1987-88; assoc. Parker, Vogelsingers & Assocs., Washington, 1988-90; pub. rels. and mktg. dir. Girl Scout Coun., Washington, 1990-99; mgr. media rels. Planned Parenthood Fedn. Am., Washington, 1999-2000; fellow Population Leadership Program, Washington, 2000—; dir. comms. and outreach USAID, Washington, 2000—. Pub. rels. cons. YWCA, Washington; judge, ad contest, Women in Comm., Iowa, 1993; workshop organizer Washington Ind. Writers, 1990; publicity com. CASE Conf., San Antonio, 1986, Smithsonian Nat. Assoc. Prog., San Antonio, 1980; panelist Women in Comms. Roundtable, 1996, Global Health Coun., Washington, 2003; presenter in field. Contbg. author: Folk Art in Texas, 1985. Prog. cons. KLRN-TV (pub.) San Antonio, 1981, 82; del. Dem. Nat. Conv., Taylor, 1976; docent Kennedy Ctr., Washington, 1989. Recipient Apex award, 1991-93, 95, 97-98, Comm. Concepts, 1991, Design honors, Tex. Assn. of Mus., 1993, IABC Silver Inkwell award, 1995, Silver Anvil award, 1996. Mem. Women in Comm. (D.C. chpt., literacy project 1992, mentoring program com., v.p. for programs 1998—), Women in Advt. and Mktg., Am. Soc. Assn. Execs., The Writers Ctr., Pub. Rels. Soc. Am. Avocations: fiction writing, quilt making. Home: 6305 E Halbert Rd Bethesda MD 20817-5409 Office: USAID G/PHN/POP The Ronald Reagan Bldg 1300 Pennsylvania Ave Washington DC 20523 Business E-Mail: sjordan@usaid.gov.

JORDAN, SASKIA A., lawyer; b. Mpls., Aug. 15, 1954; BA, Antioch Coll., 1977; JD, U. Cin., 1980. Bar: Colo. and US Dist. Ct., Dist. Colo. 1980, US Ct. Appeals, Tenth Circuit 1982, US Supreme Ct. 1986, US Ct. Appeals, Sixth Circuit 1988, US Ct. Appeals, Fifth Circuit 1996, US Ct. Appeals, Fed. Circuit 1997. Mem. editl. bd. U. Cin. Law Review, 1980; law clk. to Hon. Howard M. Kirshbaum, Colo. Ct. Appeals, 1980—81; dep. state pub. defender, 1981—86; atty. Haddon, Morgan, Mueller, Jordan, Makey & Foreman, P.C. Mem. Cmty. Corrections Bd., Adams County, Colo., 1998—2000. Mem. Adams County, Colorado Cmty. Corrections Bd., 1998—2000, 17th Judicial Dist. Commn. on Judicial Performance, 1989—91. Mem.: Nat. Assn. Criminal Def. Lawyers, Colo. Criminal Def. Bar (mem. bd. dirs. 1986—88, pres. 1989—90), Colo. Bar Assn., Denver Bar Assn.

JORDAN, SHANNON COLLEEN, medical/surgical nurse; b. Espanola, N.Mex., Dec. 5, 1952; d. William Harrison Roach and Ethel Louise (Hartsfield) Burns; m. Harweda Bruce Jordan, July 9, 1971 (div. 1991); children: Dominic, Peter, Sabian, Simon. BSN with highest honors, U. Tex., El Paso, 1992. Profl. singer, writer The Jordans, Sunrise Creations, 1971-89; staff nurse III R.E. Thomason Hosp., El Paso, Tex., 1992—2002, infection control practitioner, 2002—. Author, lyricist, composer Sunrise, 1978. Bd. dirs. Westside YMCA, El Paso, Tex., 1993-95, Hot Line of El Paso, 1992-93; vol. Reach to Recovery Am. Cancer Soc., El Paso, 1994-99. Recipient Nat. Collegiate Nursing award U.S. Achievement Acad., 1992, Outstanding Nursing award U.S. Air Force, 1992, Women of Mines award U. Tex., 1992; U. Tex. scholar, 1989-92, Teen Expo scholar, 1992, All Am. scholar U.S. Achievement Acad., 1992; Pell grantee U.S. Govt., 1989-92, Marian Meaker Aptekar grantee, 1994. Mem. Assn. Profl. Infection Control Practitioners, Sigma Theta Tau Internat., U. Tex. Alumni Assn., Golden Key Nat. Honor Soc. Alphi Chi. Republican. Protestant. Avocations: composing, writing, walking, photography, gardening. Home: 825 Somerset Dr El Paso TX 79912-4916

JORDEN, ELEANOR HARZ, linguist, educator; b. NYC; d. William George and Eleanor (Funk) Harz; m. William J. Jorden, Mar. 3, 1944 (div.); children: William Temple, Eleanor Harz, Marion Telva. AB, Bryn Mawr Coll., 1942; MA, Yale U., 1943, PhD, 1950; D.Litt. (hon.), Williams Coll., 1982; D.H.L. (hon.), Knox Coll., 1985; D. Langs. (hon.), Middlebury Coll., 1991; D. Univ. (hon.), U. Stirling, Scotland, 1993. Instr. Japanese Yale U., 1943-46, 47-48; dir. Japanese lang. program and Fgn. Service Inst. Lang. Sch., Am. Embassy, Tokyo, 1950-55; sci. linguist Fgn. Service Inst., Dept. State, Washington, 1959-69; acting head Far East langs., 1961-64; chmn., 1964-67, 69; chmn. Vietnamese lang. div., 1967-69; vis. prof. linguistics Cornell U., 1969-70, prof., 1970-87, Mary Donlon Alger prof. linguistics, 1974-87, prof. emeritus, 1987—. Bernhard disting. vis. prof. Williams Coll., 1985—86, vis. prof., 1986—87, adj. prof., 1987—92; dir. Japanese FALCON program, 1972—87; prof., Disting. fellow Nat. Fgn. Lang. Ctr. Sch. Advanced Internat. Studies Johns Hopkins U., 1987—91; acad. dir. Exchange: Japan, 1988—2004; sr. cons. prep. framework Japanese lang. curriculum and Japanese coll. bd. exam, 1991—93; sr. cons. Japanese multi-media project U. Md., 1995—97, cons. Part 2, Ohio State U., 2002—; dir. SPENG Program, 1980—; co-dir. Survey on Japanese Lang. Study, 1988—92; guest scholar Wilson Ctr. Smithsonian Instn., 1982; cons., permanent disting. dir. Nat. Assn. Self-Instrnl. Lang. Programs, pres., 1977—78, 1984—85; mem. Fulbright-Hays Com. on Internat. Exch. Scholars, 1972—75; mem. area adv. com. for East Asia, 1972—76; chmn. Social Sci. Rsch. Coun. Task Force on Japanese Lang. Tng., 1976—78; mem. adv. com. Japan Found., 1979—81; mem. Lang. Attrition Project, 1981—87; advisor Ctr. for Japanese Studies, Stirling U., Scotland, 1988—92; coun. com. langs. and lit. Yale U., 1990—98; acad. dir. Alliance for Lang. Learning and Ednl. Exch., 2004—. Author: (with Bernard Bloch) Spoken Japanese, 1945, Syntax of Modern Colloquial Japanese, 1955, Gateway to Russian, 1961, Beginning Japanese, Part 1, 1962, Part 2, 1963, (with Sheehan, Quang and others) Basic Vietnamese, vols. I, II, 1965, (with Quang) Vietnamese Familiarization Course, 1969, (with Hamako Chaplin) Reading Japanese, 1976, (with Mari Noda) Japanese: The Spoken Language, part 1, 1987, part 2, 1988, part 3, 1990, (with Richard Lambert) Japanese Language Instruction in the U.S.: Resources, Practice and Investment Strategic, 1992, (with Mari Noda) Japanese: The Written Language, Part 1, Vol. 1, 2005 Decorated Order of Precious Crown Emperor of Japan, 1985; recipient Superior Svc. award Dept. State, 1965, Japan Found. and Social Sci. Rsch. Coun. sr. fellow, 1976, Toyota award Twentieth Anniversary Fund grantee, 1978; Japan Found. award, 1985, Papalia award for Excellence Tchr. Tng., 1993, N.E. Conf. award Disting. Svc. and Leadership in Profession, 1994; honoree Eleanor Harz Jorden Festival, Portland State U., 1995. Mem. ALLEX (bd. dirs. 2004—), Assn. Asian Studies (v.p. 1979-80, pres. 1980-81), Linguistic Soc. Am., Am. Coun. Tchrs. Fgn. Langs., Nat. Assn. Self-Instrnl. Lang. Programs (pres. 1978, 85, permanent disting. dir. 1991—), Assn. Tchrs. Japanese (exec. com., pres. 1978-84), Japan Soc. N.Y. (bd. dirs. 1982-88), Exchange: Japan (bd. dirs., v.p., sec. 1998-2004). Office: 3300 Darby Rd Apt 1302 Haverford PA 19041-1067 Fax: 610-658-2563. Office Phone: 610-649-2409. Business E-Mail: ejorden@brynmawr.edu.

JORDEN, YON YOON, health services company executive; B in Acctg., Calif. State U. V.p., controller FHP Internat. Corp.; sr. v.p., CFO, WellPoint Health Networks, Inc., Blue Cross Calif., Aera Energy LLC; exec. v.p., CFO Oxford Health Plans Inc., Norwalk, Conn., 1998—. Office: AdvancePCS 750 W John Carpenter Fwy, Ste 1200 Irving TX 75039

JÖRGENSEN, BETH ELLEN, Spanish language educator; b. S.I., N.Y., Oct. 11, 1953; d. Charles William and Dorothy (Gralow) J.; m. Paul B. Watkins; children: Megan J., Benjamin J. BA in Spanish with high honors, Oberlin Coll., 1975; MA in Spanish, U. Wis., 1978, PhD in Spanish-Am. Lit., 1986. Tchg. asst. U. Wis., Madison, 1976-82, lectr. dept. Spanish and Portuguese, 1982-83; asst. prof. Spanish U. Rochester, N.Y., 1986-93, assoc. prof. Spanish N.Y., 1993—, chair dept. modern langs. and cultures N.Y., 1994-98. Assoc. chair undergrad. programs modern langs. and cultures U. Rochester, 1993-94, undergrad. advisor Spanish, mem. steering com. Multimedia Ctr., mem. study abroad com. Coll. Arts and Scis., 1993-94, dean's fellow, 1987-88; assoc. Susan B. Anthony Ctr. for Women's Studies, mem. seminar and speakers com., 1992-94; manuscript appraiser U. Tex. Press, U. Ariz. Press; book reviewer Hispanic Review, Letras Femeninas; presenter in field. Author: The Writing of Elena Poniatowska: Engaging Dialogues, 1994; co-editor: The Contemporary Mexican Chronicle, 2002; contbr. articles to profl. jours. Vilas fellow U. Wis., 1978-79, Dipman Grad. fellow Oberlin Coll., 1984-85. Mem. MLA, Am. Assn. Tchrs. Spanish and Portuguese, L.Am. Studies Assn., Assn. de Literatura Femenina Hispánica, Feministas Unidas (v.p. 2001, pres. 2002—), Phi Beta Kappa (chpt. pres. 1992-94). Office: U Rochester Modern Langs and Cultures Rochester NY 14627 Business E-Mail: bjgn@mail.rochester.edu.

JORGENSEN, DORIS JEAN, retired elementary school educator; b. July 17, 1934; d. Charles Westly Cunningham, Jr. and Pearl Anna Lula Otto; m. James Raymond Jorgensen, June 17, 1956 (dec.); children: James Lee, Judith Annn. BS, Mason City Jr. Coll., Iowa, 1954; BA, U. No. Iowa, Cedar Falls, 1973. Cert. elem. edn. Tchr. 1st grade Floyd (Iowa) Consol. Sch., 1954—55, Forest City (Iowa) Consol. Sch., 1955—56; tchr. 2d grade Thornton (Iowa) Consol. Sch., 1956—57, 1957—58, Rockwell-Swaledale (Iowa) Sch., Swaledale, 1959—60; tchr. kindergarten Ventura (Iowa) Consol. Sch., 1968—90; ret., 1990. Supervising tchr. aid Ventura Comty. Sch., 1968—90. Mem. Rep. Party Iowa, Des Moines, 2000—06, Nat. Rep. Party, Washington, 2000—06, Nat. Rep. Com., Washington, 2000—06; various offices St. Paul Evangel. Luth. Ch., 1956—; mem. Nat. Mus. Women in Arts, Washington, 1998—2006. Mem.: North Iowa Area CC Assn. (tchg. scholar 1952), Fortune Sailing Investment Club (jr. ptnr. 1999—2000). Republican. Lutheran. Avocations: painting, drawing. Home: 1815 Heather Ave Thornton IA 50479

JORGENSEN, JUDITH ANN, psychiatrist, educator; b. Parris Island, S.C. d. George Emil and Margaret Georgia Jorgensen; m. Ronald Francis Crown, July 11, 1970 (dec. Oct. 1996). BA, Stanford U., 1963; MD, U. Calif., 1968. Intern Meml. Hosp., Long Beach, Calif., 1969-70; resident County Mental Health Svcs., San Diego, 1970-73; staff psychiatrist Children and Adolescent Svcs., San Diego, 1973-78; practice medicine specializing in psychiatry La Jolla, Calif., 1973—. Staff psychiatrist County Mental Health Svcs. San Diego, 1973—78, San Diego State U. Health Svcs., 1985—87; psychiat. cons. San Diego City Coll., 1973—78, 1985—86; asst. prof. dept. psychiatry U. Calif., 1978—91, assoc. prof., 1991—96; chmn. med. quality rev. com. Dist. XIV, State of Calif., 1982—83. Fellow: Am. Soc. Adolescent Psychiatry, Am. Psychiat. Assn. (disting. life fellow); mem.: Sex Therapy and Edn., Soc. Sci. Study of Sexuality, San Diego Soc. Adolescent Psychiatry (pres. 1981—82), San Diego Psychiat. Soc. (chmn. membership com. 1976—78, v.p. 1978—80, fed. legis. rep. 1985—87, fellowship com. 1989—), Rowing Club. Office: 470 Nautilus St Ste 211 La Jolla CA 92037-5981 Office Phone: 858-459-1140. Office Fax: 858-551-0964.

JORGENSEN, VIRGINIA DYER, antique dealer, museum consultant; b. Arlington, Va., Sept. 18, 1955; d. Gordon Wade and Maureen Glesner Dyer; m. Bruce Kenneth Hopkins, Feb. 21, 1987 (div. Jan. 1992); children: Lauren Pontoni, Brett Gardner, Lacy Marie Hopkins, Dustin Kenneth Hopkins; m. William Dennis Jorgensen, Sept. 30, 1994. AA, Kellogg C.C., Battle Creek, Mich., 1977; BA magna cum laude, We. Mich. U., 1998. Pub. rels., tour guide Kellogg Co., Battle Creek, 1975—80; supply publs. writer U.S. Dept. Def., Battle Creek, 1984—88; sales team leader I.I. Stanley Automotive Lighting, Battle Creek, 1990—94; devel. coord. Mich. Maritime Mus., South Haven, 1998; antique dealer Crossroads Antique Mall, Seymour, Ind., 2000—06, Exit 76 Antique Mall, Columbus, Ind., 2000—03, Lumber Mill Antique Mall, Madison, Ind., 2006—. Trustee Kentwood (Mich.) Pub. Sch. Edn. Found., 1997—99; bd. mem. Preservation Action Alliance, Battle Creek, 1994—96; mem. design consulting bd. Housing Partnership Inc., Columbus, Ind., 2000. Recipient Edith Mange award for disting. scholarship, Western Mich.U., 1998. Mem.: Colonial Williamsburg Found., Nat. Trust for Historic Preservation, Golden Key Nat. Honor Soc., Phi Alpha Theta. Presbyterian. Avocations: breeding pugs, buying and restoring old buildings. Home and Office: 1069 Redwing Dr Columbus IN 47203 E-mail: wdandvl@earthlink.net.

JORGENSON, MARY ANN, lawyer; b. Gallipolis, Ohio, 1941; BA, Agnes Scott Coll., 1963; MA, Harvard U., 1964; JD, Case Western Res. U., 1975. Bar: Ohio 1975, N.Y. 1982. Ptnr., chair firm's corp. practice Squire, Sanders & Dempsey, 1990—2004. Office: Squire Sanders & Dempsey LLP 127 Public Sq Ste 4900 Cleveland OH 44114-1284 E-mail: mjorgenson@ssd.com.

JOSEFF, JOAN CASTLE, manufacturing executive; b. Alta., Can., Aug. 12, 1922; naturalized U.S. citizen, 1945; d. Edgar W. and Lottie (Coates) Castle; BA in Psychology, UCLA; widowed; 1 son, Jeffrey Rene. With Joseff-Hollywood, jewelry manufacture and rental and aircraft components and missiles, Burbank, Calif., 1939—, chmn. bd., pres., sec.-treas. Numerous TV appearances including CBS This Morning, Australia This Morning, Am. Movie Channel. Mem. Burbank Salary Task Force, 1979—, L.A. County Earthquake Fact-Finding Commn., 1981—; bd. dirs. San Fernando Valley area chpt. Am. Cancer Soc., treas., Genesis Energy Systems, Inc., 1993—; mem. Rep. Cen. Com.; del. Rep. Nat. Conv., 1980, 84, 88, 92, 96, 2000; active Beautiful People Award Com. Honoring John Wayne Carcer Clinic; appointed by Gov. Wilson to Barber and Cosmotology Bd; appointed br Pres. Clinton to Selective Svc. System. Recipient Women in Achievement award Soroptomist Internat., 1988, Rep. Congl. Com. award, 2004, Bus. Woman of Yr. award, 2004. Mem. Women of Motion Picture Industry (hon. life), Nat. Fedn. Rep. Women (bd. dir., Caring for Am. award 1986), Calif. Rep. Women (bd. dir., treas. 1986-90), North Hollywood Rep. Women (pres. 1981-82, parliamentarian), Nat. Fedn. of Rep (voting mem., program chair, 1994—, bylaws chair 1998—), Calif. Fedn. of Rep. Women (chaplain, Americanism chmn. so. div., regent chmn. Women of Achievement award 1988), L.A. County Fedn. of Rep. Women (scholarship chmn.). Home: 10060 Toluca Lake Ave Toluca Lake CA 91602-2924 Office: 129 E Providencia Ave Burbank CA 91502-1922 Office Phone: 323-849-2306.

JOSELL, JESSICA (JESSICA WECHSLER), public relations executive; b. Balt., June 17, 1943; d. Maury J. and Rose E. (Lodin) Snyder; m. Neil B. Josell, Apr. 30, 1965 (dec. Nov. 1967); m. Steven James Wechsler, Jan. 12, 1980. BA, U. Fla., 1965. V.p., gen. mgr. Morton Dennis Wax & Assocs., NYC, 1976-81; v.p. Raleigh Group, Ltd., NYC, 1981-87; pres. Josell Comm., Inc., NYC, 1981—. Exec. officer, bd. dirs. Bridge, Inc., NYC. Mem.: NY Women in Film and TV. Home and Office: Josell Comm Inc 185 W End Ave Ste 22C New York NY 10023-5549 Office Phone: 212-877-5560. Business E-Mail: jessica@josellpr.com.

JOSEPH, ANNE M., lawyer, law educator; BA, Williams Coll., 1992; M.Phil., Cambridge Univ., 1995; JD, Yale Univ., 2000; PhD, Harvard Univ., 2002. Law clk. U.S. Ct. Appeals (D.C. Cir.), Washington, 2000—01; atty. U.S. Dept. Just. Civil Div., Washington, 2001—03; law clk. to Ruth Bader Ginsburg U.S. Supreme Ct., Washington, 2003—04; asst. prof. Law Sch. U. Calif., Berkeley, 2004—. Contbr. articles to prof. jour. Office: Univ Calif Berkeley Law Sch 433 North Addition Berkeley CA 94720-7200

JOSEPH, DIANA JENNIFER, literature and language professor; b. New Castle, Pa., July 21, 1973; m. Allen Robert Learst, Oct. 18, 2006; m. Gary Wayne Perine, Jan. 21, 1992 (div. June 21, 1999); 1 child, Clayton Albert Perine. BA in English, Westminster Coll., New Wilmington, Pa., 1992; MFA in Creative Writing, Syracuse U., N.Y., 1996. Instr. Mesa State Coll., Grand Junction, Colo., 1996—2005; asst. prof. Minn. State U., Mankato, 2005—. Author: (short story collection) Happy or Otherwise. Dfl. Home: 418 Van Brunt St Mankato MN 56001 Office: Minn State Univ 230 Armstrong Hall Mankato MN 56001 Office Phone: 507-389-5144. Business E-Mail: diana.joseph@mnsu.edu.

JOSEPH, ELEANOR ANN, health science association administrator, consultant; b. Cleve., Mar. 6, 1944; d. Emil and Eleanor (Leelais) Dienes; m. Abraham Albert Joseph, Oct. 28, 1984 (dec.). BS in Math. cum laude, Cleve. State U., 1978, MPA in Health Care Adminstrn., 1991. Cert. profl. healthcare quality, coding specialist, accredited records technician, registered record adminstr., health info. adminstr., cert. in healthcare privacy, med. coder 2005. Asst. dir. med. records Suburban Hosp., Warrensville Heights, Ohio, 1963-77; coder Shaker Med. Ctr., Shaker Heights, Ohio, 1965, Huron Rd. Hosp., Cleve., 1965; instr. Cuyahoga C.C., Cleve., 1970-72; dir. med. records Hillcrest Hosp., Mayfield Heights, Ohio, 1977-84; med. records technician Vis. Nurse Assn., Cleve., 1985; coord. med. record svcs. Ctr. for Health Affairs Greater Cleve. Hosp. Assn., 1985-88, dir. coding svcs. Ctr. Health Affairs, 1988-89, dir. health record svcs. Ctr. Health Affairs, 1989-98; v.p. health info. mgmt. svcs. Greater Cleve. Healthcare Assn., 1999—2004, privacy officer Ctr. Health Affairs, 2001—04, v.p. revenue cycle mgmt. Ctr. Health Affairs, 2004; ind. health info. mgmt. cons., 2004—. Coding instr. cmty. edn. dept. Cleve. State U., 1998—2006; instr. cmty. edn. Lakeland C.C., adv. task force cert. program med. office mgmt., 1992—96, coding tchr., 1999; spkrs. bur. Hillcrest Hosp., Mayfield Heights, 1978—84; adv. com. Cuyahoga C.C., 1973—80, 1994—, faculty, 1999—2003; tech. adv. AHIMA Publ., 2004—05; seminar creator, presenter Corp. Coll., 2005—06; coord. seminars in field; cons. in field. Co-author: (manual) Quality Assurance Program for Medical Records Deparment, 1981, Dollars and Sense: A Reference Guide to Coding and Prospective Payment System Reimbursement Issues, 1988; co-editor: Care and Management of Health Care Records, 1988, 1992. Active Holden Arboretum, Kirtland, Ohio, 1975—, Ohio Hist. Soc., Columbus, 1975—. Recipient Outstanding Svc. award, Ctr. Health Affairs/Greater Cleve. Healthcare Assn., 1997. Mem.: N.E. Ohio Health Info. Mgmt. Assn. (chmn. coding roundtable 1993—), Ohio Health Info. Mgmt. Assn. (project leader alliances 1992—94, data quality reimbursement coun. 1992—2006, liaison to ambulatory sect. 1994—96, project leader developing coding seminars 1996—97, co-chmn. data quality and reimbursement coun. 1996—98, pres.-elect 1998—99, pres. 1999—2000, dir. and del. coord. 2000—01, del. to Am. Health Info. Mgmt. Assn. 2002—03, Disting. Mem. award 1997, Profl. Achievement award 2003), Ohio Assn. Healthcare Quality, Ohio Med. Record Assn. (alt. del. 1982, med. record coun. 1985—92, del. for state assn. mem. at nat. ann. mtg. 1989, legis. com. 1989—90, del. for state assn. mem. at nat. ann. mtg. 1990), N.E. Ohio Med. Record Assn. (treas. 1979, v.p. 1980, pres. 1982—83, counselor 1983, ednl. com. 1984, chmn. nominating com. 1986, ednl. com. 1987, cons. com. 1987—91, audit com., membership com., bylaws com., pub. rels. com.), East Ohio Med. Record Assn., Nat. Assn. Healthcare Quality, Am. Guild Patient Accts. Mgrs., Am. Health Info. Mgmt. Assn. (quality assurance and long term care sects., ambulatory records sec. 1992—2001, del. 1997—2000, item writing panel for cert. coding exams 1997—2003, accredited record tech. practitioner 2000—02, co-chmn. coun. cert. 2001, chair coun. on cert. 2002, nominating com. 2002—03, book reviewer, tech. adv. 2004—05), Am. Med. Record Assn. (cons. roster 1976, charter mem. assembly on edn. 1989), Am. Acad. Profl. Coders (treas. local chpt. 1994, endorsed as tchr. for profl. med. coder curriculum, cert.), Data Quality and Reimbursement Coun. (hon.), Holden Arboretum, Northeastern Ohio Assn. for Healthcare Quality, Cleve. City Club. Lutheran. Avocations: cultural events, nature walks, music. Personal E-mail: josephclvlnd@aol.com.

JOSEPH, GERI MACK (GERALDINE JOSEPH), former ambassador, educator, journalist; b. St. Paul, June 19, 1923; BS, U. Minn., 1946; LLD, Bates Coll., 1982; DHL (hon.), Macalester Coll., 1997; LLD, Carleton Coll., 1998; DHL (hon.). Staff writer Mpls. Tribune, 1946-53, contbg. editor, 1972-78; amb. to The Netherlands, Am. Embassy, The Hague, 1978-81; sr. fellow internat. programs U. Minn. Hubert H. Humphrey Inst. Pub. Affairs, Mpls., 1984-94, chmn. adv. bd., 1997—; dir. Mondale Policy Forum, 1990-94. Bd. dirs. Nat. Dem. Inst. for Internat. Affairs, George A. Hormel Co.; mem. U.S. President's Commn. on Mental Health, Minn. Supreme Ct. Commn. on Mentally Disabled and the Cts., mem. Coun. on Fgn. Rels., 1985—; mem. com. on Mid. East, Brookings Instn., 1987. Vice chmn. Gov.'s Commn. on Taxation, 1983-84; trustee Carleton Coll., 1975-94; mem.

Democratic Nat. Com., 1960-72, vice chmn., 1968-72; pres. Nat. Mental Health Assn., 1970-72, co-chairperson Minn. Women's Campaign Fund, 1982-84; co-chmn. Atty. Gen.'s Com. on Child Abuse within the Family, 1986. Democrat.

JOSEPH, KATHIE-ANN, biomedical researcher; b. Jamaica, 1971; BA in Sociology, Harvard Univ.; MD in Public Health, Columbia Univ. Dir. breast cancer surg. rsch. Columbia Univ. Coll. Physicians and Surgeons. Asst. prof. surgery Dept. Surgery Columbia Univ. Med. Ctr., 2003—. Recipient Hoopes Prize for Excellence in Rsch., Harvard Univ., 1991, Young Investigator award, Joanne Masin Breast Cancer Alliance, 2002, Minority Scholar award in Cancer Rsch., AACR, 2004; fellow surgical oncology, gen. surgery residency, NYU Med. Ctr., breast surgery oncology, Columbia; grantee Pilot grant, American Cancer Soc. Mem.: Assn. Acad. Surgery, Am. Soc. Clinical Oncology, Am. Assn. Cancer Rsch.

JOSEPH, MARILYN SUSAN, gynecologist; b. Aug. 18, 1946; BA, Smith Coll., 1968; MD cum laude, SUNY Downstate Med. Ctr., Bklyn., 1972. Diplomate Am. Bd. Ob-Gyn, Nat. Bd. Med. Examiners. Intern U. Minn. Hosps., 1972-73, resident in ob-gyn, 1972-76; med. fellow specialist U. Minn., 1972-76, asst. prof. ob-gyn, 1976—, dir. women's clinic, 1984—. Med. dir. Boynton Health Svc., 1993—. Author: Differential Diagnosis Obstetrics, 1978. Fellow Am. Coll. Ob-Gyn (best paper dist. VI meeting 1981); mem. Hennepin County Med. Soc., Minn. State Med. Assn., Minn. State Ob-Gyn Soc. Avocations: cooking, bird watching, travel. Office: Boynton Health Svc 410 Church St SE Minneapolis MN 55455-0346 E-mail: mjoseph@bhs.umn.edu.

JOSEPH, MICHELE BETH, special education educator, educational therapist; b. Newark, July 17, 1964; d. Allan Irwin Whitman and Carole Dee (Ratner) Chillscyzn; m. Bartlett T. Joseph, Dec. 16, 1990. BA, U. Calif., Irvine, 1985; credentials Multiple Subject, Spl. Edn., Calif. State U., Northridge, 1987, MA, 1989. Cert. spl. edn. tchr., Calif. Spl. edn. educator Newhall (Calif.) Sch. Dist., 1987-88, Simi Valley (Calif.) Unified Sch. Dist., 1988-95, Saugus (Calif.) Union Sch. Dist., 1995—. Master tchr. Simi Valley Unified Sch. Dist., 1990. Mem. NEA, Calif. Tchrs. Assn. Avocations: reading, needle point, bicycling, swimming, travel. Office: 18319 Avocet Ct Canyon Country CA 91387-8133

JOSEPH, ROSALINE RESNICK, hematologist; b. NYC, Aug. 21, 1929; d. Joseph and Malca (Rosenberg) Resnick; m. Robert J. Joseph, Jan. 2, 1954; children: Joy S., Nina B. AB, Cornell U., 1949; MD, Women's Med. Coll. Pa., Phila., 1953; MS, Temple U., 1958. Intern Kings County Hosp., Bklyn., 1953-54; resident Phila. Gen. Hosp., 1954-55, Temple U. Hosp., 1955-57; instr. dept. medicine Temple U. Med. Ctr., Phila., 1957-60, assoc. in medicine, 1960-63, asst. prof. medicine, 1963-69, assoc. prof. medicine, 1969-77; course co-coordinator Sys. Oncology Interdisciplinary Course, 1968-73; prof. medicine, dir. Med. Coll. Pa., Phila., 1977, prof. emeritus, 1999, course coordinator, 1978, prof. emeritus, 1999. Pres. med. staff Med. Coll. Pa., 1990-91. Contbr. articles to profl. jours. Del. dir. Am. Cancer Soc., 1989—. Recipient Lindback award for disting. teaching, Christian & Mary Lindback Found., 1982, Am. Cancer Soc. Div. Disting. Svc. award, 1987. Fellow ACP; mem. Am. Soc. Hematology, Am. Soc. Clin. Oncology, Alumni Assn. Med. Coll. Pa. (pres. 1988-90). Office: Med Coll Pa Hosp 3300 Henry Ave Philadelphia PA 19129-1191

JOSEPH, STEFANI ANN, art educator, painter; arrived in U.S., 1993; d. Cranog Joseph and Gladys Mary Sneyd; m. David Vincent Gale, Apr. 6, 2002. Cert. in fine art, Oxford U., Eng., 1976; MFA in Fine Art, Savannah Coll. Art and Design, Ga., 2001. Tchr. D'Overbroeks Oxford, England, 1985—93, Collingham Brown & Brown, Oxford, 1985—93; prof. Savannah Coll. Art & Design, 1993—. One-woman shows include Bender Fine Arts, Atlanta, 1999, Savannah Coll. Art and Design, 1999, Warren-Britt Galleries, Ala. State U., 2000, Stillman Coll., Tuscaloosa, Ala., 2001, Chattahoochee Valley Art Mus., La Grange, Ga., 2004, The Sallie & Harmon Boyette Gallery, 2006, The Annette Howell Turner Ctr. for the Arts, Valdosta, Ga., 2006, Represented in permanent collections St. Bartholomew's Hosp., London, exhibited in group shows at Mus. Modern Art, Oxford, Oxford Art Soc., Westgate Art Gallery, Seoul (Korea) Internat. Print Biennale, Perpignan (France)Print Biennale, Templeton Coll., Oxford, Ibiza (Spain) Grafic Print Exhbn., numerous others, Represented in permanent collections St. Hilda's Coll., Oxford, Templeton Coll., Westminster Coll., Galerie Gora, Montreal, Que., Can., Bender Fine Arts, Marietta, Ga.; contbr. articles to profl. jours.; one-woman shows include Mountain Valley Arts Coun. Home: 24 E Liberty St # 22 Savannah GA 31401 Office: Savannah Coll Art & Design Anderson St Savannah GA 31401 Office Phone: 912-525-6613. Business E-Mail: sjoseph@scad.edu.

JOSEPHIAN, JENNY ADELE, acupuncturist, artist; b. Berkeley, Calif., Mar. 5, 1959; d. Roger Eslie Josephian and Carolyn Marie Wrasse. BA, Antioch U. West, San Francisco, 1986; diploma of competence, Traditional Acupuncture Inst., Columbia, Md., 1988, M Acupuncture, 1990. Lic. acupuncturist, Calif. Mem. office staff, acupressure practitioner Acupressure Inst., Berkeley, 1981-85; pvt. practice acupressure, Berkeley, 1981-88; pvt. practice acupuncture, 1988—. Exhibited works in show at Nexus Gallery, Berkeley, Calif., 2000. Avocations: travel, gardening, dance, writing. Office: 1502 Walnut St Ste A Berkeley CA 94709-1563 Office Phone: 510-548-2261.

JOSEPHS, BABETTE, legislator; b. NYC, Aug. 4, 1940; d. Eugene and Myra A. Josephs; children: Lee Aaron Newberg, Elizabeth Master. BA, Queens Coll., 1962; JD, Rutgers U., 1976. Sole practice, Phila., 1976-78; exec. dir. Nat. Abortion Rights Action League of Pa., Phila., 1978-80, Citizens Coalition for Energy Efficiency, Phila., 1980-81; pvt. practice cons., fundraiser Phila., 1981-84; mem. Pa. Ho. of Reps., Phila., 1984—. Mem. Profl. Licensure Com., 1985—86, Ho. Health and Human Services Com., 1985—92, 1995—2002, Ho. Judiciary Com., 1987—94, 1997—2002, Ho. Appropriations Com., 1993—2002, Ho. Urban Affairs Com., 1997—98, Children and Youth Com., 2001—02, Dem. Policy Com., Common Sense Firearms Safety Caucus, Firefighters and Emergency Services Caucus, Autism Caucus, Campaign Fin. Reform Caucus, others, Pa. Commn. on Crime and Delinquency, Joint Selection Com. to Examine Election Issues, 2001—02, Agrl. and Rural Affairs Com., 2003—; mem. adv. bd. Statewide Uniform Registry of Elections, 2001—02; chair State Govt. Com., 2001—. Mem. Women's Internat. League for Peace and Freedom, LWV; hon. chair Jewish Family & Children's Services of Greater Phila.; co-founder, mem. Nat. Abortion and Reproductive Rights Action League; coord. Nat. Orgn. Women Legislators, Pa.; mem. Clean Air Coun.; Am. Jewish Com.; mem. Martin Luther King Task Force, Rebuild the Del. Valley Steering Com., Nuclear Freeze Campaign; super del. Dem. Nat. Conv., 1992; bd. dirs. ACLU; bd. mem. Save the Boyd, Franklin Paine's Skate Park. Named Legislator of Yr., Citizen Action, 1996, Dem. Woman Rep. of Yr., Capitol Area Dem. Woman's Club, 2001, Leader of Yr., Bella Vista United Civic Assn., 2004; recipient Cert. of Appreciation, AIDS WALK, 1996, President's award, Pa. Fedn. Mus. and Hist. Orgns., 1998, Disting. Pub. Svc. award, Concerned Citizens of Del. Valley, 1999, Legislator of Yr. award, Pa. Consumer Action Network, 1999, Cert. of Appreciation award, Statewide Pa. Rights Coalition, 2002, Women of Distinction award, Phila. Bus. Jour. and Nat. Assn. Women Bus. Owners, 2003, Cert. of Appreciation, Phila. 17th Police Dist., 2003, Leadership award, 2003, Disting. Achievement award, Smokefree, Pa., 2003, Spirit of Leadership award, Pathways Pa., 2004. Mem.: Center City Residents Assn., Phila. Bar Assn. (com. on civil and women's rights), Liberty City Gay and Lesbian Dem. Club. Democrat. Jewish. Office: 1528 Walnut St Philadelphia PA 19102-3604

JOSEPHS, JUDITH, counseling administrator, educator; b. Lynn, Mass., Dec. 9, 1941; d. Irvin and Frances Sarah (Glovsky) Emmerman; m. Barry David Josephs. BSc, Salem State Coll., Salem, Mass., 1963; M in Counseling, Salem State Coll., 1965, M, 1967; JD, Suffolk U., Boston, Mass., 1975. Bar:; cert. Counselor, Psychologist, Adjustment Counselor, Prin. Dir. Vocat. Schs. Counselor Lynn Pub. Schs., Lynn, Mass., 1963—. Adj. prof. Fitchburg State Coll., Fitchburg, 1990—95; prof. Salem State Coll., 1995—; bd. dirs. Salem State, Econ. Devel. Corp. Fund raiser Salem State, 2000—05, Lynn Tech. HS, 1995—2006. Recipient Toastmasters Internat. Comm. and Leadership award; grantee Easter Bach Grant, Easter Bach Chaulath Found., 2004. Mem.: Lynn Bar Assn., Mass. Sch. Counselors, Gieutu Boston Guidance. Avocations: swimming, travel, nature studies. Office: Lynn Vocat and Tech Inst 80 Neptune Blvd Lynn MA 01902

JOSEPHSON, NANCY, talent agency executive; d. Marvin J.; m. Larry Sanitsky; 3 children. BA in Economics, Brown U., 1980; JD, Harvard Law Sch., 1982. Atty. Loeb & Loeb, NY, 1982-86, Internat. Creative Mgmt., Beverly Hills, 1986, head N.Y. TV dept.; various positions as an agent, 1979-87; head TV lit. dept. Internat. Creative Mgmt., LA, 1991—95, exec. v.p. TV, 1995—2006, co-pres., 1998—2006; ptnr. The Endeavor Agy., Beverly Hills, Calif., 2006—. Developer (TV shows) Friends, Nash Bridges, Caroline in the City, The Simpsons. Named one of top twenty-five most important women in entertainment Hollywood's Reporter, 2005. Mem.: Hollywood Radio & Television Soc. (pres.). Office: The Endeavor Agy 9601 Wilshire Blvd 10th Fl Beverly Hills CA 90212*

JOSEY, DONNA ASHLEY, accountant, educator; b. LA, Nov. 17, 1958; m. Jimmy Josey; children: Jonathan Lloyd, Rebecca Blair. BSBA, Miss. Coll., Clinton, 1980, MBA, 1988. CPA Miss., 1985. Internal auditor Deposit Guaranty Nat. Bank, Jackson, Miss., 1980—84, Eastover Bank Savs., Meridian, Miss., 1985—87; coll. instr. Holmes CC, Ridgeland, Miss., 1999—. Treas. fund devel. Jr. League Jackson, 1995—2006. Office Phone: 601-605-3332. Personal E-mail: donnajosey@bellsouth.net.

JOSLIN, JANINE ELIZABETH, preservationist, consultant; b. Kansas City, Mo., Mar. 16, 1948; d. James Bryce and Isabel Quezon (Carr) Traner; m. Jack Leslie Joslin, Dec. 4, 1971; children: Jaclyn, Aaron, Amanda. BA in History, U. Mo., Kansas City, 1971; MA in Heritage Preserevation, Ga. State U., 1992. Pvt. practice cons., Rome, Ga., 1989—92; dir. Chieftains Mus., Rome, 1992—94; pres. Gaia Walkers Inc., Leawood, Kans., 1996—99; pvt. practice cons. Leawood, 1999—. Bd. mem. Women Vision Internat., Overland Park, Kans., 1996—; pres. bd. Donnelly Internat., Kansas City, Kans., 1997—98; team leader Sci. City Mus., Kansas City, Mo., 1998—99. Contbr. articles to mags. Mem. Leawood Hist. Commn., 1998—; bd. dirs. Kans. Preservation Alliance, Topeka, 2001—, pres., 2003—05, exec. dir., 2005; co-founder, pres. bd. Sharing a Vision for Generations, 2005—. Grantee, IMS, 1994, Ga. Heritage 2000, 1995, Kans. Why 150, 1999. Avocations: kayaking, hiking, rowing. Home: 12508 Catalina Leawood KS 66209 E-mail: jjoslin1@kc.rr.com.

JOSLYN, CATHERINE RUTH, art educator, artist; b. Cleve., May 18, 1950; d. Richard Owen and Mary Ellen (See) Joslyn. BA, Colby Coll., 1972; MFA, Ind. U., 1977. Owner Woven Images, Kansas City, 1973-77; vis. artist Kansas City Art Inst., 1978-79; asst. prof. Clarion (Pa.) U., 1979-85; dir. Clarion Festival of Arts, 1984-86; founding dir. univ. honors program Clarion (Pa.) U., 1986-88; assoc. prof. Clarion U., Pa., 1986—91, prof. Pa., 1992—. Commonwealth speaker Pa. Humanities Coun., Phila., 1991, art dept. chair, 1993-96; internat. lectr. and exhibitor. Contbr. articles to Grove's Dictionary Art and profl. jours.; works included in juried and solo exhibits, pvt. and corp. collections nat. and internat., 1973—. Instnl. grantee Pa. Coun. on the Arts, 1985; J. William Fulbright Sr. scholar, Peru, 2002. Mem. Surface Design Assn. (bd. dirs 1982-87, 91). Avocations: gardening, yoga, fitness. Office: Clarion U Dept Art Clarion PA 16214

JOST, KAYREN PROSSER, accountant; d. Roger Davies and Kathryn Myers Prosser; m. Robert Alan Jost. BA, Stetson U., DeLand, Fla., 1969—73, MBA Acctg. Concentration, 1983—85. CPA Bd. Accountancy, Fla., 1985. Asst. treas./asst. v.p. Coast Fed. Savs. & Loan Assn., Ormond Beach, Fla., 1975—80; sr. staff acct. Arthur Young & Co., Daytona Beach, 1985—87; sr. budget/fin. analyst, internal audit mgr. ITT Industries, ITT Cmty. Devel. Corp., Palm Coast, 1987—95; mgr., tds fin. svcs. ITT Industries, TDS Corp. Services, Palm Coast, 1995—. Sustaining mem. Jr. League, Daytona Beach, Fla., 1980—2006; mem. Am. MENSA, Ltd., Arlington, Tex., 2002—06. Recipient Hon., Nat. Mortar Bd. Orgn., 1972—73; grantee scholarship, Nat. Merit, 1969—73, Acctg. scholarship, Price Waterhouse, 1984. Mem.: Am. Inst. CPAs, Fla. Inst. CPAs, Zeta Tau Alpha (life). Democrat. Episcopal. Avocations: breeding arabian horses, boating, drawing. Office: ITT Industries; TDS Corp Svcs 2 Corporate Dr Palm Coast FL 32137 Office Phone: 386-446-6175.

JOSWIAK, RUTH ANN, retired dialysis nurse; b. Niagara, Wis., Dec. 15, 1932; d. Fred W. and Gertrude V. (Steinbauer) Gronert; m. John F. Joswiak, Nov. 27, 1954; children: Scott, Jill Banik, Jody Frazer, Jamy, Yohn. Grad., St. Mary's Hosp. Sch., Wausau, Wis., 1953; BS, St. Joseph's Coll., North Windom, Maine, 1985. Cert. BONENT. Head nurse Lakeland Manor Nursing Home, Woodruff, Wis.; staff nurse Lakeland Meml. Hosp., Woodruff, St. Mary's Hosp., Wausau; dialysis mgr. Howard Young Med. Ctr., Woodruff, unti. 1995; ret., 1995. Mem. coun. nurse mgr. Am. Heart Assn. Mem. Am. Nephrology Nurses Assn., Am. Kidney Found.

JOVANOVIC, LOIS, medical researcher; b. Mpls. BS in Biology, Columbia U., 1969; B in Hebrew Lit., Jewish Theol. Seminary, 1968, M in Hebrew Lit., 1970; MD, Albert Einstein Coll. Medicine, 1973. Intern and resident NY Hosp. Cornell U. Med. Coll., 1973—76; fellow in endocrinology and metabolism Cornell U. Med. Coll., 1976—78, instr., asst to assoc. prof., 1978—86; asst. attending physician NY Hosp., 1978—85; asst. adj. prof. and physician Rockefeller U. and Rockefeller U. Hosp., 1979—85; assoc. adj. prof. U. Calif., Irvine, 1986—88; sr. scientist Sansum Med. Rsch. Found., 1985—96; dir. and chief sci. officer Sansum Diabetes Rsch. Inst., 1996—; clin. assoc. prof. medicine U. SC- LA Med. Ctr., 1986—89, prof., 1989—; rsch. biologist U. Calif., Santa Barbara, 1990—. Author numerous books and articles on diabetes and women's health. Fellow: NY Acad. Medicine, Am. Coll. Endocrinology, Am. Coll. Nutrition, ACP. Office: Sansum Diabetes Rsch Inst 2219 Bath St Santa Barbara CA 93105*

JOVOVICH, MILLA (NATASHA MILITZA JOVOVICH), model, actress; b. Kiev, Ukraine, Dec. 17, 1975; d. Bogdanovitch and Galina Loginova Jovovich; m. Shawn Andrews, Oct. 2, 1992 (annulled Nov. 25, 1992); m. Luc Besson, Dec. 14, 1997 (div. June 12, 1999). Appeared on mag. covers including Lei, 1987, Mademoiselle, Aerna, Harper's Bazaar, Vogue, Face, i-D, Vanity Fair, W, Marie Claire; internat. spokesmodel L'Oreal; launched line of clothing with Carmen Hawk called Jovovich-Hawk, 2003. Composer: (songs in films) Gentleman Who Fell, 1993, The Rules of Attraction, 2002, The Prince & Me, 2004; costume designer: (films) Mona Lisa Smile, 2003; actor: Two Moon Junction, 1988, Return to the Blue Lagoon, 1991, Kuffs, 1992, Chaplin, 1992, Dazed and Confused, 1993, The Fifth Element, 1997, He Got Game, 1998, The Messenger: The Story of Joan of Arc, 1999, The Million Dollar Hotel, 2000, The Claim, 2000, Zoolander, 2001, Dummy, 2002, Resident Evil, 2002, The House on Turk Street, 2002, You Stupid Man, 2002, Resident Evil: Apocalypse, 2004, Ultraviolet, 2006; (TV films) The Night Train to Kathmandu, 1988; singer: (albums) The Divine Comedy, 1994. Office: c/o Spanky Taylor 3727 W Magnolia Burbank CA 91505*

JOY, CARLA MARIE, history educator; b. Denver, Sept. 5, 1945; d. Carl P. and Theresa M. (Lotito) J. AB cum laude, Loretto Heights Coll., 1967; MA, U. Denver, 1969, postgrad., 1984-87. Instr. history Cmty. Coll., Denver; prof. history Red Rocks C.C., Lakewood, Colo., 1970—. Cons. for innovative ednl. programs; reviewer fed. grants, 1983-89; mem. adv. panel Colo. Endowment for Humanities, 1985-89. Contbr. articles to profl. publs. Instr. vocat. edn. Mile High United Way, Jefferson County, 1975; participant Jefferson County Sch. Sys. R-1 Dist., 1983-88; active Red Rocks C.C. Spkrs. Bur., 1972-89, strategic planning com., 1992-97; chair history discipline Colo. Gen. Edn. Core Transfer Consortium, 1986-96, faculty transfer curriculum coun., 1997—; mem. Colo. C.C. curriculum com., 1999—; mem. history, geography, civics stds. and geography frameworks adv. com. Colo. Dept. Edn., 1995-96; steering com. Ctr. Tchg. Excellence, 1991-92, 96-97; with North Ctrl. Self-Study Process, 1972-73, 80-81, 86-88, 96-98; with K-16 Linkages Colo. Commn. for Higher Edn., 1997-98; mem. evaluation team for Colo. Awards, edn. and civic achievement for Widefield Sch. Dist. #3, 1989; mem. Red Rocks C.C.-Clear Creek Sch. Sys. Articulation Team, 1990-91; mem. Statue of Liberty-Ellis Island Found. Inc., 1987—. Ford Found. fellow, 1969; recipient Cert. of Appreciation Kiwanis Club, 1981, Telecomm. Coop. for Colo.'s Cmty. Colls., 1990-92, Master Tchr. award U. Tex.-Austin, 1982. Mem. NEA, Am. Hist. Assn., Am. Assn. Higher Edn., Nat. Coun. Social Studies, Nat. Geog. Soc., Omohundro Inst. Early Am. History and Culture, Colo. Edn. Assn., Colo. Coun. Social Studies, World Hist. Assn., Orgn. Am. Historians, The Colo. Hist. Soc., Colo. Geog. Alliance, Soc. Hist. Edn., Phi Alpha Theta. Home: 1849 S Lee St Apt D Lakewood CO 80232-6252 Office: Red Rocks C C 13300 W 6th Ave Lakewood CO 80228-1213

JOY, SUZANNE CHAUVIN, language educator; d. Wilfred Laurie Chauvin and Fernande Cecile Beaumier; m. Robert Ashley Joy, Aug. 8, 1982; children: Heather Suzanne, Adam Robert. BA, Worcester State Coll., Mass., 1972; MA, So. Ill. U., 1978. Instr. English and German Beal Coll., Bangor, Maine, 1980—86; prof. English and German Kennebec Valley C.C., Fairfield, Maine, 1986—. Fellow, U. Kans., 1972—73, So. Ill. U., 1977—78; grantee, Fullbright Found., 1973, U. Kans., 1973—74; scholar, Mass., 1969—72. Mem.: Am. Assn. Tchrs. German (treas. 2005—06), Penobscot Valley Kennel Club (chmn. edn. 2000—06). Democrat. Avocations: travel, dog training and breeding, camping, wildlife, art. Office: Kennebec Valley Community College 92 Western Avenue Fairfield ME 04937 Office Phone: 207-453-5139. Business E-Mail: sjoy@kvcc.me.edu.

JOYCE, ANN IANNUZZO, art educator; b. Scranton, Pa., May 23, 1953; d. Albert Joseph and Lucy (Giumento) Iannuzzo; m. Patrick Francis Joyce, July 23, 1977; children: Ryan Patrick, Shawn Patrick. BFA, Maryland Inst., Balt., 1975; MS, U. Scranton, 1988; postgrad., Pa. State U., 1990—. Mech. artist Internat. Corr. Schs., Scranton, Pa., 1975-77; layout artist Lynn Orgn., Wilkes-Barre, Pa., 1977-78; prodn. coord. Jewelcor Merchandising, Wilkes-Barre, 1978-82; adj. lectr. Kings Coll., Wilkes-Barre, 1981-89, asst. prof., 1989—; art dir. WVIA-TV Pub. Broadcasting, Pittston, Pa., 1985-86; publs. dir. U. Scranton, 1986-89; faculty mem. Pa. Gov.'s Inst. Faculty in Arts and Humanities, 2006—. Exec. bd. v.p. Northeastern Pa. Writing Coun., Wilkes-Barre, 1993—; edn. co-chair Northeast Pa. Ad Club, 1994-96, edn. chair, 1999-05. Contbg. author: Handbook of Classroom Assessment: Learning, Achievement, and Adjustment, 1996; group show Everhart Mus., Scranton, Pa., 1997. Cub Scout leader Boy Scouts Am., Moosic, Pa., 1992-95. Mem. ASCD, Nat. Art Edn. Assn. (Outstanding Art Educator 2004, higher edn. divsn. 2004), Am. Inst. Graphic Arts (Phila. chpt.), Calligraphers Guild, Artists for Art, Pa. Art Edn. Assn. (higher edn. divsn. chair 1998-06, Outstanding Art Educator 2003), Nat. Assn. Desktop Pubs., Seminar for Rsch. in Art Edn., Caucus for Social Theory in Art Edn. Democrat. Roman Catholic. Avocations: mixed media art, writing, vegetarian cooking. Office: King's Coll 133 N River St Wilkes Barre PA 18711-0851 Address: 148 Joyce Dr Moosic PA 18507-2113

JOYCE, ANNE RAINE, editor; b. South Bend, Ind., Oct. 2, 1942; d. James Agee and Marjorie Elizabeth (Gilstrap) Raine; m. Glenn Russell Joyce, Aug. 19, 1962; 1 child, Adam Russell. AB, Cen. Meth. Coll., 1962; MA in French, U. Mo., 1966; MA in Linguistics, U. Iowa, 1979. Cert. tchr., Mo. Tchr. Centralia (Mo.) High Sch., 1962-64; instr. Coe Coll., Cedar Rapids, Iowa, 1978-79, Georgetown U., Washington, 1980-83; asst. editor Am.-Arab Affairs, Washington, 1983-84; editor, dir. publs. Mid. East Policy, Washington, 1984—; gen. sec. Mid. East Policy Coun., Washington, 1991—, v.p., 1993—. Mem. edn. com. Fairfax County (Va.) PTA Bd., 1986-88; bd. dirs. Ams. for Middle East Understanding. U.S. Dept. Def. fellow, 1964-66; recipient Recognition award Am.-Arab Affairs Coun., 1988, Disting. Alumni award. Cen. Meth. Coll., 1990. Mem. Middle East Studies Assn., LWV (fin. chair Fairfax county chpt. 1981—). Home: 6916 Tulsa Ct Alexandria VA 22307-1730 Office: Middle East Policy Coun 1730 M St NW Ste 512 Washington DC 20036-4516 E-mail: ajoyce@mepc.org.

JOYCE, BERNITA ANNE, retired federal agency administrator; d. Albert A. and Margaret C. Joyce; m. Kenneth B. Lucas, Aug. 2, 1975. BA, Duchesne Coll.; MBA, U. Santa Clara, PhD, 1974. With Wolfe & Co. CPAs, Washington, 1971-72; fin. dir. Nat. Forest Products Assn., Washington, 1972-74; budget and fiscal officer ICC, Washington, 1974-77, Office Mgmt. and Budget, 1977-80; asst. dir. mgmt. svcs. Bur. Mines, Dept. Interior, 1980-85; asst. dir. Office Policy Analysis, Dept. Interior, 1985-96, asst. spl. trustee Am. Indians, 1996—99; asst. adminstr. S.J. Cmty. Georgetown U., 2000—05; pres. Rogers Sys., Inc., 2005—. Author: Financial Viability of Private Elementary Schools. Mem. AICPA, Sr. Execs. Assn., Assn. Govt. Accts., Cosmos Club, Beta Gamma Sigma. Home: 6001 Bradley Blvd Bethesda MD 20817-3807

JOYCE, DIANA, psychologist, education educator; d. Donald Ray and Caroline Ann Joyce. PhD, U. Fla., Gainesville, 2000. Nat. cert. sch. psychologist NASP, 2001; cert. clin. educator Dept. Edn., Fla., 2002, lic. school psychologist 2003, psychologist 2004. Affiliate asst. prof. civil and coastal coll. engring. U. Fla., 1999—2006; outside examiner Psychol. Corp., Orlando, Fla., 2001—03; sch. psychologist Hillsborough County Schools, Tampa, Fla., 2000—03; faculty ednl. psychology U. Fla., 2003—. Mem.: NASP, APA, Fla. Assn. Sch. Psychologists. Methodist. Achievements include research in temperament-based learning style preferences of students with oppositional defiant disorder and conduct disorder in psychiatric hospital and adjudicated youth programs; temperament differences between gifted and nongifted children; social-emotional assessment for behaivor disorders; sex differential in self-handicapping behaviors of male and female unergraduate students. Avocations: travel, hiking, camping, theater, art. Business E-Mail: djoyce@coe.ufl.edu.

JOYCE, JANET S., psychologist; b. Dayton, Ohio, Mar. 9, 1957; d. Jerome S. and Jane R. Sallo; m. Matthew Clark Joyce, Oct. 27, 1991; children: Rachel Leah, Sarah Anne. BA in Am. Studies, U. Calif., Santa Cruz, 1988; MS in Clin. Psychology, Pacific Grad. Sch. Psychology, 1992, PhD in Clin. Psychology, 1994. Lic. psychologist, Calif., Colo. Early childhood educator U. Calif., Santa Cruz, 1984-87; asst. editor CTB-McGraw Hill Pub. Corp., Monterey, Calif., 1987-88; predoctoral intern Alcohol and Drug Treatment Ctr. Stanford (Calif.) U. Med. Ctr., 1992-93; rsch. health scientist VA Hosp., Palo Alto, 1994—; mental health cons. U.S. Dept. Labor Job Corps Ctr., San Jose, Calif., 1993-2000; pvt. practice Los Gatos, Calif., 1994-2000, Boulder, Colo., 2000—. Mem. APA, Calif. Psychol. Assn., Colo. Psychol. Assn., U. Calif. Alumni Assn. Home: 2523 Broadway St Ste 201 Boulder CO 80304-4251 E-mail: janetsjoyce@earthlink.net.

JOYCE, JANICE ROSE, supervisor, elementary school educator; b. Vandling, Pa., July 1, 1955; d. Thomas George and Aldona J. (Kondrat) O'Boyle; m. Thomas Raymond Joyce, Oct. 17, 1981; 1 child, Michael. BS in Elem. Edn., Marywood Coll., 1977; MS in Reading Edn., 1981; MS in Elem. Adminstrn., U. Scranton, 1987. Cert. elem. edn., reading specialist, elem. adminstrn., supr. curriculum and instrn. Elem. reading tchr. Northeastern Pa. Intermediate Unit, Scranton, 1977-79; reading specialist Forest City (Pa.) Regional Sch. Dist., 1979—92, reading/fed. programs coord., 1992—99, elem. prin., 1999—2003; curriculum coord. Lackawanna Tr. Sch. Dist., Factoryville, 2003—. Spkr. Parent Awareness Tng. Conf., Pocono Mountains, Pa., 1994. Vol. Am. Heart Assn., N.E. Pa., 1989-94. Mem. ASCD, Internat. Reading Assn. (Pres.' Club award 1990-91), Pa. Assn. Fed. Program Coords. (exec. bd. 1999-), Northeastern Pa. Reading Assn. (adv. bd. mem. 1981—, membership dir. 1985—), Keystone State Reading Assn. (sec. 1985-86), Phi Delta Kappa. Home: 409 May St Mayfield PA 18433-2127 Office: Lackawanna Tr Sch dist 179 Coll Ave Factoryville PA 18419

JOYCE, MARIE CALDWELL, medical, surgical, and mental health nurse; b. Buffalo, June 29, 1927; d. Vernon Gordon and Dorothy Fleming (Sullivan) Caldwell; m. Howard C. Joyce, June 10, 1950 (dec. Dec. 27, 2003); children: Kathleen, Kristine, Kandice, Kendall. Diploma, U. Rochester, 1949; student, Loyola U., New Orleans, Our Lady of Holy Cross, William Carey Sch. Nursing. Cert. psychiat./mental health nurse. Nurse Dade Dental Hosp., Buffalo, 1963-65; staff nurse Our Lady of Victory Hosp., Lackawanna, N.Y., 1965-67, VA Med. Ctr., Buffalo, 1968-73; med.-surg. nurse Dept. Vets. Affairs, New Orleans, 1973-84, nurse in substance abuse treatment, 1985-95; ret. Mem. ANA, Nurses Orgn. Vets. Affairs (pres. New Orleans chpt. 1990-92), Am. Psychiat. Nurses Assn., Nat. Nurses Soc. on Addictions. Home: 400 Heritage Ave Terrytown LA 70056

JOYCE, PHYLLIS NORMA, principal; b. Bronx, N.Y., June 8, 1955; d. Philip Emmanuel and Dolores (Pizzolanella) Malizio; m. Thomas Patrick Joyce, June 11, 1983; 1 child, Diana. BA, CUNY, 1978; MA, Nova U., 1995. Tchr. St. Raymond's Sch., Bronx, 1980-83; tchr., head English dept. St. Anne Sch., Las Vegas, Nev., 1983-94, prin., 1994—, coord. jr. HS, 1988-94. Spl. Olympics vol. KC, Las Vegas, 1983-90; vol. Sons of Erin, Las Vegas, 1990—; pastoral coun. St. Anne Parish, 1996—. Democrat. Roman Catholic. Avocations: tennis, working out. Office Phone: 702-735-2586. E-mail: pjoyce@stanneelementary.com.

JOYCE, ROSEMARY ALEXANDRIA, anthropology educator, department chairman; b. Lackawanna, NY, Apr. 7, 1956; d. Thomas Robert and Joanne Hannah (Poth) J.; m. Russell Nicholas Sheptak, Jan. 7, 1984. BA, Cornell U., 1978; PhD, U. Ill., 1985. Instr. Jackson (Mich.) Community Coll., 1983; lectr. U. Ill., Urbana, 1984-85; asst. curator Peabody Mus., Harvard U., Cambridge, Mass., 1985-86, asst. dir., 1986-89; asst. prof. anthropology Harvard U., Cambridge, Mass., 1989-91, assoc. prof. anthropology, 1991-94, U. Calif., Berkeley, 1994—2001, prof., 2001—, chair, 2006—. Author: Cerro Palenque, 1991, Encounters with the Americas, 1995, Gender and Power in Prehispanic Mesoamerica, 2001, The Languages of Archeology, 2002, Embodied Lives, 2003; editor: Maya History, 1993, Women in Prehistory, 1997, Social Patterns in Preclassic Mesoamerica, 1999, Beyond Kinship, 2000, Mesoamerican Archeology, 2003; contbr. articles to profl. jours. NEH grantee, 1985, 86, NSF grantee, 1989, 98, 2001, Famsi grantee, 1996, Heinz Found., Wenner-Gren Found. grantee, 1997; Fulbright fellow, 1981-82. Mem. Soc. for Am. Archaeology, Am. Anthropol. Assn. Office: U Calif Anthropology Dept 232 Kroeber Hall # 3710 Berkeley CA 94720-3710 Business E-Mail: rajoyce@berkeley.edu.

JOYCE-NORRIS, ELAINE ROZELLE, elementary school educator; b. Chgo., Jan. 17, 1947; d. Ernest Chester Joyce and Margie Whitlock Joyce-Ziglor. BS in Elem. Edn., Winston-Salem State U., N.C., 1970. Tchr. early literacy Miller Elem. Sch., Huntington, W.Va., 1970—2003. Chairperson inclusion team Miller Sch., Huntington, W.Va., 1997—2003, curriculum team, 1998—2003, local sch. improvement com., 1999—2003, coord. accelerated reader, 2000—03. Mem. Walnut Hills Cmty. Action Team, Huntington, W.Va., 2005—06; mem., rschr. African Am. History and Geneal. Soc., Mt. Airy, NC, 2004—06; U.S. literacy amb. People to People Internat., 1995—2000; mem., soloist sr. choir Bethel Temple AG Ch., Huntington, W.Va., 1984—2006, mem. missions team, 2002—06. Recipient Golden Apple Tchr.'s award, Ashland Oil Co., 1993. Mem.: ASCD, Internat. Reading Assn., People to People Internat., Pro Literacy for Adults. Avocations: interior decorating, reading, genealogy, gardening, walking. Home: 190 Baer St Huntington WV 25705-1163

JOYE, AFRIE SONGCO, minister; b. Guagua, Pampanga, Philippines, Aug. 8, 1942; d. Emilio Lelay and Elmerita (Atienza) Laus Songco; m. Charles James Joye, Aug. 28, 1971. BA in Christian Edn., Harris Meml. Coll., Manila, 1963; MA in Christian Edn., Scarritt Grad. Sch., Nashville, 1970; PhD in Theology and Religious Edn., Sch. Theology at Claremont, Calif., 1990. Dir. Christian edn. First United Meth. Ch., Naga, Philippines, 1963-66; dist. Christian Edn. coord. Bicol-Palawan Region of United Meth. Ch., 1963-66; dir. Christian Edn. Cen. United Meth. Ch., Manila, 1966-68, dir. youth ministry and student ctr., 1970-71; instr. psychology and Christian edn. Philippin Christian Coll./Harris Meml. Coll., Manila, 1970-71; dir Christian Edn. Aldersgate United Meth. Ch./John Wesley United Meth. Ch., Charleston, S.C., 1971-74; instr. Palmer Coll., Charleston, S.C., 1972-74; nat. dir. Christian edn. in Asian and Native Am. chs. Gen. Bd. Discipleship, Nashville, 1976-79, nat. dir. Christian edn. in small membership chs., 1979-83; cons.-trainer in Christian edn., 1983-87; minister Christian edn. Community United Meth. Ch., Huntington Beach, Calif., 1987-90; assoc. minister Laguna Hills (Calif.) United Meth. Ch., 1990-92; co-pastor Hollywood (Calif.) First United Meth. Ch., 1992-94; sr. pastor St. Paul's United Meth. Ch., Tarzana, Calif., 1994—. Editor: Program Ideas and Training Designs for Pacific and Asian American Church Schools, 1981; contbr. articles to profl. jours. Nat. mem. Bread for the World, Fellowship of Reconciliation, Amnesty Internat. Coolidge Colloquium fellow, Assn. for Religion and Intellectual Life, 1989. Mem. AAUW (life), Nat. Christian Educators Fellowship, Am. Acad. Religion, Assn. of Profs. and Researchers of Religious Education, Nat. Fedn. Asian Am. United Meth., Religious Edn. Assn. Avocations: reading psychology, theology, organ playing, gardening, travel.

JOYNER, LORINZO LITTLE, commissioner; b. Wadesboro, N.C., May 8, 1948; BS in English Edn., N.C. A&T State U., 1969; JD, U. N.C., 1981. Tchr. English, Greensboro/Durham (NC) pub. high schs.; mem. N.C. Utilities Commn., 2001—; lawyer Office of Atty. Gen. Democrat. Office: 4325 Mail Svc Ctr Raleigh NC 27699-4325 Office Phone: 919-733-4249. Business E-Mail: ljoyner@ncuc.net.

JOYNER, MARGUERITE AUSTIN, secondary school educator; b. Memphis, Apr. 14; d. Cathey Monroe and Marguerite Victoria (Davis) Austin; m. Guy Eugene Joyner, Jr. (div. Aug. 1980); children: Marguerite Parker, Guy E. III; m. Philip O'Neil Nicar, Apr. 18, 1986. AA, William Woods Coll.; BA, So. Meth. U.; postgrad., U. Memphis, Rhodes Coll., 2003. Lic. profl. tchr. Tenn., real estate Tenn. Counselor Memphis/Shelby County Juvenile Ct., 1979—81; tchr. Briarcrest Christian Schs., Memphis, 1972—75; counselor Southaven H.S., Memphis, 1981—83; dir. recruiting ERA Sterling Realtors, Memphis, 1984—86; asst. recruiter Fed. Express/Manpower, Memphis, 1993—97; tchr. Shelby County Alt. Sch., Memphis, 2001—. Mem. Tchrs. Credit Union, Memphis; bus. cons. Melody Lane Atrium Cafe, Memphis. Trustee St. Mary's Episcopal Sch., Memphis; co-founder St. Mary's Episcopal Sch. Alumnae Assn.; asst. chmn. Rep. Precinct 44-2, Memphis. Mem.: Memphis (Tenn.) Symphony League, Les Passees Memphis, Jr. League of Memphis (chmn. day care project). Avocations: cooking, calligraphy, collecting first edition books, designing houses. Office: Shelby County Alt Sch 2911 Brunswick Rd Memphis TN 38122 Office Phone: 901-377-4700 x 250.

JOYNER KERSEE, JACKIE (JACQUELINE JOYNER KERSEE), retired track and field athlete; b. East St. Louis, Ill., Mar. 3, 1962; d. Alfred and Mary Joyner; m. Bob Kersee, Jan. 11, 1986. BA in History, UCLA, 1985; LLD (hon.), Washington U., St. Louis, 1992, Iona Coll., 1994; DHL (hon.), Harris-Stowe State Coll., 1993, Fontbonne Coll., St. Louis, 1998, Spelman Coll., 1998, Howard U., 1999, George Washington U., St. Louis, 1999. Basketball player Richmond Rage, ABL, 1996; mem. USA Track & Field Olympic Team, 1984, 1988, 1992, 1996; ret., 2001. Pres., founder JJK & Associates., Inc. Author: (autobiography) A Kind of Grace: The Autobiography of the World's Greatest Female Athlete, 1997; co-author: A Woman's Place Is Everywhere, 1994. Founder JJK Cmty. Found., 1989 (now JJK Youth Ctr. Found., 1997-), Jackie Joyner Kersee Boys & Girls Club; chmn. St. Louis Sports Commn., 1996-2000, chmn. emeritus, 2001—. Recipient Broderick Cup, 1985, James E. Sullivan Award, 1986, Jesse Owens Award, 1986, 87, Am. Black Achievement Award, Ebony mag., 1987, 1st Female Athlete of Yr. Award, Sporting News, 1988, Jim Thorpe Award, 1993, Jackie Robinson "Robie" Award, 1994, Parenting Leader Award, Parenting Mag., Jesse Owens Humanitarian Award, 1999, Humanitarian Award, Women Sports and Fitness, Pres.'s Award, Nat. Conf. Black Mayors; named Athlete of Yr., Track & Field News, 1986, Female Athlete of Yr., AP, 1987, Female of Yr., Internat. Assn. Athletics Federations, 1994, St. Louis Ambassadors Sportswoman of Yr., Hon. Harlem Globetrotter, Woman Athlete of Century, Sports Illustrated, 1999; inductee Nat. Boys and Girls Club Hall of Fame. Achievements include winner of 4 consecutive Nat. Jr. Pentathlon Championships; winner long jump, World Championships, Rome, 1987; winner Mobil Indoor Grand Prix, 1987; winner long jump, Pan Am. Games, 1987; winner heptathlon, World Championships, Stuttgart, Germany, 1993; winner hepthathlon, Goodwill Games, NYC, 1998; winner silver medal for heptathlon, LA Olympic Games, 1984; winner gold medal for heptathlon, Seoul Olympic Games, 1988; winner gold medal for long jump, Seoul Olympic Games, 1988; winner gold medal for heptathlon, Barcelona Olympic Games, 1992; winner bronze medal for long jump, Barcelona Olympic Games, 1992; winner bronze medal for long jump, Atlanta Olympic Games, 1996; set and still holds World Record for heptathlon, Seoul Olympic Games, 9/23/1988. Office: PO Box 69047 Saint Louis MO 63169-0047

JOYNES, AMELIA C., art educator; b. Bridgeport, Conn. m. Thomas J. Joynes; two children. BA, Hiram Coll., 1967; MEd, Cleve. State U., 1984. Art educator Mentor (Ohio) Sch. Dist., 1967-68, Orange Sch. Dist., Pepper Pike, Ohio, 1968-70, Kenston Sch. Dist., Chagrin Falls, Ohio, 1978—2001; instr. Cleve. State U., 1987—, lectr. edn. dept., 1987—; lectr. Case Western Res. U., 2002—. Mem. adv. bd. State of Ohio Dept. Edn.; mem. tchr. resource adv. bd. Cleve. Museum of Art; arts presenter Ohio Alliance for Art, 1998—. Textbook reviewer Harper Collins Pub. Co., 1990, 94; contbr. articles to profl. jours. Named Reg. Outstanding Art Educator Northeast Ohio, 1999. Mem. Nat. Art Edn. Assn., Nat. Mid. Sch. Assn., Ohio Art Edn. Assn. (state sec. 1984-85, elem. divsn. chmn. 1985-88), Ohio Alliance. Avocations: reading, theater, travel. E-mail: a.joynes@csuohio.edu.

JOYNES, BARBARA COLE, marketing executive; b. Rahway, N.J., Sept. 4, 1960; d. Clayton Eugene and Margaret (Fitzgerald) Cole; m. Matthew Thomas Thornhill, Oct. 15, 1983 (div. 1996); children: Allison, Clark; m. Stanley Knight Joynes III, June 24, 2000; stepchildren: Elizabeth, Alexandra. BBA in Mktg., Coll. of William and Mary, 1982. Asst. account exec. March Direct/McCann Direct, N.Y.C., 1983-84, account exec., 1984-86, account supr., 1986-87; dir. comml. client divsn. Huntsinger & Jeffer Direct, Richmond, Va., 1987-89; v.p., account supr. The Stenrich Group, Richmond, 1989-90, sr. v.p., dir. account mgmt., 1990-92, exec. v.p., dir. account mgmt., bd. dirs., 1992-95; exec. v.p. for integrated mktg. comm., mem. exec. com. The Martin Agy., Richmond, 1995-96, exec. v.p., chief adminstrv. officer, 1996—99, pnr. integrated svcs., 2000—. Mem. profit sharing com. The Martin Agy., Richmond, 1993—2003, chair mgmt. com., 1999—2002. Exec. com. bd. trustees Richmond Children's Mus., 1992-99, dir. bd. trustees, 1991-92; area coord. William and Mary Alum Admissions Network, Richmond, 1988-98; co-chair William and Mary Class of 82 Reunion com., 1997; mem. Leadership Metro Richmond Class of 1997; book fair chair Maybeury Elem. Sch., 1997—2000; cookie chair Brownie Troop #292, Girl Scouts U.S., 1996-98, bd. dirs. Commonwealth Girl Scouts Coun., 1999-2002; bd. dirs. Arts Coun. Richmond, 1998-2002; bd. dirs. Leadership Metro Richmond, 1998—2004, mem. exec. com., 1999-2004, chair devel. com., chair mem. programs com., sec. awareness/pub. rels. com., mem. recruitment com.; bd. dirs. YWCA of Richmond, 2001-, v.p., 2003-05, pres. 2005-; mem. Direct Mktg. Agy. Leaders Coun. Recipient Silver Echo award Direct Mktg. Assn., 1991, 94, Gold Echo award, 2003, 05, Richmond Area Marketer of Yr. award Am. Mktg. Assn., 1992, 93, 94, Gold Effie award, 1992, Silver Effie award, 2000, YWCA Outstanding Woman award, 1999. Mem. Greater Richmond C. of C. (mem. exec. com. 2002-04, bd. dirs. 2000—), Willow Oaks Country Club, Farmington Country Club. Avocations: travel, reading, golf. Office: The Martin Agy One Shockoe Plz Richmond VA 23219-4132

JUAN-SAUNDERS, VIVIAN, Native American tribal leader; b. San Xavier, Ariz., Nov. 27, 1959; d. Daniel and Mary Melissa (Fernando) Juan; m. Richard Saunders. AA, Ctrl. Ariz. Jr. Coll., 1977; BA in polit. sci. and secondary edn., Ariz. State U., 1984; MA in Am. Indian studies pub. policy, U. Ariz., 1992. Tutor coord. U. Ariz., Tucson, 1982-88; adminstrv. intern Tohono O'odham Nation, Sells, Ariz., 1984-85; clk. Sears, Phoenix, 1984; youth coord. Tekakwitha Conf., Great Falls, Mont., 1985-86; program coord. U. Ariz., Tucson, 1989-90, asst. dean Native Am. students; head office intergovernmental rels. Salt River-Pima Maricopa Indian cmty.; exec. asst. to chmn. Tohono O'odham Nation; v.p. edn. Tohono O'odham Cmty. Coll.; chairwoman Tohono O'odham Nation, 2003—. Pres. Inter-Tribal Coun. Ariz., 2004. Mem. Nat. Indian Edn. Assn., Nat. Tekakwitha Conf. (chair program com. 1991-92), Am. Indian Alumni Assn. (pres. 1992-93). Avocation: tohono o'odham basket weaving. Office: Tohono O'odham Nation PO Box 837 Sells AZ 85634 Office Phone: 520-383-2028. Office Fax: 520-383-3379.*

JUAREZ, MARETTA LIYA CALIMPONG, social worker; b. Gilroy, Calif., Feb. 14, 1958; d. Sulpicio and Pelagia Lagotom Calimpong; m. Henry Juarez, Mar. 24, 1984. BA, U. Calif., Berkeley, 1979; MSW, San Jose State U., 1983. Lic. clin. social worker; cert. in eye movement desensitization and reprocessing; registered play therapist; cert. alcohol and drug studies. Mgr. Pacific Bell, San Jose, Calif., 1983-84; revenue officer IRS, Salinas, Calif., 1984-85; social worker Santa Cruz (Calif.) County, 1985, Santa Clara County, San Jose, 1985—. Field instr., mem. adj. faculty San Jose State U., 1994-2000, 2005-2006; pvt. cons. 2000—; co-chair Inter-Agy. Coun. of South Santa Clara County. Recipient award Am. Legion, 1972. Mem. NASW, Nat. Coun. on Alcoholism, Assn. Play Therapists, No. Calif. Sandplay Soc., EMDR Network, Sandplay Therapists Am., Calif. Assn. Play Therapy, South County Multidisciplinary Team (co-founder), Calif. Alumni, U. Calif. Club of Santa Clara County. Democrat. Roman Catholic. Avocations: skiing, reading, writing, arts and crafts. E-mail: marettaj@hotmail.com.

JUBINSKA, PATRICIA ANN, ballet instructor, choreographer, artist, anthropologist, archaeologist; b. Norfolk, Va. d. Joseph John and Lucy (Babey) Topping; children: Vanessa Meredith, Courtney Hilary. Student, Md. State Ballet Sch., Sch. Am. Ballet, N.Y.C.; BA, R.I. Coll.; MA, Wesleyan U.; PhD, Union Inst., 1999. Mem. N.Y.C. Ballet; freelance artist Chamber Ballet of L.A., San Antonio Ballet, Md. State Ballet; artistic dir. Blackstone Valley Ballet, Harrisville, RI, 1983, Am. Ballet, Pascoag, RI, 1984—92; asst. artistic dir. Odessa Ukrainian Dancers, Woonsocket, RI, 1991—92; freelance guest artist, 1992—; mem. Mandrivka Dancers of Boston, 1993—; mem. faculty Fine Arts West Warwick Sch., 1995—; mem. faculty Roger Williams U., 2000—. Avocation: equestrian. Home: 110 Gold Mine Rd Chepachet RI 02814 Personal E-mail: pajubinska@aol.com.

JUDAS, ILSE, psychiatrist; b. Frelburg, Germany, May 5, 1924; arrived in U.S., 1938; d. Abraham Judas and Ernestine Kaufmann-Judas; m. Merton Gill (dec.); m. Jeronie Grunes (div.); children: Allen Grunes, Tina Olander. BS, U. Wis., Madison, 1947; MD, U. Wis., 1950. Diplomate Am. Bd. Psychiatry and Neurology, 1957, cert. child psychiatrist 1970, adult psychoanalyst 1965. Asst. chief child psychiatry Michael Reese Hosp., Chgo., 1954—55; assoc. clin. prof. U. Ill., Chgo., 1970—80, asst. clin. prof., 1980—89. Cons. in field. Contbr. articles to profl. jour. Vol. Chgo. Arch. Found., Chgo., 2000—04, John Howard Assn., 2000—. Avocation: knitting.

JUDD, ASHLEY, actress; b. Granada Hills, Calif., Apr. 19, 1968; d. Michael Ciminella and Naomi Judd; m. Dario Franchitti, Dec. 12, 2001. BA in French, U. Ky., 1990. Actor: (films) Kuffs, 1992, Ruby in Paradise, 1993, Smoke, 1995, Heat, 1995, The Passion of Darkly Noon, 1996, A Time To Kill, 1996, Normal Life, 1996, The Locusts, 1997, Kiss the Girls, 1997, Simon Birch, 1998, Eye of the Beholder, 1999, Double Jeopardy, 1999, Where the Heart Is, 2000, Someone Like You, 2001, High Crimes, 2002, Divine Secrets of the Ya-Ya Sisterhood, 2002, Frida, 2002, Twisted, 2004, De-Lovely, 2004, Come Early Mornings, 2006, Bug, 2006; (TV films) Till Death Us Do Part, 1992, Norma Jean & Marilyn, 1996, The Ryan Interview, 2000; (TV series) Sisters, 1991—93, Star Trek: The Next Generation, 1991. Spokesperson Youth Aids Internat. Named One of the 50 Most Beautiful People In The World, People Magazine, 1996. Mem.: Phi Beta Kappa. Office: William Morris Agy 1 William Morris Pl Beverly Hills CA 90212-2775*

JUDD, BARBARA ANN EASTWOOD, financial management professional, union activist; b. Moline, Ill., 1950; d. Albert Floyd and Ruth Eleanor (Smith) Eastwood; m. Blue Klemenz Branley, May 1978 (div. June 1982); 1 child, Chaya Branley; m. Marvin E. Judd, Nov. 1987. BS in Geo-Botany, U. Wash., 1992; MBA, Western Wash. U., 1996. Cert. fin. mgmt., 1998, mgmt. acct., 1998. Personal property tax auditor King County Dept. Assessments, Seattle, 1975-78; program adminstr. Edmonds C.C., Lynnwood, Wash., 1981-85; fixed assets acct. Stimson Lane Wine & Spirits, Woodinville, Wash., 1987-90, fin. analyst, 1990-96; tax analyst, developer SCS/Compute, Bellevue, Wash., 1996-97; sr. fin. analyst NEXTEL, Kirkland, Wash., 1997; tax analyst, developer Microsoft, Redmond, Wash., 1998-2000, enrolled agent, 2002—, fin. cons., 2000—, Eastwood Fin. Svcs., 2000—, Tax Preparation; self-employed. Active Nat. Dem. Party. Recipient Student Achievement award Wall St. Jour., 1996, Cert. Disting. Performance CFM, 1998, Washtech/CWA leadership award, 2000. Mem. NOW, Inst. Mgmt. Accts., Nat. Assn. Enrolled Agents, Calif. Soc. Enrolled Agts., NARAL, Beta Gamma Sigma. E-mail: barb_judd@earthlink.net.

JUDD, DIANE BARBAA, literature and language educator; d. Edward Raymond and Marie Hoffer Flaherty; m. Elliott Lewis Judd, Dec. 26, 1964 (dec.); children: Elizabeth Anne Taylor, James George Taylor. BS in English/Secondary Edn., U. Wis., Milw., 1964. English tchr., mus. dir. Custer HS, Milw., 1965—67; English tchr. Green Bay West HS, Wis., 1968—69; English tchr., forensics coach, yearbook asst. Arrowhead HS, Hartland, Wis., 1978—. Named Tchr. of Yr., Arrowhead HS Nat. Honor Soc., 1985, Arrowhead HS, 1978. Mem.: NEA (assoc.). Roman Catholic. Avocations: reading, travel, drawing. Home: W1087 Lewis Lane #10 Ixonia WI 53036 Office: Arrowhead HS 700 North Avenue Hartland WI 53029 Office Phone: 262-369-3612.

JUDE, CASSANDRA JOY, music educator; d. Bradley Kincaid and Nancy Iness Kiser; m. Lowell Edward Jude, Dec. 13, 1975; 1 child, Joshua Caleb. B of Music Edn., Morehead State U., 1976; M of Music Edn., Eastern Ky. U. Tchr. elem music Clark County Bd. Edn., Winchester, Ky., 1976—. Dir. plays Sch. Ch., Winchester, Ky., 1976—; dir. children's choir Ctrl. Bapt. Ch., 1982—92; tchr. advisory bd. Macmillan McGraw Hill, 1992; dir. choir Ctrl. Bapt. Ch., Winchester, Ky., 1998—2001. Dir. vacation bible sch. Ivory Hill Bapt. Ch., Irvine, Ky., 1976—79; tchr. Sunday sch. Ctrl. Bapt. Ch., Winchester, 1986—88. Grant, Clark County Edn. Found. Mem.: NEA, Ky. Orff Schulerk Assn. (Orff Schulwerk Level I cert.), Am. Orff Schulwerk Assn., Music Edn. Nat. Conf. Baptist. Avocations: reading, antiques, decorating, travel, movies. Home: 419 Skylark Dr Winchester KY 40391 Office: Providence Elem 7076 Old Boonesboro Rd Winchester KY 40391 Office Phone: 859-527-3163.

JUDGE, DOLORES BARBARA, real estate broker; b. Plymouth, Pa. m. Richard James Judge; children: Susan, Nancy, Richard Jr. Student, North Harris County Coll., 1984-85, U. Tex., 1985, Houston Community Coll., 1988-89. Real estate agt. comml. real estate cos. in area, 1981-84; owner D-J Investment Properties, Conroe, Tex., 1984—; pres., ptnr. J&M Mgmt. Co., 1996-97; pres. Judge Mgmt. Co., 1997—. Mem. first adv. bd. First Nat. Title Co., Conroe, 1989-90. Chmn. North Houston Econ. Devel. Showcase, 1990; bd. dirs. Montgomery County Crime Stoppers, Inc., 1993-2003. Mem. Conroe C. of C., Comml. Real Estate Assn. Montgomery County (pres. 1986-87, bd. dirs. 1988), Conroe Art League (exec. bd. 2003-06) Avocations: golf, travel, computers, reading. Office: D-J Investment Properties 306 Tara Park Conroe TX 77302-3756

JUDGE, MARY KATHLEEN, humanities educator; b. Oklahoma City, Sept. 26, 1967; d. William Joseph and Ruby Jean Judge. BA, Marquette U., Milw., 1989. Cert. tchr. H.S. English and humanities Okla., 1990. Camp dir. Cath. Youth Office Archdiocese of Okla., Oklahoma City, 1989; tchr. Putnam City Ctrl. Jr. H.S., 1989—93, Putnam City H.S., 1992—98; project editor Holt, Rinehart and Winston, Austin, Tex., 1998—99; tchr. advanced placement and humanities Putnam City H.S., Oklahoma City, 1999—. Leadership retreat organizer Putnam City H.S., Oklahoma City, 1993—2006; summer writing instr. Living Classrooms Found., Balt., 1993, 95; organizer student European tours Putnam City H.S., Oklahoma City, 1995, 97, 2001, 04; frelance writer Holt Rinehart and Winston, 1998; presenter Edn. Dept. State of Okla., Tulsa, 2006. Bd. mem. St. Charles Ministry Bd., Oklahoma City, 2001—; mem. St. Charles Borromeo Legis. Advocacy, 2004—; vol. educator Holy Family Home, 2003—04; freelance writer Prayer Network, Washington, 2004; leader Just Faith, 2002—03. Named Tchr. of Yr., Putnam City Ctrl. Jr. H.S., 1992—93; grantee, NEH, 2004. Mem.: Okla. Edn. Assn. (del. 2005—), Putnam City Assn. Classroom Tchrs. (bldg. rep. 2002—), St. Vincent de Paul. Roman Catholic. Avocations: reading, travel, writing. Office: Putnam City HS 5300 NW 50th Oklahoma City OK 73122 Office Phone: 405-789-4350.

JUDITZ, LILLIAN MICKLEY, retired communications educator; b. Balt., Sept. 20, 1929; d. John Hoke and Ruth Irene (Haar) Mickley; m. Robert Edward Juditz, Apr. 14, 1951 (dec.); 1 child, Victoria. BA, Gettysburg Coll., Pa., 1950. Cert. tchr. Pa., 1950. Dir. women's program WHGB ABC, Harrisburg, Pa., 1950—58; spokesman WTVN-TV, Columbus, Ohio, 1958—60; commentator WHP-TV-CBS, Harrisburg, 1960—68; educator speech and theater West Shore Sch. Dist., Camp Hill, Pa., 1966—93; ret. Author: The School, 2002. Named one of Women Who CARE, Open Stage Harrisburg, 2001; named to Honor Roll Pa., State of Pa., 1996. Mem.: AAUW, Fgn. Policy Assn. (bd. dirs.), Hist. Harrisburg (Pa.) Assn., Friends Ft. Hunter (pres. 1964—80, bd. dirs.). Democrat. Presbyterian. Avocations: gardening, photography, travel, native American poetry readings. Home: 355 S Sporting Hill Rd Mechanicsburg PA 17050

JUE, SUSAN LYNNE, interior designer; b. Berkeley, Calif., July 7, 1956; d. Howard Lynn and Rosie (Fong) J. AA with honors, Cabrillo Coll., 1977; BA, Calif. Coll. Arts and Crafts, 1979. Interior designer Lucasfilm Ltd., San Anselmo, Calif., 1980-81, Whisler-Patri Architects and Planners, San Francisco, 1982, Barry Reischmann Design Studio, San Francisco, 1983, Kaplan, McLaughlin, Diaz Architects and Planners, San Francisco, 1984-85; Gensler & Assocs., Architects San Francisco, 1985, Hirano Assocs., San Francisco, 1987-88, Clocktower Design, San Ramon, Calif., 1988-89, Reel/Grobman & Assocs., San Francisco, 1989-90; interior designer Primo Angeli Inc., San Francisco, 1990-92, Guillermo Rossello, Architect, Berkeley, Calif., 1992-94, Jean Coblentz & Assocs., San Francisco, 1995, Safeway, Pleasanton, 1996—. Chmn. Children's Discovery Mus. of San Jose, 1996; vol. Diffa - Dining by Design, 2005, Heart N Hand, 2006; house vol. SF Decorator Showcase, 2006. Recipient No. Calif. Home & Garden Design Achievement award 1992. Mem. Internat. Interior Design Assn. (newsletter editor No. Calif. chpt. 1987-88, resource index com. 1987-88, chmn. graphic com. 1987-88, Ronald McDonald House com. 1988-89, chmn. Salvation Army project com. 1990-91, chmn. Bread and Roses project com. 1991, chmn. Ctr. for AIDS, 1991-92, chmn. Maitri AIDS Hospice, 1995-97, chmn. ARIS, 1995-96, guide dogs for blind 1997-98, bd. dirs. 1991—, Cert. of Appreciation 1989, 91-92, 97-99, Cmty. Svc. Program award 1993, 97-98, pres. No. Calif. chpt. 1999-2002, bd. dirs. 2006—, v.p. philanthrophy). Avocations: travel, gardening, reading. Home: 3339 Montevideo Dr San Ramon CA 94583-2606 Office Phone: 925-467-3232.

JUENEMANN, JULIE ANN, psychologist, educator; b. Grosse Pointe, Mich., July 29, 1956; d. Joseph Guy Jr. and Betty Marjorie (Bourg) J.; m. Kurt Edward Stanley, June 21, 1980. BS with honors, Mich. State U., 1978; MA, U. Pa., 1980; PhD, Mich. State U., 1985. Lic. psychologist, Mich. Clin. child psychology intern dept. psychiatry Sch. of Medicine, U. N.C., Chapel Hill, 1983-84, vis. clin. instr. dept. psychiatry, 1985, vis. clin. asst. prof. psychiatry, 1985-86; psychologist, ind. contractor Evergreen Counseling Ctrs.-Ednl. Resources, St. Clair Shores, Mich., 1986-91; sch. psychologist Livonia (Mich.) Pub. Schs., 1989-91, student assistance and family edn. specialist, 1991—; psychologist, ind. contractor Adult-Youth Devel. Svcs., P.C., Farmington, Mich., 1991-93. Member PTA. Fellow NIMH, 1981-83; recipient Martin S. Wallach award U. N.C., 1984. Mem. NASP, Mich. Assn. Sch.

Psychologists, Phi Kappa Phi, Alpha Lambda Delta. Home: 16340 Houghton Dr Livonia MI 48154-1234 Office: Kennedy Elem Sch 14201 Hubbard Livonia MI 48154 Office Phone: 734-744-2745 x 24120. Personal E-mail: juenemann1@sbcglobal.net.

JUFFER, KRISTIN ANN, researcher; b. Omaha, Mar. 2, 1947; d. Theodore Arnold and Adeline (Brinks) J.; m. Gregory Paul Awbrey, Jan. 26, 1985 (div.); 1 child, Michael John. BA, U. Nebr., 1969; MA, U. Iowa, 1979, PhD, 1983. Cert. tchr., supt., Iowa. Tchr., acting curriculum coordinator Cedar Rapids (Iowa) Pub. Schs., 1970-80; asst. prof. then assoc. prof. edn. Western Ill. U., Macomb, 1979-86, asst. dir. bilingual edn., 1979-84, adminstrv. asst. to v.p., 1983-84, researcher, 1984-86; program officer, acad. specialist USIA, Washington, 1985-86, research analyst Voice of Am., 1986-88, dir. audience research, 1988-97; dir. U.S. radio rsch. The Arbitron Co., 1998-99; cons. HealthEducation.com; social sci. rsch. analyst Health Care Fin. Adminstrn., 2000—01; sr. study dir. Temple U., 2001—. Coordinator European Bus. Seminars, Tempe, Ariz., 1980-84; researcher, test devel. Iowa Testing Program, Iowa City, 1982-83; researcher, cons. U. Nebr., Lincoln, 1984-86; v.p. Am. Fedn. Tchrs., Cedar Rapids, 1973. Co-convenor Cedar Rapids Women's Caucus, 1970, Iowa Women's Polit. Caucus, 1972; pres. Iowa Dem. Women's Caucus, 1971. Mem. Soc. Intercultural Tng. Edn. and Research, Soc. Internat. Devel., Nat. Assn. Fgn. Student Affairs, Am. Assn. Pub. Opinion Research, Phi Delta Kappa.

JULANDER, PAULA FOIL, foundation administrator; b. Charlotte, NC, Jan. 21, 1939; d. Paul Baxter and Esther Irene (Earnhardt) Foil; m. Roydon Odell Julander, Dec. 21, 1985; 1 child, Julie McMahan Shipman. Diploma, Presbyn. Sch. Nursing, Charlotte, N.C., 1960; BS magna cum laude, U. Utah, 1984; MS in Nursing Adminstrn., Brigham Young U., 1990. RN, Utah. Nurse various positions, Fla. and S.C., 1960-66; co-founder Am. Laser Corp., 1970-79; tchg. asst. U. Utah, Salt Lake City; exec. dir. Utah Nurses Assn., 1987—89; mem. Utah Ho. of Reps., Salt Lake City, 1989-92; Dem. nominee lt. gov. State of Utah, 1992; minority whip Utah State Senate, Dist. 1, Salt Lake City, 1998—2000; health care/polit. cons. Salt Lake City, 1992—98. Mem. adj. faculty Brigham Young U. Coll. Nursing, 1987—95; bd. dirs. Block Fin. Svcs.; mem. Utah state exec. bd U.S. West Comm., 1993—96; bd. regents Calif. Luth. U., 1994—97; 2003 trustee KUED TV, 2000—03; trustee Intermountain Health Care Hosps., 2000—. Co-author (cookbook): Utah State Fare, 1995. Pres. Utah Nurses Found., 1986—88; mem. Nat. Conf. of State Legis. Com. on Families and Children, 1999—2001, The Coun. of State Govt. Com. on Health and Aging, 1999—2001, Women's Polit.Caucus, Statewide Abortion Task Force, 1990; bd. dirs. Cmty. Nursing Svc. Home Health Plus, 1992—94; mem. Planned Parenthood Assn. Utah, 1994—2991, Utahns for Choice, 1995—2002, trustee Westminster Coll., 1994—2002, HCA-St. Mark's Hosp., 1994—95; elected sen. State of Utah, 1998—2005. Recipient Utah pub. health hero award, 2000, Legislator of Yr. awrd, YWCA, 2001, Jacquelyn Erbin MD award, Planned Parenthood Action Coun., 2002, Disting. Alumni award, Coll. Nursing, U. Utah, 2002, Legislator of Yr. award, Nat. Assn. Social Workers, 2002, Eleanor Roosevelt award, Utah State Dem. Com., 2004, Women's Achievement award, Utah Commn. for Women and Families, 2005, Lucy Beth Rampton award, Utah Women's Dem. Club, 2005, Outstanding Achievement award in Govt. and Polit. Svc., YWCA, 2005, Honored Alumni award, Brigham Young U. Coll. Nursing, 2005; honored by, Govt. Commn. on Women and Families, 2005. Mem.: ANA, Women in Govt. (chair 2004), Nat Orgn. Women Legislators, Utah Nurses Assn. (legis. rep. 1987—88, Lifetime Achievement award), Phi Kappa Phi (Susan Young Gates award 1991), Sigma Theta Tau. Home: 476 B St Salt Lake City UT 84103-2544 Office Phone: 801-887-2337. Personal E-mail: paula@ulcu.com.

JULIA, MARIA C., social worker, educator, consultant; b. San Juan, P.R., Dec. 04; d. Juan and Josefa Julia; m. James Billups, Oct. 11, 1979. BA in Sociology, U. P.R., 1967, MSW, 1969; PhD in Social Work, Ohio State U., 1981. Lic. social worker, Ohio. Evaluator children's day care ctrs. Dept. Social Svcs., PR, 1966; student counselor U. P.R., PR, 1967, intern, 1968, Children's Psychiat. Hosp., Guaynabo, PR, 1969; coord. mental health program Health Dept. San Juan, PR, 1970—78; from adminstrv. assoc. to prof. Ohio State U., Columbus, 1978—89, from asst. prof. to prof. social work, 1989—; instr. social rsch. methodology Interamerican U. P.R., Hato Rey, 1979—80; pvt. practice San Juan, 1981—84. Presenter numerous meetings., confs., symposiums; guest reviewer Jour. Free Inquiry in Creative Sociology, 1998—, Rsch. on Social Work Practice, 1993-94; rsch. cons. GRUPEL Rsch. Network, U. Zambia, 1999—; mem. grant proposals evaluation com. Dept. Edn., Officer Higher Edn., Washington, 1999; mem. comms. com. and program devel. com. Ohio Commn. on Minority Health, Columbus, 1998—; grant proposals reviewer DHHS, Adminstrn. for Children, Youth, and Families, Washington, 1994—, NIMH, Pub. Health Svcs., Washington, 1994, Ohio Commn. on Minority Health, Columbus, 1988—; bd. examiners doctoral program Bharathidasan U., Tamil Nadu, India, 1994—; mem. task force on depression after delivery Ohio Dept. Mental Health, Columbus, 1990-95; trustee Columbus Internat. Program, 1991-95; mem. adv. bd. World Congress on the Family, Columbus, 1990-92; mem. rsch. and edn. com. Ohio Adv. Coun. on Newborn Screening for Hemoglobinopathies, Columbus, 1990-92. Mem. editl. bd. Jour. Social Devel. Issues, 1997—; contbr. articles to profl. jours. including Social Devel. Issues, Devel. in Practice, Internat. Social Work, Jour. Tchg. in Social Work, Jour. Global Awareness, Social Work, Adoption and Fostering, among others. Mem. internat. com. ARC, Columbus, 1989-92; mem. health and edn. com. Ohio Commn. on Spanish Speaking Affairs, Columbus, 1989-91; mem. post-partum adv. coun. Office of Gov., Columbus, 1989-90; mem. rev. com., interprofl. grant proposals Ohio Dept. Health, Columbus, 1989, mem. black infant mortality task force, 1985-89. Mem. NASW, Assn. Faculty and Profl. Women, Assn. for Rsch. on Nonprofit Orgns. and Vol. Action, Colegio de Trabajadores Sociales de P.R., Columbus Internat. Program, Coun. on Social Work Edn., Global Awareness Soc. Internat. (bd. dirs. 1991-94), Internat. Assn. Schs. Social Work, Internat. Coun. on Social Welfare, Inter-Univ. Consortium for Internat. Social Devel., Ohio State U. Alumni Soc. (Disting. Alumna of Yr. 1991), Soc. for Transcultural Family Rels., Women and Children Health Coop., Women in Internat. Devel., Phi Beta Delta, Phi Kappa Phi. Office: Ohio State U Coll Social Work 1947 N College Rd Columbus OH 43210-1123.

JULIAN, FRANCES BLOCH, volunteer; b. Indpls., July 11, 1923; d. Joseph Meyer Bloch, Roslyn Sommers (Liepold) Bloch; m. Jacob William Julian; children: William II, Jonathan, Anne Lennon. BA, Sarah Lawrence Coll., 1945. Founder, bd. mem. Ind. Repertory Theatre, 1970; bd. mem. Internat. Violin Competition, 1990—2000; bd. dirs. Indpls. Symphony Orch., 1979—82; chmn. bd. dirs. Children's Mus., Indpls., 1979—81, hon. life trustee, 1985—2001; bd. dirs. WFYI Channel 20 Pub. TV, Indpls., 1990—97; mem. fin. com. Inpls. Found., 1995—2001; bd. dirs. Athenaeum Found., Indpls., 1997—2001. Jewish. Avocations: travel, bicycling.

JULIAN, ROSE RICH, music educator, director; b. Asheboro, N.C., Sept. 9, 1937; d. Herbert C. and Esther Dennis Rich; m. Cecil Perry Julian, May 30, 1959 (div. Apr. 1977); children: Alan Perry, Keri Dawn Julian Sorensen, Derrick Kyle. AA in Voice, Mars Hill Coll., 1957; BS in Music, East Carolina U., 1959; postgrad., U N.C., 1971—79, Western Carolina U., 1995. Cert. music tchr. N.C. Dir. music USAF Chapel Choir, 1960—71; tchr. Rowan/Salisbury (N.C.) Schs., 1972—79, 1988—; dir. music Thyatira Pres Ch., Salisbury, 1982—88, Coburn U. N.C., Salisbury, 1991—97. Conductor Salisbury Choral Soc., 1993; pianist 1st Bapt. Ch., Salisbury, 1999—; judge Protestant Chapels of Europe, Frankfurt, Germany, 1970. Mem.: AOSA, NAE, Nat. Assn. Tchrs. Singing, Music Educators Assn., Piano Guild. Baptist. Home: 36 Old Farm Rd Salisbury NC 28147

JULIBER, LOIS D., manufacturing executive; b. 1949; m. John Adams. BA, Wellesley Coll.; MBA, Harvard U. Former v.p. Gen. Foods Corp.; from gen. mgr. to pres. Far East/Can. divsn. Colgate-Palmolive Co., N.Y.C., 1988-92, chief tech. officer, 1992-94, pres. Colgate—N.Am. divsn., 1994—97, exec. v.p., chief ops. developed markets, 1997—2000, COO internat. ops., 2000—02, COO L. Am. and growth functions, 2002—, vice chmn., 2004—. Bd. dirs. DuPont Corp., 1995- Bd. trustees Brookdale Found., Wellesley Coll., Girls Inc. Recipient Luminary Award, Corp. Innovator Category, Com. 200, 2002. Mem. Harvard Bus. Sch. Club N.Y. (bd. dirs.) Avocations: tennis, gardening, cooking. Office: Colgate Palmolive Co 300 Park Ave Fl 8 New York NY 10022-7499

JULICH, NANCY C., secondary school educator; d. Robert E. and Fay Presley Conner; m. Marvin Milam Julich, June 4, 1966; children: Marvin Milam Julich, Jr., Rebecca Fay Patterson. BA in English, Music, History, U. Ala., 1966; BSE in English, Music, History, Athens State U., Ala., 1982; MA in Secondary Edn., U. North Ala., 1989; EdS in Secondary Edn., U. Ala., 2003. Tchr. Horizon HS, Decatur. Bd. dirs. Morgan County Adv. Bd. For At Risk Youth, Decatur, Ala.; adj. instr. English Calhoun CC, 1989—. Child abuse prevention specialist PACT, 1984—93; bd. dirs. Decatur (Ala.) Civic Chorus, 1968—80; pres. bd. HANDS, 1992—2000. Mem.: NEA (assoc.), Ala. Million Dollar Band, Decatur Ednl. Assn., Tchrs. English Jr. Coll. (assoc.), Nat. Coll. Tchrs. English (assoc.), Ala. Edn. Assn. (assoc.), Sigma Tau Delta (assoc.), Jr. League. Office: Horizon HS 809 Church St NE Decatur AL 35601 Office Phone: 256-552-3054.

JULIEN, GAIL LESLIE, model, public relations professional; b. Long Island, New York, Apr. 13, 1940; d. David William Syme and Virginia Martha (Burth) Miller; m. Michael Louis Woodman, Sept. 12, 1958 (div.); children: Jho'meyr Renei and Sabrina Michelle; m. Francis Dana Julien, Dec. 24, 1977. Diploma in modeling, Coronet of Calif., 1960; grad., Am. Beauty Finishing Sch., 1961. Playboy bunny Playboy Club, Kansas City, Mo., 1970—72; Gremlin girl AMC, Kansas City, Mo., 1972; Dodge girl Dodge, Kansas City, Mo., 1972—73; owner, pres. Gail Woodman Enterprises Inc., Overland Park, Kans., 1972—76; sales rep. Kansas City Brit. Motors, Lenexa, Kans., 1976—78; dir. pub. rels., mktg. Downtown Air Ctr., Kansas City, Mo., 1978—80; dir. pub. rels., media rels. Bretney Corp., Kansas City, Mo., 1980—82; v.p. Nuwalters Co., Overland Park, Kans., 1983—84; regional mgr. aviation Multi Svc. Corp., Overland Park, Kans., 1984—2004. Rep. Nat. Bus. Aircraft Assn., 1984—2004, Can. Bus. Aircraft Assn., 1984-2004, Nat. Aircraft Transp. Assn., 1991, 93, 95, 98, Abbotsford Internat. Airshow, 1994-2004, Schedulars and Dispatchers Conv., 1994-2004, Internat. Operators Conf., 1984-1994, Women in Aviation, 1998-2004, Helicopter Assn. Internat., 1994-2003; internat. v.p. Women in Corp. Aviation, 2003-04, Schedulers and Dispatchers Support Com., 1999-2000. Author: Physician's Nutritional Guide, numerous poems, self improvement and modeling course; former editor WCA Newsletter; contbr. poetry to Internat. Libr. Poetry, 2006. Vol. Live On Stage '88 (AIDS), Santa Ana, Calif., 1988, St. Joseph Hosp., Kansas City; v.p. Young Dems., Midland, Mich., 1960; active Northshore Animal League, Christian Children's Fund, L.A. Mission, former bd. of dir., City of Hope, L.A., 1991; bd. dir., fundraiser Make A Wish of Tri Counties. Recipient Outstanding Sales Achievement award Brit. Leyland, 1976-77. Mem. Am. Bus. Womens Assn. Avocations: art, writing, swimming, acting. Home: 28129 Peacock Ridge Dr Apt 312 Palos Verdes Peninsula CA 90275-7121 Office Phone: 310-994-3094.

JULIEN, JOELLA L., educator; b. Omaha, Apr. 20, 1942; d. Joseph T. and Ella M. Haynes; m. Percy L. Julien, Nov. 22; children: Charles, Joel. BA, Creighton U., 1964; MS, Calif. State U., Hayward, 1974; JD, U. San Francisco, San Francisco, 1984. Adminstr., counselor to tchr. Oakland (Calif.) Unified Schs., 1971-87; chief negotiator SCCOE, San Jose, Calif., 1987-90; adj. instr. Chapman U., Orange, Calif., 1992; instr. Contra Costa Coll. Bd. dirs. San Antonio Youth Project, Oakland, 1973-76. Pub. mem. commn. for revision of rules of profl. responsibility State Bar Calif., 1989-90, 2003—; mem. assembly subcom. on ednl. reform State of Calif., 1978-80, mem. fin. aid policy study group, 1979, mem. adv. group on fin. aid problems, 1979-80. Named Disting. Educator Marcus Foster Edn. Inst., 1980. Mem. Nat. Assn. Ednl. Negotiators, Calif. Pers. and Guidance Assn., Leadership Am., Ednl. Advancement Found. (regional dir.), Alpha Kappa Alpha. Avocations: travel, reading, spoon collector, micro bear collecting.

JULIEN, KRISTIE, mathematics educator, department chairman; BA, Beloit Coll., Wis., 1990; MS, Marquette U., Milw., 1998. Cert. secondary sch. tchr. Colo. Tchr. St. Vrain Valley Schs., Longmont, Colo., 1999—, Skyline HS, Longmont, 2006—. Mem.: NEA (assoc.), Colo. Edn. Assn. (assoc.). Office: Skyline HS 600 E Mt View Ave Longmont CO 80501 Personal E-mail: cooogrrr@copper.net.

JULIFS, SANDRA JEAN, community action agency executive; b. Jersey City, July 12, 1939; d. Roy Howard and Irma Margrete (Barkhausen) Walters; m. Harold William Julifs, July 22, 1961; children: David Howard, Steven William. BA, U. Mary Wash., Fredericksburg, Va., 1961; postgrad., U. Minn., St. Paul, 1962-63, Mankato State Coll., Minn., 1963. Cert. comty. action profl. Tchr. St. James Pub. Schs., Minn., 1961-62; substitute tchr. Sleepy Eye Pub. Schs., Minn., 1963-67, home bound tutor Minn., 1967; lay reader, rater U. Wis., Stevens Point, 1968; co-founder Family Planning Service Portage County, Stevens Point, 1970-72; family planning dir. Tri-County Opportunities Coun., Rock Falls, Ill., 1971-77, energy programs coord., 1977-78, planner, EEO officer, 1978-83, pres., chief exec. officer, 1983—. Sec. Ill. Ventures for Comty. Action Springfield, 1983-91, bd. dirs. 1991-94, 96—. Active Nat. Cmty. Action Found., Washington, 1987—; bd. dirs. Twin Cities Homeless Coalition, 1989-96, Rockfalls Cmty. Devel. Corp.; adv. coun. Sauk Valley Coll. Human Svcs., 1990-99, Inst. for Social and Econ. Devel., 1992-95; mem. Sauk Valley Coll. Workforce Devel. Coun., 1999—; mem. Whiteside County Overall Econ. Devel. Coun., 1990-99; cons. com. No. Ill. Synod, Evang. Luth. Ch. Am., 1993-99, churchwide assembly del., 1995; mem. Statewide Rural Poverty Conf. Com., 1996-97; mem. Ill. State Microenterprise Initiative; cmty. svcs. adv. com. Ill. Dept. Commerce and Econ. Opportunity, 1998—, chair, 2003-; mem. Rock Falls Cmty. Devel. Coun. Bd., 2005-, mem. exec. com., 2005-. Recipient Appreciation award Western Ill. Agy. on Aging, 1980-81, Spl. Recognition award Ill. Head Start and Day Care Assn., Recognition award Ill. Cmty. Action Fund, 1984, Recognition award Ill. Ventures for Cmty. Action, 1996, Women of Achievement award YWCA, 2005 Mem. Whiteside County Welfare Assn., Lee County Welfare Assn. (sec.-treas. 1983-84), Nat. Cmty. Action Assn., Cmty. Action Partnership, Ill. Cmty. Action Assn. (com. chair 1985-88, dir. exec. com. 1986-95, treas. 1988, 89, sec. 1989, 90, v.p. 1991-93, pres. 1993-95, dir. 2000-03, Recognition award 1985-95, 2000-03). Lutheran. Avocations: travel, reading. Office: Tri-County Opportunities Coun PO Box 610 Rock Falls IL 61071-0610 Office Phone: 815-625-7830. Personal E-mail: hwjulifs@essex1.com. Business E-Mail: sjulifs@wmccinc.com.

JULMY, CAMILLE P., real estate company executive; Degree in Bus. Adminstrn., Coll. St. Michel, Fribourg, Switzerland; Degree in Econs., U. Fribourg. With Fidinam, Lugano, Switzerland, 1973—74, sr. analyst Toronto, Canada, 1974—77, v.p. Chgo., 1977—78; vice chmn., co-founder US Equities REalty, Chgo., 1978—. Mem. exec. bd. UNICEF; bd. dirs. Roosevelt U., Pomerleau Constrn. Co., Montreal, Canada. Mem.: Swiss-Am. C. of C., Ctrl. Mich. Ave. Assn. (sec., mem. exec. bd.), Greater North Mich. Ave. Assn. (sec., mem. exec. bd.), Execs. Club Chgo. Office: US Equities Realty Ste 400 20 N Michigan Ave Chicago IL 60602

JUMONVILLE, FLORENCE M., librarian, historian; b. New Orleans; d. Warren P. and Florence E. (Seither) J. BA, U. New Orleans, 1971, MEd, 1976, MA, 1988, PhD, 1997; MS, La. State U., 1972. Libr. Hist. New Orleans Collection, 1972-74, 78-82, head libr., 1982-96; libr. Belle Chasse (La.) State Sch., 1974-78; head La. and spl. collections Earl K. Long Libr., U. New Orleans, 1997—. Adj. instr. libr. sci. La. State U., Baton Rouge, 1994, 96. Author: Bibliography of New Orleans Imprints, 1764-1864, 1989, Louisiana History: An Annotated Bibliography, 2002; editor: LLA Bull., 1990—95; co-editor: A History of the Louisiana Library Association, 1925-2000, 2003; contbr. articles to profl. jours. Adv. bd. Ethel and Herman L. Midlo Ctr. for N.O. Studies, La. Hist. Records; bd. dirs. Theatre Libr. Assn. Recipient Lucy B. Foote award La. Libr. Assn., 1985, Fannie Simon award Spl. Librs. Assn. Mus., Arts and Humanities Divsn., 1997, Essae M. Culver Disting. Svc. award, La. Libr. Assn., 2005. Mem. ALA, Am. Antiquarian Soc., Am. Hist. Assn., Am. Printing History Assn., Assn. Moving Image Archivists, Bibliog. Soc. Am., Soc. for the History of Authorship, Reading and Pub., La. Hist. Assn., La. Libr. Assn. (Essae M. Culver Disting. Svc. award 2005), Beta Phi Mu, Phi Delta Kappa, Kappa Delta Pi. Avocations: needlecrafts, classic movies, reading. Office: Earl K Long Libr Univ New Orleans Lakefront New Orleans LA 70148-0001 Office Phone: 504-280-7275. Business E-Mail: fjumonvi@uno.edu.

JUN, HEESOON, psychology professor; b. Seoul, Korea (South); d. Yongduck Jun and Whangwool Kang; children: Gabriel J Aust, Eliot P Aust. PhD, U. of Wash., 1979—82. Washington State Licensed Psychologist Health Dept., State of Wash., 1987. Psychology prof. Evergreen State Coll., Olympia, Wash., 1996—. Part-time pvt. practice and consulting, Olympia, Wash. Recipient Exceptional Faculty award, Centalia Coll., 1996, NISOD Excellence award, U. of Tex. at Austin, 1996; Bilingual fellowship, U.S. Dept. of Edn., 1980—82. Mem.: APA, Deschutes Psychol. Assn. Office: Evergreen State Coll 2700 Pkwy Olympia WA 98505 Office Phone: 360-867-6855.

JUNG, ANDREA, cosmetics company executive; b. Toronto, Sept. 18, 1958; m. Michael Gould, 1993 (div.); 2 children. BA magna cum laude in English Lit., Princeton U., 1979. With Bloomingdale's; sr. v.p., gen. mdse. mgr. J.W. Robinson; sr. v.p. gen. mdse. I. Magnin, San Francisco, 1987—91; exec. v.p. women's merchandsing Neiman Marcus, 1991—92; cons. Avon Products, Inc., NYC, 1993, pres. product mktg. group, 1994—96, pres. global mktg., 1996—97, exec. v.p., pres. global mktg. & new bus., 1997—98, COO, 1998—99, pres., 1998—2001, CEO, 1999—, chmn., 2001—. Chmn. Cosmetic, Toiletry & Fragrance Found., 2001—05; bd. dirs. GE Co., 1998—, Avon Products Inc., 1998—, Cosmetic Exec. Women. Sale Corp., Donna Karan Internat., Catalyst; mem. internat. advisory bd. Solomon Smith Barney. Mem. bd. trustees NY Presbyn. Hosp. Named one of the 50 Most Powerful Women in Bus., FORTUNE mag., 1998—, Most Powerful Women, Forbes mag., 2005, Top 50 Women to Watch, Wall St. Jour., 2005, 50 Most Powerful Women in Bus., Fortune mag., 2006. Achievements include fluent in Chinese (Mandarin). Office: Avon Products Inc 1345 Ave Americas New York NY 10105-0302*

JUNG, BETTY CHIN, epidemiologist, educator, nurse; b. Bklyn., Nov. 28, 1948; d. Han You and Bo Ngan (Moy) Chin; m. Lee Jung, Oct. 1, 1972; children: Daniel, Stephanie. AA, King's Coll., Briarcliff Manor, NY, 1968; BS, Columbia U., N.Y.C., 1971; MPH, So. Conn. State U., New Haven, 1993. RN, Conn., Miss., N.Y.; cert. health edn. specialist; credentialed health info. web site rater; notary pub., Conn., 2004. Adminstrv. asst. Columbia U., N.Y.C., 1968-69; practical nurse Babies Hosp., N.Y.C., 1969-70, charge nurse, 1974-76; staff nurse Columbia-Presbyn. Hosp., N.Y.C., 1971-73; sch. nurse Nassau County Sch. System, Long Island, NY, 1984-85; grad. asst. So. Conn. State U., New Haven, 1991-92; coop. edn. intern Conn. Dept. Health Svcs., Hartford, 1991-92; intern North Ctrl. Dist. Health Dept., Enfield, Conn., 1992; epidemiologist Conn. Dept. Pub. Health, Hartford, Conn., 1992-98, health program assoc., 1998-2001, cardiovascular epidemiologist, 2003—05, cardiovascular and diabetes epidemiologist, 2005—; staff nurse Quinnipiac Coll. Student Health Svcs., 1998; mem. multicultural adv. coun. Conn. Dept. Children and Families, assoc. rsch. analyst, 2001—03. Instr. Albertus Magnus Coll., 1995—96; health columnist Baldwin Newcomers Club, NY, 1977—78; coord. Dept. Pub. Health and Svcs./Conn. EPI Info. Network, Hartford, 1994—2001; mem. Nat. Lead Info. Ctr. Spkrs. Bur., 1997—98; vol. scientist Sci.-By-Mail, 1997—98; mem. Nat. Safety Coun. Environ. Health Ctr. Spkrs. Referral Bur., 1998—2001; mem. affirmative action employee adv. com. Conn. Dept. Pub. Health, 1998—2001, mem. genetics planning com., 2004—; mem. Permanent Commn. Status of Women Talent Network, 1996—, chair news subcom., editor affirmative action newsletter, 2001; apptd. mem. multicultural adv. coun. Conn. Dept. Children and Families, 2002—03; pilot reviewer CDC Pub. Health Tng. Network, 2002—; assoc. NIH, 2004—; mem. functions workgroup EPI; dir.'s coun. pub. reps. NIH, 2004—; mem. CDC CVH Inst. planning com. Conn. Dept. Pub. Health, 2005—, lead cardiovasc. epidemiology work group, 2005—, mem. genetics edn. work group, 2006—, mem. genetics edn. nurse edn. subcom., 2006—; numerous positions So. Conn. State U., 1991—, adj. prof., 1998—, apptd. CDC cardiovascular health and bus. work group, 2005—; cons. in field; mem. grants and contracts working group Status of Women Talent Network, 2005, mem. cardiovascular state plan exec. com., 2005—; active CDC Heart Disease and Stroke Prevention Program, 2003—. Mem. editl. bd.: Data Quality, 1994—98, mem. manuscript rev. bd.: Jour. Clin. Outcomes Mgmt., 1995—, Pub. Health Reports, 1997—98; contbg. editor: Episource, A Guide to Resources in Epidemiology, 1998—99; editor/web pub.: SCSU Pub. Health E-News Bull., 2000—01, Public Health E-news, 2001—, Public Health Jobs Electronic Newsletter, 2000—, book proposal reviewer: Jossey Bass Pubs., 2003—; contbr. articles to profl. jours. Vol. nurse health educator, coord. Chinatown's First Ann. Health Fair, 1971-72; treas. Tenant Assn., Bronx, N.Y., 1976-77; pre-confirmation tchr. Bethlehem Luth. Ch., Baldwin, N.Y., 1981-85. Grantee, USPHS, 1992—98, Fed. HUD, 1995—98, U.S. Preventive Health and Health Svcs., 1998, CDC Cardiovasc. Health Program, 2003—, CDC Diabetes Prevention and Control Program, 2005—, others; Merit scholar, Kings Coll., 1968, Columbia U. scholar, 1968—69, Women's Florist Assn. scholar, 1968, Bessie Lee Gambrill scholar, So. Alumni Assn., 1992, block grantee, Maternal Child Health, 1998—2001, Adult Blood Lead Epidemiology and Surveillance Program grantee, CDC/Nat. Inst. Occupl. Safety and Health, 1992—98. Fellow: Soc. for Pub. Health Edn.; mem.: APHA (health care reform activist network, peer assistance the model stds. project), Pub. Health Expertise Network of Mentors (program dir. 2002—), Internat. Assn. Webmasters and Designers, Boston Mus. Sci., Nat. Acad. Sci. (mentor career planning ctr. beginning scientists & engrs. 1997—98), Columbia U. Sch. Nursing Alumni Assn. (survey cons. 1994—95), Internat. Assn. IT Trainers (assoc.), So. Conn. State U. Alumni Assn. (founder pub. health chpt. 1994, interim pres, then pres. 1994—98, founder, coord. pub. health alumni mentor program 1994—2002, chair coms. 1994—, numerous other positions 1994—, editor MPH Alumni Record 1995—, founder, dir., coord. pub. health alumni spkrs. bur. 1997—, founder, program dir. pub. health expertise network of mentors 2002—, Alumni Appreciation award 1998), Conn. Pub. Health Assn., Nat. Lead Info. Ctr. Spkrs. Bur., Conn. State and Territorial Epidemiologists (alternate cons. 1996—, co-leader Healthy People 2010 1999—2001, lead cardiovasc. disease 2002—), Am. Statis. Assn. (OSPA media experts list 1997—). Avocations: reading, writing, research, web development and design, bicycling. Home: 25 Driftwood Ln Guilford CT 06437-1929 Office: Conn Dept Pub Health 410 Capitol Ave Hartford CT 06106 Office Phone: 860-509-7711. Personal E-mail: bettycjung@yahoo.com.

JUNG, DORIS, soprano; b. Centralia, Ill., Jan. 5, 1924; d. John Jay and May (Middleton) Crittenden; m. Felix Popper, Nov. 3, 1951; 1 son, Richard Dorian. Student, U. Ill., Mannes Coll. Music, Vienna Acad. Performing Arts; student of Julius Cohen, student of Emma Zador, student of Luise Helletsgruber, student of Winifred Cecil. Voice tchr., NYC, 1970—. Debut as Vitellia in: Clemenza di Tito, Zurich (Switzerland) Opera, 1955, other appearances with Hamburg State Opera, Munich State Opera, Vienna State Opera, Royal Opera Copenhagen, Royal Opera Stockholm, Marseille and Strasbourg, France, Naples (Italy) Opera Co., Catania (Italy) Opera Co., NYC Opera, Met. Opera; soloist: Wagner concert conducted by Leopold Stokowski, 1971; with Syracuse (NY) Symphony, 1981; translator Birgit Nilsson Autobiography, 2007. Home: 40 W 84th St New York NY 10024-4749 Office Phone: 212-873-3147.

JUNG, NICOLE P, psychologist; b. Miss. PsyD, Fla. Inst. of Tech. Licensed Psychologist Fla. Pvt. practitioner, Orlando, Fla., 2003—. Bd. dirs. Fla. Psychol. Assn., Fla., 2005. Recipient Key Psychologist of Yr., Fla. Psychol. Assn., 2005. Mem.: APA. Office: Nicole P Jung PsyD PA 16877 E Colonial Dr #410 Orlando FL 32820 Office Phone: 407-568-6541.

JUNGBLUTH, CONNIE CARLSON, banker; b. Cheyenne, Wyo., June 20, 1955; d. Charles Marion and Janice Yvonne (Keldsen) Carlson; m. Kirk E. Jungbluth, Feb. 5, 1977; children: Tyler, Ryan. BS, Colo. State U., 1976. CPA,

Colo., Ariz. Sr. acct. Rhode Scripter & Assoc., Boulder, Colo., 1977-81; mng. acct. Arthur Young, Denver, 1981-85; asst. v.p. Dain Bosworth, Denver, 1985-87; v.p. George K. Baum & Co., Denver, 1987-91; acct. Ariz. Luth. Acad., 1994-95; sr. tax acct. Ernst & Young, LLP, Phoenix, 1995-96; mat. tax mgr. personal wealth mgmt. RSM McGladrey, Inc., Phoenix, 1996-2000; mgr. pvt. client svcs. Arthur Andersen, Phoenix, 2000—01; sr. v.p. Bank of Am. Pvt. Bank, Phoenix, 2002—06; dir. Citigroup Pvt. Bank, 2006—. Mem. adv. bd. Ariz. Cmty. Found., 2002—, Jewish Cmty. Found., 2002—, Ariz. State U. Found., 2004—05, Children's Hosp., Phoenix, 2004—, chmn., prof. adv. bd., 2006—. Active Denver Estate Planning Coun., 1981-85, Ctrl. Ariz. Estate Planning Coun., 1997-98, S. Nev. Estate Planning Coun., 2003-4; organizer Little People Am., Rocky Mountain Med. Clinic and Symposium, Denver, 1986; mem. adv. bd. Children's Home Health, Denver, 1986-89, chmn. profl. adv. bd., 2006—; fin. adv. bd. Gail Shoettler for State Treas., Denver, 1986; campaign chmn. Kathi Williams for Colo. State Legislature, 1986; mem. Sch. dist. 12 Colo. Edn. Found. Bd., 1991, Napa Sch. Dist. Elem. Site com., 1992-94; apptd. Ariz. Gov.'s Coun. Devel. Disabilities, 1998-99, chmn. planning com., 1998-99; mem. profl. adv. bd., editor Charitable Giving Guide, Ariz. Cmty. Found., 2002—. Named one of 50 to watch, Denver mag., 1988. Mem. AICPA, Fin. Planning Assn., Colo. Soc. CPAs (strategic planning com. 1987-89, instr. bank 1983, trustee 1984-87, pres. bd. trustees 1986-87, bd. dir. 1987-89, chmn. career edn. com. 1982-83, pub. svc. award 1985-87), Little People of Am., Colo. Mcpl. Bond Dealers, Ariz. Herb Assn., Metro North C. of C. (bd. dir. 1987-90), Denver City Club (bd. dir. 1987-88), Phi Beta Phi. Avocations: faith, horticulture, philanthropy, gourmet cooking. Office: Bank of America Pvt Bank 201 E Washington Ste 2300 Phoenix AZ 85004

JUNGER, PATRICIA CAROL, nurse; d. James John and Rose (Menno) Colello; m. Sept. 19, 1964 (div. 1990); children: Kevin, Steven and Paul (twins). AAS, Erie C.C., 1976. RN, N.Y. Staff nurse med. tchg. fl. Buffalo Gen. Hosp., 1977—. Mem. unit practice coun. Buffalo (N.Y.) Gen. Hosp., 2003—. Past religious edn. tchr. St. Barnabas Roman Cath. Ch. Recipient Peer Recognition award from co-workers, 1997. Mem. Comm. Workers of Am. Democrat. Roman Catholic. Avocations: piano, gardening, reading, crafts, music.

JUNKER, MIRIAM M., music educator; d. Rudolph A. and Elizabeth L. Hagen; m. Eugene William Junker, May 12, 1972; children: Jonathon David, Alexis Rebecca. BS, U. Minn., Mpls., 1968, MA, 1971. Tchr. instrumental music Benilde-St. Margaret's H.S., Mpls., 1971—75, Chaska Sr. H.S., Minn., 1975—. Choir dir. Macalester-Plymouth United Ch., St. Paul, 1971—81. Profl. Devel. in Music fellowship, Minn. Dept. of Edn., 1982. Mem.: Chaska Edn. Assn. (bldg. rep. 2005—), Minn. Band Dirs. Assn., Nat. Band Assn., Music Educator's Nat. Conf. Office Phone: 952-556-7159.

JUNKERMAN, DENISE MARIE, secondary school educator; d. George and Erma Junkerman. BS in Edn. and Secondary English, Kutztown U., Pa., 1997; postgrad., Coll. Notre Dame, Balt., 1997—98, Colegio de Mayor Santa Maria, Madrid, 2000, Keystone Coll., Pa., 2005. Cert. secondary English Commonwealth of Pa., 1997, secondary edn. English Md. State Dept. Edn., 1998, spl. edn. Md. State Dept. Edn., 1997, field hockey coach Nat. Coll. Athletic Assn., 2001. English tchr. grade 8 SE Mid. Sch., Balt., 1997—2001; head field hockey and lacrosse coach Carver Ctr. for Arts and Tech., Towson, Md., 1998—2001; English tchr. grade 12 Prep. Charter Sch., Phila., 2001—; head field hockey coach Phila. U., 2001—04. Nominee Divsn. II So. Region Coach of Yr., Nat. Collegate Athletic Assn. and Nat. Field Hockey Coaches Assn., 2002—03; named Coach of Yr., Phila. U., 2002—03. Mem.: Nat. Coun. Tchrs. English. Independent. Roman Catholic. Office: Preparatory Charter High School 1928 Point Breeze Ave Philadelphia PA 19145 Office Phone: 215-334-6144. Personal E-mail: denisejunkerman@hotmail.com.

JUNZ, HELEN B., economist; d. Samson and Dobra Bachner. BA, PhD, U. Amsterdam; MA, New Sch. Social Rsch. Acting chief consumer price sect. Nat. Indsl. Conf. Bd., N.Y.C., 1953-58; research officer Nat. Inst. Econ. and Social Research, London, 1958-60; economist Bur. Econ. Analysis, Dept. Commerce, Washington, 1960-62; adviser div. internat. fin. bd. govs. Fed. Res. System, Washington, 1962-77; dep. asst. sec. Office of Asst. Sec. for Internat. Affairs, Dept. Treasury, Washington, 1977-79; v.p., sr. advisor 1st Nat. Bank Chgo., 1979-80; v.p. Townsend Greenspan & Co., Inc., N.Y.C., 1980-82; sr. advisor European dept. IMF, 1982-87, dep. dir. exch. and trade rels. dept., 1987-89, spl. trade rep., dir. Geneva office, 1989-94; dir. gold econs. svc. World Gold Coun., Geneva, Switzerland, 1994-96; pres. HBJ Internat., London, 1996—. Adviser OECD, Paris, 1967-69; sr. internat. economist Council of Econ. Advisers, The White House, Washington, 1975-77. Author: Where did all the money go?, 2002; contbr. articles to profl. jours. Mem. Am. Econ. Assn., Coun. Fgn. Rels., Cosmos Club, Reform Club. Office: HBJ Intnat 39 Chalcot Sq London NW1 8YP England E-mail: hbjunz@planet.nl.

JUODVALKIS, EGLE (EGLĖ JUODVALKĖ), writer; b. East Chgo., Ind., Jan. 28, 1950; d. Antanas and Ona (Norkutė) J.; m. Henryk Skwarczynski, Sept. 2, 1989. BA, U. Chgo., 1973. Sr. editor Radio Free Europe/Radio Liberty, Inc., Munich, 1976-95; self-employed writer, poet, 1995—. Author: (poetry) If You Touch Me, 1972, Who Has the Ring?, 1983, The Necklace of Mnemosine, 1996, (prose) Sugar Mountain or The Adventures of a Lithuanian Diabetic in America and Other Exotic Places, 2000, (bilingual poetry and CD of author's reading) Veidrodis ir tuštuma/The Mirror and the Void, 2002 (Book of Yr. award Emigré Lithuanian Writer's Orgn., 2003). Mem. Santara-Šviesa, Korp! Neo-Lithuania, Internat. Pen Lithuanian Ctr., Lithuanian Writers Union. Avocation: touring Greece.

JURAN, SYLVIA LOUISE, retired editor; b. Chgo. d. Joseph Moses and Sadie (Shapiro) J. BA, U. Minn.; MA, Columbia U., 1960; PhD, Harvard U., 1975. Project editor Macmillan Pub. Co., N.Y.C., 1981-91; editor Ralph Appelbaum Assocs. Inc., N.Y.C., 1991—2005; ret. Faculty The New Sch., N.Y.C., 1980-82. Project editor: Ency. of the Holocaust, 1990 (Dartmouth medal ALA, 1990), Ency. of the Third Reich, 1991; editor scripts for mus. exhbns.; contbr. articles to profl. jours. Nat. Def. fgn. lang. fellow, 1960-61, 62-63. Mem. Harvard Club of N.Y.C., Harvard Grad. Sch. Alumni Assn. (N.Y. exec. com. 1984—).

JURASKA, JANICE MARIE, psychology professor; b. Berwyn, Ill., Feb. 9, 1949; BA, Lawrence U., 1971; MA, U. Ill., 1975; PhD, U. Colo., 1977. NIMH postdoctoral fellow psychology dept. U. Ill., Champaign, 1978-80; from asst. prof. to assoc. prof. psychology dept. Ind. U., Bloomington, 1980-85; from assoc. prof. to prof. dept. psychology U. Ill., Champaign, 1986-94, assoc. prof., 1986-94, prof., 1994—. Co-editor: Developmental Neuropsychobiology, 1986. Grantee NIH, NIMH, NSF, John D. and Catherine T. MacArthur Found. Fellow Am. Psychol. Soc.; mem. Soc. for Neurosci., Soc. Behavioral Neuroendocrinology, Internat. Behavioral Neurosci. Soc., Phi Beta Kappa. Office: Univ Ill Dept Psychology 603 E Daniel St Champaign IL 61820-6232 E-mail: jjuraska@uiuc.edu.

JURGELSKI, ANNETTE ELIZABETH, academic administrator; b. Newark, Nov. 12, 1930; d. Edward Charles and Elizabeth (Dick) Lanquist; m. William Jurgelski, Sept. 4, 1954; children: Susan E., William Martin. BA in Journalism, NYU, NYC, 1955; MA in Tchg., Duke U., Durham, NC, 1970. Cert. tchr. NC. Bus. corr. Book of the Month Club, Inc., NYC, 1948—55; office mgr. New Brunswick Sci. Co., NJ, 1955—57; instr. English U. PR, Mayaguez, 1957—59; jr. HS tchr. Durham Pub. Schs., NC, 1967—68; mgr. grants program Duke U., 1973—79; office mgr., vocat. instr. NCAET, Chapel Hill, NC, 1979—82; office mgr., adminstrv. asst. U. NC, Chapel Hill, 1982—89; tchr. English and Spanish Beaufort County Schs., Aurora, NC, 1989—90; libr. asst. Duke U., 1990—92, project mgr., Ctr. Clinic Health policy rsch., 1992—. Contbr. articles to profl. publs. Mem. Orange County Commn. for Environ., NC, 1990—2005; pres. PTA Thrift Shop, 1970—72; vol. ESL tutor, 1993—. Mem.: AAUW (pub. rels. worker), NC Sierra Club (state sec. 1990—95, mem. exec. com. 2000—05, chpt. svc. award 1993, 2006). Democrat. Avocations: reading, swimming, travel. Home: 3211 Oak Knob Ct Hillsborough NC 27278 Office: Duke U Ctr Clin Health Policy Rsch 2200 W Main St Durham NC 27705

JURGENS, JULIE GRAHAM, mathematics professor; b. Washta, Iowa, Mar. 8, 1950; d. Albert Harm and Thelma Ann (Johnson) Haenfler; m. Dennis Dean Graham, Mar. 16, 1969 (div. Oct. 17, 1988); children: Tracy Ann Graham-Lester, Tricia Jean Graham-Banta; m. David Dallas Jurgens, Apr. 17, 1998. Undergrad., Morningside Coll., Sioux City, Iowa, 1968—69; BA in Math. Edn./Phys. Edn., Wayne State Coll., 1969—72; MS, Marycrest Coll., Davenport, Iowa, 1985; PhD, U. Iowa, 1997. Prof. math. and computer sci. Marycrest U., 1985—97; dept. chair math., sci., and tech. Flagler Coll., St. Augustine, Fla., 1997—. Mem.: AAUP, Fla. Coun. Tchrs. Math., Fla. Assn. Computer in Edn., Nat. Coun. Tchrs. Math., Math. Assn. Am., Phi Delta Kappa. Home: 138 Creekside Rd Satsuma FL 32189 Office: Flagler Coll Saint Augustine FL 32085 Office Phone: 904-819-6267.

JURGENSEN, MONSERRATE, clinical nurse, consultant; b. Guyanailla, P.R., Oct. 25, 1945; d. Francisco and Felicita (Feliciano) Muniz; m. Timothy J. Jurgensen, Dec. 1, 1978; children: Timothy J. Jr., Jeremy J. Diploma, Presbyn. Hosp. Sch. Nursing, San Juan, P.R., 1967; BSN, Barry U., 1990; postgrad., Webster U., 1992—. RN, Fla. Surg. unit and surg. ICU staff nurse U. Hosp., PR, 1967-69; commd. 2d lt. USAF, 1969, advanced through grades to maj., 1986; pediat. unit staff nurse USAF Hosp., Sheppard AFB, Tex., 1969-70, orthopedic and psychiat. unit staff nurse Cam Ranh Bay, Vietnam, 1970-71, staff nurse obstetrics unit Torrejon AFB, Spain, 1971-74, obstetrics head nurse K.I. Sawyer AFB, Mich., 1974-78, staff nurse obstetrics unit, head nurse pediatric clinic Langley AFB, Va., 1978-81; med.-surg. nurse USAFR, Langley AFB, Va., 1984-86, staff nurse Primary Care Clinics Norfolk, Va., 1985-86; staff nurse Cigna HMO, Miami, Fla., 1986-87; staff nurse long-term care unit VA Hosp., Miami, 1988-90, med.-surg. nurse psychiat. unit, 1990-91; quality control nurse, infection control Immunization Clinic, Duke Field, Fla., 1989-91; evening-night supr., mgr. med.-surg. unit same day surgery Army Hosp., Ft. Jackson, SC, 1991-94; mgr. same day surgery med.-surg. unit Reynolds Army Cmty. Hosp., Ft. Sill, Okla., 1994—96; registered nurse Primary Care Clinics Vet. Adminstrn., 1997—. Mem. Soc. Presbyn. Hosp. Sch. Nursing. Republican. Avocations: tennis, cooking, sewing. Office: US Army VA Adminstn Tulsa Outpatient Clinic Tulsa OK 74145

JURGENSEN LACIVITA, MARY R., lawyer; b. Danville, Ky., July 6, 1972; BA cum laude, Boston U., 1994; JD cum laude, Suffolk U. Law Sch., 2000. Bar: Mass. 2000. Law clk. Mass. Probate and Family Ct., 2000—01; assoc. family law Prince, Lobel, Glovsky & Tye LLP, 2001—05; counsel Boston Law Collaborative, LLC, 2005—. Office: Boston Law Collaborative LLC Ste 1600 99 Summer St Boston MA 02110 Office Phone: 617-439-4700. Office Fax: 617-439-0700. E-mail: mjurgensen@bostonlawcollaborative.com.*

JURGUTIS, DANGUOLE, artist; b. Lithuania, Jan. 16, 1935; came to U.S., 1949; d. Jonas and Ona Seputa; m. George Jurgutis; children: Asta, Paulius, Darius (dec.). BS, Wayne State U., 1956; student, Oakland C.C., 1972-73, U. London, 1976. Exhibited in shows at Detroit Art Inst., 1997, Port Huron Art Mus., Lincoln Ctr., N.Y.C., Mich. State Fine Arts, Ellen Sharp Mus., Jackson, Miss., Chgo., Toronto, 1998; artist-in-residence Farmington Hills, City of Farmington, Mich., others; pvt. collections in U.S., Can., Lithuania, Eng., Japan. Mem. Farmington Artists Club (v.p. 1995-97, program chair 1993-95), Mich. Watercolor Soc.

JURKA, EDITH MILA, psychiatrist, researcher; b. NYC, Dec. 4, 1915; d. Charles Anton and Edith Dorothy (Schevcik) J. BA, Smith Coll., Northampton, Mass., 1936; postgrad., Charles U., Prague, Czechoslovakia, 1936-38; MD, Yale U., New Haven, Conn., 1944. Diplomate Am. Bd. Psychiatry and Neurology. Intern in children's med. svc. Bellevue Hosp., N.Y.C., 1944-45, asst. alienist, 1947-49; rotating intern Gallinger Hosp., Washington, 1945-46; intern N.Y. State Psychiat. Inst., N.Y.C., 1946-47; asst. psychiatrist Mt. Sinai Hosp., N.Y.C., 1949-51; pvt. practice N.Y.C., 1949—; asst. psychiatrist Roosevelt Hosp., N.Y.C., 1954-57; chief psychiatrist Pleasantville (N.Y.) Cottage Sch., 1961-74. Bd. dirs. intuition network Inst. Noetic Scis.; founder Wind Song Inst. Sec. Jane Coffin Childs Fund, 1938—41. Fellow Am. Orthopsychiat. Assn.; mem. Am. Psychiat. Assn., N.Y. Coun. Child and Adolescent Psychiatry, N.Y. County Med. Soc., N.Y. State Med. Soc. (psychiat. medicine com.), Westchester Psychiat. Soc. Avocations: architecture, parapsychology, travel, gardening, theater. Home: 16 Apple Bee Farm Ln Croton On Hudson NY 10520-3612 Office: 116 E 66th St New York NY 10021-6547 Office Phone: 212-737-0591.

JURKIEWICZ, MARGARET JOY GOMMEL, retired secondary school educator; b. Indpls., Sept. 5, 1920; d. Dewey Ezra and Joy Agnes (Edie) Gommel; m. Walter Stephen Jurkiewicz, Jan. 1, 1942; children: Mary Margaret, Dewey John, Walter Stephen Jr., Hugh Louis. BS, Ind. U., 1941; postgrad., U. Minn., 1942-43, Butler U., 1950-51, U. Cin., 1958-60, Ind. U., 1971-72, Ball State U., 1974-75. Cert. secondary tchr., Ind., Ohio. Tchr. home econ. Plymouth HS, Ind., 1941-42, Indpls. Pub. Sch., Ind., 1949-57, Mt. Confort-Hancock Co. Sch., Mt. Comfort, Ind., 1957-58, Cin. Pub. sch., 1958-61; tchr. 6th grade Plymouth Sch. corp., Ind., 1961-63; tchr. home econ. and art Argos Cmty. Sch., Ind., 1963-67; tchr. home econ. Penn-Harris-Madison Sch., Mishawaka, Ind., 1967-83; tchr. chpt. I South Bend Sch. Corp., Ind., 1983-85; vol. tchr. art various sch., Ind., 1985—, various sch., Mich., 1985—96, various sch., Ill., 1985-96. Author newsletter and booklet Polish Cultural Soc., 1979—. Bd. dir. Area Agy. on Aging Coun., Plymouth, Ind., 1987-94, Garden Cts. Sr. Housing, Plymouth, 1989—; mem. legis. com. Five County Area Agy. on Aging, 1994--; vol. tchr. sch., libr., children's mus. and sr. ctr., 1985—. Mem.: AARP (editor newsletter Marshall County chpt. 1993—), AAUW (pres., chair various coms.), Plymouth Pub. Libr. Friends, Marshall County Ret. Tchr. (pres. 1993—95), Ind. Assn. Family and Consumer Sci., Am. Assn. Family and Consumer Sci., Tippecanoe Audubon Soc., Ind. Polish Cultural Soc. (v.p., chair various coms.). Methodist. Avocations: gardening, camping, travel, football games, sewing. Home: 11570 9th A Rd Plymouth IN 46563-9581

JURKIEWICZ, MARY LOUISE, elementary school educator; b. Wadsworth, Ohio, May 30, 1947; d. William Nicholas and Margaret Rose (Cattin) Lieberth; m. Eugene John Jurkiewicz, Apr. 10, 1971; children: William Nicholas, Emily Johanna. BA, Marygrove Coll., Detroit, 1969; MAT in Reading, Oakland U., Rochester, Mich., 1972. Cert. permanent tchg. cert. Mich. Tchr. primary edn. Kensington Acad., Bloomfield Hills, Mich., 1969—74; tchr. 1st grade Detroit Country Day Sch., Bloomfield Hills, 1981—. Master tchr., team leader 1st grade Detroit Country Day Sch., Bloomfield Hills, 1986—2003. Sec. St. Owen Parish Coun., Bloomfield Hills, 1978—79; tchr. religious edn. St. Owen Ch., Bloomfield Hills, 1979—81. Recipient Longevity award, Mich. Coun. Tchrs. Math., 1995, Mich. Top Tchr. award, Met. Woman Mag., 1997. Mem.: Ind. Sch. Assn. of Cen. States (sch. rep. 1982—94), Assn. Ind. Mich. Schs. (sch. rep. 1982—94, pres. 1990—92). Roman Catholic. Avocations: gardening, travel, reading. Home: 6489 Wing Lake Rd Bloomfield Hills MI 48301 Office: Detroit Country Day Sch 3003 W Maple Rd Bloomfield Hills MI 48301

JURKOWSKI, KAREN EVANS, music educator; d. K. Gerald and Lois R. Evans; m. John P. Jurkowski, Apr. 3, 1993; children: Elizabeth, Erin. MusB in Edn., Crane Sch. Music, Potsdam, NY, 1983; MusM in Edn., VanderCook Coll. Music, Chgo., 1989. Cert. tchr. NY State Edn. Dept, 1989. Tchr. music Springville Griffith Inst. Ctrl. Sch. Dist., NY, 1984—. Pres. Lake Effect Harmony Chorus, Boston, 1990—92. Musician: Winter Olympics, 1980. Bd. dirs. Springville Players, NY, 1986—90; elder First Presbyn. Ch., 2006—06. Mem.: Music Educators Nat. Conf. (treas. student chpt. 1981—82), NY State Music Tchrs. Assn. (sec., treas. student chpt. 1982—83). Presbyterian. Avocations: gardening, knitting, sewing. Office: Springville Elementary Schools 283 North Street Springville NY 14141 Office Phone: 716-592-3261. E-mail: kjurkowski@springvillegi.org.

JURMAN-SHULMAN, CLAUDIA LYNNE, sales executive; b. Huntington, N.Y., Sept. 3, 1956; m. Robert (div.); 1 child, Jeremy Edward. BA, Pace U., 1991; MA, NY Inst. Tech., 2006. Cert. computer networking operation Katharine Gibbs AOS, 2004. Co-owner, mgr. Mercedes Airport Svc., NY, 1986-90; with Coach Realtors, Huntington, N.Y., 1994-96; sales assoc. UPS, Farmingdale, N.Y., 1997-99. Owner Computerized Color and Image Consultations for Men and Women, Fishkill, N.Y., Centerport N.Y., 1990— Author: A Surrender to the Man, 2005. Deacon Huntington Old First Ch., 1996-99; bd. dirs. Ketekomoke, Huntington, N.Y., 2003-05, chpt. historian, 2004-05. Recipient Westchester C. of C. Secretarial Success award, Pace U. White Plains, 1980, WPRPGA, 1981. Avocations: piano, poetry, weight training. E-mail: clshulmm@alumni.pace.edu.

JUST, GEMMA RIVOLI, retired advertising executive; b. N.Y.C., Nov. 29, 1921; d. Philip and Brigida (Consolo) Rivoli; m. Victor Just, Jan. 29, 1955. BA, Hunter Coll., N.Y.C., 1943. Copy group head McCann Erickson, N.Y.C., 1958-62; copy supr. Morse Internat., N.Y.C., 1962-67; v.p., dir. creative svcs. Deltakos divsn. J. Walter Thompson, N.Y.C., 1967-75; v.p., copy dir. Sudler & Hennessey divsn. Young & Rubicam, N.Y.C., 1980-87, sr. v.p., assoc. creative dir. copy, 1987-88, ret., 1989. Mem. Episcopal Ch. Women of Ch. of Incarnation, N.Y.C., also ch. altar guild pres. and acolyte. Recipient Aesculapius awards Modern Medicine mag., 1980-88; named Best Writer, Art Dirs. Club N.Y., 1979, Best Writer Young & Rubicam, 1981. Mem. Coun. Comms. Soc., Pharm. Advt. Coun., Am. Med. Writers Assn. (exec. com. 1973). Home: 155 E 38th St Apt 5D New York NY 10016-2663

JUST, JULIA BARNETT, newspaper editor; b. Chgo., Feb. 23, 1961; d. Ward Swift and Jean Ramsay (Bower) J.; m. Tom Reiss, May 19, 1996; 1 child, Lucy Madeline. BA, Columbia U., 1983. Editl. asst. The New Yorker, NYC, 1983-90; asst. editor NY Rev. Books, NYC, 1991-93; staff editor op-ed page NY Times, NYC, 1993-95, story editor N.Y. Times Mag., 1996-97, dep. editor N.Y. Times Book Rev., 1998—. Mem. N.Y. Book Critics Cir., 1990-97. Office: Book Review NY Times 229 W 43d St New York NY 10036*

JUSTICE, YVONNE HORTON, health facility administrator; b. Columbus, Ohio, Dec. 30; d. John Henry Horton and Alma Odessa Wright; children: Johnny Calloway, Javell Calloway. Assoc. Social Svcs., Columbus State C.C., 1977; BA, Ohio Dominican Coll., 1993; MS, U. Dayton, 1997. Cert. alcohol and drug counselor, chem. dependency counselor, master addition counselor, criminal justice specialist. Residential drug counselor CompDrug, Columbus, 1980; EEO counselor Air NG, Rickenbacker, Ohio, 1981-85; benefits coord. BancOhio, Columbus, 1983-85; adminstrv. asst. UNCF, Columbus, 1985; mgr. Kobacker Co., Columbus, 1987-89; therapist, case mgr. CompDrug, Inc., Columbus, 1993-96; Africentric program coord. Ohio State U. Hosps. East, Columbus, 1998-99; assoc. dir. clin. svcs. Project Linden, 1999—. Mentor Ohio Dominican Coll.; mem. adv. bd. MADD, Columbus, 1992, Holy Rosary, Columbus, 1990-93, United Way Project Diver, Columbus, 1997-98, Netcare, Inc., Columbus, 1997-98, Epilepsy Found., Columbus, 1991-93, Mothers Against Crack, 1984-87; vol. HIV instr. ARC, Columbus, 1991-93. Mem. Nat. Assn. Alcoholism and Drug Abuse Counselors, Nat. Bd. Addiction, Nat. Assn. Forensic Counselors. Baptist. Avocations: weightlifting, swimming, water aerobics, skating, reading. Home: 4793 Gale Way Groveport OH 43125-8933

JUSTICE-MOORE, KATHLEEN E., lawyer; m. Steven Moore. JD, Vanderbilt U. Sch. of Law, 1991. Atty., employment law and litigation, Calif., 1991—2001; rsch. dir. Gordon & Betty Moore Found., 2001—03, trustee, 2003—. Mem. Los Altos Hills Public Ed. Comm., 2004—. Avocations: scuba diving, snorkeling, kayaking, hiking, skiing. Office: Los Altos Hills Public Ed Comm 26379 Fremont Rd Los Altos CA 94022*

KABRICH, JEANINE RENEE, broadcaster, educator; b. Concord, Calif., May 29, 1963; d. Robert Nicolas and Judith Lynn (Johnson) Kabrich; m. Douglas Michael Curry, June 15, 1985 (div. Sept. 1987). BS in Mass Comm/Broadcast Journalism, Emerson Coll., Boston, 1989. Cert. broadcast specialist Def. Info. Sch. News reporter, writer, part-time anchor KDOC-TV Channel 56, Anaheim, Calif., 1990; creator, prodr., host, reporter, editor The Coachella Valley news mag. Palmer Cablevision, Palm Desert, Calif., 1992; news and airborne traffic reporter KFMB AM/FM/TV, San Diego, 1992-93; comm. and journalism instr. Palomar Coll. and Grossmont Coll., San Diego, 1993-96; helicopter traffic reporter KTTV-TV Fox 11, L.A., 1997-98; news anchor, news reproter KABC-AM 790, KNX AM 1070, L.A., 1996-98; So. Calif. media rep., media specialist team leader U.S. Census Bur. Census 2000 campaign, L.A., 1999—. Part-time actress, spokeswoman Burkett Talent Agy., L.A. Weekend co-host Ask the Builder, KSDO-AM, San Diego; prodr. radio comml. Served with U.S. Army, 1982-88. Mem. Radio and TV News Dirs. Assn., Soc. Profl. Journalists, Broacast Edn. Assn. Republican. Roman Catholic. Avocations: cooking, exercise, reading, teaching.

KACHALSKY, ELLEN, social worker; b. Bklyn., Feb. 20, 1954; d. Hyman Dave and Estelle Muriel (Schneider) K.; m. Lloyd Paul Silberman, June 12, 1977; children: Mindy Rachel, David Justin. BA in Psychology, SUNY, Binghamton, 1976; MSW, Adelphi U., 1979. Lic. MSW clin., Mich. Counselor Adelphi Social Work Clinic, Legal Aid Soc. Nassau County, Garden City, NY, 1978, West Oakland Cmty. Mental Health Ctr., 1979; social worker oncology unit and OICU Harper Hosp., Wayne State U. Sch. Medicine, Detroit, 1979-82; sr. med. social worker Henry Ford Hosp., Sinai Hosp., Detroit, 1983-84, Providence Hosp., Southfield, Mich., 1982-84; med. social worker St. Mary Hosp., Livonia, Mich., 1984-95; resident svc. coord. Jewish Fedn. Apts., Oak Park, Mich., 1995-97; sr. med. social worker Henry Ford Hosp., Hemophilia Treatment Ctr., Outpatient Hematology Oncology, Detroit, 1997—. Program vice chair Med. Social Wk. Coun., 1982-84, chair, 1984-86; social wk. cons. specializing in med. and health care; social wk. cons. for transitional care unit Straith Hosp., Southfield, Mich. Mem. Nat. Assn. Social Workers, Soc. for Social Work Leadership in Health Care (Mich. chpt. treas. 2001-). Office: Henry Ford Hosp K-13 Hem-One 2799 W Grand Blvd Detroit MI 48202-2689 Office Phone: 313-916-0470. Business E-Mail: ekachal1@hfhs.org.

KACHARABA, NICKOLETTE ATHANASIA, vocalist; b. East Meadow, N.Y., Feb. 20, 1976; d. Athanasios and Angela Glikos; m. Brian Joseph Kacharaba, Aug. 27, 2000. AAS in Music, Nassau C.C., Garden City, N.Y., 1997; BA in Music, SUNY, Stony Brook, 1999; MS in Music Edn., LI U., Brookville, N.Y., 2004. Cert. tchr. State of N.Y., 2004. Pvt. vocal tchr., Farmingdale, NY, 1995—2005; music tchr. k-6 St. Benedict Joseph Labre Sch., Queens, NY, 2001—02; music tchr. Islip Pub. Schs., NY, 2004—. Exec. dir., dir., musical dir. Kids for Kids Prodns. Inc., Port Jefferson, NY, 2001—02; drama dir., unit leader C.W. Post Summer Day Camp, Brookville, NY, 2002—05; asst. choral dir. USDAN, NY, 2004; music dir. Divsn. Ave. H.S., Levittown, NY, 2001—04. Singer: (chorus) ACDA 2 Year Coll. Nat. Honor Choir. Mem.: Spl. Edn. Parent Tchr. Assn. (assoc.), Parent Tchr. Assn. Islip (assoc.), Nat. Assocartion of Music Edn. (life), N.Y. State Sch. Music Assn. (life), Tri-M Music Honor Soc. (hon.). Baptist. Avocations: musicals and performance, cooking, digital photography, bowling. Office: Islip Public Schools 215 Main St Islip NY 11751 Office Phone: 631-859-2350. E-mail: nkacharaba@islipufsd.org.

KACHMAN, FRANCES GUIDUCCI, artist; b. Peckville, Pa., May 9, 1949; d. Joesph Guiducci and Eva Piccholi Born; m. James P. Kachman (separated); children: Darren, Dean. Student, Coll. of Art, Detroit, 1959, student, 1962; study with, Edgar Yeager, 1973—80, John Sanden, N.Y., Russer Ketter, Ctr. for Creative Studies, Joseph Maniscalco, Janice Tremp, Marie Larson. Exhibitions include Std. Fed. Bank, Scarab Club, Detroit Athletic Club, Detroit Med. Ctr., Represented in permanent collections Palms (Mich.) Mus., Dr. Larry Lloyd, Dr. Michael Busuittio, Olhand Lake Sem.,

Orchard Lake, Bon Secours Hosp., Mich., Fla., Hawaii, Jamaica, Bermuda, Mex., Eng., France, exhibited in group shows at Grosse Pointe Art Exhibit. Recipient numerous art awards. Mem.: Lakeside Pallet Club (past bd. dir.), Scarab Club (past bd. dir.). Home: 22901 Lakeshore Saint Clair Shores MI 48080

KACHUR, BETTY RAE, elementary school educator; b. Lorain, Ohio, June 12, 1930; d. John and Elizabeth (Stanko) Kachur. BS in Edn., Kent State U., 1963; MEd, U. Ariz., 1971. Cert. tchr., in reading. Tchr. Lorain City Schs., 1961-94. Bd. dirs. Habitat for Humanity Lorain County, 1997—2001, Lorain Pub. Libr., Ohio Friends LIbrs.; treas. Lorain Downtown Ministerial Assn.; profl. storyteller Northeastern Ohio Western Res. Assn. for Preservation and Perpetuation of Storytellers. Mem.: AAUW (social com., scholarship com. 1999), Daniel T. Gardner Reading Assn. (pres. 1978—79, treas. 1988—94), Internat. Reading Assn. (by-laws com. Ohio Coun.). Mem. United Ch. Of Christ. Avocations: reading, writing, quilting, travel.

KACINES, JULIETTE ROSETTE, behavior therapist; b. NYC, Nov. 26, 1943; d. Stanley and Agnes Dobeck; m. Charles James Kacines, Sept. 5, 1964; children: Steven, Jeffery, Jennifer. A.Mental Health Tech., Purdue U., West Lafayette, Ind., 1980; A.Supervision, Ind. U., Ft. Wayne, 1983, BS, 1986; MA in Marriage and Family Counseling, Adler Sch. Profl. Psychology, Chgo., 1996. Recipient Recognition award, Park Ctr., Ft. Wayne, 1996, 1997—2002. Mem.: Smithsonian Instn., Purdue U. Alumni Assn., Nature Conservancy, Am. Counseling Assn., Ind. U. Alumni Assn. (life). Avocations: gardening, reading, interior decorating.

KACZMAREK, JANE, actress; b. Milw., Dec. 21, 1955; d. Edward and Evelyn Kaczmarek; m. Bradley Whitford, Aug. 15, 1992; 3 children. BFA in Theatre, U. Wis.; MFA, Yale Sch. Drama, 1982. Actor: (TV series) Hometown, 1985, Equal Justice, 1990—91, Big Wave Dave's, 1993, Felicity, 1999—2000, Malcolm in the Middle, 2000— (nominated for 3 Golden Globe awards for best performance actress tv series, nominated for 4 Emmy awards for outstanding lead actress comedy series, Am. Comedy award, Family Friendly award, 2 Individual Achievement in a Comedy awards, TV Critics Assn., nominated best actress quality comedy, Viewers for Quality TV), Help Me Help You, 2006, (guest appearances) Touched by an Angel, Picket Fences, L.A. Law, Hollywood Division, St. Elsewhere, Party of Five, Frasier, Cybill, The Practice,; (TV films) All's Fair, 1989, Apollo 11, 1996, Educating Mom, 1996, Jenifer, 2001, The Deception, Boys Will Be Boys, I'll Take Manhattan, Something About Amelia, The Christmas Story, The Three Kings; (films) The Chamber, 1996, The Spittin' Image, 1997, Pleasantville, 1998, Wildly Available, 1999, Vice Versa, Uncommon Valor, D.O.A., The Heavenly Kid, Falling in Love; (plays, Broadway) Lost in Yonkers; (plays) Kindertransport, Raised in Captivity, Wasp, Escape from Happiness, Eve's Diary, Pride and Prejudice, The Legends of Oedipus, Loose Ends, Ice Cream/Hot Fudge, Better Living, Hands of Its Enemy. Co-founder charity Clothes off our Back.*

KADAR, KARIN PATRICIA, librarian; b. Oil City, Pa., May 30, 1951; d. Michael Joseph and Bette Lee (Painter) Kadar; divorced; 1 child, Michael L. BS, Clarion U., 1973; MLS, U. Pitts., 1975; postgrad., U. S.C. Lic. instrnl. II in libr. sci. and elem. edn., pub. libr. lic. Substitute tchr. McKeesport (Pa.) Area Schs., 1973, elem. sch. libr., 1973-75, 3d grade tchr., 1975-78, elem. sch. libr., 1978-81; adj. prof. Pa. State U., McKeesport, 1988; periodicals libr. Seton Hill Coll., Greensburg, Pa., 1986-89; dir. Penn Twp. Pub. Libr., Level Green, Pa., 1989-90; grade sch. libr. substitute St. Agnes Sch., North Huntington, Pa., 1992; mid. sch. libr. substitute Belle Vernon (Pa.) Area Sch. Dist., 1993-95; dir. West Newton (Pa.) Pub. Libr., 1993-95, Highland Cmty. Libr., Richland, Pa., 1996; libr. Ridgeland (S.C.) Elem. Sch., 1996-98; spl. orders coord. Barnes and Noble, Hilton Head Island, SC, 1998-99; mgr. Bluffton (S.C.) Cmty. Libr., 1998-99; media specialist Jasper (S.C.) County H.S., 1999—2001, dist. libr./ media specialist coord., 1999—; sch. tech. coord. West Hardeeville Sch., 2001—, media specialist, 2002—. Mem. consumer appeals bd. Ford Motor Co., 1989-92, coord. Sch. Dist. Libr. Media Svcs., 2000—; staff writer Current Diversions. Author: (booklet) Sammy the Smokeless Dragon, 1976; mem. adv. panel Pa. mag., 1992—94, staff writer Current Diversions, 1999—2000, mem. editl. bd. SCASL Media Messenger, mem. editl. bd. and SC Reading List com. Media Messenger. Panelist Scan Trak Shoppers, 1984—, Nat. Family Opinion, 1984—; vol. Am. Cancer Soc., 1969-94, pub. edn. chmn., 1974-80, cancer prevention study II chmn., 1982-88, pub. affairs chmn., 1984-86, residential area crusade chmn., 1984-85. Named Vol. of Yr. Am. Cancer Soc. Mon Youch Unit, 1983-84; recipient Crusade award Am. Cancer Soc., Mon Yough unit, 1985-86. Mem. ALA, Pa. Libr. Assn., Parent-Tchr. Guild, Pa. State Edn. Assn., Low Country Reading Assn. (pres.), S.C. Assn. Sch. Librs. (regional rep. Jasper County, writer and mem. editl. bd. Messenger), Westmoreland County Hist. Soc., McKeesport Coll. Club, Heritage Hist. Assn. (Hilton Head, S.C.). Avocations: writing, collecting books, genealogy. Office: West Hardeeville Sch Hwy 46 Hardeeville SC 29927 Office Phone: 843-717-1251. E-mail: akawindy@hargray.com.

KADEN, ELLEN ORAN, lawyer, consumer products company executive; b. NYC, Oct. 1, 1951; m. Lewis Kaden; 2 children. AB, Cornell U., 1972; MA, U. Chgo., 1973; JD, Columbia U., 1977. Bar: N.Y., 1978. Law clerk U.S. Dist. Ct. (so. dist.) N.Y., 1977-78; asst. prof. Columbia U. Sch. Law, 1978-82, assoc. prof., 1982-84; exec. v.p., gen. counsel, sec. CBS Inc., NYC, 1991-98; sr. v.p. law and govt. affairs Campbell Soup Co., Camden, NJ, 1988—. Reporter jud. coun. 2nd Cir. Adv. Comm. on Planning for Dist. Cts., 1979-81; assoc. Cravath, Swaine & Moore, 1981-86. Trustee Columbia U. Office: Campbell Soup Co One Campbell Pl Camden NJ 08103

KADIS, AVERIL JORDAN, retired librarian; b. Lucknow, Uttar Pradesh, India, Feb. 28, 1934; arrived in U.S., 1954; d. Ivan Averil and Satyavati Chitambar Jordan; m. Phillip Michael Kadis, Apr. 23, 1966. BA, Isabella Thoburn Coll., Lucknow, 1953; postgrad., U. Lucknow, 1954; MLS, We. Res. U., 1955; postgrad., Syracuse U., 1956. Young adult svc. asst. Cleve. Pub. Libr., 1956—57, young adult svc. libr., 1958—61; libr. Embassy of India, Washington, 1957—58; dir. libr. svc. Isabella Thoburn Coll., Lucknow, 1961—62; ref. libr. Enoch Pratt Free Libr., Balt., 1962—63, adminstv. asst. audio-visual dept., 1963—64, adult svc. libr., 1964—68, pub. rels. asst., 1968—82, dir. pub. rels. divsn., 1983—98; ret. Rights and permissions officer Literary Estate of H.L. Mencken, Balt., 1980—. Contbr. articles to profl. jours. Adv. bd. Friends of Sheridan Libr., Johns Hopkins U., Balt., 1998—99. Recipient Pub. Design award, Libr. Pub. Rels. Coun., 1995, 1996. Mem.: AAUW, Amnesty Internat., Nat. Orgn. for Women. Avocations: travel, writing. Home: 1734 P St NW Washington DC 20036-1300

KADISH, KATHERINE, artist, art educator; BFA, Carnegie Mellon U., Pitts., 1961; MA, U. Chgo., 1966. Co-dir. art gallery Harpur Coll. SUNY, Binghamton, 1963-66; curator, slide and print collection dept. art and art history, SUNY Binghamton, 1963-66, vis. asst. prof. dept. art and art history, 1974-82; master tchr. N.Y. State Summer Sch. Visual Arts, 1979-82; asst. prof. art Broome C.C., Binghamton, 1982-84; vis. lectr. art dept. Ohio State U., Columbus, 1985-86; artist-in-residence Montpelier Cultural Arts Ctr., Laurel, Md., 1986; adj. assoc. prof. dept. art and art history Wright State U., Dayton, Ohio, 1987-88; vis. asst. prof. dept. art Wittenberg U., Springfield, Ohio, 1989-90, vis. assoc. prof., Wright State U., 1992; vis. artist Arrowmont Sch. Arts and Crafts, Gatlinburg, Tenn., 1992—, Cleve. Inst. Art, 1994. One-woman shows include Denison U., Granville, Ohio, 1975, Hobart Coll., Geneva, N.Y., 1977, Arnot Art Mus., Elmira, NY, 1978, SUNY Buffalo, 1980, Va. Ctr. Creative Arts, Sweet Briar, 1981, Univ. Art Gallery SUNY Binghamton, 1981, SUNY Plattsburgh, 1981, Atlantic Gallery, N.Y.C., 1983, Wheaton Coll. Watson Gallery, Norton, Mass., 1984, NW La. U., Natchitoches, 1985, Leigh Gallery, London, 1985, 1987, 1989, Springfield (Ohio) Art Mus., 1986, Malton Gallery, Cin., 1986, 1988, Montpelier Cultural Arts Ctr., Laurel, Md., 1986, Nanjing (People's Republic of China) Arts Coll., 1987, Brevard Art Mus., Melbourne, Fla., 1990, Clemson (S.C.) U. Gallery, 1992, Roberta Kuhn Gallery, Columbus, Ohio, 1992, Yvonne Rapp Gallery, Louisville, 1992, Marta Hewett Gallery, Cin., 1994, Dayton (Ohio) Art Inst., 1994, Walsh Gallery, Chgo., 1995, Interchurch Ctr. Gallery, N.Y.C., 1995, Zella Gallery, London, 1996, Va. Mus.Fine Arts, Richmond, 1999, Univ. Va., Charlottesville, 1999, 2001, Fassbender Gallery, Chgo., 1999, Agama Gallery, NYC, 2000, 2002, Rawls Mus. Art, Courtland, Va., 2001, Deborah Davis Fine Art, Hudson, N.Y., 2002, Purdue U., West Lafayette, Ind., 2002, Washington State U., Pullman, 2003, Sun Gallery, Seoul, Korea, 2004, Gallery V, Columbus, Ohio, 2004, U. Cin. Galleries, 2005, Ruschman Gallery, Indpls., 2005, U. So. Miss. Mus., 2006, Wilmington Coll., Ohio, 2006, Mus. U. So. Miss., Hattiesburg, Miss., 2006, Wilmington Coll., Ohio, 2006, exhibited in group shows at Libr. Congress, Washington, 1973, Galerie de l'Esprit, Montreal, Que., Can., 1975, Evans Gallery, Toronto, Ont., Can., 1975, Pleiades Gallery, N.Y.C., 1976, Okla. Art Ctr., Okla. City, 1976, Empire State Plz., Albany, 1977, SUNY, Albany, 1981, N.Y. State Mus., Albany, 1981, Nat. Mus. Am. Art, Washington, D.C., traveling exhbn. to 13 states, 1981, U. N.D., Grand Forks, 1983, Whitney Mus. Am. Art/Downtown, N.Y.C., 1983, Quinton Green Fine Arts, London, 1984, Hopkins Gallery Ohio State U., Columbus, 1986, Cadogan Contemporary Gallery, London, 1990, Ohio Arts Coun. Invitational, Tokyo, 1991, Oxford (Eng.) Gallery, 1993, Anita Shapolsky Gallery, N.Y.C., 1995, Nat. Mus. Women in Arts, Washington, 1996, Boston Print Makers N. Am. Print Biennial, 1999, Bowling Green U., 2001, Korea Internat. Contemporary Print Exhbn., Seoul, 2003, Zimmerli Mus. Rutgers U., New Brunswick, N.J., 2003, Westmoreland Mus Am. Art, Greensburg, Pa., 2003, Cheryl Hazan Gallery, NYC, 2003, U. Alta. Mus., Can., 2004, Phila. Mus. Art, 2004, U. Cin., 2005, Anita Shapolsky Gallery, N.Y.C., 2006, Deborah Davis Fine Art, N.Y., 2006, Huntington Mus. Art, W.Va., 2006, Carnegie Mellon U., Pa., 2006, many others, Carnegie Mellon U., Pitts., Pa., 2006, Deborah Davis Fine Art, Huddson, N.Y., 2006, Represented in permanent collections Broome C.C., Binghamton, N.Y., Charter Oaks Bank, Columbus, 1st Federal of Boston, Cin., Fries and Fries Corp., GTE Corp., Indpls., Herbert F. Johnson Mus. Cornell U., Ithaca, N.Y., Marine Midland Bank, Binghamton, Merrill Lynch, Metel Corp., Cin., N.Y. State Coun. Arts, N.Y.C., Va. Ctr. Creative Arts, Brit. Mus., London, Victoria & Albert Mus, N.Y.C. Pub. Libr., Nat Mus. Women in Arts, Washington, Libr. of Congress, Pfizer Corp., N.Y.C., NYU. Recipient six awards, Ohio Arts Coun., 1st Annual Artist-in- Residency award Montpelier Cultural Arts Ctr., 1986, Creative Artists Pub. Svc. Program grantee N.Y. State Coun. on Arts, 1973, Travel grantee Unied Bd. Christian Higher Edn. in Asia, 1986; Residency fellow Yaddo, 1977, 78, 80, Tyrone Guthrie Ctr. for Arts, Ireland, 1988, Va. Ctr. Creative Arts, 1978-82, 87, 89, 95, 98, 2002, Vt. Studio Colony, 1990, Ludwig Vogelstein Found., 1990. Home: 1062 State Route 343 Yellow Springs OH 45387-9799 also: 222 W 14th St # 13A New York NY 10011-7200 Personal E-mail: kkadish123@aol.com.

KADOHATA, CYNTHIA, writer; b. Chgo. 1 adopted child. BA in Journalism, Univ. So. Calif. Author: (books) The Floating World, 1989, In the Heart of the Valley of Love, 1992, The Glass Mountains, 2002, (children's books) Kira Kira, 2004 (John Newbery Medal, 2005). Avocation: travel. Mailing: Atheneum Simon & Schuster 1230 Ave Of The Americas New York NY 10020 E-mail: cynthia@kira-kira.us.

KADOHIRO, JANE K., nurse, educator, consultant; b. Lima, Ohio, July 20, 1947; d. Howard M. and Betty J. (Johoske) Keller; m. Howard M. Kadohiro, Dec. 27, 1969; children: Christopher, Jennifer. BA in Sociology and Edn., U. Hawaii, Manoa, 1969; BS in Nursing, U. Hawaii, Honolulu, 1977, MPH, 1990; MS, U. Hawaii, 1994, DrPH, 1999; postgrad., Yale U., 2001. Staff nurse Children's Hosp., Honolulu, 1977-78; staff pub. health nurse Hawaii State Dept. Health, Honolulu, 1978-80, coord. hypertension and diabetes, 1980-85, projects adminstr., 1985-89, chief chronic diseases, 1989-91; office mgr. Hanalei Trends, Honolulu, 1985-89; clin. nurse specialist Queen's Med. Ctr., Honolulu, 1991-94; cons. Aiea, Hawaii, 1991—; nurse investigator Honolulu Heart Program, 1991-95, instr., 1991—98, asst. prof., 1998—, U. Hawaii at Manoa, Honolulu, 1991—, honors coun. mem., 2000—03, writing focus bd. mem., 2004—; awards com. chair Sch. Nursing, U. Hawaii at Manoa, 1995—98, writing across curriculum mem., 1999—2000, 2005—, mem. undergraduate curriculum com., 1999—, chair undergraduate curriculum com., 2006—; dep. dir. health State of Hawaii, 2003—04. Leader, advisor, life mem. Girl Scouts U.S., Honolulu, 1978—; mem. diabetes project Office of Hawaiian Affairs, 1993-95. Named Disting. Alumni U. Hawaii Sch. Nursing, 1987; one of Hawaii's Unsung Heroes, Honolulu Star Bull., 1993. Mem.: APHA, ANA (polit. action com. 1994—), Assn. Asian and Pacific Health Orgns. (adv. bd. 2002—06), Am. Heart Assn. (cardiovasc. nursing coun. 1985—97), Internat. Soc. Pediat. and Adolescent Diabetes (steering com. Internat. Diabetes Camping program 1989—96), Internat. Diabetes Fedn., Diabetes Advocacy Alliance Hawaii (convener and chair 1997—2000), Hawaii Assn. Diabetes Educators (founding mem., bd. dirs. 1989—, treas. 1994—95, pres. 1996—97, state legis. coord. 1996—2001, pub. affairs chair 1996—2001, state legis. coord. 2004—, pub. affairs chair 2005—, Diabetes Camp Edn. Nat. award 1995, Disting. Svc. award 2003), Am. Assn. Diabetes Educators (bd. dirs. 1997—2004, chair 1999—2001, 1st v.p. 2000—01, awards com. 2001—02, pres.-elect 2001—02, rsch. com. 2001—03, pub. affairs com. 2002—03, nat. pres. 2002—03, continuing edn. com.), Am. Diabetes Assn. (Hawaii affiliate founding bd. dirs. 1978—, camp nurse and camp dir. 1982—2004, pres. 1986—87, nat. del. yearly, nat. programs com. nat. youth congress 1993—95, nat. youth task force and design team 1996—97, nat. profl. edn. com. 1997—98, Pacific NW regional pres.-elect 1998—99, leadership coun. 1998—, pres. health care and edn. 1999—2000, nat. sci. sessions planning com. 2004—, co-chair advocacy com. 2004—, chair Safe 4 Schs. Project 2005—, outstanding contbns. to diabetes and camping nat. award 1994, Reaching People award 2002, Lifetime Achievement award 2005), Hawaii Nurses Assn. (Excellence in Clin. Practice award 1995), Sigma Theta Tau (Gamma Psi chpt. and chpt.-at-large, chmn. recognition com. 1986—89, founding mem., chair nominating com. 1995—97, Leadership award 2003). Avocation: travel. Home: 1629 Wilder Ave Apt 504 Honolulu HI 96822-4652 Office Phone: 808-956-6841. Business E-Mail: kadohiro@hawaii.edu.

KADZIELAWA, RENATA MARIA, physician; b. Zakopane, Poland, June 10, 1938; arrived in US, 1976; d. Tadeusz Gorecki and Maria Szalonka; m. Krzyszetof Kadzielawa (dec.); l child, Kris. MD, Acad. of Medicine, Krakow, Poland, 1964. Board Certified in Internal Medicine 1985. Rotating intern, Poland, 1965—66; exptl. pharmacology fellow Sch. Medicine, Warsaw, 1966—67; resident in internal medicine Marshal U., Huntington, W.Va., 1978—81; clin. pharmacology fellow Clinic Internal Medicine, Warsaw, 1967—70; staff physician Vet. Adm. Hosp., Huntington, 1981—88, Lexington, Ky., 1988—2001; ret., 2001. Attending tchr. Marshall U. Sch. of Medicine, Huntington, 1981—88, U. Ky., Lexington, 1988—2000. Home: 511 Hahaione St Apt 4B Honolulu HI 96825

KAEHELE, BETTIE LOUISE, accountant; b. Sherwood, Tenn., Oct. 29, 1950; d. James Henry and Ruby Katherine (Clark) Shetters; divorced; children: Josiah Dean, Dana Marie. AAS, Albuquerque Tech. Vocat. Inst., 1990; BSBA, Nat. Coll., Albuquerque, 1991. Acctg. clk. Am. Auto Assn., Albuquerque, 1980—81, Ryder Truck Rental, Inc., Albuquerque, 1981—82; owner Sherwood Svcs., 1982—86; bookkeeper, sec. Grants Steel Sash & Hardware, Albuquerque, 1986—87; acctg. specialist Burton & Co., Albuquerque, 1987—91, Neff & Co., Albuquerque, 1991—92; acctg. tech. U. N.Mex. Found., Albuquerque, 1992—97; acct. II dept. family and cmty. medicine U. N.Mex., Albuquerque, 1997—2002, acct. III dept. family and cmty. medicine, 2002—. Mem. Light and Liberty Jail Ministry. Mem.: Light and Liberty Jail Ministry. Republican. Avocations: reading, dance, theater, poetry, writing. Home: 7408 Desert Canyon Pl SW Albuquerque NM 87121-6424

KAELIN, JENNIFER ANN, secondary school educator; b. Miami, Fla., Sept. 11, 1975; d. George Robert Zell and Pamela Jean Kaelin. AA, Miami-Dade CC, 1995; BS cum laude, Fla. Internat. U., 1998. Cert. tchr. Fla. Physics tchr. Miami Dade County Pub. Schs., Miami, 1998—. Co-sponsor Sci. Honor Soc., Miami Killian Sr. HS, 2005—. Mem.: NSTA, United Tchrs. of Dade, Am. Assn. Physics Tchrs., Phi Theta Kappa, Phi Kappa Phi. Democrat. Avocations: reading, needlecrafts, travel. Office: Miami Killian Sr HS 10655 SW 97th Ave Miami FL 33176

KAEN, NAIDA, state representative; b. Frankenmuth, Mich., May 12, 1946; m. Fred R. Kaen; two children. BEd, U. Mich., 1968; MBA, U. N.H., 1977. Realtor; state rep. N.H. Ho. of Reps., 1995—. Mem. sci., tech. and energy com. N.H. Ho. Reps. Office: NH State Legis State House Concord NH 03301 Address: 22 Toon Ln Lee NH 03824-6507 E-mail: naidakaen@hotmail.com.

KAFOURY, ANN GRAHAM, psychotherapist; b. Spokane, Wash., Mar. 27, 1945; d. William Matheson and Gladys Irene (Swift) Graham; m. David Kafoury; children: Trevor, Kenan, Stephanie. BA, U. Oreg., 1967; MAT, Portland State U., 1976; MA in Counseling and Psychology, Lewis and Clark Coll., 1982. Tchr. U.S. Peace Corps, Ghana, West Africa, 1967-69, Tigard (Oreg.) Sr. H.S., 1970-74, Portland (Oreg.) C.C., 1976-79; cons. Oreg. Fitness & Health Ctr., Good Samaritan Hosp., Portland, 1982-83; alcohol and drug counselor, co-dependency group leader Cedar Hills Hosp., Portland, 1989-93, outpatient coord., 1990-93; pvt. practice psychotherapist Portland, 1982—. Oreg. network coord. Eye Movement Desensitization and Reprocessing, Portland, 1992-2004; facilitator, cons., trainer, coord. Humanitarian Assistance Program for India; intensive family therapist, Portland, 1993—. Chairperson Hillside Park Bd., Portland, 1977-80; mem. Friends of West Women's Hotel, Portland, 1983-88; officer, bd. mem. Burnside Cmty. Coun., Portland, 1984-87; sponsor Oreg. Counselors Polit. Action Com., Oreg., 1988—. Mem. ACA, Oreg. Counseling Assn., Nat. Bd. Cert. Counselors. Avocations: travel, reading, meditation, spiritual growth, sports. Home: 804 NW Culpepper Ter Portland OR 97210-3125 Office: 804 NW Culpepper Ter Portland OR 97210-3125 Office Phone: 503-291-9343.

KAGAN, ELENA, dean, law educator; b. 1960; BA summa cum laude, Princeton U., 1981; MPhil, Worchester Coll., Oxford, 1983; JD magna cum laude, Harvard Law School, 1986. Law clk. US Ct. of Appeals for Judge Abner Mikva of the US Supreme Ct. for the DC Circuit, 1986—87, US Ct. of Appeals for Justice Thurgood Marshall of the US Supreme Ct., 1987—88; assoc. Williams & Connolly, Wash., DC, 1989—91; faculty mem. Univ. of Chgo. Law Sch., Chgo., 1991—99; nominated to serve as judge US Supreme Ct. of Appeals, Wash., DC, 1999; asst. prof. Univ. of Chgo. Law Sch., 1991, prof. of law tenure Chgo., 1995; assoc. counsel to the Pres. White House, Wash., DC, 1995—96, dep. asst. to the Pres. for Domestic Policy, 1997—99, dep. dir. of the Domestic Policy Coun., 1997—99; vis. prof. Harvard Law Sch., Cambridge, Mass., 1999, prof., 2001—, dean, 2003—, Charles Hamilton Houston prof. of law, 2003—. Author: (article) Harvard Law Rev. Article, Pres. Admin., 2001 (honored as the year's top scholarly article by the Am. Bar Assoc. Section on Admin. Law and Reg. Pract., 2001). Kagan has also written on a range of First Amendment issues, including the role of governmental motive in different facets of First Amendment doctrine, and the interplay of libel law and the First Amendment. Mem.: Harvard Law Sch. faculty appt. comm., Harvard Law Sch. Locational options comm. (chair 2001—02). Kagan is a prof. of law at Harvard fLaw Sch. where she teaches admin. law, constitutional law, and civil procedure. Her recent sholarship focuses primarily on the role of the Pres. of the US in formulating and influencing fed. admin. and regulatory law. Office: Harvard Law Sch Griswold 200 1563 Mass Ave Cambridge MA 02138

KAGAN, ILSE ECHT, librarian, researcher, historian; b. Free City of Danzig, Sept. 23, 1927; d. Samuel and Hella Echt; m. Robert A. Kagan, Aug. 26, 1951 (dec. Oct. 1994); children: Jonathan, Miki. BA (hon.), Oxford U., MA, 1954; MLS, Columbia U., 1960. With Pira Energy, N.Y.C., 1987—; village historian Village of Gt. Neck (N.Y.) Estates, 1996—. Past pres. Gt. Neck Estates Civic Assn., sec., 2000—; past pres. Gt. Neck chpt. Hadassah; bd. dirs. Am. Jewish Com. Mem.: Oxford U. Club, Brit. Schs. Univ. Club, Harvard Club. Avocations: tennis, theater, music. Home: 25 Elm St Great Neck NY 11021 Office: Pira Energy 3 Park Ave New York NY 10016 Office Phone: 212-686-6808. E-mail: piraiek@concentric.net.

KAGAN, JULIA LEE, magazine editor; b. Nurnberg, Fed. Republic Germany, Nov. 25, 1948; d. Saul and Elizabeth J. Kagan. AB, Bryn Mawr Coll., 1970. Rschr. Look Mag., N.Y.C., 1970-71; editl. asst., asst. editor McCall's mag., N.Y.C., 1971-74, assoc. editor, 1974-78, sr. editor, 1978-79; articles editor Working Woman mag., N.Y.C., 1979-85, exec. editor, 1985-88; editor Psychology Today, 1988-90; sr. editor McCalls, 1990-91; contbg. editor Working Woman, 1991-93; editor-in-chief Lamaze Parents' Mag., 1992-93, Lamaze Baby Mag., 1993; spl. projects dir. Child Mag., 1993-94; sr. v.p. EDK Assocs., N.Y.C., 1994; psychology/health dir. Fitness Mag., N.Y.C., 1995-96; dep. editor Consumer Reports Mag., Yonkers, NY, 1996, editor, 1996-2000; v.p. and editl. dir. Consumers Union, 2000—03; v.p. content Zagat Survey, 2003—04; nat. editor-in-chief Back Stage, 2005; health dir. Ladies' Home Jour., 2005—. Vis. J. Stewart Riley prof. journalism Ind. U., 1991-93. Co-author: Manworks: A Guide to Style, 1980; contbg. author: The Working Woman Success Book, 1981, The Working Woman Report, 1984. Pres. Appleby Found., N.Y.C., 1982-84; trustee Bryn Mawr Coll., 2000-06 Recipient 2d Ann. Advt. Journalism award Compton Advt., 1983 Mem. Am. Soc. Mag. Editors, Womens Media Group (bd. dirs.), Journalism and Women Symposium (treas. 1993-94, pres. 1995-96), Princeton Club (N.Y.C.), Cosmopolitan Club (N.Y.C.). Office: Ladies Home Jour 125 Park Ave New York NY 10017-5529 E-mail: jlkagan@aol.com.

KAGAN, MARILYN D., retired architect; b. Providence, Nov. 13, 1930; d. Jacob L. and Emma Kenner Kagan. BS in Arch., Drexel U., 1972; student in Cert. Program, RI Sch. Design, 2005—. Cartographer U.S. Army Map Svc., Providence, 1952-53, Redevel. Authority, Phila., 1958-68; arch. George Ewing Inc., Phila., 1969-70, City of Phila. Water Dept., 1971-91; ret., 1991. Designer jewelry. Bd. dirs. Philly Walks-Pedestrian Safety Coalition, 1996-98; chair Soviet Jewry Com. of Society Hill Synagogue, Phila., 1980-90. Recipient Cert. of Appreciation, Jewish Family Svc. of Phila., 1993-96. Mem.: Na'Amat/Pioneer Women (pres. R.I. chpt. 2002—). Democrat. Jewish. Avocations: jewelry design, painting, photography, gardening, travel. Home: 311 Rochambeau Ave Providence RI 02906-3507 Personal E-mail: busybeaderkagan@aol.com.

KAGETSU, NAOMI J., dermatologist; BSChemE, MIT, Cambridge, 1982; MD, SUNY, Buffalo, 1986. Diplomate Am. Bd. Dermatology. Asst. prof. dermatology U. Cin., 1993—94; dermatologist Daniel Stewart and Assoc., Clinton Twp., Mich., 1990—94, Henry Ford Med. Group., Sterling Heights, Mich., 1994—95, Carolina Dermatology Ctr., Greensboro, NC, 1995—99, Chapel Hill Dermatology, NC, 1999—. Named one of Best Drs. in Am., Best Drs., Inc., Aiken, SC, 2005—06. Mem.: Am. Soc. Dermatologic Surgery, Am. Acad. Dermatology, Womens Dermatologic Soc. Office: Chapel Hill Dermatology 891 Willow Dr Ste 1 Chapel Hill NC 27514

KAGGEN, LOIS SHEILA, non-profit organization executive, advocate; b. NYC, Jan. 2, 1944; d. Elias and Sylvia (Muntner) K.; m. Harold Jay Burns, June 29, 1969 (dec. June 1975); 1 child, David Henry (dec.); m. Michael Francis McCann, Sept. 26, 1984. BS in Fine Arts, Skidmore Coll., 1964; postgrad., Cooper Union, 1967-70; MA in Art Edn., CCNY, 1973; PhD in Art Edn., NYU, 1997. Tchr. fine arts grades 7-9 Jr. HS 149, Bronx, NY, 1967-74; founder, pres. Resources for Artists With Disabilities, NYC, 1987—. Traumatic Brain Injury Consumer Adv., 1977—; mem. adv. bd. com. Art in Edn. Project, NY State Coun. on the Arts, Ctr. for Safety in the Arts, NYC, 1987; cons. Ea. Paralyzed Vets. Assn., Guggenheim Mus. Art, NYC, 1990; mem. bd. advisors Ind. Arts Gallery, Queens Ind. Living Ctr., Jamaica, NY, 1987-97, 98; mem. steering com. Ann. Disability Independence Day March, 1992-93, mem. Media Outreach, 1992; provider written and oral testimony in field to orgns.; bd. dirs. Ctr. for Independence of the Disabled of NY, Inc., NYC, 1996—, Gov.'s appt. to Traumatic Brain Injury Svcs. Coordinating Coun., Albany, 1997-2001, others; presenter NIH Consensus Devel. Conf. on Rehab. of Persons with Traumatic Brain Injury, Bethesda, Md., 1998, 5th Ann. Conf., Traumatic Brain Injury Program, NY State Dept. Health, Albany, 1998, Info. and Comm. Com. TBISEC (TBI Coun.) NYS-DOH, Delmar, NY, 2001, NY State Assembly task force on people with disabilities: pub. hearing City U. NY Grad. Ctr., NY, 2001, Am. Coun. Edn. conf. The Student with a Brain Injury: Achieving Goals for Higher Edn., DC, 2001; originator, conf. com. co-organizer, consumer panelist NYU Moses Ctr. for Students with Disabilities and Ctr. for Independence of Disabled of NY, Loeb Student Ctr., NYU, NYC, 1998; panel organizer, moderator, presenter Inst. for Rsch. on Women's 16th Ann. Celebration of Our Work Conf., Douglass Coll., Rutgers U., New Brunswick, NJ, 1998; mem. search com. for dir. Tang Tchg. Mus. and Art Gallery, Skidmore Coll., Saratoga Springs, NY, 2004; gave testimony Taxi and Limousine Commn., 2004; art presenter in field. Photography exhbns. include 80 Washington Sq. East Galleries, NYC, 1977, Soho Photo Gallery, NYC, 1978, 4th St. Photo Gallery, NYC, 1979, Womanart Gallery, NYC, 1979, Leslie-Lohman Gallery, NYC, 1980, 81, Window Gallery, Met. Savs. Bank, NYC, 1980, Cathedral St. John-the-Devine Gallery, NYC, 1980, Donnell Libr. Gallery, 1981; originator, organizer various exhbns. African-Am. Artists with Disabilities, Artists with Phys. Disabilities; contbr. articles, photographs to profl. jours. Mem. Nat. Inst. Disability and Rehab. Rsch.; mem. Office Spl. Edn. and Rehab. Svcs. US Dept. Edn., Washington, mem. per rev. registry, 1995—; active Disabled in Action of Greater N.Y., 1989—, Manhattan Borough Pres. Disability Adv. Coun., 1988—98, 1999—; access subcom. 504 Dem. Club for Persons with Disabilities, 2000—; mem. Mayor's Adv. Com. on People with Disabilities, NYC, 1991—93, Citywide Coalition on Disability, NYC, 1994—95; active in assistive signage needs Planning Meeting NYC Coun./Dept. Disabled, 2000; mem. info. subcom. NYC Coun. Planning Com. Dept. Disabled, 2000—; mem. Disabilities Network of NYC, 2000—; mem. disability rights steering com. 504 Dem. Club for Persons with Disabilities, 1987—88, mem. exec. com., 1990—2002; mem. NY County Dem. Com. 102ED/95 ED, 1995—; exec. com. The Village Independent Democrats, NYC, 2003—, v.p., 2005—; mem. The Village Independent Dems. Turns 50 com. The Village Independent Democrats 50th Anniversary Reception, 2006. Grantee Whitney Mus. Am. Art and the Smithsonian Instn., summer 1967, summer film inst. Stanford U., 1968; Cooper Union scholar, 1967-70; recipient Appreciation cert. Manhattan Borough Pres., 1991, Dean's Disting. Alumni Achievement award NYU, NYC, 1998. Mem. Coll. Art Assn. (com. mems. with disabilities for accessible programs and places 1990—), NYC Coun. dept. for disabled. Office: Resources for Artists with Disabilities 77 7th Ave Ste PH-H New York NY 10011-6645 Personal E-mail: loiskaggen@att.net.

KAHAI, JUGTA, pediatrician; State commr. NC Health & Wellness Trust Fund, 2003—; founder TRY (Tsunami Relief & You); cofounder (with Deepa Bhojwani) Seenigama Rainbow Clinic, Sri Lanka, 2005—; med. dir. Carousel Ctr.; pres., pediatrician Oak Island Pediatrics; pres. & founder AWAKEN (A Working Alliance for Kids with Exceptional Needs). Recipient Leadership award (Young Physicians), AMA Found., 2005. Mem.: NC Med. Soc. Office: Oak Island Pediatrics PA 4734 Long Beach Rd SE Southport NC 28461 also: The Carousel Center 2714 Market St Wilmington NC 28403-1218*

KAHAN, PHYLLIS IRENE, language educator, writer, editor, media consultant; b. St. Louis, Apr. 11, 1942; d. Meyer and Betty Kahan. AB in English cum laude, Washington U., St. Louis, 1964; MA, Stanford U., Calif., 1966; PhD, St. Louis U., 1986. Lifetime tchg. credential Calif., Mo. Prin., comm. cons. Phyllis Kahan Copy, St. Louis, 1981—94; sr. writer Washington U., St. Louis, 1988—91; placement dir. Kelly Law Registry, NYC, 1996—2000; adj. prof. English CUNY, NYC, 2003—05, St. Johns U., Queens, NY, 2003—06, Berkeley Coll., NYC, 2004—06, Fashion Inst. Tech., NYC, 2005—; adj. prof. English and Latin Met. Coll. of NY, NYC. Mem. lit. com. Nat. Arts Club, NYC, 1997—2004. Author: (novels) Witchita; editor: Nancy Friday, 2006—; columnist: Out & About St. Louis. Vol. Dem. Nat. Com., NYC, 2000. Recipient Book prize, Delta Phi Alpha, 1964, Flair award, Advt. Fedn. St. Louis, 1984, Hon. Mention, Hemingway Competition, 1986, Excellence in Tchg., St. John's U., 2005; scholar, Washington U., 1962—63; Merit scholar, Stanford U., 1965. Mem.: AAUP (assoc.), Phi Beta Kappa. Democrat. Jewish. Avocations: movies, opera, sports. Home and Office: 100 W 57th St New York NY 10019 Personal E-mail: phyllkah@aol.com.

KAHANA, EVA FROST, sociology educator; b. Budapest, Hungary, Mar. 21, 1941; came to U.S., 1957; d. Jacob and Sari Frost; m. Boaz Kahana, Apr. 15, 1962; children: Jeffrey, Michael. BA, Stern Coll., Yeshiva U., 1962; MA, CCNY, CUNY, 1965; PhD, U. Chgo., 1968; HLD (hon.), Yeshiva U., 1991. Nat. Inst. on Aging predoctoral fellow U. Chgo. Com. on Human Devel., 1963-66; postdoctoral fellow Midwest Council Social Research, 1968; with dept. sociology Washington U., St. Louis, 1967-71, successively research asst., research assoc., asst. prof.; with dept. sociology Wayne State U., Detroit, 1971-84, from assoc. prof. to prof., dir. Elderly Care Research Ctr., 1971-84; prof. Case Western Res. U., Cleve., 1984—, Armington Prof., 1989-90, chmn. dept. sociology, 1985—, dir. Elderly Care Research Ctr., 1984—, Pierce and Elizabeth Robson prof. humanities, 1990—. Cons. Nat. Inst. on Aging, Washington, 1976-80, NIMH, Washington, 1971-75. Author: (with E. Midlarsky) Altruism in Later Life, 1994; editor: (with others) Family Caregiving Across the Lifespan, 1994; mem. editl. bd. Gerontologist, 1975-79, Psychology of Aging, 1984-90, Jour. Gerontology, 1990-94, Applied Behavioral Sci. Rev., 1992—; contbr. articles to profl. jours., chpts. to books (recipient Pub.'s prize 1969). Bd. dirs. com. on aging Jewish Community Fedn., Cleve.; vol. cons. Alzheimer's Disease and Related Disorders Assn., Cleve. NIMH Career Devel. grantee, 1974-79, Nat. Inst. Aging Merit award grantee, 1989—; Mary E. Switzer Disting. fellow Nat. Inst. Rehab., 1992-93; recipient Arnold Heller award excellence in geriatrics and gerontology Menorah Park Ctr. for Aged, 1992, Diekhoff awrd for disting. grad. tchg., 2002; named Outstanding Gerontological Rschr. in Ohio, 1993, 04, Outstanding Gerontol. Educator in Ohio, 2004. Fellow Assn. for Gerontology in Higher Edn., Gerontol. Soc. Am. (chair behavioral social sci. com. 1984-85, chair 2000—, Disting. Mentorship award 1987, Polisher award 1997); mem. Am. Sociol. Assn. (coun. sect. on aging 1985-87, Disting. Scholar award sect. on aging and life course 1997, chair sect. on aging and life course, 2000-2001), Am. Psychol. Assn., Soc. for Traumatic Stress, Wayne State U. Acad. Scholars (life), Sigma Xi. Avocations: reading, antiques, travel.

KAHAO, MARY JANE, school librarian; b. Shanghai, July 17, 1924; d. William Anthony Fly and Edythe Clarice Redmond; m. Kenneth Hanson Kahao, June 6, 1945; children: Martin J. III, Kenneth H. Jr., Eve Redmond K. Gonzalez, Roger W. BA in Music, Newcomb Coll., 1945; MS in Libr. Sci., La. State U., 1964; MA in Children's Lit., Simmons Coll., 1982. Cert. sch. music tchr. La., sch. libr. La. Sch. music tchr. La. State Bd. Edn.; music tchr. West Baton Rouge Parish Schs., Port Allen, La., 1951—52, Holy Family Elem. Sch., Port Allen, 1951—52; payroll clk. Allendale Plantation, Port Allen, 1957—63; student worker La. State U. Libr., Baton Rouge, 1953—54, reference libr. humanities divsn., 1964—73, head Grad. Sch. Libr. and Info. Sci. Libr., 1973—82. Chmn. La. State U. Libr. Staff Assn., Baton Rouge, 1965; chmn. Modisette awards com. La. Libr. Assn., 1964—69. Home: 4916 Hwy 190 W Port Allen LA 70767

KAHLER, DOROTHY STIRLING, psychotherapist; b. Benton Harbor, Mich., May 8, 1955; d. Hugh MacNair and Dorothy May (Gregory) K. AB in Music, Bryn Mawr Coll., 1977; MA in Counseling, Western Mich. U., 1990; Doctorate in Psychology, Widener U., 1998. Lic. psychologist, Mich.; registered technologist in radiology, Mich. Revenue officer IRS, Marquette, Traverse City, Mich., 1979-81; radiographer trainee Marquette Gen. Hosp., 1981-83, mobile computerized axial tomography scan technologist, 1987-88; staff technologist Marquette Radiology, 1984-87, Kalamazoo Radiology, PC, 1988-91; outpatient therapist Blue Water Clinic, Port Huron, Mich., 1991-93; counselor PsychResource Assocs., Swarthmore, Pa., 1994—95; psychologist, neuropsychologist pvt. practice, Marquette, Mich., 2006—. Outpatient clinician Van Buren County Cmty. Mental Health, Paw Paw, Mich., 1990-91, neuropsychologist Marquette Gen. Hosp., Mich., 1999-2006; spkr. on co-dependency, dist. mtg. Mich. Soc. Radiology Technologists, Kalamazoo, 1990; keynote spkr. Mich. Huntington's Disease State Conf., 2004; rsch. asst. Child Therapy Newsletter. Music dir. St. Paul's Ch., Marquette, 1986-88; vol. election campaign for U.S. Rep., Marquette, 1984. Recipient silver medal Alma (Mich.) Highland Games, 1981. Mem. Am. Psychological Assn., Scottish Country Dance Soc. (dance instr. 1986-87, 1990-91, 2004-), Phi Kappa Phi. Democrat. Episc. Avocations: dance, singing. Home: 109 W Fairbanks St Marquette MI 49855-8915

KAHLES, CHERYL MARY, elementary school educator; b. Bklyn., Aug. 5, 1950; d. Thomas and Comelia Mary Dickson; m. B. Antonio Cherot (div.); children: Nicole Marie Cherot, Jason Anthony Cherot; m. James Francis Kahles, June 6, 1998. BS in Edn., U. Ill., 1973; MEd, Coll. Mt. St. Joseph, 1987. Tchr. Oakwood (Ill.) Elem. Sch., 1972—74, Diamond Elem. Sch., Danville, Ill., 1974—78, Monee (Ill.) Elem. Sch., 1978—79, Amelia Elem. Sch., Ohio, 1979—. Mem. The St. John Passion Play, Cinn., 1999—2006, Immaculate Heart of Mary Roman Cath. Ch., Cinn., 1979—2006. Mem.: NEA, Nat. PTA, Ohio Edn. Assn. Roman Catholic. Avocations: travel, sailing, celtic and renaissance festivals. Office: Amelia Elem Sch 5 E Main St Amelia OH 45102 Business E-Mail: kahles_c@westcler.org.

KAHLOW, BARBARA FENVESSY, statistician; b. Chgo., June 26, 1946; d. Stanley John and Doris (Goodman) Fenvessy; m. Lloyd Fitch Reese, Dec. 6, 1969 (div. 1977); m. Allan Howard Young, Mar. 31, 1979 (div. 1982); m. Ronald Arthur Kahlow, Sept. 28, 1985 (div. 1990). BA, Vassar Coll., 1968. Analytical statistician US Govt./Dept. HEW, Nat. Ctr. Health Stats., 1968-70, Nat. Ctr. Ednl. Stats., 1970-72, Exec. Office Pres. Office Mgmt. and Budget, Washington, 1972-98. Staff dir. subcom. on energy policy, natural resources and regulatory affairs House Govt. Reform Com., 1998-2005. Author: Motor Vehicle Accident Deaths in the U.S.: 1950-69, 1970; contbr. articles to profl. jours. N.Y. State Regents scholar, 1964-68. Mem. Foggy Bottom Assn., West End Citizens Assn., League of Rep. Women of DC, Friends of Kennedy Ctr., Friends of Corcoran, Smithsonian Assocs., Washington Vassar Club. Republican. Episcopalian. Home: Apt 704 800 25th St NW Washington DC 20037 Personal E-mail: barbara.kahlow@verizon.net.

KAHN, ANNMARIE, special education educator; b. Worcester, Mass., Apr. 22, 1960; d. Francis J. and Mary L. Labuski; m. Howard D. Kahn, June 14, 1958. MEd, Worcester State Coll., Mass., 1985. Tchr. spl. edn. Worcester Pub. Schs., Mass., 1987—97, behavioral specialist, 1997—. Behavioral cons. Worcester Pub. Schs. Recipient Tchr. of Yr., Worcester Pub. Sch., 2000, 2004, Thomas Jefferson award, 2004. Office: Worcester Public Schools 20 Irving Street Worcester MA 01608 Office Phone: 508-799-3594.

KAHN, BARBARA B., endocrinologist; BA, Stanford U., 1972; MS, U. Calif. Berkeley, 1975; MD, Stanford U. Sch. Med., 1977. Internal medicine intern, resident U. Calif. Davis Med. Ctr., Sacramento, 1977—80, clin. fellow, 1980—82; endocrine fellow, cellular metabolism & obesity sect. Nat. Inst. Arthritis, Diabetes, Digestive & Kidney Diseases, NIH, Bethesda, Md., 1982—85, sr. staff fellow, experimental diabetes, metabolism & nutrition sect., molecular, cellular & nutritional endocrinology branch, 1985—86; chief, div. endocrinology, diabetes, & metabolism Beth Israel Deaconess Med. Ctr., Boston; prof. medicine Harvard Med. Sch., Boston, dir. endocrinology, diabetes & metabolism fellowship program; assoc. dir. Boston Obesity Nutrition Rsch. Ctr. Vis. prof. Karolinska Inst., Stockholm, 2000; Pfizer vis. prof. U. Washington, 2001; Burroughs Wellcome vis. prof. Univ. NC, 2002; NHLB/NI working group on the pathophysiology of obesity-associated cardiovascular disease, 01; com. on diabetes Am. Heart Assn., 2001—; publications com. Am. Diabetes Assn., 2002—, steering com., 2000—02, NIH, 2002; editorial bd. Am. Jour. Physiology: Endocrinology & Metabolism, 2001—04, Jour. Biological Chemistry, 2002—. Mem.: AAP, Inst. Medicine, Interurban Clin. Club. Office: Div Endocrinology, Diabetes & Metabolism RN 380-C 330 Brookline Ave Boston MA 02215 Office Phone: 617-667-5422. Office Fax: 617-667-2927. E-mail: bkahn@bidmc.harvard.edu.*

KAHN, CAROLYN R., biotechnology executive; b. Bklyn., Apr. 24, 1952; d. Nathaniel L. and Celia Stashin Kahn; m. James A. Wilkins, Mar. 6, 1982; children: Philip Nathaniel, Sarah Elizabeth. AB, Johns Hopkins U., 1974, PhD, 1980. Staff scientist Gillette Corp., Gaithersburg, Md., 1990—93; cons. Kahn Mgmt. Cons., Woodbridge, Conn., 1993—98; mng. dir. biosci. Conn. Innovations, Rocky Hill, Conn., 1998—2003; CEO, pres. Hepaticus, Inc., New Haven, 2003—. Bd. dirs. MIT Enterprise Forum, Hartford, Conn. Justice of the Peace, Woodbridge, 1994—2000; founder, pres. Woodbridge Soccer Club, 1993—95, San Mateo (Calif.) Edn. Found., 1986—89; bd. dirs. Am. Liver Found., New Haven, 2004—; active Over 30 Conn. State Soccer Team. McClure fellow, Myastenia Gravis Found. Mem.: AAAS, N.Y. Acad. Sci., Sigma Xi. Achievements include patents for human cornea. Office: Hepaticus Inc 999 West St Rocky Hill CT 06067-3011

KAHN, CECILY, painter; d. Wolf Kahn and Emily Mason; m. David Kapp, May 24, 1986. Ed., Internat. Sch. Graphics, Venice, Italy, 1980—81, Calcografia Nazionale, Rome, Italy, 1980—81; BFA, RI Sch. Design, 1981. Exhibitions include Eighteen Graphic Artists in Venice, Segno Grafica Gallery, Italy, 1981, Brooklyn in Profile, Pan Arts Gallery, NY, 1983, Prints from the Workshop of Cone Editions, Gallery North, Setauket, NY, 1987, Family Lines, 1990, NYC Works by 21 Artists, 1 Penn Plaza, NY, 1988, Group Show, Blondies Contemporary Art, NYC, 1991, Beneath the Surface, Tribeca 148 Gallery, NY, 1992, Signs of Life, The Policy Bldg., NYC, 1993, Painters Painting II, The Painting Ctr., NYC, 1994, Emerging Artists '95, 1995, Recent Works, 1997, Maine Coast Artists, Ann. Juried Show, 1994, Selections from Scott Meml. Study Collection, Bryn Mawr Coll., Pa., 1994, PSA Showcase VIII, NYC, 1997, All In a Family, The New Britain Mus. Am. Art, Conn., 1997, Maine Debuts Since 1979, Maine Coast Artists, Rockport, 1997, Small Works, Kendall Art and Design, Hudson, 1997, Relatively Speaking: Mothers and Daughters in Art, NewHouse Ctr. Contemporary Art, Staten Island, 1994—97, A Welcome Exchange, Temple Bar Gallery, Dublin, Ireland, 1999, Assn., The Bond Market Assn., NY, 2001, The Art Showcase 16, 2001, Dialogue and Discourse, Dolan Ctr. Gallery, Long Island, 2001, Rhythmic Renderings, Elsa Mott Eves Gallery, NY, 2002, Inspired by the Land, Attleboro Mus., Mass., 2002, Abstract Dilemmas, Martin Art Gallery, Allentown, Pa., 2002, A Family Affair, Katherina Rich Perlow Gallery, NYC, 2002, Variations: Abstractions X4, 2003, The Gift of Art, 2003, Lohin Geduld Gallery, NY, 2004, A Kaleidoscope of Color: Recent Paintings, Thomas Dean Fine Art, Atlanta, 2005.*

KAHN, EIKO TANIGUCHI, artist; b. Fukuoka, Kyushu, Japan, Jan. 24, 1929; arrived in US, 1955, naturalized, 1958; d. Tosuke Yamashita and Masano Taniguchi; m. Frederick Joseph Kahn, Sept. 28, 1954; children: Karen, Miho Kahn Wiedis. Gen., Sumiyoshi Women's Sch., Osaka, Japan, 1944. Solo exhbns. include Gregg Gallery, N.Y.C., 1982, Nat. Arts Club, Celadon Gallery, N.Y.C., 1988, The Korby Gallery, Cedar Grove, N.J., 1995, AWS Salmagundi Club, N.Y.C., 1995, The Koh Gallery, Union City, N.J., 1996, AT&T Bell Lab. Gallery, Hopewell, N.J., 1996, Ocean County Artists Guild Gallery, N.J., 1996, Gratella Gallery, Princeton, N.J., 1997, Ellarslie Trenton City Mus., 2000. Recipient Pres.'s award Nat. Arts Club, 1981, Ablert Baldwin prize Nat. Acad. Design, 1983, Award for Excellence Middlesex County Mus., 1985. Mem. N.J. Water Color Soc. (award 1990), Audubon Artists (Medal of Honor 1981), Artists Fellowship. Avocations: golf, gardening. Address: 217 Cleveland Ln RD 4 Princeton NJ 08540-9517

KAHN, ELLEN IDA, physician, consultant; b. Osnabruek, Germany, Aug. 23, 1927; came to U.S., 1961; d. Abraham and Else M. (Westheimer) Levy; m. Richard M. Levy, Feb. 20, 1961; children: Ronald, Vivian. MD, Med. Sch., Lisbon, Portugal, 1953. Intern Hosp. Santa Maria, Lisbon, 1953-54, resident in pathology, 1954-57; chief dept. pathology Inst. Ophthalmology Gama Pinto, Lisbon, 1957-59; from instr. to assoc. prof. pathology Med. Sch., Lisbon, 1953-61, Cornell U. Med. Coll., N.Y.C., 1972-91, prof. clin. pathology, 1991—, clin. prof. pediatrics, 1992—; resident in pathology North Shore U. Hosp., Manhasset, N.Y., 1968-72, attending pathologist, 1972—, chief pediatric pathology, 1988—. Cons.pediatric pathology Mercy Hosp., Rockville Centre, N.Y., 1982—. Contbr. chpts. to books, numerous articles to profl. jours. Fellow Coll. Am. Pathologists, Am. Acad. Pediatrics, Nassau Acad. Medicine; mem. Gastroen. Assn., Hans Popper Hepatopathology Soc., Am. Assn. Study Liver Diseases, U.S.-Can. Acad. Pathology, Gastrointestinal Pathology Soc., Pediatric Pathology Soc., N.Y. Soc. Pathology, Nassau County Soc. Pathology, Nassau County Med. Soc., N.Y. State Soc. Medicine. Avocations: photography, music, reading. Office: 300 Community Dr Manhasset NY 11030-3801

KAHN, HERTA HESS (MRS. HOWARD KAHN), retired investment company executive; b. Wuerzburg, Germany; naturalized, U.S. d. Ferdinand and Lilly (Suesser) Hess; m. Herbert Levy (dec.); 1 child, Linda Levy; m. Howard Kahn (dec.). Student, Northwestern U. Sch. Commerce. Joined Paine, Webber, Jackson & Curtis, Inc., Chgo., 1941; registered rep. Paine, Webber Inc. (now UBS Fin. Svcs. Inc.), acct. v.p., v.p. investments; mktg. cons., 1995—. Author: (book) What Every Woman Should Know About Investing Her Money, 1968. Hon. life mem. nat. commn., hon. life. mem. Chgo. exec. com. Anti-Defamation League B;nai B'rith; bd. dirs. Found. Hearing and Speech Rehab., Chgo. Mem.: Chgo. Crime Commn., Chgo. Fin. Exch., CFA Inst., Investment Analysts Soc. Chgo., N.Y. Soc. Security Analysts, Tamarisk Country Club (Rancho Mirage, Calif.), Execs. Club (Chgo.), Econ. Club, Std. Club, Northmoor Country Club (Highland Park, Ill.).

KAHN, LINDA MCCLURE, actuary, consultant; b. Jacksonville, Fla. d. George Calvin and Myrtice Louise (Boggs) McClure; m. Paul Markham Kahn, May 20, 1968. BS with highest honors, U. Fla.; MS magna cum laude, U. Mich., 1964. Actuarial trainee N.Y. Life Ins. Co., N.Y.C., 1964-66, actuarial asst., 1966-69, asst. actuary, 1969-71; v.p., actuary U.S. Life Ins., Pasadena, Calif., 1972-74; mgr. Coopers & Lybrand, L.A., 1974-76; sr. cons. San Francisco, 1976-82; dir. program mgmt. Pacific Maritime Assn., San Francisco, 1982-97; pres., CEO P.M. Kahn & Assocs., 1997—; chmn., CEO Paul and Linda Kahn Found., 1998—. Bd. dirs. San Francisco Maritime Nat. Mus. Libr., 1998—, chmn. investment com., 2003—; chmn. Quarter Century Plan Devel. Com., 2003—, v.p., 2004—05; trustee ILWU-PMA Welfare Plan, 1982—97, SIU-PD-PMA Pension and Supplemental Benefits Plans, 1982—90, Seafarers Med. Ctr., 1982—90; bd. dirs. Pacific Heights Residents Assn., 1978—93, sec.-treas. bd. dirs., 1981; bd. dirs. Friends of St. Frances Childcare Ctr., 2002—, CFO, treas., 2003—. Fellow Soc. Actuaries (chmn. part 7 exam. com. 1973-76, chmn. com. on minority recruiting 1988-91, chmn. actuary of future sect. 1993-95), Conf. Cons. Actuaries; mem. Internat. Actuarial Assn., Internat. Assn. Con. Actuaries, Actuarial Studies Non-Life Ins., Am. Acad. Actuaries (enrolled actuary), Western Pension and Benefits Conf. (newsletter editor 1983-85, sec. 1985-88, treas. 1989-90), Actuarial Club Pacific States, San Francisco Actuarial Club (pres. 1981), Met. Club, Commonwealth Club, Soroptimists (v.p. 1973-74), Concordia-Argonaut Club, Pacific Club (Honolulu), Book Club Calif., Colophon Club. Home and Office: 2430 Pacific Ave San Francisco CA 94115-1238 Office Phone: 415-346-0643. E-mail: lmkahn@mindspring.com.

KAHN, MARGARET S., social worker, language educator; b. Nov. 12, 1915; d. Carl Samuel and Nina (Weiss) Stern; m. Journet Kahn, Feb. 15, 1947 (div.); children: David, Carl, Stephen, Judy, Elizabeth, Margaret, Jonathan. BA, U. Chgo., 1939, MA, 1940, postgrad., 1944, Columbia U., 1947. Instr. Barat Coll., Lake Forest, Ill., 1941—42; with Time Inc., NYC, 1942—43; social worker Hartford, Conn., 1945—46, South Bend, 1959—60, Ill. Dept. Children and Family Svcs., Chgo., 1970—81; biographer writer Ency. Brittanica, NYC, 1947; instr. Ind. U., South Bend, 1957—59, St. Xavier U., Chgo., 1960—62; ret., 1962. Author: Flotsam, 1993, Jetsam, 2005. Home: 1780 Ford Union Dr Santa Fe NM 87505

KAHN, NANCY VALERIE, publishing and entertainment executive, consultant; b. N.Y.C., Dec. 15, 1952; d. Alfred Joseph and Miriam (Kadin) Kahn. BA magna cum laude, Princeton U., 1974. Dir. prodn. and devel. Bus. Rsch. Publs., Inc.-MacRAE's Directories, N.Y.C., 1984—86; assoc. pub., exec. editor Leadership Directories Inc., N.Y.C., 1987—88; dir. new product devel. Gale Rsch. Inc., N.Y.C., 1988—89; pub., editorial dir. directories and info. devel. Adweek, N.Y.C., 1989—93; v.p. Everlink Corp., N.Y.C., 1993—94; prin. NVK Comm., N.Y.C., 1994—. Univ. scholar Princeton U., 1974. Avocations: arts, musical theatre, cabaret, foreign travel, walking. Office: NVK Comm PO Box 826 New York NY 10021

KAHN, RONNI M., psychologist; b. Kansas City, Mo., Mar. 27, 1949; d. Avery Lazarus Marrin and Natalie Gilda Kahn; m. Thomas Albert Carlson (div.); children: Louis Carlson, Marc Carlson, David Carlson, Nathaniel Carlson. BA, Drake U., Des Moines, 1980; MS, PhD, Iowa State U., 1990. Behavior therapist Jewish Hosp., St. Louis, 1987—89; substance abuse counselor Colonial Mental Health, Williamsburg, Va., 1990—92; psychologist Riverside Regional Med. Ctr., Newport News, Va., 1992—96; psychologist in pvt. practice Omaha, 1996—2001; psychologist Physicians Clinic, Inc., Omaha, 2001—06, St. Louis Behavioral Medicine Inst., 2006—. Recipient Outstanding Clin. Svcs. award, Riverside Regional Med. Ctr., Newport News, 1994. Mem.: APA, Am. Soc. for Bariatric Surgeons (assoc.). Avocations: quilting, singing. Office: Physicians Clinic 10060 Regency Cir Omaha NE 68114 Office Phone: 402-354-1354, 636-532-9188. E-mail: itsdrk@cox.net.

KAHN, SANDRA S., psychotherapist; b. Chgo., June 24, 1942; d. Chester and Ruth Sutker; m. Jack Murry Kahn, June 1, 1965; children: Erick, Jennifer. BA, U. Miami, 1964; MA, Roosevelt U., 1976. Tchr. Chgo. Pub. Schs., 1965-67; pvt. practice psychotherapy, Northbrook, Ill., 1976—. Host Shared Feelings, Sta. WEEF-AM, Highland Park, Ill., 1983—; author: The Kahn Report on Sexual Preferences, 1981, The Ex Wife Syndrome Cutting The Cord and Breaking Free After The Marriage Is Over, 1990; columnist Single Again mag. Mem. Ill. Psychol. Assn., Chgo. Psychol. Assn. (past pres. 1990). Jewish. Office: 801 Skokie Blvd Northbrook IL 60062-4039 Office Phone: 847-272-2228.

KAHN, SUSAN, artist; b. N.Y.C., Aug. 26, 1924; d. Jesse B. and Jenny Carol (Peshkin) Cohen; m. Joseph Kahn, Sept. 15, 1946 (dec.); m. Richard Rosenkranz, Feb. 1, 1981. Grad., Parsons Sch. Design, 1945; student, Moses Soyer, 1950-57. Subject of: book Susan Kahn, with an essay by Lincoln Rothschild, 1980; One-woman shows include Sagittarius Gallery, 1960, A.C.A., Galleries, 1964, 68, 71, 76, 80, Charles B. Goddard Art Center, Ardmore, Okla., 1973, Albrecht Gallery Mus. Art, St. Joseph, Mo., 1974, N.Y. Cultural Center, N.Y.C., 1974, St. Peter's Coll., Jersey City, 1978, Heidi Neuhoff Gallery, N.Y.C., 1989, Sindin Galleries, 1996; exhibited in group shows Audubon Artists, N.Y.C., Nat. Acad., N.Y.C., Springfield (Mass.) Mus., City Center, N.Y.C., A.C.A., Galleries, N.Y.C., Nat. Arts Club, N.Y.C., Butler Inst., Youngstown, Ohio, Islip Art Mus., East Islip. N.Y., 1989, Fine Arts Mus. of S., Mobile, Ala., 1989, Chatanooga Regional History Mus, 1989, Longview (Tex.) Mus. Art, 1990; represented in permanent collections, Tyler (Tex.) Mus., St. Lawrence U. Mus., Canton, N.Y., Fairleigh Dickinson U. Mus., Rutherford, N.J., Syracuse U. Mus., Sheldon Swope Gallery, Terre Haute, Ind., Montclair (N.J.) Mus. Fine Arts, Butler Inst. Am. Art, Youngstown, Ohio, Reading (Pa.) Mus., Albrecht Gallery Mus. Art, St. Joseph(Mo.), Cedar Rapids (Iowa) Art Center, N.Y. Cultural Center, N.Y.C., Edwin A. Ulrich Mus., Wichita, Kans., Wichita State U., Johns Hopkins Sch. Advanced Internat. Studies, Washington, Joslyn Mus., Omaha, U. Wyo., Laramie. Recipient Knickerbocker prize for best religious painting, 1956; Edith Lehman award Nat. Assn. Women Artists, 1958; Simmons award, 1961; Knickerbocker Artists award, 1961; Nat. Arts Club award, 1967; Knickerbocker Medal of Honor, 1964; Famous Artists Sch. award, 1967 Mem. Nat. Assn. Women Artists (Anne Barnett Meml. prize 1981, Solveig Stromsoe Palmer Meml. award 1987, Dorothy Schweitzer award 1990,Audrey Hope Shirk Meml. award 2006), Artists Equity, Met. Mus., Mus. Modern Art, Nat. Assn. Women Artists.

KAHN, VICTORIA ELAINE HOPKINS, special education educator; b. Grand Junction, Colo., Dec. 11, 1953; d. William Stanley Hopkins, Jr. and Bernice Irene (Porter) Hopkins; m. James Michael Humphrey, Sept. 17, 1982 (div. June 1986); m. Jerome Isidor Kahn, May 1, 1988 (div. June 2004). AA in Theatre Arts, Santa Ana Coll., 1974; BA with distinction in psychology, San Diego State U., 1985. Cert. edn. specialist Calif. State U., 2001. Owner, freelance photographer Victoria Vincent Photography, San Diego and Vista, Calif., 1984—94, Glendale, Ariz., 1993—94; enrichment instr. Felicita Found. for the Arts, Escondido, Calif., 1990—91; photographer, artist Vista (Calif.) Initiative for the Visual Arts, 1990—93; sub. tchr. and aide spl. edn. grades K-14 Orange County Dept. Edn., Costa Mesa, Calif., 1996—98; sub.

tchr. spl. edn. grades K-6 Garden Grove (Calif.) Unified Sch. Dist., 1997—2002; resource specialist tchr. grades 1-5 Long Beach (Calif.) Unified Sch. Dist., 2002—03; sub. spl. edn. tchr. grades K-6 North County Coastal Consortium Encinitas (Calif.) Union Sch. Dist., 2003—04; owner, designer Curriculum Creations, San Diego, 2003—05; cmty. trainer United Cerebral Palsy Assn.-Networks, Escondido, Calif., 2005—. Charter mem., artist Gallery Vista (Calif.) Artists' Assn., 1989—91; artist, photographer Holman Gallery, Scottsdale, Ariz., 1993—94. Editor: (book of poetry) Autumn Meditations, 1994, The Complete Poems of James L.O. Porter, 2002, (novella) The Chance, 2002. Vol. genealogy rsch. rm. Nat. Archives and Records Adminstrn., Laguna Niguel, Calif., 1998—2001; vol. South Coast Repertory Theatre, Costa Mesa, Calif., 1978—79; vol. summer stock The Magic Theatre, Berkeley, Calif., 1972. Recipient Achievement award, Nat. Archives and Records Adminstrn., 2000, 2001. Mem.: DAR (chmn. conservation com. Los Cerritos chpt. 2002—04, vol. lineage rsch. look up com. 2004—, chmn. conservation com. Rancho Buena Vista chpt. 2006—, mem. lineage rsch. com. Calif. state soc.), Know Thyself as Soul Found. S.W., Nat. Campaign for Tolerance, Dubois Family Assn., Tchrs. Assn. Long Beach, Coun. for Exceptional Children, Humane Farming Assn., Phi Kappa Phi, Pi Lambda Theta. Achievements include patents pending for a scenario method of teaching multiplication and division concepts (Cowboy Tim); a multi-sensory method of motivating students to read and write (The Reading Drum). Avocations: historial and geneaological research, writing, art, educational manipulatives and methods design, bird and nature watching. E-mail: kahnv@msn.com.

KAIGE, ALICE TUBB, retired librarian; b. Obion, Tenn., Jan. 27, 1922; d. George Easley and Lucile (Merryman) Tubb; m. Richard H. Kaige, Aug. 1952; children: Robert H., Richard C. (dec.), John S. (dec.) BA, Vanderbilt U., 1944; BS in Libr. Sci., Geo. Peabody Coll., 1947. Libr. Martin (Tenn.) High Sch., 1946-47, Demonstration Sch. Geo. Peabody Coll. Joint U. Librs., Nashville, Tenn., 1947-52; acquisitions libr. Lincoln Libr., Springfield, Ill., 1967-70; office coord. Springfield (Ill.) Chpt. ACLU, 1974; staff rep. Am. Fed. State, County & Mcpl. Employees, Springfield, 1975; libr. Ill. Dept. of Commerce and Community Affairs, Springfield, 1976-89. Vice chmn. Women's Internat. League for Peace and Freedom, 1969-70, various coms., 1970—; treas. Cen. Ill. Women's Lobby, 1971-72; com. on local govt. League of Women Voters, 1973-76; career day com. Urban League Guild, 1970-71; co-founder West Side Neighborhood Assn., Springfield, 1977. Recipient Elizabeth Cady Stanton award, Springfield Women's Political Caucus, 1982. Mem. Sangamon County Hist. Soc., Women's Internat. League for Peace and Freedom, War Resisters League, Ill. Audubon Soc., Ill. State Hist. Soc., World Affairs Coun. Ctrl. Ill. Avocations: reading, walking. Home: 1912 Turnberry Ct Springfield IL 62704-6211

KAIKOW, RITA ELLEN, library media specialist; b. Bklyn., Mar. 18, 1947; d. Solomon and Sylvia (Bitkoff) K BA, Queens Coll., 1968, MLS, 1971. Tchr., Bklyn., 1968—70; libr. media specialist Oceanside H.S., NY, 1971—. Liaison Nassau Sch. Libr. Sys., Carle Place, N.Y., 1980— (Outstanding Leadership, Dedication and Svc. as Facilitator award 1988); facilitator S.W. cluster, S.W. Nassau County, N.Y., 1985-94; mem. taskforce White House Conf. on Libr. and Info. Svcs Author: (mag.) The Book Report, 1991 Mem. ALA, Am. Assn. Sch. Librs., N.Y. State United Tchrs., N.Y. Libr. Assn. (sch. libr. media sect.), Nassau County Libr. Assn., Oceanside Fedn. Tchrs., L.I. Sch. Media Assn. (v.p. 1987-92, co-pres. 1992-97, pres. 1997—, Outstanding Recognition award 2002), Freedom to Read Found., Beta Phi Mu Avocation: computer technology. Office: Oceanside High Sch 3160 Skillman Ave Oceanside NY 11572-4495

KAILE, DAVINA K., lawyer; AB, Stanford U., 1990; JD, Georgetown U., 1994. Bar: Calif. 1994. Assoc. Pillsbury Madison & Sutro, LLP; mng. ptnr. Pillsbury Winthrop LLP, Palo Alto, Calif. Contbr. articles to profl. jours. Named one of Top 40 Lawyers Under 40, Nat. Law Jour., 2005. Mem.: State Bar Calif. Office: Pillsbury Winthrop LLP 2475 Hanover St Palo Alto CA 94304-1114 Office Phone: 650-233-4564. Office Fax: 650-233-4545. E-mail: davina.kaile@pillsburylaw.com.

KAIMAN, SARAH, retired physician; b. Omaha, June 10, 1915; d. Morris and Bertha Kaiman; children: Eric Koscove, Kristine Koscove. BS, U. Iowa, 1938, MD, 1940; LLB, Denver Sch. of Law, 1962. Bar: Colo. 1963, U.S. Dist. Ct. Colo. 1963, Ill. 1968; diplomate Am. Bd. Med. Examiners. Intern BethEl Hosp., Colorado Springs, Colo., 1941; pvt. practice family practice Denver, 1941—67, Thousand Oaks, Westlake Village and Ventura, Calif., 1973—84; med. officer Continental Assurance Co., Chgo., 1967—68, FDA, Washington, 1968—71, Dept. Health Svc., State of Calif., 1980—93; county physician Merced County, Calif., 1971; ret., 1993. Mem. staff Children's Meml. Hosp., St. Joseph's Hosp., Beth Israel Hosp, Gen. Rose Meml. Hosp., Denver Gen. County Hosp., Park Ave. Hosp., 1942—67, Merced Gen. Hosp., 1971—72, Westlake Cmty. Hosp., Westlake Village, 1972—73, Los Robles Hosp., Thousand Oaks, 1972—73, Simi (Calif.) Dr.'s Hosp., 1974—76, Simi Adventist Hosp., 1974—; cons. rsch. panel Med. World News, 1978; lectr., cons. in field; asst. med. dir. Continental Assurance Co., Chgo., 1967—68; med. examiner Cancer Detection Ctr., Chgo., 1969. Contbr. poems to lit. publs. Fellow: Am. Geriatrics Soc., Am. Acad. Family Physicians; mem.: AMA, LA Med. Assn., Cook County Med. Soc., Denver Med. Soc., Ill. Med. Assn., Colo. Med. Assn., Internat. Soc. Poets. Home: 6162 Calle Bodega Camarillo CA 93012 Personal E-mail: sktrust@aol.com.

KAINAROI, CYNTHIA D., assistant principal; b. Pitts., Oct. 7, 1953; d. Sidney Allen Wildman and Ruth Alberta King; children: Anne, Matthew. BS, U. Pitts., 1975, MA in Tchg., 1976; M in Ednl. Adminstrn., DuQuesne U., Pitts., 1997, EdD, 2005. Cert. elem. tchr. and prin. Pa., secondary prin. Pa., supr. letter of eligibility Pa. Asst. prin. mid. sch. North Allegheny Sch. Dist., Pitts., 1997—. Bd. mem. Pa. Mid. Sch. Assn. Western Region, 2001—. Mem.: Assn. Curriculum Devel. Office: Marshall Mid Sch 5145 Wexford Run Rd Wexford PA 15090 Office Phone: 724-934-6060.

KAISER, ANN CHRISTINE, magazine editor; b. Milw., Apr. 7, 1947; d. Herbert Walter and Annette G. (Werych) Gohlke; m. Louis Dan Kaiser; children: Richard L., Michael D. BS in Journalism, Northwestern U., 1969. Reporter Waco (Tex.) Tribune-Herald, 1969-71; editor Country Woman, Greendale, Wis., 1971—; mng. editor Taste of Home, Greendale, 1993—. Named among People of the Yr., Milw. Mag., 1998. Lutheran. Avocations: sailing, tennis, golf, travel. Office: Reiman Publs 5400 S 60th St Greendale WI 53129-1404

KAISER, BONNIE L., science educator, educator; b. Chgo. BS, U. Chgo., 1965, PhD, 1970. Precoll. sci. edn. dir. Rockefeller U., 1992—. Mem. NRC, Nat. Sci. Edn. Stds. Contbr. articles to profl. jours.; presenter nat. profl. orgns. Mem. AAAS, NSTA, Am. Chem. Soc., N.Y. Acad. Scis., U. Chgo. Alumni Assn., Sigma Xi.

KAISER, FRAN ELIZABETH, endocrinologist, gerontologist; b. N.Y.C., Dec. 6, 1949; d. Philip Francis and Bronia (Weiss) K. BS, CCNY, 1970; MD, N.Y. Med. Coll., N.Y.C., 1974. Diplomate Am. Bd. Internal Medicine, Am. Bd. Geriat. Intern Beth Israel Med. Ctr., N.Y.C., 1974-75, resident to chief resident, 1975-78; fellow in endocrinology and metabolism U. Minn., Mpls., 1978-81, instr. dept. medicine, 1980-81, asst. prof., 1981-86; asst. prof. in residence UCLA Sch. Medicine, 1986-89; assoc. prof. medicine St. Louis U., 1989-94, prof., 1994-97, assoc. dir. divsn. geriatric medicine, 1989-97, prof., 1994-97; sr. regional med. dir. Merck & Co., Inc., Irving, Tex., 1997—2003, exec. med. dir., 2003, 2005—; CEO, Kaiser and Assocs. Cons., 2004—05. Adj. prof. medicine St. Louis U, 1997-; chief sect. endocrinology and metabolism Dept. Internal Medicine, St. Paul Ramsey Med. Ctr./U. Minn. Hosps., St. Paul, 1981-86; John A. Hartford Geriatric Faculty Devel. award scholar Hartford Found., NYC/UCLA Sch. Medicine, 1986-87; chief geriatric medicine Olive View Med. Ctr./UCLA San Fernando Valley Program, Sylmar, Calif., 1987-89; med. dir. Hosp. Based Home Care, VA Med. Ctr., Sepulveda, 1987-89; clin. prof. medicine U. Tex. Southwestern Med. Sch., Dallas, 1999-. Former mem. editl. bd.: Jour. Clin. Endocrinology and Metabolism, ad hoc reviewer: Endocrinology, Jour. AMA, Jour. Am. Geriatrics Soc., past mem. editl. bd.: Am. Geriatric Soc., Internat. Medicine Bull., cons. editor: Am. Health Mag.; contbr. articles to profl. jours. Grantee NIH, 1980-81, 97, Genetech, 1987-89, Syntex Corp. 1990-92, Hoechst-Roussel, 1992-94, Bur. Health Professions, 1991-97, VIVUS, 1993-97, Merck, 1994-97, Upjohn, 1995-97. Fellow: Am. Geriatrics Soc. (past mem. editl. bd. Internal Medicine Bull., Jour. Geriatric Nephrology & Urology), Gerontol. Soc. Am.; mem.: Am. Assn. Home Care Physicians, N.Y. Acad. Sci., Am. Fedn.Clin. Rsch., Endocrine Soc. (mem. women in endocrinology group), Am. Diabetes Assn., AAAS. Achievements include research in hormonal changes with aging, studies of therapy of erectile dysfunction, testosterone, estrogen and frailty and women's health and sexuality. Office: 3510 Edgewater Dr Dallas TX 75205 Personal E-mail: Kaiserf@sbcglobal.net.

KAISER, KAREN SUE, elementary school educator; d. Reuben and Dorothy Ruth Miller; m. Richard Eugene Kaiser, Dec. 11, 1971; 1 child, Bryan Patrick. AA, Northeastern Jr. Coll., Sterling, Colo., 1969; EdB, U. No. Colo., 1972. K-2 tchr. Atwood (Colo.) Elem., 1972—73; kindergarten tchr. Sexson and Padroni Elems., Sterling, Colo., 1974—75, Sexson Elem., Sterling, 1976—84, Campbell Elem., Sterling, 1985—89, 4th grade tchr., 1990—. Art instr. Colo. Christian U., Denver, 2003; mem. achievement coun. RE-1 Valley Sch. Dist., Sterling, 1990—. Mem.: Colo. Edn. Assn., Alpha Delta Kappa (Silver Sister award 2002).

KAISER, LINDA SUSAN, lawyer; b. Alexandria, Va., Apr. 7, 1956; d. Thomas Raymond Kaiser and Joanne May (Wilber) Raynolds. BA, Pa. State U., 1978; JD, U. Pitts., 1981. Asst. counsel Pa. Ins. Dept., Harrisburg, 1981-85; sr. counsel Cigna Corp., Phila., 1985-92; asst. gen. counsel Reliance Ins. Co., Phila., 1992-95; ins. commr. Commonwealth of Pa., Harrisburg, 1995-97; sr. v.p., gen. counsel and sec. Reliance Ins. Co., Phila., 1997-2000; ptnr. Saul Ewing, LLP, 2000—03, Cozen O'Connor Attys., 2003—. Property casualty steering com. Ins. Fedn. Pa., Phila., 1992-95; alternate Pa. Workers Compensation Gov. Bd., 1993-95; bd. dirs. Nat. Assn. Ind. Insurers, 1997-2000, vice-chair membership com., 1999-2000; bd. dirs. Ins. Fedn. Pa., 1998-2000; exec. com., 2005—, Com. Seventy, 2003-. Pres. Huntington's Disease Soc. Am., Delaware Valley, Phila., 1993-96, v.p., 1996-2002; bd. dirs. Phila. Theatre Co., 2002— Mem. ABA, Soc. CPCU, Soc. Nat. Assn. Ins. Commrs. (vice chair N.E. zone 1997), Order of Coif, Barristers, Com. of Seventy. Office: 1900 Market St Philadelphia PA 19103 Office Phone: 215-665-2099. Business E-Mail: lkaiser@cozen.com.

KAISER, LOUISE MARTIN, elementary school educator; b. Anderson, S.C., Nov. 1, 1948; d. Charles Luther Martin and Helen Brown Whitaker; m. Paul Kaiser III, June 15, 1968; children: Paul IV, Ashley. AA, Anderson U., S.C., 1968; BA in Elem. Edn., Clemson U., S.C., 1976, M in Elem. Edn., 1992. Assoc. caseworker S.C. Dept. Social Svcs., Anderson, SC, 1968—71; math, lang. arts tchr. Anderson Sch. Dist. #5, SC, 1977—79, third grade tchr., 1980—85, fourth grade tchr., 1986—98, third grade tchr., 1999—. Grade chairperson South Font Sch., Anderson, SC, 1983—88, advisory chairperson, 1985—88; advisory com. McLees Elem., Anderson, SC, 2000—. Nominating com. First Bapt. Ch., Anderson, SC, 1986—89. Mem.: United Daughters of Confederacy (chaplain 1970—), DAR (good citizens chairperson 1987—89), S.C. Edn. Assn., NEA, Anderson Music Club. Baptist. Avocations: writing, travel, plays, sports. Home: 101 Roxbury Ct Anderson SC 29625 Office: McLees Elem Sch 4900 Dobbins Bridge Rd Anderson SC 29626 Personal E-mail: louisekaiser@anderson5.net.

KAISER, NINA IRENE, healthcare consultant; b. San Diego, Nov. 29, 1953; d. Louis Frederick and Mary Elizabeth (Wright) K.; children: Kellen Anne Kaiser, Ethan Andrew Kaiser-Klimist. BSN, BA in Women Studies, San Francisco State U., 1980; MBA, U. Phoenix, 2001. RN, Calif. RN Calif. Pacific Med. Ctr., San Francisco, 1980-81, Ralph K. Davies Med. Ctr., San Francisco, 1982-85, Planned Parenthood, San Francisco, 1985-86, Visiting Nurses and Hospice, San Francisco, 1986-88; RN supr. St. Mary's Home Care, San Francisco, 1991-93; RN dir. St. Vincent's Homecare and Hospice, Fremont, Calif., 1993-94; aux. dir. Home Health Link, San Leandro, Calif., 1994-99; mgmt. cons. Kaiser Home Health, Oakland, Calif., 1999—2002, mgr., 2003—. Regional coun. chair San Francisco Bay Area, 1999. Pres. Daus. of Bilitis, San Francisco, 1977-78; founding mem. Buena Vista Lesbian and Gay Parents Assn., San Francisco, 1985; treas., bd. dirs. Holladay Ave. Homeowners Assn., San Francisco, 1984-96; bd. dirs. Midrasha High Sch., Berkeley, Calif., 1996. With USN, 1971-74. Personal E-mail: missnynak@aol.com.

KAISER, SUSAN J., investment advisor; b. Chgo., Nov. 16, 1956; d. Henry Robert and Josephine Kaiser. BS in Engring., U. Iowa, 1978; MBA, Northwestern U., 1983. Cert. fin. advisor. Trading mgr. Nikko Securities, Osaka, Japan, 1992—93; pres. Kaiser Capital Mgmt., Watervliet, Mich., 1995—. Mem.: Naples Fin. Analyst Soc. Avocations: golf, tennis. Office: Kaiser Capital Mgmt PO Box 320 Watervliet MI 49098

KAISERLIAN, PENELOPE JANE, publishing executive; b. Paisley, Scotland, Oct. 19, 1943; came to U.S., 1956; d. W. Norman and Magdalene Jeanette (Houlder) Hewson; m. Arthur Kaiserlian, June 29, 1968; 1 child, Christian. BA, U. Exeter, Eng., 1965. Copywriter, sales rep. Pergamon Press, Elmsford, NY, 1965-68; exhibits mgr. Plenum Pub., N.Y.C., 1968-69; asst. mktg. mgr. U. Chgo. Press, 1969-76, mktg. mgr., 1976-83, assoc. dir., 1983-2001; dir. U. Va. Press, 2001—. Mem. Soc. for Scholarly Pub., Assn. Am. Univ. Presses (pres. 2006—), Soc. History Early Am. Republic, Assn. for Documentary Editing, Colonnade Club. Office: Univ Va Press PO Box 400318 Charlottesville VA 22904-4318

KAISH, LUISE CLAYBORN, sculptor, painter, educator; b. Atlanta, Sept. 8, 1925; d. Harry and Elsa Meyers; m. Morton Kaish, Aug. 15, 1948; 1 child, Melissa. BFA magna cum laude, Syracuse U., 1946, MFA, 1951; student, Escuela de Pintura y Escultura, Escuela de las Artes del Libro, Taller Grafico, Mexico, 1946-47. Artist-in-residence Dartmouth Coll., 1974; prof. sculpture and painting, 1980-93, chmn. div. painting and sculpture Columbia U., 1980-86, prof. emerita, 1993; vis. artist U. Wash., Seattle, Battelle seminars and study program, Seattle, 1979; artist-in-residence U. Haifa, Israel, 1985. One-man shows Meml. Art Gallery, Rochester, N.Y., 1954, Sculpture Ctr., N.Y.C., 1955, 58, Staempfli Gallery, N.Y.C., 1968, 81, 84, 87, 88, Minn. Mus. Art, St. Paul, 1969, Jewish Mus., N.Y.C., 1973, U. Ark., 1990, The Century Assn., 1998; exhibited (with Morton Kaish), Rochester Meml. Art Gallery, 1958, USIS, Rome, 1973, Dartmouth Coll., 1974, Oxford Gallery, Rochester, 1988; represented in permanent collections Whitney Mus. Am. Art, N.Y.C., Met. Mus. Art, N.Y.C., Jewish Mus., N.Y.C., Export Khleb, Moscow, Minn. Mus. Art, Gen. Mills Corp., Minn., Rochester Meml. Art Gallery, Smithsonian Instn., Nat. Mus. Am. Art, Washington, also numerous pvt. collections, commns., Syracuse U., Temple B'rith Kodesh, Rochester, Temple Israel, Westport, Conn., Holy Trinity Mission Sem., Silver Springs, Md., Temple Beth Shalom, Wilmington, Del., Beth-El Synagogue Ctr., New Rochelle, N.Y., Temple B'nai Abraham, Essex City, N.J., Continental Grain Co., N.Y. Trustee Am. Acad. in Rome, 1973-81, mem. exec. com., 1975-81, trustee emerita, 1994; trustee St. Gaudens Found., 1978-90, mem. exec. com., 1980-90. Recipient awards Everson Mus., Syracuse, 1947, awards Rochester Meml. Art Gallery, 1951, awards Ball State U., 1963, awards Ch. World Service, 1960, awards Council for Arts in Westchester, 1974, Emily Lowe award, 1956, Audubon Artists gold medal, 1963, Honor award AIA, 1975, Arents Pioneer medal, Syracuse U., 1989; Louis Comfort Tiffany grantee, 1951; Guggenheim fellow, 1959; Rome prize fellow Am. Acad. in Rome, 1970-72 Mem. Nat. Acad. Design, The Century Assn., Eta Pi Upsilon. Address: Kaish Studios 610 W End Ave # 9-a New York NY 10024-1605 Office Phone: 212-595-6815. Business E-Mail: lk4@columbia.edu.

KAJI, HIDEKO, pharmacology educator; b. Tokyo, Jan. 1, 1932; arrived in U.S., 1954; d. Sakae and Tsuneko Katayama; m. Akira Kaji, Aug. 23, 1958; children: Kenneth, Eugene, Naomi, Amy. BS, Tokyo U. Pharm. Scis., 1954; MS, U. Nebr., 1956; PhD, Purdue U., 1958. Vis. scientist Oak Ridge (Tenn.) Nat. Lab., 1962-63; assoc. U. Pa., Phila., 1963-64; rsch. assoc. The Inst. Cancer Rsch., Phila., 1965-66, asst. mem., 1966-76; vis. mem. Max Planck Inst. Molek. Gen., Berlin, 1972-73, Nat. Inst. Med. Rsch., London, 1973; assoc. prof. Jefferson Med. Coll., Phila., 1976-82, prof. biochemistry and molecular pharmacology, 1983—, Kimmel Cancer Ctr., 2005—; vis. prof. Wistar Inst., Phila., 1984-85. Cons. Nippon Paint Co., Ltd., Tokyo, 1990—, Coatesville (Pa.) VA Hosp., 1982-84. Contbr. articles to profl. jours. Fellow NIH (bd. dirs. 1986-89); mem. Am. Soc. Biochemistry and Molecular Biology, Am. Soc. Pharmacol. and Exptl. Therapeutics, Am. Soc. Microbiology, Sigma Xi. Home: 334 Fillmore St Jenkintown PA 19046-4328 Office: Jefferson Med Coll 1020 Locust St Philadelphia PA 19107-6731 Office Phone: 215-503-6547. Business E-Mail: Hideko.Kaji@jefferson.edu.

KAKUTANI, MICHIKO, critic; b. New Haven, Jan. 9, 1955; BA in English, Yale Univ., 1976. Reporter Washington Post, 1976—77; staff writer Time mag., 1977—79; reporter, cultural news NY Times, NYC, 1979—83, book critic, 1983—, now chief book critic. Recipient Pulitzer prize for criticism, 1998. Office: c/o NY Times Culture News 229 W 43d St New York NY 10036 Office Phone: 212-556-4874. Office Fax: 212-556-1516.*

KALAJIAN-LAGANI, DONNA, publishing executive; b. Mountainside, NJ, Feb. 8, 1955; d. Jack and Analid Kalajian; m. Ron Galotti, Oct. 14, 1981. BS, Penn State U., 1975. Internat. credit analyst Irving Trust Co., N.Y.C., 1976—77; ad sales rep. BMT Pub., N.Y.C., 1977—79, Woman's Day Mag., N.Y.C., 1979—81, cosmetics mgr., 1981—83, ea. mgr., 1984—87; v.p., advt. dir. Ladies' Home Jour., N.Y.C., 1987—89, v.p., pub., 1989—95; pub./sr. v.p. Cosmopolitan Mag., 1996—99; publ. dir. Cosmopolitan Group, N.Y.C., 1999—, sr. v.p., 1999—. Home: 100 Park Ave New York NY 10017-5516 Office: Cosmopolitan Hearst Magazines 224 W 57th St New York NY 10019-3299 Office Phone: 212-649-3282. Office Fax: 212-397-7581.*

KALATA, MARY ANN CATHERINE, architect; b. Passaic, N.J., Sept. 7, 1962; d. John Joseph Kalata and Filomena Katherine Kurnat. BS Archl. Technology, N.Y. Inst. Technology, 1984. Model builder, field coord. Perkins & Will, Russo & Sonder Architects, N.Y.C., 1984—94; archl. designer Andrew G. Antoniades Architects, N.Y.C., 1994—97; archl. coord. MIchael J. Romanik Architects, Paterson, NJ, 1997—. Mem. Rep. Nat. Com., Washington. Recipient gold medal in archl. technology, N.Y. Inst. Technology, 1984. Mem.: ASC/AIA, U.S. Navy League. Republican. Roman Catholic. Avocations: photography, travel, model building, audio technology. Home: 8 Baker Ct Clifton NJ 07011

KALAWSKI, EVA, lawyer; BA, Mount Holyoke Coll., 1977; JD, Georgetown Univ., 1981. V.p. human resources, gen. counsel, sec. Pilot Software Inc.; exec. v.p., gen. counsel, sec. Platinum Equity Inc., 1997—. Office: Platinum Equity 360 N Crescent Dr Beverly Hills CA 90210 Office Phone: 310-712-1850. Office Fax: 310-712-1848.

KALAYJIAN, ANIE, psychotherapist, educator, nurse, consultant; b. Aleppa, Syria; came to U.S., 1971; d. Kevork and Zabelle (Mardikian) Kalayjian; BS, L.I. U., 1979, DSc (hon.), 2001; MEd, Columbia U., 1981, profl. nursing tng. course, 1984, EdD, 1985; cert. photography, Pratt Inst., 1979. RN, N.Y., N.J., Conn.; cert. psychiat. mental health specialist; Dutch diplomate in logotherapy; advanced cert. in Eye Movement Desensitization and Reprocessing, advanced cert. in disaster mgmt. ARC; bd. cert. expert in traumatic stress; cert. expert in crisis mgmt., cert. Electro Magnetic Field balance practitioner. Psychiat. nurse Met. Hosp., N.Y.C., 1979-84; staff psychiat. mental health nurse Project Renewal, N.Y.C., 1978-2000; instr. Hunter Coll., N.Y.C., 1980-82; prof. Bloomfield (NJ) Coll., 1984-85; lectr. Jersey City (NJ) Coll., 1985; prof. Seton Hall U., South Orange, NJ, 1985-87; assoc. prof. grad. program St. Joseph Coll., 1987-91; prof. John Jay Coll. Criminal Justice, 1991-92, Fairleigh Dickinson U., 1991—92; vis. prof. Pace U., N.Y.C., 1994-95. Adj. prof. Coll. Mt. St. Vincent, Riverdale, NY, 1995—97; adj. prof. psychology Fordham U., 1998—; adj. prof. Coll. New Rochelle, 1998—99; disting. lectr. Columbia U., N.Y.C., 1995; spkr. in field; keynote spkr. Mid Am. Logotherapy Inst., 1995, Coll. Mt. St. Vincent, 1995, Hollins Coll., Va., 1995, UN; NGO exec. com. vice-chair, 2000—04; chair DPI/NGO annual conf., 2001; lectr., Argentina, Toronto, Ireland, U.N., 03. Author: Disaster and Mass Trauma: Global Perspectives on Post Disaster Mental Health Management, 1995; contbr. articles to profl. jours., chapters to books; reviewer: Readings: A Journal of Reviews and Commentary in Mental Health, 1990—; TV appearances ABC, CNN, NY1, MSNBC, CBS, Tokyo TV, TV Turkey, many others, —, radio appearances WSOU, WFUV, WBAI, Voice of America, —. Active com. for presdl. task force on nursing curriculum Soc. for Traumatic Stress Studies; co-founder, East coast coord. Mental Health Outreach to Earthquake Survivors in Armenia; program dir. Mental Health Outreach to Earthquake Survivors in Turkey, 1999, Mental Health Outreach to Tsunami in Sri Lanka, 2005, Mental Health Outreach to Hurrican Katrin and Rita, 2005, Mental Health Outreach in earthquake in Pakistan, 2006; dir. Julia Richman-Pace U.-N.Y. State Bd. Edn.-Vis. Nurse Svc.-Partnership program, 1991-92; UN rep. World Fedn. for Mental Health, mem. mental health/human rights com., 1996—. Recipient Clark Found. scholarship award, 1985, Outstanding Rsch. award Columbia U., 1993, ABSA Outstanding Achievement award APA, 1995; rsch. grantee Pace U., 1992; Endowed Nursing Edn. Columbia U., scholar, 1984; Armenian Relief Soc. scholar, 1976-77, Armenian Students Assn. Am. scholar, 1976-78; recipient Columbia U. Tchrs. Coll. Outstanding Rsch. award, 1993. Fellow APA (chair Hawaii program, 2004, treas. divsn. 52 Internat. Psychology, 2004-), Am. Orthopsychiat. Assn., N.Y. State Nursing Assn. (planning com. nursing edn); mem. Coun. on Continuing Edn., Psychiat. and Mental Health Nursing, Am. Psychol. Soc., Am. Psychiat. Nurses Assn., Am. Acad. Experts in Traumatic Stress, Internat. Coun. Psychologists, Internat. Trauma Counselors, Inst. for Psychodynamics and Origins of Mind, Armenian Students Assn. (treas. 1980-81, pres. 1981-83, scholarship chairperson 1983-85, v.p. ctrl. exec. com. 1987-88, pres. 1988-89, nat. pres. 1988-90), Armenian Info. Profls. (corr. sec. 1992-2000), Armenian-Am. Soc. for Studies on Stress and Genocide (founder, pres. 1988—), N.Y. RN's Assn. (chair edn. com. 1989-99), World Fedn. for Mental Health (UN rep. 1990-2006, treas., sec., UN com. on human rights 1994—, chair human rights com. 1996-2004, bd. dirs. Human Rights com., 2006—), Univ. for Peace (corr. sec. UN com.), Internat. Soc. Traumatic Stress Studies (v.p. N.Y. chpt. 1993-95, pres. 1995-2003), Assn. for Disaster and Mass Trauma Studies (pres., 2003—), Global Soc. for Nursing and Health (bd. mem., past pres., co-founder, acting treas.), N.Y. Counties RN Assn. (Jane Delano Disting. Svc. award 1994), APA (internat. divsn. treas., 2004—, chair internat. com. on disaster and mass trauma, mem. conf. planning com.), Kappa Delta Pi (advisor 1989-90), Sigma Theta Tau. Avocations: photography, acting, hiking, yoga, meditation. Office: 185 E 85th St Mezz 4 New York NY 10028 Office Phone: 201-723-9578. E-mail: kalayjiana@aol.com, ekalayjiana@aol.com.

KALFA, THEODOSIA ANASTASIOS, pediatrician, educator; arrived in U.S., 1991; d. Anastasios Kalfas and Chrysoula Kalfa; m. Stefanos Manganaris, June 15, 1994; children: Panayotis Thalis Manganaris, Anastasios Alexandros Manganaris. MD summa cum laude, Aristotle U., 1990, PhD in Biochemistry, 1997. Diplomate in oncology and hematology Am. Bd. Pediat., 2004, Am. Bd. Pediat., 2000. Gen. practitioner Ministry Health, Taxiarches, Greece, 1990—91; postdoctoral assoc. Med. Sch. U. Minn., Mpls., 1991—94; resident pediatrics U. N.C., Chapel Hill, NC, 1996—99; fellow pediatric hematology-oncology Med. Ctr. Duke U., Durham, NC, 2000—03; rsch. instr. Cin. (Ohio) Children's Hosp. Med Ctr., 2003—06, asst. prof. Cincinnati, Ohio, 2006—; rsch. instr. Coll. Medicine U. Cin., 2003—06, asst. prof. Coll. Medicine, 2006—. Scholar, NIH, Nat. Heart, Lung, Blood Inst., 2003—, NIH, Nat. Inst. Child Health and Human Devel., 2004—06. Fellow: Am. Acad. of Pediat.; mem.: Am. Soc. Pediatric Hematology Oncology (Young Investigator award 2006), Panhellenic Med. Assn., Greece, Am. Soc. of Hematology, Am. Assn. for Cancer Rsch. Office: Cin Children's Hosp Med Ctr 3333 Burnet Ave MLC 7015 Cincinnati OH 45229-3039 Office Phone: 513-636-0989.

KALIK, MILDRED, lawyer; b. NYC, Dec. 4, 1947; BA, U. Wis., 1969; JD, George Washington U. Law Ctr., 1972; LLM in taxation, NYU, 1982. Bar: N.Y. 1973, registered: U.S. Tax Ct. 1973, U.S. Dist. Ct., so. dist. N.Y. 1974, U.S. Ct. Appeals, second cir. 1975. Ptnr. Simpson Thacher & Bartlett LLP, N.Y.C. Mem.: New York State Bar Assn., Internat. Acad. Estate & Trust law, Assn. Bar City N.Y. (surrogates ct. 1999—2003), Am. coll. Trust & Estate Counsel, ABA (chmn. generation skipping tax planning 1981—88, asst. sec., probate & trust law sect. 1988—90, coun. 1990—97). Office: Simpson Thacher & Bartlett LLP 425 Lexington Ave New York NY 10017-3954 Office Phone: 212-455-2778. Office Fax: 212-455-2502. Business E-Mail: mkalik@stblaw.com.

KALIKOW, THEODORA JUNE, academic administrator; b. Lynn, Mass., June 6, 1941; d. Irving and Rose Kalikow. AB, Wellesley Coll., 1962; ScM, MIT, 1970; PhD, Boston U., 1974. From instr. to prof. Southeastern Mass. U., North Dartmouth, 1968-84; dean Coll. Arts and Scis., U. No. Colo., Greeley, 1984-87; dean of the coll. Plymouth (N.H.) State Coll., 1987-94, interim pres., 1992-93; pres. U. Maine, Farmington, 1994—. Contbr. articles to profl. jours. Chair steering com. Maine ACE/NIP, 1995—; chair Coun. Pub. Liberal Arts Colls., 1997-99; bd. dirs. Maine Humanities Coun., 1999—, Fin. Authority Maine, 2000-06, Ctr. for the Prevention of Hate Violence, 2004—, Maine Econ. Growth CouN., 2005—. Named to, Maine Women's Hall of Fame, 2002; recipient Mary Ann Hartman award, 2000;. NSF grantee, 1978, Am. Coun. on Edn. fellow, Brown U., 1983—84. Mem.: Assn. Am. Colls. and Univs. (bd. dirs. 2000—03), Western Mountains Alliance (chmn. 2000—03), Am. Coun. on Edn. (commn. on women 1994—97, 2000—03), Soc. Values in Higher Edn. (bd. dirs. 1991—94). Office: U Maine at Farmington Office of the Pres 224 Main St Farmington ME 04938-1911 Office Phone: 207-778-7256.

KALIN, D. JEAN (DOROTHY JEAN KALIN), artist, educator; b. Kansas City, Mo., Feb. 11, 1932; d. William Warner and Esther Dorothy (Peterson) Johnson; m. John Baptist Kalin, Jr., Jan. 5, 1952; children: Jean Loraine, Debra Ann, Diana Yvonne AA, St. Joseph Jr. Coll., Mo., 1951. Artist Hallmark Cards, Inc., Kansas City, 1952—53, 1973—93; freelance artist Kansas City, 1953—72; owner Portraits of Life, Kansas City, 1986—, art tchr., 1988—. Illustrator article Directory of Am. Portrait Artists, 1985; featured in Rockport Pubs. Best of Watercolor 2 and Painting Light and Shadow, 1997, Am. Artist Mag., 1998, 2000, Splash 5, 1998, Best of Collected Watercolor, 2002, Midwest Art, 2003, The Artists' Mag., 2003, Acrylic Highlights Mag., 2004, Watercolor Mag., 2005 Kansas City Art Inst. scholar, 1951-52 Mem. Nat. Oil and Acrylic Painters Soc. (signature), Internat. Soc. Acrylic Painters (signature), Kans. Watercolor Soc. (signature), Women Artists of West (signature), Am. Watercolor Soc. (assoc.), Nat. Watercolor Soc. (assoc.), Transparent Watercolor Soc. Am. (assoc.), Nat. Mus. Women in Arts (charter), Mo. Watercolor Soc. (signature, bd. dir.), We. Colo. Watercolor Soc. (signature), Internat. Platform Assn Avocations: gardening, travel. Address: 20650 State Rt 371 Platte City MO 64079-9344 Office Phone: 816-992-3744.

KALINA, EUNICE GOLDSTEIN, human services director; b. Cleve., Aug. 24, 1936; d. Philip and Bertha Goldstein; divorced; children: Mark, Nancy. BSc in Edn., Ind. U., 1958; MA in Counseling and Human Svcs., John Carroll U., 1989. Tchr. Breckville, Broadview Heights, Ohio, 1958—62; dir. human svcs. Mayfield Village, Ohio, 1987—. Bd. mem. Temple Ner Tamid, Euclid, Ohio, 1970—95, sec., edn. com. chmn., pers. com. chmn.; bd. mem. Hillcrest Meals on Wheels, Lyndhurst, Ohio, 1987—. Named Oustanding Citizen of Yr. Mayfield Village, 1998. Jewish. Avocations: walking, water aerobics, tai chi, theater, ballet. Home: 469 Blueberry Cir Mayfield OH 44143 Office: Mayfield Village 6622 Wilson Mills Rd Cleveland OH 44143-3407 Office Phone: 440-461-2210, 440-919-2332.

KALINICH, LILA JOYCE, psychiatrist, educator; BA, Northwestern Univ., Chgo., 1966, MD, 1969. Assoc. clin. prof. psychiatry Columbia U., NYC. Mem.: Assn. Psychoanalytic Medicine (pres. 2005—06). Office: Ctr for Psychoanalytic Trng & Rsch Columbia Univ 1051 Riverside Dr New York NY 10032 Office Phone: 212-866-0200. Business E-Mail: ljk1@columbia.edu.

KALISCH, BEATRICE JEAN, nursing educator, consultant; b. Tellahoma, Tenn., Oct. 15, 1943; d. Peter and Margaret Ruth Petersen; children— Philip P., Melanie J. BS, U. Nebr., 1965; MS, U. Md., 1967, PhD, 1970. Pediatric staff nurse Centre County Hosp., Bellefonte, Pa., 1965-66; instr. nursing Philipsburg (Pa.) Gen. Hosp. Sch. Nursing, 1966; pediatric staff nurse Greater Balt. Med. Center, Towson, Md., 1967; asst. prof. maternal-child nursing Am. U., 1967-68; clin. nurse specialist N.W. Tex. Hosp., Amarillo, 1970; assoc. prof. maternal-child nursing, curriculum coordinator nursing Amarillo Coll., 1970-71; chmn. baccalaureate nursing program, asso. prof. nursing U. So. Miss., 1971-74; prof. nursing, chmn. dept. parent-child nursing U. Mich. Sch. Nursing, Ann Arbor, 1974-86, Shirley C. Titus Disting. prof., 1977—, Titus Disting. prof. nursing mgmt., 1989—, dir. nursing bus. and health sys. program, 2000—; prin., dir. nursing consultation svcs. Ernst & Young, Detroit, 1986-89. Prin. investigator USPH grant to study image of nurses in mass media and the informational quality nursing news, U. Mich., 1977-86, prin. investigator to study intrahosp. transport of critically ill patients, 1991—; prin. investigator to study use of HIA nurse in N.Y.C. labor market, U. Mich.; prin. investigator to study the impact of managed care on critical care, U. Mich.; vis. Disting. prof. U. Ala., 1979, U. Tex., 1981, Tex. Christian U., 1983. Author: Child Abuse and Neglect: An Annotated Bibliography, 1978; co-author: Nursing Involvement in Health Planning, 1978, Politics of Nursing, 1982, Images of Nurses on Television, 1983, The Advance of American Nursing, 1986, revised, 1994, The Changing Image of the Nurse, 1987; co-editor: Studies in Nursing Mgmt.; contbr. articles to profl. jours. Recipient Joseph L. Andrews Bibliog. award Am. Assn. Law Libraries, 1979; Book of Yr. award Am. Jour. Nursing, 1978, 83, 86, 87, Outstanding Achievement award U. Md., 1987, Distinguished Alumni award U. Nebr., 1985, Shaw medal Boston Coll., 1986; USPHS fellow. Fellow: Am. Acad. Nursing; mem.: ANA, APHA, Am. Coll. Healthcare Execs., Am. Orgn. Nurse Execs., Sigma Theta Tau, Phi Kappa Phi. Presbyterian. Office: U Mich Sch Nursing 400 N Ingalls St Ann Arbor MI 48109-0482 Business E-Mail: bkalisch@umich.edu.

KALISH-WEISS, BETH ISAACS, psychologist, psychoanalyst, consultant; b. Nashville, Mar. 5, 1933; d. Harry A. and Eva (Friedman) Isaacs; m. Allan S. Kalish, Apr. 3, 1954 (div. 1972); children: Betsy Kalish-Hendler, David Harry; m. Harold A. Weiss, July 5, 1980 (div. 2005). BA, Sarah Lawrence Coll., 1955; PhD, Bryn Mawr Coll., 1976. Lic. clin. psychologist; registered dance movement therapist. Dance-movement therapist Phila. State Hosp., 1961-65; dance-movement therapist, rsch. assoc. Devel. Ctr. for Autistic Children, Phila., 1965-74; dir., assoc. prof. grad. program Movement Therapy Immaculate Heart Coll., L.A., 1975-80, Loyola Marymount U., L.A., 1980-83; faculty, psychotherapist L.A. Family Inst., 1983-86; asst. clin. prof. neuropsychiatr. inst. UCLA, 1986—; tng. supr. analyst, pres. L.A. Inst. and Soc. for Psychoanalytic Studies, 1986—. Cons., supr. L.A. County Dept. Mental Health, 1986-91, Asian-Pacific Counseling Ctr., L.A., 1986-. Contbr. articles to profl. jours. Recipient award for Movement Therapy with Schizophrenics, Phila. Mental Health Assn., Phila. State Hosp., 1961, Rsch. with Autism award Van Ameringen Found., Phila., 1972, Body Movement Scale for Atypical Children award Nat. Inst. for Mental Health, Phila., 1974-75, faculty rsch. grant, Immaculate Heart Coll., 1979, rsch. grant NEA, L.A., 1980. Fellow Am. Orthopsychiat. Assn.; mem. APA (mem. divsn. 39/psychoanalysis, women in psychoanalysis), Internat. Psychoanalytic Assn.; charter mem. Am. Dance Therapy Assn. (pres. 1972-74, trustee Marian Chace Meml. Fund, treas. 1980-90). Democrat. Jewish. Home: 6433 Tahoe Dr Los Angeles CA 90068-1655 Office Phone: 323-463-1844. Personal E-mail: bkalishweiss@mindspring.com.

KALLFELZ, TONYA LEIGH, secondary school educator; d. Robert Earl and Julie Darline Hill; m. David Michael Kallfelz, June 19, 1999; 1 child, Brayden Robert. B in Excercise and Sports Sci., SW Tex. State U., San Marcos, 1996. Cert. tchr. Tex. Tchr. Rebelette Dance Team and dance dept. Travis HS, Austin, Tex., 1997—2000; tchr. Diamond Dazzlers Dance Team and dance dept. Akins HS, Austin, 2000—. Staff, choreographer Halftime U.S.A, San Marcos, Tex., 1994—96; co-dir. All-City Dance Team, Austin, 1997—2003, All-City Dance Co., Austin, 2000—03. Vol. Katrina Relief, Austin, 2006, Blue Santa, Austin, 2000—06; active Akins Campus Adv. Com., Austin, Tex., 2005—06. Recipient Am. Dance/Drill Team Dir. award, Dance Educators, 1998. Mem.: Tex. Dance Educators of Am. (assoc.; com. chair nat. dance conv. 2006—). Office: Akins Diamond Dazzlers 10701 S First St Austin TX 78748 Office Phone: 512-841-9800. Office Fax: 512-841-9795. Business E-Mail: tkallfel@austinisd.org.

KALLIR, JANE KATHERINE, art gallery director, author; b. NYC; d. John Otto and Joyce (Ruben) Kallir. BA, Brown U., Providence, R.I., 1976. Asst. to dir. Lefebre Gallery, NYC, 1977, Galerie St. Etienne, NYC, 1977-78, co-dir., 1979—. Guest lectr. NYU, 1982—85, 1999, Mus. Am. Folk Art, NYC, 1982—85, Nat. Gallery Art, 1994, guest curator, 94; guest lectr. Ft. Lauderdale Mus. Art, 1996, guest curator, Fla., 96; guest lectr. Mus. Modern Art, 1997, Internat. Found. for Art Rsch., 1998, Wexner Ctr., Columbus, Ohio, 1999, San Diego Mus., 2001, Columbus Mus. of Art, 2002, Clark Art Inst., 2002, Van Gogh Mus., 2005; guest curator NY State Mus., Albany, 1983, Internat. Exhbn. Found., Washington, 1984—85, Mus. of City of Vienna, 1986, Austrian Nat. Gallery, 1990, Indpls. Mus. Art, 1994, San Diego Mus. Art, 1994, Nat. Mus. of Women in the Arts, 2001, Orlando Mus. of Art, Fla., 2001, Museo del Vittoriano, Rome, 2001, San Diego Mus. Art, 2001, Van Gogh Mus., 2005. Author: Gustav Klimt-Egon Schiele, 1980, Austria's Expressionism, 1981, The Folk Art Tradition, 1981, Grandma Moses, The Artist Behind the Myth, 1982, Arnold Schoenberg's Vienna, 1984, Viennese Design and the Wiener Werkstaette, 1986, Gustav Klimt: 25 Masterworks, 1989, Egon Schiele: The Complete Works, 1990, rev., 1998, Richard Gerstl/Oskar Kokoschka, 1992, Egon Schiele, 1994, Egon Schiele: 27 Masterworks, 1996, Grandma Moses, 25 Masterworks, 1997, Grandma Moses in the 21st Century, 2001, The Essential Grandma Moses, 2001, Egon Schiele, Watercolors and Drawings, 2003, Egon Schiele: Love and Death, 2005. Mem.: Art Dealers Assn. Am. (bd. dir. 1994—97, chmn. pub. rels. com. 2001—, v.p. 2003—06). Democrat. Office: Galerie St Etienne 24 W 57th St New York NY 10019-3918 Office Phone: 212-245-6734. E-mail: gallery@gse.art.com.

KALLMAN, MARY JEANNE, research scientist; b. Alexandria, Va., May 27, 1948; d. Ira Semon and Carol Louise (Gardinier) Davis; m. William Michael Kallman, Dec. 20, 1969. BS in Psychology, Lynchburg Coll., 1970; MS in Biopsychology, U. Ga., 1974, PhD, 1976. Post-doctoral fellow dept. pharmacology Med. Coll. Va., Richmond, 1976-79, rsch. assoc. dept. pharmacology, 1979, asst. prof., 1980-83; asst. prof. dept. psychology U. Miss., University, 1983-86; dir. grad. exptl. program dept. psychology dept. psychology and pharmacology U. Miss., University, 1986-91; assoc. prof. psychology and pharmacology U. Miss., University, 1986-91; sr. rsch. advisor Eli Lilly & Co., Greenfield, Ind., 1991—. Rsch. asst. dept. psychology U. Ga., 1970-73, 74-75, dept. psychiatry U. Miss. Med. Ctr., 1973-74; adj. asst. prof. dept. psychology Va. Commonwealth U., 1976-77; grant reviewer NIH, EPA, March of Dimes, document reviewer EPA. Contbr. chpts. to 8 books, numerous articles to profl. jours. Recipient Outstanding Rsch. Program award Miss. Psychol. Assn., 1986. Fellow APA; mem. AAAS, Am. Soc. Pharmacology and Exptl. Therapeutics, Neurosci., Behavioral Pharm. Soc., Behavioral Teratology Soc., Behavioral Toxicology Soc., SouthEastern Psychol. Assn., South Ctrl. Soc. Toxicology, Sigma Xi, Phi Kappa Phi. Methodist. Office: Eli Lilly & Co PO Box 708 Greenfield IN 46140-0708

KALNES, DONNA M. SIMONDET, retired principal, alcohol and drug abuse education program director; b. North Redwood, Minn., Jan. 24, 1934; d. Oscar Walter and Alma Mae Simondet; m. Rasmus B.A. Kalnes, Aug. 21, 1954; children: David Michael(dec.), Stephanie Kae, Eric Peter. BA in Elem. Edn., Luther Coll., Decorah, Iowa, 1953; MS in Tchg., U. Wis., Whitewater, 1979; splty. degree in ednl. adminstrn., U. Wis., Madison, 1995. Tchr. 2d grade Jackson Sch. Dist., Minn., 1953—54; 1st and 2d grade tchr. Hayfield Sch. Disst., Minn., 1954—56, Nichols Sch. Dist., Monona, Wis., 1956—57, Madison Sch. Dist., 1961; tchg. grades 1-8 Mukwonego Sch. Dist., Wis., 1966—68; tchr. grades 4, 7, 8 Palmyra-Eagle Sch. Dist., Wis., 1968—83, prin., 1978—94. Alcohol and other drug abuse coun. dir. K-12 Palmyra-Eagle Sch. Dist., 1983—94; alcohol and other drug abuse program grant reader Wis. Dept. Pub. Instrn., 1985—94, alcohol and other drug abuse prrogram coun. mem., 1988—94; pres. Four Lakes Prins. Assn., 1991; presenter in field. Bd. dirs., bd. curators Wis. Hist. Soc., Madison, 1999—2001; adult leader 4-H, Eagle, 1967—93; cookbook com. Friends of Old World Wis., 1988; vol. holiday fair Waukesha County Hist. Soc., 1990—; edn. com. Eagle Hist. Soc., 2005—; state del. Rep. Party of Wis., Madison, 1975—; co-author 100-yr. history St. John's Luth. Ch., North Prairie, Wis., adult Bible study leader; edn. officer Luth. Brotherhood Prairie Br. # 8146, 1987—95; bd. dirs. Friends of Wis. Hist. Soc., Madison, 1976—, pres., 1999—2001; bd. dirs. Palmyra-Eagle Scholarship and Ednl. Found., 2003—. Named Mother of Yr. for Wis., Mother of the Yr. Program, 1980, Citizen of Yr., Eagle Lioness, 1986; named one of Outstanding Elem. Tchrs. of Am., 1974, 1975, 1976; recipient Disting. Svc. award, Luther Coll., 1988, US Mcht. Marine Acad., 1992, Assn. Wis. Sch. Adminstrs., 1998. Mem.: Assn. Wis. Sch. Adminstrs. (pres., chair exec. dir. search com. 1995, 1998, bd. dirs. 1991—97, region 2 dir. 1991—93, pub. rels. com. 1993—97, chair regional profl. conf. 1994—95, co-chair exec. dirs. retirement celebration 1995), Nat. Assn. Elem. Sch. Prins., Phi Delta Kappa (nat. fellows program 1989). Lutheran. Avocations: Bible study, rosemaling, gardening, piano, crossword puzzles. Home: 520 E Waukesha Rd Eagle WI 53119 E-mail: dmkalnes@execpc.com.

KALOF, LINDA HENRY, sociologist, educator; b. Norfolk, Va., Dec. 17, 1946; d. William Douglas Henry and Mary Elizabeth Bailey; m. Thomas Michael Dietz; children: Alexandra Kalof, Adam Henry. BA, U. Fla., 1975; PhD, Am. U., 1989. Asst. prof. SUNY, Plattsburgh, 1989—95, assoc. prof., 1995-96, George Mason U., Fairfax, Va., 1996—2002, prof., 2002—03, Mich. State U., East Lansing, 2003—. Author: Looking At Animals in Human History, 2006; co-author: Evaluating Social Science Research, 1996, Environmental Values, 2005; contbr. articles to profl. jours. Office: Mich State U Dept Sociology East Lansing MI 48824 E-mail: lkalof@msu.edu.

KALSNER-SILVER, LYDIA, psychologist; b. Winnipeg, Can., May 26, 1964; d. Stanley and Jenny Kalsner; m. Jay Silver, Aug. 20, 1994; children: Dylan, Chloe. BS in Psychology, U. Toronto, 1987; MA, EdM, Columbia U., 1992; EdD in Counseling Psychology, Rutgers U., 2000. Dir. clin. assessment dept. psychiatry SUNY, Bklyn., 1992—97; psychology resident Jackson Meml. Hosp., Miami, 1997—98, post-doctoral fellow Juvenile Gun Offender Program, 2000—01; sch. psychologist Temple Beth Am Day Sch., Miami, 2001—02; psychologist Divsn. Alternative Outreach Miami (Fla.) Dade Country Pub. Schs., 2002—; pvt. practice psychotherapist Miami, 2002—. Grant reviewer crime prevention com. Miami (Fla.) Dade Criminal Justice Counsel, Miami, 1997; adj. faculty U. Miami, 1997—98; rsch. writer Higher Edn. Ext. Svc. Columbia U., N.Y., 1991—92; instr. Rutgers U., New Brunswick, NJ. Contbr. articles to profl. jours. Scholar, Tchrs. Coll. Columbia U., 1990. Mem.: APA, Soc. Personal Assessment, Fla. Psychol. Assn. Avocations: cooking, travel. Home: 5151 Collins Ave Miami Beach FL 33140 Office: 5151 Collins Ave Ste 223 Miami Beach FL 33140 Office Phone: 305-866-3579. Personal E-mail: kalsner@aol.com.

KALSOW-BERNHARD, KATHRYN MARIE, retired music educator; b. Chgo., Jan. 5, 1948; d. William H. and Frances C. Perkins; m. Leroy F. Bernhard, June 9, 2001; m. Stephen Allan Kalsow, Aug. 31, 1968 (div. Nov. 12, 1997); children: Sandra Kristen Moore, Jeffrey Stephen Kalsow, Julie Anne Kalsow. AA, Lyons Twp. Jr. Coll., LaGrange, Ill., 1967; BMus, Millikin U., Decatur, Ill., 1970; MA in Curriculum and Instrn., Concordia Coll., River Forest, Ill., 1988. Elem. music tchr. Ontarioville and Laurel Hill elem. schools, Ontarioville, Bartlett, Ill., 1970—72; music tchr. and choir dir. Eastview Jr. High, Bartlett, Ill., 1972—81, Canton Mid. Sch., Streamwood, Ill., 1981—97; condr. Elgin Children's Chorus-Treble Choir, Elgin, Ill., 1995—2002; choir dir. Elgin (Ill.) H.S., 1997—2004, ret., 2004. Dir. kinderchoir First Congl. Ch., Elgin, 1986—89; instr. music for elem. tchrs. Elgin C.C., 1989—96; instr. music methods Judson Coll., 1997—98; outreach program writer, coord. Elgin Choral Union, 1998—2006, tchr. voice, 2005—; guest condr. in field. Choir chair Fox Valley Music Festival, Ill., 1998—2000. Mem.: Ill. Music Educators Assn. (chair Dist. IX 1999—2002), Am. Choral Dirs. Assn. (life), Music Educators Nat. Conf. (life). Personal E-mail: kmbernhard@aol.com.

KALTER, EILEEN M., retired language educator; b. Monticello, NY, Aug. 9, 1943; d. Aaron (Harry) and Ray Spector; m. Ivan Kalter, June 26, 1966; children: Andrew Scott, Sheryl Lynn. Student, Sorbonne U., Paris, 1964; BA, Ithaca Coll., 1965; MA, SUNY, New Paltz, 1971. Tchr. Spanish, Monticello Ctrl. Schs., NY, 1980—83; tchr. French and Spanish Fallsburg Ctrl. Schs., NY, 1967—2002, tutor French and Spanish, 2002—05, ret., 2005. Bd. dirs. Sullivan County Dramatic Workshop; committeman Fallsburg Dem. Com., NY, 1993—2005. Recipient Hubert Humphrey award, Hadassah, 1978, Appreciation award, Fallsburg H.S. Student Govt., 2002. Mem.: Fgn. Lang. Assn. Sullivan County (pres. 2000—01), NY State Union Tchrs., NY State Assn. Fgn. Lang. Tchrs., Red Hat Soc., Jewish Women Internat., Catskill Nordic Ski Club (pres. 2004—05), Hadassah (life; pres. 1976—78). Avocations: reading, travel, cross country skiing. Home: PO Box 383 South Fallsburg NY 12779

KALVER, GAIL ELLEN, dance company executive, musician; b. Chgo., Nov. 25, 1948; d. Nathan Eli and Alice Martha (Jaffe) K. BS in Music Edn., U. Ill., 1970; MA in Clarinet Chgo. Musical Coll., Roosevelt U., 1974. Profl. musician, Chgo., 1970-77; assoc. mgr. Ravinia Festival, Highland Park, Ill., 1977-83; exec. dir. Hubbard Street Dance Chgo., 1984—. Bd. dirs. Chicago Dancers United, Ill. Arts Alliance; mem. dance panel Ill; music consul., Nat. Radio Theatre. Arts Council, Chgo., 1983-85; mem. grants panels Chgo. Office Fine Arts, 1985; conf. mem., DanceUSA, 2005. Editor: Music Explorer (for music edn.), 1983-86. Mem. grants panels NEA, 1992-94; cons. music Nat. Radio Theatre, Chgo., 1983—; mem. adv. coun. Dance Initiative Chgo. Cmty. Trust, Dancers Responding to AIDS; mem. exec. com. Dance for Life, 2003. Recipient Arts Mgmt. Excellence award, ABBY award, 2003. Office: Hubbard St Dance Chgo 1147 W Jackson Blvd Chicago IL 60607-2905

KALVIN-STIEFEL, JUDY, public relations executive; b. Valley Stream, Long Island; m. Lewis Stiefel; 1 child, Amy. BA in lit. and journalism, SUNY, Oneonta. Writer, editor Corp. Design mag., 1985—87; account supr. Howard J. Rubenstein Assoc.; dir. pub. rels. Gerstman+Meyers, 1989—93; v.p. pub. rels. Gerstman+Meyers (now Interbrand), 1993—97, Addison, NYC, 1997—99; v.p., dir. comm. Sterling Group, NYC, 1999—2001; founder, pres. Kalvin Pub. Rels., Forest Hills, NY, 2001. Author: Defining Woman: Natural Workout for Body and Mind, 1993. Recipient Women Achievement Pacesetter award, NYC Coun., 2002, NEAL award bus. writing, championship title, World Natural Bodybuilding Fedn., 1990. Mem.: NY Women in Comm. Avocation: bodybuilding. Office: 114 Ogden Ave Dobbs Ferry NY 10522-3312 Office Phone: 718-520-1660. Business E-Mail: jkalvin@kalvinpr.com.

KAMALI, NORMA, fashion designer; b. NYC, June 27, 1945; d. Sam and Estelle (Mariategui) Arraez. Grad., Fashion Inst. of Tech., 1965. Established Kamali Ltd., N.Y.C., 1967-78; owner, designer On My Own Norma Kamali, N.Y.C., 1978—. Designer costumes for Emerald City in The Wiz, 1978; for Twyla Tharp dance In the Upper Room, 1986; Parachute Designs displayed Met. Mus. of Art, N.Y.C., 1977; prodr., dir. (video) Fall Fantasy; dir. (video) Fashion Aid, 1985. Recipient Coun. Fashion Designers Am. award, 1982, 1985, Coty award, 1981, 82, 83, Ernie awards Earnshaw Rev., 1983, Fashion Inst. Design and Merchandising award, 1983, Annual Interiors award Interiors Mag., 1985, Salute to Women award N.Y. Fashion Group, 1986, Disting. Arch. award N.Y. chpt. AIA, 1986, Outstanding Grad. award Pub. Edn. Assn. N.Y., 1988, Award of Merit, Internat. Video Culture Competition, 1988, Am. Success award Fashion Inst. Tech., 1989, Youth Friends award Sch. Art League, 1997, Pencil award, 1999, Willow award Lower East Side Girls Club, 1999, Fashion Outreach Style award, 1999, Bus. Outreach award Manhattan C. of C., 2002, Entrepreneur award Fashion Group, 2002, Women's History Month award N.Y.C. Controllers Office, 2002, Bd. Director's Spl. Tribute award Coun. Fashion Designers Am., 2005; featured exhibit Met. Mus. Exhibit, 2001; inducted into Fashion Walk of Fame Fashion Ctr. Bus. Improvement Dist. Office: 11 W 56th St New York NY 10019-3902*

KAMAN, HELEN S., retired aerospace engineer, artist; b. Coraopolis, Pa., Jan. 5, 1918; d. Nels Sylvander and Myrtel McKee; m. Charles H. Kaman, Oct. 20, 1945; children: Charles William II, Cathleen, Steven. BS in Art, Edinboro U., 1940; MA in Am. Studies, Trinity Coll., 1982. Cert. aero. engring. Penn State U., 1944. Co-founder Kaman Corp. Helicopter Mfg., Bloomfield, Conn., 1946—50; engring. draftsman Sikorsky Aircraft, E. Hartford, Conn., 1944—45; ret. Solo and group shows. Bd. mem. Hartford Art Sch., 1983—89, Watkinson Sch., 1980—90. Mem.: Pen Women. Avocations: painting, skiing, travel. Home: 11 Sonrisa Ct Santa Fe NM 87506

KAMBERG, MARY-LANE, writer, journalist; b. Kansas City, Mo., Jan. 3, 1948; d. Frederick Kenneth and Jessie Marie (Lorenz) Ladewig; m. Kenneth Dee Kamberg, June 22, 1968; children: Rebekka Dyan, Johanna Lynne. BS in Journalism, U. Kans., 1980. Freelance writer, Olathe, Kans., 1985—; creative writing tchr. Johnson County C.C., Overland Park, Kans., 1987—95, Avila Coll., Kansas City, 1987-90; corr. Kansas City Star, 1990—. Presenter workshops in field; pres. bd. dirs. Whispering Prairie Press, Prairie Village, Kans., 1996-98, adv. bd. 1998—; mem. adv. bd. fiction editor Potpourri Publs. (hon. mention Nat. Poetry Month award, Potpourri, 1999), Prairie Village, 1994-97; contbg. editor Hydro Rev. Mag., Kansas City, 1991—. Author: From Patient to Payment, 1993, Tips from Tina, 1995, Cabin Fever Relievers, 1997, Little Star: A Christmas Story, 2001, The I Don't Know How To Cook Book, 2004; editor, author: Handprint in the Woods, 1997; editor: Alzheimer's Legal Survival Guide, 2000; contbr. articles to popular mags. Recipient 4th pl. award Writers Digest Mag., 1990, James P. Immroth Meml. award ALA, 1996, 1st pl. humor award Springfield Writers Guild, 2002, award Ozark Creative Writers Contest, 2002 Mem. Kansas City Writers Group (co-leader 1991-97, 2000—), Writers Place, Sisters in Crime, Kansas City Press Club, Soc. Profl. Journalists, Okla. Writers Fedn. (bd. dirs.), Mo. Poetry Soc., Nat. League Am. Pen Women (1st Pl. Poetry and Fiction 2003), Mo. Writers Guild (bd. dirs., Best Nonfiction Book 2005) Republican. Avocation: swimming. Home and Office: 2128 E 144th St Olathe KS 66062-2355 Personal E-mail: mlkwriter@yahoo.com.

KAMBOUR, ANNALIESE SPOFFORD, lawyer, media company executive; b. Schenectady, N.Y., Nov. 19, 1961; d. Roger Peabody and Virginia Louise (Dyer) K. BA, Harvard U., 1983, JD, 1986. Bar: Mass. 1986, N.Y. 1987, U.S. Tax Ct. 1987. Assoc. Paul, Weiss, Rifkind, Wharton & Garrison, N.Y.C., 1986—96, ptnr., 1996—2001; sr. v.p. tax Time Warner Inc., N.Y.C., 2001—. Mem. NOW, N.Y. State Bar Assn. Office: Paul Weiss Rifkind Wharton & Garrison Ste 4A 1285 Avenue Of The Americas Fl 21 New York NY 10019-6028

KAMEN, CHERYL L. HEIBERG, social worker; b. Bklyn., Sept. 29, 1959; d. Carl Harold Heiberg and Sylvia Olsen; m. Kevin Brian Kamen, June 18, 1995. BA in Sociology/Religion, Gettysburg Coll., 1982; MSW, Fordham U., 1984; postgrad., Hunter Coll., 1992. LMSW N.Y.; cert. in aging. Social worker Bay Ridge Nutrition and Home Care, Bklyn., 1984; dir. S.W. Bklyn. Sr. Svcs., Bklyn., 1984-88; exec. dir. Bay Ridge Ctr. for Older Adults/Ctr. for Cmty. Svcs., Bklyn., 1988—2004; dir. adult svcs. Hudson Guild, 2004—. Bd. dirs. Coun. Sr. Ctrs. and Svcs., NYC, 1997—2003; congl. del. White House Conf. on Aging, Washington, 1995; del. N.Y. State Gov.'s Conf. on Aging, Sarasota Springs, 1995. Pres. Bay Ridge Cmty. Coun., Bklyn., 1997—98, bd. dirs., 1998—2001, Friends and Rels. of the Institutionalized Aged, 2004—. Recipient citation for outstanding cmty. svc., N.Y. State Assembly, 1998, 2001, 2004, Resolution for outstanding cmty. svc., N.Y. State Senate, 1998, 2004, 2001, others; fellow Melvin Jones fellow, Lions Club Internat., 1997.

Mem.: NASW, Bay Ridge Coun. on Aging (pres. 1990—94, 2001—03), Lions Club Internat. (pres. 1999—2001), Bay Ridge Bus. and Profl. Women's Club (pres. 1998—99, 2002—03). Republican. Lutheran. Avocations: travel, gardening, reading. Home: 3009 Grand Blvd Baldwin NY 11510-4719 Office: Hudson Guild Settlement House 441 W 26th St New York NY 10001

KAMEN, PAULA, journalist, playwright; b. Chgo., 1967; B in Journalism, Univ. Ill., 1989. Former reporter Kenosha (Wis.) News. Vis. rsch. scholar, gender studies program Northwestern Univ., Chgo., 1994—. Author: (books) Feminist Fatale: Voices from the Twentysomething Generation Explore the Future of the Women's Movement, 1991, Her Way: The Report on Young Women's Evolving Sexual Choices, 1999, All in My Head, 2005; contributor: books Shiny Adidas Track Suits and the Death of Camp: The Best of Might Magazine, 1998; playwright: Seven Dates with Seven Writers; (plays) Jane: Abortion and the Underground, 1999; commentaries, book reviews: in NY Times, Washington Post, Salon, Ms. Chicago Tribune, In These Times. Named one of Chicago's 100 Most Influential Women, Crain's Chicago Business mag., 2004.

KAMENSKE, GLORIA L., retired psychologist; b. Battle Creek, Mo., Oct. 26, 1931; d. George W. and Edith O. Cheek; m. Bernard Kamenske, Dec. 19, 1960 (dec. Sept. 25, 2003). AB, U. Mich., 1953; MA, Mich. State U., 1955, PhD, 1965. Lic. psychologist DC. Rsch. psychologist Veteran's Adminstrn., Ann Arbor, Mich., 1957—59, Dept. Army, 1959—70, Human Resources Rsch. Office, 1970—71, Behavioral Scis. Rsch., 1971—73, Dept. Labor, 1973—74, Office of Sec., Health and Human Svcs., DC, 1974—76, Population Rsch., NIH, Bethesda, Md., 1976—88; pvt. practice Bethesda, Md., 1959—; ret., 1989. Fellow: APHA (Superior Work Performance award 1967, Superior Svc. award 1968); mem.: APA, Population Assn. Am. Avocation: reading. Personal E-mail: g.kamenske@verizon.net.

KAMERICK, EILEEN ANN, corporate financial executive, lawyer; b. Ravenna, Ohio, July 22, 1958; d. John Joseph and Elaine Elizabeth (Lenney) K.; m. Victor J. Heckler, Sept. 1, 1990; 1 child, Connor Joseph Heckler. AB in English summa cum laude, Boston Coll., 1980; postgrad., Exeter Coll., Oxford, Eng., 1981; JD, U. Chgo., 1984, MBA in Finance and Internat. Bus. with honors, 1993. Bar: Ill. 1984, U.S. Dist. Ct. (no. dist.) Ill. 1985, Mass. 1986, U.S. Ct. Appeals (7th cir.) 1988, U.S. Supreme Ct. 1993. Assoc. Reuben & Proctor, Chgo., 1984—86, Skadden, Arps et al, Chgo., 1986—89; atty. internat. Amoco Corp., Chgo., 1989—93, sr. fin. mgr. corp. fin., 1993—96, dir. banking and fin. svcs., 1996—97, v.p., treas., 1998—99, Whirlpool Corp., Benton Harbor, Mich., 1997; v.p., gen. counsel GE Capital Auto Fin. Svcs., Barrington, Ill., 1997—98; v.p., CFO BP Am., 1998—2000; exec. v.p. & CFO United Stationers Inc., Des Plaines, Ill., 2000—01; exec. v.p., CFO Bcom3, Chgo., 2001—03; CFO Heidrick & Struggles, Chgo., 2004—. Advisor fin. com. Am. Petroleum Inst., 1992; bd. dirs. Heartland Alliance, ServiceMaster, Westell Tech. Vol. adv. 7th Cir. Bar Assn., Chgo., 1987—; bd. dirs. Boys & Girls Clubs of Chicago. Mem. Phi Beta Kappa. Roman Catholic. Home: 2627 N Greenview Ave Chicago IL 60614 Office: 233 S Wacker Dr Ste 4200 Chicago IL 60660 Office Phone: 312-496-1557. Personal E-mail: eakesq@aol.com.

KAMERMAN, SHEILA BRODY, social work educator; b. Jan. 7, 1928; d. S. Lawrence and Helen (Golding) Brody; m. Morton Kamerman, Sept. 11, 1947; children: Nathan Brody, Elliot Herbert, Laura Kamerman-Katz. BA, NYU, 1946; MSW, Hunter Coll., 1966; D in Social Welfare, Columbia U., 1973; PhD (hon.), York U., Eng., 1998. Social worker N.Y.C. Dept. Social Svcs., 1966-68; social work supr. Bellevue Psychiat. Hosp., 1968-69; assoc. prof. social work Hunter Coll., 1977-79; from rsch. assoc. to sr. rsch. assoc. Columbia U. Sch. Social Work, 1971-79, assoc. prof. social policy and planning, 1979-81; prof. Sch. Social Work Columbia U., 1981—, Compton Found. Centennial prof., 1996—, interim dean Sch. Social Work, 2001—02. Dir. Columbia U. Inst. for Child and Family Policy, 1998—; chair NAS-NRC panel on work, family and cmty., 1980-82; mem. Com. Child Devel. Rsch. and Pub. Policy, 1983-88; mem. com. on prenatal care Inst. Medicine, 1986-88; cons. in field; mem. numerous social welfare coms. and adv. bds.; mem. Gov. Cuomo's Task Force on Poverty and Welfare Reform, 1986-87, adv. com. on Work and Family, 1987-88, UN Expert groups on social welfare and family policies; mem. Inst. Medicine/Nat. Rsch. Coun. bd. on children and families, 1998—. Author: (with Alfred J. Kahn) Not for the Poor Alone, 1975, Social Services in the United States, 1976, Social Services in International Perspective, 1977, Family Policy: Government and Families in Fourteen Countries, 1978, Child Care, Family Benefits and Working Parents, 1981, Parenting in an Unresponsive Society, 1980, Maternity and Parental Benefits and Leaves, 1980, Helping America's Families, 1982, Maternity Policies and Working Women, 1983, Income Transfers for Families with Children, 1983, Child Care: Facing the Hard Choices, 1987, The Responsive Work Place, 1987, Child Support: From Debt Collection to Social Policy, 1988, Mothers Alone: Strategies for a Time of Change, 1988, Privatization and the Welfare State, 1989, Social Services for Children, Youth and Families in the United States, 1990, Child Care, Parental Leave, and the Under 3's, 1991, A Welcome for Every Child, 1994, Starting Right: How America Neglects Its Youngest Children and What We Can Do About It, 1995, Children in big Cities, 1996, Confronting the New Politics of Child and Family Policies, (series of 6 reports), 1997, Family Change and Family Policies in Britain, Canada, New Zealand and the United States, 1998, Big Cities in the Welfare Transition, 1998, Contracting for Child and Family Services, 2000; editor: Early Childhood Education and Care, 2001; co-editor: (with Ronald A. Feldman) The Columbia University School of Social Work, 2001; (with Alfred J. Kahn) Beyond Child Poverty, the Social Exclusion of Children, 2002; contbr. articles to profl. jours. Fellow Ctr. Advanced Study in Behavioral Scis., 1983-84; recipient Hexter award Hunter Coll. Sch. Social Work, 1977, Nat. Leadership award in Social Policy, Heller Sch. Brandeis U., 1989, Lifetime Achievement award Social Welfare Policy and Practice, 2002, Significant Lifetime Achievement award Coun. on Social Work Edn., 2005; named to Hunt Coll. Hall of Fame, 1981, Columbia U Sch. Social Work Hall of Fame, 2003. Mem. NASW, Am. Pub. Human Svcs. Assn., Assn. Policy Analysis and Mgmt., Nat. Acad. Social Ins., Phi Beta Kappa. Home: 1125 Park Ave New York NY 10128-1243 Office: Columbia U Sch Social Work Mail Code 4600 1255 Amsterdam Ave New York NY 10027 Office Phone: 212-851-2270. Business E-Mail: sbk2@columbia.edu.

KAMIL, ELAINE SCHEINER, pediatric nephrologist, educator; b. Cleve., Jan. 26, 1947; d. James Frank and Maud Lily (Severn) Scheiner; m. Ivan Jeffery Kamil, Aug. 29, 1970; children: Jeremy, Adam, Megan. BS magna cum laude, U. Pitts., 1969, MD, 1973. Diplomate Am. Bd. Pediat., Am. Bd. Pediatric Nephrology. Intern in pediat. Children's Hosp. Pitts., 1973-74, resident in pediat., 1974-76; clin. fellow in pediatric nephrology Sch. Medicine, UCLA, 1976-79, acting asst. prof. pediat., 1979-80, asst. clin. prof. pediat., 1988-91, assoc. clin. prof. pediat., 1991-97, clin. prof. pediat., 1997—; rsch. fellow in nephrology Harbor-UCLA Med. Ctr., Torrance, Calif., 1980-82; med. dir. The Children's Clinic of Long Beach, Calif., 1984-87; med. dir. pediat. nurse practitioner program Calif. State U., Long Beach, 1984-87; assoc. dir. pediatric nephrology and transplant immunology Cedars-Sinai Med. Ctr., LA, 1990—2001, clin. dir. pediatric nephrology, 2001—. Adj. asst. prof. pediat. Harbor-UCLA, Torrance, Calif., 1983-87, UCLA, 1987-88; cons. in pediatric nephrology Hawthorne (Calif.) Cmty. Med. Group, 1981-2000. Author chpts. to books; contbr. articles to profl. jours. Pres.-elect med. adv. bd. Nat. Kidney Found. So. Calif., 2000-02, pres. med. adv. bd., 2002-04. Recipient Vol. Svc. award Nat. Kidney Found., 1998. Mem. AAUW, Am. Soc. Nephrology, Am. Soc. Pediatric Nephrology (co-chair workforce com. 2003-05, chair 2006—, mem. coun. 2006—), Internat. Soc. Nephrology, Internat. Soc. Pediatric Nephrology, So. Calif. Pediatric Nephrology Assn. (chair steering com. 1998—), Nat. Kidney Found. So. Calif. (med. adv. bd. 1987-96, rsch. com. 1987-90, chmn. pub. info. med. adv. bd. 1988-92, handbook com. 1988, co-chair med. adv. bd. cmty. svcs. com. 1992-93, chair-elect patient svcs. and cmty. edn. com. 1993-94, chair patients svcs. and cmty. edn. com. 1994-95, kidney camp summer vol. physician 1988-91, 93, 94, 97, 99-2005, Arthur Gordon award 1991, Exceptional Svc. award 1992, Exceptional Leadership and Support award 1995, bd. dirs. 1995-96, 2002—), Alpha Omega Alpha, Phi Beta Kappa. Office: Cedars Sinai Med Ctr 1165 WT 8700 Beverly Blvd Los Angeles CA 90048-1865 Office Phone: 310-423-4747. Business E-Mail: elaine.kamil@cshs.org.

KAMINSHINE, SARAH BERNE, special education educator; b. N.Y.C., June 19, 1982; d. Steven Jay Kaminshine and Amy Lynn Berne. BA summa cum laude, Colby Coll., 2004. Tchr. Summerbridge Cambridge, Cambridge, Mass., 2003; math tchg. asst. math. dept. Colby Coll., Waterville, Maine, 2001—04; spl. edn. counselor Camp Tova at the 92nd St. Y, N.Y.C., 2004; afterschool tchr. Nesher Program at the 92nd St. Y, N.Y.C., 2004—; asst. tchr. Cooke Ctr. for Learning and Devel., N.Y.C., 2004—. Mem. hiring com. math. dept. Colby Coll., Waterville, 2003—04. Actor: (play) Somewhere in Between. Vol. Big Brother Big Sister, Waterville, 2001—02; cantor Colby Hillel, Waterville, 2000—04. Recipient Linda K. Cotter grant, Colby Coll., 2003. Mem.: Phi Beta Kappa (hon.). Jewish. Avocations: dance, trapeze, singing, Spanish, Hebrew. Office Phone: 212-362-6092.

KAMINSKI, PATRICIA JOYCE, lab administrator; d. Lucile Anne Roberts and Tadeusz Kaminski; children: Grant Matthew, Joshua Alan. Cert. dental tech., So. Calif. Coll. Med. and Dental Careers, 1975. Cert. advanced dental implant lab. Germany, spl. jaw reconstruction Calif., prosthetic tng. ITI Straumann, Mass. Implant specialist Haupt Dental Lab., Brea, Calif., 1992—2002; tech. services mgr. Dentsply Friadent Ceramed, Lakewood, Colo., 2002—03; implant dept. mgr. Dynotech Dental Lab., Corona, Calif., 2003—04; owner Kaminski Dental Lab., Orange, Calif., 2004—. Tech. cons. Home Bus., Orange, 2000—. Avocations: travel, boating, yoga, gardening, running. Personal E-mail: pkaminski4043@sbcglobal.net.

KAMINSKY, ALICE RICHKIN, retired literature educator; b. NYC; d. Morris and Ida (Spivak) Richkin; m. Jack Kaminsky (dec.); 1 son, Eric (dec.). BA, NYU, 1946, MA, 1947, PhD, 1952. Mem. faculty dept. English NYU, 1947-49, Hunter Coll., 1952-53, Cornell U., 1954-57, Broome Community Coll., 1958-59, Cornell U., 1959-63, SUNY, Cortland, 1963—, prof., 1968-91, prof. emerita, 1991—; faculty exch. scholar State U. NY. Author: George Henry Lewes as Critic, 1968, Logic: A Philosophical Introduction, 1974; editor: Literary Criticism of George Henry Lewes, 1964, Chaucer's Troilus and Criseyde and the Critics, 1980, The Victim's Song, 1985; contbr. more than 75 articles and revs. to numerous jours. Mem.: MLA, Chaucer Soc.

KAMINSKY, IRENE, psychologist; b. N.Y.C., Jan. 19, 1945; d. Anatole and Lydia (Judey) K.; m. Bud Feuchtwanger III, July 21, 1995. BA, Syracuse U., 1966; MA, NYU, 1973, PhD, 1984. Diplomate Am. Bd. Cert. Counselors; lic. psychologist, N.Y. Interviewer N.Y. State Employment Svc., N.Y.C., 1968-74; counselor N.Y. Assn. for New Ams., N.Y.C., 1974-78; psychology intern Cabrini Med. Ctr., N.Y.C., 1979-80; coord. counseling svcs. Bramson ORT Tech. Inst., N.Y.C., 1977-82; psychology extern Karen Horney Clinic, N.Y.C., 1986-87; supr. learning disability CUNY, N.Y.C., 1984-90; psychologist N.Y.C., 1981—, Inst. for Psychotherapeutic Advancement, N.Y.C., 1987-92, Jewish Bd. Family and Children's Svcs., N.Y.C., 1990—. Presenter Am. Coun. for Learning Disabilities Internat. Conf., 1986. Mem. APA (presenter 1978, 80), N.Y. State Psychol. Assn. (presenter 1987), Am. Assn. Mental Health Counselors, N.Y. Soc. Clin. Psychologists. Avocations: swimming, reading, theater, music. E-mail: drkaminsky@nyc.rr.com.

KAMISCHKE, ELLEN JANE, mathematics educator, writer; b. Lansing, Mich., Apr. 6, 1957; d. Otis Donald and Martha Louise Meaders; m. Eric Lance Kamischke, Dec. 29, 1978; 1 child, Rachel. BS with honors, Mich. Tech. Univ., Houghton, Mich., 1979; MAT, Mich. State Univ., East Lansing, Mich., 1983. Math. tchr. Winthrop HS, Minn., 1979—81, Interlochen Arts Acad., Interlochen, Mich., 1983—. Workshop leader Key Cirriculum Press, Emeryville, Calif., 1993—; cons. AP calculus Coll. Bd. ETS, 2004—. Co-author: (math. text.) Advanced Algebra Through Data Exploration, 1998, Discovering Algebra, 2002, Discovering Advanced Algebra, 2004; author: (math supplement) A Watched Cup Never Cools. Mem.: Math. Assn. of Am., Nat. Coun. of Tchrs. of Math., Mich. Coun. of Tchrs. of Math. (Regional Dir. award 2004). Meth. Avocations: dance, cooking, sewing. Home: 1220 Reads Run Traverse City MI 49684 Office: Interlochen Art Acad PO Box 199 Interlochen MI 49643

KAMKAR, ROSEMARY, secondary school educator; b. Kittanning, Pa., Jan. 17, 1956; d. Jack C. and Dorothy I. Pozzuto; m. Javad Kamkar; 1 child, Sean. BS in Mental Retardation/Elem. Edn., Slippery Rock U., Pa., 1977; M in Learning Handicapped, San Francisco State U., Calif., 1979, M in Edml. Adminstrn., 2000. Adminstrv. asst. Hunters Point Boys Club, San Francisco, 1977—2000; tchr. San Francisco Unified Sch. Dist., 1980—. Student activities dir. Lincoln H.S., San Francisco, 1987—; student adv. coun. advisor San Francisco Unified Sch. Dist., 2005—. Recipient Outstanding Tchr. award, KTVU, 2003. Office: Lincoln HS 2162 24th Ave San Francisco CA 94116 Office Phone: 415-759-2700 ext. 3132/3137. Office Fax: 415-566-2224. E-mail: sfmom@hotmail.com.

KAMLAY, JANE, elementary school educator; b. Pontiac, Mich. m. Thomas Kamlay; children: Thomas, Michael. BS in Biology, Adrian Coll., Mich.; MA in Curriculum & Instrn., U. Mich., Ann Arbor. Tchr. East Hills Mid. Sch., Bloomfield Hills, Mich., 1970—. Named Master Tchr., Bloomfield Hills Schs. Mem.: Sigma Sigma Sigma (life). Avocations: travel, needlecrafts.

KAMLET, ELIZABETH OSEFF, elementary school educator; b. Detroit, Apr. 8, 1941; d. Sol and Sara (Cohen) Oseff; m. Arthur S. Kamlet, June 14, 1964; children: Michael, Leonard. BA in Elem Edn., U. Mich., 1963, MA, 1965. Tchr. Columbus (Ohio) Pub. Schs., Ann Arbor (Mich.) Pub. Schs., Summerfield Pub. Schs., Petersburg, Mich., Oak Park (Mich.) Pub. Schs. Recipient Mayor's Vol. Activities award. Mem. NEA, Ohio Edn. Assn., Columbus Edn. Assn. E-mail: ekamlet909@aol.com.

KAMM, LINDA HELLER, lawyer; b. NYC, Aug. 25, 1939; d. Seymour A. and Mary Heller; children: Lisa, Oliver. BA in History, Brandeis U., 1961; LLB, Boston Coll., 1967. Bar: Mass. 1967, D.C. 1978, U.S. Supreme Ct. 1985. Counsel Dem. Study Group, Washington, 1968-71; counsel select com. on coms. U.S. Ho. of Reps., Washington, 1973-75, gen. counsel budget com., 1975-77; gen. counsel U.S. Dept. Transp., Washington, 1977-80; ptnr. Foley and Lardner, Washington, 1980-84, of counsel, 1984-95; pvt. practice, 1995—; of counsel Boies, Schiller & Flexner, 2001—. Address: 188 E 70th St Apt 24C New York NY 10021-5170

KAMMERER, ANN MARIE, geotechnical engineer; b. Sacramento, Calif., May 24, 1968; d. Rodney Dean and Karen Christine (Hvolboll) K.; m. Brian Louis Faudoa. AS, City Coll. of San Francisco, 1994; BS, U. Calif Berkeley, 1996, MS, 1998, PhD, 2002. Cert. engr. Engr. Olivia Chen Cons., San Francisco, 1995-96, GEI Cons., San Francisco, 1996-97; grad. rschr. U. Calif. Berkeley, 1997—2002, lectr., 2002, postdoc. rschr., 2003—; sr. geotech. engr. Arup USA, San Francisco, 2002—. Contbr. articles to profl. jour. Chair City Coll. San Francisco Women's Resource Ctr., 1993—94; chair student leadership coun. Pacific Earthquake Engring. Ctr., 1999—2000; student trustee San Francisco C.C. Dist., 1994. Recipient Calif. Alumni Assn. Leadership scholarship, 1994, Howard D. Eberhart Meml. scholarship, 1996, Nat. Sci. Found. grad. fellowship, 1997-2000; Earthquake Engring. Rsch. Inst./Fed. Emergency Mgmt. Agy. Nat. Earthquake Hazards Reduction Program grad. fellow, 2001. Mem. ASCE, Earthquake Engring. Rsch. Inst., Pacific Earthquake Engring. Rsch. Ctr., Golden Key Nat. Honor Soc., Tau Beta Pi (pres. 1995). Democrat. Avocations: scuba diving, skiing, rock hunting. Office: Arup 901 Market St Ste 260 San Francisco CA 94103-0001 E-mail: annie.brian@mindspring.com, Annie.Kammerer@Arup.com.

KAMMERZELL, SUSAN JANE, elementary school educator, music educator; b. Greeley, Colo., Mar. 4, 1953; d. Carl Warren and Charlotte Josephine Strandberg; m. Arnold Henry Kammerzell, Sept. 11, 1976; 1 child, Jeffrey Scott. BA in Elem. Edn., U. No. Colo., 1975. Elem. tchr. grade 1 Ft. Morgan (Colo.) Sch. Dist., 1975—76; presch. dir., tchr. Wiggins (Colo.) Presch., 1987—89; elem. tchr. grade 1 Wiggins Sch. Dist., 1989—91, elem. tchr. kindergarten, 1991—96, elem. tchr. gen. music, 1996—. Sunday sch. tchr. grades 4 and 5 Wiggins Cmty. Ch., 1996—. Mem.: Nat. Assn. for Music Edn. Republican. Mem. United Church Of Christ. Avocations: travel, reading, music. Home: 5094 Road O Wiggins CO 80654 Office: Wiggins Sch Dist RE-50J Wiggins Elem 320 Chapman Wiggins CO 80654

KAMMEYER, SONIA MARGARETHA, real estate agent; b. Stockholm, June 21, 1942; came to U.S., 1964; d. Bengt Henrik and Margot Elsa M. (Hodin) Sjoberg; m. Whitman Ridgway, June 13, 1964 (div. 1978); children: Sean, Siobhan; m. Kenneth C.W. Kammeyer, Dec. 28, 1982. Student, Fleisher's Art Meml. Sch., Phila., 1966-69. With Ben Bell Real Estate, Lanham, Md., 1972-73, Robert L. Gruen Real Estate, Silver Spring, Md., 1973-81, Panarama Real Estate, Silver Spring, 1981-82, Long & Foster Real Estate, Inc., Silver Spring, 1982—. Named to Montgomery County Bd. Realtors Hall of Fame, 1994; recipient Nat. Sales Award, Realty Alliance, 1997. Mem. Montgomery County Bd. Realtors (life), Howard County Bd. Realtors, Swedish Profl. Women. Avocations: sculpture, painting, jewelry making, gardening, guitar playing. Home: 14600 Triadelphia Mill Rd Dayton MD 21036-1217 Office: Long & Foster Real Estate 3901 National Dr Burtonsville MD 20866-1141 Office Phone: 301-476-8656. E-mail: kammeyer@erols.com.

KAMPEN, IRENE BLANCHE, writer; b. Bklyn., Apr. 18, 1922; d. Jack and Mary (Harris) Trepel; 1 child, Christine. BA in Journalism, U. Wis., 1943. Author: Fear Without Childbirth, 1978, Nobody Calls At This Hour Just To Say Hello, 1975, Are You Carrying Any Gold or Living Relatives, 1970, Due To Lack of Interest Tomorrow Has Been Canceled, 1969, Here Comes The Bride There Goes Mother, 1967, Last Year At Sugarbush, 1966, Europe Without George, 1965, The Ziegfelds' Girl, 1964, We That Are Left, 1963, Life Without George, 1961; contbr. numerous articles to mags. Fellow MacDowell Colony; mem. Author's Guild Am.

KAMPITS, EVA, accrediting association administrator, educator; b. Budapest, Hungary, Feb. 22, 1946; arrived in U.S., 1951; d. Ernest Michael and Ilona (Gondi) K.; m. Dan Catalin Stefanescu, Aug. 4, 1979; children: Andreea N., Cristina F. Cert., U. Innsbruck, Austria, 1963; BA, Harvard U., 1968; MA, Boston Coll., 1971, PhD, 1977. Instr. freshman seminars MIT, Cambridge, 1973—80, freshman advisor, 1975-80, sophomore advisor, 1976-80, adminstrv. officer Artificial Intelligence Lab., 1967-78, asst. to dir. Lab. for Computer Sci., 1987-88, rsch. affiliate Media Lab., 1987-88; acad. dean Pine Manor Coll., Chestnut Hill, Mass., 1980-94, dir. sponsored programs, grad. sch. dean, 1994; dir., office sch./coll. relations New Eng. Assn. Schs. and Colls., Inc., Bedford, Mass., 1994—2003; dir. Office Exec. Dir., 2004—. Mem. NEARnet, 1989-94, Gov.'s Ednl. Tech. Adv. Coun., 1990-93; mem. steering com. Mass. Telecomputing Coalition, 1991-95, New Eng. Network Acad. Alliances in Fgn. Langs. and Lits., 1995-98, Eisenhower Regional Alliance for Math. and Sci. Reform, 1996-98; trustee Boston Archtl. Ctr., 1996-2000, overseer, 2000—; adv. bd. Dorcas Place, 2000; cons. Ministry of Edn., China, 2001—; advisor PBS Access to Coll. documentary, 2003; edn. task force CFP Bd., 2006. Founding mem. bd. editors NERComp Jour. Founding mem. bd. visitors Brimmer and May Sch., Chestnut Hill, Mass., 1992-97. Republican. Roman Catholic. Avocations: natural history, marine studies, arts, travel, tennis. Office: New Eng Assn Schs & Colls Inc 209 Burlington Rd Bedford MA 01730-1422 Office Phone: 781-271-0022. Business E-Mail: kampits@neasc.org.

KAMRANY, SAJIA, television producer; b. Kabul, Afghanistan; arrived in US, 1978; children: Tony, Michelle. Exec. prodr. & dir. (TV series) Afghanistan TV, KSCI 18, 1993—96, via satellite, 2004—; singer: (albums) Bacha Mashee, 2003. Home and Office: Apt 206D 17352 Sunset Blvd Pacific Palisades CA 90272 Office Phone: 310-459-0232. E-mail: sajiakam5@hotmail.com.*

KAN, DIANA ARTEMIS MANN SHU, painter, art educator, writer; b. Hong Kong, Mar. 3, 1926; came to U.S., 1949, naturalized, 1964; d. Kam Shek and Sing-Ying (Hong) K.; m. Paul Schwartz, May 24, 1952; 1 son, Kan Martin Meyer Sing-Si. Student, Art Students League, 1949—51, Beaux Arts, Paris, 1951—52, Grande Chaumiere, 1951—52, Ecole Beau Arts, 1952—54. Instr. watercolor Phila. Mus. Art, 1972, Sumi-e Soc., 1974—2003, Art Students League of NY, 1985, The Nat. Acad. Design, 2001, The Smithsonian Inst., Wash., DC. Fgn. corr., city editor Cosmorama Pictorial Mag., Hong Kong, 1968; art reviewer Villager, N.Y.C., 1960-69; lectr. Birmingham So. U., N.Y. U., Mills Coll., St. Joseph's Coll., Phila. Mus., Smithsonian Instn; keynote spkr. Wellsley's Coll. Asia Week, MA, 1993. Author: White Cloud, 1938, The How and Why of Chinese Painting, 1974, Am. Artist Magazine, 1974, 86; One-man shows, London, 1949, 63, 64, Paris, 1949, Hong Kong, 1937, 39, 41, 47, 48, 52, Shanghai, 1935, 37, 39, Nanking, 1936, 38, Macao, 1947, 48, Bankok, 1947, Casablanca, 1951, 52, San Francisco, 1950, 67, N.Y.C., 1950, 54, 59, 67, 71, 72, 74, 78, Naples, 1971, Elliot Mus., Stuart, Fla., 1967, 73, Bruce Mus., Greenwich, Conn., 1969, Nat. Hist. Mus., Taipei, Taiwan, 1971, N.Y. Cultural Center Mus., 1972, Galerie Barbarella, Palm Beach, Fla., 1972, Hobe Sound (Fla.) Galleries, 1976, 81, Nat. Arts Club, 1979, Dyansen Galleries, 1987-Shenchen Mus., China, 1996, Hong Kong Art Ctr., 1996, 90 others; exhibited in group shows Allied Artists of Am., 1957-90, Royal Acad. Fine Arts, London, 1963-64, Royal Soc. Painters, London, 1964, Nat. Arts Club, N.Y.C., 1964-90, Am. Water Color Soc., N.Y.C., 1966-90, Nat. Acad. Design, N.Y.C., 1967-2003, Charles and Emma Frye Mus., Seattle, 1968, Willamette U., Salem, Oreg., 1968, Columbia (S.C.) Mus. Art, 1969, Audubon Artist, 1974-90, Evansville (Ind.) Mus., 1991, Dyansen Gallery, Boston, 1991; represented permanent collections, Met. Mus. Art, Phila. Mus. Art, Nelson Gallery, Elliot Mus., Fla., Bruce Mus., Dalhousie U., Atkin Mus., Kansas City, Nat. Hist. Mus., Taipei, The Government House, Vancouver, BC, Can., Midtown Payson Galleries, China 2000 Fine Art Gallery; subject of film Eastern Spirit, Western World—A Profile of Diana Kan; paintings were published by UNICEF (christmas cards): Four Children Going Fishing, 1996, Lantern Festival, 1999, Flower Drum Song, 2002, Snow Mountain, 2002. Recipient Summer Festival award N.Y.C., 1959, 1st Prize Nat. Art Club, 1982; named most Outstanding Profl. Woman of the Yr., Washington Sq. chpt. N.Y. League Bus. and Profl. Women's Club, 1971, 79, Gold medal of honor Knickerbocker Artists, 1990, Gold medal of honor Audubon Artists, 1991, 2000, Salmagundi Club, Pres. Gold medal of honor, 1998, Audobon Artists Gold Medal of Honor; Diana Kan Appreciation Day proclaimed by Mayor of Boston, 1991, Diana Kan Day proclaimed by Mayor of NY, 2000; offl. citation proclaimed by Pres. Senate of Mass., 1991. Fellow Royal Soc. Arts; mem. Pen and Brush Club (dir. 1968, Brush Fund award 1968, Alice S. Buell Meml. award 1969, Margaret Sussman award 1991), Nat. Acad. Design (assoc., John Pike Meml. award 1987, cert. of merit 1991), Am. Watercolor Soc. (traveling award 1968, Marthe T. McKinnon award 1978, dir. 1975-77), Art Students League, Nat. League Pen Women, Audubon Artists (v.p. 1983), Allied Artists Am. (Barbara Vassilieff Meml. award 1969, Ralph Fabri Meml. award 1975, corr. sec. 1975-78), Catharine Lorillard Wolf Art Club (Anna Hyatt Huntington bronze medal 1970, 74, Gold medal of honor 1982), NYC Cultural Affairs Adv. Commn., 1999. Clubs: Overseas Press Am., Lotos, The Nat. Arts (NYC), The Salamagundi. Mailing: The Nat Arts Club 15 Gramercy Park S New York NY 10003-1705 E-mail: dianakan@dianakan.com.

KAN, YUE-SAI, journalist, writer, television personality, entrepreneur, humanitarian; b. Guilin, China; d. Wing-Lin Kan. Studied for a degree in music, Hawaii. Began career as asst. to casting agent in an advertising agy.; creator, founder, chmn. Yue-Sai Kan Cosmetics Ltd. (formed joint venture with Coty Divsn. in 1996-Yue-Sai Kan-Coty Cosmetics Shanghai Ltd., cosmetics and brand name sold to L'Oreal in May, 2004), Shanghai, 1992—2004; hon. vice-chmn. L'Oreal China, 2004—; founded Yue-Sai Kan Production Co., 1978—, Shanghai, 2005—. Host (TV show) Looking East (First weekly TV show in the US that introduced Eastern Cultures and Customs to the American Audience, last two years broadcasted on the Discovery Channel), 1978—90, First Five Broadcasts from China of the 35th

Anniversary of the People's Republic of China (PBS), 1984, host, prodr. (TV series) One World (First TV series ever produced and hosted by an American on China's nat. network, CCTV; First TV series that introduced the outside world to China), China, 1985, exec. prodr. (TV Series (syndicated nationally) and printed column in China's Harper's Bazaar) Yue-Sai's World, 2004—, exec. prodr., host (TV series) Yue-Sai Kan's People in a Changing China, 2005—, host (TV program) Half of Sky, Journey Through a Changing China (syndicated nationwide), 1989, Doing Business in Asia (PBS and worldwide; used by multi-national companies and bus. schools; featuring Japan, South Korea, Hong Kong, and Taiwan), 1991, Doing Business in China, 1999; prodr.: (documentary) China-Walls and Bridges (ABC), 1998 (Emmy award); author: One World, Yue-Sai's Guide to Beauty, Etiquette for the Modern Chinese, 2000, Celebrating Asian Beauty, 2002, How to be a Beautiful, Healthy and Successful Modern Women, 2004. Supports ednl. and humanitarian efforts; established scholarship fund to major Chinese Universities and Hunter Coll. (NYC); involved with Orbis, AIDS, and Mus. of the Chinese Americans. Named Queen of the Middle Kingdom, Time Mag., Modern Day Marco Polo, Money Mag., True Citizen Ambassador, US Congressional Record, the first and only Global Chinese-Say Yes Amb., UNICEF; named one of Most Famous Women in China, People Mag., Most Influential Women in China in the Last 20 Years, Xinhua News Agy.; recipient Exceptional Achievement award, UN, World's Leading Women Entrepreneur award, Star Group, 1999. Mem.: Com. of 100. Achievements include Created the first doll of Asian descent, the Yue-Sai Wa Wa doll in 1999; lead to a weekly cartoon series in the newspaper, Yue-Sai's Adventures, this was the first female cartoon heroine for China.*

KANADY, JANET, science educator; d. Bob and Genny Klein; m. Marlon Kanady; children: Joshua, Jared. BS in Agriculture, U. Ark., Fayetteville, 1988; M in Secondary Edn., Ark. Tech. U., Russellville, 2001. Quality control technician Wade Jones Co., Lowell, Ark.; sci. tchr. Dover (Ark.) Sch. Sec., com. mem. troop 343 Boys Scouts Am., Dover, 1994—. Mem.: Ark. Assn. Mid. Level. Educators, Ark. Sci. Tchrs. Assn. (membership chair 1994—), Nat. Sci. Tchrs. Assn. Republican. Roman Catholic. Avocations: reading, sewing, gardening. Office: Dover Mid Sch PO Box 325 Dover AR 72837 Office Phone: 479-331-4814. Business E-Mail: janet.kanady@dover.k12.ar.us.

KANAKAREDES, MELINA, actress; b. Akron, Ohio, Apr. 23, 1967; m. Peter Constantinades, Sept. 6, 1992; children: Zoe, Karina Eleni. Attended, Ohio State U.; BFA, Point Park Coll. Spokesperson Maybelline NY. Actor: (Broadway plays) Caberet; (films) Carts, 1987, Bleeding Hearts, 1994, The Long Kiss Goodnight, 1996, Dangerous Beauty, 1998, Rounders, 1998, 15 Minutes, 2001, Into the Fire, 2005; (TV films) Saint Maybe, 1998; (TV series) The More You Know, 1989—, The Guiding Light, 1991—95, New York News, 1995, Leaving LA, 1997, Providence, 1999—2002, CSI: NY, 2004—, (TV appearances) NYPD Blue, 1995, Due South, 1995, The Practice, 1997, Oz, 1998, CSI: Miami, 2004. Office: c/o Gersh Agency NY 41 Madison Ave 33rd Fl New York NY 10010*

KANAREK, ROBIN BETH, psychology educator, nutrition educator, researcher; b. Pitts., Apr. 8, 1946; d. Robert and Helen (Schugar) K.; m. John Orin Tovrov, Mar. 2, 1986; children: Daniel, Jacob. BA in Biology, Antioch Coll., 1968; MS in Psychology, Rutgers U., 1971, PhD in Psychology, 1974. Rsch. asst. Fels Rsch. Inst., 1967-68; instr. Jersey City State Coll., 1971; rsch. fellow in nutrition Harvard Univ., 1974-76; rsch. assoc. in Psychology Tufts Univ., 1977-79; rsch. fellow, divsn. of Endocrinology Sch. Medicine Univ. Calif., L.A., 1979; asst. prof. of Psychology, adj. asst. prof. of Nutrition Tufts U., 1979-84; assoc. prof. of Psychology, adj. assoc. prof. of Nutrition Tufts Univ., 1984-89; prof. of nutrition Tufts U., 1989—, dep. chair psychology, 1993—. Editor-in-chief Nutrition and Behavior, 1981-87; editorial bd. mem. Neurobehavioral Toxicology and Teratology, 1984-87, Tufts Diet and Nutrition Newsletter, 1984—, Journal of the Am. Coll. of Nutrition, 1988-93, Physiology and Behavior, 1990—; editorial reviewer Science, Physiology and Behavior, Pharmacology Biochemistry and Behavior, Neurobehavioral Toxicology and Teratology, Brain Rsch. Bulletin, Jour. of Experimental Psychology, Life Sciences, Psychopharmacology, Appetite, Jour. of Nutrition, Jour. of the Am. Coll. of Nutrition, Am. Jour. of Clin. Nutrition, Psychological Bulletin, Annals of Internal Medicine; mem. competitive rsch. panel USDA, 1984, Inst. of Medicine Com. of Military Nutrition, 1995—; ad hoc com. NSF, NIH, USDA Nutrition Rsch., Bunting Found. Harvard Univ.; mem. com. mil. nutrition Nat. Acad. Scis., 1994—, program com. Eastern Psychological Assn., 1992-94; cons. Protein Malnutrition Project, Boston Univ.; med./dental reccomendation com., Tufts Univ., animal care com., 1985—, adv. com. on faculty rsch., 1988—, Univ. grievance com., 1989-92, com. on reviewing sci. curriculum, 1985. Author: (book) Nutrition and Behavior: New Perspectives, 1991; contbr. chpts. to books, articles to profl. jours. NSF fellow, 1966; grantee Nat. Inst. Arthritis, 1977-80, 77-83, 83-87, Nat. Inst. Mental Health, 1980-81, 81-82, Biomed. rsch. grantee Tufts U., 1983, 84, 85, 86, 87, 88, 89, 90, 91, 92, Nat. Inst. Drug Abuse, 1987-90, 94—, Mars grantee, 1984-89, Natick Army Rsch. Labs., 1989—. Fellow Am. Coll Nutrition; mem. Am. Inst. Nutrition, N.Y. Acad. Scis., Eastern Psychol. Assn., North Am. Soc. for the Study of Obesity, Soc. for the Study of Ingestive Behavior, Behavioral Pharmacology Study, Soc. for Neurosciences. Office: Tufts Univ 490 Boston Ave Medford MA 02155-5532

KANE, AGNES BREZAK, pathologist, educator; b. Danbury, Conn., Nov. 3, 1946; d. John Edward and Mary Elizabeth (Hatfield) Brezak; m. David E. Kane, June 22, 1970. BA, Swarthmore Coll., 1968; MD, Temple U., 1974, PhD, 1976. Diplomate Am. Bd. Pathology. Resident Temple U. Hosp., Phila., 1975-76, 77-78; postdoctoral fellow Karolinska Inst., Stockholm, 1976-77; asst. prof. Temple U. Sch. Medicine, Phila., 1977-82, Brown U., Providence, 1982-87, assoc. prof. pathology, 1987-95, prof. pathology, 1995-96, chair dept. pathology and lab. medicine, 1996—. Mem. merit rev. bd. for basic scis. VA, Washington, 1984-86; cons. R.I. Commn. for Safety and Occupational Health, Providence, 1986—; commr. Commn. to Identify Occupational Diseases, Providence, 1987-88; mem. rev. com. Nat. Inst. Environ. Health Scis., Research Triangle Park, N.C., 1988—. Assoc. editor Am. Jour. of Pathology, 1992—; contbr. articles on exptl. pathology to sci. publs. Lucretia Mott fellow Swarthmore Coll., 1969-71; recipient Rsch. Career Devel. award NIH, 1981-86. Mem. Am. Assn. Pathologists (women's com. 1987—, program com. 1990—), Assn. Women Med. Faculty Brown U. (founder, coord.), Women in Medicine (faculty advisor Brown U. chpt.; Mary Putnam Jacobi award 1986), Phi Kappa, Sigma Xi. Avocation: gardening. Office: Brown Univ Box G Providence RI 02912

KANE, CAROL, actress; b. Cleve., June 18, 1952; Stage debut in The Prime of Miss Jean Brodie, 1966; other N.Y.C. theatre appearances include Ring 'Round the Bath Tub, 1972, The Tempest, 1974, 80, The Effect of Gamma Ray on Man-in-the-Moon Marigolds, 1978, Are You Now or Have You Ever Been?, 1978, Benefit of a Doubt, 1978, Tales from Vienna Woods, 1979, Sunday Runners in the Rain, 1980, Macbeth, 1980, The Fairy Garden, 1984, The Debutante Ball, 1988, Frankie and Johnny in the Clair de Lune, 1988, Wicked, 2006; film appearances include Carnal Knowledge, 1971, Desperate Characters, 1971, Wedding in White, 1972, The Last Detail, 1974, Dog Day Afternoon, 1975, Hester Street, 1975 (Acad. award nomination for Best Actress), Harry and Walter Go to New York, 1976, Annie Hall, 1977, Valentino, 1977, The World's Greatest Lover, 1977, The Mafu Cage, 1978, When a Stranger Calls, 1979, The Muppet Movie, 1979, The Sabiana, 1979, Les Jeux, 1980, Pandemonium, 1982, Norman Loves Rose, 1982, Can She Bake A Cherry Pie?, 1983, Over the Brooklyn Bridge, 1984, Racing With the Moon, 1984, The Secret Diary of Sigmund Freud, 1984, Transylvania 6-5000, 1985, Jumpin' Jack Flash, 1986, The Princess Bride, 1987, Ishtar, 1987, License to Drive, 1988, Scrooged, 1988, Sticky Fingers, 1988, Flashback, 1990, Joe Versus the Volcano, 1990, The Lemon Sisters, 1990, My Blue Heaven, 1990, Ted and Venus, 1991, In the Soup, 1992, When a Stranger Calls Back, 1993, Even Cowgirls Get the Blues, 1993, Baby on Board, 1993, Addams Family Values, 1993, The Crazysitter, 1995, Trees Lounge, 1996, Sunset Park, 1996, The Pallbearer, 1996, Big Bully, 1996, American Strays, 1996, Office Killer, 1997, Gone Fishin', 1997, The Tic Code, 1998, Jawbreaker, 1999, Man on the Moon, 1999, The Tic Code, The Office Party, 2000, D.C. Smalls, 2001, My First Mister, 2001, The Shrink is In, 2001, Love In the Time of Money, 2002, Confessions of a Teenage Drama Queen, 2004, The Pacifier, 2005; TV series Taxi, 1981-83, All is Forgiven, 1986, American Dreamer, 1990, Brooklyn Bridge, 1992, Pearl, 1996, Beggars and Choosers, 1999; TV films An Invasion of Privacy, 1983, Burning Rage, 1984, Drop Out Mother, 1988, When a Stranger Calls Back, 1993, Dad, the Angel & Me, 1995, Freaky Friday, 1995, Merry Christmas, George Bailey, 1997, The First Seven Years, 1998, Noah's Ark, 1999, Cosmopolitan, 2003, Audrey's Rain, 2003; TV appearances include Laverne & Shirley, 1982, Faerie Tale Theatre, 1983, Cheers, 1984, Tales from the Darkside, 1985, Crazy Like a Fox, 1985, Tales from the Crypt, 1990, (voice) Tiny Toon Adventures, 1990, Seinfeld, 1994, Empty Nest, 1994, Chicago Hope, 1995, Ellen, 1996, Homicide: Life on the Street, 1997, (voice) As Told by Ginger, (voice) Family Guy, 2001, Hope & Faith, 2004. Recipient Emmy award for outstanding supporting actress in a comedy series, 1981.*

KANE, GRACE MCNELLY, retired women's health nurse, pediatrics nurse; b. Auburn, Ill., Mar. 31, 1939; d. Irving Benjamin and Ruby Louise (Stinnett) McNelly; m. Robert John Kane, July 23, 1960 (dec. 1994); children: Scott Robert, Timothy Phillip, Pamela Collette, Glenn Randall, Andrew Keith, Bruce Ryan. Diploma, Mem. Hosp. Sch. Nursing, Springfield, Ill., 1960; BS in Profl. Arts, St. Joseph's Coll., North Windham, Maine, 1985. RN Ill., cert. in occpl. hearing conservation, fetal monitoring I and II, ACLS. Staff nurse nursery-newborn units Walther Meml. Hosp., Chgo., 1962-67; staff nurse rooming-in nursery Luth. Gen. Hosp., Park Ridge, Ill., 1977-85; staff nurse med.-surg. unit Swedish Covenant Hosp., Chgo., 1989; staff nurse occupational clinic Rush-Presbyn-St. Luke's, Elk Grove Village, Ill., 1988; nurse various hosps., Arlington Heights, Ill., 1989-93; staff nurse couplet care St. Joseph's Hosp., Phoenix, 1997—2004; ret., 2004; part-time ob/gyn. staff nurse Casa Grande (Ariz.) Regional Med. Ctr., 2004—06; staff nurse Paradise Valley Hosp., 2006—. Ob-gyn. Casa Grande Regional Med. Ctr., 2004—06. Address: 4201 N 20th St Unit 101 Phoenix AZ 85016-5484

KANE, HEIDI BAKER, secondary school educator; m. Dan Thomas Kane, July 27, 2002; 1 child, Thomas Andrew. AA, Hiwassee Coll., Madisonville, Tenn., 1994; BA, U. Tenn., Knoxville, 1996; MEd, East Tenn. State U., Johnson City, 1998. Cert. Profl. Tchr. Tenn., 2001. Tchr. Jonesborough Mid. Sch., Tenn., 1998—. Named Tchr. of Yr., Jonesborough Mid. Sch. Faculty, 2004, 2006; named to Who's Who Among America's Tchrs., 2006; Jordan Fundamentals Grant, Michael Jordan's Jordan Fundamentals Found., 2001. Methodist. Avocations: cooking, reading. Office Phone: 423-753-1190.

KANE, JACQUELINE, human resources specialist; Various positions in fin. svcs. industry; sr. v.p. human resources capital raising and global capial markets group Bank of Am.; dir. exec. leadership devel., dir. strategic change Hewlett-Packard, 2000—03; v.p. human resources Clorox. Co., Oakland, Calif., 2004—05, sr. v.p., 2005—. Bd. trustees Oakland Mus. Calif. Office: Clorox Co 1221 Broadway Oakland CA 94612-1888 Office Phone: 510-271-7000. Office Fax: 510-832-1463.

KANE, KAREN MARIE, public affairs consultant; b. Colorado Springs, Colo., Mar. 7, 1947; d. Bernard Francis and Adeline Marie (Logan) K. Student, Mills Coll., Oakland, Calif., 1965-66; BA, U. Wash., Seattle, 1970, MA, 1973, PhC, 1977, postgrad. Pub. affairs cons., housing subcom. Seattle Ret. Tchrs. Assn., 1981-84; pub. affairs cons. 1st U.S. Women's Olympic Marathon Trials, 1982-83, Seattle, 1985—. Adminstr. sponsorships and grants Allied Arts Found., 2004—. Contbr. articles to newsletters and mags. Trustee Allied Arts of Seattle, 1987—96, past chmn. hist. preservation com., sec. bd. trustees, mem. exec. com., 1987—96; trustee Allied Arts Found., 1999—, sponsorship application approval com., 2002—04; active Mayor's Landmark Theatre Adv. Group, 1991—93, Pike Place Market Hist. Commn., Seattle, 1992—98, chmn., 1997—98; com. to rev. the Hildt agreement Pike Place Market, 1998—99; active Market Constituency, 1999—; mem. Friends of Market, 1999—; vol. various polit. campaigns, Seattle; bd. dirs. Showboat Theatre Found./Bravo (formerly Showboat Theatre Found.), 1984—2002. Recipient Award of Honor Wash. Trust for Hist. Preservation, 1990, Recognition award Found. for Hist. Preservation and Adaptive Reuse, Seattle, 1991; Am. Found. grantee, 1989, 91. Mem. AAUW, LWV (chmn., hist. preservation Seattle chpt. 1989—, co-chmn land use com. 2001-05, chmn. 2005—), Mills Coll. Alumnae Assn., U. Wash. Alumni Assn., Nat. Trust for Hist. Preservation, Hist. Hawai'i Found., Found. for San Francisco's Archtl. Heritage, Wash. Trust for Hist. Preservation, Hist. Seattle Preservation and Devel. Authority. Office Phone: 206-323-4721.

KANE, LORIE, professional golfer; b. Prince Edward Island, Can., Dec. 19, 1964; d. Jack Kane. Student, Acadia U. Mem. Can. Internat. Team, 1989-92, Can. World Amateur Team, 1992; golfer LPGA, 1993—; du Maurier Ltd. Series champion, 1994, 95; series event winner, 1993-95; 2d place Toray Japan Queens Cup, 1997. Recipient Heather Farr Player Award, 1998, William and Mousie Powell Award, 2000. 1 LPGA career hole-in-one. Office: c/o LPGA 100 International Golf Dr Daytona Beach FL 32124-1082

KANE, LUCILE M., retired archivist, historian; b. Maiden Rock, Wis., Mar. 17, 1920; d. Emery John and Ruth (Coty) Kane BS, River Falls State Tchrs. Coll., 1942; MA, U. Minn., 1946. Tchr. Osceola (Wis.) High Sch., 1942-44; asst. publicity dept. U. Minn. Press, Mpls., 1945-46; rsch. fellow, editor Forest Products History Found., St. Paul, 1946-48; curator manuscripts Minn. Hist. Soc., St. Paul, 1948-75, sr. rsch. fellow, 1979-85, sr. rsch. assoc., 1985—, mem. hon. coun., 1988—. State archivist, 1975—79. Author, compiler: A Guide to the Care and Administration of Manuscripts, 2d edit., 1966, (with Kathryn A. Johnson) Manuscripts Collections of the Minnesota Historical Society, Guide No.2, 1955, The Waterfall That Built a City, 1966 (updated edit. pub. as The Falls of St. Anthony, 1987), (with Alan Ominsky) Twin Cities: A Pictorial History of Saint Paul and Minneapolis, 1983; transl., editor, Military Life in Dakota, The Jour. of Philippe Regis de Trobriand, 1951; editor: (with others) The Northern Expeditions of Major Stephen H. Long, 1978; contbr. articles to profl. jours. Recipient award of Merit Western History Assn., 1982, Disting. Svc. award Minn. Humanities Commn., 1983, award of Distinction Am. Assn. State and Local History, 1987; co-recipient Theodore C. Blegen award Minn. Hist. Soc., 1996. Fellow: Soc. Am. Archivists. Home: 11377 180th Ave Bloomer WI 54724-4733

KANE, MARGARET BRASSLER, sculptor; b. East Orange, NJ, May 25, 1909; d. Hans and Mathilde (Trumpler) Brassler; m. Arthur Ferris Kane, June 11, 1930; children: Jay Brassler, Gregory Ferris. Student, Packer Collegiate Inst., 1920—26, Syracuse U., 1927, Art Students League, 1927—29, N.Y. Coll. Music, 1928—29, John Hovannes Studio, 1932—34; PhD (hon.), Colo. State Christian Coll., 1973. Head craftsman sculpture, arts and skills unit ARC, Halloran Gen. Hosp., NY, 1942—43; jury mem. Bklyn. Mus., 1948, Am. Machine & Foundry Co., 1957; com. mem. An Am. Group, Inc. Exhibitions include, Phila. Mus., Chgo. Art Inst., Am. Fedn. Arts, NY Bot. Garden, 1981, 60th Anniversary Exhbn. Lever House, 1987—98, Sculptors Guild 50th Anniversary Exhbn., Lever House, 1987—96, 1st Bi-Coastal exhibits San Francisco, Collection Donald Trump, 1988, Collection Rene Anselmo, 1991, Shidoni Galleries, Santa Fe, N.Mex., 1989, Am. Sculpture, Hofstra Mus., 1990, exhibitions include nat. tour Am. sculpture by EducArt Projects Inc., 1992, exhibitions include, Stamford Mus. and Nature Ctr., 1996, Zimmerli Art Mus. Historical Exhibit, 1999—2000, Treasures from the Smithsonian Am. Art Mus., 2000—02, numerous others, Represented in permanent collections, Zimmerli Art Mus., Rutgers U., NJ, 1992, Nat. Mus. Am. Art, Smithsonian Instn., Washington, 1993, 2000, Bruce Mus., Greenwich, Conn., 1996, Packer Collegiate Inst., Bklyn., 2003, one-woman shows include sculpture, Friends Greenwich (Conn.) Library, 1962, prin. works include 18 foot carving in limewood, 2002, prin. works include six foot carving Reaching the Galaxies, 2002—, prin. works include plaque Burro Monument, Fair Play, Colo., prin. works include bronze panels Earthbound, cast by Tallix Art Foundry Beacon, NY, 2005, Symbols, 2005, Micro-macrocosm, 2005, Five episodes in human history, bronze works placed against a cosmic background, 2006; reprodns. Contemporary Stone Sculpture, 1970, Contemporary Am. Sculptures, Am. References, Chgo.; CD-ROM, Smithsonian Nat. Mus. Am. Art, Washington, 1995; contbr. articles to mags. Recipient Hyatt Huntington award, 1942, Am. Artist Profl. League and Monclair Art Assn. awards, 1943, 1st Henry O. Avery prize, 1944, Sculpture prize, Bklyn. Soc. Artists, Bklyn. Mus., 1946, John Rogers award, 1951, Lawrence Hyder prize, 1952, 1954, David H. Zell Meml. award, 1954, 1963, Hon. Mention, U.S. Maritime Commn., 1941, A.C.A. Gallery Competition, 1944, medal of Honor for Sculpture, Nat. Acad. Galleries, N.Y., prize for carved sculpture, 1955, prize for animal sculpture, 1956, 1st award for sculpture, Ann. New Eng. Exhbns., Silvermine, Conn. Fellow: Internat. Inst. Arts and Letters (life); mem.: Nat. Trust Hist. Preservation, silvermine Guild Artists, Internat. Soc. Artists (charter), Internat. Sculpture Ctr., Greenwich Soc. Artists (mem. coun.), Bklyn. Soc. Artists, Artists Coun. U.S.A., Pen and Brush (emeritus 1992), Nat. League Am. Pen Women, Inc. (OWL award for the Arts 1991), Nat. Assn. Women Artists (2d v.p. 1943—44), Sculptors Guild, Inc. (life; sec. to exec. bd. 1942—45, chmn. exhbn. com. 1942, 1944).

KANE, MARILYN A., occupational therapist, educator; b. Scranton, Pa., May 23, 1943; d. James William and Pauline Margaret (Buckavecky) K. BA, Marywood U., Scranton, 1967; MA, NYU, 1972. Cert. occupl. therapist; lic. occupl. therapist, N.Y. Chief ACT therapy, program dir. Hutchings Psychiat. Ctr., Syracuse, N.Y., 1972-80; team leader, chief occupl. therapy Willard (N.Y.) Psychiat. Ctr., 1980-95; pvt. practice occupl. thearpy, Trumansburg, N.Y., 1992-97; asst. prof., field work coord. Keuka Coll., Penn Yan, N.Y., 1992-97; asst. prof. occupl. therapy Ithaca (N.Y.) Coll., 1997—. Contbg. author: (manual) Functional Need Assessment for CHR Psychiatric Patients, 1990; co-author: (manual) FNA Treatment Guide, 1996. Mem. AAUP, AAUW, Am. Occupl. Therapy Assn., N.Y. State Occupl. Therapy Assn., Assn. for Driver Rehab. Specialists. Home: 109 Indian Creek Rd Ithaca NY 14850-1309

KANE, MARY DEELY, state official; b. Wilmington, Del., Mar. 10, 1962; d. Edward and Anna Teresa (Molloy) Deely; m. John Murray Kane, Apr. 12, 1986, 3 children BA in English, Mt. St. Mary's Coll., 1984, BS in Bus. & Fin., 1984; JD, Catholic U., 1999. Legis corr. to Senator J. R. Biden, Jr. US Senate, Washington, 1984-85; adminstr. spl. projects Am. Trucking Assn., Washington; of counsel Etheridge, Quinn, McAuliffe, Rowan & Hartinger, Rockville, Md., 2001—02; dep. sec. state State of Md., Annapolis, 2003—05, sec. of state, 2005—. Bd. dirs. Kane Co., Elkridge, Md., 1997—2003; alt. del. Rep. Party Nat. Conv., 2000; mem. Gov. Exec. Coun., Annapolis, Md., 2005—; chair. Gov. Subcabinet for Internat. Affairs, 2005—; mem. Gov. Commn. on Md. Mil. Monuments, 2005—, Bd. State Canvasers, 2005—, Gov. Interagency Coun. for Nonprofit Sector, 2005—. Mem. Adv. Com.for the Jefferson Patterson Hist. Pk. & Mus., 2005—, Parish Coun., Our Lady of Mercy Cath. Church, 2000—03; bd. trustees Mater Dei Sch., Bethesda, Md. Mem.: Md. State Bar Assn., ABA. Roman Catholic. Office: Office Sec of State State House Annapolis MD 21401 Office Phone: 410-974-5521. Office Fax: 410-974-5190.

KANE, MARY KAY, academic administrator, law educator; b. Detroit, Nov. 14, 1946; d. John Francis and Frances (Roberts) K.; m. Ronan Eugene Degnan, Feb. 3, 1987 (dec. Oct. 1987). BA cum laude, U. Mich., 1968, JD cum laude, 1971. Bar: Mich. 1971. Rsch. assoc., co-dir. NSF project on privacy, confidentiality and social sci. rsch. data sch. law U. Mich., 1971-72, Harvard U., 1972-74; asst. prof. law SUNY, Buffalo, 1974-77; mem. faculty Hastings Coll. Law U. Calif., San Francisco, 1977—, prof. law, 1979—, assoc. acad. dean, 1981-83, acting acad. dean, 1987-88, acad. dean., 1990-93, dean, 1993—2006, chancellor, 2001—06, John D. Digardi Disting. Prof. Law. Vis. prof. law U. Mich., 1981, U. Utah, 1983, U. Calif., Berkeley, 1983-84, sch. law U. Tex., 1989; cons. Mead Data Control, Inc., 1971, 74, Inst. on Consumer Justice, U. Mich. Sch. Law, 1972, U.S. Privacy Protection Study Commn., 1975-76; lectr. pretrial mgmt. devices U.S. magistrates for 6th and 11th cirs. Fed. Jud. Ctr., 1983; Siebenthaler lectr. Samuel P. Chase Coll. Law, U. North Ky., 1987; reporter ad hoc com. on asbestos litigation U.S. Jud. Conf., 1990-91, mem. standing com. on practice and procedure, 2001—; mem. 9th Cir. Adv. Com. on Rules Practice and Internal Oper. Procedures, 1993-96; spkr. in field. Author: Civil Procedure in a Nutshell, 1979, 5th edit., 2003, Sum and Substance on Remedies, 1981; co-prodr.(with C. Wright and A. Miller): Pocket Supplements to Federal Practice and Procedure, 1975—; co-author (with C. Wright and A. Miller): Federal Practice and Procedure, vol. 7, 3d edit., 2001, 10, 10A and 10B, 3d edit., 1998, vols. 7-7C, 2d edit., 1986, vols. 6-6A, 2d edit., 1990, vols. 11-11A, 2d edit., 1995, vols. 7A-B, 3d edit., 2005; co-author: (with J. Friedenthal and A. Miller) Hornbook on Civil Procedure, 4th edit., 2005; co-author: (with C. Wright) Hornbook on the Law of Federal Courts, 2002, Federal Practice Deskbook, 2002; mem. law sch. divsn. West. Adv. Editl. Bd., 1986—; contbr. articles to profl. jours. Mem. standing com. on rules of practice and procedure U.S. Jud. Conf., 2000—. Mem. ABA (mem. bar admissions com. 1995-2000, mem. coun. sect. legal edn. and admission to bar 2004—), Assn. Am. Law Schs. (com. on prelegal edn. statement 1982, chair sect. remedies 1982, panelist sect. on prelegal edn. 1983, exec. com. sect. on civil procedure 1983, 86, panelist sect. on tchg. methods 1984, spkr. new tchrs. conf. 1986, 89, 90, chair sect. on civil procedure 1987, spkr. sects. civil procedure and conflicts 1987, 91, chair planning com. for 1988 Tchg. Conf. in Civil Procedure 1987-88, nominating com. 1988, profl. devel. com. 1988-91, planning com. for workshop in conflicts 1988, planning com. for 1990 Conf. on Clin. Legal Edn. 1989, chair profl. devel. com. 1989-91, exec. com. 1991-93, 2000-02, pres.-elect 2000, pres. 2001), Am. Law Inst. (co-reporter complex litigation project 1988-93, coun. 1998—), ABA/Assn. Am. Law Schs. Commn. on Financing Legal Edn., State Bar Mich. Home: 8 Admiral Dr Ste 421 Emeryville CA 94608-1567 Office: U Calif Hastings Coll Law 200 McAllister St San Francisco CA 94102-4707 Office Phone: 415-565-4777. E-mail: kanem@uchastings.edu.*

KANE, PAMELA, psychologist; b. Phila., Mar. 2, 1946; d. Joseph Charles and Jean A. (Clark) K.; m. William Devier Harlow; children: Shannon Kane-Meddock, Derek Kane-Meddock, Charles Kane-Harlow; m. Terry D. Meddock (div. 1980). BA, Miami U., Oxford, Ohio, 1968; postgrad., U. Ill., 1971-72; EdM, Temple U., Phila., 1980; PhD, Temple U., 1988. Lic. psychologist, Pa., N.J. Counselor Adler Reg. Ctr., Champaign, Ill., 1968-69, supr., 1969-70, asst. dir., 1970-73; tchr., dir. N.W. Child Devel. Ctr., Phila., 1973; psychotherapist Delaware Valley Psychol. Clinics, Newportville, Pa., 1983-86, psychologist and reg. dir., 1986-89; staff psychologist Coché and Coché, Phila., 1989-92; psychologist dept. psychiatry Sch. Osteo. Medicine U. Medicine and Dentistry N.J., 1993, clin. asst. prof. dept. psychiatry Sch. Osteo. Medicine, 1993. Conductor workshops in field; cons. in field. Bd. dirs. Please Touch Mus., Phila., 1990. Mem. Assn. of Del. Valley Individuals Serving Edn., Soc. for Personality Assessment, Phila. Soc. Clin. Psychologists, Am. Psychol. Assn., Infant Mental Health Assn. Avocations: running, reading. Office: 505 S 22nd St Philadelphia PA 19146-1246

KANE, PATRICIA ELLEN, museum curator; b. Bridgeport, Conn., Apr. 4, 1944; d. James Edmund and Alice (Arsenault) K.; m. Walter Scott Braznell, July 21, 1977. BA, Chatham Coll., 1966; MA in Early Am. Culture, U. Del., 1968; PhD in Art History, Yale U., 1987. Asst. curator Garvan and related collections Am. art Yale U. Art Gallery, New Haven, Conn., 1968-74, assoc. curator Garvan and related collections Am. art, 1974-78, curator decorative arts, 1978—. Lectr. Yale U., 1976, 90, Boston U./Mus. Fine Arts, 1976; mem. Am. arts adv. com. Va. Mus. Fine Arts, 1977-78; mem. exec. com. Ctr. for Am. Art and Material Culture, 1979-81; mem. adv. com. Historic Deerfield, Inc., 1985—; mem. fine arts com. Mattatuck Mus., 1990—. Mem. editorial bd. Winterthur Portfolio: Jour. Material Culture, 1983—; contbr. articles to profl. jours. Bd. dirs. Chipstone Found., 1988-90. Henry Francis du Pont fellow, 1966-68; Advanced Acad. Degree Program fellow Nat. Mus. Act., 1977-78. Mem. Am. Ceramics Cir., Soc. Winterth Grads. (v.p. 15-76), Decorative Arts Soc. (chmn. Charles F. Montgomery award com. 1979-81, res. 1981-83), Furniture History Soc., Regional Furniture Soc., New Eng. Hist. Geneal. Soc., Conn. Hist. Soc. (mus. com. 1991-97), New Haven Colony Hist. Soc. (mus. com. 1970—), Winterthur Gu ild. Office: Yale U Art Gallery Office Am Arts PO Box 208271 New Haven CT 06520-8271

KANE, SUE ANN, counselor, geriatrics nurse; b. Tecumseh, Mich., Sept. 3, 1954; d. William Gustine and June Pauline Sisson; m. James Kane, Mar. 30, 1974; children: Kristen Leigh, Matthew James, Derrick Joel. AAS, Regents Coll., 1994; B in Applied Sci. cum laude, Siena Heights U., 1996, MA in Cmty. Agy. Counseling, 2001; sch. counselor endorsement, U. Toledo, 2003. RN Mich.; ltd. lic. profl. counselor Mich., lic. sch. counselor Mich. LPN Bixby Hosp., Adrian, Mich., 1975—84; clk. Herrick Hosp., Tecumseh, 1985—89; restorative nurse Herrick Manor, Tecumseh, 1990—96; unit nurse Dominican Life Ctr., Adrian, 1997—; clin. therapist Family Counseling and Children's Svcs., Adrian, 2004—05; clin. cons. Gerontology Network, Adrian, 2006—. Mem.: Assn. Mich. Sch. Counselors, Mich. Counseling Assn., Chi Sigma Iota. Democrat. Roman Catholic. Avocations: hiking, bicycling, skiing, snowshoeing, reading, scrapbooks. Home: 2907 Coral Ct Tecumseh MI 49286 E-mail: kane@tc3net.com.

KANE, YVETTE, lawyer, judge; b. Donaldsonville, La., Oct. 11, 1953; d. Thomas R. Pregeant and Julia Tucker; children: Kathleen, Madeline. BA, Nicholls State U., Thibodeaux, La., 1973; JD, Tulane U., 1976. Bar: Pa. Trial atty. US Equal Employment Opportunity Commn., 1977-78; asst. atty. gen. Colo. Atty. Gen.'s Office, 1978-80; dep. dist. atty. Denver Dist. Atty.'s Office, 1980-86; dep. atty. gen. rev. and advice sect. Pa. Office Atty. Gen., 1986-91; chief counsel Pa. Ind. Regulatory Rev. Commn., 1991-92; sr. assoc. Wolf, Block, Schorr & Solis-Cohen, Harrisburg, Pa., 1993-95; sec. state Commonwealth of Pa., 1995-98; US dist. judge US Dist. Ct. (mid. dist.) Pa., Harrisburg, 1998—2006, chief judge, 2006—. Office: US Dist Ct Box 11817 228 Walnut St 8th Fl Harrisburg PA 17108 Office Phone: 717-221-3920.

KANE HITTNER, MARCIA SUSAN, bank executive; b. N.Y.C. d. Howard Eugene and Sydell (Friedman) Kane; m. Ellis Hittner. Cert. fin. planning, NYU, BA in Comm. Cert. Nat. Ret. Plans Tng. Ctr., software capability maturity model cert. interim profile adminstr. Carnegie Mellon U. Pension specialist Union Dime Savs. Bank, N.Y.C., 1978—81; money market specialist Goldome (formerly Union Dime Savs. Bank), N.Y.C., 1981—82; mgr. customer svc. Citibank, N.A., N.Y.C., 1982—85, mgr. mktg. product, 1986—87, mgr. shareholder comm., 1988—89, asst. v.p., tax shelter conversions, 1990—93, asst. v.p. tech. client interface, 1993—95, asst. v.p. U.S., Europe consumer bank, 1995—99; with product design and devel. Software Engring. Process Group, 1995—99; v.p. mktg. strategy EAB subs. ABN-AMRO, 1999—2001, cons. bus. and mktg. strategy, 2001—04; sr. v.p. Cambridge Home Capital, LLC, Great Neck, NY, 2004—06; exec. v.p. Howard Kane Assocs., Inc., 2006—. Author: (with others) Critical Reading-Level G, 1980. Bd. dirs. Forest Hills Owners Corp., N.Y.C.

KANE-VANNI, PATRICIA RUTH, lawyer, paleontologist, educator; d. Joseph James and Ruth Marina (Ramirez); m. Francis William Vanni, Feb. 14, 1981; 1 child, Christian Michael. AB, Chestnut Hill Coll., 1975; JD, Temple U., 1985; postgrad., U. Pa. Bar: Pa. 1985, US Ct. Appeals (3d cir.) 1988. Freelance art illustrator, Phila., 1972—; secondary edn. instr. Archdiocese of Phila., Pa., 1980-83; contract analyst CIGNA Corp., Phila., 1983-84; jud. aide Phila. Ct. of Common Pleas, Pa., 1984; assoc. atty. Anderson and Dougherty, Wayne, Pa., 1985-86; atty. cons. Bell Tele. Co. of Pa., Pa., 1986-87; sr. assoc. corp. counsel Independence Blue Cross, Phila., 1987-96; pvt. practice law, 1996-97; dinosaur educator Acad. Natural Scis., Phila., 1997—. Atty. cons., 1996-2003; counsel Reliance Ins. Co., Phila., 1998-2000, contract atty., 2000-2003; atty. Westmont Assoc., Haddonfield, NJ, 2002; legal counsel, Housing Authority, Phila., Pa., 2003-05, atty. counsel 2005—; cons. Coll. Consortium on Drug and Alcohol Abuse, Chester, Pa., 1986-89; paleo-sci. educator Pa. Acad. Natural Sci., 1997—; paleontology field expdns. include Mont., 1999. 2000, Isle of Wight, Eng., 1999, Bahariya Oasis, Egypt, 2000; spkr. in field. Contbr. articles and illustrations to profl. mag.; performer: Phila. Revels., 2001 03, 04. Judge Del. Valley Sci. Fairs, Phila., 1986, 87, 98, 99; Dem. committeewomen, Lower Merion, Pa., 1983-87; ch. cantor, soloist, mem. choir Roman Cath. Ch.; bd. dir. Phila. Assn. Ch. Musicians. Recipient Legion of Honor award Chapel of the Four Chaplins, 1983. Mem. ABA, Pa. Bar Assn., Phila. Bar Assn. (Theatre Wing), Phila. Assn. Def. Counsel, Phila. Vol. Lawyers for Arts (bd. dir.), Nat. Health Lawyers Assn. (spkr. 1994 ann. conv.), Hispanic Bar Assn., Soc. Vertebrate Paleontology, Pa. Acad. Nat. Sci. (vol.), Delaware Valley Paleontol. Soc. (v.p. 1998—); Guild of Natural Sci. Illustrators, DAR Independence Hall Chpt. Democrat. Avocations: choral and solo vocal music, portrait painting and illustrating, paleontology. Home: 119 Bryn Mawr Ave Bala Cynwyd PA 19004-3012 Personal E-mail: pkv1@erols.com, Paleopatti@hotmail.com.

KANG, KYOUNG SOOK, retired special education educator; b. Seoul, May 29, 1942; came to U.S., 1972; d. Do Myung Suk and Jung Hyun Lee; m. Young Woo Kang, Feb. 26, 1972; children: Paul, Christopher. BA in Edn., Sookmyung Woman's U., Seoul, 1972; MS in Edn., Purdue U., 1987. Cert. elem. tchr., Ind. Clk., youth dept. Red Cross of Korea, Seoul, 1962-64; clk. Samho Trading Co., Seoul, 1965-67; field trainee Pa. State Office for the Blind, Harrisburg, 1967-68; assoc. exec. dir. Rehab. Ctr. for the Blind of Korea, Seoul, 1970-72; orientation and mobility tchr. for the blind Gary (Ind.) Community Sch. Corp., 1977—2004; ret. Sunday sch. tchr. Chunho-dong Meth. Ch., Seoul, 1958-59, Namsan Meth. Ch., Seoul, 1960-62, Westminster Presbyn. Ch., Munster, Ind., 1981-82. Author: I Am His Cane, He Is My Light (Korean edit.), 2004; co-author: Two Candles Shining in the Darkness of the World (in Korean), 1990. Leader Seoul Girl Scout coun., 1961-62. Recipient Cert. Appreciation, Korean Assn. Spl. Educators, 1978, Paul Harris award Rotary Internat., Evanston, Ill., 1987, Cert. Appreciation Gary Dept. Spl. Edn., 1988. Mem. AAUW (life), Coun. for Exceptional Children, Korean Womens Assn. of Chgo. (v.p. 1991-93), Alumnae Assn. Sookmyung Women's U. in Midwest (pres. 1990-91, pres. of bd. dirs., 2001-2003).

KANICH, KELLI JO, secondary school educator; b. Spangler, Pa., Jan. 4, 1978; d. Joseph and Sharon Kanich. BA in Math. Edn., Seton Hill U., Greensburg, Pa., 2000; MEd, St. Francis U., Loretto, Pa., 2006. Math tchr. United Sch. Dist., Armagh, Pa., 2003—; girls basketball coach United Jr. High, Armagh, Pa., 2004—. Eucharistic min. St. Timothy and Mark Cath. Ch., Twin Rocks, Pa., 1998—2006. Mem.: Pa. State Edn. Assn. Office Phone: 814-446-5615 ext 749.

KANICK, VIRGINIA, retired radiologist; b. Coaldale, Pa., Nov. 10, 1925; d. Martin and Anna (Pisklak) K. BA, Barnard Coll., 1947; MD, Columbia U., 1951. Diplomate Am. Bd. Radiology. Intern Western Reserve U. Hosps., Cleve., 1951-52; resident in radiology St. Luke's Hosp., N.Y.C., 1952-55, attending radiologist, 1955-74; acting dir. radiology St. Luke's Roosevelt Hosp., N.Y.C., 1981-84, dep. dir. of radiology, 1984-89; ptnr. West Side Radiology, N.Y.C., 1989—2003; ret., 2003. Clin. prof. radiology Coll. Physicians and Surgeons Columbia U., N.Y.C., 1975—; pres. Med. Bd. St. Luke's Roosevelt Hosp., 1980-82. Contbr. articles to profl. jours. Bd. dirs. Health System Agy. of N.Y.C., 1978-81. Fellow Am. Cancer Soc., 1955. Fellow Am. Coll. Radiology; mem. Am. Roentgen Ray Soc., Radiol. Soc. N.Am., N.Y. County Med. Soc. (sec., dir. 1978—), N.Y. State Radiol. Soc. (bd. dirs. 1975—). Independent. Avocations: skiing, travel, archaeology. Home: 560 Riverside Dr Apt 14B New York NY 10027-3240 Office Phone: 212-666-7258. Business E-Mail: vk3@columbia.edu.

KANIN, DORIS MAY, political scientist, consultant; b. Somerville, Mass., Mar. 28, 1928; d. Sidney J. and Ida Gail (Gelbsman) Small; m. Irving L. Kanin, June 11, 1944; children: Dennis, Erik, Lisa Hochheiser. BA in Govt., Boston U., 1966, MA in Govt., 1970, postgrad. in Polit. Sci., 1970-74. Dir. cultural activities Staff of George McGovern, 1972; legis. dir. to congressman Joe Moakley Washington, 1972-74; nat. polit. dir. Frank Church for Pres., 1975-76; spl. asst. Paul Tsongas U.S. Senate campaign, Boston, 1977-78; dir. Human Svcs. Dept. Fed. State Rels., Mass., 1979-81; nat. dir. pub. affairs Physicians for Social Responsibility, 1981-82; exec. of Pub. Rels. and Comms. Lynwood Labs. Inc., 1982—; polit. advisor Paul Tsongas for Pres. campaign, Mass., 1991—92. Inventor, creator: Spray-n-Starch aerosol, 1968; editor: Quincy Mass. Cmty. Ctr. Newsletter, 1956-58, Mass. Liberal Citizens of Mass. Bulletin; journalist Boston Daily Record, 1944; reporter Boston Daily Record-Am. Pres. LWV, Norwood, Mass., 1956—59, Mass. Citizens for Participation in Politics, Boston, 1973—74; chair, bd. dirs., mem., state bd. Mass. Civil Liberties Union, Boston, 1976—81; mem. steering com. women's caucus Capitol Hill Women's Polit. Caucus; elected del. to all Nat. Nominating Convs., 1972—92; del. Dem. Nat. Conv., 1972, 1976, 1980, 1982, 1986, 1992, Fla. Dem. Party Conf., 2002; dir. Mass. Cultural Affairs for Pres. Campaign, George McGovern; mem. Dem. Nat. Com., Mass., 1972—76, mem. women's caucus Mass., 1972—76, mem. edn. and tng. coun., 1976—80; bd. dirs. Mass. Ams. for Dem. Action, 1978—80, Mass. Pax; del. Mass. Dem. Party Conv., 2002, Fla. Dem. State Party Conf., 2002, Mass. Dem. Party Conv., 2003; chmn. Dem. Club, Breakers West; pres. Dem. Club Breakers West, 2005, founder; mem. Palm Beach County Dem. Party. Named: Woodrow Wilson Semi-Finalist, 1972-76, Mass. Spelling Bee Champion, Boston Herald Traveler, 1939. Mem. Internat. Aerosol Congress, League Women Voters. Democrat. Avocations: travel, painting, poetry writing, opera, ballet. Address: The Towers at Chestnut Hill Apt 606S Chestnut Hill MA 02467 Home (Summer): The Towers at Chestnut Hill 250 Hammond Pond Pkwy Apt 606S Chestnut Hill MA 02467-1510 Home (Winter): 1289 Breakers W Blvd West Palm Beach FL 33411

KANIN, FAY, screenwriter; b. NYC; d. David and Bessie Mitchell; m. Michael Kanin (dec.); children: Joel (dec.), Josh. Student, Elmira Coll., LHD (hon.), 1981; BA, U. So. Calif. Mem. Western regional exec. bd., judge Am. Coll. Theatre Festival, 1975-76. Writer: (with Michael Kanin) screenplays including The Opposite Sex, Teacher's Pet; Broadway plays including Goodbye My Fancy, His and Hers, Rashomon, Grind (Tony nomination 1985); writer, co-prodr. TV spls. including Friendly Fire, ABC-TV (Emmy award for best TV film, San Francisco Film Festival award, Peabody award), Hustling (Writers Guild award for best original drama), Tell Me Where It Hurts (Emmy award, Christopher award); Heartsounds (Peabody award). Recipient Humanitas prize prestigious Kieser award, 2003. Mem. Writers Guild Am. West (pres. screen br. 1971-73, Val Davies award 1975, Morgan Cox award 1976, Edmund H. North award 2005), Am. Film Inst. (trustee), Acad. Motion Picture Arts and Scis. (pres. 1979-82), Nat. Ctr. Film and Video Preservation (co-chmn.), Am. Film Preservation Bd. (chmn.).

KANNAN, SANDRA JEAN, elementary school educator, retired assistant principal; b. Lawrence, Mass., Oct. 7, 1943; d. John Anthony and Agnes Savinelli; m. William James Kannan, Feb. 20, 1970; 1 child, Cassandra Jean. BS, Suffolk U., Boston, Mass., 1967; MA in Edn., Mass. U., Salem, 1996. Tchr. Derry Sch. Dist., NH, 1967—70; tchr., asst. prin. Lawrence Sch. Sys., Mass., 1970—2002. Mem. elem. edn. curriculum com. Addison Gallery-Phillips H.S., Andover, Mass., 1992—2002. Mem.: Phi Kappa Phi. Democrat. Roman Catholic. Avocations: painting, gardening, cooking, reading, travel. Home: 14 Scotland Heights Rd Haverhill MA 01832

KANNENSTINE, MARGARET LAMPE, artist; b. St. Louis, Apr. 1, 1938; d. John Avery and Elizabeth (Phillips) Lampe; m. Louis Fabian Kannenstine, Oct. 3, 1959; children: David Edward, Emily Ann. BFA, Washington U., St. Louis, 1959; postgrad., Art Students League, N.Y.C., 1959—61. Trustee Pentangle Coun. Arts, 1982—88, 1993—96, chair, 1984—87, 1994, 95, hon. bd., 1997—; trustee Vt. Studio Ctr., 1989—94, chair, 1990—93; trustee Vt. Coun. Arts, 1994—2001, trustee, vice-chair, 2004—, chair, 1994—98, 2006—; trustee Nat. Assembly Arts Agys., 2001—, sec., 2004—05. One-woman shows include Vt. Artisans, Strafford, 1976, Gallery Two, Woodstock, Vt., 1974, 1977, 1985, Red Mill Gallery, Johnson, Vt., 1990, Green Mountain Power Corp., South Burlington, Vt., 1991, 1991, Vt. Coun. on Arts, Montpelier, 1991, Woodstock Gallery Art, 1991, 1994, Beside Myself Gallery, Arlington, Vt., 1992, Taylor Gallery, Meriden, NH, 1993, Kimball Union Acad., Dartmouth Coll., Hanover, NH, 1993, 1999, Kent (Conn.) Sch., 1993, Chittenden Bank, Burlington, Vt., 1994, Windy Bush Gallery, New Hope, Pa., 1995, NH Coll., Manchester, 1996, Flynn Theater Gallery, Burlington, 1996, 1998, Nat. Wildlife Fedn. Gallery, Vienna, Va., 1996, McGowan Fine Art, Concord, NH, 1997, Grayson Gallery, Woodstock, 1997, 1999, Spheris Gallery, Walpole, N.H., 1997, The Gallery at Johnny D's, Somerville, Mass., 1997, AVA Gallery, Hanover, Lebanon, 1998, Main Street Mus. Art, Hartford, Vt., 1999, Collis Ctr., Dartmouth Coll., 1999, Gallery of Graphic Arts, NYC, 1999, Lyndon State Coll., Lyndonville, Vt., 1999, 2002, Supreme Ct., Montpelier, 1999, Cushing Acad. Gallery, Ashburnham, Mass., 2001, Prince St. Gallery, NYC, 2003, Woodstock Town Hall, 2002, Vt. Gov.'s Office Gallery, 2003, Woodstock (Vt.) Folk Art, 2005, Gallery 2/Vt. Artisan Design, Brattleboro, 2005, Firehouse Ctr. for Arts, Burlington, 2005, Burlington Internat. Airport, 2006, Bridgewater Mill Gallery, Vt., 2006, exhibited in group shows at Gallery Two, 1973—88, Carl Battaglia Gallery, NYC, 1979—80, The Gallery, Williamstown, Mass., 1981—84, Vt. Coun. Arts, 1988, 1996, AVA Gallery, Hanover, 1989—98, Woodstock Gallery Art, 1989, Beside Myself Gallery, 1990, Fleming Mus., U. Vt., Burlington, 1991, Bennington Coll., 1992, Windy Bush Gallery, 1994, VCA, Woodstock, 1994, Riverfest, White River Junction, Vt., 1995, Firehouse Gallery, Burlington, 1995, McGowan Fine Art, Concord, 1995, Chaffee Gallery, Rutland, Vt., 1997, Helen Day Art Ctr., Stowe, Vt., 1997, Champion Internat., Stamford, Conn., 1997, New Art New Eng., Newport, NH, 1997, Gallery Graphic Art, NYC, 1998—2000, Grayson Gallery, Woodstock, 2000, Ute Stebich Gallery, Lenox, Mass., 1999—2001, Elsa Mott Ives Gallery, NYC, 2000, Arts Alive Gallery, Burlington, 2001, G. Wilson Gallery, Stonington, Maine, 2001, Patricia Carega Gallery, Sandwich, NH, 2002, 2003, 2004, Woodstock Folk Art and Prints, 2003, 2004, Firehouse Ctr. for the Arts, Burlington, Vt., 2005, Vision Festival Art Show, NYC, 2006, numerous others, Represented in permanent collections The Hood Mus., Hanover, NH, Robert Hull Fleming Mus., Burlington, Vt. Employees Credit Union, Montpelier, Champion Internat. Corp., Stamford, Conn., Union Mut. Ins. Co., Montpelier, Vt. Law Sch., South Royalton, Fletcher Allen Hosp., Burlington, Dartmouth Hitchcock Hosp., Lebanon, N.H., Dana Farber Cancer Inst., Boston, Vt. Hist. Soc., Montpelier, Cushing Acad., Ashburnham, Mass., Springfield (Mo.) Art Mus., Bennington Coll., numerous others. Apptd. by Sen. Leahy to Millenium Commn. of Friends of Art and Preservation in Embassies, 1999-2000, White House mini-conference on creative aging, 2005; trustee New Eng. Found. for Arts, 1996-2001, Nat. Assembly of State Arts Agys., 2000-05, sec. 2004-05; incorporator Upper Valley Cmty. Found., 1996-2000, trustee, 1999; founding dir. Woodstock Cty. Trust, v.p. 1998, 99, pres., 2000, 01; charter mem. Creative Economy Coun. of New Eng. Coun., Vt. Creative Economy Policy Coun., 2003—, Vt. Coun. Culture Innovation, 2003, 04; bd. dirs. Ctr. for Cartoon Studies, White River Junction, Vt., 2004-06, sec., 2006. Recipient Citation for achievement in arts, Vt. Arts Coun., 2002; Washington U. scholar, 1955. Mem. Cosmopolitan Club. Avocations: music, gardening, hiking. E-mail: mlkannen@aol.com.

KANNER, ELLEN BARBARA, clinical psychologist; b. Newark, Apr. 22, 1950; d. S. Lee and Elsie (Frumkin) K.; m. Brian R. Donovan, June 10, 1973; children: Gregory, Rebecca. BA in Psychology, Smith Coll., 1972; MA in Clin. Psychology, Fordham U., 1974, PhD in Clin. Psychology, 1980. Lic. psychologist N.Y. Psychology aide Behavior Modification Program Northampton (Mass.) State Hosp., 1972-73; psychology intern Kings County Hosp., Bklyn., 1975-76; part time psychology work various clinics, N.Y., 1976-77; psychologist Kings Park (N.Y.) Psychiat. Ctr., 1980-83; pvt. practice Huntington, N.Y., 1983—. Avocations: ice skating, swimming, gardening, reading. Office: 205 E Main St Huntington NY 11743-2923 Office Phone: 516-351-3436.

KANOFF, MARY ELLEN, lawyer; m. Chris Kanoff. BA in Econs., U. Calif., Berkeley, 1978, JD, 1984. Large systems mktg. rep. IBM, 1978—81; with Latham & Watkins, L.A., 1984—, ptnr., 1991—. Bd. trustees St. Matthews Sch., Pacific Palisades, Calif., St. John's Hosp., Santa Monica, Calif.; bd. dirs. Chrysalis. Named one of Top 25 Lawyers in Calif. under 45, Calif. Law Bus., 1993, Up and Coming Bus. Persons in So. Calif., L.A. Bus. Jour., 1997; recipient Founders Spirit of Chrysalis award. Mem.: ABA (bus. law and entertainment law sects.), L.A. County Bar Assn., Calif. Bar Assn. Office: Latham and Watkins LLP 633 W Fifth St Ste 4000 Los Angeles CA 90071 Office Phone: 213-891-8728.

KANOWSKY, JANET MARIE, secondary school educator; d. Carmen and Marie Teresa Russo; m. Stuart Randy Kanowsky, Sept. 15, 1973; children: Adam, Richard. AA in Liberal Arts, Suffolk County C.C., Selden, N.Y., 1996; BA in Natural Sci. and Math. summa cum laude, Dowling Coll., Oakdale, N.Y., 1997; MS in Secondary Edn., Dowling Coll., Oakdale, N.Y., 1998. Cert. tchr. math. grades 7-12 N.Y. Edn. Dept., 2002. Computer programmer County Fed. Savs. and Loan, Rockville Centre, NY, 1969—73; instr. Miller Place Continuing Edn., NY, 1985—86; aide computer rm. Miller Place Sch. Dist., NY, 1985—98; instr. SCOPE, Smithtown, NY, 1986—92; reading tchr. asst. Little Flower Sch. Dist., Wading River, NY, 1992—93; tchr. math. Longwood Ctrl. Sch. Dist., Middle Island, NY, 1998—. Participant intermediate math. curriculum project BOCES, 2000; tchr. Extended Day Program Longwood Jr. H.S., 2001—05. Creator Easterns Jr. Badminton Championships publs., 1993—95, Easterns Draw Booklet, 1999. Sec. Miller Place Badminton Club, 1993—95. Mem.: N.Y. State United Tchrs., Am. Fedn. Tchrs., Kappa Delta Pi, Phi Delta Kappa, Alpha Chi, Phi Theta Kappa, Pi Alpha Sigma. Avocations: gardening, jazzercise. Office: Longwood Jr HS 198 Longwood Rd Middle Island NY 11953

KANT, GLORIA JEAN, retired neuroscientist; b. Chgo., June 6, 1944; d. Hans Georg and Jo Sefa Kant; m. Philip Herbert Balcom, July 1, 1967 (div. 1976). BS in Chemistry, Mich. State U., 1965; PhD in Physiol. Chemistry, U. Wis., 1969. Chemist dept. psychiatry Walter Reed Army Inst. Rsch., Washington, 1970-71, neurochemist dept. microwave rsch., 1971-77, neurochemist dept. med. neuroscis., 1977-87, chief dept. med. neuroscis., 1987-95, dir. divsn. neuroscis., 1995—2001; ret. Mem. editl. bd. Pharmacology, Biochemistry and Behavior, 1991-2000; contbr. over 80 articles to sci. jours. Mem. AAAS, Soc. for Neurosci., Internat. Behavioral Neurosci. Soc., Women in Neurosci. Avocation: golf. Home: 1124 Dennis Ave Silver Spring MD 20901-2171

KANTACK, CATHERINE MARGARET, retired music educator, retired international broker; b. Cedar Rapid, Iowa, July 30, 1943; d. Roy William and Icel Margaret (Tiernan) Driscoll; m. Paul Wayne Kantack, Oct. 5, 1963; children: Keith C., Kelly A. Student, Creighton U., Omaha, 1961—62, Jefferson Davis Coll., 1975—76. Tchr. piano Naval Bn. Constrn. Ctr., Gulfport, Miss., 1974—84; tchr. piano pvt. studio New Orleans, 1984—2003; ret., 1986—. Pres. C.M.II Fin. Svcs., Inc., New Orleans, 1986—; vol. pianist Vets. Hosp., 1980. ARC swimming instr. Keesler AFB, Biloxi, Miss., 1975—81. Recipient Ministry award, Keesler Med. Ctr., 1984. Mem.: Keesler Med. Wives Club, Keesler Officers' Wives Club. Roman Catholic. Avocations: reading, cooking, swimming. Home: 53 Dogwood Rd Columbus MS 39705-5348

KANTARCI, KEJAL, radiologist, researcher; b. Istanbul, Turkey, Dec. 1, 1969; arrived in U.S., 1998; d. Vehbi and Gülseren Aydin; m. Orhun H. Kantarci, Nov. 25, 1994. MS, Marmara U., Istanbul, 1993. Resident Istanbul U., 1993—97; radiologist pvt. practice, 1997—98; asst. prof., assoc. cons. Mayo Clinic, Rochester, Minn., 2004—. Contbr. chapters to books; mem. editl. bd.: Neurosci. Imaging, 2004—. Fellow, Mayo Clinic, 1998—2004; scholar, NIH, 2005—. Mem.: Internat. Soc. Magnetic Resonance Medicine, Radiol. Soc. N.Am. Avocations: mountain climbing, scuba diving, bicycling. Office: Mayo Clinic 200 First St Rochester MN 55905 Office Phone: 507-284-9770. E-mail: kantarci.kejal@mayo.edu.

KANTER, STACY J., lawyer; b. NYC, 1958; d. Ronald I. and Elaine Kanter; m. Eric Martin Kornblau. BS magna cum laude, SUNY, Albany, 1979; JD cum laude, Bklyn. Law Sch., 1984. Bar: NY 1985. Law clk. to Hon. Raymond J. Dearie US Dist. Ct. Ea. Dist. NY, 1986—87; ptnr. Skadden, Arps, Slate, Meagher & Flom LLP, NYC, 1993—. Mng. editor Bklyn. Law Rev., 1983-84. Named one of NY's rising stars in bus. Crain's mag., 1997. Office: Skadden Arps Slate Meagher & Flom LLP 4 Times Sq New York NY 10036 Office Phone: 212-735-3497. Office Fax: 917-777-3497. E-mail: skanter@skadden.com.

KANTOR, JODI M., editor; Grad., Columbia U., 1996; postgrad., Harvard U., 1998. Dorot fellow, Jerusalem; Urban fellow Mayor's Office Ops., N.Y.C.; N.Y. editor Slate online mag., 1998—2003; editor Arts & Leisure N.Y. Times, N.Y.C., 2003—. Named to, Crain's N.Y. Bus. "40 under 40", 2004. Office: NY Times 229 W 43rd St New York NY 10036-3959

KANTROWITZ, JEAN, health products executive; b. Passaic, N.J., May 27, 1922; d. Nathan and Yetta (Applebaum) Rosensaft; m. Adrian Kantrowitz, Nov. 25, 1948; children: Niki, Lisa, Allen. BS, Rider Coll., 1942; MS, U. N.C., 1945; MPH, U. Mich., 1975. Adminstrv. asst. Maimonides Med. Ctr., Bklyn., 1961-70, Sinai Hosp., Detroit, 1970-78, '80-83; program coord., sr. clin. instr. child psyciatry divsn. Case Western Res. U. Sch. Medicine, Cleve., 1978-80; v.p. adminstrn. and bus. devel. L.VAD Tech., Inc., Detroit, 1983—. Mgmt. cons. NIH, Washington, 1974— Mem. Am. Soc. Artificial Internal Organs (co-chair project bionics, history, artificial organs work group). Home: 70 Gallogly Rd Auburn Hills MI 48326-1227 Office: LVAD Tech Inc 300 River Place Dr Ste 6850 Detroit MI 48207-5095 Office Phone: 313-446-2800.

KANTROWITZ, SUSAN LEE, lawyer; b. Queens, N.Y., Jan. 15, 1955; d. Theodore and Dinah (Kotick) Kantrowitz; m. Mark R. Halperin; 1 child, Jacob Joseph Kantrowitz-Sirotkin. BS summa cum laude, Boston U., 1977; JD, Boston Coll., 1980. Bar: Mass. 1982. Assoc. producer Sta. KOCE-TV, Huntington Beach, Calif., 1980-81; acct. exec. Bozell & Jacobs, Newport Beach, Calif., 1981; atty. WGBH Ednl. Found., Boston, 1981-84, dir. legal affairs, 1984-86, gen. counsel, dir. legal affairs, 1986—, v.p., gen. counsel, 1993. Co-author: Legal and Business Aspects of the Entertainment, Publishing and Sports Industries, 1984. Mem. ABA, Mass. Bar Assn., Boston Bar Assn.

KANUK, LESLIE LAZAR, management consultant, educator; b. NYC; d. Charles and Sylvia Lazar; m. Jack Lawrence Kanuk; children: Randi Kanuk Dauler, Alan Robert. MBA, Baruch Coll., 1964; PhD, CUNY, 1974; PhD (hon.), Mass. Maritime Acad., 1981, Maine Maritime Acad., 1988. Pres. Leslie Kanuk Assocs., NYC, 1965—78, 1981—; Lippert Disting. chair Baruch Coll., NYC, 1981-84; prof. CUNY, 1974—99, prof. emeritus, 1999—. Mem. maritime transp. rsch. bd. NAS, 1975—78; commr., vice chmn., chmn. Fed. Maritime Commn., 1978—81; chmn., pres., dir. Containerization and Intermodal Inst., 1981—93; panelist NRC-NAS, 1975—78, 1991; vis. prof. grad. program Maine Maritime Acad., 1984—93. Author: Mail Questionnaire Response Behavior, 1974, Toward an Expanding U.S.M.M., 1976, Consumer Behavior, Prentice Hall, 1978, rev. edits., 1983, 87, 89, 94, 97, 2000, 04, 06, India, 1988, Australia, 1997, 2001, Brazil, 2000, Japan, 2001, China, 2002, Czech Republic, 2004, Croatia, 2004, Internat. Edit., 1997, 2004; mem. editl. bd. Intermodal Forum, 1984-92 Bd. visitors Maine Maritime Acad., 1989—97; trustee United Seaman's Svc., 1988—. Recipient Connie award Containerization and Intermodal Inst., 1980, Diamond Superwoman award Harpers Bazaar mag., 1980, Person of Yr. award NY Fgn. Freight Forwarders and Brokers Assn., 1981, Person of Yr. award Baruch Fgn. Trade Soc., 1981, Disting. Alumnus award CCNY, 1984, Disting. PhD Alumni award CUNY, 1988, Townsend Harris medal, 1986. Mem. Beta Gamma Sigma. Fax: 212-717-8266.

KANY, JUDY C(ASPERSON), retired state senator; b. Ill., June 29, 1937; d. Helmer C. and Florence P. Casperson; m. Robert Kany, Aug. 16, 1958; children: Kristin, Geoffrey, Daniel. BBA, U. Mich., 1959; MPA, U. Maine, Orono, 1976. Mem. Maine Ho. of Reps., 1975-82, Maine Senate, 1982-92; project dir. for health professions regulation Med. Care Devel., Augusta, Maine, 1993—; mem. task force on health workforce regulation Pew Health Professions Commn., 1994-97; mayor Waterville, Maine, 1988-89; mem. issues and policy adv. com. Citizens Advocacy Ctr., Washington, 1994—2000; cmty. liaison Amity Circle Tree Ranch, Tucson, 2003—06. Chmn. Maine's Adv. Commn. on Radioactive Waste, 1981-87, Joint Standing Com. Legal Affairs, 1987-88, Joint Standing Com. on State Govt., 1979-82, Joint Standing Com. Energy and Natural Resources, 1983-84, 89-90, Joint

Standing Com. Banking and Ins., 1991-92, com. Maine Lakes, 1990-92, adv. com. on accountability to the Maine Health Care Reform Commn., 1994-95; mem. Commn. on Maine's Future, 1976, 87-89; project coord. Amity Found.'s Ariz Gov.'s Innovative Domestic Violence Prevention Grant, Amity, 2004-06. Democrat. Home: PO Box 508 81 Lakeshore Dr Belgrade Lakes ME 04918 also: 36832 S Stoney Flower Dr Tucson AZ 85739 Office Phone: 520-749-5980. Business E-Mail: jkany@amityfdn.org.

KAO, WINIFRED W., otolaryngologist; b. Shanghai, Jan. 12, 1961; d. Chi C. Kao and Te H. Liu. BA, Rutgers U., 1983; MD, U. Medicine and Dentistry N.J.- Robert Wood Johnson Med. Sch., 1987. Diplomate Am. Bd. Otolaryngology. Intern Temple U. Hosp., Phila., 1987-88, resident in otolaryngology, 1988-92; attending otolaryngologist Reading Hosp. Med. Ctr., West Reading, Pa., 1992—. Fellow ACS, Am. Acad. Otolaryngology, Head and Neck Surgery; mem. AMA, Am. Acad. Otolaryngology-Head and Neck Surgery, Pa. Med. Soc. Office: Berks ENT Surg Assocs 301 S 7th Ave West Reading PA 19611-1410 Home: 120 Millwyck Rd Lititz PA 17543-9021

KAO, YASUKO WATANABE, retired library director; b. Tokyo, Mar. 30, 1930; arrived in US, 1957; d. Kichiji and Sato (Tanaka) Watanabe; m. Shih-Kung Kao, Apr. 1, 1959; children: John Sterling, Stephanie Margaret. BA, Tsuda Coll., 1950; BA in Lit., Waseda U., Japan, 1955; MSLS, U. So. Calif., 1960. Instr. Takinogawa H.S., Tokyo, 1950—57; catalog libr. U. Utah Libr., 1960—67; Marriott Libr., 1975—77, head catalog divsn., 1978—90; dir. libr. Teikyo Loretto Heights U., 1991—95. Contbr. articles to profl. jours. Vol. Utah Chinese Am. Cmty. Sch., 1974—80, Asian Assn. Utah, 1981—90; mem., vol. Asian Art Mus. San Francisco, 1996—. Waseda U. fellow, 1958—59. Mem.: Beta Phi Mu. Home: 2625 Yuba Ave El Cerrito CA 94530-1443 Personal E-mail: ykao@sbcglobal.net.

KAPANKA, HEIDI, emergency physician; b. Bronxville, N.Y., Dec. 29, 1953; d. Louis John Kapanka and Orla M. Smith. BA cum laude, Boston U., 1976, MD, 1980; MPH, U. Tex., Houston, 1987. Diplomate Am. Bd. Emergency Physicians. Intern Naval Regional Med. Ctr., San Diego, 1980-81; resident in emergency medicine U. Fla. Health Svcs., Jacksonville, 1987-89, U. Ala., Birmingham, 1989-90; attending staff, physician Life Saver Helicopter, Carraway Meth. Med. Ctr., Birmingham, 1992—, dir. med. control, 1992—. Flight surgeon USN, 1982-85, NASA Space Shuttle Program, 1985-86; organizer, spkr. EMT Day, 1994-96; instr. ACL; reviewer quality assurance. Vol. emergency physician 1996 Olympic Games, Birmingham, Ala., 1996, PGA Golf Tournament, 1996, NASCAR Races, Talladega Speedway, 1996, 99, Rolling Stones concert, U. Ala. football games, BDCTA Horse Show; guest spkr. on flight medicine local schs., colls., U. Ala., Boy Scouts, Civic Leaders Breakfast Club, 1990-96; violinist, bd. dirs. Red Mountain Chamber Orch., 1990—. Fellow Am. Coll. Emergency Physicians; mem. AMA, Soc. NASA Flight Surgeons, Jefferson County Med. Soc. Mem. Lds Ch. Office: Carraway Meth Med Ctr 1600 Carraway Blvd Birmingham AL 35234-1913

KAPELMAN, BARBARA ANN, internist, hepatologist, gastroenterologist, educator; b. NYC, Apr. 30, 1949; d. Leonard A. and Helen (Hass) K.; m. Lawrence William Koblenz, Mar. 24, 1979; 1 child, Adam. BA, Barnard Coll., 1970; MS in Microbiology, Yale U., 1972; MD, Albert Einstein Coll. Medicine, 1975. Diplomate Am. Bd. Internal Medicine, Am. Bd. Gastroenterology. Clin. asst. prof. hepatology and gastroenterology Mt. Sinai Sch. Medicine Mt. Sinai Hosp., 1981—82; intern Roosevelt Hosp.-Columbia U., N.Y.C., 1975-76, resident, 1976-78, fellow gastroenterology, 1978-80; fellow liver diseases Mt. Sinai Sch. Medicine-CUNY, N.Y.C., 1980-81; attending physician liver diseases Mt. Sinai Hosp., N.Y.C., 1981—82; asst. attending physician in gastroenterology Beth Israel Hosp., N.Y.C., 1982-88, assoc. attending physician in medicine and gastroenterology, 1988-96, attending physician in medicine and gastroenterology, 1996—; clin. instr. in medicine Mt. Sinai Sch. of Medicine, N.Y.C., 1981-87, asst. clin. prof. medicine, 1987-94; bd. dirs. Beth Israel Med. Ctr., N.Y.C., 1984—, trustee, med. liaison, 1996-97; asst. clin. prof. medicine Albert Einstein Coll. Medicine, N.Y.C., 1994—. Trustee Med. Bd. Liaison, 1996-97; attending physician Beth Israel North, Beth Israel Med. Ctr., N.Y.C., 1982—, Hosp. for Joint Diseases-Orthopedic Inst., N.Y.C., 1982—; vis. clin. fellow Columbia U. Coll. Physicians and Surgeons, N.Y.C., 1975-80; cons. gastroenterology and hepatology, 2004—. Co-author: Gastroenterology for the House Officer, 1989; contbr. articles to profl. jours. Fellow ACP, Am. Coll. Gastroenterology; mem. AMA, Am. Women's Med. Assn., Women's Med. Assn. NYC (officer), Am. Gastroent. Assn., Am. Assn. for Study of Liver Diseases, Am. Soc. for Gastrointestinal Endoscopy, Am. Med. Informatics Assn., NY Acad. Gastroenterology, NY Soc. for Gastrointestinal Endoscopy. Avocations: medical computer software, culinary arts, medical informatics, educational activities, Hebrew language studies. Home: 201 E 87th St Apt 20k New York NY 10128-3217 Business E-Mail: bkapelman@pol.net.

KAPIKIAN, CATHERINE ANDREWS, artist; b. Cleve., Oct. 18, 1939; d. John Robert and Anne Alva (Cosgrove) Andrews; m. Albert Zaven Kapikian, Feb. 27, 1960; children: Albert, Thomas, Gregory. Student, Carnegie Mellon U., 1957—59; BA, U. Md., 1963; MTS summa cum laude, Wesley Theol. Sem., Washington, 1979. Gen. illustrator NIH, Bethesda, Md., 1959—61; artist-in-residence Wesley Theol. Sem., 1979—, mem. faculty, 1980—, founder, dir. Ctr. Arts and Religion, 1984—2001, dir. Henry Luce III Ctr. for the Arts and Religion, 2001—. Designer, fabricator liturgical tapestries, banners, paraments and vestments; mem. commn. on worship and the arts Nat. Coun. Chs., 1991-97; mem. com. Washington Nat. Cathedral's Fabric and Fine Arts, 2006. Works exhibited in group shows including Interfaith Forum on Religion, Art and Architecture, Phoenix, 1979, Chgo., 1981, Phila., 1987, Houston, 1989, Boston, 1990, St. Thomas More Newman Ctr. Liturg. Arts Exhibit, Bowling Green (Ohio) U., 1981, Archdiocese of Chgo., 1984, Biennial Exhbns. Liturgical Art Guild of Ohio, Columbus, 1985, 91, 93, 95, 97, 2001; author: Through the Christian Year: An Illustrated Guide, 1983, Art In Service of the Sacred, 2006; contbr. foreword to (book) Full Circle, 1988; contbr. articles and images to profl. jours. Mem. fabric and fine arts com. Washington Nat. Cathedral, 2006—; bd. dirs. Episcopal Ch. Visual Arts, 2002—. Fellow, Coll. Preachers, Washington Nat. Cathedral, 1992. Mem. Arts and Religion Forum of Washington Theol. Consortium (founder, mem. steering com.), Interfaith Forum on Religion, Art and Architecture (bd. dir. 1983-85, 87-90), Schuyler Inst. Worship and the Arts (bd. dir. 1987-90). Democrat. Avocations: opera, remote control airplanes. Office: Wesley Theol Seminary Henry Luce III Ctr for Arts and Religion 4500 Massachusetts Ave NW Washington DC 20016-5632 Office Phone: 202-885-8617. E-mail: ckapikian@wesleyseminary.edu.

KAPLAN, ALICE, humanities educator, writer; b. Mpls., June 22, 1954; d. Leonore Yaeger and Sidney Joseph Kaplan. BA, U. Calif., Berkeley, 1975; PhD, Yale U., 1981. Asst. prof. N.C. State U., Raleigh, 1981—83, Columbia U., N.Y.C., 1983—86; assoc. prof. Romance studies Duke U., Durham, NC, 1986—94, prof. Romance studies and lit., 1994—, Lehrman prof. Romance studies, 2003—; founding dir. Duke Ctr. French and Francophone Studies, 1999—2002. Author: Reproductions of Banality: Fascism, Literature and French Intellectual Life, 1986, Sources et citations dans "Bagatelles pour un massacre", 1988, French Lessons: A Memoir, 1993 (finalist Nat. Book Critics Cir. award in autobiography/biography, 1993), The Collaborator: The Trial and Execution of Robert Brasillach, 2000 (Book prize in history L.A. Times, 2001, finalist Nat. Book award, finalist Nat. Book Critics Cir. award, 2001), The Interpreter, 2005; translator: (novels) Le Pierrot Noir , 1998, Partita , 2001, OK Joe, 2003. Named Officier dans l'Ordre des Palmes Academiques, French Ministry of Edn., 2001; fellow, Nat. Humanities Ctr., 1989—90, Guggenheim Found., 1994, Stanford Humanities Ctr., 1994—95. Mem.: PEN, MLA, Am. Lit. Translators Assn., Assn. Pour l'Autobiographie et le Patrimoine Autobiographique.

KAPLAN, BARBARA JANE, retired city planner; b. NYC, Sept. 8, 1943; d. Richard S. and Fannie I. (Schutz) Benson; m. Jerry Martin Kaplan, May 29, 1966. BA, Barnard Coll., 1965; MS, U. Southern Calif., 1969. Asst. planner L.A. Regional Planning Commn., 1968-69; from asst. planner to assoc. planner San Diego Comprehensive Planning Orgn., 1969-71; asst. dir. of regional planning North Ctrl. Tex. Coun. of Govts., Arlington, 1971-73; dir. Pennsport Civic Assn., Phila., 1974; city planner III Phila. City Planning Commn., 1974-76, city planner V, 1976-80, dep. exec. dir., 1980-83, exec. dir., 1983-2000, ret., 2000. Trustee U. of the Arts, Phila., 1987—2001; pres. Ctr. for Literacy, Phila., 1991—96, bd. dirs., 1984—, Neighborhood Gardens Assn., Phila., 1987—. Mem.: Pa. Hort. Soc. (bd. dirs. 1993—, v.p. 2000—01, mem. coun.), Nat. Trust for Hist. Preservation, Am. Planning Assn. Avocations: reading, tennis. Home: 2421 Fairmount Ave Philadelphia PA 19130-2517 Personal E-mail: barbarajkaplan@msn.com.

KAPLAN, BETSY HESS, retired school board member; b. Bridgeton, N.J., Aug. 12, 1926; d. Alfred N. and Betsy (Bolton) Hess; m. Robert Leon Kaplan, June 11, 1953; children: Bruce Alfred, James Edward, Joan Ann. AB, Wesleyan Coll., 1947; BFA, Wesleyan Conservatory, 1948. Cert. tchr., Fla. Tchr. 4th grade Miami-Dade County Pub. Schs., Fla., 1950—53; edn. and cultural arts adv., 1961—88; instr. Miami Dade C.C., 1979—81; admintrv. asst. to Ethel K. Beckham Miami-Dade County Sch. Bd., 1980—82, mem. sch. bd., 1988—2004, chair, 1993—95; ret., 2004. Chair fed. rels. network Fla. Sch. Bds., Tallahassee, 1996-98; bd. dirs. New World Sch. Arts, Miami, 1996-2005, found. bd., 2004—; mem. Performing Arts Ctr. Trust, Miami, 1993-2004, student mentor; mem. Human Svcs. Coalition, 1995—. Mem. Emily's List, Washington, 1990—, Women's Emergency Network, Miami, 1990—, Women's Polit. Caucus, 1988—; cultural amb. Heart of the City cultural series Miami-Dade Parks and Recreation Dept., 2002; bd. mem. Gay Lesbian and Straight Edn. Network, 1989—2001, co-chair, 2001—. Named Woman Worth Knowing, Miami Beach Commn. on Status of Women, 1994, Woman of Yr., King of Clubs, 2000; named to Miami-Dade County Women's Park Wall of Honor, 2005; recipient Alumnae Disting. Achievement award, Wesleyan Coll., 1987, French Acad. Palms award, French Min. of Edn. of Youth and Sports, 1991, Ruth Wolkowsky Greenfield award, Am. Jewish Congress, 1993, Trailblazer award, Women's Com. of 100, 1993, Woman of Impact award, Cmty. Coalition for Women's History, 1995, Co. of Women, Pioneer award, Miami-Dade County Pks. Dept., 1997, Red Cross Spectrum award, Women in Edn., 1997, Lifetime Svc. to Music Edn. in Fla. and U.S., Fla. Music Educators Assn., 2000, Branches of Learning award, Women's Divsn. Greater Miami State of Israel Bonds Orgn., 2001, Heart of the Arts award, New World Sch. of the Arts, 2004, Pillar award, Black Heritage Planning Com., Miami-Dade County, 2004, Joseph R. Narot award, Temple Israel of Miami, 2004, Cervantes award, Nova U., 2004, Serving the Arts, Arts and Edn. award, Children's Cultural Coalition and Arts and Bus. Coun., 2004. Mem.: AAUW (Phoenix award 1999), LWV (Margery Rankin award 2004), M. Athalie Range Cultural Found. (bd. dirs. 1995—2002, exec. com. 2002—), Jewish Mus. Fla. (bd. dirs. 1999—2003, exec. bd. 2003—06, adv. bd. 2003—04, bd. dirs.), Alliance for Aging (mem. adv. bd. 1996—2004), Fla. Sch. Bds. Assn. (bd. dirs. 1990—99, Pres.'s award 2001), Phi Kappa Phi, Delta Kappa Gamma, Phi Delta Kappa. Democrat. Jewish. Avocations: studying art history, reading and interpreting poetry, studying and practicing French language, cooking. Home: 2 Grove Isle Dr # 1603 Miami FL 33133 Personal E-mail: bakaplan60@aol.com.

KAPLAN, CAROLYN SUE, elementary school educator; b. Childress, Tex., June 23, 1944; d. Irving and Juliette (Weiner) Kohn. Student, Hunter Coll. Cert. tchr., N.Y. Tchr. N.Y.C. Bd. Edn., 1966—79, 1991—; sec. Borough of Manhattan Community Coll., N.Y.C., 1975—76, N.Y.C. Housing Authority, 1984—90; with Headstart program United People's Meth. Ch., 1993; peer specialist, intern, mental health worker Met. Hosp., N.Y.C., 1998—99. Mem. legis. adv. com. N.Y. State Senate, Albany, 1991—; vol. Queens Woman's Ctr., 1994—; tutor adult literacy program Queens Librs., 1994—; bd. dirs. Venture House; mem. N.Y.C. Clubhouse Coalition; co-chmn. Queens Mental Health Coun., 1996-97; advocate The Bklyn. (N.Y.) Clubhouse, 1999—; co-chmn. Bklyn. (N.Y.) Mental Health Coun., 2003; tnr. Peer Specialist Ctr., 1999—; advocate Kingsbrook Jewish Med. Ctr., 2003— Mem. Assn. for Childhood Edn. Internat. Avocations: reading, cultural events, movies. Home: 19806 Pompeii Ave Jamaica NY 11423-1422

KAPLAN, CATHY M., lawyer; b. NYC, Jan. 22, 1953; BA, Yale U., 1974; JD, Columbia U., 1977. Bar: N.Y. 1978. Ptnr. Brown & Wood, NYC; now ptnr. and co-head securitization practice Sidley Austin Brown & Wood LLP, NYC, and mem. exec. com. Contbr. articles to profl. journals. Mem.: ABA. Office: Sidley Austin Brown & Wood 787 Seventh Ave New York NY 10019 Office Phone: 212-839-5531. Office Fax: 212-839-5599. Business E-Mail: ckaplan@sidley.com.

KAPLAN, ELAINE D., lawyer; b. Bklyn., Dec. 18, 1955; BA, SUNY, Binghamton, 1976; JD, Georgetown U., 1979. Atty. Office of the Solicitor U.S. Dept. Labor, 1979-83; atty. State and Local Legal Ctr., Washington, 1983-84; asst. dir. litigation, asst. counsel Nat. Treas. Employees Union, 1984—88, dep. gen. counsel, 1988-97; spl. counsel Office of Spl. Counsel, Washington, 1998—2003; of counsel Bernabei & Katz PLLC, Washington, 2003—. Mem., editorial bd. Journal of Pub. Inquiry, 2000—02.

KAPLAN, HELENE LOIS, lawyer; b. NYC, June 19, 1933; d. Jack and Shirley (Jacobs) Finkelstein; m. Mark N. Kaplan, Sept. 7, 1952; children: Marjorie Ellen, Sue Anne. AB cum laude, Barnard Coll., 1953; JD, NYU, 1967; LLD (hon.), Columbia U., 1990. Bar: N.Y. 1967. Pvt. practice, N.Y.C., 1967-78; ptnr. Webster & Sheffield, N.Y.C., 1978-86, counsel, 1986-90; of counsel Skadden, Arps, Slate, Meagher & Flom, N.Y.C., 1990—. Bd. dirs. The May Dept. Stores Co., Met. Life Inc. and Met. Life Ins. Co., JP Morgan Chase & Co., Exxon Mobil Corp. Trustee N.Y. Coun. for Humanities, 1976-82, chmn., 1978-82; trustee Barnard Coll., 1973-99, chair bd. trustees, 1984-94, trustee and chair emerita, 1999—; trustee Columbia U. Press, 1977-80, MITRE Corp., 1978-95, N.Y. Found., 1976-86, John Simon Guggenheim Meml. Found., 1981-98, NYU Law Ctr. Found., 1985-87, Neuroscis. Rsch. Found., 1986-92, Am. Mus. Natural History, 1989—, vice chair, 1993—; trustee Am. Trust for Brit. Libr., 1991-93, Com. for Econ. Devel., 1993-96, Commonwealth Fund, 1990-2003, vice chair, 1996-2003; trustee and chair emerita Inst. for Advanced Study, 1986-2002, trustee emerita, 2002—; trustee J. Paul Getty Trust, 1992—, vice chair 1997—; trustee Olive Free Libr.; trustee Carnegie Corp. N.Y., 1979—, vice-chair bd. trustees, 1981-84, 98-2002, chair, 1984-91, 2002-; chair, trustee Mt. Sinai Sch. Medicine, 1999-01, Mt. Sinai NYU Health, 1998-2001, vice-chair bd. trustees, 1993-99; trustee N.Y.C. Pub. Devel. Corp., 1978-83, vice-chair bd. trustees, 1978-82; mem. Adv. Com. on South Africa, U.S. Sec. of State, 1986-88; mem. N.Y. State Gov.'s Task Force on Life and the Law, 1985-90, Women's Forum, Inc., 1982—, Rockefeller U. Coun., 1984-94, Bretton Woods Com., 1985-96, Carnegie Coun. on Adolescent Devel., 1986-96; chair task force on sci. and tech. and jud. decision making Carnegie Commn. on Sci., Tech. and Govt., 1988-93; ptnr. N.Y.C. Partnership, 1987-92; bd. dirs. Am. Arbitration Assn., 1978-82. Mem.: N.Y.C. Bar Assn. (treas. 1991—93, mem. com. on philanthropic orgns. 1975—81, mem. com. on recruitment of lawyers 1978—82, mem. com. on profl. responsibility 1980—83), Am. Philos. Soc., Am. Acad. Arts and Scis., Century Assn., Cosmopolitan Club.*

KAPLAN, HUETTE MYRA, training services executive, consultant; b. Chgo., July 11, 1933; d. Max and Jeannette (Smith) Lazan; m. Jerrold M. Kaplan, Feb. 14, 1954 (dec.); children: Lawrence, Jeffrey. BS in Bus. Edn., DePaul U., 1971. Instr. Pub. Svc. Careers Program State of Ill., Chgo., 1971-72; instr., dir. Patricia Stevens Bus. Sch., Chgo., 1972; relocation mgr., tng. specialist, dir. tng. and devel. Zurich-Am. Ins. Cos., Chgo. and Schaumburg, Ill., 1972-80; pres., tng. cons. H.K. & Assocs., Lansing, Ill., 1980—. Tng. dir. Calumet Area Lit. Coun., Hammond, Ind., 1985—; trainer Chgo. Literacy Coordinating Ctr., 1988-93; instr. Purdue U.-Calumet, Hammond, 1976—; substitute tchr. Sch. Dist. 171, Lansing, 1995-2002. Mem. task force Chgo. Coalition for Edn. and Tng. for Employment, 1984—86; literacy vol. tutor; candidate Dist. 215 Sch Bd., 1999; docent, tour dir. Chgo. Architecture Found., 2001—; bd. dirs. Temple Beth El, Hammond, 1986—88, Calumet Area Literacy Coun., 1990—92, 1994—95, pres., 1995—2002, 2003—. Jewish. Avocations: reading, pet therapy programs, travel. Home and Office: HK & Assocs 2843 192nd St Lansing IL 60438-3717 Personal E-mail: huettek1@sbcglobal.net.

KAPLAN, JEAN GAITHER (NORMA KAPLAN), retired reading specialist; b. Cumberland, Md., Dec. 14, 1927; d. Frank Preston and Elizabeth (Mcneil) Gaither; m. Robert Lewis Kaplan, Dec. 4, 1959; 1 child, Benjamin Leigh. AB in Edn., Madison Coll., Harrisonburg, Va., 1950; MA in Edn., U. Va., 1956; postgrad., U. Va., William and Mary, 1958-61; reading specialist degree, U. Va., 1976. Tchr. Frederick County Sch. System, Winchester, Va., 1950-51, Washington County Sch. System, Hagerstown, Md., 1951-55, Charlottesville (Va.) Sch. System, 1955-60, York County (Va.) Sch. System, 1962, Newport News Sch. System, Denbigh, Va., 1963, Internat. Sch. Bangkok, 1965-67; tutor Reston Reading Ctr., Fairfax County, Va., 1972-74; tutor homebound, substitute tchr. Fairfax County Sch. Systems, 1974-78; pvt. practice pvt. tutor McLean/Middleburg, Va., 1978-89; ret., 1989. Pres. Tutorial Svcs., Inc., McLean, 1985-87; sec. The Rumson Corp., Middleburg, 1981—. Active No. Va. Conservation Coun., Fairfax County, 1976-81, Piedmont Environ. Coun.; bd. dirs. Nat. Environ. Leadership Coun. Mem. AAUW, LWV, Bangkok Am. Wives Assn., Tuesday Afternoon Club (pres. 1974-75, treas. 1995-96), Va. League Conservation Voters, Ayr Hill Garden Club, Soc. John Gaither Descs. Inc., Bluestone Soc., Goose Creek Assn., Kappa Delta Pi, Alpha Sigma Tau. Avocations: reading, theater, concerts, travel. Home and Office: PO Box 1943 Middleburg VA 20118-1943 Office Phone: 540-687-3308, 540-687-3309. Personal E-mail: jk9600k@earthlink.net.

KAPLAN, JILL REBECCA, publishing executive; b. Feb. 27, 1966; d. Katherine and Arnold Kaplan; m. Wayne David Katz, Jan. 23, 1999; 2 children. With Economist group, NYC, Times Mirror mag. group, NYC; internat. sales mgr. Dow Jones & Co./Wall St. Jour. (WSJ), NYC, 1997—2000; dir. US sales Dow Jones internat. mag. group, 2000—06; gen. mgr. WSJ Jour. Report, WSJ Weekend Jour., 2000—06, WSJ Personal Jour., 2002—06, WSJ Weekend Edition, 2005—06; pub. Crain's NY Bus., NYC, 2006—. Office: Crains NY Bus 711 3rd Ave New York NY 10017 Office Phone: 212-210-0277. Office Fax: 212-210-0799. E-mail: jkaplan@crain.com.*

KAPLAN, MADELINE, legal administrator; b. N.Y.C., June 20, 1944; d. Leo and Ethel (Finkelstein) Kahn; m. Theodore Norman Kaplan, Nov. 14, 1982. AS, Fashion Inst. Tech., N.Y.C., 1964; BA in English Lit. summa cum laude, CUNY, 1982; MBA, Baruch Coll., 1990. Free-lance fashion illustrator, N.Y.C., 1965-73; legal asst. Krause Hirsch & Gross, Esquires, N.Y.C., 1973-80; mgr. communications Stroock & Stroock & Lavan Esquires, N.Y.C., 1980-86; dir. adminstrn. Cooper Cohen Singer & Ecker Esquires, N.Y.C., 1986-87, Donovan Leisure Newton & Irvine Esquires, N.Y.C., 1987-93, Proskauer Rose Goetz & Mendelsohn, N.Y.C., 1993-95, Kaye Scholer LLP, N.Y.C., 1995—. Mem. adv. bd. Grad. Sch. Human Resources Mgmt. Mercy Coll., 1997—; bd. dirs. Suitability. Contbr. articles to profl. jours. Founder, pres. Knolls chpt. of Women's Am. Orgn. Rehab. Through Tng., Riverdale, N.Y., 1979-82, v.p. edn., Manhattan region, 1982-83; adv. bd. Suitability; vol. Starlight Found. Mem. ASTD, Assn. Legal Adminstrs. (program com.), MBA Alumni Assn. (bd. dirs.), Sigma Iota Epsilon (life). Office: 425 Park Ave New York NY 10022-3506

KAPLAN, MARJORIE, broadcast executive; married; 2 children. B in Semiotics, Brown U. Dir. advt. Kraft Gen. Foods; v.p. Ogilvy & Mather; exec. v.p. Lancit Media Entertainment; sr. v.p. children's programming and products Discovery Networks, U.S., 1997—. Cons. Warner Amex Satellite Entertainment; developer Discovery Kids. Office: Discovery Comm 7700 Wisconsin Ave Bethesda MD 20814

KAPLAN, MURIEL SHEERR, sculptor; b. Phila., Aug. 15, 1924; d. Maurice J. and Lillian J. (Jamison) Sheerr; BA, Cornell U., 1946; postgrad. Sarah Lawrence Coll., 1958-60, U. Calif. at Oxford (Eng.), summer 1971, U. Florence (Italy), summer 1973, Art Students League, N.Y.C., summers 1975-89, New Sch., N.Y.C., 1974-78, m. Murray S. Kaplan, June 3, 1946 (dec.); children: Janet Belsky, James S., S. Jerrold, Amy Sheerr Eckman. Exhbns. at Women's Clubs in Westchester, 1954-60, Allied Artists Am., 1958-73, Nat. Assn. Women Artists, 1966-05, Bklyn. Mus., 1968, Sculptors Guild, 1972, Bergen County (N.J.) Mus., 1974; 2-person shows: Camino Real Gallery, Boca Raton, Fla., 1980; represented in group shows at Norton Art Gallery, Palm Beach, Fla., 1980, Govt. Ctr., West Palm Beach, Fla., 1984, Northwood U. Gallery, 1993, 95, 96, 97; represented in permanent collections Columbia U., Brandeis U., U. Tex., Harvard Law Sch., 1990, Johnson Mus. at Cornell U., 1996, Weizman Inst., Israel, 1998, Portrait of Capt. David McCampbell aboard USS David McCampbell, 2002, Portrait of Itzahk Rabin in Internat. Exhibit Armory Art Ctr., 2002; executed twin 30 foot cor-ten steel sculptures, Tarrytown, N.Y., 1972, 2 large rotating steel sculptures Art Park, Trans-Lux Corp., 1978; art cons., interior designer, 1971-89; sec. commn. to establish art mus. in Westchester, 1956; chmn. Westchester Creative Arts Festival, 1956. Bd. dirs. Fedn. Jewish Philanthropies, 1956; chmn. 1st Sta. WNET, Channel 13 Art Auction; mem. com. art in pub. places, Palm Beach County, Fla., 1984; mem. art adv. com. Boca Raton Mus. Art, 1987-93; bd. dirs. Palm Beach County Cultural Coun. of Arts, 1992-94; tchr. sculpture Armory Arts Ctr., Palm Beach, 1987-92, bd. dirs., 1992—. Recipient prizes Nat. Assn. Women Artists, 1966, 96, 97, 2004, 06, Westchester Women's Club, 1955, 56, Allied Artists Am., 1969, Artists Guild, Palm Beach, 1987, 88, 90, 91, 92, 93, 94, 96, 97. Mem. NAD, Art Students League N.Y. Nat. Assn. Women Artists, Allied Artists Am., Nat. Sculpture Soc., Internat. Sculpture Ctr., Portraits Inc. N.Y. Address: 115 Lakeshore Dr North Palm Beach FL 33408 Office Phone: 561-626-1168. Personal E-mail: murielkaplan@aol.com.

KAPLAN, NADIA, writer; b. Chgo., Feb. 28, 1921; d. Peter and Aniela (Buchynska) Charydchak; m. Norman Kaplan, July 25, 1942 (dec. July 1989); children: Fawn Marie Stom, Norma Jean Martinez. BEd, Pestalozzi Froebel Tchrs. Coll, Chgo., 1948; postgrad., UCLA, 1947, L.A. City Coll., U. Hawaii, Honolulu, Pepperdine U., L.A., 1970, Santa Monica Coll., 1981-87. Cert. tchr., Calif. Photographer, mgr. Great Lakes (Ill.) Naval Tng. Sta., 1942-45; primary/kindergarten tchr. L.A. Unified Sch. Dist., 1946-81. Contbr. articles to profl. jours.; creator puzzles various mags. Vol. recreational tchr. Found. for Jr. Blind, L.A., 1956-75, vol. camp counselor Camp Bloomfield, Calif., camp dir., 1956-61, leader cross-country study tour for blind teenagers, 1962; mem. dem. Nat. Com., 1985—. Pestalozzi Froebel Tchrs. Coll. scholar, 1938-41; recipient Norman Kaplan Life Achievement award, 2003. UK Blind, 2003. Mem. AAUW, Women Writers West (membership chair 1982-84), United Tchrs. L.A., Calif. Ret. Tchrs. Assn., Assn. Ret. Tchrs. Ukrainian Orthodox. Avocations: writing, bonsai cultivation, doll collecting, travel, golf. Home: 1827 Fanning St Los Angeles CA 90026-1439

KAPLAN, PHYLLIS, artist, composer; b. Bklyn. d. Abraham and Ida (Heller) Kaplan. BFA, Cooper Union, 1972; postgrad., Domus Acad., Milan, 1985. Curator art exhibit Orgn. Ind. Artists, NYC, 1995—96, Westside Arts Coalition, NYC, 1997; artist in residence Hungarian Multicultural Ctr., Lake Balaton, Hungary, 2002, F. J. Music Sch., Balatonfured, 2002. Lectr., presenter in field. Exhibitions include Lever House, NYC, 1969, Berkshire Mus., Pittsfield, Mass., 1970, L.I. U., NYC, 1975, Internat. Female Artists Biennial, Stockholm, 1994, Nat. Mus. Women in the Arts, Beijing, 1995, Three Rivers Arts Festival, Carnegie Mus., Pitts., 1995—96, 2001, Fine Arts Mus. L.I., Hempstead, 1996—97, Cork Gallery, Lincoln Ctr., NYC, 1997, Blue Mountain Gallery Invitationals, 1996—98, Trevi Flash Art Mus., Italy, 1998, World Artists for Tibet at Blue Mountain, 1998, Halpert Biennial, Boone, NC, 1999, Blue Mountain Gallery Invitationals, NYC, 2000, 2001, Montgomery Coll. Gallery of Art, Rockville, Md., 2002, Canajoharie Libr. and Art Gallery Invitational, 2002 (Honorable Mention, 2002), City Hall, Balatonfured, 2002, Canajoharie Libr. and Art Gallery Invitational, 2003; contbr. paintings to various publs. including Kings Courier, 1974, The Villager N.Y.C., 1994, Vizivarosi Gallery, Budapest, 2004, ann. calendar Orgn. Ind. Artists; exhibitions include Biola U., La Miranda, Calif. Recipient award for patriotism, U.S. Savs. Bond Dr., 1987, Sharjah Art Mus., United Arab Emirates, 2000, hon. mention award, Open Space Gallery, 2000, Mayfair, Allentown, Pa., 2000, Art Environ. Advocacy U. Oreg., Eugene, 2000, Virtue Coll. Visual Arts Gallery, St. Paul, Minn., 2000, Snapshot Contemporary Mus., Balt., 2000, 35th Internat. Exhbn., San Bernardino County Mus., Redlands, Calif., 2000—01, U. South Fla. Coll. Marine Sci., St. Petersburg, 2001, Sharjah Internat. Arts Biennial, United Arab Emirates, 2001, Univ. Place Gallery, Cambridge Art Assn. Nat. Prize Show, Mass., 2001, pub. project, bear sculpture painting project for Black Bear Film Festival, Milford, Pa., 2001, Artists Studio Tour, Hoboken, NJ, 2001; grantee Artists Space, Ind. Project, 1999. Mem.: Monroe County Arts Coun. (instr. 2001). Avocations: travel, classical music. Personal E-mail: phylliskaplan@mymailstation.com.

KAPLAN, RACHEL, environmental psychologist, educator; b. Tel Aviv, Apr. 6, 1937; came to U.S., 1947; d. R.D. and R.C. (Mayer) Bach; m. Stephen Kaplan, June 16, 1957; 1 child, Abram Walden AB, Oberlin Coll., 1958; PhD, U. Mich., 1962. Assoc. prof. dept. psychology U. Mich., Ann Arbor, 1977-87, prof. dept. psychology, 1987—, prof. Sch. Natural Resources, 1978—. Author: Cognition and Environment, 1982, The Experience of Nature, 1989; editor: Humanscape, 1978; mem. editorial bd. Jour. Architecture and Planning Rsch., Landscape and Urban Planning; mem. editorial rev. bd. Environ. and Behavior; contbr. articles to profl. jours., chpts. to books Fellow Am. Psychol. Assn.; mem. AAAS, Environ. Design Research Assn. Home: 1213 S Forest Ave Ann Arbor MI 48104-3922 Office: U Mich Sch Natural Resources Ann Arbor MI 48109

KAPLAN, ROBERTA A., lawyer; b. Cleve., Sept. 29, 1966; AB magna cum laude, Harvard U., 1988; JD, Columbia U., 1991. Bar: Mass. 1991, NY 1992, U.S. Dist. Ct. NY (so. and ea. dists.) 1993, U.S. Ct. Appeals (3rd cir.) 1994. Law clk. to Chief Judge Judith S. Kay, NY; ptnr., chair women's initiatives com. Paul, Weiss, Rifkind, Wharton & Garrison, NYC. Mem. continuing edn. legal bd., NY. Named one of Top 40 Lawyers Under 40, Nat. Law Jour., 2005. Mem.: NY Women's Bar Assn., Assn. Bar. City of NY (mem. com. women in law 1994—96, mem. com. state courts superior jurisdiction 1997—). Office: Paul Weiss Rifkind Wharton & Garrison LLP 1285 Avenue of the Americas New York NY 10019-6064 Office Phone: 212-373-3086. Office Fax: 212-373-2037. E-mail: rkaplan@paulweiss.com.

KAPLAN, SANDRA LEE, artist; b. Cin., May 23, 1943; d. Howard and Helen (Katz) K.; m. Stanley Joseph Dragul, 1964 (div. 1974); 1 child, Sacha; m. Robert Lawrence Denerstein, 1986. Student, Art Acad. Cin., 1960-61; BFA with honors, Pratt Inst., Bklyn., 1965; student, CUNY, 1968-70. Illustrator Christian Sci. Monitor, Boston, 1991—94; drawing instr. Denver C.C., 1991—92; antique dealer Wazee Deco, Denver, 1992—2002; painting instr. Art Students League of Denver, 2001—. Com. mem. Arvada Ctr. for the Arts, 1994-96. Sole exhibits in various galleries including Dubins Gallery, L.A., 1988, Ventana Gallery, Santa Fe, 1985-90, Land-Escapes in Arvada Ctr. for the Arts, Arvada, Colo., 1991, Human and or Nature in Nicolaysen Mus., Casper, Wyo., 1992, Rule Modern & Contemporary, Denver, 1993, 96, Land-Escape in Wave Hill, Riverdale, N.Y., 1995, Great Am. Artists, Cin., Ohio, 1996—, Boulder (Colo.) Mus. Contemporary Art, 1997, Indigo Gallery, Boca Raton, Fla., 1997, Laura Paul Gallery, Cin., Ohio, 1998, Cline Fine Art, Santa Fe, N.Mex., 1999, 2000, William Havu Gallery, Denver, 2003, "Eden" Mizel Ctr. for the Arts, Denver, 2003; commd. works Hong Kong Marriott Hotel, 1988, Gt. West Life Assurance Co., 1991, Arvada City Hall, 1993, Sch. Pharmacy U. Colo., 1994. Trustee Mus. Contemporary Art, Denver, 2002—, sec., 2003—. Yaddo Corp. fellow, 1985; Ludwig Vogelstein grantee, 1986, Covisions grantee Colo. Coun. of Arts, 1992. Democrat. Jewish. Avocations: reading, movies. Studio: St Francis Sch 235 S Sherman St Denver CO 80209-1620 Office Phone: 303-882-2674. Personal E-mail: sankapl@yahoo.com.

KAPLOWITZ, KAREN (JILL), lawyer, consultant; b. New Haven, Nov. 27, 1946; d. Charles Cohen and Estelle (Gerber) K.; m. Alan George Cohen, Aug. 17, 1980; children: Benjamin, Elizabeth. BA cum laude, Barnard Coll., 1968; JD, U. Chgo., 1971. Bar: Calif. 1971, U.S. Dist. Ct. (Cen. Dist.) Calif. 1971. Assoc. O'Melveny & Myers, L.A., 1971-74; ptnr. Bardeen, Bersch & Kaplowitz, L.A., 1974-80, Alschuler, Grossman & Pines, L.A., 1980-96, of counsel, 1997—. Contbr. articles to profl. jours. Mem. vis. com. U. Chgo. Law Sch., 1990-93. Mem. ABA (chmn. employer-employee rels. com. of tors and ins. practice sect.), Assn. Bus. Trial Lawyers (pres.), Calif. Women Lawyers (Fay Stender award 1982), Women Lawyers Assn. L.A. Home: 1 Woodside Ln New Hope PA 18938-9281 Office: 100 Overlook Dr 2d Fl Princeton NJ 08540 Office Phone: 888-890-4240. Business E-Mail: kkaplowitz@newellis.com.

KAPNER, LORI, marketing professional; d. Joseph and Marion Kapner; m. Walter David Hosp, Oct. 7, 2001. BA in journalism, U. Md. Asst. editor Am. Machinst mag.; assoc. mng. editor Success mag., 1984; mgr. bus. devel. Lippincott & Marguiles Inc., NYC, v.p., 1992; sr. v.p. Addison, NYC, 1995—98, prin., 1998—99; founder, pres. Kapner Consulting Inc., NYC, 1999—. Adv. bd. Make-a-Wish Found. Mem.: NY Women in Comm.

KAPP, GLORIA JEAN, retired academic program director; b. Bismarck, N.D., Mar. 11, 1945; d. Nathaniel and Emma (Rmmich) K. BA, U. N.D., 1967; MA, Mich. State U., 1969; PhD, UCLA, 1979. Asst. head resident advisor Mish. State U., East Lansing, 1967-69; asst. dir. student devel., instr. S.W. Minn. State Coll., Marshall, 1969-71; instr. sociology Human Affairs Inst. Brookdale C.C., Lincroft, N.J., 1971-72; asst. dean students Calif. State U., Northridge, 1972, advisor activitie L.A., 1973-76, dir. activities and housing, 1976-77, assoc. dir. student devel., 1977-80, firscal mgr. student svcs., 1981-83, dir. ctr. student fin. svcs., 1983-87, dir. office fin. aid Long Beach, 1987-90, dir. admissions and fin. aid, 1990—2000, sr. dir. admissions and sys., 2000—04; cons./ret., 2004—. Conf. presenter in field. Contbr. articles to profl. jours. Bd. dirs. Wesley Found., 1974-91; state and local offices Nat. Women's Polit. Caucus Calif., 1976—, nat. steering com. rep., 1979-85, chair, 1981-82, nat. bd. dirs. 1989-91, nat. treas., 1985-87, nat. polit. planning com. 1989-91, treas. Victory fund, 1989—; bd. dirs. Friends Outside L.A. County, 1988—, treas., 1989-90, 94-96, pres. 1991-93. REcipient Elizabeth Cady Stanton award Elections Com. County or Orange, 1994; named Outstanding Young Women Am., 1975. Mem. Calif. Assn. Student Fin. Aid Adminstrs. (exec. coun. 1986, registration chair 1989, pres. 1991, conf. program chair, 1994), Nat. Assn. Student Pers. Adminstrs., Western Assn. Student Fin. Aid Adminstrs. (conf. program com. 1990, vice chair pubs., editor rev. 1989-90, rep. to exec. coun. 1991-92). Democrat. Avocations: gardening, reading, personal computer applications and games.

KAPP, NATHALIE, obstetrician, educator, gynecologist; b. Bountiful, Utah, June 11, 1974; d. Grant Wilford and Judith (VanZweden) Kapp. BS, Boise State U., Idaho, 1996; MD, U. Utah, Salt Lake City, 2000; MPH Biostats., Boston U., 2006. Clin. instr. Boston U. Med. Sch., 2001—06; asst. prof. Rsch. WHO, U. North Geneva, 2006—. Mem. adv. bd. Ctr. Health Internat., Austin, Tex., 2004—06. Recipient New Leader award, Wyeth Pharm., 2004. Mem.: Assn. Reproductive Health Profls., Nat. Abortion Fedn., Am. Coll. Ob-Gyn., Alpha Omega Alpha. Avocations: rock climbing, hiking, cooking. Office: World Health Orgn 20 Ave Appia CH 1211 Geneva Switzerland Personal E-mail: nathaliek@gmail.com.

KAPPAN, SANDRA JEAN, elementary school educator; b. Buffalo, N.Y., Sept. 25, 1961; d. Joseph Albert Sr. and Margaret Alice (Krupa) Savash; 1 child, Jason T. Cert. in dental assisting, Bd. of Coop. Ednl. Svcs., 1979; AAS in Secretarial Sci., Erie C.C., 1982; BS, Daemen Coll., 1997; MS in Edn. and Reading, St. Bonaventure U., 1998. Cert. spl. edn., pre-kindergarten, kindergarten, grades 1-6. Acctg. clk. Children's Hosp. of Buffalo, 1984-87; legal sec., receptionist Lofton, Savage, & Cain, Esqs., Charleston, S.C., 1987-88; sec., transciptionist Trident Regional Med. Ctr., Charleston, S.C., 1988-90; adminstrv. asst. Children's Hosp. of Buffalo, 1990-93; substitute tchr. Erie I Bd. Coop. Ednl. Svcs., Erie County, N.Y., 1996-97; resource room tchr. Lancaster (N.Y.) Ctrl. Sch. Dist., 1997; spl. edn. tchr. Erie I Bd. Ednl. Ednl. Svcs., Erie County, N.Y., 1997-98; elem. tchr. St. James Sch., Depew, N.Y., 1998-99, Amherst Ctrl. Sch. Dist., 1999-2000; spl. edn. tchr. Ctrl. Sch. Dist., West Seneca, N.Y., 2000—. Spl. edn. tchr. Erie I BOCES, summer 1999; presenter in field. Vol. PTA, Lancaster Ctrl. Sch. Dist., 1994—, Boy Scouts Am.; vol. after-sch. reading/math. program West Seneca Sch. Dist.; vol. Americare Kids Reading Program, 2000—01; vol., mem. St. John's Luth. Ch., Sunday Sch. and Choir, Lancaster, 1993—. Scholarship Lancaster Assn. of Svc. Pers., 1996. Mem.: Daemen Coll. Alumni Assn., Phi Delta Kappa. Democrat. Lutheran. Home: 479 Lake Ave Lancaster NY 14086-9666

KAPPES, MARCIA ANN, education educator; d. Virgil J. and Marcella F. Kappes. BS, Oklahoma City U., 1972, BA, 1977, MA in Tchg., 1981; MA, St. John's U., Collegeville, Minn., 1988; PhD, St. Louis U., 1992. Staff, cook St. Paul's Hermitage, Beech Grove, Ind., 1961—65; tchr. Villa Teresa Schs., Oklahoma City, 1966—81, St. Charles Sch., Oklahoma City, 1981—86; prof. St. Gregory's U., Shawnee, Okla., 1992—. Adj. prof. Oklahoma City U., 1981—89; adv. bd. Villa Teresa Sch., Oklahoma City, 2002—; instr. deacons formation program Archdiocese Oklahoma City; lectr. in field. Author: Track of Mystic: The Spirituality of Jessica Powers, 1994, Church History I & II, 1998, numerous poems. Fundraiser coord. Shawnee Interfaith Hospitality Network, 2005—06; bd. dirs. Ctr. for Christian Spirituality, Shawnee, Okla. Mem.: Nat. Cath. Edn. Assn., Inst. for Theol. Encounter (moderator 1993—), Theta Alpha Kappa (moderator 1992—). Roman Catholic. Avocations: Native Am. flute, cartooning. Office: St Gregorys Univ 1900 W MacArthur Shawnee OK 74804-2403

KAPPLER, KAREN L., music educator, musician; b. Maud, Okla., July 19, 1938; d. Raymond Maxwell and Verdena Mary (Caywood) Edwards; m. Samuel Houston Clifton, June 27, 1959 (div. Apr. 1, 1977); children: Mary Louise Clifton, Catherine Helen Sehorn; m. Karl Heinrich Kappler, Aug. 27, 1989. BA in Edn. and Music, U. Denver, 1965; postgrad., U. Colo., 1967, MMus in Piano performance, 1980; postgrad., U. No. Colo., 1970, U. Utah, 1971, Columbia U., 1976. Cert. tchr. Colo. Piano and remedial reading tchr. John Marshall H.S., Oklahoma City, 1954—56; tchr., piano, organ, voice, 1955—; tchr. Jefferson County Pub. Schs., Lakewood, Colo., 1965—73; tchr., tutor Colo. Dept. Social Svcs., Denver, 1973—75; instr. continuing edn. U. Colo., Boulder, 1977—78; tchr. Met. State Coll., Denver, 1978—80; paralegal specialist Solomon, Zimmerman, & Schwartz, P.C., 1978—85; paralegal John Dressler, Esq., Denver, 1982—84; prin., owner Paralegal Specialty Svcs., Denver, 1986—94; ch. music dir., 1980—. Pianist, organist, vocalist, primary tchr. Classen Blvd. Bapt. Ch., Oklahoma City, 1948—55; organist, choir soloist, dir. children's choirs Edgewater Meth. Ch., Denver, 1962—65; curriculum writer, nat. tchr. Jefferson County Pub. Schs., 1965—73, percussion ensemble coach, Colo., 2005; nat. coord., tchr. Robert Pace Piano Found., 1970—82; del. bd. edn. hearings on differentiated staffing Jefferson County Pub. Schs., 1971—73; dir. pilot program Colo. State Social Svcs., 1973—75; piano and voice coach dinner theaters, children's auditions, Denver, 1978—93; pvt. tchr. piano, organ, voice, theory, composition, improvisation Skinner Cmty. Sch., Denver Pub. Schs., 1980—93; weddings organist First Bapt. Ch., Denver, 1981—84; dir. music and choir, organist Highlands Christian Ch., Denver, 1983—87; prin. organist St. Thomas Moore Cath. Ch., Littleton, Colo., 1987—88; pvt. tchr., coach to piano and voice students Denver Sch. Performing Arts, 1998—2004; piano tchr. grades 5-6 Britton Elem. Sch., Okla.; dir. music and choirs, organist First Ave. Presbyn. Ch., Denver, 1988—, festival of praise choral dir., 2004. Numerous recitals, concerts. Exec. bd., officer, com. mem. Jefferson Symphony Orch., Golden, Colo., 1980—90; music stock advisor Jefferson County Libr., Lakewood, 1986; musician, spkr. Gideons Internat., Nashville and Denver, 1990—; cmty. capt. March of Dimes, Northglenn, Colo., 1992—, Am. Cancer Soc., 2004—06, Nat. Alzheimers Assn., 2004—06; performance music seminar leader Jefferson Symphony Orch., 1994, piano judge young artists competition, 2001; tchr. music, history Lewis and Clark Am. Indians Tour, Lewiston, Idaho, 2005; dir. music program, pianist Chaslou Acad., Denver, 1995—99. Grantee NDEA, 1963—65; NDEA Inst. fellow, 1968. Mem.: Thornton Arts, Sci. and Humanities Coun. (jr. artists festival piano divsn. judge 2000—04), Nat. Fedn. Music Clubs (judge coll. voice competition 1975, judge piano and organ 1998—99, 2003—04), Am. Guild Organists (com. chair Young Artists' Competition 1988, com. chair Denver Study Groups 1990), Colo. Music Tchrs. Assn. (tchr. state conv. 1981, judge local panels, Denver chair State Theory JExam 1979—80, group class tchr. state conv. workshop 1979—80), Music Tchrs. Nat. Assn., Hist. Needlework Guild, Steinway Performance Club, Kappa Delta Pi, Sigma Alpha Iota (coll. chpt. pres. 1958—59, chair scholarship com. 1975, rec. sec. 1976—77, chair audit com. 1983, v.p. ritual 1996—97, v.p. music programs and ritual 1996—2001, del. Denver Alumnae chpt. to internat. conv. 1997, pres. state chpt. 1997—2000, chair scholarships com. 1998—2001, honors chair 2000, ex-officio treas. 2000—01, co-chair benefit concert 2000—02, chair bylaws com. 2000—06, Mozart 250th birthday concert co-dir., pianist, organist 2006, chair meml. svc., chair accompanists, Alumnae Chpt. Nat. Achievement award 1998, Rose of Honor 2000, chpt. cert. recognition 2001, 2003). Republican. Presbyterian. Avocations: reading, travel, needlework design. Home and Office: 10449 Lafayette St Northglenn CO 80233-4249

KAPPNER, AUGUSTA SOUZA, academic administrator; b. Bronx, NY, June 25, 1944; d. Augusto and Monica Thomasina (Fraser) Souza; m. Thomas Kappner, Aug. 14, 1965; children: Tania, Diana. AB, Barnard Coll., 1966; MSW, Hunter Coll., N.Y.C., 1968; DSW, Columbia U., 1984. Cert. social worker, N.Y. Lectr., community affairs specialist Dept. Urban Affairs, Grad. Div., Hunter Coll., 1968-70; adj. instr., field supr. N.Y.C. C.C., 1970-71; instr., coord. urban leadership unit Columbia U. Sch. Social Wk., 1970-72; asst. prof., dir. admissions and student svcs. SUNY, Stony Brook, 1973-74; assoc. prof., chmn. human svcs. divsn. LaGuardia C.C., 1974-78, prof., dean continuing edn., 1978-84; dean acad. affairs Adult & Continuing Edn., CUNY, 1984, dean acad. affairs, instructional rsch., adult learning, 1984-86; pres. Borough of Manhattan C.C./CUNY, 1986-92; asst. sec. of vocat. and adult edn. Dept. of Edn., Washington, 1993-95; pres. Bank Street Coll., N.Y.C., 1995—. Former chair Adult Literacy Media Alliance; bd. dirs. Nat. Writing Project; mem. panel Edn. Policy NYC Dept. Edn, Am. Coun. on Edn. Commn. for Advancement of Racial and Ethnic Equity; former mem. Commn. Nation Lifelong Learners; commr., Commn. Higher Edn., Middle States Assn.; former mem. adv. bd. Fund for the Improvement Post Secondary Edn., US Dept. Edn.; former mem. adv. panel Nat. Ctr. Innovation in Governing Am. Edn.; cons. and lectr. in field. Trustee Marymount Manhattan Coll.; mem. N.Y. State Edn. Commr.'s Task Force for the Edn. of Children and Youth at Risk, N.Y. State Gov.'s Coun. on Literacy, N.Y.C. Bd. Edn. Chancellor's U./Schs. Collaborative steering com.; appointed by Mayor of City of N.Y. to Joint Commn. on Integrity in Pub. Schs.; bd. dirs. N.Y. Urban Coalition; mem. N.Y.C. Coun. on Econ. Edn. Whitney M. Young Jr. fellow, 1982, USPHS awardee, 1981, Ford Found. fellow, 1973, Silverman Fund awardee, 1968, NIMH fellow, 1967, others; recipient Harlem Sch. Arts Humanitarian award, 1990, Am. Assn. Women in Community and Jr. Colls. Presdl. award, 1989, Asian Ams. for Equality Community Svc. award, 1989, Columbia U. Medal of Excellence, 1988, Barnard Coll. medal of distinction, 1988, Found. for Child Devel. Centennial award, 1999, Morris T. Keeton award Coun. for Adult and Exptl. Learning, others. Mem. Am. Coun. on Edn.

KAPRIELIAN, VICTORIA SUSAN, medical educator; b. Bronx, NY, June 30, 1959; d. Walter and Julia (Hachigian) Kaprielian. BA, Brown U., 1981; MD, UCLA, 1985. Diplomate Am. Bd. Family Practice. Resident Duke-Watts Family Medicine, Durham, NC, 1985-88; fellow UCLA Family Medicine, L.A., 1988-89; asst. clin. prof. Duke U. Med. Ctr., Durham, N.C., 1989-98, chief, divsn. predoctoral edn. and faculty devel., dept cmty and family medicine, 1994-96, assoc. clin. prof., 1998—2003, clin. prof., 2003—; fellowship dir., dept. cmty. and family medicine Duke U., Durham, NC, 1994—99, 2000—04, dir. predoctoral edn. and faculty devel., 1996-99, vice chair for edn., dept. cmty. and family medicine, 2006—. Dir. inpatient svc. divsn. cmty. medicine Duke U., 1989-90, dir. sports medicine, 1989-94, dir. arts medicine, 1989-95, dir. predoctoral edn., 1990-2000; dir. quality improvement and continuing med. edn. dept. cmty. and family medicine, 1996—; dir. faculty devel. dept. cmty. and family medicine, Duke U., 2000-04; dir. intersessions program Duke U Sch. Medicine, 2004—. Fellow Am. Acad. Family Physicians (pub. com. 1985, mental health com. 1986-88); mem. NC Acad. Family Physicians (bd. dirs. 1998-2002, 2005— edn. com. 1989-90, med. sch. affairs 1990—2001, chair of com. 1991-97), Soc. Tchrs. Family Medicine (steering com., predoc. dir. working group 1995-98, chair 1998). Avocations: physical fitness, singing, science fiction, ethnic cooking. Office: Duke Univ Div Family Medicine PO Box 2914 Durham NC 27710-0001

KAPS, KAY A., physical education educator, coach; m. Richard Kaps, June 30, 1990 (dec. Feb. 3, 1998). BA in Edn., Pacific Luth. U., Tacoma, Wash., 1975, MA in Ednl. Adminstrn., 1989. Cert. tchr. K-12 Wash., 1975, secondary ednl. adminstrn. Wash., 1989. Phys. edn. tchr./volleyball/basketball/track coach/cheerleading advisor/adminstrv. asst./activities coord./attendance officer Wash. H.S., Tacoma, Wash., 1975—90; phys. edn. tchr./volleyball coach Sequim Mid. Sch., Sequim, Wash., 1991—. Office: Sequim Mid Sch 301 W Hendrickson Sequim WA 98382 Office Phone: 360-582-3554.

KAPS, SYDELLE, elementary school educator; b. Bklyn., Apr. 8, 1932; d. Louis and Rose Tanenbaum; m. Warren J. Kaps, June 29, 1958; children: Lowell Charles, Andrew Whitney. BA, Bklyn. Coll., 1953, MA, 1956. Tchr., Bklyn., 1953—58, Fort Dix Elem. Sch., 1958—59, Balt., 1959—60; sub. tchr. Tenafly, NYC, 1968—75. Mem. presidium Hadassah, Englewood/Tenafly, NJ, 1985—95. Avocation: bridge.

KAPSALIS, FRANCES HINOS, psychologist, educator; b. Chgo., Aug. 16, 1934; d. John Christodoulos Hinos and Vasiliki Bacopoulos; m. Peter Harry Kapsalis, July 31, 1968; children: Harrietta, John, James, Andrew. BA, Elmhurst Coll., Ill., 1960; M in Ednl. Psychology, U. Ill., Urbana, 1962; EdS, Nat. Louis U., Evanston, Ill., 1995; voice student, Viola Repp Elmhurst Coll., Ill., Maria Kalfopoulou, Athens, Greece, Mozarteum, Salzburg, Austria; student in Modern Greek, St. Basil's Acad., Garrison, N.Y. Cert. elem. edn. Ill., specialist ednl. psychology Ill. Tchr. Elmhurst Pub. Schs., Ill., 1960—64, Oak Park Pub. Schs., 1966—69, Am. Cmty. Schs., Athens, Greece, 1964—66, Chgo. Pub. Schs., 1989—92; intern sch. psychologist Carol Stream Sch. Dist. 94, 1992—94; sch. psychologist East Aurora Sch. Dist. 131, 1994—98, Proviso Area Exceptional Children, Maywood, 1998—. Tchr. Greek St. Basil's Acad., Garrison, NY, 1955—60, 1979—82. Leader La Leche League, Westchester, Ill., 1970—80; cub scout leader Boy Scouts Am., Hillside, Ill., 1981—82; mem. ch. choir. Mem.: West Suburban Sch. Psychologists (program chair 1996—2003, pres. 2003—05), Ill. Sch. Psychologists Assn. Greek Orthodox. Avocations: travel, gardening. Home: 443 S Westmore Lombard IL 60148-3025 Office: PAEC Proviso W HS Wolf Rd Hillside IL 60162

KAPSNER, CAROL RONNING, state supreme court justice; b. Bismarck, ND, Nov. 25, 1947; m. John Kapsner; children: Mical, Caithlin. BA in English lit., Coll. of St. Catherine; postgrad., Oxford U.; MA in English lit., Ind. U.; JD, U. Colo., 1977. Atty. Kapsner and Kapsner, Bismarck, 1977-98; justice N.D. Supreme Ct., 1998—. Mem. N.D. Bar Assn. (past bd. govs.), N.D. Trial Lawyers Assn. (past bd. govs.), Burleigh County Bar Assn. (pres. 1980, mem. Jud. Conference 1988-96). Office: Supreme Ct State Capitol 600 E Boulevard Ave Dept 180 Bismarck ND 58505-0530 Fax: 701-328-4480. E-mail: ckapsner@ndcourts.com.*

KAPTUR, MARCIA CAROLYN (MARCY KAPTUR), congresswoman; b. Toledo, June 17, 1946; BA in Hist., U. Wis., Madison, 1968; M in Urban Planning, U. Mich., Ann Arbor, 1974; postgraduate student, U. Manchester, Eng., 1974, MIT, 1981; LLD (hon.), U. Toledo, 1993. Urban planner Toledo-Lucas County Plan Commns., 1969—75; dir. planning Nat. Ctr. Urban Ethnic Affairs, 1975—77; asst. dir. urban affairs domestic policy staff Exec. Office of Pres., 1977-79; mem. US Congress from 9th Ohio dist., 1983—, mem. appropriations com., co-chair Congl. Ukrainian Caucus. Author: Women in Congress. Adv. com. Gund Found.; exec. com. Lucas County Dem. Com.; mem. Dem. Women's Campaign Assn. Named Legislator of Yr., Nat. Mental Health Assn.; recipient Americanism award, VFW, 1999, Barbed Wire award, 1999, Director's award, Georgetown U. Edmund A. Walsh Sch. Fgn. Svc., Ellis Island Medal of Honor, 2002. Mem. Am. Planning Assn., Am. Inst. Cert. Planners, NAACP, Urban League, Polish Mus., U. Mich. Urban Planning Alumni Assn. (bd. dirs.), Polish Am. Hist. Assn., Lucas County Dem. Bus. and Profl. Women's Club, Fulton County Dem. Women's Club. Democrat. Roman Catholic. Office: US Ho Reps 2366 Rayburn Ho Office Bldg Washington DC 20515-0001 Office Phone: 202-225-4146.*

KARABATSOS, ELIZABETH ANN, career counseling services executive; b. Geneva, Nebr., Oct. 25, 1932; d. Karl Christian and Margaret Maurine (Emrich) Brinkman; m. Kimon Tom Karabatsos, Apr. 21, 1957 (div. Feb. 1981); children: Tom Kimon, Maurine Elizabeth, Karl Kimon. BS, U. Nebr., 1954; postgrad., Ariz. State U., 1980; Cert. contemporary exec. devel., George Washington U., 1985; M Orgnl. Mgmt., U. Phoenix, 1994; student, Scottsdale (Ariz.) C.C., 1999. Cert. tchr. Ariz. Instr. bus. Fairbury (Nebr.) H.S., 1954—55; staff asst. U.S. Congress, Washington, 1955—60; with Karabatsos & Co. Pub. Rels., Washington, 1960—73; conf. asst. to asst. adminstr. and dep. adminstr. Gen. Services Adminstrn., Washington, 1973—76; dir. corr. Office Pres.-Elect, Washington, 1980; assoc. dir. adminstrv. svcs. Pres. Pers.-White House, Washington, 1981; dept. asst. to Sec. and Dep. Sec. Def., Washington, 1981—86, asst. to, 1987—89; dir. govt. and civic affairs McDonnell Douglas Helicopter Co., Mesa, Ariz., 1989—90, gen. mgr. gen. svcs., 1990—92, co. ombudsman, community rels. exec., 1992—95; exec. asst. to dir. adminstrn. State of Ariz., 1995—96; prin., owner Karabatsos & Assocs., bus. consulting and mediation svcs., Scottsdale, 1995—. Bur. chief Office Prevention and Health Promotion Ariz. Dept. Health Svcs., 1997-98; adj. prof. Met. Coll. Phoenix, 2004, Maricopa C.C., 2005, So. Mountain C.C., 2005 Mem. Nat. Mus. Women in Art, Washington; bd. dirs. U.S. C. of C. Com. on Labor & Tng.; mem. Gov.'s Sci. and Tech. Com.; mem. Ariz. Com. Employer Support the Guard and Res., 1991; active Gov. Com. for Ariz. Clean and Beautiful, World Affairs Coun. Ariz. Mem.: ASTD, AAUW, Maricopa County Assn. Family Mediators, Ariz. Assn. for Conflict Resolution (bd. dirs.), Assn. Conflict Resolution, Am. Arbitration Assn., Women in Def., U. Nebr. Cather Group, Internat. Friends Transformative Art, Order Ea. Star, Pi Beta Phi, Pi Omega Pi. Episcopalian. Home and Office: 4446 E Camelback Rd # 110 Phoenix AZ 85018 Office Phone: 602-956-3317. Office Fax: 602-956-3317. Personal E-mail: ebkarabats@aol.com.

KARABINUS, CYNTHIA JULIE ANN, psychology and sociology educator; d. Charles Samuel and Sirsky Irene (Marie) Miller; m. Thomas James Karabinus, July 24, 1982; 1 child, Julie Ann. BA in Sociology/Anthropology, Lycoming coll., Williamsport, Pa., 1977. Cert. tchr. social studies and psychology grades 7-12. Pharm. salesperson William H. Rorher, Ft. Washington, Pa., 1978—79; tchr. Bangor (Pa.) Jr. and Sr. H.S., 1980—83, Delaware Valley Regional H.S., Frenchtown, NJ, 1983—. Student council adviser Delaware Valley Regional H.S., Frenchtown, 1985—90, tchr. advanced placement psychology, 1985—90. Mem.: APA. Avocations: jogging, reading.

KARAFFA, REBECCA P., elementary school educator; b. Boston, May 16, 1954; d. Jacob Samuel and Judith Keith Paretsky; m. John Mark Karaffa, Aug. 14, 1976; children: John Michael, Julie Christine. BS, Va. Tech. U., 1976. Tchr. grade 3 Augusta County Schs., Fishersville, Va., 1978—88; tchr. grade 1 Staunton City Schs., Va., 1995—98, 2001—03, tchr. grade 2, 1998—2001, title I reading tchr., 2003—. Recipient Tchr. of Yr. award, Staunton City Schs., 2002, Dawbarn award, Staunton/Augusta Cmty., 2004. Mem.: NEA, Va. ASCD, Va. Edn. Assn., Shenandoah Valley Reading Coun., Staunton Edn. Assn. Avocations: music, gardening, cooking. Home: 44 Wakefield Dr Verona VA 24482 Office: Staunton City Schs AR Ware Elem Sch 330 Grubert Ave Staunton VA 24401 Office Phone: 540-332-3938. E-mail: rkaraffa@earthlink.net.

KARAHALIOS, SUE M. COMPTON, secondary school educator; b. Newport, R.I., May 8, 1949; d. Raymond F. and Elsie R. (Hall) Compton; divorced; children: Herb, Nicole, Koren, Corey. BS, U. New Orleans, 1970; MEd, Western Wash. U., 1979; postgrad., U. Wash. Cert. tchr., Wash. Instr. Skagit Valley Coll., Oak Harbor, Wash., 1971—; tchr. Oak Harbor Sch. Dist., 1971—; mem. Wash. State Ho. Reps., 1993—. Contbr. articles to profl. jours. Named Tchr. of the Yr., Oak Harbor, 1979; recipient gifted grant 1988. Mem. NEA, Wash. Edn. Assn. (pres.), Oak Harbor Edn. Assn., Phi Delta Kappa, Delta Kappa Gamma.

KARAIM, BETTY JUNE, retired librarian; b. Devils Lake, N.D., May 27, 1936; d. Erick Henry and Anna Caroline (Steen) Keck; m. William James Karaim, Dec. 7, 1955 (dec. 1983); children: Reed, Lisa, Ryan, Lynn, Rachel, Lee, Lara. BS in Edn., Mayville (N.D.) State U., 1958; postgrad., U. N.D., summer 1961; MLS, U. Okla., 1972; postgrad., No. Mont. Coll., 1979, 81. Libr. Cando (N.D.) High Sch., 1960-62; asst. libr., tchr. Mayville State Coll., 1962-79; libr. Havre (Mont.) Pub. Schs., 1979-82; libr. dir. Mayville State U., 1982-99, ret., prof. emerita, 1999. Bd. dirs. Mayville (N.D.) Pub. Libr., 1991-97, 2000—, pres., 1994-97, v.p., 2002-05, pres., 2005—; bd. dirs. Goose River Heritage Ctr., Mayville, 2000—, pres., 2002—; bd. dirs. M300 Assn. (arm of Mayville State U. Found.), 2000-06, sec., 2002—05. Recipient Orville Johnson Meritorious Svc. award, 1992, Disting. Alumni award Mayville State U. Alumni Found., 1997. Democrat. Avocations: reading, travel. Home: 320 1st St NW Mayville ND 58257-1107 Personal E-mail: bjkaraim@polarcomm.com.

KARALEKAS, ANNE, media executive; b. Boston, Nov. 6, 1946; d. Christus and Helen (Vogiantzis) K. AB, Wheaton Coll., Norton, Mass., 1968; AM, Harvard U., 1969, PhD, 1974. Chief project mgr. def. and arms control project Commn. on Govt. for Conduct of Fgn. Policy, Washington, 1974-75; sr. staff mem. Senate Select Com. on Intelligence, Washington, 1975-78; sr. assoc. McKinsey & Co., Washington, 1978-85; mktg. mgr. The Washington Post, 1985-87, dir. mktg., 1987-89; pub. Washington Post Mag., 1989-96, dir. specialty products group, 1993-96; gen. mgr. Washington Sidewalk, Microsoft Corp., Washington, 1996-99; bd. dirs. Digital Globe, Longmont, 1999—. Author: History of the CIA, 1976; contbr. articles and book revs. to profl. jours. Advisor fgn. policy Mondale-Ferraro Presdl. Campaign, Washington, 1984; trustee Wheaton Coll., Norton, 1985-88. Mem. Council on Fgn. Relations, Phi Beta Kappa. Greek Orthodox. Avocation: twentieth century art and lit.

KARAMAS, JOYCE EFTHEMIA, art educator, consultant, artist; b. Chgo., July 27, 1926; d. Nicholas Ernest Karamesoutis and Anastasia Asemake Vaselopoulos. BA in Art Edn., Sch. Art Inst., Chgo., 1951; MLS, Chgo. State U., 1961. Cert. art tchr. K-12 Ill., sch. libr. Ill. Tchr. Chgo. Pub. Schs., 1951—62, art supr., 1962—72, tchr., libr., 1972—80, art. coord. curriculum dept., 1980—85. Coord. sch. art at local mus., Chgo., 1962—72, Chgo., 1980—84; coord. organized children's exhibits at pub. places, Chgo., 1980—84. Exhibited in group shows at Mus. Contemporary Crafts, N.Y.C., 1966, Ill. State Traveling Exhbn., 1968, one-woman shows include Chgo. Pub. Libr., 1972. Recipient Merit award, Am. Craftsmen Coun., 1966, Invitational award, Ill. Craftsmen coun., 1968. Avocations: photography, travel. Home: PO Box 174 3057 Peach St Douglas MI 49406-0174

KARAN, DONNA (DONNA FASKE), fashion designer; b. Forest Hills, NY, Oct. 2, 1948; m. Mark Karan, 1971 (div.); 1 child, Gabrielle; m. Stephan Weiss, 1983 (dec. June 2001); 1 stepchild, Lisa. BFA, Parsons Sch. Design, 1987. Intern Liz Claiborne; With Addenda Co., to 1968; with Anne Klein & Co., NYC, 1968-84, assoc. designer, 1971-74, designer, 1974-84; owner, designer, ptnr. Donna Karan Co., NYC, 1984-96, created DKNY clothing line, 1988, chmn. bd., chief designer, 1996—2001; (Donna Karan merges with Louis Vuitton Moet Hennessy (LVMH), 2001); chief designer Donna Karan Co., NYC, 2001—. Launched fragrance Donna Karan for Women, 1992, Cashmere Mist, DKNY, 1994, Chaos, Donna Karan, 1996, Black Cashmere, 2002. Showed first complete collection for Anne Klein & Co. in 1974; collaborator on Anne Klein collections with Louis dell'Olio; author: DKNY: NYC, 1994. Bd. dirs. Design Industries Found. for AIDS; co-chair Kids for Kids, 1993, Ovarian Cancer Rsch. Super Saturday, East Hampton, N.Y, summers 1998, 99. Recipient Coty award, 1977, Awards Coun. of Fashion Designers of Am., 1985, 86, 92, Frontrunner award Sara Lee Corp., 1992, "Night of the Stars" Award The Fashion Group; co-recipient (with Louis dell'Olio) Coty Return award, 1981, Coty Hall of Fame citation, 1982, Coty award, 1984; named Menswear Designer of Yr. Coun. Fashion Designers Am., 1992. Mem. Fashion Designers Am. (bd. dirs.) Office: Donna Karan Internat West 40th St New York NY 10018 Office Phone: 212-789-1500.*

KARASEK, MARY HAPAC, city treasurer, community volunteer; b. Cicero, Ill., Jan. 11, 1924; d. Martin Emil and Eva (Capak) Hapac; m. Edward Anton Karasek, Apr. 20, 1952; 1 child, Edward Anton Jr. Degree in liberal arts, Morton Coll., 1944. Libr. Pub. Libr., Cicero, Ill., 1947-53; treas. City of Berwyn, Ill., 1985—. Mem. Morton H.S. Bd. Edn., Cicero, 1968—76; trustee Morton Coll., Cicero, 1976—2001; mem. Berwyn PTA, 1959—; precinct capt. Berwyn Dem. Orgn., 1985—. Named Berwyn Citizen of the Yr. for Millennium Yr., 2000; recipient Alumnus award, Ill. C.C., 1991, Women in History award, Morton Twp., 1993, Sr. Citizen of Yr. award, Congressman Lipinski, 1992, Those Who Excel award, Ill. State Bd. Edn., 1982, Robert W. Teeter award, Berwyn Cicero YMCA, 1982, Disting. Pub. Svc. award, Berwyn Homeowners, 1996. Mem. Delta Kappa Gamma. Avocations: reading, walking, basketball, baseball. Home: 7015 29th Pl Berwyn IL 60402-2941

KARASICK, ADEENA MICHELLE, literature and language professor, writer; b. Winnipeg, Manatoba, Can., June 1, 1965; d. Kenneth Brian and Frances Bettina Karasick; 1 child, Safia Fiera. BA, U. Brit. Columbia, 1987; MA, York U., 1991; PhD, Concordia U., 1997. Visiting prof. Gutenberg U., Mainz, Germany, 1992—93; asst. prof. York U., Toronto, Ont., Canada, 1994—96; prof. St. John's U., NYC, 2000—. Author: (book) The House that Hijack Built, 2004 (Spoken Word and Storytelling award), Dyssemia Sleaze, 2000 (Bumbershoot Festival award for Most Adventurous Publ., 2000). Recipient DFAIT Travel grant, Vancouver, B.C., 2004, Calgary, 2004, San Francisco, 2005, Travel award, External Affairs, London, 2003, Oxford, Paris, Spoken Word award, Can. Coun. for the Arts; DFAIT Travel grant, Hawaii, 2004, Chgo., 2004, Seattle, 2004, New York, 2004. Mem.: Writers Union Can., Assn. Writers & Writing Programs, Modern Lang. Assn. Jewish.

KARASIK, MIRIYAM BETH, artist, writer; d. Warner Newton and Aleen Mildred (Hznkne) Oberly; m. Myron Solomon Karasik; stepchildren: Ruth Jacqueline, Jacob Edwin. BA in English, Grand Valley State Coll., Allendale, 1968; MA in Comms. Writing for Film and TV, Govs. State U., Park Forest South, Ill., 1978. Band dir. Kent City Cmty. Schs., Mich.; tchr. Grand Rapids Pub. Schs.; software tester Coldframe, Inc.; artist, musician, writer Miryem's Ink Studio, Cathedral City, Calif., 1985—. Author: (poetry) Word Windows, (film script) Return to Poland, 1978. Mem. Cmty. Action Tng. Svcs., Grand Rapids. Mem.: Writers Guild, Internat. Horn Soc. Democrat. Jewish. Office: Miriyam's Ink Studio 3155 Date Palm Dr Ste 3-513 Cathedral City CA 92234

KARAYAN, ANI A., psychologist, consultant; d. Armik Mike and Ida S. Karayan; m. Armen D. Avanessian, Aug. 31, 2003. BA, UCLA, 1996; MA, Calif. Sch. of Profl. Psychology, 1999, PhD, 2002. Cert. early childhood edn. Pacific Oaks Coll., Calif., 1996. Counselor Glendale Unified Sch. Dist./Healthy Start Program, Calif., 1998—2000; dir. mental health Merdinian Sch., Sherman Oaks, Calif., 1998—2001; coord. psychosocial programs in spina bifida Childrens Hosp., L.A., 1999—2001; adj. faculty Antioch U., L.A., 1999—; cons. Ctr. for Celebration for Diversity through Edn., L.A., 2000—; child psychologist ENKI Health & Rsch. Sys., East L.A., 2002—. Cons. Transcultural Psychology Inst., Glendale, 2000—; lectr. UCLA Med. Residency Program, 2001; cons./lectr. Roosevelt Mid. Sch., Glendale, 2001—02; lectr. ENKI Health & Rsch. Sys., Commerce, Calif., 2004. Scholar, Calif. Sch. of Profl. Psychology, 1997—99. Mem.: Spina Bifida Assn. Am. (assoc.), APA (assoc.). Achievements include editing book on the topic of diversity education. E-mail: anikarayan@aol.com.

KARBEN, SHELLEY VALERIE, elementary and special education school educator; b. Mt. Vernon, N.Y., Dec. 1, 1944; d. Sidney and Helen (Minskoff) Gross; children: Ryan Scott, Lori Jennifer. BS, 1966; MA, NYU, 1971. Cert. tchr. spl. edn., N.Y. Tchr. kindergarten and elem. East Ramapo Ctrl. Sch. Dist., Spring Valley, NY, 1966—, tchr. spl. edn. all areas/levels and early intervention, 2001—; adj. Tchr. Tng. Inst. Coll. New Rochelle, 2002—. Chairperson Child Study Team E. Ramapo Ctrl. Sch. Dist., 1995-; mem. pub. rels. panel, supt.'s adv. panel, 1992; cons. Jewish Day Schs, Yeshivas Schs., Hebrew Schs. Spl Edn., 1969—; dir. summer spl. edn. program Yeshiva; pvt. practice evaluation and remediation, 2001-. Mem. Profl. Cons. Staff, N.Y. State Sen. Commn. on Child Abuse, Albany, 1974; mem. Commn. of Ethnic Studies, Westchester County, 1975-76; exec. com. Dem. Party, Town of Ramapo, N.Y., 1985—, mem. task force affordable housing, 1991, mem. bd. assessment rev., 1988—; mem. Hebrew Programs for the Disabled, Nat. Commn. on Torah Edn., Yeshiva U., 1974-76, Fleetwood Synagogue Sisterhood, Mt. Vernon, N.Y., pres., 1976-77; pres. Hillcrest Civic Assn., 1990-98; dir. Club ARC Rockland County, 1994; facilitator site-based mgmt. team, 1998-2000; v.p. Kehillat, New Hempstead, 1997-2000; pres. Sisterhood Kehillat, New Hempstead, 1999-. Mem. ASCD, Assn. Children with Learning Disabilities, Coun. Exceptional Children, B'nai Brith (pres. Mt. Vernon 1975-77). Jewish. E-mail: skarben@yahoo.com.

KARCHOV, TATYANA, psychiatrist; b. Novosibirsk, Russia, Jan. 25, 1956; d. Yuri Georgievich Grigorvski and Galina Michailovna Grigorovski; m. David Karchov; children: Ilya, Mark. MD, Novosibirsk Med. Sch., Russia, 1979. Diplomate Am. Bd. Psychiatry and Neurology. Asst. prof. Novosibirsk Med. Sch., 1981—92; residency in psychiatry Me. Med. Ctr., Portland, 1998—2002; chief, behavioral health unit Mid Coast Hosp., Brunswick, 2002—. Cons. Oasis Clin., Brunswick, 2005—. Contbr. papers to profl. jours. and pubs. Lt. Russian Army Res., 1979—91. Mem.: Am. Psychiat. Assn. (Me. br.). Avocations: piano, singing, photography, painting. Office: Mid Coast Hosp 123 Med Ctr Dr Brunswick ME 04011

KARCZEWSKI, LISA A., lawyer; b. Toledo, Ohio, Sept. 1, 1970; d. Thomas and Gloria Karczewski. BSc, Mich. State Univ., 1997; JD, Univ. of the Pacific, Sacramento, Calif., 2000. Bar: Calif. 2000, registered: U.S. PTO (patent atty.) 2002. Med. rsch. asst. Tulane Univ. Sch. of Medicine, New Orleans, 1993—94; rsch. asst. William Beumont Hosp., Royal Oak, Mich., 1994—97; law clerk Calif. Inst. of Tech., Pasadena, Calif., 1999; assoc. atty. Fulwider Patton et al, L.A., 2000—03, Chan Law Group LC, L.A., 2004—. Contbr. articles pub. to profl. jour. Nat. resource defense counsel NRDC, N.Y., 2002—; mem. L.A. County Mus. of Art, L.A., 2000—, Met. Mus. of Art, N.Y., 2004—. Mem.: Am. Intellectual Property Law Assn., Beverly Hills Bar Assn. Avocations: exercise, art, reading, writing, travel.

KARDISH, RUTH, retired elementary school educator; b. NY, NY, Apr. 27, 1936; d. Jonas Philip Kardish and Goldie Lorberbaum. BS in Edn., CCNY, 1957, MS in Edn., 1960. Tchr., New Rochelle, NY, 1957—91. Vol., mem. Met.Mus. Art, NY, 1979—98; vol. NY Philharmonic, 1985—95, Chamber Music Soc., 2004—, Asphalt Green fund raising. Avocations: doll collecting, classical music, collecting Swarovski crystal. Home: 520 East 81st St New York NY 10028

KARDON, JANET, museum director; b. Phila. d. Robert and Shirley (Drasin) Stolker; m. Robert Kardon, Nov. 19, 1955; children: Ross, Nina, Roy. BS in Edn., Temple U.; MA in Art History, U. Pa. Lectr. Phila. Coll. Art, 1968-75, dir. exhbns., 1975-78; dir. Inst. Contemporary Art, Phila., 1978-89, Am. Craft Mus., N.Y.C., 1989-95; ind. curator, 1996—. Adj. prof. Fashion Inst. of Tech., N.Y.C., Pratt Inst., Bklyn., Cooper Hewit; cons., panel mem. Nat. Endowment for Arts, 1975—; mus. panel mem. Pa. Coun. on Arts, Phila., 1988—; U.S. commr. Venice Biennale, Venice, 1980. Exhibitions include Labyrinths, Time, Artists SEts and Costumes, Laurie Anderson, Robert Mapplethorpe, David Salle, Gertrude and Otto Natzler; editor: Twentieth Century American Craft: A Centenary Project, The Ideal Home, 1900-1920, Revivals/Diverse Traditions, 1920-1945, Craft in the Machine Age, 1920-1945. Grantee Nat. Endowment for Arts, 1978. Home and Office: 150 E 69th St Apt 12G New York NY 10021-5704 Office Phone: 212-439-1803. Personal E-mail: jakardon@aol.com.

KARDOS, AMELIA MARIE PAPETTI, elementary school educator; b. Elizabeth, N.J., Mar. 7, 1953; d. John Frank Papetti Sr. and Elizabeth Marie Papetti; m. Joseph John Kardos III, July 22, 1979; children: Lisa Marie, Donna Melissa, Joseph John IV. MA in Ednl. Psychology, Kean Coll., Union, N.J., 1979, postgrad., 1979—81. Lic. tchr. elem. sch. N.J., 1975, tchr. reading N.J., 1975, tchr. Reading Recovery Coun. N.Am., 1997. Tchr. remedial reading and math. Elizabeth (N.J.) Bd. Edn., 1976—82; tchr. reading recovery Newark (N.J.) Pub. Schs., 1996—97; tchr. early literacy and basic skills Rahway (N.J.) Pub. Schs., 1997—. Home: 432 No Union Avenue Cranford NJ 07016 Personal E-mail: battin71@aol.com.

KARENBAUER, JACALYNN, science educator; d. John C. and Flora D. Voigt; m. Thomas Karenbauer, June 13, 1992; children: Lauren V., Matthew T., Andrew J. BS in Edn., Clarion U., 1989. Instrnl. II cert. Pa., 1989. Sci. tchr. Seneca Valley Alternative Sch., Zelienople, Pa., 1989—93, North Hills Sch. Dist., Pitts., 1994—. Sec. Nixon United Meth. Ch. Preschool, Butler, Pa., 2003—06. Grantee, North Hills Sch. Dist., 1998, 2005. Mem.: Nat. Earth Sci. Tchrs. Assn. (assoc.). Office: North Hills School District 55 Rochester Rd Pittsburgh PA 15229 Office Phone: 412-318-1000. Business E-Mail: karenbauerj@nhsd.k12.pa.us.

KARENTTE, BETTY, state legislator; b. Paducah, Ky., Sept. 13, 1931; m. Richard; 1 child, Mary. BA, MA, Calif. State U., Long Beach. Tchr. L.A. Unified Sch. Dist., 1961-92, cons., substitute tchr., 1994-96; mem. Calif. State Assembly, Sacramento, 1993—94, 2005—, Calif. State Senate, 1996—2004. Office: 3711 Long Beach Blvd Ste 801 Long Beach CA 90807 Office Fax: 562-997-0799. Business E-Mail: assemblymember.karnette@asm.ca.gov.

KARFS, TARA LYNN, elementary school educator; d. Michael Hopkins and Sandy Lynn Voegele; m. Chad Allen Karfs, June 15, 2002; 1 child, Madelynn Nicole. BS in Edn., McKendree Coll., Lebanon, Ill., 1999. 7th grade social studies tchr. West Jr. H.S., Belleville, 1999—. Track coach West Jr. High, Belleville, 1999—, girls' basketball coach, 1999—2003, character plus com. mem., 2000—, student asst. team mem., 2002—, homework club coord., 2005—. Office Phone: 618-234-8200.

KARG, RHONDA SUZANNE, psychologist, researcher; b. Miami, Fla., June 13, 1968; d. James Lee and Suzanne Smith Karg; 1 child, Jordan James Bray. AA, Lackawanna Coll., Scranton, Pa., 1993; BS in Psychology, U. Scranton, 1996; MS in Clin. Psychology, Auburn U., 1999, PhD in Clin. Psychology, 2002. Lic. psychologist Assn. State and Provincial Psychology Bds. Psychology resident Durham (N.C.) VA Med. Ctr., 2001—02, vol. psychology, 2004—; rsch. clin. psychologist RTI Internat., Research Triangle Park, NC, 2002—. Contbr. chapters to books, articles to profl. jours. Recipient All Am. Scholar Collegiate award, 1995, Lawrence J. Lennon award for Outstanding Svc. and Achievement in Psychology, U. Scranton, 1996, Excellence in Psychology award, Auburn U., 1996, Lair award for Outstanding Svc. and Achievement in Clin. Psychology, 1999, Outstanding Young Woman Am. award, 1997, Loan Repayment award, NIH, 2003—; scholar, U. Scranton, 1993—96; Acheivement scholar, 1991—93, Grad. Rsch. fellow, Auburn U., 1996—2001. Mem.: APA, Divsn. Psychotherapy (membership chair 2003—05), Psi Chi, Delta Tau Kappa. Home: 4510 Rollingwood Dr Durham NC 27713 Office: RTI Internat 3040 Cornwallis Rd Research Triangle Park NC 27709 Office Phone: 919-316-3516.

KARG, THELMA AILEEN, writer; b. Crawfordsville, Ind., June 30, 1918; d. Fred and Orpha Fern (Stewart) Crow; m. Henry Herbert Karg, Aug. 18, 1944 (dec. June 1982); children: Susan Marie Trissell, Karen Ann Weiss. MS, Ind. State U., 1937; BS, Taylor U., 1952. Sec. Harry N. Fine Atty. at Law, Crawfordsville, Ind., 1937—42; office control clerk R.R. Donnellys & Sons Co., 1942—43, Allisons GM, Indpls., 1943—46; accts. receivable Mid States Steel and Wire Co., 1943-46; tchr. Ind. State Tchrs. Assn.-Nat. Edn. Assn., Milw., Oreg., 1952-55, ISTA-NEA, Crawfordsville, Ind., 1955-62, Evang. United Brethren Ch., Terre Haute, Ind., 1962-65, Harrison, Ohio, 1968-70, Perrysville Highland Elem. Sch., Perrysville, Ind., 1970-74, various schs., Danville, Ill., 1975-76, Shelbyville, Ind., 1976-82, Waldron, Ind., 1983-95. Contbr. article to profl. jours. and newspapers. Mem. Nat. Rep. Congrl. Com., 1993—, senatorial com.; spkr. ladies groups United Meth.; nurse's aid ARC WWII. Recipient Editor's Choice award Nat. Soc. Poets, 1992-95. Mem. Christian Writers' (leader 1983-95), Ind. State Tchrs. United Methodist. Avocations: symphonies, plays, reading, entertaining, flowers. Home: 1004 Cottage Ave Crawfordsville IN 47933-1506

KARK, VICTORIA A., open heart clinical specialist; b. Washington, Jan. 11, 1954; d. Michele J. and Evelyn (Tucci) D'Anna; m. John A. Kark, July 2, 1978; children: Christopher, Rachel. BSN, U. Md., Balt., 1978; MSN, Cath. U. Am., 1981; postgrad., U. Md. CCRN. Staff nurse CVICU WRAMC, Washington; staff nurse intensive care unit Washington Adventist Hosp., Takoma Park, Md.; nursing educator Georgetown U. Sch. Nursing, Washington; open heart clin. specialist Washington Adventist Hosp., Takoma, 2006—. Mem. AACN. Home: 12806 Brandon Green Ct Silver Spring MD 20904-3569

KARKUT, BONNIE LEE, retired dental office manager; b. Muskegon, Mich., Feb. 7, 1934; d. Fay Henry Hohenstein and Doris Catherine (Nelson) Collins; m. Joseph Paul Karkut, DDS, Dec. 29, 1956; children: Deborah, Joseph, Bradley, Elizabeth. BA in Speech Pathology, Mich. State U., 1955; postgrad. studies, U. Hawaii, 1956, U. Mich., Saginaw, 1959. Cert. speech pathologist. Speech pathologist Pub. Schs., Muskegon, Mich., 1955-56, Saginaw, Mich., 1956-59; office mgr. Dental Office, Naples, Fla., 1984-95; retired, 1995. Pres. Saginaw (Mich.) County Dental Aux., 1978-79; vol. North Bay Civic Assn. Bd., 2001-05. Mem. AAUW, Fla. Dental Assn. (dental asst. and aux. sect.), Delta Zeta (program chmn. 1988-89), Panhellenic Soc. Republican. Roman Catholic. Avocations: skiing, boating, swimming, reading. Home: Tarpon Cove Villages #202 945 Carrick Bend Cir Naples FL 34110-3635

KARL, CAROL YVONNE, retired minister, religious studies educator, publisher; b. Nitro, W.Va., June 9, 1940; m. Julius Ewald Karl, Nov. 24, 1967 (dec. Jan. 25, 1999); children: Caroline Julia, Robert Julius. BSc, W.Va. State Coll., 1961; MA, Mich. State U., 1965; D in Ministry, Lake Charles Bible Coll., 1997. Educator Kanawha County Pub. Schs., Nitro, W.Va., 1961—64, Lansing Pub. Schs., Mich., 1965—66, Richland-Bean Blossom CSD, Ellettsville, Ind., 1968—73, Jefferson Country Pub. Schs., Louisville, 1974—76; tchg. asst. Mich. State U., East Lansing, 1964—65; pastor New Life Cmty. Ch., Westland, 1984—2001. Asst. prof. Anderson U., 1966—68; prin. New Life Christian Acad., Westland, 1982—93; pres. Alabaster Box, Inc., Westland, 1986—, editor, 1986—; educator Inkster Pub. Schs., 1993—2000; sec. Agape Gospel Mission, Inc., Manassas, Va., 2005—. Author: Handmaids in the Reign of Almighty God, 1992, East of Bethlehem, 2002, Scarecrows in my Cerebellum, 2002, Shoes, Silk and Salt, 2003, Brussels Sprouts in the Snow, 2003, Treasures in the Fire, 2003. Scholar, W.Va. Bd. Legislature, 1958-1961. R-Conservative. Protestant. Home: 6291 Hopeful Light Ave Las Vegas NV 89139 Business E-Mail: ykarl@alabasterbox.org.

KARL, KAILAH MARIE, military officer, small business owner; d. R. Zajkowski and M. Dodd-Lee; m. J. Karl, 2003; 1 child, Karl J. B in Applied Arts and Scis., Midwestern State U., Wichita Falls, Tex., 2004, postgrad., 2005—. Intelligence sgt. US Army, Los Alamitos, Calif., 1997—2003; ind. cons. Mary Kay, 2006—. Author instructional books. Pres. Family Readiness Group - Tex. Army N.G., Wellington, Tex., 2004—06. Sgt. U.S. Army, 1997—2005. Decorated Army Commendation medal, Army Achievement medal, Army Res. Component Achievement medal, Kosovo Svc. medal, War on Terrorism Svc. medal, Nat. Def. Svc. medal, Armed Forces Res. medal. Mem.: M.I. Corps Assn. Office Phone: 940-867-1066. Personal E-mail: mrskarl@gmail.com. E-mail: mrskarl@marykay.com.

KARLAN, PAMELA SUSAN, law educator; b. 1959; BA in History, magna cum laude, Yale U., 1980, MA in History, 1984, JD, 1984. Bar: US Supreme Ct., US Dist. Ct. So. Dist. NY, US Ct. Appeals 4th, 5th, 8th, 9th, and 11th Circuits. Law clk. to Judge Abraham D. Sofaer US Dist. Ct. So. Dist. NY, 1984—85; law clk. to Justice Harry A. Blackman US Supreme Ct., 1985—86; asst. counsel NAACP Legal Def. and Ednl. Fund, Inc., 1986—88; assoc. prof. law U. Va. Sch. Law, 1988—93, prof., 1993—98, Roy L. and Rosamond Woodruff Morgan rsch. prof., 1994—98; prof. law Stanford Law Sch., 1998—99, Kenneth and Harle Montgomery prof. pub. interest law, 1999—, academic assoc. dean, 1999—2000. Lectr. FBI Nat. Acad., 1990—2001; commr. Calif. Fair Polit. Practice Commn., 2003; vis. prof. Yale Law Sch., 1992, NYU Sch. Law, 1993, Harvard Law Sch., 1994—95, Stanford Law Sch., 1996, U. Va. Law Sch., 2002. Mem.: Am. Law Inst. Office: Stanford Law Sch Crown Quadrangle 559 Nathan Abbott Way Stanford CA 94305-8610 Office Phone: 650-725-4851. Office Fax: 650-725-0253. Business E-Mail: karlan@stanford.edu.

KARLE, ISABELLA L., chemist; b. Detroit, Dec. 2, 1921; d. Zygmunt Apolonaris and Elizabeth (Graczyk) Lugoski; m. Jerome Karle, June 4, 1942; children: Louise Hanson, Jean Marianne, Madeleine Tawney. BS in Chemistry, U. Mich., 1941, MS in Chemistry, 1942, PhD, 1944, DSc (hon.), 1976, Wayne State U., 1979, U. Md., 1986, Athens U., Greece, 1997, U. Pa., 1999; LHD (hon.), Georgetown U., 1984; DSc (hon.), Harvard U., 2001; Doctor honoris causa, Jagiellonian U., Cracow, Poland, 2002. Assoc. chemist U. Chgo., 1944; instr. chemistry U. Mich., Ann Arbor, 1944—46; physicist Naval Rsch. Lab., Washington, 1946—. Paul Ehrlich lectr. NIH, 1991; exec. com. Am. Peptide Symposium, 1975—81; adv. bd. Chem. and Engring. News, 1986—89. Mem. editl. bd.: Biopolymers Jour., 1975—, Internat. Jour. Peptide Rsch., 1981—; contbr. articles to profl. jours. Named to Mich. Women's Hall of Fame, 1989; recipient Superior Civilian Svc. award, USN, 1965, Fed. Women's award, U.S. Govt., 1973, Annual Achievement award, Soc. Women Engrs., 1968, U. Mich., 1987, Dexter Conrad award, Office Naval Rsch., 1980, WISE Lifetime Achievement award, Women in Sci. and Engring., 1986, award for disting. achievement in sci., Sec. of Navy, 1987, Gregori Aminoff prize, Swedish Royal Acad. Scis., 1988, Adm. Parsons award, Navy League U.S., 1988, Ann. Achievement award, CCNY, 1989, Bijvoet medal, U. Utrecht, The Netherlands, 1990, Vincent du Vigneaud award, Gordon Conf. (Peptides), 1992, Bower Sci. award, Franklin Inst., 1993, Nat. medal of sci., Pres. of the U.S., 1995. Fellow: Am. Inst. Chemists (Chem. Pioneer award 1984), Am. Acad. Arts Scis.; mem.: NAS (Chem. Scis. award 1995), Biophys. Soc., Am. Philos. Soc., Am. Phys. Soc., Am. Chem. Soc. (Garvan award 1976, Hillebrand award 1970, Ralph Hirschmann award in peptide chemistry 1998), Am. Crystallographic Assn. (pres. 1976). Home: 6304 Lakeview Dr Falls Church VA 22041-1309 Office: Naval Rsch Lab Code 6030 Washington DC 20375-5341 Office Phone: 202-767-2624. Business E-Mail: williams@harker.nrl.navy.mil.

KARLE-SWAILS, JEANINE, neuroscience clinical nurse specialist; b. Cin., 1970; d. Gerald Michel and Judith Marianne Karle. m. Christopher Swails, June 1, 2001; 1 child: Eric Michel. BSN, U. Cin., 1992; MSN, Med. U. S.C., 1996. RN; cert. neurosci. nurse. Staff nurse Med. U. S.C., Charleston, 1992-96; neurosci. clin. nurse specialist Roper Hosp., Charleston, 1996—2001; staff nurse U. Hosp. Neuroscience ICU, 2001—. Vis. clin. faculty U. Cin. Coll. Nursing, 2002—04, asst. prof. clin. nursing, 2004—. Parish nurse St. John the Beloved Cath. Ch., Summerville, S.C., 1996-98. Recipient Outstanding Achievement award Trident Area Cmty. Excellence, 1998, Elizabeth Kemble award U. Cin. Coll. Nursing, 2004; grantee Nat. Stroke Assn., 1999. Mem. Am. Assn. Neuroscience Nurses (pres. S.C. chpt.

1998-99, nominating com. 2005-, Ohio valley chpt. edn. co-chair, 2006-), Nat. Stroke Assn. (bd. dirs. S.C. Lowcountry chpt. 1998-2001), Sigma Theta Tau (Beta Iota chpt. bd. dirs., faculty counselor 2005—). Roman Catholic. Avocations: exercise, travel, pets. Office: U Cin Coll of Nursing PO Box 210038 Cincinnati OH 45221-0038 Home: 3654 Ridgewood Ave Cincinnati OH 45211 Office Phone: 513-558-2930. Business E-Mail: jeanine.swails@uc.edu.

KARLIN, SUSAN, design company executive; 1 adopted child, Mia Baixue. BA in comm., MA in spl. edn. Various positions including ptnr. AKM Assoc., 1985—92; founder, pres. Suka Design Inc, NYC, 1992—. Mem.: Fin. Women's Assn., Internat. Assn. Bus. Communicators, Am. Inst. Graphic Arts, NY Advt. and Comm. Network, NY Women in Comm. Achievements include conceived and her firm designed the World Trade Ctr. tribute poster, Americans Side By Side, after 9/11. Office: Suka Design Inc 560 Broadway Ste 107 New York NY 10012 Office Phone: 212-219-0082.

KARLL, JO ANN, retired judge, lawyer; b. St. Louis, Nov. 16, 1948; d. Joseph H. and Dorothy Olga (Pyle) K.; m. William Austin Hernlund, Sept. 9, 1990. BS magna cum laude, Maryville U.; JD, St. Louis U. Bar: Mo. 1993. Ins. claims adjuster, 1967-88; mem. Mo. Gen. Assembly dists. 104 and 105, 1991-93; dir. Mo. State Divsn. Workers' Compensation, Jefferson City, 1993-2000, adminstrv. law judge, 2000—03; pvt. practice High Ridge, Mo., 2003—. Founder, 1st pres. scholarship fund Mo. Kids' Chance, Inc., 1995-96, bd. dirs., 1995—; bd. dirs. North Jefferson Ambulance Bd., 2004-, pres. bd. dirs. 2005. Internat. Assn. of Indsl. Accident Bds. and Commns. (past pres.). Office: Karll Law Ctr LLC 1682 Old Gravois Rd High Ridge MO 63049 Office Phone: 636-677-7000. E-mail: karll.law@sbcglobal.net.

KARLUK, LORI JEAN, craft designer, copyeditor; b. Scranton, Pa., Aug. 29, 1958; d. Edward Julius and Josephine Anne (Cuozzo) K. Grad., high sch., 1976. Consignor, designer various shops, Pa., 1982-85; owner mail order bus. Loveables, 1983-85; staff designer Tradition Today, Roselle, Ill., 1985-86; designer All Occasion Crafts, Sparks, Nev., 1986-88; copy editor McCalls, N.Y.C., 1987-90; copy editor, product designer Herrschners, Inc., Schaumburg, Ill., 1988-92; designer Banar Designs, Fallbrook, Calif., 1991-92, Yarn Kits, Inc., N.Y.C., 1992-94; freelance designer, 1984-99; prin., owner Josie's Inspiration Studio, 1999—. Author: Safari Friends, 1987, Bear-E-Tale Bears, 1991. Sec. MADD, Lackawanna County, 1991. Recipient numerous spl. awards for designs. Mem. NOW, Soc. Craft Designers, People for the Ethical Treatment of Animals, United Friends of the Children, Internat. Soc. for Animal Rights, Teddy Bear Artists Assn., Good Bears of the World. Avocations: travel, reading, art. Home and Office: PO Box 68 Jessup PA 18434-0068 Office Phone: 570-383-0716. E-mail: ljkbears@aol.com.

KARLUS, MARY TERESA, elementary school educator; b. Menominee, Mich., July 15, 1957; d. John Charles and Sarah Ann Degeneffe; m. Michael Anthony Karlus; children: Eric Anthony, Sara Marie, Dana Michelle. BS in Elem. Edn., Marian Coll. Fond du Lac, 1993, MS in Tchr. Devel. and Tech., 1999. Tchr. 8th grade sci. and reading Sch. Dist. Slinger, Wis., 1994—. Home: 5980 Carolines Way Hartford WI 53027

KARMALI, RASHIDA ALIMAHOMED, lawyer; b. Uganda, May 12, 1948; arrived in US, 1978; d. Alimahomed and Sakina (Govani) K. BSc, MakerereU., 1971; MSc, Aberdeen U., 1973; PhD, U. Newcastle Upon Tyne, 1976; JD, Rutgers U., 1993. Bar: NY 1994, US Patent Office. Fellow Clin. Rsch. Inst., Montreal, 1976-78; rsch. assoc. E. Carolina U., Greenville, N.C., 1978-80, Meml. Sloan-Kettering Inst., N.Y.C., 1980-84; adj. assoc. prof. Cook Coll., New Brunswick, N.J., 1984-90; practice in tech. law N.Y.C., 1991—. Mem. ABA, Assn. Bar City N.Y., Am. Intellectual Property Law Assn., Licensing Execs. Soc. Office: 99 Wall St 13th Fl New York NY 10005 Office Phone: 212-651-9653. Personal E-mail: karmali@aol.com.

KARMEL, ROBERTA SEGAL, lawyer, educator; b. Chgo., May 4, 1937; d. J. Herzl and Eva E. (Elin) Segal; m. Paul R. Karmel, June 9, 1957 (dec. Aug. 1994); children: Philip, Solomon, Jonathan, Miriam; m. S. David Harrison, Oct. 29, 1995. BA, Radcliffe Coll.; LLB, NYU, 1962; HHD (hon.), King's Coll., 1998. Bar: N.Y. 1962, U.S. Dist. Ct. (so. and ea. dists.) N.Y. 1964, U.S. Ct. Appeals (2d cir.) 1968, U.S. Supreme Ct. 1968, U.S. Ct. Appeals (3d cir.) 1987. Asst. regional adminstr. SEC, Washington, 1962-69, commr., 1977-80; assoc. Willkie Farr & Gallagher, N.Y.C., 1969-72; ptnr. Rogers & Wells, N.Y.C., 1972-77, of counsel, 1980-85; ptnr. Kelley Drye & Warren, N.Y.C., 1987-94, of counsel, 1995—2002. Adj. prof. law Bklyn. Law Sch., 1973-77, 82-85, prof., 1985—, co-dir. Ctr. for Study of Internat. Bus. Law; trustee Practicing Law Inst. Author: Regulation by Prosecution, 1982; contbr. articles to profl. jours. Fellow Am. Bar Found.; mem. ABA, Assn. Bar City N.Y., Am. Law Inst., Fin. Women's Assn. Home: 66 Summit Dr Hastings On Hudson NY 10706-1215 Office: Bklyn Law Sch 250 Joralemon St Brooklyn NY 11201-3700 Office Phone: 718-780-7946. Business E-Mail: roberta.karmel@brooklaw.edu.

KARNES, ELIZABETH HELEN, academic professional, television producer; b. Los Angeles, July 22, 1951; d. Samuel and Shirley Ruth (Richmond) K. Student, U. Nice, France, 1970, Drew U., 1971; BA, Adelphi U., 1972. Exec. asst. to Bill Moyers PBS, N.Y.C., 1975-78, dir. research dir. Bill Moyers Jour., 1978-82; assoc. producer CBS Evening News, N.Y.C., 1982-83, CBS Crossroads, N.Y.C., 1984-86; exec. asst. to pres. Middlebury (Vt.) Coll., 1986—. Dir. research A Coversation with George Steiner, 1981 (Emmy award 1981); assoc. producer CBS Evening Analysis segment, Bill Moyers Commentary, 1982 (Emmy nominee 1983), 1982. Past pres. W. 69th St. Block Assn., N.Y.; bd. dir., treas. Interfaith Housing Corp. Addison County, Vt.; mem. Otter Creek Child Ctr., Addison County Benefit Bd., 1988. Mem. Women in Communication. Office: Middlebury Coll Old Chapel Middlebury VT 05753

KARNES, FRANCES ROZELLE, counselor, educator; b. Nashville, Dec. 9, 1925; d. Eron Clyde Reid and Norma Grace Lamb; m. Leon Karnes (dec.); children: Lisa G. Karnes Sieveke, David A., Stephen R. AA, Santa Ana Coll., 1976; BS in Child Devel./Psychology, U. Calif., Fullerton, 1978, MS in Counseling, 1981. Lic. Marriage Family Child Counselor 1984. Counselor U. Calif., Fullerton, 1977—80; counselor, asst. exec. dir. YWCA, Fullerton, 1980—88; instr. Rancho Santiago Coll., Santa Ana, Calif., 1989—93. Vol. tchr. asst. U. Calif. Child Devel. Ctr., Irvine, 1974—76; presenter in field. Democrat. Unitarian. Avocations: writing, architecture, art, reading, design. Home: 1072 N Granada Dr Orange CA 92869

KARNETTE, BETTY, state representative; b. Paduch, Ky., Sept. 13, 1931; m. Richard Karnette; 1 child, Mary. BA, MA, Calif. State U. Sec, office mgr. Terminal Island; tchr. L.A. Unified Sch. Dist., 1961—92; mem. Calif. State Assembly, 1992—94, dist. 27, Calif. State Senate, 1996—2004. Subs. tchr.; mem. Appropriations Com., Ins. Com., Rules Com., Transp. Com., Arts & Entertainment Com.; chair Select Com. on Ports. Mem. Long Beach Meml. Hosp. Children's Clinic; mem. assoc. bd. Sage House in San Pedro; bd. dirs. Young Horizon. Democrat. Mailing: State Capitol Rm 2176 Sacramento CA 95814 Office: 3711 Long Beach Blvd Ste 801 Long Beach CA 90807

KARNOWSKI, MARIA A., special education educator; b. Albuquerque, N.Mex., Jan. 24, 1951; d. Mary Mercedes Glynn; children: Anna, Melissa, Kelly. BS in Edn., U. Idaho, Moscow, 1974; MS in Edn., Boise State U., 1990. Tchr. spl. edn. Garden Valley Sch., Idaho, 1975—77, Parkview Jr. H.S., Emmett, Idaho, 1978—80, North Jr. H.S., Boise, 1980—94, Westgate TLC, Boise, 1994—2003, Borgh H.S., Boise, 2003—. Dir. Idaho Future Problem Solving, Boise, 1989—2006, Jr. High Ski Racing Recreational, Boise, 1990—2005. Recipient Lifetime of Svc. award, Idaho Coun. Behavior Disorders, 2005. Mem.: NEA, CEC, Idaho Edn. Assn. Avocations: skiing, golf.

KAROL, MERYL HELENE, medical educator, researcher, health facility administrator, science educator; BS, Cornell U., 1961; PhD, Columbia U., 1967. Rsch. asst. SUNY, Stony Brook, 1976-79, assoc. prof., 1979-85, prof. environ. and indsl. health, 1985—, assoc. dept. chair, 1993-2000; prof. environ. and indsl. health U. Pitts., 1985—, assoc. dean rsch., 2002, assoc. dean acad. affairs, 2002—. Sec.-gen. Internat. Union Toxicologists, 1998—2004; advisor numerous govt. health adv. bds., agys.; lectr. in field; advisor to sec. U.S. Dept. HHS; mem. adv. panel FDA, CDC, 2003; chair sci. adv. panel Mickey Leland Ctr., 2001—03; mem. sci. adv. bd. U.S. EPA; mem. com. on toxicology Nat. Rsch. Coun. Assoc. editor: Toxicology Sci., mem. editl. bd.: Inhalation Toxicology, Environ. Health, Toxicology and Ecotoxicology News, Biomed. and Environ. Scis.; contbr. articles to profl. jours. Recipient Women in Sci. award, U. Mich., 1986, Rachel Carson award, 1993, Outstanding Contbns. to Pub. Health, 1999; fellow NIH, SUNY, 1967—68. Mem.: AAAS, Soc. Toxicology (v.p. 1993, pres. 1994, Frank R. Blood award), Internat. Union Toxicologists (sec.-gen. 1998—2001), N.Y. Acad. Scis., Am. Conf. Govt. Indsl. Hygienists, Am. Assn. Immunologists, Am. Thoracic Soc., Am. Chem. Soc. Avocations: sports, design, travel, biotechnology. Office: U Pitts Dept Environ & Occupl Health 130 DeSoto St Rm A 730 Pittsburgh PA 15261 Business E-Mail: mhk@pitt.edu.

KARON, JAN (JANICE MEREDITH WILSON), writer; b. NC; Author (novels): At Home in Mitford, 1996, These High, Green Hills, 1996, Out to Canaan, 1997, A Light in the Window, 1998, A New Song, 1999, A Common Life, 2001, Patches of Godlight: Father Tim's Favorite Quotes, 2001, In This Mountain, 2002, Shepherds Abiding, 2003, The Trellis and the Seed: A Book of Encouragement for All Ages, 2003, A Continual Feast, 2005, Light from Heaven, 2005; (children's books) Miss Fannie's Hat, 2001, Jeremy: The Tale of an Honest Bunny, 2003; (cookbooks) Mitford Cookbook and Kitchen Reader, 2004. Mailing: c/o Viking Books Penguin USA 375 Hudson St New York NY 10014*

KAROSAS, KAREN, social worker, quality assurance specialist; b. Shenandoah, Pa., Dec. 7, 1951; d. Albert William Karosas and Patti Marguerite Myers; m. David Dwight Gressel, 1978 (div. 1981). BSW, Kans. U., 1973. Cert. level. 2 social studies tchr., Kans. Social worker Haverford (Pa.) State Hosp., 1987; child abuse investigator Social Svcs., Wellington, Kans., 1988; case mgr., utilization rev. coord., hosp. liaison Life Guidance Svcs., Sharon Hill, Pa., 1989-96; quality assurance specialist, therapist Warren E. Smith, Phila., 1997—99; quality assurance technician Intercultural Family Svcs., Phila., 1999—. Dir. music United Meth. Chs. Upper Darby, Pa., 1995—2002; organist Hope United Meth. Ch., Havertown, Pa., 2002—. Mem. ctrl. com. Rep. Party, Wellington, 1980, alt. Rep. state com., 1980, Kans. mem. rep. Mem. Am. Guild Organists. Avocations: swimming, playing piano and organ. Home: 111 N Lansdowne Ave Apt 7d1 Lansdowne PA 19050-2057 Office Phone: 215-386-1298.

KAROTKIN, ROSE A., marketing professional; d. Robert Edwin and Evelyn Rose (Carver) MacInnis; m. Mark Maynard Karotkin, Sr., Aug. 23, 2002; children: Mark Maynard Karotkin, Jr., Matthew Richard Lewis, Lisa Marie. BS in Bus. Mgmt. (hon.), Albertus Magnus Coll., New Haven, Conn., 2005. Mixology and bar mgmt. Boston Bartenders Sch., 2001. Mktg. Yankee Gas Services Co., Berlin, Conn., 2002—04; cons. Expressions by Rose, West Hartford, Conn., 2001—; mktg. coord. Phoenix Home Life, Hartford, 1997—2001; asst. to the dir. The Donaghue Found., Hartford, 1995—97; pres. M&R Auto Transport, 2004. Promotional assistance and hon. crew mem. for 2001 season Amistad Am., Mystic, Conn., 1999—2001; mktg. asst. Women's Am. Basketball League, Hartford, 1998—99. Co-author (environmental) R. Karotkin, K. Rook, S. Toelle (2002). Natural Gas Vehicle Marketing Plan 2002-2006. Yankee Gas Services Company, a Northeast Utilities System. Approved by the Connecticut Department of Utility Control August 8, 2002; contbr. criminology. Adv. Interval Ho., Hartford, 1998—2003; little league baseball coach Town of West Hartford, 1996—98; musician, singer, drama team Faith Living Ch., Plantsville, Conn.; co-chair representing Conn. Nat. Rep. Bus. Adv. Coun., Washington, 2003—04; sec. Spl. Friends Charities, Inc., East Hartford, 2002—. Recipient Nat. Leadership Award as Hon. Co-Chair of the Bus. Adv. Coun. representing Conn. small businesses, Nat. Rep. Congl. Com., 2003, 2003 Businesswoman of the Yr. Award, Nat. Rep. Congl. Committee's Bus. Adv. Coun., 2003. Mem.: Am. Assn. of Home-Based Bus. (assoc.), Nat. Assn. for the Self-Employed (assoc.), NAFE (assoc.), Am. Mktg. Assn. (assoc.), Kappa Gamma Pi. Independent-Republican. Christian. Achievements include designing, developing and publishing website for Special Friends Charities, Inc. Avocations: riding, hiking, travel, volleyball. Office: Expressions by Rose 95 Wilfred Street West Hartford CT 06110 Personal E-mail: karotkin@comcast.net.

KARP, DIANE R., art educator; b. 1948; PhD in Art Hist., U. Pa. Prof. 20th century art hist. Temple U.; curator-Ars Medica Phil. Mus. Art; dir. New Observations Mag., Santa Fe Art Inst., 2001—. Exhibitions include with Dan Fox In Time of Plague, Am. Mus. Nat. Hist., N.Y., exhibitions include Art, Med. & the Human Condition, Phila. Mus. Art, 1985; author: (exhibition catalogue) Ars Medica, 1985. Office: Santa Fe Art Institute 1600 St Michaels Dr Santa Fe NM 87505 E-mail: dkarp@sfai.org.

KARP, NAOMI KATHERINE, United States government administrator; b. Tucson, Mar. 6, 1942; d. James Jacob and Rose (Sosnowsky) Silver; m. Eugene Robert Karp, Oct. 23, 1965; children: Gail, Kevin. Student, Mills Coll., 1960-62; BA in Psychology, U. Ariz., 1964, M in Edn., 1965. Spl. edn. tchr. Tucson Pub. Schs., 1965-77, Fairfax (Va.) County Schs., 1978-80; program specialist U.S. Dept. Edn. OSERS, Washington, 1980-90; cons. Family & Integration Resources, Arlington, Va., 1990-92; pvt. practice Arlington, Va., 1992-93; spl. advisor to asst. sec. & acting dir. of early childhood learning U.S. Dept. Edn. Office Ednl. Rsch. and Improvement, Washington, 1993-95; dir., Nat. Inst. of Early Childhood Devel. and Edn. Dept. of Edn., Washington, 1995—. Cons. to universities, advocacy orgns. and profl. groups, 1990-93. Author: Advocacy for Families, 1991; author, editor: Inclusion: A Right not a Privilege, 1994. Mem. Am. Assn. on Mental Retardation (nat. bd. 1991-92); mem., co-founder Fed. of Families for Children's Mental Health (nat. sec., nat. bd. 1989-92, achievement award 1992).

KARP, ROBERTA SCHUHALTER, retail executive, lawyer; b. Livingston, NY, 1958; m. Brad Karp; children: Meredith, David. BA in environ. studies, SUNY, Binghamton; JD, Hofstra U., 1983. Bar: NY 1984. Atty. Kramer, Levin, Naftalis & Frankel, NYC, 1983—86; from legal counsel to v.p., gen. coun. Liz Claiborne Inc., NYC, 1986—96, v.p. corp affairs, gen. counsel, 1996—2000, sr. v.p. corp. affairs, gen. coun., 2000—. Co-chair White House Apparel Industry Partnership, 1996—99; bd. dirs. Bus. for Social Responsibility, Volunteers of Legal Svc., NY. David Rockefeller Fellow, 2000—01. Office: Liz Claiborne Inc 1441 Broadway New York NY 10018

KARP, STEPHANIE L., biology educator; b. Kalamazoo, Mich., Mar. 28, 1978; d. Norman J. Karp and Diane C. Lockwood. M in Secondary Edn., George Washington U., Washington, 2005. Tchr. Fairfax County Pub. Schs., Springfield, Va., 2004—06; camp counselor Pk. Dist. of Highland Park, Ill., 2002—03. Recipient Transition to Tchg. Program award, George Washington U. Mem.: Nat. Sci. Tchrs. Assn. Office Phone: 703-924-8300. Business E-Mail: stephanie.karp@fcps.edu.

KARPACK, KIMBERLEE JUNE RUSH, mental health counselor; b. Morristown, N.J., May 20, 1968; d. Robert Roy and June Rush. AS Liberal Arts, Ferrum Coll., 1988; BA Psychology, Shippensburg State Coll., 1990; MA Counseling, Montclair State U., 1994. Cert. alcohol/drug abuse counselor, N.J. Lab. asst. Sandoz Pharmaceutics, East Hanover, NJ, 1986—90; resident mgr. Project Hope Inc., Convent Station, NJ, 1991—94; counselor substance abuse St. Clares Med. Ctr., Boonton, NJ, 1994—2000; coord. family program Sunrise Ho. Found., Lafayette, NJ, 2000—03; pvt. practitioner, 2004—. Counselor mental health St. Clares Med. Ctr., Denville, NJ, 1991—. Recipient Young Am. award for bravery Pres. of U.S., 1986, Cert. of award for life saving efforts Denville Police Dept., 1986, Outstanding Citizen award Rockaway (N.J.) Elks, 1986; named Citizen of Month in N.J., Detectives Crime Clinic N.J. and N.Y., 1986. Mem. ACA, Am. Mental Health Counselors Assn. Home: 10 Fleetwood Dr Rockaway NJ 07866-2313 Office Phone: 973-634-3719.

KARPEN, MARIAN JOAN, financial executive; b. June 16, 1944; d. Cass John and Mary (Jagiello) Karpen. BA, Vassar Coll.; postgrad., Sorbonne, Paris, NYU, 1974—77. New England corr. Women's Wear Daily, 1966—68; Paris fashion editor Capital Cities Network, 1966—69; syndicated newspaper columnist, photojournalist Queen Features Syndicate, N.Y.C., 1971—73; acct. exec. Blyth Eastman Dillon (merged into Paine Webber), 1973—75, Oppenheimer, N.Y.C., 1975—76; v.p. mcpl. bond coord. Faulkner Dawkins & Sullivan (merged into Shearson Hayden Stone Smith Barney et al), 1976—77; mgr. retail mcpl. bond dept. Warburg Paribas Becker-A.G. Becker (merged into Merrill Lynch), sr. v.p., prin., 1977—84; sr. v.p., ltg. ptnr. Bear Stearns & Co., 1984—87, assoc. dir., 1987—90; pres., prin., CEO EuroEast® Group, Inc., N.Y.C., 1990—92; writer, creator newsletter Ea. European News; founder, pres., CEO WorkTalk®, Forum WorkTalk®, Inc., N.Y.C., 1992—; website creator, writer newsletter WorkTalk® Times; pres., founder, CEO, counselor Career Renewal Ctr.®, Inc. Past bus. adv. coun. U.S. Senate; lectr., presenter in field. Contbr. articles and photographs to newspapers and mags.; author: Career Crossroads: Ideas and Inspiration for Your Work/Life Journey. Mem. benefit com. March of Dimes, 1983; mem. Torchlight Ball com. Internat. Games for Disabled, 1984; vol. Whitney Mus. Am. Art. Named New Yorker of Week, Channel One, 1996. Mem.: Vassar Club NY (bd. dirs., exec. com., ex-officio chmn. corp. devel. com., chmn. benefit holiday open house 1989, chmn. major scholarship benefit 1991, chmn. scholarship fundraising raffle benefit 1992). Office: WorkTalk® 180 E 76th St at Lexington Ave New York NY 10021 Home: 233 E 69th St New York NY 10021-5414 Office Phone: 212-949-9300. E-mail: mjkarpen@aol.com.

KARPINSKI, HUBERTA, library trustee; b. Cato, NY, Jan. 4, 1925; d. Alfred Raymond and Lena Margaret (Fuller) Tuxill; m. Edward Karpinski, Nov. 17, 1956; children: Susan Tanielian, Rebecca Hitch, Amy Jaward. Student, U. Mich., Ann Arbor, 1943—45, Wayne U., Detroit, 1949—50; grad., NY Art Acad. Design, Detroit, 1972. Operator to svc. observer supr. Mich. Bell Telephone Co., Detroit, 1946—57; tchr. art Birmingham (Mich.) Pub. Sch., 1977—87; libr. trustee Redford (Mich.) Twp. Dist. Libr., 1971—. Chmn. Lola Valley Civic Assn., Redford, 1960-70; vice chmn. Redford Twp. Coun. Civic Assn., 1967-71; bd. dirs. 17th Dist. Mich. Dem. Party, Redford, 1968-71. Mem. Nat. Mus. Women in arts (charter), Mich. Porcelain Artists, Internat. Porcelain Art Tchrs. Avocation: painting. Home: 17418 Macarthur Redford MI 48240-2241

KARPINSKI, JANIS LEIGH, security manager; b. Rahway, N.J., May 25, 1953; d. Nelson Arthur and Ruth (Sorensen) Beam; m. George Frank Karpinski, Nov. 17, 1974. Ba in English and Secondary Edn., Kean Coll. of N.J., 1975; M in Mgmt., Embry-Riddle Aero. U., 1985. Commd. 2nd lt. U.S. Army, 1977, advanced through ranks to capt., 1981, resigned, 1987, commander milit. police co. Ft. McPherson, Ga., 1985-86; major USAR, brig. gen., comdr. Abu Ghraib Prison, 2003—04, col., 2005; intelligence officer 7th Spcl. Forces Group, Ft. Bragg, N.C., 1980-82; ops. and intelligence officer Anti-Terrorism Ctr., Mannheim, Fed. Republic Germany, 1982-83; ops. officer U.S. European Command, Mannheim, 1983-85; investigations mgr. Argenbright, Inc., Atlanta, 1987—; dep. to dir. plans tng., mobilization and security, chief of security and intelligence US Dept. Def., Ft. McPherson, Ga., 1987—, dirs. of plans, tng., mobilization and security, 1989—. Assoc. prof. City Coll. of Chgo., Fed. Republic Germany, 1982-85. Author: One Woman's Army, the Commanding General of Abu Ghraib Tells Her Story, 2005. Active Atlanta Zoological Soc., 1986. Mem. NAFE, Am. Soc. Indsl. Security, Embry-Riddle Alumni Assn. Republican. Avocations: running, swimming, sailing. Office: DPTMSEC-Security Bldg 65 Fort Mcpherson GA 30330*

KARPITSKAYA, YEKATERINA, orthopaedic surgeon; b. Simferopol, Russia, Feb. 18, 1977; d. Vladinicir Kevaynitskiy and Tafiyana Sauiokhralova. BA, Wash. U., St. Louis, 1998, Wash. U., 1998, MD, 2002. Diplomate fluroscopy supr. Residency, othopaedic surgery UCLA, 2006; house staff UCLA Orthopedic Surgery Dept., 2002—. Capt. USAF, 1998—. Avocations: tennis, running, weightlifting, fencing, painting.

KARR, KATHLEEN, writer; b. Allentown, Pa., Apr. 21, 1946; d. Stephen and Elizabeth (Szoka) Csere; m. Lawrence F. Karr, July 13, 1968; children: Suzanne, Daniel. BA, Cath. U. of Am., 1968; MA, Providence Coll., 1971; postgrad, Corcoran Sch. Art, 1972. Tchr. English and speech Barrington (R.I.) H.S., 1968-69; curator R.I. Hist. Soc. Film Archives, 1970-71; archives asst. Am. Film Inst., Washington, 1971-72, mem. catalog staff, 1972; gen. mgr. Washington Circle Theatre Corp., Washington, 1973-78; advt. dir. Circle/Showcase Theatres, Washington, 1979-83, dir. pub. rels., 1984-88; mem. pub. rels. staff Circle Mgmt. Co./Circle Releasing, Washington, 1988-93. Asst. prof. George Washington U., 1979, 80-81; lectr., instr. in film and comms. at various instns.; lectr. at film and writing confs.; juror Am. Film Fest., 1971, Rosebud Awards, 1991; mem. adv. bd. Children's Literature, 1994—. Author: It Ain't Always Easy, 1990 ("100 Books for Reading and Sharing" citation N.Y. Public Libr., 1990), Oh, Those Harper Girls!; or, Young and Dangerous, 1992 (Parents' Choice Story Book citation, 1992), Gideon and the Mummy Professor, 1993, The Cave, 1994, In the Kaiser's Clutch, 1995, Light of My Heart, 1984, From This Day Forward, 1985 (Golden Medallion award for best inspirational novel Romance Writers of Am., 1986), Chessie's King, 1986, Destiny's Dreamers Book I: Gone West, 1993, Destiny's Dreamers Book II: The Promised Land, 1993, Go West, Young Women!, 1996, Phoebe's Folly, 1996, Spy in the Sky, 1997, The Great Turkey Walk, 1998, The Lighthouse Mermaid, 1998, Oregon, Sweet Oregon, 1998, Gold-Rush Phoebe, 1998, Man of the Family, 1999 (notable book for 2000 award ALA), Skullduggery, 2000, The Boxer, 2000 (Best Books for Young Adults award ALA, The Golden Kite award 2000), It Happened in the White House, 2000, Playing with Fire, 2001, Bone Dry, 2002, Gilbert and Sullivan Set Me Free, 2003, The 7th Knot, 2002 (Agatha award for Best Children's/Young Adult Novel 2003), Exiled: Memoirs of a Camel, 2004; editor: The American Film Heritage: Views from the American Film Insitute Collection, 1972; author of various short films; contbr. to numerous jours. Mem. Washington Romance Writers (bd. dirs. 1985-86, pres. 1986-87), Children's Book Guild (pres. 2000-01). Office: Adams Literary 295 Greenwich St #260 New York NY 10017

KARR, SHARON KAY, psychology educator; b. Beloit, Kans., Jan. 27, 1938; d. William V. and Fern Louise (Johnson) Studer; m. Gerald Lee Karr, Oct. 18, 1959; children: Kevin L., Kelly J. BS, Kans. State U., 1959; MS, So. Ill. U., 1962, PhD, 1970. Cert. elem. tchr., Ill.; secondary educator, sch. psychologist, Kans.; nat. cert. sch. psychologist. Elem. tchr. Freeburg Sch. Dist., Ill., 1960, Crainville Sch. Dist., Ill., 1961-62; sch. psychologist intern Urbana Sch. Dist., Ill., 1971-72, Greenfield, 1972-73; sch. psychologist, counselor Wilmington Sch. Dist., Ohio, 1973-76; univ. prof. Emporia State U., Kans., 1976—2004, cons., 2005—. Lectr. Wilmington (Ohio) Coll., 1973; editorial cons. Mayfield Pub. Co., Palo Alto, Calif., 1978, Worth Pubs., N.Y.C., 1981-83, 89, 91, Holt, Rinehart & Winston, N.Y.C., 1986. Contbr. articles to profl. jours. V.p. Lyon County Dem. Women, Emporia, 1985-86; bd. dirs. Friends of the Libr., Emporia, 1989-90. Recipient Tchr. Coll. award for Svc., 2002; grantee Kans. Dept. Social and Rehab. Svcs., Topeka, 1986—88, Kans. Dept. Corrections, 1987—2000. Mem. APA, NASP, Internat. Sch. Psychology Assn. (charter), Assn. Psychol. and Ednl. Rsch. in Kans. (pres. 1987-88), Kans. Assn. Sch. Psychologists (govt. rels. 2005—; Lifetime Achievement award, 2002), Kans. Trainers Sch. Psychologists (pres. 1982-84, 86-88), Coun. Tchrs. Undergrad. Psychology, Phi Kappa Phi. Methodist. Avocations: music, prodn. agriculture. Home: 1155 N Hwy 99 Emporia KS 66801

KARRIEM, FATIMA, real estate broker; b. Houston, Feb. 12, 1955; d. Hara Lee Washington and Eudora Robbie Hannah; m. Timothy Carlsbeth Moon, July 5, 1972 (div. Aug. 2, 1987); children: Taurus Cornelius Moon, Onica

Monique Moon, Tamathy Cee Moon. Degree in Acctg., Upper Iowa U., Fayette, 1991. Lic. Real Estate Broker Tex. Real Estate Commn., 1995, Mortgage Broker Tex. Savs. and Loan, 2003. Cable splicing techician Southwestern Bell Tel. Co., Houston, 1977—92, installation techician Dallas, 1992—95; acctg. rep. We Wholesale, Dallas, 1991—95; reservationist SW Airline, Dallas, 1995—98; real estate agt. Henry S Miller Realtors, Duncanville, Tex., 1993—97, Century 21 Galloway-Herron, Dallas, 1997—2000; real estate agt. / broker ORG Realty, Dallas, 2000—01; broker Meirrak Realty / URA / Mortgage, Desoto, Tex., 2001—. Techician tng. Southwestern Bell Tel. Co., Houston, 1990—92; broker, adminstrn., tng. Meirrak Realty / URA, Desoto, Tex., 2001—. Vol. Paint the Town of Oak Cliff, 1995—2002; adminstr. Dallas Islamic Mosque, Dallas. Recipient Appreciation, Dallas Islamic Acad., 1997—2000, Volunteerism award, Greater Dallas Assn. Realtors, 1996—2002, Relocation Specialists award, Henry S Miller, Realtors, 1997. Mem.: Women's Coun. of Realtors (assoc.), Tex. Assn. Real Estare Brokers (assoc.), Nat. Assn. Real Estate Brokers (assoc.), Greater Dallas Assn. Realtors (assoc.; mem affiliate team, Volunteerism award 1996—2002), Grievance and Profl. Std. Com. (assoc.; com. mem., bd. dirs. 2001—03), Dallas Assn. Real Estate Brokers (assoc.), Paint the Town Oak Cliff (assoc.), Oak Cliff C. of C. (assoc.), Cedar Hill C. of C. (assoc.). Independent. Moslem. Avocations: martial arts, bicycling, body building, golf, creative advertising. Office Phone: 214-734-1125. E-mail: fkarriem@sbcglobal.net.

KARR-KIDWELL, P. J., education educator, writer; b. Ludlow, Mass., July 15, 1952; d. John Joseph and Margaret (Morgan) Karr; m. David Casey Kidwell, Aug. 10, 1980. BA, U. N.H., Durham, 1974; MA, Ohio State U., 1975, PhD, 1976. From asst. prof. to assoc. prof. Tex. Woman's U., Denton, 1977-89, prof., 1989—. Vis. assoc. prof. Tufts U., summer 1989; vis. lectr. Tex. Woman's U., summer 1976; adj. prof. Northeastern U., Boston, 1976-77; reviewer Hartcourt Brace Jovanovich Coll. Pubs., 1992, Delmar Publishers, 1993, 94; treas. North Tex. Federated Rsch., 1983, chair, 1978, 85-87; presenter in field Author: The Green Years, 1980, Youth and Adolescence, 1981; editorial staff Project Innovation, Chula Vista, Calif., 1977—2004; contbr. numerous articles to profl. jours Recipient Rsch. award Tex. Woman's U., 1983, Poetry award World of Poetry, Sacramento, 1986-87, 90, 92, Tex. Woman's U. finalist Minnie Stevens Piper Found. award, 1995, Disting. Career Tchr. award Ohio State U. 2001, 25 Yr. Recognition award Tex. Woman's U., 2002, Outstanding Adv./Mentor award Tex. Woman's U., 2003; named one of Outstanding Tchrs., Alpha Chi Mem. ASCD, Phi Delta Kappa. Avocations: writing, boating, Jin Jitsu. Office: Tex Woman's U Tchr Edn Edn Adminstrn PO Box 425769 Denton TX 76204-5769 Home: 2601 Mayhill Rd #31 Denton TX 76208-5919

KARSEN, SONJA PETRA, retired literature educator; b. Berlin, Apr. 11, 1919; arrived in U.S., 1938, naturalized, 1945; d. Fritz and Erna (Heidermann) K. Titulo de Bachiller, Ministerio de Educación Nacional, Bogotá, 1937; BA, Carleton Coll., 1939; MA, Bryn Mawr Coll., 1941; PhD, Columbia U., 1950. Instr. Spanish Lake Erie Coll., Painesville, Ohio, 1943-45; instr. modern langs. U. PR, 1945-46; instr. Spanish Syracuse (NY) U., 1947-50, Bklyn. Coll., 1950-51; asst. to dep. dir. gen. UNESCO, 1951-52, L.Am. Desk, tech. assistance dept., 1952-53, mem. tech. assistance mission Costa Rica, 1954; asst. prof. Spanish Sweet Briar Coll., Va., 1955-57; assoc. prof., chmn. dept. Romance langs. Skidmore Coll., Saratoga Springs, NY, 1957-61, chmn. dept. modern langs. and lits., 1961-79, prof. Spanish, 1961-87, prof. emerita, 1987; cons. Hudson-Mohawk Assn. Colls. and Univs., 1990. Faculty rsch. lectr. Skidmore Coll., 1963; mem. adv. and nominating com. Books Abroad, 1965-67; Fulbright lectr. Free U. Berlin, 1968; lectr. U. Gesamthochschule, Paderborn, Germany, 1995, 99. Author: Guillermo Valencia, Colombian Poet, 1951, Educational Development in Costa Rica with UNESCO's Technical Assistance, 1951-54, 1954, Jaime Torres Bodet: A Poet in a Changing World, 1963, Selected Poems of Jaime Torres Bodet, 1964, Versos y prosas de Jaime Torres Bodet, 1966, Jaime Torres Bodet, 1971, Ensayos de Literatura E Historia Iberoamericana/Essays on Iberoamerican Literature and History, 1988, Papers on Foreign Languages, Literature and Culture, 1982-87, 88, Bericht Über Den Vater: Fritz Karsen 1885-1951, 1993; translator: The Role of the Americas in History (Leopoldo Zea), 1992; editor Lang. Assn. Bull., 1980-83; mem. editl. adv. bd. Modern Lang. Studies, 1977-93; contbr. articles to profl. jours. Decorated Chevalier dans l'Ordre des Palmes Académiques, 1964; recipient Leadership award NY State Assn. Fgn. Lang. Tchrs., 1973, 76, 78, Nat. Disting. Leadership award, 1979, Disting. Svc. award, 1983, 86, Capital Dist. Fgn. Lang. Disting. Svc. award, 1987; recipient Spanish Heritage award, 1981, Alumni Achievement award Carleton Coll., 1982; exch. student auspices Inst. Internat. Edni. at Carleton Coll., 1938-39; Buenos Aires Conv. grantee for rsch. in Colombia, 1946-47; faculty rsch. grantee Skidmore Coll., summer 1959, 61, 63, 64, 67, 69, 70, 73, ad hoc faculty grantee, 71, 78, 85; scholar in French, Bryn Mawr Coll., 1939-41 Mem.: Am. Soc. French Acad. Palms, MLA (life; del. assembly 1976—78, Mildenberger medal selection com. 1984—86), AAUW (life), AAUP (life), Nat. Assn. Self-Instrnl. Lang. Programs (v.p. 1981—82, pres. 1982—83), Am. Assn. Tchrs. Spanish and Portuguese (life; emeritus), El Ateneo Doctor Jaime Torres Bodet (founding mem.), Fulbright Alumni, UN Assn. U.S.A., Asociación Internacional de Hispanistas, Nat. Geog. Soc., Sigma Delta Pi, Phi Sigma Iota. Home: 1755 York Ave Apt 37A New York NY 10128-6875

KARSON, CATHERINE JUNE, systems administrator; b. Salt Lake City, Jan. 26, 1956; d. Gary George and Sylvia June (Naylor) Anderson; m. Mitchell Reed Karson, June 14, 1987; 1 child, Rhonda. A in Gen. Studies, Pima CC, Tucson, 1989, AAS in Computer Sci., 1990. Night supr. F.G. Ferre & Son, Inc., Salt Lake City, 1973-76, exec. sec., 1977-79; operating room technician Cottonwood Hosp., Salt Lake City, 1976-77; customer svc. rep., System One rep. Eastern Airlines, Inc., Salt Lake City, Tucson, 1979-88; edn. specialist Radio Shack Computer Ctr., Tucson, 1988-89; programmer/analyst Pinal County DPIS, Florence, Ariz., 1989-90; systems analyst Carondelet Health Svcs., Tucson, 1990; programmer/analyst Misys Healthcare Sys., Tucson, 1990-94, sr. tech. proposal specialist, 1994-95, software developer, 1995-97, sr. sys. software specialist, 1997—99, sr. database adminstr., 1999—2005; database adminstr. Cmty. Partnership So. Ariz., 2005—. Cons. Pinal County Pub. Fiduciary, Florence, 1990, UBET, Barbados, West Indies, 1990—96, numerous clients, Tucson, 1990—93, Tucson Hebrew Acad., 2002—05. Mem. bus. adv. coun. Portable Practical Ednl. Preparation, Inc., Tucson, 1990—91. Mem.: Nat. Sys. Programmer Assn. Republican. Jewish. Avocations: reading, painting, music, opera, dance. Home: 5413 N Ventana Vista Rd Tucson AZ 85750-7203

KARTCHNER, GAYLA L., elementary school educator; d. Gaylan Clarence Roy and Dora Patterson; m. George H. Kartchner, Apr. 16, 1977. BS, No. Ariz. U., 1975; M In Edn., Ariz. State U., 2002. Post Degree Cert. No. Ariz. U., 1991. Tchrs. ast. Bloomfield Mcpl. Schs., N.Mex., 1988—90; substitute tchr. Farmington Mcpl. Schs., Farmington, N.Mex., 1990—91, tchr., 1992—. Pres. San Juan Basin Coun. of Reading, Farmington, 2004—, membership treas., 1994—2004; mem. Internat. Reading Assn., Newark, 1995—. Mem.: N.Mex Internat. Reading Assn. (assoc.), Internat. Reading Assn. (assoc.). Church Of Jesus Christ Of Latter Day Saints. Office Phone: 505-599-8606.

KARTHA, INDIRA, retired pathologist; b. Kerala, India, June 30, 1933; arrived in U.S., 1959; d. K. K. Kartha and Thotekat Nalini Amma; m. Kumaran Bahuleyan, Mar. 17, 1986; m. Gopinathan Kartha (dec.); children: Krishnan, Govindan, Sivan, Vijayan. MBBS, U. Trivandrum, 1956. Diplomate Am. Bd. Anatomical Cytological Pathology, 1968. Pathologist Deaconess Hosp., Buffalo, 1964—76, Mercy Hosp., Buffalo, 1964—76, Roswell Pk. Meml. Cancer Inst., Buffalo, 1964—76, St. Mary's Hosp., Lewiston, NY, 1976—2005, ret., 2005. Asst. prof. Sch. Medicine U. Buffalo, 1964—76. Home: 900 Delaware Ave 401 Buffalo NY 14209 Personal E-mail: indira_karkia@hotmail.com.

KARTY, KAREN S., secondary school educator; d. Daniel S. and Frances Karty; children: Ann M., David B., Rachel E. Goldman. BA in Biology, U. Mo., St. Louis, 1974, MS in Edn., 1982. Tchr. H.S. St. Louis Pub. Schs., 1986—2000; tchr. U. City H.S., University City, Mo., 2000—. Mem.: Kappa Delta Pi. Home: 1045 Groby Rd Saint Louis MO 63130

KASAKOVE, SUSAN, interior designer; b. Newark, Nov. 11, 1938; BFA, U. Buffalo, 1958, Hunter Coll., N.Y.C., 1960; postgrad., N.Y. Sch. of Interior Design, 1960—64, New Sch. for Social Rsch., 1967—68, Pratt Inst., Bklyn., 1968—69. Asst. interior designer Rodgers Assocs., N.Y.C., 1964-66; interior designer Walter Dorwin Teague Assocs., N.Y.C., 1966-70; sr. interior designer N.Y. State Facilities Devel. Corp., N.Y.C., 1970-95; Dormitory Authority for the State of N.Y., 1995—. Reading tutor Vols. for Children's Svcs., N.Y.C., 1976-82; chair Friends of White Plains (N.Y.) Symphony, 1981-83; emeritus Met. Mus. Art; vol. dept. Asian Dept. Work Endod, 1995, vol. guide edn. dept., 1978—; Rep. treas. 11th Ward, Yonkers, N.Y., 1979-81. Recipient Outstanding Svc. to Sch. award Rockland County (N.Y.) Lions Club, 1955. Mem. Environ. Design Rsch. Assn. Avocations: photography, history of art and architecture, golf, swimming. Home: 793 Palmer Rd Apt 3F Bronxville NY 10708-3337 Office: 1 Penn Plz Fl 52 New York NY 10119-5299 Business E-Mail: skasakov@dasny.org.

KASCH, MARY COURTEOL, occupational therapist; b. Chgo., Feb. 15, 1947; d. Paul and Bernice Zimmerman Courteol; children: Elizabeth Kasch Peter, David Michael. BS, Tufts U., 1970. Registered occupl. therapist, lic., cert. hand therapist. Pres. Hand Therapy Certification Commn., Rancho Cordova, Calif., 1989—2000, exec. dir., 2000—03; hand therapist Campus Commons Phys. Therapy, Sacramento, 1997—2001. Author: Rehabilitation of the Hand, 1979, 1985, 1991, 1996, 2001, Occupational Therapy: Practice Skills for Physical Dysfunction; mem. editl. rev. bd.: Jour. Hand Therapy, 1998—2005. Sec. Sacramento Choral Soc. Orch., Sacramento, 1998—2006. Recipient Award of Excellence, Occupl. Therapy Assn. Calif., 1986, Lillian Terris award, Profl. Exam. Svc., 1997, Nat. Svc. award, Arthritis Found., 1985, Pres.'s Gold award, Am. Soc. Hand Therapists, 1992. Fellow: Am. Occupl. Therapy Assn. Achievements include development of Certified Hand Therapist Credential. Avocations: singing, sewing. Office: Hand Therapy Certification Commission 11160 Sun Ctr Dr Rancho Cordova CA 95670 E-mail: mkasch@htcc.org.

KASCUS, MARIE ANNETTE, librarian; b. Boston, June 2, 1943; d. Anthony Joseph and Mildred (Lochiatto) Martucci; m. Joseph Edward Kascus, July 3, 1966. BA, Northeastern U., Boston, 1966; MSLS, U. Ill., 1969; ArtsD, Simmons Coll., 2004. Libr. asst. Boston Pub. Libr. Br., East Boston, Mass., 1961-66; rsch. asst. Hanscom AFB/Decision Scis. Lab., Bedford, Mass., 1964-66; asst. binding libr. Univ. Ill., Champaign-Urbana, 1970-72; head serials dept. Ctrl. Conn. State U., New Britain, 1972-99, collection mgmt. coord., 1984-86, libr. emerita, 1999; dir. library svcs. Newbury Coll., Brookline, Mass., 1999—2001; interim dir. acad. resources & lab. Champlain Coll., 2002—03, asst. dir., 2003—. Abstracter ABC-CLIO, Santa Barbara, Calif., 1979-2002; indexer Productivity, Inc., Stamford, Conn., Cambridge, Mass., 1981-86; mem. editl. bd. Cataloging and Classification Quar., 1984-2000; cons. Post Coll., Waterbury, Conn., 1986, State of Conn. Pers. Divsn., Hartford, Conn., 1987-88, Choice Mag., Middletown, Conn., 1990—; mem. program adv. bd. Sixth Off-Campus Libr. Svcs. Conf., 1992-93; mem. adv. bd. ASIS Thesaurus of Info. Sci. and Librarianship, 1993. Referee and contbr. articles to profl. jours.; presenter at profl. confs.; co-author: Library Services for Off-Campus and Distance Education: The Second Annotated Bibliography, 1996. Cons. New England Assn. Schs. and Colls., Newton, Mass., 1990, 92, CCSU Found./George R. Muirhead Scholarship Fund, New Britain, 1991, Harriet Kiser Opera Fund, Hartford, 1991—; apptd. to Mass. State Adv. Com. Librs., 2000-02. Recipient Sears B. Condit award for excellent scholarship Sears Roebuck, Inc., Boston, 1966, Alumni award for profl. promise Northea. U., Boston, 1966; AAUP Faculty Rsch. grantee Ctrl. Conn. State U., 1991; Higher Edn. Act fellow U.S. Govt. U. Ill., Champaign, 1969-70; honoree Women in Leadership YWCA, New Britain, Conn., 1997. Mem. AAUP, ALA, Assn. Coll. and Rsch. Librs. (extended campus libr. svcs. sect., chmn. stats. com., chmn. rsch. com., mem. nominations com., del. at large), Assn. Coll. and Rsch. Librs (mem. K.G. Saur award com. 1995-98, chair 1999-2000), Am. Soc. Indexers (Conn. chpt. pres. 1988-95, organizer, voting rep. Nat. Info. Stds. Orgn. 1995-98), Phi Delta Kappa, Phi Kappa Phi, Pi Sigma Alpha, Beta Phi Mu. Avocations: opera, reading, cooking, miniature books, walking/hiking. Office: Champlain Coll 83 Summit St Burlington VT 05401 Business E-Mail: kascus@champlain.edu.

KASENBERG, DARLENE FRANCES, psychologist; b. Rhinelander, Wis., Aug. 28, 1951; d. Glen Alfred and Carolyn Viola (Lombardo) Punches; m. Thomas P. Kasenberg, Sept. 5, 1971; children: Jamie Ellen, Jason Thomas. BA, So. Ill. U., 1972; MS, U. Utah, 1980; PhD, Colo. State U., 1985. Lic. psychologist, Colo. Customer svc. rep. Itel-Autex, Chgo., 1974-77; tchr. Pendergast Sch. Dist., Tolleson, Ariz., 1977-78; pvt. practice psychology Loveland, 1985—; psychologist Larimer County Mental Health Ctr., Loveland, Colo., 1986-89, Biodyne, Ft. Collins, Colo., 1989-91. Mem. Child Protection Team, Loveland, 1987-89; trustee Loveland Day Care Ctr., 1983-87. Pres.' scholar So. Ill. U., 1969. Mem. APA, Colo. Soc. Osteopathic Medicine Aux. (pres. 1990-91). Avocation: rollerblading. Home: 247 Rossum Dr Loveland CO 80537-7984 also: 1501 Cleveland Ave Loveland CO 80538-3835 Office Phone: 970-495-4816.

KASHDIN, GLADYS SHAFRAN, painter, educator, volunteer; b. Dec. 15, 1921; d. Edward M. and Miriam P. Shafran; m. Manville E. Kashdin, Oct. 11, 1942 (dec.). BA magna cum laude, U. Miami, 1960; MA, Fla. State U., 1962, PhD, 1965. Photographer, N.Y.C. and Fla., 1938-60; tchr. art Fla. and Ga., 1956-63; from asst. prof. to prof. humanities U. South Fla., Tampa, 1965-87, prof. emerita, 1987—. Lectr., adv. bd. Hillsborough County Mus., 1975—84. Exhibitions include The Everglades, 1972—75, Aspects of the River, 1975—80, Processes of Time, 1981—2006, Retrospective, 1941—96, Tampa Mus. Art, 1996, Appleton Mus. Art, Ocala, 1999, 2001—02, Mus. Sci. and Industry, Tampa, 2003, Represented in permanent collections, Taiwan, China, Columbus Mus. Arts, LeMoyne Art Found., Tampa Internat. Airport, Tampa Mus. Art, Appleton Mus. Art, Ocala, Mus. Sci. and Industry, Tampa, Miss. Mus. Art, Jackson, Jan Kaminis Platt Libr., Tampa, U. So. Fla. Spl. Collections Libr., Coll. Bus., Tampa Water Dept. Mem. U.S. Fla. Status of Women Com., 1971-76, chmn., 1975-76; nat. bd., Mus. Sci. and Industry, Tampa, 2003—; founder Dr. Gladys Shafran Kashdin Welcome Ctr., 2004 Recipient Women Helping Women in Art award Soroptimist Internat., 1979, Citizens Hon. award Hillsborough Bd. County Commrs., 1984, Mortar Bd. award for tchg. excellence, 1986, Recognition award for lifetime achievement in arts and scis. So. Acad. Letters, Arts and Scis., 2002. Mem. AAUW (1st v.p. Tampa br. 1971-72), Phi Kappa Phi (chpt.-pres. 1981-83, artist/scholar award 1987). Home: 441 Biltmore Ave Temple Terrace FL 33617-7207

KASI, LEELA PESHKAR, pharmaceutical chemist; b. Bombay, July 15, 1939; came to U.S., 1971; d. Subbaraman and Lakshmi (Shastri) Peshkar; m. Kalli R. Kasi, June 10, 1971. BS, U. Bombay, 1958; PhD, U. Marburg, W. Germany, 1968. Jr. chemist Khandelwal Labs., Bombay, 1958—59; trainee Farbwerke Hoechst, Frankfurt, Germany, 1960; teaching asst. U. of Marburg, Germany, 1967—68; sr. chemist Boehringer-Knoll Ltd., Bombay, 1969—71; mgr. quality control Health Care Ind., Michigan City, Ind., 1972—77, U. Tex.-M.D. Anderson Cancer Ctr., Houston, 1979—95, assoc. prof. nuclear medicine, faculty mem., 1990—95, dir. Exptl. Nuclear Medicine Lab., 1979—95; cons. Radiopharms. Devel., Houston, 1995—. Mem. grad. faculty U. Tex., 1984-90. Asst. editor Jour. Nuclear Medicine, 1984-89. Mem. AAAS, Am. Assn. Cancer Rsch., Soc. of Nuclear Medicine. Home and Office: 4710 Mcdermed Dr Houston TX 77035-3706 Personal E-mail: lkasi@earthlink.net.

KASIRER, SURI, lobbyist; b. 1958; d. Moshe and Gloria Kasirer; m. Bruce Jay Teitelbaum, Apr. 3, 1997. Grad., Yeshiva U. Spl. asst. for Jewish affairs to Gov. Mario M. Cuomo State of NY, Albany, 1992—94; founder Kasirer Consulting, NYC, 1995—. V.p. leadership devel. EDAH; mem. Women's Leadership Forum; bd. dirs. Nat. Jewish Dem. Coun. Mem.: Ansonia Dem. Club. Office: Kasirer Consulting 321 Broadway Ste 201 New York NY 10007 Office Phone: 212-285-1800.*

KASKE, CAROL MARGARET VONCKX, educator; b. Elgin, Ill., Feb. 5, 1933; d. J. Newell and Frances M. (Fitchie) Vonckx; m. Robert E. Kaske, June 4, 1958 (dec. Aug. 1989); 1 child, Richard J. BA, Washington U., St. Louis, 1954; MA, Smith Coll., 1956; PhD, Johns Hopkins U., 1955. Lectr. Peabody Conservatory, Balt., 1957-58, Duke U., Durham, N.C., 1959-60; lectr. women's campus U. N.C., Greensboro, 1961; lectr. U. Ill., Champaign-Urbana, 1961-64; lectr., asst. prof. Cornell U., Ithaca, N.Y., 1963-85, assoc. prof., 1985-92, prof., 1992—. Cons. in field. Author: Spenser and Biblical Poetics, 1999; author, editor: Edmond Spenser, The Faevie Queene, Book One, 2006; co-author, editor: Marsilio Ficino, 3 Books on Life, 1989; mem. editl. bd. Spenser Stud., Manchester Spenser; contbr. articles to profl. jours. Mem. AAUP, Internat. Assn. for Neo-Latin Studies, Modern Lang. Assn. (mem. exec. com. divsn. lit. and religion 2003-06, del. assembly 2004-06), Renaissance Soc. Am. (mem. exec. com. 2006—), Spenser Soc. (exec. coun., 1979-81). Democrat. Episcopalian. Avocations: violin, dogs, hiking. Home: 121 N Quarry St Ithaca NY 14850-4505 Office: Cornell U GS 252 English Dept Ithaca NY 14853

KASKINEN, BARBARA KAY, writer, composer, lyricist, musician, educator; d. Norman Ferdinand and Martha Agnes (Harju) Kaskinen. AA, Broward C.C., Coconut Creek, Fla., 1978; BA with honors, Fla. Atlantic U., 1981, MA, 1995; D in Mus. Arts, U. Miami, 2006. Studio musician, composer/arranger Electric Rize Prodns., Margate, Fla., 1982-94; ind. instr. piano, electronic keyboard and guitar. Margate, 1979-91. Co-founder Oasis Coffee House, Boca Raton, Fla., 1990—92; co-owner Electric Rize Publ, 1991; asst dir TOPS Piano Camp, 1994—96; mem. adj faculty Fla. Atlantic U., 1995—97, Broward C.C., Coconut Creek, 1996—, Miami Dade Coll., 2003—; adj instr., accompanist Palm Beach Atlantic U., West Palm Beach, Fla., 2003—; music dir. Calvary Presbyn. Ch., 2005—; adj. instr. Fla. C.C., Jacksonville, 2006. Musician (bass, keyboard player): Electric Rize Band, 1982—91; composer: Hansen House, 1987—88; author: Adult Electronic Keyboard Course Book I, 1988, Adult Electronic Keyboard Course Books II and III, 1989. Mem.: ASCAP, Nat. Piano Found., Broward County Music Tchrs. Assn. (treas), Fla. State Music Tchrs. Assn., Nat. Guild Piano Tchrs., Fla. Atlantic U. Alumni Assn. Home: 6601 NW 22nd St Pompano Beach FL 33063-2117 Address: 6601 NW 22 St Margate FL 33063 E-mail: neniksa@aol.com.

KASLOFSKY, WENDY ANNA, special education educator; b. Miami, Fla., Feb. 17, 1978; d. Regine Kaslofsky. BS in Spl. Edn., Fla. Internat. U., 2002. Cert. specific learning disabilites Fla., 2002. Tchr. Miami Dade County Pub. Sch., 2002—. Recipient Rookie Tchr. of Yr., Dade County Pub. Sch., 2002—03. Mem.: Coun. for Exceptional Children. Personal E-mail: wak925@aol.com.

KASLOW, FLORENCE WHITEMAN, psychologist, educator, family business consultant; b. Phila., Jan. 06; d. Irving and Rose (Tarin) Whiteman; m. Solis Kaslow; children: Nadine Joy, Howard Ian. AB in Sociology with distinction, Temple U., 1952; MA, Ohio State U., 1954; PhD, Bryn Mawr Coll., 1969. Lic. psychologist, marriage and family therapist, Fla.; bd. cert. psychologist Am. Bd. Clin. Psychology, Am. Bd. Forensic Psychology, Am. Bd. Family Psychology. Pvt. practice, Palm Beach Gardens, Fla., 1964—; dir. Fla. Couples and Family Inst., West Palm Beach, 1982—2004; pres. Kaslow Assocs., Palm Beach Gardens, 1985—. Cons. USN Dept. Psychiatry Residency Tng. Programs, San Diego, Portsmouth, Va., Phila., 1976-88, Palm Beach Inst., 1983-90; adj. prof. med. psychology Duke U. Med. Ctr., Durham, N.C., 1982-2002; vis. prof. psychology Fla. Inst. Tech., Melbourne, 1985-; disting. vis. prof. Calif. Grad. Sch. Family Psychology, 1989-92; weekly radio guest Voice of Am., Focus on Families, 1993-2003; pres. Am. Bd. Forensic Psychology, 1977-80, Am. Bd. Family Psychology, 1996-2000. Editor: Voices in Family Psychology, 1990, The Military Family in Peace and War, 1993; author (with L.L. Schwartz): Dynamics of Divorce: A Life Cycle Perspective, 1987; author: Handbook of Relational Diagnoses and Dysfunctional Family Patterns, 1996, Painful Partings: Divorce and Its Aftermath, 1997, Handbook of Couple and Family Forensics, 2000, Comprehensive Handbook of Psychotherapy, 4 vols., 2002; author: (with L.L. Schwartz) Welcome Home: an International and Non Traditional Adoption Reader, 2004; editor: Handbook of Family Business and Family Business Consultation: A Global Perspective, 2006; mem. editl. bd. Jour. Marital and Family Therapy, 1976—, Jour. Family Psychology, 1987—, Jour. Sex and Marital Therapy, 1984—2002, Jour. Clin. Child Psychology, 1986—, Jour. Psychotherapy, 1988—, Profl. Psychology, 2002—, assoc. editor Jour. Family Psychotherapy, 1990—; contbr. chapters to books, articles to profl. jours. Recipient Outstanding Family Therapy Contbn. award, Am. Assn. Marriage and Family Therapy, 1991, NIMH trainee, 1969. Mem. APA (divsn. family psychology pres. 1987, sec. 1983-85, com. mem. 1987—, pres. divsn. media psychology 1993, coun. rep. 2002-04, 2004-05, 2006-, Disting. Contbn. Applied Psychology award, 2000, Outstanding Conbtn. Internat. Advancement Psychology, 2002), Internat. Acad. Family Psychology (pres. 1998-2002), Am. Assn. Marital and Family Therapy, Am. Bd. Profl. Psychologists (trustee 2002-06, Disting. Psychology Contbn. award, 1994), Am. Family Therapy Acad., Coalition Family Diagnosis (chmn. 1989-93), Am. Assn. Sex Educators, Counselors and Therapists, Internat. Family Therapy Assn. (founding pres. 1987-90), Acad. Family Mediators (bd. dir. 1982-88, treas. 1985-87). Office Phone: 561-625-0288. Personal E-mail: drfkaslow@bellsouth.net.

KASPROW, BARBARA ANNE, biomedical researcher, writer; b. Hartford, Conn., Apr. 23, 1936; d. Stephen G. and Anna M. Kasprow. AB cum laude, Albertus Magnus Coll., 1958; postgrad., Laval U., 1958, Yale U., 1958-61; PhD, Loyola U., Chgo., 1969. Staff microbiology dept. Conn. State Dept. Health, 1957; lab. asst. dept. microbiology Yale U., New Haven, 1958—59; tng. scholar USPHS, 1959—60; asst. rsch. and editl. dept. anatomy Yale U., New Haven, 1961; rsch. assoc. N.Y. Med. Coll., 1961—62; rsch. assoc. to sr. rsch. assoc. and adminstrv. assoc. Inst. for Study Human Reprodn. St. Ann Ob-Gyn. Hosp., Cleve., 1962—67, asst. to dir. grad. med. edn., asst. dir. adminstrn. grad. rsch. endocrinology, Inst. for Study Human Reprodn., 1962—67; sr. rsch. assoc. dept. anatomy Stritch Sch. Medicine, Chgo., Hines, Ill., 1967—69; asst. prof. anatomy Loyola U., Chgo., 1969—75; asst. to v.p. University Rsch. Sys., 1975-79; v.p. med. topics Univ. Rsch. Sys., 1979—; asst. to pres. Internat. Basic and Biol.-Biomed. Curricula, Lombard, Ill., 1979—. Lectr. in field; invited U.S. del. on reprodn. to Vatican, 1964; round table leader Brazil-Israel Congress on Fertility and Sterility, Brazil Soc. Human Reprodn., São Paulo, 1972. Editl. asst. vol. VIII/3 Handbuch der Histochemie, Gustav Fischer Verlag, 1963; prodn. aide ednl. med. film The Soft Anvil, 1965-66; co-editor: Biology of Reproduction, Basic and Clinical Studies, 1973; contbr. articles to profl. jours. Recipient Certificate of Outstanding Achievement and Scholarship award Am. Assn. German Tchrs. and New Britain German Assn., 1954; named Honorary Citizen São Paulo, 1972. Mem. AAAS (life), Am. Assn. Anatomists, Am. Soc. Zoologists-The Soc. Integrative and Comparative Biology, Pan Am. Assn. Anatomy (co-organizer symposium on reproduction New Orleans 1972), Midwest Anatomists Assn. (program officer ann. meeting Chgo. 1974), Sigma Xi (life). Roman Catholic. Achievements include biological elucidation of growth horizons in uterine development, growth, and maturity; perfection of a hormonal model-system in highly controlled (surgerized) animals to ascertain quantitative relationships of purified estradiol-17beta and progesterone required for promotion of and duplication of these uterine growth horizons; development of experimental paradigms for the biomorphological elucidation of hormonally stimulated growth responses in endocrine target organs, and cyto- and histochemical elucidation of growth stimulants. Office: 607 E Wilson Ave Lombard IL 60148-4062

KASSEL, CATHERINE M., community, maternal, and women's health nurse, consultant; b. Bklyn., Dec. 18, 1953; d. Christopher Frank and Ana Rosa (Sousa) Pannone; m. David L. Kassel, Dec. 27, 1979. Diploma in nursing, Kings County Hosp., Bklyn., 1974; BA in Cmty. Health, CUNY,

1979; BSN with honors, Columbia U., 1989. RN, N.Y. V.p. Kassel Mgmt. Co., N.Y.C., 1985—; pres. Kassel & Co., LLC, N.Y.C. Bd. dirs., co-chair legis. com. N.Y. Counties of RNs, Dist. 13, trustee, treas. polit. action com.; past bd. dirs. Nat. Abortion Rights Action League; bd. dirs., treas., chmn. fundraising, nominating com., adv. coun., Global Kids Inc.; mem. Women's Leadership Forum of Dem. Nat. Com. Mem. ANA (polit. action com.), ANA Found. (founding mem.), N.Y. State Nurses Assn., PAC. Home: 145 W 67th St Apt 7H New York NY 10023 Office Phone: 212-875-9945.

KASSEL, TERRY, human resources specialist; BA, NYU; JD, Seton Hall U. Pvt. practice, NY and NJ; various leadership positions including asst. gen. counsel and v.p. Office of Gen. Counsel; v.p. human resources U.S. private client group Merrill Lynch, NYC, 1985—2000; sr. v.p. human resources, 2001—. Mem. bd. mgrs. Merrill Lynch Cmty. Devel. Co.; trustee Winthrop H. Smith Meml. Found., Merrill Lynch & Co. Found. Mem. adv. bd. NOW Legal Def. and Edn. Fund. Office: Merrill Lynch 4 World Financial Ctr New York NY 10080

KASSEL, VIRGINIA WELTMER, television producer, scriptwriter; b. Omaha; d. Tyler and Inez (Willard) Weltmer. BA, Bryn Mawr Coll. Producer Sta. WGBH-TV, Boston; producer NET, N.Y.C., coordinator nat. programs; mgr. spl. projects, exec. prodr. humanities programs WNET, N.Y.C.; sr. producer CBS Cable, N.Y.C., 1981-83; dir. devel. and prodn. East Coast Primetime Entertainment, Inc., 1983-87; v.p. East Coast Primetime Entertainment, Inc., 1987-89; assoc. dir. performance programs, prodn. exec. Great Performances Sta. WNET-TV, N.Y.C., 1989-91; producer, dir., writer Potter Prodns., 1991-92; dir. devel. Internat. Cultural Programming, 1992-94. Creator, prodr.: The Adams Chronicles; prodr.: The Soong Connection, 1995; contbr. articles to profl. jours. Recipient George Foster Peabody award, 1977, 2 Ohio State awards, 1977, Spl. Achievement award Nat. Assn. Ednl. Broadcasters, 1977, Triangle award, 1986; grantee NEH, Mellon Found Mem.: NATAS, N.Y. Women in Film and TV, Brit. Acad. Film and TV Arts (N.Y. and London), Am. Acad. TV Arts and Scis., Writers Guild Am. East, Nat. Com. on U.S. China Rels., Bryn Mawr Club N.Y. (bd. dirs.), Women's City Club N.Y. (bd. dirs.), Princeton Club (N.Y.). Home: 4 E 89th St New York NY 10128-0636 Office Phone: 212-860-4025. Personal E-mail: virkassel@aol.com.

KASSEWITZ, RUTH EILEEN BLOWER, retired public relations executive; b. Columbus, Ohio, May 15, 1928; d. E. Wallett and Helen (Daub) Blower; m. Jack Kassewitz, July 28, 1962 (dec.). BS in Journalism-Mgmt., Ohio State U., Columbus, 1951. Copywriter Ohio Fuel Gas Co., Columbus, 1951-55, Merritt Owens Advt. Agy., Kansas City, 1955-56; account exec. Grant Advt., Inc., Miami, 1956-59; account supr. Venn/Cole & Assocs., Miami, 1959-67; dir. comms. Ferendino/Grafton/Candela/Spillis Archs. & Engrs., Miami, 1967-69, Dade County dept. Housing and Urban Devel., Miami, 1969-72, Met. Dade County Govt., County Mgrs. Office, 1972-78; adminstr. pub. rels. U. Miami/Jackson Meml. Med. Ctr., 1978-90, ret., 1990. Bd. dirs. Girl Scouts USA, Tropical, Fla., 1974—76, 1981—83, Lung Assn. Dade-Monroe Counties, 1976—87, Met. YMCA, 1996—2003; exec. com. Miami-Dade C.C. Found., 1984—99; pres. Mental Health Assn. Dade County, 1982; mem. City of Miami Ecol. and Beautification Com. (now TREEmendous Miami, Inc.), 1978—2000; 1st vice-chmn., 1996—98; bd. govs. Barry U., Miami, 1981—83; trustee Nat. Humanities Faculty, 1981—83; treas., past chmn. Health, Edn., Promotion Coun., Inc.; adv. bd. Miami's For Me, 1987—88; mem. Coral Gables Cable TV Bd., 1983—86; cmty. adv. bd. Jr. League Greater Miami, Inc., 1989—92; founding mem. Nat. Honor Roll, Women in Pub. Rels., No. Ill. U., 1993; trustee emeritus United Protestant Appeal, 1992—99; ch. moderator Plymouth Congl. Ch., 1986—88, trustee, 1995—99, co-pres. Women's Fellowship, 2001—02. Recipient Disting. Svc. award Plymouth Congl. Ch., Miami, 1979; Ann Stover award, 1983; Golden Image award Fla. Pub. Rels. Assn., 1987; named Woman of Yr. Plymouth Congl. Ch., U. Miami Med. Sch., 1991, Humanitarian of Yr. YMCA of Gtr. Miami, 1998; honoree Fla. Women of Achievement. Fellow Pub. Rels. Soc. Am. (pres. South Fla. chpt. 1969-70, nat. chmn. govt. sect. 1973-74, nat. dir. 1974-76; cont. edn. coun. 1981-83; Silver anvil award 1973, del Assembly 1970-73, 86-89, Paul M. Lund Pub. Svc. award 1993, Miami chpt. Lifetime Achievement award 1995); mem. Women in Comms. (pres. Gtr. Miami chpt. 1962-63; Clarion awards 1973, 75, Cmty. Headliner 1985), Miami Internat. Press Club (bd. dirs. 1986-87, treas. 1992), 200 Club Greater Miami (v.p. 1999-2000), Rotary Club of Miami (bd. dirs. 1988-97, pres. 1993-94, Disting. Rotarian of Yr. 1996, Rotarian of Yr. internat. dist. # 6990 1999), Delta Delta Delta (pres. Miami alumnae chpt. 1997-99), U. Miami Heritage Soc. E-mail: ruthbk@bellsouth.net.

KASS-JOHNSON, SUSAN, artist; b. Fall River, Mass. d. Bernard Charles and Jeanette (Silver) K.; m. Alex Johnson; children: Nicholas, Gabriel. BS in Design, Cornell U.; cert. in art edn., CUNY, 1990, MFA in Painting, 1992. Instr. modern dance U. Va., Charlottesville, 1975-76; guest tchr. performance art SUNY, Buffalo, 1977; guest tchr. performance video RISD, Providence, 1979; guest tchr. Düsseldorf (Germany) Kunstakademie, 1980; tchr. painting and dance children's program Queens Coll., CUNY, 1990, 91, grad. asst., 1992; pvt. tchr. drawing, Merrick, 1993—. Art instr. N.Y. Inst. Tech., 1994; art educator Islip Art Mus., 1994; writer, dir., producer videotapes and films, 1975-84; founding mem. Colab Artists Group, N.Y.C., 1977; founder Point Reyes Dance Palace, Point Reyes Station, Calif., 1975. One-woman shows Anthology Film Archives, N.Y.C., 1977, Internat. Cultural Ctr., Antwerp, Belgium, 1978, RISD, 1979, Di Appel Galerie, Amsterdam, The Netherlands, 1979, U. Calif.-Berkeley Art Mus., 1979; 2-woman shows Whitney Mus., N.Y.C., 1978, Holly Solomon Gallery, N.Y.C., 1978; group shows include Art Inst. Chgo., 1979, Long Beach (Calif.) Mus. Art, 1979, Folkwang Mus., Essen, Germany, 1979, Mus. Modern Art, Paris, 1980, Venice Biennale, 1980, Mus. Contemporary Art, La Jolla, Calif., Mus. Contemporary Art, Chgo., 1981, Everson Mus., Syracuse, N.Y., 1981, Staftisches Kunstmuseum, Bonn, Germany, 1981, Neue Gesellshaft fur Bildende Kunst, Berlin, 1982, Van Abbemuseum, Amsterdam, 1983, Kroller Muller Museum, Amsterdam, 1984, Parrish Art Mus., Southhampton, N.Y., 1994; pub. and pvt. collections in U.S., Europe and Japan Queens Coll. fellow Chautauqua Sch. Art Colony, summer 1993. Mem. Coll. Art Assn., Nat. Mus. Women. Home: 30 Lincoln Blvd Merrick NY 11566-4013 Studio: 30 Lincoln Blvd Merrick NY 11566

KASSMAN, DEBORAH NEWMAN, university administrator, writer, editor; b. Elizabeth, NJ, Feb. 22, 1927; d. Arthur Hersh and Cecelia (Ginsberg) Newman; m. Herbert S. Kassman, Aug. 22, 1948 (div. Dec. 1996); 1 child, Judith K. Wexler. BA, Wellesley Coll., 1948. Editor The Writer, Inc., Boston, 1948-68; asst. to pres. Brandeis U., Waltham, Mass., 1968-70, univ. editor, 1970-75; dir. of stewardship Harvard U., Cambridge, Mass., 1975—2001; stewardship, donors rels. dept. Brandeis U., 2001—. Mem. adv. bd. Alice James Books, Boston; cons. on stewardship. Author: Holiday Plays for Little Players, 1956, also plays for U.S. Treasury Dept.; editor, writer Harvard Mag., 1968-69; editor The Parents Newsletter, Harvard Coll., 1969-97; contbr. articles to popular mags. Dir. Five Fields, Inc., Lexington, Mass., 1995—. Office: Brandeis Univ Donor Rels MS012 PO Box 549239 Waltham MA 02454-9239

KASSOY, HORTENSE (HONEY KASSOY), artist, sculptor, painter; b. N.Y.C., Feb. 14, 1917; d. Adolph and Mary (Apfel) Blumenkranz; m. Bernard Kassoy, June 30, 1946; children: Meredith, Sheila. Diploma, Pratt Inst., 1936; BS, Columbia U., 1938, MA, 1939; student, Parsons Sch. Design, Paris, U. Colo., 1966, NYU, 1966-67; studied sculpture with Sahl Swarz, Chaim Gross & Oronzio Maldarelli. Solo exhbns. include Caravan House Gallery, 1974, Women in the Arts Gallery, 1978, Ward-Nasse Gallery, 1986, Pioneer Gallery, Cooperstown, N.Y., 1987, 91, 97, 80th Birthday Retrospective Solo of Wood Sculpture Prints and Watercolors, Vladeck Hall Gallery, N.Y., 1997, 2002, Pioneer Gallery, Cooperstown, 1997, 2002; group exhbns. include Bronx (N.Y.) Mus., 1971, 75, 85-86, Toledo Mus. Art, Toronto Mus. Art, Hudson River Mus., Bklyn. Mus., New Age Gallery, Lever House, Bklyn. Coll., Fordham U., Lehman Coll., Cork Gallery, Nat. Acad. Design; permanent collections include Slater Meml. Mus. Co-chair visual arts Bronx (N.Y.) Coun. on Arts, 1973-76. Fellow Va. Ctr. for Creative Arts, 1986, 88, 89, 92, 95, 97; recipient 1st prize in watercolor Painters Day at N.Y. World's Fair, 1940, Walker prize for sculpture, Oneonta, NY, 2002. Mem. Am. Soc. Contemporary Artists (v.p. 1989-94, 99-2003, awards in sculpture 1979, 80, 83, 90, 92, 96, 2000, 02), N.Y. Artists Equity Assn. (v.p., bd. dirs. 1971-83), Internation Assn. Art (corr. sec. 1979-93), del. to 10th Congress 1983), Contemporary Arts Guild (rec. sec. 1981-89), Fedn. Modern Painters and Sculptors. Home: 130 Gale Pl Apt 6B Bronx NY 10463-2853 Home (Summer): Butternut Hill Studio 1577 County Route 16 Burlington Flats NY 13315-3211

KASTE, SUE CREVISTON, pediatric radiologist, researcher; b. Lakewood, Ohio, Feb. 25, 1952; d. Donald P. and Marion S. Creviston; m. Ronald H. Kaste, Apr. 28, 1984; children: Rebecca, Steven, Matthew. BA, Lake Erie Coll., 1974; AAS Physicians Asst., Cuyahoga C.C. and Cleve. Clin., 1977; DO, Chgo. Coll. Osteo. Medicine, 1981. Diplomate Am. Bd. Radiology, cert. pediat. radiology Am. Bd. Radiology, 2004, osteopath Osteo. Nat. Bd. Med. Examiners. Intern Chgo. Coll. Osteo. Medicine, Ill., 1981-82; diagnostic radiology U. Hosps. Cleve., 1982-86, fellow pediat. radiology, 1986-87; officer in charge pediat. radiology KTTCMC, Keesler AFB, Biloxi, Miss., 1987-90, chief diagnostic radiology, 1990-91; cons. dept. radiology LeBonheur Children's Med. Ctr., Memphis, 1991—2003; prof. dept. radiology U. Tenn. Coll. Medicine, Memphis, 1991—2003, prof., 2003—; full mem. dept. diagnostic imaging St. Jude Children's Rsch. Hosp., Memphis, 2002—. Reviewer Am. Jour. Roentgenology, 1994—, Pediat. Radiology, 1997—, others; contbr. articles to profl. jours Leader/asst. leader Girl Scouts Am., Cordova, Tenn., 1992-99; youth club asst. Advent Presbyn. Ch., Cordova, 1993-98, ch. orch. Maj. USAF Med. Corps, 1977-91. Grantee, Soc. Pediat. Radiology, 1998. Mem. Children's Oncology Group, Am. Coll. Radiology, Radiologic Soc. N.Am., Midwest Soc. Pediat. Radiology, Am. Soc. Bone and Mineral Rsch Avocations: flute, painting, drawing, swimming. Office: St Jude Childrens Rsch Hosp Dept Diagnostic Imaging 332 N Lauderdale St Memphis TN 38105-2729 Office Fax: 901-495-3962. E-mail: sue.kaste@stjude.org.

KASTER, LAURA A., lawyer; b. N.Y.C., May 24, 1948; BA, Tufts U., 1970; JD magna cum laude, Boston U., 1973. Bar: Mass. 1973, Ill. 1975. Law clk. to Hon. Frank M. Coffin, U.S. Ct. Appeals for 1st circuit, Boston, 1973-75; assoc. Jenner & Block, Chgo., 1975-81, ptnr., 1981-97; gen. atty. law and govt. affairs AT&T Corp., Bedminster, NJ, 1997—. Bd. trustees Lawyers Com. for Civil Rights. Co-author: Sanctions in Federal Litigation, 1991; co-editor: The Attorneys' Guide to the Seventh Circuit Court of Appeals, 3rd edit., 2005; note editor Law Rev. Boston U., 1973-72; contbr. chpt. to book and articles to profl. jours. Trustee Lawyers Com. for Civil Rights, 2005—. Fellow Am. Bar Found. (life); mem. ABA, 7th Circuit Bar Assn., Fed. Cir. Bar Assn Office Phone: 908-532-1888. Personal E-mail: laura.kaster@gmail.com.

KASTIEL, ELIZABETH MARIA, assistant principal; b. Chgo., Sept. 4, 1972; d. Bertha Maria and Ray William Kastiel; m. Michael DeMarke Putman, July 30, 2005. BA, U. Wis., Madison, 1994; MEd, U. San Diego, 1999. Cert. Gen. Adminstr. Lewis U., 2005. Reading coach Chgo. Pub. Schs., 2003—05; asst. prin. Tarkington Sch. of Excellence, Chgo., 2005—. Office: Tarkington School of Excellence CPS 3330 W 71st Street Chicago IL 60629 Home Fax: 773-535-4713. Personal E-mail: emkastiel@cps.k12.il.us.

KASTON, LISA MARSHA, social services administrator; b. N.Y.C., Apr. 1, 1955; d. Seymour Albert Kaston and Susan Zuckerman Kaston; children: Adam Louis Garcia, Emily Beth Garcia. MPS, New Sch. U., N.Y.C., 1987. Mgr. grants and cmty. initiatives Devereux Fla., Orlando, 1995—2002; dir. program devel. and contract mgmt. Hope and Help Ctr. of Ctrl. Fla., Winter Park, 2002—. Mem. steering com. coun. agy. execs. Heart of Fla. United Way, Orlando, 1998—2002; mem. Leadership Orlando, 1999—2000; mem. funding rev. panel Victims of Crime Assistance Program, 18th Jud. Cir., Brevard and Seminole Counties, Fla., 1999—2001; precinct leader Seminole County Dem. Exec. Com., 2005—; chmn. conflict resolution com. Ctrl. Fla. AIDS Planning Consortium, 2005—. Mem.: Grant Profls. Network Ctrl. Fla. (pres. 2000—01, Excellence in Grant Professionalism and Advocacy Award 2000). Avocations: travel, reading, arts. Office: Hope and Help Ctr of Ctrl Fla 1935 Woodcrest Dr Winter Park FL 32792 Office Phone: 407-415-4961. E-mail: lkaston@hopeandhelp.org.

KATA, MARIE L., securities dealer, brokerage house executive; b. Redwood Falls, Minn. m. M. T. Kata, 1984; children: Namue, Karwehn. BS in Bus., U. Minn., 1979. Lic. Series 24, cert. Series 65, Series 7. Stockbroker R.J. Steichen, 1992, Montano Securities, 1993—95, Res. Fin., 1996—97, Eisner Securities, 1997—2001, br. mgr., 1997—2001; stockbroker LaSalle St. Securities, Edina, Minn., 2001—, br. mgr., 2001—. Recipient Hon. Advisor award, Fidelity Investments, 2001. Avocations: skiing, reading, spirituality. Office: LaSalle St Securities LLC 7701 France Ave S #200 Edina MN 55435

KATARIA, TRIPTI CADAY, anesthesiologist; MD. Resident Brigham & Women's Hosp.; asst. prof. anesthesiology Feinberg Sch. Med. Northwestern U. Mem.: Am. Soc. Anesthesiologists (chair resident component). Office: Northwestern U Sch Med Dept Anesthesiolgoy 710 North Fairbanks Ct Chicago IL 60611 E-mail: t-kataria@northwestern.edu.*

KATEHI, LINDA P.B., engineering educator; b. Athens, Greece, Jan. 30, 1954; arrived in US, 1979; d. Vasilios and Georgia (Begni) K.; m. Spyros Tseregounis, July 10, 1980; children: Erik Tseregounis, Helena Tseregounis. BSEE, Nat. Tech. U., Athens, 1977; MSEE, UCLA, 1981, PhD in elec. engring., 1984. Teaching asst. Nat. Tech. U. of Athens Greece, 1977—78; rsch. engr. Dept. Def. Naval Rsch. Lab, GETEN, Athens, Greece, 1978—79; rsch. asst. UCLA, 1979-84; asst. prof. elec. engring. U. Mich., Ann Arbor, 1984—89, assoc. prof. elec. engring. and computer sci., 1989—94, prof. electrical engring. and computer sci., 1994—2001, coll. engring. assoc. dir. grad. program, 1994—95, mem. coll. engring. exec. com., 1995—98, assoc. dean grad. edn., 1998—99, sr. assoc. dean academic affairs, 1999—2001; John A. Edwardson Dean of Engring. Purdue U., West Lafayette, Ind., 2001—, prof. of computer and elec. engring., 2002—. Reviewer Army Rsch. Office, 1984—, NSF, 1984—; mem. fgn. admissions U. Mich., 1989—90, undergraduate advisor, 1990—91, graduate advisor for electromagnetics, 1991—94, mem., Coll. Engring. Faculty Advisory Com. on Excellence, 1991—92, mem., univ. senate assembly, 1991—94, mem. tenure com., 1992—95, EECS dept. exec. com., 1992—94, mem., Coll. Engring. Discipline Com., 1992—95, mem. domestic admissions EECS, 1994—97, mem. Coll. Engring., dean search com., 1995, bd. dir., Ctr. for Rsch. Learning and Teaching, 1996—97, mem., provost search com., 1997, chair, grad. chair com., 1998—99, chair, Task Force on MEng programs com., 1998—99, ex-officio, task force on masters programs com., 1998—99, chair, faculty search com. for electromagnetics, 1998—99, mem. com. on internat. inst., 1998, mem. strategic directions com., 1999—, mem., assoc. dean and assoc. provosts academic programs group, 1999—, chair, provost com. on faculty mentoring, 1999—; mem. adv. com. on electron devices Dept. Defense, 1999—; chair Pioneer Revolutionary Technologies Subcom., Aerospace Enterprise NASA, 2002—, mem. Aerospace Tech. Adv. Com. (ATAC), 2002—; chair. adv. com. to Engring. Directorate NSF, 2005—, mem. adv. com. to Directorate for Computer and Info. Sci. and Engring., 2002—; mem. Army Rsch. Lab. adv. com. on Sensors and Electrons Divsn. AUS, 2003—; mem. engring. adv. com. Iowa State U., 2003—; provost com. on New Facilities Purdue U., search com. for v.p. research, 2004—05, search com. for the sr. v.p. for fin. affairs, 2003—04. Contbr. articles to profl. jours. Recipient Rsch. Excellence Award, Elec. Engring. and Computer Sci. Dept., U. Mich. Ann Arbor, 1993, Humboldt Rsch. Award, 1994, Faculty Recognition Award, U. Mich. Ann Arbor, 1994. Fellow: IEEE (Antennas and Propagation Soc., Microwave Theory and Techniques Soc., Microwave Theory and Techniques Soc. 3d Millenium Medal 2000); mem.: NAE, Advanced Computational Electromagnetics Soc., Internat. Soc. Hybrid Microelectronics, Internat. Union Radio Sci. (Booker Young Scientist Award 1987), Union Radio Sci. Internat., Sigma Xi. Achievements include patents in field. Avocations: skiing, tennis, gardening. Office: Purdue U 400 Centennial Mall Dr West Lafayette IN 47907-2016 Business E-Mail: katehi@purdue.edu.*

KATEN, KAREN L., pharmaceutical company executive; b. 1948; BA in Polit. Sci. and Econ., U. Chgo., 1970, MBA in Mktg. and Fin., 1974. Mktg. assoc. pharms. Pfizer Inc., 1974, various positions Roerig divsn. product mgmt. group, 1975—78, group product mgr. Pfizer Labs., 1980, dir. product mgr. Pfizer Labs., v.p. mktg. Roerig divsn., 1983—86, v.p., dir. ops. Roerig divsn., 1986—91, v.p., gen. mgr. Roerig divsn., 1991—93, v.p., 1992—99, exec. v.p. Pfizer US Pharms. Group, 1993—95, pres. Pfizer US Pharms. Group NYC, 1995—2002, sr. v.p., 1999—2001; exec. v.p. Pfizer, Inc., 2001—05, vice chmn., 2005—06; exec. v.p. Pfizer Global Pharmaceuticals (formerly Pfizer Pharmaceuticals Group), 1997—2001, pres., 2001—05, Pfizer Human Health, 2005—06; advisor health policy Pfizer Inc., 2006. Bd. dirs. GM, Harris Corp., Catalyst, Nat. Alliance Hispanic Health, Am. Bur. for Med. Advancement in China; mem. internat. coun. J.P. Morgan Chase & Co.; mem. coun. U.S. and Italy, U. Chgo. Grad. Sch. Bus.; trustee U. Chgo.; nat. bd. trustees Am. Cancer Soc. Rsch. Found., NCAA Found.; health bd. advisors RAND Corp.; bd. corp. advisors Am. Diabetes Assn.; appointee US-Japan Private Sector/Govt. Commn., 2003, Nat. Infrastructure Adv. Com., 2003; bd. trustees Healthcare Leadership Coun. Named one of Most Powerful Women in Bus., Fortune mag., 1998—2005, Top 50 Women to Watch, Wall St. Jour., 2005; recipient Salute to Women Achievers award, YMCA, Women Yr. award, Boy Scout Am. Greater N.Y. Coun., NY Women's Agenda Star award, Bus. Leadership award, Burden Ctr. Aging, Iphigene Ochs Sulzburger award, Barnard Coll., Am. Fedn. Aging Rsch. Distinction award, Woman of Yr. award, NYC Police Athletic League, 2001, Woman With Heart award, Am. Heart Assn., 2004. Mem.: Nat. Pharm. Coun. (mem. bd. dirs.), Am. Diabetes Assn. (mem. bd. corp. advisors, Women of Valor award), Am. Cancer Soc. Rsch. Found. (mem. nat. bd. trustees), Nat. Alliance Hispanic Health, European Fedn. Pharm. Industry Assns. (bd. mem.), Health Leadership Coun., Pharm. Rsch. and Mfrs. Assn. Am.*

KATES, CAROLYN LOUISE, physical therapist; b. Ann Arbor, Mich., Dec. 11, 1949; d. Phillip Brown and Sara Louise Kates; m. Gregory Van Dreps, Sept. 23, 1986. BSc, U. Fla., 1982; MSc, U. Wash., Seattle, 2000. Phys. therapist Sunland Ctr., Gainseville, Fla., 1982—84, Metcalf Elem. Sch., Gainseville, 1983—85, Shana's Hosp. U. Fla., 1985—86, Swedish Med. Ctr., Seattle, 1994—99, Boyer Children's Clin., Seattle, 1987—. Asst. instr. Manual Therapy for the Pediatric Patient, Seattle, 1990—2002; clin. instr. for women's phys. theraphy svcs. U. Wash., 1994—; presenter in field. Author (constructing author): Clinical GMT Measurement with Pediatric, 2005; medical illustrator Management of Common Neuromolecular Disorders, 2005. Mem. Adv. for Comprehensive Early Intervention Practice, Seattle, 1999—2001. Mem.: Wash. State Phys. Therapy Assn., Am. Phys. Therapy Assn., Golden Key Nat. Honor Soc., Phi Kappa Phi. Democrat. Home: 2760 SW 116th St Seattle WA 98146 Office: Boyer Children's Clin 1850 Boyer Ave E Seattle WA 98112

KATES, CHERYL L., legal nursing consultant; b. Rochester, N.Y., July 4, 1970; d. John Edward Leavy and Jean Ellen (Boyle) Leavy-Ellis; 1 child, Markas J. LPN, SUNY, Brockport, 1991; AA, Monroe C.C., Rochester, 1998; BA, St. John Fisher Coll. Cert. EMT; LPN. LPN Unique Staffing, Rochester, 1991—94. Tutor Literacy Vols., Rochester, 1996—; co-dir. Edge of Justice; bd. dirs. legal com. NYCLU, Rochester. Avocations: ceramics, African American studies.

KATHAN, JOYCE C., retired social worker, administrator; b. Middletown, Conn., Oct. 28, 1931; d. Herbert G. and Mabel Elizabeth (Lee) Clark; m. Boardman W. Kathan, Aug. 17, 1952; children: Nancy Lee, David Wardell, Robert Boardman. BSW magna cum laude, So. Conn. State U., 1976. Dist. dir. Coun. Greater Boston Camp Fire Girls, 1969-73; dir. sr. citizen programs Town of Woodbury, Conn., 1976-97; info. officer Conn. Coalition of Aging, 1998—2005, bd. dirs., 2006—. Participant Global Assembly of Women and Environ., 1991; adv. bd. VNA health Care, 1985-95. Co-author: Youth Where the Action Is, 1970; (with others) Management of Hazardous Agents, Vol. 2: Social and Political Aspects, 1992. Active Prospect Commn. on Aging, Conn., 1979—89, chair, 1979—87; apptd. mem. Congl. Dist. 3 and 5 adv. coun. Conn. Permanent Commn. on Status of Women, 1996—; bd. dir. Robin Ridge Elderly Housing, 2001—03, E. Irene Boardman Found., 1995—, We. Conn. Area Agy. on Aging, 1986—92, pres., 1990—92, adv. coun., 2005—; bd. dir. Waterbury YWCA, Conn., 1977—83, rec. sec. Recipient Outstanding Conn. Women award, 1987, Vol. of Yr. award Conn. Coalition on Aging, 1999. Mem.: LWV (pres. Cheshire chpt. 1988—2003), AAUW (local and state coms. 1978—, Assn. Pub. Policy Com. 1985—89, pub. policy chmn. Conn. chpt. 1996—2000, pres. Greater Waterbury chpt. 2000—, pub. policy chmn. Conn. chpt. 2004—, pub. policy chmn. 2005—, Named Gift award Conn. chpt. 1981, 1985, 1997, Outstanding Cmty. Svc. award Conn. chpt. 1994), NASW, Conn. Assn. Sr. Ctr. Pers. (rec. sec. 1995—97, charter mem., Svc. award 1986), Women's Environ. and Devel. Orgn., Conn. LWV (pub. policy com. 1988—95). Personal E-mail: jckccoa@aol.com.

KATICH, ELEANOR PATIENCE, retired science educator; d. Marshall Howard Ungethuem and Geraldine Litilla McCarthy; m. Robert Katich, June 16, 1956 (dec.); children: Geraldine Becky, Robert II. BS, Pa. State U., State College, 1954. Home economist Mfrs. Light and Heat, Pitts., 1954—56; instr. Pa. State U., State College, 1956—57; tchr., dept. chair Rochester Area Sch. Dist., Pa., 1960—93; ret., 1993. Bd. dirs. Pa. Cyber, Midland, Pa., 2000—05; pres., bd. dirs. Lincoln Park Performing Arts, Midland, 2003—, pres. bd. dirs., 2005—. Sec. Carnegie Libr. Bd., Midland, 1995—2000; pres. Mikdland Devel. Corp., 1991—2001, Midland Heritage Project, 1996—, Midland Initiative, 2001—; mem. Beaver Initiative for Growth, Beavery County Indsl. Mus. Bd., 2005—; deacon First Presbyn. Ch., Midland, 2005—; bd. dirs. Children and Youth Sv cs., Beaver County, Pa., 1996—2001. Recipient Main Stl. award, Beaver County MainSt., 2002. Mem.: NEA, Pa. Assn. Sch. Retirees (bd. dirs. 1994—), Pa. Edn. Assn., Pa. State Alumni Assn., Phi Omicron Upsilon, Omicron Nu. Presbyterian. Avocations: travel, antiques, reading. Home: 865 Virginia Ave Midland PA 15059

KATICH, JANET, librarian; b. Weslaco, Tex. d. Donald Arol and Ethel Morgan; m. Nick Katich (div.); children: Alexandra, Philip. BA, Birmingham So. Coll., 1969; MLS, Ind. U., 2002. Cert. mgmt., supervisory issues, comm. and orgn. Ivy Tech. CC Leadership Acad., 2006. Auditor U.S. Treasury Dept., 1969—75; libr. Ivy Tech CC, Valparaiso, Ind., 2000—. Co-chair learning communities com. Ivy Tech CC. Bd. sch. trustees Crown Point Cmty. Sch. Corp., Ind., 1986—96; bd. dirs. The Discovery Alliance, Portage, Ind., 2005—; bd. trustees Crown Point Cmty. Libr., 2005—; bd. dirs., property com. mem., leader Drifting Dunes Girl Scout Coun., Merrillville, Ind.; sch. bldgs. holding corp. mem. Crown Point Cmty. Sch. Corp.; mem. Am. Heart Assn., Merrillville. Mem.: Ind. Libr. Fedn., ALA, Girl Scouts U.S.A. (life). Avocations: reading, travel, golf. Office: Ivy Tech Community Coll 2401 Valley Dr Valparaiso IN 46383 Office Phone: 219-464-8514. Business E-Mail: jkatich@ivytech.edu.

KATINA, ELENA SERGEJEVNA, singer; b. Moscow; Attended, Moscow State U., Faculty of Psychology. Singer t.A.T.u., 1999—. Rep. for Russia Eurovision Song Contest, 2003. Singer: (albums) 200 km/h in the Wrong Lane, 2002, Dangerous and Moving, 2005. Recipient 3rd Place for song "Ne ver', ne bojsia", Eurovision Song Contest, 2003. Mailing: tATu Interscope Records 2220 Colorado Ave Santa Monica CA 90404

KATSOULOMITIS, GEORGIA, foundation administrator, lawyer; Graduate, Tufts Univ.; JD, Catholic Univ., Washington. Spl. asst. US Labor Secy., Robert Reich, Washington; spl. asst. and counsel, oversight and investigations Dept. Labor, Washington; v.p. Robinson Lerer & Montgomery, NYC; now asst. exec. dir. Boston Bar Found. Class of 2004 LeadBoston leadership devel. program; past. exec. dir. Mass. Women's Polit. Caucus. Mem.: Women's Bar Assn. (legis. policy com.), Hellenic Bar Assn. (vice pres. 2005), Mass. Bar. Office: Boston Bar Found 16 Beacon St Boston MA 02108 Office Phone: 617-778-1948. Office Fax: 617-523-0127. Business E-Mail: gkatsoulomitis@bostonbar.org.

KATZ, ALIX MARTHA, respiratory care practitioner; b. Newark, Dec. 7, 1948; d. Leo F. and Anne (Chase) K. AS, Passaic County Community Coll., Paterson, N.J., 1982. Cert. respiratory therapy technician. Staff respiratory therapist Hosp. Ctr. at Orange, N.J., 1979-82; home care respiratory practitioner Homed Convalescent Equipment, Mountain Lakes, N.J., 1982-85; clin. respiratory supr. Elizabeth (N.J.) Gen. Med. Ctr., 1985-86; dir. respiratory therapy Paramed. Splty., Inc., Fairfield, NJ, 1986-88; respiratory therapist Ultra-Care Health Care Svcs., West Orange, NJ, 1988-94, Rahway Hosp., Rahway, NJ, 1994—2003, Advanced Life Svcs., Louisville, 2003—. Drug and Hosp. Union scholar, 1980. Mem. Am. Assn. for Respiratory Care, Nat. Soc. Cardio-Pulmonary Technologists, Respiratory Therapy Hist. Soc., Methaphys. Ctr. N.J. Democrat. Jewish. Avocations: science, medicine, language, religion, philosophy. Home: 230 Clarken Dr West Orange NJ 07052-3400

KATZ, ANNE HARRIS, biologist, educator, writer; b. Long Branch, N.J; BS, Ursinus Coll., Collegeville, Pa., 1966; MS, U. Mass., 1974, PhD, 1976. Cert. pvt. pilot. Tchr. biology Middletown (N.J.) Twp. High Sch., 1966-69; instr. biology Holyoke (Mass.) Community Coll., 1969; teaching and research assoc. U. Mass., 1969-76; asst. prof. biology Fordham U., N.Y.C., 1977-83; assoc. prof. biology, asst. dean Coll. St. Elizabeth, Convent Station, N.J., 1983-86; assoc. dean Coll. Natural Scis. and Math. Ind. U. Pa., 1987-91, interim dean Coll. Natural Scis. and Math., 1988-89; dean of the coll., prof. biology Lycoming Coll., Williamsport, Pa., 1991-93. Cert. pvt. pilot; cert. ecologist. Founder, editor, pub. Aviation Mus. & Event News, 1993; contbr. abstracts and articles to profl. jours. Vis. scholar Drew U., Madison, N.J., 1984-87; grantee Ctr. Field Rsch., Watertown, Mass., 1981-82, Geraldine R. Dodge Found., Morristown, N.J., 1981-83, N.J. DEP, 1983, Pa. Dept. Edn., 1989, GTE, 1990, CDC, 1991. Mem. AAAS, Ecol. Soc. Am., Aircraft Owners and Pilots Assn., Ninety Nines (aerospace edn.), Civil Air Patrol (aerospace edn. officer, pub. affairs officer), Soc. Study Reprodn., Am. Inst. Biol. Scis., N.Y. Acad. Sci., N.J. Acad. Sci., Pa. Acad. Sci., Ecol. Soc. Am. Avocations: hiking, travel, writing, flying small airplanes.

KATZ, BARBARA STEIN, special education educator; b. Springfield, Mass., July 22, 1933; d. Harry and Pearl (Black) Stein; m. Charles Murry Katz, July 14, 1957; children: Helen Lee, Robert Alan. BS, Am. Internat. Coll., Springfield, 1956, MA in Ednl. Psychology in Learning Disabilities, 1979. Cert. in elem. edn., moderate spl. needs, Mass. Elem. tchr. Springfield Pub. Schs., 1956-60; Jr. Great Books discussion leader, 1968-69; Gillingham remedial tchr. Pub. Schs., Longmeadow, Mass., 1975-78, spl. edn. tchr. Chicopee, Mass., 1978-98, reader, 1998—2002, Pioneer Valley Collaborative, East Longmeadow, Mass., 1998—2002; ret., 2002. Pres. Kodimoh Synagogue Women's Group, Springfield, 1972-74; troop leader Girl Scouts U.S., Longmeadow, 1967-70. Horace Mann grantee, 1988. Mem. NEA, Mass. Tchrs. Assn. Avocations: painting, reading, walking, swimming. Home: 407 Bliss Rd Longmeadow MA 01106-1538 Personal E-mail: lyncam5@aol.com.

KATZ, COLLEEN, publisher; b. Newark; BA in Math., Montclair (N.J.) Coll.; cert., Ctr. Linguistique Etrangers, Tours, France. Assoc. editor Fawcett Publs., N.Y.C., 1972-73, editor, 1973-76; editorial dir. Butterick Fashion Mktg. Co., N.Y.C., 1976-77; editor Ency. of Textiles, N.Y.C., 1979; editor in chief N.J. Monthly, Morristown, 1982-85; dir. publs. Ins. Info. Inst., N.Y.C., 1985-88; pub., editor-in-chief Journal of Accountancy, N.Y.C., 1988—. Adj. prof. Audrey Cohen Coll., 2000. Editor Ins. Rev., 1985-88; pub. mags. and newsletters AICPA, 1997—; editor Huguenot Heritage, 1999. Vol. tchr. Elizabeth (N.J.) Sch. System; vol. editor Nat. Council Jewish Women, NJ, 1967—71; vol. pub. relations worker Essex County Mental Health Assn., NJ, 1980—81. Named Woman of Yr., Cen. N.J. March of Dimes, 1984, Outstanding Alumnus, Montclair Coll., 1984; recipient Gold Cir. award Am. Soc. Assn. Execs., 1989, award for pub. excellence Comm. Concepts, 1990, Pub. Excellence award Mag. Week, 1990, Gen. Excellence award Soc. Nat. Assn. Publs., 1991, Golden Page award, 2000-01, 0102. Mem.: Conf. des Vins du Cahors, Soc. Nat. Assn. Publs. (Silver medal for gen. excellence 1997), Am. Soc. Mag. Editors, Soc. Profl. Journalists, Nat. Arts Club. Avocation: foreign languages. Office: Jour of Accountancy Harborside III Jersey City NJ 07311 E-mail: ckatz@aicpa.org.

KATZ, ELLEN D., law educator; BA summa cum laude, Yale U., JD. Judicial clk. for Justice David H. Souter US Supreme Ct.; for Judge Judith W. Rogers US Ct. Appeals, DC Cir.; dep. atty. gen. appellate div. Environment and Natural Resources Div., US Dept. Justice; asst. prof. U. Mich. Law Sch., Ann Arbor, 1999, prof. law. Contbr. articles to law jours. Mem.: Phi Beta Kappa. Office: U Mich Law Sch 909 Legal Research 625 S State St Ann Arbor MI 48109 Office Phone: 734-647-6241. Office Fax: 734-764-8309. E-mail: ekatz@umich.edu.

KATZ, ESTHER, historian, educator; b. Aug. 14, 1948; came to U.S., 1951; d. Harry and Rose (Katz) K. AB, Hunter Coll., 1969; MA, NYU, 1973, PhD, 1980. Instr. SUNY, Brockport, 1976, NYU, 1976, Coll. New Rochelle, N.Y.C., 1981; adj. asst. prof. NYU, 1983-90, rsch. scientist, 1989—, adj. assoc. prof., 1991—. Dir., editor Margaret Sanger Papers Project, 1987—; dep. dir. Inst. for Rsch. in History, N.Y.C., 1983-87; chair bd. dirs. Ctr. Lesbian and Gay Studies CUNY, 1991-94; mem. exec. bd., Nat. History Coalition, 2003—; cons., Ford Found., 1997-98; acting dir. program in archival mgmt. and hist. editing, 1993-94. Editor: The Selected Papers of Margaret Sanger, Vol. I: The Women Rebel, 1900-1928, 2003, The Margaret Sanger Microfilm Edition, 1996, 97; co-editor: Woman's Experience in American, 1980, Procs. of Conf. on Women Surviving Holocaust, 1983; contbr. articles on history of edn., birth control, and Margaret Sanger to profl. jours. Moses Coit Taylor fellow NYU, 1976; ACLS grant-in-aid, 1989. Mem.: Am. Hist. Assn., Orgn. Am. Historians (com. on rsch. and access to hist. documents 2003—05), Assn. for Documentary Editors (exec. coun. 2001—03, pres. 2003—04, exec. coun. 2005). Office: NYU Dept History 53 Washington Sq S New York NY 10012-1098 E-mail: esther.katz@nyu.edu.

KATZ, JANE, swimming educator; b. Sharon, Pa., Apr. 16, 1943; d. Leon and Dorthea Katz BS in Edn., CCNY, 1963; MA, NYU, 1966; MEd, Columbia Tchrs. Coll., 1972, EdD, 1978. Faculty Bronx C.C., CUNY, 1964—, prof. phys. edn., 1972—. Mem. U.S. Round-the-World Synchronized Swim Performance Team, 1964; synchronized swimming solo tour of Eng., 1969; founding co-organizer, coach 1st Internat. Israeli Youth Festival Games, 1970; mem. winning U.S. Maccabiah Swim Team, 1957; vice-chair U.S. Masters All-Am. Swim Team, 1974—; mem. Nat. Masters All-Am. Swim Team, 1974—, synchronized swimming solo champion, 1975; spkr. judge in field. Author: Swimming for Total Fitness, A Progressive Aerobic Program, 1981, rev. edit., 1993, Swimming Through Your Pregnancy, 1983, W.E.T. Workouts: Water Exercises and Techniques to Help You and tone up Aerobically, 1985, Fitness Works: Blueprint for Lifelong Fitness, 1988, Swim 30 Laps in 30 Days, 1991, The Workstation Workout, 1994, Aquatic Handbook for Lifetime Fitness, 1996, (video) The New W.E.T. Workout, 1994, The All-American Aquatic Handbook: Your Passport to Lifetime Fitness, 1996, The W.E.T. Workout, 1996; contbr. Ency. Britannica Med. and Health Ann., 1997, Swim Basics Video, 2001, Tri Synchro Video/DVD, 2003, Your Water Workout, 2003, Swim Basics on DVD, 2005, author papers in field. Trainee Fed. Adminstrn. Aging, 1971-72; mem. Internat. Hall of Fame, Ft. Lauderdale. Named Healthy Am. Fitness Leader U.S. Jaycees and the Pres's. Coun. on Phys. Fitness, 1987, Outstanding Masters Synchronized Swimming, 1987; recipient CCNY Towsend Harris Acad. medal, 1989, Outstanding Lifetime Leadership award Fedn. Internat. Nat. Amateur, 1999, cert. of merit Fedn. Internat. de Natation Amateur (FINA), Sydney, Australia, 2000, Lifetime Contbrn. to Swimming award Internat. Olympic Com., 2000. Mem.: AAHPERD, Internat. Aquatics (Hall of Fame Paragon award), U.S. Com. Sports for Israel (co-chmn. women's swimming com. 1970—, dir.), Internat. Swimming Hall of Fame (bd. dirs. 2002—). Address: 400 2nd Ave Apt 23B New York NY 10010-4052 Business E-Mail: drjanekatz@hotmail.com.

KATZ, JOETTE, state supreme court justice; b. Bklyn., Feb. 3, 1953; BA, Brandeis U., 1974; JD, U. Conn., 1977; LLD (hon.). Bar: Conn. 1977. Pvt. practice, 1977-78; asst. pub. defender Office Chief Pub. Defender, 1978-83; chief legal svcs. Pub. Defender Svcs., 1983-89; judge Superior Ct., 1989-92; assoc. justice Conn. Supreme Ct., Hartford, 1992—; adminstrv. judge Appellate Sys., Hartford, 1994-2000. Instr. U. Conn. Sch. Law, 1981-84, Yale U. Sch. Law, 2006-; instr. ethics and criminal law Quinnipiac Coll. Sch. Law, 1999—; chair Evidence Code Drafting Com., chair Adv. Com. Appellate Rules, Client Security Fund; Am. Inns Ct. (past pres. Fairfield County br.), Assn. Reproductive Tech. (mem. com.). Co-author: (book) Connecticut Criminal Caselaw Handbook: A Practitioner's Guide, 1989. Mem. Justice Edn. Ctr. Recipient Maria Miller Stewart award, Conn. Women's Education & Legal Fund, 1993, Harriet Tubman award, Nat. Orgn. for Women, 1993, Women of Distinction award, Nat. Council of Jewish Women, 2001. Mem. Am. Law Inst., Conn. Bar Assn. (Henry J. Naruk Judiciary award 2004). Office: Conn Supreme Ct 231 Capital Ave Hartford CT 06106

KATZ, LINDA M., social worker; b. Jersey City, Dec. 17, 1944; d. David A. and Florence (Friedlander) Moritz; m. Robert Lawrence Katz, June 19, 1965; children: Peter Moritz, Douglas Andrew. AA, Briarcliff Coll., Briarcliff Manor, N.Y., 1965; BS in Edn., Wheelock Coll., Boston, 1967; MSSA, Case Western Res. U., 1990. Lic. ind. social worker. Social worker, Cleveland Heights, Ohio, 1990—; case cons. Office on Aging, Cleveland Heights, 1990—. Trustee Schnurmann House for Sr. Adult Living, Mayfield Heights, Ohio, 1997—. Mem. women's coun. Cleve. Mus. Art, 1994—; group leader Cleveland Heights Sr. Activity Ctr., 1990—. Mem. NASW. Avocation: musical talent/singing. Home: 22099 Parnell Rd Shaker Heights OH 44122

KATZ, LOIS ANNE, internist, nephrologist; b. Rockville Centre, N.Y., Dec. 1, 1941; d. Irvin Martin and Frances (Berenstein) Fradkin; m. Arthur A. Katz, Aug. 18, 1962; children: David, Brian. BA, Wellesley Coll., 1962; MD, NYU, 1966. Diplomate Am. Bd. Internal Medicine, Am. Bd. Nephrology. Intern medicine Bellevue Hosp., NYU, N.Y.C., 1966-67, resident medicine, 1967-68; sr. resident medicine N.Y. Hosp., N.Y.C., 1968-69; from chief resident medicine to assoc. chief staff N.Y. VA Med. Ctr., N.Y.C., 1969—2000, assoc. chief of staff spl. emphasis programs and quality mgmt., 2000—; asst. prof. clin. medicine NYU Sch. Medicine, N.Y.C., 1974-79, assoc. prof., 1979-94, prof. clin. medicine, 1994—2002, prof. medicine, 2002—. Fellow: ACP; mem.: Am. Soc. Hypertension, Women in Nephrology (treas. 1985—89), Soc. Gen. Internal Medicine, Am. Med. Women's Assn., Am. Soc. Nephrology, Wellesley Coll. Alumnae Assn. (region 2 admission rep. 1997—2001), Sigma Xi, Alpha Omega Alpha. Jewish. Avocations: reading, swimming, cooking, music. Office: Dept Vets Affairs NY Harbor Healthcare System 423 E 23rd St New York NY 10010-5013 Office Phone: 212-951-6875. Business E-Mail: lois.katz@med.va.gov.

KATZ, MARTHA LESSMAN, lawyer; b. Chgo., Oct. 28, 1952; d. Julius Abraham and Ida (Oiring) Lessman; m. Richard M. Katz, June 27, 1976; children: Julia Erin, Meredith Evin. AB, Washington U., St. Louis, 1974; JD, Loyola U., Chgo., 1977. Bar: Ill. 1977, U.S. Dist. Ct. (no. dist.) Ill. 1977, Calif. 1981, U.S. Dist. Ct. (so. dist.) Calif. 1981, U.S. Dist. Ct. (no. dist.) Calif. 1982, Md. 1993, U.S. Supreme Ct. 1993, D.C. 1994. Assoc. Fein & Hanfling, Chgo., 1977-80, Rudick, Platt & Victor, San Diego, 1981-82, 84-91; asst. sec., counsel Itel Corp., San Francisco, 1982-84; ptnr. Katz & Mann, 1991—95; counsel U.S. Fidelity and Guaranty Co., 1995-99; prin. intellectual property and tech., life scis., biotech. and pharm. Miles & Stockbridge PC, Balt., 1999—. Mem. Greater Balt. Tech. Coun., Tech. Coun. Md. Mem. adv. bd. tech. incubator Howard County Econ. Devel. Authority. Mem. Calif. State Bar Assn., Md. Bar Assn. (spl. com. on tech.), Ill. State Bar Assn., Bar Assn. Balt. City (tech. com.), Bar Assn. DC, Women's Bar Assn., Phi Beta Kappa. Jewish. Office: 10 Light St Baltimore MD 21202-1435 Office Phone: 410-385-3570. Office Fax: 410-385-3700. Business E-Mail: mkatz@milesstockbridge.com.

KATZ, MIRIAM LESSER, psychotherapist, educator; b. Petah-Tikva, Israel, Aug. 29, 1942; came to U.S., 1965; d. Kurt and Ilse (Fliess) Lesser; m. Adrian Izhack Katz, Mar. 31, 1965; 1 child, Iris Ellen. Diploma in nursing, Beilinson U. Tel-Aviv, 1962; B Gen. Studies, Roosevelt U., Chgo., 1976; MA, U. Chgo., 1977. RN Ill.; lic. psychotherapist Am. bd. Med. Psychotherapist, lic. clin. profl. counselor. Head nurse Beilinson Med. Ctr. Tel-Aviv U., Petah-Tikva, 1962-65; operating room nurse Yale U. Med. Ctr., New Haven, 1965-67; surg. nurse U. Chgo. Med. Ctr., 1968-75; rsch. asst. dept. child psychiatry U. Chgo., 1976-80, child and adolescent psychotherapist, 1980—2005, lectr. in psychiatry, 1988—2005. Psychiat. cons. Head Start, Chgo., 1979-80. Contbr. articles to profl. jours. Founder, pres. Ron's Teen Group, activities and support group for adolescents with cancer, 1986—. Mem. Am. Psychol. Assn., Am. Assn. Counseling Psychologists, Am. Counseling Assn., World Fedn. Mental Health. Avocations: music, art. Home: 1125 E 53rd St Chicago IL 60615-4410 Office: 30 N Mich Ave Ste 1004 Chicago IL 60602

KATZ, PHYLLIS ALBERTS, developmental research psychologist; 2 children. AB in Psychology summa cum laude, Syracuse U., 1957; PhD in Devel. Clin. Psychology, Yale U., 1961. Assoc. prof. psychology CUNY, 1969-72, chairperson devel. psychology sect. PhD program in edn., 1969-75, acting exec. officer PhD program in edn., 1974-75, prof., 1973-76; dir. Inst. Rsch. on Social Problems, Boulder, 1975—. Adj. prof. U. Colo., Boulder, 1980—. Author: The Feminist Dollar, 1997; editor: Towards the Elimination of Racism, 1976; co-editor: Eliminating Racism: Profiles in Controversy, 1988, Health Issues for Minority Adolescents, 1995; founding editor: Sex Roles: Jour. Rsch., 1976-91; editor: Jour. Social Issues, 1996-2000; mem. editl. bd. Devel. Psychology, 1992; contbr. chpts. on racism, gender-role rsch., and only-child rsch. to books; also numerous articles. Trustee Colo. Music Festival, 1982-84, pres. bd. trustees, 1984-85; mem. Colo. Women's Forum, 1992—; bd. dirs. Women's Found., Colo., 1986-92. USPHS trainee Yale U., 1956-59; grantee NYU Arts and Sci. Rsch., 1963-66, CUNY Faculty Rsch., 1973, Nat. Inst. Child Health Human Devel., 1966-68, 68-72, 79-81, 81-83, 87-91, 92-97, Office of Child Devel., 1972-75, NIMH, 1977-79, Carnegie Found., 1996-98. Mem. APA (editor jour. 1974-77, chmn. child advocacy com. 1973, mem. fin. com. 1990-93, coun. rep. 1983-86, 89-92, divsn. pres. 1986-87, fellow divsns. 7, 8, 9, 35 and 45, pres.-elect divsn. 35, editor 1996—), Soc. Rsch. in Child Devel., Assn. Women in Sci.

KATZ, SALLY NORMA, psychologist; b. Bklyn., Feb. 22, 1938; d. Jack and Hattie (Shapiro) Kleinrock; m. Norman Katz, Sept. 6, 1958; children: Jay, Mark E., Steven F. BA in Psycholoy, Rutgers U., 1975, MS in Social Psychology, 1977, PhD in Social Psychology, 1979. Cons. AT&T, Am. Mgmt. Assn., Rutgers Coll., Thomas Edison Coll., N.J., 1979-80, project mgr. Basking Ridge, N.J., 1980-83; mgr. Bellcore Profl. and Mgmt. Devel., Piscataway, N.J., 1983-87; mem. tech. staff Bellcore Access Interconnection and Intermediary Mkts., Livingston, N.J., 1987-94. Cons. Commn. on Aging, East Brunswick, N.J., 1978-92, Recreation and Parks Adv. Bd., 1979-92; part-time prof. Rutgers U., New Brunswick, 1986-87; group facilitator Women Aware, New Brunswick, 1988-95. Contbr. articles to profl. jours. Soroptomist League scholar, 1978; recipient Silver Mercury award N.J. Profl. Videos, New Brunswick, 1987, Hometown Heroes award United Way, New Brunswick, 1993. Mem. APA, Bus. and Profl. Womens Assn., Toastmasters Internat. Avocations: tennis, Bocce, travel, tai chi. Home: 33 Springlawn Dr Lakewood NJ 08701-7320

KATZ, SHARON, lawyer; b. 1950; BA, New Sch. Social Research, 1971; MS, Columia U. Sch. Social Work, 1975; JD summa cum laude, Brooklyn Law Sch., 1981. Bar: N.Y. 1982, registered: U.S. Dist. Ct. So. & Ea. Dist. N.Y. 1982, U.S. Ct. Appeals, Second Cir. 1989. Atty. Davis, Polk & Wardwell, N.Y.C., 1982—90, sr. atty., 1990—97, ptnr., 1997—, co-chmn. firm pro bono com. Law clk. to Hon. Thomas C. Platt, U.S. Dist. Ct., Ea. Dist. N.Y., 1981—82. Mem.: ABA. Office: Davis Polk & Wardwell 450 Lexington Ave New York NY 10017 Office Phone: 212-450-4508. Office Fax: 212-450-3508. Business E-Mail: sharon.katz@dpw.com.

KATZ, SUSAN ARONS, language arts specialist, writer, poet; b. N.Y.C., Dec. 3, 1939; d. Edward Maurice and Selma (Stark) Arons; m. Donald Ira Katz, June 20, 1961; children: David Lawrence, Elizabeth Cheryl. BFA, Ohio U., 1961. Poet-in-residence N.Y. State Poets in Pub. Svc., N.Y.C., 1975-96; book rev. editor Bitterroot Internat. Lit. Mag., 1985-91. Workshop dir. Lang. Arts Nat.-Internat. Workshops, U.S. and Can., 1995—; mem. reading panel Poets in Pub. Svc.; workshop coord. sr. citizen and intergenerational workshops Finklestein Meml. Libr., Spring Valley, NY, 1989; cons. Disney Interactive, 1996; invited guest poet Donnell Libr. Ctr., N.Y. Pub. Libr., 1980—90; presenter in field. Author: Teaching Creatively by Working the Word, 2d edit., 1996, The Word in Play, 2004, (poetry books) The Separate Sides of Need, 1984, Two Halves of the Same Silence, 1985, An Eye for Resemblances, 1991. Recipient Henry V. Larom prize Rockland C.C., 1976, Blue Ribbon award So. Poetry Assn., 1988; nominee Pushcart prize, 1976. Mem. Poetry Soc. Am., Conservatory of Am. Letters, Ga. Poetry Soc., Ariz. State Poetry Soc. (judge). Avocations: skiing, hiking, bike and horseback riding, sailing, gardening. Office Phone: 203-241-1836. E-mail: poetlady@earthlink.net.

KATZ, TONNIE, newspaper editor; BA, Barnard Coll., 1966; MSc, Columbia U., 1967. Editor, reporter newspapers including The Quincy Patriot Ledger, Boston Herald Am., Boston Globe; Sunday/projects editor Newsday; mng. editor Balt. News Am., 1983-86, The Sun, San Bernardino, Calif., 1986-88; asst. mng. editor for news The Orange County Register, Santa Ana, Calif., 1988-89, mng. editor, 1989-92, editor, v.p., 1992-98, editor, sr. v.p., 1998—. Office: Orange County Register 625 N Grand Ave Santa Ana CA 92701-4347

KATZ, VERA, former mayor, former college administrator, state legislator; b. Dusseldorf, Germany, Aug. 3, 1933; came to U.S., 1940; d. Lazar Pistrak and Raissa Goodman; m. Mel Katz (div. 1985); 1 child, Jesse. BA, Bklyn. Coll., 1955, postgrad., 1955-57; PhD (hon.), Lewis & Clark Coll., Portland State U., Oreg. Market research analyst TIMEX, B.T. Babbitt, N.Y.C., 1957-62; mem. Oreg. Ho. of Reps., Salem, 1985—91; former dir. devel. Portland Community Coll.; mayor City of Portland, Oreg., 1992—2004. Mem. Gov.'s Council on Alcohol and Drug Abuse Programs, Oreg. Legis., Salem, 1985—; mem. adv. com. Gov.'s Council on Health, Fitness and Sports, Oreg. Legis., 1985—; mem. Gov.'s Commn. on Sch. Funding Reform; mem. Carnegie task Force on Teaching as Profession, Washington, 1985-87; vice-chair assembly Nat. Conf. State Legis., Denver, 1986—2003. Recipient Abigail Scott Duniway award Women in Communications, Inc., Portland, 1985, Jeanette Rankin First Woman award Oreg. Women's Polit. Caucus, Portland, 1985, Leadership award The Neighborhood newspaper Portland, 1985, Woman of Achievement award Commn. for Women, 1985, Outstanding Legis. Advocacy award Oreg. Primary Care Assn., 1985, Service to Portland Pub. Sch. Children award Portland Pub. Schs., 1985, Visionary Leadership award, 1998, Legal Citizen of Yr. award, 2002. Fellow Am. Leadership Forum (founder Oreg. chpt.); mem. Dem. Legis. Leaders Assn., Nat. Bd. for Profl. Teaching Standards. Democrat. Jewish. Avocations: camping, jogging, dance. Office: Office of the Mayor City Hall 1221 SW 4th Ave Rm 340 Portland OR 97204-1995

KATZ, WENDY JEAN, art historian; b. LA, Sept. 26, 1966; d. William Gerald and Roslyn Leona Katz. BA in History, Occidental Coll., LA, 1988; MA in Art History, U. Mich., Ann Arbor, 1989; PhD in Art History, UCLA, 1997. Asst. prof. U. Nebr. Lincoln, 2000—05, assoc. prof., 2005—. Interim dir. Plains Humanities Alliance, Lincoln, 2005—. Author: (book) Regionalism & Reform: Art and Class Formation in Antebellum Cincinnati, Thomas Kinkade: Masterworks of Light; contbr. catalogue, articles to profl. jours. Mem. Ctr. for Gt. Plains Studies, Lincoln, 2003—, Internat. Quilt Study Ctr., Lincoln, 2005—. Humanities Fellowship, Mellon Found., 1988—91, Fellowship in Am. Art, Henry Luce/Am. Coun. Learned Societies, 1993—94, Postdoctoral Short-Term Fellowship, Clark Libr. and Ctr. for 17th- and 18th-Century Studies, 1999, Andrew Oliver Short-Term Rsch. Fellowship, Mass. Hist. Soc., 2004. Mem.: Am. Studies Assn., Coll. Art Assn., Phi Beta Kappa. Democrat-Npl. Office: Univ Nebr-Lincoln Dept Art & Art History 120 Richards Lincoln NE 68588-0114 Office Phone: 402-472-5545. Office Fax: 402-472-9746. Business E-Mail: wkatz2@unl.edu.

KATZ-BEARNOT, SHERRY P., psychiatrist, educator; BA, Barnard Coll., 1973; MD, Mt. Sinai, 1977. Mem.: Am. Acad. Psychoanalysis and Dynamic Psychiatry (pres. 2005—06), Am. Psychiatric Assn. Office: Ctr Psychoanalytic Training & Rsch Columbia U 1051 Riverside Dr New York NY 10032 Office Phone: 212-927-5000. Business E-Mail: spk1@columbia.edu.

KATZEN, SALLY, lawyer, educator; b. Pitts., Nov. 22, 1942; d. Nathan and Hilda (Schwartz) K.; m. Timothy B. Dyk, Oct. 31, 1981; 1 child, Abraham Benjamin. BA magna cum laude, Smith Coll., 1964; JD magna cum laude, U. Mich., 1967. Bar: D.C. 1968, U.S. Supreme Ct. 1971. Congl. intern Senate Subcom. on Constl. Rights, Washington, 1963; legal rsch. asst. civil rights divsn. Dept. Justice, Washington, 1965; law clk. to Judge J. Skelly Wright U.S. Ct. Appeals (D.C. cir.), 1967-68; assoc. Wilmer, Cutler & Pickering, Washington, 1968-75, ptnr., 1975-79, 81-93; gen. counsel Coun. on Wage and Price Stability, 1979-80, dep. dir. for policy, 1980-81; adminstr. Office of Info. and Regulatory Affairs Office of Mgmt. and Budget, Washington, 1993-98, counselor to the dir., 1999-2000, dep. dir. mgmt., 2000-2001; dep. dir. Nat. Econ. Coun., The White House, Washington, 1998-99; sr. policy advisor Joe Lieberman for Pres., 2003—04. Pub. mem. Adminstrv. Conf. U.S., 1988—93; adj. prof. Georgetown U. Law Ctr., 1988, 1990—92, govt. mem. and vice chmn., 1993—95; resident scholar and lectr. Smith Coll., 2001—04; vis. lectr., fellow Johns Hopkins U., 2002—04, 2006; adj. prof. U. Pa. Law Sch., 2003; vis. prof. U. Mich. Law Sch., 2004—06; lectr. U. Mich., 2005—06; vis. prof. George Mason U. Law Sch., 2006. Editor-in-chief U. Mich. Law Rev., 1966-67. Mem. com. visitors U. Mich. Law Sch., 1972—. Fellow ABA (ho. of dels. 1978-80, 89-91, coun. adminstrv. law sect. 1979-82, chmn. adminstrv. law and regulatory practice sect. 1988-89, governing com. forum com. comm. law 1979-82, chmn. standing com. Nat. Conf. Groups 1989-92); mem. D.C. Bar Assn., Prettyman-Leventhal Inn of Ct. (exec. com. 1988-90, counselor 1990-91), Women's Bar Assn., FCC Bar Assn. (exec. com. 1984-87, pres. 1990-91), Women's Legal Def. Fund (pres. 1977, v.p. 1978), Order of Coif. Home: 4638 30th St NW Washington DC 20008-2127 Personal E-mail: dykatzen@earthlink.net.

KATZEN-GUTHRIE, JOY, performance artist, engineering executive; b. Memphis, Nov. 11, 1958; d. Eli and Bess (Bloomfield) Katzen; m. Mark C. Guthrie, Aug. 7, 1983. BFA in Music cum laude, Stephens Coll., Columbia, Mo., 1980, BA in Comms. magna cum laude, 1980. Traffic dir. WPLP News/Talk Radio, Pinellas Park, Fla., 1981-83, ops. mgr., 1982-83; traffic reporter WUSA-FM and WDAE-AM, Tampa, Fla., 1985-86; announcer, programmer, pub. rels. mgr. WXCR-FM Classics 92, Safety Harbor, Fla., 1983-87; v.p., dir. Katzen and Guthrie Assocs., Inc., Palm Harbor, Fla., 1987—; pres. Tune-of-the-Century Music, 1989—. Creator, designer, owner website www.JoyfulNoise.net, 1998—. Co-author, composer musical comedy Once Around Manhattan, 1985; author: (one-act play) A Murder in Pine County, 1987; composer, lyricist some 750 songs; performance artist CD/Cassette albums Seasons of Joy, 1989, Heart of Ancient Promise, 1993, New State of Mind, 1993, How Good and Pleasant, 1996, Passages, 1998, SoulStream, 1998, Favorite Melody, 2005, A Steadfast Bridge, ltd. edit., 2005; studio vocalist Jeff Arthur Prodns., St. Petersburg, Fla., 1985, 86, Studio C. Prodns., Tampa, 1991-92; studio vocalist, jingle writer West End Rec., Tampa, 1989, 90; session musician Hurricane Pass Studios, Clearwater, Fla., 1993—. Music dir. religious sch. Temple B'nai Israel, Clearwater, 1988-89; music dir. Perry-Mansfield Performing Arts Camp, Steamboat Springs, Colo., 1987; cantorial soloist B'nai B'rith Hillel Found., Tampa, 1990-93, Temple Shir Shalom, Gainesville, 1994-99, Congregation B'nai Emmunah, Tarpon Springs, 1996-99, Congregation Aliyah, Clearwater, 1999-2000, Temple B'nai Israel, Clearwater, 2000-2002, 2005, Temple Beth El, Sarasota, 2002-2004. Recipient 1st and 3d place awards Memphis Songwriters Assn. Competition, 1988, others; Pinellas County Arts Coun. grantee, 1997, 2004. Mem. AAUW (dir. pub. rels. 1985-97), ASCAP, Songwriters

Guild Am., Dramatists Guild, Nat. Acad. Songwriters, Nashville Songwriters Assn. Internat., Guild of Temple Musicians, Fla. Music Assn., Women's Musicians' Alliance (bd. dirs. 1998—), Hadassah (life). Democrat. Jewish. Avocations: photography, travel, music, theater, films, books. Home and Office: 2487 Indian Trl E Palm Harbor FL 34683-2806 Office Phone: 727-785-4568, 800-354-1302. Personal E-mail: joyfulnoise@earthlink.net.

KATZIN, CAROLYN FERNANDA, nutritionist, consultant; b. London, July 21, 1946; came to U.S., 1983; naturalized US citizen, 1992. d. John Mourier and Shelagh B. A. (Tighe) Lade; m. Anthony Arthur Speelman, Mar. 18, 1968 (div. Dec. 1984); 1 child, Zara Jane. BS with honors, U. London, 1983; MS in Pub. Health, UCLA, 1988. Nutritionist, L.A., 1985—. Chair dean's adv. bd. UCLA Sch. Pub. Health, 1997-2005; mem. profl. adv. bd. The Wellness Cmty., L.A., 1998—; pres. DNA Diet Inc., 2005—. Author: The Advanced Energy Guide, 1994, The Good Eating Guide and Cookbook, 1996, The Cancer Nutrition Ctr. Handbook, 2001, 2d edit., 2003. Mem.: Am. Cancer Soc. (pres. Coastal Cities U. chpt. 1999—2002, bd.dir. Calif. divsn. 2002—, adv. group nat. nutrition, physical activity and cancer control 2002—, v.p. cert. bd. for nutrition specialists 2005—). Democrat. Jewish. Office: 12011 San Vicente Blvd Ste 402 Los Angeles CA 90049-4946 Office Phone: 310-471-0529. Personal E-mail: carolyn@carolynkatzin.com.

KATZMAN, ANITA, writer; b. N.Y.C., Feb. 6, 1920; d. Louis and Sylvia (Fox) Butensky; m. Nathan Katzman, Mar. 29, 1942 (dec. 1965); children: Mark, Drew, Bruce, Mindi. BA, N.Y. U., 1940. Author: My Name is Mary 1975. Founders Bd. Asolo Performing Arts Ctr., Sarasota Fla.; Bd. Dirs. Asolo Theater Festival Assn.; Devel. Bd. USF Gerontology Ctr., Tampa Fla., Sarasota-Manatee Jewish Found., Sarota Fla., Fla. Council Libraries. Recipient GTE Community Adv. Panel 1973, Community Acheivement award Women's Resource Ctr. Sarasota 1988, West Coast Woman Newspaper Sarasota 1989. Mem. The Author's Guild, The Author's League Am., Pan Pacific & Southeast Women's Assn., Lotos Club, Univ. Club Sarasota, Longboat Key Club. Democratic. Avocation: historic restorations. Office: 10838 Marine View Dr SW Seattle WA 98146

KATZMAN, CHARLOTTE PHYLLIS, realtor; b. Bklyn., Dec. 26, 1937; d. Benjamin and Rose Simon Katzman; children: Jonathan Oscher, Suzanne Goldman, Andrea Frenkel. BA cum laude, Bklyn. Coll., 1958, student, 1958—59, Wayne State U., 1959—61. Speech pathologist N.Y. City Schs., 1958—59, Clarenceville Pub. Schs., Mich., 1959—62; personal asst. D.P. Bro. and Co., Detroit, 1962—64; sales Lord & Taylor, Novi, Mich., 1976—78; travel cons. Condo & Villa Authority, Walled Lake, Mich., 1985—96; realtor Century 21 Today, Inc., Bloomfield Hills, Mich., 2004—. Dir.: DRIS Drama Troupe, 1997—; chmn.: Congregation B'nai Moshe Jours., 2000—04. Mem.: North Oakland County Bd. Realtors, Women's League Conservative Judaism (past pres. Mich. br.), Sisterhood B'nai Moshe, Hadassah (life). Avocations: travel, bridge, reading, horseback riding, tennis. Office: Century 21 Today Inc 6755 Telegraph Rd Ste 200 Bloomfield Hills MI 48302 Office Phone: 248-283-2275.

KATZOWITZ SHENFIELD, LAUREN, philanthropy consultant; m. Marc Shenfield. BS in Comparative Lit. with honors, Brandeis U., 1970; MS with honors, Columbia U., 1971. With Newsweek mag.; then with Phila. Bull.; freelance writer, editor, cons., until 1975; cons. Ford Found., 1972-75; mgr. PBS programs Exxon Corp., 1978-81; mgr. Exxon Rsch. and Engring. Co., 1981-84; regional liaison for Europe and Africa, Exxon Corp., 1984-86; exec. dir. Philanthropy Advisors - A Svc. of UJA-Fedn. of N.Y., 1986—; pres. Lauren Katzowitz Cons., Croton on Hudson, NY, 1986—. Mem. profl. adv. coun. Met. Mus. of Art, 2000-06, Central Park Conservancy, 2001—; bd. dirs. N.Y. Regional Assn. of Grantmakers, 2000—, Women and Philanthropy, 2003-06. Named one of 12 Women to Watch in the Eighties, Ladies' Home Jour., 1979. Office: Philanthropy Advisors 130 E 59th St New York NY 10022 Office Phone: 212-836-1358. Personal E-mail: katzowitzl@philanthropyadvisorsny.org.

KAUFER, CONNIE TENORIO, special education educator, researcher; b. Saipan, No. Mariana Islands, June 12, 1945; d. Lino Pangelinan and Magdalena Faosto (Arriola) Tenorio; m. Leonard James Kaufer, Jan. 20, 1974; 1 child, Lucile Tenorio. AA in Elem. Edn., Chaffey Coll., 1968; BS in Lang. Arts, Calif. State Poly. U., 1971; MA in Edn., San Jose State U., 1983. Cert. tchr., Calif., Mariana Islands. Elem. tchr. Marianas Dept. Edn., Chalan Kanoa, Saipan, Mariana Islands, 1964-66, 74-76, 80-84, elem. and h.s. tchr., 1970-71, elem. sch. supr. Lower Base, Saipan, 1971-74, elem. sch. prin. Tanapag Village, Saipan, 1979-80; comprehensive lang. arts skills project dir. Pub. Sch. Sys., Lower Base, Saipan, 1984-87, reading specialist, 1984-94, trainer Marianas instrument for obs. of tchr. activities, 1986—94, trainer onward to excellence, 1988—94; ret., 1994. Part-time instr. U. Guam Ext., No. Marianas Coll., Saipan, 1993—; sec. Diocesan Bd. Edn. Saipan, 1985-90; trainer pacific region pacific effective schs. Pacific Region Edn. Lab., Honolulu and Saipan, 1991-93; presenter in field. Mem. Mariana Islands rep. Trust Ter. Curriculum Coun., Saipan, 1970-72; coord. cross cultural Peace Corps, Saipan, 1973, coord. Chamorro lang., 1975; pres. Chalan Kanoa Sch. Saipan Tchrs. Assn., 1981-83. Scholar Marianas Edn. Found., 1966-70, Bilingual Edn. scholar Trust Ter. Dept. Edn., 1975. Mem. ASCD, AAUW, Internat. Reading Assn. (Saipan chpt. pres. 1975-76), Pacific Islands Bilingual/Bicultural Assn., Phi Delta Kappa. Roman Catholic. Avocations: raising orchids, cooking, baking. Home: PO Box 7611 Saipan MP 96950

KAUFER, SHIRLEY HELEN, artist, painter; b. Bklyn., Oct. 3, 1920; m. Bernard Goldberg, Apr. 18, 1943; children: Alice, Marjorie. Art dir. Advt. Agys., N.Y.C., 1938-63; art cons. N.Y.C., 1964-73; sculptor Vero Beach, Fla., 1973-77; graphic designer Jewish Fedn. Coun., L.A., 1977-82. With Haystack Mt. Art Colony, Deer Isle, Maine, summers 1959-73; instr. advt., design, illustration Pels Art Sch., N.Y.C., 1968-71; instr. painting Indian River C.C., Vero Beach, 1973-77. Represented in permanent art collection pf UCLA Med. Ctr., L.A.; exhibited in numerous nat. and internat. galleries; 2 films produced on her life and works. Home: 1029 Via De La Paz Pacific Palisades CA 90272-3534 Office Phone: 310-454-4636.

KAUFFMAN, JENN, band director; b. Reno, Nev., Aug. 5, 1979; d. Leslie and Louis Lawson (Stepfather). B in Music Edn., U. Okla., Norman, 2003. Dir. of bands Maysville Pub. Schs., Okla., 2003—06, Blanchard Pub. Schs., Okla., 2006—. Com. head Blanchard Centennial Celebration, 2006—. Named Tchr. of Yr., Maysville Pub. Schs., 2004—05. Mem.: South Ctrl. Band Dirs. Assn. (pres. 2005—06).

KAUFFMAN, MARTA, producer, writer; m. Michael Skloff. B.A., Brandeis University, 1978. With Bright-Kauffman-Crane Prodns., Burbank, Calif. Creator, prodr., writer Dream On, 1990-96; creator, exec. prodr. Friends, 1994-2004 (Emmy nominee 1995, 96), Veronica's Closet, 1997-2000, Jesse, 1998-2000; lyricist Friends theme I'll Be There for You.

KAUFFMAN, TERRY, broadcast and creative arts communication educator, artist; b. San Francisco, Aug. 24, 1951; d. Raymond Roger and Patricia Virginia Kauffman. BA in Journalism with honors, U. Calif., Berkeley, 1974; MA in Comm. summa cum laude, U. Tex., 1980; PhD in Psychology, Comm., and Creative Expression and Therapy with distinction, Union Inst., Cin., 1996. With Alta. Ednl. TV, 1976; sr. writer, prodr., dir. Ampex Corp., Calif., 1980; writer, news prodr., reporter, anchor ABC, Tex., 1974-75; mem. faculty dept. radio, TV and motion pictures U. N.C., Chapel Hill, 1985; mem. faculty dept. comm. N.C. State U., Raleigh, 1986—2001; founder, artist Cards by Terry, N.C. Mus. Art, 2004—. Adj. prof. music, theatre and comm. dept. Meredith Coll., Raleigh, 1990—, tchr. art, 1995—; adv. bd., chmn. publicity Raleigh Conservatory Music; v.p. Wake Visual Arts Assn. and Gallery; founder, owner Creative Spaces; founder Cozy Cards by Terry Kauffman, 2003; expressive art therapist at psychiat. hosps. and pvt., 1994—; pens, ink, watercolor artist, tchr., 1996—; art for exec. dir. Auditory Learning Ctr., 2000—; featured interviewee, artist in jours., TV series; writer in field; radio talk show guest. Author: I'm Clueless, Confessions of a College Teacher, The Script as Blueprint, 1994, The Script as Blueprint: Writing for Radio, Television, Film, and Video, 1996, (book) Beside Myself, 2006, The Perfect Camellia, 2006, 8 vol. set poetry including Psalms of Teresa, Secret Place, Just Visiting, others, numerous poems; prodr., dir., writer, composer I'm One Person.Or The Other, Thanksgiving (PBS), 1980—, prodr., dir. Coming Home, 1973 (1st place, creativity in directing); writer, prodr.: Consumer Reports, ABC affiliate, Tex., 1975; writer, prodr. Consumer Hotline, PBS, Customs Operations at the Border; writer, prodr.: Consumer Hotline, PBS, Animal, Vegetable, Mineral, Chemical?, 1979; main character, vocalist, composer Little Miss Puppet Talks to the Angels, pub. (music book) Songs by Terry Kauffman, composer, prodr., dir. When the Wind Blows, The Rainbow (First Pl. Nat. award), The Seasons of Change, PBS, Woman Today, Profiles in Leadership, Little Miss Puppet Talks to the Angels, I'm One Person or Another, One, writer, prodr., dir., set designer (PBS family drama) Thanksgiving, 1980, San Francisco, Raleigh; artist for documentary series, rschr., writer, Alta., Can., 1976; prodr., set designer: (PBS comedy) The Bathroom, 1981; prodr.: (documentaries) Otters from Oiled Waters, 1991, and others; The Benefit to Raise Spirits, Hist. Oakwood Art Soc., Raleigh, Healing Spiral, N.C. State U.; contbr. articles to profl. jours. Singer/composer for chs. and retirement homes; pub. rels. vol. N.C. Mus. Art, 2002—, pub. rels. com. mem., cmty. outreach vol., 2005; vol. silver arts judge N.C. Sr. Games; vol. Univ. Pk. Nat. Hist. Dist., 2000—, N.C. Sr. Games; past bd. dirs. Tex. Consumer Assn., Wake Visual Arts. Named Outstanding Lectr. of Yr., Coll. of Humanities and Social Scis., N.C. State U., 1996; recipient Emmy nomination for documentary Otters from Oiled Waters, 1991, more than 15 1st place nat. awards in TV, including writing, producing, directing, music composition, acting, art and photography, vrious art and music shows, First Pl. award in Acrylic Painting, N.C. State U., 1995, One of Nine Finalists for Outstanding Tchr., Coll. of Humanities and Social Scis., N.C. State U., 1999, Nat. Video award, 1997, cert. from students, N.C. State U., 1999, plaque from students, 1999. Mem. APA, NATAS, Internat. TV Assn. (judge nat. contests), Nat. Broadcasting Soc. (8 1st place nat. awards 1973—, cert. merit Curriculum Devel. and Enrichment, 1993, named Outstanding Mem., 1993-94, Profl. Mem. of Yr. 1994), Internat. Expressive Art Therapists Assn., Calif. Scholastic Fedn. (life), Berkeley Honor Soc., Am. Psychol. Assn., Woman's Club of Raleigh, Phi Kappa Phi. Achievements include created early computer art animation at Ampex corporation headquarters. Home: 407 Furches St Raleigh NC 27607-4017 Office Phone: 919-612-3303.

KAUFFOLD, RUTH ELIZABETH, psychologist; b. Decatur, Ill., Sept. 5, 1946; d. James Henry and Elizabeth Opal Kauffold; m. Paul Dwight Entner, Aug. 23, 1968; 1 child, James Paul. BA, Cedarville Coll., Ohio, 1968; MEd, Wright State U., 1972; MS, U. Dayton, 1986; PhD, The Union Inst., 1997. Tchr. Springfield Pub. Schs., Ohio, 1968—72, Pomona Unified Sch. Dist., Calif., 1973—76, Bethel Sch. Dist., New Carlisle, Ohio, 1977—81; practicum Sycamore Hosp., Miamisburg, Ohio, 1994; intern, resident clin. psychology Agape Counseling Ctr., Centerville, 1995—2000. Co-hostess talk show Radio Sta. WHIO, Dayton, 1998; guest speaker Think TV, 2005—; lectr., spkr. in field. Active Missionary Project Ptnr., Lima, Peru, 1986; tchr. Far Hills Bapt. Ch., Dayton, Ohio, 1997, Fair Haven Ch., 2000-04 Jennings scholar Martha Holden Jennings Found., 1972. Mem. APA, AACC, Dayton Area Psychol. Assn. Avocations: interior design, architecture, gardening, reading, walking. Office: Agape Counseling Ctr 175 S Main St Centerville OH 45458-2372

KAUFMAN, AMY, film company executive, film producer; Degree in Internat. Rels., U. Pa. Asst. to prodr. Scott Rudin; with Miramax; dir. acquisitions Good Machine Internat., 1997—98, v.p. sales and acquisitions, 1998, v.p. acquisitions and co-prodns.; sr. v.p. acquisitions and co-prodns. Good Machine Internat. (now Focus Features), 2001—02, Focus Features, 2002—03, exec. v.p. acquisitions and co-prodns., 2003—04, exec. v.p. prodn. N.Y.C., 2004—. Assoc. prodr.: Buffalo Soldiers, 2001; exec. prodr.: Y Tu Mama Tambien, 2001. Named to, Crain's N.Y. Bus. "40 under 40", 2004. Office: Focus Features 2nd Fl 65 Bleecker St New York NY 10012

KAUFMAN, ANGELA J., music educator; b. Freeman, SD, Jan. 29, 1962; d. Larry Duane and Lois Marie Kaufman; m. Robert Ronald Perkinson, Sept. 20, 1991; children: Robert, Nyshie, Shane. AA, Freeman Jr. Coll., 1982; BA in Music Edn., U. Sioux Falls, 1984. Instr. 5-12 grade band Montrose (S.D.) H.S., SD, 1984—86; instr. 9-12 grade band Freeman Acad., 1986—87; tchr. 4-6 grade vocal/band Sioux Falls Pub. Schs., SD, 1986—96, tchr. K-5 grade vocal/band, 1996—97; tchr. music Angela's Sch. Music, Canton, SD, 1998—2001; tchr. K-4 gen. music, h.s. jazz band Canton Schs., 2001—02. Judge vocal contest and all state chorus, various cities, S.D., 1989-97. Musician (CDs) God Talks, 1999, Peace Will Come, 2002, On the Cross, 2004; co-creator (original music/drama duo) Are You Listening?, 1989. Recipient John Philip Sousa award, Marion H.S., 1980. Mem. NEA, Music Tchrs. Nat. Assn., Am. Choral Dirs. Assn., Music Educators Assn., S.D. Bandmasters Assn. Home: 1026 E 1st St Canton SD 57013 also: PO Box 159 Canton SD 57013-0159

KAUFMAN, ANTOINETTE DOLORES, information technology manager; b. Phila., Mar. 10, 1939; d. Joseph and Maria Falcone; m. John R. Kaufman, Apr. 30, 1988. Student, St. Joseph's U., 1968. With N.W. Ayer & Son, Inc., NYC, 1956-81; adminstrv. asst. N.W. Ayer ABH Internat., 1960, asst. corp. sec., 1977, corp. sec., 1978-79, stock transfer agt., 1969-79, info. specialist, 1979-81; exec. v.p., sec., creative dir., COO Help Bus. Svcs., Inc., Swarthmore, Pa., 1981—. Mem.: Pa. State U. Alumni Assn. (life), Navy League US (life), Union League of Phila. Avocations: ballroom dancing, cooking, violin, piano, gardening. Office: Help Bus Svcs Inc 110 Park Ave HBS Bldg Swarthmore PA 19081 Office Phone: 610-544-9787. E-mail: hbsswarthmore@hotmail.com.

KAUFMAN, BEL, author, educator; b. Berlin; d. Michael J. and Lala (Rabinowitz) K.; divorced; children: Jonathan Goldstine, Thea Goldstine. BA magna cum laude, Hunter Coll., 1934; DHL, Hunter Coll, 2001; MA with highest honors, Columbia U., 1936; LLD honors, Nasson Coll., Maine, 1965. Adj. prof. English CUNY; lectr. throughout country, also appearances on TV and radio. Mem. Commn. Performing Arts. Editorial bd., Phi Delta Kappan.; Author: Up the Down Staircase, 1965, Love, etc, 1979; also short stories, articles, TV play, translations from Russian, lyrics for musicals. Bd. dirs. Shalom Aleichem Found.; adv. council Town Hall Found. Recipient plaque Anti-Defamation League, award and plaque United Jewish Appeal, Paperback of Year award, Ky. Col. award, Bell Movie award, Nat. Treasure awrd Seasoned Citizens Theatre, 2001; also ednl. journalism awards; named to Hall of Fame Hunter Coll., winner short story contest sponsored by NEA and PEN, 1983. Mem. Author's Guild, Dramatists Guild, P.E.N., English Grad. Union, Phi Beta Kappa. Address: 1020 Park Ave New York NY 10028-0913 Personal E-mail: belkau@aol.com.

KAUFMAN, CHARLOTTE KING, artist; b. Balt., Dec. 5, 1920; d. Ben and Belle (Turow) King; m. Albert Kaufman, July 22, 1945; children: Matthew King, Ezra King. AB, Goucher Coll., 1969; MPH, Johns Hopkins U., 1972, MEd, 1976. Dir. pub. rels. Balt. Jewish Cmty. Ctr., 1962-67; rschr., editor Johns Hopkins U. Sch. Hygiene and Pub. Health, Balt., 1969-72, admissions officer, 1972-74, dir. admissions and registrar, 1974-86, dir. study cons. program for undergrads., 1985-89, pub. health acad. adviser, 1989-95; studio artist, Palm Desert, Calif., 1996—. Mem. APHA, Am. Assn. for Higher Edn., Am. Assn. Collegiate Registrars and Admissions Officers, Artists Equity Assn. (v.p. Md. chpt. 1988-90), Md. Printmakers (exec. bd. 1989-94), Palm Springs Desert Mus. Artists Coun. (exec. bd. 1997-2003), Delta Omega. Democrat. Jewish. Home: Monterey Country Club 159 Las Lomas Palm Desert CA 92260-2153 E-mail: kaufmanchar@dc.rr.

KAUFMAN, DONNA A., elementary school educator; b. Chgo., Ill. m. David Kaufman, July 3, 1971; children: Jonathan, Kimberly. BS in Edn., U. Okla.; postgrad., Adelphi U. 2d grade tchr. Louisa May Alcott, Chgo., 1981—96, 1st grade tchr., 1996—. Coach Chgo. area problem solving primary team, 2004—06; foundir, dir., social com. chair Sci. Club, 2004—06; tchr., leadership cohort organic sch. project DePaul U., 2005—06. Mem. Wrightwood Neighbors, 1987—, Friends Alcott, 1987—; local sch. coun. rep. DePaul U. Tchr. Leader Team. Rochelle Lee Reading grantee, Friends Alcott grantee, Park West Cmty. grantee, Wrightwood Neighbors Assn. grantee, Linking Lang. Making Music grantee. Mem.: ASCD, NEA, Nat. Sci. Tchr. Assn., Chgo. Tchrs. Union. Avocations: beading, knitting, gardening, hiking. Office: Louisa May Alcott Sch 2625 N Orchard Chicago IL 60614 Personal E-mail: dkaufman04@hotmail.com.

KAUFMAN, FRANCINE R., pediatric endocrinologist; m. Neal Kaufman; children: Adam, Jonah. B., Northwestern U., 1972; MD, Chgo. Med. Sch., 1976. Cert. pediatric endocrinology & metabolism. Intern Childrens Hosp. Los Angeles, 1976—77, resident, 1977—78, fellow, 1978—80, attending physician, head of Ctr. for Endocrinology, Diabetes & Metabolism; dir. Comprehensive Childhood Diabetes Ctr., Los Angeles; prof. pediatrics Univ. So. Calif. Keck Sch. Medicine. Diplomat Am. Bd. Pediatrics; co-principal investigator Keck Diabetes Prevention Initiative, Los Angeles; med. adv. bd. Mini-Med Technologies, 1993—2001, 2003—, Eli Lilly Corp., 1998—, Novo Nordisk, 1999—, Life Scan, Inc., 2000—01, 2003—; editorial bd. Internat. Diabetes Monitor, 1994—95, 1998—, Diabetes Forecast, 1998—, Diabetes Reviews, 1998—, Current Diabetes Reports, 2001—, Pediatric Diabetes, 2002—, DOC News, 2004—. Author: Diabesity, 2005; contbr. scientific papers, chapters to books. Del. WHO Assembly, Geneva, 2002, Calif. Task Force on Childhood Obesity; chair Los Angeles County Task Force on Children & Youth Physical Fitness, 2002; Calif. del. to Healthy Sch. Summit in Washington DC, 2003; chair Studies to Treat or Prevent Type 2 Diabetes in Youth (STOPP-T2); sci. adv. group Am. Diabetes Assn., 1997—, programs com., 1997—, bd. dirs., 1993—96, 2000, chair, Task Force on Health Care Reform, 1993—95, chair, Task Force on Signature Advocacy, 1993—94, chair, Pub. Policy Leadership Forum, 1995—96, Profl. Ed. Project Team, 1999—, Task Force on Schools, 2002—03, nominating com., 2003—04, pres., 2002—03; active Juvenile Diabetes Assn., Nat. Diabetes Ed. Program, Internat. Diabetes Fedn., Ctr. Disease Control & Prevention, UNESCO, NIH; profl. & patient ed. com. Am. Diabetes Assn. Los Angeles Chpt., 1985—, bd. dirs., 1986—, pres, 1988—90, caper com., 1986—, fundraising com., 1990—; pub. seminar com. Am. Diabetes Assn. Calif. Affiliate, 1985—, bd. dirs., 1988—, exec. com., 1991—, pres., 1996—97. Recipient Woman of Valor award, Am. Diabetes Assn., 2003, Banting Medal, 2003, Albert Renold award, European Assn. for the Study of Diabetes, 2003. Mem.: AAP (Endocrine exec. com. 1998—, Task Force on Obesity), Inst. Medicine. Achievements include invention of Extend Bar. Office: Childrens Hospital Los Angeles MS #1 4650 Sunset Blvd Los Angeles CA 90027 E-mail: fkaufman@chla.usc.edu.

KAUFMAN, NADEEN LAURIE, clinical psychology educator, writer; b. N.Y.C., Jan. 17, 1945; d. Seymour and Hannah (Chafetz) Bengels; m. Alan Stephen Kaufman, Dec. 20, 1964; children: Jennie Lynn, David Scott, James Corey. BS, Hofstra U., 1965; MA, Columbia U., 1972, MEd, 1975, EdD, 1978. Cert. tchr., sch. psychologist. Rsch. cons. Coll. Entrance Examination Bd., N.Y.C., 1970-73; psychologist Rutland Psychoednl. Ctr., Athens, Ga., 1975-78; asst. prof. edn. U. Ga., Athens, 1978-79; asst. prof. psychology DePaul U., Chgo., 1979-80; assoc. prof. psychology Nat. Coll. Edn., Evanston, Ill., 1980-82, Calif. Sch. Profl. Psychology, San Diego, 1982-84; dir. psychoednl. clinic Mesa Vista Hosp., San Diego, 1992-94; clin. psychology prof. Calif. Sch. Profl. Psychology, San Diego, 1994—97; lectr. Yale U., 1997—. Author: (with Alan Kaufman) Clinical Evaluation of Young Children, 1977, Specific Learning Disabilities and Difficulties in Children and Adolescents, 2001, K-ABC-II, KTEA-II and other tests. Fellow APA, Am. Psychol. Soc.; mem. NASP, Coun. for Exceptional Children, Am. Ednl. Rsch. Assn. Avocation: writing fiction. Office: Yale U Child Study Ctr 230 S Frontage Rd New Haven CT 06520

KAUFMAN, PAULA T., librarian; b. Perth Amboy, NJ, July 26, 1946; d. Harry and Clara (Katz) K.; m. L. Ratner, 1989. AB, Smith Coll., 1968; MS, Columbia U., 1969; MBA, U. New Haven, 1979. Reference libr. Columbia U., NYC, 1969-70, bus. libr., 1979-82, dir. libr. svcs., 1982-86, dir. acad. info. svcs., 1986-87, acting v.p., univ. libr., 1987-88; dean of librs. U. Tenn., Knoxville, 1988-99; univ. libr. U. Ill., Urbana Champaign, 1999—, interim chief info. officer, 2006—. Reference coord. McKinsey & Co., N.Y.C., 1970—73; founder, ptnr. Info. for Bus., N.Y.C., 1973—76; prin. reference libr. Yale U., New Haven, 1976—79; bd. dir. Ctr. Rsch. Libr., 1994—2000, chmn., 1996—97; bd. dirs. CAUSE, 1996—98; bd. dir. Assn. Rsch. Libr., 1997—2003, v.p., pres.-elect, 2000—01, pres., 2001—02; bd. dir. ILCSO, 2000—04, chair, 2001—02; bd. dirs. Coun. on Libr. and Info. Resources, 2001—, vice chair, 2001—. Contbr. articles to mags., 1983—. Bd. dirs. Cmty. Shares, Knoxville, 1993—97, Lincoln Trails Libr. Sys., Champaign, Ill., 2001—; bd. trustees Champaign (Ill.) Pub. Libr., 2004—. Mem. ALA, Soc. for Scholarly Pub., Solinet (bd. dirs., chmn. 1992-93). Office: U Ill 230 Main Libr 1408 W Gregory Dr Urbana IL 61801-3607*

KAUFMAN, SHIRONA, cantor, educator; b. Bklyn., Apr. 25, 1953; d. Uriel and Annette (Berger) Levy; m. Berl H. Kaufman (div.); children: Lianne, Leora. BFA, SUNY, Purchase, 1980. Music tchr. Temple Israel Ctr., White Plains, NY, 1999—2001, Westchester Reform, Scarsdale, 2001—04; Cantor Congregation KTI, Port Chester, 2004—. Cantor Ahavat Achim, Colchester, Conn., 2001—04. Composer, prodr.: songs Shirona: Judaic Love Songs, 2000 (Best Jewish Album, Jewish Week, 2001), Songs of the Heart and Spirit, 2002; composer: Shabbat Anthology; contbr. articles to profl. jours. Mem.: Hanashir Music Network, Women Cantor's Network. Home: Apt 9 20 Chestnut St Rye NY 10580-2853 Office Phone: 914-967-4338. Personal E-mail: shirona@bellatlantic.net.

KAUFMAN, SUSAN NANETTE BLAND, secondary school educator; b. Medicine Lodge, Kans., Nov. 23, 1961; d. Marvin Lee and Leora Jean (Ruggles) Bland; m. Alan Keith Kaufman, Aug. 4, 1984; children: Kristen Leigh, Kelli Bryn. BA, Bethany Coll., 1983; MS, Kans. State U., 1984. Cert. K-12 gifted elem. tchr., 7-12 English, 7-12 art, k-12 phys. edn., Tex. Gifted edn. tchr. Valley Ctr. (Kans.) Pub. Schs., 1984-88; elem. tchr. Maize (Kans.) Unified Sch. Dist. # 266, 1988—95; jr. high tchr. Hurst Euless Bedford Ind. Sch. Dist., 1995—97; art tchr., coach Trinity HS, Euless, Tex., 1997—. Mem. Crown of Life Luth. Ch. Mem. Tex. Nat. Edn. Assn. (resolution com. 1984-92, student NEA pres. 1983-84), Tex. Girls Coaching Assn., Am. Volleyball Coaches Assn. Avocations: reading, drawing, crafts, sports. Home: 3809 Horizon Dr Bedford TX 76021-2630 Office: Trinity HS 500 N Industrial Blvd Euless TX 76039

KAUFMAN, SUSAN SHIFFMAN, psychologist; b. Bklyn., Mar. 26, 1954; d. Harvey Benjamin and Shirley Shiffman; m. Steven Robert Kaufman, Sept. 24, 1978; 1 child, Samantha Eve. BS cum laude, Bklyn Coll., 1975; MS, St. John's U., 1976, PD, 1977; MPhil, CUNY, 1979, PhD, 1990. Cert. sch. psychologist N.Y., 1977. Rsch. asst. dept. psychology Bklyn Coll., 1974—75; sch. psychology intern Coney Island Hosp., Bklyn., 1976—77; psychodiagnostic screener and evaluator Glen Cove Pub. Schs., NY, 1977; cons. in sch. psychology N.Y.C. Bd. of Edn., Bklyn., Queens, 1977—83; ind. profl. reviewer N.Y. State Dept. of Mental Hygiene, 1977; learning disability tutor Kingsborough C.C., Bklyn., 1978; sch. psychologist Mid. Country Ctrl. Sch. Dist. #11, Centereach, NY, 1978, Lindenhurst Pub. Schs., NY, 1980—. Workshop presenter Lindenhurst Pub. Schs., NY, 1981—, psychology budget coord., 1984—, psychologist interview com. for new hires, 1985—, mentor to new psychologists, 1990—, inclusion com. mem., 1993—, supr. psychology interns and sch. psychology PhD students, 1995—2003, co-author psychologist policy and procedure manual, 1999—, universal presch. com., 2002—03, com. on spl. edn. chairperson, 2002—. Contbr. conf. workshop. Mem. Syosset Pk. Civic Assn., NY, 1995—, sec., bd. dirs., 1997—2004; corresponding sec., exec. bd. Village Elem. Sch. PTA, NY, 1996—98; mem. Residents for a More Beautiful Syosset, NY, 1999—. Mem.: NASP. Home: 1 Pine Rd Syosset NY 11791 Office: Lindenhurst Pub Schs 350 Daniel St Lindenhurst NY 11757 Office Phone: 631-226-6894. Office Fax: 631-226-6428. Personal E-mail: sskaufman@aol.com. Business E-Mail: skaufm@lindenhurstschools.org.

KAUFMAN, SUZANNE DRYER, art educator, artist, writer; b. Indpls., Oct. 10, 1927; d. Gerald and Iola (Callier) Mahalowitz; m. Joseph G. Dryer, Oct. 18, 1948 (div. 1964); children: Janet Dryer Perez, Jeffrey (dec.), Joel. Student, Purdue U., 1944-46; BA, Rockford Coll., 1965; MA, No. Ill. U., 1968. Cert. tchr., Ill. Asst. editor William H. Block & Co., "Block's Booster", Indpls., 1946-49; tchr. art Rockford (Ill.) Sch. Dist., 1965-70; instr., asst. prof., assoc. prof., prof. art Rock Valley Coll., Rockford, Ill., 1970-90, prof. emeritus, 1990—; lectr. Rockford Coll.; art critic New Art Examiner, Rockford Register Star, WREX-TV; cons. A.C.T.S. Inc., Glencoe, Ill.; judge for juried art competitions; lectr. in field; over 400 art works in pub. and pvt. collections including 1000 sq. ft. mosiac mural, Greater Rockford Airport (won competition 1988), 14 one man shows, 53 group and invitational exhibits, 31 juried exhibits; author essay: In Plain Sight, 1993; contbr. articles to prof. jours. including Hali Mag. Initiator gift fund and presentation Lindisfarne Gospels from Rockford Coll. to Holy Island, Eng., 1970; mem. visual arts panel Ill. Arts Council, 1975; mem. Mayor's Urban Design Rev. Com., Rockford, 1974-76, sculpture com. for Rockford Symbol, 1974-77; co-founder Rockford Gifted Child Assn.; v.p., sec. Rockford Art Assn. bd., 1972-82; mem. Rockford Hosp. Vols. bd., 1959-64; bd. dirs., v.p., sec. chmn. center mgmt. com. Jewish Community Center, 1960-65; vol. Highland Park Hosp., 1955-59; mem. Ind. Jewish Cmty. Rels. bd., 1948-52; chmn. Indpls. Jewish Community Center adult activities, 1950-52; bd. dirs. Rock Valley Coll. Found., 1990—, Riverfront Mus. Park, 1990—, Rockford Symphony Orch., 1990-96; pres. Chgo. Rug Soc., 1995-2004; mem. alumni bd. Rockford Coll., 1997-2000; mem. Winnebogo County Crime and Pub. Safety Commn., 2004—. Recipient Outstanding Vol. of Yr. award Sinnissippi Lung Assn., 1983, 84; 10 Yr. Svc. award Rockford Art Assn., 1982; numerous svc. awards from Rockford Meml. Hosp., Highland Park Hosp., Temple Beth El Sisterhood; 15 Yr. Svc. award Rock Valley Coll.; named Disting. Alumnus of Yr., No. Ill. U., 1985, also award for outstanding profl. achievement Dept. Art Alumni, 1985, award of Distinction, Rockford Coll., 1999. Home: 240 Market St Rockford IL 61107-3954

KAUFMAN, VICKI, civil rights investigator; b. Quincy, Mass., June 29, 1941; d. Edwin Manuel and Althea Beatrice (Cohen) Kaufman; m. Robert J. Carolan, June 1, 1963 (div. Sept. 25, 1970); children: Wendy Katherine Badger, Amy Elizabeth Speer; m. Kenneth H. Hill, Mar. 28, 1992. BA, Boston U., 1963. Tchr. Sch. Dists. of Rye, N.H. and Sumter, S.C., 1964-68; curriculum libr. U. Tenn., Nashville, 1969-71; sales/office mgr. The Jaques Co., Inc., Boston, 1972-88; civil rights investigator DHHS, Boston, 1989—. Site coord. Serve, Inc,. Derry, N.H., 1992—; founder, pres., bd. dirs. South Shore Coalition for Human Rights, Quincy, 1977—; pres., bd. dirs. Cmty. Ch. Boston, 1985-89, Dove, Inc., Shelter for Abused Women, Quincy, 1981-2001; ward 3 chair, bd. dirs. Quincy Rep. Com., 1975-89. Recipient Drylong-so award Cmty. Change, 1993, Regional award NCCJ, 1981. Mem. ASPA (bd. officer, treas. 1993—), Boston U. Alumni Assn. (pres. 1982-85, bd. dirs.). Avocations: reading, music, community service. Office: Office for Civil Rights Dept Health and Human Svcs JFK Bldg Rm 1875 Boston MA 02203 Home: 49 E Emerson St Melrose MA 02176-3542

KAUFMANN, VICKI MARIE, social services administrator; b. Lansing, Mich., Nov. 7, 1946; d. Frank Richard and Sophia Mary (Scieszka) Marczynski; m. Felix Kaufmann May 28, 1988. BA, Carlow Coll., Pitts., 1970; MS in Pastoral Studies, St. Paul U., Ottawa, ON., Can., 1976, MA, 1977. Cert. family life educator, fund raising exec. Tchr. Mt. Nazareth Acad., Pitts., 1969—71; family svc. dir. Mt. Nazareth Ctr., Pitts., 1971—75, 1977—78; parish outreach worker St. Casimir Ch., Lansing, 1978—81; parish outreach cons. Diocese of Lansing, 1980—83; family life educator Cath. Social Svcs., Lansing, 1981—84; agy. dir. Cath. Social Svc., Brighton, Mich., 1984—93, Cath. Charities of Archdiocese Miami, Wilton Manors, Fla., 1994—2002, COO, 2002—04, dir. capital devel., 2004—, cert. fund raising exec., 2005—. Chmn. Consortium on Aging, Howell, Mich., 1988-89; cons. (Lansing chpt.) Nat. Stepfamily Assn., 1982-84; facilitator Cath. Coun. on Aging, Livingston County, Mich., 1986-89. Co-author: Welcoming the Seasons, 1977, Parish Social Ministry, 1985. Co-chmn. Livingston County Emergency Shelter, Howell, Mich., 1988—, vice chmn., 1990; bd. dir. Livingston County United Way, Howell, 1988-89, Mich. Coun. of Family Rels., 1990-93; exec. sec. Coun. of Ch. Bd., Lansing, 1982-84; agy. rep. Energy Bank Coalition, Lansing, 1982-84. Mem. NAFE, Nat. Coun. Family Rels., Cath. Charities U.S.A., Mich. Coun. Family Rels. (bd. dir. 1990-93), Assn. Fundraising Profl. (cert.) Roman Catholic. Avocations: classical music, opera, the arts, travel. Office: Cath Charities 1505 NE 26th St Wilton Manors FL 33305-1323

KAUGER, YVONNE, state supreme court justice; b. Cordell, Okla., Aug. 3, 1937; d. John and Alice (Bottom) K.; 1 child, Jonna Kauger Kirschner. BS magna cum laude, Southwestern State U., Weatherford, Okla., 1958; cert. med. technologist, St. Anthony's Hosp., 1959; JD, Oklahoma City U., 1969, LLD (hon.), 1992. Med. technologist Med. Arts Lab., 1959-68; assoc. Rogers, Travis & Jordan, 1970-72; jud. asst. Okla. Supreme Ct., Oklahoma City, 1972-84, justice, 1984-94, 1998—, vice chief justice, 1994-96, chief justice, 1997-98. Mem. appellate div. Ct. on Judiciary; mem. State Capitol Preservation Commn., 1983-84; mem. dean's adv. com. Oklahoma City U. Sch. Law; lectr. William O. Douglas Lecture Series Gonzaga U., 1990. Founder Gallery of Plains Indian, Colony, Okla., Red Earth (Down Towner award 1990), 1987; active Jud. Day, Girl's State, 1976-80; keynote speaker Girl's State Hall of Fame Banquet, 1984; bd. dirs. Lyric Theatre, Inc., 1966—, pres. bd. dirs., 1981; past mem. bd. dirs. Civic Music Soc., Okla. Theatre Ctr., Canterbury Choral Soc.; mem. First Lady of Okla.'s Artisans' Alliance Com. Recipient Herbert Harley award, 1999, Gov.'s Arts award, 2005; named Panhellenic Woman of Yr., 1990, Woman of Yr. Red Lands Coun. Girl Scouts, 1990; named one of 10 Most Notable Women in Okla. OKC Orch. League, 2005; named to Washita County Hall of Fame, 1992, Okla. Women's Hall of Fame, 2001. Mem. ABA (law sch. accreditation com.), Okla. Bar Assn. (law schs. com. 1977—, Jud. Excellence award 1999), Washita County Bar Assn., Washita County Hist. Soc. (life), St. Paul's Music Soc., Iota Tau Tau, Delta Zeta (Disting. Alumna award 1988, State Delta Zeta of Yr. 1987, Nat. Woman of Yr. 1988). Episcopalian. Office: Okla Supreme Ct State Capitol Building Rm 242 Oklahoma City OK 73105 Office Phone: 405-521-3841. E-mail: yvonne.kauger@oscn.net.

KAUPA, CAROLINE MARQURITE, music educator; b. Carmel, Calif., May 13, 1957; d. Fred Wolfgang and Madeleine Marie Antoinette Herrmann; m. Frank Joseph Kaupa, Mar. 11, 1995; children: Jason Robert Mohlenbrock, Korinna Elise Mohlenbrock, Annalise Madeleine, Eskender Johann. BS magna cum laude in Elem. Edn., Ariz. State U., Tempe, 1994. Cert. ESL Ariz., 1996. Title one coord. Osborn Mid. Sch., Phoenix, 1994—2000; tchr. gen. music, dir. choir Desert MountainSch., Desert Hills, Ariz., 2001—. Recipient Sylvia Cox Single Parent Scholarship award, Ariz. State U., 1993, Returning Women's Scholarship award, BU chpt. P.E.O., 1993; Ariz. Regents scholar, Ariz. State U., 1992—94, Ernistine Nash scholar, 1993, Osborn Mid. Sch. Family/Cmty. Ctr. grantee, Ariz. Cmty. Found., 1999. Mem.: NEA, Ariz. Edn. Assn., Music Educators Nat. Conf., Ariz. Music Educators Assn. (corr.), Golden Key, Sigma Alpha Iota (life).

KAUTZER, SUSAN ANN, science educator; b. Highland, Ill., May 31, 1963; d. James and Bonnie Lou (Rehg) Haller; m. John Thomas Kautzer, Apr. 25, 1987; children: Emily, Sam. BS, So. Ill. U., Edwardsville, 1985; post-AB tchg. cert., Washington U., St. Louis, 1987; M in Secondary Biology Edn., So. Ill. U., Edwardsville, 2006. Tchr. 7th grade science Dupo Jr. H.S., Ill., 2001—. Presenter profl. workshops. Leader Girl Scouts U.S.A., Edwardsville, Ill., 1995—. Recipient Excellence in Edn. award, Emerson, 2003, Excellence in Engring. award, 2005, Outstanding Tchr. Sci. award, Exxon Mobile, 2006. Mem.: Nat. Sci. Tchrs. Assn., Ill. Sci. Tchrs. Assn. Office: Dupo Jr HS Dupo IL 62239 E-mail: funscience@hotmail.com.

KAVADAS-PAPPAS, IPHIGENIA KATHERINE, preschool administrator, educator, consultant; b. Manchester, N.H., Oct. 24, 1958; d. Demetrios Stefanos and Rodothea (Palaiologou) K.; m. Constantine George Pappas, July 29, 1979; children: George Demetrios, Rodothea Constance. BA magna cum laude, U. Detroit, 1980; MAT summa cum laude, Oakland U., 1985. Cert. tchr., Mich. Pre-sch. tchr. Assumption Nursery Sch., St. Clair Shores, Mich., 1977-80, interim dir., 1984, bd. dirs., 1980—; Sunday sch. tchr. Assumption Greek Orthodox Ch., St. Clair Shores, 1985—; chairperson pre-sch. curriculum com. Greek Orthodox Archdiocese Dept. Religious Edn., Brookline, Mass., 1987—. Cons. Assumption Nursery Sch., 1985—; validator preschs. program for cert. Co-author: Pre-school Curriculum Manual for Greek Orthodox Archdiocese, 1990, Pre-School Curriculum for National Use, 1991. Mem. Assumption Greek Orthodox Ch. Philoptochos Soc., 1978-87; trustee Assumption Nursery Sch., 1979—, Sunday sch. presch. tchr., 1985—; spl. events coord. Assumption Sunday Sch., 1999—; vol. svcs. Bemis Elem. Sch., Boulan Park Mid. Sch., 1991-96; mem. Nat. Ctr. for the Early Childhood Work Force; vol. Troy H.S., 1996—, Rainbow Connection Orgn. Recipient Vol. Svc. award Angus Elem. Sch., 1989. Mem. AAUW, Nat. Assn. for the Edn. Young Children (validator presch. programs for accreditation), Nat. Multiple Sclerosis (adv. bd. 2000). Office: Assumption Greek Orthodox 21800 Marter Rd Saint Clair Shores MI 48080-2464

KAVALER, REBECCA, writer; b. July 26, 1930; children: Matthias, Joshua. BA, Univ. Ga., Athens. Author: Further Adventures of Brunhild, 1978, Tiger in the Wood, 1986, Doubting Castle, 2001, A Little More Than Kin, 2002. Mem.: PEN. Home: 425 Riverside Dr 11K New York NY 10025 Personal E-mail: rkavaler@msn.com.

KAVALER-ADLER, SUSAN, clinical psychologist, psychoanalyst; b. N.Y.C., Jan. 31, 1950; d. Solomon and Alice (Zelikow) Weiss; m. Thomas Kavaler, July 12, 1970 (div. 1975); m. Saul Michael Adler, Aug. 14, 1983. PhD in Clin. Psychology, Adelphi U., 1974. Cert. in psychotherapy, psychoanalysis; diplomate in psychoanalysis, 2003. Psychologist Beth Israel Hosp., N.Y.C., 1974-76, Manhattan Psychiat. Children's Ctr., N.Y.C., 1977-80; pvt. practice psychotherapy-psychoanalysis N.Y.C., 1976—; founder, exec. dir. Object Rels. Inst. Psychotherapy and Psychoanalysis, 1991. Condr. writing and mourning groups; founding dir., supr., faculty, founder, exec. dir., tng. analyst Object Rels. Inst. for Psychotherapy and Psychoanalysis, 1991—; mem. faculty Postgrad. Ctr. Mental Health, N.Y.C., 1984-86, 90; mem. faculty, supr. Nat. Inst. Psychotherapies, N.Y.C., 1985-91; bd. dirs., supr. Bklyn. Inst. Psychotherapy and Psychoanalysis; adj. prof. Fordham U.; founding exec. dir. Object Rels. Inst. Psychotherapy and Psychoanalysis, 1991—; spkr pvt. seminars, writing groups. Author: (books) The Compulsion to Create, 1993, 2d edit., 2000, Women Writers and Their Demon Lovers, 1993, rev. edit., 2000, The Creative Mystique: From Red Shoes Frenzy to Love and Creativity, 1996, International Forum of Psychoanalysis, 1999, The Divine, the Deviant and the Diabolical: A Female Artist's Developmental Journey from Self Fragmentation to Self Integration in a Creative Process Group, 2000, Mourning, Spirituality and Psychic Change, 2003 (Nat. Gradiva award Nat. Assn. Advancement Psychoanalysis, 2004); contbr. over 49 articles to profl. jours. and books; editor: book chpts. Recipient 11 writing awards, Postgrad. Ctr. for Mental Health, Gradiva award, Nat. Assn. for Advancement of Psychoanalysis. Office: 115 E 9th St Apt 12P New York NY 10003-5420 also: 41 Central Park W New York NY 10023 Office Phone: 212-674-5425. Personal E-mail: suska674@aol.com, susan@kavaleradler.com.

KAVANAGH, CORNELIA KUBLER, sculptor; b. New Haven, Apr. 8, 1940; d. George Alexander and Elizabeth Bushnell Kubler; m. James Penniston Kavanagh, Feb. 6, 1971; children: Alexander, Elena. BA, Barnard Coll., 1962; MA, Columbia U., 1970-71. Solo shows include: Cornelia Kubler Kavanagh "The Shape of Time", Kirshenbaum, Bond, N.Y., 2002-03. Cornelia Kubler Kavanagh "bronze, Plaster, Stone", Tucker Robbins, N.Y. 2001. Qualita Fine Art, Las Vegas, Nev., 1999-2000, Artspace, New Haven, 1997, Conn. Art Competition Stamford Mus. and Nature Ctr., 1992, Art Asia, Hong Kong, 1992, The Discovery Mus., Bridgeport, Conn., 1997, Parish-Hadley Assocs., N.Y., 1996, Silvermine Guild Arts Ctr., New Canaan, Conn., 2000, Openasia, Venice, 2004; commd. works include Long Wharf Theater, Lancaster Winery, Sonoma, Calif.; represented in corp. collections at Kirshenbaum, Bond and Ptnrs., N.Y.C., Parish-Hadley Assocs., Inc., N.Y.C., So. Wine and Spirits, Miami, Sunbelt Beverage Corp., N.Y.C.; represented by Blue Mountain Gallery, N.Y., artformedia.com, PMW Gallery, Stamford, CT; group shows: La Biennale di Venezla, Venice, Italy, St. Pauls Sch., Conord, N.H., 2005,Gallery Contemporary Art, 2006, Port Warwick Art and Sculpture Festival, Newport News, Va., 2005, 51st Internat. Art Exhbn., 2005, Openasia Internat. Sculptre Exhbn., Venice, Italy, 2004; subject of articles. Sec. bd. dirs. New Canaan (Conn.) Country Sch., 1984-88; sec. Rowayton (Conn.) Civic Assn., 1984-88; vol. Mid Fairfield Hospice, Conn., 1984-99; mem. parents exec. com. Colby coll., 1990-98.; mem. cmty. outreach bd. Ctr. for Hope, Darien, Conn., 1996—. Recipient Best Sculpture award Discovery Mus. and Nature Ctr., Bridgeport, Conn., 1997, 1st Pl. award for stone sculpture Art of the Northeast Silvermine Sch. Art, Ct., 2000, Amidar Meml. award for stone sculpture, 2000. Mem. Nat. Sculpture Soc., Conn. Women Artists. E-mail: corneliakavanagh@aol.com.

KAVANAGH, EILEEN J., librarian; BA, Ladycliff Coll.; MS in Libr. Sci., Columbia U., 1969; MA in Liberal Studies, SUNY, Stonybrook, 1980. Reference libr. Farmingdale (N.Y.) Pub. Libr., 1969-70; from reference libr. to libr. dir. Bay Shore-Brightwaters (N.Y.) Pub. Libr., 1970—. Recipient Disting. Citizen of Yr. award, Bay Shore-Brightwaters, 2005. Office: Bay Shore-Brightwaters Pub Libr 1 S Country Rd Brightwaters NY 11718-1513 Office Phone: 631-665-4350. Business E-Mail: ekavanag@suffolk.lib.ny.us.

KAVANDI, JANET LYNN, aerospace power engineer, chemist; b. Springfield, Mo., July 17, 1959; d. William Winfred and Wanda Ruth (Garner) Sellers; m. Farhad John Kavandi, June 5, 1982. BS magna cum laude, Mo. So. State Coll., 1980; MS, U. Mo., Rolla, 1982; PhD, U. Wash., 1990. Project engr. Eagle-Picher Industries, Joplin, Mo., 1982-84; prin. engr. power systems tech. Boeing Def., Seattle, 1984—95; Astronaut NASA, Houston, 1995—. Mem. AIAA, Am. Chem. Soc. Avocations: skiing, horseback riding, windsurfing, sailing, camping. Office: Astronaut Office MIC CB Lyndon B Johnson Space Center Houston TX 77058

KAVNER, JULIE, actress; b. LA, Sept. 7, 1951; Grad., San Diego U., 1971. Actress: (TV series) Rhoda, 1974-78 (Emmy award 1978), Petrocelli, 1975, Lou Grant, 1977, Taxi, 1980, The Tracey Ullman Show, 1987-90, The Simpsons, (voice of Marge Simpson and others) 1990— (Emmy award, 1992), Sibs, 1991, Birdland, 1994, Tracey Takes On, 1996, (TV movies) Katherine, 1975, The Girl Who Couldn't Lose, 1975, No Other Love, 1979, Revenge of the Stepford Wives, 1980, Don't Drink the Water, 1994, Jake's Women, 1996, (feature films) National Lampoon Goes to the Movies, 1981, Bad Medicine, 1985, Hannah and her Sisters, 1985, Radio Days, 1987, Surrender, 1987, New York Stories, 1989, Awakenings, 1990, Alice, 1990, This Is My Life, 1992, Shadows and Fog, 1992, I'll Do Anything, 1994, Forget Paris, 1995, Deconstructing Harry, 1997, Doctor Dolittle (voice), 1998, A Walk on the Moon, 1999, Judy Berlin, 1999, Story of a Bad Boy, 1999, Someone Like You (voice), Barn Red, 2004, Click, 2006.*

KAVOVIT, BARBARA, entrepreneur; b. Bronx; 1 child, Zachary. Degree in fin., SUNY, Oswego, 1987. Asst. commodities trader; former founder, chief exec. Anchor Constrn. Inc., N.Y.C.; founder Barabara K Enterprises, 2002—. Mem. pres.'s adv. bd. New Rochelle Coll. Named one of Superstar Entrepreneurs of Small and Large Bus.; recipient N.Y. State Dept. Econ. Devel. award, Gov. Mario Cuomo. Mem.: Profl. Women in Constrn.

KAVRAKI, LYDIA, computer scientist, educator; BS, U. Crete, Greece, 1989; MS, Stanford U., 1992, PhD, 1995. Postdoctoral fellow Stanford U., research assoc.; assoc. prof. computer sci. Rice U., 1996—99, prof. bioengineering, 1999—; assoc. prof. structural & computational biology, molecular biophysics Baylor Coll. of Med., 1999—. Prog. com. mem. IJCAI, 1997—99; co-chair Internat. Workshop on Algorithmic Foundations of Robotics, 1998; prog. com. mem. IEEE Internat. Conference on Robotics Automation, 1999, ACM Annual Symposium on Computational Geometry, 1999; assoc. editor IEEE Transactions on Robotics and Automation, 1999—. Named one of Top 100 Young Innovators, MIT Tech. Review mag., 2002, Brilliant 10, Popular Sci. mag., 2003; recipient Career award, Nat. Sci. Found., Grace Murray Hopper award, Assn. for Computing Machinery, Early Career award, IEEE Robotics and Automation Soc.; grantee Alfred P. Sloan Rsch. Fellowship. Office: Rice U MS132 PO Box 1892 Houston TX 77251-1892

KAWAKAMI, BERTHA C., state representative; b. Honolulu, July 28, 1931; children: Wendall, Lyndall. BA in Edn., U. Hawaii, 1953; MA in Edn., NYU, 1962. Elem., resource tchr. Hawaii Dept. Edn. Eleele, Pearl Harbor Intermediate Sch., Nanaikapono, 1954—61; mem. lang. arts dist. team, 1962—65; prin., elem. intermediate Eleele and Kekaha Schs., 1965—79; ednl. specialist Kauai Dist. Office, 1980—87, dep. dist. supr. dept. edn., 1987; mem. Hawaii State Ho. of Reps., 1987—, asst. majority fl. leader, 1987—, mem. fin., human svcs, housing and health coms., vice chair fin. com., 1993—, majority whip, 2003—. Trustee Blood Bank of Hawaii, 1992—; mem. adv. com. Cmty. Health Nursing Divsn., 1991—; mem. quality assurance com. Kauai Vets. Meml. Hosp., 1991—; bd. dirs., v.p. Comml. Properties Inc., 1988—; mem. Waimea United Ch. of Christ, 1989—. Mem.: Japanese Am. Nat. Mus. (hon. chairperson), Hawaii State Found. on Culture and Arts, Delta Kappa Gamma Soc. Internat. Democrat. Office: State Capitol Rm 434 415 S Beretania St Honolulu HI 96813 E-mail: repkawakami@capitol.hawaii.gov.

KAWAMURA, GEORGINA K., finance company executive; b. Lanai City, Hawaii, Sept. 19, 1952; m. Gary Kawamura, 1973; children: Bryan, Jon. AA in Acctg., Maui CC. Clk. to office mgr., budget dir. Maui (Hawaii) County Mayor's Office, 1987—88; planner Castle and Cooke Resorts, Lanai, Hawaii, 1998—2002; dir. fin. Dept. Budget and Fin., Hawaii, 2002—. Avocations: hula, reading. Office: Dept Budget and Fin PO Box 150 Honolulu HI 96810

KAWASHIMA, HOPE NOZOMI, musician; b. Auburn, Calif., Apr. 2, 1937; d. Peter Shinichi and Mary Etsuko Omachi; m. Mas Kawashima, June 14, 1964; children: Mariya Yoshiko Yamamoto, Rebekah Kawashima Wong. BA in Rec. and Music Therapy, Calif. State U., Sacramento, 1959; MA in Sacred Music, San Francisco Theol. Sem., 1964; postgrad., Juilliard Sch. Music, N.Y.C., 1980—81. Ordained as deacon United Meth. Ch., consecrated to ministry United Meth. Ch., 1982; registered music therapist Calif., cert. dir. music. Music therapist State of Calif., Stockton, Napa, 1959—64; dir., organist 1st Presbyn. Ch., Altadena, Calif., 1964—71, Ontario (Oreg.) Cmty. Ch., 1972—80, J A United Ch., N.Y.C., 1980—88, LaTijera United Meth. Ch., LA, 1988—93, Lake Park United Meth. Ch., Oakland, Calif., 1993—2002; min. music St. Paul's United Meth. Ch., Fresno, Calif., 2002—05, United Japanese Christian Ch., Clovis, Calif., 2005—. Dir. Music Mart Acad., Santa Monica, Calif., 1988—91. Musician: (CD's) Songs of Faith, Hope & Love, 1967; composer, musician: CD's Love Wider than an Ocean, 1977, prodr., composer, musician: CD's Reflections of Faith, Hope & Love, 2002 (CLPEP grantee); author: Learning to Play Piano is as Easy as ABC. Gen. conf. del. United Meth. Ch., St. Louis, 1988, mem. hymnal com. Nashville, 1985—88; chairperson Theol. Forum, Berkeley, Calif., 1994—2002. Recipient Famous Diamond Poet award, Famous Poets Soc., 1995; Sears Roebuck & Co. scholar, 1955, Calif. Civil. Liberties grantee, 2002. Mem.: Nat. Guild Piano Tchrs. (local chair 1979—89), Clergywoman Calif., Calif. Scholarship Fedn. (life), Native Daughters Calif. Office: United Japanese Christian Ch 136 N Villa Clovis CA 93612

KAWAZOE, ROBIN INADA, federal official; b. Wilkinsburg, Pa., Jan. 13, 1959; d. George and Hanako (Nishio) Inada; children: Amy, Steven. BA, U. Md., 1982. Program analyst Alcohol, Drug Abuse & Mental Health Adminstrn., Rockville, Md., 1981-85, 85-87, com. mgmt. officer, 1985—86, extramural programs officer, 1987-88; spl. asst. Nat. Inst. on Drug Abuse, Rockville, 1988-90, dep. dir. Office Sci. Policy and Comm., 1990-96; dir. Office of Sci. Policy and Planning, 1997—2005; sr. advisor to dir. Nat. Inst. Alcohol Abuse and Alcoholism, Bethesda, Md., 2005—, acting dep. dir., 2006—, acting exec. officer, 2006—. Recipient Recognition award, Pub. Health Svc., 1992, Dir.'s award, NIH, 1994, 2004, Dir.'s Group award, 2000, 2004, 2005, Group award for Disting. Svc., HHS Sec., 2004. Office: Nat Inst Alcohol Abuse and Alcoholism 5635 Fishers Ln Rm 2000 Bethesda MD 20892

KAWEWE, SALIWE MOYO, social work educator, researcher; children: Neo, Rujeko, Godfrey, Kudakwashe. BSW, U. Zambia, Lusaka, 1974; MSW, Washington U., St. Louis, 1979; PhD, St. Louis U., 1985. Cert. edn. accreditation reaffirmation Coun. on Social Work, 2001. Adminstrv. asst. U. Zambia, Lusaka, 1974—77; social svcs. officer, probation officer Dept. Social Svcs., Bulawayo, Zimbabwe, 1979—81; instr. St. Louis Pub. Schs., 1981—83; social svc. worker II Mo. Divsn. Family Svcs., St. Louis, 1984—85; asst. prof. Southea. La. U., Hammond, 1985—88, Ctrl. State U., Wilberforce, Ohio, 1989, James Madison U., Harrisonburg, Va., 1989—91, Wichita State U., 1991—96; assoc. prof. So. Ill. U., Carbondale, 1996—2001, dir. grad. program, 1996—98, prof., 2002—. Contbr. chapters to books; mem. editl. bd.: Social Devel. Issues, 1998—, mem. guest editl. bd.: Nat. Women Studies Jour., 1997—98; contbr. articles to profl. jours. and publs. Mem. Nat. Assn. Social Workers, Bulawayo, Matabeleland, Zimbabwe, 1980—82; Africa regional rep. Inter-Univ. Consortium for Internat. Social Devel., Wichita, 1992—94; mem. Tangipohoa Parish Mayor's commn. on Needs of Women, Hammond, 1985—88, Inter-Univ. Consortium for Internat. Social Devel., Carbondale, 1995—, Ill. Hunger Coalition, Chgo., 1998—; sec. Kans. Coun. on Social Work Edn., Topeka, 1992—93; mem. Com. to Enhance Minority, Human and Civil Rights, Springfield, 2000—. Recipient Outstanding Scholastic Achievement award, George Warren Brown Sch. of Social Work, Wash. U., 1979, Superior Acad. Achievement award, St. Louis U. Internat. Student Assn., 1984, Appreciation for Continuing Svc. as a Faculty Advisor, Nat. Assn. Black Social Workers, 2001, Appreciation as Faculty Advisor, 2000, certificate of Dedication, African Student Coun. So. Ill. U. at Carbondale, 2001, Internat. Student Coun So. Ill. U. at Carbondale, 2001, Award of Appreciation of Svc., Nat. Assn. Black Social Workers, 2000, Recognition of Dedicated Svc., African Student Coun. So. Ill. U. at Carbondale, 1998, Dedication of Svc., African Student Coun., So. Ill. U. at Carbondale, 1997, Outstanding Leadership and Guidance, Student Orgn. of Social Work, Wichita State U., 1996, Outstanding Multilateral Study Del. award, World Congress on the Family, 1992; grantee Summer Rsch. Travel Grant, Wichita State U., 1994. Mem.: NASW (asst. dist. chair 1997—99), Internat. Coun. Social Welfare, Internat. Assn. for Schs. of Social Work, Soc. for Study of Social Problems, Peace and Social Justice Ctr. of So. Ctrl. Kans., Coun. on Social Work Edn., Internat. Assn. Feminist Econs., So. Ill. U. Women's Caucus, Nat. Women Studies Assn., So. Ill. HIV Care Consortium (bd. mem. 1997—2001), Internat. Fedn. Social Workers (life), Phi Alpha (hon.). Office: So Ill U Sch Of Social Work Mailcode 4329 Carbondale IL 62901 Office Phone: 618-453-3359. Business E-Mail: smkawewe@siu.edu.

KAY, BONNIE KATHRYN, management consultant; b. Indpls., Nov. 15, 1942; d. Carl Gaines Wiltshire and Evelyn Phyllis Davison; m. David Lee Kay, June 29, 1963 (div. 1970); 1 child, Pamela Jean. BA, Calif. State U., Sacto., 1985; MA, U. Ariz., 1987; PhD, Temple U., 1993. Adj. prof. U. Pa., Wharton Sch. Bus., Phila., 1988-91; asst. prof. W.Va. U., Morgantown, 1991-93; adj. prof. Calif. State U., Sacramento, 1995-99; cons., pres. Orgnl. Solutions, Sacramento, Calif., 1993—. Author: Organizational Consulting, 1992; contbr. articles to profl. jours. Bd. dirs. Huntington Beach (Calif.) Playhouse, 1991-94, Seacliff, 1992-94; vol. KVIE Auction, Sacto., 1975-85, Am. Ballet Theatre, N.Y.c., 1987-91, Huntington Beach Playhouse, 1991-94. Mem. Project Mgmt. Inst. Republican. Avocations: golf, crafts.

KAY, HERMA HILL, law educator; b. Orangeburg, SC, Aug. 18, 1934; d. Charles Esdorn and Herma Lee (Crawford) Hill. BA, So. Meth. U., 1956; JD, U. Chgo., 1959. Bar: Calif. 1960, U.S. Supreme Ct. 1978. Law clk. to Hon. Roger Traynor Calif. Supreme Ct., 1959-60; from asst. prof. to assoc. prof. law U. Calif., Berkeley, 1960-62, prof., 1963, dir. family law project, 1964-67, Jennings prof., 1987-96, dean, 1992-2000, Armstrong prof., 1996—; co-reporter uniform marriage and div. act Nat. Conf. Commrs. on Uniform State Laws, 1968-70. Vis. prof. U. Manchester, England, 1972, Harvard U.,

1976; mem. Gov.'s Commn. Family, 1966. Author (with D. Currie, L. Kramer and K. Roosevelt): Conflict of Laws: Cases, Comments, Questions, 7th edit., 2006; author: (with Martha S. West) Sex-Based Discrimination: Text, Cases and Materials, 6th edit., 2005; contbr. articles to profl. jours. Trustee Russell Sage Found., NY, 1972—87, chmn. bd. trustees NY, 1980—84; trustee, bd. dirs. Equal Rights Advs., Calif., 1987—88, chmn. Calif., 1976—83; pres. bd. dirs. Rosenberg Found., Calif., 1987—88, bd. dirs. Calif., 1978—. Recipient Rsch. award, Am. Bar Found., 1990, Margaret Brent award, ABA Commn. Women in Profession, 1992, Marshall-Wythe medal, 1995; fellow, Ctr. Advanced Study Behavioral Sci., Palo Alto, Calif., 1963. Mem.: ABA (sect. legal edn. and admissions to bar coun. 1992—99, sec. 1999—2001), Order of Coif (nat. pres. 1983—85), Am. Philos. Soc., Am. Acad. Arts and Scis., Assn. Am. Law Schs. (exec. com. 1986—87, pres.-elect 1988, pres. 1989, past pres. 1990), Am. Law Inst. (mem. coun. 1985—), Calif. Women Lawyers (bd. govs. 1975—77), Bar U.S. Supreme Ct., Calif. Bar Assn. Democrat. Office: U Calif Law Sch Boalt Hall Berkeley CA 94720-7200 Office Phone: 510-643-2671. E-mail: kayh@law.berkeley.edu.

KAY, JANE HOLTZ, writer; b. Boston, July 7, 1938; BA in History magna cum laude, Harvard Coll., 1960. Tchr. comms. Boston U., 1979-80; tchr. Grad. Sch. Design Harvard U., 1985-87. Lectr. Conservation Law Found., Sch. Arch. Washington U., Mus. Modern Art, N.Y. Hist. Soc., John F. Kennedy Libr. Author: Lost Boston, 1980, updated, 1999, Preserving New England, 1986, Asphalt Nation: How the Automobile Took Over America and How We Can Take It Back, 1997; contbr. intro. to WPA Guide to Massachusetts; contbr. chpts. to books; arch. critic to the Nation; contbr. to The Boston Globe, Architecture, The New York Times, Planning Mag., Sierra, Landscape Architecture, Orion Mag., among others; featured in Booknotes, Nat. Pub. Radio, ABC News, CNN, WGBH The Group, Living on Earth, NPR. Former town meeting mem., Brookline, Mass. Fellow NEA; recipient William H. Donaldson Editl. Achievement award, Jesse H. Neal Editl. Achievement award, Award of Excellence Boston Soc. Landscape Archs., Preservation award Historic Neighborhoods Assn., Media award AAUW. Office: 156 Milk St Boston MA 02109-3402 Office Phone: 617-426-7261. Personal E-mail: jholtzkay@aol.com.

KAY, MARCIA CHELLIS, writer; b. Boston, Mar. 13, 1940; d. Andrew Christopher and Dina Meland Quale; m. William G. Kay Jr. (dec.); m. Robert Dana Chellis (div.); children: Dana Chellis Keel, Bradford Adams Chellis. BS in Speech, Northwestern U., 1961, BS in Edn., 1961; EdM, Harvard U., 1979. With Boston Ednl. Rsch., Inc., Boston, 1970—71, Ednl. Recs. Am., Westport, Conn., Ednl. Writer's Collaborative, Cambridge, 1977—78; writer WGBH-TV (PBS), Boston, 1966—68; adminstrv. asst. to Joan Kennedy, 1979—82. Lectr. in field. Author: Living with the Kennedy's: The Joan Kennedy Story, 1985, The Joan Kennedy Story: One Woman's Victory Over Alcohol, Infidelity, Politics and Privilege, 1985, Ordinary Women, Extraordinary Lives, 1992. Bd. trustees Cantata Singers, Cambridge, 1968—96; 1st v.p., bd. mem. Jr. League Boston; chmn. program com. Harvard Club, New Bedford; storyteller Four Arts Children's Libr; active Am. Heart Assn.; bd. dirs. Harvard Club of Palm Beaches. Mem.: Nat. League Am. Pen Women, Author's Guild, Nat. Writers Union. Avocations: golf, tennis. Home: 200 N Ocean Blvd Palm Beach FL 33480

KAY, MARGARET J., psychologist; b. Washington, Apr. 16, 1951; d. Joseph Allen and Joan (Auchter) Brown; m. Jeffrey Edward Kay, Nov. 24, 1984; children: Meghan Joan, Jennifer Elizabeth BA, Ind. U., Pa., 1973, EdD; MS, U. Waterloo, Ont., Can., 1977. Lic. psychologist; cert. sch. psychologist. Diplomate Am. Bd. Med. Psychotherapists. Rsch. asst. Dept. Air Force, Washington, 1973; mgmt. trainee Hamilton Bank, Lancaster, Pa., 1973—74; psychologist Reality Home Svcs. for Children, Waterloo, 1976—77; chief psychologist, v.p. Pan Am Corp., Hershey, Pa., 1977—81; psychologist, owner Margaret J. Kay Assocs., Lancaster, 1981—. Cons. in field Author: Parent Power: Understanding Right To Education Laws, 1980 Adv. bd. The Janus Sch., 1990— Recipient Cert. of Appreciation Lancaster Assn. for Children & Adults with Learning Disabilities, 1985 Mem. APA, Orton Dyslexia Soc., Pa. Psychol. Assn Republican. Home: 600 Randolph Dr Lititz PA 17543-9091 Office: 2818 Lititz Pike Lancaster PA 17601-3322

KAY, SANDRA IRENE, special education educator, consultant; b. N.Y.C., Nov. 13, 1952; d. George Yury and Marcelle (Giberius) K. BS in Art Edn., SUNY, New Paltz, 1974, MS in Art Edn., 1979; MEd in Spl. Edn., Columbia U., 1987, EdD in Spl. Edn., 1989. Cert. art edn. tchr., N.Y. Art educator Monroe-Woodbury High Sch., Central Valley, N.Y., 1974-85, Pine Tree Sch., Monroe, N.Y., 1985-90; dist. coord. gifted/talented programs Monroe (N.Y.)-Woodbury Cen. Schs., 1990-92, 94—; assoc. prof. and program dir. of art edn. SUNY, New Paltz, 1992-94. Pvt. practice ednl. cons., N.Y., 1988—; vis. scholar Tchrs. Coll., Columbia U., N.Y.C., 1989-99; philosopher in residence Inst. for Arts in Edn., Albany, N.Y., summer 1991; adminstr. Eileen Barth Meml. Scholarship Fund, Ctrl. Valley, 1986—. Dean's grantee Columbia U., 1989, Coll. Found. grantee, 1992, N.Y. State Monroe-Woodbury grantee, 1988, 91; Alice A. Pierce scholar, 1989; named Tchr. of Yr., Monroe-Woodbury Ctrl. Sch. Dist., 1990; recipient Reston prize, 1990, Excellence in Tchg. Spl. Edn. award N.Y. State Federation Coun. Exceptional Children, 2002. Mem.: ASCD, World Coun. for the Gifted, Nat. Art Edn. Assn., Advocacy for Gifted and Talented Edn. in NY State (past sec. bd. dirs.), Coun. Exceptional Children, Nat. Assn. Gifted Children (past chair rsch. and evaluation divsn.), Am. Edn. Rsch. Assn., Delta Kappa Gamma. Presbyterian. Avocations: silver smithing, tennis, interior decorating. Home: 207 Bay View Ave Cornwall On Hudson NY 12520-1705 Office: Monroe Woodbury Ctrl Schs 9 N Main St PO Box 1033 Harriman NY 10926 Office Phone: 845-460-6100 ext. 6164. Business E-Mail: skay@mw.k12.ny.us.

KAY-ATKINS, CHEREE', elementary school educator; d. Charles and Mary Kay; m. Roger Atkins, Jan. 11, 1997; children: Summer Atkins, Spring Atkins. BS, Northwestern State U., Natchitoches, La., 1996, Masters, 2004, postgrad., 2004—05. Cert. tchr. La., 2005. Tchr. 3d grade Pickering Elem. Sch., Leesville, La., 1996—2000, tchr. 5th grade, 2000—04, tchr. academically gifted, 2004—. Cheerleader coach Pickering H.S., Leesville, La., 1996—99; student coun. sponsor Pickering Elem. Sch., Leesville, La., 2001—03, Jr. Beta Club sponsor, 2004—, sch. newspaper sponsor, 2004—, chmn. sch. improvement plan, 2006—. Tchr./helper Vacation Bible Sch., 2005—06. Mem.: Delta Kappa Gamma. Office: Vernon Parish Sch Bd 116 LeBleu Rd Leesville LA 71446 Office Phone: 337-537-3394. Personal E-mail: catkins@vpsb.k12.la.us.

KAYDANOVA, YEVGENYA, neurologist; b. Leningrad, Russia, Feb. 4, 1952; came to U.S., 1989; d. Abram and Natalya (Kernes) Baranchik; 1 child, Vladimir Kaydanov. MD, PhD, First Med. Sch., Leningrad, 1975. Diplomate in neurology Am. Bd. Psychiatry and Neurology. Asst. prof. neurophysiology and neurology Inst. Exptl. Medicine, Leningrad, 1975-89; resident in neurology U. Ill., Chgo., 1993-96, fellow in epilepsy and electrophysiology, 1996-97, clin. asst. prof. neurology, 1997—. Contbr. articles to profl. jours. Mem. Am. Acad. Neurology. Avocations: travel, skiing, classical music, literature. Home: 6949 N Keystone Ave Lincolnwood IL 60712-4607 Office: 912 S Wood St Chicago IL 60612-7325 E-mail: ykaydan@uic.edu.

KAYE, EVELYN PATRICIA (EVELYN PATRICIA SARSON), author, publisher, travel expert; b. London, Oct. 1, 1937; came to U.S., 1963; d. Max and Florence (Wright) K.; m. J. Christopher Sarson, Mar. 25, 1963 (div. Sept. 8, 2005); children: Katrina May, David Arnold. Advanced level gen. certificate of edn. in English and French, North London Collegiate Sch., Edgware, Middlesex, Eng., 1956; studied in Jerusalem, 1959-60; cert. in TESOL, Front Range C.C., Boulder, Colo., 2006. Cert. tchr. English as Second Lang. 2005. Sec., publicity asst. Elek Books Ltd., London, 1957-58; gen. reporter Southend Times, Southend-on-Sea, Eng., Willesden Citizen, London, East London News Agy., 1958-61; staff reporter Reuters News Agy., Paris, 1961-62; reporter, feature writer The Guardian, Manchester, Eng., 1962-63; co-founder, pres. Action for Children's TV, 1969-74, 89—. Pres. Blue Penguin Publs., 1989-97, Blue Panda Publs., 1997—; spkr. travel and adventurous women's issues. Author: Family Guide to Childrens Television: What To Watch, What To Miss, What To Change and How To Do It, 1974, rev. edit., 1979, The Family Guide to Cape Cod: What to Do When You Don't Want To Do What Everyone Else Is Doing, 1976, Crosscurrents: Children, Families and Religion, 1980, How To Treat TV with TLC: The ACT Guide to Children's Television, 1979; co-author: (textbook) Relationships in Marriage and Family, 1984, Write and Sell Your TV Drama, 1985, 2d edit., 1993, (with A. Loring) The Parents Going-Away Planner, 1987, (with J. Gardner) The Hole in The Sheet, 1987, College Bound: The Students Guide to Getting Ready, Moving In and Succeeding on Campus, (with J. Gardner) Travel and Learn: The New Guide to Educational Travel, 1992, 4th edit. 2001, Eco-Vacations: Enjoy Yourself and Save the Earth, 1991, Family Travel: Terrific New Vacation Ideas for Today's Families, 1993, Amazing Traveler: Isabella Bird-The Biography of a Victorian Adventurer, 1994, Free Vacations and Bargain Adventures in the U.S.A., 1995, 2d edit. 1998, Active Woman Vacation Guide, 1997; pres. Blue Panda Publs, 1989-2003; contbr. articles on family, travel, and the arts to nat. mags.; contbr. radio and TV interview on unusual travel incl. CNN TV News, Good Morning Am., ABC-TV, KATU-TV, Portland, Oreg., others. Mem. Am. Soc. Journalists and Authors (exec. coun. 1981-87, pres. 1984-85, v.p. conf. 1990), Pubs. Mktg. Assn. (bd. dirs. 1993-95), Colo. Ind. Pubs. Assn. (founder, pres. 1992-96), Boulder Media Women (founder 1991—), COTESOL. Home: 4655 Dapple Ln Boulder CO 80301-5381 E-mail: epkaye@msn.net.

KAYE, JANET MIRIAM, psychologist, educator; b. New Haven, Mar. 2, 1937; d. Al and Rose (Marcus) Sovitsky; m. Donald Kaye, June 26, 1955; children: Kenneth, Karen, Kendra, Keith. BS, NYU, 1958, MA, 1960; PhD, Med. Coll. of Pa., 1980. Clin. instr. Med Coll. Pa., Phila., 1980-82, asst. prof., 1982-86, assoc. prof., 1986-94, Med. Coll. Pa. Hahnemann Sch. Medicine, Phila., 1994-96, prof., 1996—2002; prof. coll. medicine Drexel U., Phila., 2002—. Contbr. articles to profl. jours. Mem. APA, Am. Assn. Cancer Edn., Am. Soc. Clin. Hypnosis, Soc. Health and Human Values, Gerontol. Soc. Am., Am. Soc. Psychiat. Oncology, Coll. Physicians Pa., Internat. Soc. Exptl. Hypnosis. Avocations: piano, working out, swimming, reading. E-mail: donjank@aol.com.

KAYE, JENNIFER A., elementary school educator, dance educator; b. Bridgeport, Conn., Nov. 30, 1982; d. Daniel K. and Frances L. Kaye. BA, Roger Williams U., Bristol, RI, 2005. Dance tchr. Barbettes Dance, Monroe, Conn., 1994—2000; dance instr. Youth Connection, Shelton, Conn., 1996—; sub. tchr. Shelton Bd. Edn., Shelton, 2001—05; dance tchr. Ctr. Stage, Shelton, 2004—; edn. dir. Boys & Girls Club of LNV, Shelton, 2005—. Sch. aide Byfield Elem., Bristol, RI, 2003—05; dance counselor Boys & Girls Club of LNV, 2005—. Dancer Pedestrian, 2004, Dreams of Grace, 2004. Recipient Dean's List, Roger Williams U., 2001, Achievement for Acad., Alpha Chi, Roger Williams U., 2005. Fellow: Future Tchrs. of Am.; mem.: Am. Alliance for Health, PE and Recreation, Nat. Dance Assn. Avocations: dance, scrapbooks, bowling, reading. Office: Boys & Girls Club of LNV 1 Positive Pl Shelton CT 06484

KAYE, JUDITH SMITH, state appeals court judge; b. Monticello, NY, Aug. 4, 1938; d. Benjamin and Lena (Cohen) Smith; m. Stephen Rackow Kaye, Feb. 11, 1964; children: Luisa Marian, Jonathan Mackey, Gordon Bernard BA, Barnard Coll., 1958; LLB cum laude, NYU, 1962; LLD (hon.), St. Lawrence U., 1985, Union U., 1985, Pace U., 1985, Syracuse U., 1988, L.I. U., 1989. Bar: NY State 1963. Assoc. Sullivan & Cromwell, NYC, 1962-64; staff atty. IBM, Armonk, NY, 1964-65; asst. to dean Sch. Law NYU, 1965-68; ptnr. Connelly Chase O'Donnell & Weyher, NYC, 1969-83; assoc. judge NY State Ct. Appeals, NYC, 1983-93, chief judge Albany, NY, 1993—. Pres., Conf. of Chief Justices; chair bd. dir., Nat. Ctr. for State Cts., 2002-03; bd. dir. Sterling Nat. Bank. Bd. editor, NY State Bar Journal; contbr. articles to profl. jours. Former bd. dirs. Legal Aid Soc.; chair, Permanent Jud. Commn. on Justice for Children; founding mem., hon. chair, Judges and Lawyers Breast Cancer Alert (JALBCA); trustee, William Nelson Cromwell Found. Recipient Vanderbilt medal NYU Sch. of Law, 1983, Medal of Distinction, Barnard Coll, 1987, John Marshall award, ABA, 2005. Fellow Am. Bar Found.; mem. Am. Law Inst., Am. Coll. Trial Lawyers, Am. Judicature Soc. (bd. dirs. 1980-83), ABA (co-chair, Commn. on the Am. Jury, 2004-05). Democrat. Achievements include being the first women to serve on the New York State's highest court when appointed Associate Judge of the Court of Appeals; being the first women to occupy the State Judiciary's highest office, Chief Judge. Office: NY Court of Appeals Court of Appeals Hall 20 Eagle St Albany NY 12207-1009 also: NY Court of Appeals 230 Park Ave Ste 826 New York NY 10169-0007*

KAYE, JUDY, actress; b. Dec. 11, 1948; d. Jerome Joseph and Shirley Edith (Silverman) K. Student, UCLA. Appeared in plays Fiddler on the Roof, Godspell, You're a Good Man Charlie Brown, 1968, Jesus Christ Superstar, 1972, (NY debut) Grease, 1977, On the Twentieth Century, 1978, Moony Shapiro Songbook, 1980, Oh Brother!, 1981, Four to Make Two, 1982, Love, 1984, Side by Side by Sondheim, Paper Mill Playhouse, Millburn, NJ, 1984-85, Windy City, Paper Mill Playhouse, 1985, The Phantom of the Opera (Tony award for featured actress in a musical), 1988, The Merry Widow, 1991, Mamma Mia!, 2002, Souvenir, 2004, Candide, 2005, Sweeney Todd, 2006; appeared with Santa Fe Opera, 1985, 90, NYC Opera, 1989, NY Philharm., 1990, Boston Symphony Tanglewood, 1990, Boston Pops, 1990, London Symphony, 1990. Jewish.*

KAYE, RUTH LINCOLN, historian; b. Buffalo, N.Y., Dec. 3, 1918; d. C. Arthur Lincoln and Ethel Elizabeth Green; m. B. Franklin Boan, Oct. 25, 1941 (div. 1949); m. Merwin Whitcomb Kaye, Sept. 4, 1953 (dec. 1987); children: Merrie L., Arthur Lincoln, Larisa Elizabeth. BA, Randolph-Macon Women's Coll., 1939. Author: (book) Thomas Lincoln Taunton Mass., 1972, Legends & Folk Tales of Old Alexandria, 1976—, (book) 215 histories Alexandria Va. homes, 1980—, History of St. Paul's Episcopal Church, 1984—. Mem.: Alexandria Hist. Soc., Alexandria Libr. Co., Soc. Mayflower Descendants, Alexandria Assn. & Nat. Trust Hist. Preservation, Nat. Geneal. Soc., Historic Alexandria Found. Republican. Home: 708 Braxton Pl Alexandria VA 22301

KAYTON-COURTNEY, KATHLEEN A., elementary school educator; b. Mineola, N.Y., Jan. 9, 1963; d. Charles and Judith Kayton. A.Fine Art, Nassau C.C., Garden City, N.Y., 1992; B.Art Edn., CUNY, 1996; MA in Liberal Arts, SUNY, Stonybrook, 2000, Advanced Cert. Edn. Computing, 2000. Cert. tchr. N.Y. Asst. tchr. Harbor Day Care Ctr., New Hyde Park, NY, 1995—97; elem. sch. art tchr. West Hempstead Unified Sch. Dist., West Hempstead, NY, 1997—. Editor: Chalkboard newsletter, 2001—. Mem.: West Hempstead Edn. Assn. Avocations: gardening, bicycling, hiking, art, running. Office: George Washington Elem Sch 347 William St West Hempstead NY 11552 Office Phone: 516-390-3130.

KAZEMINEZHAD, ZHABIZ, psychiatrist; b. Tehran, Iran, Mar. 21, 1973; d. Aziz and Mehrangiz Salehi Kazeminezhad; m. Roozbeh Rassadi, Dec. 11, 1999. BS, U. Calif., Irvine, 1995; MD, Drexel U., Phila., 2002. Rsch. asst. CoCensys Pharm. Co., Irvine, Calif., 1996; resident Thomas Jefferson U. Hosp., Phila., 2002—. Asst. facilitator med. student edn. Thomas Jefferson U. Hosp., Phila., 2005—; clin. asst. Dr. Akio Wakabayashi's Lab., U. Calif., Irvine, 1994—95, Dr. N.C. Morcos' Lab., U. Calif., 1993—94, Dr. James Belluzzi's Lab., U. Calif., 1992—93. Scholar, U. Calif., 1991—95, St. Joseph's Hosp., 1991; Bd. Regent's Scholarship, U. Calif. Fellow: Psychoanalytic Ctr. Phila.; mem.: Am. Psychiat. Assn., Alpha Epsilon Delta, Golden Key Nat. Honor Soc. Liberal. Atheist. Avocations: literature, movies, anthropology, music. Office Phone: 215-503-2836. Personal E-mail: zhabizk@yahoo.com.

KAZIMER, DENISE, secondary school educator; BS, Pa. State U., State College, 1993; MS, U. Tex., El Paso, 2005. 2athletic trainer Bishop McNamara H.S., Forestville, Md., 1993—2006, tchr., 1994—. Mem.: Nat. Athletic Trainers Orgn. Office: Bishop McNamara HS 6800 Marlboro Pike Forestville MD 20747 Office Phone: 301-735-8401.

KAZLE, ELYNMARIE, theater producer, performing arts executive; b. St. Paul, June 22, 1958; d. Victor Anton and Marylu (Gardner) K. BFA, U. Minn., Duluth, 1982; MFA, Ohio U., 1984. Prodn. mgr. Great Lakes Shakespeare, Cleve., 1983; prodn. stage mgr. San Diego Opera, 1984, PCPA Theaterfest, Santa Maria, Calif., 1985-86; stage mgr. Bklyn. Acad. Music, 1987; assoc. producer Assn. Am. Theater Actors, N.Y.C., 1988-89; prodn. stage mgr. Time Flies When You're Alive, West Hollywood, Calif., 1988—; asst. advt. display Wall St. Jour., L.A., 1988-89; west coast adminstr. Soc. Stage Dirs. and Choreographers, 1991-93; assoc. mng. dir. Actors Alley, North Hollywood, Calif., 1993-96; mng. ptnr., AIW Prodns., 1987—; bd. dirs. U.S. Inst. Theatre Tech., 1990—96, founder, stage mgr. mentoring project, 1991—, project dir., 1991-96, v.p. mem. devel., bd. dirs., 2000—06; exec. dir. Weathervane Playhouse, Akron, Ohio, 1997—2006. Editor, pub. The Ohio Network newsletter, 1984-90; prodr. Santa Monica Playhouse, 1988-94; writer/dir. Arts Alive Awards Show, 2001, 03. Trustee Theatre, L.A., 1992-94; mentor Firestone Visual and Performing Arts Program, 1999-. Recipient Stage Mgmt. award, U.S. Inst. Theatre Tech., 2004. Mem.: Ohio Cmty. Theatre Assn. (OCTA) (del. 1997—2001, 2005—), Akron Area Arts Alliance (v.p. 2001—03), Actors Equity Assn. (AEA), Stage Mgrs. Assn. LA (SMA), Stage Mgrs. Assn., US Inst. Theatre Tech. (USITT) (bd. dir. 1990—96, vice commr. 1992—2000, v.p. membership and devel. 2000—05), North Hollywood/Universal City C. of C. (bd. dir. 1994—96), Delta Chi Omega (pres. 1978), Phi Kappa Phi. Avocations: poetry, journalism, flying, rowing, rugby. Office: Weathervane Playhouse 1301 Weathervane Ln Akron OH 44313-5186 Office Phone: 330-836-2323. Office Fax: 330-873-2150. E-mail: emk2u@aol.com.

KAZMAREK, LINDA ADAMS, secondary school educator; b. Crisfield, Md., Jan. 18, 1945; d. Gordon I. Sr. and Annie Ruby (Sommers) Adams; m. Stephen Kazmarek, Jr., Aug. 2, 1981. B of Music Edn., Peabody Conservatory of Music, 1967; postgrad., Morgan U., Towson U. Cert. advanced profl. tchr., K-12, Md.; nat. cert. tchr. Mayron Cole piano method. Organist, choir dir. Halethorpe United Meth. Ch., Balt., min. music, 1978-92, 93-99; organist, choir dir. Olive Branch United Meth. Ch., 1973-77, 1978-83, 93—; piano tchr. Modal Cities Program, Balt., Balt. Cmty. Schs.; tchr. vocal music Balt. City Schs., 1967-99; min. music Halethorpe Meth. Ch., 1978-92, 93-99, St. John's Episcopal Parish Day Sch., 1999-2001; music specialist. Piano accompanist Witness Sing, 2000, Christian Choir, 2000-01; pianist Chestnut Ridge Bapt. Ch., 2001; pianist and performer Joppa Gospel Tabernacle, 2002-; pvt. tchr. piano and organ, concert artist. Composer, arranger, performer: A Family of Care (award, 1991, Praise Song, 1992, Thy Way, Lord, 1993, Peace and Rest, 1994, Sing Praise to Jesus, 1994, Trilogy for piano solo, 1994, Shine Your Light, 1994, Resurrection, 1995, 1-800-Heaven, 1995, God Has A Plan for You, 1995, Christmas Joy, 1998, His Name is Jesus, 1998, Only Love, 1999, Be Still and Listen, 1999, Awesome Love, 2001, The Gifts of the Vine, 2002, (piano arrangements) The First Noel, Angels We Have Heard on High, O Come All Ye Faithful, All Through the Night/Lullaby, I Heard the Bells on Christmas Day/Silent Night Christmas Medley, I Saw Three Ships; rec. Christmas CD His Name is Jesus, 2000, Gifts of the Vine, 2002; guest performer S.W. Emergency Svcs., 1999; CD Praise, Peace and Promise, 2002; rec. America the Beautiful/America, Jesus Loves Me, The Promise, Blessings, His Eye Is on the Sparrow, I Bowed on My Knees and Cried Holy, Praising My Saviour, 2002, Celebrate Christmas, 2003; original composition Celebrate Christmas Believe, 2004, Faith, Believe, 88 Keys of Praise, 2004. Concert perfomer for Halethorpe Meth. Ch., 1994, Meth. Bd. Child Care, 1989, Balt. S.W. Emergency Svcs., 1991; guest performer Balt. City Tchrs. Appreciation Banquet, 1991, S.W.E.S. 18th Yr. Celebration, 1999; concert artist and performer, 2001—. Recipient vol. award for music enrichment summer program, 1973, award for voluntarism Fund. for Ednl. Excellence, 1985; Fund for Ednl. Excellence grantee, 1988. Mem. NEA, Md. State Tchrs. Assn., Balt. City Tchrs. Assn., Md. Music Educators Assn. (award for 30 yrs. of svc. in music and music edn. 1997), Music Educators Nat. Conf., Md. State Music Tchrs. Assn., Nat. Music Tchrs. Assn., Gospel Music Assn., Peabody Alumni Assn. Office Phone: 410-931-0544. E-mail: Kazmarekl@comcast.net.

KEAIRNS, YVONNE EWING, psychologist; b. Pitts., Mar. 29, 1939; d. David and Helen Ewing; m. Dale Lee Keairns, Aug. 5, 1967; 1 child, Carter Ewing. BA, Baldwin-Wallace Coll., 1961; MS, U. Pitts., 1968; PhD, Duquesne U., 1980. Lic. psychologist, Pa. Psychologist Arsenal Family & Children's Ctr., Pitts., 1975-81, exec. dir., 1981-92; instr. Pitts. Theol. Sem., 1975-92, Carlow Coll., Pitts., 1992; pvt. practice psychology Pitts., 1989—. Cons. Westminster Coll., New Wilmington, Pa., KDKA TV, Pitts.; psychol. cons. video for nat. TV Secrets of Success, 1989. Mem. State Psychol. Bd., Commonwealth of Pa., Harrisburg, 1986—; del. 1st Internat. Quaker Women's Conf., Religious Soc. of Friends, London, 1990; People to People ambassador, Soviet Union, 1989. Named one of 200 Hardworking Women in Pa., Pa. Women's Orgn., 1987. Mem. APA, Pa. Psychol. Assn. (media award 1990), Greater Pitts. Psychol. Assn., 20th Century Club. Avocations: bicycling, cross country skiing, gardening, fly fishing. Home: 5419 Northumberland St Pittsburgh PA 15217-1128 Office: 5701 5th Ave Pittsburgh PA 15232-2703

KEALA, BETTY ANN LYMAN, computer scientist; b. Hilo, Hawaii, Apr. 14, 1931; d. Richard Ka'ilihiwa and Beatrice Ida (Culman) L.; m. Francis A. Keala, Nov. 28, 1952; children: Frances Ann Keala Rothwell, John Richard Keala, Robert Mark Keala. BA, U. Hawaii, 1952, MS, 1970. Cert. Data Processing Mgmt. Assn. Computer programmer Nat. Marine Fisheries Svc., Honolulu, 1957-73; administrator GTE Hawaiian Telephone, Honolulu, 1973-88; founder-owner Pacific Computer Assocs., Honolulu, 1989-94. Cons. Queen Liliuokalani Children's Ctr., Honolulu, 1993, St. Louis H.S., 1992, Honolulu Police Dept., 1979. Editor: (book) Mea Ho'omanao-My Thoughts, 1995. Mem. Bd. Parks and Recreation, Honolulu, 1983-90, vice-chair, 1989-90; trustee Honolulu Theatre for Youth, 1998; chair adv. coun. Coll. Arts & Scis., U. Hawaii, 1994-2004; mem. U. Hawaii Cmty. Partnership, 1997—, Hawaiian Music Hall Fame & Mus., 1998—. Personal E-mail: bkeala@hawaii.rr.com.

KEAN, BARBARA MCSWAIN, education educator, department chairman; d. Grover Cleveland and Shannon North McSwain; children from previous marriage: Melvin Rodman, Barton Eugene. BS, East Carolina U., 1967; MA, Marshall U., Charleston, W.Va., 1986; EdD, W.Va. U., 1989. Cert. prin. K-12 NC, elem. edn. K-6, grammar 4-8 NC, behavior/emotional handicapped K-12 NC, academically gifted K-12 NC, learning disabled K-12 NC. Elem. sch. tchr. NC Pub. Schs., Wilmington, 1974—77; elem. tchr. Valco Sch. Sys., Tema, Ghana, 1982—84; instr. Marshall U., 1989—90; from asst. to assoc. prof. W.Va. Wesleyan Coll., Buckhannon, 1990—99; prof., dir. elem. edn. Pfeiffer U., Misenheimer, NC, 1999—. Mem. adv. bd. Stany C.C. Early Childhood Program, Albemarle, NC, 2005. Named Tchr. of Yr., SNEA, W.Va. Wesleyan Coll., 1993; recipient Meth. Exemplary Tchg. award, Meth. Bd., 1992, Excellent Educator award, Mortar Bd. W.Va. Wesleyan Coll., 1994, Class of 1995 Disting. Faculty award, Sr. Class, W.Va. Wesleyan Coll., 1995, Recognition of Svcs. to Students of W.Va., W.Va. Coun. on Profl. Edn., 1996. Mem.: Omicron Delta Kappa, Delta Kappa Gamma, Kappa Delta Pi, Phi Delta Kappa. Avocations: travel, service learning. Office: Pfeiffer U 52 Hwy N Misenheimer NC 28109 Office Phone: 704-463-1360. E-mail: bkean@pfeiffer.edu.

KEANE, KAREN M., auction house executive; m. Dan Elias. Masters Degree, Boston U. Mng. dir., v.p., exec. v.p. Skinner, Inc., Boston, ptnr., CEO, 1997—. Regular featured appraiser Antique Roadshow, PBS, 1996—. Contbr. articles to profl. jours. Benefit auctioneer AIDS Action Com., Mass. Coll. Art, Inst. Contemporary Art, Boston; mem. bd. overseers DeCordova Mus., Lincoln, Mass. Office: Skinner INc 357 Main St Bolton MA 01740

KEANE, MARGARET A., lawyer; b. 1959; BA, Boston U., 1981; JD, U. Pa., 1986. Bar: NY 1986, Mass. 1986, Pa. 1997, US Supreme Ct. 1994. Co-mng. ptnr. Pitts. office LeBoeuf, Lamb, Greene & MacRae LLP, hiring ptnr. Pitts. office, chmn. litig. dept. Office: LeBoeuf Lamb Greene & MacRae LLP One Gateway Ctr Ste 1600 420 Fort Duquesne Blvd Pittsburgh PA 15222-1437 Office Phone: 412-594-2402. Office Fax: 412-594-5237. Business E-Mail: mkeane@llgm.com.

KEANE, MARIE JEANETTE (MARIA KEANE), art educator, artist; b. NYC, Mar. 31, 1931; d. Nicholas Joseph and Mary Christine (Passaretti) Santora; m. Thomas Roger Keane; children: Roger, Kathleen, Elisabeth, Mary, Julia. BA, Hunter Coll., N.Y.C., 1953; MA, U. Del., 1994. Cert. tchr., N.Y. Tchr. Niagara Falls (N.Y.) Pub. Sch. Sys., 1953-56; instr. watercolor DuPont Country Club, Wilmington, Del., 1975-78; tchr. Mt. Pleasant Sch. Dist., Wilmington, 1975-78; artist in residence Archmere Acad., Claymont, Del., 1979-83; sr. docent Del. Art Mus., Wilmington, 1987-88; artist in residence Del. Divsn. of Arts, Wilmington, 1983-93; adj. prof. fine arts and art history Wilmington Coll., 1986—. Workshop devel. Ctr. Arts, U. Del., Wilmington, 2004; docent Historic Howard Pyle Studio, Wilmington, 1990—; participant master workshop in art L.I. U., 1991; participant master workshop in monoprint Bennington (Vt.) Coll., 1993, printmaker, 1992, 95; juror Internat. Art Exhibit, Hercules; vol. Classes for Christian Formation of Spl. Populations, 1970-80; art chair Christ in Christmas Com., 1979-88; exec. bd. for physically challenged Cath. Diocese of Wilmington, 1980-87; exec. bd., com. Very Spl. Arts Festival, 1984-90; docent Del. Art Mus., 1987-88; juror Del. Camera Club Regional Exhbn., 1992; exhbn. chair Christ in Christmas Retrospect, 1992; juror Reflections Del. Scholastic State-wide Exhbn., 1993-94, Dover Art League (members exhbn), 2004; lectr. excellence in rsch., art history U. Del., 1993; scholarship chair Studio Group, Inc., 1992—; docent Smithsonian Tour, Howard Pyle Studio, Wilmington, pres., 1980-82; lectr. in field. Illustrator: Touch of Spring, 1976; author, illustrator: Watercolor Wings, 1976; author: Heroines and Housewives, 1994; one-person shows at Luther Towers Gallery, Wilmington, Friends Sch., Wilmington, Du Pont Country Club, Wilmington, Wilmington Drama League, 1995, 909 Gallery, Wilmington, Immaculata Coll., Exton-Paoli, Pa., 1997, Del. State Arts Coun., 1989, Goldey Beacom Coll., 1992, Wilmington Drama League, 1995, Grace Gallery, Wilmington, Del., 2004, numerous others; exhibited in group shows at Atrium Gallery, Wilmington, 1988, Wilmington Coll., 1988, 89, 90, 94, 96, 2003, 05, Del. Nature Soc., 1990, Del. Mus. Natural History, 1990, L.I. U., 1991, U. Del., 1992, 93, Howard Pyle Studio, 1993, 2001, Chester County Art Assn., 1993-2005, Wilmington Coll., 1994, Revsin Gallery, Phila., 2000, 2005, Da Vinci Art Alliance, Phila., 2004, 2005, Chester County Art Assn., 2005, others; represented in permanent collections Wilmington Coll., Newcastle, Del., U. Del., Newark, Zimmerli Mus., Rutgers State U., New Brunswick, Archmere Acad., Claymont, Del., Wilmington Divsn. Librs., So. Va. Coll. for Women, Buena Vista, Va., Del. Divsn. Arts, Wilmington, Mary Mother of Hope House, Wilmington, Del. Art Mus. Circulating Gallery, Studio Group Inc.; contbr. poetry to jours. and mags. Pub. and exhbn. curator Del. Artists, mem. coun. Barnes Found. scholar, Merion, Pa., 1978-80; recipient Jill Jones Nauta award Chester County Art Assn., 1988, J. Lanier Jordan Meml. award, 1989, awards Chester County Art Assn., 1992, 93, 95, award Ctr. for Creative Arts, 1992, 94, award Howard Pyle Studio Regional Exhbn., 1994, Mary Derrickson McCurdy award Rehoboth Art League, 1994,2004, awards Rehoboth Art League, 1995, profl. fellowship Del. Divsn. Arts and Nat. Endowment Arts, 1996-97, Grumbacher Gold medal award Phila. Sketch Club, 1997, Svc. award Del. Artists. Mem.: Nat. Collage Soc. (merit award 2003, 2004), Nat. Assn. Women Artists (silver medal, da Vinci Art Alliance 2006), Chester County Art Assn. (Excellence in Landscape award in watercolor 2005), Nat. League Am. Pen Women (curator Biennial exhbn. Diamond State and Holly brs. 2006, prizes 1985, 1987, 1989, 1991, 1993, 1995, 1997, nat. exhbn. Tampa 1998, 2 lit. awards in poetry nat. conv. 1998, prizes 1999, 2001, Lit. award 2004), Studio Group, Inc., Phila. Watercolor (assoc.), Am. Watercolor Soc. (assoc.), Phi Kappa Phi. Democrat. Roman Catholic. Avocations: photography, travel, digital art. Home: 332 Spalding Rd Wilmington DE 19803-2422 Office: Wilmington Coll 320 N Dupont Hwy New Castle DE 19720-6434

KEARFOTT, KIMBERLEE JANE, nuclear engineer, educator, health physicist; b. Oakland, Calif., Jan. 30, 1956; d. William Edward and Edith (Chamberlin) K. BSc, St. Mary's U., Halifax, N.S., Can., 1975; ME in Nuclear Engring., U. Va., 1977; ScD, MIT, 1980. Coop. engr. Babcock & Wilcox Co., Lynchburg, Va., 1975-77; rsch. asst. Mass. Gen. Hosp., Boston, 1980; asst. prof. Cornell U. Med. Sch., N.Y.C., 1980-84; rsch. assoc. Sloan-Kettering Cancer Ctr., N.Y.C., 1980-84; from asst. to assoc. prof. Ariz. State U., Tempe, 1984-89; assoc. prof. Ga. Inst. Tech., Atlanta, 1989-93; assoc. prof. Med. Sch. Emory U., Atlanta, 1990-93; prof. U. Mich., Ann Arbor, 1993—, dir. faculty devel. Coll. Engring., 1994-97. Contbr. articles to profl. jours. including Jour. Health Physics, Jour. of Nuc. Medicine, Jour. Computer Assisted Tomography, Jour. Med. Physics. Mem. IEEE, AAUW, Am. Nuc. Soc. (bd. dirs. 1996-01, Women's Achievement award 1995), Soc. Nuc. Medicine (Tetalman award 1991), Assn. Women in Sci., Soc. Women Engrs., Health Physics Soc. (bd. dirs. 1992-95, Anderson award 1992), Order of Engr. Office: U Mich Dept Nuclear Engring and Radiol Sci Ann Arbor MI 48109-2104 Office Phone: 734-763-9117. Business E-Mail: kearfott@umich.edu.

KEARNEY, IRENE SPRUILL, elementary school educator; b. Warrenton, N.C., May 17, 1937; d. Hughley and Janet (Alston) Spruill; m. Raymond Kearney, Sr.; children: Alfreda, Raymond Jr. BS, Elizabeth City State U., 1959; MEd, N.C. Cen. U., 1976; EdD, Nova U., 1987; PhD, Am. Theol. Sem., 1988. Cert. early childhood edn., supervision, adminstrn., middle sch., pastoral counseling. Camp dir. N.C. Cen. U. PTA, Durham; pvt. prac. Warrenton, N.C.; cons., tchr. Warren County Schs., Warrenton. Author: Sparking Divergent Thinking, 1985. Mem. NEA, Warren County Assn. Educators (pres.) Franklinton Assn. Univ. Women (V.p.), Alpha Kappa Alpha, Phi Delta Kappa. Home: 195 Big Woods Rd Warrenton NC 27589-9706 Office Phone: 252-257-3401.

KEARNEY, SISTER MARY JOHN, educator; b. Jersey City, Apr. 16, 1932; d. John Vincent and Mary Theresa (O'Neill) K.; BA, Caldwell Coll., 1962; MA, Cath. U., 1971; postgrad. Montclair State Coll.; MEd, Columbia U., 1993. Joined Sisters St. Dominic, Caldwell, N.J., 1949; elem. edn. cert., N.J., nursery sch. cert., N.J., cert. prin., supr., sch. adminstr., tchr. social studies K-12, N.J. Prin., St. Cassian Sch., Upper Montclair, N.J., 1965-66, Lacordaire Sch.-Elem., Upper Montclair, 1969-75, St. Philomena Sch., Livingston, N.J., 1975-80; mem. faculty, edn. dept. Caldwell Coll. (N.J.), 1980—, instr., 1980-86, asst. prof., 1986—92, assoc. prof., 1992—; chmn. dept., 1980-92, dir. field experiences, 1992—; dir. novices Caldwell Dominican Sisters, Caldwell, 1966-69. Active Paterson Diocesan Bd. of Edn., 1989—, v.p., 1991-93, pres., 1993—; sec. N.J. Assn. Coll. Tchr. Edn., 1986-92; mem. and regional rep. Nat. Assn. Bds. Coun., Commn., Com. Edn., 1995-2005. Named Irishwoman of Yr., St. Philomena Parish, Livingston, 1978. Mem. Nat. Cath. Edn. Assn. (bd. dirs. 1983-86, vice chmn. bd. dirs. 1984-86, pres. elem. dept. 1980-83, Pres.'s award Outstanding Service to Cath. Edn. 1988, Outstanding Educator of Yr. award 1989), Internat. Reading Assn., Tchr. Edn. Roundtable N.J., Am. Assn. Colls. for Tchr. Edn., N.J. Assn. Colls. Tchr. Edn. (sec. 1986-88), Phi Delta Kappa, Kappa Delta Pi, Kappa Delta Epsilon. Democrat. Roman Catholic. Home: Mount Saint Dominic Caldwell NJ 07006 Office: Caldwell College Ryerson Ave Caldwell NJ 07006

KEARNEY-NUNNERY, ROSE, nursing administrator, educator, consultant; b. Glen Falls, NY, July 8, 1951; d. James J. and Helen F. (Oprandy) K.; m. Jimmie E. Nunnery. BS, Keuka Coll., 1973; M of Nursing, U. Fla., 1976, PhD, 1987. Asst. prof. La. State U. Med. Ctr., New Orleans, 1976-87; project coord., indigent health care U. Fla., Gainesville, 1984-85; asst. prof. U. South Fla., Tampa, 1987-88; dir. nursing programs SUNY, New Paltz, NY, 1988-94; project dir. MS in gerontol. nursing advanced nursing edn. grant U.S. Health Resources and Svc. Adminstrn. Div. Nursing, 1992-94; head nursing dept. Tech. Coll. of the Low Country, Beaufort, SC, 1995-97, v.p. acad. affairs, 1997—2005, cons., adj. instr., 2005—. Author: Advancing Your Profession Concepts for Profl. Nursing, 1997, 3d edit., 2005. Bd. dirs. Beaufort Co. First Steps, 2000-01; Ulster County unit Am. Cancer Soc., 1991-94; nursing edn. com., 1990-92; bd. dir. Mid-Hudson Consortium for Advancement Edn. for Health Profl., 1988-94; nursing edn. com., 1988-92; scholarship com., 1989-93; com. chmn., 1990-93, treas., 1992-94; prof. devel. program SUNY, Albany, 1989-92; adv. coun. Ulster CC, 1989-94; adv. regional planning group for early intervention svc. United Cerebral Palsy Ulster County Inc., Children's Rehab. Ctr., 1989-91; mem. Ulster County adv. com. Office for Aging, 1991-94; state del. S.C. Conf. on Aging, 1995; bd. dir. Beaufort County Coun. on Aging, 1995; cmty. adv. bd. Hilton Head Med. Ctr. and Clinics, 1996-2000; mem. SC Bd. Nursing, 2000—, pres. 2000-03; accreditation evaluator So. Assn. Coll. and Sch. Commn. on Coll., 2000-05. Mem. ANA, Nat. League Nursing, S.C. Nurses Assn. (editl. bd. 1994-99, chair 1996-99), Nat. Coun. State Bds. of Nursing (mem. practice, regulation and edn. com. 2001-05, area II dir., 2005-), Sigma Theta Tau Roman Catholic. Home: 80 Peninsula Dr Hilton Head Island SC 29926-1119 Personal E-mail: rosekn@hargray.com.

KEARNS, BECKY, bank executive; Pres., resort banking Zions Bank (subsidiary of Zions Bancorporation), Salt Lake City, 1998—. Bd. chmn. Summit County Hospital, Utah; bd. mem. Pacific Coast Banking Sch., Park City Chamber of Commerce, Zions Bank Polit. Action Com., Park City Extreme Soccer, Summit Inst. for the Arts and Humanities, Idaho State U. Found., Sundance Institute's Utah Com. Named one of 25 Women to Watch, US Banker mag., 2005. Office: Zions Bank One S Main St Salt Lake City UT 84111*

KEARNS, ELLEN CECELIA, lawyer; b. Washington, Apr. 15, 1945; d. Lawrence Mark and Mary (Moran) K. AB, Regis Coll., 1967; JD, Boston Coll., 1976. Bar: Mass. 1977, U.S. Supreme Ct. 1989, U.S. Ct. Appeals (1st cir.) 1979, U.S. Dist. Ct. (Mass.) 1980. Ptnr. Kearns & Rubin, Boston, 1992—99, Epstein Becker & Green, Boston, 1999—2004; of counsel Foley & Lardner, Boston, 2005—. Mem. Gov.'s Commn. on Status of Women, 1983-86; del. Mass. Dem. Conv., 1988-90; trustee, Regis Coll.; mem. Reading Mcpl. Light Bd.; founder, bd. dirs. Sister Spirit, Inc., 1990-91; lector St. Agnes Ch. Recipient Cushing-Gavin award for Excellence in Labor-Mgmt. Rels., 1993, Regis Coll. Alumni Achievement award 1993, Boston Coll. Law Sch. Alumnae of Yr., 1992. Mem. ABA (chmn. fed. labor stds. legis. com. 1991-94), Mass. Bar Assn. (labor and employment sect. coun. 1990-93), Nat. Conf. Women's Bar Assns. (pres. 2004-), Women's Bar Assn. (bd. dirs. 1990-92, treas. 1993-95, v.p. 1995-96), Boston Bar Assn. (chmn. labor law sect. 1988-90), Boston Coll. Alumni Assn. (pres.), Reading Jaycees (treas.). Democrat. Roman Catholic. Home: 2 Beaver Rd Reading MA 01867-1103 Office: Foley & Lardner 111 Huntington Ave Boston MA 02199

KEARNS, ELLEN VERONICA, artist; b. Washington, Apr. 29, 1964; d. Francis E. and Ann P. Kearns AB cum laude, Smith Coll., 1986; PhD, Mich. State U., 1991. Grad. fellow Mich. State U., East Lansing, Mich., 1986-91; fellow Harvard U., Cambridge, 1992-93; USDA fellow Mass. Inst. Tech., Cambridge, 1993-95; vis. fellow Max-Planck-Inst., Golm, Germany, 1995-96; rsch. assoc. Dartmouth Coll., Hanover, NH, 1996-98; asst. mgr. Starbucks Coffee Co., Ridgefield, Conn., 1999—2000; assoc. mgr. Banana Republic, Mt. Kisco, NY, 2000—01; tng. specialist Fleet Boston Fin., N.Y.C., 2001—04; trainer software Blank Rome, LLP, 2004—. Avocations: painting, gardening, cats, knitting, art cars.

KEARNS, MERLE GRACE, state agency administrator; b. Bellefonte, Pa., May 19, 1938; d. Robert John and Mary Katharine (Fitzgerald) Grace; m. Thomas Raymond Kearns, June 27, 1959; children: Thomas, Michael, Timothy, Matthew. BS, Ohio State U., 1960. Tchr. St. Raphael Elem. Sch., Springfield, Ohio, 1960-62; substitute tchr. Mad River Green Dist., Springfield, 1972-78; instr. Clark Tech. Coll., Springfield, 1978-80; commr. Clark County, Ohio, 1981-91; mem. Ohio Senate, Columbus, 1991-2000, majority whip, 1998—2000; mem. Ohio Ho. of Reps., Columbus, 2001—05, majority floor leader, 2005; dir. Ohio Dept. Aging, 2005—. Pres. Bd. County Commrs., 1982—83, 1987, 90. Sec. County Commrs. Assn. Ohio, 1988, 2d v.p., 1989—90, 1st v.p., 1990; mem. exec. com. Springfield Reps., 1984—2001; chair Ohio Children's Trust Fund, 1995—2000; past chair Legis. Office of Edn. Oversight; active NCSL Welfare Reform Task Force, 2001—05; vice-chair Policy Consensus Initiative Bd., 2002—; chair Head Start Plus Study Coun.; bd. dirs. Springfield Symphony, 1980—86, Arts Coun., 1980—85; bd. dirs., mem. exec. bd. Nat. Conf. State Legislatures, 2000—03. Named Woman of the Yr., Springfield Pilot Club, 1981, Wittenburg Woman of Accomplishment, 1991, Watchdog of Treasury, 1991, 1996, 2000, Legislator of the Yr., Assn. Mental Health and Drug Addition Svcs. Bds., 1996, Pub. Childrens Svcs. Agys. Ohio, 1999, Ohio Cmty. Colls., 1997, Ohio Disting. Nurses, 2000, Advance Practice Nurse Assn., 2002, Legis. Co-Person of the Yr., Assn. Joint Vocat. Sch. Supts., 1996, Mental Health Adv. of the Yr., 2002, Outstanding Head Start Legislator of the Yr., Miami Valley, 2002, Legislator of Yr., Ohio Fedn. Tchrs., 2003, Advocate of Yr., Ohio County Alzheimer Assn., 2004, Alzheimer Legis. Advocate of Yr., 2004; recipient Pub. Policy Leadership award, 1997, Disting. Svc. Pub. Ofcls. award, Assn. Ohio Philanthropic Homes, 1999, 1st Ann. Jane Swart Disting. Svcs. to Nursing, 2000, Citizenship award, Ohio State U. Coll. Human Ecology, 2000, Legislator of Yr., Behavioral Health Authorities Assn., 2003, Ohio Better World award, Ohio Mediation Assn., 2004;, Ohio State U. scholar, 1957—59. Mem.: LWV (bd. dirs. 1964—78, pres. 1975—78), Ohio Nurses Assn. (Legislator of the Yr. 1995, 1999), Rotary, Omicron Nu. Roman Catholic. Avocation: reading. Office: Ohio Dept Aging 9th Fl 50 W Broad St Columbus OH 43215-3363 Office Phone: 614-466-7246.

KEARSE, AMALYA LYLE, federal judge; b. Vauxhall, NJ, June 11, 1937; d. Robert Freeman and Myra Lyle (Smith) K. BA, Wellesley Coll., 1959; JD cum laude, U. Mich., 1962. Bar: N.Y. 1963, U.S. Supreme Ct. 1967. Assoc. Hughes, Hubbard & Reed, N.Y.C., 1962—69, ptnr., 1969—79; judge U.S. Ct. Appeals (2d cir.), 1979—. Lectr. evidence NYU Law Sch., 1968—69. Author: Bridge Conventions Complete, 1975, Bridge Conventions Complete, 3d edit., 1990, Bridge at Your Fingertips, 1980; transl., editor: Bridge Analysis, 1979; editor: Ofcl. Ency. of Bridge, 3d edit., 1976; mem. editl. bd.: Charles Goren, 1974—. Trustee N.Y.C. YWCA, 1976—79, Am. Contract Bridge League Nat. Laws Commn., 1975—; mem. Pres.'s Com. on Selection of Fed. Jud. Officers, 1977—78; Bd. dirs. NAACP Legal Def. and Endl. Fund, 1977—79, Nat. Urban League, 1978—79. Named Women's Pairs Bridge Champion Nat. div., 1971, 1972, World div., 1986, Nat. Women's Teams Bridge Champion, 1987, 1990, 1991; named to, Bridge Hall of Fame, 2004. Mem.: ABA, Lawyers Com. for Civil Rights Under Law (mem. exec. com. 1970—79), Am. Law Inst., Assn. of Bar of City of N.Y. Office: US Ct Appeals US Courthouse 40 Foley Sq Rm 2001 New York NY 10007*

KEAT, JANE BLAKELY, education educator; b. Whitehall, Wis., Sept. 28, 1938; d. Burdette Dake and Sadie Amanda (Jordahl) Blakely; m. Donald B. Keat, Sept. 5, 1959; children: Russell J., Laura Keat Grindrod BA Elem. Edn., Am. U., 1960; MS Integrative Edn., Marywood Coll., 1983; PhD, Pa. State U., 2004. Tchr. Christ Lutheran Presch., York, Pa., 1970—88, dir., tchr., 1980—89, dir. Christian ed., 1983—89; instr. continuing edn. Pa. State U., York, 1989—2003, asst. prof., coord. Early Childhood Edn. Harrisburg, 2004—. Recipient first place credit category Nat. Univ. Continuing Ed. Assn. Region II, 1990 Mem. ASCD, Nat. Assn. Edn. Young Children, Nat. Assn. Early Childhood Tchr. Edn., Internat. Reading Assn., Phi Delta Kappa Lutheran.

KEATING, ANALOUISE, educator, author; b. Chgo., June 24, 1961; PhD, U. Ill., 1990. Prof. Ea. N.Mex. U., 1990-99, Aquinas Coll., 1999—2001; assoc. prof. Tex. Woman's U., 2001—06, prof., 2006—. Author: Women Reading Women Writing: Self-Invention in Paula Gunn Allen, Gloria Anzaldúa and Audre Lorde, 1996 (Choice Outstanding Acad. book 1996); editor: Perspectives: Gender Studies, 1999; editor Interviews/Entrevistas by Gloria E. Anzaldúa, 2000 (Susan Koppelman award 2001); co-editor (with Gloria E. Anzaldua) This Bridge We Call Home: Radical Visions for Transformation, Entremundos/Among Worlds: New Perspectives on Gloria Anzaldua, 2006, Teaching Transformation Transcultural Dialogues in the Classroom, 2006; contbr. articles to profl. jours. Grad. fellowship U. Ill., 1984, 86, Rockefeller Summer Rsch. fellowship S.W. Inst. for Rsch. on Women U. Ariz., 1992; Irene Kogan scholarship U. Ill., 1989; Tchg. Excellence Faculty Round Table grantee N.Mex. Ctr. for Tchg. Excellence, 1995-96. Mem. MLA, Nat. Women's Studies Assn., Am. Studies Assn., Soc. for the Study of Multi-Ethnic Lit. of the U.S. Avocation: swimming. Office: Tex Woman's U Women's Studies Program PO Box 425557 Denton TX 76204-5557 Office Phone: 940-898-2129. Office Fax: 940-898-2181. Personal E-mail: zami@mindspring.com. Business E-Mail: aKeating@twu.edu.

KEATING, CATHERINE, bank executive; JD, U. Va., 1980. Head Mid-Atlantic region JP Morgan Private Bank, Phila., global head Wealth Adv. and Fiduciary Svcs. NYC, 2003, pres. US Region. Office: JPMorgan Private Bank 345 Park Ave New York NY 10154-1002*

KEATING, ISABEL, actress; b. Savannah, Ga. Actor: (Broadway plays) Enchanted April, 2003, The Boy From Oz, 2003 (nominee Outer Critics Cir. best actress, 2004, nominee Tony award best featured actress in a musical, 2004, Drama Desk award best featured actress in a musical, 2004, Theatre World award for outstanding musical debut, 2004), (off Broadway shows) Bonnie, Once in a Lifetime, Waiting at the Waters Edge, (regional stage shows) The Rise and Fall of Little Voice, Three Sisters, Chilean Holiday, One Foot on the Floor, Indian Ink, 2000 (Helen Hayes award best actress, 2000), On the March to the Sea, 2005, Lady Windermere's Fan, 2005; (films) The Nanny Diaries, 2006; (TV films) Judy Garland: By Myself, 2004. Office: c/o Blue Ridge Entertainment 41 Union Sq W New York NY 10003

KEATING, SISTER KEVINA, nun, education educator; arrived in US, 1966; d. Patrick and Deborah Keating. BA cum laude, Dominican Coll., 1974; MA, U. San Francisco, 1985, EdD, 1987; MA, Stanford U., 1988. Joined Sisters of Charity of the Incarnate Word, 1966; cert. tchr. Tex., H.S. math. and English Tex. State Bd. Edn. Nun Sisters of Charity of Incarnate Word, Houston, 1966—; tchr. English St. Francis of Assisi, Houston, 1970—71; tchr, English and math. Jesse Jones Sr. H.S., Houston, 1973—74, Our Lady of Fatima Sch., Texas City, 1974, prin., 1984—85; tchr. English and math. St. Ann Sch., Salt Lake City, 1975—81, prin., 1981—83, Immaculate Heart of Mary Sch., Big Spring, Tex., 1983—84; dir. tchr. edn., asst. prof. U. San Francisco, 1987—96; asst. to v.p., assoc. prof. U. Incarnate Word, San Antonio, 1997—98; v.p. congl. leadership Congregation of Sisters of Charity of the Incarnate Word, Houston, 1998—2006. Dir. planning Sisters of Charity of the Incarnate Word, Houston, 1991—94, Houston, 1998—2006; presenter in field. Co-author: Pioneer Mentoring in Teacher Preparation, 2001; contbr. chpt. to book. Chair Intercongregational Literacy Ministry, Houston, 1999—2006; com. mem. U.S./Mexico border conditions Leadership Conf. Women Religious, Region 12, 1998—2006; bd. mem. McCauley Housing, Silver Springs, Md., 1999—2001, CHRISTUS Health, Dallas, 1999—2006. Multicultural Action Plan grantee, U. San Francisco, 1996. Mem.: Am. Assn. Colls. Tchrs. Edn., Assn. Tchr. Educators, Nat. Cath. Edn. Assn., Phi Delta Kappa. Democrat. Avocations: hiking, dance, reading, concerts. Office: Sisters of Charity of the Incarnate Word 6510 Lawndale Ave Houston TX 77023 Office Phone: 713-928-6053. Business E-Mail: keating@ccvi-vdm.org.

KEATING, LAURA LEE M., historian, records management professional; b. N.Y.C., Dec. 13, 1952; d. Matthew Joseph and Florence Patricia Salamone; m. Craig L. Keating, May 3, 1975. Student, Coll. of White Plains, N.Y.; cert. in records mgmt., Westchester C.C. Records mgmt. and property mgmt. AT&T, White Plains, 1970—2001; mcpl. historian Town of Cortlandt, Cortlandt Manor, NY, 2001—. V.p. Inst. of History, Arch., and Edn., Inc., 2003—. Trustee Cortlandt Hist. Soc., 1991—; pres. Bear Mtn. Bridge Toll House Vis. Ctr. Found., 2002—. Mem.: Westchester Civil War Round Table (pres. 2000—). Avocations: crafts, collecting reproductions of 18th and 19th century clothing, collecting antique books, living history interpretation. Home: 12 Cross Ln Cortlandt Manor NY 10567-5108

KEATING, REGINA G., computer analyst consultant; b. Bryn Mawr, Pa., Mar. 20, 1940; d. Francis Stanislaus and Frances Mulligan Gear; m. Frank J. Keating, Mar. 4, 1972 (div. Dec. 1978); 1 child, Frank. BBA, Temple U., 1981, MBA, 1982. Sr. staff local govt. com. Pa. Constnl. Conv., 1967-68; adminstr. Blank Rome Comisky & McCauley, Phila., 1968-72; computer programmer Lee Tire & Rubber Co., Valley Forge, Pa., 1984-86; programmer, analyst Amerigas Corp., Valley Forge, 1986-88, Am. Electronic Labs., Lansdale, Pa., 1988-93; cons. computer analyst Polin Assocs., Richboro, Pa., 1993—. Instr., adj. lectr. Temple U., Phila., 1981, 85. Sec., registration chmn. Dem. Com., Haverford Twp., Pa., 1964-71, com. woman, Abington Twp., 1978—. Mem. NAACP, NOW, NAFE, ACLU, World Affairs Coun.-Phila., So. Poverty Law Ctr., Pub. Citizen.

KEATON, DIANE, actress; b, Santa Ana, Calif., Jan. 5, 1946; Student, Neighborhood Playhouse, N.Y.C., 1968. Appeared on N.Y. stage in Hair, 1968, Play It Again Sam, 1969, The Primary English Class, 1976; appeared in numerous films including Lovers and Other Strangers, 1970, Play It Again Sam, 1972, The Godfather, 1972, Sleeper, 1973, The Godfather Part II, 1974, Love and Death, 1975, I Will, I Will.For Now, 1975, Harry and Walter Go To New York, 1976, Annie Hall, 1977 (Best Actress Acad. award 1978, Brit. Acad. Best Actress award 1978, N.Y. Film Critics Circle award 1978, Nat. Soc. Film Critics award 1978), Looking for Mr. Goodbar, 1977, Interiors, 1978, Manhattan, 1979, Reds, 1981 (Acad. award nominee), Shoot the Moon, 1982, Little Drummer Girl, 1984, Mrs. Soffel, 1984, Crimes of the Heart, 1986, Radio Days, 1987, Baby Boom, 1987, The Good Mother, 1988, The Lemon Sisters, 1990, The Godfather Part III, 1990, Father of the Bride, 1991, Manhattan Murder Mystery, 1993, Look Who's Talking Now, 1993 (voice), Father of the Bride 2, 1995, Marvin's Room, 1996, First Wives Club, 1996, The Only Thrill, 1997, The Other Sister, 1999, Hanging Up, 2000, Town and Country, 2001, Plan B, 2001, Something's Gotta Give, 2003 (Golden Globe for best actress in a musical or comedy, 2004, Acad. Award nomination for best actress, 2004, Screen Actors Guild Award nomination for best actress, 2004), The Family Stone, 2005; (TV films) Running Mates, 1992, Amelia Earhart, 1994, Sister Mary Explains It All, 2001; actor, prodr: (TV films) Crossed Over, 2002, On Thin Ice, 2003, Surrender, Dorothy, 2005; dir. film: Heaven, 1987, Wildflower, 1991, Unstrung Heroes, 1995; exec. prodr.: (TV series) Pasadena, 2001; accomplished artist and singer; author book of photographs: Reservations, 1980; editor: (with Marvin Heiferman) Still Life, 1983, Mr. Salesman, 1994; prodr.: The Lemon Sisters, 1990; exec. prodr.: Northern Lights (TV), 1997. Recipient Golden Globe award, 1978 Office: John Burnham William Morris Agy 151 S El Camino Dr Beverly Hills CA 90212-2704*

KEATON, FRANCES MARLENE, insurance sales representative; b. Redfield, Ark., July 1, 1944; d. John Thomas and Pauline (Hilliard) Wells; m. Larry Ronald Keaton, Sept. 17, 1946. Cert. in acctg., Draughon's Sch. Bus., 1972. Lic. ins. agt. Supr. acctg. Home Ins. Co., Little Rock, 1962—70; auditor St. Paul Ins. Co., Little Rock, 1970—74; spl. agt. Continental Ins. Co., Little Rock, 1974—. Vol. Ark. Sch. for the Blind, Little Rock, 1968. Mem. Little Rock Field Club, Casualty Roundtable, Auditor's Assn., Ins. Women, Underwriters Roundtable, The Exec. Female, Ind. Ins. Agts. Assn., Profl. Ins. Assn. Democrat. Methodist. Avocations: golf, tennis, racquetball, travel. Home and Office: 111 Red River Rd Sherwood AR 72120-5851 Office Phone: 501-833-9977. Personal E-mail: lizzik@comcast.net.

KEATON, JESSICA J., secondary school educator; b. Hollywood, Fla., Apr. 16, 1975; d. Joseph and Kathleen Falzone; m. Kenneth Keaton, June 5, 1999; children: Kameron, Karissa, Kalena. BA in Social Scis., Fla. Atlantic U., Boca Raton, 2000; M of Ednl. Leadership, Fla. Atalntic U., Boca Raton, 2006. Tchr. Sebastian River H.S., Fla., 1999—2006. Flag and dance team dir. Sebastian River H.S., Fla., 1994—2006. Mem. of recreation and pks. com. City of Sebastian, Fla., 2001—06. Office: Sebastian River HS 9001 90th Ave Sebastian FL 32958 Office Phone: 772-564-4351.

KEATON, MARGARET-ANN COLEMAN, education educator; d. Raymond Thomas and Virginia Elizabeth Coleman; m. Christopher Bruce Keaton, May 31, 1986; 1 child, Christopher Ray James. B in Psychology with honors, Purdue U., 1998; M in Psychology, U. Ind., 2003; post grad., U. Indpls., 2005—. Pres. Key-Frame Corp., Indpls., 1986—2000; team leader Ind. U., Indpls., 1997—2001; adj. faculty Ivy Tech. State Coll., Indpls., 2004—, U. Ind., Indpls., 2004—. Cons., dir. Key-Frame Corp., 1986—2000. Prodr. (creator): (video) Main Frame Aerobics, 1986; choreographer creator (video) Indiana Pacemates NBA video, 1992; author (interviewer): (video) Sports Psychology, 1997. Co-dir. Ruthann Popcheff Meml. Fund, Indpls., 1986—. Mem.: Am. Coll. Sports Medicine, APA. Avocations: exercise, reading, writing, crafts. Home: 4930 N Kessler Blvd Indianapolis IN 46228 Business E-Mail: keatonma@uindy.edu.

KEBBERLY, DORENE G., elementary school educator, music educator; b. Parma, Ohio, Mar. 19, 1963; d. Ronald William Claus and Carolee Heubach; m. Jeffrey R. Kebberly, Aug. 1, 1987; children: Marna Dorisa, Aleesa Lynette. MusB in Edn., Baldwin-Wallace Coll., Berea, Ohio, 1985; MA of Tchg., Marygrove Coll., Mich., 1999. Tchr. elem., mid. sch. music Wadsworth City Schs., Ohio, 1988—89, Brunswick Bd. Edn., 1985—88, tchr. learning disabled, 1993—97, tchr. elem. music, 1997—. Peer mentor Brunswick City Schs., 1998—2000. Mem. worship, music bd. Holy Trinity Luth. Ch., Brunswick, 2001—05, dir. ch. choir, 1989—92. Named Tchr. of Yr., Kidder Elem. Tchrs., 2002; recipient John Philip Sousa Band award, Brunswick H.S. Music Dept., 1981. Mem.: Brunswick Edn. Assn. (union sec. 1995—2002), Nat. Assn. Music Edn. Democrat. Lutheran. Avocations: flute lessons, cross stitch, gardening, reading. Home: 3714 Pheasants Walk Brunswick OH 44212 Office: Kidder Elementary School 3650 Grafton Road Brunswick OH 44212 Office Phone: 330-273-0485. E-mail: dkebberly@brunswickschools.org.

KECK, JUDITH MARIE BURKE, business owner, retired career officer; b. Springfield, Ohio, Feb. 24, 1938; d. John T. and Mary Elizabeth (Kaliher) Burke; m. Henry J. Reinhardt, Feb. 22, 1958 (div.); 1 child, Lucy L.; m. James E. Keck, Feb. 18, 1978. BS in Mgmt., Park Coll., 1983; MA in Mgmt., Cen. Mich. U., 1985; postgrad., Def. Systems Mgmt. Coll., 1986, Air War Coll., 1989; PhD, Pacific Western U., 1990. Commd. GM-14 USAF, 1969, billeting officer Zweibrucken AFB, Fed. Republic Germany, 1969-72; commissary officer Edwards AFB, Calif., 1972-74; procurement agt. George AFB, Calif., 1974-76; chief contract adminstrn. Nellis AFB, Nev., 1976-78; chief svcs. contracting Grand Forks AFB, N.D., 1978-81; contracting officer aero. systems div./air launched cruise missile div. Wright Patterson AFB, Ohio, 1981-85; program mgr. aero. sys. divsn./B-1 Bomber, 1985-87; program mgr. aero. sys. divsn. project Tomorrow, 1987-94; chief acquisition mgmt. HQ, aero. sys. divsn., 1990-94; pres., CEO Thread Bear Monograms, San Antonio. Instr. systems mgmt. Air Force Inst. Tech., Wright Patterson AFB, 1985, quality assurance, 1981; dir. fed. women's program George AFB, 1976. Mem. aero. systems divsn. Exec. Combined Fed. Campaign, 1989—. Mem. Am. Assn. for Artificial Intelligence, Nat. Contract Mgmt. Assn., Air Force Assn., Nat. Assn. Mil. Comptrollers, NAFE, Sigma Iota Epsilon. Democrat. Avocations: hunting, fishing, gardening. Home: 9139 Powhatan Dr San Antonio TX 78230-4401 Fax: 210-340-5616. Personal E-mail: jthreadbear@swbell.net.

KEDDERIS, PAMELA JEAN, academic administrator; b. Waterbury, Conn., May 15, 1956; d. Leo George and Evelyn Helen (Fenske) K. Student, U. Nice, 1976—77; BA, Assumption Coll., 1978; MBA, U. New Haven, 1981. Cert. fin. mgr., mgmt. acct. Credit analyst Citytrust Bank, Bridgeport, Conn., 1980-81, sr. credit analyst, 1981-82, fin. analyst, 1982-83, seminar instr., 1981-83; planning analyst Continental Ins. Co., N.Y.C., 1983-84, sr. planning analyst, 1984-85, dir. planning, 1985-87, asst. v.p., 1987-92, v.p., 1992-95; v.p., controller Marine Office of Am., Cranbury, N.J., 1995-97; exec. officer for fin. Conn. State Univ. Sys., Hartford, 1997-98, CFO, 1998—. Mem. State of Conn. Ins. and Risk Mgmt. Bd., 2002—. Mem.: Conn. Coun. Chief Fiscal Officers, Inst. Mgmt. Accts., New Eng. Resource Ctr. for Higher Edn. CFO Think Tank. Democrat. Lutheran. Avocations: music, travel. Office: Conn State Univ Sys 39 Woodland St Hartford CT 06105-2337 Business E-Mail: kedderisp@so.ct.edu.

KEDDIE, NIKKI R., education educator; b. N.Y.C., Aug. 30, 1930; d. Harry and Sarra Ragozin; m. Wells H. Keddie, 1953 (div. 1960). BA, Radcliffe Coll., 1951; MA, Stanford U., 1951; PhD, U. Calif., Berkeley, 1955. Instr. U. Ariz., Tucson, 1957; instr.-asst. prof. Scripps Coll., Claremont, Calif., 1957-61; asst. prof. UCLA, 1961-67, assoc. prof., 1967-72, prof., 1972—. Author: An Islamic Response to Imperialism, 1968, Iran and the Muslim World, 1995, Modern Iran: Roots and Results of Revolution, 2006, Women in the Middle East Past and Present, 2006; co-editor: Women in the Muslim World, 1978, Women in Middle Eastern History, 1991, Iran and the Surrounding World, 2002. Rockefeller fellow Rockefeller Found., Bellagio, 1992, Washington, 1980, 82, fellow Social Sci. Rsch. Coun., Iran, 1966, Guggenheim Found., Iran, 1963-64, Europe, 1959-60; recipient Persian History award Ency. Iranica Found., 2002, Internat. Balzan Found. prize, 2004. Fellow AAAS; mem. Am. Hist. Assn. (award for scholarly distinction 2001), Middle East Studies Assn. (Mentoring award 2001—), Soc. for Iranian Studies. Avocations: art, politics. Office: UCLA Dept Of History Los Angeles CA 90095-0001 Home: 1118 3rd St Apt 601 Santa Monica CA 90403-5047

KEDROWSKI, KAREN MARIE, political science professor; d. Henry Sylvester and Clara Jane Cooper Kedrowski; m. Timothy Patrick Fitzgerald, Oct. 5, 1991; children: Jonathan David Kedrowski Fitzgerald, Suzanne Mary Kedrowski Fitzgerald. BA, U. Minn., Mpls., 1986; MA, U. Okla., Norman, 1991—91, PhD, 1992. Legislative analyst Congl. Sunbelt Caucus, Washington, 1991—92; health policy analyst Families USA, 1992—94; dir. office effective tchg. Winthrop U., Rock Hill, SC, 1999—2001, prof. and chair polit. sci., 1994—. Advanced placement reader and table leader Ednl. Testing Svc., Princeton, NJ, 2002—. Author: Cancer Activism: Gender, Media and Public Policy, Media Entrepreneurs and the Media Enterprise in the US Congress. Officer York County Dem. Party, Rock Hill, SC, 1996—2004; flutist and soprano ch. choir Rock Hill, SC, 1998—2006; sec. south chpt. Women's Caucus Polit. Sci., Atlanta, 2006—. Named Outstanding Jr. Prof., Winthrop U., 1999; recipient Commendation, So. Assn. Colleges and Schools, 2001; grantee Visitng Scholar award, Carl Albert Ctr. Archives, 1995; Moody Rsch. grantee, Lyndon Johnson Presdl. Libr., 1995. Mem.: S.C. Polit. Sci. Assn. (jour. editl. bd. 2000—), So. Polit. Sci. Assn. (program com. 2005—), Am. Polit. Sci. Assn. (graber award com. 2006—). Roman Catholic. Avocations: music, flute, piano, travel, family activities. Office: Winthrop University Department of Political Science Rock Hill SC 29733 Office Phone: 803-323-4662.

KEECH, ANN MARIE, training design and multimedia consultant; b. Salt Lake City, July 25, 1951; d. Stanley Michael and Rose Elma (Migliore) Bachmurski; m. Michael Ross Keech, July 21, 1972 (div. 1983); 1 child, Jason Michael. BA in English, Christopher Newport Coll., 1976. Mgr. publs. Newport News (Va.) Shipbuilding, 1981-84; office mgr. Computer Scis. Corp., Newport News, 1984-86; mgr. Comsell, Atlanta, 1986-87, Crawford Comms., Inc., Atlanta, 1988-91; cons. Coastal Video Comms., Inc., Virginia Beach, 1991-93; project mgr. Star Mountain, Inc., Alexandria, Va., 1991-96; v.p. D&A World Wide, Inc., Atlanta, 1996-97; owner, cons. AMK, Newport News, 1997—. Writer, developer: (tng. materials) BTOS FSA Programming Guide, 1988 (Soc. for Tech. Comm. Cert. of Achievement 1989); developer: (multimedia tng. program) Confined Space Entry, 1993; mgr., editor, developer: (internat. tng. materials) International Technical Training for Telecommunications, 1996-97; developer, editor: (tng. program) Family Violence Prevention Program, 1997; developer Web-based Training Style Guide, 2000. Vol. Newport News Police, Cmty. Svc. Dept.; aux. mem. 106th Infantry Divsn. Assn., 76th Infantry Divsn. Assn., 2d Divsn. Assn. 13th Airborne Divsn. Assn., 18th Airborn Corps Assn., 1st Infantry Divsn. Assn., 3d Infantry Divsn. Assn. Mem. Am. Soc. for Law Enforcement (trainer). Avocations: music, horseback riding, pleasure reading. Office: AMK 824 Cascade Dr Newport News VA 23608-3223 Fax: (757) 988-0448. E-mail: amkeech@mindspring.com.

KEECH, ELOWYN ANN, interior designer; b. Berrien County, Mich., Oct. 5, 1937; d. Earl Docker and Elizabeth Hall (Paullin) Stephenson; 1 child, Robert Earl Stephenson. Print designer, 1957-75; freelance interior designer, photoset and video set designer St. Joseph, Mich., 1975—; owner Fog Horn Records & Tapes; contract & resdential interior design cons., project coord., adminstr. pvt. practice, 1978—. 1st Fed. Savs. & Loan Assn., Three Oaks, Mich., 1975, Holland (Mich.) Ctrl. Trade Credit Union, 1978, 1st Fed. Savs. & Loan, Holland, 1978, Yonker Realty Co., 1979, People's Bank of Holland, 1979, Whirlpool Corp. Exec. Offices, 1980—, St. Joe Human Resources divsn., 1985—, Claeys Residence, 1984—, Calley Dental Office, 1985—, Sarett Nature Ctr., 1985—, Imperial Printing, 1986—, Schraders Super Market, 1986—, Dave's Garage, 1987—, Miller Residence, 1986—, Merritt Residence, Kalamazoo, 1987—88, Smith Residence, 1988, Emergency Shelter Svcs., 1991, Butzbach Residence, 1992, Merritt Residence, Del Mar, Calif., 1993—94, Fister Better Homes & Gardens Conf. Rm., 1994, Vanderboegh Residence, 1994—96, S.W. Mich. regional Airport, 1994—, Berrien Hills Country Club, 1995—96, Butzbach Offices, 1995, Merritt Residence, Houston, 1996, Mich. Maritime Mus., 1996, St. Paul Episcopal Ch., 1996, Bacchiocchi Residence, 1996, Internat. Trade Assn. Greater Chgo., 1997, DeVries Residence, 1997, Kitchen Aid Small Appliance Display Whirlpool Tech. Ctr., 1998—99, Paullin Residence, Chgo., 1998—99, Pott, Laetz, Thomas & Hamilton Residences, 2000—01, Ft. Miami Heritage Soc. Exec. Offices, 2000, Benton Harbor-St. Joseph Herald-Palladium. Trustee Mich. Maritime Mus., 1994—97; bd. dirs., mem. steering and long-range planning coms. United Way Mich., 1980—87; bd. dirs. Blossomland United Way, 1981—86. Mem.: Internat. Interior Design Assn., Am. Rottweiler Club, Econ. Club S.W. Mich., Rotary Club (vol. chair 47th Ann. Rotary Track Meet S.W. Mich.). Office Phone: 269-369-4350. Business E-Mail: elowynkeech@talkamerica.net.

KEEFE, CAROLYN JOAN, tax accountant; b. Huntington Park, Oct. 11, 1926; d. Paul Dewey and Mary Jane (Parmater) Keefe. AA, Pasadena (Calif.) City Coll., 1947; BA, U. So. Calif., 1950. Tax acct. Shell Oil Co., L.A., 1950-71, Houston, 1971-91, ret., 1991. Advisor Midwest Mus. Am. Art, 1993—; vol. Houston Mus. Fine Arts, 1991—; vol. docent Houston Mus. Natural Sci., 1991—, Theatre Under the Stars, 1991—, Houston Pub. TV Channel 8, Houston, 1989—; donor Paul Dewey and Mary Jane Keefe scholarships. Mem. LWV, Inst. Mgmt. Accts. (emeritus life mem.), Desk and Derrick Club (bd. dir. 1994-95), Houston Alumni Club of Alpha Gamma Delta, USC Houston Alumni Club. Christian Scientist. Avocation: travel. Home: 1814 Auburn Trl Sugar Land TX 77479-6333

KEEFER, ELIZABETH J., lawyer; b. New London, Conn., July 3, 1948; d. Edward Boyd and Elizabeth Keefer; m. Richard A. Brown, May 13, 1978; 1 child, Andrew Boyd Keefer Brown. BA cum laude, Barnard Coll., 1969—71; JD mem. Order of Coif, U. Colo., 1966—67, George Wash. U., 1977. Trial atty. Fed. Trade Commn., Wash., DC, 1977—79; assoc. Bergson Borkland Margolis & Adler, Wash., DC, 1979—82; atty. adv. Dept. State, Wash., DC, 1982—86, asst. legal adv., 1986—89; dep. under sec. Internat. Affairs, U.S. Air Force, Wash., DC, 1989—92; ptnr. Hughes Hubbard & Reed, Wash., DC, 1992; dep. gen. counsel Teledyne, L.A., 1995—97; gen. counsel Columbia U., N.Y.C., 1997—. Bd. trustees Mitre Corp., McLean, Va., 2001—. Mem. bd. dirs. Women's Commn. for Women Refugee and Children, N.Y.C., 2003—. Mem.: Am. Corp. Counsel Assn. (mem. bd. dirs. 2001—). Avocations: hiking, theater, tennis. Office: Columbia U 412 Low Libr 535 W 116th St New York NY 10027 Business E-Mail: ejk27@columbia.edu.

KEEGAN, CATHERINE ANN, medical/surgical nurse, endoscopy nurse; b. Bryn Mawr, Pa., Mar. 12, 1960; d. Douglas and Catherine (Wiley) Cobourn; m. Francis Keegan, Sept. 29, 1984. Diploma, Chester County Hosp., West Chester, Pa., 1981. RN, Pa. Staff med.-surg. nurse Chester County Hosp., West Chester, Pa., 1981-90, endoscopy nurse, 1990—2000, clin. leader endoscopy, 2000—.

KEEGAN, JANE ANN, insurance executive, consultant; b. Watertown, N.Y., Sept. 1, 1950; d. Richard Isidor and Kathleen (McKinley) K. BA cum laude, SUNY, Potsdam, 1972; MBA in Risk Mgmt., Golden State U., 1986. CPCU. Comml. lines mgr. Lithgow & Rayhill, San Francisco, 1977-80; risk mgmt. account coord. Dinner Levison Co., San Francisco, 1980-83; ins. cons. San Francisco, 1983-84; account mgr. Rollins Burdick Hunter, San Francisco, 1984-85; account exec. Jardine Ins. Brokers, San Francisco, 1985-86; ins. cons. San Francisco, 1986-87; ins. adminstr. Port of Oakland, 1987—, risk mgr., 1989—, mgr. accts. payable, 1996—. Vol. San Francisco Ballet vol. orgn., 1981-96, Bay Area Bus., Govt. ARC disaster conf. steering com., 1987-88, 89, 90, 91-92; mem. Nob Hill Neighbors Assn., 1982—, City of Oakland Emergency Mgmt. Bd., 1990—. Mem. Safety Mgmt. Soc., CPCU Soc. (spl. events chairperson 1982-84, continuing profl. devel. program award 1985, 88, chair loss prevention), Calif. Assn. of Port Authorities (ins. chair 1998—), Risk and Ins. Mgr. Soc. (dep., sec. 1990—, dir. legis. 1993, dir. conf.). Democrat. Roman Catholic. Home: 17 Calafia Ct San Rafael CA 94903-2464 Office Phone: 510-627-1535. Business E-Mail: jkeegan@portoakland.com.

KEEKLEY, PATRICIA ANN, counselor, psychologist; b. Poughkeepsie, N.Y., Apr. 2, 1958; d. Jon Thomas and Carol Joan (Nordstrom) K. BA, Valparaiso U., 1981; MA, U. Akron, 1984. Lic. profl. counselor, Tex. Counselor Luth. Children's Aid and Family Svcs., Cleve., 1984-90; assoc. clin. psychologist Cen. Counties Ctr. for Mental Health and Mental Retardation, Temple, Tex., 1991—. Mem. ACA, AAMFT, Christian Counselors Tex., TCA, TAMFT, Chi Sigma Iota. Lutheran. Office: CCC MHMR 101 Park Hill Dr Hamilton TX 76531-1542

KEEL, BEVERLY J., journalist, educator, director; b. Nashville, Apr. 18, 1966; d. Pinckney D. Keel and Gloria Keel Coles. BS, Mid. Tenn. State U., 1988; MS, Columbia U. Grad. Sch. of Journalism, N.Y., 1989. Prof. Mid. Tenn. State U., Murfreesboro, 1995—, dir., Seigenthaler Chair of Excellence in first amendment studies, 2006—. Author (reporter): Nashville Scene Newsweekly (Assn. of Am. Newsweeklies Feature Writing award, 1998), Nashville Banner (AP Deadline Reporting award, 1989); corr. People Mag., N.Y., 1997—2006; contbg. editor: Am. Profile Mag., 2005—06; editor-in-chief CMT Mag., Nashville, 2006. Gov. NARAS, Nashville, 2002—06. Mem.: Leadership Music, Country Music Assn., Investigative Reporters and Editors, Soc. Profl. Journalists. Office: Mid Tenn State Univ PO Box 21 Murfreesboro TN 37132 Office Phone: 615-898-5150. Office Fax: 615-898-5682. Business E-Mail: bkeel@mtsu.edu.

KEELE, LUCY ANNE MCCANDLISH, communications executive, consultant; BA in Polit. Sci., U. Oreg., MA in Speech Comm., PhD. Lectr. U. Oreg., Umpqua CC; from asst. prof. to prof. Calif. State U., Fullerton, 1967—95, prof. emeritus, 1995—. Vis. prof. U. Kans., U. Mass., U. Pitts., U. Ala., U. Houston, Gonzaga U.; adv. bd. So. Calif. Urban Debate League; cons., presenter in field. Past pres. Western Forensic Assn.; past chair Com. on Internat. Discussion and Debate, 1974—96. Named Keele award in her honor, Nat. Collegiate Debate Tournament Bd. Trustees, 1996, Outstanding Debate Educator in Am., U. Utah, 1974; recipient Outstanding Contbn. award, Calif. Legis., 1983, Baylor U., 1983, George Ziegelmueller award, 2004. Mem.: English Speaking Union, Am. Forensic Assn. (past chair com. on comm. and the law, past chair, bd. trustees nat. debate tournament 1973—97, Outstanding Contbn. award 1985), Internat. Inst. for the Study Argument, Western Comm. Assn. (past pres., Disting. Svc. award 1997), Nat. Comm. Assn. (past chair commn. on comm., past chair fin. bd., past adminstrv. com. and legis. coun., Mentor award 2000), Am. Soc. Trial Cons. (charter, past pres., past bd. dirs.). Office: Newport Gateway Tower 2 19900 MacArthur Blvd Ste 850 Irvine CA 92612 Office Phone: 949-553-5096.

KEELEY, IRENE PATRICIA MURPHY, federal judge; b. 1944; BA, Coll. Notre Dame, 1965; MA, W.Va. U., 1977, JD, 1980. Bar: W. Va., 1980. Atty. Steptoe & Johnson, Clarksburg, W.Va., 1980-92; dist. judge U.S. Dist. Ct. (no. dist.), W. Va., 1992—. Adj. prof. law W.Va. U., 1990-91; bd. dirs. W.Va. U. Alumni Assn., 1995—, 1st v.p., 1997-98; mem. bd. advisors W.Va. U. Vis. com. W.Va. U. Coll. Law, 1987-91, 94-98; chmn. adv. bd. W.Va. U., 1997-98. Mem. ABA, Nat. Conf. Fed. Trial Judges (exec. com. 1996—,), W.Va. State Bar, W.Va. Bar Assn., Harrison County Bar Assn., Clarksburg Country Club, Oral Lake Fishing Club, Immaculate Conception Roman Cath. Ch. Office: US Courthouse PO Box 2808 500 W Pike St Rm 202 Clarksburg WV 26302-2808 Office Phone: 304-624-5850. Office Fax: 304-622-1928.

KEEN, RACHEL, psychology professor; b. Burkesville, Ky., Oct. 5, 1937; d. James Em and Regina Elizabeth (Simpson) Keen; m. Charles E. Clifton, Aug. 20, 1965 (div. 2002); children: Ramona, Catherine. BA, Berea (Ky.) Coll., 1959; MA, U. Minn., 1960, PhD, 1963. Fellow U. Wis., Madison, 1963-65; rsch. assoc. U. Iowa, Iowa City, 1966-68; from asst. prof. to assoc. prof. U. Mass., Amherst, 1968-76, prof., 1976—. Vis. prof. Stanford U., Palo Alto, Calif., 1975-76, U. Sussex, Brighton, Eng., 1981-82, U. Cambridge, Eng., 1989-90, Harvard U., 2002-2004; mem. rsch. rev. com. NIMH, 1983-87; mem. human devel. study sect. NIH, 1990-94. NIMH fellow U. Minn., 1961-63; grantee NIMH, NIH, NSF, 1968—; named Disting. Alumna Berea Coll., 1994, Disting. Sci. Contbn. award Soc. for Rsch. Child Devel., 2005; recipient Rsch. Scientist award NIMH, 1981-2001, Merit award NICHD, 1999—, Disting. Faculty award U. Mass., 1988. Fellow APA, AAAS, Acoustical Soc. Am., Am. Acad. Arts and Sciences; mem. Soc. Rsch. Child Devel. (sec. 1979-85, assoc. editor jour. 1977-79, editor Monographs 1993-99), Fedn. Behavioral, Psychol. and Cognitive Scis. (sec. 1987-90), Soc. Psychophysiol. Rsch. (bd. dirs. 1975-78, assoc. editor jour. 1972-75), Internat. Soc. Infant Studies (pres. 1998-00). Democrat. Congregationalist. Avocations: playing piano, reading. Office: U Mass Dept Psychology Amherst MA 01003 Office Phone: 413-545-2655.

KEEN, SUSAN LYNN, biology professor; d. Emmanuel and M. Lillian Keen. BSc with honors, U. BC, Vancouver, 1979; MSc, U. Mich., Ann Arbor, 1984; PhD, U. Calif., Davis, 1991. Lectr. U. Calif., Davis, 1993—2001, dir. introductory biology, 2001—. Author: (textbook) Animal Diversity, 4th edit., 2004 (Journals-Functional Ecology, Jour. of Arachnology, Marine Ecology Progress Series, Jour. of Exptl. Marine Biology & Ecology, Econ. Botan); contbg. author: Integrated Principles of Zoology, 13th edit., 2006. Recipient Associated Students award, U. Calif., 2004, Excellence in Tchg. award, U. Calif. Academic Fedn., 2006; fellow in life scis., Nat. Academies of Sci. USA, 2005—06. Mem.: Soc. Integrative and Comparative Biology. Office: Sect Evolution and Ecology U Calif Davis 1 Shields Ave Davis CA 95616 Office Phone: 530-754-9252. E-mail: slkeen@ucdavis.edu.

KEENAN, BARBARA BYRD, professional society administrator; b. Martinsburg, W.Va., Aug. 31, 1952; d. James Leonard and Elizabeth (Somerfield) Byrd; m. Terrence James; 1 child, Marjorie Lynn. BS, Old Dominion U., 1973, MS, 1975; postgrad., U. Maryland, 1976. Cert. assn. exec. Instr. Old Dominion U., Norfolk, Va., 1972-75; asst. prof. U. Maryland, Balt., 1975-76; assoc. dir. Am. Dental Hygienists Assn., Chgo., 1976-79; dir. edn. Am. Coll. Preventive Medicine, Washington, 1979-81; dir. profl. affairs Tex. Pharm. Assn., Austin, 1981-83; dir. edn. and research Tex. Med. Assn., Austin, 1983-86; exec. v.p. Internat. Assn. Hospitality Accts., Austin, 1986-90; pres. Community Assn. Inst., Alexandria, Va., 1990—2002; exec. v.p. Inst. Food Technologists, Chgo., 2003—. Chair Assns. Advance Am. Com., 1994—; chair Internat. Food Info. Svc., 2003—; bd. mem. Partnership for Food Safety Edn., 2006—. Mem. editl. bd.: Jour. Assn. Leadership, 2003—, vice chmn.:, 2005—. Bd. dirs. Nat. Bd. Cardiopulmonary Credentialing, Gaitersburg, N.D., 1981-82, mem. exec. com. 1982; bd. dirs. South Tex. Arthritis Found., San Antonio, 1987-89, Capital Area Arthritis Found., Austin, 1986-89; founding chmn. Travis County Adult Literacy Coun., Austin, 1984-90, chmn. emeritus 1990—; bd. dirs. Am. Hotel and Motel Assn. Research Found., 1988-90. Recipient award Internat. Assn. Bus. Communicators, 1988; named one of Outstanding Young Women Am., 1981, Top 10 Bus. Women of Yr., Am. Bus. Women's Assn., 1986, Disting. Alumni award Old Dominion U., 1999; inaugural recipient Barbara Bird Keenan award Nat. Bd. for Cert. of Comty. Assn. Mgrs. Fellow Am. Soc. Assn. Execs. (charter, vice chmn. 1991-92, planning com. 1985-88, 91-92, chair Assn. Advance Am. com. 1994, bd. dirs. 1985-86, 88—, chmn. ednl. sect. 1985-86, chmn. task force on social responsibility 1989—, chair fellows 1989-90, chair univ. com. 2002-, Excellence award 1985, 88, 94, CAE commr. 1991-93, sec.-treas. 1993-94, gov. task force 1992-93, chair rsch. com. 1996-97, Mgmt. Achievement award 1983, Key award 1996, award of excellence in edn. 1997); mem. Town Lake Bus. Women's Assn. (Woman of Yr. 1986), Tex. Soc. Assn. Execs. (com. chair 1981—), Greater Washington Soc. Assn. Execs. (CAE cert. com., instr. and tutor 1991-92, cmty. svc. com. 1996-97, bd. dirs. 1997—, chair 2001-2002, Monument award in edn. 1992), Leadership Austin, Leadership Tex. (bd. dirs., tng. group 1987—), Internat. Assn. Hosp. Accts. (hon. 1990), William Smith Assn. (mem. rsch. coun. 2003—), U.S. C. of C. (mem. Com. of 100). Home and Office: 1322 Isabella St Evanston IL 60201-1623 Office: Inst Food Technologists 525 W Van Buren St Chicago IL 60607 Office Phone: 312-782-8424. E-mail: bbkeenan@ift.org.

KEENAN, BARBARA MILANO, state supreme court justice; b. Vienna, 1950; BA, Cornell U., 1971; JD, George Wash. U., 1974; LLM, U. Va., 1992. Asst. commonwealth atty., Fairfax County, Va., 1974—76; pvt. law practice, 1976—80; judge Gen. Dist. Ct., Fairfax County, 1980-82, Circuit Ct., Fairfax County, 1982-85, Ct. Appeals, Va., 1985-91; assoc. justice Va. Supreme Court, Richmond, 1991—. Recipient Am. Jurisprudence award, Fairfax Bar Assn., 1995. Office: Va Supreme Ct PO Box 1315 Richmond VA 23218-1315*

KEENAN, CAROL, assistant principal; b. Malden, Mass., Jan. 22, 1964; d. Edward and Ruth Keenan. BEd, U. Mass., Boston, 1986, MEd, 1988. Cert. English, reading, spl. edn. tchr. Mass., mid. sch., H.S. adminstr. Mass. Tchr. Malden Pub. Schs., Mass., 0986—2000, H.S. asst. prin., 2000—. Office: Malden HS Apt 116 100 Ledgewood Dr Stoneham MA 02180-3617

KEENAN, DONNA HUMMEL, elementary school educator; b. Rockville Centre, N.Y., Sept. 13, 1950; d. Gerard A. and Muriel E. (Bender) Hummel; m. Robert J. Keenan, June 19, 1971; children: Ashley H., Michael A. BS, SUNY, Oneonta, 1972; MA in Teaching, Rollins Coll., 1982; cert. in Reading Recovery, Ohio State U., 1995. Cert. master tchr., Fla., 1984. Tchr. grade 4 Edmeston Cent. Sch., NY, 1972—73; tchr. grade 1, 2, 5, Title 1 Reading Orange County Pub. Schs., Orlando, Fla., 1977—94, reading recovery tchr., 1994—2002, reading resource tchr., 2002—03, tchr. grade 2, 2003—04; literacy coach Orange County Pub. Sch., 2004—. Mem. Internat. Reading Assn., Fla. Reading Assn., Orange County Reading Assn., Kappa Delta Pi (past 1st v.p., past sec.). Home: 548 Orange Dr Apt 22 Altamonte Springs FL 32701-5375 E-mail: keenand@ocps.net.

KEENAN, KATHLEEN, state legislator; b. Burlington, Vt., May 7, 1940; d. Roland and Madelyn M. (Cahill) K.; 8 children. Diploma, Jeanne Mance Sch. Nursing, 1961; diploma in nurse practitioner program, U. Vt., 1976. Nurse; mem. Vt. Ho. of Reps., Montpelier, 1989—, chair commerce com. Mem. Hinesburg Dem. Com., 1954-68, chair, 1965-68; mem. St. Albans Dem. Com., 1968—; mem. Vt. Econ. Progress Coun., 1994-98; bd. dirs. Efficiency Vt., Vt. Electric Power Prodrs., State Human Resources Investment Coun., Vt. Interactive TV; hon. bd. mem. Vt. Capital Insurance Assn. Mem. St. Albans Skating Assn. (charter), Emergency Nurses Assn., Nat. Conf. Ins. Legislators (mem. exec. com., former pres.), Bus. and Profl. Women. Address: 8 Thorpe Ave Saint Albans VT 05478-1834 Office Fax: 802-828-2228. E-mail: kkeenan@leg.state.vt.us.

KEENAN, MARY See LACY, MARY

KEENAN, NANCY A., pro-choice association executive; b. Anaconda, Mont., Feb. 14, 1952; d. Patrick John and Anne Keenan. BA in Elem. and Spl. Edn., Mont. State U., 1974; MA Edn. Adminstrn., U. Mont. Tchr. Yellowstone Boys' Ranch, 1974-75; tchr. spl. edn. Anaconda, Mont., 1975-88; mem. Mont. Ho. of Reps., 1982-88; supt. of pub. instrn. State of Mont.,

1988—2000; pres. NARAL Pro-Choice America, Washington, 2004—. Mem. taxation, edn., local govt. and revenue oversight coms., 1982-84; chmn. ho. human svcs. and aging com.; asst. Dem. whip 1989. Active Anaconda Local Devel. Corp.; past pres. A.W.A.R.E.; past nat. pres. & chair legis. com. Council of Chief State Sch. Officers; bd. dirs. Deer Lodge County Hospice; mem. Mont. Coun. for Exceptional Children. Recipient Pub. Svc. award Mont. Coun. for Exceptional Children, 1981. Mem. AAUW. Office: NARAL Pro Choice America 1156 15th St NW Washington DC 20005*

KEENAN, RETHA ELLEN VORNHOLT, retired nursing educator; b. Solon, Iowa, Aug. 15, 1934; d. Charles Elias and Helen Maurine (Konicek) Vornholt; m. David James Iverson, June 17, 1956; children: Scott, Craig; m. Roy Vincent Keenan, Jan. 5, 1980. BSN, State U. Iowa, 1955; MSN, Calif. State U., Long Beach, 1978. Cert. nurse practitioner adult and mental health. Pub. health nurse City of Long Beach, 1970-73, 94-96, cons., 1998, 99, 2000, coord. continuing edn., 1999, 2000. Pub. health nurse Hosp. Home Care, Torrance, Calif., 1973-75; patient care coord. Hillhaven, L.A., 1975-76; mental health cons. InterCity Home Health, L.A., 1978-79; instr. C.C. Dist., L.A., 1979-87; instr. nursing El Camino Coll., Torrance, 1981-86; instr. nursing Chapman Coll., Orange, Calif., 1982, Mt. St. Mary's Coll., 1986-87; cons., pvt. practice, Rancho Palos Verdes, Calif., 1987-89, 98, 99. Contbg. author: American Journal of Nursing Question and Answer Book for Nursing Boards Review, 1984, Nursing Care Planning Guides for Psychiatric and Mental Health Care, 1987-88, Nursing Care Planning Guides for Children, 1987, Nursing Care Planning Guides for Adults, 1988, Nursing Care Planning Guides for Critically Ill Adults, 1988. Mem. Assistance League of Temecula Valley, Calif. NIMH grantee, 1977-78. Mem. Sigma Theta Tau, Phi Kappa Phi, Delta Zeta. Lutheran. Avocations: travel, writing, reading. Home: PO Box 205 Temecula CA 92593-0205

KEENE, SYLVIA WHITE, retired reading specialist; d. George David and Lucille Estelle White; m. Floyd C. Keene, July 18, 1953; children: Donald G., Linda K. Solomon. BS, Va. State Coll., 1952; MS, U. Md., 1975, PhD, 1983. Cert. tchr., prin., supr. Md. Biologist Walter Reed Army Med. Ctr., Washington, 1952—66; reading specialist Montgomery County Pub. Schs., Md., 1975—90; ret., 1990. Co-founder, exec. dir. Met./Delta Adult Literacy Coun., Washington, 1993—98, treas., 1993—2004. Chair St. Mary's Guild Calvary Episcopal Ch., Washington. Named one of 100 Voices Across Am., Charming Shoppes, 2003; recipient Pub. Svc. award, Pittsburghers Club, 1995, Eliza P. Shippen award, Delta Sigma Theta, 1990, award, 1998. Mem.: NAACP, Internat. Reading Assn., DC Learns (charter, v.p. 1990), ProLiteracy Am. (steering com., adv. coun. 2000—04). Episcopalian. Avocations: reading, travel, bridge.

KEENE-BURGESS, RUTH FRANCES, military official; b. South Bend, Ind., Oct. 7, 1948; d. Seymour and Sally (Morris) K.; m. Leslie U. Burgess, Jr., Oct. 1, 1983; children: Michael Leslie, David William, Elizabeth Sue, Rachael Lee. BS, Ariz. State U., 1970; MS, Fairleigh Dickinson U., 1978; grad., U.S. Army Command and Gen. Staff Coll., 1986. Inventory mgmt. specialist U.S. Army Electronics Command, Phila., 1970-74, U.S. Army Communications-Electronics Material Readiness Command, Fort Monmouth, N.J., 1974-79; chief inventory mgmt. div. Crane (Ind.) Army Ammunition Activity, 1979-80; supply systems analyst Hdqrs. 60th Ordnance Group, Zweibruecken, Fed. Republic Germany, 1980-83; chief inventory mgmt. div. Crane (Ind.) Army Ammunition Activity, 1983-85, chief control div., 1985; inventory mgmt. specialist 200th Theater Army Material Mgmt. Ctr., Zweibruecken, 1985-88; analyst supply systems U.S. Armament, Munitions and Chem. Command, Rock Island, Ill., 1988-89; specialist logistics mgt. U.S. Army Signal Command, Ft. Huachuca, Ariz., 1989—. Troop leader Girl Scouts Am. Mem. Federally Employed Women (chpt. pres. 1979-80), NAFE, Soc. Logistics Engrs., Assn. Computing Machinery, Am. Soc. Public Adminstrn., Soc. Profl. and Exec. Women, AAAS. Democrat.

KEENER, CATHERINE, actress; b. Miami, Fla., Mar. 16, 1960; m. Dermot Mulroney, 1990 (separated); 1 child, Clyde. Grad., Wheaton Coll., Norton, Mass., 1983. Actor: (films) The Education Allison Tate, 1986, About Last Night, 1986, Survival Quest, 1989, Catchfire, 1990, Switch, 1991, Johnny Suede, 1991, The Gun in Betty Lou's Handbag, 1992, Living in Oblivion, 1995, Walking and Talking, 1996, The Destiny of Marty Fines, 1996, Boys, 1996, Box of Moon Light, 1996, The Real Blonde, 1997, Out of Sight, 1998, Your Friends and Neighbors, 1998, 8MM, 1999, Being John Malkovich, 1999, Death to Smoochy, 2002, Full Frontal, 2002, Simone, 2002, The Ballad of Jack and Rose, 2005 (Best Supporting Actress, Boston Soc. Film Critics awards, 2005), The Interpreter, 2005, 40 Year Old Virgin, 2005 (Best Supporting Actress, Boston Soc. Film Critics awards, 2005), Capote, 2005 (Best Supporting Actress, Boston Soc. Film Critics awards, 2005), Friends with Money, 2006; (TV films) Journeys North, 1994, Heroine of Hell, 1996, If These Walls Could Talk, 1996; (TV series) Ohara, 1987, (TV appearances) LA Law, 1986, Seinfeld, 1992. Address: c/o The Gersh Agy 232 N Canon Dr Beverly Hills CA 90210*

KEENER, ELIZABETH ANN, elementary school educator; b. Missoula, Mont., June 26, 1957; d. Roger Stephen and Helen Elizabeth Murray; m. Donald Lee Keener, Mar. 31, 1957; 1 child, Andrew Thomas. BS, U. Mont., Missoula, 1980; Masters, Ctrl. Wash. U., Ellensburg, 1992. Cert. K-8 tchr. Wash., 1980. Tchr. 6th grade Hoffstetter Elem., Colville, Wash., 1980—84, Sterling Mid. Sch., East Wenatchee, Wash., 1984—2004; dean of students Clovis Point Intermediate Sch., East Wenatchee, Wash., 2004—. Recipient Douglas County Excellence award, Eastmont Sch. Dist., 2003. Democrat. Avocations: boating, walking, working out, gardening. Office Phone: 509-888-1400. E-mail: keenere@eastmont206.org.

KEENER, POLLY LEONARD, illustrator; b. Akron, Ohio, July 14, 1946; d. George Holman and Alice June (Bolinger) Leonard; m. Robert Lee Keener, Dec. 29, 1967; children: Robert Edward Alan, June Whitney. Student, Kent State U., 1967, Princeton U., 1968, 73; BA, Conn. Coll., 1968. Cert. tchr., Ohio. Illustrator, Akron, 1969—; instr. cartooning Northeastern Ohio Univs. Coll. Medicine, 1992-94. Instr. cartooning U. Akron, 1979—, instr. soft sculpture, 1979-84; cartoon text writer Prentice Hall Pubs., Englewood Cliffs, N.J., 1985—; pres. Keener Corp., Akron, 1977—; judge arts and crafts competitions, Akron, 1982—. Creator: Hamster Alley comic strip, 1999-, Mystery Mosaic, 2001-. Trustee Stan Hywet Hall Found., Akron, 1972—; trustee and v.p. Women's History Project, Akron, 1993-96; v.p. Jr. League, Akron, 1988-89, Western Res. Acad. Women's Bd., Hudson, Ohio, 1987-88; active Women's Bd. Blossom Music Ctr., Penninsula, Ohio, 1969—. Named Woman of Yr. Women's History Project Ohio, 1989, Artist of Yr. 1998 Heidelberg Coll. honors program; recipient Unsung Hero award Jr. League Akron, 1988. Mem. DAR (trustee, vice-regent Cuyahoga-Portage chpt. 1992-99, regent 1999-2001, nat. vice-chmn. DAR Mag. 1999-2001, chair motion picture radio and tv com. 2000—04, state chmn. bylaws com. 2005—), Nat. Cartoonists Soc. (chmn. Great Lakes chpt. 1996-2000, nat. rep. and bd. dirs. 1997-2001, co-chmn. Nat. Cartoonists Day/Cartoon Appreciation Week Celebration 1999-2001), Soc. Illustrators. Episcopalian. Avocations: antiques, archaeology, miniatures, science. Home: 400 W Fairlawn Blvd Akron OH 44313-4510

KEENEY, MARISA GESINA, psychologist; b. Amarillo, Tex., Dec. 11, 1927; d. James Lesley and Anna Gesina (Reimers) K. BA, Trinity U., 1949; MRE, Princeton Sem., 1952; PhD, Mich. State U., 1966. Lic. psychologist, Mich. Edn. dir. Mt. Lebanon Presbyn. Ch., Pitts., 1952-56, First Presbyn. Ch., Ann Arbor, Mich., 1956-63; univ. counselor II Wayne State U. Counseling Svc., Detroit, 1966-72, univ. counselor III, 1972-93, asst. dir., 1984-93; ret., 1993. Chair Wayne State U. Commn. on the Status of Women, 1974-76. Instr. Furman U. Learning in Retirement program, 1994-2006; pres., bd. dir. United Campus Ministries, Wayne State U., 1982-83, treas., 1991; pres., bd. dir. Ecumenical Campus Ctr. and Internat. Residence, Ann Arbor, 1983-84, 91-92, Ecumenical Assn. Internat. Understanding, 1988-91. Recipient Proclamation of Recognition for chairing Wayne State U. Commn. on Status of Women, 1977, 87, 91, Outstanding Svc. award Ecumenical Campus Ctr. and Internat. Residence, 1987, 92, Women of Wayne State U. Leadership and Svc. award, 1990, Wayne State U. Svc. award, 1991, Profl. Achievement award, 1992. Mem. APA, AAUW, Mich. Psychol. Assn. (chmn. women's issues com. 1984-86), Mich. Women Psychologists (founding pres. 1987, leadership svc. awards 1989, 92), Greenville (S.C.) Woman's Club, Delta Kappa Gamma (pres., v.p., treas. Alpha Iota chpt. 1971-76, Internat. Women's Yr. award 1976). Avocations: travel, crafts, gardening, writing, reading.

KEENEY, VIRGINIA T., retired child psychiatrist; b. Albany, N.Y., Mar. 23, 1920; d. Leon Lyle and Mabel Alice Tripp; m. Arthur Hail Keeney (dec.); children: Steven Harris, Lee Douglas, Martha Heyburn; m. George Harrison Houston, Oct. 6, 2003. BS, Coll. of William and Mary, Williamsburg, Va., 1942; MD, U. Louisville, 1954. Dir. and creator program in ethics and humanities U. Louisville Sch. Medicine, 1974—2000, resident child psychiatry, 1979—84; assoc. prof. dept. comty. and family medicine U. Louisville, 1974—2004, asst. prof. dept. psychiatry, 1984—2002; ret., 2004. Bd. dirs. Buckhorn. Co-author (with Arthur Keeney): (book) Dyslexia, 1966. Mem. adv. bd. Salvation Army, Louisville; life bd. dirs. ARC, Louisville, 1999, Am. Printing House for the Blind, Louisville, 1998; chmn. bd. ARC, Louisville, 1994—96; life bd. dirs. Louisville Orch., 2003; chmn. bd. YWCA, Louisville, 1963—65; program dir. Sabin Oral Polio Campaign. Named Citizen Laureate of Louisville, Younger Women's Club, 1964, Woman of Distinction, Ctr. for Women and Families, 1992. Mem.: Jefferson County Med. Soc. Found., Ky. Physicians Health Found. (trustee 1998—), River Valley Club, Alpha Omega Alpha. Presbyterian. Avocations: tennis, reading, walking, swimming.

KEENUM, NANCY ELIZABETH, athletic director, coach; b. Decatur, Ala., June 16, 1957; d. Arthur Curtis and Ruthie Vest Keenum. AS, Calhoun C.C., Decatur, Ala., 1977; BS, U. Ala., Tuscaloosa, 1979; MA, U. North Ala., Florence, 1980; EdD, Nova Southea. U., Ft. Lauderdale, Fla., 2003. Instr. phys. edn., basketball and volleyball coach Judson Coll., Marion, Ala., 1980—82; instr. phys. edn., athletic dir., tennis and basketball and softball coach Calhoun C.C., Decatur, 1983—. Mem. coms. Calhoun C.C., 1983—. Mem. budget com. United Way, Decatur, 2005—; vol. Relay for Life Am. Cancer Soc., Decatur; tchr. Enon Bapt. Ch., Danville, Ala., 0974—. Named Coach of Yr. Nat. Softball, NJCAA, 1998—2000, Torchbearer, Olympic XIX, 2001—02. Mem.: Ala. Athletics. Avocation: bicycling. Office: Calhoun CC PO Box 2216 Decatur AL 35609

KEESEE, DONNA CHRISTINE, retired elementary school educator; b. Chgo., July 11, 1945; d. Robert Paul Williams and Dorothy Christine Krohe-Williams; m. Willis D. Keesee (dec.); children: Darla Christine, Deanna Carol Johnson. BS in Edn., So. Nazarene U., Bethany, Okla., 1967. Cert. tchr. Okla. 5th grade tchr. Yukon Pub. Schs., Okla., 1967—71, 6th grade tchr., 1978—79, 1981—82, 1983—2005; ret., 2005. Supr. Sunday sch. Nazarene Ch., Okla., 1978—88, mem. ch. bd., mem. choir, dir., 1972—, Bible study leader, 1998—2002, 2005—. Named Tchr. of Yr., Yukon Pub. Schs., 1995, Mother of Yr., Nazarene Ch., 1990.

KEESEE, PATRICIA HARTFORD, volunteer; b. Nashville, Apr. 29, 1928; d. William Donald and Mary Carolyn (Gwyn) Hartford; m. Thomas Woodfin Keesee Jr., June 26, 1953 (dec. Jan. 2000); children: Thomas Woodfin III, Anne Hartford Keesee Niemann; 1 stepson: Allen P.K. Keesee BA English, Radcliff Coll., 1950; BA Environ. Scis., SUNY, Purchase, 1977. Lab. asst. Rockefeller U. (formerly Rockefeller Inst. Med. Rsch.), N.Y.C., 1951—54. Chmn. Byram com. Nature Conservancy, Bedford, N.Y., 1978-81; mem. Conservation Bd. Town of Bedford, 1978-88, Westchester County Environ. Mgmt. Commn., 1979-88, Coun. N.Y. Bot. Garden, Bronx, 1982—, Wetlands Commn., Bedford, 1988-97; trustee Lower Hudson chpt. Nature Conservancy, Katonah, N.Y., 1980-90, 91-99, chmn., 1983-86, vice chmn., 1995-99; pres. Fed. Conservationists Westchester County, Purchase, 1985-87; trustee N.Y. State Bd. Nature Conservancy, Albany, 1983-91, vice-chmn., 1986-88; bd. dirs. Lady Bird Johnson Wildflower Ctr., 2000-05. Mem. N.Y. Acad. Scis., Garden Club Am. (conservation com. 1983-85, 95-97, vice chmn. conservation com. 1985-87, bd. dirs. 1989-91, vice chmn. scholarship com. 1991-94) Episcopalian. Avocations: gardening, hiking, tennis, birding, botanizing. Home: 140 Sarles Rd RD 3 Mount Kisco NY 10549-4733

KEESHEN, KATHLEEN KEARNEY, public relations consultant; b. NYC, Dec. 4, 1937; d. James William and Hannah Pauline (Mansfield) Kearney; 1 child (by previous marriage), John Christopher Day; m. Walt Keeshen Jr.; stepchildren: Michael Patrick, Walt John III, Kathleen Marie, William Thomas, Ralph Timothy. BA in English, U. Md., 1959, MA in Journalism, 1973, PhD in Am. Studies, 1983; MLA, Stanford U., 1995. Cert. profl. sec. Congl., legal, med., acad., corp. sec. various orgns., East and Midwest, 1954-63; staff and mgmt. positions IBM, Washington, Md., 1963-73, lab. comm. mgr. Systems Comm. Div. Manassas, Va., 1974-76, comm. staff corp. hdqrs. Armonk, N.Y., 1977-83, comm. and community rels. mgr. Almaden Rsch. Ctr. San Jose, Calif., 1983-92; prin. Keeshen Comm., Coyote (Calif.) Press., 1992—. Lectr. in field. Contbr. articles to profl. jours. Mem. adv. bd. Friends of San Jose Pub. Libr., 1987—, Silicon Valley Info. Ctr., 1986-92, Media Report to Women; mem. corp. task force Stanford U. Inst. for Rsch. on Women and Gender, 1990—, affiliated scholar, 1992-94, assocs. bd., 1994-96; affiliated scholar Beatrice M. Bain Rsch. Group on Gender, U. Calif., Berkeley, 1994-95; libr. commr. City of Morgan Hill, Calif., 1999-2003, commr. chair, 2001-2002; rep. Santa Clara county Silicon Valley Libr. Sys. Adv. Bd., 2004-06. Mem. Am. Journalism Historians Assn., Assn. for Edn. in Journalism and Mass Comm., Women in Comm., San Jose Rotary Club, San. Jose Profl. Womens Literary Assn., Calif. Writers Club, Alpha Xi Delta, Calif. Libr. Assn., Calif. Assn. of Libr. Trustees and Commrs., Santa Clara Art Assn., Los Gatos Art Assn., Spl. Librs. Assn., Am. Libr. Assn. Office: Keeshen Comm Coyote Press PO Box 13154 Coyote CA 95013-3154

KEESLING, KAREN RUTH, lawyer; b. Wichita, Kans., July 9, 1946; d. Paul W. and Ruth (Sharp) Keesling. BA, Ariz. State U., 1968, MA, 1970; JD, Georgetown U., 1981. Bar: Va. 1981, Fla. 1981, Ariz. 2000. Asst. dean of women U. Kans., Lawrence, 1970-72; exec. sec., sec.'s adv. com. on rights and responsibilities of women HEW, Washington, 1972-74; dir. White House Office of Women's Programs, Washington, 1974-77; head civil rights and equal opportunity sect., Gov. Div., Congl. Rsch. Svc. Libr. Congress, Washington, 1977-80; legis. aide Sen. Nancy Kassebaum, Washington, 1979-81; mem. pers. office staff Office of Pres.-elect, Washington, Jan. 1981; pvt. practice Falls Church, Va. and Peoria, Sun City, Ariz., 1981-88, 90—; dept. for equal opportunity dept. Dept. Air Force, Washington, 1981-82, dep. asst. sec. manpower res. affairs and installations, 1982-83, prin. dep. asst. sec. manpower res. affairs, 1983-87, prin. dep. asst. sec. readiness support dept. Washington, 1987-88, prin. dep. asst. sec. manpower and res. affairs, 1988, asst. sec. manpower and res. affairs, 1988-89; acting wage and hour adminstr. U.S. Dept. Labor, Washington, 1992-93; pvt. practice Falls Church, Va., Peoria, Sun City, Ariz. Bd. advisers Outstanding Young Women Am., 1983—90. Mem. Nat. Women's Polit. Caucus, Washington, 1980, Nat. Fedn. Rep. Women's Club, Washington, 1975; pers. com. chair Faith Presbyn. Ch., 2000—04, elder, 2000—05, mission com. chair, 2005—. Named One of Ten Outstanding Young Women of Am., 1975, Kans. Women's Golf Champion, 1966, Wichita Women's Champion, 1968, 1970, Outstanding Woman Golfer in Kans., 1966; recipient Alumni Achievement award, Ariz. State U., 1976, Elizabeth Boyer award, Women's Equity Action League, 1986, Meritorious Civilian award, USAF, 1987, Woman of Distinction award, Nat. Conf. Coll. Women, Student Leaders and Women of Distinction, 1988, Exceptional Civilian Svc. award, USAF, 1988. Mem.: Va. Bus. and Profl. Women's Found. (trustee 1985—93), The Women's Inst. Inc. (adv. coun. 1985—96), No. Va. Women atty.'s Assn. (steering com. 1990—95), Va. Fedn. Bus. and Profl. Women's Clubs (2d v.p. 1987—88, 1st v.p. 1988—89, pres.-elect 1989—90, pres. 1990—91), Fla. Bar Assn., Va. Bar Assn., Ariz. Bar Assn., P.E.O. (treas. 2001—02, v.p. 2002—03, pres. chptr. 2003—), U.S. Com. for UNIFEM (gen. counsel 1983—2002), Pi Beta Phi. Avocation: golf. Home: 9606 W Lindgren Ave Sun City AZ 85373 E-mail: Keeslingkr@aol.com.

KEESLING, RUTH MORRIS, foundation administrator; b. New Brunswick, NJ, Apr. 4, 1930; d. Mark Loren and Louise Weber Morris; m. Thomas Marion Keesling, June 30, 1956; children: Thomas Mark, James H., Frank M. BS in Journalism, U. Colo., 1953. Advt. dept. Burlingame Advance, Calif., 1953—54; news dept. Oakland Tribune, Calif., 1954; pub. rels. Mark Morris Assoc., Inc., Topeka, 1955; co-owner Pub. Rels., Inc., Denver, 1955—64; pres. Digit Fund, Denver, 1986—88; founder, sponsor Mountain Gorilla Vet. Project, Denver, 1986—2001; founder, pres. Mountain Gorilla Conservation Fund, Denver, 2001—. Founder Morris Animal Found., Denver, 1955—; pres. Dian Fossey Gorilla Fund, Denver, 1988—91, pres. internat., 1991—93; trustee Denver Zool. Found., Denver, 1969—; lectr. mountain gorillas; sponsor, founder Mt. Gorillas in Africa, 1987—; founder Wildlife Animal Medicine Dept. Makerene U., Uganda, 1994; head task force Rwandan Govt., 2000. Author: (brochures) Small Animal Clinical Nutrition, 1959; designer (exhibitions) Mus. Display Dian Fossey items, 1992—94. Named Woman of Distinction, Girl Scouts Am.; recipient Outstanding Alumni award, U. Colo., 1976, award for animal welfare, Collier County Humane Soc., 2002, Lifetime Achievement award, Brit. Airways, 2002, award, Collier County Humane Soc., 2002. Mem.: Port Royal Club, Naples Yacht Club, Denver Country Club, Pi Beta Phi (chmn. adv. bd. 1957—60, mem. house bd. 1958—61, Carolyn Lichtenberg Crest award 2000). Home: 3220 Cherryridge Rd Englewood CO 80113 Office: Mountain Gorilla Conservation Fund PO Box 2211 Englewood CO 80150-2211 Office Phone: 303-781-8484, 239-434-9447. E-mail: RuthKee@aol.com.

KEETER, LYNN CARPENTER, language educator; b. Charlotte, N.C. d. John Franklin and Georgiana (LaVender) Carpenter; children: John Blair, Eric William. BA in English, Gardner-Webb U., 1980, MA in Edn., 1985, MA in English, 1994; devel. educator specialist, Appalachian State U.; postgrad., The Union Inst., Cin. Instr. Taylor Finishing, Charlotte, 1970-74, Gardner-Webb U., Boiling Springs, N.C., 1980-86, prof. English, 1988—; tchr. self-devel. classes for underprivileged women Robeson County Schs., Lumberton, N.C., 1986-88. Founder, dir. personal devel. program for women; freelance writer for vintage clothing jours.; storyteller Appalachian folklore. Co-author: Fundamentals of Reading and Writing, 1997; writer children's stories. Mem. Internat. Reading Assn. (award 1997), A.C.E.I., pres. local chpt. N.C.R.A., N.C.Reading Assn. (pres. local coun. 1998—), Woman's Club Internat. (v.p., pres., Outstanding Woman 1980), Woman's Prayer Assn. (pres.), Coll. English Assn. (editor newsletter 1993—), Beta Sigma Phi (pres., v.p., sec., Woman of Yr. award 1991, 92, Alpha Omega award 1992), Sigma Tau Delta, Phi Delta Kappa. Avocations: antiques, interior decorating, dance.

KEETS, ELIZABETH, advocate, educator; b. Peoria County, Ill. d. Jack and Billie June Russell; m. Nov. 23, 1972 (div. Sept. 1989); children: John Charles (dec. 1994), Matthew Calvin. Cert. AIDS educator ARC. Dressmaker local bus., Canton, Ill., 1973-83; dental asst. Dr. John Lefebvre, Canton, 1983-98; AIDS educator John Keets Found., 1991—. Named woman of yr. YWCA, Canton, 1996, person of week WHOI-TV, Peoria, 1996, weekly hero WEEK-TV, Peoria, 1997, person of week, 1998, 99. Avocations: reading, walking, working with youth, mentoring school programs.

KEEZER, DEBORAH ANN, elementary school educator; b. Rutland, Vt., July 10, 1952; d. Ross Lester and Patricia Margaret Roberts; m. Jerel Evan Keezer, June 24, 1977. BS in Edn., Castleton State Coll., Vt., 1975, MA in Edn., 1986; specialist in edn., Simmons Coll., Boston, 2006. Tchr. Poultney Elem., Va., 1976—, reading specialist, 2002—05. Trainer Am. Reads, Vt., 2005—06. Named Outstanding Tchr., Poultney Sch. Dist., 1995. Mem.: Poultney Tchrs. Assn. (negotiator 1988—2006). Democrat. Home: 104 Church St Poultney VT 05764 Office: Poultney Sch Dist 96 School District Poultney VT 05764

KEFALAS, JESSIE AE, visual merchandiser, artist; b. Bklyn., Nov. 3, 1972; d. John Kostas and Anita Kay K. A of Fine Arts, Fashion Inst Tech., 1993; BFA, U. Del., 1997. Merchandiser GAP, Inc., N.Y.C., 1996—. Greek Orthodox. Avocation: painting. Home: 9 Laura Ln East Setauket NY 11733-1821

KEFFER, MARIA JEAN, environmental scientist; b. Sacramento, Dec. 10, 1951; d. George Edwin and Genevieve Nellie (Babuska) Scott; m. Gerry Craig Keffer, Nov. 6, 1971; children: Annemarie, Gregory, Margaret. AA in Liberal Arts, San Bernardino Valley Coll., Calif., 1973; BS in Natural Scis., U. Alaska, 1988, MS in Environ. Quality, 1995. Cert. environ. auditor Nat. Registry of Environ. Profls., prin. environ. auditor/EARA - U.K.; registered environ. health specialist, Nat. Environ. Health Assn. and State of Calif. Rsch. lab. assoc. VA/Loma Linda (Calif.) Hosp., 1988-90; environ. health specialist San Bernardino County, Calif., 1990-91, S&S Engring., Eagle River, Alaska, 1991-92; regulatory specialist ENSR Consulting and Engring., Anchorage, 1992-94; quality assurance environ. specialist Alyeska Pipeline Svc. Co., Anchorage, 1994-98; ISO 14001 project mgr. Hoefler Consulting Group, Anchorage, 1998—. Mem.: Environ. Auditing Roundtable. Home: 3401 Minnesota Dr Ste 300 Anchorage AK 99503-3684 Business E-Mail: mkeffer@gci.net.

KEGARISE, CAROL ANN, primary school educator; d. Merlyn E. and Gertrude E. Miller; m. Stephen Wayne Kegarise, June 15, 1968; children: Dyane Saenz, Michael, Mac. BAE, Ashland Coll., Ohio, 1968; MA in Curriculum/Instrn., Ashland U., 1991. Primary reading/writing tchr. Berlin-Milan Schs., Milan, Ohio, 1969—. Contbr. articles to profl. jours. and pubs. Grantee, Milan Rotary Club, 1996. Mem.: NEA, Berlin-Milan Tchrs. Assn. Home: 2713 Rte 113 E Milan OH 44846 Office: Berlin-Milan Schs 140 S Main St Milan OH 44846

KEGLEY, JACQUELYN ANN, philosophy educator; b. Conneaut, Ohio, July 18, 1938; d. Steven Paul and Gertrude Evelyn (Frank) Kovacevic; m. Charles William Kegley, June 12, 1964; children: Jacquelyn Ann, Stephen Lincoln Luther. BA cum laude, Allegheny Coll., 1960; MA summa cum laude, Rice U., 1964; PhD, Columbia U., 1971. Asst. prof. philosophy Calif. State U., Bakersfield, 1973-77, assoc. prof., 1977-81, prof., 1981—, chair dept. philosophy and religious studies. Vis. prof. U. Philippines, Quezon City, 1966-68; grant project dir. Calif. Coun. Humanities, 1977, project dir. 1980, 82; mem. work group on ethics Am. Colls. of Nursing, Washington, 1984-86; mem. Am. Bd. Forensic Examiners; chair acad. senate Calif. State U., 2000-03, exec. com., 2003-04. Author: Introduction to Logic, 1978, Genuine Individuals and Genuine Communities, 1997; editor: Humanistic Delivery of Services to Families, 1982, Education for the Handicapped, 1982, Genetic Knowledge, 1998; mem. edit. bd. Jour. Philosophy in Lit., 1979-84; contbr. articles to profl. jours. Active CSU Acad. Senate, 1999—; Bd. dirs. Bakersfield Mental Health Assn., 1982—84, Citizens for Betterment of Community. Recipinet Golden Roadrunner award Bakersfield Cmty., 1991, Wang Family Excellence award, 2000. Mem. Philosophy of Sci. Assn., Soc. Advancement Am. Philos. Soc. (chmn. Pacific divsn. 1979-83, nat. exec. com. 1974-79, 2003-), Philosophy Soc., Soc. Interdisciplinary Study of Mind, Am. Philos. Assn. (bd. mem. 1999-2003, chair com. on tchg.), Dorian Soc., Phi Beta Kappa. Democrat. Lutheran. Avocations: music, tennis. Home: 7312 Kroll Way Bakersfield CA 93309-2336 Office: Calif State U Dept Philosophy Bakersfield CA 93311 Office Phone: 661-664-2249. Business E-Mail: jkegley@csub.edu.

KEHOE, JENNIFER SPUNGIN, English language educator, writer, children's book editor; b. Princeton, N.J., Apr. 21, 1969; d. Gardner Mawney and Susan Jay Spungin; m. Christopher Michael Kehoe, May 24, 1995 (div. Jan. 1, 2003); children: Kelsey Jane, Conley Jay. BA, Skidmore Coll., Saratoga Springs, N.Y., 1991; MA, SUNY, Albany, 1993; PhD, SUNY, Buffalo, 2000. Cert. permanent 7-12 English tchr. N.Y. Tchr. English Nazareth Acad., Rochester, NY, 1992—94; lectr. English SUNY, Geneseo, NY, 1994—96; prof. English St. John Fisher Coll., Rochester, 1996—2004; assoc. prof. English Roberts Wesleyan Coll., Rochester, NY, 2004—. Adj. prof. Daemen Coll., Amherst, NY, 1994—96; dir. Ctr. Academic Excellence; Am. Disabilities Act coord.; presenter in field. Author: (book of poetry) Gallop, 1984, (book) Teacher's Handbook for Susan B. Anthony and Justice for All, 1995; contbr. poetry to anthologies. Recipient Millard Fillmore Coll. tchg. grants (2), 1995—97, SUNY-Buffalo tchg. fellowships (4), 1995—97, Elizabeth

Luce Moore award in poetry, 1989. Democrat. Avocation: dressage and combined equine training. Home: 106 Wilshire Rd Rochester NY 14618 Office: Roberts Wesleyan Coll 2301 Westside Dr Rochester NY 14624 Office Phone: 585-734-8808. E-mail: drjkehoe@rochester.rr.com.

KEHOE, KATHRYN J., science educator, researcher; b. Albion, Mich., Dec. 31, 1954; d. John D. and Pearl V. Kehoe; m. Andrew I. Manning, Aug. 28, 1982; children: Kelly Manning, Molly Manning. BS, Ea. Mich. U., Ypsilanti, 1977; PhD in Toxicology, U. Mich., Ann Arbor, 1990. Cert. secondary continuing edn. Mich. Dept. Edn., 1980. Tchr. Greenhills Sch., Ann Arbor, 1977—82; lectr. dept. chemistry Ea. Mich. U., Ypsilant, 1989—92; rsch. fellow Mayo Clinic, Jacksonville, Fla., 2000—04; tchr. chemistry Nease H.S., St. Augustine, Fla., 2004—; lectr. natural scis. U. North Fla., Jacksonville. Postdoctoral assoc. Univs. Mich. and Minn., Ann Arbor and Mpls., 1993—97; asst. prof. Jacksonville U., 1997—2004. Com. mem. Duval County Health Dept., Jacksonville, 1998—2000. Recipient Tennis Coach of Yr., Minn. Intercolliegate Athletic Assn., 1997, Outstanding Tchr. award, Am. Chem. Soc., 2006, Nat. Rsch. Svc. award, NIH, 1983—85, 1995—97. Office: Nease HS 10550 Ray Rd Saint Augustine FL 32095

KEHOE-GADWAY, NITA L., art educator, art gallery director; d. Rex and Erna Kehoe; m. Aaron Gadway, Aug. 2, 2003. MFA, U. of Cin., 1998; MA, U. of Iowa, 1996, BFA, 1993. Head Art Cen. Wyo. Coll., Riverton, 2000—, gallery dir., 2000—. Exhibitions include Millworks Gallery, Akron, Ohio, 2003, Delta Coll., Midland, Mich., 2005, Festive Gardens, Akko, Israel, 2005, UAP Gallery, Palace of Culture, Torgu-Mures, Romania, 2005. Grantee, Partnership 2000, 2004—05. Mem.: Alliance for Arts Edn. (bd. dirs. 2003—), Arts in Action (sec. 2003—04, pres. 2004—05), Coll. Art Assn. Achievements include research in Historical Anatomical Illustrations dating back to the 11th century. Office Phone: 307-855-2211. Office Fax: 307-855-2090. Business E-Mail: nkehoe@cwc.edu.

KEHRER, MICHELE ANN, physical therapist, athleic trainer; d. Daniel Francis and Carm Kehrer; m. Scott Thomas Harrison, May 28, 2005. BS in Sports Medicine/Phys. Edn., Western Ill. U., Macomb, 1993—95; PhD in Phys. Therapy, U. Ill., Chgo., 2001—04. Site coord. Healthsouth, Wilmette, Ill., 1996—98; clinic mgr. Peak Therapeutics, Ltd., Chgo., 1998—2000; rschr. Balance Therapy Rsch. Found., Chgo., 2000—02; owner Kehrer, Ltd., Chgo., 2001—, LifeStyle Phys. Therapy & Balance Ctr., Chgo., 2005—. Mem.: NATA, APTA. Office: LifeStyle Physical Therapy & Balance Ctr 3130 N Lincoln Ave Chicago IL 60657 Business E-Mail: balancechicago@yahoo.com.

KEHRET, PEG, writer; b. LaCrosse, Wis., Nov. 11, 1936; d. Arthur Robert and Elizabeth (Showers) Schulze; m. Carl Edward Kehret, July 2, 1955 (dec. 2004); children: Bob. C., Anne M. Kehret Konen. Student, U. Minn., 1954—55. Trustee Pacific Northwest Writers Conf., Seattle, 1983-86. Author: Vows of Love and Marriage, 1979, Refinishing and Restoring Your Piano, 1985, Winning Monologs for Young Actors, 1986, Deadly Stranger, 1987 (Children's Choice award, 1988), The Winner, 1988, ENCORE!-More Winning Monologs for Young Actors, 1988, Nightmare Mountain, 1989 (Young Hoosier Book award, 1992, Golden Sower award Nebr. Libr. Assn., 1993, Iowa Children's Choice award, 1994, Maud Hart Lovelace award, 1995), Wedding Vows, 1989, Sisters, Long Ago, 1990, Cages, 1991 (Maud Hart Lovelace award, 1996), Acting Natural, 1992, Terror at the Zoo, 1992 (Pacific N.W. Young Reader's Choice award, 1995, N.Mex. Land of Enchantment award, 1995, Iowa Children's Choice award, 1996), Horror at the Haunted House, 1992 (Sequoyah Children's Book award, 1995, Young Hoosier award, 1995), Night of Fear, 1994, Richest Kids in Town, 1994, Cat Burglar on the Prowl, 1995, Danger at the Fair, 1995, Bone Breath and the Vandals, 1995, Don't Go Near Mrs. Tallie, 1995, Desert Danger, 1995, The Ghost Followed Us Home, 1996, Earthquake Terror, 1996 (W.Va. Children's Book award, 1998, Children's Crown award Nat. Christian Sch. Assn., 1998, Utah Children's Book award, 1999, Va. Young Readers award, 1999), Race to Disaster, 1996, Screaming Eagles, 1996, Backstage Fright, 1996, Small Steps: The Year I Got Polio, 1996 (Soc. Children's Book Writers and Illustrators Golden Kite award nonfiction, 1997, PEN Ctr. USA West award, 1997, Dorothy Canfield Fisher award, 1998, Mark Twain award, 1999, Young Hoosier award, 2001), Searching for Candlestick Park, 1997, The Volcano Disaster, 1998 (Fla. Sunshine award, 2000), The Blizzard Disaster, 1998, The Flood Disaster, 1999, Shelter Dogs, 1999, I'm Not Who You Think I Am, 1999 (Lamplighter award), The Secret Journey, 1999, My Brother Made Me Do It, 2000, Don't Tell Anyone, 2000, The Hideout, 2001, Saving Lilly, 2001 (Henry Bergh award ASPCA, 2001), The Stranger Next Door, 2002 (Sequoyah award, 2005, Nev. Young Readers award, 2005), Five Pages a Day: A Writer's Journey, 2002, Spy Cat, 2003 (SD Prarie Pasque award, 2006), Escaping the Giant Wave, 2003 (Iowa Children's Choice award, 2006, Fla. Young Reader award, 2006, Nev. Young Reader award, 2006, Nebr. Golden Sower award, 2006), Abduction!, 2004 (Edgar award nominee, 2005), The Ghost's Grave, 2005, Trapped, 2006, (plays) Cemeteries are a Grave Matter, 1977, Let Him Sleep 'Till It's Time for His Funeral, 1978, Spirit!, 1979 (Forest Roberts Playwriting award No. Mich. U., 1979, Best New Play award Pioneer Drama Svc., 1980), Dracula, Darling, 1980, Charming Billy, 1981, (musical) Bicycles Built for Two, 1985; contbr. articles to mags., short stories to mags. Vol. Humane Soc., SPCA, Bellevue, Wash., 1975—. Recipient Achievement award Pacific N.W. Writers, Celebrate Lit. award N.W. Reading Coun. of Internat. Reading Assn., 1993; named Artist of Yr., Redmond Arts Commn., 1998. Mem.: Author's Guild, Soc. Children's Book Writers, Mystery Writers Am. Office: Curtis Brown Ltd Ten Astor Pl New York NY 10003

KEIM, BETTY LOU, actress, literary consulant; b. Malden, Mass., Sept. 27, 1938; d. Buster and Dorothy Clair (Tracy) Keim; m. Warren Berlinger, Feb. 18, 1960; children: Lisa, David, Edward, Elizabeth. Grad., Lodge Acad., N.Y.c., 1956. Appeared in films These Wilder Years, 1956, Teenage Rebel, 1956, Wayward Bus, 1957, Some Came Running, 1958; appeared on Broadway in Strange Fruit, Rip Van Winkle, Crime and Punishment, Texas Lil Darlin, The Remarkable Mr. Pennypacker, Roomful of Roses; appeared on TV in Omnibus, Playhouse 90, Alcoa Hour, Philco PlayHouse; appeared in TV series My Son Jeep, The Deputy. Assoc. Aid Project L.A., 1984-97; life mem., vol. Actors Fund of Am. Recipinet Motion Picture award Calif. Women's Club, 1956, Filmdoms Famous Five award Film Daily Critics, 1956, Laurel award, 1956.

KEIM, KATHERINE I., psychologist; d. Gary W. and Mary A. Linder; m. J. M. Keim, Sept. 26, 1998. PhD, Calif. Sch. Profl. Psychology.Alliant Internat. U., 2005. Psychological Assistant Dept. of Health and Human Services/Nebr., 2001, lic. mental health practitioner Dept. Health and Human Svcs., Nebr., 2004. Corrections officer Buffalo County Detention Ctr., Kearney, Nebr., 1997—98; child care worker II 2nd Home, Inc, Clovis, Calif., 1998—99; therapist Rape Counseling Svc., Fresno, 2000—01; therapist, psychol. asst. Beneficial Behavioral Health Svcs., Inc., Omaha, 2001—03; psychol. asst. Beatrice State Devel. Ctr., Beatrice, 2002—04; therapist Luth. Family Svcs., Bellevue, 2004—; psychologist Stankus Psychol. Svcs., Omaha, 2004—; psychologist Med. Ctr. U. Nebr., Nebr., 2006—. Mem.: Nebr. Psychol. Assn. Achievements include research in body image as mediated by self-esteem and perceived parental attachment, a cross-cultural analysis.

KEISER, MARY ANN MYERS, special education educator; b. Phila., Feb. 13, 1932; d. Edgar Miller and Mary (Bickley) Myers; m. John F. Keiser, Jr., Dec. 25, 1963 (wid. Sept. 1977); children: Jill, Kimberly, Beth (twins), Mary Ann, Meg (twins). BA, Dickinson Coll., 1954; MS, Temple U., 1957; MEd, Pa. State U., 1979. Tchr. sci. Media (Pa.) H.S., 1954-56; elem. tchr. Phoenixville (Pa.) Sch. Dist., 1956-57, Springfield (Pa.) Sch. Dist., 1957-64, Neshaminy Sch. Dist., Langhorne, Pa., 1964-65; reading tchr., cons. Main Line Day Sch., Haverford, Pa., 1971-79; spl. edn. tchr. West Chester (Pa.) Sch. Dist., 1979-97. Vol. R.S.V.P. and West Chester Sch. Dist. Ford Found. grantee Temple U., Phila., 1954-57. Mem. NEA, Pa. Edn. Assn. (life), Chester County Hist. Soc., PSEA-R, DAR (past sr. state pres. Pa.), Children Am. Revolution (past sr. state pres. Pa.), Needlework Guild Assn. (past pres. Paole, Malvern br.). Methodist. Avocations: doll collector, tutor for care children, travel, reading. Home: 423 Gateswood Dr West Chester PA 19380-6324

KEISER, NANETTE MARIE, research scientist; b. Flint, Mich., May 22, 1957; d. Charles Kenneth Jr. and Suzanne Mary (Sayan) Stevens; m. W. Jack Keiser, May 29, 1993; stepchildren: Christopher, Elizabeth, Laura. BS, Western Mich. U., 1980, MA, 1996, EdD, 2000. Edn. dir. Tandy Computer Ctr., Kalamazoo, 1980-85; dir. fin., adminstrn. Deming, Hughey et al, Kalamazoo, 1985-91; chief fin. and adminstrv. officer Kalamazoo Found., 1991-95; computer project dir. Coun. Mich. Founds., 1995-97; cons. W.K. Kellogg Found., 1997—2000; evaluator We. Mich. U., Kalamazoo, 1996—. Presenter in field. Bd. dirs., pres. YWCA. Mem.: AAUW, Am. Evaluation Assn. (bd. dirs., treas.), Mich. Assn. for Evaluation (bd. dirs., treas.), Phi Kappa Phi, Phi Delta Kappa. Avocations: sailing, reading, music, biking, computers.

KEISLING, MARY WEST, volunteer; b. Sparta, Tenn. d. Herbert Jones West and Dannie Young; m. John Kermit Keisling, Dec. 9, 1939 (dec. 1986); children: John H., Robert West. AB, George Washington U., 1938. State pres. Tenn. Fedn. Women's Clubs, 1968-70; vice chmn. Tenn. Arts Commn., 1977-82; mem. nat. bd. Med. Coll. Pa., 1977-91; county commr. Tenn. County Ct., 1978-85; pres. Plateau Mental Health Ctr., 1980-84; state historian DAR, 1987-90; nat. pres. U.S. Daughters 1812, 1988-91. Home: 427 Gaines St Sparta TN 38583-2124

KEITH, BARBARA ANN, elementary school educator, educator; b. Berwyn, Ill., June 18, 1946; d. John Williams and Clara Teresa (Novak) DeBest; m. Larry Brian Keith, Nov. 21, 1970; children: Christopher B., Alison Kathleen, Erin Alexandra. BA in Psychology, Marquette U., Milw., 1968; MS in Edn., U. So. Calif., 1976. Cert. Teaching K-4, Va. Tchr. St. Thomas Acquinas Sch., Milw., 1968-69, Ray M. Schmidt Sch., Westminster, Calif., 1969-71, DOD Sch., Seoul, Korea, 1975-76, St. Matthew's Sch., Virginia Beach, Va., 1986—. Mem. Nat. Cath. Edn. Assn. Roman Catholic. Avocations: sewing, reading, crafts. Office: St Matthews School 3316 Sandra Ln Virginia Beach VA 23464-1736 Business E-Mail: bkeith@smsvb.net.

KEITH, CAROL JEAN, writer, regional historian; b. Tarpon Springs, Fla., June 5, 1936; d. Sherrod Raymond and Irene Immoline (Boyd) Skeen; m. Walter Louis Keith,Mar. 16, 1956; 1 child, Barbara Jean. Cert., Am. Banking Inst., 1965; journalism, Ctrl. Fla. C.C., 1977. Exec. asst. Nations Banks, Tarpon Springs, 1962-68; adminstrv. asst. to spkr. Fla. Ho. of Reps., Tampa, 1968-69; exec. assn. Gen. Paul Adams, Tampa, 1969-70; coord. med. staff Munroe Regional Hosp., Ocala, Fla., 1974-78; biographer, novelist Bacalou Pub. Co., Crystal River, Fla., 1978—. Lectr. history Citrus and Pinellas counties, 1994—. Author: A Watch for Evil, 1990. Mem. Tarpon Springs Hist. Soc., Pinellas County Hist. Soc. (history lectr. 1994—). Republican. Baptist. Avocations: fishing, hunting, cooking. Home and Office: 951 SE Mayo Dr Crystal River FL 34429-9056

KEITH, COURTNEY S., lawyer; b. Waco, Tex., July 19, 1967; BS, Tex. Christian U., 1989; JD, Baylor U. Sch. Law, 1993. Bar: Tex. 1993. Asst. dist. atty. Tarrant County Criminal Dist. Atty.'s Office, 1993—95; ptnr. Keith Law Firm, P.C., Ft. Worth. Named a Rising Star, Tex. Super Lawyers mag., 2006. Mem.: Ft. Worth-Tarrant County Young Lawyers Assn., Assn. Trial Lawyers of Am., Texans for Civil Justice, Tex. Trial Lawyers Assn., Tarrant County Trial Lawyers Assn., ABA, Tarrant County Bar Assn. Office: Keith Law Firm PC Keith Bldg 1705 W 7th St Fort Worth TX 76102 Office Phone: 817-338-1400. E-mail: courtk@keithlaw.com.*

KEITH, JENNIE, anthropology educator, academic administrator, writer; b. Carmel, Calif., Nov. 15, 1942; d. Paul K. and Romayne Louise (Fuller) Hill; m. Marc Howard Ross, Aug. 25, 1968 (div. 1978); 1 child, Aaron Elliot Keith m. Roy Gerald Fitzgerald, June 21, 1980; 1 child, Kate Romayne Keith-Fitzgerald. BA, Pomona Coll., 1964; MA, Northwestern U., 1966, PhD, 1968; Dr.Letters (hon.), Pomona Coll., 2002. NIMH fellow, Paris, 1968-70; asst. prof. anthropology Swarthmore Coll., 1970-76, assoc. prof., 1976-82, prof., 1982—, Centennial prof. anthropology, 1990—, chmn. sociology and anthropology, 1987-92, provost, 1992-2001; exec. dir. Eugene M. Lang Ctr. for Civic and Social Responsibility, 2002—. Mem. rsch. edn. rev. com. NIMH, Washington, 1979-82; co-dir. workshop on age and anthropology Nat. Inst. Aging, Washington, 1980-81, task group leader nat. rsch. plan on aging, 1981; mem. human devel. rev. bd. NIH, 1985-89; mem. adv. coun. Brookdale Found., 1990-93. Author: Old People, New Lives, 1977, 2d paperback edit., 1982 (Am. Jour. Nursing Book of Yr. 1978), Old People as People, 1982; co-author: The Aging Experience, 1994 (Richard Kalish award Gerontol. Soc. Am. 1994); co-editor: New Methods for Old-Age Research, 1980, 2d edit., 1986, Age in Anthropological Theory, 1984; mem. editorial bd. Gerontologist, 1981-89, Jour. Gerontology, 1987-91, Jour. Aging Studies, 1989-98; assoc. editor Rsch. on Aging, 1981-88. Bd. dirs. Cmty. Svcs., Folsom, Pa., 1980-82, Inst. Outdoor Awareness, Swarthmore, 1980—; bd. dirs. Kendal-Crosslands, 1987-92, chmn., 1989-92, Kendal Corp., 1992-95; mem. gen. bd. Pendle Hill Quaker Study Ctr., 2005—. Conf. grantee Nat. Inst. Aging, 1980, rsch. grantee, 1982-90. Fellow Am. Anthrop. Assn., Gerontol. Soc. Am. (exec. bd. behavioral and social scis. sect. 1985-87, program chmn. 1989, chair 1989-90, publs. com. 1993-95); mem. Assn. Anthropology and Gerontology (founder, sec. 1980-81). Office: Swarthmore Coll Lang Ctr for Civic and Social Responsibi Swarthmore PA 19081 Office Phone: 610-690-5742. Business E-Mail: jkeith1@swarthmore.edu.

KEITH, KATHARINE, education educator; Prof. Santa Ana Coll., Santa Ana, Calif., 1991—.

KEITH, PATRICIA, multi-media specialist; b. Houston, Sept. 21, 1946; m. Nicholas Keith, July 19, 1968; 1 child, Nicholas (deceased) Keith. BA, Tex. So. U., 1970, MA, 1971; MS, Towson U., Md., 2002. Cert. libr. media specialist 1985. English, journalism, speech tchr. Houston Ind. Sch. Dist., 1976—86; children's libr. Alexandria Pub. Libr., Alexandria, Va., 1986—89; libr. media specialist Kettering Elem. Sch., Upper Marlboro, Md., 1989—92; libr. media/tech. specialist Benjamin Stoddert Mid. Sch., Temple Hills, Md., 1992—2000; libr. media specialist Charles H. Flowers H.S., Springdale, Md., 2000—. Libr. media adv. com. Office of Libr. Media Svcs.-Prince George's County Pub. Schs., Landover, Md., 1996—; tech. asst. Sagebrush Automation Conversion-Prince George's County Pub. Sch., Landover, Md., 2004—; sponsor Charles H. Flowers H.S. It's Acad. Team, Springdale, Md., 2000—; lectr. in field. Editor: (harmony chorus) Potomac Harmony Dispatch. Fellow Mentor Tchr. fellow, Md. Tech. Consortium and Md. Pub. TV, 2002, Md. Tech. Acad. fellow, Md. State Dept. of Edn., Johns Hopkins U. and Towson U., 1999—2000. Mem.: Md. Instrnl. Computer Coord. Assn. (workshop lectr. 1999—2002), Ednl. Media Assn. of Prince George's County (pres., v.p., historian 1993—2002), Consortium of Sch. Networks, Md. Ednl. Media Orgn. Avocations: reading, designing jewelry, theater, jazz. Office: Charles H Flowers High School 10001 Ardwick Ardmore Rd Springdale MD 20774 Office Phone: 301-636-8000 310. Office Fax: 301-636-8008. Personal E-mail: pkeith9214@comcast.net. E-mail: pkeith@pgcps.org.

KEITH, PAULINE MARY, artist, illustrator, writer; b. Fairfield, Nebr., July 21, 1924; d. Siebelt Ralph and Pauline Alethia (Garrison) Goldenstein; m. Everett B. Keith, Feb. 14, 1957; 1 child, Nathan Ralph. Student, George Fox Coll., 1947—48, Oreg. State U., 1955. Illustrator Merlin Press, San Jose, Calif., 1980-81; artist, illustrator, watercolorist Corvallis, Oreg., 1980-94. Author 6 chapbooks including Christmas Thoughts, Retelling the Story, 1985, Poems, 1999; editor: Four Generations of Verse, 1979; author numerous poems; contbr. articles to profl. jour; one-woman shows include Roger's Meml. Libr., Forest Grove, Oreg., 1959, Corvallis Art Ctr., 1960, 98-99, Human Resources Bldg., Corvallis, 1959-61, Corvallis Pastoral Counseling Ctr., 1992-94, 96, Hall Gallery, Sr. Ctr., 1993-03, Consumer Power, Philomath, Oreg., 1994, 02, 03, 04, 05, Art, Etc., Newburg, Oreg., 1995-2002; exhibited in group shows at Hewlett-Packard Co., 1984-85, Corvallis Art Ctr., 1992, Chintimini Sr. Ctr., 1992, 94, 01-04. Co-elder First Christian Ch. (Disciples of Christ), Corvallis, 1988-89, co-deacon, 1980-83, elder, 1991-93; sec. Hostess Club of Chintimini Sr. Ctr., Corvallis, 1987, pres., 1988-89, v.p., 1992-94; active Luth. Ch. Coun., 1999-2000. Recipient Watercolor 1st price Benton County Fair, 1982-83, 88-89, 91, 2d prize, 1987, 91, 3d prize, 1984, 90, 92, 3d prize Newberg Festival, 2005. Mem. Oreg. Assn. Christian Writers, Internat. Assn. Women Mins., Am. Legion Aux. (post poet), ArtVine (Pres.'s Choice, 1999-2002, honorable mention, 2005, Newburg Annual Festival art show 3d prize 2006) Republican. Avocation: walking. Office: 304 S College St Newberg OR 97132-3114

KEITH WAGSTAFF, MARY JANE, physician; b. Detroit, July 10, 1930; d. Calrence and Helen Marie Keith; m. Chester LeeRoy Wagstaff, Apr. 29, 1955; children: Suzanne, Sheryl, Chester LeeRoy II, David, Richard. BA, Mich. State U., East Lansing, Mich., 1951; MD, Northwestern U. Med. sch., Chgo., 1954. Internship Phila. Gen. Hosp., Phila., 1954—55; attending physician Labanon Sanatorium, Manipay, Sri Lanka, 1956—57; med. missionary Appalachian Regional Hosp., South Willamson, Ky., 1958—64; chief adult health svcs. Montgomery County Health Dept., Rockville, Md., 1964—69, chief tubuculosis control Silver Springs, 1972—76, clincian and cons., 1976—84. Task force mem. Montgomery County Pub. Schs., 1985, pub. health legis. coun., 80, adminstr., 68. Contbr. articles to profl. jour. Sec. PTA Longview Sch., Guthersburg, Md., 1980—89; bd. dirs. ARC, Rockville, Md., 1985—90; elder St. Matthew's Presbyn. Ch., 1970, Peace in Christ Luth., 2003—. Mem.: Torch Club Internat., Tau Kappa Alpha, Alpha Omega Alpha. Republican. Lutheran And Presbyternian. Avocations: painting, genealogy, reading, embroidery, birdwatching.

KEIZER, SUSAN JANE, artist; b. Montreal, Que., Can., Sept. 26, 1940; d. Roy Laver and Eulalia Frances (Shively) Swank; m. Joel Edward Keizer, Dec. 8, 1964; children: Sidney Jacob, Sarah Rebecca. BA, Reed Coll., 1964; postgrad., U. Calif. Davis, 1973-77, Md. Inst., 1978-79; MA, Calif. State U. Sacramento, 1981. Sci. illustrator Oreg. Health Scis. U., Portland, 1964, Santa Cruz, Davis, Calif., 1967—72; instr. drawing Davis Art Ctr., 1976-78; artist Davis, 1976—. Guest artist San Jose (Calif.) Mus. Sch., 1986; coord. West Coast Women's Conf., Heceta Head, Oreg., 1983; assoc. dir. Lester Gallery, Inverness, Calif., 1981-82; adj. faculty art Am. River Coll., Sacramento, 1997; guest instr. art Calif. State U., Sacramento, 1983, vis. lectr. U. Calif. Davis, 1989, 2000-02, 2004; mem. faculty summer Haysack Program Portland State U., 1999-2001. Exhibited in numerous one-woman and group shows, 1976—; represented in numerous corp. and pvt. collections. Mem. exec. bd. Nelson ARTfriends U. Calif., Davis, 1992-96, chair benefit exhbn. Nelson Gallery, 1994-2001. MacDowell Colony fellow, Peterborough, N.H., 1986. Mem.: AAUW. Home: 729 Kestrel Pl Davis CA 95616-0166 Office Phone: 530-758-0613. Business E-Mail: skeizer@cal.net.

KEIZS, MARCIA V., academic administrator; BA, U. Manitoba, Winnipeg, Can., 1967; MA, Columbia U., 1971, EdD, 1984. Prof. English Queensborough CC, CUNY, v.p., dean student svcs., 1988—94, acting vice chancellor student affairs; asst. dir. External Edn. Degree Prog. for Homebound Student; asst. dean External Affairs, Labor Rels., and Personnel LaGuardia CC, CUNY, 1984—88; acting pres. Borough of Manhattan CC, 1994—95, York Coll., CUNY, Queens, NY, 1996, pres., 2005—; v.p. academic affairs Bronx CC, 1997—2005. Founding editor New York Carib News. Chair bd. Morris Heights Health Ctr., Bronx. Mem.: Greenburgh Libr. Found. Office: CUNY 94-20 Guy R Brewer Blvd Jamaica NY 11451 Office Phone: 718-262-2000.

KELDER, DOROTHY MAE, science educator; b. Chgo., July 22; d. Peter Clarence and Dorothy (Vande Werken) Kelder. BA in Edn., Calvin Coll., Grand Rapids, Mich., 1964; MS in Edn., Bank St. Coll., N.Y.C., 1985; postgrad., U. Mich., Ann Arbor, 1966. Music tchr. grade 3, 7-9 Hudsonville Christian Sch., Mich., 1964—70; 2st and 2d grade tchr. Ea. Christian Sch. Assn., North Haledon, NJ, 1971—77; elem. tchr. E.C.U.M.P. Dawn Treader, Paterson, NJ, 1977—83; 5th grade tchr. Paterson Bd. Edn., 1985—2001, 7th grade tchr. sci., 2001—. Mem. Sch. Leadership Com., Paterson, 2004—06; leader sci. activity Sci. Resource #8, Paterson, 2001—; mem. ACORN, Paterson, 2004. Recipient Tchr. of the Yr. Gov.'s award, Paterson Pub. Schs., 1996. Mem.: Paterson Edn. Assn., N.J. Edn. Assn. Democrat. Christian Reformed Ch. Avocations: tennis, reading, travel, knitting, singing. Office: Paterson Board of Education 88 Church St Paterson NJ 07503

KELEHEAR, CAROLE MARCHBANKS SPANN, legal assistant; b. Morehead City, N.C., Oct. 2, 1945; d. William Blythe and Gladys Ophelia (Wilson) Marchbanks; m. Henry M. Spann, June 5, 1966 (div. 1978); children: Lisa Carole Spann, Elaine Mabry Spann; m. Zachariah Lockwood Kelehear, Sept. 15, 1985. Student, Winthrop Coll., 1963-64; grad., Draughon's Bus. Coll., 1965; cert. in med. terminology, Greenville Tech. Edn. Coll., 1972; grad., Millie Lewis Modeling Sch. Office mgr. S.C. Appalachian Adv. Commn., Greenville, 1965-68, Wood-Bergheer & Co., Newport Beach and Palm Springs, Calif., 1970-72, Dr. James B. Knowles, Greenville, 1977-78, Constangy, Brooks & Smith, Columbia, 1978-83; asst. to Dr. J. Ernest Lathem Lathem & McCoy, P.A., Greenville, 1972-75; asst. to Gov. Robert E. McNair, McNair, Konduros, Corley, Singletary and Dibble Law Firm, Columbia, SC, 1975-77; legal asst. to sr. ptnr. William L. Bethea Jr., Bethea, Jordan & Griffin, P.A., Hilton Head Island, 1983—88; legal asst. Rajko D. Medenica, MD, PhD, 1988—95; adminstr. Dibble Law Offices, Columbia, 1995-96; asst. to mng. dir. Steve A. Matthews and COO Larry B. Mack Haynsworth Sinkler Boyd, P.A., Columbia, 1997—. Notary pub.; vol. Ladies aux. Greenville Gen. Hosp., 1966—72, S. Coast Hosp., Laguna Beach, Calif., 1973, St. Francis Hosp., Greenville, 1974—76, Hilton Head Hosp., 1983—92. Mem.: NAFE, Am. Soc. Notaries, Am. Bus. Women's Assn., Profl. Women's Assn. Hilton Head Island, Hilton Head Hosp. Aux., Beta Sigma Phi.

KELER, MARIANNE MARTHA, lawyer; b. Budapest, Hungary, Oct. 2, 1954; d. Tibor and Margaret (Feja) Keler; m. Michael Richmond Kershow, Aug. 21, 1981; children: Stefan, Madeleine. BS Sch. Fgn. Svc., Georgetown U., 1976, JD, 1980. Bar: DC 1980. Law clk. to assoc. judge Hon. Catherine B. Kelly US Ct. Appeals DC cir., Washington, 1980-81; staff atty. office of gen. counsel SEC, Washington, 1981-83, asst. to chmn. John Shad, 1983-84; sr. atty. SLM Corp. (formerly Student Loan Mktg. Assn.), Washington, 1985-86, asst. gen. counsel, 1986-88, sr. asst. gen. counsel, 1988-90, v.p., assoc. gen. counsel, 1990-97, sr. v.p., gen. counsel, 1997—2001, exec. v.p., gen. counsel, 2001—. Sec. bd. trustees Cmty. Found for the Nat. Capital Region. Recipient Alumni Award, Georgetown U. Law Ctr., 2004. Mem. ABA (corp. and securities div.), Am. Corp. Counsel Assn. Office: SLM Holding Corp 12061 Bluemont Way Reston VA 20190

KELKER, NANCY LEE, art historian; b. Shreveport, La., Dec. 17, 1951; d. James Joesph Arthur and Elizabeth McGaughey Kelker. BFA, U. Okla., 1974, MA, 1976; PhD, U. Tex., Austin, 1985. Assoc. curator San Antonio Mus. Art, 1982—85; asst. prof. Appalachian State U., 1986—87; govt. contractor US Customs Svc., Can. Customs Svc., 1987—94; asst. prof. Erskine Coll., 1995—98; assoc. prof. Mid. Tenn. State U., Murfreesboro, Tenn., 1999—; asst. prof. SW Ga. State U., 1998—99. Cons. in field. Editor: America Before Columbus, 1985, Mexico The New Generations, 1985. Mem.: Assn. Latin Am. Art, Coll. Art Assn., Soc. Am. Archaeology (assoc.), Gordon Setter Club Can., Gordon Setter Club Am. (treas 1991—2001, local contact 2000—06), Phi Kappa Phi. Democrat. Avocation: showing dogs. Office: Department of Art MTSU 1500 Greenland Drive Box 25 Murfreesboro TN 37132 Office Phone: 615-904-8084. Business E-Mail: nkelker@mtsu.edu.

KELLAM, CARAMINE, volunteer; b. Painter, Va., Jan. 23, 1941; d. Emerson Polk and Amine (Cosby) Kellam; m. Isaac Somers White, Nov. 25, 1961 (div. 1975); children: Kellam White Griffin, Caramine White, Somers Farkas White; m. Harry Sherman Holcomb, III, May 12, 1979 (div. Mar. 2001); m. Fred Greenway, Apr. 1, 2006. AA, St. Mary's Coll., Raleigh, 1960; cert., Richmond Bus. Coll., Va., 1961. Bd. dirs. Kellam Energy, Inc. Contbr. articles to profl. jours. Trustee Northampton-Accomack Meml. Hosp., Nassawadox, Va., 1986—98, v.p. aux., 1986—88, pres., 1988—90, sec. bd.

trustees, 1989—91, vice chmn., 1991—94, chair, 1994—96; bd. dirs. Eastern Shore CC Found., 1998—, v.p. bd. dirs., 2001—03, pres., 2003—04; sec. E. Pol. Kellam Found., 1991—; vice chair Med. Soc. Va. Alliance, Richmond, Va., 2006—; mem. session Belle Haven Presbyn. Ch., 1999—2002; bd. dirs. Ea. Shore Hist. Soc., Onancock, Va., 1987—92, Shore Life Svcs., 1998—, pres., 2004—; bd. dirs. Med. Soc. Va. Alliance, Richmond, Va., 1984—94, v.p., 1989—91, pres., 1992—93; trustee Shore Meml., 2003—, sec., 2004—. Mem.: DAR (regent 2004—), Med. Soc. Va. Trust, AMA Alliance Bd. (mem. ERF com. 1994, AMA-ERF com. chmn. 1994—95, field dir. 1995—98, bylaws chmn. 1999—2000), Garden Club Eastern Shore (pres. 1973—75, Garden Week chmn. 2001—02). Avocations: travel, reading, flower arranging. Home: PO Box 38 Franktown VA 23354-0038

KELLAR, CHARLOTTE AVRUTIS, writer; b. N.Y.C., Nov. 15; d. Aaron and Fannie (Kantor) Avrutis; m. Harold Kellar, Feb. 14, 1947 (dec. Mar. 1980); 1 child, Jeffrey Hamilton. BA, NYU, 1951; student, Harrison Lewis Dramatic Sch. Editor Futurific Mag.; contbr. stories and articles to jours. and newspapers; appeared in films and music videos. Recipient 3d Prize Fiction Contest, West Side Spirit, 1988, First Prize Essay Contest, 1989, 4th Prize, W.O.R. Radio, 1988, 2d pl. award N.Y. Daily News, 1989, 3d prize Woman's Day, 1984. Mem. Pen and Brush Club (3d prize poetry 1982, 2d prize fiction 1985, 87, 1st prize poetry 1984, 4th prize prose 1989), West Side Arts Coalition (grantee 1987), Screen Actors Guild. Avocations: theater, music. Home: 645 W End Ave New York NY 10025-7322 E-mail: binnedy@earthlink.net.

KELLAR, MARIE TERESE, special education educator; b. St. Louis, Oct. 11, 1934; d. Paul and Frances Marie (O'Hallaron) Robyn; m. John Cullen Hagerty, Jan. 17, 1959 (dec. 1972); children: John Cullen Jr., Anne Rose; m. John W. Kellar, Dec. 26, 1974 (dec.); children: Stephen, Joyce, Robert, Barbara, Michael, Richard. BS in Elem. Edn., Maryville Coll., St. Louis, 1956; MAT, Webster U., 1975; postgrad., Fontbonne Coll., Clayton, Mo., 1981. Cert. elem. edn., social studies, English, learning disabilities, emotionally disturbed, behavior disordered. 1st grade tchr. Kratz Sch., St. Louis County, 1956-63; homebound tchr. Sch. Dist. Webster Groves, Mo., 1964-67, Spl. Sch. Dist. St. Louis County, 1965-67; tchr. Webster U., 1974-75, Miriam Sch., Webster Groves, 1980—84; adminstr., 1984-89; pvt. practice St. Louis, 1989—. Learning cons. St. Ambrose Sch., 1989—; presenter and spkr. in field. Contbr. articles to profl. jours. Active St. Gerard Majella Ch.; vol. March of Dimes, ARC, Am. Cancer Soc. Mem. Coun. for Exceptional Children, Mo. Assn. for Children with Learning Disabilities (Tchr. of Yr. 1984), Nat. Cath. Edn. Assn. (Disting. Tchr. award 2002), Adults With Learning Disabilities, Delta Epsilon Sigma, Pi Lambda Theta Roman Catholic. Avocations: drawing, painting, reading.

KELLER, ARMOR, artist, arts advocate; b. Montgomery, Ala., June 16, 1937; d. Alton Mason and Margaret Elizabeth (Bell) ARmor; m. Ronald Thomas Keller, Nov. 28, 1958; 1 child, Kimberlin Marie. Student, Huntingdon Coll., 1955-56, U. Guam, 1972-74; BA, U. Ala., 1982. Planning bd. Nat. Book Makers Conf., Tuscaloosa, Ala., 1995; panelist grant rev. Ala. State Coun. on Arts, Montgomery, 1995-96, 98; judge HS art exhibn. 6th Congl. Dist. Arts Caucus, Birmingham, 1995-96; cons. Birmingham Mus. Art, 1996. Shows include Meridian (Miss.) Mus. Art, 1986, Vanderbilt U., Nashville, 1987, Birmingham Mus. Art, 1989, Birmingham So. Coll., 1990, Kennedy-Douglas Ctr. for the Arts, Florence, Ala., 1992, Wiregrass Mus. Art, Dothan, Ala., 1993, Ctr. Cultural Arts, Gadsden, Ala., 1994, Kentuck Mus., Northport, Ala., 1994, Ch. of the Nativity, Huntsville, Ala., 1996, Huntsville Mus. Art, 1999, Heritage Hall Mus., Talladega, Ala., 2000, Masur Mus. Art, Monroe, La., 2001, Mercedes-Benz Internat., Mus. and Visitor Ctr., Tuscaloosa, Ala., 2003; spl. commns. for Ala. Symphony Orch. and Children's Aid Soc.; featured in Wild Wheels, 1992-93, Smithsonian, Japan Esquire, Spiegel; illustrator: Haiku: The Travelers of Eternity, 2001. Artist del. Sister City Commn., Japan, 1994, 2004; mem. Sister City Japan Com., Birmingham, 2002—06; project dir. Sister City Friendship, 2005; bd. dirs. Birmingham Sister City Commn., 2003—06. Fellow Escape to Create Seaside (Fla.) Inst., 1993, 94. Mem. Nat. League Am. Pen Women, Watercolor Soc. Ala. (pres. 1988-89), Birmingham Art Assn. (pres. 1982-83), Montgomery Art Guild (pres. 1976-78), Space One Eleven (pres. 1991-93), Bluff Park Art Assn. (project dir. 1997), Japan Am. Soc. Ala. (bd. dirs. 2002—). Avocations: tai chi, ikebana, travel, music. Home: 204 Vestavia Cir Birmingham AL 35216-1328

KELLER, CLARE GRAHAM MARROW, therapist, writer; b. St. Johnsbury, Vt., Aug. 12, 1937; d. George Meredith and Louise (Remick) Marrow; m. Edwin Robert Keller, II, Sept. 10, 1960; children: Geoffrey Hopkinson, Lisë Anne Reynolds, David Howard. B.A., Sarah Lawrence Coll., 1960. Research asst. McNeil Labs., Phila., 1960-62; pvt. practice counseling, Chadds Ford and Swarthmore, Pa., 1974-81, Harvard, Mass., 1983—, tchg. asst. Harvard U. Extension Sch., 2003—; freelance counselor, retreat and seminar leader, 1981—; workshop leader Pendle Hill, Wallingford, Pa., 1976—; dream group leader Ch. of Good Shepherd, Acton, Mass., 1982—; sec.-treas. Renaissance Internat. Corp., Harvard, 1983—; lectr. in field. Networker, hostess Beyond War, Newton, Mass., 1984-85. Mem. Soc. of the Cos. of the Holy Cross. Episcopalian. Club: C.G. Jung Found. (dir. 1977-83). Avocations: gardening; reading. Address: 14 Fruit St Newburyport MA 01950-2843 E-mail: clarekeller@comcast.net.

KELLER, EVELYN FOX, philosophy of science professor; b. NYC, Mar. 20, 1936; divorced; children: Jeffrey, Sarah. BA, Brandeis U., 1957; MA, Radcliffe Coll., 1959; PhD, Harvard U., 1963; doctorate (hon.), Mt. Holyoke Coll., 1991, U. Amsterdam, 1993, Simmons Coll., 1995; LHD (hon.), Rensselaer Polytech. Inst., 1995; doctorate (hon.), Tech. U. Lulea, Sweden, 1996; LHD (hon.), New Sch. U., 2000, Alleghany Coll., 2000, Wesleyan U., 2001. Prof. math. and humanities Northeastern U., Boston, 1982-88; prof. U. Calif., Berkeley, 1988-92; prof. history and philosophy of sci. MIT, 1992—. Vis. fellow MIT Program in Sci., Tech. and Soc., 1979-80, vis. scholar, 1980-84, vis. prof., 1985-86; vis. prof. math. and humanities Northeastern U., 1981-82; Kregerb Wolf Disting. vis. prof. Northwestern U., 1985; sr. fellow Soc. for the Humanities, Cornell U., 1987; mem. Inst. for Advanced Study, Princeton, 1987-88; co-chair U. Calif. Systemwide Coun. on Women's Studies. Editor: A Feeling for the Organism: The Life and Work of Barbara McClintock, 1982, 2d edit., 1993, Reflections on Gender and Science, 1985, 10th edit., 1995, Refiguring Life: Metaphors of Twentieth Century Biology, 1995, Secrets of Life, Secrets of Death, 1992, The Century of the Gene, 2000, Making Sense of Life: Explaining Development with Medals, Metaphors and Machines, 2002; co-editor Body/Politics: Women and the Discourses of Science, 1990, Conflicts in Feminism, 1990, Keywords in Evolutionary Discourse, 1992, Feminism and Science, 1996; Am. editor Fundamenta Scientiae, Internat. Jour. for Critical Analysis of Sci. and the Responsibility of Scientists; editl. bd. Women's Review of Books, Hypatia, Biology and Philosophy, Literature and Sci. Series, Jour. of the History of Biology; contbr. articles to profl. jours. Numerous grants and fellowships. Mem. History of Sci. Soc. Office: MIT E51-171 77 Mass Ave Cambridge MA 02139-4307 E-mail: efkeller@MIT.edu.

KELLER, JENNIFER L., lawyer; b. Ft. Wayne, Ind., Feb. 26, 1953; AB, U. Calif., Berkeley, 1975; JD, U. Calif., Hastings Coll. Law, 1978. Bar: Calif. 1978, U.S. Dist. Ct., Ctrl. and So. Dists., Calif., U.S. Ct. Appeals, Ninth Cir. 1984, U.S Dist. Ct., No. and Ea. Dists., Calif. 1997, U.S. Dist. Ct., Ariz. 1998, U.S. Supreme Ct. 1999, cert.: Specialist in Criminal Law. Sr. rsch. atty. Ct. Appeals, 4th Dist., Div. 3, 1986—89; sr. dep. pub. defender Orange County Pub. Defender's Office; pvt. practice Law Offices of Jennifer L. Keller, 1992—. Bd. dir. Pub. Law Ctr. Orange County, 1995—2000; lawyer rep. 9th Cir. Jud. Conf., 1996—99; lectr. Calif. Pub. Defenders Assn., Continuing Edn. of the Bar, 1996. Mem. Hastings Constl. Law Quarterly, 1976—77. Bd. visitors Chapman U. Sch. Law, 1995—2003, Dean's Coun., 2004—. Named Atty. of Yr., Orange County Women Lawyers, 2003, Pub. Law Ctr. Orange County, 1996; named one of The One Hundred Most Influential Lawyers in Calif., Calif. Law Bus., 2001, California's 30 Top Women Litigators, 2002; recipient Wiley Manuel award for Pro Bono Svc., State Bar Calif., 1998, Lawyer of Yr., Constl. Rights Found. Orange County, 1983, Criminal Defense Trial Lawyer Yr., Orange County Trial Lawyers Assn., 2000, Jurisprudence Award, Anti-Defamation League of Orange County & Long Branch, 2001. Mem.: Orange County Trial Lawyers Assn. (named Criminal Def. Atty. of Yr. 2000), Calif. Attys. for Criminal Justice (bd. govs. 1992—93, lectr.), State Bar Calif. (commr., Bd. Legal Specializtion, Criminal Law Advisory Comn. 1990—92, vice-chair, Bd. Legal Specializtion, Criminal Law Advisory Comn. 1992—93, chair, Bd. Legal Specializtion, Criminal Law Advisory Comn. 1993—94, convention lectr., White Collar Crime 1994, commr. Bd. Legal Specialization 2002—05), Orange County Bar Assn. (bd. dir. 1991—93, officer 1993—97, pres. 1996, lectr., State Bar of Calif. President's Pro Bono Svc. award for Dist. 8), Orange County Women Lawyers (life; bd. dirs. 1984—86, Atty. of Yr. 2003). Office: 18500 Von Karman Ave Ste 560 Irvine CA 92612-1043 Office Phone: 949-476-8700. Office Fax: 949-476-0900. E-mail: jkeller@prodigy.net.

KELLER, JOHANNA BEALE, writer, editor; MusB, U. Colo., 1977; MA in Lit., Antioch U., 1996. Editor Chamber Music mag., N.Y.C., 1997—2001; dir. Goldring Arts Journalism Program, Newhouse Sch. at Syracuse U., 2003—. Author: The Skull: North Carolina, 1961, 1998; contbr. articles, revs., translations, essays, and poetry to The New York Times, S.W. Rev., Chelsea, Hudson Rev., others. Recipient Editor's award in poetry Fla. Rev., 1997, DeemsTaylor award for journalism, Front Page award N.Y. Newswomen's Club, 2002; Arts fellow in poetry N.Y. Found. for the Arts, 1997; grantee Ludwig-Vogelstein Found., 1997; Banff Ctr. fellow, 2001; Journalism fellow USC Getty, 2002. Office: Newhouse Sch Syracuse U Syracuse NY 13244-2100 Office Phone: 315-443-2419.

KELLER, MARTHE, artist, painter; b. N.Y.C., Dec. 8, 1948; d. Charles and Judith (Herman) K.; m. Bradford H. Ensminger, July 12, 1989. Student, Overseas Sch. of Rome, 1961-64, St. Stephen's Sch., Rome, 1964-66, Temple U., 1968, Boston U., 1966-69; BFA, Md. Inst., 1971; postgrad., George Washington U., 1972-73. Vis. artist Whitaker Found., Palermo, Italy, 1982, U. Calif., Santa Barbara, 1987, Sch. of the Art Inst. of Chgo., 1990, R.I. Sch. of Design, Providence, 1993, Sarah Lawrence Coll., Bronxville, N.Y., 1991; instr. multi-level painting Sch. of Art Inst. Chgo., 1991, 95; lectr. in visual arts Princeton U., 1991-92, 98-99; instr. N.Y. Studio Sch. of Painting, 1992; adj. instr. Kingsborough Cmty. Coll., Bklyn., 1993, 94; guest lectr. Temple U., Tyler Sch. of Art, Rome, 1994, Parsons' Sch., 1995, 96, 97, Hunter Coll., CUNY, 96, 97, 98, 99, guest artist Ringling Sch., Fla., 1997; chair Coll. Art Assn. Conf., Toronto, 1997-98. One woman shows include Albuquerque Arts Ctr., U. N.Mex., 1978, Whitaker Found. Mus., Palermo, 1982, Stephen Rosenberg Gallery, N.Y., 1986, 87, 89, Conlon Gallery, Santa Fe, N.Mex., 1990, Galleria Plurima, Udine, Italy, 1991, Halsey Gallery, Coll. of Charleston, 1994, Turchetto Gallery, Milan, 1994, Rosenberg & Kaufman Fine Art, N.Y., 1997, 98, Atrium Gallery, U. Conn., 1999, Fold Color Replay, NY, 2001-02; exhibited in group shows at Stephen Rosenberg Gallery, 1986, 89, 90, 91, McNay Art Mus., San Antonio, 1986, Gallery 53 Cooperstown, N.Y., 1986, Carlo Lamagna Gallery, N.Y., 1988, Genovese Gallery, Boston, 1988, Dart Gallery, Chgo., 1988, Ill. Ctr. Gallery, Chgo., 1989, 55 Mercer Gallery, N.Y., 1990, Galleria Plurima, Udine and Milan, 1992, Edwin A. Ulrich Mus. of Art, Wichita, 1992, Cummings Art Ctr., Conn. Coll., 1992, 55 Ferris St, Bklyn., 1993, Jessica Berwind Gallery, Phila., 1993, Krasdale Foods Gallery and Lehman Coll., Westchester, N.Y., 1993, Lilian Heidenberg Gallery, N.Y., 1993, Werner Kramarsky, N.Y., 1993, Art in Embassies Program, Vienna, Austria, 1994, Noyes Mus., Oceanville, N.J., 1994, Art Initiatives and Bill Bace, 1995, Rosenberg & Kaufman Fine Art, N.Y., 1995, Mishkin Gallery, Baruch Coll., 1996, Bockenheimer Depot Internat. Exhbn., Frankfurt, Germany, 1996, Islip Art Mus., N.Y.,1997, Condeso/Lawler Gallery, 1997, Snug Harbor Cultural Ctr., 1997, Islip Art Museum., N.Y., 1997, Pratt Inst. Gallery, N.Y., 1999, Hillwood Art Mus., N.Y., 2000, Hunter Coll., 2000, 21st Suffragettes, Brooklyn, 2001, Les Fables de la Fontaine, France & U.S.A., 2002-03, Eleven Painters Eleven Views of Abstraction, Santa Fe, 2003, Intersections, Douglas Elliman Tribeca Gallery, N.Y., 2004; represented in permanent collection Met. Mus. Art, N.Y.C., 1996, Fogg Art Mus., Harvard U., Cambridge, Mass., San Jose Mus. Art, Whitney Mus. Art, Mus. Modern Art N.Y.C., others. Recipient fellowships The Mac Dowell Colony, 1990, Nat. Endowment for the Arts, 1989-90, The Mac Dowell Colony, 1989-90; grantee Ludwig Vogelstein Found., 1987, CETA grantee for costume design Albuquerque Dance Theatre, 1978. Home: 39 Walker St New York NY 10013-6001

KELLER, MARY BETH, lawyer; b. 1962; BA, Cath. U. Am., 1984; JD, U. Va. Sch. Law, 1987. Law clk. 5th Judicial Dist. Iowa, Des Moines, 1987—88; staff atty. Bd. Immigration Appeals, Exec. Office Immigration Review, US Dept. Justice, 1988—95, sr. panel atty., 1995—2004; gen. counsel Office Gen. Counsel, Exec. Office Immigration Review, US Dept. Justice, 2004—. Mem.: Iowa Bar Assn. Office: US Dept Justice Exec Office Immigration Review Office Di 5107 Leesburg Pike Ste 2600 Falls Church VA 22041

KELLER, MICHELLE R., science educator; b. Rolla, N.D., Aug. 15, 1951; d. Raymond Charles Halone and Yvonne M. (Klier) Edwards; m. Fred F. Keller, June 30, 1973; 1 child, Brent F. BS in Foods and Nutrition, N.D. State U., 1973; cert. sci. edn., Minot State U., 1977; MEd in Secondary Sci. Edn., N.Dak. State U., 2001. Instr. sci. Bisbee (N.D.)-Egeland H.S., 1975—. Judge Seiko Youth Challenge, 1993, 94; ND tchr. portfolio trainer, assessor. Access Excellence fellow Genentech/NSF, 1994; recipient Presdl. award for excellence in sci. tchg., 1993, Edn.'s Unsung Hero award 1998; named Hon. Mention Tchr., Radio Shack/Tandy scholars program, 1998, 99. Mem. Am. Assn. Physics Tchrs. (pres. N.D. sect. 2001—), Nat. Sci. Tchrs. Assn., N.D. Sci. Tchrs. Assn., N.D. Orienteering Alliance, Nat. Edn. Assn., N.D. Edn. Assn. Democrat. Roman Catholic. Avocations: walking, reading, gardening. Home: PO Box 265 201 3rd Ave W Bisbee ND 58317-0265 Office: Bisbee-Egeland H S P O Box 217 204 3rd Ave W Bisbee ND 58317 Office Phone: 701-656-3536. E-mail: mkeller@ndsualumni.net.

KELLER, NATASHA MATRINA LEONIDOW, nursing administrator; b. Nyack, NY, June 12, 1958; d. Paul and Matrina (Butich) L.; children: Alexandra, Mary, John. AAS, Rockland C.C., 1979; BS in Nursing cum laude, SUNY Coll. Technology, Utica, 1982; MS in Nursing magna cum laude, Syracuse U., 1985. RN, N.Y.; cert. nurse adminstr. Staff nurse Englewood Hosp., N.J., 1979-80; chare nurse Mary Imogene Bassett Hosp., Cooperstown, N.Y., 1980-82, nursing svc. coord., 1983-86, asst. dir. sys. devel., 1986-87; assoc. nursing practice coord. Strong Meml. Hosp.-U. Rochester, N.Y., 1987-88; asst. dir. nursing Bayfront Med. Ctr., St. Petersburg, Fla., 1988—, adminstr. on duty, 1998. Translator: Excellence in Russian Language, 1976 (Otrada award). Served as 1st lt. USAFR, 1990-91, Persian Gulf War, Saudi Arabia. Mem. Fla. Orgn. Nurse Execs., Tampa Bay Orgn. Nurse Execs., Sigma Theta Tau. Office: Bayfront Med Ctr 701 6th St S Saint Petersburg FL 33701-4814 Office Phone: 727-893-6162. Business E-Mail: natasha.keller@bayfront.org.

KELLER, RACHAEL See ANDERSON, RACHAEL

KELLER, SUZANNE, sociologist, psychotherapist; arrived in U.S., 1942; d. Joseph and Martha Infield; m. Charles M. Haar, July 5, 1975. PhD, Columbia U., N.Y.C., 1955; HHD (hon.), Hunter Coll., N.Y.C., 1990. Rsch. assoc. ctr. internat. studies MIT, Cambridge, Mass., 1955—58; asst. prof. of sociology Brandeis U., Waltham, Mass., 1959—62, Vassar Coll., Poughkeepsie, NY, 1963—64; fulbright scholar Athens Ctr. of Ekistics, Greece, 1964—68; prof. of sociology Princeton U., NJ, 1967. Author: (books) Beyond the Ruling Class, 1963, Community: Pursuing the Dream, Living the Reality, 2003; editor: Bldg. for Women. Pres. Ea. Sociol. Soc., 1986, Queenston Common Homeowners Assn., 1992. Recipient Hon. Fellow, AIA, 1974, Malfi prize, 2005. Mem.: AIA (life hon.), Am. Sociol. Assn. (life; v.p. 1984), World Soc. for Ekistics (life; v.p. 1991, pres. 2005), Phi Beta Kappa. Achievements include first woman granted tenure in the 226 year history of Princeton University. Avocations: reading, opera, travel, philanthropy, writing. Office: Princeton U Dept of Sociology 107 Wallace Hall Princeton NJ 08544 Business E-Mail: skeller@princeton.edu.

KELLER-AUGSBACH, LINDA JEAN, elementary school educator; b. Glendale, W.Va., June 7, 1951; d. Ernest Nelson and Pearl (Henry) Keller. AA, Minn. Bible Coll., 1971; postgrad., Ky. Christian Coll., 1973-74; BS, Malone Coll., 1975. Cert. elem. tchr., Fla., Ohio. 1st-8th grade tutor CETA program Minerva (Ohio) Local Schs., 1976-77; 1-2d grade tchr. Christian Schs. Cin., 1977-78; substitute tchr. Canton (Ohio) City Schs., 1978-82, Pasco County Schs., New Port Richey, Fla., 1982-83, chpt. I 6th grade tchr. Dade City, Fla., 1983-87, 4th grade tchr. New Port Richey, Fla., 1987-88, 6th grade tchr., 1988-91, 4th grade tchr., 1991—96, 4th, 5th grade tchr., 1996—99, Mittye P. Locke Elem. Sch., Elfers, Fla., 2000—. Attendee Gov. Bush Ann. Educators Leadership Summit, 2002. Author: Learning: It's Just A Game- Science, History, Word Structure, Grammar, Writing, and More, All Rolled Into One Exciting Unit, 1999. Mem. Concerned Women for Am. Republican. Avocations: creative teaching materials, crafts, sewing, reading, writing. Home: 1441 Wegman Dr Tarpon Springs FL 34689 Office Phone: 727-774-3100. Business E-Mail: laugsbac@pasco.k12.fl.us.

KELLERMAN, BARBARA, political science professor, writer; B, Sarah Lawrence Coll.; MA in Russian and East European studies, Yale Univ., MPhil, PhD in Polit. sci. Prof. Fordham U., Tufts U., George Washington U.; prof and dean of grad studies and rsch. Fairleigh Dickinson U.; dir. Ctr. for Advanced Study of Leadership, U. of Md.; rsch. dir. Ctr. for Public Leadership, JFK Sch. of Govt., Harvard U.; and lectr., public policy Harvard U., Cambridge, Mass. Co-founder Internat. Leadership Assn. Editl. bd. (publications) Presdl. Studies Quarterly, Leadership Quarterly, assoc. editor (books) Encyclopedia of Leadership; editor: Leadership: Multidisciplinary Perspectives, Political Leadership: A Source Book; co-editor (with Jeffrey Rubin): Leadership and Negotiations in the Middle East; co-editor: (with James D. Barber) Women Leaders in American Politics; co-author (with Byan Barilleaux): The President as World Leader; author: The Political Presidency: Practice of Leadership, Reinventing Leadership: Making the Connection Between Politics and Business, Bad Leadership: What It Is, How It Happens, Why It Matters, 2004; contbr. articles essays and reviews to profl. and comml. publications; polit. commentator on various TV networks. Grantee Danforth Fellowship, three Fulbright Fellowships. Office: Rsch Dir Ctr for Pub Leadership JFK Sch of Govt Ste 165-155 124 Mt Auburn Cambridge MA 02138

KELLERMAN, LYDIA SUZANNE (SUE), librarian; b. Bellefonte, Pa., Nov. 28, 1957; d. Paul Eugene and Janet Kathryn (Albright) K. BA, Pa. State U., 1979; MLS, U. Pitts., 1982. Asst. reference libr. U. Ky., Ashland C.C., 1982-84; Pa. newspaper project catalog libr. Pa. State U., University Park, 1985-88, serials record/binding libr., 1988-90, acting head, acquisitions receiving, 1990-91, preservation libr., 1992-98, head preservation dept., 1998—. Mem. adv. com. Pa. Preservation Consortium, Phila., 1997—; reviewer Inst. Mus. & Libr. Svcs., Washington, 1998, 99; cons. in field. Co-author: Advances in Preservation and Access, 1995. NEH grantee, 1991, 94, 96, 98, 99. Mem. ALA, Mid-Atlantic Regional Libr. Assn., Pa. Libr. Assn. Republican. Avocations: collecting newspapers, rare books and pottery, miniature furniture. Office: Pa State U Pattee Libr University Park PA 16802 Home: 830 Boalsburg Pike Boalsburg PA 16827-1103

KELLERMAN, SALLY CLAIRE, actress; b. Long Beach, Calif., June 2, 1937; d. John Helm and Edith Baine (Vaughn) K.; m. Richard Edelstein, Dec. 19, 1970; 4 step-daughters; m. Jonathan Krane, 1980. Student, Los Angeles City Coll., Actor's Studio, N.Y.C. Stage appearances include Singular Man, N.Y.C., Breakfast at Tiffany's; films include Reform School Girl, 1959, The Third Day, 1965, The Boston Strangler, 1968, The April Fools, 1969, M*A*S*H, 1970 (Acad. award nominee 1970, Golden Globe award 1970), Brewster McCloud, 1970, Last of the Red-Hot Lovers, 1972, Slither, 1973, Reflection of Fear, 1973, Lost Horizon, 1973, Rafferty and the Gold Dust Twins, 1975, The Big Bus, 1976, Welcome to L.A., 1977, The Mouse and His Child, 1977 (voice), Magee and the Lady, 1978, It Rained All Night The Day I Left, 1978, A Little Romance, 1979, Foxes, 1980, Loving Couples, 1980, Serial, 1980, Head On, 1980, September Gun, 1983, Moving Violations, 1985, Lethal, 1985, Back to School, 1986, That's Life, 1986, Meatballs III, 1987, Three for the Road, 1987, Someone to Love, 1987, Paramedics (voice), 1988, You Can't Hurry Love, 1988, All's Fair, 1989, Limit Up, 1989, The Secret of the Ice Cave, 1990, Happily Ever After, 1990 (voice), The Player, 1992, Younger and Younger, 1993, Mirror, Mirror 2: Raven Dance, 1994, Ready to Wear (Prêt-à-Porter), 1994, It's my Party, 1995, She's So Lovely, 1997, The Maze, 1997, The Lay of the Land, 1997, Live Virgin, 1998, Bar Hopping, 1999; also TV roles Chrysler Theatre, Mannix, It Takes a Thief, Columbo: Ashes to Ashes; TV films Verna: USO Girl, 1978, For Lovers Only, 1982, Dempsey, 1983, Secret Weapons, 1985, Elena, 1985, Boris and Natasha, 1992; miniseries Centennial, 1978-79. Recipient nominations Acad. and Golden Globe awards for MASH. Mem. Actor's Equity, AFTRA. also: 7944 Woodrow Wilson Dr Los Angeles CA 90046

KELLEY, BARBARA ELIZABETH, artist; b. Anchorage, Apr. 15, 1949; d. Lawrence Thomas Brighton and Doris Katherine Cumiskey; m. Jay Kelley, Aug. 14, 1971; children: Sarah, Zachary. Printmaking & painting, Twilight (Nat. Arts Program Jurors award, 2006). Mem.: North Coast Artists Guild (pres. 2004—05), Nat. Mus. Women in Arts, Sonoma County Cultural Arts Coun., Calif. Soc. Printmakers (assoc.). Office: Moon Catcher Studio PO Box 422 Gualala CA 95445 Business E-Mail: sonomawine@earthlink.net.

KELLEY, COLLEEN M., labor union administrator; b. Pitts., 1944; B Acctg., Drexel U.; MBA, U. Pitts. CPA. Agt. revenue IRS; dir. membership and benefits programs Nat. Treasury Employees Union, pres., chief steward, v.p. chpt. 34 Pitts., nat. exec. v.p., exec. v.p., pres., 1999—, sr. leadership coun. Mem. labor mgmt. coun. IRS, Dept. Health & Human Svc.; mem. Comml. Activities Panel; mem., sr. rev. com. Dept. Homeland Security. Bd. dir. Fed. Employee Edn. and Assistance Fund; bd. gov. Partnership for Pub. Svc. Mem.: Fed. Retirement Thrift Investment Bd. (employee thrift adv. coun.), Fed. Salary Coun. Avocation: skiing. Office: National Treasury Employees Union 1750 H St NW Washington DC 20006-4600*

KELLEY, DARCY B., biology professor; AB, Barnard Coll.; PhD, Rockefeller Univ., 1975. Co-dir., neural sys., behavior Marine Biological Lab, Woods Hole, Mass.; prof., biological sciences Columbia Univ. Forbes lectr. Grass Found., and Marine Biological Lab.; spl. lectr. Soc. Neuroscience; plenary lectr. Soc. Neuroethology; rsch. prof. Howard Hughes Med. Inst., 2002—. Editor: Jour. Neurobiology; contbr. articles to profl. journals. Recipient Jacob Javits Neuroscience Investigator award (twice), Howard Hughes Med. Inst. grant, 2002. Office: Biological Sciences Columbia Univ MC 2432 911 Fairchild Ctr New York NY 10027 Office Phone: 212-854-5108. Business E-Mail: dbk3@columbia.edu.

KELLEY, DELORES GOODWIN, state legislator; b. Norfolk, Va., May 1, 1936; d. Stephen Cornelius and Helen Elizabeth (Jefferson) Goodwin; m. Russell Victor Kelley, Jr., Dec. 26, 1956; children: Norma Kelley Johnson, Russell III, Brian. BA, Va. State Coll., 1956; MA, NYU, 1958, Purdue U., 1972; PhD, U. Md., 1977. Dir. religious edn. N.Y.C. Protestant Coun., Bronx, 1959-60; tchr. N.Y.C. Pub. Schs., Bklyn., 1962-64, Ctrl. Sch. Dist., Plainview, NY, 1965-66; asst. prof. Morgan State U., Balt., 1966-70; prof. speech comms. and English Coppin State Coll., Balt., 1973—2004; mem. Md. Ho. of Dels., Annapolis, 1991—94; former chmn. Joint Com. on Fed. Rels./Md. Senate, 1995—98; vice-chmn. exec. nomination com. Md. Senate, 1995—. Joint com. legis. policy, joint com. legis. ethics, co-chair joint com. on fair practices Md. State Senate, 1999—, vice chair, joint com. on health care delivery and fin., 2000—, fin. com., 1998—; senate chair Joint Com. on Adminstrv., Exec. and Legis. Rev., 2001—02; vice-chair sen. com. exec. nomination; vice-chair Balt. County Senate Delegation, 2003—; panelist, reviewer NEH, Washington, 1978—82, Nat. Inst. Justice, 1998—; dean Coppin State Coll., Balt., 1979—82; fellow Am. Coun. on Edn., Washington, 1982—83; vice-chair bd. dirs. Harbor Bank Md., 1982—; mem. Gov.'s Commn. on Adoption, 1995, Atty. Gen's. and Lt. Gov's. task force on family violence, 1996—, Md. Commn. on Criminal Sentencing Policy, 1996—, Md. Commn. on Infant Mortality, 1999—2002; mem. strategic planning com.

Balt. County Schs., 1999—2000; adv. com. Md. Medicaid, 1998—; commr. Edn. Commn. of States, 2004—. Editor (monograph) Concepts of Race, 1981; moderator (TV series) Teaching Writing: Process Approach, 1982. Sec. Md. Dem. Party, Annapolis, 1986-90; bd. dirs. Balt. Urban League, 1986-89; pres. Black Jewish Forum, Balt., 1990-92; commr. Md. Commn. on Values, Annapolis, 1980-85; bd. dirs. Balt. Mental Health Systems, 1991-95; host Internat. Visitors Ctr., 1976—; commn. mem. Md. Commn. Hereditary and Congenital Disorders, Balt., 1992-95; del. White House conf. on Aging, 1995; mem. Edn. Commn. States, 2004-; presdl. elector, 2004; vice chair nat. conf. state legislatures fin. svcs. com., 2005-. Fellow Purdue U., 1970-72; grantee Md. Com. for Humanities, Balt., 1977-78, NEH, Washington, 1988-89; recipient Racial Justice award YWCA of Met. Balt., 1995; named to Md. Top 100 Women, Warfields Bus. Record, 1995, 97, 2004, Cir. of Excellence award The Daily Record, 2004. Mem. Nat. Inst. Justice (panelist, rev. 1997), Inst. Govtl. Svcs. (bd. dirs. 1993-94), Nat. Polit. Congress Black Women (bd. dirs., Balt. chair 1993-95), Women Legislators Md. (1st v.p. 1995-96, pres. 1998-99), 10th Dist. Dem. Club Md. (founder, pres. 1995—), Alpha Kappa Alpha (life). Baptist. Avocations: travel, public speaking, reading. Office: 302 James Senate Office Bldg Annapolis MD 21401-1991 Office Phone: 410-841-3606. Personal E-mail: dkelley428@earthlink.net. Business E-Mail: delores_kelley@senate.state.md.us.

KELLEY, FRANCES A., occupational therapist, consultant; b. Cheyenne, Wyo., July 26, 1925; BSin Occupl. Therapy, U. So. Calif., 1949; Occupl. Cert. in Supervision, Los Angeles Valley Coll., 1985. Asst. chief occupl. therapy, therapist San Fernando VA Hosp., Calif., 1948-53, rehab. medicine svc. coord., chief occupl. therapy, clin. edn. supr. Calif., 1963-71; dir., bd. dirs. IDEAS Assocs., Inc., 1989-93; chief. occupl. therapy, coord. GM&S occupl. therapy VA Med. Ctr., Sepulveda, Calif., 1971-89, cons., vol. Dept. Occupl. Therapy, 1989—. HHon. clin. faculty dept. occupl. therapy U. Soc. Calif., 1992-95, 95—; presenter in field. Contbr. articles to profl. jours., video. Mem. Am. Occupl. Therapy Found., Calif. Found. Occupl. Therapy. Recipient Lifetime Achievement award Occupl. Therapy Assn. Calif., 1990, Cert. Appreciation Govt. Affairs Commn., 1995. Mem. Am. Occupl. Therapy Assn. (Cert. Recognition commn. on edn. 1994), Am. Occupl. Therapy Polit. Action Com., Occupl. Therapy Assn. (Calif. We. area chpt.), World Fedn. Occupl. Therapy, Nat. Assn. Ret. Fed. Employees, V.A. Retirees, Disabled Am. Vets. Aux., Arleta C. of C., San Fernando Valley Japanese Am. Cultural Ctr., Gold Star Wives Am., Nat. History Assn. San Luis Obispo Coast, Inc., Tau Alpha Epsilon. Home: 9427 Obeck Ave Arleta CA 91331-5521 E-mail: fkelley725@aol.com.

KELLEY, IRENE W., retired librarian, musician, artist; b. Taunton, Mass., Mar. 24, 1932; d. Joseph John and Bronislawa Apalonia (Kowal) Gesiak; m. Thomas Francis Kelley, Aug. 11, 1956; children: Steven, Kenneth, Richard. AB magna cum laude, Boston U., 1954, MA, 1955, EdD, 1992; MLS, Simmons Sch. Libr. Sci., 1972. Physical sci. libr. Brown U., Providence, 1955—57; libr. Randolph Pub. Libr., Mass., 1957—64, Milton HS, Mass., 1964—87; ret., 1987. Musician: Brockton Symphony, Wellesley Symphony. Mem.: Braintree Art Assn., Norwood Art Asn., Canton Art Assn. Democrat. Roman Catholic. Home: 7 Surrey Ln Canton MA 02021 Personal E-mail: ikgesiak@aol.com.

KELLEY, JANET GODSEY, lawyer; b. Ky., May 9, 1953; d. Paul and Christine Godsey; m. Peter Marcum (div.); m. Michael R. Kelley, Sept. 5, 1988; children: Megan Marcum, Christina Kelley. AB, Morehead State U., 1975; JD, U. Ky., 1978. Bar: Ky. 1978. Assoc. Wyatt Tarrant & Combs, Louisville, 1978-83, ptnr., 1983-94; gen. counsel Sunbeam Corp., Ft. Lauderdale, Fla., 1994—99; v.p., sr. counsel The Limited Inc., 1999—2001; exec. v.p., gen. counsel Kmart, Troy, Mich., 2001—03; sr. v.p., gen. counsel Family Dollar Stores, Charlotte, NC, 2004—05, 2005—. Notes editor Ky. Law Jour., 1990. Mem. Ky. Sch. Facilities Constrn. Com. Mem. ABA, Ky. Bar Assn. for Women, Women Laywers' Assn., Exec. Inst., Order of the Coif. Democrat. Office: Family Dollar Stores PO Box 1017 Charlotte NC 28201-1017 Office Phone: 704-849-7427. Business E-Mail: jkelley@familydollar.com.

KELLEY, KATHRYN B., actress; b. Pine Bluff, Ark., Sept. 27, 1955; d. Wallace Lockwood Briscoe III and Kathryn (Joyner) Briscoe now McCracken; m. Edward Sean Kelley, June 14, 1980; 1 child, Mikaela. BA in English, Va. Commonwealth U., Richmond, 1978; student, Studio Theatre Conservatory, Washington, 1982—85; MFA, NYU Tisch Sch. Arts, 1989. Reporter Globe Newspapers, Fairfax, Va., 1978—79; asst. editor Smithsonian Mag., Washington, 1980—82; actress Source Theatre Acting Co., Washington, 1984—86; freelance actress various theatres, London, Edinburgh, Yugoslavia, 1992—; assoc. artist Round House Theatre, Bethesda, Md., 2000—. Life x 3, The Diary of Anne Frank, Heartbreak House, The Cherry Orchard, Our Town, The Weir, Uncle Vanya, One Shoe Off, Look Back in Anger, A Doll's House, Sing Down the Moon, The Beckett Festival, All in the Timing, Pentecost, Joe Egg, Sand Mountain, Jack and Jill, The Alice Project, Yerma, The Hostage, Two Rooms, Playing for Time; actor, actor: Camille, No Exit, The Glass Menagerie; (TV series) NBC-TV Homocide: Life on the Street, HBO The Corner, (ind. films) The Arc, Persistence of Vision, A Prayer for Owne Meany, Central Park West/Riverside Drive, The Borrowers. Nominee Helen Hayes award, Washington Theatre Awards, 1989; recipient Mary Goldwater award, Theatre Lobby, Washington, 1997, PEER award, Washington Film and Video Coun., 1998. Mem.: AFTRA, SAG, Theatre Comms. Guild, Actors Equity Assn.

KELLEY, KATHY, literature and language educator; m. Gerald Kelley; 3 children. BA in Edn., Southwestern Okla. State U., Weatherford, 1975; Masters, Southwestern Okla. State U., 1978. Tchr. Granite (Okla.) Pub. Schs., 1975—76, Clinton (Okla.) Pub. Schs., 1976—. Rotary club sponsor Kiwanis Key Club Internat., Clinton, 1995—2006; mock trial sponsor Okla. Bar Assn., Clinton, 1999—. Bd. pres. Southwest Playhouse, Clinton, 2002—. Recipient SOPHI awards, Southwest Playhouse FAC, 1992—2005. Mem.: NEA, Okla. Edn. Assn., Kiwanis.

KELLEY, KITTY, writer; b. Spokane, Wash., Apr. 4, 1942; d. William V. Kelley; m. Michael Peter Edgley (div.); m. Johnathan Zucker. BA in English, Univ. Wash., Seattle, 1964. Employee Wash. Post, 1969—71. Author: The Glamour Spas, 1975, Jackie Oh!, 1978 (NY Times bestseller list), Elizabeth Taylor: The Last Star, 1981 (NY Times bestseller list), His Way: The Unauthorized Biography of Frank Sinatra, 1986 (#1 NY Times bestseller list, record sales made it best selling biography in publishing history), Nancy Reagan: The Unauthorized Biography, 1991 (NY Times bestseller list), The Royals, 1997 (#1 NY Times bestseller list, Publishers Weekly bestseller list), The Family: The Real Story of the Bush Dynasty, 2004 (Publishers Weekly bestseller list). Named one of The Most Famous, FAscinating and Influential Alumni of the Past 100 Years, Univ. Wash., 1999, the 20 Georgetowners of the Century, Georgetowner newspaper; named to Vanity Fair Hall of Fame; recipient Outstanding Author award, Am. Soc. Journalists and authors, Philip M. Stern award for outstanding svc. to writers and the writing profession, Medal of Merit, Lotos Club, NYC. Office: c/o Doubleday Author Mail Random House Inc 1745 Broadway New York NY 10019

KELLEY, KRISTINA ELIZABETH, secondary school educator; b. Frankfurt, Germany, Sept. 30, 1978; d. Lela Izzneer and Adam Charles Butler; m. Derek Steven Kelley, Jan. 29, 1961; 1 child, Lela Faith. B in Profl. Studies, U. Mary Hardin, Belton, Tex., 2001. Lic. tchr. State Bd. Educator Cert., 2004. Health unit coord. Scott and White Meml. Hosp., Temple, Tex., 1997—2004; tchr. Belton Ind. Sch. Dist., Tex., 2002—. Audio/visual dept., prayer team A New Day Fellowship Ch., Temple, Tex., 2000—06. Office Phone: 254-215-2000. Personal E-mail: kristina.kelley@sbcglobal.net.

KELLEY, LINDA ELAINE SPADAFORA, school psychologist, educator; b. Melrose, Mass., July 24, 1948; d. Guy Joseph Spadafora and Yolanda Elaine Maglio; children: Paul, Michael. BA in Sociology, Emmanuel Coll., Boston, Mass., 1970; MEd in Early Childhood & Spl. Edn., Ga. State U., 1980, EdS in Sch. Psychology, 1997. Learning disability specialist Atlanta Speech Sch., Atlanta, 1981—96; psychol. assoc. Child & Family Inst., Atlanta, 1997—99; sch. psychologist Holy Redeemer Cath. Sch., Alpharetta, Ga., 1999—. Bd. officer Kappa Delta Pi, Nat. Honor Soc. in Edn., Ga., 1982—88; ednl. cons. State Dept. Edn., Ga., 1988—90; bd. trustees Learning Disability Assn. Ga., 1998—2001; exec. bd. Ga. Assn. Sch. Psychologists, 2003—; sch. psychology del. to South Africa People to People Amb. Program, Spokane, Wash., 2005—. Grantee Rsch. in Reading Instrn., Ga. Assn. of Sch. Psychologists, 2000; scholar Dr. Kay Crouch Scholarship, Kappa Delta Pi, 1991; 1993. Mem.: NASP. Roman Catholic. Achievements include development of Prevention/detection and intervention: early reading failure. Avocations: tennis, hiking, dance, reading, calligraphy. Home: 1110 Morningside Pl NE Atlanta GA 30306 Personal E-mail: lekelley@bellsouth.net.

KELLEY, LINDA ROSE, human resources specialist; b. Memphis, Apr. 4, 1948; d. Simon Nmi and Elma Rose Leigh; children: Marvin Antone, Cheryl Monique Khouri. Student, U. of Memphis, 1966—78. Cert. mediator Tenn., 2003. Paralegal specialist EEOC, Memphis, 1979—81; EEO specialist Def. Depot Memphis, 1984—86, program analyst, 1986—87, EEO specialist, 1987—88, equal employment mgr.; mgmt. analyst Def. Indsl. Plant Equipment Ctr., Memphis, 1989—92; EEO specialist Def. Logistics Agy., Memphis, 1992—95; sr. EEO specialist Def. Distbn. Depot, Warner Robins, Ga., 1995—99; human resource specialist Navy Pers. Command, Millington, Tenn., 2000—03; EEO Ter. mgr. EEO and Diversity Office, Memphis IRS Ctr., 2003—; lead EEO counselor Robins AFB, Warner Robins, Ga. Pres. Blacks In Govt., Memphis, 2003—. Mem. Operation PUSH, Macon Jazz Assn., Ga., Black Cultural Awarenss Com., Millington; mem. cultural diversity awareness com. City of Millington; pres. Greater Memphis chpt. Blacks in Govt.; minister of music New Jackson Ave. Ch., Memphis. Mem.: Federally Employed Women, Inc., Fed. Exec. Assn. Democrat-Npl. Baptist. Avocations: travel, pianist, reading, music. Home: 2177 Heard Ave Memphis TN 38108 Office: Memphis IRS Ctr EEO & Diversity Office PO Box 30309 AMF Stop 19 Memphis TN 38130 Office Phone: 901-546-2112. Business E-Mail: Linda.L.Kelley@irs.gov.

KELLEY, LUCILLE KNIGHT, minister, retired neurology and special duty nurse; b. Tallahassee, Fla., Sept. 29, 1929; d. Godfrey and Harriet Davis Knight; m. Clarence Kelley (dec. 1964); 1 child, David. ASN, Rochester (N.Y.) C.C., 1970; lic. in ministry, Colgate Divinity Coll., Rochester, N.Y., 2002, postgrad. in masters program, 2000—02; BA in Religion, Family and Soc., Empire State Coll., Rochester, 2001. RN N.Y.; lic. minister Genesee Bapt. Ch., 2002, ordained to ministry Genesee Bapt. Ch., Rochester, N.Y., 2003. Lic. practical nurse Monroe County Hosp., Rochester, 1960—68, RN, 1970—85, foster care staff, 1991—2001; supporting minister Genesee Bapt. Ch., Rochester, 2003—. Mem. New Salem Bapt. Ch., Sanford, Fla., 1942—50, Mount Olivet Bapt. Ch., 1951—54, mem. choir, 1980—2000, treas., 1995—96, dir. social functions, 1996—2000; mem. Genesee Bapt. Ch., 2000—. Home: 149 Brooks Ave Rochester NY 14606

KELLEY, LYDIA R.B., lawyer; b. Mar. 12, 1964; m. Stephen W. Kelley. BA, Wellesley Coll., 1986; JD, U. Mich., 1989. Ptnr., chmn. firm recruiting & devel. com. McDermott Will & Emery LLP. Mem.: U.S. Dist. Ct. N. Dist. Ill., Ill. Bar Assn., Fed. Tax Inst. Adv. Com. Office: McDermott Will & Emery 227 W Monroe St Chicago IL 60606 Office Phone: 312-984-6470. Office Fax: 312-984-7700. Business E-Mail: lkelley@mwe.com.

KELLEY, MARGARET MARY, music educator, musician; b. Milw., Oct. 16, 1952; d. Thomas Crawford and Josephine (Kenney) K. BM, U. Iowa, 1975; MM, U. Idaho, 1978, MEd, 1979. Pianist, Pullman, Wash., 1980—; mem. piano faculty Lewis-Clark State Coll., Lewiston, Idaho, 1984-87, U. Idaho, 2001—03. Performed as soloist, chamber, accompanist, 1971—; author: In Good Time: College, 2000, Getting There, 2002, vol. 3, 2005, Return Flight, 2006. Spay/neuter chair Humane Soc., Moscow, Idaho, 1996—, bd. dirs. 2000—, pres. bd. dir. 2001-04. Mem. ACLU (bd. dirs. Pullman), Music Tchrs. Nat. Assn., Pullman Music Tchrs. (pres. 1982-83, 87-88, v.p. 1983-85, treas. 1990—), Amnesty Internat. Avocations: writing, running, swimming, reading. Home: 860 SW Alcora Dr Pullman WA 99163-2053 E-mail: megk@pullman.com.

KELLEY, MARY E., science educator; b. Bangkok, Aug. 29, 1970; d. Mary Gilliam and Hayward Kelley. BS biology, Va. Commonwealth U., Richmond, 1994; MAT Biology Edn., Norfolk State U., 1996. Tchr. sci. Hampton City Schools, Va., 1996—. Instr. sci. Hampton U., 1998—. Recipient Unsung Hero, Zion Bapt. Ch., 1999; Rsch. fellow, Am. Physiol. Soc., 1998. Mem.: Delta Sigma Theta (life). Office: Bethel High 1067 Big Bethel Road Hampton VA 23666 Personal E-mail: biotoonmania@yahoo.com. E-mail: mkelley@sbo.hampton.k12.va.us.

KELLEY, MARY ELIZABETH (MARY LAGRONE), information technology specialist; b. Temple, Tex., Feb. 12, 1947; d. Harry John and Mary Erma (Windham) LaGrone; m. Roy Earl Kelley, May 10, 1968; children: Roy John, James Lewis, Joanna Marylu. BS, U. Mary Hardin-Baylor, 1968. Cert. tchr. Tex. Math tchr. Killeen HS, Tex., 1977-78; clk. typist Readiness Region VIII, Aurora, Colo., 1979; statis. clk. Fitzsimons Army Med. Ctr., 1980-81, mgmt. asst., 1981-83; clk. typist Corpus Christi Army Depot, Tex., 1984; mgmt. asst. Health Care Studies and Clin. Investigation Act, Fort Sam Houston, 1984-85; computer programmer, analyst Health Care Systems Support Act, 1985-88, computer systems analyst, 1988-92, computer specialist, 1992-94, data base adminstr., 1994-96, Lotus Notes sys. adminstr., 1996-98; process integrator, asst. comdr. force integration US Army Med. Dept. Ctr. and Sch., 1998-99, computer specialist, 1999—2002, info. tech. specialist, 2002—. Tchr. Fitzsimmons Army Med. Ctr., 1978—79; cons., 1978—79. Author: (database) Health Care Management System, 1988—94. Vol. Parents Encouraging Parents, Denver, 1979—83, Friends of Safe House, Denver, 1980—83, Heidi Search Ctr., San Antonio, 1990; vol. family assistance crisis team San Antonio Police Dept., 1997—99, vol. Vols. in Policing, 1998—99; founder Top of Hill Residents' Alliance, San Antonio, 1997. Recipient achievement medal for civilian svc., Dept. Army, 1991. Mem.: DAR, Gold Star Wives, Soc. Mayflower Descs., Daus. Republic of Tex., United Daus of Confederacy Tex., Alpha Phi, Sigma Tau Delta, Delta Psi Theta, Alpha Chi. Roman Catholic. Avocations: reading, needlecrafts, genealogy, Special Olympics, poetry.

KELLEY, MARYELLEN R., economist, management consultant; b. Boston, Apr. 26, 1951; d. Albert Francis and Agnes Mary (Athy) K.; m. Bennett Harrison, Jan. 25, 1981, (dec. Jan. 17, 1999). BA, Brandeis U., 1971; M in City Planning, Harvard U., 1976; PhD in Mgmt., MIT, 1984. Harman fellow Harvard U., Cambridge, 1982-83; asst. prof. mgmt. U. Mass., Boston, 1984-88; vis. asst. prof. mgmt. and pub. policy Carnegie Mellon U., Pitts., 1988-89, asst. prof. mgmt. and pub. policy, 1989-91, assoc. prof. mgmt. and pub. policy, 1991-97; sr. economist Nat. Inst. Standards and Tech., 1997—2000; pres. Pamet Hill Assocs. Econ. Rsch. & Mgmt. Consulting, 2001—. Vis. scholar MIT Indsl. Performance Ctr., Cambridge, 1994—96; vis. assoc. prof. tech. policy dept. polit. sci. MIT, Cambridge, 1994—95. Contbr. articles to Scientific, Economic and Mgmt. jours. Mem. AAAS, Acad. of Mgmt. Office: Pamet Hill Assocs PO Box 636 Truro MA 02666-0636 E-mail: Maryellen.Kelley@direcway.com.

KELLEY, NANETTE NOLAND, business owner, entrepreneur; b. Lake Charles, La., Dec. 9, 1958; d. Amadee Wade and Helen Weber (Richard) Noland; m. Timothy E. Kelley, Mar. 18, 1989. BS, La. State U., 1980. Pres. Carlson Travel Network, Lafayette, New Orleans, La., 1982—, The Powell Group, Lake Charles, La., 1991—. Founding mem., bd. dirs. Champac, Baton Rouge, 1989-93. Acad. distinction fund bd., 1990-91; chmn. YWCA Banquet, Baton Rouge; bd. dirs. Friends of the Zoo, Baton Rouge, 1987-88. Recipient Women of Achievement award YWCA, 1987; named Sales & Mktg. Execs. Internat. Marketer of Yr., 1985, one of Outstanding Young Women Am., 1987, La. State U. Alumnus of Yr., 1990-91, Young Exec. of Yr., 1991-92. Fellow La. State U. Vis. Bus. Execs.; mem. C. of C. (bd. dirs. 1986-90, mem. exec. com. 1989-90), Baton Rouge C. of C. (bd. dirs.), Chi Omega (adv. com. 1982-85, chmn. 1983-84), La. Partnership for Tech. and Innovation (founder). Episcopalian. Avocations: piano, cooking, duck hunting, flying. Home: PO Box 788 Baton Rouge LA 70821-0788 Office: ERLY INDUSTRIES P O Box 788 Baton Rouge LA 70821

KELLEY, PATRICIA, marketing representative; b. Carrollton, Ga., Jan. 21, 1953; BA in Journalism, Ga. State U., Atlanta, 1974; BSN, West Ga. Coll., Carrollton, 1990. RN Fla. Pub. rels. asst. Grady Meml. Hosp., Atlanta, 1974—77; editl. asst. Childers & Sullivan, Huntsville, Ala., 1977—78; sales rep. AAA Employment Agy., Huntsville, 1978—80; editor Wright Pub. Co., Atlanta, 1980—82; elec./electronic drafter PRC Cons., Atlanta, 1980—87; rschr. Dept. Nursing at West Ga. Coll., Carrollton, 1989—90; med./surg. nurse Tanner Med. Ctr., Carrollton, 1989—90, Delray Cmty. Hosp., Delray Beach, Fla., 1990—91; sales rep. Innovative Med. Svcs., 1991—94; with staff devel., employee rels. Beverly Oaks Rehab. and Nursing Ctr., 1994—95; sales rep./pub. rels. rep. Columbia HCA, Melbourne, Fla., 1996—99; bus. writer/pub. rels. cons. Cocoa Beach, Fla., 2000—. Vol. Project Response, Brevard County Sexual Assault Victim Svcs. All-Am. scholar U.S. Achievement Acad., 1990, recipient Nat. Coll. Nursing award, 1989. Mem. NOW, Space Coast Bus. Writer's Guild, Omicron Delta Kappa. Democrat. Home: 768 Beacon St Palm Bay FL 32907 Personal E-mail: flgator@netscape.com.

KELLEY, PATRICIA HAGELIN, geology educator; b. Cleve., Dec. 8, 1953; d. Daniel Warn and Virginia Louise (Morgan) Hagelin; m. Jonathan Robert Kelley, June 18, 1977; children: Timothy Daniel, Katherine Louise. BA, Coll. of Wooster, 1975; AM, Harvard U., 1977, PhD, 1979. Instr. New Eng. Coll., Henniker, NH, 1979; asst. prof. U. Miss., University, 1979-85, assoc. prof., 1985-89, acting assoc. vice chancellor acad. affairs, 1988, prof., 1989-92, assoc. dean, 1989-90; program dir. NSF, Washington, 1990-92; prof., chmn. dept. geology U. N.D., Grand Forks, 1992-97; prof. U. NC, Wilmington, 1997—, chmn. dept. earth scis., 1997—2003. Editor several books; contbr. articles to profl. jours. Deacon Bethel Presbyn. Ch., Olive Branch, Miss., 1985-90. Rsch. grantee NSF, 1986-89, 90-99, 2000-03; NSF fellow, 1976-79. Fellow AAAS, Geol. Soc. Am., Paleontol. Soc. (coun. 1984-85, 95-96, 98-2004, chair S.E. sect. 1984-85, chair N.C. sect. 1995-96, pres.-elect 1998-2000, pres. 2000-02, past pres. 2002-04); mem. Assn. Women Geosci. (Outstanding Educator award 2003), Paleontol. Rsch. Inst. (trustee 2003-, pres. bd. trustees 2004-06), Soc. Econ. Paleontologists and Mineralogists, Sigma Xi, Phi Beta Kappa. Presbyterian. Avocations: writing, music, travel. Office: Dept Geography and Geology Univ NC Wilmington NC 28403-5944 Office Phone: 910-962-7406. Business E-Mail: kelleyp@uncw.edu.

KELLEY, PATRICIA T., music educator; b. Anderson, S.C., May 20, 1960; d. William R. and Joyce S. Tucker; m. Glenn E. Kelley, Nov. 16, 1990; children: Joseph Tucker, Sarah Grace. BA, Columbia Coll., S.C., 1980; M. U. S.C., Columbia, 1985. Cert. Tchr. Music Edn. Choral S.C., 1980, Tchr. Early Childhood Edn. S.C., 1985. Music specialist Johnsonville Elem. Sch., SC, 1980—. Chair elem. honors choir S.C. Music Educators. Active mem. Lynches River Free Will Bapt. Ch., Scranton, SC, 2001—06. EIA Grant, Dept. Edn. S.C., 2004, 2005. Mem.: Palmetto State Teachers Assn., S.C. Music Educators Assn. (chmn. elem. honors choir 2004—), Music Educators Nat. Conf. Baptist. Avocations: cooking, spending time with my family, singing, working with children. Home: 503 North Half Moon Road Lake City SC 29560 Office: Johnsonville Elem Sch 160 East Marion Street Johnsonville SC 29555 Home Fax: 843-386-3801; Office Fax: 843-386-3574. Personal E-mail: pkelley@johnsonvillefd.org. E-mail: pkelley@flo5.k12.sc.us.

KELLEY, SHANA O., biochemist; BS in Chemistry, Seton Hall U., 1992; PhD in Chemistry, Calif. Inst. Tech., 1999; postdoctoral rsch., Scripps Rsch. Inst., 1999—2000. Asst. prof. dept. chemistry Boston Coll., 2000—. Founding scientist and cons. GeneOhm Scis., La Jolla, Calif., 2001—. Contbr. articles to profl. jour. Named one of Top 100 Young Innovators, MIT Tech. Review, 2004; recipient NSF Career award, 2004; Alfred P. Sloan fellowship, 2004. Office: Merkert Chemistry Ctr 140 Commonwealth Ave Chestnut Hill MA 02467 Business E-Mail: shana.kelley@bc.edu.

KELLEY, SHEILA SEYMOUR, public relations consultant; b. Bronxville, NY; d. William Joseph and Jane (Seymour) K.; m. Robert Max Kaufman, 1959. BA magna cum laude, Syracuse U., 1949. Reporter Yonkers Herald Statesman, NYC, 1950; reporter, editor Close Up column Herald Tribune, NYC, 1950-53; writer, prodr. Sta. WNBC-TV, NYC, 1953-54, asst. to Alfred Gwynne Vanderbilt, 1955; media cons. to Senator Jacob K. Javits, NYC, 1956-74; press sec. Senator Jacobs K. Javits, Washington, 1958-61; account supr., v.p. Harshe Rotman Druck, NYC, 1961-76; founder, pres. VOTES, Inc., NYC, 1973-75; v.p. Doremus Pub. Rels., NYC, 1976-86, sr. v.p., 1987-90, exec. v.p., 1990, Gavin Anderson & Co., NYC, 1990-96, sr. counselor, 1996-97; prin. The Dilenschneider Group, 1997—. Mem.: Women Execs. in Pub. Rels. (pres. 1987—88, dir. found. 1999—, bd. dirs. 2005), Pub. Rels. Soc. Am. (accredited), Hon. Order Ky. Cols., Phi Beta Kappa. Republican. Avocations: skiing, golf, gardening. Office Phone: 212-922-0900. Business E-Mail: skelley@dgi-nyc.com.

KELLEY, SUDHA S., operating room nurse; b. India, May 26, 1943; d. Shamsundar I. and Rahelbai (Kale) Samudre; m. Fred H. Kelley, Dec. 29, 1969; children: Avinash, Daniel. MAH State Civil Hosp., State Civil Hosp. and Coll., 1966; student, Johns Hopkins U., Shepherd Pratt Hosp., Balt., Virginia Beach Gen. Hosp.; postgrad., Delaware C.C., 1998-99. RN, N.Y., Va., Md. Nursery nurse Virginia Beach (Va.) Gen. Hosp., 1980-81; oper. room nurse Virginia Beach Gen. Hosp., 1981-82, Greater Balt. Med. Ctr., 1983-84; exam. express dir., women's svcs. emergency room nurse Sinai Hosp., Balt., 1988-89, oper. rm. nurse, 1988-99; emergency rm. pool nurse Bon Secours Hosp., Balt., 1992-93; RN coll. instr. Home: 300 Sabal Palm Ln Apt 107 Chesapeake VA 23320-1737

KELLEY, VIRGINIA WIARD (JUDY KELLEY), dance educator; b. Washington, Nov. 17, 1937; d. David Kyle and Mary Margaret (Barber) Wiard; m. Leo Gilbert Kelley, July 2, 1960; children: Cheryl, Raymond, John, Brenda. Degree in bus. adminstrn., Miller-Motte Bus. Coll., 1958; dance edn. degree, Kent State U., 1986. Grad. Dance Masters of Am. Performer Tony Grant Stars of Tomorrow, Atlantic City, N.J., 1951-53; performer Cressetts Betty Cress Dance Studio, tour of East Coast, 1958, Jacksonville, N.C., 1958-59; instr., performer, choreographer Cuppett's Performing Arts Ctr., Vienna, Va., 1981-99, Vienna Comty. Ctr., 1982-99. Actress Wilmington (N.C.) Theatrical Soc., 1957; performer Miss Wilmington Pageant, 1958. Helper Dem. Party, Vienna, 1992. Named Ms. Senior N.C., 2000. Mem. Dance Masters of Am. (dance educator 1981—), Cameo Club. Democrat. Roman Catholic. Avocations: tap dancing, weightlifting, line dancing, swimming. Home: 153 Topsail Rd North Topsail Beach NC 28460-8242 E-mail: traintap@bellsouth.net.

KELLEY, WENDY ROCK, academic administrator; d. Jim and Kathleen Rock; m. Jim Kelley, June 21, 1997; 1 child, Maggie; children: Mari, Jack. BA in Geography and Biology, Augustana Coll., Rock Island, Ill., 1992; MA in Higher Edn., U. of Iowa, 1998. Admissions counselor Augustana Coll., Rock Island, Ill., 1992—95, asst. dir. of admissions, 1995—98, assoc. dir. of admissions, 1998—2004, asst. dir. human resources, 2005—. Liturgy mem. Our Lady of the River Cath. Ch., LeClaire, Iowa, 2001—05. Mem.: Am. Mktg. Assn., Ill. Assn. for Coll. Admission Counseling. Office Phone: 309-794-7740. E-mail: wendykelley@augustana.edu.

KELLEY, WENDY THUE, fine arts advisor, curator; b. Santa Monica, Calif., July 4, 1941; d. Horace Wendel and Marjory (Simmons) Thue; children: David Byron Jr., Christopher S., Jennifer M. AA, Stephens Coll., Columbia, Mo., 1960; BA, Phillips U., 1963; postgrad., NYU, 1996, Instituto Allende, San Miguel de Allende, 1993. Cert. tchr., Conn. Prin., owner Wendy Kelley Art Advisor, Old Greenwich, 1985—. Curator exhbns. U. So. Calif. Inst. Genetic Medicine Gallery, LCOR Devels., Home Box Office/Time

Warner, N.Y.C., 1990-2002, Hines, Inc.; cons. curator Discovery Mus., Bridgeport, Conn.; cons. Aetna, Cornell Med. Ctr., Time-Warner, Apple Computer, Marriott Corp. Bd. dirs. YMCA, 1987-93 Mem. Nat. Assn. Profl. Art Advisors, N.E. Appraisers Assn., Kappa Alpha Theta. Avocations: printmaking, photography. Home: 3132 6th St Santa Monica CA 90405 Personal E-mail: wtko@mindspring.com.

KELLEY FITCHETT, CHRISTINE RUTH, business owner, consultant; b. St. Louis, Oct. 14, 1951; d. John Weatherhead and Mary Christine (Echkout) K.; 1 child, Jennifer Christine. AS in Nursing, St. Louis Community Coll., 1975; BA in Bus. Mgmt., Webster U., 1988, postgrad., 1988—. Charge relief and staff nurse St. Luke's W., Cardinal Glennon, St. Louis, 1975-77; pub. health nurse Vis. Nurse Assn., St. Louis, 1977-78; chief flight nurse Tri-Star Aviation, St. Louis, 1978-80; agy. nurse Med. Staffing, Med.-Staff, Dallas, 1980-83; charge relief and psychiatric staff nurse/counselor St. John's Mercy Med. Ctr., St. Louis, 1983-85, adolescent psychotherapist/counselor, 1985; dir. air ambulance div. Jet Svcs., Inc., Chesterfield, Mo., 1985-87; pres., CEO Air-Med. Internat., Inc., St. Louis, 1987-96; home health nurse part-time St. Mary's Health Ctr., St. Louis, 1991—; orthopaedic nurse Aspen Valley Hosp., Aspen, Colo., 1993—. Bus. cons. Genesis Learning Systems, Creve Coeur, Mo., 1989-90; assisted Dept. Health State of Mo. in writing air ambulance regulations for fixed wing aircraft, 1988; part-time home health nurse St. Mary's Health Ctr., St. Louis, 1991—; orthopaedic nurse Snowmass Clinic, Aspen, Colo., 1993. Mem. Regional Commerce & Growth Assn., St. Louis, 1986—, 89—; State Adv. Coun. for Emergency Med. Svcs., Jefferson City, Mo., 1988—. Mem. Profl. Aeromed. Transport Assn. (bd. dirs. 1988—), Assn. Air Med. Svcs., Nat. Assn. Women Bus. Owners, Mo. Emergency Med. Svcs. Alliance, Nat. Flight Nurse Assn., Regional Commerce and Growth Assn's. Pres.'s Club, Mothers Club. Republican. Avocations: travel, water sports, skiing, photography, golf. Office: PO Box 4755 Vail CO 81658-4755

KELLEY-HALL, MARYON HOYLE, retired social worker; b. Anderson, Ind., Aug. 5, 1924; d. Arthur Dent and Mildred Madeline (Hall) Hoyle; m. Dean M. Kelley, June 8, 1946; 1 child, Lenore Wadsworth Hervey; m. Richard A. Hall, Oct. 14, 2000. AB, U. Denver, 1945; MSW, Columbia U., N.Y.C., 1967. Psychiat. social worker Rockland State Hosp., Orangeburg, N.Y., 1963-67, psychiat. social work supr., 1967-70; dir. social svcs. Rockland Children's Psychiat. Ctr., Orangeburg, 1970—72, chief child care svc., 1972—73; chief children's habilitation svc. Suffolk Devel. Ctr., Melville, NY, 1974—79; med. social worker Suffolk County Health Svcs., Hauppauge, NY, 1983-89; med. social work supr. Brentwood (N.Y.) Family Health Ctr., 1990—93. Home: 800 S 15th St # I-869 Sebring OH 44672

KELLMAN, SANDRA Y., lawyer; b. Mar. 21, 1952; BA with high honors, Univ. Ill., Urbana-Champaign, 1973; JD cum laude, Northwestern Univ., 1977. Bar: Ill. 1977. Ptnr. co-chmn. Lodging & Timeshare practice group DLA Piper Rudnick Gray Cary, Chgo. Editor (note & comment): Jour. of Criminal Law & Criminology; contbr. articles to profl. jours. Office: DLA Piper Rudnick Gray Cary Suite 1900 203 N LaSalle St Chicago IL 60601-1293 Office Phone: 312-368-4082. Office Fax: 312-236-7516. Business E-Mail: sandra.kellman@dlapiper.com.

KELLNER, TATANA, artist, art educator; b. Prague, Nov. 21, 1950; came to U.S., 1969; d. Eugene and Eva (Freund) K BA, U. Toledo, 1972; MFA, Rochester Inst. Tech., 1974. Artistic dir. Women's Studio Workshop, Inc., 1974—, artist, instr. Art in Edn. Initiative, 1986—, N.Y. State Coun. Arts, 1986—, Kingston Consol. Sch. Dist., NY, 1986—; represented by Goldstrom Gallery, N.Y.C. Artist in residence Visual Studies Workshop, Rochester, N.Y., 1987, Artpark, Lewiston, N.Y., 1987, Yaddo, Saratoga Springs, N.Y., 1988, Va. Ctr. Arts, Sweet Briar, 1992, 99, MacDowell Colony, Peterborough, N.H., 1986, 92, 2001, Banff Ctr. Arts, 1995, Ragdale, Evanston, Ill., 1986, Millay Colony, 2003, Blue Mountain Arts Ctr., 2006; tech. cons. fine arts dept. SUNY, New Paltz, 1974-75; vis. artist in residence U. So. Maine, Gorham, 1997; lectr. in field Exhibited in group shows including Everson Mus., Syracuse, N.Y., 1990, Harwick Coll., 1990, Multimedia Arts Ctr., N.Y.C., 1990, Rensselaer County Coun. for Arts, Troy, N.Y., 1992, Hera Gallery, Wakefield, R.I., 1992, Harper Collins Publs., N.Y.C., 1993, SUNY, New Paltz, 1993, Pratt Manhattan Gallery, 1993, Blum Helman Gallery, N.Y.C., Marywood Coll., Slatedale, Pa., 1994, Ohio State U., Columbus, 1994, Ormond (Fla.) Meml. Art Mus., 1995, Warren St. Gallery, Hudson, N.Y., Klutznick Nat. Jewish Mus., Washington, 1995, 494 Gallery, N.Y.C., Photographic Resource Ctr., Boston, 1995, Forman Gallery, Jamestown, N.Y., 1995, Monmouth Mus., Lincroft, N.J., 1996, U. Ariz. Mus. Art, Tucson, 1999-2000, Neuberger Mus., Purchase, N.Y., 1998, Mus. Contemporary Art, Fort Collins, Colo., 2004, Creative Concepts, Beacon, N.Y., 2003, Grossmont Coll., El Cajon, Calif., 2005, Dist. Fine Arts, Washington, 2005, Wellesley Coll. Libr., 2005, Sterling Libr. Yale U., 2005, Athens Inst. Contemporary Art, Ga., 2006; one-person exhbns. include Kleinert Arts Ctr., Woodstock, N.Y., 1989, The Queens Mus. at Bulova Corp. Ctr., N.Y.C., 1991, CEPA Gallery, Buffalo, 1993, 2002, Harwick Coll., Oneonta, N.Y., 1994, SUNY Oswego, 1994, We. Mich. U., Kalamazoo, 1995, Bloomsburg (Pa.) U., 1995, Soc. Contemporary Photography, Kansas City, Mo., 1996, Floating Gallery Ctr. Photography, Winnipeg, Man., Can., 1996, Ctr. Visual Arts U. Toledo (Ohio), 1997, Mednick Gallery U. Arts, Phila., 1997, Ft. Lewis Coll., Durango, Colo., 1997, Marist Coll., Poughkeepsie, N.Y., 1997, Gallerie Sans Nom, Moncton, Can., 1997, Lake George (N.Y.) Arts Project, 1998, Goldstrom Gallery, N.Y.C., 1998, Sarek Gallery, Bucknell U., Pa., 2001, Ceva Buffalor, 2002, Edinboro U., Pa., 2003, Wister C.C., 2003, Ulster C.C., Stone Ridge, N.Y., 2003, R&F Gallery, Kingston, N.Y., 2006; represented in permanent collections Mus. Modern Art Libr., U. Toledo, Walker Arts Ctr. Libr., Rochester Inst. Tech., Mobil Corp., Met. Mus. Libr.; author 12 artists' books Mentor Empire State Coll., 1978-81, curator art gallery, 1994 Grantee N.Y. State Coun. on Arts, 1980, Empire State Crafts Alliance, 1989, Individual Artist N.Y. Found. Arts, 1992, 96, 97, Pollock-Krasner Found., 2005; recipient Photographer's Fund award Ctr. for Photography, 1984, 2003, award Ruth Chenven Found., 1985, Arax award Dutchess C.C. 25th Ann. Competition, Purchase award, Toledo (Ohio) Mus. Art, Rochester Inst. Tech Home: 552 Binnewater Rd Kingston NY 12401-8458 Office: Women's Studio Workshop PO Box 489 Rosendale NY 12472-0489 Office Phone: 845-658-9133. Business E-Mail: tanara@wsworkshop.org.

KELLOGG, MARY MARJORIE, retired special education educator, supervisor; b. Kansas City, Mo., Sept. 17, 1949; d. Harlan Rhodes Justus and Lyda Ethel Shipman; m. Robert Russell Kellogg, June 13, 1970; 1 child, Ryan Russell. BA in Elem. Edn., U. Oreg., Eugene, 1971; EdM in Mid. Grades, Kansas State U., Manhattan, 1991; EdS in Leadership, U. Ala., Tuscaloosa, 1999. Cert. level 6 ednl. specialist Ga., tchr. grades K-12 Ga. Tchr. Springfield (Oreg.) City Schs., 1972—85; coord. spl. programs Marietta (Ga) H.S., 1986—2005; ret., 2005. Founder and coord. REACH program Marietta (Ga.) City Schs., 1987—2005; mem. exec. bd. Marietta Edn. Assn., 2003—05. Mem. Cobb and Douglas County Youth and Health Devel. Adv. Coun., 2005—; bd. dir. Ga. Breast Cancer Coalition, Atlanta, 2005—, Spiritual Democracy, 2006—. Named Nat. Educator of Yr., Milliken Found., 1991, Am. Hero in Edn. runner up, Reader's Digest, 1991, Woman of Achievement, Northwest Ga. YWCA, 2006. Avocations: mentoring students, travel, gardening, reading. Home: 2557 Old Orchard Trail Marietta GA 30062

KELLOGG FAIN, KAREN, retired history educator; b. Pueblo, Colo., Oct. 10, 1940; d. Howard Davis and Mary Lucille (Cole) Kellogg; m. Sept. 1, 1961; divorced; 1 child, Kristopher. Student, U. Ariz., 1958-61; BA, U. So. Colo., 1967; MA, U. No. Colo., 1977; postgrad., U. Denver, 1968, 72-93, Colo. State U., 1975, 91, Chadron State Coll., 1975, U. No. Ill., 1977, 83, Ft. Hayes State Coll., 1979, U. Colo., 1979, 86-87, 92, Ind. U., 1988. Cert. secondary tchr. Colo., 1967. Tchr. history and geography Denver Pub. Schs., 1967-96; tchr. West H.S., Denver, 1992-96. Area adminstr., tchr. coord. Close Up program, Washington, 1982-84; reviewer, cons. for book Geography, Our Changing World, 1990. Vol., chmn. young profls. Inst. Internat. Edn. and World Affairs Coun., Denver, 1980—; state selection com. U.S. Senate and Japan Scholarship Com., Denver, 1981-89, Youth for Understanding, Denver; active Denver Art Mus., 1970—; vol. Denver Mus. Natural History, 1989—, Am. Cancer Soc. Jail and Bail, 1996, Climb the Mountain, 1996, Denver Conv. Bur., 1997; bd. overseas Dept. Def. Dependents Sch., Guantanamo Bay, Cuba, 1990-91; screening panelist Tchr. to Japan Program Rocky Mtn. Regional Fulbright Meml. Fund, 1997; vol. tour guide Colo. State Capitol, 1997-2001; vol. aide Colo. State Rep. Nancy Todd Fulbright scholar Chadron State Coll., Pakistan, 1975; Geog. Soc. grantee U. Colo., 1986; recipient award for Project Prince, Colo. U./Denver Pub. Schs./Denver Police Dept., 1992. Mem.: AAUW, Colo. Coun. on Internat. Orgns. (mem. bd. 1999—), Colo. Geographic Alliance (steering com. 1986), Rocky Mountain Regional World History Assn. (steering com. 1984—87), Am. Forum for Global Edn., Fulbright Assn. (bd. dirs. and regional liaison Colo. chpt. 2001—), World History Assn., Nat. Coun. Social Studies (del. 1984), Colo. Coun. Social Studies (sec. 1984—86), Denver Bot. Gardens, Kappa Kappa Iota, Gamma Phi Beta. Episcopalian. Avocations: travel, hosting international visitors, swimming, reading. Home: 12643 E Bates Cir Aurora CO 80014-3315 E-mail: karenfain@hotmail.com.

KELLUMS, KAREN J., psychologist; b. St. Louis, Dec. 22, 1953; d. Eugene and Bonnie Kellums. BS in Biology, Hardin-Simmons U., 1977; MA in Clin. Psychology, George Fox U., 1993, PsyD in Clin. Psychology, 1995; cert. completion, Eating Disorder Inst., 1997. Lic. psychologist, Mo., Wash.; cert. health svcs. provider. Guest lectr. Wesley Inst. for the Arts, Sydney, Australia, 1993; psychologist New Life Clinics, St. Louis, 1997-98, Mineral Area Regional Med. Ctr., Farmington, Potosi, Mo., 1998-99, N.W. Psychol. Resources, Longview, Wash., 1999—2004, Pacific Psychol. Assocs., 2006—. Psychology instr. Pillsbury Inst. Applied Christianity, Bridgeton, Mo., 1997-99, Lindenwood U., St. Charles, Mo., 1997; adj. faculty Western Baptist Sem., 2003—; spkr. in field. Recipient loan repayment, Nat. Health Svcs. Corp., Bethesda, Md., 1998—2001. Mem. APA, Internat. Assn. Play Therapy, Christian Assn. for Psychol. Studies, Writers Internat. Network. Baptist.

KELLY, ALEDA MAE, retired secondary education educator; b. Mayfield, Ky., June 18, 1926; d. William Aubrey and Nomye (Brandon) Farmer; m. Troy Wilbert Kelly, June 5, 1948 (dec., 2003); children: Gene Michael, Patricia Jane Hendren. BA, Murray State U., 1948. Cert. tchr., Ky., Mo., Ill. Tchr. Benton (Ky.) City Schs., 1948-49, East Prairie (Mo.) Sch., 1949-52, Colusa (Ill.) Sch. Sys., 1958-60, Nauvoo (Ill.) Sch. Sys., 1961-64; tutor doctoral students So. Ill. U., Carbondale, 1964-67. Author: 20th Anniversary Aldersgate United Methodist Church, 1975, 40th Anniversary Aldersgate United Methodist Church, 1995, The Flame Still Burns, History of Memphis Conference United Methodist Women, 1995, History of Alumni Association-Memphis State University, 1996, Love Made Visible, History of Memphis McKendree District United Methodist Women, 1997. Active YWCA, Memphis, 1997; mem., officer Aldersgate United Meth. Ch., Memphis, 1967-97; mem. nominating com. McKendree Dist. United Meth. Women. Mem. United Meth. Women (v.p., historian McKendree dist.), Alpha Sigma Alpha (editor 1946-48), Kappa Delta Pi. Democrat. Avocations: reading, writing, presenting programs and workshops. Home: 4482 E Dearing Rd Memphis TN 38117-6902

KELLY, ANASTASIA D. (STASIA KELLY), telecommunications industry executive, lawyer; b. Boston, 1949; m. Mike Kelly; children: Mike, Brian. Grad., Trinity U., 1971; JD, George Washington U., 1981. Bar: Tex., DC, Va. With Air Lines Pilots Assn., Martin-Marietta Corp.; atty. Wilmer, Cutler & Pickering, Washington, Carrington, Coleman, Sloman & Blumenthal, Dallas, 1981—85; joined Fannie Mae, 1995, sr. v.p., gen. coun., sec., 1996—99; exec. v.p., gen. counsel, sec. Sears, Roebuck and Co., Chgo., 1999—2003; exec. v.p., gen. counsel MCI, Inc. (formerly WorldCom), Ashburn, Va., 2003—06, corp. sec., 2003—04; exec. v.p., gen. counsel, sr. regulatory & compliance officer Am. Internat. Group, Inc. (AIG), 2006. Bd. dirs. Ownes-Ill., 1999—2003; vice chair Equal Justice Works, Assn. Corp. Counsel, Lawyers for Children of Am.; adv. counsel mem. Woodrow Wilson Ctr. for Internat. for Internat. Scholars. Trustee Trinity Coll. Mem.: ABA (mem. Com. on Corp. Laws). Office: Am Internat Group Inc (AIG) 70 Pine St New York NY 10270 Office Phone: 703-886-5600.*

KELLY, BARBARA SUE, psychologist; b. Somers Point, N.J., June 24, 1958; d. Joseph Raymond and Catherine Agnes Kelly. BA, Muhlenberg Coll., 1980; MA, Marywood Coll., 1983; PhD, Walden U., 2001. Lic. psychologist Pa., NJ. Cmty. social worker Ctr. for Human Devel., Millville, N.J., 1984-87; counselor I Cape Counseling Svcs., Cape May Courthouse, N.J., 1987-88; biofeedback therapist Guardian Group, Inc., Plymouth Meeting, Pa., 1992-97; v.p. Psychol. Wellness Assocs., Deptford, NJ, 1996—2004; clin. psychologist/sub investigator CRI Worldwide, 2002—. Fellow Biofeedback Cert. Inst. Am.; mem. APA, Pa. Soc. Behavioral Medicine and Biofeedback. Avocations: cooking, gardening, music, reading. Office: Psychol Wellness Assocs LLC PO Box 5025 Deptford NJ 08096-0025

KELLY, BEVERLY ANN, elementary school educator; b. LA, Nov. 28, 1952; d. Irene Andrews and Jerry Kelly. BA, Calif. State U., LA, 1977; MS, La Verne U., Calif., 1985. Cert. elem. multiple subjects State of Calif., 1978, children's ctr. permit State of Calif. Weekend day camp sec. Found. for Jr. Blind, View Park, Calif., 1975—77, multi-handicapped tchr., 1978—79; classroom vol. First St. Spl. Edn. Sch., East L.A., 1977; dormitory asst. Calif. State Disgnostic Sch. for Neurol. Handicapped Children, L.A., 1977—78; spl. day class intern Marianne Frostig Ctr. Ednl. Therapy, West L.A., Calif., 1979—80; learning handicapped tchr. Queen Anne Elem. Sch., L.A., 1980—85; resource specialist tchr. Century Pk. Elem. Sch., Inglewood, Calif., 1985—, d.a.t.e. coord., 2002—04. Asst. supr. Teen Post, L.A., Calif., 1979—80; ESL tchr. Dorsey H.S., L.A., Calif., 1999—2000; asst. dir. Youth Experience Summer Program, View Park, Calif., 1981; fellow Marianne Frostig, L.A.; npi UCLA, Brentwood, Calif.; work study aide Neurol. Sch., L.A. Mem. Lambda Pi Zeta, South Bay, Calif.; sunday sch. tchr. West Angeles Ch. of God in Christ, L.A., 1978—80; vol. Willie Jordan Mission, L.A., 1998—99; mem. Voices In Praise Choir, L.A., 1999—2004, West Angeles Prison Ministry, L.A., 2004—05, Wildlife Fedn., 2005—06. Mem.: Sierra Club, Wildlife Fedn. (corr.), Four Seasons Ski Club (assoc.), West L.A. Sierra Club (assoc.), Zeta Phi Beta (assoc.; vice sec. 1998—2000). Democrat-Npl. Mem. Ch. Of God. Avocations: travel, photography, african dance, computer graphics, crocheting. Office Phone: 323-755-2800. Personal E-mail: bkellee@msn.com. E-mail: bkelly@lausd.k12.ca.us.

KELLY, CANDACE LEE, secondary school educator; b. Hartford, Conn., June 11, 1954; d. Richard Burnet Dakin and G. Barbara Clark; 1 child, Margaret Elizabeth. AA, U. Fla., Gainesville, 1978; BA, U. North Fla., Jacksonville, 1980; MEd, U. North Fla., 1990. Cert. tchr. Fla. Commd. USN, 1972, advanced through grades to lt. comdr., 1980—95; ret., 1995; naval sci. tchr. Du Fletcher H.S., Neptune Beach, Fla., 1998—2002, tchr., 1995—. Mem. sch. adv. com., Neptune Beach, 2003—; chair Shared Decision Making Com., Neptune Beach, 2002—; interpreter NPS-Castillo de San Marcos, St. Augustine, Fla., 1998—. Named Tchr. of the Yr., Du Fletcher H.S., 2005. Mem.: Am. Legion (post officer 1999—), Men of Menendez, Spanish Garrison. Republican. Episcopalian. Avocation: history. Home: 149 Belvedere St Atlantic Beach FL 32233

KELLY, CAROL A., travel company executive; married; 3 children. BS in Computer Sci. Engring., Mich. State U.; MBA, U. Chgo. CPA. With COVIA, United Airlines; v.p., CFO Apollo Travel Svcs., Rolling Meadows, Ill.; v.p., corp. svcs. Sabre Holdings, Southlake, Tex., 1998—99, sr. v.p., corp. svcs., 1999, sr. v.p., chief info. officer, 1999—. Recipient Best Marriage of IT and Bus. Processes award, Salomon Smith Barney, 2001.

KELLY, CAROL ROWDEN, psychologist; b. Carroll, Iowa, Aug. 29, 1943; d. Paul Harold and Clare Hunstock Rowden; m. William Michael Kelly, Sept. 2, 1984. BA, U. San Francisco, Calif., 1974; MA, John F. Kennedy U., Orinda, Calif., 1988; PhD, Calif. Inst. Integral Studies, San Francisco, Calif., 1994. Lic. marriage amd family therapist Calif. Bd. Behavioral Sci. Examiners, 1992, psychologist Calif. Bd. Psychology, 2003, Oreg. Bd. Psychology, 2004. Fin. analyst Levi Strauss & Co., San Francisco, 1975—79, Consol. Capital Cos., Emeryville, Calif., 1980—86; corp. cons. ReVision ReSources, San Jose, Calif., 1994—2000; staff psychologist EMQ Children & Family Svcs., Campbell, Calif., 2000—04; prin., owner LifeCourse Coaching & Consulting, Portland, Oreg., 2005—. Docent Portland Art Mus., Oreg., 2004—06. Home and Office: LifeCourse Coaching & Consulting 2898 SW Champlain Drive Portland OR 97205 Office Phone: 503-248-2163. Business E-Mail: carol.kelly@lifeccc.com.

KELLY, CAROLYN SUE, newspaper executive; b. Pasco, Wash., Oct. 25, 1952; d. Jerald Davin and Margaret Helen (Nibler) K. BBA, Gonzaga U., 1974; MBA, Seattle U., 1985. CPA, Wash., 1976. Acct. Brajcich & Loeffler, Spokane, Wash., 1972-74; auditor Peat, Marwick, Mitchell & Co., Seattle, 1974-77; fin. analyst Seattle Times, 1977-81, asst. circulation mgr., 1981-83, spl. project advt. mgr., 1983—87, dir. mktg. and new bus., 1987—89, v.p., CFO, 1989—95, sr. v.p., CFO, 1995—97, sr. v.p., gen. mgr., 1997—2001, pres., COO, 2001—. Mem. Fin. Execs. Avocation: running. Office: Seattle Times PO Box 70 Seattle WA 98111-0070

KELLY, CHRISTINA, editor; BA in English & History, Colgate U. Contbg. editor US; editor Sassy, 1988—94; dep. editor/founding editor Jane Mag., 1997—2000; exec. editor YM Mag., 2000—01, editor-in-chief, 2001—04; exec. editor ELLEgirl, 2004—05, editor-in-chief, 2005—06. Publisher: freelance articles include Rolling Stone, Spin, Premiere, The Rolling Stone Book of Women in Rock. Mem.: ASME.

KELLY, CLEO PARKER, retired bank executive; b. Moreland, Ala., Feb. 25, 1918; d. Lee Reynold and Mittie Revis; m. Albert Francis Parker, Nov. 4, 1933 (dec. Nov. 15, 1983); 1 child, Brenda Faye Floyd; m. Emmett Smith Kelly, Oct. 8, 1985. AS in Banking, Broward C.C., Ft. Lauderdale, Fla., 1980; BA in Psychology, U. Miami, Fla., 1964. Sec., clk. Morgan County Office Dep. Sheriff, Decatur, Ala.; dep. cir. ct. clk. Morgan County Cir. Ct. Clks. Office, Decatur; legal sec. Hare, Wynn & Newell, Birmingham, Nichols, Gaither, Green, Frater & Beckham, Miami; numerous secretarial positions First Nat. Bank Miami; various positions Barnett Bank (now Bank Am.), Hollywood and Miami, Fla., asst. v.p. Vol. Hospice Broward County, Ft. Lauderdale, 1988, Hollywood Hills Meth. Ch., Fla., tchr. Sunday sch. Fla. Named Woman of Yr., Hollywood Bus. and Profl. Womens Club, 1977. Democrat. Methodist. Avocations: golf, walking.

KELLY, COLLEEN ADELE, secondary school educator; b. Chgo., Feb. 4, 1934; d. Patrick Bernard and Mabel Virginia (Smith) K. BA, Pace U., 1955; MA, St. John's U., Jamaica, N.Y., 1966, NYU, 1974; PhD, U. Conn., 1983. Instr. Good Counsel Coll., White Plains, N.Y., 1955-58; tchr. St. John's Sch., Mahpac, N.Y., 1958-60, Our Lady of Sorrows Sch., White Plains, N.Y., 1960-61; chmn. dept. history John F. Kennedy High Sch., Somers, N.Y., 1961-68; tchr. Fairfield (Conn.) High Sch., 1968—; adj. prof. Cen. Conn. State U., New Britain, 1987—. Cons. McDougall, Littell & Co., 1986-87; commr. Nat. Commn. on Asia in the Schs., 1999—. Co-author: (book) Indian Summer, 1976, 2d edit., 1979; contbg. writer tchrs. manual: A World History, Links Across Time and Place, 1987; editor: A Catalogue of Asian Studies Resources in Conn., 1980, Asia in Connecticut A Catalogue of Asian Resources in Connecticut and Environments, 2nd edit., 1996; co-author filmstrip: China's Communes, 1975. Fulbright grantee, 1984, 67, U. Conn. Rsch. Found. grantee, 1981; Delta Kappa Gamma internat. scholar, 1981; named Alumni of Yr. Pace U., 1981; Pier fellow Yale U., 1996-97. Mem. Assn. for Asian Studies (exec. com. New Eng. Conf., mem. Buchanan prize com. 2003-05), Comparative and Internat. Edn. Soc., Asia Soc. Vietnam Challenge (tchr. cons. 1997-98) Democrat. Roman Catholic. Avocations: photography, writing, travel, art, music. Home: 197B Heritage Vlg Southbury CT 06488-1443 Office: Fairfield H S Melville Ave Fairfield CT 06432-2001

KELLY, DEANNA M., assistant principal; b. N.Y. BA, LeMoyne Coll., Syracuse, N.Y., 1991; MS, U. Albany, N.Y., 1993. Cert. S.A.S. N.Y., 1999, permanent tchr. cert. English 7-12 N.Y., 1993. Asst. prin. Cohoes H.S., NY, 1999—. Mem.: ESSAA. Office: Cohoes High School One Tiger Cir Cohoes NY 12047 Office Phone: 518-237-9100 1404. Office Fax: 518-238-0169. Business E-Mail: dkelly@cohoes.org.

KELLY, DIANA KAY, counselor, educator; b. Shaw AFB, S.C., July 31, 1958; d. Donald I. and Georgianna Kelly; life ptnr. Mary L. Baldwin. BA in Sociology, U. N.Mex, Albuquerque, 1979; MA in Rehab. Counseling, Calif. State U., San Bernardino, 1995. Cert. rehab. counselor Commn. Rehab. Counselor Certification, 1995. Prof. City Colls. Chgo., Brunssum, Netherlands, 1979—80; test examiner U.S. Army, Brunssum, Netherlands, 1980—81; supr. FEDCO, Ontario, Calif., 1982—88; asst. mgr./title asst. World Title Co., Colton, Calif., 1989—94; title asst. Stewart Title Co., Riverside, Calif., 1994—95; counselor/asst. prof. Bakersfield (Calif.) Coll., 1996—. Mem. adv. bd. WorkAbility III, Bakersfield Coll., 1996—; counselor coord. Calif. C.Cs., Disabled Student Programs and Svcs., Region V, Fresno, Calif., 2002—03. Advisor, student club Students for the Ethical Treatment of Humanity, Bakersfield Coll., Bakersfield, Calif., 2000—02; presenter Nat. Orgn. for the Mentally Ill (NAMI), Bakersfield, Calif., 2002—02, Kern County Mental Health In-Service, Bakersfield, Calif., 2002—02, Calif. Placement Assn. (CPA) ann. Conf., Fresno, Calif., 2003—03, Multiple Sclerosis Soc., Bakersfield, Calif., 2003—03, Calif. State Dept. of Rehab., Bakersfield, Calif., 1997—2002. Mem.: Calif. Assn. for Counseling and Devel. (assoc.), Calif. Assn. for Postsecondary Edn. and Disability (CAPED) (assoc.), Nat. Rehab. Assn. (assoc.), Nat. Rehab. Counseling Assn. (assoc.), Chi Sigma Iota (assoc.; v.p., student club 1994—95), Phi Kappa Phi (life). Avocations: reading, travel. Office: Bakersfield Coll Support Svcs 1801 Panorama Dr Bakersfield CA 93305

KELLY, SISTER DOROTHY ANN, academic administrator; b. Bronx, NY, July 26, 1929; d. Walter David and Sarah (McCauley) K. BA in History, Coll. New Rochelle, 1951; MA in Am. Ch. History, Cath. U., Washington, 1958; PhD in Am. Intellectual History, U. Notre Dame, 1970; LittD (hon.), Mercy Coll., Dobbs Ferry, N.Y., 1976; LLD (hon.), Nazareth Coll. of Rochester, N.Y., 1979; DHL (hon.), Coll. St. Rose, 1981, Manhattan Coll., 1979, LeMoyne Coll., 1990, St. Thomas Aquinas Coll., 1990, St. Joseph Coll., Conn., 1996, Iona Coll., 1997. Joined Order of St. Ursula, Roman Cath. Ch., 1952. Assoc. prof. history Coll. New Rochelle, N.Y., 1957—, chmn. dept. history N.Y., 1965-67, acad. dean N.Y., 1967-72, acting pres. N.Y., 1970-71, pres. N.Y., 1972-97, chancellor N.Y., 1997—. Mem. Interreligious Coun. New Rochelle, 1974—, exec. com., 1974-79, v.p., 1980-84, pres., 1984-88, mem. Commn. Ind. Colls. and Univs. State of N.Y., 1976-78, chmn. bd. trustees, 1978-80, mem. govt. rels. com., 1980-81; chmn. Com. Higher Edn. Opportunity, 1976-78; mem. commr. of edn. Adv. Coun. on Higher Edn. for N.Y. State, 1975-77, subcom. on postsecondary occupational edn., 1975-77; exec. com. Empire State Found. Ind. Liberal Arts Colls., 1975—, vice chmn., 1977-81, chmn., 1981—; trustee, mem. exec. com. Assn. Colls. and Univs. State of N.Y., 1976-80; mem. com. on purpose and identity Assn. Cath. Colls. and Univs., 1975-80; mem. steering com. Neylan Conf., 1978-81, mem. bishops and pres. com., 1979-84; mem. adv. coun. on fin. aid to students Office Edn., HEW, 1978-86; chmn. Women's Coll. Coalition, 1981-83; chmn. govt. rels. adv. com. Nat. Assn. Ind. Colls. and Univs., 1981-82, chair, 1987-88. Chair City-wide Confs., New Rochelle, 1977-79; bd. dirs. United Way Westchester, 1977-84, mem. planning, allocations, evaluation com., 1977-80, nominating and campaign coms., 1990—; bd. dirs. Westchester County Assn., 1980-90, New Rochelle Community Action Program, 1982-83, New Rochelle Cmty. Fund, 1989-91; mem. steering com. Westchester County Women's Hall of Fame, 1984-85; bd. dirs. Vis. Nurse Svcs. in Westchester, Inc., 1983-86, chair nominating com., 1985-86; trustee LeMoyne Coll., 1982-88, vice chairperson, 1984-87; mem. bd. govs. New Rochelle Hosp. Med. Ctr., 1987—; trustee United Student Aid Funds, 1980-90, Ursuline Sch., New Rochelle, 1988—, Cath. U. Am., 1988—, Am. Coun. on Edn., 1990—, Ind. Coll. Fund Am., 1982-85; mem. ofcl. U.S. del. to UN 4th World Conf. on Women in Beijing, 1995; mem. nat. adv. bd. Nat. Mus. Women in the Arts, 1996—. Recipient Medallion award Westchester C.C., 1978, Leadership award Am. Soc. Pub. Adminstrn., 1986, Sch. Svc. award Thornton-Donovan

Sch., 1977, Henry D. Paley award, 1994, Father Theodore M. Hesburgh award, 1998, N.Y. State Gov.'s award for excellence, 1997; inducted into Westchester County/Avon Women's Hall of Fame, 1989; Paul Harris fellow, 1997. Mem. AAUP, AAUW, NCCJ (trustee 1989—), Am. Hist. Assn., Nat. Fedn. Bus. and Profl. Women, Am. Assn. Higher Edn., Nat. Assembly Women Religious, Am. Coun. Edn. (bd. dirs. 1990), Assn. Am. Colls. (bd. dirs. 1983-86), Tchrs. Ins. and Annuity Assn. Am. (trustee 1987—, fin. com. 1987-88, exec. com. 1988—, audit com. 1990—, products and svcs. com. 1990-91, nominating and pers. com. 1991), Assn. Colls. Mid-Hudson Area (pres. 1979-81, exec. com. 1982—).

KELLY, DOROTHY HELEN, pediatrician, educator; b. Fitchburg, Mass., July 29, 1944; BS in Nursing magna cum laude, Fitchburg State Co., 1966; BS with distinction, Wayne State U., 1968, MD with distinction, 1972. Diplomate Am. Bd. Pediatrics, Pediatric Pulmonology. Intern Children's Svc. Mass. Gen. Hosp., Boston, 1972-73, resident in pediatrics, 1973-75, fellow in pediatrics pulmonary medicine, 1976-79, co-dir. pediat. pulmonary lab., 1976—83, assoc. dir. pediatric pulmonary unit, 1983—95; teaching fellow Harvard Med. Sch., Boston, 1973-75, clin. fellow, 1972-75, instr. in pediatrics, 1975-81, asst. prof. pediatrics, 1981-89, assoc. prof. pediatrics, 1989-95, U. Tex., Galveston, 1995-97, Houston, 1995—; assoc. dir. S.W. SIDS Rsch. Inst. Meml. Herman S.W. Hosp., Houston, 1995—. Cons. Bur. Community Health Svcs., NEW, 1979-80, FDA, 1986, 88-92, ECRI, 1987-88, also others; chmn. apnea adv. com. Nat. Sudden Infant Death Syndrome Found., 1979-81; mem. com. anesthesiology and respiratory devices panel Ctr. for Devices and Radiol. Health, FDA, 1990-94; chmn. physicians' com. Nat. Assn. Apnea Profls., 1990-91, also others; reviewer numerous jours. in field. Contbr. numerous articles to profl. jours. Recipient Woman of Vision award Nat. Soc. for Prevention of Blindness, Mass. Affiliate, 1981, First Disting. Alumni award Fitchburg State Coll., 1984, grants in field. Mem. Am. Med. Woman's Assn., Am. Acad. Pediatrics (task force on prolonged apnea 1978), Am. Thoracic Soc., Internat. Pediatric Soc., Assn. for Psychophysiol. Study Sleep, Soc. for Pediatric Rsch., Tex. Thoracic Soc., Tex. Med. Assn., Tex. Pediatric Soc., Am. Autonomic Soc., Am. Assn. SIDS Prevention Physicians (bd. dirs., pres.-elect), NH Pediatric Soc. Office: North Country Pediatrics Littleton Regional Hosp Littleton NH 03561 Office Phone: 603-484-2803. E-mail: dhkelly@aap.net.

KELLY, GRACE DENTINO, secondary school educator; b. Peoria, Ill., Mar. 30, 1934; d. Michael and Arnita Balagna (Barto) Dentino; m. Robert N. Kelly, Aug. 31, 1957; children: Susan, James, Stephen, Patrick. Cert. med. tech., St. Francis Sch. Med. Tech., Peoria, Ill., 1955; BS, Bradley U., Peoria, Ill., 1971, MS, 1973. Tchr. sci. St. Mark Sch., Peoria, asst. prin., 1980-83, prin., 1992-98; prin., chmn. jr. HS curriculum com. for drug edn. St. Thomas Sch., Peoria Heights, Ill., 1983-89; tchr. biology and chemistry Woodruff HS, Peoria, 1989-90; prin. Blessed Sacrament Sch., Morton, Ill., 1991-92, Trewyn Mid. Sch., Peoria, 1998—2002, mem. math. curriculum com.; lead tchr. Glen Oak Primary Sch., Peoria, 2002—06; ret. Presenter Ill. Math Tchr. Conv., Peoria, 1992; tchr. Aurora U., Ill. Mem. adv. bd. Peoria Jour. Star Newspaper, 1973-80. Bd. dirs. Spl. People Encounter Christ, 1997. Recipient Econs. Educator award Joint Coun. on Econ. Edn., NYC, 1982—, dedication to excellence in edn. and to justice and equality award NOW, 1998, Esmark Found. award Ill. Coun. Econ. Edn., 1984, Those Who Excell award Ill. State Bd., 1989, PARC award, 1989, Today's Cath. Tchr.'s Project: Sharing award, 1992, Adminstr. of Yr. award Today's Cath. Tchr. Mag., 1992, Jean Tucker award Ill. Valley Mental Health Assn., 1994, Positive Promotions 1st prize Midwest Exceptional Tchr. award, 2005; named Tchr. Who Makes a Difference, Positive Promotions, 2004, 06; grantee Nat. City Bank, 2003-06. Mem. AAUW (Outstanding Cmty. Svc. award, Justice Edn. award 1998), Nat. Sci. Tchrs. Assn., Am. Soc. Clin. Pathologists, Ill. Sci. Tchrs. Assn. (dir. region III, presenter papers), Ill. Jr. Acad. Sci. (dir. region I), Phi Delta Kappa Roman Catholic. Home: 1815 W High St Peoria IL 61606-1635

KELLY, HOLLY ANDREA, federal agency administrator, director, real estate developer; b. Cin., Dec. 1, 1963; d. Jesse and Barbara (Byers) Robinson; children: Gretchen R., Kimberly B. BA, Xavier U., Cin., 1994; MPA, No. Ky. U., 1997. Cert. econ. devel. fin. profl., 1997. Mgr. residential svcs. Metro Mgmt., Inc., Cin., 1994-96; devel. officer City of Cin., 1996—98, econ. devel. specialist, 2001—04; dep. dir. U.S. Dept. Housing and Urban Devel., Washington, 2004—. Notary Pub., Ohio, 1995—. Mem. LWV, Am. Soc. Pub. Adminstrn. (bd. dirs.), Nat. Coun. Negro Women. Democrat. Baptist. Avocations: reading, photography. Office: US Dept Housing and Urban Devel 451 7th St SW Washington DC 20410

KELLY, JANICE HELEN, elementary school educator; b. Akron, Ohio, Nov. 28, 1951; d. Joe Ralph and Barbara Ann (Goins) Long; m. W. Gary Kelly, May 10, 1973; children: Benjamin, Chad. BS in Elem. Edn., Akron U., 1984; M in Edn., Kent State U., Ohio, 1994; EdD in Ednl. Leadership, Ashland U., Ohio, 2006—. Cert. elem. tchr., Ohio; nat. bd. cert. Mid. Child. Gen., 1999. Tchr. Suffield United C.C. Coop., Suffield, Ohio, 1984-86, Mogadore (Ohio) Local Schs., 1986—. Cadre mem. Summit County Tech. Acad., Cuyahoga Falls, Ohio, 1994; classroom tchr. SBC Ameritech, Kent State, Ohio, 2000, 2002. Mem., tchr. Randolph (Ohio) United Meth. Ch., 1973—. Recipient Outstanding Educator award Somers Elem. PTA, Mogadore, 1989, Crystal Apple award Plain Dealer, 2003; Eisenhower grantee Kent State U., 1990-92, Tech., Industry, Environ. Edn. grantee Gen Corp, 1993. Mem. ASCD, Ohio Edn. Assn., Mogadore Edn. Assn. (sec. 1990-92, v.p. 1995—, co-pres. 2001-03), Sci. Edn. Coun. Ohio. Avocations: doll-making/collecting, computer technology, golf, swimming. Home: 534 Hartville Rd Atwater OH 44201-9785 Office: Somers Elementary School 3600 Herbert St Mogadore OH 44260-1199 E-mail: teach534@hotmail.com.

KELLY, JEAN SLATTER, healthcare administrator, nurse; b. Marianna, Fla., Jan. 6, 1945; d. John M. and Macie L. (Pittman) Wright; m. Marion D. Kelly, Dec. 22, 1976; 1 child, Kerry C. Slatter. Diploma, Grady Meml. Hosp., Atlanta, 1965; BS in Health Edn., U. Ga., 1987; MS in Cmty. Health Adminstrn., Calif. Coll. Health Sci., 1997. RN; cert. mental health profl. and nursing staff devel. and continuing edn. Treatment coord. Ga. Regional Hosp., Decatur, 1977-79; sr. nurse in crisis stablzn. Gwinnett Mental Health Ctr., Lawrenceville, Ga., 1979-81; aging coord. Clayton County Mental Health Ctr., Riverdale, Ga., 1984-88; mental health program specialist Ga. Dept. Human Resources, Atlanta, 1988-92, program mgr. early intervention and infant followup, 1992-95, policy-program analyst early intervention/sch. health svcs., 1995—. Mem. Ga. State Nurses Assn. Home: 2577 Glenrock Dr Decatur GA 30032-5860 Office: 2 Peachtree St NW Fl 37 Atlanta GA 30303-3181

KELLY, JUDITH REESE, literature educator; d. David William Reese and Lorraine Spenst; children: Rin Christine, Caroline Marie Reese. BA with Honors, Colo. State U., Fort Collins, 1966—70; MA, U. Colo., Boulder, 1976—78. Tchr. French, English Lake Mid. Sch., Denver, 1970—72; tchr. English, newspaper advisor Alameda H.S., Lakewood, Colo.; instr. Red Rocks C.C., Arvada/Lakewood, 1998—99; tchr. honors English, humanities Columbine H.S., Littleton, 1986—; tchr. Shakespeare, English Arapahoe C.C. H.S., Littleton, 2004—05; tchr. French Colo. Acad., Denver, 2006—. Title i adminstr. El Paso County Pub. Schs., Colorado Springs, 1972; in-svc. instr. Colo. Writing Project, Boulder/Lakewood, 1977—78; tchr. focus group Denver Ctr. for Performing Arts, Denver, 1996—2006; colo. dir., shakespeare festival English Speaking Union, 1998—99; tchr./scholar NEH, Siena, Italy, 2003; adv. bd. Opera Colo., Denver; exhibitor Nat. Coun. Tchrs. of English, Denver, 2000; spkr. in field. Author: (magazine article) Colorado Homes and Lifestyles (Colo. Press Women award Winner, 1984); contbr. articles. Bd. Kim Robards Dance, Denver, 2000—05; bd. dirs. Colo. Shakespeare Festival Guild, 2006; grant writer intern Mus. Contemporary Art, Denver, 1999—2000; grant writer Museo de las Americas, Denver, 2005—06. Recipient Sophomore/Jr. Hon. Assns., Colo. State U., 1967—69, Outstanding Woman Student Colo. State U., AAUW, 1970, Mortar Bd. Nat. Honor Soc., 1970, Cmty. Svc. award, Nat. Assn. Poetry Therapists, 2002, Tchg. Excellence in Arts, Opera Colo., 2003, Romance Lang. Hon., Nat. Romance Lang. Assn., 1969—70, Colulmbine HS Colo. Tchr. of Yr., Jefferson County Schs., 2004; grantee Gifted and Talented Am. Humanities, 1999. Mem.: Alliance Francaise. Office Phone: 303-982-4460.

KELLY, KAREN DELORIS, addiction counselor, administrator; b. Cleve., Oct. 6, 1951; d. Lawrence Childs and Doris R. (Minter) Wilder; 1 child, Kendrick Lamar Kelly. BS, Park Coll., 1984; MS, Ctrl. Mich. U., 1988. Cert. addictions counselor. Pres., CEO Circle of Recovery, Inc., Decatur, Ga., 1982—; clin. dir. DHR/Atlanta West, 1986-87; program dir. DHR/McIntosh Trail Outpatient Substance Abuse Svcs., Griffin, Ga., 1987-90; statewide coord. State Bd. Pardons and Paroles, Atlanta, 1990-92; clin. dir. Cameron & Assocs., Atlanta, 1992-95; dir. addiction tech. transfer Ctr. More House Sch. of Medicine-Psychiatry, 1995—99. Aftercare coord., cons. The Bradford, Atlanta, 1987-91; cons. More House Sch. of Medicine, 1990-95, Dept. Ga. of Corrections, Atlanta, 1990—2004; faculty U. Ga., Athens, 1990—. Contbr. articles to profl. jours. Bd. dirs. Morris Brown Criminal Justice Coun., Atlanta, Changed Living, 1994, Promise of Hope, 2003; mem. Ray of Hope Christian Ch., Decatur, 1987—. Mem. Delta Sigma Theta. Avocations: outdoor activities, reading sports, theater, travel. Home: 6064 Valley Green Rd Lithonia GA 30058-3169 Office: PO Box 360515 Decatur GA 30036

KELLY, KATHLEEN, medical researcher; PhD, U. Calif., Irvine. Postdoctoral training Harvard Med. Sch.; independent investigator Nat. Cancer Inst., 1984—; chief Cell and Cancer Biology Br. Ctr. Cancer Rsch., Nat. Cancer Inst., head Signal Transduction Sect. Office: Nat Cancer Inst Bldg 37 Rm 1068 37 Convent Dr Bethesda MD 20892 Office Phone: 301-435-4651. Office Fax: 301-435-4655. E-mail: kkelly@helix.nih.gov.

KELLY, KATHLEEN S(UE), communications educator; b. Duluth, Minn., Aug. 6, 1943; d. Russell J. and Idun N. Mehrman; m. George F. Kelly, Apr. 29, 1961; children: Jodie A., Jennifer L. AA, Moorpark (Calif.) Coll., 1971; BS in Journalism, U. Md., College Park, 1973, MA in Pub. Rels., 1979, PhD in Pub. Communication, 1989. Accredited pub. rels.; cert. fundraising exec. Dir. pub. info. Bowie (Md.) State U., 1974-77; asst. to dean, instr. Coll. Journalism U. Md., College Park, 1977-79, assoc. dir. devel., 1979-82; v.p. Mt. Vernon Coll., Washington, 1982-83; dir. devel. U. Md., College Park, 1983-85, assoc. dean, lectr. Coll. Journalism, 1985-88, asst. dean Coll. Bus. and Mgmt., 1988-90; prof. U. La., Lafayette, 1991—2003; prof., chair dept. pub. rels. U. Fla., Gainesville, 2003—. Cons. NASA, NIH, Mt. St. Marys Coll., 1986—; lectr. CASE, Pub. Rels. Soc. Am., 1987—. Author: Fund Raising and Public Relations: A Critical Analysis, 1991, Building Fund-Raising Theory, 1994, Effective Fund-Raising Management, 1998. Named PRIDE Book award winner Speech Comm. Assn., 1991, article award winner 1994, John Grenzebach award winner for rsch. on philanthropy CASE and Am. Assn. Fund-Raising Coun., 1991, 98, PRIG award winner for outstanding dissertation Internat. Comm. Assn., 1990, winner 1995 Pathfinder award Inst. for Pub. Rels. Rsch. and Edn., Staley/Robeson/Ryan/St. Lawarence prize for rsch. on fund raising and philanthropy Nat. Soc. Fundraising Execs., 1998, Jackson, Jackson & Wagner Behavioral Sci. prize, Pub. Relations Soc. Am. Found., 1999. Fellow Pub. Rels. Soc. Am. (chmn. ednl. and cultural orgn. sect. 1989, pres. Md. chpt. 1986-87, Pres.' Cup 1981, nat. bd. dirs. 1994-96, Jackson Jackson and Wagner Behavioral Sci. prize 1999); mem. Nat. Soc. Fund Raising Execs. (mem. rsch. coun.), Coun. Advancement and Support of Edn. (women's forum 1983), Phi Kappa Phi. Democrat. Avocations: travel, reading. Office: U Fla Dept Pub Rels PO Box 118400 Gainesville FL 32611-8400 Office Phone: 352-392-9359. Business E-Mail: kskelly@jou.ufl.edu.

KELLY, LOVETA BROWN, elementary school educator; b. Greenville, S.C., Feb. 12, 1951; d. Grady Andrew and Alma Jean (Adams) Brown; m. James Franklin Kelly, Jan. 19, 1971; children: Colleen Loveta Eubanks, Sean James. BA Early Childhood Edn., U. S.C. Spartanburg, 1986, MA Elem. Edn., 1989. Cert. Early Childhood Edn. and Elem. Edn. S.C. Dept. Edn., 1986. Tchr. fifth grade Startex Elem. Sch., SC, 1986—97; tchr. sixth grade lang. arts and social studies Beech Springs Intermediate Sch., Duncan, SC, 1998—. Mem. com. for incentive pay for dist. 5 tchrs. Spartanburg Sch. Dist. 5, Duncan, 1989—92; mem. act 135 team Startex Elem. Sch., 1994—95; discussion leader Jr. Gt. Books, Duncan, 1990—. Tchr. Sun. sch. Taylors First Bapt. Ch., SC, 1978—91. Mem.: NEA, Soc. for Prevention Cruelty to Animals. D-Liberal. Lutheran. Avocations: reading, interior decorating, cocker spaniel owner. Home: 18 Thames Drive Taylors SC 29687 Office: Spartanburg School District 5 PO Box 800 Duncan SC 29334-0800 Personal E-mail: kellylb@spart5.k12.sc.us.

KELLY, LUCIE STIRM YOUNG, nursing educator; b. Stuttgart, Germany, May 2, 1925; came to U.S., 1929; d. Hugo Karl and Emilie Rosa (Engel) Stirm; m. J. Austin Young, Aug. 30, 1946 (div. Feb. 1971); m. Thomas Martin Kelly, 1972 (dec. Aug. 2003); 1 child by previous marriage, Gay Aleta (Mrs. Donald Meyer). BS, U. Pitts., 1947, MLitt, 1957, PhD, 1965; D in Nursing Edn. (hon.), U. RI, 1977; LHD (hon.), Georgetown U., 1983; DSc (hon.), Widener U., 1984; D of Pub. Svc. (hon.), Am. U., 1985; DSc (hon.), U. Mass., 1989; DHL (hon.), SUNY, 1996. Instr. nursing McKeesport (Pa.) Hosp., 1953-57, asst. adminstr. nursing, 1966-69; asst. prof. nursing U. Pitts., 1957-64, asst. dean, 1965; prof., chmn. nursing dept. Calif. State U., LA, 1969-72; co-project dir. curriculum rsch. Nat. League for Nursing, 1973-74; project dir. patient edn., office consumer health edn., also adj. assoc. prof. cmty. medicine Coll. Medicine and Dentistry N.J.-Rutgers Med. Sch., 1974-75; prof. pub. health and nursing Sch. Pub. Health and Sch. Nursing Columbia U., N.Y.C., 1975-90, prof. emeritus Sch Pub. Health, Sch. Nursing, 1990—, assoc. dean acad. affairs Sch. Pub. Health, 1988-90, hon. prof. nursing edn. Tchrs. Coll., 1977-93, acting head divsn. health adminstrn. Sch. Pub. Health, 1980-81, 86-88; on leave as exec. dir. Mid-Atlantic Regional Nursing Assn., 1981-82. Cons. U. Nev., Las Vegas, 1970-72, Ball State U., Ind., 1971, Long Beach (Calif.) Naval Hosp., 1971-72, Travis AFB, Calif., 1972, Brentwood VA Hosp., LA, 1971-72, Ctrl. Nursing Office VA, Washington, 1971-94, N.J. Dept. Higher Edn., 1974-78, John Wiley Pub., 1974-76, Sch. Nursing and Sch. Pub. Health Am. U. Beirut accreditation visit, 1978; mem. spl. med. adv. group VA Dept. Medicine and Surgery, Washington, 1980-84; cons. nursing com. AMA, 1971-74, Citizen's Com. for Children, N.Y.C.; v.p. Pa. Health Coun., 1968-69; mem. adv. com. physicians assts. Calif. Bd. Med. Examiners, adv. com. Cancer Soc. L.A., 1970-72, com. nursing VA, Washington, 1971-74, chair 1975-90, regional med. programs, Pa., 1967-69, Calif. 1970-72; mem. spl. adv. com. on med. licensure and profl. conduct N.Y. State Assembly, 1977-79, mem. nat. adv. com. Encore (nat. YWCA post-mastectomy group rehab. project), 1977-83; assoc. mem. N.Y. Acad. Medicine, 1988-90; mem. ethics com. Palisades Med. Ctr., 1993-05, bd. govs., 1995-05, mem. profl. and quality rev. com., 1995-05, chair, 1998-05, exec. com., 1998-99; 2d vice chair N.Y. Presbyn. Healthcare Sys., Palisades Med. Ctr., 1999-03, 1st vice chair 2003-05; lectr., cons., guest Beijing Med. Coll., China, 1982, Aga Khan U., Pakistan, 1990; bd. visitors U. Pitts. Sch. Nursing, 1986-93; mem. editl. adv. bd. Am. Jour. Pub. Health, 1992, chair, 1993-97; nat. and internat. lectr. in field; chair adv. com. grad. program in pub. health U. Medicine and Dentistry of N.J., 1995-00; vol. cert. mediator for Hudson County mcpl. cts., 2004-05. Author: (textbooks) The Nursing Experience: Trends, Challenges, Transitions, 4th edit., 2002, Dimensions of Profl. Nursing, 9th edit., 2003; contbg. editor: (jour.) Jour. Nursing Adminstrn., 1975—82; columnist: jour. Nursing Outlook, editor-in-chief, 1982—91; mem. bd. advisors (jour.) Nurses Almanac, 1978, Nurse Manager's Handbook, 1979, Nursing Administration Handbook, 1992; editor (editl. bd.): (jour.) Am. Health, 1981—91; editl. bd. (jour.) Nursing and Health Care, 1991—95, Internat. Nursing Index, 1997—2001. Bd. dirs. ARC, LA, 1971-72; bd. dirs. Vis. Nurse Svc. N.Y., 1980-01, mem. exec. com., chmn. human resources, 1989-01; bd. dirs. Concern for Dying, 1983-89; bd. trustees Calif. State Coll. LA Found., 1971-72, U. Pitts., 1984-90, mem. exec. com. 1988-90; chair bd. visitors U. Pitts. Sch. Pub. Health, 1988-90; bd. visitors U. Miami Sch. Nursing, 1986-05; mem. health svcs. com. Children's Aid Soc., N.Y., 1978-84; v.p. Am. Nurses Found., 1980-82; mem. nat. adv. coun. on nurse tng. HRA, 1981-85; mem. nurses leadership coun. Chlorine Chemistry Coun., 1999-03; hon. bd. dirs. NOVA Found., 1998—, Health Professions Panel, Am. Legacy Found., 2000—. Named Outstanding Alumna U. Pitts. Sch. Nursing, 1966, Pa. Nurse of Yr., 1967, Roll of Honor N.J. State Nurses Assn., 1990; named to Tchrs. Coll. Columbia U. Nursing Edn. Alumni Hall of Fame, 1999; recipient Disting. Alumna award U. Pitts. Sch. Edn., 1981, Shaw medal Boston Coll., 1985, Bicentennial Medallion of Distinction, U. Pitts., 1987, R. Louise McManus Medallion for Disting. Svc. to Nursing, Tchrs. Coll. Columbia U., 1987, Dean's Disting. Svc. award Columbia Sch. Pub. Health, 1995, Second Century award in health care, Columbia U. Sch. Nursing, 1996; fellow HEW, 1965. Fellow Am. Acad. Nursing (named Living Legend 2001); mem. ANA (dir. 1978-82, Hon. Recognition award 1992), APHA (Ruth Freeman Pub. Health Nursing award 1993), Pa. Nurses Assn. (pres. 1966-69), Nat. League Nursing (bd. govs. 1991-95), Nurses Ednl. Funds Bd., U . Pitts. Sch. Nursing Alumni (pres. 1959), Vis. Nurse Assn. Ctrl. Jersey (bd. dirs. 1999-2001, mem. bd. trustees), Am. Hosp. Assn. (com. chmn. 1967-68), Assn. Grad. Faculty Cmty. Health/Pub. Health Nursing (v.p. 1980-81), Sigma Theta Tau (sr. editor Image 1978-81, pres.-elect 1981-83, pres. 1983-85, nat. campaign chair Ctr. for Nursing Scholarship 1987-89, chair devel. com. 1989-95, spl. advisor 1995-97, planned giving task force 1998-2001, Mentor award 1985, 93, 97, Spirit of Philanthropy award 1997), Pi Lambda Theta, Alpha Tau Delta (Cert. of Merit 1968). Achievements include collection of papers in Mugar Library, Boston U.

KELLY, MARILYN, state supreme court justice; b. Apr. 15, 1938; m. Donald Newman. BA, Ea. Mich. U., 1960, JD (hon.); postgrad., U. Paris.; MA, Middlebury Coll., 1961; JD with honors, Wayne State U., 1971. Assoc. Dykema, Gossett, Spencer, Goodnow & Trigg, Detroit, 1973-78; ptnr. Dudley, Patterson, Maxwell, Smith & Kelly, Bloomfield Hills, Mich., 1978-80; owner Marilyn Kelly & Assocs., Bloomfield Hills, Birmingham, Mich., 1980-88; judge Mich. Ct. of Appeals, 1989-96; justice Mich. Supreme Ct., 1997—. Tchr. lang., lit. Grosse Pointe Pub. Schs., Albion Coll., Ea. Mich. U.; past mem. rep. assembly, comms. com., family law coun. Mich. State Bar; co-chair Open Justice Commn., 1999—; mem. governing bd. Nat. Consortium for Racial & Ethnic Fairness in Cts. Active Mich. Dem. Party, 1963—; former bd. dirs. Channel 56-Pub. TV, Detroit, Women's Survival Ctr., Pontiac; former mem. citizens advisory com. Detroit Public Schools, Wayne County Community Coll., Oakland County Community Coll. Recipient Disting Alumni award Ea. Mich. U., Disting. Svc. award Mich. Edn. Assn., Eleanor Roosevelt Humanities award State of Israel Bonds Atty. Div., 2003. Mem. Soc. Irish-Am. Lawyers, Women Lawyers Assn. (past pres.), Oakland County Bar Assn. (past chair family law com.), State Bar Mich. (Michael Franck award 2003); Fellow Mich. State Bar Found. Office: Mich Supreme Ct 3034 West Grand Blvd Detroit MI 48202*

KELLY, MARY, sculptor; b. Fort Dodge, Iowa, 1941; BA, Coll. St. Teresa, Minn., 1963; MA, Piux XII Inst., Florence, Italy, 1965; post grad. diploma, St. Martins Sch. Art, London, 1968—70. Visiting artist & fellow New Hall Coll., Cambridge U., England, 1985—86; dir. studios-Ind. Study Program Whitney Mus. Am. Art, NYC, 1989—96; prof.-interdisciplinary study UCLA. One-woman shows include Santa Monica Mus. Art, Calif., Generali Found., Vienna, New Mus. Contemporary Art, NY, Power Plant, Toronto, Can., Vancouver Art Gallery, Konstmuseet Malmö, Helsinki City Art Mus., Inst. Contemporary Art, London, Herbert F. Johnson Mus., Cornell U., LA Contemporary Exhbns., Riverside Studios, London, Mus. Modern Art, Oxford, exhibited in group shows at La. Mus. Modern Art, Denmark, UCLA Hammer Mus., Mus. Contemporary Art, LA, Bronx Mus., NYC, Tate Modern, London, Kunsthalle, Vienna, Art Gallery, ON, Carnegie Mus. Art, Whitney Biennial, Whitney Mus. Am. Art, 1991, 2004, Am. Century, 1999, Inst. Contemporary Art, Boston, Yale Ctr. British Art, 4th Biennial, Gallery Sydney New South Wales, Musee d'Art Moderne de la Ville de Paris, The Hague Gemeentemuseum; author: Imaging Desire, 1996, Mary Kelly, 1997, Post-Partum Document, 1998, Rereading Post-Partum Document, 1999. Visual Arts Fellowship, Nat. Endowment Arts, 1987. Mailing: c/o Postmasters Gallery 459 West 19th St New York NY 10011

KELLY, MARY KATHRYN, special education administrator; b. Garnett, Kans., Aug. 30, 1954; d. Calvin Ansley Borror and Barbara Jane Strain; m. Danny Reid Kelly, Aug. 14, 1976; children: Brendan S., Brianna L., Bryce D. B in Music Edn., U. Kans., Lawrence, 1976; MEd, Wichita State U., Kans., 1988, Ednl. Specialist, 1989. Music therapist Topeka Pub. Schs., 1977—78; tchr. Rainbows United, Wichita, Kans., 1978; music therapist Wichita Pub. Schs., Wichita, Kans., 1978—80, sch. psychologist, 1989; asst. dir. Heartspring, Wichita, Kans., 1998—2003; sch. psychologist Wichita Pub Schs., 2003—05; spl. edn. adminstr. Derby Pub. Schs., Kans., 2005—. Mem.: NASP, NCSP (cert.), Phi Kappa Phi.

KELLY, MAXINE ANN, retired property developer; b. Ft. Wayne, Ind., Aug. 14, 1931; d. Victor J. and Marguerite E. (Biebesheimer) Cramer; m. James Herbert Kelly, Oct. 4, 1968 (dec. Apr. 1974). BA, Northwestern U., 1956. Sec. Parry & Barns Law Offices, Ft. Wayne, 1951—52, Lincoln Nat. Bank and Trust Co., 1956—58; sr. clk. stenographer divsn. Mental Health Alaska Dept. Health, Anchorage, 1958—60; office mgr. Langdon Psychiat. Clinic, 1960—70; propr. A-1 Bookkeeping Svc., 1974—75; ptnr. Gonder-Kelly Enterprises and A-is-A Constrn., Wasilla, Alaska, 1965—92; sales assoc. Yukon Realty/Gallery of Homes, Wasilla, 1989; sec. Rogers Realty, Inc., Wasilla, 1989, MMC Constrn., Inc., 1992—96. Pres., treas. Libertarian Party, Anchorage, 1968—69, Alaska Libertarian Party, 1969—70; dir. Alaska Mental Health Assn., Anchorage, 1960—61. Mem.: AAUW (life), Whittier Boat Owners Assn. (treas. 1980—84), Anchorage C. of C. Home: 8653 Augusta Cir Anchorage AK 99504-4202

KELLY, MOIRA, actress; b. Queens, NY, Mar. 6, 1968; Student, Marymount Coll. Appeared in films The Boy Who Cried Bitch, 1991, Billy Bathgate, 1991, The Cutting Edge, 1992, Mr. Saturday Night, 1992, Chaplin, 1992, Twin Peaks: Fire Walk With Me, 1992, With Honors, 1994, Little Odessa, 1994, The Tie That Binds, 1995, (voice) The Lion King, 1994, Unhook the Stars, 1996, Entertaining Angels: The Dorothy Day Story, 1996, Changing Habits, 1997, Drive, She Said, 1997, Love Walked In, 1998, Dangerous Beauty, 1998, Hi-Life, 1998, Henry Hill, 1999, The Safety of Objects, 2001, (voice) The Lion King 1 1/2, 2004; TV movies include Monday After the Miracle, 1998; television appearances include (movies) Love Lies and Murder, 1991, Daybreak, 1993, To Have and To Hold, 1998, (series) The West Wing, 1999-2000. Office: care Gersh Agy 232 N Canon Dr Beverly Hills CA 90210-5302

KELLY, NANCY FOLDEN, art association administrator; b. Fredericksburg, Va., Oct. 28, 1951; d. Virgil Alvis Jr. and Frances Virginia (DeShazo) Folden; m. Frank R. Kelly, Aug. 11, 1973; 1 child, Katherine Elizabeth Kelly. BA in Theatre Arts, Va. Poly. Inst. and State U., 1973; MFA in Theatre Directing, So. Meth. U., 1975. Coord. student programs Lincoln Ctr. Inst., NYC, 1976-79; dir. NYC Opera Nat. Co. and edn. dept. Lincoln Ctr., 1979-93, mem. coun. on ednl. programs, 1979-93; mng. dir. Broadway Arts Theatre Young Audiences, NYC, 1994-96; dir. family and cmty. programs Ctrl. Park Conservancy, NYC, 1996-98; fin. mgr., assoc. dir. devel. Film Soc. Lincoln Ctr., NYC, 1999—2005, dir ops., 2006—. Office Phone: 212-875-5208. E-mail: nkelly@filmlinc.com.

KELLY, NANCY FRIEDA WOLICKI, lawyer; b. Chgo., Sept. 8, 1953; d. Samuel and Ingrid (Rappel) W. BA in Journalism and Sociology, U. Ariz., 1974, JD, 1977. Bar: Ariz. 1977. Law clk. Ariz. Ct. Appeals, 1977-78; legis. asst. fgn. policy and armed svcs. health, staff atty. Billy Carter investigation to U.S. Sen. Dennis DeConcini, 1979-81; staff dir. Senate Subcom. on Alcoholism and Drug Abuse, Washington, 1981-84; mem. staff Senator Gordon J. Humphrey, Washington, 1984-87; coord. adv. com. Voluntary Fgn. U.S. Aid, 1987; sr. analyst legal and drug related issues president's Commn. on the HIV Epidemic, 1987-88; sr. policy analyst Commn. Exec. Legis. Jud. Salaries, 1988-89; counselor Sec. Energy, 1989-93; v.p. Kelly, Anderson & Assocs., Alexandria, Va., 1993—. Recipient William Spaid Meml. award U. Ariz. Coll. Law, 1977, Senate commendation for Billy Carter investigation,

1980. Mem. Ariz. Bar Assn., Phi Kappa Phi. Jewish. Office: 424 N Washington St Alexandria VA 22314-2312 Home: 1290 Beresford Ct Mc Lean VA 22101-2426 Office Phone: 703-518-8828. Business E-Mail: nancy.kelly@kapa.net.

KELLY, PAMELA B., lawyer; BA, U. Va., 1981; JD, UCLA, 1986. Bar: Calif. 1986. With Latham & Watkins, L.A., 1986—, ptnr., 1994—. Mem.: ABA (bus. law sect.), L.A. County Bar Assn., Calif. Bar Assn.

KELLY, PATRICIA BEYER, personal trainer; b. Torrington, Conn., Mar. 23, 1955; BS, Springfield Coll., Mass., 1977. Cert. Nat. Athletic Trainers Assn. Head athletic trainer, asst. athletic dir. Cushing Acad., Ashburnham, Mass., 1977—86; head athletic trainer Hotchkiss Sch., Lakeville, Conn., 1986—. Address: PO Box 800 Lakeville CT 06039-0800

KELLY, RUTH, state agency administrator; b. Mt. Vernon, N.Y. d. John Edwin and Ruth Elizabeth (Brady) Dowling; m. Paul Joseph Kelly Jr., June 27, 1964; children: Johanna, Paul Edwin, Thomas Martin, Christopher Mark, Heather Marie. BA, Seton Hall Coll., 1962; MA, Duke U., 1964. Assoc. tech. staff Bell Labs., N.Y., 1964-65; office mgr. Santa Fe Mountain Ctr., N.M., 1989-91, A.G. Edwards & Sons, Santa Fe, N.M., 1992-94; dir. Bds. and Commns. Office Gov., Santa Fe, 1995—. Chmn. Roswell Pub. Libr., N.M., 1975-76. Mem. bd. of Zia, Girl Scout Coun., Artesia, N.M., 1980; treas. Republican Party Santa Fe Co., 1993-94. Recipient Trustee of Yr. award, N.M. Libr. Assn., 1977. Mem. Federated Republican Women of Santa Fe. Avocations: reading, aerobics, golf, skiing. Office: Office of Gov State Capitol Bldg 400 Santa Fe NM 87503-0001

KELLY, SUE W., congresswoman; b. Lima, Ohio, Sept. 26, 1936; m. Edward W. Kelly; 4 children. BA in Botany and Bacteriology, Denison U., Granville, Ohio, 1958; MA in Health Advocacy, Sarah Lawrence Coll., Bronxville, NY, 1985. Biomedical rschr. Boston City Hosp., New Eng. Inst. Med. Rsch., 1958; tchr. sci. and math. John Jay Jr. HS, 1962-63, Harvey Sch.; real estate rehabilitator, 1963; campaign coord. Staff of US Rep. Hamilton Fish from NY, 1971-72; intern Ruth Taylor Home, 1973-74; florist, owner Somerstown Flower Shop, 1978-79; patient advocate emergency room St. Luke's Hosp., NY, 1984-87; adj. prof. grad. prog. health advocacy Sarah Lawrence Coll., 1987-92; mem. US Congress from 19th NY dist., 1995—. Vice chmn. com. fin. svcs. U.S. Ho. Reps.; mem. transp. and infrastructure com. US Congress; mem. com. small bus. U.S. Ho. Reps.; chair fin. svcs. oversight and investigations subcommittee US Congress, founder Congl. anti-terrorist financing task force. Recipient Guardian of Seniors' Rights award, Hero of the Taxpayer award, Guardian of Small Bus. award, Nat. Fed. Ind. Bus., Friend of the Farm award, Am. Farm Bur., Sgt. Charles Valenti Legislator of Yr. award, Enlisted Assn. of NY Nat. Guard, Nat. Health Care Humanitarian award, Patient Adv. Found., 1999, Friend of the Nat. Pks. award, Nat. Pks. Conservation Assn., 2005. Republican. Presbyterian. Office: US House Reps 2182 Rayburn House Office Bldg Washington DC 20515 Office Phone: 202-225-5441.*

KELLY, SUEDEEN G., commissioner; b. 1951; BA, U. Rochester; JD, Cornell U. Bar: DC 1976, N.Mex. With Leubben, Hughes & Kelly, N.Mex.; atty. Office of Atty. Gen., N.Mex.; chair N.Mex. Pub. Svc. Commn.; legis. aide to U.S. Senator Jeff Bingaman, 1999; counsel to Calif. Independent Sys. Operator, 2000; with Modrall, Sperling, Roehl, Harris & Sisk, Albuquerque, 2000—03; commr. Fed. Energy Regulatory Commn., Washington, 2003—. Office: Fed Energy Regulatory Commn 888 First St NE Washington DC 20426*

KELLY, SUSAN, writer, educator; b. N.Y.C., Apr. 10, 1949; d. William Howard and Constance Meta Kelly. BA hons. in English, U. Mass., Boston, 1970; MA, Boston Coll., Boston, 1971; PhD, U. Edinburgh, Scotland, 1975. Lectr. in English Tufts U., Medford, Mass., 1978—82; assoc. mgmt. comm. Harvard Bus. Sch., 1982—87; workshop leader Simmons Coll. New Eng. Writers workshop, Boston, 1987—93; vis. asst. prof. literary journalism Hampshire Coll., Amherst, 2003—. Cons. Mass. Criminal Justice Tng. Coun., Boston, 1985. Author: (novels) The Gemini Man, 1985, The Summertime Soldiers, 1986, Trail of the Dragon, Until Proven Innocent, 1990, And Soon I'll Come to Kill You, 1991, Out of the Darkness, (non-fiction) The Boston Stranglers, (short stories) Blue Curacao, The Healer, 1990; contbr. articles to profl. jour. Lectr. in report writing Cambridge Police Acad., Cambridge, Mass., 1983—84; trip leader Appalachian Mountain Club, Andover, Mass., 1997—2001. Business E-Mail: skelly@hampshire.edu.

KELM, BONNIE G., art museum director, educator, art appraiser, consultant; b. Bklyn., Mar. 29, 1947; d. Julius and Anita (Baron) Steiman; m. William G. Malis; 1 child, Michael Darren. BS in Art Edn., Buffalo State U., 1968; MA in Art History, Bowling Green (Ohio) State U., 1975; PhD in Arts Adminstrn., Ohio State U., 1987. Art tchr. Toledo Pub. Schs., 1968—71; ednl. cons. Columbus (Ohio) Mus. Art, 1976—81; prof. art Franklin U., Columbus, 1976—88; legis. coord. Ohio Ho. of Reps., Columbus, 1977; pres. bd. trustees Columbus Inst. for Contemporary Art, 1977—81; tech. asst. cons. Ohio Arts Coun., Columbus, 1984—88; dir. Bunte Gallery Franklin U., Columbus, 1978—88; dir. art mus. Miami U., Oxford, Ohio, 1988—96, assoc. prof., 1988—96; dir. Muscarelle Mus. of Art Coll. William and Mary, Williamsburg, Va., 1996—2002, assoc. prof. art and art history, 1996—2002; dir. Univ. Art Mus. U. Calif., Santa Barbara, 2002—06. Adj. prof. dept. art history U. Art Mus. U. Calif., Santa Barbara; grant panelist Ohio Arts Coun., Columbus, 1985—87, Columbus, 1991—95, 2006—; art book reviewer William C. Brown Pub., Madison, Wis., 1985—92; mem. acquisitions adv. bd. Martin Luther King Ctr., Columbus, 1987—88; field reviewer Inst. Mus. Svcs., Washington, 1990—; chair grant panel Art in Pub. Places, 1992—95; trustee Ohio Mus. Assn., 1993—96; adv. bd. Women Beyond Borders, 2004—; state apptd. mem. adv. com. Ohio Percent for Art, 1994—96; spkr., presenter in field. Author, editor (mus. catalogues) Connections, 1985, Into the Mainstream: Contemporary Folk Art, 1991, Testimony of Images: PreColumbian Art, 1992, Collecting by Design: The Allen Collection, 1994, Photographs by Barbara Hershey: A Retrospective, 1995, Georgia O'Keeffe in Williamsburg, 2001; contbr. chpt. to books, articles to profl. jours. Founding mem., mem. adv. coun. Columbus Cultural Arts Ctr., 1977-81; coord., curator Cultural Exch. Program, Honolulu-Columbus, 1980; mem. acad. women achievers YWCA, 1991—; mem. adv. bd. Women beyond Borders, 2004—. Recipient Marantz Disting. Scholar award Ohio State U., 1995, Gelpe award YWCA, 1987, Cultural Advancement of City of Columbus award, The Columbus Dispatch, 1984, Disting. Svc. award, Columbus Art League, 1984, Critic's Choice award Found. for Cmty. of Artists, N.Y., 1981; Fulbright scholar USIA, 1988 (The Netherlands); NEH fellow East-West Ctr., Honolulu, 1991. Mem. Am. Assn. Mus. (advocacy task force, surveyor mus. assessment program 1996—, nat. program com. 2001), Assn. Coll. and Univ. Mus. and Galleries (bd. dirs. 1998-2006), Western Mus. Assn., Fulbright Assn., Coll. Art Assn. (session chair, mus. com. 2004—), Internat. Coun. Mus., Calif. Assn. Mus Office Phone: 805-815-5198. E-mail: bgkelm@wavecable.com.

KELMAN, MARYBETH, retired health care consultant, health policy analyst; AS in Nursing, Rutgers U., 1964; BA, Douglas Coll., 1977; MA, Rutgers U., 1988. Program dir. health promotion N.J. Hosp. Assn., Princeton, NJ, 1983-87; policy analyst N.J. Dept. Human Svcs., Trenton, NJ, 1988-89; exec. dir. Eye Screening Coord. Coun. N.J., Inc., Monmouth Junction, NJ, 1989-91; health care cons. N.J. Divsn. Pensions and Benefits, Trenton, 1992—2004; ret., 2004. Trustee Forums Inst. for Pub. Policy, Princeton, 1998—, chmn., 1998—2005. Home: 1500 Sawyer Ave Manasquan NJ 08736 Personal E-mail: mbkelman@verizon.net.

KELSEY, CHRISTINE J., innkeeper, chef; b. Bennington, Vt., Nov. 4, 1948; d. Carl and Leanette Hart; m. Steven Kelsey; 2 children. Student, Fishes Jr. Coll., Hyde Park Culinary Sch., NY. Recreational therapist Great Barrington Healthcare, Great Barrington, Mass., 1975—95; innkeeper, chef Our Inn, Housatonic, 1987—. Former Brownie leader Girl Scouts USA; former den leader Boy Scouts Am. Mem.: Stockbridge C. of C., So. Berkshire C. of C., So. Berkshire Assn., Berkshire Lodgings Assn. Avocations: gardening, cooking, golf, baking. Home: 325 N Plain Rd Housatonic MA 01236 E-mail: innkeepers@christinesinn.com.

KELSEY, EDITH JEANINE, psychotherapist, consultant; b. Freeport, Ill., Oct. 15, 1937; d. John Melvin and Florence Lucille (Ewald) Anderson; divorced; children: Steven Craig, Kevin John. Student, Pasadena Coll., 1955-58; BA in Psychology, Calif. State U., San Jose, 1980; MA in Counseling Psychology, Santa Clara U., 1984. Lic. marriage, family and child counselor. Counselor, cons., cert. trainer Values Tech., Santa Cruz, Calif., 1981—, dir. research, 1982-84; intern in counseling Sr. Residential Services, San Jose, 1983-84; psychotherapist Process Therapy Inst., Los Gatos, Calif., 1983-86, Sexual Abuse Treatment Ctr., San Jose, 1984-87. Cons. in field, Santa Clara Valley, 1982-89; trainer, cons. Omega Assoc., 1987-92; teaching asst. Santa Clara U., 1994-98, supr. interns counseling high-risk students, 1997—; pvt. practice psychotherapy, cons., tng., 1986—. Contbr. articles to profl. jours. Vol. Parental Stress Hotline, Palo Alto, Calif., 1980-85. Mem. Am. Assn. Marriage and Family Therapists, Calif. Assn. Marriage and Family Therapists (clin.), Palo Alto C. of C. Democrat. Presbyterian. Avocations: skiing, hiking. Home: 431 Casita Ct Los Altos CA 94022-1774 Office: PO Box 61125 Palo Alto CA 94306-6125 Office Phone: 650-329-8223. Personal E-mail: jeanine@earthlink.net.

KELSEY, NORMA L., labor union administrator; b. Independence, Kans., Sept. 19, 1935; d. James Harrison Arnold and Mary Louise Harshman; m. Alfred J. Jones, Dec. 22, 1951 (div. Oct. 1961); m. Robert A. Kelsey, Oct. 18, 1961; children: Jack, Cathryn, James, David; stepchildren: Robert Jr., Larry Krepelka, Karen Metcalf; foster children: Patrick and Vernor Williams. Student, Am. River Coll., 1965-70. Sec. OPEIU #29, Sacramento, Calif., 1961-80, OPEIU #8, Seattle, Wash., 1980—. Bd. dirs., v.p. El Centro de la Raza, Seattle, 1986-98. Mem. Mensa (SIGHT coord. 1982-92), King County Union Retirees Coun. (pres. 1998—), King County Labor Coun. (trustee, exec. bd. 1997—), Office and Profl. Employees (sec.-treas. local #8 1985-89, pres. 1989—). Democrat. Avocations: travel, labor union activities. Home: 22316 11th Ave S Des Moines WA 98198-6923 Office: OPEIU #8 2800 1st Ave Seattle WA 98121-1182

KELSO, CHARLOTTE ELIZABETH, elementary school educator, health and physical education specialist; d. James Edward and Charlotte Anne Kelso. BS, Appalachian State U., Boone, N.C., 1979; MA, Tenn. Tech U., Cookeville, 1980. Cert. tchr. Va., 1984, athletic trainer NATABOC, 1984. Head women's basketball/prof. So. Ark. Unversity, El Dorado, 1980—82; math instr./athletic trainer/coach Richmond County H.S., Rockingham, NC, 1982—84; elem. phys. edn. specialist Roanoke City Schs., Va., 1984—89; head atletic trainer/prof. Mt. Olive Coll., Mount Olive, NC, 1989—90; head athletic trainer/prof. Morgan State U., Balt., 1990—96; health/phys. edn. specialist Swanson Mid. Sch., Arlington, Va., 1996—. Fire instr. Prince William County Fire Programs, Nokesville, Va., 1997; adj. instr. Va. Dept. of Fire Programs, Richmond, 1986; coach Roanoke Stars, Roanoke, Va., 1985—90; basketball coach Swanson Mid. Sch., Arlington, Va., 1999. Vol. fire fighter Evergreen Fire Dept., Evergreen, Va., 1997, Clearbrook Fire Dept., Roanoke, Va., 1985—89. Named Fire Fighter of the Yr., Clearbrook Vol. Fire and Rescue, 1996. Mem.: NEA., NATA, Va. Assn. Health Phys. Edn. Recreation and Dance (bd. dirs. 1997, v.p. 2003—06, Recreation Profl. of Year 2006). Avocations: travel, golf, flying.

KELSO, LINDA YAYOI, lawyer; b. Boulder, Colo., 1946; d. Nobutaka and Tai Ike; m. William Alton Kelso, 1968. BA, Stanford U., 1968; MA, U. Wis., 1973; JD, U. Fla., 1979. Bar: Fla. 1980. Assoc. Mahoney, Hadlow & Adams, Jacksonville, Fla., 1979-82, Commander, Legler, Werber, Dawes, Sadler & Howell, Jacksonville, 1982-86, ptnr., 1986-91, Foley & Lardner, L.L.P., Jacksonville, 1992—. Mem. ABA (bus. law sect.), Jacksonville Bar Assn., Phi Beta Kappa, Order of Coif. Avocations: music, gardening, cooking. Office: Foley & Lardner LLP PO Box 240 Jacksonville FL 32201-0240 Office Phone: 904-359-2000. E-mail: lkelso@foley.com.

KELTY, MIRIAM CAROL, psychologist, health science administrator; b. N.Y.C., Nov. 4, 1938; d. Charles and Lillian (Pomerantz) Friedman; m. Edward John Kelty, Nov. 6, 1966; children: Joel Paul, Ruth Ann Student, U. Paris, 1957—58, Antioch Coll., Yellowsprings, Ohio, 1955—58; BA, CCNY, 1960, MA, 1962; PhD, Rutgers U., 1965. Lic. psychologist, D.C. Lectr. CCNY, 1962—65; psychologist VA Med. Ctr., Boston, 1966—68, NIMH, Bethesda, Md., 1968—70; adminstrv. officer head sci. affairs APA, Washington, 1970—74; psychologist Nat. Commn. Protection of Human Subjects of Biomed. and Behavioral Rsch., Bethesda, 1974—78; exec. sec. human devel. Rsch. Grants divsn. NIH, Bethesda, 1978—81, asst. chief referral and rev. Rsch. Grants divsn., 1981—86; assoc. dir. extramural affairs Nat. Inst. on Aging, Bethesda, 1986—. Rsch. assoc. Sch. Pub. Health Harvard U., Boston, 1966-68; mem. social scis. and population study sect. NIH, Bethesda, 1975-78; sci. advisor Assn. for Advancement of Psychology, Washington, 1984-86 Assoc. editor Am. Psychologist, 1970-74; contbr. articles to profl. publs Bd. dirs. World Future Soc., Washington, 1968-75, Bannockburn Swimmers Club, Bethesda, 1984-90 Predoctoral fellow Pub. Health Svc., NIMH, 1962-65, postdoctoral fellow, 1965-66 Fellow AAAS (sec. nominating com.), APA (sec. fellow com. Health Psychology divsn. 1984-90, Career Contbns. award 1999, pres. Psychologists in Pub. Svc. divsn. 1982, exec. com. 1976-83, awards com., fellowship com., pres. Population and Environ. Psychology divsn. 1979) Avocations: swimming, tennis, travel. Office: Nat Inst on Aging 7201 Wisconsin Ave Rm 218 Bethesda MD 20814-4810

KEM, KATHERINE FRANCES, urban planner; b. Raleigh, N.C., Apr. 2, 1958; d. Winfield Thomas and Iris Elaine (Pearce) Fisher; m. William Earl Baker Jr., July 7, 1979 (div. Dec. 1996); children: Ryan Thomas, Heather Nicole; m. Jackie David Kem, Jan. 10, 1997. BBA, U. Tex., 1982; MPA, Troy State U., Germany, 1988. Tax preparer H&R Block, Lubbock, Tex. and Fayetteville, N.C., 1990-93, 96; Protestant music dir. 425 Air Base Squadron, Izmir, Turkey, 1994-95, dependent schs. officer, 1994-95; clk. Cumberland County Planning, Fayetteville, 1996; planner City of Fayetteville, 1996—2001. Pres. Hardwick Elem. Sch. P.T.A., Lubbock, Tex., 1992-93; Bible drill tchr. Shadow Hills Bapt. Ch., Lubbock, 1992-93; bn. coord. Family Support Group, 319th Mi, Ft. Bragg, N.C., 1997; music dir. LaGrange Park Bapt. Ch., Fayetteville, 1995—. Recipient Comdr.'s award for pub. svc. Dept. of Army, 1997. Mem. Internat. Cake Exploration Soc., Am. Planners Assn., N.C. Am. Planners Assn. Republican. Baptist. Avocations: cake decorating, cross stitching, reading, skiing. Office: City of Fayetteville 433 Hay St Fayetteville NC 28301-5537

KEMENY, M. MARGARET, oncologist, surgeon, educator, hospital administrator; b. Elizabeth, NJ, May 7, 1946; d. George Kemeny and Ellen Sagi. BS, Harvard U., 1968; MD, Columbia U., 1972. Dir. cancer ctr. Queens Cancer Ctr., N.Y.C., 2001—; divsn. chief surg. oncology SUNY Stony Brook. Prof. surgery Mt. Sinai Sch. Medicine, 2005—. Editor: Jour. Clin. Oncology. Fellow: ACS (bd. govs., vice chair bd. govs.); mem.: Assn. Women Surgeons (pres.). Home: 36 Perry St New York NY 10014 Office: Queens Cancer Ctr at Queens Hosp 82-68 164th St Jamaica NY 11432 Office Phone: 718-883-4031. Business E-Mail: kemenym@nychhc.org.

KEMMERER, SHARON JEAN, computer systems analyst; b. Sellersville, Pa., Apr. 11, 1956; d. John Musselman and Esther Jone (Landis) K. BS, Shippensburg U., 1978; MBA, Marymount U., 1982. Mgmt. analyst Navy Internat. Logistics, Phila., 1978-81; computer systems analyst Navy Supply Sys. Commn., Crystal City, Va., 1981-86, Nat. Inst. Stds. and Tech., Gaithersburg, Md., 1986—. Adult tutor, 1991-95; mem. diversity bd. Nat. Inst. Stds. and Tech., 1997-2000. Contbr. articles, poetry to newspapers; author publs. Moderator Lung Assn., Fairfax, Va., 1986; vol. Project Heart, Washington, 1986—87, Montgomery County Health Buddy, 1988—99, Stepping Stones Shelter for Homeless, 1989—91, Pets on Wheels, 1994—96, Avon 3 Day Breast Cancer 60 mile walk, 2000; cmty. family selection Habitat for Humanity, Montgomery County, 2003—04, bd. dirs., 2004—, exec. com., 2004—; vol. Burgundy Crest Vols., 2002—; dir. Global Village Mission trips Habitat For Humanity Internat., 2003—; mem. Global Village Mission Trips, 2000—04; mission trips Luthern Disaster Relief, 2005—; deacon Alexandria Ch., Va., 1985—86, v.p. coun., 1985, ch. coun., 1995—2001, band mem., 2003—; mem. adv. bd. to dean of edn. and human resources Shippensburg U., 2002—. Named to, Souderton Area H.S. Hall of Fame, 2005. Lutheran. Avocations: renovation, antiques, volleyball, power walking. Office: Nat Inst Stds and Tech Mfg Engring Lab Gaithersburg MD 20899-8260

KEMNITZ, D'ARCY, lawyer, gay lesbian association executive; b. Madison, Wis., 1963; BA, Univ. Wis., Madison; JD, Hamline Univ., St. Paul. Bar: Md. 1999. Exec. dir. Nat. Lesbian & Gay Law Assn., Washington, 2004—. Vol. fund-raiser Nat. Lesbian and Gay Legal Assn., Washington, 2000, GAY-LAW, Gay, Lesbian, Bisexual, Transgender Attys. of Washington. Office: Nat Lesbian & Gay Law Assn Ste 1170 S 601 13th St NW Washington DC 20005-3823 Office Phone: 202-637-6384.

KEMP, ANN, retired librarian; b. Providence, Ky., Aug. 2, 1941; d. Charlie and Rubye (Sigler) Kemp Page. BA, Belmont U., 1964; MLS, Vanderbilt U., 1965, postgrad., 1968-79. Cert. tchr. Ky. Libr. Nashville (Tenn.) Pub. Libr., 1965, U. Louisville Libr., 1965-67, Dawson Springs (Ky.) Ind. Schs., 1967-93; instr. Murray (Ky.) State U., 1973-78. Author: Poem, The ABC's of Parthenon. Mem.: DAR, Ky. Libr. Assoc., Ky. Edn. Assoc., Nat. Edn. Assoc., The Parthenon Patrons. Baptist. Avocations: studying architecture and folklore, poetry. Home: 703 S Clinton St Athens AL 35611

KEMP, DONNA RENEE, public administration educator, public policy educator, academic administrator; b. Idaho Falls, Idaho, Apr. 12, 1945; d. Glen E. and Maybel A. (Smith) Kemp; m. Geoffrey K. Guss, Apr. 11, 1970 (div.); 1 child, April R. Kemp Guss. Student Chapman Coll., 1963—65; BA cum laude in Polit. Sci., Coll. Idaho, 1967; MA, U. Oreg., 1970; MPA, U. Idaho, 1977; MEd, Coll. Idaho, 1978; PhD, U. Idaho, 1978. LCSW Idaho, 1982, lic. counselor Idaho, 1984. Dir. vol. services, coord. foster grandparents program Idaho State Sch. and Hosp., Dept. Health and Welfare, Nampa, 1971—75; planner Exec. Office of Gov. Div. Budget and Policy Planning, Boise, 1975; program mgr. Idaho Office Energy, Boise, 1978—80; prin. planner Idaho Dept. Health and Welfare, Boise, 1980; assoc. prof. polit. sci., coord. govt. and pub. svc. program Winthrop Coll., Rock Hill, SC, 1980—81; prof. pub. policy and adminstrn., coord. healthcare mgmt. program Calif. State Coll., Bakersfield, 1981—85; prof. pub. adminstrn. and polit. sci., advisor, coord. Calif. State U., Chico, 1985—. Adj. prof. Coll. Idaho, Caldwell, 1970—72, Boise State U., 1972—80; cons. in field, 1976—. Contbr. articles to profl. jours. Counselor Haven Counseling Ctr., Bakersfield, 1982—85. Recipient Affirmative Action Faculty Devel. program award, Calif. State U. Sys., 1983; Whittenberger fellow, U. Idaho, 1977, Stillinger scholar, 1976. Mem.: Am. Mental Health Counselors Assn., Am. Personnel and Guidance Assn., Am. Pub. Health Assn., Am. Polit. Sci. Assn., Am. Soc. Pub. Adminstrn., LWV, ACLU, NOW, Sierra Club. Office: Calif State Coll Dept Pub Policy Admins Bakersfield CA 93309

KEMP, LORI ANN, elementary school educator; b. Bad Axe, Mich., Sept. 20, 1979; d. James Ronald and Judy Kay Brown; m. John Edward Kemp, July 31, 2004. BA, Hope Coll., Holland, Mich., 2002; MA, Marygrove Coll., Detroit, 2005. Cert. elem. tchr. Tchr. Cass City Pub. Schs., Mich., 2002—. Mem.: AAUW (treas. Cass City br. 2004—). Lutheran. Avocations: travel, scrapbooks. Home: 10900 Sebewaing Rd Sebewaing MI 48759 Office: Campbell Elem 6627 Rose St Cass City MI 48726

KEMP, NANCY MARTIN, history educator; b. Memphis, Oct. 5, 1956; d. Maynard Austin and Joy (Lomax) Martin; m. Van Kemp, Oct. 14, 1994; children from previous marriage: Robert C. Brown, Andy Brown. BS, U. Tenn., Martin, 1997; MA Curriculum, Austin Peay U., Clarksville, Tenn., 1998. Cert. tchr. Tenn. Editor News Dem., Waverly, Tenn., 1980—85; dir. comm. Mid. Tenn. Electric, Centerville, 1985—86; tchr. Humphreys County Schs., Waverly, 1988—89, Crockett County Schs., Alcone, Tenn., 1989—91, Houston County Schs., Erin, Tenn., 1991—92, Benton County Schs., Camden, Tenn., 1992—93, Williamson County Schs., Franklin, Tenn., 1996—. Freelance insvc. cons., 2000—. Contbr. articles to Tennessean Newspaper. Named Tchr. of Week, Fox News Nashville, 2004. Mem.: NEA. Democrat. Methodist. Office: Centennial HS 5050 Malbry Ln Franklin TN 37067

KEMP, SUZANNE LEPPART, elementary school educator, clubwoman; b. N.Y.C., Dec. 28, 1929; d. John Culver and Eleanor (Buxton) Leppart; m. Ralph Clinton Kemp, Apr. 4, 1953; children— Valerie Gale, Sandra Lynn, John Maynard, Renee Alison. Grad. Ogontz Jr. Coll., 1949; B.S., U. Md., 1952. Elem. sch. tchr. Mem. Nat. Soc. Women Descs. of Ancient and Hon. Arty. Co., Nat. Soc. Daus. of Founders and Patriots of Am. (corr. sec.), Nat. Soc. Sons and Daus. of Pilgrims, Nat. Soc. U.S. Daus. of 1812 (chpt. organizing Md. state pres. 1977-79, chpt. v.p. 1979—), Nat. Soc. New Eng. Women (colony pres. 1978-80, Nat. Soc. Colonial Dames XVII Century (state chmn. heraldry and coats of arms 1977-79), Nat. Soc. D.A.R. (chpt. regent 1970-73, chpt. v.p., Md. soc. chmn. transp. 1976-79), Md. State Officers Club, Md. Hist. Soc., Friends of Animals, Defenders of Animal Rights Inc., U. Md. Alumni, English Speaking Union, Star Spangled Banner Flag House Assn., Potter-Balt. Clayworks, Balt. Mus. Art, Walters Art Gallery, Dames of the Court of Honor, Kappa Delta Alumni. Clubs: Baltimore Country; Lago Mar (Ft. Lauderdale, Fla.); Roland Park Women's; Woodbrook-Murray Hill Garden Club, Federation Garden Clubs. Editor; The Spinning Wheel, 1973-76. Home: 2508 Stone Mill Rd Baltimore MD 21208

KEMPER, CHRISTINA, small business owner, respiratory therapist, elementary school educator; b. St. Louis, Feb. 16, 1952; d. Edward James and Norma Helen (Renner) K.; m. Don Eichholz, Dec. 23, 1972 (div. Apr. 1994); children: Cherie L., Derek V. BS in Edn., U. Mo., St. Louis, 1976, MA in Polit. Sci., 1980; AAS in Respiratory Therapy, Maryville U., 1983. Registered respiratory therapist. Intensive and critical care specialist various hosps., St. Louis, 1974—. Tchr. Parish Sch. Religion, St. Joseph's Ch., Manchester, Mo.; leader Girl Scouts Am., St. Louis. Mem. NOW (treas.), Am. Assn. for Respiratory Care, Nat. Bd. for Respiratory Care, Kappa Delta Pi. Avocations: reading, interior decorating, jewelry designing. Home: 12930 Twin Meadow Ct Creve Coeur MO 63146-1803 Personal E-mail: gemqueen@sbcglobal.net.

KEMPER, DORLA DEAN EATON (DORLA DEAN EATON), real estate broker; b. Calhoun, Mo., Sept. 10, 1929; d. Paul McVay and Jesse Lee (McCombs) Eaton; m. Charles K. Kemper, Mar. 1, 1951; children: Kevin Keil, Kara Lee. BS in Edn., Ctrl. Mo. State U., 1952. Tchr. pub. schs., Twin Falls, Idaho, 1950—51, Mission, Kans., 1952—53, Burbank, Calif., 1953—57; sales rep. real estate Minn., 1967—68, Calif., 1971—73, Deanie Kemper, Inc. Real Estate Brokerage, Loomis, Calif., 1974—76, pres., 1976—91; sr. cons. Capital Holding Corp., Louisville, 1991—93. Pres. Battle Creek Park Elem. Sch. PTA, St. Paul, 1966-67; mem. Placer County (Calif.) Bicentennial Commn., 1976; mem. Sierra Coll. Adv. Com., 1981—; active Placer County Hist. Soc. Named to Million Dollar Club (lifetime) Sacramento and Placer County bds. Realtors, 1978-94; designated Grad. Realtors Inst., Cert. Residential Specialist. Mem. Nat. Assn. Realtor, Calif. Assn. Realtors, Nat. Assn. Real Estate Appraisers, Placer County Bd. Realtors (profl. stds. com.), DAR (chpt. regent 1971-73, organizing chpt. regent 1977—, dist. dir. 1978-80, state registrar Calif. 1980-82, state vice regent 1982-84, state regent 1984-86, nat. resolutions com., nat. rec. sec. gen. 1986-89, nat. chmn. units overseas 1983-86, nat. pres. gen. 1995-98, hon. nat. pres. gen. 1998—, nat. chmn. WWII Meml. Campaign 1998-2001, pres. Nat. Officers Club 2006-), Nat. Gavel Soc., Daus. Am. Colonists, Colonial Dames Am., Internat. Platform Assn., Hidden Valley Women's Club (pres. Loomis chpt. 1970-71), Auburn Travel Study (pres. 1979). Republican. Home: 8165 Morningside Dr Granite Bay CA 95746-8163

KEMPER DIETRICH, SHEILA, educational association administrator; d. Rufus Crosby Kemper, Jr. and Cynthia Anne Kemper; m. Walter Reich Dietrich, May 15, 1982; children: August Dietrich, Andrew Dietrich, Cynthia Dietrich. BA in Social Anthropology and African Studies, Pitzer Coll., Claremont, Calif., 1979. Tchr. English as a fgn. lang. Peace Corp, Zaire, 1979—81; asst. prodn. mgr. Playbill Mag., N.Y.C., 1981—82; asst. mgr./mktg. dir. Kansas City Symphony, Mo., 1982—84; fin. counseling rep. UMB Bank, Kansas City, Mo., 1993—94, v.p., mgr. fin. counseling divsn., 1994—96, sr. v.p., mgr. pvt. client svcs., 1996—2000, exec. v.p., mgr. personal trust svcs., 2000—01, exec. v.p., dep. head trust and wealth mgmt., 2001—02, exec. v.p., divsnl. mgr. trust and wealth mgmt., 2002—05; exec. dir. N.Am. Riding for the Handicapped Assn., Denver, 2005—. Spkr. in field. Contbr. articles to profl. jours. Named in her honor, Sheila Kemper Dietrich Pk., 1999; recipient award, Women Helping Women, 1992, Cert. of Appreciation, Mayor's Com. on Persons with Disabilities, 1993, Disability Awareness award, Easter Seals Soc., 1995, Citizen of Yr. award, CNN 1340 AM Radio, 1996, WOW award, Shawnee-Mission Med. Ctr., 2004. Mem.: Am. Horse Coun., Colo. Horse Coun., Cert. Horsemanship Assn. Office Phone: 303-452-1212. Business E-Mail: skdietrich@narha.org.

KEMPF, ANDREA CARON, librarian, educator; b. San Francisco, Oct. 15, 1943; d. Benjamin and Esther (Zelby) Caron; m. George Rushing Kempf (div.); children: Robin Jeanine, Lucas Parekh; m. Evan Ross Luskin, Mar. 20, 1993. AB, Brandeis U., Waltham, Mass., 1965; MAT, Johns Hopkins U., Balt., 1966; MSLS, Simmons Coll., Boston, 1974. H.s. English tchr. Cleve. Pub. Schs., 1966—67, N.Y.C. Pub. Schs., 1967—68; libr. asst. Columbia U., N.Y.C., 1968—69; libr. Albuquerque Pub. Libr., 1974—75, U. No. Colo., Greeley, 1975—83, Johnson County C.C., Overland Park, Kans., 1983—. Bd. dirs. KCMLIN MAART, Kansas City, 2001—; selector United We Read, Kansas City, 2002—. Contbr. articles and book reviews to profl. jours. Mem. Lyric Opera Guild, Kansas City, 1993—; mem. programming bd. Kansas City Jewish Book Fair, 1999—2003. Recipient Fiction Book Rev. of the Yr. award, Libr. Jour., 2000, Award for Excellence in Edn., Burlington-No. R.R., 1995, Disting. Svc. award, Johnson County C.C., 1996, 1999, 2001, 2005, Internat. Edn. award, 2006. Mem.: ALA, Kans. Libr. Assn., Met. Area Reading Roundtable. Avocations: cooking, opera. Home: 7600 W 100 St Overland Park KS 66212 Office: Billington Library Johnson County Community College 12345 College Blvd Overland Park KS 66210 Office Phone: 913-469-8500 x 3286. E-mail: akempf@jccc.edu.

KEMPSTON DARKES, V. MAUREEN, automotive executive; b. Toronto, Can. BA in History and Polit. Sci., U. Toronto, LLB; D in Commerce (hon.), St. Mary's U., Halifax, 1995; LLD (hon.), U. Toronto, 1996, U. Victoria, 1996, McMaster U., 1997. Bar: Ont. Mem. legal staff GM Can. Ltd., 1975-79, asst. counsel Detroit, 1979-80, head tax staff, 1980-84, mem. treas. office NYC, 1985-87, acting treas., gen. dir. pub. affairs, 1987-91, v.p. corp. affairs, 1991, bd. dirs., 1991, gen. counsel, sec., 1992, pres., gen. mgr., v.p. GM Oshawa, Ont., 1994—2001; group v.p. GM, Detroit, 2002—; and pres. GM LAAM, Detroit, 2002—. Appointed Free Trade Agreement Automotive Select Panel, 1989, Transp. Equipment Sectoral Adv. Group on Internat. Trade, 1994; bd. dirs. CAMI Automotive, CN Rail, Noranda Inc., Thomson Corp. Active Ont. Govt. Edn. Accountability Bd.; mem. arts and sci. adv. bd. U. Toronto; bd. govs. U. Waterloo; mem. adv. com. U. We. Ont.'s Richard Ivey Sch. Bus.; bd. dirs. Women's Coll. Hosp. Found., New Directions; chair major gifts fundraising campaign Women's Coll. Hosp.; mem. coun. adv. govs. YMCA Greater Toronto. Recipient Margaret Brent Women Lawyers of Achievement award, ABA, 1998, Disting. Svc. Citation, Automotive Hall of Fame, 1999, Order of Ont., 1997, Officer of Order of Can., 2000. Mem. Bus. Coun. on Nat. Issues, Can. Vehicle Mfrs. Assn., Natural Resources Can. Min. Adv. Coun. on Indsl. Energy Efficiency, Automotive Adv. Com. Office: GM Group VP & Pres LAAM 300 Renaissance Ctr Detroit MI 48265-3000*

KENAGY, CHERI LYNN, nurse; b. Houston, Nov. 12, 1958; d. Kenneth Leigh and Mary Louise Kenagy; m. William J. Balan, July 30, 1982 (dec. Jan. 15, 1991). Student, San Jacinto Coll., 1980. Lic. vocat. nurse, cert. physician asst., pediat. advanced life support. Hosp. staff relief Ace Med. Staffing, Houston, 1998—, AHA, Houston, 1998—. Conservative. Presbyterian. Avocations: travel, scuba diving. Home: Box 5885 Pasadena TX 77508-5885 Personal E-mail: txauburn2002@yahoo.com.

KENAS-HELLER, JANE HAMILTON, musician; b. Fond du Lac, Wis., June 17, 1951; d. Vern Aaron and Marilyn Jane (Bluemke) Kenas; m. Irwin L. Heller. MusB, U. Wis., Stevens Point, 1975; MA, Northeastern Ill. U., 1987. Staff accompanist dept. music Northeastern Ill. U., Chgo., 1982—. Music dir. USO Tour to Europe, Germany, 1973; music dir., composer Harlequin Players Theatre Co., Palatine, Ill.; accompanist Park Ridge (Ill.) Chorale; condr. Temple Beth El High Holiday Choir, Northbrook, Ill. Composer: (mus. play) The Adventures of Goldilocks, 1990; (one-act opera) Romance Novel, 1993. Organist Edgewater Presbyn. Ch., Chgo.; pianist Ravinia Festival, Highland Pk., Ill., 2003—. Office: Northeastern Ill U 5500 N Saint Louis Ave Chicago IL 60625-4679

KENDALL, DOROTHY IRENE, secondary school educator; d. Alger Hugh Kendall, Sr. and Adelia Irene (Rasor) Kendall. BBA, U. Tex. Austin, 1967; MEd, U. Houston, Victoria, Tex., 1980. Cert. Tchr. Tex., 1969. Tchr. Victoria Meml. H.S. (formally Victoria H.S.), 1967—. Owner Open Door Boutique, Karnes City, Tex., 1970—74, Kendall's Boutique, Victoria, 1974—77; tchr., coach Victoria H.S., 1968—73. Sponsor Student Coun. Victoria Meml. H.S., 1989—92; sponsor Meml. Christian Club, Victoria, 1993—2006; tchr. Sun. sch. Northside Bapt. Ch., Victoria, 1968—77; sponsor Bapt. Young Women's Assn., Victoria, Tex., 1968—75. Recipient Outstanding Tchr., Nat. Honor Roll's Outstanding Am. Teachers, 2006, Leadership Cert., E. I. duPont deNemours and Co., 1992. Mem.: Nat. Edn. Assn. (life), Tex. State Tchrs. Assn. (life), Tex. Exes (life). Avocations: photography, travel, horseback riding, tennis. Office: Victoria Memorial High School 1110 Sam Houston Drive Victoria TX 77901

KENDALL, JACQUELINE A., social worker; b. Detroit, May 13, 1956; d. Arnold W. and Gertrude L. Kendall. BS in Social Work, Weber State Coll., 1985; MSW, U. S.C., 1988. Lic. master social worker. Social worker Heartland Hospice, West Columbia, SC. Recipient Elizabeth Poat award of excellence, ARC, 1997, Clara Barton award for vol. leadership, 1999, 6th man award, Leukemia and Lymphoma Soc., 2000. Mem.: Nat. Assn. Nonthetic Counselors, Am. Acad. Bereavement Facilitators.

KENDALL, KAY LYNN, interior designer, consultant; b. Cadillac, Mich., Aug. 20, 1950; d. Robert Llewellyn and Betty Louise (Powers) K.; 1 child, Anna Renee Easter. BFA, U. Mich., 1973. Draftsman, interior designer store planning dept. Jacobson Stores, Inc., Chelsea, Mich., 1974-79, sr. interior designer store planning dept., 1981—98; prin., pres. Kay Kendall Designs LLC dba K.I.D.D. LLC (Kendall Interior Design and Devel. LLC), 1979—; sr. interior designer Maddalena's Inc., 1998—2002; realtor Edward Surovell Realtors, Ann Arbor, Mich., 2000—05, Citadel Group, Jackson, Mich., 2005—. Cons. in field. Big sister Big Bros./Big Sisters Jackson County. Mem. Am. Soc. Interior Designers (profl. mem., assoc. Ctrl. Mich. chpt.). Avocations: tennis, golf, gardening, skiing. Home: 701 Church St Grass Lake MI 49240-9206 Office: KIDD LLC 107 1/2 S Main St Chelsea MI 48118 Office Phone: 734-433-0811. Business E-Mail: kkendall@kidd-llc.com.

KENDALL, LYNNA MARTIN, music educator; b. Rifle, Colo., Nov. 26, 1955; d. Lee Ellis and Donna Naomi Martin; m. Gary Kendall; children: Tahlie, Shea, Sean, Sterling. BA, So. Utah State Coll., Cedar City, 1978. Dist. music specialist Uintah Sch. Dist., Vernal, 1978—80; dist. elem. music specialist Idaho Sch. District #202, Dayton, 1980—81. Dist. art coord., tchr. music Uiintah Sch. Dist., 1995—2006. Grantee, Utah State Office Edn., 2000—06, Artworks for Kids, 2006—. Fellow: Am. Orff Schulwerk Assn.; mem.: Utah Music Educators Assn., Music Educator Nat. Conf. Office: Vernal Middle School 721 West 100 South Vernal UT 84078 Office Phone: 435-781-3140. Office Fax: 435-781-3143. E-mail: lynna.kendall@uintah.net.

KENDALL, SUSAN CAROL, science educator; d. Ronald and Carolyn Comer; m. Brian Kendall, July 6, 1996; children: Emellie Ann, Braden Milan. BS in Edn., Ind. State U., Terre Haute, 1996; MS in Edn., Ind. U., New Albany, 2000. Tchr. 6th grade sci. Scottsburg Mid. Sch., Ind., 1996—. American Baptist. Office: Scottsburg Mid Sch 425 S Third Scottsburg IN 47170 Office Phone: 812-752-8926.

KENDALL HULL, MARGARIDA, art educator, painter; b. Lisbon, Portugal; Attended studied history & philosophy, U. Lisbon; BFA, Corcoran Sch. Art, 1973; MFA, Catholic U., 1982. Visiting prof. studio art Towson State U., 1986; asst. prof. studio art George Mason U., 1987, assoc. prof., 1994, 2000—. Represented in permanent collections, Art Inst. Chgo., Gulbenkian Mus. Contemporary Art, Lisbon, Portugal, one-woman shows include, Osuna Gallery, Washington D.C., 1983, Gulbenkian Found., 1984, exhibitions include, Baltimore, Chgo., N.Y., Phila., Gallery K, Dupont Cir. Office: Art Dept George Mason U 4400 University Dr Fairfax VA 22030-4444

KENDIG, FLORENCE GEERTZ (BOBBI KENDIG), retired social worker; b. Aurora, Ill., Feb. 7, 1936; d. Eric and Florence Elizabeth (Hard) Geertz; m. Edwin Walton Kendig, June 13, 1964; children: David Eric, Susan Louise, Lisa Jean. BA, Northwestern U., 1957; MSW, U. So. Calif., 1965. Lic. clin. social worker. Social caseworker Bur. Pub. Assistance, Long Beach, Calif., 1957-59, 1962-63; contract counselor Family Services, Long Beach, 1972-75; co-founder, dir. Children's program Cedar House, Long Beach, 1974-82, Sarah Ctr., Long Beach, 1984-88. Cons. Interagy. Council Child Abuse and Neglect, ICAN Assocs., Long Beach YWCA; educator filial therapy Long Beach Unified Sch. Dist., 1973-74. Chmn. bd. dirs. New Directions Sch., Long Beach, 1974-75. Recipient Cert. Appreciation Interagy. Council Child Abuse and Neglect, Los Angeles, 1985, Resolution and Key to City City of Long Beach, 1979. Mem. Nat. Assn. Social Workers, Long Beach Area Child Trauma Council (vice chmn. 1984, chmn. 1985). Democrat. Quaker. Avocations: piano music, camping, hiking.

KENDIG, LYNNE E., physician; b. Phila., Dec. 6, 1949; d. Carl M. and Marion (Conkle) Shetzley; m. William Lampe, 1969 (div. 1978); 1 child, Megan Alpert; m. Dan Spicer, Aug. 21, 1983 (div. 1998); m. Robert Kendig, Sept. 13, 2003. BS in Edn., U. Pa., 1971; MS in Computer Edn., Lesley Coll., 1985; MD with honors, U. Colo., 1994. Tchr. elem. edn. Tredyeffrin-East town Sch. Dist., Berwyn, Pa., 1976—81, Cherry Creek Sch. Dist., Englewood, Colo., 1982—87; intern, residency St. Joseph's Hosp., Denver, 1994—97; family practice physician Exempla Healthcare Orchard Family Practice, Englewood, 1997—; pvt. practice family physician Oasis Family Medicine, Denver, 2000—. IBM edn. cons., Englewood, 1986-87; resident physician St. Joseph Hosp. Family Practice, Denver, 1994-97; mem. admissions com. U. Colo. Med. Sch., Denver, 1993-94. Vol. student physician Stout Street Homeless Clinic, Denver, 1990-94; physician lectr., educator Tar Wars, Denver, 1995-96; mem. Denver Pub. Libr. Friends Found., 1996—. Mem. AMA, Am. Acad. Family Physicians, Colo. Med. Soc., Alpha Omega Alpha. Avocations: hiking, travel, gardening. Home: 635 Bellaire St Denver CO 80220-4934 E-mail: lynnekendig@earthlink.net.

KENDLE, CANDACE, pharmaceutical executive; m. Christopher C. Bergen; 2 children. BS in Pharmacy, U. Cin., 1970, PhD in Pharmacy, 1972. Resident Cin. Children's Hosp. Med. Ctr., 1972; epidemiology fellow U. N.C. Sch. Pub. Health; dir. pharmacy The Children's Hosp. Phila., 1979—81; clin. asst. prof. Phila. Coll. Pharmacy and Scis., 1979—81; clin. assoc. prof. pediat. U. Pa. Sch. Medicine., 1979—81; co-founder, CEO Kendle Internat., Inc., Cin., 1981—, chmn., 1991—. Adj. assoc. prof. U. Cin. Sch. Pharmacy, 1982—84; bd. dirs. U. Cin., H.J. Heinz Co., Isabella Venture Fund, UMD Inc. Contbr. articles to profl. jours. Named one of Nations Top 25 Female CEO's, Worth Mag., 2001; recipient Entrepreneur of Yr. award, Cin. Mag., 1998, Disting. Alumni award, U. Cin. Dept. Women's STudies, 1999, Arthur C. Glasser Disting. Alumni award, U. Cin., Coll. Pharmacy, 2001, William Howard Taft medal for notable achievement, U. Cin., 2002. Mem.: Com. of 200, Assn. Clin. Rsch. Orgns. (founder). Office: Kendle Internat Inc 1200 Carew Tower 441 Vine St Cincinnati OH 45202

KENDRICK, BEVERLY ANN, medical/surgical nurse, small business owner; b. Rupert, Idaho, July 17, 1949; d. Robert Alfred and Erna (Plocher) Dockter; m. Sidney Cannon, Aug. 22, 1967 (div.); 1 child, Lisa Ann; m. Budd Leroy Kendrick, Dec. 26, 1978; children: Cassandra Rachelle, Angela Priscilla. Assoc. of Sci., Boise State U., 1989, BS, 1993; grad. bus. program, Idaho Small Bus. Devel. Ctr., Boise, 1997. RN, Idaho; cert. staff devel. continuing edn. nurse; cert. med.-surg. nurse. Coord. infant stimulation program Adult and Child Devel. Ctr., Boise, 1974-78; parent educator St. Alphonsus Regional Med. Ctr., Boise, 1996-97, nurse educator, 1996-97, risk mgr., 1998—2002, hospice nurse, 2002—03; investigator Idaho Bd. of Medicine, 2003—. Owner Angel Essence, Boise, 1995—2005. Author: Infant Stimulation Procedure Manual, 1978. Facilitator Women's Network of Entrepreneurial Tng., 1996-97; bd. dirs. Women's Entrepreneurial Mentoring Sys., v.p., 1996-97, pres., 1998-99; co-founder Small Bus. Adminstrn. Women's Bus. Ctr., 1999. RN scholar St. Alphonsus Regional Med. Ctr., 1988; named Women in Bus. Adv. of Yr. Idaho SBA, 1998; receipent Idaho Women Making History awar, 2005. Mem. AAUW, Angel Collectors' Club Am., Idaho Coalition for Single Moms. Avocations: travel, reading, collecting angel collectibles, angel art. Home: 12912 W Baldcypress Dr Boise ID 83713-2064 Personal E-mail: ladywinsg17@aol.com.

KENDRICK, KATHERINE, lawyer; b. S.C. BA, U. Calif., Berkeley; JD, Columbia U., 1986. Assoc. Latham & Watkins, Los Angeles; with legal dept. Walt Disney Studios, 1989—96; v.p. European legal affairs Walt Disney Co.; gen. counsel DreamWorks Animation SKG, Inc., 1996—2004, bd. dirs., gen. counsel, 2004—. Bd. mem. Next Generation Coun., Motion Picture and Television Fund; adv. bd. LA Sports and Entertainment Commn., Kernochan Ctr. Law, Media and Arts, Columbia U. Sch. Law, Western Region Bd. US Ski and Snowboard Assn. Office: DreamWorks SKG 1000 Flower St Glendale CA 91201

KENDRICK, KIM, federal agency administrator; BA, Bowdoin Coll.; JD, U. Pitts. Asst. gen. counsel insured housing and cmty. devel. litigation US Dept. Housing & Urban Devel., Washington, 1990—95; legal counsel DC Housing Authority, 1995—98, regional adminstr., 1998—2002; gen. counsel Covenant House Washington; sr. counselor to sec. US Dept. Housing & Urban Devel., Washington, asst. sec. for fair housing and equal opportunity, 2005—. Office: HUD 451 Seventh St SW Rm 5100 Mail Code E Washington DC 20410 Office Phone: 202-708-4252. Office Fax: 202-708-4483.

KENDRICK, KIMPI KING, lawyer; b. Nashville, Sept. 10, 1965; d. Patricia Hicks and Kenneth K. King; m. Donald F. Kendrick, Feb. 14, 2000; children: Hilary Ann Howser, Emily N. Orbison. AS, Vol. State C.C., Gallatin, Tenn., 1985; BS, Mid. Tenn. State U., Murfreesboro, 2000; JD, Nashville U., 2004. Policy support user liaison Accenture, Nashville, 1999—2004; atty. Kimpi Kendrick, Atty. at Law, Murfreesboro, Tenn., 2004—. Pro bono work for disadvantaged clients, Murfreesboro, 2004—06. Mem.: ATLA. Avocations: scuba diving, travel, motorcycling. Office: Kimpi Kendrick Attorney at Law 301 N Spring St Murfreesboro TN 37130 Office Phone: 615-217-3560. Office Fax: 615-217-3553.

KENDRICK-HOPGOOD, DEBRA JO, small business owner; b. Mount Vernon, Ill., June 26, 1958; d. L. John and B. Jean (Stovall) K.; m. Joseph Jefferson Hopgood Jr., Jan. 10, 1981; children: Jillian Denise, Ashley Erin. Owner Balloons and Tunes, 1985-90; with Kendrick Paper Stock Co., Mt. Vernon, Ill., 1980—; owner Shenanigans Restaurant, 1990—2004. Com. mem. Mt. Vernon Civic Ctr., 1983-86, Jefferson County Crime Stoppers, Mt. Vernon, 1984-85; chaperone Loiterers Club, Mt. Vernon, 1987; mem. adv. bd. Good Samaritan Hosp., 1988-93; bd. dirs. Mt. Vernon Twp. High Sch. Bd. Edn., 1986—, Mt. Vernon Women's Crisis Ctr., 1988-91, Jefferson County, 1988; bd. suprs. Jefferson County, 1988—; bd. dirs. Bright and Beautiful, 1989—; mem. Mt. Vernon Econ. Devel. Commn., 1997—; mem. adv. bd. Jefferson County Health Dept., 1995-98; asst. leader Girl Scouts USA, 1998—, girl scout leader, 2005—; mem. Mt. Vernon Econ. Devel. Commn., 1997—. Named Woman of Yr. Mt. Vernon Bus. and Profl. Women's Club, 1998, DBE of Yr. Ill. Dept. of Transp. Bus. of Small Bus. Enterprise, 1997, Trucker of the Month, Midwest Truckers Assn. Mem. Nat. Fedn. Female Execs., Bus. and Profl. Womens Club, People Against Violent Environments (bd. dirs.), Jefferson County C. of C. (bd. dirs.). Baptist. Avocations: collecting coins, reading, tennis, old movies. Office: Kendrick Paper Stock Co PO Box 1385 Mount Vernon IL 62864-0028 Office Phone: 800-346-1326. E-mail: kendrickpaper@msn.com.

KENEALLY, KATHRYN MARIE, lawyer; b. Dayton, Ohio, Apr. 30, 1958; d. William Henry and Joanna Gertrude K.; m. Thomas Marshall, Oct. 16, 1992. BA, Cornell U., 1979; JD, Fordham U., 1982; LLM in Taxation, NYU, 1993. Bar: N.Y., 1983, U.S. Dist. Ct. (so., ea. dists.) N.Y., 1983, U.S. Ct. Appeal (2d, 3d, 11th cirs.), U.S. Tax Ct. Law clk. to Hon. E. R. Neaher U.S. Dist. Ct. (ea. dist.) N.Y., Bklyn., 1982-83; assoc. Skadden Arps Slate Meagher & Flom, N.Y.C., 1983-85, Kostelanetz Ritholz Tigue & Fink, N.Y.C., 1985-90, ptnr., 1990-93, Kostelanetz & Fink, LLP, N.Y.C., 1993-99; mem. Owen & Davis, PC, N.Y.C., 2000—02; ptnr. Fulbright & Jaworski, L.L.P., N.Y.C., 2002—. Columnist The Champion, 1996—, Jour. Tax Practice and Prodecure, 1999-; co-author: Practice Under Federal Sentencing Guidelines, 1998; contbr. articles to profl. jours. Mem. practitioners adv. group U.S. Sentencing Commn., 1993—. Mem. ABA (chmn. taxation sect., civil and criminal tax penalties com. 2000-02, stds. tax practice com., 2005-), Nat. Assn. Criminal Def. Lawyers (life). Home: 48 Charlotte Pl Hartsdale NY 10530-2602 Office: Fulbright & Jaworski LLP 660 Fifth Ave New York NY 10103 Office Phone: 212-318-3000. E-mail: kkeneally@fulbright.com.

KENNA, GAIL ANN, secondary and higher education educator; b. Fullerton, Calif., June 5, 1943; d. Robert Theron and Barbara Francis Wilson; m. Michael James Kenna, June 28, 1968; children: Michelle Donahue, Bonnie Hutchinson. BA, U. So. Calif., 1965; MA in Writing, Goddard Coll., Vt., 1982; postgrad., U. Calif., Berkeley, Oxford U. Life secondary edn.credential Calif., 1967. With LA City Schs., 1967—68, Napa (Calif.) Unified Schs., 1969—79; assoc. prof. with European program Troy State U., Germany, 1981—83; with mil. program Chapman Coll., Calif., 1983—85; with Malaysian program Ind. U., Malaysia, 1987—90; with Venezuelan program Shelton State U., Venezuela, 1991—93; with dept. lit. Am. U., Washington, 1996—97; with Ctrl. Tex. U., Bogata, Colombia, 2000; tchr. Rappahanock Edn. Found., 2005—06. Spkr. mil. orgns., DIA, industry; freelance journalist numerous newspapers and mags. Author: Along the Gold Rush Trail, 1983, Face of the Avila, 1995, Beyond the Wall, 2001 (Puffin Found. grant, 2000). Charity coord. Am. govt. orgns., 1992—95; with child abuse project City of Montgomery, Ala., 1979—80. Recipient Fgn. Svc. Vol. award, 1995, Best Svcs., USAFE. Mem.: U. So. Calif. Alumni, Audubon Soc., Delta Gamma. Democrat. Avocations: tennis, travel, reading. Home: PO Box 216 Wicomico Church VA 22579 Office Phone: 804-436-8615. Personal E-mail: gailkenna@aol.com.

KENNAN, ELIZABETH TOPHAM, academic administrator, retired historian; b. Phila., Feb. 25, 1938; AB summa cum laude, Mt. Holyoke Coll., 1960; MA, Oxford (Eng.) U., 1962; PhD, U. Wash., 1966; LHD (hon.), Trinity Coll., 1978, Amherst Coll., 1980, St. Mary's Coll., 1982, Oberlin Coll., 1983; LLD (hon.), Smith Coll., 1984; LittD (hon.), Cath. U. of Am., 1985, U. Mass., Amherst, 1988. Asst. prof. history Cath. U., Washington, 1966-70, assoc. prof. history, dir. medieval and Byzantine studies, 1970-78, dir. program in early Christian humanism, 1970-78; pres. Five Colls. Inc., 1985-94; pres., prof. history Mt. Holyoke Coll., South Hadley, Mass., 1978-95, pres. emeritus, 1996. Bd. dirs. Coun. on Libr. Resources, 1980-95; mem. com. Folger Shakespeare Libr., 1994-2001; lead dir. N.E. Utilities, Hartford, Conn.; bd. dirs. The Putnam Funds, Boston, Talbots, Hingham, Mass. Co-author: (under pseudonym Clare Munnings) Overnight Float, 2000; contbr. articles to profl. jours. including Georgetown Univ. Press, Univ. of Wash. Press, Cath. Univ. of Am., Cath. Univ. Press, Cistercian Publs., Mem. Coun. on Econ. Devel., 1991-95; mem. bd. selectors Jefferson awards Am. Inst. for Pub. Svc., 1991-96; trustee U. Notre Dame, 1985-94, Miss Porter's Sch., 1980-85; mem. higher edn. program com. Dana Found., 1986-90, Indo-U.S. Subcommn. on Edn. and Culture, 1986-91; vice chmn. 1000 Friends of Mass., 1989-91, Mass Gov.'s Nominating Coun., 1990-91; trustee Trustees for the Reservations, 1999—, Centre Coll., Danville, Ky., 2001—, Midway Coll., Midway, Ky., Nat. Trust Hist. Preservation, 2004—. Marshall scholar, 1960; Woodrow Wilson fellow (hon.), 1960. Mem. Coun. Fgn. Rels. Home and Office: Cambus-Kenneth Farm PO Box 1989 Danville KY 40423

KENNARD, JOYCE L., state supreme court justice; b. Bandung, West Java, Indonesia, May 6, 1941; AA, Pasadena City Coll., 1970, U. So. Calif., 1970, BA in German magna cum laude, 1971, MPA, JD, U. So. Calif., 1974; JD (hon.), Pepperdine Sch. Law, 1989; LLD (hon.), Calif. Western Sch. Law, 1990, Southwestern U. Sch. Law, 1991, Whittier Law Sch., 1994, Northwestern Sch. Law, Lewis and Clark Coll., 1997, Lincoln Law Sch., 1997, San Joaquin Coll. Law, 2004. Dep. atty. gen., LA, 1975—79; sr. atty. State Ct. Appeals, LA, 1979—86; judge LA County Mcpl. Ct., 1986—87; assoc. justice pro tempore State Ct. Appeal (divsn. three), LA, 1987; judge LA County Superior Ct., 1987—88; assoc. justice State Ct. Appeals (divsn. five), LA, 1988—89, Calif. Supreme Ct., San Francisco, 1989—. Chair appellate adv. com. Calif. Jud. Coun., 1996—. Recipient Contbg. Progress of Dignity and Self-Esteem Among Amputees award, Sacramento Women Amputees Group, 1990, Lifetime Achievement award, Ind. Living Ctr. So. Calif., 1990, award, Gov.'s Hall of Fame for People with Disabilities, 1990, Ernestine Stahlhut award, Women Lawyers' Assn. of LA, 1990, award, San Fernando Valley Bar, 1990, Asian/Pacific Women's Network, LA, 1991, YWCA, L.A., 1991, Justice of Yr. 1991 award, Calif. Trial Lawyers Assn., 1992 Chinese-Am. Pioneers So. Calif. Judiciary award, Chinese Hist. Soc. of So. Calif., First Ann. Women of 90's award, Robinson's Dep. Store, LA, 1992, First Ann. Netherlands-Am. Heritage award, Netherlands-Am. Arts and Cultural Found., 1992, Atty. Gen. award, Asian and Pacific Islander Employee Adv. Com., Atty. Gen.'s Office, 1992, award, ABA Task Force on Opportunities for Minorities in Jud. Adminstrn. Divsn. and Commn. on Opportunities for Minorities in Profession, 1992, Margaret Brent Women Lawyers of Achievement award, ABA, 1993, Trailblazer award, Nat. Asian Pacific Am. Bar Assn. (NAPABA), 1994, Founders award, Nat. Asian Pacific Am. Law Students Assn. (NAPALSA), 1994, Access award, LA County Commn. Disabilities, 1994, St. Thomas More Medallion award, St. Thomas More Law Honor Soc. and Loyola Law Sch., 1995, 1996 Spirit Excellence award, ABA's Commn. on Opportunities for Minorities in the Profession, award, Marin Women's Hall of Fame, 1997, San Francisco Women Lawyers Alliance, 1997, Asian Pacific Am. Legal Ctr. So. Calif., LA, 1997, Coun. Asian Pacific Islanders Together Active Leadership (C.A.P.I.T.A.L), 1997, Accompanying award, Asian Bar Assn. Sacramento, Legal Impact award, Asian Law Alliance, San Jose, Calif., 2000, First Justice Rose Bird Meml. award, Calif. Women Lawyers San Francisco, 2001, Pub. Svc. award, Asian Pacific Am. Bar Assn., 2001, Jud. Coun.'s award, San Francisco, 2004, Achieve with Inspiration and Courage award, Orgn. Chinese Ams., San Mateo, Calif., 2005, Cert. Spl. Congl. Recognition, Congressman Tom Lantos, 2005, Cert. of Recognition, Spkr. pro Tempore Leland Y. Yee Calif. State Assembly, 2005, Cert. of Commendation, Bd. Suprs. San Mateo County, 2005, Lifetime Achievement award, Japanese Am. Bar. Assn. LA, 2006. Mem.: Alpha Gamma Sigma Soc., Alpha Mu Gamma, Phi Kappa Phi, Phi Beta Kappa. Office: Calif Supreme Ct 350 McAllister St San Francisco CA 94102-4783

KENNARD, LYDIA H., airport terminal executive; BA, Stanford U.; MS, MIT; JD, Harvard U. Former pres./prin.-in-charge KDG Devel. Constrn. Consulting, L.A.; former mem. L.A. Planning Commn.; dep. exec. dir. design and constrn. L.A. World Airports, 1994-99, interim exec. dir., 1999-2000, exec. dir., 2000—03; chmn. KDG Develop. & Constrn. Cons., LA, 2003—. Mem. Calif. Air Resources Bd., 2004-; bd. dir. IndyMac Bank; lawyer in real estate and constrn. law. Active UniHealth Found. Bd.; past mem. Calif. Med.

Ctr. Found. Bd., Equal Opportunity Adv. Coun. So. Calif. Edison. Named Woman of Yr. L.A. chpt. Women's Trans. Seminar, 1995, Civic Leader of Yr. Nat. Assn. Women Bus. Owners-L.A., 2000. Home: 1055 E Colorado Blvd Ste 500 Pasadena CA 91106-2371

KENNEDY, ADRIENNE LITA, playwright; b. Pitts., Sept. 13, 1931; d. Cornell Wallace and Etta (Haugabook) Hawkins; m. Joseph C. Kennedy, May 15, 1953 (div. 1966); children: Joseph C., Adam. BS, Ohio State U., 1953; student creative writing, Columbia U., 1954-56; student playwrighting, New Sch. Social Research, Am. Theatre Wing, Circle in the Sq. Theatre Sch., 1957-58, 62; doctorate (hon.), Ohio State U., 2003. Mem. playwriting unit Actors Studio, N.Y.C., 1962-65; lectr. Yale U., New Haven, 1972-74; CBS fellow Sch. Drama, N.Y.C., 1973; lectr. Princeton (N.J.) U., 1977; vis. assoc. prof. Brown U., 1979-80. Rep. to conf. Internat. Theatre Inst., Budapest, 1978; vis. lectr. Harvard U., 1990, 91, vis. prof., 1997—. Author: (plays) Funnyhouse of a Negro, 1964, Cities in Bezique, 1965, A Rat's Mass, 1966, A Lesson in Dead Language, 1966, The Lennon Plays, 1968, Sun, Cities of Bezique, 1969; A Movie Star Has To Star in Black and White, 1976, Ohio State Murders, She Talks to Beethoven, 1990, (with Adam Kennedy) Sleep Deprivation Chamber, 1995; (play) People Who Led to My Plays, 1987 (Manhattan Borough Pres.'s award 1988), Letter to My Students, Lancashire Lad, The Vanishing Literary Club, 2005, (adaptation) Madame Bovery, 2003; commd. by Empire State Youth Inst., 1979, Onestes, Electra, Juilliard Sch. Music, 1980, Black Children's Day, Rites and Reason, Brown U., 1980, Vanishing Literary Club, 2002, Madame Bovary, 2003; represented in numerous anthologies Norton Anthology of Am. Lit. Recipient Obie award, 1964, 96, Pierre Lecomte du Novy award Lincoln Ctr., 1994, award AAAL, 1994, Anisfield-Wolf Lifetime Achievement award, 2003, PEN/Laura Pels Found. award drama, 2006; fellow Guggenheim Found., 1968, Rockefeller Found., 1967-68, NEA, 1993, Lila Wallace Readers Digest, 1994, Yale U., 1974-75; grantee Nat. Endowment Arts, 1973, Rockefeller Found., 1974, Creative Artists Pub. Svc., 1974; Disting. lectr. U. Calif., Berkeley, 1980, 86. Fellow: MLA (hon.); mem.: PEN (bd. dirs. 1976—77). Address: 325 W 89th St New York NY 10024

KENNEDY, BARBARA ELLEN PERRY, art therapist; b. Columbus, Ohio, Apr. 22, 1937; d. Donald Earl Perry and Elsie Irene (Strait) Perry Modglin; m. Marvin Roosevelt Kennedy, July 1, 1955 (div. Sept. 1969); children: Sherry Lynn Kennedy Anderson, Michelle Reneé Kennedy Byrd. AS in Mental Health Technology cum laude, Purdue U., 1975, BA in Psychology, 1976; MA in Art Therapy, Wright State U., 1990. Registered art therapist; cert. social worker; cert. marriage and family therapist. Probation officer intern Allen County Juvenile Probation Dept., Ind., 1975; prodn. supr. asst. Allen County Assn. for Retarded, Ft. Wayne, Ind., 1975, relief supr. semi-ind. living, 1975-76; occup. therapist asst. Logansport State Hosp., Ind., 1977; rehab. therapist Richmond State Hosp., Ind., 1977—, recreation therapy dir. acute intensive treatment unit Ind., 1983-85, dir. art therapy dept. Ind., 1986—, art tchr., art therapist with MIDD, adolescent and geriatric Ind., 1995—2004; ret., 2004. Pvt. counselor, 1986—; counselor Mental Health Assn., Richmond, 1986; art therapy counselor Battered Women's Shelter, Richmond, 1986; counselor Dayton (Ohio) Pub. Sch., Family Svc. Assn., 1989-90, expressive therapy counselor with Mentally Ill Chemically Addicted population, 1993—; lectr. in field of mental health and art therapy. Author, editor: Mental Stimulation Activities, 1992. Mem. com. LWV, Richmond, 1977-80; publicity officer USCG Aux., Richmond, 1985; chairperson legis. group AAUW, Richmond, 1982-84; bd. dir. Community Coun. on Disabilities Awareness, Richmond, 1985-86; vol. ARC, Muncie, Ind. and Ft. Wayne, 1969-73; vol. tutor Adult Literacy Resource Ctr., 1991—; pres. Richmond Art Club, 1996-97; active Fountain City Wesleyan Ch. Recipient Merit scholarship Purdue U., 1971-76, Gov.'s Showcase award State of Ind., 1990. Mem. Am. Art Therapy Assn., Buckeye Art Therapy Assn., Ind. Art Therapy Assn. (v.p. 1992-95), Mensa. Mem. Wesleyan Ch. Avocations: sailing, hiking, piano, reading, art.

KENNEDY, BEVERLY (KLEBAN) BURRIS, financial advisor, former television and radio personality; b. Pitts., Sept. 23, 1943; d. Jack and Ida (Davis) Kleban; m. Thomas E. Burris, Dec. 31, 1967 (div.); 1 child, Laura Danielle Burris; m. Ed A. Kennedy, Jan 14, 1984; stepchildren: Kathleen, Patricia, Thomas. BS, Pa. State U., 1964; postgrad., Va. Commonwealth U., 1967. Founder, exec. dir. Broward Art Colony, Inc., Broward County, Fla., 1978-80; dir. sales Holiday Inn, Plantation, Fla., 1980-81; agent, registered rep. Equitable Life Assurance Soc., Ft. Lauderdale, Fla., 1982—2005; pres. Fin. Planning Svcs. Assn., Inc., Ft. Lauderdale, Fla., 1984-86; owner, fin. cons. Beverly B. Kennedy & Assocs., Ft. Lauderdale, Fla., 1982—; dir. of rsch. tech. & grants adminstrn. Diversity Planning Instit., 2001—03; founder Nat. Found. Med. Liability Reform and Accountability, Inc., Ft. Lauderdale, Fla., 2005—. Mem. adv. bd. Transflorida Bank, 1983-88; mem. bd. arbitration Nat. Assn. Securities Dealers, Inc., 1992-2004. Talk show host Sta. WWNN, 1992-93. Bd. dirs. Community Appearance Bd., 1988-89, Riverwalk, Ft. Lauderdale, 1988-89, First Charter Sch. of Excellence, Ft. Lauderdale, 1997-2003; trustee Police and Fireman Fund of Fort Lauderdale, 1990-91; appointed by gov. to Fla. State Bd. Profl. Engrs., 1988-91; cons. Com. on Fin. for Nat. Coun. examiners for Engring and Surveying, 1990-91; Rep. nominee for U.S. Congress 20th dist. Fla., 1992, 94, 19th dist., 1996; appointed to silver haired legis. of Fla., 1999-2003, exec. bd. coalition of condominiums and home owners assoc., 2001-2003; chmn. bd. Sr. Housing Mgmt. Svcs. of Tex., 2004—; spokesperson Advanced Cardiac Cons., Inc., Fla., 2005; physicians adv. com. mem. Nat. Rep. Congress; founding pres., CEO Nat. Found. for Med. Liability Reform and Accountability, 2005. Named Woman of the Year (Bus. for Profit), Women in Communications, Broward County, 1986, Bus. & Profl. Women, 1988-89, Oustanding Alumni, Pa. State Univ. Coll. Edn., 1988-89, A Woman of History, Nova S.E. U., 2001. Mem. Internat. Assn. Fin. Planning, Nat. Assn. Life Underwriters, East Broward Fed. Women's Rep. Club (pres. 1992-93). Home: 3240 Seaward Dr Lauderdale By The Sea FL 33062 Office: 100 N Federal Hwy Ste 534 Fort Lauderdale FL 33301 Office Phone: 954-763-5688. E-mail: ekenn@bellsouth.net.

KENNEDY, CAROLINE See SCHLOSSBERG, CAROLINE

KENNEDY, CHERYL LYNN, museum director; b. Pekin, Ill., Nov. 25, 1946; d. Paul Louis and Ann Marie (Bingham) Wieburg; children: Kurt Alan, Kimberly Ann. Grad. high sch., Pekin, Ill.; BA, Eastern Ill. U. Prin., and profl. quilter, Mahomet, Ill., 1976-81; program coord. Early Am. Mus., Mahomet, 1981-85; dir. Early Am. Mus. Champaign County Forest Preserve, Mahomet, 1986—. Chmn. Ill. Quilt Rsch. Project Early Am. Mus. and Land of Lincoln Quilt Assn., 1986—, Ill. Historic Sites Adv. Coun., 2000-03, mem. adv. com. AAM Mus. Assessment Program, 2002-06. Historian Meth. Local History Com., Mahomet, 1984-86; mem. Looking for Lincoln Heritage Coalition, 2006-. Mem. Am. Assn. Mus., Am. Assn. State and Local History, Ill. Assn. Mus. (past pres., advocacy chair), Ill. Heritage Assn., Champaign County Hist. Soc. Avocations: quilting, women's history, walking, gardening. Office: Early Am Mus PO Box 1040 Mahomet IL 61853-1040 Business E-Mail: ckennedy@cctpd.org.

KENNEDY, COLLEEN GERALYN, nurse, social worker; b. S.I., NY, Feb. 2, 1955; d. James Martin and Eleanor S. (Dehlinger) K.; m. Edward Francis Humphries, July 21, 1990; children: Michael J. Kennedy, Stephen Edward Humphries. AAS in Nursing, Coll. S.I., 1976; BSW, Adelphi U., 1982, MSW, 1984. RN, N.Y.; cert. social worker, N.Y. Staff nurse S.I. Hosp., 1976—80, social work asst., 1980—84, clin. social worker, 1984—85; asst. dir. social work Eger Health Care Ctr., S.I., 1985—87; systems analyst program devel. and evaluation St. Vincent's Med. Ctr., S.I., 1987—89; asst. dir. Ctr. Chem. Dependency, Bayley Seton Hosp., S.I., 1989—93; med, coord., managed care, utilization mgmt., quality assurance Bayley Seton Hosp., S.I., 1993—95; dir. health and mem. svcs. Health Plus Prepaid Health Svcs. Plan, Inc., Bklyn., 1995—99; pres. Kennedy Cons., NY, 1999—. V.p. Olde Towne Cons./Compliance Gateway Inc., NY, 1999—2002; pres., CEO Aptus Compliance Tech., Inc., 2002—. Named to Outstanding Young Women of Am., 1984. Mem. NASW, ACSW, NAFE. Democrat. Roman Catholic. Avocations: calligraphy, gourmet cooking, boating. Office: 451 Manor Rd Staten Island NY 10314 Office Phone: 718-442-7874. Business E-Mail: ckennedy@si.rr.com.

KENNEDY, CORNELIA GROEFSEMA, federal judge; b. Detroit, Aug. 4, 1923; d. Elmer H. and Mary Blanche (Gibbons) Groefsema; m. Charles S. Kennedy, Jr. (dec.); 1 son, Charles S. III. BA, U. Mich., 1945, JD with distinction, 1947; LL.D. (hon.), No. Mich. U., 1971, Eastern Mich. U., 1971, Western Mich. U., 1973, Detroit Coll. Law, 1980, U. Detroit, 1987. Bar: Mich. bar 1947. Law clk. to Chief Judge Harold M. Stephens, U.S. Ct. of Appeals, Washington, 1947-48; assoc. Elmer H. Groefsema, Detroit, 1948-52; partner Markle & Markle, Detroit, 1952-66; judge 3d Judicial Circuit Mich., 1967-70; dist. judge U.S. Dist. Ct., Eastern Dist. Mich., Detroit, 1970-79, chief judge, 1977-79; circuit judge U.S. Ct. Appeals, (6th cir.), 1979-99, sr. judge, 1999—. Mem. Commn. on the Bicentennial of the U.S. Constitution (presdl. appointment). Recipient Sesquicentennial award U. Mich. Fellow Am. Bar Found.; mem. ABA, Mich. Bar Assn. (past chmn. negligence law sect.), Detroit Bar Assn. (past dir.), Fed. Bar Assn., Am. Judicature Soc., Nat. Assn. Women Lawyers, Am. Trial Lawyers Assn., Nat. Conf. Fed. Trial Judges (past chmn.), Fed. Jud. Fellows Commn. (bd. dirs.), Fed. Jud. Ctr. (bd. dirs.), Phi Beta Kappa. Address: 744 Fed Ct House 231 1st Detroit MI 48226*

KENNEDY, DEBORAH, communications executive, writer, editor; b. Wayland, Mass., Feb. 6, 1955; m. Leonard L. M. Coster (dec.). BA, MA, Boston U., 1978; M. of Theol. Studies, Harvard Divinity Sch., 1981; MA, Am. U., 1988. Instr. Dickinson Coll., Carlisle, Pa., 1985-86, Denison U., Granville, Ohio, 1986-87; asst. to dean Am. U., Washington, 1987-90; dir. ops. Lang. at Work, Washington, 1991-98; owner, prin. Key Resources, Washington, 1998—. Chair, bd. dirs. Thomas Cir. Singers, Washington, 1995-97, fund raising chair, 1995-2000; coord. concert series St. Columba's Ch., Washington, 1994-97. Mem. ASTD, Women's Nat. Book Assn., Tchrs. of English to Spkrs. of Other Langs., Washington Ind. Writers. Episcopalian. Avocations: singing, gardening. Home and Office: Key Resources 4434 Davenport St NW Washington DC 20016-4414 E-mail: drkennedy@netacc.net.

KENNEDY, DEBRA JOYCE, marketing professional; b. July 9, 1955; d. John Nathan and Drea Hannah (Lancaster) Ward; m. John William Kennedy, Sept. 3, 1977 (div.); children: Drea, Noelle. BS in Comm., Calif. State Poly. U., 1977; MA in Orgnl. Mgmt., U. Phoenix, 2003. Pub. rels. coord. Whittier (Calif.) Hosp., 1978—79, pub. rels. mgr., 1980; pub. rels. dir. San Clemente (Calif.) Hosp., 1979—80; dir. pub. rels. Garfield Med. Ctr., Monterey Park, Calif., 1980—82; dir. mktg. and cmty. rels. Charter Oak Hosp., Covina, 1983—85; mktg. dir. CPC Horizon Hosp., Pomona, 1985—89; dir. mktg. Sierra Royale Hosp., Azusa, 1989—90; mktg. rep. PacifiCare, Cypress, 1990—92; regional medicare mgr. Health Net, Woodland Hills, Calif., 1992—95; dist. sales mgr. Kaiser Permante Health Plan, Pasadena, Calif., 1995—. Contbr. articles to profl. jours. Mem.: Healthcare Pub. Rels. and Mktg. Assn., Healthcare Mktg. Assn., Am. Soc. Hosp. Pub. Rels., Covina and Covina West C. of C., Soroptimists, West Covina Jaycees. Republican. Methodist. Personal E-mail: djkennedy0709@verizon.net.

KENNEDY, DESERIEE, law educator; m. George White Jr.; children: Noelle Kennedy White, Noah Kennedy White, Nolani Kennedy White. BA in Sociology, Lehigh U., 1984; JD, Harvard U., 1987. Bar: Calif. 1988, Pa. 1992. Assoc. Bichel & Brewer, 1987—88, Pepper, Hamilton & Schertz, LA, 1988—93; asst. city solicitor Office of City Solicitor, Phila., 1993—94; assoc. prof. U. Tenn. Coll. Law, Knoxville, 1995—. Faculty senate pres. U. Tenn., Knoxville. Contbr. articles to profl. jours. Bd. dirs., chair Race Against Racism YWCA, Knoxville; pres. bd. dirs. Lisa Ross Birth & Women's Ctr., Knoxville. Recipient Extraordinary Svc. to the Univ. award, U. Tenn., 2005, Angie Warren Perkins award, Commn. for Women, U. Tenn., Knoxville, 2005. Office: U Tenn Coll Law 1505 W Cumberland Ave Knoxville TN 37996 Office Phone: 865-974-6793.

KENNEDY, DONNA CHAPMAN, counseling administrator; b. Spartanburg, S.C., Sept. 21, 1959; d. Robert Luther and Hilda Snipes Chapman; m. Joseph Whitner Kennedy, Jr., Dec. 19, 1981; children: J. Whitner III, Robert Hughes. BS, Presbyn. Coll., Clinton, S.C., 1981; EdM, U. S.C., 1984, edn. specialist, 1990. Cert. counselor Nat. Bd. Cert. Counselors. Counselor Spartanburg Sch. Dist. Two, 1981—88, Spartanburg Sch. Dist. Three, 1988—. Intern supr. U. S.C., Columbia, 1984—. Bd. mem., vol. Children's Advocacy Ctr., Spartanburg, 1996—2003; be. mem., vol. Health Resource Ctr., Spartanburg, 2004—. Mem.: S.C. Sch. Counselors Assn. (Counselor of Yr. 2004), S.C. Counseling Assn. (recognition chair). Office: Cannons Elem Sch 1315 Old Converse Rd Spartanburg SC 29307

KENNEDY, ELIZABETH MAE, musician; b. Medford, Mass., Oct. 16, 1949; d. Thomas Power and Anne Cecelia (Coyne) Sullivan; m. William David Kennedy, Oct. 12, 1970 (div. 1984); children: Mary Elizabeth, Jonathan Martin. AS, N.S. C.C., 1969; student, Aquinas Coll., 1991—92. Cert. liturgical musician music and liturgy. Retail sales mgmt. Jordan Marsh Co., Peabody, Mass., 1966—69; retail mgmt. Sears, Roebuck and Co., Lynn, Mass., 1969—70; asst. bookkeeper Henry Leather Co., Peabody, 1970—76; office mgr. Bartlett and Steadman Co. Inc., Marblehead, Mass., 1981—90. Bandleader, performer New England Area, 1983—; music dir., contract organist St. John The Evangelist Ch., Swampscott, Mass., 1985-98; cofounder New Sch. of Music and Performing Arts, Marblehead, Mass., 1994; dir. music St. Charles Borromeo Ch., Waltham, Mass., 1998-99, Incarnation Parish, Melrose, Mass., 1999-2003. Organizer Devereux Neighborhood Assn.; active North Shore Piano Tchrs. Guild, 1988—, v.p., 1998-2000, co-pres., 2000-02; chairperson Marblehead Festival of the Arts, 1998-99. Democrat. Roman Catholic. Avocations: reading, swimming, midi, computers. Home: 46 Ocean Ave Marblehead MA 01945-3616 Fax: 781-631-1519. E-mail: elizmkenn@aol.com.

KENNEDY, EVELYN SIEFERT, foundation executive, textiles executive; b. Pitts., Nov. 11, 1927; d. Carmine and Assunta (Iacobucci) Rocci; m. George J. Siefert, May 30, 1953 (dec. 2000); children: Paul Kenneth, Carl Joseph, Ann Marie; m. Lyle H. Kennedy II, Oct. 12, 1974 (dec. 1990); m. Frederick J. Commentucci, Feb. 24, 2001. BS magna cum laude, U. RI, 1969, MS in Textiles and Clothing, 1970. Accredited appraiser of personal property, Internat. Soc. Appraisers. With Pitts. Pub. Schs., 1945-50, Goodyear Aircraft Corp., Akron, Ohio, 1950-54; clothing instr. Groton (Conn.) Dept. Adult Edn., 1958-68; pres. Sewtique, Groton, 1970—, Sewtique II, New London, Conn., 1986; v.p. Kennedy Capital Advisors, Groton, 1973-85, Kennedy Mgmt. Corp., Groton, 1974-85, Kennedy Intervest, Inc., Groton, 1975-85; pres., exec. dir. PRIDE Found., Inc., Groton, 1978—. Clothing cons. Coop. Ext. Svc., Dept. Agr.; internat. lectr. on clothing for disabled and elderly; adj. faculty U. Conn., Ea. Conn. State Coll., St. Joseph Coll.; hon. prof. U. RI, assoc. prof., 1987-2000; fed. expert witness Care Label Law, FTC, 1976; mem. Major Appliance Consumer Action Panel, 1983-89. Author: Dressing With Pride, 1980, Clothing Accessibility: A Lesson Plan to Aid the Disabled and Elderly, 1983, Textiles Speak, 1996. Regional adv. coun. SBA Active Corps Execs., Hartford, 1985-2006; bd. dirs. Small Bus. Devel. Ctr., 1989—, Easter Seal Rehab. Ctr. Southeastern Conn., Southeastern Conn. Women's Ctr., 1997—, Women's Ctr. New London County, 1997—; bus. adv. coun. U. RI, 1979-89, trustee, 1985—; active LWV; mem. Groton Vocat. Edn. Adv. Coun. Recipient award of distinction U. RI, 1969, Adv. of Yr. SBA, 1984, Outstanding Svc. in Cmty., 1991; named Woman of Yr. Bus. and Profl. Women's Club, 1977, Conn. Home Economist of Yr., 1987; named to Wall of Fame U. RI, 2004. Mem. Internat. Sleep Coun. (consumer affairs rep., SBA award 1991), Internat. Soc. Appraisers (accredited appraiser personal property, panelist FMHA roster, farmer's credit mediator 1989-92), Nat. Assn. Bedding Mfrs., Conn. Home Economists in Bus. (founder 1977, Women of Yr. 1987), Nat. Home Economists in Bus. (chmn. internat. rels., nat. fin. chmn. 1986), Am. Home Econs. Assn., Coll. and Univ. Bus. Instrs. of Conn., Am. Occupl. Therapy Assn. (resource cons. 1986—), Web-Re-Stor Assn. (wedding restoration specialist 1993-2000), Southeastern Women's Network, Textile Soc. Am., Fashion Group, Costume Soc. Am., New London Zonta Club, Bus. and Profl. Women's Club (Outstanding Women of Yr. 1977), Omicron Nu. Office: 391 Long Hill Rd Groton CT 06340-3812 Office Phone: 860-445-7320. Personal E-mail: textileappraisal@aol.com.

KENNEDY, GWENDOLYN DEBRA, artist, scriptwriter, playwright; b. Daly City, Calif., Nov. 18, 1960; d. Adolphus Brooks and Ella (Robinson) K.; children: Gwendolyn Fincher, Edward James, Jr. AA in Theater Prodn., City Coll. San Francisco, 1992. Artist Walt Disney Animation Art, 1991; artist animation and fine art www.blackpantherpartypress.tv, 1994—; owner Black Panther Party Press and Pub., 1993—. Owner mail order co. La Chateau D'Gwendolyn Kennedy Co., 1991—. Author: Billie Holliday Collection Book, 1993, Kane Kut Murder Trial, 1993, Poetic Justice, 1994, No Struggle No Progress, 1995, Nyami the Sky God, 1996, Prison Secrets. Recipient Journalist of Yr. award City News Svc., Mo., 1995. Lutheran. Avocations: guitar, ballet, art, track, piano, computers. Home: 285 Bellevue Ave Daly City CA 94014-1305 Office: PO Box 135 Daly City CA 94016-1305 Personal E-mail: sareenlove@aol.com.

KENNEDY, JERRIE ANN PRESTON, public relations executive; b. Quanah, Tex. Student, Sunset Sch. Preaching, Lubbock, Tex., 1975-78, Jo-Susan Modeling Sch., Nashville, 1984, Film Actors Lab., 1986. Co-prodr. Vincent Cirrincione & Assocs., NY, 1986; paralegal Arlington Career Inst., 1998—; freelance internat. mktg. and pub. rels. exec., Papua New Guinea. Military del. NATO Allies for The French Liaison, Ft. Hood, Tex., 1992, Vietnam War (Diplomatic immunity) 1972-1975. Author screenplay, fed. and cmty. pub. spl. events prodn. US Activist Women's Rights in the State of Tex., 2003. Recipient 1st and 3d pl. awards Modeling Assn. Am., NYC, 1985.

KENNEDY, JOANIE TISKA, artist, painter; b. Pittsfield, Mass., July 12, 1950; d. Edward Francis and Jean Frances (Hayes) Tiska; m. Willard Lee Kennedy, May 25, 1974; children: Tiska Ann, Katherine Jean, Christine Ashley. Student, East Carolina U., 1968-71, N.C. State U., Raleigh, 1971-72, Lincoln Land Coll., 1976-79. Designer Stained Glass Assoc., Knightdale, N.C., 1971-74; prof. asst. Lincoln Land Coll., Springfield, Ill., 1977-79; artist Art Space Inc., Raleigh, N.C., 1984—; bd. dirs. Mem. Med. Soc. Alliance Book Club, Nat. Mus. Women in Arts (charter), Wake Visual, Charlotte Hilton Green Park Assn., Nature Conservancy, N.C. Mus. Art, N.C. Wildlife Fedn. Avocations: gardening, walking, aerobics, water sports, writing.

KENNEDY, JUDITH MARY, school psychologist; b. Custer, S.D., June 29, 1944; d. William A. and Rosaleatha K.; m. Dwane Ellis, July 3, 1993; children from a previous marriage: David R. King, Angela R. King. BS, BHSU, 1967; MS, Idaho State U., 1990, EdS, 1991. Tchr. spl. edn. Snake River Schs., Blackfoot, Idaho, 1983-88; sch. psychologist Madison Snake River, Rexburg, Idaho, 1989-91, Rapid City (S.D.) Area Schs., 1991—. Cons. in field; life coach. Author: Getting to Know You, 1995, Parenting, 1998. Pres. Snake River Tchrs. Assn., 1988-89. Mem. S.D. Sch. Psychologists (pres. elect 1996-98). Avocations: skiing, spirituality, reading, health. Office: RCAS 21 Saint Joseph St Rapid City SD 57701-2822 Home: 21326 Englewood Rd Lead SD 57754-3708

KENNEDY, KAMELA DENISE, director; b. Mobile, Ala., Dec. 28, 1968; d. Kamel William and Dorothy Johnson Kennedy. BA, U. Ala., Tuscaloosa, 1991; MEd, Ala. State U., Montgomery, 2004, EdS, 2006. Dist. recruiter Ala. State U., Montgomery, 1991—2002, asst. coord. student activities, 2002—. Mem.: Ala. Counseling Assn. (editor newsletter 2004—05, co-editor newsletter 2005—), Chi Sigma Iota, Am. Counseling Assn., Delta Sigma Theta (co-chair com. 2005—06, bd. mem. project fundraiser 2005—06). Office: Alabama State University 915 S Jackson Street Montgomery AL 36195 Office Phone: 334-229-4888. Personal E-mail: kamelakennedy@aol.com. E-mail: kkennedy@alasu.edu.

KENNEDY, KAREN SYENCE, advertising agency executive; b. Bklyn., May 7, 1943; d. Bruno Weinschel and Pearl Heyman; first marriage: Michael Syence; children: Sherry, Scott; m. Peter Kennedy, Aug. 25, 1979. BS, Boston U., 1963. Advt. mgr. Weinschel Engring., Gaithersburg, Md., 1965-68; mktg. svcs. mgr. Rixon Electronics, Silver Spring, Md., 1968-70; pres. Comm. Unltd., Chevy Chase, Ltd., 1970-74; v.p. Ehrlich Manes & Assocs., Bethesda, Md., 1974-77; pres. Rainbow Tree, St. Croix, V.I., 1978-80; advt. programs dir. GE, McLean, Va., 1980-81; pres. Karen Syence Kennedy Assocs., Fairfax, Va., 1981-83; pres., CEO, KSK Comm., LLC, Vienna, Va., 1983—2002; ptnr. EPB Comms., N.Y.C., 1999—2002; pres. Karen Syence Kennedy Assocs., Great Falls, Va., 2002—. Pres., chmn. Treasure Beach Found., 2000—. E-mail: ksk001@earthlink.net.

KENNEDY, KATHLEEN, film producer; b. Jan. 1, 1954; m. Frank Marshall, 1987; 2 children. BA in Telecommunications and Film, San Diego State U., 1975. Various posts including camera operator, video editor, floor dir. and news prodn. coord. KCST, San Diego; co founder (with Steven Spielberg & Frank Marshall) and pres. Amblin Entertainment, Universal City, Calif., 1984—92; co-founder (with Frank Marshall), pres., prodr. Kennedy-Marshall Co., 1994—. Pres. Producers Guild of Am., 2001—06. Assoc. prodr.: (films) Poltergeist, 1982, Twilight Zone-The Movie, 1983, Indiana Jones and the Temple of Doom, 1984, Reform School Girls, 1986; prodr.: (films) E.T. The Extra-Terrestrial, 1982 (Academy award nomination for best picture 1982); (with Quincy Jones, Frank Marshall, and Spielberg) The Color Purple, 1985 (Academy award nomination for best picture 1985); (with Marshall and Art Levinson) The Money Pit, 1986; (with Marshall and Spielberg) Empire of the Sun, 1987, Always, 1989; (with Richard Vane) Arachnophobia, 1990; (with Marshall and Gerald R. Molen) Hook, 1991; (with Robert Watts) Alive, 1993; (with Molen) Jurassic Park, 1993, (with Marshall) Milk Money, 1994; (with Clint Eastwood) The Bridges of Madison County, 1995, Twister, 1996; (with Steven Spielberg), The Six Sense, 1999, Snow Falling on Cedars, 1999, A Map of the World, 1999, Artifical Intelligence: AI, 2001, Jurassic Park III, 2001, Seabiscuit, 2003, The Young Black Stallion, 2003, War of the Worlds, 2005; exec. prodr.: (films)Roller Coaster Rabbit, 1990, A Dangerous Woman, 1993, Schindler's List, 1993 (Academy award for best picture 1993), Trail Mix-Up, 1993, A Far Off Place, 1993, Balto, 1995, Congo, 1995, The Indian in the Cupboard, 1995; (with Marshall and Spielberg) Gremlins, 1984, The Goonies, 1985, Back to the Future, 1985, Young Sherlock Holmes, 1985, *batteries not included, 1987, Jurassic Park: The Lost World, 1997, Dad, 1989, Back to the Future Part II, 1990, Gremlins 2: The New Batch, 1990, Back to the Future Part III, 1990, Joe Versus the Volcano, 1990, Cape Fear, 1991, We're Back! A Dinosaur's Story, 1993, (with Marshall) Fandango, 1985; (with Marshall, Spielberg, and David Kirschner) An American Tail, 1986; (with Marshall, Spielberg, Peter Guber, and Jon Peters) Innerspace, 1987; (with Spielberg) Who Framed Roger Rabbit, 1988; (with Marshall, Spielberg, and George Lucas) The Land Before Time, 1988; (with Marshall and Lucas) Indiana Jones and the Last Crusade, 1989; (with Marshall and Kirschner) An American Tail: Fievel Goes West, 1991; (with Peter Bogdanovich) Noises Off, 1992; (with Marshall and Molen); (with Molen, Kirschner, William Hanna, and Joseph Barbera) The Flintstones, 1994, Olympic Glory, 1999, Signs, 2002; exec. prodr. TV Tummy Trouble, 1989, The Sports Pages, 2001 Bd. dir. Michael J. Fox Found. for Parkinson's Rsch. Office: Kennedy-Marshall Co 619 Arizona Ave Santa Monica CA 90401-1358*

KENNEDY, KATHY KAY, library director; b. New Kensington, Pa., Oct. 21, 1942; d. Lawrence Michael Kennedy and Vivian Mae Smeltzer. BA in English, Thiel Coll., 1964; MSLS, Drexel Inst. Tech., 1967. Bibliographer Union Libr. Catalog, Phila., 1964-67; sci./tech. librarian Carnegie Libr. of Pitts., 1967-73, adult svcs. specialist, 1973-74; libr. dir. Peoples Libr., New Kensington, pa., 1974-87; adult svcs. librarian Monroeville (Pa.) Pub. Libr., 1987-89, asst. dir., 1989-93, dir., 1993—. Editor: Review of Iron and Steel Literature, 1972. Bd. dirs. Pa. Citizens for Better Librs., Greensburg, 1996—, Monroeville Arts Coun., 1989-91; mem. bd. assocs. Thiel Coll., 2002—. Mem. Pa. Libr. Assn. (pres. 1995, editor jour. 1976-78, Cert. of Merit 1982), Bus.

and Profl. Women of Pitts. (pres. 1975-77), McKeesport Bus. and Profl. Women (Woman of Yr. 1999), Pa. Fedn. Bus. and Profl. Women (dist. dir. 1984-85), Allegheny County Libr. Assn. (bd. dirs. 1999-2001). Lutheran. Avocations: music, theater, reading, travel. Office: Monroeville Pub Libr 4000 Gateway Campus Blvd Monroeville PA 15146-3381

KENNEDY, LAUREL R., secondary school educator; b. Ogallala, Nebr., Dec. 31, 1952; d. Erle D. and Mildred B. Corfield; m. Kenneth R. Kennedy, Sept. 7, 1973; children: Danielle R., Kori L. Hicks, Tana D., Jess D., Riley D. BS in History and Math., Chadron State Coll., Nebr., 1974; M in Curriculum and Instrn., U. Nebr., Kearney, 2001. Math and history tchr. Big Springs (Nebr.) H.S., 1975—83, Ogallala (Nebr.) Pub. Schs., 1983—. Mem. Nebr. History Stds. Task Force, 2002—03; ptnr. Nebr. Partnership for Am. History Edn., 2002—; mem. Curriculum Coordinating Coun., Ogallala, 2002—05. Active First Bapt. Ch., Arthur, Nebr., 1962—2006. Mem.: Nat. Coun. for Social Studies, Nebr. Assn. for the Gifted. Republican. Baptist. Avocations: travel, reading, baking, sports, games. Office: Ogallala High School 602 E G Ogallala NE 69153 Office Phone: 308-284-4029.

KENNEDY, LEILA, accounting educator; b. Murray City, Ohio, June 19, 1941; d. Carl Eugene and Jesse Marie (Mentzer) Wynegar; m. Gary Nelson Retterer, Sept. 28, 1958 (div. Jan. 1962); children: April Anne, William Eugene; m. Junior Everett Kennedy, May 31, 1963. BS in Acctg., Bluefield State Coll., 1989; MS in Acctg., Marshall U., 1992. Faculty Nat. Bus. Coll., Bluefield, Va., 1992; adj. faculty Bluefield State Coll., W. Va., 1991-92, instr. bus. W. Va., 1992-93, asst. prof. Lewisburg, W. Va., 1993-98, assoc. prof., 1998—. Cons. in field. Avocations: crochet, knitting, reading. E-mail: lkennedy@bluefieldstate.edu.

KENNEDY, LESA FRANCE, professional sports team executive; BA in Econs., Duke U., 1983, BA in Psychology, 1983. Joined Internat. Speedway Corp., Daytona Beach, Fla., 1983, sec., 1987—96, treas., 1989—96, exec. v.p., 1996—2003, pres., 2003—, also bd. dirs., 1984—, also mem. exec. mgmt. planning com. Bd. dir. NASCAR, Sun Trust Bank. Active Civic League of the Halifax Area; bd. dir. Stetson Univ. Sch. Bus.; active United Way, Seaside Music Theater, Leadership Daytona, Daytona Beach Area C. of C.; supporter London Symphony Orch., Volusia Vision, Daytona Beach Mus. Arts and Scis. Named Top Female Sports Exec., Street & Smith's SprotsBus, 1999, 2000, 2001; named one of Top 10 Secret People Who Will Change the World, AutoWeek mag., 25 Most Influential People in NASCAR, Charlotte Observer, 2001, 2002. Mem.: Daytona Beach Area C of C, NASCAR (bd. dirs.). Office: ISC 1801 W International Speedway Blvd Daytona Beach FL 32114 Office Phone: 386-254-2700. Office Fax: 386-947-6816.

KENNEDY, LOUISE AVERY, theater critic, newspaper editor, writer; b. Dayton, Ohio, Feb. 6, 1959; d. Grafton Sherwood and Gertrude Avery (Harder) K.; m. George Langdon Gibson, May 13, 1989 (div. May 1994). BA, Yale U., 1980. Reporter, asst. editor, mng. editor New Haven Advocate, 1980-83; asst. Living editor, asst. mng. editor/Living New Haven Register and Jour. Courier, 1984-86; copy editor, Living copy desk chief Boston Globe, 1988-93, asst. book editor, 1993-95, asst. Living editor, 1995, asst. Mag. editor, 1995, food editor, home editor, arts reporter, 2001—06, theater critic, 2006—. Freelance theatre, book and mag. critic Boston Globe, 1988—. Co-author: The Between the Lions Book for Parents: Everything You Need to Know to Help Your Child Learn to Read, 2004. Named Disting. Alumna, Phillips Acad., Andover, Mass., 1994. Mem. PEN New Eng., Soc. Profl. Journalists. Office: Boston Globe 135 Morrissey Blvd Boston MA 02125 Mailing: The Boston Globe PO Box 55819 Boston MA 02205-5819 Office Phone: 617-929-2839. Office Fax: 617-929-2813. E-mail: kennedy@globe.com.*

KENNEDY, LYDIA, human resources specialist; b. 1971; BA in Psych., U. Ariz.; M in Ednl. Leadership, Northern Ariz. U., Tucson. Worked in Human Resources dept. Ariz. Daily Star, Tucson Citizen, Tucson Newspaper; tng. mgr. Casino, Sun/Casino Del Sol; dir., Human Resources dept. Buffalo Exch., Tucson, 2002—. Eller Assoc. U. Ariz. Eller Coll. of Bus. and Pub. Policy. Mem. League of United Latin Am. Citizens, 1993—; mentor Wakefield Mid. Sch.; mem., Women's Leadership Conf. Com. YWCA; mem. Ariz. Compensation survey adv. steering com., Newman Cath. Cmty. Ctr. Named one of 40 Under 40, Tucson Bus. Edge, 2006. Mem.: Am. Soc. Tng. and Devel., Soc. Human Resources Mgmt., Knights of Columbus. Office: Buffalo Exchange PO Box 40488 Tucson AZ 85717 Office Phone: 520-622-2711. Office Fax: 520-622-7015.*

KENNEDY, MAGDALENE MILLER, secondary school educator; b. Buffalo, Aug. 18, 1950; d. Walter Mathias and Christina Lowrey Miller; m. Scott Kennedy, Aug. 3, 1985; children: Christina Maria, Richard Walter. BA in English Edn., Canisius Coll., Buffalo, 1972, MS in English Edn., 1975. Cert. tchr. English pre-K-12 NY, 1975. Tchr. English Grand Island HS, NY, 1972—. Recipient Celebration of Inspiration honoree, Grand Island HS. Mem.: Grand Island Tchr. Assn., Grand Island Cmty. Choir, The Notables. Roman Cath. Avocations: singing, reading. Home: 16 Delwood Rd Kenmore NY 14217 Office: Grand Island Central Sch Dist 1100 Ransom Rd Grand Island NY 14072 Office Phone: 716-773-8800.

KENNEDY, MARGARET ALEXIS, law educator, researcher; d. Lynne and Gerry Kennedy. BA, U. Toronto, Can., 1986—90; LLB, U. Man., Winnipeg, Can., 1990—93; MA, U. B.C., Vancouver, Can., 1996—98, PhD, 1998—2004. Bar: B.C. 1995. Asst. prof., dept. criminal justice U. Nev., Las Vegas, 2005—. Recipient 41 Dissertation award, APA, 2003, 37 Dissertation award, 2004. Office: Univ Nevada 4505 Maryland Pky Box 5009 Las Vegas NV 89154-5009 Office Phone: 702-895-5122. Office Fax: 702-895-0252. Business E-Mail: alexis.kennedy@unlv.edu.

KENNEDY, MARJORIE ELLEN, librarian; b. Dauphin, Man., Can., Sept. 14, 1946; d. Stanley Harrison and Ivy Marietta (Stevens) May; m. Michael P.J. Kennedy, Apr. 3, 1980. BA, U. Sask., Regina, 1972; BLS, U. Alta., Edmonton, 1974; BEd, U. Regina, 1981. Profl. A cert. edn., Sask. Elem. sch. tchr. Indian Head (Sask) Pub. Sch., 1965-66, Elgin Sch., Weyburn, Sask., 1967-68; tchr., libr. Ctrl. Sch., Prince Albert, Sask., 1970-71; elem. sch. tchr. Vincent Massey Sch., Prince Albert, 1969-70, 72-73; children's libr. J.S. Wood br. Saskatoon (Sask.) Pub. Libr., 1974-77, asst. coord. children's svcs., 1977-79; programme head, instr. libr. tech. SIAST-Kelsey Campus, Saskatoon, 1979—. Presenter workshops on reference materials for elem. sch. librs., storytelling and libr. programming for children, 1980—; vol. dir. Children's Lit. Workshops, Sask. Libr. Assn., 1979-80; mem. organizing com. Sask. Libr. Week, Saskatoon, 1988. Mem. Vanscoy (Sask.) and Dist. Agr. Soc., 1983-95. Named to Libr. Edn. Honor Roll ALA, 1987. Mem. Can. Libr. Assn. (instl. rep. 1984—), Sask. Libr. Assn. (insl. rep. 1984—, mem. children's sect. 1982-83), Sask. Assn. Libr. Techs. (instl. rep. 1984—), Can. Club (bd. mem. 1981-84). Mem. United Ch. Can. Avocations: antique doll restoration, antiques, gardening. Office: SIAST Kelsey Campus Box 1520 Libr Info Tech Program Saskatoon SK Canada S7K 3R5 E-mail: Kennedy@siast.sk.ca.

KENNEDY, MARLA CATHERINE, psychologist; b. Milw., June 28, 1935; d. Raymond G. and Catherine (Wimmer) Mueller; m. William Robert Kennedy, Mar. 2, 1957; children: Joseph, Timothy, Kristin, William, Daniel. BS, Alverno, Milw., 1956; MA, U. Minn., 1983, postgrad., 1983-1989. Lic. psychologist, lic. marriage and family therapist. Intern with mentally ill and mentally retarded Met. Clin., Mpls., 1984—85; pvt. practice psychology, marriage and family therapy Mpls., 1985—. Spkr. in field; part-time at Family Svc. Greater St. Paul, 1989-98; dir., co-counselor Adlerian Family Edn. Ctr., 1983-85. Contbr. articles to profl. jours. Bd. dirs. Books for Africa, 1997-2002; co-founder Community Line (now First Call for Help); pres. Legions of PTAs; active YWCA Shelter for Women, St. Paul; vol. Rams Juvenile Justice, 1985-2003. Mem. Am. Acad. Neurology Aux. (bd. dirs.), Minn. Assn. Marriage and Family Therapists, Minn. Assn. Group Psychotherapists (pres. 1998-00), Alfred Adler Assn. (bd. dirs. 1965-80), AAUW (bd. dirs.), New Century (pres., bd. dirs.), Women's Investment Club (treas.), Mensa, Phi Lambda Theta (named Alumni Notable Achievement, U. Minn., 2005). Unitarian Universalist. Avocations: swimming, tennis, reading. Business E-Mail: kenne402@umn.edu.

KENNEDY, MARY SUSSOCK, artist; b. Liverpool, Eng., Oct. 29, 1926; came to U.S., 1951; d. Charles Archibald and Maria (Mullin) Sussock; m. Rogers Jack Kennedy, May 18, 1946 (dec. Jan. 1987); children: Jacollyn Fenny-Maria, Beverley Gillian, Kimberley Tara. AAS with highest honors, Fashion Inst. Tech., N.Y., 1975; BA summa cum laude, Montclair State Coll., 1977; postgrad., Montclair State Univ., 1977-78. Portrait, stage and wedding photographer Wilkinson and Kennedy, Liverpool, 1943-47; freelance artist Montville, Barnegat Light, NJ, 1956-73, Key Largo, Fla., 1984—; grad. asst. in sculpture Montclair State Univ., Upper Montclair, NJ, 1977-78; diamond stylii maker Rogers Kennedy Inc., Saddle Brook, NJ, 1978-84. One woman show at Fashion Inst. Tech., N.Y., 1974; exhibited in group shows at Smithsonian Instn., Washington, 1963, Montclair Art Mus., 1964, U.S. Custom House, N.Y.C., 1979, also exhibit opened by Princess Grace in Monaco, 1960; sculpture exhibited in two person show at Montclair State Univ., 1977. Mem. Phi Kappa Phi. Democrat. Episcopalian. Avocations: anthropology, reading, travel, gardening. Home: PO Box 2560 Key Largo FL 33037-7560

KENNEDY, MARY THERESA, mental health services professional; b. N.Y.C., Dec. 4, 1940; d. Owen and Theresa B. Reilly; m. James Anthony Kennedy, Dec. 28, 1968; 1 child, James Austin. BA, St. John's U., NY, 1962; MA, St. Johns U., NY, 1964; PD, St. John's U., NY, 1968; PhD, Fordham U., NY, 1971. Asst. prof. St. John's U., Jamaica, NY, 1968—78, CUNY, N.Y.C., 1975—87; chief psychologist Office Mental Retardation and Develop. Disabilities, N.Y.C., 1980—; psychologist pvt. practice, 1989—; assoc. prof. CUNY, N.Y.C., 1975—. Forensic coord. Office Mental Retardation and Develop. Disabilities, N.Y.C., 1980—; pres. Assn. Downstate Dirs. Psychology, N.Y.C., 1992—95. Contbr. articles to profl. jours. Recipient Outstanding Educators award, City Hall, NYC, 1972. Mem.: APA, N.Y. State Psychol. Assn., Kappa Delta Phi. Office: Dr Mary T Kennedy 217-04 Northern Blvd Bayside NY 11361 Office Phone: 718-217-2765.

KENNEDY, MARY VIRGINIA, retired diplomat; b. Pocatello, Idaho, Sept. 5, 1946; d. Charles Millard and Martha Lorissa (Evans) K. BA, U. Denver, 1968, MA, 1969; MAT, U. Idaho, 1971, JD, 2001. Tchr. cert. Idaho. Recreation aide ARC, South Vietnam, 1969-70; ops. officer State Dept. Ops. Ctr., Washington, 1977-78; spl. asst. amb. Philip Habib, Washington, 1979-80, Sec. State, Washington, 1980-81; econ. officer U.S. Embassy, Cairo, 1981-84; consul Am. Consulate, Adana, Turkey, 1985-88; Pearson fellow Office Cong. Bereuter Ho. Reps., 1988-89; exec. asst. Dept. Sec. State, Washington, 1989-91; dep. chief mission Dept. State U.S. Embassy, Kuwait, 1991-93; consul gen. Am. Consulate, Karachi, Pakistan, 1994-96; dean Sch. Profl. Area Studies, Fgn. Svc. Inst., 1996-98; ret., 1998. Bd. trustees Idaho State Hist. Soc., 1999—2002. Mem. Am. Fgn. Svc. Protective Assn. (bd. dirs. 1988-91), Phi Beta Kappa, Mortar Bd. Home: 5137 Admiral Way SW Seattle WA 98116 Address: PO Box 16634 Seattle WA 98116-0634 Personal E-mail: niact@aol.com.

KENNEDY, MAYDRA JANE PENISSON (J.P. KENNEDY), poet; b. New Orleans, Aug. 31, 1938; d. Charles Christopher and Clare Elda (Walter) Penisson Jr.; m. Jacob Louis Kennedy Sr., July 17, 1974 (dec. Nov. 1995); 1 child, Wendy Jane Kennedy. Grad., West Jefferson HS, Harvey, La. Author of poetry and song lyrics. Inductee Internat. Poetry Hall of Fame, 1997. Mem. Internat. Soc. Poets (life), Am. Fedn. Police (mem. in good standing), Nat. Mus. Women in the Arts, Paralyzed Vets. Am. (hon.). Democrat. Lutheran. Avocations: painting, singing, gardening, creative activities. Home: 807 Monroe St Gretna LA 70053-2241

KENNEDY, MEGAN CATHERINE, music educator; b. Johannesburg, July 16, 1963; arrived in U.S., 1997; d. Vivian Hector and Shirley Margaret Granger; m. David Mark Kennedy, Apr. 1, 1987; children: Diana, Jane, Kimberley. Student, Trinity Coll. Music, Johannesburg, 1975—80, U. South Africa, 1985—87, student, 1988; CIDESCO diploma, Stellenbosch Acad., 1984. Instr. St. Clair Coll., Windsor, Ont., Canada, 1988—89; piano tchr. Windsor, 1992—94, Maxwell Music, White Lake, Mich., 2002—05, Piano Power, West Bloomfield, Mich., 2002—; Piano pedagogue Mich. Music Ctr, Commerce, Mich., 2005—. Mem.: West Oakland Music Tchrs. Assn., Music Tchrs. Nat. Assn., Mich. Fedn. Music Clubs, Mich. Music Tchrs. Assn., Nat. Guild Piano Tchrs., Am. Coll. Musicians. Episcopalian. Avocations: gardening, walking, travel, history, log homes. Office Phone: 248-505-8684. Personal E-mail: meegieloo@yahoo.com.

KENNEDY, MURIEL, psychologist, consultant, educator; b. Bamberg, S.C., Mar. 29, 1965; d. Harold Lee Kennedy (dec.) and Virginia Morgan Kennedy Marion. BS, U. S.C., 1987; MS, Howard U., 1993, PhD, 1995. Lic. psychologist, Va., Md., D.C. Nuc. engr. Charleston Naval Shipyard, Charleston, S.C., 1987-90; psychology assoc. Child Advocacy Network, Balt., 1996-97; clin. psychologist Child and Family Therapy Ctr., Washington, 1997—. Clin. cons. Inst. for Life Enrichment, Washington, 1997—, Baraka Pastoral Counseling Ctr., Largo, Md., 1997—; adj. prof. Howard U., Washington, 1997—; exec. dir. Perico Inst. for Youth Devel. Entrepreneurship, Inc.; co-founder New Life Enrichment Ctr., Inc. Mem. Assn. Black Psychologists (treas. 1996-97, pres.-elect 1998-99, pres. 1999-2000, immediate past pres. 2000-2001), Psi Chi. Democrat. Baptist. Avocations: inspirational writing, listening to music, poetry, the arts, sports. E-mail: murielkenn@yahoo.com.

KENNEDY, PATRICIA BERRY, retired music educator; b. Alexandria, La., May 8, 1944; d. Gerald Adair and Zennia Juanita (Francis) Berry. B of Music Edn., Va. Commonwealth U., 1968, MEd, 1974. Cert. music tchr., gen., choral and instrumental, adminstrn. and supervision, Va. Tchr. choral music Colonial Hgts. (Va.) Pub. Schs., 1968-71; tchr. choral, instrumental and gen. music King William (Va.) Pub. Schs., 1972—2002; ret., 2002; bookeeper Dominion Uniserv Unit, 2002—. Coun. chair Dominion UniServ Unit, Richmond, Va., 1987-90, 91-93, 1st v.p., 1996-98; bd. dirs. Va. Edn. Assn., 1987-90, 91-93, 96-2000, 04—. Va. Wing CAP, Civil Air Patrol, Chesterfield, Va., 1971—. Named Sr. Mem. of Yr., Civil Air Patrol Va. Wing, 1984, 2000, PTA Mem. of Yr., Hamilton-Holmes PTA, 1985, Tchr. of Yr., Acquinton Elem. Sch., 1990, 96, King William County Schs., 1990-91, Exceptional Mem. of Yr., Acquinton PTA, 1993-94, 99-2000. Mem. NEA, Va. Educators Assn. (bd. dirs.), Music Educators Nat. Conf., Va. Elem. Music Edn. Assn. (pres. 1994-96), Va. Music Educators Assn., King William Edn. Assn. (faculty rep., sec. 1992-93, pres. 1994-97), Lions Club (bd. dirs. 2020-05). Independent. Baptist. Avocation: search and rescue work. Office: Dominon UniServ Unit 8001 Franklin Farms Dr #243 Richmond VA 23229 Home: 3518 Chesdin Blvd Sutherland VA 23885-9569 E-mail: patkennedy@mindspring.com.

KENNEDY, PEGGY BOOGAARD, artist, writer; b. Longview, Wash., Nov. 12, 1945; d. Johannes Elsworth and Martha Emily (Hill) Boogaard; divorced; children: John Steven, Anjanette M. Kennedy Hage. BA, Seattle Univ., 1967; postgrad., Univ. Juneau, 1982-85. Daycare owner Boogaard's Daycare, Ketchikan, Alaska, 1961-65; tourist info. Ketchikan Visitor's Bureau, Ketchikan, Alaska, 1966; editor Fragments, Seattle, 1967; sub. tchr. Ketchikan Borough Schs., Ketchikan, 1977-84. Author short stories and poems. Charter mem. Thespian charter, Ketchikan, Ark, 1963; Sunday sch. dir. Pentecostal Ch., Saxman, 1992-94, 76-95. With Civil Air Patrol, 1961-63. Recipient Nat. Merit Scholarship medal, 1961, 62, President's award Iliad Press for poetry, 1990. Republican. Avocations: writing, swimming, walking, sewing, reading, art, music. Home: 505 Jefferson St Lowr Ketchikan AK 99901-5852

KENNEDY, RENEAU CHARLENE UFFORD, forensic psychologist, consultant; b. Weiser, Idaho, June 18, 1954; d. Eldon Luther and Iris Jean (Hetrick) Ufford; m. Allen Ken Kennedy (div. Apr. 1999). BS in Psychology and Speech, Willamette U., 1975; MS in Psychology, U. Oreg., 1981; EdD in Psychology, Boston U., 1994; postgrad., Harvard U., 1994-98. Lic. psychologist. Tchr., counselor Victorian Dept. Edn., Melbourne, Australia, 1975-78, 80; fellow in clin. and forensic psychology The McLean Hosp., Harvard Med. Sch., Belmont, 1986-87, fellow in neuropsychology dept. neurology, 1987-89; clin. fellow in forensic psychology Harvard Med. Sch./Mass. Gen. Hosp., Boston, 1992-98; cons. Mass. Dept. Youth Svcs., Boston, 1994-95, Ky. Justice Cabinet, Frankfort, 1995; pvt. practice Weston, Mass., 1996—, Honolulu, 1997—. Affiliate clin. tng. supr., course instr. Am. Sch. Profl. Psychology, Honolulu; dir. tng. Forensic and Behavioral Scis. Inst., Honolulu, 1998-2000, Honolulu Family Therapy Ctr., 2000—; clin. fellow MGH Law and Psychiatry Svc., 1992-98; cons., spkr. in field. Mem. Ky. Justice Cabinet Juvenile Task Force, Frankfort, 1994-96, Mass. Child Death Rev. Team, Boston, 1995-97, Mass. Ct. Subcom. on Risk Assessment, Dedham, 1995—; col., aide de camp Commr. of Ky. State Police, Frankfort, 1994, 95, 96. Predoctoral fellow Harvard Med. Sch., Boston, 1992-94; named to Hon. Order of Ky. Cols. Mem. APA, Soc. for Personality Assessment, Hawaii Psychol. Assn., Homicide Rsch. Working Group, Psi Chi, Phi Delta Kappa, Pi Lambda Theta. Avocations: scuba diving, triathlon events, exotic travel. Home and Office: 3001 Diamond Head Rd Honolulu HI 96815-4716 Fax: 808-923-2299. E-mail: rkennedy@lava.net.

KENNEDY, SHERYL J., elementary school educator; d. James and Norma Ostmo; m. Kerry Kennedy; children: Christopher, Douglas. BA, Wartburg Coll., Waverly, Iowa, 1986. Cert. tchr., elem. edn. K-8, reading endorsement K-8 Iowa Dept. Edn. 4th grade tchr. Elijah Buell Elem. Sch., Clinton, Iowa, 1986—2002; supportive reading tchr. Camanche Mid. Sch., 2002—04; title I tchr. Camanche Elem. Sch., 2004—. Leader Cub Scouts Am., Clinton, 2003—, ctrl. com. mem., 2004—; chair, PTA Lyons Mid. Sch., 2004—; Sunday sch. tchr. St. Paul's Luth. Ch., Clinton, 1996—. Mem.: NEA. Avocations: reading, hiking.

KENNEDY, SUSAN MARIE, music educator; b. Attleboro, Mass., Apr. 29, 1951; d. Thomas E. and Irene K. Kennedy. MusB cum laude, U. Mass., Lowell, 1973; MA in Tchg., Bridgewater State Coll., Mass., 1981; CAGS with honors, Fitchburg State Coll., Mass., 2003. Cert. music tchr. Dept. Edn., Mass., supr., dir. Dept. Edn., Mass., music tchr. Dept. Edn., Fla., Dept. Edn., Ga., Dept. Edn., RI, Dept. Edn., Conn., adminstr. Dept. Edn., Conn. Music tchr. Citrus County Pub. Schs., Inverness, Fla., 1973—76, Bourne (Mass.) Pub. Schs., 1976—81, Lee County Pub. Schs., Ft. Myers, Fla., 1981—82, Hernando Pub. Schs., Brooksville, Fla., 1982—95, Clayton County Pub. Schs., Jonesboro, Ga., 1995—99, New Bedford (Mass.) Pub. Schs., 1999—2002, Windham (Conn.) Pub. Schs., 2002—. Performing musician (electric piano) Jerry Rellman Orch., Sharon, Mass., 1969—73; accompanist Chelmsford (Mass.) Choral Soc., 1970—71; jazz and classical pianist Holiday Inn, Dedham, Mass., 1971—72; organist various chs., Spring Hill, 1973—76; performing musician (percussion) The Wave, Citrus County, 1973—88; classical pianist various restaurants, Crystal River, Fla., 1974—76; autoharp instr. Lee County Adult Edn., Ft. Myers, 1981—82; pvt. piano tchr., Brooksville, Fla., 1983—94; performing musician(synthesizer) Candlelight Orch., Brooksville, 1988—95. Composer: pieces for students; dir. and arranger pieces for steel band, dir., prodr. original musicals, dir. first elem. steel band, Ga., 1996. Performer benefit concerts Am. Cancer Soc., Ocala, Fla., 1988—95; animal abuse investigator Humane Soc., Brooksville, 1990—95. Nominee Outstanding Elem. Tchrs. Am., 1973; named Tchr. of Yr., Hernando County, Fla., 1982, Outstanding Grad. Student in Ednl. Leadership, Fitchburg (Mass.) State Coll., 2003; recipient award, Brooksville PTO, 1992—93; grantee, Grass Roots Fine Arts Orgn., 1996, Conn. Commn. on the Arts. Mem.: Music Educators Nat. Conf. (assoc.), Kappa Delta Pi (assoc.). Avocations: fine arts, farming, travel, animals, environment. Home: 37 Granite St Foxboro MA 02035 Personal E-mail: suekennedy@rcn.com.

KENNEDY, SUSAN ORPHA, physical education educator, consultant, sports official; b. Torrington, Conn., June 1, 1951; d. Sidney Robinson Jr. and Dorothy Rose (Deering) K. BS in Phys. Edn., Ithaca Coll., 1973; MS in Phys. Edn., U. Oreg., 1978; PhD in Phys. Edn., Tex. Woman's U., 1991. Cert. K-2 tchr., N.Y. Tchr., coach Regional Dist. #1, Housatonic Valley Regional H.S., Falls Village, Conn., 1973-76; grad. teaching fellow U. Oreg., Eugene, 1976-78; substitute tchr., girls basketball coach Lake County Sch. Dist. #7, Lakeview, Oreg., 1978-80; instr., coach, athletic trainer Chadron (Nebr.) State Coll., 1980-84; rsch. asst. Tex. Woman's U., Denton, 1984-86, 88-89. Adj. faculty, U. North Tex., Denton, 1988-90. Author: (video) Prevention and Care of Athletic Injuries: Taping Techniques, 1984; coord.: (puppet show) Kids on the Block, Tex. Woman's U., 1985-86.; contbr. articles to profl. jours. Sectional ofcl., 1992—; basketball ofcl., 1970-78, 1991-2000; ofcl. U.S. Field Hockey Assn.; nat. ofcl. U.S. Women's Lacrosse Assn., 1992—; bd. dirs. Conn. Field Hockey Ofcls., 1995—, sec., 1995-2004, rules interpreter, 2003—; vol. Conn. Vols. Svcs. for Visually and Physically Handicapped, 1992-2002, rec. sec., 1999-2000; chair Inland Wetlands Commn., Litchfield, Conn. 1998-05 Named to New Agenda: N.E. Women's Hall of Fame, 2005; recipient Outstanding Official, Conn. Field Hockey Coaches Assn., 2001, Vol. of Yr., Nutmeg State Games, 2000, Ofcl. of Yr., 2000; scholar Acad. All-Am., 1987, All-Am., U.S. Achievement Acad., 1989, 1991. Mem. AAHPERD, Nat. Athlete Trainers Assn., Am. Coll. Sports Medicine, Nat. Assn. Sport Ofcls., Conn. Interscholastic Athletic Conf. Avocations: sea kayaking, weight training, officiating, environmental science issues, raising orchids. Home and Office: PO Box 1426 266 Norfolk Rd Litchfield CT 06759-2517

KENNEDY, TERESA JEAN, academic administrator, educator; d. H. Frederick and Patricia Jean Kennedy. BS in Edn., U. Idaho, Moscow, Idaho, 1984, BA in Spanish, 1984, MA in Spanish, 1985, PhD in Edn., 1998. Tchr. lang. Salem (Oreg.) Sch. Dist., 1985—87, Beaverton Sch. Dist., Aloha, Oreg., 1987—89; instr. Spanish Tillamook (Oreg.) Bay C.C., 1989—90; asst. to dir. internat. programs Wash. State U., Pullman, Wash., 1991—93; tchr. Moscow (Idaho) Sch. Dist., 1994—96; prof. edn. U. Idaho, Moscow, 1996—2003; mgr. Globe Program U. Corp. Atmospheric Rsch., Boulder, Colo., 2003—. Mem. subcom. internat. edn. Com. Econ. Devel., Washington, 2004—06; mem. rev. bd. Jour. Interactive Online Learning, 2002—. Contbr. chapters to books, articles to profl. jours. Mem. steering com. Nat. Geographic Edn. Found., 2006—. Mem.: Nat. Network Early Lang. Learning (rep. Idaho 1996—2003, rep. Pacific N.W. 2001—04, mem. nat. advocacy and polit. action com. 2001—05, editor Learning Langs. 2002—05), World Meteorol. Orgn. (mem. pub. weather svcs. expert group edn. 2006—), Idaho Assn. Tchrs. Lang. (pres. 2000—01), Pacific N.W. Coun. Langs. (pres. 2003—04, Tchr. of Yr. award 2002), Am. Coun. Tchrs. Langs. (Houghton Mifflin Excellence award 2002), Nat. Sci. Tchrs. Assn. (mem. internat. adv. bd. 2004—), Phi Delta Kappa (chpt. pres. 1999—2002, Outstanding Dissertation award 1998), Gamma Phi Beta. Avocation: scuba diving. Office: Univ Corp Atmospheric Rsch 3300 Mitchell Ln Boulder CO 80307

KENNEDY, VIRGINIA FRANCES, retired education educator; b. Cleve., Oct. 1, 1925; d. William M. and Stephanie (Wing) K.; m. Nicholas Howard Kurko, Mar. 1947 (div. Mar. 1976); children: Jean, Kaye, Lee Ann and Paul Kurko (dec.). BA, Antioch Coll., 1949; MS, U. Tenn., Knoxville, 1969; EdD, Tex. A&M U., 1979. Cert. ednl. diagnostician, TEx. Tchr. Knoxville Pub. Sch. Sys., 1966-67; ednl. diagnostician Ft. Worth Ind. Sch. Dist., 1969-76; assoc. prof. Tarleton State U., Stephenville, Tex., 1976-98. Mem.: Tex. Learning Disabilities Assn. (pres. 1961—63), S.W. Unitarian Universalist Women (pres. 2001—03), Phi Delta Kappa (chpt. 2d v.p. 1998—). Democrat. Unitarian Universalist. Avocations: gardening, working with children with learning differences.

KENNELLEY, ROSARIO CATHERINE, secondary school educator; b. Corpus Christi, Tex., Apr. 22, 1955; d. Carlos García and Maria Beltran; m. Cameron Paul Kennelley, Sept. 15, 1978; children: Erika Faye, Megan Elizabeth. AA in Gen. Edn., Mt. San Antonio Coll., Walnut, Calif., 1978; BA in Liberal Studies, Calif. State U., L.A., 1984; MA in Literacy of Lang. Devel. Azusa Pacific U., Calif., 2001. Tchr. West Covina Unified Sch. Dist., Calif., 1988—. Contbg. author: mag. California Forests-Acres The Cultural Divide, 2005. Named Tchr. of Yr., Edgewood Mid. Sch. Staff, West Covina Unified

Sch. Dist., 2003. Mem.: Calif. Coun. of the Blind, Delta Kappa Gamma (chpt. pres. 2002—). Democrat. Roman Catholic. Avocations: antiques, gardening, cooking, exercise, theater. Home: 203 S Cherrywood St West Covina CA 91791

KENNELLY, BARBARA B., retired congressman, federal agency administrator; b. Hartford, Conn., July 10, 1936; d. John Moran and Barbara (Leary) Bailey; m. James J. Kennelly, Sept. 26, 1959 (dec. 1995); children: Eleanor Bride, Barbara Leary, Louise Moran, John Bailey. BA in Econs, Trinity Coll., Washington, 1958; grad., Harvard-Radcliffe Sch. Bus. Adminstrn., 1959; MA in Govt, Trinity Coll., Hartford, 1971. Mem. Hartford Ct. of Common Council, 1975-79; sec. of state State of Conn., Hartford, 1979-83; mem. 98th-105th Congresses from 1st Dist. Conn., Hartford, 1982-98; mem. ways and means com.; counselor, assoc. commr. Social Security Adminstrn., 1999-2000; sr. adv. Baker & Hostetler, Washington; currently pres. & CEO Nat. Com. to Preserve Social Sec. & Medicare. Trustee Trinity Coll., Hartford, Conn.; active in numerous polit., civic, and goft. orgns. Greater Hartford, Conn.; co-chair Ctr. for Democracy, Washington. Democrat. Roman Catholic. Office: Natl Com Preserve Social Security & Medicare 10 G St NE Ste 600 Washington DC 20004

KENNELLY, SISTER KAREN MARGARET, retired academic administrator, church administrator, nun; b. Graceville, Minn., Aug. 4, 1933; d. Walter John Kennelly and Clara Stella Eastman. BA, Coll. St. Catherine, St. Paul, 1956; MA, Cath. U. Am., 1958; PhD, U. Calif., Berkeley, 1962. Joined Sisters of St. Joseph of Carondelet, Roman Cath. Ch., 1954. Prof. history Coll. St. Catherine, 1962-71, acad. dean, 1971-79; exec. dir. Nat. Fedn. Carondelet Colls., 1979-82; province dir. Sisters of St. Joseph of Carondelet, St. Paul, 1982-88; pres. Mt. St. Mary's Coll., L.A., 1989-2000, pres. emerita, 2000—; congl. dir. Sisters of St. Joseph of Carondelet, St. Louis, 2002—. Cons. N. Ctrl. Accreditation Assn., Chgo., 1974—84, Ohio Bd. Regents, Columbus, 1983—89; trustee colls., hosps., Minn., Mo., Wis., Calif., 1972—; chmn. Sisters St. Joseph Coll. Consortium, 1979—82. Editor, co-author: Am. Cath. Women, 1989; author (with others): Women of Minnesota, 1977; author: Women Religious and the Intellectual Life: The North American Achievement, 1996; co-editor: Gender Identities in American Catholicism, 2001;; Cath. Coll. Women in Am., 2002. Bd. dirs. Am. Coun. on Edn., 1997—99, Nat. Assn. Ind. Colls. and Univs., 1997—2000, Assn. Cath. Colls. and Univs., 1996—2000, Western Region Nat. Holocaust Mus., 1997—2000; coord. History Homes Religious Nature, 1988—. Fellow Fulbright, 1964. Mem.: Western Assn. Schs. and Colls. (sr. commn. 1997—2000), Assn. Cath. Colls. and Univs. (exec. bd. 1996—2000), Am. Coun. Edn. (bd. dirs. 1997—99), Nat. Assn. Ind. Colls. and Univs. (bd. dirs. 1997—99), Am. Assn. Rsch. Historians Medieval Spain, Medieval Acad., Am. Cath. Hist. Assn. Avocations: skiing, cuisine. Office: Congl Ctr 2311 Lindbergh Blvd Saint Louis MO 63131 Office Phone: 314-966-4048. Personal E-mail: kkennelly33@hotmail.com.

KENNER, MARILYN SFERRA, civil engineer; b. Youngstown, Ohio, Oct. 16, 1959; d. Joseph James and Mary (Conti) Sferra; m. Walter Sherden Kenner, July 7, 1984. B in Engring., Youngstown State U., 1982. Registered profl. engr., Ohio. Design and constrn. engr. Mahoning County Engr.'s Office, Youngstown, 1982-89, chief dep. engr., 1989—. Mem. engring. dean search com. Youngstown State U. Mem. Mahoning Valley Soc. Profl. Engrs. (pres., v.p. 1990-93, treas. 1987-90). Democrat. Roman Catholic. Home: 6941 Lockwood Blvd Youngstown OH 44512-4014 Office: Mahoning County Engr Office 940 Bears Den Rd Youngstown OH 44511-1218 Office Phone: 330-799-1581.

KENNETT, CHRISTIE SHIH, lawyer; b. 1970; married; 2 children. BA, Univ. Ill.; JD, St. Louis Univ. Bar: 1995. Faculty fellow St. Louis Univ. Law Sch., 1995—2001; assoc., tax, real estate, corp. law Husch & Eppenberger, St. Louis, 2001—04; atty., securities law unit State Farm Ins., Bloomington, Ill., now dir., govt. affairs. Bd. mem. Zoning Bd. of Appeals, Bloomington, Ill.; bd. dir. McLean Conty YWCA, Parklands Found.; pres. Ctrl. Ill. Chapter, Orgn. of Chinese Americans. Named one of Best Lawyers Under 40, Nat. Asian Pacific Am. Bar Assn., 2004, Top Asian Am. Corp. Execs. under 45, Goldsea. Office: Govt Affairs State Farm Ins One State Farm Plz Bloomington IL 61710

KENNEY, BELINDA JILL FORSEMAN, information technology executive; b. Oak Ridge, Tenn., Dec. 18, 1955; d. Jack Woodrow and Betty Jean Forseman; m. Ronald Gene Kenney, Feb. 23, 1985; 1 child, Brandon. BS, U. Tenn., 1977, postgrad., 1977-78; MBA, Emory U., 2000. Sales rep. Xerox Corp., Nashville, 1978—82, maj. account sales mgr., 1982—83, region sales ops. mgr. St. Louis, 1984—86, dist. sales mgr. Overland Park, Kans., 1987—89, dist. mgr. San Antonio, 1989—95, v.p. Houston, 1995—97, v.p., region gen. mgr. Bus. Svcs. Atlanta, 1998—99, sr. v.p. region mgr. NASG, 2000—01; corp. officer, exec. v.p. sales and mktg. SpectraLink Corp., Boulder, Colo., 2004—. Exec. in residence Leeds Sch. Bus. U. Colo. Patron M.D. Anderson Cancer Ctr.; vol. ARC, Disaster Assistance Call Ctr.; bd. dirs. Wise Women's Coun., Women's Vision Found., Foothills United Way Boulder, United Way Found. Mem.: Foothills Mensa. Lutheran. Avocations: jogging, reading, tennis, health and fitness. Office: 5755 Central Ave Boulder CO 80301

KENNEY, BRIGID E., lawyer; b. Balt., Feb. 9, 1951; BA, Goucher Coll., 1973; student, U. N.C.; JD with honors, U. Md., 1977. Bar: Md. 1977. Law clk. to Hon. Rita C. Davidson Ct. Spl. Appeals, Md., 1977-78; ptnr. Venable, Baetjer and Howard, Balt.; now ptnr. Venable LLP, Balt. and Washington. Chair Alliance for the Chesapeake Bay, Inc., 2005. Mem. ABA, Md. State Bar Assn., Bar Assn. Balt. City, Order of Coif. Office: Venable LLP 1800 Mercantile Bank 2 Hopkins Plz Baltimore MD 21201-2930 also: Venable LLP 575 Seventh St NW Washington DC 20004 Office Phone: 410-244-7487. Office Fax: 410-244-7742. Business E-Mail: bekenney@venable.com.

KENNEY, DOLORES THERESA, home economist; b. Pitts., Pa., July 23, 1929; d. Bernard Warfield Healey and Violet Arabela DeKlavon; m. William Brendan Kenney; children: Norman, Margaret, John, Anne, Joe, Kathy; children: Terrance, Grace, Becky. 2d grade tchr. St. Anne, San Antonio, 1951, Holy Childhood, Mascoutah, Ill., 1960—65. Pres. Coun. of Cath. Women, Buffalo. Home: 15 Clinton Ave Fredonia NY 14063

KENNEY, ESTELLE KOVAL, artist, educator; b. Chgo., Feb. 15, 1928; d. Hyman English and Florence (Browman) Koval; m. Herbert Kenney, Feb. 6, 1948; children: Carla, Robert. BFA, Art Inst. Chgo., 1976, MFA, 1978; postgrad., Yale U., 1980. Art therapist Grove Sch., Lake Forest, Ill., 1973—78, New Trier H.S., Ctrl. H.S., Winnetka, Ill., 1978—79, Mosely Sch., Chgo., 1979, Cove Sch., Evanston, Ill., 1979—82; dir. art therapy concentration, instr. painting and drawing Loyola U., Chgo., 1981—; pres., art dir. Nuts on Clark, Chgo. Pres., art dir. Nuts on Clark Inc., Chgo. One-woman shows include Evanston Libr., 1971, Zaks Gallery, Chgo., 1977, 1979, 1982, Renaissance Soc.-Bergman Gallery, U. Chgo., 1980, exhibited in group shows at Ill. State Mus., 1975, Women Artists, Here and Now, 1976, Chgo. Connections traveling exhbn., 1976—77, Bat, /wineb's Caucus for Art, 1977, Nancy Lurie Gallery, 1978, Marycrest Coll. Gallery, Davenport, Iowa, 1982, Chgo. Internat. Art Expo, 1981, 1982, 1983, Notre Dame U. Gallery, South Bend, Ind., 1982, Represented in permanent collections Ill. State Mus., Springfield, Union League Club. Chgo. Mem.: Coll. Art Assn., Ill. Art Therapy Assn. (pres. 1979—), Am. Art Therapy Assn. Personal E-mail: estellekenney@nutsonclark.com.

KENNEY, KRISTIE ANNE, ambassador; b. Washington; m. William R. Brownfield. BA in Polit. Sci., Clemson U., 1977; MA in Latin Am. Studies, Tulane U.; student, Nat. War Coll. Econ. cons. US Mission, Geneva; econ. officer US Embassy, Argentina, consular officer Jamaica; dir. Ops. Ctr. US Dept. State, Washington; mem. NSC; sr. adv. to asst. sec. for internat. narcotics & law enforcement US Dept. State, 2001—02, polit. mil. officer Office NATO Affairs, exec. sec. Washington, 1999—2001, US amb. to Ecuador Quito, Ecuador, 2002—05, US amb. to the Philippines Manila, 2006—. Recipient Disting. Honor award, US Dept. State, Arnold Raphel Meml. award. Avocations: skiing, tennis. Office: DOS Amb 8600 Manila Pl Washington DC 20521-8600*

KENNEY, MARIANNE, elementary school educator; b. Idaho Falls, Idaho, Jan. 11, 1933; d. Karl and Rose Katherine (Keller) Wolff; m. Bruce Warren Kenney, June 23, 1956; children: Karl Herbert, Peter James, Mary-Rose, Joseph Paul. BS in Elem. Edn., U. Idaho, 1955; MEd in Counseling/Guidance, U. Nev., Las Vegas, 1971. Cert. elem. edn. tchr., counseling, edn. adminstrn. Elem. tchr. Elk River (Idaho) Sch. Dist., 1953-54, Clark County Sch. Dist., Las Vegas, 1955-60, English tchr. jr. high, 1968-72, core tchr., 1972-75, Title I reading tchr., 1975-77, sch. counselor, 1977-79, dean of students, 1979-85, chpt. 1 reading tchr., 1985-93; adj. faculty mem. U. Nev., Las Vegas, 1994—. Author: Clark County School District Language Arts Guide, 1977, Clark County School District Elementary Counselors' Guide, 1979. Mem. Las Vegas Child Welfare Bd., 1977-85, chmn., 1980. Fulbright fellow, India, 1976; Edn. scholar U. Idaho, Moscow, 1954; recipient Ivy Leaf award Alpha Phi, 1954. Mem. ASCD, NEA, Clark County Classroom Tchrs. Assn., Nev. State Edn. Assn., Internat. Reading Assn., Alpha Delta Kappa Internat. (mem. internat. exec. bd. 1985-87, v.p. S.W. region 1987-89, scholar S.W. region 1990), Gen. Fedn. Women's Clubs, Mesquite Club (past pres.), Assistance League Las Vegas, Phi Delta Kappa. Avocations: western art collecting, snowmobiling, crafts, porcelain dolls.

KENNY, DEBORAH, marketing professional, finance educator; b. N.J., Nov. 13, 1962; BA, U. Pa., 1983; MA, PhD, Columbia U., 1994. Publ. Dimension Mag., N.Y.C., 1987-90; pres. N.Am. opers. The Jerusalem Report, N.Y.C., 1994-97; v.p. mktg. Parenting group Time Warner, N.Y.C., 1998-99; pres. publ. divsn. Sesame St., N.Y.C., 1999—. Bd. dirs. Domestic Abuse Prevention Project. Fellow IWF-Harvard Leadership Found., 1997-98; recipient Clarion Advt. award, 1997, Echo Leader award Direct Mktg. Assn., 1989. E-mail: dkenny2222@aol.com.

KENNY, JANE M., management consulting executive; b. Jersey City; m. Greg Myer; 3 children. B, Trinity Coll., Washington, 1974; M in English and Am. Lit., Rutgers U., 1982. Cabinet sec. to Gov. Tom Ken State of NJ, 1986—90, chief policy and planning to Gov. Christie Whitman, 1994—96; v.p. corp. cmty. affairs Beneficial Mgmt. Corp., Peapack, NJ, 1990—94; commr. NJ Dept. Cmty. Affairs, 1996—2001; regional adminstr. region 2 US EPA, 2001—03; sr. v.p. The Whitman Strategy Group, LLC, Gladstone, NJ, 2004—. Bd. dirs. New Jersey Resources, 2006—. Recipient Nat. Pub. Svc. award, Women in Govt. award, Good Housekeeping. Fellow: Nat. Acad. Pub. Adminstrs. Office: Whitman Strategy Group LLC 240 Main St Gladstone NJ 07934 Office Phone: 212-637-5000, 908-719-6510. Business E-Mail: jane.kenny@whitmanstrategygroup.com.*

KENNY, SHIRLEY STRUM, academic administrator; b. Tyler, Tex., Aug. 28, 1934; d. Marcus Leon and Florence (Golenternek) Strum; m. Robert Wayne Kenny, July 22, 1956; children: David Jack, Joel Strum, Daniel Clark, Jonathan Matthew, Sarah Elizabeth. BA, BJ, U. Tex., 1955; MA, U. Minn., 1957; PhD, U. Chgo., 1964; LHD (hon.), U. Rochester, 1988, Chonnam U., 1996, Donguk U., 2000, Ajou U., 2004. Chair English dept. U. Md., College Park, 1973-79, provost Arts and Humanities, 1979-85; pres. CUNY Queens Coll., Flushing, 1985-94, SUNY, Stony Brook, 1994—; chair Brookhaven Sci. Assocs. Author: The Conscious Lovers, 1968, The Plays of Richard Steele, 1971, The Performers and Their Plays, 1982, The Works of George Farquhar, 2 vols., 1988, British Theatre and the Other Arts, 1984, Reinventing Undergraduate Education: A Blueprint for America's Research Universities, 1998; contbr. articles to profl. jours. Bd. dirs. Goodwill Greater N.Y., LI Assn. Named Outstanding Woman, U. Md., 1983, Outstanding Alumnus, U. Tex. Coll. Comm., 1989, Disting. Alumna, U. Tex., 1999; recipient Disting. Alumnus award, U. Chgo. Club Washington, 1980, Svc. and Leadership award, N.Y. Urban League, 1988. Mem.: Woodrow Wilson Found. Bd., Boyer Comm. Educating Undergrads. (chair), Assn. Am. Colls. and Univs. (bd. dirs. 1988—91, 2005—). Office: SUNY 310 Adminstrn Bldg Stony Brook NY 11794-0701 Business E-Mail: shirley.kenny@stonybrook.edu.

KENOFER, DORIS DILLON See DILLON, DORIS

KENT, AIMEE BERNICE PETERSEN, small business owner, interior designer, landscape architect, artist; b. North Vancouver, B.C., Can., Apr. 13, 1939; d. Samuel Nathaniel and Aimee Selena (Topping) Hadley; m. Gary Andrew Petersen, May 1, 1959; children: Todd William, Troy Andrew; m. Michael Douglas Kent, Aug. 1, 1998. Student, U. Wash., 1957—59, Edmonds (Wash.) C.C., 1967—74. Owner, designer The Designing Woman, Edmonds, 1979—. Pres. Ballinger Elem. PTA, 1969-71, Madrona Jr. H.S., 1973, 74; deaconess United Presbyn. Ch., Edmonds, 1967-75. Named Woman of Yr., Jr. Women Federated Women's Clubs, 1967; recipient Golden Acorn award, Ballinger Sch. PTA, 1972. Mem. Nat. Fedn. Ind. Bus. People, Better Bus. Bur., Bus. and Profl. Women, Women Investing Now (founder 1991, pres. 1997-2000, sec. 2005-), Edmonds C. of C., Sons of Norway (Lodge 130 social chmn. 1987-93), Jubilee Reveleers Dance Club (pres. 2005-). Presbyterian. Avocation: artist. Home: 23807 113th Pl W Woodway WA 98020-5204 Office Phone: 206-542-3006. Personal E-mail: mchlkent@comcast.net.

KENT, GEORGIA L., obstetrician, gynecologist, healthcare executive, educator; b. NYC, May 30, 1950; d. Harry J. and Eva R. K. BS in Biology with honors, U. Pitts., 1971; MD, U. Pa., 1975; MBA, George Washington U., 1991. Diplomate Am. Bd. Obstetricians-Gynecologists; MD, Colo., Calif., N.Y., N.J., Pa. Sr. instr. ob-gyn. Hahnemann U., Phila., 1979-82; obstetrician-gynecologist Kaiser Group Health Assn., Washington, 1982-90; med. dir. Pacificare, Fountain Valley, Calif., 1991-93, Denver, 1993-94; v.p. med. svcs. The Prudential Ins. Co. of Am., Prudential Healthcare, Roseland, N.J., 1994-96; potter, healthcare cons. self employed, West Orange, N.J., 1997-99, Pitts., 1999—; coll. chair undergrad. bus. and mgmt. degree programs U. Phoenix-Pitts. Campus, 2000—03; pvt. practice, 2006—. Guest lectr. U. Calif. Riverside, 1992-93, Denver U., 1993-94; adj. faculty Duquesne U., 1999—; dept. chair undergrad. bus. & mgmt. U. Phoenix, Pitts., 2000-03, Cmty. Coll. Allegheny County, 2001—; pvt. practice Georgia L. Kent, MD FACOG PC, 2006—. Contbg. author, featured in: (book) Women in Medicine and Management: A Mentoring Guide, 1995; exhibited in group shows at N.J. Ctr. for Visual Arts Mem. Show, 1997, 98, Sweetwater Art Ctr., 1999, North Hills Art Ctr., 2000 (hon. mention). Mem. AAUW, Am. Coll. Obstetricians and Gynecologists, Phi Beta Kappa, Beta Gamma Sigma. Avocations: greyhound rescue/adoption, potter, gardening, walking.

KENT, JILL, midwife; b. Cottage Grove, Oreg., May 22, 1953; d. Laurence Durward and Laurel Naomi Kent; m. Mark Taylor White, June 15, 1974 (div. Nov. 12, 1987); children: Darcy Michelle Shargo, Kara Naomi White, Cameron St. John White, Brendan Morrison White; m. Stashenko Emil Hempeck, Aug. 26, 1989; children: Duncan Alexandre Kent/Hempeck, Ethan Ambrosius Kent/Hempeck. Student, Ctrl. Mo. State U., 1971—72, Moorhead State U., Minn., 1990—91. Lic. midwife Bd. Med. Practice, Minn., 2000, cert. profl. midwife N.Am. Registry Midwives. Midwife, owner, operator The Stork's Nest Birth Ctr., Moorhead, 1981—. Apptd. chair Midwifery Adv. Coun. Minn. Board of Med. Practice, 2000—03. Mem. health adv. coun. for Headstart SENDCAA (SE ND Comm. Action Agy.); vol. first responder rural rescue squad, 1988—2002; vol. Hospice Red River Valley, 2004—. Mem.: Minn. Assn. Midwives (pres. 1985—88), Minn. Midwives Guild (pres. 1988—94), Minn. Coun. Cert. Profl. Midwives (treas. 2000—03), Midwives Alliance N.Am. (midwest regional rep. to bd. 1985—88). Unitarian Universalist. Achievements include first midwife in Minn. to be granted midwife lic. since 1938; opened first and only freestanding birth ctr. in Minn., ND, and SD, 2002; mem. task force that devel. Cert. Profl. Midwife credential, 1993-95. Avocations: antiques, books, travel, gardening, music. Home: 520 32d Ave S #327 Moorhead MN 56560 E-mail: jk-cpm1@juno.com.

KENT, JILL ELSPETH, entrepreneur, art appraiser, lawyer; b. Detroit, June 1, 1948; d. Seymour and Grace (Edelman) K.; m. Mark Elliott Solomons, Aug. 20, 1978. BA, U. Mich., 1970; JD, George Washington U., 1975, LLM, 1979. Bar: D.C. 1975. Mgmt. intern U.S. Dept. Transp., Washington, 1971-73; staff analyst Office Mgmt. and Budget, Exec. Office of Pres., Washington, 1974-76; legis. counsel U.S. Treasury Dept., Washington, 1976-78, dir. legis. reference divsn. Healthcare Financing Adminstrn., 1978-80; sr. budget examiner Office Mgmt. and Budget, Exec. Office of Pres., Washington, 1980-84; chief Treasury, Gen. Svcs. Office of Mgmt. and Budget, Washington, 1984-85; dep. asst. sec. for departmental fin. and planning U.S. Dept. Treasury, Washington, 1985-86, dep. asst. sec. for dept. fin. and mgmt., 1986-88, asst. sec. of treasury, 1988-89; CFO U.S. Dept. State, Washington, 1989-93, acting under sec. of state for mgmt., 1991; exec. devel. program Office of Mgmt. and Budget, Washington, 1984; CFO George Washington U. Med. Ctr., Washington, 1993-97; v.p. IPAC, 1997-98, The Columbus Group. Pres. CEO Atlantic Threadworks Inc.; gen. mgr. The Frogeye Co., 1995—; adj. prof. pub. policy U. Md., 1993—. Bd. dirs. Mobile Med. Care Inc., 1987-91; Trustee Newport Sch., 1988-91, Washington Civic Symphony, 1994-95; bd. dirs. China Found., 1997—; sr. counselor Atlantic Coun. U.S., 1997—; bd. dirs., sec. Wash. Bach Consort. Recipient Adminstrs. award Healthcare Financing Adminstrn., 1980; named on of Top 40 Performers, Mgmt. mag., 1987, Disting. Svc. award Dept. Treasury, 1989, Am. Assn. Govt. Accts. award, 1992, Disting. Svc. award Dept. State, 1993. Mem. ABA, D.C. Bar Assn., Pres's. Coun. on Mgmt. Improvement, CFO Roundtable Healthcare Forum, Fin. Execs. Inst., Exec. Women in Govt. (treas. 1991-92, pres. 1992-93), Va. Assn. of Female Execs. (adv. coun. 1990), Coun. Excellence in Govt. (prin. 1993—). Republican. Home: 2419 California St NW Washington DC 20008-1615 Office Phone: 202-483-7209. Personal E-mail: jekent@verizon.net.

KENT, JULIE, dancer, actress, model; b. Bethesda, Md., July 11, 1969; d. Charles Lindbergh and Jennifer Elsie Cox; m. Victor Barbee, 1996. Grad. high sch., Potomac, Md. Apprentice Am. Ballet Theatre, N.Y.C., 1985-86, mem. corps de ballet, 1986-1990, soloist, 1990-93, prin. dancer, 1993—. Starring role (films) Dancers, 1986, Center Stage, 2000; performed as a guest artist nationally and internationally. Recipient Prix de Lausanne Internat. Ballet competition, 1986, 1st prize at Erik Bruhn Competition in Toronto, 1993, Prix Benois de la Danse, Stuttgart, Germany, 2000; named one of 50 Most Beautiful People, People Mag., 1993. Office: Am Ballet Theatre 890 Broadway Fl 3 New York NY 10003

KENT, LINDA GAIL, dancer; b. Buffalo, Sept. 21, 1946; d. Jerol Edward and Dorismae (Kohler) K.; m. Nicholas Wolff Lyndon, June 9, 1996. BS, Juilliard Sch., 1968. Dancer Alvin Ailey Am. Dance Theater, 1968-74, then prin. dancer, 1970-74; prin. dancer Paul Taylor Dance Co., N.Y.C., 1975-89; dir. dance Perry-Mansfield Performing Arts Sch. and Camp, Steamboat Springs, Colo., 2001—. Faculty Juilliard Sch., 1984—; artist-in-residence Union Theological Seminary, N.Y. Mem. Am. Guild Mus. Artists, Actors Equity. Democrat. Unitarian Universalist. Home: 91 Payson Ave New York NY 10034-2722 Office: The Juilliard Sch Dance Divsn 60 Lincoln Center Plz New York NY 10023-6588 Office Phone: 212-799-5000 x 7057. E-mail: lgk921@aol.com.

KENT, LISA BARNETT, marketing executive, small business owner; b. July 20, 1963; d. William and Arlene Barnett; m. Richard J. Kent. BA, Yale U., 1986; M Mgmt., Northwestern U., Evanston, Ill., 1990. Brand mgmt. Proctor & Gamble, Cin., 1990—92; exec. dir. and eventures Baby and Kids divsn. Johnson & Johnson, New Brunswick, NJ, 1992—2000; pres. and CEO Netgrocercom, North Brunswick, 2000—04; founder and pres. The Luminations Group, 2004—. E-mail: lisa@luminationsgroup.com.

KENT, LYSBETH HAWKINS, artist; b. Birmingham, Ala., Aug. 30, 1931; d. William Burgin and Lysbeth Catherine (Fullan) H.; m. Raleigh Barlee Kent, Jr., Sept. 4, 1951; children: Raleigh Barker III, Burgin Hawkins, Lysbeth Dabney Kent Francis, Katherine Aylett Kent DeBuys. Student, Vanderbilt U., 1949-50, Auburn U., 1950-51; BFA, U. Birmingham, 1989. Solo and Group exhbns. include Birmingham Art Mus., 1980, 85, 86, 87, 88, 89, Kennedy Art Ctr., Birmingham, 1987, Birmingham Pub. Libr. Gallery, 1990, Montgomery Mus. Art, 1980, Visual Arts Gallery, U. Ala., Birmingham, 1980, 81, 84, Magic City Art Connection, 1984, Meridian Mus. Art, Miss., 1986, U. Ala.-Birmingham, 1982, Sokol Gallery, Birmingham, 1983, Town Hall Gallery, Birmingham, 1984, Neiman Marcus Gallery of Contemporary Am. Artworks, Beverly Hills, Calif., 1985, Atchison Gallery, Birmingham, 1985, many others; corp. collections include Dept. Ophthalmology, Norwood Clinic, Birmingham, Dept. Surgery, Breast Clinic, numerous pvt. collectoins. Bd. dirs. St. Anne's Home, Birmingham, 1989-97; vol. Birmingham Mus. Art. Mem. Birmingham Art Assn., Space One Eleven-Alternative Art Space. Home: 2805 Cherokee Rd Birmingham AL 35223-2606

KENT, SUSAN, library director, consultant; b. NYC, Mar. 18, 1944; d. Elias and Minnie (Barnett) Solomon; m. Eric Goldberg, Mar. 27, 1966 (div. Mar. 1991); children: Evan Goldberg, Jessica Goldberg; m. Rolly Kent, Dec. 20, 1991. BA in English Lit. with honors, SUNY, 1965; MS, Columbia U., 1966. Libr., sr. libr. N.Y. Pub. Libr., 1965-67, br. mgr. Donnell Art Libr., 1967-68; reference libr. Paedergaat br. Bklyn. Pub. Libr., 1971-72; reference libr. Finkelstein Meml. Libr., Spring Valley, N.Y., 1974-76; coord. adult and young adult svcs. Tucson Pub. Libr., 1977-80, acting libr. dir., 1982, dep. libr. dir., 1980-87; mng. dir. Ariz. Theatre Co., Tucson, Phoenix, 1987-89; dir. Mpls. Pub. Libr. and Info. Ctr., 1990-95; city libr. L.A. Pub. Libr., 1995—2004, N.Y. Pub. Libr., N.Y.C., 2004—. Tchr. Pima CC, Tucson, 1978; grad. libr. sch. U. Ariz., Tucson, 1995—; panelist Ariz. Commn. Arts., 1981—85; mem. bd. devel. and fundraising Child's Play, Phoenix, 1983; reviewer pub. programs NEH, 1985, panelist challenge grants, 1986—89, panelist state programs, 1988; cons., presenter workshops Young Adult Svcs. divsn. ALA, 1986—88; bd. dirs., mem. organizing devel. and fundraising com. Flagstaff (Ariz.) Symphony Orch., 1988; cons. to librs. and nonprofit instns., 1989—90, 1992—; bd. advisors UCLA Grad. Sch. Edn. and Info. Scis., 1998—2001; presenter in field. Contbr. articles to profl. jours. Chair arts and culture com. Tucson Tomorrow, 1981—85; commr. Ariz. Commn. Arts, 1983—87; bd. dirs., v.p. Ariz. Dance Theatre, 1984—86; bd. dirs. Arizonans Cultural Devel., Ariz., 1987—89, YWCA Mpls., 1991—92; bd. dirs. women's studies adv. coun. U. Ariz., 1985—90; participant Leadership Mpls., 1990—91. Recipient Libr. of the Yr., Libr. Jour., 2002, Info. Assocs. Exec. Leadership award, UCLA Anderson Sch., 2001, Interfaith Leadership award, Archdiocese of L.A., 2004; fellow, Sch. Libr. Sci., Columbia U., 1965—66. Mem.: ALA (mem. membership com. S.W. regional chair 1983—86, mem. com. appts. 1986—87, gov. coun. 1990—98, planning and budget assembly del. 1991—93, chair conf. com. 1996—97, Joseph Lippincott award 2003), Coun. Libr. and Info. Resources (bd. dirs. 2000—), Libr. Adminstrn. and Mgmt. Assn. (mem. John Cotton Dana Award com. 1994—95), Urban Librs. Coun. (mem. exec. bd. 1994—2001, treas. 1996—98, vice chair/chair elect 1998, 1999, chair 1999—2000), Calif. Libr. Assn., Pub. Libr. Assn. (mem. nominating com. 1980—82, v.p. 1986—87, pres. 1987—88, chair publs. assmebly 1988—89, chair nat. conf. 1994, chair legis. com. 1994—95). Office: NYPub Libr Fifth Ave and 42d St New York NY 10018 Office Phone: 212-642-0120. Business E-Mail: skent@nypl.org.

KENYON, CYNTHIA J., medical researcher; BS in Chemistry and Biochemistry, U. Ga., 1976; PhD, MIT, 1981. Post-doctoral fellow Med. Rsch. Coun. Lab. Molecular Biology, Cambridge, England; prof. U. Calif., San Francisco, 1986—, Herbert Boyer Disting. prof. biochemistry and biophysics. Co-founder Elixir Pharmaceuticals, Inc., Cambridge, Mass. Contbr. articles to profl. jours. Mem.: AAAS, NAS, Inst. Medicine, 2004. Achievements include suppressing a single gene in Caenorhabditis elegans worms-nematodes and doubling their normal life span; in recent research and a few more changes, their lifespan was expanded sixfold. Office: U Calif San Francisco, Genentech Hall 600 16th St Box 2200 San Francisco CA 94143-2200 Office Phone: 415-476-9250, 415-476-9864. Office Fax: 415-514-4147. E-mail: ckenyon@biochem.ucsf.edu.*

KENYON, GERALDINE MONA, psychologist, consultant; b. Niagara Falls, N.Y., Nov. 26, 1929; d. John Warner and Mona Vivian (Slone) K.; m. Stanley Paul Gluck, Aug. 4, 1953 (div. Aug. 1966); children: Ethan, Jenny, Shayna, Jody. BS, Purdue U., 1956; MS, Trinity U., 1962; postgrad., Syracuse U., 1970-73. Lic. ednl. psychologist, Calif; registered behavior analyst; cert. sch. psychologist, Calif., N.Y. Adj. faculty Onondaga C.C., Syracuse, N.Y., 1968-73; counseling asst. Syracuse U., 1971, staff psychologist Reading Clinic, 72; sch. psychologist Syracuse City Sch. Dist., 1966-73; asst. prof. Mich. Technol. U., Houghton, 1973-76; adj. prof. Calif. Luth. Coll., Thousand Oaks, 1981-83; sch. psychologist L.A. Unified Sch. Dist., 1978—. Pres. Topanga (Calif.) Dem. Club, 1993-94. Mem. NEA (del. 1993—), APA, Calif. Fedn. Tchrs. (del. 1993-96), Calif. Assn. for Behavioral Analysis, United Tchrs. L.A. (dir. health and human svcs., bd. dirs.), Calif. Tchrs. Assn. (state coun.), Nat. Assn. Sch. Psychologists, Calif. Assn. Sch. Psychologists. Jewish. Avocation: science fiction. Office: Univ High Sch 11800 Texas Ave Los Angeles CA 90025-1499

KEOGH, HEIDI HELEN DAKE, advocate; b. Saratoga, NY, July 12, 1950; d. Charles Starks and Phyllis Sylvia (Edmunds) Dake; m. Randall Frank Keogh, Nov. 3, 1973; children: Tyler Cameron, Kelly Dake. Student, U. Colo., 1972. Reception, promotions Sta. KLAK, KJAE, Lakewood, Colo., 1972-73; acct. exec. Mixed Media Advt. Agy., Denver, 1973-75; writer, mktg. Jr. League Cookbook Devel., Denver, 1986-88; chmn., coord. Colorado Cache & Creme de Colorado Cookbooks, 1988-90. Speakers bur. Mile High Transplant Bank, Denver, 1983-84, Writer's Inst., U. Denver, 1988; bd. dir. Stewart's Shops Corp., Jr. League, Denver, The Gathering Pl., chmn. gov. bd., 2005-06, co-chair capital companion, 2005-. Contbr. articles to profl. jours. Fiscal officer, bd. dirs. Mile High Transplant Bank; blockworker Heart Fund and Am. Cancer Soc., Littleton, Colo., 1978—, Littleton Rep. Com., 1980-84; fundraising vol. Littleton Pub. Schs., 1980-98; vol. Gathering Place Assn., bd. dirs., 2003—, pres., 2003—, chmn. Brown Bag benefit, 1996; vol. Hearts for Life, 1991—, Oneday, 1992, Denver Ballet Guild, 1992—, Denver Ctr. Alliance, 1993—, Newborn Hope, 1980—, Girls, Inc., 1995—, Girls Hope, VOA Guild, 1996—, Le Bal de Ballet, 1998—, The Denver Social Register and Record, 1999—. Mem. Jr. League Denver (pub. rels. bd., v.p. ways and means 1989-90, planning coun./ad hoc 1990-92, sustainer spl. events 1993-94, found. bd. 2006—), Community Emergency Fund (chair 1991-92), Jon D. Williams Cotillion at Columbine (chmn. 1991-93), Columbine Country Club, Gamma Alpha Chi, Pi Beta Phi Alumnae Club (pres. Denver chpt. 1984-85, 93-94, nat. conv. chmn. Denver 2001, Woman of Yr., 2002), Pi Beta Phi Found. (grantee 2000-05). Episcopalian. Avocations: travel, skiing, golf. Home: 63 Fairway Ln Littleton CO 80123-6648

KEOGH, MARY CUDAHY, artist; b. Milw., Nov. 11, 1920; d. John and Katherine (Reed) Cudahy; m. Frank Stephen Keogh, Jan. 17, 1947 (dec. 1980); children: Mary K., Anne C., Patricia, Margaret E.; m. Warren Stringer, July 5, 1985. Student, Smith Coll., 1939—42; BFA, Milw. Downer Coll., 1944; postgrad., Parsons Sch. Design, 1945. Artist, 1969—. Lectr. Woman's Club of Wis., 1977, workshops, Omaha, 1978-80, demo. Cape Coral (Fla.) Art League, 1991. One and two person shows include Lee County Alliance for the Arts, 1988, 90, 96, Barbara Mann Hall, Ft. Myers, 1992, Phillips Gallery, Sanibel, Fla., 1993, Uihlein-Peters Gallery, Milw., 1994, Alliance for the Arts, 1996, Phillips Gallery Sanibel, 1997, Syzygy Gallery, 2000, Retrospective Show Phillips Gallery, Sanibel, Fla., 2004, Uihlein-Peters Gallery, Milw., 2005; exhibited in group shows at Sarasota Visual Arts Ctr., 1995, Fla. Artists' Group, Winter Haven, 1996, Lee County Alliance for the Arts, 1996, Women's Caucus for Art, Longboat Key, Fla., 1997, Fla. Artists Group, Venice, 1997, Venice Biennial, 1997, Phillips Gallery, 1998, Retrospective Art House, 2003; retrospective show Big Arts, Sanibel, Fla., 2004; represented in permanent collections U. Utah, Cedar City, Northwestern Bell, Omaha, Health Park, Ft. Myers, The Endeavers Group, Milw., others. Named Best of Show, Nebr. Wesleyan Coll., Lincoln, 1988; recipient 3d pl. award, Sarasota Visual Arts Ctr., 1995, Big Arts, Sanibel, 1995, hon. mention award, Venice (Fla.) Biennial, 1997, Fla. Artist Group award, Jacksonville Mus. Contemporary Art, 1998, Best of Show, Big Arts Sanibel, 2000, 2d award, Big Arts, 2000, award, Flag Ann. Exhbn., 2001, Flag Invitational, 2002. Mem. Women Contemporary Artists (Best of Show spring show), Nat. Mus. Women in the Arts (charter), Fla. Artists Group. Roman Catholic. Avocations: cooking, travel. Home: 9439 Coventry Ct Sanibel FL 33957-4231 E-mail: wmstringer@comcast.net.

KEOGH, MOLLY DUFFY, education educator, consultant; b. Auburn, N.Y., July 10, 1971; d. Kathleen Barry and James Joseph Duffy; m. Jeffrey Mark Keogh, June 30, 2000; children: Sean Joseph children: Madeline Elizabeth. BS in Elem. Edn., Buffalo State Coll., 1993; MS in Ednl. Leadership, Fla. Atlantic U., 1999; PhD in Tchg. and Curriculum, Syracuse U., 2005. Cert. tchg. N.Y. State, 1993, Fla., 1995. Elem. sch. tchr. various sch. dists., 1993—2001; grad. asst. Syracuse U., NY, 2001, instr., 2002—04; prof. Towson U., 2005—. Cons Syracuse U., 2005—. Mem.: Assn. Tchr. Educators, Am. Ednl. Rsch. Assn. Home: 1736 Upper Forde Ln Hampstead MD 21074 Personal E-mail: mkeogh@syr.edu.

KEOHANE, NANNERL OVERHOLSER, political scientist, academic administrator; b. Blytheville, Ark., Sept. 18, 1940; d. James Arthur and Grace (McSpadden) Overholser; m. Patrick Henry III, Sept. 16, 1962 (div. May 1969); 1 child, Stephan Henry; m. Robert Owen Keohane, Dec. 18, 1970; children: Sarah, Jonathan, Nathaniel. BA, Wellesley Coll., 1961, Oxford U., Eng., 1963; PhD, Yale U., 1967. Faculty Swarthmore Coll., Pa., 1967—73, Stanford U., Calif., 1973—81; pres., prof. polit. sci. Wellesley (Mass.) Coll., 1981—93, Duke U., Durham, NC, 1993—2004, pres. emerita, 2004—; Laurance Rockefeller disting. vis. prof. Woodrow Wilson Sch., Princeton U., 2005—. Author: Philosophy and the State in France: The Renaissance to the Enlightenment, 1980; co-editor: Feminist Theory: A Critique of Ideology, 1982. Trustee Colonial Williamsburg Found., 1988—2001, Doris Duke Charitable Found., 1996—; mem. Harvard Corp., 2005—. Named to National Women's Hall of Fame, 1995; recipient Marshall Medal, 2003; fellow, Ctr. for Advanced Study in the Behavioral Scis., 1978—79, 1987—88, 2004—05; Marshall scholar, 1961—63, Dissertation fellow, AAUW. Fellow: Am. Philos. Soc., Am. Acad. Arts and Scis.; mem.: Am. Acad. Achievement, Coun. on Fgn. Rels., Phi Beta Kappa. Democrat. Episcopalian.

KEOUGH, SANDRA J., retired special education educator, retired principal, education educator; b. Niagara Falls, N.Y., Mar. 11, 1949; d. Samuel Salvadore Rotella and Aldene Jane Sdao; m. James Michael Keough, Aug. 28, 1971; children: Heather Elise Champion, Nathan Martin. BS in Elem. Edn., SUNY, Geneseo, 1971; MS in Spl. Edn., SUNY, Buffalo, 1986; Adminstrn., St. Bonaventure U., Allegany, N.Y., 1992. 4th grade tchr. Belmont Ctrl. Sch., NY, 1974; spl. edn. tchr. Bd. Coop. Edn. Svcs., Olean, 1974—75, 1981—87, staff specialist, 1987—93; dir., curriculum Wellsville Ctrl. Sch., NY, 1993—99, elem. sch. prin., 1999—2005; adj. supr., sch. of edn. St. Bonaventure U., Allegany, 2005—. Bd. dirs. United Way, Allegany County, 2005—, ARC, Allegany County, 2005—. Home: 4478 Townline Rd Cuba NY 14727

KEOUGH, SHAWN, state legislator; m. Mike Keough; 2 children. Student, North Idaho Coll.; student in bus. mgmt., Lewis Clark State Coll. In pub. rels.; mem. Idaho Senate, Dist. 1, Boise, 1996—, mem. transp. com., mem. health and welfare com., vice chair fin. com. Mem. Idaho Women in Timber, Greater Sandpoint (Idaho) C. of C. Republican. Protestant. Office: State Capitol PO Box 83720 Boise ID 83720-0081 Office Phone: 208-332-1349.

KEOWN, LINDA JANE, language educator; b. Phila. d. Kenneth K. and Helen J. Keown; m. Richard Wayne Crow, July 29, 2000. BA, Mt. Holyoke Coll., South Hadley, Mass., 1971; MA in Tchg., Emory U., Atlanta, 1976. Tchr. Spanish Fulton County Pub. Schs., Atlanta, 1971—77, Columbia Pub. Schs., Mo., 1979—2002, Ctrl. Meth. U., Fayette, Mo., 2002—06, U. Mo., Columbia, 2006—. Cons. Ednl. Testing Svc., Princeton, NJ, 1992—2004, Coll. Bd., Evanston, Ill., 1997—2006; yoga instr. Wilson's Total Fitness, Columbia, Mo., 2002—; chair Final II Spanish Exam Com., 1997—99; chair Advanced Placement section Nat. Am. Assn. Tchr. of Spanish & Portuguese, 1995. Pres. Mus. Art & Archaeology, Columbia, 2004—06; treas. King's Daus. Cir., Columbia, 1976—99, v.p., 2002—04; mem. adminstrv. bd. Mo. United Meth. Ch., Columbia, 2000—. Named Disting. Tchr. from Mo., U.S. Dept. Edn., 1994; recipient Nat. Endowment for the Humanities, Seminar Inst., Spain, 1994; grantee Fgn. Langs. fellow, Nat. Endowment for the Humanities, Spain, 1996. Mem.: Am. Coun. Tchrg. of Fgn. Langs., Am. Assn. Tchr. of Spanish & Portuguese, Lars Mikrout Cir. Democrat. United Methodist. Avocations: yoga, reading, travel, swimming. Office: U Mo Dept Romance Langs and Lit Columbia MO 65211 Office Phone: 573-882-4263. Business E-Mail: keownl@missouri.edu.

KEPCHER, CAROLYN, real estate company executive; b. Westchester, NY, 1968; d. Raymond and Marie Cassidy; m. George Kepcher; children: Connor, Cassidy. Degree in bus. mktg., Mercy Coll., Dobbs Ferry, NY. Dir. sales and mktg. Beck Summit Hotel Mgmt. Group, Boca Raton, Fla.; with Trump Orgn., 1994—2006, former exec. v.p.; former gen. mgr., COO Trump Nat. Golf Club, Briarcliff, NY, Bedminster, NJ. Featured on (TV series) The Apprentice, 2004—06; author: Carolyn 101: Business Lessons from The Apprentice's Straight Shooter, 2004—. Mem.: Nat. Golf Course Owners Assn., Profl. Club Mktg. Assn., Met. Club Mgr.'s Assn., Club Mgr.'s Assn. Am. Office: Trump Nat Golf Club 339 Pine Rd Briarcliff Manor NY 10510

KEPNER, JANE ELLEN, psychotherapist, educator, minister; b. Lancaster, Pa., July 13, 1948; d. Richard Darlington and Miriam Kepner; m. Raymond Earl Sparks Jr., July 23, 1969 (div. Apr. 1978); 1 child, Heather Elizabeth; m. Gilbert S. Seeley, July 31, 2000. AB, CCNY, 1975; MDiv, Harvard Divinity Sch., 1985; PhD, Pacifica Grad. Inst., 2003. Vol. Vista, Auburn, Ala., 1967-69; creative drama tchr. East Harlem Day Care, N.Y.C., 1972-76; editl. asst. Bantam Books, Inc., N.Y.C., 1976-78; rschr. Theseus Prodns., Greenwich, Conn., 1978-82; homeless advocate Harvard Sq. Chs., Cambridge, Mass., 1984-85; cmty. organizer So. Middlesex Opportunity Coun., Marlboro, Mass., 1985-88; emergency psychiat. clinician Advocates, Inc., Framingham, Mass., 1988-89; assoc. prof. Curry Coll., Milton, Mass., 1989-90; psychologist, mental health advocate Portland (Oreg.) Health Svc., 1991-95, bd. advisors, 1992-94. Organizer emergency food pantry Marlboro City Coun., 1987; tenants rights and housing rights advocates Tenants Action Com., Marlboro, 1985-87. Pfeiffer fellow Harvard U. Div. Sch., 1983. Mem. Am. Counseling Assn., Oreg. Friends of C.G. Jung, Club 53 (bd. dirs. 1992-94), Amnesty Internat., Oreg. Coalition to Abolish the Death Penalty. Avocations: singing, hiking, gardening, bicycling, cooking.

KEPNER, RITA MARIE (RITA MARIE KRAMNICZ), communications educator, artist; b. Binghamton, N.Y., Nov. 15, 1944; d. Peter Walter and Helena Theresa (Piotrowski) Kramnicz; m. John C. Matthiesen; 1 child, Stewart J. Matthiesen. Student, Elmira Coll., 1962-63; BA, Harpur Coll. at SUNY, 1966; postgrad., Okla. U., 1988, Seattle Pacific U., 1991, Western Wash. U., 1991, 92; MA in Mgmt., City U., Seattle, 1998; diplome of merit (hon.), Acad. Bedriacense, Calvatore, Italy, 1984; postgrad., Wash. State U., 2005—. Holder USCG capt. lic. for passenger carrying aux. sailing vessels up to 50 tons, 1980—. Instr. exptl. coll. U. Wash., 1972-74; instr. sculpture internship program Evergreen Coll., Olympia, Wash., 1974-78; informal visual arts amb. between U.S. and Poland, 1976-81; pres. fed. women's program coun. Seattle dist., 1985-86; fed. women's program mgr. Schweinfurt, Germany, 1986-87, Wiesbaden, Germany, 1988; artist-in-residence City of Seattle, 1975, 77-78; del. Internat. Sculptors Conf., Toronto, Ont., Can., 1978; writer, editor, pub. affairs specialist Seattle dist. U.S. Army Corps Engrs.; spokesperson Exxon Valdez oil spill clean-up ops.; pub. affairs officer Wiesbaden Milcom Hdqrs., 1987-88; editor Schweinfurt Crusader, 1986-87; instr. writing & editing for mgrs. Dept. of Navy, Bremerton, Wash., 1991—93; tchg. asst. Edward R. Murrow Sch. Comm. Washington State U., Pullman, 2005—. Apptd. disaster assistance spokesperson and pub. affairs reservist Hdqrs., Fed. Emergency Mgmt. Agy., Washington, mid-western floods U.S., 1993, So. Calif. firestorm, 1993, Northridge earthquake, Calif., 1994, States of Ga., Oreg., Wash. and Alaska, 1994, No. Calif. floods, 1995, Oklahoma City Bombing, 1995, W.Va. floods, 1995, Wash. State floods, 1996, N.Y. State snowstorms and floods, 1996, Pa. floods, 1996, Huricane Fran, N.C., 1996, severe storms and flooding Calif., 1997, Ohio, 1997, Ill., 1997, blizzards and floods, N.D., 1997, winter storms, N.H., 1998, El Nino earthslides and floods in Calif., 1998, Mass. floods, 1998, Hurricane Bonnie, N.C., N.Y. storms, Hurricane Georges, U.S.V.I., 1998, Okla. City tornadoes, 1999, Kans. tornadoes, 1999, Hurricane Brett, Tex., 1999, Salt Lake City tornado, 1999, Tropical Storm Floyd Floods, N.Y., 1999, Tropical Storm Floyd, Vermont, 1999, disaster response reservist; temp. reassignment to Nat. Transp. Safety Bd. Flight 990 Egyptian Airline crash, 1999, Los Alamos fire, 2000, Mont. fires, 2000, Arkansas ice storm, 2001, Oklahoma ice storm, windstorms, tornadoes and floods, 2001, Kans. ice storms, 2002, Ky. hailstorms, floods and tornadoes, 2002, La. hurricanes, 2002, Tenn. tornados and floods, 2003, reassigned to external affairs Dept. Homeland Security, FEMA, 2003, spl. assignment FEMA Reg. 3, Phila., 2004, Nebr., Mo., Fla., 2005, Hurricane Katrina, New Orleans, 2005, 06, Pa. flooding, 2006; appt. to Nat. Crisis Response Team,Washington, 2002; trainer class for lead pub. affairs officers Emergency Mgmt. Inst., Emmitsburg, Md., 2003; adj. faculty City U. Bellevue, Wash., 2006-. One-woman shows include Willoughby Wallace Meml. Gallery, Branford, Conn., 1967, Penryn Gallery, Seattle, 1970, 73, 76, Haines Gallery, Seattle, 1975, Zoliborz Gallery, Warsaw, Poland, 1981, Yorkshire 510, Norman, Okla., 1988, Women's Ctr., Port Townsend, Wash., 1995, Bruskin Gallery, 1998, Turtle Bluff, Nordland, Wash., 2001; group shows include SUNY, Binghamton, 1966, 96, Manawata Art Gallery, Palmerston North, N.Z., 1976, Modern Art Mus., Seattle, 1976, Portland (Oreg.) Art Mus., 1976, Hajnowka (Poland) Gallery, 1977, Die Roemer Gallery, Wiesbaden, Fed. Republic Germany, 1988, Blue Heron Gallery, Port Hadlock, Wash., 1991-92, Quimper Arts, Bruskin Gallery, Port Townsend, Wash., 1993, 94, Port Townsend Women's Ctr., 1995, Ichikawa, Japan, 1997, Scott Milo Gallery, Anacortes, Wash., 2000-2003, Jefferson County Arts Alliance Gallery, Port Townsend, Wash., 2002, Quimper Arts, 2003, Gallery 9, Port Townsend, Wash., 2004, 2005, Salal Cafe, Port Townsend, 2006; maj. works include Peace Pipe, Zalaegerszeg, Hungary, 1975, Human Forms in Balance Seattle Ctr., City of Seattle, 1975, Unity, City of Znin, Poland, 1976, Rough to Smooth, Hard to Soft Man to Woman In Transition is Unity, Seattle Pub. Libr., 1978, Negative Round, Seattle Pub. Libr. Art Dept., The Surveyor, Savannah, Ga.; sculpture commn. U.S. Army Corps of Engrs., 1995, 96, Medicine Man-Cowlitz Indian Tribe, 2000; contbr. articles to N.W. Arts, Seattle Post-Intelligencer, Leonardo mag., Polska Panorama, Poland mag. Founder Bainbridge Island Arts and Humanities Coun., 1984; VISTA vol., 1982-84; paramedic vol. and bd. dir. Aradia Med. Clinic, Seattle, 1972-74; founder Chimacum (Wash.) Sch. Dist. Learning Boosters, 1989; loaned exec. to govt. campaigns United Way, 1989; trainer for campaign coords. and key workers, 1989; 1st aid trainer Medic I, Seattle, 1989-91; elected chair Marrowstone Island Groundwater Com., 1989-94; mem. adv. com. Seawater Intrusion Team Dept. of Ecology, Wash. State; pres. Marrowstone Island Cmty. Assn., 1993-94; mem., sec. orgnl. task force to structure The Marrowstone Island Found., 2000, adv., cert. mem. Jefferson County Explorer Search and Rescue, 1990-2000. Recipient merit award for superior journalistic achievement U.S. Army CE, 1984, 85, 2d place news category competition award, 1985-86, Recognition letter, Nat. Trans. Safety Bd., 1999; suggestion award Dept. Army, 1984, ofcl. commendation Dept. of Army, 1985, 86, 87, 90, Dept. of Navy, Puget Sound Naval Shipyard, 1990, 91, Achievement cert. Washington Assn. Educators of the Talented and Gifted, 1990, Specialist Achievement award, 1991, Recognition cert. FEMA, 1993 (3), 1994, 95, 96, 97, 98, 99 (3), 2000, 2001, 2002, 2003, 2004, 2005, 2006; named Citizen of Yr., Marrowstone Island, Wash., 1994; Kosciuszko Found. grantee, 1975, 76, 79, 81; pres.'s scholar City U., Bellevue, Wash., 1995-98; scholar Wash. State U., Edward R. Murrow Sch. Comm., 2005-. Mem. N.W. Multihull Assn. (commodore 1974), Marrowstone Island Cmty. Assn. (pres. 1983), Quimper Arts. Home and Office: 8643 Flagler Rd Nordland WA 98358-9600 E-mail: rkepner@wsu.edu.

KEPPLER, MARY LOUISE, elementary school educator; b. Altoona, Pa., Nov. 5, 1927; d. Oscar David and Florence Marie (DeViney) K. BS in Edn., Kutztown (Pa.) State Coll., 1949. Cert. tchr. Del. Classroom tchr. Newark (Del.) Sch. Dist., 1949-78, Christiana Dist., New Castle County, Del., 1978-80, ret., 1980. Tchr. pilot program open classroom, 1972-74; instr. tchg. students to aide kindergarten students Mini-Tchrs., 1972-78, literary braillist, divsn. visually impaired, Del., 1984-2000. Mem. adminstrv. bd. Meth. Ch., Newark, Del., 1975-80, 84-, chair status/role of women, 1984-96, mem. outreach com., 1999—, task force Winterthur Mus. Ednl. Found., Wilmington, 1972, energy conservation task force Hagley Mus., Wilmington, Del., 1976. Recipient Outstanding Elem. Tchr. of Am. award, 1975, Gov.'s award Vol. Braillist, 1994. Mem. NEA (life), Retired Tchrs. Assn., Delta Kappa Gamma (regional dir. N.E. region 1980-82, internat. chmn. membership 1986-88, charter mem., state pres. 1977-79, state parliamentarian 1999—, state rules com. 1999-2003, state nomination com. 1985-90, 2001—), Libr. Assn., Nat. Braille Assn., Del. Ret. Sch. Pers. Assn. Republican. Methodist. Avocations: photography, poetry, short story book group, collecting books on local history. Home: 115 Townsend Rd Newark DE 19711-7905

KER, LORA KAY, elementary music educator; b. Denver, Apr. 4, 1947; d. Delbert Scott and Betty Laura (Allen) Van Reeth; m. Bruce Campbell Ker, Aug. 2, 1969; children: Kara, Kristen, Kevin. BFA, Ohio U., 1969; MA in New Profl. Studies, Tchg., George Mason U., 2004. Choral/gen. music tchr. Wilson Jr. H.S., Newark, Ohio, 1969-73; children's choir dir. St. Paul United Meth. Ch., Newark, 1970-77, Fields United Meth. Ch., North Ridgeville, Ohio, 1977-79; dir. youth ministries St. Paul United Meth. Ch., Woodbridge, Va., 1980-87; elem. music tchr. Prince William County Pub. Schs., Woodbridge, 1987—. Music instr. Ctr. for Arts, Manassas, Va., 1994-95. Mission chair, music leader, youth usher coord., mem. choir St. Paul United Meth. Ch., Woodbridge, 1987—, chair edn. work area, 1996. Mem. NEA, Va. Edn. Assn., Am. Orff Schulwerk Assn. (cert.), Sigma Alpha Iota. Republican. Avocations: people-watching, needlecrafts, crewel, counted cross-stitch. Home: 13008 Amesbury St Woodbridge VA 22192-3702 Office: Rosa Parks Elem Sch 13664 Knightsbridge Dr Woodbridge VA 22193

KERBEN, LAURA SARAH, middle and secondary school educator; b. Key West, Fla., Apr. 19, 1952; d. Abe Kerben and Freida Speizman. BA, U. Ctrl. Fla., Orlando, U. Fla., Gainesville. Cert. sci. tchr. Nat. Bd. Cert. Tchrs. Chair sci. dept., Galaxt, 1990—2003; tchr. sci. Volusia County Schs., Deltona, Fla., mentor tchr., 2001—06. Grantee, Volusia County Environ. Mgmt., 1997; Challenger grant, CEMAVE Entomology. Mem.: ACLU, Sierra Club. Democrat. Avocations: bicycling, hiking, reading, travel. Home: PO Box 740068 Orange City FL 32774 Business E-Mail: lskerben@vokusia.k12.fl.us.

KERBER, LINDA KAUFMAN, historian, educator; b. N.Y.C., Jan. 23, 1940; d. Harry Hagman and Dorothy (Haber) Kaufman; m. Richard Kerber, June 5, 1960; children: Ross Jeremy, Justin Seth. AB cum laude, Barnard Coll., 1960; MA, NYU, 1961; PhD, Columbia U., 1968; DHL, Grinnell Coll., 1992. Instr., asst. prof. history Stern Coll., Yeshiva U., N.Y.C., 1963-68; asst. prof. history San Jose State Coll., Calif., 1969-70; vis. asst. prof. history Stanford U., Calif., 1970-71; asst. prof. history U. Iowa, Iowa City, 1971-75, prof., 1975-85, May Brodbeck prof., 1985—. Vis. prof. U. Chgo., 1991-92, Oxford U., England, 2006—. Author: Federalists in Dissent: Imagery and Ideology in Jeffersonian America, 1970, paperback edit., 1980, 97, Women of the Republic: Intellect and Ideology in Revolutionary America, 1980, paperback edit., 1986, Toward an Intellectual History of Women, 1997, No Constitutional Right to Be Ladies: Women and the Obligations of Citizenship, 1998, paperback edit., 1999 (Littleton-Griswold prize in legal history Am. Hist. Assn., Joan Kelley prize in womens history Am. Hist. Assn.); co-editor: Women's America: Refocusing the Past, 1982, 6th edit., 2004, U.S. History As Women's History, 1995; mem. editl. bd. Signs: Jour. Women in Culture and Society, Jour. Women's History; contbr. articles and book revs. to profl. jours. Fellow Danforth Found., NEH, 1976, 83-84, 94, Am. Coun. Learned Socs., 1975, Nat. Humanities Ctr., 1990-91, Guggenheim Found., 1990-91, Radcliffe Inst. for Advanced Study, 2003. Mem. Orgn. Am. Historians (pres. 1996-97), Am. Hist. Assn. (pres. 2006), Am. Studies Assn. (pres. 1988), Am. Soc. for Legal History, Berkshire Conf. Women Historians, Soc. Am. Historians, Japan U.S. Friendship Commn., PEN Am. Ctr., Am. Acad. Arts and Scis., Am. Philos. Soc. Jewish. Office: U Iowa Dept History Iowa City IA 52242

KERBIS, GERTRUDE LEMPP, architect; m. Walter Peterhans (dec.); m. Donald Kerbis (div. 1972); children: Julian, Lisa, Kim. BS, U. Ill.; MA, Ill. Inst. Tech.; postgrad., Grad. Sch. Design, Harvard U., 1949-50. Archtl. designer Skidmore, Owings & Merrill, Chgo., 1954-59, C.F. Murphy Assocs., Chgo., 1959-62, 65-67; pvt. practice architecture Lempp Kerbis Assocs., Chgo., 1967—; lectr. U. Ill., 1969; prof. William Rainey Harper Coll., 1970—95, Washington U., St. Louis, 1977, 82, Ill. Inst. Tech., 1989-91. Archtl. cons. Dept. Urban Renewal, City of Chgo.; mem. Northeastern Ill. Planning Commn., Open Land Project, Mid-North Community Orgn., Chgo. Met. Housing and Planning Council, Chgo. Mayor's Commn. for Preservation Chgo.'s Hist. Architecture; bd. dirs. Chgo. Sch. Architecture Found., 1972-76; trustee Chgo. Archtl. Assistance Ctr., Glessner House Found., Inland Architect Mag.; lectr. Art Inst. Chgo., U. N.Mex., Ill. Inst. Tech., Washington U., St. Louis, Ball State U., Muncie, Ind., U. Utah, Salt Lake City. Prin. archtl. works include U.S. Air Force Acad. dining hall, Colo., 1957, Skokie (Ill.) Pub. Library, 1959, Meadows Club, Lake Meadows, Chgo., 1959, O'Hare Internat. Airport 7 Continents Bldg, 1963; prin. developer and architect: Tennis Club, Highland Park, Ill., 1968, Watervliet, Mich. Tennis Ranch, 1970, Greenhouse Condominium, Chgo., 1976, Webster-Clark Townhouses, Chgo., 1986, Chappell Sch., 1993; exhibited at Chgo. Hist. Soc., 1984, Chgo. Mus. Sci. and Industry, 1985, Paris Exhbn. Chgo. Architects, 1985, Spertus Mus.; represented in permanent archtl. drawings collection Art Inst. Chgo. Active Art Inst. Chgo. Recipient award for outstanding achievement in professions YWCA Met. Chgo., 1984 Fellow AIA (bd. dirs. Chgo. chpt. 1971-75, chpt. pres. 1980, nat. com. architecture, arts and recreation 1972-75, com. on design 1975-80, head subcom. inst. honors nomination); mem. Chgo. Women in Architecture (founder), Chgo. Network, Internat. Women's Forum, Arts Club Chgo., Cliff Dwellers (bd. dirs. 1987-88, pres. 1988, 89), Lambda Alpha. Office: Lempp Kerbis Assocs 172 W Burton Pl Chicago IL 60610-1310 Personal E-mail: lk172@aol.com.

KERBY, RAMONA ANNE, librarian; b. Dallas, Feb. 5, 1951; d. Raymond Richard and Bette Lee (Rudd) Nolen; m. Steve Alan Kerby, Nov. 27, 1973. BA in Elem. Edn./Spanish, Tex. Wesleyan U., 1973; MEd in Counseling Edn., Tex. Christian U., 1975; MLS, Tex. Woman's U., 1980, PhD, 1984. Elem. sch. libr. J.B. Little Elem. Sch., Arlington, Tex., 1978-93; coord. sch. libr. media program McDaniel Coll. Author: Investigating the Effectiveness of School Library Instruction, 1984, Friendly Bees, Ferocious, Bees, 1987, 38 Weeks Till Summer Vacation, 1989, Asthma, 1989, Cocroaches, 1989, Beverly Sills, America's Own Opera Star, 1989, Amelia Earhart, Courage in the Sky, 1990, Samuel Morse, 1991, Frederick Douglass, 1994, Yearbooks in Science 1950-59, 1995, Robert E. Lee: Southern Hero of the Civil War, 1997, Reading Fun: Quick and Easy Activities for the School Library Media Center, 1998, Collection Development for the School Library Media Program, 2006. Recipient Siddie Jo Johnson award State of Tex., 1990; NEH tchr.-scholar, 1993-94. Mem. ALA, Tex. Assn. Sch. Librs. (chair 1989-90), Tex. Libr. Assn., Soc. Children's Book Writers, Authors Guild, Assn. Libr. Info. Sci. Edn., Alpha Chi, Beta Phi Mu.

KERCHEVAL, PATRICIA, secondary school educator; b. Houston, Dec. 12, 1944; m. William Franklin Kercheval, June 17, 1967; children: Kristin Kay Garrison, Blake Alton. BA, Sam Houston State U., Huntsville, Tex., 1967, MEd, 1985. Tchr. Hardin County Jr. High, Radcliff, Ky., 1967—68, Austin H.S., Houston, 1967, Ft. Knox H.S., Ky., 1968—69, Spring Br. H.S., Houston, 1969—71, Willis H.S., 1978—. Chair fgn. lang. dept. Willis H.S., Tex., 2005—, coord. advanced placement, 1988—, coord. gifted and talented, 1988—, chair English dept., 1985—2004. Mem. choir and trio First Bapt. Ch., Willis, 1971, pers. com. Recipient Tex. Secondary Tchr. ofYr., Region VI Ednl. Svc. Ctr., 1997—98. Conservative. Baptist. Avocations: travel, singing, reading, horseback riding. Home: 11490 Bilnoski Road Willis TX 77378 Office: Willis High School 1201 Fm 830 Willis TX 77378 Office Phone: 936-856-1250. Business E-Mail: pkercheval@willisisd.net.

KERCKHOFF, SYLVIA STANSBURY, mayor; b. Toledo, June 7, 1928; d. Paul William Stansbury and Lass Elizabeth Hackney; m. Alan Chester Kerckhoff, June 11, 1949; children: Steven, Sharon. BS, U. Wis., 1950; MAT, Duke U., 1960. Kindergarten tchr. Madison (Wis.) Schs., 1950-52; rsch. asst. Vanderbilt U., Nashville, 1957-58; jr. and sr. h.s. tchr. City Schs., Durham, N.C., 1959-60, 69-81; mem. City Coun., City of Durham, 1981-93, mayor, 1993-99. Co-chair Violence Prevention Commn., Durham, 1993-97; mem. Chamber Commerce Bd., Durham, 1993-97; founder Mayor's Univ. Adv. Coun., Durham, 1993-97; co-chair City-County Com., Durham, 1993-97. Chair N.C. League Municipalities, Transp., Comm. and Pub. Safety, 1996-97; mem. Gov.'s Transit 2000 Commn., N.C., 1996; v.p. N.C. LWV, 1967-69, fin. chair, Durham LWV, 1960-70; co-chair Youth Coordinating Bd., 1998—; v.p. pres. bd. dirs. Durham United Way, 1998-2000; bd. dirs. Triangle United Way; co-chair Durham Cultural Master Plan, 2002—. Recipient Leadership award Duke U. med. Ctr., Durham, 1995, Durham County Women's Commn. Svc. award, 1993, Community Leadership in Arts award Durham Arts Coun., 1991; inductee DeVilbiss H.S. Hall of Fame, Toledo, 1998. Democrat. Presbyterian. Avocations: reading, tennis, music, hiking, travel. Home: 1511 Pinecrest Rd Durham NC 27705-5816

KEREN, KINNERET, biophysicist; b. Jerusalem; PhD in physics, Technion Israel Inst. Tech. Postdoctoral rschr. Theriot Lab., Dept. Biochemistry Stanford U. Contbr. articles to profl. jour. Named one of Top 100 Young Innovators, MIT Tech. Review, 2004. Office: Stanford U Dept Biochemistry Stanford CA 94305 Business E-Mail: kinneret@stanford.edu.

KERES, KAREN LYNNE, literature and language professor; b. Evanston, Ill., Oct. 22, 1945; d. Frank and Bette (Pascoe) K.; m. Walter Wilson Berg. BA, St. Marys Coll., 1967; postgrad., U. Notre Dame, 1967-68; MA, U. Iowa, 1969. Assoc. prof. English, humanities and fine arts William Rainey Harper Coll., Palatine, Ill., 1969-95, prof., 1995—, Palomar Coll., San Marcos, Calif., 1990-93. Cons. in field. Mem. MLA, Ill. Assn. Tchrs. English, Am. Fedn. Tchrs., Nature Conservancy, Mensa. Home: 222 Fairfield Dr Island Lake IL 60042-9622 Office: William Rainey Harper Coll Dept Liberal Arts Palatine IL 60067 Personal E-mail: KLK1022@comcast.net.

KERGER, PAULA ARNOLD, broadcast executive; b. Dec. 20, 1957; married. BS, U. Balt., 1979. Mgmt. positions U.S. Com. UNICEF, Washington, 1979—84; head develop. Internat. Ho., 1984—89; mgmt. positions Met. Opera, 1989—93; v.p. WNET-TV, NYC, 1993—2004, dir. govt. affairs, 1993—2002, sta. mgr., 2002—04, exec. v.p., COO, 2004—06; pres., CEO PBS, 2006—. Bd. dirs. PBS Found.; vice chair, bd. trustees Am. Pub. TV. Office: PBS 1320 Braddock Pl Alexandria VA 22314 Office Phone: 703-739-5000. Office Fax: 703-739-5777.*

KERKEMEYER, VICTORIA MARIE, physical therapist; b. St. Charles, Mo., Sept. 1, 1970; d. Paul Edward and Geraldine Theresa (Tochtrof) Kerkemeyer. BS in Phys. Therapy, St. Louis U., Mo., 1992. Cert. ATC NATA-BOC, Mo. Cert. athletic trainer City of St. Charles Sch. Dist., St. Charles, 1992—; phys. therapist Cave Springs Phys. Therapy, St. Peters, Mo., 1992—93; phys. therapist, cert. athletic trainer West Clay Phys. Therapy, St. Charles, Mo., 1993—95, Health South, St. Charles, 1995—2002, Excel Sports and Phys. Therapy, St. Peters, Mo., 2003—.

KERN, JEANNE RUSTEMEYER WOOD, retired secondary school educator; b. Washington, Dec. 8, 1939; d. Joseph Howard Rustemeyer and Jeannetta Greever Rustemeyer Jameson; m. Richard Alan Kern, Dec. 14, 2001; 1 child, Kristin C. BA, BS, U. Kans., Lawrence; MEd, U. Houston, 1965. Tchr. Bridge City (Tex.) HS, 1963—96, acad. team coach, 1990—96. Author: (novels) Trips and Whales and Puppy Dog Tales, 2005 (Golden Triangle Writers Guild romance award), (poems) Armchair Detective (Pushcart Prize nominee); proofreader: Ozarks Monthly; actor: (video) Hospice: The Caregiver (nat. award-winner). Bd. dirs. v.p. Orange (Tex.) Cmty. Players, 1988—2001; pres., sec. SE Tex. Arts Coun., Beaumont, 1995—2001; pres. Golden Triangle Writers Guild, Beaumont, Tex., 1998—2000; officer Osher Lifelong Learning Inst. Lincoln, 2002—06. Named Woman of the Yr., Bus. and Profl. Women, 1978, Tchr. of the Yr., Bridge City HS, 1980. Mem.: Am. Mensa (Chmns. award 2006), Alumni U. Kans. (life), Friends of the Lied, Welcome Wagon, Kappa Kappa Gamma (life; province dir. alumnae 2005—06). Home and Office: 2600 Cheshire North Ct Lincoln NE 68512 Office Phone: 402-423-0428. Personal E-mail: jeanne@richkern.com.

KERNAN, BARBARA DESIND, senior government executive; b. N.Y.C., Jan. 11, 1939; d. Philip and Anne (Feuer) Desind; m. Joseph E. Kernan, Feb. 14, 1973. BA cum laude, Smith Coll., 1960; postgrad. Oxford U., 1963; MA, Harvard U., 1963; postgrad. in edn. policy George Washington U., 1980. Editor Harvard Law Sch., 1960-62; tchr. English, Newton (Mass.) H.S., 1962-63; editor Allyn & Bacon Pubs., Boston, 1963-64; edn. assoc. Upward Bound, Edn. Assocs., Inc., Washington, 1965-68; edn. program specialist Title I, Elem. and Secondary Edn. Act, U.S. Office Edn., 1969-73; fellow Am. Polit. Sci. Assn., Senator William Proxmire and Congressman Alphonzo Bell, 1973-74; spl. asst. to dep. commr. for elem. and secondary edn. and dir. dissemination, sch. fin. and analysis, U.S. Office Edn., 1975-77, chief program analysis br. divsn. edn. for disadvantaged, 1977-79; chief grant program coordination staff Office Dep. Commr. for Ednl. Resources, 1979-80; chief priority concerns staff Office Asst. Sec. Mgmt., U.S. Dept. Edn., Washington, 1980-81; dir. divsn. orgnl. devel. and analysis Office of Dep. Undersec. for Mgmt., 1981-86; Sr. Exec. Svc. candidate on spl. project to improve status of women Sec. Transp., Washington, 1983-84; inducted Sr. Exec. Svc., 1986; assoc. adminstr. for adminstrn. Nat. Hwy. Traffic Safety Adminstrn., U.S. Dept. Transp., 1986-94, career devel. leader to presdl. mgmt. interns, 1989-91; trustee Capricorn Galleries, Rockville, Md., 1996-97, pres., 1997—; owner Philip Desind Collection, Am. Realism Fine Arts, 1997—. Recipient awards U.S. Office Edn., 1969, 71, 77, U.S. Dept. Edn., 1981-86, U.S. Dept. Transp., 1991, 94, Small Agy. Coun., 1990; scholarships U. Mich., 1956-58, Smith Coll., 1958-60, Harvard U., 1962-63; Am. Polit. Sci. Assn. fellow, 1973-74; Sr. Exec. fellow John F. Kennedy Sch. Govt. Harvard U., 1983. Office Phone: 301-340-6900. Personal E-mail: bkernan@prodigy.net.

KERNS, GERTRUDE YVONNE, psychologist; b. Flint, Mich., July 25, 1931; d. Lloyd D. and Mildred C. (Ter Achter) B.; BA, Olivet Coll., 1953; MA, Wayne State U., 1958; PhD, U. Mich., 1979. Sch. psychologist Roseville (Mich.) Pub. Schs., 1958-68, Grosse Pointe (Mich.) Pub. Schs., 1968-86; pvt. practice psychology, Grosse Pointe, 1980—; instr. psychology Macomb C.C., 1959-69. Author: A Second Heartbeat, 1979. Mem. Am. Psychol. Assn., Mich. Psychol. Assn., Lakeshore Psychol. Assn. (pres. 1988-89), Psi Chi. Home: 28820 Grant St Saint Clair Shores MI 48081-3207 Office: 131 Kercheval Ave Ste 140 Grosse Pointe Farms MI 48236-3630

KERNS, VIRGINIA B., anthropologist, writer; b. San Diego, 1948; d. James T. and Ruth B. Kerns; m. Ronald Adam Hallett. BA in Anthropology, Coll. William and Mary, 1970; PhD in Anthropology, U. Ill., 1977. Vis. asst. prof. Coll. William and Mary, Williamsburg, Va., 1977—78, from asst. prof. to prof., 1985—, chair dept. anthropology, 1988—93; asst. prof. Va. Tech, Blacksburg, Va., 1978—83; vis. asst. prof. U. Iowa, Iowa City, 1981; rsch. anthropologist UN Food and Agr. Orgn., Rome, 1984. Assoc. editor Am. Ethnologist Am. Ethnol. Soc., 1979—84; bd. dirs. U. Press Va., Charlottesville, 1995—98. Author: Scenes from the High Desert, 2003 (Evans Biography award, 2004); Women and the Ancestors: Black Carib Kinship and Ritual, 1983, 2d edit., 1997; editor: In Her Prime, 1985, 2d edit., 1992. Named Writer-in-residence, Mesa Refuge, 2005; recipient Faculty award for Advancement of Scholarship, Phi Beta Kappa, Alpha of Va., 1988, Thomas Jefferson Tchg. award, Coll. William and Mary, 1989, Outstanding Faculty award, State Coun. for Higher Edn. in Va., 1991; fellow, Fulbright-Hays Commn., 1974—75, Va. Found. for Humanities, 1989; grantee, Wenner-Gren Found. for Anthrop. Rsch., 1974—75, 1976; Hon. fellow, Woodrow Wilson Found., 1974. Fellow: Am. Anthrop. Assn.; mem.: Phi Beta Kappa. Office: Coll William and Mary Dept Anthropology PO Box 8795 Williamsburg VA 23187-8795 Office Phone: 757-221-1054. E-mail: vbkern@wm.edu.

KERR, BARBARA PROSSER, research scientist, educator; b. Asheville, N.C., Dec. 28, 1925; d. George Holcomb and Gertrude Berenice (Parker) Prosser; m. William Albert Kerr, June 18, 1950 (div. May 1959); 1 child, Diana. BA, U. Chgo., 1951; MSW, Ariz. State U., 1971. Cert. clin. social worker, psychiatry and mental health nursing. Exec. sec. Union Theol. Sem., N.Y.C., 1961-67; case worker Dept. Pub. Welfare, Wilmington, Del., 1967-69; psychiatric nurse St. Luke's Hosp. and Med. Ctr., Phoenix, 1969-70; emergency rm. social worker Maricopa Med. Ctr., Phoenix, 1971-82; founder, dir. Kerr-Cole Sustainable Living Ctr., Taylor, Ariz., 1983—. Adv. Solar Cookers Internat., Sacramento, 1993—. Author: The Expanding World of Solar Box Cookers, 1991; inventor Solar Box Cooker, 1976, Solar Wall Oven, 1986. Home: PO Box 576 Taylor AZ 85939 Office Phone: 928-536-2269. Personal E-mail: kerrcole@frontiernet.net.

KERR, CRISTIE, professional golfer; b. Miami, Fla., Oct. 12, 1977; Winner Longs Drugs Challenge, 2002, LPGA Takefuji Classic, 2004, ShopRite LPGA Classic, 2004, State Farm Classic, 2004, Michelob Ultra Open, 2005, Franklin Am. Mortgage Championship, 2006; tied for second U.S. Open, 2000. Winner Fla. State Jr. Girls Championship, 1993, 94, 95; mem. U.S. Curtis Cup Team, 1996, U.S. Solheim Cup Team, 2002, 03, 05. Achievements include low amateur at 1996 U.S. Women's Open; fifth place LPGA money list, 2004; nine top-ten finishes, 2004; winner, Wendy's Championship for Children, 2005, John Q. Hammons Hotel Classic, 2006. Avocations: fishing, baking. Office: c/o LPGA 100 International Golf Dr Daytona Beach FL 32124-1092*

KERR, DARLENE DIXON, electric power company executive; b. Syracuse, N.Y., Nov. 26, 1951; d. James and Mary Dixon; children: E. Kaye, J. Craig. BA, SUNY, Potsdam, 1973; MBA, Syracuse U., 1984. V.p. sys. electric ops. Niagara Mohawk Power Corp., Syracuse, 1988-91, v.p. gas mktg. and rates, 1991-93, v.p. electric customer svcs., 1993-94, sr. v.p. electric customer svc., 1994-95, sr. v.p. energy distbn., 1995—98, past mem. steering com. and past chmn. polit. action com., exec. v.p. energy delivery, 1998—99, exec. v.p., chief oper. officer, 1999—2000, pres., chief operating officer, 2000—01; sr. v.p. Nat. Grid U.S.A., 2001—, pres., Nat. Grid U.S.A. Svc. Co., 2001—. Former mem. adv. bd. Rural Metro; former mem. policy coun. Success by 6. Former trustee Onondaga C.C.; former bd. dirs. Cmty.-Gen. Hosp.; mem. Syracuse U. Thursday Morning Roundtable and Corinthian Found.; mem. task force Bus. Alliance for a New N.Y.; past pres. and bd. dirs. Onondaga Citizens League; past v.p. bd. dirs. Regional Learning Svc., Inc.; past mem. policy and planning com. Leadership Grater Syracuse; former mem. Downtown Improvement Task Force; former committeewoman and vice chmn. Onondaga Rep. Com.; former mem. numerous campaign ad. coms. and Onondaga County Rep. task forces; mem. chmn.'s coun. and fin. com. Onondaga County Rep. Com.; bd. dirs. Farmers and Traders Life Ins. Co., Utilites Mutual Ins. Co., Greater Syracuse C.C., M&T Bank, N.Y. State Women in Comm. and Energy, former pres., LeMoyne Coll., Mktg. Execs. conf., Ctrl. N.Y. Regional Compact, Greater Syracuse Econ. Growth Coun., Syracuse 20/20. Named Mover and Shaker for bus. Syracuse Herald Am., 1990, Woman of Achievement for career Post-Std., 1991, Alumni of Distinction, SUNY, 1993, Citizen of Yr. Temple Adath Yeshurun, Syracuse, Woman of Achievement N.Y. State-Gov. Pataki, Extraordinary Woman Nat. Women's Hall of Fame, Seneca Falls, N.Y.; recipient Spirit Am. Women award Girls Inc. Ctrl. N.W., 1993, Multiple Sclerosis Soc. Crusaders for a Cure award, Zonta Crystal award. Office: National Grid USA 300 Erie Blvd W Syracuse NY 13202-4250

KERR, JANET SPENCE, physiologist, pharmacologist, researcher; b. New Haven, May 30, 1942; d. Alexander Pyott and Janet Blake (Conley) Spence; m. Thomas Albert Kerr Jr., July 24, 1965; children: Sarah Patterson, Matthew Spence, Timothy Marden. BA, Beaver Coll., 1964; MS, Rutgers U., 1969, PhD, 1973. Asst. prof. Rutgers U., Camden, NJ, 1973-76; rsch. assoc. U. Pa. Sch. Medicine, Phila., 1976-79; asst. prof. U. Medicine and Dentistry N.J.-Rutgers Med. Sch., New Brunswick, 1979-84; prin. rsch. scientist DuPont Pharms. Co., Wilmington, Del., 1985—2001; prin. investigator ENANTA Pharms., 2002; sr. investigator Merck Pharm. Co., Inc., 2003—. Sec. Biochem. Pharmacology Discussion Group, 1997—; vis. scientist Med. Sch. Harvard U., 2002—03; sr. investigator Merck & Co., Inc., 2003—. Contbr. articles to profl. jours. Busch fellow Rutgers U. Mem. AAAS, Am. Heart Assn., Am. Fedn. Clin. Rsch., Am. Physiol. Soc., Am. Thoracic Soc., Am. Assn. Cancer Rsch., Inflammation Rsch. Assn. (bd. dirs. 1996-98), N.Y. Acad. Scis., Sigma Xi. Personal E-mail: janetskerr@hotmail.com. Business E-Mail: janet_kerr@merck.com.

KERR, JOAN LINDSAY, supervisor, consultant; b. Van Nuys, Calif., Nov. 13, 1948; d. Donald Ransom and Paula Helen Wilbur Lindsay; m. Robert Kerr III, June 30, 2001; children: Brian Letlow, Elizabeth Letlow. BA in History, U. Calif., Santa Barbara, 1970; MA in Edn. Adminstrn., Calif. State U., Bakersfield, 1997. Cert. secondary tchg. Calif., adminstrn. svc. Calif. Mid. sch. tchr. Bakersfield (Calif.) City Sch., 1984—94, program specialist, 1995—99; curriculum specialist Rosedale Union Sch. Dist., Bakersfield, 2000—. Program facilitator Calif. history project U. Calif., Santa Barbara, 1995—2000; cons. gifted edn. various sch. dists., Calif., 2004—. Contbr. articles to profl. jours. Lay leader Unitarian Universalist Fellowship Kern County, Bakersfield, 2003—. Recipient History Tchr. of Yr., Kern County Coun. Social Studies, 1996, Excellence in Social Sci. Edn., Bakersfield City Sch., 1998. Mem.: Calif. Assn. for Gifted (bd. dirs. 2006—, educator rep. 2006—), Phi Delta Kappa. Avocations: travel, theater, hiking. Office: Rosedale Union Sch Dist 2553 Old Farm Rd Bakersfield CA 93312 Office Phone: 661-588-6000. Office Fax: 661-588-6009. Personal E-mail: robslassie@hotmail.com. Business E-Mail: jkerr@rosedale.k12.ca.us.

KERR, LOU C., foundation administrator; d. Lem C. and M. Mae (Beck) Coker; m. Robert S. Kerr, Jr., July, 1972; children: Steven S., Laura Kerr Ogle. BS in Edn. and Health, Oklahoma City U., DHL (hon.), 1991. V.p. The Kerr Found., Inc., Oklahoma City, 1985-99, pres., chair, 1999—. Founder, dir. Red Earth, Inc., Oklahoma City; adv. com. Breast Cancer Prevention and Treatment, 1994—; mem. Commn. on the Status of Women, 1994-99, 2000—; mem. Gov.'s State White House Conf. on Aging; mem. selection com. for Truman Found. Scholars, 1991-2000; mem. Social Security Disability Task Force; chair State Capitol Preservation Commn., 1990—; adv. coun. for gov. Okla. Environ. Concerns Coun., vice chair for gov., others; pres. Ind. Coll. Fund. V.p. fundraising campaign Allied Arts, 1985, v.p. exec. com., 1988—89, sec. exec. com., 1990—; mem. adv. coun. Women's Pres. Orgn.; mem., founder Atty. Gen.'s Consumer Adv. Com.; founder Bizzell Libr. Soc., U. Okla.; exec. com., v.p. Ctr. of the Am. Indian/Red Earth, 1983—; founder, chair Okla. Internat. Women's Forum, 1990—; nat. trustee Nat. Symphony Orch., Washington, 1999—; trustee NPR Found., Washington, 2001—; chair State Capitol Preservation Commn., Oklahoma City, 1990—; women's leadership bd., exec. com. Harvard U., Cambridge, 1999; 3d v.p. Red Lands coun. Girl Scouts U.S., 1993—97; v.p. Global Family Found.; mem. exec. com. Lyric Theatre of Okla., Inc., 1992—; adv. trustee Oklahoma City U.; v.p. Sister Cities, Inc, 1989—, exec. bd.; trustee Okla. Sch. Sci. and Math Found.; adv. dir. Tulsa Ballet Theatre; chair Okla. Centennial Commn., 2006—; bd. visitors U. Okla. Coll. Nursing, 2006—, Sam Noble Okla. Mus. Natural History, 2006—; trustee United Meth. Found. for Christian Higher Edn., 1996—, others; nat. bd. Fund for Am., 1989—; bd. govs. Okla. Ctr. of Sci. and Arts, Inc., 1987—97; mem. adv. bd. U. Okla. Coll. Fine Arts, 1994—2000, U. Okla. Polit. Com., ANSER-Ctr. for Internat. Aerospace Coop., 1995—98, Hazel K. Goddess Fund for Stroke Rsch. in Women, Internat. Gymnastics Hall of Fame, 1997—; adv. bd. dirs. Okla. Breast Inst., 1992—97; bd. dirs., exec. com. Ctrl. Okla. Coun. of World Affairs; bd. dirs. Am. Cancer Soc., Oklahoma County unit, 1995—97, Internat. Women's Forum, Washington, 1992—; exec. bd. Norick Art Mus.; chair, exec. bd. Dulaney-Browne Libr. Soc.; bd. dirs., co-chair Okla. Ind. Colls. Found., 1994—; bd. trustees Totts Gap, 2000—; bd. vis. Okla. U. Health Sci. Ctr. Named to Okla. Commerce and Industry Hall of Honor, Oklahoma City U., 2000, Okla. City Pub. Sch. Found. Wall of Fame, 2001, Philanthropy World Hall of Fame, 2006; knighted into The Byzantine Order of the Holy Sepulchre; recipient Vis A Tergo award Women's Bus. Ctr., 1997, Women Who Make a Difference award Internat. Women's Forum, 1994, Cert. of Merit Vol. Action Com. of Cmty. Coun., Okla. Tourism and Recreation Indsl. Gov.'s award, Nat. Others award Salvation Army, Kirkpatrick Petree award for outstanding cmty. svc. Oklahoma City U. Music Theatre Soc., 1988, Gov.'s Arts award Okla. State Arts Coun., 1988, Woman of Distinction award, Girl Scouts Red Lands Coun., 2002, Leading Lights award Internat. Women's Forum, 2003, Urban Pioneer award, 2006; named March 2, 2005 as Lou C. Kerr Day, Okla. Gov. Henry. Fellow: Nat. Acad. Pub. Adminstrn. (hon.); mem.: Okla. Med. Rsch. Fdn. (bd. mem. 2000—), League of Hist. Am. Theatres (bd.mem. 2004—), NAPA (hon. fellow 2005). Democrat. Methodist. Office: The Kerr Foundation Inc 12501 N May Ave Oklahoma City OK 73120 Fax: (405) 749-2877. E-mail: lkerr@thekerrfoundation.org.

KERR, NANCY HELEN, psychology educator; b. L.A., June 27, 1947; d. Edmund James and Sally (Byrd) K.; m. David Foulkes, Apr. 19, 1978. BA, Stanford U., 1969; PhD, Cornell U., 1974. Asst. prof. psychology U. Wyo., Laramie, 1974-78; vis. asst. prof. psychology Emory U., Atlanta, 1978-79, vis. asst. prof. psychiatry, 1979-82; vis. asst. prof. psychology Mercer U., Macon, Ga., 1982-83; asst. prof. to prof. psychology Oglethorpe U., Atlanta, 1983—, chair div. behavioral scis., 1989-96, interim acad. dean, 1996-97, provost, 1997—. Contbr. articles to profl. jours. Recipient James McKeen Cattell award, 1990. Mem. Psychonomic Soc. Office: Oglethorpe U 4484 Peachtree Rd NE Atlanta GA 30319-2797

KERR, NANCY KAROLYN, pastor, mental health services professional; b. July 10, 1934; d. Owen W. and Iris Irene (Israel) K.; m. Richard Clayton Williams, June 28, 1953 (div.); children: Richard Charles, Donna Louise. Student, Boston U., 1953; AA, U. Bridgeport, 1966; BA, Hofstra U., 1967; postgrad. in clin. psychology, Adelphi U. Inst. Advanced Psychol. Studies, 1968-73; MDiv, Associated Mennonite Bibl. Sems., 1986. Ordained pastor Mennonite Ch., 1987; apptd. pastor Kamloops Presbytery Ch., Can., 1992. Pastoral counselor Nat. Coun. Chs., Jackson, Miss., 1964; dir. teen program Waterbury (Conn.) YWCA, 1966-67; intern in psychology N.Y. Med. Coll., 1971-72, rsch. cons., 1972-73; coord. home svcs., psychologist City and County of Denver, 1972-75; cons. Mennonite Mental Health Svcs., Denver, 1975-78; asst. prof. psychology Messiah Coll., 1978-79; mental health cons., 1979-81; called to ministry Mennonite Ch., 1981; pastor Cin. Mennonite Fellowship, 1981-83, mem. Gen. Conf. Peace and Justice Reference Coun., 1983-85; instr. Associated Mennonite Bibl. Sems., 1985; tchg. elder Assembly Mennonite Ch., 1985-86; pastor Pulaski Mennonite Ch., 1986-89; exec. dir., pastoral counselor Bethesda Counseling Svcs., Prince George B.C., 1989-99; pvt. practice, 1999—. Spl. ch. curriculum Nat. Coun. Chs., 1981; mem. Cen. Dist. Conf. Peace and Justice Com., 1981-89; mem. exec. bd. People for Peace, 1981-83. Sec. Ft. George Housing Soc., 2002—; clin. supr. St. Stevens. Sem., Edmonton, Canada; active Prince George Ministerial Assn., chmn. edn. and airport chapel coms., 1990—92; elder St. Giles Presbyn. Ch., 1996—2000; bd. dirs. Tri-County Counselling Clinic, Memphis, Mo., 1980—81, Boulder (Colo.) ARC, 1977—78, PLURA, B.C. Synod, 1995—98, Prince George Neighbor Link, 1995—99, Davis County Mins. Assn., v.p., 1988—89; mem. Waterbury Planned Parenthood Bd., 1964—67, MW Children's Home Bd., 1974—75, Mennonite Disabilities Respite Care Bd., 1981—86, Prince George Children's Svcs. com., 1992—94; adv. com. Prince George Planning Coun., 1997—98; mem. housing Prince George adv. bd. Mennonite Cen. Com., 1998—99. Mem. APA (assoc.), Can. Psychol. Assn., Soc. Psychologists for Study of Social Issues, Christian Assn. Psychol. Studies, Soc. Bibl. Lit. & Exegesis, sec. Ft. Geo. Bd., 2004-. Office: Nancy Kerr Counselling Svcs 110-154 Quebec St Prince George BC Canada V2L 1W2

KERR, SHAUNA GAY, secondary school educator; d. Frank M. Kerr and Gay Lee Davidson; m. Dennis Allen Cumin; children: Chad, Derreck. BA, Boise State U., Idaho, 1975; MEd, Mont. State U., Billings, 2000. Graphic artist Design and Lithography, Boise; art dir. Peview Mag., Billings; graphic designer Ecclemation Point Advt., Billings, Sch. Dist. 2, Billings; artist, graphic designer Graphic Impressions, Billings; tchr. Billings West H.S. Mem. sch. to cmty. com. Billings Pub. Schs., 2003—. Officer, historian Billings Arts Assn., 1993, 1994; officer, sec. North Elevation Task Force, Billings, 1996—; bd. dirs. Lesman Meml. Art Studio, Billings, 2005, 2006. Recipient hon. mention, Yellowstone Exposition, 2005. Mem.: Billings Edn. Assn., Journalism Educators Assn. Avocations: skiing, antiques, painting, photography. Home: 907 N 31st St Billings MT 59101 Office: Billings West HS 2201 St Johns Ave Billings MT 59102-4786

KERR, SYLVIA JOANN, science educator; b. Detroit, June 19, 1941; d. Frederic Dilmus and Maud (Dirst) Pfeffer; widowed; children: David, Kathleen. BA, Carleton Coll., 1963; MS, U. Minn., 1966, PhD, 1968. Asst. prof. Augsburg Coll., Mpls., 1968-71; instr. Anoka Ramsey Community Coll., Coon Rapids, Minn., 1973-74; from asst. prof. to full prof. Hamline U., St. Paul, 1974—. Contbr. articles to profl. jour. NIH fellow U. Minn., 1972, 74-75. Office: Hamline U Dept Biology 1536 Hewitt Ave Saint Paul MN 55104-1205 E-mail: sKerr@piper.hamline.edu.

KERR, TONYA, newscaster; b. Dallas; m. Rick Kerr; children: Taylor, McKenna, Ainsley. BA in Broadcast Journalism, Tex. Tech. U. Pvt. practice, Houston; press sec. US Rep. Sam Johnson, Tex.; with Prime Time Live, Washington; prodn. assoc., field prodr. Prime Time Live ABC News, London; anchor Sta. KPRC-TV, Houston, 2000—. Office: Sta KPRC-TV PO Box 2222 Houston TX 77252-2222

KERRIGAN, NANCY, professional figure skater, retired Olympic athlete; b. Woburn, Mass., Oct. 13, 1969; d. Daniel and Brenda Kerrigan; m. Jerry Solomon, 1995; children: Matthew Eric Solomon, Brian Russell Solomon. Bronze medalist World Championships, 1991, 92; U.S. nat. bronze medalist, 1991; U.S. nat. silver medalist, 1992; bronze medalist Olympic Games, Albertville, France, 1992; U.S. nat. champion, 1993; silver medalist Olympic Games, Lillehammer, Norway, 1994. Numerous commls. and product endorsements including Walt Disney Co., Reebok, Northwest Airlines, Frosted Cheerios, Ray Ban, Revlon, Aetna U.S. Healthcare, Salvino Bammers, AquaTrend, Tostitos, sportsinstruction.com; author: In My Own Words, 1996; author: (with Mary Spencer) Artistry on Ice, 2002; choreographer Halloween on Ice; performer: (video) Fairy Tales on Ice, Champions on Ice Tour, 1992—2004, (TV spls.) Dreams on Ice, Breaking the Ice, Nancy Kerrigan and Friends, Holiday Celebration on Ice, One Enchanted Evening, Divas on Ice, Nancy Kerrigan's Winter Wonderland, Colors of Winter, 2003, Grease on Ice, 1998—99, Broadway on Ice, 2000, Footloose on Ice, 2001, Skating with Celebrities, 2005; host (TV series) Lifetime TV, 2002—04, commentator Comcast, TV host Nancy Kerrigan's World of Figure Skating, 2002, 2005, Grand Prix of Figure Skating, ISU Grand Prix Lifetime TV, 2003—04; co-host: (TV series) The Insider, 2006; singer: (albums) Reflections Off the Ice, 1999, Simply the Best, 2004; actor: (TV series) Boy Meets World, 1995, The Journey of Allen Strange, 1998, Ice Angel, Hollywood Squares, 2003, Family Feud, 2003, Intimate Portrait, 2004, (voice): (TV films) The Easter Egg Adventure. Spokesperson Lions Club, 1994, Children's Trust Fund, 1997, Spalding Rehab. Hosp., MADD, Fight for Sight; founder, benefactor Nancy Kerrigan Found.; hon. chair Nancy Kerrigan Golf Classic, 2000—. Recipient Bronze medal, World Figure Skating Championships, 1991, Silver medal, 1992, Bronze medal, U.S. Pro Championships, 1997, Goodwill Games, 2000, Outstanding Mother award, Mother's Day Found., 2001, Henry Iba Outstanding Citizen Athlete award, 2002. Office: care of StarGames Bldg 1 40 Salem St Lynnfield MA 01940 Office Phone: 781-224-9655.

KERR-NOWLAN, DONNA COURTNEY, pre-school administrator; b. Wellsboro, Pa., Sept. 25, 1940; d. Sylvan LaRue and Mildred Fowler Kerr; children from previous marriage: Craig Kerr Nowlan, Brent Fowler Nowlan. Cert., Jean Summers Bus. Sch., N.Y., 1956; student, Corning C.C., Mansfield (Pa.) State Tchrs. Coll., 1960. Owner, bridal cons. Bridal Bower, 1960—63;

owner Victorian Fingerlakes Tour Guides, 1963—72; dir., owner Building Block Nursery & Pre-K, Elmira, NY, 1969—. Coord. Civil War prison camp Chemung County C. of C., Elmira, 2000—; pres. Hist. Near Westside Bd. Dirs. and Assn., 1985—89; mem. planning commn. City of Elmira; mem. Chemung County Planning Bd.; hostess Orchids and Candlelight Arnot Ogden Hosp., 1991—; dir. Found. for Ctrl. Diocese Episcopal Ch., Syracuse, NY, 1981. Named Woman of Achievement, Chemung County Coun. of Women, 1993; named to Legion of Honor, Chaplin of Four Chaplins, Valley Forge, Pa., 1994; recipient Cmty. Svc. award, Hist. Near Westside Neighborhood Assn., 1982, cert. of appreciation, Elmira Coll., 1985, 1994, Robert Goostrey award, Chemung County C. of C., 1990. Mem.: Twin Tier Jazz Soc. (bd. dirs. 1989—, pres. 2000—), Hal Roach Soc. (bd. dirs. 1987—), Soroptimist Internat. (pres. Elmira chpt. 1989—99, Outstanding Cmty. Svc. award 1994, Outstanding Club Mem. 1995, Outstanding Cmty. Vol. 1996, Outstanding Vol. Svc. award 1986). Republican. Episcopalian. Avocations: walking, gourmet cooking, reading, painting. Home: 715 Winsor Ave Elmira NY 14905 Office: Building Block Pvt Nursery Sch 308 College Ave Elmira NY 14901 Personal E-mail: dnowlan@stny.rr.com.

KERR WALKER, JOI MECHELLE, literacy educator, consultant; b. Balt., May 22, 1968; d. Jerald Michael Kerr and Rosetta Kerr Wilson; m. David Julian Walker, Jan. 22, 2000; 1 child, Justin T. Kerr. BS in Mktg., Morgan State U., Balt., 1990, MS in Transp. Mgmt., 1992; MA in Tchg., Early Childhood Edn., Towson State U., Md., 1993; PhD, U. Md., College Park, 2001. Cert. child daycare Md., 1994. Adj. prof. several colls. and univs., Balt./Wash. area, 1994—; primary sch. educator Balt. City Pub. Sch. Sys., 1993—97, cons. tchr., 1997—99; asst. prof. Morgan State U., Balt., 1999—2003; reading specialist Md. State Dept. Edn., Balt., 2003—05; ind. literacy cons. JKW Links to Literacy, LLC, Balt., 2005—. Reading course revision com. co-chair Md. State Dept. Edn., Balt., 2005, literacy cons., 05, Cecil Elem. Sch., Balt., 2005—06, Hyde Leadership Pub. Charter Sch., Washington, 2005—, Balt. City Pub. Sch. Sys., 2005—, DC Pub. Schs., 2006. Leader Girl Scouts Ctrl. Md., Balt., 1990—93; vol. cmty. svc. day Comcast Cable, Balt., 2004—05; vol. emergent literacy activity planner Balt. County Pub. Sch. Sys., Towson, 2001—03. Recipient Academic Achievement award in Mktg., Morgan State U., 1990, Best Rsch. Paper-Summer Transp. Intern Program for Diverse Groups, U.S. Dept. Transp., 1991. Mem.: Internat. Reading Assn., Internat. Reading Assn. Coun. Md., Kappa Delta Pi Internat. Honor Soc. in Edn. Democrat-Npl. Interfaith. Avocations: reading, travel, dance, attending musicals and plays. Home Fax: 410-435-4843. Personal E-mail: linkstoliteracy@comcast.net.

KERSTEN, MARY LOU, real estate broker; b. Milw., May 22, 1950; d. Oliver and Leocadia Coleman; m. David Moore Thomas, June 24, 1974 (div. 1981); m. Christian George Kersten, Jan. 5, 1985; 1 child, Hilary Coleman. BA, U. Wis., 1972. Dir. rsch. Am. U., Washington, 1974-76; dir. devel. Southeastern U., Washington, 1976-78; dir. conf. planning Coun. Advancement & Support of Edn., Washington, 1978-82; dir. ednl. programs Nat. Assn. Fund Raisers, Washington, 1982-85; adminstrv. asst. to headmaster Cate Sch., Ojai, Calif., 1985-87; real estate broker, owner Hillsdale (N.Y.) Country Realty, 1987—. Bd. dirs. Columbia Greene Bd. Realtors, Hudson, N.Y. Planning bd. Town of Hillsdale, 1996—; pres. bd. dirs. Friends Hillsdale Pub. Libr., 1994—95; pres. Columbia Greene Bd. Realtors, 2002—05; bd. dirs. Hillsdale Pub. Libr., 1996—2003, Clarion Concerts Columbia County, Copake, NY, 1998. Named Realtor of Yr., Columbia Greene Bd. Realtors, 2003, 2004; named to Realtors Honor Soc., NY State Assn. Realtors, 2004. Mem.: NYSAR Realtors Honor Soc. Avocations: country walking, travel, biking, gardening. Office: Hillsdale Country Realty PO Box 400 Hillsdale NY 12529-0400

KERWICK, COLLEEN, lawyer, artist; b. Kilkenny, Ireland, Mar. 9, 1976; d. Sean Kerwick and Eileen Brennan-Kerwick. B Corp. Law, Nat. U. Ireland, Galway, 1998, LLB, 1999. Bar: N.Y. 2001. Litig. assoc. Williamson & Williamson, N.Y.C., 2002—03; counsel Cullen and Dykman, N.Y.C., 2003—. Founder Young Irish Film Makers, Kilkenny City, Ireland, 1991—. Actor: (ctrl. character in ind. feature) Dagober; creative embroidery, The Creation of Man (Cork Internat. Film Festival, 1993). Mentor Vol. Lawyers Project, N.Y.C., 2004—06; sec. Emerald Assn. L.I., N.Y.C., 2005—06. Mem.: N.Y. State Trial Lawyers Assn. (assoc.). Avocations: painting, piano, drama, music, irish culture and language. Office: Cullen and Dykman Brklyn Heights 177 Montague St Brooklyn NY 11201 Office Fax: 718-935-1509. Personal E-mail: colleen_kerwick@yahoo.com. E-mail: ckerwick@cullenanddykman.com.

KERWIN, ELIZABETH ANDERSON, retired anesthesiologist; b. Lincoln, Nebr., Nov. 30, 1923; d. Arthur and Grethen Haslam Anderson; married, Apr. 5, 1957; children: Allison E., Charles M., Sean A. AA, Stephens Coll., Columbia, Mo., 1942; BS, U. Nebr., Lincoln, 1944; MD, U. Nebr., Omaha, 1947. Intern Phila. Gen. Hosp., 1947—48, resident in anethesia, 1948—50, Presbyn. Hosp., Phila., 1950—52; chief anesthesiology Chester County Hosp., Westchester, Pa., 1953—74; staff anethesiology Cheshire Med. Ctr., Keene, NH, 1974—76. Mem.: Am. Bd. Anesthesiology.

KERZ, LOUISE, historian; b. NYC, Sept. 16, 1936; d. Louis and Catharine Sohn; m. Leo Kerz, Apr., 1965 (dec. 1976); children: Jonathan, Antony; m. Al Hirschfeld, Oct. 1996 (dec. 2003). Student, Queens Coll., 1954-56, Marymount Coll., 1972-74. Theatre producer Leo Kerz Prodns., N.Y.C., 1960-74; theatrical curator N.Y. Cultural Ctr., N.Y.C., 1974, Theatre of Max Reinhardt, 1974, N.Y. Pub. Libr. Lincoln Ctr., N.Y.C., 1984, Calif. Mus. Sci. and Industry, L.A., 1985, The Demille Dynasty, 1984; rsch. cons. CBS: On the Air, 1978, Smith-Hemion TV Prodns., L.A., 1987—, The Phantom of the Opera, 1995. Dir. rsch. Greengage Prodns., Julie Andrews/Greengage Prodns., LA, 1988, Tony Awards Telecast 50th Anniversary Show, 1947—96; rsch. cons. TV Acad. Hall of Fame and Tony Awards telecasts, 1993—96; dir. rights and permissions The Line King (The Al Hirschfeld Story-nominated for Oscar 1996) NY Times, TV documentary; rsch. historian six-part TV series Broadway, 1997; spl. cons. The Demille Family-Documentary Am. Movie Channel, 1997; exec. cons., liaison Hirschfeld Exhbns., catalogs, books and events Mus. of City of NY, cons. Hirschfeld's NY exhibit, 2001; cons. Hirschfeld's Hollywood exhibit Acad. Motion Picture Arts & Scis., Beverly Hills, Calif., 2001; cons. catalogues to exhibits Pub. Harry N. Abrams, 2001; exhibit organizer V&A Theatre Mus., Nat. Theatre Southbank, London, 2005, Al Hirschfeld's Brits on Broadway; organizer London 2005 Hirschfeld Celebration, V&A Theatre Mus. and Royal Nat. Theatre at Southbank; curator book Hirschfeld's British Aisles, 2005. Assoc. prodr. on Broadway: Rhinoceros, 1961; contbg. editor: N.Y.C. Access, 1983; picture editor The DeMilles: An American Family, 1988, Al Hirschfeld: On Line, 1998, curator, dir. Exhibit Broadway, 1995, curator, photographer (exhibitions) Hirschfeld Celebration at Leica Gallery, N.Y.C., 2002; one-woman shows include The Leica Gallery, N.Y.C., 2002; curator, writer Hirschfelds British Aisles, 2005. Vol. Persian Gulf war Am. Jewish Congress, Israel, 1991; elected mem. Tony Awards nominating com. Am. Theatre Wing, 2000-2003; co-chair Al Hirschfeld Centennial, assoc. prodr. Al Hirschfeld 100th Birthday Salute, 2003, dir. Al Hirschfeld Found., 2004-. Mem. Theatre Libr. Assn. Democrat. Address: c/o Al Hirschfeld Found 122 E 95th St New York NY 10128-1705

KERZEE, BETH BUMPAS, music educator; b. Madisonville, Tex., Feb. 24, 1961; d. Ted Barclay and Margaret Ogle Bumpas; children: Jordan Michael, Sarah Beth. MusB, Dallas Bapt. U., 1979—85; M of Ednl. Adminstrn., Sul Ross State U., Alpine, Tex., 1995—97. Cert. Music Tchr., Prin. Tex. Dept. Edn., 1985. Head choral dir. Red Oak High, 2004—; min. of music First United Meth. Ch., Red Oak, 2005—. Orchestra director: musical theatre. V.p. C. of C., Balmorhea, 1996—97. Recipient Best Musical Dir., Stephenville Area Theatre, 1987. Mem.: Tex. Music Educators Assn. (region chair-elect 2005—06). Democrat. Methodist. Office: Red Oak HS PO Box 9000 154 Louise Ritter Blvd Red Oak TX 75154 Office Phone: 469-437-8813. Office Fax: 469-437-6768. Personal E-mail: bkerzee@hotmail.com. Business E-Mail: beth.kerzee@redoakisd.org.

KERZMANN, OLIVIA LINDSAY, music educator; b. Jonesboro, Ark., May 11, 1980; d. Jeffery Dean and Brenda Gail Emmert; m. Randy Kenneth Kerzmann, Feb. 9, 1980; 1 child, Erin Grace. BSEd in Music, Minot State U., N.D., 2002. K-12 music tchr. Granville Sch. Towner Granville Unified Schs., ND, 2003—. Music dir. 1st Presbyn. Ch., Minot, ND, 2002—04. Singer: (solo competition) Nat. Assn. Tchrs. Singing in N.D., 2001 (1st pl. sr. women). Mem. Minot Ch. of Christ, Minot, ND, 1993—2006. Scholar, Divsn. Music Minot State U., 1998—2002. Mem.: Music Educators Nat. Conf. (assoc.). Office Phone: 701-728-6641.

KES, VICKI, museum director; b. Bessemer, Ala., June 2, 1952; d. Gerald Vance and Marjorie Jean (Bush) George; m. Pieter A. Kes, Sr., Nov., 2002; children: Alissa Henson, Rebecca Hubbard. Office worker Mining Corp. of the South, Vance, Ala., 1978-79; artist, sign painter Bob's Sign Shop, Midfield, Ala., 1980—; dir. Iron & Steel Mus. of Ala., McCalla, 1980—. Program completion Office of Mus Programs, Smithsonian, Washington, 1987. Artist (book) Tannehill Crafts, 1982. Events Planner Ala. Reunion State of Ala., Montgomery, 1989. Recipient Top 20 Events in the South East award SE Tourism Soc., Atlanta, 1986-87, 88, 91, Head Start Vol. award, 1994. Mem. Ala. Preservation Alliance, Soc. Indsl. Archaeology, Nat. Trust for Hist. Preservation, Birmingham Area Mus. Assn., Am. Assn. State and Local History (program completion 1980), Am. Assn. Mus., Ala. Mus. Assn. (sec.-treas. 1983-85, chair com. Southeastern Museums Conf. 1999, co-chair com. 2000, Meritorious Svc. award 1983), Ala. State Employees Assn. (pres. Tannehill chpt. 1993-99). Democrat. Baptist. Avocations: pen, ink drawings, painting. Home: 258 Stipes Rd West Blocton AL 35184 Office: Tannehill Historical State Park 12632 Confederate Pkwy Mc Calla AL 35111-2620 Business E-Mail: tannehillmuseum@att.net.

KESHVALA, SEELPA H, secondary school educator; b. Milw., June 30, 1975; d. Hamir K and Mani M Keshvala. BS, U. Wis., Milw., 1998, MS, postgrad., U. Wis., Milw., 2000—. Prinicipal and Superintendency Licensure Wis., 2004, Professional Educator Wis. Dept. of Edn., 1998. Tchr. Milw. Pub. Schools, 1998—2002, Milw. Area Tech. Coll., 2002—. Recipient Barbara L. Jackson Scholar, UCEA, 2004, Holmes Scholar, Holmes Partnership Acad., 2005, Lura M. Currithurs Scholarship, Pi Lambda Theta, Beta Epsilon Chpt., 2000, Advanced Opportunity Program (AOP) Fellowship, Grad. Sch., 2002—03, 2003—04, 2004—05. Mem.: Holmes Partnership Acad. (Holmes Scholar 2005), U. Coun. of Ednl. Adminstrn., Am. Edn. Rsch. Assn., Pi Lambda Theta. Hindu. Home: 1100 W Wells St Apt 811 Milwaukee WI 53233 Office: Dept of Administrative Leadership Enderis Hall Room 658 Milwaukee WI 53201 Office Phone: 414-229-2868. Office Fax: 414-229-5300. Personal E-mail: keshvala@uwm.edu.

KESLER, BONNIE L., psychology professor; b. St. Petersburg, Fla., Oct. 18, 1954; d. Ruth R. Bonbrake; m. David B. Kesler; children: Sara E., Aaron B. MA, EdS, U. South Fla., Tampa. Cert. sch. psychologist Fla., 2000. Sch. psychologist Manatee County Sch. Bd., Bradenton, Fla., 1990—93, Dr. Ray L. Bowman, St. Petersburg, 1993—2004; prof. psychology St. Petersburg Coll. Sch. psychologist Dr. Patricia Shiflett, St. Petersburg, 1993—2004. Bd.dirs. Y.W.C.A., St. Petersburg, 1993—94. Mem.: APA (assoc.), Delta Kappa Gamma (assoc.; rec. sec. 2006—). Democrat. Jewish. Avocations: piano, running, travel. Office: St Petersburg Coll 6605 5th Ave North Saint Petersburg FL 33733 Office Phone: 727-341-4643.

KESSEL, BRINA, ornithologist, educator, researcher; b. Ithaca, NY, Nov. 20, 1925; d. Marcel and Quinta (Cattell) K.; m. Raymond B. Roof, June 19, 1957 (dec. 1968). BS, Cornell U., 1947, PhD, 1951; MS, U. Wis., Madison, 1949. Student asst. Patuxent Rsch. Refuge, 1946; student tchg. asst. Cornell U., 1945-47, grad. asst., 1947-48, 49-51; asst. Wis. Alumni Rsch. Found., 1948—49; instr. biol. sci. U. Alaska, summer 1951, asst. prof. biol. sci., 1951-54, assoc. prof. zoology, 1954-59, prof. zoology, 1959-96, head dept. biol. scis., 1957-66, dean Coll. Biol. Scis. and Renewable Resources, 1961-72, curator terrestrial vertebrate mus. collections, 1972-90, curator ornithology collection, 1990-95, adminstrv. assoc. for acad. programs, grad. and undergrad., dir. acad. advising, office of chancellor, 1973-80, sr. scientist, 1996-99, prof. emeritus, dean emeritus, curator emeritus, 1999—. Project dir. U. Alaska ecol. investigations for AEC Project Chariot, 1959—63; ornithol. investigations N.W. Alaska pipeline, 1976—81, Susitna Hydroelectric Project, 1980—83. Author books; contbr. articles to profl. jours. Recipient Outstanding Contbn. award Alaska Bird Conf.; U. Alaska with ann. award Brina Kessel Medal for Excellence in Sci. named in her honor; swale pond at Creamer's Field Migratory Waterfowl Refuge in Fairbanks named in her honor. Fellow AAAS, Am. Ornithologists' Union (v.p. 1977, pres.-elect 1990-92, pres. 1992-94), Arctic Inst. N.Am.; mem. Wilson Ornithol. Soc., Cooper Ornithol. Soc., Soc. Northwestern Vertebrate Biology, Pacific Seabird Group, Arctic Audubon Soc. (hon.), Assn. Field Ornithologists, Sigma Xi (pres. U. Alaska 1957), Phi Kappa Phi, Sigma Delta Epsilon. Achievements include research in European Starling in North America; biogeography, seasonality, and biology of birds in Alaska. Office: U Alaska Mus of the North PO Box 80211 Fairbanks AK 99708-0211 Business E-Mail: ffbxk@uaf.edu.

KESSEL, JOYCE B., English professor; d. William C. and Phyllis White Kessel; life ptnr. Leanna Manna. AA in Humanities, Erie CC, Buffalo, 1973; BA in English, St. Bonaventure U., NY, 1975; MA in English, SUNY, Fredonia, 1976. Assoc. prof. English Villa Maria Coll. Buffalo, 1977—, chair faculty Senate, 1990—98, 2004—. Faculty advisor creative arts mag. SKALD, Buffalo, 1977—; faculty advisor Viking at Villa Maria Coll., Buffalo, 1980—. Author: various poems; editor: Earth's Daughters: A Feminist Arts Periodical, 1989—2006; audiobook reviewer Libr. Jour., 1994—2006. Recipient Silver crown SKALD 2004, Columbia Scholastic Press Assn., 2005. Mem.: Coll. English Assn., Just Buffalo Lit. Ctr., Nat. Coun. Tchrs. English. Office: Villa Maria Coll Buffalo 240 Pine Ridge Rd Buffalo NY 14225 Business E-Mail: jkessel@villa.edu.

KESSELRING, DEBBIE ANNE, systems engineer; b. Durham, N.C., July 21, 1965; d. Henry G. and Maria K.; m. Timothy J. Dacey; 1 child, Denise. BS in Aero. Engring., U. Md., 1987; MS in Systems Engring., Va. Tech. Inst., 1995. Engring. cons. VEDA Inc., Arlington, Va., 1988-89; structural engr. Naval Air Sys. Command, Arlington, Va., 1989-93, air-to-air missile program analyst, 1993-95; sys. engr. Ballistic Missile Def. Orgn., Washington, 1995—98, Computer Scis. Corp., 1998—2001, tech. dir., 2003—; dep. dir. Anteon Corp., 2001—03. Mem. AIAA (sr.).

KESSINGER, MARGARET ANNE, medical educator; b. Beckley, W.Va., June 4, 1941; d. Clisby Theodore and Margaret Anne (Ellison) K.; m. Loyd Ernst Wegner, Nov. 27, 1971. MA, W.Va. U., 1963, MD, 1967. Diplomate Am. Bd. Internal Medicine and Med. Oncology. Internal medicine house officer U. Nebr. Med. Ctr., Omaha, 1967-70, fellow med. oncology, 1970-72, asst. prof. internal medicine, 1972-77, assoc. prof., 1977-90, prof., 1990—, assoc. chief oncology hematology sect., 1988-91, chief oncology hematology sect., 1991-99; assoc. dir. clin. rsch. U. Nebr. Med. Ctr./Eppley Cancer Ctr., Omaha, 1999—. Contbr. articles to profl. publs. Fellow ACP, Am. Assn. Cancer Edn.; mem. Am. Soc. Clin. Oncology, Am. Assn. Cancer Rsch., Internat. Soc. Exptl. Hematology, Am. Soc. Hematology, Sigma Xi, Alpha Omega Alpha. Republican. Methodist. Avocations: aviation, gardening, canning, skiing. Office: U Nebr Med Ctr 987680 Nebraska Med Ctr Omaha NE 68198-0001 E-mail: makessin@unmc.edu.

KESSLER, ANN MICHELE, dance educator, costume designer; m. Aran David Kessler; children: Andria, Alexander, Ari. BA in Theatre, U. Mich., 1988, MFA in Design, 1993. Assoc. prof. Valparaiso (Ind.) U., 1996—. Resident designer Valparaiso U. Costume designer Les Liaisons Dangereuses (Joseph Jefferson Citation, 1996), Ascending Mists (Mid-State Regional Ballet Festival Gala Participant, 2000), Three Shades of Red (Gyor Ballet Secondary Sch. Festival, Gyor, Hungary, 1997), Isadora Duncan: Image through Art (Gallery Opening, Brauer Mus., 1998), The Nutcracker, The Duel, The Book of the Dun Cow (World Premiere Prodn., 1998), Uncle Vanya (Nominee, Joseph Jefferson Citation, 1996), The Servant of Two Masters (KC/ACTF Region III Finalist, 1997), Anna Karenina (KC/ACTF Region III Finalist, 2003), Side by Side by Sondheim (KC/ACTF Region III Finalist, 2006). Mem.: Kennedy Ctr., Am. Coll. Theatre Festival, Region III (Region III respondant), U.S. Inst. Theatre Tech. Achievements include dir., choreographer Valparaiso U. dance ensemble. Office Phone: 219-464-5751.

KESSLER, DIANE COOKSEY, religious organization administrator, minister; b. Jan. 8, 1947; BA in Religion, Oberlin Coll., 1969; MA in Religion and Soc., Andover Newton Theol. Sch., 1971, postgrad., 1979—; DD (hon.), Episcopal Divinity Sch., 2001. Ordained to ministry United Ch. of Christ, 1983. Assoc. dir. for strategy and action Mass. Coun. Chs., Boston, 1975-88, exec. dir., 1988—. Ind. preacher; speaker in field. Author: Parents and the Experts, 1974, God's Simple Gift: Meditations on Friendship and Spirituality, 1988; co-author: Councils of Churches and the Ecumenial Vision, 2000; editor: Together on the Way, 1999, Receive One Another.hospitality in ecumenical perspective, 2005; co-editor Encounters for Unity, 1995; also articles; mem. editl. adv. bd. Theology and Pub. Policy, 1989, 98, Mid-Stream, 1995-98. Former mem. adv. bd. Mass. Dept. Revenue; active Wellesley Congl. Ch.; mem. coun. for ecumenism United Ch. of Christ, 1984-94, chairperson coun. 1988-89, 90-91; mem. Atty Gen.'s Adv. Com. on Pub. Charities, 1988—, World Coun. of Churches, Joint Working Group, 1998-2005, 2006—; trustee Hancock Variable Series Trust I, 1999-2005; bd. dirs. Howard Benevolent Soc., 1989-96, New Eng. Holocaust Meml. Com., 1st Ch. Legacy Fund. Recipient Outstanding Woman award Coll. Club, 1990, Focolare award, 1994, Social Action Ministries award, 1995, Patron of Christian Unity award, 1998, Spirit of Hill award Candones Newton Theol. Sch., 2006. Mem. Valiant Woman award 1991), Boston Min.'s Club. Office: Mass Coun Chs 14 Beacon St Ste 416 Boston MA 02108-3704 Business E-Mail: council@masscouncilofchurches.org.

KESSLER, GALE SUZANNE, psychologist, educator; b. Chgo., Sept. 5, 1940; d. George I. Alpert and Celia Larman-Alpert-Shaps; m. Marvin Charles Facktor, June 4, 1960 (dec.); children: Greg Facktor, Charles Facktor, Laura Meehan; m. John W. Kessler, Feb. 20, 1986 (dec. Apr. 4, 2001). BA in Edn., Roosevelt U., Chgo., 1961; MS in Orgnl. Behavior, Adminstrn., George Williams Coll., Aurora, Ill., 1980. Tchr. Chgo. Pub. Schs., 1961; dir. constituency rels. George Williams Coll., 1982—85; dir. alumni rels. Grad. Sch. Bus. U. Chgo., 1986; dir. devel. Nat. MS Soc., Chgo., 1986—87; tchr. Chgo. Pub. Schs., 1987; instr. Columbia Coll., Lake Ozark, Mo., 1993—95; exec. dir. Women's Coun., Mo., 1998—2001. Internat. liaison to human svcs. George Williams Coll., Downers Grove, Ill., 1982—85; advisor Inst. for Women's Policy Rsch., Washington, 2000—01. Columnist: Consultations, 1995—98; author: Male "Mid-Life Crisis In Relation To Job Change", 1980. Chair Elmhurst Citizens for Flood Control, Ill., 1987—90; pres. Arts Coun., Lake Ozark, Mo., 1991—93; candidate state rep. State of Mo., Lake Ozark, 1997—98. Recipient Key to City, City of Elmhurst, Ill., 1990. Fellow: World Affairs Coun. (Seattle); mem.: Women's Univ. Club (co-chair com. 2003, Seattle). Avocations: reading, travel, writing, golf, tennis. Home: 7905 W Mercer Way Mercer Island WA 98040

KESSLER, GLADYS, federal judge; b. 1938; BA, Cornell U., 1959; LLB, Harvard U., 1962. Staff atty. enforcement divsn. Nat. Labor Rels. Bd., 1962-64; legis. asst. to Senator Harrison A. Williams US Senate, 1964-66; legis. asst. to Rep. Jonathan B. Bingham US Ho. Reps., 1966-68; spl. asst. Office Staff Relations N.Y.C. Bd. Edn., 1968-69; ptnr. Berlin, Roisman and Kessler (and successor firms), 1969-77; assoc. judge D.C. Superior Ct., 1977-94; judge U.S. Dist. Ct. D.C., Washington, 1994—. Asst. lectr. law sch. George Washington U., 1971-73; del. to judicial adminstrn. divsn. D.C. Superior Ct., 1985-90; mem. adv. bd. Ctr. for Dispute Settlement Inst. for Judicial Adminstrn., State Justice Inst., mem. adv. com. nat. judicial edn. project on domestic violence; mem BNA adv. bd. Alternative Dispute Resolution Report, 1987-90; mem. family law cirriculum planning com. Georgetown U.; lead judge permanency planning project Nat. Coun. Juvenile and Family Ct. Judges; chair Nat. Conf. on Bioethics, Family and the Law, D.C., 1991; mem. faculty Nat. Inst. Trial Advocacy; exec. com. Nat. ABA Jud. Divsn./Conf. of Federal Trial Judges, 1997-2000; with U.S. Jud. Conf. Com. on Ct. Adminstrn. and Mgmt., 1999. Contbr. articles to legal jours. Recipient Women Lawyer of Yr. award Women's Bar Assn., 1983, Svc. award D.C. Coalition Against Domestic Violence, 1987, Judicial Excellence award Trial Lawyers Assn. Washington, 1987. Fellow Am. Bar Found.; mem. ABA (judicial adminstrn. divsn., com. on bioethics and AIDS, adv. com. on youth, alcohol and drug problems, nat. adv. bd. on child support and criminal justice, individual rights and responsibilities sect.), Am. Judicature Soc. (bd. dirs. 1985-89), Nat. Assn. Women Judges (v.p. 1979-81, pres. 1981-82), Nat. Ctr. for State Cts. (bd. dirs. 1984-87), Women's Legal Def. Fund (founding pres. 1971), Women Judges' Fund. for Justice (bd. dirs. 1980—), Found. for Women Judges (pres. 1980-82). Office: US Courthouse 333 Constitution Ave NW Washington DC 20001-2802

KESSLER, INGRID ANDERSON, musician, music educator; b. North Platte, Nebr., Aug. 18, 1944; d. R. Cedric and Ruby (Peterson) Anderson; m. Robert Michael Kessler, May 23, 1971; children: Jeffrey Charles, Lynn Elizabeth. BA in English Lit., U. Iowa, Iowa City, 1966; MusB summa cum laude, Vanderbilt U., 1998. Pianist, 1980—; pvt. tchr., 1983—; founding faculty W.O. Smith Music Sch., Nashville, 1984—87. Mem.: Nashville Opera Guild, Nat. Guild Piano Tchrs. (v.p. 1995—96, various other offices 1985—2001), Nashville Area Music Tchrs. Assn. (various offices 1985—2001, pres. 1999—2001). Jewish. Avocations: photography, gardening, travel, physical fitness. Home: 1247 Saxon Dr Nashville TN 37215

KESSLER, JEAN S., clinical data manager; b. New Brunswick, N.J., Oct. 20, 1954; d. John S. and Henrietta Marguerite (Pasquier de Lumeau) Kessler; m. Michael P. Gutzan, Sept. 16, 1984. AAS with highest honors, Middlesex County Coll., 1981; AS in Mgmt., Edison State Coll., 1990, postgrad., 1990—. Cert. profl. ins. woman. Underwriter Am. Reliance Ins. Co., Lawrenceville, NJ, 1989—92; bus. analyst Sprint, Bala Cynwyd, Pa., 1992—95; toxicology/med. devel. assoc. J & J Janssen, Titusville, NJ, 1995—99; adminstr. Rhodia, Cranbury, NJ, 2000—01; clin. data mgr. imaging Bio-Imaging, Newtown, Pa., 2001—02, PRA Internat., Horsham, Pa., 2002—03, ICON, North Wales, Pa., 2003—05, PharmaNet, Princeton, NJ, 2005—. Mem.: NAFE, Soc. Clin. Data Mgmt., Nat. Assn. Ins. Women, Mensa, Nu Tau Sigma.

KESSLER, JOAN BLUMENSTEIN, lawyer; AB in English, U. Mich., 1967, PhD in Speech Communication, 1973; MA in Speech Communication, UCLA, 1969; JD, Loyola U., L.A., 1986. Bar: Calif 1987. Tchr., debate coach various pub. high schs., 1967-70; instr. dept. speech Monroe CC, Rochester, NY, 1970-71; instr. communication and law Loyola U., Chgo., 1976, asst. prof., 1973-76; assoc. prof. dept. speech communication Calif. State U., Northridge, 1977-83; extern Calif. Ct. Appeal, 1985-86; assoc. Frandzel and Share, LA, 1986-90, Gold, Marks, Ring and Pepper, 1990-93; shareholder Kessler & Kessler, Century City, Calif., 1994—. Contbr. articles to profl jours. Mem. advancement com. U. Mich. Grad. Sch., 1992—; bd. govs. City of Hope, 1996—2000; bd. dirs. San Fernando Valley unit Am Cancer Soc, 1982—83; bd. dirs., chair long-range planning com. St. Vincent's Hosp. Found., 1990—. Office: Kessler and Kessler Ste 400 1901 Avenue of the Stars Los Angeles CA 90067-3002 Office Phone: 310-552-9800. Business E-Mail: jkessler@kesslerandkessler.com.

KESSLER, JOAN F., judge, lawyer; b. June 25, 1943; m. Frederick P. Kessler, Sept. 1967; 2 children. BA, U. Kans., 1961-65; postgrad., U. Wis., 1965-66; JD cum laude, Marquette U., 1968. Law clk. Hon. John W. Reynolds U.S. Dist. Ct. (ea. dist.) Wis., Milw., 1968-69; assoc. Warschafsky, Rotter & Tarnoff, Milw., 1969-71; pvt. practice Milw., 1971-74; assoc. Cook & Franke, S.C., Milw., 1974-78; U.S. atty. Eastern Dist. Wis., Milw., 1978-81; ptnr. Foley & Lardner, Milw., 1981—2004; judge Ct. Appeals Wisc., Milw., 2004—. Lectr. profl. responsibility U. Wis. Law Sch., Marquette U. Law Sch., Milw., 1994-96; mem. bd. govs. State Bar of Wis., 1985-89, 90-92, 93-95, chair, 1993, bd. dirs. family law sect., 1991-94; mem. Jud. Coun. Wis., Madison, 1989-92; mem. Milw. Bd. Attys. Profl. Responsibility,

1979-85. Bd. dirs. Legal Aid Soc., 1974-78, v.p., 1978, Urban League, 1980-82, Women's Bus. Initiative Corp., 1989-91, Girl Scouts U.S., Milw., 1994-96; bd. dirs., pres. Voters for Choice in Wis., 1989-93. Fellow Am. Matrimonial Lawyers (bd. govs. 1990-96, v.p. 1996-99), Am. Law Inst., Am. Bar Found.; mem. ABA (chair sect. individual rights and responsibilities 2003-04, coun. mem. 1997-2004, editor Human Rights 1997-99), ACLU. Office: Judge Ct Appeals Wis 633 W Wisconsin Milwaukee WI 53203 Office Phone: 414-227-4684. E-mail: joan.kessler@wicourts.gov.

KESSLER, KENDALL SEAY FERIOZI, artist; b. Washington, Nov. 4, 1954; d. Dan John and Anne Fletcher (Trotter) Feriozi; m. Clyde Thomas Kessler, June 25, 1977; 1 child, Alan. BA in Art Edn., Va. Poly. Inst. and State U., 1976; MFA in Painting and Printmaking, Radford U., 1983. Tchr. art, Spanish Cherrydale Christian Sch., Arlington, Va., 1976-77; tchr. community arts sch. Radford (Va.) U., 1980-82, adminstr., 1982-83; tchr. art Fine Arts Ctr., Pulaski, Va., 1984; instr. art Radford U., 1985-87, 88-93, interim gallery dir., 1987-88, asst. prof. art, 2000—; freelance profl. artist, tchr. Radford, 1993—. Illustrator (poetry books) Shooting Creek, 1982, Dancing at Big Vein, 1987, Preservations, 1989; promotional book jacket illustrator: The Rosewood Casket by Sharon McCrumb, 1996; exhibited in group shows Agora Gallery, Soho, N.Y., 1994, 95; exhibited and represented by The Gallery, Radford, Va., Fine Art Ctr. for the New River Valley, Pulaski, Va. Officer PEO Sisterhood, Radford, 1992—94, mem., 1989—, Lamplighters, Radford Pub. Libr., 1991—. Recipient Am. Artist award Pastel Soc. West Coast 4th Nat. Exhibit, Sacramento, Daniel Greene 1st place award for oils Paris (Tex.) Art Fair, 1991, Best in Show award Fincastle (Va.) Arts Festival, 1997. Mem. Nat. Mus. Women in Arts, Blacksburg Regional Art Assn., Lynwood Artists, Piedmont Arts Assn. Avocations: theater, literature, music, skating. Home: PO Box 3612 Radford VA 24143-3612 Office Phone: 540-231-9261. Business E-Mail: kkessler@radford.edu.

KESSLER, LYNN ELIZABETH, state legislator; b. Seattle, Feb. 26, 1941; d. John Mathew and Kathryn Eisen; m. Keith L. Kessler, Dec. 24, 1980; children: William John Moore, Christopher Scott Moore, Bradley Jerome Moore, Jamie. Attended, Seattle U., 1958-59. Mem. Wash. Ho. of Reps., 1993—. Majority leader, mem. rules com., mem. appropriations com. Exec. dir. United Way Grays Harbor, 1984-92; mem. adv. coun. Head Start, 1986-89, Cervical Cancer Awareness Task Force, 1990-91, vocat. adv. coun. Hoquiam High Sch., 1991—, strategic planning com. Grays Harbor Community Hosp., 1991-92, Grays Harbor Food Bank Com., 1991-92, Grays Harbor Dem. Ctrl. Com.; vice-chair Grays Harbor County Shorelines Mgmt. Bd., 1988-90; chair Disability Awareness Com., 1988-90, Youth 2000 Com., 1990-91; pres. Teenage Pregnancy, Parenting and Prevention Adv. Coun., 1989-91; v.p. Grays Harbor Econ. Devel. Coun., 1990-; trustee Grays Harbor Coll., 1991-2001, Aberdeen YMCA, 1991— Mem. Aberdeen Rotary (pres. 1993-94). Home: 62 Kessler Ln Hoquiam WA 98550-9742 Office: Wash Ho of Reps Legislative Bldg 3rd Fl Olympia WA 98504-0001

KESSLER-HODGSON, LEE GWENDOLYN, actress, performing company executive; b. Wellsville, N.Y., Jan. 16, 1947; d. James Hewitt and Reba Gwendolyn (Adsit) Kessler; m. Bruce Gridley, June 22, 1969 (div. Dec. 1979); m. Jeffrey Craig Hodgson, Oct. 31, 1987. BA, Grove City Coll., 1968; MA, U. Wis., 1969. Prof. Sangamon State U., Springfield, Ill., 1969-70; pers. exec. Bullock's, L.A., 1971-74; owner Brunnen Enterprises, L.A., 1982—. Author: A Child of Arthur, 1981, White King and The Doctor, 2005; prodr., writer play including Anais Nin: The Paris Years, 1986; appeared in TV movies, mini-series including Roots, 1978, Backstairs at The White House, 1979, Blind Ambition, 1980, Hill Street Blues, 1984-87, Murder By Reason of Insanity, 1985, Hoover, 1986, Creator, 1987, Our House, 1988, Favorite Son, 1988, Lou Grant 1983-84, Barney Miller, 1979, L.A. Law, 1990, Hunter, 1991, (screenplay) Settlers Way, 1988; (TV series) Matlock, L.A. Law others. Knapp Prize fellow U. Wis., 1969. Mem. AFTRA, SAG, Actors Equity Assn. Republican. Mem. Ch. Scientology. Avocations: singer, directing, motivational speaking. Mailing: PO Box 1808 Eureka MT 59917 Office Phone: 877-478-0835. Personal E-mail: kesslerl@bww.com. Business E-Mail: kesslerl@ltdkate.com.

KESTEN, BETTY LEE, retired special education educator; b. Riceville, Iowa, Oct. 27, 1921; d. Leo Adelbert and Adelaide Charlotte (Minkebige) Bathen; children: Steven F. Kesten, Gregory L. Kesten. Student, Mt. Mercy Coll., Cedar Rapids, Iowa, 1940-42; BA, Calif. State U., Long Beach, 1964; MA, U. San Francisco, 1982; postgrad., numerous colls. and univs. Cert. life elem. edn., life learning handicapped, gen. sch. svcs. credentials, resource specialist cert., Calif. Elem. tchr. McIntire (Iowa) Sch. Dist., 1942-44, Iowa City Sch. Dist., 1944-45, Bloomfield Sch. Dist., Hawaiian Gardens, Calif., 1948-51, St. Hilary's Sch., Pico Rivera, Calif., 1958-62, St. Dominic Savio Sch., Bellflower, Calif., 1962-64, Downey (Calif.) Unified Sch. Dist., 1964-89; dir., tchr. The Learning Tree, Tutoring Svc., Downey, 1989—2005. Cons. Richlore Found., Anaheim, Calif., 1989-2005. Recipient award for oustanding svc. to dept. spl. edn. Calif. State U., L.A., 1979, Tchr. of Yr. award Woman's Club Downey, 1983, Hon. Svc. award Calif. PTA, 1988. Mem. Calif. Fedn. Coun. for Exceptional Children (treas. chpt. 563, 1982-88, Outstanding Svc. award 1983), Calif. Assn. Resource Specialists. Avocations: painting, graphology, creative writing, genealogy. Office: Unit 41 16211 Downey Ave Paramount CA 90723-5562

KESTER, CHERYL L., management consultant; b. Tex., 1967; d. Melvyn R. and Virginia A. Goodwin; m. Charles M. Kester, 1968. BA, John Brown U., Siloam Springs, Ark., 1991; MA, Georgetown U., Washington, 1996. Cert. Fund Raising Exec. Cert. Fund Raising Execs. Internat., 2005. Coord. acad. computing John Brown U., 1994—95, dir. network computing svcs., 1995—97, dir. tech. planning, R & D, 1997—99, dir. grants and found. rels., 1999—2005; ptnr. Thomas-Forbes & Kester, Fayetteville, 2005—; dir. of web services John Brown U., Siloam Springs, Ark., 1999—2003. Mem. Coun. Christian Colls. & Univs. Commn. Tech., Washington, 1998—2003; mem., editl. rev. com. EDUCAUSE, 1998—2001. Contbr. articles to profl. jours. Lic. lay reader Episcopal Ch., Siloam Springs, 2003—06; mem. Habitat for Humanity Fayetteville, 2000—03, sec., 2001—03; mem. Ozark Highlanders Pipe Band, Fayetteville, 1998—2006. Scholar Presdl. Award, John Brown U., 1987—91; English Dept. Scholarship, Georgetown U., 1993—94. Mem.: Coun. Advancement and Support of Edn., Assn. Fundraising Profls. (sec. bd. dirs. NW Ark. chpt. 2003—04, pres.-elect bd. dirs. 2004—05, pres. bd. dirs. 2005—), Am. Assn. Grant Profls., Alpha Chi, Sigma Tau Delta. Avocations: Scottish tenor drumming, travel, gardening, reading. Office: Thomas-Forbes & Kester LLC 13602 White Oak Lane Fayetteville AR 72704 Office Fax: 479-582-1053.

KESTER, GUNILLA THEANDER, poet, literature educator, music educator; b. Lund, Sweden, Jan. 28, 1958; arrived in U.S., 1982; d. Sten and Siv Theander; m. Daniel John Kester, June 19, 1988; children: Anya Rebecca, Shiri Sophia. BA, U. Stockholm, 1982, U. Lund, 1982; MA, Pa. State U., 1985; PhD, U. N.C., 1991. Adj. asst. prof. Franklin-Marshall Coll., Lancaster, Pa., 1995—96, Daemen Coll., Buffalo, 1997—; classical guitar tchr. Amherst Sch. Music, Buffalo, 1997—. Asst. festival dir. Rantucci Internat. Guitar Festival and Competition, Buffalo, 1997—. Author: Writing the Subject, 1995, 1997, articles and poems; contbr. poetry to various publs. Finalist Co. Prize for Poetry, 2005; recipient first prize, Gival Press Tri-Lang. Competition in English, 2002; Fulbright scholar, 1982, Scandinavian-Am. fellow, 1986. Mem.: Am. Profl. Woman Writers, Buffalo Guitar Soc. (v.p. 1997—), Swedish Women's Edn'l. Assn., Hadassah. Office: Daemen Coll 4380 Main St Amherst NY 14226 E-mail: gkester@adelphia.net.

KESTER, HELEN MARY, minister; b. Three Springs, Pa., Jan. 19, 1953; d. James R. and Phoebe C. (Dalzell) Daniels; m. Hal W. Kester, July 5, 1975; children: Mary Beth, Timothy, William Shondelmyer. BS, Slippery Rock U., 1974, MEd, 1978; MDiv, Pitts. Theol. Sem., 2006. Cert. elem. tchr., reading specialist, Pa. 8th grade reading tchr. New Kensington (Pa.)-Arnold Sch. Dist., 1974—2006, chair reading dept., 1974—2006; pastor Derry Presbyn. Ch., Pa., 2006—. Mem. NEA, Pa. State Edn. Assn., Internat. Reading Assn., Phi Delta Kappa, Kappa Delta Pi. Office Phone: 724-694-5710. E-mail: hkester@comcast.net.

KETCHAM, SALLY ANN, historic site staff member, consultant; b. Norfolk, Nebr., Mar. 11, 1928; d. William Ralph and Sallie Gertrude (Marshall) Johnson; m. Richard W. Ketcham, Jan. 24, 1962; children: Sallie Jane, William Marshall. Student, Colo. Woman's Coll., 1946—47; BA, U. Nebr., 1950, MA, 1956. Curator of history Nebr. State Hist. Soc., Lincoln, 1951—60; furnishing curator U.S. Nat. Pk. Svc., Omaha, 1960—62, rsch. specialist San Francisco, 1962—64, Washington, 1962—67; contractor U.S. Nat. Pk. Svc. and others, 1968—96, U.S. Fish and Wildlife, Omaha, 1979. Restoration chmn. Gen. Crook House, Omaha, 1980—86, Avery House, Ft. Collins, 1985—; steering com. Amigos de la Romero House, Ft. Collins, 2001—02. Co-author: (book) Sautterhouse Five, 1983; contbr. articles to profl. jours. and newspapers. Mem. Landmark Preservation Com., Ft. Collins, 1984—90, Poudre Landmarks Fedn., Ft. Collins, 1986—2000, Colo. Hist. Soc.; v.p. Douglas County Hist. Soc., Omaha, 1980—86; pres. Ft. Collins Hist. Soc. Recipient Disting. Svc. award, Douglas County Hist. Soc., 1984, Award of Excellence, City of Ft. Collins, 1990, Superior Svc. award, Nat. Park Svc., Outstanding Cmty. Svc. award, PLF, 2003. Mem.: Ft. Laramie Assn. (hon.).

KETCHUM, IRENE FRANCES, library supporter; b. Hammond, Ind., Jan. 19, 1914; d. Peter H. and Theresa C. (Weis) Young; m. Alden W. Ketchum, Sept. 17, 1936 (dec. 1973); 1 child, William H. Grad. high sch., Hammond, 1932. Cert. mcpl. clk. Mng. editor Herald Newspapers, Gary, Ind., 1950-55; clk.-treas. Town of Highland, Ind., 1956-79; trustee, bd. sec. Lake County Pub. Libr., Merrillville, Ind., 1980-95; past trustee, 1995—; pres., 1995. Active Ind. State Libr. Adv. Com., Indpls., 1988—90; treas. Highland Cmty. Events Coun., 1975—; mem. Friends of Ind. Librs., Friends of Lake County Pub. Libr., Lake County Pub. Libr. Found.; pres. Highland Women's Dem. Club, 1978; auditor Highland Dem. Club, 1980—89. Named Sagamore of the Wabash, 1996, Fraternalist of Yr., Fraternal Congress, 2002. Mem. Internat. Inst. Mcpl. Clks., Ind. League Mcpl. Clks. and Treas. (assoc., treas., sec., v.p., pres. 1967-68), Girl Scouts USA (life). Roman Catholic. Avocations: community service volunteer, reading, travel.

KETEFIAN, SHAKÉ, nursing educator; b. Beirut, Dec. 29, 1939; d. Krikor and Zaghganoush (Soghomonian) K. BSN, Am. U. Beirut, 1963; MEd, Columbia U., 1968, EdD, 1972. From asst. prof. nursing to prof. NYU Sch. Edn., Health, Nursing and Arts Professions, N.Y.C., 1972-84; dir. continuing edn. in nursing NYU, N.Y.C.; with U. Mich., 1984—; prof., assoc. dean for grad. studies, dir. doctoral and postdoctoral studies U. Mich. Sch. Nursing, Ann Arbor, 1984—91, dir. internat. affairs, 1996—, acting dean, 1991-92. Contbr. articles to profl. jours. Fellow AAUW, Am. Acad. Nursing (governing coun.); mem. ANA, Am. Orgn. Nurse Execs., Midwest Nursing Rsch. Soc. (chair sci. integrity task force 1994-96, 2001-03), Mich. Nurses Assn., Internat. Network for Doctoral Edn. in Nursing (co-founder, pres.), Sigma Theta Tau. Office: U Mich Sch Nursing 400 N Ingalls Ann Arbor MI 48109 Office Phone: 734-763-6669. Business E-Mail: ketefian@umich.edu.

KETTERLING, DEBRA M., secondary school educator; b. Lamoure, ND, July 21, 1951; d. Harold E. and Hilda L. Weixel; m. Lynn Ketterling, Dec. 28, 1968; children: Darin, Dustin. EdM, U. Mary VCSU, Bismarck, N.D., 1974. Tchr., Killdeer, ND, Veblen, SD, 1976—80, White, SD, 1980—85, Richardton, ND, 1985—89, Century HS, Bismarck, ND, 1989—. Mem. coll. adv. bd. U. Mary Masters, Bismarck, ND, 1998; tchr., adv. bd. Century H.S., Bismarck, ND, 1989—. Home: 2905 Vancouver Ln Bismarck ND 58503

KETTERSON, ELLEN D., biologist, educator; b. Orange, NJ, Aug. 9, 1945; d. John B. and Lois (Meadows) K.; m. Val Nolan, Jr., Oct. 17, 1980. BA in Botany, Ind. U., 1966, MA in Botany, 1968, PhD in Zoology, 1974. NIH fellow Wash. State U., 1975-77; asst. prof. biol. scis. Bowling Green State U., 1975-77; vis. asst. prof. to asst. prof. biology Ind. U., Bloomington, 1977-84, from assoc. prof. to prof. biology, 1984—, co-dir. Ctr. for Integrative Study Animal Behavior, 1990—2002. Vis. scientist Purdue U., Lafayette, Ind., 1991, Rockefeller U., 1985, U. Va., 1984. Mem. editl. bd. Current Ornithology, 1989—, editor, 1994-98; mem. editl. bd. Animal Behaviour, 1997—, assoc. editor, 1991-94; mem. editl. bd. Evolution, 1994, editor, 1994-99; editor: Jour. Avian Biology, 1999—2004. NSF Rsch. grants, 1978—; Guggenheim fellow, 2004. Fellow Am. Ornithologists Union (v.p. 1995-96, coun. 1988-91, Elliot Coues award 1996), Animal Behavior Soc. (Exemplar award 2004), Royal Soc. London (sci. editor Proced 2005—); mem. AAAS, Internat. Ornithol. Com., Ecol. Soc. Am., Am. Soc. Naturalists, Assn. Field Ornithologists, Cooper Ornithol. Soc., Soc. Conservation Biology, Soc. Study of Evolution, Soc. Integrative and Comparative Biology, Soc. Behavioral Neuroendocrinology, Wilson Ornithol. Soc. (Margaret M. Nice award 1998), Sigma Xi. Office: Indiana U Dept Biology Bloomington IN 47405 E-mail: ketterso@indiana.edu.

KETTLING, VIRGINIA, retired health facility administrator; b. Toldeo, Aug. 9, 1932; d. Charles Albert and Elizabeth (Knapp) Reuthe; m. George Kettling, June 16, 1962; children: Elys, Kandys, Gynevra, Geoff. BSN, Capital U., 1955; MA, Ohio State U., 1962. Cert. nursing admin. advanced. Asst. dir. nursing Christ Hosp., Cin., 1962—65; asst. prof., dir. baccalaureate program U. Cin., 1965-71; asst. v.p., nursing dir. Bethesda Hosp. Sch. Nursing, Cin., 1971-77; clin. asst. prof. U. Wis., Milw., 1981-88; chief nurse exec. Mt. Sinai Med. Ctr., Milw., 1977-88; v.p. patient care United Samaritans Med. Ctr., Danville, Ill., 1988-97; cert. parish nurse Bethel Luth. Ch., Danville, 1997—2002; parish nurse Christ the King Luth Ch., 2003—, Advent Luth. Ch. and St. John Luth. Ch., 2004—. Cons. assoc. degree program D.A.C.C., 1998—; interim pres. Lakeview Coll. Nursing, Danville, 1999—2000, planning devel. fiscal officer, 2000. Named nominee, Wisc. Nurse Exec. Yr. Mem.: Midwest Alliance Nursing, Am. Coll. Healthcare Execs., Am. Hosp. Pub. (reviewer books), Ill. Orgn. Nurse Execs., Am. Orgn. Nurse Execs., Exec. Club Danville. Home: 958 Algoma Dr Port Washington WI 53074 Office: 1193 Lakefield Rd Grafton WI 53074 Office Phone: 262-894-9160. E-mail: vkettling@wi.rr.com.

KETTUNEN ZEGART, MAR(GARET) JEAN, artist, educator; b. Lansing, Mich., Aug. 19, 1926; d. Arne Gerald and Ruth (Cresswell) Kettunen; m. Harold Jerome Zegart, Aug. 3, 1954 (div. Dec. 1964); children: Benjamin Arne, Kathleen Anne (dec.), Johnathan Morris, Jamin Andrew. Student, Cranbrook Art Acad., Bloomfield Hills, Mich., 1946; BA cum laude, Mich. State U., 1947; MA in Painting, U. Calif., Berkeley, 1954; studied and worked in a tiller 17, in printmaking studios, 1948—53, studied with major artists, 1944—54. Cert. in gen. secondary edn., art and English; cert. in arts adminstrn. Asst. to art editor Glamor, Conde Nast Publs., N.Y.C., 1947-53; designer, sec. Smith, Tepper Sundberg, San Francisco, 1953-54; instr. painting Coll. of Marin, Kentfield, Calif., summer 1961; educator, adult educator La Serna H.S., East Whittier (Calif.) Sch. Dist., 1961-62; Fulbright exch. tchr. Testwood Hampshire Schs., Totten, Hants, Eng., 1979-80; art educator, arts cons. Tamalpais (Calif.) H.S., 1961, 62-91. One-woman shows include Wittenborne Schultz, Inc., N.Y.C., Marin County Civic Ctr., Mus. of Modern Art, San Francisco, Kings Gallery, others, exhibited in group shows at San Francisco Mus. Modern Art Rental Galleries, Kings' Gallery/UU Ctr., San Francisco, Bklyn. Mus., Phila. Print Club, Palace of the Legion of Honor, Met. Mus. Art, N.Y., others, Represented in permanent collections Suomi Coll., Mich. State U., Guggenheim Mus., Mus. Modern Art, N.Y.C., Pub. Libr., Whitney Mus., Musea de Arte Moderna, Sao Paulo, Brazil, Brit. Mus., London, Achenbach Graphic Arts Collection, San Francisco Mus., others. Cmty. planning advocate. Recipient Milley award for Cmty. Svc. and Art Achievements, 2005. Mem.: NEA (life Milly award 2005), Marin Ret. Tchrs. Assn. (bd. dirs., comm. editor, pub. rels.), San Francisco Mus. Modern Art, San Francisco Mus. Soc., Graphic Art Coun., Calif. Tchrs. Assn. (life), Friend of Del Norte, Mill Valley Outdoor Art Club (bd. dirs., civics and conservation chair, 2d v.p.). Avocations: reading, attending theatre, opera and ballet, family genealogy. Home: 118 Highland Ln Mill Valley CA 94941-3564 Personal E-mail: kettz@aol.com.

KEULEGAN, EMMA PAULINE, special education educator; b. Washington, Jan. 21, 1930; d. Garbis H. and Nellie Virginia (Moore) K. BA, Dumbarton Coll. of Holy Cross, 1954. Cert. tchr. elem. and spl. edn. Tchr. St. Dominic's Elem. Sch., Washington, 1954-56, Sacred Heart Acad., Washington, 1956-59, Our Lady of Victory, Washington, 1959-63, St. Francis Acad., Vicksburg, Miss., 1963-78, Culkin Acad., Vicksburg, 1978-91, substitute tchr. spl. edn., 1991—. Treas. PTA, Vicksburg, 1980; pres. Vicksburg Geneal. Soc., 1999. Mem.: DAR (chpt. regent 1967—69, sec. 1994, chpt. chaplain 1996, chpt. libr. 2002, chpt. membership chmn.), Daus. of United Confederacy (chpt. chaplain), Soc. Descs. of Knights of Most Noble Order of the Garter, Sovereign Colonial Soc. Am. Royal Descent, Soc. Magna Charta Dames and Barons (state chaplain 2001), Daus. of the War of 1812 (state chaplain 1998, hon. state pres. 2002—03, state pres. 2002—), Daus. Am. Colonists (chaplain 1985—89, state pres. 1992—94, hon. state pres. 1994—), Colonial Dames 17th Century (state v.p. 1987—89, state pres. 1989, hon. state pres. 1991—), Internat. Reading Assn. (pres. Warren County chpt.), Vicksburg Geneal. Soc. (pres. 2003). Republican. Roman Catholic. Avocations: needlecrafts, reading, coin collecting/numismatics, stamp collecting/philately. Home: 215 Buena Vista Dr Vicksburg MS 39180-5612

KEVILLE, TERRI DONNA, lawyer; b. Phila., Mar. 5, 1951; d. Bernard Louis and Dora Duchovnay Jacobs; m. Thomas Joseph Keville, Aug. 25, 1974; children: James Thomas, Jordan Brian, Warren Lowell, Owen Stuart. BA, U. Pa., 1972; JD, U. So. Calif., Gould Sch. Law, 1992. Bar: Calif. 1992, US Dist. Ct. (ctrl. dist.) Calif. 1992, US Ct. Appeals (9th cir.) 1992, US Supreme Ct. 2000. Summer assoc. Horvitz & Levy, Encino, Calif., 1990; assoc. Manatt, Phelps & Phillips, LLP, Los Angeles, 1992—97, ptnr., 1998—. Editor: California Health Law News. Recipient Order of the Coif, USC Chpt., 1992, Articles Editor, So. Calif. Law Rev., 1991-1992. Mem.: Calif. Soc. Healthcare Attys. (bd. editors 1995—2006, pres. 2004—05), LA County Bar Assn. (co-chair, bioethics com. 2000—02, LA County Med. Assn./LACBA joint com. on biomedical ethics, co chair), ABA Health Law Sect., Am. Health Lawyers Assn. Jewish. Avocation: classical music. Office: Manatt Phelps & Phillips LLP 11355 W Olympic Blvd Los Angeles CA 90064-1614 Office Phone: 310-312-4183. Office Fax: 310-914-5735. Business E-Mail: tkeville@manatt.com.

KEWIN, CYNTHIA MCLENDON, secondary school educator; b. Lexington, Ky., Aug. 25, 1957; d. William Watts and Olive Mershon (Johnson) McLendon; m. Kevin Jon Kewin, Apr. 5, 1986. BS in Speech and Drama, Asbury Coll., 1979; MEd, Georgetown U., 1987, postgrad., 1988; BA in English, U. Ky., 1989. Cert. tchr. grades 7-12. Substitute tchr., Lexington, 1979-82; tchr. Educare, Lexington, 1979—; sales and mktg. rep. Campbell House, Lexington, 1979—; word processing specialist A.B. Dick, Lexington, 1979-80; spl. agt. Am. Family Security, Lexington, 1980-81; fin. cons. Mass. Mut. Ins., Lexington, 1981-83; tchr. Fayette County Pub. Schs., Lexington, 1983—. Mem. Leadership Edn., Lexington, 1996—. Bd. dirs. Tend My Sheep Ministries, Lexington; drama and choir mem. Lexington; assoc. mem. Immanuel Bapt. Ch. Mem. NEA, Ky. Edn. Assn., Fayette County Edn. Assn., Nat. Coun. Tchrs. English, Ky. Coun. Tchrs. English, Ednl. Theater Assn. Democrat. Avocations: theater, music, sewing, landscaping, gardening. Home: 3208 Breckenwood Dr Lexington KY 40502-2912 Office: Lafayette HS 401 Reed Ln Lexington KY 40503-1200

KEWISH, SHARON PATRICIA, literature educator; d. Ralph and Fern Kewish. BS, We. Ill. U., Macomb, 1965, MA in English, 1966. Assoc. prof. English Cumberland C.C., Vineland, NJ, 1971—. Recipient Nat. Tchg. Excellence award. Avocations: reading, travel, theater.

KEWLEY, SHARON LYNN, systems analyst, consultant; b. Geneseo, Ill., Sept. 23, 1958; d. James Leslie and Geraldine (Myers) Kewley. BBA (hon.), U. Miami, Fla., 1988; MSc in Computer Info. Sys., U. Phoenix, 2004. 1984gen. agt. Varvaris and Associates, Cedar Rapids, Iowa, 1981; programmer, analyst U. Miami, Coral Gables, Fla., 1984—88; systems analyst Metro Dade County, Miami, Fla., 1988—91; sys. analyst Nat. Coun. on Compensation Ins., Boca Raton, Fla., 1991—93; owner Boca Byte, Boca Raton, Fla., 1993—. Mem. NAFE, Kendall Jaycees, Nat. Gold Key Honor Soc., PADI-divemaster. Republican. Lutheran. Avocations: scuba diving, cruising, world travel. Office: Boca Byte PO Box 880009 Boca Raton FL 33488-0009 Personal E-mail: kewstan@aol.com.

KEY, KRISTINA POPE, literature and language professor; b. Sapulpa, Okla., Aug. 15, 1972; d. Thomas Joe and June Kathleen Pope; m. Randall Miles Key, Aug. 17, 1972. PhD in English, U. La., Lafayette, 2003. Instr. English River Parishes C.C., Sorrento, La., 2002—04; asst. prof. English St. Andrews Presbyn. Coll., Laurinburg, NC, 2004—. Office: St Andrews Presbyterian College 1700 Dogwood Mile Laurinburg NC 28352 Office Phone: 910-277-5267. Personal E-mail: keykp@sapc.edu.

KEY, RACHEL E., literature and language professor; b. Kirkland, Wash., Nov. 16, 1973; d. John and Charlotte Key. BA in English, Ctrl. Wash. U., Ellensburg, 1998; MA in English, Ctrl. Wash. U., 2001; postgrad., Okla. State U., Stillwater, 2004—. Instr. Ctrl. Wash. U., 2000—01, Ctrl. Tex. Coll.-USN Pace Program, Killeen, 2001—02; grad. tchg. assoc. Okla. State U., 2002—04; adj. instr. No. Okla. Coll., Stillwater, 2004; asst. prof. East Ctrl. U., Ada, Okla., 2004—. Academic facilitator dept. athletics Okla. State U., 2003—05. Editor (online jour.) Write On!. Vol. English instr. Stillwater Hispanic Lang. Inst., 2004. Mem.: Popular Culture Assn. Office Phone: 580-310-5453. E-mail: rkey@mailclerk.ecok.edu.

KEY, TARA ANN, clinical social worker; b. Southfield, Mich., June 19, 1966; d. Bruce Stewart and Doris Ann (Diehl) Baldwin; m. Denman Arlan Key, Oct. 17, 1989. BSW, East Tex. State U., 1988; MS in Social Work, U. Tex., Arlington, 1992. Lic. master social worker, Tex.; advanced clin. practitioner, Tex. Intern in social work, cons. Terrell (Tex.) State Hosp., 1988-89, clin. social worker, 1989-91; dir. social svcs. Terrell Care Ctr., 1991-92; clin. social worker VA Med. Ctr., Dallas, 1992—. Vol. faculty, clin. instr. psychiatry U. Tex. Southwestern Med. Sch., Dallas, 1994-97, 2004—; field instr. masters level social work U. Tex. at Arlington, 1998—. Vol. Spl. Olympics, Commerce, Tex., 1988, Stylist, Attitudes and Attires, 2003—. Recipient Mental Health and Behavioral Scis. Svc. Dirs. award Dept. Vets. Affairs, 1994. Mem.: Alpha Delta Mu. Avocations: archaeology, travel, gardening, mountain biking, camping. Home: 541 Oxbow St Mesquite TX 75149-4851 Office: VA Med Ctr 4500 S Lancaster Rd Dallas TX 75216-7256 Office Phone: 214-857-0722. Business E-Mail: tara.key@va.gov.

KEYES, FLO, language educator; b. Rutland, Vt., Sept. 21, 1957; d. Stuart Norton and Florence Elizabeth (Ericksen) Keyes; m. Thomas Joseph Mistokowski, May 30, 1975 (div. Jan. 1991); 1 child, Thomas Anthony. AA summa cum laude, County Coll. Morris, Randolph, N.J., 1979; BA summa cum laude, Montclair State Coll., N.J., 1982; MA summa cum laude, Montclair State Coll., 1986; MPhil summa cum laude, Drew U., Madison, N.J., 1998, PhD summa cum laude, 2002. Lic. airplane pilot. Adj. prof. English Castleton State Coll., Vt., 1986—94, Warren County C.C., Washington, NJ, 1995—97, Castleton State Coll., 1998—2001, asst. prof. English, 2001—. Mem. bd. Vt. Acad. Arts and Scis., 2003—. Author: (book) Literature of Hope in the Middle Ages and Today, 2006; editor: (newsletter) V.A.A.S., 2006; author: (poetry) Mountain Troubadour, 2004—06 (various poetry prizes). Mem.: Poetry Soc. Vt. (mem. anthology com. 2005—), South Ctrl. Renaissance Conf. Independent. Presbyterian. Avocations: gardening, music, acting. Office: Castleton State Coll 6 Alumni Dr Castleton VT 05735 Business E-Mail: keyesf@castleton.edu.

KEYES, JOAN ROSS RAFTER, education educator, writer; b. Bklyn., Aug. 12, 1924; d. Joseph W. and Hermia (Ross) Rafter; m. William Ambrose, Apr. 26, 1947 (dec.); children: William, Peter, Dion, Kenzie. BA, Adelphi U., Garden City, N.Y., 1945; MS, Long Island U., Greenvale, N.Y., 1973. Prodn. asst. CBS Radio, N.Y., 1943-44; cub news reporter Bklyn. Daily Eagle, 1945-46; advt. copywriter Gimbel's Dept. Store, N.Y., 1946-47; adj. prof. L.I. U., Greenvale, NY, 1984—; tchr. Port Wash. Pub. Schs., NY, 1970-94. Lectr., cons. pub. sch. dists. nationwide, 1978—; workshop leader Tchrs. English to Speakers Other Langs. convs., 1981—; cons. Kids' Readers, 2005. Author: Beats! Conversations in Rhythm, 1983, (video program) Now You're Talking, 1987, (computer program) Quick Talk, 1990, Oxford Picture Dictionary for Kids Program, 1998; contbr. articles to ednl. mags. Lectr., catechist Our Lady of Fatima Ch., Port Washington, 1987—; vol. Earthwatch, Mallorca, 1988. Australia/New Zealand ednl. grantee Port Washington Pub. Schs., 1992. Mem. Tchrs. of English to Speakers of Other Languages, Am. Fedn. of Tchrs., N.Y. State United Tchrs., Port Wash. Tchrs. Assn. Republican. Roman Catholic. Avocations: music, painting, travel, tennis, photography. Personal E-mail: joanrosskeyes@aol.com.

KEYES, MARIA VEGA, social studies educator; b. Baton Rouge, La., Nov. 13, 1973; d. Benjamin Clark Vega, Jr. and Elmere LeBlanc Vega; m. Joe Bearre Keyes, Aug. 4, 2001. MA in History, U. Tex., Arlington, 1998. Tchr. social studies Mill Creek H.S., Hoschton, Ga., 2001—; adj. instr. Piedmont Coll., Athens, Ga., 2006—. Reader SAT Pearson Edn., 2005—. Liberal. Christian. Office: Mill Creek HS 4400 Braselton Hoschton GA 30548 Office Phone: 678-714-5850.

KEYES, SAUNDRA ELISE, newspaper editor; b. Salt Lake City, June 28, 1945; d. Vernon Harrison and Mildred K.; m. William J. Ivey, June 13, 1969 (div. 1976). BA, U. Utah, 1966; MA, Ind. U., 1969, PhD, 1976. Tchr. Salt Lake City Pub. Schs., 1966-67; asst. prof. Fisk U., Nashville, 1971-76; reporter, city editor The Tennessean, Nashville, 1976-83; staff writer The Courier-Jour., Louisville, 1983-84; dep. mng. editor Orlando (Fla.) Sentinel, 1985-88; mng. editor Phila. Daily News, 1988-90; exec. editor, sr. v.p. Press-Telegram, Long Beach, Calif., 1991-93; mng. editor The Miami Herald, 1993-96, Contra Costa Times, 1996—2000; editor Honolulu Advertiser, 2000—. Ford Found. fellow, 1978. Mem.: Am. Soc. Newspaper Editors (pres. accrediting coun. on edn. in journalism and mass comm. 2004—). Office: Honolulu Advertiser 605 Kapiolani Blvd PO Box 3110 Honolulu HI 96802

KEYS, ALICIA (ALICIA AUGELLO COOK), vocalist, musician, songwriter; b. NYC, Jan. 25, 1981; d. Craig Cook and Terri Augello. Student, Columbia U. Singer: (albums) Songs in A Minor, 2001 (Video Music Award, two Billboard Awards, two Am. Music Awards, two NAACP Image Awards, three Soul Train awards, two World Music Awards, an ECCHO award, Grammy Award for Best New Artist, Song of Yr., Best R&B Vocal Performance, Best R&B Song and Best R&B Album), The Diary of Alicia Keys, 2003 (MTV Video Music award Best R&B Video for the song "If I Ain't Got You", 2004, R&B/Hip-Hop Singles of Yr.:"If I Ain't Got You", Billboard Music Awards, 2004, R&B/Hip-Hop Airplay Single of Yr.:"If I Ain't Got You", Billboard Music Awards, 2004, Grammy Award for Best R&B Album, 2005); composer: (films) Hollywood Homicide, Dr. Dolittle 2, Ali; actor: (TV guest appearances) The Cosby Show, 1985, Saturday Night Live, 2001, Charmed, 2001, Tonight Show with Jay Leno, 2001, American Dreams, 2003, Oprah Winfrey Show, 2004; author: Tears for Water: Songbook of Poems and Lyrics, 2004. Named Female Artist of Yr., Billboard Music Awards, 2004, Hot 100 Artist of Yr., 2004, Female Hot 100 Artist of Yr., 2004, Hot 100 Songwriter of Yr., 2004; named one of Time Mag. 100 Most Influential People, 2005, 50 Most Influential African-Americans, Ebony Mag., 2004; recipient Favorite Female Artist-Soul/Rhythm & Blues Music, Am. Music Awards, 2004, Female R&B/Hip-Hop Artist of Yr., Billboard Music Awards, 2004, R&B/Hip-Hop Singles Artist of Yr., 2004, Best R&B Video for Karma, MTV Video Music Awards, 2005, Outstanding Female Artist, NAACP Image awards, 2006, Outstanding Music Video and Outstanding Song for Unbreakable, NAACP Image award, 2006. Office: BMG Entertainment 1540 Broadway New York NY 10036

KEYS, ELIZABETH A., accountant, director; b. Grosse Pointe, Mich., Jan. 6, 1969; BS summa cum laude, Boston Coll., 1991. CPA, Mich. Audit asst. Deloitte & Touche, Detroit, 1991-93, audit sr., 1993-95, audit mgr., 1995, Singapore, 1995-97; regional mgr. acctg. Gen. Motors Asia Pacific, Singapore, 1997-98, chief acctg. officer, 1998-2000; dir. investor rels. GM, Detroit, 2000—. Bd. dirs. Assn. for Retarded Citizens, Mich., 1995. Mem. AICPA, Mich. Assn. CPAs. Home: 154 W 70th St Apt 9a New York NY 10023-4405 E-mail: beth.keys@gm.com.

KEYWOOD, KAY HILL, mathematics educator, small business owner; b. Las Cruces, N.Mex., Feb. 16, 1954; d. Kenneth Wade and Barbara Ivy Hill; m. Steven Glenn Keywood, Nov. 21, 1995; children: Allen Wade Jones, Russell Ben Jones, Robert Trent Jones. BS, Tex. A&M, Commerce, 1976. Cert. life time tchr. Tex., 1976. 8th grade math tchr. Crockett Jr. H.S., Paris, Tex., 1976—, Travis Jr. H.S., 1991—. Membership bd. Bonham St. Ch. Christ, Paris, Tex., mem. directory. Grantee, TARGET Region VIII Ednl. Ctr., 2004. Office Phone: 903-737-7473.

KEZLARIAN, NANCY KAY, marriage and family therapist; b. Royal Oak, Mich., Aug. 26, 1948; d. Barkev A. and Nancy (Israelian) K.; m. Robert S. Vinetz, M.D., Aug. 1995. Student, U. Vienna, Austria, 1969; BA, Albion Coll., 1970; MA in Theatre and TV, U. Mich., 1971; MA in Clin. Psychology, Pepperdine U., 1992. Cert. secondary tchr., Mich., Calif.; lic. marriage family therapist. Tchr. West Bloomfield Hills (Mich.) High Sch., 1971-76; tchr. ESL, L.A. Pub. Schs., 1976-80; personnel dir. Samuel Goldwyn Co., L.A., 1985-86; dir. adminstrn. and human resources (Norman Lear) Act III Communications, L.A., 1986-90; dir. programs Salvation Army Booth Meml. Ctr., L.A., 1993-94; asst. exec. dir. Florence Crittenton Ctr., L.A., 1994-96, exec. dir., 1996-2000; pvt. practice marriage and family therapy, 2000—. Owner, mgr. KAZ, hand painted clothing co., L.A., 1980-85; mem. Screen Actors Guild. Actress My Seventeenth Summer, The Big Blue Marble, 1979 (Emmy award for children's TV programming). Bd. dirs. Calif. Assn. Children's Homes. Named Tchr. of Yr., West Bloomfield Hills High Sch., 1976. Mem. SAG, Pers. and Indsl. Rels. Assn. (legis. rep. dist. 5 1989, 90), Calif. Assn. of Marriage and Family Therapists, L.A. Group Psychotherapy Soc., Rotary Internat., People for the Am. Way, Psi Chi. Avocations: writing, world mythologies, theater, abstract artist, vegetarian chef. Personal E-mail: rsvinetz@pol.net.

KHABBAZ, RIMA, government agency administrator; BS, Am. U. Beirut, 1975, MD, 1979. Cert. in Internal Medicine. Internal medicine tng. Am. U. Beirut Med. Ctr., Lebanon, 1978—80; fellowship in infectious diseases U. Md.; resident internal medicine Union Meml. Hosp., Balt.; epidemic intelligence officer Centers for Disease Control, 1980; dep. dir. Divsn. Viral and Rickettsial Diseases Nat. Ctr. Infectious Diseases, Centers for Disease Control, assoc. dir. epidemiologic sci., acting dep. dir., dir., 2005—. Blood product adv. com. US Food & Drug Adminstrn., 1995—99. Contbr. chapters to books, articles to profl jours. Fellow: Infectious Disease Soc. Am. (scientific program com. 1999—2002); mem.: Am. Soc. of Tropical Medicine and Hygiene, Am. Bd. for Microbiology, Am. Epidemiologic Soc. Office: Nat Ctr Infectious Diseases CDC Bldg 1 Rm 6013 1600 Clifton Rd NE Atlanta GA 30333 Office Phone: 404-639-3401.*

KHAN, ARFA, radiologist, educator; b. Srinagar, Kashmir, India, Dec. 4, 1943; came to U.S., 1966; d. Ghulam Rasool and Ruqia Hayat; m. Faroque A. Khan, Apr. 16, 1966; children: Arif O., Shireen. B of Medicine, B of Surgery, Govt. Med. Coll., Kashmir, 1964. Diplomate Am. Bd. Radiology. Intern Barberton (Ohio) Citizen Hosp., 1966-67; resident in radiology L.I. Jewish Med. Ctr., New Hyde Park, NY, 1967-70, from instr. to assoc. prof. radiology, 1970-93, chief thoracic radiology, 1983—, prof., 1993—, assoc. chmn. radiology, 1994-2000; program dir., 1995. Contbr. over 65 articles to radiology jours. Fellow Am. Coll. Radiology; mem. Am. Coll. Radiology, Am. Soc. Neuroradiology, Am. Soc. Head & Neck Radiology, Am. Soc. Thoracic Radiology, Radiol. Soc. N.Am. Democrat. Moslem. Avocations: cooking, tennis, aerobics, gardening, skiing. Office Phone: 718-470-7177. Office Fax: 718-343-7463. Business E-Mail: khan@lij.edu.

KHAN, CHAKA (YVETTE MARIE STEVENS), singer; b. Great Lakes, IL, Mar. 23, 1953; m. Hassan Khan, 1970 (div. 1971); m. Richard Holland, 1974 (div. 1980); m. Doug Rasheed, 2001; children: Damien Holland, Milini. D (hon.), Berklee Coll. Music, 2004. Singer musical group Rufus, 1972-76; solo performer Warner Bros. Records, 1978—96. Founder, chmn. Chaka Khan Found., Beverly Hills, Calif., 1999—; founder EarthSong Entertainment, Beverly Hills, Calif. Singer (with Rufus) (albums) Rufus, 1973, Rags to Rufus, 1974, Rufusized, 1974, Rufus Featuring Chaka Khan, 1975, Ask Rufus, 1977, Masterjam, 1979, Camouflage, 1981, Stompin' At the Savoy, 1983, (solo albums) Chaka, 1979, Naughty, 1980, Whatcha' Gonna Do For Me, 1981, Echoes of an Era, 1982, Chaka Khan, 1983 (Grammy award for Best Female R&B Vocal Performance, 1983), I Feel For You, 1984 (Grammy award for Best Female Vocal R&B Performance, 1984), Destiny, 1986, CK, 1989, Life is a Dance, 1989, The Woman I Am, 1992 (Grammy award for Best Female R&B Vocal Performance, 1992), Vol. 1: Epiphany: The Best of Chaka Kahn, 1996, Come 2 My House, 1998, Chaka Khan Live, 2003, ClassiKhan, 2004; singer (songs) Tell Me Something Good (Grammy award for Best Group R&B Performance, 1974), I'm Every Woman, 1978, Be Bop Medley (Grammy award for Best Vocal Arrangement, 1983), Reading Rainbow TV theme song, 1983, Ain't Nobody (Grammy award for Best Group Vocal R&B Performance, 1983), I'll Be Good to You (Grammy award for Best Vocal Duo, 1990), What's Going On, 2001 (Grammy award for Best Traditional R&B Vocal Performance, 2002); appearances include (films) The Blues Brothers, 1980 (TV series) Hunter, 1984, New York Undercover, 1994, The Good News, 1997, Living Single, 1993, Malcolm & Eddie, 1996 (stage) Mama, I Want to Sing, 1995, Signed, Sealed, Delivered, 2002; author (autobiography) Chaka! Through the Fire, 2003. Named one of 200 Extraordinary Women Who've Changed the World, Essence mag., 1995, 100 Greatest Women of Rock 'N Roll, VH1, 1999; recipient 8 Grammy awards, Diamond Life award, Internat. Assn. African Am. Music, 1992, Lena Horne Career Achievement award, Soul Train Lady of Soul Awards, 1998, Lifetime Achievement award, Music of Black Origin (MOBO) Awards, 2002, Emerging Artist & Tech. in Music, 2002, World Music Awards, 2003, Black Entertainment TV (BET), 2006, Beverly Hills C.A.R.E.S. award, 2004, Woman of Yr. award, I'm Every Woman Conf., 2004, Humanitarian award, Chaka Khan Found., 2004. Office: Chaka Khan Found E Tower Ste 515 9100 Wilshire Blvd Beverly Hills CA 90212*

KHARINA, NINA YURIEVNA, science educator, dental assistant; b. Taganrog, Russia, Mar. 28, 1958; arrived in U.S., 1996; d. Yuriy Nikolaevich Yefimov and Galina Vasilievna Yefimova; m. Nikolay Alekseyevich Kharin, Feb. 24, 1979; 1 child, Ilya Nikolaevich Kharin. MD, Rostov-on-Don State Med. U., Russia, 1981. Physician/pediatrician State City Hosp., Taganrog, 1981—86; sr. tchr. pathophysiology Med. Coll., Taganrog, 1984—96, head dept. biomed. disciplines, 1986—96; adj. therapist Univ. Hosp., Taganrog, 1993—96; adj. faculty Cuyahoga C.C., Highland Hills, Ohio, 2003—. Maj. lt. Navy, 1981—96, Russia. Recipient Tchr. of Highest Category, State Health Dept., Rostov-on-Don, Russia, 1995, Excellent Worker, Nat. Edn. of Russian Fedn., 1995, Outstanding Adj. Faculty, Cuyahoga C.C., 2005. Russian Orthodox Christian. Avocation: reading. Home: 892 Pinewood View Rd Sagamore Hills OH 44067 Office: Cuyahoga CC 4250 Richmond Rd Highland Hills OH 44122 Personal E-mail: nkharin@aol.com.

KHATIB, KATHY, school administrator, educator; b. Chgo., July 25, 1943; d. John and Mary Samsuris; m. Ahmed Khatib, Oct. 27, 1973; children: Kate, John. BA, U. Ill., Chgo., 1968; diploma, Am. Montessori Internat., Perugia, Italy, 1973. Tchr. spl. edn. Southwest Sch., Chgo., 1968—70, Kiddie Camp Sch., Madison, Wis., 1970—72; asst. tchr. trainer Centro Internat. Montessori, Perugia, 1973—77; tchr. Alexander Montessori Sch., Miami, 1978—79; adminstr., head tchr. Johnstown Montessori Sch., Pa., 1979—82, Cmty. Montessori Sch., Glasgow, Ky., 1985—2004. Spkr., presenter in field. Mem.: Internat. Montessori Coun., Am. Montessori Soc., Assn. Montessori Internat. Avocation: boating.

KHEEL, SUSAN TALMADGE, retired reference services manager; b. Bklyn., Dec. 6, 1945; d. Benjamin and Jean Talmadge; m. Brian Selig Kheel, June 26, 1966; 1 child, Marsha Beth Goldwasser. BA, Douglass Coll., 1967; MLS, Rutgers U., 1972. Cert. secondary sch. tchr. French State Bd. Examiners Dept. Edn., N.J., 1967, pub. libr. State Bd. Examiners Dept. Edn., N.J., 1976. Tchr. French Churchill Jr. HS, East Brunswick, N.J., 1967—69, Montgomery Twp. Secondary Sch., N.J., 1969—70; reference services mgr. East Brunswick Pub. Libr., 1971—2001. Self-employed reference cons., N.J., 2001—. Treas. Rutgers Hillel: The Found. for Jewish Campus Life, New Brunswick, 2001—. Recipient Libr. Svc. award to an Individual, Libr. Assn. N.J., 2001. Mem.: ALA, N.J. Libr. Assn., Hadassah, The Women's Zionist Orgn. Am. (life), Conservative Temple Sisterhood (Highland Park, N.J.), Beta Phi Mu, Phi Beta Kappa. Jewish. Home: 345 Felton Ave Highland Park NJ 08904 Personal E-mail: skheel@aol.com.

KHIDEKEL, REGINA P., art historian, curator, educator; b. Khmelnitsky, Russia, Apr. 11, 1946; d. Peter I. and Sophie M. (Sirota) Gezunterman; m. Mark L. Khidekel, Dec. 3, 1967; 1 child, Roman M. MA, Acad. Fine Arts, St. PEtersburg, Russia, 1969, PhD, 1978. Tchr., lectr. Leningrad (USSR) U. Architecture, 1972-85; art dir. Diaghilev Art Ctr., St. Petersburg, 1990-93; founder, pres. Russian-Am. Cultural Ctr., N.Y.C., 1998—. Author: "It's the Real Thing" Soviet & Post Soviet Sots Art and American Pop Art, 1998; contbr. to Art News mag., books and catalogs. Mem. Internat. Art Critics Assn., Russian Union of Artists (awards 1975, 79). Home: 500 E 77th St Apt 316 New York NY 10162-0001 E-mail: khidart@aol.com.

KHOL, CHAREL L., psychologist; b. Cleve., Apr. 2, 1943; divorced; children: Adrienne Marie, Matthew Philip. BS in Edn., Ohio State U., 1965; MS in Edn., Ohio U., 1969; PhD, Kent State U., 1982. Lic. psychologist, Ohio. Psychologist Kevin Coleman Ctr., Ravenna, Ohio, 1983-87; pvt. practice Ravenna and Kent, 1984—; psychologist Child Guidance Ctr., Akron, Ohio, 1987—. Cons., expert witness. Named Jennings Scholar for Tchr. Excellence, Jennings Trust, 1967. Mem.: APA, State U. Varsity O, Ohio Psychol. Assn. Avocations: reading, quilting, collecting. Office: 265 W Main St Ste 102 Kent OH 44240 also: Child Guidance Ctr 312 Locust Akron OH 44305-3838 Office Phone: 330-678-9210.

KHOSH, MARY SIVERT, psychologist; b. Akron, Ohio, July 28, 1942; d. Floyd Calvin and Mattie Paul (Milwee) Sivert; m. John G.H. Khosh, Sept. 1, 1961; children: Sheila June, Deanna June, Lisa June, Lora June. BA, U. Akron, 1966, MS, 1970; PhD, Kent State U., 1976; MBA, Baldwin-Wallace Coll., 1983. Career counselor Baldwin-Wallace Coll., Berea, Ohio, 1974-75, asst. dir. counseling and advising ctr., 1975-76, assoc. dir. counseling and advising ctr., 1976-78, dir. articulation project, 1976-77, dir. counseling and advising ctr., 1978-80, dir. career counseling and field experience, 1980-83; pvt. practice indsl. and organizational psychology Cleve., 1977-93; pres. Knosh & Assocs., Cleve., 1984-93; consulting psychologist Leadership Devel. Inst. Eckerd Coll., St. Petersburg, Fla., 1993—. Mgmt. psychologist, cons. Ohio Psychol. Cons. to Industry Inc., Shaker Heights, 1983-84; mem. adj. faculty Baldwin-Wallace Coll., Bern, Ohio, 1973-83; cons. in field. Contbr. articles to profl. jours. V.p. S.W. Gen. Hosp. Jr. Bd., Berea, 1969; guest organist Akron United Meth. Ch., 1961; mem. S.W. Gen. Hosp. Med. Wives, 1966-76, pres. 1968-70. Mem. ASTD, Am. Psychol. Assn., Ohio Psychol. Assn., Cleve. Psychol. Assn. (trustee 1984-85, v.p. 1985-86), Cleve. Cons. Psychol. Assn., Soc. of Human Resource Mgrs., Fairview Gen. Hosp. Women's Aux., Greater Cleve. Human Resource Soc. (v.p. 1987—), Acad. Sr. Profl. at Eckerd Coll. Democrat. Methodist. Office: Mgt Devel Inst Eckerd Coll Saint Petersburg FL 33711 Home: 4830 Ospray Dr S #106 Saint Petersburg FL 33711

KHOURY, COLLEEN A., dean; b. 1943; BA, Colby Coll., 1964; JD, Ill. Inst. Tech., 1975. Dir. info. and devel. pvt. child welfare agy., Chgo.; pub. info. dir. Cook County Dept. Pub. Aid; assoc. Bell, Boyd & Lloyd, 1975—83, ptnr., 1983; gen. counsel Ventrex Labs.; prof. U. Maine Sch. Law, Portland, 1985—, assoc. dean, 1991—93, dean, 1998—. Bd. dirs. Justice Action Group, Banknorth Group, Inc.; chair Commn. on Gender, Justice and Cts., Maine Supreme Jud. Ct., 1993—96. Corporator Boys and Girls Clubs Greater Portland, Maine; trustee Portland Symphony Orch.; vice chair bd. trustees Colby Coll. Recipient Caroline Duby Glassman award, Maine State Bar Assn., 1997, Deborah Morton award, U. New Eng., 2002, Margaret Brent Lawyers Achievement award, ABA, 2003. Mem.: Am. Law Inst., Maine Bar Found. (bd. dirs.). Office: Univ Maine Sch Law 246 Deering Ave Portland ME 04102

KHURI, SOUMAYA MAKDISSI, mathematics professor; arrived in U.S., 1960; d. Ilyas Khuri-Makdissi and Wadia Mary Hourani; m. Raja Najib Khuri, July 8, 1959 (div. Mar. 13, 1996); children: Fadlo, Ramzi, Jananne. BS, American U., Beirut, 1960; MA, Harvard U., Cambridge, Mass., 1961; PhD, Yale U., Conn., 1974. Asst. prof. math. American U. Beirut, 1979, assoc. prof. math., 1979—85, prof. math. dept., 1985—87; vis. fellow math. Yale U., New Haven, 1984—85, 1986—87; assoc. prof. math. dept. East Carolina U., Greenville, NC, 1987—91, prof. math. dept., 1991—. Author: (rsch. papers) Jour. Algebra, Proceedings Am. Math. Soc., 1977, 1978, 1979, Com. Jour. Math., Proceedings London Math. Soc., 1980, 1981, 1982. Avocations: travel, reading. Home: 122 Longmeadow Rd Greenville NC 27858 Office: East Carolina Univ Math Dept Greenville NC 27858 Personal E-mail: khuris@ecu.edu.

KHVOST-VOSTRIKOVA, NATALIA S., art educator, consultant; d. Serg I Khvostionkov and Maya Jacob Khvostionkova; children: Kuzma Nick Vostrikov, Gavrela Nick Vostrikov. BD Arts, Tech. Inst., Moscow, 1981. Cert. Fashion design Russian Ministry of Fashion Industry, 1981. Exhibitions, perfomances, Forbidden Art-the postwar Russian Avant-gard. Achievements include Participation Biennale Internationale Firenze(Italy). Personal E-mail: nkhvost@msn.com.

KIANG, CHING-HWA, chemical engineering educator; b. Taipei, Taiwan, Jan. 20, 1965; came to U.S., June 24, 1988; d. Song Kiang and Pi-Ying Huang; m. Michael William Deem, Sept. 2, 1995. BSChemE, Nat. Taiwan U., Taipei, 1987; PhD in Chemistry, Calif. Inst. Tech., 1995. Rsch. asst. Inst. Atomic and Molecular Scis. Academia Sinica, Taipei, Taiwan, 1987-88; postdoctoral assoc. dept. Physics MIT, 1995-96; vis. asst. prof. dept. Chemistry and Biochemistry UCLA, 1996—99, cram tchr.-scholar dept. Chemistry and Biochemistry, 1996—99, rsch. asst., physicist Dept. Physics and Astronomy, 2000—02; asst. prof. dept. physics and astronomy Rice U., Houston, 2002—. Grantee NIH, 1998, U. Calif. Energy, 1998, NSF, 2005. Mem. Am. Phys. Soc., Sigma Xi. Achievements include patent in field. Office: Dept Physics and Astronomy Rice U 6100 Main St MS 61 Houston TX 77005 Office Phone: 713-348-4130. E-mail: chkiang@rice.edu.

KIBBLE-CACIOPPO, MAXINE LORRAINE, recording company executive; b. Bklyn., July 3, 1950; d. Robert Langston and Arletha Cobb; m. Robert Francis Kibble, Oct. 4, 1979 (div.); 1 child, Vanessa; m. Victor V. Cacioppo, Aug. 7, 1998. BS, NYU, 1978. Sales assoc. Saks Fifth Ave., Bergdorf, N.Y.C., 1988-92; model Sch. Visual Arts, N.Y.C., 1993-96; exec. asst. Banco Inverlat, N.Y.C., 1996—; songwriter N.Y.C., 1998; owner Sable Records, N.Y.C., 1993-97. Choreographer (modern dance) Portrait of a Shadow, 1977. Bd. dirs. Andrew Janetti and Dancers, N.Y.C., 1995-97; dance tchr. Police Athletic League, N.Y.C., 1977; mem. Broadway Fights Back (AIDS Orgn.), N.Y.C., 1998; mem. PTA, Unity H.S., N.Y.C., 1998. Recipient Hon. award Andrew Janetti & Dancers, 1998. Mem. ASCAP, NAFE. Avocations: aerobics, gardening. Office: 1518 Vista Sierra Dr El Cajon CA 92019-3583

KIBRICK, ANNE, retired nursing educator, dean; b. Palmer, Mass., June 1, 1919; d. Martin and Christine (Grigas) Karlon; m. Sidney Kibrick, June 16, 1949; children: Joan, John. RN, Worcester Hahnemann Hosp., Mass., 1941; BS, Boston U., 1945; MA, Columbia Tchrs. Coll., 1948; EdD, Harvard U., 1958; LHD (hon.), St. Joseph's Coll., Windham, Maine, 1973. Asst. edn. dir. Cushing VA Hosp., Framingham, Mass., 1948—49; asst. prof. nursing Simmons Coll., Boston, 1949—55; dir. grad. div. Boston U. Sch. Nursing, 1958—63, dean, 1963—68, prof., 1968—70; chmn. dept. nursing Boston Coll. Grad. Sch. Arts and Sci., 1970—74; founding chmn. Sch. Nursing Boston State Coll., 1974—82; founding dean Sch. Nursing U. Mass., Boston, 1974—88, prof., 1988—93, prof. emeritus, 1993—. Mem. adv. coun. Coll. Nursing and Health Scis. U. Mass., Boston, 2004—. Mem. editl. bd. Mass. Jour. Cmty. Health. Mem. Brookline Town Meeting, 1995—2000; mem. nat. adv. bd. Hadassah Nurses Coun., 1996—; bd. dirs. Brookline Mental Health Assn., Met. chpt. ARC, Children's Ctr. Brookline and Greater Boston, Inc., 1984—89, Boston Health Care for Homeless, 1988—90, Landy-Kaplan Nurses Coun., 1992—, treas., 1994—96. Named to, Nursing Edn. Alumni Assn. Tchr.'s Coll., Columbia U. Hall of Fame, 1999. Fellow: Am. Acad. Nursing; mem.: Mass. Assn. RNs (charter mem., Living Legend award 2006), Inst. of Medicine of NAS, Mass. Blueprint 2000, Mass. Orgn. Elder Ams. (bd. dirs. 1988—2000), Mass. Med. Soc. (postgrad. med. inst. 1983—96, bd. dirs. 1983—96, exec. com. 1989—96), Nat. Acads. of Practice, Mass. Nurses Found. (v.p. 1983—86), AIDS Internat. Info. Found. (founding mem. 1985), Mass. Nurses Assn. (dir. 1982—86, charter inductee Hall of Fame 2000), Nat. Mass. League Nursing (pres. 1971—73), ANA, Pi Lambda Theta, Sigma Theta Tau. Home: # 312 130 Seminary Ave Auburndale MA 02466 E-mail: akibrick@lasell.edu.

KICKISH, MARGARET ELIZABETH, elementary school educator; b. Atlantic City, Nov. 30, 1949; d. James Bernard and Margaret Elizabeth (Egan) Parlett; m. Robert Anthony Kickish, June 30, 1973; children: Eileen, Kathleen, Robert Jr. BS, Franciscan U., 1971; MEd, Coll. NJ, 1977. Cert. elem. tchr., learning disabilities tchr. cons. Tchr. Our Lady Star of the Sea Sch., Atlantic City, 1971-75, Weymouth Twp. Elem. Sch., Dorothy, NJ, 1975-89; curriculum coord. Port Republic (NJ) Sch., 1990-91; tchr. Brigantine (NJ) Bd. Edn., 1991-94, supr. curriculum and instrn., 1995—. Cognetics coach St. Joseph Sch., Somers Point, NJ, 1989—. Treas. PTA, Somers Point, 1987—89, pres., 1989—90; asst. coach Somers Point Softball Assn., 1991—; rec. sec. Parents Orgn. Mainland Regional HS, 2001—05; mem. choir St. Joseph Ch., Somers Point, 1985—. Mem.: ASCD, NEA, AAUW, Assn. Learning Cons., Coun. Exceptional Children, Prins. and Suprs. Assn., NJ Edn. Assn., South Jersey Irish Cultural Soc., Seashore Mother of Twins Club, Phi Delta Kappa (exec. v.p. 2005), Delta Zeta, Kappa Delta Pi. Democrat. Roman Catholic. Avocations: swimming, bicycling, reading, travel, crafts. Home: 526 9th St Somers Point NJ 08244-1458 Office: Brigantine Bd of Edn 301 E Evans Blvd Brigantine NJ 08203-3424 Office Phone: 609-266-2877. E-mail: mskick@aol.com.

KIDD, LOVETTA MONZA, music educator; b. Anniston, Ala., Jan. 13, 1943; d. Andrew Jackson and Velma Mildred (Duke) Traywick; m. Everett Wayne Kidd, Dec. 20, 1961 (dec. Dec. 1998); children: Michelle Kidd Belindo, Andy, David. Student, Okla. Coll. for Women, 1961-62, Southwestern Okla. State U., 1982-83. Pvt. piano tchr., Eva, Okla., 1967-69, Sickles, Okla., 1970-71, Dibble, Okla., 1971-78, Anadarko, Okla., 1979—. Pianist First Bapt. Ch., Anadarko, 1980's. Sec. Okla. Conservative Com., Norman, 1994-95; vice chmn. Caddo County (Okla.) Rep. party, 1995-97, chmn., 1997-99; alt. del. Nat. Rep. Convention, San Diego, 1996. Mem. Okla. Fedn. Rep. Women, Concerned Women for Am., Anadarko Eagle Forum (founder, pres. 1994—), Okla.'s First Ladies, Gen. Fedn. Women's Clubs Philomathic Club (sec. 1996-98, v.p. 1998—), Okla. Fedn. Music Clubs (dist. Gold Cup chmn. 1993—), Musical Key Club (founder, pres. 1981—). Avocations: reading, gardening, needlepoint, painting, drawing. Home: 701 W Alabama Ave Anadarko OK 73005-4636

KIDD, LYNDEN LOUISE, healthcare consultant; b. Laramie, Wyo., May 7, 1959; d. David Thomas and Sally Louise (Noble) Kidd; m. Jeffrey Lee Marcinowski, Sept. 5, 1998; 1 child, Sophia Lucille Marcinowski. AA, Stephens Coll., 1979; BA in Polit. Sci., Comm., U. Wyo., 1981, JD, 1986. Adminstrv. dir. Wyo. Med. Ctr., Casper, 1986—92, v.p. med. affairs, 1992—95; consultant Next Iteration, Casper, 1995—96; assoc. APM Inc., Chgo., 1996—97; prin. Next Iteration, Phila., 1998—; search cons. Ken Clark Internat., Princeton, NJ, 1998—2001, practice dir., 2000—03. Contbr.: Managing Change in Healthcare: Teaming for Innovation, 1999. Mem. Wyo. Heritage Soc., 1987-89, Gov.'s Coun. Sports and Fitness, Wyo., 1991-96; chmn., mem. Leadership Casper, 1989-91; bd. dirs., campaign chmn. United Way, Casper, 1989-96, pres., 1994-95; bd. dirs. Casper Classic, Inc., 1989-92. Mem.: Healthcare Businesswomen's Assn., Soc. Human Resources Mgmt., Regulatory Affairs Profl. Soc., Soc. Competitive Intelligence, Am. Health Lawyers Assn., Am. Coll. Healthcare Execs. (assoc.), Casper C. of C. (bd. dirs. 1991—94), Phi Alpha Delta. Avocations: volunteer work, reading, music. Home and Office: 426 Mahogany Walk Newtown PA 18940-4212 Business E-Mail: lyndenkidd@comcast.net.

KIDD, MARY JANE, literature and language educator; m. Kenneth Kidd. BS in Secondary Edn., SE Mo. State U., Cape Girardeau, 1978, MS in Secondary Edn., 1982. English tchr. Scott City HS, Mo., 1982—85, Oran HS, Mo., 1985—96, Delta R-5 HS, Mo., 1996—. Office: Delta HS PO Box 787 Delta MO 63744-0787

KIDD, RUTH PRICE, retired secondary school educator; b. New Orleans, Nov. 28, 1927; d. Author James and Louise Francis Price; m. Edward Alvin Rhone (div.); m. Wesley McMillan Kidd, Jan. 25, 1958; 1 child, Wesliane Marie Kidd-Johnson. BS in Health, So. U., Baton Rouge, 1951, MS in Health, 1963. Tchr. Orleans Parish Sch. Bd., New Orleans, 1951—90. Dir. Bethany Sr. Ctr. and Exercise for Srs. Program, New Orleans, 1990—2005. Dir. youth choir Bethany United Meth. Ch., 1981—85. Named Coach of Yr. for girls basketball, John McDonogh Sr. H.S.; recipient Svc. to Band award. Mem.: AARP (past pres., rec. sec., Andrus award), Gilbert Acad. Alumni (pres. 1986—93, 1997—2005, fin. sec. 2005—), Orleans Parish Sch. Tchrs. (rec. sec. retirees chpt. 1990—99, v.p. retirees chpt. 1999—2006), Sigma Gamma Rho (parliamentarian rec. sec. 1993—2005, Christian Svc. award). Home: 2715 W Rothland St 9B Gonzales LA 70737

KIDMAN, NICOLE, actress; b. Honolulu, June 20, 1967; d. Anthony and Janelle Kidman; m. Tom Cruise, Dec. 24, 1990 (div. Aug. 8, 2001); children: Isabella Jane Kidman, Connor Antony Kidman; m. Keith Urban, June 25, 2006. Goodwill amb. UN Devel. Fund for Women, 2006—. Film appearances include BMX Bandits, 1983, Bush Christmas, 1983, Wills & Burke, 1985, Archer's Adventure, 1985, Windrider, 1986, Watch the Shadows Dance (aka Nightmaster), 1986, Bit Part, 1987, Emerald City, 1989, Dead Calm, 1989, Days of Thunder, 1990, Flirting, 1991, Billy Bathgate, 1991 (Golden Globe Award nomination 1992), Far and Away, 1992, Malice, 1993, My Life, 1993, Batman Forever, 1995, Portrait of a Lady, 1996, To Die For, 1995 (Golden Globe award), The Peacemaker, 1997, Practical Magic, 1998, Eyes Wide Shut, 1999, The Others, 2001 (nominee Best Performance by Actress in Motion Picture-Drama Golden Globe award 2002, Best Actress KCFCC award 2001), Birthday Girl, 2001, Moulin Rouge, 2001 (Best Actress in Motion Picture Musical/Comedy Golden Globe award 2001, nominee Best Actress in Leading Role Acad. award 2002, Best Actress London Film Critics Cir. award 2001), The Hours, 2002 (Best Actress Academy award, 2003, Best Actress in Leading Role, British Acad. Film Award (BAFTA), 2003, Best Actress Golden Globe, 2003), Dogville, 2003, The Human Stain, 2003, Cold Mountain, 2003, The Stepford Wives, 2004, Birth, 2004, The Interpreter, 2005, Bewitched, 2005; prodr. (films) In the Cut, 2003; TV appearances include Five Mile Creek, 1983, Chase Through the Night, 1983, Matthew and Son, 1984, Bangkok Hilton, 1989 (Australian Film Inst. Best Actress in Miniseries), Vietnam, 1985 (Australian Film Inst. Best Actress in Miniseries); theatrical prodns. include The Blue Room, London, 1997-98, Broadway, 1998-99. Goodwill amb. UN Develop. Fund for Women, UNIFEM, 2006—. Named Australian of Yr., NSW, 2004, Companion of the Order of Australia, 2006; named one of 50 Most Powerful People in Hollywood, Premiere mag., 2003—06; recipient ShoWest Dist. Decade Achievement award, 2002, Citizen award, UN, 2004. Address: Creative Artists Agy 9830 Wilshire Blvd Beverly Hills CA 90212*

KIECOLT-GLASER, JANICE KAY, psychologist; b. Okla. City, Okla., June 30, 1951; d. Edward Harold and Vergie Mae (Lively) Kiecolt; m. Ronald Glaser, Jan. 18, 1980. BA in Psychology with honors, U. Okla., 1972; PhD in Clin. Psychology, U. Miami, 1976. Lic. psychologist, Ohio. Clin. psychology intern Baylor U. Coll. Medicine, Houston, 1974-75; postdoctoral fellow in adult clin. psychology U. Rochester, N.Y., 1976-78; asst. prof. psychiatry Ohio State U. Coll. Medicine, Columbus, 1978-84, assoc. prof. psychiatry and psychology, 1984-89, prof. psychiatry and psychology, 1989—, dir. divsn. health psychology, 1994—, active various coms. Mem. AIDS study sect. NIMH, 1988-91. Editl. bd. Brain, Behavior and Immunity jour., 1986—, Health Psychology jour., 1989—, Brit. Jour. Health Psychology, 1996—, Jour. Behavioral Medicine, 1994—, Psychosomatic Medicine, 1990—, Jour. Cons. and Clin. Psychology, 1992—, Jour. Gerontology, 1992—; reviewer Jour. Personality and Social Psychology, Psychiatry Rsch. jour.; author: Detecting Lies, 1997, Unconscious Truths, 1998, Handbook of Human Stress and Immunity, 1994; contbr. articles to profl. jours., chpts. to books. NIMH grantee, 1985—; recipient Merit award NIMH, 1993; Ohio State Disting. scholar, 1994, Devel. Health Psychology award, Divsn. Health Psychology and Adult Devel. and Aging, Norman Cousins award, Psychoneuroimmunology Rsch. Soc., 1998. Fellow Am. Psychol. Assn. (Outstanding Contbns. award 1988), Acad. Behavioral Medicine Rsch.; mem. Phi Beta Kappa, Inst. Medicine. Avocations: jogging, fiction writing. Office: Ohio State U Coll Medicine Dept Psychiatry 1670 Upham Dr Columbus OH 43210

KIEFER, CHERYL LYNN, elementary school educator; Cert. tchr. Hawaii. Sci. tchr. Keaau (Hawaii) Mid. Sch., 1997—2005, tech coord., 2005—. Office: State of Hawaii 16-565 Keaau-Pahoa Rd Keaau HI 96749 Office Phone: 808-982-4200. Business E-Mail: cheryl_kiefer@notes.k12.hi.us.

KIEFER, KIT ANNETTE, editor; b. Wausau, Wis., Dec. 18, 1958; d. Arthur Clarence and Mae Evelyn (Wagner) K.; m. Jon Andrew Brecka, Sept. 26, 1985 (div. Jan. 1990); children: J.J., Jeff, Gwinneth; m. David C. Mueller, June 27, 1991; 1 child, Gib. BA in Journalism and Polit. Sci., U. Wis., River Falls, 1981. Asst. editor 13-30 Corp., Knoxville, Tenn., 1981-85; editor Krause Publs., Iola, Wis., 1986—. Writer Search, Amherst, Wis., 1986-90, Trapper & Predator Caller, Iola, 1988-90; cons. Paul M. Green Inc., Madison, Wis., 1987-90. Author: The Post-Nuclear Collegian, 1985, The Top 100, 1990, They Called it Rock, 1991, Fantasy Baseball Guide to Fantasy Baseball, 1991. Sec. Cen. Wis. Network; advisor Stalag-Mites Jr. Spelunking Group; vol. League of Pollsters, Amherst, 1988, St. Mary of Mt. Carmel Divorcees Against Drugs, Amherst, 1989. Recipient Excellence in Design award Wis. Pottery League, 1988, Roger award Portage County Poetry Soc., 1989, Salesperson of Yr. award Wicker Plus, 1989. Mem. Daus. of Sons of Norway (hon. nat. chairperson), Amherst Range Riders (sec.-treas. 1988-90). Republican. Lutheran. Avocations: sailboarding, snowmobiling, pottery, cooking. Home: 801 9th St Plover WI 54467-2182

KIEFER, RITA BRADY, writer, educator; b. Long Branch, N.J., July 15, 1930; d. Mary Zita Padien and Alexander Joseph Brady; m. Jerry A. Kiefer, July 11, 1970. MA, U. Notre Dame, Ind., 1958. Prin. St. Francis H.S., Cleve., 1959—64; dean of studies Notre Dame Coll., South Euclid, Ohio, 1964—66; instr. English So. Colo. State Coll., Pueblo, 1967—70; prof. English and women's studies U. No. Colo., Greeley, 1970—2000, prof. emerita. Writing program dir. Gateway Shelter For Battered Women, Englewood, Colo., 2000—. Author: 3 books, 120 poems, essays, articles in profl. jour. Named Outstanding Lit. Woman of Weld County, A Woman's Pl., 1994; fellow, Danforth Found., 1976; grantee, Colo. Endowment for the Humanities, 1987, Puffin Found. Ltd., 2005; Disting. Scholar, U. No. Colo., 1993, Colo. Visions grant, Colo. Coun. on Arts, 1993. Personal E-mail: rbkiefer@comcast.net.

KIEFFER, GINA MARIE, history professor; b. Mendota, Ill., Dec. 11, 1968; d. Michael Walzer and Kay Brown; m. Donald O'Dell Kieffer, July 1, 1995; children: Devin Lewis Pletsch, Joseph Donald. MA, Ill. State U., Normal, Ill., 2002. Adj. faculty history Parkland Coll., Champaign, Ill., 2002—. Adj. faculty history Heartland Coll., Normal, 2005—. Author online courses. Roman Cath. Avocations: Tae Kwon Do, sports, travel. Home: 2810 Arrowhead Dr Bloomington IL 61704 Office: Parkland College Bradley Ave Champaign IL Office Phone: 217-351-2527. Personal E-mail: ginakieffer@msn.com. Business E-Mail: gkieffer@parkland.edu.

KIEFFER, KATHLEEN CECIL, elementary school educator; b. Hastings, Minn., Sept. 23, 1931; d. William A. and Kathryn (Brummel) Schaffer; m. Ralph W. Kieffer, Aug. 11, 1956 (div. Jan. 1972); 1 child, Joseph W. BS, Coll. St. Teresa, Winona, Minn., 1953; MA, St. Thomas Coll., St. Paul, 1968. Cert. specific learning disabilities Minn. Elem. tchr. Mpls. Pub. Schs., 1953—68, specific learning disabilities resource tchr., 1968—93, vol. tchr. grade 4 Sheridan Sch., 1996—. Treas., pres. Mpls. Women in Edn., 1982—83, 1992—93. Del. to local, state and dist. convs. DFL Party, State of Minn., 1974—, mem. local, dist. and state ctrl. coms., 1984—; sec. DFL Senate Dist. 52 and 51, Ramsey County, Minn., 1992—; bd. mem. St. John's Ch., New Brighton, 1998—. Mem.: Mpls. Ret. Tchrs., We in Svc. to Edn. (v.p. 1994—), Minn. Assn. for Childhood Edn. Internat. (sec. 1977—80, v.p. 1988—89, pres. 1990—92, com. mem. 1994—, v.p. 2002—, Promoting the Well Being of Children award 2003), St. Vincent DePaul Soc., Delta Kappa Gamma (pres. 1980—82, legis. chmn. Gamma chpt. 1984—, comm. chmn. Tau State chpt. 1983—85, nominations com. Tau State chpt. 1989—90, Woman of Achievement award Gamma chpt. 1988). Roman Catholic. Home: 5180 Bona Rd New Brighton MN 55112

KIEFFER, MARCIA S., psychotherapist; b. Buffalo, Mar. 29, 1951; d. Milford Shepherd and Doris Verna (Nerber) Smith; m. William Charles Kieffer, Nov. 25, 1972; children: Michelle L. Kieffer Kowalski. AA in Applied Sci., Hilbert Coll., 1988; BS, Buffalo State Coll., 1993; MSW, SUNY Buffalo, 1995. LCSW N.Y., cert. alcohol and substance abuse counselor N.Y. Teller, bookeeper Mfrs. & Traders Trust, Buffalo, 1969-71; accounts recieveable Peter J. Schmidt, Buffalo, 1971-72; booking Meyer SFS Niagara, Buffalo, 1972-73; teller Bank of N.Y., Buffalo, 1973-75; headcashier Tops, Markets, Buffalo, 1980-81; teller Evans Nat. Bank, Angola, N.Y., 1981-88; dir. care and devel. Luth. Svc. Soc., Buffalo, 1988; case mgr. Suburban Adult Svcs., Buffalo, 1988-95; clin. social worker, psychotherapist Cmty. Concern, Derby, NY, 1995—2000; clin. dir. Chautauqua County Chem. Dependency Clinic, Dunkirk, NY, 2000—. Student intern supr. St. Bonaventure, Hamburg, N.Y., 2002-03, Sch. Social Work, 2002-03, Hilbert Coll., 1997, Fredonia State Coll., 2000. Deacon Holy Cross Luth. Ch., Farnham, NY, 1988— Recipient Franciscan award, Hilbert Coll., 1988, McGrath award Human Svcs, Hilbert Coll., 1988, Excellency in Social Work, award, Buffalo State Coll., 1993. Mem.: NASW. Avocations: grandchildren, walking, reading, gardening, animals. Home: 6786 Wayne Dr Derby NY 14047-9737 Personal E-mail: bkieffer@usadatanet.net.

KIEL, BRENDA KAY, medical/surgical nurse; b. Osage, Iowa, Nov. 9, 1965; d. Leslie A. and Margaret L. (Troge) M.; m. Chad Kiel, Aug. 29, 1998. AS, N.E. Iowa Tech. Inst., 1986. Cert. ACLS, med.-surg. nurse, emergency rm. nurse, neonatal ruscitation. Staff nurse med./surg. wing St. Joseph Community Hosp., New Hampton, Iowa, 1986-98; clinic nurse Mercy Family Care Buffalo Ctr. (Iowa) Clinic, 1998—.

KIEL, MARTHA GUILLET, art educator; d. Nicholas Jesse and Mary Terry Guillet; children: Mary K., Bit, Drei. BS, Midwestern St. U., Tex., 1953; MEd, Abiline Christian U., Tex., 1974. Art tchr. Abilene (Tex.) ISD, 1966—2000; chair art dept. Hardin Simmons U., Abilene, Tex., 2000—. Photographs, Big Country Art Assn., 2003. Trustee Grace Mus.; pres. Big Country Art Assn., 2001—03. Mem.: Tex. Art Edn. Assn. (sec. 1999—2001, treas. 2001—03, chair 2000—03). Home: 533 Sayles Blvd Abilene TX 79605-3101

KIELY, CHRISTY E., lawyer; b. Syracuse, NY, Mar. 1, 1976; d. John C. Wetzel and Barbara E. Mosch; m. Michael A. Kiely, Sept. 7, 2002. BA in English and Psychology, Coll. William and Mary, Williamsburg, Va., 1998; JD, Duke U., Durham, NC, 2002. Bar: Va. 2002. Atty. Hunton and Williams, LLP, Richmond, 2002—. Chair pub. edn. com. Va. State Bar Young Lawyers' Conf., Richmond, 2002—05, chair admission and orientation ceremony com., 2004—06, chair domestic violence safety project, 2005—06. Author: (reference book) Model Employee Policies and Forms for Virginia Employers, 2006; contbr. poetry to lit. mags. Atty. adv. Women's Advocacy Project, Richmond, Va., 2002—06; atty. vol. Ctrl. Va. Legal Aid Hotline, Richmond, Va., 2003—06; guardian ad litem Durham County, Durham, NC. Recipient E. Randolph Williams award, Hunton and Williams, LLP, 2003—06, Svc. award, Va. State Bar Young Lawyers' Conf., 2004, 2005, 2006. Mem.: ABA, Richmond Bar Assn., Va. Bar Assn. (pro bono servant), Va. State Bar (bd. govs. young lawyers conf. 2006—, Younger Lawyer of Yr. 2006), John Marshall Inn of Ct., Women's Networking Forum (mem. exec. com. 2002—). Home: 4742 Rockfield Rd Richmond VA 23237 Office: Hunton and Williams LLP Riverfront Plz E 951 E Byrd St Richmond VA 23219 Office Phone: 804-788-8677. Office Fax: 804-788-8218. Business E-Mail: ckiely@hunton.com.

KIELY, PAULA, city librarian; Coord. children's svcs. Milw. Pub. Libr., dep. dir. Librs. Dept., dep. city librarian, ctrl. libr. svcs. mgr., interim city librarian, 2006—. Office: Milw Pub Libr 814 W Wisconsin Ave Milwaukee WI 53233 Office Phone: 414-286-3020. E-mail: pkiely@mpl.org.*

KIENBAUM, JANICE MAE, reading specialist; d. Harold James and Marilyn Mae Kienbaum; children: Jeffrey James Pagel, Jennifer Mae Buhrow. B in Elem. Edn., U. Wis., Whitewater, 1971; M in Tchg. Reading, U. Wis., Eau Claire, 1990. Lic. profl. educator reading specialist k-8 Wis. Dept. Pub. Instrn., elem. sch. libr. Wis. Dept. Pub. Instrn. Elem. sch. libr. East Troy Schs., Wis., 1971—74; substitute tchr. Rice Lake Schs., 1986—87, Prairie Farm Schs., 1986—87, Barron Area Schs., 1980—87, handicap instrnl. aide, 1987—89, Title I reading tchr. and reading specialist, 1989—. Coach Odyssey of the Mind then Destination Imagination, Barron, Wis., 1993—2003. Contbr. poetry to anthologies. Sunday sch. tchr. First Luth. Ch., Barron, Wis., 1982—95, 2006, planning com. gift from the heart, 1993—. Mem.: Internat. Soc. Poets, Internat. Reading Assn., Wis. State Reading Assn. (chair publs. com. 1999—), Northwest Wis. Reading Coun. (mem. planning com. young authors conf. 1993—, v.p. 1990, 1997, pres. 1991, 1998). Lutheran. Avocations: writing, poetry, reading, fishing. Home: 40 S 2d St Barron WI 54812 Office: Barron Area Schs Woodland Sch 808 Woodland Ave Barron WI 54812 Office Phone: 715-537-5621. Business E-Mail: kienbaum@barron.k12.wi.us.

KIENITZ, LADONNA TRAPP, lawyer, librarian, municipal official; b. Bay City, Mich. d. Orlin D. and Mary (Stanford) Trapp; m. John Kienitz, Feb. 9, 1951 (div. Dec. 1974); children: John, Jim, Rebecca, Mary, Timothy, David. BA, Westmar Coll., 1951; MA in Libr. Sci., Dominican U., River Forest, Ill., 1970; M Mgmt., Northwestern U., 1984; JD, Western State U., Fullerton, Calif., 1995; LLM in Taxation, U. San Diego, 2004. Head libr. Woodlands Acad., Lake Forest, Ill., 1973-77; project officer North Suburban Libr. Sys., Wheeling, Ill., 1977-78; libr. dir. Lincolnwood (Ill.) Pub. Libr. Dist., 1978-86; city libr. City of Newport Beach, Calif., 1986—2002, dir. cmty. svcs. Calif., 1994—2002; tax atty. Chapman U. Sch. Law Tax Law Clinic, Orange, 2003—, Tustin Law Offices, 2005—. Mem.: ALA, ABA, US Tax Ct. Bar, US Supreme Ct. Bar, Pub. Libr. Assn. (pres. 1995—96), State Bar Calif., Orange County Bar Assn. Office Phone: 949-300-6951. Business E-Mail: ladonnakienitz@sbcglobal.net.

KIER, ANN B. BURNETTE, pathology educator; b. Littlefield, Tex., June 26, 1949; d. Robert Merlin and Martha (Bond) Yarbrough; m. Friedhelm Schroeder, Dec. 9, 1978; 1 child, Hilary. BA, U. Tex., 1971; BS, Tex. A&M U., 1973, DVM, 1974; PhD, U. Mo., 1979. Diplomate, Am. Coll. Lab. Animal Medicine. NIH fellow U. Mo., Columbia, 1976-79, asst. prof., 1979-84, assoc. prof., 1984-87; assoc. prof. dept. pathology U. Cin. Med. Sch., 1987-91, prof., dir. divsn. comparative pathology, dept. pathology, 1991-93; prof., head dept. pathobiology Tex. A&M U., College Station, 1994—. Cons. NIH, Washington, 1983—, Comparative Pathology, Frann Sci., Cin., 1987—. Contbr. articles to profl. jours. NIH grantee, 1980—. Mem. AAAS, Am. Assn. Pathologists. Avocations: scuba diving, piano, reading. Home: PO Box 500 Wellborn TX 77881-0500 Office: Tex A&M Univ Dept Pathobiology College Station TX 77843-0001 Office Phone: 979-862-1509. Business E-Mail: akier@cvm.tamu.edu.

KIERNAN, MARGARET M., adult education educator; b. Ross, Calif., Feb. 18, 1944; d. William C. and Elizabeth K. Murray; m. John S. Kiernan, July 19, 1969; m. Robert K. Dwyer, June 11, 1966 (dec. July 15, 1967); children: Christopher S., Kathleen K. Dwyer, Sean R. BA in Psychology, Coll. New Rochelle, 1966; MS in Adult Edn., Old Dominion U., 1989. Postgrad. profl. tchg. lic. Commonwealth of Va., 1992. First grade tchr. St. Francis Xavier Sch., Washington, 1968—69; pre-school tchr. St. Francis Episcopal Sch., Charlotte, NC, 1971—73; ESL tchr. Virginia Beach (Va.) Adult Learning Ctr., 1980—87, ESL coordinating tchr., 1987—2002, ESL coord., 2002—. Pres. Virginia Beach (Va.) Coun. PTAs. Recipient Human Rights award, Virginia Beach Human Rights Commn., 2001. Mem.: Va. TESOL (pres. 1985—86, 1993—97, Pres. award 1990), Virginia Beach Assn. Secondary Prins., Va. Beach Reading Coun. (Literacy Tchr. of the Yr. 1991), TESOL (chair adult edn. interest sect. 2000—01), Virginia Beach Coun. PTAs (life; pres.). Avocations: reading, gardening. Home: 3812 Old Shell Rd Virginia Beach VA 23452 Office: Virginia Beach Adult Learning Ctr 4160 Virginia Beach Blvd Virginia Beach VA 23452 Office Phone: 757-306-0991. Personal E-mail: sand2448@cox.net. E-mail: mkiernan@vbcps.k12.va.us.

KIERSCHT, MARCIA SELLAND, academic administrator, psychologist; b. Rugby, ND; d. Osmund Harold and Cynthia (Thoresen) Selland; m. Charles M. Kierscht, Aug. 19, 1961 (div. 1972); children: Cynthia Ann, Matthew Mason. BA, U. Iowa, 1960, MA, 1962; PhD, Vanderbilt U., 1975. Lic. psychologist, Ill., Minn. Sch. psychologist South Suburban Cook County, Homewood, Ill., 1962-64, Dist. 108, Highland Park, Ill., 1964-65, Spl. Edn. Dist. Lake County Ill., Gurnee, 1966-72; psychol. examiner John F. Kennedy Ctr., George Peabody Coll., 1972-73; instr. in pediatrics Med. Sch. Vanderbilt U., Nashville, 1975-76; assoc. prof. Moorhead (Minn.) State U., 1976-80, asst. to pres., 1980-86; provost, chief exec. officer Tri-Coll. U., Fargo, ND, 1986-90; dean grad. and profl. sch. Hood Coll., Frederick, Md., 1990-93; v.p. Consortium of Univs. of the Washington Met. Area, 1993-94; pres. Stephens Coll., Columbia, Mo., 1994—2003, pres. emeritus, 2003—. Contbr. articles to profl. jours. V.p. Plains Art Mus., Moorhead, 1986-88; chmn. bd. govs. Fargo-Moorhead Area Found., Fargo, 1983-90; bd. dirs. United Way, Columbia, 1994-2001; mem. mgmt. coun. div. III, NAAA, 2001-03. Recipient Pembina Trail award, Minn. Hist. Soc., 1994. Mem. Am. Coun. on Edn., Coun. of Fellows, Fargo C. of C., Columbia C. of C. (bd. dirs.), Montgomery County High Tech. Coun., Rotary Club (Moorhead, Columbia, Frederick-towne), Cosmos Club, Washington.

KIEU, QUYNH DINH, pediatrician, not-for-profit developer; b. Hanoi, Vietnam, Mar. 18, 1950; m. Chan Kieu. MD, U. Saigon, Vietnam, 1975. Intern U. Calif., Irvine, Orange, 1976—77, resident, 1977—78, fellow, 1978—79, asst. clin. prof. pediat., 1985—; pvt. practice, 1979—; founder, pres. Project Vietnam, 1996—. Recipient Woman of Yr. award, Calif. Assembly's 69th Dist., 2004. Mem.: AMA Found. (Pride in Profession award 2004), Healthcare Found. Orange County (bd. dirs.), Vietnamese Med. Assn., Am. Acad. Pediat. Office: Project Vietnam 11100 Warner Ave Ste 116 Fountain Valley CA 92708-7500 Office Phone: 714-641-0850. Business E-Mail: qkieu@aap.org.*

KIFER, BRENDA A., medical/surgical and critical care nurse; b. Reading, Pa., Jan. 17, 1943; d. James Stewart and Emma Elizabeth (Belles) K. Diploma, Harrisburg Polyclinic Hosp., 1970; BSN, Messiah Coll., Grantham, Pa., 1971. Cert. med.-surg. nurse; CCRN; ACLS. Nurse Reading Med. Ctr.; nurse, instr. Pottstown (Pa.) Meml. Med. Ctr.; staff nurse in gerontology Vets. Affairs Ctr., Martinsburg, W.Va.; staff nurse med.-surg. ICU's VA Med. Ctr.; staff nurse PICU Winchester Med. Ctr., 1991—, charge nurse Va. Contbr. articles to profl. jours. Home: PO Box 201 Bunker Hill WV 25413-0201

KIFFMEYER, MARY, state official; b. Balta, N.D., Dec. 29, 1946; m. Ralph Kiffmeyer; children: Christina, Patrick, James, John. RN, St. Gabriel's Sch. Nursing, Little Falls, Minn. RN Minn. Sec. of state State of Minn., St. Paul, 1999—. Mem. Minn. State Exec. Coun., Minn. State Bd. Investment. Mem. adv. bd. The Heartland Inst., Election Assistance Commn. Standards; bd. dirs. Hope for the City, Cradle of Hope, Close-up Found., Downtown Mpls. YMCA. Recipient Leadership award, Nat. Electronic Commerce Coordinating Coun., In the Arena award, Ctr. for Digital Govt., Commitment to Absentee Voting for the Military award, Fed. Voter Assistance, Outstanding Woman in Govt. award, Minn. Women of Today, 2003. Mem.: Nat. Assn. Secs. of State (past pres., chair com. bus. services, pres. 2003). Republican. Office: Office Sec of State 180 State Office Bldg 100 Dr Martin Luther King Jr Blvd Saint Paul MN 55155-1210 Office Phone: 651-296-2079. Office Fax: 651-215-0682. E-mail: secretary.state@state.mn.us.*

KIGER, F. LOUISE, nursing administrator; b. El Paso, Tex., Aug. 5, 1938; d. LaVirgen Silva Grey; m. Charles R. Kiger, June 27, 1970; children: Stephanie, Jim, Derek. BSN, U. N.Mex., Albuquerque, 1959; MSN, U. Wash., 1979. Staff nurse Bataan Meml. Hosp., Albuquerque, 1959-60; advanced through grades to comdr. USN, various positions, 1960-71, USPHS and Indian Health Svc., 1979-93; capt. USPHS, 1993; dir., chief nurse Indian Health Svc. Divsn. of Nursing, Rockville, Md., 1993—. Recipient Bronze Star V, 1969. Mem. Nat. Alaska Native Am. Indian Nurses Assn., N.Mex. Indian Nurses Assn. Roman Catholic. Avocations: reading, gardening, travel. Office: US Dept Health and Human Svcs Indian Health Svc 5600 Fishers Ln Rockville MD 20852-1750

KIGGINS, MILDRED L., marketing professional; b. Hempstead, N.Y., Sept. 14, 1927; d. Wolfgang and Hannah Ingeborg (Olsson) Weissmann; m. Andrew Edward Kiggins, Jan. 8, 1962 (div. 1982); children: Daniel Mark, David Bruce. Diploma, Donovan Bus. Coll., Hackensack, N.J., 1945, Luther Coll. Acad., 1947. Exec. sec. Greenwich Engrng. divsn. Am. Machine & Foundry Inc., Stamford, Conn., 1954-61. Mktg. Dr. Andrew Becker MD, Becker Pharm. Cons., Redwood City, Calif., 2000— Tchr. Sunday sch. St. John's Luth. Ch., Stamford, 1948-50. Republican. Avocations: gardening, music, sports, church activities. Home: 39 Wisteria Ln Tracy CA 95377-8765 Office Phone: 209-836-6064.

KIJOWSKI, ROSEMARY JOAN, small business owner, retired music educator; b. Perth Amboy, N.J., Feb. 13, 1948; d. John Raymond and Rosaria Rosica Kijowski; children: Robert John, Edward Raymond. BA, The Coll. of N.J., Ewing, 1970, MA, 1976. Cert. Fitness Nutritionist Calif., 2004, Tchr. of Music, K-12 N.J., 1970. Vocal and music dir. Edison Bd. of Edn., NJ, 1970—2005; talent show/ advisor Woodrow Wilson M.S., Edison, NJ, 1998—2005, peer leadership advisor, 2000—01; owner, gen.mgr. fitness ctr. The Body Shoppe for Women, Edison, NJ, 2003—. Asst. coach Odyssey of the Mind, Edison, NJ, 1984—90. Mem.: N.J. Assn. Women Bus. Owners, Edison Twp. Edn. Assn. (assoc. Tchr. of Yr. 1998), N.J. Edn. Assn. (assoc.), Music Educators Nat. Conf. (assoc.), N.J. Edn. Assn. (assoc.), N.J. Ret. Educators Assn. (assoc.), N.J. Music Educators Assn. (assoc.). Home: 52 Riverview Ave Edison NJ 08817 Office: The Body Shoppe Fitness Ctr 1897 Woodbridge Ave Edison NJ 08817 Office Phone: 732-572-3953. Personal E-mail: bodyshpro@msn.com.

KIKEL, SUZANNE, patent agent; b. Pitts., Apr. 4, 1946; d. John George Kikel and Elizabeth Marie Pello; m. John Thomas Stauffer, Oct. 25, 1996. BA in Humanities, U. Pitts., 1972, BS in Mech. Engrng., 1981; A in Chemistry, C.C. Allegheny County, Pitts., 1994. Registered patent practitioner U.S.

Patent and Trademark Office, 1976. Patent agt. Wean United, Inc., Pitts., 1974-86, Eckert Seamans Cherin & Mellott, LLC, Pitts., 1986-95; intellectual property coord., patent agt. ECC Internat., Inc., Atlanta, 1995-99; patent agt. Calgon Corp., Pitts., 1999-2000, Pietrallo, Bosick & Gordon, Pitts., 2000—. Mem. Pitts. Intellectual Patent Law Assn., Pitts. Ski Club. Avocations: golf, tennis, skiing, biking, photography. Office: Pietrallo Bosick and Gordon 38th Flr 1 Oxford Ct Fl Grant38 Pittsburgh PA 15219-1407

KIKO, COLLEEN DUFFY, lawyer; BS, ND State; JD, George Mason U. Supervisory labor rels. specialist Fed. Labor Rels. Authority, 1976—83; atty. adv. Civil Rights Div., Dept. of Justice, 1986—89; spl. asst. US atty. (Ea. dist.) Va US Dept. Justice, Alexandria, 1986—89; assoc. counsel Judiciary Subcommittee of Civil and Constl. Rights, House Judiciary Com., US Ho. of Reps., 1989; atty. Law Offices of Colleen Duffy Kiko, PC; assoc. Ronald M. Cohen & Assocs., PC, Arlington, Va.; judge Employees' Compensation Appeals Bd., Dept. of Labor, 2002—05; gen. counsel US Fed. Labor Relations Authority, 2005—. Office: US Fed Labor Relations Authority 1400 K St NW Washington DC 20424

KILANKO, OYENIKE EUNICE, obstetrician, gynecologist; b. Bklyn., Mar. 5, 1972; d. Isaian Olayemi Oyedijo and Elizabeth Olayemi Tugbiyele Otedijo; m. Isaac Taiwo Kilanko, Sept. 20, 1998; children: Bolutiwi, Iyanu. BS, CUNY, 1995; MD, NYU, 1997. Diplomate Am. Bd. Ob-gyn. Assoc. attending Woodhill Med. Group, Bklyn., 2001—. Pres., co-owner Dermacare Bklyn. Hts., 2005—. Author poems. Fellow: Am. Coll. Ob-gyn. Office: Dermacare Bklyn Hts 122 Atlantic Ave Brooklyn NY 11201 Office Phone: 718-625-7546.

KILBANE, CATHERINE M., lawyer; b. Cleve., Apr. 10, 1963; BA cum laude, Case Western Res. U., 1984, JD cum laude, 1987. Bar: Ohio 1987. Ptnr. Baker & Hostetler, Cleve., 1997—2003; sr. v.p., gen. counsel, sec. Am. Greetings Corp., Cleve., 2003—. Mem. Delta Theta Phi. Office: Am Greetings Corp One American Rd Cleveland OH 44144

KILBANE, KATHLEEN ANN, stage manager; b. Cleve., Nov. 30, 1971; d. John Philip and Joan Marie Kilbane. BA in Polit. Sci., Coll. Wooster, 1994. Info. resource specialist Solid Waste Assn. N.Am., Silver Spring, Md., 1994—97; stage mgr. Horizons Theatre, Arlington, Va., 1998—2000, The Theatre Conspiracy, Washington, 1999—2000, Wash. Shakespeare Co., Arlington, Va., 2001; prodn. asst. The Shakespeare Theatre, Washington, 2002—04, asst. stage mgr., 2005—; stage mgr. African Continuum Theatre Co., Washington. Rsch. analyst Solid Waste Assn. N.Am., 1997—2002. Recipient Outstanding Vol. of Yr., Theatre J, 2004. Mem.: African Continuum Theatre Co., Actors' Equity Assn. Avocations: travel, cycling. Personal E-mail: kkilb@juno.com.

KILBERG, BOBBIE GREENE, govenment official; b. N.Y.C., Nov. 25, 1944; married; 4 children. BA, Vassar Coll., 1965; MA, Columbia U., 1966; LLB, Yale U., 1969. Former assoc. counsel Pres. Gerald Ford, 1975-77; former pvt. practice law; now dep. asst. to Pres. U.S., dir. pub. liaison The White Ho. Office: Exec Office of Pres Pub Liaison 1600 Pennsylvania Ave NW Washington DC 20500-0003

KILBOURNE, BARBARA JEAN, health and housing executive; b. Milw., Mar. 21, 1941; d. Burton Conwell and Marjorie Janet (Tufts) K.; m. Kenneth Keith Kauffman, Feb. 10, 1962 (div. 1983) BA, U. Minn., 1972; MBA, Coll. St. Thomas, St. Paul, 1980. Adminstr. Ebenezer Soc., Mpls., 1974—85; v.p., dir. housing Walker Residence and Health Svcs., Inc., Mpls., 1985—88; exec. v.p. Oblate Ministries Health and Aging, West St. Paul, Minn., 1988—94; cons., 1995—; pres. Barbara J. Kilbourne, Ltd., 1996—; exec. dir. Cath. Health Assn. Minn., 1997—2002; v.p. mem. svcs. and internal ops. Minn. Health and Housing Alliance, 2001—06. Chair Minn. State Operated Svcs., 2000-02 Author: Family Councils in Nursing Homes, 1981 Chmn. bd. dirs. LifeWorks, Eagan, Minn., 1985-96, Minn. Assn. Homes for Aging, 1991-92, Sem. Plaza, Red Wing, 1995-97; project chair Dialog 2000, Dakota County, Minn., 1988-91; bd. dirs. ARC, Mpls., 1997-2002, Common Bond Cmtys., 1999-2002, Villa Guadalupe, Chgo., chair, 1999-2006. Mem. Minn. Rural Health Assn. (bd. dirs. 1998-2001) Episcopalian. Avocations: poetry, golf, hiking. Home and Office: 435 Shelard Pky Minneapolis MN 55426

KILBOURNE, KRYSTAL HEWETT, retired rail transportation executive; b. Sandersville, Ga., Apr. 7, 1940; d. John Ray and Kathleen (Perkins) Hewett; m. Alan Arden Kilbourne, July 1, 1961 (div. May 1972); children: Arden Alan, Keith Ray. A, U. Ga., 1960. Tchr. Massey Bus. Coll., Jacksonville, Fla., 1968-72, editor, reporter, photographer, 1968-72; asst. to pres. Luter Advt. Agy., Jacksonville, Fla., 1973-74; asst. to dir. Leukemia Soc., Jacksonville, Fla., 1975-76; asst. to pres. TeleCheck Corp., Jacksonville, Fla., 1979; mgr. customer svc. railroad ops. CSX Transp., Jacksonville, Fla., 1980—2002; ret., 2002. Chair CSX Equal Employment Opportunity Coun., 1992-94. Tuition scholar U. Ga., 1958; recipient Transp. Workers Leadership award, 1995. Mem. Nat. Assn. Railway Bus. Women, Am. Coun. Railroad Women. Democrat. Presbyterian. Avocations: painting, poetry, snorkeling, travel, reading. Home: 357 Briar Bay Cir Orlando FL 32825

KILBURN, KATHERINE LYNN (KAPPY KILBURN), theater director, theater producer; b. Oskoda, Mich., June 27, 1972; d. Sandra S. and Richard Fisk Kilburn. BA, U. Mo., Columbia, 1994. Co-prodr. Directors Lab West, L.A., 1999—; spl. projects coord. Ctr. Theatre Group, 2000—05; assoc. dir. artistic devel. Pasadena Playhouse, 2004—. Freelance dir. Fremont Ctr. Theatre, L.A., Calif., 2000—; prodr. new plays artistic devel. program Hothouse at the Playhouse. Dir.: (plays) Three Hotels; prodr.: (fundraisers) Stephen Sondheim's 75th at the Hollywood Bowl, All About Gordon - tribute to Gordon Davidson at the Ahmanson; company mgr. (fundraisers) The World of Nick Adams, Kodak Theatre. Mem.: L.A. Stage Alliance, Theatre Comm. Group (assoc.), Soc. Stage Directors and Choreographers (assoc.), Lincoln Ctr. Theater Dirs. Lab (life), Kappa Kappa Gamma (life; v.p. L.A. alumni chpt. 2003). Democrat. Methodist. Avocations: travel, knitting, painting, animal care. Home: 601 Meridian Ave #E South Pasadena CA 91030 Office: Pasadena Playhouse 39 S El Molino Ave Pasadena CA 91101 Office Phone: 626-792-8672 212. E-mail: kkilburn@pasadenaplayhouse.org.

KILCHER, JEWEL See JEWEL

KILCHER, Q'ORIANKA (Q'ORIANKA WAIRA QOIANA KILCHER), actress, singer, dancer; b. Schweigmait, Germany, Feb. 11, 1990; Studies dance at the, Edge; studies acting with Gary Austin and Wendy McKenzie, studies voice with Seth Riggs. Actor: (films) How the Grinch Stole Christmas, 2000, The New World, 2005 (Best Young Actress nominee, Broadcast Film Critics Assn., 2006, Breakthrough Performance Actress, Nat. Bd. Review, 2005, Outstanding Actress in aotion Picture, Nat. Coun. La Raza ALMA award (Am. Latin Media Arts), 2006); guest appearance Madison Heights, 2002; performer: (TV) Star Search, 1983, Amahl and the Night Visitors. Recipient Ballet Hawaii's Young Choregraphers award, 1997, Best Overall Talent. Avocations: martial arts dance, Capoeira, horseback riding, sailing, acrobatics, enjoys writing music, studies wushu kung fu.*

KILCULLEN, MAUREEN, librarian, educator; b. Canton, Ohio, Oct. 29, 1954; d. Thomas Vincent and Betty Jane (Rawley) Kilcullen. BA in History, Kent State U., 1981, MLS, 1984. Libr. reference/audiovisual Barberton Pub. Libr., Barberton, Ohio, 1985—90; assoc. prof., reference libr. Stark Campus Kent State U., Canton, Ohio, 1990—. Contbr. chapters to books, articles to profl. jours. Vol. Dublin Irish Festival, Dublin, Ohio, 1995—. Recipient Regional Campus Vice Provost award Outstanding Service, Kent State U. Regional Campuses, 1997. Mem.: ALA, Acad. Libr. Assn. Ohio, Assn. Coll. and Rsch. Librs. Democrat. Roman Catholic. Avocations: reading, gardening, genealogy, photography. Office: Kent State Univ Stark Campus 6000 Frank Ave Canton OH 44720 Office Fax: 330-494-6212. Business E-Mail: mkilcullen@stark.kent.edu.

KILDAL, LORI ANN, dean; b. Ferndale, Mich., Oct. 12, 1954; d. Theodore W. and Charlotte E. Kildal. BS, Calif. State Poly. U., Pomona, 1977; MEd, Azusa Pacific U., Calif., 1987; PhD, U. N.Mex., Albuquerque, 1996. Cert. tchr. Calif., instr. ARC. Health fitness dir. YMCA, Tucson, 1981—83; athletic dir., tchr., coach Northview HS, Covina, Calif., 1983—87; asst. prof., coach Azusa Pacific U., 1987—96, exec. dir., 1999—2005; athletic dir. Peru State Coll., Nebr., 1996—97; assoc. dean Grossmont Coll., San Diego, 1997—99; dean acad. programs Victor Valley Coll., Victorville, Calif., 2006—. Co-author: (cmty. outreach program) Teachers are Heroes, 2002—. Mem. Grossman Coll. Found., San Diego, 1997—99; mem. pres.' cir. Victor Valley Coll. Found., Victorville, 2006—. Named Coach of Yr., Golden State Athletic Conf., 1991, 1995; recipient Cmty. Svc. award, Jefferson Pilot Comms., San Diego, 1999—2005, Effective Advt. on Radio award, San Diego Broadcasters Assn., 2005. Mem.: AAHPERD. Avocations: water-skiing, reading, drums. Office: Victor Valley Coll 18422 Bear Valley Rd Victorville CA 92395 Business E-Mail: kildall@vvc.edu.

KILDE, SANDRA JEAN, nurse anesthetist, educator; b. Eau Claire, Wis., June 25, 1938; d. Harry Milan and Beverly June (Johnson) K. Diploma, Luther Hosp. Sch. Nursing, Eau Claire, 1959; BA, Met. State U., St. Paul, 1976; MA, U. St. Thomas, 1981; EdD, Nova Southeastern U., 1987. RN, Wis., Minn. Oper. rm. nurse Luther Hosp., Eau Claire, 1959-61, head nurse oper. rm., 1961-63; supr. oper. rm. Midway Hosp., St. Paul, 1963-66; staff anesthetist North Meml. Med. Ctr., Robbinsdale, Minn., 1967-68, St. Joseph's Hosp., St. Paul, 1992-99, R.C. Shefland Anesthesia, Ltd., Bemidji, Minn., 2003—, St. Luke's Hosp., Duluth, Minn., 2005—. Program dir. Mpls. Sch. Anesthesia, St. Louis Park, Minn., 1968-96; adj. assoc. prof. St. Mary's U., Winona, Minn., 1982-96, adj. prof., 1996-2004, program dir. Masters Degree Program, 1984-96; nurse anesthesia cons., 1996—; ednl. cons. chmn. reviewer Coun. on Accreditation of Nurse Anesthesia Ednl. Programs, Park Ridge, Ill., 1983-92, 99-2005, elected to coun., 1992-99, vice chmn., 1994-97, chmn., 1997-99; corp. mem. Aitkin Cmty. Hosp., Inc. dba Riverwood HealthCare Ctr., 2001—, bd. dirs., 2002—; presenter in field. Choir dir. Grace Luth. Ch., McGregor, Minn., 1988—, mem. ch. coun., 1992—97, 1998—2001, pres. ch. coun., 1992—97. Recipient Good Neighbor award Sta. WCCO, Mpls., 1980, Disting. Alumni Achievement award Nova Southeastern U., 1993, Lifetime Achievement for Excellence in Edn. award Mpls. Sch. Anesthesia Class of 1999, 1999, St. John Baptist de La Salle award outstanding tchg. and profl. svc. St. Mary's U., 1999, Cert. of Appreciation Aitkin County Bd. Commrs. and Aitkin County Health and Human Svc. Adv. Com., 2001. Mem. Am. Assn. Nurse Anesthetists (pres. 1981-82, pres., bd. dirs. Edn. and Rsch. Found., 1981-83, cert. profl. excellence 1976, Program Dir. of Yr. award 1992, Helen Lamb Outstanding Educator award 2005), Minn. Assn. Nurse Anesthetists (pres. 1975-76, Agatha Hodgins Practictioner award, 2005). Lutheran. Avocations: gardening, fishing, photography, choir directing, playing guitar and piano. Home and Office: PO Box 80 Palisade MN 56469-0080 Personal E-mail: sjkilde1@juno.com.

KILDEE, JENNIFER, translator, editor; BS in Journalism, Cal Poly; MFA in Dramaturgy, SUNY, Stony Brook. Cert. in French to English translation Am. Translators Assn., Va., 2002. Tech. writer Internat. Bus. Machines, San Jose, Calif.; English tchr. Paris; project mgr./editor OST Translations, Berkeley, 1997—2000; bus. owner/translator Rive Gauche Translations, Berkeley, Calif., 2000—. Mem.: Am. Translators Assn. Avocations: travel, cooking, literature. Personal E-mail: blanchepage@aol.com.

KILE, ELIZABETH COLLIER, art educator, artist; b. NYC, Jan. 15, 1954; d. Samuel Meyer Collier and Virginia Ann Lawler, adopted d. Elton Lewis and Maud Elizabeth Lawler; children: Richard Collier, Kathryn Elizabeth. BFA cum laude, U. Mich., Ann Arbor, 1976; MA in Guidance and Counseling, Oakland U., Rochester, Mich., 1979; MEd in Art, U. Ill., Champaign Urbana, 2001. Cert. tchr. K-12 Mich., Ill., guidance and counseling Mich. Swim instr., lifeguard City of Charlevoix/Rogers City, Mich., 1975—80; art tchr. Romeo (Mich.) Cmty. Schs., 1976—80, Stephenson Elem. Sch., Des Plaines, Ill., 1987—89, Avoca Sch. Dist. 37, Wilmette, Ill., 1989—90, Kildeer Countryside SD 96, Long Grove, Ill., 1990—. Fine arts dir. St Simons Episcopal Ch., Arlington Heights, Ill., 1993—95; fine arts dir., co-chair Kaleidoscope Fine Arts Festival, Buffalo Grove, Ill., 1996, Mad About the Arts Festival, Buffalo Grove, 1998. Costume and set designer St. Simon's Christmas Prodns.; Exhibited in group shows at Crooked Tree Arts Coun. Photo Show (1st pl., 1973), BFA U. Mich. Art Show; logo designer various prodns. Judge and jury for fine arts scholarships Frontier Days Festival, Arlington Heights, 1997—2002; Sunday sch. tchr. St. Simon's Episcopal Ch., Arlington Heights, 1997; vol. Cowboy Dreams, Barrington, Ill., 2004—05. Recipient First Sch. Athletic Letter to a Female, George A. Dondero HS, 1972; Competitive scholar, State of Mich., 1972, Sch. of Art scholar, U. Mich., 1975, 1976. Mem.: NEA, Ill. Art Edn. Assn., Kildeer Edn. Assn., Ill. Edn. Assn., Mus. Contemporary Art, Art Inst. Chgo., U. Mich. Alumni Assn., Kappa Alpha Theta. Episcopalian. Avocations: art, skiing, horses, gardening, travel. Home: 107 N Kaspar Ave Arlington Heights IL 60005-1217 Office: Woodlawn Mid Sch 6362 Gilmer Rd Long Grove IL 60047 Office Phone: 847-353-8500 ext 2506. Personal E-mail: lizkile@wowway.com. E-mail: lkile@district96.k12.il.us.

KILE, PATRICIA D., retired elementary school educator; b. Nicholson, Pa. d. Wilmer Lester Darling and Sarah Alice Powers; m. Charles Wilson Kile Jr., Nov. 23, 1957; children: Charles David, Elizabeth Anne. BS in Edn., Beaver Coll., 1956, MEd in Gifted Edn., 1978. Tchr. Springfield Twp. Schs., Erdenheim, Pa., 1956-58, Upper Darby, Pa., 1958-60, Plymouth Twp. Schs., Montgomery County, Pa., 1960-62, Colonial Sch. Dist., Plymouth Meeting, Pa., 1973-93. Fund agt., class editor Arcadia U., 1986—. Author, photographer Pa. mag., 1990—; field editor Taste of Home, 1990—. Recipient Mary Louise Armstrong Wolf award, Arcadia U., 2001, Ethlyn Selner Mack award, 2001, Golden Disc award Meritorious Svc., 2006. Mem. AAUW (sec. 1995-98, Outstanding Woman of Hawley Honesdale br. 1999), Guild of Am. Paper Cutters. Avocations: crafts, scherenschnitte, photography, travelogues.

KILEY, KATIE, printmaker, painter; b. Decatur, Ill., 1951; m. John Kiley; children: Joanne, Julia. Ed., Clarke Coll., Dubuque, Iowa; BA in Art, St. Ambrose U., 1974; MA, U. Iowa, 1987; MFA, Iowa State U., 1989. Mem. advertising dept. Deere & Co., 1972—73; prof. art St. Ambrose U. Exhibitions include Drawings, Prints and Paintings, Muchnic Gallery, Atchison, Kans., 1998, Whiskey Gods and Cold Black Beads: Drawings, Paintings and Prints, Alfons Gallery, Milw., 1995, Girls! Girls! Girls!, Jacqueline Ross Gallery, Chgo., 1998, Paintings, Drawings and Prints, Dartmouth Coll., 1998, Gossamer Veils, Figge-Moss, Stoney Brook Sch., NY, 2000, Conversations, Quigley Gallery, Clarke Coll., Dubuque, Iowa, 2003, Constructing the Figure, Augustana Coll., Rock Island, Ill, 2003, Printmaker's Traveling Show: The Prairie, Grinell, Iowa, 2003, Kiley and Koiso, Midcoast Gallery, LeClaire, Iowa, 2004, Venus Envy, Midcoast Bucktown Gallery, Davenport, Iowa, 2005, Nat. Acad., 2006. Mailing: c/o del Mano Gallery 11981 San Vicente Blvd Los Angeles CA 90049*

KILGARIN, KAREN, state official, public relations consultant; b. Omaha, Mar. 12, 1957; d. Bradford Michael and Verna Jane (Will) Kilgarin; 1 child, Celeste Mattson Torrence. BA, U. Nebr., Kearney, 1979. With Real Estate Assocs., Inc., Omaha, 1979—84; capital bur. chief Sta. KETV, Omaha, 1984—92; dir. comm. and publs. Nebr. Edn. Assn., Lincoln, 1995—98, 1999—; dep. chief staff to gov., dir. pub. rels. State of Nebr., Lincoln, 1992—95, dir. dept. adminstrv. svcs., 1998—99. Mem. Nebr. Senate, Omaha, 1980—84; judicial nominating com. Gubernatorial appointment, 2000; mem. Capital Environment Comm. Mayor appointment, 2000. Mem. exec. com. Nebr. Dem. Com., Lincoln, 1995—98; trustee U. Nebr.-Kearney Found., 1992—95, mem. chancellor's adv. coun., 1995—. Recipient Outstanding Alumni award U. Nebr.-Kearney, 1993, Omaha South H.S., 1995, Wings award LWV, Omaha, 1995, President's award Nebr. Broadcasters Assn., 1995. Mem. NEA (pub. rels. coun. of states), Soc. Profl. Journalists, State Edn. Editors. Presbyterian. Avocations: photography, collecting, politics. Office: NSEA 605 S 14th St Lincoln NE 68508-2726

KILGORE, MARY HELEN, mathematics educator; b. Denison, Tex., Jan. 29, 1947; d. Bernard Joseph Mayhew and Katherine Irene Linde; m. Ronnie Gene Kilgore, Aug. 27, 1966; children: Danette Kathryn Bernard, Ronnie Gene II, Heather Elizabeth Panikkar, Brittney Leigh Walker, Barrett Joseph, Lyndsey Anne. BS Edn., U. Ark., Fayetteville, 1991. Cert. Secondary Math. Tchr. State of Ark., 1991. Tchr. secondary math. Butterfield Jr. H.S., Van Buren, Ark., 1991—. Sponsor Nat. Jr. Honor Soc. Butterfield Jr. H.S., Van Buren, 1999—, focus tchr. Math. Dept., 2005—, sponsor math counts, 1999—. Vol. Alma Performing Arts Ctr., Ark., 2005—06. Named to Who's Who Among Am. Tchrs. Roman Catholic. Avocations: stained glass, wood crafts. Home: 6315 S Atlanta Fort Smith AR 72903-4923 Office: Butterfield Jr HS 312 N 19th Van Buren AR 72956 E-mail: mkilgore@vbsd.us.

KILGUSS, ELSIE SCHAICH, small business owner, educator; b. Manhattan, NY, Aug. 04; BS in Advt., Mktg., Bryant Coll.; studied with Charles Sovek, studied with Betty Cappelli, 1968, studied with Henry Hensche, Lois Griffel; grad., RISD; student, Cape Sch. Art. With Horton, Church & Goff, Advt. Agy., Providence; represented by Gallery at Chatham (Mass.), 1990-99; owner, instr. Studio Zwei, Wickford, RI, 1991—. Art instr. Wickford Art Assn., 1990-98, Warwick Art Mus., 1990-2000, Attleboro Mus., 2000—, South County Art Assn., 1994-2004. One-woman shows include Wickford Art Festival, 1988—2004, Gallery at Chatham, 1990—99, Studio Zwei Gallery, Wickford, 1991—, Alfred Butler & Co., North Kingstown, 1992—, Fleet Bank, 1992—, RI State House, Providence, 1993—, Art in the Garden, 1995, 1997, 1999, Aszzo, 1998—99, Music on the Hill Anniversary Art Show, 1998, Cafe Gallery, 1998—99, Dodge House Gallery, Providence, 1999, 2001, 2003, Providence, 2001, 2003, Warwick Mus. Art, 2000; two-woman shows B&H Framing, 1987, Artists Gallery, Wickford, 1990, Maxwell Mays Gallery-Providence Art Club, 1991, 1993, 1995, 1997, Providence Art Club, 1993, 1995, 1997—98; Exhibited in group shows at Warwick Art Mus., 1987, 1989, 1991, 1997—99, Helme House, Kingston, RI, 1990, 1993, 1995, 1997, 2000, 2002, Woods-Gerry Gallery, Providence, 1991, Wickford Art Assn. Gallery, North Kingstown, 1991, 1993, 1995, 1997, 1999, RI Sch. Design Mus., Providence, 1992, Spring Bull Gallery, Newport, RI, 1993, 1999, 2001—02, Newport Art Mus., 1990, 1993, 1995, 1997, 1999—2001, 2003, RI Watercolor Soc., Pawtucket, 1993, 1995, 1997, 2000, 2003, South County Helme House, 2001—02, Spring Bull Gallery, 2002—03, Represented in permanent collections Alfred Butler & Co., Carribean Villas, others; catalog covers Providence Mag., R.I. Sch. Design, Cape Cod Mag., North Kingstown Villager. Mem.: Nat. Mus. Women in Arts, Warwick Mus., Boston Mus. Fine Arts, RISD Mus., Attleboro Mus., Newport Mus., Copley Soc. (Boston), Creative Arts Ctr., Newport Artist's Guild, South County Art Assn., Wickford Art Assn. (art instr. 1990—91, 1998—99, past pres. 1991), RI Watercolor Soc., Am. Soc. Marine Artists (assoc.), Am. Watercolor Soc. (assoc.), Oil Painters Am. (assoc.), Providence Art Club. Studio: Studio Zwei Gallery 2 Main St North Kingstown RI 02852-5016 Office Phone: 401-295-5907. E-mail: ekilguss@verizon.net, elsiekilguss@studiozweigallery.net.

KILIAN, JOY A., pre-school educator; d. Richard F. and Carol J. Blais; m. Scott C. Kilian, Jan. 14, 1980; children: Sean R., Andrea M. BSc in Bus. Adminstrn., Chapman U., 1995; MBA, Wayland Bapt. U., 1999, MEd, 2000. Prin., owner 2/$1 Greeting Card Shop, Clovis, N.Mex., 1996—98; educator early childhood Clovis (N.Mex.) Mcpl. Schs., 1998—, ednl. diagnostician, 2005—. Instr. Embry-Riddle Aero. U., Clovis, 2001—; adv. bd. Individuals with Disabilities in Edn. Act., 2003—; policy com. Clovis Municipal Schs., 1999—. Asst. dist. commr. Boy Scouts Am., 2000—05, unit commr., 1992—2004; asst. bingo team Sacred Heart Ch., Clovis, 1992—. Recipient Merit award, Boy Scouts Am., 1995, Silver Beaver award, 1998. Mem.: Coun. Exceptional Children (sec. Early Childhood Divsn. 1998—). Avocations: reading, sewing, gardening. Office: Clovis Mcpl Schs PO Box 19000 Clovis NM 88102-9000

KILKELLY, MARJORIE LEE, state legislator; b. Hartford, Conn., Dec. 1, 1954; d. Bruce Hamilton and Corlys Lucille (Lux) Brewer; children: Jeffrey Jr. (dec.), Robert, Sarah A.E. BS in Human Svcs., N.H. Coll., 1986, MS in Cmty. Econ. Devel., 1986; postgrad., Harvard U., 1997. Asst. to dir. Lincoln County Summer Youth Employment Program, Wiscasset, Maine, 1978; coordinator Community Food & Nutrition Program Coastal Enterprises, Inc., Wiscasset, 1978-79, Coastal Econ. Devel. Corp., Wiscasset, 1979-80, dir. Head Start Program Bath, Maine, 1980-84; asst. instr. N.H. Coll., Manchester, 1985-86; dir. Jr. Tots Wiscasset Recreation Program, 1985-88; dir. food services Boothbay Sch. Dept., Boothbay Harbor, Maine, 1985-88; owner Hurricane Hill Catering Co., Wiscasset, 1989—; mem. Maine Ho. of Reps., Augusta, 1986-96; house chair com. on agr., forestry and conservation, 1995-96; co-chmn. coastal caucus Maine Ho. of Reps., Augusta, spkr. pro tem, 1996—, candidate for speaker of house, 1992, candidate for house majority whip, 1994, chmn. agr., forestry and conservation com., 1995—; candidate Maine Senate, 1996; state senator, chmn. agriculture conservation and forestry com., island fish and wildlife com. State of Maine, 1996-98, chmn. Nat. Conf. State Legislators agr. com., 1997—; mem. Harvard state and local govt. ofcls. program Kennedy Sch. Govt., 1997—; cmty. devel. dir. Island Inst., Rockland, Maine, 1997—, community devel. dir., 1997—. Treas. Coastal Enterprises, Inc., Rundlet Block, Wis., 1981-90; rep. to Internat. Conf. on Econ. Devel., New Delhi, 1983—; 3d Selectman Town of Wiscasset, 1993-97; dir. devel. Maine Hospice Coun., 2000; owner Hurrican Hill Cons.; dir. N.E. States Assn. for Agrl. Stewardship, 1996-02. Mem. planning com. Blaine House Conf. on Families, 1979-80; active Maine Human Svcs. Coun. Sta. 23, Augusta, 1980-88; Sunday sch. tchr., lectr. St. Philips Episcopal Ch., Wiscasset, 1984-85, chmn. coord. com. food bank, 1986-88, sr. warden, 1995-98; chmn. Wis. Dem. Com., 1986; nat. chmn. Schs. S.O.S. Nat. Hunger Awareness Program, Denver, 1986; mem. exec. com. Maine Rural Devel. Coun., 1995—; spkr. pro tempere 118th Legislature, 1996; candidate Main State Senate Dist. 16, 1996; chair comm. adv. panel on decommissioning Maine Yankee Nuclear Plant, 1997, mem. legis. select com.; bd. dirs. Miles Health Care, Damanscotta, Mass., 1996—, Mid Coast United Way; chmn. Citizens Adv. Panel on Decommissioning Maine Yankee Atomic Power Plant, 1997—; lay dep. Nat. Episc. Ch. Conv., 1996—, vice chair nat. concerns com., chair Maine deputation, 2003. Recipient Good Governance award, Maine Merchants Assn., 2000; fellow New Eng. Rural, Coun. State Govts. Toll, Flemming fellow, Ctr. Policy Alternatives, 1999, Eisenhower Exch., 1999; grantee Maine Welfare Edn. Employment Tng. Program, 1983. Mem. Bus. and Profl. Women (Maine Young Career Woman award 1989), Huntoon Hill Grange Club, Lincoln County Pomona Grange Club, Sportsmans Alliance Club Maine, Am. Coun. Young Polit. Leaders, United Way Mid Coast Maine (bd. mem.), Miles Hlth. Care Bd., U. Maine Bd. Agr., Northeast States Assn. for Agrl. Stewardship (chair, dir.), Maine Farm Bur., Maine State Grange Club. Democrat. Episcopalian. Avocations: horseback riding, gourmet cooking, fishing. Office: NSAAS 5 MCCobb Rd Dresden ME 04342 Home: 5 McCobb Rd Dresden ME 04342-4023 Office Phone: 207-737-4717. E-mail: mkilkelly@csg.org.

KILLDEER, JOHN See MAYHAR, ARDATH

KILLEBREW, BETTY RACKLEY, language educator; b. Pontotoc, Miss., June 26, 1931; d. Aubrey Jesse and Odonnell (Rutledge) R.; m. Willard Wayne Killebrew, Dec. 20, 1974. BS, U. So. Miss., 1953; MA, Miss. State U., 1965, Ednl. Specialist, 1976. Jr. high English tchr. Lambert (Miss.) High Sch., 1953-56; high sch. English tchr. Tunica County (Miss.) High Sch., 1956-59; high sch. English and Spanish tchr. Benoit (Miss.) High Sch., 1959-69; English instr., chair humanities E. Miss. C.C., Scooba, Miss., 1969—. Pres. Scooba (Miss.) Music Club, 1970—. Named Outstanding Young Women of Am., Outstanding Faculty E. Miss. Community Coll., 1989. Mem. Local Faculty Assn., Southeastern Conf. for English Tchrs., Miss. Jr. and Community Coll. Assn., Order of the Eastern Star, Gideon's Aux. Democrat. Baptist. Avocations: reading, gardening.

KILLEBREW, ELLEN JANE (MRS. EDWARD S. GRAVES), cardiologist, educator; b. Tiffin, Ohio, Oct. 8, 1937; d. Joseph Arthur and Stephanie (Beriont) K.; m. Edward S. Graves, Sept. 12, 1970. BS in Biology, Bucknell U., 1959; MD, N.J. Coll. Medicine, 1965. Diplomate in cardiovasc. disease

Am. Bd. Internal Medicine. Intern U. Colo., 1965-66, resident, 1966-68; cardiology fellow Pacific Med. Ctr., San Francisco, 1968-70; dir. coronary care Permanente Med. Group, Richmond, Calif., 1970-83; asst. prof. U. Calif. Med. Ctr., San Francisco, 1970-83, assoc. prof., 1983-93; clin. prof. medicine U. Calif., San Francisco, 1992—, mem. admissions panel, 1998—. Admissions panel joint med. program U. Calif. San Francisco/U. Calif. Berkeley, 1998—; expert med. reviewer Calif. Med. Br., 1999, Bd. of Med. Examiners Calif., 1999—. Contbr. chapters to books. Contbr. Resolution Firm Calif. State Assmebly, 2005. Recipient Physician's Recognition award continuing med. edn., Lowell Beal award Permante Med. Group/House Staff Assn., 1992, Commendation State Assembly of Calif. for Contbr to Women and Heart Disease, 2005; Robert C. Kirkwood Meml. scholar in cardiology, 1970. Fellow ACP, Am. Coll. Cardiology; mem. Fedn. Clin. Rsch., Am. Heart Assn. (rsch. chmn. Contra Costa chpt. 1975—, v.p. 1980, pres. chpt. 1981-82, chmn. CPR com. Alameda chpt. 1984, pres. Oakland Piedmont br. 1995—, bd. dirs. western affiliate). Home: 30 Redding Ct Belvedere Tiburon CA 94920-1318 Office: 280 W Macarthur Blvd Oakland CA 94611-5642 also: 901 Nevin Ave Richmond CA 94801-3143 Business E-Mail: ellen.killebrew@kp.org.

KILLEEN, JOHANNE, small business owner; Degree, R.I. Sch. of Design; dates in Culinary Arts (hon.), Johson and Wales Univ. Chef, co-owner Al Forno Restaurant, Providence, 1975—. Appearances (TV series), In Julia Child's Kitchen with Master Chefs, Baking with Julia, Martha Stewart Living, David Rosengarten's Grilling, Cooking Live Primetime (Sarah Moulton); co-author: CUCINA SIMPATICA:Robust Trattoria Cooking, 1999. Actively involved Providence Pub. Libr., R.I. Food Bank, R.I. Project Aids, R.I. Ballet. Co-recipient The Ten Best Chefs in Am., Food and Wine; named World's Best Restaurant for casual dining, Internat. Herald Tribune, Scholars-in Residence; named one of top twenty women chefs in the country, USA Today; recipient nearly every honor, award and pub. recognition for orginal, innovative cuisine, Disting. Restaurants of North Am., Conde Nast Traveler's, 1992—2003, Hall of Fame award, Nation's restaurant, Insegna del Ristrante Italiano, Italian Ministries of Agrl. and of Foriegn Trade, 1999. Achievements include has taught DeGustibus (Macy's N.Y.C), Bristol Farms, Drager's, Fetzer Vineyards in Calif., La Varenne in W. Va., and in Italy teach regularly at the Capezzana Estate in Tuscany and Hotel Cipriani in V. Office: 577 S Main St Providence RI 02903

KILLEN, KATHLEEN ELIZABETH, systems engineer, retired military officer; b. Winnfield, La., Dec. 23, 1953; d. Walter Walden and Beatrice (Bright) K.; 1 child, Woodrow H. Kroll III. BSChE, La. Tech. U., 1983; BS in Aero. Engring., Air Force Inst. Tech., 1985, MS in Sys. Mgmt., 1992. Commd. 2d lt. USAF, 1983, advanced through grades to maj., 1995, armament engr. Maverick missile Wright-Patterson AFB, Ohio, 1985-88, chief global positioning system bus systems engr. L.A. AFB, Calif., 1988-91, program mgr. Spinal Cord Injury Transport Sys. Brooks AFB, Tex., 1992—96, instr. Systems Acquisition Sch., 1997—98, ret., 1998; assoc. rsch. engr. Tex. Engring. Experiment Sta., San Antonio, 1998—2003; quality engr. CACI Internat., San Antonio, 2003—. Petty officer 2d class USN, 1974-79. Decorated Achievement medal, Commendation medal, Joint Svc. Achievement medal, Meritorious Svc. medal. Avocations: reading, crafts, sewing. Office Phone: 210-735-1903 256.

KILLEN, ROSEANNE MARIE, social worker; b. Phila., Mar. 17, 1946; d. Joseph George and Lucy (Brunetti) Gentile; m. Larry R. Killen, Jan. 2, 1971; children: Rachel, Erin. BSW, Ind. U., 1976, MSW, 1978. Cert. social worker Acad. Cert. Social Workers, Tenn.; RN, Pa., Lic. Clin. Social Worker, State Tenn., 1992. Marriage and family therapist Cath. Social Svc. Indpls., 1979-89; psychotherapist Community Hosp. Diabetes Care Ctr., Indpls., 1988-90; pvt. practice clin. social work Profl. Counseling Ctr. Ind., Indpls., 1989-90; psychotherapist employee assistance program Bowater So. Div., Calhoun, Tenn., 1991-94; clin. social worker Bradley Meml. HomeHealth and Hospice, 1997-99. Pub. speaker on divorce and parenting to local schs. and ch. confs. Vol., bd. dirs. community rels. Bradley Hosp. Healthcare Found., 1991-95. Mem. NASW. Home: 3272 Chestnut Cir NW Cleveland TN 37312-2113

KILLIAN, JERRI, director, educator; BS, U. Phoenix, Colo. Springs, Colo., 1984, MBA, 1986; MPA, U. Colo., Denver, Colo., 1994, PhD in Pub. Adminstrn., 1997. Mgr. strategic planning Digital Equipment Corp., Marlboro, Mass., 1978—86; mgr. global planning Apple Computer, Cupertino, Calif., 1986—88; pvt. practice Killian Consulting, Colo. Springs, 1990—98; asst. prof. U. Utah, Salt Lake City, 1998—2000; assoc. prof. Wright State U., Dayton, Ohio, 2000—, dir. MPA Program, 2000—. Author: Handbook of Conflict Management, 2003; contbr. articles to profl. jours. Chmn. HighRise Services Co., Inc., Dayton, Ohio, 2001—. Recipient PhD Dissertation of Yr. award, U. Colo., 1997; grantee, Wright State U., 2006—. Mem.: AAUP, ASPA (mem. nat. coun. 2006—), Soc. Women in Pub. Adminstrn. (mem. exec. bd. 2004—), Nat. Assn. Schs. Pub. Affairs and Adminstrn., Pub. Adminstrn. Theory Network, Wright State U. Women's Rsch. Network, Pi Alpha Alpha (faculty advisor 2002—). Office: Wright State University 3640 Colonel Glenn Highway Dayton OH 45435 Office Phone: 937-775-3867.

KILLIAN, TIFFANY NOEL, secondary school educator; b. Garland, Tex., July 11, 1981; d. Sandra Karen and Alberto Martinez Ramirez (Stepfather); m. Joshua Wayne Killian, Sept. 3, 2005. BA in Social Sci., U. North Tex., 2003. Cert. secondary sch. tchr. Tex. Child care tchr. First Bapt. Ch., Garland, Tex., 1999—2004; secondary tchr. Newman Smith HS, Carrollton, Tex., 2003—. Mem.: Assn. Tex. Profl. Educators (corr.).

KILLINGBECK, JANICE LYNELLE (MRS. VICTOR LEE KILLINGBECK), journalist; b. Flint, Mich., Nov. 11, 1948; d. Leonard Paul and Ina Marie (Harris) Johnson; m. Victor Lee Killingbeck, Sept. 26, 1970; children: Deeanna Dawn, Victor Scott. BA, Mich. State U., 1970; postgrad., Delta Coll., 1971-72; MA in Humanities, Ctrl. Mich. U., 2002. Tourist counselor Mich. Dept. State Hwys., Clare, 1969; copy editor Mich. State News, East Lansing, 1969-70; gen. reporter Midland (Mich.) Daily News, 1970; substitute tchr. Saginaw (Mich.) Pub. Schs., 1971; pub. rels. teller 1st State Bank of Saginaw, 1971-75; crew leader spl. census in Buena Vista Twp. Detroit Regional Office, U.S. Bur. Census, 1976, interviewer ann. housing survey-std. met. statis. areas, 1977-78, interviewer on-going health surveys, 1979-85, Nat. Crime Survey, 1985-86; editor AMEN newsletter United Meth. Women, Saginaw, 1984-87, Bridgeport-Birch Run Weekly News, 1986-93; owner Have Camera Will Travel, 1993—. Accelerated reader para-profl. A.A. Claytor Elem. Sch. Buena Vista Sch. Dist., Saginaw, Mich., 1997, libr., 1998-2004, libr. Ricker Mid. Sch., 2004—; libr. Ames United Meth. Ch., Saquinaw, 2006—. Mem. Women in Comm., Sigma Delta Chi. Methodist. Home: 4946 Hess Rd Saginaw MI 48601-6809 Office: 801 State St Saginaw MI 48601 Office Phone: 989-753-6430. Business E-Mail: killingbeckj@email.bvsd.k12.mi.us.

KILLORAN, CYNTHIA LOCKHART, retired elementary school educator; b. Collinsville, Ill., June 19, 1918; d. Hugh McLelland and Estelle (Jones) Lockhart; m. Timothy Thomas Killoran, Feb. 9, 1944 (dec. Mar. 1991); children: Margaret, Kathleen, Timothy P., Cynthia, Mary. BS, U. Ill., 1940, postgrad. Home econs. tchr. LaMoille HS, Ill., 1940-41; home supr. Farm Security, Dept. Agr., Pittsfield, Ill., 1941-42; civilian instr. radio operating procedure USAAC, Sioux Falls, S.D., 1942-44, Batavia, Ill., 1944-69; kindergarten tchr. Batavia Sch. Dist. # 101, 1967-93; ret., 1993. Methodist.

KILNER, URSULA BLANCHE, genealogist, educator, writer; b. Chgo., Feb. 2, 1925; d. Frederic Russell and Blanche (Miller) Gamble; m. Glen Kilner, May 12, 1950 (dec. Feb. 1998). BA cum laude, Mt. Holyoke Coll., 1946; MA, Columbia U., 1947, postgrad., to 1951. Asst. to editor Grolier Pub., NYC, 1947; mgr. Magnamusic Inc., Garrison, NY, 1954-55; publicity and fundraising Little Guild of St. Francis Inc., Cornwall, Conn., 1957-68; lectr. U. Conn., Torrington, 1964-66; genealogist Bird Bottom Genealogy, Salisbury, Conn., 1979—. Owner, mgr. The Tenth Muse, phonograph and stereo co., 1958-60; reporter The Comml. Record, 1960-61. Author, editor: A Revolutionary Cook Book, 1985, A Cook Book for All Seasons, 1994; columnist The Voice, 1993—2003, Animal Life, 2004—06, book reviewer Heritage Books; contbr. articles to profl. jours. Mem. Planning and Zoning Commn., Salisbury, Conn., 1981-82, NY State Hist. Assn. Mem.: DAR (chpt. registrar Salisbury Arsenal 1982—2004), N.Y. State Hist. Assn., Ill. Geneal. Soc., N.Y. Hist. Assn., Essex (Mass.) Soc. Genealogists, Nat. Geneal. Soc., Soc. Genealogists, Conn. Gravestone Studies, Assn. Gravestone Studies, Vt. Genealogists Soc., Suffolk County Hist. Soc., Conn. Soc. Genealogists, Am. Coll. Genealogists (asst. nat. registrar 1990—91, cert. genealogist), N.H. Genealogy Soc. (life), Nat. Soc. Huguenots (life; adv. bd. 1993—2001, Conn. registrar 1998—2001), N.H. Soc. Genealogists (life), N.Y. Geneal./Biog. Soc. (life), New Eng. Hist./Geneal. Soc. (life), Salisbury Assn., Sons and Daus. First Settlers Newbury, Van Voorhees Family Soc., Greyhound Friends West, Inc., Nat. Soc. Colonial Dames XVII Century (organizing pres. Winthrop Fleet chpt. 1990, Conn. state registrar 1995—99, chpt. pres. 1999—2001, ret.), Sheffield Hist. Soc. (life), Morse Family Soc. (life), Piscataqua Pioneers N.H. (life), Kewanee (Ill.) Hist. Soc. (life), Andover (Mass.) Hist. Soc. (life), Nat. Soc. Daus. Am. Colonists (ret. Conn. registrar), Seeley Family Soc., Whitlock Family Soc., Ea. Star. Avocations: knitting, lecturing, saving greyhounds, greenhouse plants. Home and Office: Bird Bottom Farm RR 1 Salisbury CT 06068-9802

KILPATRICK, CAROLYN CHEEKS, congresswoman; b. Detroit, June 25, 1945; d. Marvell and Willa Mae (Henry) Cheeks; divorced; children: Kwame, Ayanna. AS, Ferris State Coll., Big Rapids, Mich., 1965; BS, Western Mich. U., 1972; MS in Edn., U. Mich., 1977. Tchr. Murray Wright High Sch., Detroit, 1972-78; mem. Mich. Ho. of Reps., Lansing, 1978-96, U.S. Congress from 13th Mich. dist. (formerly 15th), Washington, 1997—; mem. appropriations com. Del. Dem. Convs., 1980, 84, 88. Participant Mich. African Trade Mission, 1984, UN Internat. Women's Conf., 1986; del. participant Mich. Dept. Agr. to Nairobi (Kenya) Internat. Agr. Show, 1986. Recipient Anthony Wayne award Wayne State U., Disting. Legislator award U. Mich., Disting. Alumni award Ferris State U., Woman of Yr. award Gentlemen of Wall St., Inc., Burton-Abercrombie award 15th Dem. Congrl. dist.; named one of Most Influential Black Americans, Ebony mag., 2006. Mem. Nat. Orgn. 100 Black Women. Democrat. Office: House of Reps 1610 Longworth House Office Bldg Washington DC 20515-2215 also: Dist Office 1274 Library Ste 1B Detroit MI 48226 Office Phone: 202-225-2261, 313-965-9004. Office Fax: 202-225-5730, 313-965-9006.*

KILPATRICK, JENNIFER M., counseling administrator; b. Starkville, Miss., July 15, 1956; d. Keneth S. and Helen Elaine McMinn; m. Jimmy Don Kilpatrick, July 6, 1996; stepchildren: Jessica K. Bridge Water, Merri Gray; children: Anna Leigh Wilkerson, Ashley Elizabeth Wilkerson. BS, Miss. State Univ., Starkville, Miss., 1979, MA, 1984. Cert. Nat. counselor, Nat. sch. counselor. Tchr. Clay County Sch., West Point, Miss.; child devel. instr. McKellar Tech. Ctr., Columbus, Miss., special populations coord.; counselor Columbus Mcpl. sch., Columbus, Miss., Rankin County Sch. Dist., Brandon, Miss. Mem. Holcim Cmty. Adv. Bd., Crawford, Miss., 2001—, McKellar Tech. Adv. Bd., Columbus, Miss., 1988—. Charter mem. Miss. Wildlife Assn.; sponser Special Olympics, Miss. Diabetes Assn. Recipient Tchr. of the Yr., McKellar Tech. Ctr. Mem.: Assn. for CAreer and Tech. Edn., Am. Counseling Assn., Miss. Counseling Assn., Am. Vocat. Assn. Avocations: cooking, reading, travel.

KILPATRICK, JUDITH ANN, medical/surgical nurse, educator; b. Chester, Pa; m. Richard Kilpatrick. Diploma, Albert Einstein Med. Ctr., Phila., 1968; BSN, U. Pa., 1971, MSN, 1978; DNSc, Widener U., 2002. RN, Pa. Asst. prof. Widener U., Chester, 2002—. Mem. ANA, NLN, Sigma Theta Tau Internat., Pa. Nurses Assn. E-mail: jakilpatrick@mail.widener.edu.

KILPATRICK, LAURA SHELBY, music educator; b. Des Moines, Feb. 27, 1961; d. Nicholas Ligear and Barbara Slezak Shelby; m. Mark Allen Kilpatrick, July 28, 1984; children: Jennifer Morgan, Mitchell Austin. BS in music edn., U. Mo., 1983; M in edn., Lesley U., 2001. Cert. tchg. Nat. Bd. Profl. Tchrs. Standards. Exec. asst. Pebble Beach Co., Pebble Beach, Calif., 1985—91, Century Fin., Kans. City, Mo., 1992—94; office mgr. Space Developers, Callahan Constrn., Trinitas, Old Town Corp., Independence, Mo., 1994—96; children and youth choir dir. Christ United Meth. Ch., Independence, 1993—2003; music tchr. Thomas Hart Benton Elem., Independence, 1996—2001; tchr. Bryant Elem., Independence, 2001—. Dir. Independence Sch. Dist. Wide Holiday Concert, 1999, 2001, Kans. City Chorale Holiday Concert, Independence, 2002. Finalist Tchr. of the Yr., Indep. Sch. Dist., 2003, 2006; Outstanding tchr. grant, Gov. Employees Hosp. Assn., 2003, 2004. Mem.: Music Educators Nat. Conf., Mo. State Tchrs. Assn. Methodist. Achievements include Nat. Anthem soloist for Kans. City Royals Baseball Team in 1996 and 2004. Avocations: sports and health, movies and live performances. Home: 19209 E 34th St S Independence MO 64057 Office: Bryant Elem 827 W College Ave Independence MO 64050

KILPATRICK, MAUREEN, food service executive; Grad. cert., Calif. Culinary Acad. Worked with Lydia Shire Pignoli, Boston; worked with Ana Sortun and Moncef Medeb 8 Holyoke, Boston; worked with Rene Becker High-Rise Bread Co., Hi-Rise Pie Co.; with Harvest, Boston; worked with Rene Michelena La Bettolla, Boston; pastry chef Oleana, Cambridge, Mass. Office: Oleana 134 Hampshire St Cambridge MA 02139

KIM, CHEONAE, artist, educator; d. Mong Song Kim and Byung Bu Ahn. BS, Ewha Women's U., Seoul, Republic of Korea, 1975; BA, So. Ill. U., 1983, MFA, 1986. Artist in residence So. Ill. U., Carbondale, 1991—; vis. lectr. Washington U., St. Louis, 1997—2004. Exhibitions include Mils. Art Mus., UCLA. Grantee, Nat. Endowment for Arts, 1993. Mem.: Phi Kappa Phi (Outstanding Artist 2003). Home: 1925 Brown Pl Murphysboro IL 62966 Office: So Ill U 1100 S Normal Carbondale IL 62901 Office Phone: 618-453-4315. Business E-Mail: cheonae@siu.edu.

KIM, CHRISTINA, professional golfer; b. San Jose, Calif., Mar. 15, 1984; Attended, De Anza CC. Winner Longs Drugs Challenge, 2004. Achievements include shot lowest score ever at any USGA event, U.S. Girl's Amateur Championships, 2001; finished second on Futures Tour money list. Avocations: yoga, reading, writing. Office: c/o LPGA 100 International Golf Dr Daytona Beach FL 32124-1092

KIM, HAZEL, public relations executive; BA, SUNY, Buffalo; MBA, Boston Univ. Dir community rels. John Hancock Co. Mem. bd. WGBH; bd. advocates Bay Cove Human Svcs.; co-chair Mass. Asian Am. and Pacific Islanders in Philanthropy. Vol. math tutor Boston Pub. Schools; playspace activities leader Horizon for Homeless Families. Named one of Boston's Ten Young Outstanding Leaders, Jaycees, 2004, 40 Under 40, Boston Bus. Jour., 2006. Office: John Hancock Fin Svcs John Hancock Plc Boston MA 02117*

KIM, IRENE JIYUN, music professor, choral conductor; MusB, U. Calif., LA, 1992, MusM, 1995. Cert. music tchr. Calif., 1997. Music tchr. San Gabriel HS, Calif., 1997—2000; assoc. prof. music LA City Coll., 2000—. Conductor South Bay Chinese Chorus Soc., Rancho Palos Verdes, Calif., 1994—99; music tchr. Redeemer Bapt. Elem. Sch., LA, 1995—96; music dir. La Palma United Meth. Ch., 1995—97, Culver-Palms United Meth. Ch., Calif., 1998—2001; artistic dir. U. Campus Choir, LA, 1998—2001. Mem.: U. Calif. Alumni Assn., Am. Fedn. Tchrs., Music Assn. Calif. C.C., Am. Choral Dirs. Assn. Office: LA City Coll 855 N Vermont Ave Los Angeles CA 90029 Business E-Mail: kimij@lacitycollege.edu.

KIM, JEAN, psychiatrist; d. Byung-Oh and Kae-Sung Kim. BA In English, Yale U., New Haven, Conn., 1996; MD, Med. Coll. Va., Richmond, 2000. Diplomate Am. Bd. Psychiatry and Neurology. Resident in psychiatry Mt. Sinai Med. Ctr., N.Y.C., 2000—04, attending psychiatrist, 2004—06, N.Y. Presbyn. Hosp.-Westchester Divsn., White Plains, 2006—. Mem.: Am. Psychiat. Assn. Office: NY Presbyn Hosp Westchester Divsn 21 Bloomingdale Rd White Plains NY 10605 Office Phone: 914-997-5867. E-mail: jeanki@yahoo.com.

KIM, JOSEPHINE M., education educator; d. Hak Soo and Kyon Cha Kim. BS in Comm., Liberty U., 1996, MA in Profl. Counseling, 1998; PhD, U. Va., 2005. Cert. Counselors Nat. Bd. Cert. Counselors, lic. mental health counselor. Mental health clin. supr. U. Va. Counselor Edn. Program, Charlottesville, Va., 2003—05; postdoctoral, tchg. fellow Harvard Grad. Sch. Edn., Cambridge, Mass., 2005—. Clin. coord. counseling svcs. U. Va. Counselor Edn. Program, 2003—04; lectr., edn. risk and prevention program Harvard Grad. Sch. Edn. Mem.: ACA. Office: Harvard Grad Sch Edn 406 Larsen Hall Appian Way Cambridge MA 02138 Business E-Mail: fimjo@gse.harvard.edu.

KIM, LILLIAN G. LEE, retired administrative assistant; b. Toishan, Canton, China, June 17, 1919; came to the U.S., 1921; d. Yick You and Lucy Yu Oy (Louie) Lee; m. Herman Hom Kim, Oct. 12, 1941. Cert., Ea. U., 1941. Stenographer, sec. Peabody Book Shop, Balt., 1937-38; sec. Prisoners Aid Assn., Balt., 1938-41; sec. Civilian Def. Exec. Office Balt. Mcpl. Govt., 1942-44, sec. to safety dir., 1944-48; sec.-stenographer, asst. supr. stenography divsn. Ctrl. Payroll Bur., 1948-64, adminstrv. sec., supr. adminstrv. and stenographic sect., 1946-63, supr. adminstrv. sect., 1964-77; ret., 1977. Ctrl. payroll councilwoman Classified Mcpl. Employee Assn., Balt., 1949-77, columnist Hall Light, 1950-77; chair ret. employee group CHICA-Combined Health/Industry Comb. Appeal and United Way, Balt., 1970-77; bd. dirs. Women's Civic League; pres., bd. dirs. AARP (Rodgers Forge Chpt. 2360), 1996-, publicity and pub. rels. officer, corr. sec., 1997-99; lectr. in field. Author: (with Lee Yick You and Louie Yu Oy) Early Baltimore Chinese Families, 1976, Chinese Americans-A Part of America, 1977; Letters to the Editor: (tribute to Marhsall Sisters) History of Grace & St. Peter's Chinese Ch. Sch., 1975, Tien Nien Poems, Lectures, and Speeches, Gnin-Gnin's China: Our Heritage, 1980, Grace and St. Peter's Chinese Church School (founders Frances L. and Florence M. "Daisy" Marshall), Chinese Traditions, Customs, and Festivals; author short stories, essays, 1960-70; edit. publ. Wah Kue Sim Mon (bilingual news bull.), 1998, Tien Nien Chatter; cmty. news columnist Towson Times, 1978—; freelance writer Senior Digest, 1990—; Gone But Not Forgotten: Nostalgic Maryland Memories, 1993, editor-pub. Tien Nien Chatter, 1946-60; contbg. writer Hall Light, 1950-77. Founder Chinese Young People's Fellowship, sec., mem. pub. rels. sect. 1946-60, pres., 1960-65; mem. Senator Charles McMathias Jr.s' Select. Immigration Com., 1960s; founder, exec. sec. Grace and St. Peter's Bilingual Chinese Lang. Sch., Balt., 1954-73, supr., 1964-85, dir., prin., 1974—, compiler evening praryer svc. and hymn book; vestrywoman Grace and St. Peter's Ch., Balt., mem. parish activity planning, 1969—, compiler bilingual evening prayer svc.; sec. bd. trustees Grace and St. Peter's Sch., Balt., 1980-86, trustee, 1987-90; exec. bd. Boy Scouts Am., 1978-95; bd. dirs. Women's Civic League, 1979-82, exec. bd., 1999; mem. Bishop's Guild, Diocese of Md., 1960-99; mem. Holly Tour Com., Inc. of Balt., 1975-85, sec., 1978-82; sec., pub. rels. Chinese Women's Assn. Balt., 1937-46; Chinese interpreter of Am. laws, social security taxes, federal and state taxes to Chinese; represented Chinese immigrants in cts. as a vol.; advocate Family Reunionifications, Canton, Balt., 1964; participant Testimonial Dinner Tribute to Councilman Leon A. Rubenstein, Senator Charles McMathias Retirement Dinner; spkr. Tribute to Senator Barbara A. Mikulski; del. to Md. Diocesan Conv., selected lay reader Diocesan Conv. Holy Eucharist Svc., St. Anne's Ch., Annapolis, numerous other diocesan activities; cmty. advocate Dept Justice, Immigration and Naturalization Svc., 1997—; initator, coord. Grace and St. Peter's Chinese Lunar New Yr., Balt.; compiler bilingual citizenship study guide; mem. exec. bd. Boy Scouts Am., 1978-1995; organizer Tiger Club program; apptd. to serve on Senator Charles McMathias Jr.'s select immigration com., 1960s. Recipient awards, including Spl. Baltimorean award, 1976, Balt.'s Best Blue and Silver awards, numerous times, award for outstanding svc. in promoting internat. rels., Carnation Volunteerism award, Balt. City Outstanding Woman of Yr. award, Baltimore County Exec. Proclamation, 1985, Balt. County Woman of Yr., 1986, GERI award, 1990, Baltimore County Execs.'s Baltimore County Exec. citation-Humanitarian award honoree, 1993, Gold 13 medal WJZ-TV, Exec. Citation Humanitarian award Baltimore County, Golden Rule award JC Penney's, Best of Towson, 1998, First Place Best Vol. award Readers of Towson Times, 1998; Congratulatory Honors award Club 88 Tchrs. of Lyndhurst Elem. Sch. No. 88), 1999, award for outstanding svc. tchg. and promoting lang., culture, tradition, and history Coordination Coun. for N.Am. Affairs, Dist. Svc. to Balt. Chinese Cmty. award Balt. chpt. Orgn. Chinese Ams., Outstanding Achievement award Dorothy G. Reddick, 1999, Feast of the Dedication cert. of appreciation Grace and St. Peter's Parish, 1999, My Most Significant Memory of 20th Century award Dept. Aging, 2000. Mem. AARP (pub. rels. dir., bd. dirs.), Episcopal Asiamerica Ministry (parish rep. 1975-93, diocesan rep. 1994—), DAR (medal of honr.), Walters Art Mus., Balt. Mus. Art, Md. Hist. Soc., Stars Spangled Banner Assn., Johns Hopkins Alumni Assn., UCLA Alumni Assn., Washington Nat. Episcopal Cathedral Assn., Ellis Island Found.-Statue of Liberty, Chinese Hist. Soc. Am. (life), Chinese Hist. Soc. So. Calif. (life), Assn. Chinese Schs., Chinese Lang. Tchrs. Assn., Crozier Soc., Md. Assn. of Deaf, Historic Towson, Inc., Balto Coun. Fgn. Affairs, Reagan Ranch, WYPR Radio News Sta., Friends of Nat. Parks at Gettysburg, U.S. Capitol Hist. Soc., Nat. Trust for Historic Presevation, Chesapeake Bay Found., Balt. City Hist. Soc., Enoch Pratt Free Libr./State Libr. Resource. Democrat. Episcopalian. Avocations: community service, gardening, bowling, reading. Office: Grace & St Peters Chinese Lang Sch 707 Park Ave Baltimore MD 21201-4703 Home: 4901 Carroll Ct Baldwin MD 21013-9205

KIM, MICAELA, speech pathology/audiology services professional; b. Seoul, Korea; arrived in US, 1971; BA in Comm., Boston Coll., 1993; MS in Speech-Language Pathology, St. Xavier U., 2001. Documentary rschr. Seoul Broadcast System, Seoul; with ChicagoLand TV, 1994; field prodr. & rschr. WBBM-TV, 1995; gen. assignment reporter then medical anchor/reporter WBTW-TV, Myrtle Beach, 1996—97; freelance reporter WYCC-TV, Chicago, 1997—99; speech-language pathologist Lutheran Gen. Hosp., U. Chicago Hosp., Edward Hosp., Ill. Early Intervention System; now founder Smiling Star Speech & Language, Hinsdale, Ill. Recipient Mark Twain award. Mem.: Ill. Speech-Language-Hearing Assn., Am. Speech-Language-Hearing Assn., Asian Am. Journalists Assn. (treas. Chicago chapter 1995, v.p. Chicago chapter 1996). Office: Smiling Star Speech & Language 112 S Grant St Hinsdale IL 60521

KIM, SABRINA S., lawyer; b. Seoul, South Korea, Oct. 9, 1969; BA magna cum laude, UCLA, 1992; JD, Univ. Calif., Hastings, 1996. Bar: Calif. 1996. Dep. atty. gen. Calif. Dept. Justice; assoc., securities litigation Milberg Weiss Bershad & Shapiro, LA. Ad. prof. Loyola Law Sch. Named a Rising Star, So. Calif. Super Lawyers, 2006. Mem.: Assn. Bus. Trial Lawyers (bd. mem.), Phi Beta Kappa. Office: Milberg Weiss Bershad & Schulman Ste 3900 300 S Grand Ave Los Angeles CA 90071 Office Phone: 213-617-1200. Office Fax: 213-617-1975. Business E-Mail: skim@milbergweiss.com.*

KIM, SACHIKO O., music educator; b. Kyoto, Aug. 24, 1955; d. Toyokazu and Matsuko Okuno; m. Donghee Kim, Aug. 21, 1982; children: Stephen Donghee, Allison Sachiko. BA, Doshisha U., Kyoto, 1978; MA, Mich. State U., East Lansing, 1980, MEd, 1982. Cert. Tchr.-Early Childhood Edn. State of Ill., 2000, Tchr. Elementary K-9 State of Ill., 2004. Tchr. Christ Luth. Presch., Vernon Hills, 1990—97; permanent substitute tchr. Hawthorn Sch., Vernon Hills, 1998—2001; tchr. music Hawthorn Kindergarten, Vernon Hills, 2001—05, Hawthorn Elem. North, Vernon Hills, Ill., 2005—. Instr. Coll. of Lake County, Glayslake, Ill., 2004—; tchr. Futabukai Japanese Sat. Sch., Niles, Ill., 1989—97. Mem.: Greater Chgo. Orff Assn. Office: Hawthorn Elementary North 301 Hawthorn Parkway Vernon Hills IL 60061

KIM, SANGDUK, biochemistry educator, researcher; b. Seoul, Korea, June 15, 1930; came to U.S., 1954; d. Tak Won and chungHee (Kil) K.; m. Woon Ki Paik, June 15, 1959; children: Margaret, Dean, David. MD, Korea U.,

Seoul, 1953; PhD, U. Wis., 1960. Intern Evang. Deaconess Hosp., Milw., 1954-55; rsch. assoc. U. Wis., Madison, 1959-61, U. Ottawa, Ont., Can., 1961-66; rsch. assoc. Fels Inst. Temple U., Phila., 1966-73, sr. investigator Fels Inst., 1973-78, assoc. prof. biochemistry Fels Inst., 1978-90, prof. biochemistry, 1990—. Author: (monograph) Protein Methylation, 1980; editor: Protein Methylation, 1990. NIH Rsch. grantee, 1973-81, NSF Rsch. grantee, 1979-85, Nat. Multiple Sclerosis Rsch. grantee, 1985—. Mem. Am. Soc. Biol. Chemists, Am. Assn. for Cancer Rsch., N.Y. Acad. Sci., Am. Chem. Soc., Am. Soc. for Neurochemistry. Home: 7818 Oak Lane Rd Cheltenham PA 19012-1015 Office: Temple U Fels Inst 3420 N Broad St Philadelphia PA 19140-5104

KIM, SONJA CHUNG, elementary school educator; b. Seoul, Sept. 23, 1941; came to U.S., 1967; d. Sung Kwon and BoSoon (Chun) Chung; m. Man Jae Kim, Mar. 24, 1964; children: Richard S., Lesley S. BA, Seoul Nat. U., 1964; MA, Ohio State U., 1969; postgrad., Mich. State U., 1970-71, Western Mich. U., 1973-74. Cert. tchr., Mich., Korea. Tchr. Kalamazoo Korean Sch., 1987-90, prin., 1993-94; tchr., educator White Pigeon (Mich.) Community Schs., 1971—2002; ret. Pres. Kports & Co., Portage, Mich., 1985—. Mem. NEA, Mich. Edn. Assn., Mich. Music Edn. Assn., Seoul Nat. U. Alumni Assn. (pres. 1989—). Avocations: travel, reading, golf. Home: PO Box 1423 Portage MI 49081-1423

KIM, SOOK CHA, artist; b. Choong-Joo, Korea, Mar. 30, 1940; arrived in U.S., 1973; d. Kyung Nam Chai and Choon Yi Lim; m. Myung Hak Kim, Dec. 5, 1967; 1 child, Young Kyoon. BFA, Hong-Ik U., 1965, MFA, 1967. Owner Morning Star Art Gallery, Washington, 1995—2003. Featured artist Art Addiction Internat. Gallery. Recipient Gold medal--Art Addiction Internat. prize Most Talented Artists Competition, Sweden, 1997, Cert. of Merit 6th Internat. Female Artist Art Exhbn. on Internet Art Mus., 1999. Home: 6540 Braddock Rd Alexandria VA 22312-2206

KIM, WILLA, costume designer; b. LA; d. Shoon Kwan and Nora Kim; m. William Pene Du Bois. Costume designer New Theatre for Now, Mark Taper Forum, L.A., 1969-70, Goodman Theatre, Chgo., 1978-79. Set and costume designer Feld Ballet, Joffrey Ballet, Am. Ballet Theatre, San Francisco Ballet. Costume designer: (theatre) Red Eye of Love, 1961, Fortuna, 1962, The Saving Grace, 1963, Have I Got a Girl for You!, 1963, Funnyhouse of a Negro, 1964, Dynamite Tonight, 1964, A Midsummer Night's Dream, 1964, The Old Glory, 1964 (Obie award 1964-65), Helen, 1964, The Day the Whores Came out To Play Tennis, 1965, Sing to Me Through Open Windows, 1965, The Stag King, 1965, Malcolm, 1966, The Office, 1966, Chu Chem, 1966, Hail Scrawdyke!, 1966, Scuba Duba, 1967, The Ceremony of Innocence, 1967, Promenade, 1969 (Drama Desk award 1969-70), Papp, 1969, Operation Sidewinder, 1970 (Drama Desk award 1969-70), Sunday Dinner, 1970, The Screens, 1971 (Maharam award 1971-72, Drama Desk award 1971-72, Variety N.Y. Drama Critics Poll award 1971-72), Sleep, 1972, Lysistrata, 1972, The Chickencoop Chinaman, 1972, Jumpers, 1974, Goodtime Charley, 1975 (Tony award nomination best costume design 1975), The Old Glory: a trilogy, 1976, Dancin', 1978 (Tony award nomination best costume design 1978), The Grinding Machine, 1978, Bosoms and Neglect, 1979, Sophisticated Ladies, 1981 (Tony award best costume design 1981), Family Devotions, 1981, Lydie Breeze, 1982, Chaplin, 1983, Elizabeth and Essex, 1984, Song and Dance, 1985 (Tony award nomination best costume design 1986), Long Day's Journey Into Night, 1986, The Front Page, 1986, Legs Diamond, 1989 (Tony award nomination best costume design 1989), The Will Rogers Follies, 1991 (Tony award best costume design 1991), Four Baboons Adoring the Sun, 1992, Tommy Tune Tonight!, 1993, Grease, 1994, Victor/Victoria, 1995, Stage Door Charley, 1995, Terra Incognita, 1997, The Film Society, 1997, Missing Footage, 1999, An Enemy of the People, 2003, Rough Crossing, 2004, The Bay at Nice, 2004, Woman Before A Glass, 2005 (Obie award, Village Voice, 2005); (ballets) Birds of Sorrow, 1962, Gamelan, 1963, Game of Noah, 1965, Daphins et Chloe, Papillon, Scenes for the Theatre, A Song for Dead Warriors, Shinju, Rodin, Dream Dances, Dancin with Gershwin, St. Louis Woman; (TV) The Tempest, 1981 (Emmy award 1981), Le Rossignol; (TV) Gardens of Stone, 1987; (operas) The Magic Flute, Le Rossignol, Help, Help, the Gobolinks, Turnadot; (special projects) Gown for Julie Andrews, Acad. Awards, 1997, Opening Ceremonies, Winter Olympic Games, Nagano, Japan, 1998. Recipient Asian Woman of Achievement award Asian Am. Profl. Women, 1983, Irene Sharaff Lifetime Achievement award TDF, 1995, Ruth Morley Designing Woman of Yr. award, 2001, Patricia Zipprodt award for innovative costume design, 2003, USITT Disting. Achievement in Costume DEsign, 2005. Democrat. Home: 250 W 82nd St New York NY 10024-5421 Office: c/o Peter S Diggins Assoc 133 W 71 #8B New York NY 10023

KIM, YUNJIM (YUN-JIN KIM), actress; b. Seoul, South Korea, Nov. 7, 1973; Tng., HS Performing Arts, NYC, British Am. Drama Acad.; BFA in Acting, Boston U. Film location mgr., 1996. Spokesperson Kanebo. Actor: (TV miniseries) Beautiful Vacation, 1996, (miniseries) Hunch; (TV series) Wedding Dress, 1998, With Love, 1999, Lost, 2004— (Outstanding Female TV Performance, Asian Excellence Awards, 2006, Outstanding Performance by an Ensemble in a Drama Series, Screen Actors Guild award, 2006); (films) Shiri, 1999, Gingko Bed 2, 2000, Rush!, 2001, Iron Palm, 2002, Ardor, 2002, Yesterday, 2002, Journal (Diary) of June, 2005; guest host The View, 2005, published (photobook) XOXO. Avocations: dance, trained fighter, Tae Kwon Do. Office: c/o ABC Inc 77 W 66th St New York NY 10023-6298

KIM, YUN-JIN See KIM, YUNJIM

KIMBALL, CATHERINE D., state supreme court justice; b. Alexandria, La., Feb. 7, 1945; d. William H. and Jane C. (Kelley) Dick; m. Clyde W. Kimball; 3 children. JD, La. State U., 1970. Law clerk US Dist. Court, Western Dist. La., 1970; spec. coun. La. Attorney Gen. Office, 1971—73; gen coun. La. Commn. Law Enforcement & Admin. Crim. Just., 1973—81; priv. law prac., 1975—82; asst. dist. atty. 18th Jud. Dist., 1978—82; judge La. Dist. Ct. (18th dist.), 1982—92; assoc. justice La. Supreme Ct., 1992—. Adjunct prof. law Tulane Law Sch. Summer Abroad Program; chair La. Supreme Ct. Case Mgmt. Info. Sys. Task Force, La. Supreme Ct. Tech. Com., Alternative Dispute Resolution Com.; ex officio mem. Complex Litigation Com.; chair Jud. Budgetary Control Bd.; mem. La. Data Base Commn.; bd. mem. Juvenile Justice Reform Act Implementation Commn.; mem. US Dept. Justice Nat. Integration Resource Ctr. Task Force; chair Integrated Criminal Justice Info. Sys. Policy Bd., Justice Funding Commn. Named one of Top 25 Women of Achievement, Baton Rouge Bus. Report, 1997; recipient Outstanding Jud. award, Victims & Citizens Against Crime, Inc., President's award, La. CASA Assn., 2002, Amb. for Children award., 2003. Mem.: Order of the Coif, Wex Malone Am. Inn of Ct., State-Federal Jud. Council, Am. Judicature Soc., La. State Bar Assn. Office: La Supreme Ct 400 Royal St New Orleans LA 70130*

KIMBALL, DOROTHY JEAN, retired foundation executive; b. Riceville, Miss., Dec. 27, 1927; d. Hiram William and Norma Lucille (Wilson) Cutrer; m. Peter Nolan Kimball, Nov. 30, 1946; children: Donna Jean, Brenda Gail. Student, La. State U., 1947-48. With E.B. Badger & Sons Constrn. Co., Baton Rouge, 1944-45; sec. State of La. Dept. Edn., Baton Rouge, 1945-49; sec., bkpr. Better Bus. Bur. of Baton Rouge, Inc., 1950-52; pvt. sec., nat. comdt., mgr. nat. hdqtrs. Marine Corps League, Baton Rouge, 1952-54; sec., bookkeeper Louis B. Rogers Constrn. Co., Baton Rouge, 1954; sec. to pres. Crawford Corp., Baton Rouge, 1955-64; sec-v.p. Crofton (Md.) Corp., 1964-74; sec.-treas. W.H. Crawford, Baton Rouge, 1975-89; found. exec. Crawford Found., Baton Rouge, 1990-96. Named Baton Rouge High Magnet Sch. Hall of Fame, 1999. Mem. Am. Legion Aux. (Post 38), City Club, Country Club of La., Rolls Royce Club (entertainment com. 1985-87). Republican. Baptist. Avocations: fishing, reading, dance. Home: 1418 Applewood Rd Baton Rouge LA 70808-5905

KIMBALL, JULIE ELLIS, small press publisher, humorist, writer; b. Providence, Sept. 30, 1952; d. James Robert and Arlene Barker McDonnell; m. Penn T. Kimball, July 27, 1985; 1 child, Laura J. BA, Brown U., 1974; MS, Columbia U. Grad. Sch. Journalism, 1975. Reporter, copy editor, asst. Sunday editor Daily Register, Red Bank, NJ, 1975—80; headline writer NY Daily News, NYC, 1989—90; pub. Westmeadow Press, Vineyard Haven, Mass., 2001—. Adj. prof. Columbia U. Grad. Sch. Journalism, NYC, 1986—88; media critic The Woman's Reporter, NJ, 1980—87. Author: 45 Minutes to America: Dispatches from Martha's Vineyard, 2001; editor: (poetry anthology) Vineyard Poets, 2003. D-Liberal. Congregationalist. Home: PO Box 4148 Vineyard Haven MA 02568 Office: Westmeadow Press PO Box 4338 Vineyard Haven MA 02568 Office Phone: 508-696-7497.

KIMBALL, VIRGINIA MARIE, theology studies educator, writer; b. L.A., June 28, 1940; d. John Donovan and Bethany June Strong; m. Dean Fiske Kimball, June 3, 1961; children: Cheryl Marie, Laurence Dean, Lucia Marie, Mary Louise, Thomas Justin, Maura Lynn, John Clement, Elizabeth Marie, Katrina Marie. Student, Coll. Notre Dame Md., 1958—59, student, 1960—61; MA, Andover Newton Theol. Sch., 1992; student, Weston Jesuit Sch. Theology, 1992—93; STL, U. Dayton, 2000, STD, 2003. Freelance writer Chelmsford (Mass.) Newsweekly, 1971—75; freelance writer, editor Westford (Mass.) Eagle, 1975—81; tech. writer Vision Machine Rsch., Cambridge, Mass., 1981—82; journalist, reporter, corr. Lowell (Mass.) Sun, 1982—96. Tchr. evening sch. U. Mass., Lowell, 1991—95; tchr. adult edn. Franciscan Ctr., Andover, 1993—95; tchr. grad. religious studies dept. U. Dayton, 1996; adj. tchr. religious studies Merrimack Coll., North Andover, 1995—. Appeared on (TV show) ABC's 20/20 spl. In Search of Mary, 2000, 2002; contbr. articles to profl. jours.; editor: Otros Dies, Memories of "Other Days".from Mexico in Revolution to a Life of Medicine in Texas, 1984, The Seven Sacraments of the Greek Orthodox CHurch, 1988, On the Sidelines: Decisions, Skills and Training in Youth Sport, 1988, The Loom's Price, 1992; author: (poetry collection) Westford.home blossoms for forever, 1996, (plays) At the Edge, 1980 (2d pl. Lowell Play Competition). Mem. Marian Libr. Nat. Spkrs. Bur., Dayton; mem. Transfiguration of Our Saviour Greek Orthodox Ch., Lowell, Mass. Mem.: Am. Acad. Religion, Women's Orthodox Ministries and Edn. Network, Ecumenical Soc. of Blessed Virgin Mary U.S.A. (v.p., spkrs. bur.), Mariological Soc. Am. (pres.), Orthodox Theol. Soc. Greek Orthodox. Office: Merrimack Coll Turnpike Rd North Andover MA Home: 4 Wayne Rd Westford MA 01886 Office Phone: 978-837-5000 ext. 4189.

KIMBER, KAREN BEECHER, law educator; b. New Brunswick, NJ, June 3, 1945; d. Stanley and Emma Beecher Kimber. BA, The College of NJ, 1967; MA, Hunter Coll., 2005. Tv prodn. asst. Dancer Fitzgerald Sample, NYC, 1967—72; tv advt. coord. McCaffrey & McCall, NYC, 1973—76, AC and Advt., NYC, 1976—77; mng. ptnr. Kimber Bus. Machines Co., North Brunswick, NJ, 1977—83; instr. John Jay Coll. of Criminal Justice, NYC, 2005—. Advt. mgr. NY State TESOL, 2001—02. Contbr. articles to profl. jours. and mags. Hospitality coord. St. Thomas Ch., NYC, 1996—. Mem.: Ch. Club N.Y., St. George's Soc., Order of St. John of Jerusalem. Republican. Episc. Avocation: travel. Home: 200 East 33d St Apt 29A New York NY 10016 Office: John Jay Coll of Criminal Justice 445 West 59th St Rn 1201N New York NY 10019

KIMBERLY, SUSAN ELIZABETH, municipal official, writer; b. Tracy, Minn., July 23, 1942; d. Mervin Glen and Blanche Pontius (Lees) Sylvester. BA, U. Minn., Mpls., 1965. Coun. mem. City of St. Paul, Minn., 1974—78; v.p. Piper Jaffray, Mpls., 1978—82; self-employed cons. St. Paul, 1983—86; asst. to mayor City of St. Paul, 1987—88, dep. mayor, chief staff, 1999—2002; commr. Metro Waste Control, St. Paul, 1985—91; exec. dir. Coalition for Cmty. Devel., St. Paul, 1992—97; team leader St. Paul Planning Dept., 1997—98; program adminstr. City of St. Paul, 2002—03; dep. state dir. US Senator Norm Coleman, 2003—04; dir. St. Paul Planning and Econ. Devel. Dept., 2005—06. Dir.and pres. Minn. Film Bd., Mpls., 1987-98, Regiouns Hosp., 2004—; dir. St. Paul Found., 1998-, Family Housing Fund, 1999-2005. Mem.: Como Women's Golf League (pres.). Republican. Episcopalian. Avocations: running, golf. Office: 697 Laurel Ave #4E Saint Paul MN 55104 Office Phone: 612-747-7588. E-mail: susan.kimberly@comcast.net.

KIMBLE, MELINDA LOUISE, environmental administrator; m. James R. Phippard; 4 stepchildren. B in Econs., M in Econs., U. Denver; MPA in Econs., Kennedy Sch. Fgn. svc. officer Dept. of State, Washington, 1971-89, sr. fgn. svc. officer, 1989-93, min. counselor, 1993-97, dep. asst. sec. Bur. Internat. Orgn. Affairs, 1993-97, prin. dep. asst. sec. Oceans and Internat. Environ. and Sci. Affairs, 1997-99; v.p. programs UN Found., Washington, 2000—03, sr. v.p. programs, 2003—. Recipient award Global Alliance for Women's Health, Internat. Honor award USDA, Disting. Honor award Dept. State, 2000. Office: 1225 Connecticut Ave NW 4th Fl Washington DC 20036-1815

KIMBRIEL-EGUIA, SUSAN, engineering planner, small business owner; b. San Francisco, July 22, 1949; d. Scott Slaughter and Kathleen (Edens) Smith; m. Floyd Thomas Kimbriel; children: John Thomas, Tammy Lee Petersen; m. Candelario Eguia, Feb. 14, 1991; 1 child, Daniel. Accredited Nat. Assn. Family Child Care. Engring. planner, sys. adminstr. various mainframe and PC based sys. Northrop Aircraft, Hawthorne, Calif., 1982-91; owner, operator Susie's Day Care/PreSchool, Palmdale, Calif., 1995—. Mem.: Antelope Valley Child Care Assn., Nat. Assn. for Family Child Care. Avocations: handcrafts, gardening, computer graphics.

KIMBROUGH, FRANCES HARRIETT, psychologist; b. Bryan, Tex., Sept. 10, 1947; d. Wallace M. and Frances H. (James) K. BA, Tex. A&M U., 1969, MEd, 1971, PhD, 1981. Lic. psychologist; lic. profl. counselor, health svc. provider, family mediator, real estate broker; cert. secondary edn. counselor, spl. edn. counselor, Spanish/English. tchr. Head sportswear dept. Lester's Clothing Store, Bryan, 1970-71; tchr. Spanish S.F. Austin High Sch., Bryan, 1971-75, psychologist, 1982-84; counselor Bryan High Sch., 1975-76; psychology intern Tex. A&M U., College Station, Tex., 1981-82; pvt. practice psychologist Bryan, 1985—. With Desert Hills Psychiat. Ctr., College Station, 1992—. Mem. adminstrv. bd. First United Meth. Ch., Bryan, 1993-94, tchr. Sunday Sch.; mem. Brazos County A&M Club, College Station. Named to Outstanding Young Women of Am. Mem. Am. Psychol. Assn., Tex. Psychol. Assn., Brazos Valley Psychol. Assn., Am. Counseling Assn., Am. Assn. Christian Counselors, Christian Counselors of Tex. Avocations: travel, Bible study, dancing, fgn. langs., photography. Home: 501 E 29th St Bryan TX 77803-4034 Office: 403 S Houston Ave Bryan TX 77803

KIMBROUGH, JANIE, library director; b. Binger, Okla. d. Ralph and Lorraine Tyrrell; m. Jimmy O. Kimbrough; children: Dianne, Mike, Kevin. Student, OCCC, Oklahoma City. Br. mgr. Blanchard (Okla.) Pub. Libr., Pioneer Libr. Sys., 1972—. Pres. Blanchard C. of C., 2002. Office: Pioneer Libr Sys PO Box 614 Blanchard OK 73010-0614

KIMBROUGH, LORELEI, retired elementary school educator, retired secondary school educator; b. Chgo. d. Paul and Lina (Higgs) Bobbett; m. James Kimbrough; children: Denise, Devi, Paul, Jeri Lynn, Sandra, Diane, James III. BS in Edn., Ill. State U., 1947; postgrad., DePaul U., Chgo. U. Cert. tchr., Ill. Tchr. of Latin and English, Greensboro (N.C.) Pub. Schs.; spl. edn. tchr. Chgo. State Hosp./Reed Zone Ctr., Chgo., Jewish Children's Bur., Chgo.; elem. tchr. Chgo. Bd. of Edn., Pasadena (Calif.) H.S.; English tchr. Malala H.S., Madang, 1993-94; tchr. jr. H.S. Cathedral Chapel Cath. Sch., 1995-96, Holy Trinity Sch., L.A., 1998-2000; ret., 2004. Tutor to fgn. students. Missionary worker L.A. Archdiocese, Papua New Guinea; vol. ARC, Solheim Luth. Home, Glendale Meml. Hosp. 4-year scholar State of Ill., Chgo. Musical Coll. award. Mem. Nat. Coun. Tchrs. of English, Ill. Coun. of Social Studies, Nat. Coun. Social Studies.

KIMBROUGH, NATALIE, history and language educator; b. Hamburg, Germany, Jan. 24, 1970; d. Christa Renate Scholl; m. William H. Kimbrough, Apr. 1, 1999. BA in Am. Studies, U. Hamburg, 1994, PhD in History, 2003; MA in US History, George Mason U., Fairfax, Va., 1998. Adj. instr. online U. Md. U. Coll., Adelphi, Md., 2003—; asst. prof. history CC Balt. County, 2005—. Instr. German lang. US Dept. State Fgn. Svc. Inst., Arlington, Va., 1999—2005, lead curriculum developer, distance edn., 2004—06; adj. instr. online Strayer U., Newington, Va., 2002—05; adj. prof. history George Mason U., 2003—04; faculty advisor History Club, 2005—06; organizing mem. UMOJA Com., 2006; presenter in field. Vol. Friends of the Vietnam Vets. Meml., Arlington, 1994—99; bd. mem. Ea. CC Social Sci. Assn, Va., 2006—. Recipient Quadrille Ball award, Inst. Internat. Edn., NY, 1997—98, Franklin award, US Dept. State Fgn. Svc. Inst., 2001, 2002, 2003, Hon. Faculty Svc. award, Student Life and Activities, 2005—06; German Academic Exch. Program scholar, German Govt. and Johns Hopkins U., 1994—95. Mem.: N.E. Popular Culture Assn., Popular Culture Assn./Am. Culture Assn., Orgn. Am. Historians, Am. History Assn, Am. Studies Assn., CC Humanities Assn., Oral History Assn. Avocations: poetry, reading, music, dance, walking. Office: CC Balt County 800 S Rolling Rd Baltimore MD 21228 Office Phone: 410-455-6916. Business E-Mail: nkimbrough@ccbcmd.edu.

KIMES, BEVERLY RAE, editor, writer; b. Aug. 17, 1939; d. Raymond Lionel and Grace Florence (Perrin) Kimes; m. James H. Cox, July 6, 1984. BS, U. Ill., 1961; MA in Journalism, Pa. State U., 1963. Dir. publicity Mateer Playhouse, Neff's Mill, Pa., 1962, Pavillion Theatre, University Park, Pa., 1963; asst. editor Automobile Quar. Publs., N.Y.C., Princeton, N.J., 1963-64, assoc. editor, 1965-66, mng. editor, 1967-74, editor, 1975-81, The Classic Car, 1981—. Mem. bd. corp. Mus. Transp., Brookline, Mass.; trustee Nat. Automotive History Collection, Detroit Pub. Libr., Saratoga (N.Y.) Automobile Mus., Rolls-Royce Found. Author: The Classic Tradition of the Lincoln Motor Car, 1968, The Cars that Henry Ford Built, 1978; author: (with R. M. Langworth) Oldsmobile: The First Seventy-Five Years, 1972; author: (with Rene Dreyfus) My Two Lives, 1983; author: (with Robert C. Ackerson) Chevrolet: A History from 1911, 1984, The Standard Catalog of American Cars 1805-1942, 1985, The Star and the Laurel: The Centennial History of Daimler, Mercedes and Benz, 1986, The Classic Era, 2001, Pioneers, Engineers and Scoundrels, 2005 (named Best Book 2005, 2005); editor: Great Cars and Grand Marques, 1976, Packard: History of the Motor Car and the Company, 1979, Automobile Quarterly's Handbook of Automotive Hobbies, 1981, The Classic Car: The Ultimate Book about the World's Grandest Automobiles, 1990. Recipient Thomas McKean trophy, 1983, 1985, 1986, 2001, 2005, Moto award, Nat. Assn. Automotive Journalists, 1984—86, 1997, Disting. Svc. citation, Automotive Hall of Fame, 1993, Best Mag. Article and Best of the Best, Internat. Automotive Media Assn., 2002, Lifetime Achievement award, 2005. Mem.: Soc. Automotive Historians (pres. 1987—89, Cugnot award 1978—79, 1983, Friend of Automotive History award 1985, Cugnot award 1985—86, Benz award 1994, 1998, Cugnot award 2001, 2002, Benz award 2003), Internat. Motor Press Assn.

KIMMEL, ELLEN BISHOP, psychologist, educator; b. Knoxville, Tenn., Sept. 16, 1939; d. Archer W. and Mary Ellen (Baker) Bishop; divorced; children: Elinor, Ann, Jean, Tracy. BA summa cum laude, U. Tenn., 1961; MA, U. Fla., 1962, PhD, 1965. Asst. prof., rsch. assoc. Ohio U., 1965-68; asst. prof. U. South Fla., Tampa, 1968-72, assoc. prof., dean Univ. Studies Coll., 1972-73, prof. psychology and ednl. psychology, 1975-95, chair, 1992-94, disting. prof., 1996—2003, prof. emerita, 2003—. Disting. vis. prof. psychology Simon Fraser U., Vancouver, B.C., Can., 1980-81; cons. numerous sch. systems, bus. and govt. Author books; contbr. articles to profl. jours., chpts. to books. Mem. Fla. Blue Ribbon Task Force on Juvenile Delinquency, 1976-77; mem. Fla. Gov.'s Commn. on Women, 1979-83; mem. adv. bd. Stop Rape, Good Govt., Inc.; bd. dirs. NCCJ. Recipient Outstanding Svc. award State of Fla., 1975, Outstanding Tchg. award U. South Fla., 1978, Career Achievement award U. Tenn., 1983, Professorial Excellence award Fla. State U. Sys., 1997, Disting. Sr. Scholar Spl. Commendation of Honor, AAUW, 2001; 17 rsch. grants. Fellow: APA (governing coun. 1982—85, pres. divsn. 1986—88, Disting. Leadership award 1993), Am. Assn. Applied and Preventive Psychology (bd. dirs. 1994—97, charter fellow, program chair 1991, Disting. Edn. award 1994), Am. Psychol. Soc. (charter fellow, conf. chair 1990); mem.: Southeastern Psychol. Assn. (pres. 1977—79), Assn. Women in Psychology (Disting. Publ. award 2000), Athena Soc., Omicron Delta Kappa, Delta Kappa Gamma, Sigma Xi. Democrat. Office: U South Fla EDU 162 Tampa FL 33620 Business E-Mail: kimmel@tempest.coedu.usf.edu.

KIMMONS, CINDY LOU, reading specialist; b. Marion, Ind., Nov. 29, 1949; d. Jack Howard and Elsin Janice (Tillett) k. BA, Purdue U., 1971, MS, 1976, postgrad., 1978, Penn State U., 1990. Cert. reading specialist, Ind., Pa. Tchr. School City of Hammond, Ind., 1971-80, Fox Chapel Area Sch. Dist., Pitts., 1980-87; reading specialist North Allegheny Sch. Dist., Pitts., 1987—. Adminstr. Langford Learning Ctr., Pitts., 1987-89. Fundraiser Am. Cancer Soc., Hammond, 1972-74. Named Hon. Hoosier scholar State of Ind., 1967-69. Mem. ASCD, ASCPA, DAV, Western Pa. Humane Soc., Western Pa. Tchrs. of English, North Allegheny Spl. Edn. Adv. Com., Delta Kappa Gamma. Avocations: paperweight collecting, reading (mysteries, science, psychology), raising and training dogs. Home: 4101 Circle Dr Allison Park PA 15101-3461 Office: Ingomar Middle Sch Ingomar Heights Rd Pittsburgh PA 15237 Office Phone: 412-348-1470 x1600.

KIMREY, KAREN GOSS, secondary school educator; b. Oxford, NC, July 22, 1956; d. Mildred Currin Goss; m. Clay Hansen Kimrey, June 30, 2004; m. Michael McLendon, May 11, 1985 (div.); 1 child, Tracy Lynn McLendon. B cum laude, Meredith Coll., Raleigh, 1991. Tech. advisor Nortel Networks, Research Triangle Park, NC, 1995—2001; tchr. Granville County Sch., Creedmoor, 2001—04; tchr. 8th grade Heritage Mid. Sch., Wake Forest, 2004—. Chair dept. social studies Heritage Mid. Sch., 2005—, team leader aviators track 4, 8th grade, 2005—. Recipient Employee Excellence award, Granville County Schs., 2001—03. Mem.: DAR (life), United Daus. Confederacy (life), Phi Alpha Theta (life). Conservative. Baptist. Avocations: motorcycling, needlecrafts, reading. Home: 7605 Bud Morris Road Wake Forest NC 27587 Office: Heritage Middle School 3400 Rogers Road Wake Forest NC 27587 Office Phone: 919-562-6204. Personal E-mail: karenkimrey@nc.rr.com. Business E-Mail: kkimrey@wcpss.net.

KIMURA, DOREEN, psychology professor, researcher; b. Winnipeg, Man., Can. 1 child, Charlotte Vanderwolf. BA, McGill U., Montreal, Que., Can., 1956, MA, 1957, PhD, 1961; LLD (hon.), Simon Fraser U., 1993, Queen's U., 1999. Lectr. Sir George Williams U. (now Concordia U.), Montreal, 1960-61; rsch. assoc. otol. rsch. lab. UCLA Med. Ctr., 1962-63; rsch. assoc. Coll. Medicine, McMaster U., Hamilton, Ont., 1964-67; assoc. prof. psychology U. Western Ont., London, 1967-74, prof., 1974-98, coord. clin. neuropsychology program, 1983-97. Supr. clin. neuropsychology Univ. Hosp., London, 1975-83; vis. prof. psychology Simon Fraser U., 1998—. Author: Neuromotor Mechanisms in Human Communication, 1993, Sex and Cognition, 1999, French, Japanese, Swedish, Spanish, Portuguese edits.; contbr. numerous articles to profl. jours. Recipient Outstanding Sci. Achievement award Can. Assn. Women in Sci., 1986, John Dewan award Ont. Mental Health Found., 1992; fellow Montreal Neurol. Inst., 1960-61, Geigy fellow Kantonsspital, Zürich, Switzerland, 1963-64, D.O. Hebb Disting. Contbn. award, Can. Soc. Brain, Behav. & Cogn. Sciences, 2005. Fellow Royal Soc. Can., Can. Psychol. Assn. (Disting. Contbns. to Sci. award 1985); mem. Soc. Acad. Freedom and Scholarship (founding pres. 1992-93, 98-2000). Office: Simon Fraser U Dept Psychology Burnaby BC Canada V5A 1S6 Office Phone: 604-291-3356. Business E-Mail: dkimura@sfu.ca.

KINARD, CYNTHIA COCHRAN, artist, writer; b. Columbia, S.C., Dec. 8, 1952; d. Thomas Louie and Eleanor (Bannister) Cochran; m. James Borden Kinard, Oct. 5, 1948. BA in Art with honors, BA in Modern Fgn. Langs. with honors, Western Carolina U., 1975; student, Angel Acad. Art, Florence, Italy, 2005. Exec. dir. Alleghany Arts Coun., Sparta, N.C., 1995—96. Watercolor portrait, Daydreams Contentment, 2005 (Strathmore Paper award, 2004, 2nd Pl., 2003), New Arrival (3rd Pl., 2001), Poppy (Signature Status, 2002), New Arrival (Patron award, 2002), Harvest Legacy (Merit award, 2001), Raymond by Firelight (Merchants award, 1997), Wayne and Waynette (Spl. Recognition, 2000), Harvest Legacy (Grand Champion, 1999), Daydreams (Grand Champion, 2004), Blake (Spl. Recognition, 2001), floral watercolor, The

Bloom (2nd Pl., 2001); author: (novel) Castleknob, 1st in a Series called The Kudzu Clan. Pres. Friends of the Libr., Sparta, 1996—97; pastor's wife Burningtown Bapt. Ch., Franklin, N.C., 2000—06; exec. dir. Alleghany Arts Coun., Sparta, 1996—97. Mem.: Associated Artists Winston-Salem, Inc. (assoc.), Am. Soc. Portrait Artists (assoc.), Watercolor Soc. N.C. (assoc.), Portrait Soc. Am. (assoc.), Nat. Watercolor Soc. (assoc.), Mo. Watercolor Soc. (assoc.), Am. Watercolor Soc. (assoc.), Am. Soc. Classical Realism (assoc.), So. Watercolor Soc. (assoc.), Nat. Mus. Women in the Arts (assoc.). Conservative. Christian. Avocations: travel, hiking, raising dogs, photography, writing. Home: 1480 Mica City Rd Franklin NC 28734 Personal E-mail: cckinard@earthlink.net.

KINBERG, JUDY, television producer, television director; b. Freeport, NY, Sept. 15, 1948; d. Jack H. and Rose M. (Schwartz) K. BA, Hofstra U., 1970. Prodn. asst. various programs including Camera Three CBS TV, N.Y.C., 1970-75; assoc. producer PBS-WNET/Dance in America, N.Y.C., 1975-76, producer, 1977—. NBC co-producer: He Makes Me Feel Like Dancin', 1984 (Acad. award, Emmy award, Chgo. Internat. Film Festival Silver Hugo, CINE Golden Eagle award, Christopher awards); prodr., dir. Who's Dancin' Now? (AFI L.A. Internat. Film Fest. Audience award, Best Documentary, Cine Golden Eagle award, Parents' Choice award), 1999; producer: PBS Dance in America: The Feld Ballet, 1979, The Green Table (with Joffrey Ballet), 1982, The Magic Flute (with N.Y.C. Ballet), 1983, San Francisco Ballet: A Song for Dead Warriors, 1984, A Choreographer's Notebook: Stravinsky Piano Ballets by Peter Martins, 1984, Balanchine, Parts I and II, 1984 (27th Ann. Internat. Film and TV awards of N.Y., gold medal Chgo. Internat. Film Festival Silver Plaque Monitor award, Emmy nomination), San Francisco Ballet in Cinderella, 1985 (Internat. Film and TV Festival of N.Y. gold medal, CINE Golden Eagle award, Parent's Choice award), Mark Morris, 1986 (CINE Golden Eagle award, Am. Film & Video Festival Red Ribbon award), Choreography by Jerome Robbins, 1986 (Chgo. Internat. Film Festival Silver Hugo, CINE Golden Eagle award), Dance Theatre of Harlem in A Streetcar Named Desire, 1986 (Chgo. Internat. Film Festival Silver Hugo), In Memory of.A Ballet by Jerome Robbins, 1987 (Chgo. Internat. Film Festival Silver Hugo, CINE Golden Eagle award), Agnes, the Indomitable de Mille, 1987 (Emmy award, Chgo. Internat. Film Festival Silver Hugo, CINE Golden Eagle award), Paul Taylor: Roses and Last Look, 1988, Balanchine and Cunningham: An Evening at Am. Ballet Theatre, 1988, La Sylphide (with the Pa./Milw. Ballet), 1989, A Night at The Joffrey, 1989, (Emmy nomination, Gold medal Internat. Film and TV Festival of N.Y., Best Video Creation IMZ Video Danse Awards, Gold Hugo award Chgo. Internat. Film Festival), The Search for Nijinsky's Rite of Spring, 1989 (producer/dir., Best Documentary IMZ Video Danse Awards, Internat. Film & TV Festival N.Y. Bronze medal), Baryshnikov Dances Balanchine, 1989 (Emmy nomination, finalist Internat. Film and TV Festival of N.Y.), Paul Taylor's Speaking in Tongues (Gold medal Internat. Film and TV Festival N.Y. Gold Plaque award Chgo. Internat. Film Festival), 1991, The Hard Nut with Mark Morris Dance Group, 1992 (Gold medal Internat. Film and TV Festival of N.Y., Emmy nomination), Balanchine Celebration, 1993 (with N.Y.C. City Ballet, Emmy nomination), The Wrecker's Ball, Three Dances by Paul Taylor, 1996 (Rose d'or de Montreaux Festival finalist); producer, dir. Bob Fosse/Steam Heat, 1990 (Emmy award, Ohio State award, Chgo. Film Festival Silver Plaque, Festival Internat. du Film Sur L'Art, Festival Rose d'Or, Montreux), A Tudor Evening with Am. Ballet Theatre, 1990, Balanchine in Am. with the N.Y.C. Ballet, 1990, Ballerinas: Dances by Peter Martins, 1991, A Renaissance Revisited, 1996 (N.Y. Festivals finalist award), (documentary) Variety and Virtuosity/American Ballet Theatre Now, 1998 (Chris award Columbus Internat. Film & Video Festival), Am. Ballet Theatre in Le Corsaire, (Emmy award 2000)From Broadway: Fosse, 2001 (CINE Golden Eagle award); producer PBS Great Performances: Out of Our Fathers' House, 1978; co-producer PBS Dance in America: Pilobolus Dance Theatre, 1977, Trailblazers of Modern Dance, 1977 (1st pl. 9th Ann. Dance Film and Video Festival), San Francisco Ballet: Romeo and Juliet, 1978, Choreography by Balanchine, Part III, 1978 (Chgo. Internat. Film Festival Silver Plaque, Emmy nomination), Choreography by Balanchine, Part IV, 1979 (Emmy award), The Martha Graham Dance Company: Clytemnestra, 1979 (Chgo. Internat. Film Festival Golden Hugo), Two Duets with Choreography by Jerome Robbins and Peter Martins, 1980, Nureyev and the Joffrey Ballet: In Tribute to Nijinsky, 1981 (Peabody award 1981, Emmy nomination), The Tempest: Live with the San Francisco Ballet, 1981, L'Enfant et Les Sortileges, 1981, Paul Taylor: Three Modern Classics, 1982, Paul Taylor: Two Landmark Dances, 1982, Bournonville Dances (with mems. ofN.Y.C. Ballet), 1982; co-producer PBS Theater in America: When Hell Freezes Over I'll Skate, 1979; prodr., dir. PBS Great Performances: The World of Jim Henson, 1994 (Parents Choice honor, 1995, Emmy award), Born to Be Wild: The Leading Men of American Ballet Theatre, 2002 (Festival Rose d'Or Montreux, N.Y. Festivals Gold World medal, Parents' Choice Silver Honor, Berkeley Video and Film Grand Festival Winner, Chris Statuette 2003, Ojai Film Festival Jury award), 22nd Festival Internat. Du Film Sur L'Art, 4th Constellation Change Screen Dance Festival, London, (with Am. Ballet Theatre) The Dream, 2004, Swan Lake (with Am. Ballet Theatre); prodr. PBS Stage on Screen: The Man Who Came to Dinner, 2000, The Women, 2002. Mem. Dirs.' Guild Am., Acad. TV Arts and Scis. Office: Thirteen/WNET/Dance In America 450 W 33rd St Fl 6 New York NY 10001-2603

KINCAID, JUDITH WELLS, electronics company executive; b. Tampa, Fla., July 1, 1944; d. George Redfield and Louise Wells (Brodt) K.; one child: Jennifer Wells Maben. A, Stanford U., 1966, MS in Indsl. Engring., 1978. Sci. programmer med. rsch. Stanford (Calif.) U., 1972-77; info. systems mgr. Hewlett Packard Co., Palo Alto, Calif., 1978-2001, mgr. strategic systems, 1985-91; direct mktg. mgr. Hewlett Packard Corp., Palo Alto, Calif., 1991-95, dir. customer relationship mgmt., 1995-2001; pres. JK Assocs., Palo Alto, Calif., 2001—. Author: Customer Relationship Management: Getting It Right, 2003. Bd. dirs. Ecumenical Hunger Program. Mem. Inst. Indsl. Engrs., Dir. Mktg. Assn. (privacy program chair 1998—, bus. to bus. ops. coun. 1998-2005), Ecumenical Hunger Program (bd. dirs., treas. 2004-05, bd. chair 2005). Office: JK Assocs LLC PO Box 61117 Palo Alto CA 94306 Business E-Mail: jkincaid@jk-associates.com.

KINCAID, KAREN OWERS, nursing educator; d. Harold Wesley and Katherine Ophelia Owers; children: Angela Marie Fontenot, Phillip Todd. BSN, U. Tex., San Antonio, Tex., 1971, MSN, 1974; PhD in Health Scis., Tex. Woman's U., Denton, Tex., 2002. RN Tex., 1972, Alaska, 2004; cert. health edn. specialist The Nat. Commn. Health Ed Credentialing, Inc., 2002. Asst. prof. Auburn U., Montgomery, Ala., 2002—03; asst. prof. Sch. Nursing U. Alaska, Anchorage, 2004—. Vice chmn. adv. coun. Older Alaskans Program Salvation Army, Anchorage, 2004—06. Decorated Chief Nurse Officer award USPHS; named Outstanding Pub. Health Nurse, Tex. Nurse's Assn., 1986. Mem.: Commisssioned Officers Assn. (assoc.; chmn. by-laws com. 1992—94), Sigma Theta Tau (life; chmn. nominations com. 2004). Avocations: travel, reading. Office: Univ of Alaska Anchorage Sch of Nrsing 3211 Providence Drive Anchorage AK 99508 Office Phone: 907-786-4021. Business E-Mail: afkdk@uaa.alaska.edu.

KINCAID, SARAH SANDERS, mathematics educator; b. Booneville, Miss., Mar. 7, 1949; d. Joseph Daniel Sanders, I and Wanda Faye Sanders; m. Terry Lee Kincaid, Aug. 29, 1969; children: Meridith Leigh Sims, Jonathan David. MA in Edn., Austin Peay State U., Clarksville, Tenn., 1993. Math. tchr. Clarksville-Montgomery County Sch. Sys., Tenn., 1988—. Adj. faculty Austin Peay State U., Clarksville, Tenn., 1997—98. Nursery supr. Madison St. Ch. of Christ, Clarksville, 1985—2006. Named Dist. Classroom Tchr., Northwest H.S., 2000. Mem.: Clarksville-Montgomery County Educators Assn. Mem. Church Of Christ. Home: 1311 Willow Bend Drive Clarksville TN 37043 Office: Northwest High Sch 800 Lafayette Rd Clarksville TN 37042 Office Phone: 931-648-5675.

KINCH, JANET CAROLYN BROZIC, English and German language and literature educator, academic administrator; b. Cleve., Mar. 6, 1954; d. H. Joseph Brozic and Eleanor Ruth Peters; m. Timothy Lee Kinch, July 30, 1983. AB in English, Kenyon Coll., 1976; postgrad., U. Salzburg, Austria, 1976-79, 80-81; MA in English, Bowling Green State U., 1981, MA in German, 1982, PhD in English, 1986. Counselor Am. Inst. Fgn. Study, Salzburg, Austria, 1975, 76, acting dean Vienna, 1977; Fulbright tchg. asst. Austrian Fulbright Commn., St. Johann im Pongau, Pongau, Austria, 1977-79; tchg. fellow Bowling Green (Ohio) State U., 1981-86, instr. English, 1986-87, asst. prof., 1987-88; from asst. to assoc. prof. Edinboro U. of Pa., 1988—, dir. univ. honors program, 1998—2001, exec. dir. Pa.-Canadian Studies Consortium, 2000—. Founder, coord. HIV/AIDS awareness and edn. Edinboro U. of Pa., 1993—; rep., charter mem. The Pa. Canadian Studies Consortium, 1993—, dir. 2000—; advisor English and Humanities Club, 1993—, Alpha Chi Nat. Honor Soc., Pa. Zeta Chpt., 1998—; founder, advisor Sigma Tau Delta Internat. English Honors Soc., Alpha Eta Chi Chpt., 1999—; conf. coord. the Chuck Palahniak Internat. Acad. Conf., U. Pa., 2001, 03. Author: Mark Twain's German Critical Reception, 1989; contbr.: Mark Twain Encyclopedia, 1993. Mem. Erie (Pa.) AIDS Network, 1993—; mem. Univ. Senate, sec., 1995-98, mem. exec. com., 1995—2000. Univ. fellow Bowling Green State U., 1984-85. Mem. Mark Twain Cir., Can. Studies Consortium of Pa. (exec. dir., exec. mem., steering com. 1997—), Sigma Tau Delta, Phi Sigma Iota, Alpha Sigma Lambda. Avocations: community service, travel, indoor and outdoor gardening, interior design, collecting Pacific Northwest native art. Office: Edinboro U of Pa 114 Centennial Hall Edinboro PA 16444-0001

KIND, ROSALIND WEINTRAUB, special education educator; b. Phila., Oct. 22, 1948; d. Morris Leonard and Freda Weintraub; m. Richard Rogers Kind, Apr. 14, 1979; children: Michael Norman, Jeffrey Richard. BS, Trenton State Coll., Ewing, N.J., 1971; MEd, Trenton State Coll., 1973, MA, 1975, EdS, 1977. Cert. Teacher of Handicapped N.J., 1971. Tchr. of handicapped Mt. Holly Sch. Dist., NJ, 1971—75; ednl. specialist Burlington County Spl. Svcs. Sch., Mt. Holly, 1976—. Democrat-Npl. Jewish. Avocations: golf, racquetball, travel, dance. Office: Burlington County Spl Svcs Sch Woodland Rd 20 Pioneer Blvd Mount Holly NJ 08060 Office Phone: 609-261-5600 ext. 2264. Office Fax: 609-949-7419.

KIND, SUSAN J., fundraiser; BA, MA, SUNY, New Paltz. Former sr. dir. for develop. NYU Tisch Sch. of Arts; former v.p. for develop. Montefiore Med. Ctr., Continuum Health Partners, Inc.; vice dean for develop. NYU Sch. of Medicine, NYC, 2005—; v.p. for develop. NYU Hospitals Ctr., NYC, 2005—. Bd. mem. Women in Develop., NYC. Office: NYU Med Ctr and Sch of Medicine 550 First Ave New York NY 10016

KINDALL, SUSAN CAROL, music educator; b. Greenville, S.C., Feb. 26, 1967; d. Keith Lavern and Ella Joyce (Clayton) K. BMus, Bob Jones U., 1988, MMus, 1990; D of Musical Arts, U. Okla., 1994. Mem. faculty Bob Jones U., Greenville, 1988-90; mem. music faculty U. Okla., Norman, 1990-94; instr. music Ouachita Bapt. U., Arkadelphia, Ark., 1994-96; prof. music Bob Jones U., 1998—. Coord. Ouachita Bapt. U., 1995; Am. music festival and piano competition coord., Richard Cumming Concert and lectr. series U. Okla., 1993; dir Greenville Concert Piano Series. Mem. Music Tchrs. Nat. Assn., Ark. State Music Tchrs. Assn., S.C. Music Tchrs. Assn., Greenville Music Tchrs. Club, Arkadelphia Philharm. Club. Crescent music Club. Avocations: running, backpacking, hiking. Home: 2 Capewood Ct Greenville SC 29609-3910

KINDBERG, SHIRLEY JANE, pediatrician; b. Newark, Feb. 4, 1936; d. John Bertil and Mabel Jacoba (deJonge) Kindberg; m. Charles Dale Coln, May 12, 1962; children: Sara Goldstein, Eric Coln, Lois Thompson, Ruth Skipper, Mary Mielenz. BS, Wheaton Coll., 1957; MD, Baylor U., 1961. Intern Tex. Children's Hosp., Houston, 1961-62; resident Children's Med. Ctr., Dallas, 1962-63; fellow in pediat. pulmonary disease U. Tex. S.W. Med. Sch., Dallas, 1963-64, fellow in pediat. infectious disease, 1965-67; pvt. practice gen. pediat. Dallas, 1969-81; pvt. practice newborns, 1981—2004. Active Park Cities Presbyn. Ch.; mem. Dallas Symphony Assn. Republican. Presbyterian. Avocations: cooking, travel, music, exercise. Personal E-mail: colnoma@sbcglobal.net.

KINDER, SUZANNE FONAY WEMPLE, retired historian, retired educator; b. Veszprem, Hungary, Aug. 1, 1927; arrived in U.S., 1948; d. Ernest and Magda Mihalyfy F., Countess Ernest Szechenyi; m. George Barr Wemple, June 17, 1957 (dec. Apr. 1988); m. Gordon T. Kinder, May 26, 1990. B, English Sisters, Budapest, Hungary, 1945, U. Calif., Berkeley, 1953; MLS, Columbia U., 1955, PhD, 1967. Ref. asst. Columbia U., 1955—58; instr. Stern Coll. Women, N.Y.C., 1962-63; asst. prof. Tchrs. Coll., Columbia U., N.Y.C., 1964-66; from asst. prof. to prof. Barnard Coll., Columbia U., N.Y.C., 1966-92, ret., 1992. Author: Atto of Vercelli: Church, State and Christian Society, 1979, Women in Frankish Society, 1981, 1983 (Berkshire prize, 1981); co-editor: Women in Medieval Society, 1985; contbr. chapters to books, articles to ency. and profl. jours. Recipient grant NEH, 1975, 80, 81-85, Spivack summer grant Barnard Coll., 1970, 81, Fulbright grant, 1982. Mem.: AAUP. Home: 102 Moorings Park Dr Apt E104 Naples FL 34105-2142 Personal E-mail: gtkinder@aol.com.

KINDL, PATRICE, writer; b. Schenectady, N.Y., Oct. 16, 1951; d. Fred Henry and Catherine Mary (Quinlan) K.; m. Paul Fredrick Roediger, Oct. 16, 1976; 1 child, Alexander. Diploma, Niskayuna H.S., 1969. Author: (book) Owl In Love, 1993 (Notable Book award ALA 1994, Best Book for Reluctant Readers, Golden Kite award Honor Book), The Woman in the Wall, 1997, The Woman in the Wall, 1997. Foster parent Helping Hands Simian Aides to the Disabled, Boston, 1990-94; coach Olympics of the Mind, Ballston Lake, N.Y., 1985-88; counsellor Rape Crisis Svc., Schenectady, 1981-84. Democrat. Office: care Houghton Mifflin Co 222 Berkeley St Boston MA 02116-3748 also: RR 2 Box 1C Middleburgh NY 12122-9601

KING, ALISON, lawyer; BA, Wheaton Coll., 1987; JD, Tulane U., 1996. Bar: NY 1997. Counsel corp. and fin. dept. Kaye Scholer LLP, NYC. Office: Kaye Scholer LLP 425 Park Ave New York NY 10022 Office Phone: 212-736-7037. E-mail: aking@kayescholer.com.

KING, ALMA JEAN, retired physical education educator, healthcare educator; b. Hamilton, Ohio, Feb. 28, 1939; d. William Lawrence and Esther Mary (Smith) K. BS in Edn., Miami U., Oxford, Ohio, 1961; MEd, Bowling Green State U., 1963; postgrad., Fla. Atlantic U., 1969, '92, Nova U., Ft. Lauderdale, Fla., 1979. Cert. elem. and secondry tchr., Ohio, all levels incl. coll., Fla. Tchr. health, physical edn. Rogers Middle Sch., Broward County Bd. Pub. Instrn., 1963-64; assoc. prof. health, phys edn., recreation, dance Broward C.C., Fort Lauderdale, Fla., 1964-94; ret., 1994. Dir. Intramurals and Extramurals Boward C.C., Fort Lauderdale, Fla., 1964-67, chair person Women's Affairs, 1978, health and safety com., 1975, faculty evaluation com. 1980-85, mem. faculty ins. benefits com. 1993-94. Sponsor Broward County Fire Fighters, Police; active mem. Police Benevolent Assn.; Historical Soc. Grantee Broward C.C. Staff Devel. Fund, 1988. Mem. AAHPERD, NEA, Fla. Edn. Assn., Fla. Assn for Health, Physical Edn., Recreation and Dance, Am. Assn. for Advancement of Health Edn., United Faculty of Fla., Fla. Assn. of C.C., Order of the Eastern Star (past Worthy Matron), Order of Shrine. Avocations: concerts, theater, art, historic museums, recreational activities. Home: 4310 Buchanan St Hollywood FL 33021-5917

KING, AMANDA ARNETTE, elementary school educator; b. Conway, S.C., Feb. 6, 1951; d. James Hilton and Maisie (Dunn) Arnette; m. Roachel Dent King III, Dec. 31, 1972; children: Roachel Dent IV, Amanda Catherine. AB, Coker Coll., Hartsville, S.C., 1973; MEd of Early Childhood Edn., U. S.C., Columbia, 1997. Tchr. Darlington (S.C.) County Sch. Dist., 1972-75, 78-81, James F. Byrnes Acad., Florence, S.C., 1981-88, Darlington County Sch. Dist., 1988—. Part-time adult edn. instr. Rosenwald/St. David's Elem. Sch., SC, 1992—. Mem. Society Hill (S.C.) Rescue Squad, Woodmen of World, Palmetto Project; bd. dirs., vice chmn. Darlington County Libr. Sys.; bd. dirs. Mental Health Assn. Darlington County, First Steps Bd., Darlington County; chmn. bd. dirs. Darlington County Dept. Disabilities and Spl. Needs; dir. 5th-6th grade Sunday Sch.; mem. Clemson Ext. Adv. Coun. Recipient Golden Apple award, 1993-94, Tchr. of the Yr. award James F. Byrnes Acad., 1988, Rosenwald/St. David's Elem. Sch., 1990, 93, 97; named Star Tchr. Time Warner Cable, 1998, S.C. Part-Time Adult Edn. Tchr. of Yr., 2001. Mem. Nat. Coun. Tchrs. English, S.C. Coun. Tchrs. Math., Internat. Reading Assn., Palmetto State Tchrs. Assn. (mem. com., dist. rep., pres. Darlington County Sch. Dist.), Coker Coll. Alumni Assn. (2d v.p. 1988—, Outstanding Alumni com. 1989-90, 93—), Pilot Club (Hartsville, S.C.), Alpha Delta Kappa. Baptist. Home: PO Box 58 Society Hill SC 29593-0058 E-mail: amyteachus@yahoo.com.

KING, AMANDA WILHITE, science educator; b. Birmingham, Ala. d. Gerry Wiley and Bonnie Morrow Wilhite; m. Brett Alexander King, Mar. 9, 1991; children: Victoria Lynn, Alexandria Marie. AS, Wallace State CC, Hanceville, Ala., 1987; BS in Secondary Edn. Sci., U. Ala., Tuscaloosa, Ala., 1990; MA in Secondary Edn. Sci., U. Ala., 1996. Sci. tchr. Jonesboro HS, Jonesboro, Ga., 1990—91, Osborne HS, Marietta, Ga., 1991—93, Simmons Mid. Sch., Hoover, Ala., 1993—99, Muscle Shoals Mid. Sch., Muscle Shoals, Ala., 1999—. Pres. Friends Muscle Shoals Pub. Libr., Muscle Shoals, 2005—; sponsor Scholar's Bowl Team, Muscle Shoals, 2005—, Sci. Olympad Team, 2004—. Grantee Youth Svcs. grant, State Farm, 2004. Mem.: NSTA, Ala. Sci. Tchrs. Assn. Republican. Baptist. Office: Muscle Shoals Mid Sch 100 Trojan Dr Muscle Shoals AL 35661

KING, AMY CATHRYNE PATTERSON, retired mathamatics educator, researcher; b. Douglas, Wyo., Dec. 30, 1928; d. John Francis and Mabel Eloise (Wear) Patterson; m. Don R. King, Aug. 8, 1949 (dec. 1985). BS, U. Mo., 1949; MA, U. Wichita, 1960; PhD, U. Ky., 1970. Tchr. Goddard (Kans.) Pub. Schs., 1956-58, U. Wichita, 1960-62; asst. instr. U. Kans., Lawrence, 1962-65; instr. Washburn U., Topeka, 1966-67; teaching asst. U. Ky., Lexington, 1967-70; prof. math. Ea. Ky. U., Richmond, 1970-98; Found. prof. emeritus, 1998—. Presenter in field. Author: instr.'s manual for College Algebra, 1981; (with Cecil B. Read) Pathways to Probability, 1963; contbr. (with others) articles to profl. jours. Departmental rep. for United Way, 1983; pres. Cokesbury Sunday Sch., Centenary United Meth. Ch., 1995-96, tchr. 3-yr.-olds. Recipient Award in Teaching, Ea. Ky. U., Richmond, 1982, Ea. Ky. U. Found. Professorship, 1993. Mem. Am. Math. Soc., Math. Assn. Am. (mem. various coms., 1st award for Disting. Coll. or Univ. Teaching 1992), Nat. Coun. Tchrs. Math., Assn. for Women of Math., Ky. Coun. Tchrs. Math. (Maths. Edn. Svc. and Achievement award 1998), Women in Math. Edn., Ky. Acad. Computer Users' Group, AAUP (treas. local chpt. 1984-86), Pi Mu Epsilon, Kappa Mu Epsilon, Pi Lambda Theta, Sigma Delta Pi, Delta Kappa Gamma (pres. Omicron chpt., 1994-96), Sigma Xi. Phi Kappa Phi. Methodist. E-mail: amyking@infionline.net.

KING, BARBARA JEAN, nurse; b. Cape Girardeau, Mo., June 28, 1941; d. Otto Samuel and Goldie Elizabeth (Clover) Fowler; m. Charles Basil King, Jr., Sept. 4, 1972; children: Otto Samuel, Christopher Lee. Student, Weatherford Jr. Coll., 1965; nursing degree, John Peter Smith Hosp. Sch. Profl. Nursing, 1969. RN, Tex. Head nurse pediat. and isolation County Hosp.; also ICU and CCU, Small Gen. Hosp., Ft. Worth, 1969-72; dir. nursing svc. Jarvis Hts. Nursing Ctr., Ft. Worth, 1976-77; dir. nursing svcs. Ft. Worth Rehab. Farm, 1978-80; staff nurse, asst. supr. shift Decatur (Tex.) Cmty. Hosp., 1983-85; staff nurse and supr. Burdgeport Hosp., Tex., 1986—; mgr., CEO, King Cons. Group for Homecare Mgmt., 2003—. Clin. supr., patient care coord. Hospice of Tejas; instr. vocat. nursing Cooke County Coll., Gainesville, Tex., 1981; clin. care supr. home health dept. Faith Community Hosp., 1992, assoc. dir. 1993—; patient care coord. Family Svcs. Home Health Svcs., Inc., 1994, adminstrn. for choice Choice Home Health Svcs., Inc., 1995, Nocona Gen. Hosp. Home Health, 1998, asst. dir., 1999; cons. convalescent centers and hosps. Chmn. child care com. Women of Moose, 1997—; ch. organist Bethel Bapt. Ch., assoc. pianist, 1996. Served with M.C., USN, 1962-65. Mem. Dirs. of Nursing Homes Assn. Tarrant County (v.p.). Democrat. Home: 106 S Trappier St Alvord TX 76225-6015

KING, BARBARA LEWIS, minister, lecturer; b. Houston, Aug. 26, 1930; d. Lee Andrew Lewis and Mildred Marie (Jackson) Shackelford; m. Moses King, Sept. 8, 1966 (div. Sept. 1970); 1 child, Michael. BA, Tex. So. U., 1955; MSW, Atlanta U., 1957, postgrad.; DDiv, Bethune Cookman Coll., 1988. Exec. dir. South Chgo. Community Svc. Assn., Chgo., 1966-68; dean community rels. Malcolm X campus Chgo. City Coll., 1967-69; instr. Sch. Social Work Atlanta U., 1970-71; dir. South Cen. Community Mental Health Ctr., 1971-73; dean students Spelman Coll., 1973-74; founder, minister Hillside Internat. Truth Ctr., 1971—; founder, pres. Barbara King Sch. Ministry, 1977—. Host Sta. WVEU, Atlanta, 1987—, WXIA, Atlanta, 1980-85, Channel 8, Atlanta, 1980-85. Author: What is a Miracle?, 1973, Do I Need a Flood, 1983, Transform Your Little Book, 1989. Mem. nat. rules com. Dem. Nat. Conv., Ga., 1984; mem. State Com. on the Life and History of Black Georgians, Atlanta, 1986, Ethics Bd. Met. Atlanta, 1986, Joint Bd. Family Practice, Atlanta, 1986. Mem. Am. Mgmt. Assn., Internat. New Thought Alliance (v.p. 1972), Christian Coun. Met. Atlanta (trustee 1985), Internat. Congress Women Ministries (internat. pres. 1975), Acad. Cert. Social Workers, Nat. Assn. Social Workers, Women's of C. in Atlanta, Zeta Phi Beta. Office: Hillside Internat Truth Ctr 2450 Cascade Rd SW Atlanta GA 30311-3226

KING, BARBARA SACKHEIM, travel company executive; b. Chgo., Apr. 9, 1948; d. Norman Robert and Pauline Huft Sackheim; m. Michael Raymond King, May 24, 1998; children: Lauren Marissa, David Elliott Weiner, Joshua Neal. BS, Northwestern U., 1970. Realtor Prudential Henry and Burrows, Overland Park, Kans., 1990—92; pres. Gt. Getaways, Leawood, 1992—. Life mem. Nat. Coun. Jewish Women, Kansas City, Mo.; v.p. Fine Arts Guild William Jewell, Liberty, Mo., 1986—87; mem. March Dimes, 1992—93. Mem.: Ctrl. Exch., Internat. Coun. Tourism Ptnrs., Airline Reporting Corp., Internat. Airline Travel Assn., Cruise Line Internat. Assn., Am. Soc. Travel Agts., Virtuoso, Pi Lambda Theta. Home: 4416 W 150th St Leawood KS 66224 Office: Great Getaways 4600 College Blvd Ste 103 Leawood KS 66211 Office Phone: 913-338-2244.

KING, BILLIE JEAN MOFFITT, retired professional tennis player; b. Long Beach, Calif., Nov. 22, 1943; d. Willard J. and Betty Moffitt; m. Larry King (div. 1987), Sept. 17, 1965. Student, Calif. State U. at Los Angeles, 1961-64; PhD (hon.), Calif. State U., 1997; degree (hon.), Trinity Coll., 1998; PhD (hon.), U. Pa, 1999, U. Mass., 2000. Amateur tennis player, 1958-67; profl., 1968—84; mem. Tennis Challenge Series, 1977, 78; dir., ofcl. spokesperson World Team Tennis, Chgo., 1985—; commentator, analyst Wimbeldon and other tennis events HBO, N.Y.C. Winner, Singles champion tournaments include: Wimbledon, 1966-68, 72, 73,75, U.S. Open, 1967, 71, 72, 74, Australian Open, 1968, French Open, 1972; Doubles champion Wimbledon, 1961, 62, 65, 67, 68, 70-73, 79 U.S. Open, 1965, 67, 74, 80, French Open, 1972; mixed doubles champion Wimbledon, 1967, 71, 73, 74, U.S. Open, 1967, 71, 73, French, 1967, 70, Australian, 1968; winner 29 Virginia Slims singles titles, 1970-77, 4 Colgate titles, 1977, Fedn. Cup, 1963-67, 76-79, Wightman Cup, 1961-67, 70, 77, 78; World Tennis Team All-Star, 3 times; host Colgate women's sports TV spl. The Lady is a Champ, 1975; sports commentator ABC-TV, 1975-78;founder Women's Tennis Assn., 1973, pres., 1973-75, 80-81; founder, Women's Sports Found, 1974, Profl. World TeamTennis, 1974, World TeamTennis Profl. League, 1981, World TeamTennis Recreational League, 1985, World TeamTennis Charities, 1987; co-founder, pub. WomenSports mag., 1974, Kingdom, Inc., San Mateo, Calif.; founding mem., Women's Sports Legends; first woman commr. (Team Tennis League) profl. sports history, 1984; TV commentator HBO-Sports Wimbeldon coverage; capt. Fed. Cup for USA, 1995; cons. Virginia Slims World Championship Series;mem., Planned Parenthood, US Profl. Tennis Assn., US Profl. Tennis Registry, Chgo. Area Women's Sports Assn., advisory bd, Areta Sports award nomination com., Jim Thorpe Pro sports nomination com. award, sports advisory bd. for the Vic Braden Neurology Rsch. Inst., USTA Player Devel. Com.; bd. dirs. Challenger Ctr., Elton John AIDS Found., S.A.F.E., Nat. AIDS Fund, Altria Group, Inc., Women's Sports Found.; amb. Adventures in Movement Charity; coach Fed. Cup Women's Tennis Team, 1995-96, 98-2003, USA Olympic Women's Tennis Team, 1996, 2000; nat. spokesperson Literary Vols. Am.; tennis tchr. to profls. Author:

Tennis to Win, 1970, (with Kim Chapin) Billie Jean, 1974, (with Greg Hoffman) Tennis Love: A Parent's Guide to the Sport, 1978, (with Frank Deford) The Autobiography of Billie Jean King, 1982 (with Cynthia Starr) We Have Come a Long Way, The Story of Women's Tennis, 1988. Named Sportsperson of Yr., 1972, Top 40 Athletes, 1994, Sports Illustrated; Woman Athlete of Yr., A.P., 1967, 73, Top Woman Athlete of Yr., 1972; Woman of Yr., Time mag., 1976, One of 10 Most Powerful Women in Am., Harper's Bazaar, 1977, One of 25 Most Influential Women in Am., World Almanac, 1977, One of 100 Most Important Ams. of 20th Century, Life mag., 1990, woman of the Year, Women in Sports & Events, 2002; named to Internat. Tennis Hall of Fame, 1987, Nat. Women's Hall of Fame, 1990, Chgo. Gay and Lesbian Hall of Fame, 1999, Court of Champions, USTA Nat. Tennis Ctr., 2003; WTA Hon. Membership award, 1986, Female Teaching Pro of the Decade, 1994, Lifetime Achievement award, March of Dimes, 1994, Flo Hymnal award, Women's Sports Found, 1997, "Player Who Makes a Difference award", 1997, US Olympic Com. Nat. Tennis Coach of the Year award, 1997, Nat. Women's Law Ctr. honoree, 1997, Elizabeth Blackwill award for Courage, William & Hobart Smith Colleges, 1998, Arthur Ashe award for Courage, ESPN, 1999, Community Role Model award, LA Gay & Lesbian Ctr., 1999, NFL Players Assn. Lifetime Achievement award, 1999, Sports Illustrated "Athletes Who Changed the Game award, 1999, Capitol award, GLAAD, 2000, Radcliffe medal, Radcliffe Coll., 2002, Internat Olympic Com. Women & Sport World Trophy, 2002, Nat. Assn. Collegiate Women Athletic Administrators award of Honor, 2002, Pillipe Chatrier award, Internat. Tennis Fedn., 2003. Won 71 singles titles, including 12 Grand Slam singles titles; won 20 Wimbledon titles;First woman to win more than $100,000 in a single season in any sport; Highest singles ranking 1(5 times between 1966-72); defeated Bobby Riggs in "The Battle of the Sexes" tennis match, Sept. 20, 1973, Houston, Tex. Office: Billie Jean King Ste 983 960 Harlem Ave Glenview IL 60025

KING, BONNIE BESS WORLINE, writer, educator; b. El Dorado, Kans., Aug. 3, 1914; d. Robert Hite and Grace Lavera (Miller) Worline; m. Irvill King, 1937 (dec. Mar. 1987); children: Courtner, April, Waveland. AB, U. Chgo., 1935; MA, U. Pitts., 1946; PhD, U. Kans., 1961. Cert. in spl. edn., Calif. Writer fiction Chgo. Daily News, from 1933; writer catalog copy and correspondence Montgomery Ward and Co., Chgo., from 1935; continuity editor KCKN, Kansas City, Kans., 1942-44; pub. rels. and publs. dir., instr. journalism and advt. Endicott Coll., Beverly, Mass., 1945; dir. publs. and pub. rels., instr. English Gorham (Maine) State Coll., 1946-51; instr. English, U. Kans., 1951-61; publs. asst. Menninger Psychiat. Clinic, Topeka, 1956-61; tchr. journalism, English and Latin Brawley (Calif.) H.S., 1961-62, dir., instr. spl. edn., 1962-70; asst. prof. humanities Imperial Valley campus San Diego State U., 1963-84; cons. spl. edn. Imperial/San Diego Counties, 1962-84; emeritus asst. prof. humanities San Diego State U., 1984—; tchr. creative writing Calipatria State Prison, 1997—. Spkr. in field. Author: Sod House Adventure, 1956, The Sod Schoolhouse, 1996, Handicap Hut-At Camp Mary Jane, 2006; editor The Imp newsletter San Diego State U., 1965-84. Initiator, Assn. Retarded Citizens, Imperial County, 1964, Woman Haven, Imperial County, 1965, Spl. Olympics, Imperial County, 1967. Named Woman of Yr., Calif. State Legislature, 1988. Mem Calif. State Tchrs. Assn. (past pres.). Democrat. Avocations: gardening, sewing, cooking, swimming. Address: 279 J St Brawley CA 92227-2329

KING, BONNIE LA VERNE, education educator; b. Denver, Aug. 28, 1942; d. Carl A. and Myrtle Carlson; m. Hal K. King, Aug. 15, 1964 (dec. Nov. 1991); children: Mark, Christina, Peter. BA in Elem. Edn., U. Denver, 1964; postgrad., U. Colo.; MA in Ednl. Adminstrn., U. Hawaii, 1994. Tchr. Denver Pub. Schs., 1964-66, Cheyenne Mountain Pub. Schs., Colorado Springs, Colo., 1966-74, State of Hawaii Dept. of Edn., Maui, 1989—; lectr., instr. elem. reading and literacy U. Hawaii Sch. Edn., 1994—. Instr., lectr. McGill U., Montreal, 1997-98; real estate broker, Colo., 1976-89; coord. early childhood vision screening program. Contbr. poetry to anthologies. Vol. Colorado Springs Fine Arts Ctr., 1973-86; docent, art tchr. Montreal Museum of Fine Arts; vol., instr. Alzheimer's Assn.; chmn. vols. Spl. Olympics; U.S. figure skating judge, 1980—; ch. deacon; mem. Honolulu Symphony Choral. Recipient Gold Medal U.S. Figure Skating Competition, 1961. Mem. AAUW, Internat. Reading Assn. Avocations: swimming, skiing.

KING, CAROLE (CAROLE KLEIN), lyricist, singer; b. Bklyn., Feb. 9, 1942; m. Gerry Goffin; m. Charles Larkey; m. Rick Evers, 1977 (dec., 1978); m. Rick Sorensen, 1982; children: Louise, Sherry, Molly, Levi. Student, Queens Coll. Co-writer (with Gerry Goffin) numerous songs, 1960-68, including Will You Love Me Tomorrow?, Go Away, Little Girl, Up on the Roof, (with Jerry Wexler) Natural Woman, The Locomotion, Take Good Care of My Baby, (with Toni Stern) It's Too Late, 1971; albums include Music, 1971, Tapestry, 1971 (4 Grammy awards), Simple Things, Pearls: Songs of Goffin and King, Rhymes & Reasons, 1972, Fantasy, 1973, Wrap Around Joy, 1974, Really Rosie, 1975, Thoroughbred, 1975, Her Greatest Hits: Songs of Long Ago, 1978, One To One, 1982, Speeding Time, 1983, City Streets, 1989, Colour Of Your Dreams, 1993, In Concert, 1994, A Natural Woman, 1994, The Carnegie Hall Concert, 1996, Pearls/Time Gone By, 1998, Super Hits, 2000, Love Makes the World, 2001, The Living Room Tour, 2005; composer music for films Head, 1968, Murphy's Romance, 1985, The Care Bears Movie, 1985; off-Broadway theater appearance in A Minor Incident, 1989; Broadway appearance in Blood Brothers, 1994; appeared in (films) Murphy's Romance, 1985, Russkies, 1987, (TV film) Hider in the House, 1989; (TV series) The Tracy Ullman Show, Gilmore Girls, 2002, 2005. Inducted in Rock & Roll Hall of Fame, 1990. Office: Carole Kgn Prodns 11684 Ventura Blvd 273 Studio City CA 91604

KING, CAROLE WAYNE, foundation administrator; b. Pitts., Sept. 18, 1943; d. Wayne Shupe Forsythe and Elizabeth Phyllis; m. John W. King, June 6, 1993. BA, Antioch Coll., 1967; JD, Suffolk U., 1978. Bar: Md. 1981. Exec. dir. New England Spanish Am. Regional Inst., Boston, 1969—73; mgr. exceptions and appeals U.S. Dept. Energy and Hew, Boston, 1974—79; mgr. contracts Westinghouse Else Corp., Balt., 1979—83; dir. Vols. Med. Engring., Balt., 1984—92; founder, v.p. Merrythought Found., Annapolis, Md., 1993—; prin., owner Pembroke (Md.) St. Salon. Cons. in field; mem. com. leadership program Greater Balt., 1992. Contbr. columns in newspapers. Bd. dirs. Woodstock Acad., Ledminster, Mass., 1971—73, Brevard (N.C.) Little Theater, 2000—. Mem.: AAUW, Soaring Soc. Am. Avocations: painting, sailing, swimming, hiking. Home and Office: 473 Summit Ridge Lake Toxaway NC 28747

KING, CAROLYN DINEEN, federal judge; b. Syracuse, N.Y., Jan. 30, 1938; d. Robert E. and Carolyn E. (Bareham) Dineen; m. Thomas M. Reavley; children: James Randall, Philip Randall, Stephen Randall. BA summa cum laude, Smith Coll., 1959; LLB, Yale U., 1962. Bar: D.C. 1962, Tex. 1963. Assoc. Fulbright & Jaworski, Houston, 1962—72; ptnr. Childs, Fortenbach, Beck & Guyton, 1972—78, Sullivan, Bailey, King, Randall & Sabom, 1978—79; judge US Ct. Appeals (5th Cir.), 1979—, chief judge, 1999—2006; mem. U.S. Jud. Conf., 1999—2006, exec. com., 2000—05, chmn. exec. com., 2002—05. Trustee, exec. com., treas. Houston Ballet Found., 1967—70; Houston dist. adv. coun. SBA, 1972—76; Dallas regional panel Pres.'s Commn. White House Fellowships, 1972—76, mem. commn., 1977; bd. dirs. Houston chpt. Am. Heart Assn., 1978—79; nat. trustee Palmer Drug Abuse Program, 1978—79; trustee, sec., treas., chmn. audit com., fin. com., mgmt. com. United Way Tex. Gulf Coast, 1979—85; trustee, exec. com., chmn. bd. trustees U. St. Thomas, 1988—98. Recipient Smith Coll. medal, 1997, Outstanding Alumnus award, Phi Beta Kappa Alumni of Greater Houston, 1998, Margaret Brent Women Lawyers of Achievement award, ABA, 2005; rsch. fellow, Ctr. for Am. and Internat. Law, 1989—. Mem.: ABA, Philos. Soc. Tex., Houston Bar Assn., State Bar Tex., Am. Law Inst. (coun. 1991—, chmn. membership com. 1997—99), Fed. Bar Assn. Roman Catholic. Office: US Ct Appeals 11020 US Courthouse 515 Rusk Avenue Houston TX 77002-2694

KING, CODIE MARY, art center director, artist; d. Richard Heywood King and Winifred Ouderkirk; life ptnr. John F. Politano; children: Megan Marie King-Politano, Kellie Ann King-Politano, Matthew James King-Politano. BFA, Boston U., 1984; MFA, NYSCCeramics/Alfred (NY) U., 1986. Artist, Hilo, Hawaii, 1987—2000; art dir. Wailoa Arts & Cultural Ctr., Hilo, 2000—. Recipient Silver medal of honor, Brit. Royal Soc., 1984. Mem.: AAUW (assoc.). Office: State of Hawaii/DLNR/Wailoa Ctr 200 Piopio St Hilo HI 96720 Office Phone: 808-933-0416. Office Fax: 808-933-0417. E-mail: wailoa@yahoo.com.

KING, CORINNE MICHELLE, music educator; b. Jackson, Wyo., Mar. 6, 1981; d. Robert Allen and Sandra Jill Nelson; m. Robert Lyle King, July 24, 2004. BA in Music Edn. magna cum laude, U. Wyo., 2003. Tchr. elem. music Paintbrush Elem., Gillette, Wyo., 2003—05, Rock River Sch., 2005—. Mem.: Music Educators Nat. Conf., Wyo. Music Educators Assn., Pi Kappa Lambda. Avocations: scrapbooking, singing, violin. Office: Rock River Sch 262 N Morris Rock River WY 82083

KING, CYNTHIA BREGMAN, writer; b. N.Y.C., Aug. 27, 1925; d. Adolph and Elsie (Oschrin) Bregman; m. Jonathan King July 26, 1944 (dec 1997); children: Gordon Barkley, Austin Arthur (dec.), Nathaniel Bregman. Student, Bryn Mawr Coll., 1943-44, U. Chgo., 1944-46, N.Y.U., 1964-67. Assoc. editor Hillman Periodicals, N.Y.C., 1946-50; mng. editor Fawcett Publs., N.Y.C., 1950-55; creative writing tchr. The Awty Sch., Houston, 1974-75. Book reviewer, N.Y. Times Book Rev., 1976-83, Detroit News, 1980-88; dir. short story symposium Friends of Detroit Pub. Libr. and Detroit Women Writers, 1985; creative writing residencies Mich. Coun. of the Arts, Detroit, 1976-86. Author: In the Morning of Time, 1970, The Year of Mr. Nobody, 1978, Beggars and Choosers, 1980, Sailing Home, 1982; editor Fripp Island Audubon Club Natural History Publs., 1990-92 Mem. Pritchards Island adv. bd. U. SC, Beaufort, 1991—2006; pres. Fripp Island Audubon Club, 1991—92; asst. to chmn. Beaufort County Dem. Party, 1989—91. Recipient Spring Readings award, Detroit Working Writers, 2003; Creative Artist's grantee, Mich. Coun. for the Arts, 1985—86. Mem. The Authors Guild, Poets and Writers, Inc., Detroit Women Writers, Inc. (pres. 1979-81). Personal E-mail: tonibking@adelphia.net.

KING, DEBORAH IRENE, academic administrator; b. Bklyn., Sept. 3, 1952; d. Roland Burlough and Ethel Marianna (Blunt) K. BA, Richmond Coll., 1974; MS, St. John's U., Jamaica, N.Y., 1978, Pace U., 1985. Cert. elem., intermediate, jr. high sch. tchr., adminstr., N.Y. Dir. Wise Meml. Montessori Learning Ctr., St. Albans, N.Y., 1974-78; dir. reading lab. Malcolm-King Coll., N.Y.C., 1979-80; tchr. Pub. Sch. 269, Bklyn., 1978-80; aftersch. ctr. dir. Pub. Sch. 156, Laurelton, N.Y., 1980-81; tchr. Pub. Schs. 95 and 176, Jamaica and Cambria Heights, N.Y., 1981-83; music dir., intern in edn. adminstn. Pub. Sch. 176, Cambria Heights, 1984-85; aftersch. prog. asst. dir. Pub. Sch. 134, St. Albans, 1985—; tchr. Pub. Sch. 176, Cambria Heights, 1983-87; adminstr. Pub. Sch. 156, Laurelton, N.Y., 1987-91, Pub. Sch. 37, Springfield Gardens, N.Y., 1991—; prof. instrnl. staff dept. letters Coll. New Rochelle, N.Y.C., 1992—; sch. adminstr. PS 140, Queens, Jamacia, NY, 2005—. Tutor N.Y.C. Bd. Edn., Jamaica, 1980—. Mem. parish council, lector St. Pascal Baylon Ch., 1986—; mem. Civics Com., St. Albans. Mem. Am. Montessori Soc., Nat. Assn. U. Women, Assn. Black Educators N.Y., Phi Delta Kappa. Avocations: travel, theater, art. Home: 99-45 60th Ave Apt 6G Rego Park NY 11368-4411

KING, ELAINE A., curator, art historian, critic; b. Oak Park, Ill., Apr. 12, 1947; d. Casimir Stanley and Catherine Mary (Chmel) Czerwien. BS, No. Ill. U., 1968, MA, 1974; PhD, Northwestern U., 1986. Cert. Fine Arts Appraisal, 2002. Intern George Eastman House, Rochester, NY, 1977; lectr. history of photography Northwestern U., Evanston, Ill., 1977-81; curator Dittmar Meml. Gallery, Evanston, 1978-81; dir. Artemesia Gallery, Chgo., 1976-77; exec. dir., chief curator Carnegie-Mellon Art Gallery, Pitts., 1985—91; prof. critical theory and history of art Carnegie Mellon U., Pitts., 1981—. Bd. dirs. Mountain Lake Criticism Conf., Blacksburg, Va., 1982-91; ind. curator, 1991—; exhbn. rev. panel Pa. Coun. on Arts, 1991; exec. dir., chief curator Contemporary Art Ctr., Cin., 1993-95; guest curator Pitts. Cultural Trust, 1992, 93, 95, 96, Mari de Mater O'Neill mid-career survey Mus. Arts, P.R.; 10 year Retrospective of Diane Samuels, Mus. of Art, Györ, Hungary, Györ, 1999, bd. dirs. Mid-Am. Coll. Art Assn.; panel chair Midwest CAA Conf., 1997, 2003; co-coord. Wats:ON Festival, 1996-2003; adj. prof. U. Cin., 1994; art critic-in-residence U. Ariz., Tucson; guest curator Hungarian Bienale Exhbn. II, Györ, 1993, Master Graphic Arts Internat. Biennial, 1995, 97, 99, 2001, 03, 05; pres. Internat. Jury, 2003; panelist NEA Visual Arts, 1993; grant reviewer Inst. Mus. Sci., Washington, 1994, Ohio Arts Coun. fellowship and grant evaluator, 1994-95; Internat. Rev. panel AAUW internat. fellowships, Washington, 2000-03; mem. organizing com. Midwest Mus. Con., 1994-95; rep. Inter Arts Spring 1996 Budapest (Hungary) Crossroads; critic rep. Assn. Internat. Critics Art Conf. The Edge, Zagreb, Croatia; chmn. com. disting. exhbn. award Coll. Arts Assn., 1995-98, Assn. Internat. Critics Art XXXIV Congress Internat. Art Critics, Zagreb, Assn. Internat. Critics Art conf. ctrl. European cross-roads, 1996, 97, Assn. Internat. Critics Art Congress 2000, Barbados, 2003, Slovania, 2005, London; juror exhbn. 3rd Prague Internat.; nominator 4th Prague Internat., 2004; art-historian in residence internat. program Am. U., 2006, chair Sch. Visual Arts Plenary Session Conf., 2005, Internat. Popular Culture Assn. Conf., Wales, 2005, Chautauqua Inst., summer 2006; guest curator, spkr. in field. Curator, author: Crossing Borders: USA/Europe, Alleghany Coll. Art Galleries, 2000, Marking, 1999, The Figure As Fiction, 1993, Alfred DeCredico: Drawings, 1985-93, Emily Cheng: Monoprints, 1994, (exhbn. catalogues) Barry LeVa: 1966-88, Mel Bochner: 1973-85, Elizabeth Murray: Drawings: 1980-86, Michael Gitlin: Sculpture & Drawings, 1990, New Generations: Chgo., 1990, New Generations: N.Y., 1991, Magdalena Jetalová, 1991, Martin Puryear: Sculpture & Drawings, 1987, Abstraction/Abstraction, Tishan Hsu, Paintings, Drawings & Sculpture, 1987, N.Y. Painting Today, Michel Gerand: Drawings and Site Works, 1989, Drawings and Sculpture, 1990, Art in the Age of Information, 1993, Five Artists at the Airport: Insights into Public Art, 1992, Martha Rosler: In Place of the Public, 1994, Shari Zolla, 1997, Lyzabeth Bayard: 2 Installations, Light Into Art: From Video to Virtual Reality (also booklet), David Humphrey: Paintings and Drawings 1987-95 (also catalogue), others; author: The Misunderstood Patron, The National Endowment for the Arts; co-editor: Ethics and the Visual Arts, 2006; critic-in-residence Sch. Art, San Juan, PR; free lance art critic, Washington Post, Grapheion, Tema Celeste, & Sculpture, Cin. Enquirer; Grapheion; Art on Paper, Pitt. Post-Gazette, art critic in residence Delaware Contemporary Ctr. for the Arts, 1992, Mid-Atlantic Arts Fellow, 1991, No. Ill. U., 1997; corr. critic, regional editor Diaglogue, Columbus, Ohio, 1984-89; corr. critic Sculpture; co-editor: (with Gail Levin) Ethics and the Visual Arts, 2006; contbr. articles to profl. jours. Active Dem. Party, Evanston, ward judge, 1977-78, precinct capt., 1977. Recipient Hunt Art award, 1977, Disting. Art Historian Residency award Am. U., 2006; scholar Pa. Humanities Coun., 1997, Nat. Mus. Am. Art, 2000; grantee Carnegie Mellon U., 1985, 87, 89-90, 96-99, 2002, Grant Trust for Mut. Understanding, Rockefeller Found., 1994, Thendora Found., 1995, Pa. Coun. on Arts, 2000, IREX, 2000; fellow Pa. Coun. on Arts, 1985, 89, 95, 99, 2000, Smithsonian Inst., 1998, 2000—, Nat. Portrait Gallery, 2001, Inst. for Art History, Acad. Scis., Budapest, Hungary, 2002, Ctrl. European Cultural Inst., 2002; named disting. art historian Am. U., Corcino, Italy, 2006. Mem. Coll. Art Assn., Am. Assn. Mus., Assn. Historians Am. Art, Assn. Internat. Critics Art (Am. sect.), Art Table, Midwest Coll. Art Assn. Avocations: cooking, gardening, tennis, swimming, sailing. Office: Carnegie Mellon U Coll Fine Arts Pittsburgh PA 15213 Office Phone: 412-268-1970. Personal E-mail: eaking13@yahoo.com. Business E-Mail: ek06@andrew.cmu.edu.

KING, SISTER ELEACE, special education services professional; b. Greenport, N.Y., Oct. 10, 1946; d. Gerald C. King and Alice Cecelia Ward. BA, Marywood Coll., 1969; MS, Yeshiva U., 1974; EdD, Johns Hopkins U., 1983. First grade tchr. St. John the Evangelist Sch., Scranton, Pa., 1969—70; spl. edn. tchr. Archdiocese of NY, New York, 1970—74; asst. prof. Marywood Coll., Scranton, 1974—86; sr. rsch. assoc. Ctr. Applied Rsch. Apostolate/Georgetown U., Washington, 1988—94; asst. supt. spl. edn. Diocese of Bridgeport, 1994—. Adv. bd. mem. St. Catherine Acad., Bridgeport, 1999—; bd. of trustees Nat. Cath. Partnership Disabilities, Washington, 2003—, treas. bd. trustees. Contbr. chapters to books. Adv. coun. mem. State Dept. Mental Retardation, Southwest Region, Conn., 1999—2000, mem., human rights com., 1998—2003. Scholar, The Inner-City Found. Charity and Edn., 1999—2004, Pitt Found., 2004. Mem.: Coun. Exceptional Children (assoc.), Nat. Cath. Edn. Assn. (assoc.). Roman Catholic. Achievements include Founder, St. Catherine Academy, a special education school for children with intellectual disabilities. Avocations: reading, knitting, walking. Office: Diocese of Bridgeport 238 Jewett Ave Bridgeport CT 06606 Office Phone: 203-372-4301 330. Office Fax: 203-372-1961. Personal E-mail: sreleace@aol.com. E-mail: srking@diobpt.org.

KING, ELIZABETH ANN, writer; b. Malden, Mass., May 9, 1938; d. Richard H. Sheldon and Jane I. (Cotton) Killoran; m. Richard William King, 1965 (div.); children: Kathy Ann, Richard Eric. AA, Moorpark Coll., 1977; BA, Northridge (Calif.) State U., 1978. Adminstrv. sec., 1981-86; freelance writer, 1987—. Author: Corridors, Winter Solstice, (with Sam Kane Giancana) Tales of the Vanguard: The Announcer, (series of picture books) The Little Old School House; author of short stories; editor Mission Without Borders, 1999-2006; contbr. poetry to anthologies; lyricist: I Believe in Heroes, 1987, Journey's End, 1988. Avocations: astronomy, anthropology, computer graphics/design, writing.

KING, GLADIOLA TIN, retired medical technician; b. Tampa, Fla., Feb. 9, 1932; d. Charlie Sam and Rose Mary Tin; children: William S. Jr., Lisa Lee King Grant. BS, Fla. So. Coll., Lakeland, 1954. Lic. supr. in hematology, chemistry, serology, bacteriology, urinalysis, cytology and histology Fla. Med. technologist Am. Soc. Clin. Pathology, Boston, 1955; ret. Dept. head Med. Assisting Prog., Broward CC, Ft. Lauderdale, Fla., 1967—99; mediator Citizens Dispute Settlement Prog. 13th Judicial Circuit Fla., Hillsborough County, 1980—82; cons. Fla. State, Medicare, 1982—95. Contbr. scientific papers. Clk. dist. 423 State Elections, Tampa, 1999—2001; med. missionary Nativity Ch., La Victoria, Dominican Republic, 1995—; vol. Idlewild Bapt. Ch., Tampa, Fla., 1990—; bd. dirs. Seminole Presbyn. Ch., Tampa, 1980—90. Mem.: Am. Soc. Clin. Pathology, Tampa Bay Gem and Mineral Sci. Club, U. South Fla. Fossil Club, Sun City Lapidary Club, Kings Point Lapidary Club. Republican. Baptist. Avocations: archaeology, jewelry design. Home: 2201 Hayling Pl Sun City Center FL 33573

KING, GWENDOLYN S., retired utility company executive, retired federal official; b. East Orange, N.J. d. Frank M. and Henryne (Walker) Stewart; m. Colbert I. King. BA cum laude, Howard U., 1962; postgrad., George Washington U.; doctorate (hon.), U. Md., 1990, U. New Haven, 1992. Legis. asst. to Sen. John Heinz, Washington, 1978-79; dir. Commonwealth of Pa. Office, Washington, 1979-86; dep. asst. to the pres. and dir. Office Intergovtl. Affairs, The White House, Washington, 1986-88; exec. v.p. Gogol & Assocs., 1988-89; commr. Social Security Adminstrn., Balt., 1989-92; sr. v.p. corp. and pub. affairs PECO Energy Corp., Phila., 1992-98; pres. Podium Prose, LLC, Washington. Bd. dirs. Lockheed Martin, Marsh & McLennan Cos., Monsanto Corp. Mem. Pres.'s Commn. to Strengthen Social Security, 2001. Recipient Drum Major for Justice award So. Christian Leadership Conf., 1990, Disting. Alumni award Howard U., 1991, Black Achievement Bus. and Fin. award Ebony Mag., 1992. Mem. Nat. Assn. Corp. Dirs. (bd. dirs.). Office: Podium Prose LLC Ste 1012 1025 Connecticut Ave NW Washington DC 20036

KING, IMOGENE M., retired nursing educator; b. West Point, Iowa, Jan. 30, 1923; Diploma, St. John's Hosp., 1945; BSN, St. Louis U., 1948, MSN, 1957; EdD, Columbia U., 1961; PhD (hon.), So. Ill. U., 1990, Loyola U., Chgo., 1998. Instr. med.-surg. nursing, asst. DON St. John's Hosp., St. Louis, 1947-58; from asst. prof. nursing to assoc. prof. Loyola U, Chgo., 1961-66, prof., dir. grad. program in nursing, 1972-80; prof. U. South Fla., Tampa, 1980-90, dir. rsch., 1982-85, prof. emeritus, 1990—. Asst. chief rsch. grants br. divsn. nursing HEW, Washington, 1966—68; prof., dean rsch. nursing Ohio State U., Columbus, 1968—72; mem. def. adv. com. women svcs. Dept. Def., 1972—75; adj. prof. U. Miami Sch. Nursing, 1986—89; cons. VA Hosp., health care agys. Author: Toward a Theory for Nursing, 1971, transl. to Japanese, 1975, A Theory for Nursing Systems, Concepts, Process, 1981, transl. to Japanese, 1983, transl. to Spanish, 1985, Curriculum and Instruction in Nursing, 1986; mem. editl. bd. Theoria: Jour. Nursing Theorica; contbr. articles to profl. jours., chapters to books. Alderman, chmn. fin. com. Ward 2, Wood Dale, Ill., 1975—79; bd. dirs. operation PAR Inc., Pinellas County, Fla., 1990—92. Recipient Founders award, St. Louis U., 1969, Recognition of Contbns. to Nursing Edn. award, Columbia U. Tchrs. Coll., 1983, Disting. Scholar award, U. So. Fla., 1988—89, award for Outstanding Cmty. Svc., U. Tampa, 1997, Imogene King Rsch. award, 1997, Fla. Gov.'s medal for Contbn. to Nursing and Health Care, 1997, Dirs. award, Fla. League Nursing, 1997. Fellow: Am. Acad. Nursing (hon. inducted Living Legends 2005); mem.: ANA (conv. lectr. 1996, Jessie M. Scott award 1996, Hall of Fame award 2004), Fla. Nurses Found., Fla. Nurses Assn. (life; dir. region 2 1981—83, pres. dist. IC 1982—83, 2d v.p. 1983—85, bd. dirs. 1997—2001, Dist. IV bd. dirs. 2004—06, Advancing the Nursing Profl. award, Nurse of the Yr. 1984, Nursing Rsch. award 1985, Hall of Fame award 2003), Ill. Nurses Assn. (Highest Recognition award 1975, award 19th dist. 1975), Phi Kappa Phi (Scholar award 1988), Sigma Theta Tau (counselor Delta Beta chpt. 1983—85, pres-elect 1986—87, pres. 1987—89, disting. lectr. 1990—91, co-chmn. biennial conv. 1991, mem. nominating com. 1993—95, co-editor The Lang. of Nursing Theory and Metatheory 1997, Founders award for Excellence in Nursing Edn. 1989, Virginia Henderson fellow 1993). Personal E-mail: imkn@earthlink.net.

KING, JANE CONNELL, mathematics professor; b. Shelbyville, Ky., May 3, 1939; d. Charles Edward Connell and Bobbye Jane Williams; m. Jerry Porter King, Sept. 5, 1962; children: Elizabeth Robinson, David Williams. BA, U. Ky., 1961, MS, 1962. Tchr. math. Moravian Prep. Sch., Bethlehem, Pa., 1967—69; asst. prof. math. Cedar Crest Coll., Allentown, Pa., 1969—80, dir. internship program, 1974—80; vis. lectr. math. Lehigh U., Bethlehem, 1981—86, supr. math. tutoring ctr., adj. prof., 1996—. Referee Two Yr. Coll. Math. Reader, 1978; vis. instr. math. Lafayette Coll., Easton, Pa., 1988—89; vis. asst. prof. Moravian Coll., Bethlehem, 1989—90. Bd. dirs., violinist Lehigh Valley Chamber Orch., Bethlehem, 1982—88, Pa. Sinfonia Orch., Allentown, 1993—97. Mem.: Am. Fedn. Musicians, Math. Assn. Am., Lehigh U. Women's Club (treas., v.p., pres. 1981—87). Conservative. Roman Catholic. Avocations: violin, jogging. Home: 1351 Gaspar Ave Bethlehem PA 18017 Office: Lehigh U 35 Sayre Dr Bethlehem PA 18015 Business E-Mail: janeking@lehigh.edu.

KING, JANE CUDLIP COBLENTZ, volunteer educator; b. Iron Mountain, Mich., May 4, 1922; d. William Stacey and Mary Elva (Martin) Cudlip; m. George Samuel Coblentz, June 8, 1942 (dec. June 1989); children: Bruce Harper, Keith George, Nancy Allison Coblentz Patch; m. James E. King, August 23, 1991 (dec. Jan. 1994). BA, Mills Coll., 1942. Mem. Sch. Resource and Career Guidance Vols., Inc., Atherton, Calif., 1965-69, pres., CEO, 1969—. Exec. asst. to dean of admissions Mills Coll., 1994-99. Proofreader, contbr. Mills Coll. Quarterly mag. Life gov. Royal Children's Hosp., Melbourne, Australia, 1963—; pres. United Menlo Park (Calif.) Homeowners Assn., 1994—; nat. pres. Mills Coll. Alumnae Assn., 1969-73, trustee, 1975-83; bd. govs. Mills Coll. Alumnae Assn., 1966-73, 75-83, 98-2000, life bd. govs., 2006—, v.p., 2001—06. Named Vol. of Yr., Sequoia Union H.S. Dist., 1988, Disting. Woman Mid-Peninsula (forerunner San Mateo County Women's Hall of Fame), 1975; recipient Golden Acorn award for Outstanding Cmty. Svc., Menlo Park C. of C., 1991. Mem. AAUW (Menlo-Atherton br. pres. 1994-96, v.p. programs 1996-97, editor Directory and Acorn, 1994—), Atherlons, Palo Alto (Calif.) Area Mills Coll. Club (pres. 1986), Phi Beta Kappa. Episcopalian. Avocations: reading, gardening. Personal E-mail: jccking@juno.com.

KING, JANET CARLSON, nutrition educator, researcher; b. Red Oak, Iowa, Oct. 3, 1941; d. Paul Emil and Norma Carolina (Anderson) Carlson; m. Charles Talmadge King, Dec. 25, 1967; children: Matthew, Samuel. BS, Iowa

State U., 1963; PhD, U. Calif., Berkeley, 1972. Dietitian Fitzsimmons Gen. Hosp., Denver, 1964-67; NIH postdoctoral fellow dept. nutrition sci. U. Calif., Berkeley, 1972-73, asst. prof. nutrition dept. nutrition sci., 1973-78, assoc. prof. nutrition dept. nutrition sci., 1978-83, prof. nutrition dept. nutrition sci., 1983—, chair dept. nutrition sci., 1988-94; dir. USDA Western Human Nutrition Rsch. Ctr., Davis, Calif., 1995—2002; sr. scientist Children's Hosp. Oakland (Calif.) Rsch. Inst., 2003—; prof. emeritus U. Calif., 1995—, prof. nutrition and internal medicine, 2003—. Frances E. Fischer Meml. nutrition lectr. Am. Dietetic Assn. Found., 1985, Lotte Arnrich Nutrition lectr. Iowa State U., 1985; Massee lectr. U. ND, 1991, Lydia J. Roberts lectr. U. Chgo., 1995, Virginia A. Beal lectr. U. Mass., 1998; vis. prof. U. Calif., Davis, 1998—. Contbr. articles to Jour. Am. Diet. Assn., Am. Jour. Clin. Nutrition, Jour. Nutrition, Nutrition Rsch., Obstetrics and Gynecology, Brit. Jour. Obstetrics and Gynaecology. Recipient Lederle Labs. award in human nutrition, Am. Inst. Nutrition, 1989, Internat. award in human nutrition, 1996, Atwater award, Am. Soc. Nutritional Scis., 2004. Mem.: AAAS, Inst. Medicine of NAS, Am. Dietetic Assn., Am. Soc. for Nutritional Scis., Am. Soc. Clin. Nutrition. Office: Childrens Hosp Oakland Rsch Inst 5700 MKL Jr Way Oakland CA 94609 Office Phone: 510-450-7939. E-mail: jking@chori.org.

KING, JOY RAINEY, poet, executive secretary; b. Memphis, Aug. 5, 1939; d. Roy Henry and Margaret (Irvin) Rainey; m. Guy Robert King, Dec. 24, 1956; children: William Lonnie, Cheryl King Ramsey. Grad., Whitehaven H.S., Memphis, 1957. Sec. Gen. Telephone Co., Sumter, S.C., 1957-59; med. sec. L.H. Brisco, MD, Tupelo, Miss., 1963-69, James Ballard, MD, Tupelo, 1969-73; with First Nat. Bank of Southaven, Miss., 1973-79. Staff writer Majestic Records and Countrywine Pub. Co. Author: From the Gazebo, Wonder of Words, 2003 (Internat. Book of Gold prize, 2003), numerous poems, 25 poetry books, (songs) America's New Hero; singer: Majestic Records. Recipient Editor's Choice award, 1993, 94, Pres.'s recognition lit. excellence Nat. Authors Registry, 1999-2000, Poet of Month award; named Author of Yr., Edizoni U., Trento, Italy, 1999, Internat. Peace prize United Cultural Conv., 2002. Mem. Internat. Soc. Poets, Poets Guild, Internat. Poetry Hall of Fame, So. Ill. Writers Guild (sec. 1996-98), Top Recorders Songwriters Assn., Famous Poets Soc., Metverse Muse in India, World Congress of Poets. Baptist.

KING, JOY RIEMER, art educator, linguist; d. Bjarne Viggo and Thora Yrsa Xenia (Riemer) Ferdinandsen; m. Charles Banks King, Jr. IV, July 4, 1992; stepchildren: Captain Charles Pat, Dorothy Marie 1 child, Nanette Joy Xenia Riemer. Diploma, Sorbonne, 1959; BA, Principia Coll., 1961; MA, Columbia U., 1968; art specialist diploma, Fla. Internat. U., 1999. Cert. tchr. Ill., 1961, Fla., 1972. Tchrs. aide Columbia U. Team, Kabul, Afghanistan, 1961—62; tchr., curriculum coord. Parents' Coop. Sch., Jeddah, Saudi Arabia, 1967—68; prin., tchr. Latin, French, civics, arts So. Acad., Miami, 1972—77; instr. art Internat. Fine Arts Coll., Miami, 1977—78; instr. French & English Internat. Sch. Langs., Miami Shores, 1978—79; mgr./artist Frances W. Cary Antiques, 1983—89; instr. French & Danish Inlingua, Coral Gables, 1989—90; tchr., art, French, U.S. history Dade County Pub. Schools, 1990—2002; art therapist St. Mary Cathedral Sch., 2002—. Dir. Paul Abrams Found., Miami, Fla., 1998—2001, So. Acad., 1972—77. Exhibitions include Jackie Hinckey Sipes Gallery, Dublin-Kitzen Fine Arts Gallery, Coral Gables, Fairchild Tropical Garden, Bok Tower Gardens, S.E. Pastel Soc., Salmagundi Club, N.Y.C., Hispanic C.C., Miami, Paula Insel Gallery, N.Y., Stern's Gallery, Roselyn Gallery, N.C., Art Works Gallery, Miami, Nat. Art Edn. Assn. Elec. Gallery, Washington; contbr. articles to profl. jours. Pub. rels. dir. Civitan, North Miami, 2000—01. Named in U.S. Congl. Record for art edn. program with at risk students, U.S. Congress, 1992; recipient Marge Pearlson award, Dade Coalition Cmty. Edn., 1997, award of Excellence, Goya Foods, Fla., 1996, cert. of Appreciation, Metro-Dade Police Dept, Northside Sta., 1996. Mem.: ASPCA, Southeastern Pastel Soc., Fla. Watercolor Soc., Nat. Art Edn. Assn., French Teachers Am., Alliance Francaise, Fla. Art Edn. Assn., Nat. Assn. Women Artists, Dade Art Educators Assn., The Nature Conservancy, Friends the Everglades, Nat. Wildlife Fedn., Smithsonian Instn., St. Joseph's Indian Sch., North Shore Animal League, Farm Sanctuary, World Vision, Friends Bok Tower, Internat. Fund for Animal Welfare, Navy League, Nat. Gardening Club (life). Avocations: reading, swimming, painting, sculpting, writing. Office Phone: 305-799-2610. Personal E-mail: joyscapes@bellsouth.net.

KING, KATHY COOPER, music educator; b. Ackerman, Miss., Jan. 12, 1954; d. Bobby Gene and Mary Lou (McGee) Cooper; m. Kenneth A. King, Aug. 1, 1976; children: Matthew Cooper, Katherine Elizabeth. B of Music Edn., 1976, M of Music Edn., 1983, Cert. in Gifted/Talented Music Edn., 1986, ArtsD of Music Edn., Vocal Pedagogy, 1996. Vocal, choral and piano tchr. Weir (Miss.) H.S., 1976—78; dir. of music Ackerman (Miss.) United Meth. Ch., 1978—98; vocal, choral and piano tchr. Ackerman H.S., 1976—96; choral music edn. instr. U. Miss., University, 1996—97; vocal, choral and classroom tchr. Holmes C.C., Goodman, Miss., 1997—. Featured in Making the Grade, WTVA, 1990. Recipient Outstanding Cmty. Leader in Edn., Choctaw County Econ. Devel. Coun., 1991, STAR Tchr. award, Miss. Econ. Devel. Coun., 1995, Tchr. of Yr. award, Choctaw County, 1995. Mem.: Miss. Music Educators Assn., Music Tchrs. Nat. Assn., Nat. Assn. Tchrs. of Singing, Music Educators Nat. Conf., Am. Choral Dirs. Assn., Phi Kappa Phi, Sigma Alpha Iota, Pi Kappa Lambda. Republican. Methodist. Avocations: gourmet cooking, travelling, interior decorating, fitness training. Home: PO Box 413 Ackerman MS 39735 Office: Holmes CC PO Box 369 Goodman MS 39079

KING, KAY WANDER, academic administrator, design educator, fashion designer, consultant; b. Houston, Oct. 16, 1937; d. Aretas Robert and Verna Elizabeth (Klann) Wander; m. George Ronald King, Jan. 21, 1960; 1 child, Collin Wander. BA, U. North Tex., 1959; M of Liberal Arts, Houston Bapt. U., 1991. Fashion designer Kabro Houston, Inc., 1959—66, Joe Frank, Inc., Houston, 1966—68; dir. fashion Foley's, Houston, 1968—70; prin. Kay King Designer/Cons., Houston, 1970—; chair fashion dept. Houston C.C., 1981—97, chair fashion and interior design dept., 1997—2003, interim dean workforce devel., 2000—01, chmn. Dept. Applied Arts, 2003—; cultural exch. prof. fashion design Jinan, China, 2000, Tel Aviv, 2006. Mem. adv. bd. Spring (Tex.) Ind. Sch. Dist. Tech. Edn., 1990—; bd. dirs. Make it Yourself with Wool, Tex., nat. judge, Tex., 1997—2001; Tex. Workforce Edn. Course Manual Facilitator, 1997—2001; site evaluator Tex. Coord. Bd. for Higher Edn., 1994, 99, 2000. Wardrobe designer Mrs. Am., 1966, Houston Oilers Cheerleaders, 1968-92, Astroworld and The Astrodome, 1968-69, Brian Boru Opera, 1991, Design Industries Found. Fighting AIDS, 1994-96, Houston Comets/Houston Rockets, 1997. Chair Gulf Coast area United Cerebral Palsy Telethon, 1981; chair Whiteley Endowment Scholarship Awards, Houston, 1990-93, Sickle Cell Found., Houston, 1995-2000; adminstr. Bedichek Faculty Devel. Grants, 1995-96; pres. Spring Br. Ind. Sch. Dist. Coun., PTAs, Houston, 1987-88; bd. dirs. Houston C.C. Found., 1988-93, Mus. Fine Arts Costume Inst., Houston, 1991—, acquisitions com., 1993—. Named Woman to Watch, Houston Woman mag., 1991, Woman of Excellence, Fedn. Houston Profl. Women, 1992, Women's Archives honoree, U. Houston, 1998—99; recipient Exemplary Program awards for fashion design and fashion merchandising, Tex. Higher Edn. Coord. Bd., 2001, 2005, Exemplary Program award for interior design, 2005, Freedoms Found. at Valley Forge Nat. award, 2001, Yellow Rose of Tex., Gov. Tex., 1982, Nat. Inst. for Staff and Orgnl. Devel. Tchg. Excellence award, U. Tex., 1993, Award of Excellence, Houston C.C. Faculty Assn. Coun., 1995, Fin. Advisors' Excellence in Cmty. Leadership award, Am. Express, 1996, Innovation award, Houston C.C., 1996, Chancellor's Medallion award, 1996, Tony Chee Tchg. Excellence award, 1996, Bedichek Outstanding Cmty. Svc. award, 1997, Athena award, Sickle Cell Assn., 1997, Fine Arts Fashion award, Mus. Fine Arts Houston, 1999, Fashion Forum award, Foley's Dept. Store and Fashion Group Internat., 2000; Bedichek Faculty Devel. grantee, 1986, 1989, 1990, 1993, 1994. Fellow Costume Soc. Am. (awards chair 1992-93, exec. bd. dirs., sec. 1993-99, v.p. 2000-04, pres.-elect 2004-06, internat. symposium coord. 2004, internat. pres. 2006—, Pres.'s award 2004, fellow 2005); mem. Nat. PTA (life, hon., coun. pres. 1987-88), Tex. Jr. Coll. Tchrs. Assn. (sect. chair 1990-92), Fashion Group Internat. (bd. dirs., cultural exch. chair 1965-71, regional dir. 1969-70, program dir., chair career conf. 1994, retail chair 1995, Keynote address 1997, internat. conf. del. Paris 2000, Toronto 2004), Houston C.C. Women Adminstrs. Assn. (bd. dirs. 1993-95, v.p. 1994-95, Star award 1989, Keynote address 1996), Houston Fashion Designers Assn. (charter, publicity chair 1989-93, v.p. bd. dirs. 1993-97), Tex. Sheep and Goat Raisers Assn. (Achievement award 2003), Fedn. Houston Profl. Women (bd. dirs., program dir. 1993, adminstrv. sec. 1994, pres.-elect 1995, pres. 1996, past pres. 1997, travel dir. 1998—, charter Classy Clown Corps 1994-2000), Zeta Tau Alpha (charity showhouse chair 1985, Nat. Cert. of Merit 1986). Avocations: opera, ballet, travel, graphic computer design, professional football. Office: Houston CC System 1300 Holman St # 325A Houston TX 77004-3834 Office Phone: 713-718-6152. Business E-Mail: kay.king@hccs.edu.

KING, LINDA, musician, educator; b. Wichita Falls, Tex., July 30, 1940; d. Charles Ecford Jr. and Norma Reeda Collins; m. James Arthur King, Aug. 19, 1961; children: Linda Renée DeValois, James Arthur II, Jon Allen. Student, Tex. Christian U., 1958, 59, 60; MusM, Juilliard Conservatory, 1973. Judge Nat. Fedn. Music Clubs; adjudicator Nat. Guild Auditions, Austin, Tex., 1987—; founder, past pres. Piano Arts Assn., Denver, 1987; exec. dir. Rocky Mountain Duo Piano Competition, Colorado Springs, Colo., 1997-99; piano tchr., 1968—; founder, exec. dir. The Clementi Piano Festival, 1994-2000. Active Jr. League, Dallas, 1967-70; pres. Irving (Tex.) Women's Choral Club, 1968-73, PTO, Irving, 1970; bd. mem., actor Irving Cmty. Theatre, 1968-73; follies now girl Symphony Guild, Irving, 1970-73; children's choir dir. First Christian Ch., Irving, 1968; city choir dir. Girl Scouts, Irving, 1970. Named Outstanding Mem., South Suburban Christian Ch., Littleton, 1981. Mem. Am. Coll. Musicians (adjudicator), Nat. Music Tchrs. Assn., Colo. State Music Tchrs. Assn., Fedn. Music Clubs (state pres. 1998-2000), Colo. Fedn. Music Clubs (state pres. 1998-2000), Alpha Gamma Delta (pledge trainer 1962-63). Republican. Avocations: directing singing groups of high school students, teaching children piano who cannot afford lessons. Home: 6916 S Ogden Ct Littleton CO 80122-1370

KING, LINDA MARIE, art educator, director; b. Elizabeth, N.J., Apr. 8, 1962; d. George William and Marian Elizabeth King. BA in Music, Kean U., Union, N.J., 1984; MA in Music, Jersey City State U., 1994; EdD in Policy, Mgmt. and Ednl. Leadership, Seton Hall U., South Orange, N.J., 2003. Tchr. Paterson Cath. Regional H.S., NJ, 1984—85, Roselle Pub. Schs., 1985—88, Westfield Pub. Schs., 1988—97, supr. fine arts, 1997—. Grantee, Edn. Fund Westfield, 2005—06, Coalition Arts, 2005—06. Mem.: Nat. Assn. Secondary Sch. Prins., Music Educators Nat. Conf., N.J. Music Administrators (sec. exec. bd. 2006—). Roman Catholic. Avocations: performing in oldies band, sports. Office: Westfield Bd Edn 302 Elm Westfield NJ 07090-3104 Home: 50 Furber Ave Linden NJ 07036

KING, LINDA ORR, museum director, consultant; b. Washington, June 21, 1948; d. William Baxter and Jayne (Reiser) Orr; m. James McClain King (dec. Aug. 1997); children: David, Adam, Lindsay. BA, La. State U., 1970, MA in Fine Arts, 1971; postgrad., Ga. State U., 2003—. Fine arts history asst. La. State U., Baton Rouge, 1967-70, grad. asst., 1970-71; assoc. curator La. State Mus., New Orleans, 1971-74; curator Coastal Ga. Hist. Soc./St. Simons Island Lighthouse Mus., St. Simons Island, 1984-87; dir. Coastal Ga. Hist. Soc., St. Simons Island, 1987-2000; dir. exhibitions and collections Atlanta Hist. Ctr., 2000-01; ind. mus. profl., 2001—. Romanian Mus. advisor U.S. State Dept., 2002. Co-editor: (photograph essay) George Francois Mugnier, 1975. Pres. Glynn County Soc. of St. Vincent de Paul, 1990-94; mem. Glynn County Courthouse Renovation Com., 1989-2000; Ga. state dir. S.E. Mus. Conf., 1990-94, also membership chair; mem. adv. coun. Brunswick Downtown Devel. Authority; mem. Leadership Glynn, 1992; mem. Commn. on Preservation of Ga. State Capitol; chmn. adv. coun. on hist. preservation Coastal Regional Devel. Ctr., 1987-98, chmn., 1996-98. Recipient Kellogg Career Enhancement award, Kellogg Found., 1989, Leadership award, Southeastern Mus. Conf., 1995, Nat. Mus. award, 1999, Ga. History Mus. Exhibit of 2002 award, 2002; fellow Internat. Partnership Among Mus. fellow to Sierra Leone, 1992. Mem. Ga. Assn. Mus. and Galleries (treas. 1987-89, Mus. Profl. of Yr. 1993), Coastal Mus. Assn. (treas. 1987-89), Am. Assn. Mus., Low Country Mus. Network (treas. 1993-99). Roman Catholic. Home: 3472 Paces Pl NW Atlanta GA 30327 E-mail: lindaorrking@bellsouth.net.

KING, LINDSAY BRAWNER, music educator; d. Thomas Watson Brawner III and Linda Johnston; m. Brent Radford King, 2000; 1 child, Elizabeth. B Music Edn., U. Louisville, 1997; M Music Edn., Fla. State U., Tallahassee, 2001. Cert. instrumental music tchr. Ky. Mid. sch. band dir., asst. HS dir. Trigg County Schs., Cadiz, Ky., 1997—99, Calloway County Schs., Murray, Ky., 2001—02, Scott County Schs., Georgetown, Ky., 2002—. Mem. Capital City Cmty. Band, Frankfort, Ky., 1992—. Mem.: Music Educators Nat. Conf., Ky. Music Educators Assn. (Mid. Sch. Tchr. of Yr. 2005—06).

KING, LLOYD JOANN, music educator, volunteer; b. L.A., Dec. 24, 1929; d. Ray and Dorothy (Lloyd) Kerst; m. Lawrence Gilbert King, Sept. 15, 1950; children: Kathy Lynn King Scott, Kevin Paul King. AA, L.A. City Coll., 1949; BA, Calif. State U., L.A., 1951; MA in Edn., Eastern Mich. U., Ypsilanti, 1959. Tchr. 2d grade Long Beach Sch. Dist., Calif., 1951-52; tchr 1st grade Am. Sch., Pasay City, Philippines, 1953-54; tchr. 1st and 2d grade L.A. Sch. Dist., 1954; tchr. 2d grade, instrumental music, gen. music Willow Run Sch. Dist., Mich., 1954-59; dir. Christian Edn. Meth. Ch., Camarillo, Calif., 1963, 64; co-owner King's Magnavox Music Store, Thousand Oaks, Calif., 1969-74; pvt. music tchr. L.A., Ypsilanti, Mich., Thousand Oaks, Roseburg, Oreg., 1946—. Author: (History of Oreg. PEO) Yesterdays, Today and Tomorrows, 1994, also mag. articles. Elder, Presbyn. Ch., Roseburg, 1991—, treas. women's assn., clerk of session. Named Woman of Yr., Thousand Oaks/Conejo Valley C. of C., 1968; recipient scholarships and grants. Mem. AAUW (past state officer), PEO, Oreg. Music Tchrs. Assn., Nat. Music Tchrs. Assn. Republican. Avocations: travel, music, theosophy, genealogy. Home: 1779 NW Riverview Dr Roseburg OR 97470-6104 Personal E-mail: larryking@mac.com.

KING, LYNDA, counselor; d. Kenneth Dodds and Emily Marie King. BA Psychology, Tabor Coll., Hillsboro, Kans., 1995; MA Profl. Counseling, Ottawa U., Phoenix, 2002. Dir. care staff Res-Care, Mesa, Ariz., 1998—2006; therapist Mental Health Agy., Apache Junction, Ariz., 2006—. Democrat. Avocations: hiking, rock climbing.

KING, LYNDA ANNE WHITLOW, psychologist, educator; b. Danville, Va., Aug. 7, 1947; d. Detlef F. and Doris F. (Van Hook) Whitlow; m. Daniel Walter King., Nov. 29, 1969. Student Coll. of William and Mary, 1965-67; B.S., U. Md., 1969; M.A., U. Washington, 1975, Ph.D., 1979; R.N., Mich. Research asst. Bur. of Sch. Service and Research, U. Washington, Seattle, 1975-76, research assoc., 1976-77; instr. City Coll., Seattle, 1976-78; asst. prof. psychology Central Mich. U., Mt. Pleasant, 1979-83, assoc. prof., 1983-89, prof., 1989-95; rsch. psychologist Nat. Ctr. PTSD, Boston, 1995—; prof. Boston U., 1997—. Served with Nurse Corps, U.S. Army, 1969-72. Mem. Am. Psychol. Soc., Phi Delta Kappa, Sigma Theta Tau, Phi Kappa Phi. Contbr. articles on psychology to profl. jours. Office: Boston VAMC 150 S Huntington Ave Boston MA 02130-4817 Home: 31 Lothrop St Beverly MA 01915-5050

KING, LYNDEL IRENE SAUNDERS, museum director; b. Enid, Okla., June 10, 1943; d. Leslie Jay and Jennie Irene (Duggan) Saunders; m. Blaine Larman King, June 12, 1965. BA, U. Kans., Lawrence, 1965; MA, U. Minn.-Mpls., 1971, PhD, 1982. Dir. Frederick R. Weisman Art Mus., U. Minn., Mpls., 1979—; dir. exhbns. and mus. programs Control Data Corp., 1979, 80-81; exhbn. coord. Nat. Gallery of Art, Washington, 1980. Recipient Cultural Contbn. of Yr. award Mpls. C. of C., 1978; Honor award Minn. Soc. Architects, 1979. Mem. Assn. Art Mus. Dirs. (chair art issues com. 1998-2000, chair tech. comm. com. 2000, bd. trustees 1998—), Art Mus. Assn. Am. (v.p. bd. dirs. 1984-89), Assn. Coll. and Univ. Mus. and Galleries (v.p. 1989-92), Am. Assn. Mus., Internat. Coun. Mus., Upper Midwest Conservation Assn. (pres. bd. dirs. 1980—), Minn. Assn. Mus. (steering com. 1982), Am. Fedn. Arts Bd. Home: 326 W 50th St Minneapolis MN 55419-1247 Office: Weisman Art Mus 333 E River Rd Minneapolis MN 55455-0367 E-mail: wamdir@umn.edu.

KING, MARCIA GYGLI, artist; b. Cleve., June 4, 1931; d. Robert Prescott and Ruth (Farr) Gygli; m. Rollin White King, May 10, 1956 (div. 1974); children: Rollin White King Jr., Edward Prescott King. BA, Smith Coll., 1953; MFA, U. Tex., San Antonio, 1981. Docent Nat. Gallery Art, Washington, 1956-60; organizer, dir. docent program McNay Art Mus., San Antonio, 1964-76; art critic Express news, San Antonio, 1976-77; artist N.Y.C., 1979—. Lectr. Nat. Gallery Art, Washington, 1956-60, div. continuing edn. U. Tex., 1976, So. Meth. U., Dallas, 1984, McNay Art Mus., San Antonio, 1984, Washington Project for the Arts, 1985, Monserrat Coll. Art, Beverly, Mass., 1987, Whitney Mus., Phillip Morris, N.Y.C., 1988, Lehman Coll. CUNY, 1988, MTA Pub. Art Commn. for Creative Stations, N.Y., 1995; panelist Panel on Women in the Arts, Alexandria, Va., 1978, Washington Project for the Arts, 1985, Corpus Christi (Tex.) State U., 1986, Dallas Mus., 1991, New Mus., N.Y., 1993, Mus. Mod. Art, N.Y., 1995. One woman shows include McNamara O'Connor Mus., Victoria, Tex., 1975, Charleston Gallery, San Antonio, 1980, Douglas Coll. Rutgers U., New Brunswick, N.J., 1981, McNay Art Mus., San Antonio, 1984, Mattingly Baker Gallery, Dallas, 1984, White Columns, N.Y., 1985, Parker Smalley Gallery, N.Y., Manhattan Marymount, N.Y., 1986, Ferver Gallery, N.Y., 1987, Katzen Brown Gallery, N.Y.C., 1988, 90, Haines Gallery, San Francisco, 1988, Wallace Wentworth Gallery, Washington, 1988, U. N.C., 1989, Valerie Miller Gallery, Palm Desert, Calif., 1989, Cleve. Ctr. for Contemporary Art, 1989-90, Hal Katzen, N.Y., 1992, 94, Guild Hall Mus., N.Y., 1995, Renee Fotouhi Fine Art, N.Y., 1995, Arts Acad., Md., 1996, Kouros Gallery, N.Y., 1999, Parchman Stremmel Gallery, San Antonio, 2000, San Antonio Art League Mus., 2000, Bklyn. Botanic Garden, 2001, Gallery Camino, Real, Fla., 2002, Gallery 668, N.Y., 2003; represented in collections Bklyn. Mus., Cleve. Mus., Guggenheim Mus., Johnson Mus., Cornell U., Nat. Mus. Women in Arts, Newark Mus., Robert Coll., Istanbul, Ark. Art Ctr., Guild Hall, L.I., McNay Art Mus., San Antonio Art League. Recipient Internat. Women's Yr. Panel award, Tex., 1977, Artist of Yr., San Antonio, 2000, James Kirkeby Nat. Meml. award Tex. Watercolor Soc., 1976, Brewer's Digest award Lone Star Brewery Day, 1963, Annual Z.T. Scott award & cir. Tex. Fine Arts Assn., 1970, Ethel T. Drought Meml. award San Antonio Art League Exhbn., 1971, Best of Show award Tex. Watercolor Show, 1971, First Purchase Prize, Tex. Watercolor Show, 1972, First Purchase Prize, 17th Delta Annual, Ark. Art. Ctr., 1974; named Outstanding Woman in San Antonio, Women's Polit. Caucus, 1979. Avocations: swimming, bicycling. Office: 477 Broome St Apt 63 New York NY 10013-5311

KING, MARGARET ANN, communications educator; b. Marion, Ind., Feb. 27, 1936; d. Paul Milton and Janet Mary (Broderick) Burke; m. Charles Claude King, Aug. 25, 1956; children: C. Kevin, Elizabeth Ann, Paul S., Margaret C. Student, Ohio Dominican, 1953-56, U. Kans., 1980-81; BA in Communication, Purdue U., 1986, MA in Pub. Communication, 1990. Regional rep. Indpls. Juv. Justice Task Force, 1984-85; vis. instr. dept. communication Purdue U., West Lafayette, Ind., 1992-96; v.p. King Mktg. Cons., Inc., 1996—2002; adj. lectr. U. Cin., 2002—. Bd. dirs. Vis. Nurse Home Health Svcs.; adj. instr. U. Cin., 2002—. Contbr. chpt. to book. Grad. mem. Leadership Lafayette, 1983. Purdue U. fellow, 1986-87. Mem. AAUW, Ctrl. States Comm. Assn. (conf. presenter 1989), Golden Key, Phi Kappa Phi. Republican. Roman Catholic. Avocations: poetry writing, vocal and piano music. Home: 7938 Wild Orchard Ln Cincinnati OH 45242-4309

KING, MARGARET LEAH, history professor; b. NYC, Oct. 16, 1947; d. Reno C. and Marie (Ackerman) King; m. Robert E. Kessler, Nov. 12, 1976; children: David King Kessler, Jeremy King Kessler. BA, Sarah Lawrence Coll., 1967; MA, Stanford U., 1968, PhD, 1972. Asst. prof. dept. history Calif. State Coll., Fullerton, 1969-70; asst. prof. Bklyn. Coll., CUNY, 1972-76, assoc. prof., 1976-86, Broeklundian prof., 2006—; prof. Bklyn. Coll. and Grad. Ctr., CUNY, 1987—, Claire and Leonard Tow disting. prof., 2000—02. Disting. guest prof. Centre for Reformation and Renaissance Studies, U. Toronto, 1995. Author: The Renaissance in Europe, 2004, (textbook) Western Civilization: A Social and Cultural History, 2d edit., 2002, Venetian Humanism in an Age of Patrician Dominance, 1986, Women of the Renaissance, 1991, The Death of the Child Valerio Marcello, 1994, The Renaissance in Europe, 2004; editor, translator: (with Diana Robin) Complete Works of Isotta Nogarola, 2004; co-editor series The Other Voice in Early Modern Europe; contbr. articles to profl. jours. Recipient Howard R. Marraro prize, Am. Cath. Hist. Assn., 1986, Tow award for distinction in scholarship, Bklyn. Coll., 1994—95; fellow, Danforth Found., 1967—72, Woodrow Wilson Found., 1967—68, Am. Coun. Learned Socs., 1977—78, NEH, 1986—87, Leonard and Claire Tow Disting. fellow, 2000—; grantee, Am. Coun. Learned Socs., 1976, Gladys Krieble Delmas Found., 1977—78, 1980—81, 1990, Am. Philos. Soc., 1979, 1990, NEH, 1984. Mem. Am. Hist. Assn. (Howard and Helen Mararro prize 1996), Hist. Soc., Renaissance Soc. Am. (exec. dir. 1988-95, editor Renaissance Quar. 1984-88, 97-2002). Home: 324 Beverly Rd Little Neck NY 11363-1125 Office: CUNY Bklyn Coll Dept History 2900 Bedford Ave Brooklyn NY 11210-2814 Office Phone: 718-951-5303. E-mail: mking@nyc.rr.com.

KING, MARJORIE JEAN, secondary school educator; b. Morgantown, W.Va., Jan. 20, 1928; d. Herbert Leslie and Hortense (Reeder) Fisher; m. Arnold Kimsey King, Jr., June 22, 1952; children: Leslie Diane, Carole Jean, Arnold Kimsey III, Julia Paige. Student, U. Chgo., 1947; BA, W.Va. U., 1948, MA, 1950; postgrad., U. N.C., 1956. Cert. tchr., N.C. Fellow W.Va. U., Morgantown, 1948-50; dir. adult program YWCA, Durham, N.C., 1950-52; instr. English McKendree Coll., Lebanon, Ill., 1952-53; asst. chief U. N.C. Bur. Corr.Inst., Chapel Hill, 1954-55; tchr. English Durham County Schs., Durham, 1955-59; prof. English Chowan Coll., Murfreesboro, N.C., 1964-74; instr. English N.C. Ctrl. U., Durham, 1974-93; retired, 1993. Cons. N.C. Tchr. Edn. Exam, Mebane, 1983. Co-author: Paragraph Patterns, 1987. Sec. Ahoskie (N.C.) Book Clu, 1966-68; pres. Woodland (N.C.) Women's Club, 1973-74; v.p., pres. Epworth United Meth. Women, Durham, 1977-82, assoc. treas. Durham dist., 1980-85. Mem. MLA, Nat. Coun. Tchrs. English. Democrat. Methodist. Avocations: choir and piano music, creative writing and leadership seminars. Home: 5315 Yardley Ter Durham NC 27707-9740

KING, MARJORIE LOUISE, cardiologist; b. 1953; MD, Pa. State U., 1979. Diplomate Am. Bd. Internal Medicine. Intern NYU-Manhattan VA Hosp., 1979-80, resident in internal medicine, 1980-82, fellow in cardiology, 1982-84; staff Helen Hayes Hosp., West Haverstraw, NY, 1984—, dir. cardiac svcs. Mem. AMA; Am. Assn. Cardiovascular and Pulmonary Rehab. (pres. 2005-06) Office: Helen Hayes Hosp Rte 9W West Haverstraw NY 10993*

KING, MARY ESTHER, elementary school educator; b. Waterloo, N.Y., June 28, 1952; d. Arthur William and Esther Mae Kelsey; m. Charles Kenneth King, Aug. 25, 1973; children: Jessica Falcione, Matthew. BS, Oswego State U., N.Y., 2003; MED, Nazareth Coll., Rochester, N.Y., 1977, cert. in reading, 1990. Tchr. Manchester-Shortsville Ctrl. Sch., NY, 1973—93, reading tchr., 1993—. Frameworks facilitator Manchester-Shortsville Ctrl. Sch., 1990—91. Mem. Oaks Corners Presbyn. Ch., NY, 1979—2006, treas., 1979—2006; chairperson Oaks Corners Antique Show, Oaks Corners, 1991—2006. Mem.: N.Y. State United Tchr. (assoc.), Reading Recovery Coun. N.Am. (assoc.), Lakes Counties Coun. (assoc.), Red Jacket Faculty Assn. (assoc.; treas. 1981—91), Delta Kappa Gamma (life; 1st and 2nd v.p. 2004—06). Presbyterian. Avocations: reading, cross country skiing, gardening. Home: 1264 Rt 14 Phelps NY 14532 Office: Manchester-Shortsville Ctrl Sch 1506 Rt 21 Shortsville NY 14548 Office Phone: 585-289-9647.

KING, MARY-CLAIRE, geneticist, educator; b. Evanston, Ill., Feb. 27, 1946; m. 1973; 1 child, Emily King Colwell. BA in Math. (cum laude), Carleton Coll., Northfield, Minn., 1966; PhD in Genetics, U. Calif., Berkeley, 1973; PhD (hon.), Carleton Coll., Bard Coll., Smith Coll., Dartmouth Coll.

Postdoctoral tng. U. Calif.-San Francisco; prof. genetics and epidemiology U. Calif. Berkeley, 1976—95; Am. Cancer Soc. rsch. prof. genome scis. and medicine U. Wash., Seattle, 1995—. Mem. bd. sci. counselors Nat. Cancer Inst., Meml. Sloan-Kettering Cancer Ctr., mem. NRC com. to advise Dept. Def. on the Breast Cancer Rsch. Program., NIH Genome Study Sect.; served on Nat. Commn. on Breast Cancer of the President's Cancer Panel; mem. adv. bd., NIH Office of Rsch. on Women's Health, Coun. of the NIH Fogarty Ctr., Nat. Action Plan for Breast Cancer, NIH Breast Cancer Program Review Group; affiliate mem. Fred Hutchinson Cancer Rsch. Ctr., Seattle; cons. Com. for Investigation of Disappearance of Persons, Govt. Argentina, Buenos Aires, 1984; carried out DNA Identifications for the UN War Crimes Tribunial; mem. UN Forensic Anthropology Team; mem. adv. bd. Robert Wood Johnson Found. Minority Med. Faculty Develop. program Contbr. articles to profl. jours. Named Woman of Yr., Glamour Mag.; recipient Clowes award, Basic Rsch., Am. Assn. Cancer Rsch., Jill Rose award, Am. Breast Cancer Found., Brinker award, Susan G. Komen Breast Cancer Found., 1999, Genetics prize, Peter Gruber Found., 2004, Weizmann Women & Sci. award, Am. Com. for Weizmann Inst. Sci., 2006. Fellow AAAS, Inst. Medicine, Acad. Arts and Sciences; mem. Am. Soc. Human Genetics, Soc. Epidemiologic Research, NAS, Phi Beta Kappa, Sigma Xi. Achievements include identifying the close similarity of the human and chimpanzee genomes; discovery of a gene (BRCA1) that predisposes to breast cancer; introduced direct sequencing of PCR-amplified segments of mitochondrial DNA for identifying people or their remains by comparing their DNA to that of relatives. Office: Dept Medicine and Genome Sciences Health Sciences RM K-160 U Washington Box 357720 Seattle WA 98195-7720 Office Phone: 206-616-4294. Office Fax: 206-616-4295. E-mail: mcking@u.washington.edu.*

KING, MEGHAN ANNE, secondary school educator; b. Neenah, Wis., Nov. 23, 1979; d. Mark Richard and Margaret Ann Laemmrich; m. Bryan John King, June 18, 2005. BS in Secondary Edn., Drake U., Des Moines, 2002. Lic. tchr. Iowa, 2002. English/lang. arts tchr. Ottumwa H.S., Iowa, 2002—04, West Ctrl. Valley, Stuart, Iowa, 2004—. Asst. speech coach West Ctrl. Valley, Stuart, Iowa, 2004—. Office: West Central Valley HS Stuart IA 50250

KING, MOLLY ELIZABETH RUTLAND, elementary school educator; b. Sheffield, Ala., Aug. 1, 1967; d. Glen Davis and Sheila Jean (Wells) Rutland; m. Richard Allen King, Dec. 30, 1989. BS in Elem. Edn., U. No. Ala., 1989; EdS, Nat. Louis U., Germany, 2003. Cert. tchr., Ala. Ballet tchr. Bryan's Studio of Fine Arts, Florence, Ala., 1986-89; asst. tchr. Oxford (Miss.) U. Sch., 1990; tchr. Holly Springs (Miss.) Intermediate Sch., 1990-91, Care To learn Sch., Huntsville, Ala., 1991-92, Madison Acad., Huntsville, 1992-93; owner, dir., instr. King's Acad. Fine Arts, Huntsville, 1991—99; instr. U. Phoenix, 2005—. Coach, advisor Madison Acad. Acad. Bowl, 1992-93. Contbr. articles to profl. publs. Asst. dir., dir. scholarship program bd. Franklin County Jr. Miss Program, Belgreen, Ala., 1986-99, choreographer, asst. dir., 1986-92, dir., 1993-94. Mem. Profl. Dance Tchrs. Assn. (mem. state adv. bd. 1989-93), Internat. Tchrs. of Dance Inc., Sigma Tau Delta, Kappa Delta Pi. Mem. Ch. of Christ. Avocations: ballet, model building.

KING, MURIEL EILEEN, secondary school educator; b. Georgetown, Demerara, Guyana, July 2, 1924; came to U.S., 1972; d. Egbert Sinclair Harvey and Edna Mollyneau; m. Rupert Oliver King, Aug. 4, 1944; children: Egbert Samuel, Aubrey, Ancil, Rawle Oliver, Dawn Allison. BA in English cum laude, L.I. U., Bklyn., 1975, MSc in Edn., 1977. Cert. tchr., Calif., Guyana, Can. Tchr. Washington High Sch., Georgetown, 1942-44, Enterprise High Sch., Georgetown, 1944-49, Mt. Zion Luth. Sch., Georgetown, 1949-56, Schepmoed Sch., Berbice, 1959-62, Tchrs. Tng. Coll., 1962-63, Ascension Luth. Coll., 1963-69, Kyle (Sask., Can.) Composite Sch., 1969-72, Epiphany High Sch., 1972-80, Straubeamuller Jr. High. Sch., 1981. Sr. asst., Georgetown, 1963-69. Author: Juvenile Delinquency and the Part Education Can Play to Solve the Problem, 1964. Liaison officer, tchr. Aboriginal Indians, Homeless in the Mantinique Hotels, Prince George Hotel Homeless, Guyana, S.Am., 1949-56. NSF award, L.I.U., 1978-79. Avocations: art, painting, debating, needlecrafts. Home: 6075 Geremander Ave Rialto CA 92377-4023

KING, NICOLE, molecular biologist, educator; BA, Ind. U., Bloomington, 1992; AM, Harvard U., 1996, PhD, 1999. Postdoctoral fellow U. Wis., 2000—03; asst. prof., genetics and develop., dept. molecular and cell biology and integrative biology U. Calif., Berkeley, 2003—, faculty affiliate, Ctr. for Integrative Genomics. Contbr. articles to profl. jour. Named a MacArthur Fellow, John D. and Catherine T. MacArthur Found., 2005. Office: Univ Calif Berkeley Dept Molecular & Cell Biology 142 Life Sciences Addition #3200 Berkeley CA 94720-3200 Office Phone: 510-643-9395, 510-643-9417 (lab). Office Fax: 510-643-6791. E-mail: nking@berkeley.edu.

KING, NORAH MCCANN, federal judge; b. Steubenville, Ohio, Aug. 13, 1949; d. Charles Bernard and Frances Marcella (Krumm) McCann; married; 4 children. BA cum laude, Rosary Coll. (now Dominican U.), 1971; JD summa cum laude, Ohio State U., 1975. Bar: Ohio 1975, So. Dist. of Ohio 1980. Law clerk U.S. Dist. Ct., Columbus, Ohio, 1975-79; counsel Frost, King, Freytag & Carpenter, Columbus, Ohio, 1979-82; asst. prof. Ohio State U., Columbus, 1980-82; U.S. magistrate judge U.S. Dist. Ct., Columbus, 1982—, chief magistrate judge, 2000—04. Recipient award of merit Columbus Bar Assn., 1990. Mem.: Fed. Bar Assn., Coun. U.S. Magistrate Judges. Office: US Dist Ct 85 Marconi Blvd Rm 235 Columbus OH 43215-2837 Office Phone: 614-719-3390.

KING, PATRICIA ANN, law educator; b. Norfolk, Va., June 12, 1942; d. Addison A. and Grayce (Wood) K.; m. Roger W. Wilkins, Feb. 21, 1981; 1 child, Elizabeth. BA, Wheaton Coll., 1963; JD, Harvard U., 1969. Bar: D.C. 1969, U.S. Supreme Ct. 1980. Spl. asst. to chair EEOC, Washington, 1969-71; dep. dir. civil rights office HEW, Washington, 1971-73; prof. law Georgetown Law Ctr., Washington, 1973—, Carmack Waterhouse Prof. Law, Medicine, Ethics, and Public Policy. Adj. prof. Sch. Hygiene and Pub. Health Johns Hopkins U., 1990—; bd. dirs. Wheaton Coll., Womens Legal Defense Fund. Co-author: Law, Science and Medicine, 1984; contbr. articles to profl. jours. Chmn. Redevelopment Land Agy., Washington, 1976-80. Fellow Hastings Ctr.; mem. Am. Soc. Law and Medicine, Am. Law Inst., Inst. Medicine. Office: Georgetown Law Ctr 600 New Jersey Ave NW Washington DC 20001-2075*

KING, PEGGY MARSHA, special education educator, researcher; b. Chgo., May 4, 1950; d. Thomas Edgar and Rhoda Newsom Hollingsworth; m. James Francis King, Mar. 21, 1972; children: James Ryan, Jessica Marie. BA, MS; postgrad., Aurora U., 2003—05. Cert. sch. adminstr. Ill., 2004. Inclusion specialist Glen Ellyn Sch. Dist. # 89, Ill., 1996—2004, spl. edn. dir., 2004—. Presenter in field. Mem. Wall of Tolerance, So. Poverty Law Ctr., Ala., 2004—05; life mem. PTA, Bensonville, Ill., 1990—; mem. HOPE Found. Mem.: ASCD, Ill. Alliance Adminstrs. of Spl. Edn. (assoc.). Office: Ccsd # 89 22W600 Butterfield Rd Glen Ellyn IL 60137 Office Phone: 630-469-8900. Business E-Mail: pking@ccsd89.org.

KING, REBECCA JANE, nursing administrator, educator; b. Warsaw, Ind., Jan. 25, 1970; d. George Allen Chapman and Clematean Hinson Moore; m. Johnny Allen King; 1 child, Nathan John. Student, W.Va. U., Morgantown, 1988—90; BSN, U. Charleston, 1994; MS in Adult Tech. Edn., Marshall U., 2002, MSN, 2004. Cert. BLS instr. W.Va., tchr. W.Va.; RN W.Va. Charge nurse cardiac unit Charleston Area Med. Ctr. Meml., Charleston, W.Va., 1994—96, Eye and Ear Clinic, Charleston, 1996—2001; practical nursing instr. Garnet Career Ctr., Charleston, 1999—2003; HIV/AIDS coord. W. Va. Dept. Edn., 2003—. CPR instr., Charleston, 1993—; vis. nurse Charleston Area Med. Ctr. Home Care, Charleston, 1997—2000. Organizer relay for life team Am. Cancer Soc., Charleston, 2001—; blood drive organizer ARC, Charleston, 2002—; clothing drive Mildred Mitchell Bateman Hosp., Huntington, W.Va., 2002—. Mem.: W.Va. Asthma Coalition, Nat. Assn. State Sch. Nurse Cons., W.Va. Assn. Sch. Nurses, Sigma Theta Tau. Avocations: walking, bicycling. Office: W Va Dept Edn Student Svc and Health Promotions Bldg 6 Rm 309 1900 Kanawha Blvd E Charleston WV 25305 Office Phone: 304-558-8830. Personal E-mail: rjnking@earthlink.net.

KING, REGINA, actress; b. L.A., Jan. 15, 1971; m. Ian Alexander, Apr. 23, 1997; 1 child. Actor: (TV series) 227, 1985—90, Leap of Faith, 2002; (TV films) Where the Truth Lies, 1999, If These Walls Could Talk 2, 2000, Damaged Care, 2002; (films) Boyz n the Hood, 1991, Poetic Justice, 1993, Higher Learning, 1995, Friday, 1995, A Thin Line Between Love and Hate, 1996, Jerry Maguire, 1996, Rituals, 1998, How Stella Got Her Groove Back, 1998, Enemy of the State, 1998, Mighty Joe Young, 1998, Down to Earth, 2001, Daddy Day Care, 2003, Legally Blonde 2: Red, White & Blonde, 2003, A Cinderella Story, 2004, Ray, 2004, Miss Congeniality 2: Armed and Fabulous, 2005, (voice) The Ant Bully, 2006; actor, prodr.: (films) Final Breakdown, 2002.*

KING, RO, psychotherapist, educator; b. New York City, May 25, 1941; d. George and Selma King. BS cum laude, Pa. State U., 1963; MS in Sch. Psychology, CUNY, 1970; PhD, Am. Commonwealth U., 1987. Lic. clin. mental health counselor, N.Mex.; cert. sch. psychologist, N.Y., human capacities practitioner. Psychologist NYU Reading Inst., 1969-73; with gen. studies NYU, 1971-73; psychotherapist Richmond Coll. CUNY, N.Y.C., 1973-75; workshop leader Ctr. Experiential Psychotherapy, N.Y.C., 1970—96; supr. Ctr. Human Potential, Identy House, N.Y.C., 1970—; pvt. practice psychotherapy N.Y., N.Mex., 1970—. Psychology educator NYU, CCNY, Soc. Ethical Culture, 1971—; guest lectr. New Sch. Social Rsch.; leader, mem. Therapist Networking, Santa Fe, 1995—; course cons. Regis U., 1998. Leade, mem. People for Peace, Santa Fe, 1991—; organizer Multicultural exch., Santa Fe, 1992; mem. various women's orgns., N.Y.C., 1969—; leader Women's Action Coun., Santa Fe, 1993; cons. Nat. Folk Art Mus., 2005— Mem. Am. Counseling Assn., Helix Profl. Devel. Group, Associated Psychotherapists (salon leader 1978-89). Avocations: writing, hiking, gardening, crafts. Home: 10 Camino Peralta Santa Fe NM 87507-0106 Office: 10 Camino Peralta Santa Fe NM 87507

KING, ROSALYN MERCITA, social sciences educator, researcher, psychologist; b. Jacksonville, Fla., Aug. 16, 1948; d. Morris Charles and Marie (Coleman) K. BS, Howard U., 1970, MA, 1972; EdD, Harvard U., 1979. Dir. police youth project NCCJ, Washington, 1970-73; placement coord. U. North Fla., Jacksonville, 1973-74, instr., student support counselor, 1973-75; career edn. program coord. Roxbury/Harvard Sch. Program, Cambridge, Mass., 1976; rsch. analyst Spl. Commn. on Unequal Ednl. Opportunity Mass. Ho. of Reps., Boston, 1977; program coord. Freedom House, Inc., Roxbury, Mass., 1977-78; sr. program assoc. Expand Assocs., Inc., Silver Spring, Md., 1979; sr. assoc., dir. rsch. Mark Battle Assocs., Inc., Washington, 1980; dir. planning, program devel. and tech. assistance PUSH-Excel Inst. Research and Tng., Washington, 1981; rsch. assoc. So. Ctr. Studies in Pub. Policy Clark Coll., Atlanta, 1981-84; pres. Info. Rsch. Network Svc., Alexandria, Va., 1984—, Bathshua's Greetings, Alexandria, 1988—. Chief racial stats. U.S. Bur. Census, Washington, 1988; vis. prof. psychology Coppin State Coll., Balt., 1989-90; faculty rsch. assoc. U. Md., College Park, 1990-91; adj. lectr. dept. psychology George Mason U., Fairfax, Va., 1991—; adj. prof. psychology Prince George's C.C., Andrews AFB, 1991-94, Mary Washington Coll., Fredericksburg, Va., 1992-93, Catonsville (Md.) C.C., 1991-96, lectr., 1994-96; sr. pub. health analyst Agy. for HIV/AIDS Comm. Pub. Health, Washington, 1992-94; from assoc. prof. to prof. psychology and chair Ctr. for Tchg. Excellence No. Va. Region, No. Va. C.C., Loudoun campus, Sterling, Va., 1996—, planning com. Nat. Assessment Ednl. Progress, writing framework and specifications devel. ACT Inc., Nat. Assessment Governing Bd.; presenter papers in field. Contbr. articles to profl. jours. Mem. APA, Am. Psychol. Soc., Soc. for Tchg. of Psychology, Eastern C.C. Social Scis. Assn. (bd. trustees 2003—, chair bd. trustees 2005), Psi Chi, Phi Delta Kappa. Office Phone: 703-450-2629. E-mail: rosalynmercita.king@worldnet.att.net, roking@nvcc.edu.

KING, SHARON LOUISE, lawyer; b. Ft. Wayne, Ind., Jan. 12, 1932; AB, Mt. Holyoke Coll., 1954; JD with distinction, Valparaiso U., 1957; LLM in Taxation, Georgetown U., 1961. Bar: Ind. 1957, D.C. 1958, Ill. 1962. Trial atty. tax divsn. U.S. Dept. Justice, 1958—62; sr. counsel Sidley Austin LLP, Chgo. Bd. dirs., past pres. Lawyer's Com. for Better Housing, Inc.; mem. North Shore Sr. Ctr., 2006—, bd. dirs., 2006—. Fellow Am. Coll. Tax Counsel; mem. ABA (chmn. com. closely-held corps. taxation sect. 1979-81, regulated pub. utilities com. taxation sect. 1982-83, coun. dir. taxation sect. 1983-86), Chgo. Bar Assn. (bd. mgrs. 1973-75, chmn. fed. tax com. 1983-84), Ill. State Bar Assn. (counsel dir. sect. fed. taxation 1989-91), Women's Bar Found. (bd. dirs., past pres.). Office: Sidley Austin LLP One S Dearborn St Chicago IL 60603

KING, SHARON MARIE, consulting company executive; b. Clarksville, Ark., Sept. 16, 1946; d. Argie L. and Vida M. K.; m. Robert W. Warnke, Feb. 14, 1983; children: Michael R., Jenna L. AA, Coll. of Ozarks, Clarksville, 1966; BA summa cum laude, Calif. State U., Dominguez Hills, 1979. Sr. exec. asst. Computer Sci. Corp., El Segundo, Calif., 1973-79; office mgr., bookkeeper Internal Charter Brokers, Manhattan Beach, Calif., 1979-80; office mgr. Metal Box Can, Torrance, Calif., 1980-81; sec. to pres. Filtrol, L.A., 1981-82; owner, mgr. Select Secretarial Svc., Manhattan Beach, 1982-89; pres., CEO Chipton-Ross, Inc., El Segundo, Calif., 1989—. Mem. Calif. C. of C. Presbyterian. Office: Chipton-Ross Inc 1756 Manhattan Beach Blvd Manhattan Beach CA 90266-6220 E-mail: sking@chiptonross.com.

KING, SHEILA SUE, music educator, elementary school educator; b. Chgo., Aug. 23, 1949; d. Robert William and Bernette Lips; m. John W. King, June 12, 1976; 1 child, Sarah Rebecca. B in Music Edn., Mich. State U., 1971. Pvt. music tchr., Laramie, Wyo., 1971—75; music tchr. Houston Ind. Sch. Dist., Houston, 1975—76; pvt. music tchr. Huntsville, Ala., 1976—80, Gaithersburg, Md., 1976—80; music tchr. Apollo Elem. Sch., Titusville, Fla., 1981—. Dir. music Good Shepherd Luth. Ch., Titusville, Fla., 1981—; mem. leadership team Brevard County Sch., Melbourne, Fla., 1983—. Bd. dirs. Brevard Symphony Youth Orch., 2002—. Named Brevard County Tchr. of Yr., 2004, Fla. Music Educator of Yr., 2005. Mem.: Brevard Symphony Youth Orchestra (exec. bd. 2002), Am. Orff-Schulwerk Assn. (Ctrl. Fla. chpt. v.p. 1983—), Fla. Music Educators Assn. (music demonstration sch. 1996—99, 1999—, state chmn. 1999—), Music Educators Nat. Conf., Alpha Delta Kappa. Lutheran. Avocation: space coast clogger. Home: 3730 Oakhill Drive Titusville FL 32780 Office: Apollo Elementary 3085 Knox McRae Drive Titusville FL 32780 E-mail: pianoforte@mindspring.com.

KING, SHELLEY B., science educator; d. Charles E. and Rose M. Bunyea; m. Victor B. King, Nov. 26, 1975; 1 child, Katherine Laura Rose. BS, Cumberland Coll., Williamsburg, Ky., 1976; MS, U. Tenn., Knoxville, 1980. Cert. tchr. biology grades 9-12 Tenn., elem. tchr. grades 1-8 Tenn. Tchr. spl. edn. East LaFollette Elem. Sch., Tenn., 1976—81; tchr. West LaFollette Elem. Sch. and LaFollette Mid. Sch., 1981—2002; tchr. sci. grade 8 Jacksboro Mid. Sch., 2002—03; tchr. biology Campbell County H.S., 2003—. Sch. leader green schs. program Campbell County H.S., Jacksboro, Tenn., 2003—, sponsor biology club, 2005—, sponsor high schs. for Habitat, 2006. Author: Dichotomous Key of Spring Wildflowers in East Tennessee, 2005. Facilitator biology club conservation project Cove Lake State Park, Caryville, Tenn., 2005—. Grantee, Tenn. Dept. Environment and Conservation, 2003, Beta Phi, 2005. Mem.: NSTA, Tenn. Sci. Tchrs. Assn., Rocky Mountain Elk Found. Presbyterian. Avocations: hiking, photography, boating. Office: Campbell County Comprehensive HS 150 Cougar Ln Jacksboro TN 37757-5131

KING, SHERYL JAYNE, secondary school educator, counselor; b. East Grand Rapids, Mich., Oct. 29, 1945; d. Thomas Benton III and Bettyann Louise (Mains) K. BS in Family Living, Sociology, Secondary Edn., Cen. Mich. U., 1968, M in Counseling, 1971. Educator Newaygo (Mich.) Pub. Schs., 1968-72; interior decorator Sue King Interiors, Grand Rapids, Mich., 1972-73; dir. girl's unit Dillon Family and Youth Svcs., Tulsa, 1973-74; mgr. Fellowhip Press, Grand Rapids, Minn., 1974-76; educator, counselor Itasca Community Coll., Grand Rapids, 1977-81, Dist. 318, Grand Rapids, 1977—, dept. head, 1977-81, 85-87. Bd. dirs., chair program com. Marriage and Family Devel. Ctr., Grand Rapids, 1985-89. Treas. Cove Whole Foods Coop., 1978-80; chmn. bd. Christian Cmty. Sch., 1977-78; jr. high softball coach, 1983-86; issues com. No. Minn. Citizens League, Grand Rapids, 1984—, Blandin Found. Study, 1985-86; chair Itasca County Women's Consortium, Grand Rapids, 1983-87, Women's Day Conf., Grand Rapids, 1983-87; bd. dirs. audio tech. Fellowship of Believers, Grand Rapids, 1974-87, 90-98, deaconess, 1974—; bd. dir. audio tech Camp Dominion, Cass Lake, Minn., 1976-80; fitness com., chmn. aquatic com., YMCA, Grand Rapids, 1974-87; sec. Grand Rapids Libr., 2003—. Recipient 6 Outstanding Svc. awards Fellowship of Believers, 1974-79. Mem. Alpha Delta Kappa. Independent. Avocations: photography, tennis, sailing, softball, travel, writing. Home: 1914 Mckinney Lake Rd Grand Rapids MN 55744-4330

KING, SHIRLEY ANN, middle school educator; b. Joliet, Ill., Oct. 20, 1959; d. James Thomas Hall and Betty Jean Pellow; m. Douglas Wayne King, Oct. 21, 1977; children: Jennifer Lynnette Hicks, Gary Wayne. BS in Edn., Memphis State U., 1992; MS in Edn., U. Memphis, 2001. Lic. profl. educator Tenn. Tchr. Tipton County Bd. of Edn., Covington, Tenn., 1992—. Office: Munford Mid Sch 100 Education Ave Munford TN 38058 Office Phone: 901-837-1700.

KING, SUSAN BENNETT, retired glass company executive; b. Sioux City, Iowa, Apr. 29, 1940; d. Francis Moffatt Bennett and Marjorie (Rittenhouse) Sillin; m. Stephen P. Glantz. AB, Duke U., 1962. Legis. asst. U.S. Senate, Washington, 1963-66; dir. Nat. Com. for Effective Congress, Washington, 1967-71, Ctr. Pub. Financing of Elections, Washington, 1972-75; exec. asst. to chmn. Fed. Election Commn., Washington, 1975-77; chmn. U.S. Consumer Product Safety Commn., Washington, 1978-81; dir. consumer affairs Corning (N.Y.) Glass Works, 1982, v.p. corp. communications, 1983-86; pres. Steuben Glass, N.Y.C., 1987-92; sr. v.p. corp. affairs Corning Inc., 1992-94. Trustee Duke U., Durham, NC, 1987—2001, Nat. Pub. Radio Found.; chmn. bd. Making a Difference in Cmtys., Inc., 1995—, Triangle Cmty. Found., 2002—, trustee; bd. dirs. MPC, Inc., 1995—. Fellow Inst. Politics, Harvard U., 1981.

KING, SUSAN MARIE, special education educator; b. Cambridge, Mass., Feb. 10, 1956; d. V. James and Joan Frances Cannalonga; m. John Charles King, Apr. 27, 1975. Student, Valencia C.C., Kissimmee, Fla., 1996—97; student sign lang., Mid Fla. Tech, Orlando, Fla, 1987—92, Fla. Sch. for the Deaf and Blind, St. Augustine, Fla. Vocat. 7 Teaching Certificate Kissimmee, Fla., 1997, cert. QA Registry of Interpreters for the Deaf, completition Dale Carnegie. Belly dancer, Orlando, Fla., 1980—82; co-owner, mgr. Colonial Motel and Apts., St. Cloud, Fla., 1980—89; tchr. Master's Acad., St. Cloud, Fla., 1989—91, Heartland Christian Acad., Kissimmee, Fla., 1993—94, Kingsway Christian Sch., St. Cloud, Fla., 1994—95, Osceola Assn. for Retarded Citizens and Tech. Edn. Ctr. Osceola (TECO), Kissimmee, Fla., 1995—97; tchr., testing specialist TECO, Kissimmee, Fla., 1995—. Sales rep. Avon, 2000—; mystery shopper, 2003—. Co-dir. (variety shows) Variety Show; translator: (first person to interpret Nat. Anthem performance in sign lang.) Orlando Magic Game, 1990 (cert., 1990). Vol. Spl. Olympics, Kissimmee, Fla., 1994—96, Osceola Ctr.Arts, Kissimmee, Fla., 1995—96, Am. Bible Soc., New York, NY, 1984—89; interpreter Heartland Worship Ctr., Kissimmee, Fla., 1985—95. Recipient Second Pl. Nat. Essay Olympics, Assn. of Christian Sch. Internat., 1994. Mem.: Kissimmee Deaf Club (mem. 1988—91). Republican. Avocations: horseback riding, reading, puzzles and games. Office: Tech Edn Ctr Osceola-TECO 501 Simpson Rd Kissimmee FL 34744-4459

KING, TABITHA, author; b. 1949; m. Stephen King. Author: (novels) Small World, 1981, Caretakers, 1983, The Trap, 1985, Pearl, 1988, One on One, 1993, The Book of Reuben, 1995, Survivor, 1997, (non-fiction) Mid-Life Confidential, 1994, (anthologies) Shadows 4, 1981, The Best of the Best, 1998, (short stories) The Blue Chair, 1981, Djinn and Tonic, 1998; actor: (films) Knightriders, 1981. Trustee The Stephen and Tabitha King Foundation. Office: The Stephen and Tabitha King Found 49 Florida Ave Bangor ME 04401 Office Phone: 207-990-2910. Office Fax: 207-990-2975.

KING, TAMARA POWERS, music educator, musician; b. Spartanburg, S.C., Dec. 29, 1959; d. Douglas Edgar and Patricia Elizabeth Powers; m. Bryan Ray King, June 23, 1985; 1 child, Caroline Dawn. MusB in Edn., So. Missionary Coll., Collegedale, Tenn., 1982; MusM, Converse Coll., 2004. Customer svc. and sales Powers Printing Co., Inc., Spartanburg, 1982—2000; violin tchr. dept. pre-coll. Converse Coll., Spartanburg, 1982—84; violin and viola tchr. Spartanburg, 1996—, Alia Lawson Pre-Coll., Spartanburg, 2001—03; strings and orch. tchr. Spartanburg County Sch. Dist. 1, Inman, SC, 2002—04. Violinist Spartanburg Symphony Orch., 1982—95, Greenville Symphony Orch., SC, 1985—87, Greater Spartanburg Philharm., 1995—97; violinist and violist Converse Symphony Orch., Spartanburg, 2000—04. Mem. music com. Spartanburg Seventh Day Adventist Ch., 1985—2005, asst. choir dir., 2000. Mem.: Am. String Tchrs. Assn., Music Educator's Nat. Conf., Spartanburg Philharm. Music Club. Avocations: reading, birding and nature study, drawing, collecting musical instruments, painting. Home: 1099 Moore-Duncan Hwy Moore SC 29369

KING, TERESA HOWARD, special education educator, consultant; b. Clovis, N.Mex., Nov. 28, 1949; children: Heather, Matthew. BS, Ea. N.Mex. U., 1974, MA, 1981. Cert. elem. tchr., spl. edn. tchr. Tchr. 4th grade Clovis Mcpl. Schs., Clovis, N.Mex., 1975-76, tchr. 3d grade, 1976-80, tchr. 5th grade, 1980-87, tchr. spl. edn., 1987-93, facilitator enriched learning program, 1994, ednl. diagnostician, 1994—98, Arlington ISD, 1998—2002, Beford, Tex., 2002—. Co-owner Teresdan Softeware LLC, Arlington, Tex., 1998—. Co-author (computer software) Diagnostic Report Writer, 1995, R/2/4/KIDZ, 1995. Artists in Residency grantee N.Mex. Arts Divsn., 1992. Mem.: Delta Kappa Gamma, Phi Delta Kappa. Home: 2208 Hunter View Ct Arlington TX 76013-1423

KING, TRACEY GROUX, psychotherapist; b. Teaneck, N.J., Feb. 18, 1956; d. Charles Robert and Exilda May Groux; m. Robert A. King, Aug. 15, 1980; children: Audrey Renee, Ian Robert. AA, Dawson Coll., Montreal, Que., 1975; BS, Trent U., Peterborough, Ont., 1978; MA, Marymount U., Arlington, Va., 1996. LPC; lic. profl. psychotherapist Va. Counselor then psychotherapist Purcellville Counseling Ctr., Va., 2000—. Adj. prof. Marymount U., Arlington, 2004, guest lectr., 1999. Disaster mental health specialist and responder to 9/11 ARC, Arlington, 2000—; vol. Victim Witness, Leesburg, Va., 1996. Mem.: Marymount U. Alumni Assn. (adv. bd. 2000—01), Am. Counseling Assn., Psi Chi (life), Delta Epsilon Sigma (life). Democrat. Avocations: bicycling, swimming, running. Office: Purcellville Counseling Center 200 E Main St Purcellville VA 20182

KING, TRACY LYNN, science educator; b. Chgo., Jan. 15, 1966; d. Larry H. and Loretta Joyce (Yarbrough) Witherington; m. Junior Owen King, Aug. 26, 1989; children: Sara Lynn, Jefferson Allen. BS Biol. Sci., U. Tenn., Martin, 1991, History Endorsement, 1999. Tchr. sci. Starkville City Schs., Miss., 1993, Obion County HS, Troy, Tenn., 1994—95; spl. edn. asst. Weakley County Schs., Sharon, Tenn., 1997—2000; tchr. sci. and math. Carroll Acad., Huntingdon, Tenn., 2000—. Remediation tchr. Weakley County Schs., Martin, 1997—98, substitute tchr., Dresden, Tenn., 1995—96, Bradford Spl. Sch. Dist., Tenn., 1995—96. Leader Reel Foot Coun. Girl Scouts, Jackson, Tenn., 1997—99; asst. Horse Bowl and Hippology Team 4-H, Dresden, 2002—04; adv. Jr. Nat. Young Leaders Conf., Washington, 2004; parent vol. FFA chpt. Westview HS, Martin, 2003—. Mem.: Tenn. Sci. Tchrs. Assn., Order Ea. Star. Avocations: reading, horseback riding, needlecrafts, piano, gardening. Office: Carroll Academy 625 High St Ste 101 Huntingdon TN 38344-1731 Personal E-mail: double-K-ranch1@yahoo.com.

KING, VERNA ST. CLAIR, retired school counselor; b. Berwick, La.; d. John Westley and Florence Ellen (Calvin) St. C.; A.B., Wiley Coll., 1937; M.A., San Diego State U., 1977; m. Alonzo Le Roy King, Aug. 27, 1939 (dec.); children— Alonzo Le Roy, Joyce Laraine, Verna Lee Eugenia King Bickerstaff, St. Clair A., Reginald Calvin (dec.). Tchr., Morgan City, La., 1939-40; tchr. San Diego Unified Sch. Dist., 1955-67, parent counselor, 1967-78, counselor grades 1-9, 1978-86; cons. Tucson Sch. Dist., 1977—, dir. compensatory edn., 1983—. Mem. Calif. Democratic State Central Com., 1950—, Dem. County Central Com., 1972—, del. nat. conv., 1976, 84, mem. exec. bd. Dem. State Central Com., 1982—; mem. San Diego County Sander Adv. Commn., 1982; hon. life mem. PTA; bd. dirs. YWCA, 1983—, v.p., 1987-88; chair Dem. County Ctrl. fundraising, 1992—; del. Dem. Nat. Com., 1992. Recipient Key to City, Mayor C. Dail, 1955, cert. United Negro Coll. Fund dr., 1980, Urban League Pvt. Sector award, 1982, 4th Ann. Conf. on Issues in Ethnicity and Mental Health Participants award, 1982; named Woman of Dedication, Salvation Army, 1985, Citizen of Yr., City Club and Jaycees, 1985, Woman of Achievement, Pres.' Council, 1983, Henry Auerbach award San Diego Dem. Party Ctrl. Com., 1997; numerous other honors. Mem. NEA (women's council 1980-82), AAUW, Calif. Tchrs. Assn. (state council 1979—, area dir. 1985—), San Diego Tchrs. Assn. (dir. 1958, 64, sec. 1964-67), Nat. Council Negro Women, San Diego County Council Dem. Women (pres. 1986-88), Compensatory Edn. Assn. (area dir. 1982-87), Pres. Women, Inc., Alpha Kappa Alpha (pres. 1978-80), Delta Kappa Gamma. Methodist. Clubs: Women's Inc., Order Eastern Star.

KING, VIRGINIA SHATTUCK, painter, retired school nurse, educator; b. Bklyn., Feb. 8, 1921; d. Harold James Shattuck and Lillian Elizabeth Shattuck; m. Stuart G. King, May 26, 1946 (dec. July 1988); children: Richard D.(dec.), Stuart George, Harold James, Douglas Louis. BS in Nursing, Columbia U., 1944; postgrad., Adelphi U., SUNY, Stony Brook. RN N.Y., 1946; cert. sch. nurse tchr. N.Y., 1960. Head nurse, obstet. fl. Columbia - Presbyn. Hosp., NYC, 1945—46; pub. health nurse Suffolk County, NY, 1953, sch. nurse, 1959—79, tchr. health edn., 1970—79, ret., 1979. Author: From Then.To Who Knows When, 1996; one-woman shows include King Ctr. Performing Arts, 2000—01, Maxwell C. King Ctr. Performing Arts, 2001—02, exhibitions include King Ctr. Performing Arts, 1993, Fla. State Soc. Nat. Soc. DAR, 1993, Spacecoast Art League, 1996—97 (3d pl., 1996, 2d pl., 1997), Brevard Mus. Arts and Scis., 1997, 1999, Fla. Hist. Soc. Tebeau Libr., 1998, George Plimpton Zoo-to-Do, Cape Canaveral, 1998, Moffitt Cancer Rsch. Ctr., 1999, Fla. Watercolor Soc., 1999, 2001 (Strathmore award), Charlotte County Art Guild, 2000, Ridge Art League, 2000, Bayard Ho. Exhibit, 2000, Strawbridge Art League, 2002, 2004—06 (Merit award, 2006), Orlando Mus. Art, 2001, So. Watercolor Soc., 2002, 2005, Melbourn Internat. Airport, 2004, Nat. Wildlife Ctr., Merrit Island, Fla., 2004—05, Ga. Water Color Soc. Mems. Show, 2006, others, Represented in permanent collections Brevard County Libr. Second v.p. Friends of Eau Gallie Pub. Libr., 1999—. Recipient Strathmore Paper award, Fla. Water Color Soc., 2001. Mem.: DAR, Nat. League Am. Pen Women, NSDAR (chpt. regent 1990—92, vice regent 2005—06), Strawbridge Art League, Ga. Watercolor Soc. (ribbon and prize 2003), So. Watercolor Soc., P-2 Fla. Watercolor Soc., Brevard watercolor Soc., N.Y. State Tchrs. Retired in Fla. (pres. Suncoast chpt. 1992—94, Svc. award 2001). Republican. Achievements include the Virginia Shattuck Archives at Health Scis. Divsn. of Columbia U. Avocations: watercolor artist, writing, swimming, music. Home and Studio: 2419 Apache Dr Melbourne FL 32935 Office Phone: 321-259-1074. Personal E-mail: hglartiste@aol.com.

KINGERY, ALICE L., elementary school educator; b. Findlay, Ohio, Mar. 30, 1948; d. Ralph D. and Martha Lurleen Beamer; m. Mel C. Kingery, Jr., June 13, 1970; children: Melanie Peters, Adam. BS, Findlay Coll., 1970; MS, Butler U., Indpls., 1974. Tchr. North Elem., Noblesville, Ind., 1970—96, Benton (Tenn.) Elem., 1996—. Bd. dirs. Polk County Friends Libr., Noblesville, 2005—06. Mem.: NEA, Tenn. Edn. Assn., Polk County Edn. Assn. (pres., exec. commn. bldg. rep. 1997—2006). Democrat. Roman Catholic. Home: 426 Quarry Rd Benton TN 37307 Office: PO Box 613 Benton TN 37307-0613

KINGET, G. MARIAN, educator, psychologist; b. Belgium, June 2, 1910; came to U.S., 1948, naturalized, 1957; d. Rene Jules Henri and Elisa (Declercq) K. PhD summa cum laude, U. Louvain, Belgium, 1948; postdoctoral, N.Y. U., 1948-49, Columbia U., 1949-50. With U. Chgo., 1950-52; asst. prof. psychology Mich. State U., East Lansing, 1952-55, asso. prof., 1955-66, prof., 1966-81, emeritus prof., 1981. Author: On Being Human, 1975, 2d edition, 1987, Psychotherapie et Relations Humaines (transl. Spanish, Italian, and Portuguese), Vol. II, 1962, The Drawing-Completion Test, 1952, (with Carl R. Rogers) Psychotherapie et Relations Humaines (transl. Spanish, Italian and Portuguese), Vol. I, 1962, Psychotherapie en Menselijke Verhoudingen, 1959; contbr. (with Carl R. Rogers) chpts. to books. Mem. Am., Midwestern, Mich. psychol. assns., AAUP.

KING HAUSER, ANN MARIE B., retired controller, artist, realtor; b. Manila, Nov. 7, 1951; d. Antonio G. and Dalisay B. King. BS in Hotel and Restaurant Mgmt., U. of the Philippines, Manila, 1972; MBA, Northwestern U., Evanston, Ill., 1977. Analyst Pacific Vegetable Oils, San Francisco, 1978—80; fin. analyst, sr. fin. mgr. Del Monte Corp., San Francisco, 1980—84, dir. fin. planning Internat. Grocery Products Divsn., 1984—86, dir. analytical svcs. U.S.A. divsn., 1986—87, mktg. controller USA divsn., 1987—90, dir. planning, 1990—92, controller Internat. Mkts., 1992; realtor Wells & Bennett, Walnut Creek, Calif., 2003—. Featured spkr. Indonesian Batik paintings U. Philippines Alumnae Assn., Chgo., 1974. Joy Mag. website, 2001—03, one-woman shows include Philippine Consulate, San Francisco, exhibited in group shows at Blackhawk Gallery, Sebastopol Ctr. Arts, Calif., Danville Fine Arts Gallery, San Francisco Acad. Arts Gallery, Sacramento Arts Ctr., Represented in permanent collections N.W. Kellogg Sch. Bus. Dean's Office, Toshiba Corp. Mem.: Internat. Soc. Exptl. Artists, The Nat. Mus. Women in the Arts, Alamo Danville Artists Soc., Calif. Watercolor Assn. Roman Catholic. Avocations: tennis, bridge, music, opera, travel. Home: 787 Lakemont Pl # 7 San Ramon CA 94582

KINGSBURY, CAROLYN ANN, aerospace engineer, craftsman, writer; b. Newark, Ohio, Aug. 4, 1938; d. Cecil C. Layman and Orpha Edith (Hisey) Layman Dick; m. L.C. James Kingsbury, Apr. 25, 1959; children: Donald Lynn, Kenneth James. BS in Math. and Info. & Computer Scis., U. Calif., Irvine, 1979; postgrad., West Coast U., 1982-84. Systems engr. analyst Rockwell Internat., Downey, Calif., 1979-84; system and software engr. Northrop Corp., Pico Rivera, Calif., 1984-89; systems engr., rsch. engr. Hughes Aircraft Co., Long Beach, Calif., 1989-90, Fullerton, Calif., 1990—91; writer, 2001—. Pres. PTA, Manhattan Beach, Calif., 1971-73; Cub Scout den mother Boy Scouts Am., Manhattan Beach, 1972-73; mem. Fountain Valley Regional Hosp. Guild, 1993-96; radio reader Regional Audio Info. Svc. Enterprises, 1997-98; vol. computer cons. Henderson County Assessor's Office, 1997-98, Head Start program, 1998-99; with Blue Ridge Literacy Coun., 1998, 2002-03, Henderson County Pub. Libr., 2000-02. Recipient Svc. award Calif. Congress Parents and Tchrs., 1973, Leadership Achievement award YWCA, L.A., 1980, 84, NASA Achievement awards, 1983. Mem. NAFE, AAUW, Nat. Mgmt. Assn., Newtowners Club (pres. 1962). Republican. Home: 319 Mockingbird Dr Hendersonville NC 28792-6553 E-mail: kingsburys@bellsouth.net.

KINGSLAND, GRACE HARVEY, retired medical/surgical nurse, artist; b. Lovell, Wyo., Nov. 22, 1925; d. James M. Harrington and G. Esther; m. Robert G. Harvey (div.); children: James, Robert, Joan, Janet; m. Charles E. Kingsland, Sept. 10, 2005. Diploma, U. Mont., Bozeman, 1946; BS, U. Portlant, Oreg., 1982; postgrad., U. Ky., Lexington, 2001—05. RN. Nurse Corvallis Gen. Hosp., Oreg., 1946—68, St. Johns Hosp., Longview, Wash., 1966—69, Hosp., Portland, 1976—78, US Pub. Health Apple Program, Longview, 1984—86; ret., 1986; graphologist pvt. practice, RI, 1970—2005; artist Donovan Scholars Program, Lexington, 2001—05. Ptnr. Harvey Constrn., 1969—71, cons. advisor, 1972—73. Exhibitions include U. Ky., 2001—04. With U.S. Army, 1945—46. Mem.: Mus. Women in Art. Republican. Avocations: birdwatching, painting.

KINGSLEY, ELLEN, publishing executive; b. NYC, Oct. 1, 1951; d. Theodore Kingsley and Judith Kingsley-Fitting; m. Robert M.A. Hirschfeld, Jan. 21, 1984; children: Theodore, Andrew. BA, Sarah Lawrence Coll., 1973; MA, NYU, 1977. Speech writer for Elinor Guggenheimer, NYC; speech writer for commr. consumer affairs, 1974—76; speech writer for John Sawhill, (pres. NYU), 1976—77; consumer affairs reporter, anchor WJZ-TV, Balt., 1977—80; consumer affairs reporter WUSA-TV, Washington, 1980—90; pres. Kingsley Comm., 1990—97; editor, pub. ADDitude Mag., 1998—. Contbr. articles to newspapers, mags. Recipient six Emmy awards, Media award, World Hunger Yr., 1983, Best Documentary award, UPI, 1984, Consumer Journalism award, Nat. Press Club, 1984, Media award, Consumer Fedn. Am., 1985. Office: 1720 Bissonnet Houston TX 77005 also: ADDitude Magazine 39 West 37th St 15th Fl New York NY 10018

KINGSLEY, KATHRYN ALEXIS KRAH, retired elementary school educator; d. Carl Alexis and Evelyn Brown Krah; m. Noel Draeger, June 12, 1966 (div. 1973); m. David A. Walsh, July 21, 1983. BS in Edn., No. Ill. U., 1966; MA in Multicultural Edn., Calif. State U., Dominguez Hills, 1976. Std. tchg. credential grades 7-12 Calif. Tchr, Sandwich (Ill.) Sch. Dist., 1966—67, El Monte (Calif.) Sch. Dist., 1967—9069; middle sch. tchr. Torrance (Calif.) Unified Sch. Dist., 1969—, ret., 2003. Rep. Nat. Edn. Assn. Conv., Portland, Oreg., 1974. Coord., editor: poetry Poetry Through the Ages, 1996—2003. Active So. Poverty Law Clinic, 1983—, ACLU, South Bay, Calif., 2002—, Dem. Party. Mem.: NEA, Torrance Tchrs. Assn. (bd. dirs. 1969—78, sch. rep. 1985—2003), Calif. Tchrs. Assn. (WHO award 2003). Avocations: theater, travel, reading, writing, dance. Home: 1533 Espinosa Cir Palos Verdes Estates CA 90274

KINGSLEY, PATRICIA, public relations executive; b. Gastonia, NC, May 7, 1932; d. Robert Henry and Marjorie (Norment) Ratchford; m. Walter Kingsley, Apr. 1, 1966 (div. 1978); 1 child, Janis Susan. Student, Winthrop Coll., 1950-51. Publicist Fountainebleau Hotel, Miami Beach, Fla., 1952; exec. asst. ZIV TV, NYC, 1953-58; sec. to publicist Rogers & Cowan, LA and NYC, 1960-71; ptnr. Pickwick Pub. Rels., LA, 1971-80, PMK/HBH Pub. Rels. (an InterPublic Group company), LA and NYC, 1980—, London, 2005—. Adv. com. Women's Action for Nuclear Disarmament, Arlington, Mass., 1983—. Democrat. Office: PMK/HBH Pub Rels Inc 700 N San Vicente Blvd West Hollywood CA 90069 also: Pmk Hbh Public Relations 161 Avenue Of The Americas Rm 10r New York NY 10013-1205 Office Phone: 310-289-6200, 212-582-1111.

KINGSOLVER, BARBARA ELLEN, writer; b. Annapolis, Md., Apr. 8, 1955; d. Wendell and Virginia (Henry) K.; m. Steven Hopp, 1993; 2 children. BA, DePauw U., 1977; MS, U. Ariz., 1981; LittD (hon.), DePauw U., 1994. Sci. writer U. Ariz., Tucson, 1981-85; free-lance journalist Tucson, 1985-87; novelist, 1987—. Book reviewer N.Y. Times, 1988—, L.A. Times, 1989—. Author: The Bean Trees, 1988 (ALA award 1988), Homeland and Other Stories, 1969 (ALA award 1990), Holding the Line: Women in the Great Arizona Mine Strike of 1983, 89, Animal Dreams, 1990 (PEN West Fiction award 1991, Edward Abbey Ecofiction award 1991), Another America, 1992, Pigs in Heaven, 1993 (L.A. Times Fiction prize 1993, Mountains and Plains Fiction award 1993, Western Heritage award 1993, ABBY Honor Book 1994), Essays, High Tide in Tucson, 1995, The Poisonwood Bible, 1998 (ABBY Honor Book 2000, PEN/Faulkner honoree 1999, Pulitzer runner-up 1999, Orange Prize short list 1999), Prodigal Summer, 2001, Small Wonder, 2002; co-author (with Annie Belt) Last Stand: America's Virgin Lands. Recipient Feature-writing award Ariz. Press Club, 1986; citation of accomplishment UN Nat. Coun. of Women, 1989; Woodrow Wilson Found./Lila Wallace fellow, 1992-93; Andrea Egan award Nat. Writers Union, 1998, Nat. Humanities Medal, 2000, Best Am. Sci. and Nature Writing, 2001, Gov.'s Nat. Award in the Arts, Ky., 2002, John P. McGovern award for Family, 2002, Nat. award Physicians for Social Responsibility, 2002. Mem. PEN Ctr. USA West, Nat. Writers Union, Phi Beta Kappa. Avocations: human rights, environmental conservation, gardening, history. Office: PO Box 160 Meadowview VA 24361

KINGSTON, ALEX (ALEXANDRA KINGSTON), actress; b. London, Mar. 11, 1963; m. Ralph Fiennes, 1993 (div. 1997); m. Florian Haertel, 1998; 1 child. Student, Royal Acad. Dramatic Arts. T.V. and movie actress. Appeared in TV films Foreign Affairs, 1993, Woman of the Wolf, 1994, The Infiltrator, 1995, Weapons of Mass Distraction, 1997, The Poseidon Adventure, 2005; films include The Cook, The Thief, His Wife & Her Lover, 1989, A Pin for the Butterfly, 1994, Carrington, 1995, Virtual Encounters 2, 1998, Croupier, 1998, This Space Between Us, 2000, Essex Boys, 2000, Warrior Queen, 2003, Sweet Land, 2005, Alpha Dog, 2006; TV series include The Knock, 1996, ER, 1997-2004; TV miniseries include Crocodile Shoes, 1994, The Fortunes and Misfortunes of Moll Flanders, 1999; theatre appearances in Much Ado About Nothing, King Lear, Love's Labour's Lost, The Curse of the Starving Class, The Bright and Bold Design, Othello, The Alchemist, Traveling Players, Saved, Julius Caesar, See How They Run, One Flew Over the Cuckoo's Nest, 2006. Recipient SAG award for Outstanding Performance by Ensemble in a Drama Series, 1994. Office: c/o The Gersh Agy 232 N Canon Dr Beverly Hills CA 90210-5302*

KINGSTON, MAXINE HONG, writer, educator; b. Stockton, Calif., Oct. 27, 1940; d. Tom and Ying Lan (Chew) Hong; m. Earll Kingston, Nov. 23, 1962; 1 child, Joseph Lawrence. BA, U. Calif., Berkeley, 1962; D (hon.), Ea. Mich. U., 1988, Colby Coll., 1990, Brandeis U., 1991, U. Mass., 1991. Tchr. English, Sunset H.S., Hayward, Calif., 1965-66, Kahuku (Hawaii) H.S., 1967, Kahaluu (Hawaii) Drop-In Sch., 1968, Kailua (Hawaii) H.S., 1969, Honolulu Bus. Coll., 1969, Mid-Pacific Inst., Honolulu, 1970-77; prof. English, vis. writer U. Hawaii, Honolulu, 1977; Thelma McCandless Disting. Prof. Eastern Mich. U., Ypsilanti, 1986, sr. lectr. emerita U. Calif., Berkeley, 1990-2003. Author: The Woman Warrior: Memoirs of a Girlhood Among Ghosts, 1976 (Nat. Book Critics Cir. award for non-fiction; cited by Time mag., N.Y. Times Book Rev. and Asian Mail as one of best books of yr. and decade), China Men, 1981 (Nat. Book award; runner-up for Pulitzer prize, Nat. Book Critics Cir. award nominee 1988), Hawai' One Summer, 1987 (Western Books Exhbn. Book award, Book Builders West Book award), Tripmaster Monkey-His Fake Book, 1989 (PEN USA West award in Fiction), Through the Black Curtain, 1988, To Be The Poet, 2002, The Fifth Book of Peace, 2003 (Best Spiritual Book award, Spirituality and Health, 2003); editor: The Literature of California, 2001 (Commonwealth Club Book award 2001), Veterans of War, Veterans of Peace, 2006; contbr. short stories, articles and poems to mags. and jours., including Iowa Rev., The New Yorker, Am. Heritage, Redbook, Mother Jones, Caliban, Mich. Quarterly, Ms., The Hungry Mind Rev., N.Y. Times, L.A. Times, Zyzzyva; prodr. The Woman Warrior, Berkeley Repertory Co., 1994, The Huntington Theater, Boston, 1994, The Mark Taper Forum, L.A., 1995; host: (TV series) Journey to the West, 1994; subject of documentaries Talking Story, Stories My Country Told Me, Writers and Places; interviews on Dick Cavett, Bill Moyers, Ken Burns' The West, The News Hour with Jim Lehrer; actor Truck Girl, 2004. Guggenheim fellow, 1981; recipient Nat. Endowment for the Arts Writers award, 1980, 82, Mademoiselle mag. award, 1977, Anisfield Wolf Book award, 1978, Calif. Arts Commn. award, 1981, Hawaii award for lit., 1982, Calif. Gov.'s award art, 1989, Major Book Collection award Brandeis U. Nat. Women's Com., 1990, award lit. Am. Acad. & Inst. Arts & Letters, 1990, Lila Wallace Reader's Digest Writing award, 1992, Spl. Achievement Oakland Bus. Arts award, 1994; named Living Treasure Hawaii, 1980, Woman of Yr. Asian Pacific Women's Network, 1981, Cyril Magnin award for Outstanding Achievement in the Arts, 1996, Disting. Artists award The Music Ctr. of L.A. County, 1996, Nat. Humanities medal NEH, 1997, Fred Cody Lifetime Achievement award, 1998, John Dos Passos prize for lit., 1998, Ka Palapola Po'okela award 1999, Profiles of Courage honor Swords to Plowshares, 1999, Alumna of Yr. award U. Calif.-Berkeley, 2000, Gold medal Calif. State Libr., 2002, Asian Am. Writers Workshop Lifetime Achievement award, 2006. Mem. Am. Acad. Arts and Scis. (KPFA Peace award 2005, Red Hen Press Lifetime Achievement award 2006).

KINKEAD, VERDA CHRISTINE, non-profit organization executive, retired consultant; b. Plant City, Fla., Feb. 12, 1931; d. Ernest Glenn and Mina Lee (Alexander) K. Diploma, Bronson Meth. Hosp. Sch. Nursing, Kalamazoo, 1952; BA in Humanities, Adrian Coll., 1963; MA Guidance-Counseling, Mich. State U., 1964. RN, Mich. Nurse Bronson Meth. Hosp., 1952-54; 2d sr. surg. nurse West Side Med. Group, Kalamazoo, 1954-60; mentor, resident asst. Adrian (Mich.) Coll., 1962-63; head resident Alma Coll., 1964-65, asst. dean student affairs, dean women, 1965-69; co-founder, co-dir. Handicappers Info. Coun. and Patient Equipment Locker, Inc., Alma, 1981-87, pres., CEO, co-chmn. bd. dirs., 1987-95, ret., 1995, pres., CEO emeritus, founding co-chair, 1995—, bd. chmn., 1995—. Ednl. asst. East Main Meth. Ch., Kalamazoo, 1959-60. Former editor Saginaw Valley Dynamo; editor Challenger newsletter, 1986-90; contbr. poetry to various publs. Bd. dirs. Saginaw Valley br. Nat. Multiple Sclerosis Soc.; past treas.; sec. bd. dir., fair sec. Gratiot Agrl. Soc., Ithaca, Mich., 1977-83; vol. counselor Gratiot County Mental Health Ctr., Alma, 1983-90; chmn. Gratiot County Early Intervention Coun., 1989-90; organizer group facilitator Ptnrs. in Renewal, Alma, 1989-94; lay speaker United Meth. Ch.; mem. Go Grow Gratiot, 1989-94, co-chair awards com. 1989-90, chairperson, 1990-91. Recipient Outstanding Svc. award Mich. Coll. Pers. Assn., 1972, Saginaw Valley br. Multiple Sclerosis Soc., 1986, 150 First Lady award Mich. Women's Commn., 1987, vol. leadership award Greater Mich. Found., 1988, Outstanding Alumni award Adrian Coll., 1988, Order of the Tartan Alma C. of C. Outstanding Citizen award, 1993, State Mich. Helping Handicapped award, 1995, Gratiot County Bd. Commrs., 1995; Paul Harris fellow Rotary Internat., 1994. Mem. AAUW (sec. Alma br. 1965), Order Eastern Star (chaplain 1988-89, assoc. conductress 1989-91, conductress 1991-93, assoc. matron 1993-94, starpoint Ruth 1994-00, chaplain 2004-), Alma Woman's Club (life, v.p. 1990, pres. 1991-92, 92-93, publicity chair 2006-), Rotary (handicapper com. 1991-95, world community svc. com. 1992-95, project SEVA com. co-chair 1991-95, sgt. at arms 1993-94), Phi Delta Kappa. Republican. Avocations: painting, needlecrafts, writing, singing, photography. Home: 3060 N Union Rd Alma MI 48801-9740

KINLEY, CHRISTINE T., physician assistant; b. Carter County, Tenn. d. Lon Samuel and Mary (Johnson) Turbyfill; children: Amy Nikol, Michael Lon. Diploma, Johnson City Vocat. Tech. Sch., 1977; BSN, East Tenn. State U., 1988; Physician Asst., Trevecca Nazarene U., Nashville, 1997; postgrad., U. Health Scis., St. John's U., St. Lucia Sch. Medicine. LPN, RN, Tenn.; cert. physician asst. Charge nurse Four Oaks Health Care Ctr., Jonesborough, Tenn.; staff nurse VA Med. Ctr., Johnson, Tenn., nurse recruiter; physician asst. Johnson City Emergency Physicians, 1997-1999, emergency care coverage, 2000—; emergency care coverage Olde Towne Gen. Medicine, 2000—. E-mail: CKinley133@aol.com.

KINNAIRD, ELEANOR GATES, state legislator, lawyer; b. Rochester, Minn., Nov. 14, 1931; d. E. Vernon and E. Madge (Pollock) Gates; m. Richard W. Kinnaird, July 27, 1954 (div. June 1982); children: Robinson S., Michael G., Paul N. BA, Carleton Coll., 1953; MM, U. N.C., 1973; JD, N.C. Ctrl. U., 1992. Bar: N.C. 1992, U.S. Dist. Ct. (ea. and mid. dists.) N.C. 1992, U.S. Ct. Appeals (4th cir.) 1992. Staff atty. N.C. Prisoner Legal Svcs., Inc., Raleigh, 1993—2004; senator N.C. Gen. Assembly, 1997—; pvt. practice, 2004—. Mayor, Town of Carrboro, 1987-95. Mem.: Phi Alpha Delta. Episcopalian. Avocations: political and civic activities, movies, reading, gardening. Home: 207 W Poplar Ave Carrboro NC 27510-1613 Office: 211 N Columbia St Chapel Hill NC 27514 Office Phone: 919-942-4445. E-mail: elliek@ncleg.net.

KINNE, FRANCES BARTLETT, academic administrator; b. Story City, Iowa; d. Charles Morton and Bertha (Olson) Barlett; m. Harry L. Kinne, Jr. (dec.); m. Wothington Bordley, Jr. (dec.). Student, U. No. Iowa; B of Music Edn., M of Music Edn., Drake U., degree (hon.); PhD cum laude, U. Frankfurt, Fed. Republic of Germany, 1957; LHD (hon.), Wagner Coll., NY; LLD (hon.), Lenoir Rhyne Coll.; DHL (hon.), Jacksonville U., 1995; LLD (hon.), Flagler Coll.; DFA (hon.), Drake U., 1981. Tchr. music Kelley (Iowa) Consol. Sch.; supr. music Boxholm (Iowa) Consol. Sch., Des Moines pub. schs.; sr. hostess Camp Crowder, Mo.; dir. recreation VA, Wadsworth, Kans.; lectr. music, English and Western culture Tsuda Coll., Tokyo; cons. music U.S. Army Gen. Hdqrs., Tokyo; mem. faculty Jacksonville (Fla.) U., 1958—, Disting. Univ. prof., 1961-62, prof. music and humanities, 1963—, dean, founder Coll. Fine Arts, interim pres., 1979, pres., 1979-89, chancellor, 1989-94; chancellor emeritus, 1995—. Past chmn. Ind. Colls. and Univs. Fla.; mem. adv. coun. Nat. Soc. Arts and Letters; hon. mem. staff Mayo Clinic, Jacksonville; coporator Charles Schepens Eye Rsch. Inst. Havard U., Cambridge, Mass., mem. adv. bd. Women's Eye Task Force. Author: A Comparative Study of British Traditional and American Indegenous Ballads, 1958, Iowa Girl: The President Wears a Skirt, 2000, (CD) Memories (in memory of friend, Bob Hope), 2004; contbr. chapters to books, articles to profl. jours. Mem., chmn. adv. bd. Ronald McDonald House; bd. dirs., life mem. Jacksonville Symphony Assn., Bert Thomas Scholarship Found., Doug Mine Found.; bd. dirs., mem. exec. com. Eye Rsch. Found.; trustee Drake U.; past mem. bd. govs. Jacksonville C. of C., past v.p.; mem. pres.'s adv. coun. Flagler Coll. Named Eve of Decade, hon. mem., 3d Armored Divsn., U.S. Army, Woman of Achievement, Ponte Vedra Woman's Club, 2005; recipient hon. awards, Bus. and Profl. Women's Clubs, 1962, Disting. Svc. award, Drake U., 1966, 1st Fla. Gov.'s award for achievement in arts, 1972, EVE award in edn., 1973, Arts Assembly Individual award, 1978—79, Roast award, Soc. for Prevention of Blindness, 1980, Brotherhood award, NCCJ, 1981, Top Mgmt. award, Jacksonville Sales and Mktg. Execs., 1981, Alumni Achievement award, U. No. Iowa, Ann. Burton C. Bryan award, Pub. Svc. award, Physicians Edn. Network, Freedom Found. Valley Forge, Disting. Svc. award, Fla. Soc. Ophthalmology, Women of Achievement award, 1st Coast Bus. and Profl. Women's Club Jacksonville, Disting. Educator award, Internat. Longshoremen's Assn., Hope award, Nat. Multiple Sclerosis Soc., Disting. Am. award, Nat. Football Fedn., Fla. State Mus. Tchrs. award, Outstanding Civic Leader award, Civic Roundtable of Jacksonville, Vol. Jacksonville 2d Ann. Bernard Gregory Servant Leader award, Elaine Gordon Lifetime Achievement award, Fla. Fedn. Bus. and Profl. Women, 1996, Order of the South award, So. Acad. Letters, Arts and Scis., Nat. Soc. Arts and Letters, Lifetime Achievement award, Arthritis Found., 2004, Davis award for Lifetime Achievement, Outstanding Philanthropist, 2005; inducted into Fla. Women's Hall of Fame, Outstanding Svc. to Theatre Edn. Fla. Assn. for Theatre Edn., day named in her honor, Women's Club of Jacksonville and other orgns., one of six women featured on History Week posters apptd. by Mayor Jacksonville, bldgs. named in honor, Frances Bartlett Kinne Univ. Ctr. Jacksonville U., Frances Bartlett Kinne Alumni and Devel. Ctr. Drake U., Frances Bartlett Kinne Auditorium at Mayo Clinic, Jacksonville, north wing of Bertha Bartlett Pub. Libr., Kinne Garden (Wilma's Little People Sch.), Jacksonville. Mem.: AAUW, PEO, Nat. Soc. Arts and Letters (adv. coun.), Internat. Coun. Fine Arts Deans (past chmn.), So. Acad. Letters, Arts and Scis., Ind. Colls. and Univs. Fla. (past chmn.), Nat. Assn. Schs. Music (past chmn. region 7), Fla. Coll. Music Edn. Assn. (past pres., v.p.), Friday Musicale, Assn. Am. Colls. (past bd. govs., mem. exec. com.), Fla. Music Edn. Assn. (past bd. dirs.), Music Educators Nat. Conf., Fla. Music Tchr. Assn., Nat. Music Tchrs. Assn., Fine Art Forum (hon.), Jacksonville Women's Network Inner Wheel, Fla. Women's Hall of Fame (Gov.'s 1st award), Delius Assn. Fla. (life), Ret. Officers Assn. (hon.), River Club, Exch. Club (Golden Deeds award), St. John's Dinner Club (past pres.), Rotary (pres. 2000, bd. dirs. Jacksonville chpt., pres. Jacksonville 2000—, Paul Harris fellow), Green Key (hon.), Alpha Xi Delta (Woman of Distinction award), Beta Gamma Sigma, Mu Phi Epsilon, Alpha Xi Delta, Omicron Delta Kappa (hon.), Alpha Kappa Psi (hon.), Alpha Kappa Pi (hon.), Alpha Psi Omega (hon.). Home: 4032 Mission Hills Cir W Jacksonville FL 32225-4635

KINNER, NANCY E., civil engineer, educator, environmental engineer, researcher; b. Oceanside, NY, Oct. 28, 1954; d. Gilbert Floyd Kinner and Margaret Mitchell Cummings; m. T. Taylor Eighmy, June 4, 1983. BA in Biology, Cornell U., NYC, 1976; MSCE, U. NH, Durham, 1980, PhD in Engring., 1983. From asst. prof. to prof. dept. civil engring. U. NH, Durham, 1983—, Davison prof., 1991—94, Waite prof., 1999—2002. Dir. Bedrock Bioremediation Ctr., Durham, 1998—; co-dir. Coastal Response Rsch. Ctr., Durham, 2004—. Mem. editl. bd.: Microbial Ecology. Mem. com. on radon risk assessment NAS; mem. Waste Mgmt. Coun., Concord, NH, 1996—2006. Recipient Coll. Engring. Phys. Sci. Tchg. Excellence award, U. NH, 1989, Jean Brierley Teaching award, 1995; fellow Fulbright fellow, Fulbright Assn., 1997. Mem.: Water Environment Fedn., Nat. Ground Water Assn., Internat. Soc. Subsurface Microbiology (mem. exec. com. 2005—), Internat. Assn. Water Quality, Assn. of Environ. Engring. and Sci. Professors, Am. Soc. of Civil Engring., Am. Water Works Assn., Am. Soc. Microbiology, Am. Soc. Engring. Edn. Achievements include development of College of Engineering and Physical Science Teaching Excellence Award. Avocation: sailing. Home: 4 Granger Dr Lee NH 03824 Office: UNH 35 Colovos Rd 236 Gregg Hall Durham NH 03824 Office Phone: 603-862-1422. Office Fax: 603-862-3957. Business E-Mail: nancy.kinner@unh.edu.

KINNEY, BETTY CAUDILL, elementary school educator; b. Franklin, Ky., Sept. 1, 1939; d. James Donald and Margaret Irene (McReynolds) Chaddock; m. Robert Lee Kinney, Aug. 5, 1961; children: Leanne Michelle Timura, Robert Bryan. BS, Middle Tenn. State U., Murfreesboro, 1961, MEd, 1971. Tchr. 8th grade Murfreesboro City Schs., 1961-62; GED tchr. U.S. Army Edn. Ctr., Frankfurt and Hanau, Germany, 1961-66, USAF Edn. Ctr., Smyrna, Tenn., 1967-68; Title 1 reading tchr. Murfreesboro City Schs., 1968-71; reading tchr. Spartanburg (S.C.) Dist. 7, 1972; cons. Spartanburg Dist. 2, 1972-73; Model Cities project tchr. Charles Lea Ctr., Spartanburg, 1972-73; reading tchr. Sch. Dist. of Greenville County, Greenville, S.C., 1973-76; reading specialist Virginia Beach (Va.) Schs., 1976-82; reading resource tchr. Rush-Henrietta (N.Y.) Ctrl. Schs., 1982—2002; ret., 2002. Part-time test scorer Pearson Ednl. Measurments, Inc. Choir soprano 1st Presbyn. Ch. Choir, Pittsford, N.Y., 1984—; mem. Hendersonville Cmty. Chorus, 2004-06. Named Reading Tchr. of Yr. Monroe County, 1991; recipient Winner's Circle award Henrietta C. of C. Mem. N.Y. State Reading Assn., Rochester Area Reading Coun. (bd. dirs. 1983-85, v.p. 1985-86, pres. 1986-87, historian 1987-92). Democrat. Avocations: gardening, reading, travel, singing. Home: 120 Pembroke Dr Hendersonville TN 37075

KINNEY, BONNIE LOGAN, retired music educator; b. Newnan, Ga., July 11, 1951; d. James Charles and Barbara Scarborough Logan; m. Charles William Kinney, July 8, 1947; 1 child, Jeff Carlton. A in Music, Truett McConnell Jr. Coll., Cleveland, Ga., 1971; MusB, U. Ga., Athens, 1973. Cert. music tchr. K-12. Music tchr., chorus tchr. Rockmart Jr. HS, Ga., 1975—96; music tchr. Goodyear Elem., Rockmart, 1975—96, East Side Elem. Sch., Rockmart, 1975—96, Red Bird Elem., Calhoun, Ga., 1996—99; chorus tchr. Elbert County HS, Elberton, Ga., 1999—2005. Music dir. 1st United Meth., Rockmart, 1984—97; dir. Rockmart Cmty. Chorus, 1995—96, Elbert Chorale, Elberton, 2000—03. Named Tchr. of Yr., Goodyear Elem., 1987, Elbert County HS, 2004. Mem.: Ga. Music Educators. Methodist. Avocations: exercise, singing, guitar. Home: 323 Wildwood Dr Dallas GA 30132 E-mail: kinney_charles@bellsouth.net.

KINNEY, CATHERINE R., stock exchange executive; married; 2 children. BS magna cum laude, Iona Coll.; cert. advanced mgmt., Harvard Sch. Bus.; DHL (hon.), Georgetown U., 2004; degree (hon.), Rosemont Coll. Various positions NY Stock Exch., 1974—86, mgr. trading-floor opers. and tech., 1986—95, group exec. v.p., 1995—2002, pres. & co-COO, 2002—06, NYSE Group, Inc., 2006—. Bd. mem. Met Life Ins. Co., 2002—04, Depository Trust & Clearing Corp., US India Bus. Coun. Trustee Iona Coll.; bd. dirs. Georgetown U.; mem. bd. Jr. Achievement NY, NY Stock Exch. Found., Catholic Charities. Office: attn Ray Pellecchia NYSE Group Inc 11 Wall St New York NY 10005*

KINNEY, ELEANOR DE ARMAN, law educator; b. Boston, Jan. 17, 1947; d. Thomas DeArman and Eleanor Shepard (Roberts) K.; m. Charles Malcolm Clark Jr., June 25, 1983; children: Janet Marie, Brian Alexander, Margaret Louise. AB, Duke U., 1969, JD, 1973; MA, U. Chgo., 1970; MPH, U. N.C., 1979. Bar: Ohio 1973, N.C. 1977, U.S. Dist. Ct. (no. dist.) Ohio 1974. Assoc. Squire, Sanders & Dempsey, Cleve., 1973-77; estate planning officer Duke U. Med. Ctr., Durham, N.C., 1977-79; program analyst HHS, Washington, 1979-82; asst. gen. counsel Am. Hosp. Assn., Chgo., 1982-84; vis. prof. Ind. U. Sch. Law, Indpls., 1984-85, asst. prof., 1985-88, found. dir. William S. & Christine S. Hall Ctr. for Law and Health, 1987—, assoc. prof., 1988-90, Hall Render prof. law & exec. dir. Latin Am. Law Program, 1990—; adj prof. Ind. U. Sch. Public & Environ. Affairs & Sch. Medicine. Cons. Adminstrv. Conf. U.S., Washington, 1985—91; mem. exec. bd. Ind. State Bd. of Health, 1989—99; Fulbright fellow Nat. Univ. LaPlata, Argentina, 1999—2000. Author: Protecting American Health Care Consumers, 2002. Ed., Guide to Medicare Coverage Decision-Making and Appeals, 2002. Contbr. articles to legal jours., also monographs, chpts. to books. Mem.: ABA (coun. sect. on adminstrv. law and regulatory practice 1997—, vice-chair 2003—04, chair-elect 2004—05), Am. Law Inst., Am. Assn. Law Schs. (bd. mem. sect. on on adminstrv. law law 1998—, vice chair 2003—04, chair-elect 2004—05, chair 2005—), Am. Pub. Health Assn. Office: Indiana U School of Law Inlow Hall Room 136F 530 W New York St Indianapolis IN 46202-3225 Office Phone: 317-274-4091. Business E-Mail: ekinney@iupui.edu.

KINNEY, JEANNE KAWELOLANI, English studies educator, writer; b. Bayville, N.Y., Nov. 22, 1964; d. Robert Warren Stewart and Genevieve Lehuanani (Okilauea) Kinney. BA, Linfield Coll., 1986; MFA, Bowling Green State U., 1988. Tchr. Hawaii Bus. Coll., Honolulu, 1993-95; ESL tchr. GEOs Lang. Corp., Osaka and Kobe, Japan, 1996-97; English tchr. St. Joseph's H.S., Hilo, Hawaii, 2000. Poet-in-the-schs. Dept. Edn., Honolulu, fall 1994; sub. English tchr. St. Andrew's Priory, Honolulu, 1993; adj. English tchr. Chaminade U., Honolulu, spring 1993, 94; basic skills instr. Kamehameha Schs., Honolulu, 1991-92; English tchr., speech coach Punahou Sch., Honolulu, 1989-91. Contbr. to profl. publs. including Hawaii Rev., Kaimana, Ascent, Seattle Rev., Bamboo Ridge Press. Precinct ops. cood. Office Lt. Gov., Hawaii Elections Divsn., 1991-93, precinct worker trainer, 1989-91; v.p. Hawaii Lit. Arts Coun., Honolulu, 1990; pub. rels. officer Hawaii Speech League, Honolulu, 1991. Avocations: dance, swimming, writing, travel, foreign languages.

KINNEY, JOYCE P., elementary school educator; d. Bernard Michael and Doris Ethel Pleiss; m. Fred Marvin Kinney, Aug. 14, 1960; children: John, Steve, Dan. BS, Mankato State Coll., Minn., 1959. Assoc. in ministry Evang. Luth. Ch. in Am. Elem. tchr. grade 4 Owatonna Pub. Schs., Minn., 1959—62; elem. tchr. grade 3 Grand Meadow Pub. Schs., Minn., 1962—63; substitute tchr. grades K-6 Austin Pub. Schs., Minn., 1964—88; cons. Christian Edn. Ctr., Austin, 1988—2003; psychometrist Workforce Ctr. U. Minn., Austin, 1983—98; dir. Christian edn. Our Savior's Luth. Ch., Austin, 1983—98. Vol. Austin Med. Ctr., 2004—06, ARC, Austin, 2004—06, Our Savior's Luth. Ch., Austin, 1977—2006. Mem.: AAUW (treas., chair edn. found.). Avocations: scrapbooks, needlecrafts, cards, bicycling, travel.

KINNEY, LISA FRANCES, lawyer; b. Laramie, Wyo., Mar. 13, 1951; d. Irvin Wayne and Phyllis (Poe) Kinney; m. Rodney Philip Lang, Feb. 5, 1971; children: Cambria Helen, Shelby Robert, Eli Wayne. BA, U. Wyo., 1973, JD, 1986; MLS, U. Oreg., 1975. Reference libr. U. Wyo. Sci. Libr., Laramie, 1975-76; outreach dir. Albany County Libr., Laramie, 1975-76, dir., 1977-83; mem. Wyo. State Senate, Laramie, 1984-94, minority leader, 1992-94; with documentation office Am. Heritage Ctr. U. Wyo., 1991-94; assoc. Corthell & King, 1994-96, shareholder, 1996-99; owner Summit Bar Rev., 1987—2004; fin. planner VALIC, 2001—. Author: (with Rodney Lang) Civil Rights of the Developmentally Disabled, 1986; (with Rodney Lang and Phyllis Kinney) Manual For Families with Emotionally Disturbed and Mentally Ill Relatives, 1988, rev. 1991, 99, Lobby For Your Library, Know What Works, 1992, Understanding Mental Illnesses: A Family Legal Guide, 2004; contbr. articles to profl. jours.; editor, compiler pub. rels. directory of ALA, 1982. Bd. dirs. Big Bros./Big Sisters, Laramie, 1980-83, Children's Mus., 1993-97; bd. dirs. Am. Heritage Ctr., 1993-97, Citizen of the Century, 1997-99, govt. chmn. 1997-99; pres. Friends Cmty. Recreation Project, 2001—. Named Outstanding Wyo. Libr. Assn., 1977, Young Woman, State of Wyo., 1980; recipient Beginning Young Profl. award, Mt. Plains Libr. Assn., 1980, Arts and Scis. Disting. Alumni award, U. Wyo., 1997, Making Democracy Work award, Wyo. LWV, 2000. Mem.: ABA, Nat. Conf. State Legislatures (various coms. 1985—90), Laramie Area C. of C. (bd. dirs. 1996—2000, mem. 1999, Top Hand award 1997), Zonta, Kiwanis. Democrat. Avocations: photography, dance, reading, travel, languages. Home: 1415 E Baker St Laramie WY 82072 Office: PO Box 1710 Laramie WY 82073-1710 Office Phone: 307-742-6644. Personal E-mail: lfkl@aol.com.

KINNEY, NANCY THERESA, political science professor; b. Chgo., Ill., Feb. 19, 1954; d. Harold Stephen Kinney and Mary Ellen Morgan; m. Robert Anton Franken, Nov. 4, 1995. BA in Religious Studies, Regis U., Denver, 1984; MA in Mass. Comms., U. Denver, 1991; PhD in Pub. Affairs, U. Colo., Denver, 2001. Affiliate faculty mem. Regis U., 1993—2001; asst. prof. dept. polit. sci. U. Mo., St. Louis, 2001—. Mem. St. Francis Ctr. Day Shelter, Denver, 1997—2001. Mem.: Assn. Rsch. on Nonprofit Orgns. and Voluntary Action. Office: U Mo St Louis 8001 Natural Bridge Rd 347 SSB Saint Louis MO 63121 Office Phone: 314-516-5420. Office Fax: 314-516-7236. Business E-Mail: ntkinney@umsl.edu.

KINNEY, ROBIN SMITH, chemist, educator; b. Lexington, N.C., Mar. 19, 1957; d. Gilbert Lee and Ethel Swing Smith; m. Michael Robert Kinney, Nov. 20, 1977; children: Kristen Jill, Evan Michael, Galen Taylor. BA in Chemistry magna cum laude, U. N.C., Wilmington, 1979. Cert. tchr. chemistry and phys. sci. N.C. Bd. Edn., 1979. Spl. projects analyst Wright Chem. Corp., Acme, NC, 1979—85; tchr. chemistry and phys. sci. E.A. Laney H.S., Wilmington, NC, 1985—88; tchr. Wilmington Acad. Arts and Scis., 1999—. Mem. disciplinary com., curriculum com. bd. dirs. Wilmington Acad. Arts and Scis., 2001—06. Cub scout den leader Boy Scouts Am., Wilmington, 1995—96; chmn. youth dept., mem. gen. bd., vacation bible sch. crafts dir. First Christian Ch., Wilmington, 1990—93. Named North Carolina's Family Leader of Tomorrow, Gen. Mills, 1975. Mem.: N.C. Sci. Tchrs. Assn. Office: Wilmington Academy of Arts and Sciences 4126 S College Rd Wilmington NC 28412 Office Phone: 910-392-3139.

KINNIER, EMILY P., artist; d. Nelson Palmore and Elizabeth Bott; m. Eugene Howard Kinnier, Feb. 4, 1939. Grad., Pan Am. Bus. Coll., Richmond, VA, 1935; Studied, Art Students League, N.Y.C., 1953—70. Treas. patterson nj br. Nat. League of Am. Penwomen, Patterson, NJ, 1968—69; treas. Richmond br. Nat. League of Am. Pen Women (Hdgs.), Washington, 1977—78. Studied with Laura Glenn Douglas, Washington, 1950—50; studied with Vytlacil, Kantor, Hovannes, Ben Cunningham, Hale Art Students League, N.Y.C., 1953—72; studied with Burgoyne Diller Studio Atlantic Highlands, Atlantic Highlands, NJ, 1960—64; studied with Laura Pahris Richmond Printmaking Workshop, Richmond, Va., 1980—82. One-woman shows include Middle St. Gallery, Wash., Va., 1996—98, exhibited in group shows, 2000, 2002, exhibitions include Juried Show, Newark Mus., 1964 (Second Prize in Watercolor), State Juried Show, Montclair Mus., 1964 (2nd prize on watercolor), Montclair Mus., N.J., 1964, Jersey City Mus., 1965, Festival of Arts, Monmouth Coll., N.J., 1966, Middle St. Gallery, Wash., Va., 1995, 1708 Gallery, Richmond, Va., 1996—2004, Nations Bank Gallery, 1998. Arts bd. St. Pauls Episc. Ch., Richmond, Va., 1982—84. Mem.: Nat. League of Am. Pen Women Richmond Br., Art Students League N.Y.C. (life). Avocations: travel, gardening. Home: 812 N Tilden Richmond VA 23221-1517

KINSBRUNER BUSH, JENNIFER, lawyer; AB in History & Latin Am. Studies summa cum laude, Princeton U., 1996; Fulbright Scholar, Universidad Católica, Santiago, Chile, 1996—97; JD, Yale Law Sch., 2000. Bar: Calif., US Ct. of Appeals, Federal Circuit. Rsch. assoc. Wiggin & Dana; summer assoc. Kirkland & Ellis, 1998, Cleary Gottlieb, 1999; law clerk to Judge Stanley Marcus US Ct. of Appeals, 11th Circuit, 2000—01; assoc. Irell & Manella, 2001—02; assoc., intellectual property litigation Fish & Richardson, San Diego, 2002—. Office: Fish & Richardson 12390 El Camino Real San Diego CA 92130 Office Phone: 858-678-5070. Office Fax: 858-678-5099. Business E-Mail: bush@fr.com.

KINSER, CYNTHIA D., state supreme court justice; b. Pennington Gap, Dec. 20, 1951; d. Morris and Velda (Myers) Fannon; m. H. Allen Kinser, Jr., March 17, 1974; children: Charles Adam, Terah Diane. Student, Univ. of Ga., 1970-71; BA, Univ. of Tenn., 1974; JD, Univ. of Va., 1977. Bar: Va. 1977, U.S. Dist. Ct. (we. dist.) Va. 1977, U.S. Ct. Appeals (4th cir.) 1977, U.S. Supreme Ct. 1988. Law clk. to Judge Glen M. Williams U.S. Dist. Ct., 1977-78; pvt. law practice, 1978-90; commonwealth's atty. Lee County, Va., 1980-83; magistrate judge U.S. Dist. Ct. (we. dist.) Va., Abingdon, 1990-98; justice Va. Supreme Ct., Richmond, 1998—. Trustee Chapter 7 Panel, U.S. Bankruptcy Ct., 1979-90. Mem. Va. Bar Assn., Va. Trial Lawyers Assn., Am. Bar Assn. Methodist. Office: Va Supreme Ct PO Box 1315 Richmond VA 23218-1315*

KINSLOW, MONICA M., forensic specialist; b. Chgo., Feb. 19, 1956; d. Chris C. and Martha Stratton; m. Keith Kinslow, Mar. 8, 1975; children: Aisha Ebony, Naomi Alice, Miles Keith. BS in Chemistry, Chgo. State U., 1981. Criminalist Chgo. Police Dept., 1988-96; forensic scientist Ill. State Police, Chgo., 1996—. Mem. Midwestern Assn. Forensic Scientists, Am. Chem. Soc. Avocations: church activities, reading. Office: Ill State Police Forensic Sci Ctr 1941 W Roosevelt Rd Chicago IL 60608-1246

KINSOLVING, ANN ODENE, elementary school educator, musician; b. Charleston, W.Va. d. Odie and Mildred Moore Kinsolving; 1 child, Bethany Ann Simmons. BA in Elem. Edn. magna cum laude, Morris Harvey Coll., 1973; MA in Ednl. Adminstrn., W.Va. Coll. Grad. Studies, 1976. Tchr. Grandview Elem., Charleston, W.Va., 1973—78; vice prin. Cross Lanes Elem., W.Va., 1978—81, tchr., 1991—, mem. k-5 curriculum team, 1991—, mem. multicultural edn. com., 2002—04; mem. safe schs. com. Kanawha County Schs. Tech. Acad., 2005—06; prin. Midway Elem., Charleston, 1981—84, Alban Elem., St. Albans, W.Va., 1984—91. Organist First Bapt. St. Albans, 1991—; coord. W. Va. Young Writers, 2006. Contbr. essays in field. Co-sponsor youth in India Compassion Internat., Colo. Springs, Colo., 2004—; mentor Keep A Child In Sch., Kanawha County Schs., 1996—; supporter Chandler Sch. Arts, Charleston, 2002—, W.Va. State U. Marching Band and Choral Dept. Recipient Morris Harvey Coll. Key award, 1973. Mem.: Am. Guild Organists, Kanawha Educators, Pi Gamma Mu (pres.), Kappa Delta Pi (pres.), Sigma Tau Delta, Delta Kappa Gamma, Phi Delta Kappa. Republican. Baptist. Avocations: music, piano, pets, reading, photography. Home: 5010 Washington St W Charleston WV 25313-1527 Office: Cross Lanes Elem 5525 Big Tyler Rd Cross Lanes WV 25313 Office Phone: 304-776-2022. Business E-Mail: aokinsolving@access.kana.k12.wv.us.

KINSOLVING, SYLVIA CROCKETT, musician, educator; b. Berkeley, Calif., Sept. 30, 1931; d. Harold Waldo and Louise (Effinger) Crockett; m. Charles Lester Kinsolving, Dec. 18, 1953; children: Laura Louise, Thomas Philip, Kathleen Susan. AA in Voice, Piano magna cum laude, No. Va. Community Coll., 1983; BA, U. Calif., Berkeley, 1953. Solo vocalist various chs., Va., 1982—; pvt. tchr. piano Vienna, Va., 1983—. Singer, soloist Unity Ch., Oakton, Va., 1980—, St. Andrew's Anglican Ch., Alexandria, Va., 1985—; active numerous local musical prodns., 1959—. Tour leader Vienna Newcomers, 1980. Mem. PEO, U. Calif. Alumni Club, Fairfax West Music Fellowship (sec. 1990—), Phi Theta Kappa, Pi Beta Phi. Democrat. Episcopalian. Avocations: walking, swimming, music, reading. Home: 1517 Beulah Rd Vienna VA 22182-1417

KINTZ, MYRNA LUTES, retired language educator; b. Bozeman, Mont., Jan. 18, 1941; d. Robert Hill and Mary O'Hare Lutes; m. Charles Leo Kintz, June 14, 1964; 1 child, Todd Lawrence. BS, Mont. State U., Bozeman, 1963; MA, U. Mont., Missoula, 1977. Tchr., counselor East Jr. High, Great Falls, Mont., 1963—64, Burley Jr. and H.S., Idaho, 1964—65; French tchr. Cleveland H.S., Portland, Oreg., 1965—66; French instr. Dawson C.C., Glendive, Mont., 1966—89; ret., 1989. Mem. adv. bd. Investment Ctr. Am., Glendive, 2006—. Active Friends Makoshika State Park, Glendive, Congl. Ch., 1982—. Mem.: DCAU, PEO (corr. sec.), Friends of the Libr. (life), Frontier Gateway Mus. (life), Alpha Lambda Delta, Phi Kappa Phi, Morter Bd. Avocations: golf, embroidery, travel, reading, piano. Home: 412 Maple Ave Glendive MT 59330

KINZIE, BRENDA ASBURRY, counselor; b. Roanoke, Va., Oct. 25, 1945; d. Omar Lee and Nadine Myrl (Sublett) Asburry; m. Samuel Joseph Kinzie, Mar. 30, 1973. BA, Hollins U., 1990; MS, Radford U., 1991. Case mgr./counselor Total Action Against Poverty, Roanoke, 1993—95; interagy. case coord. City of Roanoke, 1995—98. Vol. Am. Cancer Soc. Mem.: ACA, Hunting Hills Garden Club. Democrat. Divine Sci. Ch. Avocations: music, reading, walking, flower gardening. Home: 1051 Starmount Ave Roanoke VA 24019-3135

KINZIE, JEANNIE JONES, radiation oncologist, nuclear medicine physician; b. Great Falls, Mont., Mar. 14, 1940; d. James Wayne and Lillian Alice (Young) Jones; m. Joseph Lee Kinzie, Mar. 26, 1965 (div. Sept. 1982); 1 child, Daniel Joseph; m. Johnson Wachira, Oct. 7, 1991. Student, Oreg. State U., 1960; BS, Mont. State U., 1961; MD, Washington U., 1965; MBA, U. Phoenix, 1997. Diplomate Am. Bd. Radiology; diplomate Am. Bd. Nuclear Medicine; cert. advanced master gardener Colo. State U., 1997. Intern. in surgery U. N.C., Chapel Hill, 1965-66; resident in therapeutic radiology Washington U., St. Louis, 1968-71, instr. in radiology, 1971-73; asst. prof. in radiology Med. Coll. of Wis., Milw., 1973-75, U. Chgo., 1975-78, assoc. prof. in radiology, 1978-80; assoc. prof. of radiation oncology Wayne State U., Detroit, 1980-85; prof. radiology U. Colo., Denver, 1985-95; dir. radiation oncology U. Hosp., Denver, 1985-91; fellow in nuclear medicine U. Colo., 1996-98, asst. clin. prof. nuclear medicine, 1998—2005; staff radiologist Denver Vets. Hosp., Denver, 2003—. Cons. Denver Vets. Hosp., 1985-98, Denver Gen. Hosp., 1985-95, Rose Med. Ctr., 1986-95, FDA Ctr. for Devices and Radiologic Health, 1986-2003; mem. sci. adv. bd. Cancer League Colo., 1985-88; examiner Am. Bd. Radiology, 1985-88; adv. physician Colo. Med. Found., 1988-98; chmn. faculty promotion com. U. Colo. Health Scis. Ctr., 1988-89. Assoc. editor Internat. Jour. Radiation Oncology Biology and Physics, 1985-95; contbr. articles to profl. jours.; chpts. to books. Mem. Faith Bible Chapel Ch. NIH grantee, 1973-75. Fellow: Am. Coll. Radiology; mem.: AMA, Am. Cancer Soc. (bd. dirs. Denver unit 1986—87), Am. Soc. Therapeutic Radiologists, Rocky Mountain Oncology Soc. (bd. dirs. 1989—93, pres. 1991—93), Colo. Radiol. Soc., Denver Med. Soc., Colo. Med. Soc. (del. or alt. del. to Colo. Med. Soc. Ho. of Dels. 1989—), Am. Coll. Nuclear Physicians. Republican. Avocations: gardening, rug latching, mountain climbing. Personal E-mail: jeannie.kinzie@att.net.

KINZLER, CHARISSA D., special education educator; b. Oakdale, Pa., Dec. 12, 1980; d. Daniel J. and Kimberly D. Kinzler. BA in Elem. and Spl. Edn., Alderson-Broadus Coll., Philippi, W.Va., 2003; post grad. in Curriculum and Instrn., Gannon U., Erie, Pa., 2003—. Cert. elem. spl. edn. Pa. Dept. Edn., W.Va. Dept. Edn., in secondary English Pa. Dept. Edn., W.Va. Dept. Edn., in mid. sch. math Pa. Dept. Edn., W.Va. Dept. Edn. Spl. edn. tchr. Bradley-Mt. Lebanon Schs., Pitts., 2003—05, resource tchr., 2005—. Mem.: Coun. Exceptional Children, Phi Delta Kappa. Personal E-mail: kinzlercd@yahoo.com.

KIPNISS MACDONALD, BETTY ANN, artist, educator; b. Bklyn., Aug. 1936; d. Samuel Simon and Stella Anita (Blackton) Kipniss; m. Gordon James MacDonald (div.); children: Gordon, Maureen, Michael, Bruce BA, Adelphi U., 1958; MA, Columbia U., N.Y.C., 1960. Instr. Montshire Mus., Hanover, NH, 1979—84, Lebanon Coll., NH, 1984, Smithsonian Instn., Washington, 1985—95. Instr. Corcoran Mus. Art, 1996-98; pres., bd. dirs. Washington Printmakers Gallery; bd. dirs. Washington Print Club Exhbns. include Nat. Mus. Women in Arts, Washington, 1994-95; permanent collections include Cmty. for Creative Nonviolence, Washington, Mus. Modern Art, Buenos Aires, Am. Cultural Ctr., New Delhi, India, Pa. State U., New Orleans Mus. Art; featured in William and Mary Rev., 1992-96 Grantee Giorgio Cini Found., 1962, NEA, 1981; recipient 1st prize printmakers Washington Women's Art Ctr., 1986, Past Pres.'s award Mus. Fine Arts, Springfield, Mass., 1982, de Cordova Mus., Soc. Am. Graphic Artists N.Y., Merit award Currier Gallery Art, 1987, Purchase prize Print Club Albany, N.Y., 1998, Purchase award Permanent Collection Ark. State U., 2001, Mus. Graphics award Washington County Mus. Fine Arts, Md., 2003, First prize Miniature Painters, Sculptors and Gravers Soc., 2005 Mem. L.A. Printmaking Soc., Soc. Am. Graphic Artist, Boston Printmakers

KIPPER, BARBARA LEVY, wholesale distribution executive; b. Chgo., July 16, 1942; d. Charles and Ruth (Doctoroff) Levy; m. David A. Kipper, Sept. 9, 1974; children: Talia Rose, Tamar Judith. BA, U. Mich., 1964. Reporter Chgo. Sun-Times, 1964-67; photo editor Cosmopolitan Mag., N.Y.C., 1969-71; vice chmn. Chas Levy Co., Chgo., 1984-86, chmn., 1986—. Trustee Spertus Inst. Jewish Studies, Chgo.(Ill.) Hist. Soc., Golden Apple Ind., Joffrey Ballet of Chgo. Recipient Deborah award Com. Women's Equality, Am. Jewish Congress, 1992, Shap Shapiro Human Rels. award The Anti-Defamation League of B'nai B'rith, Personal PAC's Leadership award, 1996, Disting. Cmty. Leadership award, ADL, Jewish Culture, 2004; named Nat. Soc. Fund Raising Execs. Disting. Philanthropist, 1995. Mem.: Nat. Found. Jewish Culture (Golden Sceptre award), Chgo. Network, Com. of 200, Internat. Women's Forum, Econ. Club of Chgo., Chgo. Network, The Standard Club. Jewish. Office Phone: 708-356-3601. Business E-Mail: bkipper@chaslevy.com.

KIRBY, HEATHER SUZANNE, music educator; b. Sellarsville, Pa., Jan. 29, 1970; d. James Dennis Ward and Suzan Elaine Goodman; m. Robert Vincent Kirby, Aug. 2, 1997; 1 child, Jasmine Tracy. MusB cum laude, U. Mass., Lowell, 1992; MusM, Temple U., 2005. Music specialist Falmouth (Mass.) Pub. Schs., 1992—2000; music specialist, elem. coord. Dedham (Mass.) Pub. Schs., 2001—. Children's choir dir. First Congl. Ch., Falmouth, 1993—96; children's choir dir., instr., early childhood specialist Todd G. Patkin Opera Performing Arts Ctr., Stoughton, Mass., 2004—; founder, dir. Family Music Learning Inst. Foster parent Mass. Dept. Social Svcs., Brockston, 2001—; mem. music ministry Holy Family Life Teen Band, Rockland, Mass., 2001—. Recipient Alan Scottgood award, U. Mass., Lowell, 1992. Mem.: Gorden Inst. Music Learning (membership commn. 2004—06, founder and pres. New Eng. chpt. 2005—), Mass. Music Educators Assn. (conf. planning com. 2003—), Soc. Gen. Music in Mass. (pres.-elect 2002—05, task force mem. 2004—, pres. 2005—, Excellence in Gen. Music award 2004), Early Childhood Music and Movement Assn., Music Educators Nat. Conf., Pi Kappa Lambda. Republican. Roman Catholic. Avocations: Tae Kwon Do, camping, dance, travel. Office: Riverdale Elem Sch Needham St Dedham MA 02026 Office Phone: 781-326-5350. E-mail: happtharmonizer@aol.com.

KIRBY, MARCIA KAREN, library and information scientist; b. Williamsburg, Va., Oct. 23, 1952; d. Marion O. and Rita S. Smith; m. Garnett E. Kirby, Jr., Aug. 18, 1979; children: Jon-David G., Phillip E. Libr. clk. Williamsburg Regional Libr., Va., 1975—80; libr. tech. Navelex Tech. Libr., Portsmouth, Va., 1982—83; libr. clk. Hampton U. Libr., Va., 1985—87; libr. tech. Internat. Telephone Telegraph, Hampton, Va., 1987—91; libr. clk. Hampton U. Libr., Va., 1992—95; tchr. resource ctr. clk. Newport News Pub. Schs., Va., 1995—96; libr. clk. Gildersleeve Mid. Sch., Newport News, Va., 1995—97; libr. practitioner I Coll. of William & Mary Libr., Williamsburg, Va., 1997—. Mem.: Classified Staff Assn. (corr.; pres. 2000—01, sec. 2003). Avocations: reading, photography, videography, piano.

KIRBY, SHERYL C., secondary school educator; b. Phila., Dec. 1, 1955; d. Harold F. and Marie V. Curtis; m. Joseph P. Kirby; children: Erin, Katelyn, Shannon. BS in Acctg., Phila. U., 1988; MA in Curriculum, Instrn. and Supervision, Rider U., 2004. Acct. Pelmor Labs., Inc., Newtown, Pa., 1978—93, mgr. customer svc., 1993—99; tchr. bus. edn. Mastbaum HS, Phila., 1999—2001; tech. tchr. leader Germantown HS, Phila., 2001—. Grantee, Perloff Found., Calif., 2000, Pa. Dept. Edn., 2004. Mem.: ASCD, Am. Fedn. Tchrs., Phi Delta Kappa.

KIRBY, SUSAN COLLINS, literature and language professor, consultant; b. North Wilkesboro, N.C., Feb. 16, 1945; d. William Bryan and Alice Hylton Collins; m. Joe G. Kirby, III, Dec. 27, 1967; children: Joe G. IV, Susan Caroline. BS, Radford Coll., Va/, 1966; MA, Wake Forest U., Winston-Salem, N.C., 1967. Assoc. prof. English Radford U., 1967—. Coord. Writing Across the Curriculum Radford U., 1989—95, dir. supplemental instrn. program, 1998—2001, dir. freshman connections, 1991—95, co-dir. Faculty Devel. Ctr., 1995—96, faculty writing cons. Waldron Coll. Health Svcs., 2003—04. Recipient Radford Univ. Svc. award, 2001. Mem.: Va. Assn. Tchrs. of English, Assn. for Tchrs. of Tech. Writing, Nat. Coun. Tchrs. of English, Assn. for Bus. Comm., Soc. for Tech. Comm. Methodist. Office: Radford Uni Main St Box 6935 Radford VA 24142 Office Phone: 540-831-5365. Personal E-mail: skirby@radford.edu.

KIRBY, VESTA ANN, artist; d. Ross Ives Kirby and Pauline Ida (Kirby) Aiello, Al Aiello (Stepfather). Cert. of Interior Arch., Parsons Sch. Design, N.Y.C., N.Y., 1959, BFA, 1995; MFA, John F. Kennedy U., Berkeley, Calif., 2000; student, Art Students League, N.Y.C., 1973—74. Interior designer Skidmore, Owings and Merrill Arch., N.Y.C., 1959—62; design cons. European and Japan Archs., 1962—68; project designer Whisler PatriArch., San Francisco, 1969—72; design cons. N.Y. Archs., 1972—76; dir. interiors MBT Archs., San Francisco, 1979—82; instr. Acad. Art Coll., San Francisco, 1988—95; instr. ext. San Francisco Art Inst. Ext., 1996—98; from instr. to prof. U. Calif. Ext., Berkeley, 1988—. Color cons., San Francisco, 1984—2004; lectr. in field; artist-in-residence Capine Found. for Arts, Newfoundland, Canada, 2002, Djerassi Resident Arts Program, Woodside, Calif., 2004. Numerous exhbns. and collections, Represented in permanent collections San Francisco Mus. Modern Art, Artists Gallery. Mem.: San Francisco Mus. Modern Art, Coll. Art Assn., Fine Arts Mus. San Francisco, Audubon Club, Sierra Club. Zen Buddhist. Avocations: music, poetry, swimming, writing. Office Phone: 415-284-1070. Home Fax: 415-771-4491. E-mail: vesta@vestakirby.com.

KIRCHMEIER, EMMALOU HANDFORD, minister, writer; b. Bklyn., Feb. 13, 1924; d. Walter Handford and Florence Alexandria Lawson; m. Otto Frank Kirchmeier, Nov. 21, 1942 (dec.); children: John, Judy, James, Walter, Kathy, Paul(dec.), William(dec.). DivM, Boston U. Sch. of Theology, 1985—88; BA, Ame Internat., 1974—77. Bur. chief The Hartford Courant, Conn., 1974—77; feature writer The Hartford Woman, 1981—84; advtg. mgr. Conn. Bus. Rev., 1981—84; sr. pastor Monroeton Charge, 1988—92; vis. chaplain, asst. pastor Myakka City, Sarasota, Fla., 1996—2001; dir. pastoral care Elizabeth Ch. Manor, Binghamton, NY, 2002; part time chaplain The Inn, Sarasota Bay Club, 2002—. Pub. dir. Fla. African Am. Cultural Acad., SAR Sr. Ctr., 2003—; bd. dirs., sec. Friends Selby Libr., 2004—. Recipient Evangelism award, Bishop and Wellsbor Dist., 1991, Pres. award, Asnuntuck Cmty. Coll., 1975, Golden B award, Hartford C. of C., award for feature writing, Conn. Editl. Assn., 1975, New England Press Assn., 1975, Yellow Jacket recognition, Am. Internat. Coll. Mem.: Am. Internat. Coll. Alumni Assn, Boston U. Alumni Assn. Democrat. United Meth. Avocations: ballroom dancing, writing, gardening, sewing, theater.

KIRCHMEIER-BOYES, MELANIE JOAN, middle school educator; b. Williston, N.D., Dec. 18, 1964; d. Kenneth Wayne and Ida Marie (Schaan) Kirchmeier; m. Mark Ian Boyes, June 18, 1988; children: Malorie, Acacia, Laykin. BS, Minot (N.D.) State U., 1987. Cert. tchr., Wyo., N.D. English tchr. grades 7 to 12 Grenora (N.D.) High Sch., 1987-89; journalist Williston (N.D.) Daily and Sunday Herald, 1989-90; English tchr. grades 10 and 11 Williston High Sch., 1990-91; English tchr. grades 7 to 9 CY Jr. High Sch., Casper, Wyo., 1991—. Advisor sch. newspaper, Grenora, 1987-89, Williston, 1990-91; evaluator Dist. Writing Assessment, Casper, 1992, spelling coach, 1992—; dist. mentor to new tchrs., 2002—; gradebook mgr.; cohort facilitator; presenter in field. Recipient 1st pl. state contest feature writing, 1991. Mem. NEA, Legal Edn. Assn. Roman Catholic. Avocations: tennis, writing, poetry, softball, reading. Office Phone: 307-577-4474.

KIRCHNER, ELIZABETH PARSONS, clinical psychologist; b. Balt., July 20, 1928; d. Wilber Fay and Marguerite Victoria (Lindsay) Parsons; m. Henry Paul Kirchner, Nov. 11, 1950; children: Peter, James, Robert. BS, Cornell U., 1950; MS, Pa. State U., 1952, PhD, 1955. Lic. psychologist, Pa. Pvt. practice, State College, Pa., 1958—. Mem. faculty dept. psychology Pa. State U., University Park, 1965-80; psychologist Buffalo State Hosp., 1959-61, U. Buffalo Med. Sch., 1961-64; cons. Pa. Correctional System, 1972-80, VA Hosp., Altoona, Pa., 1973-76, State Hosp. System Pa., 1975-78, Office of Juvenile Probation and Parole, Bellefonte, Pa., 1983-85, Centre Community Hosp., State College, 1985—, Multiple Sclerosis Soc., Pa., 1989—. Author: Assertive Training in Prison, 1973, Be Your Own Therapist, 1981, Coping with Chronic Illness, 1988; contbr. articles to profl. jours., newspapers. Bd. dirs. state and local ACLU, 1968-75; co-founder Environ. Forum, State College, 1985. Grantee NIH, 1971-73. Mem. LWV, Am. Psychol. Assn., Coun. Human Svcs., Art Alliance Cen. Pa., Farmland Preservation Artists, (founder), Pa. Guild Craftsmen, Sierra Club (officer), Sigma Xi. Avocation: arts. Office: 111 S Allen St Ste 2D State College PA 16801-4735 Office Phone: 814-237-1980.

KIRCHNER, JOANN ELAINE, psychiatrist; d. Roy Richmond and Bertha Maye Griffin; m. Jeffrey J. Kirchner, Nov. 20, 1980; children: Christen Kathleen, Jessica Leigh. BS in Math and Econs., Miss. U. Women, Columbus, 1980; MD, U. Ark., Little Rock, 1992. Resident U. Ark. Med. Scis., Little Rock, 1992—95; engr. SWBT, 1980—85; psychiatrist, health svcs. rschr. Ctrl. Ark. Vets. Healthcare Sys., North Little Rock, 1993—. Cons. VA Palo Alto Health Care Sys., Menlo Park, Calif., 2005—, VA Med. Ctr., Iowa City, 2004—; assoc. dir., clin. care South Ctrl. Mental Illness Rsch. Edn. and Clin. Care, North Little Rock, 2003—; cons. Substance Abuse Mental Health & Services Adminstrn., Tech. Adv. Ctr., Postive Aging Resource Ctr., Boston, 2002—05; assoc. dir. VA Mental Health Quality Enhancement Rsch. Initiative, North Little Rock, 1999—2000. Mentor Sci. Fair, Little Rock, 1998; soccer coach Our Lady Holy Souls Jr. High Schs., 1995—98, Little Rock Football Club, 1997—2001. Recipient Red Sash Clin. Sci. Tchg. award, U. Ark. Med. Scis., 1999; fellow, 1995—97. Mem.: AMA, Ark. Psychiat. Assn., Am. Psychiat. Assn. Office: Central Arkansas Veterans Healthcare Sys 2200 Fort Roots Drive Bldg 58 (152/NLR) North Little Rock AR 72114 Office Phone: 501-257-1719. E-mail: kirchnerjoanne@uams.edu.

KIRCHNER, LISA BETH, actress, vocalist; b. L.A. d. Leon and Gertrude (Schoenberg) K. BA, Sarah Lawrence Coll., N.Y., 1975. Picture rschr. McGraw-Hill, 1985-87, John Wiley & Sons, 1988, Simon & Schuster/Globe Book Co., 1992—2000, Chelsea House Pubs., 1987-94, Oxford Univ. Press, 1997, Facts on File, 2001—02, Greenwood Pub. Co., 1997, Lazard Freres, 1998—, The Oryx Press, 1999—, Abbeville Press, 2001—02. Songwriter, BMI. Broadway appearances include The Threepenny Opera, 1975, The Human Comedy, 1985; off-Broadway appearances include the Radiant City, 1993, Hotel for Criminals, 1974, The American Imagination, others; TV shows include Songs From the Heart, Another World, The Guiding Light, As The World Turns, Out of Our Father's House; appearances at The White House and Gracie Mansion; performed as featured soloist and back-up singer with Judy Collins (numerous TV appearances); prodr., solo vocalist CD releases (Albany Records) entitled One More Rhyme, 1999, When Lights Are Low, 2002. Mem. AFTRA, SAG, BMI, Equity, Actor's Equity Assn. Avocations: painting, crafts, poetry. E-mail: kirchl@aol.com.

KIRCHNER, MARY KATHERINE, musician, educator; b. Omaha, Apr. 22, 1937; d. Ferdinand Anthony and Loretta Agnes (Brady) Dascher; m. John Edmund Kirchner, Jr., June 20, 1959; children: J. Kevin, Mark A., Patrick D., Edmund J., Thomas J. BA, Loretto Heights Coll., 1959. Pvt. voice tchr., Edina, Minn., 1982—. Voice tchr. Performing Arts Ctr., Edina, 1982—95; adj. faculty voice tchr. Edina HS, 1982—99; pres. Thursday Musical, Mpls., 1992—94. Sec. Rep. Senate Dist. 42, 1983—85. Mem.: Minn. Music Tchrs. Assn. (adminstr. non-keyboard programs 1987—89, cert.), Nat. Assn. Tchrs. Singing, Mu Phi Epsilon (pres. 1988—90, dist. dir. 1995—98). Roman Catholic. Avocations: reading, walking. Home: 7470 Cahill Rd Edina MN 55439 Personal E-mail: jkkirchner@msn.com.

KIRCHNER, URSULA SCHWEBS, science educator; BS, Duke U., Durham, NC, 1976—80; MEd, Marymount U., Arlington, 1993—96. Course developer Tex. Instruments, Houston, 1981—85; sci. tchr. Fairfax County Pub. Schs., Reston, Va., 1997—. Cons. Am. Inst. Rsch., 1997—2002.

KIRCHOFF, MOLLY, music educator; b. Brookville, Pa., May 12, 1978; d. Arthur and Mary Ann Manfroni; m. Matthew Kirchoff. MusB, Mercyhurst Coll., D'Angelo Sch. Music, Erie, Pa., 2000. Tchr. h.s. music Villa Maria H.S., Erie, Pa., 2000—02; tchr. elem. music Sch. Dist. Lancaster, 2003—. Mem.: MENC, PSEA. Roman Catholic. Achievements include development of a music literacy curriculum. Avocations: piano, singing, sports, travel. Personal E-mail: makirchoff@lancaster.k12.pa.us.

KIRDANI, ESTHER MAY, retired school counselor; b. Nunda, N.Y., Aug. 27, 1936; d. Herbert Stewart and Sarah Edith (Veley) Stewart Kernahan; m. Rashad Y. Kirdani, Aug. 16, 1958; children: Lavinia Helen, Leila Andrea. BS in Home Econs. Edn., SUNY, Buffalo, 1958; EdM in Secondary Guidance, U. Buffalo, 1972. Permanent cert. home econs. edn. and secondary sch. guidance. Tchr. home econs. Royalton-Hartland (N.Y.) Ctrl. Sch., 1958-60; tchr. math. Grafton (Mass.) Jr. H.S., 1962-65, Clarence (N.Y.) Jr. H.S., 1967-68; sch. counselor West Seneca (N.Y.) Sch. Dist., 1973—2002; ret., 2002. Mem. ACA, Am. Sch. Counselor Assn., Western N.Y. Guidance Dirs. and Chairpersons (coord. 1987-94), Western N.Y. Sch. Counselors Consortium, Western N.Y. Sch. Counselors Assn. (Sch. Counselor of Yr. 2001-02). Avocations: gardening, travel, knitting, doll collecting. Home: 44 Buttonwood Ln East Amherst NY 14051-1642

KIRK, ARTEMIS G., university librarian; BA in Music, Vassar Coll.; M in Libr. and Info. Sci., Simmons Coll., Boston; MusM, Harvard U. Past asst. libr. Hellenic Coll., Brookline, Mass.; head libr. Pine Manor Coll., Chestnut Hill, Mass.; dir. libr. and co-dir. info. tech. Simmons Coll.; asst. dir. libr. for collections and budget U. Miami; dir. univ. libr. U. RI, 1998—2001; univ. libr. Georgetown U., 2001—. Bd. dir. RI Higher Edn. Libr. Info. Network; bd. mem. RI libr. bd. Fellow, U.S. Info. Agency, Am. Assoc. Libr. Mem.: Assn. Coll. and Rsch. Libr. Office: Lauinger Libr Georgetown U 37th and N Streets NW Washington DC 20057-1174 Office Phone: 202-687-7425. Office Fax: 202-687-7501. E-mail: agk3@georgetown.edu.*

KIRK, BONNIE LONGEST, retired elementary school educator; b. Troy, NC, Jan. 16, 1943; d. Walter Roland and Mary Frances (Cochran) Longest; m. William Thomas Kirk, June 13, 1965 (dec.); children: Kimberly Lynn, Heather Liane Kirk Pollard. BA, Elon U., NC, 1965. Tchr. Almance County Schs., Burlington, NC, 1965—66, Asheville City Schs., NC, 1966—67, Goldsboro City Schs., NC, 1967—72, Wake County Schs., Raleigh, NC, 1979—97, Almance Burlington Schs., Burlington, 1997—2004; ret., 2004. Home: 512 Francisca Ln Cary NC 27511-3746

KIRK, CHARLOTTE LEIDECKER, director; b. Sheffield, Ala., Feb. 11, 1949; d. Boyd Frank and Mildred Wiley Leidecker; m. Clinton Dale Kirk, Sept. 8, 1967 (div. Mar. 1996); 1 child, Chad E. BS magna cum laude, Murray State U., 1976, MA in Edn., 1980, MA in Sch. Adminstrn., 1986. Kindergarten tchr. Crittenden County Bd. Edn., Marion, Ky., 1977—86; primary tchr. Ft. Thomas (Ky.) Bd. Edn., 1986—88, Harrodsburg (Ky.) Bd. Edn., 1988—89; spl. edn. cons. Ky. Dept. Edn., Frankfort, 1989—94; dir. state and fed. programs Hickman County Bd. Edn., Clinton, Ky., 1994—96; dir. spl. edn. McCracken County Bd. Edn., Paducah, Ky., 1996—2000; asst. supt. Hickman County Bd. Edn., Clinton, 2000—01; dir. spl. edn. Covington (Ky.) Bd. Edn., 2001—. Charter mem. Ky. Assn. Sch. Admin. Inst. for Women in Adminstrn., 1978—2002; pres., sec. Western Ky. Assn. Sch. Adminstr., Paducah, 1995—2000; mem. adv. bd. Ky. Dept. Juvenile Justice, Frankfort, 1998—2001; cons. Trimble County Bd. Edn., Bedford, Ky., 2003; com. mem. Devel. of Ky. Adminstrv. Regulations for Spl. Edn.; presenter Ky. Assn. Gifted Edn. Rec. sec. Marion (Ky.) Woman's Club, 1980—86. Mem.: Kappa Delta Phi, Phi Delta Kappa. Democrat. Baptist. Avocations: sailing, reading, golf. Home: PO Box 8214 Paducah KY 42002-8214 Office Phone: 859-392-1137.

KIRK, DEBORAH, piano educator; b. Morehead City, N.C., Aug. 14, 1951; d. David Arthur Kirk Jr. and Judy Mann Hartford; m. Kenneth Hinso, Dec. 23, 1984. BM, U. N.C., Greensboro, 1973, MM, 1988. Nat. cert. music tchr.; cert. music tchr., N.C. Ind. piano tchr., Greensboro, 1986—. Piano tchr. Music Camp/U. N.C., Greensboro, 1997; adjudicator Raleigh Music Tchrs. Assn., 1996, Charlotte Piano Forum, NC, 1999, N.C. Fedn. Music Clubs, 1999; music specialist Peeler Open Sch. for Performing Arts. Concerto soloist Univ. Symphony Orch., Greensboro, 1973. Mem. Greensboro Music Tchrs. Assn. (v.p. 1995-98), N.C. Music Tchrs. Assn. (dist. festival chair 1996-99), Music Tchrs. Nat. Assn., Am. Coll. Musicians Guild. Avocation: feral cat management. E-mail: dkkirk@hotmail.com.

KIRK, DIANA E., bank executive; Exec. v.p. Pvt. Banking Div. Zions First Nat. Bank, Salt Lake City, mem. exec. mgmt. team. Past commr. Salt Lake City Planning Com. Bd. mem. Salt Lake Rotary Club, Planned Parenthood Assn. of Utah. Mem.: Nat. Assn. for Women and Bus. Owners. Office: Zions Bank One S Main, Ste 1134 Salt Lake City UT 84111 Office Phone: 801-524-4787.

KIRK, JANE SEAVER, municipal government administrator; b. Boston, May 12, 1928; d. Howard Wesley and Ruth (Seaver) K. BA, Duke U., Durham, N.C., 1950; MS, Springfield Coll., Mass., 1956. Ctr. dir. ARC, Korea, Japan, France, Morocco, 1951-60; dep. dir. internat. group YMCA of the U.S.A., Chgo., 1961-93; chair selectmen Town of Nelson, NH, 1997—. Bd. dirs. N.E. Delta Dental, Concord, NH; incorporator Monadnock Family Svcs., 2001—02. Trustee Hist. Soc. Cheshire County, Keene, NH, 1995—2001, Springfield Coll., 1973—2000; pres. Granite Lake Assn., Munsonville, NH, 1995—2000; bd. dirs. Duke Ctr. for Living, Durham, NC, 1995—2001. Recipient Fundraising Achievement award N.Am. YMCA Devel. Officers, 1991. Mem. AAUW, DAR, ARCOA, NAFYR, Daus. of Founders and Patriots, Order Eastern Star, Union League Club Chgo., Coll. Club of Boston, Descendants of Colonial Clergy, Women's Aux., Mass. Ancient and Honorable Artillery Co., Edmund Rice (1638) Assn., Ladies Charitable Soc., Bay State African Violet Soc., Walpole Hist. Soc., Rotary Club of Keene (Paul Harris fellow), Historical Soc. Chesire County, Alice Cir., Phi Beta Kappa. Republican. Baptist. Avocations: photography, gardening, travel, walking. Home: 543 Granite Lake Rd Nelson NH 03457-5121

KIRK, JILL, management consultant; BA, U. Oreg. Corp. dir. human resources/orgnl. devel. Tektonix, Inc., group human resources mgr.; dir. cmty. affairs Tektronix, Inc., 1994; exec. dir. Tektronix Found., 1991; founder The Kirk Group LLC, 1999—; ptnr. Lindberg/Kirk/Millar, 2000—; v.p. Oreg. Bus. Coun., 2005—. Mem. bd. dirs., exec. bd., govt. affairs com. Am. Electronics Assn.; bd. dirs. Associated Oreg. Industries; chair deputies com. Oreg. Bus. Coun., vice chair edn. com., mem. higher edn. task force, mem. pub. fin. com. Mem. Oreg. State Bd. Edn., 1996—, chairperson, 2001—, mem. exec. com., mem. joint bds. working group, mem. econ. devel. joint bds. working group; trustee Portland Art Mus., 1998—2001, 2001—; mem. adv. com. Portland Ctr. for the Performing Arts; bd. dirs. Portland Youth Philharm.; mem. strategic planning com. United Way Columbia-Willamette; active Oreg. Profl. Devel. Coun.; bd. chair Lintner Ctr. for Advanced Edn.; active Govs. Task Force on Higher Edn., Govs. Task Force on Quality Edn.; bd. dirs. Japanese Garden Soc., 2001, STARS, Portland Edn. Network, N.W. Bus. for Culture and the Arts, Nat. Alliance Bus. Western Region. Mem.: Portland C. of C. (bd. dirs.). Office: Oreg Bus Coun 1100 SW 6th Ave Ste 1608 Portland OR 97204-1090

KIRK, KATHRYN A., science educator; b. Waterloo, Iowa, Sept. 27, 1952; d. Fredric O. and Delores A. Kirk; m. Gregory H. Landis; 1 child, Anna Landis. BS in Edn., Bloomsburg State Coll., Pa., 1973; M, Phila. U., 1994. Tchr. North Pa. Sch. Dist., Lanodale, 1971—78; sbustitute tchr. various schs., 1978—85; tchr. Boyertown Area Sch. Dist., 1986—, leader sci. dept., 1992—. Mem.: NEA, Pa. Sci. Educators Assn. Avocations: bicycling, skiing, travel. Office: Bouertown Area Sr High Sch 120 N Monroe St Barto PA 19504

KIRK, LYNDA POUNDS, biofeedback therapist, neurotherapist, counselor; b. Corpus Christi, Tex., Dec. 17, 1946; d. James Arthur and Elizabeth Pauline (Sanders) Pounds; children: Leslie Jennifer, Edward Christopher. BA, U. Tex., Austin, 1977; MA, St. Edwards U., 1996. Lic. profl. counselor. Therapist Austin (Tex.) State Hosp., 1977-80; dir. stress mgmt. The Hills Med./Sports Complex, Austin, 1980-82; founder, owner Austin Biofeedback Ctr., 1982—, Health Mastery Concepts, Austin, 1982—, Optimal Performance Inst., 2000—; CEO Healthy Life Options, Inc., Austin, 1998—. Cons. State of Tex., Austin, 1983—, City of Austin, 1985—, Lower Colo. River Authority, Austin, 1984—. Author: (book/cassette series) Regenerative Relaxation, 1981; Urological Applications of Biofeedback, Stress Mastery and Peak Performance, 1986. Bd. dirs. South Austin Civic Club, 1983—, pres., 1987; bd. dirs., treas. Texans for the Preservation of Hist. Structures, 1990—; bd. dirs. Austin Ctr. for Attitudinal Healing, 1992—. Fellow Biofeedback Cert. Inst. Am. (sr.), Internat. Soc. for Neuronal Regulation (pres. 1997-98); mem. Assn. Applied Psychophysiology and Biofeedback (pres. 2003-2004, found. bd. 2005), Internat. Soc. for Study of Subtle Energies and Energy Medicine, Biofeedback Soc. Tex. (pres. 1995-97, exec. bd., citation award 1989), Behavioral Medicine Soc. Am., Am. Holistic Med. Assn., Diplomate Cert. Quantitative Electroencephalography Technologists, Acad. Cert. Neurotherapists, Phi Beta Kappa Episcopalian. Avocations: jogging, snorkeling, mountain biking, designs for world peace. Home: 420 Brady Ln Austin TX 78746-5502 Office: Austin Biofeedback Ctr 3624 N Hills Dr Ste B205 Austin TX 78731-3061

KIRK, REA HELENE (REA HELENE GLAZER), special education educator; b. N.Y.C., Nov. 17, 1944; d. Benjamin and Lillian (Kellis) Glazer; 3 stepchildren. BA, UCLA, 1966; MA, Ea. Mont. Coll., 1981; EdD, U. So. Calif., 1985. Cert. spl. edn. tchr. Calif., Mont. Tchr. spl. edn., LA, 1966—73; clin. sec. speech and lang. clinic Missoula, Mont., 1973—75; tchr. spl. edn. Missoula, Gt. Falls, Mont., 1975—82; br. mgr. YWCA LA, Beverly Hills, Calif., 1989—91; sch. adminstrn., ednl. coord. Adv. Schs. Calif., 1991—94; dir. Woman's Resource Ctr., Gt. Falls, 1981—82, Battered Woman's Shelter, Rock Springs, Wyo., 1982—84, Battered Women's Program, Sweetwater County, Wyo., 1984—88, San Gabriel Valley, Calif., 1988; with Spl. Edn., Pasadena, 1994—96, prin., 1995; asst. prof. U. Wis., Platteville, 1996—2003, assoc. prof., 2003—. Mem. Wyo. Commn. Aging, Rock Springs; vis. prof. U. Wuhan, China, 2003—04, Miss. Valley State U., Itta Bena, 2005; adv. bd. New Tchr. Advocate; sec. faculty senate U. Wis., Platteville, 2005—06. Pres., bd. dirs. Battered Women's Shelter, Gt. Falls; founder, advisor Rape Action Line, Gt. Falls; 4-H leader; hostess Friendship Force, amb. Wyo., Germany, Italy; v.p. Coun. Devel. Disabilities, Wis.; bd. dirs. Coun. Children with Behavior Disorders, Wis., Family Advs., Platteville, 1996—; organizer Women's Readers Theater, Platteville; active YWCA, Mont., Wyo., Cmty. Action Bd. City of LA; pres., bd. dirs. religious congregation, Rock Springs; founder Jewish religious svcs., Missoula. Named Advisor of the Yr., U. Wis., 2000, Woman of Yr., U. Wis., Platteville, 2006, Significant Wyo. Woman as Social Justice Reformer and Peace Activist, Sweetwater County, Wyo.; recipient honors, Missoula 4-H, Underkoffler Tchg. Excellence award, U. Wis., 2000, honor for Anti-Poverty work, LA Mayor Bradley, Support Staff award, U. Wis., Platteville, 2006; Gladys Byron scholar, U. So. Calif., 1993, Dept. Edn. scholar, 1994. Mem.: Assn. Children with Learning Disabilities (Named Outstanding Mem. 1982), Wis. Assn. Children with Behavior Disorders, Wis. Coun. Exceptional Children (bd. dirs., pres. S.W. region), Wis. Divsn. Mentally Retarded/Developmentally Disabled, Coun. Exceptional Children (v.p. Gt. Falls 1981—82, bd. dirs., Professionally Recognized Spl. Educator 1998), Pioneer Svc. Club (adv.), Pi Lambda Theta, Kappa Delta Pi (co-counselor 2000—, sec. 2002—), Phi Kappa Phi, Delta Kappa Gamma (sec. 2002—), Phi Delta Kappa. Office Phone: 608-342-1279. Business E-Mail: kirkr@uwplatt.edu.

KIRKEBYE, AMANDA STARK, art educator; b. Rochester, N.Y., Aug. 29, 1975; d. Rory Edward and Linda Newland Stark; m. Brian John Kirkebye, July 27, 2002; 1 child, Taelor Charles. A, Monroe CC, Rochester, N.Y., 1993—95; student, Nazareth Coll., Rochester, 1995—97, M of Art Edn., 1998—2000. Cert. k-12 art tchr. N.Y., 2004. 6m clk., sign shop artist Wegmans Food Markets, Rochester, 1993—99; art tchr. Greece Ctrl. Sch. Dist., Rochester, 2000—. Freelance artist, Pittsford, NY. Logo design, Pittsford Musical Prodns., 2001—04, scenic artist, 2001, menu artwork and dining rm., Schoen Place Prime Rib & Grill, 2002. Bd. mem. Pittsford Musicals, 2002—04. Independent. Avocations: painting, drawing, photography, collage, scenic art. Office: Greece Ctrl Sch Dist West Ridge 200 Alcott Rd Rochester NY 14626

KIRKGAARD, VALERIE ANNE, media group executive, radio host, writer, radio producer, consultant; b. Merced, Calif., Aug. 18, 1940; d. Basil Stuart and Audrey (Thompson) Coghlan; m. Alonzo Bryson Kirkgaard, Oct. 6, 1962 (div. Aug. 1983); children: Jennifer Alexandra, John Erik. AA, Santa Monica City Coll., 1961; BA, UCLA, 1968; M in Counseling, Goddard Coll., LA, 1982; M in Enlightenment, Sci. of Mind Ch., San Diego, 1992; PhD (hon.), Harrington U., 1999. Bd. and care organizer Norwalk State Hosp., L.A., 1976-78; liaison to bd. dirs. Gay and Lesbian Cmty. Svcs. Ctr., 1976—79; therapist in pvt. practice Kirkgaard & Assocs, Pasadena, Pacific Palisades, Santa Monica, Calif., 1975—; pvt. practice relationship cons., 1976—; CEO Kirkgaard Media. Ear coning educator, mfr., 1992—; prodr., host radio and TV Waking Up In America, 1987—; radio prodr. Terry Cole Whittaker; radio prodr./host Open Forum, Waking Up In America, 2 programs for KFNX, Phoenix, KTBL, Albuquerque, WHLD, WMNY, Buffalo; spkr. in field; also VoiceAmerica.com. Author: Breakfast At Bob's, 1982, Take Two Breaths and Call Me in the Morning, 1988,environ. editor United Fitness Mag., 1992; columnist Hollywood Times, 1976, Century City News, 1990-92, Topanga Messenger, 1996—; author numerous articles; numerous appearances and interviews; inventor in field. Founder Golden Hearts Found. Olympic Torch bearer, 1984. Mem. Calif. Assn. Marriage Family and Child Counselors, Women's Mus. of Art, Los Angeles County Mus. Art, World Vision, State of the World Forum, The Hunger Project, Mus. of Tolerance, Greater L.A. Press Club, Scriptwriters Network, Pacific Palisades C. of C., Roar Found., Global Security Inst. Avocations: horseback riding, hiking, reading, gardening. Home: 19733 Sunset Trl Topanga CA 90290 Office: Kirkgaard & Assocs 869 Via De La Paz Ste F Pacific Palisades CA 90272-5202 Office Phone: 310-459-4824, 310-455-8623. E-mail: val@wakingupinamerica.com, valerieannekirkgaard@mac.com.

KIRKHAM, M. B., plant physiologist, educator; b. Cedar Rapids, Iowa; d. Don and Mary Elizabeth (Erwin) K. BA with honors, Wellesley Coll.; MS, PhD, U. Wis. Cert. profl. agronomist. Plant physiologist U.S. EPA, Cin., 1973-74; asst. prof. U. Mass., Amherst, 1974-76, Okla. State U., Stillwater, 1976-80; from assoc. prof. to prof. Kans. State U., Manhattan, 1980—. Guest lectr. Inst. Water Conservancy and Hydroelectric Power Rsch., Inst. Farm Irrigation Rsch., China, 1985, Inst. Exptl. Agronomy, Italy, 1989, Agrl. U. Wageningen, Inst. for Soil Fertility, Haren, Netherlands, 1991, Massey U., New Zealand, 1991, Lincoln U., New Zealand, 1998, Environ. and Risk Mgmt. Group Hort. Rsch., 1998, Palmerston North, New Zealand, 1998, U. Hannover, Germany, 2003; William A. Albrecht seminar spkr. U. Mo., 1994; vis. scholar Biol. Labs., Harvard U., 1990; vis. scientist environ. physics sect. dept. sci. and indsl. rsch. Palmerston North, 1991, The Hort. and Food Rsch.

Inst. New Zealand, Ltd., Crown Rsch. Inst., Palmerston North, 1998, 2005, Landcare Rsch., Lincoln, New Zealand, 1998; mem. peer rev. panel USDA/Nat. Rsch. Initiative, Washington, 1994; mem. rev. panel USDA Office Sci. Quality Rev. Water Quality Nat. Program, 2001; apptd. mem. US Nat. Com. for Soil Sci. of NAS, 2001—04; participant confs. and symposia; spkr., presenter in field. Author: Principles of Soil and Plant Water Relations, 2004; editor: Water Use in Crop Production, 1999; co-editor (with I.K. Iskander): Trace Elements in Soil, 2001; cons. editor Plant and Soil Jour., 1979—2005, mem. editl. bd. BioCycle, 1978—82, Field Crops Rsch. Jour., 1983—91, Soil Sci., 1997—, Jour. Crop Improvement, 1996—, Jour. Environ. Quality, 2002—, Crop Sci., 2004—, mem. editl. adv. bd. Internat. Agrophysics, 2000—, Australia Jour. Soil Rsch., 2004—; contbr. more than 220 articles and papers to sci. jours. Recipient Best Reviewer award, Water Resources Engring. divsn. Jour. Irrigation and Drainage Engring., ASCE, 1996, grad. faculty tchg. award, Coll. of Agr., Kanas State Univ., 2001; grantee, NSF, USDA, US Dept. Energy, Kans. Ctr. Agrl. Resources and the Environ., Manhattan; NSF postdoctoral fellow, U. Wis., 1971—73, NDEA fellow, E.I. du Pont de Nemours and Co. summer faculty fellow, 1976. Fellow: AAAS, Crop Sci. Soc. Am. (editl. bd. 1980—84, 2004—, chair-elect crop physiology and metabolism divsn. 2006), Royal Meteorol. Soc., Soil Sci. Soc. Am. (travel grantee to internat. congress Japan 1990), Am. Soc. Agronomy (editl. bd. 1985—90); mem.: Am. Chem. Soc., Am. Math. Assn., Am. Phys. Soc., Internat. Assn. Hydrol. Sci., Royal Soc. New Zealand, Internat. Water Resources Assn., Am. Geophys. Union, Internat. Assn. Vegetation Sci., Am. Phytopathol. Soc., Water Environment Fedn., Growth Regulator Soc. Am., Soc. Exptl. Biology (London), NY Acad. Sci., Scandinavian Soc. Plant Physiology, Japanese Soc. Plant Physiology, Soc. Francaise de Physiologie Végétale, Am. Meteorol. Soc., Bot. Soc. Am., Internat. Union Soil Sci. (1st vice chmn. commn. soil physics 1994—98, sec. commn. on soils, food security and human health 2002—), Internat. Soil Tillage Rsch. Orgn., Am. Soc. Hort. Sci., Am. Soc. Plant Physiology (editl. bd. 1982—87), Sigma Xi (sec. chpt. 1997—99, Outstanding Sr. Scientist award 2002), Gamma Sigma Delta (Disting. Faculty award Kan. State U. chpt. 2001), Phi Kappa Phi (scholar award 2000). Home: 1420 McCain Ln Apt 244 Manhattan KS 66502-4680 Office: Kans State U Dept Agronomy Throckmorton Hall Manhattan KS 66505-5501 Office Phone: 785-532-0422. Business E-Mail: mbk@ksu.edu.

KIRKHORN, LEE-ELLEN CHARLOTTE, community health nurse, educator; b. Kennewick, Wash., Aug. 19, 1956; d. Ernest Arnold and Ellen Lillian Mathilda (Landstrom) Copstead. ADN, Columbia Basin Coll., 1976; BSN summa cum laude, Wash. State U., 1978; M Nursing, U. Wash., 1979; PhD, Gonzaga U., 1983. Rsch. asst. Wash. State U., Pullman, 1976-77; clinic nurse Profl. Mall, Pullman, 1976-77; charge nurse St. Brendan Nursing Home, Spokane, Wash., 1977-78; rsch. asst. U. Wash., Seattle, 1979; instr. Intercollegiate Ctr. for Nursing Edn., Spokane, 1979-81; pub. health nurse Spokane County Vis. Nurses Assn., 1980, 82, Zion Luth. Ch., Deer Park, Wash., 1993; asst. prof. Intercollegiate Coll. Nursing, Spokane, 1981-85, assoc. prof., 1985—2001; assoc. dean Western Campus U. Wis. Madison Sch. Nursing, 2001—05; assoc. prof. U. Wis., Eau Claire Coll. Nursing and Health Scis., 2005—. Cons., presenter in field; adj. clin. faculty mem. Hawaii Pacific U., Honolulu, 1994; assoc. prof. Intercollegiate Coll. Nursing U. Guam, 1991; external grant reveiwer Alta. Can. Found. for Nursing Rsch., 1991—. Editor: Perspectives on Pathophysiology, 1995, 2001, 05; contbr. articles to profl. publs., chpts. to books; mem. editl. bd. Geriatric Nursing, 1991—; rsch. cons. Spokane Planning Affiliates Network, 1989—; geriatric cons. Nehalem Valley Care Ctr., 1988, Hood River Care Ctr., 1989; expert witness Reed & Giesa, P.S., 1986. Mem. exec. bd., chair grantwriting subcom. Inland Empire br. Nat. Arthritis Found., 1991-2001; team capt. fundraising dr. Am. Heart Assn., 1988-2001; mem. task force on aging Sacred Heart Ctr., 1984-2000; co-leader fund dr. United Way, 1980. Postdoctoral fellow Gerontol. Soc. Am., 1986, 87. Mem. ANA (cert. gerontol. clin. nursing specialist), Am. Mental Health Counselors Assn. (cert. gerontol. counseling trainer), AAUP, Nat. League Nurses, Bus. and Profl. Women, Gerontol. Soc. Am., Internat. Coun. Nurses, Internat. Rehab. Inst., Wash. State Nurses Assn., Wash. State Pub. Health Assn., Inland Empire Nurses Assn. (nominating com. 1981-82), Western Gerontol. Soc., Intercollegiate Ctr. for Nursing Edn. Alumni Assn., Mensa, Sigma Theta Tau (2d v.p. Delta Chi chpt.-at-large). Lutheran. Avocations: photography, people watching, classical music. Home: 1412 Nixon Ave Eau Claire WI 54701-6575 Office: Univ Wisconsin Eau Claire Coll Nursing and Health Scis Eau Claire WI 54701 Office Phone: 715-836-5005. Personal E-mail: lecopstead@aol.com.

KIRKIEN-RZESZOTARSKI, ALICJA MARIA, academic administrator, researcher, educator; b. Lodz, Poland; came to U.S., 1965; d. Leszek Tadeusz and Francesca Irene (Mortkowicz) Kirkien. MSChemE, Polish U. Coll., London, 1951; PhD, U. London, 1955. Asst. prof. chemistry U. W.I., Jamaica, 1956-59, assoc. prof., 1959-61, Trinidad, 1961-65, Trinity Coll., Washington, 1966-68, prof. chemistry, 1968-92, chair chemistry dept., 1969-91, prof. emeritus, 1992—. Sr. rsch. assoc. George Washington U. Med. Ctr., Washington, 1984. One person show at Trinity Coll., Washington, 1994; watercolors and oils exhibited in show at Sorrento, Italy, 1994, 96, Karistos, Greece, 1993, Cade Gallery, Anne Arundel Coll., Arnold, Md., 1998; contbr. numerous articles to profl. publs. Sec., treas. Polish Vets. Assn., Washington, 1981-83. Named one of Outstanding Educators of Am., 1973, 75; sr. rsch. fellow Univ. Coll., 1965-66, 71, U. Calif., Santa Barbara, 1967. Fellow Royal Inst. Chem. (Gt. Britain); mem. Md. Fedn. Art (Critics Choice award for pottery 1992), Am. Chem. Soc. (adv. bd. Chem. and Engring. News 1978-81), Chem. Soc. Gt. Britain, Polish Inst. Arts and Scis. of N.Y., Phi Beta Kappa. Republican. Roman Catholic. Avocations: graphic painting, and ceramics. Home: 407 Buckspur Ct Millersville MD 21108-1764 Office: Trinity Coll 125 Michigan Ave NW Washington DC 20010-2916

KIRKLAND, CINDY D., paralegal; b. Dalton, Ga., Jan. 18, 1975; d. Larry Ray Childers and Wilma Jean Shampo; m. Gary Wayne Kirkland, Apr. 24, 1999; children: Ariel Breanna, Hunter Gene, Jordan Paul. Cert.: GA (Paralegal) 2002. Paralegal McCamy, Phillips, Tuggle & Fordham, LLP, Dalton, Ga., 2000—05, The McCurry Law Firm, LLC, Dalton, 2005—. Mem.: ATLA, Ga. Trial Lawyers Assn. Home: 140 Murray One Pl Chatsworth GA 30705 Office: The McCurry Law Firm LLC 402 N Selvidge St Dalton GA 30720 Office Phone: 706-279-1174. Office Fax: 706-279-1183. Personal E-mail: cindyk03@alltel.net. Business E-Mail: ckirkland@mccurrylaw.com.

KIRKLAND, NANCY CHILDS, secondary school educator, consultant; b. Ideal, Ga., July 20, 1937; d. Millard Geddings and Bessie Vioda (Forbes) C.; m. Allard Corley French, Jr., Apr. 22, 1961 (div. Dec. 7, 1978); children: Vianne Elizabeth French Marchese, Nancy Alysia French Joyce; m. Clarence Nathaniel Kirkland, Jr., Dec. 12, 1987. AB in Speech and Religious Edn., LaGrange Coll., 1959; MS, Troy State U., 1977; EdD in Child and Youth Studies, Nova U., 1993. Cert. tchr. English, Religion, instr. Profl. Refinements in Developing Effectiveness, Tchr. Effectiveness and Classroom Handling. Dir. Christian edn. First Meth. Ch., Thomson, Ga., 1959; tchr. English Flanagan (Ill.) Jr.-Sr. H.S., 1962—63; tchr. English and social studies Woodland Jr. H.S., Streater, Ill., 1963—64; tchr. 5th grade Sheridan Elem. Sch., Bloominton, Ill., 1964—65; tchr. English Samson (Ala.) H.S., 1965, Choctawhatchee H.S., Fort Walton Beach, Fla., 1966—68, Marianna (Fla.) H.S., 1972—77; dir. devel. reading lab. Chiefland (Fla.) H.S., 1979—82; tchr. English Buchholz H.S., Gainesville, 1982—. Co-founder, cons. KPS Leadership Specialists, Jonesboro, Ga., 1993—; chairperson Buchholz facilitis com., Gainesville, Fla., 1993—; instr. English Santa Fe C. C., Gainesville, Fla., 1982-87, 96; asst. chairperson Buchholz English Dept., Gainesville, Fla., 1989-92. Contbr. articles to profl. jours. Sec., co-chmn., mem. Buchholz sch. adv. coun., Gainesville, 1994-95; tchr., dir., tchr. trainer Sunday sch., vacation sch., Fla.; actress, dir. Little Theaters, ch. groups, Ill., Ga., Ala.; coord. Gainesville Sister Cities Youth Correspondence Program, 1991-93. Mem. AAUW, ASCD, Alachua Multicultural Coun. (grantee 1992), Nat. Coun. Tchrs. English, Fla. Coun. Tchrs. English, Altrusa Internat. Gainesville (sec. 2004-, dir. 2005-), Alachua Coun. Tchrs. English (v.p. 1991-92, pres. 1992-93), Gainesville C. of C., Altrusa Internat. Gainesville (sec. 2002). Methodist. Avocations: crafts, sewing, fishing, travel. Home: 1728 NW 94th St Gainesville FL 32606-5570 Office: Buchholz H S 5510 NW 27th Ave Gainesville FL 32606-6405 E-mail: Kirkland@gator.net.

KIRKLAND, REBECCA TRENT, endocrinologist; b. Durham, N.C., Dec. 27, 1942; d. Josiah Charles Trent and Mary Duke (Biddle) Trent-Semans; m. John Lindsey Kirkland III, June 24, 1965. BA, Duke U., 1964, MD, 1968. Intern Baylor Coll. Medicine, 1968-69, resident in pediatrics, 1969-70, fellow in pediatric endocrinology, 1971-73, asst. prof. dept. pediatrics, 1975-81, assoc. prof., 1981-88, prof., 1988—, sr. assoc. dean med. edn. London, 2000; registrar Guy's Hosp., Hosp. for Sick Children, London, 1970; with U. Pa. Sch. Medicine, 1973-74, fellow, 1974-75. Asst. physician divsn. endocrinology Children's Hosp. Phila., 1973-75; mem. staff Tex. Children's Hosp., 1975—, Harris County Hosp. Dist., 1975—; head ambulatory svcs. Tex. Children's Hosp., 1984—, dir. jr. league outpatient dept., 1984—. Contbr. articles and revs. to profl. jours. Active Leadership Tex., Leadership Houston; pres. Greater Houston Women's Found., 1994—96; bd. dirs. AVANCE, Inc., 1992, YWCA, 1992; trustee Mus. Med. Sci., 1984—88; pres. Josiah C. Trent Meml. Found., Inc., 1983—, v.p., 1977—83; bd. dirs. Am. Leadership Forum, 1991, mem. selection com., 1989, 1990, sec. bd. dirs. Houston/Gulf Coast chpg., 1989, 1990, pres.-elect, 1991, pres., 1991—93; bd. dirs. Mus. Health and Med. Scis., 2001—. NIH fellow, 1971-73; recipient Alumnae award Baldwin Sch., 1983, Disting. Alumni award Durham Acad., 1984, Goodheart Humanitarian award B'nai B'rith, 1986, Disting. Svc. award Duke U. Med. Alumni Assn., 1992, Recognition award Ctr. for Interaction: Man, Sci. and Culture, 1993, One Voice for Children award Tex. Network for Medically Fragile and Chronically-Ill Children, 1993; named one of five Outstanding Women of Yr. Channel 13, Houston, 1984, Woman on the move Houston Post, 1989. Fellow Am. Acad. Pediatrics; mem. Endocrine Soc., Am. Fedn. For Clin. Rsch., So. Soc. for Pediatric Rsch., Lawson-Wilkins Pediatric Endocrine Soc., Houston Pediatric Soc., Tex. Pediatric Soc., Tex. Med. Assn., Soc. for Pediatric Rsch., Pediatric Endocrinology Soc. Tex., Ambulatory Pediatric Assn., Am. Pediatric Soc., Am. Acad. Pediatrics (pediatric endocrine sect.) 1990), Tex. Diabetes and Endocrine Assn. Office Phone: 832-822-3441. Business E-Mail: rebeccak@bcm.tmc.edu.

KIRKLEY, D. CHRISTINE, not-for-profit developer; b. Horton, Ala., Aug. 28, 1932; d. Vester Boyd and Josephine Prumrytle (Parrish) K.; m. Jack Stanley I, July 4, 1952; 1 child, Jack Stanley II. Student, U. Ala., 1951-52, Samford U., 1963-65, Cathedral Coll., 1982. Svr. rep. South Ctrl. Bell, Birmingham, Ala., 1984—; dir. Helpline Christian Outreach Ministries Inc, Birmingham, 1991—. Area mgr. Operating Blessing, Birmingham, 1989—; mem. Christian Helplines Internat., 1990—, sec. exec. com., 1994—. Mem. Telephone Pioneers Am. (fund raiser 1976-78, pres. 1979, cmty. edn. coord. 1982-83, drug abuse chairperson 1982-83). Mem. Assemby of God Ch. Avocations: reading, bowling, crocheting, swimming. Office: Helpline Christian Outreach Ministries Inc 8 Roebuck Dr Birmingham AL 35215-8046 Office Phone: 205-833-7712. E-mail: hplnchrs@bellsouth.net.

KIRKLEY, VICKI, school system administrator, director; d. Roger and Paula Strahan; m. James William Kirkley, Dec. 21, 1991; 1 child, Connor. MS, U. North Tex., Denton, 1996. Cert. tchr. Tex. Theater dir. McKinney Ind. Sch. Dist., Tex., 2000—, dist. coord. for theatre. Dir.: (plays) Seussical The Musical, I Hate Hamlet, The Real Inspector Hound, Brave Navigator, Joseph and the Amazing Technicolor Dreamcoat. Vol. Music Theatre Denton, Tex., 1995—2006. Mem.: Denton Cmty. Theatre, Music Theatre of Denton, Tex. Ednl. Theatre Assn., Ednl. Theatre Assn. (internat. thespian troupe dir. 2000—), Internat. Thespian Soc. (troupe dir. 2000—06). Office: McKinney Boyd HS 600 N Lake Forest Dr Mc Kinney TX 75070 Office Phone: 817-368-8268.

KIRKPATRICK, ALICIA ANN, elementary school educator, department chairman; b. New Orleans, Jan. 25, 1977; d. Kenny and Shirley Thompson. MA, U. Ala., Tuscaloosa, 2002. Cert. T-5 educator Profl. Stds. Commn., Ga., 2003. 6th grade sci. tchr. Anita White Carson Mid. Sch., Greensboro, Ga., 2003—, sci. dept. chairperson, 2005—. Sch. coun. sec. Anita White Carson Mid. Sch., Greensboro, 2003—, track coach, 2004—06, wrestling coach, 2003—04, 6th grade team leader, 2004—05. Sec. Anita White Carson Mid. Sch. Coun., Greensboro, 2003—06. Named Tchr. of Yr., Anita White Carson Mid. Sch., 2005—06; Title II-D Wireless Classroom grantee, Ga. Dept. Edn., 2005—06. Mem.: NSTA, PAGE Tchr. Acad., Spl. Olympics Ga. (coach/vol. 2004—06), Atlanta Reef Club, Kappa Delta Pi, Kappa Delta Epsilon (Outstanding Mem. award 2003).

KIRKPATRICK, ANNE SAUNDERS, systems analyst; b. Birmingham, Mich., July 4, 1938; d. Stanley Rathburn and Esther (Casteel) Saunders; children: Elizabeth, Martha, Robert, Sarah. Student, Wellesley Coll., 1956-57, Laval U., Quebec City, Can., 1958, U. Ariz., 1958-59; BA in Philosophy, U. Mich., 1961. Sys. engr. IBM, Chgo., 1962-64; sr. analyst Commonwealth Edison Co., Chgo., 1981-97. Treas. Taproot Reps., DuPage County, Ill., 1977—80; pres. Hinsdale (Ill.) Women's Rep. Club, 1978—81. Mem.: Wellesley Chgo. (bd. dirs. 1972—73). Home: 222 E Chestnut St Unit 8B Chicago IL 60611-2376 Personal E-mail: a.kirkpatrick@sbcglobal.net.

KIRKPATRICK, DIANE YVONNE, retired speech pathology/audiology services professional; b. San Diego, Apr. 20, 1938; d. Claude Cliff Davis and Charlotte (Mulnix) Gibson; m. Richard John Prigge Sr., July 2, 1960 (div.); children: Richard John Jr., Tamsin Gail, Kimberly Ann; m. Lee Kingston Kirkpatrick, Aug. 24, 1985. BA, U. Calif., Santa Barbara, 1970, MA, 1973. Cert. clin. competency speech and lang. pathology; lifetime restricted tchg. credential, Calif. Speech pathologist Santa Barbara County Schs., 1972-98, ret., 1998. Mem. Beacon of Light Found., Santa Barbara, 1989—; elder 1st Presbyn. Ch., Santa Barbara, 1995-98, 2004-; chpt. dir. Goldwing Roadriders Assn., Santa Barbara, 1997-98; mem. Santa Barbara Civil Grand Jury, 1999-2000; mem. Master Chorale, Santa Barbara. Mem.: Am. Speech and Hearing Assn. Home: 415 N Turnpike Rd Santa Barbara CA 93111-1932 E-mail: dyksb@cox.net.

KIRKPATRICK, EDITH KILLGORE, music educator, volunteer; b. Lisbon, La., Nov. 14, 1918; d. Thomas Morton and Bess Blanche (Melton) Killgore; m. Claude Kirkpatrick, Aug. 21, 1938; children: Claude Kent (dec.), Thomas Killgore, Edith Kay, Charles Kris. BA, La. Coll., 1938; grad., Juilliard Sch. of Music, 1938; MusM, La. State U., 1965; LLD (hon.), La. Coll., 1980. Pvt. voice tchr., Sulphur, Jennings, La., 1939-59; instr. music McNeese State U., Lake Charles, La., 1955-58; choir dir., ch. soloist Bapt. Ch., Sulphur, Jennings, Baton Rouge, 1938-95. Vis. asst. prof. La. State U., Baton Rouge, 1967-68; mem. State Bd. of Trustees for Higher Edn., Baton Rouge, 1975-77; mem. La. Bd. of Regents for Higher Edn., Baton Rouge, 1978-90. Contbg. editor La. Bapt. Message, 1970-75; chmn. editl. bd., writer, critic Music Clubs Mag., 1969-95; contbr. articles to mags. Mem. exec. bd. La. Bapt., Alexandria, 1969-75; chmn. woman's divsn. Gubernatorial candidate, Jennings, 1959, Baton Rouge, 1963; candidate State Bd. Edn., Baton Rouge, 1974; bd. dirs. Baton Rouge Arts Coun. and Cmty. Fund for Arts, 1983-89, Red Cross, Baton Rouge, 1961-66, YMCA, Baton Rouge, 1961-66, PTA, Baton Rouge, 1961-66, Baton Rouge Symphony, 1961-2002; women's pres. U. Bapt. Ch., Jennings, 1992-95, 1st Bapt. Ch., Baton Rouge, 1964-68; founder, chmn. Batan Rouge (La.) Symphony Youth Orch., 1983-2002. Recipient Disting. Alumni award La. Coll., 1961, Vol. Activist award Speech and Hearing Baton Rouge, 1979, Brotherhood award Baton Rouge chpt. Conf. Christians and Jews, 1989, Disting. Alumni award La. State U., 1995. Mem. Nat. Fedn. Music (exec. bd. 1979-95), La. Arts in Edn., Baton Rouge Music Club (state pres. 1966-70), Bapt. Women's Missions (state pres. 1960-63), Mortar Bd., ODK, Sigma Alpha Iota, Phi Kappa Lambda, PEO, Phi Kappa Phi. Democrat. Avocations: cooking, gardening, reading.

KIRKPATRICK, JEANE DUANE JORDAN, political scientist, federal official; b. Duncan, Okla. d. Welcher F. and Leona (Kile) Jordan; m. Evron M. Kirkpatrick; children: Douglas Jordan, John Evron, Stuart Alan. AA, Stephens Coll.; AB, Barnard Coll.; MA, PhD, Columbia U.; postgrad., U. Paris; LHD (hon.), Georgetown U., U. Pitts., U. Charleston, Hebrew U., Colo. Sch. Mines, St. John's U., Universidad Francisco Marroquin, Guatemala, Coll. William Mary, U. Mich., Syracuse U.; degree (hon.), Loyola U., Chgo., U. Rochester. Asst. prof. polit. sci. Trinity Coll., 1962-67; assoc. prof. polit. sci. Georgetown U., Washington, 1967-73, prof., 1973—, Leavey prof., 1978—2002, prof. emeritus, 2002—; sr. fellow Am. Enterprise Inst. for Pub. Policy Rsch., 1977—; mem. cabinet U.S. permanent rep. to UN, 1981-85; mem. Def. Policy Rev. Bd. (DPB), 1985-93; chair Commn. on Fail Safe and Risk Reduction (FARR), 1990-92; mem. Pres.'s Fgn. Intelligence and Adv. Bd. (PFIAD), 1985-89; head U.S. Delegation to Human Rights Commn., 2003. Author: Elections USA, 1956, Perspectives, 1962, The Strategy of Deception, 1963, Mass Behavior in Battle and Captivity, 1968, Leader and Vanguard in Mass Society; The Peronist Movement in Argentina, 1971, Political Woman, 1974, The New Presidential Elite, 1976, Dismantling the Parties: Reflections on Party Reform and Party Decomposition, 1978, The Reagan Phenomenon, 1983, Dictatorships and Double Standards, 1982, Legitimacy and Force (2 vols.), 1988, The Withering Away of the Totalitarian State, 1990; syndicated columnist, 1985-97; contbr. articles to profl. jours.; editor, contbr. various pubs. Trustee Helen Dwight Reid Ednl. Found., 1972—, pres., 1990—. Recipient Disting. Alumna award Stephens Coll., 1978, B'nai B'rith Humanitarian award, 1982, Award of the Commonwealth Fund, 1983, Gold medal VFW, 1984, French Prix Politique, 1984, Dept. Def. Disting. Pub. Svc. medal, 1985, Bronze Palm, 1992, Disting. Svc. medal Mayor of N.Y.C., 1985, Presdl. Medal of Freedom, 1985, Jamestown Freedom award, 1990, Centennial medal Nat. Soc. DAR, 1991, Disting. Svc. award USO, 1994, Laureate of the Lincoln Acad. of Ill., Medallion of Lincoln, 1996, Jerusalem 2000 award, 1996, Casey medal of hon., 1998, Tomas Garrigue Masaryk Order, 1998, Chauncey Rose award Rose-Hulman Inst. Tech., 1999, Hungarian Presdl. Gold medal, 1999, Living Legends medal Libr. Congress, 2000, Grand Officier du Wissam Al Alaoui medal King of Morocco, 2000; Kirkpatrick professorship of internat. affairs chair established in her honor Harvard U., 1999; Coun. on Fgn. Rels. established Jeane Kirkpatrick chair in nat. security, 2002. Mem. Internat. Polit. Sci. Assn. (exec. coun.), Am. Polit. Sci. Assn. (Hubert Humphrey award 1988), So. Polit. Sci. Assn. Office: Am Enterprise Inst 1150 17th St NW Washington DC 20036-4603 E-mail: jkirkpatrick@aei.org.

KIRKSEY, AVANELLE, nutrition educator; b. Mulberry, Ark., Mar. 23, 1926; BS, U. Ark., Fayetteville, 1947; MS, U. Tenn., Knoxville, 1950; PhD, Pa. State U., University Park, 1961; postdoctoral, U. Calif., Davis, 1976; DSc honoris causa, Purdue U., Ind., 1997. Assoc. prof. Ark. Polytechnic U., Russellville, 1950—55; rsch. asst. Pa. State U., University Park, 1956—58, fellow Gen. Foods, 1958—60; assoc. prof. Purdue U., West Lafayette, Ind., 1961—69, prof. nutrition, 1970—85, disting. prof., 1985—96, disting. prof. emeritus, 1997. Prin. investigator nutrition project in rural Egypt; coord. nutrition program Indonesian Univs., 1987—91. Contbr. articles to profl. jours. Recipient Borden award, Am. Home Econs. Assn., 1980. Fellow Am. Inst. Nutrition (Lederle award 1994); mem. N.Y. Acad. Scis., Phi Kappa Phi, Sigma Xi. Office: Purdue U Dept Food Nutrition West Lafayette IN 47907 Office Phone: 479-452-2340.

KIRKWOOD, BESSIE HERSHBERGER, mathematics professor; b. Bentonville, Ark., June 22, 1950; d. Lewis Edward Hershberger and Mable Louise Hershberger Barnett; m. James Radford Kirkwood, Jan. 7, 1978; children: Katherine, Elizabeth. BS in Math., U. Ark., Fayetteville, 1972, MS in Math., 1974; PhD in Math., U. Okla., Norman, 1977; PhD in Stats., U. Va., Charlottesville, 1995. Asst. prof. Sweet Briar Coll., Va., 1988—90, assoc. prof., 1990—99, prof., 1999—. Vis. asst. prof. James Madison U., Harrisonburg, Va., 1978—79, Sweet Briar Coll., 1979—82, 1983—88, Macalester Coll., St. Paul, 1982—83. Grantee, NSF, 2004—. Mem.: Assn. Women in Math., Math. Assn. Am., Am. Statis. Assn., Jefferson Choral Soc., Phi Beta Kappa. Methodist. Office: Sweet Briar Coll Sweet Briar VA 24595

KIRKWOOD, CATHERINE, artist; b. N.Y.C., July 4, 1949; d. Kenneth Munn Kirkwood and Alexa (Dannenbaum) Hirsh; m. Craig Campbell Anderson; children: Heather Dene, Julia Suzanne. Student, Syracuse U., 1967-69, Calif. Coll. Arts and Crafts, Oakland, 1970-71; BFA, U. N.Mex., 1972, MA, 1974. Grad. instr. U. N.Mex., 1973-74; owner, designer Mei Ming Ware, Santa Fe, 1985-89. One-person shows include Medicine Woman, Taos, N.Mex., 1993; exhibited in group shows including 1972 S.W. Fine Arts Biennial Mus. N.Mex., Santa Fe, Downey (Calif.) Mus. Art Unltd. Exhibit, 1972, 19th Exhbn. Southwestern Prints and Drawings Dallas Mus., 1972, U. N.Mex., 1972, Introduction '73 Hills Gallery, Santa Fe, 1973, Gallery Modern Art, Taos, 1973, Henderson Mus., Boulder, Colo., 1974, 19th Ann. Invitational Art Exhbn., Union, N.J., 1978, Machler Gallery, Phila., 1978, Albuquerque United Artists, 1979, Faculty Show U. N.Mex., Albuquerque, 1979, Tuthill-Gimprich Gallery, N.Y.C., 1980, AIR Gallery, Austin, Tex., 1984, Mus. N.Mex., Santa Fe, Pueblo (Colo.) Art Ctr., 1985, AAUW Calendar, 1989, Cydney Payton Gallery, Denver, 1989, Gallery at the Rep, Santa Fe, 1990, Pangaea Elemental Arts, Santa Fe, 1991, Kimo Theatre, Albuquerque, 1992, Copeland-Rutherford Gallery, Santa Fe, 1992; represented permanent collections Downey Mus., AT&T Co., Chgo. Democrat.

KIRMSE, SISTER ANNE-MARIE ROSE, nun, educator, researcher; b. Bklyn., Sept. 23, 1941; d. Frank Joseph Sr. and Anna (Keck) Kirmse. BA in English, St. Francis Coll., 1972; MA in Theology, Providence Coll., 1975; PhD in Theology, Fordham U., 1989. Joined Sisters of St. Dominic, Roman Cath. Ch., 1960; cert. elem. tchr., N.Y. Tchr. elem. sch. Diocese Bklyn., 1962—73; instr. adult edn. Diocese Rockville Ctr., N.Y.C., 1974—, dir. spiritual programs, 1979—; dir. religious edn. St. Anthony Padua Parish, East Northport, NY, 1975—83; asst. to Card. Avery Dulles Fordham U., Bronx, NY, 1988—, rsch. assoc. Laurence J. McGinley chair in religion and soc., 1989—2003. Demonstration tchr. Paulist Press, N.Y.C., 1968-70; cons. Elem. Sch. Catechetical Assoc., Bklyn., 1971-73; mem. adj. faculty grad. program Sem. Immaculate Conception, Huntington, N.Y., 1979-80; adj. instr. Molloy Coll., Rockville Centre, 1985, St. Joseph's Coll., Patchogue, N.Y., 1990-91; adj. asst. prof. Ignatius Coll., Bronx, N.Y., 1996-98; adj. assoc. prof. Fordham Coll. Liberal Studies, 1998-; mem. adv. com., Pastoral Inst., Diocese of Bklyn., 2006-. Recipient Kerygma Award Diocese of Rockville Ctr., 1980; Dominican Scholar Providence Coll., 1973, Presdl. Scholar Fordham U., 1988; McGinley Fellow Fordham U., 1988, KPTC fellow, 2001, Anton J. Kaiser fellow, 2004, George F. Hixson fellow, 2004, Diamond Hixson, 2006. Mem. Cath. Theol. Soc. Am., Coll. Theology Soc., Kiwanis (pres. Fordham U. 1997-2000, Tablet of Honor 2000, N.Y. dist. chmn. Internat. Understanding Student Exch., 2001-03, lt. gov. Bronx-Westchester South divsn. 2003-04, dist. chmn. human and spiritual values, 2005-06). Democrat. Roman Catholic. Avocations: swimming, needlecrafts, cooking, travel, reading. Office: Fordham U Faber Hall 255 Bronx NY 10458 Office Phone: 718-817-4746. Business E-Mail: kirmse@fordham.edu.

KIRNAN, JEAN POWELL, psychology educator; b. Short Hills, N.J., Mar. 30, 1956; d. Bernard MacDonald and Marie (Harrity) Powell; m. John Vincent Kirnan, Aug. 23, 1980; children: Tarah, Katelyn, Patrick. BA in Psychology cum laude, Immaculate Coll., 1978; MA, Fordham U., 1980, PhD in Psychometrics, 1986. Rsch. analyst Prudential Ins. Co. Am., Newark, 1981-86; prof. psychology Coll. NJ (formerly Trenton State Coll.), 1986—, dept. chmn., 2005—. Human resources cons. Contbr. articles to profl. jours. Mem.: Soc. for Orgn. Psychologists. Avocation: spending time with family. Office: The Coll of New Jersey PO Box 7718 Ewing NJ 08628-0718

KIRNOS, DINA, technology support professional; b. Dushanbe, Russia, Oct. 6, 1953; came to the U.S., 1979; d. Sholom and Klara (Blitshteyn) Kirnos; children: Semyon Shnayderman, Mallory McCoy. BA, U. Dushanbe, 1974. Programmer Royal Ins. Co., N.Y.C., 1979-82; systems analyst Chem. Bank, N.Y.C., 1982-84, Securities Industry Automation Corp., N.Y.C., 1984-89; sr. systems analyst N.Y. Stock Exch., 1989-94, dir. support, 1994—. Mgr. customer svcs. N.Y. Stock Exch., Inc., 1994—. Mem. Assn. Info. Techs., Help Desk Inst. Republican. Jewish. Avocation: music. Office: NY Stock Exch Inc 20 Broad St New York NY 10005-2601

KIRPES, ANNE IRENE, elementary school educator; b. Dubuque, Iowa, Oct. 6, 1966; d. Raymond Louis and Norma Jean Margaret (Kern) K. BA, U. No. Iowa, 1989; EdM, Harvard U., 1997. Lic. elem. edn. Tchr. 1st grade Western Ave Sch., Sch. Dist. 161, Flossmoor, Ill., 1989-93, Serena Hills Sch., Sch. Dist. 161, Chicago Heights, Ill., 1993-96; tchr. 3rd grade Wheelock Lab. Keene (N.H.) State Coll., 1997-98; reading/lang. arts test devel. specialist Riverside Pub. Co., Itasca, Ill., 1998—2002; reading test devel. dir. Data Recognition Corp., Maple Grove, Minn., 2002—. Exch. team mem. Rotary Group, Paris, 1995. Recipient Silver Congl. award U.S.A., 1988, Gold Congl. award, 1991; Young Alumni award U. No. Iowa Alumni Assn., Cedar Falls, 1994. Mem. ASCD, Nat. Coun. Tchrs. English, Whole Lang. Umbrella, Internat. Reading Assn., Kappa Delta Pi (internat. nominations com. 1988-90), Phi Delta Kappa, Alpha Upsilon Alpha (ad hoc com. mem., 2005—), Omicron Delta Kappa. Avocations: reading, travel, puzzles, butterfly memorabilia, board games. Home: 9461 Jewel Ln North Maple Grove MN 55311

KIRSCH, ABIGAIL, culinary productions executive; b. Bklyn., Jan. 22, 1930; d. Joseph and Mollie (Langbert) Greenberg; m. Robert B. Kirsch, June 19, 1951; children: Richard, James, Billy, Jo-Ellen. BA, Adelphi U., 1951; culinary cert., Cordon Bleu, Paris, 1967, Culinary Inst. Am., 1968. Founder, owner, chef, instr. Abigail Kirsch Sch. Cookery, Chappaqua, N.Y., 1964-75; founder Abigail Kirsch Culinary Prodns., Ltd., Tarrytown, N.Y., 1975—; chef, owner Abigail Kirsch's Husband's Pl., Chappaqua, 1975; owner, operator Abigail Kirsch at Tappan Hill, Tarrytown, N.Y., 1989—. Author cookbooks: Teen Cuisine, 1968, The Bride and Groom's First Cookbook, 1996, Invitation to Dinner, 1998, The Bride and Groom's Menu Cookbook, 2002; contbr. articles to profl. publs.; appeared on TV programs on CNN, Food Network, Discovery, Our Home, 1996. Bd. dirs. Westchester County Assn., White Plains, N.Y., 1997-99, March of Dimes West Divsn., White Plains, 1989-90; mem. exec. bd. Food Patch of Westchester, Millwood, N.Y., 1993-97; ann. gala advisor Westchester C.C., Valhalla, N.Y., 1990. Recipient Small Bus. award for Women U.S. C. of C., 1987, Vol. of Yr. award March of Dimes, 1992, Headliner award Women in Comms., 1995, Woman of Distinction award roundtable for Women in Food Svc., 1995, Pacesetter award Nat. Roundtable of Women in Food Svc., 1996, Restaurateur of Yr. award N.Y. State Restaurant Assn., 1996, Silver Plate award Internat. Food Svc. Mfrs. Assn., 1997, Family of Yr. award Family Svc. of Westchester, 1997; named to New York's 100 Most Influential Women in Bus., Crain's N.Y. Bus., 1999. Mem. Culinary Inst. Am. (chair ednl. policies com. 1988-95, sec. 1991-93, vice chair 1993-95, trustee emeritus 1995—), Les Dames d'Escoffier Internat. (sec. N.Y. chpt. 1995-96, pres. 1996-98, internat. pres. 1999—). Avocations: reading, travel, swimming. Home: 18 Robin Hood Rd Pound Ridge NY 10576-2306 Office: Abigail Kirsch at Tappan Hill 81 Highland Ave Tarrytown NY 10591-4206

KIRSCHENBAUM, LISA L., portfolio manager, financial advisor; b. N.Y.C., May 7, 1971; d. J. Michael and Paulenne Lydia (Roeske) K. BA, Brandeis U., 1994. Lic. portfolio mgr. Pres., CEO Financier's Internat. Inc., Mendham, N.J., 1992-95; account exec. T.R. Winston, Inc., Bedminster, N.J., 1994-95; Quantum Portfolio Mgr., Fin. Advisor Prudential Securities, N.Y.C., 1995-97; fin. cons. Chase Investment Svcs. Corp., N.Y.C., 1997-99; v.p., sr. fin. exec. CitiGold Pvt. Banking Group, N.Y.C., 1999—. Mem. Women's Rep. Com. Somerset County, 1994—. Mem. Internat. Platform Assn., N.Y. Health and Racquet Club, Mendham Raquet Club. Republican. Avocations: skiing, chess, deep sea fishing, boating, tennis. Home: 80 Chapin Rd Bernardsville NJ 07924-1102 Office: CitiGold Fin Ctr 666 5th Ave Frnt 5 New York NY 10103-0001

KIRSCHMAN, ELLEN FREEMAN, psychologist; b. N.Y.C., Sept. 25, 1939; d. Lewis and Dorothy (Freeman) K. BA in Dance, Adelphi U., 1961; MSW, U. Calif., Berkeley, 1970; PhD in Psychology, Wright Inst., 1983. Probation officer Alameda County, Oakland, Calif., 1966-68; with dept. psychiatry Kaiser Permanent, Redwood City, Calif., 1970-78. Cons. San Jose Police Comm., 1990-92, Palo Alto (Calif) Police, 1983—, Palo Alto Fire Dept., 1991—, Drug Enforcement Agy., 1997—, others. Author: I Love A Cop: What Police Families Need to Know, 1997, I Love A Firefighter: What the Family Needs To Know, 2004. Mem. APA, Internat. Assn. Chiefs of Police (psychol. svcs. com.). Office Phone: 650-365-5794.

KIRSCHMAN, TAMMY JEAN, literature and language educator; b. South Amboy, NJ, Jan. 11, 1958; d. John F. and Gerry Edith Phillips; m. John J. Kirschman, Jan. 18, 1976; children: Jonathan, Joshua, Jeremiah, Melody. BS in Elem. Edn., U. New Mexico, 1995, MA in Secondary Edn., 1996, ABD in Language Hist., 2005. First grade tchr. Albuquerque Pub. Sch., N.Mex., 1996—; instr. U. New Mexico, 1994—; adj. prof. Lesley U., Boston, 2006; trainee West Edn., Okla., Calif., 2005—. Cons. APS, 2001, writer curriculum, 2004—06. Recipient Language Arts Tchr. of Yr., Internat. Reading Assn., 2006, Woman on the Move, ABQ C. of C., 2004, Tchg. Excellence, Superintendent of APS, 2001. Mem.: ASCD, Internat. Reading Assn., Nat. Coun. Tchrs. English. Home: 1012 Garcia St NE Albuquerque NM 87112

KIRSCHNER, BARBARA STARRELS, gastroenterologist; b. Phila., Mar. 23, 1941; m. Robert H. Kirschner (dec.). MD, Women's Med. Coll. Pa., 1967. Diplomate Am. Bd. Pediatrics; cert. in pediatric gastroenterology and nutrition. Intern U. Chgo., 1967-68, resident, 1968-70; mem. staff U. Chgo. Children's Hosp., 1977-83, asst. prof. pediatrics, 1984-88, prof. pediatrics and medicine, 1988—, mem. com. on nutrition and nutritional biology. Contbr. articles to profl. jours. Pediatric Gastroenterology fellow U. Chgo., 1975-77; recipient Davidson award in Pediatric gastroenterology Acad. Pediatrics, 1993, Joseph Brenneman award Chgo. Pediat. Soc., 2001. Mem. Am. Gastroenterologic Assn., N.Am. Soc. Pediatric Gastroenterology, Soc. Pediatric Rsch., Alpha Omega Alpha. Office: U Chgo Med Ctr 5839 S Maryland Ave # MC 4065 Chicago IL 60637-5417 Office Phone: 773-702-6152.

KIRSCHNER-BROMLEY, VICTORIA ANN, clinical counselor; b. Detroit, May 21, 1960; d. Isadore Ann and Leah (Goodman) Kirschner; m. Howard Russ Bromley, June 24, 1984. BA in Communications, U. Mich., 1983; MEd in Clin. Counseling, The Citadel, Charleston, S.C., 1990. Lic. profl. counselor; credentialed clin. counselor for alcohol and other drugs. Vol. for sexually and emotionally abused children Carolina Youth Devel. Ctr., North Charleston, 1988-89; intern in psychology VA Med. Ctr., Charleston, 1990; clin. counselor Trident Med. Ctr., 1990-92; pvt. practice specializing in couples therapy and eating disorders, 1990-92; case mgr. for chronically mentally ill Berkeley Cmty. Mental Health Ctr., 1992-93; counselor dept. alcohol and other drug abuse svcs. Charles County Clin. Counselor III, 1994-96, interim clin. supr., 1996; fiction writer, 1997—. Mem. Internat. Assn. Eatiing Disorder Profls., Am. Assn. Marriage and Family Therapists, Nat. Assn. Alcohol and Drug Abuse Counselors. Avocations: theater arts, dance, horseback riding, needlepoint, photography.

KIRSCHSTEIN, RUTH LILLIAN, physician; b. Bklyn., Oct. 12, 1926; d. Julius and Elizabeth (Berm) Kirschstein; m. Alan S. Rabson, June 11, 1950; 1 child, Arnold. BA magna cum laude, L.I. U., 1947; MD, Tulane U., 1951, LLD, PhD, Tulane U., 1997; DSc (hon.), Mt. Sinai Sch. Medicine, 1984; LLD, Atlanta U., 1985; DSc (hon.), Med. Coll. Ohio, 1986; LHD (hon.), L.I. U., 1991; PhD (hon.), U. Rochester Sch. Medicine, 1998, Brown U., 1999; DSc (hon.), Spelman Coll., 2001, Georgetown U., 2001. Intern Kings County Hosp., Bklyn., 1951-52; resident pathology VA Hosp., Atlanta, Providence Hosp., Detroit, Clin. Ctr., NIH, Bethesda, Md., 1952-57; fellow Nat. Heart Inst. Tulane U., 1953-54; asst. dir. div. biologics standards NIH, 1971-72; dep. dir. Bur. Biologics, FDA, 1972-73, dep. assoc. commr. sci., 1973-74; acting assoc. dir. woman's health NIH, Bethesda, 1974-93, acting dir., 1993, dep. dir., 1993—99, acting dir., 2000—02, sr. advisor to dir., 2003—. Chmn. grants peer rev. study team NIH; mem. Inst. Medicine NAS, 1982—; co-chair, sec. Spl. Emphasis Oversight com. on Sci. and Tech., 1989—; mem. Office Tech. Assessment Adv. Com. on Basic Rsch., 1989—; co-chair PHS Coordinating Com. on Women's Health Issues, 1990—. Recipient Superior Svc. award, 1980, 1993, Presdl. Disting. Exec. Rank award, 1985, 1995, Pub. Svc. award, Fedn. Am. Soc.s Exptl. Biology, 1993, Nat. Pub. Svc. award, Am. Pub. Adminstrn./Nat. Acad. Pub. Adminstrn., 1994, Roger W. Jones award for exec. leadership, Am. U., 1994, Georgeanna Seegar Jones Women's Health Lifetime Achievement award, 1995, Albert Sabin Hero of Sci. award, 2000, Women Achievement award, Anti-Defamation League, 2001, J. Richard Nesson award, Harvard Med. Sch., 2002, Pub. Svc. award, Am. Soc. for Biochemistry and Molecular Biology, 2003. Mem.: NAS-IOM, AMA (Dr. Nathan Davis award 1990), Am. Acad. Arts and Scis., Am. Acad. Microbiology, Am. Assn. Pathologists, Am. Assn. Immunologists. Office: NIH 1 Center Dr Msc 0148 Rm 158 Bethesda MD 20892-0001 Business E-Mail: rk25n@nih.gov.

KIRST-ASHMAN, KAREN KAY, social work educator; b. Milw., Dec. 29, 1950; d. Gary A. and Ruth G. Kirst; m. Nicolas H. Ashman, June 5, 1982. BA in Social Work, U. Wis., 1972, MS in Social Work, 1973; PhD, U. Ill., 1983. Lic. ind. clin. social worker Wis. Social worker Curative Workshop, Milw., 1973-75; pvt. therapist Juneau Acad. Residential Treatment Ctr., Milw., 1975-76; social work therapist Juneau Acad. Day Svcs., Milw., 1975-76, social svc. dir., 1976-77, asst. dir., 1977-78; teaching asst. U. Ill. Sch. Social Work, Urbana-Champaign, 1978-80; prof. U. Wis., Whitewater, 1980—, coord. sexual harassment awareness program, 1983-85, chairperson women's studies dept., 1985-88, chairperson social work dept., 1988-91. Mem. bd. Coun. on Social Work Edn., 1998—2001. Author: Understanding Human Behavior and the Social Environment, 1987, 7th edit., 2007, Understanding Generalist Practice, 1993, 4th edit., 2006, Generalist Practice with Organizations and Communities, 1997, 3d edit., 2006, The Macro Skills Workbook, 1998, 2d edit., 2000, Human Behavior, Communities, Organizations, and Groups in the Macro Social Environment, 2000, Introduction to Social Work and Social Welfare: Critical Thinking Perspectives, 2003; mem. editl. bd. Affilia: Jour. Women and Social Work, 1990—96;, author. Mem.: NASW, Wis. Coun. Social Work Edn. (exec. bd. mem. 1989—2004), Coun. on Social Work Edn. (bd. dir. 1998—2001), Acad. Cert. Social Workers. Home: 4945 Riverside Rd Waterford WI 53185-3329 Office: U Wis Social Work Dept Whitewater WI 53185

KIRTLEY, JANE ELIZABETH, law educator; b. Indpls., Nov. 7, 1953; d. William Raymond and Faye Marie (Price) Kirtley; m. Stephen Jon Cribari, May 8, 1985. BS in Journalism, Northwestern U., 1975, MS in Journalism, 1976; JD, Vanderbilt U., 1979. Bar: N.Y. 1980, U.S. Dist. Ct. (we. dist.) N.Y. 1980, DC 1982, U.S. Dist. Ct. DC 1982, U.S. Ct. Claims 1982, U.S. Ct. Appeals (4th cir.) 1982, U.S. Ct. Appeals (DC cir.) 1985, U.S. Supreme Ct. 1985, Va. 1995, U.S. Ct. Appeals (10th cir.) 1996, U.S. Ct. Appeals (5th cir.) 1997, U.S. Ct. Appeals (6th and 11th cirs.) 1998. Assoc. Nixon, Hargrave, Devans & Doyle, Rochester, NY, 1979-81, Washington, 1981-84; exec. dir. Reporters Com. for Freedom of Press, Arlington, Va., 1985-99; Silha prof. media ethics & law Sch. Journalism & Mass Comm. U. Minn., Mpls., 1999—, mem. affiliated faculty Law Sch., 2001—; dir. Silha Ctr. Study Media Ethics and Law, Mpls., 2000—. Mem. adj. faculty Am. U. Sch. Comm., 1988—98; mem. affiliated law faculty U. Minn., 2001—; disting. vis. prof. Suffolk U. Law Sch., 2004. Exec. articles editor: Vanderbilt U. Jour. Transnational Law, 1978—79; editor: The News Media and the Law, 1985—, The First Amendment Handbook, 1987, 4th edit., 1995, Agents of Discovery, 1991, 1993, 1995, Pressing Issues, 1998—99; columnist: NEPA Bull., 1988—89, Va.'s Press, 1991—99, Am. Journalism Rev., 1995—, W.Va.'s Press, 1997—99, Tenn. Press, 1997—99, mem. editl. bd.: Comm. Law and Policy. Bd. dirs. Sigma Delta Chi Found., Indpls. Mem.: ABA, Va. State Bar Assn., DC Bar Assn., N.Y. State Bar Assn., Sigma Delta Chi. Home: 3645 46th Ave S Minneapolis MN 55406-2937 Office: 111 Murphy Hall 206 Church St SE Minneapolis MN 55455-0488 Office Phone: 612-625-9038. Business E-Mail: kirtl001@tc.umn.edu.

KIRTON, JENNIFER MYERS, artist; b. Berwick, Pa., Sept. 16, 1949; d. Fred H. and Jean I. Myers; m. Timothy Kirton, Aug. 8, 1970; children: Timothy James, Andrea Jolene, Andrew Joseph. Diploma, Orange Meml. Sch. Nursing, Orlando, Fla., 1970. RN. Galleries in Paris; represented by Mt. Dora, Fla., art-exchang.com, IRRA Registry, NMWA Gallery Artisan Inn, Deland. Tchr. drawing Mt. Dora Ctr. for Arts; overseas prodn. exhibitor, Paris, 1992—; lectr. in field; chair, judge juried art shows. Exhibited in group shows at Nat. Red Cross Scholastic (Nat. award, 1961), Apopka Art & Foliage (1st Place, 1975, 1982, Purchase award, 1978, 3rd Place, 1983, Hon. Mention, 1980, 1986), Winter Park Mall (Best of Show, 1977), Longwood Artist League of Orange County / Cen. Fla. Artists (3rd Place, 1980), Colonial Plz. (Hon. Mention, 1982, 1st Place, 1988, 1989), Springs Plz. (Hon. Mention, 1983), Howell Branch Plz. (1st Place, 1984), Under the Trees (2nd Place, 1984, Special Judges award, 1985), Fashion Sq. (Hon. Mention, 1986), Artist League (Hon. Mention, 1986), Centrust (1st Place, 1988), Lake County Art Show (Hon. Mention, 1992), Working Area Artist, Altamonte Libr., Pine Hills, Fiesta in Pk., Art Addiction Sweeden, Mount Dora Ctr. Arts (hon. mention), Internat. Judeo Christian Upstream Gallery, 2005, Artists Fla., Vol. IV, 1994—95, one-woman shows include Meritor Bank, Seminole CC, 5th St., Overseas European Corp., Mayor's Show Apopka City Hall, Fruitland Park Libr., Winter Park Fine Art Gallery, 2005, Biennial Deland Mus. Art, Serious Studios, Miami, Fla., 2004, exhibited in group shows at Serious Studio, Galveston, 2005, Serious Studios, Berlin, mural, Apopka H.S. Stadium, Represented in permanent collections City of Apopka, Mt. Dora Ctr. Arts, exhibited in group shows at 1st Leesburg Art Assn. Spring Show, 2006, others. Named Artist of Month, artexchange website, 2004, artisrepublik.com, 2005, Mount Dora Mus. Art, 2006, Co-artist of Month, Legacy Fine Art, 2005; named one of Best of Fla. Artists and Artisan, Gallery Direct Am. Art Collector Book One and Two, vol. 4; named to promote Art Exch. site, Art Expo, N.Y.; recipient trophy, Fla. com. Nat. Mus. Art, 2005. Mem.: Internat. Registry Artist and Artwork, Art Exch. (rep.), Leesburg Art Assn., Ctrl. Fla. Artists, Orange County League Artists (past pres.), Nat. League Pen Women, Nat. Mus. Women Arts (mem. Fla. com., historian ecentfl.com, historian). Baptist. Avocation: collecting fine art. Home: 4700 Meadowland Dr Mount Dora FL 32757-9661 Office Phone: 407-353-8332. Personal E-mail: kirtonart@aol.com.

KIRWAN, BETTY-JANE, lawyer; b. Rockeville Center, N.Y., Feb. 4, 1947; d. Franklin Ira and Pearl Elias; m. Ralph D. Kirwan (div.); children: Katherine, Andrew, Kerrigan; m. John Terence Hanna, Sept. 15, 1985. AB, U. Calif., Berkeley, 1968, JD, 1971. Bar: Calif. 1972, U.S. Dist. Ct. (cen. dist.) Calif. Atty. McCutchen, Black, Verleger, Shea, L.A., 1972-85; founding ptnr. McClintock, Kirwan, Benshoof, Rochefort, Weston, L.A., 1985-89; environ. atty., chair dept. environment L.A. office Latham & Watkins, L.A., 1989—, ptnr., 1989—. Pres. Boalt Hall Alumni Assn., Berkeley, 1983-84; vice chair Hathaway Children's Svcs., L.A., 1984-89. Bd. dirs. Hathaway Children's Svcs., 1985-90, PLI Environ. Law Adv. Com., 1992—. Mem. ABA (vice chair air quality com. Natural Resource sect. 1980-88, chair environ. quality com. Natural Resource sect., chair environ. controls com. Bus. Law sect. 1986-90, coun. Bus. Law sect. 1990-94), Boalt Hall Alumni Assn. (pres. 1984). Office: Latham & Watkins 633 W Fifth St Ste 4000 Los Angeles CA 90071 Home: 1300 Chelten Way South Pasadena CA 91030-3912 Office Phone: 213-485-1234. Business E-Mail: bj.kirwane@lw.com.

KIRWAN, KATHARYN GRACE (MRS. GERALD BOURKE KIRWAN JR.), retired small business owner; b. Monroe, Wash., Dec. 1, 1913; d. Walter Samuel and Bertha Ella (Shrum) Camp; m. Gerald Bourke Kirwan Jr., Jan. 13, 1945. Student, U. Puget Sound, 1933-34; BA, BS, Tex. Woman's U., 1937; postgrad., U. Wash., 1941. Libr. Brady (Tex.) Sr. High Sch., 1937-38, McCamey (Tex.) Sr. High Sch., 1938-43; mgr. Milady's Frock Shop, Monroe, 1946-62, owner, mgr., 1962-93. Mem. Monroe Breast Cancer Screening Project cmty. planning group Fred Hutchinson Cancer Rsch. Ctrs., 1991-93; meml. chmn. Monroe chpt. Am. Cancer Soc., 1961-93; co-chair hon. com. YMCA Pool program, 2005-; mem. Snohomish County Police Svcs. Action Coun., 1971; mem. Monroe Pub. Libr. Bd., 1950-65, pres. bd., 1964-65; mem. Monroe City Coun., 1969-73; mayor City of Monroe, 1974-81; commr. Snohomish County Hosp. dist. 1, 1970-90, chmn. bd. commrs., 1980-90; mem. East Snohomish County Health Planning Com., 1979-81; mem. Snohomish County Law and Justice Planning Com., 1974-78, Snohomish County Econ. Devel. Coun., 1975-81, Snohomish County Pub. Utility Dist. Citizens Adv. Task Force, 1983; sr. warden Ch. of Our Saviour, Monroe, 1976-77, 89, sr. warden, 1976-77, 89-90; co-chair hon. com. pool program YMCA, 2005. With USNR, 1943-46. Recipient Malstrom award for Hist. Homes and Bldgs. of Monroe, 2000, award of project excellence Washington Mus. Assn., 2000, Pres.'s Call to Svc. award, 2006, Pres.'s Coun. on Svc. and Civic Participation award, 2006, U.S. Pres.'s Vol. Svc. award, 2006. Mem. AAUW, U.S. Naval Inst., Ret. Officers Assn., Naval Res. Assn., Bus. and Profl. Women's Club (2d v.p. 1980-82, pres. 1983-84), Washington Gens., Snohomish County Pharm. Aux., C. of C. (pres. 1972), Valley Gen. Hosp. Guild (pres. 1994, 95, 96), Valley Gen. Hosp. Found. (sec. 1993-97). Episcopalian. Home: 538 S Blakeley St Monroe WA 98272-2402

KIRWIN, BARBARA ROSA, forensic specialist; d. Ernest Joseph and Isolene Smith Rosa; m. Thomas Joseph Kirwin, Sept. 26, 1971; 1 child, Damon Thomas-Joseph. BA in Psychology, CUNY Queens Coll., 1970, MA in Psychology, 1972; PhD in Clin. Psychology, New Sch. U., 1980; postdoctoral cert., LI U., 1984. Cert. psychologist NY, 1981. Narcotics parole officer NY State Office Drug Abuse Svcs., Long Island City, 1974—76; drug abuse specialist Nat. Drug Rsch. Inst., NYC, 1976—78; psychology intern OMH Ctrl. Islip PC, Brentwood, NY, 1978—79; rsch. neuropsychologist NIMH, Creedmoor PC, Queens Village, NY, 1979—80; chief svc., svc. unit Creedmoor PC, Queens Village, 1980—82; asst. dir. adminstrn. NY State Office Mental Health Creedmoor PC, Queens Village, 1982—84, assoc. psychologist, 1984—87; dir. Harborview Psychol. Svcs., Huntington, NY, 1984—. Forensic cons. Def. Attys., 1980—; expert witness State and Fed. Cts., NYC, 1980—; forensic cons. Met. Area Dist. Attys., NY, 1981—; forensic cons., state atty. gen. Office of State Atty. Gen., Fla., 2001—. Author: The Mad, The Bad and The Innocent: The Criminal Mind on Trial; prodr.: (broadband prodn.) Madness, (documentary) The Chameleon Killer, The Queen of Cons. Bd. dirs. Ind. Living Assn., Bklyn., 1989. Fellow, Am. Coll. Forensic Examiners Internat., 2003. Mem.: APA, Nat. Register Svc. Providers in Psychology, Am. Coll. Forensic Psychology. Office: Harborview Psychol Svcs 200 W Carver St Ste 5 Huntington NY 11743 Office Phone: 631-367-4200. Personal E-mail: harborviewpsych@optonline.net, barbara.kirwin@gmail.com.

KIRY-RYAN, RITA IRENE, computer scientist, educator; b. St. Louis, July 12, 1960; d. Joseph and Annie Marie (Lorenz) Kiry; m. Thomas Ryan, May 26, 1989; children: Tommy Ryan, Jenny Ryan. BS in Mktg., St. Louis U., 1982, MBA in Internat. Bus., 1988. Maj. account rep. Konica Bus. Machines, St. Louis, 1988—90; store mgr. U.S. Shoe Corp., 1990—93, Charming Shoppes Inc., St. Louis, 1993—94; instr. Sterling Coll., St. Louis, 1996—97, Sanford Brown Coll., St. Louis, 1994—99, ITT Tech. Inst., St. Louis, 1996—2004, faculty advisor, 2001—, chair Sch. Bus., 2004—. Vol. Long Elem. Sch., Crestwood, Mo.; mem. Celiac Sprue Assn., St. Louis, 2003. Mem.: Am. Assn. Profs., St. Louis U. Alumni Assn. Roman Catholic. Avocation: travel. Office: ITT Tech Inst 13505 Lakefront Dr Earth City MO 63045 Office Phone: 314-298-7800 ext. 152. Business E-Mail: rkiry@itt-tech.edu.

KISCH, GLORIA, sculptor; b. N.Y.C., Nov. 14, 1941; d. Max Stern and Hilda Lowenthal; div.; children: Theo, Rhona. BA, Sarah Lawrence Coll., 1963; BFA, MFA, Otis Art Inst., 1969. One woman shows include Newport Harbor Mus., Newport Beach, Calif., 1974, Calif. State U., L.A., 1977, Inst. Contemporary Art, L.A., 1978, U. Calif., Irvine, 1979, Security Pacific Pla., L.A., 1980, Inst. Art & Urban Resources, P.S. 1, L.I., 1980, Milw. Art Mus., 1981, Queens Mus., Flushing, N.Y., 1983, Robert Moses Pla. at Lincoln Ctr. Fordham U., N.Y.C., 1987, Bergen Mus. Art, Paramus, N.J., 1997. Studio: 620 Broadway New York NY 10012-2616

KISER, CHÉRIE R., lawyer; b. 1958; BA, Univ. Minn., 1983; JD specialization in Comm., Catholic Univ. Am., 1987. Bar: Pa. 1987, D.C. 1988. Law clk. to Commr. Dennis R. Patrick FCC, Washington; sr. regulatory atty. Sprint Comm. Co.; ptnr. Mintz Levin Cohn Ferris Glovsky & Popeo PC, Washington, mng. ptnr. D.C. office. Chair comm. sect. Mintz Levin Cohn Ferris Glovsky & Popeo PC, chair diversity com., mem. policy com.; spkr. at numerous confs. in field. Contbr. articles to profl. jour. Mem.: Fed. Comm. Bar Assn. Office: Mintz Levin Cohn Ferris Glovsky & Popeo 701 Pennsylvania Av NW Washington DC 20004 Office Phone: 202-434-7325. Office Fax: 202-434-7400. Business E-Mail: crkiser@mintz.com.

KISER, HAZEL THERESA, educational association administrator, lawyer; b. Piedmont, Ala., Apr. 1, 1942; d. John Melvin and Nanette Ophelia Davis Rankin; m. Waylan Calvin Kiser; children: Jeffery Andrew, Valerie Theresa Kiser Chitom. BA, BS, M, Jacksonville State U., Ala.; PhD, U. Ala., Tuscaloosa, 1974; JD, Birmingham Sch. Law, 1998. Bar: Ala. 1998. Tchr. Piedmont City Sch., 1964—74, asst. supt., 1974—85, supt., 1985—96; pvt. practice Kiser Law Firm, Anniston, Ala., 1998—2001; dir. prof. devel. Coun. for Leaders Ala. Sch., Montgomery, 2001—. Found. mem. Jacksonville State U., 1987—. Apptd. mem. Ft. McClellan Reuse/Reauthorization Com.; bd. dirs. Girl Scouts Am., Anniston, 1987—92. Named Citizen of Yr., Piedmont C. of C., 1981. Mem.: DAR (regent, former treas.), Piedmont Hist. Soc. (pres. 1978), Contemporary Study Club (pres. 1976), Lions (former officer), Delta Kappa Gamma (pres. 1974, former v.p.). Methodist. Avocations: reading, antiques, exercise. Home: 101 Shamrock Ln Piedmont AL 36272 Address: Ala Coun Sch Adminstrn PO Box 428 Montgomery AL 36101 Office Phone: 256-447-2985. Office Fax: 256-447-2985. Business E-Mail: theresa@clasleaders.org.

KISER, MOLLY, musician; b. Dec. 15, 1971; d. Loren Hall and Yoko Tajima Kiser. Student, Tokyo Nat. U. of Fine Arts and Music, 1990; BM, Curtis Inst. Music, 1994; MM, New Eng. Conservatory, 1996; D of Mus. Arts, Juilliard Sch., 2003. Performer: Beethoven's 5th concerto "Emperor" with Rosenkranz Orch., Tchaikovsky's 1st Piano Concerto with NHK secondary Orch., Aspen Music Festival Student Orch., 1992, Salem Philharm. Orch., 1995, New Eng. Conservatory Symphony Orch., 1994, 1996, Ft. Collins Symphony Orch., 1996, Corpus Christi Symphony Orch., 1997, World Festival Orch., 1999, Westchester Symphony Orch., 2001, Tokyo City Orch., 2002. Recipient piano hons. audition, New Eng. Conservatory, 1991, winner concerto competition, Aspen Music Sch., 1992, New Eng. Conservatory, 1994, 1996, 1st prize, 41st Ft. Collins Symphony Orch. Young Artist Competition, 1996, 15th Kingsville Internat. Young Performers competition, 1996, Bronze medal, 6th San Antonio Internat. Piano competition, 1997, Silver medal, 47th Nina Widemann Piano competition, 1997, gold medal, World Piano competition, 1999, numerous others; fellow Tanglewood Music Festival fellow, 1993. Avocations: dancing, reading. Home: Apt 3F 33 Hamilton Ter New York NY 10031 Office: The Juilliard Sch 60 Lincoln Center Plz New York NY 10023

KISER, RUTH MARGUERITE, music educator; MusB, So. Ill. U., 1981; MS in Music Edn., U. Ill., 1984. Lic. K-12 music edn. Ill., 1980, elem. edn. Ill., 1982, lic. K-12 music edn. N.C., 1998, elem edn. N.C., 1998. Tchr. Hamilton County Schs., McLeansboro, Ill., 1981—83, Urbana Jr. H.S., Ill., 1984—85, Hickory City Sch., 1998—99, Catawba County Sch., Newton, NC, 1999—2001, Alexander County Sch., Taylorsville, NC, 2001—05, Catawba County Schs., 2006—; adj. prof. Lenoir-Rhyne Coll., Hickory, NC, 1994—2005; tchg. asst. Catawba County Sch., Hickory, 2005—06. Accompanist Mt. View Elem. Sch., Hickory, 1996—2000; vol. Foard H.S. Music Boosters, Newton, NC, 2002—06; accompanist Mt. Grove Bapt. Ch., Hickory, 2000—06.

KISER-MILLER, KATHY JOY, humanities educator; b. Dayton, Ohio, Feb. 18, 1956; d. Fred Cecil and Joyce Arlene Kiser; m. Daniel Patrick Miller, Aug. 22, 1981; children: Alexander Ross Miller, Davis Noel Miller. BA, Otterbein Coll., 1978; MFA, U. Wis., 1981. Cert. secondary theatre. Sales-kitchen design Matercraft Industries, Boulder, Colo., 1981—83; sales Ford Mktg. Inst., Denver, 1983—84; prof. humanities Colo. Mountain Coll., Steamboat Springs, 1985—. Forensic dir. Colo. Mountain Coll., Steamboat Springs, 1989—95, theatre dir., 1995—, comm. and humanities discipline coord., Glenwood Springs, 1999—; humanities state chair Colo. State Faculty, 1999—2003; adjudicator Theatre Masters, Aspen, Colo., 2003—;

judge scholarships Perry Mansfield Performing Arts Camp, Steamboat Springs; mem. adj. faculty Front Range C.C., Westminster, Colo., 1989—95, Regis U., Denver, 1990—94; artist in residence Boulder Valley Schs., 1987—88. Actor: Actors Theatre of Louisville, Midwest Playwright Lab., Germinal Stage, Nat. Pub. Radio-Shakespeare Series, The Changing Scene; mem. editl. adv. bd.: Collegiate Press, 1998—2001. Mem. performing arts guild Steamboat Springs Arts Coun., 1999—2000. Recipient Voice of Democracy Citation, VFW Womens Aux., 1990. Mem.: NEA, C.C. Humanities Assn., Colo. Edn. Assn., Nat. Women in the Arts, U.S. Ski Assn. (sec. 2002—), Theatre Comm. Guild, Kiwanis (pres. 2000—01, sec. 1998—99), Steamboat Springs Winter Sports Club (chair winter carnival sales 1999). Office: Colorado Mountain College 1330 Bob Adams Dr Steamboat Springs CO 80487

KISIEL, IDA MARIE, education educator, writer; d. Salvatore and Mary Rose Collura; m. Theodore Kisiel, Dec. 26, 1963; children: Caroline Marya, Cassandra Louisa. EdB, Duquesne U., 1949; MA, Pa. State U., 1951; PhD, U. Pitts., 1962—62. Myers-Briggs Type Indicator Ill., 1998. Drama coach/script writer Pitts. Radio Sch., 1952—54; asst. prof. Duquesne U., Pitts., 1953—62, dir. writers' workshop, 1955—60; program dir., children's lit. series WDUQ, Duquesne U., Pitts., 1955—58; program host, modern novel series Duquesne U., Pitts., 1958—61; biography reviewer Pitts. Press, 1959—60; assoc. prof. Canisius Coll., Buffalo, 1965—69; adj. prof. Mundelein Coll., Chgo., 1972—74; prof. humanities Roosevelt U., Chgo., 1974—2000, dir. discovery workshop for women, 1975—80; exec. dir. Carrus Ednl. Resources, Winfield, Ill., 1979—; freelance writer Winfield, Ill., 1980—; radio talk show host WFMT, Chgo., 1980; guest columnist for careers Chgo. Tribune, 1981; dir., job retraining programs for tchrs. DuPage Bd. Edn., Wheaton, Ill., 1982; radio program host, women in nontraditional roles WFMT, Chgo., 1988; consulting ptnr. Redirections, Inc., Chgo., 1988—91; academic dir., ptnrs. in corp. Roosevelt U., Chgo., 1990—95, prof. emeritus, 1992—2005, dir. tng. and devel. Chgo., 1995—2000, dir. in tng., 1995—2000. Writing cons. AC Davenport Co., Palatine, Ill., 1975; cons./expert vocat. witness various law firms, Chgo., 1979—; exec. dir. Carrus Ednl. Resources, Winfield, Ill., 1979—; dir. comprehensive employment tng. act job skills program U.S. Fed. Govt., Chgo., 1979—80; lectr. Women in Mgmt., North Shore Conf., Chgo., 1980—85; lectr., women's roles Women in Radio & TV, Chgo., 1982; lectr. on setting goals, linkages Coll. DuPage, Glen Ellyn, Ill., 1989; employment dir., paralegal program Roosevelt U., Chgo., 1992—98. Author: (columnist/articles) Chgo.Tribune, (memoir) Thank You, Miss Mackelroy; contbr. book/memoir; author: (book) Design for Change, Presentation Skills for Trainers; editor: Pittsburgh Festival: Special Bicentennial Issue; author: New Directions: Contemporary Issues in Career and Lifestyle Management, How to Get a Job as a Paralegal (3rd Edition), Career Strategies for Secretaries; contbr. book; author: (poems) Portraits & Promises, (nonfiction) Season of Grace; careers editor, columnist: Chgo. Tribune; author: numerous articles in newspapers, modules. Civic dir., cmty. resources program No. Ill. U. Lab Sch., DeKalb, 1972—73; mem. Citizens for a Better Environment, Winfield, 1980—89, Winfield United, 2004—05, Regional Commn. on Higher Edn. in Western Pa., 1985, 1962; judge Sec. of Yr. Profl. Secretaries Internat., Chgo., 1981—82; dir., job skills retraining program North Shore Edn. Ctr., Evanston, 1974—75; mem. Friends of Winfield Libr., Winfield, Ill., 2004—05. Recipient Woman of Yr., Sigma Lambda Phi, 1955, Recognition award, GSA, 1985, Spl. Recognition award, Diversity Coun. of Lucent Tech., 1989, Recognition award, Women in Mgmt., 1990; fellow Project for the Study of Adult Learning, State of Ill., 1995; grantee, Am. Philos. Soc., 1962. Mem.: AAUW, Nat. Career Devel. Assn., Assn. Psychol. Type (licentiate), Wellsley Ctrs. for Women (assoc.), Am. Bd. Vocat. Experts (assoc.), Nat. Assn. Women in the Arts. Avocations: reading, travel, writing, counseling young adults. Personal E-mail: mkisiel1@comcast.net.

KISLAK, JEAN HART, art director; b. 1931; d. Frank Ernest and Isabelle Tayor (Ellis) Hart; m. William I. Herendeen, Aug. 23, 1952 (div. Feb. 1956); m. Louis G. Johnson, Jan. 31, 1959 (div. Feb. 1975); 1 child, Jennifer Taylor Johnson; m. Jay Kislak, Apr. 7, 1985. Student, Peace Jr. Coll., Raleigh, N.C., Queens Coll., Charlotte, N.C. With Storer Broadcasting Co., Miami, Fla., S.E. Banks, N.A., Miami, 1974-84, art dir., 1974-84; mem. Gov. Fla. Panel Visual Arts, 1979-81; art cons., 1974—. Internat. rep. Christies, Inc., 1998—2001; mem. art and archtecture com. Libr. of Congress, Washington, 2003. Bd. dirs. Viscaya Mus., Miami, 1963, Beaux Arts, U. Miami, 1968, Theatre Art Patrons, Miami, 1968, Theatre Art Patrons, Miami, 1965, Nat. Wildflower Assn., 1991, NEH, Fla., 1992, Miami (Fla.) Humane Soc., 2006, Artisworth Mus., Rockland, Maine, 2006; trustee Dade County Zool. Soc., 1988—, Miami Art Mus., Barry Coll. Charter Sch.; mem. Bacardi Imports Art Bd., 1983-89, 98—, Fla. State Bd. Art Coun., 1987, Miami Art Mus. (formerly Dade County Ctr. for the Arts Bd.), 1989-99; mem. exec. bd. Zool. Soc. Fla., 1994; mem. Fla. Humanities Bd., 1994; mem. visual arts com. Libr. Congress, 2002. Recipient Gov. Fla. award art, 1976, 79, Miami Dade Pub. Libr. award, 1978, Bus. Com. for Arts award, 1975-79, WPBT Pub. TV award, 1976, 77, 80, Lowe Gallery, U. Miami cert. recognition, 1980, Dade County Art in Pub. Places cert. recognition, 1981, 82. Mem. 1805 Club (London) (hon. v.p. 1993—), Kislak Found. (bd. dirs. 1997—). Address: 720 NE 69th St Miami FL 33138-5738

KISLING, FANNY, counselor, educator; b. Preble County, Ohio, Jan. 14, 1931; d. William Benjamin and Anna Viola (Wing) Banis; m. Donald Robert Kisling, May 14, 1950 (dec. 1991); children: Emily Margaret, Rebecca Jane, Karen Lea, Suzanne Michele, Orval William, David Guy. BS with honors, Miami U., Oxford, Ohio, 1973, MEd, 1974, PhD, 1986. Lic. profl. counselor; cert. tchr. Commuter advisor Miami U., 1975-76, program cons., 1976-78; prof., counselor Sinclair C.C., 1978-96, retired, 1996. Lectr. Kent (Ohio) State U., 1990; presenter in field. One-woman shows include Preble County Art Ctr., Eaton, Ohio, 2006. Mayor Eaton, Ohio, 1995-97; mem. Eaton City Coun., 1993-97, Eaton Bicentennial Com.; bd. dirs. SCOPE Cmty. Action Agy., Ohio, 1993, Preble County Coun. on Aging, Preble County Art Assn., Preble County Retired Tchrs. Assn.; elder First Presbyn. Ch., Eaton, 1993. Mem. AAUW, Am. Counseling Assn., Am. Coll. Pers. Assn., Ohio Coll. Pers. Assn., Phi Kappa Phi, Kappa Delta Pi, Phi Delta Kappa. Republican. Avocations: writing, bird watching, gardening, painting, hiking. Home: 305 East Ave Eaton OH 45320-2005 Personal E-mail: fkisling@woh.rr.com.

KISS, BOGLARKA, musician, educator; b. Pecs, Hungary, Apr. 19, 1974; d. Tibor Kiss and Boglarka Torma. BA in Econs., Whittier Coll., Calif., 1996; MFA in Flute performance, U. of Calif., Irvine, 2000; postgrad., Boton U. Bus. analyst McKinsey & Co., LA, 1996—98; instr. Cerritos Coll., Norwalk, Calif., 2000—. Musician: (cds of flute works) Air, 2002, (flute concerto) US, 2006. Recipient Yamaha prize, Julius Baker Internat. Flute Seminar, 2000; scholar Academic Scholarship, Whittier Coll., 1992—96, Grad. Scholarship, U. of Calif., Irvine, 1998—2000. Mem.: Mu Phi Epsilon. Office: Cerritos Coll 11110 Alondra Blvd Norwalk CA 90650 Personal E-mail: boglarka@fuvola.com.

KISS, ELIZABETH, academic administrator, philosophy educator; d. Sandor and Eva Ilona Kiss; m. Jeffrey Holzgrefe, Mar. 18, 1989. BA magna cum laude, Davidson Coll., NC, 1983; B of Philosophy, Oxford U., UK, 1985, D. Philosophy, 1990. Instr. in politics Princeton U., 1988—89, asst. prof., 1990—96; vis. prof. of humanities Deep Springs Coll., Deep Springs, Calif., 1990—91; fellow, ethics prog. Harvard U., Cambridge, Mass., 1992—93; fellow Nat. Humanities Ctr., NC, 1995—96; vis. prof. Deep Springs Coll., Deep Springs, Calif., 1999; assoc. prof. Duke U., Durham, NC, 1997—, Nannerl O. Keohane dir. Kenan Inst. for Ethics, 1997—2006; pres. Agnes Scott Coll., Decatur, Ga., 2006—. Bd. of directors Ctr. for Documentary Studies, Durham, NC, 1997—2003; dean's adv. com. on svc. learning Duke U., Durham, NC, 1997—; co-chair Academic Integrity Assessment Com., Durham, NC, 1999—. Author: (article) Moral Ambition within and beyond Political Constraints: Reflections on Restorative Justice, Democracy and the Politics of Recognition, In Praise of Eccentricity: Character, Moral Education, and Democracy, Alchemy or Fools Gold: Assessing Feminist Doubts and Rights. Represented Hungarian Human Rights Found. Conf. on Non-Governmental Organizations and Human Rights, UN, Geneva, 1987—87; Martin Luther King day planning com. Duke U., Durham, NC, 2000—01; interpreter at Hungarian elections Alliance of Free Democrats, Budapest, Hungary, 1990—90. Recipient Bowen Presdl. Preceptorship, Princeton U., 1994-1997; grantee Postdoctoral grant, Am. Coun. of Learned Societies, 2000-2001; scholar Rhodes Scholarship, Oxford U., 1983-1986. Mem.: N. Am. Soc. for Social Philosophy, NAS (treas.), Ctr. for Academic Integrity (bd. of directors 1997—2003), Davidson Coll. (bd. of trustees 1997—2003), NC Rhodes Scholarships (sec., selection com. 1998—2003). Office: Agnes Scott Coll 141 E College Ave Decatur GA 30030 Office Phone: 404-471-6280. Office Fax: 404-471-6067. E-mail: president@agnesscott.edu.*

KISSANE, SHARON FLORENCE, writer, consultant, educator; b. Chgo., July 2, 1940; d. Bruno William and Agnes Evelyn (Payne) Mrotek; m. James Quin Kissane, July 2, 1966 (dec. June 1989); children: Laura Janine Ehrke, Elaine Marie Kissane. BA, De Paul U., Chgo., 1962; MA, Northwestern U., Evanston, Ill., 1963; PhD, Loyola U., Chgo., 1970. Cert. tchr., Ill. Tchr. Notre Dame H.S., Chgo., 1959-61, Our Lady of Solace Sch., Chgo., 1961-62; tech. writer, editor Commerce Clearing House, Chgo., 1962-63; tchr. U. Ill., Chgo., 1963-66; mgr. Amalgamated Ins. Co., Chgo., 1966-68; writer Herald Newspapers, Des Plaines, Ill., 1968-69; assoc. dir. Montague Coll. Psycho-Ednl. Clinic, Chgo., 1970-72; dir. Learning Ctr., libr. Stevenson Elem. Sch., Des Plaines, 1972-73; dir. Park Ridge Reading Ctr., Ill., 1973-78; pres. Kissane Comms. Ltd., Barrington, Ill., 1979—. Learning disabilities specialist Montessori Sch., Lake Forest, Ill.; gifted coord. Winfield Pub. Schs.; spkr. in field. Author: What is Child Abuse?, 1993, 2001, Gang Awareness, 1995, 2001; co-author: Polish Biographical Dictionary, 1992, Career Success for People With Physical Disabilities, 1996, Autobiography of Mousie Garner, Vaudeville Stooge; contbr. articles to profl. jours. and encyclopedia of advt. Bd. dirs. Barrington (Ill.) Children's Choir, 1984-85, LA FEP Student Exch. Program, Barrington, 1983-84, Barrington Area United Way, Operation Smile Internat., Chgo.; mem. task force Dist. # 220, Barrington, 1983-86; founding mem. Barrington Area Arts Coun., 1980, Park Ridge Hist. Soc., 1972; mem. curriculum com. Barrington H.S., 1981-84; elections judge South Barrington Precinct, 1989—; mem. bus. adv. coun. Nat. Rep. Congl. com.; pres. small bus. advisory council. Recipient Dale Carnegie Speech scholarship Jr. Achievement, 1958, Ronald Regan Gold Medal Winner, Pres. Small Bus. Adv. Council, 2004, La Cittá del Sole, Italy, Disting. Bus. Leader award, 2001, Ill. Businessman of Yr. award, 2003, Poetry.com award; named Hon. Citizen of Korea, 1965, Women of the Yr. Am. Biog. Assn., 2004; honored as local author, Ill. Assn. Conv., 1999; Literacy grantee, 2000. Mem. Nat. Assn. Women Bus. Owners (bd. dirs. 1982-83), Ralph Metcalfe Found. (bd. dirs.), Internat. Platform Assn., MIT Forum, Ill. Libr. Assn. (Conn. chpt.), Barrington Profl. Women, Midwest Soc. Profl. Cons., Northwestern U. Entertainment Alliance, Authors Guild, Writers Guild Am., Loyola U. Grad. Alumni Soc. (bd. mem. exec. bd.), South Barrington Hist. Soc. (chmn.), Phi Delta Kappa, Kappa Gamma Pi. Republican. Avocations: painting, post-card art, music, sports. Office: Kissane Comms Ltd 15 Turning Shore Dr South Barrington IL 60010-9597 Office Phone: 847-381-7192. Personal E-mail: kissanecom@sbcglobal.net.

KISSIRE, LISA MARIE, learning specialist; b. Jacksonville, Fla., Mar. 9, 1971; d. Naaman Dean Freeman and Karen Josie Ann Duncan, Dewey Joe Duncan (Stepfather) and Monique Freeman (Stepmother); m. Ronnie Lynn Kissire, Aug. 13, 1988; children: Severian Charles, Karissa Marie, Serech Blaine. AS in Gen. Edn., Garland County C.C., Hot Springs, Ark., 1995; BS in Edn. cum laude, Henderson State U., Arkadelphia, Ark., 1997, MS in Edn., 2004, postgrad., 2005—. Tchr. math. Lake Hamilton Jr. H.S., Pearcy, Ark., 1997—, dept. chair math., 2001—03. Mem.: Ark. Rural Tchrs. Assn. (assoc.), Nat. Coun. Tchrs. Math. (assoc.). Democrat. Roman Catholic. Avocation: dance. Office: Bryant Sch Dist 200 NW 4th St Bldg # 600 Bryant AR 72022 Office Phone: 501-653-5064. Office Fax: 501-847-7217. Business E-Mail: LKissire@bryantschools.org.

KISSLER, CYNTHIA ELOISE, geologist, consultant; b. Knoxville, Tenn., July 6, 1949; d. James Albert Jurney and Josephine Cassandra Ramsey-Jurney; m. Albert Donald Kissler, Apr. 16, 1994; children: Eric, T. Duff. AAS, Wenatchee Valley Coll., 1994; BS in Geology, Ctrl. Wash. U., 1996, postgrad. Geol. cons., E. Wenatchee, 1998. Mem. Am. Goephys. Union, Geol. Soc. Am., Wenatchee Applarians. Avocations: skiing, woodworking. Home and Office: 690 Degage St East Wenatchee WA 98802-4961 E-mail: kisslerc@nwi.net.

KISSLING, PHLEANE M., science educator; d. Carl R. Kauffman; m. Steve D. Kissling, Dec. 31, 1994; 1 child, Alexi N. BS in Biology, Ursinus Coll., Collegeville, Pa., 1989; MEd, Allentown Coll. St. Francis DeSales, Center Valley, Pa., 1998. Tchr. sci. Conrad Weiser Area Sch. Dist., Robesonia, Pa., 1990—. Deacon St. Paul's UCC, Robesonia, Pa., 2002—04. Mem.: Conrad Weiser Edn. Assn. (rep. 2002—04), Pa. Sci. Tchrs. Assn. United Church Of Christ. Achievements include development of science curriculum for middle school. Avocations: travel, gardening, cooking, boating, fishing. Home: 15 Walden West Bernville PA 19506 Office: Conrad Weiser Area School District 44 Big Spring Road Robesonia PA 19551 Office Phone: 610-693-8514. Personal E-mail: pkissling@hotmail.com. E-mail: p_kissling@conradweiser.org.

KISTHARDT, ESTELLE A., career planning administrator, educator; d. Eugene A. and Estelle M. Scopelliti; m. David B. Kisthardt, Apr. 7, 1990; 1 child, Cord B. BSBA, Bloomsburg U., Pa., 1985. Cert. tchr. Pa., 1985. Tchr. Shamokin Area Sch. Dist., Pa., 1985—88; tchr., career counselor Milton Hershey Sch., 1989—. Mem.: Assn. Curriculum Devel. (assoc.). Home: 830 Spartan Lane CH Hershey PA 17033 Office: Milton Hershey School 830 Spartan Lane Catherine Hall Hershey PA 17033 Office Phone: 717-520-2623. Home Fax: 717-520-2644; Office Fax: 717-520-2644. Personal E-mail: kisthardte@mhs-pa.org.

KISTIAKOWSKY, VERA, physical researcher, educator; b. Princeton, NJ, Sept. 9, 1928; d. George Bogdan and Hildegard (Moebius) K.; m. Gerhard Emil Fischer, June 16, 1951 (div. 1970); children: Marc Laurenz Fischer, Karen Marie Fischer. AB, Mt. Holyoke Coll., 1948, ScD (hon.), 1978; PhD, U. Calif., Berkeley, 1952. Staff scientist U.S. Naval Rsch. Def. Lab., San Francisco, 1952-53; fellow U. Calif., Berkeley, 1953-54; rsch. assoc. Columbia U., N.Y.C., 1954-57, instr., 1957-59; asst. prof. Brandeis U., Waltham, Mass., 1959-62, adj. assoc. prof., 1962-63; staff mem. MIT, Cambridge, 1963-69, sr. rsch. scientist, 1969-72, prof. physics, 1972-94, prof. emerita, 1994—. Author: Atomic Energy, 1959, One Way Is Down, 1967; contbr. articles to profl. jours Dir. Coun. for a Liveable World, 1983—2005, dir. Edn. Fund, 1983—2001, pres., 1997—2000. Recipient Centennial award, Mt. Holyoke Coll., 1972. Fellow AAAS, Am. Phys. Soc. (councilor 1974-77); mem. Assn. for Women in Sci. (pres. 1982-83), Phi Beta Kappa (vis. scholar 1983-84, senator 1988-96), Sigma Xi (lectr. 1990-92). Achievements include research in nuc. and elem. particle physics and astrophysics. E-mail: verak@mit.edu.

KISTLER, JOYCE DIANNA, secondary school educator; d. Joseph Arthur and Vada Margarett Jenkins; m. Anthony Max Kistler, June 2, 1984; children: Angela Marie, Jake Asher, Jordan Anthony. BA in English Edn., East Ctrl. U., 1977, M Secondary Edn., 1981. Tchr. Henryetta (Okla.) HS, 1977—84, Ponca City (Okla.) HS, 1984—96, Deer Creek - Lamont (Okla.) Sch., 1996—. Assessor Nat. Bd. Profl. Tchg. Stds., San Antonio, 2003—. Asst. cub master Boy Scouts Am., Lamont, 1999—2001. Mem.: NEA, Classroom Teachers Assn. (v.p. 2006), Okla. Edn. Assn. Democrat. Mem. Christ Ch. Avocations: reading, gardening, exercise, travel.

KISTLER, LORETTA M., social worker, consultant; b. Lehighton, Pa., Oct. 1, 1960; d. Wayne R. Behler and Carolyn A. Walck, adopted d. James E. Ahner and Maryellen L. Behler; m. John Kistler, Nov. 13, 1982 (div. Dec. 16, 1989). BA, Cedar Crest Coll., 1982; MSW, Marywood U., 1984. Lic. social worker Pa., LCSW N.J. Psychiat. social worker Wiley Ho., Bethlehem, Pa., 1984—88; adolescent addictions evaluator Good Samaritan Hosp., Pottsville, Pa., 1988—89; clin. coord. Renewal Centers, Quakertown, Pa., 1989—91, Vitae Ho., Glenmore, Pa., 1991—95; program coord., therapist Cath. Charities-Diocese of Metuchen, Perth Amboy, NJ, 1995—2002; chief social worker Easton (Pa.) Hosp., 2002—. Faculty liasion Marywood U., Scranton, Pa., 1995—2002; program developer Regional Devel. Corp., Pottsville, 1993; addictions group educator Bethesda Treatment Programs, Lehighton, Pa., 1984—89. Sec., past dir. LV K-9 Therapy Assn., Nazareth, Pa., 1997—2003. Mem.: NASW. Lutheran. Avocations: river rafting, camping, therapy dog community education and visiting, cooking. Office: Easton Hosp 250 21st St Easton PA 18042 Personal E-mail: rett60@yahoo.com.

KIST-TAHMASIAN, CANDACE LYNEE, psychologist; b. New Hampton, Iowa, Mar. 9, 1965; d. Kenneth Duane and Elinor Davis Kist; m. Norek Tahmasian, Dec. 18, 1987; children: Michael Tahmasian, Precious Grace Tahmasian. BA, U. No. Iowa, 1988, MEd, 1998, EdS, 2000. Tchr. Garden City (Kans.) Unified Sch. Dist. 457, 1989—94, Maricopa (Ariz.) Unified Sch. Dist., 1994—95, Pasadena (Calif.) Unified Sch. Dist., 1995—96; sch. psychologist Kestone AEA #1, Elkader, Iowa, 1999—2005, Desoto (Kans.) Unified Sch. Dist. 232, 2005—. Mem., bd. dirs. Gt. Plays Day Care, New Hampton, 1997—99; mem., vol. Toys for Tots, New Hampton, 2003—05; rec. sec. 1st Bapt. Ch., New Hampton, 2000—05. Mem.: NASP, Assn. Ednl. Therapists, Internat. Dyslexia Assn. Avocations: travel, reading.

KISVARSANYI, EVA BOGNAR, retired geologist; b. Budapest, Hungary, Dec. 18, 1935; arrived in U.S., 1957; d. Kalman and Ilona (Simon) Bognar; m. Geza Kisvarsanyi, July 3, 1956; 1 child, Erika G. Student, Eotvos Lorand U., Budapest, 1954-56; BS in Geology, U. Mo., Rolla, 1958, MS, 1960. Geologist Mo. Geol. Survey, Rolla, 1959-68; from rsch. geologist to sect. chief Mo. Dept. Natural Resources/Geol. Survey Program, Rolla, 1968-90; asst. dir. MODNR/Geol. Survey Program, Rolla, 1990-93; cons. Sarasota, Fla., 1993—; exec. dir. Hungarian-Am. Cultural Assn., Inc., 1995—; tchr. Sarasota County Pub. Sch. Sys., Sarasota, 1994-98; dir. comm. NEM, Inc., 1998—2001; ret., 2001. Editor: geol. guidebooks, 1976—; contbr. articles to profl. jours. Fellow: Soc. Econ. Geologists (mem. rsch. com. 1989—92), Geol. Soc. Am. (mem. rep. 1985—93); mem.: AAUW, Sigma Xi (pres. Rolla chpt. 1990—91). Avocations: travel, music. E-mail: evakis@prodigy.net.

KITAHATA-SPORN, AMY, movement educator; b. Kyoto, Sept. 1, 1957; came to U.S. 1960; d. Luke Masahiko and Carolyn Dawson (Massey) Kitahata; m. Lee Stuart Sporn, Sept. 26, 1981. BA, Oberlin Coll., 1979; tchrs. cert., Am. Ctr. for the Alexander Technique, 1983, Ctr. for Study of Authentic Movement, 1991. Pvt. practice in Alexander Technique, N.Y.C., 1983—; mem. faculty Am. Ctr. for Alexander Technique, N.Y.C., 1984-90, The Juilliard Sch., N.Y.C., 1984—; pvt. instr. creative movement N.Y.C., 1988—. Mem. Am. Ctr. for the Alexander Technique (bd. dirs. 1984-86), N.Am. Soc. Tchrs. of Alexander Technique, Nature Conservancy, Sierra Club. Avocations: yoga, authentic movement, hiking, biking, dance. Office: The Juilliard Sch Lincoln Ctr New York NY 10023

KITCH, TERRI LYNN, language educator; b. Pueblo, Colo., Nov. 15, 1958; d. Ronald William and Betty Jean Baker; m. David Bruce Kitch, June 21, 1997; children: Clint Calli, Cody. BA in Elem. Edn., Ctrl. Conn. State U., New Britain, 1991; MA in Literacy, Lesley Coll., Boston, 1996. Language arts, reading tchr. Rocky Ford HS, R-Z Sch. Dist., Colo., 1993—, mem. dist. accountability com., 1994—2001, mem. curriculum com., 2005—. Bd. dirs. Rocky Ford Arts Commn., 2004—. Republican. Methodist. Avocations: reading, travel, art, quilting.

KITCHEN, BARBETTE LOUISE, retired secondary school educator; b. Traverse City, Mich., Mar. 14, 1942; d. Robert Jacob and Flora Eleanor (Morse) Spinner; m. Roger William Kitchen, Jan. 25, 1964; children: Monica, Robert, Angela. AA, Northwestern Mich. Coll., 1962; BA, We. Mich. U., 1964; postgrad., Mich. State U., 1964. Tchr. French, bus. Bellaire Pub. Schs., Mich., 1965—68, Elk Rapids Schs., Mich., 1969—2001, ret., 2001—. Mem. founding com. Grand Traverse Area Spelling Bee, 1977—; founder, co-chmn. Fgn. Lang. Day, No. Lower Mich., 1986-91; charter mem. Elk Rapids Sweet Adelines, 1984, pres. 1986-90; saxophonist Grand Traverse Cmty. Band, Traverse City, 1978—; advisor Elk Rapids H.S. French Club, 1981-88. Mem. NEA, No. Mich. Fgn. Lang. Tchrs. Assn. (founder, pres. 1983—), Mich. Fgn. Lang. Assn. (v.p. 1989-92, pres. 1992-93), Cen. States Conf. Tchg. Fgn. Langs. (adv. coun.), Am. Assn. Tchrs. French, Mich. Edn. Assn., Elk Rapids Edn. Assn. Meth. Avocations: vocal and instrumental music, barbershop arranging, computer skills, camping, logic puzzles. Home: PO Box 457 Elk Rapids MI 49629-0457 E-mail: barbettek@aol.com.

KITCHENS-STEPHENS, EVELYN H., counselor, educator; d. Marcellus Sr. and Evelyn Kitchens; m. Herbert L. Stephens, Sept. 23, 1992. BS, U. Pitts., 1982, MEd, 1987; PhD, Duquesne U., 2005. Cert. counselor Nat. Bd. Cert. Counselors and Affiliates, Inc. Counselor, prof. C.C. of Allegheny County, Pitts., 1987—. Adj. faculty mem. Duquesne U., Pitts., 2003—05; adj. lectr. Chatham Coll., Pitts., 2004—05; pvt. conflict resolutionist; presenter in field; freelance choreographer, liturgical dancer New Horizons Theatre Co. Dancer: New Horizons Theatre Co. Choreographer Dance. Mem. race and reconcilliation dialogue group St. Paul's Cathedral, Pitts., 1997—2006. Mem.: AAHPERD, ACA (assoc.), Am. Fedn. Tchrs. (assoc.), Chi Sigma Iota (assoc.). Avocations: reading, travel, singing, acting. Office: CC Allegheny County 808 Ridge Ave Pittsburgh PA 15212-6097 Office Phone: 412-237-2565.

KITE, MARILYN S., state supreme court justice, lawyer; b. Laramie, Wyo., Oct. 2, 1947; BA with honors, U. Wyo., 1970, JD with honors, 1974. Bar: Wyo. 1974. Sr. asst. atty. gen. State of Wyo., 1974—78; atty. Holland & Hart, Jackson, Wyo., 1979—2000; justice Wyo. Supreme Ct., 2000—. Contbr. articles to profl. jours. Mem. ABA (nat. resources sect., litigation sect.), Wyo. State Bar. Address: Wyo Supreme Ct 2301 Capitol Ave Cheyenne WY 82002*

KITSANTAS, ANASTASIA, educational psychologist; PhD in Edn. Psychology, CUNY, 1996. Asst. prof. James Madison U., Harrisonburg, Va., 1997—99, Fla. State U., Tallahassee, 1999—2001; assoc. prof., edn. psychology program coord. George Mason U., Fairfax, Va., 2001—. Assoc. dir. Hellenic Inst. Psychology & Health, 1999—. Contbr. articles to profl. jours. Mem.: APA, Fla. Rsch. Assn., Am. Ednl. Rsch. Assn. (chair, spl. interest group officer 2001—). Office: George Mason Univ Grad Sch Edn MSN 4B3 Fairfax VA 22030-4444 Home: 2505 Popkins Ln Alexandria VA 22306-1815 Business E-Mail: akitsant@gmu.edu.

KITSKA, SUSAN ANN, retired secondary school educator; b. Akron, Ohio, Feb. 3, 1946; d. Joseph David and Cecilia Martha (Alleman) K. BS in Edn. cum laude, Kent State U., 1968, MEd with honors, 1974. Cert. permanent tchr., Ohio. Tchr. English and German, Medina Sr. HS, Ohio, 1968-73, Cuyahoga Falls Schs., Ohio, 1973-83; tchr. English, coord. writing lab. Walsh Jesuit HS, Cuyahoga Falls, 1984-88; tchr. English and German, Rittman Sr. HS, Ohio, 1988—98; with Cuyahoga Valley Career Ctr., Brecksville, Ohio, 1998—2001; ret., 2001. Instr. English, Wooster Bus. Coll., Barberton, Ohio, 198890, U. Akron, Ohio, 1988-90; substitute tchr. Cuyahoga Falls City Schs., 2005-. Vol. Inventors Hall of Fame, Akron, summer 1990. Scholar Ohio Coun. PTA, 1964, Kent State U., 1964-68. Mem. NEA, Am. Assn. Tchrs. German, Ohio Coun. Tchrs. English, Ohio Fgn. Lang. Tchrs. Assn., Ohio Edn. Assn., Rittman Edn. Assn., Delta Phi Alpha. Avocations: walking, reading, writing letters, cooking, travel. Home: 400 W Reserve Dr Cuyahoga Falls OH 44223-3785

KITSMILLER, MYRA JORDAN, elementary school educator; b. Canton, Ohio, Jan. 16, 1956; d. Carl Edward and Virginia Parrish Jordan; children: Heidi Ann, Emily Grace. B in Music Edn., Mount Union Coll., Alliance, OH, 1978; M in Art of Tchg., Marygrove U., Detroit, 2004. Cert. music educator

Ohio Dept. Edn. Music tchr. Teays Valley Schs., Ashville, Ohio, 1978—92, Pickerington Local Schs., Ohio, 1993—. Mem.: Ohio Educators Assn. Office: Pickerington Local Schools 750 Preston Trails Pickerington OH 43147 Office Phone: 614-833-3630.

KITT, EARTHA MAE, actress, singer; b. St. Matthews, S.C., Jan. 17, 1927; d. John and Anna K.; m. William McDonald, June 1960 (div.); 1 child, Kitt Shapiro. Grad. high sch. Soloist with Katherine Dunham Dance Group, 1948; night club singer, 1949—, appearing in France, Turkey, Greece, Egypt, N.Y.C., Hollywood, Las Vegas, London, Stockholm; actress: (plays) Dr. Faustus, Paris, 1951, New Faces of 1952, N.Y.C., Mrs. Patterson, N.Y.C., 1954, Shinbone Alley, N.Y.C., 1957, Timbuktu, 1978, Blues in the Night, 1985, Mimi Le Duck, 2006; (films) including New Faces, 1953, Accused, 1957, Anna Lucasta, 1958, Mark of the Hawk, 1958, St. Louis Blues, 1957, Saint of Devil's Island, 1961, Synanon, 1965, Up The Chastity Belt, 1971, Dragonard, Ernest Scared Stupid, 1991, Boomerang, 1992, Fatal Instinct, 1993, Harriet the Spy, 1996, Ill Gotten Gains (voice), 1997, (TV) The Wild Thornberrys (voice), 1998, The Emperor's New Grove (voice), 2000, Feast of All Saints, 2001, Santa Baby!, 2001, Standard Time, 2002, Holes, 2003, also 2 French films, also numerous TV appearances including Cat Woman role in Batman series, (broadway shows) The Wizard of Oz, 1998, The Wild Party, 2000 (Tony nominee), Rodgers & Hammerstein's Cinderella, 2001; star: (documentary film) All By Myself, 1982; albums include That Bad Eartha, 1953, Down to Eartha, 1955, Thursday's Child, 1956, St. Louis Blues, 1958, The Fabulous Eartha Kitt, Eartha Kitt Revisited, 1960, Bad But Beautiful, 1962, My Way: A Musical Tribute to Rev. Dr. Martin Luther King Jr., 1987, Best of Eartha Kitt, 1983, Thinking Jazz, 1991, Miss Kitt, To You, 1992, Back in Business, 1994, Sentimental Eartha, 1995, Standard/Live, 1998, The Best of Eartha Kitt: Where Is My Man, 1998, Lovin' Spree, 2005, She's So Good, 2006; author: Thursday's Child, 1956, A Tart Is Not a Sweet, Alone With Me, 1976, I'm Still Here, 1990, Confessions of a Sex Kitten, 1991; co-author: Down to Eartha, 2000, How to Rejuvenate: It's Not Too Late, 2000 Recipient Nightlife Legend award, 2006; named Woman of Yr. Nat. Assn. Negro Musicians, 1968; nominated 2 Grammys, 2 Tony awards, 1 Emmy.*

KITT, OLGA, artist; b. N.Y.C., July 29, 1929; d. Elias and Mary (Opiela) K.; m. Nicholas Rawluk, Aug. 6, 1955 (div. 1960); 1 child, Wade. BA, Queens Coll., 1951; MA, State U. Iowa, 1952; studied with Meyer Schapiro, N.Y.C., 1954; studied with Hans Hofmann, N.Y.C., Provincetown, 1954-55; postgrad., Inst. Fine Arts, NYU, 1955, NYU, 1960-62; studied with Robert Beverly Hale, N.Y.C., 1979. Gallery asst. Chappellier Gallery, N.Y.C., 1952—53; asst. to Walter Pach NY, 1953—56; tchg. asst. CCNY, 1953—58; tchr. art NY, 1962—80. One-woman shows include CCNY, 1957, Manhattan Coll., Riverdale, N.Y., 1980, Blackout Gallery, N.Y.C., 1997, Coll. Mt. St. Vincent, 2001, 2002, 2003, The Corridor Gallery of Riverdale Temple, 2001, 2002, The Corridor Gallery of Interchurch Ctr., 2002, Starving Artists Gallery, 2005, Bronx Borough Pres. Carrion's Gallery, 2005, Hall of Fame Gallery, Bronx C.C., 2006, exhibited in group shows at Whitney Mus., N.Y.C., 1954, Bronx County Hist. Soc., 1978, Mus. Modern Art, N.Y.C., 1978, Art Students League, 1979, Bronx Mus. Arts, 1979, Coll. Mt. St. Vincent, 2000, Broome St. Gallery, N.Y.C., 2002, 2003, 2004, 2005, 2006, Represented in permanent collections Bronx Council of the Arts, Bronx Arts Ensemble, Riverdale Press, Riverdale YM-YWHA, U. Iowa, Iowa City, Fordham U., Fordham Prep. Sch., Hostos Coll., N.Y.C., Harris Sch. of Art, Tenn., numerous pvt. collections. Home: Apt 4D 5610 Netherland Ave Bronx NY 10471-1703 Studio: 495 S Broadway Yonkers NY 10705-3221 E-mail: olgakitt@aol.com.

KITTEL, PAMELA RAE, education educator; b. Ann Arbor, Mich., May 5, 1955; d. Rae S. and Gwendolyn Leach Earl; m. Wayne D. Kittel, Apr. 8, 1978; children: Jonathan, Jeremy, Jessica. BS, Ea. Mich. U., 1977, MA, 1994; student, U. Mich., 2001—. Cert. tchr. Mich. Rsch. asst. U. Mich., Ann Arbor, 1979—84, rsch. assoc., 1985—87; tchr. cons. Clonlara Sch., Ann Arbor, 1994—2000. Tchg. asst. U. Mich., Ann Arbor, 2001—02, 2006, Ea. Mich. U., Ypsilanti, Mich., 2005. Mem. planning commn. City Saline, Mich., 1987—93. Fellow U. Mich., 2001—. Mem.: Learning Disabilities Assn., Am. Ednl. Rsch. Assn., Coun. Exceptional Children, East Horizons Assn. (pres. 2003—06). Home: PO Box 653 Saline MI 48176 Personal E-mail: pkittel@umich.edu.

KITTREDGE, KATHARINE OTTAWAY, literature and language professor; b. Poughkeepsie, NY, Mar. 21, 1961; d. Gerald Howard and Esther Donaldson Ottaway; m. Ronald Jan Kittredge, June 6, 1986; children: Anna Donaldson, Steen William. PhD in English Lit., Binghamton U., NY, 1992. Assoc. prof. English Ithaca Coll., NY, 1990—. Adj. prof. Broome C.C., Binghamton, NY, 1985—87; vis. prof. Cornell U., Ithaca, 1988. Editor: Lewd and Notorious: Female Transgression in the Eighteenth Century, 2001; co-editor: Power and Poverty, 2002. Mem.: Am. Soc. Eighteenth Century Studies. Office: English Department Ithaca College Dryden Road Ithaca NY 14850 Office Phone: 607-274-1575.

KITTRELL, ETHEL JEAN, musician, retired literature and language professor; b. Birmingham, June 27, 1927; d. David McCarty and Dorothy Ethel Clark McCarty; 1 child, Camille. BA in English and Music Theory, Blue Mt. Coll., Miss., 1946; MA in Philos., U. Chgo., 1954; PhD in English, So. Ill. U., Carbondale, 1973. Exec. sec. Va. Telelphone and Telegraph, Charlottesville, 1949—51; legal sec. U. Chgo., 1952—53; tchr. music Ctrl. Pk. Sch., Birmingham, 1961; instr. English So. Ill. U., Carbondale, 1962—72, asst. prof., assoc. prof. English, 1972—94; leader, performer 3 jazz bands, 1978—2006. Prodr.(performer): (CD) Chasing Rainbows, 1984, Encore, 1992, Strut, 1993, Syncopate, 1994, Incredible Draw, 1997, Out of Gate, 1999, Hymns, 2000, Shine, 2002, Choice Cuts, 2002, Running Wild, 2002, See Mama, 2003, Farm, 2004, Plane, 2004, Fast, 2004, Faster, 2005, Half Fast, 2006. Mem.: Sierra Club. Home: 1104 Florida St Edwardsville IL 62025 Personal E-mail: kittrell@sbcglobal.net.

KITZMAN, MARY THERESE, elementary school educator; b. Washington, Ind., Oct. 2, 1957; d. William Guy and Anastasia Padgett; m. Steven Milton Kitzman, Mar. 29, 1958; children: Shane Milton, Tyler William. BA, Ind. State U., Terre Haute, 1981. Kindergarten tchr. Quabache Elem. Sch., Terre Haute, Ind., 1982—86; first grade tchr. St. Dominic Sch., Northfield, Minn., 1995—. Adminstr. Kids Voting, Northfield, Minn., 2004—06; social minister, choir mem. St. Dominic Ch., Northfield, Minn., 1990—2006; chairperson Touchdown Club, Northfield, Minn., 2005—, Athletic Com., Northfield, Minn., 1997—99, Parent/Student Assn., Northfield, 1995—97. Independent. Roman Catholic. Avocations: community volunteer, tutor children.

KIVELSON, MARGARET GALLAND, physicist; b. NYC, Oct. 21, 1928; d. Walter Isaac and Madeleine (Wiener) Galland; m. Daniel Kivelson, Aug. 15, 1949; children: Steven Allan, Valerie Ann. AB, Radcliffe Coll., 1950, AM, 1951, PhD, 1957. Cons. Rand Corp., Santa Monica, Calif., 1956-69; asst. to geophysicist UCLA, 1967-83, prof., 1983—, also chmn. dept. earth and space scis., 1984-87, acting dir. Inst. Geophys. Planet Physics, 1999—2000; prin. investigator of magnetometer, Galileo Mission Jet Propulsion Lab., Pasadena, Calif., 1977—2004. Overseer Harvard Coll., 1977-83; adv. coun. NASA, 1987-93; chair atmospheric adv. com. NSF, 1986-89, Com. Solar and Space Physics, 1977-86, com. planetary exploration, 1986-87, com. solar terrestial physics, 1989-92; adv. com. geoscis. NSF, 1993-97; space studies bd. NRC, 2002-05. Editor: The Solar System: Observations and Interpretations, 1986; co-editor: Introduction to Space Physics, 1995; contbr. articles to profl. jours. Named Woman of Yr., LA Mus. Sci. and Industry, 1979, Woman of Sci., UCLA, 1984; recipient Grad. Soc. medal Radcliffe Coll., 1983, 350th Anniversary Alumni medal Harvard U., 1986, Alfvén medal European Geophys. Union, 2005. Fellow AAAS, NAS, Internat. Inst. Astronautics, Am. Geophys. Union (Fleming medal 2005), Am. Acad. Arts and Scis., Am. Phys. Soc., Am. Philosophical Soc., Royal Astron. Soc.; mem. Am. Astron. Soc. Office: UCLA Dept Earth & Space Scis 6847 Slichter Los Angeles CA 90095-0001 Office Phone: 310-825-3435. Business E-Mail: mkivelson@igpp.ucla.edu.

KIVITTER, LINDA JEAN, medical nurse; b. Oelwien, Iowa, Aug. 14, 1950; d. Clarence Earl Clark and Pearl Elizabeth (Stempfle) Clark; m. William Allen Kivitter, Feb. 8, 1975 (dec. Jan. 2000); 1 child, Tara Lee. Lic. practical nurse, Kaw Area Vocat. Tech. Sch., 1971; diploma, Stormont-Vail Sch. Nursing, 1981; BSN, St. Mary of Plains Coll., 1990. RN, Kans. Staff nurse Stormont-Vail Regional Med. Ctr., Topeka. Mem. ANA (cert. med.-surg. nurse 1982-92). Personal E-mail: lkivitter@cox.net.

KIVLAHAN, COLEEN, public health officer; m. Bernard Ewigman; children: Kevin, Nathan. BS, St. Louis U.; MD, Med. Coll. Ohio, Toledo. Intern and resident U. Mo. Med. Ctr.; med. dir. Columbia/Boone County Health Dept.; med. dir. divsn. maternal, child and family health Mo. Dept. Health, 1987-89, Mo. Dept. Social Svcs., 1989-93; dir. Mo. State Dept. Health, 1993; med. dir. Fantus Health Ctr. John H. Stroger Jr. Hosp., Chgo., family physician Fantus Health Ctr.; med. dir. spl. project Schaller Anderson Inc., Phoenix. Med. dir. Health Resources and Services Adminstrn., Washington; founder, co-med. dir. Boone County Family Health Ctr. Recipient Pride in the Profession award, AMA Found., 2005. Avocation: running. Office: Schaller Anderson Inc Bldg 1 Ste 200 4645 East Cotton Center Blvd Phoenix AZ 85040 also: Fantus Health Center 621 S Winchester Chicago IL 60612*

KIYOTA, HEIDE P., psychologist; b. Bamberg, Germany, June 6, 1942; came to U.S., 1970; m. Ronald Kiyota; children: Heather, Catherine, Michelle. Student, U. South Africa, 1970-73, NYU, 1973; BS in Psychology, U. Md., 1975; MA, U. Md., Balt., 1979; PhD in Clin. Psychology, U. Hawaii, 1986. Rsch. asst. Dr. H.E. Kaiser, Balt., 1970-76; counselor Regional Inst. for Children and Adolescents, Balt., 1976-77; tchg. asst. dept. psychology U. Md., Balt., 1976-77; supr. multiple offender alcoholism program Balt. City Hosps., 1977-80; rsch. asst. Youth Devel. and Rsch. Ctr. U. Hawaii at Manoa, Honolulu, 1980-83; psychology asst. Kukulu Kumuhana Project, Honolulu, 1981-82; psychologist asst. Dept. Edn./Spl. Edn., Honolulu, 1982; intern in clin. psychology dept. medicine and surgery VA, Honolulu, 1983-84; clin. psychologist Kalihi Palama Counseling Svcs., Honolulu, 1987-89; pvt. practice Mililani, Hawaii, 1988—. Presenter convs. in field. Mem. APA, Hawaii Psychol. Assn., Phi Kappa Phi. Home: 1812 Nahenahe Pl Wahiawa HI 96786-2627 Office: Heide P Kiyota Phd 319 N Cane St # A Wahiawa HI 96786-2109 Office Phone: 808-621-1820.

KIYOTA, MELODEE YOKO, secondary school educator; d. Stella Kiyota. BS, San Jose State U., 1997, MA, 2006. Tchr., coach Santa Clara (Calif.) H.S., 1998—. Instr. Am. Sport Edn. Program. Recipient Diversity award Tchr. of Yr., Santa Clara HS, 2005. Mem.: AAHPERD, Calif. Alliance of Health, Phys. Edn., Recreation, and Dance. Home: 2228 Calle de Primavera Santa Clara CA 95054 Office: 3000 Benton St Santa Clara CA 95051

KIZER, CAROLYN ASHLEY, poet, educator; b. Spokane, Wash., Dec. 10, 1925; d. Benjamin Hamilton and M. (Ashley) K.; m. Stimson Bullitt, Jan., 1948 (div.); children: Ashley Ann, Scott, Jill Hamilton; m. John Marshall Woodbridge, Apr. 11, 1975. BA, Sarah Lawrence Coll., 1945; postgrad. (Chinese govt. fellow in comparative lit.), Columbia U., 1946-47; studied poetry with Theodore Roethke, U. Wash., 1953-54; LittD (hon.), Whitman Coll., 1986, St. Andrew's Coll., 1989, Mills Coll., 1990, Wash. State U., 1991. Specialist in lit. U.S. Dept. State, Pakistan, 1964-65; first dir. lit. programs Nat. Endowment for Arts, 1966-70; poet-in-residence U. N.C. at Chapel Hill, 1970-74; Hurst Prof. Lit. Washington U., St. Louis, 1971; lectr. Spring Lecture Series Barnard Coll., 1972; acting dir. grad. writing program Columbia U., 1972; poet-in-residence Ohio U., 1974; vis. poet Iowa Writer's Workshop, 1975; prof. U. Md., 1976-77; poet-in-residence, disting. vis. lectr. Centre Coll., Ky., 1979; disting. vis. poet East Wash. U., 1980; Elliston prof. poetry U. Cin., 1981; Bingham disting. prof. U. Louisville, Ky., 1982; disting. vis. poet Bucknell U., Pa., 1982; vis. poet SUNY, Albany, 1982; prof. Columbia U. Sch. Arts, 1982; prof. poetry Stanford U., 1986; sr. fellow in humanities Princeton U., 1986; vis. prof. writing U. Ariz., 1989, 90, U. Calif., Davis, 1991; Coal Royalty chair U. Ala., 1995. Participant Internat. Poetry Festivals, London, 1960, 70, Yugoslavia, 1969, 70, Pakistan, 1969, Rotterdam, Netherlands, 1970, Knokke-le-Zut, Belgium, 1970, Bordeaux, 1992, Dublin, 1993, Glasgow, 1994; sr. fellow humanities council Princeton U., 1986. Author: Poems, 1959, The Ungrateful Garden, 1961, Knock Upon Silence, 1965, Midnight Was My Cry, 1971, Mermaids in the Basement: Poems for Women, 1984 (San Francisco Arts Commn. award 1986), Yin: New Poems, 1984 (Pulitzer prize in poetry 1985), The Nearness of You, 1987 (Theodore Roethke prize, 1988); Proses: On Poems & Poets, 1994, Picking & Choosing: Prose on Prose, 1995, Harping On: Poems 1985-1995, 1996, The Complete Pro Femina, 2000, Cool, Calm and Collected Poems, 1960-2000; editor: Woman Poet: The West, 1980, Leaving Taos, 1981, The Essential Clare, 1993, 100 Great Poems by Women, 1995; translator Carrying Over, 1988; founder, editor: Poetry N.W., 1959-65; contbr. poems, articles to Am. and Brit. jours. Recipient award Am. Acad. and Inst. Arts and Letters, 1985, Pres.'s medal Ea. Wash. U., 1988, 5 Gov.'s awards State of Wash., 1965, 85, 95, 98, 2001, Silver medal Commonwealth Club, 1997, 2002, Aiken Taylor prize Sewanee Rev., 1998, Patterson prize, 2002, Western State Lifetime Achievement award, 2002, 1st prize Ind. Pub. Book award, 2002, L.A. Times Top Ten Books award, 2002, Acad. prize, 2003, Poets' prize, 2003. Mem. PEN, Amnesty Internat., Poetry Soc. Am. (Masefield prize 1983, Frost medal 1988). Episcopalian. Address: 19772 8th St E Sonoma CA 95476-3849

KIZER, NANCY ANNE, music educator, musician; b. Richmond, Calif., July 30, 1940; d. Benjamin Harrison Pilgrim and Doris Mabel (Parnell) Pilgrim-Myers; children: Kevin John Keuning, Stephen Douglas Keuning. MusB, U. of the Pacific, Stockton, Calif., 1958—62. Cert. secondary music tchr. Musician/violist Stockton Symphony Orch., Stockton, Calif., 1959—; music tchr./grades 7-9 Stockton Unified Sch. Dist., Stockton, Calif., 1962—64; music tchr./grades kindergarten-12 Lincoln Unified Sch. Dist., Stockton, Calif., 1983—95; coord./summer arts program Stockton Arts Commn., Stockton, Calif., 1987—2002; instr./string ensemble San Joaquin Delta Coll., Stockton, Calif., 1995—97; music libr. Stockton Symphony Assn., Stockton, 1996—2002, pers. mgr., 1999—; instr./string ensemble San Joaquin Delta Coll., Stockton, Calif., 2002—04; music tchr./HS Stockton Unified Sch. Dist., Stockton, Calif., 2002—. Recipient Music Honor Student, Santa Cruz HS, 1958. Mem.: Mortar Bd./Sr. Women's Honor Soc. (mem. 1962), Am. Fedn. Musicians, Nat. Educators Assn. (licentiate), Music Educators Nat. Conf. (licentiate), Mu Phi Epsilon/Nat. Music Fraternity (mem. 1959—). Home: 2424 North Center St Stockton CA 95204 Office: Stockton Symphony 46 West Freemont St Stockton CA 95202 Personal E-mail: vlanancy@inreach.com. Business E-Mail: personnel@stocktonsymphony.org.

KJAR, NANCY, elementary school educator; b. Hot Springs, SD, Apr. 17, 1947; d. Kenneth Winton and Marjorie Loraine Krutsch; m. Donald Robert Kjar, June 13, 1970; children: Steven Todd, Scott Ryan. BS in Edn., Chadron State U., 1969. Cert. tchr., Minn. 5th grade tchr. Sidney (Nebr.) Pub. Schs., 1969-70; 3d grade tchr. Eden Valley (Minn.) Watkins Pub. Sch., 1970-73, 4th grade tchr., 1986—2002. Recipient Leadership in Ednl. Excellence award, Resource Tng. and Solutions (formerly Ctrl. Minn. Svc. Coop.), 2002. Republican. Avocations: reading, music, walking, travel, needlecrafts. Personal E-mail: nancy_kjar@yahoo.com.

KLAGES, CONSTANCE WARNER, management consultant; b. N.Y.C., May 29, 1934; d. Ernest Frederick and Elsie (Roedler) Klages; m. James Lotz Jr., Apr. 26, 1975. BA, Dickinson Coll., 1956. Asst. personnel dir., personnel asst. Internat. Internat. Edn., N.Y.C, 1956—62; employment supr., salary asst Sperry Rand Corp., N.Y.C, 1962—65; rsch. and survey mgr. Commerce & Indsl. Assn., Inc., N.Y.C, 1965—66; v.p., assoc., rsch. dir. Battalia Lotz & Assn., Inc., N.Y.C, 1966—75; exec. v.p., treas. Internat. Mgmt. Advisors, Inc., N.Y.C, 1975—. Vol. membership com. Sutton Area Cmty. Elmhurst Gen. Hosp., N.Y.C., 1976, dir. co-op. bd., 1987—; bd. dirs. Sag Harbor Villa Homeowners Assn.; bd. advisors Dickinson Coll., 1980—84, trustee, 1984—. Mem.: Dickinson Coll. Alumni Coun., Nat. Assn. Corp. and Profl. Recruiters, Phi Mu (N.Y.C. Alumni chpt. v.p. 1961—62, pres. 1962—63, dist. alumnae dir. 1966—68).

KLAGES, KAREN LOUISE, music educator, musician; b. Pasadena, Calif., Nov. 10, 1964; d. Henry Eugene and Marjorie Bakker Klages. MusB in Edn., Ind. U., 1986, MusM, 1989. Profl. clear tchg. credential Calif., cert. gifted and talented edn. Pasadena Unified Sch. Dist., Calif. Tchr. instrumental music Pasadena (Calif.) Unified Sch. Dist., 1987—; French horn performer Fresno (Calif.) Philharm., 1999—; freelance musician various LA area orchs., 1987—; horn instr. Pasadena City Coll., 2000—04. Creator Eliot Mid. Sch. Jazz Band, 1991—. Musician (soloist): (with La Mirada Symphony) Schumann's Konzertstuck for Horns, (with Pasadena Orch.) Mozart's Horn Concerto #2. Vol. Lake Ave. Ch., Pasadena, 1983—2005; dir. performing groups Altadena (Calif.) Arts Coun., 2003—05; precinct worker nat. elections 2000 and 2004 Pasadena, 2000—04. Recipient Cert. of Recognition for Mus. Excellence in Pasadena Schs., City of Pasadena, 2003, Cert. of Recognition for Outstanding Dedication to Pasadena Schs., Bd. of Edn., Pasadena Unified Sch. Dist., 2003; grantee, Mr. Holland's Opus Found., 2002, Pasadena Ednl. Found., 2002, 2003, 2004. Mem.: NEA (assoc.; local site rep. 2003—05), Internat. Horn Soc. (assoc.), Am. Fedn. of Musicians (assoc.), Music Educators' Nat. Conf. (assoc.), So. Calif. Sch. Band and Orch. Assn. (assoc.). Avocations: backpacking, bicycling, dog shows, travel, reading. Home: 1915 Homewood Dr Altadena CA 91001 Office Phone: 626-795-6981. Personal E-mail: usermusic2264@aol.com.

KLAGSBRUN, FRANCINE, writer, editor; b. N.Y.C. d. Benjamin and Anna Pike Lifton; m. Samuel Charles Klagsbrun, Jan. 23, 1955; 1 child, Sarah Devora. BA magna cum laude, Bklyn. Coll., 1952; B in Hebrew Lit., Jewish Theol. Sem., N.Y.C., 1952; MA, NYU, 1959; D of Hebrew Letters (hon.), Jewish Theol. Sem., 1999. Sr. editor World Book Ency., Chgo., 1957—62, mng. editor, 1962—63; exec. editor Ency. Americana, N.Y.C., 1963—65, Cowles Book Co., N.Y.C., 1965—68; editl. dir. Universal Edn. Co., N.Y.C., 1969—72. Author: (book) Sigmund Freud: A Biography, 1967, The First Book of Spices, 1968, Psychiatry: What It Is, What It Does, 1969, Freedom Now! The Story of the Abolitionists, 1972, Too Young to Die: Youth and Suicide, 1976, Voices of Wisdom: Jewish Ideals and Ethics for Everyday Living, 1980, Voices of Widom: Jewish Ideals and Ethics for Everyday Living, new edit., 2001, Married People: Staying Together in the Age of Divorce, 1985, Married People: Staying Together in the Age of Divorce, updated edit., 1992, Mixed Feelings: Love, Hate, Rivalry and Reconciliation Among Brothers and Sisters, 1992, Mixed Feelings: Love, Hate, Rivalry and Reconciliation Among Brothers and Sisters, paperback edit., 1993, Jewish Days: A Book of Jewish Life and Culture Around the Year, 1996, Jewish Days: A Book of Jewish Life and Culture Around the Year, paperback edit., 1998, The Fourth Commandment: Remember the Sabbath Day, 2002; editor: Assassination: Robert F. Kennedy, 1968, The First Ms. Reader, 1973, Free to Be.You and Me, 1974 (Graphic Arts award, 1974), Words of Women, 1975; contbr. articles to mags. and newspapers; columnist: Moment Mag., 1990—, Jewish Week, 1993—, bd. dirs.: Lilith Mag., mem. editl. bd.: Hadassah Mag. Mem. women's dialogue group Am. Jewish Com.; mem. task force Jewish woman United Jewish Appeal Fedn. Jewish Philanthropies; trustee Jewish Mus.; founding chair, bd. overseers Libr. Jewish Theol. Sem.; bd. dirs. Nat. Jewish Book Coun. Named Woman Who Made a Difference, Am. Jewish Congress, 2000, honoree, Jewish Mus. Purim Ball, 2005; recipient Eternal Light medal, Jewish Theol. Sem., 1993, Outstanding Alumna award, 1996, Disting. Alumna award, Bklyn. Coll., 2000, Centennial award, Rabbinical Assembly Am., 2000, Stanley M. Isaacs Human Rels. award, Am. Jewish Com., 2000. Mem.: Phi Beta Kappa. Office: Charlotte Sheedy Agy 65 Bleeker St New York NY 10012 Personal E-mail: fklagsbrun@aol.com.

KLAICH, DOLORES, writer, educator; b. Cleve., Aug. 9, 1936; d. Jacob and Caroline (Stampar) K. BA, Case Western Res U., 1958; postgrad., SUNY Stony Brook, 1994—. Reporter Life mag., N.Y.C., 1962-67; freelance writer, editor, lectr., 1967—; edn. coord. L.I. Assn. for AIDS Care, Huntington, N.Y., 1987-89; lectr. SUNY Sch. Health, Tech. and Mgmt., 1989—. Judge Ferro-Grumley Lit. Awards, N.Y.C., 1989, 90. Author: Woman Plus Woman: Attitudes toward Lesbianism, 1974, Heavy Gilt, 1988. Co-chmn. East End Lesbian and Gay Orgn., Southampton, N.Y., 1977-85; del. Nat. Women's Conf., Houston, 1977; bd. mem. Women's Crisis Ctr., Brattleboro, Vt. Democrat. Home: 75 Mather Rd Brattleboro VT 05301-8830

KLAMERUS, KAREN JEAN, pharmacist, researcher; b. Chgo., Aug. 10, 1957; d. Robert Edward and Jane Mary (Nawoj) Klamerus; m. Frederick P. Zeller. BS in Pharmacy, U. Ill., 1980; PharmD, U. Ky., 1981. Registered pharmacist Ky., Ill., Pa. Staff pharmacist Haggin Meml. Hosp., Harrodsburg, Ky., 1980-81, Regional Med. Ctr., Madisonville, Ky., 1982, critical care liasion, 1982; clin. pharmacist resident U. Nebr., Omaha, 1983; clin. pharmacist cardiothoracic surgery U. Ill., Chgo., 1983-88, clin asst. prof. dept. pharmacy practice, 1983-86, asst. prof., 1986-88, departmental affiliate dept. pharmaceutics, 1986-88; sr. pharmacokineticist Wyeth-Ayerst Rsch., Phila., 1988-91, asst. dir. clin. pharmacology, 1991-95, assoc. dir. clin. pharmacology, 1995-97; dir. med. rsch. Roche Global Devel., Palo Alto, Calif., 1997—2001; dir. clin. rsch. Vical, Inc., San Diego, 2002; dir. clin. pharmacology Pfizer, Inc., 2002—04, sr. dir., clin. pharmacology, 2004—. Fellow: Am. Coll. Clin. Pharmacology (indsl. rels. com. 1995); mem.: Mid-Atlantic Coll. Clin. Pharmacology (sec. 1991, pres. 1992—94), Am. Soc. Clin. Pharmacology and Therapeutics. Avocations: softball, scuba diving, gardening, sewing. Office: Pfizer-La Jolla 10777 Sci Ctr Dr CB10 San Diego CA 92121 Personal E-mail: kjklamerus@yahoo.com.

KLARK, DENISE J., special education educator, consultant; b. North Wilkesboro, N.C., May 9, 1967; d. Samuel Theron and Donna Lynn Jennings; m. John Fitzgerald Klark, Oct. 22, 1994; children: Jonathan Taylor and Brandon Tyler (twins). BA in Mental Handicaps, U. N.C., Charlotte, 1994; postgrad., Appalachian State U., 1997, 98, 99. Cert. tchf. B-K and K-12 spl. edn., N.C. Spl. edn. tchr. Wilkes County Schs., Wilkesboro, N.C., 1995-97; dir. Summer Program for Exceptional Children, North Wilkesboro, N.C., 1994—; preschool/spl. edn. tchr. Wilkes Devel. Day Sch., Wilkesboro, 1997—. Bd. dirs. Summer Program for Exceptional Children, 1994—. Office: Wilkes Devel Day Sch 1021 Welborn Ave Wilkesboro NC 28697-2223

KLARREICH, SUE FRIEDMAN, education administrator, consultant; b. Cleve., Jan. 14, 1929; d. Maurice David and Matilda Saks Friedman; children: Karin, Betsy, Kathie, Beth. BA, U. Mich., 1950; MA, Western Reserve U., 1970; PhD, Case Western Reserve U., 1973. Sch. psychologist City of Cleve., 1970—71; dir. program devel. Jewish Vocational Svc., Cleve., 1973—82; co-dir. women resource Cleve. Found., 1974—77; title IX project dir. Cleve. Hts. Schs., Palo Alto, Calif., 1979—81; project dir. Am. Assn. U. Women, Los Altos, Calif., 1992—2000; adminstr. Friedman-Klarreich Family Found., Cleve., 2000—, Miami, 2000—. Cons. Early Learning Inst., Palo Alto, Calif., 1983—92; project supr. JCC, Palo Alto, Calif., 1990—98; project cons. Apple Computer, Mt. View, Calif., 1992. Author: Dozens of Cousins, 1985, Tech Time for Girls, 1992. Bd. mem. Met. Bank, Cleve., 1973—82, Mt. Sinai Hosp., Cleve., 1978—82; bd. mem., officer JCC, Palo Alto, 1983—90; bd. mem. Am. Assn. U. Women, Palo Alto, 1989—2000. Mem.: U. Miami Inst. for Retired Profl. Avocations: drawing, painting. Home: 101 Crandon Blvd 473 Key Biscayne FL 33149

KLASFIELD, ILENE, psychologist; b. N.Y.C., Aug. 23, 1943; d. Robert Louis and Laura Mersand; m. Jon Klasfield, Dec. 24, 1962; children: Alan, Michael. BS, N.Y. State U., Old Westbury, 1978; MS, LaSalle U., Mandeville, La., 1998, PhD in Psychology, 2000. Acct., mgr. Almike Realty, Boca Raton, Fla.; therapist, psychologist, vol. JCC, Boca Raton, 1998—. Parent adv. com. Boca H.S., Boca Raton. Bd. dirs. Women's League for Peace, Queens, N.Y.; vol. Home for the Aged, Boca Raton; active Women for Alternative Medicine, 1993, Am. Cancer Soc., 1968-70, Mothers Against Drunk Driving, Boca Raton, 1990-98, United Cerebral Palsy Assn., Washington, 1990. Mem. Alzheimer's Assn. Democrat. Avocations: tai chi, writing, reading, hiking, gardening, tennis, yoga. Home: 1908 NW 4th Ave Apt 122 Boca Raton FL 33432

KLASS, PHYLLIS CONSTANCE, retired genetic counselor, psychotherapist; b. Scranton, Pa., Aug. 13, 1927; d. Max Gordon and Lina Rachel (Levine) Rich; m. Felix Klass, Sept. 27, 1952 (dec. Mar. 1988); children: Steven, Janet. BA, Syracuse U., 1947; MA, Columbia U., 1948; MS, Sarah Lawrence Coll., 1972. Diplomate Am. Bd. Med. Genetics. Asst. prof. Cornell Med. Sch., N.Y.C., 1972—; dir. genetic counseling program N.Y. Hosp., 1972—89; ret., 1989. Chair genetic counseling Prenatal Diagnosis Lab of N.Y., 1975-81. Fellow Am. Orthopsychiat. Assn.; mem. Nat. Soc. of Genetic Counselors (chair profl. issues com.), Am. Soc. of Human Genetics.

KLASSEN, MARGRETA, clinical psychologist, educator; b. L.A., May 4, 1928; d. David Charles and Jessie Irene (Asseltine) K.; m. Richard Caddell Calhoun, May 31, 1946 (div. 1962); children: Cathleen, Melissa, Nancy, Richard; m. Norman K. Dunn, July 25, 1963 (div. 1969); m. Donald Cole Wargin, Feb. 14, 1970 (dec. Jan 1984). BA, Pitzer Coll., 1968; MS, Calif. State U., L.A., 1972; PhD, Claremont (Calif.) Grad. Sch., 1982. Diplomate Am. Coll. Forensic Examiners, cert. practioner Biofeedback Inst. Am. Instr., counselor Chaffey Community Coll., Alta Loma, Calif., 1972-74; dir. bio-feedback program U. La Verne, Calif., 1974-76; owner Assocs. for Wellness, Claremont, Calif., 1979—; with Cert. Inst. of Am., Wheatridge, Colo., 1984-92; asst. prof. Calif. State Poly. U., Pomona, 1986-88; oral commr. Calif. Dept. Consumer Affairs, Sacramento, 1986-88; stress mgmt. program coord. Claremont Coll., 1988—97. Participant Golden Poet, World Congress of Poets, NYC, 1991; presenter joint meeting European Space Agy., German Rsch. Soc., Internat. Soc. for Bio-Behavioral Self-Regulation, Munich, 1991; program dir. Juvenile Connection, 1998-99; mem. adv. coun. Continuing Edn. in Mental Health, U. Calif. Irvine, 1998-2000; mem., presenter Soc. for Rsch. in Adult Devel., 2005. Editor: History of the Arabian Horse, 1968; reviewer: Jour. of the Assn. for Assessment in Counseling, Am. Counseling Assn., 1996-99. People to People del., USSR, 1989; mem. Claremont Hist. Soc., 1989-90, Internat. Soc. Police Surgeons, 2000-06; mem. steering com. Families First Collaborative of Orange County, 1998-99; mem. centennial heritage com. Newport Beach, 2005-06. Sr. fellow emeritus, Biofeedback Cert. Inst. of Am., 2002. Fellow Coll. for Advanced Practice in Psychology; mem. Am. Psychol. Assn., Assn. for Applied Psychology and Bio-feedback, Orange County Psychol. Assn. (contbr. newsletter), Internat. Stress Mgmt. Assn. (sec., treas. 2003-), Inland Empire Bus. Women's Assn. (pres. Upland (Calif.) chpt. 1984), Laguna Poets Assn. (presenter), Pitzer Coll. Alumni Assn. (mem. leadership com. Orange County chpt. 2000-01). Avocations: swimming, writing. Home: 230 Lille Ln Apt 212 Newport Beach CA 92663-2665 Office: Newport Psychology Group 20371 Irvine Ave Ste A-160 Santa Ana CA 92707 Office Phone: 714-540-5010. Personal E-mail: drpsyreal8@aol.com.

KLATZKIN, TERRI, real estate company executive; Contr. Clark Enterprises Inc., Bethesda, Md. Office: Clark Enterprises Inc 15th Fl 7500 Old Georgetown Rd Fl 15 Bethesda MD 20814-6133

KLAVITER, HELEN LOTHROP, editor-in-chief, magazine editor; b. Lima, Ohio, Mar. 5, 1944; d. Eugene H. and Jean (Walters) Lothrop; m. Douglas B. Klaviter, June 7, 1969 (div. 1982); 1 child, Elizabeth. BA, Cornell Coll., Mt. Vernon, Iowa, 1966. Communication specialist Coop. Extension Service, Urbana, Ill., 1969-71; mng. editor The Poetry Found. Poetry Mag., Chgo., 1973—. Editorial cons. Harper & Row, N.Y.C., 1983-87. Bd. dirs. Ill. Theatre Ctr., 1989-95, St. Clement's Open Pantry, 1990—, Episc. Diocese of Chgo. Hunger Commn., 1992—, Comms. Commn., 1993—. Episcopalian. Office: Poetry Mag The Poetry Found 444 N Michigan Ave Ste 1850 Chicago IL 60611 Office Phone: 312-799-8004. Business E-Mail: hklaviter@poetrymagazine.org.

KLAW, BARBARA ANNE, language educator; b. Chgo., Mar. 22, 1957; BA cum laude in French, No. Ill. U., 1979; postgrad., Northwestern U., 1982-83; MA in French lit., U. Pa., 1985, PhD in French, 1990. Teaching asst. Northwestern U., Evanston, Ill., 1982-83; teaching asst. U. Pa., Phila., 1983-84, 84-85, 1986-87; lectr. Université de Dijon, Dijon, France, 1985-86, U. Pa., Phila, 1987-88; teaching asst. Penn-in-Tours program Faculté des Lettres, Tours, France, summer 1988; asst. prof. French No. Ky. U., Highland Heights, 1990-96; assoc. prof. No. Ky. Univ., 1996—2001, prof., 2001—. Faculty advisor Internat. Student Union, No. Ky. U., 1991-98; participant com. for modification of tng. program for new tchg. assts. Northwestern U., spring 1983. Author: Le Paris de Beauvoir; editor, translator: Diary of a Philosophy Student, 2006; mem. editl. bd. Women in French Studies, 1999—; mem. adv. bd. Simone de Beauvoir Studies, 2002—; numerous presentations in French and on French subjects; contbr. articles to profl. jours. No. Ky. U. summer fellow, 1991, 94, 97, Am. Philos. Soc. grantee, 1997; NEH grantee, 2001-04. Mem. MLA, Simone de Beauvoir Soc., Alliance Française de Cin. (bd. dirs., pres. 2006-), Am. Assn. Tchrs. French, Women in French (treas. 1992—98), French-Am. C. of C. in Cin., Ky. World Lang. Assn. Business E-Mail: klaw@nku.edu.

KLAWE, MARIA MARGARET, academic administrator, engineering educator, computer science educator; b. Toronto, Ontario, Can., July 5, 1951; d. Janusz Josef and Kathleen Wreath (McCaughan) K.; m. Nicholas John Pippenger, May 12, 1980; children: Janek, Sasha. BSc in math., U. Alberta, 1973; PhD, U. Alberta, Edmonton, Can., 1977; PhD (hon.), Ryerson U., 2001, U. Waterloo, 2003, Queens U., 2004. Asst. prof. dept. math. sci. Oakland U., Rochester, Mich., 1977-78; asst. prof. dept. computer sci. U. Toronto, Canada, 1979-80; rsch. staff mem. IBM Rsch., San Jose, Calif., 1980-89, mgr. discrete math., 1984-88, mgr. dept. math., related computer sci., 1985-87; prof., head dept. computer sci. U. BC, Vancouver, 1988-95, v.p. student and acad. svcs., 1995—98, dean sci., 1998—2002; dean Sch. Engring & Applied Sci. Princeton U., 2003—, prof. dept. computer sci., 2003—06; pres. Harvey Mudd Coll., Claremont, Calif., 2006—. Spkr. in field; mem. adv. bd. univ. rels. IBM Toronto Lab., 1989; mem. sci. adv. bd. Dimacs NSF Sci. Tech. Ctr., New Brunswick, NJ, 1989-95; mem. adv. bd. Geometry Ctr., 1991-95; mem. BC Premier's Adv. Coun. on Sci. and Tech., 1993—2001, Provincial Adv. Com. on Edn. Tech., 1993; founder, dir. E-GEMS project U. BC, 1992-2002; Chair for Women in Sci. and Engring. Nat. Sciences and Engring. Rsch. Coun. of Can.(NSERC)-IBM, 1997-2002; co-founder, chmn. bd. Silicon Chalk, Vancouver.; bd. trustees Math. Sciences Rsch. Inst., chair bd. trustees Anita Borg Inst. Women and Tech. Palo Alto Calif.; trustee Inst. Pure and Applied Math. LA. Editor: (jours.) Combinatorica, 1985—, SIAM Jour. on Computing, 1986-93, SIAM Jour. on Discrete Math., 1987-93; contbr. articles to profl. jours. Named Can. New Media Educator of Yr., 2001, BC Sci. Coun. Champion of Yr., 2001; recipient Women of Distinction Award in Sci. and Tech., Vancouver YWCA, 1997, Can. Wired Woman Pioneer Award, 2001, Disting. Alum. Award, U. Alberta, 2003, Nico Habermann award, 2004; INCO scholar, 1968—71, NRC Can. fellow, 1973—77. Fellow Assn. Computing Machinery (mem. coun. 1998-2000, v.p. 2000-02, pres. 2002-04); mem. Am. Math. Soc. (bd. trustees 1992-97, chmn. 1995-96), Can. Math. Soc., Can. Heads Computer Sci. (pres. 1990-91), Assn. Women Math., Computing Rsch. Assn. (mem. bd. 1990-96), Soc. Indsl. and Applied Math. Avocations: running, painting, kayaking, windsurfing. Office: Harvey Mudd Coll Kingston Hall, Rm 201 301 Platt Blvd Claremont CA 91711 Office Phone: 909-621-8120. E-mail: klawe@hmc.edu.*

KLEBANOW, BARBARA ELAINE, secondary school educator; b. Dec. 6, 1936; d. Joseph Herman and Helen (Feldstein) Klebanow. BA, U. Conn., 1958; MS, Yeshiva U., 1960; profl. diploma, U. Conn., 1965; MS, Lehman Coll., 1977. Cert. sch. dist. adminstr. N.Y., reading specialist N.Y., spl. edn. tchr. N.Y. Tchr. elem. classroom North Rockland Ctrl. Sch. Dist., Stony Point, NY, 1960—64, reading specialist elem. level, 1964—69, reading specialist secondary level, 1969—95, adminstrv., intern, 1977—78. State coord. Internat. Reading Assn., NY, 1987—91, chair cert. reading adv. group, NY, 1987—88, chair nat. task force cert. in reading, 1993—95. Recipient Celebrate Literacy award, Rockland Reading Coun., 1987, Reading Tchr. award, N.Y. State, 1987. Fellow: Rockland Reading Coun., Assn. Women Adminstrs. Westchester; mem.: Internat. Reading Assn. (chair specialized reading profls. spl. interest group 1989—), N.Y. State Reading Assn. (pres. 1983—84), Phi Delta Kappa. Avocations: travel, reading, habdicrafts.

KLEE, ANN RENEE, lawyer; BA in Ancient History, Swarthmore Coll., 1983; JD, U. Pa., 1986. Assoc. Crowell & Moring LLP, Washington, 1986—90; ptnr., chair environ. group Preston, Gates, Ellis & Rouvelas Meeds, Washington, 1990—95; environ. counsel to Senator Dick Kempthorne US Senate, Washington; chief counsel Senate Environment and Pub. Works Com., Washington, 1995—2001; counselor, spl. asst. to sec. US Dept. Interior, Washington, 2001—04; asst. adminstr., gen. counsel US EPA, Washington, 2004—06; ptnr. nat. resources & environ. group Crowell & Moring LLP, Washington, 2006—. Office: Crowell & Moring LLP 1001 Pennsylvania Ave NW Washington DC 20004 E-mail: aklee@crowell.com.*

KLEE, CLAUDE BLENC, medical researcher; MD, U. Marsailles, France, 1959. Chief lab. chemistry, chief protein biochemistry sect. Nat. Cancer Inst., 1974—. Recipient Women's Excellence in Scis. award, Fedn. Am. Soc. for Exptl. Biology, 1997. Fellow: AAAS; mem.: Inst. Medicine, Nat. Acad. Sci. Office: Nat Cancer Inst-Biochem Lab 9000 Rockville Pike Bethesda MD 20892-0001

KLEEFELD, CAROLYN MARY, artist, writer, poet; b. Catford, Eng., May 11, 1935; came to U.S., 1939; d. Sydney Mark and Amelia (Lewis) Taper; m. Travis Kleefeld (div.); children: Carla Ann, Claudia Eve. Student, UCLA, 1955—62. Artist, Central Coast, Calif., 1985—; author, poet Malibu, Beverly Hills, Calif., 1960—, Central Coast, 1980—. Bd. dirs. Spiritual Emergence Network, Santa Cruz, Calif., Our Ultimate Investment, Hollywood, Henry Miller Libr., Big Sur, Calif.; spkr. in field. Author: Climates of the Mind, 1979, braille edit., 1979, Satan Sleeps with the Holy, 1982, Lovers in Evolution, 1983, The Alchemy of Possibility: Reinventing Your Personal Mythology, 1998; included in Mavericks of the Mind: Conversations for the New Millenium, 1993, Songs of Ecstasy, Vol. I and II, 1990-1991; co-author (with David Wayne Dunn) Kissing Darkness, 2003; artist: exhibited in one women shows at Gallerie Illuminati, Santa Monica, Calif, 1991. Supporter Plowshares, San Francisco, United Way, Ams. for Peace, PAWS, Earth Trust, Ams. for Peace Now. Recipient 1st prize Bay Area Poets Coalition, San Francisco, 1986, award of Excellence, So. Calif. Poets Pen, San Diego, 1985, Coast Weekly 101-Word Short Story Contest winner, Monterey, Calif., 2005. Avocations: swimming, hiking, inter-species communication, philosophy, genetics. Office: Atoms Mirror Atoms Inc PO Box 221693 Carmel CA 93922-1693

KLEIKAMP, BEVERLY, poet, writer, publisher; b. Iron Mountain, Mich., Apr. 15, 1953; d. Hector Joseph and Lorraine Agnes (Frisque) Dugree; m. Vernon Lee Kleikamp, Feb. 5, 1972; children: Henry J., Richard V., Carl A. Freelance writer U.P. Horse News, Florence, Wisc., 1984-91; pub. North Star Pub., 1998—. Editor mag. Northern Stars, 1997—; author: Fifth Season, 1997, Of Higher Powers, 1998; pub.: Best of 98 Anthology, 1999, Old Century/New Millennium Anthology, 2000, Shining Stars Anthology, 2001, Stars of Wonder Anthology, 2002, Stars I, 2003, Stars II, 2003, Stories for Children, 2002, Tracy and The Shadow Horse, 2003, Poetic Stars of 2004, 2005, Stars of Storytelling 2004, 2005, Short Story Stars of '05, 2006, Poetry Stars of '05, 2006. Recipient 8th Honorable Mention, Poets' RoundTable 59th Internat. Poetry Contest, 1999, 6th Hon. Mention 63d ann. contest, 2003. Mem. Upper Peninsula Publs./Authors Assn., Upper Peninsula Writers Assn. Avocations: camping, fishing, hunting, photograpy. Home: N17285 County Road 400 Powers MI 49874-9758

KLEIM, E. DENISE, city official; BA in Econs. cum laude, San Jose State U., 1975; MBA, Willamette U., 1982. Mgmt. asst. Urban Renewal Agy. City of Salem, Oreg., 1976-78, grant adminstr. dept. cmty. devel. Oreg., 1978-80, asst. to dir. dept. cmty. devel. Oreg., 1981-84, lobbyist Oreg., 1980-83; sr. mgmt. analyst Bur. Bldgs., City of Portland, Oreg., 1984-86, adminstrv. mgr. Oreg., 1986-99, mgr. adminstrv. svcs. bur. devel. svcs., 1999—. V.p. Montclair After Sch. Care Assn., Portland, 1995-96; mem. Atkinson Soc., Salem, 1995-97. Office: City of Portland Bur Devel Svc 1120 SW 5th Ave Portland OR 97204-1912

KLEIMAN, MARY MARGARET, lawyer; b. Norfolk, Va., May 26, 1959; d. William Edward and Patricia Mae Holste; m. David James Kleiman, June 29, 1991; children: Amanda Grace, Amy Elizabeth. BA in History summa cum laude, Marian Coll., Indpls., 1981; JD cum laude, Ind. U., Indpls., 1984. Bar: Ind. 1985, U.S. Dist. Ct. (no. and so. dists.) Ind. 1985. Bailiff, law clk. Marion County Mcpl. Ct., Indpls., 1983-84; counsel Am. Fletcher Nat. Bank (now Bank One, Ind. N.A.), Indpls., 1985-88; assoc. Krieg DeVault Alexander & Capehart, Indpls., 1989-95; ptnr. Krieg Devault Alexander & Capehart, Indpls., 1995-2000; v.p. and assoc. gen. counsel Federal Home Loan Bank of Indianapolis, 2000—. Bd. dirs. Ind. Bus. Devel. Corp., 1994-97; spkr. at banking confs. Contbr. articles to profl. jours. Pro bono atty. Cmty. Orgns. Legal Assistance Project, Indpls., 1994—; vol. com. chair, mem. client programs com. Ind. chpt. Nat. Multiple Sclerosis Soc., 1997-2001, trustee Ind. chpt., 1999-2001; mem. mission com. Castleton United Meth. Ch., Indpls., 1993-2000, acolyte coord., mem. worship com., 1998-99, mem. chancel choir, 1999—, chair staff-parish rels. com., 2000-02; bd. dirs. Circle Area Comm. Devel. Corp., 2000—, Downtown Area Comm. Devel. Corp., 2000—, Mass. Ave. Comm. Devel. Corp., 2000—, Naval Air Warfare Center Reuse Planning Authority. Recipient Leadership award Nat. Multiple Sclerosis Soc., 1998, Nat. Vol. of Yr. award Nat. Multiple Sclerosis Soc., 1999, Outstanding Vol. award Ind. Ronald McDonald House, 1990; named to Outstanding Young Women in Am., 1981, 87. Mem. ABA, Ind. State Bar Assn., Indpls. Bar Assn. (chair printed forms com. 1987), Phi Delta Phi. Democrat. Avocations: gardening, cross-stitch, reading science fiction, calligraphy. Office: Federal Home Loan Bank 8250 Woodfield Crossing Blvd Ste 210 Indianapolis IN 46240-4348 E-mail: mkleiman@fhlbi.com.

KLEIMOLA, SHARON LEIGH, retired elementary school educator; b. Ironwood, Mich., July 26, 1945; d. Matt R. and Ida Josephine Kleimola. BS in Elem. Edn., No. Mich. U., Marquette, 1967; MA in Edn., Ea. Mich. U., Ypsilanti, 1971; EdS, Wayne State U., Detroit, 1977. Tchr. Utica Cmty. Schs., Mich., 1967—2001; ret. Student tchr. supr. Oakland U., Rochester, Mich., 1997—2000; rev. panel mem. Dept. Edn., Lansing, Mich., 1999. Mem.: NEA, Humane Soc., Nat. Arthritis Found. Avocations: reading, bridge, golf. Home: 1052 Willow Grove Rochester MI 48307

KLEIN, BARBARA A., information technology executive; BS, Marquette U.; MBA, Loyola U., Chgo., 1977. CPA. Former exec. Pillsbury, Sears, Roebuck and Co.; former v.p., corp. contr. Ameritech Corp.; former v.p. fin., CFO Dean Foods Co.; sr. v.p., CFO CDW Computer Ctrs., Vernon Hills, Ill., 2002—. Mem.: AICPA. Office: CDW 200 N Milwaukee Ave Vernon Hills IL 60061

KLEIN, CAROL LYNNE, psychologist; b. Bklyn., Nov. 8, 1941; d. Jay J. and Rebecca Lehrman; m. Robert L. Klein, Aug. 20, 1966; children: Alisa Beth, Matthew Douglas. BS cum laude, SUNY, 1962; M of Edn., Temple U., 1975, D of Edn., 1986. Cert. sch. psychologist Pa. Elem. tchr. PS 183, Bklyn., 1962—66, West Hills Sch., Knoxville, Tenn., 1966—70; counseling psychologist B'Nai Brith Career Counseling, Phila., 1977—78; psychologist Whitmarsh Psychol. Assocs., Lafayette Hill, Pa., 1979—. Psychologist United Cerebral Palsy, Phila., 1996—97; cons. psychologist Chester Charter Sch., Pa., 1996—2004, Spring Ford Sch. Dist., 2004—05, Coatesville Sch. Dist., 2006—; bd. dirs. Phila. Soc. Clin. Psychologists and Pub. Rels. Bd. dirs. Whitemarsh Citizens Coun., 1974—75; mem. citizens advisory coun. Montgomery County Office of Children and Youth, Pa., 1986—94; trustee Colonial Found. For Ednl. Innovations, 1996—2005; LWV Pa., 1973—75. Early Childhood Specialization grant, Temple U., Pa., 1995. Mem.: APA, Pa. Psychol. Assn., Nat. Assn. Sch. Psychologist. Home and Office: 105 Hollyhock Dr Lafayette Hill PA 19444 Personal E-mail: clklein@aol.com.

KLEIN, CHARLOTTE CONRAD, public relations executive; b. Detroit, June 20, 1923; d. Joseph and Bessie (Brown) K. BA, UCLA, 1945. Corr. UPI, Los Angeles, 1945-46; staff writer CBS, Los Angeles, 1946-47; publicist David O. Selznick Studios, Culver City, Calif., 1947-49, Foladare and Assocs., Los Angeles, 1949-51; publicist to v.p. Edward Gottlieb & Assocs., N.Y.C., 1951-62; v.p. to sr. v.p. Harshe Rotman & Druck, N.Y.C., 1962-78; dir. press/govt. affairs Sta. WNET-TV, N.Y.C., 1978-79; pres. Charlotte C. Klein Assocs., N.Y.C., 1979-84; sr. v.p., group supr. Porter Novelli, N.Y.C., 1984-89; prin. Charlotte Klein Assocs., N.Y.C., 1989—2002. Adj. prof. pub. rels. NYU; bd. dirs. U.S. Trademark Assn., 1959-62, Am. Arbitration Assn., 1970-80 (exec. com. 1980-82); mem. adv. bd. Coll. and Cmty. Fellowship Grad. Ctr., CUNY, 2002-06; cons. Ctr. for Advancement of Women, 2003-04. Contbr. articles to profl. jours. Bd. dirs. Manhattan chpt. Am. Cancer Soc., 1988-92. Recipient Cine Golden Eagle, 1977, Matrix award Women in Comms., 1975, Honor award Coll. and Cmty. Fellowship, 2004, Keeper of the Flame award Nat. Women's Hall of Fame, 2005. Mem. Pub. Rels. Soc. Am. (accredited; pres. N.Y. chpt. 1985-86, Silver Anvil award 1978, John Hill award 1988), Women's Forum (bd. dirs. N.Y. chpt. 1986-87, 96-98), Internat. Women's Forum (leadership com. chair dialogue for democracy 1993-98, co-chair task force on violence against women globally, 1998-2001), Women Execs. in Pub. Rels. (pres. 1965), N.Y. Women in Comm. Avocations: painting, stamp collecting/philately. Office Phone: 212-683-3543. Personal E-mail: bettlott@earthlink.net.

KLEIN, CHARLOTTE FEUERSTEIN, art consultant; b. Stoneham, Mass., June 3, 1931; d. Harold and Esther B. (Franks) Feuerstein; m. Philipp Hillel Klein, June 21, 1953; children— Joshua David, Daniel William, Jonathan Henry. BS, Boston U., 1953. Tchr. pub. schs., Scotia, Schenectady, Niscayuna, NY, 1953-56, Newton, Mass., 1974-75; ptnr., art cons. Washington Graphics, Washington, 1979-82; dir., art adviser CFK Assocs., Washington, 1982. Mem. AAUW, LWV, Washington Opera Soc., The Phillips Collection, Friends of Kennedy Ctr., Washington, Nat. Symphony Orch. Assn., Holocaust Mus., Corcoran Gallery Art, Smithsonian Assn. Mem. Nat. Bldg. Mus., Am. for Arts Action Fund, Nat. Trust Hist. Preservation, Nat. Mus. Women, US Holocaust Meml. Mus., Nat. Parks Conservation Assn.

KLEIN, CINTHIA MARIE, parochial school educator; d. LeRoy Joseph and Jacqueline Ann Griffard; m. William John Klein, Oct. 21, 1994; children: Grant, Gavin. Student, Jefferson Coll., Hillsboro, Mo., 1989—91, Mineral Area Coll., Park Hills, Mo., 1991—92; EdB, Ctrl. Meth. Coll., Fayette, Mo., 1994; MEd, Webster U., St. Louis, 2001. Cert. tchr. Mo. Elem. tchr. Jefferson R-7 Sch., Festus, Mo., 1994—99; sci. tchr. St. Agnes Sch., Bloomsdale, Mo., 1999—. Chmn. Trash for Cash, St. Joseph Sch. PTA, Zell, Mo., 2004—06. Mem.: Nat. Cath. Ednl. Assn. Roman Catholic. Avocations: reading, swimming, gardening.

KLEIN, CRYSTAL SHELAYNE, science educator, volleyball coach; b. Loup City, Nebr., Sept. 18, 1973; d. Wayne H. and Dayle D. Klein. BS, U. Nebr., Kearney, 1996. Teaching Certificate State of Nebr., 1998. Sci. tchr. Umonhon Nation Pub. Sch., Macy, Nebr., 1999—. Home: Po Box 433 Macy NE 68039 Office: Umonhon Nation Pub Sch 100 Main St PO BOX 280 Macy NE 68039 Office Phone: 402-837-5622.

KLEIN, CYNTHIA, art appraiser; BA in Art Hist., U. Mass., Amherst, BS in Bus. Adminstrn., Mktg. with honors; grad studies in Art Hist., Rutgers U. Specialist, paintings dept. to dir., prints dept. C.G. Sloan & Co. Auctioneers, N. Bethesda, Md., 1991—2000; v.p., dir., prints dept. Doyle New York, 2000—. Prints appraiser Antiques Roadshow, WGBH-PBS. Mem.: Am. Hist. Prints Collectors Soc., Soc. for Japanese Arts, Phi Beta Kappa. Office: Doyle New York 175 E 87th St New York NY 10128 Office Phone: 212-427-4141 ext. 246. Office Fax: 212-369-0892. Business E-Mail: prints@doylenewyork.com.

KLEIN, DEBORAH LYNN, art educator; b. West Chester, Pa., June 28, 1981; d. Euguen and Margaret Hulnick Klein. BSE in Art Edn., Millersville U. Pa., 2003. Cert. art edn. grades K-12 Pa., 2003. Art tchr. grades 5-8 Octorara Area Sch. Dist., Atglen, Pa., 2003—. Office Phone: 610-593-8223.

KLEIN, DEBORAH RAE, nurse; b. Detroit, Mar. 29, 1951; d. Chester Anthony and E. Jacquelyn (Hollenbeck) Simpson; m. Robert Joseph Klein, Apr. 15, 1977; 1 child, Jeffrey. BS in Nursing, Mich. State U., 1974; MS in Health Adminstrn., U. Houston, 1984. Grad. nurse St. Mary's Hosp., Livonia, Mich., 1974; RN U.S. Army, Ft. Polk, La., 1974-78; DON Byrd Meml. Hosp., Leesville, La., 1978-79, Alvin (Tex.) Cmty. Hosp., 1979-83; adminstrn. resident Katy (Tex.) Med. Ctr., 1983-84, DON, 1984-85, COO, DON, 1985-90; v.p. Doctors' Hosp., Tulsa, 1990-97; dir. ops. improvement Okla. divsn. Columbia HCA, 1997-98; v.p., COO SouthCrest Hosp., Tulsa, Okla., 1998—2001; chief nursing officer Vaughn Regional Med. Ctr., Selma, Ala., 2002—03; dir. Tulsa Regional Med. Ctr., Tulsa, Okla., 2000—01; v.p. clin. integration Hillcrest HealthCare Sys., Tulsa, 2000—01; nurse mgr. VAMC, Salem, Va., 2003—. Cons. in field; adj. faculty Bartlesville Wesleyan Coll., 1999-2001. Sec., treas. Sam Houston coun. Boy Scouts Am., 1984-88. Capt. U.S. Army, 1972-78. With U.S. Army Nurse Corps, 1974—78. Recipient Commendation medal, U.S. Army. Mem.: Sigma Theta Tau. Republican. Roman Catholic. Avocations: reading, crafts. Home: 532 Santee Rd Roanoke VA 24019-4928 Office Phone: 540-982-2463 ext. 2485.

KLEIN, ELAINE CHARLOTTE, school system administrator; b. Herreid, S.D., June 14, 1939; d. Herman F. and Minnie (Weigum) Klein; 1 child, Erika Katherine. BA, U. Puget Sound, 1961; MA, U. Wash., 1964; cert. in adminstrn., Seattle U., 1976; postgrad., Western Wash. U., 1986. Cert. secondary sch. adminstr. Wash., K-12 tchr. Wash. Tchr. Edmonds Sch. Dist., Lynnwood, Wash., 1961-77; asst. prin. Meadowdale Jr. HS, Lynnwood, Wash., 1977-80, Mountlake Terrace (Wash.) HS, 1981-93, prin., 1993-97; exec. dir. cmty. svcs. Frederick (Md.) County Pub. Schs., 1997—. Adj. faculty Heritage Inst., Antioch U., Seattle Pacific U., Western Wash. U.; instr. Mt. St. Mary's Coll., Emmitsburg, Md.; cons. Am. Coll. Testing Passport Portfolio, Iowa City, 1995—97; presenter in field. Co-author: (book) ACT Manual for Administrators, 1997; grant writer:. Pres. Pacific N.W. region Internat. Tng. Comm., Alaska, B.C., Canada, Wash., 1993—94. Named Wash. State Prin. of the Yr., 1997, Adminstr. of the Yr., Md. Assn. Edn. Office Pers., 1999, Friend of Edn., M. St. Mary's Coll., 1999, Outstanding Contbr., Hood Coll., 2002; recipient award for Excellence in Edn., Wash. State Legislature, 1997. Mem.: ASCD, Nat. Assn. Secondary Sch. Prins. and Affiliates, Am. Assn. Sch. Adminstrs., Rotary (Mountlake Terrace pres. 1996—97). Methodist. Avocations: public speaking, reading, travel, advocating for public schools. Office: Frederick County Pub Schs 115 E Church St Frederick MD 21701-5403 E-mail: elaine.klein@fcps.org.

KLEIN, ELAYNE MARGERY, retired elementary school educator; b. L.I., N.Y., Apr. 25, 1947; d. Jack and Anne (Fialkow) K. BS, L.I. U., 1969, MS, 1972. Cert. elem. tchr., cert. in guidance edn., N.Y. Student tchr. 2nd, then 4th grades Robbins Lane Elem. Sch., Syosset, N.Y., 1968-69; tchr. 5th grade West Islip (N.Y.) Pub. Schs., 1969—2002. Co-organizer/supr. 5th and 6th grade drama club West Islip Pub. Schs., 1972. Mem. Am. Fedn. Tchrs., N.Y. State United Tchrs., N.Y. State Congress Parents and Tchrs. (hon. life), Iota Alpha Pi. Avocations: reading, opera, ballet, travel, collecting antiques.

KLEIN, FREDA, retired state agency administrator; b. Seattle, May 17, 1920; d. Joseph and Julia (Caplan) Vinikow; m. Jerry Jerome Klein, Oct. 20, 1946; children: Jan Susan Klein Waples, Kerry Joseph, Robin Jo Klein. BA, U. Wash., 1942; MS, U. Nev., Las Vega, 1969, EdD, 1978. Owner, mgr. Smart Shop, Provo, Utah, 1958-60, Small Fry Shop, Las Vegas, 1961-66; vocat. counselor, test adminstr. Nev. Employment Security Dept., Las Vegas, 1966-77, local office mgr., 1978-95; ret., 1995. Contbr. Nevada Kids Count Data Books, 2001-2004, The Linguistic Landscape of Nevada Schools, 2003, Adolescents and Substance Abuse, 2003, Internet Crimes Against Children, 2003, The Transition of Nevada Adolescents to Adulthood: A Rocky Road, 2004, articles to profl. jours.; screenwriter: 1995-1998. Exec. bd. Pvt. Industry Coun., Las Vegas, 1988—, Interstate Conf. on Employment Security Agys., Nev., 1988—90, Area Coordinating Com. for Econ. Devel., Las Vegas, 1988—95; vol. Ctr. for Bus. and Econ. Rsch., U. Nev., Las Vegas, 1995—. Recipient Achievement award Nev. Bus. Svc., 1990, Cert. of Spl. Congl.

Recognition, 1992; named Outstanding Woman, Goodwill Industries sci. and rsch. divsn., 1977; selected to be included in Wall of Women exhibit Women of Diversity, 2005. Mem. AAUW, Internat. Assn. Pers. in Employment Security, U. Nev. Las Vegas Alumni Assn., Henderson C. of C. (exec. bd. 1986-95), Soroptimist Internat. (pres. 1987-88), Phi Kappa Phi (scholastic hon.). Avocations: hiking, swimming, writing. Home: 2830 Phoenix St Las Vegas NV 89121-1312 E-mail: drfredai@aol.com.

KLEIN, GABRIELLA SONJA, retired communications executive; b. Chgo., Apr. 11, 1938; d. Frank E. Vosicky and Sonja (Kosner) Becvar; m. Donald J. Klein. BA in Comm. and Bus. Mgmt., Alverno Coll., 1983. Editor, owner Fox Lake (Wis.) Rep., 1962-65, McFarland (Wis.) Comty. Life and Monona Cmty. Herald, 1966-69; bur. reporter Waukesha (Wis.) Daily Freeman, 1969-71; cmty. rels. staff Waukesha County Tech. Coll., Pewaukee, Wis., 1971-73; pub. rels. specialist JI Case Co., Racine, Wis., 1973-75, corp. publs. editor, 1975-80; v.p., bd. dirs. publs. Image Mgmt. Valley View Ctr., Milw., 1980-82; pres. Comm. Concepts Unltd., Racine, 1983-98; ret., 1998. Past pres. Big Bros./Big Sisters Racine County; past v.p. devel. Girl Scouts Racine County, bd. dirs. Recipient award Wis. Press Assn., Nat. Fedn. Press Women, Silver medal Ad Club Racine, 1998, Outstanding Alumna award Alverno Coll., 1999, Edn. Cmty. Leader of Yr., Racine Area Mfrs. and Commerce, 2000, Thanks Badge award Girl Scouts of Racine County, 2000, Cmty. Trustee award Leadership Racine, 2004, Thanks Badge II award Girl Scouts Racine County, 2005, Oustanding Youth Adv. award Racine County Youth as Resources, 2006; named Wis. Woman Entrepreneur of Yr., 1985, Vol. of Yr. Racine Area United Way, 1994, Woman of Distinction Bus., Racine YWCA, 1995. Home: 3045 Chatham St Racine WI 53402-4001

KLEIN, GAIL BETH MARANTZ, freelance/self-employed writer, animal breeder; b. Bklyn., Dec. 1, 1946; d. Herbert and Florence (Dresner) Marantz; m. Harvey Leon Klein, Mar. 17, 1979. AB cum laude, U. Miami, Coral Gables, Fla., 1968, MEd, 1969, MBA, 1977. Cert. residential contractor, Fla.; notary pub. Asst. dir. student activities Miami-Dade Community Coll., 1969-79, instr. photography for mentally retarded adults, 1974, acting dir. student activities, 1976, acting advisor student publs., 1979; dog breeder Vizcaya Shepherds, Palm Beach Gardens, Fla., East Hampton, Conn., 1979—; trainer Dog Obedience and Conformation Show Handling, West Palm Beach, 1980—; owner, CEO Word Master Profl. Comm. Freelance writer WordMaster Profl. Comms.; mgr. proposal devel., specialist Profl. Food-Svc. Mgmt., Inc., 1994—97; spl. projects-ops. Chartwells, 1997—98; proposal and resource libr. mgmt., proposal writer Wackenhut Corp., Inc., 1998—2000; cons. Universal Staffing Svcs., 2001; sr. tech. cons. Belcan Corp., 2001—02; tech. publs. analyst-mil. engines Pratt & Whitney, 2002—04, tng. coord. Turbine Module Ctr., 2004—; spke in field; appeared on various radio talk shows. Editor (booklet) 1978 Consumers Guide to Banking, 1978, (newsletter) Newsletter of German Shepherd Dog Club Ft. Lauderdale, Inc., 1980-83, Sunshine State Shepherd, 1988-89; contbr. articles to newspapers and mags. Chair spl. events com. Third Century U.S.A., Dade County, Fla., 1976; mem. adv. com., mktg. cons. YWCA of Greater Miami, 1976-79; mem. comty. rels. com. Greater Miami Jewish Fedn., 1976-79; mem. Met. Miami Art Ctr., 1977-79; vice chair, chair appeals bd. Palm Beach County Animal Care and Control, 1989-97, mem. pet overpopulation com., 1991-93; co-developer, co-adminstr. OFA Verifications for German Shepherd Dogs, 1985—; pub. info. coord. Am. Kennel Club, Palm Beach County, 1991-94. Recipient Job Training Partnership Act Employee of Yr. award State of Fla., 1994. Mem.: Am. Sewing Guild, Palm Beach Users Group, Conformation Judges Assn. Fla., Inc., Nat. Assn. Dog Obedience Instrs., Assn. Proposal Mgmt. Profls., Fla. Freelance Writers Assn., Hadassah (life), Wolf Song of Alaska (grant/proposal writer), Treasure Coast German Shepherd Dog Club (charter), Jupiter-Tequesta Dog Club, Inc. (pres. 1984—85, bd. dirs., various other offices, Gaines Sportsmanship award 1993), German Shepherd Dog Club of Can., Inc., German Shepherd Dog Club of Greater Miami (life; rec. sec. 1977—78, corr. sec. 1978—80, bd. dirs. 1981—82, 1989—94), German Shepherd Dog Club Am., Inc. (hip dysplasia/orthopedic com. 1987—89), German Shepherd Dog Club Eastern Conn., Obedience Tng. Club Palm Beach County, Inc. (AKC Cmty. Achievement Merit award 1994), Mortar Board, Phi Kappa Phi, Epsilon Tau Lambda, Alpha Lambda Delta. Republican. Jewish. Avocations: reading, computers, crafts, photography, sewing. Home: 12 Comstock Trl East Hampton CT 06424-2304 Personal E-mail: gailklein@aol.com.

KLEIN, IRMA MOLLIGAN, career planning administrator, consultant; b. New Orleans, Jan. 5, 1929; d. Harry Joseph and Gesina Francis (Bauer) Molligan; m. John Vincent Chelena (dec. 1978); 1 child, Joseph William Chelena; m. Chris George Klein, Aug. 14, 1965; 1 stepchild, Arnold Conrad. BS in Bus., Augustine Coll.; postgrad., Mktg. Inst., Chgo., Loyola U., Realtors Inst., Baton Rouge. Mgr. Stan Weber & Assocs., Metairie, La., 1971-75, tng. dir., 1975-81; cons. Coldwell Banker Comml. Co., New Orleans, 1981; dir. career devel. Coldwell Banker Residential Co., New Orleans, 1982-85; pres. Irma Klein Career Devel., Inc., 1994-95, Klein Enterprises, Inc., 1994—. Instr. U. New Orleans, Realtors Inst., La. Real Estate Commn. Author: Training Manual, 1978, Career Development, 1982, Obtaining Listings, 1986, Participative Marketing, 1986, Marketing & Servicing Listings, 1987, Designing Training Curriculum, 1987, Participative Management. Mem. La. Hist. Assn. Meml. Hall Found. Mem.: CRS (pres. La. chpt. 1988—90), CRB (pres. La. chpt. 1982—83, chmn. edn.), Confederate Lit. (pres. New Orleans 2001—), Antique Study Group (pres. 2001—03), Les Quarante Ecolieres (pres. 1994—96), La. Dental Assts. Assn. (pres. 1964), Am. Dental Assts. Assn., Nat. Assn. Realtors (nat. conv. spkr. 1986), Realtors Nat. Mktg. Inst. (residential specialist 1977, amb. Tex. and La. 1985—, cert. broker 1980, Outstanding Achievement award 1985), Edn. and Resources (pres. La. chpt., cert.), Jefferson Bd. Realtors (v.p. 1984), La. Realtors Assn. (bd. dirs. 1973—74, grad. Realtors Inst. 1976), Metairie Woman's Club (sec. 1997—99, pres.-elect 1999, pres. 2000—01), Rsch. Club New Orleans (pres. 1984—85), Odyssey Ho. La. Republican. Roman Catholic. Avocation: antiques.

KLEIN, JENNY LYNN, neuroscientist, researcher; b. Hialeah, Fla., Apr. 10, 1979; BS, U. Fla., 2001; MS, U. Ctrl. Fla., 2005. Clinician, rschr., grad. student U. Ctrl. Fla., Orlando, Fla., 2001—, instr. psychology, 2005. Assessment specialist Lakeside Alternatives, Inc., Orlando, 2003—04; evaluator neurpsychology Maitland Psychology, P.A., Fla., 2004—05; pres. Grad. Student's Family Interactions Group U. Ctrl. Fla., 2003—; intern La Amistad Behavioral Health Svcs., Maitland, Fla., 2005—; presenter in field. Contbr. (chpt.) The parent-young child relationship: Dealing with and surviving the "Terrible Twos", Multiracial and multiethnic clients: History.; contbr. articles to profl. jours. Grantee, U. Ctrl. Fla., 2002—06; scholar, U. Fla., 2000—01; Fla. Bright Futures Academic scholarship, State Fla., 1997—2001, Delores A. Auzenne fellowship, U. Ctrl. Fla., 2002—04. Mem.: APA, Southeastern Psychol. Assn., Assn.Behavioral and Cognitive Therapies, Cuban American Student Assn. (chmn. cmty. svc. 1999—2000), Doctoral Orgn. Students in Clin. Psychology (sec. 2001—03, historian 2003—04, pres. 2004—05). Democrat. Avocations: travel, music. Office: University of Central Florida PO Box 161390 Orlando FL 32816-1390 Business E-Mail: jklein@ucf.edu.

KLEIN, JULIA MEREDITH, freelance journalist; b. Phila., Dec. 11, 1955; d. Abraham and Murielle (Pollack) Klein. BA magna cum laude, Harvard U., 1977. Copy editor J.B. Lippincott, Phila., 1977; features reporter The Oakland Press, Pontiac, Mich., 1978; freelance writer, researcher, editorial cons., 1978—; reporter, critic and editor The Phila. Inquirer, 1983-2000. Nat. Arts Journalism Program fellow, 1996-97, John J. McCloy fellow in journalism, 1998, Alicia Patterson Found. fellow, 2000, Western Knight Ctr. fellow for Specialized Journalism, 2001; Fulbright German Studies Seminar, 2004. Mem. Soc. Profl. Journalists (2d pl. award for criticism 1998, 2003, 3d Pl. award for criticism 1999), Am. Soc. Journalists and Authors, N.Am. Travel Journalists Assn., Journalism and Women Symposium, Nat. Book Critics Cir., Phi Beta Kappa Home and Office: 307 Monroe St Philadelphia PA 19147-3211 Office Phone: 215-733-0761. Personal E-mail: julklein@verizon.net.

KLEIN, KITTY R., counseling administrator; d. Naomi Klein; m. Igal Rabinovich, Apr. 9, 2006. B of Psychology, L.I. Univ., Upper Brookville, N.Y., 1993; MS, St. John's U., Jamaica, N.Y., 1995, Profl. Diploma, 1997. Dir., guidance The Acad. Environ. Sci., N.Y.C., 1997—2001; asst. prin., pupil pers. Norman Thomas HS, N.Y.C., 2001—03; dist. dir. guidance Locust Valley Sch. Dist., 2003—04, Manhasset Pub. Schs., 2004—06; dir., guidance counselor Garden City Pub. Schs., NY, 2006—. Listed under Wall of Tolerance - Rosa Parks. Contbr. Nat. Libr. Poetry, papers to profl. pubs. Mem.: ACA, Nat. Assn. Coll. Admission (counselor 2000—), Nassau Counselor's Assn., Internat. Libr. Poetry. Avocations: dance, billiards, volleyball. Office: Garden City Pub Schs Garden City NY 11530

KLEIN, LAURA COLIN, publishing executive; With Levine, Huntley, Schmidt & Beaver Advt., N.Y.C., 1985—86; nat. sales mgr. Andrew's Mag., 1986—89; acct. mgr. ELLE Mag., 1989—92; Ea. sales mgr. Woman's Day, N.Y.C., 1992—96, v.p., ad dir., 1996—2000, v.p., pub., 2002—; pub. Family Life, 2000. Office: Womans Day Mag Hachette Filipacchi Mags Inc 1633 Broadway 42d Fl New York NY 10019 Office Phone: 212-767-6000. Office Fax: 212-767-5610.*

KLEIN, LUELLA VOOGD, obstetrics and gynecology educator; b. Walker, Iowa, Oct. 24, 1924; d. Elmer De Witt and Leah (Stunkard) Bare; m. Alfred O. Colquitt. BA, U. Iowa, 1947, MD, 1949. Diplomate Am. Bd. Ob-Gyn. Intern Western Res. U., Cleve., 1949—50; resident in medicine, surgery and ob-gyn Cleve. City Hosp., 1950—55; U.S. Sr. Fulbright Rsch. scholar U. London Postgrad. Med. Sch., 1955—57; obstetric cons. Ga. Dept. Pub. Health, Atlanta, 1958—60; pvt. practice Atlanta, 1960—65; asst. dir. clin. rsch. Bristol Labs., Syracuse, NY, 1965—67; prof., dir. maternal and infant care project Emory U. Grady Meml. Hosp., Atlanta, 1967—; co-dir. Regional Perinatal Ctr., Charles Howard Candler prof., chmn. dept. ob-gyn Emory U. Sch. Medicine, Atlanta, 1986—93. Gen. bd. dirs., bd. dirs. divsn. maternal-fetal medicine Am. Bd. Ob-Gyn.; bd. dirs. Alan Guttmacher Inst., N.Y.C., chmn., vice chmn.; Maternal and Child Health Care governing coun. Am. Hosp. Assn., Chgo.; chmn. FDA Ob-Gyn Device Com., Washington, 1986—88. Recipient Elizabeth Blackwell award, Am. Women's Med. Assn., 1986, Atlanta Woman History Maker award, Am. Women's Assn., 1987, Emory medal, 1988, Daggett Harvey award, Chgo. Maternity Ctr., Northwestern U., 1991, 40th Anniversary award, Fedn. Internat. Gynecology and Obstetrics, 1994. Fellow: ACOG (pres., v.p., asst. sec. 1982—85, Disting. Svc. award 1994); mem.: AMA, Inst. Medicine, Med. Assn. Ga. (chair maternal and child health care com.), Atlanta Obstet. and Gynecol. Soc. (pres.), Ga. Obstet. and Gynecol. Soc. (pres.), Marietta (Ga.) Country Club. Office: Grady Meml Hosp DeptGyn/Ob 69 Jesse Hall Dr SE Atlanta GA 30303-3033

KLEIN, LYNN ELLEN, artist; b. San Francisco, Apr. 14, 1950; BA in Studio Arts, U. Minn., 1974, MFA in Design, 1976. Instr. art edn. U. Minn., Mpls., 1976-78, lectr. in design, 1974-84; vis. artist U. Iowa, Ames, 1984—, Textile Ctr. of Minn., 2003. Resident Cité Internat. des Arts, Paris, 1984-86, summer 1998, vis. artist Textile Arts Ctr. of Minn., 2003. One-woman shows include Rochester (Minn.) Fine Arts Ctr., 1976, Northrup Gallery, U. Minn., Mpls., 1976, Allrich Gallery, San Francisco, 1982, 1988, Coffman Gallery, U. Minn., 1982, The Print Club, Phila., 1985, Foster-White Gallery, Seattle, 1989, Carolyn Ruff Gallery, Mpls., 1994, Robert Green Fine Arts, 2000, exhibited in group shows at Mpls. Inst. Arts, 1976, 1988, Franklin Inst. Sci. Mus., Phila., 1984, Minn. Mus. Art, St. Paul, 1990, Textile Arts Internat., 1990, 1992, San Francisco Bay Area Women Artists Mentors, 1994, USART San Francisco Internat. Art Expo, I. Wolk Gallery, St. Helena, Calif., 1996, Robert Green Fine Arts, Mill Valley, Calif., 1996, 2002, Craftsman's Guild and Calif. Heritage Gallery, 1998, Ren Brown Collection, Bodega Bay, Calif., 1998, Gensler Architecture-Material Matters, San Francisco, 1998, San Jose Mus. Art, Visible Rhythm, 2001, 2003, Kala Art Inst., 2002, Pyramid Atlantic Book Arts Fair, Wash., 2002, Brave New World Print Portfolio, NY Print Fair, 2004, Neomodern Calif. Abstraction Crocker Art Mus. to Monterey Mus., Sacramento, 2005, Represented in permanent collections Mpls. Inst. Arts, Oakland (Calif.) Mus., Bibliotéque Nat., Dept. des Estampes et de lá Photographie, Paris, Phila. Mus. Art, Walker Art Ctr., Mpls., Achenbach Found., Fine Arts Mus. San Francisco, San Jose Mus. Art., Calif., NY Pub. Libr., Rutgers Univ. Ctr. for Innovative Prints, Crocker Art Mus., Sacramento, San Diego Mus. Art, Libr. Congress, Washington, Ohio Mus. Art, print publs., Double/Absent, edit. 15, 1983 (Calif. Phelan award for printmaking), Untitled, edit. 10, 1992, Wild Women Portfolio, edit. 20, 2002, Brave New World, edit. 20, 2004, commns., Miami Internat. Airport, 2000, Caesar's Palace, Las Vegas, 2001, Fairmount, Cancun, Mex., 2004, Ritz Carelton, Palm Beach, Fla., 2005, numerous others, bibliography, Memory on Cloth, 2002. Recipient J.D. Phelan award World Print Coun., 1983; Minn. State Arts Bd. Grantee, 1978; Photography fellow, St. Paul, 1984; Rockefeller Found. fellow, Am. Ctr., 1984-86, Jerome Found. Printmaking fellow, Kala Inst., Berkeley, 1989; Amity Art Found. grant, Woodbridge, Conn., 2003. Mem.: Achenbach Graphic Arts Coun.

KLEIN, MARY ANN, special education educator; b. Ridgewood, N.J., Jan. 31, 1956; d. Julius R. and Nancy M. Pascuzzo; m. Thomas F. Klein, July 16, 1983. B in Elem. Edn. & Spl. Edn., Adelphi U., Garden City, N.Y., 1978; M in Spl. Edn. & Reading, Adelphi Univ., Garden City, N.Y., 1980. Cert. in spl. edn. Learning disabilities specialist Merrick UFSD, Merrick, NY, 1978—. Swimming instr. disabled children and adults Village of Garden City, 1974—79; pvt. piano instr., NY, 1978—82; clinician & diagnostician Adelphi U. Reading Clinic, Garden City, 1980—84; ednl. cons. BOCES of Nassau County, Merrick, NY, 1993—94, SETRC of Nassau County, Westbury, NY, 1995—96; founder peer tutoring program Birch Sch., Merrick, NY; spl. edn. rep. Birch Child Study Team, Merrick, NY. Co-author: (curriculum guide) Foundations for Learning, 1991; author: (resource guide) Strategies to Assist Learning Disabled Children in the Classroom Setting, 1995. Mem. Merrick PTA, 1978—, tchr. liaison, 1994—97; mem. Merrick SEPTA, 1983—, Com. on Spl. Edn., 1983—, Nassau Reading Coun., 1996—; co-founder Students Against Destructive Decision-Making, Birch Sch., Merrick, NY; apptd. Crisis Mgmt. Team, Birch Sch. Mem.: State Congress of Parents & Tchrs. (hon.), Coun. for Exceptional Children, Kappa Delta Pi. Avocations: piano, travel. E-mail: beachbum7777777@aol.com.

KLEIN, NANCY LYNN, fine jewelry company owner, consultant; b. Syracuse, N.Y., May 9, 1961; d. Irwin Lenard and Ann Betty (Ginsburg) K. BS in Journalism, Ohio U., 1985; grad., Gem. Inst. Am., N.Y.C., 1987. Advt. coord. Henry Birks Fine Jewelry, N.Y.C., 1985-87; brand mgr. N.W. Ayer Advt., N.Y.C., 1987-90; advt. dir. Honora Jewelry Co., N.Y.C., 1991-92; asst. jewelry buyer Finlay Co., N.Y.C., 1992-94, buyer fine jewelry Washington, 1994-95; sr. buyer fine jewelry QVC Network, West Chester, Pa., 1995-96; pres., owner Antica Design, Inc., N.Y.C., 1996—. Mem. Women's Jewelry Assn. Office: Antica Design Inc 19 W 44th St Fl 9 New York NY 10036-6001 E-mail: nk5037@aol.com.

KLEIN, SAMI WEINER, librarian; b. Worcester, Mass., July 6, 1939; d. Phillip and Barbara Rose (Ginsburg) Weiner; m. Eugene Robert Klein, Oct. 22, 1961; children: Pamela, Jeffrey, Elizabeth. BS, Simmons Coll., 1961; MLS, U. Md., 1973; postgrad., Johns Hopkins U., 1976-78. Chemist Hercules, Wilmington, Del., 1961-62, FDA, Washington, 1965-66; libr. NSWC, White Oak, Md., 1973-78; chief Hdqs. Libr. EPA, Washington, 1978-82; chief rsch. info. svcs. Nat. Inst. Svcs. and Tech., Gaithersburg, Md., 1982-95; chief rsch. libr. and info. program, rsch. libr. Nat. Inst. Stds. and Tech., Gaithersburg, Md., 1995-99; retired Nat. Inst. Svcs. and Tech., Gaithersburg, Md., 1999. Cons. in field; mem. librs. exec. coun. Met. Washington Coun. of Govts., 1981-82; elected mem. com. Fed. Libr. Info. Ctr., 1993-95, chair, budget and fin. working group, 1994-98. Editor OIS Sci.-Tech Info, 1982-95; mem. editorial bd. Assn. Ofcly. Analyt. Chemists, 1985-92, Sci. and Tech. Librs., 1996—. Fed. govt. rep. Inst. for Sci. Info. Internat. Users Group, 1985—86; mem. info. tech. com. Candlelight Concert Soc.; chmn. Howard County Holocaust Remembrance Program, 2003; 2d v.p. Bet Aviv Congregation, 2004—06, pres., 2004—; mem. edn. com. Fed. Libr. and Info. Ctr. Com., 1987—91. Recipient Gold medal Am. Soc. Chemists, 1961, Engring. award Govt. Inidustry Data Exch. Program, 1997. Mem. ALA (sec.-treas. Fed. Librs. Round Table 1983-84, rep. to NTIS 1984-90, bd. dirs. 1986-89, v.p. 1991, pres. 1991-92, nominations chair 1992-93, scholar 1994-96, chair privatization com. 1995-97, chair co-awards com. 1996—, 1st FLRT Disting. Svc. award 1995), Spl. Librs. Assn. (treas. info.-tech. group 1986-87, student loan com. 1984-85), D.C. Law Librs. Soc. (NIST v.p. standards com. for women 1988, pres. 1989, bd. dirs. Comstar Credit Union 1994-2000), Fed. Libr. and Info. Network (exec. adv. com. 1989-91, sec. 1989, vice chair 1990-91), Jewish Mus. Md. (bd. dirs. 1999-2004), Beta Phi Mu. Democrat. Jewish. Home: 11041 Wood Elves Way Columbia MD 21044-1002 E-mail: swklein@comcast.net.

KLEIN, SHIRLEY SNYDERMAN, retail executive; b. Balt., Oct. 23, 1929; d. Julius Herman and Fannie (Dannenberg) Snyderman; m. Ralph Lincoln Klein, Jan. 4, 1953; children: Andrew P., Michael J., Howard S. BA, Towson State Tchr.'s Coll., 1951. Office staff accts. receivable, jr. controller Klein's Tower Plz., Inc., Forest Hill, Md., 1952-60, jr. buyer, 1960-70, v.p., buyer children's, ladies, linens, 1970—; chmn. Upper Chesapeake Health Found., 1993—2001; bd. mem. Upper Chesapeake Health Sys. (2 Hosp.), 1994. Treas. Mortgage Svc. Co., Inc., 1956—64; v.p. Klein's Supermarkets, 1979—, Colgate Investments, 1970—. Pres. Hadassah Harford County, 1966-68; v.p.;. adv. bd. John Carroll Sch., Md. Diocese, 1967, bd. mem., 1970; chmn. Retinitis Pigmentosa Found., Harford County, Md., 1971; bd. dirs. Harford Opera Theatre Guild, 1976-79; treas. Harford County Commn. for Women, 1977-82; v.p. Jewish Nat. Fund., Balt., 1990-95, bd. dirs., 1993-2000; vice chair Israel Bonds Balt., 1980-97. Recipient Goldie Myeir award, 1996. Mem.: LWV. Home: 109 W Jarrettsville Rd Forest Hill MD 21050-1319 Office: 2101 Rockspring Road Forest Hill MD 21050 Fax: 410-838-5592.

KLEIN, SOPHIA H., entrepreneur; b. Dayton, Ohio, Aug. 17, 1915; d. Felix Frank Borkowski, Helen Marie Sichujainska; children: Helen Marie, Betty Jean. Owner Oak Hill Optical, Dayton, Town & Country Water Softener, Dayton, Klein Enterprises, Dayton, Country Squire Supper Club, Dayton, Bagel Connection, Dayton, Exquisitely Yours Jewelers, Dayton. Initiator rosary ministry various chs. worldwide; program creator Radio Rosary Hour Sta. WGXM-FM; promoter Pope John Paul II Cultural Ctr., Washington, 2000. Mem.: Dayton Cath. Bus. Women's Club (pres., Dayton Woman of Yr. 1988), Holy Seplecher (Lady of the Cross 1987—, U.S. Rep. Millennium visit to Vatican 2000). Democrat. Roman Catholic. Avocation: golf. Home: 4542 Cooper Rd Cincinnati OH 45242-5617

KLEIN, SUSAN ELAINE, librarian; b. Cedar Falls, Iowa, Aug. 5, 1952; d. Elmo Calvin and Mabel Audrey (Taylor) Boone; m. Richard Joseph Klein II, Oct. 16, 1982; children: Michael Joseph, Christopher James. BA, U. No. Iowa, 1974. Reporter The No. Iowan, Cedar Falls, summer 1972; res. desk clk. U. No. Iowa Libr., Cedar Falls, summer 1974; paralegal for migrant action program VISTA, Muscatine, Iowa, 1975-76; office asst. Cedar Falls Pub. Libr., 1976-77, libr. asst., 1977—79, cataloger, 1978-86, libr. asst., 1986-87, young adult libr., 1988—. Mem. Iowa Libr. Assn. (cert.). Democrat. Avocations: cooking, bicycling, gardening, canoeing, reading.

KLEIN, VIRGINIA SUE, psychotherapist; b. Liberty, N.Y., Dec. 30, 1936; d. Abe and Lillian (Malin) Levine; m. Andrew Klein, Mar. 29, 1959; children: Earl Saul, Holly Jo. BS, Rutgers U., 1972, MSW, 1974, PhD, 1978. Lic. psychotherapist, clin. social worker, N.J. Psychotherapist N.J. Correctional Inst. for Women, Clinton, 1973-75; pvt. practice Somerville, N.J., 1974—. Prodr., host cable TV shows and series, including Growing Up in the 80's, 1986-88, Through the Looking Glass, 1988—; radio show host, presenter seminars and tng. programs; lectr., cons. in field; co-founder, chmn. interna. confs. on incest and related problems; co-founder Internat. Network Against Incest and Child Sexual Abuse; co-dir. The Tng. Inst., Switzerland, 18 yrs. of tng. profls. in Switzerland, 1989, 90. Author: How to Get Free!, 1985, Bad Mad Boy, Honey Bear, and the Magic, Waterfall (A Continuing Family Story), 1986, I-am, Pa-pah and Ma-me, 1986. Mem. NASW, Acad. Cert. Social Workers, Am. Inst. Counseling and Psychotherapy (diplomate). Home and Office: 18 S Cadillac Dr Somerville NJ 08876-1732

KLEINER, DIANA ELIZABETH EDELMAN, art historian, educator, academic administrator; b. NYC, Sept. 18, 1947; d. Morton Henry and Hilda Rachel (Wyner) Edelman; m. Fred S. Kleiner, Dec. 22, 1972; 1 child, Alexander Mark. BA magna cum laude, Smith Coll., 1969; MA, MPhil, Columbia U., 1970, 74, PhD, 1976; MA (hon.), Yale U., 1989. Lectr., asst. prof. U. Va., Charlottesville, 1975-76, 76-78; vis. asst. prof. U. Mass., Boston, 1979; Mellon faculty fellow Harvard U., Cambridge, Mass., 1979-80; asst. prof. Yale U., New Haven, 1980-82, assoc. prof., 1982-89, fellow Whitney Humanities Ctr., 1984—87, master Pierson Coll., 1986—87, dir. grad. studies dept. history of art, 1988-90, prof. history of art and classics, 1989-95, dir. grad. studies dept. classics, 1991-94, chair dept. classics, 1994-95, Dunham prof. classics and history of art, 1995—, dep. provost for the arts, 1995—2003, prin. investigator open ednl. resources video lectr. project, 2006—; liason Faculty Programs, AllLearn, 2001—06. Adv. bd. Archaeol. News, Tallahassee, 1980-2000, Am. Jour. Archaeology, Boston, 1985-98; chair program for ann. meetings com. Archaeol. Inst. Am., Boston, 1988-93. Author: Roman Group Portraiture, 1977, The Monument of Philopappos in Athens, 1983, Roman Imperial Funerary Altars with Portraits, 1987, Roman Sculpture, 1992, paperback edit., 1994, Cleopatra and Rome, 2005; editor: I, Clavdia: Women in Ancient Rome, 1996, I Clavdia II: Women in Roman Art and Society, 2000. Bd. dirs. Westville Cmty. Nursery Sch., New Haven, 1989-90, Foote Sch., New Haven, 1994-2000; regional rep. Deerfield (Mass.) Acad., 2001-06, parent's com., 2002-04, trustee, 2004-. Grantee Am. Coun. Learned Socs., 1979, NEH, 1980, 95, Am. Philos. Soc. 1982, John Paul Getty Trust, 1992, William and Flora Hewlett Found., 2006—. Mem. Archaeol. Inst. Am., Coll. Art Assn. Home: 102 Rimmon Rd Woodbridge CT 06525-1941 Office Phone: 203-432-2673. Business E-Mail: diana.kleiner@yale.edu.

KLEINER, HEATHER SMITH, retired academic administrator; b. N.Y.C., Mar. 31, 1940; d. Henry Lee Smith and Marie (Ballou) Edwards; m. Scott Alter Kleiner, Mar. 20, 1961; children: Greta (dec.), Catherine. BA in Sociology, Smith Coll., 1961; MAT in Edn., Lynchburg Coll., 1969; postgrad., U. Ga., 1974-82. Rsch. analyst Edward Weiss Advt., Chgo., 1963-65; acad. advisor U. Ga. Coll. Arts and Scis., Athens, 1982-88; asst. dir. womens studies program U. Ga., Athens, 1988-90, assoc. dir. womens studies program, 1990-2000. Co-founder, 1st pres. Jeannette Rankin Found., Athens, 1976-77, bd. dirs., hon. dir., 1977—, chair capital fund drive 1993-96; trustee Unitarian Universalist Fellowship of Athens, Ga., 2003-06. Mem.: LWV, AAUW, Jeannette Rankin Found. Avocations: reading, swimming.

KLEINER, MADELEINE A., lawyer; b. 1951; Graduate, Cornell U.; JD, Yale Law Sch. Clk. to Hon. William P. Gray U.S. Dist. Ct. for Ctrl. Dist. of Calif.; assoc. Gibson, Dunn and Crutcher, L.A., 1977—83, ptnr., 1983—95; sr. exec. v.p., chief adminstrv. officer, gen. counsel H.F. Ahmanson & Co., 1995—2001; exec. v.p., gen. counsel, corp. sec. Hilton Hotels Corp., Beverly Hills, Calif., 2001—. Bd. advisors UCLA Med. Ctr. Asst. sec. Performing Arts Coun., L.A. Music Ctr. Office: Hilton Hotels Corp 9336 Civic Ctr Dr Beverly Hills CA 90210

KLEINHENZ, NANCY ALISON, medical/surgical nurse; b. Dayton, Ohio, Mar. 10, 1960; d. William G. and Thelma J. Reeves. Diploma in nursing, Miami Valley Hosp., Dayton, 1982; BSN, U. Phoenix, 2004. RN, Ohio. Med.-surg. nurse Miami Valley Hosp., 2000—02; home care nurse, infusion nurse, 2002—04; pediatric nurse Physician's Office, 2004—.

KLEINLEIN, KATHY LYNN, training and development executive; b. S.I., NY, May 2, 1950; d. Thomas and Helen Mary (O'Reilly) Perricone; m. Kenneth Robert Kleinlein, Oct. 30, 1983. BA, Wagner Coll., 1971, MA, 1974; MBA, Rutgers U., 1984; MA in Theology, Barry U., 1998; EdD, Grad. Theol. Found., 2004. Cert. secondary tchr., N.Y., N.J., Fla. Tchr. English N.Y.C. Bd. Edn., S.I., 1971-74, Matawan (N.J.) Bd. Edn., 1974-79; instr. English

Middlesex County Coll., Edison, NJ, 1978-81; med. sales rep. Pfizer/Roerig, Bklyn., 1979-81, mgr. tng. ops. N.Y.C., 1981-86; dir. sales tng. Winthrop Pharms. divsn. Sterling Drug, N.Y.C., 1986-87; dir. tng. Reuters Info. Sys., NYC, 1987—90; pres., dir. tng. Women in Transition, 1990—98; pastoral min., dir. religious edn. St. Raphael's Ch., 1998—2001; diocesan dir. catechetical ministry Diocese of Venice, Fla., 2001—. Pres. Kleinlein Cons.; pers. mgmt. officer USAR, NJ, 1981-86; cons. Concepts & Prodrs., NYC, 1981-85; bd. regents Blessed Edmund Rice Sch. for Pastoral Ministry; bd. dirs. Campaign for Human Devel. Trainer United Way, 1982-83, polit. action com., 1982—85; mem. Rep. Presdl. Task Force, Washington, 1983—; chair Sarasota Library Adv. Bd.; sec. Intracoastal Civic Assn.; reinventing govt. coun. Sarasota County Planning Commn., exec. bd. Edn. Found., St. Joseph Bon Secours Hosp.; grievance com. Fla. Bar; bd. regents Blessed Edmund Rice Sch. for Pastoral Ministry. Mem. Sarasota County Sch. Bd., 2002—. Capt. U.S. Army, 1974—78. First woman in N.Y. N.G., 1974; first woman instr. Empire State Mil. Acad., Peekskill, N.Y., 1976. Mem.: Sarasota Women's Alliance, Rep. Women's Club, Alpha Omicron Pi. Republican. Roman Catholic. Office: Diocese Venice Cath Ctr 1000 Pinebrook Rd Venice FL 34292 Office Phone: 941-484-9543. Business E-Mail: kleinlein@dioceseofvenice.org.

KLEINMAN, NOELA MACGINN, family nurse practitioner; b. Mar. 17, 1961; m. Andrew Y. Kleinman, June 8, 2003. BSN, SUNY, Stony Brook, 1983, MS, Nurse Practitioner, 1989. RN, N.Y., 1983; cert. family nurse practitioner, N.Y., 1989, Am. Bd. Occupl. Health Nurse, 1994, Am. Acad. Nurse Practitioners, 1995, ANA family nurse practitioner, 1993. Occupl. health nurse practitioner L.I. Jewish Med. Ctr., Lake Success, NY, 1989-93; clin. mgr. for employee health NYU Med. Ctr., 1993-96; dir. Sound Shore Health Sys., New Rochelle, NY, 1996-99; nurse practitioner, officer Med. Dept. J.P. Morgan Chase, N.Y.C., 1999—2002; cosmetic nurse practitioner Dr. Andrew Kleinman Plastic Surgery Practice, Westchester, NY, 1998—; skincare practitioner SkinKlinic, N.Y.C., 2002—03; nurse practitioner, health ctr. mgr. CHD Meridan, 2003—04. Home: 257 Weaver St Apt 4D Greenwich CT 06831 Office Phone: 914-632-8500.

KLEIN-SCHEER, CATHY ANN, social worker; b. Hicksville, N.Y., Jan. 23, 1951; d. Louis and Dorothy (Levine) Klein; m. Barry Scheer, Oct. 23, 1983; 1 child, Danielle. AA, Nassau Community Coll., Garden City, N.Y., 1971; BSW, SUNY, Buffalo, 1973, MSW, 1976. Cert. social worker R-ACSW; diplomate Register Clin. Social Work. Coord. vol. svcs. Erie County Rehab. Ctr., 1972-73; alcoholism cons. Buffalo Gen. Hosp. Community Mental Health Ctr., 1976-77; psychiat. social worker Pilgram State Hosp., 1978; asst. coord. Plainview Rehab. Ctr. Family Svcs., 1978-79; psychiat. social work Beth Israel Med. Ctr., 1979-86; pvt. practice Kew Gardens, N.Y., 1984—, Croton-on-Hudson, N.Y., 1994—. Mem.: NASW. Office: 80-59 Lefferts Blvd Kew Gardens NY 11415-1715 also: 40 Irving Ave Croton On Hudson NY 10520-2644 Office Phone: 914-271-1369. E-mail: cathycsw@bestweb.net.

KLEJNOT, GETHA JEAN, school nurse practitioner, music educator; b. Stroudsburg, Pa., July 28, 1950; d. Robert Roger and Betty Wilson Snyder; m. Gerald Francis Klejnot, Sr., Feb. 14, 1986 (div. Apr. 2, 1998); 1 child, Andrew Robert. AA in nursing, C.C. Balt., 1976; MusB, Peabody Conservatory, 1980. RN Md., 1976, CPR, Am. Heart Assn., 1976. Oncology and bone marrow transplant nurse Johns Hopkins Hosp., Balt., 1976—80; head nurse Balt. City Hospitals, 1980—84; home health nurse Bay Area Home Health, Annapolis, 1984—85; icu-ccu nurse SRT Med Staff, Balt.; pvt. piano tchr. for large studio Annapolis, 1987—; sch. health nurse Anne Arundel County Health Dept, 1995—. Tchg. asst. pre-sch. music theory Eastman Sch. Music, U. Rochester, NY, 1968—70. Mem.: Nat. Guild Piano Tchrs. Achievements include Piano study with Maria Luisa Faini, Julio Esteban, Alexander Paskanov; Harpsichord study with Shirley Matthews; Piano pedagogy with Tinka Knopf; Master classes with Eugene List and Ignor Kipnis. Avocation: kayaking. Home: 1217 Plateau Pl Annapolis MD 21401 Office Phone: 410-222-7134. Personal E-mail: gesny@comcast.net.

KLEMENT, DIANE, retired educational assistant; b. Bronx, N.Y., Feb. 24, 1945; d. James Teller and Hilda (Artiano) Wright; m. Robert Francis Klement, Jan. 23, 1943; children: Debora Suzanne, James Robert. Student, Fairleigh Dickinson U., 1962-64. Tchr. aide Riverhead (N.Y.) Sch. Dist., 1976—. Pres., mem. Wildwood Acres Homeowners Assn., 1980-82, Wading River Fire Dept. Aux., 1979-81. Mem. Suffolk Ednl. Assn. (del. local 870 1989-92, v.p. 1992-95, pres. 1995—), Civil Svc. Employees Assn. (pres. Riverhead aides 1976-98; co-chairperson sch. dist. com. L.I. region I 1998—; mem. sch. rep. polit. action com. 1995-98, sen. liaison 1995—). Avocations: travel, boating, camping. Office: Civil Svc Employees Assn Suffolk Edn Local 870 1731D N Ocean Ave Medford NY 11763-2649

KLEMENT, VERA, artist; b. Gdansk, Dec. 14, 1929; d. Klement and Rose (Rakovchik) Shapiro; divorced; 1 son, Max Klement Shapey. Cert. in fine arts, Cooper Union Sch. Art and Architecture, 1950. Prof. art U. Chgo., 1969—95. Residency and stipend Camargo Found., Cassis, France. One woman shows include RoKo Gallery, N.Y.C., 1958, 60, Bridge Gallery, N.Y.C., 1965, Artemisia Gallery, Chgo., 1974, Chicago Gallery, 1976, Marianne Deson Gallery, 1979, 81, Goethe Inst., 1981, CDS Gallery, N.Y.C., 1981, 84, Roy Boyd Gallery, Chgo., 1983, 85, 87, 89, 90, 91, 92, 93, Spertus Mus., Chgo., 1987, retrospective exhbn., 1953-86, Renaissance Soc., Chgo., 1987, Brody's Gallery, Washington, 1992, Fassbender Gallery, Chgo., 1994, 95, 96, 97, Chgo. Cultural Ctr., 1999, retrospective exhbn., 1965-99, Fassbender, 1999, 2001, Ft. Wayne (Ind.) Mus. Art, 2001, Block Mus., Northwestern U., Evanston, Ill., 2001, U. Ariz. Mus. Art, Tucson, 2001, Tarble Arts Ctr., Ea. Ill. U., Charleston, 2002, Brauer Art Mus., Valparaiso (Ind.) U., 2002, Eric Yake Kenagy Gallery, Goshen (Ind.) Coll., 2003, Miami U. Mus. Art, Oxford, Ohio, 2004, Maya Polsky Gallery, Chgo., 2004, Frederick Baker, Chgo. 2004, Printworks, Chgo., 2004, Daum Mus. Contemporary Art, Sedalia, Mo., 2004, DCS Gallery, N.Y.C., 2005; group shows include Mus. Modern Art, N.Y.C., 1954, 55, Bklyn. Mus., 1950-60, Dallas Mus. Fine Arts, 1954, Tate Gallery, London, 1956, Museo de Arte Moderno, Barcelona, Spain, 1955, Musee d'Arte Moderne, Paris, 1955, U. Ky., 1959, Art Inst. Chgo., 1967, Walker Art Ctr., Mpls., 1977, U. Mo., 1978, Detroit Inst. Arts, 1978, Ukrainian Inst. Art, Chgo., 1978, Jewish Mus., N.Y.C., 1982, Kunstverein, Munich, Germany, 1987, Amerika Haus, Berlin, 1987, Terra Mus. Am. Art, Chgo., 1988, Corcoran Gallery, Washington, 1994, Cultural Ctr., Chgo., 1994, former IBM Gallery, N.Y.C., 1995, Virginia Beach Ctr. Arts, 1995, Fischer Art Gallery U. So. Calif., 1995, Portland (Oreg.) Mus. Art, Evanston Art Ctr., Mus. Contemporary Art, Chgo., 1996, Block Gallery Northwestern U., Evanston, 1996, Riva Yares Gallery, Santa Fe, 2002, Klein Artworks, Chgo., 2002, Maya Polsky Gallery, Chgo., 2002; represented in permanent collections Mus. Modern Art, N.Y.C., Phila. Mus. Art, Print Club, Phila., Ill. State Mus., Springfield, U. Tex., Nat. Mus. Am. Art, Washington, Jewish Mus., N.Y.C., Art Inst. Chgo., Philip Morris, N.Y.C., Smart Mus. U. Chgo., Sch. Social Svc. Adminstrn. U. Chgo., Mus. Contemporary Art, Chgo., Mary and Leigh Block Gallery, Evanston. Mus. Art U. Ariz., Tucson, Union Club League Chgo., Daum Mus. Contemporary Art, Sedalia, Mo., Kresge Mus. Art, East Lansing, Mich., U. Miami Mus. Art, Oxford, Ohio; also pvt. collections. Recipient Pollock/Krasner Found. award, 1998; Louis Comfort Tiffany Found. fellow, 1954, Guggenheim fellow, 1981-82, Nat. Endowment for the Arts fellow, 1987; Ill. Arts Coun. grantee, 1988. Personal E-mail: veraklement@aol.com.

KLEMP, NANCY JEAN, secondary school educator; b. Leavenworth, Kans., Aug. 29, 1943; d. Michael L. and Clara I. (Kochanowski) Buselt; m. Louis A. Klemp; children: Louis III, Jeffrey C., Jennifer R. BA, St. Mary Coll., Leavenworth, 1965; M, Webster U. Cert. secondary sch. tchr., Kans. Biology tchr. Unified Sch. Dist. 453, Leavenworth, 1988—, chair high sch. sci. dept. Sec., treas. Storage Box, Inc., Leavenworth, 1976—. Mem. St. John's Hosp. Guild; vol. mgr. C.W. PArker Carousl Mus. Gift Shop; nat. trustee Loyal Christian Benefit Assn.; bd. mem. U. St. Mary. Mem. LNEA, Ladies' C. of C. Republican. Roman Catholic. Avocations: country carving, sewing, gardening. Home: 1816 Pine Ridge Dr Leavenworth KS 66048-5416 Office: Storage Box Inc 1314 Eisenhower Rd Leavenworth KS 66048-5601

KLENK, CHRISTINE, athletic trainer, educator; b. Phila., Pa., Jan. 16, 1968; d. Vincent and Josephine Bocchinfuso; m. Shawn Thomas Klenk, July 31; children: Taylor, Jessie, Maxwell. BS, Temple U., Phila., 1990, MEd, 1993. Athletic trainer NovaCare, Phila., 1993—99, Washington Twp. HS, Sewell, NJ, 2000—02, Richard Stockton Coll., Pomona, NJ, 2002—. Adj. prof. Rowan U., Glassboro, NY, 2002—. Home: 102 Rex Rd Somerdale NJ 08083-2024

KLENKE, DEBORAH ANN, band and choral director, department chairman; b. Oak Park, Ill., May 20, 1958; d. Myron and Rita Frances Joshel; children: S. Joel, Jeremy. BS, Elmhurst Coll., 1986. Dir. music, dept. chmn. Faith Christian Elem.- Jr. HS, Geneva, Ill., 1987—2003; dir. bands St. Peter Sch., Geneva, Ill., 1991—99. Prin. flutist West Suburban Symphony, Hinsdale, 1991—2003; freelance flutist. Mem.: Ill. Grade Sch. Music Assn., Ill. Music Educators Assn., Chgo. Flute Club. Office: Faith Christian Elem - Jr HS 1745 Kaneville Rd Geneva IL 60134 Personal E-mail: debklenke@yahoo.com.

KLEPPER, ELIZABETH LEE, retired physiologist; b. Memphis, Mar. 8, 1936; d. George Madden and Margaret Elizabeth (Lee) K. BA, Vanderbilt U., 1958; MA, Duke U., 1963, PhD, 1966. Rsch. scientist Commonwealth Sci. and Indsl. Rsch. Orgn., Griffith, Australia, 1966-68, Battelle Northwest Lab., Richland, Wash., 1972-76; asst. prof. Auburn U., Ala., 1968-72; plant physiologist USDA Agrl. Rsch. Svc., Pendleton, Oreg., 1976-85, rsch. leader, 1985-96; ret., 1996. Assoc. editor Crop Sci., 1977-80, 88-90, tech. editor, 1990-92, editor, 1992-95; mem. editl. bd. Plant Physiology, 1977-92, Irrigation Sci., 1987-92; mem. editl. adv. bd. Field Crops Rsch., 1983-91; contbr. articles to profl. jours., chpts. to books. Mem. Umatilla Basin Watershed Coun., 2005—. Marshall scholar Brit. Govt., 1958-59; NSF fellow, 1964-66; Recipient First Citizen award, Pendleton, 2005, White Rose award, March of Dimes, Portland, 2005. Fellow: AAAS, Am. Soc. Agronomy (monograph com. 1983—90, bd. dirs. 1995—98), Soil Sci. Soc. Am. (fellows com. 1986—88), Crop Sci. Soc. Am. (fellows com. 1989—91, pres.-elect 1995—96, pres. 1996—97, Monsanto Disting. Career award 2004); mem.: Agronomic Sci. Found. (bd. dirs. 1993—99), Sigma Xi. Home: 1454 SW 45th Pendleton OR 97801 E-mail: klepperb@uci.net.

KLESTZICK, BARBARA R., social worker, educator; d. Meyer and Nora Rosenshein Klestzick; m. Lew Cohn, June 28, 1987; 1 child, Benjamin Moshe Cohn. BA, SUNY, Albany, 1969—73; MA, George Wash. U., DC, 1977—79; MSW, Va. Comonwealth U., Richmond, 1988—90. Cert. in brief psychotherapy DC, 1985. Family asst. NYC Bd. Ed., 1973—74; farmer, head soc. com., work organizer Kibbutz Gezer, Israel, 1974—76; project dir. Urban Sci. & Ednl. Rsch., DC, 1977—80; counselor, cmty. ed. coord., dir. counseling DC Rape Crisis Ctr., 1979—88; edn. dir. Temple Micah Religious Sch., DC, 1979—96; faculty Shepherd Pratt Hosp., Balt., 1989—91; substitute tchr., counselor Gesher Jewish Day Sch., Fairfax, Va., 1996—2005; presch. tchr. Keshet Child Devel. Ctr., Alexandria, Va., 2004—. Cons. DC Rape Crisis Ctr., 1988—89, Informatics Sys., DC, 1988—90; mem. adv. com. Arlington Bd. Ed., Va., 2003—04. Contbr. articles to profl. jours. Fundraiser Avon Breast Cancer, DC, 2000—01; child's rights worker Alexandria CASA, 1996—97; fundraiser AIDS Marathon, DC, 2006. Recipient Player of Yr. award, Arlington County Women's Soccer Assn., 1985; grantee Nat. Merit Scholarship Letter of Commendation award, NMSQT, 1969; scholar Regents Scholarship award, NYS, 1969—73. Mem.: Agudas Achim Congregation (assoc.; mem. ship v.p. 2001—03). Avocations: soccer, reading, yoga, hiking, bicycling. Home: 1121 S 18th St Arlington VA 22202

KLEVEN, LAURA, science educator; d. Janet Kreutter; m. Dennis Kleven, Aug. 3, 2002; 1 child, Brandon. MA in Tchg. Sci., Minn. State U., Mankato. Tchr. sci. Johnson H.S., St. Paul, 2000—. Grantee, Ecolab, 2001—04, 2006. Office Phone: 651-293-8890.

KLEVEN, MARGUERITE, state legislator; Mem. S.D. Senate from 29th dist., Pierre, 1995—; mem. appropriations com., chmn. govt. ops. and audit com. S.D. Senate, Pierre. Republican.

KLIEBHAN, SISTER M(ARY) CAMILLE, academic administrator; b. Milw., Apr. 4, 1923; d. Alfred Sebastian and Mae Eileen (McNamara) K. Student, Cardinal Stritch Coll., Milw., 1945-48; BA, Cath. Sisters Coll., Washington, 1949; MA, Cath. U. Am., 1951, PhD, 1955. Joined Sisters of St. Francis of Assisi, Roman Catholic Ch., 1945; legal sec. Spence and Hanley (attys.), Milw., 1941-45; instr. edn. Cardinal Stritch Coll., 1955-62, assoc. prof., 1962-68, prof., 1968—, head dept. edn., 1962-67, dean students, 1962-64, chmn. grad. div., 1964-69, v.p. for acad. and student affairs, 1969-74, pres., also bd. dirs., 1974-91, chancellor, 1991—. Mem. TEMPO, 1982—2001, bd. dirs., 1986—89; bd. govs. Wis. Policy Rsch. Inst., 1987—97; bd. dirs. Goals for Milw. 2000, 1980—83; treas. Wis. Found. Ind. Colls., 1974—79, 1987—90, v.p., 1979—81, pres., 1981—83; bd. dirs. DePaul Hosp., 1982—91, Sacred Heart Sch. Theology, 1983—2004, dir. emerita, 2004; bd. dirs. Viterbo Coll., 1990—98, Milw. Cath. Home, 1991—2001, St. Ann Ctr. for Intergenerational Care, 1991—99, Wis. Psychoanalytic Found., 1989—96, St. Coletta's of Mass., 1995—98, Internat. Inst. Wis., 1984—94, Milw. Achiever Program, Inc., 1983—2003, dir. emerita, 2004; bd. dirs. Franciscan Pilgrimage Programs, Inc., 1997—, Friends of Internat. Inst. Wis., 1994—, Mental Hea.th Assn. Milwaukee County, 1983—87, Pub. Policy Forum, 1987—90, Better Bus. Bur. of Wis., Inc., 1989—2001, YWCA Greater Milw., 1996—2001, St. Camillus Campus, 1996—2001, mem. adv. bd., 1989—96. Mem. Am. Psychol. Assn., Rotary Club of Milw. (v.p., pres. elect 1992-93, pres. 1993-94), St. Mary's Acad. Alumnae Assn., Phi Delta Kappa, Delta Epsilon Sigma, Psi Chi, Delta Kappa Gamma, Kappa Delta Pi. Business E-Mail: ckliebhan@stritch.edu.

KLIEMAN, RIKKI JO, lawyer, legal analyst; b. Chgo., May 13, 1948; d. Ben and Jeannette (Wiener) K.; m. Philip A. Brady, Sept. 20, 1987 (div.); m. William J. Bratton, April 30, 1999 BS, Northwestern U., Evanston, Ill., 1970; JD, Boston U., 1975. Bar: Mass. 1975, Colo. 1977, U.S. Dist. Ct. Mass. 1975, U.S. Ct. Appeals (1st cir.) 1976, U.S. Ct. Appeals (11th cir.) 1984. Law clk. to Hon. Walter J. Skinner U.S. Dist. Ct., Boston, 1975-76; asst. dist. atty. Middlesex County, Cambridge, Mass., 1977-79, Norfolk County, Dedham, Mass., 1979-81; assoc. Choate, Hall & Stewart, Boston, 1981-84; ptnr. Friedman & Atherton, Boston, 1984-89, Klieman & Lyons, Boston, 1989—94; of counsel Klieman, Lyons, Schindler & Gross (formerly Klieman & Lyons), Boston, 1994—; anchor Court-TV, 1994—2003, legal analyst, 2003—, The Today Show, 2003—. Instr. Bosto U. Sch. Law, 1977-79, 86-, tchr. Continuing Legal Edn., 1979—, adj. prof. Columbia Law Sch., 1996-2003 Author:(autobiography) Fairy Takes Can Come True-How A Driven Woman Changed Her Fate, 2003; Author/editor: Woman Trial Lawyers, 1987—; editor Mass. Lawyers Weekly, 1981-85; contbr. articles to profl. jours.; Film appearances include The Cable Guy, 1996, A Civil Action, 1998, 15 Minutes, 2001; TV appearances include The D.A., 2004, Dr. Vegas, 2004, Las Vegas, 2005, NYPD Blue, 2005; TV miniseries An American Tragedy, 2000 Exec. com. for civil rights Anti Defamation League, Boston, 1991—; dir., clk. Shepherd Ho., Boston, 1986—. Named One of Top Five Female Trial Attys. in U.S.A., Time Mag., 1983. Mem. ABA, Nat. Assn. of Criminal Def. Lawyers (bd. dirs. 1983-88), Boston Bar Assn., Mass. Bar Assn. (criminal justice coun. 1982-84), Women's Bar Assn., Mass. Assn. of Women Lawyers, Mass. Acad. of Trial Attys. Avocations: jogging, aerobics, theater, films. Office: Klieman Lyons Schindler & Gross 21 Custom House St Boston MA 02110

KLIMCZAK, JANICE BEVERLY, secondary school educator; b. New Britain, Conn., Jan. 25, 1944; d. Edward John and Mary Sophie (Knapp) Folcik; m. Joseph Clement Klimczak, Sept. 5, 1965 (dec.). BS, Cen. Conn. State Coll., 1965. Cert. elem. and secondary sci. tchr., Mass. Tchr. grades 7-8, Dracut, Mass., 1966—2006; ret., 2006. Cons. U. Lowell, Mass. Supt., tchr. Sunday Sch. St. Casimir's Ch., Lowell, 1965—, sec., 1968—, organist and dir. choir, 1981—. Horace Mann grantee State of Mass., 1986-88. Mem. NEA, Mass. Tchrs. Assn., Dracut Tchrs. Assn. Polish National Catholic. Avocations: reading, singing, playing organ, sewing. Home: 30 Longmeadow Dr Lowell MA 01852-3233

KLIMEK, KRISTEN M., physical therapist; d. John and Diane Klimek. M Phys. Therapy, St. Louis U., 2004. Intern Performance Bracing and Orthotics, St. Louis, 2001—04; phys. therapist Athletico, Chgo., 2005—. Mem.: Nat. Athletic Trainers Assn., Am. Phys. Therapy Assn. Office: Athletico 6255 W Archer Ave Chicago IL 60638 Office Phone: 773-284-6735.

KLIMLEY, NANCY E., volunteer; b. Chgo. d. William Peter and Flora (Sutherland) Enzweiler; m. Francis Joseph Klimley; children: Lisa, Brooks. BA, St. Mary's Coll., Notre Dame, Inc., 1951. Asst. fashion coord., dir. Carson Pirie Scott, Chgo.; asst. social dir. Lake Shore Club, Chgo., editor mag. Chmn. women's divsn. Chgo. Heart Assn., 1958—, pres. women's coun., 3 times. Bd. dirs. Chgo. Boys and Girls Club, 1970—, Brookfield Zoo, 1982—, Libr. of Internat. Rels., 1980-92, Northwestern U. Settlement, 1962-78, Great Lakes Hosp. League, 1962, Boy Scouts Am., 1965, Aides to the Handicapped, 1965, ARC, Mus. of Scis.; bd. dirs. Children's Home and Aid Soc., 3-time pres. woman's bd., sponsor parent bd. 1962—; bd. dirs. Fashion Group, treas., 1958; bd. dirs. Am. Opera Soc., 1962-76, Ill. Opera Guild, 1962-76, Artists Adv. Coun., 1970-80, Republican Women Vols., 1958; bd. dirs., mem. exec. com. USO, 1980—, benefit chmn. 5 years, founder, pres. woman's adv. bd.; founding mem., benefit chmn. Joffrey Ballet, vice chmn. emeritus of benefits; chmn., hon. chmn. The Consular Ball; hon. chmn. Lupus Found. Recipient Golden Heart award, Heart of Yr. award Am. Heart Assn., Fund Raising award Children's Home and Aid Soc., Golden Eagle award USO, others. Mem. Chgo. Hist. Soc., Guild of the Chgo. Hist. Soc., Antiquarians of the Art Inst. (life), Woman's Athletic Club (bd. dirs.), Saddle and Cycle Club. Republican. Roman Catholic. Avocations: antiques, collecting and reading books, world of fashion as an art form, interior decorating. Home: 860 N DeWitt Pl Apt 1007 Chicago IL 60611

KLINCK, CYNTHIA ANNE, library director; b. Salamanaca, NY, Nov. 1, 1948; d. William James and Marjorie Irene (Woodruff) K.; m. Andrew Clavert Humphries, Nov. 26, 1983. BS, Ball State U., 1970; MLS, U. Ky., 1976. Reference/ young adult libr. Bartholomew County Libr., Columbus, Ind., 1970-74; dir. Paul Sawyier Pub. Libr., Frankfort, Ky., 1974-78, Washington-Centerville Pub. Libr., Dayton, Ohio, 1978—. Libr. bldg. cons.; libr. cons., trainer OPLIN Task Force. Contbr. articles to profl. jours. Bd. dirs. Bluegrass Comty. Action Agy., Frankfort, Ky., 1971-73; founder, bd. dirs. FACTS, Inc., Frankfort, 1972-74; co-founder, bd. dirs. Seniors, Inc., Dayton, Ohio, 1980-81, 91—; trustee, officer South Comty., Inc. Mental Health Ctr., Dayton, 1980-89; pres. Miami Valley Librs.; govt. affairs com., ann. conf. planning com., fin. resources task force conf. presenter Ohio Libr. Coun.; program presenter Ohio Libr. Coun. Confs.; del. to Am. Libr. Assn. Congress on Profl. Edn.; mem. Create-The-Vision Cmty. Planning Task Force, com. chair. Named one of Dayton's Top Ten Women, Dayton Daily News, 2005; recipient Vol. of Yr., So. Metro Regional C. of C. Mem. ALA, Am. Soc. for Info. Sci., Am. Soc. for Pers. Adminstrn., Ohio Libr. Assn. (chmn. legis. com.), South Metro Regional C. of C. (exec. com., bd. dirs., chmn. edn. com., chair), Rotary (bd. dirs.), Pub. Libr. Assn. Mng. for Results (trainer). Office: Washington-Centerville Pub Libr 111 W Spring Valley Rd Dayton OH 45458-3761 Office Phone: 937-435-7375.

KLINE, CAROL MARLEIGH, editor, writer; d. Marcia Groch Norton and Roy Charles Kline. BA, U. So. Calif., LA, 1967; MA, Columbia U., N.Y.C., 1967. Tv anchor, talk show host Japan Cable TV, Tokyo, 1973—78; tv anchor WGHP-TV, High Point, NC, 1980—84; instr. U. NC, Greensboro, 1984—86, Wake Forest U., Winston/Salem, NC, 1985—86; writer, prodn. coord. Easton Hosp., Pa., 1988—92; pub. rels. assoc. Assn. for Childhood Edn. Internat., Olney, Md., 1993—97; program coord. The Smithsonian Assocs., Washington, 1996—97; jour. editor, dir. publs. Am. Chiropractic Assn., Arlington, 1997—. Tv cons. NHP, Washington, 1992—93. Prodr.: (md interviews for radio programming) Medical Update. Sponsor of Ugandan child's edn. Arlington Acad. of Hope, Va., 2001—; v.p. Homeowners' Assn., Falls Church, Va., 2002—04. Mem.: IONS. Office: Am Chiropractic Assn 1701 Clarendon Blvd Arlington VA 22209 Office Phone: 503-293-4343.

KLINE, KATY, museum director; Curator, coord. spl. projects List Visual Arts Ctr., MIT, Cambridge, dir., 1986—98, Bowdoin Coll. Mus. Art, Brunswick, Maine, 1998—. Review panelist Nat. Endowment for Arts, Inst. Mus. Svcs., Adolph and Esther Gottlieb Found.; juror Del. Art Mus. Biennial, Mid Atlantic Arts Found., RI Sch. Design Mus. Art, McKnight Found.; vis. com. Williams Coll. Mus. Art. Mem. City of Lowell's Pub. Art Adv. Bd. Recipient Gyorgy Kepes Fellowship Prize, 1995. Office: Bowdoin Coll Mus Art 9400 College Station Brunswick ME 04011

KLINE, KELLEY KNAPP, psychology professor; b. Phila., Pa d. Joseph Andrew and Diana Lynn Knapp; 1 child, Christopher John. BA, Richard Stockton Coll. NJ, Pomona, 1992; MA, SUNY, Stony Brook, 1995, PhD, 1998. Vis. asst. prof. U. Okla., Norman, 1998—99; adj. instr. Fla. State U., Tallahassee, 1999—2001, asst. prof. Panama City, 2002—. Faculty advisor Psychology Club, Panama City, 2003—, Pi Alpha Upsilon, Panama City, 2005—. Contbr. articles to profl. jours. Mem.: Assn. for Psychol. Sci. Lutheran. Avocations: reading, running, ice skating. Office: 4750 Collegiate Dr Panama City FL 32405

KLINE, LEONA RUTH, nurse, volunteer; b. Aliqurppa, Pa., May 21, 1920; d. Simon and Clara (Budnic) Hartstein; m. Jacob M. Kline (dec.); 1 child, Karen Sue Fox. BA, Pepperdine U., Calif., 1960. RN Montefiore Hosp. Sch. Nursing, Pitts., 1941. Pvt. nurse Hosp. and Homes; RN Office Dr. Jacob M. Kline, L.A., 1941—56. Vol. S.W. Health Ctr., 1957, asst. nurse, 66, 67. Editor monthly bulletins and so. area articles. Clerk Voting in LA, judge, inspector, precinct officer; founder Braille classes Temple; chairperson AE pri event PTA, 1967, pres. Hillcrest Dr. Elem. Sch., hon. life mem., Bluebird co-leader, editor paper; chairperson advanced gifts women's divsn. Jewish Fedn. Coun. LA, 1965, editor, 1967, pres. Crenshaw leaders, 1969; involved with Dem. Com.; v.p. B'Nai-Crenshaw Israel Sisterhood LA, mem. sch. bd.; mem. bd. Brentwood Westwood Symphony Orch., 1983—2005, pres., 1983—2005, Calif. Drs. Symphony Orch., 2004—05, mem. bd., 2004—05; bd. dirs. Diplomat, 1994—96. Avocations: painting, writing, poetry, interior decorating, knitting.

KLINE, MABLE CORNELIA PAGE, retired secondary school educator; b. Memphis, Aug. 20, 1928; d. George M. and Lillie (Davidson) Brown; 1 child, Gail Angela Page. Student, LeMoyne Coll.; BSEd, Wayne State U., 1948, postgrad. Tchr., Flint, Mich., 1950—51, Pontiac, Mich., 1953—62; tchr. 12th grade English Cass Tech. H.S., Detroit, 1962—95, coord. Study Skills program, mem. English book selection com., 1986—; ret., 1995. Mem.: ASCD, NEA (life), YWCA (life), NAACP (life), Nat. Coun. Tchrs. English, Am. Fedn. Tchrs., Sayne State U. Alumni Assn., Delta Sigma Theta. Episcopalian. Home: 555 Brush St Apt 1512 Detroit MI 48226-4354 Office: Cass Tech High Sch English Dept 2421 2d Ave Detroit MI 48201-2697

KLINE, MARGARET, chemistry professor; d. Frank M. and Shirley S. Kline. AB, U. Calif., Irvine, 1977; PhD, Brown U., Providence, 1982. Postdoctoral fellow U. Calif., Irvine, 1982—84; instr. Calif. State U., Long Beach, 1984—88; prof. Santa Monica Coll., 1988—. Named Chemistry Instr. of Yr., Calif. State U., Long Beach Undergraduate Chemistry Student Club, 1987. Mem.: Am. Chem. Soc. Avocation: horseback riding. Office: Santa Monica College 1900 Pico Blvd Santa Monica CA 90405 Office Phone: 310-434-4745. Business E-Mail: kline_peggy@smc.edu.

KLINE, NANCY MATTOON, librarian; b. Providence, Oct. 9, 1937; d. Donald Potter and Lillian Hortense (Groux) Mattoon; m. Kenneth Ernest Kline, June 20, 1959. BS, U. Conn., 1959, MS, 1961; MLS, U. R.I., 1973; PhD, U. Conn., 1994. Map libr. U. Conn. Libr., Storrs, 1970-79, dept. head, 1979-88, asst. to dir. libr., 1989-90, reference librarian, 1991-93, reference collection coord., 1993—, acting reference dept. head, 1995-96, library liaison, 2005—. Contbr. articles to profl. jours., 1973—. Bd. dirs. Mansfield (Conn.) Libr., 1978-83; libr. Mansfield Hist. Soc., 1969-79; com. mem. Planning for Year 2002, Mansfield, 1989-92 Mem. ALA, Spl. Librs. Assn. (assoc. editor bulletin 1973-77, editor 1976-79), Conn. Libr. Assn. (pres. 1980-81), Assn. Coll. and Rsch. Librs. (New Eng. chpt., chair collection devel. interest group 1995—), New Eng. Libr. Assn., Beta Phi Mu, Phi Kappa Phi, Phi Delta Kappa. Office: U Conn Libr 369 Fairfield Storrs Mansfield CT 06269-6016 Home: PO Box 577 Storrs Mansfield CT 06268-0577

KLINE, SHARON ELAINE, science educator; b. Norristown, Pa., July 10, 1955; d. Burnell Junior and Margaret Lucille Myers; m. Gerald Raymond Kline, June 9, 1979; 1 child, Natalie Rae. Bachelor's degree, Kutztown U., Pa., 1977; Master's degree, Arcadia U., Glenside, Pa., 1985; Doctorate, Immaculata U., Pa., 2002. Asst. dir. curriculum and supr. Bensalem (Pa.) Township Sch. Dist., 1977—. Prof. math. and sci. Holy Family U., Phila., 2004—, St. Joseph's U., Phila., 2006. Fundraiser Bristol (Pa.) Borough H.S., 2000—03. Mem.: Nat. Sci. Tchrs. Assn. Office: Bensalem Township Sch Dist 3000 Donallen Dr Bensalem PA 19020

KLINE, SUSAN ANDERSON, medical educator, internist; b. Dallas, June 4, 1937; d. Kenneth Kirby and Frances Annette (Demorest) Anderson; m. Edward Mahon Kline, Dec. 26, 1964 (dec. July 1990). BA, Ohio U., 1959; MD, Northwestern U., 1963. Diplomate Am. Bd. Internal Medicine, Nat. Bd. Med. Examiners (bd. dirs. 1977-81). Asst. physician NY Hosp., 1967—68, physician-to-outpatients, 1968—69, electrocardiographer, 1968—70, asst. attending physician, 1969—76, physician-in-charge cardiopulmonary lab., 1970—71, dir. adult cardiac catheterizaion lab., 1970—71, dir. adult cardiac catheterization lab., 1971—79, assoc. attending physician, 1976—85, emeritus attending physician, 1985—, emeritus dir. adult cardiac catheterization lab., 1985—; assoc. dean student affairs Cornell U. Med. Coll., NYC, 1974—78; assoc. dean admissions and student affairs Cornell Med. Sch., Ithaca, NY, 1978—80; mgr. occupl. med. programs GE Co., 1980—84; sr. assoc. dean student affairs NY Med. Coll., Valhalla, 1984—94, interim dean, v.p. med. affairs, 1994—96, exec. vice dean acad. affairs, vice provost univ. student affairs, 1996—. Mem. test com. Ednl. Commn. on Fgn. Med. Grads., Phila., 1985—92; mem. U.S. Med. Licensing Exam test accommodations com. Nat. Bd. Med. Examiners, Phila., 1992—97; chmn. unmatched student com. Nat. Residency Matching Program, 1998—2000, mem. exec. com., 2003—, chair second match com., 2003—05, pres.-elect, 2004—05, pres., 2005—06, chair nominating com., 2005—06, bd. dirs.; mem. Liaison Com. Med. Edn., 1998—2004, chair ad hoc subcom. rev. accreditation stds., 2000—01, exec. com., 2002—04, policy com., 2003—04; chmn. adv. com. Electronic Residency Application Svc., 1996—2001. Bd. visitors Coll. Arts, Ohio U., Athens, 1981—91; bd. dirs. Burke Rehab. Hosp., White Plains, 1997—2006. Recipient Leaders of the Future award, Nat. Coun. Women, N.Y.C., 1978, Cert. of Appreciation, Ohio U., 1978. Fellow: ACP, Am. Soc. Internal Medicine, Am. Coll. Cardiology; mem.: Phi Kappa Phi, Am. Assn. Med. Colls. (chmn. 1989—93, mem. sr. mgmt. adv. com. 2001—05, chmn. N.E. group on student affairs), N.Y. Cardiologists Soc., Am. Heart Assn. (fellow coun. on clin. cardiology), Cruising Club Am., Alpha Omega Alpha, Phi Beta Kappa. Avocation: sailing. Home: 561 Pequot Ave Southport CT 06490-1366 Office: NY Med Coll Sunshine Cottage Valhalla NY 10595 Office Phone: 914-594-4500. Personal E-mail: sakline@ahglobal.net. Business E-Mail: kline@nymc.edu.

KLINE, SYRIL LEVIN, writer, educator, educational consultant; b. Washington, Oct. 19, 1953; d. Irvin and Blanche Levin; children: Seth Adam Lessans, Jonathan Rafael Lessans; m. Peter Lee Kline, Dec. 28, 1989 BS, U. Md., 1975. Cert. integrative learning master facilitator, 1990. Tchr. Hebrew Washington Hebrew Congregation, 1974-80; sec., realtor Colquitt-Carruthers Inc., Montgomery County, Md., 1974-80; adminstrv. asst. Bd. Jewish Edn., Silver Spring, Md., 1980-81; tchr. presch. and kindergarten Children's Learning Ctr., Rockville, Md., 1982-89; curriculum designer, dir. integrative learning Nat. Acad. Integrative Learning, Rochester, NY, 1990-92; ednl. cons. Integra Learning Systems, South Bend, Ind., 1992—; free-lance radio and print writer South Bend, 1992—; tchr. Winchester Sch., Silver Spring, Md., 2005—. Ednl. cons. Integrative Learning Systems, Damascus, Md., 1988-89; ind. cons., course designer Prince George's County (Md.) Libr., 1989, North Syracuse (NY) Schs., 1989-92, Oswego (NY) Cmty. Schs., 1989-92, Xerox, Rochester, NY, 1990-92, Eastman Kodak, Rochester, 1990-92, Penn Yann (NY) Schs., 1991, Utica (NY) Schs., 1991, City of Rochester Schs., 1991, Bellcore, Elizabeth, NJ, 1991, Alliant Tech Sys., St. Paul, 1991, Paramus (NJ) Cmty. Schs., 1992, Govt. Can., 1992, Project Read, San Francisco, 1992, Sandia Labs, Santa Fe, 1992, City of Elkhart, Ind., 1992-94, Trinity Corp., Joliet, Ill., 1995, Scottsdale Mall, South Bend, 1995, Pathfinders, Plymouth, Ind., 1996; assessment designer Integra Learning Systems, 1995; asst. childrens program coord. Brookside Gardens, Wheaton, Md.; presenter in field Co-author: (novel) The Butterfly Dreams, 1998; featured commentator Sta. WVPE, 1995-98; columnist Action Line; soprano Ind. Opera North; author: The Changeling, 2003, 2d edit., 2005, The Fortunate Unhappy, 2003 Spkr., presenter Little Bear Child Abuse Prevention Program, Madison Ctr. Hosp., South Bend, 1993-95; vol. fundraiser Jewish Fedn. St. Joseph Valley, South Bend, 1995-96; mem. com., writer, presenter Holocaust Commemoration; actress, dir. Osceola Players, South Bend Civic Theatre, Victorian Lyric Opera Co.; cantorial soloist Temple Beth El, South Bend, 1997. Mem. Hadassah (life, corres. sec. 1994-95), Omicron Nu. Democrat. Office: 1404 Billman Ln Silver Spring MD 20902

KLINEFELTER, HYLDA CATHARINE, retired obstetrician, retired gynecologist; b. Gettysburg, Pa., Sept. 28, 1929; d. Roscoe Emanuel and Sara Catherine (Wagner) K.; m. Edward Ralph Kohnstam, June 18, 1955; children: Charles, Kathryn. Student, Gettysburg Coll., 1947-48; AB, U. Pa., 1951; MD, Med. Coll. Pa., 1955. Diplomate Am. Bd. Ob-Gyn. Rotating intern Phila. Gen. Hosp., 1955-56; resident in ob.-gyn. Presbyn. U. Pa. Med. Ctr., Phila., 1956-59; mem. teaching staff Med. Coll. Pa., Phila., 1959-62; staff ob-gyn. Riddle Meml. Hosp., 1962—99; rsch. asst. maternal and child health Pa. Hosp., Phila., 1964-66; co-supr. family planning clinic Presbyn. Hosp./U. Pa. Med. Ctr., 1967-68; ptnr. Media (Pa.) Clinic, 1969-81; pvt. practice, 1981-86; ptnr. Granite Run Ob.-Gyn. Assocs., Media, 1986—99; ret., 1999. Mem. staff Riddle Meml. Hosp., vice chmn. ob-gyn., 1989-93, chmn. ob-gyn., 1993-99. Contbr. articles to med. jours. Fellow ACOG; mem. AMA, Am. Med. Womens Assn. (past treas. dist. 25), Reproductive Medicine Assn., Am. Assn. Gyn. Laparoscopists, Internat. Soc. Gynecology Endoscopy, Delaware County Med. Soc., Pa. Med. Soc., Fox Valley Civic Assn., Soroptomist, Alpha Xi Delta. Republican. Lutheran. Avocations: singing, gardening, needlecrafts, painting. Home: 930 Hidden Hollow Dr Gap PA 17527-9562

KLINEFELTER, SARAH STEPHENS, retired dean, broadcast executive; b. Des Moines, Jan. 30, 1938; d. Edward John and Mary Ethel (Adams) Stephens; m. Neil Klinefelter. BA, Drake U., Des Moines, 1958; MA, U. Iowa, Iowa City, 1968; postgrad., Harvard U., Cambridge, Mass., 1984, U. Wis., 1987, Vanderbilt U., Nashville, Tenn., 1991-92. Chmn. humanities dept. High Sch. Dist. 230, Orland Pk., Ill., 1958-68; chmn. communications and humanities div. Kirkwood Community Coll., Cedar Rapids, Iowa, 1968-78; prof. English Sch. of the Ozarks, Point Lookout, Mo., 1978-86; gen. mgr. Sta. KSOZ-FM, Point Lookout, 1986-90; dean div. of performing and profl. arts Coll. of the Ozarks, Point Lookout, 1989-2001. Commr. Skaggs Cmty. Hosp., Branson, Mo., 1986—; chmn. Branson Planning and Zoning Commn., 1983; project dir. Mo. Humanities Bd.; commr., examiner North Cen. Assn. Higher Edn., 1978-85; commr. Iowa Humanities Bd., 1971-78; mem. Taney County Planning and Zoning Commn., 1989-98, 2005—; pres. Branson Arts Coun., 1997—2002; co-chair Taney County Bd. Adjustment; FDA noro-virus grant coord. Branson City Health Dept., 2003-04; Elderhostel instr. Ozark Adventures, 2001-06. Democrat. Presbyterian. Home: 182 Hensley Rd Forsyth MO 65653-5137 Personal E-mail: sarahk@tri-lakes.net. E-mail: klinefelter@centurytel.net.

KLING, JENNIFER RAE, music educator; b. Louisville, Ky., Mar. 11, 1972; d. Lawrence Ray and Pamela Sue Mills; m. Carl Andrew Kling, June 14, 2003; 1 child, Elizabeth Rae. B of Mus. Edn., Ind. U., Bloomington, 1995; MusM, U. Louisville, Ky., 1998. Band dir. Ctrl. Noble Cmty. Sch. Corp., Albion, Ind., 1995—96; asst. band dir. Charleston So. U., SC, 1998—99; band dir. Henry County Pub. Schs., New Castle, Ky., 1999—2001, Hardin County Schs., Elizabethtown, Ky., 2001—04, Bedford Cmty. Schs., Iowa, 2004—05, Maryville R-II Schs., Maryville, Mo., 2005—. Grad. tchg. asst. U. Louisville Sch. of Music, 1996—98; asst. clinic mgr. Ind. U. Summer Music Clinic, Bloomington, 1997—2004; travel escort Music Travel Consultants, Indpls., 1998—2004; staff instr. Louisville Male H.S. Band, 1999—2002; trumpet instr., Louisville, 1999—2004; staff mem. Ky. Ambs. of Music, Louisville, 2000; orch. dir. Floyd County Youth Orch., New Albany, Ind., 2000—02; trumpet instr. NW Mo. State U. Summer Band Camp, Maryville, 2005, band dir., 06. Musician (trumpet soloist): (performance) Concerto in E-Flat Major - Hummel (Concerto Competition winner U. Louisville Sch. of Music, 1997), My Old Kentucky Home - Goldman, A Trumpeter's Lullaby - Anderson, Let us Break Bread (Soloist with the Charleston So. U. Wind Ensemble, 1999). Recipient Young Artist award, Ball State U., 1990, scholarship, Ind. U. Summer Music Clinic, 1990, Divsn. I Concert Band Contest awards, Ind., Ky., Iowa, and Mo. State Music Orgns., 1995-2006, 1st pl. award Maryville Jazz Band, N.W. Mo. State U. Jazz Festival, 2006. Mem.: Nat. Band Assn., Mo. Music Educators' Assn., Mo. Bandmasters' Assn., Internat. Assn. of Jazz Educators. Office Phone: 660-562-4168. Personal E-mail: cakjrk03@earthlink.net.

KLING, PHRADIE (PHRADIE KLING GOLD), small business owner, educator; b. N.Y.C., July 2, 1933; d. Samuel A. and Mary Leah (Cohen) Kling; m. Lee M. Gold, Sept. 5, 1955 (div. 1976); children: Judith Eileen, Laura Susan, Stephen Samuel, James David. BA, Cornell U., 1955; MA in Human Genetics, Sarah Lawrence Coll., 1971. Genetic counselor assoc. Coll. Medicine and Dentistry N.J., Newark, 1970—73; assoc. genetic counselor Sarah Lawrence Coll., Bronxville, NY, 1970—73; genetic counselor N.Y. Fertility Rsch. Found., N.Y.C., 1971—73; staff assoc., genetic counselor depts. pediatrics, ob-gyn and neurology Columbia U. Coll. Physicians and Surgeons, N.Y.C., 1973—78; asst. in genetics St. Luke's Hosp. Ctr., N.Y.C., 1977—79; health program assoc. Conn. Dept. Health Svcs., Hartford, 1978—84; edn. cons. Conn. Traumatic Brain Injury Assn., Rocky Hill, 1984—85; office mgr. Anderson Turf Irrigation Inc., Plainville, Conn., 1986—92; owner, mgr. KlingWorks, contract adminstrn., Avon, Conn., 1992—. Spkr., instr. health and health ethics issues, Conn., NY, NJ, 1971—85; dir. confs. genetics and traumatic brain injury, 1980—85; project dir. ednl. field testing Biol. Scis. Curriculum Study, 1981—83; scientist AAAS Sci.-by-Mail, 1991—2000. Active Farmington River Watershed Assn., Simsbury, Conn., 1988—; docent Sci. Mus. Conn., West Hartford, 1989—90. Recipient citation for dedicated svc., Conn. Safety Belt Coalition, 1985. Mem.: Conn. Assn. Jungian Psychology (bd. dirs.), Bus. and Profl. Microcomputer Users Group (bd. dirs.), Am. Human Genetics Soc., Am. Mensa (chpt. coord. gifted children 1985—), Cornell Club Greater Hartford. Home and Office: 33 Hunter Rd Avon CT 06001-3618

KLINGER, GAIL GREAVES, art educator, illustrator; b. Evanston, Ill., Dec. 21, 1953; d. Harold and Darlene Peterson Greaves; m. Richard William Klinger, II, Aug. 14, 1976; children: Kimberly, Kurt, Kristen. BS in Edn. (cum laude), No. Ill. U., DeKalb, 1972—75; M, Nat. Louis U., Wheaton, Ill., 1991. K-12 art instr. Avon Cmty. Unit Dist. 176, Ill., 1976—79; 6-8 home mgmt. Oak Brook Sch. Dist. 53, 1979—83; 6-8 art instr. Butter Sch. Dist. 53, Oak Brook, 1979—. Arts & crafts instr., summer programs Elk Grove Village & Oak Brook Pk. Dists., Ill., 1968; art exhibit coord. Butter Sch. Dist. 43, 1976—, stage set designer, builder, 1976—2002, art club sponsor, 1976—2002, cheerleading coach, 1983—88, yearbook adv., 1981—92, Washington, D.C. trip coord. & planner, 1981—99. Book, Verses for Dad's Heart, 2004, Verse's for Mom's Heart, 2005. Troop leader Girl Scouts Am., Wheaton, 1995—2005; summer arts & crafts dir. Global Outreach, Wheaton Bible Ch., 2000—; mem. steering com. Friends of Elk Grove Village Pub. Libr., 1882—1984. Mem.: NEA, Soc. Children's Book Writers & Illustrators, Nat. Art Edn. Assn. Republican. Mem. Christian Ch. Avocations: scuba diving, gardening, interior decorating. Office: Butter Jr HS 2801 York Rd Oak Brook IL 60523-2334

KLINGER, MARILYN SYDNEY, lawyer; b. NYC, Aug. 14, 1953; d. Victor and Lillyan Judith Klinger. BS, U. Santa Clara, 1975; JD, U. Calif., Hastings, 1978. Bar: Calif. 1978. Assoc. Chickering & Gregory, San Francisco, 1978-81, Steefel, Levitt & Weiss, San Francisco, 1981-82, Sedgwick, Detert, Moran & Arnold, San Francisco and L.A., 1982-87, ptnr. San Francisco, 1988-98, L.A., 1998—. Guest lectr. Stanford U. Sch. Engring. Vol. atty. Lawyers Commn. on Urban Affairs, San Francisco, 1978-80. Mem. ABA (tort and ins. practice sect., chair surety and fidelity com. 2003-04, constrn. forum, pub. contracts sect.), Internat. Assn. Def. Counsel (chmn. fidelity and surety com. 1996-98), Nat. Bond Claims Assn. (spkr.), Surety Claims Inst. (spkr.), No. Calif. Surety Underwriters Assn., No. Calif. Surety Claims Assn. (lectr., pres. 1989-90), Surety Assn. L.A. (spkr.). Avocations: reading, hiking, golf. Home: 939 15th St # 10 Santa Monica CA 90403-3146 Office: Sedgwick Detert Moran & Arnold 801 S Figueroa St Fl 18 Los Angeles CA 90017-2573 Office Phone: 213-615-8038. Business E-Mail: marilyn.klinger@sdma.com.

KLINGER, SUSAN, art educator, artist; BS in Edn., Millersville U., 1979; MEd in Art Edn., Kutztown U., 1984. Cert. Instr. II Dept. Edn., Pa., 1983. Art tchr. Perkiomen Valley Sch. Dist., Collegeville, Pa., 1980—, art dept. chairperson, 1990—2004. Instr. Cabrini Coll., Radnor, 1992—93; affiliated artist Swarthmore (Pa.) Studio, 1992—, Hardcastle Gallery, Centreville, Del., 2003—. One-woman shows include Off the Wall Gallery, Skippack, Pa., Elaina Fine Art Gallery, Collegeville, Pa. Named one of Montgomery County's, Times Herald, 2000; recipient Lifetime Achievement award, Perkiomen Valley Sch. Dist. Found., 1995, cert. Spl. Congl. Recognition for Outstanding Svc. to Cmty., US Congress, 1995. Mem.: NEA, Pa. State Edn. Assn., Perkiomen Valley Art Ctr., Greater Norristown Art League (50th anniversary com. mem. 1990—91, bd. dirs. 1990—91), Phila./Tri State Artists Equity, Phila. Water Color Soc., Pa. Watercolor Soc., Md. Pastel Soc. (signature mem.).

KLINGHOFFER, JUDITH APTER, historian, consultant; b. Sept. 4, 1946; d. Abraham Apter and Rachel (Preisler) Basch; m. Arthur Jay Klinghoffer, May 18, 1969; 1 child, Joella. BA, Hebrew U., 1967; MA in Pub. History, Rutgers U., 1986, PhD in History, 1994. Pub. historian, Cherry Hill, 1986-90; asst. prof. Rowan U., Glassboro, N.J., 1991-92; staff mem. Ctr. Hist. Analysis, Rutgers U., New Brunswick, N.J., 1994-95; pres. Global Perspectives, Cherry Hill, 1997—. Vis. lectr. Beijing, China, 1992-93; Fulbright prof., Aarhus, Denmark, 1996. Co-author: Israel and the Soviet Union, 1985, International Citizens' Tribunals: Mobilizing Public Opinion to Advance Human Rights, 2002; author: The Citizen Planner, 1989, Vietnam, The Jews and The Middle East: Unintended Consequences, 1999; contbr. articles to profl. jours., to online jours. E-mail: klinghof@crab.rutgers.edu.

KLINGLER, GWENDOLYN WALBOLT, state representative; b. Toledo, May 28, 1944; d. L. Byron and Elizabeth (Brown) Walbolt; m. Walter Gerald Klingler, June 11, 1966; children: Kelly Michelle, Lance, Jeffrey. BA, Ohio Wesleyan U., 1966; MA, U. Mich., 1969; JD, George Washington U., 1981. Bar: Ill. Rsch. assoc. U. Mich., Ann Arbor, 1966-71; abstractor Year Book Med. Pub., Chgo., 1972-75; law clk. FDA, Rockville, Md., 1980; atty. Atty. Gen.'s Office State of Ill., Springfield, 1981-84, appellate prosecutor, 1984-92; ptnr. Boyle, Klingler & McClain, Springfield, 1992-95. Mem. Springfield Bd. of Edn., 1987-91, pres., 1988; alderman Springfield City Coun., 1991-95; Rep. Ill. Ho. of Reps., 100th Dist., 1995-2003. Recipient Woman of Achievement award in Govt., Women-in-Mgmt., 1994, Disting. Alumni award Leadership Springfield, 1996. Mem. AAUW, Cen. Ill. Women's Bar Assn. (chair membership com.), Sangamon County Bar Assn., Greater Springfield C. of C., Women-in-Mgmt. Republican. Presbyterian (elder). Home: 1600 Ruth Pl Springfield IL 62704-3362 E-mail: klingler@housegopmail.state.il.us.

KLINK, JOANN MARIE, clergywoman; b. Upper Sandusky, Ohio, Nov. 24, 1938; d. Ernest Robert and Hazel Fern (Snyder) Schilling; m. Joel Richard Klink, June 28, 1959; children: Brian Joel, Cara Lee. BS in Edn., Otterbein Coll., 1960; MA in Religious Studies, United Theol. Sem., New Brighton, Minn., 1984; postgrad., Shalem Inst. for Spiritual Formation, 1999; cert. completion, Christian Spiritual Guidance, 1999. Commd. min. United Ch. of Christ, 1980, cert. specialist in ch. edn. Tchr. math. Johnstown (Ohio) H.S., 1960, Worthington (Ohio) Jr. H.S., 1960-61; instr. math. Ohio No. U., Ada, 1961-63; tchr. math. Wis. State U. Campus Sch., Eau Claire, 1963-65; ch. educator 1st Congl. Ch., Eau Claire, 1972-84; coord. CANCE Sch. Christian Educators, Mpls., 1985-88; min. Christian nurture Nekoosa (Wis.) United Ch. of Christ, 1988-89; project coord. St. Bede Ctr., Eau Claire, 1993-94; coord. Spirit of Living Network, Eau Claire, 1995—2002. Spiritual dir., Eau Claire, 1996—, Labyrinth Advocacy Group, Eau Claire, 2002—, Eau Claire's Phoenix Pk. Labyrinth Project, 2004-05. Mem. adv. bd. Ctr. and Network for Christian Educators, Mpls., 1982-88; curriculum writer Wis. Conf., United Ch. of Christ, Madison, 1985-88. Former mem. human growth and devel. adv. com. Eau Claire Pub. Schs. Mem. AAUW (program chmn. 1973-75, pres. 1975-77, scholarship named in her honor 1997). Avocations: watercolor painting, birding, gardening, walking. Home and Office: 215 Corydon Rd Eau Claire WI 54701-5905 E-mail: klinkjr@uwec.edu.

KLINKE, LOUISE HOYT, volunteer; b. Rochester, N.Y., Nov. 16, 1933; d. Martin Breck Hoyt and Evelyn Louise Moone; children: Geoffrey P., David H., Debra L. Tice. AA, Rochester Bus. Inst., 1952. Dir. fin. and pers. Landmark Soc. Western N.Y., Rochester, 1965—85; ret., 1985. Vol. Landmark Soc. Preservation Issues Com., Nathaniel Rochester Soc., Rochester Inst. Tech., Arts and Cultural Coun. Devel. Com.; vol. chmn. Hillside's Bldg. Com.; mem. Meml. Art Gallery, Eastman House, Strong Mus., Nat. Trust for Hist. Preservation, Preservation League N.Y. State, Smithsonian Inst., Met. Mus., Rochester Area Cmty. Found.; treas. Rochester Contemporary; mem. adv. bd. MECA, 2005—; bd. dirs. Art Walk, Race and Reconciliation, Keuka Coll., 1982—, Hillside Children's Ctr., 1982—, treas.; former v.p. Hillside Children's Found.; bd. dirs. Women's Found. Genesee Valley, Rochester Hist. Soc., 1984—, former treas.; bd. dirs. Alzheimer's Assn., former treas.; bd. dirs. Pyramid Arts Ctr., former treas.; bd. dirs. Opera Theatre Rochester, treas.; former bd. dirs. Friends Eastman Opera; bd. dirs. Garth Fagan Dance, 2001—. Mem.: BOA, Geva Theatre Rochester City Ballet, Assn. Fund Raising Profls., Chatterbox Club. Democrat. Episcopalian. Home: 1400 East Ave #203 Rochester NY 14610 E-mail: weesie702@frontiernet.net.

KLINMAN, JUDITH POLLOCK, biochemist, educator; b. Phila., Apr. 17, 1941; d. Edward and Sylvia Pollock; m. Norman R. Klinman, July 3, 1963 (div. 1978); children: Andrew, Douglas. BA, U. Pa., 1962, PhD (hon.), 1966, degree (hon.), 2006; PhD (hon.), U. Uppsala, Sweden, 2000, U. Penna, 2006. Postdoctoral fellow Weizmann Inst. Sci., Rehovoth, Israel, 1966—67; postdoctoral assoc. Inst. Cancer Rsch., Phila., 1968—70, rsch. assoc., 1970—72, asst. mem., 1972—77, assoc. mem., 1977—78; asst. prof. biophysics U. Pa., Phila., 1974—78; assoc. prof. chemistry U. Calif., Berkeley, 1978—82, prof., 1982—, Miller prof., 1992, 2003—04, prof. molecular and cell biology, 1993—, chair chem. dept., 2000—03, Joel Hildebrand chair, 2002—03. Mem. ad hoc biochemistry and phys. biochemistry study sects. NIH, 1977—84, phys. biochemistry study sect., 1984—88. Mem. editl. bd.: Jour. Biol. Chemistry, 1979—84, Biofactors, 1991—98, European Jour. Biochemistry, 1991—95, Biochemistry, 1993—, Ann. Rev. Biochemistry, 1996—2000, Accts. Chem. Res., 1995—98, Current Opinion in Chemical Biology, 1997—, Chemical Record, 2000—, Advances in Physical Organic Chemistry, 2003—; contbr. articles to profl. jours. Fellow, NSF, 1964, NIH, 1964—66, Guggenheim, 1988—89. Mem.: NAS, Am. Philos. Soc., Am. Soc. Biochemistry and Molecular Biology (membership com. 1984—86, pub. affairs com. 1987—94, program com. 1995, pres.-elect 1997, pres. 1998, past pres. 1999), Am. Acad. Arts and Scis., Am. Chmn. Soc. (exec. coun. biol. divsn. 1982—85, chmn. nominating com. 1987—88, program chair 1991—92, Repligen award 1994, Remsen award 2005), Sigma Xi. Office: U Calif Dept Chemistry Berkeley CA 94720-0001 Office Phone: 510-642-2668.

KLOEPFER, MARGUERITE FONNESBECK, writer; b. Logan, Utah, Nov. 13, 1916; d. Leon and Jean (Brown) Fonnesbeck; m. Lynn William Kloepfer, Aug. 6, 1937; children: William Leon, Kenneth Lynn, Kathryn Kloepfer Ellis, Robert Alan. BS, Utah State U., 1937. Legal sec. Lynn W. Kloepfer, Atty., Ontario, Calif., 1958-74; freelance writer, novelist Ontario, Calif., 1974—. Author: (novels) Bentley, 1979, Singles Survival, 1979, But Where is Love, 1980, The Heart and the Scarab, 1981, Schatten in der Wuste, 1983, In A Pickle, 2003, Hope's Beat, 2003; contbr. short stories, articles. Pres. Foothill chpt. Nat. Charity League Inc., Ontario, 1965-67, nat. pres., 1968-70; pres. Interfraternity Mother's Clubs council U. So. Calif., Los Angeles, 1971-72. Clubs: Friday Afternoon (West San Bernardino County) (pres. 1986-87). Home: 306 E Hawthorne St Ontario CA 91764-1749

KLONOFF-COHEN, HILLARY SANDRA, epidemiologist; d. Harry and Mary Klonoff; m. Randy Earl Cohen, Aug. 31, 1981; 1 child, Auroraleigh Camillia Klonoff. BA in Psychology, U. B.C., Vancouver, 1976; MS in Biology, U. Bridgeport, 1985; PhD in Epidemiology, U. of NC, Chapel Hill, 1987. Cert.Human Nutrition U. of Bridgeport, Conn., 1984. Staff epidemiologist Eisenhower Med. Ctr., Rancho Mirage, Calif., 1988—89; prof. U. of Calif., San Diego, La Jolla, Calif., 1990—. Cons. San Bernardino County Med. Ctr., Calif., 1989—91, Infant Mortality Rev. Program Adv. Com., San Diego, 1994—96; com. mem. Office of Environ. Health Hazard Assessment, Devel. and Reproductive Toxicants Identification Com., Sacramento, 1999—; com. mem., sys. wide cancer rsch. coord. com. U. Calif. Office Pres., Calif., 1994—. Contbr. articles to med. and sci. jours. Recipient Career Devel. award, Calif. Tobacco-Related Disease Program, 1992—94; grantee Calif. Breast Cancer Rsch. Program, 2005—, U. of Calif. Acad. Senate award, 1996, Calif. Tobacco-Related Disease Rsch. Program. Supplemental Minority Tng. grant, 1993-1994, Calif. Tobacco-Related Disease Rsch. Program. New Investigator award, 1990-1992, EPA -Biomarkers for the Assessment of Exposure and Toxicity in Children — STAR award, 2003—, Calif. Tobacco-Related Disease Rsch. Program, 2003—, Save Our Children's Sights, Mobile Pre-school Eye Care, First Five Commn. of San Diego, 2003—05, Calif. Breast Cancer Rsch. Program. Translational Rsch. Collaboration award, 1999-2003, Calif. Tobacco-Related Disease Rsch. Program, 1998—2003, 1993-1999. Mem.: APHA, Soc. for Reproductive Endocrinology and Infertility, Am. Soc. for Reproductive Medicine, Pub. Health Alumni Assn. U. NC Chapel Hill, Assn. for Women in Sci., Soc. Epidemiologic Rsch., So. Calif. Pub. Health Assn. Office: Univ Calif San Diego Dept Family & Preventive Medicine 9500 Gilman Drive La Jolla CA 92093-0607 E-mail: hklonoffcohen@ucsd.edu.

KLONT, BARBARA ANNE, librarian; b. Eaton Rapids, Mich., May 8, 1944; BA in Elem. Edn., Mich. State U., 1966; MS in Libr. Sci., Wayne State U., 1971, postgrad., 1974, BA in Computer Sci., 1985. Reference libr. gen. info. dept. Detroit Pub. Libr., 1972-75, reference libr. sociology and econ. dept., 1976-79, reference libr. tech. and sci. dept., 1979-85, 1st asst. tech. and sci. dept., 1985-91, mgr. tech. and sci. dept., 1991—. Office: Detroit Pub Libr Tech and Sci Dept 5201 Woodward Ave Detroit MI 48202-4093

KLOPFLEISCH, STEPHANIE SQUANCE, social services agency administrator; m. Randall Klopfleisch; children: Elizabeth, Jennifer, Matthew BA, Pomona Coll., 1962; MSW, UCLA, 1966. Social worker L.A. County, 1963—67, program dir. day care, vol. svcs., 1968—71, divsn. chief children's svcs. Dept. Pub. Social Svcs., 1971—73, dir. bur. social svcs. Dept. Pub. Social Svcs., 1973—79, chief dep. dir. dept. cmty. svcs., 1980—96, dir., 1996—2001. With Area 10 Devel. Disabilities, 1981-82; bd. dirs. L.A. Fed. Emergency Mgmt. Act, 1985-91, pres., 1987; bd. dirs. L.A. Shelter Partnership, Pomona Coll. Assocs., 1988— Mem. Calif. Commn. Family Planning, 1976-79; chmn. L.A. Commn. Children's Instns., 1977-78; bd. dirs. United Way Info., 1978-79; chmn. L.A. County Internat. Yr. of Child Commn., 1978-79; bd. govs Sch. Social Welfare, UCLA, 1981-84; bd. dirs. Calif. Soc. Welfare Archives, 1999—, pres.2002—; mem. Brentwood Symphony, 1999—, bd. dirs., 2004; mem. L.A. Valley Symphony, 2004 Mem. NASW, L.A. Philharm. Affiliates, Soroptimist Internat. (bd. dirs., pres. L.A. chpt. 1993)

KLOS, SIOBHÁN LYDIA, theater director; d. Harold Alvin Klos and Edith Karinna O'Dwyer. B of Psychology, B of Speech and Theater, U. Wis., LaCrosse, 1984; Assoc. in Practical Theology, Christ for the Nations, Dallas, 1987. Exec. asst. Sal Anania Sheet Metal, LaCrosse, 1977—84; hostess, asst. mgr. Hyatt Hotels, Dallas, 1986—87; receptionist Greater Life Ch., North Dallas, Tex., 1988—90; candle carver Candles by Christy, Oakcliff, Tex., 1985—96; customer svc. profl. Sewell Village Cadillac, Dallas, 1990—93; exec. asst. Scott Hinkle Outreach Ministries, Dallas and Phoenix, 1993—96; prodn. dir. Phoenix 1st Assembly, 1996—. Costume designer Paradise Valley C.C., Phoenix, 2004—06; prodn. asst. Jewish Voice Broadcasting, Phoenix, 2000—04, costume and makeup designer, 2000—04. Playwright: mus. My Place in the World, 1988, illustrated sermon Memory of Freedom, 2004. Founder, dir. Father's Artists, Dallas and Phoenix, 1998—2005; promotor Making Your Dreams Come True Phoenix First, 2005. Recipient Quill and Scroll award, Cen. H.S., 1979—84, Higher Edn. grant, U. Wis., 1984, Pell grant, 1984. Avocations: calligraphy, weapons and stage combat, designing clothes, candle carving, filmmaking. Office: Phoenix 1st Assembly 13613 N Cave Creek Rd Phoenix AZ 85022

KLOSAWSKA, ANNA M., literature and language professor; b. Warsaw, Aug. 16, 1966; PhD in French Studies, Brown U., Providence, 1994. Vis. prof. Kenyon Coll., Gambier, Ohio, 1993—97; prof. Miami U., Oxford, 1997—. Vis. prof. Coll. Wooster, Ohio, 1995. Author: Queer Love in the Middle Ages, 2005; editor: Violence Against Women in Medieval Texts, 1998. Office: French and Italian Dept Miami Univ Oxford 500 High St Oxford OH 45056-1602

KLOSS, LINDA L., medical association administrator; B, Coll. St. Scholastica, Minn., 1968. Former sr. mgr. MediQual Systems, Inc., Mass., InterQual, Inc., Chgo.; exec. v.p., CEO Am. Health Info. Mgmt. Assn., Chgo., 1995—. Bd. dirs. Am. Health Info. Mgmt. Assn., 1980—86, pres. bd. dirs., 1985; bd. dir. Nat. Alliance for Health Info. Tech., 2004—. Recipient Sr. Alice Lamb award for achievement, Coll. St. Scholastica, 1984. Office: Am Health Info Mgmt Assn 233 N Michigan Ave Ste 2150 Chicago IL 60601-5519 Business E-Mail: lkloss@ahima.org.*

KLOSTER, CAROL GOOD, wholesale distribution executive; b. Richmond, Va., Aug. 18, 1948; d. David William and Lucy (McDowell) Good; m. John Kenneth Kloster III, Feb. 15, 1975; children: John Kenneth IV, Amanda Aileen. AB, Coll. William and Mary, 1970. Personnel supr. Charles Levy Circulating Co., Chgo., 1974-75, warehouse supr., 1976-77, warehouse mgr., 1978-80, dir. sales, 1980-83, asst. v.p., dir. mktg., 1984; v.p., gen. mgr. Video Trend of Chgo., 1985-86; v.p. gen. mgr. Levy Home Entertainment, 1986-92; pres., CEO Chas Levy Co., 1992—. Mem. bd., Family Focus Inc. Recipient Algernon Sidney Sullivan award Coll. William and Mary, 1970. Presbyterian. Home: 619 W North St Hinsdale IL 60521-3152 Office: Chas Levy Company 1930 George St Ste 1 Melrose Park IL 60160-1501

KLOSTREICH, EVA TRICULES, educational association administrator; d. Homer and Magdalene (Sathmary) Tricules; m. Julius Klostreich; children: Adam J Tricules Kiernan, Christopher J., Nathaniel Clark Tricules Andrews, Michael J., Harrison C P Tricules Andrews. BA cum laude, Kean U., Union, N.J., 1978; PhD, Union Inst. & U., Cin., 2001. Cert. addictive personalities and behavioral excesses program Rational Emotive Behavior Therapy Inst., N.Y., family, child and adolescent therapy program Rational Emotive Behavior Therapy Inst., N.Y., lic. tchr. of the handicapped State of N.J., tchr. nursery kindergarten State of N.J., tchr. of reading State of N.J., permit holder N.J. Bd. Psychol. Examiners. Resident asst. Kean U., 1975—78; child evaluation clinician Ednl. Psychol. Svcs., Matawan, NJ, 1976—78; clin. educator, rschr. Princeton Child Devel. Inst. for Severely Emotionally Disturbed and Autistic Children, Lawrenceville, NJ, 1978—79; creator, designer Spotswood Pub. Schs., Preschool Handicapped Nat. Grant, NJ, 1979—80; co-director mental health services provider Cmty. Christian Counseling Ctr., Red Bank, NJ, 1980—81; mental health svcs. provider Christian Counseling Ctr., Comty. Bpatist Ch., Somerset, 1989—91; dir., supr. Christian Nursery Sch. Day Care Ctr., Comty. Bapt. Ch., Somerset, NJ, 1990—91; dir., mental health svcs. provier Farmingdale, NJ, 1991—93; owner, corp. exec. Kings Noble Metal Inc., Long Branch, NJ, 1993—; ednl. therapeutic evaluation/remediation provider Lion of Judah Religious Mental Health Svcs., Las Vegas, Nev., 1993—97; dir., mental health svcs. provider Lion Of Judah Religious Mental Health Svcs., Las Vegas, Nev., 1993—2001, Christian Mental Health Svcs., Eatontown, NJ, 2002—04; mental health clinician Rugby Sch. at Woodfield, Belmar, NJ, 2002—03; chmn. Kings Noble Metal, Inc. Cons. for bus. orgn. Ho. of Ruth Homeless Shelter, Long Branch, 1998; theology intern for Christian psychology Br. Encouragement, Saints Program Shrewsbury (N.J.) Assembly of God Ch., 1998—99; cons. for multiple personality disorder differential diagnosis FBI, Red Bank, NJ, 1993; cons. mentor program facilitating ch. people helping the poverty population Love INC (In the Name of Christ), Long Branch, 1998; v.p. Greater Red Bank Clergy Group, Red Bank, 2004—05; contbr. to creation and support of the interfaith coun. for the homeless Hospitality Network, Scotch Plains, NJ, 1983—86; pastor of pastors, a supervision support rsch. project Am. Bapt. Churches of N.J., Hamilton Square, NJ, 2004—; state coord. Am. Bapt. Chs. N.J. Mins. Coun. Together in Ministry, Manasquan, NJ, 2002—04; commd. deacon Evang. Luth. Chs. Am., Reformation Luth. Ch., West Long Branch, NJ; adj. instr. Brookdale C.C., Lincroft, NJ, 2003—04; public spkr., seminar leader for religion/mental health; seminar leader, spkr. Race Track Chaplaincy of Am., Houston, orgl. sys. analyst; mem. exec. com., emeritus rep. Nat. Office Race Track Chaplaincy of Am. Author: (nonfiction book) The Theory Of Christian Psychology; design course, Independent Study in Design; musician (soloist) worship performances; musician: (choir) All State Choir; musician: (soloist) (profl. performance) State Arts Award Ceremony; dir., arranger: contemporary Christian music K-Sharp; author: (book chpt.) The Lutheran View of the Bible; singer, composer, arranger: duet/solo performances Living Waters; contbr. articles to mags. and newspapers; dir.: (religious skits and plays) The Living Last Supper. Organizer, contbr. to creation of ann. nat. chaplains tng. sch. Race Track Chaplaincy Am., Long Branch, 1991—92; spkr. Race Track Chaplaincy of Am., L.A., 2005; camp counselor for emotionally disturbed and spl. needs campers Am. Bapt. Chs. Bapt. Camp and Conf. Ctr., Lebanon, 1977; mem. state youth program Am. Bapt. Chs. N.J., Hamilton Square, 1978—79; mem. Am. Bapt. Chs. Women in Ministry, Hamilton Square, 2002—05; pub. spkr. list Am. Bapt. Chs. N.J., Hamiliton Square, 2003—05, approved seminar provider for 273 chs. Hamilton Square, 2003—05; author, creator, dir. full-time nursery sch. day care program Comty. Bapt. Ch., Somerset, 1990—91; organizer Comty. Christian Counseling Ctr. Red Bank Bapt. Ch., Red Bank, 1982—83; orgn. contbr. Las Vegas City Wide Prayer Initiative for Revival, Las Vegas, Nev., 2000—01; mem. missions com. Red Bank Bapt. Ch., 2003—04; deacon Reformation Luth. Ch., 2001—05; coll. student rep. search com. for dean of students Kean U., Union, 1975—76, coll. student rep. liaison with fgn. students, 1975—77, founder student orgn. of peers helping peers, 1975—77, contbr. to writing initial grant for internat. studies in St. Kitts, 1976—77. Mem.: APA, Internat. Soc. for Multiple Personality Disorder, N.J. Soc. for Study of Multiple Personality Disorder. Republican. Achievements include development of theory of Christian psychology. Home: 621 Westwood Ave Long Branch NJ 07740 Office: Kings Noble Metal Inc 621 Westwood Ave Long Branch NJ 07740 Office Phone: 732-822-7279. Personal E-mail: klostreich1@msn.com. E-mail: klostreich1@kingsnoblemetal.com.

KLOTH, CAROLYN, meteorologist; b. Lakewood, Ohio, Apr. 22, 1954; d. James Albert and Marian Lucille (Fiske) K. BS in Meteorology, Fla. State U., 1976; MS in Meteorology, U. Okla., 1980. Lic. pvt. pilot. Meteorologist intern Nat. Weather Svc., Louisville, 1980-82; meteorologist Nat. Severe Storms Forecast Ctr., Kansas City, 1982-95, Aviation Weather Ctr., Kansas City, 1995—. Part-time student scientist, coop. student Nat. Severe Storms Lab., Norman, Okla., 1977-80. Mem. Nat. Weather Assn. (Aviation Meteorologist award 2000, co-chmn. aviation weather com. 1997-2002, v.p. 2002, chmn. publs. com. 2004), Nat. Weather Svc. Employees Orgn., Am. Air Mus. in Britain (founding mem.), Fla. State U. Alumni Assn., U. Okla. Alumni Assn. Democrat. Avocations: gardening, needlecrafts, reading, history. Office: Aviation Weather Ctr 7220 NW 101st Ter Rm 105 Kansas City MO 64153-2371

KLOTTER, ELEANOR IRENE, retired social worker; b. Montra, Ohio, June 8, 1929; d. Charles James and Nina Maud (Shrigley) Faulkner; m. Harold Ray Myers (div.); children: Harold Philip Myers, Nina Louise Myers McCauley; m. John T. Klotter, June 4, 1960 (dec.). AA, Aptos Jr. Coll., Calif., 1964; BA, San Jose State U., 1966; MS, Fresno State U., 2000. Cert. rehab. counselor Calif. Social worker I Santa Cruz (Calif.) County Social Svc., 1967—72; social worker III Fresno (Calif.) County Social Svc., 1974—95; social worker III, rehab. counselor Geneseo Foster Family Agy., Fresno, 2000—03; ret., 2003. Vol. ESL tchr. Clovis Adult Sch.; vol. tutor internat. students in M program; vol. counselor suicide hot line; vol. polit. campaigns, 1994—2000. Named Social Worker of Yr., Calif. Foster Parents Assn., 1986. Democrat. Presbyterian. Avocations: politics, museums, music.

KLOTZ, ANN MARIE, director; b. Detroit, Mich., Feb. 18, 1979; d. Charles Giacolone and Katherine (Klotz) Giacalone. BA Polit. Sci., Women Studies, Grand Valley State U., Allendale, Mich., 2002; MA Student Affairs Adminstrn., Mich. State U., 2004. Dir. residence hall Ball State U., Muncie, Ind., 2004—. Named Advisor of the Yr., 2005; recipient Max Raines Most Outstanding First Yr. Grad. Student in Student Affaris adminstrn., Mich. State U., 2003. Mem.: Am. Coll. Personnel Assn., Phi Kappa Phi. Democrat. Avocations: politics, reading, musicals, exercise, entertaining. Office: Ball State Univ 400 Schmidt Hall Muncie IN 47306 Office Phone: 765-285-5042. E-mail: aklotz@bsu.edu.

KLOTZ, FLORENCE, costume designer; b. N.Y.C., Oct. 28, 1920; d. Philip K. and Hannah Kraus. Student, Parsons Sch. Design, 1941. Designer: Broadway shows Take Her She's Mine, 1960, Never Too Late, 1962, Nobody Loves An Albatross, 1963, On An Open Roof, 1963, Owl and the Pussycat, 1964, One by One, 1964, Mating Dance, 1965, The Best Laid Plans, 1966, Superman, 1966, Paris Is Out, 1970, Norman Is That You, 1970, Legends, Follies, 1971 (Drama Desk award, Tony award), A Little Night Music, 1973 (Drama Desk award, Tony award), Side By Side Sondheim, 1975, Pacific Overtures, 1976 (Drama Desk award, Tony award, Los Angeles Critic Circle award), On the 20th Century, 1978 (Drama Desk award), Broadway Broadway, Dancin' In The Streets, 1982, Grind, 1984 (Tony award), Jerry's Girls, 1985; (ballet-jazz opus) Antique Epagraph, N.Y.C.; Broadway musicals Rags, 1986, Roza, 1987; Ctr. prodns. Carousel, 1956, Oklahoma, 1956, Annie Get Your Gun, 1956, 4 Baggatelle; movies Something for Everyone, 1969, A Little Night Music, 1976 (Oscar nomination, Los Angeles Critic Circle award); ice shows John Curry's Ice Dancing, 1979; Broadway musical A Doll's Life; ballet 8 Lines, 1986, I'm Old Fashioned (Jerome Robbins), Ives Songs (Jerome Robbins), City of Angels, 1989 (Tony award nominee, Outer Critics Circle award), Kiss of the Spider Woman, 1989 (Tony award 1989, Drama Desk award 1989), Show Boat, Toronto, Can., 1993, Broadway, 1994-95 (N.Y. Outer Critics Cirlce award 1995, Drama Desk award 1995, Tony award 1995, Theatre L.A. Ovation award 1997, Jessie award 1996), Whistle Down the Wind, 1996. Recipient Life Achievement award Theatre Crafts Internat., 1994, L.A. Ovation award, 1997, award NAACP, 1997, Dramalogue, 1997, L.A. Drama Desk, 1997; inducted into Theatre Hall of Fame, 1997, Patricia Zipprodt award, Fashion Inst. of Techn., 2002, Irene Sharaff award, 2005. Democrat. Home: New York, NY. Died Nov. 1, 2006.

KLOTZ, LEORA NYLEE, retired music educator, vocalist; b. Canton, Ohio, Oct. 17, 1928; d. Clarence Karl and Nellie (Jacoby) Dretke; m. Kenneth Gordon Klotz, June 29, 1963. BMus and B.Pub. Sch. Music, Mount Union Coll., Alliance, Ohio, 1950; MA, Western Res. U., Cleve., 1954. Cert. vocal music tchr. Ohio. Elem. music supr. Canton City Schs., Ohio, 1950—60, h.s. vocal dir., 1955—60; elem. music tchr. Louisville City Schs., Ohio, 1960—71, h.s. vocal dir., 1960—81; adult choir dir. Perry Christian Ch., Canton, 1959—87; ret., 1987; mem. young artists competition com. Canton Symphony Orch. Bd., 1981—89; dir. Trirosis choir. Soprano soloist The Messiah Canton Symphony Orch., 1954—55; soprano soloist First Christian Ch., 1946—65, North Canton Cmty. Christian Ch., numerous vocal (solo) appearances N.E. Ohio. Composer choral octavos. Soprano soloist Rep. Civic Celebration, Canton, Ohio, 1950—60. Recipient Outstanding Young Ohio Composer, Ohioana Libr. Assn., 1959. Mem.: Mount Union Women, Canton Symphony League, Am. Guild Organists, ASCAP, Ohio Ret. Tchrs. Assn., Am. Choral Dirs. Assn. (life), Stark County Ret. Tchrs. Assn. (life), MacDowell Chorale (hon.), Canton Woman's Club, MacDowell Music Club (hon.), Order Ea. Star, PEO Sisterhood, Mu Phi Epsilon, Delta Kappa Gamma. Republican. Avocations: collecting Hummel figurines, reading, cooking. Home: 4009 Beechtree Cir NW Canton OH 44709

KLUGE, JANICE, art educator; b. Berwyn, Ill., July 25, 1952; d. Kenneth Leonard and Mildred Mary Kluge; m. George Cam Langley, June 30, 1984. BFA, U. Ill., 1974; MA, U. Wis., 1980, MFA, 1982. Instr., tchg. asst. U. Wis., Madison, 1977-82; asst. prof. art U. Ala., Birmingham, 1982-89, assoc. prof. art, 1989-2000, prof., 2000—, acting chair dept., 1993, dir. art edn., 1988—, interim dept. chair., 2000—. Dir. Samuel B. Barker Outdoor Scupture Competition, U. Ala., Birmingham, 1995—. Exhibited in solo show at Huntsville Mus. Art, 1998; group exhbns. at Columbus (Ga.) Mus. Art, 1998, Ormeau Baths Gallery, Belfast, No. Ireland, 1996, The Nat. Mus. for Women in the Arts, Washington, 2000, numerous others; featured in articles in Metalsmith mag., Sculpture mag. Recipient Individual Artist fellow Ala. State Coun. on Arts, 1988-89, 98-99; Andy Warhol Found. grantee Space One Eleven, Birmingham, 1997-98; U. Ala. Birmingham grantee, 1995-96, 97-98. Mem. Soc. N.Am. Goldsmiths Office: U Ala Birmingham Dept Art And Art History Birmingham AL 35294-0001 E-mail: kluge@uab.edu.

KLUGER, RUTH, German language educator, editor; b. Vienna, Oct. 30, 1931; came to U.S., 1947, naturalized, 1952; d. Viktor and Alma (Gredinger) Kluger Hirschel; m. Werner T. Angress, Mar. 1952 (div. 1962); children: Percy, Dan. BA, Hunter Coll., 1950; MA, U. Calif.-Berkeley, 1952, PhD, 1967. Asst. prof. German lang. and lit. Case Western Res. U., 1966-70; assoc. prof. U. Kans., Lawrence, 1970-73, U. Va., Charlottesville, 1973-75, prof., 1975-76, U. Calif.-Irvine, 1976-80, 86-88, dir. Göttingen Study Ctr., Edn. Abroad Program, 1988-90, prof. emeritus; prof. Princeton U., 1980-86; editor German Quar., 1977-84. Author: The Early German Epigram: A Study in Baroque Poetry, 1971, Weiter leben Eine Jugend, 1992, Katastrophen, Über Deutsche Literatur, 1994, Frauen lesen anders, 1996; corr. editor Simon Wiesenthal Ctr. Ann., 1987; contbr. articles to profl. jous. Recipient Rauriser Literaturpreis, 1993, Grimmelshausen-Preis, 1993, Niedersachsen Preis, 1993, Marie-Louise-Kaschnitz preis, 1994, Heine-Preis, 1997, Thomas-Mann-Preis, 1999; ACLS fellow, 1978. Mem. MLA (exec. coun. 1978-82), Am. Assn. Tchrs. German (exec. coun. 1976-81), Deutsche Akademie für Sprache und Dichtung, Lessing Soc. (pres. 1977-79), PEN Club. Democrat. Jewish. Home: 62 Whitman Ct Irvine CA 92612-4066 Office: U Calif Dept German Irvine CA 92697-0001 E-mail: rkluger@uci.edu.

KLUGHART, TONI ANNE, music educator, musician, singer; b. Detroit, Mich., Dec. 5, 1964; d. Eugene Stanley McGuire Jr. and Rose Marie (Williams) McGuire; m. Charles Edward Klughart, Dec. 5, 1998; 1 child, Nathaniel Edward. AA Fine Arts, No.Va. C.C., 1983. Piano and voice instr., owner Ten Fingers Piano Studio, Fairfax, Va., 1986—96; asst. mgr. Music & Arts, Springfield, Va., 1986—88; piano instr., accompanist Comm. Music Sch., Richmond, Va., 1996—97; owner Klughart Music Sch., Atlanta, 1998—2003; office asst. Mobility Products Unlimited, LLC, Sparta, Tenn., 2003—; piano, guitar, voice Klughart Music Sch., Sparta, Tenn., 2003—. Singer, composer: CD Christmas and Lullabyes and Mary's Arms. Organ Study scholarship, Am. Guild Organists, 1995. Avocations: exercise, reading, crocheting, composing. Office: El-Shaddai Ministries 337 Burley St Sparta TN 38583

KLUKA, DARLENE ANN, human performance educator, researcher; b. Berwyn, Ill., Oct. 6, 1950; d. Aloysius Louis and Lillian (Malkovsky) K. BA, Ill. State U., 1972, MA, 1976; PhD, Tex. Woman's U., 1985. Educator, coach Fenton H.S., Bensenville, Ill., 1972-73, New Trier East H.S., Winnetka, Ill., 1973-80; coach Bradley Univ., Peoria, Ill., 1980-82; grad. tchg. asst. Tex. Woman's Univ., Denton, 1982-85; prof. Newberry (SC) Coll., 1985-86; prof., rschr., dir. Human Performance Ctr. Grambling (La.) State U., 1986-90, prof., coord. kinesiology and sport studies, 1997—2005; asst. prof. human studies and sport adminstrn. U. Ala., Birmingham, 1990-94, rschr., dir. Motor Behavior and Sports Vision Lab., 1990-94; dir. grad. program U. Ctrl. Okla., Edmond, 1994-97; dir. Kennesaw State U. Global Ctr. Social Change Through Women's Leadership and Sport, Ga., 2006—. Head of del. Internat. Olympic Acad., Olympia, Greece, 1990; dep. del. U.S. Olympic Com., 1996-2000; adv. bd. Women's Sports Found., 1992—; U.S.A. Volleyball Sports Medicine and Performance Commn., 1994—; bd. dirs. U.S.A. Volleyball, v.p. rels. and human resources, 1996-2000. Author: Visual Skill Enhancement for Sport Exercises, 1989, Volleyball Drills, 1990, Volleyball, 4th edit., 2000, Motor Behavior: From Learning to Performance, 1999; founding co-editor Internat. Jour. Sports Vision, 1991-97; founding editor Internat. Jour. Volleyball Rsch., 1997—, mem. editl. bd., Coaching Volleyball Jour., 1988-2005. Dir. Internat. Coun. Health, Phys. Edn., Recreation, Sport and Dance Girls and Women in Sport Commn., 1993—2001; mem. La. Gov.'s Coun. on Phys. Fitness and Sports, 2003—05; mem. La. advocacy com. Am. Heart Assn., 2005—. Recipient Rsch. award So. Assn. Phys. Edn. Coll. Women, 1994, 96, USA Volleyball Leader award, 1998, Joseph Andera Rsch. award Internat. Acad. of SportsVision, 1999, Disting. Svc. award AAALF Internat. Rels. Coun., 1999, Disting. Achievements award Ill. State U. Alumni Assn., 1997; LAHPERD scholar, 1999-2000, Honor award 2002, So. Dist. Honor award 2003; AAHPERD Honor award, 2004; Disting. Scholar in Sport award 1995, Internat. Coun. of Health Physical Edn., Recreation, Sport and Dance, AAHPERD C.D. Henry award, 2005. Mem. AAHPERD (rsch. fellow, bd. govs. 1993-96, So. dist. scholar 2001, C.D. Henry Ethnic Minority award 2005), AAUP (Disting. scholar award 1997), JOPERD (editl. bd. 2002-05, chair 2004-04), Nat. Assn. for Girls and Women in Sport (bd. dirs., exec. com. 1989-92, 93-96, pres. 1990-91, Honor award 1996), Internat. Coun. for Sport Sci. and Phys. Edn. (exec. bd. 1997-02, treas. 2002-04, editl. bd. 1998—, editl. bd. chmn., 2005—, mem. pres.' com. 2002—), Internat. Acad. Sports Vision (adv. bd. 1989-98, v.p. 1993-01), Am. Volleyball Coaches Assn. (mem. editl. bd. Coaching Volleyball Jour., 1988-, bd. dirs. 2003—06, chmn. edn. and publs. com. 2003—06, Excellence in Edn. award 1999), IAPESGW (Kluka/Love Young Rsch. Award named in her honor 2001), Am. Volleyball Coaches Assn. (Hall of Fame inductee 2003), Women's Sports Found. (internat. coun. 1993—, edn. and rsch. coun. 1995—, Pres.'s award 1996, Darlene A. Kluka rsch. award named in her honor 2001), Internat. Assn. Phys. Edn. and Sports Girls and Women, Girls and Women in Sport (bd. cons. 2000—06, pres. 2005—). Roman Catholic. Avocations: jogging, photography, collecting olympic games memorabilia, bicycling. Office: Global Ctr for Social Change/Women's Sport Mail Drop # 5800 Kennesaw U Kennesaw GA 30144 E-mail: dkluka@kennesaw.edu.

KLUM, HEIDI, model, actress; b. Bergisch-Gladbach, Germany, June 1, 1973; d. Gunther and Erna Klum; m. Ric Pipino, Sept. 6, 1997 (div. 2003); 1 child, Leni; m. Seal, May 10, 2005; 1 child, Henry Guenther. Model Victoria's Secret Fashion Show, 2001, 2002, 2003; appeared on covers of major mags. including Elle, Sports Illustrated (Swimsuit Edit.), Mademoiselle, Glamour, Bride's, Cosmopolitan; appeared in campaigns including Bonne Bell, Finesse, Gerry Webber, Givenchy, Amerige, INC, Am. Express, Kathleen Madden, Katjes, Nike, Otto, Peek&Cloppenburg, Swatch, Victoria's Secret; launched line of perfume, 2002; co-creator jewelry collection The Heidi Klum Collection for Mouawad; designer of a line of Birkenstocks. Actor: (films) 54, 1998, Blow Dry, 2001, Ella Enchanted, 2004, The Life and Death of Peter Sellers, 2004; (TV films) Spin City, 1998—99; exec. prodr., host (TV series) Project Runaway, 2004—, TV appearances include Sex and the City, 2001, Malcolm in the Middle, 2002, Yes, Dear, 2002, CSI: Miami, 2003; author (with Alexandra Postman): Heidi Klum's Body of Knowledge: 8 Rules of Model Behavior (To Help You Take off on the Runway of Life), 2004. Charity involvements include ARC, Elizabeth Glazer Pediatric AIDS Found. Office: William Morris Agy One William Morris Pl Beverly Hills CA 90212*

KLUTHE, KATHLEEN A., elementary school educator; b. Dodge, Nebr., Sept. 24, 1943; d. Conrad Kluthe and Leona Renner. BS in Edn., Alverno Coll., Milw., Wis., 1960; MA in Religious Edn., Fordham U., N.Y.C., N.Y., 1969; MA in Culture and Spirituality, Holy Name U., Oakland, Calif., 2000. Dir. youth ministry Mother of Sorrows Ch., Tucson, 1969—80, Resurrection Ch., Tempe, Ariz., 1980—86, St. Pius Ch., Tucson, 1986—90; dir. campus ministry Salpointe Cath. H.S., Tucson, 1990—2000; team mem. Jordan Ministry, Tucson, 2000—06; pres. Sch. Sisters of St. Francis Internat. Religious Cmty., Milw., 2006. Mem.: Internat. Religious Cmty. of Sch. Sisters of St. Francis (pres. 2006—). Office: Sch Sisters of St Francis 1501 S Layton Blvd Milwaukee WI 53215 Office Phone: 414-384-4105. Personal E-mail: kathleenkluthe@hotmail.com.

KLUTTS, RHONDA ASBURY, music educator; b. Chattanooga, Nov. 10, 1965; d. Charles Ronald and Carolyn Faye Asbury; m. Joe Douglas Klutts, June 26, 1960; 1 child, Jeremy Douglas. MusB, Lamar U., Beaumont, Tex., 1988. Cert. all levels music Tex., 1988. Choral dir. Terry H.S., Rosenberg, Tex., 1997—. Mem.: Tex. Music Educators Assn. Office Phone: 832-223-3400.

KMETZ, LEAH E., elementary school educator; b. Williamsport, Pa., July 15, 1981; d. Elizabeth Kmetz. BS in Music Therapy, Slippery Rock U., Pa., 2004. Cert. music therapist, tchr. Va., Pa. Music therapist FCPS, Herndon, Va., 2004—. Mem.: Music Educators Nat. Conf., Am. Music Tchrs. Assn., Mu Phi Epsilon (gate keeper 2001—02). Office: Herndon Mid Sch 901 Locust St Herndon VA 20170 Office Phone: 703-904-4922. Business E-Mail: leah.kmetz@fcps.edu.

KMETZ-MCMILLIN, MARIANNE DENISE, secondary school educator; d. Michael John and Rose Miriam Kmetz; children: Ryan Michael McMillin, Mirielle Rosellen McMillin. BA in English, Canisius Coll., Buffalo, 1976. Cert. tchr. Va. Acct. exec. Johnston Mktg. Group, Tarrytown, NY, 1989—98; traffic mgr. D/A, Norfolk, Va., 1998—2000; media buyer Tele Video Prodns., Virginia Beach, Va., 2000—02; tchr. Chesepeake Pub Schs., Va., 2002—. Tchr. Japanese Old Dominion U., Norfolk, 2003; presenter in field. Mix it up at lunch facilitator So Law Poverty Ctr./Oscar Smith HS, Chesapeake, 2005. Recipient Excellence in Holocaust Edn. award, Jewish Fedn. Tidewater, 2005. Fellow: Tidewater Writing Project; mem.: So. Law Poverty Ctr. Avocations: writing, drawing, sports, reading.

KMIEC ROBERTS, HELEN MARIE, middle school educator; b. Bellville, Tex., Dec. 16, 1967; d. Phillip David and Mary Agnes (Svach) K. Assoc., Blinn Coll., Brenham, Tex., 1988; BA in Tchg., Sam Houston State U., 1990; MEd, U. Houston, 1996. Lic. tchr. earth/life sci., Tex. 6th grade sci. tchr. Spring Branch Mid. Sch., Houston, 1990—. Participant various workshops and insts. Mem. Am. Fedn. Tchrs., Spring Branch Edn. Assn. Republican. Roman Catholic. Avocations: reading, cooking, bicycling. Office: Spring Branch Mid Sch 1000 Piney Point Rd Houston TX 77024-2729 Home: 3715 Westerdale Fulshear TX 77441

KNACKSTEDT, MARY V., interior designer; b. Harrisburg, Pa., Oct. 26, 1940; d. Harry and Veronica Knackstedt. Student, Pratt Inst., 1957-59, Cooper Union, Phila. Coll. Art. Pres. Knackstedt Inc., Harrisburg, N.Y.C., 1958—. Adv. bd. PNC Bank, N.A., Camp Hill, Pa., 1981—; lectr. bus. practices Harvard U., 1988—; cons., speaker in field. Author: Interior Design for Profit, 1980, Profitable Career Options for Designers, 1985, The Interior Design Business Handbook, 1988, 4th edit., 2005, Marketing and Design Services: The Designer Client Rlationship, 1993, Interior Design and Beyond, 1995; prin. works include Hershey Med. Ctr., Milton Hershey Sch., founder's Hall, Hershey, Pa., Hershey Pub. Libr. Bus. devel. program founder Riverfront Peoples Park, Harrisburg, 1980-90; bd. dirs. Harrisburg Symphony Assn., 1983-89; founder, pres. Profl. Cath. Women's Forum; devel. coun. Bishop McDevitt Sch., Harrisburg. Fellow Internat. Interior Design Assn., Am. Soc. Interior Designers (past officer); mem. Internat. Furnishings and Design Assn., Illuminating Engring. Soc. N.Am., Interior Design Soc., Pres.'s Assn., Am. Mgmt. Assn. Home and Office: 2901 N Front St Harrisburg PA 17110-1223 Address: 161 E 61st St New York NY 10021-8125 Office Phone: 717-238-7548. Personal E-mail: maryknackstedt@aol.com.

KNAFF, REBECCA E., personal trainer; d. Walter James and Robin E. Knaff. BS, U. Mont., Missoula, 2001. Cert. Athletic Trainer Nat. Athletics Trainers Assn., 2001. Cert. athletic trainer Dickenson County Healthcare Sys., Iron Mountain, Mich., 2001—03, Big Horn Basin Orthopaedic Clinic, Cody, Wyo., 2006. Vol. athletic trainer Vallely Christian Sch., Missoula, Mont., 2004—05. Recipient Reinhardt Athletic Tng. award, U. Mont., 2001. Mem.: Nat. Athletic Trainers Assn. Whig Party. Office: Big Horn Basin Orthopaedic Clinic 720 Lindsay Ln Cody WY 82414 Office Phone: 307-899-2856.

KNAPP, AMY K., insurance company executive; With health maintenance orgn., Fla.; pres., CEO United Healthcare N.E., N.Y.C. Office: United Healthcare NE 2 Penn Plz Fl 7 New York NY 10121

KNAPP, ANNAMARIA LOIS, music educator; b. McCook, NB, Feb. 26, 1982; d. David Wayne and Jacquelyn Day Knapp. B Music Edn., Ctrl. Meth. Coll., 2004. Band dir. Campbell (Mo.) R-II Sch., 2004—. Mem. Poplar Bluff (Mo.) Cmty. Band, 2004—; mem. ch. bell choir Poplar Bluff, 2004—05. Recipient W.D. Settle award. Mem.: Mo. Bandmasters Assn., Music Educators Nat. Conf., Sigma Alpha Iota. Methodist. Office: Camptell R-II Sch 801 S Hwy 53 Campbell MO 63933

KNAPP, BARBARA ALLISON, financial planner, oncological nurse consultant; b. Boston, May 30, 1936; d. Henry Philip and Mary Veronica (Norton) Frank; m. John Northcott Knapp, July 27, 1963 (dec. June 12, 1994); children: Linda, David, Diana; m. James M. Nikrant, June 20, 1998. BSN, Hood Coll., 1959; MA, U. Iowa Sch. Nursing, 1981. Instr. Mass. Gen. Hosp. Sch. Nursing, Boston, 1959—63; acting dir. Aga Khan Hosp., Nairobi, Kenya, 1963—65; dir. dept. patient edn. Mercy Hosp., Cedar Rapids, Iowa, 1975—78; clin. nurse specialist Dept. Otolaryngology U. Iowa Hosp. and Clinics, Iowa City, 1981—84, clin. nurse specialist oncology, 1992—94; clin. nurse specialist surg. nursing U. Chgo. Med. Ctr., 1984—92; nursing cons., chmn. CEO SCI Fin. Group Inc., Cedar Rapids, 1994—2002. Bd. accreditation Nat. League for Nursing N.Y.C., 1993-96; adv. bd. Mercy Hosp. Women's Health Ctr., 1994—, MBA adv. bd. U. Iowa Coll. Bus. Dir., editor: (instructive films) Preoperative Teaching Film, 1976 (Am. Hosp. Assn. Film of the Yr. 1976), Learning About Diabetes, 1978, Head and Neck Postoperative Care, 1984, Psychosocial Effects of Head and Neck Cancer, 1984. Bd. dirs. United Way, Cedar Rapids, 1994—, Cedar Rapids Symphony Orch., YMCA, Cedar Rapids, Meth-Wick Retirement Cmty. (pres. bd.), Jr. Achievement; trustee Mt. Mercy Coll. (vice.-chair bd.), YMCA, 1996-2000, Mercy Hosp., Cedar Rapids, 2003— Mem. Am. Cancer Soc., Oncology Nursing Soc., Cedar Rapids C. of C. (dir. 1996—), Rotary Internat., Sigma Theta Tau. Avocations: reading, travel, skiing, golf, tennis. Home: 307 Crescent St SE Cedar Rapids IA 52403-1731 Office Phone: 319-366-4908. E-mail: bknapp@mchsi.com.

KNAPP, CANDACE LOUISE, sculptor; b. Benton Harbor, Mich., Feb. 28, 1948; d. Claire Warren and Frances Mary (Collins) K.; m. Björn Andrén, Mar. 3, 1988. BFA, Cleve. Inst. Art, 1971; MFA, U. Ill., 1974. Sculptures exhibited in numerous galleries; represented in permanent collections including Northwood Inst. Collection, West Palm Beach, Fla., Memphis Brooks Mus. Art, Mobil Oil Co., Stockholm, HageGården Music Ctr., Edane, Sweden, others; included in book Contemporary American Women Sculptors; numerous commns. including St. Peter and Paul Cath. Ch., Orlando, Fla., Padre Pio Found., Cromwell, Conn., Temple Emanuel, Dallas, West Haven, Conn., Tampa (Fla.) Gen. Hosp., Pub. Art Commn. City of St. Petersburg, Fla., Pub. Art Commn. Hillsborough County Courthouse, Tampa, Fla. Helen Greene Perry traveling scholar, 1971. Personal E-mail: candy@candaceknapp.com.

KNAPP, ELLEN M., financial company executive; 2 children. BS, U. SC, 1974. With Computer Scis. Corp. NASA Goddard Space Fligth Ctr.; with Booz-Allen & Hamilton; vice chmn., tech. Coopers & Lybrand, N.Y.C., 1992—98; chief knowledge officer, global CIO PriceWaterhouse Coopers, N.Y.C., 1998—. Mem. bd. assessment Nat. Rsch. Coun.; session chmn. Internat. Conf. on Future of Industry in Advanced Socs. MIT; guest lectr. Columbia U., Dartmouth U., Oxford U.; juror Lemelson-MIT award for Invention and Innovation, 1996, 97; keynote spkr. 10 Anniversary Symposium computer sci. and telecomms. bd. NAS, 1996; keynote spkr. numerous confs. Co-author: Every Manager's Guide to Business Processes, 1995; contbr. articles, chapters to books. Office: PriceWaterHouseCoopers 1301 Ave of Ams New York NY 10019-6022

KNAPP, LISA MARIE, music educator; b. Middletown, Conn., Aug. 22, 1971; d. David H. and Carol A. Knapp; life ptnr. David C. Raicik. BA in Music, Ctrl. Conn. State U., New Britain, 1997. Cert. tchr. Tex., 2005. Band dir. Trinity Ind. Sch. Dist., Tex., 2001—03; music tchr. Lee Acad., Maine, 2005—. Pvt. saxophone and clarinet instr. Conroe Ind. Sch. Dist., Tex., 2003—05. Recipient Faculty Merit award, 1997; scholar, Sam Houston State U., 1997—2000. Office: Lee Acad 4 Winn Rd Lee ME 04455 Office Phone: 207-738-2252. E-mail: lknapp@leeacademy.org.

KNAPP, MILDRED FLORENCE, retired social worker; b. Detroit, Apr. 15, 1932; d. Edwin Frederick and Florence Josephine (Antaya) K. BBA, U. Mich., 1954, MA in Cmty. and Adult Edn., 1964, MSW, 1967. Dist. dir. Girl Scouts Met. Detroit, 1954-63; planning asst. Coun. Social Agys. Flint and Genessee Counties, 1965; sch. social worker Detroit (Mich.) Pub. Schs., 1967-98, ret., 1998. Field instr. Alumnae bd. govs. U. Mich., 1972-75, scholarship chair, 1969-70 76-80, chair spl. com. women's athletics, 1972-75, class agt. fund raising Sch. Bus. Adminstrn., 1978-79; active Founders Soc. Detroit Inst. Art, 1969—, Friends Children's Mus. Detroit, 1978— Women's Assn., Detroit Symphony Orch., 1982-89, Mich. Humane Soc., 1991—; vol. Coun. Detroit Symphony Orch., 1990—; trustee, fin. chmn. Children's Mus.; charter mem. World War II Meml. Recipient Appreciation cert.; fellow, Mott Found., 1964; grantee, HEW, 1966. Mem. NASW, Acad. Cert. Social Workers, Nat. Cmty. Edn. Assn. (charter), Sch. Social Work Assn. Am. (charter), Outdoor Edn. and Camping Coun. (charter), Mich. Sch. Social Workers Assn. (pres. 1980-81), Detroit Sch. Social Workers Assn. (past pres.), Detroit Assn. U. Mich. Women (pres. 1980-82), Detroit Fedn. Tchrs., Madame Alexander Doll Club, WWII Meml. (charter mem.). Methodist. Home: 702 Lakepointe St Grosse Pointe Park MI 48230-1706

KNAPP, PATRICIA ANN, psychologist, educator; b. Sandusky, Ohio, June 22, 1943; d. Charles Allan and Therma Eleanor (Kincade) Moore; m. Gary Robert Knapp, Dec. 15, 1963 (div. Dec. 1983); children: Chelsea Allison, Kirby Robert; m. Ronald Tipton, Jan. 27, 1995. BS, Colo. State U., 1968; MEd, Loyola U., 1976; MA, U. Md., 1986, PhD, 1988. Lic. psychologist, Md. Speech therapist Prince George's County Pub. Sch., Bladensburg, Md., 1968-70; dir. Womanscope, Inc., Columbia, Md., 1978-82; instr. Howard (Md.) Community Coll., 1982-86; intern in psychology Mt. Vernon Ctr. for Community Mental Health, Alexandria, Va., 1986-87; pvt. practice psychologist Towson, Md., 1987-89, Columbia, 1990—. Adj. faculty U. Md. Baltimore County, 1988—; bd. dirs. Family Life Ctr. Contbr. articles to profl. jours. Mem. APA, Md. Psychol. Assn., Balt. Psychol. Assn., Nat. Register Health Svc. Providers in Psychology (registered), Phi Kappa Phi. Avocations: tennis, piano. Home: 15513 Bushy Tail Run Woodbine MD 21797-8025 Office: 10715 Charter Dr Ste 270 Columbia MD 21044-2871

KNAPP, ROSALIND ANN, lawyer; b. Washington, Aug. 15, 1945; d. Joseph Burke and Hilary (Eaves) K. BA, Stanford U., 1967, JD, 1973. Bar: Calif. 1973, D.C. 1980. Atty. US Dept. Transp., Washington, 1973—74, spl. asst. to dep. sec., 1974—77, atty.-adv, 1977—79, asst. gen. counsel legislation, 1979-81, dep. gen. counsel, 1981—, acting gen. counsel, 2006—. Mem. D.C. Bar Assn., Calif. Bar Assn. Office: US Dept Transp Office of the General Counsel 400 7th St SW Washington DC 20590-0003 Office Phone: 202-366-4713. Business E-Mail: lindy.knapp@dot.gov.

KNAPP, SYLVIA CLARE, religious studies educator, language educator; b. Schenectady, N.Y., Apr. 13, 1937; d. Theodore Karl and Margaret Blann Knapp. BS in Music Edn., Bob Jones U., SC, 1959; MS, Radford U., Va., 1992. Cert. secondary tchr. Fla., 1959. Missionary OMS Internat., Inc., 1961—2002, Taichung, Taiwan, 1961—2002; tchr. and curriculum dir. Jian Hua Sch. Fgn. Langs., Weihai, China, 2003—05; ret., 2005. Tour accompanist Taiwan Men's Choir OMS Internat., Inc., Canada, 1969; dir. Chung Tai English Inst., Taichung, Taiwan, 1970—97; tchr. broadcaster The Chungtai English Broadcast, 1970—89. Author: (bilingual textbooks) Correcting Common Mistakes in English, 1984, The Parables of Jesus, 1992, My Offering, 2002; performer: (recordings) Youth Choruses Vol 3, 1984; contbr. articles to OUTREACH mag. Vol. tchr. English to Chinese restaurant workers, 2006—. Recipient First prize 5th Ann. Music Festival, Schenectady Fedn. Women's Orgn. Mem.: TESOL (assoc.). Avocations: piano, Chinese musical instruments, singing, travel. Home: 889 Ravenwood Dr Greenwood IN 46142 Office: OMS Internat Inc 941 Fry Rd Greenwood IN 46142 Office Phone: 317-881-6751. E-mail: scknapp2003@yahoo.com.

KNAPP, VIRGINIA ESTELLA, retired secondary education educator; b. Washington, May 11, 1919; d. Bradford and Stella (White) Knapp; BA, Tex. Tech. U., 1940; MA, U. Tex. 1948; postgrad. Sul Ross Coll., 1950, Stephen F. Austin U., 1964-68. Tchr. journalism, high schs., Silverton, Tex., 1940-41, Electra, Tex., 1941-42, Joinerville, Tex., 1942-60, Carthage, Tex., 1961-69; tchr. history and journalism Longview (Tex.) High Sch., 1969-80; instr. Trinity U., San Antonio, summer 1972; fellowship tchr. Wall St. Jour., Tex. A&M U., College Station, summers 1964-67. Chmn., Rusk County (Tex.) Hist. Commn., 1980—2002; pres. Rusk County Hist. Found.; mem. Henderson Main St. Bd. Recipient Wall St. Jour. award Outstanding Journalism Tchrs. of Yr., 1965-66; Trail Blazer award Tex. High Sch. Press Assn., 1980; Woman of Yr. award, 1983. Mem. Tex. State Tchrs. Assn., Classroom Tchrs. Assn., Tex. Assn. Jour. Dirs., Rusk County Heritage Assn., Rusk County Hist. Commn., Women in Communications (pres. Longview chpt. 1972-74, Service award 1975), Tex. Press Women, bd.member Gaston Mus. (finance chmn.). Episcopalian. Contbr. hist. writing to Ala. Rev., Progressive Farmer, Rusk County C. of C. Brochure, Rusk County Heritage, numerous others. Home: 1802 Elm St Apt 301 Henderson TX 75652-6256 Office: 514 N High St Henderson TX 75652-5912

KNAUER, VIRGINIA HARRINGTON (MRS. WILHELM F. KNAUER), advocate, retired federal agency administrator; b. Phila., Mar. 28, 1915; d. Herman Winfield and Helen (Harrington) Wright; m. Wilhelm F. Knauer, Jan. 27, 1940; children: Wilhelm F., Valerie H. (Mrs. I. Townsend Burden III). BFA, U. Pa., 1937; grad., Pa. Acad. Fine Arts, 1937; postgrad., Royal Acad. Fine Arts, Florence, Italy, 1938-39; LL.D. (hon.), Phila. Coll. Textiles and Sci., St. Francis de Sales, Widener Coll., Chester, Pa., Tufts U.; Litt.D. (hon.), Drexel U.; L.H.D. (hon.), Russell Sage Coll., Pa. Coll. Podiatric Medicine; L.H.D., Jacksonville U.; LLD (hon.), U. Pa., 1971. Dir. Pa. Bur. Consumer Protection, 1968-69; spl. asst. to Pres. for consumer affairs The White House, 1969-77; dir. U.S. Office Consumer Affairs, Washington, 1971-77, 81-88; spl. adv. to Pres. for consumer affairs The White House, 1981-88; chair ABRH Inc., Washington, 1988-91; consumer cons. Haney and Knauer, Inc., Washington, 1991-93. Pres. Virginia Knauer & Assocs., Inc., Washington, 1977-81; chmn. Coun. for Advancement of Consumer Policy, 1979-81; U.S. rep., vice chmn. consumer policy com. OECD, 1970-77, 81-88; mem. Coun. Wage and Price Stability, 1974-77; vice-chmn. Philadelphia County Rep. Com., 1958-77; pres. Phila. Congress Rep. Women's Councils, 1958-77; dir. Pa. Coun. Rep. Women, 1963-80; founder N.E. Phila. Coun. Rep. Women, pres., 1956-68 Bd. dirs. Hannah Penn House, 1956—, v.p., 1971; chmn. Knauer Found. Hist. Preservation, 1963—; nat. chmn. to promote no fault automobile ins. Project New Start, 1988-91; bd. dirs. Nat. Coalition for Cancer Survivorship; mem. city coun., Phila., Pa., 1960-68. Recipient Gimbel-Phila. award, 1977, Ind. Achievement in Govt. award Soc. Consumer Affairs Profls., 1983; named Disting. Dau. Pa., 1969; named to Disting. Women's Com., Northwood U., 1997. Mem. Nat. Trust Hist. Preservation, Am. Assn. Ret. Persons, Internat. Neighbors Club, Exec. Women in Govt., Penn Women (trustees coun.), Consumers for World Trade (bd. dirs.), Zeta Tau Alpha, Kappa Delta Epsilon (hon.). Episcopalian.

KNEAVEL, ANN CALLANAN, humanities educator, communications consultant; b. Balt., Oct. 29, 1946; d. James Michael and Ann (Ijams) Callanan; m. Thomas Charles Kneavel, Jr., Dec. 18, 1970; children: Meredith Elizabeth, Thomas Charles III, Rebecca Ann. BA, Coll. Notre Dame Md., 1968; MA in Am. Lit., U. Md., 1970; PhD in Modern Brit. Lit., U. Ottawa, 1979. Instr. U. Md., College Park, 1968—71, U. Ottawa, 0971—1972, Wilmington Coll., Del., 1976—79, Del. Tech. and C.C., Dover, 1975—79; asst. prof. Widener U., Chester, Pa., 1981—82; prof. Goldey-Beacom Coll., Wilmington, 1981—; dir. satellite campuses Total Quality Master's Program, Falmouth, Mass., 1995—. Contbr. articles to profl. jours. Trustee Hockessin (Del.) Pub. Libr., 1981-93, Alpha Tau Omega Fraternity, Wilmington, 1994—; mem. Friends of Hockessin Libr., 1981—. Mem. MLA, Nat. Coun. Tchrs. English, Conf. on Christianity and Lit., Am. Culture Assn., C.C. Humanities Assn., Alpha Chi (faculty sponsor, Svc. award 1994, v.p. region VI 2000-02, pres. region VI, 2002-04, nat. coun. 2003—), Nat. Coun. 2003-. Roman Catholic. Home: 7 Arthur Dr Hockessin DE 19707-1012 Office: Goldey-Beacom Coll 4701 Limestone Rd Wilmington DE 19808-1927 Business E-Mail: kneavela@gbc.edu.

KNEBEL, ROSEMARY, secondary school educator; d. Raymond and Esther Klump; m. Gary Wayne Knebel, Sept. 30, 1978; children: Adrianne Rochelle, Brittni Linnea. AA, Blinn Jr. Coll., Brenham, 1978; BS, Tex. A&M, College Station, 1990. 12th grade English tchr. Brenham HS, 1990—. Office: Brenham High Sch 525 A H Ehrig Dr Brenham TX 77833 Office Phone: 979-277-6570. Personal E-mail: rknebel@brenhamisd.net.

KNEE, RUTH IRELAN (MRS. JUNIOR K. KNEE), social worker, health care consultant; b. Sapulpa, Okla., Mar. 21, 1920; d. Oren M. and Daisy (Daubin) Irelan; m. Junior K. Knee, May 29, 1943 (dec. Oct. 1981). BA, U. Okla., 1941, cert. social work, 1942; MA in Social Svcs. Adminstrn., U. Chgo., 1945. Psychiat. social worker, asst. supr. Ill. Psychiat. Inst., U. Ill., Chgo., 1943-44; psychiat. social worker USPHS Employee Health Unit, Washington, 1944—49; social work assoc. Army Med. Ctr., Walter Reed Army Hosp., Washington, 1949-54; psychiat. social work cons. HEW, Region III, Washington, 1955-56; with NIMH, Chevy Chase, Md., 1956-72; chief mental health care adminstrn. br. Health Svcs. and Mental Health Adminstrn., USPHS assoc. dep. adminstr., 1972-73; dep. dir. Office of Nursing Home Affairs, 1973-74; long-term mental health care cons.; mem. com. on mental health and illness of elderly HEW, 1976-77; mem. panel on legal and ethical issues Pres.'s Commn. on Mental Health, 1977-78; liaison mem. Nat. Adv. Mental Health Coun., 1977-81. Mem. edtl. bd. Health and Social Work, 1979-81. Bd. dirs. Hillhaven Found., 1975-86, governing bd. Cathedral Coll. of the Laity, Washington Nat. Cathedral, 1988-94, Cathedral Fund Com., 1997—,bd. of visitors sch. of social work, Univ. of Okla., 2000— Recipient Edith Abbott award, U. Chgo. Sch. Social Svc. Adminstrn., 2001, Disting. Alumna award, U. Okla. Coll. Arts and Scis., 1999. Fellow APHA (sec. mental health sect. 1968-70, chmn. 1971-72), Am. Orthopsychiat. Assn. (life), Gerontol. Soc. Am., Am. Assn. Psychiat. Social Workers (pres. 1951-53); mem. Nat. Conf. Social Welfare (nat. bd. 1968-71, 2d v.p. 1973-74), Inst. Medicine/NAS (com. study future of pub. health 1986-87), Coun. on Social Work Edn., Nat. Assn. Social Workers (sec. 1955-56, nat. dir. 1956-57, 84-86, chmn. competence study com., practice and knowledge com. 1963-71, presdl. award for exemplary svc. 1999), Acad. Cert. Social Workers (NASW Found. co-chair social work pioneers 1993—), Am. Pub. Welfare Assn., DAR, U. Okla. Assocs., Women's Nat. Dem. Club (mem. gov. bd. 1992-95, ednl. found. bd. 1992-2000), Cosmos Club (Washington, chair program com. 1998-2001), Phi Beta Kappa (fellow), Psi Chi. Address: 8809 Arlington Blvd Fairfax VA 22031-2705

KNEESE, CAROLYN CALVIN, retired education educator; b. Austin, Sept. 16, 1941; d. Elmer Ben and Agnes Standlee Calvin; children: Kyle Calvin, Reagan Scott. BA, U. Tex., Austin, 1962; MA, Houston Baptist U., 1990; EdD, U. Houston, 1994. Cert. real estate broker Tex., 1988. Tchr. Austin Sch. Dist., Tex., 1963—64, Highland Park Sch. Dist., Dallas, 1964—67; translator, rschr. Methodist Hosp., Houston, 1969—70; rsch. asst. U. Houston, 1993—94; rsch. assoc. Tex. A&M U., College Station, 1994, asst. prof. dept. ednl. adminstrn. Commerce, 1998—2002, assoc. prof. dept. ednl. adminstrn., 2003—04, ret., 2004. Co-author: School Calendar Reform: Learning in All Seasons, 2006; author: numerous jour. articles and publs. Bd. mem. Partnership Baylor Coll. Medicine, Houston, 2006; past bd. mem. Houston Symphony. Mem.: AAUW, Tex. Real Estate Commn., Phi Delta Kappa. Home: 1100 Uptown Park Blvd Houston TX 77056 Personal E-mail: cckneese@aol.com.

KNEWSTEP, NANCY COLEMAN, secondary school educator; b. Charlottesville, Va., Mar. 4, 1953; d. Edmund Moore Coleman, Sr. and Anne Halsey Coleman; m. Edward Alan Knewstep, Aug. 13, 1988; 1 child, Lindsey A. BS in Child Devel. Svcs., Va. Poly. Inst. & State U., Blacksburg, 1976. Salesperson, bookkeeper Moormont Orchard and Rapidan Berry Garden, Va., 1963—93; sci. tchr., sci. chair St. Luke's Luth. Sch., Culpeper, Va., 1987—. Elder Presbyn. Ch., 1995—. Mem.: Nat. Sci. Tchrs. Assn. Avocations: gardening, reading, travel. Home: PO Box 73 7322 Knewstep Ln Rapidan VA 22733

KNEZO, GENEVIEVE JOHANNA, science and technology policy researcher; b. Aug. 8, 1942; d. John and Genevieve (Sadowski) K.; 1 child, Alexandra M. AB in Polit. Sci., Rutgers U., 1964; MA in Sci., Tech. and Pub. Policy, George Washington U., 1981; grad., Nat. Def. U., 1989. With Congl. Rsch. Svc. Libr. of Congress, Washington, 1967—, specialist in sci. and tech., 1979—, head sci., rsch. and tech. sect., 1986-88, sr. level specialist in sci. and tech. policy, 1991—. Author profl. publs. Mem. Phi Beta Kappa, Pi Sigma Alpha. Avocations: white-water canoeing, hiking, gymnastics, classical music, community volunteer activities. Home: 606 Oakley Pl Alexandria VA 22302-3611 Office: Libr of Congress Congl Rsch Svc Resources Sci/Indust Divsn Washington DC 20540-7450 E-mail: gknezo@crs.loc.gov.

KNICKEL, CARIN S., oil industry executive; b. Powell, Wyo. BA in Mktg. and Stats., U. Colo.; M.Mgmt., MIT. Mktg. account mgr. ConocoPhillips, 1979—87, area dir. light oil sales product supply and trading, 1987, gen. mgr. bus. develop. for refining and mktg. in Europe London, gen. mgr. refining, mktg., and transp., pres. specialty bus. divsn., 2001—03, v.p. human resources Houston, 2003—. Chmn. rodeo run com. ConocoPhillips; bd. dirs. Colo. Spl. Olympics. Office: ConocoPhillips 600 N Dairy Ashford Rd Houston TX 77079*

KNIERIEM, BEULAH WHITE, retired elementary school educator, minister; b. Appomattox, Va., Oct. 31, 1930; d. George Harrison and Virgie Ade (Kestner) White; m. Robert William Knieriem, July 11, 1953; children: Shawn, Roxanne (dec.), Roberta. AA, Mars Hill (N.C.) Coll., 1950; BA, Lynchburg (Va.) Coll., 1952; student, Baldwin-Wallace Coll., 1964-69, Ashland Sem., 1992-93. Lic. elem. tchr., Ohio; lic. to ministry, 1995. Tchr. Bd. Edn., Cleve., 1966-79; lifetime Stephen min. United Ch. of Christ, Cleve., 1990—; interim min., 1997—99; pastor Litchfield United Ch. of Christ, Ohio, 1999—. Min. nursing homes, Cleve., 1990—; chaplain Ky. Cols., 1990—. Democrat. Avocation: running. Home: 7324 Grant Blvd Cleveland OH 44130-5351

KNIESER, CATHERINE, music educator; b. Seoul, Republic of Korea, Aug. 12, 1974; d. Thomas and Susan Knieser. MusB, U. Del., 1997; MusM, Ithaca Coll., 2000. Cert. tchr. N.Y., Nat. Bd. Early Adolescent through Young Adulthood, 2003. Tchr.-in-charge, secondary music Wappingers Ctrl. Sch. Dist., Wappingers Falls, NY, 1999—. Grantee Latin Percussion Mini grant, Wappingers Ctrl. Sch. Dist., 1998—99, African Music Mini grant, Mid Hudson Tchr. Ctr., 1999—2000, Tech. Digital grant, Wappingers Ctrl. Sch. Dist., 2002—. Mem.: N.Y. State Sch. Music Assn., Music Educators Nat. Conf., Am. Orff-Schulwerk Assn., Sigma Alpha Iota (life). Personal E-mail: krabaple@vh.net.

KNIGHT, ATHELIA WILHELMENIA, journalist; b. Portsmouth, Va., Oct. 15, 1950; d. Daniel Dennis and Adell Virginia (Savage) K. BA with honors in English, Norfolk State Coll., 1973; MA with honors in Journalism, Ohio State U., 1974. Cert. tchr. Va. Aide D.C. Coop. Extension Service, 1969-72; sub. tchr. Portsmouth Pub. Schs., 1973; reporter Virginian Pilot, Norfolk, 1973, Chgo. Tribune, 1974; met. desk reporter Washington Post, 1975-81, investigative reporter, 1981-94, sports writer, 1994-2000; asst. dir. Washington Post Young Journalists, 2000—03, dir., 2003; adj. prof. Georgetown U., 2002—. Vis. prof. journalism Hampton U., 2001. Mem. Herb Block Found. Recipient Mark Twain award, 1982, 87, Front Page award Washington-Balt. Newspaper Guild, 1982, Nat. award for edn. Edn. Writers Assn., 1987, Pub. Svc. award Md.-Del.-D.C. Press Assn., 1990, 93, 1st Pl. award for spot news, 1997; Ohio State U. fellow, 1974, Nieman fellow Harvard U., 1985-86. Maynard Mgmt. at the Kellogg Sch. of Mgmt. N.W. U., 2003. Mem.: Investigative Reporters and Editors, Nat. Assn. Black Journalists, Women in Comm. Methodist. Office: Washington Post 1150 15th St NW Washington DC 20071-0002

KNIGHT, BARBARA See GIVEN, BARBARA

KNIGHT, BILLIE-RENEE, language educator; d. Robert C. and Eleanor L. Knight. B in Edn., Ea. Mont. Coll., Billings, Mont., 1991. Fgn. lang. instr. Billings Ctrl. H.S., Mont., 1991—92, Worland Mid. Sch., Wyo., 1992—94, Hayden H.S., Topeka, 1994—. Internat. club sponsor Hayden H.S., Topeka, 1994—, nat. honor soc. sponsor, 1994—, student coun. sponsor, 1996—, fgn. lang. dept. chairperson, 1998—, vocabulary com. chair, 2004—. Recipient Pinnacle award for Tchg. Excellence, Hayden H.S., 2004. Mem.: NASC, ACTFL, FLTEACH, Kans. World Lang. Assn. Catholic. Avocations: travel, writing, reading. Office: Hayden HS 401 SW Gage Topeka KS 66606 Office Phone: 785-272-5210. Personal E-mail: knightdrk2@yahoo.com. E-mail: knightb@haydenhigh.org.

KNIGHT, BRENDA JEAN, mathematics educator; d. Herman Robert and Edith Frances Shirley; m. Larry Felix Shirley, July 7, 1981; children: Leigh Anne Prisinzano, Jason Robert, Jeremy Christopher. BS in Math., U. of Houston, 1974. Math tchr. Ross S. Sterling H.S., Baytown, Tex., 1995—2004, Stephen F. Austin H.S., Sugar Land, Tex., 2004—. Co-sponsor Stephen F. Austin Mu Alpha Theta, Sugar Land, 2004—06. Office: Stephen F Austin H S 3434 Pheasant Creek Dr Sugar Land TX 77478 Office Phone: 281-634-2000. Personal E-mail: bjknight@houston.rr.com. Business E-Mail: brenda.knight@fortbend.k12.tx.us.

KNIGHT, EILEEN QUINN, education educator, consultant; d. Charles Francis and Catherine Kelker Quinn; m. John R. Knight (dec.); children: Jack, Pat, Mike. B in Math., Siena Heights U., Mich., 1969; Masters, De Paul U., Chgo., 1975; PhD, U. Ill., 1992. Asst. prof., 1985—89; assoc. prof. St. Xavier U., Chgo., 1985—2000, prof. edn., 2001—. Recipient Outstanding Presentation award, Nat. Staff Devel. Council, 2003; scholar, Saint Xavier U., 2003; Grant, 3M, 1991, Lily Found., 1992, NSF, 1996, 2000, Ctr. for Ednl. Practice, 1996, Qualities of Mercy Grant, St. Xavier U., 1999. Home: 15302 Mallard Cir Orland Park IL 60462 Personal E-mail: eqkmath@gmail.com, knight@sxu.edu.

KNIGHT, HARRIETTE, secondary educator; Secondary tchr. Emerson Sch. Visual and Performing Arts, Gary, Ind. Named Outstanding High Sch. Tchr. Inland Steel Ryerson Found., 1992. Office: Emerson Sch for the Visual and Performing Arts 716 E 7th Ave Gary IN 46402-2699

KNIGHT, IDA BROWN, retired elementary school educator; b. Macon, Ga., Aug. 8, 1918; d. Morgan Cornelius and Ida (Moore) Brown; m. Dempsey Lewis Knight, Apr. 11, 1942; children: Lavera Knight Hughes, Eugene Charles. BS, Spelman Coll., 1940; MS, SUNY, Fredonia, 1958; postgrad., SUNY, 1974, U. Manchester, Eng., 1974. Cert. tchr. home econs. Clothing tchr. Bibb County Vocat. Sch., Macon, 1940-42; tchr. home econs. Ballard Normal Sch., Macon, 1943-45; elem. tchr. Jamestown (N.Y.) Pub. Schs., 1955-77; ret., 1977. Bd. dirs. Jamestown Girls Club, 1970-78, Jamestown Cmty. Schs., 1989-97; ch. organist, 1974-82; jr. bd. Elizabeth Marvin Cmty. House, 1994-2001, gov. bd. dirs., 1998-2000. Mem. AAUW, Chautauqua County Ret. Tchrs. Assn., N.Y. State Congress Parents and Tchrs. (hon. life), Links, Inc. (past pres. Jamestown chpt.), Delta Kappa Gamma (corr. sec. 1963-64). Avocations: flower gardening, hand crafts, playing piano, reading. Home: 5573 Place Dr South Bend IN 46614

KNIGHT, KAREN ANNE MCGEE, artist, educator, educational research administrator; b. Florence, Ala., July 5, 1956; d. Glenn Houston and Juanita May (Fowler) McGee; m. Charles Ronald Knight, June 3, 1980; 1 child, Lara-Elizabeth. AA, Fla. Coll., 1976; BS, U. N. Ala., 1978, MA in Edn., 1994. Cert. tchr., Tenn., Ala. Title I reading aide Florence City Schs., 1978—79, 1st grade tchr., 1980—83; pre-kindergarten tchr. Belmont Weekday Sch., Nashville, 1984—85; kindergarten tchr. Metro-Davidson County Schs., Nashville, 1985—87; freelance watercolorist Shoals Artist's Guild, Florence, 1992—, Westat/quality control monitor, 1997—98, Westat/assessment adminstr., 1998—2001, Westat/field supr., 2001—. Chair Shoals Artists Guild, 1993—, v.p., 1996, pres., 1998. Sunday sch. tchr. Placed in watercolor competition N. Ala. State Fair, 1993. Mem. Nat. Mus. Women in Arts, Watercolor Soc. Ala. (N.W. Ala. area rep. 1996-2000), Tenn. Valley Art Assn., So. Watercolor Soc., Tenn. Valley Art Assn. Guild Avocations: herb and perennial gardening, genealogy. Home: 111 Snell Dr Florence AL 35630-6257

KNIGHT, KAREN CHAMBERS, nurse; b. Auburndale, Fla., July 3, 1958; d. Dewey Lee and Margaret (Johnson) Dillard; m. Jim L. Chambers, June 16, 1974 (div. Sept. 1993); m. Phillip J. Knight, May 10, 1996; children: Shane Chambers, Nakia Lester, Jeremy Knight, Josh Knight. Grad., N.W. Ala. Tech., Hamilton, 1977; Diploma, North Ala. State Coll., Phil Campbell, 1987. LPN; RN; CCM, CDMS. Nurse Walker Regional Med. Ctr., Jasper, Ala., 1983-87, 90-94; occupl. health nurse West Point Pepperell, Jasper, 1987-89; rehab. specialist IntraCorp, Birmingham, Ala., 1989; med. case mgr. Directions Mgmt. Svcs., Inc., Muscle Shoals, Ala., 1989-91, 92-93; supr. corp. client svcs. Relife, Inc., Birmingham, 1991-92; mgr. case mgmt. svcs. PCA Health Plan of Ala., Birmingham, 1993-95; dir. med. mgmt. Triton Health Systems, LLC, Birmingham, 1995-96; dir. utilization mgmt. GuideStar Health Systems, Inc., Birmingham, 1996-2000; dir. health svcs. VIVA Health, Birmingham, 2000—. Contbr. articles to profl. jours.; presenter in field. Mem. Case Mgmt. Soc. Am. (sec. 1998—, pres.-elect 2001, Case Mgr. of Yr. 1995). Baptist. Office: VIVA Health 1400 21st Pl S Birmingham AL 35205 E-mail: KdKnight2@aol.com.

KNIGHT, KATHERINE ELLEN, science educator, mathematics educator; b. Sacramento, Feb. 24, 1965; d. D. Clark and Shelby A. Biggs; m. Jeffrey Charles Knight, Sept. 2, 1990; children: Clinton Clark, Erik Jeffrey. BA, U. Calif., Berkeley, 1987; EdM, Nat. U., Sacramento, 2004. Adj. prof. North Ctrl. Tex. Coll., Bowie, 1999—2000; tchr. Fairfield (Calif.) Unified, 2004—05; sci. and math tchr. Pierce Joint Unified, Arbuckle, Calif., 2005—. Sheriff's posse mem. Colusa County Sheriff, Williams, Calif., 2004—06; exec. dir. Bowie (Tex.) C. of C., 1999—2001; tutor U. Calif., Berkeley, 1984—87; sec. Cowlitz Hunter Jumper Assn., Longview, Wash., 1994—98. Mem.: AAUW (assoc.), Calif. Assn. for the Gifted (corr.). Democrat. Roman Catholic. Avocations: reading, horses. Home: 2292 Zumwalt Road Williams CA 95987 Office Phone: 530-473-3445.

KNIGHT, MARSHA DIANNE, special education educator; b. Kansas City, Mo., Dec. 13, 1954; d. William Eugene and Leona Belle (Kelton) Cox; m. Paul Ervin Knight, Mar. 24, 1978; children: Megan Dianne, Adam Christopher. AS in Secretarial Sci., Chattanooga State U., 1975; BS in Spl. Edn., U. Tenn., 1993, MEd, 1995; EdS in Adminstrn., Lincoln Meml. U., Harrgate, Tenn., 2000. Sec. to pres. So. Combustion and Controls, Chattanooga, 1975-78; engring. asst. U.S. Stove Co., Chattanooga, 1979-86; grad. asst. U. Tenn., Chattanooga, 1993-94; gtchr. spl. edn. Ridgeland H.S., Rossville, Ga., 1994—. Scholar U. Tenn., 1992. Mem. NEA, CEC, Kappa Delta Pi. Avocation: softball. Office: Ridgeland H S 2878 Happy Valley Rd Rossville GA 30741-6011

KNIGHT, PATRICIA MARIE, biomedical engineer, consultant; b. Schnectady, NY, Jan. 25, 1952; BS in Engring. Sci., Ariz. State U., 1974, MSChemE, 1976; PhD in Biomed. Engring., U. Utah, 1983. Teaching and rsch. asst. Ariz. State U., Tempe, 1974-76; product devel. engr. Am. Med. Optics, Irvine, Calif., 1976-79, mgr. materials rsch., 1983-87; rsch. asst. U. Utah, Salt Lake City, 1979-83; dir. materials rsch. Allergan Surg. Products, Irvine, 1987-88, dir. rsch., 1988-91, v.p. rsch., devel. and engring., 1991—2002; v.p. rsch., devel. Advanced Med. Optics, Santa Ana, Calif., 2002—03; cons. biomed. product rsch. and devel. Laguna Niguel, Calif., 2003—. Contbr. articles to profl. jours. Mem. Soc. Biomaterials, Am. Chem. Soc., Soc. Women Engrs., Assn. Rsch. in Vision and Opthalmology, Biomed. Engring. Soc. E-mail: pkbiomed@cox.net.

KNIGHT, REBECCA JEAN, secondary school educator; b. Oklahoma City, Nov. 8, 1949; d. G.B. and Lillian Pearl (Wright) Williams; m. Ronnie Dean (Knight), Mar. 1, 1968; children: Ronald Chad, Dustin Ryan BS, East Tex. State U., 1972, post grad., 1989—92. Cert. tchr. Tex. Tchrs. aide Bailey Inglish Elem., Bonham, Tex., 1971; tchr. Bonham H.S., 1973—. Mem. ins. com. Bonham Ind. Sch. Dist., 1975—, dist. site based com., 1992-93, campus site based com., 1993-98 chair English Dept. 2001-; tchr. adult Sunday sch. Ch. of God, Lannius, Tex., 1990—, tchr. teenage Sunday sch., 1969-90 Named Tchr. of Yr., Bonham Ind. Sch. Dist., 2003. Mem. NEA, Assn. Tex. Profl. Educators, Nat. Coun. Tchrs. English, Tex. State Tchrs. Assn., No Tex. Tchr. Left Behind, Assn. Tex. Profl. Educators, Alpha Chi. Avocations: reading, computers, walking, sewing, decorating.

KNIGHT, SHERRY ANN, art educator; b. Wash., Pa., July 8, 1955; d. Bernard P. and Angela Bernotas Miller; m. Kent Richard Knight, Jan. 2, 1980. BA, Carlow Coll., Pitts., 1977; EdM, U. Pitts., 1979. Cert. secondary principal Pa. Adj. prof. C.C. Allegheny County, Pitts., 1982—89; tchr. visual arts Trinity HS, Wash., Pa., 1977—. Sec. Pa. Coalition Arts in Edn., 1992—98; advisor and sec. Warhol Mus., Pitts., 2002—. Contbr. photographs Dog Fancy mag., 1998, articles to art pubs. Bd. sec. Pa. Crimestoppers, Wash., Pa., 1994—98; pres. bd. dirs. Pet Search, Wash., Pa., 1996—, People Animal Welfare, Wash., Pa., 1986—96. Named Outstanding Art Educator, Pa. Coalition Arts in Edn., 1996; recipient Ednl. Svc. award, Carlow U., 2004; Fulbright scholar, Japan, 2005. Mem.: Assn. Artists of Pa., Pa. Coun. Arts, Pa. Arts Edn. Assn. (registration chair 1977—, Secondary Art Educator 2001). Democrat. Roman Catholic. Achievements include 4 copyrights for art. Avocations: animals, skiing, reading, museums, gardening. Home: 257 Point View Dr Washington PA 15301 Office: Trinity Area HS 231 Park Ave Washington PA 15301 E-mail: ksam10@pulsenet.com.

KNIGHT, SHIRLEY, actress; b. Goessel, Kans., July 5, 1936; d. Noel Johnson and Virginia (Webster) K.; m. Eugene Persson, 1959 (div., 1969) m. John R. Hopkins, 1969 (dec. July 23, 1998); children: Kaitlin, Sophie. D.F.A., Lake Forest Coll., 1978. Actress theatre and films. Theater debut in Look Back in Anger, Pasadena (Calif.) Playhouse, 1958, N.Y.C. debut in Journey to the Day, 1963; other N.Y.C. theater appearances include The Three Sisters, 1964, Rooms, 1966, We Have Always Lived in the Castle, 1966, The Watering Place, 1969, Kennedy's Children, 1975 (Tony award), Happy End, 1977; with Bristol (Eng.) Old Vic Theatre in And People All Around, 1967; other appearances in Eng. include A Touch of the Poet, 1970, Antigone, 1971, Economic Necessity, 1973; other U.S. theater appearances include A Streetcar Named Desire, Princeton, N.J., 1976, Happy End, N.Y.C., 1977, Landscape of the Body, Chgo., then N.Y.C., 1977, A Lovely Sunday for Creve Coeur, Charleston, S.C., then N.Y.C., 1979, Losing Time, N.Y.C., 1979, I Won't Dance, Buffalo, 1980, Come Back Little Sheba, N.Y.C., 1984, Women Heroes, N.Y.C., 1986, The Depot, N.Y.C., 1987, Cycling Past the Matterhorn, (off-Broadway), 2005; film appearances include: Five Gates to Hell, 1959, Ice Palace, 1960, The Dark at the Top of the Stairs, 1960, The Couch, 1962, Sweet Bird of Youth, 1962, House of Women, 1962, Flight from Ashiya, 1964, The Group, 1966, Petulia, 1966, Dutchman, 1967, The Rain People, 1969, Secrets, 1971, The Counterfeit Killer, 1970, Juggernaut, 1974, Beyond the Poseidon Adventure, 1979, Prisoners, 1981, Endless Love, 1981, The Sender, 1982, The Secret Life of Houses, 1994, Benders, 1994, Color of Night, 1994, Stuart Saves His Family, 1995, Death In Venice, CA, 1994, Diabolique, 1996, As Good as it Gets, 1997, The Man Who Counted, 1998, 75 Degrees in July, 2000, Angel Eyes, 2001, The Salton Sea, 2002, P.S. Your Cat is Dead, 2002, Divine Secrets of the Ya-Ya Sisterhood, 2002, Fly Cherry, 2003, A House on a Hull, 2003, Sexual Life, 2005, To Lie in Green Pastures, 2005, Locked In, 2005, Grandma's Boy, 2006; TV films include: The Outsider, 1967, Shadow Over Elveron, 1968, The Counterfeit Killer, 1968, Majesty, 1968, The Lie, 1971, The Country Girl, 1973, Friendly Persuasion, 1975, Medical Story, 1975, Return to Earth, 1976, 21 Hours at Munich, 1976, The Defection of Simas Kudirka, 1978, Champions: A Love Story, 1979, Playing for Time, 1980, With Intent to Kill, 1984, Sweet Scent of Death, 1984, Billionaire Boys Club, 1987, Bump in the Night, 1991, Shadow of a Doubt, 1991, To Save a Child, 1991, A Mother's Revenge, 1993, Hoggs' Heaven, 1994, Baby Brokers, 1994, The Yarn Princess, 1994, A Part of the Family, 1994, Fudge-A-Mania, 1995, Dad, the Angel & Me, 1995, Children of the Dust, 1995, Indictment: The McMartin Trial, 1995 (Emmy award), Stolen Memories: Secrets From the Rose Garden, 1996, A Promise to Carolyn, 1996, Somebody Is Waiting, 1996, Little Boy Blue, 1997, The Wedding, 1998, If These Walls Could Talk, 1996, The Univited, 1996, Mary & Time, 1996, Dying to be Perfect: The Ellen Hart Pena Story, 1996, Convictions, 1997, A Father for Brittany, 1998, A Marriage of Convenience, 1998, My Louisiana Sky, 2001, Shadow Realm, 2002, Mrs. Ashboro's Cat, 2003; (TV series) Buckskin, 1958, Angel Falls, 1993, Maggie Winters, 1998; (TV mini series) When Love Kills: The Seduction of John Hearn, 1993; guest appearances includeRawhide, 1959, The Fugitive, 1964, 1965, 2001, Marcus Welby, M.D., 1974, Barnaby Jones, 1975, Spenser: For Hire, 1985, 1987, thirtysomething, 1987, Murder She Wrote, 1990, Matlock, 1990, Law & Order, 1991, 2001, Law & Order: Special Victims Unit, 2003, L.A. Law, 1993, NYPD, 1995, Ally McBeal, 2002, ER, 2002, Crossing Jordan, 2004, Cold Case, 2004, House, M.D., 2005, Desperate Housewives, 2005 and several others. Active Com. for Handgun Control, nat. civil rights orgns., worker for peace. Recipient Tony award (Antoinette Perry for Supporting or Featured Actress), 1976, Emmy award for Outstanding Guest Performer in Comedy Drama or Series, 1988, Emmy award for Outstanding Guest Performer in a Drama Series (NYPD Blue), 1995.*

KNIGHT CRANE, MARJORIE, foundation administrator; b. Miami, Fla. d. James L. Knight. Studied, Rollins Coll., Winter Park, Fla.; BA magna cum laude, Queens Coll. Trustee John S. and James L. Knight Found., 1994—, mem., grants review com.; mem., planning and program com.; exec. com. mem., president's advisory circle Queens Coll.; mem. Opera Guild of Charlotte; pres. RibbonWalk Conservancy, Inc.; bd. dirs., library Queens Coll. Mem.: Crown Soc. of Carolinas Concert Assn. Office: Knight Found Wachovia Fin Ctr Ste 3300 200 S Biscayne Blvd Miami FL 33131*

KNIGHTEN, LATRENDA, elementary school educator, consultant; d. Randolph and Dianne Judson Knighten. BA in Early Childhood Edn. and Psychology, Tulane U., 1987. Cert. tchr. La., 1987. From tchr. kindergarten to specialist math. elem. sch. East Baton Rouge (La.) Parish, 1987—2003, specialist math. elem. sch., 2003—. Contractor La. State Dept. Edn., 01, 2003; cons. in field; mem. numerous coms. East Baton Rouge (La.) Parish; presenter in field. Contbr. lessons for teacher training. Finalist Elem. Tchr. of Yr., East Baton Rouge (La.) Parish, 1996, State Tchr. of Yr. award, La., 1997, Tchr. of Yr. award, CPB Nat. Tchr. Tng. Inst., 1998; named Tchr. of Yr., Wildwood Elem., 1997; recipient Elem. Tchr. of Yr., East Baton Rouge (La.) Parish, 1997; grantee, Friends of Environmental Edn., 1994—95, Quality Sci. and Math. Equipment Fund, 1994—96, Academic Distinction Fund, 1994—96. Mem.: Nat. Sci. Educators Leadership Assn., Nat. Sci. Tchrs. Assn. (sci. program key leader La. 1997—), Nat. Coun. Tchrs. Math. (chmn. conf. program 2004, profl. devel. com. 2004—, presenter), La. Sci. Tchrs. Assn. (co-chmn. conf. program 2000, regional rep. 2003), La. Assn. Sci. Leaders, La. Assn. Computer Using Educators, La. Fedn. Tchrs., La. Assn. Tchrs. Math. (sec. 1997—99, co-chmn. conf. program 2000, rep. 2000—01, pres.-elect 2001—02, pres. 2002—04, chmn. conf. 2003, 2003, past pres. 2004—), Baton Rouge (La.) Area Coun. Tchrs. Math. (pres. 2003—, 2000—01, pres.-elect 1999—2000, v.p. elem. 1994—96), Assn. Supr. and Curriculum Devel., Phi Delta Kappa.

KNIGHTLEY, KEIRA, actress; b. Teddington, Middlesex, Eng., Mar. 26, 1985; d. Will Knightley and Sharman Mcdonald. Actor: (films) A Village Affair, 1994, Innocent Lies, 1995, Star Wars: Episode I - The Phantom Menace, 1999, The Hold, 2001, Deflation, 2001, New Year's Eve, 2002, Bend it Like Beckham, 2002, Thunderpants, 2002, Pure, 2002, The Seasons Alter, 2002, Pirates of the Caribbean: The Curse of the Black Pearl, 2003, Love Actually, 2003, King Arthur, 2004, Stories of Lost Souls, 2005, The Jacket, 2005, Pride and Prejudice, 2005, Domino, 2005, Pirates of the Caribbean: Dead Man's Chest, 2006 (Movies-Choice Hissy Fit and Choice Scream, Teen Choice Awards, 2006); (TV films) Royal Celebration, 1993, Treasure Seekers, 1996, Coming Home, 1998, Princess of Thieves, 2001; (TV miniseries) Oliver Twist, 1999, Doctor Zhivago, 2002. Named one of 50 Most Powerful People in Hollywood, Premiere mag., 2006.*

KNIZESKI, JUSTINE ESTELLE, insurance company executive; b. Glen Cove, NY, June 4, 1954; d. John Martin and Elsie Beatrice (Gozelski) Knizeski. BA, Conn. Coll., 1976; M in Mgmt., Northwestern U., 1981. Customer svc. supr. Brunswick Savs., Freeport, Maine, 1977-79; investment analyst Bankers Life and Casualty Co., Chgo., 1980-83, dir. corp. planning and analysis, 1983-87; dir. budgets, cost acctg. Blue Cross/Blue Shield of Ill., 1987-97, dir. planning, budgets and analysis, 1997—, exec. dir. budgets and analysis, 2002—, divsn. v.p. corp. budgets and procurement, 2003—04, v.p., chief procurement officer, 2004—. Sec. Alternatives, Inc., Chgo., 1991—92, vice chmn., 1987—91, 2002—04, chair fin. com., 2002—05, ad hoc fin. com., 1998—2001; active Chgo. Coun. Fgn. Rels., 2002—; ad hoc fin. com. Alternatives, Inc., 2005—, chmn. bd. dir., 1984—87, bd. dir., 1983—84, 2001—02, Non-Profit Fin. Ctr., 2000—03, treas., 2002—03. Mem.: Planning Forum. Avocations: travel, sailing, bicycling, travel, painting. Business E-Mail: knizeskij@bcbsil.com.

KNOBLAUCH, MARY REILLY (MARY LOUISE REILLY), retired music educator, writer; b. Montrose, Mo., Feb. 21, 1922; d. John Henry Welling and Sylvesta Lesmeister; m. Charles A. Knoblauch, Apr. 7, 1996; m. Barney E. Reilly, Dec. 28, 1946 (dec. July 30, 1991); 1 child, Marguerite Ann. BS in Music Edn., St. Mary Coll., Leavenworth, Kans., 1944; MA in Edn., Immaculate Heart Coll., L.A., Calif., 1956; LHD (hon.), St. Mary Coll., Leavenworth, Kans., 2002. Tchr. music French Inst. Notre Dame De Sion, Kansas City, Mo., 1944—46, L.A. City Schs., 1946—54, supr. music ctrl. dist., 1954—55; asst. prof. music L.A. State Coll., 1955—57; assoc. prof. music San Fernando State Coll., Northridge, Calif., 1957—74; prof. music Calif. State U., Northridge, 1975—92, prof. emeritus, 1992. Music cons. L.A. Parochial Schs., 1963—73; adv. bd. Cultural Ctr., Woodland Hills, Calif., 1960; v.p. edn. Opera Guild, L.A., 1970. Author: (tchr.'s materials) It's Time for Music, 1985, (textbooks) World of Music K-6, 1988, Music Connection Series K-6, 1995—98. Grant dir. L.A. Mcpl. Arts, 1978; mem. Liturgical Music Comm., L.A., 1972—79; dir. Docent Ministry, St. Francis of Assisi, 1999—; mem. Comprehensive Arts Ctr. State Dept. of Edn., Sacramento, 1976. Recipient Disting. Prof. award, Calif. State U., 1979, St. Cecilia's award Docent Ministry, 2002, Lifetime Achievement award, Calif. Music Educators Hall of Fame, 2002. Mem.: La Quinta Arts Found., Sigma Alpha Iota (award of Honor 1961), Delta Kappa Gamma (grad. scholarship 1955). Achievements include development of music framework for Calif. schs., State Dept. Edn., 1970. Avocations: reading, piano, dance, gardening. Home: 48 605 Vista Tierra La Quinta CA 92253

KNOEBEL, SUZANNE BUCKNER, cardiologist, educator; b. Ft. Wayne, Ind., Dec. 13, 1926; d. Doster and Marie (Lewis) Buckner. AB, Goucher Coll., 1948; MD, Ind. U.-Indpls., 1960. Diplomate: Am. Bd. Internal Medicine. Asst. prof. medicine Ind. U., Indpls., 1966-69, assoc. prof., 1969-72, prof., 1972-77, Krannert prof., 1977—. Asst. dean rsch. Ind. U., Indpls., 1975-85; assoc. dir. Krannert Inst. Cardiology, Indpls., 1974-90; asst. chief cardiology sect. Richard L. Roudebush VA Med. Ctr., Indpls., 1982-90; editor-in-chief ACC Current Jour. Rev., 1992-2000. Fellow Am. Coll. Cardiology (v.p. 1980-81, pres. 1982-83); mem. Am. Fedn. Clin. Research, Assn. Univ. Cardiologists Office: Krannert Inst 1701 N Senate Ave Indianapolis IN 46202 Office Phone: 317-962-0061. Business E-Mail: sknoebel@iupui.edu.

KNOLL, GLORIA JEAN, music educator; b. Bismarck, ND, Mar. 6, 1947; d. Gustav and Edna Kosanke; m. James L. Pearson (div.); children: Kristin Pearson, James K. Pearson, Erik Pearson, Erin Pearson; m. Marvin P. Knoll, June 15, 1991. BS, Minn. State U., Moorhead, 1969. Cert. tchr. ND, 1969. Vocal and instrumental instr. Grandin HS, ND, 1970—73, Prairie Rose Elem. Sch., Bismarck, 1979—89, Hagen Jr. HS, Dickinson, ND, 1989—99, Horizon Mid. Sch., Bismarck, 1999—; vocal music instr. Nathan Twining Jr. HS, Grand Forks, ND, 1973—76. Site chmn. Western Dakota Assn. Music Festival, Bismarck, 2006—; mem. Oahe Women's Orgn., Bismarck, 2004—06; mem. mission outreach McCabe United Meth. Ch., Bismarck, 2000—06. Mem.: Am. Choral Dirs. Assn. (ND state pres. 2003—, ND state membership chmn. 2000—03). Office: Horizon Mid Sch 500 Ash Coulee Dr Bismarck ND 58503 Business E-Mail: gloria_knol@educ8.org.

KNOLL, JEANNETTE THERIOT, state supreme court justice; b. Baton Rouge, La. m. Jerold Edward Knoll; children: Triston Kane, Eddie Jr., Edmond Humphries, Blake Theriot, Jonathan Paul. BA in Polit. Sci., Loyola U., 1966; JD, Loyola U. Sch. of Law, 1969; LLM in Jud. Process, U. Va. Sch. of Law, 1996; studied with Maestro Adler, Mannes Coll. of Music, 1962-63. Criminal defense atty., first asst. dist. atty. Twelfth Jud. Dist. Ct. Avoyelles Parish, 1972-82; gratuitous atty., advisor U.S. Selective Svc., Marksville, La.; judge (3d cir.) U.S. Ct. of Appeal, 1982-93; assoc. justice La. Supreme Ct., 1997—. Instr. La. Jud. Coll.; chair CLE La. Ct. of Appeal Judges; former mem. state bd. of La. Commn. on Law Enforcement & Criminal Justice; former mem. Past pres. Bus. and Profl. Women's Club; Marksville C. of C.; active Am. Legion Aux.; dir. Arts & Humanities Council of Avoyelles, Inc.; former chmn. La. March of Dimes. Named La. Crimefighters' Outstanding Jurist of Yr., 2000; named to La. Political Hall of Fame, 2000; recipient Met. Opera Assn., New Orleans Opera Guild Scholarship, Outstanding Jud. award, Victims & Citizens Against Crime, Inc., 1995, 2002. Mem.: La. State Bar Assn. Office: La Supreme Ct 400 Royal St New Orleans LA 70130*

KNOLL, ROSE ANN, radiologist, technologist; b. Marshfield, Wis., Mar. 28, 1954; d. Edward Edwin Jr. and Mary Ellen (Allen) K. BS, U. Wis., La Crosse, 1976; MSA, Cen. Mich. U., 1985; AAS, Community Coll. of USAF, 1985. Radiologic technologist Pentagon USAF Flight Medicine Clinic, Washington, 1982-85; radiology mgr. USAF Clinic, McGuire AFB, N.J., 1985; radiologic technologist Georgetown U. Hosp., Washington, 1985-86; radiology dir. Divine Savior Hosp. and Nursing Home, Portage, Wis., 1986-90; dir. imaging svcs. Douglas Cmty. Med. Ctr., Roseburg, Oreg., 1990—2000; mgr. med. imaging Meriter Hosp., Madison, Wis., 2000—. Staff sgt. USAF, 1979-85. Recipient Humanitarian award, Longevity award; U. Wis. leadershp grantee; decorated Good Conduct medal with oak leaf cluster. Mem. Am. Soc. Radiologic Technologists, Am. Healthcare Radiology Adminstrs., Am. Registry Radiologic Technologists, Ctrl. Mich. U. Alumni, UW Lacrosse Alumni, Gamma Sigma Sigma Alumni, 4-H Alumni. Roman Catholic. Home: 346 Kent Ln Apt 303 Madison WI 53713-3933 Office: Meriter Hosp Med Imaging 202 S Park St Madison WI 53715 Office Phone: 608-267-6090 ext 5933. Personal E-mail: knollr@sbcglobal.net. Business E-Mail: rknoll@meriter.com.

KNOOP, MAGGIE PEARSON, language educator; b. Pitts., July 5, 1945; d. Lawrence Thomas and Marie Barnes Pearson; m. Michael Francis Knoop, Apr. 10, 1970 (div.); children: Jamie Michael, Meagan Pearson. BA, U. South Fla., 1971, MA, 1982. Tchr., coach Acad. Holy Names, Tampa, Fla., 1971—74, Shorecrest Prep. Sch., St. Petersburg, Fla., 1974—87; prof. St. Petersburg Coll., Clearwater, Fla., 1989—. Area dir. publicity Women's State Track Honor Roll, Fla., 1981—82; exercise specialist and fitness cons. Group W Cable, St. Petersburg, 1982—86; chmn. Divsn. Girl's and Women's Sports Fla. Assn. of Health, Phys. Edn., Recreation and Dance, Fla., 1986—87; presenter in field. Co-author: (pub.svc. announcements) Drug Abuse. Mem.: NOW, AAUW, Bay Area Regional Tchrs. Second Lang. Learners (treas.), Planned Parenthood Fedn. Am., NARAL Pro Choice. Democrat. Avocations: wellness, travel, literature. Home: 610 Island Way 105 Clearwater FL 33767 Office: St Petersburg College 2465 Drew Street Clearwater FL 33765 Office Phone: 727-791-2663. Personal E-mail: mknoop@tampabay.rr.com. Business E-Mail: knoopmaggie@spcollege.edu.

KNOP, RUTH M., mathematics educator; b. St. Louis, Mo., Jan. 28, 1974; d. Michael E. and Carolyn S. Bresnahan; m. Dennis M. Knop, Dec. 29, 2001; 1 child, Jackson T. BA in Secondary Edn., St. Louis U., Mo., 1997; BA in Math, St. Louis U., 1997; MEd, U. Mo., St. Louis, Mo., 2001. PC I and PC II Mo., 1997. Math. tchr. Francis Howell Sch. Dist., St. Charles, Mo., 1997—2000, Pky. Sch. Dist., St. Louis, 2000—05, coord. math., 2005—. Nctm rep. Math. Educators Greater St. Louis, 2003—06. Mem.: ASCD (assoc.), Nat. Coun. Suprs. Math. (assoc.), Nat. Coun. Tchrs. Math. (assoc.; local arrangements com. chairperson-student hosts 2006), Mo. Coun. Tchrs. Math. (assoc.), Math. Educators Greater St. Louis (assoc.; nctm rep. 2003—06). Roman Catholic. Avocations: piano, travel, cooking. Home: 7143 Dardenne Prairie Dr Dardenne Prairie MO 63368 Office: Instnl Svcs Ctr 12657 Fee Fee Rd Saint Louis MO 63146 Office Phone: 314-415-7042. Business E-Mail: rknop@pkwy.k12.mo.us.

KNOPF, CLAIRE, editor, writer; b. Passaic, N.J., Apr. 22, 1939; d. Isadore and Helen Knopf. Student, Mich. State U., 1957—59, U. Calif., Berkeley, 1960—61, Columbia U., N.Y.C., 1962—63, Parsons Sch. Design, 1995—96. Freelance copy editor Massada Pub. Co., The Magnes Press, The Hebrew U., Israel, 1970—79; writer Edrei-Sharon Publs., Israel, 1970—79; copy editor Time Mag., Time Warner, Inc., N.Y.C., 1980—96; freelance copy editor New Woman Mag., Vogue Mag., 1997—2000, US Weekly, BabyTalk, Smart Money, In Touch Weekly, Quest, Food & Wine, Ladies' Home Jour., Psychology Today Mag., NYC2012, U.S. Candidate City for Olympic Games, others; copy editor, writer, reporter Salt Lake Olympic Winter Games and Paralympic Winter Games, Salt Lake City, 2000—02; writer, reporter, rschr. Internat. Figure Skating Mag., 2002—. Mem.: Soc. Children's Book Writers and Illustrators, Time-Life Alumni Soc., N.Y. Press Club, Inc. Avocations: art, writing children's books, ice skating, cross country skiing. Home: Apt 14M 6040 Boulevard East West New York NJ 07093 Personal E-mail: claireknopf@earthlink.net.

KNOPF, TANA DARLENE, counselor, music educator; b. Des Moines, Oct. 19, 1951; d. Charles D. Sr. and Edith D. Smith; m. James E. Knopf, Aug. 7, 1982; children: Daniel P., Chandra D. BA, Met. State Coll., Denver, 1974; MEd, U. Colo., Denver, 1983. Instrumental music tchr. Denver Pub. Schs., 1974—2000, counselor, 2001—. Business E-Mail: tana_knopf@dpsk12.org.

KNOTT, JENNIFER W., lawyer; b. Irving, Tex., May 9, 1974; BA cum laude, So. Meth. U., 1996; JD cum laude, So. Meth. U. Dedman Sch. Law, 2000. Bar: Tex. 2000, US Dist. Ct. (no. and ea. dists. Tex.). Assoc. McElree, Savage & Smith, P.C., Dallas. Comments editor: So. Meth. U. Law Rev., 1999—2000. Named a Rising Star, Tex. Super Lawyers mag., 2006. Mem.: Dallas Assn. Young Lawyers (mem. freedom run com. 2004, 2005), Dallas Bar Assn. Office: McElree Savage & Smith PC Plz of the Americas Ste 1600 600 N Pearl St Lock Box Number 175 Dallas TX 75201-2809 Office Phone: 214-979-0681. E-mail: jknott@mspc.com.*

KNOTTS, MAUREEN MARY, science educator; b. Cleve., June 1, 1978; d. Patricia and David Knotts. BS in Zoology, Ohio State U., Columbus, 2000, MEd, 2001. Cert. Secondary Sci. Educator 7-12 Ohio, 2001. Sci. educator Northland HS, Columbus, 2001—. Coach cross country/track Northland HS, 2001—. Rsch. com. Friends of the Lower Olentangy Watershed, Columbus, 2002; vol. Big Brother / Big Sister Orgn., Columbus, 2004. Mem.: NSTA, Varsity O Women's Alumni Soc. Citizens. Achievements include Varsity O Letter Awards, OSU Cross Country and Track 1996-2000. Office: Northland High School 1919 Northcliff Dr Columbus OH 43229 Office Phone: 614-365-5342. E-mail: knotts.16@osu.edu.

KNOTT-TWINE, LAURA MAE, director; b. Hartford, Conn., Nov. 11, 1946; m. Richard Graham Twine, Jan. 26, 1973; children: Edward Dean, Susan Helene. BA, Norwich U., 1996—98, MA, 1998—99. Pres. and owner Orchard Ho. Weavers, Windham Ctr., 1980—85; founder, exec. dir. & ceo Windham Textile and History Mus., Inc., 1980—95; dirctor of SBA Women's Bus. Ctr. U. of Hartford, Conn., 2000—; faculty- undergraduate Union U./Vt. Coll., Monpelier, Vt., 2002—. Pres., v.p. & sec. Handweavers Guild of Conn., Glastonbury, Conn., 1979—84; v.p. NE CT Tourism Dist., Windham, Conn., 1984—86; advisor Nat. Heritage Corrior Pk. Bd., Hartford, Conn., 1988—95; paliamentarian Assn. of Girl Scouts Exec. Staff, North Haven, Conn., 1997—98; mem. Windham, Conn. Econ. Devel. Com., Windham, Conn., 1988—95; founder Windham Textile and History Museum, Inc.; instr. bus. Vermont Coll. Handweaver, Colonial Handweaving. Mem. Nat. Heritage Corridor Bd., Hartford, Conn., 1988—95; advisor Nat. Inst. of Puppetry at U. of Conn., Storrs, Conn., 1990—96; mem. Assn. of Women's Bus. Centers, Boston, 2000—03; program officer Museums of NE Conn. Assn., 1989—95; mem. SBA Women Bus. Advocate, Conn., 2002; life mem. Girl Scouts of Am., NYC, 1998—2003. Independent. Catholic. Avocations: handweaving, handspinning, reading, travel. Home: 32 Gray Pine Common Avon CT 06001 Office: The Entrepreneurial Center U Hartford 50 Elizabeth St Hartford CT 06105 Office Phone: 860-570-0331. Personal E-mail: rltwine@comcast.com.

KNOUS, PAMELA K., wholesale distribution executive; b. Minn. Student, Carleton Coll.; BA in Math., U. Ariz., BS in Bus. Adminstrn. Ptnr. KPMG Peat Marwick, LA, 1977—91; group v.p. finance The Vons Companies, Inc., 1991—94; sr. v.p., CFO The Vons. Companies, Inc., 1994; exec. v.p., CFO The Vons Companies, Inc., 1995—97, treas.; exec. v.p., CFO Supervalu Inc., Mpls., 1997—. Bd. dir. Tennant Co., Twin Cities Pub. Television. Office: Supervalu Inc 11840 Valley View Rd Eden Prairie MN 55344 Office Phone: 952-828-4000. Office Fax: 952-828-8998.*

KNOWLES, BEYONCÉ GISELLE See BEYONCÉ

KNOWLES, ELIZABETH PRINGLE, museum director; b. Decatur, Ill., Jan. 9, 1943; d. William Bull and Elizabeth E. (Pillsbury) Pringle; m. Joseph E. Knowles; 1 child, Elizabeth Bakewell. BA in Humanities with honors, Stanford U., 1964; MA in Art History, U. Calif., Santa Barbara, 1968; grad., Mus. Mgmt. Inst., 1984; MBA, Rensselaer Poly. Inst., 1999. Cert. jr. coll. tchr. Calif. Instr. art history Murray State U., Murray, Ky., 1967-68; instr. Santa Barbara Art Inst., 1969, Santa Barbara City Coll., 1969-70, 76-78, instr. cont. edn., 1973-86; from staff coord. docents to curator edn. Santa Barbara Mus. Art, 1974-86; assoc. dir. Meml. Art Gallery, Rochester, NY, 1986-88; instr. mus. studies Calif. State U., Long Beach, 1989; exec. dir. Lyman Allyn Art Mus., New London, Conn., 1989-95; pres. Only In Conn. Spl. Interest Tours, Chester, 1995-97; supr. mus. edn. programs Mystic (Conn.) Seaport Mus., 1996-2001; exec. dir. Wildling Art Mus., Los Olivos, Calif., 2001—. Instr. continuing edn. Santa Barbara City Coll., 1973—86, 2002—. Contbr. essays to art catalogues. Bd. dirs., chmn. Met. Transit Dist., Santa Barbara, 1978—80; commr. Santa Barbara City Planning Commn., 1975—77; founding pres. Santa Barbara Contemporary Arts Forum, 1976—78. Fellow Kellogg Found., Smithsonian Inst., 1985. Mem.: New Eng. Mus. Assn. (v.p. 1993—95), Coll. Art Assn., Am. Assn. Mus. (treas. edn. com. 1986—88). Office Phone: 805-688-1082. E-mail: Penny@wildlingmuseum.org.

KNOWLES, MARILYN RAE, ballet company administrator; b. Fresno, Calif., Sept. 23, 1937; d. Lawrence Earl and Phyllis Marie (Faus) Evans; m. Lawrence Rowland, Oct. 9, 1960; children: Stuart Ashley, Paul Joseph. BFA, U. Utah, 1959; MFA, U. Utah1960. Soloist Pacific Ballet, San Francisco, 1961—71; artistic dir. Fresno Ballet, 1973—. Tchr. ballet Severance Sch. Dance, Fresno, 1971—. Mem.: La Paloma Guild Fresno City and County Hist. Soc., Delta Delta Delta.

KNOWLES, MARJORIE FINE, law educator, dean; b. Bklyn., July 4, 1939; d. Jesse J. and Roslyn (Leff) Fine; m. Ralph I. Knowles, Jr., June 3, 1972. BA, Smith Coll., 1960; LLB, Harvard U., 1965. Bar: Ala., N.Y., D.C. Teaching fellow Harvard U., 1963-64; law clk. to judge U.S. Dist. Ct. (so. dist.), NY, 1965-66; asst. U.S. atty. U.S. Atty.'s Office, N.Y.C., 1966-67; asst. dist. atty. N.Y. County Dist. Atty., N.Y.C., 1967-70; exec. dir. Joint Found. Support, Inc., N.Y.C., 1970-72; asst. gen. counsel HEW, Washington, 1978-79; insp. gen. U.S. Dept. Labor, Washington, 1979-80; assoc. prof. U. Ala. Sch. Law, Tuscaloosa, 1972-75, prof., 1975-86, assoc. dean, 1982-84; law prof., dean Ga. State U. Coll. Law, Atlanta, 1986-91, law prof., 1986—. Cons. Ford Found., N.Y.C., 1973-98, 2000-03, trustee Coll. Retirement Equities Fund, N.Y.C., 1983-2002; mem. exec. com. Conf. on Women and the Constn., 1986-88; mem. com. on continuing profl. edn. Am. Law Inst.-ABA, 1987-93. Contbr. articles to profl. jours. Am. Council Edn. fellow, 1976—77, Aspen Inst. fellow, Rockefeller Found., 1976. Mem. ABA (chmn. new deans workshop 1988), Ala. State Bar Assn., N.Y. State Bar Assn., D.C. Bar Assn., Am. Law Inst., Tchrs. Ins. Annuity Assn. (trustee 2003-). Office: Ga State U Coll Law University Plz Atlanta GA 30303 Office Phone: 404-651-2081.

KNOWLES, PATRICIA MARIE, science educator; d. Richard Lance and Alice Kay Knowles; children: Jason Zow, Ki-jana Zow, Khalitri Zow. BS in Elem. Edn., Western Oreg. U., Monmouth, 1987; MS in Secondary Edn. Health, Western Oreg. U., 1997. Cert. tchr. Fla. Dept of Edn., 2001. Tchr. Orange County Pub. Schs., Orlando, Fla., 1999—. Team leader Orange County Pub. Schs., Orlando, Fla., 2000—, sci. dept. chairperson, 2004—, athletic dir., 2005—, girls basketball coach, 2000—, girl's track coach, 2000—. Named Tchr. of the Yr., Orange County Pub. Schs., 2006; named to Athletic Hall of Fame, Western Oreg. U., 2004. Mem.: Orange County Classroom Tchrs. Assn. (assoc.), NEA (assoc.), Fla. Edn. Assn. (assoc.). Office: Walker Middle School 150 Amidon Ln Orlando FL 32809 Office Phone: 407-858-3210 289. Home Fax: 407-858-3218; Office Fax: 407-858-3218. E-mail: knowlep2@ocps.net.

KNOWLTON, GRACE FARRAR, sculptor, photographer; b. Buffalo, Mar. 15, 1932; d. Frank Neff and Esther Sargeant (Norton) Farrar; m. Winthrop Knowlton, July 8, 1960 (div. 1980); children: Eliza, Samantha. BA, Smith Coll., 1954; MA, Columbia U., 1981. Asst. to curator of graphic arts Nat. Gallery of Art, Washington, 1955-57; tchr. art Arlington (Va.) Pub. Schs., 1957-60; sculptor, photographer, painter, 1960—; tchr. art Art Students League, N.Y.C., 1999—. One-woman shows include Katonah (N.Y.) Mus., 1993, Smith Coll. Mus., Northampton, Mass., 1993, Hirschl & Adler Modern, N.Y.C., 1997, Bates Coll. Mus., Lewiston, Maine, 2002, Neuberger Mus., Purchase, N.Y., 2002, Represented in permanent collections Corcoran Gallery Art, Washington, D.C., Met. Mus., N.Y.C., Storm King Art Ctr., Mountainville, N.Y., Victoria & Albert Mus., London, Eng., Yale U. Mus. Art, New Haven, Conn., Houston (Tex.) Mus. Fine Arts. Home: 67 Ludlow Ln Palisades NY 10964-1606 Personal E-mail: graceknowlton@earthlink.net.

KNOWLTON, MARIE, retired special education educator; b. Springville, N.Y., Feb. 3, 1936; d. Frank E. and Eva (Reith) K.; children: Martha, John, Michelle, Paolillo BS, Cornell U., 1958, PhD, 1983. Cert. braille transcriber. Tchr., visually impaired Newfield Sch. Dist., NY; assoc. prof. U. Minn., Mpls., 1983—2001, ret., 2001. Developer computer-assisted graphic for blind readers; contbr. articles to profl. jours Minn. Functional Vision Assessment grantee Mem. Coun. for Exceptional Children, Assn. for Edn. and Rehab. of Blind and Visually Impaired

KNOWLTON, SYLVIA KELLEY, physician; d. Darwin and Mary Kelley (Dec.); m. R. A. Levinson, Dec., 1971 (div. 1988); 1 child, Diana Nicole Levinson; m. Donald William Knowlton, Apr. 20, 1989; children: Fred (dec.), Bill. BS, Ind. U., 1977, MD, 1975. Diplomate Am. Bd. Internal Medicine, Am. Bd. Allergy and Immunology. Intern in internal medicine Mt. Sinai Med. Ctr., Miami Beach, Fla., 1976; resident in internal medicine U. Mich., Ann Arbor, 1976, U. Calif., Davis, 1976-77; fellow Nat. Jewish Hosp., Denver, 1977-79; pvt. practice Boca Raton, Fla., 1980; physician Asthma & Allergy Associates P.C., Ithaca, NY. Republican. Avocations: singing, sailing, poetry. Home: PO Box 64 Alfred Station NY 14803-9794 Office Phone: 607-257-6563.

KNOX, BARBARA S., education educator; d. Willie E. and Lizzie Searey; children: Chederick Dion, Kiara W. BS in Sociology, Savanah State Coll., Ga., 1969; M in Edn., Berry Coll., Ga., 1978; DMin in Christian Edn., Jacksonville Theol. Sem., 2005. Cert. ednl. specialist in curriculum and instrn. Lincoln Meml. U. (Tenn.), 2003. Tchr. Adairsville (Ga.) Mid. Sch., 1988—2001, Kingston (Ga.) Elem. Sch., 1969—88; asst. prof. edn. Shorter Coll., Rome, Ga., 2001—. Mem.: Nat. Mid. Sch. Assn., Christian Women in Action, Women of Shorter, Am. Assn. Univ. Women (chair edn. fund 2002—), Delta Sigma Theta (v.p. 2004—). Baptist. Avocation: doll collecting. Home: 710 E 17th St Rome GA 30161 Office: Shorter Coll 315 Shorter Ave Rome GA 30165 Personal E-mail: bknox@shorter.edu, bsk0220@bellsouth.net.

KNOX, DANIELLE NICOLE, secondary school educator; b. Atlanta, Aug. 28, 1981; d. Robert Frederick and LaReta Darnetta Knox. BS, Stephen F. Austin State U., Nacogdoches, Tex., 2004. Cert. tchr. Tex., 2004. H.S. math tchr. Tyler Ind. Sch. Dist., Tex., 2004—; prof. Tyler Jr. Coll., 2005—. Author poetry. Office: Tyler Independent School District 1120 NNW Loop 323 Tyler TX 75702 Home: Apt D 126 E First St Tyler TX 75701 Office Phone: 903-262-2850. Personal E-mail: educatorinlife@yahoo.com.

KNOX, DEBBY, newscaster; m. Richard Triman; 2 children. Grad., U. Mich. With various stas., Elkhart, Ind., South Bend; anchor Sta. WISH-TV, Indpls., 1980—. Recipient Casper award, Ind. State Med. Journalism awards (3), Associated Press award, United Press Internat. award. Office: WISH-TV 1950 N Meridian St Indianapolis IN 46207

KNOX, DEBORAH CAROLYN, state information systems administrator; b. Manchester, Tenn., Mar. 31, 1962; d. Eugene Clarke and Myrtle Carolyn (Bell) Knox. BBA in Acctg., Middle Tenn. State U., 1984. CPA, Tenn.; cert. govt. fin. mgr. Sr. fin. planner Lincoln Fin. Group, Brentwood, Tenn., 1986; staff acct. Charles Tharp & Assocs., Nashville, 1987; staff acct. dept. treasury State of Tenn., Nashville, 1984-85, supr. pension payroll dept. treasury, 1987, compliance analyst, policy planner, 1988, dir. program acctg. dept. fin., adminstrn., 1988-93; from data adminstr. to mgr. application devel. and support Dept. of Fin. and Adminstrn., Nashville, 1993-99, asst. dir. info. sys. mgmt., 1999—2005, project mgmt. and finance office, 2006—. Mem. Assn. Govt. Accts., Nat. Assn. CPAs (John Lewis award 1984). Avocations: snow and water skiing, raising and training horses and dogs.

KNOX, GERTIE R., compliance executive, accountant; b. Rossville, Tenn., Feb. 2, 1960; d. Columbus and Mabel (Strickland) K.; m. Micheal F. Coley, Sept. 1, 1990. BBA, U. Memphis, 1982; MBA, Colo. State U., 1998. CPA, Calif. Contracts and fin. adminstr. Textron Aerostructures, Nashville, 1983-86; ptnr. PricewaterhouseCoopers LLP, Irvine, Calif., 1986-2001; COO, Global Social Compliance LLC, L.A., 2001—. Mem.: AICPA. Avocations: reading, travel.

KNOX, LORI BRICKNER, mathematician, educator; d. Michael Joseph and Teresa Jane Brickner; m. Jared Evan Knox, June 19, 2004; children: Joshua Ethan, Noah Michael. BS in Math., U. of Pitts., MA in Tchg. Tchr. Mt. Lebanon Sch. Dist., Pitts., 1999—. Office: Mt Lebanon School District 11 Castle Shannon Blvd Pittsburgh PA 15228 Office Phone: 412-344-2122.

KNOX, TRUDY, publisher, consultant, retired psychologist; b. Cape Girardeau, Mo., Aug. 11, 1926; d. Raymond Kenneth and Gertrude (McCann) K.; m. Joseph Russel Bagby, Feb. 14, 1962 (div. July 1969); children: Kenneth, Laurel, James. BS, Northwestern U., 1948; MA, U. Fla., 1951; EdD, U. Ark., 1973. Lic. psychologist, Ill. Psychologist Columbus State Sch. State of Ohio, 1952-57, Scioto Village State of Ohio, Delaware, 1957-62; psychologist, cons. Granville, Ohio, 1962-67; psychologist Ohio Reformatory for Women, Marysville, 1987-90. Adj. faculty Ohio State U., Newark, Columbus, 1974—; weekly columnist Community Booster, 2000-. Pub. book and cassette program The Music Is You by R. Perez, 1983, Turn Right at The Next Corner by Pat Vivo, 1991, Economics of Education by Martin Schoppmeyer, 1992, Sans Souci Spa Dining by Susanne Kircher, 1993, Where There's Hope by Hope Mihalap, 1994; contbr. articles to profl. jours. Co-founder Columbus Met. Club, 1975. Mem. APA, Am. Group Psychotherapy Soc., Ohio Speakers Forum (founder, charter pres. 1980-81, Trudy Knox award 1986), Funeral Consumers Alliance(pres. 1986-89). Home: 168 Wildwood Dr Granville OH 43023-1073

KNUCKLES, BARBARA MILLER, academic administrator; b. Hinsdale, Ill., Jan. 11, 1948; d. John Gillis and Anne Agatha (Albert) Miller; m. Jeffry J. Knuckles, June 7, 1969; 1 child, James Albert. BA, U. Ill., 1970, MS, 1971. Editor ctr. for advanced computation U. Ill., Urbana, 1972-73; v.p., dir. rsch. Marsteller Inc., Chgo., 1973-78; corp. v.p. mktg. rsch. Beatrice, Chgo., 1978-86; v.p., gen. mgr. The Wirthlin Group, Chgo., 1986-88; pres. NNI, Inc., Naperville, Ill., 1988-95; dir. corp. and external rels. North Ctrl. Coll., Naperville, 1992—. Bd. dirs. J.R. Short Milling Co., Chgo., Harris Bank, Naperville, Dollar Gen. Corp.; owner Naperville Nannies, Inc., 1985-95. Trustee Edward Hosp., Naperville, 1986—; elder Knox Presbyn. Ch., Naperville, 1995—; vol. Avery Coonley Sch., Downers Grove, Ill., 1988—. Named outstanding alumni U. Ill., 1986, outstanding vol. Second Harvest Food Bank, Chgo., 1986, Ill. 4-H Found., Urbana, 1988. Mem. Econ. Club Chgo., Woman's Athletic Club Chgo. (bd. dirs., com. chair), Rotary Club (Naperville). Presbyterian. Avocations: travel, books, gardening, music. Office: North Cen Coll 30 N Brainard St Naperville IL 60540-4607

KNUDSEN, CHILTON ABBIE RICHARDSON, bishop; b. Sept. 29, 1946; m. Michael J. Knudsen, May 29, 1971; 1 child, Daniel. BA, Chatham Coll., Pitts., 1968; MDiv, Seabury-Western Theol. Sem., Evanston, Ill., 1980. Ordained deacon, 1980, priest, 1981; pastoral care officer Episcopal Diocese of Chgo.; consecrated bishop, 1998; bishop Episcopal Diocese of Maine, Portland, 1998—. Episcopalian. Office: Episcopal Diocese of Maine 143 State St Portland ME 04101 Office Phone: 207-772-1953. Office Fax: 207-773-0095.

KNUDSEN, HELEN EWING ZOLLARS, librarian; b. Kittery, Maine, Apr. 5, 1939; d. Allen Marshall and Marian (Himes) Zollars; m. Arnold Christian Knudsen, June 22, 1958 (div. 1974); children: Karen Christianne, Christina Louise, Lois Kathrine. AB, Principia Coll., 1958; BA, Calif. State U., Los Angeles, 1970; MSLS, U. So. Calif., 1973. Librarian Calif. Inst. Tech., Pasadena, 1973—. Lit. search specialist, IPAC, Pasadena, 1985—, Space Telescope, Pasadena, 1987—; dir. Olivetree Assocs., Sierra Madre, Calif., 1975—. Editor/pub. Astronomy and Astrophysics Monthly Index, 1975—. Mem. Spl. Libraries Assn. (pres. elect from 1971). Avocations: backpacking, photography.

KNUTH, MARYA DANIELLE, special education educator; b. Bowling Green, Ohio, Apr. 27, 1971; d. Kerry Lee and Sandra Jean Knuth. BEd, U. Toledo, 1997; MEd (hon.), U Toledo, 2002; cert. in reading (hon.), U. Toledo, 2002. Cert. in tchg. Tchr. spl. edn. Jefferson Jr. H.S., Toledo, 1997—98, Washington Jr. H.S., Toledo, 1998—; promotion coord. J&L Mktg., 2002—. Coach intramurals Washington Local Schs., Toledo, 1998—2002; chairperson bldg. beautification com. Washington Jr. H.S., Toledo, 2001—, chairperson best practice com.; dem. exch. program Ohio - Ukraine- Hungary Ednl. Exch. Program in the Pub. Sch. Setting, Toledo, 1999—2000; reading tutor Read for Lit., Toledo, 2000—; co-chairperson 100% Homework Club, Washington Jr. High, 2002—03; promotion coord. J&L Mktg., 1999—; head coach freshman girls Whitmer HS. Author (editor): A Netherland Tour, 1998. Mem. Build Your Sch. Garden Com., 2003—; head coach freshman Broomball Team, Toledo, 2003—; mem. Sister Cities of Toledo, 2000—. Recipient Best Lesson Plans award, Teachers Orgn., 2000. Mem.: ASCD, Coun. Exceptional Children. Republican. Avocations: tutoring, travel, rollerblading. Home: 4812 W Bancroft St Apt 30 Toledo OH 43615 Office: Washington Jr HS 5700 Whitmer Dr Toledo OH 43613 Personal E-mail: MaryaK1999@aol.com.

KNUTH FISCHER, CYNTHIA STROUT, environmental consultant; b. Walpole, Mass. d. Harold A. and Doris A. (Kendall) Strout; m. Adam Knuth (dec.); m. Charles S. Fischer. BA, Middlebury Coll., 1948; MA in Internat. Law and Govt., NYU, 1965. Adminstrv. asst. FAO Mission to Iraq, Baghdad, 1950—53; internat. conf. precis-writer Copenhagen, 1954—56; exec. sec. to UN legal counsel, 1956—62; exec. sec. to pres. Gen. Assembly UN, N.Y.C., 1962—63; exec. sec. UN Devel. Program, N.Y.C., 1964—69; adminstrv. asst. Ctr. for Internat. Affairs, Harvard U., Cambridge, Mass., 1976—82; founder, pres. Friends of Native Ams., 1986—. Founder Menotomy Indian Day, Arlington, Mass., 1991, Aberjona Indian Day, Winchester, Mass., 1992; founder, pres. Ctr. for Environ. Edn., East Coast, 1990—; sec. to bd. dirs. UN Assn. Greater Phila., 1998—2002; publicity chair, bd. dirs. Valley Forge Audubon Soc., 1996—2000; environ chair Lions Club of West Chester, Pa., 1996. Vol. Chadds Ford Hist. Soc., Second Reading Bookstore to benefit Sr. Ctr. of West Chester, 1998—; founder Friends of Indigenous Peoples, 2000—; vol. Phila. Hospitality, 2002—; mem. Coalition for A Strong UN, 1980—; vol. Meals on Wheels CC Hosp., 2003—. Mem. Common Cause (exec. bd. Mass. 1986), Mass. UN Assn. (exec. bd. 1970), Boston Jazz Soc. (exec. bd. 1975), Mystic River Watershed Assn. (exec. bd. 1991), Phi Delta Kappa (2d v.p. Harvard U. chpt. 1990-92), Sierra Club/Thoreau Group (chair 1993), Walden Forever Wild (exec. bd. 1993-95). Home: 956 Conner Rd West Chester PA 19380-1810 Office Phone: 610-696-1324. Personal E-mail: cknuth@aol.com.

KNUTSON, BONNIE RAE, secondary school educator, artist; b. Perryton, Tex., Nov. 1, 1949; d. Vernon Ray and Imogene Marie Fronk; 1 child, Michael Shane. BS in Art, West Tex. A&M U., Canyon, 1972. Cert. tchr. emotionally disturbed. elem. and gen. elem., art Tex. Comml. artist KGNC Radio and TV, Amarillo, Tex., 1972-73, Traftin & Autry Printers, Amarillo, 1973-74; secondary tchr. Amarillo Ind. Schs., 1974—. Advisor La Airosa, Amarillo H.S., 1989-93. Designer, editor cookbook Something Different, 1995; designer T-shirts, golf towels, presentations; comml. artist monthly publs. Accent West, Grain Producers News, N.Mex. Stockman, Panhandle, 1973-74. Mem. Delta Kappa Gamma, Kappa Pi. Republican. Christian. Avocations: drawing and painting, commercial art and design, interior decorating, gardening. Office: Tascosa HS 3921 Westlawn St Amarillo TX 79102-1795

KNUTZEN, MARTHA LORRAINE, lawyer; b. Bellingham, Wash., Aug. 28, 1956; BA in Polit. Sci., Scripps Coll., 1978; MA in Polit. Sci, Practical Politics, U. San Francisco, 1981, JD, 1981. Bar: Calif. 1981. Lawyer, mgr. legal computer support svcs., San Francisco, 1981—. Mem. San Francisco Citizens' Adv. Com. on Elections, 1994-96; 3d vice chair Dem. Party, San Francisco, 1996-2000, treas., 1996-2000; mem. Resolution Com., Calif. Dem. Party, 2001—2005; chair San Francisco Human Rights Commn., 1996-2005; cmty. organizer. Recipient Civil Rights Leadership award Calif. Assn. Human Rights Commn., 1996. Office: San Francisco Dist Atty 850 Bryant # 322 San Francisco CA 94103 Home: Apt 44 601 Van Ness Ave San Francisco CA 94102-3263

KO, CHRISTINE J., dermatologist, educator; d. Suk Moon and Malsook Kim Ko; m. Peter G. Whang, Aug. 28, 2004. BA, Princeton U., 1995; MD, NYU, 1999. Diplomate Am. Bd. Dermatology, Am. Bds. Dermatology and Pathology. Clin. instr. UCLA and U. Calif. Irvine, Irvine, 2004—05; asst. prof. Drexel U. Coll. Medicine, Phila., 2005—06. Contbr. articles to profl. jours.; editor: Essentials of Dermatology, 2005—06. Recipient honors, Am. Med. Women's Assn., 1999, Resident Tchg. award, U. Calif. Irvine, 2003. Mem.: Am. Soc. Dermatopathology, Am. Acad. Dermatology, Phi Beta Kappa, Alpha Omega Alpha. Avocations: aerobics, writing, reading. Office Phone: 203-785-4094.

KOART, NELLIE HART, real estate investor, real estate company executive; b. San Luis Obispo, Calif., Jan. 3, 1930; d. Will Carleton and Nellie Malchen (Cash) Hart; m. William Harold Koart, Jr., June 16, 1951 (dec. 1976); children: Kristen Marie Kittle, Matthew William. Student, Whittier Coll., 1947-49; BA, U. Calif., Santa Barbara, 1952; MA, Los Angeles State Coll., 1957. Life diploma elem. edn., Calif. Farm worker Hart Farms, Montebello, Calif., 1940-48; play leader Los Angeles County parks and Recreation, E. Los Angeles, Rosemead, Calif., 1948-51; elem. tchr. Potrero Heights Sch. Dist., South San Gabriel, Calif., 1951-55, vice prin., 1955-57; real estate salesman William Koart Real Estate, Goleta, Calif., 1963-76; real estate investor Ko-Art Enterprises, Goleta, 1976—; pres. Wm. Koart Constrn. Co., Inc., Goleta, 1975-91; real estate salesperson Joseph McGeever Realty Co., Goleta, 1976-91. Adv. bd. Bank of Montecito, Santa Barbara, Calif., 1983—. Editor: Reflections, 1972. Charter mem. Calif. Regents program Calif. Fedn. Republican Women, 1989; treas. Santa Barbara County Fedn. Republican Women, Alamar-Hope Ranch, 1981-82, treas. County Bd., 1983-84, auditor, 1985, 96, 97; treas. Com. to Recall Hone, Maschke and Shewczyk, Goleta, 1984; treas. Santa Barbara County Lincoln Club, 1983-87, bd. dirs., 1983-93; assoc. mem. state cen. com. Calif. Republican Party, 1985-87. Mem.: Santa Barbara County Tax-Payers Assn., Serena Cove Owners Assn. (sec.-treas., bd. dirs. 1990—2002), Santa Barbara Apt. Assn., Santa Barbara County Lincoln Club, Antique Automobile Club of Am. (sec. treas. Santa Barbara 1980—84). Avocations: swimming, coin collecting/numismatics, genealogy, gardening, football. Office: KO-ART Enterprises PO Box 310 Goleta CA 93116-0310

KOBE, LAN, medical physicist; b. Semarang, Indonesia; naturalized; d. O.G. and L.N. (The) Kobe. BS in Physics, IKIP U., Bandung, Indonesia, 1964, MS in Physics, 1967; MS in Med. Physics and Biophysics, U. Calif., Berkeley, 1975. Physics instr. Sch. Engring. Tarumanegara U., Jakarta, Indonesia, 1968-72; rsch. fellow dept. radiation oncology U. Calif., San Francisco, 1975-77; clin. physicist in residence dept. radiation oncology UCLA, 1977-78, asst. hosp. radiation physicist, 1978-80, hosp. radiation physicist, 1980—. Instr. radiation oncology physics to resident physicians and med. physics grad. students. Contbr. articles to profl. jours. Newhouse grantee U. Calif., Berkeley, 1974-75, grantee dean grad. divsn. U. Calif., Berkeley, 1975; recipient Pres. Work Study award U. Calif., Berkeley, 1974-75, Outstanding Svc. award, 1986, Devel. Achievement award, 1988. Mem. Am. Soc. for Therapeutic Radiology and Oncology, Am. Assn. Physicists in Medicine (nat. and So. Calif. chpts.), Am. Bd. Radiology (cert.), Am. Assn. Individual Investors (life). Office: UCLA Dept Radiation Oncology Los Angeles CA 90095-6951

KOBER, ARLETTA REFSHAUGE (MRS. KAY L. KOBER), supervisor; b. Cedar Falls, Iowa, Oct. 31, 1919; d. Edward and Mary (Jensen) Refshauge; m. Kay Leonard Kober, Feb. 14, 1944; children: Kay Mary, Karilyn Eve. BA, State Coll. Iowa, 1940; MA, U. No. Iowa. Tchr. HS, Soldier, Iowa, 1943—50, 1965—67; coord. Office Edn. Waterloo (Iowa) Cmty. Schs., 1967—84; head dept. coop. career edn. West HS, Waterloo, 1974—84. Mem. Waterloo Sch. Health Coun.; mem. nominating com. YWCA, Waterloo; Black Hawk County chmn. Tb Christmas Seals; ward chmn. ARC, Waterloo; co-chmn. Citizen's Com. Sch. Bond Issue; pres. Waterloo PTA Coun., Waterloo Vis. Nursing Assn., 1956—62, 1982—, Kingsley Sch. PTA, 1959—60; v.p. Waterloo Women's Club, 1962—63, pres., 1963—64, trustee bd. clubhouse dirs., 1957—58; mem. Gen. Fedn. Women's Clubs, Nat. Congress Parents and Tchrs.; bd. dirs. United Svcs. Black Hawk County, Broadway Theatre League, St. Francis Hosp. Found., Black Hawk County Rep. Women, 1952—53; del. Iowa Rep. Convs., 1996, 1998; Presbyterial world svc. chmn. Presbyn. Women's Assn.; deacon Westminister Presbyn. Ch., 1995—98. Mem.: LWV (dir. Waterloo 1951—52), NEA, AAUW (v.p. Cedar Falls 1946—47), Black Hawk County Hist. Soc. (charter), Internat. Platform Assn., Town Club (dir.), P.E.O., Elklets, Dleta Kappa Gamma, Delta Pi Epsilon (v.p. 1966—67). Home: 3436 Augusta Cir Waterloo IA 50701-4608 Office: 503 W 4th St Waterloo IA 50701-1554

KOBLICK, JOAN LESSER, retired art educator, artist; b. N.Y.C., Mar. 28, 1932; d. Abraham Avrum and Blanche Helen (Rothbaum) Lesser; m. Mervyn Leland Cadwallader (div.); m. Daniel Cecil Koblick, July 6, 1960; 1 child, Rebecca Pauline; 1 stepchild, Laurinda Joan McKinlay. BFA, Pratt Inst., Bklyn., 1953; postgrad., San Jose State U., 1974, U. Chgo. Freelance artist/printmaker, N.Y., Oreg., Calif., Ill., 1949—; social worker Lane County Welfare Commn., Eugene, Oreg., 1953—57; tchr. fine arts, art history Lab. Schs., U. Chgo., 1970—2001, dir. HS arts/literary mag., 1979—2001, chair fine arts dept., 1979—90, 1995—2001. Dir. Art Print Studio, 2000—. Exhibitions include L'Attalla Gallery, 1971—74, Crocker Art Mus., Sacramento, 1955, Bennington Coll. Art Gallery, Vt., 1995, Represented in permanent collections, exhibitions include 57th St. Art Fair, Chgo., 1969, 1970, 1971. Mem.: Nat. Mus. Women in Arts (charter). Avocations: travel, literature, theater. Personal E-mail: jkoblick12@aol.com.

KOC, LORRAINE K(IESSLING), lawyer; b. Gulfport, Miss., Jan. 29, 1958; BA magna cum laude, Univ. Pa., 1979, MA, 1979, JD, 1983. Bar: Pa. 1983. Gen. counsel Deb Shops, Inc., Phila., 1985—, v.p., 1985—. Mem. adj. faculty Pa. State Univ., Abington, 1989—, mem. bd. advisors, 1989—. Mem.: Assn. Corporate Counsel, Pa. Bar Assn. (mem. employment law com.), Nat. Assn. Women Lawyers (pres. 2005—), ABA (chair corp. counsel com. gen. practice sect. 2004), Soc. Human Resource Mgmt., Phila. Bar Assn. (Disting. Svc. award 1988). Office: Deb Shops Inc 9401 Bluegrass Rd Philadelphia PA 19114 Office Phone: 215-676-6000 ext. 217. Business E-Mail: lkoc@debshops.com.

KOCEL, KATHERINE MERLE, psychology professor, researcher; d. Benjamin Frances and Alice Marie Kocel; m. Robert M. Loew (dec.); 1 child, Rebecca M. Loew; m. John K. Kleinjans. BA in Psychology, Antioch U., 1968; PhD in Social Psychology, U. Hawaii, 1978. Rsch. asst. U. Calif. Med. Ctr., San Francisco, 1969—71; instr., rsch. asst. U. Hawaii, Honolulu, 1972—78, instr. II, 1990—92; rsch. assoc. U. Calif.-LA, 1979—81; comm. Loew Broadcasting, Honolulu, 1982—89; prof. psychology Jackson State U., Miss., 1993—2000, Berkeley City Coll., Berkeley, Calif., 2000—. Cons. Media Rsch. Group, Honolulu, 1983—88; spkr. in field, 1995—99. Author: (book) Cognitive Abilities, 1977, Treatment Delivery System & Alcohol Abuse in Women, 1982; contbr. chapters to books, articles to profl. jours.; prodr., dir., bd. dirs. (TV show) League of Women Voters, Honolulu, 1986—90. Bd. dirs. Am. Assn. U. Women, Palo Alto, Calif., 2001—02. Recipient Tchr. of Year, Miss. Psychological Assn., 1999. Mem.: APA, Sci. Rsch. Soc. Am., Sigma Xi, Psychology Tchrs. CCs, Nat. Sci. Found. (panelist Instrumentation & Lab. Improvement Program 1996—97, panelist grad. rsch. fellowship program 1998—2000, 2004), Stanford Parents & CAL Alumni. Avocations: hiking, swimming, cooking, reading. Personal E-mail: kkocel@gmail.com.

KOCH, AIMEE HELEN, art gallery director, photographer; b. Washington, Nov. 2, 1979; d. Arthur and Kathy Caplan Koch. BA, Amherst Coll., Mass., 2001; MFA, Wash. U., 2005. Intern photography White Ho., Washington, 1998; tutor The Literacy Project, Amherst, Mass., 1998—2001; tchg. asst. Washington U., St. Louis, 2003—05, counselor admissions, 2003—05; administr. 1708 Gallery, Richmond, Va., 2006—. Dir. ops. Art4Love, NYC, 2001—02; fellowship Cooper Union, NYC, 2004, Cité Internat. Art, Paris, 2005. Numerous national exhibitions including, exhibitions include Bullivant Gallery, 2004 (Art Dimensions award, 2004), Buddy Holly Ctr., 2005 (Juror award, 2005). Fellow, Humanity in Action, 1999; grantee Armstrong Writing award, Amherst Coll., 1997—99; scholar, Sch. Art Wash. U., 2003—05; Doshia Am. Studies grantee, Amherst Coll., 2000—01, Laura and William Jens scholar, Wash. U., 2004—05. Mem.: Coll. Art Assn., Phi Betta Kappa. Home: 3509-1 Kensington Ave Richmond VA 23221 Office: 1708 Gallery PO Box 12520 Richmond VA 23241 Office Phone: 804-643-1708. Office Fax: 804-643-7839. Personal E-mail: info@aimeekoch.com. Business E-Mail: akoch@1708gallery.org.

KOCH, CAROL SUE, middle school educator; b. Detroit, July 23, 1944; d. Francis Paul and Jonnie Lucille (Glasscock) Rhodes; m. Delaine Brian Koch, Aug. 18, 1968; children: Katherine Ann-Marie, Delaine Brian II. BS in Secondary Edn., S.E. Mo. State U., 1962; MA in Edn., Nat.-Louis U., 1991; student, Nat. Ctr. for Teaching, summer 1992. Cert. tchr., Mo., Ill. Tchr. sci. Belvidere (Ill.) Schs., 1966—. Cons., course instr. Internat. Renewal Inst., Palatine, Ill., 1991—; instr. Koch's Ednl. Consulting Svc.; facilitator/instr. St. Xavier/I.R.I. field-based masters program and coursework; instr. off-site Aurora U., 1993—. Mem. ASCD, Nat. Sci. Tchrs. Assn., Ill. State Tchrs. Assn., Ill. Edn. Assn. (state and regional coms. 1979—, state com. election and bylaws 1985—), Alpha Delta Kappa. Avocations: collecting cookbooks, rocking horses and pottery. Office: Belvidere Jr High 919 E 6th St Belvidere IL 61008-4500 Home: 2617 Driftwood LN Rockford IL 61107-1114

KOCH, CARRIE S., mathematics educator; b. Elmhurst, Ill., Sept. 10, 1979; d. Robert and Eileen Mary Koch. BA in Math, Northwestern U., Evanston, Ill., 2001; MA in Math Edn., DePaul U., Chgo., Ill., 2004. Tchr. math. Hoffman Estates (Ill.) H.S., 2002—. Coach. girls' swimming Hoffman Estates HS, Ill., 2002—, coach girls' water polo, 2005—. Recipient Outstanding Achievement award, Ill. Coun. Tchrs. Math., 2005. Office: Hoffman Estates High School 1100 W Higgins Hoffman Estates IL 60195 Office Phone: 847-755-5741. Business E-Mail: ckoch@d211.org.

KOCH, CATHERINE ANN, music educator, musician; b. Manchester, N.H., July 27, 1953; d. David Milton and Clarice Joyce Cargill; children: Christopher Lawrence, Gretchen Renate. B in Music Edn., Bucknell U., Lewisburg, Pa., 1975; MS in Music Edn., Syracuse U., 1976. Cert. tchr. N.Y. Pvt. piano, voice and guitar tchr., Fayetteville, NY, 1975—; choral and gen. music tchr. Smith Rd. Sch., N. Syracuse, NY, 1976—81, Manlius Pebble Hill Sch., DeWitt, NY, 1981—89, Eagle Hill Middle Sch., Manlius, NY, 1989—. Substitute organist, soloist various chs., NY, 1993—; organist U. Meth. Ch., Manlius, 1976—93; jr. choir dir. DeWitt Cmty. Ch., 1993—2000; accompanist Syracuse U. Oratorio Soc., 1975—82; mgr., accompanist Jr. High All-County Chorus, Onondaga County, NY, 1992, Onondaga County, 95, Onondaga County, 98, Onondaga County, 2001; chmn. elem. and jr. high vocal task com. Elem. and Jr. High Schs., Onondaga County, 2001—03. Author: (pocket card) Student's Prayer, 1995; musician (pianist): Purely Percussion, 1993, 1995. Recipient Music Masters Harmony award, Soc. Preservation and Encouragement Barbershop Quartet Singing in Am., 2003. Mem.: Am. Choral Dirs. Assn., Onondaga County Music Educators Assn. (pres.), N.Y. State Sch. Music Assn. (presenter 1997, 2004, Presdl. Citation for Fayetteville-Manlius music program 1997), Music Educators Nat. Conf. Avocations: reading, swimming, biking. Home: 320 Highbridge St Fayetteville NY 13066 Office: Eagle Hill Middle Sch 4645 Enders Rd Manlius NY 13104

KOCH, CHRISTINE, legislative aide; b. Moline, ill. d. Clarence Albert and Bernadine Jeanette Grams; m. Allan Craig Koch, July 11, 1965; children: David Craig, Brian Michael. Student, U. Ill., 1963-65, Wayne State U., 1965-67. Tchr. Harper Woods Publ. Sch., Harper Woods, Mich., 1967-74; admin. asst. Congressman David E. Bonior, Mt. Clemens, Mich., 1977—2001. Pres. Comprehensive Youth Svcs., Mt. Clemens, Mich., Clinton Twp. Dem. Club; sect. Salvation Army Adv. Bd., Downtown Devel. Authority, Mich. Housing Counselors, Mt. Clemens, Mich.; recording sect. tenth dist. Dem. Com. Democrat. Methodist. Avocations: reading, gardening.

KOCH, CYNTHIA M., library director; BA, Pa. State U.; MA, U. Pa., PhD in Am. Civilization. Dir. Old Barracks Mus., Trenton, NJ, 1979—93; exec. dir. NJ Coun. for the Humanities, 1993—97; assoc. dir. Penn Nat. Commn. on Society, Culture and Cmty., U. Pa., 1997—99; dir. Franklin D. Roosevelt Presdl. Libr. and Mus., Hyde Park, NY, 1999—. Ex-officio dir. Franklin and Eleanor Roosevelt Inst. Mem.: Phi Beta Kappa. Office: Franklin D Roosevelt Presdl Libr and Mus 4079 Albany Post Rd Hyde Park NY 12538-1990 Office Phone: 845-486-7752. E-mail: cynthia.koch@nara.gov.*

KOCH, DIANNE M., language educator, music educator; b. Dubuque, Iowa, July 17, 1959; d. Harlan Joseph and Rosemary Elizabeth Noonan; m. Kevin James Koch, July 31, 1982; children: Paul, Brian, Angela. B in Music Edn., Loras Coll., 1981, MA in English, 2000. Band and choral dir. Lost Nation (Iowa) Cmty. Schs., 1981-82; band dir. Wahlert H.S., Dubuque, 1982-90; pvt. piano tchr. Dubuque, 1990—2005; instr. English Loras Coll., 2000—04, Dubuque Sr. H.S., Dubuque, 2004—. Musician for area ch., 1982—; ch. organist St. Mary's Ch., Dubuque, 1983-88; mem. Big Band Express Jazz Band, Dubuque, 1989-92; leader St. Columbkille Folk Group, Dubuque, 1991—; elem. band dir. Wahlert HS, Dubuque, 1991-2000. V.p., programming dir. Theresian Women's Prayer Group, Dubuque, 1994—97; den leader Cub Scouts, Dubuque, 1996—2000; active St. Mary's Ch., Dubuque, 1982—88, St. Columbkille Ch., Dubuque, 1989—; dir., asst. dir., spkr., musician Christian Experience Weekend Retreats, Dubuque, 1993—. Mem.: Nat. Coun. Tchrs. English, Dubuque Area Piano Tchrs. (co-pres. Dubuque chpt. 1995—2005). Avocations: biking, hiking, camping, reading, canoeing. Home: 285 S Grandview Ave Dubuque IA 52003-7226 E-mail: dkoch@dubuque.k12.ia.us.

KOCH, DOROTHY HARRIET, artist; b. Schenectady, NY, May 10, 1917; d. Morris and Anna Schmidt; m. Sidney Koch, June 6, 1943; 1 child, Barbara Koch-Eisenstein; children: Amy M., Sarah B. Student, Traphagen Sch. Fashion, 1937—38; BA in Art, Rutgers U., 1984; studied with, George Segal, 1953—58. Draftsman Diehl Co., Finderne, NJ, 1941—43, Weston Electric Co., Newark, 1943—44; instr. painting and crafts Young Men and Young Women's Hebrew Assn., Highland Park, NJ, 1972—76. Author: It's Wild, 1998; one-woman shows include Pargot Gallery, 1986, Woman's Caucus for Art, 1997, Highland Park Libr., exhibited in group shows at NJ Soc. Arch., Woodbridge, exhibitions include Boca Raton Mus. Art, Jewish Cmty. Ctr., Highland Park, Represented in permanent collections Highalnd Park Cons. Temple. Recipient 1st pl. award watercolor, Artists League Ctrl. NJ, 1992. Achievements include patents for marriage canopy. Avocations: reading, gardening, needlecrafts.

KOCH, EDNA MAE, lawyer, nurse; b. Terre Haute, Ind., Oct. 12, 1951; d. Leo K. and Lucille E. (Smith) K.; m. Mark D. Orton. BS in Nursing, Ind. State U., 1977; JD, Ind. U., 1980. Bar: Ind. 1980, U.S. Dist. Ct. (so. dist.) Ind. 1980. Assoc. Dillon & Cohen, Indpls., 1980-85; ptnr. Tipton, Cohen & Koch, Indpls., 1985-93, LaCava, Zeigler & Carter, Indpls., 1993-94, Zeigler Cohen & Koch, Indpls., 1994—. Leader seminars for nurses, Ind. U. Med. Ctr., Ball State U., Muncie, Ind., St. Vincent Hosp., Indpls., Deaconess Hosp., Evansville, Ind., others; lectr. on med. malpractice Cen. Ind. chpt. AACCN, Indpls. "500" Postgrad. Course in Emergency Medicine, Ind. Assn. Osteo. Physicians and Surgeons State Conv., numerous others. Mem. ABA, ANA, Ind. State Bar Assn., Indpls. Bar Assn., Am. Soc. Law and Medicine, Ind. State Nurses Assn. Republican. Office: Zeigler Cohen & Koch Ste 104 9465 Counselors Row Indianapolis IN 46240-3816 Office Phone: 317-844-5200. Business E-Mail: ekoch@zcklaw.com.

KOCH, FRANCES DIDATO, literature and language educator, writer; b. Akron, Ohio, Mar. 17, 1959; d. Vincent and Gypsy (Horton) Didato; m. David Michael Koch, Oct. 28, 1990; children: Kevin Woodrum, Corey Woodrum. BA English, U. Akron, Ohio, 1990; M Pastoral Counseling, Malone Coll., Canton, Ohio, 1999. Cert. Tchr. English Nat. Bd. for Profl. Tchg. Stds., 2002. Tchr. English Barberton H.S., Ohio, 1990—. Mentor praxis/pathwise Barberton City Schs., 2000—; freelance writer in field. Author: (novel/drama) Seven Curriculum Units; contbr. articles to profl. jours. Vol., trainer Project LEARN, Akron, 1987—89. Office: Barberton High School 555 Barber Rd Barberton OH 44203 Personal E-mail: dfkoch@msn.com. E-mail: fkoch@barberton.summit.k12.oh.us.

KOCH, GRETCHEN ANN, mathematics and computer science professor; b. Lawton, Okla., Nov. 20, 1979; d. James Raymond and Mary Ann Koch. BS in Math., St. Lawrence U., Canton, NY, 2001; MS in Applied Math., Rensselaer Poly. Inst., Troy, NY, 2005, PhD in Math., 2005. Rsch. asst. Rensselaer Poly. Inst., 2003—05; asst. prof. math. and computer sci. Goucher Coll., Balt., 2005—. NSF VIGRE fellow, Rensselaer Poly. Inst., 2001—02. Mem.: Am. Math. Soc., Math. Assn. Am. (Exxon-Mobil project NExT fellow 2005—06, Md.-DC-Va. sect. NExT fellow 2005—), Gamma Sigma Alpha, Pi Mu Epsilon, Omicron Delta Kappa, Chi Omega (treas. 1999—99), Phi Beta Kappa. Office: Goucher Coll 1021 Dulaney Valley Rd Baltimore MD 21204 Office Phone: 410-337-6541. Business E-Mail: gretchen.koch@goucher.edu.

KOCH, KATHERINE ROSE, communications executive; b. Pitts., Apr. 21, 1949; d. Irving Samuel Stapsy and Betty Ruth (Sachs) Blake; m. Stanley Christopher Brown, July 26, 1986; 1 child, Matthew. BFA, Rochester Inst. Tech., 1973. Instr. Ivy Sch. Profl. Art, Pitts., 1973-74; advt. dir. Buhl Optical Co., Pitts., 1974-77; pres., creative dir. Ambit Mktg. Comm., Ft. Lauderdale, Fla., 1977—. Instr. Point Park Coll., Pitts., 1977-78. Bd. dirs. United Way, Broward County, 1995—, Broward C.C. Found., 2002, Broward Coordinating Coun., 1994—, Broward Alliance, Ft. Lauderdale Mus. Art. Mem.: Tower Forum (bd. dirs. 1995—), Womens Exec. Club (pres. 1995—96). Office: Ambit Mktg Comm 2455 E Sunrise Blvd Ste 711 Fort Lauderdale FL 33304-3110

KOCH, KATRINA M., private school educator; d. Jack Nolan and Carol Ann (Albertsen) St. Clair; m. Lorin Matthew Koch, July 17, 2004. B Music Edn., Walla Walla Coll., 2004. Music and English tchr. Livingstone Adventist Acad., Salem, Oreg., 2004—. Mem.: Nat. Coun. Tchrs. English, Music Educators Nat. Conf. Seventh-Day Adventist. Avocations: oragami, volleyball, cooking. Office: Livingstone Adventist Acad 5771 Fruitland Rd NE Salem OR 97301

KOCH, LINDA BROWN, utility administrator; b. Clay County, Tenn., Nov. 1, 1947; d. Verne Robert and Erma A. Cherry; m. James M. Brown, Sept. 4, 1966 (dec. Jan. 1994); children: Melissa Brown LaFoe, James K. Brown; m. Ronald W. Koch, Oct. 26, 1996. ASA in Bus. Mgmt., Ind. U./Purdue U., Indpls., 1990; BA in Bus. Mgmt. magna cum laude, Ind. Wesleyan U., 1995; MA in Pub. Rels., Ball State U., 1999. Exec. sec. to sr. v.p. corp. affairs Indpls. Power & Light, 1984-89, cmty. investment mgr., 1989-97, dir. cmty. rels., 1997—. Bd. dirs. Flanner House, Indpls., 1992—, Girls Inc. of Indpls., 1993-98, IPL Employee Credit Union, Indpls., 1992-98; mem. children and youth impact coun. United Way Ctrl. Ind., 1999—. Recipient Keystone award IPL Women's Club, 1992. Mem. Pub. Rels. Soc. Am. (chpt. chair, Keystone award 1999-00), Ctrl. Ind. Corp. Vol. Coun. (founder, pres. 1999—), Exch. Club. (bd. dirs. 1996—). Home: 680 Hillcrest Dr Greenwood IN 46142-1827 Office: Indpls Power & Light Co PO Box 1595 1 Monument Cir Indianapolis IN 46204-2900 E-mail: lkoch@ipalco.com.

KOCH, LORETTA PETERSON, librarian, educator; b. Anna, Ill., Mar. 5, 1951; d. Vance G. and Dorothy M. (Cline) Peterson; m. David Victor Koch, Aug. 25, 1979; 1 child, Elizabeth; stepchildren: John, Victor. AB in in English with high honors, U. Ill., 1973, MS in LS, 1974; postgrad., So. Ill. U., Carbondale, 1976. Adult svcs. libr. Carbondale Pub. Libr., 1974-81; owner, operator L. Koch-Words, editing and word processing, Carbondale, 1981-85; rsch. asst. So. Ill. U., 1973, asst. humanities libr., 1985-86, libr. tech. asst. III humanities div., 1986-89, asst. humanities libr., 1989-92, acting humanities libr., 1992-93, humanities libr., 1993—, asst. prof. libr. affairs, 1989-95, assoc. prof. libr. affairs Carbondale, 1995—, mem. faculty exec. bd., 1989-91. Participant confs. and workshops; presenter in field; field reader grant proposals Ill. Coop. Collection Mgmt. Coordinating Com., 1993. Contbr. articles to profl. publs. Divsn. coord. fund drive United Way, 1989, 90; room parent Lakeland Sch., 1993-94, Parrish Sch., 1994-95, 95-96, 96-97, Thomas Sch., 1998-99, 99-2000; asst. leader troop 813, Girl Scouts U.S.A., 1993-94. Mem. ALA (chmn. poster session abstracts booklet com. 1993-94), Assn. of Coll. and Rsch. Libr. (comm. com. women's studies sect. 1993-95), Libr. Adminstrn. and Mgmt. Assn. (using stats. for libr. evaluation com.), Reference and adult svcs. divsn. Ill. Libr. Assn. (nominations com. resources and tech. svcs. forum 1993-94), Margaret Atwood Soc., Midwest Assn. for Can. Studies, Assn. for Can. Studies in U.S., Beta Phi Mu. Home: 2800 W Sunset Dr Carbondale IL 62901-2046 Office: So Ill U Humanities Div Morris Libr Carbondale IL 62901 E-mail: lkoch@lib.siu.edu.

KOCH, MARGARET RAU, writer, artist, historian; b. Sacramento; d. George James Rau and Callista Marie Martin; children: Edward James, Kathleen, Thomas C. Student, U. Calif., Berkeley, 1936-38. Mem. editl. staff Santa Cruz (Calif.) Sentinel, 1958-76. Author: Santa Cruz County, Parade of the Past, 1973, 74, 77, 81, 91, 99, They Called It Home, 1974, Walk Around Santa Cruz, 1978, Going To School in Santa Cruz County, 1978, The Pasatiempo Story, 1990, Santa Cat-Behind the Lace Curtains, 2001; exhibited in group shows at Sedona Arts Ctr., Yavapai County Arts Fair, Ft. Verde Art Show, 1997, 98, 99, 2000. Organizer, first pres. Santa Cruz Hist. Soc. Recipient 3 Mixed Media Watercolor awards Yavapai County Art Fair, Ariz., 2 Watercolor awards Fort Verde Art Show, Ariz. Mem. No. Ariz. Watercolo Soc., Pen Women, Santa Cruz Art League, Sedona Art Ctr. Home: 2307 Town Center Dr Klamath Falls OR 97601-7142

KOCH, MOLLY BROWN, retired parent educator; b. Phila., Pa., Nov. 20, 1927; d. Harry and Sarah Potash Brown; m. William Koch, June 22, 1947; children: Jessica Robin Jones, Andrea Leslie London, Richard Andrew. Continuing edn., Balt. Hebrew U., 1957—67. Tchr. Balt. Hebrew Congregation Religious Sch., 1966—74, Temple Oheb Shalom, 1979, Reform Jewish Acad., Youth Inst.; parent educator Balt. City and Balt. County Boards of Edn., 1956—65; tchr., prin. Columbia Jewish Family Sch., 1975—78. Dir. Project Yedid, Balt., 1980—87. Pub. edn. Personal Freedom Found. and Project Yedid, Balt., 1975—87; pres. Jews for Judaism, Balt., 1999—2004; bd. mem. Prisoners' Aid, Balt., 1960—62, Robert Lindner Found., Balt., 1958—62; pres., co-founder Personal Freedom Found., 1975—80; dir. Project Yedid, 1980—87. Recipient Hon. Outstanding Woman award, Woman's Day Mag., 1979, Disting. Svc. award, Mid. Atlantic-Great Lakes Organized Crime Law Enforcement Network, 1987, Ofcl. Recognition, Senate of the State of Md., 1987, 2002, Balt. County Coun., 2002, First Ann. Lipsetts award, Bd. of Jewish Edn., 1979. Avocations: public speaking, writing. Personal E-mail: mabko18@bcpl.net.

KOCH, VIRGINIA GREENLEAF (VIRGINIA M. GREENLEAF), painter; b. Chgo., Aug. 28, 1925; d. William Henry and Henrietta Irene (Moser) Greenleaf; m. Aley Allan, 1945 (div.); m. William Greenough, 1951 (dec.); m. Henry Koch, Aug. 20, 1962 (dec.); children: Diedra G., William G. Pupil of Ivan Olinsky, 1941-42; student, Yale U., 1943-45; pupil of Robert Brackman, 1946; student, Am. U., Washington; postgrad., Am. U., 1956-57; pupil of Gene Davis, 1968-70. One-woman shows include Studio Gallery, Washington, 1970, 72, 74, 76, Haslem Gallery, Madison, Wis., 1971, In Town Gallery, Cleve., 1973, World Bank, Washington, 1972, Art League No. Va., 1973, Main St. Gallery, Boston, 1976-81, 83, 87-89, Nantucket, 1977, 82-89, 91-93, 95-98, Gallery 124, NYC, 1983, Gallery at Essex Meadows, 2001, Christy Lawrence Gallery, Old Lyme, Conn., 2003; exhibited in group shows at Maritime Mus., 1990-91, Newport News, Va., 1971-72, U. No. Va., 1973, U. Richmond, Va., 1972, U. Md., 1975, Parsons Drefyss Gallery, NYC, 1976-77, Phillips Collection, Washington, 1989, Corcoran Gallery, 1975, 92-93, Cooley Gallery, 2003, 04, 05, Old Lyme, 1991-2002, Alva Gallery, New London, Conn., 2001, Rittenhouse Fine Arts Gallery, Phila., 2002, Cooley Gallery, 2005, Pet Connections Old Lyme, 2005; represented in permanent collections Dept. of State, Washington, Lyme Acad. of Fine Arts, Old Lyme, various ambassadors' residences. Active Olde Town Citizens' Com., Alexandria, Va., 1964-73, Georgetown Citizens' Assn., Washington, 1971-75, Hosp. Thrist Shop, Nantucket, Mass., 1968-71, Nat. Symphony of Washington, DC Com., 1970—; bd. dirs. Arts Council of Nantucket. Mem. Studio Gallery, Foundery Group Women Paitners, Artists' Equity, Art League Va., Art Found. Nantucket Hist. Found. Office Phone: 860-434-3272.

KOCHER, JUANITA FAY, retired auditor; b. Falmouth, Ky., Aug. 9, 1933; d. William Birgest and Lula (Gillespie) Vickroy; m. Donald Edward Kocher, Nov. 18, 1953. Grad. high sch., Bright, Ind. Cert. internal auditor and compliance officer. Bookkeeper Mchts. Bank and Trust Co., West Harrison, Ind., 1952-56, teller, asst. cashier, 1962-87, br. mgr., 1979-87, internal auditor, 1987-96, ret., 1996; bookkeeper Progressive Bank, New Orleans, 1956-58; with proof dept. 1st Nat. Bank, Cin., Ohio, 1958-59, teller Harrison, Ohio, 1959-62. Bookkeeper Donald E. Kocher Constrn., Harrison, 1981—. Mem. Am. Bankers Assn., Ind. Bankers Assn. Home: 11277 Biddinger Rd Harrison OH 45030

KOCHERIL, SOSA VARGHESE, rheumatologist; b. Bombay, Maharashtra, India, July 27, 1969; came to U.S., 1994; d. Abraham and Chinnamma Varghese; m. Paul George Kocheril, Sept. 19, 1993. MB BS, Lokmanya Tilak Mcpl. Med Coll., Bombay, India, 1993. Cert. Edl. Commn. Fgn. Med. Grads. Resident pathologist B.Y.L. Nair Charitable Hosp., Bombay, 1992-94; rsch. assoc. Wayne State U. Dept. Urology, Detroit, 1996-97; resident in internal med. Saginaw Coop. Hosps., Mich., 1997—2000; rheumatologist U. Mich. Contbr. articles to jours. in field. Winner Clin. Vignette and Rsch. Competition, 80th Ann. ACP-Am. Soc. Internal Medicine Nat. Conf., 1999. Assoc. mem. ACP, AMA. Avocations: travel, reading, music.

KOCHMAN, SUSAN M., language educator; b. Savannah, Ga., May 30, 1966; d. Daniel Howard and Louise Mary (Rodman) Kochman. BS in Edn., Duquesne U., 1988; Master's Equivalency, U. Pitts., Georgetown U., 2000—01. Tchr. English Pitts. Pub. Schs., 1988—93, Hempfield Area Sch. Dist., Greensburg, Pa., 1993—. Author: (article) English Jour., 1997; Red Carpet reporter for Star 100.7 Grammy Awards, 2004. Recipient Nat. Endowment, Nat. Endowment for the Humanities, Wash., 1998; fellowship, Nat. Writing Project, Pitts., 1990. Mem.: NEA, Nat. Coun. Tchrs. English, Nat. Forensic League. Democrat. Roman Catholic. Avocations: writing, travel, genealogy. Office: Hempfield HS 4345 Route 136 Greensburg PA 15601 Business E-Mail: s.kochman@hempfieldarea.k12.pa.us.

KOCSIS, JOAN BOSCO, elementary school educator; b. Phillipsburg, N.J., Feb. 6, 1941; d. Frederick B. and Frances (Marina) Bosco; m. Gerald S. Kocsis Sr., Dec. 30, 1961; children: Gerald S. Jr., Jacqueline Kocsis Morgan. BA, Trenton State Coll., 1962; MEd, U. N.C., Charlotte, 1987. Cert. kindergarten-4 tchr., early childhood edn., lang. arts kindergarten-12, social studies 7-12, adminstrn., supervision and curriculum, N.C. Tchr. grades kindergarten, 1, 3 Hamilton Twp. (N.J.) Bd. Edn., 1962—68; tchr. grades kindergarten, talented and gifted Hopewell Valley Bd. Edn., Pennington, 1976—79; tchr. grades 4, 2, 3 Union County Pub. Schs., Monroe, 1981—88;

tchr. grade 1 Charlotte (N.C.)-Mecklenburg Pub. Schs., 1988—89; tchr. grades 1, 2 Union County Pub. Schs., Monroe, 1989—. Presenter (TV show) "Positively for Parents", 1992. Recipient Presdl. award for excellence in tchg. sci. and math. NSF, 1994. Mem. NEA, NSTA, N.C. Sci. Tchrs. Assn., Assn. Presdl. Awardees in Sci. Tchg., Internat. Reading Assn. (Union-Monroe coun. treas. 1993—). Home: 309 Auckland Ln Matthews NC 28104-7867

KODA-KIMBLE, MARY ANNE, medical educator, pharmacologist, dean; PharmD, U. Calif., San Francisco, 1969. Lic. pharmacist Calif., 1969, cert. diabetes educator. Faculty U. Calif., San Francisco, 1970—, prof., dean Sch. Pharmacy, Thomas J. Long Endowed chair in Chain Pharmacy Practice. Mem. nonprescription drugs adv. com. FDA; mem. Calif. State Bd. of Pharmacy; lectr. and cons. in field. Co-editor (with others): Applied Therapeutics for Clinical Pharmacists, 1975, 1978, Basic Clinical Pharmacokinetics, 1980, Applied Therapeutics: Clinical Use of Drugs, 1988, Basic Clinical Pharmacokinetics, 1988, Handbook of Applied Therapeutics, 3d edit., 1996; contbr. numerous articles to profl. jours., chpts. to books.; editl. bd. Internat. Jour. Clin. Pharmacology, 1979—82, Drug Interactions Newsletter and Update, 1981, Diabetes Forecast, 1986—89, referee various jours. Numerous others. Named to Hall of Fame, CPhA; recipient Disting. Alumna award, U. Calif.-San Francisco. Mem.: Nat. Acad. of Practice in Pharmacy (founding mem., Disting. Practitioner), Am. Coun. on Pharm. Edn., Am. Coll. Clin. Pharmacy (bd. dirs., Edn. award), Calif. Soc. Health-System Pharmacists (bd. dirs., Pharmacist of the Yr.), Am. Pharm. Assn. (task force on edn.), Am. Assn. Colls. of Pharmacy (pres., commn. to implement change in pharm. edn.), Inst. of Medicine of NAS. Office: Sch Pharmacy UCSF Box 0622 San Francisco CA 94143-0622

KODZ, IRENA CHESLAVOVNA, internist; b. Lida, Belarus, Nov. 15, 1963; came to U.S., 1993; d. Cheslav Stanislavovich Kodz and Leokadia Francevna Gecevich. MD, State Med. Inst., Minsk, Belarus. Diplomate Am. Bd. Internal Medicine. Intern, resident Regional Hosp., Minsk, 1987-88, physician Staryje Dorogi, Belarus, 1988-93; intern Med. Coll. of Ohio, Toledo, 1995-96, resident, 1996-98; physician Ashland (Ohio) Internal Medicine, 1998—. Staff physician, cons. Samaritan Hosp., Ashland, 1998—. Mem. ACP, Am. Soc. Internal Medicine. Roman Catholic. Office: Ashland Internal Medicine 2111 Claremont Ave Ashland OH 44805-3547

KOEHL, MIMI R., integrative biology professor; BA in Biology with Dept. Honors, magna cum laude, Gettysburg Coll.; PhD in Zoology, Duke U. Postdoctoral fellow Friday Harbor Lab., U. Wash., U. York, England; Virginia G. and Robert E. Gill chair, natural history U. Calif., Berkeley, prof., integrative biology. Contbr. articles to profl. jours. Recipient Borelli award, Am. Soc. Biomechanics, Presdl. Young Investigator award, Young Alumni Achievement award, Gettysburg Coll., Disting. Alumni award; Phi Beta Kappa Vis. Scholar, John Simon Guggenheim Meml. Found. Fellowship, MacArthur Found. Fellowship award. Fellow: Calif. Acad. Sci.; mem.: Am. Acad. Arts & Sciences, NAS. Office: U Calif Berkeley Dept Integrative Biology Office 4116VLSB 3060 Valley Life Sciences Bldg #3140 Berkeley CA 94720-3140 Office Phone: 510-642-8103, 510-643-9048 (lab). Office Fax: 510-643-6264. Business E-Mail: cnidaria@berkeley.edu.*

KOEHLER, CHARITY MARIE, music educator; d. Rodney Lee and Cindy Inez Hamann; m. Michael Robert Koehler, July 27, 2002. BA in Music Edn., Briar Cliff U., Sioux City, 1999; MA in Edn., Briar Cliff U., 2003. Dir. vocal music Salem Luth. Ch., Dakota City, Nebr., 1998—2002, Homer (Nebr.) Cmty. Sch., 1999—2005, St. John Luth. Ch., Sioux City, 2004—, Sacred Heart Sch., Sioux City, 2005—06. Mem.: Am. Guild English Handbell Ringers, Am. Choral Dirs. Assn., Nat. Fedn. Music Clubs.

KOEHLER, IRMGARD KILB, dermatologist, educator; b. Freiburg, Germany, July 2, 1940; came to U.S., 1967; d. Johannes Ernst and Anna Magdalena (Grob) Kilb; divorced; children: Stephan Arpad, Dinah Anna. Attended, U. Munich, 1959-65; MD, Ind. U., 1969; postgrad., U. Chgo., 1975-78. Diplomate Am. Bd. Dermatology. Intern U. Munich, 1965-67, U. Chgo., 1971-73; pvt. practice Chgo., 1978; instr. Rush Med. Coll., Chgo., 1979-81; clin. assoc. prof. Chgo. Coll. Osteopathic Medicine, 1983-85; clin. asst. prof. U. Ill., Chgo., 1990—. Rsch. in photodynamic therapy for skin cancers and hyperproliferative skin disorders. Mem. AMA, Am. Acad. Dermatology, Chgo. Dermatol. Soc., Ill. Dermatol. Soc. Office: 150 N Wacker Dr Ste 2300 Chicago IL 60606-1608

KOEHLER, JANE ELLEN, librarian; b. Belleville, Ill., Oct. 18, 1944; d. Edward William and Elizabeth Ellen (Sanford) Hindman; m. Robert Philip Koehler, Feb. 18, 1936; children: Clare Anne, Beth Ellen. BS, Eastern Ill. U., 1967; MS, U. Ill., 1970. Cert. edn. educator. Library asst. Belleville (Ill.) Pub. Library, 1964-65; tchr. librarian Sch. Dist. 72, Woodstock, Ill., 1966-73; dir. library services Sch. Dist. 200, Woodstock, 1969-73; dir. youth services Woodstock Pub. Library, 1980-89, asst. dir., 1989—. Author: (short story) Northwest Herald, 1980; columnist Woodstock Ind., 2001—. Bd. dir. Auxillary Mem. Hosp.; vol. Turning Point (Crisis Intervention), 1978-88; mem. Ill. Literary Heritage Com., 1984-85; chmn. Mem. Hosp. for Mem. Library Adminstr. Coun. of Northern Ill. (sec. 1990), Woodstock Fine Arts Assn. Republican. Roman Catholic. Avocations: writing, swimming, skiing, quilting, travel, theater. Home: 13171 Hickory Ln Woodstock IL 60098-3617 Office: Woodstock Pub Library 414 W Judd St Woodstock IL 60098-3131

KOEHLER, TAMMIE, obstetrician, gynecologist; b. Tulsa, Okla., Sept. 1, 1963; d. Ronald and Roberta Carter; m. Duane Koehler, Mar. 18, 1989; children: Sarah, Rachel;children from previous marriage: Byron Long, Stacey Long, Eric Long. BS, Pittsburg State U., Kans., 1997. Chief resident Okla. U. Health Scis., Tulsa, 2001—05; physicia, owner Miami Women's Clinic, Inc., 2005—. Office: Miami Women's Clinic Inc 301 2nd SW STE 204 Miami OK 74354 Office Phone: 918-542-4300. Office Fax: 918-542-3310.

KOELLING, SHIRLEY M., mathematics educator; b. Sycamore, Ill., Nov. 8, 1948; d. Ralph L. and Marion E. Johnson; m. Vern Koelling, Dec. 14, 1974; children: Kristin, Erik. BA, Augustana Coll., 1971; MA in Math Edn., DePaul U., 1990. Math tchr. Fairmont Sch., Lockport, Ill., 1971—72, Channahon (Ill.) Mid. Sch., 1972—75, Grant Pk. (Ill.) H.S., 1975—2005. Math team coach Grant Pk. H.S., 1975—, scholastic team coach, 2000—. Bd. mem. at large Girl Scouts Trailways Coun., Joliet, Ill., 1995—2005, chair nominating com., 2006—. Mem.: Met. Math Club Chgo., Ill. Coun. Tchrs. Math., Nat. Coun. Tchrs. Math., Am. Daughters of Sweden (3rd v.p. 1999—2005, pres. 2005—), South Suburban Geneal. & Hist. Soc. (bd. dirs.). Home: 12 Lake Metonga Tr Grant Park IL 60940 Office: Grant Park High Sch 421 Esson Farm Rd Grant Park IL 60940 Office Phone: 815-465-2181. Home Fax: 815-465-2482; Office Fax: 815-465-2505. Personal E-mail: koellings@yahoo.com.

KOELLNER, LAURETTE, aerospace transportation executive; b. Bklyn., Oct. 21, 1954; B in Bus. Mgmt., U. Ctrl. Fla.; MBA, Stetson U. Cert. contracts mgr. Nat. Contracts Mgmt. Assn. Analyst contracts, advanced to various positions McDonnell Douglas, 1978—86, mgr. contracts and pricing missle sys. co. Titusville, Fla., 1986—88, bus. mgr. Tomahawk Cruise Missle prog., 1988—89, dir. strategic and bus. planning, 1989—90, head internal support and svcs. ops. missle prodn. facility, 1990—92; budget mgr. McDonnell Douglas Aerospace, St. Louis, 1992—94, dir. human resources divisn., 1994—96, v.p., gen. auditor, 1996—97, Boeing Co. (formerly McDonnell Douglas), St. Louis, 1997—99, v.p., corp. controller, 1999—2004, exec. v.p., 2004—; pres. Connexion by Boeing, 2004—06, Boeing Internat., 2006—. Bd. dirs. Sara Lee Corp., Exostar, Chgo. Coun. Fgn. Rels., Chicagoland C. of C.; mem. bd. regents U. Portland; mem. dean's exec. coun. coll. bus. adminstrn. U. Ctrl. Fla. Named to Hall of Fame, U. Ctrl. Fla., 2003. Mem.: Economic Club Chgo. Office: Boeing World Hdqs 100 N Riverside Chicago IL 60606 Office Phone: 312-544-2000.*

KOELMEL, LORNA LEE, data processing executive; b. Denver, May 15, 1936; d. George Bannister and Gladys Lee Steuart; m. Herbert Howard Nelson, Sept. 9, 1956 (div. Mar. 1967); children: Karen Dianne, Phillip Dean, Lois Lynn; m. Robert Darrel Koelmel, May 12, 1981; stepchildren: Kim, Cheryl, Dawn, Debbie. BA in English, U. Colo., 1967. Cert. secondary English tchr. Substitute English tchr. Jefferson County Schs., Lakewood, Colo., 1967—68; sec. specialist IBM Corp., Denver, 1968—75, pers. adminstr., 1975—82, asst. ctr. coord., 1982—85, office systems specialist, 1985—87, backup computer operator, 1987—; computer instr. Barnes Bus. Coll., Denver, 1987—92; owner, mgr. Lorna's Precision Word Processing and Desktop Pub., Denver, 1987—89; computer cons. Denver, 1990—. Editor newsletter Colo. Nat. Campers and Hikers Assn., 1992-94. Organist Christian Sci. Soc., Buena Vista, Colo., 1963-66, 1st Ch. Christ Scientists Thornton-Westminster, Thornton, Colo., 1994—; chmn. bd. dirs., 1979-80. Mem. NAFE, Nat. Secs. Assn. (retirement ctr. chair 1977-78, newsletter chair 1979-80, v.p. 1980-81), Am. Theatre Organ Soc. (Rocky Mountain chpt.), Am. Guild Organists, U. Colo. Alumni Assn., Avon Ind. Sales Rep and Pres. Club, Alpha Chi Omega (publicity com. 1986-88). Clubs: Nat. Writers. Lodges: Job's Daus. (recorder 1953-54). Republican. Avocations: quilting, piano, bridge, logic problems, golf.

KOENIG, BONNIE, international non-profit organization consultant; d. Bruce D. and Florence (Englander); m. Gerald N. Rosenberg. BA, Dickinson Coll., 1979; MA, Yale U., 1983. Program assoc. U.S. Dept. Commerce/ITA, Washington, 1983-85; exec. dir. Coun. Great Lakes Govs., Chgo., 1986-90, Zonta Internat., Chgo., 1990-95; pres. Going Internat. Assocs., 1995—. Mem. CIVICUS: World Alliance for Citizen Participation. Mem. Am. Soc. Assn. Execs., Chgo. Soc. Assn. Execs. (internat. sect. planning com.). Address: 11344 S Lothair Ave Chicago IL 60643-4134 E-mail: koenig@goinginternational.com.

KOENIG, ELIZABETH BARBARA, sculptor; b. N.Y.C., Apr. 20, 1937; d. Hayward and Selma E. (Rosen) Ulman; m. Carl Stuart Koenig, Sept. 10, 1961; children: Katherine Lee, Kenneth Douglas. BA, Wellesley Coll., 1958; MD, Yale U., 1962; postgrad., Art Students League N.Y., 1963-64, Corcoran Sch. Art, 1964-67. One-woman shows include St. John's Coll., Annapolis, Md., 1974, Foxhall Gallery, Washington, 1977, 85, 99, also solo retrospectives Lyman Allyn Mus., New London, Conn., 1978, Rotunda of Pan-Am. Health Orgn., Washington, 1978, Gallery Metayer, Paris, 1999; exhibited in group shows at Internat. Dedication Nat. Bur. Stds., Gaithersburg, Md., 1966, Textile Mus., Washington, 1974-75, No. Va. Mus., Alexandria, 1975, Meridian House Internat., Washington, 1980; commd. works include Free Spirit marble carving Washington Hebrew Congregation, 1978, Monumental Torso bronze for grounds George Meany Ctr. for Labor Studies, 1982, desert stone marble carving Regional Ctr. for Women in Arts, Westchester, Pa., 2003; represented in pvt. collections, U.S. and Europe. Recipient 1st prize sculpture Tri-State Regional Exhbn., Md., 1970, 2d and 3d prize sculpture, 1971. Mem. Artists Equity Assn. (v.p. Washington 1977-83), Art Students League N.Y. (life), Internat. Sculpture Ctr., New Arts Ctr. Avocations: reading, gardening. Home: 9014 Charred Oak Dr Bethesda MD 20817-1924

KOENIG, HEIDI O., public administration professor; MA in Psychology, U. Nebr., Lincoln, JD, 1989; PhD, Syracuse U., NY, 1994. Assoc. prof. divsn. pub. adminstrn. No. Ill. U., DeKalb, 1993—. Author: (book) Public Administration and Law. Mem.: Am. Soc. Polit. Sci., ASPA (chmn. sect. pub. law and adminstrn. 2002—). Office: No Ill U Divsn Pub Adminstrn Carroll Ave Dekalb IL 60115-2828 Office Phone: 815-753-6167.

KOENIG, MARGARET SUSANNE, elementary school educator; BA, Coll. Notre Dame, 1998; MEd, Loyola Coll. Md., 2002. Cert. advanced profl. tchng. Md. State Dept. Edn., Md. Elem. classroom tchr. Balt. County Pub. Schs., 1998—. Internship NOAA, Silver Spring, Md., 2004. Author: Remote Sensing and Coral Reefs: A Fifth Grade Science Unit. Mem.: NSTA, Nat. Educators Assn., Md. Coun. Tchrs. Math., Kappa Gamma Pi, Kappa Delta Pi. Home: 6433 Saint Philips Rd Linthicum MD 21090-2647 Office: Balt County Public Schs 1500 Frederick Rd Baltimore MD 21228 Office Phone: 410-887-0820. Personal E-mail: sacrevache@yahoo.com. Business E-mail: mkoenig@bcps.org.

KOENIG, MAUREEN CATHERINE, science educator; b. LA, June 11, 1949; d. Robert Curtis and Lucille Catherine Martin; m. William Richard Koenig, Sept. 12, 1970; children: Kristin Maureen, Ryan Patrick. BS in Biology, Loyola Marymount U., 1971; MS in Edn., U. So. Calif., 2001. Clear single subject tchg. credential in life sci. Commn. on Tchr. Credentialing, State of Calif., 1992. Med. technologist, bacteriologist specialist, co-dept. head bacteriology, edn. coord. sch. of med. tech. Daniel Freeman Hosp., Ingelwood, Calif., 1971—78; tchr. sci., math, computer St. Anthony Claret Sch., Anaheim, Calif., 1987—2001; 7th & 8th grade sci. tchr. Yorba Linda Mid. Sch., Calif., 2002, sci. dept. chair, 2004—. Presenter in field. Recipient ExploraVisions awards Competition - US Western Regional Winner, Nat. Sci. Tchrs. Assn., Toshiba, 1998, Innovation in Edn. award, Project Tomorrow, 2006. Mem.: NSTA (assoc.), Orange County Sci. Educators Assn. (assoc.), Calif. Sci. Tchrs. Assn. (assoc.), Phi Kappa Phi (life). Avocations: hiking, dinosaur excavation, ATV riding, snowmobiling, skiing. Office Phone: 714-528-7090. Office Fax: 714-996-2752. Personal E-mail: mo_koenig@hotmail.com. E-mail: mkoenig@pylusd.org.

KOENIG, NORMA EVANS, retired religious studies educator; b. Bloomfield, Ind., Feb. 10, 1922; d. Alexander Robert and Della E. (Stein) Evans; m. Robert Emil Koenig, July 18, 1943; children: Elsa K. Weber, Robert Evans, Richard Alexander, Martha K. Stone, Thea K. Burton, Laura K. Godinez. AM, U. Chgo., 1947. Cert. clergy United Ch. Christ, United Presbyn. Ch. Counselor Elmhurst Coll., Elmhurst, Ill., 1946—47; editor Chgo. Bapt. Assn., Chgo., 1947—48; editor, writer divsn. Christian edn. United Ch. of Christ, 1954—65; instr., asst. prof. U. Ill., Chgo., 1948—54; editor, bd. chair United Presbyn. Ch., Phila., 1968—70; editor JED Share Mag., 1970—90; interim assoc. prof. Lancaster Theological Seminary, 1989—90. Developer ElderNet. Author: All About Arthur, 1961, One Night, 1961, Tell Me the Stories of Jesus, 1957; author: (packets) Ch. & the Kindergarten Child, 1955; Ch. & the Nursery Child, 1956. Pres. Lower Merion (Pa.) HS Parents Assn., 1964—66, Interschool Coun., Lower Merion, 1967—69, Penn Wynne Libr. Bd., Lower Merion, Twp. Libr. Assn. and Bd., Lower Merion. Recipient Florence James Adams Poetry Reading award, Chgo., 1947, Children and Ch. award, St. Louis, 1992, Best Children's Bk of Yr., 1961. Democrat. Avocations: music, drama, public speaking. Home: Havertown, Pa. Died Apr. 9, 2006.

KOENIGSBERG, JUDY Z. NULMAN, psychologist; b. NYC, Apr. 21, 1951; d. Macy and Sarah (Rosenberg) Nulman; m. David I. Koenigsberg, June 18, 1972; children: Benjamin, Rachel T. Grad. summa cum laude, Yeshiva U. Tchrs. Inst., N.Y.C., 1971; BA with honors, Bklyn. Coll., 1972; MA, Northeastern Ill. U., 1980; grad. study, U. Chgo., 1980—82; MEd, Loyola U., Chgo., 1985; PhD in Psychology, Northwestern U., 1990. Lic. and reg. clin. psychologist, Ill. Clin. cons. Charter Barclay Hosp., Chgo., 1985-86; psychology extern Luth. Gen. Hosp., Park Ridge, Ill., 1987-88; psychol. testing extern Evanston (Ill.) Hosp., 1988-89, psychology intern, 1989-90; psychology postdoctoral resident Loyola U. Chgo., 1991-92; clin. psychologist U. Chgo., 1993-94; dir. Stats. Inst., 1995—. Instr. Loyola U., Chgo., 2005—. Contbr. articles to profl. jours., chapters to books. Recipient Outstanding Achievement award Nat. Culture Coun., 1972; scholar Bklyn. Coll., 1972, Kappa Delta Pi, 1972. Mem. APA, Ill. Psychol. Assn., Soc. for Computers in Psychology, Northwestern U. Alumni Assn. Sch. Edn. and Social Policy (dir. bd. 1993-94). Avocations: violin, Tae Kwon Do, table tennis. Office: 708 Church St Ste 207 Evanston IL 60201-3840 Office Phone: 312-409-4222. E-mail: jzok@earthlink.net.

KOENKER, DIANE P., history professor; b. Chgo., July 29, 1947; m. Roger Koenker; 1 child. AB in History, Grinnell Coll., 1969; AM in Comparative Studies in History, U. Mich., 1971, PhD in History, 1976. From asst. prof. to assoc. prof. in history Temple U., Phila., 1976-83; asst. prof. history U. Ill., Urbana-Champaign, 1983-86, assoc. prof., 1986-88, prof. history, 1988—, dir. Russian and East European Ctr., 1990-96, editor Slavic Rev., 1996—2006. Vis. lectr. history U. Ill., Urbana-Champaign, 1975; vis. fellow Australian Nat. U., 1989, Fulbright-Hays Faculty Rsch. Abroad, 1993; lectr. in field. Author: Moscow Workers and the 1917 Revolution, 1981, paperback edit., 1986, (with William G. Rosenberg) Strikes and Revolution in Russia 1917, 1989, Republic of Labor: Russian Printers and Soviet Socialism, 1918-1930, 2005; editor: Third All-Russian Trade Union Conference 1917, 1982, (with William G. Rosenberg and Ronald Grigor Suny) Party, State and Society in the Russian Civil War: Explorations in Social History, 1989, (with Ronald D. Bachman) Revelations from the Russian Archives, 1997; editor, translator: (with S.A. Smith) Notes of a Red Guard, 1993; mem. editl. bd. Cambridge Soviet Paperbacks; mem. adv. bd. Soviet Studies in History, 1986-89; book reviewer to numerous jours.; contbr. articles to profl. jours. Fellow Temple U., 1977, 82, Russian Inst.-Columbia U., 1977-78, NEH, 1983-84, NEH, 1984-85, 94-95, MUCIA Exch. fellow Moscow State U., 1991, Guggenheim Found., 2006; grantee Am. Coun. Learned Socs.-Social Sci. Rsch. Coun., 1977-78, Temple U., 1979-81, 82-83, William and Flora Hewlett Internat. Rsch. grantee, 1986, 91, Nat. Coun. for Soviet and East European Rsch., 1989, Arnold O. Beckman Rsch. Bd. grantee, 1990-91, 2002—, IREX Travel grantee, 1993, 2006; recipient Fulbright-Hays Faculty Rsch. award for USSR, 1989. Mem. Am. Hist. Assn. (mem. membership com. 1996-98, European History sect. chair 2001, Chester Higby prize European sect. 2003), Am. Assn. Advancement Slavic Studies (bd. dirs. 1996—), Midwest Workshop of Russian and Soviet Historians, Assn. Women in Slavic Studies. also: U Ill Dept History 810 S Wright St Urbana IL 61801-3644

KOEPP, DONNA PAULINE PETERSEN, librarian; b. Clinton, Iowa, Oct. 8, 1941; d. Leo August and Pauline Sena (Outzen) Petersen; m. David Ward Koepp, June 5, 1960 (div. June 1984). BS in Edn., U. Colo., 1967; MA in Libr., U. Denver, 1974; postgrad., U. Colo., 1984-85. Subject specialist govt. publs., map dept. Denver Pub. Libr., 1967-85; head govt. documents, map libr. U. Kans., Lawrence, 1985-2000, map and geomedia svcs. libr., 2000—02. Head govt. document, microforms, reference instrn. Soc. Sci. Program Harvard U., 2002-; apptd. Fed. Depository Libr. Coun. to Pub. Printer, 1998-2001. Prodn. mgr. Meridian Jour., 1988-93, 96-99; editor: Index and Carto-Bibliography of Maps, 1789-1969, 1995. Recipient Documents to the People award Congl. Info. Svc./Govt. Documents Round Table/ALA, 1999. Mem. Map & Geography Round Table of Am. Libr. Assn. (chmn. 1986-87, Outstanding Contbn. to Map Librarianship 1991), Govt. Documents Round Table of Am. Libr. Assn., Western Assn. Map Librs. (sec. 1983-84). Office: Govt Documents Microforms Libr Lamont Libr Lower Level U Harvard College Libr Cambridge MA 02138- Office Phone: 617-495-2105. Business E-Mail: koepp@fas.harvard.edu.

KOEPPEL, HOLLY KELLER, electric power industry executive; b. Pitts., May 17, 1958; married; 2 children. BS in Bus., Ohio State U., Columbus; MS in Bus., Ohio State U. From mgr. to v.p. Asia-Pacific Ops. Consolidated Natural Gas, Sydney, Australia, 1984—2000; v.p. new ventures for corp. devel. Am. Electric Power Co., Columbus, Ohio, 2000—02, exec. v.p. comml. ops., 2002—04, exec. v.p. AEP Utilities East, 2004—06, exec. v.p., CFO, 2006—. Office: Am Elec Power Co 1 Riverside Plz Columbus OH 43215-1000

KOEPPEL, MARY SUE, communications educator, writer; b. Phlox, Wis., Dec. 12, 1939; d. Alphonse and Emma Petronella Marx Koeppel; m. Robert B. Gentry, May 31, 1980. BA, Alverno Coll., 1962; MA, Loyola U., Chgo., 1968; postgrad., U. Wis., St. Louis U., U. N.H., U. Calif., U. North Fla., U. Minn., Jacksonville U. Tchr. St. Joseph H.S., Milw., 1962-68, Pius XI H.S., Milw., 1968-72; instr., head dept. comms., dir. learning ctr. Waukesha County Tech. Inst., Pewaukee, Wis., 1972-80; pres., exec. bd. West Suburban Coun. Tchg. Profession, 1976-80. Adv. Waukesha chpt. Parents Without Partners, 1975—80; cons. Learning Ctrs., 1976—2005, Coll. and Univ. Faculties; instr. comm. Fla. C.C., Jacksonville, 1980—2005; TV interviewer Writer to Writer, Jacksonville, Fla., 1989—; instr. Nat. Inst. for Tchrs. Writing, Greenfield, Mass., 1987—94, Westbrook Coll., Portland, Maine, 1980—84; faculty Master Tchr. Inst., 1989—2005. Editor (-in-chief): Kalliope Jour. Women's Lit. and Art, 1988—2005, Lollipops, Lizards and Literature, 1994—2005; editor: Instructional Network Notes, 1982—85; author: Writing Resources for Conferencing and Collaboration, 1989, Writing Strategies Plus Collaboration, 1997, 4th rev. edit., 2005, Write Your Life-The Memory Catcher, 1998, In the Library of Silences, Poems of Loss, 2001, Between the Bones, poems, 2005; co-founder Letters Coun., 1996, interviewer Worth Quoting, 1994—, Author to Author, 1994—; co-editor: Women of Vision, 2000; contbg. editor: State St. Rev., 1992—, 2003—; contbr. articles to profl. jours. Mem. Sherman Park Cmty. Ctr., 1975—80; co-founder, bd. dirs. Instrnl. Network for coll. Faculty, 1981—85. Recipient Red Schoolhouse award, Assn. Fla. C.C., 1983, Faculty Excellence award, 2000, Frances Buck Sherman award, 2001, Educator of Yr. award, Cultural Coun. of Greater Jacksonville, 2002, Bd. Trustees award for Cmty. Svc., Fla. C.C. at Jacksonville, 2003; grantee, NDEA, 1968, Art Ventures, 1992, Tchg. and Learning Ctr., 1999; scholar, Fla. Humanities Coun., 1999. Mem.: Am. Pen Women. Business E-Mail: skoeppel@fccj.edu.

KOERBER, DOLORES JEAN, music educator, musician; b. Martins Ferry, Ohio, Apr. 7, 1936; d. Clarence Donald and Bertha Gail (Palmer) K. B in Religious Edn., Malone Coll., 1958, BS, 1965; MEd, Kent State U., 1972; D in Religious Edn., Massillon Baptist Coll., 2000. Cert. tchr. music grades K-12, Ohio. Tchr. Coun. Religious Edn., North Canton, Ohio, 1958-60, Shelby, Ohio, 1960-62, Garaway Local, Sugarcreek, Ohio, 1965-71, Fairless Local, Justus, Ohio, 1971-73, Massillon (Ohio) Christian Sch., 1973-75; prof. Massillon Bapt. Coll., 1973—. Choir dir. Evang. United Brethren Ch., Sugarcreek, 1965-68, Westminster Presbyn., Canton, 1973-75, organist, 1981-85, Christ United Meth., Louisville, Ohio, 1985-92, St. Paul's United Meth., Canton, 1993—. Performer in programs for schs., clubs and chs. Mem. alumni exec. bd. Malone Coll., 2004—. Named first native Cantonian to graduate from Malone Coll. after its relocation in Canton, 1958. Mem.: Am. Guild Organists, Fortnightly Music Club (pres. 1970—71), MacDowell Music Club (rec. sec. 2001—03, 1st v.p. 2003—05, pres. 2005—), Malone Coll. Alumni (exec. bd. 2004). Republican. Avocations: doll collecting, handwork, swimming.

KOERBER, ERICA, photographer; b. 1970; Owner, chief photographer Evon Photography; ops. mgr. Ventana Rsch. Corp. Involved with Susan G. Komen Race for the Cure, Women's Found. Southern Ariz., Youth On Their Own, Brewster Ctr. Domestic Violence Services, Angel Charity for Children, Tucson Indian Ctr., Arts for All & Third St. Kids, Humane Soc. Southern Ariz., Child Protective Services. Named one of 40 Under 40, Tucson Bus. Edge, 2006. Office: Ventana Research Corporation 2702 S4th Ave Tucson AZ 85713 Office Phone: 520-882-8772. Office Fax: 520-882-8762.*

KOERBER, JOAN C., retired elementary school educator; b. Newark, Mar. 23, 1929; d. George Vincent and Catherine Rose (Donahue) Callanan; m. John Calvin Koerber, June 27, 1953; children: John C., Joanne C BS Elem. Edn., Newark State Coll., 1952; MA Adminstrn., Kean Coll., Union, N.J., 1984. Tchr. 15th Ave Sch., Newark, 1952—71, Lincoln Sch., Newark, 1971—78, tchr. Chpt. I, 1978—79, coord. Chpt. I, 1979—84, tchr. basic skills, 1984—95; ret., 1995. Summer sch. coord. Lincoln Sch., 1979-84; past pres. Kean Coll. Grad. Sch. Coun Sec. Essex County PTA; rec. sec., dir. Crandon Lakes Country Club Inc. Property Owners Assn.; lector and eucharist min. Our Lady of Mt. Carmel Ch., Swartswood, N.J Mem. ASCD, AAUW, PTA (hon. life), NEA, N.J. Edn. Assn., Essex County Edn. Assn., Newark Edn. Assn., Newark Tchrs. Union, N.J. State Columbiettes (supreme bd. dirs., past state pres.), Kappa Delta Phi (past pres.), Phi Delta Kappa (past pres.) Home: 17 N Bayberry Rd Newton NJ 07860-6570

KOERBER, MARILYNN ELEANOR, gerontology nursing educator, consultant, nurse; b. Covington, Ky., Feb. 1, 1942; d. Harold Clyde and Vivian Eleanor (Conrad) Hilge; m. James Paul Koerber, May 29, 1971. Diploma, Christ Hosp. Sch. Nursing, Cin., 1964; BSN, U. Ky., 1967; MPH, U. Mich., 1970. RN, Ohio, S.C.; cert. gerontologist. Staff nurse premature and newborn nursery Cin. Gen. Hosp., 1964-65; staff nurse, hosp. discharge planner Vis. Nurse Assn., Cin., 1967-69, asst. dir. Atlanta, 1976-78; instr. Coll. Nursing, U. Ky., Lexington, 1970-71; supr. Montgomery County Health Dept., Rockville, Md., 1971-74; asst. prof. Coll. Nursing, U. S.C., Columbia, 1979-86, instr., 1987-89; alzheimer's project coord. S.C. Commn. on Aging, Columbia, 1988-90; dir. edn. and tng. Luth. Homes S.C., White Rock, 1988-91; grad. asst. U. S.C. Sch. of Pub. Health, 1991-94; trainer for homemakers home health aides S.C. Divsn. on Aging, 1991-97; coord. to train homemakers home aides nursing assts. State Pilot Program, DSS and Divsn. on Aging, 1993-95; Alzheimer's trainer office aging, nurse mgr. Beaufort-Jasper Hampton Comprehensive Health, 1998—2003; allied health program mgr. Tech. Coll. of the Lowcountry, 1997—. Mem. utilization rev. bd. Palmetto Health Dist., Lexington, 1984-2000; test item writer, nurse aide cert. Psychol. Corp., San Antonio, 1989, 91, 92; bd. examiners Nursing Home Adminstrn. and Community Residential Care Facility Adminstr., chmn. of edn. com., Columbia, S.C., 1990-93; presenter gerontol. workshops and residential care facilities adminstrn. Contbg. editor: (handbook) Promoting Caregiver Groups, 1984; reviewer gerontology textbooks, 1983-91; contbr. tng. video and manuals on Alzheimers, 1988 (hon. mention Retirement Rsch. Found. 1989). Del. S.C. Gov. White House Conf. on Aging, Columbia, 1981; chmn. ann. meeting S.C. Fedn. for Older Ams., Columbia, 1989—91; v.p. Alzheimer's Family Services of Greater Beaufort, 1998—99, mem. adv. bd., 2002—; bd. dirs. Sr. Svcs. of Beaufort County, 1997—2002, Alzheimer's Family Services of Greater Beaufort, 1997—2002. USPHS trainee, 1965-67, Adm. on Aging trainee, 1969-70. Mem. ANA (cert. gerontol. nurse, cmty. health nurse), S.C. Nurses Assn., So. Gerontol. Soc., Gerontol. Soc. Am., S.C. Gerontol. Soc. (treas. 1989-91, Rosamond R. Boyd award 1986, Pres. award Mid State Alzheimers Chpt., 1993, Macy Scally Alzheimers award 2000), Soc. for Pub. Health Edn., Am. Soc. on Aging, Alzheimers Assn. (bd. dirs. Columbia chpt. 1988-93, sec. 1992, chmn. nominating com. 1991-92; bd. dirs. S.C. combined health appeal 1991-93), Nat. Coun. on Aging, Nat. Gerontol. Nursing Assn. Democrat. Unitarian Universalist. Avocations: interior decorating, wine tasting.

KOESCHE, AILEEN MARY, special education educator; b. Berwyn, Ill., July 17, 1976; d. John James and Marianne C. Flanagan. BS, Bradley U., 1998; MS in Edn., No. Ill. U., 2003. Cert. tchr. Ill. Tchr. Burbank (Ill.) Sch. Dist. #111, 1999—2000, Lincoln-Way H.S. #210, Frankfort, Ill., 2000—. Com. mem. North Ctrl. Accreditation, 2002—. Mem.: Coun. for Exceptional Children, Kappa Delta Pi. Home: 3338 Thomas Hickey Dr Joliet IL 60431 Office: Lincoln Way East HS 201 Colorado Ave Frankfort IL 60423 E-mail: aileenflanagan@msn.com.

KOESSEL, JEANNINE CARROL, retired principal; d. Clarence Frederick and Gladys Ida (Stats) Krantz; m. Donald R. Koesel, Aug. 3, 1996; stepchildren: Martin, Kathryn; m. Thomas Walter Rebentisch (div.); children: Ann Louise Rebentisch, Philip Karl Rebentisch. BMusEd, Lawrence U., Appleton, Wis., 1951; MA, Mich. State U., East Lansing, Mich., 1969. Tchr. music grades k-12 County Schs., Ohio, 1951—54; tchr. music grades k-8 Belding Pub. Schs., Mich., 1954—70; dir. fed. and state reading and math programs Coldwater Cmty. Schs., 1970—87, elem. prin., 1987—91. Mem. curriculum rev. com. Mich. Dept. Edn., Lansing, 1985—91. One-woman shows include, 2005. Mem. Santa Fe Symphony Guild, Ft. Collins Symphony Guild; instigator domestic violence shelters, 1979—2003; founding mem. and pres. Altusa Club, 1987—91; singer West Valley Chorale, 2000—; mem. Surprise Symphony Guild. Named Woman of Yr., Coldwater City Coun., 1971, Adminstr. of Yr., Mich. Reading Assn., 1989. Mem.: AAUW (officer Coldwater, Ft. Collins, SAnta Fe and Surprize chpts. 1967—), Sun City Grand Art Club (mem. program com. 2005—), West Valley Symphony Guild (chair Walling music scholarship 2002—). Avocations: painting, travel, music, reading, book discussion group.

KOESTER, BETTY JEANNETTE, retired elementary school educator; b. Albuquerque, July 15, 1940; d. James Warren and Dorothy Marguerite (VanMeter) Burton; m. Thomas L. Koester, Dec. 27, 1959 (div. June 1989); children: Brian T., Brett J., Bennett G. BS in Elem. Edn., Old Dominion U., 1966; M in Elem. Edn., reading endorsement, U. N.Mex., 1984. Tchr. 1st grade Clark Elem. Sch., Waukegan, Ill., 1966—67; substitute tchr. various schs., 1970—84; Chpt. 1 reading tchr. Adobe Acres Elem. Sch., Albuquerque, 1984—85; tchr. 2d through 4th grades Tomasita Elem. Sch., Albuquerque, 1985—92; tchr. grades 2-5, chpt. 1 reading Mary Ann Binford Elem. Sch., Albuquerque, 1992—95; tchr. 2d grade, title 1 reading Lowell Elem. Sch., Albuquerque, 1995—2000; ret., 2000. Tutor U. N.Mex., Albuquerque, 1980-84; tchr. 5th grade Las Vegas, Nev., 2000-02, Sylvan Reading Ctr., 2001-03, 2005—; reading tutor Bel-Air Elem. Sch., 2003-04; substitute tchr., 2005— Republican. Methodist. Avocations: sewing, reading, travel. Home: Apt 1211 6200 Eubank NE Albuquerque NM 87111

KOESTER, JOLENE, academic administrator; BA magna cum laude, U. Minn., 1970; MA in Communication Arts, U. Wis., Madison, 1971; PhD in Speech Communications, U. Minn., 1980. Asst. prof. speech and drama U. Mo., Columbia, 1980—83; asst. prof. communication studies Calif. State U., Sacramento, 1983—85, assoc. prof. communication studies, 1985—89, dept. chair communication studies, 1986—89, prof. communication studies, 1989—2000, asst. v.p. academic affairs, 1989—91, assoc. v.p. academic affairs, 1991—93, v.p. academic affairs, 1993—2000, provost, 1996—2000; pres. Calif. State U. Northridge, 2000—. Office: Calif State U UN 200 18111 Nordhoff St Northridge CA 91330-8230

KOESTER, LISA, principal; b. Sioux City, Iowa, July 31, 1957; d. Clifford Duane and Janet Anne Hansen; m. David John Koester, June 9, 1979; children: Andrew John, Amy Lynn. BS, Iowa State U., 1979, MS, 1994. Cert. administrator, evaluator, Iowa. Tchr., coach South Tama County Schs., Toledo, Iowa, 1979-82, 88-92, Gladbrook (Iowa) Cmty. Schs., 1982-84; grad. rsch. asst. Iowa State U., Ames, 1992-94; mid. sch. assoc. prin. Marshalltown (Iowa) Cmty. Schs., 1994-98; h.s. prin. Gladbrook-Reinbeck Cmty. Schs., Reinbeck, Iowa, 1998—. Ednl. cons., Gladbrook, 1994—. Mem. Sch. Bd., Gladbrook Cmty. Schs., 1983-86. Mem. ASCD, Nat. Assn. Secondary Sch. Prins., Alpha Delta Kappa, Phi Kappa Phi, Phi Delta Kappa. Republican. Methodist. Avocations: sports, reading, gardening, computers. Home: 513 6th St Gladbrook IA 50635-9411 Office: Gladbrook-Reinbeck HS 600 Blackhawk St Reinbeck IA 50669-1312

KOESTNER, CAROL ANN, information technology manager, consultant; d. Edward Richard and Ileita P. Koestner; adopted children: Tamera A. Hough, Sheryl D. Fox, Charles R. Shumate. BA in Math., U. of South Fla., 1969, Roanoke Coll., 1967. Programmer May Plant DuPont Data Sys., Camden, SC, 1969—71; analyst May Plant Nylon Info. Sys., Camden, 1971—74; from sr. analyst to sr. specialist DuPont Nylon Info. Sys., Camden, 1974—84, sr. specialist, 1984—89; sys. cons. DuPont Textiles & Interiors Nylon Info. Sys., Camden, 1990—2004; ret., 2004. Bus. cons. applied economics class Jr. Achievement Camden (S.C.) HS, 1987—99. Musician at various venues songs. Pres. band booster club Camden (S.C.) HS, 1979—80; campaign leader breast cancer Am. Cancer Soc., Columbia and Camden, SC, 2001—02; mem. coun. on ministries Lyttleton St. United Meth. Ch., Camden, 1980—83; vol. grant writer. Vet.'s Formation, Columbia, SC, 2002—03. Recipient Jake Watson award, United Way of Kershaw County, 1987, 1993, Svc. award, Jr. Achievement. Republican. Methodist. Avocations: travel, volunteer work, crafts. Office: DuPont Textiles & Interiors PO Drawer 7000 Camden SC 29020-7000 Home: 34 Middleton Dr Lugoff SC 29078 Personal E-mail: ckoestner@aol.com.

KOETTER, CORNELIA M., lawyer; b. Durham, NC, Apr. 25, 1958; BA, Loyola Coll., 1980; JD, U. Md., 1985. Bar: Md. 1986, DC 1990. Assoc. Nolan, Plumhoff & Williams, Chartered. Mem.: Md. Bar Assn. Office: Nolan, Plumhoff & Williams, Chartered Ste 700, Nottingham Ctr 502 Washington Ave Towson MD 21204-4528 E-mail: ckoetter@nolanplumhoff.com.

KOFF, SHIRLEY IRENE, writer; b. Oakland, Calif., Aug. 31, 1948; d. Lawrence Ray and Stella Pauline (Durham) Butler; m. Robert Allen Koff, June 12, 1971; children: Jennifer, Katherine. BA, Calif. State U., 1971, MA, 1972. Adj. prof. Pellissippi State U., Knoxville, 1989-93; asst. mgr. Adolfo II, Pigeon Forge, Tenn., 1994-98. Poet, writer; tchr. adult religious edn. classes and seminars; expert info. provider internet resource AskAnything.com. Tchr., lay min., bd. dirs. First Assembly of God Ch., Sevierville, 1996-99; core group leader, founding mem. Wellspring Congregation, United Meth. Ch., 1999-2001. Mem.: AAUW, Knoxville (Tenn.) Writers Guild, Tenn. Writers Alliance, Appalachian Writers Assn., Mensa. Democrat. Avocations: writing, speaking, teaching. Home: 1214 Amber Ln Sevierville TN 37862-6101 E-mail: sikoff@chartern.net.

KOFLER, SILVIA MARIA, writer, educator; d. Maria and Heinrich Kofler; life ptnr. David Paarmann. MA in English, U. Mo., Kansas City, 1995. Instr. Rockhurst U., Kansas City, Mo., 1998—; lectr. U. Kans., Lawrence, 1999—. Riverfront readings mem. Organize Lit. Readings, Kansas City, Mo., 2004—. Author (poet): (book of poetry) From the Suburbs with the Wedding Dress in its Coffin/Vom Vorort mit dem Hochzeitskleid im Sarg, book of poems in English and German; contbr. anthology; author: (play) Markers (Plays-In-Progress contest winner at Rockhurst U., 2003), (essay about imagination) Compromise (2nd Prize for writing about the nature of imagination from Rockhust U. Mag., 2001). Mem./vol. Writers Pl. Midwest Ctr. for Lit. Arts, Kansas City, Mo., 1992—2006. Mem.: Am. Assn. of Lit. Translators, Acad. of Am. Poets. Office: Univ Kans Jayhawk Blvd Lawrence KS 66045 Business E-Mail: relfok@ku.edu.

KOFNOVEC, DONNA ANN See HANOVER, DONNA

KOGAN, INNA, psychiatrist, educator; b. Kharkov, USSR, Sept. 5, 1940; came to U.S., 1979; d. Alexander and Fanya (Ioffe) Epelbaum; m. Boris Kogan, Nov. 22, 1962; 1 child, James B. MD, Med. Sch., Perm, USSR, 1957-59, Med. Sch., Riga, Latvia, 1964. Tng. in ophthalmology Med. Sch., Riga, 1964-65; staff ophthalmologist Outpatient Clinic, Riga, 1964-78; physician asst. to William S. Harris, M.D., Dallas, 1980-83; flexible intern U. Tex. Southwestern Med. Sch., Dallas, 1984-85, resident in ophthalmology, 1985-86, resident in psychiatry, 1987-90, clin. instr. psychiatry dept., 1990-95, clin. assoc. prof., 1995—; mem. staff Terrell (Tex.) State Hosp., Dallas, 1990-92; pvt. practice Dallas, 1992—. Head statis. divsn. Ministry Pub. Health Latvia, Riga, 1975-78; med. dir. Meth. Med. Ctr., Dallas, 1993-94. Contbr. articles to med. jours., including Contact and Intraocular Lens Med. Jour., Am. Intraocular Implant Soc. Jours. Recipient Cert. Excellence, Nancy A.A. Roeske, 2000, Cert. Appreciation, U. Tex. S.W. Med. Sch., 2002, 2004, 2005, Arthur M. Griffin award, 1997—98, Jewish Family Svc. Appreciation award, 1995, Terrell State Hosp. Appreciation award, 1987—92, Nat. Leadership award, Nat. Rep. Congl. Com. Mem. Am. Psychiat. Assn., North Tex. Soc. Psychiat. Physicians, Tex. Soc. Psychiat. Physicians, Dallas Area Women Psychiatrists. Republican. Avocations: music, art, travel, reading. Office: Ste 504 13101 Preston Rd Dallas TX 75240-5231 Office Phone: 469-791-9000.

KOGELSCHATZ, JOAN LEE, psychologist, psychotherapist; b. Detroit, Nov. 26, 1940; d. Edgar Rolfe and Helen Josephine (York) K.; B.A., U. Fla., 1963; M.S.W., Fla. State U., 1967, Ph.D., 1976. Intern, VA Hosp., Bay Pines, Fla., 1966, div. child and adolescent psychiatry, dept. psychiatry U. Fla. Med. Center, Gainesville, 1966; instr. psychiatry div. child Adolescent psychiatry U. Fla. Med. Center, Shands Teaching Hosp. & Clinics, Gainesville, 1967-72; field supr., instr. Fla. State U., 1973, field supr., instr. Psychiatric Social Work, 1973-74; pvt. practice psychology, Dothan, Ala., 1975—; guest lectr. Shands Teaching Hosp. & Clinics, 1975, Neurosis Inst., Moscow, 1992, Siriraj/Bumrongrad Hosps., Bangkok, Thailand, others; cons. Lyster Army Hosp., Ft. Rucker, Ala., 1975-78; guest lectr. Dept. Mental Health, Ft. Rucker, 1975; lectr. in field; asst. prof. U. Ala., 1976-77; cons. Bd. dirs. Ala. Soc. Crippled Children and Adults, 1981—, cons., 1981—, fin. chmn., 1983—; apptd. to adv. bd. Law Enforcement Planning Agy. Ala., State of Ala., 1980—, State of Ala. Child Abuse and Neglect Prevention, pres., chmn., 1985-91; chmn., pres. State of Ala. Children's Trust Fund Council, 1984-86, pres. Ala. 2d Congl. Dist., 1985. Diplomate Am. Bd. Psychotherapy, Am. Bd. Medical Psychotherapy, Am. Bd. Pain Mgmt., Am. Bd. Med. Psychotherapists, Am. Bd. Sexologist; lic. profl. counselor, Ala.; lic. marriage and family therapist, Ala.; lic. psychologist, Fla.; lic. clin. psychiat. social worker, Ala.; cert. emergency therapist, Fla. State U.; bd. cert. emergency crisis response, traumatic stress expert, Am. Acad. Experts in Traumatic Stress; bd. certified traumatologist, Traumatology Inst. Fla. State U.; bd. dirs. Dothan Child Abuse Prevention Bd., S.E. Ala. BBB, S.E. Ala. Symphony Assn., Ala.Soc. Crippled Children and Adults, Girls Club Dothan, S.E. Ala. Rehab. Bd., chmn. legis. com.; bd. dirs., cons. Fibromyelgia and Chronic Fatigue Support Group, Compassionate Friends, Adam Group; chmn. com. mem., bd. dirs. Landmark Found.; exec. bd. mem., chmn. judges com. Nat. Peanut Festival. Host. An Hour With Dr. Joan WWNT, WTKN-Talk Radio, 1995. Named Woman of Yr., Nat. Fedn. Bus. and Profl. Women, 1984, Model Woman of Yr., Girls Clubs of Dothan, 1998; recipient Sm. Bus. of Yr. Profl. Divsn. award Dothan C. of C., 1994, Leadership Dothan award, 1989, Treasurer, Leadership Dothan Alumni Coun., 1990. Mem. Am. Acad. Clin. Sexologists (founding clin. fellow), Am. Psychol. Assn., Acad. Psychosomatic Medicine, Am. Acad. Pain Mgmt. (cert.), Am. Orthopsychiat. Assn. (life), Am. Assn. Psychiat. Services for Children (chmn. pub. edn. com. 1984), Internat. Assn. Trauma Counselors, Internat. Soc. Clin. Hypnosis, Am. Soc. Clin. Hypnosis (cert.), Am. Assn. Marriage and Family Therapists, Nat. Assn. Social Workers, Acad. Cert. Social Workers, Nat. Council Family Relations, Southeastern Council on Family Relations, Assn. Traumatic Stress Specialists, Internat. Critical Incident Stress Found., Am. Assn. Sex Therapists, Fla. Assn. Practicing Psychologists, Counselors and Therapists, Gulf Coast Assn. Marriage and Family Therapy, Alpha Kappa Delta. Contbr. articles to profl. jours. Office: 921 Honeysuckle Rd Dothan AL 36305-1934

KOGLER, DONNA MARIE, elementary school educator; b. Milw., Oct. 16, 1956; d. Donald and Violet Wisnefske; m. Paul Lee Kogler (div.); children: Jennifer, Abigail, Elizabeth. BS, U. Wis., Oshkosh, 1993; MEd, St. Scholastica, Duluth, Minn., 2000. Tchr. Green Tree Elem. Sch., West Bend, Wis., 1993—. Recipient Top Tchr. award, WBKV TV, West Bend, 1994. Mem.: Ozaukee Cty Hist. Soc. Office: Green Tree Elem Sch 1330 Green Tree Rd West Bend WI 53090

KOHAS, ARTEMIS DIANE, guidance counselor; b. Allentown, Pa., Mar. 30, 1975; d. Elli Kohas. BS in Psychology, Lafayette Coll., Easton, Pa., 1997; MA in Applied Psychology, NYU, N.Y.C., 2001. Cert. K-12 guidance counselor N.Y., 2000, N.Y.C. Elem. sch. guidance counselor NYC Dept. Edn., 2002—. Mem.: Sandplay Therapists Am., Am. Group Psychotherapy Assn. Avocations: travel, dance, music, spa experiences, yoga, pinochle.

KOH-BAKER, JOANN BEEN, music educator; b. Kelantan, Kelantan, Malaysia, Dec. 10, 1964; d. Leng Siang Koh and Pet Peng Eng; m. William Sidney Baker, June 4, 2000; children: Victoria S. Baker, Vincent J. Baker. BA, Nat. U. Singapore, 1986; MusM in Music Theory, Boston U., 1991, PhD in Musicology, 1998; MusM in Piano Performance, Ohio U., Athens, 1989. Performer's diploma, piano licentiate Trinity Coll. Music, London, 1983, ABRSM musicianship London Royal Schs. Music, 1986, ABRSM pianoforte duet London Royal Schs. Music, 1982, ABRSM theory music grade 8 London Royal Schs. Music, 1982, ABRSM pianoforte playing grade 8 London Royal Schs. Music, 1980, Japanese language proficiency level 4 Japan Found. and Assn. Internat. Edn., 1984. Assoc. prof. music Mt. Vernon Nazarene U., Ohio, 1999—. Pianist; concert program annotator; piano accompanist; lectr. in field; presenter in field; piano judge World Piano Pedagogy Conf., 2006; scholar, rschr. in field. Recitalist (piano recital) Piano Concerto in Sundays at Five Concerts; contbr. chapters to books. Bd. mem. Nat. Assn. for Asian Am. Profl., Boston, 1997, chair profl. devel. in the arts, 1998. Recipient award of Merit in Sports Club, Nat. U. Singapore, 1986; scholar, Boston U., 1992—98; Faculty Devel. Summer grantee, Mt. Vernon Nazarene U., 2004, 2005, 2006. Mem.: Music Tchrs. Nat. Assn., Soc. For Ethnomusicology, Soc. For Music Theory (officer com. on diversity 1999—2002), Coll. Music Soc. Office: Mount Vernon Nazarene University 800 Martinsburg Rd Mount Vernon OH 43050 Office Phone: 740-392-6862.

KOHEN, MARTHA, architecture educator; Grad., U. de la Republica, Montevideo, Uruguay; postgrad. diploma, Cambridge U., Eng. Arch., tchr., Paysandu, Uruguay, 1971—76; arch., cons. Matto Grosso, Brazil, 1976—84, Sao Paulo, Brazil, 1976—84; asst. prof. Sommer and Sprechmann Studio, Sch. Arch., 1985—94; assoc. prof. Otero Studio, Sch. Arch., Montevideo, 1994—98; dir. acad. cooperation unit faculty arch. Univ. de la Republica, Uruguay, 1998—2003; dir. and prof. Sch. Arch., Coll. Design, Constrn. and Planning U. Fla., 2003—; founding mem. Kohen-Otero Archtl. Studio, Montevideo, 1989—. Dep. bd. mem. Internat. Coun. Urban Planners, 1994, nat. mem., 1995—2000; vis. prof. Internat. Seminars Arch. e Citta U. degli Studi di Napoli Federico II, Italy, 1991—93; vis. lectr. Sch. Arch., Rosario, Argentina, 1992, Rosario, 1996—98, NYU Internat. Ctr. for Advanced Studies, 2000; mem. jury Fourth Internat. Seminary, Napoli, Italy, 1992; vis. prof. 7th Internat. Seminary, Napoli, Italy, 1998; vis. prof. dept. arch. U. Hong Kong, 2002. Recipient First prize, Barao de Rio Branco Square, Rio de Janeiro, 1995, Meml. of the Disappeared Detained Citizens, City of Montevideo, 1996, Hdqrs. of URAGUA, 2000, Spl. Mention, The Cerrillos Masterplan, Portal del Bicentenario, Santiago de Chile, 2001, First prize landscape arch., Quito Internat. Biennale, 2002, First prize, Sao Paulo Biennal of Arch., 2003. Mem.: Uruguayan Archtl. Assn. (mem. Coll. Cons., mem. Coll. Juries 1995—), Soc. for Internat. Devel. (Uruguayan chpt.). Office: Univ Fla Sch Arch PO Box 115702 Gainesville FL 32611-5702

KOHI, SUSAN, bilingual educator, translator; b. San Francisco, Nov. 28, 1948; d. Maurice Winkler Levinson and Fay Patricia (Lacey) Krier; m. Mahmoud Kohi, Mar. 24, 1973, (div. May 1993); children: Kamila, Samir, Kelly. BA, Holy Name Coll., 1970; MA, Middlebury Coll., 1973. Cert. French, Spanish, bilingual edn. tchr., Ariz. Tchr. fgn. lang. Marin Cath. H.S., Greenbrae, Calif., 1970-71; tchr. English Ecole Breguet, Paris, 1971-72; fgn. exch. teller Bank of Am., Paris, 1972-73; tchr. fgn. lang. Scottsdale C.C., Scottsdale, Ariz., 1974-75; translator Nat. Semiconductor Corp., Sidi-Bel-Abbes, Algeria, 1976-77; tchr., English Société Informatique, Aix-en-Provence, France, 1992; tchr. ESL Greenway Mid. Sch., Phoenix, 1994—98; ESL Spanish North Canyon HS, Phoenix, 1998, Horizon HS, 2003, Norh Canyon HS, 2005. Recipient scholarship, Pi Delta Phi. Mem. NEA, named to Who's Who Among America's Teachers; Nat. Assn. for Bilingual Edn., Ariz. Tchrs. of ESL. Avocations: tennis, swimming, gardening. Home: 4114 E Union Hills Dr Unit 1189 Phoenix AZ 85050-3327

KOHL, DOLORES, museum director, educator; b. Milw., July 27, 1933; d. Max and Mary (Hiken) K.; children: Stephen Solovy, Jonathan Solovy. BA cum laude, Brandeis U., 1955. Tchr. Oak Terrace Sch., Highwood, Ill., 1969-74; pres. Dolores Kohl Edn. Found., Wilmette, Ill., 1972—, Kohl Children's Mus., Wilmette, 1985—. Lectr. in field; commr. White House Commn. on Presdl. Scholars. Editor, pub.: Bright Ideas in Language Arts, 1978, Teacher Centering, 1978, The Teacher Center in a Tube, Vols. I-III, 1978-80, Math Ideas, 1979, Social Studies, 1980, Teaching Shabbat and Holidays, 1980, Teachers in the 80's, 1980, Tapestry, 1982, Worthy of the Name, 1986, And Gladly Teach, 1989; producer: (films) Song of Radauti, Merry Widow, Billy Sunday, Die Fledermaus, Animation Pie. Trustee Ravinia Festival Assn.; mem. Ravinia Women's Bd., Women's Issues Network, Inst. for Ednl. Rsch.; bd. mem. Jewish Found. of Christian Rescuers, Amti-Defamation League, East Village Youth Program; mem. adv. bd. Family Network; governing mem. Chgo. Symphony Orch. Named Outstanding Tchr. of Yr. State of Ill., Outstanding Educator of Yr., Nat. Louis U.; recipient Deborah award Am. Jewish Congress, Lifetime Achievement award Midwest Women's Ctr.; named to North Shore Walk of Fame. Mem. Assn. Youth Mus., Am. Assn. Mus., Donors Forum Chgo., Brandeis U. Alumni Assn., Art Inst. Chgo., Phi Delta Kappa. Office: Kohl Childrens Museum 2100 Patriot Blvd Glenview IL 60026-8018

KOHL, JOAN, not-for-profit developer, social worker; b. N.Y.C., Mar. 28, 1952; d. Michael and Victoria Lucas; m. Donald Kohl, Aug. 12, 1978. BA, CUNY, 1974, MSW, 1978. Cert. social worker, N.Y.; cert. wildlife rehabilitator. Recreation specialist Lt. Joseph P. Kennedy Jr. Home, Bronx, N.Y., 1975-78; social worker Rofay Nursing Home, Bronx, 1978-81; dir. social svc. New Rochelle (N.Y.) Hosp. Med. Ctr., 1981-84; pres., founder Coral Springs (Fla.) Nature Ctr. and Wildlife Hosp., 1992—. Adv. bd. mem. Coral Springs Growth Mgmt. and Environ. Protection Commn., 1991—, Fla. Wildlife Rehab. Assn., Miami, 1996—, Sawgrass Springs Middle Sch., Coral Springs, 1996—; pres. bd. dirs. Wildlife Care Ctr., Inc., 1985-95. Recipient Outstanding Personal Contbn. awad Keep Fla. Beautiful, 1998, 1st Annual Legacy award Nature Conservancy, Fla., 1999; Forestry grantee Fla. Dept. Agr., 1998. Mem. Leadership Broward Found., Leadership North Broward (alumni, environ. chair 1993-94), Coral Springs C. of C. (founder 1995, Rookie of the Yr. 1997). Avocations: wildlife preservation, birding, photography, gardening, aviculturist. Office: Coral Springs Nature Ctr 3916 NW 73rd Ave Coral Springs FL 33065-2140

KOHLER, DEBORAH DIAMOND, dietitian, food service executive; b. Queens, N.Y., Nov. 5, 1960; d. Morris and Susan Erika (Pottasch) Diamond; m. Michael Henry Kohler, July 31, 1988; children: Joshua, Jacob, Abigail. BS, Mich. State U., 1982. Registered dietitian. Res. clin. dietitian South Nassau Cmty. Hosp., Oceanside, N.Y., 1982; clin. dietitian Southampton (N.Y.) Hosp., 1982-84; chief dietitian St. Luke's Hosp., Allentown Campus, 1984-86, food svc. dir., 1986—2001, St. Luke's Quakertown (Pa.) Hosp., 1996—2000, Mack Trucks World Hdqrs., 2002—. Computer cons. dist. area Sodexho, Allentown, 1991-2001. Mem. Am. Dietetic Assn., Lehigh Valley Dietetic Assn. Jewish. Avocations: volleyball, bowling, raising children, baseball fan, pinochle. Home: 5750 Woodcrest Dr Coopersburg PA 18036-2312

KOHLER, JANET SUE, artist; d. Willard Charles and Lois Grace Kohler; m. Timothy Moore Jarratt, Jan. 2, 1993; m. Peter Warren Halsey, June 24, 1984 (dec. Sept. 20, 1984); 1 child, Daniel Matthew Jarratt. Assoc., Washtenaw C.C., 1968—71; BFA, Coll. for Creative Studies, 1976—79; MFA, Ea. Mich. U., 1989—92. Treas. Detoit Focus Gallery, 1980—84; graphic designer Chrysler Corp., Detroit, 1983—98; tchr. Ann Arbor Art Ctr., 1990—, U. of Mich., 2002—. Chairperson Ann Arbor Area Pastel Group, Mich., 2003—06. Exhibitions include Lawrence St. Gallery, Ferndale, Mich., Riverside Gallery, Ypsilanti, Mich., Great Lakes Pastel Soc. Nat. Juried Pastel Competition, Midland Ctr. for the Arts, 2006. Recipient Exceptional Merit award, Ella Sharp Mus., Jackson Mich., 1993, EMU Drawing award, Ea. Mich. U., 1991, Purchase award, Krasl Art Ctr., 1993, Jurors Choice award, Ann Arbor Art Assn. Ann. Exhbn., 1982, Hon. Mention, U of M Gifts of Art/Ann Arbor Women's Artists, 2002, 1st place Pastels, Best of Mich. Artists and Artisans, 2005; Grad. Fellowship award, Ea. Mich. U., 1990, Hon. Scholarship, Ctr. for Creative Studies, 1978, Painting scholarship, Detroit Soc. of Women Painters & Sculptors, 1978. Mem.: Ann Arbor Women Artists, Gt. Lakes Pastel Soc. (hon.), Detoit Inst. of Arts (assoc.), Ann Arbor Area Pastelists (assoc.; chmn. 2003—06). Home: 797 Madouse Ct Whitmore Lake MI 48189 Home Fax: 734-449-5112. Personal E-mail: jskohler@sbcglobal.net.

KOHLER, LAURA E., human resources executive; married; 3 children. Grad., Duke U., 1984; MFA, Cath. U., 1987. Past tchr. Chgo. Pub. Schs.; past corp. team facilitator; past mgr. Nat. Players, Washington; past residence mgr. Olney (Md.) Theatre; founder Chgo.; past exec. dir. Kohler Found., Inc.; v.p. human resources Kohler Co., 1990—, past v.p. comm., 1994—99, sr. v.p. human resources, also bd. dirs. Office: Kohler Co 444 Highland Dr Kohler WI 53044-1500

KOHLER, NORA HELEN, music educator; b. Missoula, Mont., Sept. 17, 1950; d. Edwin Gibbs and Helen (Oktabec) Linderman; m. Allen L. Kohler, Jr., Aug. 23, 1969; children: Oralee, Jennifer, Benjamin, Keri, Robert. BS cum laude in Elem. Edn., We. Mont. Coll., 2001. Music aid Ramsay (Mont.) Sch. Dist., 1996—98; tchr. Powell County HS, Deer Lodge, Mont., 2001—02, coach pep band, 2001—02; tchr. music Sch. Dist. 1, Butte, Mont., 2002—. Bd. dirs. Young Musicians Club, Butte, tchr., 1989—. Co-dir. City YMCA Benefit Concert, Butte, 1996—98; co-leader Brownie Girl Scouts, 1980—81, leader, 1985—88, Dist. Boy Scouts, 1976—78; active various positions Cub Scouts, 1983—91; active LDS Ch., 1969—. Named Den Leader of Yr., Viligante Coun. Boy Scouts Am., 1985. Mem.: Treasure State Orff, Mont. Fedn. Tchrs., Mont. Edn. Assn., Mont. Gen. Music Tchrs. Assn., Music Educators Nat. Conf. Mem. Lds Ch. Avocations: fishing, hunting, sewing. Office: School Dist 1 West Elem 800 South Emmett Butte MT 59701

KOHLER, SHEILA M., humanities educator, writer; b. Johannesburg, Nov. 13, 1941; arrived in U.S., 1981; d. Max Kohler and Sheila M. Bodley; m. William M. Tucker; children: Sasha T., Cybele, Brett. BA, Sorbonne, Paris; MA, Inst. Catholique, Paris; MFA, Columbia U., 1983. Prof. New Sch., N.Y.C., 1996—99, CCNY, 2001, Bennington Coll., 2001—03, Columbia U., 2006—. Author: The Perfect Place, 1987, Miracles in America, 1990, The House on R Street, 1994, Cracks, 1999, One Girl, 1999, The Children of Pithiviers, 2001, Stories From Another World, 2002, Crossways, 2004 (Best Am. award Houghton Mifflin, 1999), Bluebird, 2004 (Antioch Review award, 2004). Recipient O'Henry Prize, 1989; Lewis B. Cullman Libr. Fellowship, N.Y. Pub. Libr. Ctr. for Scholars and Writers, 2003—. Personal E-mail: sheilakohler@hotmail.com.

KOHLHORST, GAIL LEWIS, librarian; b. Phila., Dec. 5, 1946; d. Richard Elliott and Lucille (Lampkin) Lewis; m. Allyn Leon Kohlhorst, Feb. 14, 1974; 1 child, Jennifer Marion. BA in Govt, Otterbein Coll., Westerville, Ohio, 1969; MS in L.S, Cath. U. Am., 1977. Info. classifier U.S. Ho. of Reps. Commn. on Internal Security, Washington, 1969-70; adminstrv. asst. Office of Gen. Counsel, GSA, Washington, 1971-76; chief tech. services sect. GSA Libr., Washington, 1976-79; chief GSA libr., 1979-88; acting chief, div. info. and libr. svcs. U.S. Dept. Interior, Washington, 1988-89; chief libr. svcs. br. GSA, Washington, 1989-96; chief mgmt. analysis FDA, Rockville, Md., 1996, dir. mgmt. sys. and policy, 1996-99, dir. divsn. mgmt. programs, 1999—. Author: Art and Architecture: An Annotated Bibliography, 1986, Total Quality Management: An Annotated Bibliography, 1990, 91, 93, Federal Librarians Round Table, ALA, Yearbook, 1989, Federal Librarian, 1991-94; contbr. Calendar Commn. on the Bicentennial for the U.S. Constn. Chair Trinity Evangelism Com., 2001—. Recipient Outstanding Performance awards, 1973, 75, 76, 79, 81-86, 88-89, 91-96, Spl. Achievement awards, 1982-84, Commendable Svc. award, 1984, Nat. Capital Performance award, 1985, Meritorious Svc. award, 1992, Disting. Svc. award, 1995, Dep. Commr.'s Spl. Achievement award, 1999, award of Merit, 2001. Mem. ALA (Fed. Libr.'s Achievement award 1995), Fed. Librs. Round Table (pres. 1990-91, membership chair 1994-96), Fed. Libr. and Info. Ctr. (observer 1984-96, exec. bd. 1992-94, chair 1994, membership and governance com.), Fed. Pre-Conf. on the White House Conf. on Librs. and Scis. (del. 1990), Fedlink Adv. Coun. (chair exec. adv. coun. 1988-90), Pub. Employees Roundtable (bd. dirs. 1994-96), D.C. Libr. Assn., United Meth. Women (mem. Dulin outreach com. 1994-96, pres. Joshua's Way 1995-96, mem. Naomi Circle Trinity 2001—, chair Trinity Evangelism 2001—), Beta Phi Mu. Methodist. Office: FDA 5600 Fishers Ln HFA 300 Rm 4B-03 Parklawn Bldg Rockville MD 20852-5600 Home: RR 3 Box 654 Harpers Ferry WV 25425-9307

KOHLMANN, SUSAN J., lawyer; b. Jan. 15, 1958; BA, Yale Univ., 1979; JD, Columbia Univ., 1982. Bar: NY 1983. Ptnr., chmn. Intellectual Property dept., office mng. ptnr. Pillsbury Winthrop Shaw Pittman, NYC. Editor (Casenote & Comment): Columbia Jour. Transnational Law. Mem. bd. legal adv. NOW Legal Def. & Edn. Fund. Mem.: Internat. Trademark Assn., Assn. Bar City of NY (co-chmn. Com. on Women & the Law 1999—2001, mem. exec. com.). Office: Pillsbury Winthrop Shaw Pittman 1540 Broadway New York NY 10036 Office Phone: 212-858-1707. Office Fax: 212-858-1500. Business E-Mail: susan.kohlmann@pillsburylaw.com.

KOHLSTEDT, SALLY GREGORY, historian, educator; b. Ypsilanti, Mich., Jan. 30, 1943; BA, Valparaiso U., 1965; MA, Mich. State U., 1966; PhD, U. Ill., 1972. Asst. prof. Simmons Coll., Boston, 1971-75; assoc. prof. to prof. Syracuse (N.Y.) U., 1975-89; prof. history of sci. U. Minn., Mpls., 1989—; dir. Ctr. for Advanced Feminist Studies, 1997-98. Vis. prof. history of sci. Cornell U., 1989, Amerika Inst. U. Munich, 1997; vis. assoc. Calif. Inst. Tech., 2004, lectr. in field Author: The Formation American Scientific Community: AAAS, 1848-1860, 1976; editor: (with Margaret Rossiter) Historical Writing on American Science, Osiris, 2d Series, 1, 1985, (with R.W. Home) International Science and National Scientific Identity: Australia between Britain and America, 1991, The Origins of Natural Science in the United States: The Essays of George Brown Goode, 1991, (with Barbara Haslett et al.) Gender and Scientific Authority, 1996, (with Helen Lonino) The Women, Gender, and Science Question, 1997, The History of Women in Science: An Isis Reader, 1999, (with Bruce Leavenstein and Michael Sokal) The Establishment of Science in America: The American Association for the Advancement of Science, 1999; contbr. articles to profl. jours.; mem. editl. bd. Signs, 1980-88, 90-93, Sci., 1980-81, News and Views: History of Am. Sci. Newsletter, 1980-86, Sci., Tech. and Human Values, 1983-90, Syracuse Scholar, 1985-88, chair, 1988, Minerva, 2000—, Isis, 2002-; assoc. editor Am. Nat. Biography, 2d edit., 1988-98, consulting edit., 1993-99; Gruphon Press Reprints in the History of Science, 1993-98; reviewer books, articles, proposals for NSDF, NEH, U. Chgo. Press, others; editor sci. biography series Cambridge U., 1997-2003. Grantee NSF, 1969, 78-79, 84, 93-95, 2002, 06, Smithsonian Instn. predoctoral fellow, 1970-71, Danforth Assoc., 1975-82, Syracuse U. grantee, 1976, 82, Am. Philos. Soc. rsch. grantee, 1977, Haven fellow Am. Antiquarian Soc., 1982, Fulbright Sr. fellow U. Melbourne, Australia, 1983, Woodrow Wilson Ctr. fellow, 1986, Smithsonian Instn. Sr. fellow, 1987. Fellow AAAS (nominating com. 1980-83, 96-98, sect. chair 1986, bd. dirs. 1998-2002, chair divsn. on sci., ethics and religion 2003—, coun. 2004—), Am. Hist. Assn. (profl. com. 1974-76, rep. U.S. Nat. Archives Adv. Coun. 1974-76), Berkshire Conf. Women Historians (program com. 1974), Forum on the History Sci. in Am. (coord. com. 1980-86, chair 1985, 86), History of Sci. Soc. (sec. 1978-81, coun. 1982-84, 89-91, 94-96, com. on publs. 1982-87, chair nominating com. 1985, 99, women's com. 1972-74, vis. lectr. 1988-89, chair edn. com. 1989, pres. 1992, 93, Pfizer prize com. 2006—), Internat. Congress for History of Sci. (U.S. del. 1977, 81, vice chair 1985) Orgn. Am. Historians (chair com. on status of women 1983-85, endowment fund drive, auction subcom. 1990-91). Lutheran. Home: 4140 Edmund Blvd Minneapolis MN 55406-3646 Business E-Mail: sgk@umn.edu.

KOHN, JEAN GATEWOOD, retired health facility administrator, pediatrician; b. Chgo., July 8, 1926; d. Gatewood and Esther Lydia (Harper) Gatewood; m. Martin M. Kohn, Feb. 10, 1951; children: Helen, Joel, Michael, David. BS, U. Chgo., 1948, MD, 1950; MPH, U. Calif., Berkeley, 1973. Diplomate Am. Bd. Pediatrics. Physician Permanente Med. Group, San Leandro, Calif., 1953-60; pediatric cons. Calif. Children Svcs., 1961-72; lectr. maternal and child health U. Calif., 1973-91; med. advisor rehab. engrng. ctr. Packard Children's Hosp. at Stanford, Calif., 1976-97, med. dir. child prosthetic clinic Calif., 1977-97, ret. Calif., 1997, pediatrician Mary L. Johnson Infant Devel. Unit, 2000—. Asst. neurologic diagnostic ctr. U. Calif., San Francisco, 1960-72; pediatric cons. Project HOPE, Nicaragua, 1966, Peru, 1962; pediatric cons. sch. pub. health U. Hawaii, Okinawa, 1975. Contbr. chpts. to books and articles to profl. jours. Mem. adv. panel State of Calif. Dept. Spl. Edn., Calif. Children Svcs.; bd. dirs. Mental Health Assn., United Cerebral Palsy Assn., Head Start, San Mateo County, 1993—. Recipient Lyda M. Smiley award Calif. Sch. Nurses Orgn., 1987. Fellow Am. Acad. Pediats., Am. Acad. Cerebral Palsy and Devel. Medicine; mem. Project HOPE Alumni Assn. (pres. 1988-92). Office Phone: 650-725-8995.

KOHN, MARGARET SHERMAN, music educator, pianist; b. Boston, May 4, 1928; d. Albert Case Sherman and Elizabeth Antoinette Judkins; m. Karl George Kohn, June 23, 1950; children: Susanna Margaret, Emily Elizabeth Kohn Berthel. BA, Radcliffe Coll., 1950. Instr. music Pomona Coll., Claremont, Calif., 1970; concert pianist, 1950—.

KOHN, MARY LOUISE BEATRICE, nurse; b. Yellow Springs, Ohio, Jan. 13, 1920; d. Theophilus John and Mary Katherine (Schmitkons) Gaehr; m. Howard D. Kohn, 1944; children: Marcia R., Marcia K. Epstein. AB, Coll. Wooster, 1940; M in Nursing, Case Western Res. U., 1943. Nurse, 1943-44, Atlantic City Hosp., 1944, Thomas M. England Gen. Hosp., U.S. Army, Atlantic City, 1945-46, Peter Bent Brigham Hosp., Boston, 1947, Univ. Hosps., Cleve., 1946-48; mem. faculty Frances Payne Bolton Sch. Nursing Case Western Res. U., Cleve., 1948-52; vol. nurse Blood Svc. ARC, 1952-55; office nurse Cleve., 1955-94; freelance writer. Author: Berry and Kohn's Operating Room Technique, 10th edit., 2003; asst. editor: Cleve. Physician Acad. Medicine, 1966-71. Bd. dirs. Aux. Acad. Medicine Cleve., 1970-72, officer, 1976; active Cleve. Health Mus. Aux., Am. Cancer Soc. vol.; women's com. Cleve. Orch., 1970, Sta. WVIZ-TV. Mem.: ANA, Soc. Prevention of Cruelty to Animals, Assn. Oper. Rm. Nurses, Assn. Oper. Rm. Nurses of Greater Cleve. (charter, plaque 2004), Greater Cleve. Nurses Assn., Nat. Wildlife Fedn., Cleve. Zool. Soc., Coun. World Affairs, Friends of Cleve. Ballet, Alumni Assn. Wooster Coll., Frances P. Bolton Sch. Nursing Alumni Assn. (pres. 1974—75, bd. dirs. 1997—2000), Western Res. Hist. Soc., Am. Heart Assn., Cleve. Playhouse, Internat. Fund for Animal Welfare, Cleve. Animal Protective League, U.S. Humane Soc., Smithsonian Instn., Cleve. Children's Mus., Alzheimer's Assn., Sierra Club, Antique Automobile Assn. Am., Women's City Club (Jewel award 1992), Cleve. Racquet Club (social com. 1999—2000), Sigma Theta Tau Internat. Home: 28099 Belcourt Rd Cleveland OH 44124-5615

KOHNE, HEIDI ANN, church musician; b. Salem, Oreg., Sept. 15, 1974; d. Wilmar Allison and Karen Lee Kohne. MusB in organ performance, DePauw U., 1997; MusM in organ and ch. music, Ind. U., 1999. Organist St. Paul's Cath. Ch., Greencastle, Ind., 1994—97; concert office employee Interlochen Ctr. for the Arts, Interlochen, Mich., 1996—97, stage crew employee, 1998; organist Covenant Presbyn. Ch., Gresham, Oreg., 1999—2001; Kresge auditorium stage mgr. Interlochen Ctr. for the Arts, 1999—2003; organist Mt. Tabor Presbyn. Ch., Portland, Oreg., 2001—02, dir. music ministries, organist, 2003—. Program com. mem. Am. Guild of Organists, Portland, Oreg., 2001—02, sub dean, 2002—04, dean, 2004—. Computer graphics: Interlochen Stage Charts, 2003. Stage hand Portland Baroque Orch., Portland, Oreg., 2003—; accompanist Mt. Tabor Mid. Sch. Choir, Portland, Oreg., 2003—06. Mem.: PEO, Presbyn. Assn. Musicians, Am. Guild Organists (cert. svc. playing). Presbyterian. Home: 1917 NE 77th Ave Portland OR 97213 Office: Mt Tabor Presbyn Ch 5441 SE Belmont Portland OR 97215 Office Phone: 503-234-6493. E-mail: hkohne@theinter.com.

KOHNEN, CAROL ANN, librarian; b. St. Louis, Apr. 8, 1948; d. Joseph William and Josephine (Strenfel) Licavoli; m. Richard Joseph Kohnen, May 9, 1970; children: Jill Patricia, Douglas Richard. BA, St. Louis U., 1970; MA in Libr. Sci., U. Mo., 1994. Cert. tchr., secondary English Mo., libr. K-12 Mo. Programmer, cons., Creve Coeur, Mo., 1981-90; audio-visual technician Parkway Schs., Chesterfield, 1989-92; libr. St. Joseph's Acad., Frontenac, 1992-98, Parkway No. HS, 1998—2004; coord. libr., media svc. Parkway Sch. Dist., 2004—. Co-chair telecomms, users group Coop. Sch. Dists., St. Louis County, 1995—99; dept. leader Parkway No. HS, 1999—2004; mem. tech. coun. Parkway Sch. Dist., 2002—, chmn. tech. integration and facilitation com., 2004—05. Am. memory fellow, Libr. Congress, 1998—99. Mem.: Mo. Assn. Sch. Librs., St. Louis Suburban Sch. Librs. Assn. (sec. 1993—95, membership chmn. 2001—03), Mo. Assn. Sch. Librs. (Webmaster, bd. dirs. 2003—), Am. Assn. Sch. Librs., ASCD, ALA, Beta Phi Mu, Phi Beta Kappa. Avocations: reading, genealogy, web browsing. Office: Parkway School Dist Libr Media Svcs 455 North Woods Mill Rd Chesterfield MO 63017 Business E-Mail: ckohnen@pkwy.k12.mo.us.

KOHNSTAMM, ABBY E., marketing executive; b. LA; married; 2 children. BA, Tufts U.; MA in Edn., NYU, MBA. Various mktg. positions including sr. v.p. cardmember mktg. Am. Express, 1979—93; v.p. corp. mktg. IBM, Armonk, NY, 1993—98, sr. v.p. corp. mktg., 1998—2006, cons., 2006—. Bd. of overseers Arts & Sci. Tufts U., NYU Stern Sch. of Bus.; bd. dirs. IBM Credit Corp., Tiffany & Co. Mem. Assn. Nat. Advertisers. Avocations: music, theater. Office: IBM Corp New Orchard Rd Armonk NY 10504-1722 Office Phone: 914-765-1900. E-mail: abby@us.ibm.com.*

KOHWI-SHIGEMATSU, TERUMI, research scientist; b. Tokyo, Aug. 30, 1949; d. Teruhiko and Futaba (Takamatsu) Shigematsu; m. Yoshinori Kohwi; 1 child, Minoree. BS magna cum laude, Washington Coll., 1971; MA, John Hopkins U., 1973; PhD, U. Tokyo, 1978. Sci. fellow Japan Soc. for Promotion, Tokyo, 1978-79; rsch. scientist Inst. Tuberculosis and Cancer, Sendai, Miyaginken, Japan, 1979-81; postdoctoral fellow Fred Hutchinson Cancer Rsch. Ctr., Seattle, Wash., 1981-84; asst. staff scientist La Jolla (Calif.) Cancer Rsch. Found., 1984-88, staff scientist La Jolla, 1988-94, sr. staff scientist, 1994-96; sr. staff scientist life scis. divsn. Lawrence Berkeley Lab.-U. Calif., Berkeley, 1996—. NIH Fogarty Internat. fellow, 1981-82, Leukemia Soc. Am. spl. fellow, 1983-85. Mem. NIH (chem. pathology study sect. 1992-96), Am. Cancer Soc. (Faculty award 1988-93). Office: Lawrence Berkeley Lab Univ Calif Berkeley CA 94720-0001 Home: 2620 Arlington Blvd El Cerrito CA 94530-1506

KOITA, SAIDA YAHYA, psychoanalyst, educator; b. Bombay, Jan. 5, 1945; d. A. and M. Kalvert; m. Yahya Koita; children: Zain, Selma. Student, Sophia Coll., Bombay; MD, Grant Med. Coll., Bombay, 1969; postgrad., Inst. Psychoanalysis, 1977-85. Diplomate Am. Bd. Psychiatry and Neurology, lic. psychoanalyst Fla., cert. psychoanalysis 2004, tng. and supervising analyst 2005. Resident in ob-gyn. Grant Med. Coll., Bombay, 1969-71; intern in pediats. Jackson Meml. Hosp., Miami, Fla., 1974, resident in psychiatry, 1974-77, chief resident in psychiatry, 1976-77; clin. instr. psychiatry U. Miami Sch. Medicine, 1977-79, asst. prof. psychiatry, 1979-88, assoc. prof. psychiatry, 1988—; pvt. practice, 1977—; assoc. teaching analyst Balt. Inst. Psychoanalysis, 1988—; teaching analyst Fla. Psychoanalytic Inst. Treas. Fla. Psycholoanalyst Instn., 2005—, bd. dirs., 2005—. Mem. Am. Psychoanalytic Assn., Am. Psychiat. Assn., So. Med. Assn., Fla. Psychoanalytic Soc. (chair program comm. 2000-04, chair continuing edn. 2000, pres. elect), South Fla. Psychiat. Soc. (patient rep. ethics com. 1987—, liaison to residents in psychiatry 1978-82, v.p. 1988-89, treas., panelist, moderator local symposiums). Office: 420 S Dixie Hwy Ste 4H Coral Gables FL 33146-2228

KOKES, KATHLEEN A., music educator, voice educator; d. H. Peter and Karen A. Donnelly; m. David P. Kokes, July 1, 1989; 1 child, Christopher R. BS in Music Edn., Skidmore Coll., 1988, BS in Psychology, 1988; MS in Edn., Plattsburgh State U., 1992. Cert. tchr. NY. Music educator North Colonie Schs., Latham, NY, 1988—89, Northeastern Clinton Ctrl. Schs., Champlain, NY, 1989—. Policy bd. chair North Country Tchr. Resource Ctr., 2002—04. Lobbying rep. for com. of 100 NY State United Tchrs., Albany, 2001—04, task force, 2002—04. Mem.: Clinton County Music Educators Assn. (choral chair 2005—), Music Educators Nat. Conf. (pres. coll. chpt. 1985—), Am. Choral Dirs., N.Y. State Sch. Music Assn. (mixed chorus chair zone 9 2005, choral chair zone 6 2005—06, diversity com. 2005—). Home: 431 Gilbert Rd Mooers NY 12958 Office Phone: 518-298-8638. Business E-Mail: kkokes@nccscougar.org.

KOKX, SARAH LYNN, elementary school educator; b. Muskegon, Mich., May 30, 1981; d. Linda Lou Gust and Wayne Allen Schindlbeck; m. Theodore Andrew Kokx, July 16, 2005; 1 child, Jessica Ann. BS in Edn., Ctrl. Mich. U., 2004. Cert. Provisional Tchr. Mich., 2004. Substitute tchr. Shepherd Pub. Schs., Mich., 2002—03, Mt. Pleasant Pub. Schs., Mich., 2002—03; student tchr. El Colegio Dominico Americano, Santo Domingo, Dominican Republic, 2004, Reeths-Puffer Intermediate, North Muskegon, Mich., 2004; tchr. Cantrick Mid. Sch., Monroe, 2004—. Avocations: travel, quilting, reading, scrapbooks, flute. Personal E-mail: schindls@yahoo.com.

KOLAKOSKI, DAWN LAYMOND, education educator, consultant, music educator; d. Robert F. and Marjory M. Laymond; children: Kathryn Turana, Rebecca Ashley. BS, Coll. of St. Rose, Albany, NY, 1981, MS. in Edn, 1984, MS in Early Childhood Edn., 1993; EdD, Nova Southeastern U., Ft. Lauderdale, FL, 2001. Cert. tchr. music K-12 N.Y., 1981. Music tchr. Bethlehem Ctrl. Sch. Dist., Delmar, NY, 1980—83; owner/dir. The Magic of Music, Delmar, NY, 1982—97; adj. prof. Maria Coll., Albany, 1989—97; assoc. prof. Hudson Valley C.C., Troy, 1991—; mem. nat. faculty Lesley U., Boston, 2003—. Owner and cons. Resources for Ednl. Tng., Delmar, NY, 1993—. Author: (textbook) Write It Down: A Guided Jour. of Ideas, Strategies, and Reflection for Beginning Tchrs., 2004. Mem.: N.Y. State Am. Assoc. Degree Early Childhood Educators (pres. 1999—).

KOLAKOWSKI, DIANA JEAN, county commissioner; b. Detroit, Aug. 28, 1943; d. Leo and Genevieve (Bosh) Zyskowski; m. William Francis Kolakowski, Jr., Oct. 22, 1966; children: Wiliam Francis III, John. BS, U. Detroit, Mich., 1965. Lab. asst. chemistry dept. U. Detroit, 1961-65; rsch. chemist Detroit Inst. Cancer Rsch., Mich. Cancer Found., 1965-70; substitute tchr. Warren (Mich.) Consol. Schs., 1979-81; mem. Macomb County Bd. Commrs., Mt. Clemens, Mich., 1983—2006, vice chmn., 1993-95, chmn., 1995-97; econ. devel. dir. City of Warren, 2006—. Dir. S.E. Mich. Transp. Authority, Detroit, 1983—85; trustee Macomb County Ret. System, Mt. Clemens, 1988—91, 1992—95, 2003—06; del. S.E. Mich. Coun. Govts., Detroit, 1987—2006, vice chmn., 1995—99, chmn., 1999—2000, Regional Transit Coord. Coun., 1995—97; bd. dirs. Creating a Healthier Macomb, 1996—2001, Macomb Bar Found., 1996—2006. Contbr. articles to sci. jours. Trustee Myasthenia Gravis Found., Southfield, Mich., 1964-71; dir. Otsikita coun. Girl Scouts Am., 1995-96; mem., sec. Sterling Heights (Mich.) Bd. Zoning Appeals, 1978-83; mem. Macomb County Dem. Exec. Com., Mt. Clemens, 1982—, 10th and 12th Dem. Congl. Dist. Exec. Com., Warren, 1982—, del. 1996 Dem. Nat. Conv.; mem. behavioral medicine adv. coun. St. Joseph Hosp., Warren Cmty. Chorus Named Woman of Distinction, Macomb County Girl Scouts U.S.A., 1996, Woman of Yr., Am. Fedn. State, County and Mcpl. Employees 411, 2004; recipient Leadership award, Cath. Social Svcs. Macomb, 1997, Polish Pride award, Polish Am. Citizens for Equity, 1997, Excellence in County Govt. award, 1997, Regional Ambassador award, S.E. Mich. Coun. Govt., 2005; GM scholar, U. Detroit, 1961—65. Mem.: Warren Hist. Soc., Polish Am. Congress, Alpha Sigma Nu. Roman Catholic. Avocations: singing, piano, crossword and jigsaw puzzles. Home: 33488 Breckenridge Dr Sterling Heights MI 48310-6082 Office: Mayor's Office City of Warren 29500 Van Dyke Warren MI 48093 Office Phone: 586-574-4519.

KOLAR, JANET BROSTRON, physician assistant, medical technologist; b. St. Louis, Jan. 8, 1937; d. William Olaf and Susan Ann (Dzurovcin) B.; m Robert Joseph Kolar, Sept. 21, 1957 (div. June 1976); children: John Alexander, Elizabeth Susan Hinn, Paul Daniel, Peter Nicholas. Diploma in med. tech., Century Coll. Med. Tech., 1955; diploma in physicians asst. program, St. Louis U., 1976. Bd. cert. physician asst. Biochem. rsch. technologist Argonne Cancer Rsch. Hosp., Chgo., 1955-60; cyto technician, biochem. rsch. technologist dept. medicine U. Chgo. Hosp., 1960-62, supr. surg. biochem. lab., rsch. asst. dept. surgery, 1962-65; med. technologist Overland (Mo.) Med. Ctr., 1967-89; medication counselor, physicians asst. Lipid Rsch. Ctr., Wash. U. Sch. of Medicine, St. Louis, 1976-83; physician asst., coord. cardiovascular risk reduction ctr. St. Louis U. Med. Ctr., 1983-85; physician asst. VA Med. Ctr., St. Louis, 1985-90; physician asst. in gen. surgery Barnes-Jewish-Christian Health System, St. Louis, 1990—. Mem. adv. subcom. to intervention com. NIH-Coronary Primary Prevention Trial, 1981-83. Contbr. articles to profl. jours. Co-chairwoman childhood edn. Women's Internat. League Peace and Freedom, St. Louis, 1970-73; vol. enrichment program children's folk music Flynn Park Sch., University City, Mo., 1972-73; vol. children's folk music Countryside Montessori Sch., Creve Coeur, Mo., 1968-71. Mem. Mo. Acad. Physician Assts. VA Physicians Asst., Epsilon Omicron Mu. Avocations: folk guitar, dance, drag racing, cooking, needlecrafts. Office: Barnes Jewish Christian Health System 216 S Kingshighway Blvd Saint Louis MO 63110-1026

KOLAR, MARY JANE, trade and professional association executive; b. Benton, Ill., Aug. 9, 1941; d. Thomas Haskell and Mary Jane (Sanders) Burnett; m. Otto Michael Kolar, Aug. 13, 1966; children: Robin Lynn, Deon Michael. BA with high honors, So. Ill. U., 1963, MA with highest honors, 1964. Tchr. pub. schs., Benton and Zeigler, Ill., 1960-63; grad. asst. and grad. fellow So. Ill. U., Carbondale, 1963-64; instr. Ridgewood High Sch., Norridge, Ill., 1964-67, Maine Twp. High Sch., Des Plaines, Ill., 1967-70; freelance writer plumbing, heating & cooling industry couns. Chgo., 1970-71; ednl. coord. Am. Dietetic Assn., Chgo., 1971-72; dir. profl. devel. Am. Dental Hygienists Assn., Chgo., 1972-78; dir. Learning Ctr. div. Am. Coll. Cardiology, Bethesda, Md., 1978-80; dir. edn. Nat. Moving and Storage Assn., Alexandria, Va., 1980-82; exec. dir. Women in Communications, Inc., Austin, Tex., 1982-84, Altrusa Internat., Chgo., 1984-87, Assn. Govt. Accts., Alexandria, Va., 1987-90, Bus./Profl. Advt. Assn., Alexandria, 1991-92, Am. Assn. Family and Consumer Scis., Alexandria, 1992-96, dir. Project Taking Charge Adolescent Pregnancy Prevention Program, 1993-95; pres., CEO The Alexandria Group, Inc. (charter accredited co., Am. Soc. Assn. Execs.), 1996—. Mem., chair Accreditation Commn. for Assn. Mgmt. Cos., 2005—06; cons. spkr. various profl., philanthropic and trade assns., ednl. instns. and fed agys. Contbr. articles to profl. jours. and assn. mags., chapters to books. Mem. adv. council Accrediting Commn., Assn. of Ind. Colls. and Schs., 1980-88; treas. Pub. Employees Roundtable, 1988-90, Hollin Hills Civic Assn., 1989-90. Fellow Am. Soc. Allied Health Professions (dir. 1978-79), Am. Soc. Assn. Execs. (charter accredited; cert. commr. accreditation commn. for assn. mgmt. cos. 2002—, Key Profl. Assn. coun. 1994-96, peer rev. com., 1997-2000, rsch. com. 1996-2000, strategic leadership forum com. 1996-97, awards com. 1992-93, univ. affairs commn. 1986-92, chair 1990-91, found. bd. 1987-91, chmn. edn. sect. 1982-83, bd. dirs. 1983-86, chair higher edn. task force 1990-91, chair fellows 1987, Educator of Yr. award 1978, Key award 1990); mem. Greater Washington Soc. Assn. Execs. (edn. com. 1979-82, CEO com. 1990-92, 94-96, vice chair 1995-96, strategic planning com. 1994-95, exec. search com. 1994-96), Future Home Makers Am. (bd. dirs. 1992-96), Alexandria C. of C. (assn. coun. 1990-96, steering com. 1993-96), Women in Comm. (newsletter editor, legis. and career re-entry chair, chair ERA task force, dir. Washington profl. chpt. 1981-83, program com. Chgo. chpt. 1984-86), So. Ill. U. Alumni Assn. (bd. dirs. 1984-89, v.p. 1986-89, presdl. search com. 1986-87). Office: PO Box 142089 Austin TX 78714-2089 also: 8309 Cross Park Dr Austin TX 78754 Office Phone: 512-973-0040. Business E-Mail: mjkolar@alexandriagroup.com.

KOLASA, KATHRYN MARIANNE, food and nutrition educator, consultant; b. Detroit, July 26, 1949; d. Marion J. (dec.) and Blanche Ann (Gasiorowski) K.; m. Patrick Noud Kelly, Jan. 3, 1983. BS, Mich. State U., 1970; PhD, U. Tenn., 1974. Test kitchen home economist Kellogg Co., 1971; instr. dept. food sci. and food systems adminstrn. U. Tenn.-Knoxville, 1973-74; asst. prof. dept. food sci. and human nutrition Mich. State U., East Lansing, 1974-76, assoc. prof., 1976-82; prof., chmn. food, nutrition and instn. mgmt. Sch. Home Econs. East Carolina U., Greenville, NC, 1982-86; prof., head nutrition edn. and svcs. sect. Dept. Family Medicine Brody Sch. of Medicine, 2000—, sect. head resident edn., 1995-2000. Mem. subcom. food and nutrition bd. NAS on Uses of the RDA, 1981-83; cons. food and nutrition; vice chmn. edn. subcom. Am. Heart Assn. Consumer Nutrition, 1992-93. Author: (with Ann Bass and Lou Wakefield) Community Nutrition and Individual Food Behavior, 1978, (interactive video disc, with Ann Jobe) Cardiovascular Health: Focus on Nutrition, Fitness and Smoking Cessation, CD-ROM: Images of Cancer Prevention, The Nutrition-Cancer Link. Recipient Dale Rasmann Nutrition Edn. Memorial award Soc. Tchrs. Fam. Medicine, 1998, award Excellence in Med. Edn. Dannon Inst./Am. Soc. Clin. Nutrition, 2000, Disting. Prof. for Tchg. award East Carolina U., 2001; named Master Educator, 2000; grants in nutrition and food service and med. nutrition edn., 1974—; Kellogg nat. fellow, 1985-88. Mem. Soc. Nutrition Edn. (pres. 1984, Career Achievement award 1995), Am. Soc. Nutrition, Am. Dietetic Assn., Soc. Tchrs. Family Medicine. Office Phone: 252-744-1358. E-mail: KOLASAKA@mail.ecu.edu.

KOLATA, GINA, journalist; b. Balt., Feb. 25, 1948; d. Arthur and Ruth Lillian (Aaronson) Bari; m. William George Kolata; children: Therese Bari, Stefan Matthew. BS in Microbiology, U. Md., 1969, MA in Applied Mathematics, 1973; postgrad., MIT, 1969-70. Copy editor Sci. Mag., Washington, 1973-74, writer, 1974-87; columnist GQ, Bild der Wissenschaft, 1984—87, Jour. Investigative Dermatology, 1985—87; reporter, sci. and medicine N.Y. Times, N.Y.C., 1987—. Spkr. in field. Co-author: The Baby Doctors: Probing the Limits of Fetal Medicine, 1991; author Sex in America, 1995, Flu: The Story of the Great Influenza Pandemic, 2001, Clone: The Road to Dolly and the Path Ahead, 2001, Ultimate Fitness: The Quest for Truth About Exercise and Health, 2003. Named finalist, Pulitzer prize, 2000; recipient Statis. Reporting Excellence award, Am. Statis. Assn., 2004. Avocations: bicycling, running. Office: NY Times Sci Times Sect 229 W 43rd St New York NY 10036-3959

KOLB, DOROTHY GONG, elementary school educator; b. San Jose, Calif. d. Jack and Lucille Gong; m. William Harris Kolb, Mar. 22, 1970. BA with highest honors, San Jose State U., 1964; postgrad., U. Hawaii, Calif. State U., L.A.; MA in Ednl. Tech., Pepperdine U., 1992. Cert. in elem. edn., edn. for mentally retarded, edn. for learning handicapped pre-sch., adult classes, resource specialist, English lang. devel., specially designed acad. instrn. in English, 2000, 2003. Tchr. Cambrian Sch. Dist., San Jose, 1964-66, Ctrl. Oahu Sch. Dist., Wahiawa, Hawaii, 1966-68, Montebello (Calif.) Unified Sch. Dist., 1968—. Recipient Very Spl. Person award, Calif. PTA, 1998, Hon. Svc. award, 2003; Walter Bachrodt Meml. scholar. Mem.: Tau Beta Pi, Pi Tau Sigma, Kappa Delta Pi, Pi Lambda Theta.

KOLB, GLORIA RO, medical products executive; BS in mech. engring., MIT, 1994; MS in mech. engring., Stanford U., 1995; MBA in entrepreneurship, Babson Coll., 2001. Founder, pres. Fossa Med., Inc., 2001—. Named one of Top 100 Young Innovators, MIT Tech. Review, 2004. Office: Fossa Med 13 Highland Cir Needham MA 02494

KOLB, VERA M., chemist, educator; b. Belgrade, Yugoslavia, Feb. 5, 1948; arrived in U.S., 1973; d. Martin A. and Dobrila (Lopicic) Kolb; m. Cal Y. Meyers, 1976 (div. 1986); m. Michael S. Gregory, 1997 (div. 1999). BS, Belgrade U., 1971, MS, 1973; PhD, So. Ill. U., 1976. Fellow So. Ill. U., Carbondale, 1977-78, vis. faculty lctr., 1978-85; assoc. prof. chemistry U. Wis., Parkside, 1985-90, prof. chemistry, 1990—, dept. chair, 1995-97. Vis. scientist Salk Inst. Biol. Studies U. Calif., San Diego, 1992—94; instr. San Francisco State U., 1997; vis. scholar Northwestern U., 2002—03. Editor: (book) Teratogens, Chemicals which Cause Birth Defects, 2nd edit., 1993, 1988; contbr. articles to profl. jours.; musician (violinist): Racine Symphony Orch., Parkside Cmty Orch., 2002—05. Assoc. dir. higher edn. Wis. Space Grant Consortium, 1995—97, assoc. dir. for special initiatives, 2002—05; violinist Racine (Wis.) Symphony Orch., Parkside Cmty. Orch. Recipient Rsch. and Higher Edn. awards, Wis. Space Grant Consortium, 1999—, Hall of Fame, Southeastern Wis. Educators, 2002; grantee, NIH, 1984—87, Am. Soc. Biochemistry and Molecular Biology, 1988; Fulbright grantee, 1973—76, NASA fellow, 1992—94. Mem.: Am. Chem. Soc. (task force occupl. safety and health 1980—94). Achievements include patents in field. Office: Univ Wis Parkside Dept Chemistry PO Box 2000 Kenosha WI 53141-2000 Office Phone: 262-595-2133.

KOLBE, STEPHANIE JILL, artist; b. New Ulm, Minn., Feb. 7, 1947; d. Virgil and Arline (Blomguist) Schmieseg; m. Douglas Kolbe, Mar. 16, 1968; children: Justin, Erin. BS in English magna cum laude, Minn. State U., 1969. Tchr. Appleton (Minn.) H.S., 1969-70, Owatonna (Minn.) H.S., 1970-72; daycare provider Owatonna, 1973-83; artist, 1982—. Supt. Steele County Fair, Owatonna, 1984—; artist Minn. Wildlife Heritage Found., St. Paul, 1984-98, Festival Arts, Owatonna, 1994—. Exhibitions include Owatonna Festival of Arts, Steele Co. Fair; contbr. Creative Woodworking and Craft Mag., 2004. Mem., artist Owatonna Arts Ctr., 1982—; vol., presenter, tchr. Santa's Cellar, 1978—, Straight River Wood Carver's, Owatonna, 1982—, Susquecentennial Arts Com., 2003-04. Recipient Best of Show award Minn. Art Show, 1989, award Excellence, 1992, Best of Show award, 1995, People's Choice award Minn. Wildlife Heritage Art Show, 1997, Best of Show for sculpture Owatonna Festival of Arts, Best of Show, Grand Champion, First prize in realistic birds, second prize best of show, Herb Hanson Meml. award, Royal Chislers award, Upper Midwest Wood Carver's Expo, 2006. Mem. Nat. Wood Carver's Assn., Internat. Wood Carver's Assn., Minn. Wild Fowl and Decoy Club. Avocations: dance, painting, sculpting, computer art, travel.

KOLBERT, ELIZABETH RUTH, journalist; b. July 1961; d. Gerald and Marlene Kolbert; m. John Kleiner, 1991; 3 children. Grad., Yale U. Albany bur. chief NY Times; staff writer The New Yorker mag., 1999—. Recipient AAAS Sci. Journalism award, Mag. reporting, 2005, Public Interest award, Am. Soc. Mag. Editors and Columbia Univ., 2006; Fulbright Scholar, Universitat-Hamburg, Germany. Office: The New Yorker Mag 4 Times Sq New York NY 10036*

KOLBERT, KATHRYN, lawyer, educator; b. Detroit, Apr. 8, 1952; d. Melvin and Rosalie Betty (Frank) K.; children: Samuel Kolbert-Hyle, Kate Kolbert-Hyle. BA, Cornell U., 1974; JD, Temple U., 1977. Bar: Pa. 1977, U.S. Dist. Ct. (ea. dist.) Pa. 1977, U.S. Ct. Appeals (3d cir.) 1977, U.S. Supreme Ct. 1985, U.S. Dist. Ct. N.D. 1991, U.S. Ct. Appeals (5th cir.) 1991, U.S. Ct. Appeals (10th cir.) 1994, U.S. Ct. Appeals (8th cir.) 1994. Atty. Community Legal Svcs., Phila., 1977-79, Women's Law Project, Phila., 1979-88; co-founder, dir. policy Women's Agenda, Phila., 1984-88; atty. pvt. practice, Wyndmoor, Pa., 1997. Cons. Planned Parenthood Fedn., N.Y.C., 1988-89, Nat. Abortion Rights Action League, Washington, 1987; cons. reproductive freedom project ACLU, N.Y.C., 1988-89, state coordinating counsel, 1989-92; v.p. Ctr Reproductive Law & Policy, N.Y., 1992-97; lectr. dept. women's studies U. Pa., 1978-86, 90-91, lectr. Sch. Law, 1989-91, sr. rsch. adminstr. Annenberg Pub. Policy Ctr., 1998—; Open Soc. Inst. fellow, 1998-2000. Exec. prodr. (radio series on constnl. law) Justice Talking; contbr. chpts. to books. Founder, Commn. to Elect Women Judges, Women Judges Pac, Phila, 1984; bd. dirs. Com. to Elect the Casey 5, Phila. Recipient Dedicated Advocacy award Nat. Abortion Rights Action League Pa., 1986, Pa. Coalition Against Domestic Violence, 1986, Luth. Settlement House Women's Program, 1987, Am. Dem. Action award, 1989, honoree Women's Way, 1991; named One of 100 Most Influential Lawyers in Am., Nat. Law Jour. Democrat. Jewish. Business E-Mail: KKOLBERT@asc.upenn.edu.

KOLBESON, MARILYN HOPF, holistic practitioner, artist, retired advertising executive, poet; b. Cin., June 9, 1930; d. Henry Dilg Hopt and Carolyn Josephine (Brown) Hopf; children: Michael Llen, Kenneth Ray, Patrick James, Pamela Sue Kolbeson Lang, James Allan. Student, U. Cin., 1947—48, student, 1950. Cert. holistic memory release practitioner. Interior decorator Metro Carpet, 1971-77; sales and mktg. mgr. Cox Patrick United Van Lines, 1977-80; sales mktg. mgr. Creative Incentives, Houston, 1980-81; pres. Ad Sense, Inc., Houston, 1981-87, M.H. Kolbeson & Assocs., Houston, 1987, Seattle, 1987—, The Phoenix Books, Seattle, 1987-90, METASELF Healing, Seattle, 1999—. Bd. dirs. Umbrella Prodns.; cons. N.L.P. Practitioner and Cons.; Aircraft bus. mgmt. cons., Seattle, 1988—90; holographic memory release practitioner, 1996—; cooking demonstrator, nutritional advisor Puget Consumers Coop., Seattle, 1991—2002; lectr., cons. in field. Pub.: You Make the Difference in Nat. Lit. Poetry Anthology, Morning Song, 1996,: Moving On in Nat. Libr. Poetry, 1998; contbr. poetry to A Place at the Table, 1999; Heart Button Technique, 1995, Om Art angel meditation balls, 2002; mgr., assoc. prodr.: (mus. comedy) Times Three, 1999; prodn. mgr. Of a Certain Age, 2002, 2004; Green Scythe, 2004; instrument keeper (group shows) Gentle Wind Project, 1999—, creator, artist Art in the Round, Faces on the Wall exhibit, 2006—. Vol. Seattle Pub. Schs., 1992—2005; mem. citizens adv. bd. Arcola (Ill.) Sch. Dist., 1964—66; mem. ARC, Seattle; charter mem. Rep. Task Force; mem. adv. bd. Alief Ind. Sch. Dist., 1981—87, pres., 1983—84; bd. dirs. Santa Maria Hostel, 1983—86, v.p., 1983—84; mem. citizen's adv. bd. Am. Inst. Achievement, 1986—87; bd. dirs. Breighton Found. Sr. Housing Devel., Seattle, 2000—05, S.E. Seattle Sr. Found., 2000—; founder, pres. Mind Force, Houston, 1978—87, Seattle, 1987—95; founder META Group, Seattle, 1991—, Meta-Self Healing Ministries, Seattle, 1997—. Mem.: Nat. Sch. Pub. Rels. Assn., Internat. Soc. Poets, Inst. Noetic Scis., Houston Advt. Splty. Assn. (bd. dirs. 1984—87, treas. 1985, v.p. 1986—87), Internat. Platform Assn., World Future Soc., Nat. Assn. Mentally Ill. (Wash.), Toastmasters (area gov. 1978), Galleria Area C. of C. (bd. dirs. 1986—87), Fair and Tender Ladies Book Group Seattle, Lakewood Seward Park Cmty. Club (bd. dirs.), Grand Club (v.p. 1986). Republican. Universalist. Office: 5253 S Brandon St Seattle WA 98118-2522 Office Phone: 206-723-3588. Personal E-mail: mhk99@comcast.net.

KOLBUSH, ELIZABETH ANN KUHNS, secondary educator; b. Pitts., July 8, 1965; d. Elbert Addison and Rebecca Ann (Furman) K. BS in Edn. with deptl. honor, Slippery Rock (Pa.) U., 1987; MA in English, California U., Pa., 1989; postgrad., Old Dominion U. Cert. tchr., Va., Pa., Md. Substitute tchr. Bethlehem-Center Schs., Fredericktown, Pa., 1987; instr. English writing lab. California U. Pa., 1987-89; tchr. Accomack County Schs., Accomac, Va., 1989—. Head coach varsity cheerleading squad, 1992-2005. NEH fellow, Duquesne U., 1995, Arthur Vining Davis fellow, 2002-03; named Dist. Cheerleading Coach of Yr., 1992. Mem. Nat. Coun. Tchrs. English, Va. English Assn., Alpha Psi Omega. Democrat. Roman Catholic. Avocations: reading, theater, church work, crafts, travel. Office: Arcadia High Sch PO Box 69 8210 Lankford Hwy Oak Hall VA 23416-2114 Home: PO Box 6 Nelsonia VA 23414 Office Phone: 757-824-5613. Business E-Mail: ekolbush@ahs.accomack.k12.va.us. E-mail: englishteacher83@yahoo.com.

KOLCHENS, SILVIA, science educator; PhD, U. Cologne, Germany, 1989. Rsch. assoc. U. Ariz., Tucson, 1989—94; prof. Pima C.C., Tucson, 1995—. Vis. scientist DuPont Co., Wilmington, Del., 1988, U. Ariz., Tucson, 2006—. Office: Pima CC 2202 W Anklam Rd Tucson AZ 85709 Office Phone: 520-206-6660. Office Fax: 520-206-6902. Business E-Mail: silvia.kolchens@pima.edu.

KOLINER, FRANCES ELOISE, educational administrator; b. L.A., June 6, 1949; d. Julius and Elizabeth (Pasternak) K.; m. Robert McNeil Crawford, Oct. 16, 1972; children: Rose Gabrielle, Ian McNeil Joseph. BA, Humboldt State U., 1972; learning handicapped credential, Sonoma State U., 1985, MA in Edn. Reading Specialist, 2005. Cert. resource specialist, Calif. Ind. study tchr. Willits (Calif.) Unified Sch. Dist., 1973-96, mem. adv. cabinet, 1993-96; home study coord. Anderson Valley Unified Sch. Dist., Boonville, Calif., 1996—. Mem. Calif. Arts Project, 1990-2000, Telementer, 1995-2000; mem. inst. staff drama team Redwood Arts Project, Arcata, Calif., 1992, 94; Mendocino county co-coord. Calif. Art Project, Redwood Arts Project, 1996—2000. Named State Tchr. of Yr. for Small Schs., 1994; fellow Calif. Arts Project, 1990, 92. Mem. ASCD, AAUW, Willits Tchrs. Assn. (officer negotiation com. 1993-94), Consortium Ind. Studies, Computer Using Educators. Avocations: reading, music, computers, gardening, crafts. Home: PO Box 1063 Willits CA 95490-1063 Business E-Mail: fkoliner@mcn.org.

KOLKER, SONDRA G., not-for-profit fundraiser; b. N.Y.C., Nov. 30, 1933; d. Morris Henry and Alice (Cohen) Budow; m. Justin William Kolker, Aug. 23, 1953 (div.); children: Lawrence Paul, David Brett; m. David Kern, July 2000 (dec. Sept. 10, 2003). Student, Hofstra U. Dir. N.Y.C. Office N.Y. State Dem. Com., 1977-79; v.p., exec. dir. Fund for Higher Edn., N.Y.C., 1980-88; pres. Sondra Kolker & Assocs., Halesite, N.Y., 1988-96, Miami, Fla., 1996-98, Ft. Lauderdale, Fla., 1998—. Spl. cons. Internat. Devel. Svcs. subs NMP of Am., Inc., 1989-90; dist. rep. Congressman Robert J. Mrazek, 1990-93. Speechwriter for numerous speakers at corp. banquets, 1980-88. Bd. dirs. Huntington (N.Y.) Townwide Fund, 1978-96, Single Family Homes at Sawgrass, treas., 1999-–; mem. adv. bd. Julia's Fund (divsn. Gilda's Club), 1999—; active Huntington Hosp. Aux., 1965-96, Great Gatsby Soc. for Multiple Sclerosis, 1988-96, Marble Hills Civic Assn., Halesite, 1955-96; committeewoman Huntington Dem. Com., 1974-82; fundraiser/dist. rep. Congressman Robert J. Mrazek, L.I., N.Y., 1991-93; banquet planner Temple Adath Or; active Temple Kol Ami; mem. Broward Guild, Miami City Ballet. Recipient Meritorious Svc. award Huntington Twp. C. of C., 1974, 76, 77, 78, Bicentennial Citation Town of Huntington, 1977. Mem. NAFE, MOMA, NAMI, Met. Mus. Art, Nat. Mus. Women in the Arts, L.I. Crafts Guild, Huntington Twp. C. of C., Women's Econ. Round Table, Huntington Bus. and Profl. Women, Nature Conservancy, Sierra Club, World Wildlife Fund. Jewish. Avocations: fabric painting, poetry, nature study, travel, opera. Home and Office: Sondra Kolker & Assoc 12683 NW 11th Pl Sunrise FL 33323-3119

KOLL, KATHRYN JANE, music educator; b. Manitowoc, Wis., Oct. 9, 1957; d. Wilfred E. and Mavyn L. Kleinhans; m. Greg M. Koll, June 15, 1985; children: Anna M., Kayla E. MusB Edn., Silver Lake Coll., Manitowoc, 1985, MusM Edn., 2004. Cert. music tchr. Dept. Pub. Instrn. Wis., 1980, Kodaly cert. Silver Lake Coll., Wis., 2003. Music tchr./gen. kodaly and band ACES/St. Bernadette Cath. Elem. Sch., Appleton, Wis., 1980—94; music tchr./gen. kodaly and instrumental Kimberly Area Sch. Dist., Wis., 1994—; pvt. piano tchr. Appleton, 1983—93. Mem.: Diocesan Music Educators Assn. (sec. 1983—85), Assn. Wis. Area Kodaly Educators (mem. at large 2005—), Midwest Kodaly Music Educators, Orgn. Am. Kodaly Educators, Music Educators. Roman Catholic. Avocations: gardening, songleading in church, geocaching. Home: 626 E Grant Appleton WI 54911 Office: Kimberly Area School District Kimberly WI 54136 Personal E-mail: kkoll@sbcglobal.net.

KOLLAR-KOTELLY, COLLEEN, federal judge; b. Apr. 17, 1943; m. John T. Kotelly. BA, Cath. U., 1965, JD, 1968. Law clerk to Hon. Catherine Kelly, Dist. Columbia Ct. Appeals, 1968—69; atty. criminal divsn. US Dept. Justice, 1969-72; chief legal counsel St. Elizabeth's Hosp., 1972-84; judge DC Superior Ct., 1984-97, dep. presiding judge, criminal divsn., 1995—97; dist. judge US Dist. Ct. DC, 1997—. Apptd. mem. Judicial Conf. Com. Fin. Disclosure by Chief Justice Rehnquist, 2000—02; apptd. to presiding judge US Foreign Intelligence Surveillance Ct. by Chief Justice Rehnquist, 2002—09; adj. prof. joint tchg. program on mental health and the law Georgetown U. Sch. Medicine, chair bd. art trust for superior ct. Fellow: ABA; mem.: Thurgood Marshall Inn of Ct. (founding mem.). Office: 333 Constitution Ave NW Washington DC 20001-2802

KOLLATZ, REBECCA LYNN, music educator; b. St. Francis, Wis., Mar. 4, 1978; d. Kenneth Donald and Debra Lou Kollatz. MusB, Butler U., Indpls., 2001; postgrad., Viterbo U., La Crosse, Wis., 2005—. Pool mgr., water safety instr. New Berlin Pk. and Recreation, New Berlin, Wis., 1992—2005; band, choral dir. Williams Bay Sch. Dist., Wis., 2001—02; voice instr. White Ho. of Music, Waukesha, Wis., 2002; dir. orchs. John Bullen Middle Sch., Kenosha, Wis., 2002—. Coord. sch.-wide enrichment John Bullen Mid. Sch., Kenosha, Wis., 2003—05; internship Indpls. Children's Choir, 2000; treas. Butler U. Chorale, Indpls., 1998—2000. Presenter (rsch. conf.) Luca Morenzio, Masque of the Red Death; musician: (opera) Cosi fan Tutti (2d pl. Nat. Assn. Tchrs. Singing competition, 2001). Music ministry Newman Ctr., Indpls., 1998—2001. Named Outstanding Sophomore, Pi Kappa Lambda, 1998, Gus Poulimas Outstanding Prospective String Tchr., Butler U., 2001; recipient Alta. Denk String award, Mu Phi Epsilon, 2000, Gerke Meml. Performance award, 2000; Pressor scholar, Butler U., 1998. Mem.: ASTA (assoc.), MENC (assoc.), Phi Kappa Phi, Pi Kappa Lambda, Mu Phi Epsilon (sec. Kappa chpt. 1998—2000, v.p. Kappa chpt. 2000—01). Avocations: swimming, knitting, philosophy, music. Home: 15980 W Allison Dr New Berlin WI 53151 Office: John Bullen Middle Sch 2804 39th Ave Kenosha WI 53144 Office Phone: 262-597-4058. Personal E-mail: bkollatz@sbcglobal.net.

KOLLER, BERNEDA JOLEEN, library administrator; b. Marion, SD, Dec. 23, 1935; d. Theodore Jacob Poppe and Clara Johanna Goertz; m. Dennis Eugene Koller, May 8, 1955; children: Kim Denise, Kerry Tay, Kecia Rae. BA, Augustana Coll., 1974; postgrad., U. S.D., 1976-77. Cert. pub. libr. mgmt., S.D. Sec. Turner County Soil Conservation Dist., Parker, S.D.; tchr. Freeman (S.D.) Pub. H.S., 1974-81; sec. State Farm Ins., Freeman, 1982-90; libr. dir. Freeman Pub. Libr., 1990—. Spkr. hist. lectrs., 1984-2005. Author: (book) Ironic Point of Light, 1994; columnist Freeman Courier, 1983-88. Pres. Parker (S.C.) Alumni Assn., 1959; sec. S.D. Assn. German-Russians, Pierre, 1989—; dir. Musicals at Schmeckfest, Freeman, 1976, 82, 86; mem. Am. Hist. Soc. of Germans from Russia, Lincoln, Nebr., 1986—, German Russian Hist. Soc., Bismarck, N.D., 1994—; pres. Homestead chpt. Am. Hist. Soc. of Germans from Russia, Freeman and Yankton, 1988—; historian, sec., chairperson Dorcas Soc., Freeman, 1976-96; tour guide Freeman Devel. Corp., 1997—; pres., sec., mem. Freeman Area Arts Coun. and Freeman Area Arts Alliance, 1998—; ch. del. Wellspring Wholistic Care Ctr., Freeman, 1997—. Recipient Best Local Column award S.D. Press Assn., 1985, 2d pl. statewide. Mem. S.D. Libr. Assn. Democrat. Mennonite. Avocations: writing, genealogy, travel, knitting, guitar. Office: Freeman Pub Libr PO Box I Freeman SD 57029 Fax: 605-925-7127. E-mail: bkoller85@hotmail.com.

KOLLER, DAPHNE, computer scientist; m. Dan Avida. BS in Math. and Computer sci., Hebrew U., Jerusalem, Israel, 1985, MSc in Computer Sci., 1986; PhD in Computer Sci., Stanford U., Calif., 1993. Postdoctoral fellow, computer sci. divsn. U. Calif., Berkeley, 1993—95; asst. prof., computer sci. Stanford U., Calif., 1995—2001, assoc. prof., computer sci. Calif., 2001—. Author: published in jour. such as Games and Economic Behavior, Artificial Intelligence, Science, and Nature Genetics. Named a MacArthur Fellow, 2004; recipient Young Investigator award, Office of Naval Rsch., 1999, Presdl. Early Career award for Scientists and Engineers, 1999, Fellow Internat. Joint Conf. on Artificial Intelligence Computers and Though award, 2001; Rothschild Grad. Fellowship, 1989—90, U. Calif. President's Postdoctoral Fellowship, 1993—95, Sloan Found. Rsch. Fellowship, 1996. Avocations: reading, music, hiking, sailing, scuba diving. Office: Computer Sci Dept Rm 142 Gates Bldg 1A Stanford U 353 Serra Mall Stanford CA 94305-9010 Office Phone: 650-723-6598. Office Fax: 650-725-1449. Business E-Mail: koller@CS.stanford.edu.*

KOLLMEYER, CARIE ANN, pediatrician; b. Farmington, Mo., Jan. 2, 1977; d. Kimbel Christopher and Ruth Ann Kollmeyer. BA in Psychology, St. Louis U., 1999, MD, 2003. Resident U. Ky., Lexington, 2003—. Mem. med. team Park West Med. Mission to Ecuador, Knoxville, Tenn., 2002, U. Ky. Med. Mission Ecuador, Lexington, 2005. Mem.: Am. Psychiat. Assn., Am. Acad. Pediatrics. Lutheran. Avocations: cooking, reading.

KOLODZIEJSKI, CYNTHIA F., secondary school educator; d. John and Helen Walker; m. John Kolodziejski, June 15, 2001; 1 child, Kyle. AAS, Ulster County C.C., Stone Ridge, NY, 1987; BS, East Stroudsburg U., Pa., 1991; MS in Edn., Mt. St. Mary Coll., Newburgh, NY, 1995. Tchr. health edn. Kingston City Schs., NY, 1991—. Mem.: Am. Alliance Health, Phys. Edn., Recreation and Dance. Office: Kingston City Schs 118 Merilina Ave Kingston NY 12401

KOLUMBA, KIM DALE, elementary education educator, speech and language pathologist; b. Marshfield, Wis., Dec. 11, 1954; d. Arthur and Helen (Mallek) K. BS, U. Wis., 1977, MS in Speech Pathology, 1978, cert. in tchg., 1990. Speech-lang. pathologist Sch. Dist. of Wis. Dells, 1978—90; tchr. early childhood and exceptional edn. needs Sch. Dist. Wisconsin Dells, 1990—. Cooperating tchr. U. Wis., Stevens Point, 1990—. Exec. officer PTA, Wisconsin Dells, 1990—; mem., leader Wisconsin Dells Dist. Wellness com. Mem. NEA (early childhood divsn.), Wis. Edn. Assn., South Ctrl. Edn. Assn., Wisconsin Dells Tchrs. Assn. (rep. 1981—, chair com. 1997-98). Avocations: bicycling, football, gardening, travel, walking. Office: Sch Dist Wisconsin Dells 300 Vine St Wisconsin Dells WI 53965-1826 Office Phone: 608-253-2468 123.

KOMAROFF, LINDA, curator; Joined faculty dept. art Hamilton Coll., NY, 1986; with Met. Mus. Art, NYC; joined LA County Mus. Art, 1995, curator Islamic art, head dept. ancient and Islamic art. Author: The Golden Disk of Heaven: Metalwork of Timurid Iran, 1992; Co-curator (with Stefano Carboni) (exhibitions) The Legacy of Genghis Kahn: Courtly Art and Culture in Western Asia, 1256-1353 (Alfred H. Barr Jr. Award for exhbn. catalogue, Coll. Art Assn., 2004). Recipient Media Award, Muslim Pub. Affairs Coun., 2003; Fulbright Scholar Grant, 1980—81, 1988—89. Office: LA County Mus Art 5905 Wilshire Blvd Los Angeles CA 90036

KOMECHAK, MARILYN GILBERT, psychologist; b. Wabash, Ind., Aug. 28, 1936; d. Russell and Evelyn Georgianna (Snyder) Gilbert; B.S., Purdue U., 1954; B.S., Tex. Christian U., 1966, M.Ed., 1968; Ph.D., North Tex. State U., 1975; m. George J. Komechak, Aug. 23, 1958; children— Kimberly Ann, Gilbert Matthew. Counselor clin. staff Child Study Center, Ft. Worth, 1968-74; assoc. dir. behavioral Sch. for Community Service, North Tex. State U., Denton, 1974-77; pvt. practice psychology, Ft. Worth, 1977—1996; adj. prof. Tex. Christian U., U. Tex., Arlington; dir. Jon Pierce, Inc.; bd. dirs. Dance and Theater Arts Dept., U. North Tex., 1989-96; cons. to schs. and mgmt.; presenter in field. Mem. Sanger-Harris adv. bd. for Dallas/Ft. Worth, 1983—; mem. chancellor's alumni adv. com. U. North Tex., 1987. Author: The Prairie Tree, 1987, Morals and Manners for the Millennium, 2002, Paisano Pete: Snake-Killer Bird, 2003 (named Best Juvenile Book, Okla. Writers Fedn., 2004), Aries, 2005; contbr. poetry to literary jours.; contbr. short stories to various pubs. Recipient Oustanding Alumnus award La Fontaine H.S., nd., 2004. Mem. DAR, Am. Psychol. Assn., Tex. Psychol. Assn., Tarrant County Psychol. Assn. Tex. State Poetry Soc., Ft. Worth Poetry Soc. (Mem.'s Contest award 2006), Ft. Worth Freelance Writers, Inc., Nat. League Am. Pen Women, Psi Chi, Delta Gamma. Episcopalian. Author: Getting Yourself Together, 1982; contbr. articles on counseling and psychology to profl. jours., poetry to anthologies.

KOMINS, DEBORAH, psychotherapist; d. Bernard Barnett and Reba Cobrin; children: Benjamin, Barrie, Max. MSW, Temple U., Phila., 1977; MEd, Antioch U., Phila./Ohio, 1979; cert. psychoanalysis, Phila. Sch. Psychoanalysis, 1996. Social worker Woodhaven/Temple U., Phila., 1979—84; psychoanalyst/therapist pvt. practice, Phila., 1984—. Vol. Phila. Libr., Dem. Party, Phila. Achievements include leading support groups for mothers without custody, appearing on radio and TV to address this issue. Office Phone: 215-564-1451. E-mail: dkomins@msn.com.

KOMISARCZYK, SHIRLEY THERESA, secondary school educator; b. Cascade, Md., Nov. 6, 1930; d. Raymond Thomas and Mary Nina (Coyle) Swinscoe; m. Robert Patrick Clonan, May 3, 1952 (div. 1972); children: Richard Clonan, Eileen Clonan Monesson, Brian Clonan, Shirlene Clonan Soos, Christopher Clonan; m. Michael Komisarczyk (div. Oct. 1978). BS Elem. Edn. cum laude, Fordham U., 1961; MA Ednl. Adminstrn. and Supervision summa cum laude, Seton Hall U., 1972. Lic. tchr., prin., N.J. Pvt. sec. N.Am. Reassurance Co., N.Y.C, 1949—52, 7755 Dependants Sch. Detachment, Karlsruhe, Germany, 1952—53, Bank of China, N.Y.C., 1954—57; tchr. Clark Bd. Edn., NJ, 1961, Woodbridge Bd. Edn., Colonia, NJ, 1965—68; specialist remedial reading Old Bridge Bd. Edn., NJ, 1972—94; ret., 1994. Mem. Rep. Nat. Com. Mem. N.J. Edn. Assn., Middlesex County Edn. Assn., Women In Edn. Com., Old Bridge Edn. Assn., Am. Assn. Retired Persons (life). Roman Catholic. Home: 32 Coventry Ter Marlboro NJ 07746-1738

KOMOLA, CHRISTINE T., corporate financial executive; Asst. controller Staples, Framingham, Mass., 1997, v.p. planning & control, 1997—99, CFO Staples.com, 1999—2001, sr. v.p., gen mdse. mgr., 2001—04, sr. v.p., controller, 2004—. Office: Staples 500 Staples Dr Framingham MA 01702*

KONCZAK, SANDRA M., elementary school educator; b. Baird, Tex., Aug. 29, 1950; d. Uthell Saunders; m. Edward M. Konczak, Sept. 20, 1968; children: Tamatha Jo Dayberry, Michael. BS in Curriculum and Instrn., Tex. A&M U., 1979; MEd, Stephen F. Austin State U., Nacogdoches, Tex., 1981; EdD, Concordia U., 2002. Environ. edn. endorsement Stephen F. Austin U., Tex., 1993, cert. mid-mgmt. adminstr., elem. edn., life sci., math., computer literacy (grades 7 & 8). Tchr. Grapeland Ind. Sch. Dist., Tex., 1979—81, Mexia Ind. Sch. Dist., Tex., 1981—86, asst. prin., 1986—88; tchr. Abilene Ind. Sch. Dist., Tex., 1989—. Mem. Abilene Edn. Coun., 1992—96; sponsor teen leadership coun. Girl Scouts Am., Abilene, 1997—2001; advisor Astronomy Merit Badge Troop 227 Boys Scouts Am., 1989—. Mem.: Big Country Coun. Tchrs. Math. and Sci., Nat. Coun. Tchrs. Math., NSTA, Tex. Outdoor Edn. Assn., Tex. Computer Edn. Assn., Assn. Tex. Profl. Educators, Reserve Peace Officers Tex. Avocations: travel, sewing, reading. Home: 219 Market St Baird TX 79504 Office: Madison Mid Sch Abilene TX 79504

KONCZAL, LISA, sociology educator, researcher; b. Rochester, Mich., Dec. 19, 1969; d. Daniel J. and Sharon K. Konczal, Elaine Konczal (Stepmother); m. Mohamad Reza Bahrami, Feb. 18, 2006. BA in Internat. Rels., Fla. Internat. U., Miami, 1993; MA in Comparative Sociology, Fla. Internat. U., 1997, PhD, 2001. Rsch. asst. Immigration & Ethnicity Inst., Fla. Internat. U., 1995—99, rsch. assoc. Met. Ctr., 1997—2001; postdoctoral rsch. assoc. Princeton U., NJ, 2000—02; asst. prof. sociology Barry U., Miami Shores, Fla., 2002—. Prin. investigator Barry U., 2006—. Basketball coach YMCA, Miami, 1996—97; vol. Fraternidad Nicaraguense, Miami, 1996—97; facilator Children Internat., 2003; vol. Camillas Ho., Miami, 2003—05. Recipient 1st pl. award for paper and presentation at Grad. Scholarly Forum, Fla. Internat. U., 2001, cert. profl. devel. in recognition of outstanding scholarship and svc., Barry U., 2002—03. Mem.: Soc. for Study of Social Problems, Am. Sociol. Assn., Pi Gamma Mu. Office: Barry U 11300 NE 2nd Ave Lehman 306 Miami Shores FL 33161 Office Phone: 305-899-4916. E-mail: lkonczal@barry.edu.

KONECHNE, ANN M., women's college basketball coach, director; b. Mitchell, S.D., July 15, 1977; d. David M. and Barbara J. Konechne. BS in Indsl. Engring., S.D. Sch. of Mines and Tech., Rapid City, 1999; MA, St. Cloud State U., Minn., 2004. Head women's basketball coach Dakota Wesleyan U., Mitchell, SD, 2004—, athletic dir., 2005—. NAIA nat. com. mem. Coun. of Athletic Administrs., Olathe, Kans., 2005—. Vol. Rotary Club, Mitchell, SD, 2004—06. Roman Catholic. Avocations: golf, travel, physical activity. Office: Dakota Wesleyan Univ 1200 W University Ave Mitchell SD 57301 Office Phone: 605-995-2175.

KONECKY, EDITH, writer; b. N.Y.C., Aug. 1, 1922; d. Harry and Elizabeth (Smith) Rubin; m. Murray Leon Konecky, May 14, 1942 (div. 1963); children: Michael, Joshua. Student, NYU, 1938-41. Author: Allegra Maud Goldman, 1976, reprinted 1978, 87, 90, 93, 2001, A Place at the Table, 1989, reprinted 1990, 99, Past Sorrows and Coming Attractions, 2000, View to the North, 2004; contbr. short stories to various mags. and anthologies, including Best American Short Stories of 1964; contbr. poetry to various mags. and anthologies, and essays to The Writer's Handbook, 1991, 2000; work discussed in Her Testimony, 1994 and Jewish-American Women Writers. 1994; co-prodr. Yiddish Book Ctr., KCRW, 1995. N.Y. Found. for the Arts fellow 1992; Yaddo fellow, 1962-88; MacDowell Colony fellow, 1971-98; Helene Wurlitzer Found. fellow, 1973; VCCA fellow, 1981, Djerassi Found. fellow, 1987; Blue Mountain Ctr. fellow, 1983-88; Leighton Artist Colony at the Banff Ctr. for Fine Arts fellow, 1990; recipient Mabel Louise Robinson prize for best short story of yr., Columbia U., 1961; recipient Quill award for best fiction, 1963, Mass. Rev.; recipient citations ALA, 1976, Sch. Libr. Jour., 1977 (Best Young Adult books). Mem. Authors' Guild, PEN, Poets and Writers. Personal E-mail: ekonecky@nyc.rr.com.

KONEFAL, MARGARET MOORE, health facility administrator, critical care nurse, nursing consultant, educator; b. N.Y.C., Apr. 20, 1939; d. James G. and Virgene M. (Allen) Moore; m. Walter A. Konefal, Dec. 30, 1961 (div. 1992); children: Douglas, David, Jesse, Benjamin; m. James J. Gallagher, Feb. 15, 2003. BSN, Incarnate Word Coll., 1961; MSN, Cath. U. of Am., 1969; PhD, Old Dominion U., 1991. RN Tex., cert. nurse adminstr., advanced. Clin. nurse specialist, clin. coord. newborn svcs. Children's Nat. Med. Ctr., Washington, 1972-77; assoc. DON Children's Hosp. of the King's Daus., Norfolk, Va., 1977-82; asst. prof. Norfolk State U., 1982-91; dir. critical care nursing Children's Hosp., Columbus, Ohio, 1991-94; dir. Meml. Children's Hosp., Savannah, Ga., 1994—95; dir. clin. edn. and performance devel. Meml. Healthcare Sys., Savannah, 1995—97; adminstrv. dir. child and adolescent ctr. U. Tex.-M.D. Anderson Cancer Ctr., Houston, 1997—99; sr. mgr. and healthcare industry leader Internal Audit Svcs., Gulf Coast Area, Ernst & Young LLP, 1999-2000; dir. women and infant svcs. Ben Taub Gen. Hosp., Houston, 2000—06, assoc. chief nursing officer, 2006—. Adj. faculty Ohio State U., 1992—94. Mem. ANA, Am. Coll. Healthcare Execs., Houston Orgn. Nurse Execs., Nat. Assn. Neonatal Nurses, Nat. Perinatal Assn., Assn. Womens Health, Obstet. and Neonatal Nurses, Tex. Forum on Health Safety, Sigma Theta Tau. Home: 5743 Cheena Dr Houston TX 77096-5911 Office: Ben Taub Gen Hosp Harris County Hosp Dist 1504 Taub Loop Houston TX 77030 Office Phone: 713-873-3066. E-mail: Margi1@ix.netcom.com, Margaret_Konefal@hchd.tmc.edu.

KONERSMAN, ELAINE REICH, nursing administrator; b. Macon, Ga., Aug. 12, 1949; d. Edward Allen Reich and Martha Alberta (Bridges) Kirkpatrick; m. Elijah Arlington Scott, Aug. 4, 1967 (dec. Nov. 1970); 1 child, Michael Arlington Scott; m. Gregory Lee Konersman, Mar. 29, 1985 (dec. Nov. 2002). ADN, Macon Coll., 1983. RN, Ga. Floor nurse supr. Perry (Ga.)-Houston County Hosp., 1983-85, Mangum (Okla.) City Hosp., 1985-87, Tillman County Hosp., Frederick, Okla., 1987-88; traveling nurse Kahu Malama Nurses, Honolulu, 1989-90; charge nurse nursery, fl. nurse ICU nursery Tripler Army Med. Ctr., Honolulu, 1990-92; coord. endocrinology clinic MacDill AFB, Tampa, Fla., 1991-93; clin. nurse pediat. unit South Fla. Bapt. Hosp., Plant City, 1993-96; clin. coord. nursing Pediatric Svcs. Am., Inc., Macon, 1997—2005. Gail Burdsall Cowan scholar Macon Coll., 1982-83. Baptist. Avocations: reading, stock car racing, computer programmer. Home: 121 Rocky Creek Ct NE #NE Milledgeville GA 31061-7990

KONG, LAURA S. L., geophysicist; b. Honolulu, July 23, 1961; d. Albert T.S. and Cordelia (Seu) K.; m. Kevin T.M. Johnson, Mar. 3, 1990. ScB, Brown U., 1983; PhD, MIT/Woods Hole Oceanog. Inst., 1990. Grad. rschr. Woods Hole (Mass.) Oceanog. Instn., 1984-90; postdoctoral fellow U. Tokyo, 1990-91; geophysicist Pacific Tsunami Warning Ctr., Ewa Beach, Hawaii, 1991-93; seismologist U.S. Geol. Survey Hawaiian Volcano Obs., 1993-95; rschr. U. Hawaii, Honolulu, 1996-99; environ. specialist Dept. Transp., Honolulu, 2000—05; dir. Internat. Tsunami Info. Ctr., Honolulu, 2005—. Chair Hawaii Earthquake Adv. Bd., 1994—; tsunami advisor State of Hawaii, 1999—; mem. equal opportunity adv. bd. Nat. Earth Svc. Pacific Region, Honolulu, 1992-93, Asain-Am.-Pacific Islander spl. emphasis program mgr., 1992-93; mem. steering com. U.S. Nat. Tsunami Hazard Mitigation Program; mem. Hawaii State Hazard Mitigation Forum, Hawaii Multi-Hazard Sci. Adv. Com.; legis. rschr. Hawaii Senate, 1996-98. Contbr. articles to profl. jours.; spkr., editl. reviewer in field. Rsch. fellow Japan Govt.-Japan Soc. for Promotion of Sci., 1990; recipient Young Investigator grant Japan Soc. for Promotion of Sci., 1990. Mem. Am. Geophys. Union, Seismol. Soc. Am., Hawaii Ctr. for Volcanology, Assn. Women in Sci., Sigma Xi. Avocation: sports. Office: Nat Weather Svc Internat Tsunami Info Ctr 737 Bishop St Ste 220 Honolulu HI 96813 E-mail: laura.kong@fhwa.dot.gov.

KONIGSBURG, ELAINE LOBL, writer; b. N.Y.C., Feb. 10, 1930; d. Adolph and Beulah (Klein) Lobl; m. David Konigsburg, July 6, 1952; children— Paul, Laurie, Ross. BS, Carnegie Mellon U., 1952; postgrad., U. Pitts., 1952-54; DHL (hon.), U. North Fla., 2001. Author: juveniles Jennifer, Hecate, Macbeth, William McKinley and Me, Elizabeth, 1967 (Newbery Honor Book), From The Mixed-Up Files of Mrs. Basil E. Frankweiler, 1967 (Newbery medal 1968), About the B'nai Bagels, 1969, (George), 1970, Altogether, One at a Time, 1971, A Proud Taste for Scarlet and Miniver, 1973 (Nat. Book award nominee), The Dragon in the Ghetto Caper, 1974, The Second Mrs. Giaconda, 1975, Father's Arcane Daughter, 1976, Throwing Shadows, 1979 (Am. Book award nominee), Journey to an 800 Number, 1981, Up From Jericho Tel, 1986, Samuel Todd's Book of Great Colors, 1990, Samuel Todd's Book of Great Inventions, 1991, Amy Elizabeth Explores Bloomingdale's, 1992, T-backs, T-shirts, COAT and Suit, 1993, TalkTalk, 1995, The View From Saturday, 1996 (Newbery medal 1997), Silent to the Bone, 2000, The Outcasts of 19 Schuyler Place, 2004. Recipient Regina medal, Cath. Libr. Assn., 2001; named to State of Fla. Hall of Fame, 2000.

KONNER, JOAN WEINER, academic administrator, educator, television producer, writer, retired television executive; b. Paterson, N.J., Feb. 24, 1931; d. Martin and Tillie (Frankel) Weiner; children: Rosemary, Catherine (dec.); m. Alvin H. Perlmutter. Student, Vassar Coll., 1948—49; BA, Sarah Lawrence Coll., 1951; MS, Columbia U., 1961. Editl. writer, columnist, reporter Hackensack (N.J.) Record, 1961-63; prodr., reporter WNDT Ednl. Broadcasting Corp., N.Y.C., 1963-65; prodr., writer, reporter NBC News, N.Y.C., 1965-77; exec. prodr. nat. pub. affairs programs WNET Ednl. Broadcasting Corp., N.Y.C., 1977-78, exec. prodr. Bill Moyers Jour., 1978-81, v.p. met. programming, 1981-84; exec. prodr., pres., co-founder Pub. Affairs TV with Bill Moyers PBS; prof. broadcast and journalism Columbia U., N.Y.C., 1988—97, pub. Columbia Journalism Rev., 1988-99, dean emerita Grad. Sch. Journalism, 1997—; ret. Prof. Grad. Sch. Journalism, Columbia U., N.Y.C., 1988-2006. Bd. dirs. Hudson River Found., Contemplative Mind in Society, Florence and John Schumann Found.; past trustee Providence Jour., Columbia U., Rockland Ctr. for Arts, Sarah Lawrence Coll., Religion Writers Found., Radio and TV News Dirs. Found., Pulitzer Prize Bd. Recipient 16 Emmy awards NATAS, Columbia-du Pont award, Peabody award, Gavel award ABA, Edward R. Murrow award, others. Mem. Dirs. Guild, Writers Guild, Soc. Profl. Journalists, New Spaper Women's Club of N.Y.C., Century Assn., Cosmopolitan Club. E-mail: jk25@columbia.edu.

KONRAD, CAROL JOAN, secondary school educator; b. Gas City, Ind., Aug. 16, 1957; d. Robert J. and Lily Ruth (Neville) K. BS in Secondary Edn., Millersville State Coll., 1979, MEd, 1983. Tchr. math., coach Washington & Lee High Sch., Montross, Va., 1979-82, Lebanon Cath. High Sch., Pa., 1982-83, Prince George's County Sch., Largo High Sch., Md., 1983-85; coach girl's basketball Prince George's County Sch., DuVal High Sch., Lanham, Md., 1983—91, coach softball, 1983—, tchr. math., 1985—. Dir. 9th grade aerospace team Duval High Sch. Coach Lanham Boys and Girls Club, 1991-94, athletic dir., 1998-2005. Recipient Ray A. Kroc Tchr. Achievement award McDonald's, 1991. Mem. ASCD, Nat. Tchrs. of Maths. E-mail: cjksbgold@aol.com.

KOOB, KATHRYN LORAINE, religious studies educator; b. Independence, Iowa, Oct. 8, 1938; d. Harold Frederick Koob and Elsie Muriel Woodward. BA, Wartburg Coll., 1962; MA, U. Denver, 1968; MA Religion, Lutheran Theol. Sem., Gettysburg, Pa., 1998; LHD (hon.), Gwynedd-Mercy Coll., Gwynedd Valley, Pa., 1981, Upsala Coll., 1983. Dist. parish worker Am. Luth. Ch., Denver, 1958—60; tchr. St. Paul's Luth. Sch., Waverly, Iowa, 1962—64, Newton (Iowa) Pub. Schs., Newton, 1964—68; fgn. svc. officer U.S. Info. Agy., Washington, 1969—96; motivational spkr. Waverly, Iowa, 1981—. Co-chair Nat. Adv. Bd. for Comm. Arts Dept. Wartburg Coll., Waverly, Iowa, 2001—. Author: Guest of the Revolution, 1982 (Gold Medallion Book Award presented by Evang. Christian Pub. Assn., 1984); contbr. chapters to books Heroes, 1983, articles to profl. jours. and newspapers. Pres. Wartburg Cmty. Symphony Bd., Waverly; bd. dirs. Iowa Divsn. UN Assn.-U.S.A., Iowa City, 1999—; sec. bd. dirs. ASPIRE-Therapeutic Riding Program, Waterloo. Recipient medal of valor, U.S. Dept. State, 1981, Governor's medal of valor, Iowa State Gov., 1981, Woman of Yr. award, Am. Legion Women's Aux., 2002, Wartburg medal, 2006. Mem.: AAUW (Waverly chpt.), U.S. Info. Agy. Alumni Assn. (life), Am. Fgn. Svc. Assn. (life), Rotary, Kappa Delta Gamma. Lutheran. Avocations: travel, opera, reading. Home: 608 3rd Ave NW Waverly IA 50677-2331 Office: Wartburg Coll 100 Wartburg Blvd PO Box 1003 Waverly IA 50677 Office Phone: 319-352-8408. Business E-Mail: kathryn.koob@wartburg.edu.

KOOKER, JEAN L., retired elementary school educator; b. Lampasas, Tex., Dec. 29, 1924; d. Frank L. and Jess Moss Harman; m. Earl W. Kooker, May 31, 1947 (dec.); children: Lynn Fassnacht, Cheryl Brainerd, Kirk, Candace Luedde. BA, U. North Tex., Denton, 1947, MEd, 1956. Cert. tchr. Tex., 1944, supr. Tex., 1956. Tchr. Unity Pub. Sch., Lampasas, Tex., 1943—44, Lampasas Jr. H.S., 1944—47, Pharr, San Juan, Alamo Sch. Dist., Tex., 1947—48, Denton Ind. Sch. Dist., 1953—83, ret., 1983. Mem. long term planning com. Denton Ind. Sch. Dist., 1971—74; prin., owner Women's Interracial Corp., Denton, 1963—67. Cons. Denton Girl Scouts, 1974—77; tchr., active mission program Trinity Presbyn. Ch., Denton; bd. dirs., officer Cross Timbers Girl Scouts, Denton, 1965—72; bd. dirs. Fairhaven Ret. Home, Denton, 1969—75, Child Welfare Bd., Denton, 1970—76, Denton Food Ctr., 1976—82. Recipient Thanks Badge award, Girl Scouts Am., 1970, Make It Happen award, Denton Christian Presch., 2004. Mem.: U. Women U. North Tex. (pres.), Women's Interracial Group, Denton Interracial Women, Alpha Chi. Democrat. Presbyn. Avocations: reading, bridge, travel, camping, ecology. Home: 1610 Laurelwood Dr Denton TX 76209

KOOLURIS, HORTENSE DOLAN, performing arts educator, consultant, dancer; b. NYC, Sept. 22, 1914; d. Morris and Esther (Zatz) Dolinsky; m. Spero George Kooluris, Mar. 18, 1943 (dec. Nov. 1984); children: G. Kirby, Linda Kooluris-Dobbs. Student, Hunter Coll., 1922—24; studied with, Irma Duncan, Anna Duncan, Maria-Theresa Duncan, 1922—2024. Pvt. practice, 1929—88; co-founder Centenary Dance Co., 1977—88; ret., 1988. Adv. bd. Isadora Duncan Internat. Inst., Inc., N.Y.C., 1977—2000; dance coach Artist in Conflict, Palm Beach, Fla., 1982; guest artist Isadora Duncan Birth Meml. Celebration, Tokyo, 1991; instr. NYU, 1991—94; cons., spkr. presenter in field; rep. Isadora Duncan Heritage Dance Theater of Agnes de Mille, 1976. Dancer Carnegie Hall, Madison Sq. Garden; dir., performer: Duncan Dancers, 1992; performer (soloist): Lincoln Sq. Neighborhood Assn., 1993, Isadora Duncan Studio, 1994; performer: Nat. Soc. Arts and Letters Tea, 1994; contbr. articles to profl. jours. Evaluating com. NJ Arts Coun., 1982. Named Guest of Honor, Duncan Dance Program, Great Neck, NY, 1992. Mem.: Nat. Soc. Arts and Letters (dance chair NJ chpt. 1994). Home: 3744 SE Old St Lucie Blvd Stuart FL 34996

KOOLURIS DOBBS, LINDA KIA, artist, photographer; b. Orange, NJ, 1949; m. Kildare Dobbs, 1981. AA, Pine Manor Coll., 1968; Cert., Sorbonne, 1968-69; BFA with honors, Sch. Visual Arts, 1972. Tchg. staff various colls., 1975—; tchg. staff fashion dept/ Ryerson U., 1980—2003; tchg. staff Avenue Rd. Art Sch., 1999—. Exhibitions include Mus. of Textiles, Toronto, Bronxville Art and Frame Gallery, Atrium Gallery, Chubb Group of Ins. Cos., Warren, N.J., Vancouver Art Gallery, Newbury Fine Arts, Boston and Edgartown, Mass., Art Gallery of Hamilton, Toronto Watercolour Soc., Vancouver Maritime Mus., Ceperley House of Visual Arts Burnaby, B.C., Sutton Gallery, The Granary, Port Hope, Ont., Hummingbird Centre, Carrier Gallery, Columbus Ctr., First Canadian Pl. Gallery, Toronto, U. Toronto, Regis Coll., U. Toronto, Zwicker's Gallery, Halifax, N.S., Represented in permanent collections AT&T, Artform, Norway, Glaxo Wellcome Inc., Inland Pacific Enterprises, Temple Scott & Assocs., Uniglobe, Goodman & Goodman, Advance Travel, AGF Mgmt. Ltd., Toronto Stock Exch., Ont. Govt. Art Collection, Parliament Bldg., Queen's Park, Pine Manor Coll., U.S., Mt. Sinai Hosp., Merrill Lynch, Aon Reed Stenhouse, U. Toronto, Harry Ransom Humanities Rsch. Ctr., U. Tex., Austin, Law Soc. Upper Can., Scotia McLeod, Probyn & Co., Munk Ctr. Internat. Studies, Massey Coll. Faculties of Law and Dentistry, U. Toronto, others, prin. works include portrait commns. the Hon. Henry N. R. Jackman, the Hon. Edwin A. Goodman, the Hon. Barbara McDougall, others, the Hon. David Peterson, Prof. Vern Krishna, Dr. Syvia Ostry, Brian Moore, Judge Ronald St. John MacDonald, Richard B. Wright, Karen Kain, others, Splash 3, 4, 5 & 8, Can. Bus. Mag.; contbr. photographs to popular mags. including Nat. Post, Fin. Post., Verve Mag., Can. Bus. Mag., Irish Times Mag. Recipient Ann. Art Purchase prize Pine Manor Coll., 1968, 2d prize Fin. Post Ann. Reports awards, 1981, Hon. Mention Ann. Fall Show Toronoto Watercolour Soc., 1991, Best in Architecture award Toronto Watercolour Soc. 1994. Address: 484 Avenue Rd Ste 609 Toronto ON Canada M4V 2J4 Office Phone: 416-960-8984.

KOOPERSMITH, KIM, lawyer; b. Lake Success, NY, Aug. 11, 1959; d. Kenneth and Marcia Ilene (Shapiro) K.; m. William J. Borner, June 19, 1983; children: Meredith Lee, Charlotte Jane. BA cum laude, U. Pa., 1981; JD, Fordham U., 1984. Bar: NY 1985, US Dist. Ct. (so. and ea. dists.) NY 1985, US Ct. of Appeals (2nd cir.). Ptnr. Anderson Kill Olick & Oshinsky, P.C., NYC, 1984; now ptnr. litig. and mem. mgmt. com. Akin Gump Strauss Hauer & Feld LLP, NYC. Contbr. articles to profl. publs. Mem. NY State Bar Assn., Assn. of Bar NYC Office: Akin Gump Strauss Hauer & Feld LLP 590 Madison Ave New York NY 10022-2524 Office Phone: 212-872-1060. Business E-Mail: kkoopersmith@akingump.com.

KOPEC-GARNETT, LINDA, nursing administrator, researcher; d. Frank J. and Anna Paul Kopec; m. Thomas R. Garnett, Oct. 6, 1990. BSN cum laude, Fitchburg State Coll., 1983; MS in Health Svc. Adminstrn., Ctrl. Mich. U., 1996. RN in Va. Nurse intern Med. Coll. Va. Hosp., Richmond, Va., 1983, nurse clinician in neurosci. ICU, 1984—86; terr. mgr., patient care specialist Kinetic Concepts Therapeutic Svc., Richmond, 1986—89; rsch. coord. neurology dept. Med. Coll. Va. and Va. Commonwealth U., Richmond, 1989—; adminstr. neurology dept. Va. Commonwealth U., Richmond, 2001—. Mem.: Am. Epilepsy Soc., Sigma Theta Tau.

KOPELL, NANCY, mathematician, education educator; b. N.Y.C., Nov. 8, 1942; BS in Math., Cornell U.; PhD, U. Calif.-Berkeley, 1967. C.L.E. Moore Instructorship MIT, Cambridge, 1967—69; faculty mem. Northeastern U., 1969—78, prof. math., 1978—86, Boston U., 1986—. Co-dir. Ctr. for BioDynamics Boston U.; vis. prof. Centre National de la Recherche Scientifique France, 1970, MIT, 1975, 1976—77, Calif. Inst. Tech., 1976; Volmer Fries Meml. lectr. Rensselaer Polytechnic Inst.; Mark Kac Meml. lectr. Los Alamos Nat. Labs.; Univ. lectr. Boston U., 1993. Named William Goodwin Aurelio Prof. of Math. and Sci., Boston U., 2000; fellow, Gugenheim Found., Sloan Found., MacArthur Found., 1990—95. Mem.: NAS. Office: CAS Math and Stats Boston Univ 111 Cummington St Boston MA 02215

KOPENHAVER, PATRICIA ELLSWORTH, podiatrist; Student, Columbia U., 1950-53; BA, George Washington U., 1954; MA, Columbia U., 1956; Dr. Podiatric Medicine, N.Y. Coll. Podiatric Medicine, 1963, postgrad., 1980; LLD (hon.), Barry U., 1998; MD (hon.) (hon.), Internat. U. Health Scis. Sch. Medicine, 2001; MD (hon.), Internat. Univ. of the Hlth. Sci., 2001. Diplomate Nat. Bd. Podiatry Examiners. Pvt. practice podiatry, Greenwich, Conn., 1964—; staff podiatrist Havenhealth Care Ctr., Greenwich, 2003—. Mem. staff Laurelton Convalescent Hosp., Greenwich; trustee N.Y. Coll. Podiatric Medicine, 1998. Bd. dirs. Monmouth Opera Guild, 1965; trustee Monmouth Opera Festival, 1966, v.p., 1964; mem. Greenwich Arts Coun.; program chmn. Greenwich Women's Rep. Club, 1983-84, 4th dist. rep., 1984-85, 87—; trustee N.Y. Coll. Podiatric Medicine, 1998—. Recipient Hosp. Fund award for med. research translations ARC, Alumni award of distinction N.Y. Coll. Podiatric Medicine, 1997; scholarship named in her honor N.Y. Coll. Podiatric Medicine, 1997. Mem. AAUW (v.p. 1991, pres. Greenwich br. 1992-94, bd. dirs. 1996), NOW, Conn. Podiatric Med. Assn., Hist. Soc., Asian Soc., Fairfield Podiatry Assn., Am. Assn. Women Podiatrists (founding charter pres. 1969-78), Acad. Podiatry, Am. Podiatry Coun., UN Assn. U.S.A., Acad. Podiatric Medicine (chmn. nominating com. 1981, 1st v.p. 1983-84, chmn. fundraising 1984-85, chmn. women's issues 1985, chmn. cmty. edn. 1989), Am. Acad. Sports Medicine, Am. Acad. Podiatric Sports Medicine (assoc. 1989), George Washington U. Alumni Assn., Columbia Alumni Assn., Fairfield County Alumni Assn. Columbia U., Coast Soc. of Founders Barry U. (treas. 1998), Nat. Fedn. Rep. Women, Bruce Mus., Nature Conservancy, Federated Garden Clubs Conn., St. Mary Ladies Guild, Greenwich Gardeners, Womans' Club (ways and means com. 1989, pres.), English Speaking Union, Soroptimists Internat. Am. (pres. Greenwich br. 1990—, bd. dirs. 1997-98), Inc. (vice chmn. program com. 1985—, regional med. scholarship chmn. 1987, med. scholarship chmn. N.E. region 1988, program dir. 1988—, pres. Greenwich br. 1990-92), Toastmasters, Travel Club (program com. 1984—), Soroptimist (bd. dirs. 1997, 2000—), Greenwich Woman's Club (chair gardeners judges 2001—), Pi Epsilon Chi. Home: 2 Sutton Pl S New York NY 10022-3070 also: 8 Dearfield Dr Greenwich CT 06831-5348 Office Phone: 203-661-9311. Office Fax: 203-869-5096.

KOPERSKI, NANCI CAROL, nursing consultant, women's health nurse; b. Omaha, Sept. 14, 1962; d. William S. Jr. and Ethel A. (Friday) Koperski; divorced. Student, Marquette U.; BSN cum laude, Creighton U., 1984; MBA, MHSA, Ariz. State U. RN, Ariz.; cert. women's health nurse. Staff nurse Phoenix Meml. Hosp., Phoenix Gen. Hosp., Community Hosp., Phoenix, Phoenix Indian Med. Ctr.; clin. care coord. Ahwatukee Foothills Samaritan Health Ctr., 1992—2001; staff nurse Alegent Health, Omaha, 2001—04; legal nurse cons. Omaha, 2004—. Mem. Assn. Women's Health, Obstet. and Neonatal Nurses, Ariz. Nurses Assn., Sigma Theta Tau. Office Phone: 800-421-8183.

KOPF, NANCY, special education educator; b. Bath, N.Y., May 5, 1947; d. Donald and Louise Francis; m. Raymond Kopf, Apr. 23, 1966; 1 child, John. B, M, Edinboro U., Pa., 1971. Spl. edn. tchr. Penncrest Sch. Dist., Saegertown, Pa., 1986—. Actor: (regional summer theater) Brigadoon, Carnival, Oklahoma, Mame, Anything Goes. Ofcl. bd. Sunday sch. tchr. Chapmanville (Pa.) Cmty. Ch., 1980—2005. Recipient Innovative Tchg. award. Avocations: travel, autograph collecting, theater, visiting adopted schools on the Amazon, tour guide. Home: 358 Meadville Rd Titusville PA 16354 Office: Penncrest Sch Dist 18741 Mook Rd Saegertown PA 16433 Office Phone: 814-763-2323. E-mail: nkopf@penncrest.iu5.org.

KOPF, RANDI, family and oncology nurse practitioner, lawyer; b. Jersey City, Mar. 30, 1953; d. Soloman and Sydell Kopf. BS, MS, SUNY, Stony Brook, 1978; JD, U. Md., Balt., 1989. Bar: Md., 1989, D.C., 1991; cert. family nurse practitioner. Pvt. practitioner allergy and dermatology, 1982-83; pvt. cons. practice as oncology nurse practitioner; legal intern Office of Gen. Counsel, NIH, 1988; legal assoc., health svcs. group Nixon, Hargrave, Devans & Doyle, Washington, 1990-93; prin. atty., founder Kopf HealthLaw Group, Bethesda, Md., 1995; pvt. law practice, 1995—. Lectr., cons. Am. Cancer Soc.; mem. faculty Georgetown U., U. Md., Adelphi U.; nat. lectr. on med. legal topics. Author: Handbook of Nursing Physical Assesment, 1987, Before You Sign.Managed Care Contract Review for Health Care Providers, 1996; editor, contbg. author Jour. Nursing Law, 1993—; contbr. articles to nat. profl. jours. Recipient Alumni award for Outstanding Volunteerism, Cornell U., 1998. Mem. D.C. Bar Assn., Md. Bar Assn., Am. Hosp. Atty. Assn., Chesapeake Nurse Atty. Assn. (pres., bd. dirs.), Am. Health Lawyers Assn. Home: 511 Golden Oak TER Rockville MD 20850-7801

KOPFMANN, BEVERLY JEAN, small business owner; b. Waukesha, Wis. d. Raymond Scheets and Dolores Cynthia Baumgartner; m. Richard Joseph Kopfmann; children: Victoria Lynn, David Scott, Robert Paul. V.p. Kopfmann Corp., Milw., 1955—79; minister Universal Life Ch., Modesto, Calif., 2002—06; pres./owner Beverly Kay Enterprises, Inc., Mequon, 1982—2006. Author: (book) The Blue-print of Your Soul, 2000; contbr. articles to mags. Avocation: art. Home: 8713 W Poplar Dr Mequon WI 53097 Office: 11431 No Port Washington Rd Mequon WI 53092

KOPICKI, BETH ANN, special education educator; b. N.Y. d. Thomas and Eleanor Kopicki; children: Abigayle Good, Andrew Good, Jacob Good. BS in Spl. and Elem. Edn., Kutztown State Coll., Pa., 1977; MEd in Tchg. English as a Second Lang., U. of Turabo, Gurabo, P.R., 2001. Tchr. Orleans Parish Sch. Dist., New Orleans, 1977—79, Warren County Pub. Schs., Front Royal, Va., 1979—80, Reading Sch. Dist., Pa., 1995—2003, No. Lebanon Sch. Dist., Fredericksburg, Pa., 2003—. Student assistance program team mem. So. Mid. Sch., 1996—2003, yearbook advisor, 1998—2003; student coun. advisor No.

Lebanon Mid. Sch., 2003—, peer mediation advisor, 2004—; instr. Montgomery County Intermediate Unit, Norristown, Pa., 2001—05; summer inst. facilitator Lehigh Valley Writing Project, Fogelsville, Pa., 2006—. Sunday sch. tchr. Millcreek Luth. Ch., Newmanstown, Pa., 1990—95; pres. Front Royal (Va.) Children's Ctr., 1980—82. Recipient Unsung Hero award, Caron Found., 2003. Fellow: Nat. Writing Project; mem.: AAUW, NEA. Avocations: writing, photography, gardening. Home: 2016 Jay St Lebanon PA 17046

KOPIELSKI, CAMILLE ANN, counseling administrator, volunteer; b. Chgo., Dec. 25; d. John Louis and Martha Ann Filar; m. Stanley Bernard Kopielski, May 14, 1966 (dec.). BA in History, Polit. Sci., St. Mary of the Woods, Ind., 1959; MA in History, Govt., Boston U., 1961. Cert. counseling and guidance Northeastern Ill. Nat. Bd. Cert. Counselors Assn., Chgo. Counselor, tchr. Carl Schurz HS, Chgo., 1960—93. Sec. Secondary Sch. Counselors Assn., Chgo., 1980—97; chmn. North Ctrl. Accrediting Assoc. Sch. Cmty. Team, Chgo., 1986—93; Eucharistic minister coord. Our Lady of Wayside, Arlington Heights, 1989—; trustee Holy Trinity High Sch., Chgo., 1998—; bd. mem. Gordon Tech. H.S. Judge nat. spelling bee Polish Nat. Alliance, 1994—; v.p. ill. divsn. Polish Am. Congress, 1985—2004, 2006—, nat. dir., 1990—2004, 2006, bd. mem., Am. Coun. Polish Culture, 2004—; page Nat. Polit. Conv., Ill., 1952—56; chair Chgo. Intercollegiate Coun., Scholarship, 1960—; treas. Polish Mus. Am., Chgo., 1989—; dir. Copernicus Found., Chgo., 1998—2000, Legion Young Polish Women, Chgo., 1999—2000; pres. Coalition Polish Am. Women, Polit. Advancement, Chgo., 1998—2000; bd. mem. Lira Ensemble, Chgo., 2002—, Bishop Abramowicz Sem., Chgo., 2003—; adv. council Polish Nat. Alliance Dist. 12,13, Chgo., 1999—; adv. State Congl. Ethic Cmty., Chgo., 2001—; audit mem. PNA Women's Div. Dist. 13, Chgo., 1998—, PNA Welfare Assoc, Chgo., 2000—; audit com. Polish Constn. Day Parade, Chgo., 2001—; pres. Polish Women's Civic Club, 1994—98, 2002—; bd. mem. Polish Am. Leadership Assn.; treas. Coun. 91 PNA, 1991—; nat. dir. Polish Am. Congress, Chgo., 2006—; bd. mem. Pope John Paul II Jubilee, Chgo., 2003; judge nat. spelling bee Polish Women's Alliance, 2000; mem. White House Conf. Drugs Edn., Chgo., 1995. Mem.: Am. Assn. Friends Kosciuszco, Windows Wayside, Coun. Educator Polonia, Ill. Congress Parent Tchrs. (life), Polish Falcons, Polish Roman Catholic Union Am., Polish Women's Alliance, Polish Nat. Alliance (vice chmn. conv. 1994, judge 1998—2003, pres. Love of Fatherland Soc. 2001—), St. Mary of the Woods Coll. Chgo. Club (bd. mem. 1997—), Order Malta (dame). Roman Catholic. Achievements include development of 1st Polish Bilingual program, Carl Schurz HS, 1975; Polish Am. Heritage Month, 1985-2002; coordinating Youth career conference, U. Ill., 1998; founder Polish Honor Soc., 2001. Home: 1015 Cypress Dr Arlington Heights IL 60005

KOPLOVITZ, KAY, television network executive; b. Milw., Apr. 11, 1945; d. William E. and Jane T. Smith; m. William C. Koplovitz Jr., Apr. 17, 1971. BS, U. Wis., 1967; MA in Comms., Mich. State U., 1968. Radio and TV producer, dir. Sta. WTMJ-TV, Milw., 1967; editor Comm. Satellite Corp., Washington, 1968-72; dir. cmty. svc. UA Columbia Cablevision, Oakland, NJ, 1973-75; v.p., exec. dir. UA Columbia Satellite Services Inc., Oakland, NJ, 1977-80; founder, chmn., CEO USA Networks and Sci-Fi Channel, NYC, 1977—98; CEO Koplovitz & Co., NYC, 1998—; chmn. bd Reality Central, 2003—. Founder Springboard 2000; bd. dirs. Springboard Enterprises, Liz Claiborne Inc., 1992—, non-exec. chmn., 2007—; bd. dirs. Instinet. Mem. bd. overseers NYU Grad. Sch. Bus., 1984-90; bd. dir. Nat. Jr. Achievement, 1986-1996. Named to Entrepreneur oHall of Fame, Babson Coll., 2001, Cable Hall of Fame, 2001, Broadcasting Mag. Hall of Fame, 1992; recipient Outstanding Alumnus award, Mich. State U. Grad. Sch. Bus., 1985, Outstanding Corp. Social Responsibility, CUNY, 1986, Women Who Run the World award, Sara Lee Corp., 1987, Muse award, N.Y. Women in Film and TV, 1992, Ellis Island medal of honor, 1993, Crystal award, Women in Film, 1993. Mem.: Com. of 200, Nat. Acad. Cable Programming (bd. dirs. 1984—87), Cable Advt. Bur. (bd. dirs., exec. com., treas. 1981—87, Chmn.'s award for leadership 1987), Women in Cable (founding bd. dirs., membership chmn. 1979—80, v.p. 1981—82, pres. 1982—83), Nat. Acad. TV Arts and Scis. (chmn. 1994—97, bd. dirs. 1984—93), Internat. Coun., Advt. Coun. Inc. (chmn. 1992—93, bd. dirs. 1985—94), Nat. Cable TV Assn. (bd. dirs. 1984—98), N.Y.C. Partnership (bd. dirs. 1987—), Womens Forum. Avocations: tennis, skiing, travel. Office: Koplovitz & Co 30 Rockefeller Ctr 27th Fl New York NY 10112 E-mail: kay@koplovitz.com.*

KOPLOW, ELLEN, lawyer, brokerage house executive; BA, Univ. Md.; JD cum laude, Univ. Balt. Mng. principal Miles & Stockbridge, Columbia, Md.; dep. gen. counsel Ameritrade Holding Corp., Omaha, 1999—2000, acting gen. counsel, 2000—01, exec. v.p. & gen. counsel, 2001—. Office: Ameritrade Holding Corp PO Box 2760 Omaha NE 68103-2760 Office Phone: 402-331-2744. Office Fax: 402-597-7789. Business E-Mail: ekoplow@ameritrade.com.

KOPP, CAROL ANN, special education educator; b. Willmar, Minn., Dec. 23, 1952; d. Herman Joseph and Mildred Mercele (Taylor) Hoehl; m. Daniel Ralph Kopp, July 31, 1976; children: Brian James, Jason Daniel. BA in Spl. and Elem. Edn., U. Wis., Eau Claire, 1975; learning disabilities cert., U. Wis., Whitewater, 1990, M of Spl. Edn., 1994. Cert. vocat., tchr. secondary, learning disabilities and mentally retarded, elem. tchr. mentally retarded, Wis., Spl. Population Wis. Tech. Coll., 2000. Tchr. Grant Elem. Sch., Marshfield, Wis., 1975-79; tchr. learning disabilities and mentally retarded Southwestern High Sch., Hazel Green, Wis., 1979-86, tchr. learning disabilities, 1986-91; transition coord., instr. spl. needs S.W. Tech. Coll. Wis., Fennimore, 1991—2000; assoc. dean gen. studies S.W. Wis. Tech. Coll., Fennimore, 2000—. Group home relief parent Wis. Group Home Inc., Marshfield, 1978-79; forensics coach Southwestern Community Schs., 1980-83; tchr. multi-handicapped Southwestern Elem. Sch., summer 1980; Job Tng. Partnership Act coord. Coop. Edn. Svc. Agy. 3, Fennimore, 1983-84; com. mem. Southwestern Alcohol & Other Drugs Adv. Bd., 1988-91; mem. Dodgeville (Wis.) Transition Adv. Bd., 1992—; sec. Insvc. Coun., Hazel Green, 1983-85. Pres. Calico Farm Presch. Parent Team, Hazel Green; dir. Marshfield Spl. Olympics, 1976-79; mem. Iowa County Transition Agy. Team, 1993—, Crawford County Transition Agy. team, 1993—; mem. student effectiveness com. Southwest Tech. Coll., 1992—,, chair, 1999—, sec., 1993—, Crawford County Steering Com., 2000-, Southwest Wis. Cmty. Action Program, 2001- Recipient Outstanding Contbn. to Sports award Marshfield Athletic Club, 1978. Mem. Coun. for Exceptional Children, Assn. on Higher Edn. and Disability, Wis. Fedn. Tchrs. (sec.-treas. Hazel Green 1983-84), Assn. Career & Tech. Edn., Commn. Adult Basic Edn., Wis. Literacy. Home: PO Box 413 Hazel Green WI 53811-0413 Office: SW Wis Tech Coll 1800 Bronson Blvd Fennimore WI 53809-9778 E-mail: ckopp@swtc.edu.

KOPP, NANCY KORNBLITH, state official; b. Coral Gables, Fla., Dec. 7, 1943; d. Lester and Barbara M. (Levy) Kornblith; m. Robert E. Kopp, May 3, 1969; children: Emily, Robert E. III. BA with honors, Wellesley Coll., 1965; MA, U. Chgo., 1968; LittD (hon.), Hood Coll., 1988; LHD (hon.), Towson U., 2001; JD (hon.), U. Md., Balt., 2001. Instr. polit. sci. U. Ill., 1968-69; staff spl. subcom. on edn. U.S. Ho. of Reps., Washington, 1970-71; legis. staff Md. Gen. Assembly, Annapolis, 1971-74; mem. Md. Ho. of Dels., 1974—2002, spkr. pro tem, 1991-93, chmn. appropriations subcom on edn. and devel., chmn. spending affordability joint com.; state treas. State of Md., Annapolis, 2002—. Chmn. Md. Coll. Savings Plans. Mem. State Retirement and Pension Bd.; vice chmn. Capital Debt Affordability Com., chmn.; mem. Nat. Assessment Governing Bd., Md. Supplemental Retirement Bd., Md. Higher Edn. Investment Bd. Mem.: N.E. State Treas. Assn. (chmn. capital debt affordability com., vice chmn. state ret. and pension bd.). Democrat. Jewish. Office: Treasury Building 80 Calvert St Annapolis MD 21401 Office Phone: 410-260-7160. E-mail: nkopp@treasurer.state.md.us.

KOPP, WENDY, educational association administrator; b. Austin, Tex., June 29, 1967; m. Richard Barth; 3 children. BA, Princeton U., 1998, degree (hon.), 2000, Conn. Coll., 1995, Drew U., 1995, Smith Coll., 2001, Pace U., 2004, Mercy Coll., 2004. Founder, pres. Teach For America, NYC, 1989—. Mem. Pres. Coun. on Svc. and Civic Participation, 2003—; adv. bd. mem. Ctr. Pub. Leadership, Kennedy Sch. Govt., Harvard U., 2003—, Nat. Coun. on Tchr. Quality; bd. dirs. New Tchr. Project, Learning Project, Kipp Acad. Author: One Day, All Children: The Unlikely Triumph of Teach For America and What I Learned Along the Way, 2001. Named Woman of Yr., Glamour mag., 1990; named to Time Mag. Roster of Am. Most Promising Leaders Under 40, 1994; recipient Jefferson Award for Pub. Svcs., 1991, Kilby Young Innovator award, 1991, Woodrow Wilson award, 1993, Aetna's Voice of Conscience award, 1994, Citizen Activist award, Gleitsman Found., 1994, Children's Champion Award, Child mag., 2003, Clinton Ctr. Award for Leadership and Nat. Svc., 2003, Outstanding Social Entrepreneur Award, Schwab Found., 2003; Nat. Acad. fellow, 1990. Office: Teach For America 315 W 36th St 7th Fl New York NY 10018-6404 Office Phone: 212-279-2080. Office Fax: 212-279-2081.*

KOPPEL, AUDREY FEILER, electrologist, educator; b. NYC, Sept. 25, 1944; d. Jules Eugene and Lee (Gibel) Feiler; m. Mark Alyn Koppel, May 28, 1967; children: Jason, Seth. BA, Bklyn. Coll., 1972; diploma in electrolysis, Hoffman Inst., 1975; post grad., Kree Inst., 1980, George Washington U., 1984, Essex C. C., 1984. Lic. esthetician cosmetologist, cert. corrective cosmetics paramedical tng. program Dermablend Corp. for Corrective Cosmetics, advanced aesthetics paramedical skin care and camouflage application, paramedical skin care Dermablend Corp. for Corrective Cosmetics, lic. realtor N.J., nat. bd. cert. electrolysis 1985, lic. electrolysis N.J., 205. Electrologist, Bklyn., 1976, Glemby Internat., N.Y.C., 1976—78, Island Electrolysis, Manhasset, NY, 1982—84; registrar, supr. instr. Kree Inst., N.Y.C., 1978—82; pres. North Shore Electrolysis, Manhasset, 1982—84; dir., electrologist Bklyn. Studio, 1982—; pres. Ray Internat., 1986—. Editor, author: pamphlet Glossary for Electrolysis, 1985; contbr. articles to profl. jours. Active Boy Scouts Am., 1977—84; chmn. hosp. and med. coms. Share, 1993—94. Mem.: Aesthetics Internat. Assn., Soc. Clin. and Med. Electrologists, Internat. Guild of Electrologists (Merit award 1978), N.Y. Electrolysis Assn. (corr. sec. 1983—85, pres. 1985—90, bd. trustee 1990—94, advisor 1990—94), Nat. Esthetic Rehab. Assn., Am. Electrology Assn. (v.p. 1984—, continuing edn. coord. 1985, chmn. pub. rels. com. 1989—), U.S. Power Squadron (flag lt.), Bklyn. Yacht Club (v.p. ladies aux. 1989—90, pres. 1990—94). Democrat. Jewish. Avocations: boating, swimming, music. Office: Bklyn Studio of Electrolysis 2376 E 16th St Ste 1 Brooklyn NY 11229-4471 also: Modern Touch Hair Salon 161 Lincoln Ave Elberon NJ 07740 also: Jeff Klein Realty 208 Monmouth Rd Oakhurst NJ 07755 Mailing: 83 Peasley Dr Marlboro NJ 07746 Office Phone: 732-996-3586. Personal E-mail: audreyk@optonline.net, audrey@koppel.net, ridhair@koppel.net.

KOPPELMAN, DOROTHY MYERS, artist, consultant; b. NYC, June 13, 1920; d. Harry Walter and May (Chalmers) Myers; m. Chaim Koppelman, Feb. 13, 1943; 1 child, Ann. Student, Bklyn. Coll., 1938-42, Am. Artists Sch., 1940-42, Art Students League, 1942; student of Aesthetic Realism, with Eli Siegel, 1942-78, with Ellen Reiss, 1978—. Instr. art Bklyn. Coll., 1952-75; dir. Terrain Gallery, N.Y.C., 1955-83, Visual Arts Gallery., Sch. Visual Arts, 1961-62; pres. Aesthetic Realism Found., 1973-85, cons., 1973—. Instr. Nat. Acad. Sch. of Design, 1988—89, 1996, 98. One-woman shows include Terrain Gallery, 1961, Rina Gallery, Jersey City, 1961, Atlantic Gallery, 1999; exhibited in group shows at Mus. Modern Art, N.Y.C., 1962, Balt. Mus., 1962, Bklyn. Mus., 1962, N.J. State Mus., Jersey City, 1959, San Francisco Art Inst., 1961-62, 65, Butler Art Inst., Youngstown, Ohio, 1965, 1966, Nat. Acad. of Design Juried Ann., 1986, 90, 2000, Swiss Inst., N.Y.C., Susan Teller Gallery, N.Y.C., 1993, 95, Drawing Ctr., N.Y.C., Audubon Soc. ann., N.Y.C., 1995-96, 98, Chuck Levitan Gallery, N.Y.C., 1996, Puffin Room, 1996, Washington Square East Gallery, N.Y.C., 1992, 96, Am. Soc. Contemporary Artists Anns., 1994-96, 97, 98, 99, 2000, 01, 02, 03, 04, Atlantic Gallery, 1998-2005, Beatrice Conde Gallery, 2000, Terrain Gallery, 2001, 02, 03,04, 05, Sarah Lawrence Gallery, 2001, Denise Bibro Gallery, 2001, Whitney Mus. Am. Art, 2006, Peace Tower Whitney Biennial, 2006; represented in permanent collections Hampton U., Nat. Mus. Women in the Arts, Mus. Jewish Family, Durham, N.C., Savannah Coll. Art and Design, Washington County Mus. Art, Md., Libr. Congress, Washington, N.Y. Hist. Soc.; author Poems and Prints, 2000; co-author: Aesthetic Realism: We Have Been There - Six Artists, 1969; illustrator Children's Guide to Parents (by Eli Siegel), 1971, 2d edit., 2003. Recipient Theresa Lindner award for painting ASCA, 1996, Clara Shainness award for painting, 1999; Tiffany grantee for painting, 1965. Home: 498 Broome St New York NY 10013-2213 Office: Aesthetic Realism Found Inc 141 Greene St New York NY 10012-3201 Personal E-mail: pierodella@aol.com.

KOPPERUD, MARILYN SUE, music educator; b. Windom, Minn., Aug. 6, 1948; d. William Vaupel and Doris Niffenegger; children: Bryce, Joel. MusB in Edn., Morningside Coll., 1970; cert. in Orff-Schulwerk, U. Denver, 1982; MusM in Edn., U. No. Colo., 1991. Lic. tchr. Colo. Tchr. music Storden-Jeffers (Minn.) Schs., 1972—74, Fulda (Minn.) Pub. Schs., 1974—82, Adams Sch. Dist., Northglenn, Colo., 1982—. Asst. prof. music U. No. Colo., Greeley, Colo., 1990—91; organist Northglenn (Colo.) Meth. Ch., 1988—91; dir. music, organist United Ch. Christ, Denver, 1992—98, St. John Luth. Ch., Thornton, 1998—2003, Messiah Luth. Ch., Denver, 2003—; freelance pianist, accompanist, Denver, 1988—. Vol. Habitat for Humanity, Denver, 1994. Mem.: NEA, Am. Guild Organists, Am. Choral Dirs. Assn., Phi Kappa Lambda. Democrat. Avocations: hiking, bicycling, reading, travel, shopping. Home: 11284 Decatar Cir Westminster CO 80234 E-mail: mskopperud@msn.com.

KOPPMAN, MAE Z., writer, educator; b. N.Y.C., June 22, 1922; d. Henry and Anna (Marks) Zuckerman; m. Lion Koppman, Dec. 5, 1948; children: Steve, Debbie. BS in Ednl. Psychology, NYU, 1944; MA in Humanities, Hunter Coll., NYC, 1972. Tchr. Bd. Edn., N.Y.C., 1969—84; freelance writer, 1982—; assoc. editor Jewish Digest, Houston, 1958—61. Mem. staff Sloan Kettering Cancer Ctr., 1991—2004. Contbr. articles to profl. jours., poems to anthologies. Mem.: Nat. Assn. for Poetry Therapy, Acad. Am. Poets (assoc.). Home: 4025 Pulitzer Pl #104 San Diego CA 92122 Personal E-mail: writemae@yahoo.com.

KOPROWSKA, IRENA, cytologist, medical researcher; b. Warsaw, May 12, 1917; came to U.S., 1944; d. Henryk and Eugenia Grasberg; m. Hilary Koprowski, July 14, 1938; children: Claude, Christopher. BA, Popielewska/Roszkowska, Warsaw, 1934; MD, Warsaw U., 1939. Cert. Am. Bd. Pathology, Internat. Bd. Cytology. Intern in medicine Villejuif Lunatic Asylum, Seine, France, 1940; asst. pathologist Rio de Janeiro City Hosp., Miguel Couto, Brazil, 1942-44; rsch. fellow dept. pathology Cornell U. Med. Coll., N.Y.C., 1945-46, rsch. asst. dept. pharmacology, 1949-50, rsch. fellow dept. of anatomy, 1949-54; rsch. fellow applied immunology Pub. Health Rsch. Inst. of The City of N.Y., 1946-47; asst. pathologist N.Y. Infirmary for Women and Children, N.Y.C., 1947-49; asst. prof. dept. pathology SUNY Downstate Med. Ctr., Bklyn., 1954-57; assoc. prof. pathology, dir. cytology lab./Sch. Cytotech. Hahnemann Med. Coll., Phila., 1957-64, prof. pathology dir. cytology lab., sch. cytotechnology, 1964-70; prof. pathology, dir. cytology lab. Temple U. Sch. Med., Phila., 1970-87, prof. emerita, 1987—. Cons. WHO, Switzerland, Egypt, Iran, Latin Am., India, 1960-85, Armed Forces Inst. Pathology, Air Force Cytology Rescreen Project, 1979-80. Author: Woman Wanders Through Life and Science, 1997; contbr. articles on cancer rsch. to profl. and sci. jours. Named Woman Physician of Yr., Polish Am. Med. Assn., 1977; grantee USPHS-Nat. Cancer Insts., 1954-75, rsch. grantee Bender Co., Vienna, Austria, 1983-89. Fellow Am. Soc. Clin. Pathologists (emeritus), Coll. Am. Pathologists (emeritus), Coll. Physicians of Phila., Internat. Acad. Cytology (hon.), Internat. Acad. Pathology (emeritus); mem. Am. Assn. for Cancer Rsch. Inc. (emeritus), Am. Assn. Pathologists Inc. (emeritus), Am. Med. Women's Assn., Am. Soc. Cytology (life, Papanicolaou award 1985), Am. Soc. Exptl. Pathology, Argentinian Soc. Cytology (hon.), Path. Soc. Phila. Avocations: reading, writing. Home: 334 Fairhill Rd Wynnewood PA 19096-1804

KOPROWSKI, SUZANNE MARIE, educational diagnostician administrator, educator; b. Milw., 1953; BS, U. Wis., 1975; MA, Cardinal Stritch Coll., 1982. Tchr. St. Francis Children Ctr, Milw., sch. prin.; tchr. Waukesh Sch. Dist., Wis., ednl. Diagnostician. Instr. Waukesha County Tech. Coll; cons. Paraeducator Cons., Mukwonago, Wis. Author: (books) Portfolio Development for Paraedicators, 2006. Steering com. Partnership for Youth Asset Bldg., Mukwonago, Wis., 2003—. Mem.: Internat. Reading Assn., Wis. Divsn. of Learning Disabilities, Coun. Exceptional Children. Avocation: writing. Home: 596 W 32571 Valley Ct Mukwonago WI 53149

KORAL, MARIAN, writer; b. Washington, Pa., Jan. 31, 1954; d. Charles Oscar and Grace Regina (Cook) Skoog; m. Enis Osman Koral, Sept. 8, 1990. BA, U. Pitts, 1975. Pub. rels. asst. City of Pitts., 1975-76; English tchr. Centro-Colombo Am., Bogota, Colombia, 1977-78, Point Park Coll., Pitts., 1978, Berlitz, Pitts., 1979-82; adminstrv. asst. U. Pitts., 1982-86, dir. alumni comms., 1997—; writer U. Pitts. Med. Ctr., 1986-97. Mem. Coun. for the Advancement and Support of Edn. Avocations: travel, photography, history. Office Phone: 412-624-8229.

KORB, CHRISTINE ANN, music therapist, researcher, educator; b. Milw., Aug. 9, 1943; d. Carl William and Lucille (Bell) Knoernschild; m. Mark Lee Korb, June 3, 1967 (div. May 1991); children: Tracy Lee, Amy Elizabeth. BS, Mt. Mary Coll., Milw., 1965; MMus in Music Therapy, Colo. State U., Ft. Collins, 1988. Registered and bd. cert. music therapist. Field dir. Girl Scouts of Am., Ill, Wis., 1965-69; contractual swimming tchr. YMCA, Janesville, Wis., 1970-76; contractual music tchr. YWCA, Janesville, Wis., 1971-76; music therapist inpatient/outpatient psychiat. unit Poudre Valley Hosp., Ft. Collins, 1989-92; music therapist Mary Hill Retirement Ctr., Milw., 1992-93, VA Med. Ctr., Milw., 1992-98; vis. asst. prof. music therapy Willamette U., Salem, Oreg., 1998—2000; dir of music therapy Marylhurst Univ., Oreg., 2000—. Composer (musical works) Namasté, 1988 (Art of Peace award 1985), We Are Your People of Love, 1981 (hon. mention Am. Song Festival 1981), Windseeker, 1988, Merry Christmas Day, 1994. Founding mem. Women in the Arts, Ft. Collins, 1987-88. Rsch. for music therapy grantee Helen Bader Found., Milw., 1994-95. Mem. AAUW, Am. Music Therapy Assn., Music Tchrs. Nat. Assn., Amnesty Internat., Mu Phi Epsilon. Democrat. Avocations: reading, spirituality, hiking, cross country skiing, canoeing. Home: 13538 SW 63rd Pl Portland OR 97219-8122 Office Phone: 503-636-8141. Business E-Mail: ckorb@marylhurst.edu.

KORB, ELIZABETH GRACE, nurse midwife; b. Wilmington, N.C., Mar. 1, 1951; d. Carl Wilhelm Bissenger Korb and Betty Jane Stroup; m. Joel Vincent LeFebvre, May 19, 1973 (div. June 1976); m. James Clinton Queen, June 22, 1984; 1 child, James Michael Andrew Queen. BSN, U. N.C., Greensboro, 1973; MSN, U. Utah, 1980. Cert. nurse midwife. Staff nurse, instr. New Hanover Meml. Hosp., Wilmington, N.C., 1973-76; staff nurse Meml. Mission Hosp., Asheville, N.C., 1976-78, LDS Hosp., Salt Lake City, 1978-79; practising nurse midwife Dr. Michael Watson, Bamberg, S.C., 1980, Fletcher (N.C.) Ob-Gyn. Assocs., 1981-83, Nurse-Midwifery Assocs., Fletcher, 1983-85, Asheville (N.C.) Women's Med. Ctr., 1985-86, 88; practising nurse midwife, clin. coord. Regional Perinatal Assocs., Asheville, 1986-88; perinatal clin. coord., practicing nurse midwife Mountain Area Health Edn. Ctr., Asheville, 1988—, sr. nurse-midwife, 2002—. Clin. preceptor Cmty.-Based Nurse-Midwifery Edn. Program, 1993—, East Carolina U. Nurse-Midwifery Edn. Program, 1993; mem. mgmt. team Mountain Area Perinatal Substance Abuse Program, 1993—2003; bd. dirs. Mary Benson House, Asheville; mem. adv. panel Emory U., Nurse Midwifery in Pub. Sector, Atlanta, 1988-2000; mem. strategic planning group for women's and children's svcs. Mission-St. Joseph's Health Sys., 1998—2000. Mem. birth defects task force WNC, 1998—. Named to Outstanding Young Women of Am., 1982; recipient Profl. award March of Dimes, Asheville, 1993. Mem. ANA, Nat. Perinatal Assn., N.C. Perinatal Assn. (bd. dirs. 1988-93), N.C. Nurses Assn., Am. Coll. Nurse Midwives (life, N.C. del. legis. conf. 1993, 94, nominating com. 1981-82, chpt. chair 2003—), Internat. Childbirth Edn. Assn., Am. Coll. Nurse Midwives, Mary Breckin Ridge Club (charter mem.), Phi Kappa phi, Sigma Theta Tau. Democrat. Lutheran. Avocations: exercise, swimming, fishing, sewing. Office: Mountain Area Health Edn Ctr Ob-Gyn Specialists 900 Hendersonville Rd Ste 206 Asheville NC 28803- Office Phone: 828-771-5500. E-mail: EGraceK@bellsouth.net.

KORB, JOAN, prosecutor; b. Fond du Lac, Wis., Jan. 22, 1953; d. Allen Dale Korb and Evelyn A. Schmitz-Korb; m. Frederic B. Will, June 19, 1983. BS in Biology, U. Wis., Oshkosh, 1975; JD, John Marshall Sch. Law, Chgo., 1985. Bar: Wis. 1985, Ill. 1985. Asst. corp. counsel Racine County, Racine, Wis., 1985-89, asst. dist. atty., 1990-99, Door County, Sturgeon Bay, Wis., 1999—. Commentator on fetal abuse on TV, radio, in newspapers. Author novels. Mem. Mt. Pleasant (Wis.) Zoning Bd. Appeals, 1987-99; past pres. Wis. Profl. Soc. on Abuse of Children, Milw.; treas. Bd. Children Law Sec. of State Bar of Wis., 1998-2003. Mem. NOW, AAUW (pub. policy chmn. Racine 1995-99), Sierra Club (life). Avocations: lectr. children and legal issues, reading, scuba diving, sailing, travel. Office: Door County Dist Atty's Office 421 Nebraska St Ofc Sturgeon Bay WI 54235-2249 Office Phone: 920-746-2284.

KORBEL, LINDA ANNE, language educator, educator; b. Chgo., Mar. 31, 1949; d. Joseph Edward and Jessie (Vercillo) Gentile; m. Albert J. Korbel, Apr. 28, 1973 (dec. 1997). BA, MA, Domincan U., 1971. Dean langs., humanaties and the arts Oakton CC, Des Plaines, Ill., 1971—, chmn. dept., 1985—. Exec. dir. Am. Coun. Internat. Intercultural Edn., 1993—; exec. chair Ill. Consortium for Internat. Studies and Programs, Normal, 1993-2000. Mem. Am. Coun. Teaching Fgn. Langs., Am. Assn. Tchrs. French, Ill. Coun. Teaching Fgn. Langs., Chgo. Coun. Fgn. Rels. Avocations: travel, reading, gastronomy. Office: Oakton C C 1600 E Golf Rd Des Plaines IL 60016-1234

KORBER, BETTE TINA MARIE, chemist; b. Long Beach, Calif., 1958; d. George Korber. BS in chemistry, Calif. State U., 1981; PhD in chemistry in the field of immunology, Calif. Inst. Tech., 1988. Postdoctoral fellow Los Alamos Nat. Lab., 1990, tech. staff scientist theoretical biology and biophysics (T10) group, 1993—. Elizabeth Glaser scientist Pediatric AIDS Found., 1997—2003; external faculty Santa Fe Inst., N.Mex. Nominee Rave award in Medicine, WIRED, 2005; recipient Los Alamos Nat. Achievement award, 1996, 2002, Elizabeth Glaser Scientist for the Pediatric AIDS Found., 1997—2003, Outstanding Alumnus award for Sch. Natural Scis., Calif. State U., Long Beach, 2001, Ernest Orlando Lawrence award, US Dept. Energy, 2004; fellow, Leukemia Soc., Harvard U., 1988—90, Dir. Funded Postdoctoral Fellow, Los Alamos Nat. Lab, 1990—92; grantee Los Alamos Nat. Lab. Fellow, 2002. Achievements include publishing over 100 sci. papers that have been cited over 3,700 times; conducting pioneering studies delineating the genetic characteristics of the virus population; developing the Los Alamos HIV database, a foundation for HIV research for scientific community; internationally recognized AIDS researcher. Office: Los Alamos Nat Lab MS K710 T 10 Theoretical Divsn Los Alamos NM 87545 Office Phone: 505-665-4453. Office Fax: 505-665-3493. Business E-Mail: btk@lanl.gov.

KORCHIN, JUDITH MIRIAM, lawyer; b. Kew Gardens, NY, Apr. 28, 1949; d. Arthur Walter and Mena (Levisohn) Goldstein; m. Paul Maury Korchin, June 10, 1972; 1 son, Brian Edward. BA with high honors, U. Fla., 1971, JD with honors, 1974. Bar: Fla. 1974, U.S. Ct. Appeal (2d, 5th and 11th cirs.), U.S. Dist. Ct. (so., mid. and no. dists) Fla. Law clk. to judge U.S. Dist. Ct., 1974-76; assoc. Steel, Hector & Davis, Miami, Fla., 1976-81, ptnr., 1981-87, Holland and Knight, Miami, 1987—. Author, exec. editor U. Fla. Law Rev., 1973—74; contbr. chapters to books, articles to profl. jours. Mem. U. Fla. Law Ctr. Coun., 1980-83; pres. alumni bd. U. Fla. Law Rev., 1983; bd. dirs. Fla. Film & Rec. Inst., 1982-84. Named Best of the Bar, So. Fla. Bus. Jour., 2004, 2005, 2006; named one of Fla. Trend's Legal Elite, 2004, 2005, 2006, Fla. Super Lawyers, 2006, Best Lawyers in Am., 2006; recipient Trail Blazer award, The Women's Com. of 100, 1988. Fellow: Fla. Bar Found. (subcom. legal assistance for poor 1988—90), Am. Bar Found.; mem.: ABA (sect. alternative dispute resolution, vice chmn. 1994—95, co-chmn. fed. ct. mediation com. 1995, sect. labor and employment law, sect. litig.), Fla. Bar

Assn. (vice chmn. jud. nominating procedures com. 1982, civil procedure rules com. 1984—89, 1993—95), Nat. Assn. Bank Women (TV panelist greater Miami chpt. 1987), Nat. Assn. Women Bus. Owners (adv. coun. 1987—88), Dade County Bar Assn. (bd. dirs. 1981—82, treas. 1982, sec. 1983, 3d v.p. 1984, 2d v.p. 1985, 1st v.p. 1986, pres. 1987), CPR Inst. Dispute Resolution (nat. panelist 1994—, exec. com. 2003—), Am. Arbitration Assn. (employment law panel, s.e. complex litig. panel 1993—, comml. law panel 1993—), Greater Miami C. of C. (com. profl. devel. 1988—90), Rabbinical Assn. Greater Miami (TV panelist Still Small Voice 1987), City Club (bd. dirs. 1988—93), Phi Kappa Phi, Phi Beta Kappa, Order of Coif. Office: Holland & Knight PO Box 015441 701 Brickell Ave Ste 3000 Miami FL 33131-2898 Office Phone: 305-789-7764. Business E-Mail: judith.korchin@hklaw.com.

KORDALEWSKI, LYDIA MARIA, news correspondent, municipal employee; b. Detroit, Oct. 19, 1956; d. Zygmunt and Maria Kordalewski. AA, East Los Angeles Coll., 1979. Police svc. rep. L.A. Police Dept., 1979—88; actress, casting asst. Miami, Fla., 1988—99; news corr. Polish News, Polish Am. Jour., various others, 1999—; mcpl. asst. enforcement, dir. park and recreation Bal Harbour City Hall, Fla., 2001—. Media spokesperson Haitian-Am. Law Enforcement Officers Assn., Fla., 2001—. Mem. Hall of Fame Selection Com., North Miami, Fla., 1999—; advocate mem. Fla. Local Advocacy Coun., 1999—; assoc. councillor Atlantic Coun. of U.S., Washington, 1999—; sec. Polish Am. Congress, Fla., 1999—; chair audience devel. com. Mus. Contemporary Art, 1999—; organizer, founder internat. NATO European Balls, 1999—2001; candidate for city coun. City of North Miami, 2001. Named Woman of Yr., Polish Am. Congress, Fla., 2001; recipient cert. of achievement, White Ho. Comm. Agy., Miami, 1994, cert. award, Eckerd's Salute to Women, Miami, 2000. Mem.: Am. Inst. Polish Culture, Polish-Am. Club (dir. pub. rels. 1999—). Democrat. Roman Catholic. Avocations: travel, photography, volunteering, languages. Home: 11550 NE 22nd Dr North Miami FL 33181

KORDINAK, IRMA L., piano educator, musician; b. Buffalo, Feb. 27, 1930; d. Paul Eugene Kompalla and Pauline Beuter; m. Albert Andrew Kordinak, July 18, 1964. BM, Oberlin Coll. Conservatory Music, Ohio, 1953; postgrad, Eastman Sch. Music, Rochester, N.Y., 1962. Nat. cert. tchr. music Music Tchrs. Nat. Assn. Pianist, singer Hormel All-Girl Orch., 1953—54; piano faculty Cmty. Music Sch., Buffalo, 1954-64; piano tchr. pvt. practice, 1954—. Pres. Music Forum for Piano Tchrs. of Western N.Y., 1970—72, social chmn., 2002—04; hon. mem. Music Forum for Piano Tchr. of Western N.Y., 2003; pres. dist. 8 N.Y. Fedn. Music Clubs, 1970—76; pres.-elect Amherst Symphony Orch. (Women's Com.), NY, 1999—2000, co-chair scholarship com., 2000—03; chmn. dist. 10 N.Y. State Music Tchrs. Assn., Buffalo, 1987—2006; bd. dirs. QRS Arts Found., Buffalo, 1991—98. Mem.: Music Tchrs. Nat. Assn., Am. Liszt Soc., Friends of Vienna in Buffalo, Opera Buffs of Western N.Y., Chromatic Club (hon.; life, past. pres. 1967—68). Avocations: photography, theater, concerts. Home and Office: Buffalo-Niagara Frontier MTA 265 Countryside Ln Buffalo NY 14221-1523

KOREMAN, DOROTHY GOLDSTEIN, physician, dermatologist; b. Bklyn., Nov. 1, 1940; d. Benjamin and Ida (Krenick) Goldstein; m. Neil M. Koreman, Aug. 16, 1964; children: Elizabeth Koreman Landau, Robert Stephen. BA, Bklyn. Coll., 1961; MD, SUNY, Bklyn., 1965. Diplomate Am. Bd. Dermatology. Intern pediatrics Kings County Hosp. Ctr., Bklyn., 1965-66; resident dept. dermatology Wayne State U. Sch. Medicine, Detroit, 1966-69; clin. instr. dermatology Sch. Medicine Wayne State U., Detroit, 1969-71; asst. clin. prof. dermatology U. Miami, 1971-75, assoc. clin. prof. dermatology, 1975-82, clin. prof. dermatology and cutaneous surgery, 1982—. Mem. Miami Dermatol. Soc. (pres. 1978-79). Avocations: travel, cooking, reading, skiing, needlepoint. E-mail: skinkor40@aol.com.

KORENIC, LYNETTE MARIE, librarian; b. Berwyn, Ill., Mar. 29, 1950; d. Emil Walter and Donna Marie (Harbutt) K. m. Jerome Dennis Reif, Dec. 31, 1988. BS in Art, U. Wis., 1977, MFA, 1979, MA in LS, 1981, MA in Art History, 1984; PhD in Art History, U. Claif., Santa Barbara, 2006. Asst. art libr. Ind. U., Bloomington, 1982-84; art libr. U. Calif., Santa Barbara, 1984-88, head Arts Libr., 1988-99; art libr. U. Wis., Madison, 1999—. Author articles. Mem. Art Librs. Soc. N.Am. (sec. 1983-84, v.p. 1989, pres. 1990), Beta Phi Mu. Office Phone: 608-263-2256. E-mail: lkorenic@library.wisc.edu.

KORFF, PHYLLIS G., lawyer; b. NYC, 1943; BA, Bklyn. Coll., 1964; EdM, Boston U., 1967; JD, NYU, 1981. Bar: NY 1982. Ptnr. Skaden, Arps, Slate, Meagher & Flom LLP, NYC, 1990—. Office: Skadden Arps Slate Meagher & Flom LLP 4 Times Sq New York NY 10036 Office Phone: 212-735-2694. Office Fax: 212-777-2694. E-mail: pkorff@skadden.com.

KORMAN, BARBARA, sculptor; b. NYC, Apr. 8, 1938; d. David and Rose (Katz) K. BFA cum laude, N.Y. State Coll. Ceramics, 1959, MFA, 1960. Sculptor Barbara Korman Design Studio, N.Y.C., 1960—. Educator sculpture and design N.Y.C. Bd. Edn., 1961-91; photographer, prodr. audio-visual ednl. packages, N.Y.C., 1973-89; designer, producer wearable sculpture, 1992—. One-woman shows include Overseas Press Club, N.Y.C., 1988, Tiffany & Co. Windows, 1992, U.S. Mil. Acad., West Point, N.Y., 1996, Westchester C.C., Valhalla, N.Y., 2003, Krause Gallery, Providence, 2003, Piero Gallery, South Orange, N.J., 2004, Gallery Yellow, Cross River, N.Y., 2006, exhibited in group shows at Met. Mus. Art, N.Y.C., 1976, Nat. Arts Club, 1976, Hudson River Mus., Yonkers, N.Y., 1978, Queens Mus., Flushing, N.Y., 1981, Heckscher Mus., Huntington, N.Y., 1996, Grounds for Sculpture, Hamilton, N.J., 2001, Yosemite Gallery, Yosemite Nat. Park, Calif., 2002, Hammond Mus., North Salem, N.Y., 2004, Arts Exch., Westchester Arts Coun., White Plains, N.Y., 2004, Katunah Mus., N.Y., 2006. Recipient Excaliber Foundry award for bronze casting, 1998, BRIO award for sculpture, 1997-98, Jeffrey Childs Willis Meml. prize for sculpture, 1984, Outstanding Art Educator award Sch. Art League, 1977, Internat. Woman's Yr. award for Outstanding Cultural Contbns., 1975, 76, House of Heydenryk prize for Sculpture, 1974, Yosemite Renaissance XVII award, 2002, Coun. Am. Artist Socs. award, 2002; materials grantee Formica Corp., 1985. Mem. Internat. Sculpture Ctr., Katonah Mus. Artist Assn. (bd. dirs., pres.), Bronx Coun. of Arts. Studio: 357 E 201st St Bronx NY 10458-2205 E-mail: kormanstudio@aol.com.

KORN, CAROL M., retired elementary school educator; b. Ellwood, Pa., Aug. 24, 1947; d. Harold Wesley and Mae S. Wise; m. James L. Korn, Dec. 30, 1971; children: Douglas J., David R. BA, Morehead State U., Ky., 1969; ME, Slippery Rock U., Pa., 1973. Tchr. elem. phys. edn. and health Seneca Valley Sch., Harmony, Pa., 1969—2005, ret., 2005. Adj. faculty Slippery Rock U. Coord. Sch. Health Leadership Inst. Recipient Program award, Am. Cancer Soc. Mem.: Nat. Assn. Sport and Physical Edn., Pa. State Assn. Health, Phys. Edn., Recreation and Dance (conv. mgr. 2006, creditials chair, locals assn., pres. Butler,Lawrence, Mercer county chpts., Profl. Hon. award 2001). Home: 114 Lawrence Ave Butler PA 16001

KORN, CLAIRE VEDENSKY, secondary school educator, writer; b. Berkeley, Calif., Aug. 12, 1933; d. Dmitri Nicholas and Helen Ingalls (Montmorency) Vedensky; m. Harold A. Korn, July 26, 1958 (dec. Feb. 1990); 1 child, Alexander David. Student, U. Calif., Berkeley, 1951; BA, Stanford U., 1955, PhD, 1969; MA, U. Minn., 1958. Instr. U. Minn. Sch. Medicine, Mpls., 1957-58; rsch. assoc. Dept. Psychology Stanford U., Calif., 1958-60; with Cons. Psychologists Assn., Palo Alto, Calif., 1959-69; guidance counselor Palo Alto Unified Sch. Dist., 1968-69; asst. prof. Fla. State U., Tallahassee, 1970-71; founder, dir. Natural Bridge Sch., Tallahassee, 1974-80; open sch. coord. Ann Arbor Pub. Schs., 1985-86; free-lance writer, 1984—. Co-author: Furee Sukuru: Sono Genjtan to Yume, 1984; Author: Michigan State Parks: Yesterday Through Tomorrow, 1989, Alternative American Schools, 1991, Flashes and Lies, 2002; contbr. articles to profl. jours. Mem. Detroit Women Writers (v.p. 1991—), Am. Psychol. Assn., Soc. Childrens Bookwriters. Home: 40 Arden Rd Berkeley CA 94704-1809

KORN, JESSICA SUSAN, research scientist, educator; b. L.A., Aug. 16, 1968; d. Lester B. and Carolbeth (Goldman) K. BA in Sociology, UCLA, 1990, MA in Edn., 1992, PhD in Philosophy, 1996. Actor Curb-Esquire Films, Burbank, Calif., 1984; exec. asst. Korn Capital Group, Inc., L.A., 1991; tchg. asst. Grad. Sch. Edn. and Info. Studies UCLA, 1995, rsch. analyst Grad. Sch. Edn. and Info. Studies, 1992—96, postdoctoral fellow Higher Edn. Rsch. Inst., 1996—97, tchg. assoc., 1997; rsch. scientist, affiliate asst. prof. U. Wash., 1997—99; v.p. instnl. rsch. Eckerd Coll., St. Petersburg, Fla., 1999—2005; rsch. scientist, assoc. dir. instnl. rsch. Loyola U. Chgo., 2005—. Internat. election observer Orgn. for Security and Cooperation in Europe, 1997, 98, 2000, 02. Contbr. articles to profl. jours. Jr. assoc. Big Sisters Am., L.A., 1994-98. Mem. AAUW, Am. Ednl. Rsch. Assn., Assn. Study of Higher Edn., Assn. for Instnl. Rsch., Nat. Coun. Rsch. on Women, Screen Actors Guild Am. Avocations: working with rape and other trauma survivors, humanitarian aid work, travel, yoga.

KORNAHRENS, CASEY, elementary school educator; b. Syossett, N.Y., Apr. 26, 1978; d. Howard and Dianne Kornahrens. BSc, Adelphi U., 2001, MA, 2006. Cert. phys. educator N.Y., 2001, health educator N.Y., 2006. Tchr. phys. edn. Farmingdale (N.Y.) Pub. Schs., 2002—04, PLainedge Unified Sch. Dist., Massepqua, NY, 2004—. Sports instr. Jewish Cmty. Ctr., Glen Cove, NY, 2001—. Vol. coach St. Peter of Alcantara, Port Washington, NY. Nominee Disney Tchr. of Yr., Walt Disney, 2006; recipient JB Nash award, N.Y. State, 2000, Nassau Zone award, Nassau County, 2000. Mem.: AAPE-HRED. Home: 15 West Woods Road Great Neck NY 11020 Personal E-mail: kck25@aol.com.

KORNASKY, LINDA A., literature educator; b. Southbridge, Mass., Apr. 2, 1964; d. Edward and Janet Kornasky; m. Mark Louis Hama, May 13, 1995. BA, U. RI, 1986, MA, 1988; PhD, Tulane U., New Orleans, 1994. Assoc. prof. Angelo State U., San Angelo, Tex., 1996—. Founding mem. San Angelo LWV, 2005—06; chair scholarship com. San Angelo Gifted and Talented Edn. Supporters, 2005—06; faculty advisor Angelo State University's chpt. Alpha Lambda Delta Nat. Freshman Honor Soc., San Angelo, 2000—06. Rsch. Enhancement grantee, Angelo State U., 2000. Mem.: Soc. for the Study Am. Women Writers. Avocations: bicycling, travel. Office Phone: 325-942-2273.

KORNBLAU, BARBARA L., physical therapist, educator; BS in Occupl. Therapy, U. Wis., Madison, 1977; JD, U. Miami Sch. Law, 1984. Admitted to practice: Fla., US Ct. Appeals, 11th cir., US Dist. Ct., So. Dist. Fla.; diplomate Am. Acad. Pain Mgmt., Am. Bd. Disability Analysts; lic. Occupl. Therapist Fla., Tex., rehab. svcs. provider/rehab. counselor, cert. disability mgmt. specialist, case mgr., disability analysis: sr. disability analyst. Occupl. therapist Kuakini Med. Ctr., Honolulu, 1978, Rock County Health Care Ctr., Janesville, Wis., 1978—79, Coop. Edn. Svc. Agy. #17, Janesville, Wis., 1979—80; contract occupl. therapist Prince George County Pub. Health Dept., Md., 1980; asst. to coord. disabled students affairs Cath. U., Washington, 1980; occupl. therapist South Miami Hosp., 1980—85; dir. clin. svcs., owner Innovative Therapeutics, 1985—87; assoc. dir. Occupl. Therapy Resource Svcs., Inc., 1985—87; chief occupl. therapy Bapt. Hosp. of Miami, Fla., 1986—87; atty. for various law firms in the areas of personal injury, asbestos litigation and workers' compensation, 1987—89; pres. ADA Cons., Inc., 1991—; pvt. practice law, 1985—; adj. prof. Fla. Internat. U., Sch. Health Sciences, 1986, adj. prof. occupl. therapy, 1992, vis. lectr. occupl. therapy, 1992—93; prof. occupl. therapy and pub. health Nova Southeastern U., Ft. Lauderdale, Fla., 1994—, adj. prof., Shepard Broad Law Ctr., 2003—. Cons. in field, 1982—; invited presenter in field. Contbr. numerous articles to profl. jours., chpts. to books, chapters to books; co-author (with Karen Jacobs): Principle and Practices of Work, 2001; co-author: (with Shirley Starling) Ethics in Rehabilitation, 2000; mem. editl. bd. Am. Jour. Pain Mgmt., Occupl. Therapy in health Care, Prevention Plus Newsletter, Advance for Occupl. Therapists, peer rev. panel mem. Jour. of Care Mgmt., guest appearances for TV, radio print & web-based media. Founder, former dir. Pro Bono Law Project for the Deaf; program participant Put Something Back; mem. attorney's divsn. ACLU; vol. Dade County Bar Assn. Vol. Lawyers Program; numerous other civic activities; mem. instnl. rev. bd. and ethics com. Deering Hosp.; past bd. dirs. Bus. Coalition for Americans with Disabilities; former edn. com. mem. Multiple Sclerosis Soc.; bd. dirs., chair S.E. br. Fla. chpt. Arthritis Found., 1998—2000, sec., 1999—2000, chpt. del. to nat. ho. of dels., 1999—2000, exec. bd. mem. Fla. chpt., 1999—2000; past steering com. ann. jud. reception Greater Miami Jewish Fedn.; former exec. bd. mem. Am. Occupl. Therapy Found.; former profl. adv. bd. mem. Asperger Syndrome Coalition of US; founding pres., chair bd. dirs. Friends of Occupl. Therapy, Inc.; immediate past-pres., chair bd. dirs. Fund for the Promotion of Awareness of Occupl. Therapy; former mem. bus. adv. coun., projects with industry Abilities, Inc. Named Young Achiever, Wis. State Jour., 1976, Disting. Lectr., Maine Tech. Coll. Sys., 1993, Outstanding Alumni, U. Wis.-Madison Sch. Edn., 1999; recipient Outstanding Sr. award, U. Wis., 1977, Presdl. Recognition Award for outstanding svc. to families and communities, Rotary Internat., 1995, 1996, Cmty. Advocate award, Deaf Services Bur., 1996, Vol. of the Yr. award, Arthritis Found. (Fla. Chpt.), 1998, Vanderkooi Lectureship, Tex. Women's U., 2003, Ellen Garms Lectureship, Wayne State U., 2004; fellow DeWitt Wallace fellow, NYU Inst. Rehab. Medicine, 1973; scholar Wis. State Legis. scholar, 1974—77, Henry B. Herman Meml. scholar, 1975; Robert Wood Johnson Health Policy Fellow, IOM, 2006. Fellow: Am. Occupl. Therapy Assn. (chair, work programs spl. interest sect. 1993—96, chair, commn. stds. and ethics comm. 1998—2000, immediate past pres., chair bd. dirs. 2001—04, pres.-elect, exec. bd. dirs., chair stds. and ethics commn., past chair work programs spl. interest sect., paper reviewer ann. conf., mem. adminstrn., edn., tech., & work programs spl. interest sect., former mem. governance taskforce, former mem. collaboration taskforce, former mem. representative assembly, Svc. award 1996, 2000, 2004); mem.: Internat. Assn. Rehabilitation Professionals, Am. Pub. Health Assn., Am. Soc. Pain Educators (mem. adv bd.), U. Wis. Alumni Assn. (former pres. and founding mem. S. Fla. chpt.), Fla. Bar Assn. (employment, workers' compensation and elder law sects., co-chair, com. on phys. and comm. access to the legal cmty.), Am. Soc. for Law, Medicine and Ethics, ABA (labor sect.), Nat. Assn. Rehab. Providers in the Pvt. Sector, Case Mgmt. Soc. Am., N.Am. Cervicogenic Headache Soc., Fla. Occupl. Therapy Assn. (legal cons., conf. planning com. mem., paper peer reviewer, legis. impact team capt., Svc. award 1994—97, Award of Excellence 1998), Autism Soc. Am., APHA, Am. Bd. Disability Analysts, Am. Acad. Pain Mgmt. (adv. bd. edn. com. mem., adv. bd.), U. Wis. Alumni Assn. (South Fla. chpt.) (former pres. & founding mem., organized ann. founder's day events, past alumni judge for homecoming floats in Madison), U. Miami Alumni Assn., U. Miami President's Club, South Miami Rotary Club (Paul Harris fellow, sec. and pres.-elect, numerous other com. positions), U. Miami Hurricane Club, Pi Theta Epsilon. Office: Nova Southeastern Univ 3200 S University Dr Fort Lauderdale FL 33328 Office Phone: 954-262-1238. Office Fax: 305-667-6211. E-mail: kornblau@nova.edu.*

KORNBLEET, LYNDA MAE, insulation, fireproofing and acoustical contractor; b. Kansas City, Kans., June 15, 1951; d. Seymour Gerald Kornbleet and Jacqueline F. (Hurst) Kornbleet Malka. BA, U. St. Thomas, Houston, 1979. Lic. real estate salesperson; Disadvantaged Bus. Cert., State of Tex. Temporary counselor Lyman's Pers., Houston, 1974-75; real estate salesperson Coldwell Banker, Houston, 1975-77; sales, office mgr. Acme Insulation, Dallas, also Houston, 1977-79; owner, pres. Payless Insulation Inc., Houston, 1979—; contractor City of Houston, 1985—; owner, founder Superior Air Ducts, Houston, 2002—. HVAC contractor. Active Houston Ind. Sch. Dist., 1989—. Recipient award Internat. Cellulose, 2003; named Contractor of Yr., Sears Home Improvement, 1988. Mem. Houston Air Conditioning Coun. (bd. dirs. 1982-83), Cellulose Insulation Contractors (chmn. Houston 1981-82), Houston Bus. Coun., Insulation Contractors Assn. Greater Houston (pres. 1991-94, award for Top 50 Woman-Owned Cos. 1995), Women in Constrn. (bd. dirs. 1998-2000, sec.). Democrat. Avocations: bridge, golf. Office: Payless Insulation 1331 Seamist Dr Houston TX 77008-5017 Office Phone: 713-868-1021. Business E-Mail: LMK@paylessinsulation.com.

KORN-DAVIS, DOTTIE, artist, educator, consultant; b. L.A. d. William and Anne Miller. BA, UCLA, 1961; MA, San Diego State U., 1981. Artist-in-residence Laocheng Tchrs. U., Shandong, China, 1996 El Taller de Pubilla Kasas, Barcelona, Spain, 1998-99, 2002, 05-06; active Art in the Cmty./Woman's Caucus for Arts, San Diego, 1994—, Found. for Women, San Diego; open studio artist COVA, 1995, 99, Found. for Women; invited lectr U. Miquel Hernandes, 2005; lectr. in field. Solo shows include Expressive Arts Inst., San Diego, Art Gallery/Earl and Birdie Taylor Libr., San Diego, 2002-03, Mira Costa Coll., Oceanside, Calif., Woodland Hills, Calif., Maude Kearns Art Ctr., Eugene, Oreg., SD Art Inst. Mus., Balboa Park, San Diego, Calif., East County Performing Arts Ctr., El Cajon, Caif., Spectrum Gallery, San Diego, Imperial Valley Coll., Calif., Found. for Women, San Diego; exhibited in group shows at Mus., Calif. Ctr. for the Arts, Escondido, Calif., Taos (N.Mex.) Hist. Mus., Centre for Arts, Pico Rivera, Calif., Multicultural Arts Inst., San Diego, San Diego Artists Guild, Spectrum Gallery, San Diego, Riverside (Calif.) Arts Mus., San Diego (Calif.) Art Inst., Orange County Ct. for Contemporary Art, Santa Ana, Calif., L.A. Mcpl. Art Gallery, U. Wis. Ctr., Waukesha, Art Union Gallery, San Diego, Gallery Ten, Rockford, Ill., Next Door Gallery, San Diego, USCD Cross Cultural Ctr. Gallery, San Diego, Pierce Coll., Woodland Hills, Calif., Sierra Club Gallery, San Diego, Calif., Stables Gallery, Taos, N.Mex., Pierre Coll., numerous others. Bd. dirs. Artists Guild/Mus. Art, 1991-92. Recipient 1st Prize award San Diego Artists Guild, 1983. Avocations: travel, hiking, theater, dance. E-mail: davis@mail.sdsu.edu.

KORNER, BARBARA OLIVER, academic administrator; b. Kansas City, Mo., July 26, 1950; d. Robert C and Vonda F (Jenkins) Oliver; m. James Richard Korner, July 7, 1979. PhD, Ohio U., Athens, Ohio, 1983. Asst. to dean Univ. Coll., Ohio U., Athens; spl. asst. to chancellor U. Mo., Columbia, 1985—88, asst. dir. Sch. Fine Arts, 1988—90; dean Fine and Performing Arts, Seattle Pacific U., 1990—99; interim dean Coll. Fine Arts U. Fla., Gainesville, 2000—. Founder, dir. Acad. Leadership Inst. Assn. for Theatre in Higher Edn., Downers Grove, Ill., 2000—; speakers' bur. Wash. Commn. for the Humanities, Seattle; spkr. Mo. Humanities Coun., St. Louis; dir. Leadership Inst., Assn. for Theatre in Higher Edn., Downers Grove, Ill. Editor: (book) Hardship and Hope: Mo. Women Writing About their Lives; actor: Responding to the Call: Women of Spiritual Action, Hardship and Hope: Heroines in Life and Art (Grant: Mo. Humanities Coun.), Creating Sacred Spaces. Bd. dir. Duval Sch. Arts Coun., Gainesville, Fla.; pres. Kiwanis Club, Seattle; lay spkr. United Meth. Ch. Recipient Disting. Alumni award, Coll. Fine Arts, Ohio U., 2004. Mem.: Nat. Storytelling Assn., S.E. Theatre Conf., Assn. for Theatre in Higher Edn. (v.p. for adminstrn. 1993—99), Kiwanis (Outstanding Leadership Award 1998). United Meth. Ch. Office: University of Florida PO Box 115800 Fine Arts A Gainesville FL 32611-5800 E-mail: bkorner@arts.ufl.edu.

KORNHABER, DONNA MARIE, theater educator; b. New Haven, Conn., Dec. 16, 1979; d. Donna Marie Fusco; m. David Deren Kornhaber, Jan. 9, 2005. BFA in Film and TV, NYU, NYC, 1999, MFA in Dramatic Writing, 2001; MA in English and Comparative Lit., Columbia U., NYC, 2003, MPhil in Theatre, 2005, postgrad., 2005—. Asst. to dean, artistic dir. Yale Sch. Drama/Yale Repertory Theatre, New Haven, 2001—02; faculty fellow Columbia U., NYC, 2003—. Presenter in field. Contbr. articles to profl. jours., columns in newspapers. Mem.: MLA, Mensa. Avocations: writing, music, travel. Personal E-mail: dmf2004@columbia.edu.

KORNRICH, RHODA, psychologist; b. N.Y.C., Nov. 17, 1930; d. Irving and Celia (Edlin) Adelstein; m. Seymour Warshaw (div. 1973); children: Lynne Gilman, Sheryl Kraft, Michael Warshaw; m. Milton Kornrich, 1985. BA, CUNY-Hunter Coll., 1951; MS, Queens Coll., Flushing, N.Y., 1971; PhD, Fordham U., 1978. Tchr. Long Beach (N.Y.) Pub. Schs., 1951-52, 56-71; psychologist Yonkers (N.Y.) Pub. Schs., 1971-72; psychotherapist North Suffolk Mental Health Ctr., Smithtown, N.Y., 1974-79, Commack (N.Y.) Consultation Ctr., 1979-85; psychologist Behavioral Stress Ctr., Levittown, N.Y., 1983-86, Smithtown Pub. Schs., 1975-93; pvt. practice Smithtown, 1993—; psychotherapist Inst. for Rational Counseling, Bohemia, N.Y., 1995-98; cons. Suffolk County Dept. Health Bur. Svcs. for Children with Disabilities, Hauppague, N.Y., 1998—. Mem. APA, Nassau County Psychol. Assn., N.Y. State United Tchrs. Avocations: music, travel, piano, reading, writing.

KORNS, LEOTA ELSIE, writer, mountain land developer, insurance broker; b. Canton, Okla., Jan. 19, 1916; d. James Abraham and Ida Agnes (Engel) Klopfenstine; m. Richard Francis Korns, July 1, 1943 (wid. Dec. 17, 1988); 1 child, Michael Francis. BS, Pitts. State U. of Kans., 1966. Sec. various firms, Kans. City, Mo., 1937-45; cons. Electrolux Corp., St. Paul, 1946-49; sec. health, safety and waste IAEA, Vienna, Austria, 1959-60; tchr. Montezuma-Cortez H.S., Cortez, Colo., 1966-67; ins. agent Korns Ins. Agy., Durango, Colo., 1968—; owner, pres. Korns Investments, Inc., Durango, Colo., 1970—. Bd. dirs. LaPlata County Landowners Assn., Durango, 1981-87; writer, instr. women's history course U. N.Mex., Albuquerque, Ft. Lewis Coll., Durango, Colo., and Mesa (Ariz.) C.C., 1970-75; also spkr. in field. Author: (novels) Yesterday Should Have Been Over, 1965, Somewhere Out in the West, 2002; (play) Angry Young Men, 1957; writer numerous short stories including The Combine, 1947. Convenor, mem. NOW, Durango, 1970—; precinct capt. La Plata County Rep. Party, 1981—. Mem. Unity Sch. Christianity, Trimble Hot Springs. Avocations: mountain walking, swimming, piano, cross country skiing. Home: 519 Hickory Ridge Ln Box 11 Bayfield CO 81122 Office Phone: 970-884-7051, 970-884-7051. E-mail: leotakorns@frontier.net.

KOROLOGOS, ANN MCLAUGHLIN, communications executive; b. Newark, Nov. 16, 1941; d. Edward Joseph and Marie (Koellhoffer) Lauenstein; m. John McLaughlin, 1975 (div. 1991); m. Tom C. Korologos, 2000. Student, U. London, 1961-62; BA, Marymount Coll., 1963; postgrad., Wharton Sch., 1987. Supr. network comml. schedule ABC, N.Y.C., 1963-66; dir. alumnae relations Marymount Coll., Tarrytown, NY, 1966-69; account exec. Myers-Infoplan Internat. Inc., N.Y.C., 1969-71; dir. comm. Presdl. Election Com., Washington, 1971-72; asst. to chmn. and press sec. Presdl. Inaugural Com., Washington, 1972-73; dir. Office of Pub. Affairs, EPA, Washington, 1973-74; govt. rels. and comm. exec. Union Carbide Corp., N.Y.C. and Washington, 1974-77; pub. affairs, issues mgmt. counseling McLaughlin & Co., 1977-81; asst. sec. for pub. affairs Dept. of Treasury, Washington, 1981-84; under sec. Dept. of Interior, Washington, 1984-87; cons. Ctr. Strategic and Internat. Studies, Washington, 1987; sec. labor Dept. of Labor, Washington, 1987-89; vis. fellow Urban Inst., 1989-92; pres., CEO New Am. Schs. Devel. Corp., 1992-93; ret., 1993. Mem. def. adv. com. Women in the Svcs., 1973—74; mem. Am. Coun. Capital Formation, 1976—78; mem. environ. edn. task force HEW, 1976—77; chair Pres.'s Commn. Aviation Security and Terrorism, 1989—90; bd. dirs. Kellogg Co., Host Hotels & Resorts, Inc., Am. Airlines, AMR Corp., Harman Internat. Industries, Inc., Microsoft; pres. Fed. City Coun., 1990—95; chair Aspen Inst., 1996—2000, vice-chair, 1996; chmn. RAND. Bd. dirs. Charles A. Dana Found. Mem.: Sulgrave Club, Met. Club, Cosmos Club. Republican. Roman Catholic.

KOROT, BERYL, artist; b. N.Y.C., Sept. 17, 1945; d. George and Frieda (Braunstein) K.; m. Steve Reich, May 30, 1976; 1 child, Ezra. Student, U. Wis., 1963-65; BA, Queens Coll., 1967. Chief, co-founder Radical Software, 1970-73; co-editor Video Art, 1976. Exhibitions include 4 channel video work Dachau 1974, 5 channel video work, weavings, drawings, Text and Commentary: Three Tales and the Cave:, Kitchen, N.Y.C., 1975, Everson Mus. Art, Syracuse, N.Y., 1975, 1977, Documenta 6, Kassel, Germany, 1977, Videopoints, Mus Modern Art, N.Y.C., 1978, Mickery Theatre, Holland, 1978, Whitney Mus., N.Y.C., 1980, San Francisco Art Inst., 1981, Leo Castelli Gallery, N.Y.C., 1977, Mus. Fine Arts, Montreal, 1979, John Weber Gallery, 1986, Jack Tilton Gallery, 1987, Carnegie Mus. Art, 1990, Long Beach Mus. Art, 1988, Jewish Mus., N.Y.C., 1988, Video Skuptur, Kunstverein, Koln, 1989, The Cave, 1993, Reina Sofia Mus., Madrid, 1993—94, Dusseldorf Kunsthalle, Whitney Mus. Am. Art, N.Y.C., Carnegie Mus. Art,

ICC Gallery, Tokyo, 1997, Hindenburg, 1998, Bklyn. Acad. Music, 1998, Spoleto Festival, 1998, Mass. Coll. Art, 1999, Historischen Mus., Frankfurt, 2000—01, Whitney Mus., N.Y.C., 2000, 2001, Jewish Mus. Paris, 2002—03, short commd. work, Art 21, PBS, 2002, Apex Gallery, N.Y.C., 2004, DM2, 2005, Seoul, Korea, 2005, web project, Auschwitz, PBS.org, 2005—. Fellow, N.Y. State Coun. on Arts, 1978, Creative Artist Pub. Svc., 1975, 1979; grantee, Rockefeller Found., 1989, 1998, Andy Warhol Found., 1991, NEA, 1991—92; artist fellow, 1975, 1977, 1979, Guggenheim fellow, 1994, Montgomery fellow, Dartmouth Coll., 2000. Home: 258 Broadway New York NY 10007-2315 Personal E-mail: bkorot@aol.com.

KOROW, ELINORE MARIA, artist, educator; b. Akron, Ohio, July 31, 1934; d. Alexander and Elizabeth Helen (Doszpoly) Vigh; m. John Henry Korow, Sept. 28, 1957 (div. Oct. 1980); children: Christopher, David, Daniel; m. Harry Edward Bieber, Aug. 1, 1982 (dec. May 1994). Student, Siena Heights Women's Coll., 1952-53; diploma, Cleve. Inst. Art, 1957, Sawyer Coll. Bus., 1976. Staff artist Am. Greetings Corp., Cleve., 1957-58, designer, 1970-73; owner Elinore Korow: Portraits, Shaker Heights, Ohio, 1973-94, Akron, 1994—. Instr. painting Cuyahoga CC, Cleve., 1979—, chmn. sr. excellence art exhbn.; instr. U. Akron, 1995—; dir. spl. exhbns. Massillon Art Mus., Canton Mus. Art, 2000—; lectr. in field. Exhibited in group shows at Russell Art Exhibit, Novelty, Ohio, 1992, Ohio Regional Painting Exhbn., 1993, Beck Ctr. Cultural Arts, Lakewood, Ohio, 1993, Canton Art Inst., Butler Inst. Am. Art, Youngstown, Nat. Acad. Design, N.Y.C., Lynn Kottler Galleries, World Trade Ctr., others, one-woman shows include Cuyahoga Valley Art Ctr., Cuyahoga Falls, Ohio, 1995, Akron Woman's City Club, 1996, Stow Munroe Falls Libr., Ohio, 2006, others, Represented in permanent collections Blue Cross/Blue Shield N.E. Ohio, Am. Greetings Corp., U. Akron Alumni Ctr., Cleve. Playhouse, Temple Emanuel, Cleveland Heights, Ohio, Kent State U., 1st Congl. Ch., Akron. Women's com. Cleve. Orch., 2002; rep. Women's Art League Akron Area Arts Alliance, 2001; judge Akron Arts Expo, Ohio, 2002—05; tutor artist Am. Diabetes Assn. Fund Raising Benefit, 2006; charter mem. Alliance Visual Arts, 1999—2000; bd. dirs. Akron Soc. Artists and Women's Art League, 2001—, Cuyahoga Valley Art Ctr., 2005. Recipient 2d pl., 17th Ann. Russell Show, Novelty, 1992, 1st pl. award, 1993, 3d pl., Valley Art Ctr., Cuyahoga Falls, 1994, 1st prize cash award, AIDS Benefit, Ohio, 2000, 1st prize, All Mem. Show, 2001, 1st pl., Lawrence Churski Gallery, 2002, Best in Show, Stan Hywet Hall and Gardens, Akron, Ohio, 2006, Hon. Mention, 2006. Mem.: Boardroom Group, Akron Soc. Artists (signature), Ohio Watercolor Soc. (charter), Women's Art Club Cleve. (past pres. 1970—71), Women's Art League (past pres. 1999—2000, 1st Pl. award 1st Congl. Ch. Akron 2005), Am. Soc. Portrait Artists, Pastel Soc. Am. (assoc.), Women's Network. Avocations: music, travel. Home: 923 Mayfair Rd Akron OH 44303-1317 Office Phone: 330-867-8796. E-mail: elinorekorow@neo.rr.com.

KORPAL, CHARYL ELAINE, secondary school educator; b. Emo, Ont., Can., Nov. 16, 1946; came to U.S., 1946; d. Charles Sigard and Martha Edith (Ericksen) Mark; m. Donald Paul Korpal, July 7, 1967. BS in Teaching, Mankato State U., 1976, postgrad., 1988; MEd, U. Minn., St. Paul, 1991. Tchr. Ind. Sch. Dist. 77, Mankato, Minn., 1976-77; tchr. mktg., coord., DECA advisor New Ulm Cathedral, 1977-78; mktg. tchr. coord., advisor Mankato East High Sch., 1978—2003; mktg. tchg. coord Mankato West High Sch., 2003—. Active March Dimes, Boyd Schuler's campaign for Minn. House Reps. Recipient PTA scholarship Indus High Sch., 1965, Bus. Econs. Edn. Foud. scholarship Olaf Coll., 1986; Minn. State Bd. Vocational Tech. Edn. scholar, 1987, Spirit of Youth award, 2005 Mem. NEA, Distributive Edn. Clubs Am. (bd. dirs. 1980-81, recipient scholarship 1975, Outstanding Sr. Service award 1976, Cert. Appreciation 1980—, hon. life, Minn. Secondary Mktg. Tchr. of Yr. 1983), Nat. Assn. Distributive Edn. Tchrs., Mktg. and Distributive Edn. Assn., Am. Vocat. Assn., Mktg. Educators Minn., Mktg. Edn. Assn., Nat. Fedn. Bus. and Profl. Women's Clubs, Mankato Bus. Profl. Women's Club. Lodges: Sons of Norway Elvesvingen. Home: 54 Camelot Ln Mankato MN 56001-6308 Office: Mankato W High Sch 1351 S Riverfront Dr Mankato MN 56001-6830 Office Phone: 507-387-3461 x115. Business E-Mail: ckorpal@isd77.k12.mn.us.

KORRY, ALEXANDRA D., lawyer; b. London, 1959; AB, Harvard U., 1980; MSc, London Sch. Econs./Polit. Sci., 1981; JD, Duke U., 1986. Bar: NY 1988. Assoc. Sullivan & Cromwell, NYC, 1986—93, ptnr., mergers & acquisitions practice, 1993—. Office: Sullivan & Cromwell 125 Broad St New York NY 10004-2498 Office Phone: 212-558-4370. Office Fax: 212-558-3588.

KORSGAARD, CHRISTINE MARION, philosophy educator; b. Chgo., Apr. 9, 1952; d. Albert and Marion Hangaard (Kortbek) K.; m. Timothy David Gould, June 1980 (div. Sept. 1984). BA, U. Ill., 1974; PhD, Harvard U., 1981. Instr. Yale U., New Haven, 1979-80; asst. prof. U. Calif., Santa Barbara, 1980-83; from asst. prof. to prof. U. Chgo., 1983-91; prof. Harvard U., Cambridge, Mass., 1991—, chair philosophy dept., 1996—2002. Vis. assoc. prof. Berkeley, 1989, UCLA, 1990; Tanner lectr. human values, 1992, Locke lectrs., 2002. Author: The Sources of Normativity, 1996, Creating the Kingdom of Ends, 1996; editor: (with Andrews Reath and Barbara Herman) Reclaiming the History of Ethics: Essays for John Rawls, 1997; contbr. chpts. to books, articles to profl. jours. Recipient Mellon Disting. Achievement award, 2004; Whiting fellow, 1978-79; Ctr. for Human Values fellow, 1995-96. Fellow AAAS; mem. Am. Philos. Assn., N.Am. Kant Soc., Hume Soc., Am. Soc. for Polit. and Legal Philosophy. Office Phone: 617-495-3916. E-mail: Christine_Korsgaard@Harvard.edu.

KORSHAK, SHELLEY J., psychiatrist; b. Chgo. d. Donald Korshak and Rachel Firestone; m. Laurence A. Sode, Feb. 14, 2003. BA, Barnard Coll., N.Y.C., 1971; MD, U. Ill., Chgo., 1979. Pvt. practice psychiatry, Chgo., 1983—. Instr. U. Chgo., 2005—; bd. mem. Ill. Group Psychotherapy Soc., 2005—. Office: Dr Shelley J Korshak Ste 700 30 N Mich Ave Chicago IL 60602-3814

KORSTEN, SUSAN SNYDER, science educator; b. Cherry Hill, N.C., July 28, 1944; d. Eugene Ralph and Beatrice Roggen Snyder; m. Mark Allen Korsten, Dec. 18, 1974; children: Eric Robert, Caroline Messer. AB, U. Pa., Phila., 1966; MA, Tchrs. Coll. Columbia U., N.Y.C., 1967. Cert. tchr. grades 1-6 N.Y.C. Tchr. math. Riverside Sch., N.Y.C., 1967—68; tchr. 5th grade Downtown Cmty. Sch., N.Y.C., 1968—71; tchr. math. and computer Dalton Sch., N.Y.C., 1971—94; tchr. sci. Calhoun Sch., N.Y.C., 1994—. Mem. sch. bd. Downtown Cmty. Schs., 1968—71; spkr. elem. sch. sci. Assn. Tchrs. Ind. Schs., N.Y.C., 1996—2005. Author: articles in sch. newspapers, poems in sch. archive. Mem. bd. Hastings Creative Arts Coun., Hastings-on-Hudson, 1979—87; nature guide Hastings Elem. Sch., 1981—87; founder, co-dir. Help-A-Child Program, Hastings-on-Hudson, 1992—. Named Outstanding Tchr. of Yr., Calhoun Sch., 2000; recipient Prin.'s Excellence award, Prin. Dalton 1st Program, 1993. Mem.: Assn. Tchrs. Ind. Schs. Democrat. Jewish. Achievements include first educator invited to teach at Dalton Schools in Tokyo and Nagoya; taught Japanese teachers how to instruct computer, science and mathematics; created and taught in one of the first computer laboratories for young children, 1978. Avocations: ballroom dancing, singing, travel, poetry, aerobics. Home: 2 Edgewood Ave Hastings On Hudson NY 10706 Office: Calhoun Sch 433 West End Ave New York NY 10024 Office Phone: 212-497-6500. Business E-Mail: susan.korsten@calhoun.org.

KORTE, GENEVIEVE L., music educator; b. Bluffton, Ohio, July 9, 1928; d. Orlin Schumacher and Kathryn Garber; m. Urban H Korte, Aug. 20, 1949; children: Edward(dec.), Esther E Judson, Maria, Robert, James, Betty Jean (Sister Mary Cathrine), Janet Hill, Carol Bowman, Susan Carter. B in Music Performance and Music Edn., U. Dayton, 1980. Organist St. Christopher Cath. Ch., 1965—80; supr., admissions mail U. Dayton, Ohio, 1972—80; head sec. psychology dept. Va. Commonwealth U., Richmond, 1980—81; music tchr. Dinwiddie Sch., Va., 1981—83, Dayton Christian Sch., Tipp City, Ohio, 1984—85; piano instr. Korte Keyboard, 1965—2005; organist Hillcrest Brethren Ch., 1985—2003. Recipient Merit award, Nat. Fedn. of Music Club, 1997—98. Mem.: Dayton Piano Teachers Study Club (v.p. 2002—03, pres. 2004—06), Dayton Music Club (3d v.p. 1999—2000), Ohio Music Teachers Assn. (dir. student activities 1997—98). Home: 1071 Bosco Ave Vandalia OH 45377 Office Phone: 937-890-5301.

KORTH, CHARLOTTE WILLIAMS, furniture and interior design firm executive; b. Milw.; d. Lewis C. and Marguerite Peil Brooks; m. Robert Lee Williams, Jr., Oct. 25, 1944 (dec.); children: Patricia Williams, Melissa Williams O'Rourke, Brooks Williams; m. Fred Korth, Aug. 23, 1980. Student, U. Wis., 1941. Owner Charlotte's Inc., El Paso, Tex., 1951—, chmn., CEO, 1979—; pres. Paso del Norte Design, Inc., El Paso, 1978-81; mem. adv. com. for interior design program El Paso C.C., 1981—; mem. adv. bd. S.W. Design Inst., 1982—; ptnr. Wilko Partnership, 1981-98; mem. adv. bd. Mountain Bell Telephone Co., 1976-79; mem. Sch. Architecture Found. Adv. Coun. U. Tex. Austin, 1985-91. Charter mem. Com. of 200, 1982—, Nat. Mus. Women in the Arts, 1985—; mem. Renaissance 400, El Paso, El Paso Women's Symphony Guild, El Paso Mus. Art. Recipient of Silver plaque Gifts and Decorative Accessories Mag., 1978; named Woman of Yr. by El Paso Am. Bus. Women's Assn., 1978, Outstanding Woman of Yr. by Women's Polit. Caucus, 1979. Mem. Am. Soc. Interior Designers (bd. dirs. Tex. chpt. 1977-82), El Paso Women's C. of C. (hon.), El Paso C. of C. (dir. 1976-82), Coronado Country Club, Internat. Club, El Paso Country Club, Santa Teresa Country Club (N.Mex.). Avocations: travel, antiques, collectibles. Home: 6041 Torrey Pines Dr El Paso TX 79912-2029 Office: Charlotte's Inc 5411 N Mesa St Ste 7 El Paso TX 79912-5495

KORTHUIS, KATHLEEN ELIZABETH, retired dean; b. Hancock, Minn., Mar. 29, 1934; d. Dewey J. and Theresa (Vander Meer) Hoitenga; m. Ronald J. Korthuis, Sept. 4, 1954; children: Ronald, Sara, Barbara. Student, Blodgett Meml. Hosp., 1955; BSN, Wayne State U., 1971, MSN, 1973; PhD, U. Toledo, 1982. Dept. chair gerontol. nursing Sch. Nursing Med. Coll. Ohio Sch. Nursing, Toledo, 1982-86, assoc. dean grad. program, 1992-96; dean Sch. Nursing Seattle U., 1986-92. Mem. ANA, Wash. Nurses Assn., Coun. Nursing Edn. Wash. (pres. 1989-91). Home: 3251 Ravine Hollow Ct Lambertville MI 48144-9693

KORTLANDER, MYRNA, psychotherapist; b. N.Y.C., July 12, 1934; d. Irving and Jean (Feldman) Beckenstein; children: Marc Allen, Don Richard. BA, CUNY, 1975; MSW, Fordham U., 1981. Diplomate Nat. Assn. Social Workers. Staff Alfred Adler Mental Health Clinic, N.Y.C., 1981-83; psychotherapist Lower East Side Svc. Ctr., N.Y.C., 1983-86, L.I. Cons. Ctr., Forest Hills, N.Y., 1986-87; pvt. practice Forest Hills, 1981—. Mem. NASW, N.Y. State Soc. Clin. Social Work Psychotherapists, Am. Group Psychotherapy Assocs. Home: 11020 71st Rd Apt 910 Forest Hills NY 11375-4908

KORTUM-MANAGHAN, SANTANA NATASHA, lawyer; b. Anaconda, Mont., Apr. 9, 1973; d. George Peter and Barbara Jean Kortum; m. William L. Managhan; children: Michael Managhan, Madison Managhan, Gabriella Managhan. BA in History, U. Mont., Missoula; JD, U. Mont, Missoula. Claims examiner Social Security Adminstrn., Helena, Mont.; mediator Mont. Consumer Protection Office, Helena; ptnr. Managhan & Kortum-Managhan Law Firm PLLC, Kalispell. Address: PO Box 938 Kalispell MT 59903-0938

KORY, MARIANNE GREENE, lawyer; b. NYC, 1931; d. Hyman Louis and Belle (Rome) Greene; children: Erich Marcel, Lisa. BA, CCNY; JD, N.Y. Law Sch., 1976; LLM, U. Wash., 1986. Bar: Ohio 1977, D.C. 1979, N.Y. 1983, Vt. 1994, U.S. Dist. Ct. (so. and ea. dists.) N.Y. 1983, U.S. Dist. Ct. Vt. 1994. Hearing examiner Ohio Bd. Employee Compensation, Columbus, 1977; atty. advisor Office Hearings and Appeals Social Security Adminstrn., Cin. and N.Y.C., 1977-78; gen. atty. labor Office of Solicitor U.S. Dept. of Labor, N.Y.C., 1978-82; pvt. practice N.Y.C., 1983—; adminstrv. Seattle, 1989-91, Burlington, Vt., 1994—. Founder Cin. chpt. Amnesty Internat., 1977. Alvin Johnson fellow in Philosophy; grad. faculty New Sch. for Social Rsch. Mem. NOW, Nat. Abortion Rights Action League, Feminist Majority Found., Vt. Bar Assn., Planned Parenthood, Defenders of Wildlife, Ctr. for Marine Conservation, WWF, Nat. Wildlife Fedn., Humane Soc., Emily's List, Phi Beta Kappa. Office: 1361 S Ocean Blvd #202 Pompano Beach FL 33062-8022 Office Phone: 954-781-2820. Personal E-mail: mariannekory@aol.com.

KORZENIK, DIANA, art educator; b. N.Y.C., Mar. 15, 1941; d. Harold and Lillian (Shapiro) K. BA in Art History, Vassar Coll., 1957-59; BA, Oberlin Coll., 1961; EdD, Harvard U., 1972. Tchr. art N.Y.C. Pub. Schs., 1964-69; prof. art Mass. Coll. Art, Boston, 1972-94; lectr. art grad. sch. edn. Harvard U., Cambridge, Mass., 1995—. Vis. lectr. Tufts U., Medford, Mass., 1972-73; curator exhibits Mass. Coll. Art, 1975, U. N.H., 1986-87, Manchester (N.H.) Hist. Soc., 1986-87, Fruitlands Mus., Mass., 1988. Author: (with Maurice Brown) Art Making and Education; exhibited in group show at Boston Athenaeum, 1990, 91. Named Educator of Yr., Mass. Art Edn. Assn., 1984; recipient Leab award ALA, 2006; Yale U. fellow, 1958, Woodrow Wilson fellow, 1962; Pub. Grant, Getty Trust, 1985. Mem. Am. Antiquarian Soc., Nat. Art Edn. Assn. (author Framing the Past 1990, June McFee award 1987, Lowenfeld award 1998), Internat. Soc. for Edn. through Art, Nat. Soc. for Edn. in Art and Design, U.S. Soc. for Edn. through Art (jour. bd.), Ephemera Soc. Am. (bd. dirs.), Friends of the Longfellow House (founder, pres.).

KOS, NIRVANA GABRIELA, psychologist; b. Pula, Croatia, Jan. 9, 1981; arrived in U.S., 1999; d. Miroslav and Silvana Kos. BA in Psychology, Fla. Internat. U., 2003; MS in Psychology, Fla. State U., 2006. CPA Fla. Interim counselor youth devel. program Fla. Internat. U., Miami, 2003—04; clinician BACC, Miami, 2003—04. Vol. Miami Temple Ch., 2002—05. Seventh-Day Adventist. Avocations: volleyball, tennis, reading, travel.

KOSACZ, BARBARA A., lawyer; b. Pawtucket, RI, Feb. 16, 1958; BA, Stanford U., 1980; JD, U. Calif., Berkeley, 1988. Bar: Calif. 1988. Ptnr. Cooley Goodward LLP (formerly Cooley Godward Castro Huddleson & Tatum), Palo Alto, Calif., 1995—, mgmt. com. mem., 1997—98. V.p. bus. devel., gen. counsel iScribe, Inc., 2001; guest lectr. Boalt Hall Law Sch., Santa Clara Law Sch., Stanford Law Sch. Sr. article editor High Tech. Law Jour., 1987—88. Office: Cooley Godward LLP Five Palo Alto Sq 3000 El Camino Real Palo Alto CA 94306-2155 Office Phone: 650-843-5000. E-mail: bkosacz@cooley.com.

KOSECOFF, JACQUELINE BARBARA, health care company executive; b. Los Angeles, June 15, 1949; d. Herman Plaut and Betty (Bass) Hamburger; m. Robert Henry Brook, Jan. 17, 1982; children: Rachel Brook, Davida Brook. BA, UCLA, 1970; MS, Brown U., 1971; PhD, UCLA, 1973. Prof. medicine and pub. health UCLA, 1976—; pres., co-CEO Value Health Scis., Santa Monica, Calif., 1988—98; v.p. Value Health, Inc., Avon, Conn.; pres., founder Protocare, Inc., 1998—2002; exec. v.p., Pharmaceutical Svcs. PacifiCare Health Sys., Inc., Cypress, Calif., 2002—. Author: An Evaluation Primer, 1978, How to Evaluate Education Programs, 1980, Evaluation Basics, 1982, How to Conduct Surveys, 1985; contbr. numerous articles to profl. publs. Regents scholar UCLA, 1967-71; NSF fellow, 1971-72. Mem. Am. Pub. Health Assn., Assn. for Health Services Research. Democrat. Jewish. Office: PacifiCare Health Sys Inc 5995 Plaza Dr Cypress CA 90630

KOSEL, RENÉE, state representative; b. Chgo., Apr. 3, 1943; m. Alfred Kosel; 3 children. BS in Edn., Western Ill. U. Bd. dirs. Lincoln-Way H.S. Dist. Recipient numerous awards. Mem.: local cmty. orgns. Republican. Lutheran. Office: 200 N Stratton Office Bldg Springfield IL 62706 Address: 19201 S LaGrange Rd Ste 204B Mokena IL 60448 Office Phone: 708-479-4200. E-mail: rkosel@aol.com.

KOSHEWITZ, PHYLLIS J., elementary school educator; b. Newton, N.J., Nov. 9, 1945; d. Miles J. and Emily F. Knepper; m. Robert H. Koshewitz, Oct. 21, 1967; children: Amy, Rob(dec.), Rhonda. BS in Elem. Edn., Calif. U. of Pa., Calif., Pa., 1967; MEd, St. Francis U., Loretta, Pa., 1993; student, various univs. Tchr. Berlin Brothersvalley Sch. Dist., Berlin, Pa., 1967; substitute tchr. Conemaugh Township Sch. Dist., Davidsville, Pa., 1967—72, North Star Sch. Dist., Boswell, Pa., 1967—92; tchr. Somerset Area Sch. Dist., Pa., 1982—. Presenter in field. Author: Quilts Are Forever, 2002; contbr. chapters to books; prin. works include six latch hook banners, Somerset Jr. H.S. Recipient Trip award, Nat. Tchrs. Sci. Am., Washington, D.C. Unseen Tour and Conf.; grantee, McDonalds, 1995, 1997, 1999. Fellow: Southwestern Pa. Writer's Project; mem.: PTA (life), NEA (life), Nat. Coun. Tchrs. Math., Pa. Coun. Tchrs. Math., Nat. Sci. Tchrs. Assn., Pa. State Edn. Assn. (life), Somerset Area Edn. Assn. (life), Pa. State Tchrs. Assn., Laurel Highlands Math. Alliance (chmn. nominations com. 1996—2006), Women Evang. Luth. Ch. Am. (cir. leader, sec., pres.), Kappa Delta Pi. Republican. Luth. Avocations: reading, writing, computers, interior decorating, design. Home: 2763 Penn Ave Hollsopple PA 15935-6621 Office: Somerset Area Sch Dist 191 Discovery Ln Somerset PA 15501-8754

KOSHIMITSU, KEIKO, artist; b. Tokyo, Sept. 21, 1958; arrived in U.S., 1984; d. Minoru and Sumiko Koshimitsu; m. Aldo E. Garay, June 1, 1995; children: Kazuki Aldo Garay Jr., Rina Angelica Garay. BFA, Tama Art U., Tokyo, 1981; MA in Edn., Yokohama Nat. U., Japan, 1983. Supr. The Bank of Yokohama, N.Y.C., 1997—2002, asst. v.p., 2003. One-woman shows include JTB Equitable Ctr., N.Y., 1992, exhibitions include Tokyo Prefecture Mus., 1979, 1980, 1982, Bronx Mus., N.Y., 1994, exhibited in group shows at Sanaa Gallery, Tokyo, 1981, Sumitomo Bldg. Gallery, 1981, Kanagawa Prefecture Gallery, Yokohama, 1982, Yokohama Gallery, 1982, 1983, 1984, 1985, 1986, Mitsubishi Gallery, Tokyo, 1983, Cast Iron Gallery, N.Y., 1992, 1996, El Bohio C.C., 1992, Tenri Gallery, 1992, Klein Landaw Fine Arts, 1992, Japan Consulate, 1993, 2004, Walter Wickiser Gallery, N.Y., 1993, 1995, 1999, 2000, 2001, Gallery One Twenty Eight, 1994, Liver House, 1994, Krasdale Gallery, 1995, Ise Gallery, 1996, 1997, Kaoru Gallery, Tokyo, 1997, Broome St. Gallery, N.Y., 1999, New Century Artist Gallery, 2000, Caelum Gallery, 2001, Tenri Gallery, 2001, 2002, 2003, 2004. Mem.: Japanese Artists Assn. (treas. 1991—99, pres. 2000—), Tama Art U. Alumni Assn. (v.p., treas. 2003). Home: 175 Maplewood Ave Bogota NJ 07603 Office: Japanese Artist Assn NY Inc 175 Maplewood Ave Bogota NJ 07603 E-mail: keikokoshimitsu@optonline.net.

KOSISKY, SHELLEY ANN, psychologist; b. Takoma Park, Md., Apr. 20, 1959; d. Joseph Simon and Audrey Susan (Harris) K. BS magna cum laude, U. Md., 1981; MA, Cath. U. Am., 1985, PhD, 1989. Lic. psychologist. Fed. jr. fellow child and family rsch. br. NIH, Bethesda, Md., 1977-84, rsch. psychologist Child Psychiatry, 1985-87; clin. psychology fellow Harvard Med. Sch. Childrens Hosp., Boston, 1987-88; instr. sch. medicine U. Md., Balt., 1989-90; psychology assoc. Patuxent Med. Group, Inc., Columbia, Md., 1990-91; pvt. practice Bethesda, Md., 1991—92, Annapolis, Md., 1992—; cons. Mt. Washington Pediatric Hosp., Baltimore, Md., 1991-94, Naval Med. Clinic, Annapolis, Md., 1992—98, Midshore Mental health Svcs., Eastern Shore, Md., 1999—2003, Naval Acad. Primary Sch., Annapolis, Md., 2003—. Rsch. and teaching asst. Life Cycle Inst., Cath. U. Am., Washington, 1981-87; family therapist Youth Svc. Bur., Greenbelt, Md., 1985-87, Bowie, Md., 1986-87; invited guest lectr. Anne Arundel C.C., Annapolis, Md., 2003-. Contbr. articles to profl. jours. Vol. Kidney Found., Heart Fund, March of Dimes. Mem. APA, Md. Psychol. Assn., Soc. Pediat. Psychology, U. Md. Alumni Assn. Democrat. Avocations: travel, swimming, cross country skiing, racquetball, gardening. Office Phone: 410-757-4988.

KOSKI, DONNA FAITH, poet; b. Wildwood, NJ, Aug. 18, 1935; d. Sebastian and Mildred (Shastany) Rossitto; m. Paul A. Koski, May 5, 1968 (div. June 1982); children: Danita Swift-Stearns, Darla Swift, Deanna Swift-Everett, Deena Swift Bauer, Charles Swift. Student, San Diego Jr. Coll., 1955-58, Mesa Jr. Coll, San Diego, 1993. With Pacific Telephone, San Diego, 1954-68; credit clk. Norwich (Conn.) Gas & Lights, 1968-70; clk. Navy Exch., New London, Conn., 1969-70; front desk clk. Del Webb's, San Diego, 1971-72; payroll clk. U.S.I.U., San Diego, 1974-76; facility mgr. Price Costco, San Diego, 1978-94, Price Enterprises, Inc., San Diego, 1994-97, Price Smart Vacations (Costco Travel), 1997—99; facility and maintenance mgr. The Price Club, 1999—2000; quality control and support agent Club 4 U. Worker Diversified Copier Products in San Diego, Price's, PAcific bell, Westgate (C Arnolt Smith), Alvin Strep Interiors, USIU, Norwich Gas and Electric, John Myers of Norwich, Navy Exch.-New London, Conn, several hotels and motels. Author: The Power of Love, 1995, Nights in Sedona, 1995, Faces in the Clouds, 1994, Dream Catcher, 2001, The New Heros, 2003, numerous poems, (book) Theatre of the Mind, 2003, Celebrate Poets Speak Out, 2003. Vol. Nat. Multiple Sclerosis Soc., San Diego, 1995, React-Telecom. Emergency Svcs., San Diego, 1985-93, Perot Hdqrs., San Diego, 1992, 96, Social Svcs., San Diego, 1980-82, Project Oz (runaway kids). Recipient Editor's Choice award Nat. Libr. of Poetry, 1995, Accomplishment of Merit, Creative Arts and Sci., 1994, 1st Place Browning Competition award Iliad Press, 1998, Presdl. Recognition award, 1998-99, Outstanding Achievement in Poetry award Famous Poets Soc., 1998, others. Mem. Internat. Soc. Poets, Internat. Soc. Authors and Artists, Blind Soc., Multiple Sclerosis Soc., Moose. Mem. Unity Ch. Avocations: writing, poetry, computers, music, sports. Home: 8661 Winter Gardens Blvd SP 45 Lakeside CA 92040 Personal E-mail: koskidonna@aol.com, k78@yahoo.com.

KOSS, MARY LYNDON PEASE, psychology educator, researcher; b. Louisville, Sept. 1, 1948; d. Richard Charles and Carol (Bade) Pease; m. Paul G. Koss, Aug. 3, 1968; children: John Bade, Paul Shanor. AB, U. Mich., 1970; PhD, U. Minn., 1972. Lic. psychologist, Ariz. Asst. prof. psychology St. Olaf Coll., Northfield, Minn., 1973-76; prof. psychology Kent (Ohio) State U., 1976-88; prof. dept. health promotion scis. Coll. Pub. Health, U. Ariz., Tucson, 1988—. Grantee NIMH, 1978-98, Nat. Inst. Justice, U.S. Dept. Justice, NIAAA, 1995-2005, CDC, 2002— Mem.: APA, Nat. Inst. Justice. Democrat. Office Phone: 520-626-9502. Business E-Mail: mpk@u.arizona.edu.

KOSSINA, MARY HELEN, elementary school educator; b. East Saint Louis, Ill., Oct. 7, 1950; d. Ruppert Earl and Lillian Frances (Lunnemann) Blair; m. James Louis Kossina, July 12, 1974; children: Robert James, Angela Louise. BS, So. Ill. U., 1971. Cert. tchr. Ill., 1971. Seventh grade tchr. Saints Peter and Paul Cath. Sch., Collinsville, Ill., 1971—74, 1984—2005. Supr. Saints Peter and Paul's Safety Patrol, Collinsville, 1980—2005; mem. Saints Peter and Paul Edn. Com., Collinsville, 2001—05. Active Saints Peter and Paul Booster Club, Collinsville, 1972—2005. Recipient Award of Excellence, Ill. Math. and Sci. Acad., 2002. Roman Catholic. Avocations: fantasy football, fishing, boating. Office: Saints Peter and Paul Catholic School 210 N Morrison Collinsville IL 62234 Office Phone: 1-618-344-5450.

KOSSUTH, JOANNE M., academic administrator; BA, Holy Cross Coll.; MS, Lesley U. Systems mgr. Fisher Coll.; dir. info. tech. Wheelock Coll.; dir. computer support services Boston U. Sch. Mgmt.; now chief info. officer, assoc. v.p. devel. Franklin W. Olin Coll. Engring. Named one of Premier 100 IT Leaders, Computerworld, 2005. Office: Franklin W Olin Coll Engring Olin Way Needham MA 02492-1200 Office Phone: 781-292-2431. Office Fax: 781-292-2440. E-mail: joanne.kossuth@olin.edu.

KOSTER, BARBARA, insurance company executive; Acct. Chase Manhattan Bank, 1976—87, v.p. fin. sys., 1980—85, v.p. info. svcs., 1985—88, pres., Chase Access Svcs., 1988—95; v.p., policy adminstrn. and mgmt. info. systems Prudential Financial, 1995—97, v.p., Individual Fin. Svcs., 1997—2000, chief info. officer, individual life ins. systems Newark, 2000—03, sr. v.p., chief info. officer, 2004—. Recipient award Women in Sci. & Tech., 1999. Office: Prudential Ins Co Am 751 Broad St Newark NJ 07102-3714

KOSTER, ELAINE, publishing executive; b. NYC; BA, Barnard Coll. Pres., pub. Dutton Signet, N.Y.C.; head Elaine Koster Literary Agy. LLC, N.Y.C. Office: Elaine Koster Literary Agy LLC 55 Central Park W Ste 6 New York NY 10023-6003 Personal E-mail: elainekost@aol.com.

KOSTIC, DINA, musician, music educator; b. Belgrade, Serbia-Monteneg, Jan. 18, 1977; d. Lana Peck. MusB, So. Meth. U., Dallas, 1996; MusM, Northwestern U., Evanston, Ill., 1998. Concertmaster New World Symphony, Miami Beach, Fla., 1999—2002; lectr. violin Barry U., Miami Shores, Fla., 2002—; violinist Fla. Philharm., Fort Lauderdale, 2002—03, Palm Beach Chamber Music Festival, Fla., 2003—; concertmaster Orlando Philharm., Fla., 2003; violinist Palm Beach Opera, West Palm Beach, Fla., 2004—. Digital reviewer Insight for the Blind, Fort Lauderdale, 2003—06. Scholar, So. Meth. U., 1992—96, Civic Orch. Chgo. Mem.: Am. String Tchrs. Assn. Avocations: skiing, travel.

KOSTICK, ALEXANDRA, ophthalmologist; BSc, MD, U. Man., Winnipeg, Can., 1990. Surg. intern St. Boniface Hosp./U. Man., Winnipeg, 1990-91; rsch. fellow in ocular pathology Storm Eye Inst./Med. U. S.C., Charleston, 1991-92; resident in ophthalmology U. Sask., Saskatoon, Can., 1992-95; fellow corneal diseases U. Mo., Columbia, 1995-96; practice ophthalmology specializing in cornea and external diseases, Ormond Beach, Palm Coast, Fla., 1996—. Contbr. articles to profl. jours. Fellow ACS, Am. Acad. Ophthalmology; mem. Am. Soc. Cataract and Refractive Surgeons, European Soc. Cataract and Refractive Surgeons, Royal Coll. Physicians and Surgeons Can., Castroviejo Corneal Soc., Paton Eye Bank Soc., Can. Ophthalmology Soc., Royal Acad. Dancing (London). Office Phone: 386-446-9590.

KOSTOVA, ELIZABETH, writer; b. New London, Conn., 1964; m. Georgi Kostova, 1990. BA in Brit. Studies, Yale Univ.; MFA, Univ. Mich., 2004. Author: (novels) The Historian, 2005 (debuted #1 NY Times Bestseller list, Debut Author of Yr. Quills Book awards, 2005). Mailing: Author Mail Little Brown Co 1271 Ave of the Americas New York NY 10020*

KOSTY, CARLITA, secondary school educator; b. Tampa, Fla., Jan. 30, 1944; d. Carl Chambers and Gladys (Stallings) Hughes; m. Michael Edward Lamm (div.); 1 child, Sharon Lamm Heusinger; m. Donald Paul Kosty, Dec. 19, 1975 (dec. May 2005); 1 stepchild, John. BA in History and Spanish, Southwestern U., Georgetown, Tex., 1964. Cert. tchr. Tex. Tchr. Bryan (Tex.) Pub. Schs., 1964—66, Channelview (Tex.) Ind. Sch. Dist., 1968—69, Pasadena (Tex.) Ind. Sch. Dist., 1969—72; tchr., chair hist. dept. Southside Ind. Sch. Dist., San Antonio, 1977—84, Northside Ind. Sch. Dist., San Antonio, 1984—. Participant, contbr. Whole Cloth: Discovering Sci. & Tech. through Am. History Brown U., Providence, Nat. Mus. Am. History, Smithsonian Instn., Washington, 1991—98. Author: History Fair Workbook, 2002. Mem. San Antonio Conservation Soc., 1980—. Recipient Excellence in Tchg., Trinity U., 1981. Mem.: Orgn. Am. Historians, Nat. Coun. Social Studies. Avocations: sewing, knitting. Office: Rudder Mid Sch 6558 Horn Blvd San Antonio TX 78240 Office Phone: 210-397-5000. Business E-Mail: CarlitaKosty@nisd.net.

KOTCHER, SHIRLEY J.W., lawyer; b. June 6, 1924; m. Harry A. Kotcher; children: Leslie Susan, Dana Anne. BA, NYU; JD, Columbia U. Bar: N.Y. In-house counsel Booth Meml. Med. Ctr., Flushing, N.Y., 1975-83, gen. counsel, 1983-91; v.p., gen. counsel the N.Y. Hosp. Med. Ctr. Queens, 1991-97; advisor health care Borough Pres. Queens, 1978. Author: Hidden gold and Pitfalls in New Tax Law, 1970. Mem. North Hempstead Sr. Citizen Commn., Manhasset, NY, 1999—; mem. affordable sr. housing endowment adv. com. Town of North Hempstead, 1999—; bd. dirs. Denton Green Housing Co. Inc., Garden City Park, NY, 1999—. Mem. ABA (health law forum com.), Nat. Health Lawyers Assn., Am. Acad. Hosp. Attys., Am. Soc. Law and Medicine, Am. Soc. Health Care Risk Mgmt., Assn. for Hosp. Risk Mgmt. N.Y., Greater N.Y. Hosp. Assn. (legal adv. com. 1976-97).

KOTCHKA, CLAUDIA B., consumer products company executive, accountant; b. July 11, 1951; married; 1 child. BBA, Ohio Univ., 1973. CPA. With Arthur Anderson & Co., 1973—78; mktg. & brand mgmt. positions with Proctor & Gamble Co., Cin., 1978—97, v.p. art & package design, 1997—98, v.p. design & mktg. knowledge, 1998—99, v.p., feminine care mktg., 1999—2000, v.p. eBus. ventures, 2000—01, v.p., design innovation and strategy, 2001—. Mem. adv. bd. New Zealand Trade and Investment; spkr. in field. Featured in or quoted in numerous publications, guest appearance Today Show. Named one of Best Leaders of 2005, BusinessWeek, 25 Masters of Innovation, 20 Masters of Design, Fast Company Mag., 2005. Office: Proctor & Gamble Co 1 Proctor & Gamble Plz Cincinnati OH 45202*

KOTECKI, DAWN MARIE, social studies educator; b. Cudahy, Wis., Oct. 12, 1963; d. Henry C. and Sophie J Kotecki. BS in Secondary Edn., U. Wis., 1987. Cert. tchr. Tex., 1989. Substitute tchr. Cudahy Pub. Schs., Wis., 1987—89; tchr. social studies Patrick Henry Mid. Sch., Houston, 1989—96; tchr. Tex. history W. I. Stevenson Mid. Sch., Houston, 1996—2000; tchr. social studies Ceser E. Chavez H.S., Houston, 2000—. Adviser Nat. Honor Soc., Houston, 2000—. Mem.: Nat. Coun. for Social Studies. Avocations: swimming, reading, travel, music, meeting people. Home: 1311 Diamante Dr Pasadena TX 77504 Office Phone: 713-495-6950. Office Fax: 713-495-6986. Personal E-mail: dawnkotecki@yahoo.com. Business E-Mail: dkotecki@houstonisd.org.

KOTEFF, ELLEN, periodical editor; b. Harvey, Ill. d. Walter Peter and Florence (Walz) Koteff. BS in Journalism, U. Fla. Editor Palm Beach (Fla.) Daily News; met. editor Daily Record, Parsippany, NJ; exec. editor Nation's Restaurant News, N.Y.C., editor-in-chief, 2004—. Former v.p. Internat. Foodservice Editl. Coun.; mem. jury IFMA Silver Plate; bd. mem. Elliot Leadership Inst. Bd. dirs. Women's Foodservice Forum, 2003. Recipient Jesse H. Neal award, 2002, 2004, McAllister Editl. fellowship award, 2002. Office: Nations Restaurant News 425 Park Ave New York NY 10022-3506 Office Phone: 212-756-5186. Business E-Mail: ekoteff@nrn.com.

KOTHERA, LYNNE MAXINE, psychologist; b. Cleve., Dec. 18, 1938; d. Leonard Frank and Lillian (Shackleton) K.; m. Richard Litwin, Oct. 24, 1965 (dec.). BA with hons., Denison U., Granville, Ohio, 1960; MA, NYU, 1983; PhD, L.I. U., Bklyn., 1989; postgrad. psychotherapy/psychoanalysis, NYU, 2003. Dancer Martha Graham Dance Co., N.Y.C., 1961-62, Carmen DeLavallade Dance Co., N.Y.C., 1965-68, Glen Tetley Dance Co., N.Y.C., 1965-69; prin. dancer John Butler's, N.Y.C., 1971; artist-in-residence Boston High Schs. - Title III, 1969-71, Hobart-Smith Coll./Denison U., 1973; auditor N.Y. State Council of the Arts, N.Y.C., 1974-78; predoctoral fellow clin. psychology Yale-New Haven Hosp., 1987-88; postdoctoral fellow neuropsychology Inst. of Living, Hartford, Conn., 1989-91; with dept. rehab. medicine Mt. Sinai Med. Ctr., N.Y.C., 1991—2006, co-dir. tng. in-patient, 1995—2006; adj. asst. prof. Hunter Coll., N.Y.C., 1998-99. Mem.: APA. Democrat. Avocation: the arts. Home: PO Box 1138 Bridgehampton NY 11932

KOTT, TAMA I., music educator; b. N.Y.C., Jan. 7, 1970; d. Jacob and Doris L. Kott. MusB in Performance and Edn., New Eng. Conservatory, Boston, 1992; MusM in Performance and Lit., Eastman Sch. Music U. Rochester, N.Y., 1994; DMA, Ohio State U., Columbus, 2000. Cert. tchr. Mass., 1992. Prof. music Berry Coll., Mt. Berry, Ga., 2001—05; tchr. Music Sch., Inc., N.Y.C., 2005—06; prof. West Liberty State Coll., W.Va., 2006—. Prin. bassoon Heidelberg Opera Orch., Germany, 1993; substitute bassoon Columbus Symphony Orch., 1999—2001; prin. bassoon Orquesta Sinfonica Universidad Autonomo Nueva Leon, Monterrey, Mexico, 2000; adjudicator Music Festivals, Inc., Birdsboro, Pa., 2001—; substitute bassoon Chattanooga Symphony Orch., 2001—05; prin. bassoon Chamber Players of South, 2001—05; invited performer lecture/recital Russian bassoon music Internat. Double Reed Soc. Conf., San Antonio, 2005; faculty Blue Lake Fine Arts Camp, 2006. Musician: Fischoff National Chamber Music Competition (semi-finalist); author: An Index of Excerpts and an Overview of Published Orchestral Excerpt Collections with A Comparison of Three Collections, 2004; composer: Variations on a Shaker Melody: for Woodwind Quintet, 2004, Swansea Town: for Brass Quintet, 2005, Be Thou My Vision: for Woodwind Trio, 2006, O Come Thou Font of Every Blessing: for Woodwind Trio, 2006; dedicatee Schizologue: Dialogue for Solo Bassoon; contbr. papers to jours. Rep. Coll. Music Soc., 2003—05. Recipient ASCAPLUS award, 2006—; fellow, Eastman Sch. Music, 1992—94; grantee, pARTners for the Arts, 1999, U. Mo., Columbia, 2003—04, Berry Coll., 2002—03, 2004, 2005; scholar, Aspen Music Festival, 1990, 1992. Mem.: Ala. Music Educators Assn., N.J. Music Educators Assn. (clinician 2003—04), Music Educators Nat. Conf. (assoc.), Coll. Music Soc. (assoc.; campus rep. 2003), Am. Fedn. Musicians (assoc.; clinician), Internat. Double Reed Soc. (assoc.), Pi Kappa Lambda (life), Phi Kappa Phi (life), Sigma Alpha Iota (assoc.). Office Phone: 304-336-8098. Personal E-mail: tamakott@yahoo.com. Business E-Mail: tkott@westliberty.edu.

KOTTER, RITA JOAN, theatre educator, design consultant; b. Superior, Wis., Aug. 6, 1934; d. Edward Kotter and Mernnie Geraldine Bellino; children: Rebekah West, Laura Majors, Richmond Majors. BA, U. of Wis., 1952—56; MA, U. of Colo., 1959—69. Teacher Certification Colo., 1959. Tchr., theatre, speech, English Beloit Pub. Schools, Wis., 1956—57, Roseville Pub. Schs., Mich., 1957—58, Canon City Pub. Schs., Colo., 1959—60, Brighton Pub. Schs., Colo., 1960—64, Boulder Valley Schs., Colo., 1964—91; fine arts dept. chair Fairview H.S., Boulder, Colo.; parliamentarian U. of Colo. Bd. of Regents, 1999—. Pub. speaking trainer Boulder Bus. & Profl. Women, Boulder, Colo., 1993—; theatre cons. Carousel Dinner Theatre, Ft. Collins, Colo., 1992—94; master artist-in-residence Deer Creek Elem. Sch., Bailey, Colo., 1993—93; student tchr. supr. U. of No. Colo., 1993—94. Pres. Secondary Sch. Theatre Assn., Washington, 1983—85; bd. of nominations chair Am. Theatre Assn., Washington, D.C., 1973—85; pres. Arts & Humanities Assembly of Boulder County, 1965—2005; chair Leadership Boulder-C. of C., 1993—97; parliamentarian Alliance for Colo. Theatre, Denver, 1984—97; treas. Rocky Mountain Theatre Assn., Denver, 1989—93; adjudicator Am. Coll. Theatre Festival, 1972—92, Festival of Am. Cmty. Theatres, Denver, 1980—90. Recipient Women Who Light up the Cmty., Boulder C. of C., 1999, Inaugural Hall of Fame, Colo. Thespian Soc., 2000, AMOCO Gold Medallion of Excellence, Rocky Mountain/Am. Coll. Theatre Festival, 1984, Alpha Psi Omega Outstanding Theatre Student, U. of Wis. at Superior, 1956, Disting. Svc. award, Alliance for Colo. Theatre, 1993. Mem.: Boulder Bus. & Profl. Women (parliamentarian 1994—2000), Am. Alliance for Theatre & Edn. (dir. of stds. 1987—91), Colo. Alliance for Arts Edn (v.p. 2003—04). Avocations: reading, theatre, skating, tennis, dance. Home: 1407 Bradley Dr Boulder CO 80305

KOTTLER, JOAN LYNN, counselor; b. Nashville, Mar. 28, 1943; d. Julian L. and Dorothy Rose (Schiffman) K.; m. Alvin C. Levy, Feb. 6, 1966 (div. 1982); children: Michael Andrew, Susan Elizabeth. BS, Peabody Coll., 1964; MEd, Emory U., 1965, Ga. State U., 1992. Tchr. hearing impaired Atlanta Speech Sch., 1964-66; ednl. audiologist Med. Coll. Va., Richmond, 1970-73; tchr. hearing impaired DeKalb County Sch. System, Atlanta, 1979-91, lead tchr. for student svcs./counselor, 1991—, counselor, 1991—2005; ret., 2005. Part-time liaison for deaf/hard of hearing program Dekalb Sch. Sys., 2005—. Vol. Temple Homeless Shelter, Atlanta, 1989—, Dem. Conv., Atlanta, 1988; active High Mus. Art, Atlanta, 1988. Mem. DeKalb Assn. Educators, DeKalb Sch. Counselors Assn. (Elem. Sch. Counselor of Yr. for DeKalb County 1994), Ga. Sch. Counselors Assn., Profl. Assn. Ga. Educators, Am. Sch. Counselors Assn. Avocations: gardening, aerobics, reading, tennis, walking, ballroom dancing.

KOTUK, ANDREA MIKOTAJUK, public relations executive, writer; b. New Brunswick, N.J., Oct. 19, 1948; d. Michael and Julia Dorothy (Muka) Mikotajuk. BA, Rutgers U., 1970. Pub. relations asst. Wall St. Jour. Newspaper Fund, Princeton, NJ, 1970; editorial asst. Redbook mag., N.Y.C., 1970-71; asst. pub. relations dir. Children's Aid Soc., N.Y.C., 1971-75; assoc. pub. relations dir. Planned Parenthood, N.Y.C., 1975-80; pres. Andrea & Assocs., N.Y.C., 1980—. Writer publicist for non-profit agys.; contbg. editor Arts Mag., 1970-75. Office: Andrea & Assocs 5th Floor 112 E 23rd St New York NY 10010-4518 Office Phone: 212-353-9585. Personal E-mail: andreapr@earthlink.net.

KOUFFMAN, PAULETTE, psychologist; b. N.Y., N.Y., Mar. 22, 1971; d. Marc and Miriam Kouffman. BA Cum Laude, Wash. U., St. Louis, MO; MA, Widener U., Chester, Pa., D in psychology. Lic. psychologist NY State Bd. of Edn., 2004. Therapist LaSalle U. Counseling Ctr., Phila., 1998—99; psychologist Elwyn Inc., Elwyn, Pa., 1999—2002, Psychol. Svcs. & Human Devel. Ctr., Ft. Washington, Pa., 2002—03; adj. prof. Touro Coll., N.Y., 2004—; psychologist Bklyn Ctr. for Families in Crisis, Bklyn., 2004—; psychologist & life coach pvt. practice, N.Y., 2004—. Cert. empowerment coach Inst. of Profl. Empowerment Coaching, Manalapan, NJ, 2004—. Author: 'Playing Among the Dead: How Holocaust Survivors Used Play to Survive Psychologically', 1999, (children's book) 'The Color-Blind Bower Bird', 2005; contbr. monthly column to profl. jour. Humanity team mem. Humanity Team, N.Y., 2004—05. Mem.: APA (assoc.). Achievements include Simon Simonson Leadership Award. Avocations: teaching, writing, spirituality, travel, walking the beach. Office: Dr Paulette Kouffman 205 Lexington Ave 9th Fl New York NY 10016 Office Phone: 718-593-7717. Home Fax: 212-725-1790; Office Fax: 212-725-1790. Business E-Mail: kpaulet@verizon.net.

KOURIDES, IONE ANNE, endocrinologist, researcher, educator; b. N.Y.C., Sept. 1, 1942; d. Peter T. and Anne E. (Spetseris) K.; m. Charles G. Zaroulis, Nov. 30, 1974; children: Anna Larisa, Andrew, Christina, Peter. BA, Wellesley Coll., 1963; MD, Harvard U., 1967. Diplomate Am. Bd. Internal Medicine, Am. Bd. Endocrinology and Metabolism. Intern Jewish Hosp., Washington U., St. Louis, 1967-68; resident Montefiore, Albert Einstein Med. Sch., Bronx, NY, 1968-69; fellow Beth Israel, Harvard U., Boston, 1970-72; assoc. prof. medicine Cornell U. Med. Coll., N.Y.C., 1981—; sr. med. dir., worldwide team leader endocrine care Pfizer Inc., N.Y.C., 1990—. Mem. editl. bd. Endocrinology, Jour. Clin. Endocrinol Metabolism, also others; contbr. over 100 articles to sci. jours., chpts. to books. Mem. nat. campaign Harvard Med. Sch., Boston, 1986-92; nat. bd. dirs. Philoptochos Soc. Greek Orthodox Archdiocese. Grantee NIH, 1979-84. Fellow ACP; mem. Am. Soc. Clin. Investigation, Am. Assn. Physicians, Am. Thyroid Assn. (coms.), Endocrine Soc. (coms.). Achievements include discovery of alpha-secreting pituitary tumors; measurement of amniotic fluid thyroid stimulating hormone that can be used to diagnose hypthyroidism in utero; development of insulin secretagogue Glucotrol XL. Home: 1070 Park Ave New York NY 10128-1000 Office: Pfizer Inc 235 E 42nd St New York NY 10017-5755 Office Phone: 212-573-2178. Business E-Mail: kourii@pfizer.com.

KOURLIS, REBECCA LOVE, director, former state supreme court justice; b. Colorado Springs, Colo., Nov. 11, 1952; d. John Arthur and Ann (Daniels) Love; m. Thomas Aristithis Kourlis, July 15, 1978; children: Stacy Ann, Katherine Love, Aristithis Thomas. BA with distinction in English, Stanford U., 1973, JD, 1976; LLD (hon.), U. Denver, 1997. Bar: Colo. 1976, D.C. 1979, U.S. Dist. Ct. Colo. 1976, U.S. Ct. Appeals (10th cir.) 1976, Colo. Supreme Ct., U.S. Ct. Appeals (D.C. cir.), U.S. Claims Ct., U.S. Supreme Ct. Assoc. Davis, Graham & Stubbs, Denver, 1976-78; sole practice Craig, Colo., 1978-87; judge 14th Jud. Dist. Ct., Craig, Colo., 1987-94; arbiter Jud. Arbiter Group, Inc., 1994-95; justice Colo. Supreme Ct., 1995—2006; exec. dir. Inst. Advancement Am. Legal Sys. U. Denver, 2006—. Water judge divsn. 6, 1987-94; lectr. to profl. groups. Contbr. articles to profl. jours. Chmn. Moffat County Arts and Humanities, Craig, 1979; mem. Colo. Commn. on Higher Edn., Denver, 1980-81; mem. adv. bd. Colo. Divsn. Youth Svcs., 1988-91; mem. com. civil jury instructions, 1990-95, standing com. gender and justice, 1994-97, chair jud. adv. coun., 1997-2002, chair com. on jury reform, 1996—, chair com. family issues, 2002—; co-chair com. on atty. grievance reform, 1997-2002; mem. long range planning com. Moffat County Sch., 1990; bd. visitors Stanford U., 1989-94, Law Sch. U. Denver, 1997-2002; trustee Kent Denver Sch., 1996-2002, Graland Sch., 2004—. Named N.W. Colo. Daily Press Woman of Yr., 1993; recipient Trailblazer award AAUW, 1998, Mary Lathrop award Colo. Women's Bar Assn., 2001, Jud. Excellence award Acad. Matrimonial Lawyers, 2002, Champion for Children award Rocky Mountain Children's Law Ctr., 2003, Friend of Children award Adv. for Children, 2003. Fellow: Colo. Bar Found., Am. Bar Found.; mem.: N.W. Colo. Bar Assn. (Cmty. Svc. award 1993—94), Dist. Ct. Judges' Assn. (pres. 1993—94), Colo. Bar Assn. (bd. govs. 1983—85, mineral law sect. bd. dirs. 1985, sr. v.p. 1987—88), Rocky Mountain Mineral Found. Office: U Denver Inst Advancement Am Legal Sys 1901 E Asbury Denver CO 80208 Office Phone: 303-871-6600. Business E-Mail: legalinstitute@du.edu.

KOURNIKOVA, ANNA, retired professional tennis player; b. Moscow, June 7, 1981; d. Sergei and Alla Kournikova; m. Sergei Fedorov (div.). Prof. tennis player WTA, 1995—2004. Player Russian Fed Cup team, 1996—97, 2000, Russian Olympic Team, 1996; founder Physical Culture Russian Acad., 1997. Actor: (films) Me, Myself & Irene, 2000. ITF Jr. World champion, 1995, ITF Women's Cir. Satellite Event, Midland, Mich., 1996, title ITF Women's Cir. Satellite, Rockford, Ill.; winner Orange Bowl, 1995, Italian Open Jrs., 1995, European Champaionships, 1995; semi-finalist Wimbledon Jrs., 1995, quarter finalist French Open Jrs.; recipient (with Martina Hingis) WTA Tour Doubles Team of the Year award, 1999; named 1 or top 10 Most Marketable Female Athletes, Sports Business Daily, 2003. Achievements include won 16 career WTA doubles titles including Australian Open, 1999, 2000.

KOUZEL, MILDRED, artist; b. New Haven, Dec. 21, 1922; d. Samuel Goldberg (dec.) and Martha Mitzen-Hendler (dec.); m. Bernard Kouzel, June 20, 1948 (dec. Nov. 1993); children: Ilene, Janet, Lynn. RN, Grace Hosp. Sch. Nursing, New Haven, 1944; student, NYU, 1946-48; MA, Calif. State U., 1972. Pub. health nurse Lehigh Valley Pub. Health Nursing Assn., Allentown, Pa., 1948-49. One-woman shows include Fullerton (Calif.) Libr., 1977, Brand Librs. Art Gallery, Glendale, Calif., 1982, Agoura Hills (Calif.) Mcpl. Gallery, 1984, Orange County Ctr. for Contemporary Art, Santa Ana, Calif., 1986, 88, Techline Studio, L.A., 1990, L.A. Art Core Brewery Annex, 1997, U. of Judaism, Platt Gallery, L.A., 1997, Grand Ctrl. Gallery, Santa Ana, Calif., 2002, JCC Long Beach, Calif., 2005; group exhbns. include Del Mar Coll., Corpus Christi, Tex., 1976, Century Gallery, Sylmar, Calif., 1983, Brea (Calif.) Civic Gallery, 1985, Peter Strauss Ranch, Agoura, CAlif., 1985, Seasoned Eye Nat. Traveling Exhibit AARP, Washington, N.Y.C., others, 1986, UN World Conf. on Women, Nairobi, Kenya, 1986, So. Calif. Prints and Drawings, Saddleback Coll., Calif., Downey (Calif.) Mus., 1987, Anaheim (Calif.) Cultural Ctr., 1988, Pine St. Lobby Gallery, San Francisco, 1990, Koll Ctr. Newport, Newport Beach, Calif., 1991, Orange County Ctr. for Contemporary Art, Santa Ana, Calif., 1994, Wignal Mus./Gallery, Chaffey Coll., Rancho Cucmonga, Calif., 1994, Maynard Walker Art Collection, Garnet Kans., 1995, Chapman U., So. Calif. Artists, Orange, 1998, Calif. State U., Fullerton, 1998, Anaheim Cultural Ctr., 1999, Palos Verdes Art Ctr., Calif., 2002; pub. art projects include John Wayne Airport, Newport Beach, 1990, Calif. State U., Fullerton, 1990, Fullerton Mus. Ctr., 1991, 92, City of Brea Bus Shelter Program, Brea, 1992, Hunt Libr., Fullerton, 1999; commd. works for Temple Beth Tikvah, Fullerton, 1982, 84, Temple Beth Sholom, Whittier, Calif., 1985, Home Savs. Bank, Irwindale, Calif., 1988; represented in numerous pvt. collections. Mem. scholarship fund bd. Calif. State U., Fullerton, 1994, 95. 1st lt. U.S. Army Nurse Corps, 1945-46. Fellow So. Calif. Artists, Women's Caucus for the Arts. Democrat. Jewish. Avocations: folk dancing, writing memoirs, watching films, listening to jazz.

KOVAC, CAROLINE (CAROL KOVAC), computer company executive; BA, Oberlin Coll.; PhD in Chem., U. So. Calif. Joined IBM, 1983; dir. computational biology IBM Rsch., v.p. tech. strategy, div. operations; gen. mgr. IBM Life Sci., 2000—. Mem.-emeritus IBM Acad. Tech. Named to Hall of Fame, Women in Tech. Internat., 2002. Office: IBM 1133 Westchester Ave White Plains NY 10604

KOVAC, SHIRLEY ANN, retired elementary school educator; b. Sharon, Pa., Feb. 7, 1950; d. Peter and Stella Antos; m. Donald Edward Kovac; children: Shelly, Karen, Donald Jr. BS in Edn., Slippery Rock U., 1972. Libr. aide Sharon City Schs., Pa., 1972—75, substitute tchr., 1975—76; tchr. 1st grade Hadley Elem. Sch., 1976—82, Musser Elem. Sch., 1982—83; tchr. 1st and 2d grade West Hill Elem. Sch., 1983—90; tchr. 5th grade Case Ave. Elem. Sch., 1990—93, tchr. 2d grade, 1993—2005; ret., 2005. Recipient Tchg. and Spl. Student Activities award, Adminstrn. and Bd. Edn., Sharon, 1999. Mem.: NEA, Pa. State Tchrs. Assn., Sharon Tchrs. Assn. Office: Ednl Svc Ctr 215 Forker Blvd Sharon PA 16146

KOVACS, BEATRICE, library studies educator; b. Seekirchen, Austria, June 2, 1945; came to U.S., 1948; d. Lorand and Helen (Magyary-Kossa) K.; m. Thomas Gordon Basler, Apr. 20, 1969 (div. 1979); m. Louis Edward Mitchum, Jan. 10, 1994. AB in English, Syracuse U., 1966; MLS, Rutgers State U., 1967; DLS, Columbia U., 1983. Libr. Nassau Acad. Medicine, Garden City, N.Y., 1967-70; cataloger, asst. acquisitions libr. Augusta (Ga.) Regional Libr., 1974-78; collection devel. libr. Med. Coll. Ga., Augusta, 1978-80; acct. specialist Readmore Publs., N.Y.C., 1982-83; chief collection devel. U. N.Mex. Med. Ctr. Libr., Albuquerque, 1984-85; asst. prof. U. N.C., Greensboro, 1985-91, assoc. prof., 1991—. Vis. instr. Pratt Inst. Grad. Sch. Libr., Bklyn., 1982-83; adj. prof. U. N.C. Chapel Hill Sch. Info. and Libr. Sci., 1997-98. Author: Decision-Making Process for Library Collections, 1990, ALA Fingertip Guide to National Health-Information Resources, 1995; co-author: Health Sciences Librarianship, 1977, Using Science and Technology Information Resources, 1991; contbr. articles to profl. jours. Bishop scholarship Med. Libr. Assn., 1966; recipient Meritorious Achievement award, NC Chpt. Spl. Librs. Assn., 2005. Mem. ALA, N.C. Libr. Assn., Spl. Librs. Assn., N.C. Spl. Librs. Assn. (pres. 1992-93), Assn. Libr. and Info. Sci. Educators. Office: U NC Sch Edn PO Box 26170 Greensboro NC 27402-6170 E-mail: bea_kovacs@uncg.edu.

KOVACS, CHRISTINA MARIE, music educator; b. Irvington, NJ, Oct. 17, 1976; d. Charles and Isabella Joan Kovacs. BA in English, Caldwell Coll., 2004, BA in Music, 2004. Music tchr. Archdiocese of Newark Schs. Mem.: Music Educators Nat. Conf. Roman Catholic. Home: 37 Byrd Ave Bloomfield NJ 07003-4426

KOVAL, DONITA R., bank executive; Pres. Omega Bank, State College, Pa., 2002—, CEO, 2003—, Omega Fin. Corp., Pa., 2003—, pres., 2004—, bd. dirs., 2005—. Office: Omega Fin Corp 366 Walker Dr State College PA 16801 Office Phone: 814-231-7680.*

KOVANIS, LOUKEA NAKOS, chemistry educator, researcher; d. Patricia N. and Nakos L. Kovanis. Bachelors, U. Mich., Ann Arbor, 1988; Masters, Ea. Mich. U., Ypsilanti, 1997. Cert. secondary edn. Ctrl. Mich. U., 1998. Chemistry instr. Holly HS, Mich., 1994—97, Clarkston HS, Mich., 1998—; biol. aid NOAA, Pascagoula, Miss., 2005. Home: 300 Trealout #6 Fenton MI 48430 Office: Clarkston HS 6093 Flemings Lake Rd Clarkston MI 48346 Office Phone: 248-623-3766. Personal E-mail: loukea_sea@yahoo.com.

KOVE, MIRIAM, psychotherapist; b. Chotin, Romania, Feb. 17, 1941; came to U.S., Sept. 12, 1962; d. Avrum and Riva (Nussenbaum) Wolkove; m. Marc L. Kouffman, Aug. 16, 1964 (div. Oct. 24, 1989); children: Avra, Paulette. BA in English Lit., Sir George Williams U., 1962; MA in Early Childhood, Hunter Coll., 1975; Cert. in Psychoanalytic Psychotherapy, New Hope Guild, N.Y.C., 1979; MSW, Adelphi U., 1983. Tchr. various pub. schs., Montreal, Can., 1957-58; actress N.Y.C., 1962—; tchr. early childhood Emanuel Nursery Sch., N.Y.C., 1964-74; adj. lectr. early childhood Cmty. Coll., Bklyn., 1974-75; psychotherapist, clinician New Hope Guild Ctr., N.Y.C., 1979-81; intake dir., clinician Insts. of Religion and Health, N.Y.C., 1983-84; pschotherapist N.Y.C., 1984—; faculty, supr. New Hope Guild Ctr., N.Y.C., 1990—; dir. day care on-site therapy program C.I.S. Counseling Ctr., N.Y.C., 1992-94. Author: (book) Myths and Madness. Mem. People for the Am. Way, Warsaw Gathering of Holocaust Survivors. Recipient Hebrew prize Sir George Williams U., 1962; recommended for English prize Concordia U. Fellow Nat. Orgn. Social Work, Soc. for Clin. Social Work Psychotherapists (edn. com.); mem. New Hope Grad. Soc. (steering com.), Am. Bd. Examiners in Clin. Social Work. Jewish. Home and Office: 320 E 25th St Apt 8ee New York NY 10010-3100 Office Phone: 212-689-1442. Personal E-mail: miriamkove@hotmail.com.

KOVEL, TERRY HORVITZ, writer, antiques authority; b. Cleve. d. Isadore and Rix Horvitz; m. Ralph Kovel; children: Lee R., Karen. BA, Wellesley Coll., 1950. Tchr. math. Hawken Sch. for Boys, Shaker Heights, Ohio, 1961-71; now pres. Antiques Inc.; past tchr. course in antiques Western Res. U., John Carroll U. Writer: (with Ralph Kovel) syndicated column Kovels Antiques and Collecting, 1955—, Ask the Experts, House Beautiful, 1979-00, Medio, CD-Rom mag., 1995, The Kovels on Collecting, Forbes Mag., 2000-02; editor: monthly newsletters Kovels on Antiques and Collectibles, 1974-, Kovels Sports Collectibles, 1992-97; TV series Know Your Antiques, Pub. TV, 1969-70; syndicated TV Series Kovels on Collecting, 1981, 87, Collector's Journal TV, 1989-93, Flea Market Finds with the Kovels HGTV, 2000-04; numerous appearances on radio and TV talk shows; author: (with Ralph Kovel) Kovels' Dictionary of Marks-Pottery and Porcelain, 1953, rev. edit., 1995, Directory of American Silver, Pewter and Silver Plate, 1958, American Country Furniture, 1780-1875, 1963, Kovels' Know Your Antiques, rev. edit, 1993, Kovels' American Art Pottery, 1993, Kovels' American Antiques 1750-1900, 2004, Kovels' Antiques and Collectibles Price List, 38th edit., 2006, Kovels' Know Your Collectibles, 1981, 92, Kovels' Bottle Price List, 13th edit., 2006, Kovels' Organizer for Collectors, 1978, revised, 1983, Kovels' Price Guide for Collector Plates, Figurines, Paperweights and Other Limited Editions, 1978, Kovels' Collector's Guide to American Art Pottery, 1974, Kovels' Collector's Guide to Limited Editions, 1974, Kovels' Depression Glass and Dinnerware Price List, 8th edit., 2004, Kovels' Illustrated Price Guide to Royal Doulton, 2d edit., 1984, Kovels' Collectors' Source Book, 1983, Kovels' New Dictionary of Marks Pottery and Porcelain, 1850 to the Present, 1986, Kovels' Advertising Collectibles Price List, 1986, 05, Kovels' Guide to Selling Your Antiques and Collectibles, 1987, 2d edit., 1990, Kovels' Book of Antique Labels, 1982, Kovels' American Silver Marks 1650 to the Present, 1989, Kovels' Antiques and Collectibles Fix-It Source Book, 1990, Kovels' Guide to Selling, Buying and Fixing Your Antiques and Collectibles, 1995, Kovels' Quick Tips: 799 Helpful Hints on How To Care for Your Collectibles, 1995, The Label Made Me Buy It, 1998, Kovels' Yellow Pages, 2d. edit., 2003, Kovels' Bid, Buy and Sell Online, 2001; (Video tape series) Collecting With the Kovels, 1995, Art Pottery I, Art Pottery II, Kovels' Page-A-Day Collectibles Calendar 1990, 1991, Kovels' Antiques and Collectibles 2003 Day-At-A Time-Calendar; contbr. numerous articles on antiques to publs, chapt. to books. Trustee Hiram Coll., 1989—99, hon. trustee, 2000; bd. mem. Shaker Hist. Soc. Hiram fellow; recipient Peirce award for outstanding cmty. svc. Sta. WVIZ-TV, 1980, Cleve. Emmy award for best entertainment, 1971, Cleve. Emmy award for cultural affairs programming, 1987; Laurel Sch. Alumanae of Yr. Office: PO Box 22200 Cleveland OH 44122-0200

KOVNER, KATHLEEN JANE, civic worker, portrait artist; b. Cambridge, Mass., Nov. 25, 1919; d. David Leo and Kathleen Elizabeth (Lalley) Lane; m. Benjamin Kovner (dec.), June 20, 1938; children: Kathleen Barbara (dec.), Michael Anthony, Peter Christopher. Student, Art Students League, N.Y.C., 1937-40. Owner, CEO Helen Bennett Ltd., Stamford, Conn., 1948-59; cons. Bride's Mag., N.Y.C., 1967-70; co-chair membership com. Women's Nat. Rep. Club, N.Y.C., 1980-81, chmn. membership com., 1981-87, v.p., 1986-87, also bd. dirs. Ltd. ptnr. 519 8th Ave Corp., N.Y.C., 18-19th St. Corp., N.Y.C., Kaufman Arcade Bldg., N.Y.C., 19th St. Assn., N.Y.C., dir. Nelson Tower Assoc., N.Y.C., 1998, ptnr. 450 Seventh Ave Assoc., N.Y.C. Portrait artist in oils, with various portraits in pvt. collections. Fundraiser St. Ignatius Loyola, N.Y.C., 1960-61, Jeanine Pirro-Campaign for Dist. Atty., Westchester County, N.Y., 1993, 97. Republican. Roman Catholic. Home: 62 Brookridge Dr Greenwich CT 06830-4830 also: 923 5th Ave New York NY 10021-2649

KOWAL, PENNY HOPE, educational consultant; b. Langdon, Mo., June 17, 1943; d. William Ralph and Merry Scamman Oswald; m. Frank Florian Kowal, Nov. 28, 1988; children: Christopher Cortlandt Rehberg, Mathew Addison Rehberg, Henry John Rehberg, Karan Elizabeth, Kathy Jane. BA, N.W. Mo. State U., Maryville, Missouri, 1966; MA, U. So. Fla., 1978; PhD, U. Nebr., 1989. Lic. supt. K-12 Nebr., 1989. Staff devel. specialist Ednl. Svc. Unit #3, Fremont, Nebr., 1976—78; coord. programs for gifted Millard Pub. Sch., Omaha, 1978—85, dir. instrnl. effectiveness, 1985—94, dir. staff devel., 1994—97, dir. effective sch., 1995—97, assoc. supt. ednl. svcs., 1997—2002. Trainer for 3 minute walkthru supervision various K-12 sch. dist., Nebr., 2004—; life coach, Omaha, 2004—. Pres., bd. trustees Unity Ch. of Omaha, 2003—05. Independent. Avocations: travel, gardening, music, exercise. Home: 16155 Capitol Ave Omaha NE 68118-2009 Office: Kowal and Assoc 16155 Capitol Ave Omaha NE 68118-2009 Office Phone: 402-330-1240.

KOWALSKA, MARIA TERESA, research scientist, educator; b. Wielun, Poland, June 8, 1932; arrived in U.S., 1982, naturalized, 1991; d. Jozef Ozmina and Zofia Elzbieta Pecherska; m. Wielislaw Kowalski, Apr. 19, 1954 (dec. Nov. 1991); children: Jacek Kowalski, Beata Kowalska-Ellington. BA, Lyceum Gen. Edn., Lodz, Poland, 1950; MS in Pharmacy, Med. Acad., Poznan, Poland, 1954, PhD in Pharmacy, 1964; Dr. Hab., Med. Acad., Lodz, 1978. Asst. prof. pharmacy Med. Acad., Poznan, 1955—69; postdoctoral fellow in pharmacy U. Paris, 1969—70; assoc. prof. Acad. Agr., Poznan, 1970—80; prof. pharmacognosy Nat. U. Kinshasa, Zaire, 1980—82; rsch. assoc. Rsch. Ctr. Fairchild Frop Garden, Miami, Fla., 1985—90. Adj. asst. prof. dept. biochemistry and molecular biology Sch. Medicine U. Miami, 1990—2000; counselor students Acad. Agr., Poznan, 1975—80; prin. investigator on grant Internat. Palm Soc., Miami, 1986, Miami, 87, World Wildlife Fund, Washington, 1988. Appeared (TV) ABC Miami News, 1992, CNN News, 1993; contbr. articles to profl. jours. Avocations: music, skiing, mountain climbing. Home: 6421 SW 106 St Miami FL 33156

KOWALSKI, DEBRA ATKISSON, physician; d. Thomas and Patricia Atkisson; m. Roger Geer, June 22, 2002; 1 child, Katherine. MD, Tex. Tech U. Sch. of Medicine, Lubbock, 1986. Board Certification Am. Bd. of Psychiatry and Neurology, 1991, Board Certification, Child and Adolescent Psychiatry Am. Bd. of Psychiatry and Neurology, 1993. Assoc. med. dir. Cook Children's Med. Ctr., Ft. Worth, 1992—96; med. dir. The Excel Ctr., Ft. Worth, 1996—2001, Sundance Behavioral Health Care, Ft. Worth, 2005—. Cons. Early Childhood Intervention, Ft. Worth, 2000—, CorpHealth, Ft. Worth, 1999—. Tchr. Tex. Girl's Choir, Ft. Worth, 2006, Elem. Sunday Sch. Class, Ft. Worth, 2005—06; cons. Early Childhood Mental Health Com., Ft. Worth, 2005; troop leader Girl Scouts, Ft. Worth, 2001—06. Named one of Ft. Worth Tex. Top Docs, Tarrant County Med. Soc., 2002—04, 2006; Seeley fellowship, Karl Menninger Sch. of Psychiatry, 1991. Fellow: Am. Psychiat. Assn.; mem.: Tex. Soc. of Psychiat. Physicians. Christian Meth. Avocations: travel, cooking, reading. Office: Debra Atkisson Kowalski MD PA 6410 Southwest Blvd Ste 205 Fort Worth TX 76109 Office Phone: 817-735-44430. Office Fax: 817-735-4565.

KOWALSKI, KATHLEEN PATRICIA, reporter, publishing executive; b. Detroit; d. Arthur Aloysius and Theresa Joyce (Pathe) K. BA in English Lang. and Lit., U. Mich., 1987. Sales, divsn. trainer, mktg. mgr. Encyclopaedia Britannica, Southfield, Mich., 1981-86; computer graphics, comm. and systems coord. Kelly/Kelly Tech. Svcs., Troy, Mich., 1987-95; intern WJBK-TV, Southfield, 1990-91; host on air talent Cable TV Sta. WTRY, Troy, Mich., 1993-94; pres. Kowality Writing, West Bloomfield, Mich., 1993—; quality sys. coord. Ford Motor Co., 1998—. Author: Blossoming Rose, 1995. Mem. U. Mich. Alumnae Group, Ice Skating Inst. Am., Beta Alpha Psi. Roman Catholic. Avocations: ballet, figure skating, horseback riding, skiing, piano. Home: 641 N Fairgrounds Rd Imlay City MI 48444-9490

KOWLESSAR, MURIEL, retired pediatric educator; b. Bklyn., Jan. 2, 1926; d. John Henry and Arene (Driver) Chevious; m. O. Dhodanand Kowlessar, Dec. 27, 1952; 1 child, Indrani. AB, Barnard Coll., 1947; MD, Columbia U., 1951. Diplomate Am. Bd. Pediatrics. Instr. Downstate Med. Ctr., Bklyn., 1958-64, asst. prof., 1965-66; asst. prof. clin. pediatrics Temple U., Phila., 1967-70; assoc. prof. Med. Coll. Pa., Phila., 1971-83, dir. pediatric group svcs., 1975-90, acting chmn. pediatrics dept., 1981-83, vice chair pediatrics dept., 1982-91, prof., 1983-91, prof. emeritus, 1991—. Contbr. articles to med. jours. Mem. Pa. Gov.'s Task Force on Spl. Supplemental Food Program for Women, Infants and Children, Harrisburg, 1981-83, Phila. Bd. Health, 1982-86; vol. Phila. Com. for Homeless, 1991-92, Gateway Literacy Program, YMCA, Germantown Bridge, Pa., 1992-93. Fellow Am. Acad. Pediatrics (emeritus); mem. Phila. Pediatric Soc., Cosmopolitan Club Phila., Phi Beta Kappa. Democrat. Avocations: ballroom dancing, opera, travel.

KOYLE, DENYS MARIE, motel and restaurant executive; b. Payson, Utah, Jan. 7, 1948; d. Grant William Koyle and Shirley Jayne (Garbett) Schena; m. Alexander Ray Perea, Apr. 28, 1968 (div. 1979); children: Gary A., Dennis A.; m. John Dean Baker, Oct. 21, 1981 (div. 1994); step-children: Christina, David, Craig, Tom. BA magna cum laude, U. Utah, 1970; postgrad., U. Calif.-Long Beach, 1976-77. Cert. tchr., Utah. Owner, mgr. Border Inn, Baker, Nev., 1977-81, 85—. Instr. No. Nev. Community Coll., Ely, 1990-1996. Mem. Nev. Dem. Exec. Com., 1984, Nev. Dem. Ctrl. Com.; sec. Baker Town Adv. Bd., 1985-91, 1993-1995; bd. dirs. White Pine County Libr., 1991-1997, chmn., 1992-1997; bd. dirs., pres. Great Basin Heritage Area Partnership, 2005—. Recipient Gov.'s Tourism Devel. award, 1988, 2005. Mem. Nev. Cattlewomen's Assn. (officer local sect.), White Pine County C. of C. (bd. dirs.), ACLU Nev. (bd. dirs. 1996-2005), Rotary Club of Ely (pres. 2002-2003). Avocations: piano, reading, hiking. Office: Border Inn PO Box 30 Baker NV 89311-0030 Office Phone: 775-234-7300. E-mail: borderinn@aol.com.

KOYM, ZALA COX, retired elementary school educator; b. San Antonio, July 21, 1948; d. Bruce Meador and Ruby Esther (Jordan) Cox; m. Charles Raymond Koym, July 5, 1969; children: Carol Ann, Cathy Lynn, Suzie Kay. BS Edn., SW Tex. State U., 1970; grad., Inst. Children's Lit., 2003. Cert. supervision tchr. effective practices. Elem. tchr. Schertz-Cibolo Ind. Sch. Dist., Tex., 1970—71; substitute tchr. Alamogordo Pub. Schs., N.Mex., 1973—75; tchr. elem. Round Rock Ind. Sch. Dist., Tex., 1983—96, asst. prin., 1988—91, mentor tchr., 1993—96, 1999—2001; tchr. 3-4th grade multi-age Ft. Sam Houston Elem., San Antonio, 1996—98; tchr. 3d grade Silver Creek Elem., Azle, Tex., 1998—99, tchr. 4th grade, 1999—2003, tchr. looping grades 3 and 4, 1998—2003; ret., 2003. Coord. sci. lab. Robertson Elem., Old Town Elem., 1983—89; chair, coord. 5th grade level Round Rock Ind. Sch. Dist., 1986—90, chair 2d grade level, 1990—93; textbook advisor State of Tex., 1989; coord. sci. lab. Improvement Coun. Ft. Sam Houston Dist., 1996—97, mem. campus gifted and talented com. Improvement Coun., 1997—99, dir. campus spelling bee Improvement Coun., 1998—2003, coord. campus sci. Improvement Coun., 1999—2003; vol. Lake County Christian Sch., Ft. Worth, 2004—06. Active PTA, 1981—96, v.p. programs, 1994—95, site-based decision making campus rep., 1993—95; active PTO, 1996—2003; neighborhood capt. March of Dimes, 1990, Am. Heart Assn., 1994—95, Am. Inst. Cancer Rsch., 1999; mem. Campus Student Assistance Program Team, 1990—96, Old Town Bldg. Leadership Team, 1991—92; dir. vacation Bible Sch. Fredericksburg United Meth. Ch., 1984—87, mem. scholarship com., 1992—94. Named Silver Creek Tchr. of Yr., 1999—2000. Mem.: ASCD, Assn. Tex. Profl. Educators (campus rep. 1998—2003), Phi Delta Kappa (sec. 1991—93, assoc. historian 1994—95, v.p. programs 1995—96). Home: 2202 Amberstone Fredericksburg TX 78624-6795 Personal E-mail: ckoym@aol.com.

KOZAK, HARLEY JANE, actress, writer; b. Wilkes-Barre, Pa., Jan. 28, 1957; d. Joseph Aloysius and Dorothy (Taraldsen) K.; m. Gregory Aldisert, 1997; children: Audrey, Lorenzo and Gianna. Cert., NYU, 1980. Appeared in films Parenthood, 1989, Arachnophobia, 1990, The Taking of Beverly Hills, 1990, The Favor, 1990, Necessary Roughness, 1991, All I Want for Christmas, 1991, Magic in The Water, 1995, TV series Harts of the West, 1993-94, Bringing Up Jack, 1995, You Wish, 1997; author: (novels) Dating Dead Men, 2004 (Agatha, Anthony and Macavity awards for Best First Mystery Novel, Nebr. Book award for Best Fiction, 2005), Dating is Murder, 2005. Office: Renee Zuckerbrot Lit Agy 115 W 29th St 10th Fl New York NY 10001

KOZAK, KAREN S., writer; b. Bethesda, Md., Sept. 8, 1944; d. John J. Kozak and Sarah Elizabeth Majors. BA, Wellesley Coll., Mass., 1967; MA Grad. Sch. Librarianship, U. Denver, 1969. Reference libr. Love Libr. U. Nebr., Lincoln, 1969—71; cataloger Alumni Libr. Creighton U., Omaha, 1971—75, head cataloging Alumni Libr., 1975—81; dir. libr. Bellevue Coll., Nebr., 1981—87; writer Omaha, 1987—. Sec. Coll. and Univ. sect. Nebr. Libr. Assn., 1981—82; sec. Libr. Dirs. Assn., 1983—84; docent Henry Doorly Zoo, Omaha, 1992—, bd. dirs., chair membership com., 2002—04; docent Joslyn Art Mus., Omaha, 1989—90. Author (Midwestern Reflections series): Striking the Senses, 1996, Trying on Trouble, 1998, Reaching for Rubies, 1999, Opening with One, 1999, Weaving the Wind, 2000, Climbing the Clouds, 2001, Keeping the Keys, 2002; author: (poetry) Four Seasons in Poetry, 2003, Celebrate: A Collection of Women's Writings, 2006. Pres. Nebr. Wellesley Club, 1987—97; poet laureate region 7 Am. Mensa Ltd., Arlington, Tex., 2001, proctor coord. region 7, 1996—. Mem.: Am. Soc. Interior Designers, Nebr. Writers Guild (scholarship com. 2004—05), PEO (history com. CR chpt. 1974), Nebr.-We. Iowa Mensa (proctor coord. 1988—), Phi Theta Kappa (Omaha chpt.). Democrat. Presbyterian. Avocations: gardening, writing, interior decorating.

KOZBERG, DONNA WALTERS, rehabilitation services professional; b. Milford, Del., Jan. 1, 1952; d. Robert Glyndwr and Gailey Ruth (Bedorf) Walters; m. Ronald Paul Kozberg, June 8, 1974; 1 child, Mariel Gailey. BA, U. Fla., 1973, M in Rehab. Counseling, 1974; MFA, CUNY, 1979; MBA, Rutgers U., 1986. Cert. rehab. counselor. Rehab. counselor Office Vocat. Rehab., N.Y.C., 1975-81; area dir. Lift, Inc., Staten Island, NY, 1981-83, ea. region dir. pub. relations, advt. Mountainside, NJ, 1983-85, v.p., 1985—, v.p., chief fin. officer, 1988, exec. v.p., 1991-93, pres., 1993; co-founder, mng. dir. Expert Strategies, Inc., Mountainside, NJ, 1992—; self-employed writer, editor, 1975—. Adv. bd. Rutgers Exec. Master Bus. Adminstrn. Contbr. articles to profl. jours.; assoc. editor Parachute mag., 1978; editor-in-chief (newsletter) Counselor Adv, 1980. Pres. Com. on Employment of People with Disabilities; trustee Ctr. for Creative Living; bd. dirs. N.J. Adv. Coun. for Independent Living, adv. panel NYU. Mem. Nat. Rehab. Assn. (Spl. citation 1974, grantee 1973), Nat. Rehab. Adminstrs. Assn., Nat. Rehab. Counselors Assn., N.J. Rehab. Counselors Assn. (pres. 1996), Poets and Writers. Avocations: Tennis, English lit., Tae Kwon Do. Home: 45 Dug Way Watchung NJ 07069-6011 Office: Lift Inc PO Box 4264 Warren NJ 07059-0264 E-mail: dwkozberg@aol.com.

KOZBERG, JOANNE CORDAY, public affairs consultant; b. Edmonton, Alta., Can., July 4, 1944; d. Eliot and Marian (Lipkind) Corday; m. Roger A. Kozberg, May 25, 1968; children: Lindsey, Anthony. BA in history, U. Calif., Berkeley, 1966; MA in pub. policy, Occidental Coll., 1969. Assoc. prodr. KCET Cmty. Affairs Dept., LA, 1967-68; dir. So. Calif. NAACP Legal Def. and Edn. Fund, LA, 1975-77; acting exec. dir., dir. pub. affairs and the arts program CORO Found., LA, 1978-81; sr. policy cons. to US Senator Pete Wilson, LA, 1984-88; chair Calif. Arts Coun., 1988—91, exec. dir., 1991-93; sec. state and consumer affairs State of Calif., 1993-98; pres., COO Music Ctr. of LA County, 1999—2002; now ptnr. Calif. Strategies, LA. Mem. Nat. Hwy. Adv. Comm., Washington, 1980-86; dir. Western States Arts Fedn., Santa Fe, 1991-94, Nat. Assembly of State Arts Agys., Washington, 1992-94. Pres. The Blue Ribbon, LA, 1988—91; trustee Calif. Cmty. Found.; bd. dirs. Ctr. Theatre Group, LA, 1994—99; bd. regents U. Calif., 1998—; bd. trustees J. Paul Getty Trust, LA, 2005—. Recipient Rosalie M. Stern award U. Calif., Berkeley, 1984, Crystal Eagle award for pub. affairs excellence, Coro Found., 1998; CORO fellow, 1967. Mem. Calif. Club, Hillcrest Country Club. Republican. Jewish. Avocations: bicycling, tennis. Office: Calif Strategies Ste 1025 1875 Century Pk E Los Angeles CA 90067 Office Phone: 310-843-9600.

KOZEVA, NATALIA, music educator; b. Kharkov, Ukraine, Aug. 3, 1965; d. Nikolai Glukhov and Victoria Glukhova; m. Vladimir Kozev, Oct. 19, 1985 (div. May 7, 2002); children: Jenny, Katie. Master's, Rostov State Musical-Pedagogical Inst., Rostov-on-Don, Russia, 1989. Cert. tchr. Ill. State Tchr. Certification Bd., 2005. Ch. pianist First Ch. of Christ, Scientist, Schaumburg, Ill., 2001—; music tchr. Summit Acad., Elgin, Ill., 2004—06, Liberty Elem. Sch., Carpentersville, Ill., 2006—. Office: Liberty Elem Sch 6500 Miller Rd Carpentersville IL 60110 Office Phone: 847-851-8300. Personal E-mail: nkozeva@sbcglobal.net.

KOZIK, SUSAN S., information technology executive; Grad., Bates Coll. With Cigna Corp.; sr. v.p., chief tech. officer Penn Mut. Life Ins. Co.; v.p. info. tech. ops. and svcs. Lucent Techs.; exec. v.p., chief tech. officer TIAA-CREF, N.Y.C., 2003—. Active, former trustee Bates Coll. Recipient 1st Disting. Young Alumni award, Bates Coll. Office: TIAA-CREF 730 3d Ave New York NY 10017

KOZLOFF, JESSICA S., academic administrator; b. San Antonio, Mar. 29, 1941; d. Robert John and Ann (Acklen) Sledge; m. Stephen R. Kozloff, June 12, 1965; children: Kyle Schaller, Rebecca Esther. BS, U. Nev., 1963, MA, 1964; PhD, Colo. State U., 1983. Prof. polit. sci. U. Northern Colo., Greeley, 1976-89, exec. asst. to pres., 1985-89; v.p. acad. affairs State Colls. in Colo., Denver, 1989-94; pres. Bloomsburg U., 1994—. Mem. Middle States Commn. on Higher Edn., 2000—, chair 2006-; bd. dirs. Geisinger Health Plan, 2004— Bd. dirs. United Way, Bloomsburg, 1994—2000, Boy Scouts Am., Bloomsburg, 1994—2000. Acad. Adminstrn. fellow Am. Coun. on Edn., 1985. Mem.: Pa. Compact (bd. dirs. 1998—2001), Bloomsburg C. of C., Nat. Collegiate Athletics Assn. (mem. pres. commn. 1996—2001), Am. Assn. State Colls. and Univs. (bd. dirs. 2004—), Bloomsburg Rotary Club. Avocations: golf, tennis, skiing, biking, travel. Office: Bloomsburg U 400 E 2nd St Bloomsburg PA 17815-1399 Office Phone: 570-389-4526. Business E-Mail: jkozloff@bloomu.edu.

KOZLOFF, JOYCE, artist; b. Somerville, N.J., Dec. 14, 1942; m. Max Kozloff. BFA, Carnegie Inst. Tech., 1964; MFA, Columbia Univ., 1967. Taught at Chgo. Art Inst., Sch. Visual Arts, NYC, Cooper Union, NYC. Exhibitions include Payson Galleries, NYC, 1995, DC Moore Gallery, NYC, 1996-2001, Boston Univ. Art Gallery, 2000, Whitney Mus. Contemporary Art, NYC, 1999-2000, Nat. Mus. Women in the Arts, Washington, 2001; represented in permanent collections of Met. Mus. Art, NYC, Mus. Modern Art, NYC, Nat. Gallery of Art, Washington; author of Patterns of Desire, 2000; co-author, w. Robert Kushner, of Boy's Art, 2003. Grantee Yaddo Fellowship, Sarasota Springs N.Y., Diane Wood Middlebrook Fellowship, Rockefeller Found., Bellagio, Italy, Jules Guerin Fellowship, Am. Acad., Rome, Italy, Nat. Endowment for the Arts. Mem.: NAD (academician). Home: 152 Wooster St New York NY 10012

KOZLOSKI, LISA MARIE, psychologist, director; b. Wilkes-Barre, Pa., Oct. 29, 1977; d. William Joseph and Claire Mary Jones; m. Brian Donald Kozloski, Nov. 7, 1998; children: Brian Donald Kozloski Jr, Hunter William. BS, King's Coll., 1998; MA, Marywood U., 2000, cert. in Sch. Psychology, 2002. Cert. sch. psychologist Pa., 2002. Sch. psychologist Neiu 19, Archbald, Pa., 2002—05; dir. psychol. svcs. Mid Valley Sch. Dist., Throop, Pa., 2005—. Mem.: Assn. Sch. Psychologists Pa. (assoc.), Nat. Assn. Sch. Psychologists (assoc.). Office: Mid Valley School District 52 Underwood Road Throop PA 18412 Office Phone: 570-307-2186.

KOZLOW, BEVERLY KAY, retired physical therapist, psychologist, realtor; b. Detroit, Aug. 10, 1931; d. Samuel and Genevieve Ione (Griffin) K.; m. Roy Carl Gleaves, Apr. 16, 1959 (div. 1975). BS, Eastern Mich. U., 1953; MS, UCLA, 1959; PhD, Sierra U., 1987. Registered physical therapist. Phys. therapist Walter Reed Army Med. Ctr., Washington, 1953-55, Crippled Children's Soc., Rockville, Md., 1955-56, San Bernardino (Calif.) County Hosp., 1957-59; coord. phys. therapy program UCLA, 1959-67; home health phys. therapist Vis. Nurses Assn. L.A., 1967-68; from staff to dir. phys. therapy L.A. County Med. Dept., 1968-73; dir. in-patient/out-patient acute and rehab. svcs. Valley Med. Ctr., Van Nuys, Calif., 1973-81; contract phys. therapist L.A., 1981-89; home health phys. therapist Vis. Nurses Assn., Stuart, Fla., 1992-96; CPS Great River Property, Guerneville, Calif., 1997—2002; ret., 2002. Adj. faculty U.S. Army Command and Gen. Staff Coll., Ft. Leavenworth, Kans., 1986-92. Ret. col. U.S. Army. Mem. Am. Physical Therapy Assn. (life), Ret. Officers Assn. Democrat. Jewish. Avocations: reading, travel, gardening. Home: 14317 Datetree Dr Elizabeth Lake CA 93532-1433 Personal E-mail: bkoz4u@verizon.net.

KOZLOWSKI, CHERYL M., fixed income analyst; b. Boston, July 19, 1974; d. Leo Dennis and Angeles Zenaida. BA, Middlebury Coll., 1996; postgrad., Harvard Bus. Sch., 2000—02. Lic. pilot. Fin. analyst Merrill Lynch, N.Y.C., 1996-1998; prin. Clayton, Dubilier & Rice, Inc., N.Y.C., 1998-2000; equity analyst Am. Express, 2002—04; fixed income analyst Airlie Opportunity Fund, 2004—. Treas. The Friends of Tolstoy Found., 1998—2002; chmn. Young New Yorkers of N.Y. Philharmonic, 1999—2002; bd. dirs. Shackleton Schs., 2000—05. Avocation: skiing. Home: 610 Park Ave Apt 14A New York NY 10021-7080 E-mail: ckozlowski@mba2002.hbs.edu.

KRA, PAULINE SKORNICKI, French language educator; b. Lodz, Poland, July 30, 1934; arrived in US, 1950, naturalized, 1955; d. Edward and Nathalie Skornicki; m. Leo Dietrich Kra, Mar. 10, 1955; children: David Theodore, Andrew Jason. Student, Radcliffe Coll., 1951-53; BA, Barnard Coll., 1955; MA, Columbia U., 1963, PhD, 1968; MA, Queens Coll., 1990. Lectr. Queens Coll., CUNY, 1964-65; asst. prof. French Yeshiva U., NYC, 1968-74, assoc. prof., 1974-82, prof., 1982-99, prof. emerita, 1999—; sr. programmer analyst Dept. Biomed. Informatics Columbia U., NYC, 1998—. Author: Religion in Montesquieu's Lettres Persanes, 1970; co-editor: Montesquieu, Lettres Persanes, 2004; contbr. articles to profl. jours. Mem. MLA, Am. Assn. Tchrs. French, Am. Soc. 18th Century Studies, Société Française d'étude du XVIII Siècle, Soc. Montesquieu, Assn. for Computers and Humanities, Assn. for Lit. and Linguistic Computing, Phi Beta Kappa. Achievements include invention of methods for extracting information on interactions between biological entities from natural language text data. Home: 10914 Ascan Ave Forest Hills NY 11375-5370 Business E-Mail: kra@yu.edu.

KRACHT, CHRISTINA MARIE, secondary school educator, coach; b. Flint, Mich., July 18, 1980; d. James Richard and Margaret Diane Kracht. BSc, Southwestern Assemblies of God U., 2001. Cert. self-contained classroom, English lang. arts, reading ELS supplemental tchr. Tex. Third grade tchr. McDonald Elem., Ferris, Tex., 2002—04; seventh grade tchr. Ferguson Jr. High, Arlington, Tex., 2004—06; reading tchr. R.L. Turner HS, Carrollton, Tex., 2006—. Seventh grade writing level leader Ferguson Jr. High, 2005—06. Republican. Christian. Avocations: sports, exercise, movies. Home: 1725 Crooks Ct Grand Prairie TX 75051 Office: Ferguson Jr High 600 SE Green Oaks Arlington TX 76018 E-mail: christinambracht@yahoo.com.

KRAEMER, HELENA ANTOINETTE CHMURA, psychiatry educator; Degree, Stanford U., 1963. With Stanford U., 1964—, prof. biostats. in psychiatry, Dept. Psychiatry and Behavioral Scis., 1991—, mem. Comprehensive Cancer Ctr. Mem. editorial bd. Jour. Child & Adolescent Psychopharmacology. Co-author: How Many Subjects?: Statistical Power Analysis in Rsch., 1987, Evaluating Medical Tests: Objective & Quantitative Guidelines, 1992, To Your Health: How to Understand What Research Tells Us About Risk, 2005. Recipient Harvard award in psychiat. epidemiology and biostats., 2001. Mem.: Inst. Medicine. Office: Stanford U Dept Psychiatry and Behavioral Scis 300 Pasteur Dr Stanford CA 94305 also: Stanford Comprehensive Cancer Ctr 875 Blake Wilbur Dr Stanford CA 94305 Business E-Mail: hck@stanford.edu.*

KRAEMER, LILLIAN ELIZABETH, lawyer; b. NYC, Apr. 18, 1940; d. Frederick Joseph and Edmee Elizabeth (de Watteville) K.; m. John W. Vincent, June 22, 1962 (div. 1964). BA, Swarthmore Coll., 1961; JD, U. Chgo., 1964. Bar: N.Y. 1965, U.S. Dist. Ct. (so. dist.) N.Y. 1967, U.S. Dist. Ct. (ea. dist.) N.Y. 1971. Assoc. Cleary, Gottlieb, Steen & Hamilton, N.Y.C., 1964-71, Simpson Thacher & Bartlett, N.Y.C., 1971-74, ptnr., 1974-99, of counsel, 2000—. Mem. vis. com. U. Chgo. Law Sch., 1988-90, 91-94, 97-99 Bd. mgrs. Swarthmore Coll., 1993—2005; warden St. Francis Episcopal Ch.,

Stamford, Conn., 2001-05; bd. dirs. Turtle Bay Music Sch., 2005—. Fellow Am. Coll. Bankruptcy; mem. Lawyers Alliance for N.Y. (bd. dirs. 1996-2001, co-chair capital campaign 2003-05), Assn. Bar City N.Y. (mem. various coms.), Order of Coif, Phi Beta Kappa. Democrat. Avocations: travel, reading, word games. Home: 2 Beekman Pl New York NY 10022-8058 Address: 46 Saddle Rock Rd Stamford CT 06902 E-mail: lkraemer@stblaw.com.

KRAETZER, MARY C., sociologist, educator, consultant; b. NYC, Sept. 12, 1943; d. Kenneth G. and Adele L. Kraetzer; m. Kestas E. Silunas. AB, Coll. New Rochelle, 1965; MA, Fordham U., 1967, PhD, 1975. Instr. Mercy Coll., Dobbs Ferry, NY, 1969—70, asst. prof., 1970—75, assoc. prof., 1975—79, prof., 1979—, program dir. behavioral sci., 1997—, program dir. grad. programs in health svc. mgmt., 2001—. Rsch. asst. Fordham U., Bronx, N.Y., 1965-67, tchg. asst., 1967-68, tchg. fellow, 1968-69, adj. instr., 1971-75, adj. asst. prof., 1975-76; adj. assoc. prof. L.I. U. Grad. br. Campus Mercy Coll., 1976-79, adj. prof., 1979-81, coord. MS in Cmty. Health Program, 1976-81, adj. prof. Westchester campus, 1988-94; rsch. cons. elem. schoolbooks Nat. Coun. Chs./Ch. Women United Task Force on Global Consciousness, N.Y.C., 1971; mem. adv. com. edn. and society div. Nat. Coun. Chs., 1975-78; mem. evaluation team Middle States Assn. Colls. and Secondary Schs. Commn. on Higher Edn., Monmouth, N.J., 1976; presenter in field. Contbr. chapters to books, articles to profl. jours. Recipient Tchg. Excellence award Mercy Coll., 1999; Bd. Regents scholar, 1961-65, 65-69; Fordham U. scholar, 1965-68; Fordham U. fellow, 1968-69; Mercy Coll. grantee, 1984, 85, 86, 88, 92; Mercy Coll. Faculty Devel. grantee, 1999; NSF summer intern, 1967. Mem. APHA (conf. presenter), Am. Sociol. Assn. (presenter). Office: Mercy Coll 555 Broadway Dobbs Ferry NY 10522-1134 Office Phone: 914-674-7341. Business E-Mail: mkraetzer@mercy.edu.

KRAFKA, MARY BAIRD, lawyer; b. Ottumwa, Iowa, Jan. 4, 1942; d. Glenn Leroy and Alice Erna (Krebill) B.; m. Jerry Lee Krafka, Oct. 14, 1962; children: Lisa Krafka Piper, Gregory D., Jeffrey A., Amy Krafka Pittman. BA in English and Human Rels., William Penn Coll., Oskaloosa, Iowa, 1990; JD, U. Iowa, 1993. Bar: Iowa 1993. Vol. lawyer Legal Svcs. Corp., Ottumwa, 1993-94; pvt. practice, Ottumwa, 1994—. Mem. AAUW, ABA, Iowa Bar Assn., Wapello County Bar Assn., PEO Sisterhood (Iowa chpt. HC 1973). Lutheran. Avocations: sewing, reading, walking, running, people. Home: 931 W Mary St Ottumwa IA 52501-4904 Office: 101 S Market St Ste 203 Ottumwa IA 52501-2933 Office Phone: 641-683-7515. Business E-Mail: mbkrafka@lisco.com.

KRAFT, ELAINE JOY, community relations and communications official; b. Sept. 1, 1951; d. Harry J. and Leatrice M. (Hanan) Kraft; children: Paul Kraft, Leslie Jo. BA, U. Wash., 1973; MPA, U. Puget Sound, 1979. Reporter Eastside Jour., Bellevue, Wash., 1972—76; editor Jour./Enterprise Newspapers, Wash. State, 1976; mem. staff Wash. State Senate, 1976—78, Wash. Ho. of Reps., 1978—82, pub. info. officer, 1976—78, mem. leadership staff, asst. to caucus chmn., 1980—. Pntr., pres. Media Kraft Comm.; mgr. corp. info., advt. and mktg. comm. Weyerhaeuser Co., 1982—85; dir. comm. Weyerhaeuser Paper Co., 1985—87; dir. cmty. rels. N.W. region Coors Brewing Co., 1987—95; comm. dir. King County exec. King County Ct. House, 1996—2005; dir. pub. rels. and comms. U. Wash., Bothell, 2006—. Recipient state and nat. journalism design and advt. awards. Mem.: Wash. Press Assn., Women in Comm., Nat. Fedn. Press Women. Office: U Wash 18115 Campus Way NE Bothell WA 98011-8246 Office Phone: 425-352-3395. Business E-Mail: ekraft@uwb.edu.

KRAFT, LEAH MICHELLE, art educator; b. Cleburne, May 13, 1967; d. Hugh Thomas Massey, II and Karla Jo Matthews; m. Albert David Kraft, Aug. 6, 1988. BA, BSE, Lubbock Christian U., Tex., 1990; MA, West Tex. A&M U., Canyon, 1995; PhD, Tex. Tech. U., Lubbock, 2001. Art tchr. Dunbar H.S., Lubbock, 1990—94; prof. art edn. Lubbock Christian U., 1994—. Mem. editl. rev. bd. Visual Arts Rsch. Jour., Urbana-Champaign, Ill., 2005, Visual Culture and Gender Jour., 2006. Contbr. articles to profl. jours. Vol. Vatican Fresco Exhibit, Tex. Tech. Mus., Lubbock, 2002; sponsor Student Art Edn. Assn., Lubbock Christian U., 2002—; mem. Louise Hopkins Underwood Ctr. for Arts, Lubbock, 2004—. Recipient Cultural Connections grant, Tex. Commn. on Arts, 2000, 2004, Spl. Needs Travel grant, 2002. Mem.: Tex. Assn. of Schs. of Art, Natural Art Edn. Assn., Tex. Art Edn. Assn. (chair higher edn. divsn. 2002—05). Office: Lubbock Christian U 5601 19th St Lubbock TX 79407

KRAFT, ROSEMARIE, dean, educator; b. Franklin, Pa., Nov. 18, 1936; d. Jack B. Harter and Romaine B. Shick; m. Louis R. Kraft; children: Louis W., Jack C. PhD, Ohio State U., 1976. Prof. U. Calif., Davis, 1977—, assoc. dean, 1994—. Dir., prof. for future fellowship U. Calif., Davis, 1995—. Author: Individual Differences in Cognition, 1998. Recipient McNair Scholars grant, U.S. Dept. Edn., 1995, 1999. Avocations: hiking, reading, travel. Home: 1315 Lake Blvd Davis CA 95616 Office: U Calif Davis One Shields Ave Davis CA 95616

KRAFT, YVETTE, art educator; b. Washington, Jan. 17, 1945; d. Alvin Abraham and Rena Zlotnick Kraft. Studies with Master Painter Leon Berkowitz, 1982—87; student, Corcoran Coll. of Art and Design, 1992—2004. Art dir. after-sch. program Georgetown Montessori Sch., 1988; art instr. Washington Home, Sr. Citizen Care Facility, 1989—90; art instr. students with spl. needs Horace Mann Elem. Sch., 1990; art instr. Southeast Asian Refugee Children, 4-H, Arlington, Va., 1989—90; pvt. art instr. ages 2-17, 1990—92; art instr. Janney Elem. Sch., 1991, 1998, 1999, Ben Murch Elem. Sch., 1991; artist-in-residence Anne Beers Elem. Sch., 1992—93; art instr. children and adolescents with emotional disorders Clara Aisenstein, MD, Child Psychiatrist, 1993—96; art instr. Randle Highlands Elem. Sch., 1994, Naylor Rd. Elem. Sch., 1997, Bethany Woman's Shelter, 1998—2000, S.E. Vets. Svc. Ctr., 2005—; condr. art classes N St. Village, Washington, 2003—04. Fine arts com. Washington Hebrew Congregation, 1979—82; adv. bd. New Art Examiner Mag., Washington, 1985—86; asst. mgr. Americana West Gallery; founder, dir. Project City People, 1992, 93; edn. dir. Fondo del Sol Visual Arts Ctr., 1992—93. One-woman shows include Maret Sch., Washington, 1987, Georgetown Montessori Sch., 1988, Horace Mann Sch., 1989, Fillmore Sch. of Arts, 1991, NIH, Clin. Ctr. Gallery, Bethesda, Md., 1995, Fondo de Sol Visual Arts Ctr., Washington, 1996, DC Arts Ctr., 1999, Nat. Coalition for Homeless, 2001, exhibited in group shows at Am. Art League, 1982—85, Highlights of the Yr. Exhbn., Martin Luther King Libr., 1986—87, Washington Hebrew Congregation, 1986—87, 2002—03, Capricorn Gallery, Bethesda, Md., 1987, Ctr. for Collaborative Art and Visual Edn., Washington, 1999, Capital Children's Mus., 1999, Eight Is An Octive, Nat. Theatre, 2000, Am. Oh Yes Folk Art Gallery, 2000—03, Joy of Motion, 2001, Rockville Arts Pl., Md., 2003. Grantee grant, Cafritz Found., 1990, 1991, Hattie M. Strong Found., 1991, George Preston Marshall, 1991. Independent. Jewish. Avocations: jazz, walking, art museums, sketching, clothing design and coordination. Office Phone: 202-332-0535.

KRAG, OLGA, interior designer; b. St. Louis, Nov. 27, 1937; d. Jovica Todor and Milka (Slijpecevic) Golubovic. AA, U. Mo., 1958; cert. interior design, UCLA, 1979. Interior designer William L. Pereira Assocs., L.A., 1977-80; aassoc. Reel/Grobman Assocs., L.A., 1980-81; project mgr. Kaneko/Laff Assocs., L.A., 1982, Stuart Laff Assocs., L.A., 1983-85; restaurateur The Edge, St. Lois, 1983-84; pvt. practice comml. interior design, L.A., 1981—. Mem. invitation and ticket com. Calif. Chamber Symphony Soc., 1980-81; vol. Westside Rep. Coun., Proposition 1, 1971; asst. inaugural presentation Mus. of Childhood, L.A., 1985. Recipient Carole Eichen design award U. Calif., 1979. Mem. Am. Soc. Interior Designers, Inst. Bus. Designers, Phi Chi Theta, Beta Sigma Phi. Republican. Serbian Orthodox. Home and Office: 700 Levering Ave Apt 10 Los Angeles CA 90024-2797

KRAISOSKY, ALISSA JO, psychiatrist; b. Fontana, Calif., Dec. 25, 1973; d. William Larry and Joquita Kraisosky. BS in Biology, La Sierra U., Calif.; MD, Loma Linda U., 2000. Resident U. Hawaii, Honolulu, 2000—02, U. N.Mex., Albuquerque, 2003—04; staff physician Staffcare, Inc., Martinz, Calif., 2005—. Named Chief Resident, Va., 2004. Mem.: Am. Psychiat. Assn. Avocations: skiing, reading, hiking.

KRAKOFF, DIANE ELIZABETH BUTTS, medical/surgical nurse; b. Columbus, Ohio, July 1, 1955; d. Edwin Joseph and Mary Lee (Fenstermaker) B. BSN, Ohio State U., 1978; MSN, U. Cin., 1984. Cert. critical care RN, CDE. Staff RN Riverside Meth. Hosp., Columbus, 1978-83; grad. asst. U. Cin., 1984; endocrinology clin. nurse specialist Mt. Carmel Med. Ctr., Columbus, 1985-90; rsch. assoc. II Ohio State U. Hosp., Columbus, 1990-92; diabetes nurse educator St Vincent's Hosp., Indpls., 1992-94; case mgr. Mount Carmel Health, Columbus, 2000—. Presenter in field. Contbr. articles to profl. jours. Mem. Cen. Ohio Assn. Diabetes Educators (past pres., sec. 1989-90), Am. Assn. Diabetes Educators (ann. program and meeting planning com., chairperson mini-sessions com. ann. meeting), Cen. Ohio Clin. Nurse Specialist Support Group (founder), Cen. Ohio Diabetes Assn., Am. Diabetes Assn., AACN (instr. cen. Ohio core curriculum rev. course edocrinology model 1986, 87, 89, 91). Home: 1400 Candlewood Dr Columbus OH 43235-1620 Office: 793 W State St Columbus OH 43222-1551 Office Phone: 614-898-4385.

KRALL, DIANA, musician; b. Nanaimo, BC, Can., Nov. 16, 1964; Student, Berklee Coll. Music, 1982—84; degree (hon.), U. Victoria. With Justin Time Records, Montreal, Que., Canada, 1993, GRP, Verve Records. Musician: (albums) Stepping Out, 1993, Only Trust Your Heart, 1995, All For You, 1996, Love Scenes, 1997, When I Look In Your Eyes, 1999 (Grammy award for Best Jazz Vocal Performance, 2000, Grammy award nomination for Album of Yr., 2000, Cert. Platinum, U.S. and Portugal, Double Platinum in Can., Gold, France, Juno award Best Vocal Jazz Album), The Look of Love, 2001 (Quadruple Platinum, Can., Platinum, Australia, New Zealand, Poland and Portugal, Gold, France, Singapore, Eng., Juno award for Best Artist, Best Album, Best Vocal Jazz Album, Record of Yr. award Nat. Jazz Awards), Live in Paris, 2002 (Grammy award for Best Jazz Vocal Album), Heartdrops: Vince Benedetti Meets Diana Krall, 2003, The Girl in the Other Room, 2004, Xmas Songs featuring the Clayton/Hamilton Jazz Orchestra, 2005. Named Musician of Yr., Nat. Jazz Awards, Internat. Musician. Office: Macklam/Feldman Mgmt 1505 W 2d Ave Ste 200 Vancouver BC Canada V6H 3Y4 E-mail: management@mfmgt.com.

KRALL, VITA, psychologist; b. New Haven, July 9, 1923; d. Moses Adam and Jennie (Alper) K. BA, Antioch Coll., Yellow Springs, Ohio, 1944; MA, U. Iowa, 1945; PhD, U. Rochester (N.Y.), 1951. Lic. psychologist, Conn. Instr. U. Rochester, 1948-51, Mich. State U., East Lansing, 1951-53; sr. clin. psychologist Topeka, 1953-58, Kans. Neurol. Inst., Topeka, 1959-60; staff psychologist Child Guidance Clinic of Greater Bridgeport (Conn.), Inc., 1961-62; psychologist, dir. tng. Michael Reese Hosp., Chgo., 1963-88; rsch. psychologist Hartford (Conn.) Hosp., 1989-90. Author: Developmental Psychodiagnostic Assessment of Children and Adolescents, 1989, Play Therapy Primer, 1989, Psychological Development of High Risk Multiple Birth Children, 1991. Recipient Saft award for outstanding instr. Michael Reese Hosp., Chgo., 1983, 87, Disting. Svc. award, Am. Bd. Profl. Psychologists, 1987, Disting. Psychologist, Ill. Psychol. Assn., 1983. Fellow Am. Orthopsychiatric Assn., APA; mem. Soc. for Personality Assessment. Avocation: painting. Home and Office: 18 Atwater St Milford CT 06460-7662

KRAM, SHIRLEY WOHL, federal judge; b. NYC, 1922; Student, Hunter Coll., 1940-41, CUNY, 1940-47; LLB, Bklyn. Law Sch., 1950. Atty. Legal Aid Soc. N.Y., 1951-53, 1962-71; assoc. Simons & Hardy, 1954-55; pvt. practice law, 1955-60; judge Family Ct., N.Y.C., 1971-83, U.S. Dist. Ct. (So. Dist.), NYC, 1983—93, sr. judge, 1993—. Author: (with Neil A. Frank) The Law of Child Custody, Development of the Substantive Law Office: 2101 US Courthouse 40 Centre St New York NY 10007-1581

KRAMER, ANDREA S., lawyer; b. Chgo., Mar. 15, 1955; BA summa cum laude with high distinction, U. Ill., 1975; JD cum laude, Northwestern U., 1978. Bar: Ill. 1978, U.S. Tax Ct. 1980, U.S. Ct. Fed. Claims 1982, Ill. Ct. Appeals (no. dist., 7th cir.). With Coffield, Ungaretti & Harris, Chgo.; ptnr. McDermott Will & Emery LLP, Chgo. Adj. law prof. Northwestern U. Sch. Law. Author: Financial Products: Taxation, Regulation and Design, 2000; mem. editorial bd. Jour. Criminal Law and Criminology, 1976-78; contbr. articles to profl. jours., chpts. to books. Founding mem. The Women's Treatment Ctr., Chgo., chmn. bd. dirs.; bd. dirs. Dance Art. Recipient Bronze Tablet, U. Ill., 1975, Unsung Heroine Award, Cook County Bd. Commrs., 2004. Mem. Anti-Defamation League, Internat. Bar Assn., Chgo. Bar Assn. (sect. taxation), Chgo. Fin. Exchange, Alpha Lambda Delta, Phi Alpha Theta, Phi Beta Kappa, Phi Kappa Phi. Office: McDermott Will & Emery LLP 227 W Monroe St Chicago IL 60606-5096 Office Phone: 312-984-6480. Office Fax: 312-984-7700. Business E-Mail: akramer@mwe.com.

KRAMER, BARBARA H., lawyer; b. Phila., Sept. 30, 1965; d. Mitchell and Judith Kramer; m. Steven Acker; children: Anna, Eva, Alexander. BA, Columbia U., NYC, 1987; JD, Georgetown U., Washington, 1990. Jd. clk. hon. Santiago Campos U.S. Dist. Ct. N.Mex., Santa Fe, 1990—92; ptnr. Kramer & Kramer, Ann Arbor, Mich., 1993—; atty. Morgan Stanley, Tokyo, 1997—98. Bd. dirs. J.F. Kapnek Charitable Trust, Lafayette, Calif., 1998—, Girls on the Run, Ann Arbor, 2004—. Office: Kramer & Kramer 24 Frank Lloyd Dr Ann Arbor MI 48105 Office Phone: 734-930-5452. Business E-Mail: bkramer@kramerandkramer.com.

KRAMER, CAROL GERTRUDE, marriage and family counselor; b. Grand Rapids, Mich., Jan. 14, 1939; d. Wilson John and Katherine Joanne (Wasdyke) Rottschafer; m. Peter William Kramer, July 1, 1960; children: Connie R. Kramer Sattler, Paul Wilson Kramer. AB, Calvin Coll., 1960; MA, U. Mich., 1969; PhD, Holy Cross Coll., 1973; MSW, Grand Valley State U., 1985. Diplomate Internat. Acad. Behavioral Medicine, Counseling and Psychotherapy, cert. addictions/substance abuse counselor Mich., hypnotherapist/psychotherapist, clin. certified forensic counselor 2001, critical incident stress mgmt. 2003. Elem. tchr. Jenison (Mich.) Pub. Sch., 1960-65; sch. social worker Grand Rapids Pub. Sch., 1964-81; pvt. practice marriage and family counselor Grand Rapids, 1973—; v.p. Human Resource Assocs., Grand Rapids, 1983-88; pres. bd. dirs. Telecounseling, 1996-99. Guest lectr. Calvin Coll., Mich. State U., Grand Valley State U., 1975-85; presenter in field. Co-author: Parent Involvement Program, 1993, Stop Sexual Abuse for Everyone, 1996. Apptd. fellow State Mich. Bd. Marriage Counselors, 1985—87; pres. bd. dirs. Stop Sexual Abuse for Everyone; bd. dirs. Citizens for Parental Rights, 2004—; mem. Gerald R. Ford Rep. Women, Grand Rapids, 1980—87; ruling elder 1st Presbyn. Ch., Grand Rapids, 1975—78; co-chair pastoral rels. com. Gun Lake Cmty. Ch., 1989—91, v.p. consistory, 1991—93; bd. dirs. Citizens Parental Rights, 2004. Named one of Outstanding Young Women in Am., 1974; recipient Meritorious Svc. award Kent County Family Life Coun., 1983. Fellow Am. Assn. Marriage and Family Therapist; mem. NASW, Mich. Assn. Marriage Counselors (awards com. 1988, chmn. 1991, nominations com. 1992-95), Kent County Family Life Coun. (pres. 1975), Voters Against Sexual Abuse (pres., bd. dirs. 1992—). Home: 12622 Park Dr Wayland MI 49348-9085 Office: 1251 Century Ave SW Ste 107 Grand Rapids MI 49503-8047

KRAMER, CECILE EDITH, retired medical librarian; b. NYC, Jan. 6, 1927; d. Marcus and Henrietta (Marks) K. BS, CCNY, 1956; MS in L.S., Columbia U., 1960. Reference asst. Columbia U. Health Scis. Library, N.Y.C., 1957-61, asst. librarian, 1961-75; dir. Health Scis. Libr. Northwestern U., Chgo., 1975-91, asst. prof. edn., 1975-91, prof. emeritus, 1991—. Instr. library and info. sci. Rosary Coll., 1981-85; cons. Francis A. Countway Library Medicine, Harvard U., 1974. Pres. Friends of Libr., Fla. Atlantic U., Boca Raton. Fellow Med. Libr. Assn. (chmn. med. sch. librs. group 1975-76, editor newsletter 1975-77, instr. continuing edn. 1966-75, mem. panel cons. editors Bull. 1987-90, disting. mem. Acad. Health Info. Profls. 1993—); mem. Biomed. Comm. Network (chmn. 1979-80). Home: Homewood at Boca 9591 Yamato Rd Boca Raton FL 33434 Business E-Mail: kramer@fau.edu.

KRAMER, ELEANOR, retired real estate broker, tax specialist, financial consultant; b. NYC, Feb. 18, 1939; d. Herman I. Kramer and Fay (Berger) Kramer-Levy; m. Richard H. Fitz-Gerald III, Dec. 24, 1959 (div.); m. Gregory F. Navarro, Oct. 1, 1975 (div. Mar. 1996); children: Brad, Cindy. BA in Speech and Theater, Bklyn Coll., 1975; MS in Urban Affairs, CUNY, Hunter Coll., 1976. Tchr. cultural arts Bronx (N.Y.) Bd. Edn., 1966-70; real estate broker, pres. Tritown Realty Corp., Mamaroneck, NY, 1978-83; pvt. practice tax cons. Mamaroneck, 1983—2000. Adj. prof. sociology Rockland CC, Suffern, N.Y., 1979-85, Westchester CC, Valhalla, NY, 1979-85; founder dance therapy St. Vincent's Hosp., NYC; lectr., demonstrator NYC Pub. Schs., author, prodr., performer, co-creator child edn. programs, 1967-77; ombudsman Bklyn. Coll., 1974-75. Mem. pub. rel. com. Bicentennial commn. Village of Mamaroneck, 1976; bd. dirs. Cmty. Action Program, Mamaroneck, 1977-79; ombudsman Bklyn. Coll., 1974-75. Mem.: LWV (bd. dirs. 1977—80), NOW (ad hoc chmn. 1970, co-chair, co-author women's ednl. seminar Libr. of Congress), Nat. Soc. Tax Preparers, Lions (Larchmont, NY). Avocations: puzzles, tennis, antiques, jazz, theater. Mailing: 616 Clearwater Park Rd West Palm Beach FL 33401

KRAMER, ELISSA LIPCON, nuclear medicine physician, educator; b. NYC, Feb. 22, 1951; d. Jules and Esther Ruth (Wagner) Lipcon; life ptnr. Jay Newman; children: Rachel, Aaron. BA, U. Pa., 1973; MD, NYU, 1977; postgrad., NYU Sch. Medicine, 2000—. Diplomate Am. Bd. Nuc. Medicine, Am. Bd. Radiology. Ob-gyn. intern Bellevue Hosp. Ctr./NYU Med. Ctr., 1977-78, resident in radiology, 1978-80, fellow in nuc. medicine, 1980-82; asst. prof. clin. radiology NYU, 1982-89, assoc. prof. clin. radiology, 1989-96, prof. clin. radiology, 1996—. Assoc. prof. radiology Cornell U. Med. Ctr., Ithaca, N.Y., 1989-90; assoc. Sloan-Kettering Cancer Ctr., N.Y.C., 1989-90; assoc. dir. nuc. medicine Tisch Hosp., N.Y.C., 1989-99; assoc. attending physician Tisch Hosp., 1990-99, Bellevue Hosp., N.Y.C., 1990—; dir. nuclear medicine Tisch Hosp./Bellevue Hosp., 1999—; master Lewis Thomas Soc. for the Arts and Humanities in Medicine, NYU Sch. Medicine. Author, editor: Clinical SPECT Imaging, 1995; contbr. articles to profl. jours. Nat. Cancer Inst./NIH Rsch. grantee, 1993-. Mem. Radiology Soc. N.Am., Soc. Nuc. Medicine (mem. brain imaging coun. 1982—, bd. dirs. 1992-93). Office: 550 First Ave New York NY 10016 Business E-Mail: elissa.kramer@med.nyu.edu.

KRAMER, HELENE, banking executive; Head info. security HSBC.com, Inc., Jersey City. Named one of Premier 100 IT Leaders, Computerworld, 2005. Office: Hsbc.com Inc 545 Washington Blvd Jersey City NJ 07310

KRAMER, KAREN SUE, psychologist, educator; b. L.A., Sept. 6, 1942; d. Frank Pacheco Kramer and Velma Eileen (Devlin) Moore; m. Stewart A. Sterling, Dec. 30, 1965 (div. 1974); 1 child, Scott Kramer Sterling. BA, U. Calif., Berkeley, 1966; MA, U.S. Internat. U., 1976; PhD, Profl. Sch. Psychology, 1980; MA in Asian studies, U. San Francisco, 2004. Psychometrist U. Calif. Counseling Ctr., Berkeley, 1966—67; social worker Alameda County Welfare Dept., Oakland, Calif., 1967—69; vol. coord. San Diego County Probation Dept., 1971—73, officer, 1973—76; counselor and coord. clin. and outreach programs Western Inst., San Diego, 1976—77; program coord. and counselor Women's Resource Ctr., Oceanside, Calif., 1977—78; pvt. practice psychology San Diego, 1978—81; planner/analyst San Diego County Dept. Health Svcs., 1979—81; prof. psychology Nat. U., San Diego, 1979—81; social svcs. program cons. Calif. Dept. Social Svcs., Emeryville, 1981—83; affirmative action officer State Compensation Ins. Fund, San Francisco, 1983—87; cmty. psychologist Calif. Dept. Mental Health, 1987—89; pvt. practice psychology Berkeley, 1990—. Personnel analyst State Comp. Ins. Fund, 1989-91; regional property mgr. State Compensation Ins. Fund, San Francisco, 1991-95; pres. North County Coun. Social Concerns, Vista, Calif., 1977-78; advisor USMC Camp Pendleton Human Svcs., 1977-79; mem. adv. bd. Chinatown Resources Devel. Ctr., San Francisco, 1984-87, 2000-, San Francisco Rehab., 1984-87; bd. dirs. Network Cons. Svcs., Napa, Calif.; founder QiGong in China Ednl. Svcs. Travel/Study Programs, 1999-2005, Cross Cultural Tng., 2006; asst. dir. QiGong for Children, Am. Found. Traditional Chinese Medicine; cons. Success Strategies, programs for Health, Sports, Tests, Life; prof. psychology Am. Coll. TCM, 1999; pub. chmn. Intuition Network Conf., 1997; advisor Calif.-Hawaii Inst., 1998-; founder Barefoot Doctors, 2006. Editl. advisor Alternative Medicine, 1998; host Voice Am. Radio Show on Mental Health, 2004-. Clin. dir. Pathways to Wellness Clinics, Oakland, Calif., 2002—05; chmn. pub. awareness com. Alameda County Mental Health Bd., 2000—04. Mem. Calif. Peer Counselors Assn. (adv. bd. 1987-90), Calif. Prevention Network (bd. dirs. 1989-93, editl. advisor jour. 1992-93). Office Phone: 510-527-7154. Personal E-mail: k.kramer@comcast.com.

KRAMER, LINDA KONHEIM, curator, art historian; b. NYC, Nov. 8, 1939; d. Clarence John and May (Sternberg) Konheim; m. Samuel R. Kramer, Apr. 24, 1977; 1 child, Nicholas Clarence. BA in Fine Arts and Art History, Smith Coll., 1961; BFA in Painting and Graphic Design, Yale U., 1963; MA in 19th and 20th Century European and Am. Art, NYU, 1968, PhD, 2000. Curator asst. Solomon R. Guggenheim Mus., 1963—66, program adminstr., 1966—76; cataloger modern drawings Sotheby's Park-Bernet, N.Y.C., 1980-82; expert in modern drawings Sotheby's N.Y., 1982-85; curator prints and drawings, dept. head Bklyn. Mus., 1985-94. Tchr. Sch. Visual Arts, N.Y.C., 1977-80, Manhattanville Coll., summer 1995, 96; exec. dir. Nancy Graves Found., N.Y.C., 1996—; mem. adv. bd. Coll. Fine Arts, West Wash. U., Bellingham, 1987-95. Author: books, pamphlets and catalogs; contbr. articles to profl. jours. Grantee Nat. Mus. Act, 1976, 78; Jane and Morgan Whitney fellow Met. Mus. Art, 1995-96. Mem.: Am. Assn. Mus., Print Coun. Am., Art Table, Coll. Art Assn. Home: 372 Central Park W New York NY 10025-8240 Office: Nancy Graves Found 450 W 31st St 2d Fl New York NY 10001-4608 Office Phone: 212-560-0602. Business E-Mail: mail@nancygravesfoundation.org.

KRAMER, LORA L., executive assistant; b. East Patchogue, N.Y., Aug. 11, 1966; d. Oscar Emmett and Marylin Emily Blevins; m. Eric A. Kramer, Aug. 22, 1993; children: Jake Theodore, Isabella Camille. AAS, Suffolk C.C., Selden, N.Y., 1987; student, Inst. de Touraine, Tours, France, 1988; BS in French, SUNY, Brockport, 1988. Exec. asst. U.S. Arctic Rsch. Commn., Fairbanks, Alaska, 1989; sr. editl. asst. Am. Phys. Soc., Ridge, N.Y., 1985-87, 90-95; exec. asst. The Ulanov Partnership, Princeton, N.J., 1995—. Mem. DAR (jr. mem.; registrar 1998—02), Steuben Soc. Am., Historian, 2002. Avocations: piano, sailing. E-mail: kramer@ulanov.com.

KRAMER, MARLENE DIXIE, dietician; b. Matewan, W.Va., Mar. 5, 1952; d. Starling Hull and Martha Elizabeth K. AS, Brunswick (Ga.) Coll., 1970-72; BS in Home Econs., U. Ga., 1972-75; grad. dietetic traineeship program, Greenville (S.C.) Hosp. System, 1975-76. Registered and lic. dietitian. Dietitian Greenville Hosp. System, 1976; mgr. nutritional svcs. Citrus Meml. Hosp., Inverness, Fla., 1976—. Ombudsman coun. State of Fla. Long Term Care, Inverness, 1988-90; culinary arts cons. Withlacoochee Tech. Inst., Inverness, 1984—; adj. instr. Cen. Fla. Community Coll., Ocala, 1993. Mem. Am. Dietetic Assn., Am. Hosp. Food Svc. Adminstrs. Home: 911 E Harvard St Inverness FL 34452-6726

KRAMER, MARY ELIZABETH, ambassador, former state legislator; b. Burlington, Iowa, June 14, 1935; d. Ross L. and Geneva M. (McElhinney) Barnett; m. Kay Frederick Kramer, June 13, 1958; children: Kent, Krista. BA, U. Iowa, 1957, MA, 1971. Cert. tchr., Iowa. Tchr. Newton (Iowa) Pub. Schs., 1957-61, Iowa City Pub. Schs., 1961-67, tchr., asst. supt., 1971-75; dir. pers. Younkers, Inc., Des Moines, 1975-81; v.p. Wellmark, Inc., Des Moines, 1981-99; mem. Iowa Senate from 37th dist., Des Moines, 1990—2004; pres. of the senate, 1997—2004; U.S. amb. to Barbados and Ea. Caribbean, 2004—. Mem. Olympic adv. com. Blue Cross and Blue Shield Assn., Chgo.,

1988—92; presdl. appointee White House Commn. on Presdl. Scholars, 2001, now chmn.; Bd. dirs. Polk County Child Care Rsch. Ctr., Des Moines, 1986—96, YWCA, Des Moines, 1989—94. Named Mgr. of Yr. Iowa Mgmt. Assocs., 1985, Woman of Achievement YWCA, 1986, Woman of Vision Young Women's Resource Ctr., 1989. Mem. Soc. Human Resource Mgmt. (Profl. of Yr. 1996), Iowa Mgmt. Assn. (pres. 1988), Greater Des Moines C. of C. (bd. dirs. 1986-96), Nexus, Rotary Internat. Republican. Presbyterian. Avocations: music, public speaking. Office: Iowa State Senate State Capitol Des Moines IA 50319-0001 also: Am Embassy Bridgetown CMR 1014-Exec Fpo AA 34055 Office Phone: 246-436-4950. E-mail: mkramer@legis.state.ia.us, kaynmary@aol.com.

KRAMER, NOËL ANKETELL, judge; b. Bay City, Mich., Nov. 22, 1945; d. Thomas Jackson and Ruth Genevieve (LeRoux) Anketell; m. Franklin D. Kramer, May 30, 1970; children: Katherine, Christopher. BA with honors, Vassar Coll., 1967; JD with honors, U. Mich., 1971. Bar: D.C. 1972, U.S. Supreme Ct. 1975. Assoc. Wilmer, Cutler & Pickering, Washington, 1971-76; asst. U.S. atty. D.C. US Dept. State, Washington, 1976-84; judge D.C. Superior Ct., Washington, 1984—2005, dep. presiding judge, criminal div., 1999—2003, presiding judge, criminal div., 2000—05; assoc. judge D.C. Ct. Appeals, Washington, 2005—. Recipient Judge Robert A. Shuker award, 2004. Mem. ABA., Nat. Assn. Women Judges, Women's Bar Assn. D.C. (Woman Lawyer of Yr., 2005), D.C. Bar (chair person cts., lawyers and adminstrn. justice div. 1982-84), U. Mich. Law Club Washington (pres. 1976-78). Office: DC Ct Appeals 500 Indiana Ave NW Rm 6000 Washington DC 20001-2131*

KRAMER, SUSAN See SURMAN, SUSAN

KRAMER, SYBIL JEAN, elementary school educator, writer; b. Junction City, Kans., Feb. 7, 1948; d. Elmer William and Leona Mae Kramer. BS, Concordia Tchrs. Coll., Seward, Nebr., 1969; MA in Spl. Edn., Concordia U., Riverforest, Ill., 1988. Cert. elem. tchr. State of Ill., 2002. Sec. self svc. ctr. U.S. Army, Fort Riley, Kans., 1965—65, sec. maintenance dept., 1966—66, sec. to dir. svc. clubs, 1967—67, message ctr. operator for staff judge adv., 1968—68, claims dept. for staff judge adv., 1969—69; tchr., grades 1 and 2 Messiah Luth. Ch. Sch., Memphis, 1969—78, tchr., prin., 1978—81; tchr. grade 2 St. Peter Luth. Ch. Sch., Arlington Heights, Ill., 1981—. Youth group dir. Messiah Luth. Ch., Memphis, 1970—79; sch. choir dir. Messiah Luth. Ch. Sch., 1980—81, coach volleyball, basketball, track, t-ball, softball, 1970—81; dir. glee club St. Peter Luth. Ch. Sch., Arlington Heights, 1994—99, drama coord., 1983—, dir. mid. sch. drama, 1983—90, 1995—, playwright and dir. primary operetta, 1984—, yearbook editor, designer and photographer, 1985—. Author (director): (operetta) Those Dear Old Golden Rule Days, The Toy Shop, The King Who Couldn't Laugh, Pocketful Of Dreams. Singer Raleigh Cmty. Chorus, Memphis, 1974—80, Voices Worship St. Peter Luth. Ch., Arlington Heights, Ill., 1981—. Recipient Journalism award, Junction City H.S., 1965. Mem.: Luth. Edn. Assn. Conservative. Lutheran. Avocations: photography, singing, sewing, reading, writing. Office: St Peter Luth Ch/Sch 111 West Olive St Arlington Heights IL 60004-4766 Office Phone: 847-253-6638.

KRAMNICZ, RITA MARIE See KEPNER, RITA

KRAMNICZ, ROSANNE, freelance writer; b. Binghamton, N.Y., Mar. 26, 1948; d. Peter W. and Helena T. (Piotrowski) K.; m. Colin Douglas Anable, Dec. 10, 1990. BA/BS, Reed Coll., 1970. News columnist The Am., Deer River, Minn., 1976-78, Western Itasca Rev., Bemidji, Minn., 1977-78; news feature writer Va. Pilot, Virginia Beach, 1979; film script rschr. Warner Bros., Phoenix, 1980-81; clog dance instr., 1989—; feature writer Bangor (Maine) Daily News, 1985; columnist, feature writer Peninsula Daily News, Port Angeles, Wash., 1990-92; freelance writer Nordland, Wash., 1992—. Sailed with sextant (celestial navigation) from Wash. to Hawaii, 1980, 88; writing tchr. Maine Women in the Arts, 1982, Bangor, 1985, Oahu (Hawaii) Arts, 1982; co-author: (poetry) Stylus, 1984 (Libr. award); massage therapist, 1989—, shaman healing therapist and spkr., 2001—. Contbr. articles and stories to numerous jours., periodicals, and other publs. Mem. Jefferson County Dem. Club, Port Townsend, Wash., 1996-, Marrowstone Island Cmty. Assn., Nordland, 1991-; vol. EMT and CPR instr. Squaw Lake (Minn.) Ambulance, Virginia Beach, 1979, Chimacun (Wash.) Food Bank, 1989-93; crisis clinic vol., 1969-70. Recipient Merit award Famous Poets Soc., 1995; named Select Poetry Reader/Writer, Minn. Arts Coun., 1977, USMC Platoon Queen, Parris Island, NC, 1965. Avocations: swimming, gardening, dance, travel. Home: 281 Nolton Rd Nordland WA 98358-9539

KRAMP, SUZAN MARIE, systems programmer; MusB in Music Edn., Susquehanna U., 1975; MusM, Ohio State U., 1977; AS in Bus. Data Processing, Columbus State CC, 1987. Cert. database adminstr. IBM, solutions expert IBM, specialist IBM. Programmer, analyst Franklin County Data Ctr., Columbus, Ohio, 1986—90, Nationwide Ins., Columbus, 1990—94, database adminstr., 1994—97, DB2 systems programmer, 1997—. Mem., fundraiser Nat. Audubon Soc., Columbus chpt., Ohio, 1988—2006. Mem.: Ctrl. Ohio DB2 Users Group, Am. Birding Assn., U.S. Chess Fedn., Nat. Mus. Am. Indian, Nat. Wildlife Fedn., Hawk Mountain Sanctuary, Cornell Lab. Ornithology, Columbus Zoo Colo Club, Mensa. Office Phone: 614-249-5864.

KRANE, HILARY K., lawyer; b. Chgo. m. Kelly Bulkeley; children: Dylan, Maya, Conor. Bachelor's degree, Stanford U., 1986; JD, U. Chgo., 1989. Law clk. to U.S. Dist. Judge Milton I. Shadur, 1989—90; litig. assoc. Skadden, Arps, Slate, Meagher & Flom, 1990—94; various positions including asst. gen. counsel, ptnr. PricewaterhouseCoopers, San Francisco, 1994—2005; sr. v.p., gen. counsel Levi Strauss & Co., 2006—. Office: Levi Strauss & Co 1155 Battery St San Francisco CA 94111*

KRANE, JESSICA (AIDA JESSICA KOHNOP-KRANE), writer, educator; d. Samuel Rubenstein and Esther Ginsburg; m. Louis Kohnop, Jan. 11, 1956. Student, Roosevelt U. Writer, concert pianist, lectr. Appearances on varous TV programs including The Tonight Show, To Tell the Truth, The Today Show. Author: Face-O-Metrics, 1968, The Sensuous Approach to Looking Younger, 1971, How to Use Your Hands to Save Your Face, 1969, Born Again Vision, 1995; debut as pianist: Orchestra Hall, 1956; musician: toured U.S. and Canada with Louis Kohnop, Bklyn. Mus., WNYC, NY Town Hall, cmty. concerts. Avocation: fashion design.

KRANE, SUSAN, museum director, curator; b. Gary, Ind., June 8, 1954; BA, Carleton Coll., 1976; MA, Columbia U., 1978; MBA, U. Colo., 2000. Rockefeller Found. intern Walker Art Ctr., Mpls., 1978-79; curator Albright-Knox Art Gallery, Buffalo, 1979—87, High Mus. Art, Atlanta, 1987-95; adj. faculty Emory U., 1988-95; dir. U. Colo. Art Mus., 1996—2001; adj. prof. U. Colo., Scottsdale Mus. Contemporary Art, Ariz., 2001—. Author catalogues: Judy Pfaff, 1982, Surfacing Images: The Paintings of Joe Zucker, 1982, Mario Merz, 1984, Jan Kotik: The Painterly Object, 1984, Hollis Frampton: Recollections Recreations, 1984, The Wayward Muse, 1987, Albright-Knox Art Gallery: The Paintings and Sculpture Collection, 19877, Creighton Michael, 1987, Sherrie Levine, 1988, Houston Conwill, 1989, Ida Applebroog, 1989, Lynda Benglis: Dual Natures, 1991, Joel Otterson, 1991, Max Weber: The Cubist Decade 1910-1920, 1991, Barbara Ess, 1992, Ray Smith, 1993, Alison Saar, 1993, Equal Rights and Justice, 1994, Tampering Artists and Abstraction Today, 1995; contbr. Striking Out: Another American Road Show, 1991, Graven Images, 1991, Conversations at the Castle: Changing Audiences and Contemporary Art, Out of Order: Mapping Social Space, 2000, Lesley Dill: A 10-Year Survey, 2002, Let's Walk West: Brad Kahlhamer, 2004 Office: Scottsdale Mus Contemporary Art 7380 E Second St Scottsdale AZ 85251 Office Phone: 480-874-4632. Business E-Mail: susank@sccarts.org.

KRANE, VIKKI, psychology educator; d. Mark and Penny Krane. PhD, Univ. of N.C., Greensboro, 1990. Prof. sport psychology Bowling Green State U., Bowling Green, Ohio, 1990—, dir. women's studies program, 2003—. Editor: The Sport Psychologist, 2000—04, (jour.) Women in Sport & Physical Activity, 2005—; contbr. articles to profl. jours. Fellow Rsch. consortium fellow, AAHPERD, 1992. Fellow: Assn. for the Advancement of Applied Sport Psychology (secretary-treasurer 1994—97, cert. cons.); mem.: AAHPERD (pres. 2005—), N.Am. Soc. for the Psychology of Sport and Phys. Activity. Office: Bowling Green State U Women's Studies 226 East Hall Bowling Green OH 43403

KRANICH, MARGARET MANSLEY, artist; b. Phila., Mar. 23, 1925; d. Walter Edward and Elsie Katherine (Kerth) Mansley; m. Wilmer LeRoy Kranich, July 1, 1950; children: Laurence Wilmer, Deborah Margaret, Gary Richard. BS, West Chester U., 1946; MS, U. Pa., 1949; postgrad., Pa. State U., 1949, Worcester State Coll., 1961, Sch. the Worcester Art Museum, 1978-84. Cert. secondary tchr., English, social studies, guidance counseling. English tchr. Bristol (Pa.) H.S., 1946-48; tchr. Phila. Sch. System, 1948-50; yoga tchr. Worcester (Mass.) Polytechnic Inst., 1972-78; pvt. practice portraiit artist pvt. practice, Worcester, Mass., 1982-85, Chapel Hill, N.C., 1985-92; pvt. practice Shrewsbury, Mass., 1992—. Represented in permanent collections Dr. Robert H. Goddard Rocket Pioneer Scientist, 1984, The Rev. Michael Scrogin, Four WPI Presidents, Lee Bracegirdle and French Horn, Sydney Philharm. Symphony Orch., Dr. Richard Cartwright, Dr. Benjamin Griffin, others; exhibited at Southgate at Shrewsbury, Mass., 1994. V.p., bd. dirs. Child Guidance Assn. of Worcester, Mass., 1966-70; bd. dirs. The Children's Friend of Worcester, Mass., 1966-70, Merrifield House of Worcester, Mass., 1966-70; working vol. Child Guidance Assn. Nursery Sch. for Retarded, Worcester, Mass., 1962; mem. founding com. Worcester Internat. House; chorus dir Southgate at Shrewsbury, 2003—, yoga instr, 1996—. Recipient First prize portrait Cen Mass. Art Assn., 1982, U. Mass. Med. Ctr. Solo Art Show, Worcester, 1984, 3 Person Art Exhibit Worcester Poly. Inst., 1985. Mem. AAUW, Nat. Mus. Women in the Arts (charter mem.). Avocations: travel, genealogy, music, reading. Home: 30 Julio Dr Apt 615 Shrewsbury MA 01545-3047 Personal E-mail: mkranich@townisp.com.

KRANKING, MARGARET GRAHAM, retired artist, educator; b. Dec. 21, 1930; d. Stephen Wayne and Madge Williams (Dawes) Graham; m. James David Kranking, Aug. 23, 1952; children: James Andrew, Ann Marie Kranking Eggleton, David Wayne. BA summa cum laude (Clendenin fellow), Am. U., 1952. Asst. to head publs. Nat. Gallery Art, Washington, 1952-53; ret., 2006. Tchr. art Woman's Club, Chevy Chase, Md., 1976-88, 98-2006; guest instr. Amherst Coll., 1985, The Homestead, Hot Springs, Va., 1997; judge The Miniature Painters, Sculptors and Gravers Soc. Washington, 69th Ann. Internat. Exhbn., 2002, Bethesda, Md. One-woman shows include Spectrum Gallery, Washington, 1974, 76, 78-79, 83, 85, 87, 90, 92, 95, 97, 2000, Philip Morris, U.S.A., Richmond, Va., 1982-83, 86, Forence (S.C.) Mus., 1991, Lombardi Cancer treatment Ctr., Washington, 1992, Capital Gallery, Frankfort, Ky., 1993, Acad. Arts, Easton, Md., 1999, Warm Springs (Va.) Gallery, 1997-98; exhibited in group shows at Balt. Mus., 1974, 76, Corcoran Gallery Art, Washington, 1952, 72, USIA Traveling Exhbt., C.Am., 1978-79, AARP Traveling Exhbn., 1986; represented in permanent collections U. Va., Philip Morris U.S.A., USCG, AT&T, Freddie Mac, Florence Mus., S.C., Navy Fed. Credit Union Hdqs., Vienna, Va., Marsh and McClennan Co., Washington, The Washington Hilton, D.C., USCG Hall Heroes; traveling exhbn. Nat. Watercolor Soc., Watercolor U.S.A., Am. Watercolor Soc., Am. Artist mag., North Light mag., Adirondacks Nat. Exhbn. of Am. Watercolor, Artitude Internat. Art Competition, N.Y., Shada Gallery, Riyadh, Saudi Arabia, Belle Grove Plantation Invitational, Middletown, Va., Strathmore Hall Arts Ctr., North Bethesda, Md., Wash. Woman mag., Am. Speech-Lang. Hearing Assn., mag., Govt. House, Annapolis, Md. Invitational, 1997-99, Strathmore Hall Arts Ctr., North Bethesda, Md., Montgomery Coll. Invitational, Md., Glen View Mansion Invitational, Rockville, Md., 2000, Art in Embassies, N.Y.C., 2005—; ofcl. artist USCG; commd. to do painting of military funeral of Lt. Jack Rittichier for USCG Hall of Heroes, 2004; art in embassies, Residence of John Bolton Amb. to UN and U.S. Mission, N.Y., U.S.A. Mission Office, UN; contbr. reproductions and text to numerous books. Recipient George Gray award USCG Art Program, N.Y., 1991, 98. Mem.: Western Colo. Watercolor Soc., Ala. Watercolor Soc., Balt. Watercolor Soc., Western Fedn. Watercolor Socs., Watercolor Art Soc. Houston, Transparent Watercolor Soc. Am., Am. Watercolor Soc., Washington Soc. Landscape Painters, Potomac Valley Watercolorists (pres. 1981—83), Washington Watercolor Assn., So. Watercolor Soc., Ga. Watercolor Soc., Southwestern Watercolor Soc., Nat. Watercolor Soc. Roman Catholic. Home: 3504 Taylor St Chevy Chase MD 20815-4022

KRANOWITZ, CAROL STOCK, pre-school educator, writer; b. New Haven, Conn., Dec. 3, 1945; d. Herman Edward and Doris Baker Stock; m. Alan Michael Kranowitz, June 25, 1967; children: Jeremy Lewis, David Stock. BA, Barnard Coll., N.Y., 1967; MA in Edn. and Human Devel., George Wash. U., Washington, D.C., 1995. Preschool tchr. St. Columba's Nursery Sch., Washington, 1976—2001; internat. lectr. Sensory Processing Disorder, 1998—. Author: The Out-of-Sync Child: Recognizing and Coping with Sensory Processing Disorder, 1998, The Out-of-Sync Child Has Fun, 2003 (Therapeutic Contbn. award Devel. Delay Resources, 2003), 101 Activities for Kids in Tight Spaces, 1995, The Goodenoughs Get in Sync! A Story for Kids About Sensory Processing Disorder, 2004 (I-Parenting Media award, 2005, Juvenile Non-fiction award, 2004), Preschool Sensory Scan for Educators, 2005; co-author: Answers to Questions Teachers Ask About Sensory Integration, 2001, Balzer-Martin Preschool Screening, 1992, Hear, See, Play! Music Discovery Activities for Young Children, 1989; editor-in-chief: S.I. Focus Mag., 2004—. Adv. bd. Devel. Delay Resources, Pitts., 1998—, Nat. Autism Assn., 2004—, S.I. Challenge, Dallas-Ft. Worth, 2000—. Jewish. Avocation: cello.

KRANS, MICHELLE M., publishing executive; b. Chgo. m. Michael Krans; 1 child, Sarah. With McCord Ins. Services, Studio City, Calif., 1985—90; mktg. & promotions mgr. Desert Sun, Palm Springs, Calif., 1990—2001, advt. & mktg. dir., 2001—05, pres., pub., 2005—. Named Advt. Exec. of Yr. for 2005, Gannett Co. Inc.; recipient 4 Pres.'s Rings for outstanding work in advt. & mktg., Chmn.'s Ring, 2006. Office: The Desert Sun PO Box 2734 Palm Springs CA 92263 Office Phone: 760-322-8889.*

KRANTZ, CLAIRE WOLF, artist, freelance critic, curator; b. Chgo., June 22, 1938; d. George and Etta (Shtriker) Kaplan; m. San Robert Wolf, Mar. 8, 1959 (dec. 1973); children: Richard Wolf, Deborah Wolf Blanks, Rachel Wolf; m. David L. Krantz, Dec. 19, 1976. BS in Occpl. Therapy, U. Ill., 1961; post grad., Stanford U., 1977-78; BFA, Sch. Inst. of Chgo., 1979, postgrad., 1980-83. Occpl. therapist, 1961-76. Lectr. at various universities in the U.S., Europe, and Indonesia. Solo and two-person exhbns. include Gallerie S&H De Buck, Belgium, 1989, Galerie Paula Kouwenhoven, Delft, The Netherlands, 1990, Galerie Blankenese, Germany, 1991, Sazama Gallery, Chgo., 1992, Chgo. Cultural Ctr., 1993, Perimeter Gallery, Chgo., 1997, 2002, Bade Mus., Berkeley, Calif., 1997, Wash. State U., Pullman, 1997, Kedia Kabun Gallery, Yogyakarta, Indonesia, 1998, Contemporary Art Ctr. of Peria, Ill., 2000, I. Space Gallery, 2002, Toomey-Tourell Gallery, San Francisco, 2002, Flatfile Photographic Gallery, Chgo., 2004, various others; group exhbns. include Walker Gallery Art, 1981, Art Inst. Chgo., 1981, A.I.R. Gallery, N.Y.C., 1991-2003, Spertus Mus., Chgo., 1994, NY Arts Gallery, N.Y.C., 2003, Clarke House Mus., Chgo., 20094, various others; organized exhibits for institutions including: The Spertus Mus., The State of Ill. Mus., U-Turn E-Magazine, Wood Street Gallery, Ukrainian Inst. Modern Art; freelance art critic for nat. art publs., including Art in America. Mem. Chgo. Art Critics Assn., Phi Kappa Phi. Home and Studio: 711 S Dearborn #401 Chicago IL 60605-2308 Office Phone: 312-753-5071 (also fax). E-mail: cwkrantz@rcn.com.

KRANTZ, JUDITH TARCHER, novelist; b. NYC, Jan. 9, 1928; d. Jack David and Mary (Brager) Tarcher; m. Stephen Falk Krantz, Feb. 19, 1954; children: Nicholas, Anthony. BA, Wellesley Coll., 1948. Fashion publicist, Paris, 1948-49; fashion editor Good Housekeeping mag., N.Y.C., 1949-56; contbg. writer McCalls, 1956-59, Ladies Home Jour., 1959-71; contbg. west coast editor Cosmopolitan mag., 1971-79. Author: Scruples, 1978, Princess Daisy, 1980, Mistral's Daughter, 1982, I'll Take Manhattan, 1986, Till We Meet Again, 1988, Dazzle, 1990, Scruples Two, 1992, Lovers, 1994, Spring Collection, 1996, The Jewels of Tessa Kent, 1998, Sex & Shopping: Confessions of a Nice Jewish Girl, 2000. Office: St Martin Press 175 5th Ave New York NY 10010

KRANYIK, ELIZABETH ANN, secondary school educator; b. Bridgeport, Conn., Nov. 15, 1957; d. Andrew Ladislaus and Marion Irene (Slater) K.; m. Charles Edward Porzelt III, Nov. 28, 1992; children: Charles Edward Porzelt IV, Marial Elizabeth Porzelt. BS summa cum laude, Western Conn. State U., 1979; MA, Fairfield U., 1989. Cert. h.s. tchr., gen. sci. endorsement, Conn. Tchr., program coordinator Fairfield (Conn.) Elem. Summer Sch., 1973-85; tchr. St. Maurice Sch., Stamford, Conn., 1980-82, Our Lady of Lourdes Sch., Melbourne, Fla., 1982-85, St. Pius X Sch., Fairfield, 1985-87, Bridgeport Pub. Schs., 1988-93, Bridgeport Regional Vocat. Aquaculture Sch., 1993—. Freelance tutor; cons., tchr. Mill River Wetlands Prog., Fairfield, 1985-87, honors tchr., 1991; cons. Ocean Classroom, Bridgeport, Conn., 1989-90, NASA Newest Scholar, 1991, Sound Educators Assn., 1992—. Vol. H.M.S. ROSE Found., Bridgeport, 1985-93, tour guide, 1985-93; den leader Boy Scouts Am., 1998-2003, asst. scoutmaster, 2004-; union del. BEA, 2000-, legis. chair, 2003-05, retirement chair, 2005-06. Mem. Nat. Sci. Tchrs. Assn., Alliance Francais (Merit award 1979), Sound Educators Assn., Southeastern New Eng. Marine Educators, Phi Delta Kappa. Congregationalist. Avocations: nature study, reading, swimming, carpentry. Home: 129 Jockey Hollow Rd Monroe CT 06468-1270

KRANZ, KATHLEEN NEE, pianist, music educator; b. Fontana, Calif., May 31, 1951; d. Bruce Lester Brown and Margaret JoAnne Nee; m. Tomas Patten Kranz, July 4, 1978; 1 child, Michael Alexander. AB in Music, Fla. State U., Tallahassee, 1973, MusM in Piano Performace, 1977; PhD in Music Theoretical Studies, U. Calif., San Diego, 1985. Cert. music tchr. Music Tchrs. Nat. Assn., 2004. Mus. dir. Actor's Theater of Louisville, 1973—74, Asolo State Theater, Sarasota, Fla., 1974—75; mem. faculty, piano instr. U. Calif., San Diego, 1983—87; pvt. studio tchr. piano San Diego, 1978—; prof. piano, head theory dept. Calif. Inst. of Music, San Diego, 1988—. Profl. accompanist Fairbanks Sch. for the Performing Arts, 1988—97; music theory tchr. Suzuki Assn., Calif., 1984—88; performer chamber music, San Diego, 1978—; master tchr. Am. Music Scholarship Assn., Cin., 1984—86, Batiquitos Festival, Del Mar, Calif., 1988; master accompanist, coach San Diego Children's Choir, 2003—; pres. San Diego (Calif.) Conservatory Music, 2005—. Contbr. articles to profl. jours. Recipient award, Fla. Fedn. Music Clubs, 1976, Alice Hohn scholarship, U. Calif., San Diego Grad. Sch., 1981; fellow, U. Calif., San Diego, 1981. Mem.: Music Tchrs.' Assn. Calif. (H.S. credit chmn., chmn. Bach Festival, chmn. Goodlin scholarship, chmn. composition contest), Music Tchrs.' Nat. Assn., Nat. Fedn. Music Clubs (judge 2004, adjudicator 2004). Home: 3543 1/2 Myrtle Ave San Diego CA 92104 Office Phone: 858-259-0645. Personal E-mail: drkathleenkranz@yahoo.com.

KRASEVAC, ESTHER, retired academic administrator; b. East Chicago, Ind., May 28, 1935; d. John and Veronica (Glowacki) Gruszkos; m. George J. Krasevac, June 25, 1960; children: Karin Krasevac-Lenz, Kimberly Ann Krasevac-Szekely. BS, Ind. U., 1958; MEd, Loyola U., Chgo., 1961. Cert. elem. and secondary tchr., Ind. Tchr. East Chgo. Pub. Schs., 1958-61; tchr. social studies Merrillville (Ind.) Pub. Schs. and St. Mary's Cath. Sch., Crown Point, Ind., 1963-71; coordinator Advisors for New Am. Resettlement Program for Refugees, Frackville, Pa., 1977; profl. vol., organizer various social, polit. and religious causes, Pottsville and Reading, Pa., 1968-78; dir. spl. gifts Albright Coll., Reading, 1978-85, dir. devel., 1985; exec. dir. Found. for Ind. Colls. Pa., Phila., 1987-89; v.p. devel. Centenary Coll., Hackettstown, NJ, 1989—92, Alvernia Coll., Reading, Pa., 1992—2000; ret., 2000. Trustee Reading Area C.C., 1975-82, commr. Reading Housing Authority, 1973-78; active social service agys., Reading, 1980-2000, v.p. The Classic Exch., 2001-06, hospice vol., 2003-, co-chair vol. appts. ushers Sr. Box Office, ct. apptd. advocate abused and neglected children CASA, 2004-; candidate from Berks County Pa. Legislature, 1976; TV interviewer and moderator Dems. Berks County, 1982—; v.p., originator LWV Schuylkill County, Pa., 1968-69; pres. LWV Berks County, 1971-73; state bd. LWV Pa., 1975-76; mentor My Sister's Cir., 2004-. Named Mediator City Reading, Albright Coll., 1987. Mem. Cath. Cmty. st. Francis Xavier, Citizen's Planned Housing Assn., Coun. Advancement and Support Edn. (forum participant 1983), Balt. Women's Giving Cir., Phi Lambda Theta. Roman Catholic. Avocations: politics, reading, travel. Home: 12300 Rosslare Ridge Rd Lutherville Timonium MD 21093-8207

KRASNEWICH, KATHRYN, water transportation executive; b. 1973; BS, U. Ill., 1995. Investment banker Arthur Andersen & cO., 1995—2000, Deutsche Bank, 2000—03; dir. mergers and acquisitions Brunswick Corp., Chgo., 2003—. Named one of 40 Under Forty, Crain's Bus. Chgo., 2005. Office: Brunswick Corp 1 Northfield Ct Lake Forest IL 60045-4811 Office Phone: 847-735-4700. Office Fax: 847-735-4765.*

KRASNY, PAULA J., lawyer; b. Phila., Pa., Sept. 29, 1963; Student, Harvard U., 1984; AB, Vassar Coll., 1985; JD, Northwestern U., 1988. Bar: Ill. 1988. Atty. McDermott, Will & Emery, Chgo., ptnr., 1995—99, Baker & McKenzie, Chgo., 1999—. Mem. adv. bd. Northwestern Jour. Tech. and Intellectual Property; bd. dir. Frances Lehman Loeb Art Ctr. Vassar Coll. Mem.: ABA, Internat. Trademark Assn., Am.-Israel C. of C. Office: Baker & McKenzie One Prudential Plz 130 East Randolph Dr Chicago IL 60601

KRATOVIL, JANE LINDLEY, think tank associate, not-for-profit developer; b. Boston, Nov. 25, 1952; 1 child, Lindley. BA, Lynchburg Coll., 1974. Various positions U.S. Ho. of Reps., Washington, 1974-77, The Pittston Co., Greenwich, Conn., 1977-79; assoc. dir. City Sports Mgmt. Inc., Washington, 1979-82; adminstrv. asst. to spl. asst. to pres. for adminstrn. The White House, Washington, 1982-85; exec. asst. to gen. and dep. gen. counsel U.S. Dept. Treasury, Washington, 1985-88; exec. dir., sec. Eisenhower World Affairs Inst., Washington, 1988-2000; pres. Lindley & Assoc., Alexandria, Va., 2000—. Office: 2230 Candlewood Dr Alexandria VA 22308-1505 E-mail: jkratovil@earthlink.net.

KRATZNER, JUDITH EVELYN, program manager; b. Fairmont, Minn., Sept. 4, 1942; d. Vernon W. and Evelyn B. (Jagodzinske) Schuler; m. Roland Ray Kratzner, Aug. 18, 1962; children: Mark V., Julie Ann, Jonathan R. BEd, Ill. State U., 1964; MEd, Ball State U., 1974; MS in Adminstrn., U. Notre Dame, 1986. Tchr. Sch. Dist. 117, Jacksonville, Ill., 1966-69, Harrison-Washington Sch. Dist., Gaston, Ind., 1970-73; dir. vols. St. John's Health Sys., Anderson, Ind., 1974-77, dir. human resource devel., 1977-84, asst. corporate staff, 1984-87, dir. cmty. svcs., 1987-93, dir. adult day care, 1993-96; exec. dir. Ind. Assn. Area Agys. Aging, Indpls., 1997-99; dir. ret. and sr. vol. program Anderson Pub. Libr., 1999—. Chair Ind. ElderCare Coalition, Indpls., 1993, 94; bd. dirs. Life Stream Svcs. Inc., 2000—, chair, 2002—. Pres. Anderson/Madison County YWCA, 1989, 90; pres. Mgmt. Club of Madison County, 1983-84; pres. Hist. West 8th St. Neighborhood Assn., Anderson, 1992-94; pres. LWV, Muncie, Ind., 1971-73. Recipient Women of Worth award Anderson Coun. of Women, 1994, YWCA Vol. of Yr. award, Anderson, 1992, Svc. Cmty. award Cmty. Svc. Coun., Anderson, 1989, Disting. Svc. award Internat. Mgmt. Coun., Anderson, 1987. Mem. Nat. Coun. on Aging (Nat. Adult Day Care Svcs. Assn. unit 1985), Nat. Adult Day Care Svcs. Assn. (region V. rep. 1991-96, nat. sec. 1996-98), Ind. Assn. Adult Day Care Svcs. (pres. 1986, 87). Avocations: historic preservation, photography. Home: 421 W 8th St Anderson IN 46016-1373 Office: RSVP Anderson Pub Libr 111 E 12th St Anderson IN 46016 E-mail: jkratzner@and.lib.in.us.

KRAUS, JILL GANSMAN, former jewelry industry marketing executive; b. Phila., Oct. 25, 1952; d. Lester David and Lois (Singer) Gansman; m. Peter Steven Kraus, July 20, 1980; 2 children, Jason Andrew, Benjamin Michael. BFA, Carnegie Mellon U., 1974; MFA, RISD, 1977. Designer Accesocraft, NYC, 1977-78, Cadoro, NYC, 1978-79; asst. to dir. of design Monet Jewelry, NYC, 1979-81; sr. designer Swank Inc., NYC, 1981-85; named product mktg. mgr. Marvella, NYC, 1985; cons. Liz Claiborne; named v.p. design & training Swarovski Jewelry US Ltd., NYC, 1992. V.p. associates divsn. Jewish Guild for the Blind, NYC, 1983—87; bd. trustees Carnegie Mellon U.; bd. dirs. World Studio Found., NYC; co-chair Friends of the Carnegie Internat.; commd. Kraus Campo garden for Carnegie Mellon U. campus, 2004. Named one of Top 200 Collectors, ARTnews mag., 2004. Democrat. Avocation: Collector Contemporary Art.

KRAUS, LISA MARIE WASKO, music educator, composer, musician; b. Phila., Oct. 10, 1969; d. Raymond and Muriel Joan Wasko; m. Timothy J. Kraus, Nov. 23, 2002; 1 child, Emily Victoria. AA in Music, Phila. CC, 1987; MusB Magna Cum Laude, Temple U., 1993; MusM Suma Cum Laude, Duquesne U., 2001. Cert. Music K-12 PA, 1993. Tchr. music, art, lit. tchr., program dir. Blair Christian Acad., 1993—95; tchr. orch., choir, music theory Archdiocese of Phila. St. Maria Goretti H.S., 1995—96; tchr. music, musical/vocal dir., asst. dir. musicals Bristol Twp. Sch. Dist., Levittown, 1996—. Studio musician Various Studios, 1987—; composer, arranger She Writes Music, 2001—, Martial Arts Channel, Breakthrough Comm., 2003—. Performer: Pipes and Drums of the Delaware Valley, 1987—2003, Artists Conf., 2001—02. Recipient Recognition award, Found. for Ednl. Excellence, 1997, Musical Achievement Citation, Sen. Tommy Tomlinson, 2001, Performing Arts award, Mayor Bristol Twp., 2000, 2001, award, So. Poverty Law Ctr., 2004, Supts. award/Sch. Bd. Honors for Musical, Bristol Twp. Sch. Dist., 2006; Ednl. scholar, St. Albain Swain Masonic Lodge #529, 2000. Master: TRI M Music Honor Soc. (corr.; soc. sponsor 2001—, Cert. Recognition 2002); mem.: Am. Choral Dirs. Assn., Music Educators Nat. Conf. (assoc.; collegiate chpt. treas. 1991—92), Nat. Acad. Recording Arts and Scis. (assoc.). Avocations: photography, antiques, painting, scrapbooks, voice overs.

KRAUS, MARGERY, management consultant, communications company executive; b. Franklin, NJ, May 20, 1946; d. Soland Lily (Cvern) Rosen; m. Stephen Kraus, Sept. 4, 1966; children: Lisa, Evan, Mara. BA in Polit. Sci., Am. U., 1967, MA in Govt., 1970. With Close Up Found., Arlington, Va., 1971-84, v.p., 1976-84; exec. v.p. APCO, Inc., Washington, 1984—88; pres., CEO APCO Worldwide (formerly APCO, Inc.), Washington, 1988—. Bd. dirs. Internat. Mgmt. and Devel. Inst., Northwestern Mutual Govt'l Rels. Com., chair, Coun. of PR Firms, Pub. Affairs Coun., Catherine B. Reynolds Found., Inst. for Public Rels., Creative Coalition, Meridian Internat. Ctr.; cons., speaker in field; adv. bd. Kellogg Sch. Mgmt. Bd. dirs. Close Up Found. Named Washington Businesswoman of the Year, 1998, Pub. Rels. Profl. of Yr., Pub. Rels. Week, 1997, 2004, Internat. Pub. Rels. Profl. of Yr., 2001. Mem., Adv. Bd., Terry Sanford Inst. of Public Policy, Duke Univ, Coun. on Am. Politics, George Washington Univ. Grad. Sch. of Political Mgmt. Home: 9609 Whitecedar Ct Vienna VA 22181-5423 Office: APCO Worldwide 700 12th St NW Ste 800 Washington DC 20005 Business E-Mail: mkraus@apcoworldwide.com.

KRAUS, NAOMI, retired biochemist; b. Budapest, Hungary, July 4, 1933; came to U.S., 1965; d. Jacob and Vilma (Schwartz) K.; (div.); 1 child, Daphna. MS, Hebrew U., Jerusalem, Israel, 1960; PhD, Hebrew U., 1966. Instr. U. Pa., Phila., 1968-74; asst. prof. U. Tex. Sch. Medicine, Houston, 1974-76, assoc. prof., 1976-86, prof., 1986—2000; ret., 2000. Editor: Hormonal Control of Gluconeogenesis, 1986. Pres. Gulf Coast chpt. Assn. Women in Sci., 1974-76, v.p., 1989-90. Recipient grants from NIH, NSF. Mem. AAAS, Am. Soc. Cell Biology. Achievements include rsch. in role Ca 2+ plays in the transduction of hormonal signals.

KRAUS, NORMA JEAN, human resources executive; b. Pitts., Feb. 11, 1931; d. Edward Karl and Alli Alexandria (Hermanson) K. BA, U. Pitts., 1954; postgrad., NYU, 1959—61, Cornell U., 1969—70. Pers. mgr. for several cos., 1957-70; corp. dir. pers. TelePrompter Corp., NYC, 1970-73; exec. asst., speech writer to Lt. Gov. NY Office of Lt. Gov., Albany, 1974-79; exec. officer, v.p. human resources, labor rels. and stockholder rels. Volt Info. Scics., Inc., NYC, 1979—. Co-founder Manhattan Women's Polit. Caucus, 1971; co-founder NY State Women's Polit. Caucus, 1972, vice chair, 1978; bd. dirs. Ctr. for Women in Govt., 1977-79. Lt. (s.g.) USNR, 1954-57. Pa. State Senatorial Scholar, 1950-54. Democrat. Avocations: politics, women's rights. Office: Volt Info Scis Inc 560 Lexington Ave Fl 15 New York NY 10022-6828 Office Phone: 212-704-2423. E-mail: njkideas@optonline.net, nkraus@volt.com.

KRAUS, ROZANN B., performing company executive; b. Dayton, Ohio, Oct. 7, 1952; m. Daniel Michael Epstein, Oct. 25, 1970; children: Jennah Buckaroo EpsteinKraus, Connor Bagel EpsteinKraus. MA, SUNY, Brockport, 1973. Pres./founder The Dance Complex, Cambridge, Mass., 1991—. Artistic dir./choreographer KRAUSAND., Cambridge, Mass., 1974—98. Performer (concert dance) Paul Robeson award (Creative and Concerned Participation in the Arts in the Cmty., 1982). Democrat. Avocations: running, swimming, bicycling, political activism, writing. Office: The Dance Complex 536 Massachusetts Ave Cambridge MA 02139 Office Phone: 617-547-9363.

KRAUS, RUBY JEAN, art educator; d. Grady Reese and Verna Mae White; m. Ruby Jean White, Feb. 7, 1970; 1 child, Mathew Tyson. BS in Edn., SMSU, Springfield, Mo., 1976. Cert. visual arts specialist Tenn., 1987. Title I math./lang. arts tchr. Tenn. Prep. Sch., Nashville, 1987—96; visual arts specialist Bradley County Pub. Schs.-Walker Valley H.S., Cleveland, Tenn., 1999—; art tchr. grades 1-5 Jefferson Elem. Sch., Jefferson City, Tenn., 2006—. Art cons. Lee U., Cleveland, 1999—2006. Recreational art dir. Ch. of God, Ardmore, Okla., 1981—86, pres. women's group. Recipient Mayoral award for Tchr. Excellence, City of Nashville Mayor, 1993. Mem.: NEA (bldg. rep. 1992—94). Achievements include development of Church Program for families with Special Needs. Avocation: community service. Office: Bradley County Public Schools Keith St Cleveland TN 37312 Office Phone: 423-416-2060. Personal E-mail: vernruby@charter.net.

KRAUSE, GLORIA ROSE, music educator; b. Milw., Oct. 30, 1922; d. Carl Fred and Rose (Bremeier) Runge; m. George Tanner Krause Jr., June 24, 1960; 1 child, George Henry. MusB, U. Rochester, 1946; MusM, Northwestern U., 1954. Music tchr. Livingston Manor (N.Y.) Cen., 1946-59, Monticello (N.Y.) Cen. Sch., 1959-61, Liberty (N.Y.) Cen. Sch., 1966-67, Livingston Manor Sch., 1968-79, Narrowsburg (N.Y.) Ctrl. Sch., 1979-87. Dir. Ill. Winds Chamber Ensemble, Narrowsburg, N.Y., 1975—; gen. mgr. Delaware Valley Opera, Narrowsburg, 1986—. Music dir.: (operas) HMS Pinafore, Mikado, Pirates of Penzance, Princess Ida, Patience, Amahl and Night Visitors, The Medium, Gondoliers, Marriage of Figaro, Don Pasquale, Die Fledermaus, Gypsy Baron, The Beggars Opera, La Traviata, Madame Butterfly, La Boehme, The Medium, The Merry Widow, The Barber of Seville (Rossini), Student Prince, Orphans in the Underworld, Hansel and Gretel; bassoonist with Highland Symphony Orch., Middletown, NY, 1986-90, New Sussex Cmty. Orch., Sparta, NJ, 1984-90. Pres. Del. Valley Arts Alliance, 1980—; bd. dirs. Tusten-Cochecton Librr., Narrowsburg, 1988—. Recipient Svc. award Siddha Meditation Ashram Found., South Fallsburg, NY, 1990, Recognition award Alliance NY State Arts Coun., 1995; named Woman of Yr., Catskill Mountain Bus. and Profl. Women, 1995; Gloria R. Krause Recital Hall named in her honor Del. Valley Arts Alliance, 2002 Office: Del Valley Opera PO Box 188 Narrowsburg NY 12764-0188 Business E-Mail: dvo@citlink.net.

KRAUSE, HELEN FOX, retired otolaryngologist; b. Boston, Mar. 20, 1932; d. Nathan and Frances Lena (Rich) Fox; children: Merrick Eli, Beth Riva Harper, Kim Debra Codd. BS, U. Maine, 1954; MD, Tuft U., 1958. Diplomate Am. Bd. Otolaryngology. Intern Health Ctr. Hosps. Pitts., 1958-59; resident Eye & Ear Hosp., Children's Hosp., VA Hosp., 1959-62; pvt. practice Pitts., 1962—2003; ret., 2003. Mem. otolaryngology adv. bd. U.S. Pharmacopea, 1991-96, 00—, chmn., 1995-00; prof. U. Pitts. Sch. Medicine; vis. prof. Pan Hellenic Otorhinolaryngology Soc., Crete, Greece, 1993, Panama, Argentina, 1998, China, Hong Kong, 1999, Thailand, China, Taiwan, 2000, Pan Am. Otolaryn. Soc., 2000; pres., dir. 1st World Congress of Otorhinolaryngologic Allergy, Endoscopy and Laser Surgery, Athens, 1998, 01; bd. dirs. Bayer Pharm. Women's Health Initiative; vis. prof. Thailand, Singapore; lectr. 2nd World Congress Otolaryngology, Allergy and Immunology, 2001; chairperson Nat. Hadassah Physicians Coun. Author, editor: Otolaryngic Allergy and Immunology, 1989; lectr., vis. prof. Singapore, Bangkok, Hong Kong (multiple tng. programs 1990); contbr. chpts. to books and articles to profl. jours. Pres. North Hills Jewish Cmty. Ctr., Pitts., 1973-74; cons. North Allegheny Sch. Bd., Pitts., 1977; lectr. North Allegheny Sr. High Sch., Wexford, 1979-84; chmn. Desert Storm Project, North Hills Bus. and Profl. Women, 1991. Recipient Disting. Svc. award, Pa. Acad. Otolaryngology, 1993, Hon. Achievement award, Am. Acad. Otolaryngology Head and Neck Surgery, 1993, Bd. Govs. Chair award, 2000, Bd. Govs. award, Practioner of Excellence, 2003, Presdl. citation, 2004, Bd. Govs. Volunteerism award, 2004, Bd. Govs. Vounteerism award, 2005, Recognition award, Panhellenic Soc. ORL-HNS, 2001, Lifetime Achievement award, Am. Acad. Otolaryngic Allergy, 2002; scholar Jackson Meml. Labs., Bar Harbor, Maine, 1954. Fellow ACS, Am. Acad. Otolaryngology Head and Neck Surgery (bd. govs. 1982-89, 90—, Practitioner Excellence award 2003, Presdl. citation 2004, Volunteerism award 2004, 05), Am. Acad. Otolaryngologic Allergy (pres. 2984-85, Lifetime Achievement award 2002, Svc. award 1990, cert. appreciation 1991, Pres.'s award 1997, Spl. Achievement award 1997), Am. Acad. Facial Plastic and Rsch. Surgery; mem. Pa. Acad. Otolaryngology (pres. 1989-90), Internat. Soc. Otorhinolaryngic Allergy and Immunology (pres. 1995-98), Pitts. Otological Soc. (pres. 1983-85), Phi Beta Kappa, Phi Kappa Phi. Office: 1301 Aviara Pl Gibsonia PA 15044-8042 Personal E-mail: hfk@zoominternet.net.

KRAUSE, JENNIE SUE, athletic trainer, nutrition counselor; b. Anchorage, Nov. 25, 1981; d. Lonnie Ray and Barbara Ann Napier; m. Matthew Haston Krause, July 27, 2002. BS in Sports Medicine magna cum laude, San Diego Christian Coll., El Cajon, Calif., 2003. Cert. Nat. Athletic Trainers' Assn. Bd. Cert., lic. athletic trainer Bd. Medicine, Va.; cert. personal trainer FiTour, aerobic instr. FiTour. Cert. athletic trainer, phys. therapy asst. B.b. & B., Santee, Calif., 2003—04; dir. fitness Liberty U., Lynchburg, Va., 2004—. Nutrition counselor Liberty U., Lynchburg, 2004—. Mem. Thomas Rd. Bapt. Ch., Lynchburg, 2004—06. Named Acad. All-Am., Nat. Assn. Intercollegiate Athletics, 2000—03; recipient Outstanding Grad. award, San Diego Christian Coll., 2003. Mem.: Nat. Athletic Trainers Assn. Conservative. Achievements include research in eating disorders. Avocations: sports, reading, camping, hunting, fishing.

KRAUSE, MARCELLA ELIZABETH MASON (MRS. EUGENE FITCH KRAUSE), retired secondary education educator; b. Norfolk, Nebr.; d. James Haskell and Elizabeth (Vader) Mason; student Northeast C.C., 1928-30; B.S., U. Neb., 1934; M.A., Columbia, 1938; postgrad. summers U. Calif. at Berkeley, 1950, 51, 65, Stanford, 1964, Creighton U., 1966, Chico (Calif.) State U., 1967; m. Eugene Fitch Krause, June 1, 1945; 1 dau., Kathryn Elizabeth. Tchr., Royal (Nebr.) pub. schs., 1930-32, Hardy (Nebr.) pub. schs., 1933-35, Omaha pub. schs., 1935-37, Lincoln Sch. of Tchrs. Coll., Columbia, 1937-38, Florence (Ala.) State Tchrs. Coll., summer 1938, Tchrs. Coll., U. Nebr., 1938-42, Corpus Christi (Tex.) pub. schs., 1942-45, Oakland (Calif.) pub. schs., 1945-83. Bd. dirs. U. Nebr. Womens Faculty Club, 1940-42; mem. Nebr. State Tchrs. Conv. Panel, 1940—; mem. U. Nebr. Reading Inst., 1940; speaker Iowa State Tchrs. Conv., 1941; reading speaker Nebr. State Tchrs. conv., 1941; lectr. Johnson County Tchrs. Inst., 1942; chmn. Reading Survey Corpus Christi pub. schs., 1943; chmn. Inservice Reading Meetings Oakland pub. schs., 1948-57. Mem. Gov.'s Adv. Commn. on Status Women Conf., San Francisco, 1966; service worker ARC, Am. Cancer Soc., United Crusade, Oakland CD; Republican precinct capt., 1964-70; v.p. Oakland Fedn. Rep. Women. Ford Found. Fund for Advancement Edn. fellow, 1955-56; scholar Stanford, 1964; Calif. Congress PTA scholar U. Calif., 1965, Norfolk (Nebr.) Hall of Success Northeast C.C., 1990; recipient award of Excellence, U. Nebr. Tchrs. Coll., 1998. Mem. Nat. Council Women, AAUW (dir.), Calif. Tchrs. Assn., Oakland Mus. Assn., U. Nebr. Alumni Assn. (Alumni Achievement award 1984), Californians for Nebr., Ladies Grand Army Republic, 1960, 1986-87 Ruth Assn., Martha Assn. (pres. East Bay chpt. 1979), Sierra DAR (regent), Eastbay DAR Regents Assn. (pres.), Nebr. Alumni Assn. (life, alumni achievement award 1984), Grand Lake Bus. and Profl. Women, Internat. Platform Assn., Eastbay Past Matrons Assn., P.E.O., Pi Lambda Theta (pres. No. Calif. chpt.), Alpha Delta Kappa. Methodist. Mem. Order Eastern Star (past matron). Contbr. articles to profl. jours. Home: 5615 Estates Dr Oakland CA 94618-2725

KRAUSE, MARILYN RUTH, elementary school educator; d. John and Ruth Mitchell; m. Robert Krause, Jr., Dec. 27, 1980; children: John, Phillip, Crystal. BS in Med. Tech., No. Mich. U., Marquette, 1977—81; elem. edn. cert., secondary edn. cert., U. Alaska, Fairbanks; MS in Edn., Western Oreg. U. Tchr. Ryan Mid. Sch., Fairbanks, 1996—2006, Fairbanks Dist. Summer Sch., 2003, 2005; coord. Ryan After Schs. Tutoring, Fairbanks, 2004—05. Coord. Sci. Fair, Alaska; adv. Future Farmer's Am. Recipient Agriscience Tchr. of Yr., Future Farmer's Am., Alaska, 2006; grantee Staff Incentive grant, Fairbanks Sch. Dist., 2006. Mem.: NEA. Avocations: figure skating, quilting, spinning, cooking. Home: 640 Cambridge Dr Fairbanks AK 99709

KRAUSE, MARJORIE N., biochemist; b. Chgo., July 25, 1937; d. Robert Mortimer Krause and Eleanor Driese. BS, Mich. State U., 1959; MS, Cleve. State U., 1986. Cert. tchr., Mich.; cert. medical technologist in hematology Am. Soc. Clinical Pathologists. Technician Dartmouth Coll., Hanover, N.H., 1960-66, U. Vt., Burlington, 1966-70; technologist Case We. Res. U., Cleve., 1971-75, 89-93, U. Hosps., Cleve., 1975-79; lab technologist, med. technologist Cleve. Clinic Found., 1979-89; computer lab technician Lakeland C.C., Kirtland, Ohio, 1996-97, 99; narrator Sea World Ohio, Aurora, 1998, info. technologist, 2000. Judge youth sci. fair Ohio Acad. Scis., Columbus, Ohio, 1995, 96. Vol. Cleve. Orch., 1972—, Playhouse Sq. Found., 1988—2004, Hunter Jumper Classic, 1999—2002, Internat. Children's Games, 2004. Recipient cert. recognition, Playhouse Sq. Found., 1995, 1996, 1998, 2004. Avocations: natural history, bird watching, opera, theater, classical music. Home: 27500 Bishop Park Dr Apt 316 Wickliffe OH 44092-2757

KRAUSE, PATRICIA ANN, elementary school educator; b. St. Louis, Mar. 4, 1941; d. John Melvin and Mary Ruby (Watkins) Raftery; divorced; children: Kim, Kris, Kirk, Kari, Keli. BSEd, U. Mo., St. Louis, 1980; MAEd, Maryville U., 1990. Cert. early childhood edn., elem. edn., gifted edn., Mo. Tchr. St. Louis Archdiocese, 1961-80, Community Sch., St. Louis, 1981-83, Rossman Sch., St. Louis, 1983-85, St. Louis Bd. Edn., 1988—. Tchr. Gifted Resource Coun., St. Louis, 1985-92, Talented Young Learner, St. Louis, 1990-91; dir. Horizons, 1990-92; adj. clin. instr. Maryville U., St. Louis, 1990— Cons. N.W. County Teen Coun., Maryland Heights, Mo., 1990-92; facilitator Project Construct Nat. Ctr., 1992—. Fellow St. Louis Tchrs. Acad.; mem. Nat. Sci. Tchrs. Assn. (presenter 1992, 93, 94), Nat. Assn. Edn. Young Child, Mo. Assn. Edn. Young Child, Friends of Gifted, Nat. Educator Assn., Mo. Educator Assn. (kindergarten state task force). Home: 2356 Wescreek Dr Maryland Heights MO 63043-4112 Office: St Anns Cath Sch 7532 Natural Bridge Saint Louis MO 63121

KRAUSE, SONJA, chemistry professor; b. St. Gall, Switzerland, Aug. 10, 1933; came to U.S., 1939; d. Friedrich and Rita (Maas) K.; m. Walter Walls Goodwin, Nov. 27, 1970 BS, Rensselaer Poly. Inst., 1954; PhD, U. Calif., Berkeley, 1957. Sr. phys. chemist Rohm & Haas Co., Phila., 1957-64; vol. U.S. Peace Corps, Nigeria, 1964-65; asst. lectr. Lagos U.; asst. prof. Gondar Health Coll. U.S. Peace Corps, Ethiopia, 1965-66; vis. asst. prof. U. So. Calif., L.A., 1966-67; chemistry faculty Rensselaer Poly. Inst., Troy, NY, 1967—, prof., 1978—2004, prof. emeritus, 2004—. Mem. coun. Gordon Rsch. Conf., 1981-83; mem. com. on polymers and engring. NRC, 1992-94; sabbatical Inst. Charles Sadron, Ctr. Rsch. on Macromolecules, Strasbourg, France, 1987. Author: (with others) Chemistry of Environment, 1978, 2d edit., 2002; editor: Molecular Electro-Optics, 1981; mem. editorial adv. bd. Macromolecules, 1982-84 Bd. dirs. Nat. Plastics Ctr. and Mus., Leominster, Mass., 1996-2000. Fellow Am. Phys. Soc. (coun. divsn. biol. physics 1980-93); mem. IUPAC (assoc.), Am. Chem. Soc. (chmn. ea. N.Y. sect. 1981-82, councillor 1991-95, adv. bd. petroleum rsch. fund 1979-81, assoc. mem. com. on edn. 1993-95, assoc. mem. internat. com. 1996), Biophys. Soc. (coun. 1977), N.Y. Acad. Scis., Sigma Xi (pres. Rensselaer Poly Inst. chpt. 1984-85). Office: Rensselaer Poly Inst Dept Chemistry Troy NY 12180 Business E-Mail: krauss@rpi.edu.

KRAUSER, JANICE, special education educator; b. Chgo., Apr. 30, 1951; d. John Francis and June (Fogle) K. BS, U. Tenn., 1973; MEd, Fla. Atlantic U., 1979. Tchr. John Sevier Elem. Sch., Knoxville, Tenn., 1973-76; substitute tchr. Broward County Schs., Ft. Lauderdale, Fla., 1976-78; tchr. Broward Estates Elem. Sch., Ft. Lauderdale, 1978-79, Attucks Mid. Sch., Hollywood, Fla., 1979-81; tchr., spl. edn. specialist South Broward High Sch., Hollywood, 1981-92; spl. edn. specialist New River Middle Sch., Ft. Lauderdale, 1992—. Selected mem. Fla. Spkrs. Bur., 1997—; state-wide design team mem. of inclusion materials for sch.-based adminstrs.; mem. Fla. Comprehensive Sys. Pers. Devel., 1997—. Co-author: (curriculum) Fundamental Math I and II, Consumer Math, Applied English I, II, and III, Fundamental English I, II, III; published photographer. Zone chmn. U.S.Water Polo, Colorado Springs, 1984-92, 98-2000, bd. dirs. 1998-2000; treas. Fla. Water Polo, 1982-97; dist. del. U.S. Masters Swimming, 1987-95; mem. internat. congress Internat. Swimming Hall of Fame, Ft. Lauderdale, 1994—, (bd. dirs. 1989-93); water polo referee VII World Master's Swimming Championships, Casablanca, Morocco, 1998. Named Swimming Coach of Yr. Hollywood Sun-Tattle, 1984-85, Head Water Polo Coach U.S. Olympic Festival, 1986, 90; selected to Pine Crest Sch. Athletic Hall of Fame, 1998, U.S. Water Polo Hall of Fame, 1998; 3rd place medal women 40+ U.S. Water Polo Master's Nat., 2006, 11th FINA World Championships, 2006. Mem. Coun. Exceptional Children (v.p. Broward County 1998-2000), U. Tenn. Alumni Assn. (sec. Dade Broward chpt., 2003—), Pine Crest Alumni Assn. (bd. dirs. 1993-2000, sec. 1995-97, v.p. 1999-2000, pres. 2000), Brain Injury Assn. of Fla. (event com. 2001—), Phi Delta Kappa. Avocations: needlepoint, reading, sewing, volunteering. Home: 1610 NE 43rd St Oakland Park FL 33334-5509

KRAUSKOPF, NANCY KAY, middle school educator, journalist; b. McAlester, Okla., Sept. 28, 1961; d. Howard Harold and Fairel Trammel Brown; children: Brandon Joseph, Brian Nicholas. BAT, Sam Houston State U., Huntsville, Tex., 1983. Cert. secondary educator Tex. News editor Houston Cmty. Newspapers, Channelview, Tex., 1983—84; social studies tchr. Galena Pk. Ind. Sch. Dist., Houston, 1985—88; social studies tchr. Crosby Mid. Sch., Crosby Ind. Sch. Dist., Tex., 1992—. Social studies dept. chair Crosby Mid. Sch., 1994—. Named Tchr. of Yr., Crosby Mid. Sch., 1998—99. Office Phone: 281-328-9264.

KRAUSS, DIANA S., secondary school educator; m. Jere P. LaPointe, Aug. 4, 1995. MFA, Boston U., Mass., 1980. Cert. tchr. young adult lang. arts Nat. Bd. Profl. Tchg. Standards, 2001. Tchr. English Dexter (Maine) Regional H.S., 1988—98, Mt. Ararat H.S., Topsham, Maine, 1998—. Cons. advanced placement Coll. Bd., N.Y., 1994—2003. Chmn. Monson (Maine) Libr. Bd., 1992—2006. Office Phone: 207-729-2951.

KRAUSS, JAMIE GAIL, psychologist; b. N.Y.C., Feb. 19, 1952; d. Robert and Mildred (Rothenberg) K.; m. William Scott Burgey, Oct. 18, 1987; 1 child. BA in Psychology cum laude, U. Colo., 1974; MA, U. Hartford, 1977; PhD, Boston Coll., 1986. Lic. psychologist, Mass. Staff psychologist Framingham (Mass.) Ct. Clinic, 1977-79, Worcester (Mass.) State Hosp., 1979-80; psychologist cons. Dekalb Emergency Mental Health Svc., Decatur, Ga., 1980-81; emergency svcs. clinician The Ctr. for Mental Health, Watertown, Mass., 1981-82; clin. fellow in psychology Mass. Gen. Hosp., Boston, 1983-84; prin. psychologist, team leader Met. State Hosp., Waltham, Mass., 1985-88; staff psychologist, team leader Quincy (Mass.) Mental Health Ctr., 1988-90, dir. psychology, 1991-93; forensic psychologist Bridgewater (Mass.) State Hosp., 1993—. Designated forensic profl. Commonwealth of Mass., 1995—, forensic mental health supr., 1997—; supr. APA internship program South Shore Mental Health Ctr., 1989-93; supr. psychology trainees Met. State Hosp., Waltham, 1985-88; clin. fellow in psychology Harvard Med. Sch., Boston, 1983-84; supr. Worcester Family Therapy Tng. Program, 1979-80. Grad. Teaching fellow Boston Coll., 1982, Grad. Rsch. fellow Boston Coll., 1985, Faculty, Law and Psychiatry fellow, U. Mass. Med. Sch., 2002—. Mem. Mass. Psychol. Assn. Democrat. Jewish. Avocations: musical theater, movies, antiques, travel, reading. Office: Bridgewater State Hosp 20 Administration Rd Bridgewater MA 02324-3201

KRAUSS, JUDITH BELLIVEAU, nursing educator; b. Malden, Mass., Apr. 11, 1947; d. Leo F. and Dorothy (Conners) Belliveau; m. Ronald L. Krauss, Sept. 5, 1970; children: Jennifer Leigh, Sarah Elizabeth. BS, Boston Coll., 1968; MSN, Yale U., 1970. RN, Conn. Clin. specialist Conn. Mental Health Ctr., New Haven, 1971-73; clin. instr. Yale Sch. Nursing, New Haven, 1971-73; asst. prof. rsch. Yale U. Sch. Nursing, New Haven, 1973-78, assoc. dean, 1978-85, prof., dean, 1985-98, prof., 1998—; master Yale U. Silliman Coll., 2000—, chair coun. of masters, 2004—. Cons. pharm. and pub. cons., sch., govt. agys. Author: The Chronically Ill Psychiatric Patient and the Community, 1982 (Am. Jour. Nursing Book of Yr. 1982); editor Archives of Psychiat. Nursing, 1986-2005; mem. editl. bd. Psychiat. Rehab., Psychiat. Svcs.; contbr. articles to profl. jours Trustee Boston Coll., 1991-99, trustee assoc., 2000—. Am. Nurses Found. scholar, 1978; recipient Chamberlain award Soc. Edn. and Rsch. in Nursing, 1994, Alumni Achievement award Boston Coll., 2004, medal Yale U. Sch. Nursing, 2005; named Disting. Alumna Yale Sch. Nursing, 1984; scholar Am. Acad. Nursing/Inst. Medicine, 1998-99. Mem. ANA (Disting. Contbn. to Psychiat. Nursing award 1992, Leadership citation 2002), Am. Acad. Nursing, Conn. Nurses Assn. (mem. cabinet on edn. 1987-89, bd. dirs. 1988-91, rep. to ANA house of dels. 1988-91, Josephine Dolan award 1989), Sigma Theta Tau (Disting. Lectr. award 1987), Delta Mu (Founders award 1987). Avocations: tennis, golf, hiking, skiing. Office: Yale U Sch Nursing Ste 200 100 Church St S New Haven CT 06536-0740 Business E-Mail: judith.krauss@yale.edu.

KRAUSS, MARTY WYNGAARDEN, academic administrator; BA, U. Mich., 1974; PhD, Brandeis U., 1981. John Stein prof. disability rsch. Heller Sch. for Social Policy and Mgmt. Brandeis U., Waltham, Mass., provost, sr. v.p. for acad. affairs, 2003—. Chairperson Mass. Govs. Commn. on Mental Retardation, 1993—99; mem. com. on disability determination for mental retardation NRC, 2000—01. Author: numerous books; contbr. articles to profl. jours. Recipient Christian Pueschel Meml. Rsch. award, 2000, Disting. Rsch. award, 2001. Office: Brandeis Univ Office of Provost 415 South St MS 134 Waltham MA 02454 Office Phone: 781-736-2101.

KRAUT, JOANNE LENORA, computer programmer, analyst; b. Watertown, Wis., Oct. 29, 1949; d. Gilbert Arthur and Dorothy Ann (Gebel) K. BA in Russian, U. Wis., 1971, MS in Computer Sci., 1973. Computer programmer U. Wis. Sch. Bus., Madison, 1969-72, Milw. Ins. Co., 1973-74; tech. coord. Wis. Dept. Justice, Madison, 1974-83; tech. svcs. supr. CRC Telecomm. (formerly Benchmark Criminal Justice Systems), New Berlin, Wis., 1983-89; sr. programmer/analyst Info. Comm. Corp., Pub. Safety Software, Inc., 1989-91; advanced systems engr. EDS, 1991-93; tech. specialist Time Ins., Milw., 1993-96; staff analyst Exacta Corp., Brookfield, Wis., 1996-98; prin. engr. Johnson Controls, Inc., 1998—. Mem. Lakewood Gardens Assn. (dir. 1981-83), Dundee Terrs. Condominium Assn. (officer 1983-99), Hartland Police & Fire Commn. (1998-99). Mem. Phi Beta Kappa. Office: Johnson Controls Inc 507 E Michigan St Milwaukee WI 53202-5211

KRAUTH, LAURIE D., psychotherapist, writer; b. Queens, NY, Aug. 18, 1958; d. Seymour Daniel and Phyllis Krauth; m. John D. Harding, Aug. 15, 1998; 1 child, Joshua Krauth-Harding. BA in Social Sci., U. Mich., Ann Arbor, 1981, MA in Journalism, 1985; MA in Clinical Psychology, Ctr. for

Humanistic Studies, Detroit, 1994. Cert. LLP Mich. Reporter, night city editor The Blade, Toledo, 1985—93; psychotherapist preventive and nutritional medicine program Beaumont Hosp., Birmingham, Mich., 1994—98; pvt. practice Ann Arbor, 1994—. Freelance journalist Newsweek, 1989—92, NY Times, 1989—92; psychotherapist Plymouth Family Svc., Mich., 1995—96, Eastwood Clinic, Livonia, Mich., 1996—99, Ann Arbor Cons. Svcs., 1999—; spkr., cons. in field. Contbr. articles to popular mags. Active Peace Works, Ann Arbor, 2003—; sci. adv. bd. Obsessive Compulsive Disorder Found. Mich., 2005—. Mem.: APA, Mich. Assn. Profl. Psychologists, Eye Movement Desensitization and Reprocessing Internat. Assn. (cert.), Assn. for Behavioral and Cognitive Therapies, Anxiety Disorders Assn. Am. Avocations: tennis, kayaking, dance, reading, motorcycling. Office: 2002 Hogback Rd Ste 15 Ann Arbor MI 48105 Office Phone: 734-973-3100.

KRAVEC, CYNTHIA VALLEN, microbiologist; b. Newark, Sept. 8, 1951; d. William George and Elizabeth Irene (VanAllen) K. BS, Syracuse (N.Y.) U., 1974; MS, Seton Hall U., S. Orange, N.J., 1980; MBA, Monmouth Coll., W. Long Branch, N.J., 1986. Registered microbiologist. Sr. technician GIBCO/Invenex, Millburn, NJ, 1974-79; rsch. scientist Wampole Labs. div. Carter-Wallace Inc., East Windsor, NJ, 1979-90; scientist Roche Diagnostic Systems subsidiary Hoffmann-LaRoche, Inc., Nutley, NJ, 1990-98, Schering-Plough, Kenilworth, NJ, 1998—. Contbr. articles to profl. jours. Mem. Am. Soc. Microbiology, Tissue Culture Assn., Soc. of Indsl. Microbiology. Home: 1006 Coolidge St Westfield NJ 07090-1215 Office: Schering-Plough Rsch Inst 2015 Galloping Hill Rd Kenilworth NJ 07033-1300

KRAVEC, FRANCES MARY, elementary school educator; b. Slovakia, Sept. 26, 1948; came to U.S., 1949; d. Emerick Andrew and Martha Mary (Jancosek) K. BS, California (Pa.) U., 1970, MS, 1971. Cert. elem. tchr., Pa. Phys. edn. tchr. Charleroi (Pa.) Area Sch. Dist., 1970-71, kindergarten tchr., 1971—. Mem. Charleroi Elem. PTA. Mon Valley Consortium grantee, 1988, 91, 93, 94. Mem. NEA, Pa. State Edn. Assn., Charleroi Area Edn. Assn. Democrat. Roman Catholic. Avocations: photography, sewing, travel. Home: 479 Charles St Charleroi PA 15022-1006 Office: Charleroi Elem Ctr Fecsen Dr Charleroi PA 15022

KRAVIS, MARIE-JOSEE DROUIN, economist; b. Ottawa, Ont., Can., Sept. 11, 1949; d. Gaëtan and Anne Drouin; m. Henry R. Kravis, 1994. BA in Econs, U. Que., Montreal, 1970; MA, U. Ottawa, 1973; LLD (hon.), Univ. Windsor, Laurentian Univ., Canada. Fin. analyst Power Corp. Can. Ltd., 1969-70; spl. asst. to solicitor gen. Can., also to minister supply and services Govt. of Can., 1971-73; sr. economist Hudson Inst., 1973—76; exec. dir. Hudson Inst. Canada, Montreal, 1976—94; sr. fellow Hudson Inst., 1994—, bd. mem. & exec. com. mem. Canadian Council for Rsch. on Social Sci. & Humanities, 1982—86, Canadian Govt. Comm. Adv. Bd., 1982—89, Consultative Com. on Fin. Inst., Govt. Quebec, 1984—90; vice chmn. Royal Canadian Commn. on Nat. Passenger Transp., 1990—92; bd. dir. Ford Motor Co., 1995—, Vivendi Universal, 2001—, Interactive Corp., 2001—. Co-author: Canada HAS a Future, 1978, Quebec 1985, 1980, Western European Adjustment to Structural Economic Problems; contr. articles to profl. jours.; former weekly columnist for National Post, Canada; former host of weekly Canadian TV show on economics. Bd. trustees Mus. Modern Art, N.Y.C; trustee Inst. for Advanced Study, Princeton, NJ; chmn. Robin Hood Found. Named one of Top 200 Collectors, ARTnews Mag., 2004. Fellow: Council on Fgn. Rels.; mem.: Forest and Stream (Dorval, Que.) (sr. fellow). Avocation: collector of Old Masters, Impressionism, 20th century art & French furniture. Office: Hudson Institute 1015 15th St NW Ste 600 Washington DC 20005-2605 Office Phone: 202-223-7770. Office Fax: 202-223-8537.

KRAVITCH, PHYLLIS A., federal judge; b. Savannah, Ga., Aug. 23, 1920; d. Aaron and Ella (Wiseman) K. BA, Goucher Coll., 1941, LLD (hon.), 1981; LLB, U. Pa., 1943; LLD (hon.), Emory U., 1998. Bar: Ga. 1943, U.S. Dist. Ct. 1944, U.S. Supreme Ct. 1948, U.S. Ct. Appeals (5th cir.) 1962. Practice law, Savannah, 1944—76; judge Superior Ct., Eastern Jud. Circuit of Ga., 1977—79, U.S. Ct. Appeals (5th cir.), Atlanta, 1979—81, U.S. Ct. Appeals (11th cir.), 1981—, sr. judge, 1996—. Mem. Jud. Conf. Standing Com. on Rules, 1994—2000. Trustee Inst. Continuing Legal Edn. in Ga., 1979—82; mem. Bd. Edn., Chatham County, Ga., 1949—55; mem. coun. Law Sch., Emory U., Atlanta, 1985—; mem. vis. com. Law Sch., U. Chgo., 1990—93; bd. visitors Ga. State U. Law Sch., 1994—; mem. regional rev. panel Truman Scholarship Found., 1993—2000; mem. vis. com. Goucher Coll., 2000—. Recipient Hannah G. Solomon award, Nat. Coun. Jewish Women, 1978, James Wilson award, U. Pa. Law Alumni Soc., 1992, Trailblazer award, Greater Atlanta Hadassah, 2000, Kathleen Kessler award, Ga. Assn. Women Lawyers, 2001, Shining Star award, Atlanta Women's Found., 2002, J. Ben Watkins award, Stetson Coll. Law, 2005. Fellow: Am. Bar Found.; mem.: ABA (Margaret Brent award 1991), Nat. Assn. Women Lawyers (Arabella Babb Mansfield award 1999), U. Pa. Law Soc., Am. Law Inst., Am. Judicature Soc. (Devitt award com. 1998—99), State Bar Ga., Savannah Bar Assn. (pres. 1976). Office: US Ct Appeals 11th Cir 56 Forsyth St NW # 202 Atlanta GA 30303-2205 Office Phone: 404-335-6300.

KRAVITZ, ELLEN KING, musicologist, educator; b. Fords, NJ, May 25, 1929; d. Walter J. and Frances M. (Prybylowski) Kokowicz; m. Hilard L. Kravitz, Jan. 9, 1972; children: Julie Frances, Heather Frances stepchildren: Kent, Kerry, Jay. BA, Georgian Ct. Coll., 1964; MM, U. So. Calif., 1966, PhD, 1970. Tchr. 7th and 8th grade music Mt. St. Mary Acad., North Plainfield, NJ, 1949-50; cloistered nun Carmelite Monastery, Lafayette, La., 1950-61; instr. Loyola U., L.A., 1967; asst. prof. music Calif. State U., L.A., 1967-71, assoc. prof., 1971-74, prof., 1974—99, emeritus prof., 1999—. Founder Friends of Music Calif. State U., L.A., 1976. Mem. editl. adv. bd.: Jour. Arnold Schoenberg Inst., 1977—87; editor: Jour. Arnold Schoenberg Inst., Vol. I, No. 3, 1977, Jour. Arnold Schoenberg Inst., Vol. II, No. 3, 1978; author (with others): Catalog of Schoenberg's Paintings, Drawings and Sketches; author: (book) Music in Our Culture, 1996. Guest lectr. Schoenberg Centennial Com., 1969—, mem., 1974. Mem.: Hist. Assn. L.A. Music Ctr., Am. Musicol. Soc., L.A. County Mus. Art, Pi Kappa Lambda, Mu Phi Epsilon.

KRAWCHECK, SALLIE L., bank executive; b. Charleston, SC, Nov. 28, 1964; m. Gary Appel. BA, U. N.C., Chapel Hill, 1987; MBA, Columbia U., N.Y.C., 1992. Fin. analyst Salomon Brothers, Inc.; assoc. corp. fin. dept. Donaldson, Lufkin & Jenrette; sr. rsch. analyst Sanford C. Bernstein, 1994—98, dir. rsch., 1999—2001; exec. v.p. Alliance Capital Mgmt. L.P., 2001—02; chmn., CEO Sanford C. Bernstein, 2001—02, Smith Barney, NYC, 2002—04; exec. v.p. fin., ops. & strategy, CFO Citigroup Inc., NYC, 2004—. Mem. Citigroup Mgmt. com., Citigroup Bus. Heads com. Bd. dirs. U. N.C. at Chapel Hill Foundations, Inc., Carnegie Hall; bd. overseers Columbia Bus. Sch. Named Most Influential Person Under the Age of 40, Fortune mag., 2003; named one of Global Business Influentials, Time mag., 2002, Most Powerful Women in Bus., Fortune mag., 2002, 2003, 2004, 2006, Most Powerful Women, Forbes mag., 2005—06. Office: Citigroup Inc 399 Park Ave New York NY 10022*

KRAWITZ, RHODA NAYOR, clinical psychologist, psychoanalyst; b. Bayonne, N.J., Feb. 11, 1925; d. George and Lenette Bettina (Feldman) Nayor; m. Herman Everett, Feb. 17, 1952; children: David, Joshua. BA, Cornell U., 1944; MA, The New Sch., 1954; PhD, Adelphi U., 1960; cert. psychoanalysis, N.Y. Freudian Soc., 1984. Cert. clin. psychologist, N.Y. Remedial therapist Lawrence (N.Y.) Pub. Schs., 1954-58; faculty asst. Adelphi U., Garden City, N.Y., 1955-57; psychologist Little Red Sch. House, N.Y.C., 1957-58; pvt. practice psychodiagnostics, 1958-75; asst. clin. psychologist Child Psychiatry Dept. Mt. Sinai Hosp., N.Y.C., 1961-62; rsch. psychologist Child Devel. Ctr., N.Y.C., 1963-64; staff psychologist Lincoln Inst. for Psychotherapy, N.Y.C., 1975-78; pvt. practice N.Y.C., 1975—; instr. clin. psychology dept. psychiatry St. Luke's Hosp. Columbia U., N.Y.C., 1981-86. Mem. Am. Psychol. Assn. (div. of psychoanalysis), N.Y. State Psychol. Assn., N.Y. Soc. Clin. Psychologists. Jewish. Avocations: music, art, theater, literature, antiques. Home and Office: 333 E 57th St New York NY 10022-2950 Office Phone: 212-688-5609.

KRAYNAK, MARCELLE GEORGEANN, not-for-profit developer; b. N.Y.C., N.Y., Apr. 3, 1944; d. Richard A. and Bernice (Weinberg) Kane; m. Anthony Walter Kraynak, Sept. 27, 1989; children: Marylin Kotansky, Joseph Kossmann, Bobbi Dempsey, William Kossmann. AAS in Human Svcs. magna cum laude, Lackawanna Jr. Coll., Hazleton, Pa., 1996. LPN, Pa. Buyer cosmetics F. W. Woolworth, Jamaica, NY, 1964—65; asst. dir., group supr. YMCA/YWCA; staff nurse St. Joseph's Med. Ctr., Hazleton, 1989—90; dir. Children's Rainbow Found., Hazleton, 1990—92; founder, exec. dir. Silent Santa, Hazleton, 1992—. Co-chair Vietnam Relocation Com., Wilkes-Barre, Pa., 1974; v.p. Vine Manor Resident Coun., Hazleton, 1993—. Named Nurse of Hope, Am. Cancer Soc., 1989; recipient Sam-Son award, Sam-Son Prodns. Avocations: reading, writing. Home and Office: 320 W Mine St #204 Hazleton PA 18201

KREAGER, EILEEN DAVIS, financial consultant; b. Caldwell, Ohio, Mar. 2, 1924; d. Fred Raymond and Esther (Farson) Davis. BBA, Ohio State U., 1945. With accounts receivable dept. M & R Dietetic, Columbus, Ohio, 1945—50; complete charge bookkeeper Magic Seal Paper Products, Columbus, 1950—53, A. Walt Runglin Co., L.A., 1953—54; office mgr. Roy C. Haddox and Son, Columbus, 1954—60; bursar Meth. Theol. Sch. Ohio, Delaware, 1961—86; adminstrv. cons. Fin. Ltd., 1986—. Ptnr. Coll. Adminstrv. Sci., Ohio State U., 1975-80; seminar participant Paperwork Systems and Computer Sci., 1965, Computer Systems, 1964, Griffith Found. Seminar Working Women, 1975; pres. Altrusa Club of Delaware, Ohio, 1972-73. Del. Altrusa Internat., Montreal, 1972, Altrusa Regional, Greenbrier, 1973. Fellow Am. Biog. Inst. (life); mem. AAUW, Assoc. Am. Inst. Mgmt. (exec. coun. of Inst. 1979), Am. Soc. Profl. Cons., Internat. Platform Assn., Ohio State U. Alumna Assn., Columbus Computer Soc., Air Force Assn., Fraternal Order of Police Ohio, Motts Mil. Mus., Innovation Alliance, Toastmasters Internat., Ohio State U. Faculty Club, Univ. Club Columbus, Capital Club, Delaware Country Club, Columbus Met. Club, Friends Hist. Costume & Textile Collection Ohio State U., Internat. Order Police Ohio, Inc., Kappa Delta Methodist. Home: PO Box 214 Columbus OH 43085-0214

KREBER, LISA ANN, neuroscientist, psychologist; b. Cherokee, Iowa, Nov. 24, 1976; d. Charles Francis Kreber and Sherlyn Kay Robson. BS in Psychology with honors, U. Iowa, 1999; MA in Psychology, U. Colo., 2002, PhD in Neurosci. and Psychology, 2005. Libr. asst. U. Iowa, Iowa City, 1995—99; tchg. asst. U. Colo., Boulder, 1999—2005; tutor psychology, statis. Student Acad. Svcs., 1997—2005; cognitive therapy asst. Mary Ann Keatley PhD, LLC, 1999—2005; rsch. asst. U. Colo., 1999—2005; statis. cons. Carol Newlin MD, 2002; rsch. coord. Ctr. Neuro Skills, Bakersfield, Calif., 2005—. Guest lectr. psychology U. Colo., 1999—2005, undergrad. mentor, 1999—2005; undergrad. advisor U. Iowa, 1996—99. Contbr. articles to profl. jours. Vol. Lawton Fire & Rescue Sqaud, Iowa, 1993—95. Fellow, U. Colo., 2001—05; grantee, 2000, 2002. Mem.: Women in Neurotrauma, Nat. Neurotrauma Soc., Soc. Neurosci. Avocations: running, reading, movies. Office: Ctr Neuro Skills 2658 Mt Vernon Ave Bakersfield CA 93306

KREBS, MARGARET ELOISE, publishing executive; b. Clearfield, Pa., Apr. 20, 1927; d. Henry Louis and Delia Louise (Beahan) Krebs. Grad. high sch. With Progressive Pub. Co., Inc., Clearfield, 1945—, bus. office mgr., 1959—60, bus. mgr., 1960—63, asst. to pub., 1963—69, dir., exec. v.p., 1969—77, pres., 1977—, assoc. pub., 1981—. V.p., sec. Clearfield Broadcasters, Inc., Stas. WCPA-AM and WQYX-FM, 1965—, dir., 1971—. Mem.: Pa. Newspaper Women's Assn., Lake Glendale Sailing Club (sec. 1966—), Clearfield Bus. and Profl. Women's Club (pres. 1952—53, dist. membership chmn. 1952—53). Democrat. Roman Catholic. Home: 526 Ogden Ave Clearfield PA 16830-2146 Office: 206 E Locust St Clearfield PA 16830-2423

KREBS, MARJORI MADDOX, social studies educator, consultant; b. Lubbock, Tex., Dec. 22, 1962; d. Joe Price and Peggy Barnes Maddox; m. Paul Krebs, June 2, 1984; children: Taylor, Jacob. BA in History, U. Okla., Norman, 1981; MA, Ohio State U., Columbus, 1988—91; EdD, Bowling Green State U., Ohio, 2003—06. Secondary Comprehensive Social Studies Ohio Dept. Edn., 1985. HS social studies tchr. Worthington City Sch. Dist., Ohio, 1985—99, career edn. dist. coord., 1996—99; instr. Bowling Green State U., Ohio, 1999—. Cons. Partnerships Make a Difference, Upper Arlington, Ohio, 1999—. Com. mem. Cmty. Coalition Youth and Families, Bowling Green, 2004—06, Young Life, Bowling Green, 2005—06; v.p. Bowling Green Jr. High PTO, Bowling Green, 2005—06. Recipient Young Tchr. of Yr., Rotary Club, Worthington, Ohio, 1985, Tchr. of Yr., Worthington Kilbourne HS, 1999. Home: 1528 Muirfield Dr Bowling Green OH 43402 Office: Bowling Green State Univ Education Bldg #529 Bowling Green OH 43403 Office Phone: 419-372-7345. Business E-Mail: mkrebs@bgsu.edu.

KREBS, MARTHA, physicist, federal science agency administrator; PhD in Theoretical Physics, Cath. U. America, Washington, D.C., 1975. Staff dir. House subcommittee on energy development and applications, Washington, 1977-83; assoc. dir. planning and devel. Lawrence Berkeley Lab., 1983-93; dir. office of sci. Dept. of Energy, 1993-99; sr. fellow Inst. Def. Analyses.

KREBS, MARY, art educator; d. Andrew and Mary McCaffrey; m. Richard Krebs, May 11, 1980; 1 child, Michael. BS in Art Edn., SUNY, 1972; MBA in Mktg., Adelphi U., 1980; MEd in Elem. Edn., L.I. U., 1993. N.Y. State tchg. cert. elem. edn. (N-6), N.Y. State tchg. cert Eedn. (K-12). Buyer Bloomingdales, New York City, NY, 1973—80; dir. of customer svc. El Greco Leather (Candie's Shoes), Pt. Washington, NY, 1980—81; divisional mdse. mgr. Federated Dept. Stores, New York City, NY, 1981—83; graphic artist/sculptor Self Employed, Massapequa, NY, 1983—; tchr. - pre -sch. Cmty. Meth. Sch. & Our Lady of Assumption, Massapequa, NY, 1986—93; tchr. - elem. Massapequa Schools - Birch Ln./Unqua, Massapequa, NY, 1993—95; tchr. - art secondary Massapequa Schools - Berner Mid. Sch., Massapequa, NY, 1995—. Book, Rachel's Star of David. Bldg. rep. Massapequa Fedn. Tchrs., 2003—. Named Outstanding Vol., YES Cmty. Counseling Ctr., 1996; named to Wall of Tolerance, Rosa Parks, Nat. Campaign for Tolerance, So. Poverty Law Ctr., Ala., 2003; recipient Cert. of Merit, Massapequa Bd. of Edn., 2002; M-TRACT and LINC-IT grants, NY Tchr. Ctr., Tech. Grants, 2000, 2001, 2006, Richard Gazzola Tchr. fellow, N.Y. State PTA, 2001. Mem.: Green County Coun. Arts, Massapequa S.D. (advisor 1993—), N.Y. State Art Tchr.'s Assn. (conf. presenter, spkr.'s bur. 1995—), N.Y. State PTA (life; chairperson 1985—2001, Hon. Life 2001), Massapequa PTA Coun. (life; mem. 1985—2001, Disting. Svc. 2001), Massapequa PTA (life; pres./mem. 1985—2001, tchr. rep. 1990—, Hon. Life 1996). Avocations: sculpting, bowling, tennis. E-mail: mck_art@optonline.net.

KREBS, NINA BOYD, psychologist; b. Phoenix, Sept. 9, 1938; d. Hugh Lewis and Elizabeth Bevette (Burleson) Boyd; m. Richard Lee Schafer, Aug. 13, 1960 (div. 1969); children: Erica Schafer, Karen Fleming; m. David O. Krebs, Aug. 27, 1973 BA Edn., Ariz. State U., 1960, MA Edn., 1964; EdD Counseling and Guidance, Ball State U., Muncie, Ind., 1971. Lic. psychologist, Calif. Counseling psychologist Calif. State U., Sacramento, 1971—76; ptnr. Ctr. for Family, Individual and Orgnl. Devel., Sacramento, 1976—83; pvt. practice psychology Sacramento, 1978—98; ret, 1998. Psychology examiner Calif. State Bd. Med. Quality Assurance, 1978-93; ind. contractor U.S. Bur. Reclamation, Mid-Pacific Region, 1979; cons. in field; lectr. in field; creator, presenter 7-session workshop series, Feminine Power at Work, 1990-98 Author: Changing Woman Changing Work, 1993, Edgewalkers: Defusing Cultural Boundaries on the New Global Frontier, 1999; co-author (with Robert Allen) Psychotheatrics, the New Art of Self-Transformation, 1979; contbr. articles to profl. jours Mem. Sacramento Valley Psychol. Assn. (divsn. 1 pres. 1991-92) Avocations: photography, hiking, camping, painting, digital art. Office: 4651 Breuner Ave Sacramento CA 95819-1514

KREBSBACH, JENNIFER SUSAN, nurse; b. St. Cloud, Minn., Mar. 4, 1965; d. James H. and Margaret G. (Thometz) H. BS in Nursing, Coll. of St. Benedict, St. Joseph, Minn., 1987. RN Minn.; cert. med.-surg. nursing ANCC. Staff nurse VA Med. Ctr., St. Cloud, 1987-89; staff nurse float pool St. Cloud Hosp., 1989-96, imaging svcs. RN specialist, 1996—. VA Health Profl. scholar, 1985-87. Mem. Mem. Am. Radiol. Nurses Assn., Sigma Theta Tau.

KREDELL, CAROL RUTH, artist; b. Paterson, N.J., Oct. 20, 1924; d. Robert Blee Wilhelmina and Stella K. Wilhelina. BS, Pratt Inst., Bklyn., 1946; MS in Home Econs., U. Wis., 1957; MS in Art Edn., Syracuse U., 1968. Extension home economist York County/Pa. State U., State College, 1946-60; asst. prof. interior design Cornell U., Ithaca, N.Y., 1960-65; lectr. home econs. Syracuse (N.Y.) U., 1965-67; tchr. art and home econs. Ithaca City Sch. Dist., 1968-88; artist, vol. Trumansburg (N.Y.) Conservatory of Fine Arts, 1982—. Disaster vol. Tompkins County ARC, Ithaca, 1993—; vol. Trumansburg Conservatory fine arts and other shows, 1982—. Mem. Young Ladies Radio League, Second Area Young Ladies Amateur Radio Club, Tompkins County Amateur Radio Club (operator for disasters), Epsilon Sigma Phi. Republican. Presbyterian. Home: 1 Sunrise Ter Trumansburg NY 14886-9102

KREEK, MARY JEANNE, physician; b. Washington; d. Louis Francis and Esperance (Agee) K; m. Robert A. Schaefer, Jan. 24, 1970; children: Robert A., Esperance Anne BA, Wellesley Coll., 1958; MD, Columbia U., Coll. Physicians and Surgeons, 1962; D (hon.), Uppsala U., Sweden, 2000. Med. rschr. NIH, Bethesda, Md., 1957—62; intern, resident Cornell N.Y. Hosp. Med. Ctr., N.Y.C., 1962—65, fellow, 1965—67; instr. medicine Cornell Med. Coll., 1966—67; clinician specializing in internal medicine, endocrinology, gastroenterology, hepatology, pharmacology, neurosci., molecular genetics NYC, 1966—. Mem. staff N.Y.-Presbyn. Hosp.-Weill Sch. Medicine of Cornell U., 1968—77, clin. asst. prof., asst. attending physician, now assoc. attending physician, adj. assoc. prof.; asst. prof. Rockefeller U., 1967—72, sr. rsch. assoc., physician, 1972—83, assoc. prof., physician, 1983—94, prof., sr. physician, head of lab., 1994—; head Ind. Lab. on Biology of Addictive Disease, 1975—94, head of lab., 1994—; sr. physician Rockefeller U. Hosp., 1994—; adj. prof. Beijing Med. U., 1996—2000, Peking U., 2000—, Karolinska Inst., 2001; mem. gen. medicine study sect. NIH, 1973—77; co-chmn. John E. Fogarty (NIH) Internat. Conf. Hepatotoxicity Due to Drugs and Chems., 1977, charter mem. peer rev. oversight group, 1996—2000; vis. prof. Pahlavi U., Shiraz, Iran, 1977; spl. adv. Nat. Inst. Drug Abuse, 1976—86, mem. nat. adv. coun., 1991—95, mem. molecular genetics consortium, 1999—; prin. investigator Rsch. Ctr. Biol. Basis Addictive Diseases, 1987—; mem. gastroenterology adv. com. FDA, 1975—79, 1992—96, NIH Gen. Clin.; mem. gen. rsch. ctr. study sect. NIH, 1979—83, chmn., 1982—83; mem. exec. com. Coll. Problems Drug Dependence, 1982—87, 1989—94, chmn. exec. com., 1985—87, chair sci. program com., 1991—96; fellow CPDD, 1992—; dir. NIH-Nat. Inst. Drug Abuse Rsch. Ctr., 1987—. Recipient Borden Rsch. award, 1962, Career Scientist award Health Rsch. Coun. City NY, 1974-75, Dole/Nyswander award, 1984, Rsch. Scientist award NIH Gen. Clin. sect., 1978—, Mentor of Mentors award Am. Soc. Addiction Medicine, 1995, Assn. for Med. Edn. and Rsch. in Substance Abuse-Betty Ford award for outstanding rsch., 1996, R. Brinkley Smithers Disting. Scholar award Am. Soc. Addiction Medicine, 1999, Nathan B. Eddy award, Lifetime Rsch. award Coll. on Problems of Drug Dependence, 1999, Gold Medal Lifetime Excellence award Columbia U. Coll. Physicians and Surgeons Alumni Assn., 2004, Marian Fischman award, Coll. Ptnrs., 2005, Founders award, Intenat. Narcotic Rsch. Conf., 2005 Fellow: ACP (life), Am. Coll. Psychiatry, Harvey Soc., NY Acad. Scis., Am. Fedn. for Clin. Rsch., Assn. Am. Physicians (life), Am. Coll. Neuropsychopharmacology (mem. coun. 2004—); mem.: Soc. on Neurosci s., Rsch. Soc. on Alcoholism, Coun. Fgn. Rels. (life), Internat. Narcotic Rsch. Conf. (exec. com. 1993—97, pres.-elect 2001—03, pres. 2003—06, past pres. 2006—), Internat. Assn. Study Liver, Am. Assn. Study Liver Diseases, Endocrine Soc., N.Y. Gastroent. Assn. (pres. 1987), Am. Gastroent. Assn., Shakespeare Soc. of Wellesley, Phi Beta Kappa, Sigma Xi. Office: Rockefeller U New York NY 10021

KREGG, HELEN CHRISTINE, foundation administrator; b. Buffalo, N.Y., Mar. 17, 1945; d. Harvester Land and Helen Jean Stormer; m. Joseph Michael Kregg (div. Dec. 29, 1989); children: John Michael, Kyle Edward. Degree in urban pub. policy and adminstrn., SUNY, Buffalo, 1991. Sales rep. McNeil Comsumer Products, Spring House, 1983—84, McNeil Pharm. Co., Spring House, Pa., 1984—85; workstudy student asst. SUNY, Buffalo, 1986—90; adminstrn. asst. State Farm Ins., Buffalo, 1988—89, County of Erie, Buffalo, 1990—93; adminstrv. asst. Erie County Dem. Com., Buffalo, 1991—92; outside admissions rep. Bryant & Stratton Bus. Instn., Buffalo, 1993—94. Adviser, participant project S team SUNY, Buffalo. Organizer, pres. Linwood - Oxford Neighborhood Coun., Buffalo, 1990—92; 1st class of inst. of pub. leadership workshop Western N.Y. YWCA, Buffalo, 1991; elected rep. Erie County Dem. Party, Buffalo, 1991—96; bd. dirs. Housing Opportunities Made Equal, Buffalo, 1992—2005; founder, pres. Buffalo Family Ski Club, 1985—90; co-founder, past pres. Minority Health Coalition, Buffalo, 1998—2005. Recipient Rita Webb Smith Citizen Drug Fighter of the Yr. award, N.Y. State Gov. Mario Cuomo, 1992, Bd. Dirs. award for disting. svc. in fair housing, Housing Opportunities Made Equal, 1999, Mildred Francis Lockwood Lacey award, SUNY, Buffalo, 2002, Minority Health Coalition grant, N.Y. State Dept. of Health, 2003, Affirm the Dream Cert. of Appreciation award, Office of Affirmative Action, Roswell Pk. Cancer Instn., 2004. Democrat.

KREHBIEL, JENNIFER NELL, art educator; d. Wendell Milton Smith and Janice Nell Woodley; m. Gary Clint Krehbiel, Feb. 18, 1995. BA in Edn., Boise State U., Idaho, 1990. Tchr. art Aberdeen (Idaho) Sch. Dist., 1990—. Chmn. Dept. Art Aberdeen (Idaho) H.S., 1990—, adv. sophomore class, 1990—, adv. yearbook, 1992—. Mem.: Tantphaus Pk. Zool. Soc., Nat. Home Gardening Club. Republican. Avocations: gardening, reading, sewing, drawing, remodeling. Office: Aberdeen High School PO Box 610 Aberdeen ID 83210 Office Phone: 208-397-4152.

KREIDER, KAREN BEECHY, secondary education educator, language professional; b. Fremont, Mich., Sept. 10, 1944; d. Atlee and Winifred (Nelson) Beechy; m. Gerald L. Kreider, Aug. 26, 1967; children: Katherine, Emily. BA, Goshen (Ind.) Coll., 1966; EdM, Temple U., 1969, PhD, 1981. Tchr. Sch. Dist. Phila., 1966—. Named Lindenbaum Tchr. of Yr., Phila. Schls., 1987, Tchr. of Yr., Harrisburg, Pa., 1991; Coun. of Basic Edn. fellow, 1990. Avocations: travel, reading. Home: 14 Walters Ln Royersford PA 19468-1124 Office: Central High School Ogontz & Olney Aves Philadelphia PA 19141

KREIDER, LOUISA J., biologist, librarian; b. Barberton, Ohio, May 14; d. Edward Wells and Jacqueline Simonson Kreider. BA, Cornell U., Ithaca, NY, 1989; MLS, Kent State U., Ohio, 1990; postgrad., U. Akron, Ohio, 2003—. Cert. name authority cooperative program trainer Program for Coop. Cataloging, Washington, 1995, monographic bibliographic record program trainer Program for Coop. Cataloging, Washington, 1995. Curatorial asst. Stan Hywet Hall and Gardens, Akron, Ohio, 1991—92; catalog libr. Cleve. Pub. Libr., 1992—97, reference libr., 1997—98, catalog libr., 1998—99, authority and quality control libr., 1999—2004; instr. Kent State U., Ohio, 2001; conservation intern Student Conservation Assn., Charlestown, NH, 2004; seasonal interpretive pk. ranger Cuyahoga Valley Nat. Pk., Brecksville, Ohio, 2005; seasonal biologist Metro Parks, Serving Summit County, Akron, 2006—. Presenter seminars in field. Mem. Akron Symphony Chorus, Akron, 1992—97, 1998—2006; vol. Cuyahoga Valley Nat. Pk., Brecksville, 2004—06, Metro Parks, Serving Summit County, Akron, 2002—06; docent Stan Hywet Hall and Gardens, Akron, 1987—90; clk. of vestry St. Timothy's Episcopal Ch., Macedonia, Ohio, 1998—2000. Named Outstanding Woman scholar, U. Akron Women in Higher Edn., 2006; recipient President's Vol. Svc. award, President's Coun. Svc. and Civic Participation, 2005; scholar, Buckeye Trail Assn., 2004—05; Dr. Kevin E. Kelleher Meml. Fund scholar, U. Akron, 2005, Ohio Environ. Sci. and Environ. Engring. scholar, Ohio Acad. Sci., 2006. Mem.: ALA (com. stds. 1997—99), Program Coop. Cataloging (standing com. tng. 1997—99), Ohio Libr. Coun. (sec. 2002, mem. action coun. tech. services divsn. 2003), Humane Soc. Greater Akron,

North Country Trail Assn., Buckeye Trail Assn., Nat. Audubon Soc., Nat. Soc. Collegiate Scholars, Beta Beta Beta. Episcopalian. Avocations: birdwatching, backpacking, camping, calligraphy, cats.

KREIDER, SUSAN B., elementary school educator; b. New Kensington, Pa., May 21, 1954; d. David T. and Virginia A. Burkett; m. Paul H. Kreider III, Apr. 14, 1984; children: Elizabeth, Allison. BS, Slippery Rock U., Pa., 1976; MA, U. Pitts., 1977; Reading Specialist, Pa. State U., Harrisburg, 1998. Tchr. 3d grade North Allegheny Sch. Dist., Pitts., 1978—84; tchr. elem. Derry Township Sch. Dist., Hershey, Pa., 1988—. Recipient Golden Apple award, Capital Area Assn. Edn. Young Children. Mem.: NEA (bldg. rep. 1988—), Pa. State Edn. Assn. (bldg. rep. 1988—), Derry Township Hist. Soc. (vol. Hershey Gardens/Mus. 2003—). Democrat. Methodist. Avocations: reading, gardening, yoga. Home: 1405 Woodlawn Dr Hershey PA 17033

KREIGER, BARBARA S., writer, educator; b. Derby, Conn., Oct. 25, 1948; d. Samuel and Elaine Natalie (Chausky) Kreiger; m. Alan Lelchuk, Oct. 7, 1979; children: Saul, Daniel. BA, Russell Sage Coll., 1970; MA, Boston Coll., 1973; PhD, Brandeis U., 1978. Sr. lectr. and adj. assoc. prof. Dartmouth Coll., Hanover, NH, 1983—. Author: The Dead Sea: Myth, History and Politics, 1997, Divine Expectations: An American Woman in Nineteenth-Century Palestine, 1999. Avocations: gardening, woodworking. Home: 112 Brook Hollow Hanover NH 03755

KREILICK, MARJORIE ELLEN, education educator; b. Oak Harbor, Ohio, Nov. 8, 1925; d. Rolland Chester Kreilick and Luella Mable Smith. BA, Ohio State U., Columbus, 1946, MA, 1947; MFA, Cranbrook Acad., Mich., 1952. Lectr. Toledo Mus., 1948—51; prof. U. Wis., Madison, 1953—91. Rsch. Grant, U. Wis., 1961, 1965, Design Grant, 1968, Rsch. Grant, 1970, 1976, 1979, 1980, Edwin Austin Abbey Fellowship, Am. Acad., Rome, 1961—63. Home: 2713 Chamberlin St Madison WI 53705

KREINDLER, MARLA J., lawyer; b. Cin., Feb. 20, 1963; Attended, London Sch. Econs., 1982; BA, U. Mich., 1984, JD, 1987. Bar: Ill. 1987. Ptnr., chair Employee Benefits and Exec. Compensation Dept., sr. mem. Corp. and Fin. Svcs. Dept. Katten Muchin Zavis Rosenman, Chgo. Mem.: WEB, Women in Financial Svcs. (founding mem. Chgo. chap.), Stable Value Investment Assn., Pension Real Estate Assn., Art Inst. Chgo.

KREISSMAN, STARRETT, librarian; b. NYC, Jan. 4, 1946; d. Bernard and Shirley (Relis) K.; m. David Dolan, Apr. 13, 1985; 1 child, Sonya. BA, Grinnell Coll., 1967; MLS, Columbia U., 1968. Asst. circulation libr. Columbia U., N.Y.C., 1968-70; sci. libr. N.Y. Pub. Libr., N.Y.C., 1970-71; outreach libr. Stanislaus County Free Libr., Modesto, Calif., 1971-73, Oakdale libr., 1974-79, acquisitions libr., 1979-85, br. supr., 1985-92, county libr., 1992—99; libr. dir. Ventura County Libr., 1999—. Writer book revs. Stanislaus County Commn. on Women. Mem. ALA, Pub. Libr. Assn., Calif. Libr. Assn. (legis. com. 1993-95, 2003—, Libr. of Yr. 1998), Rotary. Office: Ventura County Library 646 County Square Dr Ste 150 Ventura CA 93003 Office Phone: 805-477-7333.

KREITZ, HELEN MARIE, retired elementary school educator; b. Taylor, Tex., Aug. 22, 1929; d. Joseph Jr. and Mary Lena (Miller) K. BA, U. Mary Hardin-Baylor, 1950; MEd, U. Tex., 1959. Cert. tchr., Tex. Bookkeeper Singer Sewing Machine Co., Taylor, 1950-51; advt. salesperson Taylor Times, 1951-52; tchr. Temple (Tex.) Ind. Sch. Dist., 1952-88. Lector, eucharistic min. St. Mary's Cath. Ch., Temple, 1974—. Mem. Tex. Ret. Tchrs. (life, treas. Temple chpt. 1991-2002), Tex. State Tchrs. Assn. (life, treas. Temple chpt. 1954-55), Tex. Classroom Tchrs. Assn. (life, pres. Temple chpt. 1967-69), U. Tex. Execs. (life), Pi Lambda Theta (life). Roman Catholic. Avocations: sewing, handcrafts. Home: PO Box 3446 Temple TX 76505-3446

KREITZBURG, MARILYN JUNE, academic librarian; d. A.E. and Margaret Louise (Harvey) Kreitzburg. Student, Rockford Coll. for Women, 1948—50; AB magna cum laude, Knox Coll., 1954; MA, U. Va., 1956; cert. in philosophy, U. Edinburgh, Scotland, 1960. Copywriter, broadcaster radio and TV Black Hawk Broadcasting Co., Waterloo, Iowa, 1959—60; freelance promotion NYC, 1957; lectr. on Asia, women and fgn. affairs Ill., Iowa, 1957—59; order libr., asst. to coll. libr. Knox Coll., Ill., 1960—72; faculty librarian Johnstown Coll., U. Pitts., 1972—93, dir. library and overseer of dept. audiovisual instr. svcs., 1972—75, divisional libr. and catalogues for edn., engring., soc. sci., 1975—77, head of curriculum room, nonprint media, periodicals and reference, 1977—78, head of instr., ref., rsch., 1978—93; exhibits and instr. Urban League Pitts. prog. for Johnstown youth; judge HS regional speech contests; mem. faculty senate com. ednl. policies, 1980—93. Faculty advisor Delta Zeta, 1980—83, Johnstown Venture Club; pvt. music instr., 1946—48, 1950—52; cons. in field, 1980—93. Bd. dirs., actress Prairie Players Civic Theater, 1960—65; rescue vol. Richland Twp. Vol. Fire Dept., 1977, ARC Disaster Inquiry Svc.; mem. Inter-Svc. Club Coun., 1976—80; leader Girl Scout Songsters, Rockford, Ill., 1948—50; vol. Windber Regional Hospice, Windber Med. Ctr., 2002—; instr. Urban League of Pitts. program for Johnstown children; judge HS regional speech contests. Recipient medal, DAR, 1948, Nichols prize in history, 1954; Helen Lee Wessels fellow, 1954—56, Fulbright fellow at large, in Southeast Asia, 1957—59. Mem.: Johnstown Art League (pres. 2003, 2004, exec. com. 2005—), Women's Assn. U. Pitts. (pres. 1978—79, exec. bd.), Inter Nos, Soroptimist Internat., Pi Beta Phi, Sigma Alpha Iota, Pi Sigma Alpha, Delta Kappa Gamma Soc. Internat. (chpt. v.p. 1966—68, pres. 1989—91, World Fellowships chmn. 2002—), Phi Beta Kappa (chpt. pres. 1978—79).

KREITZER, TRICIA D., chemistry educator; d. John R. Kreitzer and Leah D. Rogers-Kreitzer; m. Sean P. Naylor, Oct. 6, 2005; children: Madison Rose Naylor, Miranda Ruth Naylor. BS, Duquesne U., Pitts., 1993, MS in Edn., 1995. Cert. tchr. Pa., 2000. Tchr. chemistry, chair sci. dept. Keystone Oaks H.S., Pitts., 1995—. Tchr. SAT prep. Keystone Oaks H.S., 2005—. Recipient Student Tchr. award, Duquesne U., 1995; scholar, 1989—93. Mem.: Nat. Sci. Tchrs. Assn. (assoc.), Spectroscopy Soc. Pitts. (assoc.), Soc. Analytical Chemists (assoc.), Am. Chem. Soc. (assoc.). Office: Keystone Oaks High School 1000 Kelton Avenue Pittsburgh PA 15216 Office Phone: 412-571-6000. Personal E-mail: kreitzer@kosd.org.

KREIZMAN-RECZEK, KAREN INGRID, librarian; b. Phila., Pa., Jan. 19, 1965; d. Bernard Kreizman and Marilyn Ann Lieberman; m. Peter R. Reczek, Aug. 28, 1999. BS in Social Sci. and Humanities, Clarkson U., 1985; MLS, SUNY, Buffalo, NY, 1987. Libr. technician R&D Devel. Ctr., Occidental Chem. Corp., Grand Is., NY, 1987-88; asst. libr. Pharm. Rsch. Inst., Bristol-Myers Squibb Co., Buffalo, 1988-90, rsch. libr., 1990-91, info. scientist, 1991-93, sr. info. scientist, 1993-96; global info. specialist Bureau Veritas, Buffalo, 1996-97, mgr., 1997—. Author: Establishing an Information Center: A Practical Guide, 1999; contbr. articles to profl. jour. Mem. Med. Libr. Assn. (sr.), Soc. of Competitive Intelligence Profls., Spl. Librs. Assn. (bull. editor 1993-95, chair elect 1994-95, chair pharm. divsn. 1995-96, bd. dir. 2001-2003, profl. devel. com. 2003—, pres.-elect 2003—), Western NY Health Sci. Librs. (past-pres. 1995-96, pres. 1994-95, v.p. 1993-94, newsletter editor 1992-94, exec. bd. 1990-91, 92-93), Western NY Libr. Resources Coun. (continuing edn. chair 1992-93, regional automation chair 1993-95, bd. trustees 2000—, pres. 2003), Beta Phi Mu. Home: 22 Towhee Ct East Amherst NY 14051-1606 Office: Bureau Veritas 100 Northpointe Pkwy Buffalo NY 14228-1884

KRELL, REBECCA DAWN, music educator; b. Springfield, Ill., Mar. 6, 1976; d. Gloria May Keeslar; m. Eric James Krell, June 3, 2000; 1 child, Elia Carolina. MusB in Edn., Ea. Ill. U., Charleston, 1998. Tchr. k-6 gen. music Hawthorne Irving, Rock Island, Ill., 2001—02; dir. k-12 music Rivermont Collegiate, Bettendorf, Iowa, 2002—03; tchr. k-6 gen. music F.V.de Coronado Elem. Sch., Nogales, Ariz., 2003—04; dir. 6-12 dist. choral Nogales Unified Sch. Dist., 2004—. Piano player and nursery asst. First Bapt. Ch., Nogales, 2003—. Mem.: Am. Choral Dirs. Assn. (assoc.), Music Educators Nat. Conf. (assoc.). R-Consevative. Avocations: walking, reading, piano, singing. Office Phone: 520-604-2474.

KRELL-MORRIS, CHERI LEE, psychologist; b. Toledo, Mar. 23, 1949; d. Leonard Charles and Doris Leone (Sharples) Krell; B.Ed., U. Toledo, 1975; M.S., U. Nev., 1979; postgrad. Immaculata U., 2003; children— Marci Lynn, Cari Ann. Lic. psychologist, Pa.; cert. sch. psychologist. Health edn. cons. Ohio Dept. Health, Div. Alcoholism, Columbus, 1975-77; dir. social services Cherry Hill (N.J.) Med. Ctr., 1979-80; mgr. StayWell Control Data Corp., Norristown, Pa., 1980-82, edn. and lifestyle change cons., 1982; counselor New Life Youth & Family Svcs., 1985-2003; sch. psychologist Spring-Ford Sch. Dist., 2003—; pvt. practice Innovative Counseling Assocs., 2001—. Dir. Ohio's Ann. Teenage Inst. on Alcohol and Other Drugs, Columbus, 1975-77; faculty Midwest Inst. Alcohol Studies, Notre Dame, Ind. and Kalamazoo, Mich., 1977. Served with USAF, 1968-72. Mem. Pa. Psychol. Assn., Nat. Assn. Sch. Psychologists, Eta Sigma Gamma. Mem. United Ch. of Christ. Home: 212 Salford Station Rd Perkiomenville PA 18074-9740 Office: Spring-Ford High Sch 350 South Lewis Rd Royersford PA 19468-2499 Office Phone: 610-326-2728, 610-705-6032. Business E-Mail: cmorr@spring-ford.org.

KREMENTZ, JILL, photographer, author; b. N.Y.C., Feb. 19, 1940; d. Walter and Virginia (Hyde) Krementz; m. Kurt, Jr. Vonnegut, Nov. 1979; 1 child, Lily Vonnegut. Student, Drew U., 1958—59; attended Art Students League. With Harper's Bazaar mag., 1959—60, Glamour mag., 1960—61; pub. rels. staff Indian Industries Fair, New Delhi, 1961; reporter Show mag., 1962—64; staff photographer N.Y. Herald Tribune, 1964—65, staff photographer Vietnam, 1965—66; assoc. editor Status-Diplomat mag., 1966—67; contbg. editor N.Y. mag., 1967—68; corr. Time-Life Inc., 1969—70; contbg. photographer People mag., 1974—; chancellor, commr. Nat. Portrait Gallery, DC. Contbr. photography numerous U.S. and fgn. periodicals; photographer (one-woman shows) Madison (Wis.) Art Ctr., 1973, U. Mass., Boston, 1974, Nikon Gallery, N.Y.C., 1974, Del. Art Mus., Wilmington, 1975, Newark Mus., 1994, Staley-Wise Gallery, 1996; one-woman shows include The Margaret Mitchell House, Atlanta, 1999; photographer (one-woman shows) The Nat. Portrait Gallery, 2003—, The Mark Twain House, Hartford, Conn, 2004, (permanent collections) Mus. Modern Art, Libr. of Congress, The Face of South Vietnam (text by Dean Brelis), 1968, Words and Their Masters (text by Israel Shenker), 1974; author: Sweet Pea: A Black Girl Growing Up in the Rural South (foreword by Margaret Mead), 1969, A Very Young Dancer, 1976, A Very Young Rider, 1977, A Very Young Gymnast, 1978, A Very Young Circus Flyer, 1979, A Very Young Skater, 1979, The Writer's Image, 1980, How It Feels When a Parent Dies, 1981, How It Feels to be Adopted, 1982, How It Feels When Parents Divorce, 1984, The Fun of Cooking, 1985, Lily Goes to the Playground, 1986, Jack Goes to the Beach, 1986, Katherine Goes to Nursery School, 1986, Jamie Goes on an Airplane, 1986, Tanya Goes to the Dentist, 1986, Benjy Goes to a Restaurant, 1986, Holly's Farm Animals, 1986, Zachary Goes to the Zoo, 1986, A Visit to Washington, D.C., 1987, How It Feels to Fight for Your Life, 1989, A Very Young Skier, 1990, A Very Young Musician, 1990, A Very Young Gardener, 1990, A Very Young Actress, 1991, How It Feels to Live With a Physical Disability, 1992, The Writer's Desk, 1996, The Jewish Writer, 1998. Recipient Nonfiction award, Washington Post/Children's Book Guild, 1984, ACCH Joan Fassler Meml. Book award, 1990, Equality, Dignity, Independence award, Nat. Easter Seals, 1992. Mem.: PEN. Address: care Alfred A Knopf Inc 201 E 50th St New York NY 10022-7703

KREMER, HONOR FRANCES (NOREEN KREMER), real estate broker, small business owner; came to U.S., 1961; m. Manny Kremer; 1 child, Patrick David. BS, CUNY; MS, Baruch Coll. Group sec. Bentalls, Ltd.; office mgr. Aschner Assocs., N.Y.C., 1961-63; pub. rels. asst. McMaster U., Hamilton, 1963-64; office mgr. Packaging Components, N.Y.C., 1965-67; head acctg. Shaller Rubin Assocs., N.Y.C., 1967-72, v.p. fin. and adminstrn., 1979-82, sr. v.p., 1982—, sec.-treas. multi-media divsn., 1972-75. Pvt. practice bus. cons., 1986-89; sr. v.p., exec. v.p., fin. officer Lewis & Gace Med. Advt., N.Y.C., 1989-91; broker, owner Malone Kremer Realty, Leonia, N.J., 1991—; bus. cons., 1991—. Mem. Nat. Assn. Realtors, N.J. Assn. Realtors, Nat. Fedn. Bus. and Profl. Women (bd. dirs., v.p.), Advt. Fin. Mgmt. Group. Roman Catholic. Office Phone: 201-461-1100.

KREMPOSKY, VICKEY DARLENE, secondary school educator; b. Connellsville, Pa., Oct. 15, 1952; d. Eugene Sturges and Dora Katheryn Shipley; m. Matthew Joseph Kremposky, Aug. 17, 1974; children: Chevonne Marie, Alicia Anne, Joshua Michael. EdM, California U. Pa., 1984. Tchr. Geibel Cath. H.S., Connellsville, 1985—2001, Adelphoi Village, Connellsville, 2001—02, Frazier Sch. Dist., Perryopolis, Pa., 2002—. Coach and mgmt. team Spl. Olympics - Fayette County, Uniontown, Pa., 1996—; soccer coach Waynesburg Coll., Pa., 1996—2001, Laurel Highlands H.S., Uniontown, 2001—; tutoring/saturday sch. Frazier Sch. Dist., Perryopolis, 2002—. Bd. mem., referee assignor Fayette County Youth Soccer Club, Uniontown, 1998—2006. Mem.: Zeta Tau Alpha (life; treas., corr. sec. 1971—73). Avocations: skiing, soccer, reading, scuba diving, travel. Home: 2126 University Dr Lemont Furnace PA 15456 Office: Frazier School District 142 Constitution St Perryopolis PA 15473 Office Phone: 724-736-4426.

KRENDL, CATHY STRICKLIN, lawyer; b. Paris, Tex., Mar. 14, 1945; d. Louis and Margaret Helen (Young) S.; m. James R. Krendl, July 5, 1969; children: Peggy, Susan, Anne. BA summa cum laude, North Tex. State U., 1967; JD cum laude, Harvard U., 1970. Bar: Alaska 1970, Colo. 1972. Atty. Hughes, Thorsness, Lowe Gantz & Clark, Anchorage, 1970-71; adj. prof. U. Colo. Denver Ctr., 1972-73; from asst. prof. to prof. law, dir. bus planning program U. Denver, 1973-83; ptnr. Krendl, Krendl, Sachnoff & Way, Denver, 1983—. Author: Colorado Business Corporation Act Deskbook, 2003—06; editor: Colorado Methods of Practice, 8 vols., 1983—2006, Closely Held Corporations in Colorado, vols. 1-3, 1981; contbr. articles to profl. jours. Named Disting. Alumna, North Tex. State U., 1985, Super Lawyer, Colo., 2006; named to Best Lawyers in Am., Corp. Law and Corp. Governance, 1995—. Mem. Colo. Bar Assn. (bd. govs. 1982-86, 88-91, chmn. securities subsect. 1986, bus. law sect. 1988-89, Professionalism award), Denver Bar Assn. (pres. 1989-90). Avocation: reading. Home: 1551 Larimer St Apt 1101 Denver CO 80202-1630 Office Phone: 303-629-2600. E-mail: csk@krendl.com.

KRENEK, DEBBY, newspaper editor; b. Tex., Dec. 11, 1955; d. Ernest Reed and Elizabeth Pendleton (Brown) K.; m. James C. Roberts Jr., Feb. 28, 1987; children: Christine Elizabeth Roberts, Taylor James Roberts. BJ, Tex. A&M Univ., 1978. Copy editor Corpus Christi (Tex.) Caller-Times, 1978-81; copy editor to news editor Dallas Times Herald, 1981-85, asst. bus. editor, 1985-86, exec. news editor, 1986-87; dep. news editor NY Daily News, 1987-88, dep. mng. editor, 1988-91, mng. editor, 1991-93, exec. editor, 1993-97, editor-in-chief, 1997-2000; assoc. editor Newsday, 2001—03, cross-media editor, 2003—04, mng. editor, 2004—. Chief creative officer Petplace.com, 2000—01. Named to Acad. of Women Achievers YWCA, NY, 1992, named to Texas Twenty (most influential Texans) Tex. Monthly Mag., 1998. Avocations: photography, tennis, home renovation. Office: Newsday 235 Pinelawn Rd Melville NY 11747-4250*

KRENEK, MARY LOUISE, political scientist, researcher; b. Wharton, Tex., Dec. 8, 1951; d. George P., Jr. and Vlasta (Zahn) Krenek. AA, Wharton County Jr. Coll., 1972; BA, Tex. A&I U., 1974; MA in Polit. Sci., St. Mary's U., 1992; Czech lang. cert., Charles U., 1994. Cert. secondary and elem. tchr. Tex. Polygraph examiner, San Antonio, 1979—81; ind. contractor market, polit. and social rschr. San Antonio, Houston, 1982—; with S.W. Casting, Houston. Substitute tchr., tchr. San Antonio Ind. Sch. Dist., 1981—82, Houston Ind. Sch. Dist., 1991—98, 2002—; instr. govt. Wharton County Jr. Coll., 1997—99; assoc. J.C. Penney Co., Inc., 1994—2000; with Am. Acad. Excellence, Houston, Southwest Casting, 2006—. Actor(movie productions, TV commercials):. Sec. Egypt Plantation Mus., 2003; del. Tex. Dem. Conv., 1971—72, 2006; precinct chair Dem. Party, Ft. Bend County, Tex. 1st lt. U.S. Army, 1975—78, lt. col. USAR, 1978—2003, ret. USAR, 2003. Mem.: AARP, Tex. Czech Heritage and Cultural Ctr., Am. Polit. Sci. Assn., Nat. Assn. Self-Employed, Point/Counterpoint (Houston chpt.), Res. Officers Assn. (sec.-treas. Alamo chpt., jr. v.p. Dept. Tex., sec. Greater Houston chpt., ROTC coord.), Wharton County Hist. Mus. Assn. (assoc.), Houston Czech Cultural Ctr., Women in Mil. Svc. Am. Meml. Found. (charter), St. Mary's U. Alumni Assn., Am. Legion, Pi Sigma Alpha. Roman Catholic. Avocations: reading, writing, travel. Home: 10502 Fountain Lake Dr Stafford TX 77477-3711 also: PO Box 310 Egypt TX 77436-0310 Personal E-mail: marykrenek01@aol.com.

KRENTZ, JANE, former state legislator, elementary school educator; b. Mpls., Dec. 24, 1952; children: Leah, Sarah, Jeremy. BA, Hamline U., 1971; MEd, U. Minn., 1996. Elem. sch. tchr.; former mem. Minn. Senate from 51st dist., St. Paul, 1993—2003; now Midwest coord. Nat. Caucus Environ. Legislators. Mem. C. of C. Stillwater, Forest Lake, Anoka County (all Minn.). Office: Nat Caucus Environ Legislators 14177 Paris Ave N Stillwater MN 55082

KREPS, MARTHA S., elementary school educator; d. Franklin A. and Margaret J. Stone; m. Lawrence A. Kreps, Aug. 23, 1975; children: Carrie, Amy, Marcus. BSc, Taylor U., Upland, Ind., 1971; MEd, U. Cin., Ohio, 1974. Tchr. Clearlake Jr. H.S., Cocoa, Fla., 1971—73; instr. North Pk. Coll., Chgo., 1975, asst. prof.; instr. Urbana Coll., Urbana, Ohio, 1979—81; mgr. cir. rider reatreat bus West Ohio Conf. United Meth. Ch., Urbana, 1979—81; tchr. St. James of the Valley, Cin., 1999—2000, St. Michael Sch., Sharonville, Ohio, 2000—. Lay leader lay speaking United Meth. Ch., Cin., 2002—. Mem.: AAHPERD, Ohio Alliance Health, Phys. End, Recreation and Dance. Meth. Home: 11992 Deerhorn Dr Cincinnati OH 45240 Office: St Michael Sch 11136 Oak St Cincinnati OH 45241

KRESS, JILL CLANCY, human resources professional, consultant; b. Washington, Oct. 11, 1949; d. John William and Barbara Lois (Smith) Costello; m. Paul W. Combs, July 27, 2001; 1 child from previous marriage, Jason Patrick. BS in Edn., Jacksonville U., 1971. Tchr. Duval County Pub. Sch., Jacksonville, Fla., 1971—73; dir. Nat. Exec. Search, Washington, 1976—85; dir. human resources Cellmark Diagnostics, Germantown, Md., 1986—89, Life Technologies, Inc., Gaithersburg, Md., 1989—97; cons. HR Concepts, LLC, 1997—98; pres. HR Concepts, 2002—; v.p. Human Resources Am. WholeHealth, Reston, Va., 1998—2000; sr. dir. Conservation Internat., Wash., 2000—02; pres. HR Concepts LLC, 2002—; founder Critters for the Cure, Inc., 2005—, pres., 2005—. Workshop trainer Va. Tech., Blacksburg, 1992—, Md. U., College Park, 1991—, Hood Coll., Frederick, 1994—; biotech. adv. bd. Montgomery Coll. Mem. Soc. for Human Resources Mgmt., Biotechnology Indsl. Orgn. (steering com. mem.), Montgomery County High Technology Coun. (steering com.), Middle Atlantic Placement Assn. (adv. bd.). Republican. Roman Catholic. Avocations: racquetball, tennis, guitar. Office: Ste 307 301 High Gables Dr Gaithersburg MD 20878 Office Phone: 301-977-3776. E-mail: clancyk10@comcast.net.

KRETCHMAR, LESLIE, medical/surgical nurse; d. Arthur Lockwood Kretchmar and Elaine Edgell Hughes; m. Salah Ghalib Husseini, Mar. 23, 1966 (div. Oct. 21, 1991); children: Ghalib Arthur Husseini, Tarik Salah Husseini, Sharif Salah Husseini. ADN, Coll. of DuPage, Glen Elyn, Ill., 1979; BA, U. Ill., Chgo., 1995. Registered Nurse, Dept. of Profl. Regulation/Ill., 1979. Staff nurse Glen Ellyn Clinic, Ill., 1979—85, Bapt. Hosp., Nashville, 1987—88; program coord. U. Ill., Chgo., 1989—2004; staff nurse Luth. Gen. Hosp., Park Ridge, Ill., 2004—05, HCR Manor Care, Naperville, 2005—. Literacy vol. Literacy Vols. Am., Wheaton, Ill., 1991—94; vol. Med. Reserve Corps, Cmty. Emergency Response Team. Mem.: Rehab. Nurses Assn. (assoc.), Am. Nurses Assoc. (assoc.). Christian - Presbyterian. Personal E-mail: lesliekretchmar@netzero.net.

KRETZSCHMAR, ANGELINA GENZER, small business owner, paralegal; b. San Antonio, July 19, 1946; d. Louis J. Genzer and Alma M. (Krause) Haase; m. Charles H. Kretzschmar, July 31, 1971. BBA cum laude, St. Mary's U., San Antonio, 1974. Budget analyst Fed. Govt., San Antonio, 1974-92, EEO specialist, 1992-96; owner, operator Kretzschmar Prop., San Antonio, 1971—. Fed. women's program mgr. Fed. Govt., San Antonio, 1992-96. Campaign treas. Citizens for Open Govt., San Antonio, 1988; polit. action com. Women's Polit. Caucas, San Antonio, 1993. Mem. Bus. & Profl. Women Inc. (com. chair), AAUW (public policy com. 1994), San Antonio Coun. of Fed. Womans Program Mgrs. (sec.), Federally Employed Women, Inc. (legis. chair). Democrat. Lutheran. Avocations: travel, reading, politics, genealogy, historic cemeteries.

KREVANS, RACHEL, lawyer; b. Balt., June 15, 1957; d. Julius Richard and Patricia (Abrams) K. BA, Dartmouth Coll., 1979; JD, U. Calif., Davis, 1984. Law clk. hon. Robert Boochever U.S. Ct. Appeals for Ninth Cir., Juneau, Alaska, 1984-85; assoc. Morrison & Foerster LLP, San Francisco, 1985-90, mng. ptnr.-San Francisco office, 1991—. Office: Morrison & Foerster LLP 425 Market St San Francisco CA 94105-2482 Office Phone: 415-677-7178. Office Fax: 415-268-7522. Business E-Mail: rkrevans@mofo.com.

KREVSKY, MARGERY BROWN, talent agency executive; b. Phila., Oct. 24, 1944; d. John Lewis and Margery Jane (Moss) Brown; m. Joseph Langdon Stearns, Oct. 19, 1968 (div. Nov. 1979); 1 child, Joseph Leland Stearns; m. Seymour Krevsky, Feb. 11, 1981. BS in Elem. Edn., Lock Haven U., 1966; MFA in Retail Adminstrn., Tobe-Colburn, 1968. Tchr. 1st grade Yardley (Pa.) Sch. Sys., 1966-67; buyer Macy's Herald Sq., N.Y.C., 1968-69; asst. editor Glamour mag. Conde-Nast Publs., N.Y.C., 1969-71; mgr. fashion bur. Hudsons, Detroit, 1971-74; fashion merchandise mgr. Alvin's, Pontiac, Mich., 1974-81; pres., CEO Prodns. Plus, Birmingham, Mich., 1981—. Bd. dirs. Northwood U., Midland, Mich., Wayne State U., Detroit. Mem. Oakland Execs. Assn. (bd. dirs. 1990—), Adcrafters, Fashion Group, Women in Comm. Avocations: cooking, reading, aerobics. Office: Prodns Plus 30600 Telegraph Rd Ste 2156 Bingham Farms MI 48025-4532

KREY, DEAN MARIE, retired education educator; b. Turtle Lake, Wis., Feb. 18, 1942; d. Henry August and Sophie Otillia Wickboldt; m. Monte Arthur Hansen, June 12, 1965 (div. 1983); m. Robert Dean Krey, Sept. 5, 1987. BS, U. Wis., River Falls, 1964, MS in Tchg., 1969; PhD, U. Minn., Mpls., 1977. Cert. tchr. Wis. 6th grade tchr. New Richmond Pub. Schs., New Richmond, Wis., 1964—65, St. Croix Falls Pub. Schs., Wis., 1965—68; instr., tchr. 2d grade lab sch. U. Wis., River Falls, 1969—71, prof. tchr. edn., 1969—2002, assoc. dean, 1982—88, prof. emerita, 2002—. Coord. Tchg. Methods Block, 1972—2002; mem. curriculum writing team State of Wis. Dept. Pub. Instrn., 1973—2000; co-leader Brit. Exch. Program for Elem. Sch. Children, 1975; social studies children's book cons. Kane Press, NYC, 2003—06; spkr. in field; cons. in field; workshop leader, Taiwan, 1974, Taiwan, 77. Author: Children's Literature in Social Studies: Teaching to the Standards, 1998; contbr. columns, articles to profl. jours. and chpts. to books. Co-chmn. Wis. Gov.'s Writing Team Social Studies Academic Stds., 1994—98; reviewer chmn. notable social studies trade books young people Children's Book Coun., NYC, 1997—2000; curriculum team mem. exploring humanitarian law ARC, Washington, 2002—06, rep. Ea. Europe and exploring humanitarian law workshop Budapest, Hungary, 2003. Named Disting. Tchr. of Yr., U. Wis.-River Falls, 1991, Tchr. Educator of Yr., U. Wis.-River Falls/Wis. Dept. Pub. Instrn., 1992, Outstanding Faculty Mem., U. Wis.-River Falls Coll. Edn., 1993; 18 grants, 1988—2000. Mem.: AAUW (moderator voter forum 2004, vol. book sale, Outstanding Woman Univ. Prof. award 1988), Wis. Coun. Social Studies (pres. 1983—85, Outstanding Svc. award 1988, Snavely award for contbns. in field of social studies 2000), Nat. Coun. Social Studies (Pres. award 1999), Phi Kappa Phi, Phi Delta Kappa. Avocations: choral singing, pastel painting, dance, reading. Home: 724 River Ridge Ct River Falls WI 54022 Personal E-mail: rdkrey@comcast.net.

KRIDER, MARGARET YOUNG, art educator; b. Pitts., Aug. 20, 1920; d. Thomas Smith and Josephine Bridget (Connelly) Y.; m. Robert Arthur Krider, May 12, 1945; children: Karen L., Ann Noel, Darcie Ellen Robbins. BFA in Art Edn., Carnegie-Mellon U., Pitts., 1942; MEd in Art Edn., Edinboro U., 1969. Tchr. art West Homestead (Pa.) Pub. Sch., 1942-44, Mt. Oliver (Pa.) Pub. Sch., 1942-44; recreational worker Valley Forge Gen. Hosp. ARC, Phoenixville, Pa., 1944-45; assoc. prof. Villa Maria Coll., Erie, Pa., 1950-87. Adj. instr. Pa. State U. Behrend Campus, Erie, Pa., 1981-87; presenter papers Ea. Arts Conv., N.Y.C., 1962, Kutztown (Pa.) State U., 1967, U. Pa. Art Conf., Pitts., 1980; condr. workshops Peterborough State Coll., Toronto, Ont., Can., 1972-73; presenter in field, 1962—. Exhibited in one and two-person shows at Chautauqua Art Gallery, William Penn Meml. Mus., Butler Mus., Patterson Gallery, Glass Growers Gallery, Kada Gallery, Erie, Sycamore Gallery, Cummings Gallery, Schuster Gallery, Adams Gallery, Dunkirk, NY, Schuster Gallery of Gannon Unit, The Gallery Place, Cleve., 2005, Gathering Pl., Cleve., Bayfront Gallery, Erie, Pa., others; juried and invitational shows incl. Erie Art Mus., Erie Summer Festivals, Agnon Fine Art and Crafts, Carlow Coll. Pa. Women's Art, Bruce Gallery, Forum Gallery, Nat. Mus. Women in Arts, Gathering Pl. at Commerce Pk., Cleve., 2005; contbr. articles to art jours. Bd. dirs., sec. Arts Coun. Erie, Pa., 1974-76, Erie Civic Ballet Co., 1970-75; bd. dirs. Erie County Hist. Soc., 1988-94; active LWV, 1950s; Girl Scout leader Cathedral Grade Sch., Erie, 1956-66; hist. restoration advisor Battles Mus., Girard, Pa., 1993-98. Recipient Community award Florence Crittenton Home, 1991; named Outstanding Tchr. Villa Maria Coll. Presdl. Award, 1987, Outstanding Art Educator PAEA, 1989. Mem. AAUW (bd. dirs., chair 1967-90, Found. Ednl. award 1984, Outstanding Woman finalist 1992), Women's Round Table, Nat. Art Edn., Northwestern Pa. Artists Assn. (chair membership), Pa. Soc. Art Edn., Erie County Hist. Soc. (hon., life), Women's Round Table, Delta Kappa Gamma (chmn. Book Alive). Independent. Roman Catholic. Home: 6130 Mistletoe Ave Fairview PA 16415-2702

KRIEG, NANCY KAY, social worker, poet, musician; b. Jefferson City, Mo., Oct. 11, 1954; d. Arlin Darrell and Doris Lee Basinger; m. Russell Hugh Krieg, Mar. 15, 1975 (div. Aug. 18, 1988). BA in Psychology, Columbia Coll., 1994. Co-owner The Melody Shop, Jefferson City, Mo., 1975—85; co-mgr. Premiere Video, Osage Beach, 1991—94; social worker Miller County Psychol. Svcs., Eldon, 1994—95; substitute tchr. Eldon Pub. Schs., 1995; tchg. counselor, supr. Overland Pk., Kans., 1995—96; substitute tchr. Oak Hill Day Sch., Gladstone, Mo., 1997—98; tchg. counselor Concerned Care, Inc., Kansas City, 1998—. Author poetry. Recipient Mo. Writers' Week award for Poetry, Mo. Writers Guild, 1994, 1995, 1996, 1997. Mem.: Am. Fedn. Musicians, Acad. Am. Poets, The Writers Pl. Avocations: jazz drummer/percussion, mandolin, guitar, songwriting, poetry. Home: 1236 E 25th Ave Kansas City MO 64116

KRIEGER, LOIS B., retired state agency administrator; b. Merritt, B.C., Can., Nov. 4, 1917; came to the U.S., Feb. 1918; d. Howard Irving and Selma (Nelson) Boylan; m. James H. Krieger, 1938 (dec. 1975); children: James B.(dec.), Tor, Terra, Lex D., W. Heath, A. Kim. Cert., U. Calif., Berkeley, 1937. Bd. dirs. The Met. Water Dist. So. Calif., 1976-2001, ret., 2001. Chairperson MWO, So. Calif., 1989-92. Trustee U. Calif., Riverside, 1978—. Mem. Assn. Calif. Water Agys. (pres. 1987-89, mem. adv. com.), Assn. State Water Agys. (life). Avocation: reading.

KRIEGER, MARCIA SMITH, federal judge; b. Denver, Mar. 3, 1954; d. Donald P. Jr. and Marjorie Craig (Gearhart) Smith; m. Michael S. Krieger, Aug. 26, 1976 (div. July 1988); children: Miriam Anna, Matthias Edward; m. Frank H. Roberts, Jr., Mar. 9, 1991; stepchildren: Melissa Noel Roberts, Kelly Suzanne Roberts, Heidi Marie Roberts. BA, Lewis & Clark Coll., 1975; JD, U. Colo., 1979. Bar: Colo. 1979, U.S. Dist. Ct. Colo. 1979, U.S. Ct. Appeals (10th cir.) 1979. Rotary grad. fellow U. Munich, Germany, 1975—76; assoc. Mason, Reuler & Peek, P.C., Denver, 1976-83, Smart, DeFurio Brooks, Eklund & McClure, Denver, 1983-84; ptnr. Brooks & Krieger, P.C., Denver, 1984-88, Wood, Ris & Hames, P.C., Denver, 1988-90; pvt. practice U.S. Bankruptcy Court, 10th Circuit, Denver, 1990-94; judge U.S. Bankruptcy Ct., 10th Circuit, Denver, 1994-2000; chief judge U.S. Bankruptcy Ct., Denver, 2000—02, U.S. Dist. Ct., 2002—. Lectr. U. Denver Grad. Tax Program, 1987—, Colo. Soc. CPA's, Denver, 1984-87, Colo. Continuing Legal Edn., Denver, 1980—, Colo. Trial Lawyers Assn., Denver, 1987—, U. Colo. Law Sch.; adj. instr. U. Colo. Sch. Law, 1999-2001; spkr. in field. Contbr. articles to profl. publs. Vestry person Good Shepherd Episcopal Ch., Englewood, 1986—, judge and coach for H.S. mock trial. Mem. Colo. Bar Assn. (past chair Com. Court Reform; past mem. Professionalism Com.), Arapahoe Bar Assn., Arraj Inn of Ct. (v.p.), Nat. Conf. Bankruptcy Judges (past chair Internat. Law Rels. Com, Ethics Com.; past mem. Newsletter Com., Program Com.), Littleton Adv. Coun. for Gifted and Talented education, Alfred A. Arraj Inn of Court (past pres.), Colo. Jud. Coordinating Coun., Kenya Children Found. (bd. dirs.). Republican. Avocations: international relations, travel, marksmanship. Office: US Dist Ct Dist Colo Alfred J Arraj US Courthouse 901 19th St A-941 Denver CO 80294

KRIEGSMAN, SALI ANN, performing arts executive, consultant, writer; b. N.Y.C., Apr. 16, 1936; d. Aaron and Charlotte (Pomeranz) Ribakove; m. Alan M. Kriegsman, Nov. 28, 1957. MA, Goddard Coll., 1976. Rsch. assoc. Scripps Clinic and Rsch. Found., La Jolla, Calif., 1961-65; exec. editor Am. Film Inst., Washington, 1969-74; asst. prof. George Washington U., Washington, 1979-80; dance cons. Smithsonian Instn., Washington, 1979—84; dir. dance program NEA, Washington, 1986-95; exec. dir. Jacob's Pillow Dance Festival, Becket, Mass., 1995-98. Writer An Evening of Dance, In Performance at the White House, Sta. WETA-TV, 1998; mem. arts acad. adv. com. Coll. Bd., 1996-97; mem. nat. dance and media project leadership group UCLA, 1996-2000; mem. steering com. Am. Assembly Art, Tech. and Intellectual Property, 2000-02; sr. advisor Digital Dance Libr., 2002-03. Author: Modern Dance in America: The Bennington Years, 1981; contbr.: Britannica Book Of The Year, 1984-86; contbg. author: International Encyclopedia of Dance, 1998. Bd. dirs. Mass. Mus. Contemporary Art, 1995-97, Meredith Monk/The House Found., 2001—; pres. Dance Heritage Coalition, 1999-2000. Recipient Flo-Bert award N.Y. Com. To Celebrate Nat. Tap Dance Day, 1997, Oklahoma City U. Preservation of Heritage Am. Dance award, 1999, Tap Preservation award, N.Y.C. Tap Festival, 2002, Tradition in Tap award, 2006; fellow Va. Ctr. for Creative Arts, 2003. E-mail: saliann@verizon.net.

KRIER, ANN O., product designer, writer; d. Charles Albert Overslaugh and Carol Jane Dann; m. James T. Krier, Apr. 22, 1995; children: Brett James, Maggie Sue. BS, Muskingum Coll., 1984. V.p. Trimark/Foodcraft, Winston Salem, NC, 1999—2005; pres. Design One World, Inc., Lewisville, NC, 2004—. Author (designer): (book) Creative Beads from Paper and Fabric, 2005. Mem.: Craft and Hobby Assn., Associated Artists, Am. Sewing Guild, Soc. Creative Designers. Independent. Avocations: kayaking, camping, collage, fiber arts, repousse, art quilting. Home: 963 Ridge Gate Dr Lewisville NC 27023 Office: Design One World Inc PO Box 382 Lewisville NC 27023 Office Phone: 336-287-5361. Business E-Mail: akrier@designoneworld.com.

KRIFTNER, GAIL LYN, choreographer, educator; b. Hackensack, NJ, Apr. 15, 1952; d. John Louis and Grace Lucille Bassano; m. Gary Richard Kriftner, July 31, 1977; children: Jessica Arbittier, Lyndsey, Lauren. BS, Trenton State Coll., 1974. Tchr. West Morris Ctrl. High Sch., Chester, NJ, 1974—80; mgr. No. NJ area Jazzercise, Inc., 1984—91; tchr. dance Hillside Elem. Sch., Montclair, 1992—. Adj. prof. dept. movement & dance scis. William Paterson U., Wayne, NJ, 2004; chmn. related arts dept. Hillside Sch., 2000—, dir., choreographer, 1992—. Creator, dir. Hillside Alumni Dance Scholarship, Montclair, 2002—. Recipient Heart of Gold award, Hillside Sch. PTA, 1998, Govs. Art Edn. award, State NJ, Trenton, 2000, Dance Tchr. of Yr. award, N.J. Assn. Health, Physical Edn., Recreation and Dance, 2000, Weston award for Excellence in Edn., Montclair, N.J., 2006. Mem.: NJ Assn. Health, Phys. Edn., Recreation and Dance (v.p. dance 2001—04), Am. Assn. Health, Phys. Edn., Recreation and Dance. Roman Catholic. Avocations: dance, skiing, walking. Office: Hillside Elem Sch 54 Orange Rd Montclair NJ 07042

KRIGSMAN, NAOMI, psychologist, consultant, photographer; b. Haifa, Israel, 1930; came to U.S., 1953, naturalized, 1961; d. Bezalel and Regina (Yacobi) Goussinsky; m. Ruben Krigsman; children: Michael W., Richard G., Jonathan H. BA, Hebrew U., Jerusalem; MS, CCNY; PhD, Hofstra U., 1983. Lic. psychologist, N.Y. Psychologist Mental Retardation Clinic, Flower-Fifth Ave. Hosp., N.Y.C., Children's Ctr., N.U.C. Dept. Welfare, Rehab. Clinic, St. Barnabas Hosp., Newark, United Cerebral Palsy Ctr., Roosevelt, N.Y., Burke Rehab. Ctr., White Plains, N.Y., New Rochelle (N.Y.) City Sch. Dist., 1970-95. Adj. asst. prof. grad. psychology dept. Coll. of New Rochelle, 1992-93; employment selection, career devel., employee relocation, quality circles, U.S. and Israel; psychol. evaluations and consultation in family ct. and supreme ct.; feature writer N.Y. Womensweek, 1978-79; mem. bus. adv. com. dept. rehab. medicine, Mt. Sinai Med. Ctr., 1991-96. Co-author tng. materials for quality circles; also author articles; exhibited in 2 person photography shows, 1990, 91, 1-person show, 1993, Israel, 1996, 2000; exhibited in group show at Mus. Photography, 1996; represented in permanent collection Mus. of Photography, Israel. Former mem. Assn. Family and Conciliation Cts. With Israeli Defense Forces, 1948—49. N.Y. State Mental Health Dept. fellow, 1958-59. Mem. APA, N.Y. State Psychol. Assn. Home: 617 West St Harrison NY 10528-2508 Personal E-mail: naomikrigsmau@yahoo.com.

KRILL, KAY (KATHERINE LAWTHER KRILL), apparel executive; b. Wilmington, NC, Mar. 27, 1955; d. James Wyatt and Katherine (King) L.; m. Charles Philip McEvoy III, Sept. 12, 1981 (div. Oct. 1985); 2 children. BA in Psychology and Econs., Agnes Scott Coll., Atlanta, 1977. From asst. buyer to buyer Macy's Dept. Store, Atlanta, 1977-81; buyer Talbot's, Hingham, Mass., 1981-84, dir. catalog merchandising, 1984-88; v.p. merchandising Mark Shale, Burr Ridge, Ill., 1988—90; exec. v.p. gen. merchandising mgr. women's ops. Hartmarx Corp., 1990—92; pres. Carroll Reed, 1992—94; merchandising v.p. separates, dresses and petites Ann Taylor Stores Corp., 1994—96, sr. v.p. gen. merchandise mgr. Ann Taylor Loft, 1996—98, exec. v.p. Ann Taylor Loft, 1998—2001, pres. Ann Taylor Loft, 2001—04, pres., 2004—, mem. bd. dirs., 2004—, CEO, 2005—. Mem. Jr. League Atlanta, 1977-81, Boston, 1981-88, Chgo., 1988; mem. bd. trustees Agnes Scott Coll., 1994-00; chairperson bd. visitors Bolles Sch., Jacksonville, Fla., 1992-98. Mem. Fashion Group Boston, Nat. Assn. Female Execs., Direct Mktg. Assn. Clubs: East Bank (Chgo.). Republican. Episcopalian. Avocations: tennis, aerobics, shopping. Office: Ann Taylor Stores Corp 7 Times Sq New York NY 10036

KRIM, EILEEN Y., physician; b. N.Y., 1951; MD, N.Y. Medical Coll., 1975. Intern Beth Israel Medical Ctr., N.Y., 1975-76, resident ob-gyn, 1976-79; fellow North Shore Univ. Hosp., Manhasset, N.Y., 1979-81, staff; asst. clinical prof. ob-gyn N.Y. Univ. Sch. Medicine. Fellow Am. Coll. Obstetricians & Gynecologists; mem. Am. Fertility Soc. Office: Northern Obs-Gyn 2110 Northern Blvd Ste 207 Manhasset NY 11030-3500

KRIM, MATHILDE, medical educator; b. Como, Italy, July 9, 1926; came to U.S. BS, U. Geneva, Switzerland, 1948, PhD, 1953; DSc (hon.), Long Island U., 1987; LLD (hon.), Columbia U., 1988; DSc (hon.), Brandeis U., 1989; DHL (hon.), Southeastern Mass. U., 1990; DSc. (hon.), Tulane U., 1990; DHL (hon.), SUNY, Stonybrook, 1991; DSc (hon.), Columbia Coll., 1992, Dartmouth Coll., 2005. Asst. genetic sect., dept. exptl. biology Weizmann Inst. Sci., Rehovot, Israel, 1953-54, jr. scientist, 1954-57, rsch. assoc., 1957-59; rsch. assoc.divsn. virus rsch. Cornell Med. Coll., N.Y.C., 1959-62; rsch. assoc. Sloan Kettering Inst. Cancer Rsch., N.Y.C., 1962-68, assoc., 1968-75, assoc. mem., 1975-85, co-head interferon evaluation program, 1975-81, head interferon lab, 1981-85; assoc. rsch. scientist dept. pediatrics St. Luke's-Roosevelt Hosp. Ctr. and Columbia U., N.Y.C., 1986-90; adjunct prof. pub. health Columbia U., N.Y.C., 1990—; founding co-chair, chmn. bd., CEO Am. Found. for AIDS Rsch., N.Y.C., 1985—2005, founding chmn., bd. dir., 2005—. Bd. dirs. AIDSFILMS, Am. Com. for Weizmann Inst. Sci., Nat. Biomed. Rsch. Found.; trustee Scientists' Inst. for Pub. Information, Feinberg Grad. Sch. Weizmann Inst. Sci., African-Am. Inst.; mem. adv. panel on higher edn., New York, 1965, President's Com. on Mental Retardation, 1966-69, jury Albert D. Lasker Rsch. awards 1968-71, 78—, adv. bd. Health Profls. for Polit. Action, 1968-70, adv. com. to Sec. of HEW on Health Proteciton and Disease Prevention, 1969-70, Coun. NEH, 1969-73, Panel of Cons. on Cancer, Com. Labor and Pub. Welfare, U.S.Senate, 1970-71, adv. com. Nat. Colorectal Cancer Program NIH, 1971-73, working group develo. rsch. segment Virus Cancer Program NIH, 1971-74, review com. "A" Virus Cancer Program NIH, 1974-77, adv. com. Inst. Internat. Edn., 1974—, adv. com. Program of Sci., Tech., and Human Values NEH, 1974-78, U.S. Nat. Commn. for UNESCO, 1979-80, adv. com. World Rehabilitation Fund, 1978-82, Interferon Clin. Adv. Com. Schering-Plough Corp., 1980-85, Bristol Labs. Adv. Panel on Biological Response Modifiers, 1981-84, sci. adv. com. Am. Found. AIDS Rsch., 1985—, Com. of 100 for Nat. Health Ins., AIDS task force Am. Assn. Sex Educators, Counselors and Therapists, 1985—, rsch. adv. coun. Nat. Orgn. for Rare Disorders Inc., 1985—, AIDS Health Edn. Risk Reduction Consultation, Ctrs. for Disease Control, 1986, task force on Chemotherapeutics, Nat. Inst. of Allergy and Infectious Diseases, NIH, 1986, met. area adv. com. Lower Manhattan AIDS consortium, 1986—, scientific adv. bd. Nat. Coalition on Immune System Disorders, 1986—, adv. com. The Village Nursing Home, 1986—, sect. for the study of ethical, legal and social issues HIV Ctr. for Clin. and Behavioral Studies, 1987—, AIDS Rsch. Ctr., 1987—, bd. advisors Nat. Lawyers Guild AIDS Network, 1987—, AIDS adv. panel Planned Parenthood Fed. Am., 1988—, nat. adv. com. Nat. Communtiy AIDS Partnership, 1988—, adv. com. Women and AIDS Resource Network, 1988—; commr. Pres.'s Commn. for the Study of Ethical Problems in Medicine and Biomedical and Behavioral Rsch., adv. bd. LOVE HEALS, 1989—, adv. bd. Internat. Alliance for Haiti, 1989—, adv. bd. AIDS-AUFKLARUNG, Frankfurt, Germany, 1990—, internat. com. Lottare Informare Formare Educare, Rome, Italy, 1990—, adv. coun. Columbia Sch. Pub. Health, 1990—, AIDS adv. panel, Med. Soc. State of New York, 1992—. Editor (with others) Mediation of Cellular Immunity in Cancer by Immune Modifiers: Progress in Cancer Research and Therapy, 1981;mem. editorial bd. The Aids Record; assoc. editor Cancer Investigation, Interferon Newsletter, Aids Care; contbr. articles to profl. jours. Bd. dirs. Nat. Med. Assn. Found., 1968-69, Inst. of Soc., Ethics, and the Life Scis. (The Hastings Ctr.), 1979-89; trustee Nat. Urban League, 1966-72, The Rockefeller Found., 1971-84, AIDS Med. Found. 1983-89, chairperson; vice chmn. Citizens Organized Against Drug Abuse, 1966; exec. sec. Am. Com for Assistance to Tunisia, 1968-69; dir. at large Am. Cancer Soc., 1970-72. Fellow NAS 1977; scholar, U. Geneva, 1947-52; recipient Spirit of Achievement award Nat. Women's Divsn. Albert Einstein Coll. Medicine, 1972, Humanitarian award Fund for Human Dignity, 1985, award for contbns. to civic life Women's City Club, 1986, John and Samuel Bard award in medicine and sci., 1986, Human Rights Campaign Fund award, 1986, Elizabeth Cutter Morrow award, City of New York YWCA, 1986, Jack Dempsey Humanitarian award St. Clare's Hosp. and Health Ctr., 1986, 10 Ams. Who've Made a Difference award Better Health and Living Mag., 1987, Eleanor Roosevelt Leadership award NOW, 1987, Achievement award Am. Assn. of Physicians for Human Rights, 1987, Humanist Disting. Svc. award Am. Humanist Assn., 1987, Hall of Fame award Internat. Women's Forum, 1987, Commitment to Life award, AIDS project L.A., 1987, Frontrunner award Sara Lee Corp., 1988, Exceptional achievement award, Women's Project and Prodns., 1988, Pres.'s award Am. Equity Assn., 1988, Medical award Hassadah, New York, 1988, award for Pioneering Achievements in Health and Higher Edn. Charles A. Dana Found., 1988, gold medal of honor Casita Maria, 1988, Caring award Stewart McKinney Found., 1988, Outstanding Mother award Nat. Mother's Day Com., 1989, Myrtle Wreath Humantiarian award Nat. Hassadah, 1991, Edwin C. Whitehead award Nat. Ctr. Health Edn., 1991, M. Carey Thomas award Bryn Mawr Coll., 1991, Scientic Freedom and Responsibility award AAAS, 1994; named Woman of Distinction Birmingham (Ala.) So. Coll., 1987, Dallas Cares Benefit honoree, 1989, 100 New York Women Barnard Coll., 1989. Mem. NAS, NAACP, Am. Assn. Advancement of Sci., Soc. Biological Therapy, Am. Soc. Microbiology, Internat. Soc. for Interferon Rsch., Am. Humanists Assn.

KRINER, SALLY GLADYS PEARL, artist; b. Bradford, Ohio, Jan. 29, 1911; d. Henry Walter and Pearl Rebecca (Brubaker) Brant; m. Leo Louis Kriner, Feb. 28, 1933; children— Patricia Staab, Jane Palombo. Grad. Arsenal Tech. sch. Indpls.; student Ind. U.-Indpls., 1954, Herron Sch. Art, Indpls., 1958. Exhibited in one woman shows Hoosier Salon, Indpls., 1960, Village Art Gallery, Southport, Ind., 1967, 70, 73, Brown County Art Guild, Nashville, Ind., 1970, 74, 77, 80, 83, 87, 92; group shows include South Side Art League, Indpls., 1959-74, Indpls. Art League, 1959-64, Brown County Art Guild, 1969—, Hoosier Salon, 1961, 65, 67-68, 73, 75-77, 82, 86-87, 91, 95, Frames and Things Gallery, 1995; represented in permanent collections Riley Hosp., Indpls., others. Founder Southside Women's Symphony Com., Indpls., 1958; treas. Perry Twp. Republican Club, Ind., 1960-65; pres. State Assembly Women's Club, 1965-67; bd. dirs. ARC, Indpls., 1942-45, Southside Civic Orgn., Indpls., 1954, Clowes Hall Women's Com., Indpls., 1963. Recipient citation ARC, 1946; citation Marion County Meritorious Svc. award, 1959; citation Greater Southside Civic Orgn., 1961; Art award Kappa Kappa Kappa, 1967-68, 70-71. Fellow Indpls. Art League Found. (awards 1960-66); mem. Southside Art League, Inc. (pres. 1964-65, awards 1964-75, founder), Ind. Artists Club, Inc. (Purchases award 1978), Ind. Heritage Arts, Inc., Rutland Art Assn., Brown County Art Guild (pres. 1980-83, v.p. 1983—), Ind. Fedn. Arts Clubs (bd. dirs. 1963-73), Ind. Artist (chmn. prize fund 1974-75), Consignment and appraisal of fine arts, Hoosier Salon, Indpls. Mus. Arts, Nat. Soc. Arts and Letters, Nat. Mus. Women in Arts, Hoosier Group Women in Arts, Oil Painters of America (Master of Art award for contbg. to heritage Brown County Indiana Art Colony 1997, cert. of appreciation, Southside Art League, Inc, 2004). Presbyterian. Avocation: growing flowers. Home: 394 E Freeman Ridge Rd Nashville IN 47448-8871

KRINGEL, DEANNA LYNN, music educator; b. Dundalk, Md., Mar. 18, 1974; d. Arthur Dale and Dorothy Ann Kringel. BA, James Madison U., 1996. Lic. tchr. Va., 1996. Tchr., band dir. Fairfax County Pub. Schs., Springfield, Va., 1996—97; tchr., orch. dir. Roanoke (Va.) City Pub. Schs., 1998—99, Hanover County Pub. Schs., Ashland, Va., 1999—2000, Chesapeake (Va.) City Pub. Schs., 2000—; condr. Williamsburg (Va.) Youth Orch., 2000—05; dir. Oscar Smith H.S. Strolling Strings, 2000—. Pvt. music tchr., 1996—2005; freelance profl. violinist, violist and flutist, Va., 1996—; cons. in field; condr. in field, Va.; clinician in field, Va. Musician: Gov. Dels. Inaugural Banquet, 1986, Summer Del. Govs. Sch. Excellence, 1990, Va. Music Educators Assn. Conf., 2005. Vol. musician Local Chs. and Hosps., Va., 1992—. Scholar Ben Wright Music scholarship, James Madison U., 1992, Second Pl. award Littman Music Competition, Concordia Coll., Bronxville, N.Y., 1992. Mem.: Am. String Tchrs. Assn., Music Educators Nat. Conf., Va. Band and Orch. Dirs. Assn., Va. Music Educators Assn., Sigma Alpha Iota. Lutheran. Avocations: fitness training, music. Office: Oscar F Smith HS 1994 Tiger Dr Chesapeake VA 23320 Home: 900D St Andrews Reach Chesapeake VA 23320-8518 Office Phone: 757-548-0696. Business E-Mail: director@osmith-orchestra.org.

KRINSKY, CAROL HERSELLE, art historian, educator; b. NYC, June 2, 1937; d. David and Jane (Gartman) Herselle; m. Robert Daniel Krinsky, Jan. 25, 1959; 2 children. BA, Smith Coll., 1957; MA, NYU, 1960, PhD, 1965. Mem. faculty NYU, 1965—, assoc. prof. art history, 1973-78, prof., 1978—; Frederic Lindley Morgan prof. U. Louisville, 2001. Author: Vitruvius de Architectura, 1521. 1969, Rockefeller Center, 1978, Synagogues of Europe, 1985, rev. edit., 1996, Gordon Bunshaft of Skidmore, Owings & Merrill, 1988, Europas Synagogen, 1988, Contemporary Native American Architecture, 1996; contbr. articles to profl. jours. Bd. dirs. Internat. Survey Jewish Monuments, Syracuse, N.Y., 1981—, Soc. Archtl. Historians, 1978-80, 86-89, The Mac Dowell Colony, Inc., 1989—, Jewish Heritage Coun. World Monuments Fund; co-chair seminar on the city Columbia U., 1993-95. Am. Coun. Learned Socs. grantee, 1981, Nat. Endowment for the Arts grantee, 1993; recipient Arnold Brunner award N.Y.C. chpt. AIA, 1990. Fellow Soc. Archtl. Historians (pres. 1984-86, pres. NYC chpt. 1977-79); mem. Coll. Art Assn. (Disting. Tchg. of Art History award 2004), Planning History Group, Am. Urban History Assn., Internat. Ctr. Medieval Art, Women's City Club, Phi Beta Kappa. Office: NYU Dept Fine Arts 100 Washington Sq E New York NY 10003-6688 Office Phone: 212-998-8186. Business E-Mail: chk1@nyu.edu.

KRINTZMAN, B. J., lawyer, real estate broker, television show host; b. Worcester, Mass., Dec. 30, 1946; d. Sumner B. and Shirley R. (Sigel) Cotzin; m. Steven Krintzman, Aug. 9, 1969 (div. Jan. 1978); children: Douglas Andrew, Joshua Barrett. AB, Vassar Coll., 1968; MBA, Harvard U., 1970; JD, Boston Coll. Law Sch., 1991. Lic. real estate broker, Mass. Mng. dir. Boston Shakespeare Co., 1979-82; dir. planning Boston Symphony Orch., 1982-84; talk/game show hostess Newton Continental Cablevision, Mass., 1984-85; real estate broker Hughes Assocs., Newton, 1984-91; atty. Hale and Dorr, 1991—; host Law Line with Atty. BJ Krintzman, 1996—. Mem. adv. bd. WBZ-TV Fund for the Arts, 1982-85; mem. adv. bd. Boston Shakespeare Co., 1982-84, bd. dirs., 1979-82; bd. govs. Harvard Bus. Sch. Alumni Assn., 1983-86; trustee Mass. Cultural Alliance, 1980-84; mem. scholarship com. Worcester County Vassar Club, 1976-82, chairperson, 1982; commr. Human Rights Adv. Bd., Worcester, 1977-78. Named 1 of 10 Outstanding Young Leaders of Greater Boston, Boston Jaycees, 1980. Mem. Boston Bar Assn., Mass. Bar Assn., Am. Bar Assn., Greater Boston Real Estate Bd., Harvard Bus. Sch. Assn. (bd. govs. 1983-86). Jewish. Club: New Eng. Backgammon (Boston). Avocations: crossword puzzles, antiques, theater, tennis. Home and Office: 30 Avalon Rd Newton MA 02468-1610

KRIPKE, MARGARET LOUISE, immunologist, health facility executive; b. Concord, Calif., July 21, 1943; d. Clyde Charles and Vivian Faith (Leighter) Cook; m. Bernard Kripke, Dec. 28, 1966 (div. 1974); 1 child, Katharine; m. Isaiah J. Fidler, Oct. 18, 1975; children: Morli, Daniel. BA in Bacteriology, U. Calif., Berkeley, 1965, MA in Bacteriology, 1967, PhD in Immunology, 1970; postdoctoral, Ohio State U., 1970-72. Asst. prof. dept. pathology Coll. Medicine, U. Utah, Salt Lake City, 1972-75; head immunobiology of phys. and chem. carcinogenesis sect. Cancer Biology Program, NCI-Frederick Cancer Rsch. Facility, Frederick, Md., 1975-82; assoc. dir. Cancer Biology Program, NCI-Frederick (Md.) Cancer Rsch. Facility, 1979, dir., 1979-82; dir. immunobiology of phys. and chem. carcinogenesis lab. NCI-Frederick Cancer Rsch. Facility, Md., 1982-83; prof., chmn. dept. immunology U. Tex. M.D. Anderson Cancer Ctr., Houston, 1983—, v.p. for academic programs, 1998, sr. v.p. and chief academic officer, 1999—2001, exec. v.p. and chief academic officer, 2001—; Kathryn O'Connor rsch. prof. U. Tex. Med. Sch., Houston, 1983-86, rsch. prof. dept. pathology, 1984-87, rsch. prof. dept. dermatology, 1984—, Vivian L. Smith chair in immunology, 1986—. Edna Roe Meml. lectr. VIIIth Internat. Congress on Photobiology, Strasbourg, 1980, Chancellor's Disting. lectr. U. Calif., Berkeley, 1980; chmn. Gordon Conf. on Cancer, New London, N.H., 1983; Warner-Lambert lectr. U. Mich., Ann Arbor, 1983; dir. program in immunology U. Tex., Grad. Sch. Biomedical Scis., Houston, 1989-92; bd. sci. counselors div. cancer biology and diagnosis and ctrs. Nat. Cancer Inst., Bethesda, Md., 1989-93; chair EPA sci. adv. bd. subcom. on the causes and effects of the stratospheric ozone depletion, Washington, 1987, 1995-96, mem. exec. com. 1991-96; mem. Nat. Cancer Adv. Bd. subcom. to review Nat. Cancer Program, 1993; Estee Lauder lectureship Johns Hopkins Univ., Balt., 1983; Grace Faillace lectureship Northridge Hosp., Ft. Lauderdale, Fla., 1985; Meyerhoff Professorship, Weizmann Inst. Sci., Rehovot, Israel, 1985; Pharma-Medica lecture, Danish Dermatological, Arhus, Denmark, 1987; spl. lecture 17th World Cong. Dermatology, Berline, 1987; Maruice S. Segal lecture, Tufts Univ. Sch. Medicine, Boston, 1989; serves on UN Environ. Program Subcom. on stratospheric ozone depletion; mem. subcom. C (IRG-C) of Cancer Ctrs. and Rsch. Programs Review Com., Nat. Cancer Inst., 1995; mem. Am. Cancer Soc. Coun. for Extramural Grants, 1997-2000; lectr. in field. Contbr. chpts. to books and articles to profl. jours. Recipient Calif. Alumni Assn. scholarship, 1961, Lila Gruber award for cancer rsch. Am. Acad. Dermatology, 1984, Herman Pinkus award for basic rsch. on the skin, Am. Soc. Dermatopathology, 1985, Past State Pres.'s award Tex. Fedn. of the Bus. and Profl. Women's Club, 1991, Maria T. Bonazinga award, 1999, Raymond Bourgine award, 1999; fellow AAAS Mem. Am. Soc. for Photobiology (sec. coun. 1991—, pres. 1997-98, rsch. award, 1998), Am. Assn. for Cancer Rsch. (pres.-elect 1992, pres. 1993-94), Am. Assn. Immunologists, Soc. for Leukocyte Biology (coun. 1985-89), Soc. for Investigative Dermatology. Achievements include pioneering the field of photoimmunology and expert on skin cancer. Avocations: cross country horseback jumping, gardening, pianist. Office: M D Anderson Cancer Ctr 1515 Holcombe Blvd Houston TX 77030-4009 Office Phone: 713-792-8578, 713-792-6161.

KRISCHER, DEVORA, writer, editor; b. Oak Park, Ill., Mar. 20, 1947; d. John Joseph and Frances Elizabeth (Kirke) Lang; m. Charles Krischer, Dec. 19, 2005. BA cum laude, Beloit Coll., 1969; postgrad., Boston U., 1971—72. Tchr, elem. and presch., Boston, Oak Park, 1968—72; regional adminstr. TRW Fin. Sys., Wellesley, Mass., 1972—76; mgr. mktg. comm. Computer Sharing Svcs., Denver, 1976—82; dir. corp. comm. Corp. Mgmt. Sys., Denver, 1982—85; sr. copywriter On-Line Software Internat., Ft. Lee, NJ, 1985—86; mgr. corp. comm. Health Mgmt. Sys., N.Y.C., 1986—89; dir. pub. rels. Am. Sephardi Fedn., 1989—92; pres. Mitrell Group, 1982—84; dir. U.S. mktg. Best of Israel, 1994—95; publs. specialist PCS Health Sys., Inc., 1995—98; mgr. sci. publs. AdvancePCS, 1998—2002; cons. med. editor Caremark, 2002—. Press release chmn. Nassau Region Hadassah, 1992—94; bd. dirs. Chabad Women, 1995—98, Companion Animal Assn. Ariz., 1999—2000. Dir. pub. rels. Bus. Roundtable Nat. Security, Colo., 1983—84; bd. dirs. Talia Hadassah, 1986—94, co-pres., 1990—92; v.p. edn. Long Beach Hadassah, 1992—94. Named Woman of Yr., Talia Hadassah, 1993; recipient Nat. Leadership award, Long Beach Hadassah, 1991—92, Talia Hadassah, 1993—94, Vol. of Yr. award, Assisted Living Fedn. Am., Ariz., 2004. Mem.: Am. Sephardi Fedn. (edn. com. 1987—89), Colo. Conf. Communicators, Denver Advt. Fedn. (bd. dirs. 1981—83, Alfie award 1984), Coun. Sci. Editors (sponsorship com. 1999—2005, program com. 2000—, chmn. sponsorship com. 2002—05, chmn. program com. 2005—06, chair 50th anniversary com. 2006—07, Disting. Svc. award 2006), Am. Med. Writers Assn. (biomed. communicators task force 2001—04, chair 2003—04). Business E-Mail: devora.krischer@caremark.com.

KRISE, PATRICIA LOVE, automotive industry executive; b. Indpls., July 28, 1959; d. John Bernard and Ann (Emmons) Love; m. Thomas Warren Krise, Sept. 5, 1987. BA magna cum laude, Hanover Coll., Ind., 1981; MBA honors, Miami U., Oxford, Ohio, 1982. Substitute tchr. Henry County Sch. Dist., Knightstown, Ind., 1982—83; project mgr. Servaas Labs., Inc., Indpls., 1983—84; sales analyst Ford Motor Co., Mpls., 1984, outstate field mgr., 1984—86, met. field mgr., 1986—87, mgr. truck merchandising, 1987—88, mgr. merchandising, 1988—89, met. field dir. Denver dist., 1989, market representation specialist Denver dist., 1990—91; mgr. regional market rep. Infiniti divsn. Nissan Motor Corp., Naperville, Ill., 1991—92, mgr. regional merchandising Infiniti divsn., 1992—93, dealer ops. cons. Infiniti divsn., 1993—97, mgr. dealer ops. Infiniti divsn., 1995—97; mgr. adminstrv./remktg. Fairlane Credit subs. Ford Motor Credit, Colorado Springs, 1997—99, mgr. nat. expansion, remktg. and adminstrn. Fairlane Credit subs., 1999, mgr. acct. svcs., 1999—2004, mgr. process and quality, 2004, mgr. spl. projects Orlando, Fla., 2005—. Advisor/presenter Ford Dealer Advt. Fund, Mpls., 1987-88. Nat. sponsorship liaison Race for the Cure, Colorado Springs, 2002—04; vol. Marian House Soup Kitchen, 1997—2000; adult lit. tutor Jr. Achievement, 1998, bd. dirs. Colorado Springs, 2002—04; mem. fund-raising com. Race for the Cure, Colorado Springs, 1999, co-chair ops. com., 2001, co-chair Fairlane Credit, 1998. Recipient Outstanding Mktg. award Ctrl. Region Ford Motor Co., 1987, Wall St. Jour. award, 1982; named Internat. Woman of Yr., 1992. Mem. NAFE, Twin Cities Sales Mgrs. Club, Hanover Coll. Alumni Assn., Women's Athletic Assn. (treas. 1979-80), Pre-Law Club (pres. 1980-81), Alpha Delta Pi Office Phone: 407-667-3948. Personal E-mail: pkrise@peoplepc.com. Business E-Mail: pkrise@ford.com.

KRISSEL, SUSAN HINKLE, transportation company executive; b. Miami, Fla., Nov. 21, 1947; d. Jack Boyd and Carolyn (Frates) Hinkle; m. Richard Krissel, Mar. 19, 1972; children: John Boyd, Carolyn Frates. BA, U. Miami, 1970, MEd, 1977. Grad. admissions counselor Fla. Internat. U., Miami, 1971-74, budget coord. external degree program, 1974-78, transcript officer, 1978-82; owner, dir. Southeastern Consolidated Industries, Inc., 1982—. Bd. dirs. Jr. League Miami, 1985-86, Beaux Arts, U. Miami, Coral Gables, 1980-84, Parents Assn. Trinity Episcopal Sch., Miami, 1988-91; pres. Woman's Cancer Assn., U. Miami, 1980-81, Palmer Trinity Parents Assn., 1992-93; trustee Palmer Trinity Sch., 1992-93; mem. Young Patronesses of the Opera, bd. govs., 1999-2004. Mem. The Flamingo Forum, Jr. League Miami, Beaux Arts. Episcopalian. Avocations: reading, boating, travel, needlepoint, golf. Home: 8750 SW 63rd Ct Miami FL 33143-8069

KRISTENSEN, KATHLEEN HOWARD, music educator; b. Salt Lake City, May 10, 1939; d. Erin Neils and Verdis Eliza (Berrett) Howard; m. Karl G. Topham (div. 1968); children: Stephanie T. Fullmer, Amelia T. Curtis, Suzanne T. Jones, David Howard Topham; m. Paul Kristensen, Jan. 21, 1983. Student, Brigham Young U., 1957-59, U. Utah, 1970-72. Mem. Mormon Tabernacle Choir, 20 yrs. Mem. Am. Guild Organists (sub-dean), Nat. Assn. Tchrs. Singing, Nat. Assn. Music, Utah Music Tchrs., John Birch Soc. Republican. Mem. Lds Ch. Home: 2146 E 7420 S Salt Lake City UT 84121-4925

KRISTIN, KAREN, artist; b. LA, Aug. 27, 1943; d. Earle Barnard and Ann Maxine (Taylor) Immel; m. Richard Edward Amend, Aug. 21, 1976 (div. Aug. 1981); m. Gary Marchal Lloyd, Oct. 1, 1985 (div. Sept.1989). Student, Art Ctr. Coll. Design, 1961, Valley Jr. Coll., 1962, Pierce Jr. Coll., 1967—68, UCLA, 1969—70. Lectr. UCLA Ext. Program, 1973-76; scenic artist Hollywood, Calif., 1978-83; ptnr., designer, lead painter Sky Art Scenic Art Svcs., Hollywood, Calif., 1983-88; owner, pres., lead painter, designer Sky Art Karen Kristin, Inc., Englewood, Colo., 1989—. Spkr., lectr. in field. Co-author (under Karen Kristin Amend): Handwriting Analysis: The Complete Basic Book, 1980, Achieving Compatibility with Handwriting-Analysis, vol. I, Understanding Your Emotional Relationships, 1992, vol. II, Exploring Your Sexual Relationships, 1992; prin. murals include The Cirque Du Soleil Theater, Las Vegas, 1993, N.Mex. Mus. Natural History, 1989, 90, Forum Shops at Caesars, Las Vegas, 1992, 97, Kansas City Station Hotel and Casino, Kansas City, Mo., 1996, Sunset Station Hotel and Casino, Las Vegas, 1997, Venetian Hotel Grand Canal Shoppes, Las Vegas, 1998, Chaitanya Joti Mus., Puttaparthy, India, 2000, Hyatt Casino, Blackhawk, Colo., 2001, Argosy Casino, Kans. City, Mo., 2003, Rangeeli Mahal, Barsara, India, 2003, Boulder Sta. Casino, Las Vegas, 2004, Charlestown Race and Sports Book, 2005, The Bismarck Airport, 2005; sky art backdrops for numerous movies, commls., and TV. Mem. Am. Assn. Handwriting Analysts (spkr. 1991—), Am. Handwriting Analysis Found. (spkr. 1991—), Human Graphics Ctr., Graphex Internat. and Gold NIBS, Universal Soc. of Integral Why (mentor 1994—). Democrat. Avocations: photography, reading, travel, camping, fishing. Office: Sky Art Karen Kristin Inc 125 N Sligo Cortez CO 81321-2939 Office Phone: 970-565-8965. Personal E-mail: skyartkk@aol.com.

KRISTOF, KATHY M., journalist; b. Burbank, Calif., Feb. 4, 1960; d. Joseph E. and Frances S. Kristof; m. Richard R. Magnuson, Jr., Jan. 4, 1986 (div.); 2 children. BA, U. So. Calif., L.A., 1983. Reporter L.A. Bus. Jour., 1984-88, Daily News, Woodland Hills, Calif., 1988-89, L.A. Times, 1989—; syndicated columnist L.A. Times Syndicate, 1991—. Author: Kathy Kristof's Complete Book of Dollars and Sense, 1997, Investing 101, 2000, Taming the Tuition Tiger, 2003; contbr. articles to mags. and profl. jours. Recipient John Hancock Fin. Svcs. award, 1992, Personal Fin. Writing award ICI/Am. U., 1994, Consumer Adv. of Yr., Calif. Alliance for Consumer Edn., 1998. Mem. Soc. Bus. Editors and Writers (pres. 2003), Calif. Newspapers Pubs. Assn. (2nd pl. Bus. and Fin. Story award 1999). Office: Los Angeles Times 202 W 1st St Los Angeles CA 90012 E-mail: kathy.kristof@latimes.com.

KRIZER, JODI, performing arts executive; Mng. dir. Bill T. Jones/Arnie Zane Dance Co., NYC, exec. dir.; dir. Mktg. and Pub. Rels. Alvin Ailey Dance Found., Inc., NYC. Office: Alvin Ailey Dance Found, Inc Joan Weill Ctr for Dance 405 W 55th St New York NY 10019

KROBATH, KRISTA ANN, pharmacist; b. Pottsville, Pa., July 8, 1962; d. James Joseph and Gaye Diane (Anderson) E.; m. Gilbert Krobath; 1 adopted child, Kelleigh Ann. BS in Pharmacy, Temple U., 1985. Registered pharmacist. Pharmacist People's Drug, Harrisburg, Pa., 1985-86; pharmacist, mgr. Amcare Health Svcs., Harrisburg, 1986-96; pharmacist Pharmerica, Harrisburg, 1996-99, Express Scripts, Harrisburg, 1999—. Mem.: Capital Area Pharm. Assn., Pa. Pharm. Assn.

KROEGER, CATHERINE C., writer, educator, editor; b. St. Paul, Minn., Dec. 12, 1925; d. Homer Pierce Clark and Elizabeth Turner Dunsmoor; m. Richard Clark Kroeger, Dec. 22, 1950; children: Paul, Robert, Elizabeth, Marjorie, Mary. AB, Bryn Mawr Coll., 1947; MA, U. Minn., 1982, PhD, 1987. Founding pres. Christian for Bibl. Equality, Mpls., 1987-95; pres. emerita Christians for Bibl. Equality, Mpls., 1995—; Protestant chaplain Hamilton Coll., Clinton, N.Y., 1987-88; adj. assoc. prof. Gordon Conwell Theol. Sem., South Hamilton, Mass., 1992—. Founding organizer Women in the Bibl. World sect. Soc. Bibl. Lit., 1980-89. Author, editor: Women, Abuse and the Bible, 1996, Healing the Hurting, 1998; co-editor: Study Bible for Women, 1996; editor: InterVarsity Press Women's Bible Commentary, 2002; mem. editl. bd.: Jour. Religion and Abuse, 1999—; co-author (with Nancy Nason-Clark): No Place for Abuse: Biblical and Practical Resources to Counteract Domestic Violence, 2001; co-author: (witn Nancy Nason-Clark) Beyond Abuse, 2004; author: I Suffer Not A Woman, 1992. Bd. dirs. St. Paul Philharm Soc., 1964-66, Evangels. for Social Action, Phila., 1987-93; bd. dirs., pres. Minn. Sch. Missions, St. Paul, 1959-79; bd. dirs. emerita Whitworth Coll., Spokane, Wash; pres. Peace and Safety in the Christian Home. Fellow Inst. Bibl. Rsch. (exec. bd. 1995-97); mem. Am. Acad. Religion/Soc. Bibl. Lit., Women's Classical Caucus, Archaeol. Inst. Am., Am. Philological Assn. Presbyterian. Avocation: conducting study tours. Home: 1073 Stony Brook Rd Brewster MA 02631-2448 Office: Gordon Conwell Theol Sem 130 Essex St South Hamilton MA 01982-2317 E-mail: ckroeger@world.std.com.

KROGFOSS, KIMBERLY JEAN, elementary school educator; b. Devils Lake, N.D., Jan. 13, 1970; d. Peter Martin and Jeanette Evelyn Ripplinger; m. Karl V. Krogfoss Jr., June 13, 1992; children: Karli M., Kale D. B in Elem. Edn., Valley City State U., 1992; MEd, U. N.D., 2002. Tchr. 3d grade Prairie View Elem. Sch., Devils Lake, ND, 1995—99, Sweetwater Elem. Sch., 1999—2002, reading coord., 2002—. Office: Sweetwater Elem Sch 1304 2d Ave W Devils Lake ND 58301 Office Phone: 701-662-7630. E-mail: kimberly.krogfoss@sendit.nodak.edu.

KROHLEY-GATT, PATRICIA ANNE, marketing professional, sales executive; b. NYC, Feb. 13, 1954; d. Casper and Ann Marie (Calise) Inzerillo; m. Richard John Krohley Sr., June 10, 1977 (div. 2001); m. Alfred Gatt, 2006; 1 child, Richard John Krohley Jr. Grad., Bklyn. Mus. Art Sch., 1971, Queens Coll., 1972, Fashion Inst. Tech., 1974. Lic. real estate salesperson, N.Y. Realtor Weichert Bonus Realty, Woodhaven, NY, 1988—96; account exec. Met. Life Ins. Co., Lake Success, NY, 1996—98; inside sales rep. GE Plastics, 1998—2001; account exec. Laird Plastics, Westbury, NY, 2001—03; dir. mktg. Corcon Developers, West Hempstead, NY, 2003—06; with Al Gatt Signs & Graphics, Valley Stream, NY, 2006—. Mem. Agt. Adv. Panel, Century 21 Broker's Coun., L.I., NY, 1990; key communicator Re/Max of N.Y., 1993—96. Recipient scholarship Bklyn. Mus. Art, 1971. Mem. Nat. Assn. Life Underwriters, Nat. Assn. Realtors, N.Y. State Assn. Realtors, N.Y.C. Assn. Life Underwriters, L.I. Bd. Realtors, Women in Transition (founder, pres. 1993—), Nat. Art League, Alliance of Queens Artists. Avocations: environmental and social issues, children's advocate, writing, photography, painting.

KROIS, AUDREY, artist; b. Boston, Mar. 14, 1934; d. Henry and Lillian Marie (Mueller) Haeberle; m. Richard Gamage, May 14, 1966 (div. Mar. 1975); m. Joseph E. Krois Jr., June 17, 1978. BA, Syracuse U., 1956; MSW, Columbia U., 1958; postgrad., Fashion Inst. Tech., 1964-66, Art Students League, 1973-76. Social worker Pleasantville (N.Y.) Cottage Sch., 1958-62; cons. to UNICEF UN, Bangkok, Thailand, 1963; supr. vol. program Henry St. Settlement, N.Y.C., 1964-66; dir. cmty. devel. program Anti Poverty Funding, N.Y.C., 1966-68; supervising dir., asst. v.p., cons. Divsn. Homemaker, Home Health Care, G.H.I., Inc., N.Y.C., 1969-78. One-woman shows include Clayton Liberatore Gallery, Bridgehampton, N.Y., 1995, 1996, 1999, 2002, South Palm Beach Town Hall Gallery, 1998, Southampton Town Hall, 1998, exhibited in group shows at Access to the Arts, Jamestown, N.Y., 1981, Embroiderers Guild Abigail Adams Smith Mus., N.Y.C., 1982, Arrowmont Sch., Gatlinburg, Tenn., 1982, Gayle Wilson Gallery, Southampton, N.Y., 1983, 1988, Discovery Art Gallery, Glen Cove, N.Y., 1989, Decatur House, Washington, 1990, Mus. Am. Quilter Soc., Paducah, Ky., 1992, Vanderbilt Mus., Centerport, N.Y., 1992, 1994, Wellspring Gallery, Santa Monica, Calif., 1993—94, Aullwood Audubon Ctr., Dayton, Ohio, 1996 (Best of Show), South Fla. Fair, 2002, Northern Trust Bank, 2002, Everglades Vis. Ctr., 2002, Water Mill Mus., Water Mill, N.Y., 2002, West Palm Beach Internat. Airport, 2002—03. Recipient 2d Pl. award Brookhaven Arts and Humanities Coun., 1997, 2d Pl. award East End Arts Coun., 1998. Mem. South Fork Craft Assn., Southampton Artists Assn. (bd. dirs. 1990-96, fin. dir. 1992-93, pres. 1994, Award of Excellence in Watercolor, 1994-96), Goodman Design Gallery (Award of Merit in Watercolor 1993), Palm Beach Watercolor Soc. Home: PO Box 2482 Palm Beach FL 33480-2482

KROKEN, PATRICIA ANN, health science association administrator; b. Sturgis, Mich., June 26, 1947; d. Jesse W. and Dorothy Beth (Hollister) Penn; m. Bruce Edward Kroken, Jan. 28, 1967; children: Christina, Jennifer. BS in English cum laude, No. Mich. U., 1970. V.p., account supr. Rick Johnson & Co., Albuquerque, 1984-87; expansion sales mgr. Bueno Foods, 1987-89; bus. devel. dir. Radiology Assocs., Albuquerque, 1990-93, exec. dir., 1993-2000; v.p. compliance solutions div. Telemedix, Inc., Albuquerque, 2000—01; pres. Healthcare Resource Providers, LLC, 2001—. Adj. prof. U. N.Mex., Albuquerque, 1983—94; spkr. in field. Contbr. articles to various jours. Lectr. N. Mex. Womens Polit. Caucus, Albuquerque, 1986. Fellow Am. Coll. Med. Practice Execs.; mem. Radiology Bus. Mgmt. Assn. (chair publs. com. 1997-99, pres. 1999, Calhoun award 1996, 99), N.Mex. Med. Group Mgmt. Assn. (pres. 1995). Avocations: writing, horseback riding, public speaking. Home: PO Box 90190 Albuquerque NM 87199-0190

KROKOS, KELLEY JOAN, psychologist, consultant; b. Columbia, S.C., Sept. 13, 1963; d. Stanley Bernard and Jo Allen Krokos. BA, Furman U., 1985; MS, NC State U., 1999, PhD, 2003. Sr. rsch. scientist Am. Inst. Rsch., DC, 2003—. Mem.: Soc. Indsl. - Orgnl. Psychologists, Soc. Human Performance Extreme Environments (assoc.; bd. dirs. 2004—), Phi Kappa Phi (life). Office: Am Insts Rsch 1000 Thomas Jefferson St NW Washington DC 20007 Office Phone: 202-403-5259. Office Fax: 202-403-5033. Business E-Mail: kkrokos@air.org.

KROLEWSKI, BOZENA K., molecular biologist, researcher, cell biologist; b. Warsaw, Jan. 18, 1949; came to the U.S., 1981; d. Stefan and Zdzislawa M.S. (Zabielski) Checinski; m. Andrzej S. Krolewski, June 3, 1972; children: Martin A., Adam W. BA, Warsaw Med. Sch., Poland, 1971; MS, Warsaw Med. Sch., 1972, PhD, 1979. Rsch. asst. Warsaw Med. Sch., 1972—74; vis. fellow Harvard Sch. Pub. Health, Boston, 1981-84, rsch. fellow, 1984-87, scientist, 1987-92, sr. scientist, 1992—; rsch. assoc., cons. Joslin Diabetes Ctr., Boston, 1992—. Contbr. articles to profl. jours. Recipient Rsch. award NIH, Boston, 1984. Mem. Radiation Rsch. Soc., Cancer Rsch. Soc. Roman Catholic. Avocations: collecting antiques, walking, climbing, history, politics. Home: 639 Great Plain Ave Needham MA 02492 Office: Joslin Diabetes Ctr Genetics/Epidemiology 3d Flr One Joslin Pl Boston MA 02215 Office Phone: 617-732-2668. Business E-Mail: bozena.krolewski@joslin.harvard.edu.

KROLL, CONNIE RAE, librarian, information services consultant; b. Karlstad, Minn., June 12, 1955; d. Rudolph Julius and Irene Eleanor K. AAS, U. Minn., Crookston, Minn., 1975; BA, U. N.D., 1992; MLIS, U. Okla., 1993; postgrad. studies, Tex. Woman's U., 1993—96. Circulation svcs. asst. N.W. Regional Libr., Thief River Falls, Minn., 1979-84, br. libr. substitute Warren, Hallock, Minn., 1985-88; libr. rsch. asst. U. N.D., Grand Forks, 1988-90; circulation asst. Grand Forks Pub, Libr., 1990-91; supr. interlibr. svcs. U. N.D. Med. Libr., Grand Forks, 1988-92; grad. asst. reference Bizzell Libr. U. Okla., Norman, 1993; grad. asst., vol. Tex. Woman's U., Denton, 1993-96; libr., dir. LRC Howard Coll., San Angelo, Tex., 1996—; med. libr. Reynolds Army Hosp, Lawton, Okla., 2003—. Grant reviewer LSCA, State of Wash., Olympia, 1994; rsch. cons. Haynes & Boone Law Firm, Dallas, 1995-96; planning com., Tex. Tech. Visions of the Future, Lubbock, Tex., 1996—, instrl. coun. Howard Coll., San Angelo, Tex., 1996—; presenter: How to Avoid Vertical Stripes and an Empty Pocketbook, 1997. Vol. Christmas at Old Ft. Concho, San Angelo, Tex., 1996, 97, 99; catalog sale rep. Concho Kennel Club, San Angelo, 1997, hospitality chair, 1998, chair state employees contbn. campaign, 1998, chair Ann. Dog Show, 1999. Recipient Title IIB fellowship Dept Edn., Norman, Okla., 1993, Title IIB Dept. Edn., Denton, Tex., 1994-96, Mayo Drake scholarship State Employees Contbn. Campaign, Albuquerque, N. Mex., 1997. Mem. ALA, Tex. Libr. Assn. (com. mem.), Assn. Libr. and Info. Sci. Educators, N.D. Libr. Assn., Med. Libr. Assn. (s. ctrl. chpt. 1997). Home: 407 NW 5th St Lawton OK 73507-6934

KROLL, LYNNE FRANCINE, artist; b. San Mateo, Calif., Dec. 18, 1943; d. Nathan and Dorothy (Smith) Cole; m. Jeffrey Joseph Kroll, June 9, 1963; children: Beth, Lisa, Andrew. AAS, Bklyn. C.C., 1963. Exhibited at Ann Kolb Nature Ctr., Hollywood, Fla., So. Watercolor Soc. 21st Ann. Exbhn.; works featured in The Best of Watercolor II, 1997, The Best of Watercolor II Painting and Composition, 1998, Citilinks mag., 1997; juried exhibitions Lincoln Ctr. for Performing Arts, Cork Gallery, 2005, 7th Annual Bakers Dozen Collage Exchange, Plymouth, 138th Annual Internat. Exhibit Am. Watercolor Soc. (Traveling award, 2005), 139th, 2006, Aqueous USA Kty. Watercolor Soc. (Camlin Merchandise award, Color Q award, 2005), 23rd Annual Juried Exhibit Palm Beach Watercolor Soc. (First Place award, 2006), 63rd Annual Exhibit, Salmagundi Club, NY Audobon Artists Art Students League NY award, 2006, and many others; exhibited in permanent collection Jane Voorhees Zimmerli Art Mus., Rutgers U., Nat. Assn. Women Artists Permanent Collection, Internat. Mus. Eollage and Assemblage, Mexico, The Mus. and Gallery of Collage, France; contb. articles to profl. jours. Recipient Moses Worthman Meml. award Allied Artists Am., 1994, Dick Blick Materials award Audubon Artists ann. Exhibit, 1996, Curators Excellence award Ariz. Aqueous 11th Ann. Watermedia Exhibit., Judges Recognition award Mus. of New Art, 1996, Materials and Travel award Ky. Watercolor Soc., 1996, 5th Pl. Pitts. Watercolor Soc., 1996, South Fla. Cultural Consortium Fellowship Grant award for artistic excellence, 1998. Mem. Nat. Soc. Painters Casein & Acrylic, Nat. Assn. Women Artists (Distinction award 1995), Soc. Layerists Multi-Media, Fla. Watercolor Soc. (Strathmore Excellence award 1994), Tex. Watercolor Soc. (Laredo Nat. Bank award, 2006), La. Watercolor Soc., Western Colo. Watercolor Soc., Watercolor Soc. Ala., Southern Watercolor Soc. (Holbein Merchandise award, 2006), Calif. Watercolor Assn., Goldcoast Watercolor Soc. (Grumbacher Gold medallion 1994, Sax Arts & Crafts award 1994), Artist Orgn., Profl. Artist Guild, Nat. Coll. Soc., Audobon Artists, Allied Artists Am., 2+3 the Artists's Organ., Boca Raton Mus. Art Artist Guild, Catherine Lorillane Wolfe Art Club. Home: 3971 NW 101st Dr Coral Springs FL 33065-1589 Personal E-mail: butterflynne@myacc.net.

KROLL, SUE, broadcast executive; Pres. internat. mktg. Warner Bros. Pictures. Office: Time Warner 4000 Warner Blvd Burbank CA 91522 Office Phone: 818-954-6000. E-mail: sue.kroll@warnerbros.com.*

KROMINGA, LYNN, cosmetics executive, lawyer; b. L.A., May 16, 1950; d. Dale E. and Phyllis M. Krominga; m. Amnon Shiboleth, Apr. 9, 1992; 1 child, Karen Lee Shiboleth. BA in German, U. Minn., 1972, JD, 1974. Bar: Minn. 1974, N.Y. 1976. Assoc. firms in Mpls. and N.Y.C., 1974-77; assoc. counsel Am. Express Co., N.Y.C., 1977-80; sr. internat. counsel Revlon, Inc., N.Y.C., 1981-92, v.p. law, 1988-92, gen. counsel to exec. com., 1991-92, pres. licensing divsn., 1992-98, mem. exec. com., 1993-94, 97-99, exec. v.p. bus. devel., 1998-99; mem. bd. advisors MakeoverStudio.com, 1999—2001; bd. advisors Salonforce.com., 1999—2002; CEO Fashion Wire Daily, Inc., 2002; ptnr. KLS Mgmt. LLC, 2002—04, Krominga Holdings LLC, 2004—. Bd. dirs. StructuredWeb.com., 2000-02, Avis Budget Group, Inc, 2006- Mem. ABA, Internat. Bar Assn. Cosmetic, Toiletry and Fragrance Assn. (vice chmn. govt. rels. com. 1991-92), Am. Arbitration Assn. (corp. counsel com. 1986-92, panel of arbitrators for large complex cases 1993-94, internat. panel of arbitrators 1997—), Phi Beta Kappa. E-mail: lkrominga@aol.com.

KROMMINGA, AN-MARIE, special education educator; b. Yakima, Washington, Mar. 23, 1936; d. Fred Henry and Edith Bessie Jackson; m. William Reynold Kromminga, Aug. 23, 1956. BA in Edn., Walla Walla College, 1958. Cert. profl. educator K-12 spl. edn., K-8 elem. edn., P-3 early childhood spl. edn., early childhood edn. Washington. Tchr. grades 1-7 Upper Columbia Conf. of Seventh-Day Adventist, Toppenish, Wash., 1955—56, tachr. grades 1-4 Wapato, Wash., 1959—60; tchr. grades 5-6 Ill. Conf. of Seventh-Day Adventist, Aurora, 1963—64, tchr. grades 1-8 Canton, 1972—74; substitute and homebound tchg. various schs., Ill., 1974—79; homemaking skills tchr. Ill. Dept. Children and Family Svcs., Sterling, 1979—81; home products ind. dealer, unit sales leader, to dist. leader Stanley Home Products Inc., Ill. and Wash., 1975—; presch./kindergarten tchr. Upper Columbia Conf. of Seventh-Day Adventists, Pasco, Wash., 1986—90; life skills spl. edn. tchr. Kiona-Benton Sch. Dist. 52, Benton City, Wash., 1990—. Chair Work Opportunities for Rural Kids, Benton City, 1990—96, Spl. Edn. Parent Group, Benton City, 1990—96; mem. Tri-Cities (Wash.) Transition Team, 1990—. Author: History of Benton City, Washington, 2000; contbr. articles to ch. newsletters and publs. Active disaster relief and cmty. svc. Seventh-Day Adventist Ch., 1963—79; leader for children's clubs and recreation programs for cmty. and ch., 1963—79. Recipient Tri City Crystal Apple award for excellence in edn., various cmty. svc. groups, bus., and orgns., 2002. Mem.: Coun. for Exceptional Children. Seventh Day Adventist. Avocations: dolls, music boxes, leathercraft, travel. Home: 1004 Frontier PR NE Benton City WA 99320

KRONENBERG, MINDY ELLEN, psychologist, psychology professor; d. Joel and Suzie Kronenberg. BA, Washington U., St. Louis, 1996; PhD, U. Memphis, 2003. Lic. clin. psychologist La., 2004. Clin. asst. prof. La. State U. Health Scis. Ctr., New Orleans, 2004—. Mem.: APA.

KRONOWITZ, PAMELA RENEE, music educator; b. Manhattan, NY, Dec. 3, 1954; d. Harold Arthur and Frieda (Kahn) Simmons; children: Lauren, Damon. BA, York Coll., 1976; MA, Queens Coll., 1978. Orch. tchr. Massapequa Pub. Schs., NY, 1994—. Coach Greenwich Youth Orch., 1995—97; adjucator N.Y. State Sch. Music Assn. Home: 6 David Ave Hicksville NY 11801 Personal E-mail: freeatlaztt@optonline.net.

KROP, LOIS PULVER, psychologist; b. Scranton, Pa., Dec. 24, 1930; d. Samuel Max and Esther Golden Pulver; m. Michael Morris Krop, June 14, 1953; children: Pamela Sue, Daniel Steven, Judith Mary, David Ralph. BA, Pa. State U., 1952; MSW, U. Pa., 1954; PhD, Nova Southeastern U., 1976. LCSW; lic. sch. psychologist Fla., cert. family ct. mediator Fla., lic. marriage and family therapist Fla., 1986, cert. clin. hypnotherapist, sports counselor, hypnotherapist 1995, county ct. mediator Fla. Supreme Ct. Family therapist Alexandria Family Svcs., Va., 1954—58; treatment specialist Cath. Family Svcs., Miami, Fla., 1960—85; pvt. practice Marriage and Family Svcs., Inc., Aventura, Fla., 1985—; qualified supr. MFT-CSW and MHL, Tallahassee, 2000—. Prof. acad. lifelong learning Fla. Internat. U., Miami, Fla., 1998—; cons. Mgmt. Tng. Inst., Ft. Lauderdale, 1996—; lectr. Inst. for Ret. Profls., U. Miami, 2002—; prof. Univ. Miami Inst. for Ret. Profl., 2001—. Author: (book) Family Hour/Family Power, 2000; contbr. articles to profl. jours. Bd. trustees U. Pa. Dade Alumni, Miami, Fla., 1985—; pres. Majestic Towers, Bal Harbour, Fla., 1999—, Hadassah Chai Chpt., Miami, 1990—92. Mem.: NASW (pres. 1965), Barry U. Field Instrs. (pres. 1985—87), Assn. of Fla. Sch. Psychologists, Mensa (cert. sports instr. 1998—), Phi Beta Kappa, Mortar Bd., Phi Kappa Phi. Avocations: tennis, scuba diving, bridge, reading, travel. Home: 9601 Collins Ave #1710 Bal Harbour FL 33154 Office: 19495 Biscayne Blvd #203 Aventura FL 33180 Office Phone: 305-937-4500. Personal E-mail: drloiskrop@aol.com.

KROPF, NANCY P., social worker, educator, director; b. Detroit, June 9, 1959; d. Charles J. and Eunice I. Kropf; life ptnr. Stephanie Kay Swann. BA, Hope Coll., Holland, Mich., 1981; MSW, Mich. State U., East Lansing, 1983; PhD, Va. Commonwealth U., Richmond, 1990. Prof. U. Ga., Sch. Social Work, Athens, 1990—2006; prof., dir. Ga. State U., Sch. Social Work, Atlanta, 2006—. Vis. chair gerontology St. Thomas U., Fredericton, New Brunswick, Canada, 2000. Co-author: (text book) Gerontological Social Work. Scholar, John A. Hartford Found., 2000—02. Fellow: Gerontology Soc. Am.; mem.: Assoc Gerontology Edn. (pres. 2000—03). Office: Georgia State University Social Work 140 Decatur St Atlanta GA 30303 Office Phone: 404-371-4147. Business E-Mail: nkropf@gsu.edu.

KROPF, SUSAN J., retired cosmetics executive; married. BA in English, St. John's U.; MBA in Fin., NYU. Adminstrv. asst. Avon Products, Inc., N.Y.C., 1970, various mgmt. positions, 1970-85, v.p. purchasing and package devel., 1985-90, v.p., sr. officer product devel., 1990-92, v.p. R&D and mfg., 1992-97, sr. v.p. global ops. and bus. devel., 1992-97, exec. v.p., 1998-99, COO N.Am. & Global Bus. Ops., 1999—2006, pres., 2001—06. Bd. dirs. Green Point Savs. Bank, Avon Products Inc., MeadWestvaco Corp., Sherwin Williams Co., Wallace Found. Mem.: Fashion Group Internat., Cosmetic Exec. Women. Office: Avon Products Inc Ste C2-04 1251 Avenue Of The Americas New York NY 10020-1196*

KROTZ, JANET M. TRAHAN, artist, former gallery owner, art educator; b. Rockville Centre, NY, May 28, 1951; d. James Joseph and Dorothy Agnes Ball; m. Scott Trahan, Feb. 10, 1973 (div.); children: Mandy A., Kate M.; m. James J. Krotz, June 12, 2006. Student, C.W. Post Coll., 1970-71, Suffolk C.C., 1972. Ptnr., owner, artist Bellport Ln. Art Gallery, NY, 1996—2000; adminstrv. asst. Gateway Performing Arts, 1999—2001; bus. owner Janet M. Trahan, Artist, 1994—; represented by Art Reps., Calif., 2001—03, Intercontinental Greetings, Ltd., NYC, 2002—; art tchr. Studio Music and Art, Sayville, NY, 2002—03; mural artist Sayville, 2002—. Exhbns. at Longwood Libr., Middle Island, NY, 1996, Bald Hill Gallery, L.I., NY, 1996, Salmagundi Club, NYC, 1996, 97, 99, 2000, 01, 02 (A.E.S. Meml. award 1996), Fed. Hall, NYC, 1996, Hutchings Gallery, Brookville, NY, 1997, Woodbury (NY) Cmty. Ctr., 1997, Bayport Blue Point (NY) Libr., 1997, 98, 99, 2000, 01, 02, 03, Nat. Art League Open Art Exhbn., Douglaston, NY, 1997, Stage Gallery, Merrick, NY, 1997, Islip (NY) Art Mus., 1996, 97, 98, 99 (1st Pl. Oil 1999), 2000, 01, 02, Nat. Soc. Painters in Casein and Acrylics, Inc., NYC, 1996-2004, Huntington (NY) Arts Coun., 1998, Heckscher Mus. Art, Huntington, 1998, Houston Watercolor Soc., 2000, Watermedia, 2000, A Victorian on the Bay, Eastport, NY, 1998-2005, Chrysalis Gallery, Southampton, NY, 2001-04, Art League L.I. Mems. Exhbn., 2003, Cactus Girls, Sayville, N.Y., 2003, Nat. Soc. Painters in Casein and Acrylic 50th Ann. Banana Factory, Bethlehem, Pa., 2003, Ann. Show, 2004, Salon du Nord, St. Paul, Minn., 2004—; scenic painter Airport Playhouse, Bohemia, NY, 2002 Grants and awards judge Sayville (NY) Mus. Boosters for Arts, 1998-99; juror of selection Nat. Soc. of Painters in Casein and Acrylic, N.Y., 2004; costumer designer Ballet L.I., Bohemia, NY, 1987-90, set designer, 1989-90; costumer designer Sayville Mid. Sch., 1996, 97. Recipient 1st pl. oil and acrylic category West Hampton Beach Annual Outdoor Show, 1998, North Shore Art League 1st place in acrylics, Most Popular award and Hon. Mention, Arts Coun. E.I. Pub. Libr. Mem. Nat. Soc. Painters in Casein and Acrylics (life signature, A.E.S. Peterson Meml. award 1996, Antonio Cirino Meml. award 1996, Hon. Mention award 1997), Audubon Artist Assn. (assoc.), Art League of L.I. (hon. mention), South Bay Art Assn. (1st prize acrylic 1997, hon. mention 1999, Best in Show 2001), Wet Paints Studio Group (1st pl. oil 1998, hon. mention 1998, 2d pl. Acrylic 1999, 2d pl. Acrylic 2002). Roman Catholic. Avocations: art, music, theater, travel, theology. Personal E-mail: janettrahan@yahoo.com.

KROUPA, BETTY JEAN, medical/surgical nurse; b. Pikeville, Ky., Feb. 13, 1958; d. Donald B. and Gloria Ann (Roberts) Bartley; m. Joseph John Kroupa Jr., Oct. 17, 1981; children: Lisa Nicole, James Eric and Joseph John III (twins). ADN, Daytona Beach (Fla.) Community Coll., 1980. Grad. nurse Halifax Hosp., Daytona Beach; staff RN Our Lady of Mercy, Dyer, Ind., Park Plaza Hosp., Houston; charge nurse West Houston Med. Ctr.

KROUPA, DIANE LYNN, federal judge; b. Mitchell, S.D., Oct. 12, 1955; d. Edwin Raymond and Delores Ilene (Duncan Burg) K.; m. Robert Eugene Fackler, Sept. 12, 1981; children: Erin Elizabeth, Sara Marie. BS in Fgn. Svc., Georgetown U., 1978, postgrad., 1981-83; JD, U. S.D., Vermillion, 1981. Bar: S.D. 1981, D.C. 1984, Minn. 1986. Atty., advisor IRS legis. and regulation divsn. Office of Chief Counsel, Washington, 1981-84; atty., advisor to Judge Joel Gerber U.S. Tax Ct., Washington, 1984-85; assoc. Dorsey & Whitney, Mpls., 1985-87, Parsinen Bowman Levy, Mpls., 1987-90, ptnr., 1990-95; judge Minn. Tax Ct., St. Paul, 1995—2001, chief judge, 1998—2001; judge U.S. Tax Ct., Washington, 2003—. Chair tax sect. Hennepin County Bar, Mpls., 1985—; mem. adv. bd. Hamline U., St. Paul, 1995—. Editor multi-vol. treatises on corps., 1995; contbr. articles to profl. jours. Legal advisor Minn. Women's Polit. Caucus, Minn. Women's Edn. Coun., St. Paul, 1989-91, Jr. League Mpls., 1991-93. Recipient Volunteer of Year Award, Jr. League of Minn., 1993. Mem.: Am. Judicature Soc., Nat. Assn. of Women Judges, Minn. State Bar Assn. (Disting. Service Award 2001, Cmty. Vol. of Year 1998), ABA. Avocations: children activities, computers, furniture refinishing, reading. Office: US Tax Ct 400 Second St Washington DC 20217

KRUC, ANTOINETTE CAMPION, family physician; b. Scranton, Pa., May 9, 1939; d. Robert Francis and Mary Elizabeth (Boyle) Campion; m. Peter John Kruc, Mar. 2, 1962 (div. Sept. 1973); children: Kathryn Anne, David Campion. BS, Phila. Coll. Pharmacy & Sci., 1961; DO, Phila. Coll. Osteo. Medicine, 1977. Rotating intern Osteo. Hosp., Phila.; physician/owner Spruce Hill Med. Assocs., Phila., 1978-95, Kruc/Palmerio Part, Phila., 1982-94; physician Allegheny Health Edn. and Rsch. Found., Phila., 1995—. Corp. mem. Pa.Blue Shield, Harrisburg, 1995—. Bd. dirs. West Cath. H.S., Phila., 1994—; spkr. Optimists-Overbrook, Phila., 1985—. Recipient Cmty. Svc. award Pa. House of Reps., 1983, Optimists Internat., 1993. Mem. POMA, POFPS, AC of GP, PCOS, Alpha Omega Alpha. Avocations: antiques and collectibles, sports memorabilia, reading, hiking.

KRUEGER, ANNE, economist; b. Endicott, NY; BA, Oberlin (Ohio) Coll., 1953; MS, U. Wis., 1956, PhD, 1958, Georgetown U., 1992; PhD (hon.), Hacettepe U., Ankara, Turkey, 1990, Monash U., 1995; D of Bus. (hon.), Melbourne Bus. Sch., 2004. From asst. prof. to prof. econs. U. Minn., Mpls., 1959—82; v.p. econs. and rsch. The World Bank, Washington, 1982-86; art and scis. prof. econs. Duke U., Durham, NC, 1987-93; Herald and Caroline L. Ritch prof arts and scis. in econs. Stanford (Calif.) U., 1993—2003, dir. Ctr. Rsch. Econ. Devel. and Policy Reform, 1996-2001; 1st dep. mng. dir. Internat. Monetary Fund, Washington, 2001—06, spl. adv. to mng. dir., 2006—. Vis. cons. dept. econs. Harvard U., 1990-98; sr. non-resident fellow Brookings Inst., 1990-92; rsch. assoc. Nat. Bur. Econs.; hon. prof. Acad. Nat. Economy, Moscow, 2004. Author: Trade Policies and Developing Nations, 1995, Economic Policies at Cross Purposes, 1993, Economic Policy Reform in Developing Countries, 1992, The Political Economy of Agricultural Pricing Policy, Vol. 5: A Synthesis of the Political Economy in Developing Countries, 1992, Economic Policy Reform: The Second Stage, 2000; co-author (with O. Aktan): Swimming Against the Tide: Turkish Trade Reform in the 1980s, 1992; editor: (with R.H. Bates) Political and Economic Interactions in Economic Policy Reform, 1993, The World Trade Organization as an International Institution, 1998, Economic Policy Reform: Second Stage, 2000, A New Approach to Sovereign Debt Restructuring, 2002, Economic Policy Reform and the Indian Economy, 2003, (with Jose Antonio Gonzales, Vittorio Corbo and Aaron Tornell) Latin American Macroeconomic Reform: The Second Stage, 2003, (with Sajjid Z. Chinoy) Reforming India's Economic, Financial and Fiscal Policies, 2003. Mem. N.Y. State Regents Commn. on Higher Edn., 1992-93. Recipient Robertson prize NAS, 1984, Bernhard Harms prize Inst. for World Economy, Kiel, 1990, Enterprise award Kenan Inst., 1990, Seidman prize, 1994; named Hon. Prof., Acad. Nat. Economy, Moscow, 2004. Fellow AAAS, Econometric Soc. (award 1984); mem. NAS, Am. Econ. Assn. (disting. fellow, chmn. com. rsch. 1988-92, chmn. commn. on grad. edn. in econs. 1989-90, v.p. 1977, pres.-elect 1995, pres. 1996, rep. to Internat. Econ. Assn. and mem. IEA exec. com. 1992-98, v.p. Internat. Econ. Assn. 1994-98). Office: Internat Monetary Fund 700 19th St NW Washington DC 20431

KRUEGER, BETTY ADEL, county official; b. Bellville, Tex., May 31, 1934; d. Roland Christian Krueger and Flora Margaret Stalbaum. Student, Blinn Jr. Coll., Tex. A&M U. Adminstrv. asst. to county sch. supt., Bellville, Tex., 1952-78; adminstrv. asst. to county judge, 1979-83; county treas. Austin County, Bellville, 1983—. Pres. Bellville Pub. Libr. Bd., 1992—; mem. Austin County Civic Chorale, 1989—. Named Woman of Yr. Bus. and Profl. Women Dist. 3, 1981. Mem. Pilot Club of Bellville (sec., pres. 1986—), Bellville VFW Aux., Woodmen of the World (dir.). Democrat. Lutheran. Avocations: bowling, playing cards, dominos, travel. Home: PO Box 723 Bellville TX 77418-0723

KRUEGER, BONNIE LEE, editor, writer; b. Chgo., Feb. 3, 1950; d. Harry Bernard and Lillian (Soyak) Krueger; m. James Lawrence Spurlock, Mar. 8, 1972. Student, Morraine Valley Coll., 1970. Adminstrv. asst. Carson Pirie Scott & Co., Chgo., 1969-72; traffic coord. Tatham Laird & Kudner, Chgo., 1973-74, J. Walter Thompson, Chgo., 1974-76, prodn. coord., 1976-78; editor-in-chief Assoc. Pubs., Chgo., 1978—, Sophisticate's Hairstyle Guide, 1978—, Sophisticate's Beauty Guide, 1978—, Complete Woman, 1981—; pub., editorial svcs. dir. Sophisticate's Black Hair Guide, 1983—, Sophisticate's Soap Star Styles, 1994-95. Active Statue of Liberty Restoration Com., NYC, 1983, Chgo. Architecture Found.; campaign worker Cook County State's Atty., Chgo., 1982; poll watcher Cook County Dem. Orgn., 1983. Recipient Exceptional Woman in Pub. award, Women in Periodical Pub., 2000. Mem. Soc. Profl. Journalists, Am. Health and Beauty Aids Inst. (assoc., Communicator of Yr. award), Lincoln Park Zool. Soc., Landmarks Preservation Coun. of Ill., Art Inst. Chgo., Chgo. Hist. Soc., Mus. Contemporary Art, Peta, Headline Club, PAWS (Pets Are Worth Saving), Sigma Delta Chi, City Club Chgo. Lutheran. Office: Complete Woman 875 N Michigan Ave Chicago IL 60611-1803 Office Phone: 312-266-8680. Business E-Mail: krueger@associatedpub.com.

KRUEGER, DEBORAH A. BLAKE, school psychologist, consultant; b. Chgo., Aug. 22, 1954; d. Stanley Walter and Maryanne Lois Blake; m. Darrell George Krueger, May 31, 1986; children: Sarah, Joshua. BA, DePaul U., 1976, MEd, 1980; PhD, Loyola U., 1998. Lic. sch. psychologist Ill. Learning disabilities specialist Assocs. in Family Therapy, Lake Bluff, Ill., 1980-85; reading and learning disabilities specialist Proviso West H.S., Hillside, Ill., 1980-82; edn. therapist Hartgrove Hosp., Chgo., 1982-85; dir. spl. edn. Old Orchard Hosp., Skokie, Ill., 1985-87; program coord. One-to-One Learning Ctr., Northfield, Ill., 1995-98; sch. psychologist Winnetka (Ill.) Pub. Schs., 1997—. Cons. Naperville and Woodridge Schs., 1998—; lectr. Loyola U., Chgo., 1997—; pvt. practice, Northbrook, 2000—; third party cons. hartgrove Psychol. Hosp., Chgo., 1985—88, Old Orchard Psychol. Hosp., Skokie, 1987—89; co-founder Baby N'Me Mother-Infant Dyad Groups, 1991; spkr. Resolve Orgn., Good Samaritan Hosp., Downers Grove, Ill., 1991; global initiative del. partipant to Eastern Europe, 2004. Founder Living with Infertility and Experimentation, Evanston, Ill., 1990—96, mem. steering com., 1990—94. Grantee, Loyola U., 1996. Mem.: APA, Ill. Assn. Infant Mental Health, Ill. Sch. Psychol. Assn., Soc. Personality Assessment, Nat. Assn. Sch. Psychologists, Assn. Advancement Therapeutic Edn. Avocations: piano, exercise, reading, local school involvement. Home: 2434 Ridgeway Ave Evanston IL 60201-1858 Office: Winnetka Pub Schs 520 Glendale Ave Winnetka IL 60093-2135 also: 910 Skokie Blvd Northbrook IL 60062 Office Phone: 847-604-4160. Personal E-mail: DbKrueger@aol.com.

KRUEGER, MARLO BUSH, retired lawyer; b. Little Rock, Sept. 5, 1956; d. James Shepherd Bush and Frances Rosannah Davidson; m. James Robert Krueger, Sept. 15, 2001. BS in Pub. Adminstrn., U. Ark., Fayetteville, 1978, JD, 1981. Bar: (Ark.) 1981. Asst. reporter decisions Ark. Supreme Ct. and Ct. of Appeals, Little Rock, 1982—88, reporter decisions, 1988—95, interim reporter decisions, 2006. Articles editor (jour.) The Saline (Best Edited Documentary award, 1994, Dale Bumpers award for best Civil War article, 1994, Best Comty. History Pub. in Local Jour. award, 2000). Mem., sec. Saline County History and Heritage Soc., 1994—95; mem. various bds. and coms. 1st Meth. Ch., Benton, 1984—89, 1992—93. Mem.: Ark. Bar Assn., Assn. Reporters of Jud. Decisions (various coms., exec. bd. 1987—94, pres. 1992—93, Devoted Svc. award 1995), Phi Delta Phi (clk. 1980—81). Meth. Avocations: genealogy, fishing, computers, photography, history. Home: 4011 Hwy 5 Benton AR 72015-8277 Personal E-mail: krueger@uplink.net.

KRUEGLER, CATHERINE A., sister, parochial school educator; d. James Lawrence Kruegler and Rose Mary Catherine Maloney. AS, Hudson Valley C.C., 1972; BS cum laude, Coll. St. Rose, 1977; MA, Boston Coll., 1988. Cert. tchr. N.Y. Educator St. Paul's Sch., Norwich, NY, 1972—75, Mechanicville, NY, 1977—79; pastoral minister St. Anthony's Ch., Syracuse, NY, 1979—86, Sacred Heart Ch., Mercedes, Tex., 1986—87, Prince of Peace Ch., Lyford, Tex., 1987—91; dir. religious edn. St. Patrick's Ch., Albany, NY, 1991—97; theology tchr. Cohoes (N.Y.) Cath. Sch., 1997—98, Saratoga (N.Y.) Cath. Sch., 1999—2002; liason labor Free the Children, Albany, 2001—02; svc. learning coord. Acad. of Holy Names, Albany, 2003—05. Bd. dirs. Urban Ministry Bd., Syracuse, 1982—86; del. mem. Witness for Peace, Nicaragua, 1985, 1990, s. ctrl. coord. Brownsville, Tex., 1990, Sisters Coun. Leadership, 1987—91; bd. dirs. St. Casimir's Sch., Albany, 1992—94. Recipient Svc. award, St. Patrick's Ch. and Hispanic Apostolate, N.Y., 1997; scholar, Hispanic Apostolate, N.Y., 1994. Mem.: Pax Christi. Democrat. Roman Catholic. Achievements include internat. observer election, Nicaragua, 1990; mem. del. kidnapped Flotilla for Peace, 1985. Avocations: reading, photography, pottery, gardening, skiing. Office: Acad of Holy Names 1075 New Scotland Rd Albany NY 12208 Office Phone: 518-438-7895. Business E-Mail: sckruegler@ahns.org.

KRUGER, BARBARA, artist, art critic; b. Newark, Jan. 26, 1945; Student, Syracuse U., Parsons Sch. Design, N.Y.C., Sch. Visual Arts. Illustrator Condé Nast Publs., N.Y.C., 1967-68, chief designer Mademoiselle mag., 1968-72. Film critic Artforum; vis. artist Calif. Inst. Art, Art Inst. Chgo., U. Calif., Berkeley; prof. art dept. UCLA; arranger collections Pictures and Promises, The Kitchen, N.Y.C., 1981, Artists' Use of Lang., Franklin Furnace, N.Y.C., 1983, Creative Perspectives in Am. Photography, Hallwall's Gallery, Buffalo, 1983. Author: Picture/Readings, 1979, No Progress in Pleasure, 1982; one-woman shows Crousel/Hussenot Gallery, Paris, 1987, Monika Spruth Gallery, Cologne, Germany, 1987, 90, Nat. Art Gallery, Wellington, New Zealand, 1988, Mary Boone Gallery, N.Y.C., 1989, Galerie Bebert, Rotterdam, The Netherlands, 1989, Fred Hoffman Gallery, Santa Monica, Calif., 1989, Duke U. Mus. Art, Durham, N.C., 1990, Whitney Mus. Modern Art, Mus. Contemporary Art, Chgo., Mus. Contemporary Art, L.A., 1999, numerous others; exhibited in group shows Whitney Mus. Am. Art, N.Y.C., 1973, 82, 83, 85, 87, 89, Castello di Rivoli, Turin, Italy, 1989, Pa. Acad. Fine Arts, Phila., 1989, Denver Art Mus., 1989, Mus. 20th Century, Vienna, Austria, 1989, Ctr. Georges Pompidou, Paris, 1989, Mus. Contemporary Art, L.A., 1989, Rheinhalle, Cologne, 1989, Frankfurt (Germany) Kunstverein and Schirn Kunsthalle, 1989, also numerous others; work represented in various publs. Grantee Creative Artists Svc. Program, 1976-77, Nat. Endowment Arts, 1983-84; Golden Lion award lifetime achievement, Venice Biennial, 2005. Office: Mary Boone Gallery 745 5th Ave Ste 405 New York NY 10151-0401 also: UCLA Department of Art Ste 245 11000 Kinross Ave Los Angeles CA 90095*

KRUGER, LEONDRA R., lawyer; AB magna cum laude, Harvard Univ., 1997; JD, Yale Univ., 2001. Bar: Calif. Law clk. U.S. Ct. Appeals (D.C. cir.), Washington, 2002—03; law clk. to Hon. John Paul Stevens U.S. Supreme Ct., Washington, 2003; assoc. Jenner & Block, Washington, Wilmer Cutler Pickering Hale & Dorr, Washington, 2004—. Editor-in-chief The Yale Law Joun. Mem.: Phi Beta Kappa. Office: Wilmer Cutler Pickering Hale & Dorr 2445 M St NW Washington DC 20037

KRUGER, PAULA, telecommunications industry executive; b. Bklyn., July 31, 1950; d. Jean Jacques Kruger and Jo Campione; m. Lawrence C. Heller; children: Michael, Tracy, Jessica. BA, CW Post, 1972, MBA, 1976. V.p. customer rels. Cablevision, Woodbury, NY, 1994—97; corp. v.p. customer svc. Am. Express, N.Y.C., Citibank, N.Y.C., v.p. devel. divsn.; v.p. consumer svcs. group South Korea; v.p. teleservices Excel Comm., 1997—99, exec. v.p., customer and independent representative ops., 1999; gen. mgr. customer relationship mgmt. service line Electronic Data Systems Corp., 2002—03; exec. v.p. consumer markets group Qwest Comm., 2003—. Office: Qwest Comm Internat 1801 California St Denver CO 80202

KRUGMAN, MARIAN G., retired librarian; d. Samuel and Bertha Gold; m. Arnold David Krugman (dec.); children: Janet, Neil, Craig, Meredith. BA, L.I. U., Bklyn., 1948; MSLS, N.C. U., Chapel Hill, 1968. Cert. poetry therapist Nat. Assn. Poetry Therapy. Sch. libr. Durham Acad., NC, 1968—69; libr. Sch. of Pub. Health, Dept. Environmental Scis., U. N.C., Chapel Hill, 1969—74; patent libr. VA Med. Ctr., Lyons, NJ, 1975—96. With USMC, 1944—46. Mem.: Nat. Assn. Poetryy Therapy. Home: 76 Forest Dr Durham NC 27705 Personal E-mail: mkrugman@nc.rr.com.

KRULEWICZ, RITA GLORIA, special education educator; d. Charles Lewis and Gloria Edna Perrine; m. Donald Joseph Krulewicz; 1 child, Clare. BS, Coll. Misericordia, 1976; MEd, Trenton State Coll., 1979. Multihandicapped tchr. The Woods Sch., Langhorne, Pa., 1976-79, Mercer County Spl. Svcs. Sch. Dist., Hamilton, NJ, 1979-86; resource ctr. tchr. Princeton (N.J.) Regional Sch. Dist., 1992—, John Witherspoon Mid. Sch., Princeton, 1992—. Worker Dem. Orgn., Pa., 1976—; mem. Morrisville Hist. Soc., 1976—. Named Tchr. of Yr. Mercer County Spl. Svcs., 1986. Mem.: NEA, Coun. Exceptional Children (professionally recognized spl. edn. 1999—), N.J. Edn. Assn., Kappa Delta Pi. Roman Catholic. Avocations: reading, gardening, surfing the net, going to movies, travel. Home: 136 Carlisle Ave Yardville NJ 08620-1244 Office: John Witherspoon Mid Sch 217 Walnut Ln Princeton NJ 08540-3484

KRULFELD, RUTH MARILYN, anthropologist, educator; m. Jacob Mendel Krulfeld, 1964; 1 child, Michael David. BA cum laude, Brandeis U., 1956; PhD, Yale U., 1974. Field rschr. micro-geog. rsch. farms, Singapore, Malaya, 1951-53; anthrop. rschr., Jamaica, 1957, Costa Rica, Nicaragua, Panama, 1958, Sasak of Lombok, Indonesia, 1960—63, 1993; anthrop. rschr. S.E. Asian refugees to U.S., 1981—; anthrop. rschr., Lombok, Indonesia and N.E. Thailand, 1993; asst. prof. anthropology, dir. grad. students George Washington U., Washington, 1964-72, 93-97, assoc. prof., 1973-76, prof., 1976-2000, chmn. dept. anthropology, 1984-87, founder spl. grad. program in internat. world devel., prof. anthropology, internat. affairs, prof. emeritus anthropology, human scis., internat. affairs, 2000—. Bd. dir. No. Va. Humanities Coun., Internat. Buddhist Com.; rschr. Laotian refugees in U.S., 1981-, also rschr. on culture change in villages in Indonesia; bd. dirs. Newcomers Cmty. Svc. Ctr.; mem. bd. advisors Lao-Am. Women's Assn., Lao Cmty. Forum; mem. faculty Semester At Sea, 1999, 2003; bd. dir. Successful New Ams. Project, S.E. Asian Resource Action Ctr Co-author: Reconstructing Lives, Recapturing Meaning: Refugee Identity, Gender and Culture Change, 1994, Beyond Boundaries: Selected papers on Refugees and Immigrants, 1997, Power, Ethics, and Human Rights: Anthropological Studies of Refugee Research and Action, 1998; contbr. articles to profl. jours.; editl. bd. com. on refugees and immigrants. Currier scholar Yale U., 1958; Ford fellow, 1960-62; grantee Found. for Study of Man, 1957, Am. Coun., 1963, Cotlow faculty rsch. grantee, 1992-93, faculty rsch. grantee George Washington U., 1992-93, rsch. grantee Va. Found. for Humanities and Pub. Policy, 1995-96; recipient Banneker award Ctr. for Washington Area Studies, 1996, George Washington U. award for Pedigogical Rsch. and Devel. in Edn., award for Outstanding Contributions to U. and Wider Soc., 2000. Mem. AAAS (com. on sci. freedom and responsibility), Anthrop. Soc. Washington, Am. Anthrop. Assn. (nominating com., com. on refugee issues gen. anthropology divsn., vice chair com. on refugee issues 1992-94, gen. anthropology divsn. 1993-94, exec. bd. com. on refugees and immigrants 1994-99, CORI editl. bd. 1998-99, CORI award for best paper on refugees issues 1992, Pedagogical Rsch. and Innovative Devel. in Edn. award 1994, award for leadership and contbn. to refugee studies com. on refugees and immigrants 2000). Office: George Washington U Dept Anthropology Washington DC 20052-0001

KRULIK, BARBARA S., prodution manager, curator, art director, writer; b. N.Y.C., June 13, 1955; d. Herbert Arnold and Irene Sylvia K. BA in Art History, Pa. State U., 1976; MA in Museology, Reinwardt Acad., Amsterdam, The Netherlands, 2000. Asst. to dir. NAD, N.Y.C., 1976—78, acting dir., 1977-78, coord. exhbns., 1978-83, asst. dir., 1983-89, interim dir., 1989-90, dep. dir., 1990-92; assoc. dir. Forum Gallery, N.Y.C., 1992-94; dir. Grad. Sch. Figurative Art New York Acad. Art, N.Y.C., 1994-97; owner, dir. KCCS (Krulik Cultural Cons. Svs.), 2001—; mgr. Magpie Music Dance Co., Amsterdam, Netherlands, 2003—, Streettheater Co. Warner en Consorten, Amsterdam; mem. steering com. Found. Exhbn. Man, Amsterdam, Netherlands, 2004—; prodn. mgr. No Apology, Amsterdam, 2004—05, Cinedans, 2006, Bodies Anonymous, Amsterdam, 2006. Ind. curator, 1997—; cons., 1997—. Author, editor exhbn. catalogues. Mem. Am. Assn. Mus. (curators and registrars coms.), Internat. Coun. on Mus. Office Phone: 011 31 6 29242947. Personal E-mail: b.krulik@chello.nl.

KRUM, DEE, secondary school educator; b. Maquoketa, Iowa, Jan. 6, 1958; d. Wayne Richard and Marilyn Joyce Williams; m. Roy Leon Krum, Dec. 6, 1980; children: Bobby Lee, Joey Leon. BA in English Edn., Iowa Wesleyan Coll., Mt. Pleasant, 1980, postgrad., 1980. Jr. high lang. arts tchr. St. Joseph Sch., DeWitt, Iowa, 1983—91; English, theater tchr. West Ctrl. HS, Maynard, Iowa, 1991—2005; speech, theater tchr. Maquoketa (Iowa) HS, 2005—. Libr. bd. Maynard Pub. Libr., 1994—98; adv. bd. West Central Sch., Maynard, 1996—2002, sch. to work adv., 1996—2005. Mem.: Iowa HS Speech Assn., Educators of Theater Arts, Nat. Forsenics League. Democrat. Home: 309 W Monroe Maquoketa IA 52060

KRUMHOLZ, MIMI, human resources administrator; b. N.Y.C., Aug. 7, 1954; d. Jack Walter and Ida Judith (Intrator) Jerome; m. Andrew Jay Krumholz, Aug. 15 1991; children: Matthew, Aaron, Paul. BA in Edn., SUNY, Stony Brook, 1976, BS in Psychology, 1976; MS in Clin. Psychology, Towson State U., Md., 1982. Paralegal Donovan, Leisure, N.Y.C., 1976-77; human resource mgr. Dynatech Data sys., Springfield, Va, 1977-80; human resource dir. Calif. Milling Corp., L.A., 1980-81, Providence Ctr., Arnold, Md, 1986-88, Dewey, Ballantine, Washington, 1988-90; legal adminstr. Latham & Watkins, Washington, 1990—, dir. profl. devel., 1999—, dir. human resources, 2000—. Mem. Assn. Legal Adminstrs, Soc. Human Resources Mgmt., Am. Soc. Training and Devel. Avocations: reading, swimming, writing. E-mail: mimi.krumholz@lw.com.

KRUMREY, CAROLYN, mechanical engineer; married. BSME, U. Tex.; M in Environ. Mgmt., U. Houston. Divsn. chief engr. space shuttle NASA Johnson Space Ctr., Houston. Avocations: aerobics, weightlifting, hiking, skiing, running. Office: NASA Johnson Space Ctr 2101 NASA Rd 1 Houston TX 77058-3696

KRUPANSKY, BLANCHE ETHEL, retired judge; b. Cleve., Dec. 10, 1925; d. Frank and Anna K.; m. Frank W. Vargo, Apr. 30, 1960. AB, Flora Stone Mather Coll., 1943-47; JD, Case Western Res. U., 1948, LLM, 1966. Bar: Ohio 1949. Gen. practice law, 1949-61, 83-84; asst. atty. gen. State of Ohio; asst. chief counsel Ohio Bur. Workmen's Compensation; judge Cleve. Mcpl. Ct., 1961-69; judge Common Pleas Ct. Cuyahoga County, 1969-77, Ct. Appeals Ohio 8th Appellate Dist., 1977-81; justice Supreme Ct. Ohio, 1981-83; judge 8th Dist. Ct. Appeals, 1984—95, chief justice, 1991; ret.,

1995. Vis. com. Case Western U. Law Sch., 1974-78, bd. govs., 1975-76; mem. adv. com. Akron State U., 1982-85, vis. com., 1982-86. Mem. adv. com. Akron State U., 1982—85, mem. vis. com., 1982—86. Recipient Outstanding Jud. Service award Supreme Ct. Ohio, 1972-76, Law Book scholar award Cuyahoga Women's Polit. Caucus, 1981, outstanding contbn. to law award Ohio Assn. Civil Trial Attys., 1982, Disting. Alumna award, 1982, Disting. Service award Women's Space, 1982, award Democratic Women's Caucus, 1983, award Women's Equity Action League Ohio, 1983; Personal Achievement and Community Svc. award Case We. Res. U., 1988, Margaret Ireland award Women's City Club, 1984; named Woman of Achievement Inter-Club Council Cleve., 1969; inducted into Ohio Women's Hall of Fame, 1981 Mem. Nat. Assn. Women Lawyers, Nat. Assn. Women Judges, Ohio Bar Assn. (Cronise Lutes award 1997), Bar Assn. Greater Cleve., Cuyahoga County Bar Assn., Cleve. Women Lawyers, LWV, Ohio Ctrs. of Appeals Assn., Ohio Assn. Attys. Gen., Ohio Appellate Judges Assn., Soc. of Benchers (chair 1994-95), SAR (Silver Medal award 1995). Republic. Roman Catholic. Club: Woman's City (Woman of Achievement award 1981) (Cleve.).

KRUPCHAK, TAMARA, artist; b. Lake Station, Ind., Apr. 15, 1956; d. John Charles Krupchak and Rose Marie Maretich-Krupchak. BS, Ball State U., 1978. Artist, spkr., creativity coach Tamara Krupchak Fine Art, San Diego, 1988—. Group shows include San Diego Tijuana Yokohama Art Exchange, 1992, San Diego Mus. Art, 1994, 97, 98, 99; artist (book) Getting Exposure, 1995. Bd. dirs. artist guild San Diego Mus. Art, 1994-97, trustee, 1996-97; mem. nat. devel. com. Coll. Fine Arts, Ball State U., 2001. Recipient art commn. St. Mary's Health and Learning Ctr., Grand Rapids, Mich., 1998, Sunland Christian Sci. Healing Ctr., San Diego, 1998. Mem. Toastmasters Internat. (winner Area 21 Internat. Speech Contest 1998). Home: 12869 Starwood Ln San Diego CA 92131-4211

KRUPIT, ALISON, elementary school educator; b. Orange, NJ, Aug. 4, 1958; d. Bert and Barbara Krupit; children: Troy Kuersten, Kyle Kuersten. Degree in Acctg., Penn State, 1980. Cert. clear multi-subject Dept. Edn., CA, tchr. Simpson U. Acct. Fed. Res. Bank, N.Y.C., 1980—82; tchr. Cmty. Edn., Quakenbruck, Artland, Germany, 1985—87; tchr. aide Enterprise Sch. Dist., Redding, Calif., 1990—94; tchr. Bella Vista (Calif.) Elem. Sch., 1996—2000, Redding Sch. Arts, 2000—. Acct. World Savs., Oakland, Calif., 1988—89. Publicity Friends of Shasta County Libr., Redding, 1992—2004. Recipient Acctg., Penn State, 1980. Mem.: AAUW (assoc.). Avocations: paddling, hiking, reading, travel. Office: Redding Sch of Arts 2200 Eureka Way Redding CA 96001 Office Phone: 530-247-6933. Business E-Mail: akrupit@suhsd.net.

KRUSA-DOSSIN, MARY ANN, military officer; m. Paul F. Dossin; 1 child, Michael. BA in Psychology and Sociology, Tex. Christian U., 1974; MS in Human Rels., Golden Gate U., 1981; MS in Nat. Resource Planning, Nat. Def. U., 1995. Commd. 2d lt. USMC, 1975, advanced through grades to brig. gen., platoon comdr. security dept. MCAS El Toro, 1976—79, tng. and human affairs officer Aircraft Group 15, 1st Marine Aircraft Wing, 1979—81, ops. officer provost marshal's office Iwakuni, Japan, 1979—81, dir. family svc. ctr. Camp Lejeune, 1981—84, with provost marshal's office, 1984—85, provost marshal MCAS Yuma, Ariz., 1988—91, exec. offier Hdqrs. and svc. battalion MCB Camp Smedley D. Butler Okinawa, Japan, 1992—93, comdr., 1993—96, action officer joint staff J-7 operational plans and interoperability directorate Pentagon, 1996—98, comdr. security battalion MCB Camp Pendleton, 1998—2000, asst. chief of staff cmty. svcs. MCB Camp Pendleton, 2000—02, dep. dir. Marine Corps Pub. Affairs, 2002—03, dir. Marine Corps. Pub. Affairs, 2003—. Decorated Legion of Merit. Home: 1200 Crystal Dr Apt 412 Arlington VA 22202-4305

KRUSE, ANN GRAY, computer programmer; b. Oklahoma City, Jan. 4, 1941; d. Floyd and Bernice Florence (Follansbee) Gray; m. Roy Edwin Kruse, Mar. 20, 1971 (dec.). AB, Randolph Macon Woman's Coll., 1963; MBA, U. Chgo., 1973. Programming mgr. Ind. Info. Controls, Valparaiso, Ind., 1966-67; systems programmer Am. Steel Foundries, Hammond, Ind., 1970-73; engr. applications programming Bell Helicopter Textron, Fort Worth, 1974-76; lead systems programmer Harris Data Communications, Dallas, 1976-81; sr. systems programmer Lone Star Gas Co., Dallas, 1981-82; sr. software specialist Raytheon, Dallas, 1982—. Republican. Episcopalian. Home: 6128 Black Berry Ln Dallas TX 75248-4909 Office: PO Box 660023 Dallas TX 75266-0023 E-mail: akruse@gsb.uchicago.edu.

KRUSE, DORIS EVELYN, counselor; b. Marion, Ky., Aug. 9, 1942; d. Bartley R. and Edith M. Winters; children: Richard E., Timothy W.; m. Terry A. Kruse, May 26, 1984. Cert. domestic violence counselor, addiction counselor, criminal justice specialist, master addiction counselor. Prison counselor RMBH, Canon City, Colo., 1977-81; social svcs. counselor El Paso County, Colorado Springs, 1981-82; DUI counselor Uplift Awareness, 1980-83; outpatient dir. Penrose Hosp., Colorado Springs, 1984-88; program developer Mercy Hosp., Denver, 1988-91; program dir. Running Creek Counseling, Franktown, Colo., 1988—, program dir., edn. specialist, 1988—. Mem. Douglas County DV Task Force. Recipient Bonnie Forguer award Sch. of Addictive Behavior, 1997. Mem. Nat. Assn. Alcoholism and Drug Abuse Counselors, Substance Abuse Counselors of Colo., Rocky Mountain Behavioral Health. Avocations: reading, writing, gardening, grandmothering. Office: Running CreeK Counseling Svc PO Box 776 Franktown CO 80116-0776

KRUSE, MARGARET M., art educator; b. Cape Girardeau, Mo., June 9, 1935; d. Arthur Lawrence Fuerth and Corona Ann Heisserer; m. Frederic Wallace Kruse, Nov. 25, 1960; children: Constance Katheryn, Valerie Anne. BS in Secondary Edn., State U. S.E. Mo., 1957; MEd in Art, Webster U., 1994. Tchr. art St. Charles (Mo.) HS, 1958—59, Bayless HS, St. Louis, 1959—66, Parkway S. Jr. HS, St. Louis, 1967—69, Ladue Sch. Dist., St. Louis, 1969—73, Immacotata Sch., St. Louis, Our Lady of Pillar, St. Louis, 1985—. Mem.: Nat. Cath. Edn. Assn., Mo. Art Edn. Assn., Nat. Art Edn. Assn. Home: 164 Saddleford Dr Chesterfield MO 63017

KRUSE, MARYLIN LYNN, retired language educator; b. Kansas City, Mo., June 26, 1940; d. Mildred Marie Goetsch; m. Richard Lee Weinberg, Dec. 26, 1962 (div. Oct. 1988); children: Eric H., Kerstin I; m. Leon Edward Kruse, Dec. 28, 1998. BA, Cornell Coll., Mt. Vernon, Iowa, 1962; MA, Marycrest Coll., Davenport, Iowa, 1982. Tchr. English Galesburg Cmty. Schs., Ill., 1962—63, Grant Cmty. Schs., Fox Lake, Ill., 1963—64, Saydel Cmty. Schs., Des Moines, 1965—66; instr. English Grandview Coll., Des Moines, 1966—76; behavior disorders cons. We. Ill. Assn., Galesburg, 1976—77; coord. prevocational Knox-Warren Spl. Edn. Dist., Galesburg, 1977—78; tchr. Spanish Winola Cmty. Schs., Viola, Ill., 1979—80; tchr. spl. edn. Pleasant Valley Cmty. Schs., Iowa, 1980—86; instr. English Ea. Iowa C.C. Dist., Davenport, 1983—86; tchr. spl. edn. Davenport Cmty. Schs., 1986—94, tchr. fgn. lang., 1994—2002, ret., 2002. Adj. instr. English Daytona Beach C.C., Fla. Co-author: Parent Prerogatives, 1979. Recipient Tchr. Incentive award State of Iowa Dept. Edn., 1982; chpt. II grant U.S. Office of Edn., Williams Jr. High, 1988. Mem.: Audubon Soc. Republican. Presbyterian. Avocations: bird watching, reading. Home: 3023 S Atlantic Ave 807 Daytona Beach FL 32118-6157 Office Phone: 386-506-3912. E-mail: krusel@dbcc.edu.

KRUSE, RONIA, information technology executive; b. 1970; MS in Taxation, Wayne State U., 1994. Lectr. Wayne State U.; sr. tax cons. Deloitte & Touche L.L.P., 1995—99; pres., CEO OpTech L.L.C., Detroit, 1999—. Named one of 40 Under 40, Crain's Detroit Bus., 2006. Office: OpTech LLC Guardian Bldg 500 Griswold Ste 1690 Detroit MI 48226 Office Phone: 313-962-9000. Office Fax: 313-962-9001.*

KRUSEMARK, JANICE WELLS, physicial education educator; d. James and Mary Wells; m. Steven W. Krusemark, Nov. 25, 1983; children: Elyana Wells, Justin Wells, Jacqueline Wells. BA, Mich. State U., 1978. Cert. tcht. Mass., 1983. Physical edn. tchr. Newburyport (Mass.) Pub. Schs., 2000—. Com. mem. Elem. Space Needs Com., Newburyport, Mass., 2000—02. Mem.: MAHPERD (assoc.; sec. 2004—05). Home: 78 Lime St Newburyport MA 01950 Personal E-mail: janicewk@comcast.net.

KRUSICK, MARGARET ANN, state legislator; b. Milw., Oct. 26, 1956; d. Ronald J. and Maxine C. K. BA, U. Wis., 1978; postgrad., U. Wis., Madison, 1979-82. Legal asst. Milw. Law Office, 1973-78; teaching asst. U. Wis., Milw., 1978-79; staff mem. Govs. Ombudsman Program for the Aging & Disabled, Madison, Wis., 1980; administrv. asst. Wis. Higher Edn. Aids Bd., Madison, 1981; legis. aide Wis. Assembly, Madison, 1982-83, state rep., 1983—. Author: Wisconsin Youth Suicide Prevention Act, 1985, Wisconsin Nursing Home Reform Act, 1987, Wisconsin Truancy Reform Act, 1988, Elder Abuse Fund, 1989, Stolen Goods Recovery Act, 1990, Fair Prescription Drug Pricing Act, 1994, Anti-Graffiti Act, 1996, Caregiver Criminal Background Checks and Abuse Prevention Act, 1997, Child Abuse Prosecution Act, 1998, Nursing Home Resident Protection Act, 1998, Seniorcare Prescription Drug Program, 2002, Criminal Background Checks for School Van and Bus Drivers, 2003, Child Protection and Clergy Abuse Reporting Act, 2004, Child Support Collection Act, 2004. Mem. St. Gregory Great Cath. Ch., Milw., 1960—, Dem. Party, Milw., 1980—; bd. dirs. Alzheimer's Assn., 1986-88. Named Legislator of Yr. award Wis. Sch. Counselors, Madison, 1986, Wis. County Constnl. Officers Legislator of Yr., 1999; recipient Sr. Citizen Appreciation Allied Coun. for Sr. Milw., 1987, Crime Prevention award Milw. Police Dept., Milw., 1988, Cert. Appreciation, Milw. Pub. Sch., 1989, Friends of Homecare award, 1989, Environ. Decades' Clean 16 award, 1986-90, 95-96, Badger State Sheriff's Law and Order award, 1993, Appreciation award Coalition of Wis. Aging Groups, 1998, 2001. Mem. Jackson Park Neighborhood Assn.(Wis. Coun. Sr. Citizens award, 2003), U. Milw. Alumni Assn. (trustee 1986-90). Achievements include development of Alliance for attendance truancy abatement task force, which led to the Govenores state call to action to end child abuse and neglect. Office: Wis Assembly State Capitol Madison WI 53702-0001 Home: 128 N State Capital PO Box 8952 Madison WI 53708 Business E-Mail: rep.kusick@legis.state.wi.us.

KRUTSCH, PHYLLIS, academic administrator; MS, U. Wis. Regent U. Wis., 1990—97, 2000—, chmn. edn. com., 1994—97, chmn. com. bd. effectiveness. Grantee, Bradley Found. Mailing: 727 Superior Ave Washburn WI 54891

KRYGER, JERRI RENEE, elementary school educator; b. Tucson, Oct. 27, 1961; d. Arthur Alex and Donna Lee Elias; m. Richard C. Kryger, June 28, 1986. BA, Ariz. State U., Tempe, 1985. Cert. elem. edn. Ariz., ESL endorsment Ariz. Classroom teacher 1st and 2d grades Gadsden Dist. #32, San Luis, Ariz., 1985—2004; computer tchr. K-6 Ariz. Desert Sch., San Luis, 2004—05; computer tchr. SW Jr. High, San Luis, 2005—. Asst. swim coach Yuma HS, Ariz., 1986—93; head swim coach So. Ariz. Sandsharks, Yuma, 1995—2002; swim coach Kofa HS, Yuma, 1995—2005. Pres. Gadsden Edn. Assn., San Luis, 2004—06. Fellow: Ariz. Edn. Assn. (assoc.). Home: 2218 W Brook St Yuma AZ 85364 Office: SW Jr High 963 N 8th Ave San Luis AZ 85349 Office Phone: 928-627-6580.

KRYSHTALOWYCH, HELEN ZWENYSLAWA, lawyer; b. Fed. Republic Germany, Nov. 27, 1945; came to U.S., 1950; d. Jaroslaw Gregory and Jaroslawa (Czorniak) K. BABS, Ohio State U., 1967; EdM, Kent State U., 1971; JD, Cleve. State U., 1980. Bar: Ohio 1980, U.S. Dist. Ct. (no. dist.) Ohio 1981, U.S. Ct. Appeals (6th cir.) 1981. Tchr. English East Tech. High Sch., Cleve., 1967-69; psychiat. social worker Fallsview Mental Health Ctr., Cuyahoga Falls, Ohio, 1971-73; counselor Chagrin Falls (Ohio) High Sch., 1973-80; assoc. Squire, Sanders & Dempsey, Cleve., 1980-89, ptnr., 1989—. Trustee Epilepsy Found. N.E. Ohio, Cleve., 1989; dir. Ukrainian-Mus. Archives, Cleve., 1991. Mem. ABA (internat. law and practice sect.), Ohio State Bar Assn. (employment law and sch. law coms.), Cleve. Bar Assn. (internat. law group), Ukrainian Am. Bar Assn. Avocation: languages. Office: Squire Sanders & Dempsey 4900 Society Ctr 127 Public Sq Ste 4900 Cleveland OH 44114-1304 E-mail: hkryshtalowych@ssd.com.

KRZTON, NANCY L., lawyer, writer; d. Henry Charles and Jane Daly Wechsler; children: Alicia, Amelia. BA in Speech Comm. cum laude, Allegheny Coll., 1975; JD magna cum laude, U. Pitts., 1984. Bar: Pa. 1984. Pub. svc. dir., copy writer Sta. WLIO-TV, Lima, Ohio, 1975—76; news dir. Sta. KDLK-FM, Del Rio, Tex., 1976—78; reporter Del Rio News-Herald, 1978—79; editor, reporter Ben Lomond Beacon, Roy, Utah, 1979—80; assoc. atty. Kirkpatrick & Lockhart, Pitts., 1984—88; ptnr. Krzton & Krzton, Tarentum, Pa., 1988—2003; law clk. Ct. Common Pleas, Kittanning, Pa., 2004—. Mem. law review U. Pitts., 1982—83, law review note editor, 1983—84. Bd. dirs. Allegheny Valley Hosp., Natrona Heights, 1995—98, Allegheny Valley YMCA, Natrona Heights, Pa., 1988—90, Adv. Bd. on Autism and Related Disorders, Pitts., 1998—99. Recipient 1st pl. newspaper feature series, AP Mng. Editors Assn. Tex., 1979, Edwin O. Ochester Undergrad. Poetry award, U. Pitts., 2002. Mem.: Order of Coif. Democrat. Avocations: poetry, travel. Home: 1410 Pacific Ave Natrona Heights PA 15065 Office: Armstrong County Ct Common Pleas Kittanning PA

KRZYKOWSKI, JAMIE LEE, education educator; d. James and Jean Calman; m. Mark Allen Krzykowski, July 3, 1999; children: Savannah, Sydney. BS in Pre-Physical Therapy and Athletic Tng., NW Nazarene U., Idaho, 1996; MS in Sports Medicine and Exercise Physiology, U.S. Sports Acad., Ala., 1999; PhD in Holistic Nutrition, Clayton Coll. of Natural Health, Birminham, 2004—. Cert. Athletic Trainer Nat. Athletic Trainer's Assn., 1997, Profl. Rescuer, AED, and First Aid Instr. ARC, 1999, EMT Nat. Registry of EMT's, 2001, Nutritional Specialist Lifestyle Mgmt. Inc., 2001. Instr. phys. edn. Mt. Vernon Nazarene Coll., Ohio, 1998—99; grad. asst. athletic trainer, med. asst. U. Wis. Hosps. and Clinics, Madison, 1999—2001; head athletic trainer Mt. Horeb HS, Wis., 1999—2001; assoc. prof., athletic trainer Olivet Nazarene U., Bourbonnais, Ill., 2001—03; athletic trainer, adj. prof. kinesiology Elmhurst Coll., Ill., 2003—06; adj. prof. natural and health scis. Carroll Coll., Waukesha, Wis., 2006—. Presenter (nutrition presentation) Making Healthy Lifestyle Choices that will Last a Lifetime. Advisor, participant Elmhurst Coll. Habitat for Humanity, Oklahoma City, 2004—05, Albany, Ga., 2005—06. Mem.: Wis. Athletic Trainers Affiliated Credentialing Bd., State of Ill. Dept. Profl. Regulation, ARC, Nat. Registry of Emergency Med. Technicians, Wis. Athletic Trainers Assn., Ill. Athletic Trainers Assn., Gt. Lakes Athletic Trainers Assn., Nat. Athletic Trainers Assn. Achievements include research in Adolescent Female Use of Creatine; Study Coordinator, Covance Success IIa Celebrex Ankle Sprain Study; Case study Knee Injury - Football.

KRZYZAN, JUDY LYNN, automotive executive; b. Buffalo, Sept. 1, 1951; d. James Lambert and Janet Lucille (Grabau) McKellar; m. Ronald Edward Krzyzan, Dec. 21, 1974 (div. Jan. 1989); 1 child, Brian Edward. Student, Erie C.C., 1969-70. With counter and delivery M & H Auto Supply, Orchard Park, N.Y., 1973-75; parts counter person Crest Dodge Inc., Orchard Park, 1975-81; parts mgr. Case Chrysler Plymouth, Hamburg, N.Y., 1981-87, Mancuso Chrysler Plymouth, Hamburg, 1987-91, Transitowne Dodge, Williamsville, N.Y., 1991—. Supr. Profl. Inventory Assn., N.H., 1976-85. Named Mopar Parts Master, 1996. Mem. Chrysler Parts and Svc. Mgrs. Guild (v.p., sec. 1986-87, 89-92). Avocations: scuba diving, horseback riding, downhill skiing, kayaking, trap shooting. Office: Transitowne Dodge 7408 Transit Rd Williamsville NY 14221-6091 Home: 222 Park Forest DR Williamsville NY 14221-4351 E-mail: partzladi@aol.com.

K-TURKEL, JUDITH LEAH ROSENTHAL (JUDI K-TURKEL), writer, editor, publisher; b. N.Y.C., Jan. 3, 1934; d. Samuel S. and Pauline (Turkel) Rosenthal; m. Franklynn Peterson; children: Joseph, Jeffrey Kesselman, David, Kevin Peterson. BA, Bklyn. Coll., 1955. Story and mng. editor Dell Publs., N.Y.C., 1955-58, 62-65; editor-in-chief Sterling, Stearn & KMR Publs., N.Y.C., 1959-62; sr. editor Macfadden-Bartell Publs., N.Y.C., 1966-68; freelance writer N.Y.C. and Wis., 1968—2005; pres. P/K Assocs., Inc., Madison, Wis., 1977—. Instr. adult edn. Great Neck (N.Y.) Pub. Schs., 1973-76, U. Wis., Madison, 1977-82; instr. journalism Madison Area Tech. Coll., 1984-87; lectr. nonfiction writing CW Post Ctr., L.I. U., Manhasset, N.Y., 1976-77; tchr.-in-residence Rhinelander (Wis.) Sch. Arts, 1984-86. Author: (writing as Judi Kesselman) Stopping Out, 1976, (writing as Judi Kesselman-Turkel with Franklynn Peterson) The Do-It-Yourself Custom Van Book, 1977, Vans, 1979, (with others) Eat Anything Exercise Diet, 1979, Snowmobile Maintenance and Repair, 1979, I Can Use Tools, 1981, (textbook) Good Writing, 1980—, Test Taking Strategies, 1981, 2d edit., 2004, Study Smarts, 1981, 2004, Homeowner's Book of Lists, 1981, How to Improve Damn Near Everything Around Your Home, 1981, The Author's Handbook, 1982, rev., 1986, 2006, The Grammar Crammer, 1982, 2004, Research Shortcuts, 1982, 2004, Note-Taking Made Easy, 1982, rev. edit. 2004, The Vocabulary Builder, 1982, rev. edit. 2004, Getting it Down: How to Get Your Ideas on Paper, 1983, rev. edit.(as Secrets to Writing Great Papers), 2004, Spelling Simplified, 1983, 2004, The Magazine Writer's Handbook, 1983, rev. edit., 1986, 2006; syndicated computer newspaper columnist, 1983—; editor (newsletter) CPA Micro Report, 1985-92, CPA's PC Network Advisor, 1991-92; pub. CPA Computer Report, 1994—; contbr. articles to profl. jours. Chmn. non-partisan Citizens Nominating Com., Great Neck, 1972-75. Recipient Bus. Press. award, 1977, Nat. Press Club award, 1984, 85. Mem. Am. Soc. Journalists and Authors, Coun. Wis. Writers (pres. 1982-85), Authors Guild, Authors League. Avocations: travel, music. Office: P/K Assocs Inc 3006 Gregory St Madison WI 53711-1847 E-mail: info@booksthatteach.com.

KUBIC, M(ARCIA) SYLVIA, elementary school educator; b. Athens, Tenn., Sept. 10, 1936; d. Roy Thomas Fuller and Essie May (Powell) Gross; m. Gerald Merlin Kubic, Nov. 23, 1963 (div. 1975); children: Gerald Jr., Matthew, Kenneth. BS, Carson-Newman Coll., 1958. Tchr. East Brainerd Elem. Sch., Chattanooga, 1958-64, Bess T. Shepherd, Chattanooga, 1974—. Cons. Book Selection Com., Chattanooga, 1975; mem. Selected Task Force, 1989-90, City Schs. Tech. Plannning Commn., 1990-91. Mem., tchr. East Ridge Bapt. Ch., Chattanooga, sec. Sunday sch. Mem. NEA (del. nat. conv. 1961), Internat. Reading Assn., Tenn. Edn. Assn., Hamilton County Edn. Assn. (sec. 1963-64), Chattanooga Edn. Assn., Delta Kappa Gamma. Home: 7441 Hamilton Run Dr Chattanooga TN 37421-1871 Office: Bess T Shepherd Sch 7126 Tyner Rd Chattanooga TN 37421-1094

KUBISTAL, PATRICIA BERNICE, educational consultant; b. Chgo., Jan. 19, 1938; d. Edward John and Bernice Mildred (Lenz) Kubistal. AB cum laude, Loyola U., Chgo., 1959, AM, 1964, AM, 1965, PhD, 1968; postgrad., Chgo. State Coll., 1962, Ill. Inst. Tech., 1963, State U. Iowa, 1963, Nat. Coll. Edn., 1974-75. With Chgo. Bd. Edn., 1959-93, tchr., 1959-63, counselor, 1963-65, adminstrv. intern, 1965-66, asst. to dist. supt., 1966-69, prin. spl. edn. sch., 1969-75; prin. Simpson Sch., 1975-76, Brentano Sch., 1975-87, Roosevelt H.S., 1987, Haugan Sch., 1989; prin. Cook County Juvenile Temporary Detention Ctr. Sch. Jones Met. H.S. Bus. and Commerce, 1989-90, adminstr. dept. spl. edn., 1990-93; supr. Lake View Evening Sch., 1982-92, ednl. cons., 1993—. Lectr. Loyola U. Sch. Edn., Nat. Coll. Edn. Grad. Sch., Mundelein Coll., 1982-91, DePaul U., 1998-99; coord. Upper Bound Program of U. Ill. Circle Campus, 1966-68. Book rev. editor of Chgo. Prins. Jour., 1970-76, gen. editor, 1982-90. Active Crusade of Mercy; mem. com. Ill. Constnl. Conv., 1967-69; mem. Citizens Sch. Com., 1969-71; mem. edn. com. Field Mus., 1971; ednl. advisor North Side Chgo. PTA Region, 1975; gov. Loyola U., 1961-87; pres. St. Matthews Parish Coun., 1995-98. Recipient Outstanding Intern award Nat. Assn. Secondary Sch. Prins., 1966, Outstanding Prin. award Citizen's Sch. Com. of Chgo., 1986; named Outstanding History Tchr., Chgo. Pub. Schs., 1963, Oustanding Ill. Educator, 1970, one of Oustanding Women of Ill., 1970, St. Luke's Logan Sq. Cmty. Person of Yr., 1977; NDEA grantee, 1963, NSF grantee, 1965, HEW Region 5 grantee for drug edn., 1974, Chgo. Bd. Edn. Prins.' grantee for study robotics in elem. schs.; U. Chgo. adminstrv. fellow 1984. Mem. Ill. Personnel and Guidance Assn., NEA, Ill. Edn. Assn., Chgo. Edn. Assn., Am. Acad. Polit. and Social Sci., Chgo. Prins. and Adminstrs. Assn. (pres. aux.), Nat. Coun. Adminstrv. Women, Chgo. Coun. Exceptional Children, Loyal Christian Benevolent Assn., Kappa Gamma Pi, Pi Gamma Mu, Phi Delta Kappa, Delta Kappa Gamma (paliamentarian 1979-80, pres. Kappa chpt. 1988-90, Lambda state editor 1982-92, chmn. Lambda state comm. com. 1992, Internat. Golden Gift Fund award), Delta Sigma Rho, Phi Sigma Tau. Home and Office: 5111 N Oakley Ave Chicago IL 60625-1829

KUBO, KIMBERLY ANNETTE, entrepreneur; b. L.A., Calif., Apr. 30, 1969; d. Arnold Toshio Kubo and Sheryl J. Jai; children: Leah Marie Mortenson, Sarah Grace Mortenson. BA, U. Phoenix; Assoc. of Arts, Fashion Inst. Design and Merchandising. Sales exec. Tardus Fin. Group, Honolulu, 2002—; bus. owner jazziegirl.com, Honolulu, 2002—. Former dir. Dress for Success Worldwide, Honolulu, mem. adv. bd. Make-up artist He Did It Just For You, 1999. Mem. Kailua Christian Women's Club, 2001. Named Cmty. Servicewomen of Yr. for Hawaii, Soroptomist Internat. Local Chpt. Venture Club of Honolulu, 2004; named one of 40 Under 40, Pacific Bus. News, 2003. Avocations: reading, pilates, walking. Address: Dress for Success Worldwide YWCA of Oahu 1040 Richard St Honolulu HI 96813 Personal E-mail: shinko25@hotmail.com. E-mail: kim@kimkubo.com.

KUBY, BARBARA ELEANOR, personnel director, management consultant; b. Medford, Mass., Sept. 1, 1944; d. Robert William and Eleanor (Frasca) Asdell; m. Thomas Kuby, July 12, 1969. BS in Edn./ Psychology, Kent State U., 1966, MEd, 1987. Tchr. Nordonia/Euclid (Ohio) Pub. Schs., 1966-78; chief tng. officer United Bldg. Factories, Manama, Bahrain, 1979-81; mgr. tng. and devel. Norton Co., Akron, Ohio, 1981-85; v.p. Kuby and Assocs. Inc., Chagrin Falls, Ohio, 1973-91, pres., 1992—2002; corp. dir. human resource devel. and systems TransOhio Savs. Bank, Cleve., 1985-88; asst. v.p. human resources and adminstrv. sys. Leasing Dynamics, Inc., Cleve., 1988-90; dir. human resources, orgnl. devel. GOJO Industries, Akron, 1990-93, v.p. human resources and orgnl. devel., 1993—2006, v.p. orgnl. devel., 2006—. Adj. faculty cons. Buffalo State U., 1972—92, Lake Erie Coll., Cleve., 1985—95; lectr., cons. Cleve. State U., 1978—2000; program dir. Ctr. Profl. Advancement, East Brunswick, NJ, 1978—99. Cons., lectr. Girl Scouts U.S., Cleve., 1981—90; colleague Creative Edn. Found.; cons. project bus. Jr. Achievement, 1992—93; trustee Ohio Ballet, 1996—2002; bd. dirs. Apollo's Fire Baroque Orch. Friends Bd., 2003—. Recipient Svc./Commitment award, Creative Edn. Found., 2001, Athena Award Finalist, 2003. Mem.: ACLU, Cleve. Coun. on World Affairs, Soc. Orgnl. Learning, Human Resource Planning Soc., Holocaust Meml. Mus., Greenpeace. Avocations: travel, gardening, photography. Home: 7236 Chagrin Rd Chagrin Falls OH 44023-1102

KUBY, PATRICIA J., mathematics professor; d. Edward and Betty Seidewand; m. Joseph J. Kuby, Jr.; children: Jason J., Jessica A. BS in Math., Rochester Inst. Tech., N.Y., 1977, MS in Quality & Applied Stats., 1984. Adj. instr. math. Monroe C.C., Rochester, NY, 1978—81; programmer Rochester Product Divsn. GM, 1975—78; adj. instr. math. Rochester Inst. Tech., 1981—92; assoc. prof. math. Monroe C.C., 1991—. Co-author: Elementary Statistics, 10th edit. Recipient Excellence in Adj. Tchg. award, Rochester Inst. Tech., 1990, Inst. award of Merit, GM Automotive Svc. Ednl. Programs, 2003. Home: 838 Bradington Cir Webster NY 14580 Office: Monroe CC 1000 E Henrietta Rd Rochester NY 14623 Office Phone: 585-292-2937. E-mail: pkuby@monroecc.edu.

KUCHARSKI, KATHLEEN MARTIN, secondary school educator; b. Los Banos, Calif., Feb. 10, 1948; d. Clarence Lewis Martin and Amy Irene Clark; m. Stephen Joseph Kucharski, Feb. 12, 2005; m. Jerold Glenn Raley, June 12, 1971 (div. Dec. 0, 1992); children: Patrick Martin Raley, Daniel Frazier Raley, Shain Kathleen Jeffares. BA, Humboldt State U., Arcata, Calif., 1971. Single (English) and multiple subjects tchg. credentials Calif., 1974, std. secondary tchg. credential (Language Arts) Oreg., 1987, profl. tech. credential (comm. journalism) Oreg., 1999. Edn. dir. North Coast Cooperatives, Inc., Arcata, Calif., 1977—85; English/journalism tchr. Brookings-Harbor H.S., Oreg., 1987—, Bruin players drama advisor, 1988—93, Bruin Hunter student newspaper advisor, 1989—, 1998—, forensics coach, 2003—04, freshman acad. coord., 2005—. Dir. Calif. Coop. Fedn., Sacramento, 1982—84; state focus team for arts and comm. Oreg. Dept. Edn., Salem, 1996—97. Author: (curriculum) Making the Connection: From School to Work. Recipient First Freedom award, Greater Oreg. Soc. Profl. Journalists, 2000; grantee Classrom Grant Program, LeadAmerica Found., 2005; Student/Newspaper Partnership grantee, Newspaper Assn. Am. Found., 2000. Avocations: gardening, animal husbandry, travel. Home: 275 Allen Ln Brookings OR 97415 Office: Brookings-Harbor School District 17-C 629 Easy St Brookings OR 97415 Office Phone: 541-469-2108. Business E-Mail: kathleer@brookings.k12.or.us.

KUCK, LEA HABER, lawyer; b. Lockport, N.Y., 1965; AB magna cum laude, Hamilton Coll., 1987; JD, NYU, 1990. Bar: N.Y. 1991, U.S. Dist. Ct. (ea. dist.) Mich. 1992. Law clk. HOn. Steven D. Pepe U.S. Dist. Ct. (ea. dist.) Mich., 1990—92; atty. Skadden, Arps, Slate, Meagher & Flom LLP, N.Y., 1992—98, ptnr., 1998—. Office: Skadden Arps Slate Meagher & Flom LLP Four Times Square New York NY 10036

KUDDES, KATHRYN M., fine arts director; b. Midland, Tex., July 11, 1960; d. Fred M. and Dale M. Springer; m. Kenton C. Kuddes. MusB, Millikin U., 1983; Master in Music Edn., U. North Tex., 1995. Cert. provisional all-level music tchr. Tex., tchr. Kodály tng. Tex., profl. supr. Tex. Choral dir. 6-12 Stafford Mcpl. Sch. Dist., Stafford, Tex., 1983—86; elem. music specialist Killeen Ind. Sch. Dist., Killeen, Tex., 1986—89, Coll. Sta. Ind. Sch. Dist., College Station, Tex., 1989—94; grad. tchg. fellow U. North Tex., Denton, Tex., 1994—95; elem. music specialist Plano Ind. Sch. Dist., Plano, Tex., 1995—98, K-12 coord. vocal music, 1998—, dir. fine arts. V.p. Kodály Educators Texas, 1992—97; pres. so. divsn. Orgn. Am. Kodály Educators, 1997—2001. Editor: (profl. newsletter) KET Encounter, 1997. Mem. P.E.O. Sisterhood, Allen, 1987—2002. Named nationally registered music educator, Music Educators Nat. Conf., 1993. Mem.: Assn. Supervision and Curriculum Devel., Am. Orff-Schulwerk Assn., Texas Music Adminstrs. Conf., Orgn. Am. Kodály Educators (pres. so. divsn. 1997—2001), Kodály Educators Tex. (v.p. 1992—97), Am. Choral Dirs. Assn., Tex. Choral Dirs. Assn., Music Educators Nat. Conf., Tex. Music Educators Assn. Avocations: music, folk instruments, travel. Office: Plano Ind Sch Dist 2700 W 15th St Plano TX 75075 Office Phone: 469-752-8049. Business E-Mail: kkuddes@pisd.edu.

KUDO, IRMA SETSUKO, not-for-profit executive director; b. Ica, Peru, Feb. 25, 1939; arrived in U.S., 1944; d. Seiichi and Angelica (Yoshinaga) Higashide. Asst. dir. coun. annual session ADA, Chgo., 1971-80; exec. dir. Am. Assn. of Endodontists, Chgo., 1980—. Recipient Warren Wakai medal Japan Endodontic Assn., 1992. Mem. ADA Alumni Assn. Student Clinicians (hon.), Am. Assn. Endodontists (hon.), Am. Soc. of Assn. Execs., Profl. Conv. Mgmt. Assn., Assn. Forum Chicagoland. Office: Am Assn of Endodontists 211 E Chicago Ave Ste 1100 Chicago IL 60611-2687 E-mail: ikudo@aae.org.

KUDROW, LISA (LISA MARIE DIANE KUDROW), actress; b. Encino, Calif., July 30, 1963; d. Lee and Nedra Kudrow; m. Michael Stern, May 27, 1995; 1 child, Julian Murray. BS in Biology, Vassar Coll., Poughkeepsie, N.Y., 1985. Actress (TV series) Mad About You, 1991-99, Friends, 1994-2004 (Emmy award outstanding supporting actress, 1998, SAG award outstanding performance female, 2000, Am. Comedy award, 2000, Golden Satellite award best actress, 2000), Hopeless Pictures, 2005; (TV guest appearances) Cheers, 1989, Newhart, 1990, Life Goes On, 1990, Coach, 1993-94, Flying Blind, 1993, Hope & Gloria, 1996, The Simpsons (voice), 1998; (films) The Crazysitter, 1995, Romy and Michele's High School Reunion, 1997, Clockwatchers, 1997, The Opposite of Sex, 1998 (NY Film Critics Circle award, 2000), Hercules (voice) 1998, Analyze This, 1998, Hanging Up, 2000, All Over the Guy, 2001, Dr. Dolittle 2 (voice), 2001, Analyze That, 2002, Marci X, 2003, Wonderland, 2003, Happy Endings, 2005; exec. prodr.: (TV films) Picking Up and Dropping Off, 2003; actress, exec. prodr., writer (TV series) The Comeback, 2005; (music video) The Rembrandts I'll Be There For You, 1995. Named one of 50 Most Beautiful People in World, People mag., 1997. Mem.: Groundlings Improv Group.

KUDRYASHEVA, ALEKSANDRA A., microbiologist, nutritionist; b. Tula, Russia, Jan. 1, 1934; d. Andrew P. and Neonila K. (Volkonogova) Chernozhukov; m. Michael N. Kudryashev (dec.); m. Dan B. Chopyk, Dec. 19, 1990. BS in Biology, All-Union Inst. Food Industry, Moscow, 1965, DSc, 1969; PhD in Tech. Biol. Scis., Russia, 1983; PhD (hon.), Volgograd Tech. Inst., 1996. Technologist Glavkonserv Food Ministry, Govt. of USSR, Eisk, Krasnodar Region, 1954-61, head. of lab. irradiation microbiology Tula, 1962-71; from asst. prof. to prof. Russian Acad. Economy, Moscow, 1971-93, dean tech. and commodities, 1983-85, head dept. biotech., 1985-93; head food resources Inst. of Human Ecology, Moscow, 1993-97; pres. Internat. Ctr. Nutrition and Health Rehab., Toms River, NJ, 1997—; cons. UNO, 2001—03. V.p. radiology of food products, Russian Acad. Agr., Moscow, 1976-89; pres. Assn. of Commodities Specialists of USSR, 1985-91; chmn. cert. com. Coun. of Ministers of USSR, 1989-96; sec. commodities sect. Ministry of Edn., Govt. of USSR, 1978-85. Author: Humanity, Biodiversity and Environment (in Russian), 2004; contbr. more than 400 articles to sci. and profl. jours., books; holder more than 50 patents. Mem. Russian Acad. Natural Scis. (silver medal), Union of Concerned Scientists, N.Y. Acad. Scis., Internat. Info. Acad. (internat. prize 1996). Achievements include radiobiological and microbiological methods of food preservation; new technologies of manufacture and application of natural bio-correctors for food, medicine, agriculture and ecology. Avocations: travel, photography, ethnic cooking, poetry. Home and Office: 106 Guadeloupe Dr Toms River NJ 08757

KUEBLER, BARBARA CAMPBELL, science educator; b. Jefferson City, Mo., Aug. 3, 1951; d. Donald Lee and Virginia Lee (Williams) Campbell; m. John Wilson Kuebler, May 15, 1971; children: John Wilson II, Julia Kathryn. BS in Edn., U. Ga., 1973; MEd, Lincoln U., 1993. Tchr. home econs. Madison County H.S., Daniellsville, Ga., 1973-76; tchr. sci. Jefferson City Pub. Schs., 1976—. Recipient Select Tchr. as Regional Resources, State of Mo., 2001—03. Mem. ASCD, NSTA (conv. presenter 1996), Nat. Mid. Sch. Assn., Mo. Mid. Sch. Assn. (conv. presenter 1993, 94), Regional Profl. Devel. Com., Delta Kappa Gamma. Mem. Christian Ch. (Disciples Of Christ). Avocations: reading, knitting, needlecrafts, computers. Office: Lewis & Clark Mid Sch 325 Lewis And Clark Dr Jefferson City MO 65101-5586 E-mail: barbara.kuebler@jcps.k12.mo.us.

KUEHL, SHEILA JAMES, state legislator, department chairman; b. Tulsa, Feb. 9, 1941; d. Arthur Joseph and Lillian Ruth (Krasner) K. BA, UCLA, 1962; JD, Harvard U., 1978. Actress, 1950-65; assoc. dean of students UCLA, 1969-75; pvt. practice LA, 1978-85; law prof. Loyola U. LA, 1985-89; mng. atty. Calif. Women's Law Ctr., LA, 1989-93; mem. Calif. State Assembly, Sacramento, 1995-2000, spkr. pro tem, 1997-99, chair jud. com., 1999-2000; mem. Calif. State Senate, 2001—, chmn. natural resources and water com., 2001—06, 2006—. Chair Select Com. on Calif.'s Healthcare Crisis, 2005-. Appeared in TV series Broadside, 1964-65, as Zelda Gilroy in Dobie Gillis, 1959-63, as Jackie Erwin in Trouble with Father, 1950-56. Bd. overseers Harvard U., 1997-05. Named One of 20 Most Fascinating Women in Politics, George Mag., 1996, named One of 100 Most Influential Attys. in Calif., Calif. Law Bus., 1998; recipient Barry Goldwater Human Rights award, 1998, Legislator of Yr., Calif. Pks. and Recreation Soc., 1999, Pub. Svc. award UCLA Alumni Assn., 2000, Liberty award Lambda Legal Def. Edn. Fund, 2002, Women in Govt. award Good Housekeeping, 2003, Courageous Leader award Women Against Gun Violence, 2005, Matthew O. Tobriner Pub. Svc. award Legal Aid Soc., 2005; named Legislator of Yr., Congress Calif. Srs., 2006. Office: State Capitol Sacramento CA 95814-4906 Office Phone: 916-651-4023.

KUEHN, LUCILLE M., retired humanities educator; b. NYC, May 26, 1924; d. David and Hilda Maisel; children: Susan, Robert, David. BA magna cum laude, U. Minn., Mpls., 1948; MA, U. Calif., Irvine, 1969. Humanities educator U. Calif., Irvine, 1966—78; govtl. cons. Corona Del Mar, Calif., 1979—96. Lectr. Radcliffe Coll. Inst., 1972. Founding pres. LWV of Orange County, Newport Beach, 1961—63; bd. dirs. Orange County Grand Jury, Santa Ana, Calif., 1964—65, Orange County Juvenile Justice Commn., Santa Ana, 1965—66; mem. Orange County Mental Health Commn., Santa Ana, 1966—67, Newport Beach City Coun., 1974—78, Newport Harbor Art Mus., Newport Beach, 1974—87, South Coast Repertory Theatre, Costa Mesa, Calif., 1974—83, Town Hall of Calif., LA, 1975—85; pres. Town Hall Orange County Forum, 1981—84; co-chair Newport Beach Conservancy, 1987—90; pres. Irvine Town & Gown U. Calif., Irvine, 1989—90, mem. Sch. of the Arts, 1992—2005, mem. Humanities Assocs., 1995—2000; mem. Newport Beach Pub. Libr. Found., 1989—94, Newport Beach Pub. Libr., 1992—96, Newport Beach Gen. Plan Com., Calif., 2002—. Named Newport Beach Citizen of Yr., 1966; recipient Leadership in Bus. and Industry award, No. Orange County YWCA, 1982, Lauds and Laurels for Cmty. Svc. award, U. Calif., Irvine Alumni Assn., 1990; fellow, US Office of Edn., 1970. Jewish. Avocations: education, reading, gardening.

KUEHN, MILDRED MAY, retired social worker; b. Milw., June 24, 1933; d. Frederick Kuehn and Mildred Leona Josslyn; m. Donald Tebay, Feb. 28, 1953 (div. June 22, 1994); children: Kim Tebay, Leslie Tebay, Jennifer Tebay. BS, U. Wis., Milw., 1981. Social worker Heritage Nursing Home, Port Washington, Wis., 1984—85; tchr.'s aide Grafton (Wis.) H.S., 1985—87, ret., 2003—. Mem. Jewish Cmty. Ctr., 1997—. Mem.: Nat. Trust for Hist. Preservation, U. Wis. Alumni. Methodist. Avocations: painting, reading, guitar, sewing, Sheepshead and Bridge.

KUEHN, NANCY ANN, retired secondary school educator; b. Monessen, Pa., Mar. 21, 1950; d. John Joseph and Grace Patricia Radacsy; m. John Kuehn. BS, Calif. U., Calif., Pa., 1971; Master's, U. Pitts., 1979. Tchr. English Pemberton Bd. Edn., NJ, 1971—77; tchr. English, gifted Fox Chapel Bd. Edn., Pa., 1977—2006; ret., 2006. Sponsor lit. arts mag. Tapestry, 1977—2006; sponsor sch. newspaper Fox Tales, 1977—2006; creator career program for students Pittsburghers Who Make a Difference, 2001—06. Mem.: PSEA, NEA, Nat. Coun. Tchrs. of English, Pa. Edn. Assn. Avocations: animal rescue, travel, gardening, reading.

KUEHNE, HELENIRENE ANNE, art educator; b. Douglasville, Pa., Nov. 7, 1941; d. John Julius Dusco and Helen Kathryn Rogosky; m. Paul Howard Kuehne, June 28, 1980; 1 child, John Paul. BS, Kutztown U., 1964, MEd, 1968; postgrad., U. No. Colo., 1978, LaSalle U., 1994. Tchr. elem. art Kutztown (Pa.) Area Schs., 1964-83, tchr. secondary art, 1983—, chair fine arts dept., mem. curriculum coun., 1993—. Tchr. coop. tchr. program Kutztown U., 1970—, mem. program adv. com., 1972. Works exhibited in various art shows, 1978-81. Sec. Muhlenberg Twp. Arts Bd., Laureldale, Pa., 1991—; merit badge counselor Boy Scouts Am., Laureldale, 1993—; active Friends of Reading Pub. Mus., 1991. Grantee Pa. Coun. Arts, 1993-94. Mem. AAUW (chair 1979-80, 88-89), Wyomissing Inst. Fine Arts, Delta Kappa Gamma. Avocations: gourmet cooking, music. Home: 3512 Kent Ave Laureldale PA 19605 Office: Kutztown Area Sr High 50 Trexler Ave Kutztown PA 19530-9700

KUEHNE, KELLI, professional golfer; b. Dallas, May 11, 1977; Student, U. Tex. Profl. golfer, 1998—; tied for 20th pl. First Union Betsy King Classic, 1998; participant 24 tournaments, 1998. Named 6th in standings Rolex Rookie of Yr., 1998; placed 1st Corning Classic. Avocations: fishing, hunting. Office: care LPGA 100 International Golf Dr Daytona Beach FL 32124-1082

KUEHNER, DENISE ANN, music educator, musician; b. Evanston, Ill., July 6, 1953; d. Alice Catherine Langan and Albert Edward Delgado; m. Eric Lee Kuehner, Oct. 26, 1954; children: Jeffrey Allen, Katherine Elizabeth. BME, Valparaiso U., 1977; MM in cello performance and lit., U. Notre Dame, 1984. Tchr., string specialist South Bend Cmty. Sch. Corp., Ind., 1984—; lectr./adj. faculty St. Mary's Coll., Notre Dame, Ind., 1986—. Sect. cellist NW Ind. Symphony, Gary, Ind., 1972—83; cellist Carlson String Quartet, South Bend, 1978—; sect. cellist SW Mich. Symphony, St. Joseph, Mich., 1979—84, South Bend Symphony Orch., Ind., 1981—; choir dir. St. Paul Luth. Ch., South Bend, Ind., 1984—; acad. youth orch. dir. Ind. U. at South Bend, South Bend, Ind., 1986—; guest condr. Ind. all-region orch. Am. String Tchrs. Assn., La Porte, Ind., 1987; sect. cellist/soloist Borderline Philharm. and Chamber Music Festival, Waubun, Minn., 1989—2003; cellist Whitewater String Trio, South Bend, 1996—; orch. guest condr. Gt. Lake Music Camp, Ind., 1998; orch. dir. Summer Symphonette, South Bend, Ind., 2000—; condr. SBCSC Firefly Proms., South Bend, Ind., 2000—. Editor: (newsletter) Michiana Cello Society News of Note. Worship com. St. Paul Ch., South Bend, Ind., 1990—. Mem.: Nat. Educators Assn., Ind. Music Educators Assn., Nat. Sch. Orch. Assn., Am. String Tchrs. Assn., Sigma Alpha Iota (musical dir. 1975—76, Sword of Honor 1976). Lutheran (Ms). Avocations: reading, art, dance, singing. Home: 19576 Paxson Drive South South Bend IN 46637 Office: Clay High School 19131 Darden Rd South Bend IN 46637 Office Phone: 574-243-7037. E-mail: dkuehner@sbcsc.k12.in.us.

KUENN, MARJORIE ASP, music educator; b. Moorhead, Minn., Dec. 26, 1951; d. Robert Louis and Violet Rose Asp; m. Brent Jay Kuenn, Feb. 25, 1978 (div. Jan. 2001). EdB in Violin, U. So. Miss., 1973, EdM, 1974. Violinist Fargo-Moorhead Symphony, 1967—69, Meridian Symphony, Miss., 1969—79, Jackson Symphony, Miss., 1969—79, Jackson Mini-Orch., 1969—79, Miss. Opera South, 1969—79, Miss. Opera, 1969—79, Gulfcoast Symphony, Miss., 1969—79, Miss. Ballet Orch., 1969—79, Mobile Opera, Ala., 1969—79, Tupelo Symphony, Miss., 1969—79, Greenville Symphony, Miss., 1969—79, Monroe Symphony, La., 1969—79, U. So. Miss. Symphony, Opera, Chamber & Ensemble, 1969—74; tchr. Jackson Symphony Orch., 1974—79; dir. orch. Hickman Mills Sch. Dist., Kansas City, Mo., 1979—; chair dept. music Smith-Hale Mid. Sch., Kansas city, 1990—; choir dir. Grace Bapt. Ch., Lee's Summit, Mo., 2005—. Author: Vocal Techniques, vol. I, 1998, Vocal Techniques, vol. II, 2003, Choir Warm-up Exercises, 2002. Music scholar, U. So. Miss., 1969—73, Grad. Music Studies fellow, 1973—74. Mem.: U. So. Miss. Alumni Assn., Am. Fedn. Tchrs., Music Educators Nat. Conf., Mu Phi Epsilon, Alpha Lambda Delta. Avocations: sewing, reading, exercise. Office: Smith-Hale Mid Sch 8925 Longview Rd Kansas City MO 64134 Office Phone: 816-316-7663. Business E-Mail: marjoriek@hickmanmills.org.

KUGELMAN, STEPHANIE, advertising executive; married; 1 child. BA in Psychology and Sociology, Elmira Coll., 1969. With creative rsch. group Young & Rubicam NY, 1971—, dir. insights group, 1991, mng. dir., vice chmn., mng. ptnr., dir. br. planning group, chmn., CEO, 1999—2001; vice chmn., chief strategic officer Young & Rubicam, 2001—. Office: Young & Rubicam 285 Madison Ave New York NY 10017-6486

KUH, CHARLOTTE VIRGINIA, economist; b. Apr. 13, 1944; d. Peter Greenebaum and Frederica Angela (Coerr) K.; m. Roy Radner, Jan. 22, 1978; children: Siobhan Frederica, Michael Edwin. BA magna cum laude, Radcliffe Coll., 1967; MPhil (Univ. fellow), Yale U., 1969, PhD (Dept. Labor grantee), 1976. Rec. sec.-treas. Econometric Soc., New Haven, 1970-75; acting asst. prof. engring. econ. systems Stanford U., 1974-76; asst. prof. Harvard U. Grad. Sch. Edn., 1976-79; staff mgr., dist. mgr. AT&T Corp., 1979-87; exec. dir. grad. records exams program Ednl. Testing Svc., 1987-95; exec. dir. Office of Sci. and Engring. Personnel Nat. Rsch. Coun., 1995—2001; dep. exec. dir. policy & global affairs divsn. Nat. Rsch. coun., Washington, 2001—. Mem. rev. panel NSF, 1979, 81, mem. adv. panel policy rsch. and sci. resource studies, 1983-87; mem. rev. panel Nat. Inst. Edn., 1978-85; mem. com. study nat. needs for biomed. and behavioral research pers. NRC, 1980-85, mem. adv. panel Office Sci. and Engring. Pers., 1983-90, mem. panel on stats. on supply and demand for precoll. sci. and math. tchrs., com. on nat. stats., 1986-89, mem. com. Women in Sci. and Engring. NRC, 1991-95, vice chair, 1993-95, mem. com. to study strategies to strengthen excellence of the N.I.H. Intramural Research Program, Inst. of Medicine, 1988; mem. exec. com. of dels. Am. Coun. Learned Socs., 1999—2002, chmn. 2001-02, treas., bd. dirs., 2002—; mem. adv. com. Bunting Inst., Radcliffe Coll., 1998—2001; cons. in field. Author articles in field. Grantee Carnegie Coun. Higher Edn., Ford Found., Spencer Found. Fellow Assn. Women in Sci.; mem. Am. Econ. Assn., Econometric Soc. Office: Natl Research Council 500 5th St Washington DC 20001 Office Phone: 202-334-2700. E-mail: ckuh@nas.edu, cvkuh@earthlink.net.

KUHFUSS, LISA A., mathematics educator; b. Peoria, Ill., Mar. 14, 1978; d. Lee and Cheryl Kuhfuss. BA in Bus. Adminstrn. and Acctg., Ill. Coll., Jacksonville, 2000; BS in Mid. Sch. Math., U. Mo., St. Louis, 2004. Group acct. Maritz, St. Louis, 2000—02; tchr. Carr Ln. Mid. Sch., St. Louis, 2004—. Vol. tchr. WorldTeach, Namibia, 2006. Activities co-chair Am. Cancer Soc., St. Louis, 2001—06; big sister Big Bros. Big Sisters Am., St. Louis, 2001—06; class agt. Ill. Coll., Jacksonville, 2001—06. Avocations: travel, reading, water sports. Office Phone: 314-231-0413.

KUHL, JUDITH ANNETTE, retired science educator; d. Edgar William and Isabelle Lucy (Tyler) Kuhl; children from previous marriage: Sharon Annette, Martha Amy. BS in Biology, Indiana U. Pa., 1960; MS in Biology, Troy State U., Dorthan, Ala., 1987. Advanced profl. tchg. cert. Md. Tchr. Arlington County Sch. Bd., Arlington, Va., 1967—78; sci. tchr. Houston Acad., Dothan, 1980—81, W. T. Woodson HS, Fairfax, Va., 1982—83, Houston County HS, Columbia, Ala., 1984—85; instr. Wiregrass Rehab. Ctr., Dothan, 1985—87; sci. tchr. Prince George's County Schs., Suitland, Md., 1988—2003; substitute tchr. Escambia County Sch. Bd., Pensacola, Fla., 2003—06; ret., 2006. Tax prepaper H & R Block, Enterprise, Ala., 1984, Enterprise, 85; pest survey technician Md. Dept. Agr., 1989—91, 2000—01; rsch. fellow ARC, Rockeville, Md., 1993; instr. animal sci. Johns Hopkins U., Frederick, Md., 1998, Frederick, 99, Hood Coll., 1998, 99. Juvenile/sch. probation officer Arlington County Juvenile Ct., Va., 1969—70; camp dir. Youth Conservation Corps., Quantico, Va., 1977—80; mem. ASPCA, Audobon Soc.; bd. dirs. Pensacola Civitan Club, 2004—. Recipient Citizen of the Yr. award, Outstanding Biology Tchr. Hon. Mention award, Assn. Biology Tchrs., 1992; Am. Physiol. Soc. Summer Rsch. grantee, U. Md., 1995. Mem.: NEA, Md. State Tchrs. Assn., Eastern Star, Alpha Sigma Alpha (life). Avocations: gardening, reading, microscopy. Home: 1860 Ponderosa Dr Pensacola FL 32534

KUHL, PATRICIA K., science educator; b. Mitchell, S.D., Nov. 5, 1946; d. Joseph John and Susan Mary (Schaeffer) K.; m. Andrew N. Meltzoff, Sept. 28, 1985; 1 child, Katherine. BA, St. Cloud State U., Minn., 1967; MA, U. Minn., 1971, PhD, 1973. Postdoctoral research assoc. Cen. Inst. for Deaf, St. Louis, 1973-76; from rsch. assoc. to prof. U. Wash., Seattle, 1976—82, prof., 1982—, William P. and Ruth Gerberding prof., 1997—, dept. chair, 1994—, dir. Inst. Learning and Brain Scis., 2003—. Gov. bd. Am. Inst. Physics, 1994-96; trustee Neurosci. Rsch. Found., 1994—; bd. dirs. Wash. Tech. Ctr., U. Wash., 1994-96; invited presenter White House Conf. on Early Learning and the Brain, 1997, Early Childhood Cognitive Devel., 2001. Editor Jour. Neurosci., 1989-96. Recipient Women in Research citation Kennedy Council, 1978, Virginia Merrill Bloedel Scholar award, 1992-94. Fellow AAAS, Am. Psychol. Soc., Acoustical Soc. Am. (assoc. editor Jour. 1988-92, chair medals and awards, 1992-94, v.p. 1997, Silver medal 1997, pres. 1999—); mem. Am. Acad. Arts and Scis. Office: Inst Learning and Brain Sci Dept Speech & Hearing Sciences 357988 Seattle WA 98105-6247 Office Phone: 206-685-1921. Business E-Mail: pkkuhl@u.washington.edu.

KUHL, TONYA L., science educator; BS Chem. Engring., U. Ariz., 1989; PhD Chem. Engring., U. Calif., Santa Barbara, 1996. Postdoctoral fellow U. Calif., Santa Barbara, 1996—97, asst. rsch. engr., 1997—2000, asst. prof. chem. engring. Davis, Calif. Office: One Shields Ave Davis CA 95616

KUHLER, DEBORAH GAIL, grief therapist, retired state legislator; b. Moorhead, Minn., Oct. 12, 1952; d. Robert Edgar and Beverly Maxine (Buechler) Ecker; m. George Henry Kuhler, Dec. 28, 1973; children: Karen Elizabeth, Ellen Christine. BA, Dakota Wesleyan U., 1974; MA, U. N.D., 1977. Outpatient therapist Ctr. for Human Devel., Grand Forks, ND, 1975-77; mental health counselor Community Counseling Services, Huron, SD, 1978-88, 91-93; owner, dir. bereavement svcs. Kuhler Funeral Home, Huron, 1978—; adj. prof. Huron U., 1979—83, 1990—2002; mem. from dist. 23 S.D. Ho. Reps., Pierre, 1987-90; mem. House Judiciary com., chair House Health and Welfare Com., Pierre, 1990. Active First United Meth. Ch. Named Young Alumnus of the Yr., Dakota Wesleyan U., 1989, Bus. and Profl. Women, 1989. Mem. ACA, PEO, Am. Mental Health Counselors Assn., Assn. for Death Edn. and Counseling. Avocations: reading, breadmaking, sewing, piano. E-mail: kuhlerdg@yahoo.com.

KUHLMANN-WILSDORF, DORIS, materials scientist, inventor, retired educator; b. Bremen, Germany, Feb. 15, 1922; came to U.S., 1956. d. A. Friedrich and Elsa S. (Dreyer) K.; m. Heinz G.F. Wilsdorf, Jan. 4, 1950; children: Gabriele, Michael. BS in Physics, U. Göttingen, Germany, 1944, MS, 1946, PhD in Materials Sci., 1947; DSc in Physics-Materials Sci., U. Witwatersrand, South Africa, 1954; DSc in Physics (hon.), U. Pretoria, South Africa, 2004. Postdoctoral fellow U. Göttingen, 1947-48; postdoctoral fellow in physics U. Bristol, Eng., 1949-50; lectr. physics U. Witwatersrand, Johannesburg, 1950-56; from assoc. prof. metall. engring. to prof. U. Pa., Phila., 1957-63; prof. engring. physics U. Va., Charlottesville, 1963-66, univ. prof. applied sci., 1966—2005; prof. emeritus, 2005—. Co-founder, co-owner HiPerCon; inventor in field. Editor: 4 materials sci. books; contbr. articles to profl. jours. Recipient J. Shelton Horsley award Va. Acad. Sci., 1966, Americanism medal DAR, 1966, Heyn medal German Metall. Soc., 1988, Achievement award Soc. Women Engrs., 1989, Ragnar Holm Sci. Achievement award IEEE, 1991. Fellow Am. Soc. Materials Internat. (life, Edward DeMille Campbell Meml. lectr. 2002), Am. Phys. Soc.; mem. Am. Soc. Women Engrs. (life), Am. Soc. Engring. Edn. (medal for excellence 1965, 66), AIME Metall. Soc., Nat. Acad. Engring. Achievements include development of metal fiber brushes; invention of multipolar motors; patents in field. Business E-Mail: dw@virginia.edu.

KUHLS, BARBARA SUE, medical/surgical nurse; b. Platteville, Wis., Nov. 29, 1950; d. Marion Lyle and Dorothy Louise (Manuel) Humphrey; m. Ronald Edward Kuhls, June 6, 1970; children: Kara Marie Morrison, Aaron Lee, Ionut Kuhls. BSN, U. Wis., 1979; M of Ministry, Bethany Theol. Sem., 1995. Med.-surg. staff nurse St. Agnes Hosp., Fond Du Lac, Wis., 1979-80, perinatal staff nurse, 1980-83, mobile unit staff nurse, 1983-85, minor surg. and gastrointestinal procedure asst., 1985-91, phys. rehab. charge nurse, 1991-94; pregnancy counselor Bethany Christian Svcs., Fond Du Lac, 1993-98; innkeeper Dixon House B&B, 1999—2005; G.I. staff nurse, 1999—. Support group leader Women in Ramah, Fond Du Lac, 1987-89; mem. adv. bd. Fond Du Lac chpt. Wis. Right to Life, 1986-92, 95. Vol. nurse Samaritan Free Clinic, Fond Du Lac, 1993-94. Mem. Nat. Christian Counselors Assn., Am. Assn. Christian Counselors, Nurses Christian Fellowship (chpt. leader). Baptist. Avocations: reading, writing, gardening. Home: N7585 Deer Path Rd Fond Du Lac WI 54935-9512 E-mail: bkuhls@charter.net.

KUHN, ANNE NAOMI WICKER (MRS. HAROLD B. KUHN), foreign language educator; b. Lynchburg, Va.; d. George Barnett and Annie (Hicks) Wicker; m. Harold B. Kuhn. Diploma Malone Coll., 1933, Trinity Coll. Music, London, 1937; AB, John Fletcher Coll., 1939; MA, Boston U., 1942, postgrad., 1965-70; postgrad. (fellow) Harvard U., 1942-44, 66-68; hon. grad. Asbury Coll., 1978. Instr., Emmanuel Bible Coll., Birkenhead, Eng., 1936-37; asst. in history John Fletcher Coll., University Park, Iowa, 1938-39; librarian Harvard U., 1939-44; tchr. adult edn. program U.S. Armed Forces, Fuerstenfeldbruck Air Base, Germany, 1951-52; prof. Union Bibl. Sem., Yeotmal, India, 1957-58; lectr. Armenian Bible Inst., Beirut, Lebanon, 1958; prof. German, Asbury Coll., Wilmore, Ky., 1962—, co-dir. coll. study tour to East Germany and West Germany, 1976, 77, 78, co-dir. acad. tours, 1979, 80; dir. acad. tour, Russia, 1981, 85, Scandanavia, 1982, Indonesia, Singapore, 1983, Hong Kong and Thailand, 1983, 85, East Germany, West Germany, France and Austria, 1983, Russia and Finland, 1984, 85, 89, China, 1979, 84, 85, 89,

Estonia, Latvia, 1985, 89, Poland, 1989, 91, 92, Portugal, Spain, France, Ireland, Scotland, Norway, England, 1987, The Balkans, Hungary, Czech Republic, Slovak Republic, Bulgaria, Romania and Turkey, 1992, alumni academic tour Malta, Sicily, Greece, Macedonia, 1995; tchr. Seoul Theol. Sem., fall 1978. Author: (pamphlet) The Impact of the Transition to Modern Education Upon Religious Education, 1950; The Influence of Paul Gerhardt upon Wesleyan Hymnody, 1960, Light to Dispel Fear, 1987; transl. German ch. records, poems, letters; contbr. articles to profl. jours. Del. Youth for Christ World Conf., 1948, 50, London Yearly Meeting of Friends, Edinburgh, Scotland, 1948, World Council Chs., Amsterdam, 1948, World Friends Conf., Oxford, Eng., 1952, World Methodist Conf., Oslo, Norway, 1961, Deutscher Kirchentag, Dortmund, Germany, 1963, German Lang. Congress, Bonn, W. Ger., 1974, Internat. Conf. Religion, Amsterdam, Netherlands, Poland, West Berlin, Fed. Republic Germany, 1986, Internat. Missionary Conf., Eng., 1987, Congress on the Bible II, Washington, 1987; participant Internat. Congress World Evangelization, Lausanne, Switzerland, 1974; del., speaker Internat. Conf. on Holocaust and Genocide, Oxford and London, 1988; speaker Founders Week Malone Coll., Ohio, 1989, Nat. Quaker Conf., Denver; mem. acad. tour Poland, 1988; vol. of various special assignments in Ctrl. and Eastern Europe. Recipient German Consular award, Boston, 1965, Thomas Mann award Boston U., 1967; named Ky. Col., 1978. Fellow Goethe-Institut for Germanisten, Munich, 1966-68, 70-71. Mem. AAUW, Am. Assn. Tchrs. German, NEA, Ky. Ednl. Assn., Lincoln Lit. Soc., Protestant Women of Chapel, Harvard Univ. Faculty Club (Cambridge, Mass.), Harvard Univ. Club Eastern and Ctrl. Ky. (Lexington), United Daughters of the Confederacy, Delta Phi Alpha (award 1963, 65). Mem. Soc. of Friends. Home: 406 Kenyon Ave Wilmore KY 40390-1033

KUHN, AUDREY GRENDAHL, graphic designer, printmaker, fiber artist; b. Chgo., May 3, 1929; d. Arthur Bertram Grendahl and Louise Margaret (Scholz) Carr; m. Thomas Mansfield Kuhn, Dec. 31, 1955; children: Thomas Jr., Rhonda Reynolds, Kristyn Stout, Karen. BA in Design, U. Mich., 1952; postgrad., Russell Sage Coll., 1975. Cert. tchr., N.Y. Tech. illustrator Ford Motor Co., Dearborn, Mich., 1952-56, asst. to art dir., 1956; art tchr. Shenendehowa Cen. Sch., Clifton Park, N.Y., 1973; pres. Audrey Grendahl Kuhn Graphics/Articoats, Clifton Park, 1974—. Exhbns. include Saratoga (N.Y.) Performing Arts Ctr., 1977, Hudson Valley C.C., Troy, N.Y., 1979, Gallery Assn. N.Y. Traveling Exhibits, 1978-79, Grover Gallery, Denver, 1982, Artexpo, N.Y.C., 1979-89, San Francisco, 1981, So. Vt. Art Ctr., 1984-86, Cen. Galleries, Albany, N.Y., 1985, Schoolhouse Gallery, Sanibel, Fla., 1986; juried shows include Mohawk-Hudson Regional, SUNY Art Gallery, Albany, 1973, Albany Inst., 1978, Albany Artists Show, 1976, Shenendehowa Arts Festival, 1976, J.R. Barker Gallery, Palm Beach, Fla., 1977, SUNY Art Gallery, Albany, 1978, Arena Art Open, Binghamton, N.Y., 1978, Cooperstown Nat. Art Show, 1978, Terrance Gallery, Palenville, N.Y., 1983, Saratoga Performing Arts Ctr., 1983-89, Phila. Art Show, 1983-89, Mindscape Gallery, Evanston, Ill., 1994, Am. Crafts Coun., Columbus, Ohio, 1994; exhibited in galleries including Attic Gallery, Portland, Oreg., Artex, Ltd., Hong Kong, Concept Art Gallery, Pitts., Corp. Art West, Seattle, Dan Greenblat Gallery, N.Y.C., others; represented in collections Georgetown Stes., Washington, Delco Battery Renaissance Ctr., Detroit, Toshiba, Tokyo, Mus. Modern Art, Haifa, Israel, Norton Simon, N.Y.C., others. Mem. Print Club Albany (bd. dirs., treas., presentation print chair 1987-91), Schenectady Mus. (designer arts coun.), Rehoboth Art League (Juror's award of excellence 1992), Kappa Delta (pres. alumnae group 1992-94), Christians in the Visual Arts, Saratoga County Arts Coun., Syracuse Printmakers. Democrat. Methodist. Avocations: aerobics, swimming, cross country skiing, sewing, knitting. Home and Office: 10 Valdepenas Ln Clifton Park NY 12065-5810

KUHN, HARRIET LURENSKY, school psychologist; b. Arlington, Va., Sept. 12, 1962; d. Robert Lee and Eleanor Vivian (Goldman) L. BA, Simmons Coll., 1984; MA, Cath. U. of Am., 1990; MEd, George Mason U., 1995. Nat. cert. sch. psychologist; lic. profl. counselor, Md., D.C. Residential social worker Reliance Social Care, London, 1985; sch. psychologist D.C. Pub. Schs., Washington, 1991—. Robert Porter scholar, 1993; recipient Downtown Jaycees Grant award, 1993. Mem. Am. Assn. Sch. Psychologists, D.C. Assn. Sch. Psychologists, Washington Rowing Assn. Democrat. Jewish. Avocations: rowing, swimming, bicycling, gardening, soccer. Home: 8705 Lowell St Bethesda MD 20817-3217 Office: Ross Elem Sch 1730 R St NW Washington DC 20009-2410 Office Phone: 301-379-8705.

KUHN, JOLYN, artist; b. Newark, Dec. 12, 1946; d. Joseph Roger and Evelyn Dorothy (Raimando) Tartaglia; m. Richard Francis Kuhn, July 16, 1966; children: David, Daniel, Chalena, Athena, Richard. Student, Newark Sch. Fine/Indsl. Arts, 1966; BFA, Md. Inst. Coll. At, Balt., 1989; student, Anne Arundel C.C., Arnold, Md., 1988, Schuler Sch. Fine Art, 2004. Fashion illustrator Banbergers, Newark, 1966; photographer Siegal Majestic, Catonsville, Md., 1980s; sports photographer The Picture Man, Md., 1990s; owner Kuhns Photography, Pasadena, Md., 1989—; freelance artist, 1969—. Substitute tchr. Anne Arundel Pub. Sch. Sys., 1973-87; dir. Parks and Recreation Dept., 1980-86. Works include clay sculpture, jewelry, stained glass windows, etchings, prints, portraits. Recipient numerous awards for artwork. Avocations: painting, sewing, bicycling, swimming, gardening. Home: 616 Riverside Dr Pasadena MD 21122-5046 Personal E-mail: Jolyndk@aol.com.

KUHN, KATHLEEN JO, accountant; b. Springfield, Ill., Aug. 9, 1947; d. Henry Elmer and Norma Florene (Niehaus) Burge; m. Gerald L. Kuhn, June 22, 1968; children: Gerald Lynn, Brett Anthony. BS Bus., Bradley U., 1969. CPA Ill. Contr. Byerly Music Co., Peoria, Ill., 1969—70; staff acct. Clifton Gunderson & Co., Columbus, Ind., 1970—71; acct. Dept. Transp., State of Ill., Springfield, 1972—76, Gerald L. Kuhn & Assocs., Springfield, 1976—78, ptnr., 1979—, mgr. quality control, 1990—, human resources mgr., 1996—. Grad. asst. Dale Carnegie courses, 1979—80; writer, editor co. policy guideline, 1979—80; editor co. quality control manual, 1990; chair internal auditing com. CID/CEF, 2003—. Chair fin. com. Lutheran H.S., Springfield, 2002—, bd. dirs., 2003—04; pianist Trinity Luth. Ch. Recipient Attendance award, Continuing Profl. Edn. for Accts., 1979—. Mem.: AICPA, Nat. Bus. & Motivational Assn., Am. Woman's Soc. CPA, Ill. Soc. CPA, Met. Federated Jr. Women's Club, Springfield Art Assn., Olympic Swim Club. Office: 2659 Farragut Dr Springfield IL 62704-1462 Home: 1901 Grist Mill Springfield IL 62718 Office Phone: 217-698-8400.

KUHN, MELANIE R., literature educator, consultant; d. Emma Gertrude and Raymond Joseph Kuhn; m. Jason Edward Chambers, Mar. 18, 2003. BA magna cum laude, Boston Coll., 1984; EdM, Harvard Grad. Sch. of Edn., Cambridge, MA, 1988; MPhil, Cambridge U., Eng., 1993; PhD, U. Ga., Athens, 2000. Clinician Ctr. Acad., London, 1989—92; asst. prof. literacy edn. Rutgers Grad. Sch. of Edn., New Brunswick, NJ, 2000—. Author: (chapter) Theoretical Models and Processes, 2004, Literacy: Major Themes in Education, 2004; contbr. articles to profl. jours. and books. Reviewer Am. Ednl. Rsch. Assn., 1997, Nat. Reading Conf., 1999—2003, Jour. of Ednl. Psychology, 2002, Internat. Reading Assn., Newark, Del., 2001—03; principle investigator Effectiveness of Recording for the Blind and Dyslexics Learning Through Listening Program; reviewer Jour. Literacy Rsch., 2001—; ad hoc reviewer Jour. of Spl. Edn., 2003. Recipient Finalist, Outstanding Dissertation of the Yr., Internat. Reading Assn., 2002, Finalist, Outstanding Student Rsch., Nat. Reading Conf., 2000; grantee full Grant for study at Cambridge U., ESRC, 1992-93, Eisenhower Grant for Profl. Devel. Across Districts, NJ. Dept. of Edn., 2001-03, RFB&D Learning Through Listening Study, 2004—05. Mem.: Assn. of Reading Grad. Students (assoc.; pres. 1995—96), Nat. Reading Conf. (assoc.), Am. Ednl. Rsch. Assn. (assoc.), Internat. Reading Assn. (assoc.), Alpha Upsilon Alpha (assoc.). Independent. Catholic. Achievements include research in IERI Grant The Development of Fluent and Automatic Reading: Precursor to Learning from Text. Avocations: swimming, travel, walking. Office: 144 Morris St #1 Jersey City NJ 07302 E-mail: melaniek@rci.rutgers.edu.

KUHN, ROSE MARIE, language educator; b. UCCLE, Belgium; arrived in USA, 1974; m. Thomas H. Zynda. BA, Facultes Universitaires St. Louis, Brussels, 1971; MA, Universite Catholique de Louvain, Belgium, 1974, Catholic U., Washington, D.C., 1977, PhD, 1988. Tchr. in French Nat. Cathedral HS, Wash., DC, 1977—79; lectr. in French Oberlin Coll., Oberlin, Ohio, 1979—80; lectr. in German Cath. Univ., Wash., DC, 1980—82; vis. lectr. of German Hope Coll., Holland, Mich., 1982—83; asst. prof. of French Rhodes Coll., Memphis, 1983—; vis. asst. prof. of French Christian Bros. Univ., Memphis, 1987—88; prof. of French Calif. State Univ., Fresno, Calif., 1988—. Office: Calif State Univ Fresno EE96 Dept Modern & Classical Langs and Lits Fresno CA 93740-8030

KUHRT, SHARON LEE, nursing administrator; b. Denver, July 20, 1957; d. John Wilfred and Yoshiko (Ueda) Kuhrt. BSN, Loretto Heights Coll., 1982; MSN, Regis U., 1992. RN Colo., Mass., Maine. RN level III Porter Meml. Hosp., Denver, 1981-87; transport supr. Kapiolani Med. Ctr. Women & Children, Honolulu, 1987-89; dir. patient care unit Aspen Valley Hosp., Colo., 1989-91; dir. clin. practice Ctrl. Maine Med. Ctr., Lewiston, 1991-2000, dir. Sch. Nursing, 1998—. Home: 873 Oak Hill Rd North Yarmouth ME 04097-6242 E-mail: skhurts@cmhc.org.

KUIKEN, DIANE (DEE) MARIE, science educator; b. Ridgewood, N.J., Apr. 23, 1967; d. Diane Judith and Jerald Steven Boldezar; m. Brian Howard Kuiken, Aug. 15, 1992; children: Brian Nicholas, Brett Howard. BA, Boston Coll., Chestnut Hill, Mass., 1989; MS, Montclair State U., Montclair, New Jersey, 1992—94. Cert. supr. N.J., 2006. Technician Beacon Med. Lab., Brighton, Mass., 1987—89; tchr. sci. George Wash. Mid. Sch., Ridgewood, NJ, 1989—. Facilitator/test preparation N.J. Performance Assessment Assn., Monroe Township, 2003—. Author: (children's book) Jack's Daddy. Team mem. Cornerstone, Franklin Lakes, NJ, 2006—. Recipient Tchr. of Yr. award/Gov.'s Tchr. award, State of N.J., one. Home: 448 Weymouth Dr Wyckoff NJ 07481 Office: George Washington Mid Sch 155 Washington Pl Ridgewood NJ 07450 Office Phone: 201-280-8722. Personal E-mail: deesplace@optonline.net. E-mail: dkuiken@ridgewood.k12.nj.us.

KUJAWA, SISTER ROSE MARIE, academic administrator; b. Detroit; d. Francis and Anne Kujawa. BS in math., Madonna U., Livonia, Mich., 1966; MS in edn. and math., Wayne State U., Detroit, 1971, PhD in higher edn. adminstrn., 1979. Dept. chair math. Bishop Borgess H.S.; asst. prin. and curriculum coord. Ladywood H.S.; prof. Madonna U., Livonia, Mich., 1975, academic dean, academic v.p., acting dean Coll. of Arts and Sci., pres., 2001—. Office: Madonna U 36600 Schoolcraft Rd Livonia MI 48150-1173

KUJAWA-HOLBROOK, SHERYL, theology studies educator, academic administrator; m. Paul BA, Marquette U.; MA, Sarah Lawrence Coll.; MTS, Harvard Div. Sch.; MDiv, Episcopal Div. Sch., 1983; EdD, Columbia U.; PhD, Boston Coll. & CUNY. Dir. ministries with young people Episcopal Ch. Ctr.; asst. Ch. Incarnation, NYC; youth missioner Diocese Mass.; asst. Cathedral Ch. of St. Paul, Boston; chaplain Dorchester Mental Health Ctr. & McLean Hosp., Mass.; assoc. prof. pastoral theology Episcopal Div. Sch., Cambridge, Mass., 1998—2004, Suzanne Radley Hiatt Chair in Feminist Pastoral Theology & Ch. History, 2004—, academic dean, 2005—. Chair anti-racism com. Episcopal Ch. Exec. Coun., 1998—. Author: A House of Prayer for All Peoples: Congregations Building Multiracial Community, By Grace Came Incarnation: A Social History of the Church of the Incarnation, Murray Hill, NY, 1952-2002; editor: A Documentary History of Women in the Episcopal Church; co-editor (with Fredrica Harris Thompsett): Deeper Joy: Lay Women and Vocation in the 20th Century Episcopal Church. Office: Episcopal Div Sch 99 Brattle St Cambridge MA 02138 E-mail: skujawa@eds.edu.

KUJAWSKI, ELIZABETH SZANCER, art curator, consultant; b. N.Y.C., Feb. 7, 1951; d. Henryk and Irene (Zilz) Szancer; children: Melissa, Stephanie. BA cum laude in Art History and Italian, Douglass Coll., 1972; MA in Art History, Queens Coll., 1975. Info. asst. Whitney Mus. Am. Art, N.Y.C., 1972-75; asst. curator Collection of Nelson A. Rockefeller, N.Y.C., 1975-79; asst. dir. SKT Galleries, Inc., N.Y.C., 1979-82; prin., art curator, cons. Elizabeth Szancer Kujawski Art Advisors, N.Y.C., 1982—. Mem. exhbn. com. Internat. Ctr. Photography, N.Y.C. Mem.: Art Table, Inc., Internat. Assn. Profl. Art Advisors (pres. 1998—2000, bd. dirs. 2000—). Avocations: tennis, languages, travel. Office: 767 5th Ave Ste 4200 New York NY 10153-0023 Office Phone: 212-572-3867. Personal E-mail: eartsk@aol.com.

KUK, MARY HALVORSON, secondary school educator; b. Puyallup, Wash., Oct. 31, 1954; d. Raymond W. and Ruth A. Halvorson; m. Gregory L. Kuk, Feb. 5, 1983. BA, Ea. Wash. U., 1977; EdM in Health Edn., Oreg. State U., 1988. Educator South Umpqua Sch. Dist., Myrtle Creek, Oreg., 1977—. First aid/CPR instr. ARC, Roseburg, Oreg., 1995—; mem. Prevention Coalition, Roseburg, 1999—. Mem.: NEA, Nat. Multiple Sclerosis Soc., South Umpqua Edn. Assn. (bldg. rep.). Avocations: camping, photography, sewing, reading. Home: 425 W Maple Roseburg OR 97470-2926 Office: S Umpqua Sch Dist 501 NW Chadwick Myrtle Creek OR 97457

KUKER, GINA JOANNE, education educator; b. Waterloo, Iowa, Oct. 3, 1969; d. Eugene Louis and Janice Louise (Malquist) Matthias; m. Brent James Kuker, July 2, 2000; children: Jocelyn Maria, Braxton James. BA, Concordia Coll., St. Paul, 1992; MA, U. North Tex., Denton, 2000; post grad., U. No. Iowa, Cedar Falls, 2002—. Tchr. jr. high Grace Luth. Sch., Arlington, Tex., 1992—96; tchr. social studies Duncanville Ind. Sch. Dist., Tex., 1996—2000; asst. prof. edn. Upper Iowa U., Fayette, 2000—. Scholar, U. No. Iowa, 2003. Mem.: Internat. Soc. Tech. in Edn., Iowa Assn. Colls. Tchr. Edn., Phi Delta Kappa. Lutheran. Office: Upper Iowa Univ 605 Washington St PO Box 1857 Fayette IA 52142-1857

KUKLIN, SUSAN BEVERLY, law librarian, lawyer; b. Chgo., Nov. 25, 1947; d. Albert and Marion (Waller) K. BA in English and History with honors, U. Ariz., 1969, JD, 1973; MLS, Ind. U., 1970; LLM in Taxation, DePaul U., 1981. Bar: Ariz. 1973, Ill. 1980, Calif. 1984, U.S. Dist. Ct. (no. dist.) Ill. 1980. Asst. city atty. City of Phoenix, 1974-75; dep. county atty. County of Pima, Ariz., 1975-76; polit. sci., law libr. asst. prof. law No. Ill. U., 1976-78; law libr., assoc. prof. U. S.D., 1978-79; dir. law libr., asst. prof. DePaul U., 1979-83; law libr., dir. Santa Clara County, San Jose, Calif., 1983—2004; faculty libr. Pima Cmty. Coll., Tucson, 2005—. Sec. bd. trustees Law Library Santa Clara County. Editor: Desert Vista Campus Newsletter, 2006—. Mem. Am. Assn. Law Libr. (cert. law libr.), Coun. Calif. County Law Libr. (newsletter editor 1983-84), No. Calif. Assn. Law Libr., Phi Beta Kappa, Phi Kappa Phi, Alpha Lambda Delta, Phi Alpha Theta, Phi Delta Phi. Office: Pima Cmty Coll Desert Vista Libr 5901 S Calle Santa Cruz Tucson AZ 85709 Business E-Mail: skuklin@pima.edu.

KUKLINSKI, JOAN LINDSEY, librarian; b. Lynn, Mass., Nov. 28, 1950; d. Richard Jay and M. Claire (Murphy) Card; m. Walter S. Kuklinski, June 17, 1972. BA cum laude, Mass. State Coll., Salem, 1972; MLS, U. R.I., 1976; CAGS in Pub. Adminstrn., Clark U., 2002. Classified librarian U. R.I. Extension Divsn. Libr., Providence, 1974-75, U. R.I. Cataloging Dept., Kingston, 1975-79; original cataloger Tex. A&M U. Libr., College Station, 1979-82; cataloger Goldfarb Libr., Braindeis U., Waltham, Mass., 1982-83, automation coord., 1983-85; exec. dir. Minuteman Libr. Network, Framingham, Mass., 1985-96, C/W Mars, Inc., Paxton, Mass., 1996—. Mem. Town of South Kingstown (R.I.) Women's Adv. Commn., 1977-79; trustee Princeton (Mass.) Pub. Libr., 1994—; mem. strategic planning com. for libr. svc. in yr. 2000 Mass. Bd. Libr. Commrs. Mem. ALA (resources and tech. svcs. divsn. 1980-85), Mass. Librs. Assn., New Eng. Libr. Assn., Libr. Info. Tech. Assn., Assn. Specialized Libr. and Coop. Groups (NELINET Bd. 1994—), Am. Contract Bridge League, Delta Tau Kappa. Office: Cw Mars Inc 67 Millbrook St Ste 201 Worcester MA 01606-2843

KULIK, ROSALYN FRANTA, food company executive, consultant; b. Wilmington, Del., Aug. 29, 1951; d. William Alfred and Virginia Louise (Ellis) Franta. BS in Voc. Home Econs. Edn., Purdue U., 1972, MS in Foods and Nutrition, 1974; postgrad. in advanced mgmt. program, Harvard Bus. Sch., 1990. Registered dietitian. Home economist Kellogg Co., Battle Creek, Mich., 1974-75, nutrition and consumer specialist, 1975-77, mgr. advt. to children, 1977-79, corp. adminstrv. asst., 1979, dir. nutrition, 1979-82, dir. nutrition and analytical services, 1982, v.p. nutrition and chemistry, 1983, v.p. quality and nutrition, 1983-87, v.p., asst. to chmn., 1987-88; exec. v.p., gen. mgr. Fearn Internat., Franklin Park, Ill., 1988-90; cons., 1991—. Adj. faculty U. Tampa, Fla., 2001—05. Contbr. articles on food sci. and nutrition to profl. jours. Tampa Bay regional coord. Camp Invention, Inc., 2004—05; mem. ch. coun. Grace Luth. Ch., Tampa, Fla., 2000—03, 2004—, v.p., 2004—; bd. dirs. State Arthritis Found., County Vol. Ctr., Neighborhood Property Owners Assn., 2002—06. Recipient Ada Decker Malott Meml. scholarship, Purdue U., 1970, disting. alumna award Purdue U. Sch. of Consumer and Family Sci., Excellence in Svc. award Nutrition in Complementary Care Dietetic Practic Group, 2005. Fellow Am. Dietetic Assn. (cofounder, exec. officer nutrition in complementary care dietetic practice group 1998-2004, chair 2002-03, author position statement 2005); mem. Inst. Food Technologists (profl. mem.), Am. Dietetic Assn., Homeowners Property Assn. Avila (bd. dirs. 2002-06), Phi Kappa Phi, Gamma Sigma Delta, Omicron Nu, Alpha Omicron Pi. Republican. Lutheran. Avocations: music, church work, travel, jr. league volunteerism. Personal E-mail: kulikcon@msn.com.

KULIKOWSKI, CHERYL E., music educator; b. Pleasant Mount, Pa., Sept. 27, 1978; d. John and Cynthia Kulikowski. BS in Music Edn., Clarion U., 2001, BS in Elem. Edn., 2001; M in Music Edn., Ithaca Coll., 2006. Dir. bands, instrumental tchr. Sayre (Pa.) Area Sch. Dist., 2002—05, Cedar Crest HS, Cornwall-Lebanon Sch. Dist., Pa., 2005—. Author: The Clarinet, 2001. Mem.: NEA, Lancaster-Lebanon County Music Educators Assn., Internat. Clarinet Assn., Pa. State Educators Assn., Bradford-Sullivan County Music Educators Assn. (treas. 2002—05), Pa. Music Educators Assn. (William Nash Continuing Edn. scholar 2004), Music Educators Nat. Conf. Address: 2135 Penn St Lebanon PA 17042 Personal E-mail: cekulikows@hotmail.com.

KULKARNI, KAVITA-VIBHA ARUN, chemist; b. Dharwad, Karnataka, India, Aug. 12, 1945; arrived in U.S., 1971; d. Ratnakar and Chhaya Ratnakar Joshi; m. Arun Pandurang Kulkarni, June 30, 1971 (dec.); children: Arvind Kulkami, Aparna Kulkami. BSc, Pune U., India, 1965, MS, 1968, U. South Fla., 1998. Sci. and math. tchr. Adarsha Vidya Bhavan HS, Pune, 1968—69; quality control chemist Dai-ichi-Karkaria Pvt. Ltd., Pune, 1969—71; cashier Roses Dept. Store, Raleigh, NC, 1974—75; lectr. in chemistry NC State U., Raleigh, 1975—80, Ea. Mich. U., Ypsilanti, 1984—85; rsch. tech. in biology U. Tampa, Fla., 1989—90; rsch. asst. in internal medicine U. South Fla., Tampa, 1990—91, tchg. asst. organic chemistry, 1994—95, sci. advisor, 1999—2003; rsch. chemist Belmac Pharm. Co., Tampa, 1991—94. Contbr. articles to profl. jours. Non-backward class scholar, Maharastra State Govt., India, 1961—63, open merit scholar, 1963—65, merit scholar, Pune U., 1966—68. Mem.: Am. Chem. Soc., Phi Lambda Upsilon. Avocations: reading, travel, crocheting. Home: 18422 Dorman Rd Lithia FL 33547

KULKARNI, SHAILA V., secondary school educator; b. Annapolis, Md., Aug. 14, 1977; BS, U. Md., College Park, 1999. Project mgr. Am. Mgmt. Systems, Fairfax, Va., 2000—03; tchr. South River H.S., Edgewater, Md., 2003—. Scholar Banneker Key scholar, U. of Md., 1995—99. Mem.: Golden Key (life). Office Phone: 410-956-5600.

KULLEN, SHIRLEY ROBINOWITZ, psychiatric epidemiologist, consultant; b. Balt., Sept. 6, 1922; d. Joseph and Rose (Collins) Robinowitz; m. Joseph Stephen Reff, Sept. 14, 1941 (div. 1958); children: Richard Brian, Robert Alan; m. Sidney Irving Margolis, Oct. 28, 1973 (dec. Dec. 1988); m. Sol Kullen, Jan. 10, 1993. BS, Am. U., 1959, MBA, 1961, PhD, 1972. Statistician NIMH, Bethesda, Md., 1964-72, health scientist adminstrn., 1972-93; cons. psychiatric epidemiologist, Chevy Chase, Md., 1993—. Adj. prof. Am. U. Washington, 1961, 69, 70, 74, 87, seminar developer, 1987; lectr. Howard U., Washington, 1963-67. Bd. dirs. Jewish Cmty. Ctr. Greater Washington, Rockville, Md., 1979—90, Hebrew Home Washington, Rockville, 1980—85, Fed. Credit Union, Rockville, 1987—93; exec. v.p. S-K Family Partnership, 1996—2005. Recipient Helen Palmer Kettler Soc. award, Am. U., 2004. Mem. APHA (adv. bd. mental health sect. 1990-93), AAUW. Avocations: golf, music, writing. Office: 5610 Wisconsin Ave Chevy Chase MD 20815 Office Phone: 301-652-3655. Personal E-mail: sugar906@aol.com.

KULLMAN, ELLEN JAMISON, chemicals executive; b. Jan. 22, 1956; m. Michael Kullman; 3 children. BS in Mech. Engring., Tufts U., 1978; MBA, Northwestern U. Various bus. devel., mktg. and sales positions GE; mktg. mgr. med. imaging DuPont, 1988—90, bus. dir. x-ray film, 1990—92, global bus. dir. electronic imaging Printing & Pub., 1992—94, global bus. dir. White Pigment & Mineral Products, 1994—95, v.p., gen. mgr. White Pigment & Mineral Products, 1995—98, v.p., gen. mgr. Safety Resources, 1998—99, v.p., gen. mgr. Bio-Based Materials, 1999—2000, v.p., gen. mgr. DuPont Flooring Systems & DuPont Surfaces, 2001—02, group v.p. DuPont Safety & Protection, 2002—06, exec. v.p. Dupont Safety & Protection; Dupont Coatings & Color Tech.; Mktg. & Sales & Safety & Sustainability, 2006—. Bd. dir. Gen. Motors Corp., 2004—. Trustee Christiana Care Corp.; mem. bd. overseers Tufts U.; bd. dirs. Del. Symphony, Wellness Cmty. Named one of 50 Most Powerful Women in Bus., Fortune mag., 2006; recipient Aiming High award, 2004. Office: DuPont Bldg 1007 Market St Wilmington DE 19898*

KULP, BETTE JONEVE, retired educator, wallpaper installation business owner; b. Pomona, Calif., Jan. 5, 1936; d. John M. and Eva Kathleen (Lynch) Beck; m. Edwin Hanaway Kulp, Sept. 12, 1957 (div. Apr. 1972); m. Frank Harold Little, Oct. 8, 1977. BS in Home Econs., UCLA, 1957, GPPS credential, 1972. Credential C.C. counselor, gen. pupil personnel svcs., tchr. homemaking. Social worker L.A. County DPSS, 1957-59; tchr., counselor L.A. City Sch. Dist., 1959-81; wallpaper installer West Los Angeles, Calif., 1981-87. Mem. UCLA Scholarship Com. West L.A., San Luis Obispo, Calif., 1978—; judge Acad. Decathalon, San Luis Obispo County, 1989-90, 92, 98-2004. Vol. Daffodil Days Am. Cancer Soc., San Luis Obispo, 1992—, Am. Heart Assn., San Luis Obispo, 1992, Sr. Nutrition Program, San Luis Obispo, 1993-2002; runner Spl. Olympics, San Luis Obispo, 1992; participant Audubon Bird-A-Thon, San Luis Obispo, 1993; locator nesting birds Audubon Breeding Bird Atlas, San Luis Obispo, 1992; fundraiser Womens Shelter Program, San Luis Obispo, 1993-94; precinct clk., judge San Luis Obispo County Election Bd., 1989—; mem. Sch. Dist. Orgn. Com. San Luis Obispo County Schs., 1995—; aide Dist. 3 San Luis Obispo County Bd. Suprs., 1994-96; campaign com. Marie Kiersch for Cuesta Coll. Bd. Trustees, 1994; vol. 22nd Congl. Dist., 1997, Neighborhood Vol. March of Dimes, 1998; mem. San Lusi Obispo County Grand Jury, 2003-2004. Recipient Appreciation award Women's Shelter Program, 1993, Unsung Heroine award San Luis Obispo Commn. Status Women, 1995. Mem. AAUW (treas. San Luis Obispo br. 1989-91, pres.-elect 1991-92, pres. 1992-93, bylaws revision com. 1993, San Luis Obispo Interbr. chair 1993-94, chair state resolutions 1994-95, Grant Honoree 1994, membership co-v.p. 1994-95, herstory coord., 1995-96, Cuesta scholarship chair 1995-96, scholarship treas. 2000—, parliamentarian 1993-94,interbranch rep., 2003-04; dual mem. five cities Pismo 1994, endorsement com. 1995, scholarship com. 1995-2005, chair 1996-2002, 2003-2005, bylaws chair 1996-97, 99, 2001, co-pres. 1998-99, tech. trek com. 2001, scholarship fundraising v.p., 2002-04, interbranch rep., 2003-04), Santa Lucia Bridge Club, Phi Mu Alumnae (founder Calif. Ctrl. Coast chpt.), Newcomers Club, Morro Coast Audubon Soc. Avocations: bridge, birding, travel, reading, puzzles. Home: 2362 Meadow St San Luis Obispo CA 93401-5628

KULYK, KAREN GAY, artist; b. Toronto, Can., July 19, 1950; d. Joseph and Natalie Melanie (Solowski) K. BFA with honors, York U., 1973. Founder, curator Seedlings Gallery, Toronto, 1973-75; established studios worldwide, 1975—. Tchr. various instns., Can., Thailand, Bermuda, Eng., Mexico. One-woman shows include Kitchener-Waterloo Art Gallery, 1994, Rodman Hall, St. Catharines, Ont., 1995, Harbinger Gallery, 1994—, Marianne Friedland Gallery, 1974-1996, Masterworks Found. Gallery, Hamilton, Bermuda, 1997, Henry Dyson Fine Art, London, 1996—, Carnegie Gallery, Dundas, Ont., Can., 1996, Nancy Poole's Studio, Toronto, 1996-99, Gallery on the Bay, Hamilton, Ont., 1997—, Wallack Gallery, Ottawa, Can., 1996—, Zwicker Gallery, Halifax, N.S., Can., 1999—, Nat. Gallery Thailand, Grey Coll. U. Durham, Eng., 2000; exhibited in group shows at Harbinger Gallery, Waterloo, Ont., Touchstone Gallery, Hong Kong, Marianne Friedland Gallery, Fla., Sotheby's, Toronto, Chgo. Internat. Art Exhbn., York U., U. Toronto, Offices of Gov. Gen. of Can., Carleton U. Art Gallery, numerous others; represented in collections at Kitchener-Waterloo Art Gallery, Wilfred Laurier U., Waterloo, Art Gallery of Hamilton, Carleton U., York U., Agnes Etherington Art Gallery, Nat. Gallery of Bermuda, Hartford Coll., Md., Can. Trust, Dominion Trust, Shell Can., Thai Airways Internat., Can. Airlines Internat., Dalhousie U., N.S., Aliant Atlantic Telecom., Can., others, pvt. collections; illustration: Orff, 27 Dragons and a Snarkel, Dalhouseie U. Art Gallery, Halifax, Nova Scotia; subject of several newspaper articles. Recipient Grollo d'Oro, award Treviso Internat. Art Competition, 1983; grantee Sheila Hugh Mackay Found., 1996. Home and Office: 5270 Morris St Halifax NS Canada B3J 1B4 Personal E-mail: mgoodyear@dal.ca. E-mail: karenkulyk@hotmail.com.

KUMANYIKA, SHIRIKI K., nutrition epidemiology researcher, educator; b. Balt., Mar. 16, 1945; m. Christiaan B. Morssink; children: Chenjerai, Annoesjka. BA, Syracuse U., 1965; MS in Social Work, Columbia U., 1969; PhD in Human Nutrition, Cornell U., 1978; MPH, Johns Hopkins U., 1984. Asst. prof. nutrition Cornell U., Ithaca, NY, 1977-84; from asst. prof. to assoc. prof. epidemiology Johns Hopkins U. Sch. Hygiene and Pub. Health, Balt., 1984-89, asst. prof. internat. health, 1984-89; assoc. prof. nutritional epidemiology Pa. State U., University Park, 1989-92, prof. epidemiology, 1993-96; assoc. dir. for epidemiology Pa. State U. Coll. Medicine, Hershey, 1992-96; prof. epidemiology, prof. human nutrition and dietetics U. Ill. at Chgo., 1996-99, head dept. human nutrition and dietetics, 1996-99; chief of svc. U. Ill. Hosp. Nutritional Svcs., 1996-99; prof. epidemiology Children's Hosp. Phila., U. Pa. Sch. Med., Phila., 1999—, assoc. dean health promotion and disease prevention, 1999—, dir., grad. program, pub. health studies; dir. Penn-Cheyney Export Ctr. Inner City Health, Phila. Sr. scholar, Ctr. Clin. Epidemiology & Biostatistics (CCEB) U. Pa., sr. fellow, Inst. Aging, Leonard Davis Inst. Health Economics, adj. prof. epidemiology dept. health evaluation scis. Coll. Medicine, Pa. State U., Hershey, 1996-99; mem. adv. bd. Women's Health Alliance. Contbr. articles to profl. jours. Bd. dirs. Nat. Rural Ctr., 1978-82, Nat. Black Women's Health Project, 1994-99; mem. Women's Health Initiative adv. com. 1993-, US Dietary Guidelines Com., 1995, 2000, Nat. Heart, Lung, & Blood Inst. adv. coun., 1996-2000, NIH Obesity Task Force, 2001-, Nat. Children's Study adv. com., 2002-2003; active WHO. NIH grantee; recipient Bolton L. Corson medal Franklin Inst., 1997. Fellow Am. Coll. Epidemiology, Am. Coll. Nutrition; mem. AAUP, APHA, Am. Diabetes Assn., Am. Dietetic Assn., Am. Inst. Nutrition, Am. Soc. for Clin. Nutrition, Assn. Black Cardiologists, Internat. Soc. on Hypertension in Blacks, Nat. Med. Assn., N.Am. Assn. Study of Obesity, Soc. for Epidemiol. Rsch., Soc. for Nutrition Edn., Internat. Soc. and Fedn. Cardiology, Inst. Medicine. Office: Ctr Clin Epidemiology and Biostats U Pa Sch Med 8th Fl Blockley Hall 423 Guardian Dr Philadelphia PA 19104-6021 E-mail: skumanyi@cceb.med.upenn.edu.*

KUMAR, FAITH, clinical professional counselor; b. South Haven, Mich., May 12, 1960; d. Norris Kendall and Verna Ann (Jeffries) Curtis BS, Western Mich. U., 1990, M Counseling Psychology, 1993. Lic. clin. profl. counselor, Ill. Nursery supr. Child Devel. Ctr., Kalamazoo, 1988-90; tchr. Kalamazoo Pub. Sch. Sys., 1990-93; supr. Victor C. Neuman, Chgo., 1993-94; mentor counselor IL Mentor, Schaumburg, Ill., 1994-97; pvt. practice Chgo., 1997—. Counselor Lakeside Boys and Girls Home, Kalamazoo, 1990-93; therapist Ctrl. Bapt. Family Svcs., Chgo., 1994; peer supr. for pvt. therapists, Chgo., 1998—. Author: (juvenile) Legend of Hun, 1986. Vol. Big Bros.-Big Sisters, Kalamazoo, 1989-93; vol. probation officer, Kalamazoo, 1989-92. Avocations: swimming, dance, travel, reading, stamp collecting/philately.

KUMAR, RAMYA, academic administrator; d. Brinda Kumar. BA in Psychology, U. Mass., 2001, MS in Biol. Scis., 2003. Cert. rape aggression defense instr. Rape Aggression Defense Sys. Resident advisor U. Mass., Lowell, 1999—2000, asst. resident dir., 2000—02, resident dir., 2002—03, Mich. State U., East Lansing, Mich., 2003—04, assoc. dir. student affairs, Lyman Briggs Sch., 2003—04; hall dir. U. Ariz., Tucson, 2004—. Culture fest mktg. chair U. Mass., 2000—01, safety com., 2000—01, yearbook prodn. com., 2000—02; coord. residence hall orientation Mich. State U., 2003—04, advisor, Lyman Briggs ambassadors, 2003—04, com. mem. women's history banquet and conf., 2003—04; advisor, coalition Indian undergrad. students Mich. State. U., East Lansing, Mich., 2003—04; regional conf. programming advisor affiliated coll. and univ. residence halls Inter Mountain, Tucson, 2004—04; freshman seminar instr. U. Ariz., Tucson, 2004—, advisor, residence hall coun., 2004—05, staff selection, tng. com., 2004—, acad. initiatives com., 2004—. Vol. tunnel of opression U. Ariz., 2004—, sexual assault awareness marathon organizer, 2004—; yound adult coord., tchr. children's spirituality class Sri Sathya Sai Baba Ctr. Tucson, 2005. Recipient Resident Advisor of Yr., U. Mass., 1999, Programmer of Yr., 1999, Psi Chi Inductee, Psi Chi Nat. Honors Soc. Psychology, 2001. Mem.: Assn. Internat. Mountain Affiliated Housing Ofcrs., Nat. Assn. Student Pers. Adminstrs., Am. Coll. Pers. Assn., Psi Chi. Achievements include research in Alzheimer's using mazes and diet patterns, published in the Journal of Neuromolecular Medicine.

KUMAR, RITA, literature and language educator; m. Pawan Kumar; children: Aarti, Aman. PhD in English, U. of Lucknow, India, 1991. Postgrad. cert. tchg. English Cen. Inst. of Langs., India, advanced diploma in French U. of Lucknow, cert. in French Alliance Francaise de Calgary, Can. Asst. prof. English U. of Cin., Cin., 2001—. Owner, trainer, cons. Impact Internat., Dryden, Ont., Canada, 1993—98; adj. prof. English Mercyhurst Coll., Erie, Pa., 1998—2001; adj. lectr. Behrend Coll., Pa. State U., 2000. Mem. Police Svcs. Bd., Dryden, 1993—95. Recipient grad. scholarship for PhD, Univ. Grants Commn., 1987—91, Gold Medal for all-India level essay competetion, Gandhi Found., 1989, Future of Learning award. Mem.: 2-Yr. Coll. Assn., Nat. Assn. of Devel. Edn., Nat. Coun. Tchrs. of English.

KUMIN, LIBBY BARBARA, speech language pathologist, educator; b. Bklyn., Nov. 11, 1945; d. Herbert H. and Berniece (Shuch) K.; m. Martin J. Lazar, Jan. 18, 1969; 1 child, Jonathan Kumin Lazar. BA summa cum laude, LIU, 1965; MA, NYU, 1966, PhD, 1969. Lic. speech pathologist, pathology. Asst. prof. speech pathology U. Md., College Park, 1972-76, cons., 1976-80; assoc. prof. Loyola Coll., Balt., 1980-88, prof., 1988—, chmn. dept. speech and lang. pathology, 1983—99, dir. MS program, 1983—2003, dir. grad. programs, 1999—2003. Adj. prof. Loyola Coll., 1976-80; specialist in speech and language in Down Syndrome; mem. profl. adv. bd. Nat. Down Syndrome Cong.; leader of parent and profl. seminars; mem. Down Syndrome Med. Interest Group. Author: Aphasia, 1978, Classroom Language Skills in Children with Down Syndrome, 2001, Early Communication Skills for Children with Down Syndrome, 2003; therapies editor: Down Syndrome Quar.; contbr. articles to profl. jours. Recipient Outstanding Individual of Yr. award Howard County Assn. Retarded Citizens, Nat. Meritorious Svc. award Nat. Down Syndrome Congress, 1987, Rsch. award Christian Pueschel Meml., 2004, The Pres.'s award Nat. Down Syndrome Soc., 2005; grantee Loyola Coll., 1983, 91, 97, 99, 2002, 04, Aaron and Lillie Straus Found., 1983-89, 99-2005, Taishoff Family Found., 2005, 06, Columbia Found., Joseph P. Kennedy Found., 1995, 2002, Shriver Ctr., 1996-98, 2002 Mem. ARC, Nat. Down Syndrome Soc. (Pres.'s award 2005), Nat. Down Syndrome Congress, Am. Speech/Lang./Hearing Assn. (cert.), Md. Speech and Hearing Assn., Taishoff Family Found., Sigma Tau Delta, Pi Lambda Theta. Office: Loyola Coll Dept Speech Pathology 4501 N Charles St Dept Speech Baltimore MD 21210-2601 Business E-Mail: lkumin@loyola.edu.

KUMIN, MAXINE WINOKUR, poet, writer; b. Phila., June 6, 1925; d. Peter and Doll (Simon) Winokur; m. Victor Montwid Kumin, June 29, 1946; children: Jane Simon, Judith Montwid, Daniel David. AB, Radcliffe Coll., 1946, MA, 1948; LHD (hon.), Centre Coll., 1976, Davis and Elkins Coll., 1977, Regis Coll., 1979, New England Coll., 1982, Claremont Grad. Sch., 1983, U. N.H., 1984, Bowdoin Coll., 2002. Instr. Tufts U., Medford, Mass., 1958-61, lectr. English, 1965-68. Scholar Radcliffe Inst. for Ind. Study, 1961-63; vis. lectr. U. Mass., Amherst, 1973, Princeton U., 1977, 79, 81-82; adj. prof. Columbia U., 1975; Fannie Hurst prof. of literature Brandeis U., 1975, Wash. U., St. Louis, 1977; Carolyn Wilkerson Bell vis. scholar Randolph-Macon Woman's Coll., 1978; poet in residence Bucknell U., 1983; vis. prof. MIT, 1984, U. Miami, 1995, Pitzer Coll., 1996; McGee prof. of writing Davidson Coll., 1997; writer in residence Fla. Internat. U., 1998-2000; master artist Atlantic Ctr. for Arts, New Smyrna Beach, Fla., 1984-2002; staff mem. Bread Loaf Writers' Conf., 1969-71, 73, 75, 77; poetry cons. Library of Congress, 1981-82; elector The Poet's Corner, The Cathedral of St. John the Divine, 1990-1996; mem. staff Sewanee Writer's Conf., 1993-94, Bucknell U. visiting poet, 2001. Author: (poetry) Halfway, 1961, The Privilege, 1965, The Nightmare Factory, 1970, Up Country: Poems of New England, 1972 (Pulitzer Prize for poetry 1973), House, Bridge, Fountain, Gate, 1975, The Retrieval System, 1978, Our Ground Time Here Will Be Brief, 1982, Closing the Ring, 1984, The Long Approach, 1985, Nurture, 1989, Looking for Luck, 1992 (Poets' Prize), Connecting the Dots, 1996, Selected Poems 1960-1990, 1997, The Long Marriage, 2001, Bringing Together, 2003, Jack and Other New Poems, 2005; (novels) Through Dooms of Love, 1965, The Passions of Uxport, 1968, The Abduction, 1971, The Designated Heir, 1974; (essays) To Make A Prairie: Essays on Poets, Poetry, and Country Living, 1980, In Deep: Country Essays, 1987, Women, Animals and Vegetables: Essays and Stories, 1994, Inside the Halo and Beyond, 2000, Always Beginning, 2000; (short stories) Why Can't We Live Together Like Civilized Human Beings?, 1982; (juvenile) Sebastian and the Dragon, 1960, Spring Things, 1961, A Summer Story, 1961, Follow the Fall, 1961, A Winter Friend, 1961, Mittens in May, 1962, No One Writes a Letter to the Snail, 1962, Archibald the Traveling Poodle, 1963, (with Sexton) Eggs of Things, 1963, (with Sexton) More Eggs of Things, 1964, Speedy Digs Downside Up, 1964, The Beach Before Breakfast, 1964, Paul Bunyan, 1966, Faraway Farm, 1967, The Wonderful Babies of 1809 and Other Years, 1968, When Grandmother Was Young, 1970, When Great-Grandmother Was Young, 1971, (with Sexton) Joey and the Birthday Present, 1971, (with Sexton) The Wizard's Tears, 1975, What Color Is Caesar?, 1978, The Microscope, 1984; contbr. poems to nat. mags. Recipient Lowell Mason Palmer award, 1960, William Marion Reedy award, 1968, Eunice Tietjens Meml. prize Poetry Mag., 1972, Borestone Mountain award, 1976, Radcliffe Coll. Alumnae Recognition award, 1978, Am. Acad. and Inst. Arts and Letters award for excellence in literature, 1980, Levinson award Poetry mag., 1987, The Poets' prize, 1994, Aiken Taylor Poetry prize, 1995, Centennial award Harvard Grad. Sch. Arts and Scis., 1996, NH Writers Project Lifetime Achievement award, 1998, Ruth Lilly Poetry Prize, 1999, Charity Randall award, 2000, Robert Frost award, Plymouth Coll., 2001, Harvard U. Arts medal, 2005; grantee Nat. Endowment for the Arts, 1966; fellow Nat. Coun. on Arts and Humanities, 1967-68; fellow Acad. Am. Poets, 1986-2002; fellow Woodrow Wilson, 1979-80, 91-93. Mem. Acad. Am. Poets (chancellor), Poetry Soc. Am., PEN Am., Authors Guild, The Writers Union.

KUMISKI, CHERYL MARIE, artist; b. Cambridge, Mass., Oct. 25, 1955; d. John Joseph and Pauline Armand (Valois) K.; m. Timothy Leo White, Dec. 25, 1995 (div.). Grad. high sch., Medford, Mass. Owner, designer Cheryl Kumiski Stained Glass, Rochester, NH, 1985—. Cons. in field. Mem. Maine Crafts Assn., ExeterLeague N.H. Craftsmen (v.p., coun. mem.), League N.H. Craftsmen (scholar 1990, 92, 94), Exeter Assn. Arts, Internat. Glass Guild (founding pres.). Avocations: biking, hiking, gardening. Home and Office: 37 N Main St Rochester NH 03867 Office Phone: 603-335-3577. Personal E-mail: info@cherylkumiski.com.

KUMMETH, PATRICIA JOAN, nursing educator; b. Libertyville, Ill., Mar. 7, 1949; d. Francis Alphonse Kummeth, Elizabeth Claire Kummeth. BSN, Coll. St. Teresa, 1970; MSN, U. Wis., Eau Claire, 1988. Registered nurse. Staff nurse St. Marys Hosp., Rochester, Minn., 1970—72, clin. insvc. educator, 1972—76, head nurse med., 1976—78, staff nurse hematology/nephrology, 1978—81; nursing edn. specialist Mayo Clinic Hosp., Rochester, 1982—. Mem. commn. on accreditation Am. Nurses' Credentialing Ctr., Washington, 1998—2002. Author: (booklet) Problem-Oriented Charting: A Study Guide, 1976. Sec. Rochester Women's Softball Assn., 1994—98. Recipient Breaking Barriers award, Minn. Coalition to Promote Women in Athletic Leadership, 2001. Mem.: ANA (congress on nursing practice and economics 1998—2002), Minn. Nurses Assn. (commn. on edn. 1991—92, sec. 1992—93, commn. nursing practice 1999—2003), Acad. Med.-Surg. Nurses (sec. Upper Miss. River Valley chpt. 1999—2001), Am. Soc.Healthcare Educators and Trainers (info. mgr. Minn. affiliate 1993—95), Minn. Nurses Assn. (pres. 6th dist. 1988—92, sec. 1995—99, 1995—99, dir. 2000—02), Sigma Theta Tau (Kappa Mu chpt.). Roman Catholic. Avocations: reading, golf, travel. Office: Mayo Clinic Hosp 1216 Second St SW - 7 Marian Hall Rochester MN 55902 Home: 5162 3rd St NW Rochester MN 55901-4418 Office Phone: 507-255-5722.

KUMOJI, IDA, art educator; d. John Larweh and Diana Tsotso Kumoji; m. Maxwell Ankrah, Aug. 12, 1968. BA (hon.), Coll. St. Catherine, St. Paul, 2001; MFA, U. Minn., Duluth, 2005. Grad. instr. U. Minn., Duluth, 2002—05; asst. prof. Ea. Ky. U., Richmond, 2005—. Recipient Jr. Faculty Rsch. award, Ea. Ky. U., 2006. Mem.: Am. Inst. Graphic Arts (assoc. scholar 2004), Phi Beta Kappa (hon.). Home: 319 kristen Dr Apt # 3 Richmond KY 40475 Office: Eastern Kentucky University 521 Lancester Ave Richmond KY 40475 Office Phone: 859-622-8235. Personal E-mail: ida.kumoji@eku.edu.

KUMOR, MICHELLE, special education educator; b. Park Ridge, Ill., June 5, 1978; d. Raymond and Barbara Dombroski; m. Kumor John, July 24, 2004. BS in Edn., Ea. Ill. U., Charleston, 2000; MA in Tchg. and Leadership, St. Xavier U., Chgo. Cert. spl. tchg. Ill. State Bd. Edn., 2001. Spl. edn. tchr. Schaumburg Sch. Dist. #54, Ill., 2001—02, Glenview Sch. Dist. #34, Ill., 2002—04; spl. edn. inclusion tchr. Ridgewood H.S. Dist. #234, Norridge, Ill., 2004—. Camp counselor Elk Grove Village Pk. Dist., Ill., 1997—2000; head cheerleading coach Ridgewood H.S. Dist. #234, Norridge, 2004—, head softball coach, 2006—. Achievements include research in how the use of multiple intelligences in teacher planning and student choice empowers students to take charge of their own learning. Home: 8711 W Bryn Mawr Ave #708 Chicago IL 60631 Office Phone: 708-456-4242.

KUMPATY, HEPHZIBAH J., chemistry professor; m. Subha K. Kumpaty. PhD, U. Miss., 1996. Assoc. prof. U. Wis., Whitewater, Wis., 1996—. Rschr. U. Wis., Milw., 2006, dir. women and sci. program, Oshkosh, Wis., 1999—2002. Contbr. articles to profl. jours. Recipient Chancellor's award, U. Wis. Whitewater, 2005. Mem.: Am. Chem. Soc. (advisor local student chpt. Wis. Whitewater, 2005. Mem.: Am. Chem. Soc. (advisor local student chpt. award 2005). Avocations: travel, reading, cooking. Office: UW Whitewater 800 West main st Whitewater WI 800 W Office Phone: 262-472-1097. Business E-Mail: kumpatyh@uww.edu.

KUNC, KAREN, artist, educator; b. Omaha, Dec. 15, 1952; BFA, U. Nebr., Lincoln, 1975; MFA, Ohio State U., 1977. Assoc. prof. printmaking U. Nebr., Lincoln, 1983-97, full prof. printmaking, 1997—, gallery dir., 1988-91. Prof., art, Univ. Neb., 1983-, vis. asst. prof. U. Calif., Berkeley, 1987; vis. artist, instr. Carleton Coll., Northfield, Minn., 1989; rsch. fellow Kyoto Seika U., Japan, 1993; vis. artist Icelandic Coll. Arts & Crafts, Rekyavik, 1995. One-woman show Columbus (Ohio) Mus. Art, 1983, Sheldon Meml. Art Gallery, Lincoln, 1984, Mus. Art, U. Iowa, City, 1994, Joslyn Art Mus., Omaha, 1995, Gallery APA, Nagoya, Japan, 1995, Kutna Hora, Czech Republic, 1996, Galleria Harmonia, Jyvasklya, Finland, 1996; exhibited in group shows San Francisco Mus. Modern Art, 1980, Honolulu Acad. Arts, 1985, Mednorodini Graficni Likovni Ctr., Ljubljana, Yugoslavia, 1987, Zimmerli Art Mus., Rutgers U., New Brusnwick, N.J., 1988, Greenville (S.C.) County Mus. Art, 1988, Calif. Palace Legion of Honor, San Francisco, 1989, Nat. Mus. Women in Arts, Washington, 1991, Elvehjem Mus. Art, U. Wis., Madison, 1993, 9th Seoul Internat. Print Biennale, 1994, Tama Art Mus., Japan, 1995, Graphicstudio Gallery, Tampa, Fla., 1996, Nat. Mus. Am. Art, Washington, 1997; represented in permanent collections Mus. of Modern Art, N.Y., Nat. Mus. Am. Art, Smithsonian Instn., Washington, Libr. Congress, Washington, Worcester (Mass.) Art Mus., Sheldon Meml. Art Gallery, U. Nebr., Nat. Art Libr., Victoria and Albert Mus., London, Mus. Modern Art, N.Y.C., Bklyn. Mus. Art, Fogg Art Mus. Harvard U.; commns. include woodcut print Madison Print Club, 1994, Benziger Winery Imagery Series, Glen Ellen, Calif., 1996, prints Zimmerli Art Mus., 1995, Rutgers Archives Printmaking Studios, 1995, artists book Nat. Mus. Women Arts, Washington, 1996; co-author, editor: Polish Prints: A Contemporary Graphic Tradition, 1989; author: Woodcut and the Contemporary Impressions, 1993; represented by Jane Haslem Gallery, Washington. Recipient 1st prize Graphica Atlaantica, Reykjavik, Iceland, 1987, purchase award U. Del., 1988, prize Machida City Mus. Graphic Art, Tokyo, 1993; fellow Nat. Endowment Arts, 1984, 96; Fulbright scholar, 1996. Mem. NAD (academician, 1994-), Mid-Am. Print Coun., Coll. Art Assn., Ctr. Book Arts, Calif. Soc. Printmakers, Boston Printmakers, Print Club. Office: Art & History 303B NCW Univ Nebraska Lincoln NE 68588-0114 also: Atrium Gallery 4729 Mcpherson Ave Saint Louis MO 63108-1918 Office Phone: 402-472-5541. E-mail: kkunc@unlserve.unl.edu.

KUNCL, KIMBERLY A., obstetrician, gynecologist; b. Chgo. BA, Grinnell Coll., Iowa, 1987; MD, Morehouse Sch. of Medicine, Atlanta, Ga., 1995. Lic. Medical Doctor Ga., 2001. Resident St. John's Hosp. and Med. Ctr., Detroit, 1995—99; attending physician Douglas Women's Ctr., Lithin Springs, Ga., 1999—, Wellster Cobb Hosp. and Med. Ctr., Arstell, Ga., 1999—. Asst. prof. of family practice Emory U., Atlanta, 2001—03; spkr. in field. Mem. Old Fourth World Neighborhood Assn., Atlanta, 2004—. Mem.: ACOG, Nat. Med. Assn. Achievements include vocational interests in minimally invasive surgery including laparoscopy and hystroscopy. Avocations: hiking, tennis. Office: Douglas Womens Ctr 880 Crestmark Ave Ste 200 Lithia Springs GA 30122

KUNDERT, JUDY A., writer; b. Denver, Sept. 19, 1944; d. Lloyd I. and Evelyn A. Rebuck; m. Donald P. Kundert. BA, Loyola U., 1976; MA, DePaul U., 1984. Cert.: (legal asst.). Real estate analyst Aerial Comm., Inc., Chgo., 1996—97; paralegal Holme Roberts Owen, Denver, 1997—2000, Brownstein, Hyatt, Faber, Denver, 2000—03, Jacob, Chase et al, Denver, 2003—05, Dufford & Brown, P.C., Denver, 2005—. Sec. Chgo. Women in Govt. Rels., 1993—95. Author: Talking With Trees, 2006, Understanding Your Personality With Trees, 2006. Bd. dirs. Ctrl. City Opera Pros, Denver, 1997—98, Broomfield (Colo.) Pub. Libr., 2005—. Mem.: Colo. Ind. Pubs. Assn., Rocky Mountain Fiction Writers. Avocations: needlepoint design, bicycling, tennis, reading, movies. Home: 14184 Waterside Ln Broomfield CO 80020 Office: Dufford Brown PC Ste 2100 1700 Broadway Denver CO 80290 Office Phone: 303-837-6351. Business E-Mail: judy@judykundert.com.

KUNDRAT, VIRGINIA LYNN, science educator; b. Urbana, Ill., May 10, 1959; d. Addison Gilbert and Nancy Lois Cook; m. Albert Ted Kundrat, Apr. 13, 1985; children: Sarah Hope, Norah Joy. BA, Wheaton Coll., 1981; MS, Ind. U., 2004. Teaching License in Chemistry & Physics Ind. Profl. Standards Bd., 1999. Chemist, asst. metallographer Nat. Intergroup, Inc., Midwest Steel divsn., Portage, Ind., 1981—89; interim gen. chemistry lab instr. Valparaiso U., Ind., 1990; chemistry and physics tchr. Carmel H.S., Ind., 1999—. Musician Carmel Symphony Orch., Ind., 1992, Ind. Horn Ensemble, 2001; musician and tchr. Coll. Pk. ch., Indpls., 2001. Mem.: NSTA, Hoosier Assn. of Sci. Teachers, Inc., Am. Chem. Soc. Avocations: music, gardening, reading, sewing. Home: 4816 Pebblepointe Pass Zionsville IN 46077 Office: Carmel HS 520 E Main St Carmel IN 46032 Office Phone: 317-846-7721 1190. E-mail: vkundrat@ccs.k12.in.us.

KUNES, ELLEN, magazine executive; m. David Freeman; 2 children. Grad., U. NH, 1981. Cons. editor Mademoiselle Mag.; contbg. editor Omni Mag.; exec. editor Self Mag.; lifestyle dir. McCall's, 1991—94; exec. editor Redbook Mag., 1994—98, Cosmopolitan, 1998—99; editor O Mag., 1999; editor-in-chief Redbook Mag., 2001—04; with mag. devel. group Hearst Magazines, 2004—. Author: Living Well - Or Even Better - On Less, 1991. Office: Hearst 250 W 55th St New York NY 10019-5201

KUNG, CANDIE, professional golfer; b. Kaohsiung, Taiwan, Aug. 8, 1981; Attended, U. So. Calif. Winner U.S. Pub. Links Championship, 2001, State Farm Classic, 2003; Wachovia LPGA Classic, 2003, LPGA Takefuji Classsic, 2003. Two-time NCAA All-Am.; winner Pac-10 Championships, 2000; three-time Am. Jr. Golf Assn. All-Am. Named Am. Jr. Golf Assn. Player of Yr., 1999. Office: c/o LPGA 100 International Golf Dr Daytona Beach FL 32124-1092*

KUNIN, JACQUELINE BARLOW, retired art educator; b. Harrisburg, Pa., Apr. 20, 1941; d. Rodney Kipton and Marie (Trunk) Barlow; m. Richard Henry Kunin, June 17, 1967. BFA, Pratt Inst., 1963; MEd, Temple U., 1967. Comml. artist Dock and Kinney Co., NYC, 1963-64; art libr. Norcross, Inc., NYC, 1964; tchr. graphic arts Jones Jr. H.S., Phila., 1964-66; tchr. art John Bartram H.S., Phila., 1966-86; tchr. painting and drawing H.S. for Creative and Performing Arts, Phila., 1986—2006; ret., 2006. Named Disting Tchr. White House Commn. Presdl. Scholars, Washington, 1994, Outstanding Educator award Phila. Coll. Textiles and Sci., 1997. Mem. AAUW, Pa. Art Edn. Assn., Victorian Soc. Am. (Phila. chpt. bd. dirs. 1986-96), Valley Forge Civic Assn. Avocations: painting, collecting american costumes 1850-1950.

KUNIN, MADELEINE MAY, former ambassador to Switzerland, former governor; b. Zurich, Switzerland, Sept. 28, 1933; arrived in U.S., 1940, naturalized, 1947; d. Ferdinand and Renee (Bloch) May; m. John W. Hennessey, Jr., Feb. 12, 2006; children: Julia, Peter, Adam, Daniel. BA, U. Mass., 1956; MS, Columbia U., 1957; MA, U. Vt., 1967; degree (hon.). Newspaper reporter Burlington Free Press, Vt., 1957-58; guide Brussels World's Fair, Belgium, 1958; TV asst. producer Sta. WCAX-TV, Burlington, 1960-61; freelance writer, instr. English Trinity Coll., Burlington, 1969-70; mem. Vt. Ho. of Reps., 1973-78; lt. gov. State of Vt., Montpelier, 1979-82, gov., 1985-91; disting. vis. in Pub. Policy Bunting Inst., Cambridge, Mass., 1991-92; Montgomery fellow Dartmouth Coll., Hanover, NH, 1992; dep. sec. edn. Dept. Edn., Washington, 1993-96; U.S. amb. to Switzerland, 1996-99; scholar in residence Middlebury Coll., 1999; disting. vis. prof. St. Michael's Coll. and U. Vt., 2003—. Fellow Inst. Politics, Sch. Govt. Harvard U., 1983, pub. policy fellow Bunting Inst., Radcliffe Coll., 1991—92; lectr. Middlebury Coll., St. Michael's Coll., 1984; disting. pub. policy visitor Rockefeller Ctr., Dartmouth Coll., 1992; mem. Vt. Joint Fiscal Com., 1977—78; mem. exec. com. Nat. Conf. Lt. Govs., 1979—80; founder, pres. Inst. Sustainable Cmtys., Montpellier, 1991—; mem. 3 person com. to recommend v.p. to Bill Clinton; mem. transition team, co-chair nat. com. Women for Clinton, 1992; commentator TV and Pub. RAdio. Author: Living a Political Life: A Memoir, 1994, The Big Green Book, 1976; contbr. articles to profl. jours., mags. and newspapers. Commentator Vt. Pub. Radio. Named Outstanding State Legislator, Eagleton Inst. Politics, Rutgers U., 1975; Montgomery fellow, Dartmouth Coll., 1991, scholar in residence, Middlebury Coll., 1999—. Fellow: Am. Acad. Arts and Scis.; mem.: New Eng. Gov.'s Conf. (chairperson), Nat. Gov.'s Conf. (chair com. energy and environ.), Nat. Gov.'s Assn. (mem. exec. com.). Democrat. Office: Univ Vt Burlington VT 05401 Business E-Mail: madeleine.kunin@uvm.edu. E-mail: mkunin@smcvt.edu.

KUNKEL, BARBARA J., law firm executive; Chief info. officer Nixon Peabody LLP. Named one of Premier 100 IT Leaders, Computerworld, 2005. Office: Nixon Peabody LLP 1100 Clinton St Rochester NY 14604 Office Phone: 585-263-1000. Office Fax: 585-263-1600.

KUNKEL, GEORGIE BRIGHT, freelance writer, retired counselor; b. Chehalis, Wash. d. George Riley and Myrtia (McLaughlin) Bright; m. Norman C. Kunkel, Apr. 25, 1946; children: N. Joseph D.C.(dec.), Stephen Gregory, Susan Ann, Kimberly Jane Waligorska. BA in Edn., Western Wash. U., 1944; MEd, U. Wash., 1968. Tchr. pub. schs., Vader, Centralia, Seattle, Wash., 1941-67; counselor Highline Pub. Schs., Seattle, 1967-82. Sch.

counselor rep. State of Art Conf., Balt., 1980; spkr. on women's issues, humor, and the Holocaust. Author: You're Damn Right I Wear Purple! Color Me Feminist, 2000; co-author (with Norman C. Kunkel): WWII Liberator's Life: AFS Ambulance Driver Chooses Peace, 2006; editor: Women and Girls in Edn., 1972—75; columnist: West Seattle Herald and Northwest Prime Time; contbr. articles to profl. jours. Organizer Women and Girls in Edn., Wash. State, 1971; pres. Wash. State NOW, 1973; past pres. West Seattle Dem. Women's Club. Grantee Women Adminstrs. Wash. State, 1971, Edn. Svc. Dist., Seattle, 1980; recipient Woman of Achievement award Past Pres. Assembly, 2000; winner essay contest and appeared on Oprah show. Mem. NEA (sec. pub. rels.), ACA (pres. state br. 1982-83), Am. Sch. Counseling Assn. (pres. state divsn. 1980-81), Seattle Counselors Assn. (organizer, past pres. office exec., Counselor of Yr. award 1990). Unitarian Universalist. Avocation: singing. Home and Office: 3409 SW Trenton St Seattle WA 98126-3743 Office Phone: 206-935-8663.

KUNKEL-CHRISTMAN, DEBRA ANN, secondary school educator; b. Palmerton, Pa., Sept. 11, 1967; d. Rosalie Meridith and Eugene William Kunkel; m. Kevin Douglas Christman, Aug. 9, 1997. EdM (hon.), Kutztown U., 2000. Cert. tchr. Pa., 1991. Tchr. Saucon Valley Sch. Dist., Hellertown, Pa., 1994—2005. Mem.: Coun. Exceptional Children. Office: Saucon Valley Sch Dist 2095 Polk Valley Rd Hellertown PA 18055 Home: 2025 Brown St Allentown PA 18104-1415

KUNKLE, MARY LOU, counselor; b. Norborne, Mo., Aug. 22, 1937; d. William J. and Hazel Irene (Lungren) McLaughlin; m. John K. Kunkle, Jan. 27, 1956; children: Cindy Canzanella, John W., Karen Reynolds, Nancy Harvest. BA, Millersville U., 1984, MS, 1988; PhD, Walden U., 1994. Lic. profl. counselor, cert. addictions counselor; diplomate Pa. Chem. Abuse Cert. Bd. Legal sec. Stein, Storb, Mann & O'Brien, Lancaster, Pa., 1970—74; city treas. City of Estell Manor, NJ, 1977—78; with Estell Manor Ch., 1974—78; legal sec. Shreiner & Patterson, Lancaster, Pa., 1978—81; sec. RR Donnelly & Sons. Co., 1981—89; counselor Christian Counseling Svcs., Ephrata, 1988—94, Pa. Counseling Svcs., East Petersburg, 1994—. Cons. Manor Care Nursing Care, Dallastown, Pa., 1999. Avocations: choir, music. Home: 2487 Carriage Dr Lancaster PA 17601 Office: Pa Counseling Svcs 6079 Main St East Petersburg PA 17520 Office Phone: 717-560-1908.

KUNSTADTER, GERALDINE SAPOLSKY, foundation executive; b. Boston, Jan. 6, 1928; d. Harry Herman and Nettie Sapolsky; m. John W. Kunstadter, Apr. 23, 1949; children: John W., Lisa, Christopher, Elizabeth Student, MIT, 1945-48. Draftsman U. Chgo. Cyclotron Project, 1948; engrng. asst. Gen. Electric Corp., Lynn, Mass., 1948-49; pres. Capricorn Investments Corp., 1971—; chmn., pres., dir. A. Kunstadter Family Found., N.Y.C., 1966—. Host family program dir. N.Y.C. Commn. for UN, 1971-86; pres. Nat. Inst. Social Scis., 1979-81; adv. coun. hospitality com. UN Delegations. Mem. internat. hospitality com. Nat. Coun. Women; chmn. N.Y.-Beijing Sister City Com.; mem. Com. Mgmnt. of Network 20/20; bd. dirs. Bridge to Asia Found., Atlantic Coun. of U.S., Ctr. US.-China Arts Exch., Inst. World Affairs; bd. dirs Nat. Com. on. US-China Rels. Recipient Windham award, 1970, Silver medal, Nat. Inst. Social Sci., 1981, Pres.'s medal, Archtl. Soc. China, 2001. Mem. Inst. Current World Affairs, Nat. Com. US-China Rels., Coun. on Fgn. Rels., Hurlingham Club, Lansdowne Club (London), Cosmopolitan Club N.Y.(Internat. com.).

KUNTZ, CAROL B., psychologist, educator, marriage and family therapist; b. Dickinson, N.D., Oct. 13, 1952; d. J. N. Kuntz and Veronica Decker; divorced; children: Rick, Jess, Kristy. ADN, Dickinson State U., 1983; BS in Psychology, U. N.D., 1988; MA in Psychology, Ctrl. Mich. U., 1990, D in Psychology, 1993. Diplomate Am. Psychotherapy Assn., cert. profl. qualification psychology Assn. State and Provincial Psychology Bd. RN St. Joseph's Hosp., Dickinson, ND, 1983, Minot, ND, 1983—86, United Hosp., Grand Forks, 1987—88, Ctrl. Mich. Hosp., Mt. Pleasant, 1988—92; rsch. asst. to Dr. David Stein U. N.D., Grand Forks, ND, 1987—88; psychologist Cath. Family Svcs., Mt. Pleasant, 1991—92; clin. psychologist Univ. Physicians, Sioux Falls, SD, 1993—2002, Avera McKennan Hosp., Univ. Health Ctr., Sioux Falls, 2002—. Cons. Healthy Solutions, Sioux Falls, 1992—93; asst. prof. U. S.D., Sioux Falls, 1994—, supr. psychiatry residents, 2002—; presenter in field. Mem.: APA, Am. Assn. Marriage and Family Therapy, Am. Psychol. Assn. Clin. Psychology, Am. Psychotherapy Assn., Am. Bd. Disability Analysts (diplomate), Internat. Neuropsychological Soc., Nat. Acad. Neuropsychology, S.D. Psychol. Assn., Clin. Neuropsychology, Psychology of Women, Nat. Register health SVc. Providers Psychology, Psi Chi. Roman Catholic. Avocations: ceramics, painting, poetry, bicycling, hiking. Office: Univ Psychiatry Assocs 4400 W 69th St #1500 Sioux Falls SD 57108 Office Phone: 605-322-5700. Personal E-mail: drcbk52@aol.com.

KUNTZ, MARION LUCILE LEATHERS, classicist, educator, historian; b. Atlanta, Sept. 6, 1924; d. Otto Asa and Lucile (Parks) Leathers; m. Paul G. Kuntz, Nov. 26, 1970; children by previous marriage: Charles, Otto Alan (Daniels). BA, Agnes Scott Coll., 1945; MA, Emory U., 1964, PhD, 1969. Lectr. Latin Lovett Sch., Atlanta, 1963-66; from mem. faculty to prof. Ga. State U., 1966—75, Regents' Prof., 1975—, chmn. dept. fgn. langs., 1975-84, Fuller E. Callaway prof., 1984—, rsch. prof., 1984—. Author: Colloquium of the Seven About Secrets of the Sublime of Jean Bodin, 1975, Guillaume Postel, Prophet of the Restitution of All Things: His Life and Thought, 1981, Jacob's Ladder and the Tree of Life: Concepts of Hierarchy and the Great Chain of Being, 1987, Postello, Venezia e Il Suo Mondo, 1988, Venice, Myth and Utopian Thought, 1999, The Anointment of Dionisio: Prophecy and Politics in Renaissance Italy, 2002; also scholarly articles; mem. editl. bd. Library of Renaissance Humanism. V.p. acad. affairs Am.-Hellenic Found.; patron Atlanta Opera. Named Latin Tchr. of Yr. State Ga., 1965; Am. Classical League scholar, 1966, Gladys Krieble Delmas scholar, 1991; Am. Coun. Learned Socs. grantee, 1970, 73, 76, 81, 87, 90; recipient Alumni Disting. Prof. award Ga. State U., 1994, medal for excellence in Renaissance studies Pres. of Coun. Gen., Tours, France, 1995, Disting. Career Alumna award Agnes Scott Coll., 1995 Master: Soc. for Values in Higher Edn., Philosophy and Religion; mem.: Am. Cath. Hist. Assn., Classical Assn. Midwest and South (Semple award 1965), Am. Philol. Assn., Archaeol. Inst. Am., Soc. di Philosophique Medievale, Soc. Medieval and Renaissance Philosophy (exec. bd. 1988—90), Medieval Acad. Soc. de Culture Europèenne, Soc. des Seizièmistes, Soc. Christian Philosophers (exec. bd. 1987—), Internat. Soc. Neo-Latin Studies, Internat. Soc. Neo-Platonic Studies, Am. Hist. Assn., Am. Soc. Ch. History, Am. Cath. Philos. Assn., Am. Soc. Aesthetics, Renaissance Soc. Am. (coun. 1994—97, trustee 2003—), Michael C. Carlos Mus. (patron), Friends of the Vatican Libr., Italia Nostra, Fondazione Ambiente Italiana, Amici di Querini-Stampalia Galleria e Biblioteca, Coun. Amici di Biblioteca Nazionale di San Marco, Italian Cultural Soc., Nat. Trust Hist. Preservation, Atlanta Hist. Soc., High Mus. of Art, Friends of the Warburg Inst., World Monuments Fund, The Atlanta Opera, The Atlanta Symphony, Am. Acad. Rome (sec.-treas. 1970—74), The Commerce Club, Omicron Delta Kappa, Phi Kappa Phi, Phi Beta Kappa. Roman Catholic. Home: Villa Veneziana 1655 Ponce De Leon Ave Atlanta GA 30307 also: San Marco 4157 Venice Italy Business E-Mail: marion@gsu.edu.

KUNZ, ALEXANDRA CAVITT, physician, anthropologist, researcher; b. Waukegan, Ill., Aug. 3, 1944; d. Howard Hamilton Cavitt and Evelyn Lucille (Becker) Goding; m. Louis William Kunz, Jan. 27, 1968 (div. July 1981); children: Jacob Alexander (dec.), Carmen Rachel. BS with Distinction, U. Nebr., 1966; MD, Ea. Va. Med. Sch., 1991; CPH, Harvard U., 1992, post-grad. Evolutionary Anthropology, 1995—2000. Registered dental hygienist. Mem U.S. Pub. Health Team, Hawaii, 1966; periodontal hygienist Nebr., Hawaii, Calif. Ariz., Mass., Va., 1966—91; med. rschr. Harvard U., Boston, 1992—. Rschr. Wampumpeag, Inc. Mem.: AMA (mem. com. on alcohol and health), AAAS, Women in Neurosurgery, Am. Found. AIDS Rsch., Mass. Med. Soc., Internat. Neurotrauma Soc., Am. Assn. Neurol. Surgeons Rsch. Found., Physicians Social Responsibility, Physicians Human Rights. Avocations: ice skating, cross country skiing, piano. E-mail: arkunz@post.harvard.edu.

KUNZ, APRIL BRIMMER, state legislator, lawyer; b. Denver, Apr. 1, 1954; divorced. AA, Stephens Coll., 1974; BS, U. So. Calif., 1976; JD, U. Wyo., 1979. Bar: Wyo. Pres. K and R Enterprises; mem. Wyo. Ho. Reps., Cheyenne, 1985-86, 90-92, Wyo. Senate, Cheyenne, 1992—, chair jud. com., v.p., 1999—2000, majority floor leader, 2001—02, pres., 2003—04. Mem. Laramie County Rep. Women's Club. Mem. Wyo. State Bar Assn, Laramie County Bar Assn. Republican. Home: PO Box 285 Cheyenne WY 82003-0285 Office: Wyo Senate State Capitol Cheyenne WY 82002-0001

KUNZ, HEIDI, healthcare company executive; Grad., Georgetown U., 1977; MBA, Columbia U. Dir. overseas financing, asst. treas., then treas. GM Can.; treas. GM, White Plains, N.Y., 1993-95; exec. v.p., CFO ITT, 1995-99, Gap Inc., 1999—2003, Blue Shield Calif., San Francisco, 2003—. Bd. dirs. Agilent Technologies, Inc., 2000—. Office: Blue Shield 50 Beale St San Francisco CA 94105-1808

KUO, CHARLENE, finance professional; b. Taiwan, July 11, 1964; d. Kirk H. and Stella S. Kuo. BS, U. Calif., Berkeley, 1986; MS, MIT, 1989; JD, Coll. William & Mary, 1994. Cons. Standard & Poor's, N.Y.C., 1994-95; sr. cons. Summit Systems, Inc., N.Y.C., 1995-97; v.p. Goldman Sachs & Co., N.Y.C., 1997—. Vol. N.Y.C. Jr. League, 1996—, Nat. Dem. Com., N.Y.C., 1999—; mem. N.Y. Met. Mus., 1998—. ITT scholar, U. Calif., 1982-86. Mem. Princeton Club N.Y., Tau Beta Pi, Eta Kappa Nu. Avocations: painting, music. Office: Goldman Sachs & Co 85 Broad St New York NY 10004-2456

KUPELIAN, LOUISE PAULSON, musician, educator; b. Swarthmore, Pa., Jan. 9, 1922; d. Paul Michael and Annastasia Paulson; m. Vahey S. Kupelian, June 23, 1943; children: Theodore Paul, David Ralph, Diane Louise. Grad., Phila. Conservatory Music, 1941. Master piano tchr. Louise Kupelian Piano Studios, Chevy Chase, Md., 1938—2006, concert pianist, 1940—. Master: Music Tchrs. Nat. Assn. (life; master piano tchr.); mem.: Md. State Music Tchrs. Assn. (life; co-chair program planning 1989—91), Friday Morning Music Club (life; judge 1990—92), Phi Kappa Phi (life).

KUPER, DANIELA F., writer; b. Chgo., June 18, 1950; d. Harry W. and Anne F. (Fisher) K.; children: Judah E., Sahra J. BA, So. Ill. U., 1971. Pres., creative dir. Kuper-Finlon Advt., Boulder, 1982-88. Writer, spkr., 1988—. Author: (novel) Hunger and Thirst, 2004; contbr. fiction to newspapers and mags. Ucross Found. fellow, Djerassi Found. fellow. Mem. Colo. Author's League, Denver Ad Fedn., Boulder C. of C., Art Dirs. Club Denver (award 1985, 86).

KUPETS, COURTNEY, Olympic athlete; b. Bedford, Tex., July 27, 1986; Mem. U.S. Nat. Gymnastics Team, 1999—; gymnast Team USA, Athens Olympic Games, 2004—. Named TOPs Athlete of the Yr., 2002. Achievements include World Champion, Uneven Bars, World Gymnastics Championships, Hungary, 2002; U.S. Champion, All-Around, U.S. Nat. Championships, 2003; mem. U.S. World Championships Gold medal team, 2003; U.S. co-champion, All-Around, U.S. Nat. Championships, 2004. Avocations: reading, shopping, diving. Office: c/o USOC One Olympic Plz Colorado Springs CO 80909

KUPIEC, SUZANNE L., utilities executive; BBA in Fin. and Acctg., Tex. A&M U. CPA Tex. Joined Ernst & Young, LLP, 1989, ptnr.; v.p., chief risk and corp. compliance officer Reliant Resources, Inc., Houston, 2003—. Mem.: AICPA, Tex. State Soc. CPA. Office: Reliant Energy Exec Offices PO Box 2286 Houston TX 77252-2286

KUPKA, NANCY ELYSE WYATT, dance educator; b. Honolulu, Jan. 24, 1947; d. Clarence Arthur Wyatt and Janet Mae Wullschleger-Wyatt; m. Craig Leigh Kupka, July 27, 1974; children: Gregory Mykal Wyatt, Colin Kia'i. BA, Calif. State LA, 1975; MA, UCLA, 1979. Prof. dance Calif. State U., LA, 1976—; prof. child devel. Glendale C.C., Calif., 2001—. Resource specialist in dance LA County Sch. Dists., 1976—. Dir. (children's dance concert) Moving Dance Images; dancer (ballet) Ballet Russe de Monte Carlo, dancer (modern dance) Celebration, For the Love of Gregory's Grandparents, numerous venues in US and Europe; author: Developing Dance Arts Literacy, 1996, Cross Cultural Themes in Dance, 2004, Dancing Core Curriculum in the Elementary Classroom, 2005, Multicultural Approach to Dance, 2006. Home: 5151 State University Dr Los Angeles CA 90032 Office: California State U 5151 State University Dr Los Angeles CA 90032 Office Phone: 323-343-5125. Home Fax: 323-343-5567; Office Fax: 323-343-5567. Business E-Mail: nkupka@calstatela.edu.

KUPOVITS, JENE IRENE, special education educator; d. Vincent Dennis and Susan Jane Lajiness; m. Joseph Ste Kupovits, June 18, 1993; children: Alexis Nicole, Joseph Vincent. Bachelors Degree, U. Toledo, 1991; Masters Degree, Ea. Mich. U., 1998. Cert. tchr. gen. edn. K-6, spl. edn. K-12 learning disabilities and emotional impairments. Tchr. self-contained Monroe (Mich.) County Intermediate Sch. Dist., Monroe, Mich., 1991—; cross-categorical tchr., 2001—06. Least restrictive environment facilitator Monroe County Intermediate Sch. Dist., 1997—2000. Mem.: Coun. for Exceptional Children. Avocation: running.

KUPPER, KETTI, artist; b. L.A., Oct. 14, 1951; d. Charles Parnell Kupper and Donna Corrine Callen; m. Steven Robert Ford Feb. 9, 1978 (div. Mar. 1994); children: Ashley Elizabeth, Kimberly Brianna. BS, Brigham Young, 1974; student, Acad. Art, San Francisco, 1974-76; MFA in Visual Art, Norwich U., 1994. Freelance painter, illustrator, 1980—; prin., co-owner Fordesign Mktg., Wilton, Conn., 1990-93; chmn. of art U. Bridgeport, 1991-96; ind. cons. Milford, Conn., 1994-98; mentor, tchr. Conn. Commn. Arts, Hartford, Conn., 1996-98; non resident studio tchr. Vt. Coll., Monpelier, 1998—; pres. Ketti Kupper's Art & Design Inc., L.A. Featured garden designer Beverly Hills Garden and Design Showcase, Hist. Greystone Mansion, 2004. Commd. paintings include portrait Clint Murchison for Dallas Times Herald Mag., 1984, Am. Express Olympiadas Barcelona for commercial, 1992, portrait U. Bridgeport Pres. Edwin Eigel, 1995; collections include: Nestle Corp., Ptnrs. Nat. Health Plans, Tex. Instruments; designer, Romantic Backyard Getaway (winning designer, HGTV Landscaper's Challenge); art pub. in Times, Newsweek, Conn. Mag., Dallas Life Mag., Readers Digest. Curator Focus on Environ. U. Bridgeport Coll.; cmty. environ. activist Bridgeport Area Arts Coun.; dir. contest Smithsonian Nat. Mus. Am. Indian, N.Y.C., 1994; grantwriter, mural dir. Conn. commn. Arts, 1995; bd. dirs. Women's Caucus for Art, L.A. Recipient Addy 14th Dist. Region award Am. Adv. Fedn., 1984, Painting award The Discovery Mus., 1995, Painting award Silvermine Artists Guild, 1996, Painting award Artworks Gallery, 1997, One of 10 Landscape Designers Beverly Hills Hist. Greystone Estate Garden & Design Showcase. Mem. AIA, Coll. Art Assn., Women's Caucus for Arts (chpt. pres. 1996-98), N.Y. Soc. Illustrators, Calif. Lawyers for Arts, Nat. Art Educators Assn., Assn. Profl. Landscape Designers. Democrat. Avocations: writing, gardening, remodeling, construction design. Office: 4208 1/2 Camero Ave Los Angeles CA 90027-4519 Office Phone: 323-660-7756. E-mail: info@kettikupper.com.

KUPST, MARY JO, psychologist, researcher; b. Chgo., Oct. 4, 1945; d. George Eugene and Winifred Mary (Hughes) K.; m. Alfred Procter Stresen-Reuter Jr., Aug. 21, 1977. BS, Loyola U., 1967, MA, 1969, PhD, 1972. Lic. psychologist, Ill., Wis. Postdoctoral fellow U. Ill. Med. Ctr., Chgo., 1971—72; rsch. psychologist Children's Meml. Hosp., Chgo., 1972—89; assoc. prof. psychiatry and pediatrics Northwestern U. Med. Sch., Chgo., 1981—89; prof. pediatrics Med. Coll. Wis., Milw., 1989—, dir. pediatric psychology, 1995—. Practice clin. psychology, Chgo., 1975-89, McHenry, Ill., 1987-89; co-chair pediat. oncology group psychology com., 1995-2001, vice chair psychology discipline Children's Oncology Group, 2002-06. Editor: (with others) The Child with Cancer, 1980; contbr. articles to profl. jours. V.p. McHenry County Mental Health Bd., 1997—2001; co-chair Alliance for Childhood Cancer, 2005—. Fellow: APA (pres. divsn. 54 2004—05, charter fellow); mem.: Wis. Psychol. Assn. Office: Med Coll Wis Dept Pediats 8701 W Watertown Plank Rd Milwaukee WI 53226-3548 E-mail: mkupst@mcw.edu.

KURIANSKY, JUDY, television personality, radio personality, reporter, clinical psychologist, writer, educator; b. NYC, Jan. 31, 1947; d. Abraham and Sylvia (Feld) Brodsky; m. Edward Kuriansky, Aug. 24, 1969. BA, Smith Coll., 1968; EdM, Boston U., 1970; PhD, NYU, 1980. Diplomate Am. Bd. Sexology, 2003. Reporter Sta. WABC-TV, N.Y.C., 1980-82, Sta. WBZ-TV, Boston, 1981-82, Sta. WCBS-TV, 1982-86, N.Y.C., 1986-88, Sta. WPIX-TV, N.Y.C., 1987-89, Sta. CNBC-TV, Ft. Lee, NJ, 1989-93; host Total Wellness for Women program Sta. WDBB-TV, Birmingham, Ala., 1988-89; program host Sta. WABC-AM, N.Y.C., 1980-87, Sta. WOR-AM, 1987-88; temp. program host ABC Talk Radio, N.Y.C., 1988-90; host Modern Satellite Network, 1981; TV host J.C. Penney Golden Rule Network, Dallas, 1988-90; feature contbr. Attitudes Show LifeTime, 1992-94; host Love Phones, nat. syndicated Premiere Radio Networks, N.Y.C., 1992-97; host Dr. Judy Show, Winstar Radio, 1998-99. Spokesperson Universal Studios Fla., 1993—94, Church and Dwight, 2000—01; cons. Lily of France, Charles of the Ritz, The Rolland Co., Taylor-Gordon Arons Advt., Clairol, Durex, London Internat., 1995, Organon, 1999—, Ky. Married for Life Survey, 2003—; tchr. Columbia U. Med. Sch., 1974—79, Inst. for Health and Religion, 1980—82; adj. prof. clin. psychology NYU, 1993—95; adj. prof. psychology Columbia U. Tchrs. Coll., 2001—; vis. prof. Beijing U. Health Sci. Ctr., 2002—; judge Most Unforgettable Women contest Revlon, 1990; judge Close-Up N Roll Contest, 1993, Cooney Waters P.R., Herpes Awareness Contest, 1996; therapy coord. Nat. Inst. for Psychotherapists, 1977—79; therapist Ctr. for Marital and Family Therapy, 1986—; cons. Shanghai Inst. Reproductive Health Instrn., China, 1999—; trainer marital cons. China Sexology Assn., 2000—; v.p. Quezon Corp., 1978—79; sr. rsch. scientist N.Y. State Psychiat. Inst., 1970—78; lectr. Blanton Peale Inst., 1979—81; mem. adv. bd. Single Living mag., 1997—98, Lane Bryant, 1997—98; adj. prof. psychology Yeshiva Univ., 2003—; asst. clin. prof. psychiatry Columbia Med. Ctr., 2003—; vis. prof Peking U. Health Scis. Ctr.; instr. dept. psychiatry Hong Kong U.; mem. exec. bd. Internat. Assn. Applied Psychology, 2006—; mem. at large UN Com. Mental Health, 2006—. Author: Sex, Now That I've Got Your Attention, Let Me Answer Your Questions, 1984, How to Love a Nice Guy, 1990, Italian and Japanese transls., Generation Sex, 1995, The Complete Idiots Guide to Dating, 1996, 2d edit., 1999, 3rd edit., 2003, The Complete Idiots Guide to a Healthy Relationship, 1997, 2d edit., 2001, The Complete Idiots Guide to Tantric Sex, 2001, 2d edit., 2004, China Reproductive Health Hotline Professionals Solve Problems on Sex and Emotions, 2001, Terror in the Holy Land: Inside the Anguish of the Israelis and Palestinians, 2006, Beyond Bullets and Bombs: Grassroots Peace building between Israelis and Palestinians, 2006; columnist Family Circle mag., 1984—89, Whole Life Times, 1986—87, King Features Newspaper, 1984—86, N.Y. and L.I. Newsday, 1993—2000, Penthouse mag., 1995—, Soap Opera Update, 1995—96, Telluride Daily Planet, 1995—98, Cosmo Girl mag., 2001—03, Singapore Straits Times, 2002—, N.Y. Daily News website, 2004—; columnist: China Trends Health mag., 2004—; writer New Woman, Ad Age, Boardroom Reports, Am. Advt. Fedn. mag., Chgo. Tribune Woman News, South China Morning Post, 2001—; contbg. editor: Beauty Mag., 1989—90; guest editor Ladies Home Jour., 1993, AOL On-Line Show, Keyword: Dr. Judy, 1996—97, www.cameraplanet.com, 2001—02, www.matureamerica.com, 2002—03, mem. adv. bd. Single Living mag., 1997—99; author: Goodbye My Troubles, Hello My Happiness, 1997. UN NGO rep. Internat. Assn. Applied Psychology and World Coun. for Psychotherapy, 2004—; bd. dirs. Scientists Com. for Pub. Info., 1977—79; mem. adv. bd. N.Y. City Self Help Orgn., 1983—85; mem. benefits com. Mental Health Svcs. for Deaf, 1980—82; bd. advisors Planned Parenthood, 1998—. Recipient Civilian Commendation, N.Y.C. Police Dept., 1984, Cert. for Unique Pub. Svc. AWRT, 1984, Star award for individual achievement in radio, 1997, Sabo Media Programming Visionary award, 1984, Maggie award Planned Parenthood, 1985, 93, Freedoms Found. award Children for a Better Soc., 1986, Olive award Coun. of Chs., 1986, Mercury award Larimi Comm., 1987, Lifetime Achievement in Sexology medal, AACS, 2004. Fellow APA; mem. Am. Women in Radio and TV (pres. N.Y. chpt. 1988-89, nat. found. vice chair 1988-90, nat. bd. treas. 1995-98, Internat. Outreach award 2003), Soc. Sex Therapy and Rsch. (charter), Am. Assn. Sex, Educators, Counselors and Therapists (exec. bd. 2004-05), TV Acad. of N.Y. (gov. 1987-91), Friars Club. Office Phone: 212-445-3995. Personal E-mail: drjudyaide@aol.com. Business E-Mail: apollack@premiereradio.com.

KURKUL, WEN WANG, musician, educator, administrator; b. Taipei, Taiwan, Oct. 30, 1964; arrived in U.S., 1986; d. Shih-Ming and Hsieh-Chu Wang. MusM, Ohio U., 1988; MusD, U. Mo., 1995; D in Music Edn., Ind. U., 2000. Prof., adminstr. Sch. Music Tainan (Taiwan) Woman's Coll. Arts & Tech., 1989—92; prof. Nat. Taiwan Acad. Arts, 1989—92, Nat Sun Yat-Sen U., Kaohsiung, Taiwan, 1990-92; vis. faculty Sch. Music Ind. U., Bloomington, 1999—2000; prof. dept. music George Mason U., 2000—03, dir. music edn. dept. music Coll. Visual and Performing Arts, 2001—03, exec. dir. Orff Schulwerk Tchr. Tng. and Cert. Program, 2001—03; prof. dept. music Montgomery Coll., 2004—, also music dir., condr. symphony orch.; founder, exec. dir. Empowered to Excel program Montgomery Coll and Montgomery County Pub. Schs. Symphony Orch. Partnership Program, 2005—06. Music dir., condr. Montgomery Coll. Symphony Orch. Soloist-in-residence Nat. Chiang Kai Shek Cultural Ctr., Taipei, 1991-94; flutist Asian Composers League, Taipei, 1990-92; asst. prin. flutist Taiwan Symphony Orch., Taichung, 1984-86; founder, dir. Empowered to Excel, Montgomery Coll. and Montgomery Pub. Schs. Symphony Orch. Partnership Program, 2005-06; contbr. articles to profl. jours. Nat. Art and Sci. Coun. scholar, Taiwan, 1989-92; Nat. Rsch. grant Ministry of Edn., Taiwan, 1989-92; named New Performing Star of Yr. Nat. Theatre and Concert Hall Planning and Mgmt. Coun., Taiwan, 1991. Mem.: APA, AAUP, Nat. Assn. Student Personnel Adminstrs., Nat. Assn. Student Affairs Profls., Internat. Soc. Philosophy Music Edn. (founding), Pub. Rels. Soc. Am., Am. Edml. Rsch. Assn., Am. Orff-Schulwerk Assn., Internat. Soc. for Music Edn. (Eng.), European Recorder Tchrs. Assn., Soc. for Rsch. in Music Edn., Music Edn. Nat. Conf., Coll. Music Soc., Nat. Flute Assn. (life), Am. Symphony Orch. League, Phi Kappa Lambda. Home: 403 Misty Knoll Dr Rockville MD 20850-2879 Personal E-mail: wenyi.kurkul@verizon.net. Business E-Mail: Wen.Kurkul@montgomerycollege.edu.

KURLI, MADHAVI, ophthalmologist; b. Madanapalli, Andhra Pradesh, India, Mar. 9, 1974; d. Parthasarathy and Janaki Devi Katukota; m. Vineel Kurli, Jan. 22, 1999. MB, BS, Chennai Med. Coll., India, 1998. Diplomate Royal Coll. of Ophthalmologists, London, 2002. Ho. officer in internal medicine Hull Royal Infirmary, Hull, Yorkshire, England, 1999—2000; extern in ophthalmology St. James' U. Hosp., Leeds, Yorkshire, England, 2000; sr. ho. officer in ophthalmology Stepping Hill Hosp., Stockport, Chesire, England, 2000—01, Wolverhampton and Midland Counties Eye Infirmary, West Midlands, England, 2001—03; rsch. fellow in ophthalmic oncology N.Y. Eye Cancer Ctr., N.Y.C., 2003—. Author: (book chapt.) Ophthalmology Clinics of North America, 2005, Progress in Kidney Cancer Research, 2005; presenter: in field; contbr. articles to profl. jours. Mem.: Royal Coll. of Ophthalmologists, London, N.Y. Acad. Scis., Assn. for Rsch. in Vision and Ophthalmology, Am. Acad. of Ophthalmology. Office: NY Eye Cancer Ctr 115 E 61st St New York NY 10021 Personal E-mail: mkurli@hotmail.com. Business E-Mail: mkurli@eyecancer.com. E-mail: mkurli@gmail.com.

KURMAN, JUTA, music educator; b. Wändra, Parnu, Estonia, Nov. 7, 1912; d. August and Maria (Reier) Tomberg; m. Alexander Pooman, Sept. 17, 1938 (dec. 1938); m. Hugo Kurman, Jan. 18, 1940; children: Jaan, Juri-George. Tchrs. Lic., Tchrs. Sem., Estonia, 1934; Artist Dipl., State Conservatory of Music, Estonia, 1940, N.Y. Coll. of Music, 1952. Tchr. Tallinn (Estonia) Pub. Schs., 1934-38; performing artist concerts, state radio, and theater Estonia, 1932-40; TV voice soloist Maj. Bowes Original Amateur Hour, Radio City, NY, 1949-50; with Claire Mann Show, Channel 5, N.Y.C., 1952; pres.

Estonian Music Ctr., N.Y.C., 1973—. Club and ch. soloist; lectr in field; music critic Free Estonian Word, 1948—, Baltic Papers; lector Estonian Lang. Course, NYC, 1993—. Co-editor: Haapsalu Shawl, 1972, Kompiling Mart Saar VocalAlbum, 1965, Kompiling Kaljo Raid Estonian Volksongs Album, 1991; contbr. articles to profl. jurs. Sustaining mem. Rep. Nat. Com., 1990—; mem. Ronald Reagan Presdl. Found., 1987—; mem. Pres. Bush Task Force; presdl. coun. Rep. Party Decorated White Star V Orden, Estonian Republic; named Laureate of Estonian Letters and Scis. Found.; N.Y. Coll. Music grantee, 1948. Mem. Estonian Music Sorority (pres. 1951-63), Estonian Women's Club of N.Y. (pres.), Estonian Ednl. Soc. (hon. mem. elders coun.), Federated Estonian Women's Clubs Estonian Republic (hon.), World Fedn. Estonian Women's Clubs in Exile (West) (founding pres. 1966—), Baltic-Am. Women's Coun. (past pres.). Republican. Lutheran. Avocations: music, poetry, writing. Home: 68-50 Juno St Forest Hills NY 11375-5728 Office: Estonian Music Ctr 243 E 34th St New York NY 10016-4852

KURTH, JENNIFER LYNN, osteopath; d. Paul Kurth and Barbara Kurth-Schuldt. DO, Western U. Health Scis., Pomona, Calif., 2002. Lic. Calif., 2003, Ill., 2005. Resident U. Calif. Irvine Med. Ctr., Orange, 2002—05; fellow Children's Meml. Hosp., Chgo., 2005—. Recipient Janet M. Glasgow award, Western U. Health Scis., 2002. Mem.: AMA, Am. Osteo. Assn., Am. Acad. Child and Adolescent Psychiatry, Am. Psychiat. Assn. Office: Children's Memorial Hospital 2300 Children's Plaza Chicago IL 60614 Office Phone: 773-880-3503.

KURTZ, DOLORES MAY, civic worker; b. Reading, Pa., Oct. 27, 1933; d. Harry Claude and Ethel Gertrude (Fields) Filbert; m. William McKillips Kurtz, Oct. 26, 1957. Sec. cert., Pa. State U., 1980. Legal sec. Snyder, Balmer & Kershner, Reading, 1951-53; head teletype operator E. duPont de Nemours, Reading, 1953-56; exec. sec. Ford New Holland (Pa.) Inc. (formerly Sperry New Holland), 1956-91; ret., 1991. Active Lancaster County Rep. Com., 1983-85; pres. New Holland Area Womans Club, 1982-84; bd. dirs. Cmty. Meml. Park Assn., New Holland, 1957-82, Lancaster County Fedn. Womens Clubs, 1982—, 2d v.p., 1984-86, 1st v.p., 1986-88, pres. 1988-90; founding mem. Summer Arts Festival, New Holland, 1980—, bd. dirs., 1985-91; membership chair S.E. dist. Pa. Fedn. Womens Clubs, 1984-86; area rep., bd. dirs. Womens Rep. Club Lancaster County, 1982-84; com. mem. New Holland Boro, 1983-85; v.p. Lancaster-Lebanon Arthritis Found. Guild, 1992, pres., 1993. Recipient Outstanding Vol. for Pa. award Pa. Fedn. Womens Clubs, 1984, Woman in the Arts award, 1998. Mem. Gen. Fedn. Womens Clubs Pa. (conservation divsn. chair 1996-98, credentials com. 1998-2000, chmn. Caps for Kids project Lancaster County chpt. 1999—2006). Methodist. Avocations: arts and crafts, travel, photography.

KURTZ, MARY DENISE BATES, secondary school educator; d. Herbert Leo and Mae Bates; children: Sarah Elizabeth, Laura Marie, James Gregory. MEd, Nat. Coll. of Edn., Evanston, Ill., 1976. Cert. T5 in edn.:E nglish 7-12, mid. sch., reading specialist, learning disabled Ga. Tchr. English Marillac H.S., Northfield, Ill., 1973—77, St. Francis H.S., Mountain View, Calif., 1977—78; chpt./title 1 tchr. Ames H.S., Iowa, 1979—86; tchr. English and spl. edn. Clarke County Schs., Athens, Ga., 1986—96; tchr. alternative sch. Barrow County, Winder, Ga., 1996—98; chair mid. sch., lang. arts St. Joseph Cath. Sch., Athens, 1998—. Pres. Green Acres Swim Team, Athens, 1987—89; vol. 4-H, Athens, 1990—2006; pres., mem. St. Joseph Cath. Sch. Bd. of Edn., Athens, 1996—99; sec. Athens United Soccer, 1989—91. Named Athens-Clarke County 4-H Tchr. of Yr., Clarke County 4-H. Mem.: Ga. 4-H Vol. Leader Assn. (pres., various offices). Office: St Joseph Cath Sch 134 Prince Ave Athens GA 30601 Office Phone: 706-543-1621. Personal E-mail: mkurtz1@hotmail.com. Business E-Mail: mkurtz@sjsathens.org.

KURTZ, MAXINE, personnel director, writer, lawyer; b. Mpls., Oct. 17, 1921; d. Jack Isadore and Beatrice (Cohen) K. BA, U. Minn., 1942; MS in Govt. Mgmt., U. Denver, 1945, JD, 1962; postdoctoral student, U. Calif., San Diego, 1978. Bar: Colo. 1962, U.S. Dist. Ct. Colo., 1992. Analyst Tri-County Regional Planning, Denver, 1945-47; chief rsch. and spl. projects Planning Office, City and County of Denver, 1947-66; dir. tech. and evaluation Model Cities Program, 1966-71; pers. rsch. officer Denver Career Svc. Auth., 1972-86, dir. pers. svcs., 1986-88, sr. pers. specialist, 1988-90, pub. sector pers. con., 1990-95, atty., 1990—, pers. and human resources cons., 1996-98. Expert witness nat. com. on urban problems, U.S. Ho. of Reps., U.S. Senate. Author: Law of Planning and Land Use Regulations in Colorado, 1966, Invisible Cage: A Memoir, 2005; co-author: Care and Feeding of Witnesses, Expert and Otherwise, 1974; bd. editors: Pub. Adminstrn. Rev., Washington, 1980-83, 88-92; editl. adv. bd. Internat. Pers. Mgmt. Assn.; prin. investigator: Employment: An American Enigma, 1979. Active Women's Forum of Colo., Denver Dem. Com.; chair Colo. adv. com. to U.S. Civil Rights Commn., 1985-89, mem. 1989-2002. Sloan fellow U. Denver, 1944-45; recipient Outstanding Achievement award U. Minn., 1971, Alumni of Notable Achievement award, 1994. Mem. ABA, Am. Inst. Planners (sec. treas. 1968-70, bd. govs. 1972-75), Am. Planning Assn., Am. Soc. Pub. Adminstrn. (nat. coun. 1978-81, Donald Stone award), Colo. Bar Assn., Denver Bar Assn., Order St. Ives, Pi Alpha Alpha. Jewish. Home and Office: 2361 Monaco Pky Denver CO 80207-3453

KURTZ, SWOOSIE, actress; b. Omaha, Sept. 6, 1944; d. Frank and Margo (Rogers) K. Student, Acad. Music and Dramatic Art, London, U. So. Calif. Appeared on TV series As the World Turns, 1956, Mary, 1978, Love, Sidney, 1981-83 (nominated Best Actress in Comedy Series 1982-83), Sisters, 1991-96 (Emmy nominee Lead Actress in Drama 1993, 94, SAG award nominee 1995), Suddenly Susan, 1996, 97, Touched by an Angel, 1997, ER, 1998, Love and Money, 1999, That's Life, 2000-01, Huff, 2004-06; (TV films) Ah, Wilderness!, 1976, Walking Through the Fire, 1979, Uncommon Women and Others, 1979, Marriage is Alive and Well, 1980, The Mating Season, 1980, Fifth of July, 1982, A Caribbean Mystery, 1983, Guilty Conscience, 1985, A Time to Live, 1985, The House of Blue Leaves, 1987, Baja Oklahoma, 1988 (Golden Globe nominee 1987), Terror on Track 9, 1992, The Image (Emmy nominee, Ace award nominee), 1990, The Positively True Adventures of the Alleged Texas Cheerleader-Murdering Mom, 1993, And the Band Played On, 1993 (Emmy award nominee 1994, Ace award nominee), One Christmas, 1994, Betrayed: A Story of Three Women, 1995, A Promise to Carolyn, 1996, Little Girls in Pretty Boxes, 1997, More Tales of the City, 1998, My Own Country, 1998, Harvey, 1999, The Wilde Girls, 2001, Nadine in Date Land, 2005, Category 7: The End of the World, 2005; TV guest appearances on Kojak, Carol and Co. (Emmy award); (films) Slap Shot, 1977, The World According to Garp, 1982, Against All Odds, 1984, Wild Cats, 1986, True Stories, 1986, Vice Versa, 1988, Bright Lights, Big City, 1988, Dangerous Liaisons, 1988, Stanley and Iris, 1989, A Shock to the System, 1990, Reality Bites, 1994, Citizen Ruth, 1996, Liar, Liar, 1997, Outside Ozona, 1999, Cruel Intentions, 1999, The White River Kid, 2000, Sleep Easy, Hutch Rimes, 2000, Get Over It, 2001, Bubble Boy, 2001, The Rules of Attraction, 2002, Duplex, 2003; (theater) Ah Wilderness!, 1975, Children, 1976, Tartuffe, 1977 (Tony award nominee), A History of the American Film, 1978 (Drama Desk award), Uncommon Women and Others, 1978 (Obie award, Drama Desk award), Who's Afraid of Virginia Woolf, 1980, Summer, 1980, Fifth of July, 1980-82 (Tony award, Drama Desk award, Outer Critics Circle award), Michael Bennett's Scandal, 1985, Beach House, 1986, The House of Blue Leaves, 1986-87 (Tony award, Obie award), Hunting Cockroaches, 1987 (Drama Logue award nominee), Love Letters, 1989-90, Six Degrees of Separation, 1990, Lips Together, Teeth Apart, 1991, The Mineola Twins, 1999 (Obie award, Drama Desk award nominee, Outer Critics Circle award nominee), The Vagina Monologues, 2000, Imaginary Friends, 2002-03, Frozen, 2004 (Tony award nominee, Best Actress in a Play), Heartbreak House, 2006.*

KURTZBERG, JOANNE, pediatrician, educator; b. N.Y.C., Nov. 18, 1950; d. Lawrence Kurtzberg; m. Henry S. Friedman; children: Joshua, Sara. BA, Sarah Lawrence Coll., 1972; MD, N.Y. Med. Coll., 1976. Intern in pediats. Dartmouth Med. Ctr., Hanover, NH, 1976—77; resident in pediats. Upstate Med. Ctr., Syracuse, NY, 1977—79, clin. rsch. fellow in pediat. hematology/oncology, 1979—80; mem. faculty Duke Comprehensive Cancer Ctr., Durham, NC, 1983—; sr. rsch. fellow in pediat. hematology/oncology Duke U. Med. Ctr., Durham, NC, 1980—86, asst. prof., assoc. prof. pediat., 1983—88, prof. pediat., 1993—, dir. pediatric bone marrow lab., 1989—, dir. pediat. blood and marrow transplant program, 1989—2004, mem. grad. faculty Grad. Sch. pathology dept., 1993—, assoc. prof. pathology, 1991—2003, prof. pathology, 2003—, dir. Carolinas cord blood bank, 1996—, chief divsn. pediatric blood and marrow transplant, 2004—. Recipient R. Wayne Rundles award for excellence in cancer rsch., 1993, Basil O'Connor Starter Scholar Rsch. award, 1985-87. Fellow Leukemia Soc. Am. (spl. fellow, scholar 1986-89); mem. Internat. Soc. for Hematotherapy and Graft Engring., Am. Soc. for Blood & Marros & Transplantation, Am. Soc. Pediat. Hematology/Oncology, Am. Soc. Hematology, Soc. for Pediat. Rsch., Pediat. Oncology Group, Alpha Omega Alpha. Home: 1808 Faison Rd Durham NC 27705-2439 Office: Duke U Med Ctr PO Box 3350 Durham NC 27702-3350 Office Phone: 919-668-1119.

KURZ, DIANA, artist, educator; b. Vienna; d. Benjamin and Lillian (Hellreich) K BA cum laude, Brandeis U.; MFA, Columbia U. Mem. faculty Phila. Coll. Art, 1968—73, CUNY, Queens, 1971—76, Pratt Inst., Bklyn., 1973, U. Colo., Boulder, 1978, SUNY, Stony Brook, 1979, Va. Commonwealth U., Richmond, 1980, Cleve. Inst. of Art, 1980—81, Sch. of Art Inst. Chgo., 1987. One-woman shows include Green Mountain Gallery, N.Y.C., 1972, 74, 77, 79, Snug Harbor Cultural Ctr., 1982, Alex Rosenberg Gallery, N.Y.C., 1984, 87, Bklyn. Botanic Garden, 1989, Bienville Gallery, New Orleans, 1989, Palais De Justice-Aix-En-Provence, France, 1986, Rider Coll., 1984, Mercer County C.C., 1990, Thomas Ctr. Gallery, Gainesville Fla., Kavehaz, N.Y.C., 1995, Austrian Consulate Gen., N.Y.C., 1995, Synagogue for Arts, N.Y.C., 1996, Santa Fe C.C., Gainesville, 1998, Bezirksmuseum Josefstadt, Vienna, 1998; U. Minn., Mpls., 2000; Seton Hill Coll., Greensburg, Pa., 2000; Trenton City Mus., N.J., 2002; Seton Hall U., South Orange, N.J., 2002; Purdue U. Ft. Wayne, Ind., 2003; Holocuast Mus. & Study Ctr., Spring Valley, N.Y., 2003; St. Joseph's Coll., Pat Chauph, N.Y., 2003; group shows include: CUB Space, N.Y., 2006, Hudgins Ctr. Arts, Duluth, Ga., 2005, Mercer County C.C., N.M. Denver Internat. Airport, 2004, Broom St. Gallery, N.Y.C., 2005, CVB Space, N.Y.C., 2006, Vision Festival, N.Y.C., 2005, Denver Internat. Airport, 2004, Gallery South Orange, 2001; Blue Mountain Gallery, N.Y., 1998, 2002; Glasgow Sch. Art, Scotland, 2002; Rose Art Mus., Mass., 1974, L.I. U., Queens, 1975, Bklyn. Mus., 1975, Westminster Coll., 1976, Ind. U. Art Mus., 1977, Pub. Sch. 1, N.Y., SUNY Stony Brook, 1978, U. Colo., 1979, Boston Mus. Sch., 1980, U. Hartford, Conn., 1980, Weatherspoon Gallery, N.C., 1981, Rosenberg Gallery, N.Y., 1982, Sachs Gallery, N.Y., 1983, Artist Choice Mus., N.Y., Louisville Gallery, 1984, Ingber Gallery, N.Y., 1985, Koslow Gallery, L.A., 1988, Transco, Tex., 1988, Grand Ctrl. Gallery, N.Y., 1989, Ceres Gallery, N.Y., 1990, Soviet Exch. Exhibit, USSR, 1990—, Tweed Gallery, N.Y.C., 1993, Thomas Ctr. Gallery, Gainesville, 1993, Bergen Mus. Art, 1993, Trenton City Mus., 1994, U. Tex., San Antonio, 1995, Clymer Mus., Ellensburg, Wash., 1995, Broome St. Gallery, N.Y.C., 1996, 99, 2004, Nat. Mus. Women in Arts, 1997, MMC Gallery, N.Y.C., 1999 Bd. dirs. Fine Arts Fedn., N.Y. Fellow Yaddo, 1968-69, MacDowell Colony fellow, 1976, Vt. Studio, 1987; Fulbright grantee, 1965-66, CAPS grantee N.Y. State Coun. Arts, 1977; recipient award Am. Ctr. Residency, Paris, 1985-86, Atlantic Ctr. Arts, 2005; artist-in-residence Austrian Fed. Ministry Arts, Vienna, 1997 N.Y. Artists Equity (bd. dirs.), Fine Arts Fedn. N.Y.C. (bd. dirs.) Home and Office: 152 Wooster St New York NY 10012-5330

KURZWEIL, EDITH, social sciences educator, editor; b. Vienna; d. Ernest W. and Wilhelmine M. (Fischer) Weiss; widowed; 1 child, Allen J. BA, Queens Coll., CUNY, 1967; MA, New Sch. Social Rsch., 1969, PhD, 1973. Asst. prof. sociology Hunter Coll., N.Y.C., 1972-75, Montclair State Coll., Upper Monclair, NJ, 1973-78; assoc. prof. Rutgers U., Newark, 1979-85, prof., chmn., 1985-92; Disting. Olin. Prof. Adelphi U., 1993, univ. prof., 1994—2001, prof. emeritus, 2001—. Vis. prof. Goethe U., 1984. Author: The Age of Structuralism, 1980, Italian Entrepreneurs, 1983, The Freudians: A Comparative Perspective, 1989, Freudians and Feminists, 1995, Briefe aus Wien: Nazi Laws & Jewish Lives, 1999, English lang. edit., 2005, The Partisan Century: 60 Years of Partisan Review, 1996; author: (with others) Literature and Psychoanalysis, 1983, Writers and Politics, 1983, Cultural Analysis, 1984; exec. editor: Partisan Rev., 1978—94; editor, 1994—2003; mem. editl. bd.: Psyche, 1990—, Psychoanalytic Books, 1990—2000, series editor: Psychiatry and Psychology Transaction, 1995—2004. Adv. bd. N.Y. Civil Rights Coalition, 2001—; bd. govs. New Sch. U., 1999—. Recipient Nat. Humanities medal, 2003; Rockefeller Humanities fellow, 1982—83, NEH fellow, 1987—88, NEH grantee, 1989—90, 1991—92, NYCH grantee, 1995. Mem.: PEN, Internat. Sociol. Assn., Internat. Assn. History Psychoanalysis, Tocqueville Soc., Am. Sociol. Assn., Women's Freedom Network (bd. dirs. 1994—). Home: 1 Lincoln Plz New York NY 10023-7129 Personal E-mail: ekurzweil@rcn.com.

KUSHINSKY, JEANNE ALICE, humanities educator; b. Reading, Pa, Jan. 12, 1937; d. Otis Jacob and Alice Elizabeth (Kurtz) Rothenberger; m. Sheldon Melvin Wallerstein, May 9, 1959 (div. July 1978); children: Seth, Gail Wallerstein Melichar; m. David Lazar Kushinsky, Apr. 11, 1987. BS, Cedar Crest Coll., 1958; postgrad., Kean U. N.J., 1978—92, Rutgers U., 1993. Tchr. East Orange Bd. Edn., NJ, 1958—60; editor Dept. Testing and Assessment State Dept. Edn., Trenton, NJ, 1974—76; tchr. Edison Township Bd. Edn., NJ, 1974—2000; pvt. tutor SAT verbal sect. Edison, NJ, 1980—. Mem. Citizen's Adv. Coun. Edn., Edison, NJ, 1991—93. Fashion show com. Rahway Hosp. Found., 2002—; chairperson gala Edison Arts Soc., 2003—, bd. trustees NJ, 2000—; active Dist. VIII Middlesex County Bd. Atty. Ethics, Trenton, NJ, 2000—. Grantee grant, N.J. Coun. for Humanities, 1996. Mem.: Brandeis Univ. Nat. Women's Comm., NJ Edn. Assn., NEA, Metuchen-Edison Hist. Soc., Proprietary House, Nat. Trust for Hist. Preservation, Borough Improvement League. Democrat. Jewish. Avocations: historic preservation architecture, feminist issues, mentoring young people, film studies, reading. Home: 9 Ayers Ct Metuchen NJ 08840-1172

KUSHLIS, PATRICIA HOGIN, foreign affairs writer, analyst; b. Fall River, Mass., Oct. 5, 1944; d. James Edgar and Frances Marston Hogin; m. William Joseph Kushlis, Apr. 3, 1971; 1 child, Christopher James. BA in Liberal Arts, U. of the Pacific, 1965; MA in Internat. Rels., Syracuse U., 1969, PhD in Polit. Sci., 1978. U.S. fgn. svc. officer U.S. Info. Agy. (now U.S. Dept. State), Athens, Greece, 1970—71, 1981—84, Bangkok, 1972—75, Moscow, 1978—80, Helsinki, Finland, 1988—92, Manila, 1992—94; adj. prof. U. N.Mex., Albuquerque, 1999—2005; N.Mex. state mgr. Voter News Svc., Albuquerque, 2000—02. Cofounder World Affairs Forum, Santa Fe, 2003—. Asst. editor: quarterly mag. Dialogue, 1976; editor: (internet mag.) U.S. Fgn. Policy Agenda, 1996—98, (weblog) www.whirledview.typepad.com. Bd. dirs. U.S.-Philippine Fulbright Commn., Manila, 1992—94. Mem.: U.S.-Indonesia Soc., Pub. Diplomacy Coun., Albuquerque Com. on Fgn. Rels. (bd. dirs. 2001—06), Santa Fe Coun. on Internat. Rels. (bd. dirs. 1998—2000), Am. Fgn. Svc. Assn. Avocations: skiing, music, travel. Home: 12704 Osito Ct NE Albuquerque NM 87111

KUSHNER, AILEEN F., elementary school educator; d. Richard V. and Nina M. Jackman; m. Thomas A. Kushner; children: Christopher, Amanda, Erin, Bryan. BA, Marygrove Coll., Detroit, 1988, MA in Tchg., 2001. Substitute tchr. Bridgeport-Spaulding Cmty. Schs., Mich., 1991—99; tchr. Bridgeport-Spalding Cmty. Schs., 1999—. Freelance artist, Bridgeport, 1981—. Coord. Hoops for Huntingtons Bridgeport-Spaulding Mid. Sch., 2004—. Grantee, Saginaw Cmty. Found., Mich., 2001, Mich. State U., 2004—. Mem.: NEA, Mich. Art Edn. Assn., Nat. Art Edn. Assn., Mich. Edn. Assn. Avocations: music, bowling, art, gardening. Office: Bridgeport-Spalding Mid Sch 4221 Bearcat Blvd Bridgeport MI 48722

KUSHNER, EVE, writer; b. Winston-Salem, N.C., Sept. 22, 1968; d. Jack and Annetta Esther (Horwitz) Kushner; m. Haroon Khalid Chaudhri, Apr. 12, 1992. Student, U. Calif., San Diego, 1988, U. London, 1988-89, U. Denver, 1990; BA summa cum laude, Dartmouth Coll., 1990. Proofreader Dharma Enterprises, Oakland, Calif., 1991-92; pres. Spruced Up Manuscripts, Berkeley, Calif., 1991—99, Profiles and More, Berkeley, 1999—. Author: Experiencing Abortion: A Weaving of Women's Words, 1997. Dartmouth Gen. Award Com. fellow, 1991. Mem. Phi Beta Kappa. Office: Profiles and More 1730 Martin Luther King Jr Way Berkeley CA 94709 Personal E-mail: evekushner@yahoo.com.

KUSMIERSKI, JANET LOUISE, painter, graphics designer, illustrator; b. Queens, N.Y., Oct. 22, 1953; d. Henry Kusmierski and Irene Mastro; m. Greg G. Singer, Jan. 24, 1985; children: Avery K. Singer, Calder K. Singer. BFA, Parsons Sch. Design/New Sch. for Social Rsch., 1974; MA, Hunter Coll. of CUNY, 1978. One-woman shows include Elizabeth Harris Gallery, 1999, exhibited in group shows at Snug Harbor Cultural Ctr./Newhouse Gallery, 1997, Aisling Gallery, 1996, Artwalk-Studio Tours, 1995, Heckscher Mus., 1995, Women's Caucus for Art, N.Y.C. chpt., 1992, Everson Mus., 1986 (Honorable Mention), The Drawing Ctr., 1982. Artist grantee Artists Space, 1985; recipient Mary Duke Biddle Found. honorarium Mary Duke Biddle Found., 1981. Democrat. Roman Catholic. Office: 9 Murray St 6 SE New York NY 10007-2243

KUSSMAN, ELEANOR (ELLIE KUSSMAN), retired educational superintendent; b. Bklyn., Mar. 17, 1934; d. Mortimer Joseph and Eleanor Mary (O'Brien) Gleeson; m. Karl Kussman, June 30, 1956 (dec. Oct. 1988); children: Katherine Ann, Kristine Sue. BA, Wheaton Coll., Norton, Mass., 1955; MS, LaVerne Coll., Claremont, Calif., 1974. Cert. tchr. K-C.C., cert. in pupil pers. and adminstrn., Calif. Tchr. sci. and math. Norwood (Mass.) Jr. H.S., 1955-56; tchr. phys. edn. Brawley (Calif.) Union H.S., 1956-58, Ctrl. Union H.S., El Centro, Calif., 1958-74, tchr. health careers, 1974-80, state and fed. project dir., 1980-85; instr. horse husbandry and equitation Imperial Valley Coll., Imperial, Calif., 1974-76; supr. Imperial Valley (Calif.) Regional Occupational Program, 1985-95. Cons. Calif. Joint Gender Equity Com., Sacramento, 1991-96, State of Calif. Gender Equity, Sacramento, 1986-96; grad. instr. program in counseling and guidance U.Calif., Redlands, 1989 Mem. fin. com. United Way, El Centro, 1987-93; sec.-treas. Pvt. Industry Coun., El Centro, 1985-95; past sec.-treas. Calif. Regional Occupational Ctrs./Programs, 1986-88; bd. dirs. Imperial Valley Coll. Desert Mus., 1998-2000. Named Educator of Yr. Imperial Valley Chpt. Phi Delta Kappa, 1995. Mem. AAUW, ASCD, Assn. Calif. Sch. Adminstrs. (past local and regional officer), Rotary Internat. (bd. dirs. 1994-97). Avocations: camping, travel, gardening, reading, horses. Home: PO Box 83 El Centro CA 92244-0083

KUSSROW, NANCY ESTHER, educational association administrator; BA, Valparaiso U., 1952; MA, U. N.C., 1954. Exec. dir. Nat. Assn. prins. of Schs. for Girls; ret., 1996.

KUTLAR, FERDANE, genetics educator, researcher; b. Turkey, Apr. 15, 1945; came to U.S., 1984; d. Mehmet and Sidika Tanrikulu; m. Abdullah Kutlar, Feb. 7, 1975. MD, Istanbul (Turkey) Med. Sch., 1971. Bd. cert in internal medicine, Turkey, 1976. Resident in internal medicine Istanbul U. Sch. Medicine, 1972-76; chief resident dept. medicine Istanbul Hosp., 1977-81; rsch. fellow Med. Coll. Ga., Augusta, 1982; hematology fellow Istanbul U. Sch. Medicine, 1983; rsch. fellow Med. Coll. Ga., Augusta, 1984, asst. prof., 1985-99, assoc. prof. medicine, 1999—. Dir. DNA lab. Med. Coll. Ga., Augusta, 1994—; presenter in field. Contbr. articles to profl. jours. Mem. Am. Soc. Hematology, Am. Soc. Human Genetics, Med. Coll. Ga. Pres.'s Club. Avocations: painting, gardening, decorating, chess. Home: 623 Sawgrass Dr Martinez GA 30907-9137 Office: Med Coll Ga Dept Medicine 15th St AC-1000 Augusta GA 30912-2100 Office Phone: 706-721-9768. Business E-Mail: fkutlar@mail.mcg.edu.

KUTLER, ALISON L., lawyer; d. Stuart and Sandy Kutler. BA in Govt., cum laude, Georgetown U., 1993; JD, Stanford U., 1999. Bar: DC, Nebr. 1999. Mem. staff US Rep. Peter Hoagland, 1991—93; various positions with Clinton Adminstrn., 1993—96; asst. to US Sec. Commerce Ron Brown; Congl. affairs specialist US Dept. Commerce Bur Export Adminstrn., Small Bus. Adminstrn.; dep. chief of staff to Hadassah Lieberman Gore-Lieberman Presdl. Campaign, 2000; assoc. Arent Fox Kinter Plotkin & Kahn, Washington; assoc., pub. law & policy strategies group Sonnenschein Nath & Rosenthal LLP, Washington, 2002—. Office: Sonnenschein Nath & Rosenthal LLP Ste 600, E Tower 1301 K St NW Washington DC 20005 Office Phone: 202-408-9142. Office Fax: 202-408-6399. Business E-Mail: akutler@sonnenschein.com.

KUTNER, JANET, art critic, book reviewer; b. Dallas, Sept. 20, 1937; m. Jonathan D. Kutner, Jan. 15, 1961. Student, Stanford U., 1955-57; BA in English, So. Meth. U., 1959. Asst. dir. Dallas Mus. Contemporary Arts, 1959-61; art critic, book reviewer Dallas Morning News, 1970—; Dallas/Ft. Worth corr. ARTnews Mag., 1975—. Mem. arts adv. panel Dallas Mcpl. Libr., 1981-91; mem. adv. bd. Arts Magnet H.S. of Dallas, 1980-92; mem. adv. com. Sch. Architecture and Environ. Design, U. Tex., Arlington, 1985-87; mem. long range planning com. Dallas Mus. Art, 1985-86; mem. visual arts and architecture adv. panel Tex. Com. on Arts, 1980-82. Contbr. articles to profl. jours.; juror various art exhbns. Bd. trustees Greenhill Sch., Dallas, 1980-81. Art critics grantee Nat. Endowment for Arts, 1976-77, art critic's fellow Nat. Gallery Art, 1991-; recipient Legend award Dallas Ctr. Contemporary Art, 2005. Mem. Am. Assn. Museums, Dallas Mus. Art, Internat. Coun. Museums, ArtTable, Dallas Press Club (Critics award 1997). Office: Dallas Morning News PO Box 655237 Dallas TX 75265-5237

KUTOSH, SUE, artist; b. Elizabeth, N.J., Dec. 25, 1947; d. Stephen and Irene (Ribecky) K. BFA, Carnegie-Mellon U., 1971; MA, Kent State U., 1973. One-woman shows include Keane Mason Gallery, N.Y.C., 1978, West Broadway Gallery, N.Y.C., 1981, Kristen Richards Gallery, N.Y.C., 1983, Mussavi Arts Gallery, N.Y.C., 1987, N.Y. Bot. Garden, Bronx, 1992, Montserrat Gallery, N.Y.C., 1996, Pleiades Gallery, N.Y.C., 1997; art included in books: The Films of Jane Fonda, 1981, Hispanic Hollywood, 1990, The Lavender Screen, 1993, Hollywood Babble On, 1994, New Art Internat., 1998-2000, Direct Art mag., 2005; scenic art contbns. Sesame Street Recipient Daytime Emmy for Seseame Street, 1993-94. Mem. United Scenic Artists, Local 829, Catharine Lorillard Wolfe Art Club, N.Y. Artists Equity, Nat. Assn. Women Artists. Avocation: photography. Home: 200 E 16th St Apt 2-d New York NY 10003-3708

KUTRYB, SUSAN L., mathematician, educator; d. William M. and Lillian T. Leslie; m. Stanley G. Kutryb, June 28, 1975; children: Nicholas S., Matthew B., Adam B. BS, SUNY, Plattsburgh, 1975; MA, SUNY, Albany, 1977. Cert. secondary math. tchr. NY. Asst. prof. Hudson Valley C.C., Troy, NY, 1993—. Mem.: NY State Math. Assn. Two Yr. Colls. (legis. chmn. 2005—), An. Math. Assn. Two Yr. Colls. Office: Hudson Valley CC 80 Vandenburgh Ave Troy NY 12180 Office Phone: 518-629-4867. Business E-Mail: kutrysus@hvcc.edu.

KUTSCHINSKI, DOROTHY IRENE, elementary school educator; b. Denison, Iowa, Feb. 19, 1922; d. Gustave Waldemar and Wilhelmina Louisa (Stahl) Wiese; m. Alvin Otto Kutschinski; children: Karen E. Kutschinski Christensen, Linda K. Kutschinski Nepper. BA, Morningside Coll., 1965, MA in Teaching, 1970. Tchr. Crawford County (Iowa) Rural Schs., 1940-53, Charter Oak (Iowa) Community Schs., 1953-90; substitute tchr., 1990—. Apptd. to Crawford County Coun. Local Govt. for Hist. Preservation, 1992—, chair 1996—; tchr. Bible class St. John Luth. Ch., Charter Oak, Iowa, 1956—; sec. Crawford County Rep. Ctrl. Com., 1980-91, 98—; pres. Crawford County Rep. Women, 1978-86 trustee Iowa N.W. Regional Libr., 1991-2001; co-founder, sec., charter Oak-Ute Cmty. Sch. Edn. Found., 1994—, apptd. to adv. com., sec., 1993-2001. Named Outstanding Elem. Tchr. of Am., 1973; recipient Tchr. of Yr. award, Denison Newspapers, 1985, Women of Excellence award, Women Aware, Inc., 2001. Mem. AAUW (treas. 1985-90, pres. 1991-93), Iowa State Hist. Soc., Crawford County Hist. Soc. (life), The Smithsonian Assocs., The Audubon Soc., Living History Farms, Iowa Natural

Heritage, Crawford County Arts Assn. (pres. 1986-88, bd. dirs. 1972—, sec. 1996—), Delta Kappa Gamma, Alpha Delta (sec. 1984—). Avocations: reading, sewing, bird watching, walking, writing. Home: 103 Pine Ave Charter Oak IA 51439-7453

KUTTLER, JUDITH ESTHER, retired psychotherapist; b. Paterson, NJ, Feb. 26, 1938; d. Theodor Herzl and Roslyn Unterman; children: Hillel Moshe, David Eli, Nadine Eve. BA, Marymount Manhattan Coll., NYC, 1974; MSW, Hunter Coll. Sch. Social Work, NYC, 1978, post-masters cert. in adv. clin. social work in family therapy, 1982. RN Beth Israel Hosp. (now known as Beth Israel Med. Ctr.), NYC, 1960. Psychotherapist Creedmoor Psychiatric Ctr., Queens, NY, 1972—84, social worker, Manhattan Children's Psychiatric Ctr., Ward's Island, NY, 1986—88, Creedmoor Psychiatric Ctr., Queens, 1988—94; self-employed psychotherapist Adv. Ctr. for Psychotherapy, Jamaica Estates, 1994—2002. Docent Jewish Mus., NYC; com. mem. Penn South Housing Complex, NYC; mentor Manhattan Comprehensive Day/Night HS. Jewish. Avocations: reading, hiking, poetry, travel, writing. Home: 365 W 25th St Apt 20H New York NY 10001-5825

KUYKENDALL, CRYSTAL ARLENE, educational consultant, lawyer; b. Chgo., Dec. 11, 1949; d. Cleophus Avant and Ellen (Campbell) Logan; m. Roosevelt Kuykendall, Apr. 10, 1969 (dec. Aug. 1972); children: Kahlil, Rasheki, Kashif. BA, Southern Ill. U., 1970; MA, Montclair State U., 1972; EdD, Atlanta U., 1975; JD, Georgetown U., 1982; LHD (hon.), Lewis and Clark Coll., Portland, 2002; MDiv, Va. Union U., 2005. Bar: D.C. 1988. Instr. Seton Hall U., South Orange, N.J., 1971-73; adminstrn. intern D.C. Pub. Schs., 1974-75; dir. citizens tng. inst. Nat. Com. for Citizens in Edn., Washington, 1975-77; dir. urban and minorities rels. dept. Nat. Sch. Bd. Assn., Washington, 1977-79; edn. dir. PSI Assocs., Inc., Washington, 1979-80; exec. dir. Nat. Alliance of Black Sch. Educators, Washington, 1980-81; dir. mktg. Roy Littlejohn Assoc., Inc., Washington, 1983—; pres., gen. counsel K.I.R.K., Inc. (Kreative and Innovative Resources for Kids), Washington, 1981—. Cons. to Ministry of Sport and Recreation, Western Australia Govt., 1990; chmn. U.S. Pres. Nat. Adv. Coun. on Continuing Edn., Washington, 1978-81; cons. U. Pitts. Race Desegregation Assistance Ctr., 1982-87, J.H. Lowry Assn., Chgo., 1982, U.S. Dept. of Edn. Transition Team, Washington, 1980. Author: Developing Leadership for Parent/Citizen Groups, 1975, You & Yours: Making the Most of this School Year, 1987, Improving Black Student Achievement by Enhancing Self Image, 1989, From Rage to Hope: Strategies for Reclaiming Black and Hispanic Students, 1992, 2d edit., 2004, Dreaming of a PHAT Century, 2000, 2nd edit., 2003, 2005 Mem. adv. bd. Inst. of the Black World, Atlanta, 1975-81; mem. steering com. Nat Conf. on Parental Involvement, Denver, 1977-78; mem. edn. task force Martin Luther King Jr. Ctr. for Social Change, Atlanta, 1978-80; mem. bd. dirs. Health Power, Inc., 1995-2001; chairperson, bd. dirs. Henry C. Gregory III Family Life Ctr. Found. of Shiloh Bapt. Ch. of Washington, 2003—, bd. mem., 1996—; mem. bd dirs. Md. Mentoring Partnership; assoc. min. Shiloh Bapt. Ch., Washington, 2005—. Named Honorary Citizen of New Orleans, Mayor's Office, 1976; Ford found. fellow, 1973-74; Honorary Ky Colonel award, 1993, 99, 2002; Cert. Congl. Recognition, 2001. Mem. Nat. Bar Assn., Nat. Alliance of Black Sch. Edn., Alpha Kappa Alpha. Democrat. Baptist. Avocations: poetry writing, card playing, swimming, jogging, skiing. Office: KIRK Inc PO Box 60115 Potomac MD 20859-0115 Office Phone: 301-299-4189. Personal E-mail: ckuykendal@aol.com.

KUYPER, JOAN CAROLYN, foundation administrator; b. Balt., Oct. 22, 1941; d. Irving Charles and Ethel Mae (Pritchett) O'Connor; m. William Kuyper, Dec. 20, 1964; children: Susan Carol, Edward Philip. BA in Edn., Salisbury State U., 1963; postgrad., Columbia U., 1978; MA in Arts Mgmt. and Bus., NYU, 1988. Elem. sch. tchr. Prince Georges County Schs., Md., 1963—68; freelance singer, opera, oratorio, chamber music Amato Opera, N.Y.C., 1967—80; owner, mgr. Privette Artists' Registry, Placement for Svc. for Singers, Teaneck, NJ, 1969—78; exec. dir. Teaneck Artists Performing Chamber Music Series, 1975—80; bd. dirs. Pro Arte Chorale and adv. bd. on arts, Teaneck, 1976—81; program dir. Vols. in Arts & Humanities Vol. Bur. Bergen County, NJ, 1978—81; dir. Bergen Mus. Art and Sci., 1981—83; cons. Am. Soc. Prevention Cruelty to Animals, 1984, Am. Coun. for Arts, 1987; dir. ops. Isabel O'Neil Found. and Studio, 1984—85; dir. vol. svcs. March of Dimes Birth Defects Found. of Greater N.Y., 1985—88; dir. chpt. devel. Huntington's Disease Soc. Am., 1988—91; mgmt. cons. Girl Scouts Am., 1992—2000; dep. dir. for orgnl. advancement Soc. Women Engrs., 2000—03; CEO, exec. dir. The Netherland-Am. Found., 2003—. Sr. counsel The Forbes Group. Mem.: PEO, Exec. Women in Golf Assn., SearchNet, Orgnl. Devel. Network, Nat. Soc. Fund Raising Execs., Assn. for Vol. Adminstrn. (author handbook), Am. Mktg. Assn. (bd. dirs. 1990—96), Mus. Coun. N.J., Assn. Mus., Am. Soc. Assn. Execs. (cert.), N.Y. Soc. Assn. Execs. (membership com. 1991—94, Cert. Assn. Execs. chair 1995—96, program planning com. 1996—98, chmn. profl. devel. com. 1998—), Altrusa Club (bd. dirs. 1984—86, pres. 1986—88, bd. dirs. 1990—93, 1996—), Phi Alpha Theta. Democrat. Presbyterian. Home: 345 W 58th St Apt 14X New York NY 10019-1142 also: 1275 Pebble Beach Rd Tobyhanna PA 18466-9119 Office Phone: 212-825-1221. E-mail: kuyper@thenaf.org.

KUZAN, KATHLEEN, speech pathology services professional, educator; b. East Orange, N.J., July 2, 1955; d. James and Angela (Poeta) Massotto; m. Roman Michael Kuzan, Aug. 14, 1977; children: Larissa Marie, Michael Nicholas. BA, Montclair U., Upper Montclair, N.J., 1977, MA, 1983. Cert. speech lang. pathologist, speech lang. specialist, tchr. of the handicapped, reading tchr., CCC. Supplemental speech correctionist Bd. of Edn., Union, NJ, 1977—78, reading tchr. Irvington, 1978—80, speech cons. pre-sch. summer screening Union Twp., 1978—90; adj. prof. Kean U., Union, 1990—94; speech - lang. pathologist Bd. of Edn., Union Twp., NJ, 1980—. Supr. clin. fellowship yr. ASHA - Union Twp. Schs., 2001—02; speech lang. pathologist pvt. practice, 1985—. Mem. Holy Spirit Ch., Union, religion tchr., 1996—. Mem.: N.J. Edn. Assn., Am. Speech Lang. Hearing Assn., Alpha Delta Kappa (epsilon chpt.) (sec. 1998—), Phi Kappa Phi. Achievements include development of k-12 curriculum guide for speech and language svcs; program integrating speech and lang. svcs. in self-contained and regular classrooms. Avocations: reading, needlepoint, soccer mom. Office: Union Twp Bd of Edn Wash Sch Washington Ave Union NJ 07083

KUZIEMSKI, NAOMI ELIZABETH, educational consultant, counselor; b. Phila., Dec. 22, 1925; d. Andrew Raymond and Elizabeth M. (Graham) Hartman; m. Walter William Kuziemski, Dec. 28, 1943 (dec. Feb. 2000); children: Nancy Kuziemski Simpson, Sandra Ruth McElroy. BS in Bus. Edn., Temple U., Phila., 1945; MS in Counseling, Temple U., 1949. Tchr. Sch. Dist. Phila., 1945-58; coll. counselor Phila. H.S. for Girls, 1958-96; ednl. cons., 1996—. V.p. Nat. Assn. Coll. Admissions Counselors, Alexandria, Va., 1985-87, dir. Tools of the Trade workshop, 1992-95; pres. Pa. Assn. Coll. Admissions Counselors, 1991-93; focus group mem. U.S. News and World Report, Washington, 1995-96; panelist and presenter in field. Del., instnl. rep. Coll. Bd., N.Y., 1978-96. Recipient Bernard P. Ireland award Coll. Bd., Phila., 1996, Gayle C. Wilson award Nat. Assn. Coll. Admission Counselors, Alexandria, 1996, Recognition award PASSCAC, 1998; named Counselor of the Yr., Inroads, Phila., 1982. Mem. AAUW (Phila. br., v.p. 1997-99), Coll. Bd.-Middle States (planning com. 1995-97). Home: 7 Lawnside Rd Cheltenham PA 19012-1812 Personal E-mail: enkuz@aol.com.

KUZNETSOVA, EKATERINA G., theater educator, dancer; d. Gennadi Ivanovich Kuznetsov and Larissa Mihailovna Kravtsova. MA in Dance and Adult Edn., U. Alaska, Anchorage, 2006. Founder, artistic dir., choreographer Ritmovida Dance Partnership, Anchorage, 2000—; instr. Dept. Theatre and Dance U. Alaska, Anchorage, 2002—. Choreographer UAA Dance Ensemble, 2000—. Office Phone: 907-569-4706. Business E-Mail: anegk@uaa.alaska.edu.

KUZNETSOVA, SVETLANA, professional tennis player; b. St. Petersburg, Russia, June 27, 1985; d. Alexandr Kuznetsov and Galina Tsareva. Profl. tennis player WTA Tour, 2001—. Named WTA Tour Newcomer of Yr., 2002. Achievements include winning 8 career singles titles, 13 doubles titles, WTA; winning 1 career singles title, ITF; mem. Russian Fed Cup Team, 2004, Russian Olympic Team, 2004. Office: c/o WTA Tour Corp Hdqs One Progess Plz Ste 1500 Saint Petersburg FL 33701*

KUZNIK, RACHELLE LEE, science educator, writer; d. Robert and Sandra Kuznik. BA, Wichita State U., 1997; MA, Calif. U. Pa., 2004. Tchr. sci. Wichita Pub. Schs. North H.S., 1997—99, McKeesport Area Sch. Dist., Pa., 1999—2000, Hempfield Area Sch. Dist., Greensburg, 2000—. Curriculum writer PBS Jim Lehrer Newshour, 2005—; web evaluator NetTrekker, 2005—; network educator astronaut tchrs. NASA, 2004—. Recipient Triple T award, Wichita North H.S., 1999; grantee, Spectroscopy Soc. Pitts., 2002. Mem.: Nat. Earth Sci. Tchr. Assn., Nat. Sci. Tchr. Assn., Delta Kappa Gamma (hon.). Methodist. Avocations: writing, cooking, travel, weightlifting, gardening. Home: 165 Stone Church Rd Hunker PA 15639 Office: Hempfield Area High School 4345 Route 136 Greensburg PA 15601 Office Phone: 724-834-9000. Personal E-mail: saoblack@comcast.net. E-mail: r.kuznik@hempfieldarea.k12.pa.us.

KWAK, EUN-JOO, musician, educator; b. Seoul, Korea; d. Wan-Shin and Yi-Soon (Shin) Kwak; m. James F. Crowley, June 6, 1998. BMusic, Seoul Nat. U., 1987; MMusic, Roosevelt U., Chgo., 1990; DMusic, Northwestern U., 1995. Mem. piano faculty Northwestern U., Evanston, Ill., 1995-96, N.E. Mo. State U., Kirksville, 1995-96, Truman State U., Kirksville, 1996-98, Coll.of DuPage, Glen Ellyn, Ill., 1998-99; dir. piano studies New Canaan Conservatory of Music, Glenview, Ill., 1998—2000, program mgr., bd. dirs., 1998—2000; mem. piano faculty Cardinal Stritch U., Milw. Solo pianist: live recital and radio broadcast Dame Myra Hess Meml. Concerts, WFMT, 1998, duo pianist, prodr.: CD The Cheng and Kwak Piano Duo, 1997, solo pianist: radio broadcast Young Artists Live Concert Series, KBS-FM, 1994, ensemble performacne radio broadcast Musical Garden Christian Radio Taiwan, 2001; performer: (chamber music performance) Pine Mountain Music Festival, 2000; live recital and radio broadcast Sunday afternoons: The Elvehjem Concert Series, Wis. Pub. Radio, 2005, solo and duo pianist: recitals and performances with orchs. Recipient Bronze medal Tokyo Internat. Piano Duo Competition, 1994, Emily Boettcher Artists award Northwestern U., 1994, Theodor Bohlman award Internat. Beethoven Sonata Competition, Memphis, 1990; Korean Embassy scholar, 1991. Mem. Steinway Soc., Music Tchrs. Nat. Assn., Coll. Music Soc., Sigma Alpha Iota. Avocations: movies, drawing, interior decoration. Office: Cardinal Stritch U 6801 N Yates Rd Milwaukee WI 53217-4569 Office Phone: 414-410-4662. Business E-Mail: ekwak@stritch.edu.

KWAN, MICHELLE WING, professional figure skater; b. Torrance, Calif., July 7, 1980; d. Danny and Estella Kwan. Attends, UCLA. Spokesperson Walt Disney Co., 2006—. Published (book series) Michelle Kwan Presents Skating Dreams, guest appearances Disney and ABC Specials; performer: (TV special) based on the music of Disney's animated film, Mulan, 1998. Nat. spokesperson, Champions Across Am. Children's Miracle Network, 1996—, co-chair, ProKid's Program; founder Chevrolet/Michelle Kwan R.E-.W.A.R.D.S. scholarship program. Recipient Skating Mag. Readers' Choice award for figure skater of yr., 1993-94, U.S. Figure Skating Skater of Yr. award, 1994-96, 98, 99, 2001-03, Dial award, 1997, Sullivan award for top amateur athlete in Am., 2001, Kids' Choice award, 2002, 03, Teen Choice award, 2002, Skating Mag. Reader's Choice award, 2003; named Female Athlete of Yr. U.S. Olympic Com., 1996, 98-2001, 2003, Women's Sports Found. Sportswoman of Yr., 2003, CosmoGirl of Yr., 2002. Achievements include being the youngest World Champion in US history; most decorated figure skater in US history; third youngest World Champion; received 50 perfect 6.0 marks in major competitions; victories include: World Junior Championships, 1994, 96, Nations cup, 1995, U.S. Postal Svc. Challenge, 1995, State Farm U.S. Championships, 1996, 1999, 2001, 2003, Champions Series Final, 1996, Japan Open, 1997, 1999, Skate Am., 1995, 1997, 1999, 2000, Skate Can., 1995, 1997, 1999, US Championships, 1996, 1998-2004, World Championships, 1998, 1999, 2000, 2001, 2003, Goodwill Games, 1998, 1998 Ultimate Four, 1998, Grand Slam Figure Skating, 1998, US Pro Classic, 1998, Masters of Figure Skating, 1998, 1999, 2000, Silver Medal, Olympics, 1998, Bronze Medal, 2002; Michelle Kwan Trophy named in her honor, 2004. Office: US Figure Skating Assn 20 1st St Colorado Springs CO 80906-3624 Mailing: Proper Marketing Assoc c/o Shep Goldberg 44450 Pinetree Dr Ste 103 Plymouth MI 48170*

KWAN-RUBINEK, VERONIKA, broadcast executive; Pres. internat. distbn. Warner Bros. Pictures, 2001—. Office: Warner Bros Pictures International Distribution 4000 Warner Blvd Burbank CA 91522 Office Phone: 818-954-1663. Office Fax: 818-954-6112. E-mail: veronika.kwan-rubinek@warnerbros.com.*

KWIATKOWSKI, TONIA, former professional figure skater; b. Cleve., Feb. 12, 1971; Degree in psychology and comms., Baldwin-Wallace Coll. Coach Winterhurst Figure Skating Club; mem. U.S. Nat. Figure Skating Team. Recipient 3d pl. U.S. Sr. Nats., 1993, Bronze medal U.S. Nat. Figure Skating Championships, 1995, 1st pl. World Univ. Games, 1995. Mem. Phi Gamma Mu. Address: Winterhurst Figure Skating Club 14740 Lakewood Heights Blvd Cleveland OH 44107-5901

KWIK, CHRISTINE IRENE, physician, retired military officer, retired foreign service officer; b. Lvov, Poland, Sept. 12, 1939; d. Karol Stanislaus and Leonarda Fryderica (Seniuk) Kostek; widowed; children: Christine and Catherine. Grad. summa cum laude, Med. Acad. Cracow, Poland, 1956-62; grad. primary flight medicine, Brooks AFB, Tex., 1985; completed chief of profl. staff, Sheppard AFB, Tex., 1988. Diplomate Am. Bd. Emergency Medicine, Am. Bd. Internal Medicine, Poland; cert. Ednl. Coun. Fgn. Med. Grad.; re-cert. Extended Allergy Care Provider. Intern. Med. Acad., Cracow, Poland, 1962-63; residency internal medicine II Clinic Internal Diseases, Cracow, Poland, 1963-66; staff II Clinic of Internal Diseases, Cracow, Poland, 1966-69; gen. med. officer Gen. Hosp., Sokoto, Nigeria, 1969-72; intern. Frankford Hosp., Phila., 1972-73; house physician Holy Redeemer Hosp., Meadowbrook, Pa., 1973-74; emergency room physician John F. Kennedy Hosp., Phila., 1974-76, Emergency Rm. dir., 1976-78; commd. capt. USAF Med. Corp, 1978, advanced through grades to colonel, 1993; primary care physician USAF Clinic Emergency Rm., Ramstein, Germany, 1978-81; officer in charge Emergency Rm. and Gen. Practice Clinic, Peterson Field, Colo., 1981-84; primary care physician Malcolm Grow Med. Ctr., Andrews AFB, Md., 1984-88; chief clinic svc. 63d Med. Group/SGH, Norton AFB, Calif., 1988-93; staff physician 60h Med. Group, Travis AFB, Calif., 1993-96, Occupl. and Environ. Health and Safety Svc., Ft. George Meade, Md., 1996-99; ret. USAF, 1999; regional med. officer Dept. of State. Asst. tchr., sr. asst. tchr. Inst. Descriptive Anatomy, Cracow, Poland 1963-69; emergency physician on call First Aid Sta., Cracow, Poland 1966-69. Fellow: Am. Coll. Emergency Physicians; mem.: AMA, World Med. Assn. Avocations: photography, travel, gourmet cooking. E-mail: kwikci@yahoo.com.

KWONG, EVA, artist, educator; b. Hong Kong, 1954; came to the U.S., 1967; d. Tony and Ivory Kwong; m. Kirk Mangus, 1976; children: Una, Jasper. BFA, RISD, 1975; MFA, Tyler Sch. Art/Temple U., Phila., 1977. Vis. artist, 1977—; vis. faculty Cleve. Inst. Art, 1982-83; part-time faculty U. Akron, Ohio, 1987, 89, 95, Kent (Ohio) State U., 1990—. Lectr. in field. Works in over 300 exhbns. Visual Arts Regional fellow Arts Midwest, Mpls., 1987, Visual Arts fellow Nat. Endowment for the Arts, Washington, 1988, Ohio Arts Coun., Columbus, 1988, 94, 99, 2004, Ohio Arts Coun. fellow in visual arts, 2004; recipient Internat. award China NCECA, 2003. Mem. Nat. Coun. on Edn. for the Ceramic Arts (dir.-at-large 1995-97).

KYBAL, ELBA GÓMEZ DEL REY, economist, not-for-profit developer; b. Santa Fe, Argentina, Apr. 1, 1915; came to U.S., 1942; d. J. Ignacio and Concepción (del Rey) Gómez; m. Milic Kybal, July 16, 1950 (dec. July 1977); children: Cynthia, Alexander. BA in Internat. Rels., U. Litoral, Rosario, Argentina, 1940; MA in Econs., Harvard U., 1945, PhD in Econs., 1946. Economist Fed. Res. Bank, N.Y.C., 1946-47; economist, polit. affairs officer UN, N.Y.C., 1947-56, sr. economist; head specialized conf., chief L.Am. econ. integration Orgn. Am. States, Washington, dir. under secretariat for econ. and social affairs, 1956—80. Advisor InterAm. com. of women OAS, Washington, 1960—80; vol. cons. Pan Am. Devel. Found., Washington, 1980—82; vol. Argentine, Ecuadorian and Peruvian Found., Washington, 1988—90; pres. Pan Am. Roundtable, Washington, 1999—, Pan Am. Liaison Com. of Women's Orgns., 1999—2005, Retirees Assn. Orgn. Am. States, Washington, 2001—; bd. dirs. Gala Hispanic Theatre, Washington, 1997—2005. Named Vol. of the Yr., Pan Am. Devel. Found., 1981, Bus. and Profl. Women's Club, 1984. Mem.: Phi Beta Kappa. Roman Catholic. Avocation: travel. Home: Watergate South # 801 700 New Hampshire Ave NW Washington DC 20037-2406

KYGER, BRENDA SUE, intravenous therapy nurse; b. Balt., Nov. 18, 1947; d. Charles and Betty (Weese) Reynolds; m. William H. Kyger, Jan. 30, 1967; children: Jennifer Lee, Jeffrey Lee. Grad., Balt. City Hosps., 1966; ADN, Essex Community Coll., Balt., 1970; BSN, U. Md., Balt., 1991; MSN, U. Md., 1997. Cert. intravenous nurse; PICC certification. Nurse Balt. City Hosps., 1966-70, nurse, head nurse, 1970-71; staff nurse CCU/ICU Franklin Sq. Hosp., Balt., 1971-72, staff nurse intravenous therapy, 1972-92, instr. IV therapy, 1976—, clin. leader, 1988-90, clin. care coord. of IV therapy, 1998—, patient care coord. for IV therapy, 1999—. Active Clin. Practice Coun., 1988-90, 94—, quality assurance coun. Franklin Sq. Hosp. Ctr., 1991-93, Nursing Edn. Coun. Contbr. articles to profl. jours. Former mgr. girls under 16 soccer team Sharp Shooters II; former registrar Md. State Youth Soccer Assn., Inc.; past sec. Recreation and Parks Coun. Baltimore County; past. sec. Balt. Metro Soccer League. Mem. Intravenous Nurses Soc., Am. Soc. Parenteral and Enteral Nutrition, Nat. Assn. Vascular Access Networks, Oncology Nursing Soc., Sigma Theta Tau. Avocations: gardening, writing. Home: 23 Propeller Dr Baltimore MD 21220-4545 Office: Franklin Sq Hosp Ctr Franklin Square Dr Baltimore MD 21237 E-mail: DaisyJ3250@aol.com.

KYLE, CORINNE SILVERMAN, management consultant; b. N.Y.C., Jan. 4, 1930; d. Nathan and Janno (Harra) Silverman; m. Alec Kyle, Aug. 29, 1959 (div. Feb. 1969); children: Joshua, Perry (dec.), Julia. BA, Bennington Coll., 1950; MA, Harvard U., 1953. Assoc. editor Inter-Univ. Case Program, N.Y.C., 1956-60; co-founder, chief editor Financial Index, N.Y.C., 1960-63; rsch. analyst McKinsey & Co., N.Y.C., 1963-64; sr. rsch. assoc. Mktg. Sci. Inst., Phila., 1964-67; founding ptnr. Phila. Group, 1967-70; sr. assoc. Govt. Studies and Systems, Phila., 1970-72, cons. program planning and control, 1972-78; sr. assoc. Periodical Studies Svc., 1978-81; v.p., dir. rsch. Total Rsch. Corp., Princeton, NJ, 1981-82; mgr. social rsch. The Gallup Orgn., Princeton, 1982-86; v.p. Response Analysis Corp., 1986-91; dir. rsch. Gallup Internat. Inst., 1991-97; assoc. Krog & Ptnrs., Inc., 1997-99; survey rsch. cons., 1999—. Lectr. rsch. methods Temple U., 1981-82; vis. prof. Fairleigh Dickinson U., 1990-91, 93; dir. Verbena Corp., N.Y.C. Contbr. numerous articles to profl. publs. Mem. adv. coun. to 8th Dist. city councilman, Phila., 1971-79; mem. 22nd Ward Dem. Exec. Com., 1971-78, State Dem. Com., 1974-76; mem. Pa. Gov.'s Council on Nutrition, 1974-76; v.p. Miquon Upper Sch. Bd., Phila., 1977-78; trustee Princeton Regional Scholarship Found., 1982-85, pres., 1984-85; mem. bd. edn. Princeton Regional Sch. Dist., 1984-93, pres. 1987, 89; mem. exec. bd. Mercer County (N.J.) Sch. Bds. Assn., 1987-92, v.p., 1991-92; mem. exec. com. Princeton Community Dem. Orgn., 1992-97; mem. Princeton Regional Planning Bd., 1994-99, chair, 1997-99, Princeton Environ. Commn., 1994-97; chair Princeton Borough task force on consolidation, 1995; chair One Princeton, 1996-97; mem. West Orange Bd. Edn., 2002-, pres., 2004-05. Mem.: West Orange Advocates. Home: 32 Randolph Pl West Orange NJ 07052-4808 Personal E-mail: cskyle@earthlink.net.

KYLE, GENE MAGERL, merchandise presentation artist; b. Phila., Oct. 11, 1919; d. Elmer Langham and Muriel Helen (Magerl) Kyle. Student, Ctr. for Creative Studies, Detroit, 1938—45. Mdse. presentation artist D.J. Healy Shops, Detroit, 1946—50, Saks Fifth Ave., Detroit, 1950—58, J.L. Hudson Co., Detroit, 1958—84, Grosse Pointe, Mich., 1989—95; freeland mdse. presentations for windows Grosse Point, 1989—. Papercraft Detroit Artists Mkt. Holiday Shows, 1997—2003; tchr. workshop classes. Exhibited in group shows at Mich. Watercolor Soc., 1944, 1953, 1974, Mich. Artists Exhbn., 1962, 1964, Scarab Club, 1948—49, 1952, Detroit Artist Mkt., 1946—97, Mich. Gallery, 1989—92, Coach House Gallery, 1980, 1990, Cmty. House, Birmingham, Mich., 1993—94, First Fed. Mich. Bank, 1994, 1995, Swann Gallery, 1996—97, Detroit Artists Mkt., 1997—2000. Vol. presentation work. Recipient various art awards. Mem.: Grosse Pointe Artists Assn., Windsor Art Gallery, Mich. Watercolor Soc., Detroit (Mich.) Inst. Arts Founders Soc.

KYLE, PENELOPE WARD, academic administrator; b. Hampton, Va., Aug. 6, 1947; d. Lanny Astor and Penelope (Ward) K.; m. Charles L. Menges, Oct. 10, 1981; children: Kyle Ward, Penelope Whitley, Patricia Lee. BA, Guilford Coll., 1969; postgrad., So. Meth. U., 1969-71; JD, U. Va., 1979; MBA, Coll. William and Mary, 1987. Bar: Va. 1979, U.S. Ct. Appeals (4th cir.) 1979. Asst prof. Thomas Nelson C.C., Hampton, 1970-76; assoc. McGuire, Woods Battle & Boothe, Richmond, Va., 1979-81; assoc. counsel CSX Realty, Inc., Richmond, 1981-83, asst. v.p., asst. to pres., 1987-89, v.p., 1989-92; asst. corp. sec. CSX Corp., Richmond, 1983-87, v.p., 1993-94; exec. dir. Va. Lottery, Richmond, 1994—2005; pres. Radford U., Va., 2005—. Mem. exec. com. N.Am. Assn. State and Provincial Lotteries, 1997—, treas., 1998—. Trustee Hist. Richmond Found., 1983-94, 1st v.p., 1987-89, pres., 1989-91, chmn., 1991-93; mem. bd. visitors James Madison U., Harrisburg, Va., 1984-92; mem. Port of Richmond Commn., 1985-94; bd. dirs. Ctrl. Richmond Assn., 1988-96, vice-chair, 1991-93, chair, 1993-96; mem. Indsl. Devel. Authority City of Richmond, 1990-94, vice-chair, 1991-93, chair, 1993-94, bd. dirs. Richmond Childrens Mus., 1992-96, sec., 1995-96; bd. dirs. Cornerstone Realty Income Trust, Inc., Apple Residential Income Trust, Inc., Maymont Found., 1996—; commr. Richmond Redevel. and Housing Authority, 1994—; trustee Richmond United Way, 1996-97, exec. com. 1996-97; trustee Va. Commonwealth U. Found., 1994—; mem. U. Val. Law Sch. Alumni Coun., 1998—. Mem. ABA, Va. Bar Assn. (pres. young lawyers conf. 1984-85, mem. coun. 1984-85), Richmond Bar Assn., Jr. League Richmond, Greater Richmond C. of C. (bd. dirs. 1998—), Bear and Bull Club (bd. dirs. 1986-89, sec. 1987-88), The Country Club of Va. Home: 4706 Charmian Rd Richmond VA 23226-1706 Office: Radford U Office of Pres PO Box 6890 Radford VA 24142 Office Phone: 540-831-5401.

KYOFSKI, BONELYN LUGG, retired education educator; b. Nelson, Pa., Mar. 16, 1941; d. Robert Preston Lugg and Ila Hess Lugg Wiley; m. Joseph Theodore Kyofski, Nov. 22, 1979. BS, Mansfield U., 1962; MA in English, Pa. State U., 1966, PhD in English, 1976. Cert. secondary tchg. Pa. Dept. Edn. H.s. tchr. Otto Eldred Sch. Dist., Duke Center, Pa., 1962—63; tchg. asst. Pa. State U., University Park, 1963—64; asst. prof. English Harrisburg (Pa.) Area C.C., 1964—66; assoc. prof. English Lehigh County C.C., Allentown, Pa., 1967—73; dir. pub. rels. and alumni affairs Mansfield U., 1973—75; instr. English Pa. State U., University Park, 1976; coord. pub. rels., assoc. prof. Jefferson C.C., Louisville, 1977—80; h.s. tchr. No. Tioga Sch. Dist., Elkland, Pa., 1980—81, dir. fed. programs and curriculum svcs., 1981—84; prof. edn. Mansfield (Pa.) U., 1984—2003; ret.; assoc. Travel Places, Inc. Pres. Mansfield U. Senate, 1992—94; co-founder, bd. pres. No. Tier Cultural Alliance, Mansfield, 1995—; commonwealth spkr. Pa. Humanities Coun., Phila., 1999—; storyteller schs. in No. Pa., 1980—. Co-author, co-editor: cultural history Headwaters and Hardwoods: the folklore, cultural history and traditional arts of the Pennsylvania Northern Tier, editor, co-author: teachers' resource collection Northern Pennsylvania Freedom Trails: a k-12 guide to the Underground Railroad in the region. Pres. Domestic Violence Resource Ctr. Tioga County Women's Coalition, Wellsboro, Pa., 1990—92; bd. Pa. Humanities Council, 2006—; mem. Mansfield Univ. Alumni Bd., 2006—; candidate Pa. Gen. Assembly Dem. Party, 68th Assembly Dist., 1974; county committeewoman Dem. Party, Tioga County, 1980—; vice chair Tioga County Dem. Com., 2006—; elder, lay spkr. Beechers' Island Presbyn. Ch., Nelson, Pa., 1980—2005. Named Outstanding Vol. in Ky. for coll. program in women's prison, Gov. Julian Carroll, 1979; recipient founding and support grants for No. Tier Cultural Alliance, Pa. Coun. on Arts, 1995—2005, program grants for No. Tier Cultural Alliance, Dept. of Conservation and Natural Resources, 1999—2005, Pa. Gov.'s Office internship, Falk Found., 1960, grant for proposal of establishment of Displaced Homemaker Ctrs. in Ky. cmty. colls., Ky. Senate, 1980, founding and support grants for No. Tier Cultural Alliance, Ctr. for Rural Pa., 1996, 1997. Mem.: Friends of Laurel Health Sys. (hon. chair 2005), Mansfield U. Ret. Faculty (pres. 2005—), River City Bus. and Profl. Women (pres., bd. dirs. 1977—79), Hamilton Gibson Prodns. (endowment bd. trustees 2005), Coates Heritage Ho. (bd. trustees 1998—), Tioga County Hist. Soc. (publs. com. 2003—05), Lumber Heritage Region (adv. bd. 2005—), Endless Mountains Heritage Region (adv. bd. 1996—). Democrat. Presbyterian. Avocations: reading, travel, historical preservation, theater and the arts. Home: 1 Thornbottom Road Nelson PA 16940

KYRIAKOU, LINDA GRACE, communications executive; b. NYC; d. Frank T. and Dolores Helen Lagamma; m. Konstantinos G. Kyriakou, 1 child, Christina Elena. BA, Hunter Coll. Acct. exec., dir. rsch. Booke and Co., N.Y.C., 1969-75; mgr. pub. rels. CIT Fin. Corp., N.Y.C., 1975-79; dir. corp. comm. Sequa Corp., N.Y.C., 1979-88, v.p. corp. comm., 1988—. Recipient Twin award, 1985. Mem. Pub. Rels. Soc. Am., Nat. Investor Rels. Inst. (bd. dirs. 1981-82, Sr. Roundtable), Women's Bond Club N.Y. (bd. govs. 1978-80). Office: Sequa Corp 200 Park Ave Rm 4401 New York NY 10166-4400 Business E-Mail: Linda_Kyriakou@sequa.com.

KYTE, SUSAN JANET, lawyer, consultant; b. Riverhead, N.Y., Nov. 17, 1956; d. Bruce Whiteman Kyte and Barbara Jean (Clark) Goldberg. BA cum laude, Southampton Coll. divsn. L.I. U., 1978; JD, Capital U., 1984. Bar: Ohio, 1984. Assoc. atty. Matan & Smith, Columbus, Ohio, 1984-90; econ. devel. dir. City of Columbus, 1990-91; chief counsel, legis. dir. Ohio Sec. State, Columbus, 1991-95; pvt. practice Columbus, 1996—. Del. Am. Coun. Young Polit. Leaders, Columbus, 1997; mgr. Drake for Congress, 1998; founder JoAnn Davidson Ohio Leadership Inst., 1999. Vice-chair Franklin County Rep. Party, Columbus, 1992—, chair doorbbell blitz, 1988-90; founder, 1st pres. Ohio Rep. Womens Campaign Fund, Columbus, 1994—, treas., 1997—; bd. dirs. Actors Theater, Columbus, 1996—; vol. Rinehart for State Treas., Columbus, 1982, Rinehart for Mayor of Columbus, 1983, Race for the Cure, Columbus, 1995—; coord. Franklin County coalitions Voinovich for Senate, Columbus, 1988, co-chair, 1997—; treas. Keep Ohio Working Ballot Issue Commn., 1997, Every Child Counts Ballot Issue Commn., 1998, Deters for Ohio's Future, 1998—; legal counsel Teater for Mayor, 1999; treas. Tanner for City Coun., 1999; co-mgr. Browell for Judge, Columbus, 1997—; policy com. Pryce for Congress, Columbus, 1992, 94; coord. Taft for Sec. of State, Columbus, 1990; trustee Cap City Young Rep., 1984-96; active Com. for 2000, 1993; asst. legal counsel Young Rep. Nat. Fedn., 1993-95; rep. Renews Congrl. Adv. Com., D.C., 1995, 97; v.p. Columbus Literacy Coun., Columbus, 1984-92; chair comm. com. Oktoberfest, Columbus, 1992-96; steering com. Kaleidoscope Conf. for Women, Columbus, 1994—; state coord. McCain 2000 Campaign, 2000. Mem. ABA, Columbus Bar Assn., Nat. Fedn. Ind. Businesses, Nat. Assn. Polit. Cons., Ohio State Bar Assn., Coun. Govt. Ethics Lawyers. Republican. Lutheran. Avocations: cooking, travel, reading, politics. Office: 660 Bonanza TRL Clarksville VA 23927-4211 E-mail: suekyte@aol.com.

KYTLE, CAROLINE ELIZABETH, writer; b. Charleston, S.C., July 25, 1913; d. Alfred Oswald and Anna Belle (Linn) Larisey; m. David Calvin Kytle, Jan. 23, 1946. AB in English, Ga. State Womans Coll., 1935. Clerical position Office of the Pres. Ga. State Womans Coll., Valdosta, 1936-39; clk. materials bur. Nat. Youth Adminstrn., Atlanta, 1939-41; sec. Citizens' Fact Finding Movement of Ga., Atlanta, 1941-42; staff writer pub. relations Bell Aircraft, Marietta, Ga., 1942-45; produced a house organ with no asst. Davison-Paxon Dept. Store, Atlanta, 1945-46. Author: Willie Mae, 1958 (NY Times Notable Book of Yr. 1958, Ohioana Book award 1958), paperback edit., 1993, Home on the Canal, 1983, paperback edit., 1996, The Voices of Robby Wilde, 1987, paperback edit., 1995; author, editor: Time Was: A Cabin John Memory Book, 1976; author, photographer: Four Cats Make One Pride, 1978. Democrat. Unitarian Universalist. Home: Health Ctr # 106 Carolina Meadows Chapel Hill NC 27517 E-mail: ckekcm@mindspring.com.

LABARGE, MARGARET WADE, medieval history professor, historian, writer; b. NYC, July 18, 1916; arrived in Can., 1940; d. Alfred Byers and Helena (Mein) Wade; m. Raymond C. Labarge, June 20, 1940 (dec. May 1972); children: Claire Labarge Morris, Suzanne, Charles, Paul. BA, Radcliffe Coll., 1937; LittB, Oxford (Eng.) U., 1939; LittD (hon.), Carleton U., Ottawa, Ont., Can., 1976; LLD (hon.), U. Waterloo, Ont., Can., 1993; HHD (hon.), Mount St Vincent U., Halifax, N.S., 2003. Lectr. history U. Ottawa, Carleton U., 1950-62; adj. prof. history Carleton U., Ottawa, 1983—2005. Author: Simon de Montfort, 1962, A Baronial Household, 1965, Gascony, 1980, A Small Sound of the Trumpet, 1987, A Medieval Miscellany, 1997, others; contbr. articles to profl. jours. Bd. dirs. St. Vincent's Hosp., Ottawa, 1969-81; chmn. 1977-79; pub. rep. bd. dirs. Can. Nurses Assn., 1980-83; bd. dirs. Carleton U., 1984-93, Coun. on Aging, 1986-93 (pres., 1989-91). Recipient Alumnae Recognition award Radcliffe Coll., 1987, Founders award, Carleton U., 2001 Fellow Royal Soc. Can.; mem. Medieval Acad., Soc. of Can. Medievalists (pres. 1993-94), Order of Can., Phi Beta Kappa. Roman Catholic. Avocations: travel, reading, walking. Home and Office: 402-555 Wilbrod St Ottawa ON Canada K1N 5R4 E-mail: mwlabarge@sympatico.ca.

LABBE-WEBB, ELIZABETH GERALYN, performing company executive; b. Akron, Ohio, Oct. 7, 1966; d. Edward James and Ruth Carolyn (Petree) L. BA in Theatre Arts, Kent State U., 1989; MBA in Mktg. and Strategic Leadership, Ohio State U., 2003. Contract prodn. technician Players' Theatre Columbus, Ohio, 1989-91; asst. prodn./co. mgr. Phila. Festival Theatre, 1991-92; costume asst. Am. Music Theatre Festival, Phila., 1991-92; office asst. Players' Theatre Columbus, 1992-93; audio description coord. Ohio Theatre Alliance, Columbus, 1993-94; sr. devel. assoc., grants mgr. Opera Assn. Ctrl. Ohio, Columbus, 1994-99, assoc. dir. devel., 1998-2000; freelance stage mgr., freelance arthy tchr., 1994—; project mgr. The Bus. of Art, 2000—02; CEO Blue Path Group, Ltd. V.p. Rosebriar Shakespeare Co., Columbus, 1995-96, pres. 1997-98 Chpt. leader, chpt. arts officer Soc. for Creative Anachronism, 1995-2002; adv., vol. Canine Companions for Independence; creative cons. Found. for Environ. Edn., 2001-02; fundraising cons. Columbus Light Opera, 2000-2001. Personal Devel. grant Jefferson Ctr. for the Arts, 1994. Mem.: VSA Arts Ga. (exec. dir.), Ohio Prospect Rsch. Network (bd. dirs. 1997).

LABBIENTO, JULIANNE MARIE, mathematics professor; d. David Hurst and Carol Ann Landis; m. Michael L. Greenholt; 1 child, Jason Patrick. BS in math and actuarial sci., Clarion U., 1985—89; MS in math., Youngstown State U., 1992—94. Forecasting specialist Balt. Life Ins. Co., Balt., 1989—92; adj. prof., math. Youngstown State U., Youngstown, Ohio, 1992—95; adj. prof., math. and computer sci. Westminster Coll., New Wilmington, Pa., 1995—98; instr., math. Clarion U., Pa., 1998—2002; assoc. prof., math. Lehigh Carbon C.C., Schnecksville, Pa., 2002—. Mem.: Pa. State Math. Assn. Two-Yr. Colls. Office: Lehigh Carbon Community College 4525 Education Park Dr Schnecksville PA 18078 Office Phone: 610-799-1074. E-mail: jlabbiento@lccc.edu.

LABELLA, JANICE MARIE, peri-operative nurse; b. Pittston, Pa., July 29, 1966; d. Ludwig Sr. and Dorothy Manganiello; m. Michael LaBella, 1995; children: Christina, Gianna. AAS, Luzerne County C.C., Nanticoke, Pa., 1989; student, Coll. Misericordia, Dallas, Pa., 1989—; cert., Luzerne County C.C., 1992. RN; cert. first asst. CNOR, nat. cert. peri-operative nurse. Emergency svcs. nurse Pittston Med. Emergency Ctr., 1989; obstetrics nurse Wilkes Barre (Pa.) Gen. Hosp., 1989, surg. svcs. nurse, 1989-91; RN first asst. Office of Sam C. DePasquale, 1992-93; perioperative nurse, charge nurse urology/renal transplant Temple U. Hosp., Phila., 1993—, clin. specialist laser surgery, 1993—, clin. coord. for students, 1993—. Instr. continuing edn. planning Luzerne County C.C., 1993. Vol. Big Bros./Big Sisters, Am. Cancer Soc., Valley Santa; religious edn. tchr. St. Rocco's Ch., Pittston; mem. long range planning com. Pittston Area Sch. Dist., 1992. Recipient St. John Neumann award, St. Pius X award religious edn. Mem. ANA, NAFE, Am. Heart Assn., Assn. Operating Rm. Nurses (chair project Alpha 1990-91, chair rsch. 1993-94, RN 1st asst. interest group), Soc. for Urology Nurses Assn., Orgn. for Advancement Assoc. Degree Nurses, Nat. League for Nursing, Soc. Peripheral Vascular Nursing, Nat. Assn. Orthopaedic Nurses, Couns. Cardiovascular Nursing and Circulation.

LABELLE, PATTI (PATRICIA LOUISE HOLTE), singer, entertainer; b. Phila., May 24, 1944; d. Henry and Bertha Holte; m. Armstead Edwards, 1969 (div. 2000); 5 children. PhD (hon.), Berkeley Sch. Music, 1996, Cambridge U., Drexel U. Singer Patti LaBelle and the BlueBelles, 1961—70; lead singer musical group LaBelle, 1970-76; solo performer, 1977—; entrepreneur Patti LaBelle's Fragrances & Cosmetics, 1995. Established clothing line Patti LaBelle Clothing, 2003—. Albums (with the BlueBelles) Sweethearts of the Apollo, 1963, Over the Rainbow, 1967, (with LaBelle) LaBelle, 1971, Moon Shadows, 1972, Pressure Cookin', 1973, Nightbirds, 1974, Phoenix, 1975, Chameleon, 1976, (solo) Patti LaBelle, 1977, Live at the Apollo, 1980, Gonna Take A Miracle-The Spirit's in It, 1981, I'm in Love Again, 1983, Winner in You, 1986, The Best of Patti LaBelle, 1987, Patti, 1985, Be Yourself, 1989, Burnin', 1991 (Grammy award best r&b vocalist, 1991), Live (Apollo Theater), 1992, Gems, 1994, Live! One Night Only, 1998 (Grammy award best trad. r&b vocal perf., 1998), Greatest Hits, 1996, Flame, 1997, When a Woman Loves, 2000, Timeless Journey, 2004, Patti Labelle: Classic Moment, 2005; actress (films) A Soldier's Story, 1984, Sing, 1989, On the One, 2005, Idlewild, 2006; (TV movies) For Colored Girls Who Have Considered Suicide, 1982, Working, 1982, Unnatural Causes, 1986, Fire and Rain, 1989, Parker Kane, 1990, Santa Baby! (voice), 2001, My Life in Idlewild, 2005; (TV series) A Different World, 1990-93, Out All Night, 1992; (guest appearances) Dolly, 1987, The Nanny, 1994, Cosby, 1997, All of Us, 2004; (TV specials) Live Aid, 1985, The Patti LaBelle Show, 1985, Sisters in the Name of Love, 1986 (CableACE award best perf. music special, 1987) Motown 30: What's Goin' On!, 1990, Sinatra Duets, 1994, The Remarkable Journey, 2000, Born to Diva, 2003, Nina Simone: A Tribute, 2003, VH1 Divas Live, 2004, (plays) Your Arms Too Short to Box with God (revival), 1980; author Don't Block the Blessings: Revelations of a Lifetime, 1997, LaBelle Cuisine: Recipes to Sing About, 1999, Patti's Pearls: Lessons in Living Genuinely, Joyfully & Generously, 2001, Patti LaBelle's Lite Cuisine; host (TV show) Living It Up with Patti LaBelle, 2004—. Spokesperson Am. Diabetic Assn., Nat. Minority AIDS Council, Nat. Cancer Inst., founder The Patti LaBelle Med. Ed. Scholarship Fund. Recipient award of Merit, Phila. Art Alliance, 1987, Soul Train Lifetime Achievement award, 1997, Walk of Fame honoree Black Entertainment TV, 2000; Entertainer of Yr. Image award NAACP, 1992. Office: Def Soul Classics 825 8th Ave 29th Fl New York NY 10019*

LABENZ-HOUGH, MARLENE, mediator; b. St. Edward, Nebr., May 25, 1954; d. Ralph Labenz and Lorene (Laudenklos); m. Jeff Hough, Mar. 5, 1983. Assocs., Platte Coll., 1974; BS in Social Work magna cum laude, U. Nebr., 1976; MA in Clin. Psychology, Trinity U., 1980. Adminstrv. asst., mgmt. analyst II City of San Antonio Dept. Human Resources and Svcs., 1980, adminstrv. asst. II, 1980-82, casework supr., Victims of Crime Program, 1982-89, program coord., Children's Resources Divsn., 1989-90; asst. dir. Bexar County Dispute Resolution Ctr., San Antonio, 1990-92, dir., 1992—. Bd. dirs. KidShare, 1993-96, YWCA, 1990-93; mem. ADR sect. coun. State Bar Tex., 1996-99. Recipient Liberty Bell award, San Antonio Young Lawyers Assn., 2003, Recognition award, San Antonio Bar Found., 2004, Appreciation award, 2005, Recognition award for leadership. Mem.: ABA (chmn. conf. com. ADR sect. 2002), Tex. Bar Assn. (ADR sect.), Assn. Family and Conciliation Cts., Tex. Mediators Credentialing Assn., Alamo Area Mediators Assn., Tex. Dispute Resolution Ctrs. Dirs. Coun., Tex. Mediation Trainers' Roundtable, Assn. Conflict Resolution, Conflict Resolution and Peer Mediation Coun., Nat. Assn. Cmty. Mediation (founding dir.), Soc. Profls. in Dispute Resolution (co-chair S.W. region chpt. 1993, co-chair nat. conf. 1995, Profl. Dedication award 1994), Acad. Family Mediators, Tex. Assn. Mediators (chair conf. 1998, bd. dirs. 1998—2001), Alpha Xi Delta. Home: 2518 Ashton Village Dr San Antonio TX 78248-2200

LABERTEAUX, JENNIFER CLAIRE, secondary school educator; d. Gary Wayne and Melody Claire Richardson; m. Jeffrey Nelson LaBerteaux, Dec. 14, 1991; children: Jacob Nelson, Jacquelin Claire, Jamie Michelle. BS in Math., Sul Ross State U., Alpine, Tex., 1996. Cert. tchr. La. Tchr. Alpine (Tex.) Mid. Sch., 1996—97, Chico (Tex.) Mid. Sch., 1997—98, Beau Chene HS, Arnuadville, La., 1998—99; tchr., cheer coach Westminster Christian Acad., Opelousas, La., 2000—. Choreographer (musical) Annie; actor: (musical) Annie. Bible sch. tchr. Riverside Ch. of Christ, Lafayette, La., 1998—2004. Mem.: Alpha Psi Omega (life). Home: 207 St Pierre Blvd Carencro LA 70520 Office: Westminster Christian Acad 186 Westminster Dr Opelousas LA 70570

LABINER, ADRIA, psychotherapist; b. Queens, N.Y., May 15, 1953; d. Jack and Mary (Rosen) Mazarsky; m. Paul S. Labiner, June 12, 1983 (div.); children: Brandon, Arielle. BA in Speech Pathology, SUNY, New Paltz, 1974; MSW, Hunter Coll., 1988. Cert. social worker, NY, lic. clin. social worker, 1993. Social worker Summit Sch., Forest Hills, NY, 1985-88; outside cons. Vol. Counseling Svc., NYC, 1986—; psychotherapist in pvt. practice Suffern, NY, 1988—; psychotherapist Family Svc. Agy., Ft. Lauderdale, Fla., 1994—; clin. assoc. Child and Family Psychologists, Weston, Fla., 2004. Mem. Nat. Assn. Social Workers, Acad. Cert. Social Workers. Jewish. Avocations: reading, sports, theater. Home: 2665 Meadowood Ct Fort Lauderdale FL 33332-3434

LABINER, CAROLINE, architect; b. Los Angeles, CA, Mar. 29, 1958; d. Gerald Wilk and Suzanne Solov Labiner; m. Franklin George Moser, Aug. 29, 1984; children: Claire, Julia. AB, Harvard Coll., 1980; MArch, MIT, 1984. Designer Kohn Pederson Fox, N.Y.C., 1983; architect Kohn Pederson Fox Conway, N.Y.C., 1984—85; project architect The Entrenkrantz Group & Eckstot, N.Y.C., 1985—86; owner, designer CSLM Design/Big Pink Hair, Los Angeles, 1984—; owner, architect Caroline Labiner Architect, Los Angeles, Calif., 1993—.

LABOUFF, JACKIE PEARSON, retired personal care industry executive; b. Wilmington, Calif., June 26, 1936; d. Maurice Emerson and Juanita Armstrong Pearson; m. John Robert LaBouff, Oct. 5, 1957; children: Margaret C., Mark J., Thomas F., Joan. BA, Calif. State U., Domingez Hills, 1972, MA, 1987. Tchg. credential Calif., 1982, counseling credential Calif., 1987. Flight attendant Am. Airlines, LA, 1956—57; pre-sch. tchr. Hickory Tree, Torrance, Calif., 1972—77; adult edn. tchr. Torrance (Calif.) Unified Sch Dist., 1977—84, Calif. State U., Domingez Hills, 1984—94; grant dir. Lawndale (Calif.) Sch. Dist., 1991—95; exec. dir. Project Touch, Hermosa Beach, Calif., 1996—2005, ret., 2005. Tchr. adult edn. anger mgmt. Beach Cities Health Dist., Redondo Beach, Calif., 2000—; sch. bd. candidate Torrance (Calif.) Unified Sch. Dist., 1995; cons. in field. Commr. Cmty. Svcs. Commn., Torrance, Calif., 1991—99. Recipient Magnificent Woman, Carson Coord. Co., 2003. Mem.: Am. Assn. Univ. Women (pres. 1991—94, Ednl. Found. Honor award 1994). Democrat. Roman Catholic. Avocations: travel, knitting, crocheting, needlecrafts. Home: 3810 W 173 St Torrance CA 90504 Office: Project Touch 710 Pier Ave Hermosa Beach CA 90254 E-mail: sticher61@hotmail.com.

LABOVITZ, SARAH JANE, musician, educator; b. Meyersdale, Pa., Jan. 24, 1982; d. Paul Robert and Susan Lee Labovitz. MusB, Bowling Green State U., 2004; student in music edn., Ind. U., 2006—. Sr. counselor Cuyahoga Valley Nat. Pk. Environ. Edn. Ctr., Penninsula, Ohio, 2001—03; band libr. Bowling Green State U., 2003—04; head band dir. Adm. King HS Lorain City Schs., Ohio, 2004—06; dir. Firelands Symphony, 2004—06. Condr. clarinet choir Bowling Green State U., 2003—04; assoc. instr., coord. Young Winds. Musician (soloist): Sr. Recital; musician: Firelands Symphony, 2004—06. Music amb. Coll. Musical Arts Bowling Green State U., 2001—04. Recipient Music Edn. Talent award, Bowling Green State U., 2003; scholar, Ohio Bd. Regents, 2000—04, Ohio Collegiate Music Educators Assn., 2001; Univ. Prof.'s scholar, Bowling Green State U., 2000—04, Brecklen Found. Instrumental scholar, 2003, Richard and Annette Ecker scholar, 2003. Mem.: Internat. Assn. Jazz Educators (assoc.), Ohio Music Educator's Assn. (assoc.), Sigma Alpha Iota (life; treas. 2003—04, Alumni award 2004). Lutheran. Avocations: travel, sports, writing. Office: Firelands Symphony 1201 E Third St Bloomington IN 47405 Business E-Mail: slabovit@indiana.edu.

LABRIOLA CURRAN, JOANNE ELIZABETH, orthopedist; b. Pitts., Aug. 27, 1974; d. Leonard Louis and Mary Ann Theresa Labriola; m. James Drew Curran, Oct. 30, 2004; 1 child, Nathaniel James Curran. BS, Duke U., 1996. Lic. physician Pa. Rsch. fellow Duke U., Durham, 1995—96; alumni rsch. fellowship U. Pitts., 1997; rsch. fellow, Stanley J. Sarnoff endowment Scripps Rsch. Inst., San Diego, 1999—2000; resident, orthop. surgery U. Health Ctr. Pitts., 2001—06; rsch. fellow Musculoskeletal Rsch. Ctr., Pitts., 2002—03; clin. instr. U. Pitts., 2006—. Substitute team physician Pitts. HS Football Teams, 2001—02; team physician Serra Cath. HS Football Team, Pitts., 2002—; resident liaison Pa. Orthop. Soc., Pitts., 2004—; team physician Robert Morris U. Women's Hockey Team, Pitts., 2005—; resident coun. rep. Dept. Orthop., Pitts., 2005—. Contbr. articles various profl. jours., scientific papers. Com. mem. Jr. League Pitts., 2002—06. Nominee Little Golden Apple award, U. Pitts. Sch. Medicine, 2002; named Student Marshal, Duke U., 1995; named to Dean's List with Distinction, 1992-1996; recipient Harold Henderson Sankey award, U. Pitts. Sch. Medicine, 2001, Brinton prize; Rsrch. Fellowship grant, Howard Hughes, 1995, Orthopaedic Fund Rsch. grant, Albert B. Ferguson, Jr. MD, 2003-2004. Mem.: AMA, Allegheny County Med. Soc., Orthop. Rsch. Soc., Am. Acad. Orthop. Surgery, Orthop. Rsch. Lab. Alumni Coun., Pa. Orthop. Soc. (resident liaison 2004—), Golden Key Nat. Honor Soc. (hon.), Phi Eta Sigma (hon.), Phi Lambda Upsilon Nat. Hon. Chem. Soc. (hon.), Phi Beta Kappa (hon.). Avocations: dance, singing, sports. Home: 309 Cross Creek Ct Pittsburgh PA 15237 Office: U Health Ctr Pitts 3471 Fifth Ave Ste 1010 Pittsburgh PA 15213 Office Phone: 412-605-3262. Office Fax: 412-687-3724. Business E-Mail: labriolaj@upmc.edu.

LACAVA, LAURA L., elementary school educator; b. Fairfax, Va., Sept. 27, 1965; d. John W. and Sallie M. LaCava. MA, Radford U., Va., 1987; MEd, George Mason U., Fairfax, Va., 1994. Tchr. grade 6 Conner Elem. Sch., Manassas Park, Va., 1994—96, tchr., 1996—2000, tchr. grades 4 and 5, 2000—01; tchr. social studies grade 4 Manassas Pk. Elem. Sch., 2001—06, ESL tchr., 2006—. Soccer coach T.C. Williams HS, Alexandria, Va., 1993—94, Edison HS, Alexandria, Va., 1995—96; volleyball coach Manassas Pk. HS, 1995—96. Named Tchr. of Yr., Conner Elem. Sch., 1996—97; recipient Agnes Meyer Outstanding Educator of Yr. award, Manassas Pk. City Schs., 2001, Dedicated Tchr. award, Optimist Club of Manassas, 2001. Christian. Avocations: soccer, running, reading, writing. Office Phone: 703-368-2032. Personal E-mail: lllacave@aol.com.

LACEY, DOROTHY ELLEN, theology studies educator, religious organization administrator; b. Urbancrest, Ohio, Feb. 24, 1931; d. Charles Franklin Nesbitt and Clifford (Dickerson); m. Joseph W. Lacey; 1 child, Michael Clifford. B in Christian Edn., M in Christian Edn., Grace Internat. Coll., 1996, ThD, 2002, D in Christian Edn., Adminstrn. and Org., 2002. Ednl. dir. Emmanuel Tempe Ch. of Rochester N.Y., Inc., 1962—, adminstr., 1985—. Women's ministry evangelistic seminar tchr. Pentecostal Assemblies of the World, Indpls., 1960—; pres., founder Lacey's Travel Agy., Rochester, 1983—88; pres. women's ministry N.Y. Coun., 1990—96; bd. trustees Grace Internat. Coll., 2003—; dean of ministries Grace Coll., 2000. Pres. of trustee bd. Emmanuel Temple Ch. of Rochester, N.Y., 1962—. Mem.: NAACP, Profl. Bus. Women, Urban League. Pentecostal Assemblies. Avocations: singing, playing musical instruments. Home: 3500 Brown Rd PO Box 148 Caledonia NY 14423 Office: Emmanuel Temple Ch Rochester 1 Seneca Pkwy Rochester NY 14613

LACEY, RUTHANN P., lawyer; d. Duane E. and Marilyn J. Pramberg; m. Craig A. Lacey; 1 child, Kevin R. JD, Emory U. Sch. of Law, Atlanta, Ga., 1992. Cert.: Nat. Elder Law Found. (elder law atty.) 2000. Atty. elder and spl. needs law Ruthann P. Lacey, P.C., Tucker, Ga., 1995—. Presenter in field. Contbr. articles to profl. jours. Bd. mem. Ga. Cmty. Trust, Smyrna, 1998—2006, Family Initiative Residences, Inc., Atlanta, 2003—06; sec. Spl. Needs Alliance, New York, 2005—06; chair Elder Law Sect., Ga. Bar Assn., Atlanta, 2005—06. Named one of Ga. Super Lawyers, Nat. Elder Law Found., 2006. Mem.: DeKalb Estate Planning Coun., Coun. of Advanced Practitioners, Nat. Acad. of Elder Law Attorneys, Atlanta Bar Assn., Ga. Bar Assn. Conservative. Anglican. Avocations: reading, travel, photography. Office: Ruthann P Lacey PC 3541-E Habersham at Northlake Tucker GA 30084 Office Phone: 770-939-4616.

LACEY, TRUDI, professional athletics coach; Grad., N.C. State U., 1981. Asst. coach Manhattan Coll., 1981, James Madison Coll., 1982, N.C. State U., 1983—84; head coach Francis Marion Coll., SC, 1987—88, U. South Fla., 1989—96; asst. coach U. Md., 1996—97; asst. dir. women's program USA Basketball, 1997—2003; head coach, asst. gen. mgr. Charlotte Sting, NC, 2003—. Mem. women's player selection com. USA Basketball, 1993—96; asst. coach R. William Jones Cub team, 1995, Olympic Festival East team, 1994; participant USA Select Team, 1978, World U. Games team, 1981, USA Nat. eam, 1982, USA World U. Games Team, 1983; profl. player, Italy, 1985—87; founding pres. Life Coach Designs, LLC; analyst ESPN, FoxSportsNet. Named Sun Belt Conf. Coach of the Yr., 1989; recipient All-ACC honoree. Office: Charlotte Sting 100 Hive Dr Charlotte NC 28217

LACH, ALMA ELIZABETH, food and cooking writer, consultant; b. Petersburg, Ill. d. John H. and Clara E. Satorius; m. Donald F. Lach; 1 child, Sandra Judith. Diplome de Cordon Bleu, Paris, 1956. Feature writer Children's Activities mag., 1954-55; creator, performer childrens cooking TV show Let's Cook, 1955; food editor Chgo. Daily Sun-Times, 1957-65; hostess weekly food program on CBS, 1962-66; pres. Alma Lach Kitchens, Inc., Chgo., 1966—; performer TV show Over Easy, PBS, 1977-78. Dir. Alma Lach Cooking Sch., Chgo.; lectr. U. Chgo. Downtown Coll., Gourmet Inst., U. Md., 1963, Modesto (Calif.) Coll., 1978, U. Chgo., 1981; resident master Shoreland Hall, U. Chgo., 1978-81; food cons. Food Bus. Mag., 1964-66, Chgo.'s New Pump Room, Lettuce Entertain You, Bitter End Resort, Brit. V.I., Midway Airlines, Flying Food Fare, Inc., Berghoff Restaurant, Hans' Bavarian Lodge, Unocal '76, Univ. Club Chgo. Author: A Child's First Cookbook, 1950, The Campbell Kids at Home, 1953, Let's Cook, 1956, Candlelight Cookbook, 1959, Cooking a la Cordon Bleu, 1970, Alma's Almanac, 1972, Hows and Whys of French Cooking, 1974, reprint, 1998; contbr. to World Book Yearbook, 1961-75, Grolier Soc. Yearbook, 1962; columnist Modern Packaging, 1967-68, Travel & Camera, 1969, Venture, 1970, Chicago mag., 1978, Bon Appetit, 1980, Tribune Syndicate, 1982; inventor: Curly-Dog Cutting Bd., 1995, Alma's Walker Tray, 1996; one woman show: 50 pixellist art pictures, 1999, Tavern Club, Chgo., 2002-2004. Recipient Pillsbury award, 1958, Grocery Mfrs. Am. Trophy award, 1959, certificate of Honor, 1961, Chevalier du Tastevin, 1962, Commanderie de l'Ordre des Anysetiers du Roy, 1963, Confrerie de la Chaine des Rotisseurs, 1964, Les Dames D'Escoffier, 1982, Culinary Historians of Chgo., 1993. Mem. Am. Assn. Food Editors (chmn. 1959), Tavern Club, Quadrangle Club (Chgo.). Home and Office: 5750 S Kenwood Ave Chicago IL 60637-1744 Fax: 773-363-2875. Office Phone: 773-684-4906. E-mail: alma@almalach.com.

LACH, ELIZABETH, science educator; d. Michael L. and Pauline I. Lach. BS in Edn., Ill. State U., Normal, 1983. Health educator Lincoln-Way Comty. H.S., New Lenox, Ill., 1986—87; sci. educator East Aurora H.S., Aurora, Ill., 1987—. Named to Outsanding Am. Tchrs., 2006. Mem.: Nat. Sci. Tchrs. Assn. Avocations: reading, creating jewelry, crafts. Home: 314 E Victoria Cir North Aurora IL 60542 Office: East Aurora H S 500 Tomcat Ln Aurora IL 60505

LACHANCE, JANICE RACHEL, professional association administrator, retired federal agency administrator, lawyer; b. Biddeford, Maine, June 17, 1953; d. Ralph L. and Rachel A. (Desnoyers) L. BA, Manhattanville Coll., 1974; JD, Tulane U., 1978. Bar: Maine 1978, D.C. 1982, U.S. Supreme Ct. 1999. Staff dir. subcom. on antitrust Ho. of Reps., Washington, 1982-83; adminstrv. asst. Congresswoman Katie Hall, 1983-84; asst. pres. sec. Mondale-Ferraro Campaign, Washington, 1984; press sec. Congressman Tom Daschle, 1985; ptnr. Lachance and Assocs., Washington, 1985-87; dir. communications and polit. action Am. Fedn. Govt. Employees (AFL-CIO), Washington, 1987-93; dir. policy and communications U.S. Office Pers. Mgmt., Washington, 1993-96, chief of staff, 1996-97, dep. dir., 1997, dir., 1997—2001; mgmt. consultant Analytica Inc., Alexandria, Va., 2001; exec. dir. Spl. Librs. Assn. (SLA), Washington, 2003, now CEO. Vis. scholar Cornell U., 1972-73. Editor newsletter Govt. Standard, 1987-93. Mem. Delta Delta Delta, Phi Alpha Delta; fellow Nat. Acad. Pub. Admin. Democrat. Roman Catholic. Office: Spl Libraries Assn 331 South Patrick St Alexandria VA 22314 Office Phone: 703-647-4933. E-mail: janice@sla.org.

LACHANZE, (R. LACHANZE SAPP, RHONDA SAPP), actress; b. St. Augustine, Fla. m. Calvin Gooding (dec. Sept. 11, 2001); children: Celia, Zaya; m. Derek Fordjour, July 2005. BA in Theatre & Dance, U. Arts, Phila. Actress (Broadway plays) Uptown.It's Hot, 1986, Dreamgirls, 1987, Once on This Island, 1990—91 (Theatre World award, 1991, Tony award nominee, best featured actress in musical, 1991), Ragtime, 1999, Dessa Rosa, 2005, The Color Purple, 2005 (Tony award, best performance by leading actress in a musical, 2006), (plays) Playhouse, 1992, Hercules, Out of This World, Jesus Christ Superstar, 1991, Company, 1995, The Bubbly Black Girl Sheds Her Chameleon Skin, Funny Girl, 2002, Baby, 2004. Mailing: c/o Barbara Lawrence 19264 Pacific Coast Hwy Malibu CA 90265 Business E-Mail: lachanze@lachanze.com.*

LACHER, MIRIAM BROWNER, neuropsychologist; b. Bronx, N.Y., Dec. 30, 1942; d. Philip and Ruth Frieda (Rabinowitz) Browner; m. Maury Lacher, Aug. 17, 1963. AB, Cornell U., 1963; PhD, U. Mich., 1970; postgrad., Columbia U., 1981. Asst. prof. psychology Carleton Coll., Northfield, Minn., 1970-77; vis. rsch. assoc. U. Calif., Berkeley, 1976-77; vis. lectr. Vassar Coll., Poughkeepsie, N.Y., 1978-79; assoc. neuropsychology Columbia-Presbyn. Med. Ctr., N.Y.C., 1980-81; cons. N.Y. State Psychiat. Inst., N.Y.C., 1981; chief cognitive rehab. Children's Specialized Hosp., Westfield, N.J., 1982-84; cons. Vassar Coll. Counseling Svc., Poughkeepsie, 1984-90, First Step Nursery Sch., Hyde Park, N.Y., 1988; pvt. practice Poughkeepsie, 1984—. Contbr. articles to profl. jours. Sci. advisor on bd. dirs. Mid-Hudson chpt. Children and Adults with Attention Deficit Disorders, 1989-1999, Mid-Hudson Assn. for the Learning Disabled, 1992-1996. Woodrow Wilson fellow, U. Mich., 1963-64. Mem. Am. Psychol. Assn., Internat. Neuropsychol. Soc., Hudson Valley Psychol. Assn. (sec. 1984-85, 86-87, program chair 1985-86), N.Y. State Psychol. Assn., N.Y. Neuropsychol. Group. Avocation: bird-watching.

LA CHIUSA, CAROL See DISANTO, CAROL L.

LACHMAN, MARGUERITE LEANNE, real estate investment advisor; b. Vancouver, B.C., Can., Mar. 16, 1943; came to U.S., 1955; d. Wilfred Harry and Claire Elisha (Silverthorn) L. BA, U. So. Calif., 1964; MA, Claremont U., 1966. With Real Estate Rsch. Corp., 1965-87, sr. v.p., 1977-79, pres., CEO, 1979-87; mng. dir. Schroder Real Estate Assocs., 1987-99, Schroder Mortgage Assocs., 1992-98; prin. Lend Lease Real Estate Investments, 1999—2003; pres. Lachman Assoc., 2003—. Bd. dirs. Lincoln Nat. Corp., Liberty Property Trust; frequent lectr. seminars and profl. groups; exec.-in-residence Columbia Bus. Sch., 2000—. Author: (with Al Smith and Anthony Downs) Achieving Effective Desegregation, 1973, (with Susan Olson) Tax Delinquency in the Inner City, 1976, Emerging Trends in Real Estate, 1981, 82, 83, 84, 85, 86, 87, Decade to Decade, 1988, A Nation of Niches: Real Estate's Demand Demographics, 2002, Homeownership: Too Much of A Good Thing? 2003, The New Exports: Office Jobs, 2004, Global Demographics and Their Real Estate Investment Implicaitons, 2006; contbr. articles to profl. jours. Gov. Urban Land Found. Mem. Urban Land Inst., WX-N.Y. Office: Ste 19E 870 United Nations Plaza New York NY 10017 E-mail: lachmanassoc@aol.com.

LACOFF, CHERYL KLEIN, writer, artist; b. Bronx, Mar. 14, 1948; d. Bernard and Betty (Stecher) Klein; m. Martin S. Lacoff, June 15, 1969; children: Stefanie Lauren, Brandon Eric. BA in History, SUNY, 1970. Pres. Cheron Originals, Greenwich, Conn., 1980—, Reference Press Internat., Greenwich, 1988—. Author: Parapsychology, New Age and the Occult - A Source Encyclopedia, 1993, Who's Who in the Peace Corps, 1993, 98, So You're Finally Getting Married, 1999, Congratulations! Now You're Half A Century Old, 1999. Mem. Nat. Assn. Jewelry Appraisers, Allied Bd. Trade. Avocations: goldsmithing, painting, poetry, crafting, sculpting. Office: Reference Press Internat PO Box 4126 Greenwich CT 06831-0403

LACOMB-WILLIAMS, LINDA LOU, community health nurse; b. Galion, Ohio, Oct. 1, 1948; d. Horace Allen and Roberta May (Black) Braden; m. Robert Earl LaComb, Feb. 1, 1970 (div. Aug. 1984); children: Robin Marie, Patrick Alan; m. Robert Allen Williams, Aug. 30. 1991; children Erin, Megan. BSN, Capital U., 1970; MPH, U. South Fla., 2002. RN, Fla., Ohio; cert. health edn. specialist. Staff nurse St. Anne's Hosp., Columbus, Ohio, 1970; pub. health nurse Hillsborough County Dept. Health, Tampa, Fla., 1970-80, community health nurse supr., 1980-87; sr. community health nurse Polk County Dept. Health, Lakeland, Fla., 1987-88; sr. RN supr. Children's Med. Svcs., Tampa, 1988-91, Lakeland, 1991-99; sr. cmty. health nurse supr. Polk County Health Dept., Lakeland, Fla., 1999—2003; RN supr. Joyce Ely Health Ctr. Hillsborough County Health Dept., 2003—. 1st lt. flight nurse res. USAF, 1971-75. Recipient Boss of Yr. award, Strawberry chpt. Am. Bus. Women's Assn., 1985. Mem.: ARC, ANA, Fla. Nurses Assn. (grievance rep. state employees prof. bargaining unit 1976, pres. 1984—87, 1st v.p. 1989—91, dist. 2d v.p. 1998, Undine Sams award 1987, Nurse of Yr. award Dist. Four 1987), Eta Sigma Gamma, Sigma Theta Tau, Phi Kappa Phi. Republican. Presbyterian. Avocations: walking, nurses' rights, writing. Home: PO Box 1491 Valrico FL 33595-1491 Office: Hillsborough County Health Dept Joyce Ely Health Ctr 205 14th Ave SE Ruskin FL 33570 Office Phone: 813-307-8056. Personal E-mail: lacombwilliams@aol.com.

LACROIX, SOPHIA MARIE, artist; b. Port-au-Prince, Haiti, Mar. 1, 1969; arrived in U.S., 1984; d. Felix and Yanick Lorette LaCroix. BS Natural Scis., U. Fla., 1992. Pub. assistance specialist Fla. Dept. Children & Families, Miami, 1993—; artist, 1993—. Exhibitions include Afrika Fete, Miami, Fla., 1994, Coral Gables Internat Arts and Crafts Festival, Fla., 1994, Gallier Hall, New Orleans, 1995, exhibited in group shows, Queens, N.Y., 1995, exhibitions include Nat. urban League Conf., Miami, 1995, Young, Bowers and Brown Cultural Art Ctr., Opa Locka, Fla., 1995, Nat. Black Arts Festival, Atlanta, 1996, PIAA Regional Fina Art Juried Exhibition, Gulf Shores, Ala., 1997, Zora Neal Hurston Festival, Orlando, Fla., 2000, Nat. Black Fine Art Show, Manhattan, N.Y., 2001, one-woman shows include Old Capitol Complex, Tallahassee, Fla., exhibitions include numerous others. Recipient Proclamation by Miami, Fla. declaring October 26, 2000 as Sophia LaCroix Day. Mem.: KUUMBA Artist Assn. Miami, Alliance African Am. Artists, Art on Tour, LLC.

LACY, ANN MATTHEWS, geneticist, educator, researcher; b. Boston, May 29, 1932; d. Clive Willoughby and Mona Bellingham (Matthews) L. BA in Botany, Wellesley Coll., 1953; MS in Microbiology, Yale U., 1956, PhD in Microbiology, 1959. Rsch. asst. Carnegie Inst. Washington, Cold Spring Harbor, N.Y., 1953-54; instr. genetics Goucher Coll., Towson, Md., 1959-61, asst. prof. genetics, 1961-67, assoc. prof. genetics, 1967-73, prof. genetics, 1973-98, prof. emerita, 1998—, Elizabeth Connolly Todd prof., 1994-98, chmn. dept. biol. sci., 1969-72, 86-87, 89, chmn. faculty natural sci. & math., 1988-91; sr. rsch. fellow botany dept. U. Glasgow, Scotland, 1968-69. Sr. investigator NSF rsch. grants Goucher Coll., 1960-70. Contbr. articles to profl. jours. Mem. AAAS, Genetics Soc. Am., Am. Inst. Biol. Scis., Sigma Xi. Unitarian Universalist. Avocations: gardening, reading, theater, fine arts. Address: 21 Leighton Rd Wellesley MA 02482 Office Phone: 781-237-1059.

LACY, ELIZABETH BERMINGHAM, state supreme court justice; b. 1945; BA cum laude, St. Mary's Coll., Notre Dame, Ind., 1966; JD, U. Tex., 1969; LLM, U. Va., 1992. Bar: Tex. 1969, Va. 1977. Staff atty. Tex. Legis. Coun., Austin, 1969-72; atty. Office of Atty. Gen., State of Tex., Austin, 1973-76; legis. aide Va. Del. Carrington Williams, Richmond, 1976-77; dep. atty. gen. jud. affairs div. Va. Office Atty. Gen., Richmond, 1982-85; mem. Va. State Corp. Commn., Richmond, 1985-89; justice va. Supreme Ct., Richmond, 1989—. Office: Va Supreme Ct PO Box 1315 Richmond VA 02321-1315*

LACY, KAREN S., special education educator; b. Winchester, Ind., Oct. 21, 1959; d. W. Ray and Margaret Warnes; 1 child, Eva. BS, Ball State U., 1982, MA, 2003. Spl. edn. tchr. Muncie (Ind.) Cmty. Schs., 1998—2000, Monroe Ctrl. Sch. Corp., Parker City, Ind., 2000—. Mem.: Coun. for Exceptionsl Children. Avocations: bicycling, reading, singing. Office: Monroe Ctrl Elem 10421 W St Rd 32 Parker City IN 47368 Personal E-mail: karen5432@aol.com.

LACY, LUCILE C., music educator; b. Huntsville, Ala., Oct. 16, 1945; d. Ulysses and Gladys (Jacobs) L. BA, Oakwood Coll., Huntsville, Ala., 1968; M Edn, George Peabody Coll., Nashville, 1971; PhD, Ohio State U., 1985. Exec. sec. Oakwood Coll., Huntsville, 1970-71, assoc. prof. music edn., 1971—2003, prof. music, 2004—, chairperson arts and lectr., 1985—94, chairperson music dept., 1990—2000, 1996—2004; music tchr. Oakwood Acad., Huntsville, 1985-86; prof. music edn. Oakwood Coll., 1993—. Vis. prof. Ala. A&M U., Huntsville, 1980-82; minister music Oakwood Coll. Ch., Huntsville, 1987-1999. Recipient Olivetti Underwood award of merit, 1983, Partners in Excellence award Oakwood Coll., 1986, Thomas and Violet Zapara award, 1988; Lily Endowment Faculty Devel. grantee, 1983-85 Mem. Music Educators Nat. Conf., Music Tchrs. Nat. Assn., Nat. Assn. Sch. Music, Coll. Music Soc., Am. Assn. Choral Dirs., Assn. Coll. Univ. and Community Arts Adminstrs., Internat. Adventist Musician Assn., Nat. Assn. Univ. Profs., Ala. Music Edn. Assn., Huntsville Art Coun. (bd. dirs., 2001-). Seventh-day Adventist. Office: Oakwood Coll Music Dept 7000 Adventist Blvd Huntsville AL 35896-0001 Office Phone: 256-726-7284. Business E-Mail: llacy@oakwood.edu.

LACY, MARY T. (MARY KEENAN), prosecutor; b. 1950; m. Jack Lacy; 5 children. JD with honors, U. Iowa, 1978. Pvt. practice; asst. v.p., trust officer Iowa, Boulder, Colo.; with Boulder County Dist Atty.'s Office, 1983—, dep. dist. atty., dist. atty., 2000—. Established Boulder County Sexual Assault Team; nat. instr. on Acquaintance Rape; exec. bd. mem. Colo. Dist. Atty.'s Coun.; mem. Colo. Sex Offender Mgmt. Bd.; adv. bd. mem. Boulder County Ptnrs. Founder Blue Sky Bridge Child Advocacy Ctr.; bd. dirs. Chestor House, YWCA of Boulder County. Named to YWCA Hall of Fame, 1999; recipient Colo. Coalition Against Sexual Assault Award for Excellence, 1998; honored by, Colo. Juvenile Coun. Avocations: gardening, bicycling. Office: Boulder Dist Atty PO Box 471 Boulder CO 80306 Office Phone: 303-441-3700. Office Fax: 303-441-4703.*

LACY, SHEILA PATRICIA, language educator; b. Atlanta, Nov. 30, 1955; d. Gregory Edward Flynn and Margret Laraine Nugent-Flynn; m. David Milton Lacy, Jr. (div.); children: Erin Michael, Shannon Cara. BS in Early Childhood Edn., Ga. State U., 1986. ESOL endorsement Berry Coll., 1996. Tchr. Peachtree Presbyn. Ch., Atlanta, 1986—90; tchr. ESL Fulton County Bd. Edn., Atlanta, 1991—. Mem. discipline com. High Point Elem. Sch., Atlanta, 1989—. Founding mem. Nat. Campaign for Tolerance, Montgomery, Ala., 1991—. Named on Wall of Tolerance for Rosa Parks, Atlanta, 2004; grantee English tchg. grant, Fulton County, 1993. Fellow: PTA. Avocations: buidling wildlife habitats, coaching. Office: Fulton County Bd Edn 530 Greenland Rd Atlanta GA 30342 E-mail: sheilalacy@hotmail.com.

LACY, TERRI, lawyer; b. Dillon, Mont., 1953; BA with highest honors, So. Meth. U., 1975, JD, 1978. Bar: Tex. 1978. Ptnr., Estates & Estates Planning Andrews & Kurth LLP, Houston. Mng. editor Southwestern Law Jour., 1977—78. Mem.: Houston Estate & Fin. Forum, Houston Bus. & Estate Planning Coun., Houston Bar Assn., State Bar Tex., ABA, Order of Coif. Office: Andrews Kurth LLP 600 Travis St Ste 4200 Houston TX 77002-3090 Office Phone: 713-220-4482. Office Fax: 713-238-7220. Business E-Mail: tlacy@andrewskurth.com.

LADAGE, JANET LEE, education educator; b. Moline, Ill., May 2, 1949; d. Earl O. and Crystal I. (Bengston) Peterson; divorced; 1 child, Ryan T. Student, Black Hawk Coll., 1969; BSEd, Western Ill. U., 1971, MSEd, 1974. Instr. Carl Sandburg Coll., Galesburg, Ill., 1974—, chair bus. div., 1987—97, coord. bus. programs, 2005—. Mem. com. for local improvements City of Galesburg, 1990-95. Recipient Carl Sandburg Coll. Outstanding Faculty Mem. awarad Ill. Trustees Assn., 1992. Mem. NEA, Ill. Edn. Assn., Nat. Bus. Edn. Assn. Lutheran. Home: 766 N Academy St Galesburg IL 61401-2639 Office: Carl Sandburg Coll 2232 S Lake Storey Rd Galesburg IL 61401-9574 Business E-Mail: gladage@sandburg.edu.

LADANYI, BRANKA MARIA, chemist, educator; b. Zagreb, Croatia, Sept. 7, 1947; arrived in U.S., 1969; d. Branko and Nevenka (Zilic) Ladanyi; m. Marshall Fixman, Dec. 7, 1974. BSc, McGill U., Montreal, Can., 1969; MPhil, Yale U., 1971, PhD, 1973. Vis. prof. of chemistry U. Ill., 1974; postdoctoral research assoc. Yale U., 1974-77, research assoc., 1977-79; asst. prof. chemistry Colo. State U., Ft. Collins, 1979-84, assoc. prof. chemistry, 1985-87, prof. chemistry, 1987—. Vis. fellow Joint Inst. for Lab. Astrophysics, 1993—94. Assoc. editor Jour. Chem. Physics, 1994—, referee articles to profl. jours., —; contbr. articles to profl. jours. Fellow, Sloan Found., 1982—84, Dreyfus Found., 1983—87; grantee, NSF, DOE, NATO, 1983—89. Fellow: AAAS, Am. Phys. Soc.; mem.: Assn. Women in Sci., Am. Chem. Soc. (PRF grant 1979—82, 1989—91, 1995—98), Sigma Xi. Office: Colo State U Dept Chemistry Fort Collins CO 80523-1872 Business E-Mail: bl@lamar.colostate.edu.

LADAS-GASKIN, CAROL, therapist, educator, artist; b. San Bernardino, Calif., Feb. 15, 1941; d. George Haralambus and Cecelia Marie (Axdahl) Ladas; m. Stephen F. Gaskin (div. 1965); 1 child, Dana Gaskin Wenig. BA, Columbia Pacific U., Calif., 1986, MA, 1988. Reg. counselor. Clay artist, Winlaw, B.C., 1973—; Progoff Intensive jour. cons. U.S. and Can., 1986—; massage practitioner, 1989—; creative process instr., 1990-94; massage instr. Brenneke Sch. Massage, Seattle, 1990—; reg. therapist integrative therapy Seattle, 1990—; integrative psychology tchr. Leadership Inst. Seattle, 1995—. Dir. and founding mem. Paradise Valley New Family Soc., Winlaw, 1968—, Kootenay Boundary Artisan's Alliance, Winlaw, 1980-84. Sculptor: clay murals, 1993-95; clay artist: vases, 1980-95; author: Instant Stress Relief, 1998; poet: (poems) Metro Arts Program, various mags. Recipient Editor's Choice award for outstanding achievement in poetry Nat. Libr. Poetry, 1998, First Place Poetry award, Pacific Northwest Writers Competition, 2000. Democrat. Taoist. Avocations: tai chi, reading, hiking, walking, writing, journal. Home: 19557 1st Ave NW Shoreline WA 98177-2502

LADD, DIANE, actress; b. Meridian, Miss., Nov. 29, 1942; m. Bruce Dern (div.); 1 child, Laura; m. William Shea, Jr. (div.); m. Robert C. Hunter, Feb. 14, 1999; step-children: Brandon Hunter, Amy Oleson, Emily Hunter. Grad., St. Aloysius Acad. Appearances include (films) The Wild Angels, 1966, The Reivers, 1969, Macho Callahan, 1970, Rebel Rousers, 1970, WUSA, 1970, White Lightning, 1973, Alice Doesn't Live Here Anymore, 1974, Chinatown, 1974, Embryo, 1976, The November Plan, 1976, All Night Long, 1981, Something Wicked This Way Comes, 1983, Black Widow, 1987, Plain Clothes, 1988, National Lampoon's Christmas Vacation, 1989, Wild at Heart, 1990, A Kiss Before Dying, 1991, Rambling Rose, 1991, Cemetery Club, 1992, Hold Me, Thrill Me, Kiss Me, 1992, Code Name: Chaos, 1992, Carnosaur, 1993, Father Hood, 1993, Spirit Realm, 1993, Obsession, 1994, Mrs. Munck (also dir., writer, co-prodr.), 1994, The Haunted Heart, 1995, Raging Angels, 1995, Ghosts of Mississippi, 1996, Mother (also exec. prodr.), 1996, Citizen Ruth, 1996, James Dean: Race With Destiny, 1997, Primary Colors, 1998, Daddy N Them, 1999, 28 Days, 2001, Rain, 2001, Law of Enclosures, 2001, Charlies War, 2002, World's Fastest Indian, 2004-05, When I See the Ocean, 2005-06, Come Early Morning, 2005-06, Woman Inside, 2006-; (TV series) Alice, 1980-81; (TV movies) The Devil's Daughter, 1973, Thaddeus Rose and Eddie, 1978, Black Beauty, 1978, Willa, 1979, Guyana Tragedy: The Story of Jim Jones, 1980, Desperate Lives, 1982, Grace Kelly, 1983, I Married a Centerfold, 1984, Crime of Innocence, 1985, Celebration Family, 1987, Bluegrass, 1988, The Lookalike, 1990, Rock Hudson, 1990, Shadow of a Doubt, 1991, Hush Little Baby, 1994, Ruby Ridge: An American Tragedy, 1996, Breach of Faith: Family of Cops II, 1997, The Waiting Game, 1997, The Staircase, 1998, Sharing the Secret, 2000, Christy: The Movie, 2001, Aftermath, 2001, Damaged Care, 2002, Gracie's Choice, 2004; (TV mini-series) Cold Lazarus, 1996, Kristy, James Van Praag Story, (15 hour TV spl.) Christy, Choices of the Heart, Part I & II, 2001, Stephen King's Kingdom Hospital, ABC, 2003. Recipient award Brit. Acad., Spirit award, Golden Globe award, 3 Acad. award nominations, 4 Golden Globe nominations, 3 Emmy nominations for Guest Actress in a Series (Grace Under Fire), 1994, Dr. Quinn, Medicine Woman, Touched by an Angel; named Woman of Yr. City of Hope, 1992; recipient Achievement award Women in Film, 1992, PATH Angel award, 1992, Dist. Artist award L.A. Music Ctr., 1994, Hollywood Legacy award, 1994, 1st Time Dir. award Dla. Film Festival, 1996, Tribuate award Newport Festival, 1996. Office Phone: 805-640-8920.

LADEN, MARY ELLEN, literature and language educator; b. June 29, 1956; d. Edgar Dewey and Elizabeth Lou (Anderson) Laden. BA in Writing, Southwest Mo. State U., Springfield, 1979; MEd, U. Mo., Columbia, 1987. Tchr. English Jefferson City Pub. Schs., Mo., 1981—. Mem.: NEA, Heritage Doll Club, Delta Kappa Gamma. Avocations: miniatures, doll collecting, reading, writing. Office: Jefferson City High Sch 609 Union St Jefferson City MO 65101

LADEWIG GOODMAN, JEANNE MARGARET, artist; b. Grand Rapids, Mich., June 26, 1923; d. Roland Adolph and Margaret Francis (Palmer) Ladewig; m. Larry Goodman, June 1963 (div. 1966). BEd, Concordia Coll., 1945; MS in Art Edn., Ill. Inst. Tech., 1970; postgrad., Chgo. Art Inst., 1959—68. Tchr. Luth. Schs., Chgo., 1952—62; tchr. art Park Ridge Pub. Sch. Dist. 64, Ill., 1962—74, coord. art, 1974—88. Workshop presenter NAEA-IAEA; guest lectr. U. Ill., 1971-72; adv. bd. Contemporary Art Workshop, Chgo.; hiring cons. Evanston (Ill.) Schs., 1985; chair art bd. biannual art show Nat. Am. Pen Women, Denver, Colo., 2005-06. One-woman shows include Scottsdale Art Show, 2005, Gallery Z, Providence, 2005, exhibited in group shows at Ditmar Gallery Northwestern, 1972, Abney Galleries, 1973, Concordia U., 1996, Ariz. State U. Gammage Auditorium, 1998, World Fine Art, NY, 1997—2003, San Bernardino Ann. Ariz. Watercolor Art Show, 1999, 2001, 2003, Ariz. State down town, 2004, Meyers Gallery, Scottsdale; designer life-size horse for Scottsdale Parade Horses, 2001; contbr. articles to profl. jours. Vol. free meals Luth. Ch., Chgo., 1990-95; vol. Terra Mus. of Art, Chgo., 1989-95. Grantee Helene Wurlitzer Found., 1972; 1st prize water color show Artist Guild of Chgo., 1986; recipient Best of Show award, 1999, Vista Show Merit award, 2001, 2002. Mem.: AAUW, Nat. League Am. Pen Women. (art bd. chair 2004—, pres. Scottsdale br.), Chgo. Artists Coalition, Chgo. Soc. of Artists. Lutheran. Avocations: travel, writing.

LADIGES, LORI JEAN, learning disabilities specialist; b. Sheboygan, Wis., Feb. 25, 1956; d. Donald William and Marion Margaret (Henning) L. BS in Edn., U. Wis., 1978; MA in Learning Disabilities, Cardinal Stritch Coll., 1984. Cert. tchr. elem. (grades 1-8), Cognitive disorders (K-12) and learning disabilities (K-12), reading tchr. (K-12). Learning disabilities specialist Kohler (Wis.) Pub. Sch., 1978-99; tchr. Cardinal Stritch U., Milw., 1989, from adj. asst. prof. to asst. prof., 1996—, reviewer Sch. Evaluation Consortium, 1995. Part-time instr. Silver Lake Coll., Manitowoc, Wis., 1984-92; sch. evaluation consortium chair spl. edn. Kohler Pub. Schs., 1989-99, learning disabilities specialist, rep. long-range planning com., 1992-96, cheerleading advisor, 1981-84, yearbook advisor, 1985-86, edn. assn. negotiating team, 1998-99. Chair grad. admissions com. Cardinal Stritch U., 2004—, student affairs com., 1999—2004. Mem. Kohler Edn. Assn. (v.p. 1997-98), Sch. to Work com., Learning Disbilities Assn. Wis., Alpha Sigma (Grace Alvord award 1978). Lutheran. Avocations: travel, reading, fashion design/coordination. Home: 2236 N 23rd St Sheboygan WI 53083-4443 Office: LJL Ednl Consulting LLC 2236 N 23rd St Sheboygan WI 53083-4443

LADNER, APRIL C., lawyer; b. Hattiesburg, Miss., Feb. 4, 1979; d. Ronnie L. and Belinda C. Crane; m. Aaron A. Ladner, Nov. 19, 2005. BS in Bus. Adminstrn., U. So. Miss., Hattiesburg, 2001; JD, U. Miss., Oxford, 2004. Bar: Miss. 2004, Ala. 2005. Assoc. Hortman Harlow Martindale Bassi Robinson & McDaniel, PLLC, Laurel, Miss., 2004—. Mem. First Bapt. Ch., Hattiesburg, 2005. Mem.: ABA, ATLA, Ala. Bar Assn., Jones County Bar Assn. (sec. 2006—), Miss. Bar Assn. Office: Hortman Harlow Martindale Bassi Robinson PO Drawer 1409 Laurel MS 39441 Office Phone: 601-649-8611. Office Fax: 601-649-6062. Personal E-mail: aladner@hortmanharlow.com.

LADUKE, BETTIE, academic administrator; b. Parsons, Kans. d. Leonard and Betty LaDuke. BSBA, U. Tulsa, Okla., 1973; MS, Iowa State U., Ames, 1976. Engagement mgr. Datalogix, Inc., Atlanta, 1993—95, presales cons., 1995—97; dir./mgr. edn. SynQuest, Inc., Norcross, Ga., 1997—2003; instr. econs. Perimeter Coll., Atlanta, 2005—06, asst. dir. faculty devel., online campus, 2006—. Author: (how-to book) Dusty, Here! Understanding a Dog's Point of View. Tchr. Sunday sch. Peachtree Presbyn. Ch., Atlanta, 2002—04. Mem.: Ga. Assn. Econs. and Fin. Achievements include development of online classes in private industry and several colleges and universities. Office: Perimeter Coll Atlanta GA

LAEGER, THERESE ROACH, performing arts educator; b. Birmingham, Ala., Aug. 30, 1956; d. Robert Ernest and Jeanette Stephens Roach; m. Kenneth Edward Laeger, June 28, 1980; children: Brittany Anne, Colleen Jeanette. BA, Birmingham So. Coll., Ala., 1975—79. Soloist dancer Birmingham Ballet, 1974—76; dancer Cleve. Ballet, 1978—79; soloist/prin. dancer Ala. Ballet, Birmingham, 1980—87, ballet mistress/asst. to the artistic dir., 1980—96; dance instr. Ala. Sch. Fine Arts, Birmingham, 1980—96, dance chair, 1996—. Chmn. regional dance competition Nat. Soc. Arts & Letters, Birmingham; scholarship chair Ala. Dance Coun., Birmingham, 2003—05. Dancer (ballet performance) Firebird (Obelisk award, 1978). Chmn. adminstrv. coun. Avondale United Meth. Ch., Birmingham, 2006—. Methodist. Home: 3114 Whitehall Rd Birmingham AL 35209 Office: Ala Sch Fine Arts 1800 8th Ave N Birmingham AL 35203 Office Phone: 205-252-9241. Home Fax: 205-251-9541; Office Fax: 205-251-9541. Business E-Mail: tlaeger@asfa.k12.al.us.

LAFANTANO, ELIZABETH, music educator; d. John Joseph and Joan Theresa Bestercy; m. Pascal Marc LaFantano, Apr. 11, 1992; 1 child, Mary Elizabeth. MusB in Music Edn., SUNY, Fredonia, 1978—82; MA in Liberal Studies in Music & Edn., SUNY at Stony Brook, Stony Brook, New York, 1985—87; Profl. Diploma in Sch. Adminstrn., SUNY, Stony Brook, 2004—06. Cert. in music edn. NY, 1987, sch. dist. adminstrn. NY, 2006. Music tchr. St. Anastasia's John Carroll HS, Fort Pierce, Fla., 1982—84, Kings Pk. Sch. Dist., NY, 1984—2005, supr. fine & applied arts, 2005—. Religious educator St. Joseph's Ch., Kings Park, 2002—06. Mem.: NY State Sch. Music Assn., Kings Pk. Classroom Tchrs. Assn. (assoc.; v.p. 2000—02, Saturn/ Am. Fedn. Tchrs. Partners in Leadership award 2002), Suffolk County Music Educators Assn. (assoc.), NY State Coun. Adminstrs. Music Edn. (assoc.), Music Educators Nat. Conf. (assoc.). Office: William T Rogers Mid Sch 97 Old Dock Rd Kings Park NY 11754 Office Phone: 631-269-3289. Business E-Mail: lafantanoe@mail.kpcsd.k12.ny.us.

LAFARGUE, MELBA FAYE FULMER, credit manager, realtor; b. Baton Rouge, July 13, 1937; d. Harry Geon and Alice (Peters) Fulmer; m. Leo Wallace LaFargue, Aug. 13, 1953 (div. Aug. 1983). BS in Acctg., La. State U., 1959; postgrad., Am. Sch. Banking, 1962. Cert. fin. mgr., realtor. Co-owner Newspaper Crossroads, Kinder, La., 1958-74; loan officer Great So. Mktg. and Loan, 1959-60; office mgr. Savant Constrn. Co., Kinder, 1960-74; cons. Baton Rouge Recreation and Park Commn., 1975-77; realtor Sherwood Realty, Inc., Baton Rouge, 1974—; service mgr. Campus Fed. Credit Union, Baton Rouge, 1980—. Fin. counselor Displaced Homemakers, Baton Rouge, 1983. Mem. Women in Politics, Baton Rouge; cons. fin. Cath. Daus. Am., 1960—. Mem. Nat. Assn. of Bank Women, Nat. Assn. Realtors, Am. Mgmt. Assn., Investors Assn. Democrat. Roman Catholic. Office: AmSouth Investment Svcs Inc 201 NW Railroad Ave Hammond LA 70401-3249 Home: 6323 Westridge Dr Baton Rouge LA 70817-3452

LAFEVOR, KIMBERLY ANN, human resources specialist, educator; b. Detroit; d. Robert Lee and Mary Kathleen Calloway; m. Paul Earle Lafevor; children: Lauren, Meghan. BS in Psychology and Pers. Psychology, Athens State U.; MS in Human Resource Mgmt., Troy State U.; PhD in Bus. Adminstn. and Edn., U. Sarasota; cert. in human resources, Human Resource Cert. Inst. Human resources mgr. GM, Spring Hill, Tenn., leadership develop. advisor, tng. & develop. team leader; mem. faculty Athens State U., Ala., 2006—. Adj. faculty Columbia State Cmty. coll., Bethel Coll.; sr. human resources cons. Helton, Umberger & Assoc., Nashville. Contbr. articles to profl. jours. Leader Girl Scouts Am., Cumberland Valley Coun., Nashville. Mem.: Tenn. Employment Rels. Rsch. Assn., Indsl. Rels. Rsch. Assn., Soc. Human Resources Mgmt., Rotary. Avocations: softball, travel. Office: Athens State U 300 N Beaty St Athens AL 35611 Office Phone: 256-233-8159. Business E-Mail: kim.lafevor@athens.edu.

LAFFERTY, CHRISTINE ELIZABETH, science educator; b. Erie, Pa., Apr. 5, 1976; d. Leigh Edgar and Jean Louise Ewell; m. Sean Dillon Lafferty, Nov. 6, 1994; 1 child, Keagan. BS in Natural Resources, Colo. State U., 1999; MA in Earth Sci., U. No. Colo., 2000. Counselor Remington House, Ft. Collins, Colo., 1999; snowboard instr. Winter Park Resort, Colo., 1999; logistics coord. Outward Bound, Sierra, Calif., 2000; tchr. sci. Colo. Kines & Alternative Sch., Englewood, 2001—; curriculum devel., mem. leadership team, village coord. LeFriends, Englewood, 2005—. Vol. cmty. svc. various orgns. Mem.: Nat. Sci. Tchr. Found. Avocations: skiing, travel, reading.

LAFITTE, MARISSA B., coach; b. Bossier City, La., Mar. 14, 1973; d. Teo S. Bermillo and Gwendolyn F. Anderson; 1 child from previous marriage, Jordan Brianne. BS in Biology and Kinesiology, E. Tex. Bapt. U., Marshall, 1996; MEd, Stephen F. Austin State U., Nacogdoches, Tex., 2000. Lic. athletic trainer, nat. cert. athletic trainer. Head volleyball, asst. softball coach, athletic trainer, instr. E. Tex. Bapt. U., Marshall, 1996—98; athletic trainer E. Tex. Med. Ctr., Tyler, 1999—2001; head volleyball/softball, instr. Onachita Bapt. U., Arkadelphia, Ark., 2001—04, Winston Sch., Dallas, 2004—. Athletic trainer mentor E. Tex. Med. Ctr., Tyler, 1999—2001; club volleyball coach Victory Volleyball, Frisco, Tex., 2004—06; coach, trainer mentor Winston Sch., Dallas, 2005—. Mem.: Nat. Coaches Assn., South Water Athletic Trainers Assn., Nat. Athletic Trainers Assn. Office: Winston Sch 5707 Royal Ln Dallas TX 75224

LAFLAMME, JULIE LYNN, secondary school educator; b. Owosso, Mich., Jan. 27, 1972; d. Dale George and Barbara Ann Walter; m. Jason Ivan LaFlamme, Nov. 26, 1994; children: Jaylyn Rose, Joslyn Noelle, Jaron Nickolas. BSc, Bob Jones U., Greenville, S.C., 1994. Tchr. Faith Bapt. Schs., Davison, Mich., 1995—96, Munising Bapt. Sch., Wetmore, Mich., 1996—. Mem. clarinetists Munising Cmty. Bd., Mich., 2003—. Avocations: music, piano, sports.

LAFORGE, CAROL ANNE, secondary school educator; b. Espanola, N.Mex., May 16, 1951; d. Donald Franklin and Alice Elaine LaForge. BA, So. Utah U., Cedar City, 1973. Cert. profl. educator Utah State Bd. Edn. Tchr. Tooele (Utah) H.S., 1973—. Mem.: NEA (assoc.), Tooele Edn. Assn. (assoc.), Utah Edn. Assn. (assoc.). Home: 328 N Coleman Tooele UT 84074 Office: Tooele High School 301 West Vine St Tooele UT 84074 Office Phone: 435-833-1978 2189. Office Fax: 435-833-1984. Personal E-mail: jancarol@wirelessbeehive.com. Business E-Mail: claforge@m.tooele.k12.ut.us.

LAFORGIA, JEANNE ELLEN, performing arts educator; b. Ho-Ho-Kus, NJ; d. Jerry and Eileen LaForgia; m. James Joseph Zambuto. High Honors, Phillips Exeter Acad., 1988; BA in English and Drama with honors, Dartmouth Coll., 1992; MM in Vocal Performance, Boston U., 1995; vocal studies with Metropolitan Opera soprano Phyllis Curtin. Stage dir. and voice tchr. BU Tanglewood Inst., Lenox, Mass., 1994—97; head of drama Convent of the Sacred Heart, Greenwich, Conn., 1996—99; head of performing arts Boston U. Acad., 1999—. Singer: (cd recording) Night at the Moulin Rouge (Boston Globe Calendar Pick), Our Kinda Guys: the Music of Sinatra, Chevalier, and Montand (Boston Globe Critics Choice), (Operas) Aspen Music Festival, Tanglewood Music Ctr., Manhattan Sch. Music, Moscow Art Theater Sch. Dramatic Studies. Recipient Excellence in Tchg. prize, Harvard U., 2004. Roman Catholic. Home: 8 Wellington Rd Winchester MA 01890 Office: Boston U Acad 1 University Rd Boston MA 02115 Office Phone: 617-353-9000.

LAFRAMBOISE, JOAN CAROL, middle school educator; b. Bklyn., June 23, 1934; d. Anthony Peter and Nellie Eva (Zaleski) Ruggles; m. Albert George Laframboise, Aug. 5, 1961; children: Laura J., Brian A. BS in Edn., Springfield (Mass.) Coll., 1956. Cert. tchr. social sci., and mid. sch.; cert. tchr. support specialist; cert. tchr. gifted. Tchr. Meml. Jr. H.S., Wilbraham, Mass., 1956-61, Midland Park (N.J.) Jr./Sr. H.S., 1961-63, Luke Garrett Middle Sch., Austell, Ga., 1983-93; tchr. lang. arts Pine Mountain Middle Sch., Kennesaw, Ga., 1993-2001; ret., 2001. Coun. pres. Knights of Lithuania, Westfield, Mass., 1973-75, Holyoke, Mass., 1975-76, New Eng. dist. pres., 1976-77; mem. Wistariahurst Mus. Assocs., Holyoke, 1975-77. Jr. League minigrantee, 1991. Mem. ASCD, NEA, Ga. Assn. Educators, Cobb County Assn. Educators, Nat. Coun. Tchrs. English, Nat. Coun. Social Studies. Home: 2891 Dara Dr Marietta GA 30066-4009

LAFRANCIS, NICOLE MARIE, secondary school educator; b. McHenry, Ill., Sept. 20, 1947; d. Raymond Robert and Jude Marie LaFrancis. BS in Corp. Fitness, Western Ill. U., Macomb, 1996; MS in Phys. Edn., No. Ill. U., DeKalb, 2006. Cert. ACE, 2004. Fitness specialist The Meadow Club, Rolling Meadows, Ill., 1996—97; profl. dancer Milw. Bucks, 1997—98; grad. asst. No. Ill. U., DeKalb, 1998—2000; substitute tchr. Cook County Schs., Palatine, Ill., 2000—01; tchr. phys. edn., dance Palatine H.S., Ill., 2001—05, Wheaton Wartenville South H.S., Ill., 2005—. Coach dance team Palatine H.S. and Wheaton Warrenville South H.S., 2001—. Avocations: personal training, exercise, dance, travel, spending time with family and friends. Office: Wheaton Warrenville South HS 1993 Tiger Tr Wheaton IL 60139 Office Phone: 630-784-7005. E-mail: nlafrancis@yahoo.com.

LAFRENTZ, LAVERNE B., elementary school educator; b. Burlington, Kans., Jan. 28, 1953; d. Martin A. and Lois M. Stohs; m. Randall W. Lafrentz, Aug. 1, 1976; children: Justin, Sarah, Aaron. AA, St. John's Coll., Winfield, Kans., 1973; BS, Lutheran tchrs. diploma, Concordia Tchrs. Coll., Seward, Nebr., 1975. Lic. elem. edn. tchr. Ind. Tchr. grades 1-2 St. Paul-St. Peter Sch., Watertown, Minn., 1975—81; lic. day care/presch. provider Carver County Daycare, Watertown, Minn., 1981—89; latch key dir. East Allen County Schs., New Haven, Ind., 1990—92; case worker, social worker Assn. Retarded Citizens of Allen County, Ft. Wayne, Ind., 1992—94; tchr. grade 2 St. John's Luth. Sch., Monroeville, Ind., 1994—. Bldg. Bridges team Ball State U., Muncie, Ind., 1995—99. Spl. edn. Sunday sch. tchr. St. John Luth. Ch., Monroeville, Ind., 1990—, choir, 1989—. Recipient Follower of the Lamb award, Bethesda Luth. Homes, Watertown, Wis., 1996. Mem.: Luth. Edn. Assn., N.E. Allen County Easter Seals. Lutheran. Avocations: reading, piano, embroidery, walking. Office: St John Luth Sch 12912 Franke Rd Monroeville IN 46773 Office Phone: 260-639-0123.

LAGANA, LAURA A., medical/surgical nurse, orthopedics nurse, volunteer; b. Traverse City, Mich., Mar. 15, 1948; d. Melville John and Lucille Anne (Shreatte) Hayes; m. Thomas Lagana, Jr., Feb. 28, 1970; children: Brandon, Daniel. Diploma in nursing, Bryn Mawr (Pa.) Hosp., 1969. RN, Del., La. Nurse ICU, Del. div. Wilmington Med. Ctr.; staff nurse med.-surg. unit Lake Charles (La.) Meml. Hosp.; nurse med.-surg. nurse, team leader St. Francis Hosp., Wilmington; orthopaedic officer nurse Del. Orthopaedic Ctr., Wilmington. Recruitment speaker to local high sch.; spkr. in field. Co-author: Chicken Soup For The Volunteer's Soul, Serving Time, Serving Others; author: Touched By Angels Mercy. Vol. nurse local parochial sch.; mem. Friends Bryn Mawr Hosp. Mem. Nat. Assn. Orthopedic Nurses, Alumni Assn. Bryn Mawr Hosp. Home: PO BOX 7816 Wilmington DE 19803

LAGANGA, DONNA BRANDEIS, dean; b. Bklyn., June 27, 1950; d. Sidney L. and Sylvia (Herman) Brandeis; m. Thomas LaGanga, Aug. 11, 1974. BS in Bus. Edn., Ctrl. Conn. State Coll., 1972, MS, 1975; EdD in Ednl. Adminstrn.-C.C. Leadership, U. Tex., 1999. Various secretarial positions, 1969-72; tchr. bus. Lewis S. Mills Regional H.S., Burlington, Conn., 1972-78; cons. nat. accounts Southwestern Pub. Co., Pelham Manor, N.Y., 1978-84, dist. sales mgr., 1984-89; pres. DBL Industries, Inc., Torrington, Conn., 1989—. Nat. accounts mgr. South-Western Pub. Co., Cin., 1989—93, from sr. sales and mktg. mgr. to nat. career sch. mgr., 1993—95; dir. admissions and records Tunxis C.C.-Bristol Career Ctr., Farmington, Conn., 1995—2000, dir. cmty. alliances, 2000—04, dir. continuing edn. and workforce devel., 2002—, dean workforce devel. and continuing edn., 2004—; v.p. adminstrv. svcs. Human Resource Devel. Assocs., 1996—; co-owner Colonial Welding Svc., seminar condr., 1980—; pres. DBL Industries, Inc.; mem. adv. bd. secretarial sci. dept. LaGuardia C.C., L.I. City, NY, 1982—95; mem. adv. bd. Krissler Bus. Inst. EDPA grantee, 1973; mem. non-partisan ednl. reform task force Pres. George Bush. Named Disting. Alumni, NY CC Bd. Trustees, 2006; recipient Visionary Leadership award, Criminal Justice Command Inst.: Supervisory Leadership Program, 2006. Mem. NAFE, Assn. Info./Sys. Profls., Am. Mgmt. Assn., Nat. Bus. Edn. Assn., Profls. Secs. Internat., Eastern Bus. Edn. Assn., Conn. Bus. Edn. Assn., New Eng. Bus. Edn. Assn., Profl. Secs. Assn., N.Y., Nat. Assn. Cert. Profls. Secs. (cert. profl. sec.), U.S. Golf Assn., Delta Pi Epsilon, Phi Kappa Phi. Avocations: reading, bicycling, golf. Home: 2929 Torringford St Torrington CT 06790-2332 Office: 430E N Main St Bristol CT 06010

LAGANKE, ALLYSON ANN, psychologist; b. Cleve., Dec. 3, 1974; BA in English, Journalism, Miami U., 1997; MEd in Spl. Edn., U. Nev., Las Vegas, 2000, EdS in Sch. Psychology, 2001. Nationally Cert. Sch. Psychologist 2001. With mktg. dept. Cleve. Metroparks, Zoo, and Rainforest, 1995—96; editor Grad. Student Newsletter, 1996—97; editl. asst. Locomotive Engrs. Jour., 1997—99; grad. asst. U. Nev., Las Vegas, 2000—01; psychometrist Disability Resource Ctr., Las Vegas, 2000—01; sch. psychologist Clark County Sch. Dist., Las Vegas, 2001—. Mem.: NASP (assoc.), Nev. Assn. Sch. Psychologists (assoc.), Tri Delta (life). Avocations: travel, dance, swimming, hiking, horticulture.

LAGANO, DANEEN WESTPHAL, elementary school educator; b. Buffalo; d. Roy Howard and Cordula (Schoenlain) Westphal; m. Tom Lagano, June 21, 1959 (dec.); children: Lenore, Lance, Larry. BS in Edn., NY State U., Buffalo, 1952; MA in Edn., Long Beach State U., Calif., 1956. Cert. tchr. Calif. Kindergarten tchr. Camp Harvey Sch., Santa Ana, Calif., 1952—54, US Army, Germany, 1954—59, Tustin Elem., Calif., 1960—62; pre-sch. tchr. Tustin Presbyn. Ch., 1962—69; kindergarten tchr. Santa Ana Schs., Calif., 1969—86; ret., 1986. Sunday sch. supt. Tustin Presbyn. Ch., 1962—63. Avocations: painting, tennis, art, bowling. Home: 394 Gravenstein Terr Brentwood CA 94513-2652

LAGARDE, CHRISTINE, French government official, lawyer; b. Paris, Jan. 1, 1956; d. Lallouette Robert and Carre Nicole; m. Wilfrid Lagarde, June 17, 1982 (div. Apr. 1992); children: Pierre-Henri, Thomas. BA, U. Avignon, France, 1979; M of Law, U. Paris, 1979; M Polit. Scientist, Polit. Scis. Inst., 1977. Assoc. Baker McKenzie, Paris, 1981-87, ptnr., 1987-91, mng. ptnr., 1991-95, chmn. exec. com. Chgo., 1999—2004, chmn. policy com., 2004—05; min. of trade Govt. of France, Paris, 2005—. Author: Breaking New Ground, 1991, Into France, 1993. Mem. French Prime Min. Adv. Bd. on Attractivity of France. Decorated chevalier de la Legion d'Honneur; named one of 100 Most Powerful Women in World, Forbes mag., 2005—06. Mem. Cercle Interallie (Paris), Athenaeum Club (London). Office: Min of Trade 139 rue de Bercy 75572 Paris France Office Phone: 3315384600.

LAGARES, PORTIA OCTAVIA, music educator; b. Bklyn., May 8, 1950; d. Henry Lee and Ellen Thomasina Smith; m. Peter Lagares, Dec. 19, 1976; children: Michael Andre, Matthew David. MusB, MusM, Manhattan Sch. Music, NY, 1973. Pvt. flute instr. Williamsburg Settlement Music Sch., Brooklyn, NY, 1966—71; music educator Pub. Sch. 156, Bronx, NY, 1972—, project arts liaison, 2000—. Choir dir. World Wide Ch. of God, Queens, Westchester, festival choir dir., Saratoga Springs, NY, 2000; vol. flutist piano acompanist Ruth Taylor Nursing Home, Westchester, 1999—2005, Hospice Meml. Services/ Caring Cir., Westchester, 2001—. Musician (flute, piccolo): Queens Symphony Orch., 1967—71; musician: NY Philharm., 1970. Office: Pub Sch 156 750 Concourse Village W Bronx NY 10451 Office Phone: 718-292-5070. Home Fax: 845-628-7161; Office Fax: 718-292-5071. Personal E-mail: plagare2@aol.com. Business E-Mail: plagare@schools.nyc.gov.

LAGEMANN, ELLEN CONDLIFFE, history professor, education educator, dean; b. NYC, Dec. 20, 1945; d. John Charles and Jane Grace (Rosenthal); m. Jonathan Kord Lagemann, June 28, 1969; 1 child, Nicholas Kord. AB cum laude, Smith Coll., 1967; MA, Columbia U., 1968, PhD with distinction, 1978. Tchr. Roslyn H.S., Roslyn, NY, 1967-69; exec. dir. WMCA: Call for Action, N.Y.C., 1969-71; asst. dir. Bank Street Sch. for Children, N.Y.C., 1971-72; tching. and rsch. asst. Inst. Phil. and Politics of Edn., Tchrs. Coll. Columbia U., N.Y.C., 1974-78; asst. prof., then assoc. prof. Tchrs. Coll. Columbia U. Dept. Hist., N.Y.C., 1978-87, prof. history and edn., 1987-94, NYU, N.Y.C., 1994—2000; pres. Spencer Found., 2000—02; dean Harvard Grad. Sch. Edn., Cambridge, Mass., 2002—05, Charles Warren prof. history of Am. edn., 2002—. Trustee Concord (Mass.) Acad.; bd. dirs. Jobs for the Future, Boston, Oasis Children's Svcs., N.Y.C. Author: A Generation of Women: Education in the Lives of Progressive Reformers, 1979, Private Power for the Public Good (Outstanding Book award), 1983, The Politics of Knowledge, 1989, An Elusive Science: The Troubling History of Education Research, 2000; editor: Nursing History: New Perspectives, New Possibilities, 1983, Jane Addams on Education, 1985, Teachers College Record, 1990-95, Brown v. Bd. of Education: The Challenge for Today's Schools, 1996, Philanthropic Foundations: New Scholarship, New Possibilities, 1999, Issues in Educational Research, Problems and Possibilities, 1999; many articles and book chpts. Grantee Carnegie Corp., Spencer Found, Carnegie Found. for Advancement of Teaching, Kettering Found., Lilly Endowment, fellow Ctr. for Advanced Study in Behavioral Scis. Mem. Nat. Acad. Edn. (pres. 1998-2001), History of Edn. Soc. (pres. 1987-88), Am. Hist. Assn., Orgn. Am. Historians, Am. Ednl. Rsch. Assn., Century Assn., Cosmopolitan Club, Office: Harvard Grad Sch Edn Dean's Office Appian Way Cambridge MA 02138 Office Phone: 617-495-3401. E-mail: ellen_lagemann@harvard.edu.

LAGNADO, JENNIFER M., assistant principal; b. NYC, Oct. 9, 1974; d. Joseph and Mary A. Lagnado. BS, Cornell U., Ithaca, NY, 1996, MA Tchg., 1997; EdD, Columbia U., NYC, 2004. Sci. tchr. Lawrence H.S., Cedarhurst, NY, 1999—2005, asst. prin., 2005—. Mem.: NSTA, ASCD, NY State Assn. Women in Adminstrn. Office: Lawrence High School 2 Reilly Rd Cedarhurst NY 11516 Office Phone: 516-295-8012. Business E-Mail: jlagnado@lawrence.k12.ny.us.

LAGO, ADEENA C., performing arts educator; b. Logan, Utah, Oct. 24, 1961; d. Ronald L. and Linda H. Webster; m. Baldomero S. Lago, Sept. 16, 1989; children: Brianna C., Mckay M., Kristi E. BS in Dance Edn., Brigham Young U., Provo, Utah, 1984; MFA, U. Utah, Salt Lake City, 1991. Cert. secondary tchr. Utah State Bd. Edn., 1984. Dance tchr. Uintah H.S., Vernal, Utah, 1984—88; lectr. dance Utah State U., Logan, 1989—90; dance tchr. Granger H.S., West Valley City, Utah, 1990—. Dance co. advisor Granger H.S., West Valley City, Utah, 1990—, drill team dir., 1990—. Named Outstanding Dance Educator, Utah Assn. Health, Phys. Edn., Recreation and Dance, 1999, 5A Drill Team Coach of Yr., Utah Dance and Drill Assn., 1999, 2000, Honored Alumnus, Brigham Young U. Dance Dept., 2005, Excel Outstanding Educator, Granite Edn. Found., 2005, 4A Drill Team Coach of Yr., Utah Dance and Drill Assn., 2006. Mem.: Utah Dance Educators Orgn. (sec. 2001—06, h.s. rep. 2001—). Mem. Ch. Lds. Office: Granger HS 3690 S 3600 W West Valley City UT 84119 Office Phone: (801)646-5320. E-mail: adeena.lago@granite.k12.ut.us.

LAGOMASINO, MARIA ELENA, retired bank executive; b. Havana, Cuba, Mar. 27, 1949; B in French Lit., Manhattanville Coll.; MLS, Columbia U.; MBA, Fordham U. Joined Citibank, 1976, v.p., 1977—83; mgr., divsn. exec. Chase Pvt. Banking Internat., 1983—89, mgr. Western Hemisphere ops., 1989—94, mktg. exec. Ams. region, 1994—97; sr. mng. dir. Chase Manhattan Pvt. Bank, 1997—2000; chmn., CEO J.P. Morgan Pvt. Bank, N.Y.C., 2001—05; CEO, Asset Mgmt. Advisors, LLC, N.Y.C., 2005—. Bd. dirs. Avon Products, Coca-Cola; trustee Synergos Inst. Named one of 25 Women to Watch, US Banker Mag., 2003; named to 2004 Hispanic Bus. Corp. Elite, Hispanic Bus. Mag., 2004. Mem.: Coun. on Fgn. Rels. Office Phone: 212-881-1018. E-mail: mlagomasino@amagobal.com.

LAGON, CYNTHIA BOSTIC, librarian; b. Jackson Springs, N.C., July 8, 1949; d. William Andrew and Thelma Ester (Ewings) Bostic; children: Chante, Cheronda. BA, N.C. Ctrl. U., 1971, MLS, 1975. Libr. I Duke U., Durham, N.C., 1971-75; asst. libr. U. Ill., Chgo., 1985-87, Coll. of Chiropractic, Lombard, Ill., 1988-89; ref. libr. Triton Coll., River Grove, Ill., 1990—, prof. coll. 101, 1993, mem. acad. senate, 1992—; chmn. Quality of Life, 1996—. Sec. Hist. Soc. Original Bapt. Ch., Chgo., cons., 1991—; ref. libr. Oak Park Pub. Libr., 1995--; capt. Women's Aux. Mem. ALA, Ill. Libr. Assn. (mentor networks program 1992—), Assn. Women in Cmty. Colls. (v.p. 2001--), Sisters Investing for Success (treas.), Black Caucas Am. Libr. Assn. Avocations: reading, travel, cooking. Office: Triton Coll 2000 N 5th Ave River Grove IL 60171-1907

LAGOWSKI, BARBARA JEAN, writer, editor; b. Adams, Mass., Nov. 9, 1955; d. Frank Louis and Jeanette (Wanat) L.; m. Richard Dietrich Mumma III, Oct. 11, 1980; 1 child, Adam Dietrich. BA, U. South Fla., 1977; MA, Johns Hopkins U., 1978. Asst. editor Fred Jordan Books Grossett and Dunlap Pubs., N.Y.C., 1978-80; mng. editor Methuen Inc., N.Y.C., 1980-81; mng. assoc., sr. editor Bobb-Merrill Co Inc., N.Y.C., 1981-84; editor New Am. Libr., N.Y.C., 1984-85. Poet-in-the-schs. Hillsborough County Arts Council, Tampa, Fla., 1976-77; poet-in-residence Cloisters Children's Mus., Balt., 1977-78 Author: Silver Skates series, 1988—89; co-author: Good Spirits, 1986, Teen Terminators, 1989, How to Get the Best Public School Education for Your Child, 1991, The Sports Curmudgeon, 1993, How to Attract Anyone, Anytime, Anyplace, 1993, Daily Negotiations: A Malcontent's Book of Meditations for Every Interminable Day of the Year, 1996, 101 Ways to Flirt: How to Get More Dates and Meet Your Mate, 1997, Cyberflirt: How to Attract Anyone, Anywhere on the World Wide Web, 1999; singer: Angel Signs: A Celestial Guide to the Powers of Your Own Guardian Angel, 2002, Lucky in Love: 52 Fabulous Foolproof Flirting Strategies, 2006. Mem. Authors Guild, Phi Kappa Phi Home: 237 Lenox Ave Long Branch NJ 07740-5022 Office Phone: 732-610-1569. Personal E-mail: blagowski@aol.com.

LAGOY, MARY ELIZABETH, sister; d. Gilbert Joseph and Clara Malvine (Coash) Lagoy. BS in Edn., Medaille Coll., Buffalo, 1967; MS in Social Studies, SUNY, Albany, 1972. Joined Sisters of the Holy Names, 1955; cert. tchr. NY, Fla. Sec., teletype operator Strathmore Paper Co., Wornoco, Mass., 1950—54; tchr. pvt. and parochial schs., 1957—72; fin. and devel. asst. Sisters of Holy Names, Albany, NY, 1972—73; contr. Universal Press Syndicate, Kansas City, Mo., 1973—78; coord. Native Am. ministry St. Lucy's, Syracuse, NY, 1979—82; acct., bookkeeper Gallagher/Wald, Inc., NYC, 1983—85; dir. outreach and pantry Cathedral Parish, Albany, 1987—91; campus bus. mgr. Acad. Holy Names, Albany, 1991—93; educator Native Am. ministry Seminole Brighton Reservation, Okeechobee, Fla., 1993—98; clinical pastoral edn. resident, chaplain St. Anne's Hosp., Fall River, Mass., 1999—2000; chaplain St. Clare's Hosp., Schenectady, NY, 2000—02. Mem. evangelization and peace and justice commns. Syracuse Diocese; mem. pastoral team St. Lucy's Ch., Syracuse; mem. Multicultural Comm. Sisters of the Holy Names; mem. bd. dirs. Syracuse Native Am. Club. Democrat. Roman Catholic. Avocations: reading, travel. Home: 475 Yates St Apt 303 Albany NY 12208-3341

LA GRASSE, CAROL WINTER, property rights activist, retired civil engineer; b. Flushing, N.Y., July 31, 1942; d. Henry Ernest and Caroline (Kunkel) Winter; m. Peter Jordan La Grasse, Apr. 25, 1965. B in Engring., CCNY, 1965. Registered profl. engr., N.Y. Structural engr. James Ruderman Co., N.Y.C., 1965; civil engr. Am. Sugar Co., N.Y.C., 1966-69; civil engr., dir. contracts Leonard S. Wegman, Inc., N.Y.C., 1969-73, 74-80; corr. Adirondack Jour., Warrensburg, N.Y., 1987-92; councilman Stony Creek (N.Y.) Town Bd., 1985-93; organist Ch. of St. Cecelia, Warrensburg, N.Y., 1988-98; pres. Property Rights Found. Am., Inc., Stony Creek, N.Y., 1994—. Expert witness Ho. of Reps., Washington, 1994-97, U.S. Senate, Washington, 1999-2004, N.Y. State Senate and Assembly Eminent Domain hearings, 2005-2006; spkr. Nat. Conf. Editl. Writers, Madison, Wis., 1997, Westchester Builders Inst., White Plains, N.Y., 1998, 06, Phyllis Schafly Forum, Washington, 1998, Nat. Hardwood Lumber Assn. Symposium, Cambridge, Ohio, 1999, Alliance for Am., Washington, 1999, 2000, Citizens for Property Rights, Waterbury, Vt., 2001, Boone & Crockett Club, Ryetown, N.Y., 2001, N.Y. State Coalition of Property Owners, Rochester, 2002, Austerlitz Citizens Together, Spencertown, NY, 2006; interviewed on talk shows; featured in and interviewed for articles; planned ann. confs. on pvt. property rights, 1995, 96, 98, 99, 00-05; spkr. in field. Editor: The Moral High Ground, 1996, New York: A Mirror of the Nation, Proceedings 2nd Annual New York Conference on Private Property Rights, 1997, Real People: Their Property Under Attack, Proceedings 3rd Annual N.Y. Conf. on Pvt. Property Rights, 1998, 4th, 1999, 5th, 2000, 6th, 2002, 7th, 2003, 8th, 2004, 9th, 2005, Prfamerica website, 2001—, Proceedings 4th-9th Annual Confs. on Pvt. Property Rights, 1999-2005; editor, co-author: An Enduring Heritage: A Study of Prominent Buildings in Stony Creek Center, 1989; mem. editl. bd. (quart. jour.) Positions on Property, 1994—; editor newsletter NY Property Rights Clearinghouse, 1994-2006; contbr. numerous articles to profl. jours. Councilman Stony Creek Town Bd., 1985-93; sec., treas. Adirondack chpt. Am. Lung Assn., Hudson Falls, N.Y., 1978-90. Recipient Patriot's award Adirondack Park Local Govt. Rev. Bd., 1997. Mem. ASCE, Tau Beta Pi, Chi Epsilon. Republican. Reformed Ch. Am. Achievements include raising a national debate over environmental land designations, national heritage areas, conservation easements. Office: Property Rights Found Am Inc PO Box 75 Stony Creek NY 12878-0075 Office Phone: 518-696-5748. Business E-Mail: lagrasse@prfamerica.org.

LAGRECA, CARLA IRENE, activist; b. Poughkeepsie, NY, Jan. 5, 1952; d. Anthony Salvatore LaGreca and Gloria Marie Carloss. BA cum laude in English, Marist Coll., 1974; MA in English Lit., Fordham U., 1980. Shop steward, clk. Am. Postal Workers Union, Wappingers Falls, NY, 1980—82; change agent U.S. Postal Svc., Wappingers Falls, 1984—. Postmasters equal opportunity adv. bd. U.S. Postal Svc., Poughkeepsie, 1985; adj. prof. english dept. Marist Coll., Poughkeepsie, 1986—. Campaign vol. Labor 2000 for Hillary Clinton, NY, 2000, Ulster County Dem. Party, Ulster County, NY, 2001. Mem.: ACLU, Inst. Noetic Sci., Global Edn. Assoc., Pub. Citizen, Women's Action Coun., Amnesty Internat. Avocations: literature, theater, films, exercise. Home: PO Box 2434 Poughkeepsie NY 12603 Office: Marist College Sch of Liberal Arts North Rd Poughkeepsie NY 12601 Business E-Mail: carla.lagreca@marist.edu.

LAGUNA, ASELA RODRÍGUEZ, Spanish language and literature educator; b. San Germán, P.R., Dec. 6, 1946; came to U.S., 1968; d. Ramon Rodriguez and Eugenia Seda; m. Elpidio Laguna, June 21, 1975; children: Asela M., Maria E., Alexandra. BA, U. P.R., Mayaguez, 1968; MA, U. Ill., 1971, PhD, 1973. Asst. prof. Spanish Rutgers U., Newark, 1973-79, assoc. prof. Spanish, 1979—2002, prof. Spanish, 2002—. Dir. study abroad program in Spain, Rutgers U., 1992, 94, 96, 99, acting dir. dept. Puerto Rican and Hispanic Caribbean Studies, 2001-02, 04-05, chair dept. classical and modern langs. and lit., 2005— Author: G.B. Shaw en el Mundo Hispánico, 1981; editor: Images and Identities: The Puerto Rican in Two World Contexts, 1987, The Global Impact of Portuguese Language and Culture, 2001. Mem. exec. com. N.J. Coun. for Humanities, New Brunswick, 1987-92. Recipient Paul Robeson Faculty award, 2001; named Prof. of Yr., 2001; grantee NEH, N.J. Coun. Humanities, Dodge Found., 1983, Delmas Found., Luso-Am. Found., 1998. Mem. MLA, Am. Assn. Tchrs. of Spanish and Portuguese, Latin Am. Studies Assn., Lions. Home: 283 Newman St Metuchen NJ 08840-2643 Office Phone: 973-353-5594. E-mail: arlaguna@andromeda.rutgers.edu.

LAHAR, CINDY J., psychologist, educator; b. Concord, Mass., June 1, 1962; d. Henry Leo and Priscilla Moore Lahar. PhD, Brandeis U., 1991. Asst prof. dept. psychology U. Calgary, Alta., Canada, 1993—99; prof. psychology Miyazaki (Japan) Internat. Coll., 1998—2001; Fulbright scholar, lectr., rschr. Kingdom of Cambodia, 2003—; chair social scis. York County C.C., 2001—. Carnegie scholar, Carnegie Found. for Advancement of Tchg., 2003—, Fulbright scholar, 2003—04, Fulbright sr. specialist, Cambodia, 2006. Mem.: APA, Am. Psychol. Soc. Office: York County Cmty Coll 112 College Dr Wells ME 04090 E-mail: clahar@yccc.edu.

LAHAYE, BEVERLY, cultural organization administrator; m. Tim LaHaye; 4 children. Founder, chmn. Concerned Women for Am., Washington, 1979—; founder, radio talk show host Beverly LaHaye Live (now Concerned Women Today). Author: The Spirit Controlled Woman, The Desires of A Woman's Heart, Who Will Save Our Children?; co-author (with Dr. Janice Crouse): The Strength of a Godly Woman, 2001; co-author: (with Terry Blackstock) (fiction series) Seasons Under Heaven. Bd. dirs. Internat. Right to Life Fed., Liberty U., Childcare Internat. Recipient Christian Woman of the Year, 1984, Church Woman of the Year, 1988, Religious Freedom Award, S. Baptist Convention, 1991, Thomas Jefferson award, 2001.

LAHIFF, MARILYN J., nursing administrator; b. Youngstown, Ohio; d. Jack L. and Lila J. (Webb) Mills; m. Lawrence C. Lahiff, Apr. 26, 1974. AAS, Lorain County C.C., Elyria, Ohio, 1973; student, Youngstown U., 1960-61. RN, Fla., Ohio; lic. rehab. svc. provider, Fla.; cert. rehab. nurse, cert. ins. rehab. specialist, cert. case mgr. Team leader pediatrics Lakewood (Ohio) Hosp., 1973-75; adminstr. Upjohn HealthCare Svcs., Reno, N.Y., 1977-78, 83-84; occupational health/sch. nurse Medina (Ohio) County Achievement Ctr., 1979-83; regional mgr. Beverly Enterprises, Torrance, Calif., 1984-87; program mgr. RehabCare Corp., Cleve., 1988-89; supr. med./vocat.rehab Feisco, Sarasota, Fla., 1989-92; cons., med. case mgmt. Riscorp, Sarasota, 1993-94; chief operating officer Prime Managed Care Svcs., Inc., Sarasota, 1994—. Mem. editl. bd. Directions in Rehab. Counseling, 1994. Mem. Assn. Rehab. Nurses, Fla. State Assn. Rehab. Nurses, Phi Theta Kappa. Avocations: boating, reading. Home: 35760 Ithaca Dr Avon OH 44011

LAHIRI, JHUMPA (NILANJANA SUDESHNA), writer; b. London, Eng., July 1967; m. Alberto Vourvoulias, 2001; 2 children. BA in English Lit., Barnard Coll., 1989; MA in English, Boston U., MA in Creative Writing, MA in Comparative Lit., PhD in Renaissance studies. Author: (short stories) The New Yorker, 1998, (collection of short stories) Interpreter of Maladies, 1999 (O. Henry award, Pulitzer prize for fiction, 2000, PEN/Hemingway award, New Yorker Debut of Yr. award, Am. Acad. Arts and Letters Addison Metcalf award), (photography collection) India Holy Song, 2000, The Namesake: A Novel, 2003, (short stories) The Third and Final Continent, 1999 (Nat. Mag. award for Fiction, 2000). Named one of Best Young Writers in Am., New Yorker Mag.; recipient M.F.K. Fisher Disting. Writing award, James Beard Found. Speaks Bengali. Office: c/o Houghton Mifflin 222 Berkeley St Boston MA 02116*

LAHOOD, JULIE ANN, small business owner; b. Martins Ferry, Ohio, May 31; d. Joseph Noah LaHood and Thelma Marie Rafful LaHood. Student, Ray Coll. Design, Chgo., 1954—55, Loyola U., 1974—79. Jr. exec. Bonwit Teller, Chgo., 1959—62; asst. dept. mgr. Saks Fifth Ave., Chgo., 1962; owner Historic Properties, Monroe, Mich., Julie's Trading Post, Monroe, St. Charles, Ill. Author: numerous poems. Mem Monroe County Hist. Soc., Mich., Nat. ProLife Alliance, Washington, 2005—; humane amb. Neglected Animals, St. Charles, 1999. Recipient Best Poems and Poets award, Internat. Soc. Poets, 2002, 2003, 2005, Outstanding Achievement in Poetry award, 2006. Mem.: USAF Assn., USN League, Nat. Trust for Historic Preservation, Chgo. Hist. Soc. Republican. Roman Catholic. Avocations: gardening, cooking, poetry, music. Home: 707 Monroe Ave Saint Charles IL 60174

LAHTI, CHRISTINE, actress; b. Detroit, Apr. 4, 1950; d. Paul Theodore and Elizabeth Margaret (Tabar) L.; m. Thomas Schlamme, Sept. 4, 1983; children Wilson, Joseph, Emma. BA in Lang., Speech, Drama, U. Mich., 1972; MFA, Fla. State U., 1972-73; studies with William Esper, Uta Hagen, Herbert Berghof Studios. Actress: (stage prodns.) The Woods, 1978 (Theater World award 1979), Division Street, 1980, Loose Ends, 1981, Present Laughter, 1983, Landscape of the Body, 1984, The Country Girl, 1984, Cat on a Hot Tin Roof, 1985, Little Murders, 1987 (Obie award), The Heidi Chronicles, 1989, Three Hotels, 1993; regular mem. cast (TV series) Dr. Scorpion, 1978, The Harvey Korman Show, 1978, Chicago Hope, 1995-1999 (Golden Globe award, best actress in a leading role drama series, 1998, Emmy award, 1998), Jack & Bobby, 2004 (TV films) The Last Tenant, 1978, The Henderson Monster, 1980, The Executioner's Song, 1982, Single Bars, Single Women, 1984, Love Lives On, 1985, Amerika, 1987, No Place Like Home, 1989 (Golden Globe award, best actress in a leading role mini-series or TV movie, 1989), Crazy from the Heart, 1991, The Fear Inside, 1992, The Good Fight, 1985, The Four Diamonds, 1995, Subway Stories: Tales from the Underground, 1997, Hope, 1997, An American Daughter, 2000, The Pilot's Wife, 2002, Out of the Ashes, 2003 The Book of Ruth, 2004, Revenge of the Middle-Aged Woman, 2004 (feature films).And Justice For All, 1979, Whose Life Is It, Anyway?, 1981, Swing Shift, 1984 (N.Y. Film Critics Circle award for best supporting actress 1985, Acad. award nominee 1985, Golden Globe award nominee 1985), Ladies and Gentlemen: The Fabulous Stains, 1985, Just Between Friends, 1986, Housekeeping, 1987, Season of Dreams, 1987, Stacking, 1988, Running on Empty, 1988, Gross Anatomy, 1989, Miss Firecracker, 1989, Funny About Love, 1990, The Doctor, 1991, Leaving Normal, 1992, Hideaway, 1995, Pie in the Sky, 1995, A Weekend in the Country, 1996; prodr. short action film, actress: Lieberman in Love, 1995 (Oscar award, 1995, Acad. award nominee for best live action short film, 1996). Recipient Susan B. Anthony Failure is Impossible award, High Falls Film Festival, 2005. Office: ICM c/o Toni Howard 8942 Wilshire Blvd Beverly Hills CA 90211-1934*

LAHTINEN, SILJA LIISA, artist; b. Lumivaara, Finland; arrived in U.S., 1978; d. Vaino Lambertinpoika and Katri Elisa (Tirri) Talikka; m. Pentti Kalervo Lahtinen; children: Karoliina, Katriina, Antti. BFA, MA, U. Helsinki, Finland, 1969; BFA, Atlanta Coll. Art, 1983; MFA, Md. Inst. Coll. Art, 1986. Tchr. Teknillinen Oppilaitos, Lahti, Finland, 1969-78; teaching asst. Md. Inst., Coll. of Art, Balt., 1986; artist, owner Siljas Fine Art Studio, Marietta, Ga., 1987—. V.p., creative advisor Pentec Internat. Inc., Marietta, 1994—; tchr. etching, painting Atlanta Coll. Art, 1997—. Solo exhbns. include Ariel Gallery, NYC, 1987, 350th Anniversary Swedish/Finnish Art, Atlanta, 1988, Callanwolde Arts Ctr., Atlanta, 1988, Morin-Miller Gallery, NYC, 1989, La Chapelle de la Sorbonne, Paris, 1990, TaideArt Gallery Helsinki, 1987, 88, 91, 92, Internat. Exhbn., Ward-Nasse Gallery, NYC, 1991, Pihagalleria, Lahti, Finland, 1995, Ars Arrakoski, Padasjoki, Finland, 1999, 2000, Nuutti Galleria, Virrat, Finland, 2002 Ward-Nasse-Chelsea, NYC, 2003; group exhbns. include Scandinavian Artists, Savannah Coll. Art & Design, 1989, La Chapelle de la Sorbonne, Paris, 1990, Ariel Gallery Group Exhbns., NYC, 1987, 89, 90, Med. Coll. Ga., Augusta, 1992, 93, 94, Abney Gallery, NYC, 1993, U. Alaska, Anchorage, 1993, Ward-Nasse Gallery, NYC, 1989-99, Ward-Nasse Gallery Yr. Round Salon, 1999-2002, New Visions Gallery, Atlanta, 1993, Seaside Art Gallery, Nags Head, NC, 1993, Spruill Ctr. Gallery, Atlanta, 1993, New Ams. Selected by Coca Cola Co., 1996, Telfair Mus. Art, Savannah, 1995, Albany Mus. Art, 1994, San Bernardino Art Mus., 1995, Orgn. of Ind. Artists, NYC, 1995, Rutgers Nat., 1994, Stedman Gallery, City of Atlanta Gallery, Chastain Pk., 1994, Rolling Stone Press Gallery, Printmakers Renaissance, 1996, Atlanta Coll. of Art Juried Alumni Exhbn., 1987, 96, Chattahoochee Valley Art Mus., La Grange, Ga., 1997, Barbara Archer Gallery, Atlanta, 2001, Fabulous Finishes, Inc. and Biasucci Co., 2002, Seminole Coll., Sanford, Fla., 2003 (Award of Merit 2003), Greenbelt (Md.) C.C., 2003, Kennesaw State U., Atlanta, 2003, other shows; selected collections include Barbara Archer Gallery, 2001, Trinity Sch., Dr. Weisman Ctr., Lahden Rautateollisuus, Rauma, Vuorineuvos Tauno Matomaki, Helsinki, Pentec Internat. Inc., Markku af Herlin, Helena Jaakonmaki Collection, Hugh and Sirkka Barbour, Boston and others; contbr. various articles to profl. jours. Recipient Internat. Art Competition, Cert. of Excellence in Printmaking, NYC, 1988, Award from FINNAIR to transport exhibit round trip Finland/USA, The State of Ga. award for achievement Ga. Women in the Visual Arts, 1997, Avery Gallery, 2 Painting awards, 1988. Mem.: Womens Caucus Art, Ward Nasse Gallery, Four Winds Soc., Roswell Fine Arts Alliance, Orgn. Ind. Artists, Am. Art Therapy Assn. Lutheran. Avocations: shamanism, trance dance, zen buddhism, haiku, yoga. Office: Siljas Fine Art Studio 5220 Sunset Trl Marietta GA 30068-4740 E-mail: pentec02@bellsouth.net.

LAI, FENG-QI, instructional designer, educator; b. Shanghai, Mar. 25, 1948; arrived in U.S., 1992; d. Zheng-Zhong Lai and Yao-Zhang Zhu; m. Qun Zhang, Oct. 22, 1984. BA, Changsha (China) Railway Inst., 1982; MS, Purdue U., 1994, PhD, 1997. Asst. lectr. Shanghai Tiedao U., 1982-86, lectr., assoc. dir., 1986-91; instrnl. designer Nat. Edn. Tng. Group, Naperville, Ill., 1998; sr. instr., dir. tng. Advanced Tech. Support, Inc., Schaumburg, Ill., 1998-2000; sr. instrnl. designer, project mgr. Cognitive Concepts, Inc., Evanston, Ill., 2000—02; asst. prof. Ind. State U., Terre Haute, Ind., 2002—. Guest prof. Shanghai Normal U., 2006—. Transl.: Writing Scientific Papers in English, 1983; co-author: Applied Cryptography, 1999, Fundamental Computer Skills, 2004. Mem.: Soc. Internat. Chinese in Ednl. Tech. (pres. 2005—06), Phi Kappa Phi. Avocations: music, reading, Chinese poetry, photography, crafts. Business E-Mail: flai@indstate.edu.

LAI, LIWEN, geneticist, educator; b. Taipei, Taiwan, 1957; d. Kwan-Long Lai. BS, Nat. Taiwan U., 1980; MS, U. Calif., San Francisco, 1983; PhD, U. Tex., Dallas, 1987. Diplomate Am. Coll. Med. Genetics. Postdoctoral fellow NIH, Bethesda, Md., 1987-89; asst. rsch. sci. U. Ariz., Tuscon, 1990-94, asst. dir. Molecular Diagnostic Lab., 1992—, rsch. asst. prof., 1995-97; rsch. assoc. prof., 1997—2003; rsch. prof., 2003—. Rsch. grantee Elks, 1994-96, Dialysis Clinic Inc., 1994-96, So. Ariz. Found., 1996—, NIH, 1997—. Mem. Am. Soc. Human Genetics, Am. Soc. Gene Therapy, Am. Soc. Nephrology, Am. Soc. Cell Biology. Office: U Ariz Dept Medicine 1501 N Campbell Ave Tucson AZ 85724-0001

LAING, KAREL ANN, magazine publishing executive; b. Mpls., July 5, 1939; d. Edward Francis and Elizabeth Jane Karel (Templeton) Hannon; m. G. R. Cheesebrough, Dec. 19, 1959 (div. 1969); 1 child, Jennifer Read; m. Ronald Harris Laing, Jan. 6, 1973; 1 child, Christopher Harris Grad., U. Minn., 1960. With Guthrie Symphony Opera Program, Mpls., 1969-71; account supr. Colle & McVoy Advt. Agy., Richfield, Minn., 1971-74; owner The Cottage, Edina, Minn., 1974-75; salespromotion rep. Robert Meyers & Assocs., St. Louis Park, Minn., 1975-76; cons. Webb Co., St. Paul, 1976-77, custom pub. dir., 1977-89; pres. K.L. Publs., Inc., Bloomington, Minn., 1989—. Contbr. articles to profl. jours. Community vol. Am. Heart Assn., Am. Cancer Soc., Edina PTA; charter sponsor Walk Around Am., St. Paul, 1985 Mem. Bank Mktg. Assn., Fin. Instn. Mktg. Assn., Advt. Fedn. Am., Am. Bankers Assn., Direct Mail Mktg. Assn., Minn. Mag. Pub. Assn. (founder, bd. govs.), St. Andrews Soc. Republican. Presbyterian. Avocations: painting, gardening, reading, travel. Office: KL Publs 2001 Killebrew Dr Minneapolis MN 55425-1865

LAIOU, ANGELIKI EVANGELOS, history professor; b. Athens, Greece, Apr. 6, 1941; came to U.S., 1959; d. Evangelos K. and Virginia I. (Apostolides) Laios; m. Stavros B. Thomadakis, July 14, 1973; 1 son, Vassili N. BA, Brandeis U., 1961; MA, Harvard U., 1962, PhD, 1966. Asst. prof. history Harvard U., Cambridge, Mass., 1969-72, Dumbarton Oaks prof. Byzantine history, 1981—; assoc. prof. Brandeis U., Waltham, 1972-75; prof. Rutgers U., New Brunswick, NJ, 1975-79, disting. prof., 1979-81; chmn. Gennadeion com. (Am. Sch. Classical Studies), Athens, Greece, 1981-84; dir. Dumbarton Oaks, 1989-98; prof. history Harvard U., Cambridge, 1998—. Mem. Greek Parliament, 2000-2002; dep. min. fgn. affairs, Greece, 2000. Author: Constantinople and the Latins, 1972, Peasant Society in the Late Byzantine Empire, 1977, Mariage, amour et parenté à Byzance, XIe-XIIIe siècles, 1992, Gender, Society and Economic Life in Byzantium, 1992, The Economic History of Byzantium, 2002. Guggenheim Found. fellow, 1971-72, 79-80, Dumbarton Oaks sr. fellow, 1983—, Am. Coun. Learned Socs. fellow, 1988-89. Fellow: Acad. des Inscriptions et Balles Lettres, Am. Acad. Arts and Scis., Acad. Athens, Medieval Acad.; mem.: Am. Hist. Assn., Medieval Acad. Am., Greek Com. Study of South Eastern Europe. Office: Harvard U Dept History Cambridge MA 02138 Office Phone: 617-495-5108. E-mail: laiou@fas.harvard.edu.

LAIRD, CHERYL F., mental health services professional, paralegal; d. Wallace F. Stalnaker, Sr. and Faith M. Stalnaker; children: Craig H., Christine Vickers, Tracy Wheeler, John T. BA in Psychology, U. Ctrl. Fla., Orlando, 1989; MA in Counseling and Human Devel., Liberty U., Lynchberg, Va., 1996; EdD in Human Sexuality, Inst. Advanced Study of Human Sexuality, San Francisco, 2001. Diplomate Am. Bd. Sexology; lic. mental health counselor Fla., cert. sex. therapist Fla., forensic addictions examiner, compulsive gambling treatment specialist, hypnotherpaist Fla., leader Active Parenting of Teens, substance abuse profl., comprehensive assessor, child and adolescent needs and strengths, juvenile assessor Health Svcs. Assn., juvenile sex offender evaluator. Intern, therapist Ctr. for Drug Free Living, 1995; mental health dir., therapist Altamonte Ctr. for Counseling, 1996—98; therapist Summit Counseling Group, 1998—. Fellow: Am. Bd. Forensic Sexologists; mem.: APA, Nat. Guild Hypnotists, Am. Assn. Christian Counselors, Fla. Assn. for Treatment of Sexual Abusers, Am. Profl. Soc. on Abuse of Children, Fla. Mental Health Counselor Assn. (bd. dirs., edn. chair), Mental Health Counselors of Ctrl. Fla. (pres.), Assn. of Family and Conciliation Cts., Am. Assn. Sex Educators, Counselors, and Therapists, Assn. for Treatment of Sexual Abusers (clin. mem., diplomat). Avocation: parrot foster care. Office Phone: 407-325-1350. Fax: 407-332-8943. E-mail: cslaird@cfl.rr.com.

LAIRD, DORIS ANNE MARLEY, retired humanities educator, musician; b. Charlotte, NC, Jan. 15, 1931; d. Eugene Harris and Coleen (Bethea) Marley; m. William Everette Laird Jr., Mar. 13, 1964; children: William Everette III, Andrew Marley, Glen Howard. MusB, Converse Coll., Spartanburg, S.C., 1951; opera cert., New Eng. Conservatory, Boston, 1956; MusM, Boston U., 1956; PhD, Fla. State U., 1980. Leading soprano roles S.C. Opera Co., Columbia, 1951-53, Plymouth Rock Ctr. of Music and Art, Duxbury, Mass., 1953-56; soprano Pro Musica, Boston, 1956, New Eng. Opera Co., Boston, 1956; instr. Stratford Coll., Danville, Va., 1956-58, Sch. Music Fla. State U., Tallahassee, 1958-60, dept. humanities, 1960-68; tchr. Fla. State U., 1973-79; asst. prof. Fla. A&M U., Tallahassee, 1979-89, assoc. prof., 1990—2002; ret., 2002. Vis. scholar Cornell U., 1988; participant So. Conf. on Afro-Am. Studies, Inc. Author: Colin Morris: Modern Missionary, 1980; contbr. articles to profl. jours. Soprano Washington St. Meth. Ch., Columbia, SC, 1951-53, Copley Meth. Ch., Boston, 1953-56; soloist Trinity United Meth. Ch., Tallahassee, 1983—; mem. Saint Andrews Soc., Tallahassee, 1986—; judge Brain Bowl, Tallahassee, 1981-84; alumnae bd. Converse Coll., 2004— Named subject of article, Glamour mag., 2001, Self mag., 2003; recipient NEH award, 1988, Disting. Alumna award, Converse Coll., 2001; scholar Phi Sigma Tau, 1960. Mem. AAUP, AAUW, Nat. Art Educators Assn., Tallahassee Music Tchrs. Assn., Tallahassee Music Guild, Am. Guild of Organists, DAR (mus. rep. 1984-85, registrar 2005-), Colonial Dames of 17th Century (music dir. 1984-85), Nat. Assn. Humanities Edn., U. Wyo. Women's Club, Woman's Club Tallahassee (v.p. 2004), Converse Coll. Alumni (bd. dirs. 2003—) Republican. Achievements include subject of article Self Magazine, 2004. Avocations: travel, dance, music. Home: 1125 Mercer Dr Tallahassee FL 32312-2833 Personal E-mail: dorisamlaird@comcast.net.

LAIRD, JEAN ELOUISE RYDESKI (MRS. JACK E. LAIRD), author, adult education educator; b. Wakefield, Mich., Jan. 18, 1930; d. Chester A. and Agnes A. (Petranek) Rydeski; m. Jack E. Laird, June 9, 1951; children: John E., Jayne E., Joan Ann P., Jerilyn S., Jacquelyn T. Bus. Edn. degree, Duluth Bus. U., Minn., 1948; postgrad., U. Minn., 1949-50. Tchr. Oak Lawn (Ill.) H.S. Adult Evening Sch., 1964-72, St. Xavier U., Chgo., 1974—. Lectr., commencement address cir.; writer newspaper column Around The House With Jean, A Woman's Work, 1965-70, Chicagotown News column The World As I See It, 1969, hobby column Modern Maturity mag., travel column Travel/Leisure mag., beauty column Ladycom mag., Time and Money Savers column Lady's Circle mag., consumerism column Ladies' Home Jour. Author: Lost in the Department Store, 1964, Around the House Like Magic, 1968, Around the Kitchen Like Magic, 1969, How to Get the Most from Your Appliances, 1967, Hundreds of Hints for Harassed Homemakers, 1971, The Alphabet Zoo, 1972, The Plump Ballerina, 1971, The Porcupine Story Book, 1974, Fried Marbles and Other Fun Things to Do, 1975, Hundreds of Hints for Harassed Homemakers: The Homemaker's Book of Time and Money Savers, 1979, =Homemaker's Book of Energy Savers, 1981, also 427 paperback booklets; contbr. articles to mags. Mem.: Marist, Mt. Assissi Acad., St. Linus Guild, Queen of Peace Parents Clubs, Oak Lawn Bus. and Profl. Women's Club, Canterbury Writers Club Chgo. Roman Catholic. Home: 10540 Lockwood Ave Oak Lawn IL 60453-5161 also: Vista De Lago Lake Geneva WI 53147 also: Harbor Towers Yacht Club Siesta Key FL 34242

LAIRD, MARY See WOOD, LARRY

LAJE, ZILIA L., writer, publisher, translator; b. Havana, Cuba, Feb. 1, 1941; came to U.S., 1961; d. Luis B. Laje and Zilia Isabel Bello; divorced; 1 child, Alberto Luis Dominguez. Comml. acct., Escuela Profl. de Comercio, Havana, 1959-61; AA in Bus. Adminstrn., Miami-Dade C.C., 1989. Export documentation clk. Pittsburgh Plate Glass Internat., Havana, 1959-60; agy. sec. Occidental Life Ins. Co., Miami, 1962-67; sec. to v.p./br. mgr. Chgo. Title Ins. Co., Miami, 1972-76; corp. banking asst. S.E. Bank, N.A., Miami Springs, Fla., 1978-90; writer, transl. Miami, 1991—. Exhibitor Miami Book Fair Internat., 1995—. Author: (novels) La Cortina de Bagazo, 1995, The Sugar Cane Curtain, 2000, Cartas Son Cartas, 2001, Love Letters in the Sand, 2002, Divagaciones, 2003, 100 Recetas de Cocina Tradicionales, 2004, Genealogía-Laje, 2006. Mem.: PEN Ctr. Writers in Exile, Writers, N.Y., Cuban Writers in Miami (founder, assoc.), Women's Nat. Book Assn. (corr.), Cuban Geneal. Soc., Alliance Française de Miami. Republican. Roman Catholic. Avocations: needlepoint, photography, travel, genealogy. Office: Escritores Cubanos de Miami PO Box 45-1732 Miami FL 33245-1732 E-mail: guarinapub@juno.com.

LAJOUX, ALEXANDRA REED, editor-in-chief, educator; b. Washington, Mar. 4, 1950; d. Stanley Foster and Stella Swingle Reed; m. Bernard Jacques Lajoux, Aug. 14, 1982; 1 child, Franklin Alberto; stepchildren: Valerie Corinne, Sylvia Patricia. BA, Bennington Coll., Vt., 1972; MA, Princeton U., N.J., 1974, PhD, 1978; MBA, Loyola Coll., Balt., 1981. Asst. prof. French lang. and lit. SUNY Coll. Oswego, N.Y., 1977-78; sr. editor Dirs. and Bds. Info. for Industry, McLean, Va., 1978-80; editor Mergers and Acquisitions The Hay Group, Phila., 1980-83; editor Export Today Export Info. Group, Washington, 1983-87; editor-in-chief Nat. Assn. Corp. Dirs., Washington, 1987—2004, dir. rsch. and publs., 1992-2000, sr. rsch. analyst, 2001—04, chief knowledge officer, 2005—. Pres. Alexis & Co., Arlington, Va., 1987—; Washington bur. co-chief N.E. Internat. Bus., Washington, 1987-90; dir. M&A rsch. E-Know, Inc., Arlington, 2000-01; mem. Nat. Infrastructure Adv. Coun. - Risk Mgmt. Study Group, 2005; mem. adv. bd. E-Know, Inc., Arlington, 2005—, M&A Ptnrs., Dallas, 2005-. Author: The Art of M&A Integration, 1997, 2006; co-author (with J.F. Weston): The Art of M&A Financing and Refinancing, 1999; co-author: (with S.F. Reed) The Art of M&A: A Merger/Acquisition/Buyout Guide, 3d edit., 1999; co-author: (with C.M. Elson) The Art of M&A Due Diligence, 2000; co-author: (with H.P. Nesvold) The Art of M & A Structuring, 2004; editor-in-chief: HR Dir.: The Arthur Andersen Guide to Human Capital, 1998, 1999, 2000, 2001, recording artist: album My Country, 2006; contbr. articles to profl. jours. Co-dir. Gunston Mid. Sch. Chorus, 2000; drama and music tchr. Commonwealth Acad., Falls Church, Va., 2000—02, music tchr., spring, 2003; music tchr. Lab Sch., Washington, 2003—04; cantor, children's music asst. St. Ann Cath. Ch., Arlington, 1988—, catechist, 1999—2001; alto sect. leader St. James Ch., Falls Church, 2001—; bd. dirs. Arlington Little League, 1992—94. Princeton fellow, 1972-74, French Govt. fellow, 1975-76, Mrs. Giles Whiting fellow, 1976-77. Mem. Toastmasters Internat. (v.p. local club membership 1999-2000), Assn. Princeton Grad. Alumni (trustee 1999-2002), Nat. Assn. Pastoral Musicians, Songwriters Assn. Washington, Mil. Writers Soc. Am. Republican. Roman Catholic. Avocations: singing, composing and professionally recording songs, organizing musical performances, learning foreign languages, teaching youth and adults. Home: 2256 N Nottingham St Arlington VA 22205-3344 Office: Nat Assn Corp Dirs Ste 700 1133 21st St NW Washington DC 20036 Office Phone: 202-775-0509. Personal E-mail: arlajoux@aol.com. Business E-Mail: arlajoux@nacdonline.org.

LAKE, CAROL LEE, anesthesiologist, physician, educator; b. Altoona, Pa., July 14, 1944; d. Samuel Lindsay and Edna Winifred (McMahon) L. BS, Juniata Coll., 1966; MD, Med. Coll. Pa., 1970; MBA, U. Calif., Irvine, 1997; MPH, U. Mich., 2000. Intern Mercy Hosp., Pitts., 1970-71, resident in anesthesiology, 1971-73; staff anesthesiologist Pitts. Anesthesia Assocs., 1973-75; asst. prof. anesthesiology U. Va., Charlottesville, 1975-80, assoc. prof., 1980-89, prof. anesthesiology, 1989-94; prof. anesthesiology, chair U. Calif., Davis, 1994-95, prof. clin. anesthesiology, 1996; chief of staff Roudebush VA Med. Ctr., 1997-99; asst. dean, prof. anesthesia Ind. U., Indpls., 1997-99; prof. anesthesiology, chair U. Louisville, 1999—2004, assoc. dean for continuing med. edn., 1999—2004, asst. v.p. for health affairs/continuing edn., 2002—04; CEO Verefi Techs., Inc., Elizabethtown, Pa., 2005—. Sr. assoc. examiner Am. Bd. Anesthesiology, 1981—2005. Author: Cardiovascular Anesthesia, 1985; editor: Pediatric Cardiac Anesthesia, 1988, 4th edit., 2004; Clinical Monitoring, 1990, 2d edit., 2000; editor Seminars in Cardiothoracic and Vascular Anesthesia, 1999—; co-editor: Blood: Hemostasis, Transfusion and Alternatives in the Perioperative Period, 1995; editor Advances in Anesthesia, 1993—. Fellow Am. Coll. Cardiology; mem. Assn. Cardiac Anesthesiologists (pres. 1987-88), Soc. Cardiovascular Anesthesiologists (bd. dirs. 1988-92), Assn. Univ. Anesthesiologists, Am Coll. Physician Execs., Alpha Omega Alpha. Presbyterian. Avocations: music, entomology, gardening. E-mail: carol.lake@verefi.com.

LAKE, CONSTANCE WILLIAMS, psychologist, public health administrator; b. Cleve., Aug. 16, 1949; d. Fredrick and Helen (Martin) Williams; m. Michael J. McCargo, Sept. 1, 1973 (div. Oct. 1989); children: Courtney McCargo, Jarad McCargo; m. Kenneth Paul Lake, Sept. 7, 1997. BA, Elmhurst (Ill.) Coll., 1971; MA, U. Conn., 1973; PhD, Kent State U., 1983. Psychologist Mile Sq. Health Ctr., Chgo., 1984-86, exec. dir., 1986-90; clin.

assoc. Cmty. Mental Health Ctr., Chgo., 1985-90; AIDS cons. Assn. Black Psychologists, 1988—; instr. psychology Northeastern U., Chgo., 1989; dir. cmty. svc. Binghamton (N.Y.) Psychiat. Ctr., 1990-91; clin. assoc. Ramey & Assocs., Atlanta, 1991-92; bur. chief mental health City of Chgo. Joint Commn. Health Care Orgns., 1999—. V.p. profl. devel. Hamilton Behavioral Health, Chgo., 1992; cons./trainer Wells Cmty. Initiative, Chgo., 1992-93; trainer HIV Office, APA, Chgo., 1993—. Mem. long range planning bd. dirs. Trinity United Ch. of Christ, Chgo., 1992-99; mem. Renaissance Women, 1985-97. Honoree, Alpha Gamma Pi, Chgo., 1995; Woman of Achievement honoree broome County Status of Women, Binghamton, 1992. Mem. APA, APHA, Assn. Black Psychologists (conv. chair 1996-97), Delta Sigma Theta. Avocations: film, theater, dance. Office: Chgo Dept Pub Health 333 S State St Chicago IL 60604-3900

LAKE, JANE BURFORD, special education educator, hypnotherapist, small business owner; b. Pitts., Oct. 9, 1937; d. Henry Isaac and Emily Louise (Castore) Burford; m. Howard Kenneth Lake, Jr., Aug. 20, 1960 (!div. 1983); children: Karen Lake Ray, Christopher Kenneth. BS in Elem. Edn., U. Del., 1960; Ryan specialist, U. Calif., Irvine, 1983; PhD, Am. Inst. Hypnotherapy, Santa Ana, Calif., 1986; MEd in Adminstrn., U.S. Internat. U., Irvine, Calif., 1991. Elem. tchr. Penn Delco Union Sch. Dist., West Chester, Pa., 1960-63, Sugartown Elem. Sch., Malvern, Pa., 1963-65; substitute tchr. Oceanview-Westminster Sch. Dist., Huntington Beach, Pa., 1979-83; mem. faculty Am. Inst. Hypnotherapist, 1986-90; tchr. spl. edn. Santa Ana Unified Sch. Dist., 1983—; owner, pres. For Heaven's Sake. Pvt. practice hypnotherapy, Tustin, Calif., 1986—; mem. staff for devel. stress mgmt. Century High Sch., Santa Ana, 1991-92; fellow Nat. B d. Hypnotherapy and Hypno Anesthesiology, 1986—, Am. Bd. Hypnotherapy, 1986—; symposium speaker Nat. Head Injury Found., 1986. Cons. vol. art edn. program Jr. League, Irvine, 1976. Recipient Outstanding Contbns. to Edn. in Hypnotherapy award Nat. Bd. Hypnotherapy and Hypno Anesthesiology, 1989. Mem. NEA, Santa Ana Edn. Assn. (grievance com. 1983—), Calif. Tchrs. Edn. Assn., Calif. Assn. Neurologically Handicapped, Assn. for Children and Adults with Learning Handicaps, Tchr. Advs. for Spl. Kids, So. Calif. Head Injury Found., AAUW (edn. advisor Tustin 1990-91), LWV. Avocations: gardening, writing journals, travel, singing, creating meditations. Home: 27945 Chiclana Mission Viejo CA 92692-1223 Personal E-mail: drjlake@cox.net.

LAKE, JUDITH ANN, nurse; b. Detroit, May 6, 1944; d. William D. and Helene L. (Cook) Duckett; m. Dennis C. Lake, Apr. 23, 1966; children: Bradley W., Pamela D., Amanda L. Diploma, Harper Hosp. Sch. Nursing, 1965. RN Mich., Tenn. Staff nurse St. Mary's Hosp., Livonia, Mich., 1967; office nurse Drs. Richards and Askins, Jackson, Mich., 1970-71; staff nurse ICU Kent Gen. Hosp., Dover, Del., 1979-80; charge nurse ICU Deborah Heart & Lung Ctr., Browns Mills, N.J., 1980-83; staff nurse ICU Chelsea (Mich.) Cmty. Hosp., 1983-84, Cumberland Dialysis Ctr., Clarksville, Tenn., 1988-89; asst. head nurse Ren Ctr., Clarksville, Tenn., 1989; sr. transplant coord., nurse mgr. Transplant Ctr. Centennial Med. Ctr., Nashville, 1989-99. Avocations: sewing, tennis, gardening. Office: Nursing Edn 2300 Patterson St Nashville TN 37203

LAKE, KATHLEEN COOPER, lawyer; b. San Antonio, Jan. 11, 1955; d. Herschel Taliaferro and Virginia Mae (Hylton) Cooper; m. Randall Brent Lake, Apr. 9, 1977; 1 child, Ethan Taliaferro. AB in Polit. Sci. magna cum laude, Middlebury Coll., 1977; JD with high honors, U. Tex., 1980. Bar: Tex. 1980, U.S. Ct. Appeals (5th cir.) 1981, U.S. Ct. Appeals (D.C. and 3rd cirs.) 1984. Assoc. atty. Vinson & Elkins, Houston, 1980-88; ptnr. Vinson & Elkins, LLP, Houston, 1989—. Bd. advisors, columnist Utilities, Y2K Advisor, 1998-99. Adult leader, com. mem. Sam Houston Area Coun.-Golden Arrow dist. Boy Scouts Am., 1993—, chair troop com., 1998-2001. Recipient Unit Svc. award Sam Houston Area Coun.-Golden Arrow dist. Boy Scouts Am., 1996, 98, 2005. Fellow Tex. Bar Found. (life), Houston Bar Found.; mem. ABA (vice-chair com. 1997-99), Energy Bar Assn., Electric Coop. Bar Assn., State Bar Tex., Coll. State Bar Tex., Tex. Law Rev. Assn. (life), Houston Bar Assn., Middlebury Coll. Alumni Assn. (com. mem. 1980-2000, Houston com. chair 2001—), Order of Coif, Phi Beta Kappa, Phi Kappa Phi. Office: Vinson & Elkins LLP 2500 First City Tower 1001 Fannin St Houston TX 77002-6760 Office Phone: 713-758-3826. E-mail: klake@velaw.com.

LAKE, NOREEN L., retired accountant; b. Chicago, Ill., Jan. 4, 1956; d. Howard H. Perry and Isabelle Coninx; m. Michael E. Lake, July 19, 1986. Acctg. Cert., Oakton C.C., Des Plaines, Ill., 1983. Acctg. specialist W W Grainger, Niles, Ill., 1974—78; staff 1 acct. A B Dick Co., Niles, Ill., 1978—87; biblofile conversion Maine East H.S., Park Ridge, Ill., 1988—88; bookkeeper Advertisers Broadcast Svcs., Des Plaines, Ill., 1989—96; fin. dir. Ashley Ct. Ret. Cmty., Des Plaines, Ill., 1997—2001. Author: (written essay) Best Boss, Worst Boss (Contest winner, essay was pub., 1994), (poem) The Mind's Sunset (Editor's Choice Award, 2003). Pres. - libr. bd. trustees Des Plaines Pub. Libr., Des Plaines, Ill., 2004—; commr. Keep Des Plaines Beautiful, Des Plaines, Ill., 1994—2001; trustee Des Plaines Pub. Libr., Des Plaines, Ill., 2001—; mayoral campaign treas. Citizens for Anthony W Arredia, Des Plaines, Ill., 2001—; bd. trustee Des Plaines Healthy Cmty. Partnership, Des Plaines, Ill., 2004—. Recipient NSLS Libr. Trustee of the Yr., North Suburban Libr. Sys., 2004, Beautification Award, 1994, Theodore A Krause Sr. Meml. Award, 1994, Good Neighbor Super Star Vol. award, City of DesPlaines, 2005; Nat. Legis. Day scholar, North Suburban Libr. Sys., 2005. Mem.: Des Plaines Sr. Ctr., Friends of the Des Plaines Pub. Libr. Bapt. Achievements include Lake Pk. Golf Open Women's Scratch Champion 2002-06. Avocations: golf, couponing and refunding, reading. Home: 1538 Campbell Ave Des Plaines IL 60016 Personal E-mail: nllake@hotmail.com.

LAKE, RICKI (RICKI PAMELA LAKE), talk show host, actress; b. NYC, Sept. 21, 1968; m. Rob Sussman (separated); children Milo Sebastian, Owen Tyler Syndicated talk show host Ricki Lake, 1993—. Movie appearances include: Hairspray, 1988, Working Girl, 1988, Cookie, 1989, Cry-Baby, 11990, Last Exit to Brooklyn, 1989, Where the Day Takes You, 1992, Inside Monkey Zetterland, 1993, Serial Mom, 1994, Cabin Boy, 1994, Skinner, 1995, Mrs. Winterbourne, 1996, Cecil B. DeMented, 2000, Park, 2006; TV appearances include (series) China Beach, 1990, Kate and Allie, Fame, King of Queens, 2001, (spls.) A Family Again, 1988, Starting Now, 1989, Gravedale High, 1990, (movies) Babycakes, 1989, The Chase, 1991, Based on an Untrue Story, (pilot) Starting Now; stage actress: A Girl's Guide to Chaos, 1990, (off-Broadway) The Early Show, Youngsters, 1983; host Game $how Marathon, 2006. Recipient Gracie Allen award, Am. Women in Radio & TV, 2001, Angel award (2), Excellence in Media. also: WMA 151 S El Camino Dr Beverly Hills CA 90212-2704 also: 8530 Wilshire Blvd Beverly Hills CA 90211*

LAKE, SHELLEY, artist; BFA, RI Sch. Design, 1976; MS, MIT, 1979; D of chiropractic, Cleve. Chiropractic Coll. Teacher, aesthetics, Northampton, Mass.; and profl. photographer. Tech. dir.: (films) The Last Starfighter. Recipient three CLIO awards, Nicograph award, Japan, first place, AT&T Image Competition; grantee, Ctr. for Advanced Visual Studies. Office: 116 Pleasant St #1114 Easthampton MA 01027 Office Phone: 413-527-5350. Business E-Mail: drshelleylake@aol.com.

LAKE, SUZANNE, singer, music educator; b. Palisade, NJ, June 26, 1929; d. Mayhew Lester and Suzanne Louise (Robin) Lake; m. George A. De Vos, Nov. 19, 1974. Pvt. tchr., Oakland, Calif., 1976-86, univ. extension U. Calif., Sacramento State U., 1981-84. Featured roles opera, NYC, 1948-51; appeared in Broadway plays The King and I, 1951-54, (TV) History of Musical Comedy with Leonard Bernstein, 1957 (Emmy award 1957), Flower Drum Song, 1960-61; featured singer with Guy Lombardo, 1964-65, Experiencing Music, Expressing Culture, Oxford U. Press; concert and supper club appearances in U.S., Can., Carribbean, Japan, Korea, Taiwan and Europe, 1955-91, recs. include the Soul of Chanson, Potpourri, others; also TV appearances. Mem. Actors Equity, AFTRA, Am. Guild Mus. Artists, Am. Guild Variety Artists. Home: 2835 Morley Dr Oakland CA 94611-2547

LAKE, TINA SELANDERS, artist, educator; b. London, Sept. 12, 1953; came to U.S., 1956; d. Leslie Martin Selanders and Doris Kirk; m. Paul Saunders Lake III, Dec. 30, 1971; children: Rachel, Alexander. BS, Towson State U., 1977; MFA, San Francisco Art Inst., 1980; postgrad., Ark. Arts Ctr., 1985. Teaching asst. Towson State U., Balt., 1977; grad. teaching asst. San Francisco Art Inst., 1979; instr. drawing and painting, summer arts camp, adult drawing Ark. River Valley Art Ctr., Russellville, 1986, instr. beginning drawing for children, painting and drawing, 1991. Vis. instr. U. Ozarks, 1987, Ark. Tech. U., Russellville, 1987; part-time instr. Ark. Tech. U., 1986, vis. lectr., 1982, 83; guest speaker 3d Ann. Young Author's Conf., Ark. Tech. U., 1991; pub. rels. asst. San Francisco Art Inst., 1980; lectr. Berkeley (Calif.) Art Ctr., 1981, Ark. Arts Ctr., 1992; co-juror inaugural art exhbn. Rockefeller Ctr. U. Ark. Petit Jean Mountain, Ark., 2006. Exhibited in group shows at Holtzman Gallery, Balt., 1976, Balt. Arts Festival, 1977, San Francisco Art Inst., 1979, The Woman's Bldg., L.A., 1980, The Goodman Bldg., San Francisco, 1981, Ark. River Valley Arts Ctr., Russellville, 1981, 91, Ark. Arts Ctr., Little Rock, 1985, 86, 89, 91, 92, 93, 94, U. Ark. Fine Arts Ctr. Gallery, Fayetteville, 1986, Ark. Tech. U., 1991, Ark. Territorial Restoration Exhbn., Little Rock, 1992, 93, Russell Fine Arts Ctr., Henderson State U., Arkadelphia, Ark., 1992, 94, Treishmann Gallery Hendrix Coll., Conway, Ark., 1993, Springfield (Mo.) Art Mus., 1994, Ark. Art Ctr., Little Rock, 1995 (Jungkind Photographic Art Material award), Ft. Smith (Ark.) Art Ctr., 1996 (hon. mention), Hist. Ark. Mus., Littlerock, Ark., 2005,; one woman shows: Walton Fine Arts Ctr., U. Ozarks, 1997; represented in Ctrl. Ark. Libr. Sys., and numerous pvt. collections; graphic designer: (design and layout literary mag.) Occident, 1980-81; art adv. (literary mag.) Nebo, 1984-86. Recipient numerous Best of Show awards and Purchase awards. Home: 2802 Honeysuckle Ln Russellville AR 72801-5520 Office Phone: 501-977-2076. Business E-Mail: lake@uaccm.edu.

LA LIBERTE, ANN GILLIS, graphics designer, educator; b. St. Paul, Nov. 10, 1942; d. Edward Robert and Frances Caroline (S.) Gillis; m. Paul Henry La Liberte, Aug. 22, 1964; children: Paul E., Elizabeth La Liberte Collins, Stephen A., Helen La Liberte Gallagher, Peter N., Marc H. Student, Am U., Washington, 1963-64, Cardinal Stritch Coll., Milw., 1960-63; BA, Coll. St. Catherine, St. Paul, 1985. Artist, owner Ann La Liberte Papers and Posters, Minnetonka, Minn., 1968-71, A.L. Graphic Design and Drawings, Minnetonka, Minn., 1987-2001; artist-in-residence Tara Tonka Studio, Minnetonka, 1987-2001, Tara Claire Studio, Gordon, Wis., 2001—. Artist Arts in Schs., Minn., 1985-2001; pvt. art tchr., dir. creativity and problem solving seminars, 1991—. Liturgical design cons. Midwest, 1977—; paintings, drawings, photography and sculpture exhibited Mpls. and St. Paul area, 1983—; sculpture Life Exhibit, Paul VI Inst. for the Arts, Washington, 1988, on tour Vt., Ohio, Mo., Ill., Wis., 1988. Del. Minn. Ind. Reps., 1969, vice chmn. Minnetonka, 1970; promotional artist Soc. for Preservation Human Dignity, Palatine, Ill., 1973, Minn. Citizens Concerned for Life, 1980-88, Secular Franciscans, St. Paul, 1985; deanery rep. Pastoral Coun. Archdiocese of St. Paul and Mpls., 1978-82; chmn. devel. task force out-reach program Resurrection Ch., Mpls., 1980-81, cons. artist, 1983-87; dir. liturg. design ch. of Immaculate Heart of Mary, Minnetonka, 1989-2001; liturgical art and environ. cons. Mem. Nat. Assn. Liturgical Mins., Mpls. Inst. of Arts, Nat. Mus. Women in Arts (charter), Walker Art Ctr., Coll. of St. Catherine Alumna Assn., Artists for Life Nat. Slide Registry, Delta Phi Delta. Roman Catholic. Avocations: art history, environmental protection, gardening, travel, sculpture. Studio: Tara Claire Studio 13709 S Fowler Cir Gordon WI 54838-9039 Personal E-mail: taraclaire01@hotmail.com.

LA LIME, HELEN R. MEAGHER, ambassador; married; 2 children. BS, Georgetown U.; MS, Nat. Def. U. Consul gen., Zurich, Switzerland, 1993; with Bur. Internat. Orgnl. Affairs in Dept. of State, 1993—95; dep. chief of mission U.S. Embassy, N'djamena, Chad, 1996—99, dir. office of ctrl. African affairs, 2000—01, dep. chief of mission Rabat, 2001—03; U.S. amb. to Mozambique, 2002—. Office: DOS Amb 2330 Maputo Pl Washington DC 20521-2330

LALKA, MONICA JEAN, music educator, consultant; b. Melrose Park, Ill., May 18, 1976; d. Jean M. and John P. Lalka. B in Music Edn., Wheaton Coll., Ill., 1994—98. Music/band /choir tchr. Plainfield Dist. 202, Ill., 1999—. Ind. cons. Arbonne Internat., Irvine, Calif., 2006—. Recipient Educator of Yr., PTA, 2002. Office: Lakewood Falls Elem Sch 14050 S Budler Rd Plainfield IL 60544 Office Phone: 815-439-4560. Personal E-mail: harmonica518@yahoo.com. Business E-Mail: mlalka@learningcommunity202.org.

LALONDE, ANGELA J., primary school educator; b. Manistique, Mich., Aug. 31, 1970; d. Ann Marie and Allen Joseph LaVigne; m. Dwayne E. LaLonde, July 29, 1995; children: Brett R., Alex J. B in Elem. Edn., No. Mich. U., Marquette, 2000; MS in Reading and Literacy, Walden U., Minn., 2005. Kindergarten, readiness tchr. Big Bay de Noc Sch., Cooks, Mich., 2002—. Athletic coach Big Bay de Noc Sch., 2002—06. Mem.: Basketball Coaches Assn. Mich., Mich. Edn. Assn. Home: 1268N County Rd 437 Manistique MI 49854 Personal E-mail: ajlalonde@uplogon.com.

LAM, CAROL C., prosecutor, lawyer; b. NY; BA in Philosophy, Yale U., 1981; JD, Stanford U., 1985. Law clk. to Hon. Irving R. Kaufman US Ct. Appeals (2nd cir.), 1985—86; asst. US atty. (so. dist.) Calif. US Dept Justice, 1986—90; chief, major fraud sect. US Dept. Justice, 1997—2000, interim US atty. (so. dist.) Calif., 2002, US atty. (so. dist.) Calif., 2002—; judge Calif. Superior Ct., San Diego, 2000—02. Recipient Spl. Achievement award, US Dept. Justice, 1990—94, 1997—99, Dir.'s award for Superior Performance as an Asst. US Atty., 1994, Health & Human Svc. Inspector Gen.'s Integrity award, 1995, Atty. Gen.'s award for Disting. Svc., 1997, Health & Human Svc. Inspector Gen.'s award for Exceptional Achievement, 1997. Mem.: Stanford Law Sch. bd. visitors, Stanford Alumni Assn. Office: US Attys Office 880 Front St Rm 6293 San Diego CA 92101-8893

LAM, PAULINE POHA, library director; b. Hong Kong, Oct. 21, 1950; came to U.S., 1971; d. Cheung and Kam-Chun (Mo) Li; m. Frank Sung-Lun Lam, Nov. 28, 1973; children: Candace See-Win Lam, Megan See-Kay Lam. BA, U. B.C., 1977; MLS, U. Tex., 1980; cert. City Mgmt. Acad., Austin C.C., 1994; grad., Cedar Park Leadership Class, 2004. Libr. dir. City of Cedar Park (Tex.). Bd. dirs. Cedar Park Pub. Libr. Found., 1994—. Mem. Work Force Literacy Com. Literacy Coun. of Williamson County, 1995, Cedar Park Leadership Class 2004, Williamson County Children's Advocacy Ctr. Bd., 2003; bd. dirs. ARC of Ctrl. Tex., Austin, 1995—97, Williamson County Children's Advocacy Ctr., 2003. Mem. ALA, Tex. Libr. Assn., Tex. Mcpl. League Libr. Dir. Assn. Avocations: reading, crocheting, painting. Office: Cedar Park Pub Libr 550 Discovery Blvd Cedar Park TX 78613-2200

LAMARCA, MARY MARGARET, elementary school educator; b. Pitts., Pa., Feb. 16, 1953; d. James Joseph and Elizabeth Jane LaMarca. BS in Elem. Edn., Slippery Rock U., 1975; MEd, California U. of Pa., 1985. Cert. elem. tchr., adminstr., Md., Pa. Kindergarten and 2d grade tchr. Conchita Espinosa Acad., Miami, Fla., 1975-77; 1st grade tchr. Nativity Sch., Pitts., 1977-80; 1st and 2d grade tchr. Westinghouse-Kori Day Sch., Pusan, Republic of Korea, 1980-82; 5th and 6th grade tchr. Lake Valley Sch., Dept. of Interior, Crownpoint, N.Mex., 1983; 1st and 2d grade tchr. Westinghouse-Philippine Day Sch., Bagac, 1983-84; head tchr. Bechtel Internat.-Kori Day Sch., Republic of Korea, 1984-86, Bechtel Internat.-Korea 7-8 Sch., Republic of Korea, 1986-87; kindergarten tchr. Prince George's Cty., Md., 1987-92, Beginnings II Daycare, Seattle, 1992-93; primary tchr. Ft. Washington Forest, Md., 1993-97, tchr. reading recovery Md., 1997-99, sch. instrnl. specialist Prince George's Cty., Md., 1999—. Republican. Roman Catholic. Avocations: aerobics, quilting, crocheting. Home: 8555 Greenbelt Rd E-4 Greenbelt MD 20770

LAMARCHINA, MARILYNNE MAY, elementary school educator; b. Tustin, Calif., Oct. 11, 1932; d. William Stimson and Elizabeth Myrtle (McCarter) Hatch; m. Robert Antonio LaMarchina (dec.); children: Lisa, Vita, Floria, Adriana. AA, Fullerton Jr. Coll., 1950—52; BA, San Jose State Coll., 1952—54; studied with Philip Zimbardo, Stanford U., Calif., 1984. Elem. tchr. Newport Mesa Dist., Newport Beach, Calif., 1954—67, Dept. Edn., Honolulu, 1968—95, sub. tchr., 1995—2005. Mem. Women's Support Group, Honolulu, 1984—2000. Bd. dirs. Hawaii Philharmonic, Honolulu, 1984. Mem.: Am. Business Women's Assn., Outrigger Canoe Club. Democrat. Avocations: writing, gardening. Home: 44-749 Malulani St Kaneohe HI 96744

LAMARQUE, NATALIE GHISSLAINE, psychologist; b. Aurora, Ill., June 10, 1979; d. Harry and Ginette Lamarque. BA, U. Rochester, 2001; MA, SUNY, Buffalo, N.Y., 2004. Cert. sch. psychologist Nat. Assn. Sch. Psychologists, 2005, lic. psychologist N.C., 2004. Psychologist Gaston County Schs., Gastonia, NC, 2004—05, Wake County Pub. Sch. Sys., Raleigh, NC, 2005—. Home: 2050-314 Brentmoor Dr Raleigh NC 27604 Office: Wake County Public School System 3600 Wake Forest Rd Raleigh NC 27609 Office Phone: 919-266-8454. Personal E-mail: natalie_lamarque@yahoo.com. Business E-Mail: nlamarque@wcpss.net.

LAMB, DARLIS CAROL, sculptor; b. Wausa, Nebr. d. Lindor Soren and June Berniece (Skalberg) Nelson; m. James Robert Lamb; children: Sherry Lamb Sobh, Michael, Mitchell. BA in Fine Arts, Columbia Pacific U., San Rafael, Calif., 1988, MA in Fine Arts, 1989. Exhibitions include Nat. Arts Club, N.Y.C., 1983 (Catherine Lorillard Wolfe award sculpture, 1983, 1997, C.L. Wolfe Horse's Head award, 1994, Anna Hyatt Huntington cash award, 1995, honorable mention, 1996, medal of honor, 1998, 2005, Anna Hyatt Huntington bronze medal, 2000, Paul Manship Meml. award, 2001, Harriet W. Frishmuth Meml. Sculpture award, 2002), 1985, 1989, 1991—93, 1995—97, 1998, 2000—05, 2001, N.Am. Sculpture Exhibit, Foothills Art Ctr., Golden, Colo., 1983—84 (Pub. Svc. Co. of Colo. sculpture award, 1990), 1986—87, 1990—91, Nat. Acad. of Design, 1986, Nat. Sculpture Soc., 1985 (C. Percival Dietch Sculpture prize, 1991), 1991, 1995, 1997, 2003—06, exhibitions include Loveland Mus. and Gallery, 1990—91, Audubon Artists, 1991, Allied Artists Am., 1992, 1995, Pen and Brush, 1993 (Roman Bronze award, 1995), 1995—97, 1999, 2000, 2001, Colorado Springs Fine Arts Mus., 1996 (Award of Merit), 1998, 2000, All Colo. Exhibit, 2001 (1st prize sculpture), Represented in permanent collections Nebr. Hist. Soc., Am. Lung Assn. of Colo., Benson Park Sculpture Garden, Loveland, Space Found., Colorado Springs Osteo. Found., Thomas Jefferson H.S., Council Bluffs, Iowa (Hall of Fame, 2004), one-woman shows include Curtis Arts & Humanities Ctr., Greenwood Village, Colo., 2002. Named to Hall of Fame, Thomas Jefferson H.S., 2004. Mem. Catherine Lorillard Wolfe Art Club, N.Am. Sculpture Soc. Office Phone: 303-779-4527. Personal E-mail: dlambsculpture@usa.net.

LAMB, IRENE HENDRICKS, medical researcher; b. Ky., May 9, 1940; d. Daily P. and Bertha (Hendricks) Lamb. Diploma in nursing, Ky. Bapt. Hosp.; student, Berea Coll., Ky., Calif. State U. L.A. RN, Ky. Charge nurse, head nurse acute medicine, med. ICU, surgical ICU, emergency room various med. ctrs., 1963—67; staff nurse rsch. CCU U. So. Calif./L.A. County Med. Ctr., 1968, nurse mgr. clin. rsch. ctr., 1969—74; sr. rsch. nurse cardiology Stanford U. Sch. Medicine, Calif., 1974—85, rsch. coord. pvt. clin., 1988; dir. clin. rsch. San Diego Cardiac Ctr., 1989—92; sr. cmty. health nurse Madison County Health Dept., Berea, Ky., 1993—97; sr. clin. rsch. mgr. stroke program U. Ky. Coll. Medicine, Lexington, 1997—2001. Contbr. articles to profl. jours., chapters to books. Bd. dirs. Ky. Stroke Assn., 1998—2000. Mem.: Am. Heart Assn. Home: 107 Lorraine Ct Berea KY 40403-1317 Personal E-mail: lambmeadows@msn.com.

LAMB, ISABELLE SMITH, manufacturing executive; b. Charteris, Que., Can., Dec. 14, 1922; arrived in U.S., 1948; d. Gordon R. and Beatrice L. (Dale) Smith; married, Oct. 2, 1948 (dec.); 1 child, David E. Student, Gowling Bus. Coll., Ottawa, Ont., 1939, Carleton U., 1940—42. Sec. Gatineau Power, Ottawa, 1942; sec. to city treas. Ottawa, 1943; sec. Can. Internat. Paper, Gatineau, Que., 1943-48; adminstrv. asst. to C/B Enterprises Internat., Inc., Hoquiam, Wash., 1948-84, pres., 1984—2000, br. chmn., 2001—. Bd. dirs. U.S. Bank Washington, Seattle, Export Assistance Ctr. Wash., Seattle, N.W. Burn Found., Seattle, Wash. Coun. for Econ. Edn., Seattle, Ind. Colls. of Wash., Seattle. Participant spl. gifts United Way, Aberdeen, Wash., 1988—; active scholarships and philanthropic causes E.K. and Lillian Bishop Found., Seattle, 1985—. Avocations: reading, horseback riding. Office: Enterprises Internat Inc Blaine And Firman St Hoquiam WA 98550

LAMB, JO ANN P., geriatrics nurse; b. Glenwood, Ga., Mar. 9, 1947; d. Roy and Lucille (Mercer) Powell; m. Henry Gene Lamb, Dec. 3, 1965 (div. 1984); children: Henry G. Lamb, Jr., Roy, Melinda, Jody; m. Robert Eugene Joyner, June 14, 1991 (div. 1999). Diploma, Swainsboro Vocat./Tech., 1979; student, Ga. So. Coll., 1980. LPN, Ga. Staff nurse Meadows Meml. Hosp., Vidalia, Ga., 1980-82; staff nurse in ICU and critical care unit Toombs Alcohol and Drug Abuse Ctr., Vidalia, 1982-84; charge nurse Conners Nursing Home, Glenwood, Ga., 1984-85; supr. Bethany Nursing Ctr., Vidalia, 1990-92, charge nurse, 1985-92; nurse Claxton (Ga.) Nursing Home, Toombs Nursing and Intermediate Care Home, Lyons, Ga., 1992-93; staff nurse Laurens Convalescent Ctr., Dublin, Ga., 1994, 1994, Meadow Brook Manor, 1994—, Dublin, 1994-95; relief house supr. Dublinair Healthcare and Rehab. Ctr., Dublin, 1995-96; staff nurse Telfair State Prison, 1997—; staff charge nurse, 3-11 house supr. Bethany Nursing Ctr., Vidalia, Ga., 1999—. Mem. ind. nursing registry, Claxton; nurse Meml. Med. Ctr., Savannah, Ga.; office nurse Montgomery County Correctional Inst., Mt. Vernon, Ga., Laurens Convalescent Ctr., 1994-95, Meadowbrook Manor, 1994—; 3-11 relief house supr., supr. medicare spl. unit Gray (Ga.) Nursing Home, 1995-97, 98—, staff nurse. Democrat. Apostolic. Avocations: swimming, walking, singing, dance.

LAMB, JULIE WALSH, elementary school educator; b. Martinsville, Va., Dec. 27, 1976; d. Richard Nelson and Betty Baptist Walsh; m. Kevin Wade Lamb, May 10, 1977; children: Mason Charles, Marshall Walsh. BS in Child Devel., Meredith Coll., Raleigh, NC, 1999. Lic. tchr. Va., 1999. Tchr. Franklin City Pub. Schs., Franklin, Va., 2000—. Mem.: Va. Edn. Assn. Home: 22486 Scojo Dr Franklin VA 23851 Office: Franklin City Pub Schs Franklin VA 23851 Personal E-mail: jawlamb@yahoo.com.

LAMB, M. ELIZABETH, athletic trainer; d. Buck and Margaret E. Windham; m. Derek M. Lamb, May 17, 2003. BS in Sports Medicine and Athletic Training, Valdosta State U., Ga., 2002. Cert. athletic trainer 2002. Cert. athletic trainer Rehab. Svcs. of Tifton, Ga., 2002—04, Doctors Hosp., Augusta, Ga., 2004—. Mem.: Nat. Athletic Trainers Assn. Office: Doctors Hospital Sports Medicine 3624 J Dewey Gray Cir Ste 302 Augusta GA 30909 Office Phone: 706-651-2218. Office Fax: 706-651-2271. E-mail: elizabeth.lamb@hcahealthcare.com.

LAMB, PATSY (PAT) LEE, retired adult education educator, real estate broker; b. Verona, Mo., Oct. 19, 1936; d. Ernest Salee and Ethel Violet (Bougher) Haddock; m. Keith O'Neil Lamb, Dec. 28, 1959; children: Kenneth O'Neil, David Lee, Patricia Ann, Charles Keith. BS in Edn., Mo. Univ., 1958. Cert. in adult edn. Mo., life tchg. cert. in vocat. home econs. Mo., temporary elem. tchg. cert. N. Mex. Vocat. home economics. tchr. Sanders (Ariz.) H.S., 1958—60; tchr.-guidance Lukachukai, Ariz., 1960—62; dir. Office Navajo Econ. Opportunity Pre Sch., Ramah, N.Mex., 1966; kindergarten, 2d grade tchr. Ramah (N. Mex.) Pub. Schools, 1967—71; substitute tchr. Albuquerque (N. Mex.) Pub. Schools, 1973—75, Independence, Lee's Summit, Mo., 1978; broker, co-owner Century 21 Real Estate, Denver, 1981—88; adult edn. tchr. Crowder Coll., Neosho, Mo., 1988—2004; ret. Substitute tchr. Excelsior Youth Ctr. for Troubled Girls, Denver, 1981; outreach dir. First Baptist Ch., Albuquerque, 1975—78, acting children's dir., 1977; ch. sec. Oakwood Baptist Ch., Lee's Summit, Mo., 1980—81; organist Gospel Lighthouse Baptist Ch., condr. children's worship svc. Recipient Mo. Disting. Adult Basic Edn. Svc. award, 1998. Republican. So. Baptist.

Achievements include development of a program to involve several churches in the area in outreach called "Know Your Neighbor". Avocations: gardening, sewing, piano, organ. E-mail: keithpat@centurytel.net.

LAMB, STACIE THOMPSON, elementary school educator; b. Abilene, Tex., Nov. 9, 1965; d. George Lyman and Shirley Elizabeth (Burton) T.; m. Dennis A. Lamb; children: Lane, Logann. BS in Edn., Lubbock Christian Coll., 1986; postgrad., Tex. Tech U. Elem. Edn. grades 1-6, Tex. 1st grade tchr. Lubbock Ind. Sch. Dist. Brown Elem., Tex., 1986—87; 3rd grade tchr., chairperson Morton Ind. Sch. Dist., 1987—89; 5th grade lang. arts tchr. Whiteface Consolidated Ind. Sch. Dist., 1990—98; pre-kindergarten tchr. White Consolidated Ind. Sch. Dist., 1998—2003; tchr. 1st grade Lubbock Ind. Sch. Dist., 2003—. Mem. ASCD, Classroom Tchrs. Assn. (sec. 1988-89, elem. rep. 1991-92). Office: PO Box 117 Whiteface TX 79379-0117 Home: 5212 CR 7350 Lubbock TX 79424

LAMB, TERYANA R., secondary school educator; b. Texas City, Tex., Oct. 8, 1974; d. Frederick W. and Sophia L. Lamb; 1 child, Meshach Z. Sullivan. BA in Biology, U. Houston, Clear Lake, 1998—99. Cert. Tchr., Secondary Edn. Tex. Edn. Agy., 2002. Tchr. Milby HS, Houston, 1999—. Lead tchr. Milby HS, Houston, 2003—. Office: Milby HS 1601 Broadway Houston TX 77012 Office Phone: 713-928-7401. Business E-Mail: tlamb@houstonisd.org.

LAMBACHER, KATHLEEN HARTWELL, retired education educator; b. Muskegon, Mich., Aug. 7, 1935; d. Shattuck Wellman and Kathleen Beatrice; m. Allen H. Lambacher; children: Philippe Pezet, Anne-Marie Pezet Dorfner. BA in History, Wheaton Coll. Tchr. history Lincoln Sch., Providence, 1957—59; sub. tchr. Forest Hills Jr. HS, 1968—70; legal asst. Rankin Thompson Hine and Flory, Cleve., 1977—83; cons. Mary Kay Cosmetics, 1984—92; with Squires Constrn. Co., 1997—99; tchr.-trainer Chinese tchrs. English Shanghai, 2003, Fouling, 2004, Harbin, China, 2005; ret., 2005. Co-dir. Le Cercle Francais d'Amerique, 1964—75; tchr. ESL New Sch. Social Rsch., NYC, 1969; translator Berlitz Schs. of Lang. of Am., Inc., Cleve., 1983; ESL tchr. Wives of Diplomats. Mem. Hudson League Svc., Cleve. Town Com.; diplomat Terra Em-Pachen UN Hospitality Com.; moderator Diaconite First Presbyn. Soc., Cleve. Mem.: Philanthropic Ednl. Orgn. (chaplain), French Heritage Soc. (chpt. v.p. 2005—), Soc. Mayflower Descendants, Wheaton Coll. Alumni Assn. (R.I. state pres. 1963—65), Col. Dames Am. in State of Ohio. Avocations: bicycling, kayaking, gardening, bridge, French and German languages. Home: 70 S Hayden Pkwy Hudson OH 44236 Personal E-mail: klambacher@windstream.net.

LAMBERSON, CAROLYN JANE HINTON, music educator; b. Wake County, N.C., Feb. 1, 1939; d. Avon Battle and Ollie (Lewis) Hinton; m. Dale Allen Lamberson, Aug. 22, 1964; 1 child, David Allen. MusB, East Carolina Coll., 1961; MusM, Ind. U., 1963. Tchr. piano Smithfield Pub. Schs., NC, 1963, Mars Hill Coll., NC, 1963—. Home: PO Box 296 77 Woodland Dr Mars Hill NC 28754 Office: 138 Moore Auditorium Smithfield NC Office Phone: 828-689-1209. Business E-Mail: clamberson@mhc.edu.

LAMBERT, CHRISTINA, telecommunications executive; b. Panama; m. Jim Lambert; children: Bill, Christine, Monica. BA in bus. mgmt., Ind. U.; M in bus. adminstrn., Ind. Wesleyan U. Joined Contel (merged with GTE in 1991), 1974; asst. v.p. process planning GTE, asst. v.p. customer care; v.p., gen. mgr. wireline svcs. PR Telephone, 1999—2003, pres., CEO, 2003—.

LAMBERT, DEBORAH KETCHUM, public relations executive; b. Greenwich, Conn., Jan. 22, 1942; d. Alton Harrington and Robyna (Neilson) Ketchum; m. Harvey R. Lambert, Nov. 23, 1963 (div. 1985); children: Harvey Richard Jr., Eric Harrington. BS, Columbia U., 1965. Researcher, writer The Nowland Orgn., Greenwich, Conn., 1964-67; model Country Fashions, Greenwich, Conn., 1964-67; freelance writer to various newspapers and mags., 1977-82; press sec. Va. Del. Gwen Cody, Annandale, Va., 1981-82; assoc. editor Campus Report, Washington, 1985—; adminstrv. asst. Accuracy in Media, Inc., Washington, 1983-84, dir. pub. affairs, 1985—. TV producer weekly program The Other Side of the Story, 1994-2004; editor Why You Can't Trust the News; bd. dirs. Accuracy in Academia, Washington; film script cons. The Seductive Illusion, 1988-89. Columnist: The Eye, The Washington Inquirer, 1984—, Squeaky Chalk, Campus Report, 1985—; contbr. articles to various mags.; producer: The Other Side of the Story, 1993—. Co-founder, mem. Va. Rep. Forum, McLean, 1983—; mem. Rep. Women's Fed. Forum. Mem. Am. Bell Assn., Pub. Rels. Soc. Am., DAR., World Media Assn., Am. Platform Assn. Republican. Presbyterian. Home: 809 Gatestone St Gaithersburg MD 20008 Office: Accuracy in Media Inc 4455 Connecticut Ave NW Washington DC 20008-2328 E-mail: DLam530483@aol.com.

LAMBERT, EMILY JENKINS, elementary school educator; b. Nashville, May 11, 1977; d. Gerald Freeman and Jane Jenkins Lambert. BS in Multidisciplinary Studies, Tenn. Technol. U., Cookeville, 1999; MA in Instructional Leadership, Tenn. Technol. U., 2000. Cert. level 5 tchg. cert. 1-8. Grad. asst. Tenn. Technol. U., Cookeville, 1999—2000; tchr. Cobb County Schs., Marietta, Ga., 2000—. Tutor Cobb County Schs., Marietta, Ga., 2002—, mem. tech. com., 2005—06. Mem. Jr. League Cobb-Marietta, 2002—; vol. Wellstar Hosp., Marietta, 2003—04; children's ch. tchr. Hillside United Meth. Ch., Woodstock, Ga., 2005—06. Named Lost Mountain Tchr. of the Yr., Cobb County Schs., 2005, Ga. Sci. Tchr. of Promise, Ga. Sci. Tchrs. Assn., 2003; grantee Edn. for a Sustainable Future grantee, Cobb County Schs., 2002—03. Mem.: Nat. Sci. Tchrs. Assn., Phi Delta Kappa. Methodist. Avocations: reading, gardening, travel. Office: Lost Mountain Middle School 700 Old Mountain Rd Kennesaw GA 30152

LAMBERT, JOAN DORETY, elementary school educator; b. Trenton, N.J., Oct. 21, 1937; d. John William and Margaret (Fagan) Dorety; m. James E. Lambert Sr., June 25, 1960; children: Margi, Karen, James E., Kevin. BA, Georgian Ct. Coll., Lakewood, N.J., 1958. Cert. tchr., Pa., N.J. Tchr. 2d and 3d grades combined Washington Elem. Sch., Trenton, 1958-61; tchr. kindergarten music St. Genevieve Sch., Flourtown, Pa., 1968-78, tchr. 3d grade, 1978—. Producer, dir. musical shows for St. Genevieve Sch., 1970-78; demonstration classroom for writing process on computers Chestnut Hill Coll. Mem. Jr. League of Trenton, 1960-68, Jr. League of Phila., 1968-70. Teleflex Internat. grantee, 1989-92, Anna B. Stokes Meml. scholar, 1960, Met. Opera grantee, 1958-60. Mem. NEA. Republican. Roman Catholic. Avocations: walking, theater, reading, swimming. Office: St Genevieve Sch 1237 Bethlehem Pike Flourtown PA 19031-1902 Home: 604 Horseshow Dr Chester View Apts Royersford PA 19468

LAMBERT, JUDITH A. UNGAR, lawyer; b. NYC, Apr. 13, 1943; d. Alexander Lawrence and Helene (Rosenson) Ungar; m. Peter D. Leibowits, Aug. 22, 1965 (div. 1971); 1 child, David Gary. BS, U. Pa., 1964; JD magna cum laude, U. Miami, 1984. Bar: NY 1985, Fla. 1990. Assoc. Proskauer Rose Goetz & Mendelsohn, NYC, 1984—86, Taub & Fasciana, NYC, 1986—87, Hoffinger Friedland Dobrish Bernfeld & Hasen, NYC, 1987—88; pvt. practice NYC, 1988—. Mem. ABA, NY State Bar Assn., Assn. Bar City of NY, NY Women's Bar Assn. (family law and trusts and estates com.), NY County Lawyers Assn. Avocations: travel, music, theater. Office: 245 E 54th St New York NY 10022-4707 Office Phone: 212-888-7727. E-mail: jalesq1@aol.com.

LAMBERT, MEG STRINGER, construction executive, architect, interior designer; b. Selma, Ala., Aug. 10, 1941; d. John Bryant and Margaret Vandiver (Clark) Stringer; m. George Edward Buchner, June 30, 1962 (div. 1972); children: Susan Mayo Buchner, George Bryant Buchner, Robert Carson Buchner; m. Joseph Smith Lambert, June 20, 1975. BS, Auburn U., 1961, postgrad., 1972-73. Lic. real estate broker Ala., home builder Ala., master builder cert. Nat. Assn. Home Builders, cert. constrn. assoc. Nat. Assn. Women in Constrn. Math tchr. Selma (Ala.) Pub. Sch., 1961-62, Oscoda (Mich.) Pub. Sch., 1963-64; real estate sales Stower's Gallery of Homes, Montgomery, Ala., 1974-75; constrn. mgr. Lambert Constrn. Co., Inc., Montgomery, 1975-80, home builder, designer Prattville, Ala., 1984—; sec. estimating dept. Aesco Steel Co., Montgomery, 1981-82; steel bridge estimator and sales assoc. Trinity Industries, Montgomery, 1983-84; pres. Home Touch Builders, Inc., 2000—. Chmn. parade homes Prattville/Millbrook chpt. Home Builders, 1985—87, program chmn., 1985—90; masonry adv. bd. Prattville Vocat. Sch., Prattville, 1994—2001. Author: (book) A History of the Pleasant Hill Baptist Church (1840-1990), 1990. Vice-chmn. Prattville Planning Commn., 1992—95; mem. land use com. City Comprehensive Plan, Prattville, 1994—95; mem. leadership steering com. Autagua County, 1995—98, bd. equalization, 1995—99; chmn. health and welfare com. 1st United Meth. Ch., 1993; mem. beautificiation com. Prattville C. of C., 1992—95; pres. Pleasant Hill Cemetary Assn., 1990—98, 2000—02, South Dallas Hist. Preservation Assn., 2002—. Named Woman of the Yr., Montgomery chpt. Nat. Women in Constrn., 1990. Mem.: Greater Montgomery Home Builders Assn. (mem. longe range planning com. 1986, bd. dirs., exec. com. 2001, Named Builder of the Yr. 1989), Autauga County Heritage Assn. (pres. 1992). Republican. Avocations: genealogy, painting, historical preservation activities, working in political campaigns. Home: 394 Kingston Ridge Rd Prattville AL 36067-1725 Office: Lambert Construction Co Inc PO Box 680656 Prattville AL 36068-0656

LAMBERT, VICKIE ANN, retired dean, nursing consultant; b. Hastings, Nebr., Oct. 28, 1943; d. Victor E. and Edna M. (Hein) Wagner; m. Clinton E. Lambert, Jr., June 30, 1974; 1 child, Alexandra. Diploma, Mary Lanning Sch. Nursing, 1964; BSN, U. Iowa, 1966; MSN, Case Western Res. U., 1973; DNSc, U. Calif., San Francisco, 1981. RN, Ga. Acting chair dept. nursing adminstrn. Med. Coll. Ga., Augusta, 1982-84, coord. doctoral program nursing, 1984-85, George Mason U., Fairfax, Va., 1986-88; assoc. dean Case Western Res. U., Cleve., 1989-90; dean Sch. Nursing Med. Coll. Ga., Augusta, 1990-2001, Internat. vis. prof., 2001—. Contbr. articles to profl. jours. Fellow Am. Acad. Nursing; mem. ANA, Sigma Theta Tau Home: 8608 Wandering Fox Trail Unit 403 Odenton MD 21113 E-mail: Vlambert@mcg.edu.

LAMBERT, WILLIE LEE BELL, mobile equipment company owner, educator; b. Texas City, Tex., Oct. 23, 1929; d. William Henry and Una Oda (Stafford) Bell; m. Eddie Roy Lambert, July 2, 1949; (dec. Mar. 1980); children: Sondra Kay Lambert Bradford, Eddie Lee. Degree in bus., Met. Bus. Coll., 1950; AAS, Coll. of Mainland, 1971; BS, Sam Houston U., 1976. Cert. hand and foot reflexologist, Hatha Yoga instr. Sec. Judges Reddell & Hopkins, Texas City, 1945-47, Union Carbide Chemicals, Texas City, 1947-48, John Powers Modeling, 1948—49, Charles Martin Petroleum, Texas City, 1948-50; acct. Goodyear Co., La Marque, Tex., 1968-70; instr. Coll. of the Mainland, Texas City, 1970—, serials libr., 1970-77, instr., 1970; exec. dir., office mgr. Mobile Air Conditioning, La Marque, 1977-80; owner Kivert, Inc., La Marque, 1982—; ptnr., exec. dir. A/C Mobile Equipment Corp., La Marque, 1988—94. Owner Star Bell Ranch, 1985—. Vol. Union Carbide Chems., Texas City, 1970—, Carbide Retiree Corp., Inc., Texas City, 1980—, Hospice, Galveston, Tex., 1985—, various polit. campaigns, Texas City, 1951-62, MD Anderson Cancer Inst., U. Tex., 1995—; v.p. Coalition on Aging Galveston County, Tex. City, 1990-92; vol. Baylor Coll. Medicine, Houston, 1990—; mem. adv. coun. bd. Galveston County Sr. Citizens, Galveston, 1990—; mem. planning bd. Heart Fund and Cancer Fund, Texas City, 1953-62, Santa Fe (Tex.) St. Citizens, 1990—; benefactor mem. Mainland Mus., Texas City, Tex., 1994—; sec. YMCA, 1947-55; sec. Ladies VFW, 1950-59; leader Girl Scouts Am., 1958-65; v.p. PTA, 1957-60; counselor Bapt. Ch. Camp, 1960-64; v.p. Santa Fe Booster Club, 1963-67; mem. Internat. Platform Assn., 1995—. Named Vol. of Yr., Heights Elem. Sch., Texas City Sch. Dist., 1959, Most Glamorous Grandmother, 1985, Mother of Yr., Texas City/La Marque C. of C., 1990, Unsung Hero award Texas City, 1995, 96, 97, 99, 2001-04; named to Tex. Women's Hall of Fame, 1984. Mem. Internat. Platform Assn. Republican. Baptist. Avocations: making porcelain dolls and soft sculpture dolls, painting china portraits, sewing, needlecrafts, volunteer work. Home: PO Box 1253 Santa Fe TX 77510-1253

LAMBERTI, MARJORIE, retired social studies educator; b. New Haven, Sept. 30, 1937; d. James and Anna (Vanacore) L. BA, Smith Coll., 1959; MA, Yale U., 1960, PhD, 1965. Prof. history Middlebury Coll., Vt., 1964—84, Charles A. Dana prof., 1984—2002, ret., 2002, full-time scholar, 2002—. Author: Jewish Activism in Imperial Germany, 1978, State, Society and the Elementary School in Imperial Germany, 1989, The Politics of Education: Teachers and School Reform in Weimar Germany, 2002; mem. editl. bd.: History of Edn. Quar., 1992—94; contbr. articles to profl. jours. Mem. exec. com. Friends of Smith Coll. Librs., 1995—2001. NEH fellow, 1968-69, 81-82, Inst. for Advanced Study, Princeton, 1992-93, The Woodrow Wilson Ctr., Washington, 1997-98; German Acad. Exch. Svc. rsch. grantee, 1988, Rockefeller Archive Ctr. rsch. grantee, 2003. Mem. Am. Hist. Assn., Conf. Group for Ctrl. European History, Leo Baeck Inst., Phi Beta Kappa. Home: 8 S Gorham Ln Middlebury VT 05753-1002 Office: Middlebury Coll Library Middlebury VT 05753 E-mail: Lamberti@middlebury.edu.

LAMBETH, JUDY (E. JULIA LAMBETH), lawyer; b. Winston-Salem; m. Jerry L. McAfee. BA in English, Hollins U., 1973; JD, Wake Forest U., 1977. Atty. focused primarily on environmental issues DuPont, 1977—92, asst. gen. counsel Conoco Houston, 1992, lead atty. environmental, safety and health regulatory and litigation counsel, 1993—97, assoc. gen. counsel, mng. dir. Asia-Pacific region Hong Kong, 1997—2001; corp. sec., deputy gen. counsel Conoco Inc., 2001—02; corp. sec., deputy gen. counsel corp. services ConocoPhillips, 2002—06; exec. v.p., gen. counsel Reynolds American Inc., Winston-Salem, NC, 2006—, R.J. Reynolds Tobacco Co., Winston-Salem, NC, 2006—. Bd. dirs. Child Advocates, Houston. Mem.: NC Bar Assn. Office: Reynolds American PO Box 2990 Winston Salem NC 27102-2990*

LAMBRECH, RÉGINE M., academic administrator, language educator; b. White Plains, NY, Nov. 21, 1950; arrived in France, 1978; d. Matthew André and Winifred Dorothy (Blaney) L. BA, Ladycliff Coll., 1972; MA, Pa. State U., 1975, PhD, 1985. Tchg. asst. Pa. State U., University Park, Pa., 1972-78; vis. prof. French and English U. Lyon (France) II, 1978-79; asst. prof. French and English U. Lyon III, 1979-83; assoc. prof. French and English École Centrale de Lyon, Écully, France, 1983-2000, dir. internat. rels., 1989-2000; dir. internat. edn. Quinnipiac U., Hamden, Conn., 2000—03; head cons. Internat. Edn. Consulting, New Fairfield, Conn., 2003—. Cons. internat. rels. U. Timisoara, Romania, 1995, Rector of Poly. U. Lodz, Poland, 1993, U. Warsaw, 1994, Rector of U. Salford, Eng., 1991-92, European Commn.'s Task Force for Human Resources, Edn. and Youth, 1995-2000; adv. bd. humanities dept. U. Salford, 1990—; presenter and invited spkr. in field at various confs. and workshops; bd. dirs. Rhone-Alpes Internat. Enterprises, Lyon Internat. Mem. editl. bd. Jour. Profl. Studies, 1996—, Internat. Jour. of Leadership in Edn., 1998—, Jour. for Acad. Leadership, 2000—; book and manuscript reviewer Lang. Planning and Lang. Learning Jour., 1992—; book manuscript reviewer on 2d lang. acquisition, Cambridge U. Press, 1992—; contbr. articles to profl. jours. and conf. procs. Chair New Fairfield Youth Commn., 2001—; bd. dirs. Healing the Children Northeast, 2005—; dir. youth leadership program New Fairfield. Recipient Disting. Alumna award Pa. State U., 1996, Irena Galewska-Kielbasinski award, Tech. Univ. Darmstadt, Germany, 1993, Outstanding People of the 20th Century, 1998, Women of Achievement, 2002, Outstanding Intellectuals of the 21st Century, 2002, Cambridge Biog. Soc.; named Erasmus scholar in residence, French Dept. Trinity College, Dublin, Ireland, 1991; recipient Tchr. of Yr. award Nat. Conservatory of Arts and Profns., 1991. Mem. MLA, NAFSA, Assn. Internat. Educators (overseas ednl. advisors spl. interest group), European Assn. Internat. Edn. (chair internat. rels. mgrs. sect. 1989-94, mem. study abroad and fgn. student advisors/langs. for ednl. mobility profl. sects.; elected bd. lang. educators, chair working group on intercultural issues 1996-98, chair ICT Group), Union des Profs. de Langues Étrangéres dans les Grandes Écoles (internat. commn.), Internat. Soc. Intercultural Edn., Tng. and Rsch., Lyon Assn. Dirs. Internat. Rels. (bd. dirs. 1996-2000), Lions Club Internat., Pa. State U. Alumni Club of France (founder, pres. 1985-2000), Phi Sigma Iota, Alpha Mu Gamma, Phi Kappa Phi, Phi Beta Delta. Roman Catholic. Avocations: reading, sports, crafts, volunteer work. Home and Office: 6 Bayview Ter New Fairfield CT 06812-3402 Office Phone: 203-746-1074. Personal E-mail: reginelambrech@juno.com.

LAMBRIGHT, MARILYN, elementary school educator; b. Bklyn., N.Y., Sept. 17, 1940; d. Anthony Joseph and Betty N. Aragona; m. Hayden Lambright, May 26, 1978; 1 child, Russell;children from previous marriage: Peter Trunk, Michael Trunk. BA, Coll. of Mt. St. Vincent, Riverdale, N.Y., 1962; MA, CUNY, 1978. Tchr. Pub. Schs. Dist. 102, Bklyn., 1962—67, Pub. Schs. Dist. 90, Richmond Hills, 1971—77, Pub. Schs. Dist. 199, N.Y.C., 1977—87, Walterboro H.S., SC, 1987—92, Ruffin Mid. Sch., Ruffin, SC, 1992—. Site coord. after sch. program 21st Century Cmty. Learning Ctr., Smoaks, SC, 2000—03; dir. summer sch. Ruffin Mid. Sch., 1999—. Grantee, Impact II grantee, 1981—82. Mem.: United Fedn. Tchrs., S.C. Edn. Assn. Avocations: reading, gardening, walking. Office: Ruffin HS 155 Patriot Ln Ruffin SC 29475 Office Phone: 843-562-2291.

LAMEL, LINDA HELEN, professional society executive, retired insurance company executive, lawyer, arbitrator, retired college president; b. NYC, Sept. 10, 1943; d. Maurice and Sylvia (Abrams) Treppel; 1 child, Diana Ruth Sands. BA magna cum laude, Queens Coll., 1964; MA, NYU, 1968; JD., Bklyn. Law Sch., 1976. Bar: N.Y. 1977, U.S. Dist. Ct. (3d dist.) N.Y. 1977. Secondary sch. tchr. Farmingdale Pub. Sch., NY, 1965-73; curriculum specialist Yonkers Bd. Edn., Yonkers, 1973-75; program dir. Office of Lt. Gov., Albany, 1975-77; dep. supt. N.Y. State Ins. Dept., N.Y.C., 1977-83; pres. CEO Coll. of Ins., 1983-88; v.p. Tchr.'s Ins. and Annuity Assn., 1988-96; exec. dir. Risk and Ins. Mgmt. Soc., 1997-2000; CEO Claims on Line, Inc., 2000—02; adj. assoc. prof. Bklyn. Law Sch., 2005—. Bd. dirs. Universal Am. Fin. Corp. Contbr. articles to profl. jours. Campaign mgr. lt. gov.'s primary race, NY State, 1974; v.p. Ednl. Found., 1997-2000; bd. dirs. Greater NY coun. Boy Scouts Am., 2006—. Mem. ABA (tort and ins. sect. com. chmn. 1985-86), N.Y. State Bar Assn. (exec. com. ins. sect. 1984-88), Assn. of Bar of City of N.Y. (chmn. med. malpractice com. 1989-91, ins. law com. 1997-98), Am. Mgmt. Assn. (ins. and risk mgmt. coun.), Am. Soc. Workers Compensation Profls. (bd. dirs. 1999—), Fin. Women's Assn., Assn. Profl. Ins. Women (bd. dirs. 2002—04, Woman of Yr. 1988), Bklyn. Law Sch. Alumni Assn. (pres.), Phi Beta Kappa Assocs. (bd. dirs. 1992—2002). Office Phone: 212-371-8257. Personal E-mail: artemisbeach@yahoo.com.

LAMERE, MELISSA JO, biomechanics educator; b. Plattsburgh, NY, Mar. 2, 1982; d. Randy David and Lynn Doran LaMere. BS, SUNY, Brockport, 2004; MS, SUNY, Cortland, 2006. Cert. tchr. phys. edn. NY. Prof. biomechanics SUNY, Cortland, 2004—. Mem.: AAHPERD, Am. Coll. Sports Medicine. Office Phone: 651-753-2966. Personal E-mail: mel12star@yahoo.com. Business E-Mail: lamere25@cortland.edu.

LAMI, JUDITH IRENE, advertising executive; b. St. Louis, Nov. 4, 1949; d. Melvin Charles William and Mildred Neva (Kayhart) Linders; m. William George Tomkiel, Dec. 15, 1972 (div.); children: Soteara Tomkiel, William Tomkiel, Kimberli Tomkiel Fitts, Jennifer Tomkiel Allen, Christopher Tomkiel; m. Craig Harmon Lami, Apr. 22, 2003; stepchildren: Mike, Brian, Justin, Amber. Order filler Baker & Taylor Co., Sommerville, N.J., 1972-74; owner, founder Idea Shoppe, Garden Grove, 1983-90; seamstress, crafts person Cloth World, Anaheim, Calif., 1987-89; mgr. S.M.T. Dental Lab., San Clemente, Calif., 1990-94, pres., 1994—; founder, owner Creative Realm, Creative Printing, Etc., North Franklin, Mo., 2005—. Author: numerous poems; pub., editor: newsletter Shoppe Talk, 1987—90; editor: Perfectional Smiles, 1999; pub.: Fakatale, 1988. Vol. Reading is Fundamental Program, Garden Grove, 1988—89; freedom writer Amnesty Internat., Garden Grove, 1988—91. Fellow: World Lit. Acad.; mem.: NAFE, Dental Lab Owners Assn., Soc. Scholarly Pub., Nat. Writer's Club, Women, Inc. Avocations: sewing, writing, music, printmaking, gardening. Personal E-mail: judy_lami@yahoo.com.

LAMIAUX, RITA, pre-school educator, secondary school educator; b. Fargo, ND, Oct. 13, 1973; d. David and Marlys Bald; m. Greg LaMiaux; children: Haley, Dustin. BS in Secondary Edn., Western Mont. Coll., Dillon, 1995, AS in Early Childhood Edn., 2002. Dir., owner Kiddie Korner Early Learning Child Care and Preschool, Butte, 1998—; secondary bus. tchr. Butte H.S., Butte, Mont., 1998—2006; info. tech. instr. Mont. Tech. U. Mont., Butte, 2006—. Child care mentor Mont. Early Childhood Bur., Butte, 2004—. Grantee, Best Beginnings Mont. Early Childhood, 2004—06. Mem.: Nat. Assn. Family Child Care, Nat. Assn. Edn. of Young Children (pres. SW Mont. chpt. 2004—). Avocations: travel, photography, scrapbooking. Home: 3119 Bayard St Butte MT 59701 Office: Mont Tech U Mont 5 Basin Creek Rd Butte MT 59701

LAMKIN, CELIA BELOCORA, physician; b. Dinalupihan, Bataan, Philippines, Mar. 10, 1957; d. Crispiniano Tumulac and Rufina Paule Belocora; m. Ronald Phillip Lamkin, Feb. 14, 1997; children: Jericho Belocora Santos, John Raymond Belocoro Sablan. BS in Biol. Scis., U. Philippines, Manilla, 1978; MD, De La Salle U., Cavite, Philippines, 1984; post grad. in Occupl. Health and Safety, Coll. Pub. Health U. Philippines, Manila, 1989. Cert. physician Profl. Regulation Commn., Philippines, 1986, specialist in assistive tech. Calif. State U., Northridge, 2003. Intern U. Philippines, Philippines Gen. Hosp, Manila, 1984—85; physician Cainta Rural Health Ctr., Cainta Rizal, 1986; cons. and med. examiner Anthony Med. Clinic, Manila, 1987—88; med. examiner Insular Life Ins. Co., Makati City, 1988—93; co. physician M. Greenfield Garment Factory, Paranaque City, 1989, Drugmakers Laboratories, Inc., Paranaque City, Philippines, 1989; pvt. practice gen. practitioner Ermita, Manila and Cainta Rizal, 1986—93; HIV/ADS specialist and program coord. Pub. Sch. Sys., Saipan, Commonwealth No. Marianas Islands, 1995—96; human svcs. provider Philippine Consulate, Saipan, 1996—97; assistive tech. program coord. Coun. on Devel. Disabilities, 1997—2003; counselor and disability svcs. coord. No. Marianas Coll., 2003—05; temp. disability ret., 2005—. Workshop condr. disabilities and assistive tech.; vis. cons. Med. Ctr. Manila, 1988—91; translator U.S. Dist. Ct., 2002—05; spkr. in field. Vol. HIV instr. Am. Red Cross, first aid and CPR instr. Recipient cert. appreciation, No. Marianas Coll., 2005, Gov.'s Coun. Devel. Disabilities, Commonwealth No. Marianas Islands, 1998, 2003, Organizing Com. Internat. Biophilia Rehab. Acad., Philippines, 2004, Ho. Reps. Commonwealth No. Marianas Islands, 2004, Saipan and No. Islands Mcpl. Coun., 2004. Mem.: AMA, Internat. Biophilia Rehab. Acad. (cert. appreciation 2004), Biophilia Rehab. Acad. Japan, Am. Diabetes Assn., U. Philippines Alumni Assn. Roman Catholic. Avocations: piano, organ, cooking. Home: PO Box 7497 Saipan MP 96950-7497

LAMKIN, MARTHA DAMPF, lawyer, foundation administrator; b. Talladega, Ala., May 20, 1942; d. Keith J. and Neva (Magness); m. E. Henry Lamkin Jr., Aug. 24, 1968; children: Melinda Lamkin Magaddino, Matthew Davidson. BA in English summa cum laude, Calif. Baptist U., 1964; MA in English and Am. Lit., Vanderbilt U., 1966; JD, Ind. U., 1970. Bar: Ind. 1970. Assoc. Joseph D. Geeslin, Indpls., 1971-72, Lowe, Gray, Steele & Hoffman, Indpls., 1976-82; field office mgr. U.S. Dept. Housing and Urban Devel., Indpls., 1982-87; exec. dir., corp. rep. responsibility and govtl. affairs Cummins Engine Co., Inc., Columbus, Ind., 1987-91; exec. v.p. corp. advancement USA Group, Inc., Indpls., 1991-2000; pres., CEO, bd. dirs. USA Group Found., Inc., 2000-2001; CEO, pres., bd. dirs. Lumina Foundation for Education Inc., 2001—. Pres., bd. dirs. Cummins Engine Found., 1989-91; bd. dirs. Meridian Mut. Ins. Co., Indpls., USA Group, Inc., USA Group Loan Svcs., Inc., United Student Aid Funds, 1994-2000; bd. dirs. Citizens Gas & Coke Utility, Inc., vice chair, 1990-, bd. dirs. Coun. on Founds., 2005-. Commr., sec., chmn. Indpls. Human Rights Commn., 1971-79; commr. Indpls. Housing Authority, 1979-82; chmn. exec. com. S.K. Lacy Exec. Leadership Alumni, Indpls., 1986-87; chmn. Ind. Leadership Celebration, Indpls., 1985-87; sec. Gov.'s Mansion Commn., Indpls., 1981-89; bd. dirs. Great Indpls. Progress Commn., 1986-87, Indpls. Symphony Orch., 1983-89, 98-99, Indpls. Project, 1986-91, Ind. Fiscal Policy Inst., 1998-2003, Ind. Colls. Ind., 1997-2000; bd. dirs., sec. COMMIT, Inc., COMMIT Found., 1990-97; chmn. bd. trustees Christian Theol. Sem., Indpls., 1983-93; hon. gov. Richard C. Lugar Excellence Pub. Svc. Series, 1990—; chair, 1997,

2003, trustee Indpls. Found., 1992-2003; mem. exec. com. Mayor's Task Force on Housing, 1987, exec. com., Ind. Sports Corp., 1997-2000; sec., bd. dirs. Indpls. Econ. Devel. Corp., 1997-2000; chair, dir. Ctrl. Ind. Cmty. Found., 1998-2003; mem. Hoosier Capitol Girl Scouts Adv. Bd., 1996-2002. Recipient Presdl. Rank award 1985, Mental Health Initiative Gov. Ind., 1986, Matrix award Women in Communication, 1987, Women in the Lead Indpls. Bus. Journ. 1999, Outstanding Alumni award, Ind. U. Sch. Law-Indlps., 2000; named Hon. Dr. Christian Theol. Sem. 1999. Mem. State Assembly Women (pres. 1977-79), Indpls. Jr. League, Indpls. C. of C. (bd. dirs. 1986-87). Mem.(Disciples Of Christ). Office: Lumina Found for Edn 30 S Meridian Ste 700 Indianapolis IN 46204*

LAMM, CAROLYN BETH, lawyer; b. Buffalo, Aug. 22, 1948; d. Daniel John and Helen Barbara Lamm; m. Peter Edward Halle, Aug. 12, 1972; children: Alexander P., Daniel E. BS, SUNY Coll. at Buffalo, 1970; JD, U. Miami, 1973. Bar: Fla., 1973, D.C., 1976, N.Y. 1983. Trial atty. frauds sect. civil div. U.S. Dept. Justice, Washington, 1973-78, asst. chief comml. litigation sect. civil div., 1978, asst. dir., 1978-80; assoc. White & Case, Washington, 1980-84, ptnr., 1984—. Mem. Sec. State's Adv. Com. Pvt. Internat. law, 1987—; arbitrator US Panel of Arbitrators, Internat. Ctr. Settlement Investment Disputes, 1994-02, Uzbekistan, 2003-; mem. com. on pvt. dispute resolution NAFTA Mem. editl. adv. bd. Inside Litigation; contbg. editor: Internat. Arbitration Law Rev., 1997—; contbr. articles to legal publs. Mem. Holy Trinity Parish Coun., 1998—2001. Fellow Am. Bar Found., Am. Coll. Trial Lawyers; mem. ABA (chmn. young lawyers divsn. 1982-83, bd. govs. 2002-05, chair opers. com., exec. com., rules and calendar com., chmn. house membership com., chmn. assembly resolution com., sec. 1984-85, chmn. internat. litigation com. coun. 1991-94, sect. litigation, ho. dels. 1982—, nomination com. 1984-87, chair 1995-96, D.C. Cir. mem. 1992-95, standing com. fed. judiciary 1992-95, chmn. com. scope and correlation of work 1996-97, commn. on multidisciplinary practice, bd. govs. 2002-, steering com. 2005-, state del. D.C., co-chair ABA Day, state del. 2005—), Am. Arbitration Assn. (bd., arbitrator, adv. com. internat. arbitration, exec. com.), Fed. Bar Assn. (chmn. sect. on antitrust and trade regulation), Bar Assn. D.C. (bd. dirs., sec., found. bd.), D.C. Bar (pres. 1997-98, bd. govs. 1987-93, steering com. litigation sect., found. bd. 2001—), Am. Law Inst. (coun.), Women's Bar Assn. D.C. (Woman Lawyer of Yr. 2002), Am. Soc. Internat. Law (co-chair Interest Group Dispute Resolution), Am. Indonesian C. of C. (bd. dirs.), Am. Uzbekistan C. of C. (bd. dirs., v.p., gen. counsel), Am. Turkish Friendship Coun. (bd. dirs.), Women's Forum, Columbia Country Club, Manchester Country Club, Stratton Mountain Club. Democrat. Office: White and Case 701 13th St NW Washington DC 20005-3807 Business E-Mail: clamm@whitecase.com.

LAMONT, LEE, music company executive, communications executive; b. Queens, N.Y. m. August Tagliamonte, Apr. 30, 1951; 1 child, Leslie Lamont. With Nat. Concerts & Artists Corp., N.Y.C., 1955-58; asst. Sol Hurok Concerts, N.Y.C., 1958-67; person rep. for concerts, rec. and TV Isaac Stern, N.Y.C., 1968-76; v.p. ICM Artists Ltd., N.Y.C., 1976-85; pres. ICM Artists Ltd. and ICM Artists (London) Ltd., N.Y.C., 1985-95, chmn. bd. dirs., 1995—2002, chmn. emeritus, 2002—. Former mem. adv. com. Hannover (Germany) Internat. Violin Competition. Former mem. bd. overseers Curtis Inst. Music. Mem. Ams. for the Arts, Japan Soc., Asia Soc., Am. Symphony Orch. League (bd. dirs.), Bohemian Club. Avocations: painting, sculpture. E-mail: llamont@icmtalent.com.

LAMONT, MARILYN LAREE CLAUDEL, reading specialist, accountant; b. Cedar, Kans., July 19, 1931; d. James Vincent and Edythe Faye (Scott) Claudel; m. Charles J. Lamont, Feb. 7, 1950; children: Charles E., James F., Melinda G. Schnoes. BA in History, No. Adams (Mass.) State Coll., 1969, MS in Edn., 1971; reading and psychology student, Ft. Hays (Kans.) U., 1970, 71, 72. Cert. reading specialist, sch. psychologist, histry, spl. needs. Elem. tchr. Willimastown (Mass.) Pub. Schs., 1970-72; reading tchr. Lanesboro (Mass.) Elem. Sch., 1972-82, elem. tchr., 1982-89, reading specialist, 1989—; ret., 1996. Presenter in field. Auditor, acct. Town of New Ashford, Mass., 1984-86, treas., 1986—, tax collector, treas., 1987—. Mem. Berkshire Reading Coun. (pres. 1982-84), Mass. Reading Assn., Internat. Reading Assn. Congregationalist. Avocations: reading, knitting, sewing, gardening.

LAMONT, ROSETTE CLEMENTINE, language educator, journalist, translator; b. Paris; arrived in US, 1941, naturalized, 1946; d. Alexandre and Loudmilla (Lamont) L. BA, Hunter Coll., 1947; MA, Yale U., 1948, PhD, 1954. Tutor Romance langs. Queens Coll., CUNY, 1950-54, instr., 1954-61, asst. prof., 1961-64, assoc. prof., 1965-67, prof., 1967-96; mem. doctoral faculties, comparative lit., theatre, French and women's studies cert. program CUNY, 1968-96, prof. emeritus PhD program in theater, 1996—. State Dept. envoy Scholar Exch. Program, USSR, 1974; rsch. fellow, 1976; lectr. Alliance Francaise, Maison Francaise of NYU; vis. prof. Sorbonne, Paris, 1985-86; vis. prof. theatre Sarah Lawrence Coll., 1994—. Author: The Life and Works of Boris Pasternak, 1964, De Vive Voix, 1971, Ionesco, 1973, The Two Faces of Ionesco, 1978, Ionesco's Imperatives: The Politics of Culture, 1993, Women on the Verge, 1993; translator: Days and Memory, 1990, Auschwitz and After, 1995 (ALTA prize), Brazen, 1996, The Storm, 1999; also contbr. to various books; author, guest editor The Metaphysical Farce issue Collages and Bricolages, 1996-97; mem. editl. bd. Western European Stages, also contbg. editor; European corr. Theatre Week: Columbia Dictionary of Modern European Literature; fgn. corr. Stages; reviewer France-Amérique-Le Figaro. Decorated chevalier, then officier des Palmes Academiques, officier des Arts et Lettres (France); named to Hunter Coll. Hall of Fame, 1991; Guggenheim fellow, 1973-74; Rockefeller Found. humanities fellow, 1983-84. Mem. PEN, MLA, Am. Soc. Theatre Research, Internat. Brecht Soc., Drama Desk (voting mem.), Internat. Assn. Theatre Critics, Phi Beta Kappa, Sigma Tau Delta, Pi Delta Phi. Clubs: Yale. Mailing: 683 Main St PO Box 568 Falmouth MA 02541-0568

LA MONT, TAWANA FAYE, camera operator, video director, foundation administrator; b. Ft. Worth, May 12, 1948; d. Jerry James and Roberta Ann (Wilkinson) La M. AA, Antelope Coll., 1979; BA in Anthropology, UCLA, 1982. Forest technician, trail constrn. supr. Angeles Nat. Forest, Region 9 U.S. Forest Svc., Pear Blossom, Calif., 1974-79; trail constrn. supr., maintenance asst. Calif. State Parks, 1979-81; cable TV installer Sammons Comm., Glendale, Calif., 1981-83, camera operator, 1983-87; video studio and ENG remotes dir., mgr., program mgr. channel 6 Sammons Cable, Glendale, Calif., 1981-97; video dir., prodr. LBW & Assocs. Internat., Ltd., 1988—; pres., CEO Chamblee Found., Ltd., 1995—. Mem. ednl. access channel satellite program evaluation com., Glendale and Burbank, 1990-92; mem. Foothill Cmty. TV Network, Glendale and Burbank, 1987-95. Prodr., dir. (homeless video) Bittersweet Streets, 1988; dir., camera operator, 1988—; editor over 1000 videos. Active Glendale Hist. Soc., 1992-96; bd. dirs. Am. Heart Assn., 1992-96, comms. chair; exec. om., bd. dirs. ARC, 1993—, mem. disaster svcs. team, cultural diversity chair, 1994-95, exec. com. sec., 1998—; mem. mktg. com. Burbank YMCA, 1994-96; bd. dirs. Glendale Rose Float Assn., 1995-99, pub. chmn., 1997-98; bd. dirs., rec. sec. Glendale Symphony Orch. Assn., 1998—. Recipient awards of appreciation LBW and Assocs. Internat., 1988, Bur. Census, 1990, USMC, 1991, Verdugo Disaster Recovery Project, 1995, ARC, 1995, 96, 97, 98, 99, 2000, 01, ARC Spl. citation for exceptional vol. svc., 1995, award of outstanding pub. svc. Social Security Adminstrn. HHS, 1989, dedicated svc. award Am. Heart Assn., 1992, cert. of appreciation, 1994, 95. Mem. NAFE, NRA, Internat. Alliance Theatrical Stage Employees, Moving Picture Technicians, Artists and Allied Crafts, Internat. Cinematographic Guild (local 600), Am. Women in Radio and TV, Am. Bus. Women Assn., Internat. Pvt. Investigators Union, UCLA Alumni Assn. (life), Wildlife Waystation, Alpha Gamma. Avocations: photography, animals, flying, sailing, travel. Office: PO Box 800 Lake Hughes CA 93532-0800 Office Phone: 818-749-4512. E-mail: chambleefoun@mindspring.com.

LAMONTAGNE, CAROLE HEGLAND, retired art educator; b. Greensburg, Pa., July 28, 1948; d. Edward Carl and Emma Louise (Bitner) Hegland; m. Roger Gerard Lamontagne, July 31, 2001. BA with high honors, Seton Hill Coll., Greensburg, Pa., 1970; MEd with high honors, U. Pitts., Pa., 1980. Advt. specialist, Pitts., 1970—75; visual merchandiser Macys, NYC, 1975—79; curator Salem Crossroads Hist. Soc., Delmont, Pa., 1979—81; instr. sculpture Seton Hill U., Greensburg, Pa., 1970—71; assoc. dir. Recreation Bd. City Greensburg, Pa., 1981—83; tchr. art Greater Latrobe Sch. Dist., Latrobe, 1983—2006, Baggaley and Latrobe Elem. Sch., Latrobe, Latrobe Sr. H.S., Pa., 2004—05; ret., 2006. Recipient Outstanding Creativity award, Seton Hill Coll., 1969, 1970. Mem.: Pa. State Edn. Assn. Avocations: music, gourmet cooking, French language, interior design.

LAMONT-GORDON, MELISSA LYNNE, orchestra director, music educator; b. Elmhurst, Ill., Aug. 1, 1965; d. Lawrence Michael and Lynne Laughlin Lamont; m. Steven Howard Gordon, July 19, 1992. Attended, Carnegie-Mellon U., 1983—85; MusB, U. Pitts., 1986; post grad., Va. Commonwealth U., 1992—93, Ohio State U., Columbus, 1997, Ind. U., Bloomington, 2004. Cert. in Music Edn. Va. Commonwealth U., Advanced Placement Music Theory Instr. Ind. U. Orch. dir. Henrico County Schs., 1992—94, Hanover County Schs., 1994—98; dir. orchs., chamber ensembles Clover Hill HS, Chesterfield County Schs., 1998—, advisor student coun. assn., 2000—02. Dir. all county orchs. Chesterfield County Schs., 1997; dir. youth concert orch. Richmond Symphony Young Performers Program, 2003—05; Celtic and pedal harpist; music festival judge; guest condr., composer, arranger. Named Gov.'s Sch. Outstanding Educator, 2005. Mem.: Music Educator's Nat. Conf., Va. Band and Orch. Dir. Assn. Home: 8535 Chester Forest Ln Richmond VA 23237 Office: Clover HS 13900 Hull St Rd Midlothian VA 23112 Office Phone: 804-739-6230. E-mail: Melissa_Gordon@ccpsnet.net.

LAMORTE, JOYCE E., music educator; b. Buffalo, June 8, 1962; d. Wayne A. and Eva M. Dodge; m. David S. LaMorte, Aug. 12, 1995. BFA in Music Edn., SUNY, Amherst, NY, 1985; MA in Music Edn., Penn. Sate U., State Coll., 1989. Cert. music edn. NY, piano adjudicator. Choral/music tchr. Belfast Ctrl. Sch., NY, 1985—87; grad. assistantship music edn. Penn. State U., 1987—89; choral music tchr. Tangier Smith Elem. Sch., Mastic Beach, NY, 1989—99, The Michael J. Petrides Sch., SI, NY, 1999—. Coop. tchr. for music student tchrs. The Michael J. Petrides Sch., SI, 1999—2005; music edn. elem. edn. Wagner Coll., SI, 2001—; music edn. facilitator NYC Dept. Edn., 2002—; elem. edn. adj. lectr. Coll. SI, 2002—; NYSSMA piano adjudicator NY State Sch. Music Assn., LI, 2003—; music edn. cons. Arts Connection, NYC, 2005—06; choir dir. vocal instrn. SI Ballet Summer Inst, 2006. Asst. minister Trinity Luth. Ch., SI, 2002—, flower deliverer to shut-ins, 2003—. Mem.: Music Educator's Assn. NYC, LI Am. Orff schalwerk Assn., NYS Sch. Music Assn. Avocations: horseback riding, reading, exercise, bowling.

LAMOTHE, JOANNE LEWIS, library director, consultant; b. Boston, Mass., Nov. 24, 1956; d. William H and Virginia R Lewis; m. Joseph R. Lamothe, Apr. 21, 1979; children: Cameron Joseph, Devon Virginia, Jordan William. BA in commn., Bridgewater State Coll., 1974—78; MLIS, U. of RI, 1995—2000. Cert. of Librarianship Mass. Bd. of Libr. Commissioners, 2000. Corp. sec. Scituate Fed. Savs. and Loan Assn., Scituate, Mass., 1979—84; libr. Duxbury Free Libr., Duxbury, Mass., 1984—94, libr. dir., 1994—2000; dir. of libr. services Weymouth Pub. Libraries, Weymouth, Mass., 2000—. Pres. Old Colony Libr. Network, Braintree, Mass., 1999—2000; clk. Southeastern Mass. Libr. Sys., Lakeville, Mass., 2002—04; pres. New Eng. Libr. Assn., Gloucester, Mass., 2004—; v.p., pres. elect Southeastern Mass. Libr. Sys., Lakeville, Mass., 2005—. Mem.: Mass. Libr. Assn., New Eng. Libr. Assn., Pub. Libr. Assn., Am. Libr. Assn. Home: 40 Mill Pond Lane Duxbury MA 02332 Office: Weymouth Pub Libraries 46 Broad St Weymouth MA 02188 Office Phone: 781-337-1402. E-mail: jlamothe@ocln.org.

LAMOTTA, CONNIE FRANCES, public relations executive; b. Bronx, N.Y., Oct. 10, 1942; d. Salvatore Charles and Mary Moscatiello LaMotta; children: Raphael, Peter, David. BA, SUNY, Albany, 1969. Activities coord. San Diego Assn. for the Retarded, 1970-72; edn. program dir. Edn. Ctrs. of Newark Archdiocese, 1973-79; dir. comm. tng. Riverside Eating Disorder Clinic, Secaucus, N.J., 1979-84; comm. coord. Sun Chem. Corp., N.Y.C., 1984-86; pub. rels. dir. Nat. Coffee Assn., N.Y.C., 1986-87; v.p. pub. rels. comms. Direct Mktg. Assn., N.Y.C., 1987-99, sr. v.p. pub. rels. comms., 1987-99; pres. La Motta Strategic Comms., Inc., Nyack, NY, 1999—. Office Phone: 845-358-6301. Personal E-mail: conniela@mac.com.

LAMOTTE, JANET ALLISON, retired management consultant; b. Norfolk, Va., Mar. 3, 1942; d. Charles Nelson Jr. and Geneva Elizabeth (Baird) Johnson; m. Larry LaMotte, Aug. 30, 1964 (div. Aug. 1979); children: Lisa Renee LaMotte Buchholz, Lori Louise. AA, Rose State Coll., 1982; BA, U. Ctrl. Okla., 1984; MA in Human Rels., U. Okla., 1986. Clk./typist U.S. Army, Washington, 1960, Fort Belvoir, Va., 1961, Dallas, 1961, IRS, Dallas, 1962, Richmond, Va., 1962—63, sec., 1963—64; pers. asst. State Bd. Control, Austin, Tex., 1964—65; procurement clk. FAA, Oklahoma City, 1965—66; clk./typist DLA, Alexandria, Va., 1978, IRS, Oklahoma City, 1978—79, clk./stenographer, 1980—81; sec., Tinker AFB, 1979; acctg. clk., 1980—81; clk./stenographer, 1980—81; sec., 1981—82; supply specialist, 1982—87; worldwide inventory mgmt. specialist, 1987—98. Safety chmn. Kensler Elem. Sch. PTA, Wichita, 1974-75; vol. CONTACT Crisis Helpline, 1986-89. Federally Employed Women scholar, 1984. Mem.: AARP, AAUW, Tinker Mgmt. Assn. (membership, ticket monitor 1994—98, scholar 1981—85), Okla. Air Force Assn. (v.p. comm. 1995—97, exec. sec. 1996—97, Okla. Mem. of Yr. 1996, Nat. Exceptional Svc. award 1996), Air Force Assn. (v.p. pub. rels. Gerrity chpt. 1994, v.p. comm. 1995—98, Nat. medal of Merit 1995, Nat. Exceptional Svc. award 1996, Chpt. Exceptional Svc. award 1998), Nat. Assn. Ret. Fed. Employees, Am. Bus. Women's Assn. (v.p. membership downtown reflections chpt. 1992—93), Nat. Women's History Mus. (charter mem.), Nat. Air Force Meml. (charter), Wythe County Hist. and Gen. Assn., Okla. Geneal. Soc., Nat. WWII Meml. (charter), Okla. Hist. Soc., Toastmasters (edn. v.p. 1988, pres. Tinker chpt. 1989, area gov. 1991—92, area editor K-3 Newsletter 1992—93, awards), Rural Retreat Hist. Soc., Morrow County Geneal. Soc., Pulaski County Hist. Soc., Nat. Trust for Hist. Preservation. Methodist. Avocations: history, writing, genealogy, computers, reading. Home: 9525 Ridgeview Dr Oklahoma City OK 73120-3419 Personal E-mail: jlamott99@msn.com.

LAMOUREUX, GLORIA KATHLEEN, nurse, consultant, retired military officer; b. Billings, Mont., Nov. 2, 1947; d. Laurits Bungaard and Florence Esther (Nielsen) Nielsen; m. Kenneth Earl Lamoureux, Aug. 31, 1973 (div. Feb. 1979). BS, U. Wyo., 1970; MS, U. Md., 1984. Staff nurse, ob-gyn DePaul Hosp., Cheyenne, Wyo., 1970; enrolled USAF, 1970, advanced through grades to col.; staff nurse ob-gyn dept. 57th Tactical Hosp., Nellis AFB, Nev., 1970-71, USAF Hosp., Clark AB, Republic Philippines, 1971-73; charge nurse ob-gyn dept. USAF Regional Hosp., Sheppard AFB, Tex., 1973-75, staff nurse ob-gyn dept. MacDill AFB, Fla., 1976-79; charge nurse ob-gyn dept. USAF Med. Ctr., Andrews AFB, Md., 1979-80, MCH coord., 1980-82; chief nurse USAF Clinic, Eielson AFB, Alaska, 1984-86, Air Force Systems Command Hosp., Edwards AFB, Calif., 1986-90; comdr. 7275th Air Base Group Clinic, Italy, 1990-92, 42d Med. Group, Loring AFB, Maine, 1992-94; 347th Med. Group, Moody AFB, Ga., 1994-96; chief nursing svcs. divsn. Hdqrs. Air Edn. and Tng. Command, Randolph AFB, Tex., 1996-2000. Ind. cons. Customers First Cons., Universal City, 2000—, v.p., 2000—; sr. cons. Karta Tech., Inc., San Antonio, 2002—. Mem. Assn. Women's Health, Obstetric, and Neonatal Nurses (sec.-treas. armed forces dist. 1986-88, vice-chmn. armed forces dist. 1989-91), Air Force Assn., Bus. and Profl. Women's Assn. (pub. rels. chair Prince George's County chpt. 1981-82), Sigma Theta Tau. Republican. Lutheran. Avocations: reading, needlecrafts, piano, photography. Home: 383 Indigo Run Bulverde TX 78163 Office Phone: 210-365-3015. Business E-Mail: glamoureux@gvtc.com.

LAMPELA, LAUREL ANN, art educator; b. Superior, Wis., Oct. 15, 1952; d. Eugene Paul and Viola Alvina (Efraimson) L. BS, U. Wis., Madison, 1975; MEd, Wright State U., 1988; PhD, Ohio State U., 1990. Commd. 2d lt. USAF, 1979, advanced through grades to capt., ret., 1989; tchr. art Queen of Apostles High Sch., Madison, 1976-79; art specialist Springfield (Ohio) City Schs., 1983-87; teaching asst. Wright State U., Dayton, Ohio, 1987-88; rsch., teaching asst. Ohio State U., Columbus, 1988-89; asst. prof. Marshall U., Huntington, W.Va., 1990-91, Cleve. State U., 1991—2001; asst. prof. art edn. U. N.Mex., 2001—02, assoc. prof. art edn., 2002—. Advisor Student Orgn. for Visual Arts, Cleve., 1991-2001; program coord. art edn. U. N.Mex., 2005-06. Contbr. articles to ednl. jours. Rsch. grantee Cleve. State U., 1991, grantee Gund Found., 1992, Women's Community Found., 1992. Mem. Nat. Art Edn. Assn. (caucus for social theory), Women's Caucus for Art, Ohio Art Edn. Assn., Ohio Women's Caucus for Art. Avocation: running. Home: 4931 Pershing Ave SE Albuquerque NM 87108-3531 Office: U NMex Masley Hall Rm 205 Albuquerque NM 87131

LAMPERT, ELEANOR VERNA, retired human resources specialist; b. Porterville, Calif., Mar. 23; d. Ernest Samuel and Violet Edna (Watkins) Wilson; m. Robert Mathew Lampert, Aug. 23, 1935; chidren: Sally Lu Winton, Lary Lampert, Carol R. John. Student in bus. fin., Porterville Jr. Coll., 1977-78; grad., Anthony Real Estate Sch., 1971; student, Laguna Sch. of Art., 1972, U. Calif., Santa Cruz, 1981. Bookkeeper Porterville (Calif.) Hos., 1956-71; real estate sales staff Ray Realty, Porterville, 1973; sec. Employment Devel. Dept. State of Calif., Porterville, 1973-83; orientation and tng specialist CETA employees, 1976-80; ret. Sec. Employer Adv. Group, 1973-80, 81—. Author: Black Bloomers and Han-Ga-Ber, 1986. Mem. U.S. Senatorial Business Adv. Bd., 1981-84, Rep. Nat. congl. Com., 1982-88, Sierra View Hosp. Vol. League, 1988-89 (pres.); charter mem. Presdl. Republican Task Force, 1981—, Republican National Committee; vol. Calif Hosp. Assn., 1983-89, Calif. Spl. Olympics Spirit Team, Sonora Cmty. Hospital Oak Plus League, Special Olympics Northern Calif. partner. Recipient Merit Cert., Gov. Pat Brown, State of Calif., 1968. Mem. Lindsay Olive Growers, Sunkist Orange Growers, Am. Kennel Club, Internat. Assn. Personnel in Employment Security, Calif. State Employes Assn. (emeritus Nat. Wildlife Fedn., NRA, Friends of Porterville Library, Heritage Found., DAR (Kaweah chpt. rec. sec. 1988—), Internat. Platform Assn., Dist. Fedn. Women's Clubs (recording sec. Calif. chpt. 1988—), Ky. Hist. Soc., Women's Club of Calif. (pres. Porterville chpt. 1988-89, dist. rec. sec. 1987-89), Mo. Rep. Women of Taney County, Internat. Sporting and Leisure Club, Ladies Aux, VFW (No. 5168 Forsyth,Mo.), Ozark Walkers League, Women of the Moose Lodge, Humane Soc. U.S., History Channel Club. Republican.

LAMPHERE, BARBARA L., construction executive; b. Rochester, Dec. 15, 1945; d. Ermelinda Angelina Parsons; m. Fred Warner Jr., Oct. 12, 1996; m. Robert J. Lamphere (div.); children: Nathan W., Eric C. BA, Nazareth Coll., 1967. Vol. VISTA, Marshall, Tex., 1967—69; cmty. organizer Cayuga County Action Program, Auburn, NY, 1969—72; exec. dir., founder Cayuga County Homsite Devel. Corp., Auburn, 1972—87; v.p. devel. Two Plus Four Constrn. Co., East Syracuse, 1988—. Founder, mem., former bd. dirs. N.Y. State Rural Housing Coalition, Albany, NY, 1979—; bd. dirs. N.Y. State Rural Adv., Albany, 1981—. Mem.: Nat. Low Income Housing Coalition, Counc. for Affordable Rural Housing, Nat. Rural Housing Coalition. Democrat. Roman Catholic. Avocations: singing, horseback riding, reading, antiques, travel. Office: Two Plus Four Constrn Co 6320 Fly Rd East Syracuse NY 13057 Office Phone: 315-437-1808. Personal E-mail: lamwarn@verizon.net.

LAMPL, ANNIE WAGNER, psychotherapist; b. Vienna, Oct. 27, 1917; came to U.S., 1939; d. Carl and Martha (Frankl) Wagner; m. Josef Lampl, Jan. 26, 1939; children: John W., Lanny J. MS in Psychology, Goddard U., 1968. Lic. marriage, family, child counselor, Calif. Counselor Epihap Industry, L.A., 1963-68; sr. counselor Braille Inst., L.A., 1969—93. Counselor Visually Handicapped of the Valley, L.A., 1971—, So. Calif. Counseling Ctr., L.A., 1971—; vol. counselor Felicia mahood Sr. Ctr., 1993-2002. Recipient Penney Vol. award, 1990, Vol. award State of Calif., 1991. Mem. Analytical Psychology Club, Jung Inst.

LAMPL, PEGGY ANN, public information officer; b. N.Y.C., Dec. 12, 1930; d. Joseph and Alice L. BA, Bennington Coll., 1952. Dir. program devel. dept. mental health AMA, Chgo., 1962-66; spl. asst. NIMH, HEW, Washington, 1967-69; public relations dir. LWV, Washington, 1969—73, exec. dir., 1973—78; dep. asst. Sec. of State for congressional relations Dept. State, Washington, 1978-81; dep. dir. Iris Systems Devel., 1982-83; exec. dir. Children's Def. Fund, Washington, 1984-89, LWV, Washington, 1989—90; project mgr. Crimes of War, W.W. Norton, 1999; founder Project Vote Smart, Washington, 1993—; bd. dirs. Crimes of War Project, Washington, 1998—. Home: 2500 Q St NW Washington DC 20007-4373

LANAM, LINDA LEE, lawyer; b. Ft. Lauderdale, Fla., Nov. 21, 1948; d. Carl Edward and Evelyn (Bolton) L. BS, Ind. U., 1970, JD, 1975. Bar: Ind. 1975, Pa. 1979, U.S. Dist. Ct. (no. and so. dists.) Ind. 1975, U.S. Supreme Ct. 1982, Va. 1990. Atty., asst. counsel Lincoln Nat. Life Ins. Co., Ft. Wayne, Ind., 1975-76, 76-78; atty., mng. atty. Ins. Co. of N.Am., Phila., 1978-79, 80-81; legis. liaison Pa. Ins. Dept., Harrisburg, 1981-82, dep. ins. commr., 1982-84; exec. dir., Washington rep. Blue Cross and Blue Shield Assn., Washington, 1984-86; v.p. and sr. counsel Union Fidelity Life Ins. Co., Am. Patriot Health Ins. Co., etc., Trevose, Pa., 1986-89; v.p., gen. counsel, corp. sec. The Life Ins. Co. Va., Richmond, 1989-97, sr. v.p., gen. counsel, corp. sec., 1997-98, also bd. dirs.; v.p., dep. gen. counsel Am. Coun. Life Insurers, Washington, 1999—. Chmn. adv. com. health care legis. Nat. Assn. Ins. Commrs., 1985-87, chmn. long term care, 1986-87, mem. tech. resource com. on cost disclosure and genetic testing, 1993-98; mem. tech. adv. com. Health Ins. Assn. Am., 1986-89; mem. legis. com. Am. Coun. Life Ins., 1994-96, mem. market conduct com., 1997-98. Contbr. articles to profl. jours. Pres. Phila. Women's Network, 1980—81; chmn. city housing code bd. appeals Harrisburg, 1985—86; bd. dirs. Shakespeare Theatre Guild, 2001—. Mem. ABA, Richmond Bar Assn. Republican. Presbyterian.

LANARO, CLARA MARRAMA, music educator, writer; b. Aquila, Abruzzi, Italy, Oct. 26, 1920; came to U.S., 1946; d. Daniele Marrama and Giovanna Galli; children: Severo, Francesco, Augusto, Goffredo, Ginerva, Manlio, Oberto, Clara. BA in organ, Liceo Musicale Luisa D'Annunzio, Pescara, Italy, 1939; degree in music, Scuola Statale di Musica Luisa D' Annunzio, Pescara, Italy, 1942. Tchr. undergrads. Scuola Statale Di Musica & D'Annunzio Pescara, 1942—43; tchr. piano Liceo Musicale Luisa D'Annunzio, Pescara, Italy, 1943, San Francisco, 1948-51, U.S., Northwest Africa, 1954-61. Author: Time Signature in Super Games, The Grand Staff XL, The Staff XL, The Grand Staff XL Book I, Book II (Private/Class), The Staff XL Book I, Book II (Private/Class), Music for Piano Volume I-II, Rhythms and Insufficient Rhythms, From Games to Songs, Amplified, 2003; patentee Musical Toy Teaching Device, Directly on the Keyboard, 1972, 2000. Achievements include patents for Super Learning; a music-teaching device which shows a student of piano exactly the keys to reproduce each note on the grand staff and where notes written on the grand staff belong on the keyboard. Avocations: languages, reading. Home: Apt 1 1183 Ayala Dr Sunnyvale CA 94086-5734

LANCASTER, JEANETTE (BARBARA LANCASTER), dean, nursing educator; BSN, U. Tenn.; MSN, Case Western Res. U.; PhD, U. Okla. Staff nurse U. Tenn.; nurse clinician Univ. Hosps. of Cleve.; assoc. prof. psychiat. nursing Tex. Christian U.; coord. cmty. health nursing U. Ala., Birmingham, chair master's degree program Sch. Nursing; dean, prof. Sch. Nursing Wright State U., Dayton, Ohio; now dean, prof. nursing U. Va., Charlottesville; assoc. dir. patient care svcs. U. Va. Health Scis. Ctr., Charlottesville. Former chmn. bd. dirs. Va. Statewide Area Health Edn. Ctr.; former pres. Charlottesville and Albemarle divsn. Am. Heart Assn.; presenter in field. Author: Community and Public Health Nursing: Nursing Issues in Leading and Managing Change; editor: Family and Cmty. Health; contbr. Bd. dirs. U. Va. Women's Ctr., Hospice of the Piedmont. Recipient Disting. Alumni award Frances Payne Bolton Sch. Nursing, Case We. Res. U., 1984, Outstanding Alumni award, U. Tenn. Coll. Nursing, 1985, honored with establishment of Jeanette Lancaster Professorship in Nursing, 1999. Fellow: Am. Acad. Nursing; mem.: Am. Assn. Colls. Nursing (pres. elect). E-mail: lancaster@virginia.edu.

LANCASTER, JENNIFER NICOLE, athletic trainer, educator; d. Clayton Lee and Dorothy Anne Lancaster. BS in Edn., East Ctrl. U., Ada, Okla., 2001; MS, SE Mo. State U., Cape Girardeau, 2003; postgrad., Tex. Woman's U., Denton, 2005—. Cert. tchr. Okla., 2001. Grad. asst. athletic trainer SE Mo. State U., 2001—03; asst. athletic trainer, instr. Midwestern State U., Wichita Falls, Tex., 2003—05, dir. athletic tng. edn., 2005—, chmn. dignified lecture series, 2005—; faculty sponsor Sharing Profession of Athletic Tng., Wichita Falls, 2006—. Contract athletic trainer Breland Health & Fitness, Wichita Falls, 2003—05; athletic trainer St. Jo HS, Tex., 2005—06; presenter in field. Vol. Adopt-A-Hwy., Wichita Falls, 2006—. Mem.: SW Athletic Trainers Assn. (student rsch. and edn. com. 2005—), Nat. Athletic Trainers Assn. (cert.). Avocations: outdoor activities, reading. Office: Midwestern State U 3410 Taft Blvd Wichita Falls TX 76308

LANCASTER, JOAN ERICKSEN, judge; b. 1954; BA magna cum laude, St. Olaf Coll., Northfield, Minn., 1977; spl. diploma in social studies, Oxford U., 1976; JD cum laude, U. Minn., 1981. Atty. LeFevere, Lefler, Kennedy, O'Brien & Drawz, Mpls., 1981-83; asst. U.S. atty. Dist. Minn., Mpls., 1983-93; shareholder Leonard, Street and Deinard, Mpls., 1993-95; dist. ct. judge 4th Jud. Dist., Mpls., 1995-98; assoc. justice Minn. Supreme Ct., 1998—2002; judge U.S. Dist. Ct., St. Paul, 2002—. Office: US District Court 316 N Robert St Saint Paul MN 55101

LANCASTER, KARINE R., retired city health department administrator; b. Australia; MPH, U. Tex. Health Sci. Ctr., Houston, 1994. Pvt. practice, pediatrician, Dallas, 1978—; med. dir., health authority Dallas Co. Dept. Health and Human Svcs., Dallas, 1997—2004.

LANCASTER, KIRSTEN KEZAR, psychologist; b. Lincoln, Nebr., May 22, 1964; d. Edward Fraze and Lois Paulson Kezar; m. John Talmadge Lancaster, June 20, 1987. BSBA, High Point U., N.C., 1985; MBA, Am. U., Washington, 1987; MA, Pepperdine U., Malibu, Calif., 1991; MS, Nova Southeastern U., Ft. Lauderdale, Fla., 1995; PsyD, Nova Southeastern U., Ft. Lauderdale, 1999. Lic. psychologist N.C. Asst. coord., rsch. asst. child trauma program Nova Southeastern U. Cmty. Mental Health Ctr., Ft. Lauderdale, 1995—96, psychology resident, 1998—99; evening counselor The Renfrew Ctr., Coconut Creek, Fla., 1996—98, postdoctoral psychology resident, 1999—2000; psychologist pvt. practice Raleigh, NC, 2003—04; psychologist Holly Hill Hosp. Crisis and Assessment, Raleigh, 2003—05; sr. psychologist Wake County Human Svcs., Raleigh, 2000—05; psychologist Harbin & Assocs., 2005—. Grants com. mem. Susan G. Komen Breast Cancer Found., 2003—05; planning com. mem. WCHS Pink Ribbon Campaign, Wake County, NC, 2004—05; rschr., editor Breast Cancer Resource Directory N.C., 2004—; contbr. domestic violence legis. NC, 2004—05. Mem.: APA, N.C. Psychol. Assn. Methodist. Avocations: walking, reading, travel. Office Phone: 910-609-1990. Business E-Mail: klancaster@harbinandassociates.com.

LANCASTER, SALLY RHODUS, retired non-profit executive, consultant; b. Gladewater, Tex., June 28, 1938; d. George Lee and Milly Marie (Meadows) Rhodus; m. Olin C. Lancaster, Jr., Dec. 23, 1960; children: Olin C. III, George Charles, Julie Meadows. BA magna cum laude, So. Meth. U., 1960, MA, 1979; PhD, Tex. A&M, Commerce, 1983. Tchr. English pub. schs., 1960-61, 78-79; exec. v.p., sr. advisor Meadows Found., Inc., Dallas, 1979-96, also trustee and dir. Trustee So. Meth. U., 1980—88, East Tex. State U., regent, 1987—93; Tex. del. White House Conf. on Tourism, 1995; dir. Inst. Nautical Archaeology, 1988—2001; dir. emeritus Meadows Found.; mem. adv. bd. Cmtys. Found. Tex., 1987—2002. Named Disting. Alumni, So. Meth. U., Tex. A&M, Commerce; recipient Ruth Lester award Tex. Hist. Commn., 1998; grant-making and evaluations coms. Jacksonville Cmty. Found., 2000-01. Mem. Plantation Ladies Assn. (pres. 2000-01), Philos. Soc. Tex., Phi Beta Kappa. Presbyterian. E-mail: srhodusl@aol.com.

LAND, JUDITH BROTEN, stockbroker; b. Newark, July 27, 1951; d. Robert Allan and Marjorie (Frederickson) Broten; m. Andre Paul Land, Jan. 6, 1973; children: Ian Sherard, Margo Caryn. Student, Hood Coll., 1969-70, Denver U., 1970-71, Monmouth Coll., 1971-72, Fla. Atlantic U., 1976-77. Lic. ins. agent Fla. Brokerage ops. Fahnestock & Co., Red Bank, NJ, 1973; with ops. dept. Thomson McKinnon, South Orange, N.J., 1973-75, Boca Raton, Fla., 1977-80; sales trainee Butcher & Singer Inc., Boca Raton, 1980-81, stockbroker, 1981-85, A.G. Edwards & Sons, Inc., Boca Raton, 1985—. Lectr. Palm Beach County Schs., Boca Raton, 1987-95, Palm Beach County Librs., 1990-91; daily stock market radio reporter Sta. WDBF-AM, Delray Beach, Fla., 1979-81. Cmty. theater performer, song composer; mem. Singing Pines Children's Mus., Boca Raton, Fla., 1989, Young Women of the Arts, Boca Raton, 1989, C. of C., 1990—92, Guardianship Assn., Palm Beach, 2001—03, C. of C., 2004. Republican. Episcopalian. Avocations: golf, photography. Office: AG Edwards & Sons Inc 1900 Glades Rd Ste 451 Boca Raton FL 33431-8548 Office Phone: 800-945-8271. Business E-Mail: Judith.Land@agedwards.com.

LAND, JUDY M., real estate broker; b. Phoenix, Oct. 6, 1945; d. Sanford Karl Land and D. Latanne (Hilburn) Land Krauss; divorced; children: Neal McNeil III, Latanne. AA in Econs., Merritt Coll., 1967; MBA, Brklyn Bus. Sch., 1984. Cert. real estate developer, broker and appraiser. With real estate sales dept. Odmark/Welch Co/Mesa Realty, San Diego, 1971-76; v.p. Brehm Communities, San Diego, 1977; mgr. investment div. Ayers Realty, Encinitas, Calif., 1978-79; asst. v.p. Harry L. Summers Inc., La Jolla, Calif., 1982-85; pres. The Land Co., Carlsbad, Calif., 1979-90; nat. mktg. dir. Nat. Safety Assocs., San Diego, 1990—93; pres. Land Divsn. Prudential Calif. Realty, Rancho Santa Fe, Calif., 1996—. Fundraiser Hunger Project, 1979-86, Youth at Risk, 1984-86, Multiple Sclerosis Soc., 1984; mem. exec. com. U.S. Olympics, 1984; bd. dirs. Polit. Policies Com., San Diego, 1986. Mem. Nat. Assn. Real Estate Appraisers, Nat. Assn. Women Execs., Nat. Assn. Home builders, Home Builders Council (pres. 1985), Building Industry Assn. San Diego (bd. dirs. 1985, sale and mktg. coun.), Econ. Devel. Corp. San Diego (membership com. 1984), Women Comml. Real Estate, Life Spike Club. Avocations: tennis, skiing, swimming. Home: PO Box 676114 Rancho Santa Fe CA 92067-6114

LAND, TERRI LYNN, state official; m. Dan Hibma; children: Jessica Hibma, Nicholas Hibma. BA in Political Sci., Hope Coll., Holland, MI. Clerk Kent County, 1992—2000; sec. of state State of Mich., 2003—. Atty. Grievance Commn., 1999—2002; sec. Atty. Grievance Commn., 2001—02; mem. Secchia Millennium Commn., 2000, Cmty. Archives & Rsch. Ctr., 1997—, 54 Jefferson Study Com., 1997—. Mem. Grandville Rotary, 1990—99; mem. bd. dirs. Am. Heart Assn., 1995—99, Junior Achivement Alumni Bd., 1997—99, Project Rehab Found., 1997—98. Mem.: Mich. Supreme Ct. Hist. Soc., US Supreme Ct. Hist. Soc., Women's Resource Ctr. (v.p., bd. of dirs. 2001—02), Grand Rapids Pub. Mus. Found. Bd., Grand Rapids Rotary, Grand Rapids Early Morning Riser's Club, Friends of John Ball Zoological Park, Byron Ctr. Fine Arts Found. (pres. 1999—), Friends of Van Andel Mus., Frederick Meijer Gardens, Grand Rapids C. of C., Byron Ctr. Hist. Soc. (pres. 1990—92), Byron Ctr. Cmty. Fine Arts Coun., Potters House Found. (mem., bd. dirs. 1997—). Office: Office Sec of State Treasury Bldg First Floor 430 West Allegan St Lansing MI 48918 Office Phone: 517-373-2510. Office Fax: 517-373-0727.*

LANDAU, ANNETTE HENKIN, writer, librarian; b. N.Y.C., Apr. 7, 1921; d. Bernard and Bessie (Diamond) Henkin; m. Philip Landau (dec.); children— Harriette, Robert, Jessica (dec.). B.A., Queens Coll., 1941; M.A., Columbia U., 1943, M.Phil., 1973; M.S., C.W. Post Coll., 1969. Instr. English, Queens Coll., N.Y.C., 1943-48; libr. E.M. Pub. Library, East Meadow, N.Y., 1969-83; libr. The Klein Libr. Stephen Wise Free Synagogue, N.Y.C., 1988-95, Nat. Coun. Jewish Women N.Y. Sect. Libr., 1997—. Author short stories various mags.; contbr. articles to profl. jours. Mem. Poets and Writers, Internat. Women's Writing Guild, NOW, Nat. Coun. Jewish Women. Home: 301 E 66th St New York NY 10021-6205 Office Phone: 212-687-5030 ext. 33. Business E-Mail: alandau@ncjwny.org.

LANDAU, EMILY FISHER, art collector, foundation administrator; b. Glen Falls, N.Y., Aug. 23; d. Samuel and Cecelia (Greene) Lanzner; m. Martin A. Fisher (dec.); children: Richard L. Fisher, M. Anthony Fisher (dec.), Candia Fisher; m. Sheldon Landau. Ptnr. Fisher Bros., N.Y.C.; prs. Fisher Landau Found., N.Y.C., 1984—; founder Fisher Landau Ctr. Art, Long Island City, 1991; PhD (hon.) Yeshiva U., 1998—. Trustee Whitney Mus. Am. Art, N.Y.C., 1987—, co-chmn. contemporary com., 1994—; mem. chmn.'s coun. Mus. Modern Art, N.Y.C., 1992—, mem. com. on painting and sculpture, 1997—, mem. com. on prints and illustrated books, 1985—; bd. dirs. The Georgia O'Keeffe Mus., Santa Fe, 1996; adv. dir. Met. Opera Assn., N.Y.C., 1986-88, mng. dir., 1988—; sponsor Emily Fisher Landau professorship of neurology Harvard Med. Sch., Cambridge, Mass., 1995—; founder Fisher Landau Ctr. for Treatment of Learning Disabilities, Albert Einstein Coll. Medicine/Yeshiva U., N.Y.C., 1997—; founding mem. Nat. Mus. Women in the Arts, 1987; charter mem. U.S. Holocaust Meml. Mus., 1992; bd. dirs. Site Santa Fe, 1994. Pub. exhbn. catalog Jasper Johns: The Screenprints, 1996; Mishoo Cosmopolitan Cat (children's storybook), 2000. Vice chmn. Anti-Defamation League of B'nai B'rith, N.Y.C.; sec. Anti-Defamation Found., N.Y.C.; sponsor Music Outreach, West End Symphony Pub. Sch. Project, N.Y.C. Decorated Chevalier Order Arts and Letters (France); named one of Top 200 Collectors, ARTnews mag., 2004. Mem. Met. Club, Doubles, Palm Beach Country Club. Avocation: collector of contemporary Am. art.

LANDAU, LAURI BETH, accountant, consultant; b. Bklyn., July 21, 1952; d. Jack and Audrey Carolyn (Zuckernick) L. BA, Skidmore Coll., 1973; postgrad., Pace U., 1977-79. CPA, N.Y. Mem. staff Audrey Z. Landau, CPA, Suffern, N.Y., 1976-78, Ernst & Whinney, N.Y.C., 1979-80, mem. sr. staff, 1980-82, supr., 1982-84; mgr. Arthur Young & Co., N.Y.C., 1984-87, prin., 1987-89; sr. mgr. Ernst & Young, N.Y.C., 1989-92; ptnr. Landau & Landau, Pomona, N.Y., 1992—. Ptnr. Audrey Z. Landau & Co., Wilmington, Vt., 1995—; spkr. World Trade Inst., N.Y.C., 1987—, Nat. Fgn. Trade Coun., N.Y.C., 1989—. Composer songs. Career counselor Skidmore Coll., Saratoga Springs, N.Y., 1977—; mem. leadership com. Class of 1973, 83-85, pres., 1985-93, fund chmn., 1987-88, mem. planned gift com., 1989—. N.Y. State Regents scholar, 1970. Mem. Nat. Conf. CPA Practitioners, N.Y. State Soc. CPAs, Rockland Bus. Assn., Skidmore Coll. Alumni Assn. (mem. nominating com. 1989-92). Skidmore Alumni Club. Democrat. Avocations: music, ballet, photography, sports. Office: 26 Firemans Memorial Dr Pomona NY 10970-3553 Business E-Mail: lauri@landauandlandau.com.

LANDAU, NORMA BEATRICE, historian, educator; b. Toronto, Ont., Can., Sept. 13, 1942; d. Julius and Anne L. BA, U. Toronto, 1964, MA, 1965; PhD, U. Calif., Berkeley, 1974. Lectr. Duke U., Durham, NC, 1972-74, UCLA, 1975-76; prof., history U. Calif., Davis, 1976—. Author: The Justices of the Peace, 1984; contbr. articles profl. jours. Mem. Pacific Coast Conf. on Brit. Studies, North Am. Conf. on Brit. Studies. Office: History Dept 4210 Soc Sci & Humn Bldg U Calif Davis CA 95616

LANDAU, YVETTE E., lawyer, resort company executive; b. Milwaukee, Wis., Nov. 26, 1956; BS magna cum laude, Ariz. State U., 1979; JD, Northwestern U., 1984. Bar: Ariz. 1984, Nevada 1991. Assoc. Snell & Wilmer, Phoenix, 1984—89, prtnr., 1990—93; assoc. gen. counsel Mandalay Resort Group, 1993—96, v.p., gen. counsel, sec., 1996—. Mem. exec. com. Circus/Eldorado Joint Venture; mem. mngmt. com. Detroit Entertainment. Mem.: ABA, Internat. Assn. of Gaming Attys. (trustee 1997—), Nevada State Bar Assn., Ariz. State Bar Assn. Office: Mandalay Resort Group 3950 Las Vegas Blvd Las Vegas NV 89119

LANDAU-CRAWFORD, DOROTHY RUTH, retired social services administrator; b. Staten Island, N.Y., Oct. 5, 1957; d. Robert August and Dorothy Faith (Schaut) Landau; m. John W. Crawford, Oct. 21, 1989; 1 child, Jacqueline Lauren. AS, SUNY, Farmingdale, 1977; BS in Biology, Wagner Coll., 1979. Sci. tchr. Bais Yaakov, S.I., 1979-81; dental asst. Dr. Marvin Freeman, S.I., 1981-82; office mgr. Dr. Bennett C. Fidlow, S.I., 1982-85; polit. aide to S.I. Borough Pres. S.I. Borough Pres., 1985-89; exec. dir. Richmond Sr. Svcs. Project Share, 1990—2000; ret., 2000; v.p. Marty Moose Party Pl. LLC, 2006—. V.p. N.J. Shared Housing Assn., regional dir. Nat. Shared Housing Resouces Ctr., 1995—; environ. chmn. S.I. League for Better Govt., 1984—; pres. Tottenville Improvement Council Inc., Staten Island, 1985—. Dem. candidate N.Y. State Assembly 60th Dist., 1986, dist. leader; dir. cmty. bds. S.I. Borough Pres.'s Office; founder, pres. environ. group S.I.L.E.N.T., S.I., 1985; 1st v.p. 123d Cmty. Coun., L.I., 1986; social chmn. South Shore Dem. Club; founding mem. Friends of Clay Pit Pond Park; active Protectors of Pine Oak Woods Inc., Roserio Alliotta Dem. Club, Dem. Orgn. Richmond; trustee S.I. Bd. Leukemia Soc. Am., 1988—, chair Celebrity Waiters Luncheon; spl. election candidate for 51st Councilmatic Dist., 1994. Recipient Cmty. Activist award Office of pres. S.I. Borough, 1987. Mem. NAFE, Bus. and Profl. Women (young careerist for S.I.). Avocations: photography, sports, ceramics, youth programs. Home: 5 Boulder Creek Ct Jackson NJ 08527 Office Phone: 732-431-8775. E-mail: bsa65@aol.com.

LANDER, JOYCE ANN, retired nursing educator, retired medical/surgical nurse; b. Benton Harbor, Mich., July 27, 1942; d. James E. and Anna Mae Remus LPN, Kalamazoo Practical Nursing, Ctr., 1967; AAS, Kalamazoo Valley C.C., 1981, Grad. Massage Therapy Program, 1995. LPN-RN Bronson Meth. Hosp., Kalamazoo, 1972-82; RN med./surg. unit Borgess Med. Ctr., Kalamazoo, 1982-84; RN pediat. Upjohn Home Health Care, Kalamazoo, 1984-88; supr. nursing lab Kalamazoo Valley Comm. Coll., 1982—2005, ret., 2005. Therapeutic massage therapist in client homes with Business Kneading Peace Therapeutic Massage, Kalamazoo, 1995—; nursing asst., instr. State of Mich. Observer, 1990-96. Author: What Is A Nurse, 1980. Address: 3300 Woodstone Dr E Apt 108 Kalamazoo MI 49008-2548

LANDER, RUTH A., medical association administrator; b. Fitchburg, Mass., Dec. 13, 1948; d. H. Allison and Violet K. (Erickson) Linné; m. C. Stephen Lander, June 28, 1968; children: Timothy, Mary. BA, Ohio State U., 1978. Dir. fin. Luth. Svc. Assn. New England, Natick, Mass., 1973—76; gen. mgr. Logos, Columbus, Ohio, 1976—87; practice adminstr. Columbus Oncology Assocs., Inc., 1987—. Sec., treas. Adminstrs. Oncology Hematology Assembly, Englewood, Colo., 1994-95, legis. liaison, 1994-95, pres.-elect, 1995-96, pres., 1996-97; spkr. med. group mgmt. issues. Editor Adminstrs. in Oncology Hematology Assembly News, 1994-95; mem. editl. bd. Oncology Issues Mag., 1998-2000; mem. editl. adv. bd. for coding and reimbursement Oncology & Hematology, 2001; contbr. articles to profl. jours. Mem. task force Cmty. Oncology Alliance, 2004-05. Fellow Med. Group Mgmt. Assn., Am. Coll. Med. Practice Execs. (nat. chair membership devel. com. 1999, nat. bd. dirs. 2004—); mem. Am. Soc. Clin. Oncology (assoc.), Nat. Oncology Soc. Network, Ctrl.-Ohio Med. Group Mgmt. Assn. (pres. 1993-94, sec. 1992-93, program dir. 1991-92, exec. com. 1990-97), Assn. Cmty. Cancer Ctr. (editl. bd. mag. 1998-2000), Ohio Med. Group Mgmt. Assn. (exec. com. 1994-2001, sec. 1995-96, pres. 1998, rep. to Medicare PCOM adv. group 2003—, grass roots legis. group 1994—), Ohio Oncology Med. Group Mgmt. Assn. (pres. 1997), Ohio State Med. Assn. (assoc.; group practice task force 2000—), Columbus Med. Assn. (group practice mgrs. task force 2002—). Republican. Avocations: reading, computers, crafts, knitting, bible study. Office: Columbus Oncology Assocs 810 Jasonway Ave Ste A Columbus OH 43214-2329

LANDERHOLM, ELIZABETH JANE, early childhood education educator; b. Oak Park, Ill. d. Daniel R. and Dorothy E. LaBar; m. Wayne A. Landerholm, June 6, 1964; 1 child, Arthur Scott. BA in Sociology, DePauw U., 1963; MS in Tech., U. Chgo., 1966; EdD in Curriculum and Instrn., No. Ill. U., 1980. Cert. early childhood and elem. edn., Ill. Tchr. Chgo. Bd. Edn., 1966-69; student tchg. supr. Nat. Coll. Edn., Chgo., 1970-79; asst. prof. Roosevelt U., Chgo., 1980-83; project dir. Children's Devel. Ctr., Rockford, Ill., 1984-86; assoc. prof. Northeastern Ill. U., Chgo., 1986-92, prof., 1993—. Therapist Theraplay Inst., Chgo., 1980—84; project dir. McCosh Even Start, 1994—2003; project coord. Early Childhood Cohort/Ill. Profl. Learning Ptnrships. (TQE grant), 1999—2004; prin. investigator Early Reading First Grant, 2004—. Contbr. articles to profl. jours. McCosh Even Start grant Ill. State Bd. Edn., Chgo., 1994—, Ill. Profls. Learning Partnerships grant, 1999—. Home: 325 N Humphrey Ave Oak Park IL 60302-2516 Office: Northeastern Ill Univ 5500 N Saint Louis Ave Chicago IL 60625-4699 Office Phone: 773-442-5383. Personal E-mail: eland325@aol.com. E-mail: e-landerholm@neiu.edu.

LANDERS, AUDREY, actress, singer; b. Phila., July 18, 1959; d. Ruth Landers; m. Donald Berkowitz, May 1988; 2 children. BA, Barnard Coll. Records singles and albums with sister Judy Landers. Actress (films) 1941, 1979, Underground Aces, 1981, Tennessee Stallion, 1982, Deadly Twins, 1985, A Chorus Line, 1985, Getting Even, 1986, Johann Strauss: The King Without a Crown, 1987, California Casanova, 1991, Last Chance Love, 1997, Island Forever, 2005, (TV films) Our Voices Ourselves, 1982, Popeye Doyle, 1986, Ghost Writer, 1989, Dallas: J.R. Returns, 1996, (TV series) The Secret Storm, 1972—73, Somerset, 1974—76, Highcliffe Manor, 1979, Dallas, 1981—84, 1989, Lucky/Chances, 1990, One Life to Live, 1990—91, The Huggabug Club, 1995. Office: care Jo-Ann Geffen & Assocs 3151 Cahuenga Blvd W Ste 235 Los Angeles CA 90068-1749

LANDERS, HEATHER RENEE, elementary school educator; b. Bklyn., Nov. 9, 1970; d. Veronica (Jadusingh) and Glen Landers; children: Veronica Jasmine Lawrence, Ayannah Ananda Lawrence. BS, Tuskegee U., Ala., 1992; M in Secondary Social Studies (hon.), Adelphi U., Garden City, NY, 1998; postgrad., Nova Southeastern U., Ft. Lauderdale, Fla., 2004—06. Cert. tchr. NY, Ga. Tchr. NYC Dept. Edn., Bklyn., 1999—2004, Fulton County Bd. Edn., Atlanta, 2004—. Counselor, tutor Jackie Robinson Program, Bklyn., 1999—2002; tutor Platform Learning, Bklyn., 2002—04. Scholar, United Negro Coll. Fund, 1988—92. Office: Sandtown Mid Sch 5400 Campbellton Rd Atlanta GA 30331 Office Phone: 404-346-6500. Business E-Mail: landersh@fulton.k12.ga.us.

LANDERS, PATRICIA GLOVER, language educator; b. Pine Bluff, Ark., Nov. 15, 1945; d. Maurice Alexander Glover and Ruth Wells-Glover Wimberly; 1 child, Wendolynn. BS in Edn., Ark. State U., 1967; MS in Edn., OBU, 1976; postgrad., U. Ark., 1980—81, U. Ariz., 1980—81, Ariz. State U., 1983—88, U. Phoenix, 1988—89. Cert. tchr. English, reading specialist K-12 Ariz., C.C., English, lang. arts, composition Ariz. Elem. music supr. Greene County Tech. Schs., Paragould, Ark., 1967—68; band and choir dir. Naylor (Mo.) Schs., 1968—70; elem. tchr. Poughkeepsie (Ark.) Schs., 1970—72; reading specialist Sheridan (Ariz.) Schs., 1975—82, Casa Grande Union High Sch., Casa Grande, Ariz., 1982—; assoc. prof. Pima C.C., Tucson, 1982—94, Centra Ariz. Coll., Coolidge, Ariz., 1983—93; English tchr. Casa Granda Regional Med. Ctr. Alternative, Casa Grande, 1994—2001; lang. arts tchr. Toltec Jr. H.S.; owner Landers' Tutoring Svc., Casa Grande, 2001—. Test supr. SAT, ACT Testing Svcs., Casa Grande, 1997—. Author: Making English Make Sense, 1996. Invited rep. U.S. to China People to People Amb. Program, 2000; French hornist CAC Cmty. Concert Band, Coolidge, Ariz., 1984—2000; organist North Trekell Bapt. Ch., Casa Grande, 1996—, founder instrumental music founds. group, 2001; chair babysitting com. Casa Grand Regionl Med. Ctr., Casa Grande, 1995—98. Mem.: NEA, Ark. Reading Coun., Ctrl. Ariz. Reading Coun., Ariz. Reading Coun., Ariz. Edn. Assn., Casa Grande Edn. Assn. (pres. 1985—86, Outstanding Svc. award 1985—86), Sheridan Ednl. Assoc. (pres. 1978—79), Internat. Reading Assoc., CGRMC Aux. (com. chairperson 1995—98, Vol. of Month 1995). Democrat. Baptist. Avocations: reading, jogging, musical instruments. Home: PO Box 589 Arizona City AZ 85223 Office: CGUHS 2730 N Trekell Rd Casa Grande AZ 85222 Office Phone: 520-466-5747, 520-836-8500 4179. Personal E-mail: langders@egmailbox.com. Business E-Mail: planders@cguhs.org. E-mail: landers@egmailbox.com.

LANDERS, SUSAN MAE, psychotherapist, professional counselor; b. Houston; d. James Edward and Frances Pauline (Braunagel) L. BS in Advt., U. Tex.; MS in Psychol. Counseling, U. Houston, Clearlake, 1994; cert. in sales, Dale Carnegie Inst. Lic. profl. counselor. Mktg. rep. K.C. Products, Houston, 1981-83; account exec. Williamson County Express, Austin, Tex., 1984; advt. cons. Stas. KMMM/KOKE, Austin, 1985; key account sales rep. GranTree Furniture Rental, Austin, 1986-89; individual habilitation counselor Ctr. for the Retarded Inc., Houston, 1990; case mgr. Mental Health and Mental Retardation Authority Harris County, Houston, 1991-92; primary therapist Riceland Psychiat. Hosp., 1994-96, Planned Behavioral Healthcare Inc., 1996-98, Continuum Healthcare, Houston, 1998—2000; pvt. practice, 1998—2006; with United Behavioral Health Clinic, 2006—. Mem.: ACA, Am. Mental Health Counselors Assn. Avocation: photography. Home: 7915 Westbank Ave Houston TX 77064-8048

LANDERS, TERESA PRICE, librarian; b. NYC, Dec. 28, 1954; d. Stanley and June Ethel (Novick) Price; m. Gary David Landers, Sept. 2, 1979; children: Joshua Price, Alisha Rose. BA in History cum laude, Williams Coll., 1976; MA in LS, U. Denver, 1978; postgrad., Ctrl. Wash. U., 1980; MA in Orgnl. Mgmt., U. Phoenix, 1999. Libr., asst. analyst Earl Combs, Inc., Mercer Island, Wash., 1979; reference libr. Yakima (Wash.) Valley Regional Libr., 1981-83, coord. youth svcs., 1983-84; libr. Tempe (Ariz.) Pub. Libr., 1984-85; supervisory libr. Mesa (Ariz.) Pub. Libr., 1985-90; head telephone reference Phoenix Pub. Libr., 1990-91, head bus. and scis., 1991-95, info. svcs. mgr., 1995-99; dep. dir. Corvallis-Benton County Pub. libr., 1999—. Cons. Fed. Dept. Corrections, Phoenix, 1993. Mem. ALA, Oreg. Libr. Assn., Nat. Wildlife Fedn. (life), Altrusa, Beta Phi Mu. Democrat. Unitarian Universalist. Avocations: cooking, horseback riding, gardening. Office: Corvallis-Benton County Pub Libr 645 NW Monroe Ave Corvallis OR 97330-4722 E-mail: teresa.landers@ci.corvallis.or.us.

LANDES, GERALDINE STEINBERG, psychologist; d. Otto and Lillie (Goldman) Steinberg; m. Bernard A. Landes, Jan. 30, 1954; children: Sharon Landes Turner, Jodie Landes Corngold. BS, Northwestern U., Evanston, Ill., 1954; MA, Tex. Tech. U., Lubbock, 1960; PhD, Alliant U., San Diego, 1988. Cert. sch. psychologist Calif., lic. ednl. psychologist Calif., nat. cert. sch. psychologist, cert. marriage family therapist. Child caseworker Child Welfare, Lubbock, Tex., 1960—61; counselor Jewish Family Svc., Long Beach, Calif., 1962; sch. psychologist Bellflower (Calif.) Unified Sch. Dist., 1966—98, Paramount (Calif.) Unifed Sch. Dist., 1998—. Mem.: Assn. Calif. Sch. Adminstrs., Haddassah, Delta Kappa Gamma (treas. 1983—85). Home: 3320 Julian Ave Long Beach CA 90808 Office: Paramount Unified Sch Dist 15110 S California Ave Paramount CA 90723 Personal E-mail: landesgs@aol.com.

LANDEY, FAYE HITE, consultant; b. Atlanta, May 12, 1943; d. Irving and Sophia (Held) Hite; m. Benjamin Landey, Aug. 30, 1964; children: Leah, Sharon. Student U. Ill., 1961, Hebrew U., Jerusalem, 1962; BA, Emory U., 1964. Cert. housing mgr. Office mgr. Grolier Interstate, Atlanta, 1969-72; asst. adminstr. Campbell-Stone, Atlanta, 1972-78; owner Cupboard Gift Shop, Atlanta, 1974-78; adminstr. Campbell-Stone North, Atlanta, 1978-81; sales mgr. Apex Supply Co., Atlanta, 1981-83; owner Landey & Assocs., Atlanta, 1983—; chief exec. officer Retirement Dimensions, Atlanta, 1986—; advisor Fulton County Council on Housing, 1982. Treas., charter mem. Sandy Springs (Ga.) Arts and Heritage Soc., 1981; dir. Sandy Springs C. of C., 1982; founder Coalition Fulton County Civic Assns., 1983; mem. bd. com. Sandy Springs Benefit Ball, 1978-83; bd. dirs. Cath. Social Services; state del. Republican Party. Author: The Graying of America; It's Effects on Developers and Land Sales, 1987. Mem. Am. Assn. Homes for Aging (nat. house del. 1981), Ga. Assn. Homes for Aging (pres. elect 1982), Nat. Council on Aging, Am. Soc. on Aging, Ga. Gerontology Soc. Jewish. Club: Woman's Forum (Atlanta). Home and Office: 495 Tahoma Dr Atlanta GA 30350-4011

LANDGREBE, MARILYN ANN, nutritionist, chemicals executive; b. N.Y.C., June 8, 1935; d. Charles J. and Marie L. Osterwald; m. Albert R. Landgrebe, June 14, 1958; children: Marie Pilz, Albert C. PhD, U. Md., 1977. Nutritionist Children's Brain Rsch. Clinic, Washington, 1974—80; dir. rsch. Almar Rsch. Lab., Beltsville, Md., 1980—88; v.p. Internat. Electrochem. Systems & Tech., Long Neck, Del., 1990—. Cons. Autistic Soc., 1974-77.

Contbr. articles to profl. jours. Pres. PTA, Calverton, Md., 1967. Mem. Am. Assn. Ret. Persons, Mariner's Cove Assn. (beautiful and landscape com. 1999). Avocations: gardening, boating, reading, travel. E-mail: albert@dmv.com.

LANDIS, DONNA MARIE, nursing administrator, women's health nurse; b. Lebanon, Pa., Sept. 5, 1944; d. James O.A. and Helen Joan (Fritz) Muench; m. David J. Landis, Feb. 4, 1967 (div. Jan. 1985); children: Danielle M. Landis Barry, David J., Derek J.; m. John C. Broderick, May 8, 1990 (div. Jan. 1995). RN, St. Joseph's Hosp. Sch. Nursing, Reading, Pa., 1965. RN 1993, cert. densitometry technologist. DXA technologist Osteoporosis Diagnostic and Monitoring Ctr., Laurel, Md., 1985-95, owner, 1995—; clin. dir., clin. rsch. coord. Osteoporosis Assessment Ctr., Wheaton, Md., 1985-95; owner, clin. dir., clin. rsch. coord. Women's Health Rsch. Ctr., Laurel, Md., 1996—2006; pvt. practice as cons. in osteoporosis, bone densitometry and women's health Donna M. Landis, LLC, 2004—. Mem. nurses adv. bd. NPS Pharms., 2005—06; cons. P&G Pharms., 2006—. Mem. task force on osteoporosis State of Md., 1996—2006. Named one of Md.'s Top 100 Women in Bus., 2002. Mem.: Nat. Osteoporosis Risk Assessment Project (specialist practice and lead technologist trainer 1997—98), Allied Health Profls./Arthritis Found. (pub. policy contact), Nat. Osteoporosis Found. (pub. policy contact), Internat. Soc. Clin. Densitometry (steering com. 1993—94, contbg. editor SCAN newsletter 1994—2002, cert. com. technologists and physicians 1995—2000, sci. adv. com. 1996—2006, trustee 1999—2002, technologist edn. subcom. 2000—03, facility accreditation coun. 2004—), St. Joseph's Hosp. Alumni Assn., Balt. Bone Club, Washington Met. Bone Club (steering com. 1996, bd. dirs. 1999—2001, sec. 1999—2001), Kiwanis Internat. (bd. dirs. Prince Georges County 1997—2002, pres. Prince Georges County 2000—01, Capital dist. lt. gov. 2003—04). Office: 14201 Laurel Park Dr Laurel MD 20707-5203 Personal E-mail: dmlandis@verizon.net.

LANDIS, STORY CLELAND, federal agency administrator, neurobiologist; m. Dennis Landis; 1 child, Michael. BA in biology, Wellesley Coll., 1967; MA, Harvard U., 1970, PhD, 1973. Mem. faculty Dept. Neurobiology Harvard Med. Sch.; mem. faculty Dept. Pharmacology Case Western Res. U. Sch. of Medicine, Cleve., 1985—95, chair Dept. Neurosciences, 1990—95; sci. dir. Nat. Inst. Neurol. Disorders and Stroke, NIH, 1995—2003, dir., 2003—. Contbr. articles to profl. jours. Fellow: Am. Neurol. Assn., AAAS, Am. Acad. Arts and Sciences; mem.: Soc. Neuroscience (pres.-elect 2002). Achievements include research in the study of the developmental interactions required for the formation of functional synapses. Office: Nat Inst Neurol Disorders and Stroke Bldg 31 Rm 8A52 31 Center Dr MSC 2540 Bethesda MD 20892 Office Phone: 301-496-9746. Office Fax: 301-496-0296. E-mail: landiss@ninds.nih.gov.*

LANDO, MAXINE COHEN, circuit judge; b. Atlantic City, May 12, 1950; BA, U. Mich., 1971; JD, U. Miami, 1974. Bar: Fla. 1974, U.S. Dist. Ct. (so. dist.) Fla. 1979. Asst pub. defender Dade County Pub. Defender's Office, Miami, Fla., 1974-85; pvt. practice, 1985-91; county ct. judge 11th Jud Cir. Dade County, Miami, Fla., 1991—; elected cir. judge, 1994—. Mem. faculty New Judges Trial Skills Coll., Advanced Jud. Coll. Active Greater Miami Jewish Fedn., 1975—; mem. Young Patroness of the Opera, Miami, 1988. Police Found. grantee, 1973 Mem. ABA, Am. Judges Assn., Nat. Assn. Women Judges, Dade County Bar Assn. (criminal ct. com. 1987-88), Coral Gables Bar Assn., South Dade-Kendall Bar Assn., Fla. Criminal Def. Attys. Assn. (bd. dirs.), Fla. Assn. for Women Lawyers, B'nai B'rith. Avocations: music, theater. Office: 11th Jud Cir Dade County 1351 NW 12th St Ste 400 Miami FL 33125-1630

LANDOLFI, JENNIE LOUISE, nursing administrator; b. Warren, Ohio, Apr. 19, 1955; d. Gregory A. and Antonette (Cervone) L. Diploma, Trumbull Hosp. Sch. Nursing, Warren, 1978; cert., Brentwood Hosp. Paramedic Sch., Cleve., 1982; MSN in Adult Health, Akron U., 1997. RN, Ohio; cert. provider and instr. ACLS, BLS, PALS, instr. and coord. pre-hosp. trauma life support. Staff nurse Trumbull Meml. Hosp., Warren, 1978-82, charge nurse, 1982, coord. emergency med. svc. edn., 1986; coord. emergency med. svc. Kettering (Ohio) Med. Ctr., 1982-83; staff nurse Warren Gen. Hosp., 1984-85; home health care nurse Nurses House Call, Warren, 1987-90, emergency med. svcs./emergency dept. edn. coord., 1990—2001; nurse mgr. emergency dept. Forum Health-TMH. Hosp. rep. Trumbull County Joint Com. for Emergency Med. Svcs.; instr., course coord. pre-hosp. trauma life support Nat. Assn. EMT's. Contbr. articles to profl. jours. Apptd. State of Ohio EMS bd., 1992-97, chmn. accreditation com., 1995; pres. Trumbull County Emergency Med. Svc. Com. Mem. Emergency Nurses Assn. (N.E. Ohio chpt.), John F. Kennedy H.S. Alumni Assn. Democrat. Roman Catholic. Home: 114 Morningside Rd Niles OH 44446-2112 Office: 1350 E Market St Warren OH 44483-6608

LANDON, COLLEEN, elementary school educator; b. Wichita, Kans., Dec. 18, 1975; d. John and Norma Cregan; m. Shawn Landon, June 17, 2000; 1 child, Ashlynn. Elem. Edn., Emporia State U., Kansas, 1994—98. 7th grade math tchr. Haysville Mid. Sch., Kans., 1998—2000; 8th grade math tchr. Oreg. Trail Jr. High, Olathe, 2000—. Math dept. head Oreg. Trial Jr. High, 2003—. Grantee Clicking into the Future, Sprint, 2004—05. Independent. Roman Catholic. Avocations: swimming, volleyball. Office: Orgon Trail Jr High 1800 W Dennis Olathe KS 66061 Office Phone: 913-780-7250.

LANDON, SUSAN MELINDA, petroleum geologist; b. Mattoon, Ill., July 2, 1950; d. Albert Leroy and Nancy (Wallace) L.; m. Richard D. Dietz, Jan. 24, 1993. BA, Knox Coll., 1972; MA, SUNY, Binghamton, 1975. Cert. profl. geologist; cert. petroleum geologist. Petroleum geologist Amoco Prodn. Co., Denver, 1974—87; mgr. exploration tng. Amoco, Houston, 1987—89; ind. petroleum geologist Denver, 1990—. Editor: Interior Rift Basins, 1993. Mem., chmn. Colo. Geol. Survey Adv. Com., Denver, 1991-98; mem. Bd. on Earth Sci. and Resources-NRC, 1992-97, chair com. on earth resources, 1998-2003; mem. Nat. Coop. Geologic Mapping Program Fed. Adv. Com., 1997—. Recipient Disting. Alumni award Knox Coll., 1986. Mem. Am. Assn. Petroleum Geologists (hon., treas., Disting. Svc. award 1995), Am. Inst. Profl. Geologists (pres. 1990, Martin Van Couvering award 1991, Ben H. Parker medal 2001), Am. Geol. Inst. (pres. 1998), Rocky Mountain Assn. Geologists (pres. 2000, Disting. Svc. award 1986, Disting. Pub. Svc. to Earth Sci. award 1995). Achievements include frontier exploration for hydrocarbons in U.S. Home: 780 Ballantine Rd Golden CO 80401-9503 Office: Thomasson Ptnr Assocs 1410 High St Denver CO 80218-2609 Office Phone: 303-436-1930. Personal E-mail: susanlandon@att.net.

LANDON, SUSAN N., humanitarian, arts and environmental advocate, poet; b. Pitts., Feb. 20, 1946; d. Kenneth L. and Nina H. Landon. BA cum laude, Tufts U., 1967; MA in Counseling Psychology, Lesley U., 1988. Assoc. staff software engring. MIT Lincoln Lab., Cambridge, Mass., 1967—78; tech. staff software engr. Adaptive Optics, Cambridge, 1978—81; program office mgr. software engring. Intermetrics, Inc., Cambridge, 1981—85; compiler group mgr. software engring. Boston Systems Office, Waltham, Mass., 1985—86; pvt. practice Cambridge, 1989—92; freelance journalist focusing on environment and edn., 1991—95; sr. mem. of tech. staff (software engring.) Draper Lab., Cambridge, Mass., 1995—98. Founder & pres. Data Acquisition & Lab. Control SIG of Data Gen. Users Group, 1979—82; founder Intermetrics Women's Network, Cambridge, Mass., 1984—85; self-image subgroup leader MIT Lincoln Lab. Women's Forum, Lexington, Mass., 1973—78; counseling intern Horizons Transitional Housing Program, 1985—86. Author: numerous poems. Del. People to People Internat. Mission Understanding to South Africa, 2004; vol. Somerville Environ. and Recycling Vol., 1995—96; vol. tutor Somerville Cmty. Adult Learning Experiences, Somerville, Mass., 1998—2001; com. mem. Hoyt-Sullivan Com., Somerville, 1999—2001; writer for cmty. newspaper funded to stabilize the neighborhood after subway expansion disrupted it. North Cambridge News, Cambridge, Mass., 1991—92; Boston coord. Found. for Shamanic Studies, 1986—91; internat. friendship del. Global Peace Initiative to Egypt, 2003; clk. First Congl. Ch. of Somerville, 1997—98; writer Nat. Orgn. for Women (Boston chpt.), Cambridge, 1982—85; internat. friendship del. to Egypt: Women in Soc. trip People to People Internat., Kansas City, Mo., 2000, internat. friendship del., a Mission in Understanding to Cuba, 2002; Transcendental Meditation tchr. Students Internat. Meditation Soc., Cambridge, Mass., 1971—75; vol. computer aide Somerville Cmty. Computing Ctr., 1998—2004; activist Mass. Choice, Cambridge, Mass., 1979—81; vol. computer cons. Cambridge Multicultural Arts Ctr., Cambridge, 1999—2004; vol. Ten Thousand Villages, Cambridge, 1999—2004. Named to Wall of Tolerance, So. Law Poverty Ctr., 2002; recipient Poetry prize, Spare Change News, 2001, Peace Medal, So. Sinai Governorate/Egypt, 2003, Cambridge Poetry award Best Modern Poem, Cambridge Ctr. Adult Edn., 2003, Cambridge Poetry award Best Traditional Poem, 2004. Mem.: New Eng. Poetry Club. Avocations: reading, languages, travel, yoga. Personal E-mail: landon_susan@hotmail.com.

LANDOVSKY, ROSEMARY REID, figure skating school director, coach; b. Chgo., July 26, 1933; d. Samuel Stuart and Audrey Todd (Lyons) Reid; m. John Indulis Landovsky, Feb. 20, 1960; children: David John, Linette. BA in Psychology, Colo. Coll., 1956. Profl. skater Holiday on Ice Touring Show, U.S., Mex., Cuba, 1956-58; skating dir. and coach Paradice Arena, Birmingham, 1958-62, Les Patineurs, Huntsville, Ala., 1960-62; coach competitive (Ice Skating Inst. Am., U.S. Figure Skating Assn.) Michael Kirby and Assocs., River Forest, Chgo., Ill., 1962-63; rink mgr., skating dir. Lake Meadows Ice Arena, Chgo., 1963-68; coach (ISIA, USFSA) Rainbo Arena, Chgo., 1968-73; skating dir. Northwestern U. Skating Sch., Evanston, Ill., 1968-73, Robert Crown Ice Ctr., Evanston, 1973-75; dir. instl. programs Skokie (Ill.) Park Dist., 1975-87. Competition dir. ISIA All America Competition, 1985-86. Dir., producer, choreographer Ice Show: Nutcracker Ballet, 1973, Ice Extravaganza III, 1985, Ice Lights '86, '87. Election judge, worker, Ind. Dems., Chgo., 1964-68. Mem. AAUW, Profl. Skaters Guild, Ice Skating Inst. Am., Coll. Coll. Alumni Assn., Gamma Phi Beta. Avocations: building cabin, travel, golf, tennis, hiking. E-mail: rodysk8@earthlink.net.

LANDOW-ESSER, JANINE MARISE, lawyer; b. Omaha, Sept. 23, 1951; d. Erwin Landow and Beatrice (Hart) Appel; m. Jeffrey L. Esser, June 2, 1974; children: Erica, Caroline. BA, U. Wis., 1973; JD with honors, George Washington U., 1976. Bar: Va. 1976, DC 1977, Ill. 1985. Atty. U.S. Dept. Energy, Washington, 1976-83, Bell, Boyd & Lloyd, Chgo., 1985-86, Seyfarth, Shaw, Fairweather & Geraldson, Chgo., 1986-88, Holleb & Coff, Chgo., 1988-2000, Quarles & Brady, Chgo., 2000—. Contbr. articles to profl. jours. Bd. dirs. Bernard Zell Anshe Emet Day Sch. Parent-Tchr. Orgn., 1991-95. Mem. ABA, Chgo. Bar Assn. (vice chmn. environ. law com. 1990-91, chmn. 1991-92), Nat. Brownfield Assn. (Ill. chpt. chmn. legis. and policy com. 2005—), Am. Jewish Congress (bd. dirs., pres. Midwest Region 2001-04). Office: Quarles & Brady 500 W Madison St Ste 3700 Chicago IL 60661-2592 Office Phone: 312-715-5055. Business E-Mail: je3@quarles.com.

LANDRAM, CHRISTINA LOUELLA, librarian; b. Dec. 10, 1922; d. James Ralph and Bertie Louella (Jordan) Oliver; m. Robert Ellis Landram, Aug. 7, 1948; 1 child, Mark Owen. BA, Tex. Woman's U., 1945, BLS, 1946, MLS, 1951. Preliminary cataloger Libr. of Congress, Washington, 1946—48; cataloger U.S. Info. Ctr., Tokyo, 1948—50, U.S. Dept. Agr., Washington, 1953—54; libr. Yokota AFB, Japan, 1954—55, St. Mary's Hosp., West Palm Beach, Fla., 1957—59, Jacksonville H.S., Ark., 1959—61; coord. Shelby County Librs., Memphis, 1961—63; head catalog dept. Ga. State U. Libr., 1963—86, libr., assoc. prof. emeritus, 1986—. Contbr. articles to libr. jours. Mem. ALA (chmn. cataloging norms 1979-80, nominating com. 1977-78), Ga. Libr. Assn. (chmn. resources and tech. svcs. sect. 1969-71), Metro-Atlanta Libr. Assn. (pres. 1967-68), Southeastern Libr. Assn. (govtl. rels. com. 1975-78, intellectual freedom com. 1984-86, Rothrock awards com. 1987-90). Presbyterian. Home: 15201 Olive Blvd Apt 495 Chesterfield MO 63017-1819 Personal E-mail: bobland2@juno.com.

LANDRETH, BARBARA BUGG, librarian; b. Lousiville; d. Marvin and Marianna Moss Bugg; children: Matthew Samuel, Benjamin Moss. BA in Am. Studies, U. Md., 1971; MA in Libr. Sci., U. Ky., 1972. Libr. U. of Louisville Health Sci. Libr., Louisville, 1972—76, U. of Wash. Health Sci. Libr., Seattle, 1976—80, W.Va. U. Libr., Morgantown, 1990—97, Nat. Inst. for Occupl. Safety and Health, Morgantown, W.Va., 1997—. Mem.: Med. Libr. Assn., Spl. Lib. Assn. Office: National Inst for Occup Safety & Health 1095 Willowdale Rd Morgantown WV 26505-2845 Office Phone: 304-285-5887. Business E-Mail: blandreth@cdc.gov.

LANDRIEU, MARY LORRETTA, senator; b. Arlington, Virginia, Nov. 23, 1955; m. E. Frank Snellings. BA, La. State U., 1977. Real estate agt.; La. state rep. from dist. 90, 1980—88; La. state treas., 1988—96; US Senator from La., 1997—; mem. small business com.; mem. energy and natural resources com.; mem. appropriations com. Del., Dem. Nat. Conv., 1980 Author: (novels) Nine and Counting: The Women of the Senate, 2000. Mem. LWV, Women Execs. in State Govt., Fedn. Dem. Women, Delta Gamma. Democrat. Roman Catholic. Office: 724 Hart Senate Off Bldg Washington DC 20510-0001

LANDRIGAN, CYNTHIA SCHEER, mathematician, educator; b. Lockport, N.Y., July 7, 1954; d. Everett F. and Vera Carlson Scheer; m. John R. Landrigan, June 5, 1982; children: Christopher Ryan, Elisha Renée, Renée Cherise. BS in Math., SUNY, Brockport, N.Y., 1976, MEd, 1980. Tchr. math. H.S. Wheatland Chili Ctrl., Scottsville, NY, 1976—78; tchr. math. Mid. Sch. and H.S. Elba (N.Y.) Ctrl. Sch., 1978—80; prof. math. Erie C.C., Orchard Pk., NY, 1980—. Mem.: N.Y. State Math. Assn. Two Yr. Colls., Math. Assn. Am. Office: Erie Community Coll South 4140 Southwestern Blvd Orchard Park NY 14127

LANDRO, LAURA, editor; b. Aug. 20, 1954; m. Richard Salomon, 1996. BS in Journalism, Ohio U., 1976. Entertainment reporter, sr. editor Wall St. Jour., Bus. Week, 1981—. Author: Survivor: Taking Charge of Your Fight Against Cancer. Recipient Gerald Loeb award, 1986, Nat. Print Journalism award, Leukemia Soc. Am., 1997, Matrix award, N.Y. Women in Com., Inc., 1997, Life Achievement award, Italian Am. Cancer Found., 1998. Office: Wall St Journal 200 Liberty St New York NY 10281

LANDRÓN, ANA, school psychologist; d. Sidney Kruset and Carlina Figueroa; m. Jose R. Landron, June 29, 1974; children: Rafael A. Landron, Miguel O. Landron. BS in Psychology, Queens Coll. CUNY, 1969; MS in Sch. Psychology, St. John's U., 1995, postgrad., 1999—. Cert. in sch. psychology U. State NY, 1996, lic. bilingual sch. psychologist NYC Dept. Edn., 1996, primary and advanced practicum in rational emotive behavior therapy Albert Ellis Inst. Family counselor Children's Aid Soc., Sloane Head Start, NYC; sch. psychologist NYC Dept Edn., Forest Hills; bilingual sch. psychologist Oyster Bay-East Norwich Sch. Dist., NY, 1995—. Mem. Sen. Marcellino's Mental Health Adv. Com., Nassau County, NY, 2001; bd. advisor Centro Cultural Hispano de Oyster Bay-East Norwich y Vecinidades; mem. majority task force on children's health and safety NY State Senate. Recipient cert. acad. excellence, St. John's U., 1995, Woman of Distinction, Humanitarian award, Town of Oyster Bay, 2001. Mem.: APA, Soc. for Study of Peace, Conflict, and Violence, Soc. for Psychol. Study of Ethnic Minority Issues, Nat. Assn. Sch. Psychologists. Avocations: reading, hiking, gardening. Office: Roosevelt Elem Sch 150 W Main St Oyster Bay NY 11771

LANDRUM, ANN LOUISE, physical education educator; b. St. Louis, Mo., Apr. 20, 1964; d. Clarence Keith and Marie Elizabeth Simons; m. Ronald Keith Landrum, Nov. 16, 1996; children: Dustin, Haley; children: Zackery Bryon, Cody Bryan. Lic. phys. edn. K-12 Pittsburg State U., Kans., Mo. So. State U., edn. secondary adminstrn. William Woods U., cert. health K-12 Praxis. Instr., freshman coach, asst. volleyball and track coach Carl Junction Sch. Dist., Mo., 1993—94; instr., varsity volleyball, basketball and track head coach Cabool Sch. Dist., Mo., 1994—97; instr., varsity volleyball, freshman boys and girls basketball and varsity swimming Lamar Sch. Dist., Mo., 1997—. Recipient Curci E. White PFP grant, 2003—04, 2004—07. Mem.: LCTA, MSTA (sponsor Mid-Step Club 2003—), Mo. Alliance for Health Phys. Edn. Recreation and Dance (bd. dirs. Action and Drug Abuse Prevention Team 2003—), Am. Alliance for Health Physical Edn. Recreation and Dance (bd. dirs. About our Kids youth svcs. 2003—). Office: Lamar R I Sch Dist 202 W 7th Lamar MO 64759

LANDRUM, BEVERLY HOLLOWELL, nurse, lawyer; b. Goldsboro, N.C., Jan. 28, 1960; d. Joseph Bryant and Doris Helen (Barnett) Hollowell; m. Tim Landrum; children: Amber, Justin, Caitlyn. ADN with honors, Florence-Darlington Tech., 1989; BSN summa cum laude, Med. U. S.C., 1995; JD, U. S.C., 2001. Bar: S.C. 2002, U.S. dist. ct. 2004, 4th cir. ct. appeals 2004; RN S.C., cert. BLS, ACLS, NALS. Charge nurse Carolinas Hosp. Sys., Florence, SC, 1989—98; with Health South Rehab. Hosp., 1998—99; atty. S.C. Judicial Dept., 2002—03; asst. solicitor Fifteenth Jud. Cir., 2003—. Neighborhood campaign organizer March of Dimes, Am. Heart Assn., Atlantic Beach, Fla. and Florence, 1982—; active Assn. Parents and Tchrs., Florence, 1993—. Mem.: ABA, ANA, S.C. Am Bar Assn., S.C. Nurses Assn., Health Law Soc., Women in Law, Sigma Theta Tau.

LANDRUM-NOE, MADELEINE ELISE, accountant; b. Memphis, Tenn., Feb. 20, 1972; d. Kenneth Edward and Betty Landrum Noe; life ptnr. Rachel Ann Davis, May 14, 2000; 1 child, Nicholas Landrum. BBA, U. of Memphis, 1998, MS in Acctg., 2003. Acct. Fed. Express Corp., Memphis, 2000—04, sr. acctg. rsch. analyst, 2004—. Database mgr. Komen-Memphis Race for the Cure, Memphis, 2003—04. Liberal. Avocations: travel, reading, literature. Office: Federal Express Corporation 2007 Corporate Ave Fl 5 Memphis TN 38132 Office Phone: 901-395-7948. Personal E-mail: melangel0220@bellsouth.net.

LANDRY, ABBIE VESTAL, librarian; b. Martinsville, Va., Oct. 29, 1954; d. Samuel Raynor and Grace Loraine (Cochrane) Vestal; m. Michael Ray Landry, Aug. 4, 1979. Assoc. Gen. Edn., Patrick Henry C.C., Martinsville, Va., 1975; BA in History, Longwood Coll., Farmville, Va., 1977; M in Libr. and Info. Sci., U. Tenn., Knoxville, 1981. Grad. asst. history dept. U. Tenn., Knoxville, 1977-78, grad. teaching asst., 1978-80, grad. asst. libr. and info. sci., 1980-81; reference libr., coord. online svcs., coord. biog. instrn. Watson Libr., Northwestern State U., Natchitoches, La., 1981-87, head reference divsn., supr. reference, 1987—, interim dir., 2000—01. Adv. bd. Bowker Publ. Topical Reference Books, Princeton, N.J., 1988-89; sec. La. Assn. for Acad. Competition, 1991—; chmn. faculty-staff devel. com. Watson Libr., 1983-88, chmn. devel. com. collection, 1988-89, chmn. quiz bowl com., 1989—, automated circulation sys. com., 1984-85, centennial com. 1983-84, chmn. libr. evaluation com., 1997—; cons. Best Books for Academic Librs. Vol. 4, American History, subject specialist Bookers' Best Reference Books. Contbg. author: Booktalking the Award Winners, Vols. 1, 2, 3; mem. editl. bd. Alumni Reviewer for Reference Books Bull., 1991—; co-editor newsletter Libr. Users Edn., 1991-92; editor Online Svcs. Interest Group Newsletter, 1986-87; editor Watson Libr. Newsletter Ex Libris, 1983-2005; contbr. articles to profl. jours. Mem. Assn. for Preservation Historic Natchitoches, 1985—, Natchitoches Humane Soc., 1983—. Recipient Sigma Xi award, Natchitoches, 1986. Mem. ALA, La. Libr. Assn. (vice chair acad. sect. 1988-89, chair 1989-90, mem. exec. bd. 1988-90, coord. online svcs. interest group 1985-86), Southeastern Libr. Assn., Phi Kappa Phi, Beta Phi Mu, Phi Alpha Theta. Episcopalian. Avocations: reading, needlecrafts, travel. Office Phone: 318-357-4574.

LANDRY, JANE LORENZ, architect; b. San Antonio, Feb. 12, 1936; d. John Henry and Lulie Amanda (Sample) L.; m. Duane Eugene Landry, Sept. 8, 1956; children: Rachel, Claire, Ellyn, Jean. Student, U. Tex., 1952-55, Yale U., 1955-56; BArch, U. Pa., 1957. Registered arch., Tex. Project arch. O'Neil Ford & Assoc., San Antonio, 1959-65; prin. Duane Landry, Arch., San Antonio, 1965-68, Dallas, 1968-76; ptnr. Landry & Landry, Archs. & Planners, Dallas, 1976—, Meyer, Landry & Landry, Archs. & Planners, Dallas, 1977-80. Instr. San Antonio Coll., 1965. Dir. at large Interfaith Forum on Religion, Art and Architecture, 1991—; mem. Liturgical Commn. Diocese of Dallas, 1978-90. Recipient design awards Interfaith Forum on Religion, Art and Architecture, 1985, 89, 90, 97, 98, 2000, 2003. Fellow AIA (mem. hist. resources com., design awards Dallas chpt. 1970, 75, 76, 77, 80); mem. Tex. Soc. Architects (design award 1969, 81), The Liturgical Design Consultancy. Roman Catholic. Office: Landry & Landry Archs & Planners 6319 Meadow Rd Dallas TX 75230-5140 Office Phone: 214-265-8398.

LANDRY, MARY CATHERINE, dance instructor, choreographer; b. West Memphis, Ark., May 26, 1956; d. William Eugene and Catherine Ann Landry; m. John O'Bert Beasley, III, Dec. 29, 1984 (div. Mar. 31, 1999); 1 child, Sarah Catherine Beasley; m. Daniel Wayne Cocke, Apr. 17, 2004; children: Jonathan Cocke, Erin Cocke, Adam Cocke. BE with high honors, U. Tenn., 1985. Dancer New Repertory Dance Co. U. Tenn., Knoxville, 1982—84; soloist dancer Knoxville Met. Dance Theatre, Tenn., 1983—85; choreographer Bijou Theatre, Knoxville, 1984—84, Fountain City Sch. Performing Arts, Knoxville, 1985—92, dir., instr., 1985—92; prin. dancer Victoria Bolen Dance Theatre, Knoxville, 1985—88; featured dancer West Side Story Clarence Brown Theatre, Knoxville, 1986; profl. dancer Dolly Parton's Dixie Stampede, Pigeon Forge, Tenn., 1989; dir., choreographer, instr. Dance For Joy!, Knoxville, 1993—; dir., choreographer Liturgical Dance Co. Joy!, Knoxville, 1993—. Soloist Holston Meth. Conf., Knoxville, 1998—2001. Dancer (performance) Opening Worship Service Holston Meth. Annual Conference. At-large del. Holston Meth. Ann. Conf., Lake Junaluska, NC, 2004; drama dir. Fountain City United Meth. Ch., Knoxville, 1999—, dir. angel choir, 1993—96, dir. music makers choir, 2003—, altar guild mem., 2003—; instr. Music & Workshop Arts, Southeastern Jurisdiction Fellowship United Meth., Lake Junaluska, 2000—02; choreographer Beaver Dam Bapt. Ch., Knoxville, 2002, Smithwood Bapt. Ch. Youth Choir, Knoxville, 2002. Mem.: Fountain City Bus. & PA. United Methodist. Avocations: singing, horseback riding, travel. Home: 2525 Fair Dr Knoxville TN 37918-2324 Office: Dance For Joy 2525 Fair Dr Knoxville TN 37918-2324 Personal E-mail: marycatherine@danceforjoy.info.

LANDRY, SANDRA DENISE, secondary school educator; b. Grantsburg, Wis., Oct. 9, 1965; d. David Phillip and Melva Sue (Dodd) Carnal; children: Rebekah, Stephen. BS in Edn., Ark. State U., 1989, MS in Edn., 1997. Cert. tchr. Mo. Tchr. Pemiscot County Spl. Schs., Hayti, Mo., 1989-91, Osceola (Ark.) Pub. Schs., 1991-93, Senath-Hornersville High Sch., Senath, Mo., 1993-2000; prin. Osecola (Ark.) Pub. Schs., 2000—. Instr. Senath-Hornersville Schs., 1993—2000. Mem. Ark. Assn. Spl. Edn. Aminstrs., Coun. Exceptional Children, Learning Disabilities Assn., Delta Kappa Gamma, Beta Sigma Phi (treas. 1996-97), Kappa Delta Pi. Baptist. Avocations: bicycling, reading. Office: 1230 W Semmes Osceola AR 72370 Home: 102 W Greenbriar Dr Osceola AR 72370-2825 Business E-Mail: slandry@seminoles.k12.or.us.

LANDRY, SHERRY S., lawyer; BA, Univ. New Orleans; JD summa cum laude, Loyola Univ., New Orleans. Bar: La. 1996. Atty. Locke Liddell & Sapp; sr. chief dep. Law Dept., New Orleans, 2002—03, city atty., 2003—. Mem.: United Way for Greater New Orleans Area. Office: City Atty City Hall 1300 Perdido St Room 5E03 New Orleans LA 70112-2125 Office Phone: 504-658-9800. Office Fax: 504-565-7691.

LANDRY, TRACEY KATHERINE, social studies educator; b. Oak Lawn, Ill., May 25, 1972; d. Walter Andrew and Esther Elizabeth Lueder; m. Daniel Joseph Landry, Dec. 27, 1997; children: Paige Katherine, Ethan Daniel. MA in History, Northeastern Ill. U., Chgo., 2004; MS in Ednl. Leadership, No. Ill. U., Dekalb, 2005. Tchr. social studies Dist. 127 Grayslake Cmty. H.S., Ill., 1995—. Mem.: DAR, Nat. Coun. Social Studies. Independent. Avocations: travel, reading. Office: Grayslake Central HS 400 N Lake St Grayslake IL 60030 Office Phone: 847-223-8621 4410.

LANDSBERG, JILL WARREN, lawyer, educator, arbitrator; b. N.Y.C., Oct. 11, 1942; d. George Richard and Evelyn (Schepps) Warren; m. Lewis Landsberg, June 14, 1964; children: Alison, Judd Warren. BA, George Washington U., Washington, 1964; MAT, Yale U., 1965; JD, Boston Coll.,

1976. Bar: Mass., 1977, Ill., 1991. Assoc., dir. (ptnr.) Widett, Slater & Goldman PC, Boston, 1976-90; pvt. practice Chgo., 1991-94; faculty Med. Sch. Ethics and Human Values Dept. Northwestern U., Chgo., 1991-94; exec. asst. spl. counsel for child welfare svcs. Office of the Gov., Chgo., 1994-95, acting spl. counsel for child welfare svcs., 1995-96; cons. in field, 1996—2002; adj. prof. law Northwestern U., 2000—. Govt. agys. cons.; mem. Legis. Com. on Juvenile Justice, Chgo., 1995—96, Task Force on Violence Against Children, Chgo., 1995—99, Citizens Com. on the Juvenile Ct., Chgo., 1995—. Tutor Ptnrs. in Edn., 4th Presbyn. Ch., Chgo., 1993—; mem. steering com. Ill. Ct. Improvement Program, 1995-99; Ill. Jud. Inquiry Bd., 2000—; adv. bd. Libr. Internat. Rels., Chgo., 1993-94; bd. trustees Children's Home and Aid Soc. of Ill. Mem. Chgo. Bar Assn., Ill. State Bar Assn., Am. Arbitration Assn. (cons. 1989—),Phi Beta Kappa, Order of the Coif. Home and Office: 70 E Cedar St Chicago IL 60611-1179 Business E-Mail: j-landsberg@northwestern.edu.

LANDSTROM, ELSIE HAYES, retired editor; b. Kuling, Kiangsi, China, June 22, 1923; came to the U.S., 1935; d. Paul Goodman and Helen Mae (Wolf) Hayes; m. Victor Norman Landstrom, Jan. 21, 1953 (dec. Oct. 1989); children: Peter S., Ruth H. BA magna cum laude, Hamline U., 1945. Writer, editor adminstrv. staff Am. Friends Svc. Com., Phila., 1946-52, MIT, Cambridge, Mass., 1952-53; mem. editl. bd. Approach Mag., Phila. and Needham, 1947-67; sr. editor Word Guild, 1976-82; freelance writer and editor Conway, Mass., 1976-98; ret., 1998. Author: Closing the Circle—An American Family in China, 1998; editor: Propaganda and Aesthetics, 1979, Taoism and Chinese Religion, 1981, Hyla Doc in China 1924-1949, 1991, Hyla Doc in Africa 1950-1961, 1994; artists (exhibits) Greenfield, Mo., 1996, Book Mill, Montague, Mass., 1997. Newsletter editor, draft resisters support com. Wellesley (Mass.) Friends Meeting; chair Fair Housing Com., Needham. Avocations: birding, reading, painting. Home: 86 Kendal Dr Kennett Square PA 19348-2327

LANDVOGT, PENNY LUCILLE, psychotherapist, educator; b. Janesville, Wis., May 19, 1946; d. John Lenard and Marion Lucille Piekarski; m. William Landvogt. BS, U. Wis., 1968, MS, 1969, PhD, 1986. Assoc. prof. U. Wis., Madison, 1969-83, evaluation specialist, 1983-86; psychotherapist pvt. practice, Madison, 1985—. Avocations: multi-media art, arabian horse breeding.

LAND-WEBER, ELLEN, photography professor; b. Rochester, NY, Mar. 16, 1943; d. David and Florence Epstein; 1 child, Julia. BA, U. Iowa, 1965, MFA, 1968. Faculty mem. UCLA Extension, 1970-74, Orange Coast Coll., Costa Mesa, Calif., 1973, U. Nebr., Lincoln, 1974; asst. prof. photography Humboldt State U., Arcata, Calif., 1974-79, assoc. prof., 1979-83, prof., 1983—. Photographer Seagram's Bicentennial Courthouse Project, 1976-77, Nat. Trust for Hist. Preservation/Soc. Photographic Edn., 1987. Author: The Passionate Collector, 1980, To Save a Life: Stories of Holocaust Rescue, 2000; contbr. sects. to books; photographs pub. in numerous books and jours. Named Humboldt State U. Scholar of Yr., 2004-2005; Nat. Endowment for Arts fellow, 1974, 79, 82; Artist's support grantee Unicolor Corp., 1982, Polaroid 20X24 Artist's support grantee, 1990, 91, 93, 94; Fulbright sr. fellow, 1993-94. Mem. Soc. for Photog. Edn. (exec. bd. 1979-82, treas. 1979-81, sec. 1981-83) Avocation: weaving. Office: Humboldt State U Art Dept Arcata CA 95521

LANDY, LISA ANNE, lawyer; b. Miami, Fla., Apr. 20, 1963; d. Burton Aaron and Eleonora Maria (Simmel) L. BA, Brown U., 1985; JD cum laude, U. Miami, 1988. Bar: Fla. 1988, U.S. Dist. Ct. (so. dist.) Fla. 1988. Atty. Paul, Landy, Beiley & Harper, P.A., Miami, Fla., 1988-94, Steel Hector & Davis, Miami, 1994-97, ptnr., 1996-97; shareholder Akerman Senterfitt & Eidson P.A., Miami, 1997—. Bd. dirs. Miami City Ballet, 1992-97, pres., 1996, Women in Internat. Trade, Miami, 1992—, pres., 1995, Orgn. Women in Internat. Trade, 1994—, v.p., 1997, 98, pres. 1998-2000; bd. dirs. Women in Tech. Internat. South Fla.; bd. dirs., v.p. Commonwealth Inst. So. Fla.; chmn. The Next Step Youth Cmty. Ctr., Inc., 2000-02, IT Women, Inc., 2002—; co-chair Women of interlaw, 2004—. Mem. ABA, Inter-Am. Bar Assn. (asst. sec. 1997-2000). Avocations: sports, arts, languages.

LANE, ALLYSON C., elementary school educator; b. Canandaigua, N.Y., Aug. 13, 1976; d. Jo Ann and David Milton Lane; 1 child, Adrienne Amanda DeMarco. MS, Nazareth Coll., Rochester, 2005. Cert. lit. birth-grade 6 N.Y., 2006, lit. grade 5-12 N.Y., 2006. Lit. specialist Midlakes Mid. Sch., Clifton Springs, NY, 2000—. Mem.: Internat. Reading Assn. Office Phone: 315-548-6600.

LANE, ANN JUDITH, history professor, women's studies educator; b. N.Y.C., July 27, 1931; d. Harry A. and Elizabeth (Brown) Lane; children: Leslie Patricia, Joni Alexandra. BA, Bklyn. Coll., 1952; MA, NYU, 1958; PhD, Columbia U., 1968. Mng. editor Challenge Mag., NYU, 1953-56; asst. prof. Douglass Coll., Rutgers U., New Brunswick, N.J., 1968-71; prof. John Jay Coll., SUNY, 1971-83; vis. prof. Wheaton Coll., Norton, Mass., 1981-82; prof. history, dir. women's studies Colgate U., Hamilton, N.Y., 1983-90, U. Va., Charlottesville, 1990—. Author: To Herland and Beyond, 1990, Mary Ritter Beard: A Sourcebook, 1977, 2d edit., 1988, The Brownsville Affair, 1971; editor: Charlotte Perkins Gilman Reader, 1980, Herland: A Lost Utopian Novel, 1979. Chair Com. on Status of Women in the Profession, Orgn. of Am. Historians, 1992-95; dir. History Tchr. Inst., N.Y. Coun. for Humanities, summer 1985; mem. historians adv. com. Nat. Women's Hall of Fame, 1986—; bd. dirs. Louis M. Rabinowitz Found., 1972-76. Recipient Va. Soc. Sci. Outstanding History scholar, 2005; fellow, Berkshire Conf. Women Historians, 1988, Ford Found., 1981—82, Nat. Endowment for Humanities, 1980—81, Lilly Endowment, Inc., 1977—79, AAUW, 1959—60. Mem. AAUP (mem. com. on women 1987—), Orgn. Am. Historians (mem. Frederick Jackson Turner prize com. 1979), Women in Hist. Profession (exec. bd., coordinating com. 1971-74). Home: 2603 Jefferson Park Cir Charlottesville VA 22903-4133 Office Phone: 434-982-2961. E-mail: annlane@virginia.edu.

LANE, BARBARA MILLER (BARBARA MILLER-LANE), humanities educator; b. NYC, Nov. 1, 1934; d. George Ross Rede and Gertrude Miller; m. Jonathan Lane, Jan. 28, 1956; children: Steven Gregory, Eleanor. BA, U. Chgo., 1953, Barnard Coll., N.Y.C., 1956; MA, Radcliffe Coll., 1957; PhD, Harvard U., Cambridge, Mass., 1962. Tutor history and lit. Harvard U., Cambridge, Mass., 1960-61; lectr. to prof. history Bryn Mawr Coll., Pa., 1962-75, dir. Growth and Structure of Cities Program, 1971-89, Andrew W. Mellon prof. humanities, 1981-99, Katherine McBride prof., 1999—2005, dir. grad. group in archaeology, classics and history of art, 2004. Vis. prof. architecture Columbia U., 1989; cons. NEH sr. fellowships, Washington, 1971-73, Time-Life Books, N.Y.C., 1975; advisor Macmillan Ency. of Architects, N.Y.C., 1979-82; vis. examiner U. Helsinki, 1991; vis. lectr. Technische Universität, Berlin, 1991, Royal Inst. Tech., Stockholm, 2002. Author: (books) Architecture and Politics in Germany, 1968, 1985, National Romanticism and Modern Architecture in Germany and the Scandinavian Countries, 2000, Housing and Dwelling, 2006; co-author: Nazi Ideology Before 1933, 1978; contbg. author: books Growth and Transformation of the Modern City, 1979; author (contbg.): Macmillan Encyclopedia of Architects, 1982, Urbanisierung im 19. und 20. Jahrhundert, 1983, Perspectives in American History, 1984, The Evidence of Art: Images and Meaning in History, 1986, Art and History, 1988, Nationalism in the Visual Arts, 1991, Moderne Architektur in Deutschland: Expressionismus und Neue Sachlichkeit, 1994, Ultra terminum vagari: Scritti in onore di Carl Nylander, 1997, Oxford Companion to Architecture, 2006; contbg. editor: Urbanism Past and Present, 1980—85; bd. editors Archtl. History Found., 1988—, (journal) Ctrl. European History, 1992—97; contbr. articles to profl. jours. Co-founder, dir., chmn. bd. dirs. New Gulph Child Care Ctr., Bryn Mawr, 1971-75; mem. Mid. Atlantic Regional Com., Mellon Fellowships in the Humanities, 1985-87; mem. vis. com. Harvard U. Dept. History, 1986-92, Berlin Stadtforum (adv. coun. to Senator for Urban Devel. and Environment) 1991-96; mem. nat. screening com. Inst. Internat. Edn., 1999-2004; mem. com. NEH sr. fellowships, 2002. Recipient Lindback award for excellence in tchg., 1988, medal of honor U. Helsinki, 1996; fellow AAUW, 1959-60, Fels Found., 1961-62, Am. Coun. Learned Socs., 1967-68, Guggenheim Found., 1977-78, sr. fellow Ctr. for Advanced Study in Visual Arts, Nat. Gallery Art, Washington, 1983; Am. Scandinavian Found. fellow, 1989, Wissenschaftskolleg zu Berlin fellow, 1990-91; NEH grantee, summer 1989; NEH sr. fellow, 1998; emeritus fellow Mellon Found., 2005—. Mem. Soc. Archtl. Historians (bd. dirs. 1977-80, Alice Davis Hitchcock award 1968, chmn. awards coms. 1976, 82, chmn. jour. com. 1982-83), Conf. Group on Ctrl. European History (bd. dirs. 1977-79, chmn. awards com. 1987), Am. Hist. Assn. (mem. coun. 1979-82, chmn. com. on Popular Mag. of History 1982), Coll. Art Assn., Phi Beta Kappa. Office: Bryn Mawr Coll Bryn Mawr PA 19010

LANE, CARRIE BELLE (HAIRSTON), retired music educator; b. Columbus, Ohio, Nov. 12, 1936; d. Samuel Arthur and Carrie Belle Hairston; m. LeRoy Elsworth Lane, June 27, 1964; children: Peter Kevin, Samuel Elsworth, Todd Lucien. BS in Edn., Ohio State U., 1960. Cert. music tchr. Ohio, Wash., N.J., 1960. Music tchr. Ctrl. Local Schs., Farmer, Ohio, 1961—64, Cleve. Pub. Schs., 1964—66, Clover Pk. Pub. Schs., Tacoma, 1969, Columbus Pub. Schs., 1968—69, Mt. Laurel Pub. Schs., NJ, 1967, Pemberton Twp. Schs., NJ, 1974—77, Willingboro Pub. Schs., NJ. Pvt. voice and piano tchr., Willingboro, 1977—2002, Delanco, NJ, 2004—. Dir.: Messiah, 2005. Charter mem. and sec., v.pres. Willingboro Chpt. NAACP, 1977—88; mem. adv. bd. for Burlington County mentally ill and their families Cath. Charities, 2005—; v.p. Willingboro Dem. Com., 1982; pres. Willingboro Zoning Bd. of Adjust., 1978—94; committeewoman dist. 26 Willingboro Dem. Club, 1992—94; sr. choir soloist and dir. Willingboro Presbyn. Ch., 1977—90; soloist and asst. dir. Christ Bapt. Ch. Sr. Choir, Burlington, NJ, 1991—. Recipient Cmty. and Edn. award, Willingboro NAACP, 1982, Ft. Dix Mil. Wife of the Yr., Ft. Dix Post Comdr. and Cmty., 1974, Edn. award, Nat. Orgn. Black Law Enforcement, Camden, NJ, 1992, Edn. plaque, Camden/Phila. chpt. The Hairston Clan, Inc., 2002, Edn. and Cmty. award, Nothing But the Word Deliverance Ch., Florence, NJ, 2002, Retirement cert., NJ Senate and Assembly, WEA, Willingboro Bd. Edn., 2002. Mem.: N.J. Ret. Edn. Assn., NEA Ret. Tchrs. (assoc.), N.J. Edn. Assn. (assoc.; union rep. jr. hs 2001—02), Alpha Kappa Alpha (assoc.; charter mem. treas. 1978—, philactor 2006—, corres. sec., asst. sec., parliamentarian). Democrat-Npl. Baptist. Avocations: reading, travel, singing, teaching, directing. Home: 11 Shipps Way Delanco NJ 08075 Office Phone: 856-764-0428. Personal E-mail: chlane29@comcast.net.

LANE, COLETTE MARIE, writer; b. Cambridge, Eng., Aug. 14, 1958; arrived in U.S., 1960; d. George V. and Sheila V. Lane; 1 child, Jessica Ann. Student, Fullerton Jr. Coll., Calif. Quality control insp. ACT Connector, Anaheim, Calif., Acra Aerospace, Anaheim, Norton Auto Wheel Divsn., Fullerton. Author: Tribute to the Redwoods Poem, 2001, California Sunset Photo, 2001, Northern Lights, 2003. Avocations: music, writing, poetry, painting, psychic reading.

LANE, DARLENE KELLEY, history educator; b. Ft. Oglethorpe, Ga., Nov. 28, 1956; d. Woodie R. and Nettie E. Kelley; m. Daryl W. Lane, Apr. 19, 1975; children: Jennifer Lane Poteet, Sarah Lane Kubler. BS in Secondary Edn., U. Tenn., Chattanooga, 1998. Tchr. Ringgold (Ga.) Mid. Sch., 1998—2001, Lakeview-Ft. Oglethorpe (Ga.) H.S., 2001—, head dept., 2001—. Named Page Region I Star Tchr., Profl. Assn. Ga. Educators, 2004. Mem.: Ga. Coun. Econ. Edn., Ga. Coun. Social Studies, Nat. Coun. Social Studies. Avocations: piano, reading, home remodeling. Office: Lakeview Ft Oglethorpe High Sch 1850 Battlefield Pkwy Fort Oglethorpe GA 30742

LANE, DIANE, actress; b. N.Y.C., Jan. 22, 1965; d. Burt Lane and Colleen Farrington; m. Christopher Lambert, Oct. 1988 (div. Mar. 1994); 1 child, Eleanor; m. Josh Brolin, Aug. 14, 2004. Actress: (stage prodns.) Medea, 1972, Agamemnon, 1977, The Cherry Orchard, 1977, Runaways, 1978, Electra, The Trojan Woman, As You Like it, The Good Woman of Setzuan, (films) A Little Romance, 1979 (Young Artist Award for best juvenile actress motion picture, 1980), Cattle Annie and Little Britches, 1981, National Lampoon Goes to the Movies, 1981, Six Pack, 1982, Ladies and Gentlemen, The Fabulous Stains, 1982, The Outsiders, 1983, Rumble Fish, 1983, The Cotton Club, 1984, Streets of Fire, 1984, Lady Beware, 1987, The Big Town, 1987, Vital Signs, 1990, Chaplin, 1992, Knight Moves, 1992, Indian Summer, 1993, Wild Bill, 1995, Judge Dredd, 1995, Jack, 1996, Mad Dog Time, 1996, The Only Thrill, 1997, Murder at 1600, 1997, Over the Moon, 1998, GunShy, 1998, A Walk on the Moon, 1999, The Setting Sun, 1999, My Dog Skip, 1999, The Perfect Storm, 2000, Hard Ball, 2001, The Glass House, 2001, Unfaithful, 2002 (Acad. Award nomination for best actress, 2003, Golden Satellite award for best actress, 2003, Nat. Soc. of Film Critics award for best actress, 2003, NY Film Critics Circle award for best actress, 2003), Under the Tuscan Sun, 2003, Fierce People, 2005, Must Love Dogs, 2005, Hollywoodland, 2006; (TV movies) Child Bride of Short Creek, 1981, Miss All-America Beauty, 1982; (TV miniseries) Lonesome Dove, 1989, The World's Oldest Living Confederate Widow Tells All, 1994, A Streetcar Named Desire, 1995, Grace and Glorie, 1998. Named Actress of Yr., Hollywood Film Festival, 2003. Mem. Actors' Equity Assn., AFTRA. Office: The Endeavor Agy 9601 Wilshire Blvd Beverly Hills CA 90212*

LANE, DOROTHY SPIEGEL, preventive medicine physician; b. Bklyn., Feb. 17, 1940; d. Milton Barton and Rosalie (Jacobson) Spiegel; m. Bernard Paul Lane, Aug. 5, 1962; children: Erika, Andrew, Matthew. BA, Vassar Coll., 1961; MD, Columbia U., 1965, MPH, 1968. Diplomate Am. Bd. Preventive Medicine, Am. Bd. Family Practice. Resident in preventive medicine NYC Dept. Health Dist., 1966-68, project dir. children and youth project Title V, HHS Rockaway, 1968-69; med. cons. Maternal and Child Health Svc. HHS, Rockville, Md., 1970-71; asst. prof. preventive medicine Sch. Medicine SUNY, Stony Brook, 1971-76, assoc. prof., 1976-92, prof., 1992—2002, Disting. Svc. prof., 2002—, assoc. dean, 1986—; chair dept. cmty. medicine, dir. med. edn. Brookhaven Meml. Hosp. Med. Ctr., Patchogue, NY, 1972-86. Contbr. articles to profl. jours. Exec. com. LI divsn. Am. Cancer Soc., 1975—96, pres. LI divsn., 1982, mem. nat. assembly, 1996—2001, nat. bd. dir., 1994—96; corp. mem. Nassau Suffolk Health Sys. Agy, 1977—97; bd. dir. Cmty. Health Plan Suffolk, Hauppauge, NY, 1986—91. Grantee, HHS-USPHS, 1977—2002, 2004—, Nat. Cancer Inst., 1987—, Nat. Heart, Lung and Blood Inst., 1994—, Ctrs. for Disease Control, 2005—. Fellow: APHA, Am. Bd. Preventive Medicine (trustee 1991—2000, chair 1998—2000), NY Acad. Medicine, Am. Acad. Family Physicians, Am. Coll. Preventive Medicine (regent 1988—96, sec.-treas. 1994—96, pres.-elect 1998—2001, pres. 2001—03, immediate past pres. 2003—05, past pres. 2005—), Assn. Tchrs. Preventive Medicine (pres. 1996—98); mem.: Accreditation Coun. for Continuing Med. Edn. (bd. dirs. 2002—, exec. commn. 2005—). Office: SUNY at Stony Brook Sch Medicine Health Scis Ctr L 4 Stony Brook NY 11794-8437 Office Phone: 631-444-2094. Business E-Mail: dorothy.lane@stonybrook.edu.

LANE, ELIZABETH ANN, genealogist, researcher; b. Horton, Kans., Mar. 9, 1957; d. Dale D. Sheets and Marlene E. Kletchka; m. Rex L. Lane; children: Laura, Catherine. BSW, U. Kans., 1983. Dir. CASA, Atchison, Kans., 1997—98; asst. dir. Juvenile Intake and Assessment, Oskaloosa, Kans., 1998—2001. Mem.: AAUW, Atchison Preservation Alliance (bd. dirs. 1999—2001, treas., bd. dirs. 2004—05), Friends Atchison Libr. (pres. 2001—03), Atchison County Hist. Soc. (bd. dirs. 1998—2002, pres. 2001—02). Avocations: gardening, reading, music, travel. Home: EA Lane Rsch Svcs 841 S Fourth St Atchison KS 66002-2904 Office Phone: 913-367-0391. Personal E-mail: llane1@charter.net.

LANE, GLORIA JULIAN, foundation administrator; b. Chgo., Oct. 6, 1932; d. Coy Berry and Katherine (McDowell) Julian; m. William Gordon Lane (div. Oct. 1958); 1 child, Julie Kay Rosewood. BS in Edn., Cen. Mo. State U., 1958; MA, Bowling Green State U., 1959; PhD, No. Ill. U., 1972. Cert. tchr. Assoc. prof. William Jewell Coll., Liberty, Mo., 1959-60; chair forensic div. Coral Gables (Fla.) High Sch., 1960-64; assoc. prof. No. Ill. U., DeKalb, 1964-70; prof. Elgin (Ill.) Community Coll., 1970-72; owner, pub. Lane and Assocs, Inc., San Diego, 1972-78; prof. Nat. U., San Diego, 1978-90; pres., chief exec. officer Women's Internat. Ctr., San Diego, 1982—. Founder, dir. Living Legacy Awards, San Diego, 1984—. Author: Project Text for Effective Communications, 1972, Project Text for Executive Communication, 1980, Positive Concepts for Success, 1983; editor Who's Who Among San Diego Women, 1984, 85, 86, 90—, Systems and Structure, 1984. Named Woman of Accomplishment, Soroptimist Internat., 1985, Pres.'s Coun. San Diego, 1986, Center City Assn., 1986, Bus. and Profl. Women, San Diego, 1991, Woman of Yr., Girls' Clubs San Diego, 1986, Woman of Vision, Women's Internat. Ctr., 1990, Wonderwoman 2000 Women's Times Newspaper, 1991; recipient Angel in Action award, 1999, Independence award Ctr. for Disabled, 1986, Founder's award Children's Hosp. Internat., Washington, 1986, Making Difference for Women award, Soroptimist Internat., 1998, Women Who Mean Business Courage Award San Diego Bus. Jour., 1998. Avocations: computers, painting, writing. Home and Office: 6202 Friars Rd Unit 311 San Diego CA 92108-5000 E-mail: gloria311@aol.com.

LANE, HANA UMLAUF, editor; b. Stockholm, Mar. 14, 1946; came to U.S., 1951, naturalized, 1957; d. Karel Hugo Antonin and Anatolia (Spitel) Umlauf; m. John Richard Lane, Feb. 16, 1980; 1 stepchild, Matthew John AB magna cum laude, Vassar Coll., 1968; AM in Russian and East European Studies, Yale U., 1970. Asst. to exec. editor Newspaper Enterprise Assn., N.Y.C., 1970-72, sr. asst., asst. editor World Almanac divsn., 1972-75, assoc. editor World Almanac, 1975-80, spl. project editor, 1977-80; editor World Almanac and World Almanac Publs., N.Y.C., 1980-85; editor in chief Pharos Books, N.Y.C., 1984-91, sr. editor, 1991-93, John Wiley & Sons, 1993—. Editor: World Almanac Book of Who, 1980, World Almanac and Book of Facts, 1981-85; editor: (with others) The Woman's Almanac, 1977. Democrat. Home: 140 Fairview Ave Stamford CT 06902-8040 Business E-Mail: hlane@wiley.com.

LANE, HOLLY DIANA, artist; b. Cleve., Sept. 13, 1954; d. Edwin Joseph and Ursula Anna (Neustadt) Selyem; m. L.A. Lane, Apr. 20, 1975. AA in 2-Dimensional Art, Cuesta Coll., San Luis Obispo, Calif., 1982; BFA with great distinction, San Jose State U., 1986, MFA in Pictorial Art, 1988. One-woman shows include Ivory/Kimpton Gallery, San Francisco, 1989, Rutgers Barclay Gallery, Santa Fe, 1990, Bingham Kurts Gallery, Memphis, 1992, (solo survey show with catalog) Art Mus. S.E. Tex., Beaumont, 1995, Natalie & James Thompson Gallery, San Jose State U., 2001, Yellowstone Art Museum, 2001, Lyman Allyn Mus. Art, 2001, Schmidt Bingham Gallery, NYC, 1991, 93, 95, 97, 99, 2001, Forum Gallery, NYC, 2003, 06(with catalog); exhibited in group shows at Eiteljorg Mus., Indpls., 1995, 2000, Yerba Buena Ctr. for the Arts, San Francisco, 1994, Knoxville (Tenn.) Mus. Art, 1993-94, Fine Arts Ctr. U. RI, Kingston, 1992, Contemporary Mus., Honolulu, 1993, 2002, Boise (Idaho) Art Mus., 1994, Castle Gallery-Coll. New Rochelle, NY, 1996, Kennedy Mus. Am. Art, Athens, Ohio, 1996, Calif. Ctr. for the Arts Escondido Mus., 1996, Samuel P. Harn Mus., U. Fla., Gainesville, 1996, Whitney Mus. Am. Art, Champion, Conn., 1997-98, Arnot Art Mus., Elmira, NY, 1997-98, Susan H. Arnold Art Gallery Lebanon Valley Coll., Anneville, Pa., 1997-98, Pelham (NY) Art Ctr, 1998, Art Mus. Western Va., 1999-2000, San Jose Mus. Art, 1999-2000, Santa Cruz Art Mus., 2000, Brevard Mus. Art and Sci., Melbourne, Fla., 2000, Gallery of Contemporary Art, Sacred Heart U., Fairfield, Conn., 2002, NJ Ctr. For Visual Arts, Summit, 2002, Javitz Ctr., NYC, 2002, Forum Gallery, NYC, 2002, 04, 05, 06, Internat. Art and Design Fair, NYC, 2004, San Francisco Internat. Art Exposition, 2005, N.Y. 7th Regiment Armory, 2005, Palm Beach, Palm Beach County Conv. Ctr., Fla., 2006, Forum Gallery, L.A., 2006, others; represented in permanent collections Art Mus. S.E. Tex., Contemporary Mus., Honolulu, A.R.A. Svcs., Phila., Dow Jones & Co., NYC, Detroit Zool. Gardens, Prin. Fin. Group, Des Moines, IDS, Mpls., Memphis Cancer Ctr., Seven Bridges Found., Greenwich, Conn.; works reproduced in books, mags., calendars, jours., including ARTNews, Art in America, NY Times, NY Sun, 2003, 06, NY Press, Where NY, Art Papers, Art & Antiques, New Yorker Mag., Artweek, Christian Sci. Monitor, Pvt. Arts, Forensic Examiner, NYarts Mag., The Wilson Quar., Review Mag., NYC, 1999, Women Artists calendar 1996-98, San Raphael, Calif., The Sciences, NY Acad. Scis., 1992-93, (textbook) Artist and Audience, (London) 1996, Dreams 1900-2000, CAA News, 2003: Sci., Art and the Unconscious Mind (book), 1999, Wilson Quar., 1998, Rev. Mag., 1999, Dreamworks: Twentieth-Century Artistic and Psychological Perspectives, 1999; works presented in TV documentaries including Welcome to Nocturnia, 1993, Women in Art, Time-Warner, Manhattan Cable, NYC, 1993-94; in books accompanying TV show Bill Moyers Genesis, A Living Tradition, PBS, 1996, Healing and the Mind, 1993. Named Alumna of Yr., Cuesta Coll., 1992; pres.'s scholar San Jose State U., 1986, Johanna Rietz scholar Art Assn. of Morro Bay, Calif., 1981. Mem. Coll. Art Assn. Avocations: nature walks, contemplation, reading. Studio: 182 Brian Ln Santa Clara CA 95051 Office Phone: 212-355-4545. Personal E-mail: hlane42@earthlink.net.

LANE, IRIS MARY, retired elementary school educator; b. Kellogg, Idaho, June 24, 1934; d. Ivan John and Dorothy Vivian (McKinney) Green; m. C. Clayton, Dec. 19, 1959 (div. 1962); 1 child, Mark Andrew. AA, North Idaho Jr. Coll., Coeur d'Alene, 1955; BS, U. Idaho, Moscow, 1964; postgrad., Whitworth Coll., Spokane, 1967, Eastern Wash. U., Cheney, 1967. Tchr. Sch. Dist. 391, Kellogg, Idaho, 1955-57, Sch. Dist. 81, Spokane, Wash., 1958-93; ret., 1993. Master tchr. Local Colls., Spokane, 1962-85. Vol. Am. Heart Assn., Spokane, 1988-93, orphan and foster children assns., illiteracy improvement programs; mem. PTA Recipient Golden Acorn award Garfield Parent Tchrs. Assn., Spokane, 1978. Mem. NEA, Wash. Edn. Assn., Spokane Edn. Assn., Alpha Delta Kappa Honor Soc., Alpha Delta Kappa. Republican. Lutheran. Avocation: church activities. Home: 3405 W Francis Ave Spokane WA 99205-7427 Office Phone: 509-328-6894.

LANE, KATHY S., information technology executive, consumer products company executive; Dir. tech. svcs. Pepsi Cola Internat., 1997—98; mgr. corp. initiatives group Gen. Electric Co., 1998—99, sr. v.p. and chief info. officer, vendor fin. svcs., 1999—2000; gen. mgr. e- bus. and info. tech. Gen. Electric Oil & Gas, 2000—02; sr. v.p. corp. info. tech. and applications Gillette Co., Boston, 2002—, chief info. officer, 2002—. Named one of Premier 100 IT Leaders, Computerworld, 2006. Office: The Gillette Co Prudential Tower Boston MA 02199-8004*

LANE, LILLY KATHERINE, museum staff member; b. Inverness, Fla., Mar. 25, 1934; d. Robert Joseph and Edna Lee (Rooks) Lane; children from previous marriage: James D. Nichols, Gayle Patricia Nichols. RN, St. Luke's Hosp., Jacksonville, Fla., 1955; BFA in Ceramics cum laude, U. Fla., 1984, BA in Asian Studies, 1985, MFA in Ceramics, 1994; grad. cert. in mus. studies, Fla. State U., 2000, PhD, 2005. RN Fla., Va., Ill., Morocco. Swimming tchr., Port Lyautey, Morocco, 1962-63; RN various, 1955-83; English tchr. South China Normal U., Guangzhou, 1987-88; Chinese Calligraphy tchr. St. Augustine, Fla., 1992-93; asst. collections Harn Mus. Art, Gainesville, Fla., 1994—. Contbr. articles in Chinese and English to profl. jours. Pres. Naval Officers Wives Club, Washington, 1973—74. Named to Chancellor's List, Ednl. Comms. Inc., 2005; recipient Fed. Nursing traineeship, 1964; scholar Winn-Lovett Nursing, 1950, Fla. State Nursing, 1963. Mem.: UDC, DAR, AAUW, Fla. Assn. Mus., Am. Assn. Mus., Asian Ceramic Rsch. Orgn., Fla. Craftsmen, Asia Soc., Nat. Art Edn. Assn., Phi Delta Kappa.

LANE, MARGARET BEYNON TAYLOR, librarian; b. St. Louis, Feb. 6, 1919; d. Archer and Alice (Jones) Taylor; m. Horace C. Lane, Jan. 6, 1945; children: Margaret Elizabeth, Thomas Archer. BA, La. State U., 1939, JD, 1942; BS in Libr. Sci., Columbia U., 1941. Reference and circulation asst. Columbia Law Libr., N.Y.C., 1942-44; law libr., asst. prof. U. Conn. Sch. Law, Hartford, 1944-46; law libr. La. State U. Law Sch., Baton Rouge, 1946-48; recorder documents La. Sec. of State's Office, Baton Rouge, 1949-75; law libr. Lane Fertitta, Lane Janney & Thomas, 1976-96. Mem. depository libr. coun. to Pub. Printer, 1972-77; mem. plan devel. com. La. Fed. Depository Libr., 1982-83. Author: State Publications and Depository Libraries, 1981, Selecting and Organizing State Government Publications, 1987. Treas. Delta Iota House Bd. of Kappa Kappa Gamma, 1965-68; rep. emeritus La. Adv. Coun. State Documents Depository Program, 1990—. Inductee La. State U. Law Ctr. Hall of Fame, 1987. Mem.: ALA (interdivisional com. pub. documents 1967—74, chmn. 1967—70, govt. documents round table, state and local documents task force 1972—, coord. 1980—82, James Bennett Childs award 1981, anniversary honor roll 1996, Hoduski Founders award 1997), Baton Rouge Bar Assn., La. Bar Assn., La. Libr. Assn. (Essae M. Culver Disting. Svc. award 1976, Lucy B. Foote award 1986, Margaret T. Lane award named in her honor 1994), Mortar Bd., Baton Rouge Libr. Club, Kappa Kappa Gamma, Phi Delta Delta. Home: 333 Lee Dr Apt 274 Baton Rouge LA 70808 Personal E-mail: mtlane@cox.net.

LANE, MARSHA K., medical/surgical nurse; b. Glendale, Calif., Mar. 22, 1942; m. Albert Lane, Sept. 16, 1961; children: Alan, Mike, Shawn, Eric. LVN, Mira Costa Coll., 1971; ADN, San Diego City Coll., 1975; BS in Health Scis., Chapman Coll., 1986, postgrad., 1991. Head RN CCU Humana Hosp., Huntington Beach, Calif.; supr. ICU/CCU, TELE Tri City Med. Ctr., Oceanside, Calif., asst. unit mgr. ICU/CCU, staffnurse, dir. med./surg. svcs., developer patient diabetes tchg. program; DON LifeCare Ctr. Vista SNF.

LANE, MARY WINSTON, secondary school educator; b. Middlesboro, Ky., Oct. 10, 1923; d. Shelton and Rena (Ward) Evans; m. Richard Alan Lane, Aug. 15, 1965 (dec.); children: Barbara Ann Lane Partin, John Brian BS, Ea. Ky. U., Richmond, 1944; MS in Chemistry, U. Mo., Rolla, 1966; postgrad., Ohio State U., Columbus, 1971—73. Cert. secondary chemistry, math. and physics tchr., Ohio, Ky., gifted and talented tchr., Ky. Chemist med. physics rsch. Donner Lab. U. Calif., Berkeley, 1944—59; tchr., head dept. Bell County H.S., Pineville, Ky., 1959—66; tchr. Ottiville Schs., Ohio, 1969—71, Bath H.S., Lima, Ohio, 1974—79, Middlesboro H.S., Ky., 1979—99; ret., 1999. Prof. Lincoln Meml. U., summers 1988-89, 91; organizer, dir. Southeastern Regional Sci. Fair, 1962-66; organizer Southeastern Alliance Sci. Tchrs., 1991; workshop presenter Chem 93; presenter Woodrow Wilson Workshop, 1993 Recipient Award of Excellence in Tchg. Chemistry for Ky., Am. Chem. Soc., 1995, award for rsch. and tng. Brazilian rschrs. Brazilian Sociol. Soc., 2005; named Tandy tchr., 1992, 93 Mem. NEA, NSTA, Middlesboro Edn. Assn., Ky. Sci. Tchrs. Assn. (state bd. dirs., Disting. Svc. award 1994), Alliance 5th Dist. Sci. and Math. Tchrs. (co-dir. 1989—), Delta Kappa Gamma Democrat. Baptist. Avocations: gardening, designing and building geo solar homes. Home: RR 1 Box 519A Rose Hill VA 24281-9720

LANE, MICHELE JEANNE, special education educator; b. Portland, Oreg., Apr. 25, 1953; d. Robert William and Ann Emeline (Austin) L.; m. Edward Brien McDonough, May 14, 1983; children: Tim, Megan, Justin. AA in Pre-Sch. Edn., College of Marin, 1975; BA in Liberal Studies, Calif. State Coll., 1977; MS in Spl. Edn., Dominican Coll., 1980. Cert. multi-subject tchr., Calif., learning-handicapped specialist, Calif., severely-handicapped specialist, Calif.; bd. cert. ednl. therapist. Pres-sch. tchr. Corte Madera (Calif.) Larkspur Co-op., 1973, Beginning Sch., Marin City, Calif., 1974, Tamalpais Nursery Sch., Mill Valley, Calif., 1975-76; teacher's aide 1st grade Forestville (Calif.) Sch., 1976-77; student tchr. 2d, 3rd and 6th grades Hamilton Sch., Novato, Calif., 1978; tutor Dominican Coll. Learning Ctr., 1978-80; learning disabilities specialist, music and movement instr. Arena Learning Ctr., 1979-82; dir., learning disabilities specialist Lane's Learning Ctr., Novato, 1981—. Intern Magnolia Park Sch., St. Vincent Boys Sch., Casa Allegra; intern speech pathologist Sonoma (Calif.) State Hosp.; developer "Music in Motion" programs Recreation for the Gifted; coord. Red Ribbon Week, Novato, 1992-93. Speaker Morning Star Farm, Novato, 1992. Spl. edn. del. to People's Republic of China with Citizens Ambassador Program Internat., 1994. Mem. Assn. Ednl. Therapists (profl.), Educators in Pvt. Practice (profl.). Avocations: equestrian, gardening, hiking, cross country skiing, dance. Home and Office: Lane's Learning Ctr 1 Gustafson Ct Novato CA 94947-2882 Office Phone: 415-892-7706. Personal E-mail: michlane@aol.com.

LANE, NANCY, advocate, editor; b. N.Y.C., Dec. 20, 1938; d. Morton and Lillian (Gelb) L. AB in Am. Civilization, Barnard Coll., 1960. Mem. staff N.Y. Times, 1959—61; from asst. to assoc. editor Polit. Sci. Quar. and Procs. Acad. Polit. Sci., Columbia U., N.Y.C., 1962—70; from assoc. editor to mng. editor Am. Hist. Rev. Am. Hist. Assn., 1970—74; from sr. editor to exec. editor Oxford U. Press, N.Y.C., 1974—97; cons., 1997—98. Vol. Bellevue-NYU Program for Survivors of Torture, 1998-99. Mem.: ACLU, Ams. United for Separation of Ch. and State, Amnesty Internat. U.S.A. (vol. 1995—, torture-abolition coord. for USA Group 11, mem. Turkey Regional Action Network Group 11). Home: 45 W 10th St New York NY 10011-8731

LANE, NICOLE, dancer, educator; b. Nashville, Tenn., July 30, 1975; d. Robert Lee and Brenda Gail Boyd; m. Joe Lane Jr., July 30, 2004. AS, Columbia State CC, Tenn., 2000. Dance instr. Pat Parker Dance Sch., Old Hickory, Tenn., 1994—2006; owner Nicole Boyd Sch. Dance, Mt. Juliet, Tenn., 2006—. Home: 3981 A Vesta Rd Lebanon TN 37090-1500

LANE, PAMELA LYNN, language educator; b. LaGrange, Ga., Mar. 16, 1979; d. Jodie Starling Paschal and Mamie Jeanette Shelnutt Paschal; m. Terry Lee Lane, Nov. 26, 2005. BS in Edn., State U. West Ga., Carrollton, 2001, MEd, 2002. Educator sci. Ephesus Elem. Sch., Franklin, Ga., 2001; educator English as 2d lang. Carrol County Schs., Carrollton, 2002—. Tutor Tavernacle Bapt. Ch., Carrollton, 2005—. Mem.: Ga. Tchrs. English to Spkrs. Other Langs., Ga. Assn. Educators, Phi Theta Lambda. Republican. Baptist. Avocations: travel, photography, softball, tennis. Home: 484 Nutt Rd Franklin GA 30217 Office: Ctrl Mid Sch 155 Whooping Creek Rd Carrollton GA 30116

LANE, PATRICIA PEYTON, retired nursing consultant; b. Danville, Ill., Oct. 5, 1929; d. Louis Weldon Sr. and Ruth Jeanette (Meyer) Peyton; m. H.J. Lane, Dec. 23, 1950 (div.); children: Jennifer Lane-Carr, Peter Lane, Amelia Ozog. Diploma, St. Elizabeth Hosp., 1950; BA in Psychology magna cum laude, Rosary Coll., 1974; postgrad., Lakeview Coll. of Nursing, Danville, Ill., 1987-88; student, Triton Jr. Coll., River Grove, Ill., 1969-72. Staff nurse St. Elizabeth Hosp., Danville, Ill., 1950; staff nurse nursery Ill. Rsch. and Ednl. Hosp., Chgo., 1951, charge nurse tumour clinic, 1951-54; res. sch. nurse elem. schs., Oak Park, Ill., 1969-78; sta. mgr. Oak Park-River Infant Welfare, Oak Park, Ill., 1972-76; vision and hearing screener suburban elem. schs., Ill., 1980-82; sch. nurse West Subrban Assn. Spl. Edn., Cicero, 1978-80; caseworker, counselor Vermilion County Mental Health and Devel. Disabilities, Inc., Danville, 1983-86; case coord., nurse cons. Crosspoint Human Svcs., Danville, 1986-88; staff nurse psychiat. acute care unit Community Hosp. of Ottawa, Ill., 1988-89; dir. social svcs. Pleasant View Luther Home, Ottawa, 1989-93; clin. case coord. Access Svcs., Inc., Mendota, Ill., 1993-97; cmty. ombudsman LaSalle County Alternatives for the Older Adult, Peru, Ill., 1993-97; ret., 1997. Cons. in field. Recipient Ill. Gov.'s award for exceptional achievement in cmty. svc. and svc. to elderly, 1997, Vol. of Yr. award Residence at Oak Ridge, 2002, Vol. Appreciation award, 2004. E-mail: PatLane456@msn.com.

LANE, ROBIN, lawyer; b. Kerrville, Tex., Nov. 28, 1947; d. Rowland and Gloria (Benson) Richards; m. Stanley Lane, Aug. 22, 1971 (div.); 1 child, Joshua; m. Anthony W. Cunningham, Nov. 22, 1980; 1 child, Alexandra Cunningham. BA in Econs. with honors, U. Fla., 1969; MA, George Washington U., 1971; JD, Stetson U., 1978. Bar: Fla. 1979, NY 2002, DC 2002, U.S. Ct. Appeals (11th cir.) 1981, U.S. Supreme Ct. 1986, U.S. Ct. Appeals (D.C. cir.) 1992, U.S. Ct. Appeals (3d cir.) 1993. Mgmt. trainee internat. banking Gulf Western Industries, N.Y.C.; internat. rsch. specialist Ryder Systems, Inc., Miami, 1973, project mgr., 1974; assoc. Wagner, Cunningham, Vaughan & McLaughlin, Tampa, Fla., 1979—85; pvt. practice law, 1985—. Guest lectr. med. jurisprudence Stetson U. Coll. Law, 1982—91, also mem. exec. coun. law alumni bd. Contbr. articles to various revs. Recipient Am. Jurisprudnce award-torts, Lawyers Co-op. Fla., 1979; Scottish Rite fellow, 1968—69. Mem.: ATLA, ABA, Fla. Bar Assn., Acad. Fla. Trial Lawyers (mem. com. 1983—84), Fla. Women's Alliance, Omicron Delta Epsilon. Office: PO Box 10155 Tampa FL 33679-0155 Home: 345 Bayshore Blvd #1805 Tampa FL 33606-2388 Office Phone: 917-312-6773. Personal E-mail: RRL1128@aol.com.

LANE, ROSALIE MIDDLETON, extension specialist; b. Savannah, Ga. d. Freddie and Willie Blanche (Jones) Middleton; m. Martin Luther Jones, Apr. 24, 1964 (div. July 1977); children: Regina Veronica, Sharon Yolanda; m. Woodie Lane, Sr., Dec. 6, 1985; 1 stepchild, Woodie M., Jr. BA, Western Mich. U., 1989; M in Urban and Regional Planning, Ala. A&M U., 1995. Exec. sec. Curtis Brown, Ltd., N.Y.C., 1959-64; adminstrv. sec. Bronx (N.Y.)-Lebanon Hosp. Ctr., 1971-76; adminstr. IBM Corp., Savannah, Ga. and Huntsville, Ala., 1980-95; ext. specialist, rschr., educator Coop. Ext. Sys., Ala. A&M U., Normal, 1995—. Past mem. customer interface task force USDA, Washington. Author: (with others) A Directory of Resource for Low Income, Elderly, and Homeless Citizens in North Ala., 1995; author poems. Vol. Coalition/On- At-Risk Minority Males, Huntsville, Ala., 1992; bd. dirs. ARC Minority Initiatives Com., Huntsville, 1994. Mem. NEA, Am. Planning Assn., Com. Minorities in Pub. Transp. Orgn., Alpha Zeta. Presbyterian. Avocations: creative writing, song writing. Office: Ala Cooperative Extension Sys of Ala A&M Univ and Auburn Univ Meridian St Normal AL 35762

LANE, SOPHIA, art gallery director; b. Amesbury, Mass., Jan. 17, 1930; d. George and Mary Kostaras; m. Charles Stuart Lane, Aug. 30, 1953. BA in Psychology, Boston U., 1952; degree in Math., Boston Coll., 1961, Boston U., 1973. Cert. tchr. Mass., 1952. Lab. technician MIT, Cambridge, Mass., 1952—53; tchr. math. Bennington HS, Vt., 1953—55, Meredith HS, NH, 1955—57, Concord HS, 1957—58, Winnacunnet HS, Hampton, NH, 1958—60; co-founder, tchr. math. Dunbarton Acad., New Hampton, NH, 1959—68; tchr. math. Brookline HS, Mass., 1961—84; dir., ptnr. Old Print Barn-Art Gallery, New Hampton, NH, 1976—. Mem. social com. fulbright grantees Bennington Coll., Vt., 1954—55; v.p., treas. Jour. Print World, Meredith, NH, 1977—; lectr. in field; cons. in field; judge debates. Pub. New Hampshire's First Tourists in the Lakes and Mountains, 1993. Recipient Recognition award, Meredith C. of C., 2002; grantee, NSF, 1960—61. Avocations: bowling, coin collecting/numismatics, archaeology. Home and Office: The Old Print Barn Art Gallery PO Box 978 Meredith NH 03253

LANE, SUE ALISON, literature and language educator; b. Wichita Falls, Tex., Aug. 21, 1953; d. Robert Emil and Eloree Ogle Lane. BBA, Midwestern State U., Wichita Falls, Tex., 1976. Sec., keypunch operator City of Wichita Falls, Tex., 1976—83; lit., remedial reading tchr. City View Jr./Sr. H.S., Wichita Falls, 1983—2006. Mem.: Assn. of Tex. Profl. Educators (v.p. 2004—06). Avocations: reading, art. Home: 1208 Taylor Wichita Falls TX 76309 Office: City View Jr Sr H S 1600 City View Dr Wichita Falls TX 76306

LANE, SYLVIA, economist, educator; b. NYC; m. Benjamin Lane, Sept. 2, 1939; children: Leonard, Reese, Nancy. AB, U. Calif., Berkeley, 1934, MA, 1936; postgrad., Columbia U., 1937; PhD, U. So. Calif., 1957. Lectr., asst. prof. U. So. Calif., 1947—60; assoc. prof. econs. San Diego State U., 1961-65; assoc. prof. finance, assoc. dir. Ctr. for Econ. Edn. Calif. State U., Fullerton, 1965-69, chmn. dept. fin., 1967-69; prof. agrl. econs. U. Calif., Davis, 1969-82, prof. emerita, 1982—; prof. emerita and economist Giannini Found., U. Calif.-Berkeley, 1982—; vis. scholar Stanford U., 1975-76. Cons. Calif. Adv. Commn. Tax Reform, 1963, Adv. Office Consumer Affairs, Exec. Office of Pres., 1972-77, FAO, UN, 1983, Consumer food Subsidiaries Project, 1993. Author: (with E. Bryant Phillips) Personal Finance, 1963, rev. edit., 1979, The Insurance Tax, 1965, California's Income Tax Conformity and Withholding, 1968, (with Irma Adelman) The Balance Between Industry and Agriculture in Economic Development, 1989; author video: Women in Agriculture - Africa, 1994; editl. bd. Agrl. Econs., 1986-92; also articles, reports in field. Project economist Los Angeles County Welfare Planning Coun., 1956-59; del. White House Conf. on Food and Nutrition, 1969, Pres.'s Summit Con. on Inflation, 1974; mem. adv. com. Ctr. for Bldg. Tech., Nat. Bur. Stds., 1975-79; bd. dirs. Am. Coun. Consumer Interests, 1972-74; exec. bd. Am. Agr. Econ. Assn. 1976-79. Ford Found. fellow UCLA, 1963; Ford Found. fellow U. Chgo., 1965; fellow U. Chgo., 1968; fellow Am. Agrl. Econ. Assn., 1984; fellow Sylvia Lane Fellowship Fund, 1993. Mem. Am. Econ. Assn., Am. Coun. Consumer Interests, Omicron Delta Epsilon (pres. 1973-75, trustee 1975-83, chmn. bd. trustees 1982-84). Home and Office: Pacific Regent - La Jolla 3890 Nobel Dr #1508 San Diego CA 92122 Personal E-mail: blane5@san.rr.com.

LANES, SELMA GORDON, critic, author, editor; b. Boston, Mar. 13, 1929; d. Jacob and Lily (Whiteman) Gordon; BA, Smith Coll., 1950; MS in Journalism, Columbia, 1954; m. Jerrold B. Lanes, Nov. 21, 1959 (div. Mar. 1970); children— Andrew Oliver, Matthew Gordon. Asst. to publicity dir. Little Brown & Co., Boston, 1950-51; assoc. editor Focus Mag., NYC, 1951-53; travel page editor Boston Globe, 1953; spl. editorial asst., rschr. Look Mag., 1956-60; children's entertainment editor Show Mag., 1961-63; critic children's books for Book World (NY Herald-Tribune, later World Jour. Tribune, Wash. Post and Chgo. Tribune), 1965-71, NY Times Book Rev., 1966—; articles editor Parents Mag., 1971-74; editor-in-chief Parents Mag. Press, 1974-78; editl. dir. Western Pub. Co.; cons. to Penguin Books, 1967, Starstream Books, 1980-81; lectr. New Sch./Parsons Sch. Design, 1975-77, Del. Art Mus., 1979, Simmons Coll., 1988; dir. Schiller-Wapner Galleries, 1983-84; freelance writer, 1984—. Judge, Children's Spring Book Festival, 1970, dir., 1972; judge NY Times Ten Best Illus. Children's Books, 1973, 79, 80. Trustee Fund for Art Investment, NYC. Mem. Phi Beta Kappa. Author (juvenile) Amy Loves Good-byes, 1966; The Curiosity Book, 1968; Down the Rabbit Hole, A critical work for adults on children's literature, 1971, paperback, 1976; The Art of Maurice Sendak, 1980, Through the Looking Glass, 2004; selector-adapter: A Child's First Book of Nursery Tales, 1983, Windows of Gold, 1989; co-author: Lillian Gish: An Actor's Life for Me!, 1987.

LANE STONE, NANCY ANN, elementary school educator; b. Montague, Mass., Oct. 23, 1945; d. John Henry Adams and Helen Ann (Yez) Lane; m. Richard F. Koscinski, June 8, 1968 (dec. June 1980); children: Todd Lane Koscinski, Michael Lane Koscinski; m. David Lewis Stone, Feb. 26, 1984. BA, U. Mass., 1981; M in Human Svcs., Keene State Coll., 1990, Cert. in Ednl. Adminstrn., 1999. Cert. tchr., Mass.; cert. experienced educator, N.H. Substitute tchr. Montague Pub. Schs., 1981-84, Keene (N.H.) Pub. Schs., 1985-96; v.p. Beck Mfg., Keene, 1986—; dir. Good Mourning Children, Keene, 1988-98; dir. children's svcs. Hospice of Monadnock Region, Keene, 1992-94; elem. sch. tchr. Marlborough (N.H.) Sch. Dist., 1997—. Cons. to staff adv. com. Franklin County Tech. Sch., Turners Falls, Mass., 1977-84; intern, vol. Hospice of Cheshire County, Keene, 1989-90; mem. adj. clin. faculty Antioch New Eng. Grad. Sch., 1993-94; mem. adj. faculty Keene State Coll., 1999-2001, site supr. for student tchrs., 1999—. Dir. Big Bros./Big Sister Orgn. Recipient Sch. Vol. award Symonds Sch., Keene, 1984-85. Mem. AAUW, Assn. for Death Edn. and Counseling, Keene Woman's Club (v.p. 1986-88), Keene Bus. and Profl. Women's Club, N.H. Hospice Orgn., Children's Hospice Internat. Roman Catholic. Avocations: photography, travel, reading, exercise, mahjong.

LANE-TRENT, PATRICIA JEAN, social worker; b. Belleville, Ill., Apr. 3, 1970; d. Lawrence R. and Nola Jean (Bosick) L.; m. Jerry J. Trent Jr. (div.); 1 child, Corey Andrew. AA, AS, Belleville Area Coll., 1992; BS, So. Ill. U., 1994; student, Women's Campaign Sch., 1995. Cert. info. rsch. specialist. Co-owner Jerry's Lawncare and Landscaping, Trent's Quality Constrn., Belleville, Ill., 1993—; youth specialist Mo. Dept. Social Svcs., St. Louis, 1994-95; owner Tracks & Traces Infosource, Belleville, 1997—98; social worker Royal Hts. Nursing and Rehab., 1999—2001. Mem. NOW, NAFE. Democrat. Avocations: fishing, softball, music, singing, writing. Home: 2309 Frank Scott Pkw W Belleville IL 62223-4655 Office: 907 Martin Luther King East Saint Louis IL 62205 Office Phone: 618-482-7376.

LA NEVE, SHANNON BETH, healthcare educator; b. Atlantic City, N.J., Jan. 8, 1974; d. John Richard and Sue Marie Morgan; m. Edward James La Neve; children: Morgan Taylor, Mackenzie Marie. BS, Trenton State Coll., N.J., 1996; M in Edn. and Adminstrn., U. Phoenix, 2006. Health and phys. edn. tchr. Clark County Sch. Dist., Las Vegas, 1996—2005, k-12 health project facilitator, 2005—. Recipient Tchr. of Yr., Klassy 100FM, 1997, Rave Rev., Clark County Sch. Dist., 2006; scholar Patrica Chamberlain award, Trenton State Coll., 1996. Mem.: AAHE, AAHPERD (assoc.). Independent. Roman Catholic. Avocations: softball, travel, swimming. Office: Clark County Sch Dist 3950 S Pecos-McCleod Ave Ste C Las Vegas NV 89121 Office Phone: 702-799-2348. Office Fax: 702-855-6179. Personal E-mail: health_wellness2002@yahoo.com. E-mail: slaneve@interact.ccsd.net.

LANEY, SANDRA EILEEN, information technology executive; b. Cin., Sept. 17, 1943; d. Raymond Oliver and Henrietta Rose (Huber) H.; m. Dennis Michael Laney, Sept. 30, 1968; children: Geoffrey Michael, Melissa Ann. AS in Bus. Adminstrn., Thomas More Coll., 1988, BA in Bus. Adminstrn., 1993. Adminstrv. asst. to chief exec. officer Chemed Corp., Cin., 1982, asst. v.p., 1982-84, v.p., 1984-91, v.p., chief adminstrv. officer, 1991-93, sr. v.p., chief adminstrv. officer, 1993-2001, bd. dirs., 1986—, exec. v.p. chief adminstrn. officer, 2001—02; CEO, chmn. Cadre Computer Resources Co., 2001—. Bd. dirs. Omnicare Inc., Covington, Ky. Mem. bd. advisors Sch. Nursing U. Cin., 1992—; bd. overseers Cin. Symphony Orch., 1998; trustee Lower Price Hill Cmty. Sch., Cmty. Land Coop. of Cin. Mem. AAUW, NOW, Internat. Platform Assn., Amnesty Internat., World Affairs Coun., Women's Action Coun. Roman Catholic. Office: Cadre Computer Resources Co 1200 Chemed Ctr 255 E 5th St Cincinnati OH 45202-4700 Business E-Mail: sandra.laney@cadre.net.

LANG, ANNA JOYCE, geography professor; d. Murray and Florence Kandel Lang; m. Harold Marshall Elliott, Jan. 24, 1975; children: Dora Louise Elliott, Sarah Ariel Elliott. AB with honors, UCLA, 1969, MA, 1970, PhD, 1977. Cert. tchr. Calif. CC, 1970. Rsch. asst. UCLA, L.A., 1969—73, tchg. asst./assoc., 1971—73; rschr. Deep Canyon Desert Rsch. Ctr., Palm Desert, Calif., 1973—74; vis. instr. U. Okla., Norman, 1974—75; asst. prof. U. Miami, 1977—80; adj. prof. Weber State U., Ogden, Utah, 2003—. Author: numerous jour. articles and book revs.; author: (and actor) numerous ednl. videos. Mem. adv. com. Ogden City Schs., 2005—; donor Astrocamp, Ogden, 1993—2006; scholarship sponsor Weber State U., 1998—. Recipient J. C. Cook scholarship, UCLA, 1968—69, Faculty Prize disting. tchg., 1971—72, Instrnl. Support award, U. Miami, 1978; grantee, UCLA, 1973, 1974, Shell Co. Found., 1979, U. Miami, 1979; Chancellor's Dissertation fellow, UCLA, 1973—74. Mem.: Assn. Am. Geographers (Outstanding Tchr./Scholar 1995), Pi Gamma Mu, Phi Beta Kappa. Jewish. Achievements include research in Landscape Ecology/Desert Vegetation. Avocations: writing, reading, gardening, travel. Home: 1475 S Oakcrest Dr Ogden UT 84403 Office: Weber State Univ 1401 Univesity Cir Ogden UT 84408-1401 Office Phone: 801-626-6207. Business E-Mail: alang@weber.edu.

LANG, CHRISTINE JOANN, elementary school educator; b. Monmouth Beach, NJ, Oct. 27, 1979; d. Peter James and JoAnn Elizabeth Lang. BA in Psychology, Marist Coll., 2002; postgrad., Monmouth U., 2002—03, Western Conn. State U., 2003—. 1st grade tchr. Margaret Vetter Elem. Sch., Eatontown, NY, 2002—03, 2d grade tchr. aide, 2002; head tchr. infants and toddlers Merryhill Child Care, Newtown, Conn., 2004; spl. edn. tchr. grades 6-8 North End Mid. Sch., Waterbury, Conn., 2004—. Mem.: Pi Lambda Theta. Avocations: reading, movies. Office: North End Mid Sch 534 Bucks Hill Rd Waterbury CT 06704 E-mail: CJLang2003@aol.com.

LANG, COLLEEN ANNE, secondary school educator; b. Alexandria, Va., Apr. 17, 1968; d. Wayne Lawrence and Catherine (Ludwig) Dolan; m. Gregory Todd Lang, June 2, 1990. BA in Phys. Edn., Western Md. Coll., Westminster, 1990; cert. in edn., Fayetteville (N.C.) State U., 1996. Cert. tchr., N.C., Md. Asst. S-3 U.S. Army, Ft. Bragg, N.C., 1990-92, platoon leader, 1992, exec. officer, 1992-93, co. comdr., 1993-94; phys. edn. educator Francis Scott Key Mid. Sch., Silver Spring, Md., 1996—. Home sch. tchr. Capt. U.S. Army, 1990-94. Recipient Meritorious Svc. medal U.S. Army, 1994, Army Commendation medal 1992, 93, 94. Roman Catholic. Avocations: camping, reading, travel, bicycling, swimming. Home: 329 Jonaquin Cir Hopkinsville KY 42240-4884

LANG, JANELLE J., accountant; b. Oelwein, Iowa, May 11, 1948; d. Arthur and Esther Louise (Moeller) Andrew; m. Robert Martin Lang, Sept. 4, 1971; children: Sybil, Jacqueline. BA in Bus. and Music Edn., Upper Iowa Coll., 1970; BA in Acctg., Buena Vista Coll., 1993. Tchr. Davenport Cmty. Schs., Iowa, 1971-72, Bennett Cmty. Schs., Iowa, 1972-73, Madison Cmty. Schs., Wis., 1973-74; acct. Robert M. Lang, M.D., P.C., Ottumwa, Iowa, 1976—. Mem. governing bd. S.E. Iowa Symphony Orch., 1995—; bd. dirs. Ottumwa Civic Music, 1996; violist S.E. Iowa Symphony, 1996—, Ottumwa Symphony Orch., 1996—; pianist 1st Luth. Ch., Ottumwa, 1995. Mem. NAFE, Am. Mgmt. Assn., Nat. Soc. Accts. Lutheran. Avocation: gardening. Home: 818 E Highland Ave Ottumwa IA 52501-2134 Office: Robert M Lang MD PC 1106 Pennsylvania Ave Ottumwa IA 52501-2109 Personal E-mail: janellejlang@pcsia.net.

LANG, LAURA SMITH, lawyer; m. John Lang. BA cum laude in Speech-Lang. Pathology and Music, Butler U., Indpls., 1997; JD, So. Meth. U. Dedman Sch. Law, 2000. Assoc. Brewer, Anthony & Middlebrook, P.C., Irving, Tex. Vol. Dallas Mus. Natural Hist., Habitat for Humanity, Dallas. Named a Rising Star, Tex. Super Lawyers mag., 2006. Mem.: Dallas Assn. Young Lawyers, Tex. Young Lawyers Assn., Dallas Bar Assn., Jr. League Dallas. Office: Brewer Anthony & Middlebrook 5201 N O'Connor Blvd 5th Fl Irving TX 75039-3768 Office Phone: 972-870-9898. E-mail: llang@bamlawyers.net.*

LANG, LINDA A., food service executive; B in Fin., U. Calif., Berkeley; MBA, San Diego State U. Joined Jack in the Box Inc., 1985, divsn. v.p. new products and promotions, 1994—96, v.p. products, promotions and consumer rsch., 1996—99, v.p. mktg., 1999—2001, sr. v.p. mktg., 2001—02, exec. v.p. mktg. and ops., human resources, restaurant devel., quality assurance and logistics, 2002—03, pres., COO San Diego, 2003—05, chmn., CEO, 2005—. Bd. dir. WD-40 Co. Office: Jack in the Box Inc 9330 Balboa Ave San Diego CA 92123*

LANG, LISA ANN, music educator; b. Mt. Vernon, Ohio, Dec. 5, 1952; d. Kenneth Richard and June Pauline Auskings; m. Kenneth Ray Lang, Feb. 27, 1951; children: Natalie Ann, Christie Nicole, Matthew Ryan. Student, St. Andrews U., 1971; B of Music Edn., Baldwin-Wallace Conservatory, 1974; MA, Ohio State U., 1987. Cert. k-12 music specialist Ohio Bd. Edn., 1984. Dir. bands, jr. high and high sch. Pickerington Local Schools, Ohio, 1974—. Asst. dir. high schs. marching band Macy's Thanksgiving Day Parades, N.Y.C., 1990, 2001; asst. dir. high sch. Fiesta Bowl Parades & Nat. Band Championships, Phoenix, 1999, 2003, Orange Bowl Parades & Nat. Band Competitions, Miami, 1995, 2000, 2001, Miss Am. Pageant, Atlantic City, Md., 1994, Cotton Bowl Parade, Dallas, 1989; asst. dir. high schs. marching band Tournament of Roses, Rose Bowl Parade, 2006; host chmn. Fairfield All County Music Concerts, Pickerington, 1974—2005; concerts elderly health care facilities Pickerington Jr. High Bands, 1975—2006; curriculum chm.n.gifted program Pickerington Schools/Fairfield County, 2000—03; asst. dir. high sch. Nations Day Parade, N.Y.C., 2003, Rep. Rally Performance Pres. George Bush Sr., Columbus, 1988—88, Rep. Rally Performance Pres. Ronald Reagan, 1984—84, Rep. Rally Performance Pres. George W. Bush, 2004. Named Lead Marching Band for Parade, Macy's Thanksgiving Day Parade Com., 2001; recipient Adjudicators Choice award, Music in Parks Competitions, 1999, Outstanding Concert Band Awards, 2000, 2003, 2006, Alumni award, Baldwin Wallace Coll. Conservatory, 2003. Mem.: NEA (assoc.), Am. Schools Band Directors Assn. (hon.), Ohio Music Educators Assn. (assoc.; marching band adjudicator 1992—, solo and ensemble adjudicator, concert band adjudicator), Pickerington Edn. Assn. (assoc.; sec. 1986), Ohio Edn. Assn. (assoc.), Music Educators Nat. Conf. (assoc.), Phi Beta Mu (hon.), Phi Mu (assoc.), Tau Beta Sigma (assoc.; sec. 1973—74). Avocations: travel, reading, art. Office: Pickerington Local Schs 130 S Hill Rd Pickerington OH 43147 Office Phone: 614-833-2100. Personal E-mail: langbndldy@aol.com. E-mail: lisa_lang@fc.pickerington.k12.oh.us.

LANG, MABEL LOUISE, classics educator; b. Utica, N.Y., Nov. 12, 1917; d. Louis Bernard and Katherine (Werdge) L. BA, Cornell U., 1939; MA, Bryn Mawr Coll., 1940, PhD, 1943; Litt.D., Coll. Holy Cross, 1975, Colgate U., 1978; L.H.D., Hamilton Coll. Mem. faculty Bryn Mawr Coll., 1943-91, successively instr., asst. prof., 1943-50, assoc. prof., 1950-59, prof. Greek, 1959-88, chmn. dept., 1960-88, acting dean coll. 2d semester, 1958-59, 60-61; chmn. mng. com. Am. Sch. Classical Studies, Athens, 1975-80, chmn. admissions and fellowship com., 1966-72; Blegen disting. rsch. prof. semester I Vassar Coll., 1976-77; Martin classical lectr. Oberlin Coll., 1982. Co-author: Athenian Agora Measures and Tokens; author: Palace of Nestor Frescoes, 1969, Athenian Agora Graffiti and Dipinti, 1976; Herodotean Narrative and Discourse, 1984, Athenian Agor Ostraka, 1990; contbr. articles profl. jours. Guggenheim fellow, 1953-54; Fulbright fellow Greece, 1959-60 Mem. Am. Philos. Soc., Am. Acad. Arts and Scis., German Archaeol. Inst., Am. Philol. Assn., Soc. Promotion Hellenic Studies (Eng.), Classical Assn. (Eng.). Home: 905 New Gulph Rd Bryn Mawr PA 19010-2941 Office: Dept Greek Bryn Mawr Coll Bryn Mawr PA 19010

LANG, MARY ANN, special education educator, administrator; b. N.Y.C., Sept. 9, 1941; d. Raymond Joseph and Frances Dorothy (Campbell) Haefner; children: Diane Elyse, Linda Ann. BA, Queens Coll., CUNY, 1963; MS, Hunter Coll., CUNY, 1969; MPhil, CUNY, 1983, PhD, 1984. Lic. psychologist, N.Y.; cert. in elem. edn. and blindness and visual impairment, N.Y. Tchr. N.Y.C. Bd. Edn., 1963-68; adj. faculty Hunter Coll., CUNY, 1969-76; dir. child devel. ctr. The Lighthouse Inc., N.Y.C., 1976-78, dir. profl. tng., 1983-85, dir. program devel., 1985-88, dir. Nat. Ctr. for Vision and Child Devel., 1988—, coord. internat. programs, 1993-96, dir. Internat. Ctr. on Low Vision, 1996—, v.p. internat. programs, 1998—2005; advisor Internat. Agy. Prevention of Blindness, 2005—. Vis. prof. U. Talca, Chile, 1983-85; mem. adv. bd. Head Start-Resource Access Project, N.Y., N.J., P.R., V.I., 1980-94; advisor pub. rels. com. Internat. Agy. Prevention of Blindness, 2005- . Author: (book and video) A Special Start, 1991; co-author: AIDS, Blindness, and Low Vision: A Guide for Service Providers, 1990, Getting in Touch with Play, 1991, AIDS, Blindness, and Low Vision: A Manual for Health Organizations, 1992, Technology for Tots, 1992, Toys and Play, 1995; editor-in-chief: Lighthouse Handbook on Vision Impairment and Vision Rehabilitation, 2000; editor: Rehabilitation: Assessment, Intervention and Outcomes, 2000. Recipient Elena Gall medal, Hunter Coll., 1969, cert. Disting. Svc., Internat. Agy. Prevention of Blindness, 1999, N. Am. Achievement award, 2004. Mem.: NEA, APA, APHA, Assn. Edn. and Rehab. People with Impaired Vision, Assn. Edn. and Rehab. Blind and Visually Impaired (bd. dir. N.Y. state chpt. 1985—91, Meritorious Achievement award 1993, Lit. in Field of Low Vision award 2002). Home: 205 West End Ave Apt 14C New York NY 10023-4810 Office: Lighthouse Internat 111 E 59th St New York NY 10022-1202

LANG, NAOMI, ice skater; b. Arcata, Calif., Dec. 18, 1978; Tng. with, Igor Shpilband & Liz Coates, Detroit, 1997—2000, Alexander Zhulin, N.J., 2000—02, Tatiana Tarasova, Conn., 2002, Nikoli Morozov, 2002—. Ice dancer Naomi Lang and Peter Tchernyshev; mem. Team USA Keri Lotion Classic, 1999, Goodwill Games, 2001; U.S. skating team Olympic Winter Games, 2002. Mem. Grand Rapids (Mich.) Ballet Co. Recipient 5th, State Farm U.S. Championships, 1997, 3d, 1998, 1st, 1999, 2000, 2001, 2002, 4th, Goodwill Games, 2001, 2d, Challenge Lysiane Lauret, 1998, 5th, Cup of Russia, 1998, Skate Am., 1998, 3d, 1998, 5th, 2000, 3d, Four Continents Championships, 1999, 1st, 2000, 2d, 2001, 1st, 2002, 3d, 2003, 10th, World Championships, 1999, 8th, 2000, 9th, 2001, 2002, 8th, 2003, 2d, Keri Lotion Classic, 1999, 5th, Trophee Lalique, 1999, 4th, 2000, 1st (team), Hershey's Kisses Challenge, 2002. Office: US Figure Skating Hdqs 20 First St Colorado Springs CO 80906

LANG, PEARL, dancer, choreographer; b. Chgo., May 1922; d. Jacob and Frieda (Feder) Lack; m. Joseph Wiseman, Nov. 22, 1963. Student, Wright Jr. Coll., U. Chgo.; DFA (hon.), Juilliard Sch. Music, 1995; PhD (hon.), Juilliard Sch., 1995, DFA, 1995. Formed own co., 1953; faculty Yale, 1954-68; tchr., lectr. Juilliard, 1953-69, Jacobs Pillow, Conn. Coll., Neighborhood Playhouse, 1963-68, Israel, Sweden, Netherlands. Founder Pearl Lang Dance Found.; mem. Boston Symphony, Tanglewood Fest. Soloist, Martha Graham Dance Co., 1944-54; featured roles on Broadway include Carousel, 1945-47, Finian's Rainbow, 1947-48, Danced Martha Graham's roles in Appalachian Spring, 1974-76, El Pentitente, 1954, Primitive Mysteries, 1978-79, Diversion of Angels, 1948-70, Herodiade, 1977-79; role of Solvieg opposite John Garfield Broadway include, ANTA Peer Gynt; choreographer: TV shows CBC Folio; co-dir. T.S. Eliot's Murder in the Cathedral, Stratford, Conn., Direction, 1964-66, 67, Lamp Unto Your Feet, 158, Look Up and Live TV, 1957; co-dir., choreographer: full length prodn. Dybbuk for CBC; dir. numerous Israel Bond programs; assumed roles Emily Dickinson: Letter to the World, 1970; Clytemnestra, 1973; Jocasta in: Night Journey, 1974, for Martha Graham Dance Co.; choreographer: dance works Song of Deborah, 1952, Moonsung and Windsung, 1952, Legend, 1953, Rites, 1953, And Joy Is My Witness, 1954, Nightflight, 1954, Sky Chant, 1957, Persephone, 1958, Black Marigolds, 1959, Shirah, 1960, Apasionada, 1961, Broken Dialogues, 1962, Shore Bourne, 1964, Dismembered Fable, 1965, Pray for Dark Birds, 1966, Tongues of Fire, 1967, Piece for Brass, 1969, Moonways and Dark Tides, 1970, Sharjuhm, 1971, At That Point in Place and Time, 1973, The Possessed, 1995, Prairie Steps, 1975, Bach Rondelays, 1977, I Never Saw Another Butterfly, 1977, A Seder Night, 1977, Kaddish, 1977, Icarus, 1978, Cantigas Ladino, (10 sephardic songs), 1978, Notturno, 1980, Gypsy Ballad, 1981, Hanele The Orphan, 1981, The Tailor's Megilleh, 1981, Bridal Veil, 1982, Stravinsky's opera Oedipus Rex, 1982, Song of Songs, 1983, Shiru L'adonay, 1983, Tehillim, 1983, Sephardic Romance and Tfila, 1989, Koros, 1990, Eyn Keloheynu, 1991, Schubert Quartetsatz No. 12, 1993, Schubert Quartet 15 1st Mov., 1994, And Again a Begining, 1994, Dream Voyages, 1996, Memories and Dreams of Isaac the Blind, 1997, A Bouquet of Love Song Waltzes, 1998, Song of Azerbaijan, 1999, Icarus, 1999, The Time Is Out of Joint, 2000, Dance Panel #7, 2000, Cityscape, 2000. Recipient 2 Guggenheim fellowships; recipient Goldfadden award Congress for Jewish Culture, Achievement award Artists and Writers for Peace in the Middle East, Cultural award Workmen's Circle, Queens Coll. award, 1991, Jewish Cultural achievement award Nat. Found. for Jewish Culture, 1992; named to Hall of Fame, Internat. Com. for the Dance Libr. of Israel, 1997. Mem. Am. Guild Mus. Artists. Home and Office: Dance Foundation Inc 382 Central Park W New York NY 10025-6054 Office Phone: 212-866-2680.

LANG, PING, former professional volleyball player; head coach Olympic volleyball team; b. Beijing, Dec. 10, 1960; Student in English, Beijing Normal Univ., 1986. Profl. volleyball player Beijing Municipal Women's Volleyball Team, 1976—78, Chinese Women's Nat. Team, 1978—88, head coach, 1999—2002, Italy Modelo Club Women's Team, 1989—90, USA Women's Nat. Team, 2005—. Named Outstanding Athlete, SPCSC, 1981, Best Player, World Cup, 1985, Best Women's Coach, Internat. Volleyball Fedn., 1997; named one of Nat. Top Ten Athletes Yr., 1981—86; recipient Prize for Outstanding Results Achieved in the Yr., State Physical Culture and Sports Commission, 1980, Master of Sports award, 1980, Nat. Sports Medal, SPCSC, 1981, 1983, 1985, Gold Medal Women's Volleyball, Summer Olympics, 1984. Achievements include being leader on Championship team Asian Championships, 1979, World Women's Volleyball Championships, 1982, Asian Games, 1982, Summer Olympics, 1984, World Cup, 1985. Office: USA Womens Volleyball 715 South Circle Dr Colorado Springs CO 80910 Office Phone: 719-228-6800.

LANG, ROBERTA LYNN, food products company executive, lawyer; b. South Bend, Ind., Oct. 16, 1958; d. Robert Aschielle and Charlene Theresa (Leffert) Plasschaert; m. Richard Alan Lang, Dec. 2, 1991; 1 child, Daniel Marek; 1 stepchild, Cole. BA, Ind. U., South Bend, 1987; JD, Valparaiso U., 1990. Bar: Ind. 1990, U.S. Dist. Ct. (no. and so. dists.) Ind. 1990, Ill. 1992, U.S. Dist. Ct. (no. dist.) Ill. 1992. Assoc. Krisor & Nussbaum, South Bend, 1990-91, Momkus, Ozog & McCluskey, Downers Grove, Ill., 1992-94; pvt. practice, 1994—98; v.p., gen. counsel Whole Foods Mkt. Inc., 1998—. Gen. counsel Animal Compassion Found., 2005—; bd. dirs. Whole Planet Found. Vol. Legal Svcs. Program No. Ind., Inc., South Bend, 1985-87. Mem. DuPage County Assn. Women Lawyers. Roman Catholic. Office: Whole Foods Mkt Inc 550 Bowie St Austin TX 78703*

LANGAN, MARIE-NOELLE SUZANNE, cardiologist, educator; b. White Plains, N.Y., Aug. 4, 1960; Grad., U. Toronto, Can., 1980, MD, 1984. Diplomate Am. Bd. Internal Medicine, Am. Bd. Cardiology, Am. Bd. Clin. Electrophysiology. Intern St. Mary's Hosp./ McGill U., Montreal, Can., 1984-85; resident U. Toronto/ St. Michael's Hosp., 1985-87; cardiology fellow Phila. Heart Inst./ U. Pa. Med. Ctr., 1988-90, 1990-91; clin. instr. medicine Sch. Medicine U. Pa., 1988-89, fellow dept. medicine, 1990-91; asst. prof. medicine, dir. electrophysiology lab. George Washington U., Washington, 1991-93; asst. prof. medicine Mt. Sinai Med. Ctr., N.Y.C. Contbr. chpts. to books and articles to profl. jours. Fellow Am. Coll. Cardiology, Royal Coll. Physicians and Surgeons Can.; mem. N.Am. Soc. Pacing and Electrophysiology, Am. Heart Assn. (Clinician Scientist award 1996), Coll. Physicians and Surgeons Can. Office: Mt Sinai Med Ctr 1 Gustave L Levy Pl Box 1054 New York NY 10028-0007

LANGANKI, DEBRA LYNN, secondary school educator; d. George Thomas Verootis and Susan Marie Ukura, adopted d. William Alfred Ukura; m. Mark Harold Langanki; children: Charlotte Marie, Colton Harold. BS in Tchg., St. Cloud State U., Minn., 1992. Tchr. sci. Hibbing H.S., Minn., 1993—. Fin. sec. Bethel Luth. Ch., Warba, Minn., 2006. Named NE Divsn. Advisor of Yr., Minn. Assn. Student Councils, 1999—2000, 2005—06; recipient Minn. Forest Educator of Yr., Minn. Forest Industries, 2004; fellow, GTE, 2000. Office: Hibbing High School 800 E 21st St Hibbing MN 55746 Office Phone: 218-263-3675.

LANGAN-SATTENSPIEL, F. CANDY, medical/surgical nurse, writer; b. Jersey City, Apr. 30, 1945; adopted d. George Palangio and d. Florence Palangio-Boyer, d. John Boyer; m. Sigmund L. Sattenspiel, May 20, 2004; children: Stacy J. Panaccione, E. Sean Langan. AD, Brookdale Coll., N.J. RN N.J. Adminstr. and surg. asst. Sattenspiel Surg. Arts Pavilion, Freehold, NJ, 1978—; pres. Clin. Aesthetic Cosmetology, Freehold, NJ, 1985—; profl. model; profl. photographer. Author: (book on photography and poetry) I Am My Own Thoughts (Monmouth County Art Exhbn., 2006). Achievements include development of founder and formulator Academy Medical Skin Care Products. Office: Sattenspiel Surgical Arts Pavilion 1050 W Main St Freehold NJ 07728 Office Phone: 732-780-1333. E-mail: candylangan@aol.com.

LANGE, BILLIE CAROLA, video specialist; b. Cullman, Ala. d. John George and Josephine (Richard) Luyben; m. Harry E. Lange (dec.); children: JoAnne Lange Graham, Linda Jean Lange Reeve; m. Melvin A. Coble (dec.). Grad., Long Beach City (Calif.) Coll.; BMus, U. So. Calif. Chief piano accompanist Long Beach Civic Opera Assn.; tchr./creator aquatic exercise program U. Ala., Huntsville, 1984-87; advisor Aquatic Exercise Assn., Port Washington, Wis., 1988—; creator, prodr. aquatic video exercise tapes Billie C. Lange's Aquatics, Palm Beach, Fla., 1979—. Creator: (aquatic exercise video tapes) Slim and Trim Yoga with Billie In and Out of Pool, 1979, Slim and Trim with Billie In Pool, 1994 (televised on Today Show, NBC 1995); pianist Organ-Piano Duo and various audio tapes; instrumental, audio Tranquility, 1992. Mem. Nat. Acad. Recording Arts and Scis. Avocations: classical pianist, politics. Office: 1920 Compass Cove Dr Vero Beach FL 32963-2820

LANGE, JESSICA PHYLLIS, actress; b. Cloquet, Minn., Apr. 20, 1949; d. Al and Dorothy Lange; m. Paco Grande, 1971 (div. 1981); 1 child with Mikhail Baryshnikov, Alexandra; children with Sam Shepard: Hannah Jane, Samuel Walker Student, U. Minn.; student mime, with Etienne DeCroux, Paris. Dancer Opera Comique, Paris; model Wilhelmina Agy., N.Y.C. Film appearances include King Kong, 1976, All That Jazz, 1979, How to Beat the High Cost of Living, 1980, The Postman Always Rings Twice, 1981, Frances, 1982 (Acad. award nominee 1982), Tootsie, 1982 (Acad. award 1983), Country, 1984, Sweet Dreams, 1985, Crimes of the Heart, 1986 (Acad. award nominee 1987), Everybody's All American, 1988, Far North, 1988, Music Box, 1989 (Acad. award nominee 1990), Men Don't Leave, 1990, Cape Fear, 1991, Night and the City, 1992, Blue Sky, 1994 (Golden Globe award Best Actress in a Drama 1995, Acad. award for Best Actress 1995), Losing Isaiah, 1995, Rob Roy, 1995, A Thousand Acres, 1997, Hush, 1998, Cousin Bette, 1998, Titus, 1999, Big Fish, 2003, Broken Flowers, 2005, Don't Come Knocking, 2005, Neverwas, 2005; TV movies: Cat on a Hot Tin Roof, 1984, O' Pioneers!, 1992, A Streetcar Named Desire, 1995 (Golden Globe award 1996), Prozac Nation, 2001, Normal, 2003; in summer stock prodn. Angel on My Shoulder, N.C., 1980, A Streetcar Named Desire, 1992; prodr. Country, 1984; TV guest appearance Inside the Actors Studio, 1994; theatre: The Glass Menagerie, 2005.*

LANGE, KAREN R., music educator; d. Vincent F. and Joanne C. Hemberger; m. Stephen J. Lange, Aug. 7, 1981; children: Paul, Phillip, Emily, Allen. B in Music Edn., Wichita State U., 1972, MusM, 1977. Music educator Ferguson-Florissant Sch. Dist., Mo., 1972—78, Newton Sch. Dist., Kans., 1978—81, Wichita Sch. Dist., Kans., 1981—82, Conway Springs Sch. Dist., Kans., 1982—. Choir dir. St. Joseph Ch., Conway Springs, 1978—81, organist, 1978—; cmty. chorus dir. Kans. Fine Arts Recital Series, Conway Springs, 1999—. Mem.: Kans. Music Educators Conf., Music Educators Nat. Conf. Republican. Roman Catholic. Avocations: reading, shuttle tatting, piano. Office: USD 356 Conway Springs 607 W St Louis Conway Springs KS 67031

LANGE, LIZ, apparel designer, director; b. N.Y. m. Jeffrey Lange; 2 children. BA in Comparative Lit., Brown U., 1988. Asst. editor Vogue; fashion designer Stephen DiGeronimo; founder Liz Lange Maternity Clothing Line, N.Y.C., 1997—. Named one of 40 Under 40, Crain's NY Bus. Jour., 2006. Office: Liz Lange Maternity Corp Office 2nd Fl 347 W 36th St New York NY 10018

LANGE, LYNN MARIE, music educator; b. Janesville, Wis., May 10, 1950; d. Armita Mae Mabie; m. Fred Lawrence Lange, Mar. 10, 1973; children: Jared Steven, Jennifer Lynn, Andrew James. BMusEd, Ill. State U., Normal, 1973. Cert. mid. sch. endorsement Viterloo Coll., 2000. Band dir. Wilton Jr. H.S., Iowa, 1974—83, North Scott Jr. H.S., Eldridge, 1983—88, Woodside Mid. Sch. Saydel Schs., Des Moines, 1989—. Dir. 7-8 jazz band Woodside Mid. Sch., Des Moines, 1996—. Finalist Disney Am. Tchr., 2000; recipient Educator Excellence award, 1996. Mem.: NEA, Saydell Edn. Assn., Iowa Band Masters Assn. (dist. mid. sch. chair 2000—05). Office: Woodside Mid Sch 5810 NE 14th St Des Moines IA 50313 Office Fax: 515-265-0950. E-mail: langel@saydel.k12.ia.us.

LANGE, MAGGIE A., lawyer; b. Bay City, Mich., Feb. 18, 1952; Attended, Berkee Coll. Music; BA, U. Mich., 1991; JD, Northeastern, 1994. Bar: Mass. 1994, N.Y. 1995. Of counsel Perkins, Smith & Cohen LLP, Boston. Asst. prof. Berklee Coll. Music; frequent lectr. Practicing Law Inst., Mass. Continuing Legal Edn., Boston Bar Assn., Suffolk Law Sch., Boston Coll., U. Mass., Northeastern U. Named one of Boston's top lawyers, Boston Mag., 2002. Mem.: Women's Bar Assn., Mass. Bar Assn., Boston Bar Assn. (co-chairperson arts & entertainment com.), ABA. Office: Perkins Smith & Cohen LLP One Beacon St 30 th Floor Boston MA 02108 Office Fax: 617-854-4040, 617-854-4284. Business E-Mail: mlange@pscboston.com.

LANGE, MARY CHRISTINE, music educator; d. Frederick E.E. and Mary Norton (Barr) Lange. BS in Edn., Ea. Ill. U., Charleston, 1971, MA in Music Conducting, 1976. Dir. band Altamont Cmty. Unit #10, Ill., 1971—75, Ashmor Sch., 1975—76, Effingham Cmty. Unit #40, 1976—2005. Mem.: Ill. Music Educators Assn. (dist. V pres. 1988—94, 1999—), Ea. Star, Sigma Alpha Iota. Avocations: music, gardening, doll collecting, travel.

LANGE, NATALIE LAUREN, social studies educator; d. Michael Eugene and Aileen Janette Hyser; m. Jeremy Joseph Lange, May 28, 2004. BS in Bus. Econs., Ariz. State U., Tempe, 2004; BS in Justice Studies, Ariz. State U., 2004. Tchr. John Taylor Williams Mid. Sch., Charlotte, NC, 2004—. Corps mem. Teach For Am., Charlotte, NC, 2004—. Scholar Sun Devil scholar, Ariz. State U., 2000—04. Office Phone: 980-343-5544.

LANGE, SUSAN ALICE See STOESSER, SUSAN

LANGE-CONNELLY, PHYLLIS, musician, educator; b. Elgin, Ill., Oct. 14, 1935; d. William Carl and Freide Ricka Helena (Reimer) Werneke; children: Catherine Mary Gathman, Debra, Mark William. AA, Elgin (Ill.) C.C., 1985; BA, Nat. Lewis U., 1988; MM, No. Ill. U., 1995. Dir. music, organist Bethlehem Luth. Ch., Dundee, Ill., 1961-79, St. John's Luth. Ch., Algonquin, Ill., 1979-89, Trinity Luth. Ch., Huntley, Ill., 1990-92, St. Paul U.C.C. Ch., Barrington, Ill., 1992-94, St. James Episcopal Ch., Dundee, 1994—; assoc. organist, handbell dir. Holy Trinity Luth. Ch., Elgin, 1995-98; dir. worship and music, 1998-99. Para-profl. tutor Sch. Dist. 300, Dundee, Ill., 1979-85; music educator; mem. AGO del. to Ea. Europe through People-to-People Internat., 1998. Mem. United Way Dundee Twp., 1999, Dundee Main St. Orgn. Mem. Am. Guild Organists (dean N.W. chpt. 1999, Fox Valley chpt.), Am. Guild English Handbell Ringers, Music Tchrs. Nat. Assn., Elgin Choral Union (mem. edn./outreach com. 1999), Pi Kappa Lambda Music Soc. Democrat. Episcopalian. Avocations: reading, golf. Home: 4154 Whatehall Ln Algonquin IL 60102

LANGEL, TERESA LYNN, music educator; b. Carmichael, Calif., Jan. 21, 1981; d. Terrance and Susan Langel. MusB in Edn., VanderCook Coll. Music, Chgo., 2003. Cert. tchr. type 10 Ill. Choral music & music tech. tchr. grades 9-12 Bremen Cmty. Sch. Dist. #228, Midlothian, Ill., 2003—05; choral music tchr. grades 7-12 North Chgo. Cmty. Sch. Dist. #187, 2005—. Personal E-mail: chicago.langel@inbox.com.

LANGENHEIM, JEAN HARMON, biologist, educator; b. Homer, La., Sept. 5, 1925; d. Vergil Wilson and Jeanette (Smith) Harmon; m. Ralph Louis Langenheim, Dec. 1946 (div. Mar. 1962). BS, U. Tulsa, 1946; MS, U. Minn., 1949, PhD, 1953. Rsch. assoc. botany U. Calif., Berkeley, 1954-59, U. Ill., Urbana, 1959-61; rsch. fellow biology Harvard U., Cambridge, Mass., 1962-66; asst. prof. biology U. Calif., Santa Cruz, 1966-68, assoc. prof. biology, 1968-73, prof. biology, 1973-93, prof. biology emerita, 1993—, rsch. prof. ecol. and evolution biology, 2001—. Acad. v.p. Orgn. Tropical Studies, San Jose, Costa Rica, 1975—78; chmn. com. humid tropics U.S. Nat. Acad. Nat. Rsch. Coun., 1975—77; mem. com. floral inventory Amazon NSF, Washington, 1975—87; mem. sci. adv. bd. EPA, Washington, 1977—81. Author: (Book) Botany-Plant-Biology in Relation to Human Affairs, 1988, Plant Resins: Chemistry, Evolution, Ecology and Ethnobotany, 2003 (Klinger Best Ethnobotany Book award, Soc. Economic Botany, 2004); contbr. articles to profl. jours. Recipient Disting. Alumni award, U. Tulsa, 1979, Dedication of Madrono, Calif. Bot. Soc., 2004; grantee, NSF, 1966—88. Fellow: AAUW, AAAS, Bunting Inst., Calif. Acad. Scis.; mem.: Soc. Econ. Botany (pres. 1993—94), Assn. Tropical Biology (pres. 1985—86), Internat. Soc. Chem. Ecology (pres. 1986—87), Ecol. Soc. Am. (pres. 1986—87), Bot. Soc. Am. (Centennial award 2006). Home: 191 Palo Verde Ter Santa Cruz CA 95060-3214 Office: Univ California Dept Ecol and Evolutionary Biology Earth and Marine Scis Bldg Santa Cruz CA 95064 Office Phone: 831-459-2918. Business E-Mail: lang@darwin.ucsc.edu.

LANGENKAMP, MARY ALICE (M.A. LANGENKAMP), artist, educator; b. N.Y.C., Feb. 19, 1939; d. Horace Ralph and Pattie Lera (Turner) Myers; m. Robert Dobie Langenkamp; children: Heather, Matthew, Daniel, Lucinda. BA, George Washington U., 1962, MFA, 1985. Prof. art George Washington U., Washington, 1992-96. Exhbn. juror Arts Club Washington, 1996, George Washington U. Gallery, 2002; lectr. art law seminar Harvard Law Sch., 2002; vis. prof. art Tulsa U.; rsch. archivist Smithsonian Mus. Hist. and Tech.; instr. Philbrook Mus. Exhibited paintings and prints at U.S. Capitol, State Capitol of Okla., U.S. Embassy to Vatican, Galerie Schneider, Rome, Grand Palais, Paris, Hotel de Ville of Malaucene, France, Citibank, Washington; pvt. collections. in U.S. and Europe; work pub. in Nimrod Mag., Joyce Quar., Tulsa Tribune, Washington Post, others. Founding mem. Friends Brady Gallery, George Washington U.; mem. Tulsa County Libr. Book Review Bd., Martin Luther King's March on Washington, 1963; staff U.S. Congress; chmn. Dem. Precinct. Recipient Alfandre prize George Washington U., 1982, Gov.'s award Gov. of Okla., 1989, Air France prize, 1981; donor M.A. Langenkamp prize in Design, George Washington U. Mem. ACLU, LWV, Coll. Art Assn., F St. Hist. Soc., U.S. Capital Hist. Soc., Tulsa Shakespeare Soc., Friends Historic Village Malaucene. Democrat. Roman Catholic. Avocations: travel, films, theater, history, politics. Office: Fontalys Malaucene Vaucluse 84340 France Office Phone: 011 33 4 90 65 22 64. E-mail: malartist@yahoo.com.

LANGENKAMP, SANDRA CARROLL, retired human services administrator; b. St. Joseph, Mo., Feb. 10, 1939; d. William Harry Minger and Beverly (Carroll) Lee; m. R. Hayden Downie, June 1, 1963 (div. Feb. 1979); children: Whitney Downie, Timothy Downie, Allyson Downie; m. R. Dobie Langenkamp, Aug. 1993. BS, Tex. Women's U., 1960. Adjunctive therapist Menninger Meml. Hosp., Topeka, 1960-66; asst. adminstr. Hillcrest Med. Ctr., Tulsa, 1977-82; dir. Vol. Action Agy., Tulsa, 1982-83; exec. dir. Tulsa Bus. Health Group, 1983-95; v.p. Met. Tulsa C. of C., 1985-95; exec. dir. Tulsa Program Affordable Health Care, 1986-96; ret., 1996. Cons. mem. Okla. Employment Security Commn., Oklahoma City, 1988—; exec. dir. Tulsa Cmty. Found. Indigient Health Care, 1986—96, Long-Term Car Authority, 1999—; officer State of Okla. Basic Health Benefits Bd., 1985—96, chmn., 1992—93; mem. health benefit com. Okla. Ins. Commn., 1994—; mem. Gov.'s Com. Health Care, 1993; bd. dirs. Exec. Svc. Corps Tulsa, Associated Ctrs. Therapy. Editl. columnist: Point of View, 1985—, Tulsa Mag., 1985—. Count commn. appointee Tulsa Met. Area Planning Commn., 1973—81; mayor's appointee Tulsa Housing Authority, 1985—88; vol. Police Svc. Homicide Divsn., Police Svc. Detective Divsn., 1999—; exec. dir. Tulsa Met. Literacy Coalition, 1998—; apptd. mem. Okla. Health Care Auth., 2005—; pres. Tulsa Met. Ministry, 1980—83; bd. dirs. ARC, Tulsa, 1971—73, 1984—85, Okla. Arts Inst., 1995—, Simon Estes Found., 2000—, Tylsa Philharm., Inc., 2000—, City of Tulsa Arts Commn., 2003—. Mem.: Met. Tulsa C. of C. (v.p. 1983—95), Am. C. of C. (exec. dir. Okla. chpt.), Tulsa Tennis Club. Democrat. Roman Catholic. Avocations: reading, gardening, knitting, drawing, pottery, painting.

LANGER, ELLEN JANE, psychologist, educator, writer, artist; b. NYC, Mar. 25, 1947; d. Norman and Sylvia (Tobias) L. BA, NYU, 1970; PhD, Yale U., 1974. Cert. clin. psychologist. Asst. prof. psychology The Grad. Ctr. CUNY, 1974-77; assoc. prof. psychology Harvard U., Cambridge, Mass., 1977-81, prof., 1981—. Cons. NAS, 1979-81, NASA; mem. div. on aging Harvard U. Med. Sch., 1979—, mem. psychiat. epidemiology steering com., 1982-90; chair social psychology program Harvard U., 1982-94, chair Faculty Arts and Scis. Com. of Women, 1984-88. Author: Personal Politics, 1973, Psychology of Control, 1983, Mindfulness, 1989, The Power of Mindful Learning, 1997, On Becoming an Artist: Reinventing Yourself Through Mindful Creativity, 2005; editor: (with Charles Alexander) Higher Stages of Human Development, 1990, (with Roger Schank) Beliefs, Reasoning and Decision-Making, 1994; contbr. articles to profl. and scholarly jours.; exhibits at Julie Hellery Gallery, Provincetown, Mass., J&W Gallery, New Hope, Pa. Guggenheim fellow; grantee NIMH, NSF, Soc. for Psychol. Study of Social Issues, Milton Fund, Sloan Found., 1982; recipient Disting. Contbn. of Basic to Applied Psychology award APS, 1995. Fellow Computers and Soc. Inst., Am. Psychol. Assn. (Disting. Contributions to Psychology in Public Interest award 1988, Disting. Contributions of Basic Sci. to Applied Psychology 1995); mem. Soc. Exptl. Social Psychology, Phi Beta Kappa, Sigma Xi. Democrat. Jewish. Avocations: tennis, horseback riding. Office: Harvard U Dept Psychology 33 Kirkland St Cambridge MA 02138-2044 Business E-Mail: langer@wjh.harvard.edu.

LANGER, JUDITH ANN, language educator; b. N.Y.C. BA, CUNY, 1962, MSEd, 1965; PhD, Hofstra U., 1978; PhD (hon.), U. Uppsala, Sweden, 2005. Asst. prof. L.I. U., 1973-78; asst. prof. edn1. psychology NYU, 1978-80; sr. rschr. lang. behavior rsch. lab. U. Calif., Berkeley, 1980-84; assoc. prof. sch. of edn. Stanford U., 1984-87; prof. SUNY, Albany, 1987—, disting. prof., 2001—. Dir. Albany Inst. for Rsch. in Edn., Nat. Rsch. Ctr. on English Learning & Achievement; co-dir. Nat. Rsch. Ctr. Lit. Tchg. and Learning; trustee Rsch. Found.; task force mem. Nat. Commn. on Edn. Stds. and Testing; adv. com. New Stds. in Edn. Project, Literacy Unit, LRDC and Nat. Ctr. on Edn. and the Economy; adv. bd. Nat. Coun. of Chief State Sch. Officers, Nat. Objective in Reading, Nat. Assessment of Ednl. Progress, Reading and Writing Assessments, 1980—; cons. Calif. Assessment Program, N.C. English Lang. Arts Standards, Calif. State Dept. Edn., Ctr. for Lang. Edn. and Rsch., Ctr. for the Study of Writing, Rev. of Rsch. on Reading and Writing Relationships, Mich. State Edn. Dept. Author: Reader Meets Author/Bridging the Gap, 1982, Understanding Reading and Writing Research, 1985, Children Reading and Writing: Structures and Strategies, 1986, Language, Literacy, and Culture, 1987, Issues of Society and Schooling, How Writing Shapes Thinking: Studies of Teaching and Learning, 1987, Literature Instruction: A Focus on Student Response, 1992, Literature Instruction: Practice & Policy, 1994, Envisioning Literature, 1995, Effective Literacy Instruction: Building Successful Reading and Writing Programs, 2002, Getting To Excellent: How to Create Better Schools, 2004; contbr. articles to profl. jours.; editor: Research in the Teaching of English, 1984-92; editl. bd. English Internat., Discourse Processes, Jour. of Reading Behavior, Newsletter, Lab. of Comparative Human Cognition, Jour. of Reading and Writing, Internat. Jour. of Reading and Writing; reviewer in field. Recipient numerous grants, Presdl. award for lifetime achievement, Hofstra U., 1992, Chancellor's award for Exemplary Contbns. to Rsch., 2001, Albert J. Harris award, 2003; fellow, Rockefeller Found.; Benton fellow, U. Chgo., 1997. Fellow Am. Psychol. Assn., Nat. Conf. on Rsch. in English; mem. MLA, Am. Ednl. Rsch. Assn., Am. Psychol. Soc., Conf. on Coll. Composition and Comm., Internat. Reading Assn., Nat. Reading Conf., Nat. Coun. of Tchrs. of English (trustee), Soc. for Rsch. in Child Devel., Soc. for Text and Discourse, Kappa Delta Pi. Office: Univ at Albany 1400 Washington Ave Albany NY 12222-0100

LANGEVIN, PATRICIA ANN, mathematics educator; d. John and Dolores Grimes. M in Math. Secondary Edn., Calif. State U., Fullerton, 1982. Tchg. credential State of Calif., 1977. Instr. math., calculus and geometry Irvine H.S., Calif., 1981—. Advisor Irvine High Math Team, Irvine, 2004—. Home: 6 Palagonia Aisle Irvine CA 92606 Office: Irvine HS 4321 Walnut Irvine CA 92604 Office Phone: 949-936-7070.

LANGFORD, LAURA SUE, corporate financial executive; b. Evansville, Ind., Sept. 28, 1961; d. Lee Denmar Miller and Susan E. (Morton) Reitz; m. John E. Langford, May 15, 1992; 1 child, Rowan Diane. BFA in Drama, U. So. Calif., L.A., 1983; MBA in Fin. & Pub./Non-Profit, Columbia U., 1992. Credit mgr. Super-Freeze Co., Inc., Burbank, Calif., 1984-86; asst. Salomon Bros. Inc., L.A., 1986-87; rsch. analyst Bank of Calif., N.A., L.A., 1987, pub. fin. officer, 1988-90; intern Citizens Budget Commn., N.Y.C., 1991; analyst Standard & Poor's Ratings Group, N.Y.C., 1992-93, assoc., 1993-94, assoc. dir., 1994-95, dir., 1996-98; v.p. Duff & Phelps Credit Rating Co., N.Y.C., 1998—2000; dir. HypoVereinsbank, N.Y.C., 2000—; CFO HVB Global Assests Co., 2003—. Contbr. to periodical Standard & Poor's Credit Week, 1993—98, Duff & Phelps Credit Rating Co. Issues Update, 1998—2000; founder, editor: GAA Gazette, 1985—. Fellow Divsn. Rsch. Assn. Student Officer fellow, Columbia U., 1991—92; scholar Pres.'s scholar, U. Evansville, 1979—81. Avocations: skiing, rollercoaster riding, science fiction. Office: HVB Group 150 E 42nd St New York NY 10017 Office Phone: 212-672-5614. Business E-Mail: Laura_Langford@HVBAMERICAS.com.

LANGFORD, LINDA KOSMIN, library consultant; b. Phila., Nov. 7, 1939; d. Edward I. and Ruth (Blumfield) K.; m. Jonathan P. Meyerson, Aug. 7, 1960 (div.); m. George Langford, Oct. 31, 2000. BA, U. Pa., 1961; MSLS, Drexel U., 1966, MS in Environ. Sci., 1974. Chemistry instr. U. Md., College Park, 1961-63; libr. sci. instr., engring. libr. Drexel U., Phila., 1963-78; dep. dir. biomed. libr. U. Pa., Phila., 1979-80; libr. sect. supr. applied physics lab. The Johns Hopkins U., Laurel, Md., 1980-94; sec. mgr. libr./archives/records NASA Jet Propulsion Lab., Pasadena, Calif., 1994—2000; libr. cons., 2001—. Contbg. editor (author): (Quarterly Jour.) IEEE Engring. Mgmt. Rev., 1999—. Nat. sec. Friends of Danilo Dolci, Inc., Phila., 1971-72, bd. dirs., Short Hills, N.J., 1972-73. Recipient Exceptional Achievement medal NASA, 1998. Mem. IEEE (PCS adminstrv. com. 1995-96, EMS bd. govs. 1998-2003), Spl. Librs. Assn. (v.p., pres.-elect Phila. chpt. 1968-69). Avocation: painting. Home: 32 Bodine Rd Berwyn PA 19312-1237 E-mail: l.kosmin@ieee.org.

LANGGUTH, MARGARET WITTY, health facility administrator; b. Evanston, Ill., June 21, 1950; d. LeRoy and Catherine Ann (Conrad) Witty; m. Gregory Bryce Bukar, June 5, 1971 (dec. 1989); children: Michael Bryce, Caroline Nicole; m. Franklin James Langguth, Feb. 2, 2002. BS, DePaul U., 1972, MBA, 1981; MS, Rosalind Franklin U. Medicine and Sci., 1996. Staff med. technologist The Evanston Hosp., 1972-75, immunopathology lab. supr., 1975-77, lab. mgr., 1977-84, dir. lab. adminstrn., 1984-85; bookkeeper Ronald Knox Montessori Sch., Wilmette, Ill., 1986-87; beauty cons. Mary Kay Cosmetics, 1990-96; sec. Northwestern U., Evanston, 1991-94; physician asst. Women's Med. Group, P.C., Skokie, Evanston, Ill., 1996-98; ind. sales assoc. Mannatech, Inc., 1998—2001; adminstrv. dir. clin. lab. Rush North Shore Med. Ctr., Skokie, Ill., 1999—, six sigma facilitator. Den leader Cub Scouts, Boy Scouts Am., Wilmette, 1985—87, den leader coach, 1987—88; active PTA of St. Francis Xavier Sch., 1985—94, chair rummage sale, 1987—88, scouting coord., 1991—92, sch. bd., 1986—90, sec., 1988—89, vice chmn., 1989—90; troop co-leader, song leader Girl Scouts Am., 1992—98; mem. women's bd. Rush North Shore Med. Ctr., 2000—, mem. exec. bd., co-chair edn. com., 2005—06; campaign 2001 com. mem. United Way of Skokie Valley-Rush North Shore, co-chair for campaign 2002; eucharistic min. sick St. Francis Xavier Ch., 1990—93, liturgical song leader, 1993—2002. Recipient Emily Withrow Stebbins award, Evanston Hosp., 1985. Mem.: Clin. Lab. Mgmt. Assn., Am. Soc. Clin. Pathologists, Wilmette Hist. Soc. Avocations: knitting, interior design, reading. Office: Rush North Shore Med Ctr Clin Labs 9600 Gross Point Rd Skokie IL 60076 Office Phone: 847-933-6611. Business E-Mail: mlangguth@rsh.net.

LANGHAM, GAIL B., writer; b. Cin., Jan. 25, 1944; 3 children. BA, North Ctrl. Coll., 1989. Columnist Arts Scene, 1988-92; performing arts critic, features writer SUN Press, Naperville, Ill., 1988-92; freelance theatre critic Cin. City Beat, 1994-96; freelance writer Cin., 1993—. Founding mem. Naperville Writers Group, 1986-92. Avocations: travel, reading.

LANGHINRICHS, RUTH IMLER, playwright, writer; b. Chgo., Oct. 30, 1922; d. Roy Franklin Imler and Susan Martha Smith; m. Richard Alan Langhinrichs, May 31, 1958 (dec. July 31, 1990); children: Julia Marie Lewis-Langhinrichs, Jennifer Florence Langhinrichsen-Rohling. BS cum laude, Northwestern U., Evanston, IL, 1944. Rsch. asst. LOOK Mag., N.Y.C., 1944—46; asst. editor Sci. Illus., N.Y.C., 1946—49; asst. feature editor Scholastic Mag., N.Y.C., 1949—51; assoc. editor Ladies Home Jour., Phila., 1951—58; faculty Purdue U., Fort Wayne, Ind., 1966—76; instr. Channing Sch. for Girls, London, 1974—75; writer Fort Wayne Fine Arts Found., Ind., 1977—79; pub. rels. Pk. Ctr., Fort Wayne, Ind., 1979—84; writing cons. Ind.-Purdue U. a, Fort Wayne, Ind., 1998—. Facilitator: memoir writing workshops Friends of the Libr., Fort Wayne, Ind., 1998—. Playwright (play) Feathers, The Heart of the Limberlost: Gene Stratton-Porter, Mermaids in the Basement; author: (book) Boy Dates Girl, You're Asking Me?, (novel) The Maiden and the Crone; playwright (play) A Night on Walden Pond. Charter mem. Fort Wayne Civic Youtheatre, Ind., 1973—77; bd. mem. Martin Luther King Montessori Sch., Fort Wayne, Ind., 1975—78; founding mem. Cinema Ctr., Fort Wayne, Ind., 1976—80; bd. mem. Citizen's Cable, Fort Wayne, Ind., 1981—84; pres. Aging and In Home Svcs. of N.E. Ind., Fort Wayne, Ind., 1976—2001; bd. mem. Ft. Wayne Women's Bur., Ind., 1991—97, N.E. Ind. Coun. of Tchrs. of English, Fort Wayne, Ind., 1969—73. Recipient Four-year scholarship, Chgo. Women's Ideal Club, 1940, Woman of the Yr. award, Ft. Wayne Women's Bur., 2001, Summit award, Zonta Club Internat., 2003. Mem.: Internat. Assn. of Bus. Communicators (charter mem. 1978—79), Zonta Club Internat. (v.p. 2003), Fortnightly Club, Delta Delta Delta (life). Unitarian Universalist. Avocations: gardener, artist, commissioned clown. Home: 4422 S Wayne Ave Fort Wayne IN 46807 Personal E-mail: ruthlangx@aol.com.

LANGHOLZ, REBECCA SUE, music educator; b. Marshalltown, Iowa, May 4, 1962; d. Ralph Gerald Cooper and Charlotte Elaine Miller; m. Kelly Joe Langholz; children: Katriana, Avery. BA in Music Edn. (cum laude), Northwestern Coll., Orange City, Iowa, 1984. K-12 music tchr. Clay Ctrl. Cmty. Schs., Royal, Iowa, 1984—86; 7-12 music tchr. Interstate 35 Cmty. Schs., Truro, 1986—2001; k-12 music & band tchr. Ankeny Christian Acad., 2001—05; 6-8 music tchr. Des Moines Pub. Schs., Hoyt Mid. Sch., 2005—. Soloist: Messiah Performance. Mem.: Profl. Educators Iowa, Iowa Choral Dir.'s Assn. Office: Des Moines Pub Schs - Hoyt Mid Sch 2700 E 42nd Des Moines IA 50317

LANGHOUT-NIX, NELLEKE, artist; b. Utrecht, The Netherlands, Mar. 27, 1939; came to U.S., 1968, naturalized, 1978; d. Louis Wilhelm Frederick and Geertruida Nix; m. Ernst Langhout, July 26, 1958; 1 son, Klaas-Jan Marnix. MFA, The Hague, The Netherlands, 1958. Head art dept. Bush Sch., Seattle, 1969-71; dir. creative projects Project Rsch., Seattle, 1971-72; artist-in-residence Fairhaven Coll., Bellingham, Wash., 1974, Jefferson Cmty. Ct., Seattle, 1978-82, Lennox Sch., N.Y.C., 1982, 2002—03; tchr. summer children's art class Noble Collection, S.I.; dir. NN Gallery, Seattle, 1970—. Guest curator Holland-U.S.A. Bicentennial Show, U. Wash., 1982; project dir. Women in Art Today, Wash., 1989, Wash. State Centennial Celebration; Washington to Washington traveling exhbn., 1989; bd. dirs. Soho 20 Artists Galleries, N.Y.C., 1997-99. Executed wall hanging for King County Courthouse, Seattle, 1974; one-woman shows include Nat. Art Center, 1980, Gail Chase Gallery, Bellevue, Wash., 1979, 80, 83, 84, Original Graphics Gallery, Seattle, 1981, Bon Nat. Gallery, Seattle, 1981, Kathleen Ewing Gallery, Washington, 1986, Ina Broerse Laren, Holland, 1992, Charlotte Daneel Gallery, Holland, 11992, Christopher Gallery, Tucson, 1992, Mercer Island Cmty. Arts Ctr., 1992, Lisa Harris Gallery, Seattle, 1994, Jacques Marchais Mus. Tibetan, S.I., N.Y., 1995, 4th World Conf. on Women, China, 1995, Global Focus, Beijing, 1995, Elite Gallery, Moscow, 1995, Soho 20, N.Y.C., 1998, 99, 2000, 01, 02, 03, 04, Soul Sails Antarctica, 2005, Noble Maritime Mus., S.I., NY; exhibited in group shows, including Cheney Cowles Mus., Spokane, 1977, Bellevue Art Mus., 1978, 86, Renwick Gallery, Washington, 1978, Kleinert Gallery, Woodstock, N.Y., 1979, Artcore Meltdown, Sydney Australia, 1979, Tacoma Art Mus., 1979, 83, 86, 87, Ill. State Mus., Springfield, 1979, Plener Sandomierz, Poland, 1980, Western Assn. Art Mus. travel show, 1979-80, Madison Square Garden, N.Y.C., 1981, Exhbn. Space, N.Y.C., 1982, Lisa Harris Gallery (solo exhbns.), 1985, 87, 88, 94, Wash. State Centennial, Tacoma, 1989, Nordic Heritage Mus., Seattle, 1994, Balch Inst. Ethnic Studies, Phila., 1997, Ctr. Contemporary Art, Seattle, 1997, Zaaijer Gallery, Amsterdam, The Netherlands, 1998, Orihon and More, S.I., 2002; solo exhbns. include SoHo20, N.Y.C., 1998, 99, 2003, 05, NYC Gallery, Plener Collection, Sandomierz, Bell Tel. Co. Collection, Seattle, U. Wash., Seattle, Children's Orthopedic Hosp., Seattle, Nat. Mus. Women in Arts, Washington, Studio D'Ars Gallery, Milan, Italy, 2001, Nat. Mus. Women in Arts, Washington, 2002, Collins Gen. Ctrl. Libr., Portland, Oreg., 2002, John Noble Maritime Collection, Staten Island, N.Y.; installations Tacoma Art Mus; solo exhbns. include: Noble Maritime Collection, SI, NY; author: (with others) Step Inside the Sacred Circle, 1989, An Artist's Book 1940-45 Remembered, 1991; author: Tsoek: Earthly Writings by a Fourpaw, 1996, Cicada, the Brood of 1996, Zones of Time, Sand and Rain, 2000; writer, designer Papua New Guinea-Where She Invented Bow and Arrow, 1996; pub., editor: (Chelsea Rhodes) A Girl and Her Cat as a Matter of Fact, 2000, (artist's book) Septembereleven o-one, 2002, To Anne Frank, 2002. Bd. dirs. Wing Luke Mus., Seattle, 1978-81, Wash. State Trust Hist. Preservation, 1990-93, Soho 20, 1997-2000; v.p. Denny Regrade Cmty. Coun., 1978-79; mem. Seattle Planning Commn., 1978-84; mem. nat. adv. bd. dirs. Nat. Mus. Women in Arts, Washington, 1996—. Recipient wall hanging award City of Edmonds, Wash., 1974, Renton 83 merit award, 1984; merit award Internat. Platform Assn. Art Exhibit, 1984, silver medal 1st place, 1985, 87, gold medal, 1989; Year 2000 grant Libr. Book Fellows, Nat. Mus. of Women in the Arts, Washington. Mem. Denny Regrade Arts Coun. (co-founder), Internat. Platform Assn., Women in Arts N.Y.C., Nat. Mus. Women in Arts (founding, Libr. fellow, chmn. Wash. State com. 1988-89, mem. nat. adv. bd. 1993—), Seattle-King County Cmty. Arts Network (bd. dirs. 1983-85, chmn. 1984-85), Nat. Artist Equity Assn. Address: PO Box 375 Mercer Island WA 98040-0375 Personal E-mail: nixnelleke@hotmail.com.

LANGLAND, LAURIE LYNNE, archivist, director, educator; b. Mitchell, S.D., Mar. 21, 1964; d. Courtney John Hall and Mary Ann Klinger Hall; m. Byron Allen Langland, June 29, 1986 (div. June 2003). BS magna cum laude, U. S.D., 1985; JD, U. Wis., 1988; MA, U. Ariz., 1997. Law clk. Nelson, Rosholt, Robertson, et. al., Boise, Idaho, 1988—89, Ada County, Boise, 1989—91; libr. asst. Idaho State Law Libr., Boise, 1992—94; instr. New Careers Coll., Boise, 1993; libr. Idaho State Libr., Boise, 1994—99; newsroom staff mem. Daily Republic, Mitchell, 1999—2000; archivist Dakota Wesleyan U., Mitchell, 2000—, dir. learning svc., asst. prof., 2003—. Co-author: George McGovern: A Political Life, A Political Legacy; contbr. articles to profl. jours. Recipient Pro Bono award, Idaho State Bar, 1992. Mem.: AAUW (membership v.p. Mitchell, S.D. br.), Mitchell Assn. U. Women, S.D. Assn. U. Women, S.D. State Hist. Soc., Midwest Archives Conf., S.D. Libr. Assn., Mitchell Area Hist. Soc., Twentieth Century Club, Beta Phi Mu, Phi Beta Kappa, Alpha Phi Sigma. Democrat. Methodist. Home: PO Box 45 100 E 3rd St Fulton SD 57340 Office: Dakota Wesleyan U 1200 W University Ave Mitchell SD 57301 Office Phone: 605-995-2134. Office Fax: 605-995-2893. Business E-Mail: lalangla@dwu.edu.

LANGLEY, DONNA, film company executive; Sr. v.p. prodn. New Line Cinema, 1994—2001, Universal Pictures, 2001—03, exec. v.p. prodn., 2003—05, pres. prodn., 2005—. Exec. prodr.: (films) Austin Powers: The Spy Who Shagged Me, 1999, Drop Dead Gorgeous, 1999, The Astronaut's Wife, 1999, The Bachelor, 1999, The Cell, 2000, Lost Souls, 2000, Highway, 2002. Office: Universal Pictures 100 Universal City Plz Universal City CA 91608*

LANGLEY, PATRICIA ANN, lobbyist; b. Butler, Pa., Feb. 13, 1938; d. F.J. and Ella (Serafine) Piccola; m. Harold D. Langley, June 12, 1965; children: Erika, David. BA, U. Pitts., 1961; postgrad., Georgetown U., 1967, Cath. U. Am., 1985, George Mason U., 1990—. Legis. staff U.S. Congress, Washington, 1961-63; dir. social studies Am. Polit. Sci. Assn., Washington, 1963-65; legis. specialist U.S. Congress, Washington, 1965-67, caseworker, 1967-68; polit. staff Dem. Study Group U.S. Congress, Washington, 1969; Washington rep. Family Services Am., 1975-82, dir. Washington hdqrs., 1989-92, v.p. for govt. rels., 1992; pres. Policy Directions, Arlington, Va., 1992—. Vis. lectr. in sociology George Mason U., Fairfax, Va., 1994; bd. dirs. Coalition for Children and Youth, Washington, 1977-78; chmn. steering com. for the Coalition on White House Conf. on Families, 1979-80, Ad Hoc Coalition on A.F.D.C., 1981-82; co-founder Ptnrs. in Change Group, 1996. Active Donaldson Run Civic Assn., Arlington, Va., 1980—; bd. dirs. Va. Chamber Orch.; vol. docent Hillwood Mus., Washington, 1995—. Recipient Service Recognition award, U.S. Dept. Health and Human Svcs., 1980. Mem.: Nat. Coun. Family Rels., Women in Govt. Rels., Am. Soc. Assn. Execs., Arnova, Groves Conf., N. Va. Assn. Female Execs. Roman Catholic. Avocations: gardening, reading, old movies, community organizing. Home and Office: 2515 N Utah St Arlington VA 22207-4031 Business E-Mail: plangley@aol.com.

LANGLOIS, LORI A., human resources specialist; MEd, Plymouth State U., NH, 2001. Co-dir. profl. devel. ctr. North Country Edn. Svcs., Gorham, NH, 2003—. Bd. mem. No. White Mountain C. of C., Berlin, NH, 2003—05; treas. N.H. Staff Devel. Coun., Manchester. Office: North Country Education Services 300 Gorham Hill Road Gorham NH 03581 Office Phone: 603-466-5437.

LANGMAID, BARBRA KAY, elementary school educator; b. Chgo., Ill., Nov. 17, 1966; d. Donald Ray Olson and Sharon Kay Holm Olson; m. Gary P. Langmaid, May 24, 1992. BA in History, U. Houston, 1989; MS in Counseling, Okla. State U., Stillwater, 1992. Pers. mgr. Prostaff Pers., Little Rock, 1992—94; svc. learning mgr. Brevard CC, Cocoa, Fla., 1995—96; tchr. Brevard County Schs., Melbourne, Fla., 1996—97, Valdosta (Ga.) City Schs., 1998—2000; counselor Pasco County Schs., New Port Richey, Fla., 2000—03; tchr. Carolina Foothills Schs., Tucson, 2003—, dept. chair, curriculum resource coord., 2005—. Dept. chair, leadership team J. W. Mitchell HS, New Port Richey, 2001—03. Named Tchr. of the Yr., J. W. Mitchell HS, 2002. Mem.: ASCD, Nat. Coun. Social Studies.

LANG-MIERS, ELIZABETH ANN, judge; b. Mpls., Nov. 26, 1950; BA, U. Mo., 1972, JD, 1975. Bar: Mo. 1975, Tex. 1977, U.S. Ct. Appeals (5th cir.), U.S. Supreme Ct. Law clk. to presiding justice Mo. Supreme Ct., Jefferson City, 1975-76; ptnr. Locke Liddell & Sapp, LLP, Dallas, 1976—2003; judge Ct. Appeals, 5th Dist. Bd. dirs. Tex. Bar. Mem. Dallas County Med. Soc. Aux., bd. dirs. Met. YWCA; bd. dirs., chairperson adv. bd. Women's Resource Ctr. Leadership Dallas, Leadership Tex., Leadership Am. Recipient Am. Jurisprudence awards 1973, 74. Fellow Am. Bar Found., Tex. Bar Found. (trustee), Dallas Bar Found. (trustee, chair); mem. ABA (mem. ho. dels), Am. Law Inst., Dallas Bar Assn. (v.p. adminstrn., v.p. activities, sec.-treas., chair, vice chair bd. dirs., pres. 1998), Dallas Found. (vice chair bd. govs.), Tex. Young Lawyers Assn. (com. chair), Dallas Assn. Young Lawyers (com. chair), State Bar (bd. dirs., com. chair, Pres.'s citation 1996, 98, Woman of Excellence award, 1998, Louise Raggio award 1998, Judge Sam Williams Leadership award). Office: Ct of Appeals 600 Commerce Ste 200 Dallas TX 75201 Office Phone: 214-712-3403.

LANGRANA, ANITA, financial analyst, personal trainer; b. Ithaca, NY, July 13, 1975; d. Noshir A. and Dinaz Langrana. BS, Rutgers U., New Brunswick, NJ, 1998; MBA, Pace U., NYC, 2004. Cert. athletic trainer NJ. Human resources coord. Sports Phys. Therapy Inst., Princeton, NJ, 1998—2002, cert. athletic trainer, 2000—02; procurement divsn. intern UN, NYC, 2003; ad sales and stewardship intern Universal TV Group, NYC, 2003; fin. analyst Bristol-Myers Squibb, Princeton, 2004—05, Wyndham Worldwide, Parsippany, NJ, 2005—. Athletic Tng. scholar, Rutgers Sports Medicine Club, 1997—98. Mem.: Nat. Athletic Trainers Soc. (assoc.), Lubin Grad. Soc. (v.p. 2003—04), Lubin Bus. Sch. Alumni Assn. (bd. dirs., award 2004), Omicron Delta Epsilon, Sigma Iota Epsilon, Beta Gamma Sigma (hon.). Zoroastrian. Avocations: sports, exercise, travel, reading. Office: Wyndham Worldwide 7 Sylvan Way Parsippany NJ 07054 Office Phone: 973-496-7333. Personal E-mail: anita.langrana@gmail.com. Business E-Mail: anita.langrana@rci.com.

LANGSLEY, PAULINE ROYAL, psychiatrist; b. Lincoln, Nebr., July 2, 1927; d. Paul Ambrose and Dorothy (Sibley) Royal; m. Donald G. Langsley, Sept. 9, 1955; children: Karen Jean, Dorothy Ruth Langsley Runman, Susan Louise. BA, Mills Coll., 1949; MD, U. Nebr., 1953. Cert. psychiatrist, Am. Bd. Psychiatry and Neurology. Intern Mt. Zion Hosp., San Francisco, 1954; resident U. Calif., San Francisco, 1954-57, student health psychiatrist Berkeley, 1957-61, U. Colo., Boulder, 1961-68; assoc. clin. prof. psychiatry U. Calif. Med. Sch., Davis, 1968-76; student health psychiatrist U. Calif., Davis, 1968-76; assoc. clin. prof. psychiatry U. Cin., 1976-82; pvt. practice psychiatry Cin., 1976-82; cons. psychiatrist Federated States of Micronesia, Pohnpei, 1984-87; fellow in geriatric psychiatry Rush-Presbyn./St. Luke Hosp., Chgo., 1989-91. Mem. accreditation rev. com. Accreditation Coun. for Continuing Med. Edn., 1996-98. Trustee Mills Coll., Oakland, 1974-78, 2001—; bd. dirs. Evanston Women's Club. Fellow Am. Psychiat. Assn. (chair continuing med. edn. 1990-96); mem. AMA, Am. Med. Womens Assn., Ohio State Med. Assn., Ill. Psychiat. Soc. (sec. 1993-95, pres.-elect 1995-96, pres. 1996-97, accreditation coun. 1996-98). Home and Office: 1111 Race St 10A Denver CO 80206 Office Phone: 303-321-4193.

LANGSTON, JESSI LEA, music educator; b. N.J., Aug. 19, 1981; d. Robert E. Tranter and Lorraine E Buhrman. MusB cum laude, Ithaca Coll., N.Y., 2003. Cert. music educator K-12 N.Y., 2003, Va., 2003, N.J., 2003. Mid. sch. band and chorus dir. Orange County Pub. Schs., Orange, Va., 2003—04; band dir. Hammonton Mid. Sch., NJ, 2004—. Marching band music dir. Hammonton H.S., NJ, 2006—. Named Group II All State Champions, USSBA, 2006. Mem.: N.J. Music Educators Assn., Music Educators Nat. Conf., South Jersey Band and Orch. Dirs. Assn., NJ. Edn. Assn. Achievements include Excellent Rating at Music in the Parks Festival for Middle School Chorus; Excellent Rating at Trills and Thrills Festival for Middle School Band. Office: Hammonton Pub Sch 75 North Liberty St Hammonton NJ 08037

LANGSTON, SHEILA ANNETTE, special education educator, consultant; b. Pampa, Tex., Oct. 12, 1959; d. Marian Taylor and Bob Frazier Giles; children: Barrett Lee-Taylor, Sarah Kathleen-Annette. BS, West Tex. A&M U., 1983; MEd, U. Tex., 1997. Elem. tchg. Tex., 1983, spl. edn. tchg. birth - Grade 12 Tex., 1983. Spl. edn. tchr. Pub. Schs., Various, Tex., 1983—96; supr. of preschool programs for children with disabilities Bastrop Ind. Sch. Dist., Bastrop, Tex., 1996—99; agy. planner Tex. Early Childhood Intervention Agy., Austin, Tex., 1999—2000; coord. of svcs. for young children with disabilities Ga. Dept. of Edn., Atlanta, 2000—04; dir. Imagine IDEA, 2001—. Spkr. in field. Author professional writing. Mem. Coun. of Exceptional Children, Washington DC, 1983—2005. Grad Study fellow, U. Tex., 1995—97. Mem.: Nat. Assn. for Young Children (life), Coun. for Exceptional Children (life), Honor Soc. Women Educators. Christian. Avocations: travel, community service, gardening. Office: Imagine IDEA 3377 Glenrose Point Atlanta GA 30341 Office Phone: 770-715-0937. Business E-Mail: imagineidea@comcast.net.

LANGTON (TOMASIEWICZ), DAWN THERESA, literature and language educator; d. John Donald and Pam Theresa Tomasiewicz; m. Kevin John Langton, June 7, 2003. BA in English, Elmhurst Coll., Ill., 1997; MA in Tchr. Leadership, Roosevelt U., Chgo., 2000; M, Aurora U., Ill., 2003, St. Xavier U., Chgo., 2006. Tchr. English Barking Abbey Sch., Essex, England, 1997—97, Driscoll Cath. H.S., Addison, Ill., 1997—2000, Prospect H.S., Mount Prospect, 2000—. Coord. Saturday acad. Prospect H.S., 2001—04; coach volleyball Driscoll Cath. H.S., Addison, 1998—2000, dir. theater tech., 1997—98; advisor student coun. Prospect H.S., 2002—04, world lit. and composition team facilitator, 2005—, mgr. theater ho., 2000—02. Author: (literary criticism) Exam on the Victorian Age, (plays) So In Love. Avocations: travel, reading, exercise, theater, photography. Office Phone: 847-718-5553.

LANGUM, TERESA MARIE, elementary school educator; b. Kansas City, Mo., Oct. 6, 1954; d. Clyde Herbert Houghton (Stepfather); m. Kent Langum, May 22, 1976; children: Leslie Marie Miles, Stephanie Lynn McClain, Mary Katherine. BS in Elem and Spl. Edn., Univ. Ark., Fayetteville, Ark., 1976. Cert. tchr. Ark., 1976. Tchr. Lewisville (Tex.) Ind. Sch. Dist., Lewisville, Tex., 1984—95, Westside Elementsry, Rogers, Ark., 1995—2001, Lingle Mid. Sch., Rogers, 2001—. Tutor Rogers (Ark.) Schs., 2005—. Grantee, Rotary Club. Republican. Avocations: crocheting, gardening, travel. Office Phone: 479-631-3590.

LANHAM, BETTY BAILEY, anthropologist, educator; b. Statesville, N.C., Aug. 12, 1922; d. Clyde B. and Naomi (Bailey) L. BS, U. Va., 1944, MA, 1947; PhD, Syracuse U., 1962. Mem. faculty River Falls State Tchrs. Coll., 1948-49, U. Md., 1949-50, Wakayama U., Japan, 1951-52, Randolph Macon Women's Coll., 1954-55, Oswego State Tchrs. Coll., 1956-58, Hamilton Coll., 1961-62, Ind. U., 1962-65, Western Mich. U., 1965-67, Albany Med. Coll., 1967-70, U.Guyana, 1969-70; prof. anthropology Indiana U. of Pa., 1970-88, prof. emeritus, 1988—. Contbr. articles to jours. Wenner-Gren Found. for Anthrop. Rsch. predoctoral fellow, 1951-52, AAUW predoctoral rsch. fellow, 1959-60. Mem. Am. Anthrop. Assn., Assn. for Asian Studies Democrat. Home: 2529 Willard Dr Charlottesville VA 22903-4225

LANICCA ALBANESE, ELLEN, public relations executive; Co-founder, pres. Patrice Tanaka & Co., N.Y.C., 1990—94, pres., 1994—, head Home, Healthcare and Fin. Svcs. account groups; v.p. Lumin Collaborative. V.p. bd. dirs. League of Women Voters Edn. Found., NY. Mem.: Pub. Rels. Soc. Am. NY (exec. com. bd. dirs.). Office: Patrice Tanaka & Co Inc 320 W 13th St Fl 7 New York NY 10014-1200

LANIER, ELIZABETH K., lawyer; m. Addison Lanier; 3 children. BA with honors, Smith Coll.; JD, Columbia U.; Degree (hon.), Cin. State Tech. C.C., Coll. Mt. St. Joseph. Assoc. Davis Polk & Wardell, N.Y.C.; assoc., ptnr. Frost & Jacobs (now Frost Brown Todd LLC), Cin.; gen. counsel S.W. Ohio Regional Transit Authority; dir. Star Gas Corp.; v.p., chief of staff Cinergy Corp., 1996—98; v.p., gen. counsel GE Power Sys., 1998—2002; sr. v.p., gen. counsel Trizec Properties, 2002; exec. v.p., corp. affairs and gen. counsel US Airways Group, Inc. US Airways, Inc., Arlington, Va., 2003—, corp. sec., 2004—. Bd. dirs. Patina Oil & Gas Corp. Chmn. Aronoff Ctr.; vice chmn. Cin. Arts Assn.; mem. adv. bd. Civic Forum; bd. dirs. Ohio Bd. Regents, 1990, sec. of the bd., 1994, 1995, chmn., 1996; bd. dirs. Cin. Parks Found., Greater Cin. Conv. and Visitors Bur., Lighthouse Youth Svcs., World Affairs Coun., Children's Svcs. Levy Com. Harlan Fiske Stone scholar, Columbia U. Sch. Law. Office: US Airways 2345 Crystal Dr Arlington VA 22227

LANIER, JACQUELINE RUTH, curator, artist; b. Boston, Dec. 15, 1947; d. John Stanley and Mary Elizabeth (Porter) L.; 1 child, Raymond Rashad Lanier. BS in Edn., Morgan State U., 1976. Drama specialist Day in Arts Boston Symphony, 1971; drama specialist Balt. City Cultural Arts & Urban Svcs., 1974-78; prodr., host Sta. WEAA-FM, 1985-90; with ACTION, 1987-89; R & D implementer Abell Found., 1988-89; developer, curator Lanier Mus. African-Am. History, 1983—; bus. mgr. League for Handicap-Camp Greentop, 1997; cons., development, program design. Being Reunited with Opportunity, 1998—. Seminar staff developer dept. edn. Balt. Cith Sch., 1988; lectr., presenter IRS, 1988; R & D implementer Lady Md. Found., 1989; lectr. D.C. Pub. Libr., 1990; asst. devel. coord., collections mgr. Heritage Mus. Art, 1990—, Lanier Enterprises Internat., 1997—; curator, lectr. Benjamin Banner Mus. and Park, 1998—; lectr. in field. Prodr. Call of the Ancestor, 1992; exhbts. include Counciling Ctr., 1992, Internat. Black Women Congress, 1992, Morgan State U., 1992, Busterizing, Inc., Md. Commn. African Am. History & Culture, 1992, City Life Mus., 1992, Encore Theatre Co., 1992, Social Security Adminstrn., 1992, New Shiloh Bapt. Ch., 1992, Enon Bapt. Ch., 1992, St. Peter Clavers Ch., 1992, Immaculate Conception Ch., 1994, Martin Luther King Ch., 1994, Heritage Mus. Art, 1994, Chesapeake Coll., 1994, 97, Native Am. Mus., 1994, Nat. Assn. Black Vets., 1994, Dept. Equal Employment Devel., 1994, Perry Point Vets. Hosp., 1994, UN, 1995, D.C. Country Club, 1995, Howard County C.C., 1995, Cambridge Coll., 1995, Johns Hopkins Rsch. Inst., 1995, Hist. Sharp. St. Ch., 1995, Balt. Aquarium, 1996, Chesapeake Coll., 1996, Allaganey County Arts Coun., 1996, Heritage Mus., 1996, Md. Humanities Coun., 1996, Nat. Aquarium Balt. 1996, Mobil Corp. Hdqrs., 1996, 97, Health Care Fin. Adminstrn., 1996, 97, League Serving People with Disabilities, 1997. Mem. exec. com. Broadway East Cmty. Assn.; bd. dirs., 2d dist. rep. Citizen Plabning & Housing Assn.; chmn. East Balt. Coun. Neighborhoods, Inc.; mem. Empowerment Zone Devel. Bd.; gen. ptnr. Gay St. Housing Partnership Ltd.; bd. dirs., pres. Housing Assistance Corp.; v.p. Mid. East Cmty. Devel. Corp.; vol. Balt. City Commn. Women, Urban Svcs. Agy., Balt. City Youth Fair, WAVR Radio; com. mem. Democratic State Ctrl. Com.; mem. substance abuse prevention coun. Mayor's Coordinating Coun. Criminal Justice, Voices of Electorate; mem. Black Single Parents; mem., pres. Ira Aldridge Players; adv. com. minority bus. tourism Md. Dept. Econ. Employment Devel. Office Tourism; mem. Sankofa exhb. adv. com. Md. Hist. Soc., bd. dirs. Seventh Sons Prodn. Co. Recipient Outstanding Svc. award Campfire, Inc., Fifteen Yr. Svc. award, 100 Hours Vol. Svc. award VA, Outstanding Svc. award Md. House Dels., Citation City of Balt. Citizens, Svcs. Agy. & Citizens Balt. award Urban Svcs. Agy., Svc. to Jazz Cmty. award Gemini Prodns., Inc., Outstanding Cmty. Svc. award African Am. Women's Expo, Outstanding Leadership award AFRAM, 1995; inducted into Black Collectors Hall of Fame, 1992, Wall of Fame, 1994, Health Care Fin. Adminstrn., 1997. Mem. Nat. Assn. Fundraising Execs., Nat. Assn. Black Collectors & Dealers, New Gay St. Improvement Assn. (pres.), Black Ethnic Collectibles Mag. (adv. bd.), Transitional Housing Program (adv. com.). Democrat. Lutheran. Avocations: environmentalist, synchronized swimming, writing, reading, storytelling. Home: 3817 Clifton Ave Baltimore MD 21216-2428

LANIER, SUSIE MAE, mathematics professor; b. Millen, Ga., July 16, 1960; d. Henry Grady Lanier, Jr. and Mildred Portwood Lanier. BS IN EDN., Ga. So. Coll., 1981, MS in tchg., 1983; PhD, U. Ga., 1999. Math instr. Ga. So. U., Statesboro, Ga., 1984—96, asst. prof., math., 1996—; math. tchr. Screven County Acad., Sylvania, Ga., 1981—84. Participant U. Sys. of Ga. Math. Consortium, Ga., 2003—, U. Sys. of Ga. Partnership for Reform in Sci. and Math., Ga., 2004—. Author: When Will I Ever Teach This: An Activities Manual For Mathematics For Elementary Teachers, (online instructional resource) Demos with Positive Impact; contbr. articles to profl. jours. Recipient Assoc. Membership on Grad. Faculty, Ga. So. U., 2003—; fellow Faculty Devel. in Ga., U. Sys. of Ga., U. of Ga., 1996 - 1999; grantee Improving Tchr. Quality, U. of Ga., 2004. Mem.: Ga. Assn. for Devel. Edn. (treas. 2001—03), Nat. Coun. of Tchrs. of Math., Math. Assn. of Am., Ga. Coun. of Tchrs. of Math. (life), Phi Kappa Phi. Methodist. Avocations: travel, photography, needlework. Home: 2302 Camelia Dr W Statesboro GA 30461 Office: Ga So U P O Box 8093 Statesboro GA 30460 Office Phone: 912-681-0168. E-mail: slanier@georgiasouthern.edu.

LANIGAN, SUSAN S., lawyer; b. May 1962; BA, U. Ga.; JD, U. Ga. Law Sch. Assoc. gen. counsel Zale Corp., Irving, Tex., 1996—97, sr. v.p., gen. counsel, sec., 1997—2002; v.p., gen. counsel, corp. sec. Dollar Gen. Corp., Goodlettsville, Tenn., 2002—03, sr. v.p., gen. counsel, corp sec., 2003—. Office: Dollar General Corp 100 Mission Ridge Goodlettsville TN 37072

LANK, EDITH HANDLEMAN, journalist, educator; b. Boston, Feb. 27, 1926; m. Norman Lank; children: Avrum, David, Anna. BA magna cum laude, Syracuse U. Columnist L.A. Times Syndicate, 1976—2000; TV host Sta. WOKR-TV, Rochester, NY, 1983-84; radio host Sta. WBBF-AM, Rochester, 1984-85; columnist Tribune Media Svcs., 2000—02, Creators Syndicate, 2003—. Lectr. St. John Fisher Coll., Rochester, 1977-89; commentator Sta. WXXI-FM, Rochester, 1977—; guest Pub. Radio Internat., St. Paul, 1987—; speaker in field. Author: Home Buying, 1981, Selling Your Home, 1982, Modern Real Estate Practice in New York, 1983, rev. 9th edit., 2006, The Home Seller's Kit, 1988, rev. 4th edit. 1997, The Complete Home Buyer's Kit, 1989, rev. 4th edit., 1997, Dear Edith, 1990, Essentials of New Jersey Real Estate, rev. 9th edit., 2006, 201 Questions Every Homebuyer and Seller Must Ask, 1996, Jane Austen Speaks to Women, 2000, I've Heard It All, 2006; co-author: Your Home as a Tax Shelter, 1993; contbr. articles to Time, New Yorker, McCall's, Real Estate Today, Persuasions, Modern Maturity, others. Recipient media award Bar Assn. Monroe County, 1982, Matrix award Women in Comm., 1984; named Woman of Distinction Gov. of NY, Communicator of Yr. SUNY, Brockport, 1986. Mem. Real Estate Educators Assn. (bd. dirs., Consumer Edn. award 1982, 83, 86, 96, Real Estate Educator of Yr. 1984), Nat. Assn. Real Estate Editors (bd. dirs), Jane Austen Soc. N.Am. (dir.), Phi Beta Kappa. Avocation: scuba diving. Home and Office: 240 Hemingway Dr Rochester NY 14620-3316 E-mail: edithlank@aol.com.

LANKARD DEWEY, JUDITH MARGARET, library director, lawyer; b. Culver City, Calif., Apr. 10, 1942; d. Dorothy Harmon Brown; m. Rowland Earl Felt, Nov. 26, 1966 (div. Apr. 16, 1989); children: Scott Alan Felt, Brian Earl Felt, Keith Irvin Felt, David Merle Felt, Emily Margaret Felt; m. Fredric Allen Dewey, Oct. 30, 1999. BA, U. Redlands, 1964; MA, Ind. U., 1965; JD, U. Idaho, 1993. Bar: Idaho 1996. Catalog, reference libr. Battelle N.W., Richland, Wash., 1965—67, Richland Pub. Libr., 1967—74; legal sec., paralegal law firms Idaho Falls, Idaho, 1989—96; pvt. practice, 1996—2002; constrn. loan closing officer Zions Bank, Idaho Falls, 1998—2000; dir. Madison Libr. Dist., Rexburg, Idaho, 2001—. Mem.: Am. Libr. Assn., Law Revision Task Force, Idaho State Libr. Law, Idaho Libr. Assn. Leg. Com., Idaho Libr. Assn. Office: Madison Libr Dist 73 North Ctr Rexburg ID 83440 Office Phone: 208-356-3461.

LANKFORD, JANNA LOUISE, social studies educator; b. Stamford, Tex., Mar. 16, 1954; d. James Bryson and June Mary Lena Clark; m. Stephen Lynn Lankford, May 25, 1952; children: Matthew Lynn, Kimberly Michelle, Stephanie Leigh Schwartzenburg. BS, Angelo State U., San Angelo, Tex., 1972—75. Cert. Tchr. Tex. Dept. Edn., 1975. Kindergarten tchr. Pk. Forest Ind. Sch. Dist., Ill., 1977—79; 3rd grade tchr. Ector County Ind. Sch. Dist., Odessa, 1976—77; 4th grade tchr. Andrews Ind. Sch. Dist., 1980—82; 5th grade tchr. Am. Sch. of Warsaw, 1993—96; 6th grade social studies tchr. Ft. Bend Ind. Sch. Dist., Sugarland, Tex., 1997—. Home team leader River Pointe Ch., Sugar Land, 2004—06. Mem.: Houston Ladies Tennis Assn. (assoc. Doubles Club Championship Winner 1996, 1998, 2000, 2002). Republican. Mem. Christian Ch. Avocations: tennis, travel. Office: Sugar Land Mid Sch 321 7th St Sugar Land TX 77478 Office Phone: 281-634-3080.

LANNAN, MAURA ANNE KELLY, reporter; b. Bridgeport, Conn., Apr. 2, 1971; d. Richard Francis and Margaret Mary Kelly. BA, Boston Coll., Mass., 1993; MS in Journalism, Northwestern U., Evanston, Ill., 1994. Intern The Patriot Ledger, Quincy, Mass., 1993; corr. Conn. Post, Bridgeport, 1993; reporter Naugatuck bur. Waterbury Rep.-Am., Conn., 1994—95, edn. reporter, 1995, city hall reporter, 1995—96, state capitol reporter, 1996-99; reporter Chgo. Tribune, 2000—01, AP, 2001—05; freelance reporter, 2005—. Mem. reporters' roundtable discussion Conn. Jour. on Conn. Pub. TV, Hartford, 1998-99 and WFSB's CT '97, CT '98, Ct '99 in Hartford. Co-recipient Explanatory Reporting-Team Coverage, Pulitzer Prize, 2001. Mem. Soc. Profl. Journalists (Reporting awards Conn. chpt. 1998, 99, 2000, co-recipient Peter Lisagor award for deadline reporting, Headline Club chpt. 2003, Peter Lisagor award for business reporting, 2005), Investigative Reporters and Editors, Boston Coll. Alumni Assn., Northwestern U. Alumni Club Conn. Roman Catholic. Avocations: photography, travel, skiing, tennis, swimming. Home: PO Box 341740 Bethesda MD 20827 Personal E-mail: makelly42@hotmail.com.

LANNING, YVONNE BRADSHAW, elementary school educator; b. Smithville, Mo., Mar. 12, 1956; d. Arbeth McKinley and Frances Valjean (Whelan) Bradshaw. AA, Kansas City C.C., 1976; BS, St. Mary Coll., Leavenworth, Kans., 1985; MS, Kans. State U., 2002; PhD, St. Regis U., 2003. Cert. tchr., Kans., Kans. Assn. for Edn. Young Children. Paraprofl. St. Peter's Cathedral Sch., Kansas City; elem. and kindergarten tchr. Holy Family Sch., Kansas City; tchr. kindergarten Unified Sch. Dist. 500, Kansas City, Kansas City (Mo.) Sch. Dist. Pres. Mid-County Dem. Club, 1988; mem. Kans. Fedn. Dem. Women, Southside Dem. Club. Mem. Cath. Edn. Assn., Kans. Edn. Assn. (chmn. polit. action commn. 1988-89), Quill and Scroll, Southside Ladies Club, Women of the Moose (chpt. 1562), Am. Legion (aux. post #327), Ladies Aux. VFW (post #111), Slavic Am. Citizens Club.

LANPHER, KATHERINE, radio personality, columnist; b. May 27, 1959; BA, Northwestern U.; MA in Am. Cultural History, U. Chgo. Columnist St. Paul Pioneer-Press, Minn.; host Weeknights with Katherine Lanpher, KSTP-AM 1500, Mpls., 1995—96, Midmorning, Minn. Pub. Radio, 1988—2004, Talking Volumes; co-host The Al Franken Show, Air Am. Radio, NYC, 2004—. Guest host Talk of the Nation, Nat. Pub. Radio, 1999; commentator CNN, MSNBC, CNBC. Author: (memoir) Leap Days: Chronicles of a Midlife Move, 2006. Office: Air America Radio 641 Avenue Of The Americas Fl 4 New York NY 10011-2038*

LANQUETOT, E. ROXANNE, retired special education educator; b. Kansas City, Nov. 29, 1933; d. Myron Lewis and Bonnie (Goldberg) Leiser; m. Guy Alfred Lanquetot, Oct. 3, 1958; 1 child, Serge Normand. Student, Stanford U., 1951-53; cert. in French Pronunciation, Inst. de Phonetique, Sorbonne, Paris, 1954; BS, Columbia U., 1956, MA, 1957, CCNY, 1976; postgrad., CUNY, 1980-83. Asst. tchr. English Lycee Fenelon, Paris, 1960-62; tchr. kindergarten Lycee Francais N.Y., N.Y.C., 1964-65; dir. nursery & kindergarten Lyceum Francais, N.Y.C., 1965-66; tchr. 2d grade Pub. Sch. 113 M, N.Y.C., 1966-69; tchr., jr. guidance counselor Pub. Sch. 87 M, N.Y.C., 1969-71; tchr. emotionally handicapped Pub. Sch. 106, Bellevue Hosp., N.Y.C., 1971-99; ret., 1999. Contbr. articles to profl. publs., Newsday, Wall St. Jour., France-Amerique, others. Fellow Am. Orthophyschiatric Assn.; mem. Nat. Alliance for Rsch. on Schizophrenia and Depression (mem. leadership coun.). Avocations: classical music, theater, creative writing, travel, ballet, classical music, theater. Home and Office: 315 W 106th St New York NY 10025-3445 Personal E-mail: rglanquetot@yahoo.com.

LANSAW, TRACI LYNN, mathematics educator; d. Donald Lee and Carol Joanne Hannah; m. Jeff Lansaw, Aug. 22, 1992; children: Trent Jeffrey, Troy Anderson, Jake Matthew. BS in Math. Edn., Ohio U., Athens, 1992. Tchr. math. Colraine H.S., Colraine, Ohio, 1996—97, West Bloomfield H.S., Mich., 1997—. Scholar, Ohio U., 1988—92. Mem.: West Bloomfield Edn. Assn. Office: West Bloomfield High School 5810 Commerce Road West Bloomfield MI 48324 Office Phone: 248-865-6438. Personal E-mail: jlansaw@peoplepc.com.

LANSBURY, ANGELA BRIGID, actress; b. London, Oct. 16, 1925; came to U.S., 1940; d. Edgar and Moyna (Macgill) L.; m. Richard Cromwell, Sept. 27, 1945 (div. Aug. 1946); m. Peter Shaw, Aug. 12, 1949 (dec. Jan. 29, 2003); children: Anthony, Deirdre. Student, Webber-Douglas Sch. Drama, London, 1939-40, Feagin Sch. Drama, N.Y.C., 1940-42; LHD (hon.), Boston U., 1990. Host 41st-43d Ann. Tony Awards, 45th Ann. Emmy Awards. Actress with Metro-Goldwyn-Mayer, 1943-50; films include: Gaslight, 1944 (Acad. award nomination), National Velvet, 1944, The Picture of Dorian Gray, 1944 (Golden Globe award, Acad. award nomination), The Harvey Girls, 1946, The Hoodlum Saint, 1946, Till the Clouds Roll By, 1946, The Private Affairs of Bel Ami, 1947, If Winter Comes, 1948, Tenth Avenue Angel, 1948, State of the Union, 1948, The Three Musketeers, 1948, The Red Danube, 1949, Samson and Delilah, 1949, Kind Lady, 1951, Mutiny, 1952, Remains to be Seen, 1953, A Life at Stake, 1955, The Purple Mask, 1956, A Lawless Street, 1956, Please Murder Me, 1956, The Court Jester, 1956, The Long Hot Summer, 1958, Reluctant Debutante, 1958, A Breath of Scandal, 1960, Dark at the Top of the Stairs, 1960, Season of Passion, 1961, Blue Hawaii, 1961, All Fall Down, 1962, Manchurian Candidate, 1962 (Golden Globe award, Acad. award nomination), In the Cool of the Day, 1963, Dear Heart, 1964, The World of Henry Orient, 1964, The Greatest Story Ever Told, 1965, Harlow, 1965, The Amorous Adventures of Moll Flanders, 1965, Mister Buddwing, 1966, Something for Everyone, 1970, Bedknobs and Broomsticks, 1971, Death on the Nile, 1978, The Lady Vanishes, 1980, The Mirror Crack'd, 1980, The Pirates of Penzance, 1982, The Company of Wolves, 1983, Beauty and the Beast, 1991, Your Studio and You, 1995, Beauty & the Beast: Enchanted Christmas (vioce), 1997, Anastasia (voice), 1997, Nanny McPhee, 2005; star TV series Murder, She Wrote, 1984-96 (Golden Globe awards 1984, 86, 91, 92, 12 Emmy nominations, Lead Actress - Drama), Murder, She Wrote: A Story to Die For, 2000, Murder, She Wrote: The Last Free Man, 2001, Murder, She Wrote: The Celtic Riddle, 2003; appeared in TV mini-series Little Gloria, Happy at Last, 1982, Lace, 1984, Rage of Angels, part II, 1986; other TV movies include: The First Olympics-Athens 1896, A Talent for Murder, Gift of Love, 1982, Shootdown, 1988, The Shell Seekers, 1989, The Love She Sought, 1990, Mrs. 'Arris Goes to Paris, 1992, (musical) Mrs. Santa Claus, 1996; appeared in plays Hotel Paradiso, 1957, A Taste of Honey, 1960, Anyone Can Whistle, 1964, Mame (on Broadway), 1966, 83 (Tony award for Best Mus. Actress 1966), Dear World, 1968 (Tony award for Best Mus. Actress 1969), All Over (London Royal Shakespeare Co.), 1971, Prettybelle, 1971, Gypsy, 1974 (Tony award for Best Mus. Actress 1975, Sarah Siddons award), The King and I, 1978, Sweeney Todd, 1979 (Tony award for Best Mus. Actress 1979, Sarah Siddons award), Hamlet, Nat. Theatre, London, 1976, A Little Family Business, 1983; TV appearances Law & Order: SVU, 2005. Named Woman of Yr., Harvard Hasty Pudding Theatricals, 1968, Comdr. of British Empire by Queen Elizabeth II, 1994; named to Theatre Hall of Fame, 1982, TV Hall of Fame, 1996; recipient British Acad. award, 1991, Silver Mask Lifetime Ach. award, British Acad. Film and TV Arts, 1992, Lifetime Achievement award, Screen Actors' Guild, Hollywood, 1997, 16 Emmy Award Nominations, 8 Golden Globe Nominations; Won 6 Golden Glode Awards; received Nat. medal of the Arts from President Clinton, 1997. Office: c/o William Morris Agy 151 El Camino Dr Beverly Hills CA 90212*

LANSDOWNE, KAREN MYRTLE, retired English language and literature educator; b. Twin Falls, Idaho, Aug. 11, 1926; d. George and Effie Myrtle (Avotte) Martin; m. Paul L. Lansdowne, Sept. 12, 1948; children: Michele Lynn, Larry Alan. BA in English with honors, U. Oreg., 1948, MEd, 1958, MA with honors, 1960. Tchr. Newfield (N.Y.) H.S., 1948-50, S. Eugene (Oreg.) H.S., 1952; mem. faculty U. Oreg., Eugene, 1958-65; asst. prof. English Lane C.C., Eugene, 1965-82, ret., 1982. Cons. Oreg. Curriculum Study Center. Co-author: The Oregon Curriculum: Language/Rhetoric, I, II, III and IV, 1970; rsch., co-author: Lansdowne Family Genealogy Center Studies, 1995-99. Rep. Calif. Young Neighborhood Assn., 1978—; mem. scholarship com. First Congl. Ch., 1950-70. Mem. MLA, Pacific N.W. Regional Conf. C.C.s, Nat. Coun. Tchrs. English, U. Oreg. Women, AAUW (sec.) Jaycettes, Pi Lambda Theta (pres.), Phi Beta Patronesses (pres.), Delta Kappa Gamma. Home: 2056 Lincoln St Eugene OR 97405-2604

LANSING, JEWEL BECK (JEWEL ANNE BECK), writer, auditor; b. Ronan, Mont., May 13, 1930; d. Lars Martin and Julia Syla Beck; m. Ronald B. Lansing, June 16, 1956; children: Mark, Alyse, Annette. BA in Journalism, U. Mont., Missoula, 1952; MA in Edn., Stanford U., Calif., 1954. CPA, Oreg. Elected auditor Multnomah County, Portland, Oreg., 1975-82, City of Portland, 1983-86; adj. prof. Lewis and Clark Coll., Portland, 1989-92; interim exec. dir. William Temple Ho., Portland, 1994, YWCA, Portland, 1995; interim pres. Oreg. Coll. of Arts and Crafts, Portland, 1996; writer Portland, 1987—. Author: Campaigning for Office, 1991, 101 Campaign Tips, 1991, Deadly Games in City Hall, 1997. Portland: People, Politics, and Power, 1851-2001, 2003, 05. Candidate state treas. Dem. Party, 1976, 80; pres. Oreg. Fedn. of Dem. Women, 1977-78; city-county consolidation task force City of Portland, 1997-98; active Pacific N.W. local govt. rep. Nat. Intergovtl. Audit Forum, Washington, 1982-85. Recipient Woman of Achievement LWV, 1995, Disting. Leadership award Assn. of Govt. Accts., 1987, Pub. Svc. award Oreg. Soc. of CPAs, 1987, Taxpayers Champion award Oregonians for Cost Effective Govt., 1987; named to Silver Hall Fame, 2004. Mem. Womens Investment Network (polit. action com. exec. com., bd. dirs., founder), Oreg. Women's Polit. Caucus (First Woman award 1987), Portland Women's Polit. Caucus (Svc. award 1987), Oreg. Hist. Soc., Oreg. Environtl. Coun., Portland LWV. Unitarian Universalist. Avocations: hiking, playing cards, reading, canoeing, golf.

LANSING, MARTHA HEMPEL, physician; b. New Haven, 1942; Degree in music, Houghton Coll.; MD, U. Okla., 1982. Diplomate Am. Bd. Family Practice, cert. psychoanalytic psychotherapist. Resident in family practice U. Tenn., 1982—84, Williamsport (Pa.) Hosp.-U. Pa., 1984—85; group family practice physician, 1985—95; dir. family practice residency program Wood Johnson Med. Sch. U. Medicine and Dentistry N.J., 1997—; program dir., dir. family health ctr., assoc. prof. U. Medicine and Dentistry N.J. Staff physician Capital Health Sys.-Fuld Campus. Author (with Carol D. Goodheart): Treating People with Chronic Disease: A Psychological Guide, 1996; contbr. chpt. to book. Named one of Top Drs. 2002, Castle Connolly and N.J. Monthly Mag., Top Drs. 2003. Fellow: Nat. Inst. Program Dir. Devel. Office: Family Health Ctr 666 Plainsboro Rd # 640 Plainsboro NJ 08536-3019 Office Phone: 609-275-0487.

LANSING, SHERRY LEE, former film company executive; b. Chgo., July 31, 1944; d. Norton and Margo L.; m. William Friedkin, July 6, 1991. BS summa cum laude in Theatre, Northwestern U., 1966; DFA (hon.), Am. Film Inst. High sch. tchr. math., L.A., 1966-69; model TV commls. Max Factor Co., 1969-70, Alberto-Culver Co., 1969-70; story editor Wagner Internat. Prodn. Co., 1972-74, dir. west coast devel., 1974-75; story editor MGM, 1975-77, v.p. creative affairs, 1977; senior v.p. prodn. Columbia Pictures, 1977-80; pres. studio 20th Century Fox Prodns., Hollywood, 1980-82; founder Jaffee-Lansing Prodns., 1983—92; pres. Paramount Communications, 1990—2005; chmn. Paramount Motion Pictures Group, L.A., 1992—2005; CEO The Sherry Lansing Found., 2005—. Bd. dirs. QUALCOMM Inc., 2006—. Actress (films) Loving, 1970, Rio Lobo, 1970; (TV appearances) Ironside, 1971, Frasier, 1996; exec. prodr. (films) Racing With the Moon, 1984, Firstborn, 1984; prodr. (films) Fatal Attraction, 1987, The Accused, 1988, Black Rain, 1989, School Ties, 1992, Indecent Proposal, 1993; exec. prodr. (TV movies) When the Time Comes, 1987, Mistress, 1992. Bd. dirs. ARC; bd. regents U. Chgo., U. Calif., 1991—; bd. trustees The Carter Center, 2005—, Am. Assn. Cancer Rsch. Named one of 100 Most Powerful Women in Entertainment, Hollywood Reporter, 2003, 2004; recipient Producers Guild of Am. Milestone award, 2000, Horatio Alger Humanitarian award, 2004, Woodrow Wilson award for Corp. Citizenship, Alfred P. Sloan, Jr. Meml. award, Disting. Community Svc. award, Brandeis U.*

LANSNER, GABRIELLE, choreographer, dancer, performing company executive, actress; Attended, Juilliard, SUNY, Purchase, NYU Exptl. Theatre Wing. Assoc. mem. and performer Wooster Group; founder Gabrielle Lansner and Dancers, 1980—87; founder, artistic dir. Gabrielle Lansner and Co. Mem. Lincoln Ctr. Directors Lab., NYC, 1998—; tchr. movement for actors Am. Acad. Dramatic Arts, Mint Theatre Co. Performer: (plays) Three Places in Rhode Island, Query, 1978, Holocaust Stories, 2003, The Jewish Wife, 2003; dancer Black and White in Color, 1987; dir. and choreographer (plays) The Boy With the Glasses, 2001; choreographer (plays) Him & Her, NY Internat. Fringe Festival, 2002; dir., choreographer, book adaptation (musical) River Deep: A Tribute to Tina Turner, 2006—. Office: Artistic Director Gabrielle Lansner and Co 32 West 38th St #2 New York NY 10018 Office Phone: 212-768-0644. E-mail: gabrielle_lansner_company@yahoo.com.*

LANTER, LANORE, writer, educator; b. Argenta, Ill., Apr. 30, 1928; d. Floyd Depin Lanter and Goldie May Elkins; m. Andrew Kasparian, Oct. 17, 1948 (div. July 1976); children: Andra Kay, Dana Lee, Mark Scott, David Andrew. BA in English, Fresno State Coll., 1969. Cert. std. elem. tchr., 1972, early childhood, 1972, registered Calif., 1972. Tutor lang. skills Fresno County, Calif., 1972; co-dir. curriculum N.W. Ch. Day Care, Fresno, 1972—73; writer curriculum, head tchr. First Presbyn. Ch., Fresno, 1973—74; owner, tchr., writer curriculum Children's Corner Presch., Fresno, 1977—83; educator (older adults writing) Clovis Adult Edn./Clovis Unified Sch. Dist., Calif., 1995—; columnist Wryte Rite Tips Win Win Writing Orgn., Fresno, 2001—05. Editor, cons. San Joaquin Valley Sr. Writers, Fresno, 1994—. Author: (textbook) You Can Wryte Rite Series, 1994, (columns) Wryte Rite Tips, 2005; editor: (6 book anthologies) Inklings, 1994, 1995, 1996, We Remember When, 1997, Flights of Fantasy, 2000, Poemscapes, 2005. Vol. tchr., writing educator (55 yrs. and older) St. Agnes Hosp. Club 55 Plus, Herndon, Fresno, 1994—; mem. task force Muscular Dystrophy Assn., Shaw, Fresno, 1994; vol. Win Win Writers Orgn., 2002—05. Named Highest Achiever with muscle disease, Muscular Dystrophy, Shaw, Fresno, 1995; recipient Best Tchr. plaque, San Joaquin Valley Sr. Writers, 1997, Tolerance award, So. Poverty Law Ctr., Mont., Ala., 2003, First Pl. Srs. of William Saroyan Writing Contest, 1992, Cert. of Recognition for Outstanding Contbn., Muscular Dystrophy Assn., Calif. Legis. Assembly, 1995. Independent. Protestant. Avocations: reading, flower arranging, painting, poetry writing. Home: 2934 E Ashlan Ave Fresno CA 93726-3304 Office Phone: 559-243-1156. Personal E-mail: lanore22@aol.com.

LANTIS, DONNA LEA, retired banker, artist, art educator; b. Medford, Oreg., Oct. 12, 1931; d. James Warren Fader and Amy Bell (Crump) Fader-Snyder; m. Victor Earl Lantis, July 9, 1950 (div. Apr. 1975); children: Deborah Ann Hayes, Diana Lorraine Keaton. BS, So. Oreg. U., 1966; postgrad., Otis Art Inst., L.A., 1969; 5th yr. cert., U. Oreg., 1974. Art tchr., Oreg., Tenn., Ky.; cert. banker Am. Inst. Banking. Banker First Nat. Bank, Ashland, Oreg., 1951-62; tchr. art, history Klamath County Sch. Dist.,

Klamath Falls, Oreg., 1966-68; tchr. art Ashland Sch. Dist., 1968-75; banker First Interstate Bank, Medford, Oreg., 1979-92. Supr. student tchrs. So. Oreg. U., Ashland, 1968-75, work with traumatized children, 1968-69. Author illustrated poetry; exhbns. include Oreg. State Fair, So. Oreg. U., Portland, Monmouth Rogue Art Gallery, Medford, Oreg., banks, librs.; dollmaker. Asst. founder lupus support group, Ashland, Oreg., 1977, 78, 79. Elks scholar, 1950, John Dickey Art scholar So. Oreg. U., 1966; recipient Voice of Democracy 1st Place Hon. Mention Broadcasters and Radio Dealers of Am. KWIN, 1949. Mem. AAUW, So. Oreg. Alumni Assn., Libr. of Congress, Women in Arts. Avocations: music, history, writing, gardening, dolls, glass-blowing.

LANTZ, JOANNE BALDWIN, retired academic administrator; b. Defiance, Ohio, Jan. 26, 1932; d. Hiram J. and Ethel A. (Smith) Baldwin; m. Wayne E. Lantz. BS in Physics and Math., U. Indpls., 1953; MS in Counseling and Guidance, Ind. U., 1957; PhD in Counseling and Psychology, Mich. State U., 1969; LittD (hon.), U. Indpls., 1985; LHD (hon.), Purdue U., 1994; LLD (hon.), Manchester Coll., 1994. Tchr. physics and math. Arcola (Ind.) High Sch., 1953-57; guidance dir. New Haven (Ind.) Sr. High Sch., 1957-65; with Ind. U.-Purdue U., Fort Wayne, 1965—, interim chancellor, 1988-89, chancellor, 1989-94, chancellor emeritus, 1994—. Bd. dirs., hon. dir. Ft. Wayne Nat. Corp.; bd. dirs. Foellinger Found. Contbr. articles to profl. jours. Mem. Ft. Wayne Econ. Devel. Adv. Bd. and Task Force, 1988-91, Corp. Coun., 1988-94; bd. advisors Leadership Ft. Wayne, 1988-94; mem. adv. bd. Ind. Sml. Bus. Devel. Ctr., 1988-90; trustee Ancilla System, Inc., 1984-89, chmn. human resources com., 1985-89, exec. com., 1985-89; trustee St. Joseph's Med. Ctr., 1983-84, pers. adv. com. to bd. dirs., 1978-84, chmn., 1980-84; bd. dirs. United Way Allen County, sec., 1979-80; bd. dirs. Anthony Wayne Vocat. Rehab. Ctr., 1969-75. Mem.: AAUW (Am. women fellowship com. 1978—83, program com. 1981—83, chmn. 1981—83, internat. fellowship com. 1986—88, trust rsch. grantee 1980), APA, Southeastern Psychol. Assn. (referee conv. papers 1987—88), Ft. Wayne Ind.-Purdue Alumni Soc. (hon.), Ind. Sch. Women's Club (v.p. program chair 1979—81), Delta Kappa Gamma (leadership devel. com. 1978—82, dir. N.E. region 1982—84, exec. bd. 1982—84, adminstrv. bd. 1982—84, gen. chair conv. 1985—86, editl. bd. 1986—88, bd. trustees ednl. found. 1996—2002, nominating com. 2002—06), Sigma Xi, Pi Lambda Theta. Avocations: swimming, reading, knitting, boating. Personal E-mail: joalantz@aol.com.

LANYON, ELLEN (MRS. ROLAND GINZEL), artist, educator; b. Chgo., Dec. 21, 1926; d. Howard Wesley and Ellen (Aspinwall) L.; m. Roland Ginzel, Sept. 4, 1948; children: Andrew, Lisa. BFA, Art Inst. Chgo., 1948; MFA, U. Iowa, Iowa City, 1950; Fulbright fellow, Courtauld Inst., U. London, 1950-51. Tchr. jr. sch. Art Inst. Chgo., 1952-54; past tchr. day sch., tchr. Rockford Coll., summer 1953, Oxbow Summer Sch. Painting, Saugatuck, Mich., 1961-62, 67-70, 71-72, 78, 88, 94, U. Ill., Chgo., 1970, U. Wis. Extension, 1971-72, Pa. State U., 1974, U. Calif., 1974, Sacramento State U., 1974, Stanford U., 1974, Boston U., 1975, Kans. State U., 1976, U. Mo., 1976, U. Houston, 1977; assoc. prof. Cooper Union, N.Y.C., 1980-93; ret., 1993. Founder, sec.-treas. Chgo. Graphic Workshop, 1952-55; participant Yaddo, 1973, 75, 76, Ossobow Island Project, 1976; adj. vis. prof. So. Ill. U., 1978, No. Ill. U., 1978, SUNY, Purchase, 1978, Cooper Union, N.Y.C., 1978-79, Parsons Sch. Design, N.Y.C., 1979; disting. vis. prof. U. S.D., 1980, U. Calif. Davis, 1980, Sch. Visual Arts, N.Y.C., 1980-83; vis. artist U. N.Mex., 1981, So. Ill. U., 1984, Sch. Art Inst., Chgo., 1985, U. Tenn., Md. Inst., Northwestern Grad. Sch., 1988, U. Pa., U. Iowa, 1991, 92; instr. workshops Anderson Ranch Workshop, Snow Mass, Colo., 1994, 96, Aspen Design Conf., 1994; vis. prof. U. Iowa, 1991-92; bd. dirs. Oxbow Summer Sch. Painting, 1972-82, emeritus, 1982—, instr., 1960, 72-82, 88, 94,2005; vis. artist, instr. workshops Vt. Studio Sch., 1996, 97, 2001, 2005, Oxbow, 2005, Vt. Studio, 2005, U. Costa Rica, San Pedro and San Ramon, 1995; instr. Interlaken Sch. of Art, 1996; tchr. master class Nat. Acad. Design, 1999, Nat. Acad. Abbey Mural Workshops, 2001-2005. One woman shows, Superior St. Gallery, Chgo., 1960, Stewart Richart Gallery, San Antonio, 1962, 65, Fairweather Hardin Gallery, Chgo., 1962, Zabriskie Gallery, N.Y.C., 1962, 64, 69, 72, B.C. Holland Gallery, Chgo., 1965, 68, Ft. Wayne Art Mus., 1967, Richard Gray Gallery, Chgo., 1970, 73, 76, 79, 82, 85, Madison Art Center, 1972, Nat. Collection at Smithsonian Instn., 1972, Odyssia Gallery, Rome, 1975, Krannert Performing Arts Center, 1976, Oshkosh Pub. Mus., 1976, U. Mo., 1976, Harcus Krakow, Boston, 1977—, Fendrick Gallery, Washington, 1978, Ky. State U., 1979, Ill. Wesleyan U., 1979, U. Calif., Davis, 1980, Odyssia Gallery, N.Y., 1980, Landfall Press, 1980, Alverno Coll., Milw., 1981, Susan Caldwell, Inc., N.Y.C., 1983, N.A.M.E. Gallery, Chgo., 1983, Printworks, Ltd., Chgo., 1989, 93, 99, 2002, 03, Pretto Berland Hall, N.Y.C., 1989, Struve Gallery, Chgo., 1990, 93, Berland Hall Gallery, N.Y.C., 1992, Sioux City Art Mus., Iowa, 1992, U. Iowa Mus. Art, 1994, Andre Zarre Gallery, N.Y.C., 1994-97, TBA, Chgo., 1996, Centrocultural Costarricense Norteamericano, San Jose, Costa Rica, 1997, Jean Albano Gallery, 1997, 99, 2001, Jan Abrams Fine Arts, N.Y.C., 2005, Valerie Carberry Gallery, Chgo., 2005; retrospective exhibitions, Krannert Art Mus., McNay Art Mus., Chgo. Cultural Ctr., Stamford Mus., U. Tenn., Nat. Mus. for Women in the Arts, 1999; exhibited group shows, 1946—, including numerous traveling exhbns., Am. Fedn. Arts, 1946-48, 50, 53, 57, 65, 66, 69; Art Inst. Chgo., 1946-47, 51-53, 55, 57-58, 60-62, 64, 66-69, 71, 73, Corcoran Gallery Art, 1961, 76, Denver Art Mus., 1950, 52, Exhbn. Momentum, Chgo., 1948, 50, 52, 54, 56, Libr. Congress, 1950, 52, Met. Mus. Art, 1952, Mus. Modern Art, 1953, 62, Phila. Mus. Art, 1946, 47, 50, 54, San Francisco Mus. Art, 1946, 50, U. Ill., 1953, 54, 57, Drawing Soc., 1965-66, Mus. Contemporary Art, Chgo., 1969, Graham Gallery, N.Y.C., 1969-71, Ill. Arts Council, 1968-71, HMH Publs. Europe, 1971, Chgo. Imagists, 1972, Chgo. Sch. Art, 1972, Am. Women, 1972, Artists Books, 1973; Downtown Whitney, N.Y.C., 1978—, Queens Mus., 1978, Dayton Art Inst., 1978, Odyssia Gallery, N.Y.C., 1979, Chgo. Cultural Center, 1979, Aldrich Mus. Contemporary Art, 1980, Bklyn. Mus., 1980, Walker Art Ctr., 1981, also Lisbon, Venice biennales, Voorhees Mus. Rutgers U., Mus. Contemporary Art, Chgo., Milw. Art. Mus., Berkeley Art Mus., 1987, Cooper Union, 1989, Randall Gallery, St. Louis, 1991, Printworks Ltd., Chgo., 1989-96, 97-98, 99, 2003, 05, Berland Hall, N.Y.C., 1991, The Cultural Ctr., Chgo., 1992, Matnan Locks Gallery, Phila., 1992, Art Inst. Chgo., 1992, Nat. Mus. Women in Arts, Washington, 1994-97, Wadsworth Atheneum, Hartford, Conn., 1996, Mus. Contemporary Art, 1996, Block Gallery, Northwestern U., 1996, Rockford Art Mus., Ill. State Mus., 1997, Nat. Acad. Design, 1999, 2001, 03, 05, CUNY, Neuberger Mus. Art, 1999, Nat. Acad. Biannuals, N.Y., Am. Acad. Arts and Letters, N.Y., 2004 Racine Art Mus., Wis., 2001, 02, 03, 05, Pa. Acad., 2006, David Findlay Fine Arts, NYC, 2006; represented in permanent collections Art Inst. Chgo., Denver Art Mus., Libr. Congress, Inst. Internat. Edn., London, Finch Coll., N.Y., Krannert Mus., U. Ill., U. Mass., N.J. State Mus., Ill. State Mus., Bklyn. Mus., Mus. Contemporary Art, Chgo., Nat. Coll. Fine Arts, Walker Art Ctr., Mpls., Boston Pub. Libr., Des Moines Art Ctr., Albion Coll., Met. Mus., McNay Art Inst., Albion Coll., Kans. State U., U. Dallas, U. Houston, Cornell U., Racine Art Mus., Grand Rapids Mus. Art, Mich., U. Iowa Mus. Art, Nat. Mus. Women in Arts, Washington, Williams Coll. Mus., Mass., Pa. Acad. Fin. Arts; also numerous pvt. collections.; mural paintings: Working Men's Coop. Bank Boston, 1979, Boston Pub. Libr., 2000, State of Ill. Bldg., Chgo., 1985, State Capitol, Springfield, Ill., 1989, City of Miami Beach, Art in Public Places project, Police and Court Facility, 1993; also commns.: City Of Chicago, 1999, Riverwalk Gateway Project, 1999, St. Patrick's Ch., Chgo, 1999, Hiawatha-LRT, Mpls., 2004; published: Wonder Production Vol. I, 1971, Jataka Tales, 1975, Transformations, 1976, Transformations II (Endangered), 1983, Index, 2003; editorial bd.: Coll. Art Jour., 1982-92; illustrator:The Wandering Tattler, 1975, Perishible Press, 1976—, Red Ozier Press, 1980—. Recipient Armstrong prize Art Inst. Chgo., 1946, 55, 77, Town and Country purchase prize, 1947, Purchase prize Denver Art Mus., 1950, Purchase prize Libr. of Congress, 1950, Blair prize, 1958, Chan prize, 1961, Palmer prize, 1962, 64, Vielehr prize, 1967, Cassandra Found. award, 1970, Logan prize, 1981; grantee NEA, 1974, 87, Herewood Lester Cook Found., 1981, Florsheim Found., 1999, Purchase prize Am. Acad. Arts and Letters, 2004; named to Nat. Acad., 1997. Mem. Nat. Acad. (mem. coun. 2002-2005, chair exhbn. com. 2004-2005, elected treas. 2005), Coll. Art Assn. (dir., exec. com. 1977-80), The Century Assn. (elected), Delta Phi Delta Address: 138 Prince St New York NY 10012-3135 Office Phone: 212-966-9758. Personal E-mail: ellenlanyon@earthlink.net.

LANZINGER, JUDITH ANN, state supreme court justice; b. Toledo, Ohio, Apr. 2, 1946; m. Robert C. Lanzinger, Jr., 1967; 2 children. BA in Ed., U. Toledo, 1968; JD, U. Toledo Coll. of Law, 1977; Ms of Jud. Studies, Nat. Jud. Coll. & U. Nev., 1992. Bar: Ohio, U.S. Supreme Ct., U.S. Dist. Ct. for Northern Dist. of Ohio, U.S. Dist. Ct. for Eastern Dist. of Mich., Sixth Circuit Ct. of Appeals. Atty. environmental law Toledo Edison Co., 1978—81; atty. employment law and litigation Shumaker, Loop and Kendrick, 1981—85; judge Toledo Municipal Ct., 1985—88, Lucas County Common Pleas Ct., 1989—2003, Ohio Sixth Dist. Ct. of Appeals, 2003—04; justice Ohio Supreme Ct., 2005—. Adjunct prof. U. Toledo Coll. of Law, 1988—; prof. Nat. Jud. Coll., 1990—; mem. Ohio Criminal Sentencing Commn., 1991—97; co-chair Public Ed. and Awareness Task Force Ohio Cts. Futures Commn., 1996—2000; chair Ohio Jud. Coll., 2000—01; former mem. Ohio Supreme Ct. Bd. of Grievances and Discipline; chair Commn. Rules of Superintendence, Ohio Cts., 2006—. Recipient Superior Jud. Service award, Ohio Supreme Ct., 1985, Arabella Babb Mansfield award, Toledo Women's Bar Assn., 1995, Service to Judicial Ed. award, Ohio Jud. Coll., 2002, Golden Gavel award, Ohio Common Pleas Judges' Assn., 2002. Fellow: Ohio Bar Found.; mem.: Thurgood Marshall Assn., Am. Judicature Soc., Nat. Assn. of Women Judges, Am. Judges Assn., Ohio Bar Assn., Morrison R. Waite Am. Inn of Ct. (pres. 2000—02). Office: Ohio Supreme Ct 65 S Front St Columbus OH 43215-3431 Office Phone: 614-387-9090.

LAPADOT, GAYLE K., nursing administrator; b. Pontiac, Mich., Oct. 18, 1944; d. Addison Spencer and Phyllis Mary (Bays) Prout; m. James Ross Marshall (dec.); m. Robert Lapadot, Oct. 3, 1998; children: Kelly Lynn Davis-Collins, Kimberly Renee Cohen. Attended Pre-Nursing Program, St. Clair Coll., Port Huron, Mich., 1962—63; attended, Port Huron Practical Nursing Sch., 1963—64. LPN. Nurse Mercy Hosp., Port Huron, 1964—66; surg. nurse Bon Secour Hosp., Grosse Pointe, Mich., 1979—85; office nurse Elizabeth Brenner, Grosse Pointe, 1985—87, Vitro Retinal Cons., Detroit, 1987—95; nurse, nursing supr., clin. trial coord. Mich. Neurology Assocs., Clair Shores, 1995—. Avocations: gardening, antiques, interior design. Home: 61 Muir Rd Grosse Pointe MI 48236 Office: Mich Neurology Assocs 19699 E Old 8 Mile Rd Saint Clair Shores MI 48080 E-mail: gblapadot@comcast.net.

LAPADOT, SONEE SPINNER, retired automobile manufacturing company official; b. Sidney, Ohio, Apr. 19, 1936; d. Kenneth Lee and Helyn Kathryn (Hobby) Spinner; divorced; 1 child, Douglas Cameron Proud; m. Robert Stephen Lapadot, May 4, 1974 (div. Mar. 1994). Student, U. Cin., 1954—56, U. Akron, 1966; BS in Mgmt. Human Resources, Spring Arbor Coll., 1991; MBA, U. Phoenix, 1995. Mgr. engrng. change implementation Terex divsn. GM, Hudson, Ohio, 1975-77, mgr. prodn. scheduling, 1977-78, gen. adminstr. product purchasing, 1978-79; sr. staff asst. non-ferrous metals GM, Detroit, 1979-80, mgr. tires and wheels, 1980-83, mgr. staff purchasing, 1983-85, mgr. corp. constrn. contracting, 1985-86; mfg. techs. adminstr. Chrysler Motors, Detroit, 1986-87, mgr. mfg. prodn. control adminstrn. and svcs., 1988, mgr. advanced planning and prodn. systems, 1988-89, mgr. advanced planning and control power train, 1989-90, mgr. Mound Rd. engine prodn. control, 1990-95, mgr. corp. project systems, 1995-96, platform exec. material handling engring., 1996-99, platform exec. spl. projects, 2000-01; ret., 2001. Bd. dir. SeaChase, chmn. bldgs. & maintenance, 2003—, pres., 2004—06. Active fundraising Boy Scouts Am., Grosse Pointe, Mich., 1980-82, Detroit, 1985-96, United Fund, Detroit, 1980-99, Jr. Achievement, Detroit, 1984, 90-96, Leukemia Soc., 2004-2004, Am. Inst. Cancer Rsch., 2002-2004. Mem. NAFE, Soc. Automotive Engrs., Am. Soc. Profl. and Exec. Women, Am. Prodn. and Inventory Control Soc., Automotive Industry Action Group (returnable containers and packaging team), Mensa, Seachase Bd. (pres. 2004-06), Women's Econ. Club of Detroit. Home: 1941 Squirrel Rd Bloomfield Hills MI 48304-1162

LAPALOMBARA, CONSTANCE, artist; m. Joseph LaPalombara, June 13, 1971. BA, Manhattanville Coll., Purchase, N.Y., 1953—57; MFA, Tyler Sch. of Art, Temple U., Elkins Pk., Pa., 1980—82. Instr., fine arts So. Conn. State U., New Haven, 1984—85. One-woman shows include First St. Gallery, N.Y.C., 1990, Munson Gallery, New Haven, Conn., 1992, Il Gabbiano Gallery, Rome, Italy, 1993, Randall Tuttle Fine Arts, Woodbury, Conn., 1999, Ezra Stiles Coll., Yale U., New Haven, 2000, Wash. Art Assn., Wash. Depot, Conn., 2003, Bachelier Cardonsky Gallery, Kent, Conn., 2004, Fenn Gallery, Woodbury, 2005, Kehler Liddell Gallery, New Haven, 2005, Gallery 195, New Haven, Conn., 2006. Recipient Painting award, Ingram Merrill Found.; grantee Univ. fellowship, Tyler Sch. of Art, Temple U., 1981—82, fellowship, Conn. Commn. for Arts, 2000. Mem.: Conn. Watercolor Soc., Conn. Acad. Fine Arts, Coll. Art Assn.

LAPARLE, PAULETTE GAGNON, music educator; b. Woonsocket, R.I., Nov. 14, 1957; d. Lawrence William and Bertha Rose Gagnon; m. Eugene Frederick LaParle, Jr., Apr. 30, 1983; 1 child, Leanne Marie. BS in Music Edn., R.I. Coll., Providence, 1979, Master's in Art and Tchg., 1985. Tchr. Barrington Elem., RI, 1979—81, Barrington H.S., RI, 1981—. Co-chair dept. music K-12 Barr Schs., RI, 2001—; coop. tchr. R.I. Coll. and U. R.I., 1997, 99, 2001, 03, 06. Named Barrington Tchr. of Yr., 2005; recipient Anna Maria Coll. Excellence in Counseling/Tchg. award, 2002, Olmsted Prize for Superior Tchg., Williams Coll., 2005. Mem.: Music Educators Nat. Conf., Am. Choral Dirs. Assn. (chair repertoire and stds. 2004—05). Avocations: gardening, restoring 18th-century houses, creating jewelry.

LAPHAM, MARY ELLEN, elementary school educator; b. Manchester, Iowa, Jan. 19, 1933; d. Alfred George and Wilma Helen (Anderson) Billhorn; m. Lyle Lincoln Lapham, July 3, 1954; children: Deborah Lapham Wray, Loren L., Wesley A., Steven A., Coleen L. Cert., Iowa State Tchr.'s Coll., 1952; BS, Winona U., 1971; MEd, U. Minn., 1987. Cert. elem. tchr., kindergarten tchr., Minn. Kindergarten tchr. Dundee (Iowa) Pub. Schs., 1952-53, Waukon (Iowa) Pub. Schs., 1953-55, Dorchester (Iowa) Pub. Schs., 1965-67; 1st grade tchr. Caledonia (Minn.) Pub. Schs., 1967—. Tchr. Vols. in Overseas Coop. Assistance U.S. AID, Yamassoukro, Cote d'Ivoire, 1988; oral English tchr. Wenzhou Tchrs. Coll., Zhenjiang Province, China, 1998-99, 2000-2001. Asst. chair governance bd. Hiawatha Valley Uniserve Dist., Rochester, Minn., 1987. Mem. NEA, Minn. Edn. Assn., Caledonia Edn. Assn. (pres. 1972-73), Order Ea. Star (worthy matron 1979). Methodist. Avocations: collecting antiques, travel, gardening, sewing. Home: 204 W Main St Caledonia MN 55921-1162 Office: Caledonia Pub Schs 311 W Main St Caledonia MN 55921-1165

LAPIERRE, EILEEN MARIE, technical services manager; b. Chgo., June 1, 1966; d. Vernon Francis and Lucille Marie (Hickey) L. AAS in Comml. Art with honors, Harold Washington Coll., 1994; AA in Restaurant Mgmt., Triton Coll., 1987. Cert. photofinishing engr. Soc. Photofinishing Engrs., 2000, A+ cert. computer technician 2003. Sr. photo lab. technician Wolf Camera, Oak Park, Ill., master photo lab. technician Niles, Ill., 2000—. Press photographer Lambda Publs., Chgo., 1996-97. Photographer Garland Ct. Rev., 1993, 94-95. Recipient semi-finalist award N.Am. Open Amateur Photo, 1998, finalist 14th ann. Best of Coll. Photography, 1994, Nat. Deans List 16th ann., Vol. 2, 1992-93, Nat. Deans List 17th ann., Vol. 2, 1993-94, Outstanding Achievement in Photofinishing award Wolfpro Printoff, 1997, 2000. Mem. Internat. Freelance Photographers Assn. (life), Ilfo Pro Photographers Assn., Fuji Film Profl. Pronet, Kodak Viewfinder Forum, Soc. Photofinishing Engrs., Computing Tech. Industry Assn. Personal E-mail: thirdeyecandy@comcast.net.

LAPIERRE, KATHERINE ANN, psychiatrist, educator; b. Haverhill, Mass., Mar. 8, 1956; AB, Coll. of the Holy Cross, Worcester, Mass., 1978; MD, Tufts U., Boston, 1982. Asst. prof. Tufts U. Sch. Medicine, Boston, 1988—94, U. Mass. Med. Sch., Worcester, 1994—2002; asst. psychiatrist Harvard U., Cambridge, 2001—. Mem.: APA, Am. Soc. Clin. Psychpharmacology. Office: 1340 Ctr St Ste 204 Newton Center MA 02459

LAPOINTE, LUCIE, research institute executive; b. Valleyfield, Que., Can., Dec. 23, 1954; d. Paul and Jeannette (Gagne) LaPointe; 1 child, Lauren LaPointe-Shaw. BSc in Biol. Scis., McGill U., Montreal, Can., 1977; MBA, U. Ottawa, Can., 1982. Tech. officer divsn. biol. scis. NRC, Ottawa, 1977—80, officer program svcs. secretariat, 1982—84, exec. mgr. pub. rels. and info. svcs., 1984—87, dir. mgmt. svcs. br., 1987—89, sec. gen., 1989—2001; v.p. adminstrn., sec.-treas. Pulp and Paper Rsch. Inst. Can., Pointe-Claire, Que., 2001—; exec. mem. Internat. Coun. for Sci. Contbr. articles to profl. jours. Avocations: reading, skiing. Office: PAPRICAN 570 boul St-Jean Pointe-Claire PQ Canada H9R 3J9 Office Phone: 514-630-4103. Business E-Mail: llapointe@paprican.ca.

LAPOINTE, SABRINA ANN, music educator; b. Glenns Falls, N.Y., Mar. 3, 1980; d. Robert Francis and Laween Ann Lamb; m. Anthony David LaPointe, June 19, 2004. MusB in Music Edn., SUNY, Fredonia, 2002; MS in Curriculum and Instrn., SUNY, Plattsburgh, 2005. K-12 music cert. K-12 vocal music tchr. Minerva Ctrl. Sch., Olmsted, NY, 2004—. Honors vocal recital: SUNY Fredonia, 2002. Recipient Rena Mazzeo Vocal Music award, Sweet Adelines Internat., Troy, N.Y., 1998. Mem.: Nat. Assn. Music Educators, N.Y. State Sch. Music Assn. Democrat. Roman Catholic. Avocations: scrapbooks, professional chorus, community theater. Office: Minerva Ctrl Sch PO Box 39 Olmstedville NY 12857

LAPOLT, MARGARET, librarian; b. Austin, Pa., June 9, 1931; d. Thomas Wilbur and Frances Leona (Smith) Bennett; m. Sanford Howard LaPolt, Apr. 14, 1957 (dec. Nov. 1996); children: Cheryl Lynn LaPolt Remson, Mark Alan LaPolt. BSEd, Mansfield (Pa.) U., 1953; MSEd, Western Conn. State U., Danbury, 1963; MSLS, So. Conn. State U., New Haven, 1973. Tchr. 5th grade Bd. Edn., Clearfield, Pa., 1953-54; tchr. 6th grade Emporium (Pa.) Bd. Edn., 1954-58; tchr. 5th grade Darien (Conn.) Bd. Edn., 1958-64; tchr. 3d grade Stratford (Conn.) Bd. Edn., 1965-69, libr., 1969-70, Norwalk (Conn.) Bd. Edn., 1973-92, part-time libr., 1993—2005, ret., 2002. Singer, Norwalk Cmty. Chorus, 1961-73; singer Cmty. Bapt. Ch., Norwalk, 1958—, bd. deacons, 1993-99, trustee, 1981-87. Computer grantee, Norwalk Bd. Edn., 1985. Mem. ALA, Kappa Delta Phi, Kappa Pi. Avocations: knitting, embroidery, travel, walking.

LAPORTA, SARA, retail executive; Grad, U. Sussex; PhD, Kings Coll. U. London; grad, Mass. Inst. Tech. V.p. Boston Cons. Group, 1986—2002; sr. v.p. chief strategy officer Sears, Roebuck and Co., 2002—.

LAPORTE, ADRIENNE AROXIE, nursing administrator; b. Oceanside, NY, Sept. 29, 1938; d. Leonide and Grace (Ajamian) LaP. Diploma in nursing, St. John's Episc. Hosp., 1960; BA in Behavioral Scis., Lesley Coll., 1986; MA in Counseling, Liberty U., 1994. RN, NY, Fla., Mass., La., Ala.; cert. psychiat., mental health nurse Am. Nurses Credentialing Bd.; cert. legal nurse cons.; lic. alcohol and drug counselor I. Supr. Creedmoor State Hosp., Queens Village, NY, 1960-66, Taunton (Mass.) State Hosp., 1985-87, Mental Health Resources, Jacksonville, Fla., 1990-92, Staff Builders Home Health Agy., New Bedford, Mass., 1996-99; supr. psychiat. unit Univ. Hosp. of Jacksonville, 1977-79, Parkwood Hosp., New Bedford, 1980-84; dir. nursing Care Unit of Jacksonville Beach, Fla., 1987-90, Bradford Adult & Adolescent, Pelham, Ala., 1992-93, 94-95; program dir. Bowling Green Hosp., Mandeville, La., 1993; nurse mgr., therapist Ctr. for Health and Human Svcs., Inc., New Bedford, 1999—; pvt. practice as substance abuse therapist New Bedford, Mass., 2003—. Nurse cons. Seven Hills Found., 1996—. Lt. col. Nurse Corps U.S. Army, 1966-87, Vietnam. Decorated Bronze Star, Legion of Merit, Armed Forces Res. medal, Army Commendation medal, Combat Readiness medal, Meritorious Svc. medal, Presdl. and Unit citation, Republic of Vietnam Campaign medal, Vietnam Svc. medal. Mem. ACA, VFW, Internat. Nurses Soc. on Addictions, Fla. Nurses Assn., Am. Legion, Vietnam Vets. Am., Internat. Soc. Psychiat.-Mental Health Nurses, Internat. Nurses Soc. on Addictions.

LAPORTE, KATHLEEN DARKEN, venture capitalist; b. N.Y.C., Sept. 23, 1961; d. John Edward and Sheila Anne (Keane) Darken; m. Brian Edward LaPorte, July 30, 1988. BS in Biology summa cum laude, Yale U., 1983; MBA, Stanford U., 1987. Fin. analyst First Boston Corp., N.Y.C., 1983-84, fin. analyst San Francisco, 1984-85; assoc. Asset Mgmt. Co., Palo Alto, Calif., 1987-90, prin., 1990-92; gen. ptnr. The Sprout Group, Menlo Park, Calif., 1994—. Bd. dirs. Onyx Pharms., Richmond, Calif., CIBUS Pharms., Sequana Therapeutics, Intrabiotics Pharms., Lynx Therapeutics. Founder Phil Larson Fund, Stanford U., 1988; mem. Cmty. Impact Vol. Group, Palo Alto, 1988—. Recipient Eleanor Dawson award Yale U., 1982, MacLeish Meml. trophy Yale U., 1983. Mem. Nat. Venture Capital Assn., Western Assn. Venture Capitalists (past pres.), Bay Area Bioscience Women's Group (founding), Phi Beta Kappa. Avocations: swimming, golf. Office: The Sprout Group 3000 Sand Hill Rd Menlo Park CA 94025-7113

LAPP, ALICE WEBER, secondary school educator, editor; b. Lititz, Pa., July 29, 1931; d. Benjamin Franklin and Sarah (Hostetter) Weber; m. John Allen Lapp, Aug. 20, 1955; children: John Franklin, Jennifer W., Jessica W. BA, Ea. Mennonite U., 1955; MA, James Madison U., 1970. Tchr. English Brownell Jr. High Sch., Cleve., 1955-56; tchr. English Elkton (Va.) High Sch., 1956-58, Eisenhower Sr. High Sch., Norristown, Pa., 1958-60; art tchr. Eastern Mennonite High Sch., Harrisonburg, Va., 1962-64; lectr. English Eastern Mennonite Coll., Harrisonburg, 1964-69; substitute tchr. Ephrata (Pa.) Pub. Schs., 1970-72; lectr. English Bethlehem U., West Bank, Israel, 1978-79, Goshen (Ind.) Coll., 1983; substitute tchr. Lancaster (Pa.) Mennonite High Sch., 1987—; copy editor Pa. Mennonite Heritage, 1988—. Lectr. English, Bishop's Coll., Calcutta, India, 1996-97. Contbr. book revs. and articles to church mags. Sec. adv. bd. Salvation Army, Goshen, 1975-85; mem. bd. ARC, Elkhart County, Elkhart, Ind., 1975-85, vol., Goshen, Ephrata, 1975—. Mem. AAUW (v.p. Va. br. 1965-68, pres. Ind. br. 1981-84). Mennonite. Avocations: restoring antiques, reading, gourmet cooking. Home and Office: 13 Knollwood Dr Akron PA 17501-1113

LAPP, CAROL ANNE, oral biology educator; b. Phila. d. Joseph Henry and Ellen Veronica Schellman; m. David Frank Lapp, June 26, 1965; children: Jennifer Lynn, David Joseph. BS, Bucknell U., 1963; MS, U. RI, 1968; PhD, Med. Coll. Ga., 1985. Rsch. scientist dept. pathology M.D. Anderson Hosp. and Tumor Inst., Houston, 1965-70; tchg. asst. dept. endocrinology Med. Coll. Ga., Augusta, 1980-85, asst. rsch. scientist dept. medicine, 1985-88, postdoctoral fellow dept. pharmacology and toxicology, 1988-90, asst. prof. dept. oral biology Sch. Dentistry, 1990-96, assoc. prof. oral biology Sch. Dentistry, 1996—. Contbr. numerous articles to sci. jours. Violinist Augusta Symphony Orch., 1972-2002; tchr. Suzuki method violin instrn., Augusta, 1974-1985; elder Presbyn. Ch. U.S.A., Augusta, 1993-96, 2005—. Named one of Outstanding Young Women of Am., 1967, 73. Mem. Am. Physiol. Soc., Endocrine Soc., Internat. Cytokine Soc., Med. Coll. Ga. Grad. Studies Alumni Assn. (pres.-elect 1994-95, pres. 1995-1996), Phi Beta Kappa, Sigma Xi, Phi Kappa Phi. Avocations: violin, sailing, genealogy. Office: Med Coll Ga Dept Oral Biol & Maxillofacial Pathology AD 1434 Augusta GA 30912

LAPP, KATHRYN S., social studies educator; b. Port Clinton, Ohio, July 12, 1941; d. Norton Carl and Emma Katherine (Fisher) Rosentreter; m. Conrad Lee Lapp, Jan. 1, 1969; 1 child, Aaron Carl. BS, U. Colo., 1963; Peace Corps cert. (hon.), Columbia U., 1963; MA, NYU, 1968. Peace Corps vol. Kaduna (Nigeria) Govt. Coll., 1964-66; secondary sch. tchr. N.Y.C. Pub. Schs., 1966-69, Sch. Dist. II, Colorado Springs, Colo., 1969-89, instrnl. specialist, 1989-98, grant coord., 1997-2001; instr. tchg. methods U. Colo., Colorado Springs, 1999—2003, Colo. Coll., 2003—. Tchr. cons. Nat. Geog. Soc., Washington and Colo., 1989-99; cons., instr. for Japan studies Colo. Coll. Summer Program, Colorado Springs, 1991-92; mem. writing task force Colo. geog. stds. Colo. Dept. Edn., Denver, 1994-95. Contbr. author: Geographic

Inquiry into Global Issues, 1992; contbr. articles to profl. jours. Coord. Washington and Colo. Close Up, Colorado Springs, 1990-98; coord. Colo. congl. dist. 5, U.S. Congress and Ctr. for Civic Edn., Calabasas, Calif., 1990-2001; mem. steering com. Kids Voting, Colorado Springs, 1995-2001; active Womens Edn. Soc., Colo. Coll., 1999—; mem. Nat. Geog. Soc. adv. com. Colo. Geography Edn. Fund, 2000-05; team leader Civic Edn. Profl. Devel. Colo. Dept. Edn., 2006. Mem.: Colo. and Colorado Springs Assn. Sch. Execs. (Educator of Yr. 1998), Colo. Coun. for the Social Studies (pres. 1998—99), Nat. Coun. for the Social Studies (Outstanding Svc. award 2004), Nat. Coun. for Geog. Edn., Nat. Coun. for Hist. Edn., Colo. Geog. Alliance (Cram Maps Outstanding Contrn. to Geog. Edn. award 1998), Alpha Delta Kappa (pres. 1984—85). E-mail: lappkc@earthlink.net.

LAPUZ-DE LA PENA, ERLINDA LARON, pathology professor; b. Nov. 26, 1933; d. Eriberto Mallari and Teodora Quiero (Laron) Lapuz; m. Cordell De La Pena, Apr. 1, 1957; children: Leslie, Nina, Cordell. MD, U. Santo Tomas, 1957. Diplomate Am. Bd. Pathology. Intern St. John's Hosp., Lowell, Mass., 1959—60; attending physician Tewksbury (Mass.) Hosp., 1960—63; resident in pathology Mercy Hosp., Pitts., 1967—71; instr. pathology U. Pitts. Med. Sch., Pitts., 1967—71; chief lab. svc. VA Hosp., Clarksburg, W.Va., 1971—, chief of staff, 1983—99; courtesy staff United Hosp. Ctr.; prof. pathology W.Va. U. Sch. Medicine, 1994—; asst. prof. Coll. Nursing Salem (W.Va.) Coll., 1978; asst. prof. Coll. Nursing and Physician Assts. Alderson Broadus Coll., Phillipi, W.Va. Contbr. articles to med. jours. Fellow: Am. Soc. Clin. Pathology, Am. Coll. Pathologists; mem.: W.Va. Assn. Pathologists (bd. dirs. 1983—, pres. 1987—89, 1997—98), W.Va. Med. Assn., AMA, Clarksburg Country Club. Roman Catholic. Home: 209 Candlelight Dr Clarksburg WV 26301-9725

LAQUALE, KATHLEEN MARIE, physical education educator; b. Providence; d. John A. and Patricia Cerra; m. William E. Laquale, May 15, 1982. BS, U.R.I., Kingston, 1976; PhD, U. R.I., 1994; MS, Ind. State U., Terre Haute, 1977. Cert. athletic trainer, lic. dietary nutritionist. Asst. athletic trainer Ind. State U., Terre Haute, 1976—77; head athletic trainer Providence Coll., 1977—84; head athletic trainer, tchr. R.I. Coll., Providence, 1984—97; assoc. prof.l Bridgewater State U., Mass., 1997—. Chair adv. bd. R.I. Interscholastic Sports Medicine, Providence, 1996—2005. Contbr. chapters to books; column. editor, author Athletic Therapy Today, 2006. Sec. R.I. Interscholastic Injury Fund, Providence, 1977—; vol. med. staff 1996 Olympics, Atlanta, 1996, Preolympic Congress, Australia, 2000, World Cup Soccer, Boston, 2000, Nat. Figure Skating Championship, Boston, 2004. Named to Hall of Fame, R.I. Athletic Trainers Assn., 2006, St. Mary's Acad.-Bayview, 2005. Mem.: R.I. Nutrition Coun., Ea. Athletic Trainers Assn. (sec.-treas. 1996—98), Nat. Athletic Trainers Assn. (dist. dir. 1998—2004, named to Hall of Fame 2005). Avocations: photography, writing, cycling. Office: Bridgewater State College MAHPLS Dept Tinsley Bldg Bridgewater MA 02325

LARAYA-CUASAY, LOURDES REDUBLO, pediatrician, pulmonologist, educator; b. Baguio, Philippines, Dec. 8, 1941; came to U.S., 1966; d. Jose Marquez and Lolita (Redublo) Laraya; m. Ramon Serrano Cuasay, Aug. 7, 1965; children: Raymond Peter, Catherine Anne, Margaret Rose, Joseph Paul. AA, U. Santo Tomas, Manila, Philippines, 1958, MD cum laude, 1963. Diplomate Am. Bd. Pediatrics. Resident in pediatrics U. Santo Tomas Hosp., 1963-65, Children's Hosp. Louisville, 1966-67, Charity Hosp. New Orleans-Tulane U., 1967-68; fellow child growth and devel. Children's Hosp. Phila., 1968-69; fellow pediatric pulmonary and cystic fibrosis programs St. Christopher's Hosp. for Children, Phila., 1969-71, rsch. assoc., 1971-72; clin. instr. Tulane U., New Orleans, 1967-68; asst. prof. pediatrics Temple Health Scis. Ctr., Phila., 1972-77; assoc. prof. pediatrics Thomas Jefferson Med. Sch., Phila., 1977-79, U. Medicine & Dentistry N. J., Robert Wood Johnson Med. Sch., New Brunswick, 1980-85, prof. clin. pediatrics, 1985-98, prof. pediat., 1998—2005; med. dir. pediat. asthma ctr. K. Hovnanian Children's Hosp., Jersey Shore U. Med. Ctr., Neptune, NJ, 2004—. Dir. pediatric pulmonary medicine and cystic fibrosis ctr. U. Medicine and Dentistry, Robert Wood Johnson Med. Sch., New Brunswick, 1981-2004 Co-editor: Interstitial Lung Diseases in Children, 1988. Recipient Pediatric Rsch. award Mead Johnson Pharm. Co., Manila, 1965. Fellow Am. Coll. Chest Physicians (steering com., chmn. cardiopulmonary diseases in children 1976—), Airways Network, Am. Acad. Pediatrics (tobacco free generation rep. 1986-92); mem. Am. Ambulatory Pediatric Soc., Am. Thoracic Soc., Am. Sleep Disorder Assn., N.J. Thoracic Soc. (chmn. pediatric pulmonary com. 1986-91, governing coun. mem. 1981-94), European Respiratory Soc. Avocation: piano. Home: 100 Mercer Ave Spring Lake NJ 07762-1208 Office: Med Arts Bldg Ste 204 1944 State Hwy East 33 Neptune NJ 07754 Office Phone: 732-776-4860. Business E-Mail: llarayacuasay@meridianhealth.com.

LARCH, SARA MARGARET, healthcare executive; b. Des Moines, Iowa, Feb. 14, 1956; d. William Arthur and Beverly Frances (Klanjac) L. BA in Pub. Adminstrn., Miami U., Oxford, Ohio, 1978; MSHA, VCU, Richmond, 1992. Personnel clk. City Nat. Bank, Detroit, 1978-79; econ. anlyst asst. Cargill, Inc., Mpls., 1979-81; ob-gyn. adminstr. Ind. U. Med. Ctr., Indpls., 1981-88; adminstr. Georgetown U. Med. Ctr., Washington, 1988-94, dir. quality and capitation sys., 1995; COO Univ. Physicians, Inc. Univ. Md., Balt., 1995—. Author: The Physician Billing Process: Avoiding Potholes in the Road to Getting Paid, 2004. Mem. Assn. Mgrs. Gynecology and Obstetricians (pres. 1986-87), Med. Group Mgmt. Assn. (bd. dirs. 1995-96, 98—, chmn. 2001-02), Acad. Practice Assembly (pres. 1994-95), Am. Coll. Med. Prac. Exec. (fell., 1995), Women Bus. Leaders of the U.S. Health Care Industry Found. Avocations: piano, reading, travel, public speaking. Office: Univ Physicians Inc 419 W Redwood St Ste 220 Baltimore MD 21201-7004 Office Phone: 410-328-1722. E-mail: slarch@upi.umaryland.edu.

LARD, PAMULA D., special education educator; b. Salem, Mass., Dec. 30, 1961; d. Claude F. and Joyce A. Lard. BS in Edn., Midwest State U., Wichita Falls, Tex.; MA in Tchg., Spl. Edn., LLD, Angelo State U., San Angelo, Tex., 1985—87. Cert. athletic trainer Nat. Athletic Trainers Assn., 1989. Adaptive behavior tchr. Kingwood H.S., Kingwood, Tex., 2001—; personal trainer/fitness dir. Wellbridge, Kingwood, Tex., 1988—2005. Personal trainer Quantum Lifestyles, Kingwood, Tex., 2005—. With U.S. Army, 1993—97. Decorated Army Commendation medal; scholar Athletic Tng. scholar, Midwestern state U., 1982—84. Mem.: Nat. Athletic Trainers Assn. (licentiate). Church Of Christ. Avocations: travel, camping, reading. Office: Kingwood High School 2701 Kingwood Dr Kingwood TX 77345 Office Phone: 281-641-7082. Office Fax: 281-641-7259. Business E-Mail: pam.lard@humble.k12.tx.us.

LARDENT, ESTHER FERSTER, lawyer, consultant; b. Linz, Austria, Apr. 23, 1947; arrived in US, 1951; d. William and Rose (Seidweber) Ferster; m. Dennis Robert Lardent, July 27, 1969 (div. Dec. 1981). BA, Brown U., 1968; JD, U. Chgo., 1971. Bar: Ill. 1972, Mass. 1975, admitted to practice: US Dist. Ct. (Ill.) 1972, US Dist. Ct. (Mass.) 1975. Civil rights specialist Office of Civil Rights U.S. HEW, Chgo., 1971-72; staff dir. individual rights ABA, Chgo., 1972-74; staff atty., supr. Cambridge (Mass.) Problem Ctr., 1975-76; exec. dir. Vol. Lawyers Project Boston Bar Assn., 1977-85; legal and policy cons. Santa Fe and Washington, 1985—; ind. legal and policy cons. Ford Found., Washington, 1990—96; pres. and CEO Pro Bono Inst., 1996—. Vis. prof. U. N.Mex. Sch. Law, Albuquerque, 1985; cons. Nat. Vets. Legal Svcs. Program, Washington, 1991—; vis. scholar ethics program Boston U. Sch. Law, 1991—92; reporter ABA/Tulane Law Sch., New Orleans, 1988—90; adj. prof. law Georgetown U., Washington. Contbr. Vis. com. U. Chgo. Law Sch., 1992—. Recipient Founder Award, Phila. Bar Assn., 1991, Outstanding Pub. Interest Adv. Award, Nat. Assn. Pub. Interest Law, 1992, Exemplar Award, Nat. Legal Aid and Defender Assn., William Reece Smith Jr. Award, Nat. Assn. Pro Bono Coordinators. Mem.: DC Bar (spl. adv. pub. svc. activities rev. com. 1990—), Nat. Legal Aid and Defenders Assn. (bd. dirs. 1990—), ABA (Ho. of Dels. 1991—, cons. 1974—76, legal cons. postconviction death penalty 1987—96, legal cons. law firm pro bono project 1989—96, bd. gov. 1996—99). Office: Pro Bono Institute at Georgetown Univ Law Ctr 600 New Jersey Ave NW Washington DC 20001

LARDY, SISTER SUSAN MARIE, academic administrator; b. Sentinel Butte, N.D., Nov. 9, 1937; d. Peter Aloysius and Elizabeth Julia (Dietz) L. BS in Edn., U. Mary, Bismarck, N.D., 1965; MEd, U. N.D., 1972. Entered Order of St. Benedict, Bismarck, 1957. Elem. tchr. Cathedral Grade Sch., Bismarck, 1958-67, Christ the King Sch., Mandan, N.D., 1967-68, 70-72, St. Joseph's Sch., Mandan, 1968-70; asst. prof. edn. U. Mary, Bismarck, 1972-80; adminstr., asst. prioress Annunciation Priory, Bismarck, 1980-84, prioress, major superior, 1984-96; dir. U. Mary-Fargo (N.D.) Ctr., 1997—. Dir. Fargo Ctr. U. Mary, 1997—. Mem. Delta Kappa Gamma. Home: 1101 32nd Ave S Fargo ND 58103-6036 Office: U Mary Fargo Ctr 3001 25th St S Fargo ND 58103-5055

LARE, JANE CAMERON, school psychologist; b. Harvey, Ill. d. Howard C. and Daisy Catherine (Cameron) Lare. BA, Occidental Coll., 1957; MEd in Guidance, U. Ill., Champaign-Urbana, 1958; MEd in Sch. Psychology, Loyola U., Chgo., 1984. Counselor Oak Park (Ill.) Elem. Schs. Dist. 97, 1958-63, tchr., 1963-83, 84-86, tchr., sch. psychologist, 1986—. Mem. NEA, Nat. Assn. Sch. Psychologists, Ill. Edn. Assn., Ill. Sch. Psychologists, Oak Park Tchrs. Assn., Alpha Sigma Nu. Democrat. Presbyterian. Avocations: travel, langs. Office: Oak Park Elem Schs Dist 97 970 Madison St Oak Park IL 60302-4430

LARGENT, MARGIE, retired architect; b. Adrian, Mo., Feb. 28, 1923; d. Arlie Everett Largent and Ruby Lacey Grosshart; m. Creighton A. Anderson, May 10, 1954; children: Michael Creig, Jon William Everett. Student, Capital Bus. Coll., 1942, Art Ctr. Sch. of Design, L.A., 1944, 45, 46, Willamette U., 1946-47; BArch, U. Oreg., 1950. Registered arch., Wash., Oreg., Alaska. Sr. structural draftsman Stone & Webster Engrs., L.A. and Boston, 1950-52; prodn. coord. Jon Konigshofer, Carmel, Calif., 1953-54, Daniel-Mann-Johnson, Archs., L.A., 1954-55, Gordon Cochran, Arch., Portland, Oreg., 1956-57, John Groom, Arch., Salem, Oreg., 1958-60; designer Largent & Anderson, Lake Oswego, Oreg., 1961-63; arch. Margie Largent, Lake Oswego, 1964—. Prin. works include Shon Tay Profl. Ctr., Lake Oswego, 1965-78, Jackson Residence, Warm Springs Reservation, Oreg., 1974, Crosby-Earth Shelter, San Juan Island, Wash., 1975, Anderson Tri-Plex, Cordova, Alaska, 1983. Active Land Use Com., Lake Oswego, 1970—, Park Adv. Bd., Clacksmas County, Oreg., 1975-79, Bldg. Bd. Appeals, Lake Oswego, 1978-98; pres. Associated C. of C., Clackamas County, 1970. Mem.: Constrn. Specifications Inst. (Portland chpt. pres. 1977, 1986, editor 1979, 1984, archivist 1980, Capital chpt. archivist 1995—2003).

LARIMORE-ALBRECHT, DENI DENISE, social worker; b. Auburn, Calif., Apr. 20, 1954; d. Woodrow Franklyn and Shirley Arvada (Hougе) Larimore; m. Milton Joseph Albrecht, Apr. 11, 1985; stepchildren: Shawna Penelope (dec.), Racheal Constance, Joshua Clayton. Student, U. Nev., 1971-72, Sierra Coll., 1973; BA in Anthropology, U. Calif., Berkeley, 1975; MSW, Calif. State U., Sacramento, 1984. Social worker, Auburn, Calif., 1984—; bookkeeper Mac's Machine Shop, Auburn, Calif., 1986-88; med. social worker Auburn Faith Community Hosp., 1987-88; counselor, caseworker Alta Calif. Regional Ctr., 1987-88. Co-founder Bowen Therapy Internat., 1997, CEO, 1997—; prodr. Getlois Prodns., 2000—. Active vol. work. Auburn Faith Hospice, 1981-85; group facilitator Am. Cancer Soc., Auburn, 1984, vol. 1987; dir. music Bethlehem Luth. Ch., Auburn, 1977-83; active various local political campaigns, Placer County, Calif., 1976—; bd. dirs. Auburn Community Concert Assn., 1976—, Sierra Coll. Disabled Students Adv. Com., Rocklin, Calif., 1978-81; mem. People for the Ethical Treatment Animals. Mem. Nat. Assn. Social Workers, Smithsonian Instn., Elisabeth Kubler-Ross Ctr., Nat. Humane Edn. Soc., Calif.-Berkeley Alumni Assn., Calif. State U.-Sacramento Alumni Assn., Greenpeace, Cal Band Alumni (Berkeley). Democrat. Avocations: water sports, camping, photography, music, calligraphy. Home: 177 Valley View Dr Auburn CA 95603-5617 Business E-Mail: deni@bowentherapy.com.

LARK, SYLVIA, artist, educator; b. N.Y., Nov. 8, 1947; MFA, U. Wis., 1972. Asst. prof. U. Calif., Berkeley, 1977-81, assoc. prof., 1981-85, prof., 1985—. One woman shows include Mus. Modern Art, N.Y.C., galleries in San Francisco, Los Angeles, Frankfurt, West Germany; exhibited in over 15 major pub. mus., corp. and U. collections. Recipient Humanities Research award U. Calif., 1982, 86; Fulbright Hays fellow, 1977. Mem. Nat. Women's Caucus for Art (nat. adv. bd. 1981-84, 1986-89), Coll. Art Assn., Women's Forum West. Office: U Calif Art Dept 238 Kroeber Hall Berkeley CA 94720-3750

LARKAM, BEVERLEY MCCOSHAM, social worker, marriage and family therapist; b. Vancouver, Can., Mar. 3, 1928; arrived in U.S., 1951; d. William Howard and Marjorie Isobel (Jerome) McCosham; children: Elizabeth, Charles, Daphne, Peter, John. A Royal Conservatory of Mus., U. Toronto, Toronto, 1948; BA, U. B.C., Can., 1949; BSW, U. B.C., 1950, MSW, 1951. Bd. cert. diplomate in clin. social work; LCSW; lic. marriage and family therapist, Tex. Psychiat. social worker Brackenridge Hosp., 1952-54; chmn. dept. sr. high. sch. Univ. Presbyn. Ch., Austin, Tex., 1952-55, mem. Christian edn. com., 1961-67, bd. dirs. developing and organizing nursery sch., 1967-70; social worker Counseling-Psychol. Svcs. Ctr., U. Tex., 1971-72; psychiat. social worker, chief supr. Adult, Children's Mental Health Human-Devel. Ctr.-South, Austin, Tex., 1972-79; pvt. practice marriage and family therapy, sex therapy and individual and group psychotherapy Austin, Tex., 1975—. Field supr. Sch. Social Work U. Tex.; cons. in field. Mem. cmty. orgn. to establish classes for mentally retarded children, 1966-68; active City of Austin Commn. for Women, 1978—, chmn., 1982-84, emeritus, 1985—; organizer Austin Assn. for Marriage and Family Therapy, 1980-82, bd. dirs. Tex. Assn. for Marriage and Family Therapy, 1980-82, Nat. Assn. Commns. for Women, 1985-88; vol. usher Austin Symphony Orch. Soc., 1972—; mem. Heritage Soc. Austin, Georgetown Heritage Soc., Women's Symphony League of Austin, Austin Art Mus.; mem. Dean Sch. Social Work, profl. linkage com., 1993—; vol. family therapist Child Inc./Headstart Ranch Weekends, 1995-96; mem. Williamson County Hist. Mus. Mem. NASW, Am. Assn. Marriage and Family Therapy (approved supr., com. on racial, ethnic and cultural diversity 1992-95), Am. Group Psychotherapy Assn. (cert. group psychotherapist), Southwestern Group Psychotherapy Soc. (sr. faculty), Austin Group Psychotherapy Soc., Am. Assn. Sexuality Educators, Counselors and Therapists (cert. therapist, supr.), Acad. Cert. Social Workers, Register Clin. Social Workers, Diplomate Internat. Conf. Advancement of Pvt. Practice of Clin. Social Work, Tex. Soc. for Clin. Social Work (bd. dirs. 1990—, pres. 1997-99, chmn. Austin study group 2006—), Clin. Social Work Fedn. (fin. chmn. 1998-2000), PEO Sisterhood, Austin Woman's Forum (pres. 1994-95, 2002-03). Presbyterian (elder, session of Univ. Presbyterian Ch. 1997—). Home and Office: 2102 Raleigh Ave Austin TX 78703-2128 also: 207 E 9th St Georgetown TX 78626-5908 Office Phone: 512-476-4182. Personal E-mail: blarkam@earthlink.net.

LARKIN, BARBARA MILLS, state agency administrator; b. Dubuque, Iowa; BA magna cum laude, Clarke Coll., 1973; JD with distinction, U. Iowa, 1977. Bar: Iowa, N.C., D.C. Ptnr. Sanford, Adams, McCullough and Beard, Raleigh, N.C.; chief counsel, fgn. policy advisor to Senator Terry Sanford, 1986-92; legis. dir. Sen. Diane Feinstein, 1993; dep. asst. sec. legis. affairs U.S. Dept. State, Washington, 1993-96, asst. sec. for legis. affairs, 1996—2001; v.p. policy and advocacy CARE, Washington, 2004—. Legis. asst. Dem. rep. Michael T. Blouin, Iowa, 1974-75, coord. Blouin for Congress com., 1974. Office: CARE Ste 500 1625 K St NW Washington DC 20006 Office Phone: 202-296-5696.

LARKIN, JOAN, poet, literature and language educator; b. Boston, Apr. 16, 1939; d. George Joseph and Celia Gertrude (Rosenberg) Moffitt; m. James A. Larkin, Dec. 23, 1966 (div. 1969); 1 child, Kate. BA, Swarthmore Coll., 1960; MA, U. Ariz., 1969; MFA, Bklyn. Coll., 2005. Asst. prof. English CUNY-Bklyn. Coll., 1969—94, ret., 1994, adj. faculty MFA program, 1997—98; assoc. faculty MFA program Goddard Coll., 1994—96, 2002. Mem. guest faculty poetry writing Sarah Lawrence Coll., Bronxville, NY, 1984—86, 1988, 1997—2006; mem. core faculty MFA program New Eng. Coll., 2002—; disting. vis. poet Columbia Coll., Chgo., 2006. Author: (poems) Housework, 1975, A Long Sound, 1986, Cold River, 1997, (rec. poetry reading) A Sign I Was Not Alone, 1980, (prose) If You Want What We Have, 1998, Glad Day, 1998; co-editor: Gay and Lesbian Poetry in Our Time: An Anthology, 1988 (Lambda Lit. award 1988), Amazon Poetry, 1975, Lesbian Poetry, 1981; editor: A Woman Like That, 1999; co-translator: Sor Juana's Love Poems, 1997; contbr. poems to periodicals including Am. Poetry Rev., Conditions, Ms., Paris Rev., Sinister Wisdom, The Village Voice, Aphra, Endymion, The Lamp in the Spine, Global City Rev., Am. Rev., Genesis West, Sojourner, Margie, Hanging Loose. NEA fellow in poetry, 1987-88, 96, N.Y. Found. for Arts fellow in poetry, 1987-88; Creative Artists Pub. Svc. Program grantee N.Y. State Coun. Arts, 1976, 80; Mass. Cultural Coun. grantee in playwriting, 1995. Personal E-mail: larkin7@earthlink.net.

LARKIN, JOAN See JETT, JOAN

LARKIN, MARY SUE, financial planner; b. Kansas City, Kans., Sept. 29, 1948; d. Claude Dewey Jr. and Mildred Elaine (Foster) Wyrick; m. James Donald Larkin, June 5, 1971; children: Michael James, David Kirk. BA in Elem. Edn., Baker U., 1970; MA in Edn., Ariz. State U., 1980. CFP. Tchr. Bonner Springs (Kans.) Unified Sch. Dist., 1970-71, Finney County Unified Sch. Dist., Garden City, Kans., 1971-73, Deer Valley Unified Sch. Dist., Phoenix, 1974-80; fin. planner Larkin & Assocs., Sun City, Ariz., 1980—; co-founder, registered rep. Fin. Network Investment Corp., El Segundo, Calif., 1983, co-regional dir., 2000—. Co-author: The Larkin Guide-Enjoying the Riches of Retirement, 1987. Bd. dirs. Mingus Mountain Estate Residential Ctr., Inc., 1993, sec., 1994—. Recipient creative programming award Nat. Univ. Continuing Edn. Assn., 1994, Fin. Network Circle of Achievement award, 1999. Mem.: Fin. Planning Assn. (pres. Greater Phoenix chpt. 1994—95), Atrusa (Sun City pres. 1987—89, Dist. 11 svc. chair 2003—05, Sun City pres. 2005—), Phi Theta Kappa, Alpha Delta Sigma, Zeta Tau Alpha. Republican. Roman Catholic.

LARMORE, CATHERINE CHRISTINE, university official; b. West Chester, Pa., Apr. 8, 1947; d. Ashby Morton and Catherine (Burns) L.; m. Thomas Henry Beddall, May 2, 1994 BA, Earlham Coll., 1969. Tchr. Westtown (Pa.) Sch., 1969-75, asst. dean girls, 1971-73, dean girls, 1973-75; sec. U. Pa., Kennett Square, 1976-78; media coord. New Bolton Ctr U. Pa. Sch. Vet. Medicine, Kennett Square, 1978-83, dir. external affairs, 1983-88, dir. devel., 1988-99; dir. devel. for equine programs Va. Tech. U., 1999—. Mem. London Grove (Pa.) Twp. Planning Commn., 1990-2000, Chester County (Pa.) Women's Task Force, 1992-93, Chester County Women's Commn., 1994-95; v.p. White Clay Watershed Assn., Landenburg, Pa., 1994-95, pres., 1997-2000; sec. White Clay Creek Bi-State Preserve Adv. Coun. Commonwealth of Pa., 1996-98, v.p. 1998-99, pres. 1999-2000; chmn. steering com. for Ad Hoc Task Force on White Clay Creek, 1990; bd. dirs. Coalition for Natural Stream Valleys, 1996—, Pa. Vet. Med. Hist. Soc., 1997-99. Recipient Take Pride in Pa. award Commonwealth of Pa., 1991. Mem. Nat. Soc. Fund Raising Execs., So. Chester County C. of C. (bd. dirs. 1989-91). Avocations: gardening and horticulture, equine carriage driving, environment and open space. Office: Va Tech Middleburg Agrl Rsch and Extension Ctr 5527 Sullivans Mill Rd Middleburg VA 20117-5207

LAROBARDIER, GENEVIEVE KRAUSE, lawyer; d. Allan Joseph and Genevieve Ferington Krause; m. Lamont Marcell LaRobardier; children: Lamont Jr., Allan Lamont, Suzanne, Marie Bernadette, Genevieve. BA, Barnard Coll., NYC; MAT summa cum laude, Fairleigh Dickenson U., Teaneck, NJ, 1966; JD, Rutgers U, NJ, 1983. Bar: N.J. 1983, N.Y. 1985, U.S. Dist. Ct. N.J. 1983, U.S. Ct. Appeals (3d cir.) 1985, U.S. Ct. Appeals (2d cir.) 1987, U.S. Dist. Ct. (ea. dist.) N.Y. 1987, U.S. Dist. Ct. (so. dist.) N.Y. 1987, U.S. Supreme Ct. 1989. Asst. to dir. Latin Am. affairs Nat. Fgn. Trade Coun., N.Y.C.; legal intern, assoc. Margolis Law Firm, Verona, NJ, 1983—90; spl. counsel Hannoch Weisman Law Firm, Roseland, NJ, 1990—93; assoc. to ptnr. Bressler, Amery & Ross, P.C., Florham Park, NJ, 1993—. Editor and mem. jud. bd. Rutgers Law Rev., Newark; adj. faculty lang. Fairleigh Dickenson U., Teaneck, NJ. Contbg. author: N.J. Federal Civil Practice Handbook, N.J. Federal Civil Procedure Handbook; contbr. articles to profl. jours. Mem.: ABA, N.Y. State Bar Assn., N.J. State Bar Assn. (first vice chair internat. litigation and arbitration com., mem. internat. law orgns. sect., chair 2006—, Disting. Legis. Svc. award 1997).

LA ROCCA, ISABELLA, artist, educator; b. El Paso, Apr. 14, 1960; d. Remo and Alicia Estela (Gonzalez) La Rocca. BA, U. Pa., 1984; MFA, Ind. U., 1993. Freelance photographer, NYC, 1986—90; assoc. instr. Ind. U., Bloomington, 1991—93; instr. Herron Sch. Art, Indpls., 1992; vis. asst. prof. Ind. U., 1994—; asst. prof. DePauw U., Greencastle, Ind., 1994—95; vis. asst. prof. Bloomsburg (Pa.) U., 1995—96; freelance photographer, designer, animator San Francisco, 1996—. Instr. art Vista C.C., 1998—, Coll. of Marin, 1999—2000, Calif. State U., Hayward, 1999—2001, City Coll. San Francisco, 2000—. One-woman shows include Haas Gallery, Bloomsburg, 1996, Ctr. Photography Woodstock, N.Y., Moore Coll., Pa., 1994, Emison Art Ctr., Greencastle, 1996, exhibited in group shows at 494 Gallery, N.Y.C., 1993, Kala Art Inst., Berkeley, Calif., 2000; prodr., dir.: (films) Mariana of the Universe, 2004. Ind. U. CIC Minority fellow, 1990-91; Jewish Found. Edn. Women scholar, 1990; recipient Friends of Photography Ferguson award, 1993, Serpent Source Grant for Women Artists, 1998. Office Phone: 510-704-9521. Personal E-mail: ilr@isabellalarocca.com.

LAROCCA, PATRICIA DARLENE MCALEER, middle school educator; b. Aurora, Ill., July 12, 1951; d. Theodore Austin and Lorraine Mae (Robbins) McAleer; m. Edward Daniel LaRocca, June 28, 1975; children: Elizabeth S., Mark E. BS in Edn./Math., No. Ill. U., 1973, postgrad., 1975. Tchr. elem. sch. Roselle (Ill) Sch. Dist., 1973-80; instr. math. Coll. DuPage, Glen Ellyn, Ill., 1988-90; tchr. math. O'Neill Mid. Sch., Downers Grove, Ill., 1995—. Pvt. cons., math. tutor, Downers Grove, Ill., 1980-88, 90-95. Bd. dirs. PTA, Hillcrest Elem. Sch., Downers Grove; active Boy Scouts Am.; mem. 1st United Meth. Ch. Ill. teaching scholar, 1969. Methodist. Avocations: antiques, softball, organ, dance. Home and Office: 5648 Dunham Rd Downers Grove IL 60516-1246 Personal E-mail: roc4meep@comcast.net.

LAROCCO, THERESA M., social studies educator; b. Roanoke, Va., Feb. 25, 1954; d. John Francis Campbell and Gertrude Claire Corbett; m. Joseph C. LaRocco, Aug. 12, 1978; children: Jacqueline Downs, Catherine. BA, Roanoke Coll., Salem, Va., 1976; MA in Liberal Studies, Hollins U., Va., 1997. Cert. postgrad. profl. Commonwealth Va., 2006. Bookmobile libr. Roanoke Pub. Libr., 1976—77; tchr. social studies Roanoke Cath. Schs., 1977—83, City Salem Schs., Va., 1983—88, coordinating tchr. social studies, 1988—. Bd. dirs. Salem Hist. Soc., 2006—, Tchg. Am. History Grant, Roanoke, 2006—. Named Tchr. of Yr., Salem H.S., 1997; named to Tchr. Exch. with Germany, Armonk, 1991; NEH grantee, U. Oreg., 1993, Temple U., 1996. Mem.: NEA (PAC chmn. 1997—2000), Va. Consortium Social Studies Specialists and Coll. Educators (state pres. 2006—), Va. Coun. Social Studies (state pres. 1994—96), Va. Edn. Assn. (pac com. 1997—2000), Alpha Delta Kappa (hospitality chmn. 2004—06, scholarship chairpaerson 2002—04). Office: City of Salem Schools 510 S College Ave Salem VA 24153 Office Phone: 540-387-2437. Business E-Mail: tlarocco@salem.k12.va.us.

LAROCHELLE, WANDA CARLENE, science educator; b. Corpus Christi, Sept. 7, 1942; d. K. D. and Hermanda Carla (Knief) Atkinson; m. Raymond A. LaRochelle, June 10, 1967; children: Clayton Dean, Courtney Dawn Baumgartner. AA, Del Mar Jr. Coll., Corpus Christi, 1963; BS, Sam Houston State U., 1965. Cert. Vocat. Home Economics Sam Houston State U., 1965, Bus. Edn. Instr. Sam Houston State U., 1965, Vocat. Office Edn. Instr. North Tex. State U., 1980, Kindergarten and Pre-School Tchr. SW Tex. State U., 1983, Driver's Edn. Instr. State of Tex., 1996. Bus. tchr. East Ctrl. Ind. Sch. Dist., San Antonio, 1965—67, Odem Ind. Sch. Dist., Tex., 1967—73, Houston Ind. Sch. Dist., Tenn., 1974—78; vocat. office duplication tchr. Bastrop Ind. Sch. Dist., Tex., 1979—82; kindergarten tchr. Flatonia Ind. Sch. Dist., Tex., 1982—87; dir. student svcs. Pacific Coast Coll., Chula Vista,

Calif., 1988—94; family, consumer sci. tchr. Katy Ind. Sch. Dist., Tex., 1994—. Recipient Star of Yr., Bastrop HS, 1982. Mem.: Flatonia Parent Tchrs. Assn. (assoc.; pres. 1986—88). Avocations: reading, cooking, needlepoint. Office Phone: 281-237-4236.

LAROCQUE, GERALDINE ANN, literature educator; b. Belcourt, ND, Jan. 7, 1949; d. Sarah Grandbois; m. Carris LaRocque, Aug. 31, 1967; children: Frank, Jacqueline, Chad, Alison. BS, U. ND, Grand Forks, 1990. Language arts tchr. Belcourt (ND) Sch. Dist., 1990—. Advisor. Mem.: Assn. Improvement Tchg. Roman Cath. Avocations: gardening, sewing, cooking, reading, travel. Office: Turtle Mt Cmty HS Box 440 Belcourt ND 58316 Business E-Mail: geri.larocque@sendit.nodak.edu.

LAROSE, KATHERINE STENCEL, music educator; b. Croswell, Mich., Oct. 3, 1945; d. Jacob Stanley and Catherine Marie Stencel; m. Alan Roger LaRose; children: Renee Catherine, Alan Gregory. MusB, We. Mich. U., 1969; MusM, U. Mass., 1971. Tchg. asst. U. Mass., Amherst, Mass., 1969—71, lectr. piano, 1972—80; pvt. piano tchr. San Lorenzo, Calif., 1981—87, Fremont, Calif., 1987—. Dir., organist St. Christopher's Episc. Ch., San Lorenzo, 1993—2000; dir. music St. Barnabas Ch., Alameda, Calif., 2000—. Musician: numerous recitals, 1963—, Isabella Stewart Gardner Mus., 1974—. Mem.: Music Tchrs. Assn. Calif. (coord. theory site, bd. dirs. 1984—2004), Am. Guild Organists. Home: 4265 Jacinto Dr Fremont CA 94536 Office: St Barnabas Church 1427 Sixth St Alameda CA 94501

LAROSE, MELBA LEE, performing company executive, actress, playwright, theater director; d. Kenneth Lee and Melba Lauren LaRose; m. Elson Jose de Faria, July 14, 1987. AAS in Bus. Mgmt., SUNY, Cobleskill, 1962; at, HB Studios, N.Y.C., 1963—65, Free U. of L.A., 1972—74; pvt. tng., Acting, Dance, Voice, N.Y.C., 1977—90. Freelance actress, playwright, dir., N.Y.C., 1965—; actress, playwright and dir. Group Repertory Theatre, L.A., 1972—76; adminstrv. asst., fundraiser and actress N.Y. St. Theatre Caravan, N.Y.C., 1990—96; adminstrv. asst. The Actors Studio, N.Y.C., 1992—94; founder, artistic and adminstrv. dir. N.Y. Artists Unlimited, Inc., N.Y.C., 1982—, Downeast Arts Ctr., 2004—. Panelist A.R.T. New York, Lower Manhattan Cultural Coun., Theatre Resources Unlimited, N.Y.C., 2000—; fulbright sr. specialist roster candidate Coun. for Internat. Exch. of Scholars, Washington, 2002—. Playwright-director: (plays) Rime Ice; Who's There?; Voices of the Town - A Vaudeville Salute; Song of the Simple Truth; actor, playwright, dir.: (3 one-act plays) Cityscapes 3; (plays) Little Red - Girl from the Hood; actor, playwright A Builder of Dreams, based on the poems & life of Myrtle Evelyn Lawrence (1893-1963); Tables I Have Danced On; actor: La Ronde, The Love of Don Perlimplin & Belisa in the Garden, Glamour, Glory & Gold (the Life & Legend of Nola Noonan, Goddess & Star), Blues in Rags, The Grand Inquisitor; (films) Eyes of a Blue Dog (Best Actress - Town Hall's First Run Film Festival, 1994), Dadetown, Working Girl; (plays) Lucky Wonderful, Sganarelle, The Fugitives, The Adding Machine; dir.: The Prince & The Moon. Recipient Disting. Alumnus award, SUNY, 1987; grantee, Fund for Creative Cmtys., Lower Manhattan Cultural Coun., 1998—, Nancy Quinn Fund, 1998—, N.Y.C. Dept. of Cultural Affairs, 1999—, Puffin Found., 1999—, N.Y. Coun. for Humanities, 1999—, NEA, 2003, Gannett Found., 2004—. Mem.: AFTRA, SAG, Actors' Equity Assn., Dramatists Guild of Am., Drama League, Theatre Resources Unlimited, Alliance of Resident Theatres N.Y., Phi Theta Kappa. Avocation: travel. Office: NY Artists Unlimited Inc Ste #2A 212 W 14 Street New York NY 10011 Office Phone: 212-228-2886. E-mail: nyartunltd@aol.com.

LARRABEE, BARBARA PRINCELAU, retired intelligence officer; b. Oakland, Calif., Sept. 21, 1923; d. Paul and Mary Emilie (Rueger) Princelau; m. John Joseph Boyle, Oct. 21, 1950 (dec.); m. Donald Richard Larrabee, Nov. 2, 1996. BA, U. Calif., Berkeley, 1948. Intelligence officer CIA, Langley, Va., 1954-82. Bd. dirs. The Thift Shop, Washington, 1988-92; mem. Women's Bd. Columbia Hosp. for Women, Washington, 1986-2001, mem. exec. com., 1989-91, 96-98; mem. com. Washington Antiques Show, 1989-2004; active Rep. Womens Fed. Forum, Washington, League of Rep. Women of D.C., Inc. Recipient Cert. of Distinction CIA, 1982. Mem.: Assn. Former Intelligence Officers (bd. dirs. 1993—99, v.p. 1997—99, exec. com. 1997—99), Ctrl. Intelligence Retiree Assn., Evergreen Garden Club (v.p. 2001—02), Sulgrave Club, Nat. Press Club, U. Calif. Berkeley Alumni Club of Washington (rec. sec. 1976—77, v.p. 1984—86), Sigma Kappa (v.p. No. Va. alumnae 1992—95, devel. com. Sigma Kappa Found., Inc. 1993—95). Episcopalian. Avocations: aerobics, needlecrafts, travel. Home: 4956 Sentinel Dr Apt 304 Bethesda MD 20816-3562

LARRABEE, VIRGINIA ANN STEWART, education educator; b. Jacksonville, Fla., Nov. 21, 1923; d. Edwin Homer and Clara Victoria (Anderson) Stewart; student Pine Manor Jr. Coll., 1941-43; B.A., Wellesley Coll., 1945; M.Ed., U. Vt., 1961; Ed.D., Boston U., 1969; m. Wesley Campbell Larrabee, May 4, 1947; children— Susan Ann, Diane Elaine, Linda Jane, Judith Ann. Asst. buyer B. Altman & Co., N.Y.C., 1945-46; tchr. public schs., Forest Dale, Vt., 1955-59, Shoreham, Vt., 1959-62; audiovisual dir., Shoreham, 1959-62; elem. supr., Castleton, Vt., 1962-64; instr., master tchr. Harvard, summers 1963-65; elem. supr. public schs., Rutland, Vt., 1964-66; asst. prof. edn. Castleton State Coll., 1966-68, assoc. prof., 1969-74, prof., 1974-92, prof. emerita, 1992, chmn. dept. edn., 1972-92, dir. grad. program in reading, 1974-92, dir. Edn. Computer Ctr., 1984-92; visiting prof., Harvard U., 1986-87; mem. adv. com. Right to Read, Vt., 1974-80; mem. Vt. Edn. Commr.'s Forum, 1981—, Vt. Health Policy Coun., 1988-94; owner, operator farm and Larrabee's Point Orchard, 1953—; pres. Vt. Consortium Ednl. Tech., 1988-92; tech. cons. Rutland S.W. Supervisory Dist., 1992—. Sunday Sch. supt. Congregational Ch., Shoreham, 1948-60, choir dir., 1958-64; Pres. Vt. Coun. Ednl. Tech., 1988-92; bd. dirs Vt. Applefest, 1988; bd. trustees Helen Porter Nursing Home, 1994—. Mem. New Eng. (past dir.), Vt. (dir., pres. 1978-80, editor newsletter 1980-85) reading councils, Internat. Reading Assn., Nat., Vt. (past pres.), New Eng. (past dir.) assns. supervision and curriculum devel., Phi Delta Kappa (v.p. Vt. chpt. 1988-89), Phi Delta Kappa (pres. Vt. chpt. 1989-90), Delta Kappa Gamma, Pi Lambda Theta., Vt. Wellesley Club, Shoreham Hist. Club Home: RFD Box 56 Shoreham VT 05770 Office: Castleton State Coll Castleton VT 05735

LARRICK, PAMELA MAPHIS, marketing executive; married; 3 stepchildren. Various positions Ogilvy Mather, 1978—92; gen. mgr. O&M Direct, 1992—94; joined as mng. dir. MRM (then McCann Direct), NYC, 1994; reg. dir., N. Am. MRM; COO MRM Worldwide; pres., CEO MRM, NYC, 2001; chmn. MRM Ptnrs. (McCann customer rels. mktg.), NYC; chmn., CEO Foot Cone & Belding Worldwide, customer rels. mktg. (FCBi), NYC, 2005—. Named one of 25 Women Leaders of Advt. Industry, Ad Age, 1997, Global Power 100, 2002; recipient Emerson Lifetime Achievement award for Innovation in and Svc. to direct mktg., John Caples awards orgn. Office: FCBi 100 W 33rd New York NY 10001 Office Phone: 212-885-3000. Office Fax: 212-885-2903.

LARRIMORE, JUDITH RUTLEDGE, nurse; b. Jackson, Ala., Sept. 6, 1943; d. Kirxie Eugene and Frankie Jewel (Walters) Rutledge; m. Lennox Wilson Larrimore, Nov. 27, 1969; children: Jonathan, Jason, Jennifer, Julie. BA, U. South Ala., Mobile, 1966. RN, Ala. Charge nurse Thomasville (Ala.) Hosp., 1966-67, 86-89, nurse ob./surgery, 1989-90, mem. patient edn.-social svc. advocacy, vol. svcs. coord., 1990—; charge nurse Escambia Gen. Hosp., Pensacola, Fla., 1967-68; patient advocate Thomasville Mental Health Rehab. Ctr., 1987-88; sch. nurse Thomasville City Sch. Sys., 1988—90; patient adv., bd, dirs. Vis. Nurse Assn., 1990—. Sch. nurse Thomasville City Sch. Sys., 1988-90. Bd. dirs. Thomasville Hosp. Vis. Nurses. 1st lt. USAF, 1968-70. Baptist. Avocations: reading, piano, geneology research. Home: 811 Moncrief Dr Thomasville AL 36784-2750

LARRUBIA, EVELYN, reporter; Reporter South Fla. Sun-Sentinel, Ft. Lauderdale, Fla.; county govt. reporter, metro desk LA Times, investigative writer. Co-recipient Livingston award for local reporting, Livingston Found., 1996, Joseph L. Brechner Freedom of Information award, 1997, Ursula & Gilbert Farfel prize for investigative reporting, Scripps Howard Found., 2006, Local Watchdog Reporting award, Am. Soc. Newspaper Editors, 2006. Office: LA Times 202 W 1st St Los Angeles CA 90012 Office Phone: 213-237-7847. Office Fax: 213-237-4712. E-mail: evelyn.larrubia@latimes.com.*

LARSDOTTER, ANNA-LISA, retired translator, artist; b. Uddevalla, Bohus Län, Sweden, May 12, 1932; d. Lars Helge Svensson and Signe Ingeborg Jacobsson-Svensson; m. Erich S. Weibel, Aug. 17, 1956 (div. 1962). Student, Tchrs. Coll. for Women, Stockholm, 1951—52, Art Student's League, N.Y.C., 1953—55, New Sch. for Social Rsch., 1963—66, Summit Art Ctr., N.J., 1964—68, Academie des Beaux-Arts, Lausanne, Switzerland, 1960—62. Sec., translator internat. program Mus. Modern Art, N.Y.C., 1956; archivist Lawrence-Myden Collection, N.Y.C., 1963—64; archivist, translator Frederick Kiesler Catalogue, N.Y.C., 1979; freelance translator Data Profls. Inc., Ft. Lauderdale, Fla., 1986—97. Mem. exec. com. Summit Art Ctr., 1967—69. Contbr. articles to profl. jours.; performer: (dances) Byrd Hoffman Sch., 1969—75; appeared in: (films) Strong Medicine, 1984; (plays) Life and Times of Sigmund Freud, 1969—74; Life and Times of Joseph Stalin, 1973; Attic Clouds, 1973; A Letter for Queen Victoria, 1974; Festival d'Automne, 1974; Overture in N.Y.C., 1972; actor: (tour) Theatre des Nations, 1973; organizer: (exhbns.) with Summit Art Ctr. and Bell Tel. Labs., 1964—69; preparer: catalogue pvt. collection of composer Jack Lawrence and Walter Myden, 1963. Lutheran. Avocations: art, music, history, genealogy. Personal E-mail: allarsdotter@yahoo.com.

LARSEN, BRENDA JOYCE, elementary school educator; d. Kenneth Louis and Ina Mae Larsen. BS in Elem. Edn., No. Ariz. U., Flagstaff, Ariz., 1976. Cert. tchr. Ariz., 1998. Tchr. kindergarten Flagstaff Christian Schools, 1978; tchr. grades 4-10 Flagstaff Indian Christian Schs., 1978; tchr. elem. sch. Cmty. Christian Ctr., Cudahy, Calif., 1979—82, Pilgrim Christian Schs., Maywood, Calif., 1982—83, Huntington Pk. Bapt. Sch., Calif., 1983—91, Temecula Christian Sch., Calif., 1991—92, Hemet Christian Sch., Calif., 1992—94, Mountainside Christian Sch., San Bernardino, Calif., 1994—97; reading specialist tchr. Indian Oasis Sch. Dist., Sells, Ariz., 1998—. Coach reading Indian Oasis Sch. Dist. Mem.: Nat. Tchrs. Assn. Republican. Office Phone: 520-383-2312.

LARSEN, KRISTINA ANN, elementary school educator; b. Edmonds, Wash., Jan. 6, 1979; d. James Thomas and Katherine Ann Gooderhan; m. Luke Edward Larsen, Aug. 30, 2005. BS in Edn., U. Cen. Ark., 2002. Lic. tchr. elem. edn. P-4 Ark. Substitute tchr. Mayflower (Ark.) Elem. Sch., 2002—03; tchr. 4th grade Pulaski County Spl. Sch. Dist., Little Rock, 2003—04; tchr. 4th grade math. and sci. Lonoke (Ark.) Elem. Sch., 2004—. Chair theme com. Lonoke Elem. Sch., 2005—06, mem. textbook selection com., 2005—06, mem. leadership com., 2005—06. Mem.: Nat. Sci. Tchrs. Assn.

LARSEN, LETITIA (TISH) HOYT, history educator; b. Lincoln, Nebr., June 9, 1946; d. Edgar Charles and Gladys Pearl Hoyt; m. Gary Loy Larsen, Dec. 22, 1967; children: Kari Larsen Davidson, Amy Larsen Nash. BS, U. Nebr., 1968; MS, Columbia U., N.Y., 1972, Denver U., 2001. Program dir., med. svc. order unit Columbia-Presbyn. Med. Ctr., N.Y.C., 1968—70; adminstrv. officer Colo. Dept. of Health, Denver, 1972—74; classroom tchr. Denver Pub. Schs., 1992—2006, lead tchr. U.S. history, 2005—06; adj. prof. history U. Colo., Denver, 1998—2006. History chair Denver Sch. of Arts, 1997—2005, humanities dept. chair, 2002—04, social studies adv. coun., 2006; co-facilitator for U.S. history refinement team Denver Pub. Schs., 2005—06. Facilitator Jr. League of Denver, 1983—84; pres. Les Cygnettes, Denver, 1987—88, Denver Ballet Guild, 1989—90; women exec. bd. Augustana Luth. Ch., Denver, 1982—83. Recipient Governor's Sch. Vol. award, State of Colo., 1980; Hollingshea Fellow, Columbia U., 1970, 1971, Donnell Kay Fellow, Denver U., 2000, 2001. Achievements include Served for three years on the committee to re-design Denver Public School's U. S. History high school curriculum. Avocations: running, cooking, swimming, reading. Home: 1804 W Cape Cod Way Littleton CO 80120 Office: Denver Public Schs 900 Grant St Denver CO 80203 Office Phone: 720-423-7000. Office Fax: 720-423-7058. Personal E-mail: wahoowest@comcast.net. Business E-Mail: tish_larsen@dpsk12.org.

LARSEN, PAULA ANNE, operating room nurse; b. Norfolk, Va., Oct. 2, 1962; d. Larry Gene and Sue Frances (Williams) P. ADN, Labette C.C., 1982. RN, Mo.; CNOR. Lab. asst. Labette County Med. Ctr., Parsons, Kans., 1979-82; oper. rm. nurse St. John's Regional Med. Ctr., Joplin, Mo., 1982-85, oper. rm. nurse, shift coord., 1989-94; head nurse Mason Gen. Hosp., Shelton, Wash., 1994—2000; operating room nurse Harrison Silverdale, 2000—01, Surgery Ctr. Plano, Tex., 2001—. With Mo. Lions Eye Bank, 1989-94. Vol. RN Faith in Practice Guatemala Mission Team, 2001—. Mem. Assn. Operating Rm. Nurses (del. 1991). Republican. Baptist. Avocations: antiques, home remodeling, sign language, travel. Office: Surgery Ctr of Plano 1620 Coit Rd Plano TX 75075 E-mail: paula_larsen@sbcglobal.net.

LARSEN, SYLVIA B., state legislator; b. Troy, Ohio, July 1949; m. Robert M. Larsen; 2 children. Student, Briarcliff Coll., 1968-69; BA, U. Wis., 1972. Bd. dirs. NH Healthy Kids, Child Trust Fund, Land and Com. Heritage, Ctrl. Sr. Ctr., Concord, 1984-2000; chmn. NH Unique Coll. Savs. Program; cons. pub. rels. Concord; mem. Concord City Coun., 1989-98; mem. Dist. 15 NH Senate, Concord, 1994—, mem. fin., exec. depts. and adminstrn. com., internal affairs com., Dem. leader, 2002—. Named Servant of Yr. Pineconia Grange, 1992, Legislator of Yr., NH Grange, 2001, Woman of Yr. Bus. and Profl. Women, Concordia, Athena award Concordia Chamber. Democrat. Address: 23 Kensington Rd Concord NH 03301-2528

LARSEN HOECKLEY, CHERI LIN, language educator; BA, U. Calif., Riverside, 1984; MA, U. Tex., Austin, 1986; PhD, U. Calif., Berkeley, 1997. Assoc. prof. English Westmont Coll., Santa Barbara, Calif., 1997—. Dir. Writers' Corner Westmont Coll., 1998—2006; mem. governance coun. Cesar Chavez Charter Sch., Santa Barbara, 2002—06; program chair Conf. on Christianity and Lit., Western Region, 2005. Editor (and author of introduction): (book) Shakespeare's Heroines, or The Characteristics of Women: Moral, Poetic and Historical by Anna Murphy Jameson; author: (multiple reviews) Christianity and Lit., Religion and Lit., (multiple presentations) 18th- & 19th-Century Brit. Women Writers Conf. Founding mem., parents' coun. Cesar Chavez Charter Sch., Santa Barbara, 2001—04; mem. St. Andrews' Presbyn. Ch., Santa Barbara, 1997—. Named Outstanding Grad. Student Instr., U. Calif. Berkeley, 1996; recipient Tchg. Effectiveness award, 1996, Tchr. of Yr. Humanities Divsn., Westmont Coll., 2001; fellow, Mellon Found., 1994—95; grantee, Irvine Found., 2002, 2004. Mem.: MLA. Protestant. Office: Westmont Coll 955 La Paz Rd Santa Barbara CA 93108-1011 Office Phone: 805-565-7084.

LARSGAARD, MARY LYNETTE, librarian, writer; b. Dickinson, N.D., Aug. 4, 1946; d. Martin Vilhelm and Helen Maud (Brooks) L. BA in Geology, Macalester Coll., 1968; MALS, U. Minn., 1969; MA in Geography, U. Oreg., 1978. Asst. documents/maps libr. Ctlr. Wash. State Coll., Ellensburg, 1969-76; map libr. Colo. Sch. Mines, Golden, 1978-86, asst. head spl. collections, 1986-88; asst. head map & imagery lab. U. Calif., Santa Barbara, 1988—. Author: Map LIbrarianship: an Introduction, 1978, 3d edit., 1998, Topographic Mapping of the Americas, Australia and New Zealand, 1984, Topographic Mapping of Africa, Australia & Eurasia, 1992. Recipient SLAG&M Honors award, 1995, ALCTS Presdl. Citation, 2002. Mem.: ALA (Magert Honors award 1983, MAGERT Honors award 1983), We. Assn. Map Librs. (pres. 1975—76, SLAG & M Honors award 1995, ALCTS Presdl. citation 2002), Beta Phi Mu., Phi Beta Kappa. Avocations: walking, reading, dance. Office: U Calif Santa Barbara Davidson Libr Map and Imagery Lab Santa Barbara CA 93106 Office Phone: 805-893-4049. Business E-Mail: mary@library.ucsb.edu.

LARSON, AMY F., nurse; b. Anderson, Ind., June 9, 1965; BSN, Mich. State U., 1988; postgrad., Cath. U. Am.; MSN, U. Mich., 1992, postgrad., 1997. RN; cert. adult nurse practitioner. Nurse tech. William Beaumont Hosp., Royal Oak, Mich., 1987-88; clin. staff nurse NIH, Bethesda, Md., 1988-90; staff nurse St. Joseph's Hosp., Ann Arbor, Mich., 1990-96; edn. coord. nursing practice svcs. St. Joseph's Mercy Hosp., Ann Arbor, 1994-98; nurse practitioner dept. neurology HealthPtnrs., Mpls., 1998—. Mem. Am. Assn. Neurosci. Nurses, Sigma Theta Tau.

LARSON, ANGELA R., secondary school educator; d. Ivan P. and Rose Ann Opperman; m. Gary L Larson, Apr. 27, 1954; children: Lindsay M, Jennifer A, Jonathan L, Travis A. BS in English Edn., U. No. Iowa, Cedar Falls, 1999; BS in Journalism/Pub. Rels., U. of Nebr., Omaha, 1991. H.s. English tchr. Midland CSD, Wyoming, Iowa, 1999—. Recipient Promising Young Tchr. award, Iowa Coun. of Teacher's of English, 1999; scholar Belfer Teacher's Conf., US Holocaust Meml. Mus., 2005. Mem.: Midland Edn. Association (pres. 2003—06), Iowa Coun. of Tchrs. of English, Nat. Coun. of Tchrs.s of English, Phi Delta Kappa. Office Phone: 563-488-2292.

LARSON, AUDRA, elementary school educator; b. Hartford, Conn., July 9, 1968; d. Charles E. and Marylin C. Thomas; m. Dan Larson, Oct. 23, 1993; children: Sarah Rae, Scott Thomas. BS, Ithaca Coll., Ithaca, N.Y., 1990; MS, So. Conn. State U., New Haven, 1991. Cert. tchr. Conn., 1990. Tchr. Griswold Jr. H.S., Rocky Hill, Conn., 1990—92; phys. edn./health tchr. Chippens Hill Mid. Sch., Bristol, Conn., 1993—. Coach basketball, softball Chippens Hill Mid. Sch., Bristol, Conn., 1995—2001, unified arts team leader rep., 2004—, Washington coord., 1999—; health edn. assessment program, steering com. SCASS, State Dept Of Edn., Hartford, Conn., 2000—. Grantee Bristol Bus. Edn. grantee, Bristol Bus. Edn. Found., 2006. Mem.: AAPHERD (assoc.). Achievements include development of State of Conn. curriculum framework phys. edn., health and wellness. Office: Chippens Hill Middle School 551 Peacedale St Bristol CT 06010 Office Phone: 860-584-3881. E-mail: audralarson@ci.bristol.ct.us.

LARSON, BARBARA JEAN, art history professor; d. Chester Albert and Delores Vivian Larson; m. John Andrew Johnson, Feb. 14, 1999 (div. Nov. 8, 2001); 1 child, Vivian Johnson. BA, Northwestern U., Evanston, Ill., 1978; MA, NYU, N.Y.C., 1989, PhD, 1996. Nat. Heritage Trust fellow Bklyn. Mus., 1984—85; editor Abaris Books, N.Y.C., 1985—87; NEA Sr. Rsch. fellow Guggenheim Mus., N.Y.C., 1987—89; sr. mus. educator Mus. Modern Art, N.Y.C., 1989—93; vis. asst. prof. U. No. Mich., Marquette, 1996—97; asst. prof. Syracuse U., NY, 1997—2005; assoc. prof. U. West Fla., 1996—. Author: The Dark Side of Nature: Science, Society and the Fantastic in the Work of Odilon Redon, 2005; contbr. articles to profl. jours. Grantee, Cantor Found., 2004, NEH, 2006; Rsch. fellowship, Nat. Endowment for Arts, 1987—88. Mem.: Assn. of Historians of 19th Century Art, Soc. for Art, Lit. and Sci., Coll. Art Assn. Achievements include illuminating connections between the history of science and trends in art and literature; the way in which transformations in science effect culture, society and art imagery. Avocations: hiking, movies. Home: 1602 Governors Dr # 2217 Pensacola FL 32514 Office: Univ West Fla 11000 University Pky Pensacola FL 32514 Office Phone: 850-474-2482. Fax: 850-474-2043. E-mail: blarson@uwf.edu.

LARSON, BEVERLY ROLANDSON, retired elementary school educator; b. Oklee, Minn., May 30, 1938; d. Orville K. and Belle A. (Anderson) Rolandson; m. Roland K. Larson, June 29, 1962; children: Amy Jo, Ann Marie, Carl Lee. BS, Concordia Coll., 1962; MA, Mankato State U., 1984. Cert. elem., spl. edn. tchr., Minn. Tchr. Hudson Sch. Dist., LaPuente, Calif., 1961-62, Thief River Falls Sch. Dist., Minn., 1962-63, Sch. Dist. 271, Bloomington, Minn., 1964-69, 71-72, Valley View Sch., Bloomington, Minn., 1989—2001; spl. edn. tchr. Sch. Dist. 271, Bloomington, Minn., 1975-79, 86-89; supr. student tchrs. Luther Coll., 2001—. Youth leader, Sunday sch. tchr. Christ the King Luth. Ch., Bloomington, 1969-82; precinct co-chair Rep. Party, Bloomington, alt., del. Recipient Svc. award Walk for Mankind, 1976, Golden Apple Achiever award Ashland Oil, 1994. Mem. NEA, Assn. Childhood Edn. (pres. Bloomington br. 1992-94), Minn. Edn. Assn., Nat. Learning Disabilities Assn., Minn. Learning Disabilities Assn., Bloomington Edn. Assn. Republican. Lutheran. Avocations: crafts, reading, plays and musicals, golf. Home: 7800 Pickfair Dr Bloomington MN 55438-1380

LARSON, CAROL S., foundation administrator, lawyer; BA, Stanford U.; JD, Yale Law Sch. Law clerk to Judge Warren J. Ferguson U.S. Dist. Crt., Central Dist. of Calif.; former atty., civil litigation O'Donnell and Gordon; dir. rsch., grants, law and public policy, Ctr. for Future of Children David and Lucile Packard Found., 1989—94, dir. prog., 1995—2003, v.p., 2000—03, pres., CEO, 2004—. Special asst. and speechwriter for pres. Am. Bar Assn., 1998; lecturer Stanford Law Sch., 1994—96; coordinator of advocacy Exceptional Children's Found., Los Angeles, 1980—81. Former bd. mem. Grantmakers for Children, Youth and Families; bd. mem. No. Calif. Grantmakers, Am. Leadership Forum, Silicon Valley. Office: David and Lucile Packard Found 300 Second St Los Altos CA 94022*

LARSON, DIANE LAVERNE KUSLER, principal; b. Fredonia, ND, July 28, 1942; d. Raymond Edwin and LaVerne (Mayer) Kusler; m. Donald Floyd Larson, Aug. 14, 1965. BS, Valley City (N.D.) State U., 1964; MS, Mankato (Minn.) State U., 1977; EdS, U. Minn., 1987. Cert. tchr. Minn. Tchr. elem. Cokato (Minn.) Elem. Sch., 1962-64, Lakeview Elem. Sch., Robbinsdale, Minn., 1964-66; vocal tchr. Wheaton (Minn.) High Sch., 1966-67; tchr. Owatonna (Minn.) Elem. Sch., 1967-88, prin., 1988—. V.p. Cannon Valley Uniserv, Mankato, 1981-83; NEA del. World Confederation of Orgns. of the Teaching Professions, Melbourne, 1988. Named Woman of Yr., Owatonna Bus. and Profl. Women, 1990. Mem. NEA (bd. dirs. 1986-88), Minn. Edn. Assn. (bd. dirs. 1983-88, Outstanding Woman in Leadership award 1983), Minn. Reading Assn. (bd. dirs. 1983-97, Pres. award 1984), Internat. Reading Assn. (coord. for Minn. 1990-97, bd. dirs. 1997-2000, Celebrate Literacy award 1998), Minn. Elem. Prins. Assn., Valley City State U. Alumni Assn. (Cert. of Merit 1998), Delta Kappa Gamma (legis. chmn. 1986-88, pres. 1992, Woman of Achievement award 1989, Tau leadership chair, Tau State 1st v.p. 1997-99). Congregationalist. Home: 19654 Bagley Ave Faribault MN 55021-2246 Office: Washington Sch 338 E Main St Owatonna MN 55060-3096 Office Phone: 507-334-8289. Personal E-mail: dianedl@clear.lakes.com.

LARSON, ELLEN R., health sciences instructor; m. Larry W. Larson, June 21, 1980; 1 child, Torrey. BS in Phys. Edn., SUNY, Cortland, 1977; MS in Health Edn., U. N.Mex., Albuquerque, 1989. Cert. health edn. specialist. Health and phys. edn. tchr. Haines (Alaska) Borough Sch. Dist., 1977—2000; health scis. instr. No. Ariz. U., Flagstaff, 2000—. Panel mem. Nat. Health Edn. Stds. Rev. Com., 2005—; presenter nat. confs. in field. Named Health Promotion Dept. Tchr. of Yr., No. Ariz. U., 2002. Mem.: AAHPERD, Ariz. Assn. Health, Phys. Edn., Recreation and Dance, Am. Sch. Health Assn. Avocations: kayaking, hiking, outdoor activities. Office: No Ariz U Box 15095 Flagstaff AZ 86001

LARSON, ILENE KAY, elementary school educator; b. Alpena, Mich., July 27, 1946; d. Roy A. and Dora Jean Williams; m. John Freer Larson, June 15, 1968; children: Carolyn Grace Larson Waite, Doreen Kay Larson Fisher. AA, Alpena C.C., 1966; BA (hon.), Mich. State U., 1968; MA, Ctrl. Mich. U., 1976. Elem. tchr. Alpena Pub. Sch., 1967—2005. Presentor, spkr. in field. Vol. Friends of Libr., Alpena, 2002. Named Tchr. of Week, Sta. WHSB, Alpena, 1980, Woman of Yr., Zonta Club Internat., 2004; grantee, Besser Found. Mem.: NEA, Mich. Asn. Edn. Young Children, Thunder Bay Reading Assn., Mich. Edn. Assn., Cmty. Concert Assn., Delta Gappa Gamma. Protestant. Avocations: reading, camping, travel. Home: Box 16 12110 Clinton St Ossineke MI 49766 Office Phone: 989-358-5800. Personal E-mail: larson@m33access.com.

LARSON, JANECE S., elementary school educator; d. Richard D. and Ione C. Scow; m. Scott A. Larson, July 7, 1973; children: Katie, Mandy, Adam, Holly, Jesse. BS in Elem. Edn., Ariz. State U., Tempe, 1973; MA in Ednl.

Adminstrn., No. Ariz. U., Flagstaff, 1993. Tchr. Tempe Elem. Dist., Ariz., 1989—92; 6th gr. tchr. Mesa Pub. Sch., 1992—. Owner Amigo Presch. Inc., Phoenix, 1984—. Cub den leader Boy Scouts Am., Mesa, 1985—89, 1995—2000, coach, 1992—98, cub com. chmn., 2000—02, scout com. chmn., 2002—04; pres. Booker T. Washington Elem. PTA, Mesa, 1989—90. Named to Den Leader Hall of Fame, Boy Scouts Am., 1999; recipient Newell award, Tempe, 1990, Scouter of Yr. award, Boy Scouts Am., 2001, Woodbadge award, 2003. Mem. Lds Ch. E-mail: larsonsfamily@cox.net.

LARSON, JANICE TALLEY, application developer; b. Houston, Sept. 29, 1948; d. Hiram Peak Talley and Jennie Edna Donahoo; m. Harold Vernon Larson Jr., Apr. 8, 1977; children: Randall Neil, Christopher Lee. AA in Computers, San Jacinto Coll., 1981; BA in Computer Info. Systems, U. Houston, Clear Lake, 1984, MA in Computer Info. Systems, 1988; EdD in Instrnl. Tech., U. Houston, 1999. Programmer Control Applications, Houston, 1985-86, Tex. Eastern Pipeline, Houston, 1988-90; instr. computer sci. San Jacinto Coll., Houston, 1990-94; computer sci. reader Ednl. Testing Svc., Houston, 1996—2000; programmer for shuttle cockpit avionics upgrade United Space Alliance, 2000—02; programmer Creative Process Cons., League City, Tex., 2003—06. Adj. instr. U. Houston, Clear Lake, Tex., 1996, 99, 2003-05; sponsor Computer Sci. Club, Houston, 1992-94. Mem.: AIAA, IEEE (assoc.), U. Houston Clear Lake Alumni Assn., U. Houston Alumni Assn., Kappa Delta Pi, Phi Delta Kappa. Personal E-mail: burnwuffie@aol.com.

LARSON, JOAN ISBELL, musician, educator; b. Seattle, Wash., May 14, 1934; d. Robert Lyle and Lillian Darnall (Soward) Isbell; m. Carl Frithiof Larson, May 31, 1956; children: Dale James, Linda Darleen, Brian Carlyle, Mark Edward. BA magna cum laude Edn with music major, U. Ariz., Tucson, 1956, postgrad. studies, 1965—69; master counseling courses, Liberty U., Lynchburg, Va. Cafeteria food server Yellowstone Nat. Park, Wyo., 1955; tchr. 3d grade Lineweaver Sch., Tucson, 1956—57; substitute tchr. Owego-Appalachian Schs., 1966—69; saleswoman Worldbook-Childcraft, Field Entrpises, Owego, NY. Accompanist, performer religious services Chs. of Many Christian Denominations and charity events, 1985—; ch. pianist and singer Nichols United Meth. Ch., NY, 1978—; private music tchr. self-employed, Owego, NY, 1959—. Contbr. poetry to Poetic Voices of Am. Trainee to be mediator and emergency responder Broome and Tioga Counties, NY, 2005—; peformer with comty. groups and local bands, 1995—; spiritual dir. and guide Candlehouse Teen Challenge, Owego, NY, 1996—, edn. dir., 1995—2003. Recipient Gold Ring award, Sherwood Music Sch., Chgo., 1952; scholar summer session, 1951. Mem.: Am. Coll. Musicians (Internat. Piano Recording Competition, 6th place Tchr. Divsn. 1986, Paderewski medal 1996), Nat. Guild of Piano Tchrs. (adjudicator), Am. Assn. Christian Counselors., Phi Kappa Phi, Pi Lambda Theta, Sigma Alpha Iota. Avocations: art, gardening, dance.

LARSON, JUDY L., museum director, curator; b. Glendale, Calif., Mar. 9, 1952; d. John Arthur and Lorraine V. Larson. BA, UCLA, 1974, MA, 1978; PhD, Emory U., 1998. Acting asst. curator Los Angeles County Mus. Art, L.A., 1978; sr. cataloguer Am. Antiquarian Soc., Worcester, Mass., 1978-85; curator High Mus. Art, Atlanta, 1985—98; exec. dir. Art Museum of W. Va., W.Va., 1998—2002; dir. Nat. Museum of Women in the Arts, Washington, 2002—. Author: (catalogue) Am. Illustration 1890-1925, 1986; co-author: (catalogue) Am. Paintings at High Mus. Art, 1994; editor: Graphic Arts and the South, 1993. Office: Nat Museum of Women in the Arts 1250 New York Ave NW Washington DC 20005

LARSON, LAVONNE FAY, education educator; b. Hettinger, N.D., July 18, 1944; d. J. Hilton Larson and Cordelia M. Larson-Wegner. BA, North Ctrl. Bible Coll., 1967; BS in Edn., Greenville Coll., 1971; MS, N.D. State U., 1981; EdD, U. N.D., 1991. Tchr. h.s. Assemblies of God H.S., Suva, Fiji, 1974-78, Baker (Mont.) Pub. Schs., 1978-80; prof. Trinity Bible Coll., Ellendale, N.D., 1981—. Office: 50 6th Ave S # 196 Ellendale ND 58436-7105 Business E-Mail: llarson@trinitybiblecollege.edu.

LARSON, LYNN WOOD, artist, musician; b. Twin Falls, Idaho, Mar. 22, 1935; d. Harvey Edgar and Carrie Lane (Meiden-Powel) Wood; m. Donald Keith Larson; children: Angela Lynne, Gregory Donald. Student, U. Idaho, Moscow, Idaho, 1954. Artist, 1967—. One-woman shows include, Bozeman, Mont., 1967, Gooding Libr., 1967, War Meml. Hall, Montana, Md., Idaho, 2000. Recipient Best of Fair, Oil painting, 1993, 1995, 1999, 2002, 2005. Mem.: Sage Brush Art Guild (pres. 1992—93), Am. Legion Aux. Avocations: music, piano, auto harp, organ. Home and Office: 1105 Calif St Gooding ID 83330-1726 Business E-Mail: lynnanddkl@onewest.net.

LARSON, MARILYN J., retired music educator; b. Lindstrom, Minn., July 20, 1933; d. Reuben and Dorothy (Holm) L.; m. Harold P. Cohen, Aug. 4, 1957 (div. Dec. 1975); children: Paul, Morrie, Robert. BS with distinction, U. Minn., 1955, MA with honors, 1957. Nat. cert. tchr. music; cert. tchr., Minn.; lic. realtor. Tchr. U. Minn., Mpls., 1955-57, Mpls. Jr. High Sch., 1957-60; piano tchr. pvt. studio, Fridley, Minn.; tchr. Mpls. Pub. Schs., 1976-78, St. Paul Pub. Schs., 1978-97. Designed music curriculum Mpls. Pub. Schs.; mem. INS Roundtable, 2000-04; accompanist Adult Day Care, St. Mary's Home, 2001-04; piano music for vets., 2000-03. Accompanist U. Minn. Chorus, 1953-56, Berkshire Music Ctr. at Tanglewood, Mass., 1953. Mem. Music Tchrs. Nat. Assn., Fedn. for Am. Immigration Reform, Minnesotans for Immigration Reform (founder, exec. dir. 1999—). Independent. Luth. Avocations: reading, music. Home: 5890 Stinson Blvd Fridley MN 55432-6002 E-mail: marilynmusic@webtv.net.

LARSON, NANCY CELESTE, information technology manager; b. Chgo., July 17, 1951; d. Melvin Ellsworth and Ruth Margaret (Carlson) L. BS in Music Ed., U. Ill., 1973, MS in Music Edn., 1976; postgrad., Purdue U., 1982—86. Vocal music educator Consol. Sch. Dist., Gilman, Ill., 1975-77; elem. vocal music tchr. Sch. Dist. 161, Flossmoor, 1977-87; instr. Vander Cook Coll., Chgo., 1980-88; systems programmer analyst Sears, Roebuck & Co., 1987-92, tech. instr., 1989-90, project leader, 1990-91, sr. systems analyst, 1991-92, Trans Union LLC, 1992-94, mgr., 1994—2005, sr. mgr., 2006—. Tchr. adult computer edn. Homewood-Flossmoor HS, 1986—90. Chmn. Faith Luth. Ch., 1982-87, pres. bd., 1988-91, vocal soloist and voice-over performer. Mem. Ill. Music Educators Assn., Music Educators Nat. Conf., Ill. Educators Assn., Nat. Educators Assn., Am. ORFF Schulwerk Assn., Flossmoor Edn. Assn. (negotiator 1983-86). Republican. Avocations: swimming, reading, antiques. Home: Apt 904 1960 N Lincoln Park W Chicago IL 60614-6528 Office: Trans Union LLC 555 W Adams St Fl 4 Chicago IL 60661-3696

LARSON, SANDRA B., nursing educator; b. Chgo., Apr. 21, 1944; d. Richard Milward and Eldred Gertrude (Piehl) Blackburn; m. Eric Richard Larson, Nov. 25, 1967; children: Sarah, Keith. BS, No. Ill. U., 1966, MS, 1978. RN, Ill. Nursing educator Luth. Hosp., Moline, Ill., 1968-70; charge nurse ICU Peninsula Hosp., Burlingame, Calif., 1970-72; staff nurse Illini Hosp., Silvis, Ill., 1972-76; nursing educator Black Hawk Coll., Moline, 1976—. Co-author: Anatomy and Physiology Testbank, 1994, 97, 99. Mem. ANA, Ill. Nurses Assn. (5th dist. treas. 1982-84, pres. 1984-86, 1st v.p. 1986-87, pres. 1988-92, 2nd v.p. 1993-95), Sigma Theta Tau. Democrat. Roman Catholic. Avocations: reading, quilting. Home: 3009 29th St Moline IL 61265-6950 Office: Black Hawk Coll 6600 34th Ave Moline IL 61265-5870 Business E-Mail: larsons@bhc.edu.

LARSON, SANDRA PAULINE, music educator; b. Milw., Jan. 27, 1944; d. Arthur Herman and Pauline Frances (Schneck) Voss; m. Dale Edwin Larson, Jan. 20, 1968; children: Eric Dale, Stephan Harold, Jonathan Arthur. MusB, Cardinal Stritch Coll., 1966; MusM, Southeastern La. U., 1992. Cert. Am. Coll. Musicians. Pvt. piano tchr., Slidell, La., 1974—; adj. faculty Delgado C.C. North Shore. Piano adjudicator Am. Coll. Musicians Nat. Guild, 1994—. Piano accompanist Slidell Little Theater, 1994, 2002, 2003, 2005. Named to Order of St. Louis, Archdiocese of New Orleans, 1989. Mem. Music Tchrs. Nat. Assn. (nat. cert., piano adjudicator 1990—), Nat. Guild of Piano Tchrs. (local chair 1993-2003), La. Music Tchrs. Assn. (state cert., piano adjudicator 1990—, chmn. electronic music 1994-97), North Shore Music Tchrs. Assn. (pres. 1993-96), La. Fedn. of Music Clubs (local co-chmn. 1996-2004). Roman Catholic. Avocations: sewing, crafts, reading. Home and Office: 1130 Rue La Tour Slidell LA 70458-2220

LARSON, VICKI LORD, academic administrator, communication disorders educator; b. Prentice, Wis., Sept. 21, 1944; d. Edward A. and Stella Mae (Hilton) Lord; m. James Roy Larson, Sept. 3, 1966. BSEd, U. Wis., Madison, 1966, MS, 1968, PhD, 1974. Speech-lang. pathologist Coop. Ednl. Svc. Agy. 2, Minoqua, Wis., 1967—69; instr. U. Wis., Whitewater, 1969—71, rsch. asst. Madison, 1971—73, asst. prof. Eau Claire, 1973-77, assoc. prof., 1977—81, prof. communication disorders, 1981—91, dept. chair, 1978—83, asst. dean grad. studies and univ. rsch., 1984—89, assoc. dean grad. studies and univ. rsch., 1989—91, interim chancellor, 2005—, prof. comm. Oshkosh, 1991—2000, dean Grad. Sch. Rsch., 1991—94, provost, vice chancellor acad. affairs, 1994—2000. Acquistions editor Thinking Publs., Eau Claire, 2001—04, acquistions mgr., 2004—. Author: Adolescents: Communication Development and Disorder, 1983, Communication Assessment and Intervention Strategies for Adolescents, 1987; contbr. Handbook of Speech-Language Pathology and Audiology, 1988, Language Disorders in Older Students, 1995, Working Out With Listening, 2002, Communication Solutions for Older Students, 2003, S-MAPs curriculum-based assessment, 2004, Aspergers Syndrome: Strategies for Solving the Social Puzzle, 2005; contbr.: Working Out With Writing, 2005. Fellow: Am. Speech, Lang., Hearing Assn. (councilor); mem.: Wis. Speech, Lang., Hearing Assn. (pres. 1976, honors 1991, pres. found. 2000—04, v.p. 2005—, treas. 2005—), Golden Key, Phi Kappa Phi, Omicron Delta Kappa. Avocations: traveling, quilting, reading. Office Phone: 800-225-4769. E-mail: larsonvl@uwec.edu.

LARSON, WANDA Z., writer, poet; b. Cle Elum, Wash., Aug. 26, 1926; d. Stanley Aloysius and Anele (Valente) Zackovich; m. Glen B. Larson, Nov. 18, 1950 (div. Mar. 1967); children: Karen Holk, Margot Huffman, Lisa Larson Landrey (dec. 1998). BA, U. Wash., 1949. Columnist North Bend Herald, Snoqualmie, Wash., 1955-61, Goldendale (Wash.) Sentinel, 1962-67; news editor West Seattle Herald, 1950-51; editor employee newsletter Alaska Steamship Co., Seattle, 1951; editl. asst. Associated Publs., Portland, Oreg., 1970-72, staff writer, 1974-78; pub. Blue Unicorn Press Inc., Portland, 1990—; poet Sta. KOPB, Portland, 1991—. Author: Portlandia, 1991, Miracle at Blowing Rock, 1992, Elisabeth: A Biography, 1997, 2nd edit., 2002, Our Flag - Born Through Valor, 1999, Bird Woman/Mojave (Sacajawea), 2001, of poems. Co-recipient 2nd pl. award Poetry Forum Quar., 1990; hon. mention Still Water Press, 1990. Avocations: humanitarian interests, history. Home and Office: PO Box 40300 Portland OR 97240-0300

LARSON-MILLER, JULIE KATHLEEN, English educator; d. Donn Samford Larson and Deonna Lee Wager; m. Merle Eugene Miller, Jr., June 24, 1989; children: Adam Merle Miller, Connor Larson Miller. BA in English, Ariz. State U., Tempe, 1987; MEd in Secondary Edn., Ariz. State U., 1991. Tchr. English Rhodes Jr. H.S., Mesa, Ariz., 1989—94, Santan K-8 Sch., Chandler, Ariz., 2003—04; 'tchr. English Stapley Jr. H.S., Mesa, 1994—2003, 2004—. Mem. curriculum rev. com., AA English tchr., mem. A+ applications com. Mesa Pub. Schs., 2004—, gifted tchr., 1989—2005. Mem.: Nat. Coun. Tchrs. English. Avocations: reading, writing, cooking. Home: 21422 S 140th St Chandler AZ 85249-9307 Office: Mesa Public Schools 3250 E Hermosa Vista Dr Mesa AZ 85213

LARUE, EVA MARIE, actress; b. Long Beach, Calif., Dec. 27, 1966; d. Luis and Marcie LaRue; m. John O'Hurley, 1992 (div. 1994); m. John Callahan, Nov. 30, 1996 (div.); 1 child, Kaya McKenna. Actor: (films) Dangerous Curves, 1988, Crash and Burn, 1990, Heart Condition, 1990, Legal Tender, 1991, Ghoulies II: Ghoulies Go to College, 1991, RoboCop 3, 1993, Mirror Images II, 1994, Little Pieces, 2000; (TV series) Santa Barbara, 1988, All My Children, 1993—97, 2002—05 (Outstanding Performace in a Daytime Drama, Nat. Coun. La Raza, ALMA award (Am. Latin Media Arts), 2006), Head Over Heals, 1997, Third Watch, 2000—01, Soul Food, 2000—01, George Lopez, 2005, CSI: Miami, 2005—, (guest appendences) Charles in Charge, 1989, Perfect Strangers, 1989, Married with Children, 1990, Dallas, 1991, Dark Justice, 1992, Nurses, 1993, Diagnosis Murder, 1998, Soldier of Fortune, Inc., 1999, Grown Ups, 1999, For Your Love, 1999,: (TV films) A Dream Is a Wish Your Heart Makes: The Annette Funicello Story, 1995, Remembrance, 1996, Out of Nowhere, 1997, One Hell of a Guy, 1998, Ice, 1998; host (TV series) New Candid Camera, Weddings of a Lifetime, The World's Funniest Videos, Above-the-Line Beauty, 2005. Recipient Gracie Allen Award, Found. Am. Women in Radio and TV. Avocation: Tae Kwon Do.*

LARUSSA, LUANN, small business owner; b. Scranton, Pa., Apr. 3, 1954; d. Dominick Anthony and Anita Marie (Piraino) LaR.; m. Charles S. Lehnert, June 21, 1975; children: Charles L., Keith L. BFA, Kutztown U., 1972-75. Camera supr. Pinwheel, N.Y.C., 1975-80; owner, pres. Parsippany (N.J.) Pinwheel, 1987—. Grad. asst. Dale Carnegie, N.Y.C., 1978. Mem. Assn. Graphic Arts, Morris County C. of C. (chmn. amb. com.), Rotary (pres.-elect Parsippany Troy-Hill chpt.). Republican. Roman Catholic. Avocations: drawing, painting, camping. Office: Pinwheel Grxphix PO Box 573 Mount Bethel PA 18343-0573 Office Phone: 973-227-2000.

LARWOOD, LAURIE, psychologist; b. NY, 1941; PhD, Tulane U., 1974. Pres. Davis Instruments Corp., San Leandro, Calif., 1966—71; cons., 1969—; asst. prof. orgnl. behavior SUNY, Binghamton, 1974—76; assoc. prof., chair dept. psychology Claremont (Calif.) McKenna Coll., 1976—83, assoc. prof. bus. adminstrn., 1976—83, Claremont Grad. Sch., 1976—85; prof., head dept. mgmt. U. Ill., Chgo., 1983—87; dean sch. bus. SUNY, Albany, 1987—90; dean Coll. Bus. Adminstrn. U. Nev., Reno, 1990—92, prof., 1990—2003, prof. emerita, 2003—; dir. Inst. Strategic Bus. Issues, 1992—2003; mng. ptnr. Quail Lane Studios, Reno, 2003—. Western regional adv. coun. SBA, 1976-81; dir. Mgmt. Team; pres. Mystic Games, Inc.; mng. ptnr. Quail Lane Studios, 2003-. Author: (with M.M. Wood) Women in Management, 1977, Organizational Behavior and Management, 1984, Women's Career Development, 1987, Strategies-Successes-Senior Executives Speak Out, 1988, Women's Careers, 1988, Managing Technological Development, 1988, Impact Analysis, 1999; mem. editl. bd. Sex Roles, 1979-2003, Consultation, 1986-91, Jour. Orgnl. Behavior, 1987-2003, Jour. Vocat. Behavior, 1999-, Group and Orgn. Mgmt., 1982-84, editor, 1986-91; founding editor Women and Work, 1983, Jour. Mgmt. Case Studies, 1983-87; contbr. articles to profl. jours. Mem. Acad. Mgmt. (editl. rev. bd. Rev. 1977-82, past chmn. women in mgmt. divsn., managerial consultation divsn., tech. and innovation mgmt. divsn.), Am. Psychol. Assn., Assn. Women in Psychology. Office: Quail Ln Studios 10225 N Quail Ln Tucson AZ 85742 Mailing: Box 89789 Tucson AZ 85752 Personal E-mail: larwood@earthlink.net.

LARWOOD, SUSAN ELIZABETH, elementary school educator; d. Edward Wayne and Marianna Larwood. AA in Human Svcs., Golden West Jr. Coll., Huntington Beach, Calif., 1979; BA, Calif. State U., Long Beach, 1984; MA, U.S. Internat. U., San Diego, 1990. Lic. psychol. nurse, Calif.; Calif. State Tchg. Credential. Educator Del Obispo Elem. Sch., San Juan Capistrano, Calif., 1986—89, George White Elem. Sch., Laguna Niguel, Calif., 1989—2001, Don Juan Avila Elem. Sch., Aliso Viejo, Calif., 2001—. Mem. various coms., curriculum leader and exercise path designer Capistrano Unified Sch. Dist.; yearbook advisor George White Sch., 1991—2001, student coun. advisor, 1986—. Recipient Tchr. of Yr., Capistrano Unified Edn. Assn., 1995, hon. svc. award, PTA, 1995, Star Fish award, 2001. Mem.: Calif. Tchrs. Assn. (corr.). Office: Capistrano Unified Sch Dist San Juan Capistrano CA 92675 Personal E-mail: suelarwood@cox.net.

LARY, LYNN M., computer scientist, educator; b. Oxnard, Calif., May 13, 1966; d. Benjamin Eli and Judith Ellen Lary. B.S. Applied Math., Calif. State Poly. U., Pomona, Calif., 1988, Tchg. Credential, 1988—89, MA Edn., Computer Tech. emphasis, 1991; PhD, U. Oreg., Eugene, Oreg., 2002. Cert. Ryan Single Subject Tchg. Credential Calif., 1989, lic. Standard Advanced Math. Tchg. Oreg., 1992. Math. instr. Claremont H.S., Claremont, Calif., 1988—92, Thurston H.S., Springfield, Oreg., 1992—93, Ln. C.C., Eugene, Oreg., 1993—94; instrnl. tech. specialist Ln. Edn. Svc. Dist., Eugene, Oreg., 1994—. Online mentor HP Tech. for Tchg. Program, Nationwide, 2004—; online mentor coord. Oreg. US West/NEA Tchr. Network, Oreg., 1997—98; preparing tomorrow's tchr. to use tech. inservice tchr. component facilitator U. Oreg., Eugene, Oreg., 2002—03; oreg. content standards and tech. web site developer U. Oreg., Eugene, Oreg., 1999—2001; eisenhower tech. leadership cadre coord. Oreg. US West/NEA Tchr. Network, Eugene, Oreg., 1998—99, tech. leadership cadre workshop inst. trainer, 1997—97, outreach trainer, Oreg., 1997—98, online mentor, Oreg., 1996—97, staff devel. cons. & inst. trainer, Eugene, Oreg., 1996—97. Past pres., pres., regional rep. Orgn. for Ednl. Tech. and Curriculum, Wilsonville, Oreg., 1996—2005; edn. svc. dist. rep. NW Coun. for Computer Edn., Coeur d'Alene, Idaho, 1998—2002; poster session coord. 2003 necc poster session coord. Nat. Ednl. Computing Conf. (NECC), Seattle, Wash., 2002—03; conf. program com. co-chair NW Coun. for Computer Edn., Portland, Oreg., 2002—03; treas. Ln. County Edn. Assn., Eugene, Oreg., 1997—98, co-president, 2001—03, sec., 2003—04. Recipient Mem. of the Yr., Ln. County Edn. Assn., 2001, Jaime Escalante Award, LA Ednl. Partnership/ARCO, 1991, Tchr. of the Month, Claremont H.S., 1989, Mem. of the Yr., Ln. County Edn. Assn., 2001-02; grantee Tech. Literacy Challenge Fund, Oreg. Dept. of Edn., 2000, No Child Left Behind (NCLB) Title IID: Enhancing Edn. Through Tech., 2004, Tech. Grant, NEA, 2002, Local Leader Grant, Oreg. Edn. Assn., 2001, 2002. Mem.: Internat. Soc. for Tech. in Edn., NW Coun. for Computers in Edn. Avocations: geocaching, passport in time projects, road trips. Office: Ln Edn Svc Dist 1200 Highway 99 North Eugene OR 97402 Office Phone: 541-461-8216. Office Fax: 541-461-8298. Personal E-mail: llary@lynnlary.com. Business E-Mail: llary@lane.k12.or.us.

LASAK, JANICE UNDERHILL, elementary school educator; d. Charles A. and Dorothy Stahl Underhill; m. Frank A. Lasak, July 19, 1986; children: Sarah Elizabeth, Johanna Marie, Catherine Frances. BS, Westminster Coll., New Wilmington, Pa., 1978. Cert. tchr. Pa., Va. Elem. tchr. Warren County Sch., Front Royal, Va., 1978—85; mid. sch. math. tchr. Oxford (Pa.) Area Sch. Dist., 1985—. Costume coord. Oxford Ctr. for Dance; choir Penningtonville Presbyn. Ch., Atglen, Pa., 1992—2006; handbell choir dir. Penningtonville Ringers, Atglen, 2001—06; session mem. Penningtonville Presbyn. Ch., Atglen; planning com. Chester County Buddy Walk, West Chester, Pa., 2003—06. Mem.: Chester County Down Syndrome Interest Group. Presbyterian. Avocations: singing, reading. Office Phone: 610-932-6615. Business E-Mail: jlasak@oxford.k12.pa.us.

LASALLE, DIANA MARGARET, consulting company executive, author; b. Akron, Nov. 9, 1949; d. Frank Charles and Margaret Audrey (Penzenik) LaSalle; m. William Joseph Sanders, Mar. 25, 1972 (div. 1979); children: Aaron Michael, Phillip Andrew; m. Richard Lee Deterding, Apr. 4, 1981 (div. 2001). AA, U. Akron, 1972. Sec. U. Akron, 1969-72; office mgr. Buckeye Fence Co., Akron, 1979-84; designer/writer Dymar Agy., Akron, 1980-83; pres. Dymar Agy., Inc., Gurnee, Ill., 1984-97, Dymar Group, Gurnee, Ill., 1997—2000, Diana LaSalle & Assocs., Savannah, Ga., 2002—. Cons. Smithsonian Nat. Mus. Natural History, Washington, 1989—91. Author: Priceless: Turning Ordinary Products into Extraordinary Experiences, 2002; contbr. articles to profl. jours. Bd. dirs. No. Ill. Coun. for Alcoholism and Substance Abuse, 1994-97, adminstrv. v.p. women's bd., 1994-97. Recipient Design award HOW Mag., 1990; named Woman of the Yr. Wadsworth Jaycee Women, 1979, 83; named to Ohio Jaycee Women Hall of Fame, 1981. Mem. U.S. Equine Mktg. Assn. (pres. chmn. bd. 1989-90), Women's Bus. Exch. (pres. 1988-89), Horse Coun. of Ill. (bd. dirs. 1991-94), Am. Horse Pubs., Am. Horse Coun. Republican. Lutheran. Avocation: writing. Office: Diana LaSalle & Associates 66 Palmer Blvd Savannah GA 31410

LASAROW, MARILYN DORIS, artist, educator; b. Seattle, Oct. 23, 1928; d. Samuel Irving and Molly Pearl Powell; m. William Julius Lasarow, Feb. 4, 1951; children: Richard Michael, Elisabeth Hollins Lasarow Tozzi. BA cum laude in Philosophy, Stanford U., 1950. Pvt. art tchr., L.A., 1968—2003. One-woman shows include Feigen Palmer Gallery, L.A., 1967, exhibited in group shows at Purdue U., Ind., 1965, L.A. County Mus. Art, 1966, Feigen Palmer Gallery, L.A., 1966, Occidental Coll., Eagle Rock, Calif., 1967, Lytton Gallery, L.A., 1968, featured, in L.A. Times, Art Forum and Art in Am., work appeared on cover, Home Sect., L.A. Times, 1967. Mem.: AAUW, Nat. Mus. Women in Arts, L.A. Mus. Contemporary Art, L.A. County Mus. Art (award 1966—67), Cap and Gown, Phi Beta Kappa. Avocations: gardening, tennis, photography, filmmaking. Home: 11623 Canton Pl Studio City CA 91604 E-mail: wlasarow@mindspring.com.

LASATER, JENNIFER A., history educator, dance educator; b. Huntsville, Ala., July 29, 1981; d. Ray and Diane Brown Lasater. BA in History, U. Ala., Huntsville, 2003. Dance instr. Cmty. Ballet, Huntsville, 2001—, The Dance Co., Madison, Ala., 2002—05; history tchr. Sparkman H.S., Harvest, Ala., 2004—, dance team coach, 2005—. Choreographer (contemporary jazz dance) Forsaken, (tap/jazz dance) Dixie Chicken (winner Panoply of the Arts Choreography Competition), Tennessee Valley Vipers Dance Team, dancer, choreographer (musical theater) Chorus Linebackers, Sparkman H.S. Show Choir. Tchg. students about the constn. and citizenship We the People, Harvest, Ala., 2005—06. Office: Sparkman High School 2616 Jeff Rd Harvest AL 35749 Office Phone: 256-837-0331. Office Fax: 256-837-7673. Personal E-mail: jalasater@gmail.com. Business E-Mail: jlasater@madison.k12.al.us.

LASHER, ESTHER LU, minister; b. Denver, June 1, 1923; d. Lindley Aubrey and Irma Jane (Rust) Pim; m. Donald T. Lasher, Apr. 9, 1950 (dec. Mar. 1982); children: Patricia Sue Becker, Donald T., Keith Alan, Jennifer Luanne Oliver. A of Fine Arts, Colo. Women's Coll., 1943; BA, Denver U., 1945, MA, 1967; MA in Religious Edn., Ea. Bapt. Sem., 1948; grad., Jerusalem Ctr. for Bibl. Studies, 1995. Ordained to ministry Bapt. Ch., 1988. Christian edn. dir. 1st Bapt. Ch., Evansville, Ind., 1948-52; min. Perrysburg Bapt. Ch., Macy, Ind., 1988-95; min.-at-large Am. Baptist Conv./USA, 1996—; interim pastor United Bapt. Ch., Lewiston, Maine, 1997-98. Libr. Peru (Ind.) Pub. Schs., 1990—91; sec. Ind. Ministerial Coun., Indpls., 1990—92; chairperson Women in Ministry, Indpls., 1988—93; min. Kairos Ministry to Women in Prison, 2002; chmn. Fellowship Mission Circle, Rochester, Ind., 1988—93; mem. Partnership in Ministry, Indpls., 1990—94; bd. mgrs. Am. Bapts./Ind., 1991—93; asst. dir. Greenwood Pub. Libr., 1978—84; dir. Fulton County Pub. Libr., 1984—90; ch. & cmty. chair Am. Bapt. Conv. of Maine, 2002—06; caregiver Edge Nursing Home, Damariscotta, Maine, 2002—, chaplain, 2004—. Mem. Evansville Symphonic Orch., 1948—55, Denver Civic Orch., 1955—65, Augusta Symphony Orch., 1998—, Midcoast Cmty. Orch., 1999—; founder Fulton County Literacy Coalition, Rochester, 1989—90; tutor/trainer Peru Literacy Coalition of Peru Pub. Libr., 1994—95; active CASA Lincoln Co., Maine, 1996—; vol. libr. Rutherford Libr., South Bristol, Maine, 1996—, So. Bristol Libr., Lincoln Retirement Home; mem. Sea Coast Cmty. Orch., 1999—; chair for ch. and cmty. ABC of Maine, 2002—; chmn. diaconate bd. Damariscotta Bapt. Ch., 2004—; tutor Literacy of Lincoln County, 2005—, Lincoln County Literacy Damariscotta, 2005—; chaplain Coves Edge Nursing Home, Damariscotta; sec.-treas. North Miami County Mins. Fellowship, 1993—95; chmn. Christian Edn. Bd. and ch. planter, Denver, 1953—59, Colorado Springs, 1959—68; chaplain vol. Miles Hosp., 1997—; prayer advisor Christian Women's Club Damariscotta Bapt. Ch., 1997—2002, hostess, 1995—97, exec. bd., 1995—, chair missions com., 1997—, small group, 2003—, Sunday sch. tchr., 2006—; pres. Women's Mission Cir., Damariscotta Bapt. Assn., 1997—; chaplain-on-call Miles Meml. Hosp.; sec. Lincoln County Clergy, 1998—; ch. planter Indpls. and Zionsville, 1970—82; bd. dirs. Manitau Tng. Ctr., Rochester, 1988—90, Peru Civic Ctr., 1995; pres. Toastmasters, Rochester, 1984—90, 1995, edn. v.p., 1992—93; v.p. Mental Health Ctr., Rochester, 1987—90; sec. Northwest Area ABC/IN, 1994—95. Named Outstanding Libr., Biog. Inst., 1989, Profl. Woman of Year, 2005. Mem. Leadership Acad. (bd. dirs., sec.), Bus. and Profl. Women (pres. Greenwood, Ind. chpt.

1984-86), Rochester Women's Club (pres. 1989-92), Fulton County Mins. Assn. (treas. 1993-95), Logansport Assn. Bapt. Women, Peru Lit. Club (v.p.-elect 1995), CASA Miami County, Rotary, Sigma Alpha Iota (adv.), Christian Edn. (chmn. 1996-98), Damariscotta Assn. Women (pres. 1998—, mem. small ch. com. 1998-2003, chmn. diaconate bd. 2001—), Christian Women's Club (prayer group 1999—); Success 6 Reader Program, 2004-, Tutoring to Read Literacy Program. Republican. Home and Office: 2063 State Route 129 South Bristol ME 04568-4317

LASHER, LORI L., lawyer; b. June 16, 1960; BA in polit. sci. magna cum laude, Westminster Coll., 1981; JD cum laude, Dickinson Sch. Law, 1984. With Reed Smith LLP, Phila., 1994—, mem. exec. com., head mergers & acquisitions/gen. corp. practice group. Mem. exec. bd. Homeless Advocacy Project. Mem.: Phila. Bar Assn., Pa. Bar Assn., ABA. Office: Reed Smith LLP 2500 One Liberty Pl 1650 Market St Philadelphia PA 19103-7301 Office Phone: 215-851-8136. Office Fax: 215-851-1420. Business E-Mail: llasher@reedsmith.com.

LASHER, SANDRA LEE, minister, artist; b. Buffalo, Feb. 14, 1943; d. Jeremiah Charles and Margaret Henry Lasher; children: William Charles Ronolder, Christin Elizabeth Ronolder. BS in Art Edn., SUNY, New Paltz, 1964; MA in History, St. Bonaventure U., 1973; MDiv, Wesley Theol. Sem., Washington, 2002. Ordination 2005. Tchr. art Jenny F. Snap Jr. H.S., Endicott, NY, 1964—66, Hinsdale Ctrl., NY, 1972—98; pastor Limestone United Meth. Ch., NY, 1993—98, Gerraddstown/Ganotown, W.Va., 1998—2002; min. Belmont-SCLD United Meth., NY, 2002—. Pres. Olean Art Assn., NY, 1976; elder United Meth. Ch. Avocations: calligraphy, parament designs. Home: 17 Willets Ave Belmont NY 14813 Office: United Meth Ch 7 Park Cir Belmont NY 14813 Office Phone: 585-268-5471.

LASHLEY, BARBARA THERESA, psychologist, educator, mental health counselor; b. Cambridge, Mass., Feb. 26, 1944; d. Frederick Karl and Theresa Sarah (Greelish) Petersen; m. Leonard A.G.O. Lashley Jr., Oct. 1, 1964 (div. 1972); children: Leonard A.G.O. III, Matthew Adrian. AS in Psychology, Massasoit Community Coll., Brockton, Mass., 1977; BS in Phys. Geog., Bridgewater State Coll., 1979, MEd in Counseling Psychology, 1989. Therapist Mass. Treatment Ctr., Bridgewater, 1982-83; pers. dir. Dept. of Mental Health, Plymouth, Mass., 1983-84; maximum tier priviledge coord. Mass. Treatment Ctr., Bridgewater, 1985-88; guidance intern Martha Burwell Lab. Sch., Bridgewater, 1988; guidance counselor Epping (N.H.) Elem. Sch., 1989-90; cons. to nursing homes Heritage Hosp., Somerville, Mass., 1991—; counselor, tchr. Nutri System, Kingston, Mass., 1991-92; fee for svc. clinician South Shore Mental Health, Plymouth, 1992—; owner, therapist Children's and Family Guidance, 1989—. Cons. Easton (Mass.) Children's Mus., 1991; tchr. coll. gate summer program, Easton, 1989-91. Sec. Rocky Nook Point Improvement Assn., Kingston, 1984, treas., 1985; mem. adv. bd. Red Cloud Indian Sch., Pineridge, S.D., 1992—. Mem. AACD. Mem. Christian Ch. Avocations: gardening, cross country skiing, reading, birding. Home and Office: 64 Industrial Pk Rd Plymouth MA 02360

LASHLEY, FELISSA ROSE, dean, nursing educator, researcher; b. NYC, Apr. 6, 1941; d. Jack and Ruth (Dorbin) Lashley; divorced; children: Peter, Heather, Neal. BS, Adelphi Coll., 1961; MA, NYU, 1965; PhD, Ill. State U., 1973. Cert. Am. Bd. Med. Genetics., Am. Coll. Med. Genetics. Dean Coll. Nursing, Rutgers U., Newark, 2002—. Author: Clinical Genetics in Nursing Practice, 1998 (book of yr. award); editor: The Person with AIDS: Nursing Perspectives, 1987 (Book of Yr. award), Tuberculosis: A Sourcebook for Nursing Practice and Women, Children and HIV/AIDS (Book of Yr. award, 1993), Emerging Infectious Diseases: Trends and Issues, 2002, The Person with HIV/AIDS: Nursing Perspectives, 2000. Mem.: AAAS, ANA (coun. nurse researchers), Am. Coll. Med. Genetics, Ill. Nurses Assn., Midwest Nursing Rsch. Soc., Nat. League Nursing, Am. Acad. Nursing, Am. Soc. Human Genetics. Office Phone: 973-353-5293 ext. 647. Business E-Mail: flashley@rutgers.edu.

LASHOF, JOYCE COHEN, public health service officer, educator; b. Phila. d. Harry and Rose (Brodsky) Cohen; m. Richard K. Lashof, June 11, 1950; children: Judith, Carol, Dan. AB, Duke U., 1946; MD, Women's Med. Coll., 1950; DSc (hon.), Med. Coll. Pa., 1983. Dir. Ill. State Dept. Pub. Health, 1973—77; dep. asst. sec. for health programs and population affairs Dept. Health, Edn., and Welfare, Washington, 1977—78; sr. scholar in residence IOM, Washington, 1978; asst. dir. office of tech. assessment U.S. Congress, Washington, 1978—81; dean sch. pub. health U. Calif., Berkeley, 1981—91; prof. pub. health U. Calif. Sch. Pub. Health, Berkeley, 1981—94, prof. emeritus, 1994—. Co-chair Commn. on Am. after Roe vs. Wade, 1991—92; mem. Sec.'s Coun. Health Promotion and Disease Prevention, 1988—91; chair Pres.'s Adv. Com. on Gulf War Vets. Illnesses, 1995—97. Mem. editl. bd.: Wellness Letter, 1993—, Ann. Rev. of Pub. Health, 1987—90. Recipient Alumni Achievement award, Med. Coll. Pa., 1975, Sedgewick Meml. medal, APHA, 1995. Avocation: hiking. Home: 601 Euclid Ave Berkeley CA 94708-1331 Office: U Calif Sch Pub Health 140 Earl Warren Hl Berkeley CA 94720-7360 Office Phone: 510-642-2493. Business E-Mail: jlashof@berkeley.edu.

LASKARZEWSKI, DEBRA SUE, language educator; b. Bklyn., Apr. 26, 1968; d. Barry Charles and Frances Marilynn Blumen; m. James John Laskarzewski, July 13, 1996; children: Daniel John, Amy Rose. BA in French summa cum laude, U. N.H., 1990, MA in Tchg. summa cum laude, 1991. Level II profl. educator's lic. in French Vt. State Bd. Edn., level II profl. educator's lic. in Spanish Vt. State Bd. Edn. Summer field hockey camp coach U. N.H., Durham, 1987—95; tchr. English as 2d lang. Lycee Professionnel Robert Garnier, La Ferte Bernard, France, 1991—92; world lang. tchr. French and Spanish Missisquoi Valley Union Jr./Sr. H.S., Swanton, Vt., 1993—95; summer field hockey camp coach U. Vt., Burlington; head field hockey coach U.S. Field Hockey Assn. Future's Program (Olympic Devel.), Hanover, N.H., and Burlington, Vt., 1991—98; asst. field hockey coach U. Vt., Burlington, 1993—2000; world lang. and cultural comm. tchr. Union 32 Jr. /Sr. H.S., Montpelier, Vt., 1995—97; world lang. tchr. French and Spanish Williston (Vt.) Cen. Sch., 1997—; asst. field hockey coach U.S. Field Hockey Assn. Future's Program, Burlington, Vt., 1999—2001. Transl. computer installation manual Hallam Assocs., South Burlington, Vt. Team coord. Nat. Multiple Sclerosis Soc. and Williston Cen. Sch., 2001—05; vol. walker, fund raiser Nat. Multiple Sclerosis Soc., Burlington, 1999—2005; vol. mailer, fundraiser Am. Heart Assn., Essex Junction, Vt. Named one of 50 Greatest Sports Figures of Century (1900 - 2000) from Vt., Sports Illus., 1999; recipient athletic scholarship, U. N.H., 1986—91, 1989—91. Mem.: NEA, Phi Beta Kappa, Phi Kappa Phi (life). Avocations: field hockey, travel, running. Home: 1 Mohawk Ave Essex Junction VT 05452 Office: Williston Cen Sch 195 Central School Dr Williston VT 05495 Office Phone: 802-878-2762. Personal E-mail: skimail1@verizon.net. E-mail: laskarzewsd@wsdvt.org.

LASKOSKY, DONNA MARIE, secondary school educator; b. Hazleton, Pa., Apr. 1, 1977; d. Anthony Stephen and Wilma Florence Laskosky. B, Pa. State U., State College, 1999; M, Wilkes U., Wilkes Barre, Pa., 2003. Tchr., tennis coach Boyertown (Pa.) Area Sch. Dist., 2000—. Mem. NHS nomination com., mem. mid. state com. Boyertown Area Sch. Dist., 2002—. Mem.: NEA, Nat. Sci. Tchr. Assn., Pa. Sci. Tchr. Assn. Avocations: tennis, volleyball. Home: 533 E 4th St Apt 3 Boyertown PA 19512

LASPADA, CARMELLA, government agency administrator; BS in Psychology and TV Comm., Pa. State U., 1960. Founder No Greater Love, 1971; White House liaison and exec. dir. White House Commn. on Remembrance, 2001—. Initiator Nat. Moment of Remembrance, 2000. Named Washingtonian of Yr., Unsung Heroine, VFW Women's Aux.; recipient U.S. Spl. Ops. Command medal, Ellis Island Medal of Honor, Dickey Chapelle award, USMC League, Spirit of Enterprise award, U.S. C. of C., Rotary Club Humanitarian award, Outstanding Alumni award, Pa. State U., Woman of Yr. award, Christopher Columbus Assn. Office: White House Commn on Remembrance 1750 New York Ave NW Washington DC 20006

LASS, DIANE, counselor; b. Vermillion, S.D., June 26, 1957; d. Donald and Eunice Purvis; m. Steve Lass, Oct. 15, 1994; children: Steve, Chris, Jon Williams, Brandon Williams, Dustin Williams, Jonathan. BA in Psychology (hon.), Point Loma Nazarene U., 2000; MA in Psychology, Calif. Sch. Profl. Psychology, 2002; post grad. in Clin. Psychology, Alliant Internat. U., 2002—. Real estate sales and property mgmt. Purvis Realty, San Diego, 1983—97; crisis intervention counselor Halcyon Crisis Ho., El Cajon, Calif., 2001—02; therapist and sex offender group facilitator Calif. Dept. Corrections, San Diego, 2002—03; domestic violence counselor San Diego Family Justice Ctr., 2004—. Scholar, Alliant Internat. U., 2000—05; Presidents scholar, Point Loma Nazarene U., 1998—2000. Mem.: APA (assoc.). Personal E-mail: lassoct1015@aol.com.

LASSALETTA, ANTONIA MIR, language educator; b. Arecibo, P.R., Mar. 25, 1936; m. Manuel C. Lasaletta, Oct. 12, 1962; children: Margarita, Maria, Teresa, Manuel, Antonio. BA, U. Del Sagrado Corazión, San Juan, 1958; MA, Middlebury Coll., 1964. Exec. sec., home svc. dir. ARC, Mayaguez, PR, 1958—61; instr. Spanish Kimball Union Acad., Meriden, NH, 1963—64, Roanoke Coll., Salem, Va., 1965, U. Va., Roanoke, 1966, grad. instr. Charlottville, 1969; instr. Spanish Inter-Am. U., Bayamon, PR, 1976—78, Hawthorne Jr. High Sch., Charlotte, NC, 1984—; asst. prof. Johnson C. Smith U., 1984—92; instr. Spanish Indpendence High Sch., 1993—; asst. prof. Ctrl. Va. C.C., Lynchburg, 1993—. Mentor Johnson C. Smith U., 1985—92. Author: Intimo mundo compartido, 1986, short stories, poems; contbr. articles to profl. jours. Recipient frist prize, Sociedad Cultural Hispana, 1979, Santa Teresa medal, Colegio U. del Sagrado Corazon, P.R., 1958, 1st and 2d prizes, Cath. Daus. Am., San Juan, P.R., 1957; fellow Gov.'s fellow, U. Va., Dept. Romance Langs., Charlottesville, 1969—70.

LASSEN-FELDMAN, WENDY ANNE, sales executive, lawyer; b. Washington, Apr. 17, 1968; d. Allan Norris and Sylvia Judith (Wolf) L.; m. Evan Jay Feldman, Aug. 20, 1994; children: Harley Allyn, Nicholas Ryan. BA, U. Mich., 1990; JD cum laude, U. Balt., 1993. Bar: MD, 1993. Attorney Howell, Gately, Whitney & Carter, Towson, MD, 1993-94; placement coord. Attorneys Per Diem, Balt., 1994-95; applications cons. Lexis-Nexis, Washington, 1995-96, acct. mgr., 1996—. Bd. mem., application cons. adv. bd. Lexis-Nexis, Wash., 1995-96; corr. sec. U. Balt. Law student govt., Balt., 1992-93; mem. U. Balt. Faculty Appointment com.,1992-93. Exec. editor U. Balt. Law Rev., 1992-93, author, 1993; contbr. to legal publs. Pres. Child Study, Balt. chpt., 1999-2001; com. mem. Women's Leadership Coun. of The Associated Jewish Fedn. Balt., 2000-01; precinct chairperson Dem. Party, Md., 1995-96. Recipient Turner Svc. award, U. Balt., 1997, 98. Bd. mem. U. Balt. Law Sch. Alumni (co-chair); mem. ABA, Md. State Bar Assn. Democrat. Jewish. Avocations: art, guitar. Home: 2824 Quarry Heights Way Baltimore MD 21209-1060 Office: LEXIS-NEXIS 1150 18th St NW Washington DC 20036-3816 E-mail: wendy.lassen-feldman@lexis-nexis.com.

LASSER, GAIL MARIA, psychologist, educator; b. Saddle River, N.J., Feb. 29, 1960; d. Dominick A. and Genevieve M. Sanzo; children: Michael, Jason, Jonathan. BA, Seton Hall U., 1971; postgrad., Seton HaLL u., 1975—77; tchg. cert., William Paterson Coll., 1973; MA, Montclair State Coll., 1975. Cert. staff clin. psychologist N.J., 1977; lic. real estate agt. N.J., 1977, notary pub. Pub. rel. rep. European Health Spa, 1970—71; med. asst. Sci. Prevention and Rehab. Assn., 1973; grad. tchg. and rsch. asst. Montclair State Coll., 1973—74; clin. asst. Dr. Brower, 1974; instr. psychology Essex County Coll., 1976—77; clin. psychologist intern Cmty. Mental Health Ctr., Mt. Carmel Guild, Newark, 1976—77; lectr. St. Michaels Med. Ctr.-N.J. Coll. Medicine, 1977—80; instr. psychology Bergen Cmty. Coll., Paramus, NJ, 1977—. Asst. to ct. adminstr. Bergen County Cts., 1977—78; cons. telecom., 1994. Vol. Am. Heart Assn. Mem.: Am. Soc. Phy. Rsch., Am. Psychol. Assn., Psi Chi, Pi Lambda Theta. Home: 234 E Saddle River Rd Saddle River NJ 07458-2614

LASSITER, SHERI L., insurance company executive; b. Orange, N.J., Sept. 16, 1968; d. Robert and Joan Dixon; m. James E. Lassiter III, May 18, 1997. MBA, Rutgers U., 1992. Sr. bus. analyst AT&T, Morristown, 1992-95, fin. analyst, project mgr. Pitts., 1995-96, fin. analyst Bridgewater, N.J., 1996-97, sr. bus. analyst Short Hills, N.J., 1997-98; sr. bus. analyst/project mgr. Paragon Computer Profls., Cranford, N.J., 1998-2000; project mgr. Metlife, N.Y.C., 2000, project mgr. web develop., 2001. Mem. devel. program AT&T, Morristown, N.J., 1992-96. Author: (booklet) Order of the Eastern Star, 1999. Mem. choir Black History Celebration, 1995; mem. fundraising team Jr. Achievement, 2003. Mem. Order of the Ea. Star (officer 1998-2000, Outstanding Leadership award 1999), Drew Alumni, Black MBA Assn. Office: Metlife One Madison Ave New York NY 10010 E-mail: shersher68@yahoo.com.

LASSMANN, MARIE ELIZABETH, education educator, consultant; b. San Antonio, Mar. 13, 1945; d. William Taft and Ruby Elizabeth (Ward) Henry; children: Angela Smith, Molly Michaels, Honee Aylmer; m. Richard Allan Lassmann, Jan. 2, 1993. BS, Tex. A&I U., 1973, MS, 1979; PhD, U. Tex., 1991. Tchr. Sinton (Tex.) Ind. Sch. Dist., 1974-78, Kingsville (Tex.) Ind. Sch. Dist., 1978-89; tchg. asst. U. Tex., Austin, 1989-91; counselor Presbyn. Pan Am. Sch., Kingsville, 1992-94; assoc. prof. dept. curriculum and instrn. Tex. A&M U., Kingsville, 1994—, cons. continuing edn., 1984-95. Asst. adj. prof. Embry-Riddle Aero. U., Kingsville, 1992-94; author test questions for dental and optometry schs., 1991-92. Recipient scholarship Tex. Woman's Club, 1990-91. Mem. ASCD, Nat. Coun. Tchrs. Math. (referee 1994), Phi Kappa Phi, Delta Kappa Pi. Avocations: crocheting, painting, fishing, sewing. Business E-Mail: kfmel00@tamuk.edu.

LAST, MARIAN HELEN, social services administrator; b. L.A., July 2, 1953; d. Henry and Renee (Kahan) Last. BA, Pitzer Coll., 1975; postgrad., U. So. Calif., 1975-84; MS, Long Beach State U., 1980. Lic. marriage therapist. Coordinator City of El Monte, Calif., 1975-76, project dir. Calif., 1976—; pvt. practice psychotherapist Long Beach, Calif., 1982—; div. mgr. City of El Monte, 1982—. Cons. U. So. Calif. Andrus Ctr., L.A., 1977-78; bd. dirs. Coord. Coun., City of El Monte, 1975—, Sr. Pres.'s Coun., 1982—; Congl. del. White House Conf. on Aging, 1995; chair Nutrition Focus Group, L.A. Co. Area Agy. On Aging, 1993-2002, L.A. Long Term Care Coord. Coun., 2003—; mem. adv. coun. L.A. County Nutrition. Co-author rape survival guide, 1971. Dir., co-founder Rape Response Program, Pomona, San Gabriel Valley, Calif., 1971-80; cons. on sexual assault Pitzer Coll., Claremont, Calif., 1975-78; past pres. El Monte-South El Monte Coord. Coun. Recipient Susan B. Anthony award NOW, Pomona, 1976, Gold award Calif. Emergency Svcs. Assn., 1995, Founders award Project Sister sexual assault ctr., 2002. Mem. Am. Soc. on Aging, Calif. Assn. Sr. Ctr. Dirs. (dist. dir. XIII), Calif. Parks and Recreation Soc. (Profl. Citation award 1993), Calif. Assn. Marriage and Family Therapists, Women's Club, Civitan, Chi Kappa Rho Gamma. Democrat. Jewish. Avocations: golf, advocating rights of elderly. Office: City of El Monte 3120 N Tyler Ave El Monte CA 91731-3354 Office Phone: 626-258-8613.

LASYS, JOAN, medical/surgical nurse, educator; b. Siauliai, Lithuania, Sept. 1, 1924; arrived in Can., 1948; came to U.S., 1960; d. Joseph-Apolinarius and Elena (Šlapokaite) Barcevičius; m. Bill Lasys, July 31, 1949. RN degree, Lithuanian Red Cross Sch. Nursing, 1945; student, Ariz. State U., Tempe, 1981—86, Ea. Ariz. Coll., Thatcher, 1981—86. RN, Can., Nebr.; cert. nursing tchr., Ariz.; C.C., occupl. tchg. cert. Ariz. Staff RN St. Mary's Hosp., Montreal, Canada, 1949—51, Montreal Gen. Hosp., 1951—53, 1959—60; pvt. duty Nurses Registry, Montreal, 1953—56; Can. civil svc. RN R.H.O. Ctr. Dept. Vets. Affairs, Ottawa, 1956—57, Queen Mary Vets. Hosp., Montreal, 1957-58; staff RN St. Joseph's Hosp., Omaha, 1968—69, Meryvale Hosp., Phoenix, 1969—71, Valley View Hosp., Youngtown, Ariz., 1971—72, Boswell Hosp., Sun City, Ariz., 1972—76; RN Kivel Care Ctr., Phoenix, 1986—93, 2000—02. Past v.p. and officer Pine-Strawberry (Ariz.) Health Svcs.; columnist/reporter Payson (Ariz.) Roundup. Pub. (mag.) Small Town U.S.A.; prodr. audio tapes: Time Management, Nursing Communications; author numerous poems Mem. Payson Regional Med. Ctr. Aux.; mem Rep. Presdl. Task Force. Recipient Bronze Poet of Merit medal, Poetry Conv. and Symposium Intl. Soc. Poets, 2005, Silver bowl Outstanding Achievement in Poetry, 2005. Mem.: AAUW, Libr. Congress, Nat. Mus. Women in the Arts, Payson Libr., County Attys. and Sheriffs Assn. (hon.), Kivel Geriatric Ctr. Aux. (life), Arbor Day Found., Nature Conservancy, Cooking Club of Am. (charter). Republican. Roman Catholic. Avocations: cooking, poetry, public speaking, arts and crafts. Home: 506 N William Tell Cir Payson AZ 85541-4050

LATEGNO-NICHOLAS, CRISTYNE, travel company executive; d. Joseph and Mary Lategano. BA in Polit. Sci., Rutgers U., 1987. Press sec. Former Pres. George Bush; campaign spokeswoman Bill Bradley's 1992 Campaign; press sec. Mayor Rudy Giuliani, 1993—95, dir. comm., 1995—99, acting chief of staff; pres., CEO NYC & Co., N.Y.C., 1999—. Mem. arts, edn. and tourism adv. coun. Lower Manhattan Devel. Corp.; bd. dirs. Big Apple Greeter, Yale Women's Campaign Sch., NYU Tisch Sch. for the Arts, NYC2012. Named to, Crain's N.Y. Bus. "40 under 40", 2004. Mem.: N.Y. Soc. Assn. Execs. (bd. dirs.), Broadway Assn. (bd. dirs.), Internat. Assn. Conv. and Visitors Bur. (bd. dirs.). Office: NYC & Co 810 Seventh Ave New York NY 10019

LATENDRESSE, CHESSY NAKAMOTO, small business owner; b. Ashiya, Hyogo, Japan, Sept. 16, 1943; d. Eiji and Hideko (Nakamoto) Nishibayashi; m. John Robert Latendresse, Dec. 17, 1965; children: Gina Chiharu, John Robert Koji, Renee Nakamoto. Student, Japan, 1965, St. Michel, Kobe, Japan, 1965; Grad. Gemologist, Gemological Inst. Am., Calif. Cert. colon hygienist, clin. hypnotherapist, Japanese Reiki III master tchr. Co-owner Am. Pearl Co., Nashville, 1965—, Am. Pearl Farm, Camden, Tenn., 1979. Contbr. articles to profl. jours. Mem. Benton County Rep. Club, Camden, 1970—; pres. Camden Garden Club, 1969—; vol., tchr. spl. edn. Camden, 1970-86, Tenn. State Mus., Nashville, 1989. Named Outstanding Young Woman of Yr. for Working with Mentally Retarded, Camden, 1971; recipient Outstanding Display award Pacific Jewelry Show, 1974, Creativity award Benton County Fair, 1974, 75, 86, 89. Avocations: swimming, stringing beads, herbal healing. Office: 807 Watts Ln Nashville TN 37209 Office Phone: 615-353-1231. Business E-Mail: fancipearl@aol.com.

LATENDRESSE, LANELLE, financial services company executive; b. Bowie, Tex. d. Homer Warren and Florence (Bruce) Ward; children: Mary Burnette, James R. Asst. sec., exec. v.p. Lomas Fin. Corp., Dallas, 1960—. Mem. adv. bd. Operation Lift, 1984—. Mem.: Exec. Women Dallas (dir. 1983—), Toastmasters (Dallas), Downtowners Club.

LATHAM, CYNTHIA, elementary school educator; b. New Haven; d. Frederick and Beatrice Stevenson Latham. BA, U. Mary Hardin Baylor, Belton, Tex.; MA, U. Bridgeport, Conn. Cert. tchr. Conn., 2004. Health and fitness tchr. Post Coll., Waterbury, Conn., 1982; health tchr., phys. edn. tchr. Bridgeport Pub. Sch., 1987—97; phys. edn. tchr. Bridgeport Cath. Diocese, 2004—. Athletic advisor USA Track & Field. Author: Adventures of Frosty. Coach New Haven Age Group Track Club; track ofcl. World Para-Olympics; mem. task force Nat. Com. Phys. Edn.; mem. com. phys. fitness City of West Haven. Named Indoor and Outdoor Nat. Champion in Track and Field, Indoor Nat. Champion 20 pound weigh throw and shot put, 2005, Conn. State Champion 20 pound weight throw and shot put, 2005, Indoor Nat. Champion 20 pound weigh throw and shot put, 35 pound weight, 2006, Conn. State Champion 20 pound weight throw and shot put, 2006; recipient Olympic Silver medal, Outstanding Achievement award, State of Conn., 1986, Valuable Contbn. award, 1986. Mem.: AAHPERD (mem. Jour. Health Phys. Edn. 2006—), West Haven Hist. Soc. Avocations: nature, gardening, animals, running, weightlifting. Home: 444 Main St West Haven CT 06516

LATHAM, LAVONNE MARLYS, physical education educator; b. Garrison, Iowa, Mar. 17, 1942; d. Harry August and Vona Irene (Loveless) Hilmer; m. Robert Allen Latham Jr., July 21, 1979. BA, U. Iowa, 1964; postgrad., No. Ill. U., 1985, Western Ill. U., 1970-88, Bemidji State U., 1979. Cert. tchr., Ill. Tchr. phys. edn., elem. computer coord. Erie (Ill.) Community Unit 1, 1964—, Head counselor Camp Lenore Owaissa, Hinsdale, Mass., 1964-78. Mem. NEA, AAHPER, Ill. Assn. Health, Phys. Edn. and Recreation, U. Iowa Alumni Assn., Ill. Edn. Assn., Erie Tchrs. Assn. (pres. 1982-83), Nat. Audubon Soc., Nature Conservancy, Delta Kappa Gamma. Baptist. Avocations: violin, computers, photography, travel, outdoor activities. Home: 1002 6th St Erie IL 61250 Office: Erie Community Unit 1 605 6th Ave Erie IL 61250-9452

LATHAM, PATRICIA HORAN, lawyer; b. Hoboken, N.J., Sept. 5, 1941; d. Patrick John and Rosemary (Moller) Horan; m. Peter Samuel Latham, June 12, 1965; children: John Horan, Kerry Patricia. BA, Swarthmore Coll., 1963; JD, U. Chgo., 1966. Bar: D.C. 1967, U.S. Dist. Ct. D.C. 1967, U.S. Ct. Appeals 1967, U.S. Supreme Ct. 1970, Va. 1989, U.S. Dist. Ct. (ea. dist.) Va. 1989, U.S. Dist. Ct. Md. 1991. Assoc. Fried, Frank, Harris, Shriver & Kampelman, Washington, 1966-69; atty. Office of Gen. Counsel, SEC, Washington, 1969-71; assoc. Martin & Smith, Washington, 1971—, ptnr., 1974-85, Latham & Latham, Washington, 1986—. Lectr. Columbus Sch. Law, Cath. U. Am., Washington, 1978-92; mem. panel of arbitrators N.Y. Stock Exch., 1985—; co-founder, co-dir. Nat. Ctr. Law and Learning Disabilities, 1992—; mem. disability adv. com. GED Testing Svc., 1999—. Co-author: Attention Deficit Disorder and the Law, 1992, Attention Deficit Disorder and the Law, 2d edit., 1997, Learning Disabilities and the Law, 1993, Learning Disabilities and the Law, 2d edit., 2000, Succeeding in the Workplace, 1994, Higher Education Services for Students with Learning Disabilities and Attention Deficit Disorder: A Legal Guide, 1994, Documentation and the Law, 1996, Tales from the Workplace, 1997, Terrorism and the Law: Bringing Terrorists to Justice, 2002; contbg. author: ADD and the College Student, 1993, A Comprehensive Guide to ADD in Adults, 1995, Managing Attention and Learning Disorders in Late Adolescence and Adulthood, 1996, Textbook of Pediatric Neuropsychiatry, 1998, Learning Disabilities and Employment, 1997, ADD in Children and Adults, 1999, Pediatric Neuropsychiatry, 2006. Co-founder, trustee Beacon Coll., 1989-93, chmn. bd. trustees, 1990-92; mem. adv. bd. Disability Law Reporter Svc., 1996-2001; bd. dirs. Watergate West, 2006—. Mem.: ABA, Learning Disabilities Assn. Am. (nat. adv. bd. 1996—2000, nat. bd. dirs. 2000—), Nat. Attention Deficit Disorders Assn. (bd. dirs. 1993—98, nat. adv. bd. 1998—), Am. Arbitration Assn. (panel arbitrators and mediators 1982—), Va. Bar Assn., DC Bar Assn., Ft. Myer and Ft. McNair Club. Roman Catholic. Home: The Watergate 2700 Virginia Ave NW # 707 Washington DC 20037 Office: Latham & Latham The Watergate 2700 Virginia Ave NW Washington DC 20037 Office Phone: 202-333-1713. Business E-Mail: latham_law@earthlink.net.

LATHAM, TAMARA BERYL, chemist, researcher; b. Brisbane, Australia, July 31, 1944; arrived in U.S., 1946; d. James Samuel and Beryl (Holzheimer) Latham. BS in Chemistry, CUNY, 1979, postgrad., 1979—81. With Novocol Chem. Co., Bklyn., 1980, Sloan Kettering Inst. Cancer Ctr., N.Y.C., 1984; chemist BOC Group, Murray Hill, NJ, 1984—95, Bayer Corp., West Haven, Conn., 1995—99; with Grolier/Scholastic, West Haven, 1999—2001; rsch. recruiter 20/20 Rsch., Nashville, 2002—05; tchr. Ansonia Mid. Sch., Ansonia, Conn., 2000—; sub. tchr. Nashville Metro Pub. Sch., Nashville, 2004—. Forum moderator metric poetry Moontown Cafe Website, 2001; sci. tchr. summers Schooner S/V Quinnipiack, New Haven, 1997, 98. Author: (poetry) Mirror Of My Soul, 1999, The Poet, 2003; contbr. articles to profl. jours. With USN, 1963—66. Recipient Amos Alonzo Stagg award, U.S. Navy, 1965, Editors Challenge award for poetry, Internat. Soc. Authors and Artists, 1996. Mem.: Am. Chem. Soc., Am. Legion, The Workshop Poets. Achievements include patents for cancer anti-emetic. Avocations: singing, reading, gardening, chess. E-mail: tblatham@yahoo.com.

LATHAN, CORINNA ELISABETH, aerospace engineer; b. Nov. 7, 1967; m. David Kubalak. BA in Biopsychology and Math., Swarthmore Coll., 1988; PhD in Neurosci., MIT, 1994, SM in Aeronautics and Astronautics, 1995. Asst. prof. biomed. engring. Cath. U., Washington, 1995—99, assoc. prof. biomed. engring., 1999—2000, assoc. adj. prof.; adj. prof. aerospace engring. U. Md., 2002—; founder, pres., CEO AnthroTronix, College Park, Md., 1999—; CEO AT KidSystems, 2005—. Mem. adv. bd. Cath. U. Am. Mem. editl. bd.: Jour. Human Performance in Extreme Environs., 1998—. Founder Keys to Empowering Youth; spl. projects advisor FIRST, Inc. Named Top Innovator of Yr., Md. Daily Record, 2002, Tech. Pioneer, World Econ. Forum, 2004; named one of Top 100 World Innovators Under the Age of 35, Tech. Review-MIT's Mag. of Innovation, Top 100 Women, Md. Daily Record, 2003, Young Global Leaders, Forum of Young Global Leaders, 2006; recipient Creating a Future of Opportunity award, Dept. Aeronautics and Astronautics, MIT, 2000, Women in Tech. Leadership award for entrepreneurship, 2002. Mem.: Assn. for Advancement of Med. Instrumentation (mem. human engring. stds. com. 1997—). Office: AnthroTronix Inc 387 Technology Dr Ste 1101 College Park MD 20742*

LATHAN, MONICA J., health science association administrator, epidemiologist; b. Columbia, S.C., Aug. 24, 1972; d. Thomas and Jannie MS Lathan. BS in Psychology, Univ. Md., Coll. Park, 1993; MPH, The George Wash. Univ., Washington, 1996. Cert. health edn. specialist. Crisis therapist Terros, Inc., Phoenix, 1994; outreach counselor Ednl. Talent Search Program, Coll. Pk., Md., 1995; rsch. asst. Share Our Strength, Washington, 1995—96; project coord. Am. Pharmacists Assn., Washington, 1997—98; epidemiologist Dept. of Health & Mental Hygiene, 1998—2001; health sci. analyst Am. Pub. Health Assn., Washington, 2001—. Contbr. articles numerous pub. to profl. jour. Fellow, DHHS. Fellow: Soc. of Pub. Health Educators; mem.: Met. Wash. Pub. Health Assn., Am. Nat. Svc., Drug and Alcohol Peer Educator, Am. Pharmacists Assn., Healthy Md. Project 2010, Am. Pub. Health Assn., Alpha Kappa Alpha. Avocations: painting, aerobics, travel, writing, perfoming arts. Business E-Mail: monica.lathan@apha.org.

LATHON, SHERAINE, clergyman; b. Chicago Heights, Feb. 20, 1952; d. Roosevelt Willingham and Norma L. Cobb; m. Willie Lathon, Jr., June 11, 1983; children: Eric, Christopher. AAS, Prairie State Jr. Coll., 1972; BS, Friends Internat. U., 1992, MS, 1994, PhD, 1997. Ordained to ministry, 1999. Collection mgr. Donnelley Directory, Chgo., 1973-87; ch. adminstr. Liberty Temple Full Gospel Ch., Chgo., 1987—, sr. pastor, 1999—. Assoc. prof. Logos Ministerial Tng. Inst., Friends Internat. U. Co-author: Recovery, 2000. Sec.-treas. Bushido-Kan Acad.; pres. Sheraine Lathon Evangelistic Ministries. Mem. NAFE. Office: Liberty Temple Full Gospel Ch 2233 W 79th St Chicago IL 60620-5803 E-mail: slathon1063@aol.com.

LATHROP, ANN, retired librarian, educator; b. LA, Nov. 30, 1935; d. Paul Ray and Margaret W.; divorced; children: Richard Harold, John Randolph, Rodney Grant. BA in History summa cum laude, Ea. N.Mex. U., 1957; MLS, Rutgers U., 1964; PhD, U. Oreg., 1988. Cert. elem. tchr., Calif.; cert. libr., Calif; adminstrv. credential, Calif. Elem. sch. tchr. Chalfont (Pa.) Boro Sch., 1960-61, Livingston Elem. Sch., New Brunswick, N.J., 1961-63, Rosedale Elem. Sch., Chico, Calif., 1964-65; libr. Chico (Calif.) H.S., 1965-72, Princeton (Calif.) H.S., 1972-73, Santa Maria (Calif.) H.S., 1973-77; libr. coord. San Mateo County Office Edn., Redwood City, Calif., 1977-89; assoc. prof. Calif. State U., Long Beach, 1989-92, prof., 1993—99; ret., 1999. Author: Online Information Retrieval as a Research Tool in Secondary School Libraries, 1988, Student Cheating and Plagiarism in the Internet Era: A Wake-Up Call, 2000, Guiding Students from Cheating and Plagiarism to Honesty and Integrity, 2005; co-author: Courseware in the Classroom, 1983. Mem. ALA, NEA, Am. Assn. Sch. Librs., Assn. State Tech. Using Tchr. Educators, Calif. Faculty Assn., Calif. Sch. Libr. Assn., Computer Using Educators, Internat. Soc. for Tech. in Edn. Avocations: travel, camping. E-mail: alathrop@csulb.edu.

LATIMER, ALLIE B., retired lawyer; b. Coraopolis, Pa. d. Lawnye S. and Bennie Latimer BS, Hampton Inst.; JD, MDiv, DMin, Howard U.; LLM, Cath. U.; postgrad., Am. U., 1960—61. Bar: N.C. bar 1955, D.C. bar 1960. Vol. in projects Am. Friends Svc. Com., N.J. and Europe, 1948—49; correctional officer Fed. Reformatory for Women, Alderson, W.Va., 1949—51; pers. clk. NIH, Bethesda, 1953—55; realty officer Mitchell AFB, NY, 1955—56; with Office Gen. Counsel, GSA, Washington, 1957—76, chief counsel, 1966—71, asst. gen. counsel, 1971—76, gen. counsel, 1977—87; asst. gen. counsel NASA, 1976—77; spl. counsel Gen. Svcs. Adminstrn., Washington, 1987—96. Past chmn. central office com. Fed. Women's Program, GSA; mem. membership and budget com. Health and Welfare Council, 1967-72 Bd. dirs. D.C. Mental Health Assn., pres., 1977-79; bd. dirs. Friendship House, Washington; elder Presbyn. Ch.; mem. com. on office of Gen. Assembly, Presbyn. Ch. USA; pres. Interacial Council, 1964-75; chmn. Presbyn. Econ. Devel. Corp., 1975-81; mem. governing bd. Nat. Council Chs. of Christ in U.S.A.; bd. trustees Johnson C. Smith Theol. Sem. Recipient GSA Sustained Superior Service award, 1959, Meritorious Svc. award, 1964, Commendable Svc. award, 1964, Pub. Svc. award, 1971, Outstanding Performance award, 1971, Presdl. Rank awards, 1983, 95, Disting. Svc. award, 1984. Mem. ABA, Nat. Bar Assn. (sec. 1966-74, Hall of Fame award 1999), Fed. Bar Assn., Washington Bar Assn. (Ollie M. Cooper award 1998, Hall of Fame award 2004), N.C. Bar Assn., Nat. Bar Found. (dir. 1970-71, pres. 1974-75), Hampton Alumni Assn. (pres. Washington chpt. 1970-71), Howard Law Alumni Assn. (v.p. alumni assns. 1962-63), Links (pres. Washington chpt. 1971-74, nat. v.p. 1976-80), Federally Employed Women (co-founder, 1st pres.). Home: 3050 Military Rd NW #520 Washington DC 20015-1364

LATIMER, HELEN, retired information resource manager, writer, researcher; b. Elizabeth, N.J. d. Raymond O. and Minna A. Mercner; divorced; children: Alexander, Victoria. AB, Duke U.; MS in Journalism, Columbia U.; cert. in bus. adminstrn., Harvard-Radcliffe; MBA in Mktg., Am. U.; attended, U. Calif., Berkeley, Rutgers U.; cert. in MBA Upgrade, Syracuse U., 1995. Instr. mktg. Am. U., Washington; mgr. info. resources Burdeshaw Assocs., Ltd., Bethesda, Md., 1985-94, assoc., 1994—; commr. Mayor's Commn. on Violence Against Women, Washington, 1996—2001, D.C. Commn. Women, 1996-99. Initiated publ. specialists program George Washington U., Washington; officer alumni bds. Harvard-Radcliffe Program in Adminstrn., Am. U.; comm., info. resource mgmt. cons., tech. editor MIT Servomechanisms Lab.; AA to editor Reinhold Pub. (former subs. McGraw-Hill); facilitator, subgroup on mktg. The White House Conf. on Libr. and Info. Svcs., 1991. Past leader Troop 1907, Girl Scouts Am.; mem. Troop 100 com. Boy Scouts Am.; pres. D.C. Unit Ch. Women United, 2003-05. Mem. Spl. Librs. Assn., Harvard Bus. Sch. Club D.C. (past v.p., bd. dirs.).

LATIMER, KATHARINE RUTH, lawyer; b. Lafayette, La., Apr. 5, 1961; d. Ewing Craig and Beverly Elise (Dalferes) L. BA magna cum laude, U. Tenn., 1983; JD cum laude, Georgetown U., 1986. Bar: D.C. 1986, US Dist. Ct., Md., DC, US Ct. Appeals, Third Cir., Fourth Cir., Sixth Cir., Seventh Cir., Eighth Cir., Ninth Cir., Tenth Cir., Eleventh Cir. Jud. clk. 19th Jud. Cir. Va., Fairfax, 1986-87; assoc. then ptnr. Spriggs & Hollingsworth, Washington, 1987—. Consulting editor, adv. mem. Expert Evidence Reporter; mem. Toxic Tort Adv. Council. Mem. ABA (litig. sect.), DRI, Bar Assn. D.C. Office: Spriggs & Hollingsworth 1350 I St NW Washington DC 20005-3399 Office Phone: 202-898-5800. Office Fax: 202-682-1639. Business E-Mail: klatimer@spriggs.com.

LATIOLAIS, MINNIE FITZGERALD, retired nurse, health facility administrator; b. Dec. 26, 1921; d. Thomas Ambrose and Mildred Surita (Nagle) Fitzgerald; m. Joseph C. Latiolais Jr., July 19, 1947; children: Felisa, Diana, Sylvia, Mary, Amelia, Joseph Clifton III. RN La. Asst. night supr. Touro Infirmary, New Orleans, 1943; orthopaedic surg. nurse Ochsner Clinic, New Orleans, 1943-47; asst. DON Ochsner Found. Hosp., 1947; supr. Lafayette (La.) Gen. Hosp., 1960-64; adminstrv. asst., supr. oper. rm. Abbeville (La.) Gen. Hosp., 1964-68; gen. mgr., neurol. surg. nurse J. Robert Rivet, neurol. surgeon, Lafayette, 1968-78; hosp. cons. assoc. B.J. Landry & Assocs.; hosps. cons. Lafayette, 1979-90; DON Acadia St. Landry Hosp., Church Point, 1981-82; supr. supplies, processing and distbn. Univ. Med. Ctr., Lafayette, 1982-90, ret., 1990. Pres. SW La. Rehab. Assn., 1979-80; mem. Mid-La. Health Systems Agy., 1977-82, project rev. chmn., 1978-80; vice chmn. Acadica Regional Clearing House, 1984-86; mem. crafts and practical nurse com. Lafayette Regional Vocat.-Tech. Inst., 1980-84, chmn. 1983-84. Roman Catholic.

LATNER, SELMA, psychoanalyst; b. Bronx, Aug. 11, 1920; d. Isidore and Jennie (Reisman) Levy; m. Harold Latner, Feb. 23, 1959 (dec. 1972); children: Gail, Karan, Irwin. BBA, CCNY, 1942; MSW, U. Pitts., 1945; PhD Psychoanalysis, Heed U., 1984. Cert. psychoanalyst; diplomate clin. social work, lic. marriage and family therapist N.J. Caseworker Clin. Social Worker, NJ, Jewish Family Svcs., N.Y.C., 1949—53, Cmty. Svc. Soc., Queens, 1950—60; sr. caseworker Jewish Family Svcs., Hackensack, NJ, 1965—68; sr. family and marriage therapist Bergen County Family Counseling Svc., Hackensack, 1968—83; pvt. practice psychoanalyst Teaneck, NJ, 1981—. Recipient Outstanding Profl. Human Svcs. plaque, Am. Acad. Human Svcs., 1974—75. Mem.: NASW (Gold Card), N.J. Inst. Tng. Psychoanalysis, Nat. Assn. Advancement Psychoanalysis, N.J. Soc. Clin. Social Work, Am. Anorexic and Bulimia Assn. (bd. dirs. Teaneck chpt. 1984—88, v.p., Eating Disorders Outstanding Svcs. award 1991), Nat. Alliance Family Life. Avocations: tennis, music, art, dance. Home: 27 Oakdale Ct North Haledon NJ 07508-2920

LA TORRE, CARISSA DANITZA, counselor; d. Luis Francisco and Elia Danitza La Torre. AA in Spanish, Saddleback C.C., Mission Viejo, Calif., 1995, AA in Psychology, 1995, AA in Bus. Adminstrn., 2002; BA in Spanish, Calif. State U., Fullerton, 1998, BA in Psychology, 1998, MS in Edn., 2000. Lic. Behavior Modification Case Mgr./Specialist Calif., 1999, cert. Specialist Mild/Moderate/Severe Disabilities Calif., 1999, Multiple Subject Calif., 1999, Single Subject Calif., 1999. Educator Capistrano Unified Sch. Dist., San Juan Capistrano, Calif., 1997—99; bilingual grad. rschr. UCLA/Calif. State U., 1998—2003; office/human resource mgr. GlobalStar Electronics, Inc., Aliso Viejo, Calif., 2002—03; birth mother counselor Adoption Network Law Ctr., Inc., Lake Forest, Calif., 2003—. Presenter in field of infant devel. Rep. and spkr. MADD, Tustin, Calif., 1996—; youth group ministry leader Mission San Juan Capistrano, 2001—. Recipient Dedication and Svc. in Counseling award, Outreach Concern, Inc., 1997, 1998. Mem.: Coun. Children with Behavioral Disorders (assoc. presenter internat. conf. 2001), Divsn. Early Childhood (assoc. presenter internat. confs. 2000—01), Harley Owners' Group (life), Phi Kappa Phi (life), Zeta Tau Alpha (life; pres. and v.p. 1995—97). Office Phone: 800-455-6055, 800-455-6055. Personal E-mail: xclatorre@collegeclub.com. Business E-Mail: carissal@adoptionnetwork.com.

LATORRE, DEBI, medical/surgical nurse; b. Mt. Vernon, Ohio, Nov. 25, 1956; d. Myron Gene and Lillie Frances (Nunn) Horn; m. Carmen Latorre, Mar. 29, 1980; children: Michael Brandon, Nicholas Daniel AS, Ctrl. Ohio Tech. Coll., Newark, 1983. RN, cert. med.-surg. nurse. Nurse Licking Meml. Hosp., Newark, Knox Cmty. Hosp., Mt. Vernon, staff nurse; charge nurse Mt. Carmel East Hosp., Columbus, Ohio. Recipient Excellence in Nursing award, Mt. Carmel East Hosp., 2004. Home: 3975 Miller Paul Rd Galena OH 43021-9474

LATORRE, MARIA JOANNE, health and physical education educator; b. Phila., Mar. 13, 1966; d. Daniel Romeo and Janet Marie Daddario; m. Peter Louis Latorre, June 15, 1991; 1 child, Gabriella Denise. BS in health, West Chester U., Pa., 1988. Health and physical edn. tchr. Pennsville Mid. Sch., NJ, 1990—. Soccer coach Pennsville Meml. HS, NJ, 1990—94; class advisor Pennsville Mid. Sch., NJ, 1992—. Roman Catholic. Avocations: dance, swimming, reading, travel. Home: 411 Sheffield Ct Runnemede NJ 08078 Office: Pennsville Mid Sch 4 William Penn Ave Pennsville NJ 08070

LATOURETTE, AUDREY WOLFSON, law educator; d. Benjamin and Ann Wolfson; m. John Latourette, May 26, 1974; 1 child, Joshua W. BA magna cum laude, Rutgers U., 1968; MA, Rowan U., 1971; JD cum laude, Temple U., 1975. Bar: N.J. 1975, Pa. 1975, Supreme Ct. of NJ. 1975, U.S. Dist. Ct. (ea. dist.) Pa. 1975. Tchr. elem. sch. Pennsauken (N.J.) Pub. Schs., 1968—72; atty. Wolf, Block, Schorr & Solis-Cohen, Phila., 1975—77, Audrey Wolfson Latourette, Esq., sole practitioner, Woodbury, NJ, 1977—83; prof. bus. law Richard Stockton Coll. N.J., Pomona, NJ, 1977—. Mem. dean's external adv. coun. Rutgers U., 1999—2003; presenter in field. Editor: Temple Law Qua., 1974—75; contbr. articles to profl. jours. Judge Nat. Mock Trial Competition, Phila., 2005; mem. Pa. parents vol. program U. Pa., Phila., 2004—06; mem. adv. panel affordable housing Mayor, Cherry Hill, NJ, 1988—94; mem. Sch. Age Child Care Com., Cherry Hill, 1986—87; bd. dirs. Italian Lang. Preservation Found., Phila., 2000—05. Named one of Five Notable Faculty, Richard Stockton Coll. N.J., 2005; named to Hall Finest Alumni, Rutgers U., 2006; recipient Sadie and Nathan Kessler award, Temple U. Sch. Law, 1973, Barenkopf award, 1973, Am. Jurisprudence Criminal Law, Adminstrv. Law and Constl. Law award, 1975, Merit award, Richard Stockton Coll. N.J., 1986, Outstanding Svc. award, Rutgers U., Camden, 2003, Best Paper award, McGraw Hill, 2006; fellow, Richard Stockton Found., 1989, 1992, 1996; grantee, Richard Stockton Coll. N.J., 1979, 1981, 1987, 1986, 1988, 1993, 1993, 1993, 1994, 1996, 2004, 2006, N.J. Dept. Higher Edn., 1985; scholar, Temple U. Sch. Law, 1973, Faculty Resource Network, NYU, 2004—05. Mem.: N.E. Acad. Legal Studies in Bus. (pres. 1989—90, co-editor Jour. Legal Studies 1992—95, Best Paper award 1994, 2005). Office: Richard Stockton College of New Jersey PO Box 195 Pomona NJ 08240-0195 Office Phone: 609-652-4426. Business E-Mail: audrey.latourette@stockton.edu.

LATSCH, NICOLE L., elementary school educator; b. Fort Atkinson, Wis., Sept. 25, 1978; d. Randy Latsch and Roxanne Shultz. AAS, AAS in Horse Sci. Tech., Blackhawk East Campus, Kewanee, Wis., 1999; BEd, U. Wis., Whitewater, 2005. Cert. tchr. Idaho, Wis. Self-employed riding instr., horse trainer, Fort Atkinson, 2001—05; tchr. Aberdeen Elem. Sch., Idaho, 2005—. Pvt. 1st class U.S. Army, 2000—01. Recipient 3d High Ind. Judge award, Am. Quarter Horse Assn., Okla. City, 1998. Mem.: Am. Quarter Horse Assn., Nat. Barrel Horse Assn., Am. Legion. Mailing: PO Box 107 Aberdeen ID 83210 E-mail: latschn@aberdeen58.org.

LATTA, DIANA LENNOX, retired interior designer; b. Lahaina, Maui, Hawaii, Aug. 5, 1936; d. D. Stewart and Jean Marjorie (Anderson) Lennox; m. Arthur McKee Latta, Jan. 26, 1957 (dec.); children: Mary-Stewart, Marion McKee Davidson. Grad., The Bishop's Sch., La Jolla, Calif., 1954; student, U. Wash., Seattle, 1954—56. Dir. Vero Beach (Fla.) br. of Wellington Hall Ltd., Thomasville, NC, 1970—72; asst. to chief designer Rablen-West Interiors, Vero Beach, 1972—75; design and adminstrv. asst. to pres. Design Studio Archtl. & Interior Design Concepts, Inc., Vero Beach, 1975—82; owner, designer The Designery, Vero Beach, 1983—87; designer's asst. Frank J. Lincoln Interiors, Inc., Vero Beach, Locust Valley, NY, 1987—90; sr. staff designer Chancellor's Inc., Bellingham, Wash., 1992—93. Leading actress (Vero Beach Theatre Guild prodns) The Laughmaker, 1964, Oklahoma, 1966, model Holly Fashion Show, Vero Beach, 1962—69. Mem. Indian River Meml. Hosp. Women's Aux., Vero Beach, 1957—70, chmn. charity ball and gift shop, 1960, v.p., 1962—64; advisor to steering com. The Malt Shoppe After-Sch. Program, Mill Creek, 1995—97; founding mem. McKee Jungle Gardens Preservation Soc., Inc.; mem. coun. Snohomish County Federated Health and Safety Network, 1999—2003; founding mem. Indian River Land Trust, Vero Beach, 1989—90; chmn. Mill Creek for Youth Com., 1994; bd. dir. and chmn. hospitality com. Vero Beach Mut. Concert Assn., 1973—76; mem. adv. bd. Indian River 4-H Horsemaster's Club, 1973—76; treas. bd. dir. McKee Jungle Gardens Preservation Soc., Inc., chmn. fundraising com., pub. rels. com., 1988; bd. dir. Vero Beach Theatre Guild, 1964; mem. adv. com. Safe and Drug Free Schs. Edmonds Sch. Dist., Wash., 1996—2002; mem. key leaders bd. Cmtys. That Care Project Edmonds Sch. Dist., 2001—. Mem.: Internat. Platform Assn., Riomar Bay Yacht Club (chmn. tennis com. 1964—66, club tennis champion 1964, 1966), Kappa Kappa Gamma (founding mem. Indian River Alumnae Club 1968—90, mem. adv. bd. U. Wash., Seattle chpt. 1997—2000, founding mem. N. Sound Alumnae Assn. 2002—). Republican. Episcopalian. Home: 16018 Village Green Dr # B Mill Creek WA 98012-5874

LATTIMORE, BARBARA, health facility administrator, consultant; b. Birmingham, Ala., June 11, 1961; d. Butler and Alfreda (Kelley) Jackson; m. Ernest Eugene Lattimore, June 7, 1980; children: Kendra, Kimberly, Kandis. BS in Psychology, U. Md., 1988; MEd in Counseling, Boston U., 1990; MSA in Health Svcs., Ctrl. Mich. U., 1998. Lic. profl. counselor; nat. cert. counselor. Sta. mgr. ARC, Hanau, GErmany, 1986-89; program mgr. Sci. Applications Internat., Hanau, 1989-93; behavioral health clinician South Fulton Mental Health, East Point, Ga., 1993-96; program mgr. Child and Adolescent Program, Atlanta, 1996-98; dir. substance abuse Alcohol and Drug Treatment Ct., Atlanta, 1998—. Founder, CEO, Alternative R&D, Decatur/Stone Mountain, Ga., 1993-99; CEO, Therapeutic Managed Care, Decatur/Stone Mountain, 1999—; cons. Gwinnett County Juvenile Ct., Lawrenceville, Ga., 1998—, Daus. Endowed With Wisdom, Decatur, 1998—, ACE Check Casing, Inc., Atlanta, 1999—. Social Work Svcs., Frankfurt, Germany, 1991-93. Treas., NAACP, Hanau, 1990, v.p., 1991, pres., 1992; troup leader Girl Scouts U.S., Mannheim, Germany, 1989-92; Sunday sch. tchr. Christ Temple Fellowship, 1980—. Recipient Comdr.'s award for cmty. svc. U.S. Army, 1990. Mem. Am. Coll. Healthcare Execs., Sigma Iota Epsilon, Delta Sigma Theta. Home: 7052 Shore Rd Lithonia GA 30058-8214 Office: Fulton County Alcohol and Drug Treatment Ctr 265 Boulevard NE Atlanta GA 30312-1284

LATTIMORE, LOUISE JOAN, elementary school educator; b. Wattis, Utah, July 3, 1934; d. John T. and Ruth A. (Craven) Maulsby; m. Roy Jay Lattimore, Jan. 29, 1955; children: Karen Lattimore, Katherine, John. BA in Edn. with honors, Fresno State U., 1956; MA in Adminstrv. Services with honors, Sonoma State U., 1985. Cert. lifetime elem. tchr. and administr., Calif. Tchr. Panama Sch. Dist., Bakersfield, Calif., 1956-57, Fresno (Calif.)-Scandinavian Sch. Dist., 1957-58, Petaluma (Calif.) City Schs., 1966-68; tchr.-in-charge Liberty Sch. Dist., Petaluma, 1969-94, ret., 1994. Condr. workshops No. Calif. Kindergarten Conf., San Francisco, 1987, 89, Sonoma County Consortium, Santa Rosa, Calif., 1987, Petaluma City Schs., 1988, No. Calif. Sch. Leadership Acad., 1991; cons. in field. Vol. classroom sci. presenter; vol. tchr. sci. edn. Margaret Thomas scholar Delta Zeta, 1956. Mem. Calif. Tchrs. Assn. (dist. negotiator 1985-94, chmn. adminstrv. coun. 1994-98), Hon. Soc. for Key Women Educators, Sierra Club, Sonoma County Land Trust, Delta Kappa Gamma. Methodist. Avocations: travel, geology, bicycling, spending time with family, quilting.

LATZA, BEVERLY ANN, accountant; b. Pompton Plains, N.J., June 10, 1960; d. George and Helen Mae (Ryan) L. BA in Acctg., Bus. Adminstrn., Thiel Coll., Greenville, Pa., 1982. Internal auditor Monroe Systems for Bus., Morris Plains, N.J., 1983-85; acct. Am. Airlines, Tulsa, 1985-86, Accountemps, Tulsa, 1986-87; credit investigator Denrich Leasing, Inc., Kansas City, Mo., 1987-89; with accounts receivable dept. Coca Cola Bottling Co. Am., Lenexa, Kans., 1989; with acctg. and accounts payable depts. Wolferman's Fine Breads, Lenexa, Kans., 1992-93; tax examining asst. IRS, Kansas City, Mo., 1989-98, customer svc. rep., 1998—2001, collection due process/collection appeals case worker, 2001—05, contact rep./automated collection system, 2005—. Vol., disaster action team mem. ARC, 1996-97; reading tutor Literacy of Kansas City, 2001—02. Lutheran. Avocations: reading, movies, singing, counted cross stitch. Home: 8323 W 108th St Apt C Overland Park KS 66210-1625 Office: IRS 2306 E Bannister Rd Kansas City MO 64131-3011

LAU, CHRISTINA SIELCK, librarian; b. Orange, Calif., Dec. 14, 1955; d. Franz Johann Hinrich and Carol Felton Sielck; 1 child, Andrea. Ba in Religion, So. Calif. Coll., 1979; MLS, UCLA, L.A., Calif., 1987. Tech. svc. libr. Cuesta Coll., San Luis Obispo, Calif., 1991—2004, north county libr. Paso Robles, Calif., 2004—. Democrat. United Ch. Of Christ.

LAU, CONSTANCE H. (CONNIE LAU), electric power industry executive; b. Honolulu; BS, Yale Univ.; JD, Univ. Calif. Hastings Coll. Law; MBA, Stanford Univ. With Hawaiian Elec. Industries, Honolulu, 1984—99; treas. Hawaiian Elec. Industries, Hawaiian Elec. Co., 1989—99; fin. v.p., CFO HEI Power Corp.; sr. exec. vice-pres., COO Am. Savings Bank, 1999—2001, pres., CEO, 2001—06, Hawaiian Elec. Industries, Honolulu, 2006—. Mem. bd. Punahou Sch., Kamehameha Sch., Charles Reed Bishop Trust, Alexander & Baldwin Inc. Mem.: Maunalani Found., Hawaii Bus. Roundtable, Hawaiian Bankers Assn. Office: Hawaiian Elec Industries Bldg 1 900 Richards St Honolulu HI 96813 Office Phone: 800-272-2566.*

LAU, JENNY KWOK WAH, theater educator, consultant, film educator, consultant; arrived in U.S.A., 1979; d. Wai-Wing and Yau-Ying L.; children: Daniel, Esther. BSc in Physics, U. Hong Kong, 1976; MA in Mass Comm., Bowling Green (Ohio) U., 1981; PhD in Cinema Studies, Northwestern U., 1989. Lectr. dept. T.V. and film Hong Kong Bapt. Coll., 1983-85, asst. prof., 1990-91; vis. prof. dept. radio, T.V., film Northwestern U., 1991-92; asst. prof. Ohio U., 1992-96, assoc. prof. sch. film, 1997; assoc. prof. cinema dept. San Francisco State U., 2005—. Radio culture critic Radio Hong Kong, 1983-86; prodr., dir. Sta. 32, Chgo., 1988-89; spkr. in field; presenter numerous confs. Contbr. articles to books and profl. jours.; creator numerous exptl. films. Recipient Best Short Film Award PBS, Chgo., Boston, 1990, Baker Award, 1995; grantee for Libr. Acquisition, 1992-93, Hong Kong Office Econ. Trade, 1995, for Devel. of Web Based Courses in Film, 1997, Coll. Fine Arts, 1997, David C. Lam Inst. for East West Studies, 1998. Mem. Hong Kong Film Scholar Assn., Soc. Cinema Studies (co-chair Asian-Asian Pacific caucus, exec. coun. mem.). Achievements include being the first Chinese national (men or women) to receive a PhD degree in Cinema Studies. Avocations: singing, piano, photography, films, debates with friends. Office: San Francisco State U Cinema Dept San Francisco CA 94132

LAU, MICHELLE, mathematics educator; d. Jack Wong and Wong Ching; m. Kerman Lau, Apr. 7, 2001; 1 child, Kira. MA, Stanford U., Calif., 1999. Math tchr. Silicon Valley Essential H.S., Mountain View, Calif., 2001—02, Irvington H.S., Fremont, Calif., 2002—. Adv. coord. Irvington H.S., 2002—05. Author: (leadership guide) Survival Guide for Activity Directors. Youth leader Tri-City Chinese Bapt. Ch., Fremont, Calif., 2002—06. Mem.: Nat. Coun. Tchrs. Math. Home: 35501 Dante Pl Fremont CA 94536 Office: Irvington HS 41800 Blacow Rd Fremont CA 94538 Office Phone: 510-656-5711.

LAUBER, PATRICIA GRACE, writer; b. NYC, Feb. 5, 1924; d. Hubert Crow and Florence (Walker) Lauber; m. Russell Frost III, Apr. 11, 1981. BA, Wellesley Coll., 1945. Rsch., writer book dept. Look Mag., N.Y.C., 1945-46; staff writer Scholastic Mags., N.Y.C., 1946-48, editor, 1948-54, freelance editor, 1954-56, Challenge Books, Coward-McCann, N.Y.C., 1955-59, Good Earth Books, Garrard, Scarsdale, NY, 1973-79; founding editor, editor-in-chief Science World, Street & Smith, N.Y.C., 1956-59; chief editor Science and Mathematics, The New Book of Knowledge, Grolier, N.Y.C., 1961-67. Cons. editor Sci. Am. Books, N.Y.C., 1977—80; cons. Nat. Sci. Resources Ctr., NAS-Smithsonian Instn., 1992—94. Author: (children's book) Volcano: The Eruption and Healing of Mount St. Helens, 1986 (Newbery Honor Book, 1987, N.Y. Acad. Scis. Hon. Mention, 1987), From Flower to Flower: Animals and Pollination, 1986 (N.Y. Acad. Scis. Hon. Mention, 1988), Dinosaurs Walked Here and Other Stories Fossils Tell, 1987, Snakes are Hunters, 1988, Lost Star, the Story of Amelia Earhart, 1988, Meteors and Meteorites: Voyagers from Space, 1989, The News About Dinosaurs, 1989 (N.Y. Acad. Scis. Hon. Mention, 1990), Living with Dinosaurs, 1989 (Orbis Pictus Hon. Mention Nat. Coun. Tchrs. English, 1990), Seeing Earth from Space, 1990 (Orbis Pictus Hon. Mention Nat. Coun. Tchrs. English, 1991), Summer of Fire, 1991, Fur, Feathers, and Flippers, 1994, How Dinosaurs Came To Be, 1996, Hurricanes, 1996, Flood: Wrestling with the Mississippi, 1996, Painters of the Caves, 1998, Purrfectly Purrfect, 2000, Tubs, Toilets and

Showers, 2001, Who Came First? New Clues to Prehistoric Americans, 2003. Recipient award for Overall Contbn. to Children's Lit., Washington Post/Children's Book Guild, 1983, Eva L. Gordon award, Am. Nature Study Soc., 1988, Lit. award, Ctrl. Mo. State U., 1989, Lifetime Achievement commendation, Nat. Forum Children's Sci. Books, Carnegie-Mellon U., 1992, Alumnae Achievement award, Wellesley Coll., 1998, Kerlan award, 2000, Sci. Books and Films prize excellence in sci. books, AAAS/Subaru, 2005. Mem.: PEN, Soc. Children's Book Writers, Authors Guild. Democrat. Congregationalist. Avocations: reading, music. Office: care Scholastic Press 555 Broadway New York NY 10012-3919

LAUCK, DONNA L., mental health nurse; b. Berwick, Pa. d. Earl Andrew and Catherine Arlene Kreiser; m. Ronald Joseph Lauck, Oct. 21, 1966; 1 child, Ronadl Joseph Jr. BSN, U. Pa., 1973, MSN, 1982, DNSc, 1991. Diplomate Am. Bd. Forensic Examiners; RN Pa., cert. cert. clin. nurse specialist, ANA, adult psychiat. and mental health nursing, 94, founding certificant, Nat. Registry of Certified Group Psychotherapists, 95, BLS instr., Am. Heart Assn., sexual assault nurse examiner, 96, cognitive behavioral therapist, 01. Oper. room staff nurse Lower Bucks County Hosp., Pa., 1959-60; charge nurse Boron (Pa.) Cmty. Hosp., 1960; part-time staff nurse Barstow (Calif.) Cmty. Hosp., 1960-65; office nurse S.W. French, III, M.D., Barstow, 1960-65; IV team nurse Jefferson Hosp., Pa., 1966; staff nurse critical care unit Presbyn. Hosp., Pa., 1966; head nurse ICU/CCU Meth. Hosp., Pa., 1966-69; head nurse ICU Frankford (Pa.) Hosp., 1970-76; dir. nursing Geriat. and Med. Ctrs., Inc., 1977-79; staff nurse, asst. sr. nurse, charge nurse Friend's Hosp., Phila., 1971-86, relief 11-7 supr., 1971-86; nursing staff devel. specialist Inst. of Pa. Hosp., Phila., 1986-92, clin. nurse specialist, 1992-96; dir. clin. svc. Kirkbride Ctr., Phila., 1997; clin. nurse specialist, sr. nurse in-charge admissions Friend's Hosp., Phila., 1998-2000, sr. nurse therapist Cognitive Behavioral Unit, 2000, clin. nurse specialist, therapist Adult Svcs., 2000—03, advanced practice nurse Adult Svcs., 2000—03, unit mgr. women's unit, 2002—03; therapist Collaborative Care Abington, Phila., 2002—. Spkr. in field. Chmn. fundraising telethon U. Pa. Sch. Nursing, 1981, 1982, active mem.; mem. adv. bd. West Phila. Coalition Neighborhoods and Bus., Advanced Practices Nurses Coun., Pa. Hosp., 1994—96; active mem. liaison program for undergrad. freshman students U. Pa., 1990—, facilitator comm. workshop sr. student nurses, 1999—. Mem.: Am. Coll. Forensic Examiners, Internat. Soc. Hypnosis, Eastern Pa. Assn. Nurses Diagnosis (mem. psychiat.-mental health spl. interest group), Psychiat. Advanced Practice Nurses Pa., Internat. Assn. Study Dissociative Disorders, Am. Soc. Clin. Hypnosis, Presbyn. Hosp. Alumni Orgn. Office: 1369 Old York Rd Abington PA 19001

LAUDENKLOS, TERRY LYNN, elementary school educator; b. Glendive, Mont., Oct. 11, 1956; d. Donald James and Florence Almond Dvorak; m. David Laudenklos, June 5, 1982; 1 child, April Lynn. Student, Pillsbury Bible Coll., 1976-78; BS, Westminster Coll., Salt Lake City, 1980. Cert. elem. tchr. Okla. Tchr. 2d grade Mingo Valley Christian Sch., Tulsa, 1980-82; tchr. 5th and 6th grade Tulsa Christian Schs., 1987-89; tchr. 5th grade Southpark Christian Sch., Tulsa, 1995—.

LAUDER, AERIN, cosmetics executive; d. Ronald and Jo Carole Lauder; 2 children. Degree, U. Pa. From dir. mktg. Prescriptives to v.p. global adv. Estée Lauder Inc., NYC, 1992—2001, v.p. global adv., 2001—04, sr. v.p. global creative directions, 2004—. Jr. assoc. Mus. Modern Art, NYC; bd. trustees Thirteen WNET, NYC; costume inst. visiting com. Met. Mus. Art, NYC; bd. trustees Animal Med Ctr.; advisory bd. NY Botanical Garden. Office: Estée Lauder Inc Corp HQ 767 Fifth Ave New York NY 10153

LAUDER, EVELYN H., cosmetics executive; b. Vienna; arrived in U.S., 1940; m. Leonard A. Lauder, 1959; children: William, Gary. BA, Hunter Coll.; degree (hon.), Muhlenberg Coll., 1996. Joined as edn. dir. Estée Lauder Cos., N.Y.C., 1959, v.p., sr. corp. v.p., 1989—. Photographer: (book) The Seasons Observed, 1994, An Eye For Beauty, 2002. Founder, chmn. Breast Cancer Rsch. Found., 1993—; mem. bd. overseers Meml. Sloan-Kettering Cancer Ctr.; trustee Ctrl. Pk. Conservancy Inc.; trustee emirata The Trinity Sch., N.Y.C.; bd. dirs. New Yorkers for Parks. Named Disting. Fgn. Born Citizen, Internat. Ctr., 1987; named one of 75 Most Influential Bus. Women, Crain's Newspaper, 1996, Women of Yr., Glamour mag., 1999, Top 200 Collectors, ARTnews Mag., 2004; recipient Spirit Achievement award, Albert Einstein Coll. Medicine, 1991, Mary Waterman award, Breast Cancer Alliance, 1998, Humanitarian award, Coun. Fashion Designers Am., 2001, award for excellence in philanthropy, Soc. Meml. Sloan-Kettering, 2001, Ellis Island Medal of Honor, Nat. Ethnic Coalition Orgns., 2001. Achievements include founder of The Breast Cancer Research Foundation, the largest national organization dedicated solely to breast cancer research; implementing breast cancer awareness programs from Pink Ribbon campaigns to illuminating world landmarks in a pink glow for Breast Cancer Awareness Month. Avocation: Collector of Modern art especially Cubism. Office: Estée Lauder Cos 767 5th Ave New York NY 10153-0023

LAUDER, JO CAROLE, art association administrator; m. Ronald S. Lauder, July 1967; children: Aerin, Jane. Mem. bd. dirs. The Ronald S. Lauder Found.; pres. internat. coun. Mus. of Modern Art; mem. bd. trustees Ind. Curators Internat., Mt. Sinai Medical Ctr.; chmn. bd. dirs. Friends of Art & Preservation in Embasies. Named one of Top 200 Collectors, ARTnews Mag, 2004. Avocation: Collector of Old Masters; 19th and 20th century art, especially German. Office: Mus Modern Art 11 W 53rd St New York NY 10019

LAUDER, VALARIE ANNE, editor, educator; b. Detroit, Mar. 01; d. William J. and Murza Valerie (Mann) L. AA, Stephens Coll., Columbia, Mo., 1944; postgrad., Northwestern U. With Chgo. Daily News, 1944-52, columnist, 1946-52; lectr. Sch. Assembly Svc., also Redpath lectr., 1952-55; freelance writer for mags. and newspapers including New York Times, Yankee, Ford Times, Travel & Leisure, Am. Heritage, 1955—; editor-in-chief Scholastic Roto, 1962; editor U. N.C., 1975-80, lectr. Sch. Journalism, 1980—. Gen. sec. World Assn. for Pub. Opinion Rsch., 1988-95; nat. chmn. student writing project Ford Times, 1981-86; pub. rels. dir. Am. Dance Festival Duke U., 1982-83, lectr., instr. continuing edn. program, 1984. Contbg. editor So. Accents mag., 1982-86. Mem. nat. fundraising bd. Kennedy Ctr., 1962-63; bd. dirs. Chapel Hill Mus., Inc., 1996-98. Recipient 1st place award Nat. Fedn. Press Women, 1981, 1st place awards Ill. Women's Press Assn., 1950, 51. Mem. Pub. Rels. Soc. Am. (treas. N.C. chpt. 1982, sec. 1983, v.p. 1984, pres.-elect 1985, pres. 1986, chmn. coun. of past pres., chmn. 25th Ann. event 1987, del. Nat. Assembly 1988-94, S.E. dist. officer, nat. nominating com. 1991, 1st pres.'s award 1993), Women in Comms. (v.p. matrix N.C. Triangle chpt. 1984-85), N.C. Pub. Rels. (mem. Hall of Fame com.), DAR, Soc. Mayflower Desc. (bd. dirs. Ill. Soc. 1946-52), Chapel Hill Hist. Soc. (bd. dirs. 1981-85, 94-2001, chmn. pub. com. 1980-85, pres. 1996-2001), Chapel Hill Preservation Soc. (bd. trustees 1993-96, nominating com. 1994), N.C. Press Club (3d v.p. 1981-83, 2d v.p. 1983-85, pres. 1985, 1st pl. awards 1981, 82, 83, 84), Univ. Women's Club (2d v.p. 1988), The Carolina Club, The Nat. Press Club. Office: U NC Sch Journalism and Mass Comm CB 3365 Chapel Hill NC 27599-0001 Office Phone: 919-843-8297.

LAUDERDALE, KATHERINE SUE, lawyer; b. Wright-Patterson AFB, Ohio, May 30, 1954; d. Azo and Helen Ceola (Davis) L. BS in Polit. Sci., Ohio State U., 1975; JD, NYU, 1978. Bar: Ill. 1978, U.S. Dist. Ct. (no. dist.) Ill. 1978, Calif. 1987. Assoc. Schiff, Hardin & Waite, Chgo., 1978-82; from dir. bus. and legal affairs to sr. v.p. Sta. WTTW-TV, Chgo., 1982—2000, sr. v.p. strategic partnerships and gen. counsel, 2000—02; sr. v.p. and gen. counsel PBS, Alexandria, Va., 2002—. Mem. Lawyers Com. for Harold Washington, Chgo. 1983; bd. dirs. Midwest Women's Ctr., Chgo., 1985-94; active Chgo. Coun. Fgn. Rels., 1981-99, mem. fgn. affairs com., 1985-99; mem. adv. bd. Malcolm X Coll. Sch. Bus., 1996-99 Mem. ABA, Chgo. Bar Assn. (bd. dirs. TV Prodns., Inc. 1986-2002), Lawyers for Creative Arts (bd. dir. 1984-2002, v.p. 1998-2002), ACLU (bd. dirs. 1987-94), Nat. Acad. TV Arts and Scis., NYU Law Alumni Assn. Midwest (mem. exec. bd. 1982-86), The Ohio State U. Pres.'s Nat. Adv. Coun. on Pub. Affairs (Chgo. com., 1994-98), The History Makers (nat. adv. bd. 2003—), Hands on Network (nat. bd., 2005—, sec. exec. com. 2006) Democrat. Office: PBS 2100 Crystal Dr Arlington VA 22202 Office Phone: 703-739-5063.

LAUDIN, RIZA ANN, elementary school educator; b. Bklyn., Apr. 7, 1952; d. Judith Heller; m. Alan Laudin, Aug. 22, 1976; children: Matthew, Jillian. BA in Internat. Studies, Miami U., Oxford, Ohio, 1973; MS in Secondary Edn., Hofstra U., Hempstead, NY, 1975. Cert. tchr. NY. Tchr. Herricks Pub. Schs., New Hyde Park, NY, 1985—. Mem.: LWV (pres. Nassau County chpt. 2006—), Herricks Tchrs. Assn. (treas. 1999—2006). Home: 91 Ivy Ln Lido Beach NY 11561 Office: Herricks Public Schs 100 Shelter Rock Rd New Hyde Park NY 11040 Office Phone: 516-248-3177. Business E-Mail: rlaudin@herricks.org.

LAUDONE, ANITA HELENE, lawyer, business executive; b. 1948; m. Colin E. Harley; children: Clayton T. Harley, Victoria Spencer Harley. B.A., Conn. Coll., 1970; J.D., Columbia U., 1973. Admitted to N.Y. State bar, 1974, practiced in N.Y.C., 1973-79; asst. sec. Phelps Dodge Corp., N.Y.C., 1979-80, sec., 1980-84, v.p., sec., 1984-85. Editor Columbia Law Rev., 1973. Mem. Phi Beta Kappa.

LAUENSTEIN, ANN GAIL, librarian; b. Milw., Nov. 8, 1949; d. Elmer Lester Herbert and Elizabeth Renatta (Bovee) Zaeske; m. Mark Lauenstein, Aug. 16, 1986; 1 child, Maria. MA, U. Wis., 1972. Asst. libr. U. Wis., Wausau, 1972—73; cataloger, libr. MacMurray Coll., Jacksonville, Ill., 1973—76; corp. libr. Anheuser-Busch Cos. Inc., St. Louis, 1976—. Facilitator Anheuser-Busch Quality Circle, St. Louis, 1984—. Treas. Friends of Kirkwood Libr., 1986-98; mem. adv. coun. Sch. Info. Sci. U. Mo., 1987-95. Mem. AAUW (editor jour. 1981-84, publicity chmn. 1985-87, scholar 1984), Spl. Librs. Assn. (network liaison 1981-83, chmn. employment com. 1983-84, chmn. hospitality com. 1984-85, membership chmn. 1988-89, newsletter editor 1992-94, advt. editor 1995-97, bus. mgr. 1999—), St. Louis Regional Libr. Network (coun. 1981-83), St. Louis Online Users Group, Women in Bus. Network (adv. panel 1980-82, 86-87, programs planner 1987-88, asst. coord. 1988-89), Ohio Coll. Libr. Consortium Acquisitions Users Coun. Avocations: stamp collecting/philately, cooking, cookbook collecting. Office: Anheuser-Busch Co Inc 1 Busch Pl Saint Louis MO 63118-1852

LAUER, CASSIE LYNN, mathematics educator, department chairman; b. Mexico, Mo. M Edn., U. Mo. Columbia, 2004. Tchr. math. Holden Pub. Schs., Mo., 1998—2000, North Callaway H.S., Kingdom City, Mo., 2000—. Chair math. dept. North Callaway H.S., Kingdom City, 2003—, A+ coord., 2005—. Named to Who's Who Among Am. Tchrs., Who's Who.

LAUER, JEANETTE CAROL, dean, history educator, writer; b. St. Louis, July 14, 1935; d. Clinton Jones and Blanche Aldine (Gideon) Pentecost; m. Robert Harold Lauer, July 2, 1954; children: Jon, Julie, Jeffrey. BS, U. Mo., St. Louis, 1970; MA, Washington U., St. Louis, 1973, PhD, 1975. Assoc. prof. history St. Louis C.C., 1974-82, U.S. Internat. U., San Diego, 1982-90, prof., 1990-94, dean Coll. Arts and Scis., 1990-94, rsch. prof., 1997—. Author: Fashion Power, 1981, The Spirit and the Flesh, 1983, Til Death Do Us Part, 1986, Watersheds, 1988, The Quest for Intimacy, 5th edit., 2002, 6th edit. 2006, No Secrets, 1993, The Joy Ride, 1993, For Better of Better, 1995, True Intimacy, 1996, Intimacy on the Run, 1996, How to Build a Happy Marriage, 1996, Sociology: Contours of Society, 1997, Windows on Society, 1999, 7th edit., 2005; Becoming Family: How to Build a Stepfamily that Works, 1999, How to Survive and Thrive in an Empty Nest, 1999, Troubled Times: Readings in Social Problems, 1999, Love Never Ends, 2002, The Play Solution: How to Put the Fun Back into your Relationship, 2002, Social Problems and the Quality of Life, 10th edit., 2005, Marriage and the Family: The Quest for Intimacy, 6th edit., 2005. Woodrow Wilson fellow, 1970, Washington U. fellow, 1971-75. Mem.: Am. Hist. Assn., Orgn. Am. Historians. Democrat. Presbyterian.

LAUGHLIN, JO ANN, retired elementary school educator; b. Faucett, Mo., Aug. 8, 1939; d. Louis and Mary Evelyn (Horton) Smither; m. Robert Everett Laughlin, June 21, 1959; children: Mary Ruth, Ann Kathryn, Jonathan Everett. BS in edn., U. Mo., 1961. Tchr. Moberly Sch. Dist., Mo., 1961-63, Miami Sch. Dist., Amoret, Mo., 1966-67, Rich Hill Sch. Dist., Mo., 1969—2004; ret., 2004. Project leader 4-H, Foster, Mo., 1968—87; sponsor Jeff Laughlin Meml. Scholarship; lay leader Hume Meth. Ch., 1998—, pianist. Recipient Bates County Ext. Coun. Leaders Honor Roll cert., 1995. Mem.: Mo. State Tchr. Assn., Cmty. Tchr. Assn. (pres. 1977—78, 1998—99, 2002—03, chmn. health ins. com. 1995—2001, Tchr. of the Yr. 1990—91), Alpha Delta Kappa (sec. 1994—95, treas. 2002—04). Methodist. Home: RR 1 Box 276 Rich Hill MO 64779

LAUGHLIN, LINDA R., psychoanalyst, psychotherapist; b. Chgo., Apr. 21, 1945; d. Paul Laughlin and Gertrude K. Silver, William T. Silver (Stepfather); m. Charles Stephen Levy, Aug. 11, 1968 (div. Mar. 1975); m. Erwin Flaxman, Oct. 1980. AB, Smith Coll., 1967; MAT, Northwestern U., 1968; MPA, Harvard U., 1974; PhD, U. Mich., 1982. Lic. psychologist, N.Y. Tchr. Senn H.S., 1967-68, Wakefield H.S., Arlington, Va., 1968-69; project officer DHEW, 1969-72; rsch. assoc. Nat. Inst. Edn., Washington, 1972-75; study dir. Inst. for Social Rsch., Ann Arbor, Mich., 1975-82; dir. rsch. Girl Scouts USA, N.Y.C., 1982-89; exec. dir. Nat. Youth Employment Coalition, N.Y.C., 1989-93; dir. continuing edn. Postgrad. Ctr. for Mental Health, N.Y.C., 1997—2001; pvt. practice N.Y.C., 1993—. Cons. Dewitt Wallace-Readers Digest Fund, N.Y.C., 1994-99; mem. nat. adv. bd. Ensure, 2005-; lectr. in field. Contbr. articles to profl. jours. Bd. dirs. Metro Librs., N.Y.C., 1993-97; commr. Chancellor's Commn. on Stds., N.Y.C. Schs., 1986-89. Mem. APA. Democrat. Jewish. Avocations: Iyengar yoga, swimming, theater. Office: # 1B 17 E 96th St New York NY 10128 Office Phone: 212-426-6573. Business E-Mail: llaughlin@nyc.rr.com.

LAUGHLIN, MONIQUE MYRTLE WEANT, mental health counselor; b. Paton, Iowa, Aug. 30, 1924; d. Irving Leroy Weant and Ella Florence (Bauer) Blaylock; m. Gerald Dean Laughlin, July 15, 1944 (div. July 1975); children: Roy Melvin, Owen Willard, James Byron. BA, William Penn Coll., Oskaloosa, Iowa, 1949; MS, So. Ill. U., 1975; PhD, U. Okla., 1980. Lic. profl. counselor Okla. State Dept. Health, marital and family therapist; cert. alcohol and drug counselor Okla. State Bd. Alcohol and Drug Counselors, Okla. State Bd. Mental Health; nat. cert. counselor Nat. Bd. Cert. Counselors; nat. cert. alcohol and drug counselor Drug and Alcohol Profl. Counselor Cert. Bd., internat. alcohol and drug counselor Internat Cert. and Reciprocity Consortium, Alchohol and Drug Abuse Inc., biofeedback therapist Neurotherapy and Biofeedback Cert. Bd., clin. hypnotherapist, Am. Coun. Hypnotist Examiners. Asst. v.p. 1st Nat. Bank, Higgins, Tex., 1962-74; alcohol and drug counselor Mercy Health Ctr., Oklahoma City, 1975-76; pub. rels./counselor Cmty. Counseling Ctr., Oklahoma City, 1977-79; tng. cons. and counselor in pvt. practice Oklahoma City, 1979-80; petroleum landman Johnco Inc., Oklahoma City, 1981; tng. officer, staff devel. Dept. Human Svcs., Oklahoma City, 1981-85; developer counseling svcs., exec. dir. Break-Through, Oklahoma City, 1985—; owner, dir. Pathfinders, Inc., Oklahoma City, 1990—. With Citizen's Amb. program People to People, Spain and Portugal, 1991. Mem. Am. Assn. Marriage and Family Therapy (clin.), Okla. Psychol. Assn., Okla. Drug and Alcohol Profl. Counselor Assn., Nat. Assn. Adult Children of Dysfunctional Families. Avocation: travel. Home: 14126 Springhill Rd Edmond OK 73013-4734

LAUPER, CYNDI, musician; b. Queens, N.Y., June 20, 1953; Studied with Katie Agresta, N.Y., 1974. Toured with Doc West's Disco Band Flyer; mem. musical group Blue Angel, N.Y.C., 1980. Featured in German TV music program; rec. artist: (album) She's So Unusual, 1983, A Night To Remember, 1989, Hat Full of Stars, 1993, Twelve Deadly Cyns.and Then Some, 1995, Sisters of Avalon, 1997, Merry Christmas.Have a Nice Life, 1998, Feels Like Christmas, 2001, Shine, 2002, The Essential Cyndi Lauper, 2003, At Last, 2003, The Body Acoustic, 2006; co-writer: (songs) Girls Just Want to Have Fun, She Bop, Money Changes Everything, Time After Time, Goonies R Good Enough, 1985, True Colors, 1986, A Night to Remember, 1989; contbr. A Very Special Christmas, 1992, vol. 2, 1993; star: (videos) Girls Just Want to Have Fun, Time After Time, others; appearance (film) Vibes, 1988, Off and Running, 1991, Life with Mikey, 1993; (TV movie) Mother Goose Rock n' Rhyme, 1990; TV appearances include The Tonight Show, The David Letterman Show, Mad About You (Emmy award, Guest Actress - Comedy Series, 1995); concert tours in Japan, Australia, Hawaii and Eng.; (Broadway) The Three Penny Opera, 2006. Named one of Women of Yr., 1984, Best Female Video Performer, MTV Video Music Awards, 1984, Best Female Performer, Am. Video Awards, 1985; recipient 6 Grammy awards, 1985, 2 Am. Video awards, 1985.*

LAUPHEIMER, ANN B., lawyer; b. Phila., July 5, 1959; AB in Comparative Lit., Princeton U., 1979; JD summa cum laude, U. Penn. Law Sch., 1984. Bar: Pa. 1984. Law clerk to Judge James Hunter III US Ct. of Appeals, Third Circuit, 1984—85; assoc. Blank Rome LLP, Phila., 1986—94, ptnr., corp. litigation practice group, 1994—. Mem. Civil Justice Reform Act Advisory Com., 1994—; lecturer, continuing legal ed. Trade Secrets in New Economy, IT Systems Failure Conference, Fed. Ct. Practice, Antitrust Develop., Prisoner Civil Rights, 1994—2002. Mem.: Phila. Bar Assn. (organizer, federal bench bar conference 1994, chair, federal ct. com. 1995, mem. Sandra Day O'Conner award subcom. 1996—97), Internat. Assn. of Insurance Receivers. Office: Blank Rome LLP One Logan Sq Philadelphia PA 19103-6998 Office Phone: 215-569-5758. Office Fax: 215-569-5694. Business E-Mail: laupheimer@BlankRome.com.

LAURENCE, AMY REBECCA, music educator, composer; b. Florence, Ala., Feb. 14, 1958; MusB, Ohio State U., 1979; MA, Calif. State U., Carson, 1998. Cert. Nat. Piano Guild. Entrepreneur Amy R. Laurence Music, Dublin, Ohio, 1994—. Liaison Columbus, Ohio and Associated Bd. of the Royal Schs. Music, 1998-99. Author, arranger (folios of piano music) The Little Hands Series: Christmas, Classics, Historic Hymns, Hymns, Seasons, 1990-99, (piano rec. and printed folio) Hymns in Black and White, 1990, (piano music series) The Amateur Virtuoso, 1995—; author, composer (musical rec. and printed folio) Songs In The Night, 1990, (piano music series) Amy's Animal Tales, 1999—, Amy's Keyboard Critters, 1999—; author, composer, arranger (printed and recorded music) Music Arch. Series, 1999—; originator, co-author, composer (musical drama) The Adventures of Wallace in Wonderland, 1988; arranger (vocal music) Choral Reef Series, 1994—, (music series) Instrumental Pianist, 1995—, (piano music series) Court Musician Series, 1997—, Gold Medal Series, 2000—; arranger Miss Am. Teen 2000; pub., arranger (operettas) The Parables, 2002, The Prophets, 2002, Wrestling Jacob, 2003. Active Northwest Chapel, Dublin. Recipient Tchrs. award, Nat. Piano Guild Internat. Composition Contest, 2002. Mem. ASCAP, Music Tchrs. Nat. Assn. (nat. cert. tchr. music), Am. Coll. Musicians, Suzuki Assn. Am., Leschetizky Assn. (life), Ohio Music Tchrs. Assn. (Ohio state composition chmn. 1998-99, sec. exec. bd. ctrl.-east divsn. 1998-2000), Nat. Fed. Music Clubs (life), Delta Omicron (life). Office: Amy R Laurence Music PO Box 426 Dublin OH 43017-0426 E-mail: Amy@AmyRLaurence.com.

LAURENT, JERRY SUZANNA, communications executive; b. Oklahoma City, Dec. 28, 1942; d. Harry Austin and M. LaVerne (Barker) Minick; m. Leroy E. Laurent, July 2, 1960; children: Steven, Sandra, David, Debra. AS in Engr. Tech., Okla. State U., 1986. Owner, CEO Technically Write, Mustang, Okla., 1989-95; sr. tech. comm. specialist Applied Intelligence Group, Edmond, Okla., 1995-98, DCA Svcs., Oklahoma City, 1998—2003; owner, CEO Comm. Design Group, 2003—, pres. Oklahoma City, 2003—. Fellow: Soc. Tech. Comm. (assoc.; Superscript editor 1985, v.p. 1985, feature editor 1986, student chpt. pres. 1986, program coord. Okla. chpt. 1992—93, sec. 1993—94, v.p. 1994—95, state pres. 1995—96, state treas. Okla. chpt. 1998—99, dir./sponsor region 5 1999—2002, bylaws com. mgr. 2001—02, Region 5 conf. mgr. 2002, 2nd v.p. 2003—04, 1st v.p. 2004—05, internat. pres. 2005—06, internat. immediate past pres. 2006—, INTECOM v.p. 2006—, Disting. Chpt. Svc. award 1997, Outstanding Achievement award 2001, Vol. of Yr. award 2006); mem.: Internat. Coun. Tech. Comm. (v.p. 2006—), Am. Bus. Women's Assn. (area coun. pres. 1987—89, v.p. dist. III 1988—89, sec. 1990—91, conf. gen. chair 1992, chmn. bd. dirs. Help Us Grow Spiritually 1993—95, editor Smoke Signals, Bull. award 1977, Woman of Yr. 1978, Bull. award 1981, 1983, Bus. Assoc. of Yr. 1983—84, Bull. award 1984, 1993, 1995, Woman of Yr. 1996, 1997, named One of Top Ten Bus. Women in Nation 1997, Bull. award 1997—99, Nat. Newsletter award 1999, Bull. award 2003—04, 2006). Democrat. Baptist. Avocations: reading, public speaking, motivating people, volunteer activities. Home and Office: Comm Design Group 347 W Forest Dr Mustang OK 73064-3430

LAURENT, LYNN MARGARET, nurse; b. New Orleans, July 2, 1963; d. Thomas Joachim and Marilyn Viola (Green) K. BSN, Dillard U., 1985. Nurse Hotel Dieu Hosp., New Orleans, 1985-89, Meth. Hosp., 1989-91, Charity Hosp., 1991-92, So. Bapt. Hosp., New Orleans, 1992-94, Excellent Home Health Care, 1994—, Laurent & Assocs., 1996—. Recipient Great 100 Nurses award, New Orleans Dist. Nurses Assn., 1994, Spirit of Greatness award, Christian Faith Ministries of New Orleans, La., 1997. Republican. Roman Catholic. Avocations: reading, arts, collecting coins and antiques. Home: 3843 Coventry St Slidell LA 70458-5207

LAURO, SHIRLEY MEZVINSKY, playwright, educator; b. Des Moines, Nov. 18, 1933; d. Phillip and Helen Frances (Davidson) Shapiro; m. Norton Mezvinsky, Aug. 22, 1956 (div. 1967); 1 child, Andrea Mezvinsky; m. Louis Paul Lauro. BS cum laude, Northwestern U., Evanston, Ill., 1955; MS, U. Wis., 1957; postgrad., Columbia U., 1970—73. Instr. speech and theatre CCNY, NYC, 1967—71; instr. speech, theatre and playwriting Yeshiva U., NYC, 1971—76; instr. creative writing Manhattan Marymount Coll., NYC, 1978—79; instr. speech and drama Manhattan Cmty. Coll., NYC, 1978—79; instr. playwright Tisch Sch. of Arts NYU, 1989—; lit. cons. Ensemble Studio Theatre, NYC, 1975—80, prodn. critic, 1975—, mem. coun., 1975—. Author: (novel) The Edge, 1965, Money for Women, 1990 (Barbara Deming award, 1990), (plays) The Contest, 1975 (Nat. Found. for Jewish Culture playwright's award, 1981), The Coal Diamond, 1979 (Heidemann Prize Actors Theatre of Louisville's Fesitval of New Am. Plays, 1980, Best Short Plays of 1980), Open Admissions-one act version, 1984 (NY Dramatists Guild Hull-Warriner Playwrights award, 1981, Samuel French Playwrights award, 1979, Ten Best Plays of 1981, NY Times), Nothing Immediate, 1979 (Samuel French Playwrights award, 1979), Margaret and Kit, 1980, I Don't Know Where You're Coming From at All, 1980, In the Garden of Eden, 1984, Sunday Go To Meetin', 1987, Open Admissions-full length version, 1984 (Theatre World award), Pearls on the Moon, 1987 (Residency Alley Theatre, 1987), A Piece of My Heart, 1988, All Through the Night, 2005, (screenplays) Open Admissions, 1988. NY Found. Arts Playwrights Fellow, 1985, John Guggenheim Playwrights Fellow, 1986, NEA Playwrights Fellow, 1987. Mem.: Writers' Guild, Authors' Guild, Authors' League, Dramatists' Guild, League Profl. Theatre Women, Ensemble Studio Theatre, PEN. Democrat. Jewish. Office: care Gilbert Parker William Morris Agy 1350 Avenue Of The Americas New York NY 10019-4702

LAUTENSCHLAGER, PEGGY A., state attorney general; b. Fond du Lac, Wis., Nov. 22, 1955; d. Milton A. and Patsy R. (Oleson) L.; m. Rajiv M. Kaul, Dec. 29, 1979 (div. Dec. 1986); children: Joshua Lautenschlager Kaul, Ryan Lautenschlager Kaul; m. William P. Rippl, May 26, 1989; 1 child, Rebecca Lautenschlager Rippl. BA, Lake Forest Coll., 1977; JD, U. Wis., 1980. Bar: Wis., U.S. Dist. Ct. (we. dist.). Pvt. practice atty., Oshkosh, Wis., 1981-85; dist. atty. Winnebago County Wis., Oshkosh, 1985-88; rep. Wis. Assembly, Fond du Lac, 1988-92; U.S. atty. U.S. Dept. of Justice, Madison, Wis., 1992—2000; atty. gen. State of Wis., 2003—. Apptd. mem. Govs. Coun. on Domestic Violence, Madison, State Elections Bd., Madison; bd. dirs. Blandine House, Inc. Active Dem. Nat. Com., Washington, 1992-93; com. Wis., 1989-92. Named Legislator of Yr., Wis. Sch. Counselors, 1992, Legislator of Yr., Wis. Corrections Coalition, 1992. Mem. Wis. Bar Assn., Dane County Bar Assn., Fond du lac County Bar Assn., Phi Beta Kappa. Democrat. Avocations: gardening, house renovation, sports, cooking. Office: Office of Atty General 114 E State Capitol Madison WI 53702

LAUTENSCHLAGER, YETTA ELIZABETH, clinical social worker; b. New Haven, Jan. 23, 1942; d. Theodore Mikolinski and Yetta Christina (Zdanovich) Meehan; m. Charles M. Lautenschlager, Dec. 11, 1982 (div.); children: Yetta Ann Auger, Kristin M. Wetmore. BS, So. Conn. State U., 1964, MS, 1973; MSW, U. Conn., West Hartford, 1983. LCSW; cert. co-active coaching, employee assistance profl. Educator Bd. Edn., Hamden, Conn., 1964-81; cmty. educator Lower Naugatuck Valley Coun. Alcohol and Drug Abuse, Ansonia, Conn., 1983-84; outpatient clinician Shirley Frank Found., New Haven, 1984-85; dir., clinician Personal Growth Ctr., Hamden, 1984—; employment assistance program cons. Johnson & Johnson Med., Southington, Conn., 1995—, Midstate Med. Ctr., Meriden, Conn., 1998—. Cons. Village for Families and Children, Hartford, Conn., 1992—. Participant Mary Mashinsky campaign, Wallingford, Conn., 1984. Mem.: ASTD, NASW, Network Inc. (pres.), Internat. Fedn. Coaches, NY Women in Comm. Inc., Conn. Soc. Clin. Social Workers, Acad. Lic. Social Workers, Internat. Soc. for New Identity Process (tchg. fellow, pres.), Menninger Found. Avocations: hiking, cross country skiing, biking, reading, attending the theater.

LAUTIGAR, LINDA L., lawyer; m. A. Jerald Lautigar. BS in acctg., Metro. State Coll., Denver, 1986; JD, U. Colo., 2001. Bar: N.Mex., DC, Colo. Enforcement specialist Dept Interior, Minerals Mgmt Svc., Lakewood, Colo., 1984—. Vol. atty. Faculty Fed. Adv., Denver, 2002—; ct. appointed spl. adv. CASA Jefferson, Gilpin Counties, Golden, Colo., 2003—; vol. atty. Metro Vol. Lawyers, Denver, 2005—. Mem. Mountain Foothills Rotary Club, Evergreen, Colo., 2005—06. Recipient Best Performance by a Trial Adv. award, U. Colo., Sch. Law, 2001. Office: Dept Interior-Minerals Mgmt Svc P O Box 25165 MS-370B2 Lakewood CO 80225-0165 Office Phone: 303-231-3494.

LAUTTENBACH, CAROL, artist; b. New Haven, Nov. 26, 1934; d. Gustav Fredrick and Wanda M. (Eshner) Stolze; m. Francis John Lauttenbach; children: Daniel M., William J. Grad. with honors in oils, watercolors, Washington Sch. Art, Chgo., 1967. One-woman shows include Greene Art Gallery, Guilford, Conn., Carriage House Gallery Ltd., Guilford, Gallery 53, Meriden, Conn., John Slade Ely House Gallery, New Haven, exhibited in group shows at Conn. Classic Arts, Fairfield, 1984 (Gabriel D. Luchetti award), 1986—87 (Gabriel D. Luchetti award, 1986), 1993—95 (1st prize, 1993, 3d prize, 1994, Rosemary Landina Meml. award, 1995), 1997—98 (Westport Framing & Art Gallery award, 1997, 2d prize acrylic and oils, 1998), Mt. Carmel Art Assn., Inc., 1986—88 (Best in Show, 1986, Elizabeth Greeley Meml. award, 1987, Donald L. Perlroth, Inc. award, 1988), 1990 (Marc D. Rosenberg Meml. award), 1998 (New Haven Savings Bank award), 2002 (Mayor Carl Amento award), Arts and Crafts Assn. Meriden, Inc., 1986—88 (Jerry's Artarama award, 1988), 1990, 1993, 1995, 1997—98, 2001, 2004—05 (Best Theme award, 2005), exhibitions include Mary Lou Fischer Gallery, Guilford, 2005, Hamden Art League, 2004—05 (Utrech art Supplies award, 2004, Dusa Chiropractic Ctr. award, 2005). Recipient numerous awards including most recently, Beazley Realtors award, Mt. Carmel Art Assn., 2000, Harvey Fuller award, Arts and Crafts Assn. Meriden, Inc., 2001, Mayor Carl Amento award, Mt. Carmel Art Assn., 2002, Artist's Alternative award, Arts and Crafts Assn. Meriden, 2004, Utrech Art Supplies award, Hamden Art League, 2004, Dusa Chiropractic Ctr. award, 2005, Best Theme award, Arts and Crafts Assn. Meriden, 2005. Mem.: Arts and Crafts Assn. Meriden (First prize 1976, Best in Show award 1982, Grumbacher Silver medal 1983—84, Hon. mention 1986, 1987, Henry T. and Stella King Meml. award 1990, Jerry's Artarama Cert. award 1990, Gold medal 1993, Grumbacher Gold medal 1993, Merriam Motors award Jubilee 325 Wallingford Theme 1995, Stella King Meml. award 1997, Artist's Alternative award 2004, Best Theme award 2005, Harvey Fuller award 2001), Conn. Classic Arts, Inc. (Third prize 1981, First prize 1982, Third prize 1983, Gabriel D. Luchetti award 1984, 1986, First prize 1987, 1993, Third prize 1994, Rosemary Landino Meml. award 1995, Westport Framing and Art Gallery Award 1997, Second prize in acrylic and oils 1998), Internat. Soc. Artists, Provincetown Art Assn., New Haven Paint and Clay Club (Members' Show award 1978, Hon. mention 1996), Wadsworth Athenium (life), Conn. Acad. Fine Arts (life), Wallingford Hist. Soc. (life). Home: 39 Ridgewood Rd Wallingford CT 06492-2116

LAUTZENHEISER, BARBARA JEAN, insurance company executive; b. LaFeria, Tex., Nov. 15, 1938; d. Fred E. and Verna V. L. BA with high distinction, Nebr. Wesleyan U., 1960. Actuarial trainee Bankers Life Ins. Co. Nebr., Lincoln, 1960-64, programmer and systems analyst, 1964-65, asst. actuary, 1965-69, assoc. actuary, 1969-70, 2d v.p., actuary, 1970-72, v.p., actuary, 1972-80; sr. v.p. Phoenix Mut. Life Ins. Co., Hartford, Conn., 1980-84; pres. Montgomery Ward Life Ins. Co., Montgomery Ward Ins. Co., Forum Ins. Co., Schaumberg, Ill., 1984-85; prin., CEO Lautzenheiser & Assocs., Hartford, 1986—. Spokesperson for ins. industry, witness U.S. Senate and Ho. of Reps. coms., commns. and state legislatures; featured on TV, nat. mags. and newspaper articles; mem. Interim Actuarial Std. Bd., 1986-88, Actuarial Std. Bd., 1989-90; chmn. Com. for Fair Ins. Rates, 1983-86; mem. adv. com. Nat. Assn. Ins. Commrs. Life Disclosure (A) Com. working group, 1993; bd. dirs. LifeUSA Holding Co. Contbr. articles to profl. jours. Mem. Lincoln Electric Sys. Adminstrv. Bd., 1977-79; bd. dirs. Nebr. Wesleyan U., 1977-82, 89-93, Am. Coll., 1987-97. Recipient Young Alumni svc. award Nebr. Wesleyan U., 1971, Corp. Woman award Women Bus. Owners of N.Y., 1983, C.H. Poindexter award for disting. achievement and exceptional svc. to the assn. and ins. industry Nat. Assn. Life Cos., 1989. Fellow: Conf. Cons. Actuaries (dir. 1997—98), Soc. Actuaries (dir. 1975—80, exec. com. 1978—80, chmn. adminstrn. and fin. com. 1981—82, exec. com. 1981—84, dir. 1981—85, pres. 1982—83, assoc. editor The Actuary 1992—93, life nonforfeiture task force 1995—96); mem.: Am. Coun. Life Ins. (risk classification com. 1973—81), Life Office Mgmt. Assn. (corp. fin. planning com. 1974—81, chmn. 1976—78), Nat. Alliance Life Companies (bd. dirs. 1992—95), Soc. of Actuaries Found. (founding trustee 1994—98, trustee emeritus Actuarial Found. 1998—), Am. Acad. Actuaries (dir. 1974—77, chmn. com. on publs. 1980—81, disclosure working group 1994—2001, nonforfeiture working group 1994—, com. on life ins. 1995—98, life practice coun. vice chair 1998, co-chair 1998—99, v.p. life 1999—2001, pres.-elect 2002—03, editl. adv. bd. mem. Contingencies mag. 2002—, pres. 2003—04, immediate past pres. 2004—05, task force revise ASOP no.12 2004—, past pres. 2005—), Greater Hartford C. of C. (nat. policies panel 1980—84), Nebr. Actuaries Club (dir. 1969—70, sec.-treas. 1971—72, dir. 1971—74, pres. 1972—73, chmn. 1973—74, dir. 1992—94). Home: 17 Huntingridge Dr South Glastonbury CT 06073-3614 Office: Lautzenheiser & Assocs 235 East River Dr #306 East Hartford CT 06108-5018 Office Phone: 860-246-0893. Personal E-mail: lautzenheiser@aol.com.

LAUTZENHISER, NIANN KAY, psychologist, real estate broker; b. Bryan, Ohio, Jan. 29, 1945; d. Kermit Arden and Luella Marie (Keppler) L. Student, Bowling Green State U., Ohio, summers 1963-65; BS in Edn., Miami U., Oxford, Ohio, 1966; MS in Edn., St. Francis Coll., Ft. Wayne, Ind., 1971, MS, 1975; postgrad., Purdue U. Extension, Ft. Wayne, 1974, N.W. Tech. Coll., Archbold, Ohio, 1976-78, 80. Lic. sch. psychologist, Ind.; lic. sch. counselor, Ind.; lic. tchr. math., Ind., lic. psychology tchr., Ind.; nat. cert. counselor. Math. tchr. John F. Kennedy Jr. High Sch., Kettering, Ohio, 1966-69, Angola (Ind.) High Sch., 1969-70, guidance counselor, 1970-75, counseling psychologist, 1975-77, Angola Middle Sch., 1977—2000; dept. chair Metro. Sch. Dist. Steuben County Student Svcs., 1996—2000. Bd. dirs. Switchboard, Inc., Angola, 1974-75, Angola Community Service, Inc., 1974-76, Edon (Ohio) Community Pre-Sch., Inc., 1981-85, Steuben County Waste Watchers, Inc., 1998-2005. Recipient Master Sch. Counselor cert. Nat. Assn. Sch. Counselors, 1976. Mem. NEA, Ind. State Tchrs., Assn.

LAUZON, LAURA M., middle school educator; b. Chgo., Apr. 16, 1951; d. John Anthony and Barbara Jean (Bunche) Lauzon; children: Melissa Jean, Kimberly Anne. BS in Biology, DePaul U., 1973. Cert. tchr., Ill. Tchr. St. Viator H.S., Arlington Heights, Ill., 1973-76; sales rep. E.R. Squibb & Sons, Princeton, N.J., 1976-77; fin. analyst Motorola, Inc., Schaumburg, Ill., 1978-81; substitute tchr. Palatine, 1990; substance abuse prevention coord. Lake Zurich (Ill.) Schs., 1991-94; tchr. earth sci. and chemistry Grant Cmty. H.S., Fox Lake, Ill., 1994-97; sci. tchr. Lake Zurich Mid. Sch. North, 1997—2000; asst. ch. sec. St. Matthew Luth. Ch., Hawthorn Woods, Ill., 2003—. Bd. dirs. Lake Zurich Mid. Sch.-North PTO, 1991-98, sec., 1994-95, pres., 1995-97, hospitality chmn., 1997-98; music parent coord. Seth Paine Sch. PTO, 1993-94, vol. coord., 1992-93; vol. coord. Thomas Jefferson Sch. PTA, 1985-90; vol. tchr. Palatine and Lake Zurich Schs., 1989-98; vol. Bear Boosters, 1995-99; project co-dir. Ela Area Cmty. Partnership, Lake Zurich, 1991; referendum co-chmn. Citizens for New Schs., 1990-91, head spkrs. com., 1991; vol. St. Matthew Luth. Ch., 2000—; bd. dirs., v.p. Townhome Assn., 2004-05; vol. town home assn. Co-recipient Partnership award Lake County Fighting Back Project, 1991. Avocations: church volunteer work, tutoring, dance.

LAVALLY, REBECCA JEAN, research editor, journalist; b. Danville, Ill., Dec. 9, 1949; d. Nelson Charles and Mary (Hayes) L.; m. William Warner Kirby, June 7, 1975 (div. 1988); 1 child, Sarah Jean; m. Jeffery Manuel Raimundo, Nov. 16, 1991; stepchildren: Scott, Amy, Todd. BA in Journalism, Calif. State U., 1971, MA in Comm. Studies, 2005; postgrad., U. Tex., 2004—. Reporter Lorain (Ohio) Jour., 1972-73; reporter, copy editor Cleve. Plain Dealer, 1973-75; reporter San Jose (Calif.) Mercury News, 1975-77, UPI, Sacto., 1977-85, bur. mgr., 1985-89, Gannett News Svc., Sacto., 1989-90; editor State of Calif., Senate Office of Rsch., Sacto., 1990—2004; asst. instr. U. Tex., Austin, 2005—. Co-author newspaper column Stepfamily Tips. Mem.: Am. River Natural History Assn. (bd. dirs. 1998—2001). Avocations: running, writing, travel. Business E-Mail: rlavally@mail.utexas.edu.

LAVE, JUDITH RICE, economics professor; b. Campbellton, May 18, 1939; d. J.H. Melville and G.A. Pauline (Lister) Rice; m. Lester Bernard Lave, June 21, 1965; children: Tamara Rice, Jonathan Melville. BA in Econs., Queen's U., Kingston, Ont., Can., 1957-61; MA in Econs., Harvard U., 1964, PhD, 1967; LLD, Queen's U., 1994. Lectr., asst. prof. econ. Carnegie Mellon U., Pitts., 1966-73, assoc. prof., 1973-78; dir. econ. analysis Office of Sec., Dep. of Asst. Sec. Planning and Evaluation, Washington, 1978-79; dir. office of rsch. Health Care Fin. Adminstrn., Washington, 1980-82; prof. health econ. U. Pitts., 1982—, co-dir. Ctr. for Rsch. on Health Care, 1996—, chair dept. health policy and mgmt., 2003—. Cons. Nat. Study Internal Medicine Manpower, Chgo., 1976, Wash. State Hosp. Assn., 1984, Horty, Springer & Mattern, Pitts., 1984, Hogan and Hartson, Washington, 1989, Ont. Hosp. Assn., Conn. Hosp. Assn., 1991; cons. various agys. U.S. HHS (formerly U.S. HEW), 1971-89; mem. adv. panel Robert Wood Johnson Found., Princeton, N.J., 1983-84, 96—. Leonard Davis Inst., Phila., 1984, U.S. Congress, 1977, 82, 83—; com. mem. Inst. Medicine Coms., Washington, 1975-, Project 2000 Commn. on Future of Podiatry, Washington, 1985-86. Editl. bd. Wiley Series in Health Svcs., 1989-90, Health Svcs. Rsch., 1970-74, Inquiry, 1979-82, AUPHA Press, 1986, Jour. of Health Policy Politics and Law, Health Affairs, 1998—; co-author: Hospital Construction Act - An Evaluation of the Hill Burton Program, 1948-73, 74, Health Status, Medical Care Utilization and Outcome: A Bibliography of Empirical Studies (4 vols.) 1989, Providing Hospital Services, 1989; contbr. numerous articles to profl. jours. Mem. Prospective Payment Assessment Commn., 1993—97, Medicare Payment Adv. Commn., 1997—2000; mem. planning com. ARC, Pitts., 1986—; mem. rev. com. United Way, Pitts., 1988—90, Bd. Health Svcs., Inst. Medicine; bd. dirs. Craig House, Pitts., 1976—77, Presbyn. Sr. Care, Pitts., Jewish Health Care Found., 2002—. Woodrow Wilson fellow, 1961—62. Disting. fellow Acad. Health (pres. 1977-88, bd. dirs. 1983-93); mem. Found. for Health Svcs. Rsch. (pres. 1988-89, bd. dirs. 1983—), Am. Pub. Health Soc., Am. Econ. Soc. (com. mem.), Inst. Medicine (bd. health svcs. 2000-), Nat. Acad. Social Ins., Robert Wood Johnson Found. (com. on econ. impact of health sys. change 1996—), Internat. Health Eco Assn. Democrat. Home: 1008 Devonshire Rd Pittsburgh PA 15213-2914 Office: U Pitts A620 Pub Health Pittsburgh PA 15213 Office Phone: 412-624-0898. Business E-Mail: lave@pitt.edu.

LAVECCHIA, JAYNEE, state supreme court justice; b. Paterson, NJ, Oct. 9, 1954; m. Michael R. Cole. Grad., Douglass Coll., 1976, Rutgers U., 1979. Bar: N.J. 1980. Pvt. law practice; dep. atty. gen. divsn. of law State of NJ; asst. counsel to Gov. Thomas H. Kean Office of Counsel, dep. chief counsel to Gov. Thomas H. Kean; dir. divsn. of law dept. law anf pub. safety State of NJ, 1984-98; dir., chief adminstrv. law judge Office of Adminstrv. Law, 1989-94; commr. banking and ins. State of NJ, 1998-99; assoc. justice NJ Supreme Ct., Trenton, 2000—. Chair various N.J. Supreme Ct. Coms. Fellow ABA. Office: Supreme Ct PO Box 970 25 Market St Trenton NJ 08625*

LAVELLE, AVIS, consulting firm executive; b. Chgo., Mar. 5, 1954; d. Adolph Eugene and Mai Evelyn (Hicks) Sampson. BS in Comms. cum laude, U. Ill., 1975. Announcer, pub. affairs dir. Sta. WTAX Radio, Springfield, Ill., 1977-78; news dir., anchor Sta. WLTH Radio, Gary, Ind., 1978-79; reporter, anchor Stas. WJJD/WJEZ, Chgo., 1979-84; chief polit. reporter Sta. WGN-Radio/TV, Chgo., 1984-88; campaign press sec. Richard M. Daley for Mayor, Chgo., 1988-89; mayoral press sec. Officer of the Mayor, Chgo., 1989-92; nat. press sec. Clinton/Gore for Pres., Little Rock, 1992; spl. asst. to chmn. Vernon Jordan Presdl. Transition, Washington, 1992-93; asst. sec. pub. affairs U.S. Dept. Health and Human Svcs., Washington, 1993—95; v.p. comm. Waste Mgmt. Inc., 1995—99; v.p. govt. and pub. affairs U. Chgo. Hosps., 1999—2001; sr. ptnr. bus. devel. The Foster Group, Chgo., 2001—04; pres. A LaVelle Consulting Svcs. LLC, Chgo., 2004—. Mem. Delta Sigma Theta Pub. Svc., Chgo., 1973—; mem. steering com. Black Adoption Taskforce of Ill., Chgo., 1987; v.p. Chgo. Bd. Edn., 1997-2003; bd. dirs. Project Image, Inc., Chgo., 1988-89, Human Resources Devel. Inst., Chgo., 1988; founding mem. bd. dirs. After Sch. Matters Found.; mem. resource com. Met. Planning Coun.; campaign mgr. Mayor Richard M. Daley's Re-election, 1999; commr. Chgo. Cable Commn., 2003—; state dir. Ill. Kerry for Pres. Campaign, 2004. Recipient African Am. Bus. and Profl. Women award Dollars and Sense Mag., 1989, Women at Work award Nat. Commn. Working Women, 1980, First Place Team award AP, 1984; named one of Chicago's 100 Most Influential Women, Crain's Chgo. Bus., 2004. Democrat. Office: A LaVelle Consulting Svcs LLC 25 E Washington St #908 Chicago IL 60602 Office Phone: 312-223-0581.

LAVENDER, CHERYL ANN, music educator, composer, writer; b. Lincoln Park, Mich., June 18, 1951; d. Thomas Joseph and Gwendolyn Ann Umlauf; m. Charles Paul Lavender, June 1, 1974; children: Charles Eric, Brandon Thomas, Krista Leigh. BS in Edn., Ctrl. Mich. U., 1973. Cert. tchr. Wis. Music educator, choral dir. Beal City (Mich.) Pub. Schs., 1974—76, St. Joseph Sch., Beal City, 1974—76, Flushing (Mich.) Cmty. Schools, 1977—81, Warwick Pointe Acad., Grand Blanc, Mich., 1981—82, Fox Point (Wis.)-Bayside Sch. Dist., 1982—86, Brookfield (Wis.) Acad., 1982—84, Sch. Dist. Elmbrook, Brookfield, 1986—. Clinician Oakland U., Rochester, Mich., 1980—81, Mich. Schs. Vocal Music Assn., Lansing, U. Mich., Flint, 1983, Stanton's Music, Columbus, Ohio, 1991—, Oreg. Music Educators Assn., Eugene, 1992, Karnes Music, Chgo., 1992—2004, Pender's Music, Dallas, 1992—2002, JW Pepper, Billings, Mont., 1992—2000, Fargo, ND, 1992—2000, Moorhead, Minn., 1995—2000, Indpls., 1999, Mpls., 2001, Ward-Brodt Music, Madison, Wis., 1992—2003, JW Pepper / Wingert-Jones Music, Kansas City, Mo., 1992—2004, Schmitt Music, Mpls., 1994—2004, Fargo, ND, 2002, NW Music Svcs., Vancouver, British Columbia, Canada, 1994—2001, Ill. Music Educators Assn., Peoria, 1996—2001, SD Am. Choral Directors Assn., Sioux Falls, SD, 1996, Marquette U., Milw., 1996—2001, Tex. Music Educators Assn., San Antonio, 1997—2003, Onandoga Music Svcs., Washington, 1997, VanderCook Coll. Music, Chgo., 1997—98, Onandoga Music Svcs., NYC, 1997, Ohio Music Educators Assn., Columbus, Ohio, 1998, SD Music Educators Assn., Brookings, SD, 1998, Orff Chpt. of Iowa, Cedar Falls, Iowa, 1998, Tri-City Music, Bay City, Mich., 1999, Hal Leonard Corp., Milw., 2002—04, Iowa Music Educators Assn., Mason City, Iowa, 2002, Shattinger's Music, St. Louis, 2003, Popplers Music, Grand Forks, ND, 2005; composer, author Jensen Publications, New Berlin, Wis., 1986—89, Hal Leonard Corp., Milw., 1989—; keynote spkr. Ctrl. Mich. U., Mount Pleasant, Mich., 2003. Author: Skills Evaluation Kit, 1986, Elementary Form Pack, 1986, The Song-Writing Kit, 1986, Help! I'm a Substitute Music Teacher!, 1987, Staging a Children's Musical, 1987, See, Sing, and Play, 1987, Making Each Minute Count, 1991, The Ultimate Music Assessment and Evaluation Kit, 2000; composer: (CD) Rhythm Bingo Level 1 and Level 2, 1986, Instrument Bingo, 1987, It's Your Turn!, 1988, Composer Bingo, 1988, Music Round Robin, 1989, Music Symbol Bingo, 1989, Melody Bingo, 1990, Moans, Groans, and Skeleton Bones, 1991, Music Listening Bingo, 1992, A Spring Song Sing-Along, 1993, Come Dance a Jig, 1994, Melody Flashcard Kit Vol. I, 1994, Melody Flashcard Kit Vol. II, 2005, Rhythm Flashcard Kit Vol. I, 1994, Rhythm Flashcard Kit Vol. II, 2005, Lines and Spaces Bingo, 1996, Rockin' Rhythm Raps, 1996, It's Your Turn. Again!, 1997, Songs of the Rainbow Children, 1998, Rock 'n Raps Rhythm Tracks Vol. 1, 1999, Rock 'n Raps Rhythm Tracks Vol. II, 2005, World Instrument Bingo, 1999, Americans All, 2000, Music Styles Bingo, 2002, John Jacobson's Music Express, 2002, Solfege Bingo, 2003, Friendship Family, 2005. Del. US-South Africa Edn. Conf. Citizens Ambassador Program, Johannesburg, 1996; co-founder Swanson Sch., Loehmann's Plz. Ednl., Corp. Partnership, Brookfield, Wis., 1995—99. Recipient Disting. Alumni award, Ctrl. Mich. U., 2005; grantee, NEA Found. for Improvement of Edn., 2004. Mem.: NEA (assoc.), ASCAP (life), Elmbrook Edn. Assn., Music Educators Nat. Conf. (assoc.), Alpha Lambda Delta. Home: 20230 Liberty Ct Brookfield WI 53045 Personal E-mail: clavender@wi.rr.com.

LAVENSON, SUSAN BARKER, hotel corporate executive, consultant; b. L.A., July 26, 1936; d. Percy Morton and Rosalie Laura (Donner) Barker; m. James H. Lavenson, Apr. 22, 1973 (dec. Sept. 1998); 1 child, Ellen Ruth Stanclift. BA, Stanford U., 1958, MA, 1959; PhD (hon.), Thomas Coll., 1994. Cert. gen. secondary credential tchr., Calif. Tchr. Benjamin Franklin Jr. H.S., San Francisco, 1960; tchr. French dept. Lowell H.S., San Francisco, 1960-61; v.p. Monogram Co., San Francisco, 1961-62, creative dir. N.Y.C., 1973-86; pres. SYR Corp., Santa Barbara, Calif., 1976-89; mng. ptnr. Lavenson Ptnrs., Camden, Maine and Scottsdale, Ariz., 1989—; founding mem. The Piper Group, 2006—. Mem. commn. on co-edn. Wheaton Coll., Norton, Mass., 1985-87; mem. Relais et Chateaux, Paris, 1978-89; cons. World Bank Recruit Divsn., 1993. Author: Greening of San Ysidro, 1977 (Conf. award 1977). Trustee Camden Pub. Libr., 1989—95, v.p., 1991—93; vice chair bd. trustees Thomas Coll., Waterville, Maine, 1990—2001, trustee emerita, 2001—; trustee Atlantic Ave. Trust, 1989—91; founding pres. Maine chpt. Internat. Women's Forum, 1991—; mem. Coun. of Advisors Coll. of the Atlantic, Bar Harbor, Maine, 1996—2001, Ariz. Women's Forum; chair dean's adv. coun. Ariz. State U., 2002—04, chair coun. advisors Virginia Piper Creative Writing Ctr., 2004—05. Recipient Piper award for entrepreneurial excellence, 2002. Mem. Advice Inc., Camden Yacht Club, Stanford Alumni Assn., Com. of 200 (treas. 1985-86), Women's Entrepreneur Corps, Phi Delta Kappa (Stanford U. chpt., founding mem.). Home and Office: 7841 E Shooting Star Way Scottsdale AZ 85262 Office Phone: 480-575-7722. E-mail: sbl1@cox.net.

LAVERDIERE, CLAUDETTE MARIE, nun, head of religious order; BS in Edn., Mary Rogers Coll., Maryknoll, N.Y., 1967; M Theol. Studies, Cath. Theol. Union, Chgo., 1986; licentiate in Sacred Theology, Weston Jesuit Sch. Theology, 2000. Joined Maryknoll Sisters Congregation, 1956. Tchr. Nganza Secondary Sch. for Girls, Mwanza, Tanzania, 1967-71; with devel. dept. Maryknoll Sisters Congregation, 1972-74; tchr. religious edn. dept. secondary schs. Nakuru, Kenya, 1974-76; cathechetical dir. Nakuru Diocese, Kenya, 1976-79; team mem. devel. edn. program Mombasa Diocese, Kenya, 1980-84; registrar, tchr. Theol. Centre Religious, Nairobi, Kenya, 1987-90; pres. Maryknoll Sisters Congregation, 1991-97, student, 1997-2000; tchr. Theological Ctr. Religious, Nairobi, Kenya, 2000-01; tchr. sacred scripture Religious Sisters Inst., Kenya, 2001—03; family ministry Winslow, Maine, 2003—.

LAVERTU, MONIQUE THERESE, music educator; b. Berlin, NH, Sept. 20, 1964; d. J. Paul Cusson and Lucille Regina LeClerc; m. Robin Lee Lavertu, Aug. 9, 1986; children: Monica Lea, Ryan Alan, Brandon Patrick. BS in Music Edn., 1986. Cert. Cert. tchr. N.H., 1986. Suppy and fiscal date entry profl. Rodman Naval Sta., Panama, 1987—88; music tchr. Valent Recreation Ctr., Ft. Clayton, Panama, 1986—88; presch. music tchr. Air Force Preschs., APO, Panama, 1986—87; tng. dept. sec. James River Corp., Berlin, NH, 1988—90; gen. music tchr. Berlin Jr. H.S., Berlin, NH, 1990—96; Title 1 Reading tutor Brown Elem. Sch., Berlin, 1998—2000; vis. instrumental tchr. St. Michael Sch., Berlin, 1997—2000; music educator Gorham (N.H.) Sch. Dist., 2000—. Prin. alto saxophonist Berlin Jazz, Berlin, 1988—; bell ringer St. Paul Luth. Ch., Berlin, 1994—96; flutist area churches, Berlin, 1988—; guest condr. Balboa Honors Band, Balboa, Panama, 1986, North Country Music Festival, Whitehead, NH, 2005. Mem.: Gorham Tchrs. Assn., N.H. Music Educators Assn., Music Educators Nat. Conf. Republican. Roman Catholic. Avocation: jazz band, bell choir, snow mobiling, golf. Home: 113 Shepard St Berlin NH 03570

LAVERY, ELIZABETH J., music educator; BS in Music Edn., West Chester U., 1998. Colorguard dir. Ridgewood (N.J.) H.S., 1998—; music tchr. Franklin Ave. Mid. Sch., Franklin Lakes, NJ, 1998—, Colegio Internacional de Carabobo, Valencia, Carabobo, Venezuela, 2002—03. Vol. tchr. WorldTeach, Namibia, 2005—05; pvt. flute instr., NJ, 1996—. Active mem. Ridgewood (N.J.) United Meth. Ch., 1978—2006. Named Master Tchr., N.J. Symphony Orch., 2001—02. Mem.: N.J. Music Educators Assn., N.J. Edn. Assn., Bergen County Edn. Assn., Kappa Delta Pi (Tchr. Edn. Coun. Scholar 1999), Pi Kappa Lamba (Sr. of Yr. 1998).

LAVEY, SARAH, assistant principal; d. Leonard Pleasant and Maydell Gregory; m. Michael Allen Lavey, Oct. 27, 2001; m. John David Pinkston, Apr. 3, 1969 (dec. Nov. 27, 1990); children: John Gregory Pinkston, Stefanie, Shannon Lea Pinkston. BSE, Northeastern U., 1981; MS in Edn., U. Ark., 2000. Cert. elem. adminstr. Ark. Elem. tchr. Ft. Smith Pub. Schs., Ark., 1984—2004, asst. elem. prin., 2004—. Co-chair Trusty Elem., Fort Smith, Ark., 1994—2004. Vol. ARC, Spiro, Okla. Named Outstanding Educator, Assn. of Childhood Educators Internat., 1997—98. Mem.: ASCD, Fedn. Tchrs. Econ. (charter), Ark. Assn. Elem. Educators, Internat. Reading Assn., Phi Delta Kappa. Office Phone: 479-785-5606.

LAVIGNE, AVRIL, singer; b. Napanee, Ont., Can., Sept. 27, 1984; d. John and Judy Lavigne; m. Deryck Whibley, July 15, 2006. Singer: (albums) Let Go, 2002 (nominee Grammy award Best New Artist, 2002, nominee Grammy award Best Pop Vocal Album, 2002, nominee Grammy award for Song of Year for Complicated, 2002, nominee Grammy award for Best Female Pop Vocal Performance for song Complicated, 2002, nominee Grammy award for Best Female Rock Vocal Performance for song Sk8er Boi, 2002), Under My Skin, 2004; voice actor: (films) Over the Hedge, 2006. Achievements include signed with L.A. Reid of Arista Records at age 16. Avocations: hockey, basketball, skateboarding. Office: Network Mgmt 1650 W 2nd Ave Vancouver BC Canada V6J 4R3*

LAVIK, ERIN, chemical engineer; BS, MIT, 1995, MS, 1997, PhD, 2001. Asst. prof. biomedical and chem. engring. Yale U. Author: (plays) The Reception, 2000. Named one of 100 Top Young Innovators, MIT's Tech. Review, 2003; recipient Grad. Student Gold award, Materials Rsch. Soc., 2000. Office: Yale Univ Chem Engring Dept PO Box 208286 New Haven CT 06520

LAVIN, BERNICE E., cosmetics executive; b. 1925; m. Leonard H. Lavin, Oct. 30, 1947; children: Scott Jay (dec.), Carol Marie, Karen Sue. Student, Northwestern U. Vice chairperson of bd., sec.- treas. Alberto-Culver Co.; dir., v.p., sec.- treas. Alberto-Culver U.S.A., Inc. Sec.-treas., dir. Alberto-Culver Internat., Inc.; sec.-treas. Sally Beauty Co., Inc. Office: Alberto-Culver Co 2525 Armitage Ave Melrose Park IL 60160-1163 E-mail: blavin@alberto.com.

LAVIN, LINDA K., counselor; b. Elizabeth, N.J., Mar. 1, 1952; d. James Vincent and Madeleine (Berka) Lavin; children: Alyssa, Valerie. Student, U. Md., 1970-72; BS in BA, Ctrl. Mich. U., 1977; MS in Counseling, L.I. U.,

1991. Nat. cert. counselor, NY, neuro emotional tech., distance cert. counselor. Office mgr. Baton Rouge Family Med. Ctr., 1978-79; pers. officer Bergen State Bank, Bergenfield, N.J., 1979-81; owner Fancy Florals, Florida, N.Y., 1981-89; office mgr. Margaret Verhagen, D.C., Warwick, N.Y., 1989-91; substitute tchr. Chester Sch. Dist., 1990-91; hypnotherapist Hypnosis for Health, Florida, N.Y., 1990—; counselor Michael B. Schachter, M.D., P.C. and Assocs., Suffern, N.Y., 1991—, Dr. Joseph Roman, Warwick, 1993-94; counselor, workshop presenter Windows to the Sky, 1994—97. Lectr. quest group Theosophical Soc. Am., 1986-91; adj. prof. Marist Coll., 2004-; trainer Capital EAP, 2005-. Leader Girl Scouts U.S., Fla., 1987-91, resource person, 1989-92; mem. Found. for Advancement of Innovations in Medicine, Suffern, 1992—; vol. Hospice of Orange Hudson Valley, Inc., Newburgh, N.Y., 1991-93; religious edn. dir. Unitarian Soc. of Orange County, 1989-92, trustee, 1994-95. Mem. Am. Counseling Assn., Nat. Assn. for Clin. Application of Behavioral Medicine, Internat. Assn. Counselors and Therapists, Inst. of Noetic Scis., Assn. for Rsch. and Enlightenment, NY Mental Health Counselors Assn. (chpt. sec.), Eye Movement Desensitizational & Processing Internat. Assn., Hummingbird Manor HOA (exec. com. mem. 2004-06). Avocations: sewing, kinesiology, needlecrafts, reiki, gardening. Office: 46 Oakmont St Niskayuna NY 12309-6550 also: 211 Fishkill Ave Ste 207 Beacon NY 12508 Office Phone: 518-393-7993. Business E-Mail: transformationnow@earthlink.net.

LAVIN, SHARON RENAI, secondary school educator; b. Ypsilanti, Mich., May 24, 1974; d. Mike Lavin and Roxanna Maddox; m. Joseph DeVault (div.); 1 child, Alexandra Grace DeVault. BA, Olivet Coll.; Masters, Saginaw Valley U. Tchr. Fitzgerald Pub. Sch., Warren, Mich. Office: Fitzgerald HS 23200 Ryan Rd Warren MI 48091-4551

LAVINE, THELMA ZENO, philosophy educator; b. Boston; d. Samuel Alexander and Augusta Ann (Pearlman) L.; m. Jerome J. Sachs, Mar. 31, 1944; 1 child, Margaret Vera. AB, Radcliffe Coll., 1936; A.M., Harvard U., 1937, PhD, 1939. Instr. Wells Coll., 1941-43, asst. prof., 1945-46; asst. prof. philosophy Bklyn. Coll., 1946-51; asst. prof. U. Md., 1955-57, assoc. prof., 1957-62, prof., 1962-65; Elton prof. George Washington U., 1965-85, chmn. dept., 1969-77; Clarence J.Robinson Univ. prof. George Mason U., Fairfax, Va., 1985—. Lectr., seminar cons. Inter-Am. Def. Coll., 1975—; exec. bd. Jour. of Speculative Philosophy, 2000—. Author: From Socrates to Sartre, 1980; co-author: introduction to Collected Works of John Dewey, Vol. 16, 1990, contbg. author: Reading Dewey, 1998, contbg. editor: Free Inquiry, 1980—, exec. bd.: Jour. of Speculative Philosophy, 2000—; contbr. articles to profl. jours., chpts. to books; author: (TV course) From Socrates to Sartre: The Philosophic Quest, 1984; co-author: History and Anti-History Philosophy, 1989, contbg. author: Philosophy of Paul Ricoeur, 1995, Rorty and Pragmatism, 1996, contbg. author: Perspectives on Habermas, 2000, contbg. author: Philosophy of Paul Ricoeur, 1995, mem. exec. bd.: Jour. Speculative Philosophy, 2000—; contbr. articles to profl. jours., revs., chpts. to books; series editor Transaction, 2003. Recipient Outstanding Faculty award U. Md., 1965, Outstanding Faculty award George Washington U., 1968, Alumnae Achievement award Radcliffe Coll., 1991; NEH sr. rsch fellow, 1980; Am. Enterprise Inst. Public Policy Research fellow, 1980-81, Va. Found. Humanities fellow, 1990; Herbert W. Schneider award contbns. to Am. Philosophy, 2000. Mem. Am. Philos. Assn. (5th Ann. Romanell lectr. 1991), Soc. Advancement Am. Philosophy (exec. com. 1979-82, pres. 1992-94), Internat. Soc. Sociology Knowledge, Internat. Soc. Polit. Psychology, Metaphys. Soc. Am., Washington Philosophy Club (pres. 1967-68), Washington Sch. Psychiatry, Forum Psychiatry and Humanities (exec. bd.), Cosmos Club, Harvard Club, SOPHIA, Phi Beta Kappa (pres. chpt. 1978-80). Home: 1625 35th St NW Washington DC 20007-2316 Office: George Mason U Robinsons Profs E 207 Fairfax VA 22030 Office Phone: 703-993-2171. E-mail: tzlavine@awol.com.

LAVIN-PENNYFEATHER, ROSE, artist; b. Perth Amboy, N.J., Oct. 16, 1952; d. James V.P. and Emma (Kiblosh) Lavin; m. Franco Casentini, Feb. 14, 1974 (div. 1978); 1 child, Franco K. Casentini; m. Stefano Corti, Oct. 24, 1984 (div. 1997); 1 child, Sandro J. Corti; m. Wayne Pennyfeather, May 8, 1999. Student, Georgian Ct., 1970-72, U. Florence (Italy), 1972-73. Saleswoman Correges, Rome, 1977-78; sec. McDonnell-Douglas, Rome, 1978-80, McCann-Erickson, Rome, 1980-82, RAI TV and Radio Corp., N.Y.C., 1983-84; mgr. Benetton, Woodbridge, N.J., 1984-85; sole proprietor Art Studio LC, Woodbridge, 1990-99; art tchr. Perth Amboy Cath. Schs. K-8, 1999—. Artist drawing logo contest, Tarquinia, Italy (Silver medal 1978). Directress St. Peter's Altar Guild, Perth Amboy, 1991-2005. Mem. NOW, Nat. Mus. of Women in the Arts. Democrat. Episcopalian. Avocations: karate (brown belt), swimming, cooking. Home: 677 Parker St Perth Amboy NJ 08861-2913 Office: Perth Amboy Cath Schs 680 Catherine St Perth Amboy NJ 08861-2802

LAVIOLETTE, CATHERINE PATRICIA, librarian; b. Ely, Minn., Aug. 16, 1935; d. Joseph and Mary Rose (McCarthy) Gerzin; m. Gene LaViolette, Aug. 19, 1958; children: Mary Shawn, Barbara. BA, Coll. St. Scholastica, 1957; MLS, U. Wis., 1959. Cert. elem. and secondary sch. libr., Wis., pub. libr., Wis. From children's libr. to adminstr. cen. pub. svcs. Brown County Libr., Green Bay, Wis., 1960-86, dir., 1986—. Instr. children's lit. St. Norbert Coll., De Pere, Wis., 1967-69, 74-75. Sec. Coun. on Libr. and Network Devel., 1989—; bd. dirs. St. Mary's Hosp., Green Bay, Greater Green Bay Area Found., Univ. Bank Bd., Green Bay Sypmhony Bd. Recipient John Cotton Dana Spl. award ALA and H.W. Wilson Co., 1975, 79, 82, Community Achievement award Green Bay Jaycette, 1970. Mem. Wis. Libr. Assn. (Librarian of Yr. 1981, Library of Yr. 1993-94, numerous coms. and chairs 1960—). Office: Brown County Libr 515 Pine St Green Bay WI 54301-5194

LAVIZZO-MOUREY, RISA JUANITA, medical foundation administrator, academic administrator; b. 1954; MD, Harvard U., 1979; MBA, U. Pa., 1986. Dep. adminstr. Agy. Healthcare Policy and Rsch., U.S. Dept. Health and Human Svcs., 1992—94; Sylvan Eismann prof. of medicine U. Penn, Phila., 1995—2001, dir. Inst. of Aging, 1995—2001, chief, div. geriatric med., assoc. exec. v.p., health policy, 1995—2001; associate chief of staff for geriatrics and extended care Phila. Veterans Admin. Med. Ctr.; sr. v.p., dir., Health Care Group Robert Wood Johnson Found., Princeton, NJ, 2001—03, pres., CEO, 2003—, also mem. bd. trustees. Mem. Pres.'s Commn. on Consumer Rights and Quality in the Healthcare Industry, 1997-98; mem. advisory com. Task Force on Aging Rsch., Office of Tech. Assessment Panel on Preventive Services for Medicare Beneficiaries, Inst. of Medicine's Panel on Disease and Disability Prevention Among Older Adults, Nat. Com. for Vital and Health Statistics. Mem., IOM, Nat. Acad. Sciences, Amer. Geriatrics Soc., The Assn. of Acad. Minority Physicians, Nat. Med. Assn., Acad. for Health Services Rsch. & Health Policy, Gerontological Soc. Amer. Office: The Robert Wood Johnson Foundation PO Box 2316 College Road East and Route 1 Princeton NJ 08543-2316

LAVORI, NORA, real estate executive, lawyer; b. S.I., N.Y., Aug. 11, 1950; d. William P. and Mary E. Lavori; div. 1990; children: Liana Sterling, Alexander O. Sterling. BA, Bryn Mawr Coll., 1971; JD, Bklyn. Law Sch., 1976. Bar: N.Y. 1977. Atty., N.Y.C., 1977—; ptnr. Orleans Realty, N.Y.C., 1978—; officer The Culture Ctr., N.Y.C., 1990—. Author: Living Together, Married or Single: Your Legal Rights, 1976. Mem. real estate coun., maj. gifts com. Met. Mus. Art, N.Y.C., 1998—; trustee Bryn Mawr (Pa.) Coll., 1999-2005; vice-chair Columbus Ave. Bus. Improvement Dist., N.Y.C., 2000; bd. advisors Syracuse U., 2005—. Mem. Women's City Club N.Y. (pres. 1995-96; hon. dir.). Home: 100 W 80th St New York NY 10024

LAW, CAROL JUDITH, medical psychotherapist; b. N.Y.C., May 1, 1940; d. Aldo and Jennie (Feldman) Settimo; m. Perry J. Koll, Dec. 26, 1967 (div. Nov. 1974); 1 son, Perry J.; m. Edwin B. Law, June 1, 1979. BA, Upsala Coll., 1962; postgrad., Rutgers U., 1964-66; MA, Columbia Pacific U., 1982, PhD, 1984. Diplomate Am. Bd. Med. Psychotherapy. Pers. dir. Hotel Manhattan, N.Y.C., 1961; supr. social work Essex County, Newark, 1962-67; exec. dir. USO, Vung Tau, South Vietnam, 1967-68; dir. Dept. Health and Rehab. Svcs., Pensacola, Fla., 1968-79; therapist, tchr. Franciscan Renewal Ctr., Scottsdale, Ariz., 1982-92; pvt. practice Scottsdale, 1982-92; drug free workforce cons. Pensacola C. of C., Fla., 1992—; pres. Drug Free Workplaces, Inc., 1993—. Mem. Healthy Start of N.W. Fla.; dist 1 chmn. Alcohol, Drug Abuse and Mental Health Planning Coun. Mem. state adv. bd. Parents Anonymous, Phoenix, 1982; chmn. Gov.'s Adv. Commn. Drugs and the Elderly, Tallahassee, 1978; pres. Jaycettes, Pensacola, 1969; chmn. social com. United Way Fund, Pensacola, 1977; mem. adv. bd. USO, Pensacola, 1973, H.R.S. Dist. 1 Community Collaboration Project; trustee ORME Sch. Fellow Am. Acad. Polit. and Social Sci.; mem. Am. Assn. Pub. Adminstrs., Pensacola Country Club, Escambia County Drug Court Coalition, Fla. State C. of C. (drug issues com.,), Nat. Drugs Free Workplace Alliance (bd. dirs.), Partnership for a Drug Free Fla. (bd. dirs.), Pensacola Downtown Rotary, ESCA Rosa Work Force Bd. (chmn. personnel comm.). Roman Catholic. Home: 27 Mar Vista Cir Pensacola FL 32507-3486

LAW, CLARENE ALTA, small business owner, retired state legislator; b. Thornton, Idaho, July 22, 1933; d. Clarence Riley and Alta (Simmons) Webb; m. Franklin Kelso Meadows, Dec. 2, 1953 (div.); children: Teresa Lin Meadows, Charisse Meadows Haws, Steven Riley; m. Creed Law, 1973. Student, Idaho State Coll., 1953. Sec., sub. tchr. Grand County Schs., Cedar City, Utah, 1954-57; UPI rep. newspaper agy. Moab, Utah Regional Papers, Salt Lake City and Denver; auditor Wort Hotel, Jackson, Wyo., 1960-62; innkeeper, CEO Elk Country Motels, Inc., Jackson, Wyo., 1962—; rep. Wyo. Ho. of Reps., Cheyenne, 1991—2004. Bd. dirs. Jackson State Bank, Snow King Resort; mem. bank bd. Wyo. State Ho. Reps., 1991-98, chmn. travel com., 1993-2000, chmn. minerals and econ. devel. com., 2001-04. Chmn. sch. bd. dirs. Teton County Schs., Jackson, 1983-86; bd. dirs. Wyo. Taxpayers Assn., Bus. Coun., 1998—2004. Named Citizen of Yr. Jackson C. of C., 1976, 99, Bus. Person of Yr. Jackson Hole Realtors, 1987, Wyo. Small Bus. Person SBA, 1977. Mem. Wyo. Lodging and Restaurant Assn. (pres., chmn. bd. dirs. 1988-89, Big Wyo. award 1987), Soroptimists (charter), Bus. Profl. Womens Orgn. (Woman of Yr. 1975, mem. Heritage steering com. 1996—), Gov.'s 15-Mem. Bus. Coun. Republican. Avocations: travel, study. Address: PO Box 575 Jackson WY 83001-0575 Office: Elk County Motels Inc Box 575 43 W Pearl Jackson WY 83001 E-mail: antlerjh@aol.com.

LAW, JANE HINTON, artist, small business owner; b. Dayton, Ohio, Dec. 26, 1928; d. William Guy and Nelle Grant (Royse) Hinton; m. Lillard E. Law, Feb. 5, 1928; children: Melinda Talbot, Laurie Jorgensen, Thomas W. Hinton, Jonathan S. BA, Otterbein Coll., 1947; MA, NYU, 1970. Art supr. Worthington (Ohio) Schs., 1947-51; tchr. Gambler Schs., Mt. Vernon, Ohio, 1954-59; asst. prof. fine arts Union Coll., Elizabeth, N.J., 1969-74; tchr. So. Regional High Sch., Manahawkin, N.J., 1975-78; instr. Ocean County Coll., Toms River, N.J., 1975-76; owner Jane Law Art Studio and Gallery, Surf City, N.J., 1976—. State judge Fed. Art Assn., Westfield, N.J., 1984—; bd. dirs. Internat. Miniature Exhibit, Surf City, Nat. Watercolor Exhibit, Surf City. Editor: Long Beach Island Cookbook, 1981; artist several featured articles in cultural events, Art. Bus. News on show, calendar and cover photos. Remor judge Stafford Twp. Founders Day, MAnahawkin, N.J., 1987, state contest posters Women's History Month, 1990. Recipient Outstanding Community Bus. award Tax Payers Assn., 1988; named one of Outstanding Artists Ocean County Cultural and Heritage Commn., 1989; named Woman of Yr. AAUW, 1990. Mem. AAUW (v.p. 1985—), N.J. Assn. Sch. Adminstrs. (aux. pres. 1972—), Internat. Soc. Marine Painters, N.J. Watercolor Soc. (assoc.), Island Singers (pres. 1984—), Soroptimists (pres. 1983-84), Phila. Watercolor Club. Republican. Episcopalian. Home: 2005 Long Beach Blvd Ship Bottom NJ 08008-5552 Office: Jane Law Art Studio & Gallery 20th St & Long Beach Blvd Surf City NJ 08008

LAW, JENNIFER, middle school educator, director; d. Ronald and Joan Sheppard; m. Gregg Law, Oct. 16, 1993; children: Kaitlin, Hayley. BA in History, U. Calif., Riverside, 1992. Tchr. Waggoner Elem., Winters, Calif., 1998—99; tchr., activities dir. Wilson C. Riles Mid. Sch., Roseville, Calif., 1999—. Activities dir. Wilson C. Riles Mid. Sch., Roseville, Calif., 2004—06. Named Tchr. of Yr., Wilson C. Riles Mid. Sch., 2005—06. Mem.: Calif. Assn. Activities Dirs. Conservative. Avocations: swimming, volleyball. Office: Wilson C Riles Mid Sch 4747 PFE Rd Roseville CA 95747 Office Phone: 916-787-8100. Office Fax: 916-773-4131. Personal E-mail: jlaw@centerusd.k12.ca.us.

LAW, JERRIANN MARCELLA, artist, poet, writer; b. Franklin, Ky., Mar. 22, 1958; d. Charles Utah and Sylvia Martine (Cassetty) Law. Exhibitions include Medical Ctr. Gallery, Bowling Green, Ky., 2003; author: (anthology) Noble House Labours of Love, 2005, Goose River Press, 2005, co-author songs with Ramsey Kearney. Mem. Civil War Preservation Trust, 2002—05; mem., Tchrs. Against Hate So. Poverty Law Ctr., Birmingham, Ala., 2004—05; mem. Nat. Com. to Preserve Social Security & Medicare, 2004—05; founding mem. Nat. Mus. US Army, Washington, 2005—06, Nat. Mus. of the Am. Indian, America's Nat. WWII D-Day mus., New Orleans, 2005—06. Recipient 5th Place for Children's Fiction, Writers Digest Writing Competition, 2001. Mem.: ACLU, Acad. Am. Poets, Internat. Libr. Poetry, Cherokee Wolf Clan, Sierra Club. Avocations: scrapbooks, doll collecting. Home: PO Box 755 Franklin KY 42135

LAW, KATHLEEN SUE, elementary school educator; b. Stapleton, Nebr., Oct. 13, 1955; d. Davis Joseph and Dorothy Ora Law. AA, U. N.D., Branch Williston, 1975; BA, U. Wyo., Laramie, 1977. Cert. profl. tchr. Nat. Bd. Profl. Tchg. Stds. Tchr. Moorcroft Elem., Moorcroft, Wyo., 1977—81; tchr., dir. Rainbow Day Care, Williston, ND, 1981—85; tchr. Irving Kindergarten Ctr., Blackfoot, Idaho, 1985—. Co-author: Preparing to Read, 2002, Phonics 1, 2 and 3, 3 vols., 2004. Walk dir., treas. Idaho Walk to Emmaus, Idaho, 1996—98; presenter workshops at edn. confs. Recipient Teacher of Yr., Walmart, 2003, Phi Delta Kappa, 2003, Idaho Teacher of Yr., 2003. Mem.: Idaho Edn. Assn. (delegate 1996—97), Delta Kappa Gamma (pres. 2006—). Methodist. Avocations: singing, reading, travel. Office: Irving Kindergarten Ctr 440 W Judicial Blackfoot ID 83221

LAW, LOUISE DISOSWAY, education educator; b. Norfolk, Va., June 23, 1935; d. William Webster Disosway and Helen Marie (Benton) Mangum; m. Ralph Lee Law, June 30, 1956 (div. 1985); children: Joy, Denise, Daryl. BS magna cum laude, William and Mary Coll., 1957; MEd, U. Va., 1966, EdD, 1977. Tchr. Norfolk (Va.) Sch. System, 1957-61, Charlottesville (Va.) Sch. System, 1966-67; dir. Christian Ch. Pre-Sch., Charlottesville, 1967-72; tchr. Model Sch. Program Albermarle County (Va.) Sch. System, 1972-74; prof. Randolph-Macon Woman's Coll., Lynchburg, Va., 1974-88, chair edn. dept., 1988—2006; ret. Presenter in field. Contbr. articles to profl. jours. Mem. Internat. Reading Assn., Va. Assn. Tchr. Educators (sec. 1970-74), S.E. Assn. Tchr. Educators, South Cen. Assn. Tchr. Educators, Phi Theta Kappa. Democrat. Baptist. Avocations: reading, gardening, fishing, painting. Office: Randolph-Macon Womans Coll 2500 Rivermont Ave Lynchburg VA 24503-1555 Home: 1328 Creekside Dr Charlottesvle VA 22902-7223

LAW, MARCIA ELIZABETH, rehabilitation services professional; b. Spokane, Wash., Oct. 9, 1950; d. John Glen and Jean Carolyn (Lines) L.; 1 child, Michael Sean. AA, Spokane C.C., 1973. Notary public. Data entry operator, controller CyCare Sys., Spokane, Wash., 1974-78, tape libr., 1978-79; data entry operator Wash. state Dept. Employment Security, Spokane, 1986-87, Cath. Charities, Spokane, 1987, Cath. Diocese Spokane, 1987-90, Divsn. Vocat. Rehab. Dept. Health & Social Svcs., Seattle, 1990-95, sec. sr., 1994-99, counselor aide, 1999—2003, rehab. tech., 2003—. Mem. adv. com. Divsn. Vocat. Rehab. Dept. Health & Social Svcs., Seattle; state internal adv. com. Stakeholders Commn. Avocations: reading, movies, cross stitch, crafts, travel. Office: 18000 International Blvd Ste 1000 Seattle WA 98188-4251 E-mail: lawm@dshs.wa.gov.

LAW, PHYLLIS HAMPTON, secondary school educator; b. Killarney, W.Va., Feb. 1, 1941; d. Lynn J. Hampton and Sybil I. Pennington Hampton; m. David H. Law (div.); children: David A., Ron L. BS, W.Va. Wesleyan U., 1962; MS, W.Va. U., 1974. Fifth grade tchr. Follanshee (W.Va.) Mid. Sch., 1970—81; head HS tchr. Alternative Learning Ctr., Wellsburg, W.Va., 1981—91; tchr. Brooke HS, Wellsburg, 1991—. Sec. 4H Found., Brooke County, W.Va., 1970—, bd. dirs., 1991—. Mem.: W.Va. Edn. Assn. Democrat. Methodist. Avocations: reading, pets. Home: 137 Loretta Ave Follansbee WV 26037

LAW, SYLVIA A., law educator; b. 1942; BA, Antioch Coll., 1964; JD, NYU, 1968. Bar: NY 1968, Pa. 1970. Reginald Heber Smith Cmty. Lawyer Columbia Ctr. Social Welfare Policy & Law, 1968-69; lectr. London Sch. Econ. & Polit. Sci., 1969-70; staff dir. Pa. Health Law Project, 1970-73; asst. prof. NYU Sch. Law, NYC, 1973-76, assoc. prof., 1976-79, prof. law, 1979—94, Elizabeth K. Dollard prof. law, medicine and psychiatry, 1994—, also co-dir. Arthur Garfield Hays Civil Liberties Program. Vis. prof. Harvard U., 1984, CUNY at Queens, 1989; Hon. Phyllis W. Beck prof. law, Beasley Sch. Law Temple U., 2005. Author: Blue Cross: What Went Wrong?, 1973; co-author: (with Steve Polan) Pain and Profit: The Politics of Malpractice, 1978, (with R. Rosenblatt and S. Rosenbaum) Law and the American Health Care System, 1997. Sec. Alan Guttmacher Inst., 1978-90; chmn. Non-Traditional Employment for Women, 1985; bd. mem Ctr. Reproductive Rights, 1993-, Compassion in Dying (now Compassion & Choices), 1996-. MacArthur Fellow, 1983. Fellow Am. Soc. Arts & Sciences; mem. ACLU, SALT (treas. 1974-75, pres. 1988-90; named Lawyer of Yr., 2001), Nat. Lawyer's Guild. Office: NYU Sch Law Vanderbilt Hall Rm 429 49 Washington Sq S New York NY 10012-1099 Office Phone: 212-998-6265. Office Fax: 212-995-4526. E-mail: sylvialaw@aol.com.

LAWER, BETSY, banker, small business owner, vintner, director; b. Anchorage, July 27, 1949; d. Daniel H. and Betti Jane Cuddy; m. David A. Lawer, June 9, 1972; 1 child. Vice chair bd., COO 1st Nat. Bank Alaska, 1974—; pres. Lawer Family Winery Inc., 2005—. Emeritus bd. dirs. Providence Health Care Found., 2001; bd. dirs. Commonwealth North. Named one of the Top 25 Most Powerful Alaskans Alaska Jour. Commerce, 1999-2003, one of 25 Women to Watch US Banker, 2003. Mem.: Anchorage Athena Soc. (Athena award 2001).

LAWHON, CHARLA, editor; Grad., Drake U. With Apt. Life Mag., Des Moines; dir. editl. svcs. Meredith Design Group, 1990; exec. editor Met. Home, 1992; dep. editor InStyle Mag., N.Y.C., 1994—98, exec. editor, 1998—2002, mng. editor, 2002—. Office: InStyle Mag 1271 Ave of the Ams New York NY 10020

LAWHON, PATRICIA PATTON, literature and language professor, writer educator; b. Edgewood Arsenal, Md., Jan. 10, 1924; d. Jack Murray Patton and Elizabeth Cotter; m. Zim E. Lawhon, Dec. 23, 1944; children: Elizabeth Cotter, Mary Jane, Zim Edan, John Patton, Margaret Arnold, Bridget Jamieson, Martha Kone, Mary Benedict, Patricia Titus, Catherine Chad, Rebecca Anne, Rachel Julia, James Newton. BA, U. N.C., 1944; MA, U. Scranton, 1976. Instr. Keystone Coll., La Plume, Pa., 1974—76; adj. faculty U. Scranton, Pa., 1976—2006; instr. Marywood U., Scranton, 1977—82. Former mem. bd. Women's Resource Ctr. Mem.: Lackawanna River Corridor Assn., Archtl. Heritage Assn. (bd. dirs.), Friends of Libr., Lackawanna Hist. Soc., Alpha Sigma Nu. Address: 1527 N Washington Ave Scranton PA 18509-2361 E-mail: lawhonp1@aol.com.

LAWHON, TOMMIE COLLINS MONTGOMERY, humanities educator; b. Shelby County, Tex., Mar. 15; d. Marland Walker and Lillian (Tinsley) Collins; m. David Baldwin Montgomery, Mar. 31, 1962 (dec. Aug. 1964); m. John Lawhon, Aug. 27, 1967; 1 child, David Collins. BS, Baylor U., 1954; M in Home Econs. Edn., Tex. Woman's U., 1964, PhD in Child Devel. and Family Studies, 1966. Cert. tchr., Tex.; cert. family and consumer scis.; cert. family life educator. Tchr. Victoria Pub. Schs., Tex., 1954-55; stewardess, supr. Am. Airlines, Dallas/Ft. Worth, 1955-62; assoc. prof. home econs. Ea. Ky. U., Richmond, 1966-67, U. North Tex., Denton, 1968—, head divsn. child devel. and family studies, 1974—77, univ. tenure com., 1978—84, program head devel. in CDHE, 1993-94, mem. faculty senate, 1984-90, chmn. com. on coms., 1987-88, mem. com. status on women, 1984-87, mem. faculty salary com., 1989-95, chmn., 1989-91, mem. tradition com., 1989-95, recorder, 1989-91. Bd. dirs. U. North Tex., Univ. Union, 1985-88, mem. student mentor com., 1990-00, mem. benefits com., 1994-00, vice chair, 1994-95, chair, 1997-98, mem. faculty sen. Faculty Handbook com., 1998-2004, mem. faculty sen. mentor com., 1990-96, mem. coll. edn. greivance com., 2003-, chair, 2003-06; presenter in field. Co-author: Children are Artists, 1971, Hidden Hazards for Children and Families, 1982; editor: What to Do with Children, 1974, Field Trips for Children, 1984; contbr. articles to profl. jours. Chmn. United Way North Tex. State U., 1980-81; chmn. crusade Am. Cancer Soc., Denton County, 1982-83; chmn. nominating com. First Bapt. Ch., Denton, 1983-84, 84-85; mem. career action adv. com. Girls Inc. of Met. Dallas, 1999, chmn., 2000-01; advisor North Tex. Student Coun. on Family Rels., 1993—. Recipient Presdl. award Tex. Coun. on Family Rels., 1979, Fessor Graham award North Tex. State U., 1980, Svc. award Am. Cancer Soc., 1983, Outstanding Home Economists Alumni award Baylor U., 1985, Outstanding Event award, 12th Ann. State Conf., U. North Tex., 2006; named Hon. Prof. North Tex. State U., 1975, Meritorious award Nat. Coun. on Family Rels. Assn. of Couns., 2004; Disting. Svc. award Outstanding Orgn. Advisor, U. North Tex., 2005. Mem. Tex. Coun. on Family Rels. (pres. 1977-79, chmn. policy advisor com. 1986-88, nominating com. 1986-88, 94-96, chair 1994-96, family life edn. com. 1994-97, Moore-Bowman award 1994), Denton Assn. for Edn. Young Children (pres. 1970-72, 84-85, 85-86, v.p. 1986-87), Tex. Assn. Coll. Tchrs. (nominating com. 1988-89, 89-90, v.p. 1990-92, v.p. U. North Tex. chpt. 1987-88, pres. 1988-89, 89-90), Tex. Home Econs. Assn. (chmn. FLCD nominating com. 1983-84, chmn. child devel. and family rels. sect. 1988-90, sec. rep. bd. 1989-90), Nat. Coun. Family Rels. (com. 1982-83, cert. family life's continuing edn. com. 1996-99, chair elect cert. family life continuing edn. com. 1996, chair 1997-98, cert. family life edn. focus group and regional-state coord., chair 1996-97, coord. of all student asst. annual conf., 2001-02), Nat. Assn. Early Childhood Tchr. Educators (membership com. 1995-97), North Tex. Home Econs. Inter-orgnl. Coun. (adviser 1983-85), Phi Delta Kappa (pres. local chpt. 1991-92), Alpha Iota/Phi Upsilon Omicron (advisor 1970-82, chmn. nat. com. 1984-87, nat. bd. dirs. edn. found. 1990-94, com. pubs. 1991-92, vice chair ednl. found. 1992-94), Tri D Club (v.p. Baylor U. chpt. 1953-54), Univ. Grad. Club (pres. Tex. Woman's U. chpt. 1965-66). Democrat. Office: U North Tex Coll Edn Denton TX 76203

LAWHORN, SHANNON HIBBS, science educator; b. Chattanooga, Tenn., Jan. 28, 1972; d. Horace William and Shirley Marie Carolyn Hibbs; children: Brittany McClain, Brooke McClain, Rex. BS, U. Tenn., Tenn., 1996. Profl. Tchr. Lic. Tenn. Dept. Edn., 200. Sci. tchr. Richard Hardy Meml. Sch., South Pittsburgh, Tenn., 1996—. Recipient Conservation Tchr. of Yr., Maron County Soil Conservation, 1998, Tchr. of Yr., Richard Hardy Meml. Sch., 2002, 2004. Mem.: NEA, NSTA, Tenn. Edn. Assn. Republican. Avocations: reading, hiking, camping. Office: Richard Hardy Meml 1620 Hamilton Ave South Pittsburg TN 37380

LAWLER, CRYSTAL ANN, special education educator, consultant; b. Dearborn, Mich., Aug. 14, 1956; d. Carter McDonald and Janet Gail (Alexander) Hill; m. Ronald Lee Lawler, Sept. 11, 1976; 1 child, Hillary LeeAnn. BS in edn., Southern Ill. Univ., 1991; M in Edn., So. Ill. U., 1998. Cert. elem. tchr., learning disabilities tchr., Ill. Sec., office mgr. C.J.H. Construction Co., Fillmore, Ill., 1973-78; nurse's aide Fayette County Hosp., Vandalia, Ill., 1978-80; mgr. Dairy Queen, Hillsboro, Ill., 1982-84; tchr.'s aide in learning disabilites resource room Hillsboro (Ill.) High Sch., 1984-89; tchr. behavior disorders, learning disabilities Mid-State Spl. Edn. Coop., Hillsboro, 1991—. Tchr. Sunday sch., 1985-94, youth choir dir., 1985-91; asst. coach girls' softball, 1991. Mem. ASCD, Coun. Exceptional Children, Tchrs. Applying Whole Language, Phi Kappa Phi. Republican. Baptist. Avocations: horseback riding, running, reading, art, music. Office: Mid State Sp Edn Coop 1510 Sunset Dr Vandalia IL 62471

LAWLER, JEAN MARIE, lawyer; b. San Francisco, Aug. 7, 1954; d. Jack Wofford and Evelyn Mary (Matkovich) Suggs; m. Timothy Lawler, May 20, 1978; children— Kathleen, Megan, Colleen. A.A., Riverside City Coll., 1974; B.B.A., Loyola Marymount U., Los Angeles, 1976; J.D., Loyola U. Law Sch.-Los Angeles, 1979. Bar: Calif. Supreme Ct. 1979, Oreg. Supreme Ct. 1981. Assoc. law firm David L. Rosner, Los Angeles, 1979-80; instr. Lane Community Coll., Eugene, Oreg., 1981-82; sole practice law, Eugene, 1981-82, and Beaverton, Oreg., 1982-93, ptnr. Murchison & Cumming, LA, 1993-97, sr. ptnr and chair ins. law and risk mgmt. practice group, 1997-. Editor: Copyright Law, 1979-80; Business Associates Review, 1974; contbr. poetry to Coll. Poetry Rev., 1974, 76. Chmn. legal asst. adv. com. Lane Community Coll., 1981-82. Recipient Riverside County Bar Assn. scholarship, 1977; Loyola U. Jesuit Community scholarship, 1978; Named Calif. Super Lawyer, 2006. Mem. State Bar of Calif., Oreg. State Bar Assn., ABA, Washington County Bar Assn., Fedn. Def. & Corp. Counsel (bd. dir, 1996-, pres. 2004-2005), Assn. So. Calif. Def. Counsel (bd. dirs. 1994-2000), Def. Rsch. Inst. (bd. dirs. 2003-06), Lawyers for Civil Justice (bd. dirs. 2003-06). Democrat. Roman Catholic. Club: Jonathon Club. Office: Murchison & Cumming 9th Fl 801 S Grand Ave Los Angeles CA 90017 Office Phone: 213-630-1019. Office Fax: 210-623-6336. Business E-Mail: jlawler@murchisonlaw.com.

LAWLER, MARITA A., addiction therapist; b. Albany, Calif., July 14, 1947; d. Albert J. and Bonnie Davilla; m. David G. Lawler, June 2, 1990 (dec. Sept. 2004). BS of Human Svcs., Thomas Edison State Coll., 1998; MSc of Human Svcs., Capella U., 2000, postgrad., 1999—. Diplomate Am. Coll. Profl. Mental Health Practitioners, Am. Coll. Cert. Forensic Counselors; internat. cert. alcohol and drug counselor; nat. cert. master addictions counselor Nat. Bd. Add; nat. cert. criminal justice addicition specialist; registered addiction specialist Breining Inst.; cert. chem. dependency clin. supr. counselor II, Alaska. Lead substance abuse counselor and program developer Lassen County, Susanville, Calif., 1988-1990; lead substance abuse counselor MODOC County Alcohol and Drug Dept., Alturas, 1990—91; clin. counselor Youth and Family Svcs., 1991—94; substance abuse counselor Sundown M Ranch, Selah, Wash., 1994—95; substance abuse counselor, tng. supr. Barth & Assocs. Clinic, Yakima, 1996; cons.-owner Lawler Consulting, Alturas, Calif., 1996—98; clin. chem. dependency counselor MatSu Recovery Ctr., Wasilla, Alaska, 1998—2000; CEO, therapist, cons. Lawler Consulting, Palmer, 2000—. Bd. dir. Calif. Conf. on Alcohol Problems, Sacramento, Calif., 1989-91; cons. Calif. Dept. Corrections, Susanville, Calif., 1989-91, Modoc County Mental Health, Alcohol & Drug Svcs., Alturas, 1996-98. Actor: (theatrical prodns.) Brigadoon, 1998, A Mid-Summer Nights Dream, 1998; singer: (theatrical prodn.) HMS Pinafore, 1997; contbr. poetry to Anthology of Poetry, 1997. Chair worship com. St. Bartholomew's Episcopal Ch., Palmer, Alaska, 2000—02. Mem. APA, Internat. Assn. Addictions and Offenders Counselors, Am. Counseling Assn., Nat. Bd. Addiction Examiners, Nat. Assn. Alcoholism and Drug Abuse Counselors. Episcopalian. Avocations: reading, camping, rock and fossil hunting, travel, lifelong learning. Home: Ste 3 PMB #352 1150 S Colony Way Palmer AK 99645-6967 Office: Lawler Consulting PMB 352 1150 S Colony Way Ste 3 Palmer AK 99645 Office Phone: 907-232-8237. Home Fax: (907) 746-2926. E-mail: marita_lawler@hotmail.com, RevDrLawler@myway.com.

LAWLER, MARY LUCILLE, secondary school educator; b. Anderson, Ind., June 29, 1955; d. Thomas J. and Patricia Ann (Lawrence) L. BS, Ind. U., 1977; MA, Ball State U., 1982. Cert. tchr., Ind. Tchr., coach Delta High Sch., Muncie, Ind., 1977-78, Kouts (Ind.) High Sch., 1978-81; tchr. Greenfield (Ind.) Central High Sch., 1981—. Mem.: NEA, Nat. Assn. Nouthetic Counselors, Ind. Tchrs. Assn. Avocations: horse-back riding, reading, arts, crafts. Home: 5426 East Blue Ridge Rd Shelbyville IN 46176

LAWLER, ZARA DU PONT, musician, actor, dancer; arrived in U.S., 1972; d. Patrick Joseph and Judith Anderson Lawler. At, Ind. U., Bloomington, 1989—90; BA in Music, Barnard Coll., N.Y.C., 1992; MusM in Flute Performance, Juilliard Sch. Music, N.Y.C., 1994. Asst. prin. flute Hong Kong Philharmonic Orch., 1995—98; founder and flutist Full Fathom, N.Y.C., 1998—2000; flutist and performer Tales & Scales, Evansville, Ind., 2000—. Soloist in recitals, 1987—; collaborator Tales & Scales, Evansville, Ind., 2000—. Adult vol. Tri-State Alliance Gays and Lesbians Youth Group, Evansville, Ind., 2004—; bd. dir. Patchwork Ctrl., 2004—. Recipient First prize Concerto Competition, Ima Hogg and Houston Symphony, 1995, N.Y.C. Debut award, Artist's Internat., 2000. Avocations: folk music, banjo, house maintenence. Office: Tales and Scales PO Box 3672 Evansville IN 47735 Office Phone: 812-425-8741.

LAWLIS, PATRICIA KITE, military officer, computer consultant; b. Greensburg, Pa., May 5, 1945; d. Joseph Powell Jr. and Dorothy Theresa (Allshouse) Kite; m. John Charles Ryan, Feb. 6, 1965 (div. 1973); m. Mark Craig Lawlis, Sept. 17, 1976 (div. 1983); 1 child, Elizabeth Marie. BS in Math., East Carolina U., 1967; MS in Computer Sci., Air Force Inst. Tech., 1982; PhD in Computer Sci., Ariz. State U., 1989. Cert. secondary math. tchr. Employment counselor Pa. State Employment Svc., Washington, 1967-69; math. tchr. Fort Cherry Sch. Dist., McDonald, Pa., 1969-74; commd. 2d lt. USAF, 1974, advanced through grades to lt. col., 1974—94; data base mgr. Air Force Space Command, Colorado Springs, 1974-77; computer sys. analyst USAF in Europe, Birkenfeld, Germany, 1977-80; prof. computer sci. Air Force Inst. Tech., Wright-Patterson AFB, Ohio, 1982-86, 89-94; ret. USAF, 1994; computer cons., pres. C.J. Kemp Systems, Inc., Fairborn, Ohio, 1983—2003; women's dir. Sr. Softball USA, Sacramento, 2002—; pres. 2d Chance Sports, Inc., Phoenix, 2002—; engring. specialist Jacobs Sverdrup, San Antonio, 2003—. Ada cons., Ada Joint Program Office, Washington, 1984-94. State treas. NOW, Pa., 1973-74; active women's adv. coun. Nat. Sr. Softball Summit, Sacramento, 2003—. Recipient Mervin E. Gross award Air Force Inst. Tech., 1982, Prof. Ezra Kotcher award, 1985. Mem. Computer Soc. of IEEE, Tau Beta Pi (v.p. chpt. 1981-82), Upsilon Pi Epsilon. Office: 2nd Chance Sports Inc PO Box 93514 Phoenix AZ 85070-3514 also: Jacobs Sverdrup 1107 Crossbrook San Antonio TX 78253 Office Phone: 210-733-3383. E-mail: lawlis@aol.com.

LAWRENCE, DEBORAH JEAN, quality assurance professional; b. San Jose, Calif., June 25, 1960; BA in Math., San Jose State U., 1982; MS in Stats., Stanford U., 1985. Math. aide Info. Mgmt. Internat., Moffet Field, Calif., 1980-82; group engr. Lockheed Missiles and Space Co., Sunnyvale, Calif., 1982-89; mgr. quality assurance Analog Devices, Inc., Santa Clara, Calif., 1989—. Reengring. spl. interest group leader Coun. for Continuous Improvement, 1994-96, QS 9000 spl. interest group leader, 1995-97. Author tech. papers. Mem. Am. Soc. for Quality Control (sr. mem., cert. engr.), Am. Statis. Assn. Office: Analog Devices Inc 3550 N 1st St San Jose CA 95134

LAWRENCE, DEIRDRE ELIZABETH, librarian; b. Lawton, Okla., Mar. 15, 1952; d. Herbert Thomas and Joan Roberta (McDonald) L. BA in Art History, Richmond Coll., 1974; MLS, Pratt Inst., 1979; postgrad., Harvard U., 1981-82. Head cataloging and tech. svcs., coord. rsch. svcs. Mus. Fine Arts, Boston, 1980-83; prin. libr., coord. rsch. svcs. mus. and libr. archives Bklyn. Mus., 1983—. Mem. Rsch Libr. Group, bd. nominating com., 1994, adv. com. Getty Projects, 1996—, N.Y. Met. Reference and Rsch. Libr. Agy, conservation preservation adv. coun., 1988-92, bd. trustees, 1995—; grant reviewer fed. and state agys.; cons. in field; lectr. in field. Author: New York and Hollywood Fashion, 1986, Dressing the Part: Costume Sket, 1989, Modern Art--The Production, 1989, Guide to the Culin Archival Collection, 1996, Formation of an Islamic art library collection in an Am. museum, 1996, Culin: Collector and Documentor of the World He Saw, Fashion and How It Was Influenced by Ethnographic Collections in Museums, Native American Art and Culture: Documentary Resources, Access to Visual Images-Past and Present; contbr. articles to profl. jours.; lectr. at internat. and nat. libr. confs.; curator various collections including Bklyn. Mus., 1989, 96, 97, others. Mem. conservation, preservation adv. coun. N.Y. Met. Reference and Rsch. Libr. Agy., 1988-92, bd. trustees, 1995—. Recipient Samuel H. Kress Travel grant, 1993, 95. Mem. Art Librs. Soc. N.Am. (mem. internat. rels. com. 1996-97, other offices), Spl. Librs. Assn., Native Am. Art Studies Assn., Internat. Fedn. Libr. Assns. Office: Brooklyn Mus 200 Eastern Pkwy Brooklyn NY 11238-6099

LAWRENCE, ESTELENE YVONNE, musician, transportation executive; b. Lynch, Ky., Aug. 10, 1933; d. Samuel Coleridge and Florence Estelle (Gardner) Taylor; m. Otto Lee Lawrence, Sept. 14, 1957; children: Stuart, Neil, Adelbert. Student, Fenn Coll., 1953—60, Cleve. Inst. Music, 1955—56, John Carroll U., 1977—78, Northeastern U., Boston, 1979—80; BA, Cleve. State U., 1993. Stenographer Cleve. Transit Sys., Regional Transit Authority, 1951—76, tng. asst., 1976—78, personal devel. asst., 1978—82, dist. adminstr., 1983—86, supr., mgmt. skills instr., 1976—86, dir., tng. and career devel., 1986—88; assoc. in profl. mgmt. John Carroll U., 1977—78. Dir. music Friendly United Baptist Ch., 1947—95; piano tchr., 1953—73; minister of music Mt. Nebo Baptist Ch., 1995—; pianist, organist Nat. Baptist Convention, 1971, 80; chmn. adv. bd. Baldwin Wallace Coll., 1984—88; chief musician Regional Transit Authority Choir; mem. Cleve. Choral Union. Publicity chmn. Moses Cleve. Sch. PTA, 1965—75; audit chmn. Regional Transit Authority Main Office Credit Union, 1980—83; dist. sec. Boy Scouts Am., 1982—83; mem. adv. bd. Cleve. Mgmt. Devel. Consortium, 1985—88. Mem.: Greater Cleve. Pan-Hellenic Choir, Conf. Minority Transp. Ofcls., Cleve. Mgmt. Seminars (treas. 1979—81, pres. 1981—83), Am. Choral Dirs. Assn., East 153rd St. (v.p. 1980—), Alpha Kappa Alpha, Mu Phi Epsilon (historian 1990—91, chorister 1991—92, pres. 1992—93), Phi Kappa Gamma (pres. 1966—69). Home: 4066 E 153rd St Cleveland OH 44128-1926

LAWRENCE, EVELYN THOMPSON, retired music educator, researcher; b. Marion, Va., Nov. 13, 1919; d. John Emmett and Susie Barnett (Madison) Thompson; m. Joseph John Lawrence, Oct. 5, 1946; 1 child, Sheila Ann (dec.). BS in Edn., W. Va. State Coll., 1941; student, Va. State U., 1946, Hampton U., 1948; M of Music, U. Mich., 1952. Elem. sch. tchr., music tchr. Carnegie High Sch., Marion, Va., 1941-65; tchr. Marion Primary Sch., 1965-84; judge art, storytelling, and creative writing Smyth County Schs., Marion, Chilhowie, Va., 1984-96, rocking reader Marion, 1994—; producer, dir. plays Supporters Enriched Edn. and Knowledge, Marion, 1983-92. Music and recreation dir. Douglass Ctr., Toledo, Ohio, summer, 1953; instr. ch. music Va. Union U., Richmond, summer 1960, 61; judge Sherwood Anderson Lit. Contest, 1989-91. Author: Directoy of African-American Students and Teachers in all Smyth County Schools, 1906-1965. Organist and choir dir. Mt. Pleasant Meth. Ch., Marion, 1994—; bd. dirs. Blue Ridge Job Corps., Marion, 1994—; v.p., past pres. Church Women United, Marion, 1985-86; co-res., Smyth County Univ. Assn., 1997—; parade marshal Marion Christmas Parade, 1994; music leader Red Hat Soc., 2002—; music dir. Greenwood Meth. Ch., 2003—. Recipient 2 nominations Tchr. of Yr. award, S.W. Va. Coun. of Internat. Reading Assn., Abingdon, Va., 1981, 82, Svc. to Youth award Carnegie Sch. Alumni, Marion, 1983, Citizen of Yr. award Marion Rotary Club, 1985. Mem. AAUW (chmn. cultural rels. com. 1966-96), Alpha Kappa Alpha (1940—), Alpha Delta Kappa (tchrs. sor. 1987—). Avocations: travel, crossword puzzles, gardening. Home: 312 Broad St Marion VA 24354-2804

LAWRENCE, JANICE FLETCHER, psychologist; d. Charlie J. and Garnet Roberts Fletcher; 1 child, Vicci Leigh. AB, Marshall U., 1955, MA, 1957, MA, 1979; EdD, Va. Polytechnic Inst. & State U., 1979. Lic. sch. psychologist W.Va. Dept. Edn., 1978, Nat. Sch. Psychology, 1989, sch. psychologist, ind. practioner W.Va. Bd. Psychologists, 1995. Psychologist Kanawha County Schs., Charleston, W.Va., 1967—74; coord. psychologists W.Va. State Dept., Charleston, 1974—89; sch. psychologist Kanawha County Schs., Charleston, 1984—89; adj. clin. prof. psychology Marshall U., South Charleston, W.Va., 1978—2001; pvt. practice Cmty. Behavioral Svcs., Inc., Dunbar, W.Va., 1990—. Trustee Nat. Sci. Bd., Charleston, 1974—84. Gifted Edn. grant, W.Va. Dept. Edn., 1978—83, Handicapped Children grant, 1981—84. Mem.: Nat. Assn. Sch. Psychologists. Avocations: gardening, reading.

LAWRENCE, KAREN K., mathematics educator; d. Walt and Geraldine Kopp; m. James Randall Lawrence; children: Jana M Kellogg, Justin, Shannon, Joshua Leonard, Brian, Jared Leonard. Degree in edn., Tex. A&M U., College Station, 1978; MA in Edn., Pan Am. U., Brownsville, Tex., 1984. Instr. phys. edn. instr., coach Brownsville Ind. Sch. Dist., Tex.; tchr. elem. sch. Rockwall Ind. Sch. Dist., Tex.; instr. math. and sci. Christian Fellowship Sch., Lakewood; math. instr. Jefferson County, Lakewood, Cherokee County Schs., Canton, Ga. With USMC, 1972, Washington. Named Star Tchr., 2004; recipient Kiwanis Tchr. award, 2003. Mem.: Ga. Coun. Tchrs. of Math., Nat. Coun. Tchrs. of Math. Office: Dean Rusk Mid Sch 4695 Hickory Rd Canton GA 30115 Office Phone: 770-345-2832. Business E-Mail: karen.lawrence@cherokee.k12.ga.us.

LAWRENCE, KRISTINE GUERRA, project engineer; married. MS in Aerospace Engring., U. Colo. Gravitational biology facility engr. NASA Ames Rsch. Ctr. Mem. adv. com. women NASA Ames Rsch. Ctr. Flight medic USAF Res. Business E-Mail: klawrence@mail.arc.nasa.gov.

LAWRENCE, LAUREN, psychotherapist, writer; b. N.Y.C., June 26, 1950; d. Jack and Elaine (Gaumont) Soefer; m. David Lawrence, June 24, 1972; 1 child, Graham. MA in Psychology, New Sch. for Social Rsch., N.Y.C., 1993. Psychoanalyst, N.Y.C., 1992—. Author: Dream Keys: Unlocking the Power of Your Unconscious Mind, 1999, Dream Keys for Love, 1999, Dream Keys for the Future: Unlocking the Secrets of Your Destiny, 2000, La Llave De Los Suenos, 2001, A Quoi Revent Les Stars, 2002, Private Dreams of Public People, 2002; contbr. sci. papers and articles to profl. jours. and mags.; performer: (TV series) The Dream Zone, RISE TV, BBC; appeared on numerous TV and radio shows; contbr. columns in newspapers and mags. Friend N.Y. Psychoanalytic Soc. Achievements include founding of a third person analysis, a new method of analysis in clinical practice, which provides the analysand a narrational objectivity; the covert seduction theory, which expounds the dangers of a non-physical parental seduction, the Actualized Dream, a conscious behavioral manifestation of symbolic material-unconscious desires that manifest themselves during consciousness through extreme behavioral acts, the undisclosed visual cliche, as an attribute or assessment drawn from a visual that leads to a cliche, and the externalized dream as a manifestation of a vision. Home and Office: 31 E 72d St New York NY 10021-4146 Office Phone: 212-737-3911. E-mail: LaurenLawrence@aol.com.

LAWRENCE, MADALENA JOAN VIGNOCCHI, accountant; b. Lake Forest, Ill., July 2, 1952; d. Anthony and Juanita Dolly (Thompson) V.; m. Thomas Stanley Lawrence, Nov. 21, 1981; children: David, Michael. BS in Fin., U. Ill., 1973. CPA, Ill. Staff acct. Ernst & Ernst, Chgo., 1974-75, in-charge acct., 1975-76; semi-sr. internal auditor McGraw-Edison Co., Elgin, Ill., 1976-77, tax acct., 1977-79; sr. tax analyst Safety Kleen Corp., Elgin, 1980-84, acctg. supr., 1984-85, mgr. capital budget, property acct., 1985-91; owner Lawrence Enterprises, 1991—. Mem. Am. Inst. CPA's, Women in Mgmt. (pres. No. Fox Valley chpt. 1984-86), Ill. CPA's. Roman Catholic. Avocations: bicycling, photography. Office: Lawrence Enterprises 330 W Morse Ave Bartlett IL 60103-4068 Personal E-mail: tmlaw@quixnet.net.

LAWRENCE, MARILYN EDITH (MARILYN GUTHRIE), association executive; b. Oct. 5, 1946; d. George Nelson and Marjorie Estelle (Field) G. AAS, SUNY, Morrisville, 1966. Various secretarial positions, 1966—75; exec. asst. Northeastern Retail Lumbermens Assn., Rochester, NY, 1975—79, sr. v.p. Wellesley, Mass. and Rochester, 1979—86; placement specialist Renda Pers. Cons., Rochester, 1986—89; exec. dir. Oil Heat Inst. Upstate N.Y., Rochester, 1989—92; owner Profl. Bus. Svcs., Newark, NY, 1992—94; program dir. Assn. Mgmt. Svc., Rochester, 1992—94; exec. dir. Internat. Mcpl. Signal Assn., 1994—. Mem.: Am. Soc. Assn. Execs. Republican.

LAWRENCE, MARY JOSEPHINE (JOSIE LAWRENCE), artist, retired library official; b. Carbondale, Pa., Mar. 9, 1932; d. Domenick Anthony and Teresa Rose (Zaccone) Gentile; m. John Paul Lawrence, Apr. 25, 1953 (dec. June 1977); children: Mary Josephine, Jane Therese, Susan Michele. BFA, Mass. Coll. Art, 1989; postgrad., Chelsea (Eng.) Sch. Art, 1989, San Pancrazio Art Sch., Tuscany, Italy, 1990, 91, 92; cert. in grad. studies, Guangzhou Acad. Fine Arts, China, 1993; postgrad., Md. Inst. Fine Art, Sorrento, Italy, 1994, Ctrl. Acad. Arts and Design, Beijing, 1997, Skopelos, Greece, 1998, N.Y. Sch. Visual Arts, Barcelona, Spain, 1999, Internat. Sch. Art, Umbria, Italy, 2000. Sales clk. Gorins, 5&10, Jordan Marsh, Boston, 1946-49; clk.-typist, sec. John Hancock Ins. Co., Boston, 1950-53; machine operator, quality control supr. Rust Craft Greeting Cards, Dedham, Mass., 1961-69; restaurant hostess Tony's Villa, Waltham, Mass., 1972-73; mus. sales clk., artist John F. Kennedy Libr., Boston, 1979-87, mgr. mus. store, supr., 1988-2000; freelance artist, 2000—. Tchr.'s asst. San Pancrazio Art Sch., 1992; guest appearance TAKE TWO cable TV, Channel 11, 1996, Walpole Cmty. TV, 2001, WEZE Family 590 Talk Show, 2001. One woman shows include de Havilland Fine Art Gallery, Boston, 1997, Dr. James McDermott Gallery, Boston, 1996, Cranberry Cafe, Boston, 1997; exhibited in group shows at South Shore Arts Ctr., Cohasset, Mass., 1991, North River Arts Soc., Marshfield Hills, Mass., 1994 (Best of Show), de Havilland Fine Art Gallery, Boston, 1997, United South End Open Studios, 1998, Artana Gallery, Framingham, Mass., 2000. Juror Quincy Art Assn., 1996, 98, 2002, 2005, Weymouth Art Assn., 1995, 97, Arts Affair, 1999. Recipient Outstanding Achievement award, Nat. Archives and Rsch. Adminstrn., 1989, 1994, 1996—97, Svc. award, 1990, Blue Ribbon Mems. award, 2003, Best of show award, De Havilland Fine Arts Gallery, 1992, honorium, Weymouth Art Assn., 1995, 1997, Quincy Art Assn. award, 1996, 1998, 2002, 2005; grantee Vt. Studio Ctr., 2002, 2004. Mem. de Havilland Fine Art Gallery, South Shore Art Ctr., North River Arts Soc., Nat. Mus. Women in Arts (charter), Milton Art Mus., United S. End Artists, Fuller Mus. Art., South Boston Arts Assn., Portland Mus. Art, Farnsworth Art Mus. Democrat. Roman Catholic. Personal E-mail: josielawrence@comcast.net.

LAWRENCE, MERLOYD LUDINGTON, editor; b. Pasadena, Calif., Aug. 1, 1932; d. Nicholas Saltus and Mary Lloyd (Macy) Ludington; m. Seymour Lawrence, June 21, 1952 (div. 1984); children: Macy, Nicholas; m. John M. Myers, 1985 AB, Radcliffe Coll., 1954, MA, 1957. With Houghton Mifflin Co., 1955-57; freelance translator, 1957-65; editor, treas., v.p. Seymour Lawrence Inc., Boston, 1965-83; pres. Merloyd Lawrence, Inc., Boston, 1983—. Translator works of Flaubert and Balzac, modern French fiction, German and Swedish children's books. Treas., v.p. Milford House Properties, Ltd., N.S., Can., 1975-80; trustee Milton (Mass.) Acad., 1974-82; mem. com. clin. investigations Beth Israel/Deaconess Hosp.; bd. dirs. Northeast Wilderness Trust, 2002—, Woods Hole Rsch. Ctr., 2004—. Mem. Am. Translators Assn., New Eng. Forestry Found. (exec. bd. officer 1989—), Mass. Audubon Soc. (dir. 1974-2001, exec. com. 1992-2001, hon. dir. 2001—), Tavern Club, Phi Beta Kappa. Home: 102 Chestnut St Boston MA 02108-1120 Office: 102A Chestnut St Boston MA 02108-1120

LAWRENCE, NINA, publishing executive; married; 2 children. B cum laude, Middlebury Coll., 1982. Media planner Benton & Bowles, Inc., 1983—85; with Mag. Sales Develop. Program Time Inc., 1985—86, with advt. sales dept., 1986—87; advt. sales dir. Diversion mag. Hearst Publishing, 1987—89, pub. Hearst Profl. Magazines, 1989—90; pres. Family Publishing Concepts, 1991—92; advt. dir. Discover mag., 1992—93; pub. Disney Adventures mag., 1993—94; assoc. pub. Mademoiselle mag. Conde Nast Pubs., NYC, 1994-96; pub. Modern Bride mag. Primedia Inc., NYC, 1996-98; pub. Bride's mag. Conde Nast Pubs., NYC, 1999—2005; v.p. & pres. W mag., NYC, 2005—. Office: W Mag 7 West 34th St New York NY 10001*

LAWRENCE, RUTH ANDERSON, pediatrician; b. NYC; d. Stephen Hayes and Loretta (Harvey) A.; m. Robert Marshall Lawrence, July 4, 1950; children, Robert Michael, Barbara Asselin, Timothy Lee, Kathleen Ann, David McDonald, Mary Khalil, Joan Margaret, John Charles, Stephen Harvey. BS in Biology summa cum laude, Antioch Coll., 1945; MD, U. Rochester, 1949. Internship and residency in pediatrics Yale New Haven (Conn.) Hosp., 1949-50; asst. resident in Medicine Yale New Haven (Conn.) Community Hosp., 1950-51; postdoctoral fellow Yale New Haven Hosp., 1951, chief resident newborn svc., 1951; cons. in medicine U.S. Army, Ft. Dix, N.J., 1952; from clin. instr. to sr. instr. in pediatrics U. Rochester, N.Y., 1952-64, assoc. resident N.Y., 1957-58, asst. prof. N.Y., 1964-70, assoc. prof. N.Y., 1970-85, prof. pediatrics, ob.-gyn. N.Y., 1985—. Rsch. pediatrician Monroe County Health Dept., Rochester, 1952-58; dir. Finger Lakes Regional Poison Control Ctr., 1958—; chief nursery svc. Strong Meml. Hosp., Rochester, 1960-73, chief dept. pediatrics, The Highland Hosp., Rochester, 1960-91; adj. prof. Sch. Pub. Health, SUNY, Albany, 1996-99; rsch. in field. Author: Breastfeeding: A Guide for the Medical Profession, 6th edit., 2005; editor: various periodicals; contbr. numerous articles to profl. publs. Mem. Safety Coun. Rochester and Monroe County, also past pres.; bd. dirs., past pres. Life Line. Recipient Gold Medal award U. Rochester Alumni Assn., 1979, William Keeler award Rochester Safety Coun., 1982, Civic Contribution citation Rochester Safety Coun., 1984, Career Achievement award Girl Scouts U.S. of Genesee Valley, 1987, Rochester Diocesan award for women, St. Bernard's Inst., 1989, Albert David Kaiser medal, 1991, Chamber Civic Health Care award, 1996, Humanism in Medicine award Am. Assn. Med. Colls., 1999, Edward Mott Moore award, Monroe County Med. Soc., 2001, Nat. Best Physician award, 2002-03, Lifetime Achievement award Healthy Children, 2003, 1st Annual Leading Lady award Leading Lady Cos., Beachwood, Ohio, 2003, numerous svc. awards; named Woman of Yr. Girl Scouts U.S. of Monroe County, 1968; hon. fellow Am. Sch. Health Assn., 1960, rsch. fellow Jackson Meml. Rsch. Labs., 1945. Fellow Am. Pediatric Soc., Am. Acad. Clin. Toxicology (past trustee, Lifetime Achievement award 2002); mem. Internat. Soc. for Rsch. in Human Milk and Lactation (exec. com. 1995-98), Human Milk Banking Assn. N.Am. (adv. bd. 1980-2005), NAS (subcom. on nutrition during lactation), Acad. Breastfeeding Medicine (founding bd. dirs. 1994—, pres. 1997-98), Alpha Omega Alpha. Roman Catholic. Office: U Rochester Sch Medicine 601 Elmwood Ave Box 777 Rochester NY 14642 Office Phone: 585-275-4354. Business E-Mail: ruth_lawrence@urmc.rochester.edu.

LAWRENCE, SALLY CLARK, retired academic administrator; b. San Francisco, Dec. 29, 1930; d. George Dickson and Martha Marie Alice (Smith) Clark; m. Henry Clay Judd Jr., July 1, 1950 (div. Dec. 1972); children: Rebecca, David, Nancy; m. John I. Lawrence, Aug. 12, 1976; stepchildren: Maia, Dylan. Grad., Castilleja Sch. Girls, 1948; attended, House in the Pines Jr. Coll., Norton, Mass., 1948—49, Stanford U., 1949—50. Docent Portland Art Mus., Portland, Oreg., 1958-68; gallery owner, dir. Sally Judd Gallery, Portland, Oreg., 1968-75; art ins. appraiser, cons. Portland, Oreg., 1975-81; from interim dir. Mus. Art Sch. to pres. Pacific NW Coll. Art, Portland, Oreg., 1981—2003, pres. emerita, 2003—. Bd. dirs. Contemporary Crafts Gallery, Portland, 1970—73, Art Coll. Exch., 1982—91, Portland Arts Alliance, Portland, Oreg., 1987—2003, Portland Inst. Contemporary Art, 2005—, sec., 2006. Fellow: Nat. Assn. Sch. Art and Design (life; bd. dirs. 1984—91, 1994—2002, pres. 1996—99); mem.: Assn. Ind. Coll. of Art and Design (pres. 1995—96, sec. 1996—2001), Oreg. Ind. Coll. Assn. (bd. dirs. 1981—2003, exec. com. 1989—94, pres. 1992—93, v.p. 2001—03), Pearl Arts Found. (chair bd. dirs. 2000—03). Personal E-mail: sallyl@carrollsweb.com.

LAWRENCE, SARAH ANNE, social studies educator; b. Hartford, Conn., Jan. 5, 1974; d. Marcia D. and Mark R. Lawrence. BA in Asian Studies, Mt. Holyoke Coll., South Hadley, Mass., 1991—95; Tchr. Cert., Ctrl. Conn. State U., New Britain, 1999—2003. Asst. English tchr. Aoya HS, Aoya-cho, Japan, 1995—98; social studies tchr. Hall HS, West Hartford, Conn., 2003—. Mem.: NEA, Conn. Edn. Assn. Democrat. Avocations: travel, photography, music, reading, scrapbooks. Home: PO Box 42 New Hartford CT 06057 Office: Hall HS 975 N Main St West Hartford CT 06117 Personal E-mail: sarahalawrence@hotmail.com. Business E-Mail: sarah_lawrence@whps.org.

LAWRENCE, SHARON, actress; b. Charlotte, N.C., June 29, 1962; Appeared in (TV series) NYPD Blue, 1993, The Shaggy Dog, 1994, The Heidi Chronicles, 1995, Star Trek: Voyager, 1995, Degree of Guilt, 1995, A Friend's Betrayal, 1996, Five Desperate Hours (co-prodr.), 1997, The Only Thrill, 1998, Gossip, 1999, Blue Moon, 1999, Desperate Housewives, others; starred in sitcom, Fired Up, 1997; (stage) No Time For Comedy, 2005, Anything Goes, 2006. Nominated for Emmys, 1995, 96, SAG awards 1996, 99, Q award, 1998.*

LAWRENCE, SHARON LYNN, director, educator; d. Joseph Richard and Florence Soucie Lawrence; m. Daniel Brian Garvey, Dec. 30, 1995; children: Sebastian Antonio Perez Lawrence, Maria Alejandra Perez Lawrence, Emma Rose Garvey. BA, Siena Coll., 1980; M of edn. adminstrn., U. Mass., 2006. Tchr. English as 2d lang. Instituto Chileno-Norteamericano de Cultura, Santiago, Chile, 1990—92, Rankin County Schs., Brandon, Miss., 1995—98; chair fgn. lang., English as 2d lang. and fine arts NY Mil. Acad., Cornwall-on-Hudson, 2000—. Coach Cornwall Youth Soccer, 2005, Cath. Youth Orgn., Nashua, NH, 1999, NW Rankin Athletic Assn., Brandon, Miss., 1996—97, YMCA - YMCA, Brandon, 1995—98, Lenox Youth Sports, Lenox, Mass., 1993—95. Fellow, US Govt., Ind. U., 1981—82, 1983—84, Ind. U., 1984, Berlin Senate, 1985, 1986; Fulbright Hays fellow, US Govt., Ind. U., 1982, Fulbright Meml. fellow, Japanese Govt., 2004. Mem.: Am. Coun. Tchg. Fgn. Langs. (assoc.), Tchrs. English Spkrs. Other Langs. (assoc.). Office: NY Military Acad 78 Acad Ave Cornwall On Hudson NY 12520 Office Phone: 845-534-3710. Business E-Mail: slawrence@nyma.ouboces.org.

LAWRENCE, WENDY B., astronaut; b. Jacksonville, Fla., July 2, 1959; d. William P. Lawrence and Anne Haynes. BS in Ocean Engring., U.S. Naval Acad., 1981; MS in Ocean Engring., MIT and Woods Hole Oceanographic Institution, 1988. Naval aviator USN, 1982; with Helicopter Combat Support Squadron SIX (HC-6); officer in charge of detachment ALFA Helicopter Anti-Submarine Squadron Light THIRTY HSL-30; physics instr., novice women's crew coach U.S. Naval Acad., 1990-92; mission specialist, astronaut NASA, 1992—, flight software verifier Shuttle Avionics Integration Lab., astronaut office asst. tng. officer, ascent/entry flight engr., blue shift orbit pilot on STS-67, 1995, dir. ops. Gagarin Cosmonaut Tng. Ctr. Star City, Russia, with crew on STS-86 on space shuttle Atlantis, 1997, with crew on STS-91 on space shuttle Discovery, 1998, mission specialist 4 (MS-4) for STS-114 (Discovery) Return to Flight mission, 2005. Recipient Defense Superior Svc. medal, Defense Meritorious Svc. medal, NASA Space Flight medal, Navy Commendation medal, Navy Achievement medal, Capt. Winifred Collins award for inspirational leadership Nat. Navy League, 1986. Mem. Assn. Naval Aviation, Women Mil. Aviators, Naval Helicopter Assn., Phi Kappa Phi. Avocations: running, rowing, triathlons. Office: NASA Lyndon B Johnson Space Ctr Houston TX 77058

LAWRENCE-LIGHTFOOT, SARA, education educator, sociologist; EdD, Harvard U. Faculty mem. Harvard U., 1978—, Emily Hargroves Fisher prof. of ed. Author Worlds Apart: Relationships Between Families and Schools, 1978, Beyond Bias, 1979, Good High School: Portraits of Character and Culture, 1983, Balm in Gilead: Journey of a Healer, 1989 (Christopher award), I've Known Rivers: Lives of Loss and Liberation, 1993, Art and Science of Portraiture, 1997, Respect: An Exploration, 1999, The Essential Conversation: What Parents and Teachers Can Learn From Each Other, 2003. Bd. dirs. John D. and Catherine T. MacArthur Found., 1991—, chair, bd. dirs., 2002—; bd. dirs. Berklee Coll. of Music, Boston Globe, Bright Horizons Family Solutions. Recipient MacArthur prize, 1984, George Ledlie prize, 1993, Spencer Sr. Scholar award, 1995, Crossing the River Jordan award, Public Ed. Network, 2003, Ferguson award for Svc. to Children and Families, Nat. Louis U., 2004. Mem.: Nat. Acad. of Ed. Office: Harvard Grad Sch Ed Gutman 463 Cambridge MA 02138*

LAWSON, BARBARA SLADE, elementary school educator, artist; b. Kobe, Japan, Dec. 16, 1930; arrived in US, 1940; d. Ewell William and Michaela Carpenter Slade; m. Alvin H. Lawson, Jan. 31, 1953; children: Lawrence-(dec.), Leslie, Leigh(dec.), Katherine(dec.). BA, San Francisco State Coll., 1952. Tchr. Calif. Pub. Elem. Sch. Dist., 1953, Hayward Pub. Elem. Sch. Dist., Calif., 1954, So. San Francisco Sch. Dist., 1956, Los Lamites Sch. Dist., Calif., 1957—58, Los Altos Sch. Dist., 1960—61, Cypress Sch. Dist., 1964—86. Mem.: Watercolor West (sec. bd. dirs. 1998—2004), San Diego Watercolor Soc., Eastern Wash. Watercolor Soc., Northwestern Watercolor Soc., Pa. Watercolor Soc. Democrat. Avocation: swimming. Home: 5861 Huntley Ave Garden Grove CA 92845-2041 Office: Showcase Gallery 3851 South Bear St Ste B15 Santa Ana CA 92707 Office Phone: 714-540-6430.

LAWSON, BETH ANN REID, lawyer, strategic planner; b. NYC, Jan. 9, 1954; d. Raymond Theodore and Jean Elizabeth (Frinks) Reid; m. Michael Berry Lawson, Jan. 29, 1983; children: Rayna, Sydney. BA, Va. Tech., 1976; MPA, Golden Gate U., 1983; JD, Regent U. Law, 2004. Bar: Va. 2005. From systems analyst I to support ops. asst. City of Virginia Beach, Va., 1977-93, water conservation coord., 1993-94; owner Strategic Planning and Teamwork, Virginia Beach, 1993—; cons. Resort Leadership Coun., 1998-99; ptnr., pvt. practice law Lawson, Bryan, Johnson, Edwards-Talbot PLLC, Virginia Beach, 2006—. Cons., 1996-2000, Lifesaving Mus. Va., 1994, 98, Virginia Beach C.A.R.E. Com., 1995, Virginia Beach Rescue Squad, 1992—, Virginia Beach Mcpl. Employees Fed. Credit Union, 1992—, Virginia Beach Resort Area Adv. Commn., 1993, Virginia Beach Conv. and Visitors Devel. Bur., 1991-93, 98—; customer svc. trainer Virginia Beach Hotel/Motel Superhost, 1995-2001. Sunday sch. tchr. Wycliffe Presbyn. Ch., Virginia Beach, 1996—, softball coach, 1997. Mem. Virginia Beach Rescue Squad (hon., life), Va. Tech. Alumni Assn. (pres. 1982-83), Rotary (mediator 2001, atty. 2005, Outstanding Employee award 1993). Avocations: movies, football. Home: 701 Earl Of Warwick Ct Virginia Beach VA 23454-2910 Office: Beth Ann Lawson Atty at Law 701 Earl Of Warwick Ct Virginia Beach VA 23454-2910 Personal E-mail: balawson@aol.com.

LAWSON, BONNIE HULSEY, psychotherapist, consultant; b. Dunnellon, Fla., July 7, 1932; d. Guy Wilton and Katrina (Lanier) Hulsey; 1 child, Christopher Paul. BS, Wake Forest U., Winston-Salem, 1954; MA, Stetson U., Deland, Fla., 1970; PhD, U. Ga., 1980. Asst. prof. med. tech. Brunswick (Ga.) Coll., 1970-73; assoc. prof. med. tech. Cen. Fla. U., Orlando, 1974-75; head human rels. sect. U. Ga., Athens, 1980-93, head humanities and social scis., 1993-97; pvt. practice Hosp. Consultation, 1998—. Author TV prog.: Controlling Stress, 1981, A Step Ahead in Caring, 1981, Premenstrual Syndrome, 1985, HyperCard prog. Working with Adult Learners, 1989, Patient Relations Certificate Program, 1991. Bd. dirs., Hospice of Athens, 1986-88. Home: 2003 Needle Palm Dr Edgewater FL 32141-3913 E-mail: doconcall@webtv.net.

LAWSON, CAROLINA DONADIO, language educator, translator; b. Naples, Italy, Mar. 11, 1920; d. Joseph and Concetta (Bartolomeo) Donadio; m. Allan Leroy Lawson, Sept. 15, 1945; 1 child, John. Laurea in European langs., lit., instns., We. Group Instituto Universitario Orientale, Naples, 1946; PhD in French and Italian, Tulane U., 1971. Lectr. overseas divsn. U. Md., Leghorn, Italy, 1952; tchr. Warren Easton H.S., New Orleans, 1958—61; tchg. asst. Newcomb Coll. Tulane U., New Orleans, 1961—64; instr. Tex. Christian U., Ft. Worth, 1964—65; lectr. Downtown Ctr. U.Chgo., 1967—73; lectr. U. Akron, Ohio, 1975—76; pvt. practice lectr., translator, ind. scholar, freelance writer Moncks Corner, SC, 1985—. Vis. prof. Kent (Ohio) State U., 1977-84; mem., lectr. S.C. Humanities Coun., 1989-93. Author: (textbook) Nuove Letture di Cultura Italiana, 1975; fgn. lang. editl. reviewer Ency. Brit. Chgo., 1971; rev. editor: Italian Culture, 1981-84; contbr. many articles and revs. in lit. criticism, art history, textbooks of fables, fairy tales and biographies to profiles of famous Italians. Recipient cert. of proficiency in Japanese lang. and culture Tokyo Coll., 1958. Mem. MLA, Am. Assn. Tchrs. of Italian, Am. Assn. Italian Studies, Am. Assn. Tchrs. of French, Nat. Italian-Am. Found. Republican. Roman Catholic. Avocations: classical music, painting, sports, travel. Office Phone: 843-761-3968.

LAWSON, CORLISS SCROGGINS, lawyer; b. Topeka, Kans., Oct. 4, 1962; d. Troy Gene and Irma Leatrice Mae Scroggins; children: Tony Ray Worford II, Courtney Nichelle Worford. BA in Computer Info. sci., Washington U., Topeka, Kans., 1989; JD, Vanderbilt U., Nashville, 1992. Bar: Ga. 1992, U.S. Dist. Ct. (no. dist.) Ga. 1993, U.S. Ct. Appeals (11th cir.) 1993. Ptnr., ptnr-in-charge Lord, Bissell & Brook, LLP, Atlanta, 1992—. Spkr. in field. Contbr. articles to profl. jours. Mem. minority recruitment bd. ARC. Named one of Ga.'s Super Lawyers, 2005. Mem.: ATLA, ABA (mem. TIPS brief editl. bd. 1999—2000, mem. minority counsel demonstration program 1992—), Ga. Women's Bus. Coun., Nat. Bar Assn., Ga. Assn. Women Lawyers, Ga. Assn. Black Women Attys., Atlanta Bar Assn. Democrat. Office: Lord Bissell & Brook LLP 1170 Peachtree St Atlanta GA 30309

LAWSON, DIANE MARIE, counselor; b. Dallas, July 21, 1947; d. Michael and Clara Mae (McGuire) Maida; m. Howard Lynn Lawson, July 22, 1966; children: Scott M., Stephen L. BA, North Tex. State U., 1971, MEd. Cert. secondary English, history, learning disabilities tchr., secondary sch. counselor, vocational counselor, spl. edn. counselor, mid-mgmt. adminstr., Tex. Tchr. Italy (Tex.) Ind. Sch. Dist., 1972-80, instrnl. leader, 1984-89, elem. prin., 1989-91, h.s. counselor, 1992—; tchr. Red Oak (Tex.) Ind. Sch. Dist., 1980-81; instrnl. leader ESC Region 10, Richardson, Tex., 1981-84; GED instr. Navarro Coll., Coriscana, Tex., 1991-92. City election judge, City of Italy, 1993-95, sch. election judge, Italy, 1992; primary election clk., Ellis County, Italy, 1991. Mem. Tex. Counseling Assn., Assn. Tex. Profl. Educators. Avocations: reading, gardening, Broadway shows. Office: Italy ISD 300 S College Italy TX 76651

LAWSON, DONNA YVETTE, special education educator; b. Bklyn., N.Y., Mar. 2, 1960; d. Richard James and Dorothy Lawson; children: Dionna Y. Shinn, Brionna A. Edmundson. BA, Pace U., N.Y.C., 1983; MA, Norfolk State U., Va., 2001. Postgrad. lic., cert. adminstr. supervision k-12, emotional disturbance K-12, specific learning disabilities K-12. Dir. instr. Va. Sch., Hampton, dir. student life, spl. edn. prin., IEP coord.; spl. edn. tchr. Hampton City Schs. Dir. Advanced Devel. Learning Ctr., Hampton, Both Worlds Inc., Hampton; treas. Soleria Christian Resource Ctr., 2004. Advocate Va. Sch., Hampton. Mem.: CEC, Assn. Christian Schs. Avocation: reading. Home: 101 Montrose dr Hampton VA 23666

LAWSON, JANE ELIZABETH, retired bank executive; b. Cornwall, Ont., Can. d. Leonard J. and Margaret Lawson. BA, U. N.B., Can., LLB, 1971. With law dept. Royal Bank Can., Montreal, Que., 1974-78, sr. counsel, 1978-84, v.p., corp. sec., 1988-92, sr. v.p., sec., 1992—, ret., 2005—. Mem.: Am. Soc. Corp. Secs., Inst. Corp. Dirs., Inst. Chartered Secs. and Adminstrs., N.B. Bar Assn., Can. Bar Assn., Royal Can. Yacht Club, Mt. Royal Tennis Club. Office: Royal Bank Plz PO Box 1 Toronto ON Canada M5J 2J15

LAWSON, JANICE RAE, retired elementary school educator; b. Chgo., Jan. 22, 1938; d. Ramon Joseph and Anne Joan (Seaquist) Wallenborn; m. Ralph Dreben Lawson, Jr. BEd, Beloit Coll., Wis., 1960; MEd, George Washington U., Washington, DC, 1966; postgrad., George Mason U., Fairfax, Va., 1987-88, U. Va., Charlottesville, 1965-85; Degree in Theol. Edn., U. of South, 1989. Cert. tchr. Va. Tchr. Quantico Marine Base, Va., 1960-62; elem. tchr. Pearl Harbor Elem. Sch., Honolulu, 1962-64, Quantico Dependents Sch. System, 1964-95, ret., 1995. Counselor Diet Ctr., Springfield, Va., 1979—89; lay Eucharistic min. and lectr. Kingston Parish, vestry-stewardship warden, 2000—03. Mem. NEA (life), Quantico Edn. Assn. (treas. 1968-72), Va. Edn. Assn., Pi Lambda Theta (life), Kappa Alpha Theta (treas. 1979-81, pres. North Va. chpt. 1981-85, alumni dist. pres. 1989-95, nat. fraternity historian 2000—). Republican. Episcopalian. Avocations: golf, tap dancing, cooking, aerobics, travel. Home: PO Box 427 Cobbs Creek VA 23035-0427

LAWSON, JENNIFER, broadcast executive; b. Birmingham, Ala., June 8, 1946; d. Willie DeLeon and Velma Theresa (Foster) L.; m. Elbert Sampson, June 1, 1979 (div. Sept. 1980); m. Anthony Gittens, May 29, 1982; children: Kai, Zachary. Student, Tuskegee U., 1963—65; MFA, Columbia U., 1974; LHD (hon.), Teikyo Post U., Hartford, Conn., 1991. Assoc. producer William Greaves Prodns., N.Y.C., 1974-75; asst. prof. film studies Bklyn. Coll., 1975-77; exec. dir. The Film Fund, N.Y.C., 1977-80; TV coord. Program Fund Corp. for Pub. Broadcasting, Washington, 1980-83, assoc. dir. TV Program Fund, 1983-89, dir. TV Program Fund, 1989; exec. v.p. programming PBS, Alexandria, Va., 1989-95; broadcast cons. Md. Pub. TV, 1995—98, exec. cons., 1996—, exec. prodr. Africa, 1998-2001; pres. Magic Box Mediaworks, 1996—; gen. mgr. WHUT-TV32, 2004—. V.p. Internat. Pub. TV, Washington, 1984-88; panelist Fulbright Fellowships, Washington, 1988-90. Author, illustrator: Children of Africa, 1970; illustrator: Our Folktales, 1968, African Folktales: A Calabash of Wisdom, 1973. Coord. Nat. Coun. Negro Women, Washington, 1969. Avocations: painting, reading. Office: 1838 Ontario Pl NW Washington DC 20009-2109 Office Phone: 202-806-3010. Business E-Mail: j_lawson@howard.edu.

LAWSON, KAREN E., mathematics educator; d. Carl H. and Gladys E. Larson; m. Timothy J. Lawson, Dec. 9, 1996; children: Gracie L., Marie C. BS in Math., Black Hills State Coll., Spearfish, S.D., 1987. Lic. tchr. Nev. Dept Edn., 1987. Tchr. Churchill County Jr. H.S., Fallon, Nev., 1989—, Churchill County H.S., Fallon, 1994—, regional profl. devel. trainer, 2000—01, math dept. chairperson, 2005—. Camp cook Rodeo Bible Camp, Winnemucca, Nev., 2005—06. Mem.: Churchill County Edn. Assn. (licentiate Tchr. of Yr. 2000—01). Avocations: sewing, crafts. Office: Churchill County High Sch 1222 S Taylor Fallon NV 89406 Office Phone: 775-423-2181.

LAWSON, KELLI, communications executive; b. 1967; m. Keith Lawson; 2 children. B in Econ., Howard U., 1989. Brand mgr. Procter & Gamble; v.p., publisher, BET Books Black Entertainment TV, 1998, exec. v.p., Corp. Mktg., 1999—; owner 9 Maternity, Rockland, Md. Named one of 40 Executives Under 40, Multichannel News, 2006. Mem.: Women in Cable & Telecom. (Betsy Magness fellow 1999—2000), Nat. Black MBA Assn., Nat. Assn. Minorities in Cable, Jr. League of Wash., Delta Sigma Theta. Office: BET Holdings 1200 W Pl NE Washington DC 20018*

LAWSON, MARY CAROLYN, elementary school educator; b. Ironton, Ohio, Nov. 23, 1941; d. Jesse Wilon Johnson and Elizabeth Alice (Fields) Fleck; children: Adam Wade Roach, Seth Joseph Roach, Paul Edwin Roach (dec.), Margaret Lawson Johnson. BA, U. South Fla., Tampa, 1965, MA, 1988; student, East Carolina U., Greenville, 1969-70, student, 1982, UNC-Chapel Hill, 1970. Tchr. Washington County Schs., Plymouth, N.C., 1967-71, Hillsborough County Schs., Tampa, Fla., 1982-83, 1986—. Sec. S.W. Fla. Coalition for Social Studies, 1990—95; team leader Buchanan Mid. Sch. Steering Com., 2003—06. Author various poems, monographs; painter, photographer. Chmn., CFO Scotland Coun. Ring Camps Farthest Out Internat., 2006—; altar guild St. John's Episcopal Ch., Tampa, 1995—96; convener Internat. Order of St. Luke the Phys., Tampa, 1996; participant Coun. Rings Camps Farthest Out Resurrection Retreat, 2000—, chairperson, 2002—05. Mem. Internat. Reading Assn., Hillsborough County Reading Assn., Phi Delta Kappa. Democrat. Episcopalian. Avocations: reading, golf, writing, painting. Home: USF 30907 Tampa FL 33620 Office: Hillsborough Cty Schs 901 E Kennedy Blvd Tampa FL 33602-3507 Office Phone: 813-975-7600 ext. 457.

LAWSON, MELANIE CERISE, newscaster; d. Bill and Audrey (Hoffman) Lawson; m. Geary Broadnax, 1986 (separated 2001). B in Politics, Princeton U.; degree in Law and Journalism, Columbia U. Bar: NY, Tex. Reporter, anchor Sta. KTRK-TV, Houston, 1982—. Office: KTRK-TV 3310 Bissonnet Houston TX 77005

LAWSON, NANCY P., retired county official; b. Manassas, Va., Apr. 23, 1926; d. Edgar goodloe and Alverda Reita (Jennings) Parrish; m. Richard Challice Haydon, Jr., June 19, 1948 (dec. Oct. 1964); children: Victoria Lucille Haydon Bonifant, Richard Challice III, Geoffrey Jennings; m. Garland Loyd Lawson, Sept. 15, 1979 (dec. June 29, 2002). BA in Edn., Longwood Coll., 1947. Gen. registrar Prince William County, Manassas, 1965-91; organizer Voter Registrars Assn. Va., 1971, pres., 1972, 73, 74, parliamentarian, 1975-99. Bd. dirs., sec. Commonwealth Savs. and Loan Assn., 1980-91. Active Manassas Jr. Womans Club, 1953-61, pres., 1956; membership chmn., parliamentarian Aux. to Prince William Hosp., 1962-; bd. dirs. Manassas Cmty. Concert Assn., 1985-; trustee Manassas United Meth. Ch., 1986-. Mem.: Sudley Swim and Tennis Club (pres., bd.dirs.), Evergreen Country Club (bd. dirs. 1995—2005). Avocations: tennis, golf, piano, bridge. Home: 9007 Longstreet Dr Manassas VA 20110-4904

LAWSON, PATRICIA BOWMAN, physician, educator; b. Jackson, Miss., Nov. 8, 1966; d. Robert Pelton and Deborah (Kaye) Bowman; m. Samuel Todd Lawson, June 11, 1994; children: Margaret Ann, Sarah Elizabeth. AA, Cottey Coll., Nevada, Mo., 1987; BA in Biology cum laude, U. Miss., 1989, MD, 1994. Cert. instr. ACLS, Am. Heart Assn.; diplomate Am. Bd. Internal Medicine. Intern, resident in internal medicine Sch. Medicine U. Miss., Jackson, 1994-97, instr. Sch. Medicine, 1997-99, asst. prof. Sch. Medicine, 1999—; staff physician, chmn. utilization rev. com. G.V. Montgomery Med. Ctr., Jackson, Miss., 1997—, key physician provider profiling, cons., 1997—. Author: Quick Medical Consult Pocket Guide, 2000. Mem. ACP, AMA, Am. Soc. Internal Medicine. Office: Jackson VAMC Med Svc (111A) 1500 E Woodrow Wilson Ave Jackson MS 39216-5116 Home: 118 Norfleet Way Madison MS 39110-8528

LAWSON, RHEA BROWN, library director; 1 child, Ebony. BA, Morgan State U.; MLS, U. Md., College Park; PhD in Libr. and Info. Studies, U. Wis., Madison. Chief Ctrl. Libr. Bklyn. Pub. Libr., NY, 1999—2003; dep. dir. Detroit Pub. Libr., Mich., 2003—05; dir. Houston Pub. Libr., Tex., 2005—. Bd. dirs. Pub. Libr. Assn.; exec. bd. mem. Black Caucus of Am. Libr. Assn.; mem. Money Smart adv. bd. Fed. Reserve Bank; adv. bd. mem. Ctr. for Black Lit., Medgar Evers Coll. Office: Houston Pub Libr 500 McKinney St Houston TX 77002 Office Phone: 832-393-1300. E-mail: library.director@cityofhouston.net.*

LAWSON, SHARIANNE RENEE, political science educator; d. Halford and Reneta Lawson. BA, U. Miami, Coral Gables, 2002. Substitute tchr. Sch. Dist. Palm Beach County, West Palm Beach, Fla., 2004—05; tchr. Am. govt. Royal Palm Beach H.S., 2005—. Asst. coach Boca Raton H.S., Fla., 2004—05. Author: (children's book) Charlie the Caterpillar; poet (poetry) Tracing the Infinate: Musical Touch (Internat. Libr. of Poetry Editors' Choice Award, 2004). Recipient Come Back Athlete Yr., U. Miami Womens Track and Field, 2003. Mem.: CTA (assoc.). Office Phone: 561-753-4001.

LAWTON, BARBARA, lieutenant governor; b. Wis. m. Cal Lawton; children: Joseph, Amanda Krupp. BA summa cum laude, Lawrence U., 1987; MA, U. Wis., 1991. Lt. gov. State of Wis., Madison, 2003—. Founding mem. Ednl. Resource Found.; founding trustee Cmty. Found.; founding mem. Latinos Unidos; mem. adv. bd. Green Bay Multicultural Ctr., Women's Polit. Voice; mem. bus. planning and resource team Entrepreneurs of Color; bd. mem. Planned Parenthood Advs. Wis., Northeastern Wis. Tech. Coll. Edn. Found. Named Feminist of the Yr., Wis. Chpt. NOW, 1999; recipient Ft. Howard Founds. Humanitarian award. Mem.: AAUW, LWV, Nat. Women's Polit. Caucus. Democrat. Office: Office of Lt Governor 19 East State Capitol PO Box 2043 Madison WI 53702 Office Phone: 608-266-3516. Office Fax: 608-267-3571. E-mail: ltgov@ltgov.state.wi.us.*

LAWTON, LORILEE ANN, small business owner, accountant; b. Morrisville, Vt., July 17, 1947; d. Philip Wyman Sr. and Margaret Elaine (Ather) Noyes; m. Lee Henry Lawton, Dec. 6, 1969 (dec. Nov. 2004); children: Deborah Ann, Jeffrey Lee. BBA, U. Vt., 1969. Sr. acct., staff asst. IBM, Essex Junction, Vt., 1969-72; owner, pres., chmn. bd. Red-Hed Supply Inc., Colchester, 1972-2001; owner, pres. Firetech Sprinkler Corp., Colchester, 1992—. Bd. dirs. Mchts. Bank, Burlington, Mchts. Bankshares. Mem. Am. Fire Sprinkler Assn., Nat. Fire Protection Assn., Vt. Subcontractors Assn. Republican. Avocations: reading, gardening. Home: 571 Middle Rd Colchester VT 05446-7310 Office: Firetech Sprinkler Corp 340 Hegeman Ave Colchester VT 05446-3173 Office Phone: 802-655-1800.

LAWTON, NANCY, artist; b. Gilroy, Calif., Feb. 28, 1950; d. Edward Henry and Marilyn Kelly (Boyd) L.; m. Richard Enemark, Aug. 4, 1984; children: Faith Lawton, Forrest Lawton. BA in Fine Art, Calif. State U., San Jose, 1971; MFA, Mass. Coll. Art, Boston, 1980. Artist-in-residence Villa Montalvo Ctr. Arts, Los Gatos, Calif., 1971, Noble & Greenough Sch., Dedham, Mass., 1990. One-woman shows include The Bklyn. Mus., 1983, Victoria Munroe Gallery, N.Y.C., 1993, Hirschl & Adler Galleries, N.Y.C., 2002-05; group shows include San Francisco Mus. Modern Art, 1973, The Bklyn. Mus., 1980, 83, Staempfli Gallery, N.Y.C., 1984, The Ark. Art Ctr. Mus., Little Rock, 1984, 88, 92, 93, Victoria Munroe Gallery, 1985, 87, 88, 92, Butler Inst. Am. Art, Ohio, 1988, Smith Coll. Mus. Art, 1988, NAD, N.Y.C., 1988, Reynolds Gallery, Richmond, 1994, Nancy Solomon Gallery, Atlanta, 1995, Arnot Art Mus., Elmira, N.Y., 2001-03, Hunt Inst. for Bot. Documentation, Carnegie Mellon U., Pitts., 2001-02, Hirschl and Adler Galleries, N.Y.C., 2002-06, John Pence Galleries, San Francisco, 2004, Vose Galleries, Boston, 2004, Telfair Mus. Art, Savannah, 2006; pub. collections include The Ark. Art Ctr. Mus., Art Inst. Chgo., Bklyn. Mus., Met. Mus. Art, Smithsonian Am. Art Mus., Washington. Scholar Mellon Found., 1982; N.Y. State Creative Artists grantee, 1983, N.Y. State Arts Devel. Fund grantee, 1989. Home and Office: 78 Willett St Albany NY 12210-1001 Office Phone: 518-449-7022. E-mail: nancydraws@aol.com.

LAWTON, THELMA CUTTINO, mathematics professor, consultant; b. Suffolk, Va., Sept. 10, 1949; d. John and Hazel Cuttino; children: Althea Katrice Lawton-Thompson, Henry Iii Carlos. BS, SC State U., 1971; MS, Ind. U., 1978; EdD, U. Ctrl. Fla., 1999. Tchr., dept. chair Ind. Pub. Sch., Indpls., 1972—79; tchr. Richland County Schs., Columbia, SC, 1979—81, Houston Ind. Schs., Houston, 1981—83; prof. Seminole CC, Sanford, Fla., 1983—99, Fla. Meml. Coll., Miami, Fla., 2000—. Dir. Cities In Schs., Houston, 1982—83. Author: Math Fun Pages For Elementary Schools, Strategies For The Class Math Test, (paper) What Should Schools Teach ?. Treas. Alpha Kappa Alpha Sorority, Chgo., 2001—03; com. chair Union Of Black Episc.; pres. SC State U. Nat. Alumni Assn., Orangeburg, SC, 2003; trustee SC State U., Orangeburg, SC, 2003. Delores A. Auzenne fellowship, Fla. Dept. Of Edn., Workshop To Encourage Women In Math. grant, Math. Assn. Of Am. Mem.: Nat. Coun. Of Tchrs. Of Math., Assn. For Sch. Curriculum And Devel., Fla. Assn. Of Tchr. Educators, Math. Assn. Of Am. (com. chair 2003—04). Episcopalian. Avocations: travel, physical fitness, math. puzzles, shopping, fashion. Home: 4964 Sw 128th Ave Miramar FL 33027 Office: Florida Meml Coll 15800 NW 42nd Ave Miami FL 33054 Office Phone: 305-623-4253. Home Fax: 305-623-4283; Office Fax: 305-623-4283. E-mail: tlawton@fmc.edu.

LAWTON, VIOLET, writer; b. Cumberland, R.I., Oct. 11, 1925; d. John Arthur and Emma (Butterworth) Grayson; m. Donald Morrison, Aug. 6, 1950 (div. Feb. 1952); 1 child, Darcy Louise; m. Charles Dean Lawton, Nov. 30, 1968 (dec.); stepchildren: Peter E., Mark D. Student, Tabbot-Hubbard Bus. Sch., 1944. Bookkeeper Lonsdale Co. Berkeley Mill, Cumberland, R.I., 1943-45; purchasing sales, house newsletter advt. The Fram Corp., East Providence, R.I., 1945-50; accts. receivable, sr. credit adminstrn. The Foxboro (Mass.) Co., 1952-85; corr. The Alameda (Calif.) Jour., 1999—. Contbr. articles to mags. Mem. Writers West Alameda, Inc. (pres. 1999, sec. 1995-97). Episcopalian. Avocations: swimming, walking, dance, gardening, group singing.

LAY, JANICE AMELIA, special education educator; b. Phoenix, Nov. 24, 1962; d. Joseph Allen and Helen Doris (Morris) Beatty; children: Nickolas, Tyler, Max; m. George J. Jr., Mar. 13, 2004. BS in Edn., No. Ariz. U., 1984, M in Special Edn., 2001. Tchr. spl. edn. Oak Creek Boarding Sch., Cottonwood, Ariz., 1984-85; tchr. Maryland Sch., Phoenix, 1985-87; tchr. spl. edn. Success Sch., Mo., 1987-99, Plato Sch., 1999—2002, Mignus Union HS,

Cottonwood, Ariz., 2002—. Coord. Success Sch. Substance Abuse Prevention Program, 1987—. Mem. NEA, Mo. State Tchrs. Assn., Ariz. Edn. Assn., Mingus Union Edn. Assn., Coun. Exceptional Children. Mem. Lds Ch. Avocations: softball, cross stitch. Home: 1627 E Sandy Ln Cottonwood AZ 86326-4971

LAY, MARION, sports association executive; M of Sociology, Calif. State U., Hayward. Mem. exec. com. Can. Olympic Assn.; founder, chair Nat. Sport Ctr., Greater Vancouver; chair PacificSport Group; co-chair BC Games com.; mem. WomenSport Internat. Former Can. Olympic swimmer; founding mem. Can. Assn. for Advancement of Women in Sport & Phys. Activity; pres. 2010 LegaciesNow Society (Vancouver Olympic bid), 1998—. Recipient Women of Distinction award Recreation and Sport, YWCA, 1991, Herstorical award, CAAWS, 1994, Bryce Taylor Meml. award Outstanding Contbn. Amateur Sport, 1995, Can. Citizenship award, 1996, Bobbie Steen award Excellence Leadership Sport Cmty., 1998, Bronze medal 4x100 metre relay, Olympics, Mexico City, 1968, Internat. Olympic Com.'s Women and Sport Trophy, 2001, Leadership in Sports award, Can., 2001, Carole Anne Letheren Internat Sport Leadership award, COC & CAAWS, 2002, History Breakthrough award award, CAAWS, 2002. Office: Can Assn Adv Women & Sport & Phys Act N202 801 King Edward Ave Ottawa ON K1N 6N5 Canada

LAYBOURNE, GERALDINE B., broadcast executive; b. Plainfield, NJ, 1947; m. Kit Laybourne; children: Emily, Sam. BA art history, Vassar Coll., 1969; MS elem. ed., U. Pa., 1971. Former high sch. tchr.; joined Nickelodeon as program manager, 1980; created Nick at Nite, 1985; exec. v.p./gen. mgr. Nickelodeon/Nick at Nite, 1986—89, pres., 1989—96; vice chmn. MTV Networks, 1993—96; pres. Disney/ABC Cable Networks, NYC, 1996—98; co-founder, CEO Oxygen Media, NYC, 1998—. Bd. dirs. Insight Comm. Co., The YES Network, Nat. Coun. Families and TV, Move, Inc. Bd. dirs. Nat. Coun. Families and TV, Children Affected by AIDS Found., Nat. Ctr. Children's TV, The Nat. Cable TV Assn., Vassar Coll. Named one of 25 Most Influential People in Am., Time mag., 1996; named to, Broadcasting Hall of Fame, 1995, Broadcasting and Cable Hall of Fame, 1995; recipient Idell Kaitz award, Nat. Cable and Telecom. Assn. Vanguard Awards, 1990, Film Muse award, NY Women, 1991, Entrepreneur of Yr. award, U. Mo., Kans. City, 1991, Women in Cable award, 1992, Genii award, Am. Women in Radio and TV, 1992, Govs. award, Nat. Acad. Cable Programming, 1993, Grand Tam award, Cable TV Adminstrn. and Mktg. Com., 1994, Spotlight award, Creative Coalition, 1995, Matrix award for broadcasting, N.Y. Women in Comm., 1996, award for disting. lifetime contbn. to children and TV, Annenberg Pub. Policy Ctr., 1997, Crystal Apple award, Mayor Rudy Giuliani, 2001, award for disting. lifetime contbn. to children and TV, Annenberg Pub. Policy Ctr., Matrix award for broadcasting, N.Y. Women in Comm., Spotlight award, Creative Coalition. Mem.: Nat. Cable TV Assn. (bd. dirs.), Cable Positive (hon. chair), NY Women in Film and TV (adv. bd.). Office: Oxygen Media 75 9th Ave Fl 7 New York NY 10011-7006*

LAYMON, CYNTHIA J., artist, educator; b. Gary, Ind., Feb. 17, 1948; d. Michael and Norma (MacLaverty) Semanchik; m. Terrance E. Laymon, 1972. BA, Ind. U., 1970; MFA, So. Ill. U., 1977. Asst. prof. art Lake Erie Coll., Painesville, Ohio, 1977—79; assoc. prof. U. N.C.-Greensboro, 1979—. One-man shows include Weatherspoon Gallery, Greensboro, N.C., 1982, C. Corcoran Gallery, Muskegon, Mich., 1983, Contemporary Crafts Gallery, Louisville, 1989, exhibited in group shows at Columbus (Ohio) Mus. Fine Arts, 1975, 1977, Gathering Gallery, Kansas City, Mo., 1979, Green Hill Gallery, Greensboro, 1982, mus. in Spain and Morocco, 1982—83, Redding (Calif.) Mus., 1983, Ga. State Art Gallery, 1984, Mindscape Galleries, Chgo., 1984—85, Iowa Arts Ctr., 1984, N.C. Art Mus., 1984, Roanoke Art Mus., 1984, Tampa Art Mus., 1985, Soc. Arts and Crafts, Boston, 1985, Longwood Coll., Va., 1985, Tampa (Fla.) Mus., 1986, Weatherspoon Gallery, Greensboro, 1980—80, Fayetteville (N.C.) Mus. of Art, 1989, Fridholm Fine Art, Asheville, N.C., 1990, Mus. of York County, Rock Hill, S.C., 1990, The Art Ctr., Iowa City, Iowa, 1990. Recipient Best of Show award Columbus Inst. for Contemporary Art, 1978, Merit award Survey of Ill. Fiber, Lakeview Mus., Peoria, 1978, Handweavers Guild of Am. award, 1978, Belding Lily award North/South Carolina Fibers Competition, Charlotte, 1980, award of excellence, 1980, Am. and Efrid Mills award North/South Carolina Fibers Exhbn., 1981, Juror's Merit award Meadows Gallery, 1990. Mem.: Suface Design Assn. (S.E. rep. 1989—), N.C. Fiber Art Assn. (treas. 1979—81), Am. Craft Coun. Office: 16428 S 46th Way Phoenix AZ 85048-0155 also: 16428 S 46th Way Phoenix AZ 85048-0155

LAYTON, CAROL EICHERBERGER, dentist; b. Chambersburg, Pa., Mar. 10, 1947; d. Eugene Curtis Eichelberger and Ura Alzene Mountain; m. Daniel G. Layton (div. 1980); children: Aaron Eichelberger, Heather Page Layton Duffey; m. Joseph R. Cenname (div. 1980); children: Nicholas Tabor Cenname, Zachary Curtis Cenname. BA, Slippery Rock U., Pa., 1970; DMD, U. Pitts., 1977; postgrad., Clayton Coll. Natural Health, Birmingham, Ala., 2004—. Assoc. gen. dentist Office of Dr. F. Dale Acklin, Grove City, Pa., 1971—73, 1977—79, Office of Dr. Laurence Dietz, Beaver, Pa., 1977—79, Office of Drs. Christpher Wichmann and Linda Hamerski, Beaver Falls, Pa., 1981—83, Tri-County Dental, Cranberry, Pa., 1992—93, Davis and Davis, PC, Pitts., 1997—98, Office of Dr. Judith Davenport, Pitts., 1996—98, Office of Dr. John Gustafson, Greensburg, Pa., 1997—98; pvt. practice Coraopolis, Pa., 1979—90; employee gen. dentist Soster Dental Assn., PA, Monroeville, Pa., 1991—96; gen. dentist, dental hygienist Dental Power of Western Pa., Pitts., 1996; assoc. gen. dentist, office mgr. Nova Dental Assocs., Tarentum, Pa., 1996—97; gen. dentist Pa. Group Practice affiliate Chestnut Hills Dental Group, McKees Rocks, Pa., 2000—05, Fields Family Dentistry, Mechanicsburg, Pa., 2005—. Presenter, cons. in field; dental examiner North Versailles Sch. Dist., 1992—96, Cornell Sch. Dist., Coraopolis, St. Joseph Sch., Coraopolis; intern in med. photography Mercy Hosp., Pitts., 1991; co-owner, dir., instr. Dental Careers Ctr., Inc., 1997—2000. Master: Acad. Gen. Dentistry (pres. Sigma Rho chpt. 1968—70, bd. dirs. Pa. chpt. 1998, publs. chmn., assoc. editor newsletter 1999, editor Keystone Explorer mag. 2000—03, 2006—); fellow: Acad. Dentists Internat., Internat. Coll. Dentists; mem.: ADA, AAUW, Am. Assn. Women Dentists (treas. western Pa. chpt. 1980, pres. 1988—89, newsletter editor 1989—90), Internat. Soc. Photographers, Pa. Dental Assn., Dental Soc. Western Pa. (bd. dirs. 1989—91), Chartiers Valley Dental Soc. (pres. 1988—89), Biographical Photographers Assn., U. Pitts. Sch. Dental Medicine Alumni Assn. (bd. dirs. 1994—96), Alpha Omicron Pi. Home: 1912 Daybreak Cir Harrisburg PA 17110-9003 Office: 2101 Aspen Dr Mechanicsburg PA 17055

LAYTON, GEORGIANNA VICIK, mathematics educator; b. Riverhead, N.Y., Oct. 28, 1956; d. George Raymond and Kay Andrea Vicik; m. Thomas Paul Layton, Aug. 11, 1984; children: Brett Andrew, Chelsea Katherine. BS with honors, State U. Coll., Oneonta, N.Y., 1978; MS with honors, U. Md., College Park, 1981. Advanced profl. cert. Charles County Bd. Edn. Md., 1978. Math tchr. Charles County Bd. Edn., La Plata, Md., 1978—. New tchr. mentor Charles County Bd. Edn., La Plata, Md., 1984—; presenter to profl. confs. Author (with others): U. Md. Connected Math Project, 1993. Leader Appalachian mission Mt. Vernon Presbyn. Ch., Alexandria, Va., 2004. Named Outstanding Math Tchr., George Wash. U., 1985, Outstanding Employee, Charles County Bd. Edn., 1984, 2004, Tri-County Outstanding Math Tchr., So. Md. Elec. Coop., 1994; recipient Agnes Meyer Outstanding Tchg. award, Wash. Post, 2006, Achievement Initiative Md. Minority Student Excellence award, Md. State Dept. Edn., 2006. Mem.: Md. Coun. Tchrs. Math. (assoc. Outstanding Math. Tchr. award 2005—06). Home: 8218 Ackley St Alexandria VA 22309 Office: Matthew Henson Mid Sch 3535 Livingston Rd Indian Head MD 20640 Office Phone: 301-753-1784.

LAYTON, POLLY KERSKER, mathematics educator, language educator; b. St. Petersburg, Apr. 15, 1945; d. Peter Benjamin and Marjorie Wheeler Kersker; m. Roger Keith Layton, Nov. 27, 1965; children: James Keith, Peter Kersker. Grad., U. South Fla., 1969. 1st grade tchr. Campbell Park Elem., St. Petersburg, 1969—70; 5th grade and 3d grade tchr. Perkins Elem., St. Petersburg, 1971—93; 3d grade tchr. Perkins Fine Arts Mgmt., St. Petersburg, 1993—97; math specialist Bay Point Magnet For Math, Sci., Tech. and Spanish, St. Petersburg, 1997—2006. Tchr., coach Tchr. Enrichment Network, St. Petersburg, 1989—96; presenter New Tchrs. on Positive Discipline, U. South Fla., Tampa, 1997. Recipient Math. Tchr. of Yr., Pinellas County, Fla., 1997. Mem.: Oebutante Club (St. Petersburg), PEO, Jr. League of St. Petersburg (vol. 1970—2006). Republican. Episcopal. Avocations: piano, travel, reading. Home: 1056 Snell Isle Blvd NE Saint Petersburg FL 33704 Office: Bay Point Elem 5800 22d St S Saint Petersburg FL 33712 Business E-Mail: klayton@tampabay.rr.com.

LAYZELL, JUDY KATHLEEN, secondary school educator, writer; d. Horace Ley and Frances Maye Klauser; m. Robert M. Layzell, May 1, 1965 (dec. Dec. 1968); 1 child, Midori Anne. BS, U. Minn., 1970, MS, 1985. Cert. English tchr. Minn. English tchr. Edina (Minn.) Pub. Schs., 1970—2003; owner, tutoring svc. My Own English Tchr., 2002—. Mag. judge Nat. Scholastic Press Assn., Mpls., 1988, Mpls., 1990—91; advisor Images on Wind mag, 1985—92, 1996—2002. Author (editor): Should Juveniles Be Tried as Adults?, 2005. Vol. Big Sisters, Mpls., 1968; coach Childbirth Edn. Assn., Mpls., 1977-78; troop leader Girl Scouts U.S.A., Mpls., 1982-84; foster parent, 1990-99.

LAZAR, LUDMILA, concert pianist, music educator; b. Celje, Slovenia; married; two children. MusB, Roosevelt U., 1963, MusM, 1964; D of Musical Arts, Northwestern U., 1987. Faculty Roosevelt U., Chgo., 1967—, prof. piano Chgo. Musical Coll., 1988—, prof. emerita, 2003—, chmn. keyboard dept., 1983—2003. Lectr., demonstrator in field. Roosevelt U. rsch. grantee, 1988, 96; recipient Goethe Inst. award, 1987, Outstanding Coll. Tchr. award Roosevelt U., 1981; named to All Star Profs. Team Chgo. Tribune, 1993. Mem. AAUP, Music Tchrs. Nat. Assn. (master tchr. cert. 1991), European Piano Tchrs. Assn., Ill. State Music Tchrs. Assn., Soc. Am. Musicians (pres., v.p.), Coll. Music Soc., Musicians Club of Women (v.p.), Mu Phi Epsilon (pres., v.p.). Office: Roosevelt U 430 S Michigan Ave Chicago IL 60605-1394 Office Phone: 312-341-3779.

LAZAR, MARIOARA, psychiatrist; b. Traian, Romania, Nov. 4, 1957; arrived in U.S., 1991; d. Constantin and Cristina Conda; m. Stefan Lazar, Feb. 19, 1994 (div.); 1 child, Emanuel. MD with honors, U. Medicine, Timisoara, Romania, 1994. Resident Harlem Hosp., N.Y., 1989—2001, fellow child and adolescent psychiatry, 2001—03; psychiatrist Fla. Med. Ctr., Ft. Lauderdale, Fla., 2003—04, Broward Gen. Hosp., Ft. Lauderdale, 2003—04, Parkway Hosp., Miami, 2003—04, Aventura Hosp., Fla., 2003—04; pvt. practice psychiatrist Weston, Fla., 2004—; psychiatrist South Fla. Reception Ctr., Miami, 2004—; med. dir. child psychiatry Meml. Regional Hosp., Hollywood, Fla., 2006—. Contbr. articles to profl. jours. Mem.: Am. Acad. Child and Adolescent Psychiatry, Am. Psychiat. Assn. Avocations: classical music, history, travel. Office: 1040 Weston Rd 210 Weston FL 33326

LAZARIS, PAMELA ADRIANE, community planning and development consultant; b. Dixon, Ill., Oct. 13, 1956; d. Michael Christ and Ellen Euridice (Eftax) L.; m. Eugene Dale Monson, Oct. 17, 1987; children: Anthony Edward, Anna Adriane. BFA in Fine Arts, U. Wis., Milw., 1978; MS in Urban and Regional Planning, U. Wis., 1982; MBA, U. St. Thomas, 1992. Analyst planning Wis. Dept. Natural Resources, Madison, 1979-82; asst. city planner City of Albert Lea, Minn., 1982-83; specialist community devel. City of Winona, Minn., 1983-85; dir. community devel. City of Waseca, Minn., 1985-98; assoc. Real Estate Dynamics, Inc., Madison, Wis., 1998-99; prin. Planning Svc. and Solutions, Lake Mills, Wis., 1999—. Vol. spl. events Farmam-Minn. Agrl. Interpretive Ctr., Waseca, 1985—86; mem. Waseca County Econ. Devel. Commn., 1989—98; com. dir. Waseca Area Found., 1989—98; mem. dist. 2 city coun. City of Lake Mills, 1999—, city plan commn., 1999—, city coun. v.p., 2003—; troop 148 advancement coord. Boy Scouts Am., 2002—. Named one of Oustanding Young Women of Am., 1986. Mem. Am. Inst. Cert. Planners (cert.), Am. Planning Assn. (chpt. bd. dirs. 1986-89), Minn. Planning Assn. (v.p. 1989-90, dist. bd. dirs. 1985-89), Toastmasters (chpt. sgt.-at-arms 1987, ednl. v.p. 1988, 91-98), Lake Mills Area C. of C. Avocations: public speaking, travel, art. Home: PO Box 17 Lake Mills WI 53551-0017 Office: 110 E Madison St Lake Mills WI 53551-1644 Business E-Mail: pal@gdinet.com.

LAZARUS, ADRIENNE, retail executive; Asst. merchant Ann Taylor Stores, 1991, various merchandising positions, 1991—97; merchandising mgr. Ann Taylor Loft, 1997—2001, sr. v.p., gen. merchandising mgr., 2001—04, Ann Taylor Stores, 2004—05, exec. v.p. merchandising and design, 2005, pres., 2006—. Office: Ann Taylor Stores Corp 7 Times Square 15th Fl New York NY 10036*

LAZARUS, LILA, announcer; m. Jeff Lazarus, June 7, 1997. BA in Polit. sci., German, Kalamazoo Coll., 1984; MA in Journalism, U. Mich.; MA in Polit. sci., U. Mass.; postgrad., U. Freiburg, German, U. Bonn, Hebrew U., Israel. Prin. primet time anchor New Eng. Cable News, Boston, 1994—96; anchor Fox 25 News at 10, Boston, 1994—96; gen. assignment reporter WBAL-TV, Balt.; anchor/reporter/prodr. WJRT-TV, Flint, Mich.; anchor/reporter WWTV, Cadillac, Mich.; fgn. corr./staff reporter Ann Arbor News, Mich. Recipient award, Am. Soc. Colon and Rectal Surgeons, 1998, 1999, Emmy, 2001, Best News Spl. award, Mich. Assn. Broadcasters, 2002; fellow Hanns-Seidel, West Germany; scholar Fulbright. Office: WDIV-TV 550 W Lafayette Blvd Detroit MI 48226

LAZARUS, SHELLY (ROCHELLE BRAFF LAZARUS), advertising executive; b. NYC, Sept. 1, 1947; d. Lewis L. and Sylvia Ruth (Eisenberg) Braff; m. George M. Lazarus, Mar. 22, 1970; children: Theodore, Samantha, Benjamin. AB, Smith Coll., 1968; MBA, Columbia U., 1970. Product mgr. Clairol, NYC, 1970-71; account exec. Ogilvy & Mather, NYC, 1971-73, account supr., 1973-77, mgmt. supr., 1977-84, sr. v.p., 1981—, account group dir., 1984-87; gen. mgr. Ogilvy & Mather Direct, NYC, 1987-88, mng. dir., 1988-89, pres., 1989-91, Ogilvy & Mather, NYC, 1991-94, pres. N. Am., 1991-94; pres., COO Ogilvy & Mather Worldwide, NYC, 1995-96, CEO, 1996—, chmn., 1997—. Bd. dirs. GE, 2000—, Merck & Co., Inc., 2004—, Com. to Encourage Corp., Philanthropy, NY Presbyn. Hosp., Advt. Edn. Found., Am. Mus. Nat. History, World Wildlife Fund; mem. bd. overseers Columbia Bus. Sch. Mem. adv. bd. Judge Inst. Mgmt. Studies Cambridge U., England, Women's Forum, Yale Pres.'s Coun. Internat. Activities, Bus. Coun., 4A's Adv. Coun., Coun. Fgn. Rels., Advt. Women NY, Com. 200. Recipient YWCA Women Achievers award, 1985, Matrix award, 1995; named Businesswoman of Yr. NYC Partnership and C. of C., 1996; named one of 100 Most Powerful Women in World, Forbes mag., 2005, 50 Most Powerful Women in Bus., Fortune mag., 2006. Mem.: Am. Assn. Advt. Agys. (vice chmn. 1998—99, chmn. 1999—2000, bd. dirs.), Advt. Women N.Y. (coun. fgn. rels., com. to encourage corp. philanthropy, Woman of Yr 1994). Home: 106 E 78th St New York NY 10021-0302 Office: Ogilvy & Mather Worldwide 309 W 49th St New York NY 10019-7316

LAZERWITZ, KATHERINE CHRISTINE, retired reading specialist, educator; b. Gary, Ind., June 24, 1926; d. Constantine and Christine Coveris; m. James Arthur Lazerwitz, Jan. 21, 1955; children: Lori Rachel Solon, Jay Alan, Mark Harry, David Jack. BSBA, Ind. U., 1949, MS in Elem. Edn., 1971; BS in Elem. Edn., Ind. U. N.W., Gary, 1968; reading specialist endorsement, Ind. U. N.W., 1973. Jr. mdse. exec. Mandel Bros., Chgo., 1949—52; mgr., buyer Hudson's Women's Apparel, Gary, 1952—55; reading specialist Gary Cmty. Sch. Corp., 1973—88. Developer Art in Action program, 1975. Life v.p. Jewish Fedn. N.W. Ind. Named Woman of Distinction, YWCA, 1995, Woman of Valor, Jewish Fedn. N.W. Ind., 1990; recipient Hurst Family Leadership award, 1986, 1987, spl. recognition for exceptional commitment, 1986, 1991, Anne Kirschner Meml. award, 1988, award for chairing women's campaign, 1989, 1990, 1991, fundraising award, N.W. Ind. Symphony Soc., 1989—90, award for vols., Legacy Found., Inc. Lake County, Ind., 1997, Pres. Disting. Alumni award, Ind. U., 1997, Chancellor's Medallion, Ind. U. N.W., 1998, Disting. Alumni award, Ind. U. N.E., 1997. Mem.: Friends of Art Ind. U., Ind. U. Colloquiun Soc., Friends of Music Ind. U., Friends of Theatre Ind. U., Well Ho. Soc. Ind. U., Ind. U. President's Cir., Hadassah (life), Ind. U. Alumni Assn. (life), Varsity Club Ind. U., The Arbutus Soc. Ind. U., Newcomer's Club, Univ. Club Ind. U., Bloomington Worldwide Friendship Club. Avocations: travel, reading, volunteerism, cultural events. Home: 3704 Bridgewater Ct Bloomington IN 47401-4569 E-mail: kcl@alumni.indiana.edu.

LAZIO, LISA ANN, psychotherapist; b. Grand Rapids, Mich., Feb. 26, 1948; d. Charles John Lazio and Helen Ione Murphy. BA, Avila U., Kansas City, Mo., 1972; MA, St. Louis U., 1978, MEd, 1992, PhD, 1999. Diplomate Am. Psychotherapy Assn. Program dir. Cath. Youth Svcs., Denver, 1971—76; staff Ho. of Prayer, St. Louis, 1976—78; dir. campus ministry St. Joseph's Academy, 1978—92; couselor Holy Family Sch., 1993—96; pvt. practice CSJ Ministries, 1997—. Adj. faculty St. Louis U., 2004; bd. mem. Family Devel. Ctr., 1996—, Ctr. Counseling and Family Therapy, 1998—2005, Women in Charge, 2006—. Recipient Pro Deum et Juventutum Meam, Nat. Cath. Youth Orgn., 1972. Mem.: ACA, Am. Assn. Marriage and Family Therapists, Am. Psychotherapy Assn. Home: 9900 Harwich Dr Saint Louis MO 63126-2318 Office: CSJ Ministries 6400 Minn Ave Saint Louis MO 63111 Office Phone: 314-678-0316.

LAZO, CAROLINE EVENSEN, writer; BA in Art History, U. Minn., Mpls., 1978. Author: Jimmy Carter: On the Road to Peace, Gloria Steinem: Feminist Extraordinaire, Wilma Mankiller, 1994 (Tchr.'s choice award, 1995), Arthur Ashe, 1999 (Notable Social Studies Trade Book for Young People, 1999), Alice Walker: Freedom Writer, 2000 (Soc. Sch. Librs. Internat. Honor Book award, 2001), Leonard Bernstein: In Love with Music, 2003, F. Scott Fitzgerald: Voice of the Jazz Age, 2003, Frank Gehry, 2005.

LAZOVSKY, LORNA DEANE, minister; b. Harrisburg, Ill., Nov. 24, 1936; d. Curtis James Williams and Lillian May Rigsby; m. Daniel Lazovsky; children: David Eli, Michael Lyndon; m. Fred Plyler (div.); children: Scott Gregory Plyler, James Kevin Plyler, Susan Jane Plyler, Leslie Lorriane Plyler, Lily Ann Plyler. Founder Youth for Jesus, Desert Hot Springs, Calif.; minister state prisons; internat. pres. Women's Agape. Sr. pastor Desert Christian Fellowship Ch., Desert Hot Springs, Calif. Avocation: singing. Office Phone: 760-288-3739. Personal E-mail: lorna@macmail.com.

LAZZARA, BERNADETTE See PETERS, BERNADETTE

LAZZARA, MARGO VALENTINE, counselor, writer; b. N.Y., Jan. 23, 1958; d. Francisco Santos Valentine and Maria Guzman; m. Sebastian Lazzara, Feb. 7, 1998. Student in Gestalt Therapy, Ziegler Inst., 1990; student in Human Behavior, Psychology, NYU; degree, Am. Inst. Hypnotherapy, 1993; degree in Aromatherapy, Sch. Essentials, 1995. Cert.; hypnotherapist Johnson Inst. Hypnotherapy, 1994. Med. technician Diagnostic Ctr. Preventive Medicine, N.Y.; assoc. prodr. WOR Radio, N.Y.; sex therapist Am. Assn. Sex Educators, Counselors and Therapists, N.Y., hypnotherapist. Rape crisis counselor St. Vincents Hosp., N.Y., NY; couselor HEAL Orgn., N.Y., NY; cons. in field. Author: The Healing Aromatherapy Bath, 1999 (Best Book award, 2000), Blissful Bathtimes, 2000 (Best Book award, 2001); contbr. articles to mags. Vol. Salvation Army, N.Y., 1997. Named Miss Puerto Rico, 1976. Mem.: Am. Assn. Sex Educators, Counselors and Therapists, Internat. Assn. Counselors and Therapists, Nat. Guild Hypnotherapists. Democrat. Roman Cath. Avocations: painting, decoupage. Home and Office: Aromatica 1075 Father Capodanno Blvd Staten Island NY 10306 E-mail: margolazzara@aol.com.

LÊ, AN-MY, photographer, educator; BA with honors in Biology and French, Stanford U., 1982, MS in Biology, 1985; MFA in Photography, Yale U., 1993. Rsch. asst. in immunology Blood Ctr., Med. Ch. Stanford (Calif.) U., 1981—86, lectr. photography art dept., 1996—97, lectr. photography continuing studies dept., 1997; tchg. asst. photography dept. Yale U. Sch. Art, New Haven, 1992; lectr. photography Fordham U., NYU, Bard Coll., N.Y.C., 1998; free-lance photographer, 1993—; asst. prof. photography Bard Coll. Staff photographer Compagnons du Devoir, France, 1986—91; vis. asst. prof. Bard Coll., 1999. Author: Small Wars, 2005; Exhibited in group shows at Canton (China) Cultural Ctr., 1993, Lowinski Gallery, N.Y., 1994, Houston Ctr. for Photography (traveled to Webster U., St. Louis and Silver Eye Ctr. for Photography, Pitts.), 1994—96, 1997, Mus. Modern Art, N.Y.C., 1997, Fotofest, Houston, 1998, Scott Nicols Gallery, San Francisco, 1999, Represented in permanent collections Mus. Fine Arts, Houston, Mus. Modern Art, N.Y.C., San Francisco, Met. Mus., N.Y.C., Bibliotéque Nationale, Paris. Fellow Photography fellow, N.Y. Found. for Arts, 1996; CameraWorks Inc. grantee, 1995, Guggenheim fellow, 1997, 1998—. Office: Dept Photography Bard Coll PO Box 5000 Annandale On Hudson NY 12504-5000

LE, DAI-TRANG, mathematics educator; d. Ngoc Le and Minh Phan. MS, U. Utah, Salt Lake City, 2004; MS in Stats., U. Utah, 2006. Tchr. West H.S., Salt Lake City, 1999—2002; math instr. Davis Applied Tech. Coll., Kaysville, Utah, 2003—; math and stats. instr. Salt Lake C.C., Salt Lake City, 2005—. Scholar various scholarships, 1998. Mem.: Nat. Coun. Tchrs. Math. (assoc.), Am. Statis. Assn. (assoc.). Office: Davis Applied Technology College 550 E 300 S Kaysville UT 84037 Office Phone: 801-593-2500.

LE, DUY-LOAN, electrical engineer; b. Vietnam; arrived in U.S., 1975; BSEE magna cum laude, U. Tex., 1982; MBA, U. Houston. With Tex. Instruments, Dallas, 1982—, sr. fellow. Contbr. articles to profl. publs. Named One of Houston's Women on the Move, Tex. Exec. Women, Nat. Technologist of Yr., Women of Color, Asian Am. Engr. of Yr., WITI; named to Internat. Hall of Fame. Achievements include 22 patents in field. Office: MS 722 12203 SW Freeway Stafford TX 77477 Office Phone: 281-274-3714. E-mail: zlon@Ti.com.

LE, VIET V., lawyer; b. 1964; married; 2 children. BS, Univ. Pa.; JD, Univ. Ariz. Bar: Ariz. 1994. Assoc. gen. counsel Avnet Inc, Phoenix, 2001—. Bd. dir. Phoenix Symphony. Named one of Best Lawyers Under 40, Nat. Asian Pacific Am. Bar Assn., 2004. Mem.: State Bar Ariz., Ariz. Asian Am. Bar Assn. (dir. 2005—). Office: Assoc Gen Counsel Avnet Inc 2617 S 46th St Phoenix AZ 85034 Office Phone: 480-736-7000.

LEA, FILOMENA, English language educator, writer; b. Milw., Sept. 14, 1929; d. Peter and Noemi Volpintesta; m. Merlyn Bud Lea, Dec. 6, 1928; children: Dean, Perry. BA in Interior Design, Mount Mary Coll., 1986, postgrad.; PhB in Journalism, Marquette U., 1951. Women's feature writer Milw. Sentinel, 1952—54, home furnishing editor, 1956—64; interior designer Designed Interiors, Milw., 1964—90; writing instr. Milw. Area Tech. Coll., 1958—; instr. interior design Waukesha (Wis.) County Tech. Coll., 1989—99; feature writer 50 Plus Mag., Hartland, Wis., 1996—, Today's Wis. Woman Mag., Hartland, 1998—. Author: (personality features) Milw. Ethnic Coun. Vol., 2002—. Mem.: Milw. Area Acad. Alliance in English, Future Milw. Home and Office: 6700 N Range Line Rd Milwaukee WI 53209 Personal E-mail: filomena_lea@yahoo.com.

LEA, KAREN, elementary education educator; b. Pueblo, Colo., Feb. 19, 1962; d. Gale and Janet L. BA, N.W. Nazarene Coll., 1984; MA, U.S. Internat. U., San Diego, 1990; PhD, Walden U., 1999. Math./computer tchr. Nampa Christian Schs., Nampa, Idaho, 1984-87; math. tchr. North High Sch., Salinas, Calif., 1987-92; math. chair Roosevelt Jr. H.S., 1992-99; dean sch. edn. Olivet Nazarene U., 1999—2006; prof. edn. Trevecca Nazarene U., 2006. Bd. examiners Nat. Coun. for Accreditation of Tchr. Edn., 2005—.

LEACH, JANET C., publishing executive; b. 1956; m. John Leach; 3 children. Degree in Journalism, Bowling Green State U. Mng. editor The Cin. Enquirer, until 1998; editor Akron Beacon Jour., 1998—2003; profl. in residence Sch. Journalism and Mass Comm. Kent State U., 2003—; police reporter The Rev. Times, Fostoria. Mem. staff Ariz. Republic, Phoenix (Ariz.) Gazette; instr. journalism No. Ky. U., U. Cin. Mem. Knight Found. Recipient 4 Pulitzer prizes, Golden medal Meritorious Svc., 1994. Mem.: Am. Soc. Newspaper Editors, Akron Press Club, Soc. Profl. Journalists.

LEACHMAN, CLORIS, actress; b. Des Moines, Apr. 30, 1926; m. George England, April 19, 1953 (div. 1979); 5 children. Attended, Northwestern U. Actress: (films) including Kiss Me Deadly, 1955, Butch Cassidy and the Sundance Kid, 1969, W.U.S.A., 1970, The People Next Door, 1970, Lovers and Other Strangers, 1970, The Steagle, 1971, The Last Picture Show, 1971 (Acad. award for best supporting actress 1971), Charles and the Angel, 1972, Happy Mother's Day.Love, George, 1973, Dillinger, 1973, Daisy Miller, 1974, Young Frankenstein, 1974, Crazy Mama, 1975, High Anxiety, 1977, The Mouse and His Child, 1977 (voice), Foolin' Around, 1979, The North Avenue Irregulars, 1979, The Muppet Movie, 1979, Scavenger Hunt, 1979, Yesterday, 1979, Herbie Goes Bananas, 1980, History of the World, Part 1, 1982, Shadow Play, 1986, My Little Pony, 1986 (voice), Walk Like a Man, 1987, Hansel and Gretel, 1987, Prancer, 1989, Love Hurts, 1990, Texasville, 1990, Walter and Emily, 1991, My Boyfriend's Back, 1993, The Beverly Hillbillies, 1993, A Troll in Central Park, 1994 (voice), Storytime, 1994, Nobody's Girls, 1994, Now and Then, 1995, Music of the Heart, 1999, Hanging Up, 2000, Manna From Heaven, 2002, Alex & Emma, 2003, Bad Santa, 2003, Spanglish, 2004, The Longest Yard, 2005, Sky High, 2005, Scary Movie 4, 2006, Beerfest, 2006; TV series including Lassie, 1957, Mary Tyler Moore Show, 1970-75, Phyllis, 1975-77, Facts of Life, 1986-88, The Nutt House, 1989, Walter & Emily, 1991, Thanks, 1999; TV movies including Silent Night, Lonely Night, 1969, Suddenly Single, 1971, Haunts of the Very Rich, 1972, Brand New Life, 1973, Dying Room Only, 1973, Crime Club, 1973, Death Sentence, 1974, Thursday's Game, 1974, Hitchhike!, 1974, The Migrants, 1974, A Girl Named Sooner, 1975, Ladies of the Corridor, The New Original Wonder Woman, 1975, Death Scream, 1975, Someone I Touched, 1975, It Happened One Christmas, 1977, Long Journey Back, 1978, Mrs. R.'s Daughter, 1979, Willa, 1979, S.O.S. Titanic, 1979, The Acorn People, 1981, Advice to the Lovelorn, 1981, Miss All-American Beauty, 1982, Dixie: Changing Habits, 1983, The Demon Murder Case, 1983, Ernie Kovacs, Between the Laughter, 1984, Deadly Intentions, 1985, Love is Never Silent, Danielle Steele's Fine Things, 1990, In Broad Daylight, 1991, A Little Piece of Heaven, 1991, Fade to Black, 1993, Without a Kiss Goodbye, 1993, Spies, 1993, Miracle Child, 1993, Double, Double, Toil and Trouble, 1993, Between Love and Honor, 1995, Crazy Love, 2003, Mrs. Harris, 2005; (TV miniseries) Backstairs at the White House, 1979, Beach Girls, 2005; theater appearance in Grandma Moses: An American Primitive, Washington, 1990; TV appearances include: Alfred Hitchcock Presents, 1955, 58, 62, Gunsmoke, 1956, 61, Zane Grey Theater, 1956, Rawhide, 1960, The Twilight Zone, 1961, 2003, The Untouchables, 1962, Dr. Kildare, 1965, Perry Mason, 1966, Rhoda, 1974, Wonder Woman, 1975, The Muppet Show, 1977, The Love Boat, 1985, (voice) The Simpsons, 1991, The Nanny, 1994, Touched by an Angel, 1997, 2003, The Norm Show, 2000, Malcolm in the Middle, 2001, 2003-06, Joan of Arcadia, 2004, Two and a Half Men, 2005. Recipient 6 Emmy awards; named Miss Chicago in Miss America contest 1946.

LEADBETTER, TIFFANY, hotel executive; b. Tex., 1976; BA, Cornell U., 1998; MBA, U. Chgo. Grad. Sch. Bus. Sales mgmt. trainee Hyatt Regency McCormick Place, Chgo., 1998; from intern to dir. devel. Global Hyatt Corp., Chgo., 1999—2006, asst. v.p. N.Am. acquisitions & devel., 2006—. Named one of 40 Under 40, Crain's Chgo. Bus., 2006. Office: Global Hyatt Corp 71 S Wacker Dr Chicago IL 60606*

LEAF, RUTH, artist; b. N.Y.C. d. Max and Ida (Rothman) L.; div. June 1966; children: Karen Casino, Anita Lerner. Student, Bklyn. Coll., 1939-41, Atelier 17, 1945-47, New Sch. for Social Research, 1950-52. Dir. Ruth Leaf Studio, Queens, N.Y., 1966—. Cons. Colby Coll.; monotype demostrator Calif, Wash., Pa., N.Y., Md. Author: Intaglio Printmaking techniques, 1976, Etching Engraving & Other Intaglio Techniques, 1984. Recipient Libr. Congress Pruchase award, 1946, Am. Soc. Color Prints Tonner awards, Audubon-Silver Medal for Creative Graphics, 1979, Nassau C.C. Purchase award, 1981. Mem. Soc. Am. Graphic Artists, Boston Printmakers, Artist Equity, Nat. Soc. Lit. and the Arts, Nat. Assn. Women Artists.

LEAFGREN, RITA F., education educator; b. Chgo. d. Anthony and Lucile Kapp Rotunno; m. Donald D. Leafgren; 1 child, Douglas M. BA, U. Colo., Boulder, 1960; MA, U. Northern Colo., Greeley, 1965. Secondary level sci. tchr. Weld County Sch. Dist RE-1, LaSalle & Platteville, Colo., 1960—64; biology and earth sci. instr. U. No. Colo., Greeley, 1965—71, earth scis. lectr., 1989—; cons. Desegration Inst., 1972—73; cons. coord. Gen. Assistance Ctr., 1973—74; sci. and math. instr. Aims Cmty. Coll., Greeley, Colo., 1985—89.

LEAHEY, LYNN, editor-in-chief; married; 1 child, Jack. BA in English, Colgate U., 1981. From asst. editor, to mng. ed then editor-in-chief Soap Opera Digest, NYC, 1984—91, editor-in-chief, 1991—; editl. dir. Soap Opera Weekly, NYC, 2001—. Office: Soap Opera Digest 261 Madison Ave Fl 10 New York NY 10016-2303*

LEAHY, CHRISTINE A., information technology executive; b. Providence, June 1964; m. Adam Weinberg; children: Annika, Sammantha. BA, Brown U., 1986; JD, Boston Coll., 1991. Ptnr. Sidley Austin Brown & Wood, Chgo., 1991—2001; v.p., gen. counsel, corp. sec. CDW Corp, Vernon Hills, Ill., 2002—. Office: CDW Corp 200 N Milwaukee Ave Vernon Hills IL 60061*

LEAHY, JEANNETTE (JEANNETTE OLIVER LEAHY TINEN KAEHLER), actress; b. Sept. 9, 1927; d. Kenneth A. and Berthe Hortence (Borie) Oliver; m. Thomas J. Leahy (dec.); children: Denyse Leahy Karsten Feeney, Thomas J.; m. Wallace W. Kaehler, Jan. 13, 1980. Student, various acting workshops. TV personality Jeannette Lee Sta. WFBM-TV, Indpls., 1950-53; actress Peninsula Players Summer Stock Theatre, Door County, Wis., 1960—. Numerous radio, TV, stage, film, commls. appearances. V.p. Evanston Drama Club, 1961-62; dir. Wilmette Children's Theatre, 1960-65; bd. dirs. Easter Seal Soc., 1070-75. With U.S. Army, WWII. Mem. AFTRA, SAG, Equity Union, Mich. Shores Club, Wilmette-Kenilworth Club (pres. 1956-57, 1999-2001), North Shore Assocs. Club (pres. 1982-83, 94-95, 2002-2003). Republican. Roman Catholic.

LEAK, NANCY MARIE, artist; b. Takoma Park, Md., Nov. 24, 1931; d. George Morton and Ella (Oberholtzer) Hinkson; m. Thomas Clayton Leak Jr., Dec. 30, 1950; children: Suzanne M. Street, Sharon Leak-Hayden, Stephen, Scott. Grad. h.s., Washington. Co-illustrator: The Kissing Hand, 1993; exhbns. include Olney Art Assn., Internat. Exhbn. of the Miniature, Fla., Ga., Washington, N.J., Nev., Wash., Oreg., N.H., Mont. and Wyo., W.Va. and Pa., Cider Painters Am. Nat. Exhbn., Hunterdon Art Ctr., N.J., Sumner Mus., Washington, Gurmukhs Gallery, Aspen Hill, Md., Worldwide Miniature Exhbn., London, 1996, Australia, 2000, Hoffberger Gallery, Balt., Ocean City (Md.) Art League, Rockville (Md.) Art League, Md. Printmakers, Md. Ho. of Dels., Annapolis, NIH, Bethesda, Md., Johns Hopkins Space Telescope Sci. Inst., Balt., Del Bello Gallery, Ont., Can., Rockville Art League, Pinneberg, Germany, Gov.'s Mansion, Annapolis, 1999, George Mason U. Art Gallery, Arlington, Va., 2000, The Women's Nat. Dem. Club, Washington, 2003, Sandyspring Mus., Md., 2003, Sumner Mus., 2004, Fairhaven Juried Art Exhbn., Sykesville, Md., 2004, Worldwide Miniature Exbhn., Smithsonian Mus., Washington, 2004, Ratner Gallery, 2005, Strathmore Arts Ctr., Bethesda, Md., 2005, Playhouse Theatre Gallery, NJ, 2005, Nat. Miniature Soc. Mont., 2005, Ratner Mus., Bethesda, Md., 2006, Sandy Spring Mus., Md., 2006, Fels Point Gallery, Md., 2006, Chevy Chase Womens Club Gallery, Md., 2006, 73rd Ann. Internat. Exhbn. Fine Art, Miniature Painters, Sculptors & Gravers Soc. Washington, 2006; participated in numerous juried or invitational exhbns. Recipient numerous awards for art. Mem.: Strathmore Arts Ctr. of Bethesda, Cider Painters Am., Olney Art Assn., Rockville Art League, Miniature Art Soc. Fla., Miniature Painters, Sculptors and Gravers Assn. Washington, Md. Printmakers Assn., Nat. League Am. Pen Women. Democrat. Methodist. Avocations: crafts, reading, designing notecards, genealogy, photography.

LEAKAS, DIANA BROD, interior designer, educator; b. Mich., Oct. 14, 1954; d. Edmund and Barbara Brod; m. James T. Leakas, Aug. 18, 1979. BS, Miami U., 1976. Interior designer Town and County Furniture, Dayton, Ohio, 1976—80, Federated Stores, Dayton, 1980—82; showroom mgr. Payne Fabrics, Dayton, 1982—85; interior design instr. U. Dayton, 1987—98, Sinclair C. C., 1979—. Faculty adv. Am. Soc. Interior Designers, Dayton, Ohio, 2002—. Office: Sinclair CC 444 W 3rd ST Dayton OH 45402-1421 Office Phone: 937-512-2051.

LEALE, OLIVIA MASON, small business owner, import marketing executive; b. Boston, May 5, 1944; d. William Mason and Jane Chapin (Prouty) Smith; m. Euan Harvie-Watt, Mar. ll, l967 (div. Aug. l979); children: Katrina, Jennifer; m. Douglas Marshall Leale, Aug. 29, l980. BA, Vassar Coll., 1966. Cert. paralegal, beginning yoga instr. Sec. to dir. Met. Opera Guild, N.Y.C., 1966; sec. to pres. Friesons Printers, London, 1974—75; guide, trainer Autoguide, London, 1977—79; ptnr. Inmark Internat. Mktg. Inc., Seattle, 1980—. Owner and mgr. Argus Ranch Facility for Dogs, Seattle, 2001—. Social case worker Inner London Ednl. Authority, l975-76. Democrat. Presbyterian. Avocations: reading, making doll house furniture, painting, knitting, dog agility. Home and Office: 1233 Shenandoah Dr E Seattle WA 98112-3727 Office Phone: 253-333-2347. Personal E-mail: oleale@comcast.net.

LEAMY, NANCY M., professional athletics coach; b. Phila., Dec. 3, 1938; d. John E. and Anna Cecilia Madden; children: Anne Marie-Elizabeth Frances, Charles John, Catherine. BA, Boston Coll.; postgrad., Fairfield U. Dir. Greenwich Skating Sch. Dorothy Hamill Rink, Conn., 1971—; dir. Skating Greenwich Skating Club, Conn., 1971—95; internat., nat., sectional, regional figure skating coach, 1973—; head skating dir. Darien (Conn.) Ice Rink, 1997—2001; coach U.S. internat. team, Milan, 1997; U.S. nat. coach 2001 N. Am. Cup Challenge, 2000—01. Powerskating coach N.Y. Rangers Orgn., 1996—98; coach gold medalist Spl. Olympics, 1996; jr. olympic coach, 1995—2000; dep. governing coun. United States Figure Skating Assn., 2004—. Named to Hall of Fame, New Country Day Sch., Newton, Mass., 2004. Mem.: Profl. Skaters Assn., U.S. Figure Skating Assn., Williams Club. Republican. Roman Catholic. Avocation: horseback riding. Home: 15 Mead Ave Cos Cob CT 06807 Office Phone: 203-622-6634.

LEAN, JUDITH, physicist, researcher; BSc in Physics with honors, Australian Nat. U., 1974; PhD in Atmospheric Physics, U. Adelaide, Australia, 1980. Rschr. space sci. div. Naval Rsch. Lab., 1986—. Expert on sun's role in global climate change; mem. panels and adv. groups NASA; mem. adv. com. geosciences NSF; mem. panels and adv. groups NRC. Fellow: Am. Geophysical Union; mem.: NAS, Am. Meterol. Soc., Am. Astron. Soc. (mem. solar physics div.), Internat. Assn. Geomagnetism and Aeronomy.

LEANDRO, PATRICIA J., mathematics educator; b. New Bedford, Mass., Dec. 10, 1956; d. Adolph F and Joyce I Walecka; m. John J Leandro, Apr. 3, 1982; children: John J, Ryan C, Sara K. BA, Boston Coll., Chestnut Hill, Mass., 1978. Cert. tchr. Mass., 1978. Tchr. New Bedford Pub. Schs., Mass., 1978—2002, Dartmouth Pub. Schs., Mass., 2002—. Math coach Math Counts Math Team, Dartmouth, 2004—. Tchr. liaison Mass. Pre-engring. program, Boston, 1990—91. Mem.: Mass. Tchrs. Assn. Avocations: swimming, walking, travel, skiing. Office: Dartmouth Middle School Slocum Rd Dartmouth MA 02747 Office Phone: 508-997-9333. Personal E-mail: pleandro@dartmouthps.org.

LEAR, LYN DAVIS, psychologist; m. Norman Lear; children: Benjamin, Brianna, Madeline. BA in Psychology, Calif. State Univ., Sacramento; M in Psychology, Calif. State Univ., Northridge; PhD in Clin. Psychology, Profl. Sch. Psychological Studies, San Diego. Family therapist NY Found. for Manic Depression and Depression; tchr., humanities, psychology, philosophy Brentwood Sch., LA; private practice Beverly Hills; ptnr., co-founder Graham and Statton public rels., San Francisco. Co-founder, bd. dir. Environ. Media Assn., 1989—; assoc. bd. mem. Woodshole Oceanographic Inst.; bd. dir. Rape Treatment Ctr., Women's Polit. Com., Earth Day; founder Retain Our Am. Rights (ROAR), LA, 2003. Grantee Rockefeller Fellow in Humanities, Univ. Mass., Amherst. Office: Environmental Media Assn Ste 210 10780 Santa Monica Blvd Los Angeles CA 90025

LEAR, MARY CATHERINE, music educator; b. Pitts., Apr. 10, 1954; d. Joseph Edward and Marie Ann Erdeljac; m. Richard Allen Lear, June 12, 1992; children: Jennifer, Jonathan, Stephen, Zachary. BS in Music Edn., Duquesne U., 1976, postgrad., 1976—82. Tchr., vocal dir. Carlynton Sch. Dist., Carnegie, Pa., 1976—; vocal music dir., musicals Carlynton HS, Carnegie, 1985—. Dir., performer (female vocal quintet) Generations 2. Chairperson Relay for Life Am. Cancer Soc., Carnegie, 2001—. Mem.: Pa. Music Educators Assn. (host Dist. I Jr. HS 1993, host Dist. I Chorus Sr. HS 2000, host Region I Chorus Sr. HS 2001). Avocations: gardening, crafts, interior decorating, church cantor. Home: 418 California Ave Oakmont PA 15139 Office: Carlynton Jr Sr HS 435 King's Hwy Carnegie PA 15106

LEARNED, MICHAEL, actress; b. Washington, Apr. 9, 1939; m. Peter Donat (dec.); children: Caleb, Christopher, Lucas; m. William Parker, Dec. 18, 1979. Student, Eng. Apprentice, Conn. Shakespeare Festival; with resident and touring cos., Can. Stratford Shakespeare Festival, Am. Conservatory Theatre, also San Diego Shakespeare Festival; theatrical film debut Touched By Love, 1980; (theater appearances) Richard III at Mark Taper Forum, Los Angeles, 1982-83 season, The Loves of Anatol, Broadway, 1983, Sally's Gone, She Left Her Name, off-Broadway, 1985, The Sisters Rosensweig, Broadway, 1993, On Golden Pond, 2006; (films) Hurricane, 1974, It Couldn't Happen to a Nicer Guy, 1974, Widow, 1976, Little Mo, 1978, Off the Minnesota Strip, 1980, All My Sons, 1986, Picnic, 1986, Life During Wartime, 1997, For the Love of May, 2000, Loggerheads, 2005, others, Lethal Eviction, 2005, others; (TV series) The Waltons, 1972-79, Nurse, 1980-82, Hothouse, 1988; (TV movies) A Christmas Without Snow, 1980, Mother's Day on Walton's Mountain, 1982, The Parade, 1984, Deadly Business, 1986, Mercy or Murder, Gunsmoke: The Last Apache, 1990, Aftermath: A Test of Love, 1991, The Walton Thanksgiving Reunion, 1993, A Walton Wedding, 1995, A Walton Easter, 1997, A Father for Brittany, 1998, others; (TV appearances) Police Story, 1974, Gunsmoke, 1973, St. Elsewhere, 1984, Living Dolls, 1989, Who's the Boss?, 1989, Wiseguy, 1990, Law & Order: Special Victims Unit, 2003, All My Children, 2005, One Life to Live, 2005, Scrubs, 2006. Recipient Emmy award Nat. Acad. TV Arts and Scis., 1973, 74, 76, 82*

LEARY, CAROL ANN, academic administrator; b. Niagara Falls, NY, Mar. 29, 1947; d. Angelo Andrew and Mary Josephine (Pullano) Gigliotti; m. Noel Robert Leary, Dec. 30, 1972. BA, Boston U., 1969; MS, SUNY, Albany, 1970; PhD, Am. Univ., 1988. Asst. to v.p. for student affairs, dir. women's programs Siena Coll., Loudonville, NY, 1970-72; asst. dir. housing Boston U., 1972-78; dir. residence Simmons Coll., Boston, 1978-84, assoc. dean, 1984-85; assoc. dir. The Washington Campus, Washington, 1985-86; adminstrv. v.p., asst. to pres. Simmons Coll., Boston, 1988-94; pres. Bay Path Coll., Longmeadow, Mass. Bd. dirs. Mass. Mut. Fin. Group, United Bank. Past pres., bd. govs. Colony Club; past pres. Cooperating Colls. of Greater Springfield; exec. com., chmn. Cmty. Found.; treas. Women's Coll. Coalition; past pres. WGBY; bd. dirs. Frank Stanley Beveridge Found., Go Fit Found. Mem.: Assn. Ind. Colls. and Univs. Mass. (past chair). Avocations: art, traveling overseas, hiking. Office: Bay Path Coll Office of the President 588 Longmeadow St Longmeadow MA 01106-2212 Office Phone: 413-565-1241. Business E-Mail: cleary@baypath.edu.

LEARY, MARGARET A., law librarian, library director; b. 1942; BA, Cornell U., 1964; MLS, U. Minn., 1966; JD, William Mitchell Coll. Law, St. Paul, 1973. Bar: Minn. 1973, Mich. 1974. Chpt. cataloger U. Minn. Law Libr., 1968—69; cataloger William Mitchell Coll. Law, 1970—72; atty. Legal Aid Soc., Mpls., 1972—73; lectr. U. Mich. Sch. Info. and Libr. Studies, 1974—88; asst. dir. U. Mich. Law Sch. Libr., 1973—81, assoc. dir. Ann Arbor, 1982—84, dir., 1984—. Exec. com. mem. Inst. for Continuing Legal Edn., 2004, Am. Assn. Law Libraries, 1983—86, pres., 1988—89. Contbr. articles to profl. jours. Trustee William Mitchell Coll. Law, 1993—2002; vice chmn. Planning Commn. City of Ann Arbor, 1994—2002, mem. Planning Commn., 1994—2002. Named Volunteer of Yr., Habitat for Humanity, Huron Valley, 2002. Achievements include being first woman to head a library at one of the top 5 US law schools. Office: Office of Dir Univ Mich Law Library 801 Monroe Ann Arbor MI 48109-1210 Office Phone: 734-764-4468. Fax: 734-615-0178. Business E-Mail: mleary@umich.edu.

LEARY, MARY DEBORAH, language educator; b. Buffalo; d. Nelson E. and Harriet K. Oldman; m. Daniel F. Leary, Sept. 3, 1971; children: Shane, Shannon, Skye, Sara. BA, Lake Erie Coll., 1969; MEd, Allegheny Coll., 1972. Fgn. lang. educator Cleve. Mcpl. Sch. Dist. Mem.: Ohio Modern Fgn. Lang. Assn. (Best Fgn. Lang. Dept. in Ohio 2000). Avocations: cooking, reading. Office: John Marshall HS 3952 W 140th St Cleveland OH 44111

LEASOR, JANE, religious studies educator, humanities educator, musician; b. Portsmouth, Ohio, Aug. 10, 1922; d. Paul Raymond Leasor and Rana Kathryn (Bayer) Leasor-McDonald. BA, Wheaton Coll., 1944; MRE, N.Y. Theol. Sem., 1952; PhD, NYU, 1969. Asst. prof. Belhaven Coll., Jackson, Miss., 1952-54; dept. chmn. Beirut Coll. for Women, 1954-59; asst. to pres. Wheaton (Ill.) Coll., 1961-63; dean of women N.Y. Theol. Sem., N.Y.C., 1963-67; counselor CUNY, Bklyn., 1967-74; assoc. prof. Beirut U. Coll., 1978-80; tchr. internat. sch., Les Cayes, Haiti, 1984-85; pvt. tutor, 1985—; tchr. Fayette County (W.Va.) Schs., 1993—; prof. religion dept. U. Charleston, W.Va., 1999—. Author religious text for use in Syria and Lebanon, 1960; editor books by V.R. Edman, 1961-63, Time and Life mags. Mem. Am. Assn. Counselors, Am. Guild Organists. Episcopalian. Avocations: reading, gardening, golf, travel, history Islam religion.

LEATH, CHERYL LYNN, retired pre-school educator, poet, painter; b. Chgo., Apr. 10, 1961; d. Wayne Lee Cutliff and Judith Louise Edwards, Sharron Cutliff (Stepmother); m. Thomas Richard Leath, Dec. 6, 1980 (div. Nov. 4, 1987); children: Cristin Lynnette McCoy, Dustin Scott, Allison Rene German. AA in applied sci., Carl Sandburg Coll., 1987—90. Practicum/internship Creative Childhood Ctr., Galesburg, Ill., 1990; preschool tchr./child care provider Children's Sch., Galesburg, Ill., 1991; child care provider Teddy Bear Day Care Ctr., Monmouth, Ill.; preschool tchr./child care provider Cameron Christian Care Ctr., Cameron, Ill., 1994—94; lead early childhood preschool tchr./child care provider Spires Child Care Ctr., Galesburg, Ill., 2003; ret. Painting in acrylics, Back Upon A Time; author: (poetry) A Veteran's Day Poem, Our World's Rainbow (editor's choice award cert., 2004), Pain, A Day Spent With Depression (editor's choice award cert., 2004), From the Heart Poetry, 2005, Creative Expressions, 2005, Thoughts and Design, 2006, Uniquely Created Poetry, 2006. Vol. Relay for Life. Mem.: Coalition of Citizens with Disabilities in Ill. Conservative-R. Avocations: writing, painting, reading, volunteering, walking. Personal E-mail: cherieskids@yahoo.com.

LEATH, MARY ELIZABETH, medical/surgical nurse; b. Cochran, Ga., Aug. 12, 1949; d. Warren Shaw Leath and Hattie Mae (Blackshear) Sterling; divorced; children: Myisha Renee, Shamara Antonea. Diploma, City Hosp., 1972; BS, Johns Hopkins U., Balt., 1988; ADN, Catonsville C.C., 1990; BSN, U. Md., 1993; MS, Johns Hopkins U., Balt., 1995; PhD, Cath. U., 1997. Cert. ACLS, critical care, ICU/trauma specialist, med./surg., phlebotomy and respiratory therapy, PICC lines, IV therapy and maintenance, cardiac care, peripheral intravenous cardiac catheterization. LPN staff MIEMSS, Balt., 1973-80, Ft. Howard (Md.) VA Med. Ctr., 1981-90; staff nurse Ft. Howard (Va.) VA Med. Ctr., 1990-96, Washington Trauma Ctr., 1996—; legal nurse cons., 1998—. Mem. ANA, Black Nurses Assn., Woodmoor Cmty. Health Assn. (instr. 1984—), Pres.'s Coun. on Physical Fitness, D.C. Nursing Assn., Phi Beta Kappa, Alpha Kappa Phi.

LEATHER, VICTORIA POTTS, college librarian; b. Chattanooga, June 12, 1947; d. James Elmer Potts and Ruby Lea (Bettis) Potts Wilmoth; m. Jack Edward Leather; children: Stephen, Sean. BA cum laude, U. Chattanooga, 1968; MSLS, U. Tenn., 1978. Libr. asst. East New Orleans Regional Libr., 1969-71; libr. Erlanger Nursing Sch., Chattanooga, 1971-75; chief libr. Erlanger Hosp., Chattanooga, 1975-77; dir. Eastgate Br. Libr., Chattanooga, 1977-81; dir. libr. svcs. Chattanooga State Tech. C.C., 1981-95, dean libr. svcs., 1996—. Mem. ALA, Southeastern Libr. Assn., Tenn. Libr. Assn. (past chair legis. com.), Chattanooga Area Libr. Assn. (pres. 1978-79), Tenn. Bd. Regents Media Consortium (chair 1994-95), Phi Delta Kappa. Episcopalian. Avocations: reading, needlecrafts, travel. Office Phone: 423-697-2576. Business E-Mail: vicky.leather@chattanoogastate.edu.

LEATHERBERRY, ANNE KNOX CLARK, architect; b. Geneva, Ill., Jan. 19, 1953; d. Donald William and Margaret Lorraine (Johnson) Clark; m. David Boyd Leatherberry, Aug. 5, 1978; children: Elizabeth Anne, Laura Knox. BS in Bus., Miami U., Oxford, Ohio, 1975. With Carson, Pirie, Scott & Co., Chgo., 1975-77; health care sales specialist Gen. Foods Corp., Northlake, Ill., 1977-78; account mgr. Cin., 1978-79; pres., owner Annie's Originals/Kids Collectables, Ltd., Waukesha, Wis., 1979—; mktg. rep./demonstrator mktg. Waukesha, 1988-91; owner Dreamhouse Designs, Waukesha, 1990—, Creative Enterprises Inc., Waukesha, 1990—; jewelry designer Creative Gem Jewelry, Waukesha, 2003—. Cons. Lamb's Quarters, Hartford, Wis., 1982-83, Ungerwear, West Alexandria, Ohio, 1982-84, Little Bits, Waukeshaw, 1984-90, Evelyn's Creations, East Troy, Wis., 1986-90, The Queen's Empire, Inc., Pitts., 1989-90, DRC Co., Mukwonago, Wis., 1990—, Don Belman Builders, 1991-92, Millikin Homes, 1992—, Opportunity Homes, 1993—, Affordable Homes, 1993—, Gemini Homes, 1993, Nelson Remodeling, 1993. Active Waukesha Area Symphonic Band, 1979—, 98, 99, sec. bd. dirs., 1987-89, 99-02, v.p.; active Carroll Coll. Cmty. Orch., 1985-86; vol. tchr.'s aide Clarend on Avenue Sch., Mukwonago, 1988-89; asst. leader Girl Scouts U.S.A., 1988, leader, 1988-89; vol. staff aide Jim Thompson for Gov. Campaign, 1975-76; dir. Children's Choir, 1986; summer music dir. Luth. Ch., 1986, 88; events chmn. Edgewood Golf League, 1988-92; vol. Rose Glen Reading Rams, Waukesha, 1990-92, Health Room, 1990-91, tchr.'s aid, 1991-92; pres. archtl. rev. bd. Red Wing Hills Assn., 1993-96; instr. architecture mentor program Waukesha Sch. Dist., 1995—; spirit wear sales chmn., 1998-2002, Waukesha West H.S. Band Boosters, 1997—, bd. dirs., 1999-2002. Recipient Ptnrs. for Edn. award, 1998; named Parent Vol. of Yr. Waukesha C. of C., 1998. Mem. NAFE, PEO (officer 1980-82), Direct Mktg. Assn., Soc. Craft Designers, Met. Builders Assn., Nat. Assn. of Remodeling Industry, Kappa Kappa Gamma. Republican. Lutheran. Avocations: painting, sewing, reading, golf, gardening. Home and Office: W241S5910 Autumn Haze Ct Waukesha WI 53189-9512 Office Phone: 262-542-1498. Business E-Mail: creativefleece@cs.com.

LEATHERS, KATHERINE ANNE, education educator; b. Lynn, Mass., July 13, 1950; d. William Charles and Grace Rena (Hobbs) L. AA, Miami (Fla.) Dade C.C., 1970; BA in Edn., Fla. Atlantic U., 1971, postgrad., 1974; MS in Edn., U. Miami, 1980, EdD in Elem. Edn., 1987. Cert. tchr., Fla. Tchr. South Miami Heights (Fla.) Elem. Sch., 1972-83; tchr. Ctr. for the Expressive Arts South Miami (Fla.) Elem. Sch., 1986—2003, curriculum writer, summer 1986, asst. program planner and implementer, 1983-87; grad. asst. U. Miami, Coral Gables, 1983-86; asst. prin. intern Dade County Pub. Schs., Miami, 1988; adj. prof. elem. edn. Fla. Internat. U., Miami, 1993—98, 2001, St. Thomas U., Miami, 1993—98. Presenter U. Ga., Athens, 1987, Dade County Reading Conf., Miami, 1994, Fla. Reading Assn. Conf., Orlando, 1994; tchr. Tchg. with Toys, Miami, summer 1984, Mus. of Sci., Miami, summer 1984, 85. Contbr. articles to profl. jours. Mem. Granada Presbyn. Ch., Coral Gables, Fla., 1976-78, 81, Sunday sch. tchr., Bible study tchr., jr. H.S. advisor, counselor, mem. coll.-career activities com.; mem. Youth for Christ, Miami and Ft. Lauderdale, Fla., 1977, 80, 81, Christmas counselor; info. table vol. Key Biscayne (Fla.) Presbyn. Ch., 1991-92; nursery fol. Old Cutler Presbyn. Ch., 2001-04. Mem. ASCD, Internat. Reading Assn., Dade County Reading Assn., United Tchrs. Dade, Nat. Coun. Tchrs. English, Phi Delta Kappa, Alpha Delta Kappa. Presbyterian. Home: 11837 SW 99th St Miami FL 33186-8516

LEAVELL, ELIZABETH BOYKIN, retired pediatrician; b. Sumter, S.C., 1924; d. William deSaissire and Elizabeth (Hood) Boykin; m. Seth Eugene Latham (dec.); children: Seth Eugene Latham Jr., Margaret Elizabeth Latham Davis, Richard Boykin Latham, William deSaussure Latham; m. Lewis Edward Leavell, Jr., Aug. 16, 1985 (dec.). BS Biology, Winthrop U., Rock Hill, S.C., 1946; MD, Med. U. S.C., Charleston, 1950. Diplomate Am. Bd. Pediat., 1956. Rotating intern Roper Hosp., Charleston, 1950—51, resident Pediat., 1951—53, chief resident, 1953—54; pediatrician Civil Svc. Tripler Army Hosp., Honolulu, 1954—55; pediatrician Aiken, SC, 1955—86, Atlanta, 1955—86; ret., 1986. Chief pediat. Holy Trinity Hosp., Atlanta, 1967, South Fulton Hosp., Atlanta, 1970; clinic pediatrician Crippled Children's Clinic, Atlanta, 1980—85; dir. med. edn. Pediat. St. Joseph Hosp., Atlanta, 1962—68; med. dir. Ctrl. Presbyn. Baby Clinic, Atlanta, 1962—68. Recipient Mary Mildred Sullivan Outstanding Alumna award, Winthrop U., 1970; tchg. fellow, Med.U. S.C., 1953—54. Fellow: Am. Acad. Pediat. (chmn. Fetus and Newborn com. Ga. chpt.). Home: 320 Loring Mill Rd Sumter SC 29150

LEAVELL, TAUSHA DAWN, social studies educator; d. Walter (Bud) Richard Leavell and Bettie Jean Taylor. BS in Elem. Edn., Southeastern Okla. State U., Durant, 2000. Cert. tchr. Tex., 2003. Tchr.- 6th grade social studies Sherman ISD, Tex., 2001—. Tex. support group leader Endometriosis Rsch. Ctr. Office Phone: 903-891-6495.

LEAVITT, BETH MEADE, science educator, department chairman; b. Teaneck, NJ, July 13, 1960; d. Robert E. and Maryann Meade; m. Thomas W. Leavitt, Jr.; children: Nicholas F., Austin W. BS in Biol. Scis., Clemson U., SC, 1984; EdM in Secondary Edn., Converse Coll., Spartanburg, SC, 1999. Nat. bd. cert. tchr. Environ. chemist Rogers & Callcott Engrs., Greenville, SC, 1986—98; dept. chair sci. Wade Hampton HS, Greenville, 1999—. Planetarium educator Roper Mt. Sci. Ctr., Greenville, 2001—; ptnr. NASA Edn. Program Network Educator Astronaut Tchrs. Named Outstanding Sci. Tchr. of Yr., Greenville County Schs., 2005—06, Tchr. of Yr., Wade Hampton H.S., 2006—. Mem.: NEA, Greenville County Sci. Tchrs. Assn. (sec. 2005—), Nat. Sci. Tchrs. Assn., Am. Assn. Physics Tchrs. Office: WHHS 100 Pine Knoll Dr Greenville SC 29609

LEAVITT, LYNDA, school system administrator, educator; d. Herbert and JoAnn Dollus; m. Dan Leavitt, Aug. 22, 1981; children: Shelby, Kelly, Andrew. BS in Polit. Sci., Ctrl. Mo. State U., Warrensburg, 1980; BS in Elem. and Spl. Edn., U. Mo., St. Louis, 1994; MEd, Nat. Louis U., Chgo., 1998; D in Ednl. Leadership, St. Louis U., Mo., 2003. Cert.: (paralegal) 1983; sch. adminstr. Mo., human and orgnl. devel. Fielding Univ., 2006. Elem. tchr. Ft. Zumwalt Sch. Dist., Saint Peters, Mo., 1994—99; asst. prin. Parkway Sch. Dist., Saint Louis, 1999—2003; adj. prof. Lindenwood U., St. Charles, Mo., 2003—; area coord. Spl. Sch. Dist., St. Louis, 2003—; adj. prof. Fontbonne U., St. Louis, 2004—. Mem.: ASCD, Coun. Adminstrs. of Spl. Edn., Coun. Exceptional Children, Phi Delta Kappa, Sigma Sigma Sigma. Achievements include research in Leadership Initiatives in School Reform; U.S. Delegate to the China and U.S. Conf. on educating students with special needs Beijing, China. Office: Special Sch Dist 12110 Clayton Rd Saint Louis MO 63131 Office Phone: 314-989-8324 2766. Business E-Mail: lleavitt@ssd.k12.mo.us.

LEBARRON, SUZANNE JANE, librarian; b. Tyndall, S.D., May 29, 1945; d. Ford and Eunice (Venne) LeB. BA, Coll. of Great Falls, 1967; MA, U. Minn., 1972. Prin. libr. asst. Stanford (Calif.) U., 1967-68; reference asst. Great Falls (Mont.) Pub. Libr., 1968-70; pre-profl. Mpls. Pub. Libr., 1970-72, community libr. Sumner Community Libr., 1972-74, libr., 1974-78; NEH project dir. Minn. Office Libr. Devel. and Svc., Mpls., 1978-79; assoc. libr. N.Y. State Libr., Albany, 1979-81; div. dir. Ky. Dept. for Librs. and Archives, Frankfort, 1981-86; dep. state libr. Conn. State Libr., Hartford, 1986-89; state libr. Wyo. State Libr., Cheyenne, 1990—. Author: Humanities in Minnesota, 1979; co-author: Serials for Libraries, 1979, Networking in Kentucky, 1981; editor: Directory of Humanities Research People in New York, 1980. Mem. ALA (councilor 1978-80, 84-88, 89—, chair com. on orgn. 1990-92), Wyo. Libr. Assn. Avocations: reading, swimming. Office: Wyo State Libr 2301 Capitol Ave Cheyenne WY 82001-3656

LEBECK, CAROL E., artist, educator; b. Spokane, Wash., Sept. 8, 1931; d. Birger John and Cecile Lebeck. BA, MA, UCLA, 1958; postgrad., Swedish State Sch. DEsign, Stockholm, 1958—59. Tchg. asst. dept. art UCLA, 1956—57; art tchr. Grossmont H.S., San Diego, 1959—66; art instr. Grossmont Coll., El Cajon, Calif., 1962—85. Exhibitions include include Spectrum Gallery, San Diego, 1983, exhibitions include Gallery 8, LaJolla, 1980, Fine Arts Gallery, San Diego, 1979, Celebrations Gallery, 1979, San Diego Acad. Fine Art, 1978, Grossmont Coll. Gallery, El Cajon, Calif., 1978, Mus. Contemporary Crafts, N.Y.C., 1978, L.A. Inst. Contemporary Art, 1977, The Sculpture Gallery, San Diego, 1977, Wise and Wesler Gallery, Encino, Calif., 1977, Crocker Art Gallery, Sacramento, 1977, numerous others, one-woman shows include Spectrum Gallery, San Diego, 1981, Triad Gallery, 1976, 1975, Represented in permanent collections Ariz. State U. Fellow, Swedish Am. Soc. fellow, Stockholm, 1958—59. Home: 10436 Russell Rd La Mesa CA 91941-4391

LEBEDOFF, RANDY MILLER, lawyer; b. Washington, Oct. 16, 1949; m. David Lebedoff; children: Caroline, Jonathan, Nicholas. BA, Smith Coll., 1971; JD magna cum laude, Ind. U., 1975. Assoc. Faegre & Benson, Mpls., 1975-82, ptnr., 1983-86; v.p., gen. counsel Star Tribune, Mpls., 1989—2001; asst. sec. Star Tribune Cowles Media Co., Mpls., 1990—98; pvt. practice Mpls., 2001—02; v.p., gen. counsel Twin Cities Public Television, 2002—. Bd. dirs. Milkweed Editions, 1989-96. Bd. dirs. Minn. Opera, 1986-90, YWCA, 1984-90, Planned Parenthood Minn., 1985-90, Fund for Legal Aid Soc., 1988-96, Abbott-Northwestern Hosp., 1990-94. Mem. Newspaper Assn. Am. (legal affairs com. 1991-2002), Minn. Newspapers Assn. (bd. dirs. 1995-2002, pres. 2002). Home: 1738 Oliver Ave S Minneapolis MN 55405-2222 Office: 172 E Fourth St Saint Paul MN 55101

LEBENTHAL, ALEXANDRA, investment firm executive; d. James and Jacqueline Beymer Lebenthal; m. Jeremy Diamond, 1991; children: Benjamin, Charlotte. AB history, Princeton U., 1986. Municipal bond dept. Kidder Peabody & Co., 1986—88; joined sales department Lebenthal & Co., NYC, 1988, bd. dirs., 1992—2005, v.p., dir. mut. fund dept., 1993—94, v.p., dir. sales, 1994—95, pres., CEO, 1995—2005; chmn. Lebenthal Funds Inc., NYC; bd. dirs. Advest Inc., NYC; CEO broker dealer unit Alexandra & James Israel Discount Bank of New York, NYC, 2006—. Mem. adv. bd. Barbara K. Enterprises. Trustee Nightingale Bamford Sch., Citizen's Budget Commn.; co-founder, bd. dirs. The Women's Exec. Cir.; bd. dirs. United Jewish Appeal Fedn. N.Y. Named one of New York's 100 most influential women, Crain's N.Y. Bus., 1999. Mem.: Bond Market Assn. (bd. dirs. 2004), The Com. of 200, The Young Pres. Orgn. Office: IDB Bank 511 Fifth Ave New York NY 10017*

LE BLANC, ALICE ISABELLE, academic administrator; b. New Orleans, Dec. 23, 1949; d. Joseph and Mary Elizabeth (Welsh) Le B.; divorced; 1 child, Matthew. BA in Drama & Comm., U. New Orleans, 1971; MPH, Tulane U., 1996. Sect. editor, feature writer Las Vegas Rev.- Jour., 1972-74; asst. dir. pub. rels. Touro Infirmary, New Orleans, 1980-82; dir. cmty. rels. AMI Riverside Hosp., Corpus Christi, Tex., 1982-84; dir. comm. United Way of the Coastal Bend, Corpus Christi, 1984-86; dir. pub. rels. & devel. Ada Wilson Hosp. Phys. Medicine Rehab., Corpus Christi, 1986-89; mktg. mgr. nat. sexual trauma program River Oaks Psychiat. Hosp., New Orleans, 1989-90; mktg. cons./physician recruitment contract Eye, Ear, Nose and Throat Hosp., New Orleans, 1990; mgr. prog. svcs./exec. MHA recruitment, dept. health sys. Tulane U. Sch. Pub. Health and Tropical Medicine, New Orleans, 1990-96; instr., dir. admissions and student affairs Sch. Pub. Health La. State U. Health Scis. Ctr., New Orleans, 1996—. Bd. dirs., bd. exec. com., chmn. standing com. United Way of the Coastal Bend, Corpus Christi, 1986, 87; bd. dirs. Early Childhood Devel. Ctr., Corpus Christi, 1988. Recipient Cert. of Appreciation, Gov. of Nev., 1974, Mayor of New Orleans, 1981, First Pl. award La. Hosp. Assn., 1982, Addy award of Excellence, Corpus Christi Advt. Fedn., 1986, 87, Addy First Place awards, 1988, Cert. of Recognition, United Way of the Coastal Bend, 1986, Cert. of Appreciation, Corpus Christi Jr. League, 1987. Avocations: gardening, carpentry, writing. Business E-Mail: alebla@lsuhsc.edu.

LEBLANC, DOTSIE L., retired vocational school educator; b. Abbeville, La., Jan. 14, 1932; d. Esta A. Langlinais and Ouida M. Brasseaux; m. Dale P. LeBlanc (div.); children: Karen Domingue(dec.), Lisa Boudreaux, Jan Wicks, Victor, Steven. Degree in home econs., U. South La., Lafayette, 1971. Vocat. rehab. instr. State of La., Lafayette, 1967—73, vocat. rehab. counselor Lafayette and New Orleans, 1974—79, vocat. rehab. tng. coord. Baton Rouge, 1979—82, vocat. rehab. tng. dir., 1982—94; ret., 1994. Author: Le Petit Cajun, 1977, The Little Ant, 1976. Mem.: Vocat. Evaluation and Work Adjustment Assn. (award), La. Rehab. Assn. (pres.). Avocations: antiques, art. Home: 655 Marie Antoinette St Apt 327 Lafayette LA 70506 Personal E-mail: dotsi@bellsouth.net.

LEBLANC, JEAN EVA, writer, poet, educator; b. Leominster, Mass., Apr. 16, 1961; d. J. Camille and Sydne Grace (Lloyd) LeB. BS in Biology summa cum laude, Fitchburg State Coll., 1986; MA in English, Middlebury Coll., 1993. Adj. instr. English Sussex County C.C., Newton, NJ, 1999—. Contbr. poetry, book revs., and essays to various periodicals, mus. revs. to Classical disCDigest; contbr. natural history articles to Appalachian Trailway News, Gen. Store Mag. Avocations: hiking, visiting museums, reading, art.

LEBLANC, JEANNE MARIE, psychologist, educator; b. Tallahassee, Fla., May 19, 1965; d. Joseph Wilfred Jr. and Annalois (Jackson) LeB.; m. William Robert Hitch, Dec. 17, 1983 (div. Mar. 1992); 1 child, Jessica Elaine; m. Patrick Henry Bogan III, Oct. 8, 1994. AA, Richland Coll., 1987; BA summa cum laude, U. Tex., Dallas, 1989; PhD, U. Tex. Southwestern Med. Ctr., 1997. Lic. psychologist, Tex. Clin. psychology intern Parkland Meml. Hosp., Dallas, 1990-93, Terrell (Tex.) State Hosp., 1990-91, Scottish Rite Hosp., Dallas, 1991-92, So. Meth. U., Dallas, 1992-93; assessment specialist, neurocognitive therapist Pate Rehab., Dallas, 1993-99, neuropsychol. resident, 1997-99; asst. prof. counseling and human behavior Amber U., Garland, Tex., 1998—; program mgr. Marshall (Tex.) Youth Svcs. Sabine Valley Ctr., 1999—. Test examiner The Psychol. Corp., San Antonio, 1999—. Presenter (symposium) Ecologically Valid Treatment, 1998. Vol. crisis worker The Family Place, Dallas, 1986-88; vol. family facilitator Divert Ct.—Dallas County, 1999. Mem. APA, Tex. Psychol. Assn., MENSA. Avocations: playing clarinet, travel, attending cultural events, literary discussions.

LEBLANC, MARIANNE CAMILLE, lawyer; b. Boston, June 19, 1968; d. Norman Roger and Barbara Ann (Camille) L.; m. John Joseph Cummings III, Sept. 18, 1993. BA with honors, Wellesley Coll., 1990; JD with honors, Boston Coll., 1993. Bar: Mass. 1993, U.S. Dist. Ct. Mass. 1994. Assoc. Sugarman and Sugarman, P.C., Boston, 1993—2000, ptnr., 2000. Co-editor Jour. Mass. Acad. Trial Attys., 1998-2001. Bd. dirs. Support Com. for Battered Women, 1993-98, pres. 1994-96; bd. trustees Ursuline Acad., 2003—. Named one of Lawyers Yr., Mass. Lawyers Weekly, 1999, Top Boston Lawyers, Boston Mag., 2004, Mass. Super Lawyers, Law & Politics, 2004, Top 100 Mass. Super Lawyers, 2005, Top 50 Female Mass. Super Lawyers, 2004, 2005; recipient 40 Under 40 award, Boston Bus. Jour., 2002. Mem. ATLA (new lawyers divsn. gov., 1996-98), New. Eng. Bar Assn. (bd. dirs. 2002—), Mass. Acad. Trial Attys. (co-editor jour., bd. govs. 1999—, exec. com. 2006-, recipient New Lawyers award, 1996), Mass. Bar Assn. (civil litig. sect. coun. 2000-02, ho. dels. 2001-02, chair civil litig. sect. coun. 2001-02), Women's Bar Assn. Mass. (bd. dirs., 1999-, co-chair legis. policy com. 2001-02, ann. gala chair 2003, v.p. 2002-03, pres-elect 2003-04, pres. 2004-05), Women's Bar Found. Mass. (bd. trustees 2001—, pres.-elect 2006), New Eng. Bar Assn. (bd. dirs. 2002-05), Ursuline Acad. (bd. trustees 2003-), Children's Law Ctr. Mass. (pro bono atty. program). Democrat. Roman Catholic. Avocations: running, golf. Office: Sugarman and Sugarman PC 1 Beacon St Boston MA 02108-3107 Office Phone: 617-542-1000. Business E-Mail: mleblanc@sugarman.com.

LEBLANC, MELINDA ANNE, voice educator; b. Ga., Oct. 16, 1979; d. Tommy Dale and Beverly Carol Frost; m. Tim LeBlanc, July 10, 1999; 1 child, Caroline. MusB in Edn., U. La., Monroe, 2000. Choir tchr. St. Fredericks's HS, Monroe, 2001, Riser Mid. Sch., West Monroe, 2001—. Chair jr. high divsn. Dist. I Choral Dirs., Monroe, 2001—. Named Outstanding Am. Tchr., 2006. Office: Riser Mid Sch 100 Price Dr Monroe LA 71201 Office Phone: 318-387-0567.

LEBLANC, TINA, dancer; b. Erie, Pa. m. Marco Jerkunica, May 1988; children: Marinko James, Sasha Johan. Trained, Carlisle, Pa. Dancer Joffrey II Dancers, NYC, 1982-83, The Joffrey Ballet, NYC, 1984-92; prin. dancer San Francisco Ballet, 1992—. Guest tchr. Ctrl. Pa. Youth Ballet, 1992, 94—. Work includes roles in (with San Francisco Ballet) Con Brio, Bizet Pas de Deux, Swan Lake, Nanna's Lied, Handel--A Celebration, La fille mal gardée, Rubies, Tchaikovsky Pas de Deux, Seeing Stars, The Nutcracker, La Pavane Rouge, Company B, Romeo and Juliet, Sleeping Beauty, The Dance House, Terra Firma, Lambarena, Fly by Night, In the Night, Ballo della Regina, The Lesson, The Tuning Game, Quartette, Etudes, Western Symphony, Maelstrom, Pacific, Criss-Cross, Giselle, Theme and Variations, Gala Performance, The Vertiginous Thrill of Exactitude, Taiko, Sandpaper Ballet, La Bayadere, Night, Serenade, Celts, Stars & Stripes, Tarantella, Symphony in C, Dances at a Gathering, Don Quixote (full length), Square Dance, Apollo, Rush, Paquita, Who Cares, Study in Motion, 7 for Eight, Symphonic Variations, Two Bits, Valses Poeticos, Sea Pictures, Elite Syncopations, Smile with Your Heart, Falling, Harlequinade, Rodeo, Other Dances, Blue Rose, Quaternary, Chaconne, Artifact Suite, The Death of a Moth; (with other companies) The Green Table, Les Presages, Le sacre du printemps, Les Noces, Light Rain, Romeo and Juliet, Runaway Train, Empyrean Dances, La Vivandière, L'air D'esprit, Corsaire Pas de deux, Don Quixote pas de deux, Lacrymosa, Confetti, Kettentanz Le Beau Danube, Offenbach in the Underworld, Suite Saint Saens, Forgotten Land, Dream Dances, Postcards, Coppelia, Remembrances, Reflections, Cotillion. Recipient Princess Grace Found. award, 1988, Princess Grace Statuette award, 1995, Isadora Duncan award, 1998-99, 2000-01. Office: San Francisco Ballet Assn 455 Franklin St San Francisco CA 94102-4471 Office Phone: 415-861-5600.

LEBOFF, BARBARA, elementary school educator; b. Apr. 11, 1949; Children: Darcie, Cory. MS, Fla. State U., 1977; EdD, Tex. So. U., 1994. Tchr. various schs., Houston & Tallahassee, 1977—, MacArthur Elem. Sch., Houston, 1997—, math. lead tchr., 1999—2006; ret., 2006. Presenter Tex. Computer Edn. Assn., Tex., 1999-2002, Nat. Coun. Tchrs. Math., 2003, Houston ISD workshops in Math. and Tech.; owner The Wine Spot. Author: Affirmation Journal: Positive Thinking for Beginners, 1997. Sec., membership chmn., Cypress Falls Band Boosters, Tex., 1996-98, People to People Ambassadors Tching. Standards Del. to China, 2001. Outstanding Coll. Students of Amer., 1989, Master Tchr., Gregg Elementary Sch., 1994, Nominee Tchr. of Yr., 2002-03. Avocations: writing, sewing, alternative health, photography, quilting. Home: 7519 Andiron Cir Houston TX 77041-1516 E-mail: bleboff@yahoo.com.

LEBOUTILLIER, JANET ELA, writer, real estate developer, minister; b. Marshfield, Mass., May 10, 1936; d. Preston Carleton and Barbara (Higgins) Ela; m. John Walter McNeill, Oct. 10, 1959 (div. 1970); children: Duncan Davis McNeill, Sarah McNeill Treffry; m. Martin LeBoutillier, May 10, 1986 (dec. Feb. 2001). AA, Briarcliff Jr. Coll., 1956; BA in English Lit., U. Colo., 1958; postgrad. Real Estate/Mortgage Banking, NYU, 1973-78; AA, Wagner Leadership Sch., 2004; grad., Gateway ARC Bible Min. Sch., 2004. Lic. N.Y. (1969) and Conn. (1986) real estate broker; cert. property mgr. Sales, leasing agt. L.B. Kaye Assocs., Ltd., N.Y.C., 1969-74; comml. leasing agt. Kenneth D. Laub & Co., N.Y.C., 1975; dir. leasing, asst. bldg. mgr. Douglas Elliman Gibbons & Ives Co., N.Y.C., 1975-76; adminstr. REIT adv. unit Chase Manhattan Bank, N.A., N.Y.C., 1976-78; asst. dir. real estate investments Mass. Mut. Life Ins. Co., Springfield, Mass., 1978-80; dir. real estate investments Yale U., New Haven, Conn., 1980-81; ind. cons. N.Y.C., 1981-83; sr. analyst, equity mgmt., sales and devel. Aetna Realty Investors, Inc., Hartford, Conn., 1983-84, dir. pub. involvement unit, 1984-86; sr. asset mgr. Cigna Investments, Inc., Hartford, 1986-87; v.p. Wm. M. Hotchkiss Co., New Haven, Conn., 1987-88; pres., prin. LeBoutillier & LeBoutillier, Inc., Lyme, Conn., 1989-93. Author: Mediations on Joy, 1995. Past mem. pastoral care and healing commn., prayer team ministry leader/tng., Grace Episcopal Ch., 1991-2002; co-founder, mem., convener Heart of Compassion chpt. Internat. Order of St. Luke, 1993-2002; mem. prayer, healing ministry team Gateway Apostolic Resource Ctr., 2004, lead traveling intercessor; missionary, tchr., Living Waters Revival Ctr., 2004. Mem. Soc. Mayflower Descs., Nat. Soc. Colonial Dames (bd. mgrs., sec. 1998-2000). Independent. Avocations: writing, prophetic healing prayer ministry, walking, swimming, sports. Home and Office: 11 Acad Ln Old Lyme CT 06371-2312

LEBOWITZ, CATHARINE KOCH, state legislator; b. Winchester, Mass., June 30, 1915; d. William John and Carolyn Sophia (Kistinger) Koch; m. Murray Lebowitz, Sept. 21, 1971 (dec. Oct. 1978). Student, Northwestern U., 1948-49, Boston Coll., 1949-52; degree (hon.), Ea. Main Tech. Coll., 2003. Sec. ERA, Bangor, Augusta, Maine, 1935-38, WPA, Portland, Maine, 1938-42; pers. officer, exec. sec. USN, Portland, 1942-47; exec. sec. Clark Babbitt, Boston, 1947-48; adminstrv. asst. Moore Bus. Forms, Boston, 1948-52; apt. mgr., wholesale appliance divsn. Coffin-Wimple Inc., 1952-62; clk. U.S. Dist. Ct. Bangor (no. dist.), 1962-79; sec. Portland Credit Bur., 1980-86; mem. Bangor City Coun., 1985-87, Maine State Legislature, 1982-92. Bd. dirs. Eastern Transp., 1989—94; mem. Bus. Adv. Coun., 1991—; active Program Rev. Subcom., 1991—; mem. adv. coun. Ea. Maine Tech. Coll., 1992—; bd. dirs. Rural Health Ctrs. Maine, Inc., 1992—99; chair, adv. bd., Gala decorating com. Maine Ctr. for Arts, U. Maine, 1992—2003. Sec. Symphony Women, Bangor, 1964—84; bd. dirs. Opera House Com., 1978—94; legis. com. United Way of Penobscot Valley, 1988—93, bd. dirs., 1993—99; adv. com. Maine Devel. Found., 1988—90; adv. bd. Aftercare, Cmty. Health & Counseling Svc., 1992; planning bd. St. Joseph Hosp., 1987—92; dir., v.p. St. Joseph Hosp. Aux., 1994—99, Maine Ctr. Arts Adv. Bd., 1994—2002; apptr. by gov. Maine Commn. Cmty. Svc., 1996—2002; mem. Bangor City Hosp. Aux., 1988—99; bd. dirs. Penobscot Theater, 1990; accredited Beauty Pageant judge, 1986—; mem. Eastern Main Commn. Cmty Svc., 1996; del. Rep. Nat. Conv., 1984, 1988. Recipient Civilian Meritorious Svc. award USN, Portland, Maine, 1946, Paul Bunyan award, C. of C., 1997, Cmty. Spirit award Sr. Star recognition Merrill Merchants Bank Bangor, 1999; named Hon. Alumnus Secretarial Sci., Husson Coll., 1980, Ea. Main Tech. Coll. Champion award, 2002. Mem.: Ea. Maine Med. Ctr. Aux., Ret. Fed. Employees (v.p. 1994—, pres. 1996), Newcomb Soc., Penobscot County Reps., Bangor C. of C. (mem. comsumer rels. coun., 1981-90, gov. affairs com. 1996—, coord. 150th ann. prodn. Music Man 1984), Bangor Dist. Nursing Assn. (corp. mem. at large), Credit Women Bangor (sec. 1965—67), Nat. Assn. Ret. Fed. Employees (v.p. bd. dirs. 1993—, sec. 1994), Credit Profls. Bangor Cmty. Theater (treas. 1973—98), Credit Women Internat. (treas. 1975—77), Penobscot County Ext. Svc. (hon.; bd. dirs. 1995—), Main Art N.G. (hon.), Maine N.G. Assn. (hon.), Bangor Hist. Soc. (bd. dirs. 1993—, exec. bd. sec. 1994—99, pres. 1999—2002), Maine Maine Masque Theater (judge 1983—90), Mgmt. Club, Bangor City Rep. Club (bd. dirs., treas. 1993—97), Penobscot County Rep. Women's Club (sec. 1979), Zonta Club (pres. Bangor 1962—64, 1980—82, v.p. 1994, adv. bd. Maine migrant health program 2001—, cooperator cmty. health and counseling svcs. 2001—, Outstanding Leader 1991).

LEBOWITZ, CHARLOTTE MEYERSOHN, social worker; b. Germany, Dec. 22, 1924; arrived in U.S., 1938, naturalized, 1943; d. Franz and Magda (Wellisch) Meyersohn; m. Marshall Lebowitz, Aug. 7, 1949; children: Wendy, Marian, Mark (dec.). BA, Brown U., 1946; MSW, Simmons Coll., 1948. Psychiat. social worker Jewish Family and Children's Svc., Boston, 1948-49, ARC Home Svc. Dept., Boston, 1949-53, Youth Guidance Ctr., Framingham, Mass., 1962-69, Brandon Sch., Natick, Mass., 1969-74, Natick Pub. Schs., 1975-92. Adj. clin. instr. Boston Coll. Sch. Social Work, 1981-82; mem. exec. bd. Natick Svc. Coun., 1982-95; cons. YWCA, 1970-71. Mem. exec. bd. PTA, 1955-71, chmn. pre-sch. unit, 1955-56, mem. coun., 1956-70; trustee coun. Leonard Morse Hosp., 1976-91. Fellow: Am. Orthopsychiat. Assn.; mem.: NASW, Boston Inst. Devel. Infants and Parents, Social Workers Employed Less than Full Time, Sch. Adjustment Counselors Assn., Acad. Cert. Social Workers, Sisterhood of Temple Israel of Natick, Nonesuch Pond Improvement Assn., Brown U. Alumni Assn., Simmons Coll. Sch. Social Work Alumni Assn. Home: 2 Abbott Rd Natick MA 01760-1913

LEBRETON, MARJORY, senator; b. City View, Ont., Can., July 4, 1940; m. Douglas LeBreton; children: Linda Marlene(dec.), Michael Bruce. Student, Ottawa Bus. Coll. Campaign worker Progressive Conservative Nat. Hdqrs., 1962—63, Office of Rt. Hon. John G. Diefenbaker, 1963—67; office supr. Hon. Robert L. Stanfield, 1967—75; tour coord. Office of Rt. Hon. Joe Clark, 1976—79; dir. scheduling Office of Prime Min. Clark, 1979—80; dir. leader's tour and spkrs. bur. Progressive Conservative Nat. Hdqrs., 1981—83; tour coord., co-dir. nat. campaign tour Rt. Hon. Brian Mulroney, 1983—84; gen. mgr., dir. ops. Ottawa office Progressive Conservative Party, 1985; spl. asst. Office of Prime Min., 1986—87, dep. chief staff, spl. asst., 1987—93; senator The Senate of Can., Ottawa, 1993—, leader of the govt. Bd. dirs. Manotick Watsons Mill Millenium Fund. Mem.: MADD (nat. chair), Nepean Carleton Riding Assn., Nat. Press Club, Albany Club. Conservative. Avocation: gardening. Office: The Senate of Can 275-S CB Ottawa ON Canada K1A 0A4

LECHER, BELVADINE (BELVADINE REEVES), museum curator; b. Plainview, Nebr., Nov. 14, 1921; d. Robert Ancil and Myrtle Ivian (Rodgers) Reeves; m. Raymond Ralph Lecher, June 6, 1943; children: Krissa R. Lecher Randall, Pamela G. Lecher Hersh, Kim N. Lecher. Cert. in Hosp. Adminstrn., St. Louis U., Mo., 1967. Sec. Baird Law Office, Gordon, Nebr., 1938-39; cashier, bookkeeper, receptionist Western Pub. Svc. Co., Gordon, 1939-41, Consumers Pub. Power Co., Chadron, Nebr., 1941-45; cashier, bookkeeper, med. records Luth. Hosp. Homes Soc., Crawford, Nebr., 1952-62, adminstr., 1962-70; rate auditor, acct. Ross Transfer, Inc., Chadron, 1970-90; curator, dir. Dawes County Hist. Soc. Mus., Chadron, 1992—. Editor: (newspaper) Golden Age Courier, 1994—, (newsletter) Dawes County Hist. Soc., 1981—; co-editor: (book) Man of Many Frontiers - The Diaries of Billy the Bear Iaeger, 1994. Active Am. Cancer Soc., Dawes County, 1981—2003; tutor adult basic edn., Chadron, 1990—95; bd. dirs. Habitat for Humanity, Chadron, 1993—95. Recipient Cmty. Svc. award Rotary, Chadron, 1985, Good Neighbor award Ak-Sar-Ben/Omaha World Herald, Omaha, 1994, Woman of the Yr. award Chadron Bus. and Profl. Women's Club, Chadron, 1996, Recognition of Vol. Svc. award Am. Legion Aux., Chadron, 1994. Mem. Nebr. Mus. Assn., Nebr. State Genealogy Soc. (query editor 1982-84), Northwest Genealogy Soc. (county dir. 1992-94), Dawes County Hist. Soc. (pres. 1981-92, mus. curator 1992—), DAR (regent 1978, 80, 2000-02, registrar, 1982-95, 2004-06, treas. 1972-82), Area C. of C. (vis. com. 1996—2005). Republican. Methodist. Avocations: historic and lineage research, reading, writing, handcrafts, hiking. Office: Dawes County Hist Soc PO Box 1319 Chadron NE 69337-7329 Office Phone: 308-432-4999.

LECHEVALIER, MARY PFEIL, retired microbiologist, educator; b. Cleve., Jan. 27, 1928; d. Alfred Leslie Pfeil and Mary Edith Martin; m. Hubert Arthur Lechevalier, Apr. 7, 1950; children: Marc E.M., Paul R. BA in Physiology-Biochemistry, Mt. Holyoke Coll., 1949; MS in Microbiology, Rutgers U., 1951. Rsch. fellow Rutgers U., New Brunswick, NJ, 1949-51, rsch. assoc. inst. microbiology, 1962-74, from asst. to assoc. rsch. prof., 1974-85, rsch. prof. Waksman inst. microbiology, 1985-91, prof. emerita, 1991—; ind. rschr., 1955-59; microbiologist steroid preparative lab. E.R. Squibb and Sons, New Brunswick, 1960-61; vis. investigator Inst. Biology Czechoslovak Acad. Scis., Svc. de Mycologie Pasteur Inst., Prague, Paris, 1961-62. Cons. in field. Contbr. over 100 chpts. to books and articles to rsch. jours.; mem. adv. com. actinomycetes Bergey's Manual of Determinative Bacteriology, 8th edit.; chair adv. com. muriform actinomycetes Bergey's Manual, 9th edit. Assoc. mem. Bergey's Trust, 1989—92. Recipient Charles

Thom award, Soc. Indsl. Microbiology, 1982, Waksman award, Theobald Smith Soc., 1991. Mem. AAAS, Am. Soc. Microbiology (former mem. com. actinomycetales), US Fedn. Culture Collections (exec. com. 1982-85, J. Roger Porter award nominating com. 1983-84, 87-88, chair 1989-90, J. Roger Porter award 1992), N.Am. Mycol. Assn., Soc. for Actinomycetes Japan, Sigma Xi (pres. Rutgers U. chpt. 1977-78). Achievements include patents in field. Home: 131 Goddard-Nisbet Rd Morrisville VT 05661-8041

LECHMAN, SHARON ELIZABETH, elementary school educator; b. Manahattan, NY, Apr. 11, 1975; d. Fedele Albert and Elizabeth Anne Grisolia; m. Kris Matthew Lechman, Nov. 8, 2003. MS, Montclair U., NJ, 2005. Cert. tchr. NJ. Math. tchr. Teterboro (NJ) Vocat. Sch., 1998—99, Teaneck (NJ) Bd. Edn., 1999—. Mem.: Assn. for Curriculum Devel. Office: Teaneck High Sch 100 Elizabeth Ave Teaneck NJ 07666

LECHTANSKI, CHERYL LEE, chiropractor; b. Elizabeth, N.J., Dec. 27, 1961; d. Leo Joseph and Barbara Frances (Sullivan) Lechtanski. BA in Biology and Journalism, NYU, 1985; DC, N.Y. Chiropractic Coll., 1989; AAS in Acctg., Brookdale CC, 1998; MBA, Monmouth U., 2002. Lic. chiropractor N.J., N.Y., Pa., Del., Mich. Chiropractic assoc. Chiropractic Arts Ctr., Downingtown, Pa., 1990—91; pvt. practice Newark, 1992-93; with Morganville (N.J.) Family Chiropractic Office, 1993—. Mem.: Marine Mammal Stranding Ctr., Save the Manatee Club, Ocean Conservancy, Box Turtle Coalition N.E. (founder), Beta Gamma Sigma, Phi Chi Omega. Buddhist. Avocations: horseback riding, hiking, herpetology, softball, swimming. Home: 1 Kennedy Ct Middletown NJ 07748-3531 Office: Morganville Family Chiropractic Office 52 Tennent Rd Morganville NJ 07751-4153 Office Phone: 732-591-1223. E-mail: paboxies@hotmail.com.

LECKEY, DOLORES R., religious organization administrator, writer; b. N.Y.C., Apr. 12, 1933; d. Joseph Francis and Florence Marie Conklin; m. Thomas Philip Leckey, June 22, 1957 (dec.); children: Mary Kate Marcellus, Celia E., Thomas Joseph, Colum. BA, St. John's U., Bklyn., 1954; MA, George Washignton U., 1971. English tchr. Delahanty H.S., N.Y.C., 1954-56; elem. tchr. Oliver Sch., South Bend, Ind., 1957-58; sem. prof., adminstr DeSales Sch. Theology, Washington, 1971-77; TV prodr. Pub. TV/WNVT, Annandale, Va., 1974-76; ch. exec. Nat. Conf. Cath. Bishops, Washington, 1977-97; sr. fellow WTC, Georgetown U., Washington, 1998—. Author: The Ordinary Way, 1982, Laity Stirring the Church, 1987, Practical Spirituality, 1987, Women and Creativity, 1991, Winter Music, 1992, 7 Essentials for the Spiritual Journey, 1999, Blessings All Around, 1999; co-author: Facing Fear with Faith, 2002, Spiritual Exercises for Church Leaders, 2003; gen. editor: Just War, Lasting Peace, 2006; exec. prodr. videos. Founder Arlington Partnership for Affordable Housing, 1989—; mem. Arlington Com. of 100, 1976—; mem. adv. bd. Arlington Street People Assistance, 1998—; trustee U. Dayton, 1991-2001, St. Mary's U. and Sem., Balt., 1989-95 Recipient Cardinal Bernardin award Cath. Common Ground Initiative, Disting. Svc. award Washington Theol. Union, 1988; Louisville Inst. grantee, 1998. Mem. Assn. for Religion and Intellectual Life. Democrat. Roman Catholic. Achievements include 12 honorary degrees. Avocations: piano, theater and opera, hiking, reading. Office: Georgetown U Woodstock Theol Ctr Washington DC 20052-0001 Home: Apt 601W 3835 9th St N Arlington VA 22203-4083

LECLAIR, ELIZABETH JANE, elementary school educator; b. St. Paul, Minn., Aug. 12, 1950; m. James Michael LeClair, July 31, 1970; children: Kelli Odden, Jamie, Andrew. BSN, Abbott Hosp. Sch. Nursing, Mpls., 1971; BS in Elem. Edn., Mayville State U., ND, 1990; MS in Edn., U. N.D., Grand Forks, 2000. RN St. Michael's Hosp. Bethesda, Grand Forks, 1971—72, Luther Meml. Home, Mayville, 1990; tchr. Northwood (N.D.) Sch., 1990—91, Hatton (N.D.) Sch., 1991—92, Mayfort CG Sch., Mayville, 1992—. RN Portamedic, Mayville, 1994—96; mem. core group Mayfort CG Sch., 1998—. Named Student Tchr. of Yr., Mayville (N.D.) State U., 1990. Office: Mayfort CG Sch Peter Boe Jr Elem 20 2nd St NW Mayville ND 58257

LECLAIR, SUSAN JEAN, hematologist, clinical laboratory scientist, educator; b. New Bedford, Mass., Feb. 17, 1947; d. Joseph A. and Beatrice (Perry) L.; m. James T. Griffith; 1 child, Kimberly A. BS in Med. Tech., Stonehill Coll., 1968; MS in Med. Lab. Sci., U. Mass., 1977; PhD in Clin. Hematology, Walden U., 2001. Cert. clin. lab. scientist; cert. med. technologist. Med. technologist Union Hosp., New Bedford, Mass., 1968—70; supr. hematology Morton Hosp., Taunton, Mass., 1970—72; edn. coord., program dir. Sch. Med. Tech. Miriam Hosp., Providence, 1972—79; hematology technologist R.I. Hosp., Providence, 1979—80; asst. prof. med. lab. sci. U. Mass., Dartmouth, 1980—84, assoc. prof. med. lab. sci., 1984—92, prof. med. lab. sci., 1992—. Instr. hematology courses Brown U., Providence, 1978-80; cons. bd. Div. Clin. Hematology, Charlton Meml. Hosp., St. Luke's Hosp., 1984-2000, Nemasket Group, Inc., 1984-87, Gateway Health Alliance, 1985-87, Pawtucket Meml. Hosp., 1999-2001; chair hematology/hemostasis com. Nat. Cert. Agy. for Med. Lab. Pers. Exam. Coun., 1994-98. Editor-in-chief, Clin. Lab. Sci., 2000; contbr. articles to profl. jours.; contbr. articles to jours and chpts. to books; author computer software in hematology; creator, dir. consumer info. web page, 2000-. Reviewer Nat. Commn. Clin. Lab. Scis., 1986-89; chairperson Mass. Assn. Health Planning Agys., 1986-87; bd. dirs. Southeastern Mass. Health Planning Devel. Inc., (1975-88, numerous other offices and coms.); planning subcom. AIDS Edn. (presentor Info Series). Mem. Am. Soc. Clin. Lab. Sci. (editor clin. practice sect. CLS jour. 1996-2000, editor-in-chief CLS jour. 2001—, creator and dir. Consumer Info. Web Page), Am. Soc. Med. Tech. Edn. and Rsch. Fund, Inc. (chair 1983-85), Mass. Assn. for Med. Tech. (pres. 1977-78), Southeastern Mass. Soc. Med. Tech. (pres. 1975-76), Alpha Mu Tau (pres. 1993-94). Avocations: choral singing, cooking, reading. Office: U Mass Dept Med Lab Sci Dartmouth MA 02747 E-mail: sleclair@umassd.edu.

LECOCQ, KAREN ELIZABETH, artist; b. Santa Rosa, Calif., Nov. 4, 1949; d. Maynard Rodney and Lois May (Lessard) LeC.; m. David Lawrence Medley, Sept. 7, 1995. BA, Calif. State U., Fresno, 1971, MA, 1975; postgrad., Calif. Inst. of the Arts, L.A., 1971-72. Founding mem. Feminist Art Program, Fresno, Calif., 1971, Calif. Inst. of the Arts, L.A., 1972. Instr. Mead Coll., 2000-; grad. instr. Calif. State U., Fresno, 1976-78. One-woman shows include Calif. State U. Art Gallery, Fresno, 1970, 76, Merced (Calif.) Coll., 1969, 77, 91, Calif. Inst. of the Arts, L.A., 1972, Womanart Gallery, N.Y.C., 1980, Amos Eno Gallery, N.Y.C., 1994, 97, 750 Gallery, Sacramento, 1995, Meridian Gallery, San Francisco, 1993, Wild Gallery, Sacramento, 1999, Multicultural Arts Ctr., 2000, 04, Sorensen Gallery, 2004, Club Jinnaka Gallery, Fresno, Calif., 2006; group shows include Womanhouse, L.A., 1972, Off Centre Centre, Calgary, Alta., Can., 1985, 86, Ryosuke Gallery, Osaka, Japan, 1986, Gallery Six Oh One, San Francisco, 1989, Fresno Art Mus., 1989, Pro arts Gallery, Oakland, Calif., 1991, Calif. Mus. Art, Santa Rosa, 1991, Harbs Gallery, Lexington, Va., 1992, Russell Sage Gallery, Troy, N.Y., 1992, Amos Eno Gallery, NYC, 1994, 97, ARC Gallery, Chgo., 1993, 96, Lengyel Gallery, San Francisco, 1995, 750 Gallery, Sacramento, 1994-96, L.A. Mus. Contemporary Art, 1995, Armand Hammer Mus., L.A., 1996, Whitney Mus. Am. Art, N.Y.C., 1999, numerous others; commns. include Absolut Vodka, 1993. Artistic dir. Black and White Ball, Merced Regional Arts Coun., 1989-2005. Democrat. Home and Office: 8697 Cotton Creek Rd Mariposa CA 95338 Business E-Mail: karen@karenlecocq.com.

LECORGNE, LISETTE MARY, family practice nurse practitioner; b. New Orleans, La., Aug. 11, 1955; d. Louis Constant and Nodileen LeCompte LeCorgne. RN, No. Ariz. U., 1978; nurse practitioner, U. of Colo., 1980—82; BS in Health Arts, U. St. Francis, 1982, MS in Healthcare Adminstrn., 2004. NP, Ariz., ANCC, 1983. Med. coord. Hozhoni Found., Flagstaff, Ariz., 1979—83; nurse practitioner U. of Ariz. Campus Health, Tucson, 1983—, coord. urgent care, triage/radiology. Past pres., bd. mem. Flying Samaritans, Tucson, 1996—. Delivery of health care to indigent, Tucson, 1996—2003. Recipient Appreciation award, Associated Students with Disabilities, 1998. Mem.: ANA (assoc.). Episcopal. Avocations: woodworking, travel. Home: 5133 E Adams St Tucson AZ 85713-4105 Office: University of Arizona Campus Health PO Box 210063 Tucson AZ 85721-0063 Office Phone: 520-621-6490. Personal E-mail: lisettelecorgne@hotmail.com. E-mail: lecorgne@health.arizona.edu.

LE COUNT, VIRGINIA G., communications company executive; b. L.I. City, N.Y., Nov. 22, 1917; d. Clifford R. and Luella (Meier) LeCount. BA, Barnard Coll., 1937; MA, Columbia U., 1940. Tchr. pub. schs., P.R., 1937-38; supr. HOLC, N.Y.C., 1938-40; translator Guildhall Publs., N.Y.C., 1940-41; office mgr. Sperry Gyroscope Co., Garden City, Lake Success, Bklyn. (all N.Y.), 1941-45; billing mgr. McCann Erickson, Inc., N.Y.C., 1945-56; v.p., bus. mgr., bd. dirs. Infoplan Internat, Inc., N.Y.C., 1956-69; v.p., bus. mgr. Communications Affiliates Ltd., Communications Affiliates (Bahamas) Ltd., N.Y.C., 1964-69; bus. mgr. Jack Tinker & Ptnrs., Inc., N.Y.C., 1969-70; mgr. office services Interpublic Group of Cos., Inc., N.Y.C., 1971-72, corp. records mgr., 1972-83, mktg. intelligence data mgr., 1975-83. Mem. Alumnae Barnard Coll., N.Y. Health and Racquet Club Spa. Mem. Marble Collegiate Ch. Home: 6532 Copper Ridge Tr University Park FL 34201

LECOUNTE, LOLA HOUSTON, literature and language professor, educational consultant; d. Simpson and Lillian Edna Houston; widowed; children: Ernest Jerome, Karen Yvette, Mark Houston. BA, U. Md. Eastern Shore, 1956; MA, Trinity U., 1974; EdD, George Washington U., 1982. Tchr. English and French Accomack (Va.) County Pub. Schs., Va., 1957—59; tchr. English and history Fairfax (Va.) County Pub. Schs., 1959—67; tchr. English D.C. Pub. Schs., Washington, 1967—76, supr. English, 1976—81, asst. dir. English, 1981—92; asst. prof. Bowie (Md.) State U., 1996—, chair dept. tchg., 2001—04. Ednl. cons. E & L Consultants, Washington, 1976—88, Scholastic Book Co., N.Y.C., 1991—96, D.C. Pub. Schs., Washington, 1992—97; presenter papers at confs. Co-author: (hist./ednl. kit) Black Women in America Contribute to Our Heritage, 1983, Black Women for Social Change, 1984. Named Disting. Alumnus, Nat. Assn. Equal Opportunity in Higher Edn., 1987; named to Hall of Fame for Disting. Alumni, U. Md. Eastern Shore; recipient Outstanding Svc. award, Alpha Kappa Alpha, 1994, Outstanding Svc. in Edn. award, U. Md. Eastern Shore alumni chpt., 1992; grantee, NSF, 2004—05. Mem.: Nat. Coun. Tchrs. English, Assn. Supervision and Curriculum Devel., Assn. Tchr. Educators. Avocations: reading, poetry, singing, theater. Office: Bowie State U 14000 Jericho Park Rd Bowie MD 20715

LEDBETTER, MERRY W., mathematics educator; d. Eldridge and Pauline Willoughby; children: Brandy N., Brent S. BS in Edn., 1977; M in Math. Edn., Troy State U., Phenix City, Ala., 1991. Cert. math. tchr. Ala. State Dept. Edn., 1991. Math. tchr. Beauregard H.S., Suwanee, Ga., 1993—2004, Peachtree Ridge H.S., Suwanee, 2004—. Mem. HSGE updating com. State Dept. Edn., Montgomery, Ala., 1989—90. Jr. cabinet advisor Relay for Life, Lawrenceville, Ga., 2005—06. Nominee Golden Apple award, Channel 9 News, 2002. Avocations: swimming, reading, travel. Office Phone: 678-957-3145.

LEDBETTER, SHARON FAYE WELCH, retired educational consultant; b. L.A., Jan. 14, 1941; d. James Herbert and Verdie V. (Mattox) Welch; m. Robert A. Ledbetter, Feb. 15, 1964; children: Kimberly Ann, Scott Allen. BA, U. Tex., Austin, 1963; learning disabilities cert., Southwestern U., Tex., 1974; MEd, Southwest Tex. State U., 1979, prin. cert., 1980, supt. cert., 1984. Speech pathologist Midland (Tex.) Ind. Sch. Dist., Tex., 1963, Austin (Tex.) Ind. Sch. Dist., Tex., 1964-72; speech pathologist, asst. prin. Round Rock Ind. Sch. Dist., Tex., 1972-84; prin. Hutto Ind. Sch. Dist., 1984-88; asst. dir. divsn. med. sch. edn. Tex. Edn. Agy., 1989-94. Pres. Berkman PTA, 1983-84; v.p. Round Rock Women's Club, 1977, pres., 1978-79; sponsor Jr. Woman's Club, 1980-82; vol. Round Rock Ind. Sch. Dist., 1984; mistress ceremonies Hutto Beauty Pageant, 1986-87. Recipient Meritorious Svc. award Round Rock Ind. Sch. Dist., 1984, St. Judes Children's Rsch. Hosp., 1985, Soc. Disting. Am. H.S. Students, 1984, Disting. Svc. award Tex. Edn. Agy., 1994. Mem. ASCD, Phi Delta Kappa. Home: 43 Woodland Loop Round Rock TX 78664-9776 Personal E-mail: sledbet338@aol.com.

LEDER, MIMI, television director, film director, film producer; b. NYC, Jan. 26, 1952; d. Paul and Etyl Leder; m. Gary Werntz, Feb. 6, 1986; 1 child, Hannah. Student, Los Angeles City College, Am. Film Inst. Dir. (TV films) A Little Piece of Heaven (also known as Honor Bright), 1991, Woman with a Past, 1992, Rio Shannon, 1992, Marked for Murder, 1992, There Was a Little Boy, 1993, House of Secrets, 1993, The Sandman, 1993, The Innocent, 1994, John Doe, 2002; dir. (TV series) L.A. Law, 1986, Midnight Caller, 1988, A Year in the Life, 1988, Buck James, 1988, Just in Time, 1988, Crime Story, 1988, ER, 1994-95 (Emmy award 1995, 96), John Doe, 2002, China Beach (also prodr.), The Beast (also exec. prodr.), 2001, Jonny Zero (also prodr.), 2005, Vanished, (also exec. prodr.), 2006, (films) The Peacemaker, 1997, Deep Impact, 1998, Sentimental Journey, 1999, Pay it Forward, 2000; supervising prodr. China Beach, 1988-91 (Emmy nominations for outstanding drama series 1989, 90, and outstanding directing in drama series 1990, 91), Nightingales, 1989. Mem. Dirs. Guild Am. Office: c/o Creative Artists Agy 9830 Wilshire Blvd Beverly Hills CA 90212-1804 also: United Talent Agy 9560 Wilshire Blvd Beverly Hills CA 90212*

LEDERER, LAURA J., educational association administrator; b. Detroit, Dec. 12, 1951; d. Creighton C. and Natalie Irene (Mattson) L. Student, U. Mich., 1975. Asst. to dir. program on studies in religion U. Mich., Ann Arbor, 1971-75; exec. dir. Women Against Pornography, San Francisco, 1976-80; program dir. The L.J. and Mary C. Skaggs Found., Oakland, Calif., 1980-91; dir. protection project Kennedy Sch. Govt. Harvard U., 1993—. Editor: Take Back the Night: Women on Pornography, 1980. Bd. dirs. Global Fund for Women, Los Altos, Calif., 1987-95; mem. adv. bd. The Women's Found., San Francisco, 1980-95. Office: John F Kennedy Sch Govt 1717 Massachusetts Ave NW Ste 610 Washington DC 20036

LEDERER, MARION IRVINE, cultural administrator; b. Brampton, Ont., Can., Feb. 10, 1920; d. Oliver Bateman and Eva Jane (MacMurdo) L.; m. Francis Lederer, July 10, 1941. Student, U. Toronto, 1938, UCLA, 1942-45. Owner Canoga Mission Gallery, Canoga Park, Calif., 1967—, cultural heritage monument, 1974—. V.p. Screen Smart Set women's aux. Motion Picture and TV Fund, 1973, pres., 2002—03; founder sister city program Canoga Park-Taxco, Mex., 1963. Mem. Mayor's Cultural Task Force San Fernando Valley, 1973—, LA Cultural Affairs Commn., 1980—85; pres. Women's Aux. of Motion Pictures, TV Fund. Recipient Pub. Svc. award, mayor, city council, C. of C. Mem. Canoga Park C. of C. (cultural chmn. 1973-75, dir. 1973-75) Presbyterian. Home: PO Box 32 Canoga Park CA 91305-0032 Office: Canoga Mission Gallery 23130 Sherman Way Canoga Park CA 91307-1402

LEDERMAN, SALLY ANN, nutritionist, researcher; b. NYC, July 8, 1937; d. Joseph Edward and Leanora Rossi; m. Lawrence Lederman, Jan. 26, 1958 (div. Feb. 1991); children: Leandra, Evin. BS in Chemistry, Bklyn. Coll., 1957; MS in Nutrition, Columbia U., 1976, PhD, 1980. Analytical chemist U.S. FDA, N.Y.C., 1957—62; lectr. dept. chemistry Bklyn. Coll., 1962-66, 74; postdoctoral fellow Inst. Human Nutrition Columbia U., N.Y.C., 1980—82, postdoctoral fellow obstetrics and biochemistry, 1983, asst. prof. Sch. Pub. Health, 1983—90, assoc. prof. Sch. Pub. Health, 1990—94, prof. Tchrs. Coll., 1994—97, rschr. Tchrs. Coll., 1997—99; rsch. assoc. divsn. endocrinology, diabetes, nutrition St. Luke's-Roosevelt Hosp. Ctr., N.Y.C., 1998—2003. Spl. lectr. Mailman Sch. Pub. Health, Inst. of Human Nutrition, Columbia U., 2000—. Editor: Controversial Issues in Public Health Nutrition, 1983; contbr. articles to profl. jours. Mem. APHA, AAAS, Am. Nutrition Soc., Am. Women in Sci., N.Y. Acad. Scis. Office: CCCEH Mailman Sch Pub Health 100 Haven Ave Ste 25F New York NY 10032 Office Phone: 212-304-7280. Business E-Mail: sal1@columbia.edu.

LEDERMAN, SUSAN STURC, public administration professor; b. Bratislava, Slovakia, May 28, 1937; came to U.S., 1948; d. Ludovit and Helen Sturc; m. Peter Bernd Lederman, Aug. 25, 1957; children: Stuart, Ellen. AB in Polit. Sci., U. Mich., 1958; MA in Polit. Sci., Rutgers U., 1970, PhD in Polit. Sci., 1978. Vis. instr. Fairleigh Dickinson U., Madison, NJ, 1973-74, Drew U., Madison, 1975-76; from asst. prof. to assoc. prof. pub. adminstrn. Kean U., Union, NJ, 1977-89, prof., dir. MPA program, 1989-97; exec. dir. Gateway Inst. Regional Devel. Kean U., Union, NJ, 1997-2000; prof. Kean U., Union, NJ, 1990—. Vis. fellow Woodrow Wilson Sch., Princeton (N.J.) U., 1988-89. Co-author: (book) Elections in America—Control and Influence in Democratic Politics, 1980, (monograph) Campaign Watch: A Report on the 1992 Campaign Watch Project, 1993; editor: (book) The SLERP Reforms and Their Impact, 1989; contbr. articles to profl. jours. Mem. nat. gov. bd. Common Cause, Washington, 1994-2000; bd. dirs., sec.-treas. The Jefferson Ctr., Mpls., 1992-2002; dir. Regional Plan Assn., N.Y.C., 1991—; pres. LWV of N.J., 1985-89, program v.p., 1983-85, sec., fiscal policy dir., 1981-83, fiscal policy dir., 1979-81, adminstrn. of justice dir., 1976-79; pres. LWV of U.S., 1990-92, chair edn. fund., 1990-92; mem. bd. trustees exec. com., sec. N.J. Future, 1993—; pub. mem. Supreme Ct. of N.J. Disciplinary Oversight Com., 1994-98, Coun. of Engrng. and Sci. Splty. Bds., 1996-2002; mem. Property Tax Commn., 1998; mem. N.J. Legis. Coun. of Acad. Advisors; commr. N.J. State and Local Expenditure Revenue Policy Commn., 1985-88, N.J. Election Law Enforcement Commn., 2000-04; pres. Northeastern Polit. Sci. Assn., 1984-85; bd. dirs., sec. NJ Apple Seed, 2002—. Recipient Disting. Svc. award N.J. Polit. Sci. Assn., 1984, Pub. Svc. award ASPA, 1993, Eric Neisser Pub. Svc. award Pub. Interest Law Ctr., 2001; rsch. grantee Fund for N.J., 1981, Florence and John Schumann Found., 1988-89. Mem. Internat. Women's Forum (N.J. Forum bd. dirs. 1998—, bd. trustees 2002-,v.p. 2005-), Phi Kappa Phi, Pi Sigma Alpha, Pi Alpha Alpha. Office: Kean U 1000 Morris Ave Union NJ 07083-7131 Office Phone: 908-737-4311. Business E-Mail: slederma@kean.edu.

LEDESMA-NICHOLSON, CHARMAINE, psychotherapist; b. L.A., Aug. 29, 1943; d. Louis Edgar Dern and Reba Marie Willis; m. Raymond Cano Ledesma, May 4, 1968 (div. June 1992); 1 child, Michael; m. Steven Nicholson, Aug. 7, 1993. BA, Calif. State U., 1966; MA, Pepperdine U., 1982. Lic. marriage, family, child counselor, Calif.; lic. clin. profl. counselor, Mont. Social worker Dept. Pub. Social Svcs., L.A., 1967-70; child protection svcs. social worker County of Orange (Calif.) Pub. Social Svcs., 1970-88; supr. child protection svcs. Riverside (Calif.) County Pub. Social Svc., 1988-92; psychotherapist for sex offenders Parents United, Beaumont, Calif., 1988-92, Mont. State Prison, Deer Lodge, 1992-96, Crossroads Correctional Ctr., Shelby, Mont., 1999—2002; pvt. practice Great Falls, Mont., 1999—. Self-employed cons., supr., Great Falls, 1999—. 1st responder Avon (Mont.) Quick Response Unit, 1992-99; mem. Lewis & Clark Search & Rescue, Helena, Mont., 1994-99; vol. Eaglemount, Great Falls, 1999— (profl. ski instr. of Am.), ARC, Great Falls, 1990—. Mem. Am. Assn. of Marriage Family Therapists (clin. mem.), Assn. for Treatment of Sex Abusers (clin. mem.), Mont. Sex Offender Treatment Assn. (clin. mem.), Profl. Ski Instrs. Am. Democrat. Roman Catholic. Avocations: horseback riding, sewing, skiing, mountain climbing, canoeing. Home: 5705 62d Ave SW Great Falls MT 59404 Office Phone: 406-788-1977. Personal E-mail: stevecharm1@yahoo.com.

LEDET, PHYLLIS L., assistant principal; b. Delcambre, La., Apr. 10, 1942; d. John and Claire (Landry) LeBlanc; children: Lonny Ledet, Leah Ledet Terro, Elizabeth Ledet Romero, Laurie. BA in Elem. Edn., U. Southwestern LA, 1963, MEd in Ednl. Counseling, 1989, EdS in Ednl. Adminstrn. and Supervision, 1992. Asst. prin. L. J. Alleman Mid. and Arts Acad., Lafayette, La., 1993—2002, Scott Mid. Sch., 2002—. Bd. dirs. Jr. League Lafayette; mem. Am. Cancer Soc. (Spring Family Fair Chmn.), Govs. Commn. Goals 2000, La. State Dept. Edn. Panel VIII Com., United Way of Acadiana; leader Girl Scouts Am.; pres. Edgar Martin PTC; religious tchr. Holy Cross Cath. Ch. Mem. Assn. Profs. Edn. of La. (state pres. 1996-97), Leadership Lafayette C. of C. (class XI), Univ. La. Coll. Edn. Alumni Assn. (charter). E-mail: pledet@lft.k12.la.us.

LEDFORD, BARBRA LYNNE, elementary school educator; d. John Lewis, Sr. and Paula Clara Threadgill; m. Joseph Dane Ledford, Dec. 19; children: Jourdan Michaela, Kilian Dane. BS in elem. edn., Lincoln U., 1989; MS in curriculum and instrn., Lincoln Meml. U., 1991. Cert. K-12 adminstrn. and supervision Union Coll., Ky., 1999, nat. bd. cert. tchr., mid. childhood generalist Ky. Elem. tchr. Harlan Ind. Sch., Ky., 1989—2006. Home: 210 Ross Dr Baxter KY 40806-8325

LEDFORD, SHIRLEY LOUISE, practical nurse; b. Jasper, Ga., July 25, 1952; d. Laymon James and Edna Louise (Buchanan) Pendley; m. Kenneth Weldon Ledford, Nov. 20, 1976; 1 child, Letisha Lynn. LPN, Pickens Tech. Inst., 1977. cert. integrated computer applications; cert. CNA tchr., Ga.; cert. IV, Tex., restorative nursing, Tex. Practical nurse, asst. dir. nursing Grandview Healthcare, Jasper, 1979-93; practical nurse, infection control nurse, nurse, employee health nurse performance improvement coord., med. records coord. Mountain Side Nursing Home, Jasper, 1993—. Home: 249 Sunset Ln Ellijay GA 30536-7645 Office: Mountain Health Care PO Box 490 Jasper GA 30143-0490

LEDIN, PATRICIA ANN, nurse, legal consultant; b. Downey, Calif., May 6, 1959; d. Clyde Burdette and Estelle Angelina (Acceturo) Bornhurst; m. Scott Richard Ledin, Sept. 9, 1989. BSN, U. Ariz., 1981; postgrad., U. Phoenix, 2000. Cert. electronic fetal monitoring, inpatient obstetrics, ACLS, PALS, NRP; RN Ariz., cert. instr. PALS. Labor and delivery nurse Tucson Med. Ctr., 1981-86, childbirth instr., 1983-95, nurse, mother-baby unit, 1995-97, clin. educator obstetrics, 1986—95, CPR instr., 1986—, learning and devel. specialist, 2001—02, clin. nurse specialist, 2001, clin. educator obstetrics, 1997—2001, nurse recruiter, 2002—03, mgr. student placement program, 2004, clin. educator nursing informatics, 2004—. Adj. faculty preceptor U. Ariz., Tucson, 1988—; expert witness for legal cases, 1992—; expert reviewer Lifelines mag., 2002-; faculty, Az. Perinatal Edn. Coalition, 2000—. Contbr. articles to profl. jours. Mem. adv. com. March of Dimes, 1991—95; mentor Nat. Cert. Corp., 2001. Bristol-Meyers fellow, 1994. Mem.: Nat. Nursing Staff Devel. Orgn., Assn. Women's Health, Obstet. and Neonatal Nursing (edn. coord. 1991—98, sec.-treas. 1999—2002, Recognition award for fin. budget submission 2001, 2002, award for outstanding performance in fin. responsibility 2001), Beta mu, Omicron Delta, Sigma Theta Tau (chair nominations 2002—). Avocations: water-skiing, nascar races, boating, travel, aerobics. Office: Tucson Med Ctr 5301 E Grant Rd Tucson AZ 85712-2805

LEDONNE, DEBORAH JANE, secondary school educator; b. Darby, Pa., Mar. 4, 1956; d. Peter Anthony and Camella Jean (Perrone) LeD. Undergrad. credits in Spanish, U. Madrid, 1977; BA in Modern Langs., BS in Edn., Villanova U., 1978; Sorbonne U. Paris, U. Paris, 1979; MA in Modern Langs., Villanova U., 1982. Tchr. French/Spanish Marple Newtown Sch. Dist., Newtown Square, Pa., 1978—. Tutor Phila. area, 1978—; sec. Faculty Adv. Coun., 1990—. Mem. Phila. Mus. Art, Annenberg Ctr. of Phila. Recipient Maria Rosa award for Excellence Am. Inst. Italian Culture, 1978; chosen to attend Nat. Debutante Ball, N.Y.C., 1974, Internat. Debutante Ball, Vienna, 1975; named a Woman of Yr. Am. Biog. Inst., 1993, one of 2,000 Notable Am. Women, 1994. Mem.: NEA, Pa. State Modern Lang. Assn., Alliance Francaise, Pa. State Edn. Assn., Kappa Delta Pi. Avocations: tennis, swimming, dance, gourmet cooking. Office: Marple Newtown Sch Dist 120 Media Line Rd Newtown Square PA 19073-4614

LEDOUX, ELLEN G., music educator; b. Lake Charles, La., July 2, 1963; d. Charles Allen and Diane Elizabeth Gay; children: Roberto William Rodriguez, Suzanne Kathleen Rodriguez, Eduardo Christopher Rodriguez. MusB, U. So. Miss., Hattiesburg, 1996; M in Secondary Edn., William Carey Coll., Gulfport, Miss., 2001; attending, Walden U., 2005—. Cert. music tchr. Tex., 2004. Asst. band dir. Ocean Springs H.S., Miss., 1997—2002, North Garland H.S., Tex., 2002—. Named Most Influential Tchr., 2005; named an Outstanding Instrumentalist, Dept. Music, Coll. of Ozarks, 1990—91, Outstanding Instrumentalist, U. So. Miss., 1995—96, All Star Tchr., Ocean Springs H.S., 2001—02; recipient Semper Fidelis award, 1981, John Philip Sousa award, Coll. of Ozarks, 1991—92; Jean Cantwell scholar, 1991—93. Home: PO Box 496178 Garland TX 75049-6178 Office: North Garland High School 2109 W Buckingham Rd Garland TX 75042 Office Phone: 972-675-3136. Personal E-mail: percussiondr@yahoo.com. Business E-Mail: egledoux@garlandisd.net.

LEDOUX, PATRICIA RENEE, elementary school educator, science educator; b. Superior, Mont., Sept. 3, 1963; d. Gary Marshall and Margaret Lee O'Hara; m. James William LeDoux, June 10, 2000; children: Kyle Patrick, Cameron James; m. Stephen Edward West, Aug. 10, 1985 (div. July 15, 1996); 1 child, Robert Edward West. BA in Elem. Edn., Boise State U., Idaho, 1987, MS in Ednl. Tech., 2006. Tchr. elem. sch. Kuna Sch. Dist., Idaho, 1989—99; tchr. mid. sch. Meridian Sch. Dist., 1999—. Mem.: NEA. Office: Meridian School District 4141 E Pine Ave Meridian ID 83642 Office Phone: 208-377-1353 159.

LEDWIK, GRETCHEN MARIE, elementary school educator, art educator; b. Giddings, Tex., Nov. 10, 1965; d. Michael Harold Schmidt and Marilyn Marie Zschech; m. Warren Wayne Ledwik, Aug. 1, 1987; children: Ethan, Zachary, Elana. BS Edn., SW Tex. State U., San Marcos, 1988; Bilingual endorsement, Edn. Svc. Ctr., San Marcos, 1987. Tchr. 3d grade LaGrange Ind. Sch. Dist., Tex., 1988—2003, curriculum facilitator, 2004—06, tchr. art, 2005—. Participant N.J. Writing, Spring, Tex., 1998—2006; trainer Project Tex., Manor, 2000. Coach Fayette Area Swim Team, LaGrange Little League Softball. Named J. Ralph Outstanding Sr., SW Tex. State U., 1987. Mem.: Tex. Art Edn. Assn. Avocations: gardening, reading, needlecrafts. Office: Hermes Elem Sch PO Box 100 La Grange TX 78945-0100

LEE, ALICE INEZ, retired nurse; b. Washington, Oct. 18, 1924; d. Philip Lee and Minnie Byrd Boyd. At, Morgan State Coll., Balt., 1942—44; BSN, Meharry Med. Coll., Nashville, 1948. RN 1948. Nurse's aide Johns Hopkins Hosp., Balt., 1942; vol. nurse's aide Am. Red Cross, 1945; staff nurse Meharry Hosp., Nashville, 1948—54, supr., 1954—57, asst. dir. nursing, 1957—58; staff nurse Johns Hopkins Hosp., Balt., 1960—61, head nurse, 1961—86; ret., 1986. Vol. Balt. City Cmty. Coll., Huber Ch.; mem. Disability Found., 2005—, Nat. Mus. Am. Indian, Washington, 2005—, Animal Rights, 2005. Named to Wall of Tolerance, So. Poverty Law Ctr., 2006. Home: 1521 Lakeside Ave Baltimore MD 21218-3006

LEE, AMY, singer; b. Riverside, Calif., Dec. 13, 1981; d. John and Sara (Cargill) Lee. Co-founder & lead singer Evanescence, 1998—. Singer: (albums) Origin, 2002, Fallen, 2003 (album went Double Platinum, Grammy award best new artist, 2003), Anywhere But Home, 2004, The Open Door, 2006, (songs) Breathe, 2000, Broken, by Seether, 2002, Bring Me To Life, 2003 (Grammy award best hard rock performance, 2003), Call Me When You're Sober, 2006. Office: Wind-Up Records 72 Madison Ave New York NY 10016 Office Phone: 212-895-3100.

LEE, ANDREA JANE, academic administrator, nun; 1 adopted child, Lahens. AA in Italian, Villa Walsh Coll.; BA in music and elem. edn., Northeastern Ill. U.; MEd, Pa. State U., PhD in edn. adminstrn. Instr. tchr. edn. Pa. State U.; dean continuing edn. and cmty. svcs. Marygrove Coll., 1981—84, exec. v.p. and COO, 1984—97, interim pres., 1998; pres. Coll. of St. Catherine, St. Paul, 1999—. Office: Coll of St Catherine 2004 Randolph Ave Saint Paul MN 55105

LEE, ANITA COMBS, writer, speaker, consultant; b. Pt. Arthur, Tex., Apr. 5, 1945; d. Bruce Harrison and Thelma Viola (Turner) Combs; m. Daryl Otis Lee, Aug. 9, 1969; children: Meredith, Adam. BS, Lamar U., 1967; postgrad., Nat. Geog. Summer Inst., 1988; MA, U. North Tex., 1995. Cert. personalities workshop trainer CLASSvcs. Tchr. Hiroshima (Japan) Internat. Sch., 1967-68, Kyoto (Japan) Internat. Sch., 1968-69, Richardson (Tex.) Ind. Sch. Dist., 1969-70, Fairfax County (Va.) Schs., 1970-72; tchr. English Hefei (People's Republic China) Poly. Inst., 1982-83; tchr. world cultures Plano (Tex.) Ind. Sch. Dist., 1987-94, curriculum writer, 1987-94; asst. to headmaster PACE Acad., Atlanta, 1996—2000; asst. dir. children's ministry Roswell (Ga.) United Meth. Ch., 2000—03. Mem. tchr. exch. program, Vilnius, Lithuania, 1990; instr. writing Profl. Writers Ctr. Lamar U., 2005—06; features writer Northside Neighbor, Atlanta, 1996. Weekly columnist Plano Star Courier, 1985-87. Avocations: music, watercolor, international travel. Personal E-mail: alee@altaregos.com.

LEE, ANN MCKEIGHAN, curriculum specialist; b. Harlan, Iowa, Nov. 18, 1939; d. Earl Edward and Dorothy Elizabeth (Kaufman) McK.; m. Duane Edward Compton, Aug. 13, 1960 (div. 1985); children: Kathleen, David, Anne-Marie, John. Cert. in med. tech., Creighton U., 1960; BA in Art History, Ind. U., 1984; MA, U. South Fla., 1992, PhD, 2002. Cert. secondary tchr., Fla.; cert. med. technologist. Realtor Savage/Landrian Realty, Indpls., 1978-84; lectr. Marian Coll., Indpls., 1987-88; tchr. Sarasota (Fla.) County Schs., 1989-92, rep. faculty coun., 1991-92; lectr. curriculum & instrn. U. South Fla., 1993—2000. Vis. prof. U. South Fla., 2001—03, adj. prof., 2004; docent Historic Spanish Point, Osprey, Fla., 1989—93, Ringling Mus. Art, 1993—2004, Indpls. Mus. Art, 1968—88; presenter panel Bibliographic Instrn. Art History; ESE cons. Marion Charter Sch. Contbr. articles to profl. jours. V.p. fin. LWV, Indpls., 1971-73; v.p. dist. IV aux. ADA, 1976-78, comptr., 1978-89; coord. Gold Coun. and Ambs. U. South Fla., 1990-92. Recipient Silver Svc. award Crossroads Guild, 1981. Mem.: Sarasota Arts Coun., Gulf Coast Heritage Assn. (co-chmn. pub. rels.), Soc. Archtl. Historians (tchr. rep. 1990), Coll. Art Assn., Phi Delta Kappa, Phi Kappa Phi. Roman Catholic. Avocations: photography, tennis, landscape architecture, swimming. Home and Office: 12026 SE 178th St Summerfield FL 34491

LEE, ANNE, music educator; b. Taipei, Taiwan, July 19, 1951; d. William Chiang and Su-Chen Wu; married, Jan. 20, 1979; children: Joseph, Matthew. Degree, Shih Chien Univ., 1972. Tchr. Yamaha Music Found., Taipei, Taiwan, 1974—81; co-founder Polyphony Chamber Orch., Cupertino, Calif., 1998—. Music judge Taiwan TV music program, Taipei, 1978, Cupertino Sch. Dist., 1998—99. Ch. organist. Recipient 1st prize Composition, Shih Chien U., 1972. Mem.: Nat. Guild Piano Tchrs. (tchr. divsn. am. coll. musicians, Nat. Honor Roll Piano Tchr. 1999, 2000, 2001), Music Tchr. Nat. Assn., Music Tchr. Assn. Calif., Chinese Music Tchr. Assn. Calif. (music judge internat. music competition 1999, chmn. bd. dir. 1997—99, pres. 1996—97), Calif. Assn. Profl. Music Tchr. Avocations: chamber music, shopping, movies, church choir.

LEE, BARBARA, congresswoman; b. El Paso, Tex., July 16, 1946; m. Michael Millben (div.); children: Tony, Craig. BA, Mills Coll., 1973; M in Social Welfare, U. Calif. Berkeley, 1976. Chief of staff U.S. Rep. Ron Dellums, 1975—87; rep. Calif. State Assembly, 1990-96; mem. Calif. State Sen., 1996-98, U.S. Congress from 9th Calif. dist., Washington, 1999—; mem. fin. svcs. com., internat. rels. com. Co-chmn. Progressive Caucus; chmn. Congl. Black Caucus Task Force HIV/AIDS; whip Congl. Black Caucus, mem. Minority Bus. Task Force; mem. adv. bd. Alameda Boys Club; bd. dirs. Bay Area Black United Fund; with Black Women Organized Polit. Action; founder Calif. Commn. Status African Am. Male; mem. Calif. Commn. Status Women; mem. bd. Calif. Coastal Conservancy/Dist. Export Coun. Recipient Most Influential Black Americans, Ebony mag., 2006. Democrat. Office: US Ho Reps 1724 Longworth Ho Office Bldg Washington DC 20515-0509 also: Dist Office Ste 1000 N 1301 Clay Oakland CA 94612 Office Phone: 202-225-2661. Fax: 202-225-9817. Office Phone: 510-763-0370. Office Fax: 510-763-6538.*

LEE, BARBARA, political activist, foundation administrator; b. July 1945; d. Sidney and Ruth Fish; m. Thomas Lee, 1968 (div. 1996); children: Zach, Robbie. BA, Simmons Coll., 1967; MSW, Boston U.; degree (hon.), Pine Manor Coll., 2004. Pres., treas., dir. Barbara Lee Family Found., Cambridge, Mass.; vice chair bd. dirs. Inst. Contemporary Art, Boston; pres., treas. Revolutionary Women, Cambridge. Founding chair contemporary arts program Isabella Stewart Gardner Mus., Boston; co-founder The White House Project, 1997. Named one of Top 200 Collectors, ARTnews Mag., 2004, 21 Leaders for the 21st Century, Women's E News, 2005; named to The 100 Women Who Run this Town, Boston Mag., The 100 People Who Run this Town, 2004; recipient Opening Doors award, Women's Inst. for Housing and Econ. Devel., 2003, George Alden Dean Leadership award, Women's Campaign Sch., Yale U., 2003. Democrat. Avocation: Collector of Modern and contemporary art by women. Office: 131 Mt Auburn St, Ste 2 Cambridge MA 02138 Office Phone: 617-234-0355. Office Fax: 617-234-0357.*

LEE, BARBARA ANNE, law educator, dean; b. Newton, NJ, Apr. 9, 1949; d. Robert hanna and Keren (Dalrymple) L.; m. James Paul Begin, Aug. 14, 1982; 1 child, Robert James. BA, U. Vt., 1971; MA, Ohio State U., 1972; JD, Georgetown U., 1982; PhD, Ohio State U., 1977. Bar: NJ 1983, US Dist. Ct. NJ 1983. Instr. Franklin U., Columbus, Ohio, 1974—75; rsch. asst. Ohio State U., Columbus, 1975—77; policy analyst US Dept. Edn., Washington, 1978—80; dir. data trands Carnegie Found., Washington, 1980—82; asst. prof. Grad. Sch. Edn. Rutgers U., Brunswick, NJ, 1982—84, asst. prof. Sch. Mgmt. and Labor Rels., 1984—88, assoc. prof., 1988—94, prof., 1994—, assoc. provost, 1995—96, dean, 2000—. Mem. Study Group on Excellence in Higher Edn., Nat. Inst. Edn., 1983-84; project dir. Carnegie Corp., NYC, 1982-84. Author: Academics in Court, 1987; co-author: The Law of Higher Education, 3d edit., 1995; contbr. numerous articles to profl. jours. Corse fellow U. Vt., 1971; recipient John F. Kennedy Labor Law award Georgetown U., 1982; grantee Bur. Labor-Mgmt. Rels. and Coop. Programs, 1985-86. Mem. ABA, NJ Bar Assn. (mem. exec. com. labor and employment law sect. 1987—, women's rights sect.), Am. Ednl. Rsch. Assn., Indsl. Rels. Rsch. Assn., Acad. Mgmt., Assn. Study Higher Edn. (legal counsel 1982-88), Nat. Assn. Coll. and Univ. Attys. (vice chair editl. bd. 1986-89, chair 1995-96, chair publs. com. 1988-91, bd. dirs. 1990-93). Office: Rutgers U Office of Dean Sch Mgmt and Labor Rels 94 Rockafeller Rd Piscataway NJ 08854-8054 Office Phone: 732-445-5993. Business E-Mail: lee@smlr.rutgers.edu.

LEE, BARBARA MAHONEY, career officer, educator; b. Roanoke, Va., July 25, 1942; d. Archer W. and Marie Adeline (Gray) Mahoney; m. Walter Kenneth Lee, Aug. 5, 1956 (div. 1969); children: Kenneth Michael, Alan David. AS, Va. Western C.C., Roanoke, 1970; BA, Hollins (Va.) Coll., 1972; MS, Va. Commonwealth U., Richmond, 1979; postgrad., Am. U. Commd. ed lt. U.S. Army, 1973, advanced through grades to col., 1995; asst. prof. U.S. Mil. Acad., West Point, N.Y., 1979-83; orgnl. effectiveness staff officer Army Materiel Command, Alexandria, Va., 1983-88, Cong. liaison officer, 1988-90; v.p. human resources INTEGRATEC, Inc., Atlanta, 1990-92; orgnl. devel. cons. in pvt. practice, Atlanta, 1992-93; mil. asst. U.S. Army, Pentagon, Washington, 1993—2002; ret. USAR. Decorated Legion of Merit. Mem.: Alliance for Nat. Def., Am. Sociol. Assn., Women in Internat. Security (exec. bd. 1999—), Alpha Kappa Delta. Episcopalian. Home: 11957 Holly View Dr Woodbridge VA 22192-1040

LEE, BARBARA S., special education educator; b. Long Beach, Calif., Oct. 25, 1942; d. George Hubert Staley and Doris Emma Geer/Staley; m. Stanley Yau Ning Lee, Sept. 7, 1963; children: Tracey Golden, Linda Samuels, Tanya Prucher. BS in Phys. Sci., U. N.D., 1964; tchg. cert., Nat. U., Irvine, Calif., 1988; M in Spl. Edn., U. Phoenix, 2005. Cert. tchr. Ariz., ELL cert. 1997. Tchrs. aide Fountain Valley Sch. Dist., Calif., 1979—89; tchr. Pk. Pvt. Day Sch., Costa Mesa, Calif., 1990—96, Laveen Sch. Dist., Ariz., 1997—2000, Ariz. Dept. Corrections, Phoenix, 2000—. Mem. curriculum com. Adobe Mountain Sch., Phoenix. Life mem. PTO-Moiola Sch., Fountain Valley, 1985. Mem.: ASCD, Ariz. Pub. Employees Assn., Assn. for Rsch. and Enlightment. Avocations: dance, hiking, camping, reading, quilting. Home: 10251 W Snead Cir N Sun City AZ 85351 Office: Adobe Mountain Sch 2800 W Pinnacle Peak Phoenix AZ 85027 E-mail: thebobbiwobbi@msn.com.

LEE, BOK SIN See POWELL GEBHARD, JOY

LEE, BRANDI GREMILLION, elementary school educator; b. Lake; A in Gen. Studies, BA in Elem. Ed., McNeese State U., Lake Charles, La., 2002. Tchr. Calcasieu Parish Sch. Bd., Lake Charles, La., 2002—. Tap mentor Calcasieu Parish Sch. Bd., Lake Charles, La., 2005—. Tchr. advancement program mentor Calcasieu Parish Sch. Bd., Lake Charles, La., 2005—06. Mem.: La. Fedn. of Tchrs. (assoc.). Avocations: reading, travel. Office: Oak Park Mid Sch 2200 Oak Park Blvd Lake Charles LA 70601 Office Phone: 337-478-3310.

LEE, CAROL, lyricist, artist; b. Quanah, Tex., Oct. 20, 1946; d. Luther Benjamen and Elsie Ethel (Roman) Atwood; m. Cecil Ross Lee, Jr., Feb. 4, 1966 (div. Feb. 1994); children: Kevin Shawn, Dayna Michelle. Grad. h.s. Staff songwriter Purple Haze Music, Beckley West, Va., 1990—, artist, repertoire, 1991—. Co-writer (with Jimmie Crane) 5 songs; writer for Elvis, Doris Day, Bobby Vinton. Recipient award for short stories Robert W. Shields Editor, Washington, 1985, Semi Finalist Song, Starquest Contest, Tyler, Tex., 1993. Mem. Beckley Art Group. Avocations: flea marketing, collecting. Home: 906 Bryant Rd Quanah TX 79252

LEE, CAROL FRANCES, lawyer; b. Montreal, Que., Can., Sept. 17, 1955; came to U.S., 1966; d. Frank B. and Mary Lee; m. David John Seipp, Sept. 10, 1994. BA, Yale U., 1976, JD, 1981; BA, Oxford (Eng.) U., 1978. Bar: D.C. 1982, U.S. Ct. Appeals (D.C. cir.) 1982, U.S. Dist. Ct. D.C. 1984, U.S. Supreme Ct. 1986. Law clk. to judge U.S. Ct. Appeals (D.C. cir.), Washington, 1981-82; law clk. to justice U.S. Supreme Ct., Washington, 1982-83; assoc. Wilmer, Cutler & Pickering, Washington, 1983-88, ptnr., 1989-93; gen. counsel Export-Import Bank U.S., Washington, 1993-95; v.p., gen. counsel Internat. Fin. Corp. (World Bank Group), Washington, 1995—2002. Lectr. law Harvard U., Cambridge, Mass., 1989-90, 92, Yale U., New Haven, Conn., 1991. Contbr. articles to profl. jours. Marshall scholar U.K., Oxford, 1976. Fellow Am. Bar Found.; mem. ABA, Am. Soc. Internat. Law, Am. Soc. Legal History, Phi Beta Kappa.

LEE, CATHERINE, sculptor, painter; b. Pampa, Tex., Apr. 11, 1950; d. Paul Albert and Alice (Fleming) Porter; m. B. R. Mangham, 1967 (div. 1976); 1 child, Monk Parker; m. Sean Scully, 1977 (div. 2004). BA, San Jose State U., 1975. Asst. prof. sculpture U. Tex., San Antonio, 2000. Artist-in-residence Mpls. Coll. Art and Design, Minn. Inst. Art, 1982; vis. asst. prof. painting U. Tex., San Antonio, 1983, vis. asst. prof. sculpture, 2001; adj. asst. prof. Columbia U., N.Y.C., 1986-87. Group exhbns. include Albright-Knox Mus., Buffalo, 1987, Mus. Art, Carnegie Inst., Pitts., 1988, Am. Acad. and Inst. Arts and Letters, N.Y.C., 1988, Mus. Folkwang, Essen, Germany, 1992, Stadtische Galerie im Lenbachhaus, Munich, 1992, Neue Galerie Der Stadt Linz, Austria, 1992, Cleve. Mus. Art, 1993, Galleria Nazionale d'Arte Moderna, San Marino, Italy, 1996, The Tate Gallery, 1994, U. R.I. Art Gallery, 1996, Sonoma State U. Art Gallery, 1997, Bemis Ctr. for Contemporary Art, 1998, Städtische Gallery, Lenbachhaus, Munich, 1999, Lafayette Coll. Art Ctr., Easton, Pa., 1999, San Diego State U. Art Gallery, San Diego, 1999, Lyman-Allen Art Mus., New London, Conn., 2000, Grounds for Sculpture, The Johnson Atelier, 2002, S.W. Sch. Arts and Crafts Gallery, 2004, Irish Mus. Modern Art, Dublin, 2005, Hotel des Arts Musee, Toulon, France, 2006, Musee d'Art Moderne, St. Etienne, France, 2006. Creative Artists Pub. Svc. fellow, 1978, NEA grantee, 1989. Office: 106 Spring St New York NY 10012-3814 also: Galerie Karsten Greve Drususgasse 1-5 5000 Koln Germany also: Galerie Lelong 528 W 26th St New York NY 10001 E-mail: catherlee@aol.com.

LEE, CATHERINE TERRI, psychiatrist; d. J. Robert and Georgia Lee. BA cum laude, Smith Coll., 1974; MD, U. Pa., 1984. Bd. cert. psychiatry 1989, bd. cert. child and adolscent psychiatry 1991. Chief resident Yale Child Study Ctr., New Haven, 1989—90, clin. instr. child psychiatry, 1990—91; staff psychiatrist Highline West Seattle, 1991—93; psychiatrist pvt. practice, 1991—, psychoanalyst, 2000—; faculty Seattle Psychoanalytic Soc. and Inst., 2005—; clin. instr. child psychiatry U. Wash. Sch. Medicine, Seattle, 1991—. Cons. child and adolscent psychiatry Friends of Youth, Redmond, Wash., 1993—2001. Named one of Seattle's Best Doctors, Seattle Mag., 2002; named to Best Drs. in Am., 2005—06; recipient Albronda award, U. Calif., San Francisco, 1988. Mem.: Am. Acad. Child and Adolescent Psychiatry, Am. Psychiat. Assn., Am. Psychoanalytic Assn. Avocations: creative writing, skiing, tennis, travel. Office: 4033 E Madison St Ste 109 Seattle WA 98112 Office Phone: 206-324-4601.

LEE, CECILIA HAE-JIN, artist, writer; b. Seoul, Nov. 14, 1970; came to U.S., 1977; d. Daniel Pal-Woo and Julia Mi-Ja Lee. BA, U. Calif., San Diego, 1992; postgrad., Inst. Allende, San Miguel de Allende, Mex., 1992, Seoul Nat. U., 1994. Writer, artist, poet, photographer, and designer; resident Artist Residencies Transforming Cottages at Hedgebrook, Langley, Wash., 1999; Artist Residencies Transforming Seattle's Urban Places. Pub. art, César Chavéz Meml., U. So. Calif., L.A., 1998, City of L.A. Parks & Recreation Dept., Pecan Pk. Gymnasium, 2006, exhibitions include Rita Dean Gallery, San Diego, 1992, 1993, Installation Gallery, 1992, Loyola Law Sch. Gallery, L.A., 1993, Artspace Gallery, Woodland Hills, Calif., 1993, SITE Gallery, L.A., 1993, Mus. Contemporary Art, San Diego and Centro Cultural de la Raza, San Diego, 1992—94, L.A. Mcpl. Art Gallery, 1996, Gallery 825, L.A., 1997, Barnsdall Art Ctr. Gallery, 1998, Galeria Asociacion de Bancarios del Urugua y, Montevideo, Uruguay, 1998, Piazza Risorgimento, Sergno, Italy, 1998, Sabina Lee Gallery, 1999, Jr. Arts Gallery, L.A., 1999, Gallery Prince, 1999, Galeria de la Historia de Concepcion, Chile, 1999, UCC Gallery (2nd pl., 2002), Pierce Coll. Gallery, 2002, Hollywood Libr. Gallery, 2002, Long Beach Arts, 2006; author: Eating Korean, 2005; contbr. articles to encys., newspapers, mags., profl. jours. and periodicals, chapters to books. Recipient hon. mention Iliad Press, 1995. Mem.: WriteGirl, Women in Photography Internat., Ind. Writers So. Calif., Archive Korean Am. Artists, Soc. Children's Book Writers and Illustrators. Avocations: travel, building furniture, learning languages, cooking. Address: PO Box 36673 Los Angeles CA 90036-0673 Personal E-mail: cecilia@littlececilia.com.

LEE, CHIEH-CHI, elementary school educator; b. Taipei, Taiwan, Mar. 31, 1976; d. Jui-Long and Mei Lee; m. Dennis Star Lin, May 2, 1977. MA in Edn., Alliant Internat. U., San Diego, 2001. Cert. multiple tchg. with CLAD emphasis Calif. Commn. Tchr. Credentialing, 1999. Educator Del Valle Elem. Sch., La Puente, Calif., 1999—2003; educator math. and computer skills Orange Grove Mid. Sch., Hacienda Heights, Calif., 2003—. Grantee, Cal T, 1998—99. Avocation: travel. Office: Orange Grove Mid Sch 14505 Orange Grove Ave Hacienda Heights CA 91745 Office Phone: 626-933-7000. Personal E-mail: cclee331@yahoo.com. E-mail: clee@hlpusd.k12.ca.us.

LEE, CLAUDIA S., retired elementary school educator; b. Yonkers, NY, May 29, 1944; d. Cornell and Corrine B. Lee. BA, Morgan State U., 1966; MS, CUNY, 1971, Manhattan Coll., 1983; postgrad., L.I. U., 1988. Cert. history tchr., spl. edn. tchr., adminstr., supr. NY. Spl. edn. tchr. Union Free Dist., Dobbs Ferry, NY, 1966—71, City Sch. Dist. New Rochelle, NY, 1971—2000; ret., 2000. Adj. instr. adults Westchester C.C. Edn. Opportunity Ctr., Yonkers, NY, 1970—2001; adj. instr. Manhattan Coll., Riverdale, NY, 1972, 75; ret.: mem. adv. bd. Ann. Multicultural Bus. Youth Embarkment, Danbury, Conn., 1983—2003. Mem. allocation com. United Way of Westchester, White Plains, NY; bd. dirs. YWCA of Yonkers, 2000—01. Recipient Sojourner Truth Meritorious Svc. award, Nat. Assn. Negro Bus. and Profl. Women, Inc., 2002, Dr. Martin Luther King Svc. award, Nepperhan Cmty. Ctr., Yonkers, 2004, Franore award, Franore Svc. Orgn., White Plains, 2004. Mem.: NAACP, Nat. Assn. Negro Bus. and Profl. Women, Westchester Alliance Black Sch. Educators, Nat. Coun. Negro Women (life), Wesley and Friends (treas. 1992—2004), Westchester County Club (life). Avocations: travel, decorating, reading, museums. Home: 1116 Warburton Ave Yonkers NY 10701

LEE, CORINNE ADAMS, retired English teacher; b. Cuba, N.Y., Mar. 18, 1910; d. Duston Emery and Florence Eugenia (Butts) Adams; m. Glenn Max Lee, Oct. 30, 1936 (dec.). BA, Alfred U., 1931. Cert. tchr. N.Y. Tchr. English Lodi (N.Y.) H.S., 1931—36, Ovid (N.Y.) Ctrl. Sch., 1936—67. Author: (light verse) A Little Leeway, 1983, (anecdotes, light verse, quips) A Little More Leeway, 1984, (essays, short stories, poems) Still More Leeway, 1986. Trustee Montour Falls Meml. Libr. Mem.: LWV, Elmira and Area Ret. Tchrs. Assn., Schuyler County Ret. Tchrs. Assn., N.Y. State Ret. Tchrs. Assn., Nat. Ret. Tchrs. Assn., PTA (life). Avocations: reading, travel, writing.

LEE, DAPHNE PATRICE, special events coordinator, academic administrator; BSBA, Va. State U. Customer svc. rep. Bank of Am., Richmond, Va.; claims rep. Anthem Blue Cross Blue Shield, Richmond; spl. events coord. Va. State U., Petersburg, 2001—. Mem.: Assn. Collegiate Conf. and Events Dirs. Internat. (corr.), Delta Sigma Theta. Avocations: travel, community service. Business E-Mail: dplee@vsu.edu.

LEE, DEBRA LOUISE, cable television company executive; b. Columbia, SC, Aug. 8, 1954; d. Richard M. and Delma L. Lee; children: Quinn Spencer, Ava. BA in Polit. Sci., Brown U., 1976; MPP, JD, Harvard U., 1980. Law clk. to Hon. Barrington Parker U.S. Dist. Ct. D.C., 1980—81; atty. Steptoe & Johnson, Washington, 1981—86; v.p., gen. counsel BET (Black Entertainment TV), 1986—92, exec. v.p. legal affairs dept., gen. counsel, 1992—96, corp. sec., pres., pub. pub. divsn., 1992—96; pres., COO BET Holdings, Inc., 1996—2005, pres., CEO, 2005—, chmn., 2006—. Bd. dirs. Revoln, Inc., 2005—, BET Holdings, Inc., Eastman Kodak Co., Marriott Internat., Wash. Gas & Light Co.; nat. bd. dirs. Nat. Cable & Telecom. Assn., Cable & Telecom. Assn. for Mktg., Alvin Ailey Dance Theater, Nat. Symphony Orch., Telecom. Devel. Fund, Ctr. for Comm., Kennedy Ctr. Community & Friends Bd., Nat. Women's Law Ctr.; trustee emeritus Brown U. Bd. dirs. Kennedy Ctrs. Comty. Bd., Women in Cable, Telecom Devel. Fund, Nat. Symphony Orch. Bd. Named Woman of Yr., Women in Cable and Telecom., 2001; named one of Hundred Heavy Hitters, Cable Fax Mag., 100 Most Powerful Women in Washington, Washingtonian Mag.; recipient Eva A. Mooar award, Brown U., 1976, Nat. Achievement award, Area Chapter of the Nat. Alumnus Assn., 1992, Tower of Power Trumpet award, Turner Broadcasting Sys., 2000, Vanguard award, Nat. Cable & Telecom. Assn., 2003, Quasar award, Nat. Assn. Minorities in Communication, 2003, Silver Star award, Am. Women in Radio and TV, Par Excellence award, Dollars and $ense Mag., Wonder Woman award, Cablevision Mag. Office: BET Holdings Inc One BET Plaza 1235 W St NE Washington DC 20018-1211

LEE, DONNA A., telecommunications industry executive; b. Norfolk, Va. BS in Math., Mary Washington Coll.; MBA, Ga. State U.; postgrad. in advanced Mgmt., Harvard U. With AT&T, 1988—98; pres. Managed Network Solutions Inc., BellSouth Corp., Atlanta, 1998—2000, chief mktg. officer, 2000—. Bd. dirs. Atlanta Coll. Art, BellSouth Found. Named finalist Woman of Yr. in Tech. award, Women in Tech., 2001; named one of Top 25 Unsung Heroes of the Net, Inter@ctive Week mag., 2000; recipient Ovations award, tele.com mag. and ComNet, 2000. Avocations: tennis, swimming.

LEE, DONNA JEAN, retired nurse; b. Huntington Park, Calif., Nov. 12, 1931; d. Louis Frederick and Lena Adelaide (Hinson) Munyon; m. Frank Bernard Lee, July 16, 1949 (dec. Jan. 2006); children: Frank (dec.), Robert, John. AA in Nursing, Fullerton Jr. Coll., Calif., 1966; student, U. Calif., Irvine, 1966—74, U. N.Mex., 1982. RN, Calif.; cert. Intraventous Therapy Assn. U.S.A. Staff nurse Orange (Calif.) County Med. Ctr., 1966-71, staff and charge nurse relief ICU, CCU, Burn Unit, ER, Communicable Disease, Neo-Natal Care Unit, 1969-71, charge nurse communicable disease unit, 1969-70; staff and charge nurse ICU, emergency rm., CCU, med./surg. units Anaheim (Calif.) Meml. Hosp., 1971-74; charge and staff nurse, relief Staff Builders, Orange, 1974-82; agy. nurse Nursing Svcs. Internat., 1978-89; asst. DON Chapman Convalescent SNF, Orange, 1982; geriat. and pediat. nurse VNASS, 1985-93; hospice/respite nurse VIA Upjohn Home Healthcare Svcs and VNA Support Svcs. of Orange, 1985-93; ret. Staff relief nurse ICU/CCU various hosps. and labs, including plasmapheresis nurse Med. Lab. of Orange, 1978. Life mem. in honor of spouse Republican. Presdl. Task Force, 1982—,

Nat. Rep. Senatorial Com., Nat. Rep. Com. Ocean Conservancy, Natl. Park Trust, Wildlife Land Trust, Sierra Club. Named 25th Anniversary Honoree Calif., RATF, 2006. Mem. AACN, Harvard Med. Sch. Nurses, Am. Lung Assn., Am. Heart Assn., Arthritis Found., Life Extension Found. Baptist. Home: 924 S Hampstead St Anaheim CA 92802-1740

LEE, DOROTHY ANN, comparative literature educator; b. Columbia, Mo., Jan. 22, 1925; d. Victor Lanier and Helen Marie (Lee) Hicks; m. George Ernest Lee, June 18, 1950; children— George Victor, Helen Elaine. BA in French, Wayne State U., 1945, MA in English, 1947; MA in Comparative Lit., Radcliffe Coll., 1948; PhD. in Comparative Lit., Radcliffe Coll.-Harvard U., 1955. Instr. English Wayne State U., Detroit, 1950-51, asst. prof., 1955-57, 1960-63; instr. English Henry Ford Community Coll., Dearborn, Mich., 1963-72; asst. prof. U. Mich., Dearborn, 1972-74, assoc. prof., 1974-78, prof. comparative lit., 1979—. Contbr. articles to profl. jours. Founding mem. Your Heritage House Mus., Detroit, 1983— Recipient Disting. Teaching award U. Mich., 1985, Susan B. Anthony award Women's Commn., U. Mich., 1985, Disting. Faculty award Mich. Governing Bds., 1987; Wayne State U. fellow, 1948, Delta Sigma Theta fellow, 1948 Mem. MLA, AAUW, Detroit Study Club Clubs: Radcliffe (Detroit). Democrat. Office: U Mich-Dearborn 4901 Evergreen Rd Dearborn MI 48128-2406

LEE, ELIZABETH YOUNJU, apparel designer, design educator; b. Seoul, Rep. of Korea, June 25, 1933; arrived in U.S., 1966, naturalized; d. Chin Kap Kim and Keun Ok Bang; m. Benjamin Namkee Lee, Nov. 10, 1956; children: Chong Suh, Chong Man, Margaret. BSc, Seoul Nat. U., Republic of Korea, 1956; BS in Fashion, SUNY, 1972. Tchr. fashion design Seoul (Rep. of Korea) Nat. U., 1956—58, lectr. fashion design, 1962—66, 1972—77; tchr. home econs. Choonju (Rep. of Korea) Normal H.S., 1958—60; asst. prof. fashion design Kook Min U., Seoul, 1961—66; fashion designer Page Boy Inc., Seoul, 1970—72; prof. fashion design Dong Duk Women's U., Seoul, 1972—77; pvt. practice fashion designer Santa Monica, Calif., 1977—. Editor: Kyunghyang Daily Press, 1972—75. Pres. Korean Am. Parent Alliance Autistic Children, 2004—. Recipient Cert. Appreciation award, Mayor City of L.A., 2001, Mother of the Year award, City of L.A., 2005. Mem.: Children's Parent Assn., L.A. (Calif.) 3.1 Women's Assn. (pres. 2001—03, vice chmn. bd. dirs. 2003—). Home and Office: Elizabeth Lee Fashion Inst 528 11th St Santa Monica CA 90402

LEE, ELLA LOUISE, librarian, educator; b. Pitts., Aug. 15, 1929; d. Louis C. and Ida Lily (Ward) Lee; 1 child, Lily I. Lee-Braithwaite. BA in French Lang., History & Culture, San Francisco Coll. for Women, 1971; MA in History, U. San Francisco Jesuit U., 1978; MLS, San Jose State U., 1993. Cert. tchg. K-12 Calif., tchg. 13-14 Calif. Clk. U.S. Fgn. Svc., Japan, Denmark, Germany, Paris, 1951—61; adult ednl. profl. UN - UNESCO, Paris, 1961—67; tchr. French and history San Francisco Unified Sch., 1972—80; instr. San Francisco C.C., 1994—96; assoc. libr. Richmond Calif. Pub. Libr., 1997—99, U. San Francisco Jesuit U., 2000—05. Home and Office: 415 MacArthur Blvd #3 Oakland CA 94610 Office Phone: 510-832-8267. Personal E-mail: ella.lee@sbcglobal.net.

LEE, EMILY LIN, director, real estate company executive; b. Taipei, Taiwan, Apr. 3, 1943; arrived in U.S., 1966; d. Chai-on and Yu-shia Lin; m. Ching-tse Lee; children: Bernard Travis, Eileen May. AA, Shih-Chien Home Econ. Coll., 1964; BA, Bowling Green State U., Ohio, 1968; student, U. Tex., Austin, Tex., 1969—71. CEO Vencap Internat. Inc., N.Y.C., 1990—91; prin., owner Vencap Realty Inc., N.Y.C., 1991—; acct. rep. Metlife, Flushing, NY, 1991—2002; dir. edn. programs Golden Eagle Inst., Flushing, 1999—. Home: 4310 Kissena Blvd Apt 23 Flushing NY 11355

LEE, ESTHER BORA, elementary school educator, gifted and talented educator; b. Seoul, Mar. 13, 1980; d. Young Kil and Young Duk Lee; m. Michael David Lee, July 4, 2005. BS in Elem. Edn., U. Ill., Champaign, 2002. Tchr. grade 1 gifted edn. Prussing Elem. Sch., Chgo., 2002—. Vacation Bible sch. tchr. Teachus Missions, Felipe Neri, Mexico, 1997, English tutor Gambia, 1998, Senegal, 1999—99, gift distbr. N.Mex., 2003—03, team mem. Nev., English tutor and visitor to orphanages Chiang Rai, Thailand, 2005, tutor univ. students Chaing Rai, 2006—06. Scholar, Glenbrook Edn. Assn., 1998; James scholar, U. Ill., 2000. Mem.: Human Interest Professions Club, Alpha Lamda Delta, Kappa Delta Pi, Epsilon Delta. Conservative. Avocations: international travel, music, photography, social justice. Office Phone: 773-534-3460.

LEE, EUNICE, music educator; b. Yong San, Seoul, Republic of Korea, Mar. 16, 1967; d. Jung In and Byung Joo Lee; m. Steve Rhee, July 5, 2000. MusB, San Francisco Conservatory of Music, 1991; MusM, U. So. Calif., 2000; grad., Am. Coll. Musicians, Calif., 2005. Accompanist San Jose Korean Bapt., San Jose, 1985—92; keyboard collaborator various univs., LA, San Francisco, NY, Aspen, Ohio, 1987—2000; accompanist Foothill Coll., Palo Alto, Calif., 1988—89; dir. San Jose Piano Studio, Santa Clara, Calif., 1991—95; condr. Ch. of Love, San Jose, Calif., 1993—94; faculty De Anza Coll., Cupertino, Calif., 1993—94; tchg. asst. U. So. Calif., L.A., 1995—2000, Aspen Summer Music Festival, Colo., 1998—98; accompanist Santa Monica First Christian Ch., Santa Monica, Calif., 1999—2002; pvt. piano tchr. Bakersfield, Calif., 2004—. Adjudicator Nat. Guild Piano Audition, Am. Christian Sch. Instn. Piano Festival, 2004—05. Music dir., organist, LA, 1994—2002. Recipient Grand prize, Concerto Competitions, 1989, Leo Poldofsky award, 1996—99, Keyboard Ensemble, 1996-2000; scholar, San Francisco Conservatory of Music, 1986—91, U. of So. Calif., 1995—2000. Mem.: Nat. Guild Piano Tchrs. (assoc.), Music Tchrs. Assn. Calif. (assoc.; first v.p. 2004—). Mem. Citizens Party. Avocations: breeder, cooking, interior decorating. Office Phone: 661-205-9300. Home Fax: 661-654-0398. Personal E-mail: e.rhee04@yahoo.com.

LEE, EVA, medical educator; b. Kaohsiung, Taiwan; B, M, Nat. Taiwan Normal U.; D in Cell Biology, U. Calif., Berkeley, 1984. Mem. faculty U. Calif., San Diego, 1984—91; rsch. positions, 1984—91; prof. molecular medicine Inst. Biotech. U. Tex.; prof. dept. developmental and cell biology Sch. Biol. Scis. and dept. biol. chemistry Coll. Medicine U. Calif., Irvine, 2001—. Program dir. two nat. programs for rsch. on tumor-suppressor genes Nat. Cancer Inst.; mem. Cancer Rsch. Inst. U.Calif., mem. Chao Family Comprehensive Cancer Ctr. Recipient Presdl. Outstanding Scientist award, Soc. Chinese Bioscientists in Am., Merit award, Nat. Cancer Inst. Office: U Calif Irvine Coll Medicine Irvine CA 92697

LEE, EVELYN MARIE, elementary school educator, secondary school educator; b. Germantown, Ohio, Dec. 17, 1931; d. Robert Orlandus and Edna Cathern (Durr) Stump; m. John Henry Lee, Dec. 16, 1956; children: Mark Douglas, David Matthew, Lori Ann Lee Delehoy. BS in Edn., Otterbein Coll., 1954; EdM with emphasis in reading, U. Alaska, 1979. Dept. store tng. supr., asst. mdse. mgr. The Home Store, Dayton, Ohio, 1954-55; tchr. Parma Pub. Sch., Ohio, 1955-56; math aide civil svc. Nat. Adv. Com. for Aeros. Ames Lab., Moffett Field, Calif., 1956-57; substitute tchr. Warren Pub. Sch., Ohio, 1957-59, tchr. Ohio, 1959-60, Gwinn Pub. Sch., Mich., 1960-64, Anchorage Sch. Dist., 1964-65, 68-87, substitute tchr., 1987-96. Hon. life mem. Alaska PTA; vol. City of Loveland, The Lincoln Ctr., Fort Collins Mem. NEA (ret.; life), NEA-Alaska (ret.; life), Alaska Hist. Soc. (life), Tulpehocken Settlement Hist. Soc., Hist. Soc. Germantown, The Alaskans, Queen Mother of the Loveland Red Hattitudes (Red Hat Soc.), Loveland New Friendship Club, Order Eastern Star. United Methodist. Avocations: travel, reading, arts and crafts, genealogy. Home: 1521 Park Dr Loveland CO 80538-4285

LEE, FRANCES HELEN, editor; b. NYC, Jan. 6, 1936; d. Murray and Rose (Rothman) Lee. BA, Queens Coll., 1957; MA, NYU, 1962. Editl. asst. Christian Herald Family Bookshelf, N.Y.C., 1957-62; with Gordon and Breach Sci. Pubs., Inc., N.Y.C., 1964-66, Am. Electric Power Svc. Corp. AEP Operating Ideas, N.Y.C., 1966-69, Indsl. Water Enging. Mag., N.Y.C., 1969-71; directory editor photographic divsn. United Bus. Publs., N.Y.C., 1971-80; editor Am. Druggist Blue Book Hearst Books/Bus. Publs. Group, 1980-81; spl. projects coord. motor manuals Hearst Book Divsn., 1981-82; editor New Price Report, 1982-84, Am. Druggist Blue Book, 1982-88; freelance editor, cons., 1988—. Supr. Bronx divsn. NY State Civil Defense, 1953-59; com. on NYC charter revision Citizens Union, 1975, com. on city mgmt., 1977-92, bd. dirs., co-chmn. com. on NYC cultural concerns, 1979-97, chmn., 1997-98; vol. NYC Opera, 1988—, info. project mgr., 2001—. Recipient cert. of honor NYU Alumni Fedn., 1985, Meritorious Svc. award, 1986. Mem. N.Y. Bus. Press Editors (bd. dirs. 1988-90, sec. 1990-91), Women's Equity Action League (chmn. rsch. com.), NYU Alumnae Club (dir. 1976-78, rec. sec. 1978-80, v.p. 1980-82, pres. 1982-84, rep. to bd. dirs. fedn. 1984-86), NYU Alumni Fedn. (dir.-at-large 1986—), Villa-Lobos Music Soc. (sec. 1989-91, treas. 1992-95), NYU Club (bd. govs. 1987-89). Home: 170 2nd Ave New York NY 10003-5754 Personal E-mail: franceslee397@hotmail.com.

LEE, GRACE H., lawyer; b. 1969; BA, Calif. State Univ., Northridge; JD, New England Sch. Law. Bar: Mass. 1996. Asst. dist. atty., chief, civil rights divsn. Norfolk County Dist. Atty. Off.; atty., civil rights office US Dept. Edn.; assoc., employment discrimination, labor law Morgan Brown & Joy; dep. treas., gen. counsel Mass. State Treas., Boston, 2003—. Named one of Best Lawyers Under 40, Nat. Asian Pacific Am. Bar Assn., 2004; recipient Minority Student Assn. Distinguished Alumni award, New England Sch. Law., 1999, Timothy J. Spillane Jr. award for outstanding dist. ct. prosecution. Office: Dep Treas & Gen Counsel 12th Fl Mass State Treas Dept 1 Ashburton Pl Boston MA 02133

LEE, GWENDOLIN KUEI, retired ballet educator; b. Shanghai, The People's Republic of China, Nov. 17, 1932; came to U.S., 1978; d. Din-Yuan and Ching (Chu) L.; m. C.T. Yu, May 1955 (div. 1965); children: Aldin, Marline. Diplomate, St. Mary's Hall, Shanghai, 1952; cert., Shanghai Inst. Arts, 1955. Instr, Shanghai People's Acad. Arts, 1954-56; dir. The Lee Sch. Ballet, Shanghai, 1955-66, dir., instr. Champaign, Ill., 1981-99; instr. Shanghai Gymnastic Inst., 1960-63, Shanghai Children's Palace, 1970-78, Parkland Coll., Champaign, 1979-80, McKinley YMCA, Champaign, 1979-81; ret., 1999; instr. Refinery Ballet, Champaign, Ill., 2003—. Cons. Chgo. City Ballet, 1984-85; artistic dir. Ill. Children's Expo, sponsored by Mercy Hosp., Champaign, 1986-88. Participant, Dayton Ballet, Tulsa Ballet, Cincinnati Ballet, North Carolina Ballet's Nutcracker, The Night Before Christmas; choreographer, artistic dir. numerous ballet recitals including Grandmother's Fairy Tales, 1982, An Evening of Children's Ballet, Cinderella, Faust-The Walpurgis Night Scene, 1984, Magic Key, Swan Lake Act II, 1986, Little Red Riding Hood, The Beautiful Blue Danube, 1988, Persian Market, The Dream Scene from Don Quixote, 1990, It's a Small World, The Nutcracker, 1992, An Enchanting Evening of Children's Ballet, 1994, Grandma's Golden Book, 1996, Don Quixote, 1996; photographer sch. calendars. Mem. Vintage Champaign Coun., 1983-87. Avocations: photography, opera, drama, music. Office Phone: 217-355-4444.

LEE, HARPER (NELLE HARPER LEE), writer; b. Monroeville, Ala., Apr. 28, 1926; d. Amasa Coleman and Frances (Finch) L. Student, Huntingdon Coll., Montgomery, Ala., 1944-45; law student, U. Ala., 1945-49; student, Oxford Univ.; D (hon.), U. Ala., 1990; LHD (hon.), Spring Hill. Coll., Mobile, Ala., 1997. Reservation clk. Eastern Airlines, NYC, BOAC, NYC. Author: To Kill a Mockingbird, 1960 (Pulitzer prize for fiction 1961, made into Oscar-winning feature film starring Gregory Peck, 1962); contbr. to Vogue mag., McCall's mag. Mem. Nat. Coun. on Arts, 1966-72. Recipient Ala. Libr. Assn award, 1961, Nat. Coun. Christians and Jews Brotherhood award, 1961. Avocation: golf.*

LEE, HELIE, writer; b. Seoul, S. Korea, Aug. 29, 1964; arrived in US, 1970; BS in Polit. Sci., UCLA, 1986. Mem. Asian Am. Writers Workshop. Writer (TV series) In Living Color, Saved By The Bell, Martin Lawrence Show; author: (novels) Still Life With Rice, 1996, In The Absence of Sun, 2002, (articles) Mademoiselle, Essence, KoreAm Journal. Office: c/o Harmony Books 1745 Broadway New York NY 10019

LEE, JAN LOUISE, nursing educator; b. Grundy Center, Iowa, Oct. 30, 1953; d. Robert L. and B. Lucille (Frey) Thede; m. Henry M. Lee (div.). BSN, U. Iowa, 1975; MN, UCLA, 1980; PhD, U. So. Calif., 1988. Patient care coord. Queen of the Valley Hosp., West Covina, Calif., 1977-78; rsch. clin. nurse specialist Wadsworth VA Med. Ctr., L.A., 1980-83; asst. prof. nursing U. So. Calif., L.A., 1983-88, UCLA, 1988-95; dir. undergrad. and non-traditional programs U. Mich. Sch. Nursing, Ann Arbor, 1995—2003; prof., assoc. dean U. Tenn. Coll. Nursing, Knoxville, 2003—. Mem. ANCC Commn. on Cert. Contbr. articles to profl. jours. Grantee NIH, U. So. Calif., UCLA, others. Mem. Tenn. Nurses Assn., Sigma Theta Tau (past chpt. pres.). Home: 9746 Dawn Chase Way Knoxville TN 37931 Office: U Tenn Knoxville Coll Nursing 1200 Volunteer Blvd Knoxville TN 37996-4180 E-mail: jlee39@utk.edu.

LEE, JANET MENTORE, psychologist, educator; b. NYC, July 21, 1972; d. Percy Edward and Celina Mentore (Stepmother); m. Ryan Todd Lee, Aug. 5, 2000; 1 child, Jordyn Olivia. BA, Ithaca Coll., 1994; MS in Edn., Fordham U., 1997, PhD, 1999. Lic. psychologist Conn., 2001, N.Y., 2001, cert. sch. psychologist Conn., 2000, N.Y., 1999. Psychologist Westport (Conn.) Pub. Schs., 2000—. Psychologist Hawthorne (N.Y.) Union Free Sch. Dist., 1999—2000; adj. asst. prof. Fordham U., N.Y.C., 2000—03, Fairfield (Conn.) U., 2002—03; panelist Conn. State Advanced Learning Disability Seminar, 2002—03; presenter in field. Advisory editor: The School Psychologist-APA; contbr. articles to profl. jours. Bd. mem. Cmty. Free Dems., N.Y.C., 1997—99. Grad. Assistantship, Fordham U., 1995—99, Internat. Congress on Obesity scholar, Pfizer Pharmaceuticals, 1998. Mem.: NASP, APA (Hon. Mention Outstanding Dissertation award Divsn. 16 2000), Conn. Assn. Sch. Psychologists, Conn. Psychol. Assn., N.Y. Assn. Sch. Psychologists (Ted Bernstein Outstanding Student award 1999), N.Y. State Psychol. Assn. (future psychologists sect. chair 1997—99, Conv. scholar 1998, Spl. Citation award 1999). Democrat. Achievements include co-investigator baseline levels of obesity and weight gain among patients taking antipsychotic medications. Office: Westport Public Schs/Long Lots Elem 13 Hyde Ln Westport CT 06880 Home: 111 Barcelona Dr Jupiter FL 33458 Office Phone: 203-341-1933. Personal E-mail: jmentore@yahoo.com. E-mail: jmlee@westport.k12.ct.us.

LEE, JANIE C., curator; b. Shreveport, La., Apr. 22, 1937; d. Birch Lee and Joanna (Glassell) Wood; m. David B. Warren, Jan. 2, 1980. Student, Nat. Cathedral Sch., 1951-55; BA, Sarah Lawrence Coll., 1959. Asst. to Cheryl Crawford, Actors Studi o, N.Y.C., 1962-63; co-prodr. Off Broadway Theatre Co., N.Y.C., 1963-65; owner, pres. Janie C. Lee Gallery, Dallas, 1967-74, Houston, 1973-96, Janie C. Lee Master Drawings, N.Y.C., 1983-96; curator of drawings Whitney Mus. Am. Art, 1997—2004. Mem. art appraisal panel IRS, Washington, 1987-94; trustee Menil Found., Inc., 2000—. Prodr. ann. catalogue on 20th Century drawings, 1979-93. Mem. Alumnae Bd. Sarah Lawrence Coll. (1972-74); pres. Nancy Graves Found., 1996—. Mem. Art Dealers Assn. Am. (bd. dirs. 1980-88, 92-94, v.p. 1984-88). Office: 3711 San Felipe St # 4E Houston TX 77027 Office Phone: 713-355-5300. E-mail: janieclee@aol.com.

LEE, JEANETTE, professional pool player; b. Brooklyn, NY, July 9, 1971; Appearances: (on several television shows including) Arli$$; David Letterman; HBO Real Sports; Regis and Kelly. Achievements include highest ranking for female pool player, 1994; gold medal, Akita World Games, Japan, 2001; several event championships including Ladies Tournament of Champions, 2003, Atlanta Women's Open, 2004, Ladies Trick Shot Championship, 2004, Cuetec Cues, 2004; earned nickname Black Widow due to her ability to devour opponents. Office: c/o Octagon 7th Fl 8687 Melrose Ave Los Angeles CA 90069*

LEE, JEANNE KIT YEW, retired administrative officer; b. N.Y.C., July 31, 1959; d. Tat Yuen and Yow Seum (Chu) Lee. BBA, Baruch Coll., N.Y.C., 1982. Clk. typist U.S. Dept. Health and Human Svcs., N.Y.C., 1980-83, U.S. Consumer Product Safety Commn., N.Y.C., 1983-85, adminstrv. asst., 1985-90, sys. adminstr., 1986-93, adminstrv. officer N.Y.C., 1990—2005, ret., 2005. Mem. NAFE, Humane Soc., Nat. Wildlife Fedn. (assoc.), Am. Humane, DAV (Commanders Club 1988—). Personal E-mail: jeanneklee@yahoo.com.

LEE, JOELLE L.K., elementary school educator; b. Honolulu, Mar. 20, 1969; d. Joseph David and Bernadette Ann Ahuna; m. Edward E. Lee, Jr., July 22, 1989; children: Jasmine K., Jordan Kamalei. EdB, U. Hawaii- Manoa, Honolulu, 1991, EdM, 1999, profl. diploma, 1994. After sch. care leader Maryknoll Sch., Honolulu, 1990—91, tchr. grade 2, 1992—97, tchr. kindergarten, 1997—2004, Kamehameha Sch., 2004—. Co-chair math. curriculum Maryknoll Sch., Honolulu, 1998—2004, co-chair curriculum and articulation com. Maryknoll coord. Thanksgiving luncheon drive Salvation Army, Honolulu, 1995—2003; Eucharistic minister coord. Resurrection of the Lord Cath. Ch., Waipahu, 2003—. Mem.: Assn. Supervision Curriculum and Instrn., Nat. Assn. Edn. Young Children, Nat. Coun. Tchrs. Math. Office: Kamehameha Schs Kapālama 1887 Makuakāne St Honolulu HI 96817

LEE, JOSELYN C.R., physician, researcher; b. Hong Kong, June 7, 1961; came to U.S., 1979; d. Joseph Mui Hok and Myra Jeannon (Yip) L. BS in Chemistry, Stanford (Calif) U., 1983, MS in Biology, 1984; MD, U. Chgo., 1990. Diplomate Am. Bd. Pediatrics; lic. physician, Calif., S.C. Tchr. asst. dept. chemistry Stanford U., 1983-84; rsch. asst. pharmacology and physiology U. Chgo., 1987-89; intern dept pediatrics Harbor UCLA Hosp., Torrance, Calif., 1990-91, resident in pediatrics, 1991-93; temporary clin. lectr. pediatrics Hong Kong U. Sch. Medicine, 1993-94; pediatric cardiology fellow Med. U. S.C., Charleston, 1994—; asst. prof., pediatric cardiac electrophysiology Tulane U. Med. Sch.; dir. Children's Heart Rhythm Inst., L.A. Recipient Bristol-Myers Squibb Affiliate Travel award Am. Coll. Cardiology, 1997, Young Investigator award Am. Acad. Pediatrics, 1995, Nat. Rsch. Svc. award NIH, 1995, 97; Grantham scholar, Dr. and Mrs. Charles Yau scholar, Hong Kong Govt. scholar. Mem. AAAS, Am. Acad. Pediatrics, Am. Coll. Cardiology, N.Y. Acad. Sci., Phi Beta Kappa, No. Am. Soc. of Pacing and Electrophysiology, Phi Lambda Upsilon. Avocations: piano, singing. Office: Children's Heart Rhythm Inst PO Box 24854 Los Angeles CA 90024

LEE, JUDITH, state legislator; b. Redding, Calif., Mar. 7, 1942; m. Duane Lee, 1964; 2 children. BS, U. N.D., 1964. Real estate broker; mem. govt. & vet. affairs com. N.D. Senate 13th dist., West Fargo, ND, 1994—, human svcs., chair human svcs. com. Mem. West Fargo (N.D.) Planning and Zoning Com., 1982—94; bd. dirs. United Way of Cass-Clay, 1987—93, 2005—06, Hospice of Red River Valley, 1997—2002, Fargo-Moorhead Symphony, 2000—. Named Realtor of Yr., Fargo-Moorhead Area Assn. Realtors, 1988, YWCA Woman of the Yr. in Vol. Category, 1994, Legislator of Yr., N.D. Assn. Township Officers, 1998, N.D. Mental Health Assn., 2003; recipient Guardian of Sm. Bus. award, Nat. Fedn. Ind. Businesses, 1998, Legislator of Yr., N.D. Assn. Nurses, 2003, Legislator Svc. award, ARC, N.C., 2004, NDAR Polit. Improvement award, 2005. Mem.: Park County Realtors, Fargo-Moorhead C. of C. (bd. dirs. 1993—99), West Fargo C. of C. (bd. dirs. 1985—88). Office: PO Box 89 Fargo ND 58107-0089 Office Phone: 701-237-5031.

LEE, JUNE WARREN, dentist; b. Boston, Feb. 24, 1952; d. Earl Arnold and Rosemary Regina (Leary) Warren; m. William Lee, July 25, 1976; children: Jaime Michelle, Daniel William. BA, Brandeis U., 1973; DDS, Georgetown U., 1977; student, U.S. Dental Inst., 1985-87. Pvt. practice, Boston, 1977—. Mem. Dorchester Bd. of Trade, 2000—. Active Pierce Mid. Sch. PTO, 1997-2000, Cunningham Sch. PTO, Milton, Mass., 1987-97, Parent-Adv. Coun., Collicot Elem. Sch., Milton, 1986-87; dental instr. Cunningham Sch., 1987-97; dental screening Healthworks, Neponset Health Ctr., Boston, 1981-84; bd. dirs. Delta Dental Plan Mass., 1995-2001, Delta Dental Found. Mass., 1995-2001; vol. Dentist for SmileLine On-Line, 2001-02, Masons Child Identification Program, 2000-2005. Master Acad. Gen. Dentistry (coun. ann. meetings and internat. confs. 1993-98, 2002-, chmn. 1998 local arrangements com., past pres. New Eng. Mastertrack program, pres. Mass. chpt. 1998-2001, past chmn. editl. rev. bd. Audiodent, coun. constn. and bylaws and jud. procedures 2001-02, region one dir. 2003—); fellow Am. Coll. Dentists, Internat. Coll. Dentists, Acad. Dentistry Internat.; mem. ADA, Mass. Dental Soc. (allied profl. liaison com. 1998-99, 2000-01, amb. 2000), Yankee Dental Congress (mem. steering com. 1998-2001, 2004—, chmn. steering com. 2005-06, chmn. ednl. continuum 2005—, gen. chmn. 2003-04, co-chmn. social and cultural com., 2001, co-chmn. sci. com., 1998, co-chmn. gen. arrangements, 1996, allied sci. co-chmn. 1994), South Shore Dist. Dental Soc. (chmn.-elect 1991, chmn. 1992, chmn. program com. 1995-96), Am. Orthodontic Soc., Am. Assn. for Functional Orthodontics (master 2005), Am. Assn. Women Dentists (sec. 1987, v.p. 1988, pres. 1990, A.T. Cross Co. Women of Achievement award 1985, bd. dirs., treas. Gillette Hayden Meml. Found. 1996-2000, Lucy Hobbs Taylor award 2004), Women's Dental Soc. Mass. (sec. 1978, v.p. 1979-81, pres. 1981-83, advisor to bd. 2003—), Mass. Dentists Interested in Legislation, Chestnut Hill Rsch. Study Club. Roman Catholic. Avocations: travel, genealogy, reading, writing, celtic music. Office: 383 Neponset Ave Dorchester MA 02122-3104 Office Phone: 617-288-2680. Personal E-mail: drsinelee@hotmail.com.

LEE, KATHERINE **See JOEL, KATIE**

LEE, KATRINA LASHAWN, health insurance business consultant; b. Jacksonville, Fla., June 20, 1966; d. Kelly Lucas and Hattie Lee. AA, Fla. C.C., 1987; AS in Med. Lab. Tech., Fla. Jr. Coll., 1986; BS in Health Sci., U. North Fla., 1992, M in Health Adminstrn., 1997. Cert. Clin. Lab. Scientist Nat. Cert. Agy. Med. Lab. Personnel, Med. Lab. Tech. Am. Soc. Clin. Pathologists Bd. Registry. Sr. med. tech. U. Med. Ctr., Jacksonville, Fla., 1987—97; project cons. Blue Cross, Blue Shield Fla., Jacksonville, 1997—; adj. prof. Fla. Met. U., Orange Park, 2004—. Sec. U. North Fla. Coll. Health Alumni Assn., Jacksonville, 2005—. Mem.: Am. Alliance Health, Phys. Edn., Recreation, Dance (assoc.).

LEE, KRISTA, secondary school educator; b. Dayton, Ohio, July 20, 1968; d. Nancy Ann and Dwayne Goldsmith Lee. BS, Auburn U., Ala., 1990; MS, U. Ill., Chgo., 1992. Cert. tchr. biology Calif., NC. Tchg. asst. Auburn U., Auburn, Ala., 1989—90, U. Ill., Chgo., 1991—92, La. State U., Baton Rouge, 1992—94; intern Am. Sch. Lima, Peru, 1995—96; tchr. Bolsa Grande HS, Garden Grove, Calif., 1996—97; sci. tchr. Santa Fe Springs (Calif.) HS, 1998—99, Newport Harbor HS, Newport Beach, Calif., 1999—2001, Ontario (Calif.) HS, 2001—02, Colony HS, Ontario, Calif., 2002—06, Riverside HS, Durham, NC, 2006—. Girls cross country coach Colony HS, Ontario, 2002—04; rain forest guide Rainforest Expeditions, Puerto Maldonado, Peru, 1994—96. Contbr. chapters to books. Dive vol. Aquarium of the Pacific, Long Beach, Calif., 2003—05; bd. dirs. So. Calif. Dive Club of the Inland Empire, Claremont, Calif., 2003—05. Fellow Molecular Evolution, Mus. Natural Sci., La. State U., 1993; Tchr. grant, Newport Harbor Found., 2000, Newport-Mesa Schools Found., 2000. Mem.: Nat. Sci. Tchrs. Assn. (assoc.), Girl Scouts Am. (life), Beta Beta Beta (assoc.; pres. 1989—90). Office Phone: 919-560-3965. Personal E-mail: kristalee4@aol.com.

LEE, KRISTIN H., state agency administrator; Sr. asst. atty. gen. State of Wyo., 1988—96; commr. Wyo. Pub. Svc. Commn., Cheyenne, Wyo., 1996—. Office: Wyoming PSC Hansen Bldg 2515 Warren Ave Ste 300 Cheyenne WY 82002

LEE, LEAH RAYNELLA, elementary school educator; b. Paris, Tex., Sept. 19, 1964; d. Robert Lemanuel and Sandra Jan Lewis; m. James Richard Lee, July 31, 2004. AS, Paris Jr. Coll., 1990; BS in Interdisciplinary Studies, East Tex. State U., 1992, MS, 1996. Lic. cosmetologist Tex. Classroom sci. tchr. Blue Ridge (Tex.) Ind. Sch. Dist. Jr. High, 1992—97, Rivercrest Ind. Sch. Dist. Jr. High, Bogata, Tex., 1997—. Tex. Space grantee, NASA and U. Tex., Austin, 1999, X-Treem Sci. Curriculum grantee, Region 8 Ednl. Svc. Ctr., 2004—05, Target grantee, 2005—06. Mem.: Sci. Tchrs.' Assn. Tex., Order

Ea. Star (assoc. conductress 2006—, Star Points 2004—06), Alpha Lambda Alpha Phi. Office: Rivercrest Ind Sch Dist Junior High 4100 US Hwy 271 S Bogata TX 75417 Office Phone: 903-632-0878. Business E-Mail: llee@rivercrestisd.net.

LEE, LILLIAN ALDRIDGE, music educator; b. Greenwood, Miss., Mar. 29, 1934; d. Joseph Everette and Virginia (Gillespie) Aldridge; m. Robert G. Lee, June 24, 1956; children:Virginia Louise Lee McMurray, Dicey Gay Lee. B in Mus. Edn. magna cum laude, Miss. U. for Women, 1956; MusM, Miss. Coll., 1971, MusM in Vocal Performance, 1976. Music edn. tchr. Van Winkle and Clinton Blvd. Elem. Schs., Jackson, 1956-57, Terry (Miss.) Consol. Sch., 1962-70; choral dir. Jackson (Miss.) Preparatory Sch., 1970-77, First Presbyn. Day Sch., Jackson, 1978-96. Pvt. instr. voice and piano, Jackson and Terry, Miss., 1956-84; instr. voice Miss. Coll., 1973; dir. children's choir and youth choir Ctrl. Presbyn. Ch., Jackson, 1976-80; guest condr. Hinds County Elem. Music Festival, 1991, Miss. Pvt. Sch. Edn. Assn. State Jr. High Choral Festival, 1991; coord. children's choirs First Presbyn. Ch., Jackson, 1982-84, dir. Minnesingers Women's Ensemble, 1985-93, dir. jr. high choir, 1987-90. Soprano soloist Ctrl. Presbyn. Ch., Jackson, 1974-82. Soloist Jackson Choral Soc., 1972-75, 95-2003; asst. dir. Miss. Youth Chorale Summer Tour to Europe, 1976-78; active St. Andrews Chamber Soc., 1977-78, Miss. Opera Chorus, 1977-78; judge Capital City Jr. Miss Program, 1982. Recipient Miss. Music Educator of Year award, 1995, Blue Cross/Blue Shield Miss Ageless Hero award, 2004, Dist. Alumnae award Miss. Coll., 2005. Mem. Am. Choral Dirs. Assn. (Ernestine Ferrell award 2001), Miss. Music Educators Assn. and Music Educators Nat. Conf. (dist. VI choral chmn. 1964-65, elem. textbook selection com. 1965-66, dist. VI elem. chmn. 1966-67, state choral chmn. 1969-70, state sec. 1970-71, state treas. 1993-95), Miss. Pvt. Sch. Edn. Assn. (state choral chmn. high sch. divsn. 1971-73, 76-77, state choral chmn. jr. high divsn. 1984-85, founder, artistic dir. Miss. Girlchoir 1995-98), Sigma Alpha Iota, Kappa Delta Pi. Republican. Methodist. Avocations: sewing, needlecrafts, quilting, reading. Home: 1329 Simwood Pl Jackson MS 39211-6352

LEE, LINDA M., technical recruiter; b. L.A., Dec. 28, 1972; d. Jack K. C. and Grace K. C. Lee. BA, U. Calif., Berkeley, 1995; cert. in human resource mgmt., cert. in tng. and human resource devel. Tech. recruiter Microsoft Corp., Mountain View, Calif. Vol. Asian Women Shelter, 1998—; mentor Chinatown Leo Club, San Francisco, 1998—, Children and Family Social Svcs., 1999—. E-mail: lindalee00@msn.com.

LEE, MARCELLA, announcer; BBA, U. Mich. Photographer/reporter WLNS-TV, Lansing, Mich.; with WBNS-TV, Columbus, Ohio, KCNC-TV, Denver. Recipient, 3 Emmy award, 2003, Cmty. Svc. award, Filipino Am. Cmty. Coun. of Metro Detroit. Office: WDIV-TV 550 W Lafayette Blvd Detroit MI 48226

LEE, MARGARET BURKE, college president, language educator; b. San Diego, Dec. 28, 1943; d. Peter John and Margaret Mary (Brown) Burke; m. Donald Harry Lee, June 30, 1973 (dec. June 2002); children: Katherine Louise, Kristopher Donald. BA summa cum laude, Regis Coll., 1966; MA with honors, U. Chgo., 1970, PhD, 1978; IEM Cert., Harvard U., 1992, Seminar for New Pres., 1996. Asst. to humanities MIT, Cambridge, 1969; instr. Dover-Sherborn H.S., Dover, 1973-75, Alpena (Mich.) C.C., 1975-80, dean liberal arts, 1980-82; dean instrn. Kalamazoo Valley C.C., 1982-85; v.p. Oakton C.C., Des Plaines, Ill., 1985-95, pres., 1995—. Vice chair Am. Coun. on Internat. Intercultural Edn., 2000—, chair, 2002-05; cons., field faculty Vt. Coll., Montpelier, 1982-85; mem. admissions com. Ill. Math and Sci. Acad., 1988—; bd. govs. North Cook Edni. Svc. Ctr., 1988—2004, bd. dirs., 1989—, vice chair, 1990-91, chair, 1992-94; bd. dirs. Academic Search Cons. Svcs., 2001—. Mem. Bd. Edn. Dist. 39, Wilmette, Ill., 1990-92, Des Plaines Sister Cities, 1995—; mem. 50th ann. leadership cir. Sister Cities Internat.; bd. dirs. Ill. C.C. Atty.'s Assn., 1994—; mem. Career Edn. Planning Dist., Kalamazoo, 1982, Kalamazoo Forum/Kalamazoo Network, 1982, Needs Assessment Task Force, 1984. Ford Found. fellow, 1969—73, Woodrow Wilson Found. fellow, 1975, fed. grantee, 1978—84. Mem. Am. Assn. of C.C.'s (bd. dirs. 2000-03), Am. Assn. Cmty. and Jr. Colls., Mich. Assn. C.C. Instrnl. Adminstrs. (pres. 1983-85), Mich. Occupl. Deans Adminstrs. Coun. (exec. bd. 1983-85), Mich. Women's Studies Assn. (hons. selection com. 1984), North Ctrl. Assn. Acad. Deans (pres. 1988-90, cons. evaluator Chgo., 1982—, commr.-at-large, 1988-92, commn. on inst. of higher edn. bd. dirs., 1992—, vice chair, 1996-98, chair, 1998-2001, v.p.), Kalamazoo Consortium Higher Edn. (pres.'s coun. coord. com. 1982-85), Kalamazoo C. of C. (vocat. edn. subcom. indsl. coun. 1982), North Ctrl. Assn. Acad. Deans (v.p., pres. 1985-87), Des Plaines C. of C. (mem. bd. dirs. 1995—). Democrat. Lutheran. Avocations: quilt collecting, reading, listening to classical music, sports spectating, theatre-going. Home: 2247 Lake Ave Wilmette IL 60091-1410 Office: Oakton CC 1600 E Golf Rd Des Plaines IL 60016-1234 Business E-Mail: plee@oakton.edu.

LEE, MARGARET NORMA, artist; b. Kansas City, Mo., July 7, 1928; d. James W. and Margaret W. (Farin) Lee; PhB, U. Chgo., 1948; MA, Art Inst. Chgo., 1952. Lectr., U. Kansas City, 1957-61; cons. Kansas City Bd. Edn., Kansas City, Mo., 1966-86; guest lectr. U.Mo.-Columbia, 1983, 85, 87, 89, 91, 93-95, 97; one-woman shows Univ. Women's Club, Kansas City, 1966, Friends of Art, Kansas City, 1969, Fine Arts Gallery U. Mo. at Columbia, 1972, All Souls Unitarian Ch. Kansas City, Mo., 1978; two-Woman show Rockhurst Coll., Kansas City, Mo., 1981 exhibited in group shows U. Kans., Lawrence, 1958, Chgo. Art Inst., 1963, Nelson Art Gallery, Kansas City, Mo., 1968, 74, Mo. Art Show, 1976, Fine Arts Gallery, Davenport, Iowa, 1977; represented in permanent collections Amarillo (Tex.) Art Center, Kansas City (Mo.) Pub. Library, Park Coll., Parkville, Mo. Mem. Coll. Art Assn. Roman Catholic. Contbr. art to profl. jours.; author booklet. Home: 4109 Holmes St Kansas City MO 64110-1127

LEE, MARTHA, artist, writer; b. Chehalis, Wash., Aug. 23, 1946; d. William Robert and Phyllis Ann (Herzog) L.; m. Peter Reynolds Lockwood, Jan. 25, 1974 (div. 1982). BA in English Lit., U. Wash., 1968; student, Factory of Visual Art, 1980-82. Reporter Seattle Post-Intelligencer, 1970; personnel counselor Theresa Snow Employment, 1971-72; receptionist Northwest Kidney Ctr., 1972-73; proprietress The Reliquary, 1974-77; travel agt. Cathay Express, 1977-79; artist, 1980—. Painter various oil paintings; exhibited in numerous one-woman shows; numerous group shows including most recently: Columbia River Artists Gallery, Chinook, Washington, Blackwood Beach Cottages, Ocean Pk., Washington, Baker Bay Gallery, Ilwaco, Wash.; author: To The Beach and Other Poems, 1998. Avocations: horseback riding, reading, music. Home: PO Box 1157 Ocean Park WA 98640-1157 Office Phone: 360-665-4579. E-mail: arowhead@pacifier.com.

LEE, MARVINA SUE, science educator; d. William Marvin and Cymbeline Moss Keltner; m. Gary John Lee, Dec. 28, 2002; children: Laurie Jones Binder, Brent Robert Jones. Assocs.' degree, Lindsey Wilson Coll., Columbia, Ky., 1966; BS, Western Ky. U., Bowling Green, 1970; MS, So. Ill. U., Edwardsville, 1977. Mid. sch. tchr. Whiteside Sch., Belleville, Ill., 1971—. Dir. Svc. Learning Grant, Belleville, 2003—04. Communion steward Union United Meth. Ch., Belleville, 1980—2000, bd. trustees, 1999—2002, chmn. bd. trustees, 2002—. Recipient Emerson Excellence in Tchg. award, Emerson Electric, 2005. Mem.: Ill. Sci. Tchrs. Assn., Nat. Sci. Tchrs. Assn., Whiteside Fedn. Tchrs. (co-pres. 1996—97). Methodist. Avocations: painting, golf, travel, sewing, home decorating.

LEE, MELINDA FAYE, mathematics educator; b. Camden, S.C., Nov. 20, 1963; d. Jacqueline Polson and William Randolph Lee. BA in Math., Columbia Coll., S.C., 1986; MEd, U. S.C., Columbia, 1990. Cert. tchr. S.C. Tchr. math. Lexington H.S., SC, 1988—96, Dutch Fork H.S., Irmo, SC, 1996—. Dir. Miss Silver Fox pageant Dutch Fork H.S., Irmo, SC, 1999—2006. Office: Dutch Fork HS 1400 Old Tamah Rd Irmo SC 29063 Office Phone: 803-732-8050. Personal E-mail: mlee@lex5.k12.sc.us.

LEE, MICHELLE ANNE, financial analyst; b. Binghamton, NY, Feb. 29, 1980; d. Thomas and Patricia Lee. BS in Fin. Econs., Binghamton U., Vestal, NY, 2002, MBA, 2004. Fin. analyst Lockheed Martin Systems Integration, Owego, NY, 2000—03, program mgr., 2004—. Coach Boys and Girls Club, Owego, 2002—04, STNY Flyers Basketball Club, Binghamton, 2003—03. Recipient Lockheed Martin Honors award, Lockheed Martin, 2002, Presdl. Vol. Svc. award, 2003. Avocations: golf, basketball, travel, shopping. Home: 3360 Vestal Road A-14 Vestal NY 13850 Office Phone: 607-751-2436.

LEE, NANCY RANCK, management consultant; b. Yonkers, N.Y., Oct. 31, 1932; d. William Edward and Marion Edna Ranck; children: John Gregory, Paul Edward. BS, Cornell U., 1953; postgrad., Boston U., 1974-75. Social worker Tompkins County, Ithaca, N.Y., 1953-54; pers. adminstr. GE Advanced Electronics Ctr., Ithaca, 1954-55; fashion publicist Macy's, N.Y.C., 1956-59; mgr. advt. and pub. rels. Josiah Wedgwood & Co., N.Y.C., 1959-65; dir. comms. Gregory Fosella Assocs., Boston, 1969-71; dir. mktg. Kuras & Co., Boston, 1971-73; internat. sales mgr. Laser Focus Mag., Boston, 1973-75; pres. Lee Assocs., Boston, 1975-82; exec. v.p. Infotech, Boston, 1982-92; pres. Requisite Orgn. Assoc., Sarasota, Fla., 1992—. Lectr. Simmons Coll. Author: Targeting the Top: Everything a Woman Needs to Know to Succeed in Business, 1980. Mem. Cornell Cb, Ivy League Club, Phi Kappa Phi. Avocation: skiing. Home: 1590 1st St Sarasota FL 34236

LEE, NELDA S., art appraiser, art dealer, film producer; b. Gorman, Tex., July 3, 1941; d. Olan C. and Onis L.; 1 dau., Jeanna Lea Pool. AS (Franklin Lindsay Found. grantee), Tarleton State U., Tex., 1961; BA in Fine Arts, N. Tex. State U., 1963; postgrad., Tex. Tech. U., 1964, San Miguel de Allende Art Inst., Mexico, 1965. Head dept. art Ector H.S., Odessa, Tex., 1963-68. Group exhbns. include El Paso, Tex., New Orleans; contbr. articles to profl. jours. Bd. dir. Odessa YMCA, 1970, bd. dirs. Am. Heart Assn., Odessa, 1975; fund raiser Easter Seal Telethon, Odessa, 1978-79; bd. dir. Ector County (Tex.) Cultural Ctr., Tex. Bus. Hall of Fame, 1980-85; bd. dir., mem. acquisition com. Permian Basin Presdl. Mus., Odessa, 1978; bd. dir., chairperson acquisition com. Odessa Art Mus., 1979—; pres. Mega-Tex. Prodns., TV and movie prodrs.; pres. Ector County Dem. Women's Club, 1975, Nelda Lee, Inc., Odessa; appointee Tex. Commn. Arts, 1993—. Recipient Designer-Craftsman award El Paso Mus. Fine Arts, 1964. Mem. Am. Soc. Appraisers (sr.), Nat. Tex. Assn. Art Dealers (pres. 1978—), Odessa C. of C. Office Phone: 432-366-8426. E-mail: neldasl@cableone.net.

LEE, PAMELA ANNE, bank executive, accountant, financial analyst; b. San Francisco, May 30, 1960; d. Larry D. and Alice Mary (Reece) L. BBA, San Francisco State U., 1981. CPA Calif. Typist, bookkeeper, tax acct. James G. Woo, CPA, San Francisco, 1979-85; tutor bus. math. and stats. San Francisco State U., 1979-80; from teller to ops. officer Gibraltar Savs. and Loan, San Francisco, 1978-81; sr. acct. Price Waterhouse, San Francisco, 1981-86; corp. acctg. mgr. First Nationwide Bank, Daly City, Calif., 1986-89, v.p., 1989-91, v.p., project mgr., 1991-92, sr. conversion and bus. analyst, 1992-93; sr. bus. analyst, asst. v.p. Bank of Am., 1993—98, mktg. cons., v.p. San Francisco, 1998-99, sr. cons. bus. automation, v.p., 1999-2001, sr. v.p., 2001—. Acctg. cons. New Performance Gallery, San Francisco, 1985, San Francisco Chamber Orch., 1986; treas. Golden Gate chpt. Team Bank of Am., 2000-02, co-chmn., 2003-04, treas, 2005—. Founding mem., chair bd. trustees Asian Acctg. Students Career Day, 1988-89; vol. Mickaboo Cockatiel Rescue, 1998—, CFO, 2002--. Mem.: AICPA, Calif. Soc. CPAs, Toastmasters Internat. (co-v.p. membership Tower of Talk chpt. 2000—01, co-v.p. edn. 2001, competent toastmaster status 2001, v.p. membership 2002, competent leader status 2002, advanced toastmaster silver status 2004, pres. Everybody Speaks chpt. 2004—, v.p. edn. United We Speak chpt. 2005—). Republican. Avocations: reading, music, personal computing, crafting. Office: 1455 Market St 13th Fl San Francisco CA 94103

LEE, SALLY A., editor-in-chief; m. Rob Niosi. Grad., Durham U., Eng.; MA, Clark U., Mass. Tchr. writing and lit. Clark U.; reporter Worcester (Mass.) Telegram; mng. editor Worcester (Mass.) Monthly; spl. features editor Woman's World mag., NYC; articles editor Woman's Day mag., NYC; sr. editor Redbook mag., NYC; editor-in-chief YM, NYC, 1994—96, Fitness Mag., NYC, 1996—98, Parents Mag., NYC, 1998—; editl. dir. YM mag., NYC, 2004. Corr. E! Entertainment Network. Author: The Best Advice I Ever Got, 2001. Bd. dirs. Room to Grow, Women for Women Internat. Mem.: Parenting Network. Office: Parents Mag 375 Lexington Ave Fl 10 New York NY 10017-5514 Office Phone: 212-499-2050, 212-449-2083.

LEE, SUN MYUNG, physician; b. Seoul, Korea, July 9, 1940; d. Jong Suk and Soo Nam Lee; m. Hi Young; children: Sandra Shon, Grace, David. BS, Yonsei U., Seoul, 1961, MD, 1965; cert. in lay ministry, Whitworth Coll., 2001. Diplomate Am. Acad. Family Practice; ordained elder Korean Presbyn. Ch., 1999; commisioned lay pastor, 2003. Intern Riverside Methodist Hosp., Columbus, Oh., 1967-68; resident Veteran's Adminstrn. Hosp., Dayton, Oh., 1968-69; intern Riverside Meth. Hosp., Columbus, Ohio, 1966-67; resident Ohio State VA Hosp., Dayton, 1967-70; pvt. practice family medicine Drs. Lee & Lee PS, Spokane, Wash., 1974—. Mem. med. staff Ea. State Hosp., Medical Lake, Wash., 1972-74; pres. Drs. Lee & Lee P.S., 1974—. Author: Best Poetry of 1997, 1997; columnist Rainier Forum, Korea Post, 1995-96. Pres. Korean Lang. Sch., Spokane, 1974; Guwonsa, Korean Presbyn. Ch. Spokane, 1989-99; trustee Korean Assn. Inland Empire, Spokane, 1995; elder Korean Presbyn. Ch., Spokane, 1999, chair music ministry team, 2001; lay pastor, Mission Cmty. Ch., Spokane, Wash., 2003-04. Recipient Editors Choice award Nat. Libr. Poetry, 1996. Fellow Am. Acad. Family Physicians. Avocations: choral music, poetry, gardening. Office: Drs Lee and Lee PS 17 E Empire Ave Spokane WA 99207-1707 Office Phone: 509-328-3430. Business E-Mail: drsunleemd@yahoo.co.kr.

LEE, SUSAN, dentist, microbiologist; b. Jellico, Tenn., June 2, 1943; d. Roy Pickerell and Florida Maybell (Weaver) Savage; m. Joseph James Lee, Dec. 30, 1969 (dec. Dec. 1980); 1 child, Susan. BS, Cumberland Coll., 1965; DMD, U. Louisville, 1976. Lic. real estate agt., Ky. Asst. head dept. microbiology Norton Children's Hosp. (formerly Norton Meml. Infirmary, Louisville, 1964-69; head dept. microbiology St. Anthony's Hosp., Louisville, 1969-72; mgr. office, cons. Drs. Med. Plaza, Louisville, 1976-82; dentist Office Richard S. Bonn, DMD, Louisville, 1982-86; hygienist, dentist, cons. Office James Lewis, DMD, Louisville, 1986—. Cons. in field, 1982—. Named Hon. Order Ky. Cols. Mem. Louisville Soc. Physicians and Surgeons (sec., treas.), So. Med. Soc., Fraternal Order Police. Republican. Baptist. Avocations: tennis, gardening, boating, quilting, cooking. Home and Office: 6303 Crest Creek Ct Louisville KY 40241-5801 Personal E-mail: leemissmarco@aol.com.

LEE, SUSAN C., state legislator, lawyer; b. San Antonio, Tex., May 14, 1954; BA in Polit. Sci., U. Md., Coll. Park, 1976; JD, U. San Francisco Sch. of Law, 1982. Bar: DC 1983, Calif. 1983. Law clerk to Judge Richard Figone San Francisco Superior Ct., 1981—82; exec. dir. Nat. Dem. Council of Asian and Pacific Am., 1983—86; atty. Alexander, Bearden, Hairston, & Marks, LLP, 1993—97; of counsel Pena & Assoc., 1997—2001; legislative asst. to pres. Montgomery County Council, 2000—01; of counsel Gebhardt & Assoc., 2001—; mem. Md. Ho. of Delegates, 2002—, mem. judiciary com., 2002—, deputy majority whip, 2003—. Atty. US Commn. on Civil Rights, 1983—86, US Patent and Trademark Office, 1988—93; mem. US Patent and Trademark Public Adv. Com., Dept. of Commerce, 2000—01; co-founder Asian Pacific Am. Inst. for Congressional Studies, bd. dirs., 1995—2001. Mem.: Asian Pacific Am. Bar Assn. of Greater Wash. (pres. 1985), Nat. Asian Pacific Am. Bar Assn. Office: Md Ho of Delegates Lowe Ho Office Bldg Rm 221C 84 College Ave Annapolis MD 21401-1991

LEE, SUSAN S., mathematics educator; d. Max H. and Cora S. Stevens; m. Jeffrey S. Lee, Dec. 28, 1985; children: Whitney N., Jeffrey Alexander, Kacie B. BS, Palm Beach Atlantic Coll., Fla., 1985; M in Math. Edn., U. Ctrl. Fla., Orlando, 1999. Cert. tchr. Fla. Tchr. Liberty Mid. Sch., Orlando, 1986—2001, Timber Creek HS, Orlando, 2001—. Named Tchr. of Month, 2005, County Math. Tchr. of Yr., 2005; recipient Tchr. of Month, 2004; grantee, Supts.' Com., 1999, 2000, PTA, 2000, 2002, SAC, 1999, 2000; Darden grantee, 1999, 2000, 2001. Mem.: Nat. Coun. Tchrs. Math. Republican. Baptist. Office: Timber Creek HS 1001 Avalon Park Blvd Orlando FL 32828 Office Phone: 321-235-7800. E-mail: lees2@ocps.net.

LEE, TABIA (T. LEE), social studies educator; b. Lodi, Calif. d. Lloyd Laughlin and Ann Melton. BA in Sociology, U. Calif., Davis, 1999; MA in Edn., U. Phoenix, 2004; EdD, U. Calif., Irvine, 2006—, Calif. State U., LA, 2006—. Cert. Social Studies Tchr. Nat. Bd. Profl. Tchg. Stds., 2004. Tchr. LA Unified Sch. Dist., 1999—. Profl. reviewer Corwin Press, Thousand Oaks, 2004—. Mem.: ACLU, United Tchrs. LA, Internat. Reading Assn., Nat. Coun. Social Studies, Assn. Supervision and Curriculum Devel., Pi Lambda Theta. Avocations: reading, writing, music, dance, cooking. Personal E-mail: nbctresearch@aol.com.

LEE, THERESA K., chemicals executive; b. Gary, W.Va., Nov. 21, 1952; BS in Polit. Sci. and History, East Tenn. State U., 1974; JD, U. Tenn., 1977; postgrad., Harvard U., 1999. Staff atty. Legal Svcs. Upper East Tenn., 1977—79; sr. law clk. to Judge H. Emory Widener, Jr. U.S. Ct. Appeals (4th cir.), 1979—87; atty. Eastman Chem., 1987—91, asst. to pres., 1991—92, asst. sec., sr. counsel Tex. Eastman divsn., 1992—93, asst. sec., asst. gen. counsel legal dept. health safety and environ. group, 1993—95, asst. sec., asst. gen. counsel legal dept., corp. group, 1995—97, v.p., sec., asst. gen. counsel, 1997—2000, chief legal officer, 2000—; sr. v.p. Eastman Chem. Co., 2002—. Recipient Outstanding Alumna award, East Tenn. State U. Nat. Alumni Assn., 2002. Mem.: ABA (gen. counsel com.), Soc. Corp. Secs. & Governance Profls., Kingsport Bar Assn., Tenn. Bar Assn. (ho. of dels.), Am. Corp. Counsel Assn. (bd. dirs.). Office: Eastman Chem Co PO Box 431 Kingsport TN 37662-5280 Home: 200 S Wilcox Dr Kingsport TN 37660-5280

LEE, VIRGINIA M. -Y., medical educator, health science association administrator; PhD, U. Calif., San Francisco, 1973; MBA, U. Pa., 1984. Prof. dept. pathology and lab. medicine U. Pa. Sch. Medicine, co-dir. neurodegenerative disease rsch., 1992—2002, dir. neurodegenerative disease rsch., 2002—. Mem. grant rev. com. NIH Study Sect., others; mem. med./sci. adv. com. Alzheimer's Assn., S.E. Pa. Contbr. papers to profl. jours. Recipient John H. Ware 3d Chair for Alzheimer's Disease Rsch., Stanley N. Cohen Biomed. Rsch. award, 2000. Mem.: Inst. Medicine, Soc. for Neurosci. (elected councilor). Achievements include research in Alzheimer's disease; neuronal cytoskeleton. Office: Ctr for Neurodegenerative Disease Rsch 3d Fl Maloney Bldg 4283 3600 Spruce St Philadelphia PA 19104-4283*

LEE, VIVIAN S., radiologist; MD with hon., Harvard Med. Sch.; PhD, Oxford Univ. Gen. surgery resident Duke Univ., Chapel Hill, NC, 1992—93, chief resident diagnostic radiology, 1993—97; fell. in Body and Cardiovascular Magnetic Resonance Imaging NYU, 1997, mem. med. faculty, 1998—, named vice chmn. research, dept. Radiology, 2002, prof., depts. Radiology, Physiology, Neuro Science. Vis. prof., lectr. several nat. univ. Contbr. articles to numerous profl. med. jours.; mem. edl. bd.: Jour. Computer Assisted Tomography. Named one of 40 Under 40, Crain's NY Bus. Jour., 2006; recipient Orloff award, NYU, 2001. Mem.: Internat. Soc. Magnetic Resonance in Medicine (elected to bd. 2002, v.p. 2005, chmn. 2005). Office: Tisch Hospital Rusk 225 530 First Ave New York NY 10016*

LEE, WINNIE SITA, dentist; b. Loma Linda, Calif., Mar. 20, 1978; d. Stanley Tak and Rita Sook Lee. BA in Applied Scis., U. of Pacific, Calif., 2003; DDS, U. Pacific Sch. Dentistry, Calif., 2001. Dental Lic. Calif., 2001. Pre-clin. instr. U. Pacific Sch. Dentistry, San Francisco, 2002—04; dentist pvt. practice, Sunnyvale, 2003—. Presenter in field. Recipient Athena award, San Jose Alumni Panhellenic, Calif., 1996. Fellow: Internat. Congress Oral Implantologists, Am. Acad. Implant Dentistry (assoc.); mem.: Acad. Gen. Dentistry, Santa Clara Dental Soc., Alpha Lambda Delta. Avocations: running, exercise. Office Phone: 408-830-0888.

LEE, YEU-TSU MARGARET, surgeon, educator; b. Xian, Shensi, China, Mar. 18, 1936; m. Thomas V. Lee, Dec. 29, 1962 (div. 1987); 1 child, Maxwell M. AB in Microbiology, U. S.D., 1957; MD, Harvard U., 1961. Diplomate Am. Bd. Surgery. Assoc. prof. surgery Med. Sch., U. So. Calif., L.A., 1973-83; commd. lt. col. U.S. Army Med. Corps, 1983, advanced through grades to col., 1989; chief surg. oncology Tripler Army Med. Ctr., Honolulu, 1983-98; ret. U.S. Army, 1999; assoc. clin. prof. surgery Med. Sch., U. Hawaii, Honolulu, 1984-92, clin. prof. surgery, 1992—. Author: Malignant Lymphoma, 1974; author chpts to books; contbr. articles to profl. jours. Pres. Orgn. Chinese-Am. Women, L.A., 1981, Hawaii chpt., 1988; active U.S.-China Friendship Assn., 1991—. Decorated Nat. Def. Svc. medal, Army Commendation medal, Army Meritorious Svc. medal, Army Humanitarian Svc. medal; recipient Chinese-Am. Engrs. and Scis. Assn., 1987; named Sci. Woman Warrior, Asian-Pacific Womens Network, 1983. Mem. ACS, Soc. Surg. Oncology, Assn. Women Surgeons. Avocations: classical music, movies, hiking, ballroom dancing. Address: PO Box 29726 Honolulu HI 96820 E-mail: ytm_lee@hotmail.com.

LEECH, DIANE J., publisher; b. SI, NY, Nov. 8, 1943; d. Ivar S. Idzahl and Marion T. Immitt; m. Donald Schettini (div.); children: Alexis Schettini-Calabrese, Damien V. Schettini; m. Raymond E. Leech, Sept. 25, 1984. BS in Nursing, St. Francis, Trenton, NJ. Visiting nurse svc. supr. Pub. Health, NYC; sales mgr. Am. Jour. Nursing, NYC; assoc. publisher Jobson Publishing, NYC, M. Shanken Comm., NYC. Mem.: Am. Cancer Soc., Adv. Women NY. Republican. Roman Cath. Avocations: golf, antiques, movies, theater. Home: 448 E 20th St New York NY 10009 Office: M Shanken Comm 387 Park Ave New York NY 10016

LEECH, KATHARINE (KITTY LEECH), costume designer, educator; b. Phila., Jan. 10, 1957; d. Noyes and Louise Leech; m. Scot Campbell Galliher, Sept. 20, 1986. BA, U. Pa., Phila., 1979; MFA, NYU, NYC, 1983. Resident costume designer, costume coord. NYU Tisch Sch. Arts, NYC, 1984—2002; resident costume designer Opera Festival NJ, Princeton, 1985—88, Emelin Libr. Theatre, Mamaroneck, NY; tchr. Parson's Sch. Design, NYC, 1995—98, Playwright's Horizon's Theatre sch., 1999—2004; assoc. tchr. NYU Tisch Sch. Arts, 2002—. Chair costume design exam com. IATSE United Scenic Artists Local 829, NYC, 1988—; mem. Theatre Devel. Fund Costume Collection Adv. Com., 1995—; guest artist Am. Internat. Sch., Salzburg, Austria, 2002; guest lectr. Pratt Inst. Design, NYC, 2003—04. Costume designer (plays) Gross Indecency, The Three Trials Of Oscar Wilde, Waitng for My Man, The Novelist, A Romantic Portrait Of Jane Austen, The Gas Heart, (musical) Goblin Market, The Beautiful Lady written and directed by Elizabeth Swados, exhibitor (exhibition) The Leech- Gallagher Family Three Generations/ Five Artists, The Family Bus. Susan Teller Gallery, 2005, San Francisco Print Fair (Achenbach Found. Curator's Choice, 2002), World Stage Design; contbr. on line exhibition; costume designer (concert series) Lyrics and Lyricists, designer (window display) Greenberg and Hammer. Recipient award, U. Pa. Alumnae Club, 1979. Mem.: Soc. Children's Books Writers and Illustrators, NY Women Film and TV, Children's Book Illustrating Group. Avocations: children's book writing and illustration, photography. Office: New York University 721 Broadway New York NY 10003

LEECH, MARLA RENÉE, media specialist, educator; b. San Diego, Calif., Apr. 6, 1961; d. Thomas Franklin Leech and Margaret Vernon Blaisdel-Johnson. BA in Psychology, U. Calif., Davis, Calif., 1983; cert. in Film, U. Calif., Santa Cruz, Calif., 1987; MA in Broadcasting, U. Calif., San Francisco, Calif., 1993; B in Tchg., New Coll., 1996, MFA in Exptl. Performing Arts, 2006. Prof. broadcasting City Coll., San Francisco, 1996—. Self employed video prodr., editor, San Francisco, 1993—; prof. media Laney Coll., Oakland, Calif., 2003—; instr. online Nat. Acad. TV Arts and Scis., San Francisco, 1999; prodn. mgr. Mission Movie, San Francisco, 2003; bd. dirs. Women in Film and TV, 2004. Prodr.: (films) Breakin' The Glass, 1999, It's A Boy! Journeys From Female to Male, 2000; editor: (films) Love Makes a

Family, 1993, 2004, Strings Attached, 1998, Radical Harmonies, 2002 (Best Documentary award Frameline Fest, 2002); dir., writer, actor: CBS Reports: Tirade of the Transvisual, 2004; dir., actor: (plays) 8 Bullets, 2004; dir., writer, actor Knockers, 2005. Outdoor educator Environ. Travel Companions, San Francisco, 1999—; vol. Film Arts Found., San Francisco, 1993—95. Named Woman of Vision, Coll. San Mateo, 1999; grantee Sheldon Fay grant, Nat. Acad. TV Arts and Scis., 1993. Democrat. Avocations: drums, kayaking, guitar, politics, meeting people. Home: PO Box 460542 San Francisco CA 94146-0542 E-mail: orr40@hotmail.com.

LEEDER, ELLEN LISMORE, literature and language professor, literary critic; b. Vedado, Havana, Cuba, July 8, 1931; came to U.S., 1959; d. Thomas and Josefina (Jorge) Lismore; m. Robert Henry Leeder, Dec. 20, 1957 (dec. 1994); 1 child, Thomas Henry. D of Pedagogy, U. Havana, Cuba, 1955; MA, U. Miami, 1966, PhD, 1973. Lang. tchr. St. George's Sch., Havana, 1952-59; from part-time instr. to full prof. Spanish Barry U., Miami Shores, Fla., 1960—75, prof. Spanish, 1975—, chmn. dept. for lang., 1975-76, coord. fgn. lang., 1976—89; dir. Spanish immersion program, 1986-88. Part-time prof. Miami-Dade C.C., 1974-75; vis. prof. U. Madrid, 1982; prof. Forspro Program Studies Abroad, 1989, 90; cons. HEH, 1981-83; judge Asociación Críticos y Comentaristas del Arte, Miami, 1985—; judge Silver Knight Awards, 1979-83; oral examiner juror Dade County Pub. Schs., Miami, 1986-87. Author: El Desarraigo en Las Novelas de Angel María de Lera, 1978, Justo Sierra y el Mar, 1979, Dimensión Existencial en la Narrativa de Lera, 1992; co-editor: El arte narrativo de Hilda Perera, 1996. Bd. dirs. Vis. Nurse Assn., 1978-80. Mem. MLA, South Atlantic MLA, Am. Coun. Tchg. Fgn. Langs., Am. Assn. Tchrs. Spanish and Portuguese (pres. 1978-84, v.p. 1984-87, pres. Southeastern Fla. chpt.), Fla. Fgn. Assn., Círculo de Cultura Panamericano, Assn. Internat. Hispanistas, Assn. Cubana de Mujeres Universitarias (pres.), Cuban Women Club, Phi Alpha Theta, Kappa Delta Pi, Sigma Delta Xi, Alpha Mu Gamma, Coral Gables Country Club. Avocations: tennis, piano, singing, coin collecting/numismatics. Home: 830 SW 101st Ave Miami FL 33174-2836 Office: Barry Univ 11300 NE 2nd Ave Miami FL 33161-6695 E-mail: eleeder@mail.barry.edu.

LEEDOM-ACKERMAN, JOANNE, writer, educator; b. Dallas, Feb. 7, 1947; d. John Nesbit and Joanne (Shriver) Leedom; m. Peter Ackerman, June 3, 1972; children: Nathanael Leedom Ackerman, Elliot Leedom Ackerman. BA, Principia Coll., Elsah, Ill., 1968; MA in Creative Writing, Johns Hopkins U., 1969; MA in English, Brown U., 1974. Reporter The Christian Sci. Monitor, Boston, 1969-72; asst. prof. NYU, N.Y.C., 1976-77; lectr. CUNY, N.Y.C., 1974-76, Occidental Coll., L.A., 1978-81, UCLA Extension, 1985-87. Author: No Marble Angels, 1985, The Dark Path to the River, 1988. Bd. dirs. Save the Children, Conn., 1994-2000, Human Rights Watch, N.Y.C., 1999—, Internat. Crisis Group, Brussels and Washington, 1996—, Albert Einstein Inst., Boston, 1984-2001; trustee Brown U., 1996-2002 Johns Hopkins U., 1996—; mem. nat. adv. bd. Woodrow Wilson Nat. Fellowship Found., 1999-2002. Mem. PEN Am. Ctr. PEN USA West (pres. 1988-89), Authors Guild, English PEN, Internat. PEN (v.p. 1997—, internat. sec. 2004—), PEN Faulkner Found. (v.p., bd. dirs. 1998—), Poets and Writers (bd. dirs. 1985—), Internat. Ctr. for Journalists (bd. dirs.). E-mail: jlaajoanne@aol.com.

LEEDS, DOROTHY, author, lecturer, consultant; d. Hyman and Tonia (Perkins) Adelsberg; m. Arnold D. Weinstock, Dec. 19, 1955; children: Laura, Ian. BA, Adelphi U., 1955; MA, Columbia U., 1956. Tchr. Great Neck (N.Y.) High Sch., 1956-57, Martin Van Buren High Sch., N.Y.C., 1957-58; actress Broadway tour Stop the World I Want to Get Off, 1960-66; pres. Dorothy Leeds Knits, N.Y.C., also Ireland, 1970-77; sr. account exec. Chislovsky Design div. Grey Advt., N.Y.C., 1977-78; cons. Am. Mgmt. Assn., N.Y.C., 1978—. Bd. dirs. The Fashion Group, N.Y.C., 1980-82, The Lighthouse, N.Y.C., 1986—; cons. Mobil Oil, Citibank, Equitable, Digital Equipment, Conde Nast. Author: Smart Questions, 1987, Power Speak, 1988, Marketing Yourself, 1991, Smart Questions to Ask Your Doctor, Lawyer, Broker and Insurance Agent, 1992, Smart Questions to Ask About Your Children's Educations, 1994, Smart Questions for Savvy Shoppers, 1994; author, performer Good Lessons From Bad Women (in history). Mem. River Park Assn., N.Y.C., 1990—, Save the Children, 1985—, Concerned Citizens of Montauk, N.Y., 1969—; founder Theater for Learning. Mem. NATAS, ASTD, AFTRA, Nat. Speakers Assn., Nat. Women's Studies Assn. Home: 800 W End Ave 10A New York NY 10025-5467 Office: Organizational Techs 800 W End Ave 10A New York NY 10025-5467

LEEDS, NANCY BRECKER, sculptor, lyricist; b. N.Y.C., Dec. 22, 1924; d. Louis Julius and Dorothy (Faggen) Brecker; m. Richard Henry Leeds, May 9, 1945; children: Douglas Brecker, Constance Leeds Bennett. BA, Pine Manor Coll., 1944. Pres. Roseland Ballroom, N.Y.C., 1977-81. One-woman shows include Andrew Crispo Gallery, N.Y.C., 1979, Jeannette McIntyre Gallery Fine Arts, Palm Springs, Calif., 1987-88; exhibited in group shows at Bond St. Gallery, Great Neck, N.Y., Gallery Ranieri, N.Y.C., 1978, Country Art Gallery, 1984, Nature Conservatory Show, Country Art Gallery, 1985, Bonwit Teller, Manhasset, N.Y., 1985, Jeanette C. McIntyre Gallery, Palm Springs, Calif., 1987, The Empire Collection, N.Y.C., 1988, 89, Nassau County Mus. of Art, 1992, Chrysalis, East Hampton, 1998, Christmas Miniature Art Show at Chelsea, Nassau County Mus. of Art "Dance Dance", 2000; represented in permanent collections at New Orleans Mus. Art; writer lyrics for musical Great Scot, 1965, score for Scrooge Musical Theatre of Ariz., 1989; lyricist for popular music; lyricist for off-Broadway children's show, 2004. Trustee Floating Hosp., N.Y.C., 1975—, v.p.; mem. Upper Brookville (L.I., N.Y.) Planning Bd., 2000-01. Mem. ASCAP, Dramatist Guild, Songwriters Guild.

LEEDS, ROBIN LEIGH, transportation executive; b. Athens, Ohio, Jan. 4, 1942; d. Clarence Thomas and Jean B. (Foster) Flowers; m. John A Cornwell, Oct. 28, 1957 (div. Jan. 1968); children: Michael John, Brian Arthur; m. Barry H. Leeds, Apr. 20, 1968; children: Brett Ashley, Leslie Robin. BS in Edn., Ohio U., 1967. Cultural arts dir. Regional Sch. Dist. # 10, Burlington, Conn., 1978-81; exec. dir. Conn. Sch. Transp. Assn., Newington, Conn., 1982, ret. Exec. sec. N.E. Sch. Transp. Safety Inst., West Hartford, 1987—; regulatory liaison Nat. Sch. Transp. Assn., Alexandria, Va., 2000-; columnist Sch. Transp. News, Redondo Beach, Calif., 2002—; bd. dir., Pupil Transportation Safety Inst., Syracuse, NY, 2003-, chmn. Conn. Sch. Transp. Safety Commn., 1990-1994; state del. Nat. Standards Congress, Warrensburg, 1990, 95, 2000; mem. Gov.'s Motor Carrier Adv. Com., Conn., 1989—, Dept. Motor Vehicles Safety Task Force, Conn., 1991-96. Contbr. articles to profl. jours.; mem. adv. bd. Sch. Transp. News, 1994—. Chmn. gifted edn. task force, Regional Sch. Dist., 1976-78; arbitrator Dept. Consumer Protection, Conn., 2002—. Named Contractor of Yr., Sch. Bus Fleet Mag., 1990, Exec. of Yr., Conn. Soc. Assn. Execs., 1993. Mem. Nat. Sch. Transp. Assn., Nat. Assn. Pupil Transp., Nat. Safety Coun., Conn. Soc. Assn. Execs. (Assn. Exec. of Yr. award). Avocation: ballroom dancing. Home: 36 Church St Noank CT 06340 E-mail: leeds@costa.necoxmail.com.

LEEDS, SUSANNE, special education educator, writer; d. Joel and Hilda (Reiss) Leibowitz. BA, Queens Coll. of CUNY, 1972; MA, NYU, 1978. Cert. spl. edn. tchr. N.Y., 1978. Spl. edn. tchr. N.Y.C. Bd. Edn., 1972—82; tchr. Palm Beach County Sch. Bd., Boca Raton, Fla., 1994—. Author: (poem) Illumination (In Honor of Ethiopian Jews), 1999, At The U.S. Holocaust Meml. Mus., 2002, Gone (In Memory of Victims of 9/11), 2001; contbr. numerous poems publ. in jours. and mags.; singer: (performed with Barry Harris Jazz Ensemble) Beacon Theater, N.Y.C., 1984. Recipient 3rd prize Vi Bagliore Mem. award, Nat. League Am. Pen Women, 2000, 1st prize, 11th Ann. Sylvia Wolens Jewish Heritage Writing Competition, 2002, finalist, 15th Ann. Robert Penn Warren Poetry awards, 2002, 1st prize Grandmother Earth Nat. Writing awards (Haiku category), 2002, Wall of Tolerance honoree, Civil Rights Meml. Ctr., 2005. Mem.: Nat. Fedn. State Poetry Socs., Fla. State Poetry Assn., Nat. League of Am. Pen Women. Avocations: music, singing, opera, piano. Home: 6507 Royal Manor Cir Delray Beach FL 33484-2411 Personal E-mail: susanneleeds@yahoo.com.

LEEDY, EMILY L. FOSTER (MRS. WILLIAM N. LEEDY), retired education educator, consultant; b. Jackson, Ohio, Sept. 24, 1921; d. Raymond S. and Grace (Garrett) Foster; MEd, Ohio U., 1957; postgrad. Ohio State U., 1956, Mich. State U., 1958-59, Case Western Res. U., 1963-65; m. William N. Leedy, Jan. 1, 1943; 1 son. Dwight A. tchr. Frankfort (Ohio) schs., 1941-46, Ross County Schs., Chillicothe, Ohio, 1948-53; elem. and supervising tchr. Chillicothe City Schs., 1953-56; dean of girls, secondary tchr. Berea City Schs., 1956-57; vis. tchr. Parma City Schs., 1957-59; counselor Homewood-Flossmoor High Sch., Flossmoor, Ill., 1959-60; teaching fellow Ohio U., 1960-62; asst. prof. edn., 1962-64; assoc. prof., counselor Cuyahoga Community Coll., 1964-66; dean of women Cleve. State U., 1966-67, assoc. dean student affairs, 1967-69; guidance dir. Cathedral Latin Sch., 1969-71; dir. women's service div. Ohio Bur. Employment Svcs., 1971-83; cons. in edn., 1983-87. Mem. adv. com. S.W. Community Info. Svc., 1959-60; youth com. S.W. YWCA, 1963-70, chmn., 1964-70, bd. mgmt., 1964-70; group svcs. coun. Cleve. Welfare Fedn., 1964-66; chmn. Met. YWCA Youth Program study com., 1966, bd. dirs., 1966-72, v.p., 1967-68; chmn. adv. coun. Ohio State U. Sch. Home Econs., 1977-80, chmn., 1978-80. Named Cleve. area Woman of Achievement, 1969; named to Ohio Women's Hall of Fame, 1979, Chillicothe Ross Women's Hall of Fame, 1988; recipient Outstanding Contbn. special award Nat. Assn. Commns. for Women, 1983, Meritorious Svc. award Nat. Assn. Women Deans, Adminstrs. and Counselors, 1984. Mem. AAUW (Berea-Parma br. v.p. 1995-97), Am., Northeastern Ohio (sec. 1958-59, exec. com. 1963-64, pub. rel. chmn. 1962-64, newsletter chmn., editor 1963-64, del. nat. assembly 1959-63) personnel and guidance assns., LWV, Am. Assn. Retired Persons (Ohio women's initiative spokesperson 1987-89, state legis. com. 1989-90, AARP/VOTE state coord. Ohio 1990-94), Nat. Assn. Women Deans and Counselors (publs. com. 1967-69, profl. employment practices com. 1980-82, Meritorious Svc. award 1984), Ohio (program chmn. 1967, editor Newsletter 1968-71), Cleve. Counselors Assn. (pres. 1966), Zonta Internat. (exec. bd. 1968-70, treas. 1970-72, chmn. dist. V Status of Women 1980-81), Nat. Assn. Commns. for Women (dir. 1980-81, sec. 1981-83), Rio Grande Coll. Alumni Assn. (Atwood Achievement award 1975), Bus. and Profl. Women's Club (Nike award 1973, Berea treas. 1996-97), Ohio Retired Tchrs. Assn., Svc. Corps of Retired Execs. Delta Kappa Gamma, Women's City Club (Cleve.). Home: 699 Rocky Rd Chillicothe OH 45601

LEEGE, LISSA MARIA, biology professor; b. Columbia, Mo., Apr. 14, 1966; d. David and Patricia Leege; m. Frank Robert D'Arcangelo, June 26, 1999; 1 child, Micah Anthony D'Arcangelo. BA with distinction, St. Olaf Coll., Northfield, Minn., 1984—88; PhD in Botany, Mich. State U., East Lansing, 1992—97. Vis. asst. prof. dept. plant biology Ohio State U., Columbus, 1997—98; asst. prof. biology Ga. So. U., Statesboro, 1998—2004, assoc. prof. biology, 2004—; faculty U. Mich., Pellston, 1999—2001. Author: (lab. manual) Biological Science 110 Laboratory Manual; contbr. articles to profl. jours. Sec. pub. rels., ch. coun. St. Pauls Luth. Ch., Statesboro, 2002—06; pres. Statesboro chpt. Thrivent Fin. Lutherans, 2003—06; chair recycling com. Keep Bulloch Beautiful, Statesboro, Ga., 2001—06; mem., bd. advisors edn. com. Ga. So. Bot. Garden, Statesboro, 2001—06. Rsch. grant, Battelle Endowment Tech. & Human Affairs, Ohio State U., 2000, Nat. Pk. Svc., 2000—02, Mich. Dept. Natural Resources, 2004—05, Ga. Dept. Natural Resources, 2004—, US Fish & Wildlife Svc., 2005—06, Ga. Dept. Natural Resources, 2005—06, NSF, 2005—, Ga. So. U. Rsch. Found., 2005—06, NSF, 2006. Mem.: Ga. Acad. Sci., Bot. Soc. Am., Ecol. Soc. Am., Blue Key Nat. Honor Soc., Sigma Xi, Phi Beta Kappa. Lutheran. Achievements include research in invasive plant/rare plant interactions and model plant population dynamics. Office: Ga So Univ Biology Dept Box 8042 Statesboro GA 30460 Business E-Mail: leege@georgiasouthern.edu.

LEE JOEL, KATIE See JOEL, KATIE

LEEK, PRISCILLA, social sciences educator; BA, Brigham Young U., Provo, Utah, 1984; MA, Grand Canyon U., Phoenix, 2003. Cert. Educator State Utah, 1984. Tchr. social sci. Springville HS, Utah, 1984—85, 1987—, Spring Branch Jr. HS, Houston, 1985—86, Springville Jr. HS, 1986—87. Justice of peace, Springville, 1978—84. Mem.: APA. Office: Springville High School 1205 E 900 S Springville UT 84062 Office Phone: 801-489-2870. E-mail: p.leek@nebo.edu.

LEEKLEY, MARIE VALPOON, b. Honolulu, Mar. 28, 1941; d. Amil Richard and Florence Haruko (Soken) V.; m. John Darwin Leekley, Jr., June 26, 1965; children: Katherine Joan, Tracy Ann Kehaunani. BS, Carroll Coll., Waukesha, Wis., 1963; MEd, Nat. Coll. Edn., Evanston, Ill., 1990; PhD, Marquette U., 2002. Dir. Christian edn. Kamehameha Sch. for Girls, Honolulu, 1963-64; elem. tchr. Milw. Pub. Schs., 1965-67; vol. Marianas Edn. Dept. Peace Corps, Saipan, Mariana Islands, 1967-69, dist. coord. tchr. edn., 1969-71; tchr. Ethan Allen Sch. for Boys, Wales, Wis., 1977-96. Tchr. adult basic edn. Waukesha County Tech. Coll., Pewaukee, Wis., 1977—. Mem. Menomonee Falls (Wis.) Pub. Schs. Bd. Edn., 1990-2004; bd. dirs. Comprehensive Ednl. Svcs. Agys., West Allis, Wis., 1991-96 Recipient vol. appreciation award Greater Menomonee Falls Com., 1991, Boardmanship award Wis. Assn. Sch. Bds., 1991, 92, 93, Disting. Svc. award Menomonee Falls Sch. Dist., Human Rels. award, 2004, Friend of Edn. award, 2004, Achievement in Edn. award Waukesha County C. of C., 2005; named Edn. Leader of Yr. AAUW, 1996. Mem. ASCD, Correctional Edn. Asn., Nat. Sch. Bd. Assn., Wis. Assn. Adult and Continuing Edn., Wis. Vocat. Assn., Wis. Edn. Assn. Methodist. Home: W148N7590 Woodland Dr Menomonee Falls WI 53051-4522 Office: Waukesha County Tech Coll 327 E Broadway Waukesha WI 53186-5008 Office Phone: 262-695-2523. E-mail: mleekley@wctc.edu.

LEEMAN, EVE, psychiatrist; b. Boston, Mass., May 29, 1960; d. Cavin Philip and Susan (Epstein) Leeman; m. Alberto Jose Villar, June 23, 1990; children: Elena, Claudia, Alejandro. BA magna cum laude, Harvard U., 1982, MD, 1987. Diplomate Am. Bd. Psychiatry and Neurology. Intern Overlook Hosp., Summit, NJ; psychiat. chief resident Columbia U., NYC, 1991; pvt. practice psychiatry NYC, 1991—; instr. clin. psychiatry Columbia U., NYC, 1991—94, asst. clin. prof. psychiatry, 1994—; psychiatrist Washington Heights Cmty. Svc., NYC, 1991—2000. Rschr. NY State Psychiat. Inst. Rsch. Found., NYC, 2000—04; psychotherapy supr. residency program NY State Psychiat. Inst., NYC, 1991—; presenter in field. Contbr. revs., articles to profl. publs. Recipient Horowitz award for clin. excellence, NY State Psychiat. Inst., 1991; Laughlin fellow, Am. Coll. Psychiatrists, 1990. Mem.: Am. Acad. Psychoanalysis and Psychodynamic Psychiatry, Am. Psychiat. Assn. Avocations: tennis, jogging, reading. Office: 161 Fort Washington Ave New York NY 10032 Office Phone: 212-781-2237. Business E-Mail: el7@columbia.edu.

LEEMAN, SUSAN EPSTEIN, neuroscientist, educator; b. Chgo., May 9, 1930; d. Samuel and Dora (Gubernikoff) Epstein; m. Cavin Leeman (div.); children: Eve, Raphael, Jennifer. BA, Goucher Coll., 1951; MA, Radcliffe Coll., 1954, PhD, 1958; DS (hon.), SUNY, Utica, 1992; degree (hon.), Goucher Coll., 1993. Instr. Harvard Med. Sch., Boston, 1958-59; postdoctoral fellow Brandeis U., Waltham, Mass., 1959-62, 62-66; rsch. assoc., adj. ast. prof., asst. rsch. prof. Brandieis U., Waltham, Mass., 1966-68, 68-71; asst. prof. Harvard Med. Sch., 1972-73, assoc. prof., 1973-80; prof. U. Mass. Med. Ctr., Worcester, 1980-92, dir. interdept. neurosci. program, 1984-92; prof. dept. pharmacology Boston U. Sch. Medicine, 1992—. Burroughs Wellcome vis. prof. U.Ky., 1992. Fogarty scholar NAS, 1994; recipient Women in Sci. award N.Y. Acad., 1995. Mem. NAS (197th Lilly lectr. 1994, Fred Conrad Koch award 1994, Women in Sci. award 1995), Am. Acad. Arts and Scis. (Isadore Rosenberg lectr. 1999). Office: Boston U Sch Medicine Dept Pharmacology 715 Albany St # R-616 Boston MA 02118-2526 Office Phone: 617-638-4364. E-mail: sleeman@bu.edu.

LEEPER, KATHLEEN MARIE, elementary school educator; b. L.A., Dec. 5, 1962; d. Carl L. and Mary E. (Parker)_L. BA, Calif. Poly. Inst., 1985, MEd, 1988. Cert. adminstrn. 2001. Tchr. New Lexington Sch., El Monte, Calif., 1985—2001; asst. prin. Frank M. Wright Elem. Sch., El Monte, Calif., 2001—06; co-prin. Columbia Sch., El Monte, 2006—. Mem. leadership team New Lexington Sch.; tchr. transition English, 1990-2001; grant writer El Monte City Sch. Dist., 1990-2001. Sunday sch. tchr. El Monte 1st Presbyn. Ch., 1980-2001, elder; mem. Village Presbyn. Ch., 2005-. Mem. Delta Kappa Gamma. Presbyterian. Avocations: travel, reading, swimming, walking, spanish.

LEES, MARJORIE BERMAN, biochemist, neuroscientist; b. NYC, Mar. 17, 1923; d. Isadore I. and Ruth (Rogalsky) Berman; m. Sidney Lees, Sept. 17, 1946; children: David E., Andrew, Eliot. BA, Hunter Coll., 1943; MS, U. Chgo., 1945; PhD, Harvard U./Radcliffe Coll., 1951. Assoc. biochemist, asst. biochemist McLean Hosp., Belmont, Mass., 1953-62; rsch. assoc. Dartmouth Med. Sch., Hanover, 1962-66; assoc. biochemist McLean Hosp., Belmont, 1966-76; prin. and sr. rsch. assoc. Harvard Med. Sch., Boston, 1966-85; biomed. scientist E.K. Shriver Ctr., Waltham, Mass., 1976-98; prof. biochemistry (neurology) Harvard Med. Sch., Boston, 1985-94, prof. emerita, 1994—; biochemist Mass. Gen. Hosp., Boston, 1976-98; assoc. dir. biochemistry E.K. Shriver Ctr., Waltham, 1982-90, dir. biochemistry, 1990-93, assoc. dir. mental retardation rsch. ctr., 1994-97, sr. biomed. sci., 1998—; prof. emerita U. Mass. Med. Sch., 1999—. Mem. adv. com. biomed. and behavioral rsch. NASA/NIH, 1993—; mem. sci. adv. com. Nat. Multiple Sclerosis Soc., 1988-93. Chief editor Jour. of Neurochemistry, 1986-90; author (with others) books; contbr. articles to profl. jours. Mem. adv. coun. Nat. Inst. Neurological Disorders, Bethesda, Md., 1979-82; chmn. Radcliffe Grad. Soc., Cambridge, Mass., 1978-80. Predoctoral fellow USPHS, 1947-50, postdoctoral fellow Am. Cancer Soc., 1951-53; Javits Neurosci. grantee NIH, 1983-90, 91-97, prin. grantee NIH, 1962-98; named to Hunter Coll. Hall of Fame, 1982. Mem. Am. Soc. Biochemistry and Molecular Biology, Internat. Soc. Neurochemistry, Am. Soc. Neurochemistry (treas. 1975-81, pres. 1983-85), Soc. for Neurosci., Am. Assn. Neuropathology (assoc.), Phi Beta Kappa. Office: Shriver Ctr U Mass Med Sch Neurobiology Program 200 Trapelo Rd Waltham MA 02452-6332 Office Phone: 781-642-0129. Business E-Mail: marjorie.lees@umassmed.edu.

LEESE, JESSICA, language educator; b. New Haven, Conn., May 21, 1980; d. John and Julie Leese. MA in Edn., U. Conn., Storrs, 2003. Tchr. Spanish Wethersfield H.S., Conn., 2003—04; spl. edn. paraprofl. Clark Ln. Mid. Sch., Waterford, 2004—05; tchr. English as 2d lang. k-12 Putnam Pub. Schs., Putnam, 2005—. New Eng. scholar, U. Conn., 2003. Mem.: Conn. Edn. Assn., Conn. Tchrs. English to Spkrs. Other Langs. Avocations: travel, theater, dance, reading. Home: 2 Riverside Street Putnam CT 06260 Office Phone: 860-798-4632.

LEESON, JANET CAROLINE TOLLEFSON, cake specialties company executive; b. L'Anse, Mich., May 23, 1933; d. Harold Arnold and Sylvia Aino (Makikangas) Tollfeson; children by previous marriage: Warren Scott, Debra Delores; m. Raymond Harry Leeson, May 20, 1961 (dec. Jan. 2002); 1 child, Barry Raymond. Student, Prairie State Coll., Chgo. Heights, Ill., 1970—76; grad., Wilton Sch. Cake Decorating, Woodridge, Ill., 1974, Cosmopolitan Sch. Bus., Chgo., 1980. Mgr. Peak Svc. Cleaners, Chgo., 1959; co-owner Ra-Ja-Lee TV, Harvey, Ill., 1961-66; founder, head fgn. trade dept. Wilton Enterprises, Chgo., 1969-75; tchr. cake decorating J.C. Penney Co., Matteson, Ill., 1975; office mgr. Pat Carpenter Assocs., Highland, Ind., 1975; pres. cake supplies and cake sculpture and decorating co. Leeson's Party Cakes, Inc., Tinley Park, Ill., 1975—. Lectr. in field. Active Boy Scouts Am. and Girl Scouts U.S., 1957-63; bd. dirs. Whittier PTA, 1962-70, South Suburban Parkinson's Support Group, 1983—; adv. bd. Suburban Parkinson's Support Group, 1983—; active Bremen Twp. Rep. Com. Recipient numerous awards for cake sculpture and decorating, 1970—. Mem. Internat. Cake Exploration Soc. (charter, Outstanding Mem. Ill. 1984), Retail Bakers Am., Chgo. Area Retail Bakers Assn. (1st pl. in regional midwest wedding cake competition 1978, 80, 1st pl. nat. 1982, others), Am. Bus. Women's Assn. (chpt. publicity chmn., hospitality chmn. 1982-83, membership chmn. 1988-90, Woman of Yr. 1986), Ingalls Meml. Hosp. Aux., Lupus Found. Am. Lutheran. Home and Office: 6713 163rd Pl Tinley Park IL 60477-1717

LEET, MILDRED ROBBINS, social welfare administrator, consultant; b. NYC, Aug. 9, 1922; d. Samuel Milton and Isabella (Zeitz) Elowsky; m. Louis J. Robbins, Feb. 23, 1941 (dec. 1970); children: Jane, Aileen; m. Glen Leet, Aug. 9, 1974 (dec. 1998). BA, NYU, 1942; LHD (hon.), Coll. Human Svcs., 1988; LLD honoris causa, Marymount Coll., Tarrytown, N.Y., 1991; HHD, Lynn U., 1993; D Humanitarian Svc. (hon.), Norwich U., 1994; DHL, Conn. Coll., 1996; DHL (hon.), Wilson Coll., 2003. Pres. women's div. United Cerebral Palsy, N.Y.C., 1951-52, bd. dirs., 1953-55; rep. Nat. Coun. Women U.S. at UN, 1957-64, 1st v.p., 1959-64, pres., 1964-68, hon. pres., 1968-70; sec., v.p. conf. group U.S. Nat. Orgns. at UN, 1961-64, 76-78, vice chmn., sec., 1962-64, mem. exec. com., 1961-65, chmn. hospitality info. svc., 1960-66; vice chmn. exec. com. NGO's UN Office Public Info., 1976-78, chmn. ann. conf., 1977; chmn. com. on water, desertification, habitat and environment Conf. NGO's with consultative status with UN/ECOSOC, 1976-77; mem. exec. com. Internat. Coun. Women, 1960-73, v.p., 1970-73; chmn. program planning com., women's com. OEO, 1967-72; chmn. com. on natural disasters N.Am. Com. on Environment, 1973-77; N.Y. State chmn. UN Day, 1975; ptnr. Leet & Leet (cons. women in devel.), 1979—98. Co-founder Trickle Up Program, 1979—, pres., 1991—2000, chair, 2001—; mem. task force on Africa UN, 1995—. Contbr. articles to profl. jours.; editor UN Calendar & Digest, 1959-64, Measure of Mankind, 1963; editorial bd.: Peace & Change. Co-chmn. Vols. for Stevenson, N.Y.C., 1956; vice chmn. task force Nat. Dem. Com., 1969-72; commr. N.Y. State Commn. on Powers Local Govt., 1970-73; chmn. Coll. for Human Svcs. Audrey Cohen Coll., 1985-2000; former mem. bd. dirs. Am. Arbitration Assn., New Directions, Inst. for Mediation and Conflict Resolution, Spirit of Stockholm; bd. dirs. Hotline Internat.; v.p. Save the Children Fedn., 1986-93 rep. Internat. Peace Acad. at UN, 1974-77, Internat. Soc. Cmty. Devel., 1977-98, del. at large 1st Nat. Women's Conf., Houston, 1977; chmn. task force on internat. interdependence N.Y. State Women's Meeting, 1977; mem. Task Force on Poverty, 1977; chmn. Task Force on Women, Sci. and Tech. for Devel., 1978; U.S. del. UN Status of Women Commn., 1978, UN Conf. Sci. and Tech. for Devel., 1979, Brazzaville Centennial Celebration, 1980; mem. global adv. bd. Internat. Expn. Rural Devel., 1981—; mem. Coun. Internat. Fellows U. Bridgeport, 1982-88; trustee overseas edn. fund LWV, 1983-91; v.p. U.S. Com. UN Devel. Fund for Women, 1983-94, trustee, 1998-2000; mem. Nat. Consultative Com. Planning for Nairobi, 1984-85; co-chmn. women in devel. com. Interaction, 1985-91; mem. com. of cooperation Interam. Commn. of Women, 1986; bd. dirs. Internat. Devel. Conf., 1991-2001; mem. UN task force informal sector devel. Africa, 1995—. Recipient Crystal award Coll. Human Svcs., 1983, Ann. award Inst. Mediation and Conflict Resloution, 1985, Woman of Conscience award Nat. Coun. Women, 1996, Temple award Inst. Noetic Scis., 1987, Presdl. End Hunger award, 1987, Giraffe award Giraffe Project, 1987, Woman of the World award Eng.'s Women Aid, 1989, Mildred Robbins Leet award Interaction, 1995; co-recipient Rose award World Media Inst., 1987, Human Rights award UN Devel. Fund for Women, 1987, Leadership award U.S. Peace Corps, Woman of Vision award N.Y.C. NOW, 1990, Matrix award Women in Comm., Inc., Spirit of Enterprise award Rolex Industries, 1990, Ann. Bush's Ann. Points of Light award, 1992, Internat. Humanity award ARC Overseas Assn., 1992, Excellence award U.S. Com. for UNIFEM, 1992, Champion of Enterprise award Avon, 1994, Achievement award NYU-Washington Sq. Coll. Alumni. Assn., 1995, Lizette H. Sarnoff Vol. Svc. award Yeshiva U., 1996, Disting. Svc. award N.Y. African Studies Assn., 1996, Disting. Svc. award 50th Anniversary United Cerebral Palsy, 1997, Eleanor Schnurr award UN Assn./USA, Women of Distinction honoree Birmingham So. Coll., Spirit award Nat. Assn. Women Bus. Owners, 1998, Nat. Caring Inst. award, 2001, Nat. Women's Hall of Fame, 2003, Met. Coll. NY Leadership award, 2004, Philippine Kalayan award, 2004, Global Summit of Women Internat. Hall of Fame award, 2005. Mem. AAAS, Women's Forum, Coun. on Fgn. Rels., Cosmopolitan Club, Princeton Club. Home and Office: 54 Riverside Dr New York NY 10024-6509 E-mail: millieleet@aol.com.

LEETE, ANGELA MARIE, athletic trainer, educator; b. Oelwein, Iowa, Aug. 17, 1979; d. Donald R. and Barbara A. Ehlers; m. Daniel Charter Leete, Aug. 3, 2002; 1 child, Payton Eileen. BS in Exercise and Sports Sci., Iowa State U., Ames, 2002; MS in Health, Phys. Edn. and Recreation, Emporia (Kans.) State U., 2006. Lic. athletic trainer Iowa. Asst. athletic trainer Wartburg Coll., Waverly, Iowa, 2003—04, Upper Iowa U., Fayette, 2004—06, dir. athletic tng. edn, asst. prof. athletic tng., 2006—. Mem.: Nat. Athletic Trainers Assn. (cert. athletic trainer). Office: Upper Iowa U 605 Washington St Fayette IA 52142 Office Phone: 563-425-3355. E-mail: leetea@uiu.edu.

LEETE, ELISABETH BOURQUIN, retired language educator; b. Geneva, Oct. 18, 1929; arrived in U.S., 1953; d. Marcel and Dora Brooke Bourquin; m. Gurdon W. Leete, July 6, 1963 (dec.); 1 child, Lucy. Student, U. Geneva, 1951; BA in French, U. Mass., 1976. NY corr. France-Soir, Paris, 1958—68; French tchr. Sch. Internat. Living, Putney, Vt., Hampshire Coll., Amherst, Mass., Greenfield (Mass.) CC, Acad. Charlemont, Md., 1981—90; ret., 1990. Contbr. articles to newspapers; author: Learn French the Fast and Fun Way, 1981. Hospice vol. Avocations: cello, yoga, writing, knitting, reading. Home: 1484 Hawley Rd Ashfield MA 01330

LEEVES, JANE, actress; b. Ilford Essex, England, Apr. 18, 1961; m. Marshall Coben, Dec. 21, 1996; 2 children. Actress (TV series) The Benny Hill Show, 1983-84, Double Trouble, 1984, Throb, 1986-88, Murphy Brown, 1989-1993, Just Deserts, 1992, Frasier 1993-2004 (Emmy award nom. sup. actress, 1998, SAG award outstanding performance ensemble, 2000); (TV movies) Red Dwarf, 1992, Pandora's Clock, 1996, Just Deserts, 1999; (films) The Hunger, 1983, To Live and Die in L.A., 1985, Miracle on 34th Street, 1994, The Meaning of Life, 1983, Mr. Write, 1994, James and the Giant Peach (voice), 1996, Don't Go Breaking My Heart, 1999, Music of the Heart, 1999, Adventures of Tom Thumb and Thumbelina (voice), 2002, The Event, 2003, Garfield: A Tail of Two Kitties (voice), 2006; (TV guest appearances) Murder, She Wrote, 1987, It's a Living, 1989, Hooperman, 1989, Mr. Belvedere, 1989, My Two Dads, 1990, Who's the Boss?, 1990, Blossom, 1991, Seinfeld, 1992-93, 98, Caroline in the City, 1995, Hercules (voice), 1998, The Simpsons, 2003; (Broadway show) Cabaret, 2002. Avocations: reading, cooking, sports, dance. Office: Talent Group Inc 5670 Wilshire Blvd #820 Los Angeles CA 90036-5602*

LEE-WHITING, THERESA A., music educator, conductor; d. Warren E. Lee and Haroldean R. Schmidt, Carol Lee (Stepmother) and William Schmidt (Stepfather); m. Rodney Buell Whiting, Jan. 23, 1993 (dec. Jan. 10, 2002); 1 child, Drucilla Mary Whiting. MusB, W.Va. U., Morgantown, 1976—81; MusM in Choral Conducting & Music History & Lit., Binghamton U., NY, 2001—05. Choral music tchr. Hancock Ctrl. Schs., NY, 1999—2002; dir. music ministries Tabernacle United Meth. Ch., Binghamton, 2002—; music dir. German Choir of Binghamton, 2004—; adj. music instr. Binghamton U., 2005—; adj. instr. music Broome CC, Binghamton, 2006—. Cmty. theater dir., Delhi, NY, 1995—98; pvt. voice tchr., NY, 2003. Massed choir conductor 34th Triennial Saengerfest of NY, NY, 2006. Mem. German Club Birmington, 2004—. Fellow Grad. Tchg. Assistantship, Binghamton U., 2002—04. Fellow: Am. Choral Dirs. Assn. Achievements include being the first female conductor in 109 year history. Avocations: yoga, theater. Office: Tabernacle United Methodist Ch 83 Main St Binghamton NY 13905 Office Phone: 607-723-8983. Personal E-mail: tleewhiting@earthlink.net.

LEFCO, KATHY NAN, law librarian; b. Bethesda, Md., Feb. 24, 1949; d. Ted Lefco and Dorothy Rose (Fox) Harris; m. Stephen Gary Katz, Sept. 2, 1973 (div. May 1984); m. John Alfred Price, Nov. 24, 1984 (dec. Jan. 1989); m. Richard Louis Edmonds, Apr. 12, 2002. BA, U. Wis., 1971; MLS, U. Wis., Milw., 1975. Rsch. asst. Ctr. Auto Safety, Washington, 1971-73; asst. to dir. Ctr. Consumer Affairs, Milw., 1973-74; legis. libr. Morgan, Lewis & Bockius, Washington, 1976-78; dir. library Mulcahy & Wherry, Milw., 1978; paralegal Land of Lincoln Legal Assistance, Springfield, Ill., 1979-80; reference and interlibrary loan libr. So. Ill. U. Sch. Medicine, Springfield, 1980; reader svcs. libr. Wis. State Law Library, Madison, 1981-83; ref. libr. Mudge Rose Guthrie Alexander & Ferdon, N.Y.C., 1983-85; sr. legal info. specialist Cravath, Swaine & Moore, N.Y.C., 1985-86; asst. libr. Kaye, Scholer, Fierman, Hays & Handler, N.Y.C., 1986-89; head libr. Parker Chapin Flattau & Klimpl, N.Y.C., 1989-94; dir. libr. svcs. Winston & Strawn LLP, Chgo., 1994—. Author: (with others) Mobile Homes: The Low-Cost Housing Hoax, 1973. Mem. Chgo. Assn. Law Librs., Am. Assn. Law Librs. Democrat. Jewish. Avocations: biking, backgammon, politics. Home: 543 Oakdale Ave Glencoe IL 60022 Office: Winston & Strawn LLP 35 W Wacker Dr Ste 4200 Chicago IL 60601-1695 Office Phone: 312-558-5813. E-mail: klefco@winston.com.

LEFEVRE, CAROL BAUMANN, psychologist; b. Pierron, Ill., Nov. 26, 1924; d. Berhard Robert and Eunice Leone Baumann; m. Perry Deyo LeFevre, Sept. 14, 1946; children: Susan LeFevre Hook, Judith Ann LeFevre-Levy, Peter Gerret. AA, Stephens Coll., 1944; MA in Sociology, U. Chgo., 1948, MST, 1965, PhD in Human Devel., 1971. Asst. tchr. Chgo. Theol. Sem. Nursery Sch., 1962-63, U. Chgo., Lab. Sch., 1965-66; asst. prof. psychology St. Xavier Coll., Chgo., 1970-74, assoc. prof., 1974-86, acting chmn. dept. psychology, 1970-71, chmn. dept. psychology, 1971-77, asst. dir. Inst. Family Studies, 1973-82, dir., 1982-85; intern in clin. psychology with Adlerian pvt. practitioner, Chgo., 1973-75; pvt. practice clin. psychology, Chgo., 1975-85, ret., 1985; speaker in field. Author, researcher on subjects including returning women grad. students' changing self-conceptions, women's roles, inner city children's perceptions of sch., aging and religion. Pub. Health Svc. tng. grantee NIMH, 1969. Mem. Phi Beta Kappa. Mem. United Ch. of Christ. Home: 1314 Foulkeways Gwynedd PA 19436-1032

LEFEVRE, GERALDINE, librarian; b. Seminole, Okla., Nov. 18, 1925; came to U.S., 1959, naturalized, 1979; d. Hernan Cecil and Mary Elizabeth (Hill) Sullivan; m. Matthias Damian LeFevre III, Jan. 17, 1948 (dec. Dec. 1972); 1 child, Kathleen Ed. in library sci., U. Okla., 1947. Children's librarian San Antonio Pub. Library, 1950-55, librarian-in-charge, 1955-61, children's coordinator, 1961-70, asst. library dir., 1970—. Mem. San Antonio Council Pres., 1978-80; bd. dirs. Beautify San Antonio Recipient award of appreciation San Antonio Ind. Tchrs. Council, 1979, award of appreciation San Antonio Youth Orgn., 1979, spl. recognition San Antonio Council pres., 1979 Mem. Bexar Library Assn. (chmn. 1960-61, Julia Grothaus award 1982), Tex. Library Assn. (past chmn. dist. 10, chmn. local arrangements 1982) Lodges: Zonta (pres. local club 1978-80). Home: 15118 Circle Oak St San Antonio TX 78232-4560 Office: San Antonio Pub Library 600 Soledad St San Antonio TX 78205-1200

LEFF, DEBORAH, foundation administrator, former library director; b. Washington, Oct. 25, 1951; d. Sam and Melitta Leff. AB, Princeton (NJ) U., 1973; JD, U. Chgo., 1977. Trial atty. Civil Rights divsn. U.S. Dept. Justice, Washington, 1977-79; dir. office of pub. affairs Fed. Trade Commn., Washington, 1980-81; sr. producer Nightline-ABC News, Washington and London, 1983-89, World News Tonight-ABC News, N.Y.C., 1990-91; pres. The Joyce Found., Chgo., 1992-99; pres., CEO Am.'s Second Harvest, Chgo., 1999-2001; dir. John F. Kennedy Presdl. Libr., Boston, 2001—06; pres. Pub. Welfare Found., Washington, 2006—. Bd. dirs. Sound Portraits; chmn. Midwest Rhodes Scholars Selection Com., Chgo., 1992. Bd. dirs. Am. Bd. Internal Medicine Found., Smith Barney Charitable Fund, Inc. Office: Pub Welfare Found 1200 U St NW Washington DC 20009-4943 E-mail: dleff@publicwelfare.org.

LEFF, ILENE J(AFNEL), corporate executive, federal official; b. N.Y.C., Mar. 29; d. Abraham and Rose (Levy) L. BA cum laude, U. Pa., 1964; MA with honors, Columbia U., 1969. Statis. and computer analyst McKinsey & Co., N.Y.C., 1969-70, rsch. cons., 1971-74; mgmt. cons. N.Y.C. and Europe, 1974-78; dir. exec. resources Revlon, Inc., N.Y.C., 1978-81, dir. human resources, 1981-83, dir. pers., 1983-86; cons. APM Inc., 1986-88; mgmt. cons. The Estee Lauder Cos., 1988-92; dep. asst. sec. for mgmt. HUD, Washington, 1993-94; pres. Leff Mgmt. Cons., N.Y.C., 1995-97; mng. dir. Eisner LLP, N.Y.C., 1997-2000; pres. Leff Mgmt., 2000—. Rsch. asst. U. Pa., Phila., 1964-65; employment counselor State of N.J., Newark, 1965-66; tchr., Newark, 1966-69; lectr. Grad. Program in Pub. Policy, New Sch. for Social Rsch., Wharton Sch., Duke U.; chmn. com. on employment and unemployment, mem. exec. com. Bus. Rsch. Adv. Coun., U.S. Bur. Labor Stats., 1980; sr. del. econ. rels. and trade Sino-U.S. Conf., 1986; mem. nat. adv. bd. First Book. Contbr. issues papers and program recommendations to candidates for U.S. Pres., U.S. Senate and Congress, N.Y. State gov., mayor N.Y.C. Mem. ops. coun. Jr. Achievement Greater N.Y., 1975-78; cons. Com. for Econ. Devel., N.Y. Hosp., Regional Plan Assn., Am. Cancer Soc.; vol. for dep. mayor for ops. N.Y.C., 1977-78 Mem. N.Y. Human Resource Planners (treas. 1984), Fin. Women's Assn. N.Y. (exec. bd. 1977-78, 83-84), Fashion Group (treas. 1989). Office Phone: 212-674-1140. Personal E-mail: ileneleff@aol.com.

LEFF, REBECCA A., gifted and talented educator; b. Seattle, Aug. 24, 1953; d. Waldo B. and Corinne B. Lyden; m. Dean B. Leff, July 8, 1979; children: Benjamin P., Jamie R. MusB, Eastman Sch. Music, 1975; MusM, Northwestern U., 1979; MEd, DePaul U., 2001. Cert. tchg. Ill., 1997. Mgr. Stormfield Theatre, Chgo., 1984—86; writer, editor The Instrumentalist, Northfield, Ill., 1986—88; tchr. Quest Acad., Palatine, Ill., 1998—. Presenter various ednl. orgns., 2001—. Contbr. articles to profl. jours. Bd. dirs. Congregation Beth Am, Buffalo Grove, Ill., 2003—05. Fellow, NASA, 2002. Mem.: Nat. Coun. Tchrs Math., Nat. Storytelling Network, Ill. Assn. Gifted Children, Nat. Assn. Gifted Children, Phi Delta Kappa, Phi Kappa Phi. Avocations: yoga, reading, walking. Office: Quest Acad 500 N Benton St Palatine IL 60067 Office Phone: 847-202-8035.

LEFF, SANDRA H., art gallery director, consultant; b. NYC, Dec. 24, 1939; d. I. Bernard and Rose (Kupfer) L. BA, Cornell U., 1960; MA, Inst. Fine Arts, N.Y.C., 1969. Editorial asst. Indsl. Design Mag., N.Y.C., 1960-61; instr., asst. Mus. of City of N.Y., 1962-65; assoc. print dept. Sotheby Parke Bernet, N.Y.C., 1969-73; rsch. asst. Daniel Chester French Exhibit, Washington, 1975-77; dir. Am. painting Graham Gallery, N.Y.C., 1977-93. Author: (exhbn. catalogs) Thomas Anshutz: Paintings, Watercolors and Pastels, 1979, Guy Pène du Bois: Painter, Draftsman and Critic, 1979, Helen Torr, 1980, John White Alexander: Fin-de-Siècle American, 1980, Jan Matulka & Vaclav Vytlacil, 1992. Ford Found. fellow, 1967. Mem. Phi Beta Kappa. Avocations: reading, travel, jogging, films, photography. Office: 11 W 17th St Apt 10 New York NY 10011-5500 E-mail: sanmichkan@earthlink.net.

LEFFELL, MARY SUE, educator; b. Knoxville, Tenn., Oct. 12, 1946; d. W.O. and Katherine (Warren) L BS highest honors, U. Tenn., 1968; PhD, U. N.C., 1973. Diplomate Am. Bd. Med. Lab. Immunology, Am. Bd. Histocompatibility Immuno-genetics. Prof. dept. molecular microbiology and immunology Johns Hopkins U. Sch. Pub. Health, Balt., 1991—; prof. dept. medicine Johns Hopkins U. Sch. Medicine, 1989—, dir. Immunogenetics Labs., 1989—. Mem. sec.'s adv. coun. Organ Transplantation Dept. Health and Human Svcs., 2006—. Contbr. articles to profl. jours., chpts. to books Woodrow Wilson fellow, 1968 Mem. Am. Soc. Histocompatibility and Immunogenetics (pres. 1994-95, Disting. Svc. award 2003), United Network Organ Sharing (bd. dirs. 1991-92, 1994-96, chair Histocompatability 2006) Office: Johns Hopkins U Sch Medicine Immunogenetics Lab Baltimore MD 21205

LEFFINGWELL, DENISE C., social worker; b. Pasadena, Calif., Dec. 8, 1975; d. Richard and Sharon Rice; m. Ryan Leffingwell, Nov. 18, 2001. MSW, Calif. State U. San Bernardino, 2001; B in Sociology, U. La Verne, 1997. Lic. social worker. Sr. child care worker Family Solutions, Santa Ana, Calif., 1997—98, social work asst., 1998—99; in-home counselor Cmty. Svc. Programs, Santa Ana, 1999—2000, counselor, 2000—02; med. social worker St Mary Corwin Med. Ctr., Pueblo, Colo., 2002—03; cmty. connector Resource Exch., Colorado Springs, Colo., 2003—; caseworker Kids Crossing, Colorado Springs, 2003—. Mem.: NASW. Office: Kids Crossing 1440 E Fountain Blvd Colorado Springs CO 80910 Personal E-mail: denisericе@hotmail.com. E-mail: dleffingwell@kidscrossing.tv.

LEFFLER, CAROLE ELIZABETH, retired mental health nurse, women's health nurse; b. Sidney, Ohio, Feb. 18, 1942; d. August B. and Delores K. Aselage; children: Veronica, Christopher. ADN, Sinclair C.C., Dayton, Ohio, 1975. Cert. psychiat. nurse supr. Nurse Grandview Hosp, Dayton, 1961—76; substitute sch. nurse Fairborn City Schs., Ohio, 1981—82; dir. nursing Fairborn Nursing Home, 1983; supr. psychiat. nurse Twin Valley Behavioral Health Ctr., 1984—; ret., 2006. Mem. exec. bd. 1199; chmn. disaster mental health com. ARC Ohio. Vol., instr., disaster health nurse ARC, chmn. State of Ohio disaster mental health com.; officer, leader, camp nurse for Girl Scouts, Boy Scouts; Ch. Parish Coun. Recipient Fleur de Lis award Girl and Boy Scouts, Svc. award ARC, Fairborn Mayor's Cert. of Merit for Civic Pride, State of Ohio Govs. award Innovation Ohio, Ohio State Gov.'s award for assistance in N.Y.C. disaster, 2001. Mem. ANA, Ohio Nurses Assn., BPOE and Women of the Moose. Home: 1711 Port Jefferson Rd Sidney OH 45365-1939

LEFKOW, JOAN HUMPHREY, federal judge; b. Kans., Jan. 9, 1944; d. Otis L. and Donna Grace (Given) Humphrey; m. Michael F. Lefkow (dec. 2005), June 21, 1975 AB, Wheaton Coll., 1965; JD, Northwestern U., 1971. Bar: Ill. 1971, U.S. Dist. Ct. (no. dist.) Ill. 1972, U.S. Ct. Appeals (7th cir.) 1972, U.S. Ct. Appeals (5th cir.) 1980. Law clerk to Hon. Thomas E. Fairchild U.S. Ct. Appeals (7th cir.), 1974—75; atty. Legal Assistance Found. Chgo., 1975—79; adminstrv. law judge Ill. Fair Employment Practices Commn., 1975—77; instr. sch. law U. Miami, Fla., 1980—81; exec. dir. Cook County Legal Assistance Found., 1981—82; magistrate judge U.S. Dist. Ct. (no. dist.) Ill., 1982—96; judge U.S. Bankruptcy Ct. (no. dist.) Ill., 1997—2000. Mem. editl. bd. Northwestern U. Law Rev. Mem. Chgo. Bar Assn. (Alliance for Women 1992—), Chgo. Coun. Lawyers (gov. bd. 1975-77), 7th Cir. Bar Assn. Episcopalian. Office: Everett McKinley Dirksen Bldg Ste 1956 219 S Dearborn St Chicago IL 60604

LEFKOWITZ, MARY ROSENTHAL, ancient language educator; b. NYC, Apr. 30, 1935; d. Harold L. and Mena (Weil) Rosenthal; m. Alan L. Lefkowitz, July 1, 1956 (div.); children: Rachel, Hannah; m. Hugh Lloyd-Jones, Mar. 26, 1982. BA, Wellesley Coll., 1957; AM, Radcliffe Coll., 1959, PhD, 1961; LHD (hon.), Trinity Coll., Hartford, Conn., 1996, Grinnell Coll., 2000; PhD (hon.), U. Patras, Greece, 1999. Instr. Greek Wellesley Coll., Mass., 1960—63, asst. prof. Greek and Latin, 1964—69, assoc. prof. Greek and Latin, 1969—75, prof. Greek and Latin, 1975—79, Andrew W. Mellon prof. in humanities, 1979—2005, Andrew W. Mellon prof. emerita, 2005—. Vis. prof. U. Calif., Berkeley, 1978; vis. fellow St. Hilda's Coll., 1979-80, Corpus Christi Coll., 1991; trustee Am. Sch. Classical Studies, Athens, 2004-. Author: Heroines and Hysterics, 1981, Lives of the Greek Poets, 1981, Women in Greek Myth, 1986, First Person Fictions, 1991, Not Out of Africa, 1996, 2d edit., 1997, Greek Gods, Human Lives, 2003; co-editor: Women's Life in Greece and Rome, 1982, 2d edit., 1992, Black Athena Revisited, 1996. Recipient Radcliffe Grad. Soc. medal, 2004; fellow, NEH, 1979—80, 1991, ACLS, 1972—73; hon. fellow, St. Hilda's Coll. Oxford, 1994—. Mem. Am. Philol. Assn. (bd. dirs. 1974-77), Class Assn. New Eng. (pres. 1972-73). Home: 15 W Riding St Wellesley MA 02482-6914 E-mail: mlefkowi@wellesley.edu.

LEFLER, SHERRY LYNETTE, elementary school educator; d. Charles William and Mary Jones Ridge; m. David Donald Lefler, July 28, 1973; children: Jamie Lynn Irvin, Jacob Alan. BS in Edn., SW Tex. State U., 1972; M in Elem. Edn., Prairie View A&M U., Tex., 1977. Kindergarten endorsement SW Tex. State U. Educator Needville (Tex.) Consol. Ind. Sch. Dist., 1973—82, Lamar Consol. Ind. Sch. Dist., Rosenberg, Tex., 1982—. Trainer NJ. Writing Project in Tex., Rosenberg, 1999—; mem. Districtwide Student Improvement Coun. Lamar Consol. Ind. Sch. Dist., Rosenberg, 2002—. Named Tchr. of Yr., Travis Elem. Sch., 1992. Mem.: West Houston Area Coun. Tchrs. English (pres. 2004—), Tex. State Tchrs. Assn. (rec. sec. 1973—74), Tex. Classroom Tchrs. Assn. (assoc.), Delta Kappa Gamma (rec. sec. 1993—95). Home: 1500 Band Rd Rosenberg TX 77471 Office: Lamar Consolidated Independent School Di 3911 Avenue I Rosenberg TX 77471

LEFRANC, MARGARET (MARGARET SCHOONOVER), artist, illustrator, editor, writer; b. NYC, Mar. 15, 1907; d. Abraham and Sophie (Teplitz) Frankel; m. Raymond E. Schoonover, 1942 (div. 1945). Student, Art Students League, NYC, Kunstschule des Westerns, Berlin, NYU Grad. Sch., Andre L'Hote, Paris, Acad. Grande Chaumiere, Paris. Tchr. art Adult Edn., Los Alamos, 1946, Miami Mus. Modern Art, Fla., 1975-76. One-woman shows include Mus. N.Mex., Santa Fe, 1948, 1951, 1953, Philbrook Art Ctr., Tulsa, Okla., 1949, 1951, Okla. Art Ctr., 1950, Recorder Workshop, Miami, Fla., 1958, St. John's Coll., Santa Fe, N.Mex., 1993, 1997, A Lifetime of Imaging (works on paper), 1921—95, Figurative Works, 1920—30, Cline Fine Art Gallery, 1997, exhibited in group shows at Salon de Tuileries, Paris, 1928, 1929, 1930, Art Inst. Chgo., 1936, El Paso Mus. Art, 1964, Mus. Modern Art, 1974, North Miami Mus. Contemporary Art, 1984, Miami Collects, 1989, Women's Caucus Invitational, 1990, Gov.'s Gallery, Santa Fe, 1992, Gene Autry Western Heritage Mus., 1995, Gilcrease Mus., Tulsa, 1996, Mus. N.Mex., Santa Fe, 1996, Brigham Young U., Provo, Utah, 1996, Art in the Embassies Program, Paris, 1998—2001, Miami Dade CC Kendall Campus, Miami, Fla., 1999—2000, Modernistic Peaks, Gerald Peters Gallery, Santa Fe, 1999, Ind. State Univ. and Swope Art Mus. Women Artists, Terre Haute, Ind., 1999, Gerald Peters Gallery, 2001, 2003, Purdue U. Women Artists of the Am. West: Past and Present, 2004, Panhandle-Plains Hist. Mus., Canyon, Tex., 2004—05, St. George Art Mus., St. George Utah, 2005, Hall of Fame, Okla. City, 2006, Archives Am. Art Smithsonian Mus., Washington, DC, Represented in permanent collections Gerald Peters Gallery, Santa Fe, Belles Artes, Mex. City, Mus. Fine Arts, Santa Fe, pvt. collections, exhibitions include Women Artists of Santa Fe 1914-1964. Bd. dir., pres. Artist Equity of Fla., 1964-68; v.p. Miami Art Assn., 1958-60; founder, dir. Guild Art Gallery, NYC, 1935-37. Recipient Illustration award Fifty Best Books of Yr., Libr. of Congress, 1948, Hon. Mention award Rodeo Santa Fe, Mus. N.Mex., 1949, others, Gov.'s award for Excellence and Achievement in the Arts, 1996. Personal E-mail: McKenzieHi@aol.com.

LEGACE, KATHRYN JANE, principal; b. LaMesa, Calif., Apr. 28, 1967; d. James Leroy and Mary Elizabeth Lothringer; m. Edwin Thomas Legace, June 22, 1991. BA in English, San Diego State U., Calif., 1990; MA in Tchg., Lewis and Clark Coll., Portland, Oreg., 1998. Lic. tchr. lang. arts Calif., cert. tchr. Oreg., lang arts, standard adminstrn. Oreg. Tchr. lang. arts Grossman & Union H.S. Dist., San Diego, 1991—93; tchr. lang. arts/social studies Redmond Sch. Dist., Oreg., 1994—97; asst. prin. Bend LaPine Sch. Dist., Oreg., 1997—2004, prin., 2004—. Business E-Mail: klegace@bend.k12.or.us.

LEGATO, MARIANNE, internist, medical educator; b. N.J., Aug. 17, 1935; MD, NYU, 1962. Bd. cert. internal medicine. Intern Columbia U. Coll. Physicians and Surgeons, N.Y.C., 1962—63, resident internal medicine, 1963—64, Presbyn. Hosp., N.Y.C., 1964—65, fellow cardiology, 1965—68, assoc. attending physician, 1993—; sr. attending physician St. Luke's/Roosevelt Hosp., N.Y.C., 1980—; founder, dir. Partnership for Gender Specific Medicine Columbia U., N.Y.C., 1997—; prof. clin. medicine Columbia U. Coll. Physicians and Surgeons, 1998—. Charter mem. adv. bd. Office Rsch. on Women's Health, NIH. Author: The Female Heart: The Truth About Women and Heart Disease, 1992; author: (with Carol Colman) What Women Need to Know: From Headaches to Heart Disease and Everything in Between, 1997; author: Eve's Rib: The New Science of Gender-Specific Medicine and How It Can Save Your Life, 2002, Why Men Never Remeber and Women Never Forget, 2005; editor: The Principles of Gender Specific Medicine, 2004; founder, editor: Gender Medicine, mem. editl. bd.: Cardiovasc. Risk Factors, Prevention Mag. Named Am. Health Hero, Am. Health for Women, 1997, Heroine of Women's Health, Ladies Home Jour., 2000; named one of 300 Am. Women Changing the Face of Medicine, Nat. Libr. Medicine, 2004; named to 1,000 Women for the Nineties, Mirabella Mag., 1994; recipient Howard W. Blakeslee award, Am. Heart Assn., 1992, Leadership in Action award, Women's Action Alliance, 1994, Woman in Sci. award, Am. Med. Women's Assn., 2002, Heart of Gold award, L.I. Heart Coun., J. Murray Steele award, Sr. Investigator award, Am. Heart Assn., N.Y. Affiliate, Rsch. Career Devel. award, NIH; Martha Lyon Slater fellow. Home and Office: Partnership for Gender-Specific Medicine 962 Park Ave New York NY 10028-0313 Office Phone: 212-737-5663. Business E-Mail: mjl2@columbia.edu.

LEGATT, HADASSA, language educator; b. N.Y.C. m. Jerome Legatt. PhD, NYU, 1980. Tchr. English, Queens Secondary Schs., N.Y.C., 1960-66; prin., adminstr. N.Y.C. Schs., Queens, Bklyn., Bronx, 1979—91. Adj. asst. prof. Queensborough C.C., CUNY, N.Y.C., 1993—; adj. assoc. prof. St. John's U.; owner, pres. Speak Up, Great Neck, N.Y., 1991—; presenter and consultant in field. Mem. AAUW, NYU Alumni Assn., Toastmasters, Pi Lambda Theta. Home: 8 Parkside Dr Great Neck NY 11021-1023 Office Phone: 516-829-2978.

LEGENDRE, JACLYN, psychologist; BA magna cum laude, Nicholls State U., 2001, Specialist Degree in Sch. Psychology, 2005. Lic. specialist in sch. psychology Tex. State Bd. Examiners Psychologists, 2005. Sch. psychologist Brazosport Ind. Sch. Dist., Freeport, Tex., 2004—. Dept. Psychology scholar, Nicholls State U., 2001. Mem.: NASP (nat. cert. sch. psychologist 2005), Psi Chi (life). Achievements include research in curriculum-based measures. (Office Phone: 979-730-7230. Business E-Mail: jlegendre@brazosportisd.net.

LÉGER, VIOLA, Canadian senator; b. June 29, 1930; BA, BEd, U. Moncton; MFA, Boston U. Tchr. drama, NB; star of theatre, films, tv; senator The Senate of Can., Ottawa, 2001—. Founder La Compagnie Viola Léger Inc., 1985—. Named Officer of Order of Can., 1989; recipient Chevalier de l'Ordre de la Pléiade, 1978, Dora Mavor Moore award, 1981, Médaille du Conseil de la vie française en Amérique, 1987, Chevalier de l'Ordre française des Arts et des Lettres, 1991, Masque de l'interprétation féminine de l'Academie québécoise du théâtre. Liberal.

LEGG, HILDA GAY, former federal agency administrator; b. 1952; BS in Sociology, Campbellville Coll.; MEd, We. Ky. U. Tchr. social sci. jr. and sr. hs, Adair County, Ky., 1974—81; acting exec. dir. nat. coun. on handicapped US Dept. Edn., Washington, 1981—83; field rep. to Senator Mitch McConnell, Bowling Green, Ky., 1985—87; dir. admissions Lindsey Wilson Coll., Columbia, Ky., 1987—90; alt. fed. co-chmn. Appalachian Regional Commn., Washington, 1990—93; exec. dir., CEO Ctr. for Rural Develop., Somerset, Ky., 1994—2001; adminstr. Rural Utilities Svcs. USDA, Washington, 2001—05. Republican.

LEGGE KEMP, DIANE, architect, landscape architect; b. Englewood, N.J., Dec. 4, 1949; d. Richard Claude and Patricia (Roney) L.; m. Kevin A. Kemp; children: Alloy Hudson, McClelland Beebe, Logan Roney. BArch, Stanford U., 1972; MArch, Princeton U., 1975. Registered arch., Ill., landscape arch., Ill. Arch. Northrop, Kaelber & Kopf, Rochester, NY, 1971—73, Michael Graves, Architect, Princeton, NJ, 1973—75, The Ehrenkrantz Group, NYC, 1975-77; ptnr. Skidmore Owings & Merrill, Chgo., 1977-89; pres. Diane Legge Kemp Architecture and Landscape Consulting, Riverside, Ill., 1993—, DLK Architecture, 1993—, DLK Civic Design. Mem. bd. govs. Sch. of Art Inst., Chgo., 1991—; dir., past pres. Soc. for Contemporary Art, Chgo., 1991—. Office: DLK Civic Design 410 S Michigan Ave Chicago IL 60605-1308 Office Phone: 312-322-2550. Business E-Mail: dleggekemp@dlkinc.com.

LEGGETT, DIANE, nurse, educator; b. Belleville, Ill., Aug. 20, 1953; d. Richard and Joan Kimber; children: John, Lisa Hunziker, Bryan, Brad. MS in Nursing, U. Phoenix, 1998—2000. RN Utah, 1974. Staff nurse Pioneer Nursing Home, Brigham City, Utah, 1973—74, Brigham City Cmty. Hosp., 1974—, educator, 1975—; staff nurse Creekside Home Health, Brigham City,

1990—96; asst. prof. Weber State U., Ogden, Utah, 2000—03, assoc. prof., 2003—. Nurse ARC, Utah, 1980—2006. Mem.: ANA, Sigma Theta Tau Internat. (officer 2000—06, pres. 2002—06), Ladies Cmty. Club (officer 1976—2005). Office: Weber Sate Univ 3903 University Cir Ogden UT 84408-3903 Business E-Mail: dleggett@weber.edu.

LEGGETT, ROBERTA JEAN (BOBBI LEGGETT), retired social services administrator; b. Kankakee, Ill., Nov. 30, 1926; d. Clyde H. and Sybil D. (Billings) Karns; m. George T. Leggett, Aug. 25, 1956. Sec. Cardov div. Chemetron Corp., Chgo., 1951-60; sec., asst. mgr. Ravisloe Country Club, Homewood, Ill., 1961-65; sec. Nationwide Paper Co., Chgo., 1966-68; exec. dir. Am. Bd. Oral and Maxillofacial Surgery, Chgo., 1969-87. Mem. Chgo. Soc. Assn. Execs., Conf. Med. Soc. Execs. of Greater Chgo., Profl. Secs. Internat. Methodist.

LEGINGTON, GLORIA R., retired elementary school educator; BS, Tex. So. U, Houston, 1967; MS, U. So. Calif., L.A., 1973. Cert. adminstr. (life) Calif. Program coord. L.A. Unified Sch. Dist., 1967—2001, tchr., mentor, 1991—93, speech coach, 1992—2000, ret., 2002. Tchr. insvc. classes for area colloquim, parents and tchrs. L.A. Unified Sch. Dist., faculty shared decision making coun., 1993—94, mem. faculty senate, 1992—93, mem. sch. improvement, 1993—94, sponsor 8th grade, 1994—97; del. U.S. Spain Joint Conf. on Edn., Barcelona, 1995; coord. Elementary and Sec. Edn. Act, L.A. Unified Sch. Dist., 2001. Named semi-finalist, Nat. Libr. Poetry, 1997; recipient Editor's Choice award, 1997; grantee State Libr. award, 2000. Avocations: painting, writing, collecting black memorabilia, reading, travel.

LEGOHN, LISA MARIE, vocational school educator; d. Lawrence John and Lucille Gladys Legohn; m. Keith Lamont Stephens (div. Oct. 8, 2001); 1 child, Lisa Marie Hamilton. Completion cert., L.A. Trade Tech. Coll., 1981; Vocat. edn. instr. credential, Calif State U., Long Beach, 1987; Calif C.C. instr. credential, UCLA Ext., L.A., 1984, UCLA, 1984. Welder Komax Systems, Inc, Long Beach, 1981—87; welding instr. Compton (Calif.) C.C., 1983—2003; welder fabricator Unique Ennocations, Inglewood, Calif., 1987—89; assoc. prof. L.A. C.C. Dist., 1990—. Welding dept. adv. bd. Compton C.C., 1983—2003; constrn. tech. adv. bd. L.A. Trade Tech. Coll., 1994—; risk mgmt. cons. J. Paul Getty Mus., L.A., 2005. Welder, fabricator and builder (documentaries) BIG, welder, fabricator & builder Monster Garage. Active Jerusalem Missionary Bapt. Ch., L.A., 1999—2006. Named Welder of the Yr., L.A. Trade Tech. Coll. Catercraft Award, 1981, Tchr. of Yr., L.A. Trade Tech. Coll. Tools for Success, 1998. Mem.: Am. Welding Soc. (assoc.). Achievements include nine Guiness World Records. Avocations: cooking, swimming, investments. Office: L A Community College District LATTC 400 West Washington Blvd Los Angeles CA 90012 Office Phone: 213-763-3942. Business E-Mail: legohnlm@lattc.edu.

LEGRO, PATRICE, museum director; b. Dec. 1953; m. Alan Legro. BA in Art History, Old Dominion U., 1977; MA in internat. transaction, George Mason U., 1996. Program officer Office Internat. Affairs Nat. Acad., Wash., DC, 1987—93, mgr. Nat. Sci. Edn. Standards Project, co-study dir. Tchg. About Evolution and Nature of Sci., 1998, dir. Divsn. Comm. and Special Projects Ctr. Sci., Math., and Engring. Edn., 1998, dir. Philanthropy Svcs., 1998—2002; dir. Marian Koshland Sci. Mus. Nat. Acad. Scis., Wash., DC, 2002—. Office: Marian Koshland Sci Mus Nat Acad 500 Fifth St NW Washington DC 20001 Office Phone: 202-334-2728.

LEGROS, CHRISTY CALLAGHAN, art educator; b. Mobile, Ala., Oct. 27, 1972; d. Woodrow Benjamin Callaghan, Sr. and Mary Agnes Callaghan; m. David Frederick LeGros, Mar. 1, 2003. BS in Art Edn. K-12, U. South Ala., Mobile, 1997, MEd in Art and Edn., 2002. Art tchr., chair fine arts Theodore (Ala.) H.S., 1998—; facilitator fed. programs Mobile, Ala., 2000—; dir. hands-on art City of Mobile, 2003—. Watercolor series, Mobile Landscapes, 2006 (Key to City, 2006), acrylic paintings, Bayfest '04 Poster, 2004, Bayfest '05 Poster, 2005. Mem. prodn. com. United Cerebral Palsey, Mobile, 2006; organizer, chairperson Celebrate the Arts, Mobile, 2004, 2005; sponsor Nat. Art Honor Soc., Theodore, 2000—06. Recipient Greater Mobile Arts award, Ala. Arts Forum and Mobile Arts Coun., 2004; grantee, Mid South Edn. Found., 2006. Mem.: Bay Area Art Educators (pres. 1996—), Ala. Art Edn. Assn. (State Art Tchr. of Yr. 2005—06), Nat. Art Edn. Assn. Avocations: concerts, drawing, painting, home restoration. Office: Theodore H S 6201 Swedetown Rd Theodore AL 36582

LE GUIN, URSULA KROEBER, writer; b. Berkeley, Calif., Oct. 21, 1929; d. Alfred Louis and Theodora (Kracaw) Kroeber; m. Charles A. Le Guin, Dec. 22, 1953; children: Elisabeth, Caroline, Theodore. BA, Radcliffe Coll., 1951; MA, Columbia, 1952; 9 hon. degrees. Vis. lectr. or writer in residence numerous workshops and univs., U.S. and abroad. Author: Planet of Exile, 1966, Rocannon's World, 1966, City of Illusion, 1967, A Wizard of Earthsea, 1968, The Left Hand of Darkness, 1969, The Tombs of Atuan, 1970, The Lathe of Heaven, 1971, The Farthest Shore, 1972, The Dispossessed, 1974, The Wind's Twelve Quarters, 1975, A Very Long Way from Anywhere Else, 1976, Orsinian Tales, 1976, The Word for World is Forest, 1976, The Language of the Night, 1989, Leese Webster, 1979, Malafrena, 1979, The Beginning Place, 1980, Hard Words, 1981, The Compass Rose, 1982, The Eye of the Heron, 1983, Cobbler's Rune, 1983, King Dog, 1985, Always Coming Home, 1985, Buffalo Gals, 1987, Wild Oats and Fireweed, 1988, A Visit from Dr. Katz, 1988, Catwings, 1988, Solomon Leviathan, 1988, Fire and Stone, 1989, Catwings Return, 1989, Dancing at the Edge of the World, 1989, 1992, Tehanu, 1990, Searoad, 1991, Fish Soup, 1992, A Ride on the Red Mare's Back, 1992, Blue Moon Over Thurman Street, 1993, Wonderful Alexander and the Catwings, 1994, Going Out With Peacocks, 1994, A Fisherman of the Inland Sea, 1994, Four Ways to Forgiveness, 1995, Unlocking the Air, 1996; author: (with Diana Bellessi) The Twins; author: The Dream, 1997, Lao Tzu: Tao Te Ching: A Book About the Way and the Power of the Way, 1997, Steering the Craft, 1998, Jane on Her Own, 1999, Sixty Odd, 1999, The Telling, 2000, The Other Wind, 2001, Tales From Earthsea, 2001, The Birthday of the World, 2002, Tom Mouse, 2002; author: (transl. by Angelica Gorodischer) Kalpa Imperial, 2003; author: (transl.) Selected Poems of Gabriela Mistral, 2003, Changing Planes, 2003, The Wave in the Mind, 2004, Gifts, 2004, Incredible Good Fortune, 2006; author: (numerous) short stories, poems, criticism, screenplays. Recipient Jupiter award 1975, 76, Lewis Caroll Shelf award 1979, Internat. Fantasy award 1988, Howard D. Vursell award Am. Acad. Arts and Letters, 1991, Pushcart prize, 1991, Boston Globe-Hornbook award for excellence in juvenile fiction, 1968, Newbery Honor medal, 1972, Nebula award (novel) 1969, 75, 90, (story) 1975, Hugo award (novel) 1969, 75, (story) 1974, 88, Gandalf award, 1979, Kafka award, 1986, Nat. Book award, 1972, H.L. Davis award Oreg. Inst. Literary Arts, 1992, Hubbub annual poetry award, 1995, Asimov's Reader's award, 1995, 03, James Tiptree Jr. award, 1995, 97, Retrospective award, 1996, Theodore Sturgeon award (story), 1995, Locus Readers award (novel), 1973, (story) 1995, 02, 03, (collection) 1984, 96, (novel and collection) 2001, 02, Prix Lectures-Jeunesse award, 1987, Bumbershoot Arts award, Seattle, 1998, Lifetime Achievement award Robert Kirsch/L.A. Times, 2000, Lifetime Achievement award Pacific NW Booksellers Assn., 2001, Endeavor award, 2001, 03, Willamette Writers Lifetime Achievement award, 2002, PEN/Malamud award for short fiction, 2002, World Fantasy award, 2002, Grandmaster SWFA, 2003, Margaret A. Edwards Award for lifetime contbn. in writing for young adults, 2004; Arbuthnot lectr. ALA, 2004. Mem. NARAL, Amnesty Internet. USA, Environ. Def. Fund, Nat. Resources Def. CTEE, Planned Parenthood Fedn. Am., Oreg. Nature Conservancy, Sci. Fiction Rsch. Assn., Sci. Fiction Writers Assn. (Grand Master 2003), Authors League, PEN (PEN/USA award 2005), Writers Guild West, Phi Beta Kappa. Office: care Virginia Kidd Lit Agy PO Box 278 Milford PA 18337-0278 also: c/o William Contandi 244 Madison Ave #E1 New York NY 10016-4702

LEHMAN, BARBARA ALBU, foreign language educator, translator; b. Vineland, N.J., July 7, 1950; d. Kurt Gunther and Ruth (Landau) Albu; children: David, Kara. BA, Douglass Coll., 1972; MS in Ceramic Engring., Rutgers U., New Brunswick, N.J., 1992; degree in Holocaust Edn. (hon.), Hebrew U., Jerusalem, 1994. Cert. educator French and German. French/German lang. educator Mount Olive Township Schs., Flanders, N.J., 1973-81; French lang. educator Upper Freehold Schs., Allentown, N.J., 1984—. Translator Internat. Congress on Glass, Albuquerque, 1980, Hamburg, Germany, 1983; travel guide EF Tours, Europe, 1984—; mem. N.J. Adv. Commn. on Status of Women, 1998-2003; bd. dir. Nat. Assn. Commn. on Status of Women. Vice-chmn. Somerset County Commn. on Women, Somerville, N.J., 1985—; apptd. mem. N.J. Adv. Commn. on Status of Women, 1998-2004; elected bd. mem. Nat. Assn. Commns. Women, 2001, 03, 05. Meml. scholar Lihn Family, 1968, Grauel scholar Brookdale Holocaust Studies, 1994. Mem.: Keramos Honor Soc., Kappa Delta Pi.

LEHMAN, ELLEN J., psychologist; b. Pitts., Feb. 21, 1944; d. Alan George and Jane (Anathan) L.; m. Charles Kennel. AB, Vassar Coll., 1966; PhD, Cornell U., 1975. Lic. psychologist, Calif. Trainee James J. Putnam Children's Ctr., Boston, 1968-69; fellow Reiss-Davis Child Study Ctr., Los Angeles, 1972-74; contract instr. Calif. Sch. Profl. Psychology, L.A., 1975-76; instr. Ctr. Early Edn., L.A., 1979-80; clin. supr. Wright Inst., L.A., 1983—; pvt. practice psychology Santa Monica, Calif., 1976—; instr., bd. mem., Grad. Ctr. Child Devel., 1997—; asst. clin. prof. UCLA, 1990—; mem. Inst. Contemporary Paychoanalysis, 1991—, supervising and tng. analyst, 1993—. Docent Topanga Canyon, Nat. Park Svc., L.A., 1982—. NIMH fellow L.A., 1972-74. Mem. APA, Soc. Rsch. in Child Devel., Vassar Coll. Alumnae Assn. (chmn. admissions com. So. Calif. 1980-84), Phi Kappa Phi. Office: 1132 26th St Santa Monica CA 90403-4621 Office Phone: 310-393-0800.

LEHMAN, JOAN ALICE, real estate company executive; b. Jamaica Queens, N.Y., May 8, 1938; d. Hans Newman and Margot (Deutsch) Senen; m. Eugene Lehman, June 17, 1956 (div. Mar. 1990); children: Joel, Peter, Alan, Ira, Helen Ann, Helen Beth, Robert, Jacqueline, John, Steven, Robin, Elizabeth, Jody, Lisa, David, Andy, Jeremy, Jay. AA, Nassau C.C., East Meadow, N.Y., 1971; BS, Nova U., 1982. Lic. real estate broker, Fla. Owner Joan Lehman Real Estate Mgmt. Co., Old Bethpage, NY, 1961-82; tchr. Broward County Schs., Ft. Lauderdale, Fla., 1982-86; owner Joan Lehman Real Estate, Pompano Beach, Fla., 1986—; pres. Jo Al 1 Inc., Pompano Beach. Mem. Sunset Sch. Adv. Bd., Ft. Lauderdale, 1994-96; pres. The Pointe Condo Assn., 2001—; bd. dirs. Property Owners Ctrl. Lauderhill, Fla., 1996; den mother Boy Scouts Am., Old Bethpage, N.Y.; leader Girl Scouts U.S., Old Bethpage. Avocations: bowling, travel, theater.

LEHMAN, SHANON LEVIN See LEVIN, SHANON

LEHMAN, SHARI JOAN, music educator; b. Ft. Dodge, Iowa, Nov. 4, 1961; d. Darryl Zane and Joan Phillis Stensland; m. Curtis Alan Lehman, July 14, 1984; children: Hallie, Seth, Isaac. AA, Iowa Ctrl. C.C., Ft. Dodge, 1982; BS, Iowa State U., 1984. Cert. English as Second Lang. instr. 2004. Piano instr., accompanist, Ft. Dodge, 1989—. Instrument tchr. Cmty. Christian Sch., Ft. Dodge, 1997—2001; choir dir., Sunday sch. accompanist St. Olaf Luth. Ch., Ft. Dodge, 2000—04, bell player Maranatha Ringers, 2001—06; music dept. accompanist Ft. Dodge Sr. High, 2002—. Floutist: St. Olaf Orch., 2000—, pianist: Ft. Dodge Symphony, 2001—. Vol. Duncombe Elem. Sch., Ft. Dodge, 1994—2004; contemporary worship svcs. leader St. Olaf Luth. Ch., 2005—. Mem.: Iowa Music Tchrs. Assn., Music Tchrs. Nat. Assn. Lutheran. Avocations: walking, tennis, college basketball, travel. Home: 417 N 17th St Fort Dodge IA 50501

LEHMAN, SHARON MALANI, physical education educator; b. Honolulu, Hawaii, Feb. 5, 1960; d. Harold F. and Elizabeth A. Lehman. BPE, Azusa Pacific U., 1982, MEd, 1990; EdD, U.S. Sports Acad., 2002. Faculty coach Linfield Christian Sch., Temecula, Calif., 1984—88; prof., head softball coach Azusa Pacific U., Calif., 1988—94, asst. athletic dir., 1994—2005, chair, exercise sports and sci., 1994—, prof., 2005—. Named to Academic Hall of Honor, Azusa Pacific U., 2002; recipient Nat. Coach. of Yr., Nat. Fast Pitch and Coaches Assn., 1997, 2000. Mem.: Calif. Assn. for Health, Physical Edn., Recreation and Dance, Am. Alliance for Health, Physical Edn., Recreation and Dance. Republican. Avocations: reading, walking. Office: Azusa Pacific U 901 E Alosta Ave Azusa CA 91702

LEHMANN-CARSSOW, NANCY BETH, secondary school educator, coach; b. Kingsville, Tex., Sept. 9, 1949; d. Valgene William and Ella Mae (Zajicek) Lehmann; m. William Benton Carssow, Jr., Aug. 1, 1981. BS, U. Tex., 1971, MA, 1979. Freelance photographer, Austin, Tex., 1971-99; geography tchr., tennis coach Austin Ind. Sch. Dist., 1974-98, geography tchr., instrnl. specialist, girls' wrestling coach, 1999—. Founder Custom Pet Wheels, 1997; salesperson, mgr. What's Going On-Clothing, Austin, 1972-78; area adminstr. Am. Inst. Fgn. Study, Austin, 1974-81; area rep. World Encounters, Austin, 1981—, tour guide, Egypt, Kenya, 1977, 79, 81, 87, 92, 97-2000; tchr., cons. Nat. Geog., 1986—; tchr. Leader for People in Soviet Union, 1989, 90; vol. First Internat. Environ. Expedition to Antarctica, 1995; presenter Population Edn., 1995—; creater curriculum materials. Photographer (book) Bobwhites, 1984. Co-chair PeaceWorks. Recipient Merit award Nat. Coun. Geog. Edn., 1975, Creative Tchg. award Austin Assn. Tchrs., 1978, study grant to Malaysia and Indonesia, 1990, Excellence award for outstanding H.S. tchr. U. Tex., 1997, Edn.'s Unsung Hereos award No. Life, 1998, Outstanding Tchg. of the Humanities award, 1998, Excellence award Tex. State Bd. Edn., 1995, Peacemaker award Austin Dispute Resolution Ctr., 1998; Fulbright scholar, Israel, 1983. Mem. NEA, Nat. Coun. Geog. Edn., Earthwatch (participant archaeol. dig in Swaziland 1984, Romania 2003), World Wildlife Fund, Rotary, Tex. PTA (hon. life mem., life), Delta Kappa Gamma (pres. 1986-88), Phi Kappa Phi. Democrat. Roman Catholic. Avocations: stained glass, photography, tennis, gardening, needlepoint. Home: 1025 Quail Park Dr Austin TX 78758-6749 Office: Lanier High Sch 1201 Payton Gin Rd Austin TX 78758-6699 Office Phone: 512-414-7449. Personal E-mail: nlehmann3764@sbcglobal.net.

LEHNER, REMY D., publishing executive; b. NYC, 1956; m. Danny Lehner (dec. 1997); 1 child, Andrew. Pres., CEO Inflight Newspapers & Mags., Inc., Valley Stream, NY, 1997—. Bd. trustees Franklin Hosp. Med. Ctr.; mem. Long Island Hispanic C. of C.; various other charity and cmty. orgns.; fundraiser for over 40 local and nat. charities; established TALI Edn. Program, Alona Pub. Sch., Israel; mem. U.S. Hispanic C. of C., Long Island Breast Cancer Coalition, Lawrence Spl. Edn. PTA; mem. nat. com. Furtherance Jewish Edn. Named a sch. in honor of, TALI Edn. Fund & Sem. Judaic Studies, Israel, 1996; named one of Long Island Top Women (Hall of Fame Honoree), Business News, 2004. Mem.: NAACP (life).

LEHNER-QUAM, ALISON LYNN, library administrator; b. Oak Harbor, Wash., Apr. 25, 1960; d. Paul Elias and Johanna Marie (Vinson) Q.; m. Matthias Karl-Eugen Lehner, Oct. 3, 1997; 1 child, Peter Elias Bernhard Lehner. BA, U. Wash., 1983; cert. tech. theater, Yale U., 1985; MS in Libr. Sci., Columbia U., 1991. Freelance costumer various prodns., N.Y.C., 1984-90; cataloging asst. Fashion Inst. of Tech., N.Y.C., 1986-91; intern Bank St. Sch., N.Y.C., 1991; asst. dir. Columbia Children's Lit. Inst., N.Y.C., 1990; libr. dir. Lincoln Ctr. Inst., N.Y.C., 1991—. Project dir. Arts Edn. Reference Window on the Work, 1992—. Pub. mgr.: (periodical) The Institute View, 1996—, website mgr. www.lcinstitute.org, 2000—; resource round-up editor Teaching Artist Jour., 2002-2003. Vol. mgr. Lincoln Ctr. Inst., N.Y.C., 1995-2001. Recipient Dirs.' Emeriti award Lincoln Ctr. for Performing Arts, 1997; scholar Sch. Libr. Svcs., Columbia U., 1989, 90. Mem. ALA, N.Y. Arts in Edn. Roundtable (steering com. 1995-98), Theater Libr. Assn., Beta Phi Mu (bd. dirs. Theta chpt. 1997-2004, v.p. 1994-96). Avocations: reading, the arts. E-mail: alquam@lincolncenter.org.

LEHRMAN, MARGARET MCBRIDE, broadcast executive, television producer; b. Spokane, Wash., Sept. 25, 1944; d. John P. and Ruth A. McBride; m. Michael L. Lehrman, June 27, 1970. BA, U. Oreg., 1966; MS, Columbia U., 1970. Staff Peace Corps, Washington, 1966-69; with The Morning News Co., Washington, 1970-72; radio and newspaper reporter Albright Comms., Washington, 1973-74; tv assignment editor ABC News, Washington, 1974; press asst. Senator Robert P. Griffin, Washington, 1975-79; rschr. Today Show, NBC News, Washington, 1979, assoc. prodr., 1979—83, Washington prodr., 1983-89, dep. bur. chief, 1989-95, sr. Washington prodr. spl. coverage and events, 1995—. Trustee U. Oreg. Found., 1990-2000; adv. bd. Internat. Women's Media Found., Women's Fgn. Policy Group, World Affairs Coun. Recipient Edwin M. Hood award for diplomatic reporting (China), Nat. TV News Emmy award. Office: NBC News 4001 Nebraska Ave NW Washington DC 20016-2733 Business E-Mail: margaret.lehrman@nbc.com.

LEHRMAN, PATRICIA JAYNE, literature and language educator; b. Iowa City; d. Laurence Laughlin and Kathleen JoAnn Calvin; m. Daren Louis Lehrman, Apr. 5, 1997; 1 child, Brady Laurence. BA, Mt. Mercy Coll., Cedar Rapids, Iowa, 1987. Tchr. h.s. English Moulton-Udell H.S., Iowa, 1987—93, East Union H.S., Afton, 1993—94, Pekin H.S., Packwood, 1994—96; copy editor Bankers Advt. Co., Iowa City, 1996—97; tchr. h.s. English North Cedar H.S., Stanwood, 1997—. Mem.: NEA, Iowa Edn. Assn., Iowa Coun. Tchrs. English, Nat. Coun. Tchrs. English, Lions Club Internat. Roman Catholic. Avocations: reading, sports, writing, piano. Home: 308 Preston St Stanwood IA 52337 Office: North Cedar High School 102 E North St Stanwood IA 52337 Business E-Mail: plehrman@north-cedar.k12.ia.us.

LEIBER, ANNETTE PERONE, artist, art association administrator; b. Chgo., June 1, 1941; d. Vincent James and Micheline Frances (Przewrocki) Perone; m. Donald C. Leiber, Sept. 21, 1963; children: Michael Donald, Lynne M. BA, No. Ill. U., 1963. Chmn., dir. Addison (Ill.) Cultural Arts Commn., 1975—; grants writer A.C.A.D.C., 1982—; art tchr., lectr. Addison Pk. Dist., 1985—. Exhibited throughout Chgo. suburbs. Bd. dirs., treas. Addison Cmty. Theatre, 1990-; bd. dirs., dir., treas. Addison Children's Theatre, 1993—; pres., dir. Addison Ctr. Arts, 1994—. Named Citizen of the Month Lerner-Voice Newspapers, 1980, Outstanding Women Leader in Arts & Culture YWCA, 1989, Studs Terkel Ill. Humanities Svc. award, 1999; numerous art awards, 1970—, Woman of Distinction award AAUW, 2003. Mem. Ill. Arts Alliance (Yates Arts Advocacy award 1993), Addison Art Guild (founder, pres.), Elmhurst Artists' Guild (pres., sec. edn. 1985-90), DuPage Art League (jury chmn. 1989-92). Avocations: art, music, theater. Office: Addison Ctr Arts One Friendship Plz Addison IL 60101 Home: One Friendship Plz Addison IL 60101

LEIBMAN, FAITH H., lawyer, psychologist; b. Phila., Pa., July 24, 1953; d. Neil and Louise Leibman. BA, Temple U., 1974; JD, Widener U., 1977; MA, John Jay Coll. Criminal Justice, 1985; PhD, Maimonides U., 2001; postgrad., CUNY. Bar: Pa., US Dist. Ct. (ea. dist.) Pa., US Dist. Ct. (no. dist.) NY. Psychol. specialist Dept. Corrections, Graterford, Pa.; atty. Immigration Law Clinic, Bala Cynwyd, Pa.; capt. 15th Airborne JAG, Ft. Bragg, NC; legal advisor to adm./comdr. naval base USN, Phila. Expert witness Nat. Forensic Consultants, Narberth, Pa., 1977—; dir. Continuing Legal Edn. Inst., Phila., 1999—. Contbr. articles to profl. jours. Svc. officer Am. Legion, Ardmore, Pa.; adjutant VFW, Gladwyne, Pa. Lt. USN, 1981—85, cpl. U.S. Army, 1990—95. Mem.: Am. Acad. Clin. Sexology (clin. supr.), Am. Immigration Lawyers Assn., ATLA. Home: 304 Melrose Rd Merion Station PA 19066 Office: 11 Bala Ave Bala Cynwyd PA 19004 Office Phone: 610-664-9442. Office Fax: 610-664-9441.

LEIBOVITZ, ANNIE, photographer; b. Waterbury, Conn., Oct. 2, 1949; children: Sarah, Susan Anna, Samuelle Edith. BFA, San Francisco Art Inst., 1971. Photographer Rolling Stone, 1970-83, chief photographer, 1973-83; photographer Conde Nast Vanity Fair, Vogue, 1980—; proprietor Annie Leibovitz Studio, N.Y.C. Works exhibited in various galleries and mus. including the National Portrait Gallery, Washington DC, 1991, The Corcoran Gallery, 1999; author: Photographs: Annie Leibovitz 1970-1990, 1992, Olympic Portraits: Annie Leibovitz, 1996, Annie Leibovitz: Women,(with essay by Susan Sontag) 1999, American Music, 2003, A Photographer's Life: 1990-2005, 2006; creator offcl. portfolio for 26th Olympic Games, Atlanta, 1995. Recipient Photographer of Yr. award Am. Soc. Mag. Photographers, 1984, Innovation in Photography award Am. Soc. Mag. Photographers, 1987, Clio award, 1987, Campaign of Decade award Advt. Age mag., 1987, Infinity award for applied photography Internat. Ctr. for Photography, 1990; named one of Top 10 Living Artists, ARTnews mag., 1999. Achievements include first woman and second photographer to have a solo exhibit at The National Portrait Gallery. also: Art & Commerce Care Jim Moffat 755 Washington St New York NY 10014-1746 Office: Annie Leibovitz Studio 311 W 11th St New York NY 10014-2368 E-mail: als@leibovitzstudio.com.

LEIBOWITZ, BERNICE, artist, educator; b. Bklyn., Nov. 2, 1929; d. Nathan and Shirley (Gilman) Ottenstein; m. Herbert J. Leibowitz, Jan. 28, 1950; children: Kenneth, Lori, Paul BA, Hunter Coll., 1950, MA, 1953. Cert. art tchr., N.Y. Instr. art Hunter Coll. High Sch., N.Y.C., 1950-53, Bergenfield (N.J.) Adult Sch., 1967-74, Ft. Lee (N.J.) Adult Sch., 1969-73; community svcs. lectr. Bergen Community Coll., Paramus, N.J., 1981-83, lectr. fine arts, 1983-85, instr. art, 1974-83, 85—. Mem. edn. com. Arts Ctr. No. N.J., New Milford, 1987-91, chmn. edn. com., 1987-91, bd. dir., 1987-91; cover painting class, 1997. One-woman shows include Pleiades Gallery, N.Y.C., 1983, 85, 87, 90, 92, 94, 98, 2005; exhibited in group shows Silvermine Guild, Conn., 1990, gallery in Barcelona, Spain, 1990, Ambiente Gallery, Gelhausen, Germany, 1992, Robeson Ctr. Gallery Rutgers, Newark, 1992, Four Painters Invitational Bergen Mus., 1992, Touchstone Gallery, Washington, 1993, Art at the Northeast U.S.A. Silbermine Guild Ats Ctr., Conn., 1994, Muse Gallery, Phila., 1995, Johnson and Johnson World Hdqs., New Brunswick, N.J., 1997, Highlights Bergen Mus. Collection, 1998, Galerie Rossler, Munich, 2000, City Without Walls Seton Hall Law Sch., Newark, 2000, Interchurch Gallery, N.Y.C., 2004; represented in permanent collection in Bergen Mus. Art and Sci. Mem. Nat. Assn. Women Artists (Molly M. Canaday award for painting 1991, Belle Cramer prize, 1992), Artists Equity. Avocations: reading, travel, concerts, ballet, theater.

LEICK, CAROL LYNN, retired special education educator; b. Belleville, Ill., May 9, 1950; d. Wilbur Glenn and Jeannene Eloise Fritz; m. John Kenneth Leick, Nov. 7, 1992; children: Terry Glenn, Patrick Ryan. BS in Edn., S.W. Mo. State U., 1975; cert., Drury Coll., 1976. Lic. tchr. Mo., N.J. Tchr., Springfield, Mo., 1971—77, Mansfield Twp., Port Murray, NJ, 1977—79, Vigo County Sch. Corp., Terre Haute, Ind., 1979—80; tutor, daycare provider Terre Haute, 1981—85; tchr. Park Ctrl. Hosp., Springfield, Mo., 1986, Springfield R-12 Sch., 1986—90, Gasconade R-12 Sch., Owensville, Mo., 1990—2005; family educator for 1st Steps Franklin County Bd. for Handicapped, Union, Mo., 1991—92; ret., 2005. Recorder for pilot behavioral modification program, Springfield, 1969; mentor York Elem. and Owensville H.S., 1989, 1994—. Vol. tchr. Delaware Elem. Class for Deaf/Blind, Springfield, 1968; sponsor, leader Say No to Drugs Club, Springfield, 1989—90; mem. adv. team, discipline com., at-risk com. York Elem., Springfield, 1988—90; mem. adv. com. Owensville H.S., 1994—2005; leader Boy Scouts Am.; mem. cert. team Support Dogs, Inc.; tchr. Sunday Bible Sch., 1963—89; bd. dirs. Learning Disabilities Assn., Springfield, 1989—90. Recipient Top 100 Curriculum Ideas award, Am. Sch. Bd. Jour./The Exec. Educator, 1989, Indirect Support award, Mo. Spl. Needs Assn., 2005. Mem.: Cmty. Tchr. Assn. Avocations: reading, canoeing, travel. Office: Owensville HS Gasconade County R-2 Box 536 Owensville MO 65066

LEICKLY, PORTIA ELAINE, science educator; b. Isleta, Ohio, Aug. 13, 1944; d. Vergil Heber and Sara Jean Sergeant; m. David William Leickly (dec. Feb. 21, 2006); children: Linda Diteman, Darleen Kimbrell, Jane King. BA, Ohio Wesleyan U., Delaware, 1962—66; MS, Ball State U., Muncie, Ind., 1970—76. Tchr. of perceptually handicapped New Phila. City Schs., Ohio, 1966—68; sci. tchr. Lakewood City Schs., 1968—2006. Bd. mem. Cleve. Regional Coun. Sci. Tchrs., 1995—2004, pres., 2000. Author: Sci. & You Curriculum Guide, 1981. Unit leader/coun. Girl Scouts Am., Cin., 1965. Grantee, NSF, Ball State U., 1970—71; scholar, Martha Holden Jennings Found., Cleve., Ohio, 1982. Mem.: NEA, Sci. Edn. Coun. Ohio, Ohio Edn. Assn., Am. Assn. Sci., Nat. Assn. Biology Tchrs., Lakewood Tchr.'s Assn.

(corr. sec., membership chairperson), Delta Kappa Gamma (membership chairperson). Avocations: reading, birdwatching, camping, photography, travel. Home: 4186 W 210 Fairview Park OH 44126

LEIDEL, KATHERINE, journalist, newscaster; b. Vienna, June 28, 1954; arrived in U.S., 1956; d. Donald Charles and Beverly (Broy) Leidel; 1 child, David Michael Harris. Student, Santa Clara (Calif.) U., 1972-73, Inst. European Studies, Madrid, 1973, George Washington U., 1974; BS in Orgnl. Mgmt., Palm Beach Atlantic Coll., 1998. Mgr./developer The Country Store, Knoxville, 1976-77; cons. Southeastern Sight & Sound, Raleigh, 1977-79; producer Capitol Broadcasting Co., Raleigh, 1979-80; newsanchor Mann Media Broadcasting, Raleigh, 1980-81, Fairbanks Broadcasting, West Palm Beach, Fla., 1981-83; writer West Communications, Orlando, Fla., 1987-88; artist-in-residence Sch. Arts Palm Beach County, Fla., 1991-94; writer WeekDay Newspaper, Palm Beach Gardens, Fla., 1996-97. Mgr. Nutrition World, 1996—98; writer WeekDay Newspaper, Palm Beach Gardens, Fla., 1996—97; pub. rels. dir. Am. Lung Assn. S.E. Fla., 1998—2004; dir. comm. Am. Lung Assn. Fla., 2003—04; instr. N.Am. Riding for Handicapped Assn. Contbr. articles to profl. jours. Vol. Nassau County Humane Soc. Recipient Working Women's award, The White House, 1980. Mem.: Fla. Motion Picture and TV Assn. (v.p. 1987—88, bd. dirs. 1988—91, pres. Palm Beach area chpt. 1990, state v.p. 1991, pres.), Palm Beach County Film Adv. Coun. (hon.; chmn. 1991—93), Fla. Congress Lung Assn. Staff. Avocations: horseback riding, skiing, travel.

LEIDIG, MARGOT HELENE, retired elementary school educator, retired secondary school educator; b. Fresno, Calif., May 31, 1945; d. Euvelle R. and Anita S. Enderlin; m. Leigh Arthur Leidig, June 11, 1972; children: Bonnie Chrisman, Kimberly Minnick BA, Chico State U., 1967, MA, 1970. Faculty appt. phys. sci. dept. Chico (Calif.) State Coll., Calif., 1967—68; tchr. math., sci. Oak Grove Intermediate Sch. Mt. Diablo Unified Sch. Dist., Concord, Calif., 1968—73; tchr. resource math. John Still Jr. H.S. Sacramento City Unified Sch. Dist., 1973—80, tchr., math. Kit Carson Mid. Sch., 1980—86, tchr. math. John F. Kennedy H.S., 1986—96, tchr. math., sci. Capital City Schs., 1996—2002; ret., 2002. Presenter No. Calif. Math. Conf., Asilomar; chair No. Calif. Math. Project U. Calif., Davis, 1985 Author: 5 math. books Mem. AAUW, Calif. Math. Coun., Order Ea. Star (# 150, 25 Yr. Pin), Daus. of Nile, Phi Delta Kappa Avocations: golf, gardening, travel, reading, bridge.

LEIGH, CHERI J., engineering consulting executive; BS Civil Eng., Southern Methodist U.; MS Eng. Mgmt., Kansas U. Positions with GM, Norfolk & Western Railway; founder and principle partner Leigh & O'Kane LLC, 1983—. Volunteer Reach to Recovery. Fellow: Soc. Women Engineers (Entrepreneur award 2003); mem.: Missouri Soc. Profl. Engineers. Achievements include being the first woman engineer to be appointed to the Missouri Board for Architects, Professional Engineers, and Land Surveyors. Office: Leigh & O'Kane LLC 9201 Ward Pkwy Kansas City MO 64114-3339

LEIGH, JENNIFER JASON (JENNIFER LEIGH MORROW), actress; b. LA, Feb. 5, 1962; d. Barbara Turner and Vic Morrow; m. Noah Baumbach, Sept. 3, 2005. Student, Lee Strasberg Inst. Appearances include (films) Eyes of a Stranger, 1980, Fast Times at Ridgemont High, 1982, Wrong is Right, 1982, Easy Money, 1983, Grandview U.S.A., 1984, Flesh & Blood, 1985, The Hitcher, 1986, The Men's Club, 1986, Sister, Sister, 1987, Under Cover, 1987, Heart of Midnight, 1988, The Big Picture, 1989, Last Exit to Brooklyn, 1989 (Critic Soc. award 1990), Miami Blues, 1990 (Critic Soc. award 1990), Fire Princess, 1990, Crooked Hearts, 1991, Backdraft, 1991, Rush, 1992, Single White Female, 1992, The Prom, 1992, Short Cuts, 1993, The Hudsucker Proxy, 1994, Mrs. Parker and the Vicious Circle, 1994, Dolores Claiborne, 1994, Georgia, 1995, Kansas City, 1996, Bastard Out of Carolina, 1996, A Thousand Acres, 1997, Washington Square, 1997, eXistenZ, 1998, The King is Alive, 2000, Skipped Parts, 2000, Beautiful View, 2000, The Quickie, 2001, The Anniversary Party, 2001, Hey Arnold! The Movie, (voice) 2002, Road to Perdition, 2002, In the Cut, 2003, The Machinist, 2004, Palindromes, 2004, Childstar, 2004 (Genie award 2005), The Jacket, 2005, Easter Sunday, 2005, Rag Tale, 2005; (TV movies) Angel City, 1980, I Think I'm Having a Baby, 1981, The Killing of Randy Webster, 1981, The Best Little Girl in the World, 1981, The First Time, 1982, Have You Ever Been Ashamed of Your Parents?, 1983, Girls of the White Orchid, 1983, Picnic, 1986, Buried Alive, 1990, The Love Letter, 1998, Crossed Over, 2002 (mini series) Thanks of a Grateful Nation, 1998; prodr., actress Georgia, 1995; writer, dir., prodr., actor The Anniversary Party, 2001; TV guest appearances include The Waltons, 1972, Tracey Takes On., 1996, King of the Hill, 1997; (TV series) Hercules (voice), 1998; appeared in music video Last Cup of Sorrow by Faith No More; (theatre) Cabaret, Proof, Abigail's Party, 2005. Named one of America's 10 Most Beautiful Women, Harper's Bazaar mag., 1989. Office: ICM c/o Tracey Jacobs 8942 Wilshire Blvd Beverly Hills CA 90211-1934 also: care Elaine Rich 2400 Whitman Pl Los Angeles CA 90068-2464*

LEIGHMAN, MARILYN RUST, school counselor; d. Roy Parker and Norma Laverne Cummins, Eleanor Cline Cummins (Stepmother); m. Robert Alan Rust, June 18, 1965 (div.); children: Wade Taylor Rust, Jay Mac Rust; m. Earl Lee Leighman, July 4, 2002. BS in Home Econ. Edn., Tex. Tech U., 1966; MEd, Prairie View A&M U., 1995; postgrad., Tex. A&M U., 2005—. Lic. profl. counselor Tex. Dept. Health, 2004, cert. vocat. home econs. tchr. Tex. Edn. Agy., 1966, sch. counselor Tex. Edn. Agy., 1995. Home econ. tchr. Del Rio (Tex.) H.S., 1966—68; kindergarten and home econ. tchr. McDonald County Consol. Sch. Dist., Anderson, Mo., 1970—72; home econ. tchr. Dublin (Tex.) H.S., Dublin, Tex., 1972—73; home econ. tchr. NE Area Vocat. Tech. Sch., Afton, Okla., 1975—76; dance tchr. Marilyn Rust's Sch. of Dance, Junction, Mason, and Rocksprings, Tex., 1976—92; home econs. tchr. Rocksprings (Tex.) H.S., 1982—92; jr. high sci. tchr. Bellville (Tex.) Jr. H.S., 1992—95; sch. counselor K-12 Iola (Tex.) Ind. Sch. Dist., 1995—2005. V.p., pres. and past pres. Brazos Valley Counseling Assn., Bryan, Tex., 1998—2001. Facilitator for divorce care program A&M Ch. of Christ, College Station, Tex., 2001—02. Named Outstanding Drill Team Dir., So. Meth. U. Drill Team Camp, 1971. Mem.: Vocat. Home Econ. Tchrs. Assn. Tex. (bd. dirs. 1984—90), Brazos Valley Counseling Assn., Kappa Delta Pi, Chi Sigma Iota. Mem. Church Of Christ. Avocations: interior decorating, landscaping, travel. Personal E-mail: mcrl1963@wmconnect.com.

LEIGHTON, ANNE RENITA, writer, educator; b. Queens, N.Y., Oct. 15, 1957; d. Richard Eli Leighton and Halin Pryves. Student, Fredonia State U., 1976—80, Lehman Coll., 2002—. Radio personality WBUZ, Fredonia, NY, 1976—80, WZIR, Buffalo, 1980—81, WRNW, Briarcliff Manor, NY, 1981—82; editor Hit Pardder, NYC, 1986—94; publicist Leighton Media-Motivation-Mktg., Bronx, NY, 1993—; tchr. Baruch Coll., NYC, 1996—. Mentor Just Plainfolks, 1998—2003. Author: (plays) Reach for the Sun, 1976, One Way to Heaven, 2004, (nonfiction book) Using Your Art & The Media to Comfort People, 2005; contbr. articles to jours. Writer, event planner City Critters, N.Y.C., 1998, 2003; writer Poor Friends St. Francis, Bronx, 2003. Mem.: Cat Writers Assn. Democrat. Avocations: art, films, music. Home: 3050 Decatur Ave #1D Bronx NY 10467 Office Phone: 718-881-8183.

LEIGHTON, CAROLYN, foundation administrator; b. Providence, R.I. BS in Human Devel., Pacific Oaks Coll. Founder Leighton Corp., 1978—82, Legal Talent Directory, 1982—; chmn. Core Competency Database Project Stanford (Conn.) U., 1982—84; founder Criterion Rsch., Sherman Oaks, Calif., 1984—89, Women in Tech. Internat., Sherman Oaks, 1989—. Office: Women in Tech Internat 13351 0 Riverside Dr 441 Sherman Oaks CA 91423

LEIMAN, JOAN MAISEL, university administrator, hospital administrator; b. Rochester, Minn., Apr. 26, 1934; d. John Josiah and Ida (Rubenstein-)Maisel; m. Leonard M. Leiman June 26, 1955; children: Elizabeth, Alan. BA, Wellesley (Mass.) Coll., 1955; MA, Columbia U., 1958, MPhil, 1976, PhD, 1977. Prog. analyst N.Y.C. Bur. Budget, 1966-68, sr. budget examiner, 1968-69, asst. budget dir., 1969-71; advisor to Mayor N.Y.C. Govt., Office of Mayor, 1972-74; v.p. prog. devel. and budget Manpower Demonstration Research Corp., N.Y.C., 1977-81; v.p. planning Interfaith Med. Ctr., N.Y.C., 1982-84; exec. dep. v.p. Columbia U. Health Scis., N.Y.C., 1984-2001; chief of staff to the pres. and CEO, N.Y. Presbyn. Hosp. and Healthcare Sys., 2001—. Clin. prof. pub. health Columbia U., 1991—; pres. past. pres. Grad. Facules, Alumni of Columbia U., 1985-91; dir., vice chair N.Y. Found., 1985-93; del. White House Conf. on Aging, 1995; exec. dir. Commonwealth Fund Commn. on Women's Health, 1993-99; cons. in field. Durant scholar, 1954-55. Fellow: N.Y. Acad. Medicine (chair sect. health care delivery); mem.: Women's Health Forum, Am. Med. Women's Assn. Found. (bd. dirs. 1999—2001), Am. Assn. Med. Colls., Health Care Exec. Forum (v.p. 1986—87), YMCA Acad. Women Achievers, Women's City Club, Phi Beta Kappa. Office: NY Presbyn Hosp AP-1466 161 Ft Washington Ave New York NY 10032-3795

LEINFELLNER, RUTH, strategic planner; d. Elisabeth and Werner Leinfellner; m. Francis Coleman, Sept. 10, 2000. BA, U. Nebr., 1990, M in Cmty. and Regional Planning, 1996. Nongovernmental mgmt. advisor US Peace Corps, Roseau, Commonwealth of Dominica, Dominica, 1996—98; hiv prevention evaluation specialist State of NE HIV Prevention Program, Lincoln, Nebr., 1998—2000; policy analyst Governor's Office of Planning and Budget, Atlanta, 2001—04; strategic planner State of GA Dept. of Transp., 2004—. Guest lectr. dept. of innovation and mgmt. Tech. U. Vienna. Editor: (magazine) Power Tool Magazine ('Zine of the month - Sassy Mag., 1995); owner and moderator (internet discussion list) Urban-L Planning Discussion List, elected rep. Am. Planning Assn. Student Rep. Coun. Region 5. Office Phone: 404-483-2562.

LEININGER, MADELEINE MONICA, nursing educator, consultant, retired anthropologist, editor, writer, theorist; b. Sutton, Nebr., July 13, 1925; d. George M. S. and D. Irene (Sheedy) L. BS in Biology, Scholastic Coll., 1950, LHD, 1976; MS in Nursing, Cath. U. Am., 1953; PhD in Anthropology, U. Wash., 1965; DSc (hon.), U. Indpls., 1990; PhDN (hon.), 1990, U. Kuopio, Finland, 1991. RN; cert. transcultural nurse FAAN/Am. Acad. Nursing. Instr., mem. staff, head nurse med.-surg. unit, supr. psychiat. unit St. Joseph's Hosp., Omaha, 1950-54; assoc. prof. nursing, dir. grad. program in psychiat. nursing U. Cin. Coll. Nursing, 1954-60; research fellow Nat. League Nursing, Papua New Guinea, 1960—62, 1978, 1992, 1994; research assoc. U. Wash. Dept. Anthropology, Seattle, 1964-65; prof. nursing and anthropology, dir. nurse-scientist PhD program U. Colo., Boulder and Denver, 1966-69; dean sch. nursing, prof. nursing, lectr. anthropology U. Wash., Seattle, 1969-74; dean coll. nursing, prof. nursing and anthropology U. Utah, Salt Lake City, 1974-80; Anise J. Sorell prof. nursing Troy (Ala.) State U., 1981; prof. nursing, adj. prof. anthropology, dir. Ctr. for Health Research, dir. transcultural nursing offerings Wayne State U., Detroit, 1981-95, prof. emeritus, 1995—; prof. Coll. Nursing U. Nebr. Med. Ctr., 1997—2001; ret., 2001—. Adj. prof. anthropology U. Utah, 1974-81; adj. prof. nursing U. Nebr., 1997—; disting. vis. prof. over 200 univs., U.S. and overseas, 1970—; docent Boys and Girls Town of Am., Omaha Father Flanaghan Ctr., 1996; cons. and lectr. in field. Author: 30 books including Nursing and Anthropology: Two Worlds to Blend, 1970, Contemporary Issues in Mental Health Nursing, 1973, Caring: An Essential Human Need, 1981, Reference Sources for Transcultural Health and Nursing, 1984, Basic Psychiatric Concepts in Nursing, 1960, Care: The Essence of Nursing and Health, 1984, Qualitative Research Methods in Nursing, 1985, Care: Discovery and Clinical-Community Uses, 1988, Ethical and Moral Dimensions of Caring, 1990, Culture Care, Diversity and Universality: A Theory of Nursing, 1991, 3d edit., 2005, Care: The Compassionate Healer, 1991, Caring Imperative for Nursing Education, 1991, (co-authored with Marilyn McFarland and James Bartlett) Transcultural Nursing, 3d edit., 2005, Transcultural Nursing Concepts, Theories, Research and Practice, 3d edit., 2004, Transcultural Nursing Culture Care Theory Diversity and University. a Worldwide Theory, 3d edit., 2005; editor, founder Jour. Transcultural Nursing, 1988-00, 05 (AJN award 2003); contbr. over 400 articles to profl. jours., chpts. to books; prodr. Leininger Nursing Autobiography, 2005. Recipient Outstanding Alumni award Cath. U. Am., 1969, Hon. award Am. Assn. Colls. Nursing, 1976, 96, Nurse of Yr. award Dist. 1 Utah Nurses Assn., 1976, Lit. award Utah Nurses Assn., 1978, Trotter Disting. Pub. Lectr. award U. Tex., 1985, Disting. Faculty Tchg. Recognition award Wayne State U., 1985, Outstanding Faculty Rsch. scholar award Wayne State U. and Gerontology Inst., 1985, Gershenson Rsch. award Wayne State U., 1985, Pace Inst. Rsch. award, 1992, Hewlett Packard Rsch. award, 1992, award for Acad. Excellence AAUW-Detroit, 1986, Disting. award Bd. Govs., 1987, Pres. Excellence in Tchg. award, 1988, Women of Sci. award U. Calif., Fullerton, 1990, Outstanding U. Grad. Mentor award Wayne State U., 1995, 97, Nightingale Rsch. award Oakland U., 1995, Outstanding Nursing Leader Russell Sage Coll, Sigma Theta Tau Intl. Disting. scholar award Russell Sage Coll., 1995, Nobel prize nominee, 1999, Can. Outstanding Rsch. award Can. Nurses Assn., 2003, Deans award Wayne State U. Coll. Nursing, 2005, Outstanding Public Nursing Svc. award Wayne State U., 2005, others; Womens Hall of Fame, 2004, Leininger Learning and Transcultural Nursing Collection libr. and reading sects. at Madonna U., Livonia, Mich. named in her honor, 1996; Leininger Archival Room at Trinity Coll., Moline, Ill. named in her honor, 2002; Mary Boynton Disting. lectr., 1998; Disting. vis. scholar Jimmy Crockett Lectr. Series, Disting. Vis. scholar U. Nebr., 1999, U. (Fresno) Calif. State U., 2005; named Disting. scholar U. Wis., 2001-02, Disting lectr. Arab Am. Internat. Conf., 2005, Deana Excellence Pub. Svc. award Wayne State U., 2005, Outstanding Achievement Health Care award Wayne State U., 2005, others; Worldwide Transcultural Nursing Ctr. named in her honor, 2001; Dist. honoree Worldwide Transcultural Nursing Soc., 2003; nominee Women's Hall of Fame, 2003, Nobel Peace prize, 2000. Fellow ANA, Am. Anthropol. Soc. for Applied Anthropology (exec. com. 1980-84, nominee Nobel Perce award), Am. Acad. Nursing (Living Legend award 1998), Royal Coll. Nursing Australia (First Internat. Achievement award 2000, First Qualitative Achievement award 2003); mem. Am. Assn. Humanities, Am. Applied Anthropol. Soc., Royal Coll. Nursing Australia, Mich. Nurses Assn. (Bertha Culp Human Rights award 1994), Ctrl. States Anthropology, Amnesty Internat., Transcultural Nursing Soc. (founder, bd. dirs., pres. 1974-80), Cultural Cmty. Group Assn. (ethics, humanities heritage study group), Australian Nat. Rsch. Care Confs. (leader human care rsch.), Internat. Assn. Human Caring (founder, pres., bd. dirs.), Nordic Caring Soc. Sweden (hon.), Sigma Xi, Pi Gamma Mu, Sigma Theta Tau (Lectr. of Yr. 1987—, Disting. Spkr. at conf. 1995-2005), Delta Kappa Gamma, Alpha Tau Delta.

LEINO, DEANNA ROSE, business educator; b. Leadville, Colo., Dec. 15, 1937; d. Arvo Ensio Leino and Edith Mary (Bonan) Leino Malenck; 1 adopted child, Michael Charles Bonan. BSBA, U. Denver, 1959, MS in Bus. Adminstrn., 1967; postgrad., C.C. Denver, U. No. Colo., Colo. State U., U. Colo., Met. State Coll. Cert. tchr., vocat. tchr., Colo. Tchr. Jefferson County Adult Edn., Lakewood, Colo., 1963-67; tchr. bus., coord. coop. office edn. Jefferson HS, Edgewater, Colo., 1959-93, ret., 1993; sales assoc. Joslins Dept. Store, Denver, 1978—89; mem. ea. team. clk. office automation Denver Svc. Ctr., Nat. Pk. Svc., 1993-94; wage hour tech. US Dept. Labor, 1994—. Instr. C.C. Denver, Red Rocks, 1967-81, U. Colo., Denver, 1976-79, Parks Coll. Bus. (now P, 1967—81, U. Colo., Denver, 1976—79, Parks Coll. Bus. (now Everest Coll.), 1983—, Front Range C.C., 1998—2000; dist. advisor Future Bus. Leaders Am. Author short story. Active City of Edgewater Sister City Project Student Exch. Com., Opera Colo. Assocs. and Guild, I Pagliacci; pres. Career Women's Symphony Guild, sec.; treas. Phantoms of Opera, 1982—; pres. Colo. Symphony Guild, 2006—; ex-officio trustee Denver Symphony Assn., 1980—82, 2006—. Recipient Disting. Svc. award Jefferson County Sch. Bd., 1980, Tchr. Who Makes a Difference award Sta. KCNC/Rocky Mountain News, 1990, Youth Leader award Lakewood Optimist Club, 1993; named to Jefferson HS Wall of Fame, 1981, Jefferson County Hist. Commn. Hall of Fame, 2000, countess of the Wheat Ridge Carnation Festival, 2001. Mem. NEA (life), Colo. Edn. Assn., Jefferson County Edn. Assn., Colo. Vocat. Assn., Am. Vocat. Assn., Colo. Educators for and about Bus., Profl. Sec. Internat., Career Women's Symphony Guild, Profl. Panhellenic Assn., Colo. Congress Fgn. Lang. Tchr., Wheat Ridge C. of C. (edn. and scholarship com.), Federally Employed Women, Tyrolean Soc. Denver, Delta Pi Epsilon, Phi Chi Theta, Beta Gamma Sigma, Alpha Lambda Delta. Republican. Roman Catholic. Avocations: decorating wedding cakes, crocheting, sewing, music, world travel. Home: 3712 Allison St Wheat Ridge CO 80033-6124 Office Phone: 720-264-3257. Personal E-mail: deannaleino@comcast.net.

LEIPER ESTABROOKS, ESTHER, writer, artist, illustrator; b. West Chester, Pa., Nov. 18, 1946; d. John Ashurst and Hannah Mather (Shelly) L.; m. Peter H. Estabrooks, Nov. 23, 1972; children: Hannah Margaret, Thomas. BA in English, Va. Commonwealth U., 1970; BS in Edn., St. Joseph's Coll., 1971. Freelance writer, Jefferson, N.H., 1976—. Author: Christmas Colt, 1974, How to Enter Poetry Contests To Win, 1984, The Inkling Selection, 1984, The Wars of Faery, 1987, Tamar's Son, 1987, Children in December, 1988, Home From the Wars, 1989, A Flatlander's Guide To North Country Cooking, 1989, Stone Country, 1993, Winter Story, 1995, The Book of Lilith, 2006; illustrator: Mushrooms and Marshmallows, 1989, Hi, Sky!, 1990, Coverings, 1991, The People's of Melsea, 1996, Fables, 1999; columnist. Avocations: cats, gardening, stones/rocks, cooking, reading. Home: PO Box 87 747 Presidential Hwy US Rt 2 Jefferson NH 03583-0087

LEIRER, MARGARET (PEGGY) L., communications educator; b. St. Louis, Dec. 30, 1945; d. Henry G. and Lorene M. (Weber) Geerdes; m. Kenn L. Leirer, Nov. 27, 1965; children: Emily, Jessica. BS in Edn., Southeast Mo. State U., Cape Girardeau, 1967; MAT in Comm., Webster U., St. Louis, 2002. Cert. elem. and secondary edn., life cert. English 9-12, art 7-9, social studies 7-9 Mo. Dept. Edn., secondary edn. Ill. Tchr. Gideon Jr. HS, Mo., 1967—68, Willow Springs Sch. Dist., Mo., 1971—72, Gideon HS, 1972—73, Valmeyer CUSD, Ill., 1991—92, Grandview R-II Sch. Dist., Hillsboro, Mo., 1994—; grad. asst. tchr. Southeast Mo. State Coll., Cape Girardeau, 1969—71; sub. tchr. Gideon, Malden, and St. Eustachius High Schs., 1974—90. Adv. coun. Jefferson County Tech Prep, 1997—2006; mem., local rep. Jefferson Coll. Continuing Edn. Adv. Bd., Hillsboro, 1999—. Troop leader Cotton Ball Area Girl Scouts, Sikeston, Mo., 1967—68, 1972—76, bd. dirs, sec., 1986—92, coun. trainer, 1986—92. Recipient St. Ann Medal, Nat. Cath. Conf., 1992. Mem.: Grandview Mo. NEA (pres. 1999—2005, mem. leadership coun. 2000—02). Roman Catholic. Avocations: gardening, cardmaking, travel, camping. Office: Grandview HS 11470 Hwy C Hillsboro MO 63050 Personal E-mail: kennmar@sbcglobal.net.

LEISETH, PATRICIA SCHUTZ, educational technology specialist; b. Menomonie, Wis., Dec. 13, 1942; d. Herb D. and Dorothy F. (Husby) Schutz; m. Keith M. Leiseth, June 12, 1964; children: Kjrsten Leiseth Bobb, Jon. BA, Macalester Coll., 1964, MEd, 1972; MS, St. Cloud State U., 1994. Elem. music coord. Hopkins (Minn.) Pub. Schs., 1964-65; English instr. Bloomington (Minn.) Pub. Schs., 1965-67, Maple Lake (Minn.) Pub. Schs., 1974-90, vocal music tchr., 1990-93, K-12 technology coord., 1993-98; info. tech. specialist Dist. 279 Osseo (Minn.) Pub. Schs, Buffalo, 1998—. Vol., Buffalo (Minn.) Pub. Libr., 1993-94, Nat. Forest Svc., 1991, Okla. State Parks, 1997. Mem. NEA, Minn. Ednl. Media Orgn., Phi Kappa Phi. Avocations: reading, cross country skiing. Home: 6051 Laurel Ave Golden Valley MN 55416 Office: Osseo Public Schs Dist 279 15900 Weaver Lake Rd Maple Grove MN 55311-1432 E-mail: Kpleiseth@aol.com.

LEISHNER, JANE CARLSON, retired director; b. Dallas, Sept. 9, 1941; d. Virgil Harry and Katherine Staring Carlson; m. Stanley Louis Leishner, Aug. 3, 1963; children: Glenn Thomas, Katherine Jane, Mark Louis. BA, Midwestern U., Wichita Falls, Tex., 1963; EdM, Midwestern State U., Wichita Falls, Tex., 1991. Dean students Midwestern State U., Wichita Falls, 1993—2001, assoc. v.p., 2001—02; ret. Bd. mem. Norcentex Coun. Girl Scouts, Wichita Falls, 1995—2001; mem. North Tex. Ctr. for Non-Profit Mgmt., Wichita Falls, 1997—2002; vol. Meals on Wheels, Wichita Falls, 2000—06. Avocation: genealogy. Home: 2909 Radney Ln Wichita Falls TX 76309

LEISTER, KELLY M., lawyer; b. Allentown, Pa., Apr. 30, 1972; BA, Am. U., 1993; JD, DePaul U., 1998. Bar: Ill. 2000, Pa. 2001, NJ 2001. Ptnr. Swartz Campbell LLC, Phila. Recipient Inst. for Humane Studies Award, Cali Award. Office: Swartz Campbell LLC 1601 Market St, 34th Fl Philadelphia PA 19103 Office Phone: 215-299-4254. Office Fax: 215-299-4301. E-mail: kleister@swartzcampbell.com.*

LEISTNER, MARY EDNA, retired secondary school educator; b. Evanston, Ill., Apr. 13, 1929; d. Joseph W. and Edna C. (Moe) Cox; m. Delbert L. Leistner, Sept. 30, 1950; children: David, Martha, Joseph. BS Chemistry, Purdue U., 1950; MEd, Miami U., Oxford, Ohio, 1964. Tchr. sci. and math. Ctrl. Jr. H.S., Sidney, Ohio, 1962—66; tchr. chemistry, biology, advanced chemistry Sidney H.S., 1966—93; ret., 1993. Mem. high sch. chemistry test com. Am. Chem. Soc., 1983-85 Exec. com. Ohio Dist. Luth. Women's Missionary League, Columbus, 1978-82, conv. chmn., 1988; pres. Miami Valley zone, 1985-87; pres. Redeemer Ladies Soc., Sidney, 1980-91, 94-98, treas., 1998-2003, St. John's Luth. Joy Circle 2003—, Thrift & Shop Leader 2005—; mem. gift shop com. Wilsom Meml. Hosp., Sidney, 1994-96, aux. sec., 1997-98, membership chair, aux. v.p., 1999, aux. pres., 2000 Mem. NSTA (Cadre 100 award, H.S. chemistry test com.), We. Ohio Sci. Tchrs. Assn. (pres. 1972-73), Sci. Edn. Coun. Ohio (dist. rep. exec. bd. 1984-86, treas. 1986-90, pres. elect 1991-92, pres. 1992-93, immediate past pres. 1993-94, chair retirees/hist. com. 1995-2000), Sidney Edn. Assn. (treas. 1980-82, 85-86, Tchr. of Yr. 1988), Ohio Acad. Scis. (Jerry Acker Outstanding Tchr. of Yr. award 1988-89, Exemplar 1993), Shelby Co. Ret. Tchrs. Assn. (v.p. 2003-2004, pres. 2005-2006), Delta Kappa Gamma (2d v.p. 1992-94, 1st v.p. 1994-96, pres. 1996-98, past pres. 1998—) Republican. Lutheran.

LEITCH, SALLY LYNN, social studies educator; b. Jacksonville, Fla., Aug. 5, 1967; d. Niles Dewitt and Bebe Dianne Jester. MA in Tchg., Nat. Louis U., Evanston, Ill., 1998. Instr. Nat. Coll. Edn., Evanston, 1991—98, Waukegan Pub. Schs., Ill., 1998—2000; tchr. social studies Norfolk Pub. Schs., Va., 2000—. Tutor ROTC, Norfolk, 2001—. Author: (young adolescent fiction) My Thelma. Vol. Bayview Civic League, Norfolk, 2003. Mem.: APERD (corr.). Conservative. Christian. Office: Norfolk Pub Schs 1384 Kempsville Rd Norfolk VA 23502 Office Phone: 757-892-3200. Personal E-mail: g8trgrl88@yahoo.com. Business E-Mail: sleitch@nps.k12.va.us.

LEITER, AMANDA C., lawyer; BS, M Engring., Stanford Univ.; MS Oceanography, Univ. Wash.; JD, Harvard Univ., 2000. Law clk. to Hon. John Paul Stevens U.S. Supreme Ct., Washington, 2003—04; atty. Natural Resources Def. Council, Washington, 2004—. Editor (mng.): Environmental Law Rev. Grantee Beagle Harvard Law Sch. Fellowship, 2004. Office: Natural Resources Defense Council Suite 400 1200 New York Ave NW Washington DC 20005 Office Phone: 202-289-2398.

LEITES, BARBARA L. (ARA LEITES), artist, educator; b. Hamilton, Ohio, June 3, 1942; d. Wilbur Frank and Alice Marie (Butts) Mayer; m. William Michael Whitley, Oct. 29, 1972 (div. Nov. 1977); 1 child, Rachel Sutton; m. Andre Leo Leites, Dec. 15, 1981 (div. Mar. 2000); chldren: David, Bevin; 1 stepchild, Daniella Soto de Leites. BFA, Miami U., Oxford, Ohio, 1964, MFA, 1967. Tchr. Madison Elem. Sch., Hamilton, 1964—65; tchr. art and humanities Key West (Fla.) H.S., 1967—70, tchr. adult edn. in art, 1968—70; instr. Fla. Keys Jr. Coll., Key West, 1969—70; co-dir. Kleinert Gallery, Woodstock, NY, 1977—80; self employed artist under the name Ara Leites, 1981—. Bd. dirs. Woodstock Guild of Craftsmen, 1978—79; instr. drawing and painting, divsn. head visual arts Georgiana Bruce Kirby Preparatory Sch., Santa Cruz, Calif., 1998—2001; owner Ara Fine Art Giclee Studio; workshop instr. painting, Tuscany, 2001, ARA Fine Art Studio, Tuscany, 2002; instr. art Georgiana Bruce Kirby Prep. Sch., 2005—. Exhibited at Gallery El Ciruelo, Tepoztlan, Mex., Club 209 Gallery, Cuernavaca, Mex., Black Sheep Art Gallery, Eng., Westminster Gallery, London, Cin. Art Mus., Dayton Art Inst., Springfield (Mo.) Art Mus., Miami U., Cynon Valley Mus., Aberdare, South Wales; U.S. nat. exhbns. of over 200 shows and 70 awards including Rocky Mountain Nat., Watercolor USA, Adirondacks Nat., Nat. Watercolor Soc., Am. Watercolor Soc., Audubon Artists, Phila. Watercolor Club, Allied Artists, N.Y.C., Calif. Nat. Watercolor Soc.; subject of articles in publs. Treas., bd. dirs. Internat. Soc. Acrylic Painters, 2004—06. Mem. AAUW, Internat. Soc. Exptl. Artists (signature), Am. Artists Profl. League (signature), Nat. Watercolor Soc. (signature), Nat. Soc. Painters in Casein and Acrylic (signature), Internat. Soc. Acrylic Painters (signature, treas. 2004-06, bd. dirs. 2004-06), Watercolor USA Honor Soc. (signature), Soc. Watercolor Artists (signature), Ky. Watercolor Soc. (signature), Tex. Watercolor Soc. (signature), Ga. Watercolor Soc. (signature), Mo. Watercolor Soc. (signature), Miss. Watercolor Soc. (signature), Phila. Watercolor Club Soc. (signature), Audubon Artists (signature), Mont. Watercolor Soc. (signature), Rocky Mountain Nat. Watercolor Soc. (signature), Fedn. of Can. Artists (signature), Soc. Layerists in Mixed Media (signature), Watercolor Soc. Ala. (signature), Pa. Watercolor Soc. (signature), Taos Nat. Watercolor Soc. (signature), Ea. Washington Watercolor Soc., Delta Delta Delta Alumnae Assn. Democrat. Avocations: gardening, carpentry, skiing, surfing. Home: 168 Oxford Way Santa Cruz CA 95060-6447 Office Fax: 831-454-9777. Personal E-mail: araleites@sbcglobal.net.

LEITH, KAREN PEZZA, psychologist, educator; b. Providence, Sept. 27, 1948; d. Henry and Lucy Maria (Bevilacqua) P.; m. James Robert Leith, June 6, 1970; children: Douglas Clay, Cara Beth. BA, Brown U., Providence, R.I., 1970; MA in Religious Studies, John Carroll U., University Heights, Ohio, 1988; MA in Psychology, Case Western Res. U., Cleve., 1995, PhD, 1997. Substitute elem. tchr. City of Chgo., 1970; math. tchr. Lane Tech. HS, Chgo., 1971; instr. preschool art and coordination programs Pk. Dist. Deerfield, Ill., 1973-75, coord. preschool day camp Ill., 1975-80; jr. high religious edn. coord., catechist trainer Holy Cross, Deerfield, 1975-80; H.S. religious edn. coord. St. Mary parish, Hudson, Ohio, 1981-85, youth min., dir. religious edn., 1985-88, pastoral assoc., 1988-91; pvt. math. tutor Hudson, Aurora sch., Ohio, 1980-88; cons. for ministry devel. Diocese of Cleve., 1989—, steering com., instr., Faith and Justice Leadership Inst., 1995—; adj. faculty John Carroll U., 1988—97, 1998—99; rsch. asst. Case Western Res. U., 1993-97; adj. faculty Baldwin Wallace Coll., 1997—2006; assoc. dir. Cath. Commn. Summit County, 2006—. Editor and contbr., chair com. manual on parish and sch. partnerships, Diocese of Cleve., 1997; adv. bd. Office on Women in Ch. and Soc., Diocese of Cleve., chair 1993-97; steering com. Cath. Diocese of Cleve. Social Justice Leadership Inst., 1995-98; coord. tng. Justice Tng. Diocese of Cleve., 2000-03; dir. Call to Renewal of Summit County, 2000-, exec. dir., 2001-; presenter in field. Contbr. articles to profl. jours. Recipient Bishop Anthony M. Pilla Leadership award Roman Cath. Diocese Cleve., 1998, 2002; faculty rsch. grantee Baldwin Wallace Coll., 1997, grad. alumni travel grantee Case West Res. U., 1993-95. Mem. APA (grad. student travel award 1994), Am. Psychol. Soc., Midwestern Psychol. Assn., Soc. for Personality and Social Psychology, Cath. Commn. (bd. dir. 1984-2001, chair 1997-2001), Hudson LWV (bd. dir. 1980-92, v.p., treas.), Holy Ground (founder, spiritual dir.), mem., FutureChurch Leadership Coun., 2000-04. Avocations: reading, needlecrafts. Personal E-mail: KPL7@aol.com.

LEITZEL, JOAN RUTH, retired academic administrator; BA in Math., Hanover Coll., 1958; MA in Math., Brown U., 1961; PhD in Math., Ind. U., 1965. Instr. math. Oberlin (Ohio) Coll., 1961-62; asst. prof. math. Ohio State U., Columbus, 1965-70, assoc. prof., 1970-84, prof., 1984-92, vice-chmn. dept., 1973-79, acting chmn., 1978, assoc. provost, 1985-90; prof. dept. math. and stats. U. Nebr., Lincoln, 1992-96, sr. vice chancellor for acad. affairs, 1992-96, interim chancellor, 1995-96; pres. U. N.H., Durham, 1996—2002, pres. emerita, 2002—. Adv. com. Griffith Ins. Found., 1979-82; cons. Ohio Dept. Edn., 1980-83; participant Am. Coun. on Edn., 1980, 82; cons. Nat. Commn. on Excellence in Edn., U.S. Dept. Edn., 1982; univ. math. edn. del. to China, 1983; dir. divsn. materials devel., rsch. and info. sci. edn. NSF, 1990-92; presenter in field, 1980—; bd. dirs. Am. Assn. Higher Edn., chmn.-elect, 1996-97, chmn., 1997-98; mem. interpretive reports adv. bd. Nat. ssessment Ednl. Progress, 1995-98; trustee Consortium on Math. and Its Applications, 1994-95; mem. exec. coun. com. on acad. affairs Nat. Assn. State Univs. and Land-Grant Colls., 1994-96, bd. dirs., 1997-99, chmn. com. on faculty, 1994-96; coord. coun. for edn. NRC, 1993-95, mem. bd. on math. scis. edn., 1985-87, math. scis. edn. bd., chmn. 2000-05. Bd. dirs. United Way Lincoln, 1995-96, 1st Plymouth Ch., 1996, Lincoln Partnership for Econ. Devel., 1996, N.H. Charitable Found., 1998-02, Durham Cmty. Ch., 1996-02. Recipient Disting. Alumni award Hanover Coll., 1986, dir.'s award for mgmt. excellence NSF, 1991; Disting. Tchg. award Ohio State U., 1982, Disting. Svc. award Ohio State U., 2002, Pettee medal U. N.H., 2002; grantee NSF, 1976-798, 84-88, Battelle Found., 1981-83, SOHIO, 1983-85. Mem. AAAS (edn. com. 1981-84), Am. Math. Soc. (com. on excellence in scholarship 1993-95), Assn. for Women in Math., Math. Assn. Am. (nominatinig com. 1978-79, com. on tchr. tng. and accreditation Ohio sect. 1976-79, nat. com. on undergrad programs 1982-85, chmn. joint task force on curriculum for grades 11-13 with Nat. Coun. Tchrs. Math. 1986-88), Nat. Coun. Tchrs. Math., Mortar Bd., Sigma Xi, Phi Kappa Phi. Business E-Mail: joan.leitzel@unh.edu.

LEIVE, CYNTHIA, editor-in-chief; m. Howard Bernstein; 1 child, Lucy. BA in English Literature, Swarthmore Coll., 1988. With The Paris Rev, The Saturday Rev.; editl. asst., then dep. editor Glamour Mag., 1988—99; editor-in-chief Self Mag., 1999—2001, Glamour Mag., 2001—. Named one of Top 40 Under 40 Executives in NY, Crain's NY Bus., 2002; recipient Matrix award for magazine work, NY Women in Comm. Inc., 2006. Mailing: Glamour Mag 4 Times Square 17th Floor New York NY 10036*

LEKAS, MARY DESPINA, retired otolaryngologist; b. Worcester, Mass., May 13, 1928; d. Spyridon Peter and Merciny S. (Manoliou) Lekas; m. Harold William Picozzi (dec.). Student, Boston U.; BA, Clark U., 1949, DSc, ScD, Clark U., 1997; MD, Athens (Greece) U., 1957; MA, Brown U., 1986. Diplomate Am. Bd. Otolaryngology. Sci. instr. Hahnemann Hosp. Sch. Nursing; rotating intern Meml. Hosp., Worcester, 1957-58; resident in otolaryngology R.I. Hosp., Providence, 1958-62; resident in otolaryngology and otorhinolaryngology U. Pa. Grad. Sch. Medicine, 1960; surgeon in chief, dept. otolaryngology R.I. Hosp., 1984-96, surgeon-in-chief emerita; pvt. practice Providence, 1962—. Chmn. dept. otolaryngology Brown U., Providnce, 1984, clin. prof. emerita surgery divsn. otolaryngology, head and neck; cons. Cleft Palate Clin. and Craniofacial of R.I. Hosp., 1964—, VA Hosp., Providence, 1967—, St. Joseph Hosp., Providence, 1983—, Miriam Hosp., Providence, 1984—; lectr. profl. orgns.; mem. Project Hope in Columbia, Ceylon/Sri Lanka, SS Hope Hosp. Ship, People-to-People, Inc., Washington, 1968-69. Mem. editl. bd. Am. Jour. Rhinology, 1987—; contbr. articles to profl. jours. Mem. alumni coun. Clark U.; pres. Providence Med. Assn., 1987-88. Named R.I. Woman Physician of Yr., 1992; recipient Disting. Svc. award, Providence Med. Assn., 1996, Emeriti award, Brown U., 1999, Outstanding Svc. award, Brown Med. Alumni Assn., 1999, cert. of recognition, People-to-People, Inc.; fellow Jonas Clark fellow. Fellow ACS, Soc. Univ. Otolaryngologists-Head and Neck Surgeons, Triological Soc. (ea. sect. sec., Presdl. Citation 1993), Am. Acad. Otolaryngology-Head and Neck Surgeons (gov. R.I. chpt. bd. of govs. 1985-), Am. Acad. Facial Plastic and Reconstructive Surgeons, Am. Acad. Broncho-Escophalogy (treas., v.p. 1990); mem. AMA, Assn. Acad. Dept. Otolaryngology-Head and Neck Surgery, Deafness Rsch. Found., Am. Cleft Palate Assn., Am. Med. Women's Assn. (R.I. Woman Physician of Yr. 1992), Am. Broncho-Esophagological Assn. (hon.), New Eng. Otolaryng. Soc. (pres. 1987-88, Cert. of Recognition 1980-81), Centurion Club. Greek Orthodox. Avocations: bicycling, swimming, church choir. Home: 129 Terrace Ave Riverside RI 02915-4726 Home Fax: 401-433-0941.

LEKBERG, BARBARA, sculptor; BFA, MA, Univ. Iowa; DFA (hon.), Simpson Coll. Instr. Univ. of the Arts, Phila., Nat. Acad. Sch. of Fine Arts, NYC. Exhibitions include Sculpture Ctr., NYC, Marmara Manhattan, NYC, Mt. Holyoke Coll, Glass Art Gallery, Toronto, Pa. Acad. Fine Arts, Whitney Mus. Am. Art, Mus. Modern Art; represented in collections of NAD, Whitney Mus. Am. Art, George Washington Univ., Des Moines Art Ctr., General Electric Corp., Birmingham Mus. Art, New Sch. Univ., NY, Bayfield Clark Collection, Bermuda, Michener Mus., Pa., Brookgreen Gardens, SC. Grantee 2 Guggenheim Fellowships, Inst. Arts & Letters, Richard Florsheim Art Fund. Mem.: Century Assn., NAD (academician, Saltus Gold medal 1990), Nat. Sculpture Soc. (sec., Gold medal 1991, Fellow). Studio: Apt 2A 195 Stanton St New York NY 10002 Office Phone: 212-996-1908, 212-529-8370.

LEKUS, DIANA ROSE, librarian; b. Washington, Feb. 5, 1948; d. Max and Eleanor (Kruger) L. Student, Hofstra U., Hempstead, N.Y., 1965-66; BA, Emerson Coll., Boston, 1969; MLS, U. Pitts., Pa., 1970. Asst. dept. head. search dept. Temple U., Phila., 1970-71; cataloging supr. weekly record sect. R.R. Bowker, N.Y.C., 1972-75; cataloger, asst. prof. U. Ill., Champaign-Urbana, Ill., 1975-78; customer svc. rep. Res. Fund, N.Y.C., 1979-81; list libr. Kleid Co., N.Y.C., 1981-94; subject classifier Reed Pub. Co., New Providence, N.J., 1995-99; with Am. Lung Assn., N.Y.C., 1997; libr. Queens Borough Pub. Libr., Jamaica, N.Y., 1999—. Sr. editor Am. Book Pub. Record, 1974; book reviewer Libr. Jour., 1979. Devel. asst. Pearl Theatre Co., 1995-96. Mem. ALA, Nat. Hist. Preservation and Trust, N.Y. Sheet Music Soc., Hadassah (life). Democrat. Avocations: travel, theater, reading. Home: 28-05 37th St Astoria NY 11103-4350 E-mail: dlekus@queenslibrary.org.

LELAND, DOROTHY, academic administrator; BA in English, MA in Am. studies, PhD in Philosophy, Purdue U. Vis. asst. prof. Calif. State U., Northridge, 1977—81, U. Calif., Santa Cruz, 1981—82, Calif. State U., Chico, 1982—83; dir. interdisciplinary doctoral program in English and philosophy Purdue U., 1984—93, inaugural dir. Women's Resource Office, 1993—95; dir. Women's Studies Ctr., exec. dir. Pres.'s Commn. on Status of Women Fla. Atlantic U., 1995—98, exec. dir. univ. strategic planning, 1998—2001, assoc. provost, 2000—01, v.p., prof. philosophy Boca Raton campus, 2001—04; pres. Ga. Coll. and State U., Milledgeville, 2004—. Named a protégé, Am. Assn. State Colls. and Univs. Millennium Leadership Initiative, 2002—03. Office: Pres's Office Ga Coll & State U Campus Box 20 Milledgeville GA 31061

LELAND, JANET K., social work therapist; b. Saginaw, Mich., Dec. 6, 1954; d. Ward Coville and Betty Jane (Brown) Leland; m. Loren Jeremy Young, June 5, 1982 (div. Apr. 1994); 1 child, Amanda R. Leland-Young. BA, Mich. State U., 1977, MSW, 1981. Cert. social worker, Mich. Instr. Lansing (Mich.) C.C., 1979-93; instr. social work Mich. State U., East Lansing, 1979-81; therapist Sanctuary for Runaways, Royal Oak, Mich., 1981-83; residential dir. Haven Battered Women's Shelter, Pontiac, Mich., 1983-84; family therapist, instr. Cath. Social Svcs. of Oakland County, Royal Oak, Mich., 1983-2000; with Oakland Family Svcs., Berkeley, Mich., 2000—. Bd. dirs. Listening Ear Crisis Ctr., East Lansing, 1979-80; cons. Ingham County Women's Commn., Lansing, 1980-81, Ingham County Prosecutors Office, Lansing, 1981-82; founder REACT-Rape Edn. and Counseling Team, East Lansing, 1981-82. Contbg. author: Women, Power and Therapy, 1988; author articles. Founding mem. Coun. Against Domestic Assault, Lansing, 1979; cmty. organizer Mich. State U. Rape Crisis Ctr., 1980. Recipient Cert. of Appreciation, Cooley Law Sch./Ingham County Women's Commn., 1994, NOW, 1981, others. Mem. Acad. Cert. Social Workers. Democrat. Avocations: garage sales, furniture painting, cooking. Office: Oakland Family Svcs 2351 W 12 Mile Rd Berkley MI 48072-1826 Home: 582 Liberty Pointe Dr Ann Arbor MI 48103-6806

LELAND, JOY HANSON, retired anthropologist, researcher; b. Glendale, Calif., July 29, 1927; d. David Emmett and Florence (Sockerson) Hanson; m. David A. Riegert, Nov. 14, 1993. BA in English Lit., Pomona Coll., Claremont, Calif., 1949; MBA, Stanford U., 1960; MA in Anthropology, U. Nev., 1972; PhD in Anthropology, U. Calif., Irvine, 1975. Sec. Office Spl. Rep., Paris, 1951—53; dir. pers. Libyan Am. Tech. Assistance Svc., Tripoli, Libya, 1953—56; with Desert Research Inst. U. Nev., 1961—; asst. research prof. Desert Research Inst., U. Nev., 1975-77, assoc. research prof., 1977-79, rsch. prof., 1979-89, rsch. prof. emerita, 1990—. Author: monograph Firewater Myths, Frederick West Lander-A Biographical Sketch; contbg. author: Smithsonian Handbook of North American Indians; also articles, book chpts. Founding trustee Robert and Joy Leland Charitable Trust, 1992—2005. NIMH grantee, 1972-73; Nat. Inst. Alcohol Abuse and Alcoholism grantee, 1974-75, 79-81 Mem. Am. Anthrop. Assn., Southwestern Anthrop. Assn., Soc. Applied Anthropology, Soc. Med. Anthropology, Gt. Basin Anthrop. Conf., Phi Kappa Phi. Address: 6126 Carriage House Way Reno NV 89529-7326

LELAS, SNJEZANA, pharmacologist, researcher; b. Zagreb, Croatia, Apr. 29, 1971; d. Srdan and Jasmina Lelas. BA, U. Oxford, 1989—92, DPhil, 1993—96. Postdoctoral fellow La. State U. Med. Ctr., New Orleans, 1996—98, Harvard Med. Sch., Southborough, Mass., 1999—2001; sr. rsch. investigator Bristol-Myers Squibb, Wallingford, Conn., 2001—. Contbr. articles to profl. jours. Scholar, U. Oxford, 1991. Mem.: Am. Soc. for Pharmacology and Exptl. Therapeutics, Behavioral Pharmacology Soc., Soc. for Neuroscience. Avocations: travel, writing, sports, theater. Home: 3B Oak Hill Dr Clinton CT 06413 Office: Bristol-Myers Squibb 5 Research Pkwy Wallingford CT 06492 Office Phone: 203-677-7441. Office Fax: 203-677-7569. Business E-Mail: snjezana.lelas@bms.com.

LELYVELD, GAIL ANNICK, actress; b. Boston, May 22, 1948; d. Edward I. and Beatrice Elizabeth (Hewitt) L. BA in Polit. Sci., Boston U., 1970; MA in Polit. Sci., Goddard Coll., 1974; studied with Paul Barry, Peter Donat, Ray Reinhardt, Darrell Lauer, others. Actress, 1970—; tech. staff USA Prodns. and Midseason, Hempstead, NY, 1986-87, prodn. stage mgr., 1987—. Tech. staff Gray Wig, Hempstead, 1986, 87; cons. Talking With prodn. M.A., C.W. Post. Appeared in numerous films including Frances, Halloween III, Children On Their Birthdays, Project 1917, Rocky II, Happy Endings, Seeds of Innocence, Bonfire of the Vanities, The Music of the Heart, The Bird's Eye View, Insomnia, Monster Math, The Lesson, I'm Not Rappaport, City Hall, The House of the Venus Flytrap (ind. film), Believe for Hofstra University (film), Baby Buyer (NYU short film); (TV): Archie Bunker's Place, Mister Clown Says, White Noise, The Gentle Creature, (ABC Afterschool Spl.) Summer Stories: The Mall, Mathnet, Bill Cosby Murder Mystery, Cosby: You're OK, I'm Hilton, Upright Citizen Brigade; actor: Alice in Wonderland, Not So Grimm Fairytale Players; actress (Littletop Theater Co.) Toby Tyler, Marmalade Gumdrops, Bohemian Lights, King Lear - Tenant, Doctor & Knight Plainedge Playhouse, The Hostage, USA Prodns., The Cherry Orchard, Broadhollow Theater Bay Way Art Ctr., The House of Blue Leaves, The Lady of Larkspur Lotion, Broadhollow Theatre Bay Way Arts Ctr., Sarah Good and the Voice of Martha Corey, BDR Repertory Co., The Worst Play in the World, Women's Theatrical Collective, The Man Who Came to Dinner, U.S.A. Prodns., Holocaust Survivor-Columbia U.; Singer: Gospel Oedipus at Colonus evangelist, townsperson, choir, Musicum Collegium Hofstra U., Pala Opera Assn., St. Patrick's Cathedral Choir, Temple Emanuel New Hyde Park Choir; singer and leader Christmas Carols Garden City Group Christmas Party, Garden City Group Chorus Holiday Songs and Soloist; soloist piano recital, solo singer Ecumenical Thanksgiving Svc.; one-person performance, Dona Gracia Nasi, Memoirs of Glüchel of Hameln, Temple Emanuel of New Hyde Park, Karen Finley Workshop Performance Arts, Actors Bootcamp, Purple Rose Theatre Co.; theater tech. involvement includes stage mgr., sound asst. Wings; sound asst. Danton's Death; asst. stage mgr. props, fx, dresser Accomplice; cons. on reading The Sisters Rosenweig. Reader Yom Kippur svcs. Temple Emanuel, San Francisco. Mem. AFTRA Jewish. Avocations: reading, knitting, walking. Home: 4 Grafton St Greenlawn NY 11740 Personal E-mail: berrydoor863@yahoo.com. Business E-Mail: gail_lelyveld@gardencitygroup.com.

LEMAIRE-JENKINS, ELIZABETH ANNE, psychotherapist; b. Boston, Mar. 30, 1969; d. Henry Paul and Theresa Mary Lemaire; m. Gregory Alan Jenkins, May 24, 1989; 1 stepchild, Zachary Dilon Jenkins. BA, U. Vt., 1991, BA in Music Performance, 1991, MS cum laude, 1995. Lic. clin. mental health counselor Vt. Behavioral health care psychotherapist Cmty. Health Plan, Burlington, Vt., 1995—98; pvt. practice Winooski, Vt., 1998—; behavioral health care psychotherapist Otter Creek Assoc./Matrix Health Sys., Burlington, 1998—2004; nat. cert mental health counselor Pvt. Practice, 2004—. Guest lectr. St. Michael's Coll., Colchester, Vt., U. Vt., Burlington; presenter in field. One-woman shows include (mixed media exhibit) The Daily Planet Restaurant, 2005. Mem.: Am. Counseling Assn., Vt. Mental Health Counselors Assn., Assn. for Anorexia Nervosa and Associated Disorders, Nat. Bd. Cert. Counselors, Am. Mental Health Counselors Assn., Phi Beta Kappa. Democrat. Office: The Woolen Mill 20 W Canal St Winooski VT 05404 Office Phone: 802-655-0585. Office Fax: 802-655-0585. Personal E-mail: eljtherapist@adelphia.net.

LEMARK, NOREEN ANNE, retired neurologist; b. Esther, Mo., Apr. 14, 1921; d. James Monroe Appleberry and Eldridge Davis; m. Leslie Louis Lemak, May 19, 1944; children: Michael Lemak, Margaret Lemak, Robert Lemak. MD, Wayne State U., Detroit, 1947. Physician U. Tex. Med. Sch., Houston, 1974—96; ret., 1996. Author: A History of Stroke, 1989, Statistics in Medical Research, 1994; co-author: Werner's Syndrome, 1995. Mem.: Tex. Med. Assn., Harris County Med. Soc., Alpha Omega Alpha. Home: 5457 Sugar Hill Dr Houston TX 77056

LEMASTER, KATHY LYNN, elementary school educator; d. Robert Newton and Minnie Bell Williamson; m. Jake Alan LeMaster, June 26, 1981; children: Jason Robert, Jonathan Reed, Jessica Renae. BA, La. Tech U., Ruston, 1979. Cert. tchr. Tex., 1980. Tchr. Port Arthur Ind. Sch. Dist., Tex., 1979—87; tchr. K and grade 1 Frenship Ind. Sch. Dist.-Casey Elem. Sch., Wolfforth, Tex., 1987—95; tchr. music Frenship Ind. Sch. Dist.-Westwind Elem. Sch., Wolfforth, 1995—. Leader Girl Scouts USA, Lubbock, Tex., 1999—2004; ch. musician - orch. First Bapt. Ch., Lubbock, 1989, children's choir dir. asst., 2003, youth leader, 2004. Recipient Outstanding Leader award, Caprock Girl Scout Coun. Girl Scouts USA, 2002. Mem.: Tex. Music Educator's Assn. (corr.), Frenship Band Parents (corr.; v.p. 2000—01). Baptist. Avocations: reading, camping. Home: 3207 80th St Lubbock TX 79423 Office: Frenship ISD - Westwind Elem 300 Main St Wolfforth TX 79382 Office Phone: 806-799-3731. Business E-Mail: klemaster@frenship.us.

LEMASTER, SHERRY RENEE, not-for-profit fundraiser, foundation administrator, consultant; b. June 25, 1953; d. John William and Mary Charles LeMaster. BS, U. Ky., 1975; MS in Higher Edn. Adminstrn., Bryn Mawr Coll. Inst. for Women, 1984. Cert. fund raising exec. Lab. technician Cen. Ky. Animal Disease Diagnostic Lab., Lexington, 1975—76; grant coord., environ. specialist Commonwealth Ky. Dept. for Natural Resources and Environ. Protection, Frankfurt, 1976—78; coord. residence hall program Murray (Ky.) State U., 1978—80; dean students Midway (Ky.) Coll., 1980—81, v.p. devel. alumnae affairs, 1981—86; dir. devel. Wilderness Road Coun. Girl Scouts U.S., Lexington, 1986—88, Coll. of Agr. and Life Scis. Va. Tech., Blacksburg, Va., 1988—94; sr. major gifts officer Sch. Medicine Wake Forst U.; sr. major gifts officer NC Bapt. Hosp., Inc., Winston-Salem, 1994—98; exec. dir. devel. and alumni affairs U. Okla. Health Scis. Ctr., Oklahoma City, 1998—2000; owner, cons. LeMaitre Fundraising and Found. Mgmt., 2001—. Amb. U. Ky. Coll. Agr.; cons. U.S. Dept. Edn., 1987—. Charter mem. planning com. Nat. Disciples Devel. Execs. Conf., 1984; chmn. Midway chpt. Am. Heart Assn., 1981; active Coun. for Advancement and Support Edn., 1981—, chmn. Ky. conf., 1982; active East Ky. First Quality of Life Com., 1987—88; adminstrv. bd. First United Meth. Ch., Lexington, 1982—84, 1987. Named hon. sec. state, 1984; named to Hon. Order of Ky. Cols., 1977; recipient Young Career Woman award, Bus. and Profl. Women's Club, Frankfurt, 1981. Mem.: Advancement Women in Higher Edn. Adminstrn. (past state planning com. Ky.), Assn. Fundraising Profls. (bd. dirs. Lexington chpt. 1986), Jr. League, Ninety-Nines Internat. Assn. Women Pilots (vice chmn. Ky. Bluegrass chpt. 1986—87, chmn. bd. dirs. 1987—88, dir. South Ctrl. sect. 2000—02), U. Ky. Alumni Assn. (life), P.E.O. (charter mem. chpt. X Ky. 1990—92, amendments and recommendation com. Va. state chpt. 1990—92), Rotary, Pi Beta Phi Nat. Alumnae Assn. (alumnae province pres. 1980—81, sec. bd. dirs. Ky. Beta chpt. 1982—84, pres. Va. Zeta chpt. house corp. 1991—94). Avocations: needlepoint, swimming. Office: 396 Hwy DD Defiance MO 63341 Office Phone: 314-440-3671.

LEMASTER, SUSAN M., marketing executive, writer; b. Cody, Wyo., May 9, 1953; d. Floyd Morris and Virginia Kristena (Renner) LeM. AA, Casper Coll., 1977; BA, U. Wyo., Casper, 1979. Reporter, night editor Casper Star Tribune, 1972-76; copy editor, editor In Wyo. mag., Casper, 1979; info. dir. Wyo. Rural Electric Assn., Casper, 1980-81; story editor Wyo. Horizons mag., Casper, 1981-82; asst., instr. English lab. Casper Coll., 1982-84; mktg. mgr. Chen & Assocs., Inc., 1984-87; mktg. cons., 1987-90; dir. mktg. KaWES and Assocs., Inc., 1990-91, pub. rels. and mktg. cons., 1992-95; comm. mgr. Arthur Andersen, L.A., 1995-97, assoc. dir. sales and mktg., 1997-99, mktg. dir., 1999-2000, Pacific Region Bus. Consulting, 2000—01, mktg. mgr. healthcare, 2001—02; mktg. dir. PacifiCare Dental & Vision, Santa Ana, Calif., 2002—03; west unit mktg. leader Mercer HR Consulting, L.A., 2003—04, U.S. mktg. strategist, 2004—05, global mktg. strategist, 2005—. Freelance writer and editor, 1982—; night sch. instr. Casper Coll., 1983-84, summer sch. instr., 1984. Editor Casper Jour., 1983-84. Recipient 1st Place News Story award Wyo. Press Assn., 1973, 1st Place Editing award Wyo. Press Women, 1980. Mem. L.A. Press Club, Phi Theta Kappa, Phi Kappa Phi, Alpha Mu Gamma. Democrat. Home: 1059 E Cypress Ave Burbank CA 91501-1309 Office: Mercer HR Consulting 777 S Figueroa St Los Angeles CA 90017 Office Phone: 213-346-2522. Business E-Mail: susan.lemaster@mercer.com.

LEMAY, GAYLA DENISE, elementary school educator; b. Birmingham, May 8, 1963; d. Willard D. and Jean Shaw; m. Jeff LeMay. MEd, Walden U. Tchr. Lilburn Mid. Sch., Ga., 1999—2004, Radloff Mid. Sch., Duluth, Ga., 2004—, Salem Mid. Sch., Lithonia, Ga. Office Phone: 678-245-3400.

LE MAY, MOIRA KATHLEEN, retired psychology educator; b. N.Y.C., Apr. 12, 1934; d. Bernard Howard and Kathleen (Sullivan) Fitzpatrick; m. Joseph Albert Le May, June 14, 1958; children: Valerie H. (Le May) Teal, Joseph B. BS, Queens Coll., 1956; MS, Pa. State U., 1960, PhD, 1970. Engrng. psychologist USN Rsch. Lab., Washington, 1960-62, ITT Fed Labs., Nutley, N.J., 1962-64; instr. psychology Manhattanville Coll., Purchase, N.Y., 1964-68; asst. prof. Skidmore Coll., Saratoga Springs, N.Y., 1968-70; prof. Psychology Montclair State Coll., Upper Montclair, NJ, 1970—98; ret. Cons. in engring. psychol. USAF-WPAFB, Human Resources Lab., Dayton, Ohio, 1978-79, NASA Calif. Tech. Jet Propulsion Lab., Pasadena, 1982-83, USN Air Devel. Ctr. Warminster, Pa., 1986-87, NASA Langley Rsch. Ctr., Hampton, Va., 1989-90, NASA-Ames Rsch. Ctr., Moffett Field, Calif., 1994 Contbr. numerous artticles to profl. jours and papers to sci. meetings. Campaign worker, Ridgewood (N.J.) Dem. Orgn., 1974-89, com. rep. corresponding sec. 1978-86. Fellow Am. Psychol. Soc.; mem. IEEE, AAAS, APA, Human Factors Soc. (liaison to AAAS 1984-91). Roman Catholic. Avocations: historical preservation, antiques, architecture. Home: 1023 Hillcrest Rd Ridgewood NJ 07450-1030

LEMAY, NANCY, graphics designer, painter; b. NYC, Sept. 7, 1956; m. Harry Adrian LeMay, Jan. 24, 1986. BFA with honors, Sch. Visual Arts, 1978; postgrad., NYU, 1981-84. Admissions counselor Sch. Visual Arts, N.Y.C., 1979-81, acad. advisor, 1981-84; asst. art dir. NYU, N.Y.C., 1984-87; graphic designer J. C. Penney, N.Y.C., 1987-89; art dir. Catch A Rising Star, N.Y.C., 1989; graphic designer WNBC TV News Graphics, N.Y.C., 1989-90; graphics engr. NBC Network News Graphics, N.Y.C., 1990-91, KCOP TV News, L.A., 1991-94, supervising graphic designer, 1994—2000; graphic designer KNBC-TV, 2000—01; tchr. Rustic Canyon, Santa Monica, Calif., 2001—, Abram Friedman Occupational Ctr., LA, 2001—. Exhibited in group show Wings N Water Festival (poster winner), 1990; designer: (logotype design) Art Direction Mag. (Award of Merit), 1985; author: White Graphics, 2001; contbr. MacWeek Mag., 1989. Recipient 5 L.A. Area Emmy awards, 1996-99, Art Times award, Catherine Lorillard Wolfe Art Club's, 108th Annual Nat. Juried Show, 2004. Avocations: painting, bird watching, sculpture, photography. E-mail: NancyLeMayCo@aol.com.

LEMBKE, JANET, writer; b. Cleve., Mar. 2, 1933; d. Joseph Randolph and Sarah Howell (East) Nutt. AB in Classics, Middlebury Coll., 1953. Author: River Time, 1989, Looking for Eagles, 1990, Dangerous Birds, 1992, Shake Them Simmons Down, 1994, Skinny Dipping, 1996, Touching Earth, 2001, Soup's On, 2001, Tuscan Trees, 2001, The Quality of Life, 2004, From Grass to Gardens, 2006; translator: Aeschylus, 1973, 2d edit., 1981, Euripides, 1991, 2d edit., 94, Virgi, 2005; poet: Bronze and Iron, 1973; contbr. articles and poems to profl. jours. Mem. PEN Am. Ctr. Home: 210 N Madison St Staunton VA 24401-3359

LE MÉE, KATHARINE WILBUR, author, educational consultant, educator; b. Albany, N.Y., July 8, 1939; d. Howard Cornell and Margaret (Heath) Wilbur; m. Jean M. Le Mée, Aug. 15, 1964; 1 child, Hannah Thérèse. BA in French, U. Rochester, 1961, MA in Gen. Linguistics, 1964; PhD in Romance Linguistics, Columbia U., 1971. Tchr. French E. Rochester (N.Y.) H.S., 1961-63; instr. French Columbia Coll., N.Y.C., 1965-72; lectr. Columbia Grad. Faculties, N.Y.C., 1972; asst. prof. French Baruch Coll., CUNY, N.Y.C., 1979-85; tchr. French Ridgewood (N.J.) H.S., 1986-89; adminstr. St. Paul's Ch., Englewood, N.J., 1989-94; pres. The Eastern Connection project Le Mée Assocs./Host Family Assn. St. Petersburg, Russia, Englewood, N.J., 1992-97; author Englewood, N.J., 1992—. Presenter chant workshops Omega Inst. for Holistic Studies, Rhinebeck, N.Y., The Learning Annex, N.Y.C., 1995. Author: Chant, 1994, The Benedictine Gift of Music, 2003; guest Today Show NBC. Home and Office: 16 Mevan Ave Englewood NJ 07631-3863 Business E-Mail: jklemee@verizon.net.

LE MENAGER, LOIS M., incentive merchandise and travel company executive; b. Cleve., Apr. 25, 1934; d. Lawrence M. and Lillian C. (Simicek) Stanek; m. Charles J. Blabolil (dec. 1982); children: Sherry L., Richard A.; m. Spencer H. Le Menager, Mar. 23, 1984. Grad. high sch. Travel counselor Mktg. Innovators Internat. Inc., Rosemont, Ill., 1978-80, mktg. dir., 1980-82, chmn., CEO, owner, 1982—. Dir. Northwest Commerce Bank, Rosemont. Featured in (articles) Crain's Chgo. Bus. Recipient Entrepreneurial Success award U.S. Small Bus. Adminstrn., 1999; named Supplier of Yr., J.C. Penney Co., Inc. Mem. NAFE, Am. Inst. Entrepreneurs (Entrepreneur of Yr. 1988), Am. Mktg. Assn., Internat. Soc. Mktg. Planners, Soc. Incentive Travel Execs., Am. Soc. Travel Agts., Nat. Fedn. Ind. Bus., Nat. Assn. Women Bus. Owners, Des Plaines C. of C., Rosemont C. of C., Chicagoland C. of C. (dir.), The Chgo. Network, Exec. Club (Chgo.). Congregationalist. Office: Mktg Innovators Internat Inc 9701 W Higgins Rd Rosemont IL 60018-4717 Office Phone: 847-696-1111.*

LEMIEUX, ANNETTE ROSE, artist; b. Norfolk, Va., Oct. 11, 1957; d. Joseph and Margaret (Merci) L. BFA, Hartford Art Sch., 1980. One-person shows include U. Hartford, 1980, Artists Space, N.Y.C., 1984, Cash/Newhouse, N.Y.C., 1984, 86, 87, Josh Baer Gallery, N.Y.C., 1987, 89, Daniel Weinberg Gallery, L.A., 1987, Lisson Gallery, London, 1988, Wadsworth Atheneum, 1988, Rhona Hoffman Gallery, Chgo., 1988, John and Mable Ringling Mus., 1989, Ctr. for Fine Arts, Miami, 1989, Rhona Hoffman Gallery, 1990, Monika Spruth Galerie, Cologne, Germany, 1990, Galerie Montenay, Paris, 1991, Stichting de Appel, Amsterdam, 1991; exhibited in numerous group shows, 1979—; represented in permanent collections Mus. Modern Art, N.Y.C., Mus. Fine Arts, Boston, Wadsworth Atheneum, Hartford, Conn., Whitney Mus. Am. Art, N.Y.C., Okla. Art Mus., Oklahoma City, Israel Mus., Jerusalem. Trustee Hartford Art Sch., 1989—; mem. bd. overseers Inst. Contemporary Art, Boston. N.Y. fellow, 1987, others.

LEMIEUX, JAIME DANIELLE, physical therapist; b. Wheat Ridge, Colo., Oct. 4, 1977; d. John Curtis and Cherie Sue Lemieux. BA, U. Colo., Boulder, 2000. Cert. athletic trainer. Phys. therapy aide Colo. Phys. Therapy Inst., Broomfield, 2000—02; asst. athletic trainer Cherry Creek H.S., Greenwood Village, Colo., 2002—03; athletic trainer Healthone Broncos Sports Medicine, Denver, 2003—05, Physiotherapy Assoc., Arvoch, Colo., 2005—. Clin. instr. Met. State Coll., Denver, 2006. Mem.: Colo. Athletic Trainers Assn., Nat. Athletic Trainers Assn. Avocations: soccer, softball.

LEMIEUX, LINDA DAILEY, museum director; b. Cleve., Sept. 6, 1953; d. Leslie Leo LeMieux Jr. and Mildred Edna (Dailey) Tutt. BA, Beloit Coll., 1975; MA, U. Mich., 1979; A cert., Mus. Mgmt. Program, Boulder, Colo., 1987. Asst. curator Old Salem, Inc., Winston-Salem, NC, 1979-82; curator Clarke House, Chgo., 1982-84, Western Mus. Mining and Industry, Colorado Springs, Colo., 1985-86, dir., 1987—. Author: Prairie Avenue Guidebook, 1985; editor: The Golden Years--Mines in the Cripple Creek District, 1987; contbr. articles to mags. and newspapers. Fellow Hist. Deerfield, Mass., 1974—. Rsch. grantee Early Am. Industries Assn., 1978. Mem. Am. Assn. Mus., Am. Assn. State and Local History, Colo.-Wyo. Mus. Assn., Colo. Mining Assn., Mountain Plains Assn. Mus., Women in Mining, Colo. Mont. Wyo. State Conf. Edn. Com. NAACP. Mem. First Congl. Ch. Home: 1337 Hermosa Way Colorado Springs CO 80906-3050 Office: Western Mus Mining & Industry 1025 N Gate Rd Colorado Springs CO 80921-3018 E-mail: director@wmmi.org, lindalemieux1@aol.com.

LEMKE, CAROL ANN, music educator, pianist, accountant; b. Crivitz, Wis. d. Martin G. and Una B. (Dupey) Larson; m. Allan J. Lemke, 1968; children: Blake Betsy, Allan J. II. BMus, Wis. Conservatory of Music, 1965; degree in liberal arts, Marquette U., 1966, postgrad., U. Wis. Cert. piano tchr. Am. Coll. Musicians. Instr. Wis. Conservatory of Music, Milw., 1965—71; comptroller IGIC, Milw., 1969—71; pvt. piano and voice tchr., 1963—2006. Music judge. Performer of piano & voice. Founder North Shore Music Festival. Named to, ACM Hall of Fame, 1989. Mem.: Wis. Sch. Music Assn., Nat. Music Tchrs. Assn., Nat. Guild Piano Tchrs., Wis. Fedn. Music (bd. dirs.), Wis. Music Tchrs. Assn., Milw. Music Tchrs. Assn. (bd. dirs. 1978—2006, pres. 1986—92).

LEMKE, JILL, city planner; b. Buffalo, Jan. 17, 1967; d. James Paul and Lynne Marie Lemke. BS in Comm., SUNY, Brockport, 1989; M of Regional Planning, Cornell U., 1997. Legis. intern Monroe County Legislature, Rochester, N.Y., 1989-90; comm. coord. N.Y. State Asembly, Rochester, 1991-94; rsch. and tchg. asst. Cornell U., Ithaca, N.Y., 1994-96; govt. rels. officer Greater Buffalo Partnership, 1997; planning specialist Buffalo Gen. Health Sys., 1997-98; outreach coord. Heart of the City Neighborhoods, Buffalo, 1998-99; dir. cmty. planning City of Buffalo, 2001—03; planning cons. Lemke Freelane Group, 2003—05; mainstreet mgr. Town of Mout Airy (Md.), 2005—. Rsch. asst. Neighborhood Reinvestment Corp., Buffalo, 1996. Contbr. chpt. to book. Sec. 23d Legislature Dem. Com., Rochester, 1993-94; polit. organizer Dem. Com. and campaigns, Rochester and Buffalo, 1989-2005; mem., vol. Western N.Y. Hispanics and Friends Civic Assn., Buffalo, 1997-2005; vol. Habitat for Humanity, 1992-96; mem. housing com. Allentown Assn., Buffalo, 1996-99; bd. dirs. West Side Neighborhood Housing Svcs. Acad. All-Am. scholar, 1985-86; Dem. Women of the Legislature grantee, 1994. Avocations: music, politics, painting, rollerblading, art. Office: Mount Airy Main Street Assn Mount Airy Town Hall 110 S Main St Mount Airy MD 21771 E-mail: jlemke@ch.ci.buffalo.ny.us, jlemke17@mac.com.

LEMKE, JUDITH A., lawyer; b. New Rochelle, N.Y., Sept. 28, 1952; d. Thomas Francis and Sara Jane (Blish) Fanelli; m. W. Frederick Lemke, Apr. 1, 1980; 1 child, Morgan Frederick. Student, Manhattanville Coll., Purchase, N.Y., 1970-72; BA, Case Western Res. U., Cleve., 1974, MA, 1975, JD, 1978. Sr. cert. pub. acct. Price Waterhouse, Cleve., 1978-81; assoc. Benesch Friedlander Coplan & Aronoff, Cleve., 1981-85; adj. faculty Cleve. Marshall Coll. Law, 1982-86; ptnr. Benesch Friedlander Coplan & Aronoff, Cleve., 1986-94; prin. Kahn Kleinman Yanowitz & Arnson Co., Cleve., 1994-95; tax mgr. N.Am./L.Am. tax planning and compliance Chiquita Brands Internat., Cin., 1995-97, tax mgr. Europe, Colombia, Panama, 1998—, asst. v.p. taxation, 1998-99; v.p. tax Pepsi Bottling Group, Somers, NY, 1999—2005, Alltel Corp., Little Rock, 2005—. Adj. faculty Case Western Res. U. Sch. of Law, 1993-95. Recipient Elijah Watt Sells award for highest distinction AICPA, N.Y.C. 1979. Mem. ABA, Ohio State Bar Assn., Internat. Fiscal Assn., Case Western Res. U. Undergrad. Alumni Assn. (exec. com. 1987-95, trustee 1987-95, chmn. spl. events com. 1989-90, pres. 1990-92, v.p. 1993-94). Avocations: wilderness canoe camping, guitar. Office: Alltel Corp One Allied Dr MS B4F06-SA Little Rock AR 72202 Home: 18 Chenal Cir Little Rock AR 72223 Office Phone: 501-905-5094. Office Fax: 501-905-5096. Personal E-mail: jude.lemke@alltel.com.

LEMKE, STACY J., secondary school educator; d. Richard W. and Barbara J. Lemke; m. James W. Krehbiel, July 8, 1989. MusB in Edn. summa cum laude, U. Cin., 1986; MEd, Ashland U., Columbus, Ohio, 1999. Orch. dir., music dept. chair, suzuki violin tchr. Del. City Schs., Ohio, 1984—. Violin instr. Suzuki, 1984—; adjudicator Ohio Music Edn. Assn., 2005—. Mem.: NEA, ASTA/OOSTA, SAA, MENC/OMEA (music adjudicator 2005—). Avocations: mountain climbing, travel. Office: Rutherford B Hayes HS 289 Euclid Ave Delaware OH 43015 Office Phone: 740-833-1000 ext. 2863. Office Fax: 740-833-1899. Business E-Mail: lemkest@dcs.k12.oh.us.

LEMKE, TRACY A., music educator; b. Ocala, Fla., Oct. 26, 1975; d. Dennis Rae and Judy Ann Lemke. AA, Bethany Luth. Coll., Mankato, Minn., 1996; BS in Vocal Music Edn., Minn. State U., Mankato, Minn., 1999; synodical cert., Martin Luther Coll., New Ulm, MN, 2000. Tchr. music and art Gt. Plains Luth. H.S., Watertown, SD, 2000—. Lutheran. Avocations: singing, songwriting, art. Office: Gt Plains Luth HS 1200 Luther Ln NE Watertown SD 57201-8200 Home: 114 6th Ave NW Watertown SD 57201 Office Phone: 605-886-0672.

LEMLECH, JOHANNA KASIN, education educator; BA, UCLA, 1952; MA, Calif. State U., Northridge, 1961; EdD, U. So. Calif., 1970. Cert. elem. tchr. (life); cert. edn. adminstr. Tchr. Los Angeles Unified Sch. Dist., 1952-67; prof. U. So. Calif., Los Angeles, 1970—. Instrn. cons. sch. dists., pvt. schs., Calif. Author: Handbook for Successful Urban Teaching, 1977, Curriculum and Instructional Methods for Elementary Schools, 1984, Classroom Management: Techniques and Methods for Elementary and Secondary Teachers, 2d edit., 1988. Mem. Assn. Tchrs. Edn. (nat. higher edn. del. 1985—), Am. Ednl. Research Assn., Assn. Supervision & Curriculum Devel., Nat. Council Social Studies (edit. bd. 1984—). Avocation: cooking. Office: Univ of So Calif Sch of Edn University Park Los Angeles CA 90007

LEMMON, NICOLETTE, small business owner, marketing professional; b. Phoenix, Sept. 23, 1956; d. Stanley Vaughn and Emma Lou (Nims) L.; m. Dennis Koepke, Dec. 31, 1996; 1 child, Amanda. BS, Ariz. State U., 1978, MBA, 1983. Sales rep. Cort Furniture Rental, Phoenix, 1978-79; advt. dir. Sun Lakes (Ariz.) Mktg., 1979-80; mktg. dir. Ariz. Telco FCU, Phoenix, 1980-84; pres. LemmonTree Enterprises, Tempe, Ariz., 1984—. Author: Successful Product Development: From Research to Results, 1995, Almost Famous: How to Market Yourself for Success, 1996. Bd. dirs., past pres. MBA Coun., Coll. of Bus., Ariz. State U., Tempe, 1992-96; bd. dirs. WalkAmerica chair, March of Dimes, Phoenix, Tempe Impact Edn. Found., 1992-94. Named one of Top 50 Women Bus. Owners in Ariz., Today's Ariz. Woman Success Mag., 1995; nominee Entrepreneur of Yr., Inc. Mag., Ariz., 1996. Mem. Am. Mktg. Assn. (bd. dirs. 1989—, pres. 1996-97), Nat. Spkrs. Bur., Credit Union Exec. Soc. Suppliers Forum, Ariz. State U. Alumni Assn. (bd. dirs. 1993—. chair 2001—02, Young Alumni Achievement award 1994). Republican. Presbyterian. Office: LemmonTree Enterprises Ste 101 3010 S Priest Dr Tempe AZ 85282 Office Phone: 480-967-1405. Business E-Mail: 7solutions@lemmontree.com.

LEMONCELLI, LORINE BARBARA, counselor, elementary school educator; b. Pittston, Pa., Sept. 28, 1958; d. Lawrence and Valerie (Mislevy) Dalessandro; m. Peter Jerome Lemoncelli, Oct. 24, 1987; 1 child, Violetta Enrica. BA in Tchg., Coll. Misiercordia, 1981; MA in Counseling, Marywood Coll., 1996; phlebotomy cert., Allied Med. Career, Scranton, Pa., 1986. Elem. tchr. Montessori Sch./ Scranton Sch. Dist., Scranton, 1990-92; counselor Act 1, Wilkes-Barre, Pa., 1995, Friendship House, Scranton, 1995, Keystone City Residence, Scranton, 1996-97, Scranton Counseling, 1997-2000, Cath. Social Svcs., 2000—02; tchr. Little People, 2003—04; therapist Safety Net Counseling, Honesdale, Pa., 2006—; retail bus. owner, 2004—. Mem. PTA Riverside H.S., Taylor, Pa., 1995—; religious studies tchr. St. Ann, 1997—. Mem. Am. Counseling Assn., Marywood Counseling Assn. (pres. 1995-96), Wyoming Valley Mental Health Assn., Chi Sigma Iota. Democrat. Roman Catholic. Avocations: walking, music, travel, reading. Home: PO Box 3061 Scranton PA 18505-0061 Personal E-mail: lemonpl1@peoplepc.com.

LEMONE, MARGARET ANNE, atmospheric scientist; b. Columbia, Mo., Feb. 21, 1946; d. David Vandenberg and Margaret Ann (Meyer) LeMone; m. Peter Augustus Gilman; children: Patrick Cyrus, Sarah Margaret. BA in Math., U. Mo., 1967; PhD in Atmospheric Scis., U. Wash., 1972. Postdoctoral fellow Nat. Ctr. for Atmospheric Rsch., Boulder, Colo., 1972-73, scientist, 1973-92, sr. scientist, 1992—; chief scientist Globe, 2003—. Mem. bd. on atmospheric sci. and climate NRC, 1993-97, 2001-04; mem. sci. adv. com. U.S. Weather Rsch. Program, 1997-99. Contbr. articles to profl. jours.; contbg. author: D.C. Heath Earth Science, 1983-93; editor Jour. Atmospheric Scis., 1991-95. Woodrow Wilson fellow, NSF fellow, NDEA fellow, 1967. Fellow AAAS, Am. Meteorol. Soc. (councillor, mem. exec. com. 1992-96, Editor's award, Charles Anderson award); mem. Am. Geophys. Union, Nat. Acad. Engring. Achievements include research in dynamics of linear convection (roll vortices) in daytime atmospheric boundary layer and its relationship to clouds; demonstrating that bands of deep convection (like squall lines) can increase the vertical shear of horizontal wind (contrary to conventional wisdom at that time); developing technique to estimate small fluctuations in air pressure from aircraft flying over land, used to estimate pressure field around clouds and storms. Home: 2048 Balsam Dr Boulder CO 80304-3618 Office: Nat Ctr Atmospheric Rsch PO Box 3000 Boulder CO 80307-3000 Business E-Mail: lemone@ucar.edu.

LEMOS, GLORIA ELLIOTT, soft drink company executive; b. Royston, Ga., Apr. 29, 1946; d. Richard F. Elliott and G. Maxine (Brown) Elliot; 1 child, Joseph David. AA, Emmanuel Jr. Coll., Franklin Springs, Ga., 1966; postgrad., Oglethorpe U., 1966—68. With Coca-Cola Co., 1967, mem. exec. staff group Atlanta, 1972—77, asst. to chmn. bd Washington, 1977—79, v.p. internat. govt. affairs, 1979. Bd. dirs. Inst. for Study of Diplomacy, Georgetown U., Community Found. Greater Washington, 1980, Am. Com. for East-West Accord; trustee Fed. City Coun., 1978, Am. U., 1983, Meridian House Internat. Mem.: Internat. Women's Forum., Internat. Mgmt. and Devel. Inst. So. Ctr. for Internat. Studies, UN Internat. Bus. Coun., Washington Internat. Bus. Coun., World Trade Club, Internat. Club. Episc. Office: Coca-Cola Co 1 Coca Cola Plz NW Atlanta GA 30313-2420

LEMOS, MARGARET H., lawyer; BA, Brown Univ.; JD, N.Y.U., 2001. Law clk. U.S. Solicitor Gen., Washington, 2001, 2003, U.S. Ct. Appeals (1st cir.), Portland, Maine, 2002—03; law clerk to Hon. John Paul Stevens U.S. Supreme Ct., Washington, 2003—04; vis. faculty N.Y.U. Law Sch., New York, 2004—. Editor (sr. notes): N.Y.U. Law Rev. Bristow fellow, 2002, Furman fellow, 2004. Office: NYU Law School 40 Washington Sq So New York NY 10012

LEMY, MARIE EDITH, psychologist, educator; d. Josette Jean-Louis and Andre Louis. MPH, Hunter Coll., NY; PhD, Seton-Hall U., NJ. Lic. Psychologist N.Y. Psychologist So. Westchester BOCES, Rye, NY; asst. prof. CUNY, NY. Cons. Nassau BOCES, Seacliff, NY. Translator legal documents. Mem.: APA (assoc.). Independent. Roman Catholic. Avocations: travel, reading. Mailing: 59 New Drop Ln Hopewell Junction NY 12533 Personal E-mail: m-lemy@msn.com.

LENARD, MARY JANE, finance educator; b. York, Pa., July 8, 1955; d. Martin and Anne Ruth (Zimmerman) Kondor; m. Robert Louis Lenard, July 9, 1977 (div. 2004); children: Kevin, Kelsey. BS in Econ. and Adminstrv. Sci., Carnegie Mellon U., 1977; MBA in Fin., U. Akron, 1982; PhD in Bus. Adminstrn., Kent State U., 1995. Cert. mgmt. acct. Mgmt. trainee Equibank, NA, Pitts., 1977-78; acct., auditor Goodyear Tire and Rubber Co., Akron, Ohio, 1978-86; instr. U. Akron, 1986-93; mem. adj. faculty Cleve. State U., 1994-97; assoc. prof. Barton Coll., Wilson, NC, 1997—2001; asst. prof. U. N.C., Greensboro, 2001—05; assoc. prof. Meredith Coll., Raleigh, NC, 2005—. Author procs.; contbr. articles to profl. jours. Pres. Hillcrest Elem. PTA, Richfield, Ohio, 1992—93; v.p. Summit County PTA, Akron, 1994—96; mem., newsletter dir. Wakefield Mid. Sch. PTSA, 2000—02; coord. Vol. Income Tax Assistance, Barton Coll., Wilson, 1998—2001; active Revere Schs. Computer Curriculum Com., 1994—95; mem. Wakefield HS PTSA, 2002—; mem. and chair IT Com. for Acctg. Dept. at UNC, 2001—05; mem. Bryan Sch., UNC Greensboro Planning Com., 2002—05, Bryan Sch., UNC Greensboro Faculty Develop. Com., 2002—05, Bryan Sch., UNC Greensboro Undergraduate Programs Com., 2004—05. Grantee Faculty Devel. grant, Barton Coll., 1997, 1999. Mem.: Assn. Cert. Fraud Examiners, Decision Scis. Inst., Akron Women's Network, Assn. for Info. Systems, Inst. Mgmt. Accts. (dir. mem. retention 1994—96), Am. Acctg. Assn. (Best Paper award 1998), Beta Gamma Sigma. Home: 3049 Imperial Oaks Dr Raleigh NC 27614-7001 Office: Meredith Coll Sch Business Raleigh NC 27607 E-mail: lenardmj@meredith.edu.

LENDSEY, JACQUELYN L., foundation administrator; BS, Adelphi U.; MEd, Howard U. With pub. sch. sys., Prince George County, Md.; v.p. corp. and cmty. devel. Greater S.E. Healthcare; v.p. pub. policy Planned Parenthood Fedn. Am., N.Y.C., 1998—2001; pres., CEO Women in Cmty. Svc., Alexandria, Va., 2001—. Bd. dirs. Nat. Assembly Health and Human Svcs. Orgns., Reproductive Health Tech. Project. Mem.: Leadership Washington. Office: 1900 Beauregard St Ste 103 Alexandria VA 22311

LENEHAN, PAMELA FARRELL, financial executive; b. Stamford, Conn., May 19, 1952; d. John R. and Elsie M. (White) Lenehan; m. Lawrence F. Guess, July 11, 1999; children: Sarah, Paul. BA in Math. Econs. magna cum laude, Brown U., 1974, MA in Econs. with honors, 1974. V.p. electronics divsn. corp. banking Chase Manhattan Bank, N.Y.C., 1974-81; mng. dir. investment banking tech. Credit Suisse Group First Boston Corp., 1981-94; sr. v.p. corp. devel., treas. Oak Industries Inc., Waltham, Mass., 1995—2000; v.p. & CFO Convergent Networks, Inc., 2000—01; self-employed pvt. investor, 2001—02; pres. Ridge Hill Consulting, LLC, 2002—. Forum co-chair Springboard: New England, 2002, 2003, mem. forum com., 2004, 2005; dir. Avid Technology, Inc., 2001—, compensation com., chair audit com.; bd. Ctr. for Women & Enterprise, fin. com., strategic planning com., chair planning com., chair, strategic planning com.; bd. Spartech Corp., compensation com., audit com., chair strategic planning com. Mem.: Fin. Exec. Internat., Nat. Assn. Corp. Dir., The Boston Club, Brae Burn. Republican. Roman Catholic. Office: Ridge Hill Consulting LLC 22 Pheasant Landing Rd Needham MA 02492-1000 Office Phone: 781-449-9665. Office Fax: 781-449-0634.

LENGEL, ELIZABETH HILSCHER, behavior specialist; b. Ripon, Wis., Dec. 19, 1953; d. Frederick Albert and Patricia Ann (Westbrook) Hilscher; m. David Wayne Lengel, Nov. 18, 1978; children: John David, James Thomas, Elizabeth Ella. BA, Tift Coll., Forsyth, Ga., 1976; postgrad., Ga. Coll., 1977-80. Behavior disorders tchr. Bibb County Pub. Schs., Macon, Ga., 1976-81; sr. behavior specialist State of Ga. Dept. Youth Services, Macon, 1984-88; k-5 tchr. Vineville North Weekday Presch., Macon, Ga., 1999—. Cons. pvt. and pub. hosps. Macon, 1984—. Active Troubled Children Coun., Bibb County, Twiggs County, Jones County, Ga., 1985-90. Mem. Ga. Coalition on Consultation, Edn., and Prevention, Ga. Juvenile Services Assn., Mid. Ga. Council for Children and Youth. Baptist. Avocations: reading, needlecrafts, youth services. Home: 6725 Moseley Dixon Rd Macon GA 31220-8516

L'ENGLE, MADELEINE (MRS. HUGH FRANKLIN), writer; b. NYC, Nov. 29, 1918; d. Charles Wadsworth and Madeleine (Barnett) Camp; m. Hugh Franklin, Jan. 26, 1946 (dec., 1986); children: Josephine Franklin Jones, Maria Franklin Rooney, Bion. AB, Smith Coll., 1941; postgrad., New Sch., 1941-42, Columbia U., 1960-61; holder 19 hon. degrees. Tchr. St. Hilda's and St. Hugh's Sch., 1960—; mem. faculty U. Ind., 1965-66, 71; writer-in-residence Ohio State U., 1970, U. Rochester, 1972, Wheaton Coll., 1976—, Cathedral St. John the Divine, N.Y.C., 1965—. Author: The Small Rain, 1945, Ilsa, 1946, Camilla Dickinson, 1951, A Winter's Love, 1957, And Both Were Young, 1949, Meet the Austins, 1960, A Wrinkle in Time, 1962, The Moon by Night, 1963, The 24 Days Before Christmas, 1964, The Arm of the Starfish, 1965, The Love Letters, 1966, The Journey with Jonah, 1968, The Young Unicorns, 1968, Dance in the Desert, 1969, Lines Scribbled on an Envelope, 1969, The Other Side of the Sun, 1971, A Circle of Quiet, 1972, A Wind in the Door, 1973, The Summer of the Great-Grandmother, 1974, Dragons in the Waters, 1976, The Irrational Season, 1977, A Swiftly Tilting Planet, 1978, The Weather of the Heart, 1978, Ladder of Angels, 1980, A Ring of Endless Light, 1980, Walking on Water, 1980, A Severed Wasp, 1982, And It Was Good, 1983, A House Like a Lotus, 1984, Trailing Clouds of Glory, 1985, A Stone for a Pillow, 1986, Many Waters, 1986, Two-Part Invention, 1988, A Cry Like a Bell, 1987, Sole Into Egypt, 1989, From This Day Forward, 1988, An Acceptable Time, 1989, The Glorious Impossible, 1990, Certain Women, 1992, The Rock That Is Higher: Story As Truth, 1993, Anytime Prayers, 1994, Troubling a Star, 1994, Penguins and Golden Calves, 1996, A Live Coal in the Sea, 1996, Glimpses of Grace, 1996, Wintersong, 1996, Mothers and Daughters, 1997, Friends for the Journey, 1997, Bright Evening Star: Mystery of the Incarnation, 1997, The Other Dog, 2001, Madeleine L'Engle Herself: Reflections on a Writing Life (with Carole Chase), 2001 Pres. Crosswicks Found. Recipient Newbery medal, 1963, Sequoyah award, 1965, runner-up Hans Christian Andersen Internat. award, 1964, Lewis Carroll Shelf award, 1965, Austrian State Lit. award, 1969, Bishop's Cross, 1970, U. South Miss. medal, 1978, Regina medal, 1985, Alan award Nat. Coun. Tchrs. English, 1986, Kerlan award, 1990, Margaret Edwards award, 1998; collection of papers at Wheaton Coll. Mem. Authors Guild (mem. council), Authors League (mem. council), Writers Guild Am. Episcopalian. Office: Cathedral Libr St John the Divine 1047 Amsterdam Ave New York NY 10025-1747 also: care Random House Children's Media 1540 Broadway New York NY 10036-4039

LENHARD, SARAH, advertising executive; Mng. dir., head account svcs. SFGT, Phila. Fundraiser Phila. Zoo, Acad. of Music Restoration. Named one of 40 Under 40, Phila. Bus. Jour., 2006. Office: SFGT 2215 Walnut St Philadelphia PA 19103 Office Phone: 215-509-7700. E-mail: slehhard@sfgt.com.*

LENHART, CYNTHIA RAE, conservation organization executive; b. Cheverly, Md., Nov. 3, 1957; d. Donald Edward and Vesta Jean Lenhart. BS in Environ. Studies, Coll. William & Mary, 1979; MS in Environ. Sci., SUNY, Syracuse, 1983. Asst. to pres. Environ. Policy Inst., Washington, 1979-81; wildlife policy analyst Nat. Audubon Soc., Washington, 1984-90; exec. dir. Hawk Mountain Sanctuary, Kempton, Pa., 1990—2004; prin., owner Salamander, Saluda, NC, 2004—. Bd. dirs. Am. Bird Conservancy, Washington, Pa. Environ. Coun., Phila. Contbr. chpts. to Audubon Wildlife Report, 1985, 87, 88, 89. Chair Everglades Coalition, Washington, 1986-88.

LENHART, LORRAINE MARGARET, county official; b. Schuylkill County, Pa., Nov. 18, 1944; d. Thomas Edward and Margaret Elizabeth (Klinger) Kimmel; m. William Charles Reber II, May 10, 1964 (div. 1968); 1 child, William Charles II; m. Kenneth Edward Lenhart, June 30, 1972; children: Vickie Elaine Lenhart Marino, Sonya Lynn Lenhart Yost. Grad. H.S., Mifflinburg, Pa., 1962; Cert. sect. I, II, III, Pa. Land Title Inst., 1988; instrn. course cert., Pa. State Mcpl. Ofcl. Instrn., 1992; Newly Elected Officials Tng. I, II Cert., Commonwealth of Pa., 1994, Mcpl. Fin. Elected Officials, 1995; genealogy cert., Williamsport Area C.C.; estate planning course cert., Pa. State Co-op Ext. Various positions; deputy register and recorder Union County Pa., Lewisburg, 1978-95, register of wills, recorder of deeds, 1996—. Mem. Preservation Mifflinburg Inc.; former dir. Am. Cancer Soc., Susquehanna Valley, Lewisburg, Pa.; past coun. mem. Postal Customer Adv. Coun., Mifflinburg; past mem. Union County Hist. Soc., Lewisburg, Bald Eagle State Forest Roundtable, Mifflinburg, OUE, Allenwood, Pa.; vol. Union County Emergency Svcs., Lewisburg; past dir. Ctrl. Susquehanna unit

Am. Cancer Soc., Union County Found., Lewisburg, 1997—2003; former councillor and v.p. Mifflinburg Borough Coun., 1992—95; cert. Leadership Susquehanna Valley; past treas. Mifflinburg Hist. Soc.; past dir. Buffalo Creek Watershed Alliance; mem. Union County Coun. of Rep. Women, 1978—, Pa. Coun. Rep. Women; committeeperson Union County Rep. Com., East Ward, Mifflinburg; past bd. dirs. Mifflinburg Hist. Soc. Mem.: Register of Wills and Clk. of Orphan's Ct. Assn. Pa., Pa. Recorder of Deeds Assn., Internat. Assn. Clks., Recorders, Election Ofcls. and Treas., Mifflinburg Buggy Mus., Kiwanis Club (1st v.p. 2004—05, pres. 2005—06, sec. 2001—02, Internat. George F. Hixson award 2003). Republican. Lutheran. Avocations: reading, needlecrafts, gardening. Office: Union County Court House 103 S 2d St Lewisburg PA 17837-1996 Office Phone: 570-524-8761. E-mail: llenhart@unionco.org.

LENHART, SUZANNE, mathematician, education educator; Prof. math. U. Tenn., Knoxville. Rschr. Oak Ridge Nat. Lab. Mem.: Assn. for Women in Math. (pres. 2001—03). Office: Univ Tenn Math Dept 317 C Ayres Hall Knoxville TN 37996

LENKE, JOANNE MARIE, publishing executive; b. Chgo., Aug. 27, 1938; d. August Julian and Dorothy Anna (Gold) L. BS, Purdue U., 1960; MS, Syracuse U., 1964, PhD, 1968. Tchr. pub. schs., Evanston, Ill., 1960-63; editor Test Dept. Harcourt, Brace & World, Inc., N.Y.C., 1967-70; rsch. psychologist Harcourt Brace Jovanovich, Inc., N.Y.C., 1970-73, exec. editor, 1973-75; asst. dir. ednl. measurment divsn. The Psychol. Corp., N.Y.C., 1975-83, dir. ednl. measurement and psychometrics Cleve., 1983-85, San Antonio, 1986, v.p. dir. measurement divsn., 1986-88, sr. v.p., 1988-91, exec. v.p., 1991-97, pres., 1997-99; cons., 1999—2002; assoc. v.p. Ednl. Testing Svc., 2002—06, v.p., 2006—. Field reader U.S. Office Edn., 1972. Adv. editor Jour. Ednl. Measurement, 1974-78. NSF grantee, 1963-64. Mem. APA, Nat. Coun. Measurement in Edn., Am. Ednl. Rsch. Assn. Home: 2534 Winding VW San Antonio TX 78258-7257 Personal E-mail: jlenke@usa.net.

LENN, MARJORIE PEACE, educational association administrator, consultant; b. Bowling Green, Ohio, Jan. 17, 1946; d. Frederick Elwynn and Nelvia P. Peace; m. D. Jeffrey Lenn; 1 child, Rebecca. BA, Transylvania Coll., 1968; M in Arts and Religion, Yale U., 1970; MEd, U. Mass., 1973, EdD, 1978. Dir. student svcs. U. Mass., Amherst, 1970-79, dir. residential life, 1979-82; dir. profl. svcs. Coun. on Postsecondary Accreditation, Washington, 1982-89, v.p., 1989-92; exec. dir. Ctr. for Quality Assurance in Internat. Edn., Washington, 1992—, Global Alliance for Transnat. Edn., Washington, 1996—2000. Cons. govts. China, India, Indonesia, South Africa, Mex., Belize, Argentina, Chile, Mauritius, Romania, Hungary and others in higher edn. reform, 1991—; spl. adviser on trade in edn. svcs. U.S. Govt., 2000—. Author: International Developments in Assuring Quality in Higher Education, 1994, Ambassadors of U.S. Higher Education: Quality Credit Bearing Programs Abroad, 1997, Globalization of the Professions and the Quality Imperative, 1997, Multinational Discourse on Professional Accreditation, Certification, and Licensure: Bridges for the Globalizing Professions, 1998, The Foundations of Globalization of Higher Education and the Professions, 1999, The Globalization of the Professions in the United States and Canada: A Survey and Analysis, 2000, Higher Education and Training in the Global Marketplace: Exporting Issues and the Trade Agreements, 2002; author: (with others) Ethics in Higher Education, 1990; editor: New England Consultation Network, 1978, Site Visitors in the Accreditation Process: A Guide to Issues and Practical Concerns, 1988, International Education and Accreditation: Uncharted Waters, 1990, Conflicts of Interest in the Accreditation Process, 1991, Distance Learning and Accreditation, 1991, Diversity, Accessibility, and Quality: An Introduction to Education in the United States for Educators for Other Countries, 1995; editor, contbr. Globalization of Higher Education and the Professions: The Mobility of Students, Scholars, and Professionals, 1993, Globalization of Education and the Professions: The Case of North America, 1994, (series) Studying in the United States, 1994; contbr. articles to profl. jours. Bd. dirs. Regents Coll., 1996-98, Hong Kong Coun. Acad. Accreditation, 1989-92; v.p. adminstrv. Women's Nat. Dem. Club, Washington, 1990-91; elder Old Presbyn. Meeting House, Alexandria, Va., 1983—. Recipient Outstanding Alumni award Transylvania U., 1998, Outstanding Contbn. to Global Higher Edn. award Assn. Christian Colls. and Univs., Internat. Ecumenical Forum, 1998. Fellow Soc. for Values in Higher Edn. (bd. dirs. 1994-95); mem. Women Adminstrs. in Higher Edn. (bd. dirs. 1984-90), Internat. Network Quality Assurance Agys. in Higher Edn. (bd. dirs. 1994—), Sigma Kappa (Colby award for outstanding svc. 2000). Democrat. Presbyterian. Avocations: choral music, travel. Office: Ctr for Quality Assurance in Int Edn Nat Ctr for Higher Edn 1 Dupont Cir NW Ste 515 Washington DC 20036-1135 E-mail: cqaie@aacrao.org.

LENNON, ELIZABETH MARIE, retired special education educator; b. Chgo., Apr. 29; d. John Joseph and Johanna Amelia (Pfaff) L. AB, Ind. U., 1941; postgrad., Butler U., 1946, N.C. State U., 1956, San Francisco State U., 1960; MA in Edn. of Physically Handicapped, Columbia U., 1947. Elem. tchr., typing tchr. Ind. Sch. for the Blind, 1941-51; lower sch. tchr. Perkins Sch. for the Blind, 1951-53; tchr., insvc. coord. Gov. Morehead Sch., Raleigh, N.C., 1953-64; staff devel. specialist N.C. Commn. for the Blind, 1964-67; asst. prof. blind rehab. Western Mich. State U., Kalamazoo, 1967-78, part-time asst. prof. blind rehab., 1978-81, 88. Author publs. in field. Bd. dirs. Nat. Accreditation Coun. for Agys. Serving the Blind and Visually Impaired, 1976-83; vice chair Mich. Commn. for the Blind, 1978-84; vice chair bd. dirs Shepherd's Ctr. of Greater Kalamazoo, 1989-90, chmn., 1990—; sec. Affiliated Leadership League of and for the Blind of Am., 1978-91; bd. dirs. Southcentral Mich. Commn. on Aging, 1978-91, sec., 1986-88; sec. Am. Coun. of the Blind, 1988-90; bd. dirs. Voluntary Action Ctr. of Greater Kalamazoo, 1986—; bd. dirs., mem. com., founder Kalamazoo Ctr. for Ind. Living, 1980—; pres. Coun. of Citizens with Low Vision, 1985-88. Recipient Robert D. Mahoney award for Outstanding Svc. to Visually Impaired of Mich., Mich. Assn. of Blind and Visually Impaired, 1978, Clare Lynch award Kalamazoo Coun. of the Blind, 1981, George Card award for Outstanding Svc. to Visually Imparied Nationwide, Am. Coun. of the Blind, 1983, Spl. Tribute, State of Mich., 1984, Lifetime Achievement award Kalamazoo Ctr. for Ind. Living, 1987, Outstanding Svc. to the Older Citizens of S.W. Mich., Mich. Legislature, 1990, Jim Neubacher Lifetime Achievement award Kalamazoo Ctr. for Ind. Living, 1991, Golden Bell award J.C. Penney, 1992. STAR award, Volutary Action Ctr. of Kolonozoo for Cmty. svc., 2002. Mem. Assn. for Edn. and Rehab. of the Blind and Visually Impaired (mem. various coms. on state and nat. levels), Coun. for Exceptional Children, Mich. Assn. of Transcribers for the Visually Impaired (past pres., editor newletter, bd. dirs., founding mem.). Avocations: reading, music, travel. Home: 1400 N Drake Rd Apt 218 Kalamazoo MI 49006-3951

LENNOX, HEATHER, lawyer; b. Cleve., Sept. 22, 1967; d. Rand Tru and Leilani Marie L.; m. Douglas Robert Krause, Sept. 17, 1994. BA summa cum laude, John Carroll U., 1989; JD cum laude, Georgetown U., 1992. Bar: Ohio 1992, US Dist. Ct. (no. dist.) Ohio 1993, US Ct. Appeals (6th cir.) 2006. Ptnr. Jones Day, Cleve., 1992—. Contbr. articles to profl. jours. Named an Outstanding Young Prof., Turnarounds & Workouts, 2006, Ohio Super Lawyer, Law Politics & Pubs. of Cin. mag., 2005, 2006; named one of The Best Lawyers in Am., 2006. Mem.: Ohio State Bar Assn., Am. Bankruptcy Inst., Cleve. Bar Assn. Office: Jones Day N Point 901 Lakeside Ave E Cleveland OH 44114-1190 Office Phone: 216-586-7111. Office Fax: 216-579-0212. Business E-Mail: hlennox@jonesday.com.

LENOIR, GLORIA CISNEROS, secondary school educator, consultant; b. Monterrey, Nuevo Leon, Mex., Aug. 18, 1951; came to U.S., 1956, naturalized; d. Juan Antonio and Maria Gloria (Flores) Cisneros; m. Walter Frank Lenoir, June 6, 1975; children: Lucy Gloria, Katherine Judith, Walter Frank IV. Student, Inst. Am. Univs., 1971-72; BA in French Art, Austin Coll., 1973, MA in French Art, 1974; MBA in Fin., U. Tex., 1979, student in Ednl. Policy and Planning, 2001—. Cert. region XIII behavior coach Tex., 2005, mediator Tex., 2006. French tchr. Sherman (Tex.) H.S., 1973-74; French/Spanish tchr, dept. chmn. Lyndon Baines Johnson H.S., Austin, 1974-77; legis. aide Tex. State Capitol, Austin, Tex., 1977-81; stock broker Merrill Lynch, Austin, 1981-83, Schneider, Bernet and Hickman, Austin, 1983-84; bus. mgr. Holleman Photographic Labs., Inc., Austin, 1984-87, 88-90; account exec., stock broker Eppler, Guerin & Turner, 1987-88; ind. distbr. Austin, 1990-93; owner, cons. Profl. Cons. Svcs., Austin, 1991—2001; adj. faculty Spanish for internat. trade St. Edwards U., 1991-99; bilingual interviewer The Gallup Orgn., 1997-98; Spanish tchr., club sponsor Hyde Park Bapt. Schs., 1997-99; tchr. computer applications Travis H.S. Comm. Acad., 1999-2000, 9th grade coord., 2000—01; tchr. langs. Travis H.S., 2001—, chmn. dept. langs. other than English, 2005—, cons. region XIII, 2006—. Group counselor, organizer Inst. Fgn. Studies, U. Strasbourg, France, 1976; mktg. intern IBM, Austin, 1978; mktg. cons. Creative Ednl. Enterprises, Austin, 1980-81; hon. spkr. Mex.-Am. U. Tex., Austin, 1984; coord. small bus. workshops, 1985; group sponsor, advisor Travel Selections, 1997-03, Explorica, Inc., 2003-06; mem. campus adv. coun. Travis H.S., 1999-02; S.W. area rep. Travel Selections from Campbell, Calif., 2000-03; presenter Space Econs., NASA Educator's Conf. on Space Exploration, 2006-; spkr. in field. Photographs pub. in Women in Space, 1979, Review, 1988; exhibited in group shows, Tex. and US, 1979, 88-89, 99, 2005. Neighborhood capt. Am. Cancer Soc., Austin, 1982-86, 90, Am. Heart Assn., 1989; active Advantage Austin, 1988; dep. registrar Travis County, 2004—; liaison leads program Austin Coll., 1983-00; peer panelist Maj. Art Insts., Austin; elder Ctrl. Presbyn. Ch., 1988-90, 00-02, 06—, tchr. H.S. Sunday sch., 2002-03; Megaskills leader Austin Ind. Sch. Dist., 1991-96; bd. dirs. Magnet Parents Coalition, 1995-98; participant NASA Urban and Rural Cmty. Enrichment Program, 2002; mem. smaller learning cmtys. com. Travis HS, Austin, Tex., 2002-04, mem. partnership behavior success com., 2003-06, mem. com. HS redesign, 2005—; active Inst. Civility Govt., 2005—. Recipient Night on the Town award IBM, 1978. Mem.: NEA, Tex. Fgn. Lang. Assn., Am. Assn. Tchrs. of French, Edn. Austin, Pi Lambda Theta. Democrat. Home and Office: 1801 Lavaca St Apt 11E Austin TX 78701-1331 Personal E-mail: mrs_lenoir@hotmail.com.

LENOX, ADRIANE, actress; b. Memphis, Sept. 11, 1965; m. Zane Mark; 1 child, Crystal Joy. Performer: (Broadway plays) Ain't Misbehavin', 1978—82, Dreamgirls, 1981—85, How To Succeed in Business Without Really Trying, 1995—96, The Gershwins' Fascinating Rhythm, 1999, Kiss Me, Kate, 1999—2001, Caroline, or Change, 2004, Doubt, 2005— (Outer Critics Circle award nomination for Outstanding Featured Actress in a Play, 2005, Drama Desk award for Outstanding Featured Actress in a Play, 2005, Tony award for Best Performance by a Featured Actress in a Play, 2005), Buddy Holly Story, (off-broadway plays) Spunk, 1981, The American Play, 1994, Merrily We Roll Along, 1994, Identical Twins from Baltimore, 1995, The Venus, 1995, Broken Sleep: Three Plays, 1997, Dinah Was, 1998 (Obie award for Performance, 1998, Audelco award), The Broadway Musicals of 1943, 2001, Miss Evers Boys, 2002, Crowns, 2002, Our Town, 2002, Cavedweller, 2003, Caroline, or Change, 2004, Beehive, 1986, On the Town, 1989 (Helen Hayes award for Outstanding Lead Actress in a Musical), The Color Purple, 2004, Doubt, 2004 (Lucille Lortel award for Outstanding Featured Actress, 2005); actress (TV series) Third Watch, 2000, 2004, Law and Order, 1999, Law and Order: Special Victims Unit, 2001, 2003, (films) Forever, Lulu, 1987, On the One, 2004, (TV films) Double Platinum, 1999. Mem.: Actors Equity Assn. Office: Walter Kerr Theatre PO Box 944 New York NY 10108-0944

LENOX, ANGELA COUSINEAU, healthcare consultant; b. Vergennes, Vt, Dec. 12, 1946; d. Romeo Joseph and Colombe Mary (Gevry) C.; m. Donald Allen Lenox, Oct. 5, 1969 (div.); 1 child, Tiffanie Jae. RN diploma, Albany Med. Ctr. Sch. Nursing, 1969; BS, Barry U., 1982; M of Health Mgmt., St. Thomas U., 1990. Cert. in profl. healthcare quality. Intravenous therapist Holy Cross Hosp., Ft. Lauderdale, Fla., 1979-91; utilization review coord. North Broward Hosp., Pompano Beach, Fla., 1984-89; med. staff quality mgr. Humana Bennett, Plantation, Fla., 1990-91; med. resource analyst Hermann Hosp., Houston, 1991-93; assoc. mgr. quality improvement The Prudential, Sugar Land, Tex., 1993-95; quality dir. United Healthcare of Tex., 1999—. Contbr. articles to profl. jour. Capt. US Army res., 1991—. Mem. Tex. Gold Coast Assn. Healthcare Quality, Tex. Soc. Quality Assurance, Nat. Assn. Healthcare Quality. Avocations: skiing, running, reading, writing. Home: 4506 Evanston Dr Evans GA 30809-3006 E-mail: angeler.lenox@sbcglobal.net.

LENOX, CATHERINE CORNEAU, volunteer; b. Evanston, Ill., Sept. 16, 1920; d. Joseph Addison and Catherine Roberts Corneau; m. Lionel R. Lenox II, Dec. 9, 1945 (dec. Jan. 1994); children: Ruth Lenox Jones, Nancy, Catherine L., Elizabeth L. Howey. BA in English, Wellesley Coll., 1941; BA in Early Childhood Edn., Mills Coll., 1946; cert. in applied social gerontology, San Jose State U., 1983. Adult edn. credential San Jose State U. Tchrs. asst. Rivers Country Day Sch., Boston, 1941—42, Chestnut Hill Country Day Sch., Bethesda, Md., 1942—48; dir. Day Care Ctr., Springfield, Ill., 1943—44; tchr. Mills Coll. Childrens Sch., Oakland, Calif., 1944—45. Mem.: Sisters of Hiram (past pres., mem. sunshine com.). Republican. Baptist. Avocations: music, reading. Home: 210 Old Graham Hill Rd Santa Cruz CA 95060-1427

LENOX, GINA MARIE, music educator; b. Meadowbrook, Pa., July 12, 1979; d. David Richard and Eileen Marie Lenox. BS cum laude in Music Edn., Ind. U. of Pa., 2001. Cert. tchr. Pa., 2002. Tchr. gen. music Coun. Rock Sch. Dist., Holland, Pa., 2002; tchr. instrumental music Centennial Sch. Dist., Warminster, Pa., 2002—. Musician: Warminster (Pa.) Symphony Orch., 2001—, Ea. Wind Symphony, 2001—, Landis Mills Quintet, 2003—05, Anemos Winds, 2004—. Fellow, U. North Tex., 2006—, U. Minn., 2001. Mem.: Nat. Band Assn. (fellow 2005), Bucks County Music Educators Assn., Pa. Music Educators Assn., Music Educators Nat. Conf., Sons of Italy, Sigma Alpha Iota (life; pres. 1999—2001, corr. sec. 1999—2001, Sword Honor award 2001, Sword of Honor 2001). Home: 662 Paddock Drive Southampton PA 18966

LENTZ, BELINDA ANN, elementary school educator; b. Dover, Ohio, June 19, 1951; d. Donald Jacob and Alice Mae (Watkins) Lentz. BS in Edn., Kent State U., 1973; MS in Elem. Edn., U. Akron, 1983. Cert. elem. tchr. Tchr. elem. grades Indian Valley Local Schs., Tuscarawas, Ohio, 1973-88; tchr. Midvale (Ohio) Elem. Schs., 1988—2005; elem. sch. tchr. Tuscarawas Elem. Sch., Ohio, 2005—. Advisor Sr. High Youth Group; tchr. Sunday sch. St. John's United Ch. of Christ, 1989—, mem. ch. coun., past deacon, elder. Mem. Ohio Edn. Assn., NEA, Ohio Coun. Outdoor Educator Assn., Ohio Coun. for Social Studies, Coll. Club, Order Eastern Star (Star Point). Democrat. Avocations: reading, counted cross stitching, crafts, basketry, outdoor activities. Home: 1205 2nd St NW New Philadelphia OH 44663-1320 Office: Tuscarawas Elem Sch 361 School St Tuscarawas OH 44653 E-mail: blenz@tusco.net.

LENTZ, CHERIE LYNN, nurse; b. Oshkosh, Wisc., July 16, 1949; d. Harold H and Geraldine E Meske; m. Gregory Michael Lentz, Jan. 13, 1968; children: Gregory M Jr., Jeffrey Allen. AA, Fox Valley Tech. Coll., 1984. RN night supr. Oakridge Gardens Nursing Home, Menasha, Wis., 1984—85, Good Shepherd Svcs., Seymour, 1985—. Author: (book) The Castle's Call, 2000, A Star for Candi, 2003. Avocations: sewing, writing, cross stitch. Home: N7662 Hwy 45 New London WI 54961 Office: Good Shepherd Services 607 Bronson Rd Seymour WI 54165

LENZ, DEBRA LYNN, auditor; b. Watertown, Wis., June 8, 1973; d. Ron Floyd and Sandy Jean Lenz. BS in Acctg., Marquette U., Milw., 1996, MBA, 2003. CPA Wis., cert. Internal Auditor; CIA, 2005. Sr. auditor Deloitte & Touche LLP, Milw., 1996-99; sr. fin. analyst Rockwell Automation, Milw., 1999-2000, Harley-Davidson, Milw., 2000—. Mem. AICPA, Bus. Profl. Women, Wis. Inst. CPAs, Alpha Sigma Nu, Beta Gamma Sigma. Office: Harley-Davidson 3700 W Juneau Ave Milwaukee WI 53208 Home: W398 N5937 Autumn Woods Dr Oconomowoc WI 53066 Office Phone: 414-343-8764. Business E-Mail: debra.lenz@harley-davidson.com.

LENZ, DOLLY (IDALIZ DOLLY LENZ), real estate broker; b. Feb. 1957; d. Manuel and Lucy Camino; m. Aaron D. Lenz, 1980; children: Joseph, Jenny. Student in Acctg., Baruch Coll.; M in Acctg & Mgmt. Auditing, The New Sch. Auditor United Artists; with Sotheby's Internat. Realty; mng. dir. Prudential Douglas Elliman Real Estate, NYC, 2000—. Achievements include fluency in English, French, Italian, Portuguese, and Spanish. Avocation: running. Office: Prudential Douglas Elliman Real Estate 575 Madison Ave New York NY 10022 Office Phone: 212-891-7113. E-mail: DLenz@elliman.com.*

LENZ, MARY LYNN, bank executive; b. 1955; Undergraduate, Niagara Univ. Pres., CEO Slade's Ferry Bank, Somerset, Mass., with, 1982. Exec. bd. dir. SouthCoast Leadership Conf.; mem. adv. bd. Gabelli Sch. Bus. Roger Williams Univ., RI; spkr. in field. Named one of 50 Most Powerful Women, Fortune Mag., 2004, The 25 Most Powerful Women in Banking, US Banker mag., 2004, 2005. Office: Slades Ferry 100 Slades Ferry Ave Somerset MA 02726 Office Phone: 401-732-3222.

LEO, JACQUELINE M., editor-in-chief; Feature writer AP; sr. editor Modern Bride; co-founder Child, N.Y.C., 1986, editor-in-chief, 1987-88, Family Circle, N.Y.C., 1988-94; editl. dir. women's mags. group N.Y. Times Co., N.Y.C., 1994, dir. mag. and media devel., 1994-95; editl. dir. Good Morning America ABC-TV News, N.Y.C., 1995—97; editl. dir. Consumer Reports, 1997-99; v.p., editl. dir. Interactive Media/Meredith Corp., 1999—2001; v.p., US editor-in-chief Reader's Digest, Pleasantville, NY, 2000—. Author: New Woman's Guide To Getting Married. Recipient Matrix award Women in Comm., 1993. Mem. Am. Soc. Mag. Editors (bd. dirs., pres.), N.Y. Acad. Scis. (bd. govs.). Office: Office of Editor-in-Chief Reader's Digest Reader's Digest Rd Pleasantville NY 10570 Fax: 914-244-5900. Office Phone: 914-238-1000, 914-244-5567. Office Fax: 914-238-4559. E-mail: jacqueline_leo@rd.com.*

LEO, MARTHA E., advocate, counselor; b. Bronxville, N.Y., May 26, 1955; d. Joseph S. Leo, Robert (Stepfather) and Nancy (Lombard) Hudock. B in Social Work, R.I. Coll., Providence, 1983; MS in Counseling, So. Conn. State U., New Haven, 1989. Lic. profl. counselor Conn., cert. substance abuse counselor, rehab. counselor Nat. Rehab. Counseling Assn. Statisician Dept. Transp., Wethersfield, Conn., 1983—84; counselor Ctr. Ind. Living, Bridgeport, Conn., 1984—86; trainer mentally retarded Easter Seals, New Haven, 1986; vocat. rehab. counselor State of Conn. Dept. Social Svcs., New Haven, 1987—2001; advocate and investigator Children in Placement, New Haven, 2006—. Guardian ad litem, 2006—. Commr. Office Handicap Svcs. and Advocacy City of New Haven, 1995—97; vol. raising svc. animals. Recipient Dedicated Svcs. to Individuals with Disabilities award, State of Conn. Dept. Social Svcs., 2001. Mem.: Am. Counseling Assn. Avocations: literature, writing, dance, travel, baking. Home: 361 Lenox St New Haven CT 06513

LEON, NELLIE, health educator; d. Jesus Leon and Celia Rivas; m. Joachim M. Brown, Oct. 9, 2004. BS in Kinesiology and Health Promotion, Calif. State Poly. U., Pomona, 2003; M in Health Scis., Western U. Health Scis., Pomona, 2005; postgrad., Loma Linda U., Calif., 2005—. Grad. rsch. asst. Loma Linda U., Calif., 2005—; svc. learning instr. Western U. Health Scis., Pomona, 2005—. Health edn. cons. Calif. State Poly. U. Pomona, 2006—. Recipient Outstanding Health Promotion Grad. award, Calif. State Poly. Pomona U., 2003, Judy Ann Oliver Meml. award, Western U. Health Scis., 2005, Outstanding Thesis/Spl. Project award, 2005; Hilda Solis scholar, Calif. State Poly. Pomona U., 2005. Mem.: APHA, Am. Coll. Health Assn., Soc. Pub. Health Edn.

LEÓN, ROSEMARY CARRASCO, gynecologist; b. Hanford, Calif., Jan. 24, 1951; d. Benjamin Villasenor and Dina (Carrasco) León; m. James Dennis Albera (div.); children: Liliana Albera Thomas, Carlo Jaime Albera. Student, UCLA, 1969—71, MD, 1980; PharmD, U. Calif., San Francisco, 1975. Intern Harbor UCLA Med. Ctr., Torrance, 1980—81, resident in ob-gyn., 1983—84; ob-gyn. Porterville Family Health Ctr., Calif., 1984—88, Rosemary C. León, Inc., Visalia, Calif., 1988—2001, Tyle River Indian Cmty. Health Ctr., Porterville, 2004—05, Rene Charles, MD, Dinuba, Calif., 2006—. Mentor Chicanos for Health Edn., 1971—80, pres., 1973—75. Named Physician of Yr., Kaweah Delta Dist. Hosp., Visalia, Calif., 1991. Fellow: AMA, ACOG; mem.: Am. Fertility Soc. Democrat. Roman Catholic. Avocations: crocheting, swimming. Office: Rene Charles MD 342 Vermont AVe Dinuba CA 93618

LEONARD, ANGELA MICHELE, librarian, educator; b. Washington, June 26, 1954; d. Walter Jewell and Betty (Singleton) L. AB, Harvard U., 1976; MLS, Vanderbilt U., 1982; MPhil, George Washington U., 1987, PhD, 1994; postgrad., Dartmouth Sch. Criticism and Theory, 1996, NEH Inst., 1998, Chesapeake Regional Scholars Inst., 1999, Gilder Lehman Inst. Am. History, 2003. Cons. Seigenthaler Assocs., Nashville, 1979-81; instr. Trevecca Nazarene Coll., 1979, Nashville State Tech. Inst., 1980-81; rschr., learning libr. program Fisk U. Libr., 1981-82; cataloguer Howard U. Librs., 1983; reference libr. Founders Grad. Libr., 1983-89; tchg. asst. George Washington U., 1986-90; lectr. Bowdoin Coll., 1990-91; instr. St. Cloud State U., 1991; asst. prof. Dickinson Coll., 1992-94, Bucknell U., 1994-95; lectr. UMCP, 1995; asst. prof. Loyola Coll., Md., 1996—. Vis. prof. Johns Hopkins U., 1998; corp. and spl. ref. libr., 1988-90, 95-97; vis. scholar Wolfson Coll., Oxford U., 2005. Copy editor Am. Quarterly, 1988-90; editor: Boorstin Bibliography, Antislavery Materials; contbr. articles to books, profl. jours. Coolidge scholar, 2003, Hedgebrook fellow, 2006. Mem. ALA, NAACP, AAUW, Am. Hist. Assn., Orgn. Am. History, Semiotics Soc. Am., Nat. Soc. Exptl. Edn., Nat. Urban League, Assn. Black Women Historians (eastern regional dir.), Assn. Study African Am. Life and History, Links, Inc., Nat. Assn. Women Cath. Higher Edn., Translantic Studies Assn., Am. Soc. Environ. Historians, Black and Asian Studies Assn., Alpha Kappa Alpha, Beta Phi Mu. Roman Catholic. Office: Loyola Coll Dept Hist 4501 N Charles St Baltimore MD 21210-2601 E-mail: aleonard@loyola.edu.

LEONARD, SISTER ANNE C., school system administrator; b. N.Y.C., Dec. 22, 1936; d. Patrick A. and Mary T. (McAlpin) L. BS in Edn. and Social Sci., Fordham U., 1962, MA, 1965; CAGS, Boston U., 1972; postgrad., Hunter Coll., U. San Francisco, U. Northern Ill., Notre Dame U. Cert. tchr. K-12, adminstr. N.Y. Tchr., asst. prin., prin. Notre Dame Acad., Staten Island, NY, 1957-68; prin. Maternity B.V.M. Sch., Bourbonnais, Ill., 1968-69, St. Jude the Apostle Sch., South Holland, Ill., 1969-78; dir. Cath. Elem. Schs. Archdiocese of Chgo., 1978-83, dir. ednl. svcs., mem. Cardinal Bernadin's cabinet, 1983-90, exec. officer commn. ednl. svcs., 1983-90; supt. schs., dir. edn. Archdiocese of Okla. City, 1990-96; U.S. province leader Congregation of Notre Dame, Ridgefield, Conn., 1996—2005, leadership team Montreal, Canada, 2006—. Chair edn. divisn. Cath. Conf. Ill., 1988-90; del. gen. chpt. Congregation Notre Dame, mem. provincial coun., mem. leadership team, 2006—; mem. edn. com. U.S. Cath. Conf. Bishops, Washington, 1985-88; mem. Nat. Cath. Bishops' Millennium Com.; spkr. in field; lectr., presenter workshops; mem. Fortune 500 panel edn. and bus.; devel. mission statement, just principles compensation, new models compensation for prins., 1987-91; initiated, organized Dirs. Edn. Wis., Ill., Ind., Ohio, Mich.; attended symposia in field; mem. com. prep. Office of Cath. Edn. Conciliation Process; exec. officer local sch. bds.; initiated individually guided edn. program St. Jude Sch. Cons. textbooks William H. Sadlier, Inc.; contbr. articles to profl. jours. Trustee DePaul U., 1986—; trustee Midwestern U., 1999—, bd. dirs., vice chair acad. affairs com.; bd. dirs. Jr. Achievement, Chgo., 1984-90, Oklahoma City, 1991-96; mem. NCCJ, 1992-96, Gov. Ill. adv. com. on non-pub. schs., Springfield, 1978-82, planning com. Big Shoulders Project, officer Leadership Conf. of Women Religious (Region I), 1997-2005; mem. Congregation of Notre Dame, 2006. Mem. ASCD, Nat. Cath. Ednl. Assn. (pres. chief adminstrs. Cath. edn. 1991-94, v.p. 1989-91, vice chair bd. 1991-94, task force 1990-91, centennial com. 1997—2002, supervision, pers., curriculum, Educator of Yr. award 1990), Archdiocesan Prins. Assn. (pres. 1973-78), Nat. Religious Retirement Bd. (grant com.), Chgo. Coun. Fgn. Rels., Phi Delta Kappa (Educator of Yr. 1984). Avocations: reading, swimming, travel. Office Phone: 514-931-5891. Business E-Mail: aleonard@cnd-m.com.

LEONARD, BETSY ANN, director, writer; d. Herbert Douglas Baker, Jessie Lee and Beverly W. Koeppel (Stepfather); m. Dale Forrest Leonard, Nov. 7, 1981. BS, Fla. State U., Tallahassee, 1975; M in Curriculum and Instrn., San Diego State U., 1992. Cert. tchr. Calif. Calif. coord. Golden State Environ. Edn. Consortium, Sacramento, 1997—98; environ. edn. coord. San Diego Nat. History Mus., 1997—2001; project leader Calif. Inst. for Biodiversity, Oakland, 2002; project coord. hs curriculum project Tijuana River Nat. Estuarine Rsch. Res., Imperial Beach, Calif., 2003—05. Cons. in field. Coord. US Info. Agy., San Diego, 1997; EE grant evaluator Calif. State Dept. Edn., Sacramento, 1993—97; chair edn. com. Project Wildlife, 1986—90; del. U.S./Spain Joint Conf. Edn., Barcelona, 1995; scorer Ednl. Testing Svc., 2003; coord. North Am. Assn. Environ. Edn., 2000. Recipient 1st Pl. Nat. award, YMCA Armed Svcs., 1981, Outstanding Leadership award, Calif. Alliance Enviorn. Edn., 1997. Mem.: Nat. Assn. for Interpretation (bd. dirs. 1997—98, cert., chair environ. edn. sect. 1992—99, Environ. Edn. Svc. award 2002). Democrat. Episcopalian. Avocations: skiing, reading, writing, bicycling. Home: 71 River View Pl Parachute CO 81635 Personal E-mail: betsleon@msn.com.

LEONARD, CAROLYN BRANCH, editor, writer; b. Buffalo, Okla., Aug. 21, 1937; d. Ernest S. and Imogene (Parsons) Branch; m. John C. Leonard, Apr. 15, 1956 (div. June 1984); children: Judith G., James C.; m. Jon Heavener, Feb. 14, 1993. BA, Oklahoma City U., 1991. Pub. SAGEst PRESS, Oklahoma City, 1990—. Pub. affairs asst. U.S. Treas., Oklahoma City, 1988-94. Asst. editor: Woodward County Jour., 1982-83; editor: Harper Co. Jour., Buffalo, Okla., 1983-88, News U Can Use, Nat. Treas. Employees Union, Oklahoma City, 1994-96. Senate encoder Okla. State Capitol, 1996-99; area rep., bd. dirs. Briarcreek Neighborhood Assn.; active Meth. Ch. of the Servant; coord. Dutch Cousins Gathering, Harrodsburg, Ky., 2005 Recipient numerous awards; named Hon. Ky. Col., 2005-2006. Mem. DAR (1st v.p. Okla. Prairies 2006-), Writers of the Purple Sage (past pres.), Oklahoma City Writers (past pres. 1993, 2005), Okla. Writers Fedn. (exec. bd. 2005-), Mayflower Descs. Soc., Okla. Hist. Soc., Okla. Geneal. Soc. (newsletter editor), Mo. Hist. Soc., Ohio Hist. Soc., Ill. Hist. Soc., Bentonville Anti-Horse Thief Soc., Friends of the Libr., Servants Dinner Club.

LEONARD, JACQUELYN ANN, retired elementary school educator; b. Hollister, Okla., Apr. 2, 1931; d. Alex and Dolly M. (McCurty) McKinney; m. Malvin Paul Leonard, Feb. 6, 1952 (div. Apr. 1993); children: Diana, Andrea. BA in Art Edn. and Pub. Sch. Music, Ctrl. State U., 1955; postgrad., U. Mich., 1955—62, Mich. State U., 1955—62. Pres. Jacquelyn-Jackie Leonard Corp., Lake Orion, Mich., 1994—. Contbr. articles to profl. jours. Contbr. Am. Cares, The Law Enforcement Officers Meml. Fund, Washington. Mem.: Mich. Assn. Ret. Personnel, Nat. Trust. Avocations: reading, singing, piano, swimming. Home: 3091 Oakridge Ct Lake Orion MI 48360

LEONARD, JO ANN WARNER, social sciences educator; d. Brooks E. and Carolyn F. Warner; m. George F. Leonard, July 22, 1978; children: Christopher Michael, Ryan Patrick. BA, Marywood U., Scranton, Pa., 1973; MA, U. Scranton, Pa., 1975. Cert. comprehensive social sci. Pa. Dept. Edn., 1973. Secondary tchr. Montrose Area Sch. Dist., Pa., 1973—. Adj. faculty Luzerne C.C., Nanticoke, Pa., 2001—04. Lector Holy Name of Mary Ch., Montrose, 1986—2006. Democrat-Npl. Roman Catholic. Avocations: reading, swimming, writing.

LEONARD, JUDITH PRICE, educational advisor; b. Milw., July 10, 1941; d. Ralph H. and Sylvia (Shames) Price; m. Richard Black Leonard Jr., Dec. 15, 1962 (dec. Dec. 1978); m. Norman Crasilneck, Aug. 31, 1991. BS in Math., Antioch U., 1963; MS in Math., St. Louis U., 1970. Tchr. math. Ferguson Florissant (Mo.) Schs., 1963—94, coord., 1971—73; mentor, co-dir., faculty advisor Engelmann Math. & Sci. Inst., U. Mo., St. Louis, 1988—96; supr. student tchrs. U. Mo., St. Louis, 1995—96; coord. Regional Inst. Sci. Edn., St. Louis, 1996—2000; evaluator and cons. math. programs St. Louis Pub. Schs., 1994—2005; cons. math. programs Riverview Gardens Schs., 2006; faculty advisor NSF Young Scholars, U. Mo, St. Louis, 1997, NSF Students & Tchrs. as Rsch. Scientists, U. Mo., St. Louis, 1998—99. Co-dir. Post Dispatch and Monsanto Greater St. Louis Sci. Fair, 1998—99; adv. bd. Greater St. Louis Sci. Fair, 1997—2006, Intel Internat. Sci. and Edn. Fair, 1996—99, adults in charge, 1997—99, fair dir., 1999, mem. leadership coun., 2005—06; chair Discovery Young Scientist Challenge, St. Louis, 1999—2006; sec. exec. bd. Math. Educators Greater St. Louis, 2001—06; mem. Math. Sci. Network of Greater St. Louis, 1995—2006; math. cons. U. Mo., St. Louis, 2002—03; presenter, judge, chmn. judges for math. computer sci., physics and enging. Jr. Sci., Engring. and Humanities Symposium, 1995—2001, 2003—06. Author: Word Problems, Basic Skills Instructional Fair, 1996; author, editor: (brochure) Teacher Linking Collaborative, 1997, 2002; editor 3 Math. Books, 2002, 5th and 6th Pre Algebra, 2002. Hon. Engelmann scholar Engelmann Math. and Sci. Inst., St. Louis, 1993, NSF Young scholar U. Mo., St. Louis, 1997; recipient Math. Edn. award Math. Educators Greater St. Louis, 1994, NSF STARS award U. Mo., St. Louis, 2000, Recognition award Acad. Sci. St. Louis, 2006. Mem. NEA, Nat. Coun. Tchrs. Math., Nat. Coun. Suprs. Math., Mo. Coun. Tchrs. Math. (life), Ferguson Florissant NEA (life). Avocations: tennis, biking, walking. Home: 22 Bellerive Acres Saint Louis MO 63121-4321 Personal E-mail: judy@judyleonard.net.

LEONARD, KANDI, language educator; b. Oxnard, Calif., Jan. 13, 1959; d. Ron and Bobbie Jo Seaman; m. Ralph Hanna; 1 child, McGee Jeordi. BA, San Francisco State U., 1984, MA, 1986; PhD, U. Calif., Riverside, 1993. Cert. secondary sch. English tchr., Calif. Assoc. prof. Nat. U., L.A., 1996-98; English tchr. Ontario (Calif.) H.S., 1997—. Exec. v.p. YWCA, San Bernardino, Calif., 1993-94; fundraiser Dem. Party, Riverside, Calif., 1994. Mem. Nat. Assn. Tchrs., Sisters in Crime. Home: 932 N Crescent Heights Blvd Los Angeles CA 90046-6916

LEONARD, KRISTI, education educator, director; d. Jim and Kathy Leonard. BA, Ctrl. Coll., Pella, Iowa, 1994—97; MA, U. Iowa, Iowa City, 1998—2000, U. No. Iowa, Cedar Falls, 2002—05. Area coord./, wellness team mem. Luther Coll., Decorah, Iowa, 2000—05; asst. prof. wellness, wellness dir. Waldorf Coll., Forest City, Iowa, 2005—. Coord. Luther Coll., Decorah, Iowa, 2000—05. Mem.: Am. Alliance Health, Phys. Ed., Recreation, and Dance, Nat. Wellness Inst. Office Phone: 641-585-8264.

LEONARD, LAURA L., lawyer; b. 1956; AB, U. Calif., Davis, 1978; JD, Loyola U., Chgo., 1983. Bar: Ill. 1983. With Sidley & Austin, Chgo., 1983—, ptnr., 1991—. Lectr. on environ. aspects of bus. trans., including Northwestern U. Kellogg Grad. Sch. Mgmt.; mem. adv. bd. BNA's Environ. Due Digigence Guide. Office: Sidley & Austin Bank One Plz 10 S Dearborn St Chicago IL 60603 Fax: 323-853-7620. E-mail: lleonard@sidley.com.

LEONARD, LINDA FAYE, secondary school educator; b. Crowley, La., Nov. 3, 1948; d. Grady and Beulah (Melancon) Lapearous; m. Russell Lynn Leonard, Dec. 26, 1947; four children. BA, McNeese State U., 1974, MEd, 1975. Tchr. Sam Houston HS, Lake Charles, La., 1975-76, Welsh HS, La., 1976-77, Washington-Marion HS, Lake Charles, 1983-95; tchr., speech/debate coach Iowa HS, La., 1995—. Yearbook adviser Iowa HS, 1997—. Mem. Nat. Assn. Parliamentarians, Nat. Forensic League, Nat. Coun. Tchrs. English, Nat. Debate Coaches Assn., La. HS Speech League, La. Scholastic Pres Assn., Columbia Scholastic Press Assn., Nat. Scholastic Press Assn., Quill and Scroll. Avocations: drawing, painting, theater, quilting, camping. Home: 711 Hardy St Iowa LA 70647-3929 Office: Iowa HS 401 W Miller Ave Iowa LA 70647-3922 Office Phone: 337-582-1752. Personal E-mail: lapleonard@yahoo.com. Business E-Mail: linda.leonard@cpsb.org.

LEONARD, MARTHA GAIL, elementary school educator; b. Middlesboro, Ky., Apr. 22, 1954; d. Dana and Ester Novella (Keller) McDaniel; m. Stanley Howard Leonard, May 30, 1987; 1 child, Ashley Elizabeth. BA, Lincoln Meml. U., 1975, BS, 1978, MS, 1987. Cert. tchr., Tenn. Tchr. Tazewell New Tazewell (Tenn.) Primary Sch., 1975—2006; headmaster Heritage Bapt. Acad., New Tazewell, Tenn., 2006—; career ladder level III tchr. Tenn. Edn. chair New Tazewell United Meth. Ch., 1990, mem. adminstrv. bd., 1990-91. Mem. NEA, Tenn. Edn. Assn., Claiborne County Edn. Assn. (assn. rep. 1979-80), Nat. Geographic Soc., Am. Humane Soc., Profl. Educators of Tenn. (pres. Claiborne County Chpt., 2004-). Republican. Avocations: reading, gardening, tennis, basketball, writing. Home: 415 Russell Rd S New Tazewell TN 37825-6921 Office: Heritage Bapt Acad PO Box 1467 428 Harmon Rd New Tazewell TN 37825 Office Phone: 423-526-2807. Personal E-mail: laig@hotmail.com.

LEONARD, MONA FREEMAN, communications educator; d. Jack Robinson and Ruth Olivia Freeman; m. Jeffrey Allen Leonard, Oct. 27, 1989; 1 child, Jared Alexander. BA, Howard U., 1986, MA, 1989; postgrad., U. Ky., 1994—97. Adj. prof. U. Louisville, 1991—2002; assoc. prof. Jefferson C.C., Louisville, 1993—2005, prof., chmn., 2005—. Author (chpt.): Our Voices: Essays in Culture, Ethnicity and Communication, 2004. Mem.: Nat. Comm. Assn. Office: Jefferson CC 109 E Broadway Louisville KY 40202 Business E-Mail: mona.leonard@kctcs.edu.

LEONARD, NAOMI EHRICH, aerospace engineer, engineering educator; BSE, Princeton U., NJ, 1985; MS, U. Md., College Park, 1991, PhD, 1994. Engr. elec. power ind.; asst. prof., mech. and aerospace engring. Princeton U., 1994—99, assoc. prof., 1999—2003, prof., 2003—. Author: of numerous sci. jour. articles, including Journal of Dynamical Control Systems, Physica D, and Automatica. Named a MacArthur Fellow, 2004. Office: Dept Mech and Aerospace Engring D 234 Engring Quadrangle Princeton Univ Princeton NJ 08544 Office Phone: 609-258-5129. Office Fax: 609-258-6109. Business E-Mail: naomi@princeton.edu.*

LEONARD, PAMELA DIAN, architect, artist; b. Corpus Christi, Tex., Mar. 25, 1968; d. John David and Loretta Kay Leonard. BArch, Miss. State U., 1991. Cert. Nat. Coun. Arch. Registration Bds., 1997, registered architect, Miss., 1996. Intern architect BSW Internat., Tulsa, Okla., 1991—93, Canizaro Trigiani Architects, Jackson, Miss., 1993—96; architect Canizaro Cawthon Davis, Jackson, Miss., 1993—. Accreditation rev. team Nat. Coun. Accreditation Bd., 1989—90. Watercolor painting, St. Mark's, 1987, The Girl, 1990. Mentor Jackson Pub. Schs. VAST Mentor Program, Jackson, 1999—2000; big sister Big Brothers / Big Sisters of Green Country, Tulsa, 1992—93; catechumenate adminstr. St. Andrew's Episcopal Cathedral, Jackson, 1999—, facilities study com., 2001—, adult formation com., 2000—01, Christmas alternate giving program chair, 1999—; mem. Episcopal Diocese Miss. Young Adults Task Force; bd. dirs. Miss. Children's Mus., Jackson, 1997—99, pres. bd. dirs., 1998—99, founding sec., pres. elect bd. dirs., 1997—99, bldg. com. chair, 1997—99, jubilee jam com. chair, 1999, founding com., 1995—97. Mem.: AIA (cmty. enhancement program design competition team leader 1993, cont. edn. com. 1997—98), Angel Flight Alumni Assn., Mortar Bd. Alumni Assn. Episcopalian. Avocations: painting, drawing, writing, cooking, walking. Office: Canizaro Cawthon Davis 129 S President St Jackson MS 39201

LEONARD, PAULA LEAVY, school disciplinarian; b. New London, Conn., Sept. 15, 1950; d. Paul Matthew and Jeanne Marie Leavy; m. J. Peter Leonard (div.); 1 child, Alexander Robert; m. Dale Victor Bauman, Dec. 30, 2000. Bachelor in Liberal Arts, Northeastern U., 1973; specialist, La. State U., 1995. Cert. Nat. Assn. Sch. Psychologists. Editl. asst., staff writer New England Telephone, Boston, 1969—72; mgr. editl. svcs. Boys Clubs Am., N.Y.C., 1974—79; instr. Dept. Psychology La. State U., Shreveport, 1993—94, 1999, examiner, Assessment Ctr., 1994; sch. psychologist Caddo Parish Schs., Shreveport, 1994—. Bd. mem. Shreveport Symphony Orch., 2000—06, pres., 2002—05. Named Top Fund Raiser, Am. Walk for Diabetes, 1999; recipient Academic award, La. State U., 1995, Handicap award, Rapid Appraisal Svcs., 1997. Mem.: Caddo Assn. Edn., La. Sch. Psychologist Assn., Nat. Ass. Sch. Psychologists, Kappa Delta Phi. Home: 539 Hunters Run Bossier City LA 71111 Office: Caddo Parish Spl Edn Ctr Pupil Appraisal Svc 3004 Knight St Bldg 6 Shreveport LA 71105

LEONARD, SHEILA ANN, former government agency executive, consultant; b. Greenwich, Conn., Oct. 21, 1940; d. George Sterling and Virginia Lois Coxon; m. Sheila Ann Leonard, Oct. 14, 2000. BA, Purdue U., West Lafayette, Ind., 1974; PhD, Oreg. State U., Corvallis, Oreg., 1980; MBA, Willamette U., Salem, Oreg., 1983. Cert. level III unltd. warrant supervisory contracting officer EPA, 1993, Dept. Homeland Security, USCG, 2002. Procuring contracting officer and contract specialist Contracts Directorate, Undersea Warfare Systems Contracts Divsn., Naval Sea Systems Command, Washington, 1984—90; supervisory contract specialist. sr. contract specialist EPA, Washington, 1990—98, sr. contract specialist region 9 San Francisco, 1990—2000; sr. contract specialist GSA, Fed. Tech. Services/ANSWER Sollutions Devel. Ctr., Oakland, Calif., 2000—02; supervisory contract specialist Dept. Homeland Security, USCG, Alameda, Calif., 2002—05. Sr. rschr. sr. svcs. divsn. Dept. Human Resources, Salem, Oreg., 1980—81; fin. analyst, auditor Bonneville Power Adminstrn., Portland, Oreg., 1983—83. Chmn. 3-state conf. task force on aging United Ch. of Christ, Portland, 1980—82; vice moderator First Congl. Ch., Corvallis, 1980—82; bd. dirs. Watergate at Landmark Conco. Assn., Alexandria, Va., 1991—95; dir. Garden Isle Homeowners Assn. Bd. of Directors, Alameda, Calif., 2001—03; mem. adv. bd. Alameda Mastick Sr. Ctr., Calif., 2006—06; crisis intervention vol. Crisis Ctr., West Lafayette, Ind., 1970—72. Recipient Book award, Purdue U. Alpha Lambda Delta, 1974; Alpha Xi Delta Top Woman scholar, Purdue U., 1974, Gene Huntley Meml. scholar, Willamette U., 1982, Adele Hagnes Stamp fellow, Alpha Lambda Delta, 1974—75, Gen. Foods Fund fellow, Oreg. State U., 1974—76. Mem.: Sigma Xi, Omicron Nu, Phi Kappa Phi, Phi Beta Kappa. Democrat. Avocations: gardening, travel. Home: 1017 Kingston Ln Alameda CA 94502 Office: 1017 Kingston Ln Alameda CA 94502 Office Phone: 510-521-3696. Home Fax: 510-521-3696; Office Fax: 510-521-3696. Personal E-mail: saleonard@alamedanet.net.

LEONARD, VIRGINIA KATHRYN, financial manager; b. Street, Md., Aug. 31, 1944; d. Elbert Monroe and Mildred Rudolph (Patrick) Joines; m. James Richard Leonard, Aug. 31, 1963; children: James Richard II, Raymun Bradley. Student, Ea. Nazarene Coll., 1962-63; AA, Harford Community Coll., 1976; BS in Bus. Mgmt., U. Md., 1983; grad., U.S. Army Mgmt. Staff Coll., 1988, Fed. Exec. Inst., 1992, Harvard/JFK Sch. Govt., 1996. Program analyst Facilities Engring., Aberdeen Proving Ground, Md., 1976-79; budget analyst Aberdeen Proving Ground Command, 1980; program analyst officer Facilities Engring., Aberdeen Proving Ground, Md., 1981; budget analyst Test and Evaluation Command, Aberdeen Proving Ground, Md., 1982-83; budget analyst, budget officer Dept. of Army, Washington, 1984; budget officer test and evaluation command U.S. Army, Aberdeen Proving Ground, Md., 1985-89, fin. mgr. test and evaluation command, 1989-94, dir. resource mgmt. test and evaluation command, 1994-97, dir. resources and pers. test and evaluation, 1997-2000; ret., 2000. Avocations: travel, camping, reading. E-mail: jjplumtree@aol.com.

LEONARDO, ANN ADAMSON, marketing and sales consultant; b. Hamilton, Lanark, Scotland, Jan. 4, 1944; d. James Walker and Margaret Patterson (Burnside) Adamson; m. John Constantine Leonardo, Jr., Mar. 29, 1975; 1 child, Elizabeth Margaret. BA in Bus., McGill U., Montreal, Que., Can., 1970. Market rsch. mgr. MacLaren Advt., Toronto, Ont., Can., 1965-70; group product mgr. Menley & James, Montreal, 1970-74; mktg. mgr. Maybelline divsn. Plough, Toronto, 1074-75; v.p. mktg. Van De Kamp's Bakery, Glendale, Calif., 1976-80; v.p. mktg. and sales Cal West Periodicals, Oakland, 1980-84; mktg. cons., San Francisco, 1984-87; pes., owner Micro-Cosmic Rsch., Ketchum, Idaho, 1988—. Founding dir., bd. dirs. Family House Inc., San Francisco, 1981—90. Bd. dirs. Sagebrush Equestrian Training Ctr. Handicapped, Hailey, Idaho, 2004—, Sun Valley Summer Symphony, Idaho, 2005—. Home: 77 6516 Alii Drive Kailua Kona HI 96740 Personal E-mail: AAL5711@aol.com.

LEONARD-ZABEL, ANN MARIE T., psychologist, educator; d. Thomas M. Leonard, Sr. and Gertrude A. Leonard; m. Raymond G. Zabel, Sept. 16, 1979; children: Jessica Zabel, Steve Zabel. BA, U. Mass., Boston, 1979, CAGS in Sch. Psychology, 1991; EdM in Counseling, Bridgewater State Coll., 1981; EdD in Child and Youth Studies-Exceptional Svcs., Nova Southeastern U., 1996. Lic. ednl. psychologist Mass., mental health counselor Mass., cert. sch. psychologist Mass., Nat., diplomate Am. Psychotherapy Assn., Am. Bd. Soc. Neuropsychology; lic. social worker Mass., cert. sch. social worker/sch. adjustment counselor, internat. cert. alcohol and drug counselor, nat. cert. masters addictions counselor, nat. cert. criminal justice specialist, nat. cert. counselor, nat. cert. cognitive behavioral therapist, nat. cert. cognitive forensic therapist; cert. alcohol and drug abuse counselor Mass. Asst. dir., counselor Project Friend, Inc., Plymouth, Mass., 1982; counselor, dir. Alcoholic Family Rehab., Plymouth, 1983; psychologist Middleboro (Mass.) Pub. Schs., 1991; owner, dir. New Eng. Attentional Clinic, Plymouth, 1996; prof. Bridgewater (Mass.) State Coll., 1996; lead psychologist Foxboro (Mass.) Pub. Schs., 1999; prof. Curry Coll., Milton and Plymouth, 2002. Mem.: Am. Psychotherapy Assn. (bd. dirs., membership com.), Coun. for Exceptional Children, Nat. Assn. Sch. Psychologists, Mass. Sch. Psychologist Assn. (bd. dirs. 1997—, co-chairperson Cape and Islands Sch. Psychologist Chpt. 1994—98). Office: New Eng Attentional Clinic Park Ave Trust Bldg 7 S Park Ave 2nd Fl Plymouth MA 02360 Office Phone: 508-746-5666. E-mail: dramlz@yahoo.com.

LEONE, JEANNE, artist; b. Revere, Mass., June 8, 1946; d. Gerard Leone and Jeanne Irene DeSimone. BA Polit. Sci. with highest honors, Adelphi U., 1968. Lic. real estate broker, Mass. Dir. advt., mktg., publ. rels. Keydata Corp., Watertown, MA, 1970-74; founding and managing editor The Jour. Technol. Horizons in Edn., Acton, MA, 1974-76; pres. M & M Constrn., Chestnut Hill, MA, 1978-82; cons. F.L. Putnam Brokerage Ho., Boston, 1981; dir. advtg., mktg., publ. rels. Gould Computer Sys., Plantation, FL, 1983; cons. Northern Telecom, Toronto, Canada, 1984-85; closing and title officer Malibu Escrow Corp., Malibu, CA, 1986-87; cons. Wespac Investors Trusts, Santa Monica, CA, 1988-90, The Marquardt Co., Van Nuys, CA, 1990-95, Philip R. Gustlin, Esq., 1994-95, Technol. Renaissance Corp., Atlanta, 1996, Microtrends, Inc., Pasadena, CA, 1996-97, Bklyn., 1999. Founder Greenpoint Riverfront Artists, 1999. One-woman shows include Univ. Pl. Gallery, Harvard U., Cambridge, Mass., 1991, Wilshire Landmark Bldg,. L.A., 1993-94, Margaret Crow Gallery, Pasadena, Calif., 1995-96; commn. to create art book on the Earl Gales Jr. Collection of West African Art, Art on the Loose, 1998. Bd. dirs. Cmty. Champions, San Francisco. Mem. MENSA. Fax: 718-383-9658. E-mail: leonejean@aol.com.

LEONE, MICHELE CASTALDO, secondary school educator; b. Bethpage, N.Y., July 10, 1956; d. Raime Andrew and Rose Marie (Salegna) Castaldo; m. James Blase Leone, July 25, 1992. AS, Nassau C.C., 1976; BA, Hofstra U., 1978, MA, 1982. Tchr. math. St. Dominic High Sch., Oyster Bay, N.Y., 1978-99, chair dept. math., 1988-99; math. tutor Bethpage, N.Y., 1999—. Adj. prof. math. Nassau C.C., Garden City, N.Y., 1990—; tchr. Cath. Edn. Coop. Exam. prep. class, SAT prep. class St. Dominic H.S., 1999—. Mem. ASCD, Nat. Coun. Math. Tchrs., N.Y. State Math. Tchrs. Assn., Nassau County Tchrs. Assn. Roman Catholic. Avocations: computers, cooking, dance. Home and Office: 3939 Hahn Ave Bethpage NY 11714-5010

LEONG, CAROL JEAN, electrologist; b. Sacramento, Jan. 9, 1942; d. Walter Richard and Edith (Bond) Bloss; m. Oliver Arthur Fisk III, Apr. 12, 1964 (div. 1973); 1 child, Victoria Kay. BA in Sociology, San Jose (Calif.) State Coll., 1963; degree, Western Bus. Coll., 1964; cert. in electrolysis, Bay Area Coll. Electrolysis, 1978; degree in esthetics, Zenzi's Coll., 1998. Registered and cert. clin. profl. electrologist, Calif. Model various orgns., Calif., 1951-64; employment counselor Businessmen's Clearinghouse, Cin., 1966-67; dir. personnel Kroger Food Corp., Cin., 1967-68; prin. Carol Leong Electrolysis, San Mateo, Calif., 1978—. Prin. Designs by Carol, San Mateo, 1987—; mem. Profl. Women's Forum, 1988—. Contbr. articles to profl. publs. Pres. Peninsula Aux. Lighthouse for the Blind, 1984-85, 95-2002, 1st v.p., 1993-95, pres., 1999, 2000, 01, 02, 03; mem. Civic Garden Club, 1995—, Best Friends Animal Orgn., 1992—, The Nature Conservancy, 1995—, Nat. Fedn. Rep. Women, 1996; vol. Nat. Kidney Found. No. Calif., 1995—. Recipient Cert. of Appreciation San Francisco Lighthouse for the Blind, 1981-82, 83. Mem. Internat. Guild Profl. Electrologists (mem. continuing edn. com.), NAFE, Profl. Women's Forum, Peninsula Humane Soc., San Francisco Zool. Soc., Friends of Filoli, Am. Electrologists Assn., Electrologists Assn. Calif., Internat. Platform Assn, Order of Eastern Star, Chi Omega. Republican. Presbyterian. Avocations: golf, tennis, ballet, theater, photography. Home: 1447 Woodberry Ave San Mateo CA 94403-3712 Office: Carol Leong Electrolysis 359 N San Mateo Dr Ste 4 San Mateo CA 94401-2584 Personal E-mail: jeanssk8@aol.com.

LEONHART, MICHELE MARIE, federal agency administrator; BS in Criminal Justice, Lakewood C.C., Minn., 1978. Police officer Balt. Police Dept., Md.; spl. agt. Drug Enforcement Adminstrn., Mpls., 1980—85, spl. agt. recruiter St. Louis, 1986—88, group supr., intelligence supr. San Diego, 1988—93, OPR (internal affairs) inspector Arlington, Va., 1993—94, bd., 1994—95, asst. spl. agt. in charge of field divsn. L.A., 1995—96, sr. exec. svc. mem. spl. agt. recruitment program, 1996—97, spl. agt. in charge field divsn. San Francisco, 1997—98, L.A., 1998—2003, acting dep. adminstr. Alexandria, 2003—04, dep. adminstr., 2004—. Office: Drug Enforcement Adminstrn Mailstop AXS 2401 Jefferson Davis Hwy Alexandria VA 22301

LEONI, TEA (ELIZABETH TEA PANTALEONI), actress; b. NYC, Feb. 25, 1966; m. Neil Tardio, Feb. 1992 (div. Oct. 1995); m. David Duchovny, May 6, 1997; children: Madeline West, Kyd Miller. Attended, Sarah Lawrence Coll. Actor (TV series): Santa Barbara, 1989, Flying Blind, 1992-93, The Naked Truth, 1995-98; (TV movies) The Counterfeit Contessa, 1994; (films) Switch, 1991, A League of Their Own, 1992, Wyatt Earp, 1994, Bad Boys, 1995, Flirting with Disaster, 1996, Deep Impact, 1998, There's No Fish Food in Heaven, 1998, The Family Man, 2000, Jurassic Park 3, 2001, Hollywood Ending, 2002, People I Know, 2002, House of D, 2004, Spanglish, 2004, Fun with Dick and Jane, 2005. Recipient Saturn award best actress for "The Family Man", 2001.*

LEON RIVERA, AIDA I., language educator; b. Santurce, P.R., Jan. 20, 1944; d. Juan Elias Leon and Guillermina Rivera; married; children: Lydia I. Colon Romani, Jose Angel Colon. MS in Edn., Bank St. Coll., NYC, 1977; MA in Bilingual Edn., Hofstra U., 1977, profl. diploma in Reading, Language, and Cognition, 1979, PhD in Reading and Lang. Cognition, 1992. Cert. sch. dist. adminstr. N.Y. State Edn. Dept., sch. adminstr. N.Y. State Edn. Dept., prin. jr. h.s. N.Y.C. Sch. Dist., prin. DES N.Y.C. Sch. Dist., asst. prin. jr. h.s. N.Y.C. Sch. Dist., tchr. grades K-6 N.Y. State Edn. Dept., bilingual tchr. sch. and comty. rels. N.Y.C. Sch. Dist. Asst. prof. N.Y.C. Inds. Sch. Dist. 162, Bklyn., 1971—91; dist. dir. Dist. 32, Bklyn., 1991—92; prin. Intermediate Sch. Dist. 162, Bklyn., 1992—97; dep. chair edn. dept. Touro Coll., N.Y.C., 1997—2001; assoc. prof. edn. Fla. Meml. Coll., Miami, 2001—. Mem. adv. bd. N.Y. Inst. Bus. Tech., N.Y.C., 1998—99; v.p. Assn. Coun. Asst. Prins. of Supervisors and Adminstrs., Bklyn., 1991—92. Author: Success with Cloze-Level A, 1992, Success with Cloze-Level B, 1992. Recipient Appreciation on Tchr.'s Day award, Educators of Am., Fla. Meml. Coll., 2002, Appreciation and Dedication award, Halsey Mid. Sch., 1999, Appreciation award, Intermediate Sch. Dist. 162, 1997, 25-Yr. Svc. award, Coun. Suprs. and Adminstrs., 1996, Devotion and Guidance to Children and Parents of Intermediate Sch. Dist. 162 award, Parent Tchrs. Assn., 1996, Pub. Svc. and Contbn. to Furtherance of Good Govt. award, Good Govt. Com., Inc., 1995, Devotion and Guidance award, Intermediate Sch. Dist. 162, 1994, Patience and Dedication award, Intermediate Sch. Dist. 162 Parent Tchr. Assn., 1994, Dedication, Hard, Work and Loyalty award, Intermediate Sch. Dist. 162, 1994, Disting. Svc. and Dedication award, 1994, Dr. Aida I. Leon-Rivera award presented annually, 1993, Women's History Month award, Bushwick Outreach Ctr., 1992. Mem.: ASCD, Southeastern Regional Assn. Tchr. Educators, N.Y. State Reading Assn., Internat. Reading Assn. Avocation: travel.

LEPAGE, EILEEN MCCULLOUGH See MCCULLOUGH, EILEEN

LEPKE, CHARMA DAVIES, musician, educator; b. Delavan, Wis., Oct. 1, 1919; d. Ithel B. and Florence Mary (Jones) Davies; m. John Richard Lepke, Dec. 22, 1949 (div. July 1974). BA, Wellesley Coll., 1941, MA, 1942; MMusic, Am. Conservatory of Music, Chgo., 1946. Piano tchr., organist Fairfax Hall Jr. Coll., Waynesboro, Va., 1942-44; piano tchr. U. Nebr., Lincoln, 1946-50; ch. organist Trinity Methodist, Unitarian, Lincoln, 1946-50; missionary Am. Bd. Congl. Ch., Durban, Johannesburg, South Africa, 1950-56; ch. organist, choir dir. Congl. United Ch. of Christ, Oconomowoc/Sheboygan, Wis., 1957-70; organist Coloma, Mich., 1970-73; ch. organist Brick Bapt. Ch., Walworth, Wis., 1974, United Meth. Ch., Delavan, 1974-77, Congl. United Ch. of Christ, Delavan, 1977—; with Walworth County Arts Coun. Music editor revised Zulu hymnal Amagama Okuhlabalela, South Africa, 1951-56; composer preludes for organ, piano pieces, song and anthem. Recipient 1st prize for song Wis. Fedn. Music Clubs, 1960, others. Mem. Am. Guild of Organists, Music Tchrs. Nat. Assn., Wis. Alliance for Composers, Delavan Musical Arts Soc. (founder, pres.), Phi Beta Kappa. Congregationalist. Home: # 311 1025 S 2d St Delavan WI 53115

LEPKOWSKI, SUZANNE JOY, language educator; b. Newfane, NY, Dec. 27, 1971; d. Rockwood K. and Rose M. Chambers; m. David C. Lepkowski, 1997. BS in English, SUNY Brockport, 1997, MS in English Edn., 2003. Cert. tchr. English NY. Reading tchr. Charlotte Mid. Sch., Rochester, NY, 1997—98; tchr. English Gates-Chili Sr. HS, Rochester, 1998—99, Holley Jr. HS, NY, 1999—. Student tchr./mentor SUNY Brockport, 2002; sr. class advisor Holley Jr. HS, 2001—, tchr. SAT prep course, 2005. Recipient Florence Brasser scholarship, United Meth. Ch. North Chili, NY, 1992. Mem.: United Meth. Women (pres., sec. 2002). Republican. United Methodist. Avocations: gardening, reading. Home: 667 Whittier Rd Spencerport NY 14559 Office: Holley Jr HS 3800 N Main St Holley NY 14470

LEPORE, DAWN GOULD, Internet company executive; BA, Smith Coll. With Cin. Bell, Informatics, San Francisco, Charles Schwab Corp., San Francisco, 1983—2004, exec. v.p., chief info. officer, 1993—99, vice chmn. tech., operations and admin., 1999—2004; CEO drugstore.com inc., 2004—. Bd. dirs. Wal-Mart Stores, Inc., 2001—, eBay. Bd. dirs. Catalyst; trustee Smith Coll. Named one of Bay Area's Most Powerful Corp. Women, San Francisco Chronicle, Top 100 Women in Computing, Open Computing mag., Ten Hottest CIOs, Future Banker mag., 1999, 50 Most Powerful Women in Am. Bus., Fortune mag., 2000, 2001, 2002; recipient Aiming High Conf., NOW, 2003.

LEPORE, JILL, history professor, writer; BA in English, Tufts Univ., 1987; MA in Am. Culture, Univ. Mich., Ann Arbor, 1990; MPhil in Am. Studies, Yale Univ., 1993, PhD in Am. Studies, 1995. Asst. prof., history dept. Univ. Calif., San Diego, 1995—96, Boston Univ., 1996—2001, assoc. prof., history dept., 2001—03; prof., history dept. Harvard Univ., 2003—, and chair, history and lit. program, 2005—. Bd. dir. Boston History Collaborative, 1999—2000. Author: Encounters in the New World, 2000, The Name of War: King Philip's War and the Origins of American Identity, 1998 (Bancroft Prize, Ralph Waldo Emerson Prize, Berkshire Prize, New England Hist. Assn. Book Prize), A is for American, 2002 (Kahn award), New York Burning: Liberty, Slavery and Conspiracy in Eighteenth-Century Manhattan, 2005; co-founder, co-editor Common-place, 1999—2004, adv. bd. (TV series) History of America, American Experience, WGBH-TV, 2003, cons. TimeLab 2000, Smash Prodn./The History Channel, 1998—99, The Murder of Dr. Parkman, Spy Pond Prodn., 1999, writer Out of Time, Partners in Time Prodn., 1993—94, American Families: A History of Change, Paradise Prodn/SCETV, 1994—95, editl. bd. Penguin History of Am. Life, 2003—. Named a Disting. Lectr., Orgn. Am. Historians, 2002—05; grantee Gilder Lehrman Inst. Am. History fellowship, 2002, Nat. Endowment for Humanities fellowship, 2003—04. Mem.: Cambridge Hist. Soc., Soc. Am. Historians, Am. Antiquarian Soc. Office: History Dept Harvard Univ 209 Robinson Hall Cambridge MA 02138 Office Phone: 617-496-5083. Office Fax: 617-496-3425. Business E-Mail: jlepore@fas.harvard.edu.

LEPORE, LISA, principal; d. Ann Nancy and Anthony Nicholas Lepore. BA, R.I. U., Providence, 1981, MA, 1987. Cert. tchr. R.I., 2000. Tchr. St. Leo the Gt. Sch., Pawtucket, RI, 1985—2001, prin., 2001—. Substance abuse coord. St. Leo the Gt. Sch., Pawtucket, RI, 1987—. Pres. Girls Softball League; appeals com. chairperson Cath. Athletic League, Providence, 2003. Named Coach of Yr., Cath. Youth Orgn. League, 1995. Mem.: Nat. Cath. Edn. Assn. Home: 32 Cambridge Cir Smithfield RI 02917 Office: St Leo the Great Sch 723 Central Ave Pawtucket RI 02861 E-mail: llepore@cox.net.

LEPOW, MARTHA LIPSON, pediatric educator, consultant; b. Mar. 28, 1927; d. Harry A. and Anna (Miller) Lipson; m. Irwin H. Lepow, Feb. 7, 1958 (dec. 1984); children: Lauren, David, Daniel. BA, Oberlin Coll., 1948; MD, Case Western Res. U., 1952. Intern, resident in pediats. Case Western Res. U., Cleve., 1952—56, fellow, asst. prof. pedit., 1958—67; from assoc. prof. to prof. pediats U. Conn., Farmington, 1967—78; prof. pediats. Albany (NY) Med. Coll., 1978—, dir. Clin. Studies Ctr., 1979—87, vice chmn. pediats, 1981—94, chmn. pediats., 1994—97; attending physician Albany Med. Ctr. Hosp., NY, 1979—. Cons. pediat. infectious disease St. Peter's Hosp., 1978—82; spl. fellow USPHS, Oxford, England, 1961—62; bd. dirs. Albany Coll. Pharmacy, 1987—89; mem. study sect. NIH Epidemiology & Disease Control, 1972—76. Contbr. more than 95 articles to profl. jours.; mem. editl. bd.: Pediats., 1976—81. Sec. HEW Task Force on Immunization Practices, 1977—78; mem. Conn. Acad. Sci. and Engring., 1977; mem. adv. com. Inst. Allergy and Infectious Disease, NIH, 1978—82; bd. dirs. Whitney Youhg Health Ctr., Albany, 1985—2004; mem. profl. adv. com. Ctr. for Disabled, Albany; bd. dirs. WYHCR Found., 2005—. Mem.: Infectious Diseases Soc., Am. Soc. for Microbiology, Am. Pediat. Soc., Am. Soc. Pediat. Rsch., Am. Soc. Immunology (com. on status of women 1982—85), Com. on Vaccines, Inst. Medicine, Capital Dist. Pediat. Soc., Am. Acad. Pediats. (com. infectious diseases 1985—91, assoc. editor report), Alpha Omega Alpha, Sigma Xi. Home: 217 Milner Ave Albany NY 12208 Office: Albany Med Coll MC 88 47 New Scotland Ave Albany NY 12208 Office Phone: 518-262-5332.

LEPPARD, STEPHANIE JEAN, systems analyst, artist; b. Fairbury, Nebr., Nov. 18, 1943; d. Robert Lee (Stepfather) and Marjorie Bloyd Martin, William Flavel Peters; m. Ronald Francis Aaron, Oct. 15, 1963 (div. May 12, 1965); m. Larry Dee Leppard, Feb. 21, 1967 (div. May 25, 1975); children: Adrian Allen Aaron, Michael Jay, Danielle Lynn Leppard-Gullo. Student, Riverside City Coll., 1961—64. Pub. Svc. Supr. San Bernardino Valley Coll., 1980. Eligibility worker San Bernardino Dept. of Pub. Social Svcs., Calif., 1969—71; automated sys. analyst ISAWS - Calif. State Wide Automated Sys., Sacramento; eligibility worker supr. San Bernardino Dept. Pub. Social Svcs., 1972—75; quality control supr. San Bernardino Count Dept. of Pub. Social Svcs., San Bernardino, Calif., 1975—76; staff devel. - trainer San Bernardino County Dept. of Pub. Social Svcs., 1976—79, program mgr., 1979—93; sys. analyst State of Calif. NAPAS Automated Welfare Sys., Napa, Calif., 1993—96, San Bernardino County Dept. of Pub. Social Svcs., San Bernardino, 1996—2000, LA County LEADER Automated Sys., LA, 2000—01, CalWIN Automated Sys., Sacramento, 2001—. Tng. cons. Imperial County, Calif., 1997. Colored pencil, paintings, Haley's Bath, pencil, The Egg and the Sea Horse, colored pencil, Man In Boat, The Christmas Tree, Decorated Joshua Tree, Pippen in Trouble, Self Portrait - My grandmother, Myself, The Vacationer, water color, Sea Turtle for Noelle. Dir. Beginning Experience, San Bernardino, Calif., 1980—90; bishop's coun. mem. San Bernardino Diocese, 1990—91; peer councilor Beginning Experience, 1980—90, coord., 1980—90. Mem.: Daughter's of Am. Revolution. Avocations: needlework, colored pencil artist, consultant.

LEPPERT, ANDREA, science educator; d. Ron and Linda Turner; m. Steve Leppert, Sept. 19, 1998; children: Katelynne, Kamryn. MS in Tchg., Aurora U., Ill., 2002. Sci. tchr. Plano H.S., Ill., 2002—03, St.Charles East H.S., Ill., 2003—. Named Educator of Distinction, Nat. Soc. of H.S. Scholars, 2004—06; grantee ASSET grantee, SETI and NASA, 2006. Mem.: ASCD, Nat. Sci. Tchrs. Assn. Office: Saint Charles East HS 1020 Dunham Rd Saint Charles IL 60174 Office Phone: 630-377-4792. Personal E-mail: aleppert@d303.org.

LEPPIK, MARGARET WHITE, municipal official; b. Newark, June 5, 1943; d. John Underhill and Laura (Schaefer) White; m. Ilo Elmar Leppik, June 18, 1967; children: Peter, David, Karina. BA, Smith Coll., 1965. Rsch. asst. Wistar Inst., U. Pa., Phila., 1967-68, U. Wis., Madison, 1968-69; mem. Minn. Ho. Reps., St. Paul, 1991—2003, chair higher edn. fin. com.; mem. Met. Coun., 2003—. Active Golden Valley (Minn.) Planning Commn., 1982—90, Golden Valley Bd. Zoning Appeals, 1985—87; commr. Midwest Higher Edn. Commn., 1999—2003; bd. dirs. Minn. Partnership Action Against Tobacco, 1998—2003. Named Citizen of Distinction, Hennepin County Human Svcs. Planning Bd., 1992, Legislator of Yr., U. Minn. Alumni Assn., 1995, 1998—2001, Minn. State U. Student Assn., 1999; recipient Presdl. medallion, North Hennepin CC, 2003. Mem.: LWV (v.p., dir. 1984—90), Hubert H. Humphrey Inst. (adv. coun. 2003—), Nature Conservancy (bd. trustees 2003—), Minn. Opera Assn. (pres. 1986—88), Optimists, Rotary. Republican. Avocations: gardening, bicycling, canoeing. Home: 7500 Western Ave Golden Valley MN 55427-4849 Personal E-mail: peggy@leppik.net.

LERBS, LEAH LYNN, special education educator; b. Washington, Mo., June 28, 1967; d. Kenneth W. and Judith M. (Willis) L. BSEd, U. Mo., 1989; MAT in Spl. Edn., Webster U., St. Louis, Mo., 1994. ALC tchr. Sperreng Mid. Sch., St. Louis, 1990-91; spl. edn. paraprofl. Truman Elem. Sch., St. Louis, 1991-92; spl. edn. tchr. Gasconade County R-1 Schs., Hermann, Mo., 1992—. Mem. local sheltered workshop bd. Bergen City Coun. Mem. Mo. State Tchrs. Assn., Coun. for Exceptional Children (bd. rep. to Mo. chpt.), Coun. for Children with Behavioral Disorders, DAR. Home: PO Box 36 Berger MO 63014-0036 Office: Hermann Mid Sch 164 Blue Pride Dr Hermann MO 65041

LERCH, CAROL M., mathematics professor; b. Revere, Mass., Dec. 18, 1947; d. John P Hennessey and Olive F (Swain) Hennessey; m. Bruce F Lerch, Feb. 14, 1971; children: Bruce F Lerch, II, Kelly A, Jamie. Ph. D., Boston Coll., Chestnut Hill, MA, 2000; MA in Tchg., Bridgewater State Coll., Bridgewater, MA, 1991; BA, Regis Coll., Weston, MA, 1970. Instr. Newbury Coll., Brookline, Mass., 1991—2000; assoc. prof. math. Daniel Webster Coll., Nashua, NH, 2000—. Contbr. articles and papers to jours. Vol. Womens Golf Assn. of Mass., Norton, Mass., 2001—. Recipient Student Life Award, Newbury Coll., 1996, Athletic Director's Award, 1996, Outstanding Contributions to Newbury Coll. Men's Basketball, 1996; fellow Presdl. Fellowship, 1999. Mem.: Info. Resources Mgmt. Assn., Internat. Soc. For Cultural and Activity Rsch., Nat. Coun. of Teachers of Math., Am. Edn. Rsch. Assn., Am. Math. Assn. of Two Yr. Colleges. Avocations: golf, travel. Office: Daniel Webster College 20 University Drive Nashua NH 03063 Office Phone: 603-577-6642. E-mail: lerch@dwc.edu.

LERMAN, HANNAH, psychologist; b. N.Y.C., Mar. 7, 1936; d. Ephraim and Lillian (Harris) L.; m. Bartin T. Smith, Jan. 17, 1957 (div. 1960). BA, CCNY, 1957; MA, Mich. State U., 1961, PhD, 1963. Lic. Psychologist, Calif. Clin. psychology intern VA Hosps., Mich., 1958-61; counselor Mich. State U., East Lansing, 1961-63; clin. psychologist II Topeka State Hosp., Kans., 1963-66, L.A. County-So. Calif. Univ. Med. Ctr., 1966-70; dean academic affairs Calif. Sch. Profl. Psychology, L.A., 1970-73; pvt. practice L.A., 1973-96, Las Vegas, 1997—. Author: A Mote in Freud's Eye, 1986, Pigeonholing Women's Misery, 1996; editor Feminist Ethics in Psychotherapy, 1990; contbr. articles on women's psychology to numerous publs. CCNY fellow, 1957-58. Mem. L.A. Soc. Clin. Psychologists (pres. 1979), Am. Psychol. Assn. (pres. div. 35 psychology of women 1984-85), Am. Psychol. Assn. (fellow 1986, leadership award 1987). Office: PO Box 28339 Las Vegas NV 89126-2339 Office Phone: 702-262-9581. Business E-Mail: hlerman@earthlink.net.

LERMAN, ZAFRA MARGOLIN, science educator, public policy professor; b. Haifa, Israel, Jan. 27, 1937; came to U.S., 1969; d. Lipa and Sara (Chervinsky) Jacobi; 1 child, Yoav Margolin. BSc in Chemistry, Technion-Israel Inst. Tech., Haifa, 1960, MSc in Chemistry, 1964; PhD in Chemistry, Weizmann Inst. Sci., Rehovot, Israel, 1969. Rsch. assoc. Cornell U., Ithaca, NY, 1969-72, Northwestern U., Evanston, Ill., 1972-76; vis. scholar Swiss Fed. Inst. Tech., Zurich, Switzerland, 1976-77; mem. faculty sci. and math. dept., chmn. dept. Columbia Coll., Chgo., 1977-91, disting. prof. sci. & pub. policy, head Inst. Sci. Edn. & Sci. Communication, 1991—. Mem. organizing com. Albert Einstein Peace Prize Found., participant Internat. Conf. on Arid Lands, Corsica, France, 1981-82, mem. exec. com., 1981—; mem. Pyramid Conf. on Sci. Edn., 1984, Triangle Coalition on Sci. Edn., 1984-85; symposia and seminar lectr. Contbr. articles to profl. jours. Bd. dirs. Com. Concerned Scientists, 1989—. Recipient gold medal Coun. for Advancement and Support Edn., 1989, Nat. Catalyst award Chem. Mfrs. Assn., 1990, Jose Vasconcelos World Award in Edn., World Cultural Coun., 2000; grantee NSF, 1990. Mem. AAAS, Am. Chem. Soc. (bd. dirs. Chgo. sect. 1983-84, 87—, com. on internat. activities div. chem. edn. 1990—), Internat. Union Pure and Applied Chemistry, Am. Inst. Chemists, Nat. Sci. Tchrs. Assn., Am. Soc. for Technion (bd. dirs. 1986—), Chgo. Coun. on Fgn. Rels., Execs. Club Chgo., Sigma Xi. Office: Columbia Coll 600 S Michigan Ave Chicago IL 60605-1900 Office Phone: 312-344-7180. Office Fax: 312-344-8051.

LERNER, BARBARA, writer, researcher; b. Chgo., Mar. 31, 1935; d. Jacob Israel and Mary (Turen) Lerner. BA with honors, U. Ill., 1956; MA, U. Chgo., 1961, PhD, 1965, JD, 1977. Bar: Ill. 1977. Intern U. Chgo. Hosp. and Clinic, 1962-63; instr. Coll. Medicine U. Ill., 1963-64; clin. psychologist Ill. Mental Health Ctr., Chgo., 1965-68; assoc. prof. Ohio U., Athens, 1968-70; pvt. practice clin. psychologist Chgo., 1970-78; assoc. prof. Roosevelt U., Chgo., 1972-74; study dir. Nat. Acad. Scis., Washington, 1977-78; pres. Lerner Assocs., Princeton, NJ, 1981-96. Vis. scholar Ednl. Testing Svc., Princeton, 1978—79, sr. rsch. scientist, 1980—81; expert witness fed. cts. Debra P. vs. Turlington, Tampa, Fla., Marshall vs. Ga., 1983; vis. prof. U. Tex., Austin, 1989. Author: Therapy in the Ghetto, 1972, Minimum Competence, Maximum Choice, 1980; assoc. editor: U. Chgo. Law Rev., 1975—77, columnist: Phila. Inquirer, 1992—93; contbr. articles to profl. jours., newspapers and mags. Mem. U.S. Commn. Civil Rights, NJ, 1985—87; Pres. nominee U.S. Dept. of Edn., Washington, 1986. Recipient Cert. of Appreciation award for outstanding svc., U.S. Dept. of Edn., 1985. Mem.: Sigma Xi, Phi Beta Kappa. Avocation: gardening. Office: 5050 S East End Ave Chicago IL 60615-5901 E-mail: xlerner@ameritech.net.

LERNER, BETH M., non-profit consultant; b. Phila., Dec. 9, 1972; d. Craig and Zena Lerner; m. Kartik Krishnaiyer. BA, Temple U., 1995. Cmty. svc. coord. SE Fla. chpt. Alzheimer's Assn., Palm Beach, 2001—02; resource devel. dir. United Way of Palm Beach County, Boynton Beach, Fla., 2002—04; polit. cons. JKRB Inc., Coral Springs, Fla., 2003—04; legis. asst. State Rep. Mary Brandenburg, Palm Beach, Fla., 2004—05; non-profit cons. Am. Cancer Soc., 2005—; v.p. Palm Cons. Group, 2004—. Exec. com., Jewish cmty. rels. coun. Jewish Fedn. South Palm Beach County, Boca Raton, 2004; pub. affairs com. Planned Parenthood of Palm Beaches and Treasure Coast, West Palm Beach, 2004; team devel. chair Am. Cancer Soc., West Palm Beach, 2004; pres. Palm Beach County Young Democrats, Boynton Beach, Fla., 2003—05, Lake Worth (Fla.) Dem. Club, 2005; precinct capt. Palm Beach County Dem. Party, Lantana, Fla., 2002—; bd. dirs. Children's Case Mgmt. Orgn., Inc., West Palm Beach, 2005—. Recipient Svc. Award, Fla. Young Democrats, 2003. Mem.: NOW, AAUW, Nat. Assn. Notaries, LWV. Democrat. Jewish. Avocations: travel, politics, history. Personal E-mail: bethrenrel@aol.com.

LERNER, HARRIET GOLDHOR, psychologist, writer; Pvt. practice psychoanalyst; psychologist Menninger Clinic, Topeka. Author: The Dance of Anger, 1985, Women in Therapy, 1988, The Dance of Intimacy: A Woman's Guide to Courageous Acts of Change in Key Relationships, 1989, The Dance of Deception: Pretending and Truth Telling in Women's Lives, 1993. Office: Harper Collins Pubs Inc 10 E 53rd St Fl Cellar1 New York NY 10022-5299

LERNER, JILL, architect; BArch with hons., Cornell U., 1976. Lic. N.Y., Pa. Sr. v.p., project dir. Ellerbe Becket; prin. Kohn, Pedersen, Fox Assocs., N.Y., 1994—. Mem.: AIA (fin. com. 1995, 1996, chmn. fin. com. 1997, bd. dirs. 1999—2000). Office: KPF Assocs 111 W 57th St New York NY 10019

LERNER, LINDA JOYCE, human resources executive; b. N.Y.C., Aug. 19, 1944; d. Morris and Victoria (Mizrahi) L. BS in Bus., U. Bridgeport, 1966. Asst. dir. pers. Bridgeport (Conn.) Hosp., 1969-73; dir. pers. Tufts U., Boston, 1973-80; sr. v.p. human resources Provident Instn. Savs., Boston, 1981-88; sr. v.p. UST Corp. Bank Holding Co., Boston, 1988—. Mem. allocations com. Combined Jewish Philanthropies; v.p. bd. dirs. Horizons for Youth, Boston, 1991—; bd. dirs. Operation A.B.L.E. Fellow Internat. Mktg. Inst., Boston, 1978. Mem. ASTD, N.E. Human Resources Assn., Am. Bankers Assn. (human resources exec. com. 1991—), Mass. Bankers Assn. (human resources com. 1989—, chmn. human resources com. 1993-94), Fin. Women Internat., Boston Human Resources Assn. (chmn. sr. practitioners, bd. dirs.), The Boston Club. Avocations: photography, international travel. Office: UST Corp 40 Court St Boston MA 02108-2202

LERNER, SANDRA, artist; one-woman shows: Mercer Gallery, N.Y.C., 1969, Nassau County Mus. Fine Arts, Roslyn, N.Y., 1976, Soho Ctr. Visual Artists, N.Y.C., 1977, Betty Parsons Gallery, N.Y.C., 1982, Kampo Mus., Kyoto, Japan, 1983, 84, Gallery Don, Fukuoka, Japan, 1984, Tokyo Mus. Art, 1984, 86, 87, 89, Kampo Mus., Kyoto, 1984, 93, June Kelly Gallery, N.Y.C., 1992, 92, 96, 99-2000, June Kelly Gallery, NYC, 2004, Washington Assn. Gallery, Conn., 2005; group shows include: NAD, 1966, 72, 73, Heckscher Mus., Huntington, N.Y., 1963, 68, 69, 74, Guild Hall Mus., Easthampton, N.Y., 1974, N.Y. Carlsberg Blyptotek Mus., Copenhagen, 1980, N.Y.C. Cultural Ctr., 1983, Mus. Stoney Broook, NY, 1996, Zimmerli Mus., NEw Brunswick, N.J., 1999, Jeollabuk-do, Republic Korea, 2003, Art in Embassies Program, Bangladesh, Washington, 2004; represented in permanent collections: Aldrich Mus. Contemporary Art, Kampo Mus., Fukuoka, Japan, Zimmerli Mus., Rutgers U., Heckscher Mus., Huntington. ICA lectr., Japan, 1981; stage designer LAND Dance Performance, 1991, slide image for ECHO Japan Soc., 1995. Recipient Purchase award Nassau Community Coll., 1970, 74, Anne Eisner Putnam prize Nat. Assn. Women Artists, 1973, Benjamin Altman prize NAD, 1972; grantee ICA, 1981. Mailing: 10 E 18th St 6th Fl New York NY 10003 Office Phone: 212-929-2721. E-mail: sandralerner@aol.com, sandra@sandralearner.com.

LEROUX, TESSA, sociology professor, director; b. Rustenburg, South Africa, Dec. 28, 1954; d. Juan and Hester Heyns; m. Johann D. LeRoux, July 31, 1982; children: Michelle, Nicole. BA in Comm., Rand Afrikaans U., Johannesburg, South Africa, 1974; BA in Sociology with honors, Rand Afrikaans U., 1976, D.Litt et Phil., 1990; MA in Sociology, U. South Africa, Pretoria, 1981; higher edn. diploma, U. South Africa, 1986. Liaison officer family planning Dept. of Health, Pretoria, 1976—77; from jr. lectr. to sr. lectr. U. South Africa, 1977—89; substitute tchr. Austin Sch. Dist., Tex., 1993; assoc. prof. sociology U. Pretoria, 1993—97, prof. sociology, 1994—97; dir. Donahue Inst. Values and Pub. Life, assoc. prof. sociology Lasell Coll., Newton, Mass., 2000—, dir. Donahue Inst. Values and Pub. Life, dir. internat. programs, assoc. prof. sociology, 2001—; rsch. coord. PXE Internat., Sharon, Mass., 2000—01. Chair rsch. com. dept. sociology U. Pretoria, 1995—97; chair Gauteng Regional Com. for Nat. Rsch. Program on Global Change and Social Transformation, Pretoria, 1996—97; exec. bd. PXE Internat., Washington, 2002—05. Grantee, HHS, 1985—86, Human Scis. Rsch. Coun., 1994—95; Merit scholar, Rand Afrikaans U., 1972—76. Mem.: Ea. Sociol. Assn., Groves Conf. on Marriage and Family, Internat. Sociol. Assn., Com. on Family Rsch. Office: Lasell Coll 1844 Commonwealth Ave Newton MA 02466 Office Phone: 617-423-2104.

LEROY, BETH SEPERACK, jazz musician, music educator; b. Bridgeport, Conn., Feb. 18, 1964; d. Reinhold Joseph and Marjorie Louise (Lundahl) Seperack; m. Jonathan Paul LeRoy, Feb. 8, 1994; children: Jessica Michelle, Jonathan Paul Jr. BMusic in Jazz Studies, Ind. U., 1989. Lic. kindermusik educator. Piano instr. DeSantis Music Schoolhouse, Syracuse, N.Y., 1986-91, Carondelet Music Ctr., Latham, N.Y., 1994-96; pianist Nelson Riddle Orch., Watertown, N.Y., 1999; keyboardist Nat. Touring Co. of Annie, Schenectady, N.Y., 1997; owner, instr. Creative Keyboard Studio, Latham, 1996—; owner, artist Keyboard Occasions, Latham, 1996—. Piano accompanist Syracuse Opera Co., 1989. Mem.: Albany Music Tchrs. Assn., Music Tchrs. Nat. Assn. (auditions asst. 1999, chmn. fall recital 1999, 2000, 2001), Am. Fedn. Musicians. Avocations: running, making hand-hooked rugs, baking, weight training. Office: Keyboard Occasions PO Box 962 Latham NY 12110-0962

LEROY, JUDY WRIGHT, middle school educator; d. Johnny Leonard and Mildred Lucille Wright; m. Charles Ray LeRoy, July 22, 1994; children: Hannah Nicole Everett, Michelle Lane Everett. BS in Edn., Shorter Coll., Rome, Ga., 1999; MS in Edn., Jacksonville State U., Ala., 2002. Tchr. Pepperell Mid. Sch., Lindale, Ga., 1999—. Recipient Tchr. of Yr., Pepperell Mid. Sch., 2003—04. Office: Pepperell Middle Sch 200 Hughes Dairy Rd Lindale GA 30147 Office Phone: 706-236-1849.

LEROY, MISS JOY, model, apparel designer; b. Riverdale, Ill., Sept. 8, 1927; d. Gerald and Dorothea (Wingebach) Reasor. BS, Purdue U., 1949. Model, sales rep. Jacques, Lafayette, Ind., 1950; book dept. sales rep. Loebs, 1951-52; window trimmer Marshall Fields and Co., Evanston, Ill., 1952-53; sales and display rep. Emerald House, 1954-55. Model, narrator, designer J. L. Hudson Co., GM Corp., Coca Cola Co., Hoover Vacuum Co., Jam Handy Orgn., Rambler and Kelvinator divsn. Am. Motors Corp., Speedway Petroleum Corp., Ford Motor Co., auto, tractor & implement divsn., Sykes Co., Detroit, 1956—61; tour guide, model, freelance writer Christian Sci. Publ. Soc. and Monitor; spl. events coord. Prudential Ins. Co.; model Copley 7, Boston, 1962—70. Author: Puzz-its, 1986—2002. Founding angel Asolo Theatre, Sarasota, 1960; mem. Ft. Lauderdale Internat. Film Festival, 1990, Mus. of Art, 1978, Fla. Conservation Assn., Rep. Senatorial Com. Inner Cir., 1990, Rep. Nat. Hall of Honor, 1992, Congl. Com., 1990, Nat. Trust for Hist. Preservation, 1986, Fla. Trust for Hist. Preservation, 1987; one of founding friends 1000 Friends of Fla., 1991; life mem. Rep. Presdl. Task Force, 1993; mem. Grand Club Rep. Party Fla., 1996. Recipient Rep. Presdl. Legion Honor medal, 1993, Rep. medal of Freedom and Wall of Honor, 1994, Disting. 20th Century Rep. Leader, 1994, 1998, Founder's Wall award, 1995, World Laureate of Eng., 1999, Rep. Presdl. Roundtable, 2000—06, Internat. Order of Merit, Am. Order of Excellence, 2000, Order of Internat. Ambs., 2000, Congl. medal of excellence, 2002, Hallmark medal of honor, 2002, Rep. Senatorial Millennium medal of freedom, Lifetime Achievement award, World Congress of Arts, Sci. and Comm. Mem.: Friends of Fla. 1000, Am. Rivers, Am. Queen Inaugural Soc., Stratford Shakespearean Festival of Can., Libr. of Congress (nat. mem.), Wilderness Soc., Heritage Found., The Crystal Soc., Ellis Island Found. (charter), Cousteau Soc., Heralds of Nature Soc., Purdue U. Alumni Assn. (pres.'s coun.), USS Constn. Mus., Paddlewheel Steamboatin' Soc. Am., Nat. Corvette Owners Assn., Soc. Honorary Mariners, INTRAV-Pinnacle-Elite Explorer Club, Internat. Gov.'s Club (continental gov.), Maupin Travelers Club, Captain's Cir., Ducks Unltd., Skald Club, Seabourn Club, Cunard World Club, Magic Kingdom Entertainment Club, Zeta Tau Alpha. Avocations: travel, art, education, design, photography. Home: 2100 S Ocean Ln Apt 2104 Fort Lauderdale FL 33316-3827

LERTORA, JOANNE MARIE, psychologist; b. Holyoke, Mass., Jan. 19, 1960; d. James R. and Shirley A. (Durocher) L. BA in Psychology, U. Conn., 1981; MA in Psychology, U. Mo., 1985, PhD in Psychology, 1989. Lic. psychologist, Conn. Psychologist Newington Children's Hosp., Conn., 1989-92; pvt. practice specializing in child psychology, 1994—. Mem. APA (sport psychology divsn.). Avocations: sports, music.

LERUD-CHUBB, DIANNE KAY, secondary school educator; b. Glasgow, Mont., Apr. 10, 1942; d. William Francis and Esther Myrtle (Kollman) Brosseau; m. David Allen Lerud, Oct. 28, 1961 (div. 1985); children: Donald, DeAnne; m. James Arnold Chubb, July 20, 1990. BS, Valley City State Coll., 1964; MAE, Wayne State Coll., 1967. Cert. secondary sch. tchr. English tchr. Weston (Nebr.) High Sch., 1964-65, Wisner (Nebr.) High Sch., 1965-66, Southeastern CC, Burlington, Iowa, 1975-78, 2001—, Mediapolis (Iowa) High Sch., 1967—2000. Chairperson Phase III Ednl. Excellence Program, Mediapolis, 1987-91; mem. Gov.'s Rep. Educators Adv. Coun., Des Moines, 1987-93. Mem. Burlington Plan Commn., 1990-95, pres. 1989-91; active Nat. Women's Polit. Caucus, 1990-93, state 2d v.p., 1994-1996; fin. sec. Faith Luth. Ch., 1991-93; mem. steering com. of ERA Iowa, 1992. Recipient Vol. Appreciation award Burlington Am. Little League, 1986, Burlington YWCA Woman of Yr. award, 1992. Mem. NEA, AAUW (treas. 1991—, pres. 1994-1996), Iowa Edn. Assn., Mediapolis Edn. Assn. (pres. 1984-91), Bus. and Profl. Women (pres.-elect Burlington chpt. 1990-91, pres. 1994-1996), Burlington Alliance Women (chair 1991-1993), Optimists (co-chair internat. and local Dragonboat festival 1996-2000, Outstanding Svc. award 1993-94), DAR (regent Stars and Stripes chpt. 1996-1998, state regent, 2006—), Eastern Star, Women of Moose, Burlington Steamboat Days (pres., 2004-2005). Avocations: reading, golf, socializing, dance. Home: 2429 Gnahn St Burlington IA 52601-4415 Office: Mediapolis High Sch Northfield Ave Mediapolis IA 52637-9434

LESACK, BEATRIZ DÍAZ, secondary school educator; b. Arequipa, Peru, Dec. 2, 1948; came to U.S., 1977; d. Jésus Heradio Díaz Vargas and Elisa (Huamán) Díaz Peralta; m. Federico Vera Ponce de León, May 22, 1965 (div. 1977); 1 child, Edson Giovanni; m. Leo Pap Dorn, Oct. 27, 1977. BS in Spanish, San Agustin U., 1974; MS in Gen. Edn., SUNY, New Paltz, 1978-81, postgrad. Cert. elementary and secondary tchr., French and Spanish lang. tchr., N.Y. Tchr. Spanish Huguenot Nursery Sch., New Paltz, N.Y., 1983; tchr. elem. bilingual Ellenville (N.Y.) Sch. Dist., 1984-85; tchr. Spanish Poughkeepsie (N.Y.) Sch. Dist., 1985-86, Liberty (N.Y.) Sch. Dist., 1986-88, Fla. Unified Sch. Dist., Fla., N.Y., 1988-89; tchr. Spanish-French Hyde Park (N.Y.) Sch. Dist., 1989-91; tchr. Spanish Greenburgh Eleven Unified Sch. Dist., Dobbs Ferry, N.Y., 1991—, Copake-Taconic Hills Sch., Hillsdale, N.Y., 1995-96, FDR Sch., Bristol Twp., Pa., 1996-97; tax examiner U.S. Treasury, 1998-99, rschr., 1999—. Substitute tchr. Newburgh, Wallkill, Onteora Sch. Dists., Poughkeepsie, N.Y., 1982-83; exec. sec. Hotels and Restaurants Assn., Arequipa, 1972-73; mem. asst. Radio Club Dr. Oscar Guillen, Arequipa, 1971; tax examiner U.S. Treasury, 1998-99, rsch., 1999-2000. Fund chairman Dem. Com., New Paltz, 1991-92; mem. fundraising com. Multicultural Edn., New Paltz, 1992; mem. Mid. Sch. Steering Com., 1989-91, Multicultural Edn. Com., 1991—, steering com. Maurice Hinchey Nat. Bilingual Edn., 1980—; candidate for Phila. Bd. Edn., 2000. Fulbright Hays fellow to Dominican Rep., 1991; faculty grantee SUNY, 1978, 83-84. Mem. NAFE, Am. Assn. Tchrs. Spanish, N.Y. Fgn. Lang. Tchrs. Assn. (pres.), N.Y. Union Tchrs., Faculty Wives and Women (pres. 1989-92). Avocations: photography, video production, handicrafts, reading, golf. Home: 5411 Vicaris St Philadelphia PA 19128-2823 Office: Greenburgh Eleven Unified Sch Dist PO Box 501 Dobbs Ferry NY 10522-0501

LESCH, ANN MOSELY, political scientist, educator; b. Washington, Feb. 1, 1944; d. Philip Edward and Ruth (Bissell) Mosely. BA, Swarthmore Coll., 1966; PhD, Columbia U., 1973. Rsch. assoc. Fgn. Policy Rsch. Inst., Phila., 1972-74; assoc. Middle East rep. Am. Friends Svc. Com., Jerusalem, 1974-77; Middle East program officer Ford Found., N.Y.C., 1977-80, program officer Cairo, 1980-84; assoc. Univs. Field Staff Internat., 1984-87; prof. Villanova U., 1987—2004, assoc. dir. ctr. Arab and Islamic studies, 1992-95; dean humanities & social scis. Am. U. Cairo, 2004—. Author: The Politics of Palestinian Nationalism, 1973, Arab Politics in Palestine, 1979, Political perceptions of the Palestinians on the West Bank and Gaza, 1980, (with Mark Tessler) Israel, Egypt and the Palestinians, 1989, Transition to Palestinian Self-Government, 1992, (with D. Tschirgi) Origins and Development of the Arab-Israeli Conflict, 1998, The Sudan: Contested National Identities, 1998, (with Steven Wondu) Battle for Peace in Sudan, 2000, (with Osman Fadl) Coping with Torture: Images from Sudan, 2004, (with Ian Lustich) Exile & Return, 2005; contbr. articles to profl. jours. Co-chair Middle East Program Com., Am. Friends Svc. Com., 1989—94; mem. Quaker UN Com., 1979—80; U.S. adv. com. Interns for Peace, 1978—82; bd. dirs. Am. Near East Refugee Aid, 1980—86, Middle East Report, 1989—93, Human Rights Watch/Middle East, 1989—. Fellow Catherwood Found., 1965; NDFL, 1967-71; Am. Rsch. Ctr. grant Egypt, 1988, U.S. Inst. of Peace Rsch. grants, 1990-91, 97, 2002-03, Wilson Ctr. Guest scholar Smithsonian, 1990, Rockefeller Fdn. Bellagio Ctr., 1996, Fulbright scholar, Cairo, 1999-2000, Beirut, 2003. Mem.: Palestinian Am. Rsch. Ctr. (co-chair 1998—2001, U.S. dir. 2001—04), Coun. on Fgn. Rels., Sudan Studies Assn. (sec. 1993—96, pres. 1998—2000), Am. Polit. Sci. Assn., Mid. East Inst., Mid. East Studies Assn. (bd. dirs. 1988—91, pres. 1993—96, bull. editor 1997—99). Unitarian Universalist. Office: American Univ HUSS Dean 113 Qasr al-Aini Cairo Egypt

LESCINSKI, JOAN, higher education administrator, English educator; b. Albany, N.Y., June 27, 1947; BA, Coll. St. Rose, 1970, MA, 1974; PhD, Brown U., 1981. Cert. secondary tchr., N.Y. Prof. Coll. St. Rose, Albany, N.Y., 1974-91; assoc. academic dean Avila Coll., Kansas City, Mo., 1991-93; v.p., dean Fontbonne Coll., St. Louis, 1993-98; pres. St. Mary-of-the-Woods (Ind.) Coll., 1998—. Avocation: organic vegetable gardening. Office: St Mary-of-the-Woods Coll Office of Pres Saint Mary Of The Woods IN 47876 Office Phone: 812-535-5296. Business E-Mail: presofc@smwc.edu.

LESER, ANNE ELIZABETH, education educator; d. Stark William and Ann Moloney Leser. BA, Ohio No. U., 1972; MA, Ohio State U., 1984, PhD, 1989. Cert. elem. and secondary tchr. Tchr. Gallipolis (Ohio) City Schs., 1973—74, Hancock Hardin Wyandot Putman Head Start, Findlay, Ohio, 1974—76, edn. dir., 1976—81; cons. Upper Sandusky, Ohio, 1981—83; grad. asst. Ohio State U., Columbus, 1984—88; asst. prof. U. Fla., Gainesville, 1988—89; faculty devel. Ohio State U., Columbus, Ohio, 1989—90, U. Ill., Champaign, 1990—92; from asst. to assoc. prof. Maryville U., St. Louis, 1992—2003; assoc. prof., dir. Early Childhood Studies Bowling Green State U.-Firelands, Huron, Ohio, 2003—. Condr. workshop for tchrs. Amy Biehl Found., Cape Town, South Africa, 1999, 2005; cons. pub. schs., Cape Town, South Africa, 00; presenter nat. confs., 1994—. Co-author: (handbook) Handbook for Clinical Instructors, 1990. Mem. ACLU, So. Poverty Law Ctr., Birmingham, Ala.; vol. Rape Crisis Ctr., St. Louis, 1995—98, CASA, Ohio, 2005—; leader student group Cape Town, South Africa, 2005. Mem.: Nat. Assn. Multicultural Edn., Ohio Assn. Early Childhood Tchr. Edn. (pres.), Nat. Assn. Early Childhood Tchr. Edn., Nat. Assn. Edn. Young Children, Ohio State Alumni Club (pres. 2001, sec. 2002), Phi Delta Kappa. Avocations: travel, social justice activities, reading. Office: Bowling Green State U-Firelands 1 University Dr Huron OH 44839 Office Phone: 419-372-0928. Business E-Mail: aleser@bgnet.bgsu.edu.

LESH-LAURIE, GEORGIA ELIZABETH, academic administrator, biology professor, medical researcher; b. Cleve., July 28, 1938; d. Howard Frees and Josephine Elizabeth (Taylor) Lesh; m. William Francis Laurie, Aug. 16, 1969. BS, Marietta Coll., 1960; MS, U. Wis., 1961; PhD, Case Western Reserve U., 1966. Asst. prof. SUNY, Albany, 1966-69; asst., then assoc. prof. Case Western Reserve U., 1969-77, asst. dean, 1973-76; interim dir. Cleve. State U., Ohio, 1980, prof., chairperson, 1977-81, dean grad. studies, 1981-86, dean arts and scis., 1986-91, interim provost, v.p. academic and student affairs, 1989-90; vice chancellor acad. and student affairs U. Colo., Denver, 1991-95, interim chancellor, 1995-97, chancellor, 1997—2003, chancellor emerita, 2003—. Cons. in field; reviewer numerous granting agencies, profl. jours., 1968—; advanced placement exam. Edn. Testing Service, Princeton, N.J., 1982-83. Contbr. sci. articles to profl. pubs. Trustee Marietta Coll., Ohio, 1980-84, 85-95; mem. city/univ. interchange com., Cleve., 1983-91; chmn. commn. on women Am. Coun. Edn., 2002-2003; bd. mem. Girl Scouts Mile High Coun., Found. for Edn. Excellence, Rocky Mountain Inst. for Internat. Edn., Arapahoe C.C. Fellow NSF, NIH; grantee NIH, Am. Cancer Soc., Am. Heart Assn., Research Corp., 1968—; recipient Wright fellowship Bermuda Biol. Station; named among AAUW Women of Distinction; named to Girl Scouts Women's Leadership Cir. Fellow AAAS; mem. Am. Soc. Zoologists, Soc. Devel. Biology, Am. Soc. Cell Biology, Phi Beta Kappa. Home: 5677 S Park Pl Unit 311B Greenwood Village CO 80111 E-mail: georgia.lesh-laurie@cudenver.edu.

LESIEGE, ANNETTE, music educator, composer; b. Oakland, Apr. 28, 1947; d. Armand J. LeSiege, Mabel and Raymond D. Phelps (Stepfather). BA, San Jose State U., 1968, MA, 1970; PhD, Eastman Sch. Music, 1975. Tchr. Wake Forest U., Winston-Salem, NC, 1975—82; mng. dir. Symphony U.N., N.Y.C., 1982—86; devel. officer Cmty. Hosp., Monterey, Calif., 1986—92; tchr. Santa Catalina Sch., Monterey, 1992—96; devel. officer Audrey Cohen Coll., N.Y.C., 1996—98; tchr. New Jersey City U., Jersey City, 1998—. Composer in residence U. N.C., Chapel Hill, 1977; adj. Internat. Music Festivals, 1977—93; clinician Monterey County Youth & Honor Orch., 1987—90; faculty mem. Summer Music Monterey, 1989—94; bd. dirs. Imani Winds, N.Y.C., 2001—. Guest composer: Reynolda House Mus. Am. Art., 1976—82, N.C. Sch. of Arts, 1980, Monterey Peninsula C.C., 1987—91, Youth Music Monterey, 1990, 1992; editor: Five Improvisations, 1997; guest composer: Rockland Mid. and H.S., 2004—05; composer: Montage, 1976, Four Bagalelles, 1976, Phidian, 1977, Piano Sonata #1, 1978, Ordinary Things, 1978, Outside the Frame, 1978, Dialogue, 1978, Ricercare, 1979, Suite for Saxophone & Piano, 1979, Airs & Dances, 1980, Five Miniatures, 1980, Five Bagalelles, 1980, Woodwind Quintet, 1980, In the Silence, 1981, Confusion Breathes, 1982, Star Gazers and Other Pilgrims, 1983, Intermezzo, 1984, Suite #2, 1984, Baniff's Legacy, 1985, Night Songs, 1987, Sapphire Seesaw, 1988, Sarphinian Suite, 1988, Ten Eludes, 1989, A Curious Dialogue, 1990, Fireflies, 1992, Book Lice, 1992, Water Striders, 1992, Cicadas, 1992, Shadow Dancer, 1993, Burgundian Suite, 1995, The Waking, 1996, Piano Sonata #2, 1996, Serenade, 1997, I Did Not Know the River Would Bend, 1997, A Little Ballet for Pice, 1998, Cascades, 1998, Boutade, 1999, Genese, 1999, Reflections, 2000, Materia, 2001, Capriccio, 2002, Ode for St. Godric, 2002, Dream Load, 2003, Three Movements, 2004, Incantation & Dance, 2004, Divertimento, 2005, I Know What I Know, 2005, Five Bagatelles, 2005, Hoops and Angels, 2006, Boynton's Quest, 2006. Mem. project pool com. Winston-Salem Arts Coun., 1976; bd. dirs. Reynolda House Mus. Am. Art Chamber Music Series, 1978—82. Fellow, MacDowell Colony, 1977—. Mem.: Am. Music Ctr., Coll. Music Soc. (bd. dirs. 1980—82), Am. Soc. Composers, Authors and Pub. (pub. 1976—). Office: New Jersey City Univ 2039 Kennedy Blvd Jersey City NJ 07305 Personal E-mail: lesiege@msn.com.

LESK, ANN BERGER, lawyer; b. NYC, Feb. 7, 1947; d. Alexander and Eleanor A. (Dickinson) Berger; m. Michael E. Lesk, June 30, 1968. AB cum laude, Radcliffe Coll., 1968; JD with high honors, Rutgers U., 1977. Bar: N.Y. 1979. Law clk. to justice N.J. Supreme Ct., Mountain, 1977-78; assoc. Fried, Frank, Harris, Shriver & Jacobson LLP, NYC, 1978—84, ptnr., 1984—. Editor-in-chief Rutgers Law Rev., 1976—77. Mem.: ABA, Assn. of the Bar of City of N.Y. (com. trusts, estates and surrogates cts. 1992—95, com. estate and gift taxation 1997—2000, com. trusts, estates and surrogates cts. 2000—03, com. estate and gift taxation 2004—06, com. trusts, estates and surrogates cts. 2006—), N.Y. State Bar Assn. (mem. ho. of dels. 2003—), New York County Lawyers Assn. (co-chair com. trusts and estates legislation and govtl. affairs 1995—98, co-chair com. trusts and estates sect. 1998—2001, bd. dirs. 2001—04, sec. 2004—06, v.p. 2006—). Office: Fried Frank Harris Shriver & Jacobson LLP 1 New York Plz Fl 22 New York NY 10004-1980 Office Phone: 212-859-8113. Business E-Mail: ann.lesk@friedfrank.com.

LESKE, M. CRISTINA, medical researcher, educator; MD with highest honors, U. Chile, 1964; MPH, Harvard U., 1966; DSc (hon.), U. West Indies, 2004. Resident preventive medicine Harvard Sch. Pub. Health, Boston, 1966; resident pub. health Mass. Dept. Pub. Health, Boston, 1966—67, asst. dir. divsn. local health svcs., 1967—68; resident preventive medicine U. Rochester, NY, 1974, asst. prof. preventive medicine, 1975; asst. clin. prof. epidemiology and biostats. SUNY Coll. Optometry, N.Y.C., 1976—77, assoc. clin. prof., 1977—79; asst. prof. preventive medicine SUNY Sch. Medicine, Stony Brook, 1979—82, assoc. prof., 1982—89, prof. preventive medicine and ophthalmology, 1989—97, disting. svc. prof., 1997—, disting. prof., 2001—, head divsn. epidemiology, 1986—2002, chair dept. preventive medicine, 1991—2002; med. staff Univ. Hosp., Stony Brook, 1981—. Nat. adv. eye coun. NIH, 1987—91. Contbr. over 300 articles to profl. jours. Named Woman of the Yr. in Health, Three Village Times, N.Y., 1996, Outstanding Woman of Yr. in Sci., Town of Brookhaven, N.Y., 1998, Local Legend, Am. Med. Women Assn.; recipient Bicentennial medal, U. Cath. Chile, 1988, Disting. Achievement award in rsch., N.Y. Optometric Assn., 2000, Alumni Merit award, Harvard Sch. Pub. Health, 2004; Pub. Health fellow, Orgn. Am. States, 1965—67. Fellow: Am. Coll. Epidemiology, Am. Coll. Preventive Medicine; mem.: Inst. of Medicine of NAS. Achievements include research in in breast cancer; epidemiology of eye diseases, especially open-angle glaucoma and cataract. Office: 086L3 Health Sciences Ctr Stony Brook NY 11794-8036

LESKO, DIANE, museum director, curator; BA, Harpur Coll., 1971; MA in Art History, SUNY, Binghamton, 1975, PhD in Art History, 1982. Part-time instr. Sch. Gen. Studies SUNY, Binghamton, 1974-75, acting curator Univ. Art Gallery, 1975-76; vis. lectr. art history Hartwick Coll., Oneonta, N.Y., 1976-77; asst. prof. art history, co-dir. Coll. Art Gallery Lycoming Coll., Williamsport, Pa., 1978-85; curator of collections Mus. of Fine Arts, St. Petersburg, Fla., 1985-89, sr. curator collections and exhbns., 1989-93, asst. dir./sr. curator; exec. dir. Telfair Mus. Art, Savannah, Ga. Lectr. in field; on-site evaluator Fla. Maj. Cultural Instn. Program. Author: Gari Melchers: A Retrospective Exhibition, 1990, Jon Corbino: An Heroic Vision (mus. catalogues); author: (book) James Ensor, The Creative Years, 1985; contbr. articles and essays to profl. jours.; editor: Catalogue of the Collection of the Museum of Fine Arts, 1993, Gari Melchers: A Retrospective Exhibition, 1990, Album Amicorum Kenneth C. Lindsay, 1989, Jon Corbino: An Heroic Vision, 1987, Binghamton Collects, 1974; editor Pharos, 1984-85, 86-87. Harpur Coll. Found. scholar, 1968-71; SUNY-Binghamton grad. fellow in art history, 1971-73, doctoral fellow in art history, 1978-79; Lycoming Coll. Doctoral Dissertation grantee, 1981, faculty profl. devel. grantee, summer 1982; recipient AAM Excellence in Peer Review Service Award, 2004, Visionary Award, Savannah Area Tourism and Leadership Coun., 2004. Mem. NOW, Women's Caucus for Art, Coll. Art Assn., Am. Assn. Mus. (reviewer), Phi Beta Kappa. Office: Telfair Mus Art PO Box 10081 Savannah GA 31401

LESLIE, LISA DESHAUN, professional basketball player; b. Gardena, Calif., July 7, 1972; m. Michael Lockwood. Grad., U. So. Calif., 1994. Basketball player USA Women's Nat. Team, 1996, L.A. Sparks WNBA, 1997—. Mem. gold medal winning 1994 Goodwill Games Team, US Women's Basketball Team, Athens Olympics, 2004; color commentary USC Basketball Games; guest corr. NBA Inside Stuff. Named 1993 USA Basketball Female Athlete of Yr.; recipient gold medal Atlanta Olympics, 1996, Sydney Olympics 2000; named MVP 1st WNBA All-Star Game, 1999; named MVP of season, WNBA Championship & All-Star Game, 2001, MVP WNBA Championship and All-Star Game, 2002, WNBA Defensive Player of the Yr., 2004; named 2003 Sportswoman of the Year for a team sport, Women's Sports Foundation; named to All-WNBA First Team, 1997, 2000, 01, 02. Office: Los Angeles Sparks 555 N Nash St El Segundo CA 90245

LESLIE, MAUREEN HEELAN, university director; b. Bronx, N.Y. d. James Joseph, Sr. and Evelyn (McDonald) H.; m. Bruce Allan Leslie; children: James Christopher, Michael Patrick. BA in Bus. Mgmt. cum laude, Molloy Coll., 1997. Adminstrv. asst., A placement dir., counselor Berkeley Coll., N.Y.C., 1965—71; entrepreneur The Silk Floral Gallery, Huntington, 1984-86; gen. orgn. treas. South Huntington Sch. Dist., 1984-98; devel. assoc. Molloy Coll., Rockville Ctr., 1998-99, dir. alumni rels., 1999—2002; exec. dir. L.I. (N.Y.) Ctr. Bus. and Profl. Woemn, 2003—04; asst. dir. off-campus programs Adelphi U., Garden City, NY, 2004—. Mem. industry adv. bd. South Huntington Sch. Dist., 1998—, Mt. Sinai (N.Y.) Sch. Dist., 1999—; bd. dirs. L.I. (N.Y.) Ctr. Bus. and Profl. Women V.p. St. Hugh of Lincoln Sch. Bd., Huntington Sta., N.Y., 1983; mem. LIA/Long Isalnd Works Coalition, Melville, N.Y., 1998—. Mem. AAUW (mem. com. industries initiatives 2005—), Exec. Women's Golf Assn., Long Island Women's Agenda, Long Island Ctr. Bus. and Profl. Women, L.I. Regional C. of C. to Bus. Partnership (mem. industry adv. bd. 2001—), Young Profls. C. of C. (mem. industry adv. bd. 1998—, edn. and tng. com. 2005—), Soc. Human Resource Profls., Delta Epsilon Sigma, Delta Epsilon Pi, Lambda Pi Eta, Phi Delta Kappa Roman Catholic. Avocations: tennis, golf, swimming, dance, reading.

LESMES, STEPHANIE BROOKS, lawyer; b. Stuttgart, Germany, Sept. 16, 1971; BS summa cum laude, Tex. Christian U., 1994; JD, Tex. Tech U. Sch. Law, 1998. Bar: Tex. 1998, US Dist. Ct. (no., we. and so. dists. Tex.). Atty. Baron & Budd, P.C., Dallas, 2001—. Named a Rising Star, Tex. Super Lawyers mag., 2006. Mem.: ABA, Am. Trial Lawyers Assn., Dallas Assn. Young Lawyers, Trial Lawyers for Pub. Justice, Dallas Trial Lawyers Assn., Tex. Trial Lawyers Assn., Assn. Trial Lawyers of Am., Dallas Bar Assn. (mem. judiciary com.), Phi Beta Kappa. Avocations: travel, horseback riding. Office: Baron & Budd PC 3102 Oak Lawn Ave Ste 1100 Dallas TX 75219 Office Phone: 214-521-3605. E-mail: slesmes@baronbudd.com.*

LESONSKY, PAULA MARLENE, elementary school educator; d. Seymour and Margaret Lesonsky; m. Chad Douglas Lesonsky, June 23, 2006. M in Tchg. Arts, Garnd Canyon U., Phoenix, 2002. Cert. multiple subjects, art, CLAD Calif., 1996. Tchr. Fruitvale Elem. Sch., Hemet, Calif., 1996—2004, Diamond Valley Mid. Sch., Hemet, 2004—. Academic scholar, Soroptomists, 1983. Mem.: Delta Kappa Gamma. Office Phone: 951-925-2899.

LESONSKY, RIEVA, editor-in-chief; b. NYC, June 20, 1952; d. Gerald and Muriel (Cash) L. BJ, U. Mo., 1974. Rschr. Doubleday & Co., N.Y.C., 1975-78, Entrepreneur Mag., L.A., 1978-80, rsch. dir., 1983-84, mng. editor, 1985-86, exec. editor, 1986-87, editor Irvine, Calif., 1987-90; sr. v.p., editor dir. Entrepreneur Media, Inc., Irvine, 1990—; rsch. dir. LFP Inc., L.A., 1980-82; editor-in-chief Entrepreneur Mag., Irvine. Spkr., lectr. in field. Author: Start Your Own Business, 1998, 3d edit., 2004, Young Millionaires, 1998, Get Smart!, 1999, 303 Marketing Tips, 1999, Ultimate Guide to Franchises, 2004; editor: Complete Guide to Owning a Home-based Business, 1990, 168 More Businesses Anyone Can Start, 1991, 111 Businesses You Can Start for Under $10,000, 1991; contbr. articles to mags. Mem. adv. bd. disting. counselors Women's Leadership Exch.; nat. adv. coun. SBA, 1994—2000; bd. dirs. Students in Free Enterprise, Jr. Achievement, Orange County. Named Dist. Media Adv. of Yr., SBA, 1993, Dist. Women in Bus. Adv., SBA, 1995; Bus. Luminaries award. Mem. Women's Network for Entrepreneurial Tng. (bd. dirs., advisor, nat. steering com.). Avocations: books, magazines, baseball. Office: Entrepreneur Media Inc 2445 Mccabe Way Irvine CA 92614-6244 Office Phone: 949-261-2325. Business E-Mail: rieva@entrepreneur.com.

LESOURD, NANCY SUSAN OLIVER, lawyer, writer; b. Atlanta, Aug. 22, 1953; d. Carl Samuel and Jane (Meadows) Oliver; m. Jeffrey Alan LeSourd, Oct. 18, 1986; children: Jeffrey Luke, Catherine Victoria. BA in Polit. Sci., Agnes Scott Coll., 1975; MA in History, Edn., Tufts U., 1977; JD, Georgetown U., 1984. Bar: Pa. 1985, D.C. 1986, Va. 1992, Fed. Cir. Ct. Appeals., 1988, U.S. Claims Ct., 1988, U.S. Supreme Ct. Instr. Newton H.S., Mass., 1976—78, Stony Brook Sch., NY, 1978—81; assoc. Gammon and Grange, Washington, 1984—88; shareholder Gammon and Grange, P.C., 1988—; mgr. Marshall-LeSourd L.L.C., 1996—. Legal commentator (radio shows) UPI News, Washington, 1985-91, Focus on the Family (Washington corr.), Colorado Springs, Colo., 1987-94; legal columnist Christian Mgmt. Rev., Downers Grove, Ill., 1987-90; spkr. in field. Author: No Longer The Hero, 1992, Liberty Letters: Underground Railroad, 2003, Liberty Letters: The Story of Pocahontas, 2003, Liberty Letters: Civil War Spies, 2004, Liberty Letters: Pearl Harbor, 2004, Christy: Christmastime in Cutter Gap, 2003; editor: Georgetown Law Jour., 1982-84; contbr. articles to profl. jours.; cons., prodr. three TV movies based on Christy, 2000—. Founder, vice-chmn. bd. trustees Ambleside Sch., 1998—2001; Bd. dirs. Arlington County Equal Employment Opportunity Commn., 1985. William Robertson Coe fellow SUNY, Stony Brook, 1978. Mem. D.C. Bar Assn., Va. Bar Assn., Christian Legal Society (bd. dirs. 1990-93). Republican. Office: Gammon and Grange PC 8280 Greensboro Dr Fl 7 Mc Lean VA 22102-3807 Home: 18456 Lincoln Rd Purcellville VA 20132 Office Phone: 703-761-5000. Business E-Mail: nol@gg-law.com.

LESSER, JOAN L., lawyer; b. LA; BA, Brandeis U., 1969; JD, U. So. Calif., 1973. Bar: Calif. 1973, U.S. Dist. Ct. (cen. dist.) Calif. 1974. Assoc. Irell and Manella LLP, L.A., 1973-80, ptnr., 1980—. Bd. dirs. In2Books.org; spkr. profl. confs. Trustee Windward Sch., 1994-00, bd. dirs. UCLA Design for Sharing, 2005—, v.p. fin. Mem. Orgn. Women Execs. (past pres., bd. dirs.), Order of Coif. Office: Irell & Manella LLP 1800 Avenue Of The Stars Los Angeles CA 90067-4276 Office Phone: 310-203-7577. Business E-Mail: jlesser@irell.com.

LESSER, MIMI KORACH, painter, illustrator; b. N.Y.C., Apr. 25, 1922; d. Dean and Viola (Weinberg) Korach; m. Bert Lesser, Apr. 17, 1951; children—Steven Dean, Robin Deane. Student Sch. Art, Yale U., 1940-43. One woman shows: Barbizon Plaza Gallery, N.Y.C., 1948, Silvermine Guild, New Canaan, Conn., 1977, Pindar Gallery, N.Y.C., 1980, 83, 86; group shows include Am. Acad. Arts and Letters, N.Y.C., 1976, Silvermine Guild, 1976, 78, 81, Hudson River Mus., Yonkers, N.Y., 1976, 78, 81, Butler Inst. Am. Art, Youngstown, Ohio, 1979; freelance illustrator for books and mags., 1945-70; sketched over 1000 servicemen for USO in France, Belgium and Ger., 1945. Recipient numerous awards from art orgns. including Hudson River Mus., 1981. Jewish. Home: 24 Stonewall Ln Mamaroneck NY 10543-1024 E-mail: mimil5858@aol.com.

LESSER, WENDY, editor, writer, consultant; b. Santa Monica, Calif., Mar. 20, 1952; d. Murray Leon Lesser and Millicent Dillon; m. Richard Rizzo, Jan. 18, 1985; 1 child, Nicholas 1 stepchild, Dov Antonio. BA, Harvard U., 1973; MA, Cambridge (Eng.) U., 1975; PhD, U. Calif., Berkeley, 1982. Founding ptnr. Lesser & Ogden Assocs., Berkeley, 1977-81; founding editor Threepenny Rev., Berkeley, 1980—. Bellagio resident Rockefeller Found., Italy, 1984. Author: The Life Below the Ground, 1987, His Other Half, 1991, Pictures at an Execution, 1994, A Director Calls, 1997, The Amateur, 1999, Nothing Remains the Same, 2002, The Pagoda in the Garden, 2005; editor: Hiding in Plain Sight, 1993, The Genius of Language, 2004. Fellow, NEH, 1983, Guggenheim Found., 1988, NEH, 1992, ACLS, 1996, Open Soc. Inst., 1998, Columbia U., 2000—01, Am. Acad. Berlin, 2003, Remarque Inst., 2004, Cullman Ctr. for Scholars and Writers, 2005—06. Democrat. Office: The Threepenny Rev PO Box 9131 Berkeley CA 94709-0131

LESTENKOF, AQUILINA DEBBIE, environmental advocate; Co-dir. Ecosystem Conservation Office Tribal Govt. of St. Paul Island, Alaska. Dir. Pribilof Islands Stewardship Prog., 1994; mem. steering com. Pacific Northwest Crab Industry Adv. Com. Recipient Conservation Merit award, WWF, 2001, Eva Haller award for humanity, Wings WorldQuest Women of Discovery Awards, 2006. Mem.: Aleut Internat. Assn. Office: Ecosystem Conservation Office Tribal Govt St Paul PO Box 107 Saint Paul Island AK 99660 E-mail: aquilina@tdxak.com.*

LESTER, ALICIA LOUISE, financial analyst; b. Niagara Falls, NY, Aug. 28, 1955; d. Belmira Hinto Harris and James Lester; children: Deláno Thompson, Michael, Jr. Thompson. BS in Commerce, Niagara U., 1977. Underwriting cert. Robert Morris Assn., 1997. Mktg., acctg. analyst Carborundum Abrasives Co., Niagara Falls, NY, 1978—87; pvt. practice contractor Buffalo, 1990—96; comml. fin. analyst Fleet Boston Financial - Corp. Banking, Buffalo, 1996—2000; fin. analyst Motorola Inc., Elma, NY, 2000—02; fin. analyst II, banking officer M & T Bank, Buffalo, 2002—05; sr. fin. analyst, asst. v.p. fin. ops. Hong Kong and Shanghai Banking Corp. Ltd.,

Bank NA, Buffalo, 2005—. Owner Thunder Solutions Programming and Mktg., Buffalo, 1997—. Bd. dirs. Buffalo Prenatal-Perinatal Network, 2005—; chair Clark Acad. Performing Arts, 1990—. Mem.: Inst. Mgmt. Accts., Harriet Tubman 300, Inc., Fin. Women Internat. (comm. chair 1997—99), The Links, Inc. (Niagara Falls chp., co-chair tech. 1997—2002, chair arts facet 1997—2002, fin. sec. 2003—). Office Phone: 716-447-9400. Personal E-mail: A.Lester@verizon.net.

LESTER, JUNE, library and information scientist, educator; b. Sandersville, Ga., Aug. 25, 1942; d. Charles DuBose and Frances Irene (Cheney) L.; 1 child, Anna Elisabeth Engle. BA, Emory U., 1963, M in Librarianship, 1971; D in Libr. Sci., Columbia U., 1987, cert. in advanced librarianship, 1982. Asst. prof., cataloger U. Tenn. Libr., Knoxville, 1971-73; libr. divsn. libr. and info. mgmt. Emory U., Atlanta, 1973-81, asst. prof. div. libr. and info. mgmt., 1976-80, assoc. prof., 1980-87; accreditation officer Am. Libr. Assn., 1987-91; assoc. dean, assoc. prof. Sch. Libr. and Info. Scis. U. North Tex., Denton, 1991—93; prof. U. Okla., Norman, 1993—, dir. Sch. Libr and Info. Studies, 1993—2000. UCLA sr. fellow, 1987. Mem. ALA (coun. mem. 1987), Assn. for Libr. and Info. Sci. Edn. (bd. dirs. 1985-87, 94-97, pres. 1995-96), Am. Soc. Info. Sci. and Tech. (treas., 2004—, bd. mem., 2004—), Okla. Libr. Assn., Phi Beta Kappa, Beta Phi Mu. Unitarian Universalist. Home: 2006 Trailview Ct Norman OK 73072-6654 Office: U Okla Sch Libr and Info Studies 401 W Brooks St Norman OK 73019-6030 Office Phone: 405-325-3921. E-mail: jlester@ou.edu.

LESTER, MARSHA I., chemistry professor; BA, Rutgers U., 1976; PhD, Columbia U., 1981. NSF postdoctoral fellow AT&T Bell Laboratories, 1981—82; faculty positions through prof. Univ. Pa., 1982—, Edmund J. & Louise W. Kahn prof. nat sciences, chem. dept. chair. Miller vis. rsch. prof. Univ. Calif., Berkeley, 2003. Contbr. articles to profl. jours.; mem. editl adv. bd. Jour. Physical Chemistry, 1995—2000, mem. editl. adv. bd. Molecular Physics, 1998—2000, Chemical Physics Letters, 1997—. Recipient Camile & Henry Dreyfus Teacher Scholar award, 1986, Career Advancement award, NSF, 1988, Broida prize, Internat. Symposium on Free Radicals, 1995; Alfred P. Sloan rsch. fellow, 1987, John Simon Guggenheim fellow, 2002—03. Fellow: AAAS, Am. Physical Soc. (chair divn. laser sci. 2000—01). Office: Univ Pa Dept Chem 262T 231 S 34th St Philadelphia PA 19104-6323*

LESTER, PAMELA ROBIN, lawyer; b. N.Y.C., Aug. 5, 1958; d. Howard M. and Patricia B. Lester; married; 1 child. Student, Princeton U., 1978—79; BA cum laude, Amherst Coll., 1980; JD, Fordham U., 1983. Bar: NY 1984, DC 1985. With Advantage Internat., Inc., Washington, 1984—89, gen. counsel, 1987—89; assoc. Akin, Gump, Strauss, Hauer & Feld, Washington, 1989—90; sr. v.p. bus. affairs and gen. counsel Time Warner Sports, N.Y.C., 1991—99; COO HBO Properties, 1998—2000; pres. Lester Sports and Entertainment, Inc., 2001—. Adj. lectr. sports law Am. U. Law Sch., Washington, 1989—91; adj. faculty sports law 1992-96 Fordham U. Law Sch., Bronx, NY, 1992—96; bd. advisors Ctr. Protection of Athletes Rights, 1994—97; co-chair Am. Law Inst.-ABA Entertainment, Arts and Sports Law Program, L.A., 2006—. Contbr. chpts. on athletic mktg. and endorsement contracts to books. Head girls varsity lacrosse coach and vol. asst. field hockey coach Montgomery H.S., NJ, 2001—04; mid. sch. lacrosse coach Princeton Day Sch., Princeton, NJ, 2005—. Recipient Profl. Sports Lawyer of Yr., Fordham Law Sch., 2004. Mem. ABA (program and sports divsn. chair forum entertainment and sports industries' governing com. 1992-96, chair elect 1996, chair 1997-99, immediate past chair 1999-2001, governing com. standing com. on forum-coms. 1994), Assn. Bar City N.Y. (sports law com. 1991-94, 2004—), Sports Lawyers Assn. (bd. dir., pres.-elect 2000-01, pres. 2001-03), N.Y. State Bar Assn., Women's Sports Found. (bd. adv. 1991-99), Va. Commonwealth U. Sportscenter (adv. bd. 1999-2000), U.S. Field Hockey (mktg. com. mem.) Office: Lester Sports and Entertainment, Inc PO Box 481 Hopewell NJ 08525 Business E-Mail: pam.lester@lestersports.com.

LESTER, SANDRA KAY, social worker; b. Kalamazoo, Mich., Sept. 18, 1944; d. LeRoy Clifford and Maxine Blenn (Stafford) Butcher; m. Edward Bernard Lester, Sept. 1, 1978; children: Kevin Craig, Julie Kathleen, Nicholas Edward. BS, We. Mich. U., 1970, postgrad., 1979. Case mgr. Mich. Dept. Social Svcs., Kalamazoo, 1971, liaison interagy. foster care, 1973—77, recruiter, trainer foster care, 1977—80, specialist purchase svc. contract, 1980—83, counselor employment and tng., 1983—97; ret., 1997. Mgr. contract Mich. Dept. Social Svcs., 1984—86, specialist weatherization and home repair, 1986—; instr. Kalamazoo Valley C.C., 1976—77. Bd. dirs. Continuing Edn. Young Families, Strong Families, Safe Children, Office of Aging; pres., bd. dirs. Regional Interagy. Coun. for Developmentally Disabled, 1973—76; mem. Greater Kalamazoo United Way, 1997—2000; pres. Kalamazoo County Adv. for Sr. Issues, 2004—. Mem.: Am. Soc. Aging, Internat. Pers. Mgmt. Assn., Network, Internat. Platform Assn. Democrat. Mem. Ch. Of God. Home: 3822 Mt Olivet Rd Kalamazoo MI 49004-2048

LESTER, STACY A., chemistry educator; Degree in chemistry, U. Ctrl. Okla., Edmond, 1996. Chemist Okla. Labs., Oklahoma City, 1997; instr. chemistry Heritage H.S., 1997—. Office: Heritage High Sch 1800 NW 122d St Oklahoma City OK 73120

LESTER, STEPHANIE, elementary school educator, education educator; d. Robert Fleischmann and Donna Woods; m. Jim Lester, Mar. 0, 1981; children: Joshua, Nicholas, Rebecca. MA, Chapman U., Orange County, Calif., 1997. Multiage educator Lancaster (Calif.) Sch. Dist., 1996—; child and family edn. coll. instr. Antelope Valley Coll., Lancaster, 1998—. Spkr. and presenter in field. Youth sports coach Little League, AYSO, Quartz Hill, Calif., 1988—2005. Named Tchr. of the Yr., Lancaster Sch. Dist., 1999, Vol. of Yr., PTA, 2004; recipient Antelope Valley Bridge award, Regional Occupl. Program, Antelope Valley, 2001. Mem.: Regional Occupl. Program (assoc.; chmn. child and cmty. classroom program 1998—2006). Avocations: softball, hiking.

LESTER, VIRGINIA LAUDANO, academic administrator; b. Phila., Jan. 5, 1931; d. Edmund Francis and Emily Beatrice (Downes) Laudano; children: Pamela Lester Golde, Valerie Lester Greer. BA, Pa. State U., 1952; MEd, Temple U., 1955; PhD, Union Grad. Sch., 1972; JD, Stanford U. Law Sch., 1988. Tchr. pub. schs., Abington, Pa., 1952-55, Greenfield Center, NY, 1956; instr. edn. dept. Skidmore Coll., Saratoga Springs, NY, 1962-64, dir. ednl. research, 1967-72, asst. to the pres., 1968-72; asst. dir. Capitol Dist. Regional Supplementary Edn. Ctr., Albany, NY, 1966-67; assoc. dean, asst. prof. state-wide programs Empire State Coll., State U. NY, Saratoga Springs, 1973-75, sr. assoc. dean, assoc. prof., 1975-76, acting dean state-wide programs, 1976; pres., prof. interdisciplinary studies Mary Baldwin Coll., Staunton, Va., 1976-85, cons. to bd. trustees, 1985-88; assoc. Hunton & Williams, Richmond, Va., 1988-90; interim pres. Friends World Coll., Huntington, NY, 1990-91; dir. presdl. search consultation svc. Assn. of Governing Bds. of Univs. and Colls., 1991-94; of counsel spl. projects office of exec. dir. Am. Assn. Retired Persons, 1994—2001. Mem. cons. core faculty Union Grad. Sch., Union for Experimenting Colls. and Univs., Cin., 1975—82; vis. faculty fellow Harvard U. Grad. Sch. Edn., 1976; bd. dirs. So. Bankshares, So. Bank, Coun. Advancement of Small Colls., 1977—81, Am. Council Edn., 1983-85; adj. faculty mem. Grad. Sch. George Washington U., 1996, 2002—; cons. Nat. Exec. Svc. Corp., 1991—; state legis. lobbyist AARP, 2004—05. Mem. com. on criminal sexual assault Va. State Crime Commn., 1976; v.p. Costume Collection, Inc., 1971-73; v.p. Warren, Washington, Saratoga Counties Planned Parenthood, 1972-74, bd. dirs., 1970-74; mem. Saratoga Springs Housing Bd. Appeals, 1966-76, Commn. on Future of Va., 1982-84; bd. dirs. Nat. Urban League, 1979-86; pres. commn. NCAA, 1984-85. Mem. Am. Acad. Polit. and Social Scis., Va. Found. Ind. Colls. (trustee, exec. com.), Va. Council Ind. Colls., Am. Council on Edn. (commn. on women in higher edn. 1977-80, bd. dirs. 1981-85), Nat. Assn. Ind. Colls. and Univs. (dir.), Assn. Va. Colls. (sec.-treas. 1978-79, pres. 1980-81, dir.), Assn. Ch. Related Colls. and Univs. of South (pres. 1983), Pi Lambda Theta, Pi Gamma Mu, Chimes. Mem. Soc. Of Friends. E-mail: vlester55@msn.com.

LESTIKOW, NORMA JEAN, nursing educator; b. Freeport, Ill., July 4, 1948; d. Robert Daniel and Elizabeth Grace Shippy; m. Russell William Lestikow, July 8, 1972; children: Faith E., Matthew R. RN, Freeport Meml. Hosp., 1969; BSN, Alverno Coll., Milw., 1989; MS, No. Ill. U., DeKalb, 1998. Staff nurse Freeport Meml. Hosp., 1968—91; mem. nursing faculty Highland C.C., Freeport, Ill., 1990—. Recipient Faculty Excellence award, Highland C.C., 2002. Mem.: Nat. Orgn. for AD Nursing. Avocation: stamping and making cards. Home: 317 N Walnut Ave Freeport IL 61032 Office: Highland Community Coll 2998 W Port City Rd Freeport IL 61032 Business E-Mail: norma.lestikow@highland.edu.

LESYINSKI, DIANE M., elementary school educator; b. Taylorville, Ill., Nov. 6, 1950; d. Arthur and Christine Scott; m. Mark Matthew Lesyinski, June 28, 1971; children: Brian, Kevin. BSc, Ill. State U., Normal, Ill., 1972; M, St. Mary's, Winona, Minn., 2001. Tchr. reading, Mosseheart, Ill., 1972—74; title I Sandcreek Sch., Coon Rapids, Minn., 1978—80, Champlin Sch., Champlin, Minn., 1980—93, classrooom tchr., 1993—2006. Recipient Outstanding Young Am., Women of Today, 1985, Tchr. Outstanding Performance award. Mem.: Minn. Edn. Assn. Office Phone: 763-506-2000.

LETCHER, NAOMI JEWELL, quality engineer, educator, counselor; b. Belle Point, W. Va., Dec. 29, 1924; d. Andrew Glen and Ollie Pearl (Meadows) Presley; m. Frank Philip Johnson, Oct. 5, 1945 (div. Dec. 1953); m. Paul Arthur Letcher, Mar. 6, 1954; children: Frank, Edwin, Richard, David. AA, El Camino Jr. Coll., 1964; BA, Calif. State U., 1971. Inspector N. Am. Aviation, Downey, Calif., 1964-71; substitute tchr. ABC Unified sch. Dist., Artesia, Calif., 1971-72; recurrence control rep. Rockwell Internat., Downey, Calif., 1972-80, quality engr., 1981-86; counselor Forest Lawn Cemeteries, Cerritos, Calif., 1980-81; tech. analyst Northrop, Pico Rivera, Calif., 1986-89; ret. Gov. divsn. D-2 area T.M. Internat., Downey, Calif., 1978-79. Author: History of the Letcher Family, 1995. Docent Temecula (Calif.) Valley Mus., 1994—. Mem. AAUW, Nat. Mgmt. Assn., NOW, Srs. Golden Yrs. Club, Alpha Gamma Sigma. Democrat. Baptist. Avocations: genealogy, needlecrafts, stamp collecting/philately, dance, bowling. E-mail: OMIE8@aol.com.

LETT, CYNTHIA ELLEN WEIN, customer service administrator; b. Takoma Park, Md., Dec. 24, 1957; d. Arthur Benjamin and Mary Louise (Barker) Wein; m. Gerald Lee Lett, June 1, 1991; 1 child, Cameron Barker Wein Lett. BS, Purdue U., 1979; M, Antioch Sch. Law, 1982-83. Mktg. researcher Sheraton, Washington, 1979-80; sales mgr. Sea Pines Plantation Co., Hilton Head Island, SC, 1980-81; dir. sales Sheraton Potomac Hotel, Rockville, Md., 1981-82, Ritz Carlton Hotel, Washington, 1982-83; pres. Creative Planning Internat., Washington, 1983—; dir. The Lett Group, 1983—. Dir. mem. Great Inns Am., Annapolis, 1987-89; etiquette cons., 1989—; dir. meetings Am. Healthcare Inst., 1991-92; corp. affairs mgr., chief protocol MCI Telecom Corp., 1992-95; pres. The Lett Group, 1996—. Author: Getaway Innstyle, America's Fifty Best Inns, 1990; editor Travel Inn Style Newsletter, 1990-91, Apropos!, 1996—. Mem. ASTD, Profl. Conv. Mgmt. Assn., Found. for Internat. Meetings (bd. govs. 1985-86), Nat. Spkrs. Assn., Washington Conv. Visitors Assn., Purdue Club, Univ. Club, Internat. Soc. of Protocal & Etiquette Profls. (ISPEP) (exec. dir. 2002-), Platform Soc. Avocations: classical music, amateur photography, country inns, foreign travel, gardening. Office: Lett Group 13116 Hutchinson Way Ste 100 Silver Spring MD 20906-5947 Office Phone: 301-946-8208. Business E-Mail: info@lettgroup.com.

LETZIG, BETTY JEAN, financial consultant; b. Feb. 18, 1926; d. Robert H. and Alina Violet (Mayes) L. BA, Scarritt Coll., 1950, MA, 1968. Ednl. staff The Meth. Ch. Ark., Okla., Tex., 1953-60; with Internat. Deaconess Exch. Program, London, 1961-62; staff exec. nat. divsn. United Meth. Ch., N.Y.C., 1962-95, cons. current and deferred giving, 1995—. Coord. Mission Pers. Support Svcs., 1984-88; exec. sec. Deaconess Program Office, 1989-95. Contbr. articles to profl. jours. Bd. dirs. Global Health Action, Atlanta, 1974-88, Vellore Christian Med. Coll., N.Y.C., 1984-94; mem. U.S. com. Internat. Coun. Social Welfare, Washington, 1983-89; active Nat. Interfaith Coalition on Aging, Athens, Ga. and Washington, 1972—, pres., 1981-85. Mem.: LWV, AAUW, Older Women's League, Nat. Coun. Social Welfare, Nat. Voluntary Orgns. Ind. Living for Aging, Nat. Coun. Aging. Avocations: travel, photography, needlecrafts. Home: 266 Merrimon Ave Asheville NC 28801 Office: St Paul's United Meth Ch 223 Hillside St Asheville NC 28801

LEUCHOVIUS, DEBORAH, advocate, special education services professional, consultant; b. Litchfield, Minn., Dec. 22, 1954; d. David Robert Leslie and Corinne Ardell Shiell; m. James Raphael Poole, Aug. 18, 1979; 1 child, Frederick Winston Leuchovius Poole. BA, Hamline U., 1978; MA, Rutgers U., 1981. Americans with Disabilities Act specialist PACER Ctr., Inc., Mpls, tech. assistance specialist Mpls., 1994—96, project dir. TATRA project, 1996—, nat. coord., transition tech. assistance programs, 2001—. Cons. Change Agy., St. Paul, 1990—. Editor: (newsletter) Point of Departure, (book) The Americans with Disabilities Act: A Guide for People with Disabilities, Their Families and Advocates. Advisor to nat. leadership team Assn. Sci. and Tech. Ctrs., Mus. and Access; mem. Spina Bifida Assn. Minn., 1994—, sec., 2000; advisor VSA Arts Minn., Mpls., 1995—99; advisor to access com. Walker Art Ctr.; bd. dirs. ADA Minn., St. Paul, 1992—95; founding mem. Minn. Ind. Scholars Forum, 1981—89. Mem.: Nat. Rehab. Assn., Coun. Exceptional Children (parent rep. divsn. career devel. 1997—99). Office: PACER Ctr 8161 Normandale Blvd Minneapolis MN 55437 Office Phone: 952-838-9000. Business E-Mail: tatra@pacer.org.

LEUENBERGER, BETTY LOU, psychologist, educator; b. Detroit, Sept. 21, 1947; d. Stanley Ray and Lillian Elizabeth Nichols; m. Jerry Lee Leuenberger, Aug. 10, 1968; children: Cameron Lee, Justin L. BS in Edn., Ctrl. Mich. U., Mt. Pleasant, 1969, MA in Health Edn./Adminstrv. Curriculum Design, 1987. Tchr. Hemlock Pub. Schs., Mich., 1969—71, Meridian Pub. Schs., Sanford, Mich., 1971—77; tchr. adult edn. Kingsley Pub. Schs., Mich., 1978—93; tchr. jr. and sr. HS Traverse City Area Pub. Schs., Mich., 1978—. Mem. dist. adv. bd. Traverse City Area Pub. Schs., 1985—95, site leader, chair dept. social studies, 1985—2005. Named Tchr. of Yr., Traverse City Area Pub. Schs., 1989; named to, Nat. Honor Roll Am. Tchrs. Mem.: NCSS, ASCAID. Democrat. Avocations: motorcycling, gardening, gourmet cooking, travel. Office: Traverse City Ctrl HS PO Box 32 Traverse City MI 49685 Office Phone: 231-933-3500. Business E-Mail: leuenberbe@csh.tcaps.net.

LEUKART, BARBARA J. J., lawyer; b. N.Y.C., Nov. 24, 1948; BA, Barnard Coll., 1971; JD, Case Western Reserve U., 1975. Bar: Ohio 1975, U.S. Ct. Appeals (6th, 5th and 3d cirs.). Ptnr. Jones, Day, Reavis & Pogue, Cleve. Mem.: ABA (labor and employment law sect.), Celebrezze Inn of Ct., Ohio State Bar Assn., Order of Coif. Office: Jones Day Reavis & Pogue North Point 901 Lakeside Ave E Cleveland OH 44114-1190 Office Phone: 216-586-7190. Office Fax: 216-579-0212. E-mail: bjleukart@jonesday.com.

LEULIETTE, CONNIE JANE, secondary school educator; b. Buckhannon, W.Va., Mar. 07; d. Audie Nelson and Sadie Laura (Gregory) Ware; m. Charles Benjamin Leuliette, Jr., Sept. 5, 1964; 1 child, Eric Wesley. BS, W.Va. U., 1963, MA, 1965. Tchr. grades 1-4 Point Mountain Elem. Sch., Webster Springs, W.Va., 1959-60; tchr. gen. sci. Webster Springs (W.Va.) High Sch., 1963-64; tchr. 2d grade Norwood Elem. Sch., Clarksburg, W.Va., 1965-66, tchr. 6th grade, 1966-67; circulation clk., librarian Clarksburg-Harrison Pub. Library, 1981-83, reference librarian, 1983-89; tchr. sci. South Harrison High Sch., Lost Creek, W.Va., 1989-90, Roosevelt-Wilson Middle Sch., Nutter Fort, W.Va., 1990-96, Washington Irving Mid. Sch., Clarksburg, W.Va., 1996—2003. Pres. Nutter Fort PTA, 1978-79; elder Presbyn. Ch. NSF grantee, 1964-65. Mem. NEA, AAUW (sec. W.Va. divsn. 1981-83, conv. chmn. 1978-80, treas. 1992-96, br. pres. 1983-85, chair W.Va. Ednl. Found. 2000-02, chair W.Va. internat. rel. 2006—), W.Va. Sci. Tchrs. Assn., W.Va. Assn. Parliamentarians (unit sec. 1986-90, treas. 1991-94, 99-01, 1st v.p. 2005-), W.Va. Fedn. Woman's Club (chmn. edn. dept. 1982-86, continuing edn. divsn. 1990-92, cmty. improvement program 1992-94, dist. edn. dept. 1990-92, dist. treas. 1994-98, dist. 2d v.p. 1998-2000, dist. 1st v.p. 2000-02, dist. pres. elect 2002-04, North Ctrl. dist. pres. 2004-2006, chmn. conservation dept. 2006—), Woman's Club Nutter Fort (pres. 1990-92), Alpha Delta Kappa (W.Va. chpt. v.p. 1992-94, chpt. pres. 1994-96, state historian 2000-02, state treas. 2002-2006, state chaplain 2006—). Democrat. Presbyterian. Avocations: reading, crosswords, walking, photography, stamp collecting/philately. Home: 107 Arbutus Dr Clarksburg WV 26301-4301

LEUNER, JEAN D'MEZA, nursing educator, director; d. Jay and Marilyn Sprigg D'Meza; m. Richard Joseph Leuner; children: Kirstyn Jean, Kyle Joseph. Diploma in nursing, St. Lukes Hosp., 1972; BSN, Seton Hall U., 1975; MSN, Boston Coll., 1979, PhD, 1994. Staff nurse Nyack (N.Y.) Hosp., 1972—75; instr. St. Anselm's Coll., Manchester, NH, 1976—78; assoc. prof., interim dir. MGH Inst. Health Prof., Boston, 1980—95; assoc. dean Med. U. S.C. Coll. Nursing, Charleston, 1995—2003; dir. Sch. Nursing U. Cen. Fla., Orlando, 2003—. Chair adv. com. S.C. Bd. Nursing, Columbia, 2002—03; chair Deans and Dirs. Coun. Nursing Programs in S.C., 1999—2001. Author: (book) Mastering the Nursing Process: Case Method Approach, 1990. Mem. Def. Adv. Com. on Women in the Svcs., 2000—02. Recipient Palmetto award, S.C. Nurses Found., Twin award, Charleston S.C. YWCA. Mem.: ANA, Fla.Assn. Colls. of Nursing (chair elect), Phi Delta Kappa, Sigma Theta Tau (pres. elect Theta Epsilon chpt.). Avocations: tennis, golf, reading. Office: U Cen Fla Orlando FL 32816 Home: 2014 Wayhaven Ct Maitland FL 32751-4924

LEUPP, EDYTHE PETERSON, retired education educator; b. Mpls., Nov. 27, 1921; d. Reynold H. and Lillian (Aldridge) Peterson; m. Thomas A. Leupp, Jan. 29, 1944 (dec.); children: DeEtte(dec.), Patrice, Stacia, Roderick, Braden. BS, U. Oreg., Eugene, 1947, MS, 1951, EdD, 1972. Tchr. various pub. schs., Idaho, 1941-45, Portland, Oreg., 1945-55; dir. tchr. edn. N.W. Nazarene Coll., Nampa, Idaho, 1955-61; sch. adminstr. Portland Pub. Schs., 1963-84; dir. tchr. edn. George Fox Coll., Newberg, Oreg., 1984-87; ret., 1987. Vis. prof. So. Nazarene U., Bethany, Okla., 1988—95, Asia Pacific Nazarene Theol. Sem., 1996, prof., 2000; adj. prof. Warner Pacific Coll., Portland, 1996—97; pres. Portland Assn. Pub. Sch. Adminstrs., 1973—75; dir.-at-large Nat. Coun. Adminstrv. Women Edn., Washington, 1973—76; state chmn. Oreg. Sch. Prins. Spl. Project, 1978—79; chair Confdn. Oreg. Sch. Adminstrs. Ann. Conf.; rschr. 40 tchr. edn. programs in colls. and univs.; designer tchr. edn. program George Fox Coll. Author: tchr. edn. materials. Pres. Nampa PTA, 1958, Idaho State Aux. Mcpl. League, 1957. Named Honored Tchr. of Okla., 1993; recipient Golden Gift award, 1982; fellow, Charles Kettering Found., 1978, 1980, 1987, 1991, 1992, 1993, 1994; scholar Hazel Fishwood, 1970. Mem.: Am. Assn. Colls. Tchr. Edn., Pi Lambda Theta, Phi Delta Kappa, Delta Kappa Gamma (pres. Alpha Rho State 1986—88). Republican. Nazarene. Avocations: travel, crafts, photography. Home: 8100 SW 2nd Ave Portland OR 97219-4602

LEUZZI, LINDA, writer; b. NYC, Aug. 1, 1947; d. Benjamin DeClara, Palma DeClara; m. Vincent Leuzzi, Oct. 24, 1970. BS in Journalism, St. John's U., 1986. Coord. pub. rels., mgr. pub. rels. Avon Products Inc., N.Y.C., 1979—83; freelance corr. N.Y. Newsday, Rego Park, 1985—87; assoc. copy editor King Features Syndicate, N.Y.C., 1987—88; freelance journalist, author Sayville, NY, 1988—; reporter Suffolk County News and Islip (NY) Bull., 2002—03, editor, 2003—05. Author: To the Young Environmentalist, 1997, A Creative Life: The Young Person's Guide, 1997; author: (series) Life in America: 100 Years Ago-Vol. on Transportation, 1995, Life in America: 100 Years Ago-Vol. on Urban Life, 1995, Life in America: 100 Years Ago-Vol. on Industry, 1997, Life in America: 100 Years Ago-Vol. on Education, 1997; author: The Portuguese Boy, 2001, A Matter of Style: Women in the Fashion Industry, 1997 (Books for the Teenage List, 1997), Life Connections: Pioneers in Ecology (Books for the Teenage List, 2001); contbr. chapters to books. Former trustee Sci. Mus. L.I., Plandome, NY, 1996—2001; former trustee, mem. adv. bd Splashes of Hope, Huntington, NY, 2004—06; mem. bus. adv. bd. Sayville Sch., 1999—2002. Recipient 2d place and 3d place awards and hon. mention, N.Y. Press Assn., 2002, Sports Feature 1st Pl. award, 2005. Mem.: Am. Soc. Journalists and Authors, Rotary (host Rotary exchange students). Avocations: hiking, jogging, travel, music. Home and Office: 131 Gillette Ave Sayville NY 11782 E-mail: lindaleuzzi@aol.com.

LEVACK, EDNA BEVAN, music educator, choir director; b. Cheyenne, Wyo., Sept. 21, 1922; d. Christopher Henry Droegemueller and Charlotte Adelheit Mueller; m. Elmer Wayne Bevan, Nov. 4, 1944 (div. Dec. 1988); children: David Wayne, Ronn Merrill, Paul Bevan (dec.), Philip Neal; m. John B. Humphries, Feb. 18, 1989 (dec. Aug. 2003); m. Norman T. Levack, June 18, 2004 BS, U. Minn., 1943. Nat. and state cert. piano tchr. Freelance writer, Seattle, 1955—; piano tchr., 1955—; organist Luth. Ch., Seattle, 1950—80, choir dir., 1965—80; dir. bell choir John Knox Presbyn. Ch., Seattle, 1989—2002, Glendale Luth. Ch., Seattle, 1989—, Southminster Presbyn. Ch., Seattle, 2002—. Handbelll choir dir. Lutheran and Presbyn. chs., Seattle; conductor adult and children choirs Lutheran Chs., 1980—95. Author: Christian Finger Plays and Games, 1955. Mem.: Wash. State Music Tchrs. Assn. (past treas., past pres. South King County chpt.). Avocation: square and folk dancing. Home: 830 SW Shoremont Ave Normandy Park WA 98166-3646

LEVALLIANT, DEBBIE, information technology executive; BS in Bus. Admin., Acadia Univ. Stockbroker; pres., CEO Amirix Systems, Halifax, Canada, 1990—. Exec. com. NovaKnowledge; mem. Halifax Chamber Commerce. Mem.: Soc. Mgmt. Accts. Nova Scotia (mem. bd. dir.), CMA Soc. (adjudication panel for CMA candidates case presentation). Achievements include leading devel. global lic. program, AMIRIX; negotiating company transition from non-profit to for-profit status. Office: Amirix Systems 77 Chain Lake Dr Halifax NS B3S 1E1 Canada

LEVAN, DEBORAH JO, internist; b. Louisville, Ky., Dec. 10, 1949; d. James Walter LeVan and Martha Koenig; m. Ross Gail Parker, May 5, 1984; children: Sarah LeVan Parker, Alexander LeVan Parker. BA, Chatham Coll., 1971; MPH, U. Pitts., 1973; DO, Mich. State U., 1976. Diplomate Am. Bd. Internal Medicine. Intern Detroit Osteo. Hosp., Highland Park, Mich., 1976-77, resident in internal medicine 1977-80, internist, 1980-92; program mgr. internal medicine Bi-County County Hosp., Warren, Mich., 1988-94, Detroit Riverview Hosp., 1994—, dir. med. edn., 1996—, internist, 1992—. Clin. prof. Mich. State U., East Lansing, 1984-98; prof. medicine Kirksville Coll. Osteopathic Medicine, 1994-99. Bd. dirs. Night to Care Charity, Detroit, 1997—. Fellow Am. Coll. Osteopathic Internists; mem. ACP. Presbyterian. Avocations: running, reading. Home: 54 Merriweather Rd Grosse Pointe Farms MI 48236-3623 Office: Motor City Internists 11447 Joseph Campau Hamtramck MI 48212 Office Phone: 313-365-9740.

LEVANDOWSKI, BARBARA SUE, education educator; b. Mar. 16, 1948; d. Earl F. and Ann (Klee) L. BA in Edn. and Spanish, North Park Coll., 1970; MS in Elem. Edn., No. Ill. U., 1975, degree in curriculum and supervision/, 1977, EdD, 1979, cert. elem. tchr.; cert. secondary tchr.; cert. in adminstrv. with supt. endorsement; cert. sv. reviewer, Ill. Tchr. Round Lake (Ill.) Sch. Dist., 1970-75, Schaumburg (Ill.) Sch. Dist., 1975-87, asst. prin., 1977-87; prin., staff devel. dir. Dist. 200 Northwood Elem. Sch., Woodstock, Ill., 1987-94, dir. curriculum and instrn., 1994—2002; developer, dir. Woodstock Mentor-Instrn. for Tchrs., 1998—2002; prof. Sch. Edn., North Park U., Chgo., 2003—. Curriculum cons. Spring Grove (Ill.) Sch. Dist., 1980-81; instr. various courses, Schaumburg, 1984-86; dir. Einstein Sch. Writing Project, 1986-87; dir. Dist. 200 Thinking Thinking Skills, 1988—; co-instr. Dist. 200 Tchg. Thinking Skills Across the Curriculum, 1992—, dir. curriculum and instrn.; chair north ctrl. assn. visitation team Huntley Sch. Dist, 1989; co-developer 4 yr. tchr. mentor program, 1994—. Mem. editorial bd. Ill. Sch. R & D Jour., 1981—; contbr. articles to profl. jours. Chair Computer/Tech. Strategic Action Team, Woodstock, 1988-89. Recipient numerous awards for excellence in teaching, Those Who Excel award State of Ill., 1979; fed. grantee. Mem. NAESP, NAFE, ASCD (insvc. presenter 1984—, presenter state and nat. conv. 1989—), Am. Biog. Rsch. Assn. (bd. dirs. 1985—, publs.

com. 1983), Nat. Staff Devel. Coun., Nat. Coun. of States for Insvc., Ill. Staff Devel. Coun., Ill. Assn. for Supervision and Curriculum Devel. (chair rsch. com. 1982), Ill. Computer Educators, Inst. Ednl. Rsch. (editorial bd. advisors, co-chair effective teaching characteristics observation 1990—, Omega award), Ill. Prin. Assn. Phi Delta Kappa, Delta Kappa Gamma. Home: 426 Normandie Ln Round Lake IL 60073-3711 Office: North Park Univ 3225 W Foster Ave Chicago IL 60625 Office Phone: 773-244-5789. E-mail: blevandowski@northpark.edu.

LEVASSEUR, JANICE THONI, mathematician, educator; b. Santa Clara, Calif., July 22, 1971; d. James Casper and June Fujikawa Thoni; m. Tiernan Jerome Levasseur, Sept. 25, 1999; children: Ashley Akemi, Tanner Takashi. BS in Math. and Stats., Sonoma State U., Rohnert Park, Calif., 1994; MS in Applied Stats., U. Calif., Riverside, 1998. Group exercise instr. 24 Hr. Fitness, Moreno Valley, Calif., 1997—2002; aerobis instr. dept. phys. edn. U. Calif., Riverside, 1997—2000; instr. math. Mt. San Jacinto Coll., Menifee, Calif., 1999—, math ctr. coord., 2005—. Scholar pre-doctoral scholar, Sonoma State U., 1993—94. Mem.: Math. Assn. Am. Republican. Buddhist. Avocation: scrapbooks. Office: Mount San Jacinto College 28237 La Piedra Rd Menifee CA 92584 Office Phone: 951-639-6752. E-mail: jlevasseur@msjc.edu.

LEVEE, BARBARA POE, artist; b. N.Y.C., Mar. 4, 1922; d. Bernard Joseph and Rebecca Greenberg Reis; m. James W. Poe, 1943 (dec. 1968); children: Adam Poe, Lorna Poe(dec.); m. Michael Levee, 1984 (dec. 1988). Student, Temple U., 1940—42. Exhibitions include Surrealist Show, 1942, Art of this Century, N.Y.C., 1943, U. Calif., Santa Barbara, 1966, one-woman shows include Wakefield Gallery, 1943, PVI Gallery, N.Y.C., 1963, Rex Evans Gallery, L.A., 1970, 1972, 2 person show, J. Brown Studio Gallery, 1976, exhibitions include Glazer Gallery, La Jolla, Calif., 1974, one-woman shows include Art Space, L.A., 1978, exhibitions include Swope Gallery, 1983, 1984, Sharon Truex Fine Arts, 2000, 2001. Bd. dirs. UCLA Art Coun., Plaza de la Raza, Lincoln Park; villa coun. Getty Mus. East L.A., Malibu. Home: 2110 Mandeville Canyon Rd Los Angeles CA 90049

LEVEEN, PAULINE, retired history professor, government professor; b. NYC, Mar. 5, 1925; d. Aaron and Sophie (Karp) Ugelow; m. Seymour Leveen, Nov. 5, 1944; children: David Ian, Amy Frances, Adriane Beth. Student, Coll. City N.Y., 1941-44; BA, Elmira Coll., 1963, MS, 1965; postgrad., Cornell U., 1967, 71-72, Syracuse U., 1981-82. Cert. tchr. permanent secondary social studies. Substitute tchr. Elmira (N.Y.) Sch. Dist., 1960-65; prof. history and govt. Corning (N.Y.) C.C., 1965-92, prof. emeritus, 1992—, dir. paralegal program, 1975-93, chmn. div. social scis., 1984-91, liaison Accelerated Coll. Edn. Lectr. Elderhostel, Painted Post, N.Y., 1982—. Mem. AAUW (pres. Elmira-Corning br. 2003-06), Phi Alpha Theta, Beta Chi/Delta Kappa Gamma Corning (profl. affairs 1968, 75, legis. 1989—). Avocation: reading. Home: 60 Ohio Ave Elmira NY 14905-1822

LEVEILLE, NANCY ANNE, mathematics professor; b. Fall River, Mass., Oct. 15, 1949; d. Augustine James Paul and Leona (Beauparlant) Gancarski; m. Jacques Pierre Leveille, Aug. 18, 1973; 1 child, Nicole Therese. BA, Bridgewater State Coll., Mass., 1971; MA, Boston U., 1974; EdD, U. Houston, 2005. Cert. secondary math. tchr. Mass. Tchr. Ste. Anne Sch., Fall River, 1971—72; instr. Bristol C.C., Fall River, Mass., 1972—74, RI Coll., Providence, 1974—75; telephonist Keir and Cawder Mgmt. Svcs., London, 1977; tchr. Godolphin and Latymer, London, 1977—78; faculty asst. U. Wis., Madison, 1978—80; estimating specialist Edwards Bros., Ann Arbor, Mich., 1980—82; lectr. U. Houston-Downtown, 1983—2005, asst. prof., 2006—; instr. Houston C.C., 1985; tchr. Am. Sch. of the Hague, Wassenaar, Netherlands, 1990—91. Coord. Houston Pre-engring. Program, 1993. Judge Sci. Engring. Fair of Houston, 1985—2006; extraordinary eucharistic min. St. Theresa, Houston, 2000—06. Grantee, Ohio State U., 2006; grad. asst., Boston U., 1973—74. Mem.: AAUW, Am. Statis. Assn., Nat. Coun. Tchrs. Math., Math. Assn.Am., Pi Mu Epsilon, Kappa Delta Pi. Avocation: travel. Office: U Houston-Downtown One Main St Houston TX 77002-1001 Office Phone: 713-221-2723. Office Fax: 713-221-8086. Business E-Mail: leveillen@uhd.edu.

LEVEN, ANN RUTH, financial consultant; b. Canton, Ohio, Nov. 1, 1940; d. Joseph J. and Bessie (Scharff) L. AB, Brown U., 1962; cert. with distinction in Bus. Adminstrn., Harvard-Radcliffe U.s, 1963; MBA, Harvard U., 1964. Product mgr. household products div. Colgate-Palmolive, N.Y.C., 1964-66; account exec. Grey Advt., 1966-67; fin. asst. Met. Mus. Art, 1967-69, asst. treas., 1970-72, treas., 1972-79; v.p., sr. corp. planning officer Chase Manhattan Bank, 1979-83; pres. ARL Assoc., NY, 1983—; treas. Smithsonian Instn., Washington, 1984-90; dep. treas. Nat. Gallery Art, 1990-94, treas. and CFO, 1994-99. Adj. asst. prof. Grad. Sch. Bus. Columbia U., N.Y.C., 1975—77, adj. assoc. prof., 1977—79, adj. prof., 1980—93; exec.-in-residence Amos Tuck Sch. Dartmouth Coll., Hanover, NH, 1976, 84; bd. dir. Del. Group Family of Funds, Systemax; bd. gov. Investment Co. Inst., 1997—2004. Artist (awarded prizes for painting and graphic arts); contbr. articles to profl. jours. Exec. bd. new leadership divsn. Fedn. Jewish Philanthropies, 1968-70; coun. mem. N.Y. Pub. Libr., exec. com., 1976-79; mus. adv. panel N.Y. State Coun. Arts, 1977-79; bd. dirs. Camp Rainbow, 1970-84, v.p., 1976-78, treas., 1982-84; bd. overseers Amos Tuck Sch., 1978-84, chmn. ednl. affairs com., 1979-84; trustee Brown U., 1976—, fin. and budget com., student life com., devel. com., adv. and exec. coms., bd. dirs. Ctr. Fgn. Policy Devel.; bd. dirs. Am. Arts Alliance, 1990-92, Twyla Tharp Dance Found., 1982-87, Reading Is Fundamental, 1987-91, adv. coun., 1991-94; trustee Carnegie Corp. N.Y., 1981-1987, Artists' Choice Mus., 1979-87; vis. com. Harvard U. Bus. Sch., 1979-84; bd. overseers Hood Mus.-Hopkins Ctr. Dartmouth Coll., 1984-91, chmn., 1988-91; trustee ARC Endowment Fund, 1985-90, N.Y. Sch. Interior Design, 1996—, Andy Warhol Found., 1999—; staff Presdl. Task Force on Arts and Humanities, 1981. Recipient Young Leadership award Council Jewish Fedns. and Welfare Funds, 1968; named N.Y. State's Outstanding Young Woman, 1976. Mem. Harvard Bus. Sch. Alumni Assn. (exec. coun. 1976-79, v.p. 1978-79), Women's Fin. Assn., Women's Forum, Econ. Club of N.Y., Cosmopolitan Club, Harvard Bus. Sch. Club, Radcliffe Club, Brown Club, Art Table, Century Assn. Home: 785 Park Ave New York NY 10021-3552

LEVENSON, CAROL A., corporate bond research company executive; BA, New Coll.; MA in English, Univ. Chgo., MBA. Sr. bond analyst, portfolio security selection Harris Investment Mgmt. Co., 1984—94; co-founder, dir. rsch. Gimme Credit, Chgo., 1994—; and editor Gimme Credit daily newsletter. Named one of 100 Most Influential Women, Crain's Chicago Bus., 2004. Office: Gimme Credit Ste 210 333 W Wacker Dr Chicago IL 60606 Office Phone: 847-920-9286, 312-781-1036. Business E-Mail: clevenson@gimmecredit.com.

LEVENSON, LAURIE L., law educator; b. Inglewood, Calif., Dec. 7, 1956; d. Daniel and Irene (Moses) L.; m. Douglas E. Mirell, Sept. 3, 1984; children: Solomon, Hava. AB, Stanford U., 1977; JD, UCLA, 1980. Bar: Calif. 1981, U.S. Dist. Ct. (cen. dist.) Calif. 1981, U.S. Ct. Appeals (9th cir.) 1981. Law clk. to Hon. James Hunter III US Ct. Appeals (3rd cir.), LA, 1980-81; asst. U.S. atty., criminal sect. U.S. Dept. of Justice, LA, 1981-89; adj. prof. Southwestern U., LA, 1982—89; prof. law Loyola U., LA, 1989—, assoc. dean, acad. affairs, 1996—99, William M. Rains fellow and dir. Ctr. for Ethical Advocacy. Mem. Calif. Bar Assn. (sec., treas. exec. com. criminal law sect. 1988—), LA County Bar Assn., 1994-. Democrat. Jewish. Office: Loyola Law Sch 919 Albany St Los Angeles CA 90015-1211 Office Phone: 213-736-1149. Office Fax: 213-380-3769. E-mail: laurie.levenson@lls.edu.

LEVENTER, TERRI, psychologist; b. N.Y.C., Sept. 13; d. David and Stella Akrish; divorced; children: David, Jerry. BA, Hunter Coll., 1944; MA, NYU, 1951; EdD, UCLA, 1969. Lic. psychologist, Calif. Psychology intern San Fernando Valley Child Guidance Clinic, Van Nuys, Calif., 1968-70; psychologist Northridge (Calif.) Hosp., 1970-77; pvt. practice Sepulveda, Calif., 1977—. Mem. APA, Calif. Psychol. Assn., Los Angeles County Psychol. Assn., Group Psychoptherapy Assn. So. Calif. (bd. dirs. 1990—), San Fernando Valley Psychol. Assn. (pres. 1980), Assn. Child and Ednl. Psychologists (pres. 1976), Women's Referral Svc. Avocations: painting, writing.

LEVENTHAL, ELAINE A., internist; MD, U. Wis., 1974; PhD, Yale U., 1966. Diplomate Am. Bd. Internal Medicine. Resident in gynecolory U. Hosps., Madison, Wis., 1974—77; resident in internal medicine Mt. Sinai Med. Ctr., Milw., 1977—79; fellow in geriat. Williams S. Middleton Vets. Meml., Madison, 1979—81; prof. divsn. gen. internal medicine Robert Wood Johnson U. Med. Group, New Brunswick, NJ, 1988—. Office: Robert Wood Johnson U Med Group Clinical Acad Bldg 125 Paterson St Ste 5100A New Brunswick NJ 08901-1977 Office Phone: 732-235-6577. Business E-Mail: eleventh@umdnj.edu.

LEVENTHAL, RUTH, retired parasitology educator, university official; b. Phila., May 23, 1940; d. Harry Louis Mongin and Bertha (Rosenberg) Mongin Blai; children: Sheryl Anne, David Alan. BS, U. Pa., 1961, PhD, 1973, MBA, 1981; HHD (hon.), Thomas Jefferson U., 1995; student, Pa. Acad. Fine Arts, 2000—03. Cert. med. technologist, clin. lab. scientist. Trainee NSF, 1971, USPHS, 1969-70, 73; asst. prof. med. tech. U. Pa., Phila., 1974-77, acting dean, 1977-81; dean Hunter Coll., CUNY, 1981-84; provost, dean, prof. biology Capital Coll., Pa. State U., Middletown, 1984-95; prof. biology Pa. State U. Hershey Med. Ctr., 1996—2002; ret., 2002. Site visitor Mid. State Assn. Colls. and Secondary Schs., Phila., 1983—98. Author (with Creadle): Medical Parasitology: A Self Instructional Text, 1979; author: 5th edit., 2002. Chmn. founds. Tri-County United Way, South Central Pa., 1996, 97; mem. health found. bd. Harrisburg Hosp., Pa., 1984-92; pres. bd. dirs. Open Stage Harrisburg, 1996-97, bd. dirs. 1996-2000; bd. dirs. Tri-County Planned Parenthood, 1984-87, Harrisburg Acad., Wormleysburg, Pa., 1984-88, Metro Arts of Harrisburg, 1984-87, Tech. Coun. Ctrl. Pa., 1996-99; founding chmn. Coun. Pub. Edn., 1984-99. Recipient Alice Paul award Women's Faculty Club, U. Pa., 1981; Recognition award NE Deans of Schs. of Allied Health, 1984, Athena award Capital Region C. of C., 1992, John Baum Humanitarian award Am. Cancer Soc., 1992, Lifetime Achievement award Family and Children's Svcs., 1996, Coll. and Cmty. Svc. award Harrisburg Area C.C., 1993; named Disting. Dau. Pa. by Gov. of Pa., 1995. Avocations: painting, sculpture.

LEVENTHAL-STERN, BARBARA LYNN, artist, marriage and family counselor; b. Springfield, Ohio, Feb. 16, 1948; d. Harry Edwin and Shirley (Ungar) Leventhal; m. Michael David Stern, Sept. 12, 1970; children: Joshua Meyer, Nathaniel Benjamin. BFA, Boston Mus. Sch.-Tufts U., 1972; MA in Art, San Jose State U., 1985; MA in Counseling and Ednl. Psychology, U. San Francisco, 1989. Lic. marriage and family counselor, Calif. Instr. Morris Stulsaft Found., Pacific Art League, Palo Alto, Calif., 1986, project coord. traveling art project, 1987-89. Illustrator: The Adventures of Judah and Yona, 1975; one-woman show Springfield (Ohio) Art Ctr., 1988; exhibited in group shows Fresno (Calif.) Art Mus., 1987, Mus. Modern Art, Ljubljana, Yugoslavia, 1987, U. Wis., Milwaukee, 1987, Hard Times Gallery, Bristol, England, 1988, Barbicon Ctr., London, 1989, Taipei Fine Arts Mus., Taiwan, 1990, Fitchburg (Mass.) Art Mus., 1990, Banner Spangenberg Gallery, Palo Alto, 1991, Banska Bystrica, Czech Republic, Davis (Calif.) Art Ctr., 1991, Euphrat Gallery De Anza Coll., Cupertino, Calif., 1991, Prieto Gallery Mills Coll., Oakland, Calif., 1992, Palo Alto Cultural Ctr., 1993, Triton Mus., Santa Clara, Calif., 1993, Bade Mus. Pacific Sch. Religion, Berkeley, Calif., 1994, Michael Himovitz Gallery, Sacramento, 1995, Nat. Mus. Women in the Arts, Washington, 2003, Exploding Head Gallery, Sacramento, 2004, Stellar Somerset Gallery, Palo Alto, Calif., 2006. Rep. human rels. com. Palo Verde Sch., Palo Alto Unified Sch. Dist., 1994-95; mem. planning com. Project Dialogue, Jewish Cmty. Ctr., Palo Alto, 1996; bd. dirs. Women's Alliance, Jewish Cmty. Fedn., Palo Alto, 1996-97; com. mem. disability task force Jewish Family Svcs., San Francisco, 1996-97. Recipient 1st place award for woodcut No. Calif. Print Competition, 1984, purchase award Purdue U., 1984, Rank-Xerox Corp., Eng., 1985, young leadership award Albert L. Schultz Jewish Cmty. Ctr., Palo Alto, 1984; grantee Conn. Com. on Arts, 1975-76, Pensinsula Cmty. Found., 1986, Peninsula Cmty. Found., San Francisco, 1989, Santa Clara Arts Coun., 1995, Philanthropic Venture Found., Oakland, 2001; Ann Flanagan fellow Kala Inst., 1985; fellow to visual artists Arts Coun. Silicon Valley, San Jose, 2003. Mem. Nat. Assn. Women Artists, Womens Caucus for Art, Am. Print Alliance, Calif. Soc. Printmakers (publicity coord. 1987-88), Calif. Assn. Marriage and Family Counselors, Arts and Healing Network, L.A. Printmaking Soc., Jewish Art Cmty. of Bay. Avocations: movies, poetry, literature, gardening.

LEVERETT, DAWN R., disability education consultant; d. George R. and Wilma J. Leverett; life ptnr. Der Hsien Chang, May 10, 1997. AA, Yuba C.C., Marysville, Calif., 1993; BA in Social Work, Calif. State U., Sacramento, 1996, postgrad., 2002—; MS in Edn., Nat. U., Sacramento, 2000. Disability counselor New Directions Edn. Ctr., Sacramento, 1998—99; disability edn. cons. Yuba County Office Edn., Marysville, 2000; tech. support agt. Earthlink, Inc., Sacramento, 2000—01; resource specialist tchr. (long -term substitute) Marysville H.S., 2001—02; after hours help desk agt. Volt Info. Sciences-Hewlett Packard, Roseville, Calif., 2003—04; disability edn. cons. A.C.E. Consulting, Yuba City, 2004—; vocat. rehab. rsch. asst. Calif. Dept. Rehab., Sacramento, 2005. Associated Students Inc. rep. U. Com. for Disabled Persons, Calif. State U., Sacramento, 2005—. Author: (manual) The Diabetes Survival Guide for K-12 Teachers, The Guide to Pre-Diabetes, Type 1 Diabetes, and Type 2 Diabetes for Vocational Rehabilitation Counselors. CPR and first aid instr. ARC, Yuba City, 1991—93; leader Girl Scouts USA, Tierra Del Oro Girl Scout Coun., Olliyuma Svc. Unit, Yuba City, 1992—93; mem. Sutter County Hist. Soc., Yuba City, Calif., 2004—06. Recipient Appreciation award, Girl Scouts USA, Olliyuma Svc. Unit, Troop 1187, 1991—92, Support and Dedication award, Girl Scouts USA, Olliyuma Svc. Unit, Troop 1239, 1992—93, Adult Leadership Devel. Pin, Girl Scouts USA, 1993, Adult Leadership Devel. Leaf, 1993. Mem.: ACA, Nat. Rehab. Assn., Nat. Rehab. Counseling Assn. (pres. 2004—06), Am. Rehab. Counseling Assn., Nat. Career Devel. Assn. Office: ACE Consulting Ste 630 #315 1282 Stabler Ln Yuba City CA 95993 Office Phone: 530-701-7335. Personal E-mail: blu_mu@yahoo.com. Business E-Mail: leverett.aceconsulting@gmail.com.

LEVERING, KATHRYN H., lawyer; b. Providence, Apr. 6, 1950; BA, Wheaton Coll., 1972; MA, Byrn Mawr Coll., 1973; JD, U. Pa., 1976. Bar: Pa. 1976. Joined Drinker, Biddle & Reath, Phila., 1976, sr. ptnr., labor, employment practice group, mng. ptnr., mem. mgmt. com., and chair, litig. dept., 2002—. Mem.: ABA (mem., labor, employment sect.), Phi Beta Kappa. Office: Drinker Biddle & Reath One Logan Sq 18th & Cherry Sts Philadelphia PA 19103-6996 Office Phone: 215-988-2919. Office Fax: 215-988-2757. Business E-Mail: kate.levering@dbr.com.

LEVERMORE, MONIQUE A., psychologist, educator; b. Montreal, Quebec, Can., Oct. 29, 1966; d. Oswald and Claudette Levermore; m. Mark Bartolone, Oct. 17, 1998; children: Nino, Kai. BA, U. Miami, Fla., 1988, MS in Edn., 1990; MS, Howard U., Washington, 1993, PhD, 1995. Cert. Fellow Am. Bd. Psychol. Specialties. Clin. fellow Harvard U., Cambridge, Mass., 1994—95; resident Psy-Eckerd Youth Devel. Ctr., Okechobee, Fla., 1995—96; asst. prof. Palm Beach Atlantic U., West Palm Beach, Fla., 1996—97; pvt. practice Melbourne, Fla., 1997; asst. prof. Fla. Inst. Psychology, Melbourne, 1998—2004; pres. Adolescent Behavioral Inst., Melbourne, 2004—. Pres. Martique Corp. Chmn. adv. bd. With a Brush of Love, Md., 2002—; active Together in Partnership, Broward County, Fla., 2001—, Links, Inc., Brevard County, Fla., 2003; founder Growing Into Young Ladies Successfully; bd. dirs. Salvation Army, Melbourne, Fla., 2002—. Miami Tchg. fellow, 2006. Mem.: APA. Democrat. Episcopalian. Avocations: singing, flute. Office Phone: 321-724-2161. Office Fax: 321-952-1809. E-mail: drl@levermore.com.

LEVEY, JUDITH S., lexicographer, publisher, editor; b. New Haven, Conn., Oct. 2, 1936; d. Morris and Betty Sweetkind; m. Lawrence Levey, Sept. 9, 1961. BA, Mt. Holyoke Coll., 1958; MA, Adelphi U., 1968. Copy editor, publications Am. Heart Assn., N.Y.C., 1958-62; sr. editor and copy chief, special projects Macmillan Pub. Co., N.Y.C., 1962-68, exec. editor, lexicographer, 1968-72; editor, encyclopedias Columbia U. Press, N.Y.C., 1972-83, editor-in-chief, reference books, 1983-85; editor-in-chief, dictionaries Macmillan Pub. Co., N.Y.C., 1985-92; editorial dir. Chambers Pub./CKG, N.Y.C., 1992-93; book developer, pub. cons. Montclair, NJ, 1993—. Exec. editor Macmillan Dictionary for Students, 1973; mng. editor The New Columbia Encyclopedia, 4th edit., 1975, The New Illustrated Columbia Encyclopedia, 1978; co-editor The Concise Columbia Encyclopedia, 1st edit.; editor-in-chief Macmillan School Dictionary 2, 1989, Macmillan Dictionary for Children, 2d edit., School Dictionary 1, 1989, Macmillan First Dictionary, 1990, Macmillan Picture Word Book, 1990, Macmillan/McGraw-Hill School Dictionary 3, 1993, Scholastic First Dictionary, 1998, 2d edit., 2006; editor: The 1996 World Almanac for Kids, 1995, The 1997 World Almanac for Kids, 1996, The 1998 World Almanac for Kids, 1997. Mem.: Soc. Children's Book Writers and Illustrators, Dictionary Soc. N.Am.

LEVI, BARBARA GOSS, physicist, editor; b. Washington, May 5, 1943; d. Wilbur H. and Mildred C. (Wallin) Goss; m. Ilan M. Levi, Sept. 10, 1966; children: Daniel S., Sharon R. BA, Carleton Coll., 1965; MS, Stanford U., 1967, PhD, 1971. Assoc. editor Physics Today Am. Inst. Physics, N.Y.C., 1969-70, cons. editor Physics Today, 1970-89, assoc. editor Physics Today, 1987-88; sr. assoc. editor Physics Today, N.Y.C., 1989-93, sr. editor, 1993—2003, cons. editor, 2003—; mem. tech. staff Bell Labs, Holmdel, NJ, 1982-83; mem. rsch. staff Ctr. for Energy and Environ. Studies Princeton (N.J.) U., 1981-82, 83-87. Lectr. Fairleigh Dickinson U., Madison, NJ, 1970—75, Ga. Tech., Atlanta, 1976—80; cons. U.S. Office Tech. Assessment, Washington, 1976—93; vis. prof. Rutgers U., Piscataway, NJ, 1988—89; adj. assoc. prof. physics U. Calif., Santa Barbara, 1998—. Editor (with others): (book) Energy Sources: Conservation and Renewables, 1985, The Future of Land-Based Strategic Missiles, 1989, Global Warming: Physics and Facts, 1992. Treas. LWV, Holmdel and Colts Neck, NJ, 1983—94. Fellow: AAAS (mem. steering com. physics group 1997—), Am. Phys. Soc. (chmn. forum on physics and soc. 1988—89, edn. com. 1989—91, forum councilor 1992—95, Lilienfeld prize com. 1993—95, mem. exec. bd. 1994—95, com. on coms. 1994—96, chair 1995, 1996, mem. exec. com. forum edn. 1997—98, mem. Nicholson medal com. 1998—99, chair 1999, pub. affairs panel 2002—05); mem.: AAUW (mem. nuc. energy task force 1975—77), Am. Assn. Physics Tchrs., Fedn. Am. Scientists (gov. bd. 1985—89). Avocations: tennis, travel, hiking, skiing.

LEVI, MARINA J., language educator, theater educator; b. Glen Cove, NY, Mar. 28, 1977; m. Darrin T. Levi, July 17, 2004. BFA, Va. Commonwealth U., Richmond, 2000. Tchr. drama, English Loudoun County Pub. Schs., Ashburn, Va., 2000—. Tchr. arts camp drama Performing And Visual Arts NW, Winccchester, Va., 2000—. Director/producer (high school drama production) Plaza Suite, Fools, Cinderella, An Evening with the Bard, You're a Good Man, Charlie Brown, Odd Couple (Male & Female Versions), Funny Girl Icarus All Over Again, The Wizard of Oz.

LEVI, VICKI GOLD, picture editor, historical consultant, writer, actress; b. Atlantic City, Sept. 16, 1941; d. Albert and Beverly Valentine Gold; m. Alexander Hecht Levi, May 31, 1970; 1 child, Adam Hecht Levi. Student, Montclair State Coll., 1959-60, New Sch. Social Rsch., N.Y.C., 1970-73, Sch. Visual Arts, 1972, Lee Strass Berg Sch. Acting, 1961. Actress, Atlantic City, N.Y.C and L.A., 1945—; asst. to pres. Family Fare, Inc., N.Y.C., 1966; advt. rep. Cosmopolitan Mag., N.Y.C., 1967; publicity dir. Misty Harbor, Ltd., N.Y.C., 1968; freelance picture researcher, 1972—; contbg. picture editor Esquire Mag., N.Y.C., 1980—, Mirabella Mag., N.Y.C., 1991-93, Atlantic City Mag., 1988-2000, New Woman Mag., 1995—, Family Cir., 2000—. Story cons. Alvin Cooperman Prodns., N.Y.C., 1985—; hist. cons. various Atlantic City, N.Y.C., 1994—; lectr. on Atlantic City, 1979—; guest exhibitor Internat. Ctr. Photography, N.Y.C., 1979; guest exhibitor and lectr. Cooper Hewitt, N.Y.C., 1980; guest curator Songwriters Hall of Fame, N.Y.C., 1979; guest lectr. Mcpl. Art Soc., N.Y.C., 1979; co-founder Atlantic City Hist. Mus., 1985—, bd. dirs., exhibit dir., 1995—; hist. cons. Toast to Times Square Com., N.Y.C., 1988—; curator Atlantic City Playground of the Nation, Atlantic City Hist. Mus., 1994; co-curator Charles K. Doble's Atlantic City, 1994, Images of African Americans in Atlantic City, 1995, Seventy-Five Years of Miss America in Pictures, 1995, The Al Gold Years, 1996, Bettmann on the Boardwalk, 1997, 360 Degrees of Atlantic City, 1998, Stompin' at the Shore, 1999, Star Shine, 2001, Atlantic City Hist. Mus., 1996, Noyes Mus. Through the Lens, 1998, Up From the Boardwalk, Down by the Sea, 1998, The Illustrated World of Atlantic City, Atlantic City Art Ctr., 1999; bd. dirs. Hecht-Levi Found.; preliminary judge Miss America, 1997. Co-author: Atlantic City: 125 Years of Ocean Madness, 1979, rev. edit., 1994, Live and Be Well: A Celebraton of Yiddish Culture in America, 1982, rev. edit., 2000, You Must Have Been a Beautiful Baby, 1992, Cuba Style, 2002, Times Square Style, 2004; columnist Phila. Bull., The Way It Was, 1980, The Shore Thing, Talk of the Boardwalk, 1997—99, AC Insider's Guide, Then and Now, 1997; prodr., dir.: (hist. video) Boardwalk Ballyhoo, 1992 (Am. Assn. State and Local History award, 1995, Atlantic City Tourism Coun. Resolution award, 1995, Tourism Advocacy award Greater Atlantic City Region Tourism Coun., 1996); rschr.: Miss America, The Dream Lives On, 1995; hist. cons.: (prodn.) Atlantic City Experience, 1995; (Broadway prodn.) Having Our Say, 1995; Time an Again; hist. image cons. (PBS prodn.) I Hear America Singing, 1996; hist. rschr.: (Disney World prodn.) BoardWalk Resort, 1996; hist. cons. (Broadway prodn.) Steel Pier, 1998; hist. pictorial editor The Civil-War, 1999; commentator (PBS) There She Is: The History of Miss America, 2002, Behind the Scenes: VH-1, 2003. Named an Atlantic City Treasure, Atlantic City Women's C. of C., 1989; named to Atlantic County Woman's Hall of Fame, 1997; recipient Author's citation, N.J. Inst. Tech., Divsn. Continuing Edn., 1980, Senate Resolution, N.J. State Senate, 1979, Outstanding Achievement award, Atlantic City Women's C. of C., 1981, Proclamation from mayor of Atlantic City, 1981, Encore award, 2000, Spirit of Hospitality award, Atlantic City Conv. and Visitors Assn., 2004. Mem. NATAS (Emmy judge 1987-89, spl. events com. 1989-90), SAG, Am. Fedn. TV and Radio Artists, Am. Soc. Picture Profls. (bd. dirs. 1984). Democrat. Jewish. Avocations: world travel, memorabilia collecting. Home and Office: 211 Central Park W New York NY 10024-6020 E-mail: AC08401@aol.com.

LEVICK, MYRA FRIEDMAN, art psychotherapist, educator; b. Aug. 20, 1924; d. Louis and Ida (Segal) Friedman; m. Leonard J. Levick, Dec. 26, 1943; children: Bonnie, Karen, Marsha. BFA, Moore Coll. Art, 1963; MEd, Temple U., 1967; PhD, Bryn Mawr Coll., 1982. Lic. psychologist; cert. med. psychotherapist. Art psychotherapist Albert Einstein Med. Ctr., Phila., 1963-67; dir. adjunctive therapies and grad. tng. program art therapy Hahnemann Med. Coll. and Hosp., Phila., 1967-73, dir. masters creative arts in therapy tng. program, 1973-86; prof., cons. mental health scis. dept. Hahnemann U., 1977—. Cons. affiliated clinics and instns.; dir. So. Fla. Art Psychotherapy Inst. Author: They Could Not Talk and So They Drew, Children's Styles of Coping and Thinking, 1983, Mommy, Daddy, Look What I'm Saying: What Children Are Telling You Through Their Art, 1986, See What I'm Saying: What Children Tell Us Through Their Art, 1998, 2nd edit. 2003; contbg. author: Current Psychotherapies, 1975, Handbook of Innovative Psychotherapies, 1981, The Psychiatric Therapies, 1984; sr. editor: The Arts in Psychotherapy, 1975-81, editor-in-chief, 1982-86, emeritus, 1986—; contbr. articles to profl. lit. Recipient Humanitarian award Ronald Bruce Nippon Assn., 1976; NIMH grantee, 1975-78. Mem. APA, Internat. Soc. Psychopathology of Expression, Am. Ortho-Psychiat. Assn., Am. Soc. Psychopathology of Expression, Am. Art Therapy Assn. (founder, 1st pres. hon. life mem.), Family Inst. Phila. (exec. bd. 1982-84), Pa. Psychol. Assn. Achievements include development of Leuick emotional and coquiche art therapy assessment. Home and Office: 21675 Cypress Rd Apt 15g Boca Raton FL 33433-3220

LEVICOFF, VALERIE ANN, music educator; b. Phila., Feb. 13, 1961; d. Edward Joseph and Maryann (nee Adams) Lynch; m. Jerold Stephen Levicoff, Aug. 11, 1990; children: Alexander William, Edward Justin. BA in violin performance, Phila. Coll. of Perfoming Arts, 1983; MA in edn., La Salle U., Phila., 1990. Cert. music edn. K-12 Pa. Dept. Edn. Section violinist N.Y. Harlem Opera Co., 1985—86; social rehab. counselor Charles Drew Mental

Health, Phila., 1986—87; asst. prin., 2d violinist Reading Symphony Orch., Pa., 1986—; music educator Sch. Dist. of Pa., Phila., 1987—; concert mistress Warminster Symphony, Pa., 1996—; adj. prof. music Arcadia U., Glenside, Pa., 2003—. Judge, adjudicator Warminster Symphony, Pa., 1997—, Reading Youth Symphony, Pa., 2001—; validator, benchmark Nat. Bd. Profl. Tchg. Stds., Phila. and San Antonio, 2003. Contbg. author (curriculum material) Sounds of Learning, Phila. Opera Co., 2005, 2006; editor: String Quartet Arranging, 2001—; facilitator Reading Symphony Orch., 2001—; musician (violinist): (TV commercial) Reading Symphony, 1999—; musician: (first violinist) Strings Fantastique, 1990. Nominee Tchr. of Yr., Phila. Sch. Dist., 2004; recipient Am. Legion award, 1975, Outstanding Educator Rose Lindenbaum award, 2005. Mem.: MENC, Pa. Music Educators Assn., ASTA, Reading Musician's Union, Phila. Fedn. Musicians. Avocations: travel, knitting, reading, music, art. Home: 1979 Audubon Dr Dresher PA 19025 Personal E-mail: violinval@comcast.net.

LEVIN, CAROL ARLENE, adult education educator; b. L.A., Apr. 4, 1945; d. Harold Allen and Sally (Salter) L. AA, Santa Monica Coll., 1965; BA, UCLA, 1967; MS, Pepperdine U., 1990. Cert. tchr., 1969, bilingual tchr., 1977. Tchr. L.A. Unified Sch. Dist., 1969-89, asst. prin., 1998—2001; master tchr. UCLA, 1985-89; tchr., adviser bilingual editor newspaper D.A.R.E. to Read, 1989-94; adviser drug, alcohol and tobacco edn., 1994—98; learning support faculty Calif. State TEACH, 2001—. Pres., v.p. Calif. Assn. Childhood Edn., Los Angeles, 1977-81; chmn. workshop Calif. State Assn. for Childhood Edn. Internat. Conf., Universal City, 1979; invited observer Assn. for Childhood Edn. Internat. White House Conf.-Families, Los Angeles, 1980; tchr., adviser elem. news Sta. KTTV, Los Angeles, 1980-82. Editor: (with others) Our Los Angeles, 1976; contbr. articles to profl. jours. Treas. Dickens Towers Homeowners Assn., Sherman Oaks, Calif., 1978-80; sec. Sherman Villas Homeowners Assn, Sherman Oaks, 1981-83; mem. Sherman Oaks Homeowners Assn., 1986—, Palm Springs (Calif.) Tennis Club Owners Assn., 1981—; mem. Los Angeles Music Ctr. Theatre Group Vols., 1987-88. Recipient P.I.E. award Los Angeles Schs., 1978, 79, 80, 81. Mem. Women in Ednl. Leadership, Delta Kappa Gamma, Unihi Edn. Found. Avocations: swimming, boating, reading, rug hooking, piano. Office: Calif State U 5151 State University Dr Los Angeles CA 90032

LEVIN, CAROLYN BIBLE, volunteer; b. Dayton, Ohio, Aug. 31, 1948; children: Jennifer Levin Atocha, Brittany Levin Vogel. AS, Monticello, 1968; AB, Inst. of Merchandising., 1969. Spl. events mgr. Nat. Multiple Sclerosis Soc., 1988—89; freelance fashio coord. self-employed, 1979—90; publ. rep. freelance, Bloomfield Hills, Mich., 1989—2001; exec. dir. gifts Jules R. Schubot Jewelers, 2001—. Vol. coun. Hospice of Mich.; mem. women's com. Hospice Care, Cranbrook Acad. Art and Art Mus.; entertainment chair Oakland Family Svcs., 2003; mem. vol. coun. Detroit Symphony Orch., chmn. auction, 2003; vol. ArtServe Mich.; bd. dirs. Founders Jr. Coun., Detroit. Home: 6028 Hickory Tree Trl Bloomfield Hills MI 48301

LEVIN, DEBBE ANN, lawyer; b. Cin., Mar. 11, 1954; d. Abram Asher and Selma Ruth (Herlands) Levin. BA, Washington U., St. Louis, 1976; JD, U. Cin., 1979; LLM, NYU, 1983. Bar: Ohio 1979. Staff atty. US Ct. Appeals (6th cir.), Cin., 1979—82; shareholder Schwartz, Manes & Ruby, Cin., 1983—2002; of counsel Drew & Ward Co., LPA, Cin., 2002—04; shareholder Graf, Stiebel & Moyers Co., LPA, Cin., 2004—05, Schwartz Manes Ruby & Slovin, LPA, 2006—. Editor: U. Cin. Law Rev., 1972—79. Active Cin. Estate Planning Coun. Mem.: ABA, Nat. Acad. Elder Law Attys., Cin. Bar Assn. (chair advanced estate planning inst. 2001), Ohio Bar Assn., Greater Cin. Planned Giving Coun., Order of Coif. Jewish. Office: Schwartz Manes Ruby and Slovin LPA 441 Vine St Ste 2900 Cincinnati OH 45202-3090 Office Phone: 513-579-1414. Business E-Mail: dlevin@smrslaw.com.

LEVIN, ELIZABETH, freelance/self-employed writer; b. Plum City, Wis. d. Clarence and lillie (Bradley) Wiskerchen; children: Sherri Doolittle Mulligan, Scott Johnson, Aaron Levin. BS in Eng., Speech, U. Wis., 1958; postgrad., U. Minn., 1963-68. Head writer NBC, 1979, 80, 81; assoc. writer NBC, ABC, CBS, 1981-86; Spencer prof. Telecommunications U. Syracuse, N.Y., 1983. Instr. speech and acting U. Minn.; guest writer, speaker NYU, New Sch., Newhouse Benchmark, U. Wis., others. Creator, writer: (TV series) The Piper's Song, CBS, Sunday's-Child; developer, writer TV program A Teacher's Guide, CBS; writer: (feature film) Toxic Toys, (TV film) Boxcars and Buttercups, 1983-86, (plays) A Bad Play for an Old Lady, A Jester in the Hall of Dying Kings, Here Comes "the Chopper.", Sand, Carny Man, How to Catch a Sea-Gull in a Paper Bag, And the Old Man Had 2 Sons, The Female Entertainer; author: Nellie Pear, 1988, numerous short stories and poems. Developer creative arts programs for disturbed adolescents, Westchester Med. Ctr. Recipient O'Neill Playwright award, Carnegie award; Rockefeller grantee. Mem. Writers Guild Am. (exec. council). Home and Office: 18 Banks Farm Rd Bedford NY 10506-1914

LEVIN, EVANNE LYNN, lawyer, educator; b. L.A., Nov. 6, 1949; d. Marshall Levin and Rose (Tolchin) Levin Albert; m. Jeffrey Neal Oliver, 1992 (div. 1996); m. Al Gerisch Jr., Sept. 2005. BA in Polit. Sci. cum laude, UCLA, 1971; JD, Loyola Law Sch., L.A., 1974. Bar: Calif. 1995; lic. real estate broker Calif. Assoc. Ervin, Cohen & Jessup, Beverly Hills, Calif., 1977-78, Mason & Sloane, LA, 1978-82; atty. Orion Picturs Corp., LA, 1982-84; v.p. TV prodn. legal affairs Twentieth Century Fox Film Corp., Beverly Hills, 1986-89; of counsel Weinberg, Zipser, Arbiter & Heller, L.A., 1990; v.p., gen. counsel Zodiac Entertainment, Studio City, Calif., 1991-95; prin., owner Law Offices Evanne L. Levin, LA, 1995—; instr. entertainment law UCLA, 1999—; prin. Levin Realty, 2004—. Instr. personal mgmt. pub. and music career courses Learning Network, 1985—86; instr., asst. atty. UCLA, Learning Network, Entertainment Law Tng. Program, 1999—; devel. and fund-raising cons. Acad. for Jewish Religion, Calif., 2004—. Contbr. articles to profl. jours.; columnist: LA Women in Music Newsletter, 1986—88. Mem. Planned Giving Round Table So. Calif.; maj. gifts officer Woodbury U., 2002—04; v.p. event chair City Live!, 2003; mem. Sherman Oaks Neighborhood Coun., 2006; bd. dir. arts festival Hollywood Women's Coalition, 1985, bd. dir., 1985—86; bd. mem. and officer Woodman Manor Homeowners Assn., 1988—2005; mem. exec. bd. Wellness Guild; mem. exec. com. bd. dir. Weingart Ctr. Assn. Ptnrs., 2001—04. Mem.: Calif. Copyright Conf., LA Women Music (bd. dirs. 1986—88, mem. adv. com.), Women Entertainment Law, Beverly Hills Bar Assn. (former bd. govs., barristers bd. govs., founding mem./co-chair com. arts, mem. entertainment law com., del. to state bar and ABA convs.), Los Angeles County Bar Assn. (vols. in parole, exec. bd. intellectual property sect.), Assn. Profl. Fundraisers, Coun. Advancement Support Edn., Sherman Oaks Homeowners Assn. Avocations: scuba diving, collecting kaleidoscipes, travel. Office: 14937 Rhinestone Dr 1st Fl Sherman Oaks CA 91403 Personal E-mail: ellesq@adelphia.net. E-mail: ellesq@yahoo.com.

LEVIN, GAIL, writer, educator, photographer; d. Barron and Shirley Levin. BA, Simmons Coll., 1969, D (hon.), 1996; MA, Tufts U., 1970; PhD, Rutgers U., 1976. Instr. New Sch. for Social Rsch., N.Y.C., 1973—75, Baruch Coll., CUNY, 1974; asst. prof. art history Conn. Coll., New London, 1975—76; vis. prof. art history Grad. Ctr. CUNY, 1979—80; curator Whitney Mus. Am. Art, N.Y.C., 1976—84; vis. prof. Nesbit Coll. Design, Drexel U., 1985—86; asst. prof. art Baruch Coll. CUNY, 1986—87, assoc. prof. art, 1988—89, prof., 1990—. Will and Ariel Durant prof. humanities St. Peter's Coll., Jersey City, 1987—88; chair excellence U. Tenn., Chattanooga, 1995—96. Prodr., host Art at Issue, Manhattan Cable TV, 1985—86; author: Synchromism and American Color Abstraction, 1910-25, 1978, Edward Hopper: The Complete Prints, 1979, Edward Hopper as Illustrator, 1979, Edward Hopper: The Art and the Artist, 1980, Edward Hopper, 1984, Twentieth Century American Painting The Thyssen-Bornemisza Collection, 1987, Edward Hopper: An Intimate Biography, 1995, Edward Hopper: A Catalogue Raisonné, 1995; co-author: Abstract Expressionism: The Formative Years, 1978, Aaron Copland's America: A Cultural Perspective, 2000, Theme and Improvisation: Kandisky and The American Avant-garde 1912-1950; co-editor, contbr.: Ethics and the Visual Arts, 2006; editor: The Poetry of Solitude: A Tribute to Edward Hopper, 1995, Silent Places: A Tribute to Edward Hopper, 2000; author, photographer Hoppers Places, 1985, Marsden Hartley in Bavaria, 1989, film Edward Hopper, 1981; contbr. articles to profl. jours. and exhibition catalogues; one-woman shows include Kingston Artists Group, Gallery Rondout, 1984, Kennedy Galleries, Inc., N.Y.C., 1985, Jane Voorhees Zimmerli Art Mus., 1985, Meml. Art Gallery, U. Rochester, 1985, Fay Gold Gallery, Atlanta, Barridoff Gallery, Portland, 1986, Cedar Rapids Art Mus., 1986, Hopper House Art Ctr., Nyack, NY, 1986, Hilton Head Art League, SC, 1986, U. Iowa Art Mus., 1987, St. Peter's Coll. Art Gallery, Jersey City, 1987, Pa. Acad. of Fine Arts, 1987, Ariz. State U., Tempe, 1988, Emerson Gallery, Hamilton Coll., Clinton, NY, 1989, Milw. Art Mus., 1990, Bowdain Coll. Art Mus., 1990, Cress Gallery U. Tenn., Chattanooga, 1995, Trustman Art Gallery Simmons Coll., Boston, 1995, Provincetown (Mass.) Monument Mus., 1996, exhibited in group shows at Catskill Ctr. for Photography in Woodstock, N.Y., 1985, A.I.R. Gallery, N.Y.C., 1985, 1986, 1987, 2002, The 9th Precinct Gallery, 1986, Baruch Coll. Art Gallery, 1987. Recipient Alumnae Achievement award, Simmons Coll., 1986, The Hadassah Internat. Rsch. Inst. on Jewish Women at Brandeis U. Rsch. award, 2001—02, Rsch. award, Schlesinger Libr. Harvard U., 2005—; fellow, Pollock-Krasner/Stonybrook Found., 2006—07; grantee, Rockefeller Found., 1993, Smithsonian Inst., 1993; Rsch. grantee, NEH, 1984, 1989, 1992, 1993—95, Am. Coun. Learned Socs., 1988, U. Prof. fellow, NEH, 1998—99, 2006—, Fulbright Sr. scholar, 2006. Mem.: Coll. Art Assn., Pen Freedom to Write, Internat. Assn. Art Critics. Address: CUNY Baruch Coll B7-235 1 Bernard Baruch Way New York NY 10010-5518 Office Phone: 646-312-4062. Business E-Mail: gail_levin@baruch.cuny.edu.

LEVIN, HOLLY J., science educator; d. Gloria Miller; m. Arthur G. Levin, June 29, 1980; children: Ian S., Dana B. BS, N.J. City U., 1979. Cert. Tchr. Sci. N.J., 1979. Tchr. sci. Bayonne Bd. Edn., NJ, 1986—. Tchr. fellow of molecular biology rsch. Mem. shared decision-making team com. Bayonnne H.S., 2005—06. Recipient James Coleman Character Edn. Award, IMTT, 2005. Achievements include research in published DNA sequences of C. remanei and A. fransiscana at National Center for Biotechnology Information. Office: Bayonne High School 667 Avenue A Bayonne NJ 07002

LEVIN, JANNA J., physicist, educator; b. 1968; BS in Astronomy and Physics, Barnard Coll., 1988; PhD in Theoretical Physics, MIT, 1993. Postdoctoral fellow Canadian Inst. for Theoretical Astrophysics, 1993—95; postdoctoral fellow, Ctr. for Particle-Astrophysics U. Calif, Berkeley, 1995—98; advanced fellow, Dept. of Applied Mathematics and Theoretical Physics (DAMTP) Cambridge U., 1999—2003; Nat. Endowment for Sci. Technol. and Arts (NESTA) fellow, Astophysics Dept. Oxford U., 2003; asst. prof. astronomy & physics Barnard Coll., NYC, 2004—. NESTA Dream Time Fellow, Scientist-in-Residence Ruskin School of Drawing and Fine Art, Oxford, 2003. Author: How the Universe Got Its Spots: Diary of a Finite Time in a Finite Space, 2002, (novels) A Madman Dreams of Turing Machines: A Story of Coded Secrets and Psychotic Delusions, of Mathematics and War Told by a Physicist Obsessed by the Lives of Turing & Gödel, 2006. Recipient Kilby award, 2003. Achievements include first official scientist in residence at the Ruskin School of Drawing and Fine Art at Oxford U. Office: Barnard Altschul 505 Dept Physics & Astronomy 3009 Broadway New York NY 10027 Business E-Mail: jlevin@barnard.edu.

LEVIN, PHILLIS, education educator, writer; Prof. English, poet in residence Hofstra U., Hempstead, NY, 2001—. Fellow The MacDowell Colony, Yaddo, The Liguria Study Ctr. for the Arts and Humanities, Bogliasco, Italy. Author: (books of poetry) Temples and Fields (Poetry Soc. of Am. Norma Farber First Book award), The Afterimage, Mercury, 2001; editor: (anthology) The Penguin Book of the Sonnet, 2001., John Simon Guggenheim Meml. Found. fellow, 2003, Amy Lowell Poetry Travelling scholarship, Fulbright fellowship, Slovenia, grant, Ingram Merrill Found., 1995. Office: Rm 200 Hofstra Hall 101 Hofstra U Hempstead NY 11549-1010

LEVIN, SHANON S. (SHANON LEVIN LEHMAN), lawyer; b. Phila., 1975; BA with high honors, Pa. State U., 1997; JD magna cum laude, Temple U., 2000. Bar: Pa. 2000, NJ 2000, US Dist. Ct., NJ 2000, US Dist. Ct. (ea. dist.) Pa. 2001, US Ct. Appeals (3rd cir.) 2001, US Dist. Ct. (middle dist.) Pa. 2005. Law clk. to Hon. Berle M. Schiller US Dist. Ct. (ea. dist.) Pa., 2000—01; assoc. litig. Hangley Aronchick Segal & Pudlin, P.C., Phila. Trial team coach Temple U. Sch. Law, 2002, 06. Mem. Mann Ctr. for the Performing Arts Corp. Ptnrs., 2006—. Mem.: ABA, Pa. Bar Assn., Phila. Bar Assn. Office: Hangley Aronchick Segal & Pudlin One Logan Sq 18th & Cherry Streets, 27th Fl Philadelphia PA 19103-6933 Office Phone: 215-493-7038. Office Fax: 215-568-0300. E-mail: slevin@hangley.com.*

LEVIN, SUSAN BASS, lawyer; b. Wilmington, Del., July 18, 1952; d. Max S. and Harriet C. (Rubin) Bass; children: Lisa, Amy. BA, U. Rochester, 1972; JD, George Washington U., 1975. Bar: DC 1975, U.S. Ct. Claims 1975, N.J. 1976, Pa. 1981, U.S. Ct. Appeals (3d cir.) 1983, U.S. Supreme Ct. 1984. Law clk. to assoc. justice U.S. Ct. Claims, Washington, 1975—76; assoc. Covington & Burling, Washington, 1976—79; pvt. practice Cherry Hill, NJ, 1979—87; counsel Ballard, Spahr, Andrews & Ingersoll, Phila., Camden, 1993—96, Pepper Hamilton LLP, Phila. and Cherry Hill, 1996—2000; spl. counsel Fox Rothschild OBrien Frankel, 2001—02; commr. N.J. Dept. Cmty. Affairs, 2002—. Chair N.J. Redevel. Authority, 2002—; COO Corzine for Gov., 2005; mem. Corzine Transition Team, 2005. Trustee N.J. Coalition Small Bus. Orgns., 1985—87; del. to Pres.'s Summit Am.'s Future, chair Pam's List; chair N.J. Coun. Affordable Housing; del. Dem. Presdl. Conv., 1992, 1996, 2000, 2004; pres. Cherry Hill Twp. Coun., 1986—88; mayor City of Cherry Hill, 1988—2002; bd. dirs. N.J. Alliance Action, S. Jersey Devel. Coun., U.S. Holocaust Coun., Big Bros./Big Sisters, Boys and Girls Club, trustee; bd. dirs. N.J. League Municipalities. Recipient Woman of Achievement award, Camden County Girl Scouts, 1986, Barbara Boggs Sigmuno award, N.J. Women Polit. Caucus, 1996, Gov.'s award on volunteerism, 1998. Mem.: N.J. Assn. Women Bus. Owners (state pres. 1984—85, named Woman of the Yr. 1985), Tri County Women Lawyers (pres. 1984—85), Order of Coif, Phi Beta Kappa. Office: 1001 Broad St Trenton NJ 08002 Office Phone: 609-273-5574. Personal E-mail: brook@voicenet.com, brook168@comcast.net.

LEVIN BARONESS VON GLEICHEN, TOBE, language educator, editor, volunteer; b. Long Beach, NJ, Feb. 16, 1948; d. Morris William and Janice Metz; m. Christoph Freiherr Baron Von Gleichen, Dec. 17, 1985; 1 child, Rosa Frances Helena. BA Summa Cum Laude, Ithaca Coll., 1970; MA, NYU, Paris, 1973, U. Paris, 1974, Cornell U., 1976, PhD, 1979. Tchg. asst. Cornell U., Ithaca, NY, 1973—79; prof. U. Md., Heidelberg, Germany, 1979—. Adj. prof. U. Frankfurt, Germany, 1986—; editor-in-chief Wise Women's News, Nicosia, Cyprus, 1990—, European Jour. Women's Studies, London, 1995—, Feminist Europa, Heidelberg, Germany, 1998—; assoc. Five Coll. Women's Studio Rsch. Ctr., 2004; scholar in residence Brandois U. Editor: Women's Studies Quar., 1992—. Pres. Forward Germany, 1998—. Recipient Drazek Tchg. award, 1999, Pres. award, U. Maryland, 2003; fellow, W.E. B. Dubois Inst., Harvard U., 2006. Mem.: MLA. Avocations: reading, travel, swimming. Home: Martin Luther St 35 Frankfurt Germany 60389 Business E-Mail: levin@em.uni-frankfurt.de.

LEVINE, ALISON, entrepreneur, leadership development consultant, adventurer; b. Apr. 5, 1966; Undergraduate degree, U. Ariz.; MBA, Duke U., 2000. Positions in sales and mktg. in the healthcare industry in US and Asia, 1989—2000; with Goldman Sachs, 2000—03; founder, pres. Daredevil Strategies, San Francisco, 2003—. Dep. fin. dir. for Arnold Schwarzenegger, 2003; invited spkr. Guest appearences on Today Show, CNN, CNBC, Fox ABC News, CBS Evening News and other nat. programs, subject of articels in Oprah Mag., National Geographic, Lifetime Mag., Sports Illustrated Women, Outside and other publications, host of blog womenclimbhigh.spaces.inc.com, featured in More Than 85 Broads, Smart Moves; performer: The Vagina Monologues, Calif. Theater, 2005. Participant North Pole Leadership Challenge, 2004; founder The Climb High Found., 2005—; founding mem. World Wildlife Fund's Young Partners in Conservation. Named one of San Francisco's Top Bus. Leaders Under 40, Arizona's Most Interesting People; recipient Courage in Sports award, Anaheim Angels, 2003. Mem.: Assn. of Women MBAS, 85 Broads (co-chair). Achievements include climbing mountains in 1998 after a second heart surgery to repair a life threatening condition called Wolff Parkinson White Syndrome; serving as team captain of the first American Women's Everest Expedition in 2002; climbed highest peaks on six continents-Kilimanjaro, Aconcagua, Elbrus, Carstensz Pyramid, McKinley and Vinson, also Rainier, Muir, Whitney and Shasta, Cotopaxi (Ecuador), Ixta and Orizaba (Mexico); skied more than 100 miles to reach the top of the world-the North Pole; created Climb High Foundation for improving the lives of jobless women in third-world countries by training them to be trekking guides or porters for the local mountains; involvment in Western Uganda was groundbreaking because it was the first time the local women had climbed mountains because it was forbidden due to cultural beliefs (subordinate status of women); raised funds to build two schools in Nepal; helped to fund the construction of a school for AIDS orphans in Uganda. Avocations: mountaineering, adventure travel, philanthropy, women's initiatives, theater, reading. Office: Daredevil Strategies 1538 Filbert St #4 San Francisco CA 94123 Office Phone: 415-595-3966. Business E-Mail: alison@daredevilstrategies.com.*

LEVINE, ALLISON, psychotherapist; b. Bayshore, NY, Apr. 26, 1955; d. Leonard and Barbara Wexler; m. Martin Smietanka, Mar. 4, 1990; children: Kayla Smietanka, Tali Smietanka. BA, Ind. U., Bloomington, 1977; MA, Pepperdine U., Culver City, Calif., 1991. Psychotherapist pvt. practice, Sherman Oaks, Calif. Fellow, Wright Inst. L.A., 1992—94. Mem.: Am. Coll. Forensic Examiners (diplomate), Am. Psychotherapy Assn. (diplomate). Avocations: camping, hiking. Office: 14622 Ventura Blvd #327 Sherman Oaks CA 91403-3600

LEVINE, AUDREY PEARLSTEIN, foundation administrator; b. NYC, July 6, 1934; d. Irving and Flora Malkin Pearlstein; m. Arthur Levine, Mar. 15, 1958; children: Michael S., Charles T., Andrew S. Student, Hofstra U., 1952, student, 1957. Sec., treas. Pearlstein Found., 1976—; gen. ptnr. Adams County Realty LLP, McSherrystown, Pa., 2003—. Specialist trade shows Stone Care Internat. Inc., Owings Mills, Md., 1991—; adminstr., gen. ptnr. Pearlstein Partnership, Palm Beach, Fla., 1998—; gen. ptnr. Audrey Realty, Pikesville, Md., 2003—07. V.p. PTA Ft. Garrison Sch., Pikesville, Md., 1968—69; chmn. Hadassah Ho. & Garden Tour, Balt., Palm Beach, 1969, 1970, 1999, Booster Club Pikesville H.S., Pikesville, 1970, 1971, 1975—76, 1980—82; v.p. PTA Pikesville Sr. H.S., Pikesville, 1970, 1976, 1980—82; v.p. parents-student bd. Am. U., Washington, 1978—79, 1984—86; chmn. Save Ft. Garrison, Pikesville, 1965—66, 2001; mem. com. Senator Henry Jackson Save Soviet Jews, Washington, 1972—73; v.p. Jewish Nat. Fund Women, Balt., 1973—75; pres. Balt. (Md.) Suburban Hadassah, 1963—64; dedication chmn. Jerusalem stone wall for peace and freedom and for victims of 9-11 Har Sinai Congregation, Owings Mills, 2005; bd. dirs. Women's Aux. Sinai Hosp., Balt., 1985—88, Nat. Coun. Johns Hopkins, Balt., 1990—92, Pikesville Recreation Coun., Pikesville, 1968—71; chmn. Rededication of Fort Garrison, Pikesville, Md. Mem.: Nat. Mus. Women in the Arts (charter). Republican. Jewish. Avocations: sculpting, painting, flower arranging, boating, tennis. Home (Winter): Bldg 1 Apt 2A 2500 S Ocean Blvd Palm Beach FL 33480 Home (Summer): 3421 Garrison Farms Rd Pikesville MD 21208 Office: Audrey Levine Trust 2500 S Ocean Blvd Apt 1a2 Palm Beach FL 33480-5401 Personal E-mail: levineaa@aol.com.

LEVINE, ELAINE PRADO, psychologist, music educator, artist, small business owner; b. Inglewood, Calif., Feb. 16, 1962; d. John Franklin, Jr. and Carolyn Mae (Cable) Walter; m. Paul David Prado, Mar. 2, 1985 (div. 1994); children: Paul David Prado, Lauren Mae Prado; m. Leonard Ralph Levine, Jan. 8, 2000 (dec. May 2001); m. Jonathan Walter Achtemeier, May 31, 2005. BA in Music Composition and Theory, Flute, UCLA, 1986; MA in Edn. Counseling, Calif. State U., 1999. Tchr. multiple subjects Torrance (Calif.) Unified Sch. Dist., 1994-96, tchr. music, dir. band and choir, 1996-99, counselor, 1999-00; sch. psychologist Hemet (Calif.) Unified Sch. Dist., 2000—02, Palm Springs (Calif.) Unified Sch. Dist., 2002—04; music tchr., dir. band and choir Temecula Valley Unified Sch. Dist., 2003—04; pres., CEO J&E Long Haul Transp., Inc., 2004—. Part-time asst. prof. Calif. State U., Dominguez Hills, 1999—2000; prodr., dir., pub. Prado Prodn. and Publ., Hemet, 2000—. Author: He Always Goes First!, 1998; prodr., dir. (CD) Dreams of the Jaguar, 1999. Sec., faculty rep. Jefferson Sch. Site Coun., Torrance, 1998—99. Mem.: SAG, Owner Operators Ind. Drivers Assn., Nat. Assn. Ind. Truckers, Wiseburn Faculty Assn. (scholar 1985), So. Calif. Vocal Assn., Calif. Tchrs. Assn., Calif. Assn. Sch. Psychologists, Nat. Assn. Sch. Psychologists, UCLA Alumni Assn., Phi Kappa Phi. Avocations: tennis, skiing, swimming, travel, gardening. Home and Office: Long Haul Transp Inc 4340 State Hwy 74 Ste F-289 Hemet CA 92544 Office Phone: 951-663-9762. E-mail: elaine@jnelonghaul.com.

LEVINE, ELLEN R., editor-in-chief; b. NYC, Feb. 19, 1943; d. Eugene Jack and Jean (Zuckman) Jacobson; m. Richard U. Levine, Dec. 21, 1964; children: Daniel, Peter. Student, Wellesley Coll. Reporter The Record, Hackensack, NJ, 1964—70; editor Cosmopolitan mag., NYC, 1976—82; editor-in-chief Cosmopolitan Living mag., NYC, 1980—81, Woman's Day mag., NYC, 1982—91, Redbook mag., NYC, 1991—94, Good Housekeeping, NYC, 1994—2006; editorial cons. O, The Oprah Mag., 2000—; editl. dir. Hearst Magazines, NYC, 2006—. Commr. U.S. Atty. Gen.'s Commn. on Pornography, 1985—86; bd. dirs. Finlay Enterprises, Inc., Lifetime TV; bd. adv. NY Women in Comm.; bd. dir. Gaylord Entertainment, 2004—. Author: Planning Your Wedding, Waiting for Baby, Rooms That Grow With Your Child; mem. editl. bd. O mag.; contbr. articles to profl. jours. Bd. dirs. Lifetime TV, Christopher Reeve Paralysis Found., NY Restoration Project. Named to Writers Hall of Fame, 1981, Acad. Women Achievers, YWCA, 1982; recipient Outstanding Profl. Achievement award, N.J. Fedn. Women's Clubs, 1984, Matrix award, N.Y. Women in Comm., Inc., 1989, Am. Health Found., 1996, 2d Century award, Columbia U. Sch. Nursing, 1997, Nat. Mag. award for personal svc., 1999. Mem.: Am. Soc. Mag. Editors (named to Hall of Fame). Achievements include being first woman named editor-in-chief of Good Housekeeping. Office: Hearst Magazines 959 8th Ave New York NY 10019 E-mail: elevine@hearst.com.*

LEVINE, FELICE, educational association administrator; AB in Psychology, U. Chgo., AM in Sociology and Psychology, PhD in Psychology. Sr. rsch. social scientist Am. Bar Found., 1974—79; program dir. NSF, 1979—91; exec. officer Am. Sociol. Assn., Washington, 1991—2002; exec. dir. Am. Ednl. Rsch. Assn., Washington, 2002—. Mem. nat. human rsch. protections adv. com. U.S. Dept. Health and Human Svcs., co-chair social and behavioral sci. working group; exec. com. Consortium of Social Sci. Assns., chair, 1997—2000; mem. adv. com. Decennial Census; bd. mem. Nat. Humanities Alliance; mem. adv. com. Nat. Consortium of Violence Rsch. Fellow: AAAS, Am. Psychol. Soc. Office: Am Ednl Rsch Assn 1230 Seventeenth St NW Washington DC 20036

LEVINE, IRENE S., journalist, psychologist; d. Joseph and Helen Waldman; m. Jerome Levine, Apr. 12, 1982; 1 child, Andrew R. BA, Queens Coll. CUNY, 1968; PhD in Clin. Psychology, St. John's U., Jamaica, NY, 1981. Dir. office programs homeless NIMH, Rockville, Md., 1979—92; dep. dir. U.S. Ctr. Mental Health Svcs., Rockville, 1992—94; commn. dir., rsch. scientist Nathan Kline Inst. Psychiat. Rsch., Orangeburg, NY, 1994; prof. psychiatry N.Y. U. Sch. Medicine, 1994—. Freelance journalist. Fellow, HEW, 1978. Mem.: Authors Guild, Nat. Assn. Sci. Writers, Am. Med. Writers Assn., Assn. Healthcare Journalists, Am. Soc. Journalists and Authors. Home: 15 Stony Hollow Chappaqua NY 10514 Office Phone: 845-398-6503. E-mail: Irene@IreneLevine.com.

LEVINE, JANICE R., clinical psychologist; b. Cleve., Mar. 4, 1954; d. Bennett and Lenore (Tracht) L.; m. Brian Richard Igoe, Aug. 31, 1980; children: Brennan Joseph, Sarah Ann. BA cum laude, Yale U., 1976; MA, Harvard U., 1979, PhD, 1983. Lic. psychologist, Mass. Sr. ptnr., cons. Cambridge Consortium, Mass.; staff psychologist Ayer Clinic, Mass.; lectr.

psychology Harvard U., Cambridge, Mass. Sch. Profl. Psychology, Boston; pvt. practice clin. psychologist Lexington, Mass. Lectr., pub. speaker, workshop leader, cons. in field. Author: (book) The Couples' Health Program; co-author: (books) Beyond the Chuppah, 2000, (with Howard Markman) Why Do Fools Fall in Love, 2001. Founder Third Thursday Parent Edn. Series, Lexington, dir.; bd. dirs. Terezin Chamber Music Found. Margaret Yardley fellow, 1980, Devel. Trainee fellow NIH, 1978-79. Mem. APA, MPA. Office: 76 Bedford St Ste 19 Lexington MA 02420-4640

LEVINE, MADELINE GELTMAN, literature and language educator, translator; b. N.Y.C., Feb. 23, 1942; d. Herman and Nettie (Kritman) Geltman; m. Steven I. Levine; children: Elaine, Daniel. BA, Brandeis U., 1962; MA, Harvard U., 1964, PhD, 1971. Asst. prof. Grad Sch. CUNY, N.Y.C., 1971-74; assoc. prof. U. N.C., Chapel Hill, 1974-80, prof., 1980-94, Kenan prof. Slavic lits., 1994—, chmn. dept. Slavic langs., 1979-87, 94-99. Chmn. joint com. on Ea. Europe, Am. Coun. Learned Socs.-Social Sci. Rsch. Coun., 1989-92; chmn. bd. govs. U. N.C. Press, 1999-2005. Translator: A Memoir of the Warsaw Uprising (Miron Bialoszewski), 1977, 2d edit. 1991, The Poetry of Osip Mandelstam: God's Grateful Guest (Ryszard Przybylski), 1987, Beginning With My Streets: Essays and Recollections (Czeslaw Milosz), 1992, A Year of the Hunter (Czeslaw Milosz), 1994, Bread for the Departed (Bogdan Wojdowski), 1997, Lost Landscapes: In Search of Isaac Bashevis Singer and the Jews of Poland (Agata Tuszynska), 1998, Milosz's ABCs (Czeslaw Milosz), 2001, The Woman from Hamburg and Other True Stories, (Hanna Krall), 2005, Legends of Modernity: Essays and Letters From Occupied Poland, 1942-1943, 2005; translator with Francine Prose: A Scrap of Time and Other Stories (Ida Fink), 1986, 2d edit., 1995; author: Contemporary Polish Poetry, 1925-75, 1981; co-editor (with Bogdana Carpenter): To Begin Where I Am: Selected Essays (Czeslaw Milosz), 2001. NEH fellow, 1984, 2000; recipient (with Francine Prose) award for lit. translation PEN-America, 1988. Mem. Am. Assn. for Advancement of Slavic Studies, Polish Inst. of Arts and Scis. Am., Am. Assn. Tchrs. of Slavic and East European Langs., Am. Literary Translators Assn., Pen-Am. Home: 5001 Whitehorse Rd Hillsborough NC 27278-9399 Office: U NC CB # 3165 425 Dey Hall Chapel Hill NC 27599-3165 Office Phone: 919-962-7553. Business E-Mail: mgl@unc.edu.

LEVINE, MARILYN MARKOVICH, lawyer, arbitrator; b. Bklyn., Aug. 9, 1930; d. Harry P. and Fannie L. (Hymowitz) Markovich; m. Louis L. Levine, June 24, 1950; children: Steven R., Ronald J., Linda J. Morgenstern. BS summa cum laude, Columbia U., 1950; MA, Adelphi U., 1957; JD, Hofstra U., 1977. Bar: NY 1978, U.S. Dist. Ct. (no. and ea. dists.) NY 1978, DC 1979, U.S. Supreme Ct. 1982. Sole practice, Valley Stream, NY, 1978—. Panel arbitrator Retail Food Industry, NYC, 1980—; arbitrator NY Dist. Cts., Nassau County, 1981—; contract arbitrator Bldg. Svc. Industry, NYC, 1982—. Panel arbitrator Suffolk County Pub. Employee Rels. Bd., 1979—, Nassau County Pub. Employee Rels. Bd., 1980—, Nat. Mediation Bd., 1986—; mem. adv. coun. Ctr. Labor and Indsl. Rels. NY Inst. Tech., 1985—; counsel Nassau Civic Club, 1978—. Mem.: ABA, Nat. Acad. Arbitrators, Fed. Mediation Bd. (arbitrator 1980—), Am. Arbitration Assn. (arbitrator 1979—), NJ Bd. Mediation (panel arbitrator), Nassau County Bar Assn., DC Bar Assn., NY State Bar Assn.

LEVINE, NAOMI BRONHEIM, academic administrator; b. N.Y.C., Apr. 15, 1923; d. Nathan and Malvina (Mermelstein) Bronheim; m. Leonard Levine, Apr. 11, 1948; 1 child, Joan. BA, Hunter Coll., 1944; LLB, Columbia, 1946, JD, 1970. Bar: N.Y. 1946. With Scaadrett, Tuttle & Chalaire, N.Y.C., 1946-48, Charles Gottleib, N.Y.C., 1948-50, Am. Jewish Congress, 1950-78, exec. dir., 1972-78; v.p. to sr. v.p. external affairs NYU, N.Y.C., 1978—2002, spl. advisor to pres., 2002—; chmn., dir. Heyman Ctr. for Philanthropy and Fund Raising, 2002—. Asst. prof. law and police sci. John Jay Coll., N.Y.C., 1969—73, L.I. U., 1965—69. Author: (book) Schools in Crisis, 1969, The Jewish Poor-an American Awakening, 1974, Politics, Religion and Love, 1990; mem. editl. bd. Columbia Law Rev., 1945—46; author: For Her Days Not Her Nights. Chmn. N.Y.U. Bronfman Ctr., N.Y.U. Ctr. for Israeli Studies; com. on character and fitness N.Y. Supreme Ct.; co-chair Taub Ctr. for Israel Studies, NYU; bd. dirs. N.Y. Ctr. Philanthropy and Fund Raising. Named to Hunter Coll. Hall of Fame, 1972; recipient NY U. Presdl. medal, 2005. Office: NYU 29 Washington Square West New York NY 10011 Office Phone: 212-998-2380, 212-998-2384.

LEVINE, PAMELA, film company executive; Pres. Marketcast, 1985—95; sr. v.p. mkting., planning and rsch. Twentieth Century Fox Film Corp., 1995—2002, co-pres. domestic theatrical mktg. LA, 2002—. Office: Twentieth Century Fox Film Corp 10201 W Pico Blvd Los Angeles CA 90035 Office Phone: 310-277-2211. Office Fax: 310-203-1558.*

LEVINE, PEGGY AYLSWORTH, psychotherapist, poet, writer; b. Newark, May 2, 1921; d. Roscoe Nichols and Helen (Dorsen) Aylsworth; m. Samuel Schultz, Mar. 29, 1950 (div. 1979); children: Christie Romero, Ronald M. Schultz; m. Norman Philip Levine, Sept. 20, 1986. BA in Psychology, Lindenwood Coll., 1977; MA in Psychology, Antioch West Coll., L.A., 1978. Rschr. Carl Byoir & Assocs., N.Y.C., 1941-43; rsch. editor True Mag., Fawcett Publs., N.Y.C., 1944-45; adminstr. Valley Ctr. of Arts, Encino, Calif., 1966-69; pub. rels. dir. Comsky Gallery, L.A., 1970; pvt. practice psychotherapy Santa Monica, Calif., 1980—. Author: (children's album) The Glooby Game, 1949, (poetry) Letters to the Same Address, 1989, Along These Lines, 1995, Small Lightning, 2006, (novels) Morning in the Long Night City, 1992, Among These Several, 1996 (pub. on 1st books website 2001), This Water, This Dry Land, 2003; exhibited art boxes, Howell Green Fine Art Gallery, 2001, (collage) Mini Collage books, 2005; contbr. poems to various mags., revs. V.p. Valley Ctr. of Arts, 1956-57, publicity dir., 1955-65; publicity dir. Alliance for Survival, Santa Monica, 1979-81. Avocations: reading, ephemera and stamp collecting, reading plays, photography, art. Office Phone: 310-399-0976. Personal E-mail: poetsrx@webtv.net.

LEVINE, RUTH HANNAH, retired sculptor; b. Bronx, N.Y., Feb. 5, 1915; d. Harry and Tillie Blum; m. Philip Levine; children: Howard A., Michael, Maxine Franklin. Student, Lowell Tech. Inst., Mus. Sch., Boston, Internat. Barkhardt Akademia, Italy; studied with George Aarons, Peter Abate, Arthur Roberts. Sculptor, Rome, 1965; tchr. sculpture Whistler House, Lowell, 1964-68. One man shows include Lexington Arts and Crafts Soc., 1968, Lowell City Libr., Showcase Cinemas, 1968—; group exhbns. include Lowell Art Assn. (1st prize 1962, 64, 68), Weeden Gallery, Prudential, Boston, MIT, Loeb Drama, Harvard Coop., Concord Art Assn., 1966-68, So. Vt. Arts Ctr., Cape Cod Art Assn. (honorable mention 1967), Addison Gallery, Springfield Mus., Winterfest, Boston, Pittsfield Mus., Candle Art Gallery, Nantucket, Marblehead Art Assn., Wayside Inn, Newport Art Assn., New Bedford Festival, Nat. Iron and Steel, Washington, 1966, Chapman Gallery, N.Y.C. Mem. New England Sculptors Assn. (pub. chmn. 1968, 1st prize 1997), Lowell Art Assn. (bd. dirs., festival chmn. 1966), Cambridge Art Assn., Lexington Arts and Crafts Soc., Concord Art Assn., So. Vt. Arts Ctr., Cape Cod Art Assn. Avocations: flower arranging, golf, aerobics.

LEVINE, SARA POLLAK, psychology professor; b. Atlanta, June 24, 1970; d. Pollak Ira Edward and Faith Pollak Karen; m. Steven Howard Levine, June 29, 1996; children: Eli Lewis, Ariel Shoshana. BA, Brandeis U., 1992; MS, U. Mass., 1995, PhD, 1998. Coll. prof. Hampshire Coll., Amherst, 1998—2000, Fitchburg (Mass.) State Coll., Fitchburg, Mass., 2000—. Office: Fitchburg State Coll 160 Pearl St Fitchburg MA 01420 Office Phone: 978-665-3611. Business E-Mail: slevine@fsc.edu.

LEVINE, SARAH LOEWENBERG, developmental psychologist, school director; b. N.Y. m. Randolph H. Levine, June 21, 1970; children: Seth Jason, Johanna Beth. BA, Sarah Lawrence Coll., 1968; EdM, Harvard U., 1977, EdD, 1980. Cert. tchr., adminstr., Mass. Grade head Shady Hill Sch., Cambridge, Mass., 1969-72; coord. career edn. Roxbury-Harvard Sch. Program, Cambridge, 1977-78; teaching fellow Grad. Sch. Edn. Harvard U., Cambridge, 1978-80; assoc. dir. Prins.'s Ctr. Principals' Ctr. Harvard U., Cambridge, 1983-89; dir. prins.'s cert., lectr. edn. Harvard U., Cambridge, 1984-89; lectr. Lesley Coll., Cambridge, 1980; rsch. assoc. Edn. Devel. Ctr., Newton, Mass., 1980-83; sch. head Belmont (Mass.) Day Sch., 1989—. Cons. in field. Author: Promoting Adult and Growth in Schools, 1989; contbr. articles to profl. jours. Mem. APA, ASCD, Nat. Staff Devel. Coun. (editorial bd. 1985—), NAt. Assn. Ind. Schs., Assn. Ind. Schs. New England. Avocations: exercise, reading, movies. Office: Belmont Day Sch 55 Day School Ln Belmont MA 02478-2030

LEVINE, SHERRIE, conceptual artist; b. Hazelton, Pa. BFA, U. Wis., 1969, MFA, 1973. Exhibitions include Newborn galerie deux Co., Ltd., Tokyo, 1995, Hiram Butler Gallery, Houston, 1995, 2003, Mus. Contemporary Art, LA, 1995, Galerie Jablonka, Cologne, Germany, 1996, Frac des Pays de la Loire, Nantes, France, 1996, Mus. Modern Art, NYC, 1996, 1999, 2000, 2001, Whitney Mus., 1996, Phila. Mus. Art, 1996, Mus. Fine Arts, Boston, 1996, Campbell-Thiebaud Gallery, San Francisco, 1997, Margo Leavin Gallery, LA, 1997, 1999, 2000, 2001, XXIV Bienal de Sao Paulo, 1998, Hamburger Kunstverein, Hamburg, 1998, Pitts. Ctr. for the Arts, Pitts., 1998, Mus. Ludwig, Cologne, 1998, Walker Art Ctr., Mpls., 1998, 2002, 2005, Whitechapel Art Gallery, London, 1999, Rena Bransten Gallery, NYC, 1999, Paula Cooper Gallery, 1999, 2000, 2002, Coll. New Rochelle, NJ, 2001, Getty Rsch. Inst., LA, 2001, Centre des Arts Saidye Bronfman, Montreal, 2002, MIT List Visual Arts Ctr., Cambridge, Mass., 2003, Faggionato Fine Arts, London, 2004, Bard Coll., Annandale-on-Houston, NY, 2005, numerous others. Office: c/o Paula Cooper Gallery 534 & 521 W 21st St 2d Floor New York NY 10011*

LEVINGS, CHRISTINE ROMANO, secondary school educator, real estate developer; b. Joliet, Ill., Mar. 4, 1956; d. Frank A. and Jessie A. Romano; m. Robert G. Levings, Aug. 9, 1975; children: Rachel M. Youngers, Christopher R., Emily M. BS, Stephen F. Austin State U., Nacogdoches, Tex., 1978; MEd, Nova Southeastern U., Fort Lauderdale, Fla., 2000. Cert. profl. educator Fla. Literacy coach Seminole County Pub. Schs., Sanford, Fla., 2001—. Sec. Lake Winnemissett Civic Assn., Deland, Fla., 2001—06; mem. Fla. Reading Coun., Sanford, 2004—06. Recipient Disney's Terrific Tchr. award, Walt Disney World, 2002. Mem.: Coun. on Gifted Edn., Internat. Reading Assn. Avocations: travel, triathlons. Office: Crooms Acad Info Tech 2200 W 13th St Sanford FL 32771 Office Phone: 407-320-5764. Personal E-mail: levings25@hotmail.com.

LEVINGS, THERESA LAWRENCE, lawyer; b. Kansas City, Mo., Oct. 24, 1952; d. William Youngs and Dorothy (Neer) Frick; m. Darryl Wayne Levings, May 25, 1974; children: Leslie Page, Kerry Dillon. BJ, U. Mo., 1973; JD, U. Mo., Kansas City, 1979. Bar: Mo. 1979, U.S. Dist. Ct. (we. dist.) Mo. 1979, U.S. Ct. Appeals (8th cir.) 1982, U.S. Ct. Appeals (10th cir.) 1986, U.S. Dist. Ct. (ea. dist.) Mo. 1989, U.S. Dist. Ct. Kans. 1995. Copy editor Kansas City Star, 1975-78; law clk. to judge Mo. Supreme Ct., Jefferson City, 1979-80; from assoc. to ptnr. Morrison & Hecker, Kansas City, 1980-94; founding ptnr. Badger & Levings, L.C., Kansas City, 1994—. Mem. fed. practice com. U.S. Dist. Ct. (we. dist.), 1990-95; mem. fed. adv. com. U.S. Ct. Appeals (8th cir.), 1994-97, Kans. 2006, U.S. Supreme Ct. 2006. Mem. ABA (house dels., 2006—), Mo. Bar (bd. govs. 1990—03, pres. 2001-02), Assn. Women Lawyers Greater Kansas City (pres. 1986-87, Woman of Yr. 1993), Kansas City Met. Bar Assn. (chair civil practice and procedure com. 1988-89, chair fed. practice com. 1990-91, Inns of Court (master 1996-2000, 2002-06). Office: Badger & Levings LC Ste 1920 920 Main St Kansas City MO 64105 Office Phone: 816-421-2828. Business E-Mail: tlevings@badgerlevings.com.

LEVINS, MARY CLARE, science educator; d. William George and Kathryn Rita Bahrt; m. Peter J. Levins, Dec. 17, 1972; children: Kathryn Marie, Ruth Ann. BS, Coll. Mt. St. Vincent, N.Y.C., 1967; MS, Seton Hall U., South Orange, N.J., 1971; MAT, Kean U., Union, N.J., 1973. Tchr. sci. Holy Trinity H.S., Westfield, NJ, 1967—72; tchr. and dept. chair sci. Union Cath. H.S., Scotch Plains, 1972—77; tchr. sci. St. Agnes Sch., Clark, 1986—2000; tchr. and dept. chair sci. St. Bartholomew Sch., Scotch Plains, 1985—. Tchr. sci. and summer coord. Oak Knoll Sch., Summit, NJ, 1991—95; participant Schering Plough Summer Inst., Kenilworth, 1998. Named Tchr. of Yr., Archdiocese of Newark, 1992. Mem.: Nat. Cath. Educators Assn., Nat. Sci. Tchrs. Assn., Coll. Club Scotch Plains (1st v.p., 2d v.p., sec.). Avocations: travel, needlecrafts. Home: 166 Burns Way Fanwood NJ 07023 Office: St Bartholomew Interparochial Scotch Plains NJ 07076 Office Phone: 908-322-4265.

LEVINSKY, FRIEDA LIBBY, language educator; b. Belz, Poland, Jan. 25, 1932; came to U.S., 1949; d. Moses and Esther Bodenstein; m. Ely S. Levinsky, May 24, 1953 (div. Oct. 1980); children: Steven A., Jeff L. BA in History and Spanish, San Diego State U., 1969, postgrad., 1972. Tchr. Clairemont Adult Sch., San Diego, 1960-61, 64-65; tchr. Spanish and English adult edn. program San Diego C.C. Dist., 1971-91; tutor Kate Sessions Elem. Sch., San Diego, 1991; tutor ESL La Jolla (Calif.) Elem. Sch., 1992. Owner rental units, San Diego, 1980-2006; appeared on KPBS radio sta., and TV Channel 8; tutor English U. Calif., San Diego, 1994; asst. judge poetry contest Women in Lit., 1999. Editor: Women, Gifted Gazette; contbr. over 250 poems to lit. publs.; editor Gifted Gazette, 1972-74; poem housed at Nat. Mus. Woman in Arts, Brandeis U., Stanford U., San Diego (Calif.) Pub. Libr.; publ. judge (poetry manuscript by Pat Clark) North of Wandering; author Enlightened Ambiance, 2006. Publicity chmn. North Shores chpt. B'nai B'righ Women, San Diego, 1974-78, chmn. adult edn. com., 1972-74; publicity chmn. Coun. Jewish Women, 1980-84; chmn. reporting com. San Diego Assn. Gifted Students, 1971-72; nat. women's com. Braindeis U., 1999; mem. Pacific Beach Town Coun. Recipient Golden Poet award World of Poetry, 1986, 87, 88, 90, 91, Mentor Poetry award N.Am. Mentor, Friendly Exch. cert. Farmers Ins. Mag., Prose award Dame Lit. Soc., award San Diego County Apt. Assn. Mem. Acad. Am. Poets, Poetry Assn. Am. (Honorable Mention award 1985), Poetry Soc. Am., Nat. Collegiate Fgn. Lang. Soc., Poets and Writers, Pacific Beach Town Coun., Adams Avenue Bus. Assn., Friends La Jolla (Calif.) Libr., The Atheaneum Libr., La Jolla Hist. Soc., Nat. Collegiate Fgn. Lang. Soc., Alpha Mu Gamma. Independent. Jewish.

LEVINSON, MARINA, information technology executive; arrived in US, 1980; BS in computer sci., Leningrad Inst. Precision Mechanics and Optics. Various positions with TRW, San Jose, Calif., Tandem Computers (now part of HewlettPackard), SpectralPhysics; sr. dir. global integration 3Com Corp., Mass.; v.p., CIO PalmOne Inc., Milpitas, Calif., 1999—. Named one of Premier 100 IT Leaders, Computerworld mag., 2004.

LEVINSON, RASCHA, psychotherapist; b. N.Y.C., Nov. 27, 1930; d. Frank Alfred and Goldye Dena (Preiser) Cohen; m. Monroe Louis Levinson, Oct. 6, 1955 (div. 1973); 1 child, Nadia Levinson Fogel. BA, NYU, 1960; MSW, Columbia U., 1962; Tng. in Hypnosis, Milton Erickson Soc., N.Y.C., 1992-93. Lic. social worker, N.Y. Pvt. practice, N.Y.C., 1970—. Psychotherapist Washington Sq. Inst., N.Y.C., 1973-74; intake therapist Women's Psychotherapy Referral Svcs., N.Y.C., 1973-76, co-pres., 1997-98; supr. psychotherapy Mid-Hudson Cons. Ctr., Wappinger Falls, N.Y., 1974-83; workshop leader New Sch. Social Rsch., N.Y.C., 1980-87. Fellow Soc. Clin. Social Workers (pres. Westchester chpt. 1986-88); mem. Assn. for Women in Psychology, N.Y.C. Coalition for Women's Mental Health (bd. dirs. 1986-89), Advanced Feminist Therapy Inst. (editor newsletter 1990-92). Avocations: writing, motorcycle riding, reading, movies. Office: 441 West End Ave Ste 1B New York NY 10024 also: 149 Central Dr # 3 Briarcliff Manor NY 10510 Office Phone: 914-941-0463.

LEVINSON, RIKI, art director; b. Bklyn. d. Samuel Eliezar and Anna Sarah (Blau) Friedberg; m. Morton Levinson. BA, Cooper Union Sch. Arts, N.Y., 1943. Graphic designer Riki Levinson Design Studio, N.Y.C., 1945-69; art dir. edn. div. Western Pub. Co., N.Y.C., 1970, dir. design, mfg. edn. div., 1970-72; art dir. E. P. Dutton Inc., N.Y.C., 1972-85; asst. pub., art dir. E.P. Dutton Inc., N.Y.C., 1986-87, assoc. pub., art dir., 1987-91; freelance cons. N.Y.C., 1991—95. Author: Watch the Stars Come Out, 1985, I Go With My Family to Grandma's, 1986, DinnieAbbieSister-r-r!, 1987, Touch! Touch!, 1987, Our Home is the Sea, 1988, Me Baby!, 1991, The Emperor's New Clothes (retelling), 1991, Country Dawn to Dusk, 1992, Boys Here--Girls There, 1992, Soon, Annala, 1993, Grandpa's Hotel, 1995. Fellow: Va. Ctr. Creative Arts.

LEVISAY, JOY ELICE, art educator; b. Hamlin, Tex., Feb. 4, 1955; d. William Grady and Mary Alice (Howle) Ferguson; m. Thomas Lloyd Levisay, July 22, 1978; children: Thomas Derek, Alyson Nichole, Jenna Racquel. BA, Howard Payne U., Brownwood, Tex., 1979. Cert. tchr. elem. edn. Tex., 1979. Tchr. kindergarten Bangs Ind. Sch. Dist., Tex., 1978—98, tchr. elem. fine arts, 1998—. Mem.: Delta Kappa Gamma. Home: PO Box 336 Bangs TX 76823 Office: Bangs Ind Sch Dist PO Box 969 Bangs TX 76823 Office Phone: 325-752-7236. Business E-Mail: joy.levisay@bangsisd.net.

LEVIT, HÉLOÏSE B. (GINGER LEVIT), art historian, journalist, art dealer, consultant; b. Phila., Apr. 2, 1937; d. Elmer and Claire Frances (Schwartz) Bertman; m. Jay Joseph Levit, July 14, 1962; children: Richard Bertman, Robert Edward, Darcy Francine Honker. BA in French Literature, U. Pa., 1959; MA in French Literature, U. Richmond, 1975; MA Art History, Va. Commonwealth U., Richmond, 1998; Cert., Alliance Française, Paris, 1991, Chambre de Commerce et d'Industrie de Paris, 1991, La Sorbonne, Paris, 1994, Istituto Lorenzo di Medici Firenze, Italy, 1996, Ecole du Louvre, 1998, Cert., 2005. Arts broadcaster, Richmond, Va., 1976-82; dir. Fine Arts Am., Inc., Richmond, 1982-84; tchr. Henrico County Pub. Schs., Richmond, 1984-88; dir. devel. Sta. WVST-FM Va. State U., Petersburg, 1987-88; mgr., dir. devel. Richmond Philharm. Orch., 1988-99; fine arts and media cons. Art-I-Facts, Richmond, 1988—; cons., 1997-98. Author: Moments, Monuments & Monarchs, 1986 (Star award, 1986); arts writer: Richmond Rev., 1989—90, Mid Atlantic Antiques mag., Mid-Atlantic Antiques News, Washington Jewish Week, Tidewater Women, Va. Jewish News; anchor, prodr. (syndicated radio series) Va. Arts Report, 1978—83, Va. Women, 1984. V.p. Va. Mus. Collectors Cir., Richmond, 1986-91, mem. steering com.; pres. Richmond Area Dem. Women's Club, 1992-93; mem. Va. Mus. Coun., Richmond; rec. sec. Richmond Symphony Orch. League, 1998-2000, dir. pub. rels., 2000—, guest condr., 2000. Mem. Va. Press Women (2d pl. award 2001, 02, 03), U. Pa. Alumni Club (v.p. 1980-90, Ben Franklin award 1990), Am. Symphony Orch. League, L'Accueil Francais, Alliance Francaise, La Table Francaise (chmn. 1996—), World Affairs Coun. Avocations: antiques, art collecting, classical music, travel. Home and Office: Art-I-Facts 419 Dellbrooks Pl Richmond VA 23238-5559 Office Phone: 804-740-1471. Business E-Mail: ginger@vcu.org.

LEVITAS, MIRIAM C. STRICKMAN, documentary filmmaker; b. Aug. 3, 1936; d. Morris and Bella (Barsky) Cherrin; m. Bernard Strickman, June 3, 1956 (dec. Jan. 1975); children: Andrew, Brian, Craig, Deron; m. Theodore Clinton Levitas, Apr. 25, 1976; children: Steven, Leslie, Anthony. Student, Temple U., 1953-56; studied interior design, LaSalle U., Chgo., 1968; cert. in gerontology/cmty. svc., Ga. State U., 1988. Intergenerational Connections Contact State of Ga., 1989—. V.p. programming interior design Nat. Home Fashions League, Atlanta, 1974—75, Ga. Bd. Realtors, 1971—; founding adminstr. Stanley H. Kaplan Ednl. Ctr., Atlanta, 1974—84; owner, pres. Levitas Svcs. Inc. (Internat. Destinations), Atlanta, 1984—85; owner, v.p. Nat. Travel Svcs. and Internat. Destinations, Atlanta, 1984—85; realtor Philip White Properties Inc./Sotheby's Internat. Realty, 1985—91, Coldwell Banker Previews, 1991—; intergenerational programs and events cons.; interior designer for loft living. Solo pianist: Paul Whiteman TV, Radio City Music Hall, Phila. Youth Orch., Frankford Symphony Orch., 1950, condr.: Atlanta Symphony Orch., 1962, condr. TV spl.: Salute to Am.; prodr.(host cmty. svc. videos TV cable broadcast):, 1988—91. Pres. Ahavath Achim Sisterhood, Atlanta, 1977—79, 1996—98; bd. dirs. Jewish Family Svcs., 1993—96; bd. dirs. Atlanta chpt. Nat. Osteoporosis Found., 1990—91, Outings in the Park, 1989—91; chmn., coord. Tea at the Ritz Scottish Rite Children's Med. Ctr., 1987—90; chmn. women's divsn. Israel Bond, Atlanta, 1987, 1988, 1989, mem. aux.; chmn., coord. Who's Bringing in the Great Chefs Scottish Rige Children's Med. Ctr., 1990, 1991, 1992; mem. Atlanta Symphony, High Mus. Art, Nat. Mus. of Women in Arts, William Bremen Jewish Heritage Mus., Alliance Theater Atlanta, Atlanta Hist. Ctr.-Atlanta Hist. Soc., Alliance No. Dist. Dental Soc.; charter mem. U.S. Holocaust Mus.; bd. dirs. Jewish Ednl. Loan Fund, 2001—; nat. bd. advisors Brevard Mus. Ctr., 1993—. Named Woman of Achievement, Atlanta Jewish Fedn., 1993; scholar, Phila. Bd. Edn. Music, 1952. Mem.: NAFE, Nat. Assn. Realtors, Image Film and Video Ctr., Am. Women in Radio and TV, Women in Film (Atlanta chpt.), Internat. Furnishings and Design Assn., Spl. Children of the South (chmn. 1991—93), Atlanta Bd. Realtors, Ga. Gerontology Soc., Scots (life), B'nai Brith (life), Nat. Coun. Jewish Women (life), Hadassah (life), Brandeis Nat. Women (life), Ga. Dental Assn. Aux., Children's Med. Ctr. Aux. Office Phone: 404-431-9846. Personal E-mail: mslprod2@biltmorecomm.com.

LEVITEN, RIVA SHAMRAY, artist; b. L.A., Oct. 26, 1928; d. Peter Leo and Edythe (Smith) Shamray; m. Paul Leviten, Oct. 15, 1950 (dec. Oct. 19, 1988); children: Priscilla Leviten Warner, Marcia Leviten, Peter Leviten. BS in Apparel Design, UCLA, 1950; postgrad., Cal Arts, L.A., 1949-50, Exptl. Etching Studio, Boston, 1980-90. 1st v.p. R.I. chpt. Nat. Mus. Women in the Arts, 1997-99. Visual Rev. Bd. Newport Rev., 1997-98, R.I. Women Speak, Nat. Mus. Women in the Arts, Crone elderwoman, 1997, Monotype Printmaking and Painting Travel Show, 1998—; represented in collections at R.I. Sch. Design Mus., Danforth Mus., Slater Mus., El Paso Mus., Midwest Mus. Am. Art, Mass. Coll. Art, R.I. Coll., Tougaloo Coll., U. Ark., Marist Coll., Muscatine Art Ctr., Laura Musser Mus. Dickenson State U., Art in Embassies U.S. Dept. State, Saginaw Art Mus.; exhibited Russia, Australia, Mex., Can. Founding mem. Gallery of Social and Polit. Justice, Boston, 1996—. Recipient Herbert Cross prize South County Art Assn., Kingston, R.I., 1979. Founding mem. Showcase for Collage; elected artist mem. Mystic Art Assn.; mem. Providence Art Club, Monotype Guild of New Eng., Providence Art Club (Providence Art Club award 1998, J. Bannigan Sullivan award 1995, Bradford Swan award 1987), Nat. Assn. Women Artists (Martha Reed award 1994). Avocations: urban gardening, interior design, poetry, innkeeping, public speaking at art symposiums. Home and Office: 425 Benefit St Providence RI 02903-2933

LEVITT, B. BLAKE, writer, medical writer; b. Bridgeport, Conn., Mar. 25, 1948; d. John Joseph and Beatrice Blake; m. Andrew Levitt, Dec. 20, 1968 (div. May 1977); m. Jon P. Garvey, Nov. 19, 1983. BA in English magna cum laude, Quinnipiac Coll., 1972, BA in History summa cum, 1972; postgrad., Yale U., New Haven, 1988. Instr. English as fgn. lang. U. Khon Kaen, Thailand, 1968-69; market researcher Lyons Bakeries Ltd., London, summer 1971; traffic mgr., copywriter Provocatives Advt. Agy., Danbury, Conn., 1976-78; tech. writer tng. divsn. Jack Morton Prodns., N.Y.C., 1978-82; freelance feature and med. writer Litchfield County Times, New Milford, Conn., 1982-85, N.Y. Times, N.Y.C., 1985-89; freelance writer med. and sci. books, 1989—. Author: Electromagnetic Fields: A Consumer's Guide to the Issues and How to Protect Ourselves, 1995 (Will Solimene Book Award of Excellence 1996), 50 Essential Things to Do When the Doctor Says It's Infertility, 1995; co-author: (with John R. Sussman M.D.) Before You Conceive, The Complete Pre-Pregnancy Guide, 1989 (Will Solimene Book Award of Excellence 1991); editor: Cell Towers-Wireless Convenience? or Environmental Hazard? Proceedings of the Cell Towers Forum, State of the Sci./State of the Law, 2001; contbr. articles to N.W. Hills Mag., New Eng. Monthly, Con. Mag., Orion Afield; contbr. chpt. to book. Founding mem., bd. dirs. Warren (Conn.) Land Trust, 1989-91, Lake Watch, Inc., Lake Watch Ednl. Inst., 1996-2004; mem. exec. com. Berkshire-Litchfield Environ. Coun., 1999—; mem. Dem. Town Com., Warren, 1993—; vice chmn. zoning bd. appeals Town of Warren, 1993-95. Mem.: Nat. Assn. Sci. Writers, Bioelectromagnetics Soc., NY Acad. Scis., Am. Med. Writers Assn., Author's Guild, Author's League. Avocations: architecture, reading, hiking, gardening.

LEVITT, MIRIAM, pediatrician; b. Lampertheim, Germany, June 10, 1946; came to U.S., 1948; d. Eli and Esther (Kingston) L.; m. Harvey Flisser, June 25, 1967; children: Adam, Elizabeth, Eric. AB, NYU, 1967; MD, Yeshiva U.,

1971. Diplomate Am. Bd. Pediatrics. Intern Montefiore Med. Ctr., Bronx, N.Y., 1970-71, resident in pediatrics, 1971-73, attending pediatrician, 1975—; instr. pediatrics Albert Einstein Coll. Medicine, N.Y.C., 1973-76, asst. prof. clin., 1976—; med. staff Lawrence Hosp., Bronxville, NY, 1978—, dir. pediatrics, 1988—2003, pres. med. staff, 2002—05, mem. bd. govs., 2002—05; med. dir. Bronxville Sch. Dist., 2003—. Sch. physician Bronxville Bd. Edn., 1983—; mem. faculty coun. faculty of medicine health scis. divsn. Columbia U., 2002—04. Expert office profl. med. conduct N.Y. State Dept. Health, 1996—. Named Hon. Founder, Albert Einstein Coll. Medicine, 1995, hon. founder, 1995—. Fellow Am. Acad. Pediatrics; mem. Westchester County Med. Soc., Albert Einstein Coll. Medicine Alumni Assn. (nat. bd. govs. 1999—2005). Office: 1 Pondfield Rd Bronxville NY 10708-3706

LEVITZ, I. S., artist, educator, curator; b. Bklyn., Aug. 24, 1943; d. Irving Jacob and Mary (Matts) Steiner; m. Martin N. Levitz, June 19, 1965; children: Robin, David, Jodi. Grad., Vesper George Sch. Art, Boston, 1965; student, Trinity Coll., Hartford, 1970—72, Hartford Art Sch., 1975—77; grad. student, Wesleyan U., Middletown, Conn., 1978—79. Artist-in-residence Brandeis U. Women's Commn.,1994. Juried exhibits include Mattatuck Mus. "Conn. Vision", 1992, Silvermine Guild, Norwalk, Conn., 1983, New Britain Mus. Am. Art, 1982, 85, 87, 90, Conn. Acad. Fine Arts, 1988-91, 95, 96, Three Women Artists - Chase Freedom Gallery, Hartford Jewish Ctr., 1994, Women in the Arts, Wave Gallery, New Haven, 1995, Yale-New Haven Hosp. The Arts in Health Care, 1995. Vol. Toys for Tots, Bloomfield, 1989-92; active Hartford Arts Coun., 1976; chmn. Ann Randall Arts Com., 1978-80. Recipient Garfield award New Haven Paint and Clay 1982, Purchase award Town of Bloomfield, 1991. Mem. West Hartford Art League (chmn. selection com. for exhbns. 1983-84), Conn. Watercolor Soc.(mem.), Conn. Acad. Fine Arts (bd. dirs. 1995-96), New Britain Mus. Am. Art. Avocations: hiking, skiing, ice skating, travel, family. Office: 27 Arts Center Lane Avon CT 06001 Office Phone: 860-805-7238. E-mail: info@islevitz.com.

LEVY, CHARLOTTE LOIS, law librarian, educator, lawyer; b. Cin., Aug. 31, 1944; d. Samuel M. and Helen (Lowitz) Levy; m. Herbert Regenstreif, Dec. 11, 1980; 1 child, Cara Rachael Regenstreif. BA, U. Ky., 1966; MS, Columbia U., 1969; JD, No. Ky. U., 1975. Bar: Colo. 1979, NY 1985, Ky. 1985, U.S. Ct. Appeals (6th cir.) 1986. Law libr. No. Ky. U., 1971—75; law libr., assoc. prof. law Pace U., 1975—77; mgr. Fred B. Rothman & Co., Littleton, Colo., 1977—79; law libr., prof. Bklyn. Law Sch., 1979—85; adj. prof. Pratt Inst. Grad. Sch. Libr. and Info. Sci., 1982—85; atty. Cabinet for Human Resources, Frankfurt, Ky., 1985—87; atty., pres. Vantage Info. Cons., Inc., Frankfurt, 1983—. Cons. to various librs., pubs. Author: The Human Body and the Law, 1974 (Am. Jurisprudence Book award in domestic rels., 1974, in trusts, 1975), 2d edit., 1983, Computer-Assisted Litigation Support, 1984; mem. editl. bd.: No. Ky. U. Law Rev., 1974—75. 1st v.p. Ohavay Zion Synagogue; pres. bd. trustees Syncopated, Inc. Mem.: ABA, Fayette County Bar Assn., Ky. Bar Assn., Am. Assn. Law Librs. (cert. law libr.). Democrat. Jewish. Home: 7325 Indian Hill Rd Cincinnati OH 45243-4021

LEVY, DARA MICHELE, secondary school educator; b. L.A., Sept. 30, 1976; d. Steven Robert and Miriam Ruth Levy. BS in Biochem. and Cell Biology, U. Calif., La Jolla, 1997; MS in Biol. Scis., Stanford U., Calif., 2000. Tchr. Fremont Union High Sch. Dist., Cupertino, Calif., 2001—. Participant, master tchr. Fulbright Meml. Fund, 2003; participant Santa Clara County Biotech. Edn. Partnership, San Jose, Calif., 2002—. Mem.: Nat. Orgn. Sci. Tchrs.

LEVY, ELLEN J., writer, educator; d. Seymour and Virginia Mae (Riggs) Levy. BA magna cum laude, Yale U., 1986; MFA, Ohio State U., 2002. Editor, founder Common Lang. Newspaper, Taos, N.Mex., 1988—90; mng. editor Ind. Film and Video Mag., N.Y.C., 1991—93; dir. outreach Amigos Bravos: Friends of Rivers, Taos, 1997—99; asst. prof. Am. U., Washington, 2003—. Vis. asst. prof. Colo. Coll., Colorado Springs, 2002. Editor: Tasting Life Twice, 1995 (Lambda Lit. award, 1995); contbr. articles to popular mags. Co-coord. media Lesbian Avengers, N.Y.C., 1992—93. Recipient award, Loft-McKnight Found., 1995—96, Nelson Algren award, Chgo. Tribune, 2002; Presdl. fellow, Ohio State U., 2001—02. Mem.: ACLU, MLA, Associated Writing Programs. Democrat. Jewish. Office: Dept Lit Am Univ 4400 Mass Ave NW Washington DC 20016

LEVY, HELEN E., director; d. Harry Jacob and Rae Helene Lipkin; m. Martin B. Levy, June 6, 1954; children: Elizabeth Marie, Patricia Lynn. BA, Queens Coll., NY, 1950; MEd, U. Cin., 1971. Libr. Princeton City Sch. Dist., Cin., 1968—93, dir. Learning Ctr., 1993—2006; ret., 2006. Prodr.: (TV series) Book Sharing Time. Vol. Meals on Wheels. Mem.: AAUW, NEA (life), Ohio Edn. Assn. (life), Ohio Ret. Tchrs. Assn., Kappa Delta Pi, Phi Delta Kappa. Democrat. Jewish. Avocations: travel, reading, gardening, exercise. Home: 840 Yornhaven Rd Cincinnati OH 45240

LEVY, JERRE MARIE, psychobiology educator; b. Birmingham, Ala., Apr. 7, 1938; d. Jerome Milton and Marie (Ullman) L.; children: Marie Basch, Todd Basch. BA, U. Miami, 1962, MS, 1966; PhD, Calif. Inst. Tech., 1970. Postdoctoral fellow U. Colo., Boulder, 1970-71, Oreg. State U., 1971-72; asst. to assoc. prof. U. Pa., Phila., 1972-77; assoc. prof. to prof. U. Chgo., 1977—. Cons. editor Jour. Exptl. Psychology: Human Perception and Peformance, 1972-84; assoc. editor Brain and Cognition, 1982-92, Neuropsychologia, 1988—, The Journal of Neuroscience, 1990—; editorial bd. Human Neurobiology, 1985-87; contbr. articles to profl. jours. and books. Grantee Spencer Found. 1979—, NIMH, 1979—. Mem. Internat. Neuropsychol. Symposium, Soc. Exptl. Psychologists. Avocations: reading, traveling. Office: U Chgo Dept Psychology 5848 S University Ave Chicago IL 60637-1515

LEVY, JILL SONDRA, educational association administrator; b. Bronx, N.Y., July 13, 1938; d. Abe and Ruth (Fischer) Waltzer; m. Joseph Wilbur Levy, June 14, 1957; children: Allan Mark, Bruce Michael. BA, Queens Coll., 1959; MS, Hunter Coll., 1973; postgrad., Columbia U., 1991. Cert. sch. adminstr. and supr., N.Y. Tchr., dir. early childhood Hilltop Village, Queens, N.Y., 1962-65; tchr. N.Y.C. Bd. Edn., 1959-62, tchr., coord. spl. edn., 1975-81, supr. spl. edn., 1981-89; coord. Supervisory Support Program, NYC, 1989-94; treas. Am. Fedn. Sch. Adminstrs., Washington, 2000—03, exec. v.p., 2003—06, nat. pres., 2006—; v.p. Coun. of Suprs. and Adminstrs., NYC, 1989—92, exec. v.p., 1992—2000, pres., 2000—. Mem. exec. bd. N.Y. State Fedn. Sch. Adminstrs., N.Y.C., 1994—; dir. Leadership Inst. for Educators, N.Y.C., 1991—; mem. adv. bd. Annenberg Found., N.Y.C., 1996—; cons. Life Skills Coop., Great Barrington, Mass., 1990—. Editor newsletter ANIBIE; creator/author audio tape; author articles. Trustee Page and Otto Marx Jr. Found., N.Y.C., 1996—; mem. labor subcom. Pres.'s Com. on Employment of Poeple with Disabilities, Washington, 1996—; mem. NY. State Regents Select Com. on Disabilities, 1989-96. Recipient Outstanding Ednl. Leadership award Adminstrv. Women in Edn., 1993, Edn. Leadership award Jewish Tchrs. Cmty. Chest, 1990, 94, Outstanding Leadership award Joint Assn. Suprs., 1992, 93, Disting. Svcs. award Assn. Jewish Profls., 1997. Mem. ASCD, Coun. for Exceptional Children, Assn. for Neurologically Impaired/Brain Injured Children (pres., dir. 1975-92). Office: CSA 16 Court St 4th fl Brooklyn NY 11241-0102 also: Am Fedn Sch Adminstrs 1101 17th St NW Ste 408 Washington DC 20036 E-mail: jill@csa-nyc.org.*

LEVY, JULIA, immunology educator, researcher; b. Singapore, May 15, 1935; arrived in Can., 1940; d. Guillaume Albert and Dorothy Frances (Brown) Coppens; m. Howard Bernard Gerwing, Oct. 8, 1955 (div. 1962); children— Nicholas, Benjamin; m. Edwin Levy, June 13, 1969; 1 child, Jennifer BA with honors, U. B.C., 1955; PhD, U. London, 1958; Dr. of Univ. (hon.), U. Ottawa, 1993; DLitt (hon.), Mt. St. Vincent's U., 1994; DSc (hon.), U. Western Ont., 1997; LLD (hon.), Simon Fraser U., 1999; DSc honoris causa (hon.), U. B.C., 2001; DSc (hon.), U. Victoria, 2002; LLD (hon.), Concordia U., 2002; D of Tech. (hon.), B.C. Inst. Tech., 2002. Asst. prof. U. B.C., Vancouver, 1959-65, assoc. prof., 1965-72, prof. immunology, 1972—99, prof. emeritus, 1999—; pres., CEO QLT Inc., Vancouver, 1996—2002, exec. chmn. sci. adv. bd., 2002—. Dir. v.p. rsch. and devel. Quadra Logic Techs., Vancouver, 1980—2002; cons. Monsanto Chems., Mo., 1978—80; mem. Prime Minister's Nat. Adv. Bd. on Sci. and Tech., 1987—; exec. chmn. sci. adv. bd. QLT, Inc., 2002—. Decorated Officer of Order of Can.; named Pacific Can. Entrepreneur of Yr., 2000, Pioneer of Innovation, Bd. of Trade, 2001, Person of Yr., B.C. Tech. Industries Assn., 2001; recipient award, Can. Women Entrepreneur in Internat. Bus., 1998, Vision and Leadership award, BCBA, 1999, Amb.'s award for outstanding achievement of Can. women entrepreneurs, 1999, Nat. Merit award, Ottawa Life Scis. Coun., 1999, Future of Vision award, Found. Fighting Blindness, 2001, Women of Distinction award, YWCA, 2001, Friesen-Rygiel prize, 2002, Prix Galien Can. 2002 Rsch., 2002, award of leadership in Can. pharm. rsch. and devel., Can. Soc. Pharm. Scis., 2002, Helen Keller award, The Helen Keller Found. Rsch. and Edn., 2003, Leadership award, BC Export, 2003, Lifetime Achievement award, BC Biotech, 2004. Fellow: Royal Soc. Can.; mem.: Am. Soc. Immunology, Can. Soc. Immunology (pres. 1983—85), Can. Fedn. Biol. Sci. (pres. 1983—84). Achievements include endowed Julia G. Levy chair professorship of ophthalmology John's Hopkins Hospital, Wilmer Eye Institute. Office: QLT Inc 887 Great Northern Way Vancouver BC Canada V5T 4T5

LEVY, LEAH GARRIGAN, federal official; b. Miami, Fla., Apr. 29, 1947; d. Thomas Leo and Mary (Flaherty) Garrigan; m. Roger N. Levy, May 2, 1977; children: Philip, Aaron. BA in Polit. Sci., George Mason U., 1998, MA, 2006. Mem. legis. staff U.S. Ho. Reps., 1973-75; mem. scheduling staff U.S. Senate, 1975-77, mem. administrv. scheduling staff, 1977-81; staff asst. pub. liaison The White House, 1982-84; spl. asst. U.S Dept. Transport, Washington, 1984-89, U.S. Dept. Housing, Washington, 1989—; scheduling asst. Empower Am., Washington, 1993-94; scheduler majority leader Dick Armey U.S. Ho. of Reps., Washington, 1995-2001; dir. scheduling and advance Sec. of Labor, Washington, 2001—03, spl. asst. Office of the Sec., 2002—03; dir. scheduling U.S. Senator Elizabeth Dole, Washington, 2003—; v.p. devel. Empower Am., Washington, 2003—05; dir. scheduling and advance US Dept. Labor, Washington, 2005—, dir. operations, 2005—. Contbr. to Rep. Nat. Com., Washington. Contbr. Rep. Nat. Conv. Va. Rep. Party, Washington; del. Va. State GOP Conv., Richmond, 1994. Mem. Alpha Chi. Roman Catholic. Avocations: tennis, golf, reading. Office: US Dept Labor 200 Constitution Ave NW Washington DC 20210 Office Phone: 202-693-6073. Personal E-mail: thelevys@aol.com. Business E-Mail: levy.leah@dol.gov.

LEVY, LESLIE ANN, application developer; b. N.Y.C., Dec. 25, 1941; d. Paul and Ruth Candace (Tachna) Bauman; m. Marc Gersan Gerard Levy, Oct. 1962 (div.); children: Benjamin Gerard, Remy Marcel Gerard. BA summa cum laude in philosophy and history, Smith Coll., 1962; MBA, Harvard U., Boston, 1976, DBA, 1980. Cert. French Fashion Acad., 1964. Tchg. asst. in philosophy UCLA, 1962-63; pres. Commonwealth Collaborative, Inc., Cambridge and Sarasota, Fla., 1976—99; sr. rsch. assoc. Harvard Sch. Bus. Adminstrn., Boston, 1979-81; asst. prof. mgmt. policy, industry analysis Case Western Res. U., Cleve., 1981-84; pres., CEO Acad. for Corp. Governance, Fordham U. Grad. Sch. Bus., 1990-91; pres., dir., treas., sec. Directors, Data, Inc., 1999—; pres., sec. Life Choices and Death Wishes, 2000—. Sr. advisor, pres., dir. Inst. Rsch. on Bd. Dirs., 1998-; with Honeywell Info. Sys., Boston, 1971-75; former cons. and lectr. in field. Author: Director Motivation: Incentives and Disincentives to Board Service, 1996, Separate Chairmen of the Board: Their Roles, Legal Liabilities, and Compensation; editor, coauthor: Boards of Directors Part II; columnist: Directors and Boards, 1996-97; contbr. aricles to profl. jours. Mem. Boston and Tampa Bay Com. on Fgn. Rels. Acad. Corp. Governance rsch. fellow; Fulbright scholar. Mem. Am. Soc. Corp. Secs., Nat. Assn. Corp. Dirs., Acad. Mgmt. (article reviewer), Nat. Investor Rels. Inst., Inst. of Dirs., Federalist Soc., Women in Pensions, So. Fin. Assn., Harvard Club of Sarasota, Am. Jewish Com., Am. Jewish Congress, Nat. Coun. Jewish Women. Avocations: hiking, art history, construction, whitewater canoeing. E-mail: dirsdata@drleslielevy.com, irbd@drleslielevy.com.

LEVY, ROCHELLE FELDMAN, artist; b. N.Y.C., Aug. 4, 1937; d. Harry and Eva (Krause) Feldman. m. Robert Paley Levy, June 4, 1955; children: Kathryn Tracey, Wendy Paige, Robert Paley, Angela Brooke, Michael Tyler. Student, Barnard Coll., 1954—55, U. Pa., 1955—56; BFA, Moore Coll. Art, 1979, HHD (hon.), 1998. Mgmt. cons. Woodlyn Sch., Rosemont, Pa., 1983—2003; sr. ptnr. DRT Interiors, Phila., 1983—2003; ptnr. Phila. Phillies, 1981—94. One-woman shows include Watson Gallery Wheaton Coll. Norton, Mass., 1977, U. Pa., 1977, Med. Coll. Pa. Phila., 1982, Aquaduct Race Track, 1982, Phila. Art Alliance, 1983, Paley Gallery, Moore Coll. Art and Design, 1984, 2003, Art Alliance, 1994, Frost & Reed Gallery, Saratoga, NY, 2000-05, Frost & Reed Ltd, NYC, 2004, Cross Gate Gallery, Saratoga, 2005, 06, Reef Gallery, Ocean Reef, Fla., 2006. Pres. League of Children's Hosp. Phila., 1969-70; bd. overseers Ctr. for Judaic Studies U. Pa., 1993-96; bd. mgrs. Moore Coll. Art and Design, 1970—, chmn. exec. com., 1982-99, trustees 1979-99, chmn. emerita bd. trustees, 1999-2004. Recipient G. Allen Smith Prize Woodmere Art Gallery, Chestnut Hill, Pa., 1979, Disting. Alumni award Moore Coll. Art, 2005, Woman honoree Samuel Paley Day Care Ctr., Phila., 1990, Jefferson Bank Declaration award, 1991, Nat. Philanthropy honoree Nat. Soc. Fund Raising Execs. Greater Phila. chpt., 1994, Hon. Alumni award Moore Coll. Art, 2005. Mem. Pa. Acad. Fine Arts (selections and acquisitions com. 1970—, bd. mgrs. 1975—, chmn. exec. com. 1982—, trustee 1990—), Artist's Equity, Phila. Art Alliance, Phila. Mus. Art (assoc.), Phila. Print Club. Office: 200 W Montgomery Ave Ardmore PA 19003

LEVY, VALERY, publisher; b. Khartoum, Sudan, Feb. 16, 1946; came to U.S., 1959; d. Robert and Victorine (Malka) Braunstein; m. Joseph Levy, Aug. 24, 1968; children: Nomi, Berti. BA in Polit. Sci., Fairleigh Dickinson U., 1976, MA in Internat. Studies, 1978. Eng. tchr. Am. Inst. Cultural Affairs, Barcelona, 1965-66; Montessori tchr. Ft. Lee (N.J.) Community Ctr., 1974-81; project coord. Friends of Hebrew U., N.Y.C., 1981-83; devel. cons. Ft. Lee, 1983-85; editor, sr. editor Holt, Rinehart & Winston, N.Y.C., 1986-88; sr. editor, exec. editor Simon & Schuster Edn. Co., Morristown, Englewood, N.J., 1988-90; pres. Wonder Well Publishers, Ft. Lee, 1990-98; v.p., mng. editor Sch. divsn. McGraw-Hill, 1999—2001; assoc. pub. Macmillan-McGraw Hill, 2003—05, pub., 2005—. Author: Alphabet Connections, 1990; editor: Room Of Mirrors, 1991.

LEVY, WENDY, psychologist; b. Sao Paulo, Brazil, Sept. 21, 1956; d. Merwin Ronald and Edith (Pressburger) L.; m. Leo Massarani, Sept. 4, 1993; children: Julian, Marcel. BA, Coll. William and Mary, 1978; MA, MEd, Columbia U., 1985; D of Psychology, Yeshiva U., 1995. Lic. psychologist, Conn. Dual diagnosis therapist Gracie Square Hosp., N.Y.C., 1991-94; psychologist Karen Horney Clinic, N.Y.C., 1992-94; intern Yale Sch. Medicine, New Haven, 1994-95; coord. domestic violence program Hill Health Ctr., New Haven, 1995-96; clin. instr., clin. supr. Yale Sch. Medicine, 1997—; pvt. practice Westport, Conn., 1998—. Mem. APA, Conn. Psychol. Assn. Avocations: choral singing, biking, hiking. Office: 31 Imperial Ave Westport CT 06880-4303 Office Phone: 203-221-8377. E-mail: wlevyma@hotmail.com.

LEW, GINGER, lawyer; b. San Mateo, Calif., Nov. 3, 1948; d. Bing and Suey Bow (Ng) Lew; m. Carl Lennart Ehn Lew, Feb. 2, 1984; children: Melissa, Jeremy. BS, UCLA, 1970; JD, U. Calif., Berkeley, 1974. Bar: Calif. 1974, DC 1980. Dep. city atty. City of Los Angeles, 1974—75; asst. regional counsel Dept. Energy, San Francisco, 1975—77; chief counsel, 1978—80; dep. asst. sec. of state of East Asia Dept. of State, Washington, 1980—81; spl. advisor, 1981—82; ptnr. Stovall, Spradlin, Armstrong & Isreal, Washington, 1983—86, Arthur Young Co., Washington, 1986—93; gen. counsel US Dept. Commerce, Washington, 1993; CEO Telecommunications Investment Fund. Recipient Outstanding Achievement award, Dept. State, 1980, Meritorious Svc. award, 1981. Mem.: Nat. Lawyers, Orgn. of Chinese-Am., Women's Bar Assn., Asian Pacific Am. Bar Assn., ABA, Commonwealth, Pi Sigma Alpha. Office: US Dept Commerce Office Gen Counsel 14th & Constitution Ave NW Washington DC 20230-0001

LEW, JOYCELYNE MAE, actress; b. Santa Monica, Calif., Feb. 25, 1962; d. George and Mabel Florence (Lum) L. BA in Theatre Arts, UCLA, 1981, teaching credential, 1982; MA in Urban Edn., Pepperdine U., 1984; bilingual cert., U. So. Calif., 1983; postgrad., Stella Adler Acad., 1988; studied with, The Groundlings Improv Group, 1987. Exec. com. Acad. T.V. Arts & Scis., 2000-01. Appeared in films Tai-Pan, 1987, Fatal Beauty, 1989, The Royal Affair, 1993, Shattered Image, 1993, Dr. Boris and Mrs. Duluth, 1994, Hindsight, 1996, Fire in My Heart, 1996, Ginseng Power, 1998; TV programs The Young and the Restless, 1990, Phil Donahue Show, 1993, Hard Copy, 1994, Current Affair, 1995, Gordon Elliott, 1995, Married With Children, 1997, True Hollywood Stories, 1997, Nat. Enquirer TV, 2000, Arrest & Trial, 2000, Extra, 2001, Men are from Mars, Women are from Venus, 2001, Sins of Hollywood, 2002; (theater) Mary Tape, 2000; voice over artist, mag. model, body double, dancer; appeared in comml. Good Seasons, 1996, Pillsbury Doughboy, 1996, Pacific Bell, 1996, Beefsteak Rye Bread, 1998, Miller Beer, 1998; co-writer film script They Still Call Me Bruce, 1986 (award); song lyricist Nighttime Blues (award Allure Mag., 2002). Mem. judging com. for film grants Nat. Endowment for Arts, 1986; mem. L.A. Beautiful, 1993. Mem. AFTRA, SAG, AEA, ATAS (exec. com. performer's branch, 2000, blue ribbon com. for Emmy awards 1986-96), Assn. Asian Pacific Am. Artists (treas. 1983-89), Nat. Asian Am. Telecomms. Assn., Am. Film Inst. Conservatory Workshop, Calif. PTA (life). Avocations: calligraphy, makeup art and hair, charcoals, fashion and interior design. Home and Office: 1952 N Van Ness Ave Los Angeles CA 90068-3625 E-mail: Joycelyne@finalprint.com.

LEWALLEN, DONNA G., elementary school educator; b. Anadarko, Okla., Mar. 21, 1959; d. Eugene D. and Joycle L. King; m. Danny L. Lewallen, Mar. 14, 1980; 1 child, Brandon J. BS in Edn., SW Okla. State U., Weatherford, 1980, EdM, 1982. Cert. tchr. Okla. Dept. Edn., 2006. 4th grade tchr. Clinton (Okla.) Pub. Schs., 1985—89, gifted and talented tchr., 1989—2002, extended math tchr., 2002—. After sch. hoops coord. SW Elem., Clinton, 2000—, yearbook advisor, 2001—, math stds. testing coord., 2004—; curriculum com. Clinton Pub. Schs. Pianist, organist Oakdale Missionary Bapt. Ch., Lookeba, Okla., 2000. Named Model Educator in Math, Renaissance Learning, 2003, 2004, 2005, Master Educator in Math, 2003, 2004, 2005; grantee Found. Grants for Edn., Clinton Pub. Schs. Founds., 1988, 1989, 2000, 2002. Democrat. Baptist. Avocations: quilting, travel, working in the yard and on the farm, raising registered puppies. Home: Rt #1 Box 60-B Colony OK 73021 Office: Clinton Public Schools PO Box 729 Clinton OK 73601 Office Phone: 580-323-1290.

LEWALLEN REYNOLDS, CYNTHIA MAIRE, city administrator, small business owner; b. Oneida, Tenn., Feb. 13, 1955; d. Reason Henderson and Dorothy D. Cross; m. Ray Lewallen; children: Bradley Shane, Keisha Rae; m. Jeffrey D. Reynolds; 1 child, Akeia Grace. Student, Roane State C.C., Harriman, Tenn.; cert. pub. supervision, U. Tenn., cert. mcpl. ofcl.; cert. clk., Mid. Tenn. State U.; diploma in bus. adminstrn., Tenn. Tech., 1991. Salesclk., buyer Conastsers Dept. Store, Oneida, Tenn., 1977-97; owner day care ctr., Huntsville, Tenn., 1979-84; city recorder, adminstr. Town of Huntsville, 1984—; co-owner Tri-Tech. Environ., Huntsville, 1996—. Mem. adv. bd. Plateau Electric Coop., Oneida, 1990-91; promoter, recruiter Appalachian Ednl. Ctr., Tazewell, tenn., 1986-90. Mem. Huntsville Planning Commn., 1996—; cmty. devel. dir. Town of Huntsville, 1986-88; chmn. Tenn. Bicentennial; mem. Scott Leadership Class of 2000, 1999—; co-founder Scott County Jr. Pro Youth Program, 1986; mem. festival com. Firemen 4th Celebration, Huntsville; cheerleader coach Huntsville Jr. Pro League, 1986-96; mem. New River (Tenn.) Bapt. Ch. Mem. Tenn. Assn. Mcpl. Clks., Internat. Inst. Mcpl. Clks., Advanced Acad. Recorders, Scott County C. of C. (bd. dirs. 1998-99). Democrat. Baptist. Avocations: hiking, spending time with family, bowling, working with children. Office: Town of Huntsville PO Box 150 3053 Baker Hwy Huntsville TN 37756-4014

LEWELLEN, MELISSA DAWN, elementary school educator; b. Springfield, Mo., Aug. 19, 1971; d. Ross Eugene and Lois Evelyn Lewellen; 1 child, Mercedes Michelle. BS, Chowan Coll., NC, 2004. Cert. tchr. Fla., 2001. Asst. mgr. Metro Diesel Power, Inc., Fort Myers, Fla., 1999—2001; tchr. Lee Mid. Sch., Fort Myers, 2001—. Sci. cadre Lee County Schs., Fort Myers, 2004—. Active Girl Scouts SW Fla.; leader single parents group Grace United Meth., Cape Coral, Fla., 2002—03. Mem.: Fla. Educator's Assn. Republican. Methodist. Avocation: swimming. Office: Lee Middle School 1333 Marsh Ave Fort Myers FL 33905 Office Phone: 239-337-1333. Office Fax: 239-334-4144. Business E-Mail: melissadl@leeschools.net.

LEWENT, JUDY CAROL, pharmaceutical executive; b. Jan. 13, 1949; BS in Econs., Goucher Coll., 1970; MSc in Mgmt., MIT, 1972; LHD (hon.), Goucher Coll., 1998; DEng (hon.), Stevens Inst. Tch., 2000; DSc (hon.), NJ Inst. Tech., 2004. With corp. fin. dept. E.F. Hutton & Co., Inc., 1972—74; asst. v.p. for strategic planning Bankers Trust Co., 1974—75; sr. fin. analyst corp. planning Norton Simon, 1975—76; divsn. contr. Pfizer, Inc., 1976—80; dir. acquisitions and capital analysis Merck & Co., Inc., Whitehouse Station, NJ, 1980—83, asst. contr., 1983—85, exec. dir. fin. evaluation and analysis, 1985—87, v.p., treas., 1987—90, v.p. fin., CFO, 1990—92, sr. v.p., CFO, 1992—2001, exec. v.p., CFO, 2001—02, exec. v.p., CFO, pres., human health Asia, 2003—05, exec. v.p., CFO, 2005—. Bd. dirs. Dell Inc., Motorola Inc., Nat. Bur. Econ. Rsch., PENN Medicine; life mem. MIT Corp. Trustee Rockefeller Family Trust. Named one of 10 Most Powerful Women in NJ Bus., Star-Ledger, 2006. Mem.: Am. Acad. Arts and Scis. Office: Merck & Co Inc PO Box 100 One Merck Dr Whitehouse Station NJ 08889-0100

LEWICKE, BETTE, psychologist, writer; b. Toledo, Aug. 4, 1952; d. Louis George and Mary Helen (Nash) DeBauche; children: Sara Catherine Graves, John Paul. BA, Cath. U., 1974; MA, U. Conn., 1979, PhD, 1982. Rsch. asst. NIMH, Adult Psychiatry, Bethesda, Md., 1974-75; rsch. assoc. Brandeis U., Waltham, Mass., 1981-83; instr. Rivier Coll., Nashua, N.H., 1984-88; biofeedback clinician Behavioral Medicine Inst., Merrimack, N.H., 1987-88; psychology intern Nashua (N.H.) Brookside Hosp., 1989-91; staff psychologist Ctr. for Family Devel., Lowell, Mass., 1994; postdoctoral fellow in neuropsychology Fairlawn Rehab. Hosp., Worcester, Mass., 1994—95; neuropsychologist South Bay Mental Health, 1995—99, Crotched Mountain Rehab. Ctr., 1999—. Dir. N.H. Psychol. Orgn., Concord, 1990-92; presenter Stress Mgmt. Workshop, 1988; dir. rsch. Traumatic Brain Injury Transition Project, 1993. Contbr. articles to profl. jours. Trustee Mason (N.H.) Pub. Libr., 1991-1997; leader troop 5 Girl Scouts U.S.A., Mason, 1991-93; chpt. lead Disaster Mental Health, ARC, N.H. West chpt. Mem. APA (div. 19: Psychotherapy, div. 40: Clin. Neuropsychology), N.H. Psychol. Orgn. (fellow 1991, chmn. 1990-92), Mensa (bd. dirs. N.H. chpt.). Avocations: gardening, skiing. Home: 19 Granite Cir Dublin NH 03444-8208 Office: Crotched Mountain Rehab Ctr Brain Injury Ctr and Outpatient Svcs Iverney Dr Greenfield NH 03047 Office Phone: 603-547-3311 282.

LEWIE, REVA GOODWIN, artist, educator; b. Balt., Feb. 14, 1930; d. William Milton Goodwin Sr. and Edith Elizabeth (Koon) Goodwin; m. Lemuel Arthur Lewie Jr., Aug. 28, 1948; 1 child, Reva Marcia Lewie-Thompson, MD. BS, Morgan State U., 1956; MA, NYU, 1961; postgrad., U. Md., Towson State U. Tchr. art and geography Balt. City Pub. Schs., 1956, coord. art, 1966; instr. art Morgan State U., 1968; tchr. art resource Balt. City Pub. Schs., 1959—67, chair art dept., 1967—71, head art dept., 1971—87; v.p. Lewie Consol. Enterprises, 1990—. Docent Walters Art Mus., Balt., 1993—2004, mem. adv. bd. African Am. steering com., 1990—98, docent emeritus, 2004—; mem. Baltimore County Commn. Arts and Scis., 1990—2004. Represented in permanent collections James E. Lewis Collection, Morgan State Univ., Balt., Md., exhibitions include Loeb Ctr., NYC, Washington County Mus., Hagerstown (Artists Equity Shows), Md., State Capital, Annapolis, Md., James E. Lewis Mus. Morgan State Univ., Balt., Md., Walters Art Mus., commn., Madison Med. Ctr., Balt., Md, DHIS Inst., Lanham, Md., Commn., Garwyn Med. Ctr., Balt., Md., commn., Mercy Med. Ctr. Mem. WAM Womens Com., 1993—. Named Woman of Yr. Cmty. Svc. award, U.S. Senator Barbara Mikulski, 2003; recipient Tchr. of the Yr. award, Nat. Art Edn. Assn., 1985, Md. Art Edn. Assn. award, 1986, Walters Art

Gallery award, 1996, NAACP ACTSO award, 1992, Mary Fritzpatrick award, Federated Garden Clubs of Md. Inc., 1998, 2001, 2004, Patapsco River Links Art award, 1999, Woman of the Yr. in Cultural Arts, Balt. City's Mayoral award, City Coun. awards, Md. State awards, 1998—2003. Mem.: Md. Ret. Tchrs. Assn., Nat. Educators Assn., Les Grandes Dames (pres. 1999—2004), The Pierians, Inc. of Baltimore County, Nat. Coalition of 100 Black Women, Inc., Beautiful Balt. (bd. dirs.), Federated Garden Clubs Md. (sec. 2000), The Links (charter), For-Win-Ash Garden Club (pres. 2000—04), Zeta Phi Beta Sorority, Inc. Avocations: travel, floral design, art. Personal E-mail: rglewie@verizon.net.

LEWIN, BETSY R., illustrator; b. Pa., May 12, 1937; m. Ted B. Lewin. Grad., Pratt Inst. Illustrator: Itchy, Itchy Chicken Pox, 1992, Ho, Ho, Ho: The Complete Book of Christmas Words, 1993, Somebody Catch My Homework, 1993, Mattie's Little Possum Pet, 1993, Yo, Hungry Wolf, 1995, The Classroom Pet, 1995, My Tooth is About to Fall Out, 1995, A Thousand Cousins, 1996, Recess Mess, 1996, No Such Thing, 1997 (SLJ Honor Book, 1997, Bulletin for Ctr. on Childrens Books Blue Ribbon, Nebr. Golden Sower award), Snake Alley Band, 1998, Araminta's Paint Box, 1998, The Class Trip, 1999, Aunt Minnie McGrannahan, 1999, Click, Clack, Moo: Cows That Type, 2000 (N.Y,. Times best-seller, Soc. Illustrators Original Art, 2000, Caldecott Honor, 2003), Purrfectly Purrfect, 2000, Promises, 2000, Is It Far To Zanzibar?, 2000 (Parents Choice Gold award, 2000), Dumpy La Rue, 2001 (10 Best Illustrated Books N.Y. Times, 2001), A Houseful of Christmas, 2001, Giggle, Giggle, Quack, 2002, Aunty Minnie and the Twister, 2002, Two Eggs Please, 2003, Duck for President, 2004, author, illustrator: Booby Hatch, 1995, Walk a Green Path, 1995, What's the Matter Habibi?, 1997, Animal Snackers, 2004, co-author with Ted Lewin and illustrator: Gorilla Walk, 1999 (Smithsonian Notable Books, 1999, NSTA CB Outstanding Sci. Trade Book, 2000, N.Y. Pub. Libr. Children's Books, 1999), Elephant Quest, 2000 (NSTA CBC Outstanding Sci. Trade Book, 2001, John Burroughs award for outstanding nature book for young readers); exhibitions include Bklyn. Pub. Libr., N.Y., 2004, Children's Mus. Manhattan, 2004. Avocation: travel. Office: c/o Simon & Schuster Childrens Pub 1230 Ave of the Americas New York NY 10020

LEWIN, CYNTHIA M., lawyer; b. Boston, 1957; m. Arthur Fox; children: Courtney, Lowell, Miranda. Grad., Wellesley Coll., 1978; JD, Yale U., 1984. Bar: Colo. 1984. Law clk., LA; with Arnold & Porter, Lichtman, Trister, Singer & Ross, Washington; exec. v.p., gen. counsel Volunteers of Am., Alexandria, Va., 1998—. Office: Volunteers of Am Inc 1600 Duke St Alexandria VA 22314-3421 Office Phone: 703-341-5000. Office Fax: 703-341-7000.

LEWIN, NANCY S., actress; d. Derek Jonathan Lewin and Harriet Ria Lihs. BA in Humanities, U. Calif., Berkeley, 1988, MA in History, 1989; voice cert., John Ford Sch. Voice, 1992. Musician various bands, San Francisco, 1986—94; cons. Fore-1, San Francisco, 1992—2002; pvt. practice psychic Houston, 1992—2002; model Wilhelmina Scouting Network, Houston, 2000—02, actress, 2003. Contbr. poetry to anthologies; composer: (songs) Music Folios I and II, 2000; musician, performer: benefits Amnesty Internat., 2000, musician, performer: S.E. Texans Organized for Peace. Mem. ACLU, Beaumont, 2003—. Mem.: Acad. Am. Poets, Inst. Noetic Sci., The Art Studio, Inc., Beaumont Art League, BMI Music Club. Achievements include discovery of answer to Einstein's theory of relativity; invention of Synopses. Avocations: exhibiting art, poetry, bicycling, metaphysics, musicals. Office Phone: 409-466-8636. Personal E-mail: nlewin@gt.rr.com.

LEWIN, PEARL GOLDMAN, psychologist; b. Bklyn., Apr. 25, 1923; d. Frank and Anna Goldman; m. Seymour Z. Lewin, Oct. 17, 1943; children: David, Jonathan. BA, Hunter Coll., N.Y.C., 1943; MS, U. Mich., Ann Arbor, 1947; PhD, NYU, 1980. Lic. psychologist, N.Y. Insp. chemist quarter master corps U.S. Army, 1943-45, chemist chem. warfare Edgewood Arsenal, Md., 1945; asst. psychologist Bur. Psychol. Svcs., U. Mich., Ann Arbor, 1947-48; freelance rsch. asst. chemistry N.Y.C., 1955-71; adj. lectr. CUNY, Bklyn., 1973-74, instr., 1974-79, asst. prof., 1979-80; psychologist Creedmore Psychiat. Ctr., N.Y.C., 1980-82; sr. psychologist Manhattan Family Ct., N.Y.C., 1982-87; cons., 1987—. Mentor Peer Counseling Orgn., Bklyn. Coll., 1976-80, coord. student svcs. New Sch. Liberal Arts, 1974-76, adminstr. acad. regulations, 1974-76. Author: Sexist Humor, 1979. Mem. APA, Pi Lambda Theta, Phi Kappa Phi. Avocations: management, woodworking. Home and Office: 4231 N Walnut Ave Arlington Heights IL 60004-1302

LEWIS, AMY BETH, newswriter, reporter, writer, photographer; b. Silver Creek, N.Y., Dec. 12, 1964; d. Jon Michael Lewis and Elizabeth Jean Chodacki-Berns, Mary Lewis (Stepmother) and Charles Johnson (Stepfather); life ptnr. Michael Ohl. Degree in Comm. and Media Arts, Erie C.C. South, 2000. Supr. sheltered workshop Suburban Adult Services, Inc., Sardina, NY, 1996—98; sec., receptionist William Shoemaker Associates, Inc., Hamburg, 1996—98. Reading tutor Erie C.C., Boston, 1999—2001; writer-reporter, freelance photographer Dunkirk Observer, 2000—03. Author of poems. Orgnl. mem. Bus. and Profl. Women, Silver Creek, NY, 2001—02. Recipient Outstanding News Writing, Irving-Chautauqua County C. of C., 2002. Avocations: horseback riding, gardening, creative writing, travel, movies. Office: Dunkirk Observer 10 East Second St Dunkirk NY 14048-1602

LEWIS, ANNE MCCUTCHEON, architect; b. New Orleans, Oct. 15, 1943; d. John Tinney and Susan (Dart) McCutcheon; m. Ronald Burton Lewis, Oct. 2, 1971; children: Matthew, Oliver. BA magna cum laude, Radcliffe Coll., 1965; MArch, Harvard U., 1970. Registered architect, D.C., Md., Va., Pa. Architect Skidmore, Owings & Merrill, Washington, 1969—72, Keyes, Lethbridge & Condon, Washington, 1972—75; ptnr. McCartney Lewis Architects, Washington, 1981—98; prin. Anne McCutcheon Lewis AIA, Washington, 1976—81, 1999—. Mem. Harvard U. Grad. Sch. Design Alumni Coun., Cambridge, Mass., 1979-82; bd. dirs. Friends Non-Profit Housing, Washington, 1981-98, Washington Humane Soc., 1990—2006, D.C. Hist. Preservation Rev. Bd., 2003—. Fellow: AIA (dir.-at-large Washington chpt. 1982—84, Design awards 1979, 1983, 1989, 1990, 1991, 1992, 1993, 1996, 1998, 2000, 2001). Office: Anne McCutcheon Lewis FAIA 3400 Reservoir Rd NW Washington DC 20007-2328

LEWIS, ARLENE JANE QUIRING, music educator; b. Mt. Lake, Minn., Aug. 19, 1934; d. Emil Quiring and Mary (Schmidt) Quring; m. James Edgar Lewis, Dec. 30, 1936; children: Brenda Janelle, Barry Jonathan, Bethamy Janine. BS, Bob Jones U., 1952-57; postgrad., S.D. State U., 1964-65, Mankato State U., 1970-72. Accredited piano tchr. Nat. Guild Musicians. Tchr. English and music Huron (S.D.) Pub. Sch., 1962-63, tchr. elem. music supr., 1963-64; tchr., music supr. Forestburg S.D. Sch., 1969-84; pvt. piano tchr., Enid, Okla., 1984-96, Sioux City, Iowa, 1996—; tchr. band, vocal and elem. music Sioux City Morningside Christian Sch., 1996—2000. Music cons. and workshops Am. Christian Sch. Internat., Dallas, 1986-88; pvt. piano tchr. Pillsbury Bapt. Bible Coll., 1959-84, tchr. music edn., 1984-96; founder Piano Monster Ensemble, Sioux City, 2004. Editor Compiler: Hymns with Classical backgrounds Resource, 1982, Literacy Works found in Hymnals Resource, 1986. Founder Enid Home Scholars Choir, 1989-96; dir. children's choir Enid Mennonite Brethren Ch., 1990-94, ch. organist, 1984-96, Grace Bapt. Ch., Owatonna, 1970-84; music dir., organist Billy Sunday Meml. Tabernacle, Sioux City, 1996—2000. Named to Nat. Guild's Hall of Fame, 1991. Mem. Nat. Fedn. Musicians (founder Enid group), Nat. Piano Guild (area chmn. 1971-84, 86-96), Nat. Choristers Guild (Oklahoma City chpt.), Nat. Music Tchrs. Assn., Okla. Music Tchrs. Assn., Enid Area Music Tchrs. (sec.-treas. 1989-91, pres. 1991-92), Iowa Music Tchrs. Assn., Iowa Fedn. Music Clubs (state pres. 2000-04), Siouxland Federated Music Clubs. Republicans. Avocations: electronic knitting, quilting, painting, handcrafts. Home and Office: 3612 Cheyenne Blvd Sioux City IA 51104-1850 E-mail: arlenelewis@juno.com.

LEWIS, AUDREY GERSH, marketing professional, public relations executive, consultant; b. Phila., Dec. 1, 1933; d. Benjamin and Augusta (Fine) Gersh; divorced; children: Jamie Lewis Keith, Ruth-Ellen Lewis. Student, Temple U., Phila., 1951—53. Asst. mgr. accounts payable/receivable Turner Constrn. Co., Louisville, 1953—55; rep. sales, mktg., fin. depts. Benjamin Gersh Wholesaler Jeweler, Wyncote, Pa., 1955—69; registered rep. Seaboard Planning Corp. (formerly B.C. Morton Broker Del.), Greenwich, Conn. and Wyncote, 1969—72; placement counselor sales and mktg. dept. Greyhound Permanent Pers. subs. Greyhound Corp., Stamford, Conn., 1974—77; asst. v.p., mgr. investor rels.l, mktg. Am. Investors Corp., Greenwich, 1977—85; founder, pres. Audrey Gersh Lewis Cons. Ltd., Greenwich, 1985—, Corp. Exec. Coach, LLC, Greenwich, 2002—, Strategic Comm. Planning. Chair Cancer Fund, Wyncote, United Fund Leadership Award, Wyncote, 1963-68; asst. treas. Rep. Town Com., Greenwich, 1981-82; mem. Greenwich rep. Town Meeting, 1981, 82; mem. Greenwich Town Alarm Appeals Bd., 1985-98. Mem. Assn. Corp. Growth (bd. dirs., v.p. mktg. and pub. rels. N.Y. chpt. 1989-92, mem. nat. ann. meeting planning com. 1992, 93, 94), Assn. Corp. Growth (N.Y. chpt.), Forum Club. Avocations: antiques, walking, reading. Office: Audrey Gersh Lewis Cons Ltd Corp Exec Coach LLC 88 Parsonage Rd Greenwich CT 06830-3941 Office Phone: 203-629-0802.

LEWIS, BARBARA-ANN GAMBOA, chemistry educator; b. Manila, Jan. 9, 1934; d. Felipe Brewster and Doreen Barber Gamboa; m. Roy Stephen Lewis; children: Gilita Star Thomas, Marya Curie Hirsch, Stephen Berkeley. BS in Chemistry, Philippine Women's U., Manila, Philippines, 1949—53; MS in Soil Sci., U. Calif., Berkeley, 1963, PhD in Soil Sci., 1971. Soil technologist Bur. of Soils, Manila, 1953—64; postdoctoral appointee Argonne Nat. Lab., Ill., 1972—73, environ. scientist, 1973—79; assoc. prof. Northwestern U., Evanston, Ill., 1979—. Author: Pocket Stones. Recipient Palladium medal for engring. and conservation, Nat. Audubon Soc. and Am. Assn. of Engring. Soc., 1984. Mem.: Am. Soc. Agronomy, Am. Chem. Soc., Soil Sci. Soc. Am., Union of Concerned Scientists. Jewish. Avocations: history, violin. Home: 923 Asbury Evanston IL 60202 Office: Northwestern University 2145 Sheridan Rd Evanston IL 60208 Office Phone: 847-491-4027. Business E-Mail: b-lewis@northwestern.edu.

LEWIS, BRENDA C., secondary school educator; d. James Wesley II and Ellen Virginia Crosslin; m. Joe Robert Kimbrough; children: Joe Earl Kimbrough, Sonya Cherie Gann; m. Kenneth Lane Lewis. Student, MTSU, Murfreesboro, Tenn., 2002. Culinary educator Blackman HS, Murfreesboro, 2000—. Advisor Skills USA Blackman HS, 2000—; culinary judge, Knoxville, Tenn., 2000—05. Mem.: ACTE, NEA, Ea. Star (worthy matron 1996, 1999). Baptist. Avocations: crafts, flowers, cooking. Home: 124 Sugar Creek Ln Smyrna TN 37167 Office: Blackman HS 3956 Blaze Dr Murfreesboro TN 37129 Office Phone: 615-904-3850. Office Fax: 615-904-3851. E-mail: lewisbr@acs.k12.tn.us.

LEWIS, CARLA SUSAN, psychology educator; b. Bklyn. d. Harry Aaron and Mildred Lewis. BA summa cum laude, Fordham U., 1979; MA in Psychology, CUNY, 1984, MPhil, 1986, PhD in Psychology, 1988. Asst. rsch. scientist N.Y. State Psychiat. Inst., N.Y.C., 1987-88; rsch. scientist Columbia Sch. Pub. Health, N.Y.C., 1988-90; adj. asst. prof. MA in program in forensic psychology John Jay Coll. Criminal Justice, N.Y.C., 1990; mem. faculty psychology rsch. lab. Princeton U., NJ, 1992-93; adj. asst. prof. psychology Fordham U., N.Y.C., 1993-95; dir. planning Project Hospitality, S.I., NY, 2004—. Rsch. scientist, cons. Columbia Sch. Pub. Health, N.Y.C., 1993-94; rsch. cons. dept. environ. medicine NYU Med. Ctr., 1994, Nat. Devel. and Rsch. Inst., Insts. for Therapeutic Cmty. Rsch., N.Y.C., 1995; sr. rsch. analyst Beth Israel Medical Ctr., 2000-02; presenter in field; chief evaluator Urban Resource Inst., 2002-06, Domestic Violence Shelters U. R.I.; Mt. Sinai Pub. Advocate, 2002; presenter in field. Contbr. articles to profl. jours. Mem. task force against domestic violence City N.Y.; mem. HIV prevention planning group N.Y.C. Dept. Health; mem. quality care steering com. N.Y. AIDS Inst. Recipient Disting. Rsch. award Psi Chi Nat. Honor Soc., 1991. Mem.: APA. Office: Porject Hospitality 100 Park Ave Staten Island NY 10302 Business E-Mail: carla_lewis@projecthospitality.org.

LEWIS, CORINNE HEMETER, psychotherapist, educator; b. N.Y.C., Nov. 28, 1925; d. Leslie Hall and Frances Pope Hemeter, m. Aug. 22, 1947 (div. 1984); children: Anne Marie, Richard Allyn, Timothy Hall; m. Ceylon S. Lewis Jr., Aug. 6, 1999. BSN, U. Pitts., 1947; MSW, U. Okla., 1978. Diplomate in clin. social work. Staff nurse St. Joseph's Hosp., Buckhannon, W.Va., 1947; head nurse Myer's Clinic, Phillipi, W.Va., 1948; clin. instr., supr. Allegheny Valley Hosp., Tarentum, Pa., 1949; coord. psychiat. nursing edn. Hillcrest Med. Ctr., Tulsa, 1966-67; clin. staff mem. Tulsa Psychiat. Ctr., Tulsa, 1968-77; tchr. principles personality devel. Hillcrest Med. Ctr., Tulsa, 1966-75; supr., interns in psychotherapy Tulsa Psychiat. Ctr., 1971-77; pvt. practice psychotherapist Tulsa, 1978—2002. Dir. Drug Day Hosp., Tulsa Psychiat. Ctr., 1969, dir. nursing, 1970-71; adminstrv. cons. Family and Children's Svcs., Tulsa, 1978; renal dialysis unit cons. Hillcrest Med. Ctr., 1978; dir. Am. Cancer Soc. funded program Tulsa Psychiat. Ctr., 1977-79, cons. to dept. internal medicine, Tulsa Med. Coll., 1977-98. Jr. bd. mem. Women's Assn., Tulsa Boys Home, 1957-59; mem. Mental Health Assn. Tulsa, 1968-83, bd. dirs., 1982-83; vol. Jr. Assn., Tulsa Boys Home, 1958-59, Children's Med. Ctr., 1953-56; bd. dirs. Nursing Svc. Inc., Tulsa, 1982-83. Mem. Nat. Assn. Social Workers, Acad. Cert. Social Workers, Sigma Theta Tau. Democrat. Presbyterian. Avocations: classical music, reading. Home: 2300 Riverside Dr Apt 8F Tulsa OK 74114-2403

LEWIS, DEBORAH ALICE, tax company executive, writer; b. Griffin, Ga., Mar. 26, 1947; d. Durward and Imogene Hinds L. AA, Miss. Gulf Coast Jr. Coll., Gulfport, 1973; student, William Carey Coll., 1973; BA in English cum laude, U. So. Miss., 1978. Vets. counselor Miss. Gulf Coast Jr. Coll., Gulfport, 1973-76; spl. agt. Dept of Def., 1976-84; instr., adj. faculty Phillips Coll., Gulfport, 1979-81; mgr. H&R Block Inc., Jacksonville, 1984—, tax edn. specialist Anniston, Ala., 1986—; owner Village Tax Team, 2004—. Author: Duty, 1992, (poetry) Dan River Anthology, 1988; regional editor Feminist Lit., 1984. With USMC, 1965—68, with USMCR, 1968—75. Recipient Outstanding Young Women of Am. award, 1980. Mem. Nat. Tax Preparers Assn., Women Marines Assn., League for Animal Welfare (life mem.), Lambda Iota Tau, Nat. Assn. Tax Profls. Avocation: historian. Office: The Village Tax Team 100 Church St North Jacksonville AL 36265 Fax: 256-435-4189. E-mail: dlewis2233@aol.com.

LEWIS, DIANE, announcer; m. Glenn Lewis; 2 children. Grad., Ctrl. State U., Wilburforce, Ohio. With WPVI, Phila., KABC, L.A.; co-anchor WXYZ, Southfield, Mich., 1977—85; career in TV and film industry Calif., 1985—88; co-anchor WXYZ, Southfield, Mich., 1988—. Actor: (plays) Rocky, Rocky 5 and others. Recipient Silver Cir. award, 1995, 2 Emmy awards, 2002, Gov.'s Lifetime Achievement award, 2002, Best News Anchor, 2002. Office: WXYZ-TV 20777 W Ten Mile Rd Southfield MI 48037

LEWIS, DIANE, educator; M, Harvard U., Cambridge. Mass., 1992. Instr. Middlesex C.C., Lowell, Mass., 1997—, U. Mass. Lowell, Lowell, Mass., 1998—. Office: Middlesex Comty Coll 33 Kearney Sq Lowell MA 01852 Office Phone: 978-656-3200. E-mail: lewisd@middlesex.mass.edu.

LEWIS, DORIS ANN, principal; d. Levan Jones; m. Mickey Jerome Lewis, June 29, 2004; 1 child, Cyril Bapteese Noland. M +30, Grambling State U., La., 2002. Child care supr. Meth. Children's Home, Ruston, La., 1992—98; tchr. Crawford Elem. Sch., Arcadia, La., 1998—99, I. A. Lewis Sch., Ruston, 1999—2005, guidance counselor, 2005—06; prin. Career Acad., Ruston, 2006—. Youth leader, tchr. Sun. sch. Mt. Zion C.M.E Ch., Choudrant, La., 2000. Office: Career Academy 1435 Mayberry Street Ruston LA 71270

LEWIS, ELEANOR ADAMS, financial consultant; b. Balt., Md., Sept. 14, 1950; d. Charles Scott Adams and Eleanor Abell Owen; m. David Murch, July 6, 2002; 1 child from previous marriage, Davidson W. AA, Briarcliff Coll., 1970; BA in Art History, Old Dominion U., 1974. Cert. Coll. Fin. Planning. Adminstrv. asst. Auslew Gallery, Norfolk, Va., 1985—90, A&B Propane, Chesapeake, Va., 1992—95; fin. advisor Waddell & Reed, Virginia Beach, Va., 1995—. Chmn. programs, treas. Hermitage Found. Aux., Norfolk, 1990—; treas., mem. exec. Hermitage Found., Norfolk; mem. Chrysler Mus. Mem.: Fin. Planning Assn. (sec. 2000). Avocations: travel, museums, reading, needlepoint. Office: Waddell & Reed 2901 S Lynnhaven Rd # 340 Virginia Beach VA 23452 Home: 285 Fadley Rd Weyers Cave VA 24486-2116

LEWIS, ELEANOR ROBERTS, lawyer; b. Detroit, Jan. 5, 1944; m. Roger Kutnow Lewis, June 24, 1967; 1 child, Kevin Michael. BA, Wellesley Coll., 1965; MA, Harvard U., 1966; JD, Georgetown U., 1974. Bar: DC 1975. Atty. HUD, Washington, 1974-76, asst. gen. counsel, 1979-82; atty. Brownstein Zeidman & Schomer, Washington, 1976-79; chief counsel internat. commerce U.S. Dept. Commerce, Washington, 1982—. Author, editor (with others): book Street Law, 1975; contbr. chapters to books, articles to legal and fin. jours. Bd. dirs. Dana Pl. Condominium, Washington. Mem.: ABA (U.S. govt. liaison to internat. sect.), Sr. Execs. Assn. (bd. dirs. local chpt.), DC Bar Assn. Home: 5034 1/2 Dana Pl NW Washington DC 20016-3441 Office: US Dept Commerce 14th & Constitution Ave NW Washington DC 20230-0001

LEWIS, JAN PATRICIA, education educator; b. Seattle, Mar. 6, 1954; d. James Alfred and Jean Louise (Hamilton) L. BA in Edn., Oreg. State U., 1976; MA in Tchg., Lewis & Clark Coll., 1979; PhD in Curriculum and Instrn., U. Oreg., 1989. Cert. tchr. K-8 elem., 4-12 English, K-12 reading, Wash. Elem. tchr. Boring (Oreg.) Sch. Dist., 1976-86; grad. tchg. fellow U. Oreg., Eugene, 1986-89; from asst. prof. to prof. Pacific Luth. U., Tacoma, 1989—2005, prof., 2005—, dir. Ctr. for Tchg. and Learning, 1998—2003, co-dean sch. edn., 2006—. Mem. adj. faculty Lewis and Clark Coll., Portland, Oreg., 1984-89; literacy cons., 1984—. Co-editor N.W. Reading Jour., 1993-2000; co-author: Building a Knowledge Base in Reading, 1997, Building a Knowledge Base in Reading: Teachers at Work, 1999, 2d edit., 2005 Mem. Internat. Reading Assn., Nat. Coun. Tchrs. of English, Wash. Orgn. Reading Devel. Office: Pacific Luth U Sch Edn Tacoma WA 98447-0001 Office Phone: 253-535-7283. Business E-Mail: lewisjp@plu.edu.

LEWIS, JOAN CAROL, chemist, educator; b. Dayton, Ohio, May 4, 1960; d. Hillary Garfield and Patsy Ann Lewis. BS in Chemistry and Edn., Ea. Ky. U., Richmond, 1982, MA in Edn., 1983; postgrad. in Comprehensive Sci., No. Ky. U., Highland Heights, 1997. Tchr. chemistry Bellevue H.S., Ky., 1983—91, Roger Bacon H.S., Cin., 1991—97, West Clemant Schs., Amelia, Ohio, 1997—. Mem.: NEA (del), West Clement Edn. Assn. (v.p.), Southwest Ohio Edn. Assn. (zone rep.), Ohio Edn. Assn. (del). Office: Amelia HS 1351 Clough Pike Batavia OH 45103 Office Phone: 513-947-7491.

LEWIS, JULIETTE, actress; b. San Fernando Valley, Calif., June 21, 1975; d. Geoffrey L. and Glenis Batley; m. Stephen Berra, 1999. TV appearances include The Wonder Years, 1987, The Facts of Life, 1988, Dharma & Greg, 2001; TV Movies include Homefires, 1987, I Married Dora, 1988, Too Young To Die, 1989, A Family For Joe, 1990, My Louisiana Sky (Emmy nominee), Hysterical Blindness, 2002, Chasing Freedom, 2004; films include My Stepmother is an Alien, 1988, Runnin' Kind, 1989, Meet the Hollowheads, 1989, National Lampoons Christmas Vacation, 1989, Cape Fear, 1991 (Academy Award and Golden Globe nomination best supporting actress 1991), Crooked Hearts, 1991, Husbands and Wives, 1992, Kalifornia, 1993, That Night, 1993, What's Eating Gilbert Grape, 1993, Romeo is Bleeding, 1994, Natural Born Killers, 1994, Mixed Nuts, 1994, Strange Days, 1995, The Basketball Diaries, 1995, Audition, 1996, From Dusk Till Dawn, 1996, The Evening Star, 1996, Full Tilt Boogie, 1997, Somegirl, 1998, The 4th Floor, 1999, The Other Sister, 1999, Way of the Gun, 2000, Room to Rent, 2000, Picture Claire, 2001, Gaudi Afternoon, 2001, Armitage: Dual Matrix, 2001, Enough, 2002, Old School, 2003, Cold Creek Manor, 2003, Blueberry, 2004, Starsky & Hutch, 2004, Grilled, 2005, Aurora Borealis, 2005, Daltry Calhoun, 2005; singer, Juliette Lewis and the Licks. Involved with Fight for Kids. Office: William Morris Agy care Norman Brokaw 151 S El Camino Dr Beverly Hills CA 90212-2775 Home: 8687 Melrose Ave West Hollywood CA 90069-5701

LEWIS, KAREN MARIE, human services administrator, writer; b. Syracuse, N.Y., Oct. 29, 1965; d. Stephan Joseph and Mary Josephine (Scully) L. Student, Simon's Rock of Bard Coll., 1982—83; BA in Linguistics cum laude, Barnard Coll., 1986; MA in Psychology, Brandeis U., 1989; Cert. in Human Svcs. with honors, Berkshire C.C., 2003, AS in Human Svcs. with high honors, 2006. Prodn. asst. Claremont Rsch. and Pub., N.Y.C., 1984—86; tchg. asst. Barnard Coll., N.Y.C., 1984—86, Brandeis U., Waltham, Mass., 1988; freelance writer Great Barrington, Mass., 1989—97; editl. asst. o.blek, Great Barrington, 1992—93; ESL algebra tutor Lenox Meml. H.S., Mass., 1995; editor Construct, Inc., Great Barrington, 1994—97, tutor adult edn., 1996—98, resident advisor, 1999—2002, head resident advisor, 2002—, case mgr. and asst. dir. shelter, 2004—; intern The Artful Mind, Great Barrington, 1996, office mgr., contbg. writer, editor, 1997—98; calendar prodr., 1999—2002. Intern College Internship Program, Lee, Mass., 2003, Brien Ctr. for Mental Health and Substance Abuse, 2004. Author: numerous poems; contbr. articles to local newspapers. Mem.: Phi Theta Kappa. Roman Catholic. Home: 309 Main St Apt D Great Barrington MA 01230-1616 Office Phone: 413-528-1985, 413-528-5858.

LEWIS, KAY, interior designer, consultant; b. Greenbackville, Va., July 11, 1921; d. Charles E. Lewis and Catharine E.B. Sharpley; m. Mano G.G. Eftimiadi, Dec. 20, 1967; 1 child, Peter Gibb Cropper Nemiroff. Diploma, Lycoming Coll., Williamsport, Pa., 1940; BA, Pa. State U., University Park, 1942. Jr. exec. squad Macy, NYC, 1942—44; designer Scott Wilson Indsl. Design Studio, NYC, 1944—47; assoc. stylist Seneca Textile Co., NYC, 1947—48; stylist Elmer P. Scott Co., NYC, 1948—49, Mead and Montague, Linen Guild, Inc., NYC, 1949—53; head textile design dept. Moore Inst. Art., Phila., 1954—60; pres. Kay Lewis Inc., NYC, 1959—79; textile design instr. Arts Students League NY, NYC, 1959—79; dir. design Dalbolt, Inc., NYC, 1962—65; v.p., dir. product and design United Merchants, NYC, 1978—81. Art show judge Art Inst. and Gallery, Salisbury, Md., 1987—, Ea. Shore Art League, Onancock, Va., 1999—, Tiffany, Ford and Fulbright Founds., NYC; spkr. in field. One-woman shows include Ea. Shore Art League, Onancock, Va., 1998, watercolors and oil paintings, Textile Designs and Fabrics, 1944—2003. Recipient Alumna of Yr., Lycoming Coll., 1979. Mem.: Nat. Soc. Daus. of Am. Revolution (2d vice regent 1998—2003), Colonial Dames 17th Century, Pa. State U. Alumni Assn. (Disting. Alumna 1978). Democrat. Home: PO Box 185 Greenbackville VA 23356-0185 Personal E-mail: kaylewis23356@peoplepc.com.

LEWIS, KRISTEN R., mathematics educator; d. Ronald J. and Irene M. Helms; m. Karl A. Lewis, June 28, 1997; children: Jonathon D., Andrew J. BS, U. Ill., Urbana-Champaign, 1991; M in Curriculum and Instrn., Nat. Louis U., Evanston, Ill., 1995; M in Edn. Adminstrn., No. Ill. U., DeKalb, 2002. Spanish tchr. Barrington H.S., Ill., 1993—95, math tchr., 1993—. Mem. Cary Sch. Dist. #2 Sch. Bd., Ill., 2006—. Office Phone: 847-842-3243.

LEWIS, LINDA KATHRYN, librarian; BA, U. Okla., 1968, MLS, 1969. Reference libr. U. N.Mex., Albuquerque, 1969-88, dir. collection devel., 1988—. Co-author: The Complete Guide to Acquisitions Management, 2003; contbr. chpts. to books, articles to profl. jours. Mem. ALA, N.M. Libr. Assn., N.Am. Serials Interest Group, Assn. Coll. and Rsch. Libs Office: U N Mex MSC 05 3020 Univ Libr Albuquerque NM 87131-0001 Business E-Mail: llewis@unm.edu.

LEWIS, MARCIA, actress; b. Melrose, Mass., Aug. 18, 1938; d. Edwin Parker and Bernice (Lamb) Lewis; m. Richard Alan Woody, Nov. 19, 1966 (div. 1990); m. Fred D. Bryan, 2001. RN, Jewish Hosp. Sch. Nursing, Cin., 1959; student, U. Cin., 1961-64. Actress (broadway plays) Hello Dolly!, 1964-70, The Time of Your Life, 1969, Annie, 1977-83, Rags, 1986, Roza, 1987, Orpheus Descending, 1989, Fiddler on the Roof, 1990-91, Grease, 1994-98 (nominee for best featured actress in a musical, Tony Award, 1994),

Chicago 1996-2001 (nominee for best featured actress in a musical, Tony Award, 1997), Funny Girl, 2002, Cabaret, When She Danced, Lorene in The Time of Your Life, Romance Language, Miami; stock roles include Mae in Bye Bye Birdie, Clairee in Steel Magnolias, Sister Mary Hubert in Nunsense, Jan in Woman of the Year, Rose in Gypsy, others; films include Curtain Call (Japanese prodn.), Night Warning, 1983, Ice Pirates (cameo/co-star), 1984; TV films include The Great Ice Rip-Off, 1974, The Night They Took Miss Beautiful, 1977, When She was Bad., 1979, How to Survive a Happy Divorce, Bobby and Sarah, 1984, Orpheus Descending, 1990, Legs; (TV series) Who's Watching the Kids, 1978, Goodtime Girls, 1980; guest appearances on All My Children, Ryan's Hope, One Life to Live, Loving, Kate and Allie, Mr. Belvedere, Happy Days, The Bob Newhart Show, The Bionic Woman, others; first solo CD, Marcia Lewis Nowadays. Office: The Gage Group Inc 315 W 57th St Frnt 4H New York NY 10019-3158

LEWIS, MARGARET MARY, marketing professional; b. Bridgeport, Conn., Sept. 27, 1959; d. Raymond Phillip and Catherine Helen (Gayda) Palovchak; m. William A. Lewis Jr., Oct. 4, 1980. BS summa cum laude, Sacred Heart U., 1986; postgrad., U. Bridgeport; AS, Katherine Gibbs Sch., 1980. Program mgr. sales svc. group Newspaper Coop. Couponing, Inc., Westport, Conn., 1985-87; sales adminstr. Supermarket Communication Sys., Inc., Norwalk, 1987—88, mr. mktg. support, 1988—89; asst. project mgr. sales promotion Mktg. Corp. Am., Westport, 1989—91, account exec., 1991—92; mgr. program svcs. Ryan Partnership, 1992—93, sr. program mgr., 1993—95, mng. dir., 1995—96; account dir. Creative Alliance, 1996—97; promotion mktg. cons. CSC Weston Group, Wilton, 1997—98; account dir. TLP Inc., 1998—2000, group account dir., 2000—01; sr. dir. Source Mktg., Westport, 2001—02; mng. dir. Ryan Partnership, Wilton, 2002—04, v.p., 2004—05; exec. v.p., ptnr. Catapult Mktg. subs. D.L. Ryan Cos., Wilton, 2005—. Democrat. Roman Catholic. Home: 16 Nickel Pl Monroe CT 06468-3010 Office: Catapult Mktg 55 Post Rd W Westport CT 06880 E-mail: mlewis@catapultmarketing.com.

LEWIS, MARGARET SHIVELY, retired librarian; b. Indpls., Sept. 27, 1925; d. William E. and Florence (Knox) Shively; m. Phillip Fenton Lewis, Sept. 10, 1948; children— David William, Catharine, Fredrick, Thomas BA, Oberlin Coll., 1947; M.L.S., St. John's U., Jamaica, N.Y., 1971. Librarian Optometric Ctr. N.Y., N.Y.C., 1971; head librarian Coll. Optometry, SUNY, N.Y.C., 1971-90. Mem. exec. com. SUNY Council Head Librarians, Albany, 1977-79; chairperson Faculty Orgn., SUNY Coll. Optometry, N.Y.C., 1980-82; mem. SUNY/OCLC Network Adv. Com., 1986-90. Pres. residents assn. Forest at Duke, 1997—99; mem. Durham County Bd., United Way, 1999—2002; sr. warden St. Stephen's Ch., 2001—03; bd. dirs. Forest at Duke, 1997—2002, Coun. Sr. Citizens, 2003—. Library fellow St. John's U., Jamaica, N.Y., 1969 Fellow Am. Acad. Optometry; mem. ALA, Assn. Vision Sci. Librs. (chairperson 1977-78), N.Y. Regional Med. Librs., N.Y. State Optometric Assn. (Disting. Achievement award 1989), Phi Beta Kappa. Democrat. Episcopalian. Avocations: gardening, swimming. Home: 50 Forest At Duke Dr Durham NC 27705-5603

LEWIS, MARIANNE H., psychiatric nurse practitioner; b. Frankfurt, Germany, Feb. 8, 1921; d. Emil B. and Jessie (Falk) Horkheimer; m. Harold S. Lewis, July 10, 1943; children: Harold S., Jr., Dale G. AAS in Nursing, Pace U., White Plains, N.Y., 1970; BS, 1976; MSN in Adult Psychiatric Nursing, Yale U., 1980. Registered profl. nurse, Conn., advance nurse practitioner, Fla., cert. ANA specialist in psychiatric-mental health nursing, 1983. Sr. staff nurse Psychiatry N.Y.U. Med. Ctr., 1971-73; dir. White Plains (N.Y.) Med. Ctr. Day Hosp., 1973-78; asst. clin. prof. Yale U. Sch. Nursing, 1981-91; clin. specialist Dept. Psychiatry VA Med. Ctr., West Haven, Conn., 1980-83; nurse counseling group Norwalk, Conn., 1983-88; clin. specialist Grand View Psychiatric Resource Ctr. Waterbury (Conn.) Hosp., 1988-90; psychiatric review specialist Aetna Life and Casualty Ins. Co., Middletown, Conn., 1991-92; advanced registered nurse practitioner Vis. Nurse Asn. of Southwest Fla., 1995-96. Ombudsman for long term care patients State of Fla., 1999-2001, Commonwealth of Mass., 2002—. Spkr. Pace U. Dedication of Lienhard Sch. Nursing Bldg., Pleasantville, N.Y., 1974. Avocation: early music. Home: Kimball Farms Apt267 235 Walker St Lenox MA 01240 Personal E-mail: pooh2821@aol.com.

LEWIS, MARJORIE EHRICH, lawyer; b. Nov. 21, 1954; BA magna cum laude, Tufts U., Mass., 1976; JD, NYU, 1979. Bar: Calif. 1979. Law clk. to Hon. Warren J. Ferguson U.S. Ct. Appeals (9th cir.), 1979-80; joined Gibson, Dunn & Crutcher, 1981—, ptnr. bus. litig. LA, 1988—, now ptnr.-in-charge, LA and Century City offices. Mem. exec. com. Gibson Dunn & Crutcher, 1996—2000, mem. mgmt. com., 1999—2000. Mem. NYU Law Rev., 1977—78. Office: Gibson Dunn & Crutcher 333 S Grand Ave Ste 4400 Los Angeles CA 90071-3197 Office Phone: 213-229-7462. Office Fax: 213-229-6462. Business E-Mail: mlewis@gibsondunn.com.

LEWIS, MARTHA NELL, Christian educator, lay minister, expressive arts therapist; b. Atlanta, Mar. 4, 1944; d. Clifford Edward and Nell (Shropshire) Wilkie; m. Jeffrey Clark Lewis, Aug. 20, 1966 (div. Aug. 1986); children: John Martin, Janet Michelle Teal. BA, Tex. Tech. U., 1966; massage therapy, The Winters Sch., 1991; MA, Norwich U., 1994; MTS, Ch. Divinity Sch. Pacific, 2000. Cert. music practitioner, expressive therapist, massage therapist, music instr. Geophys. analyst Shell Oil Co., Houston, 1966-68; photogravity specialist Photogravity, Inc., Houston, 1972-80; tchr. music Little Red Sch. House, Houston, 1974-75; sec., treas. Lewis Enterprises, Inc., Houston, 1976-83; regulatory supr. Transco Energy Co., Houston, 1983-92; expressive arts therapist Shalom Renewal Ctr., Splendora, Tex., 1995, River Oaks Health Alliance, Houston, 1995—96; co-founder, past nat. exec. dir., pres., tchr. Music for Healing and Transition Program, 1994—. Massage therapist, expressive therapist, Houston, 1991-2000, Calif., 1996-2000; adj. prof. Holy Names Coll., Oakland, Calif., 1998-99; Sunday sch. coord. St. Stephen's Episc. Ch., Belvedere, Calif., 2000; min. Christian edn. St. Paul's Episc. Ch., Waco, Tex., 2000-05; children's min. Trinity Episc. Ch., Houston, 2006—. Vol. youth advisor Corpus Christi Cath. Ch., Houston, 1970-80; vocalist, instrumentalist Sounds of Faith Folk Group, Houston, 1978—; harpist Houston Harpers Harp Ensemble, 1990-92; liturgical dancer Random Dance, Berkeley, Calif., 1997-2000; instr. exercise, body awareness Transco Energy Co. Fitness Ctr., Houston, 1990-92; vol. The Inst. for Rehab. and Rsch., Houston, 1989-90, Houston Hospice, 1992-96, Houston Healing Healthcare Project, 1993-96; vol. Healing Environ. Coun. St. Luke's Episc. Hosp., 1993-96; lay chaplain Cmty. of Hope, 1994—; founder The Winters Sch. Massage Therapy Care Team, Houston, 1991-96; vol. Ctr. for AIDS Svcs., Oakland, 1996-2000, Hillcrest Hospice, 2003-05. Mem.: Nat. Assn. for Episcopal Edn. Dirs., Nat. Network Lay Profls., Christian Dance Fellowship USA, Nat. Sacred Dance Guild, Am. Massage Therapy Assn., Internat. Folk Harp Assn., Internat. Expressive Arts Therapy Assn., Sigma Kappa Alumnae Sorority (pres. Houston chpt. 1974—76, nat. collegiate province officer 1981—85, Houston Alumnae of Yr. 1981, Tex. Alumnae of Yr. 1980, Pearl Ct. award 1991), Houston Sigma Kappa Found. (bd. dirs.), Space City Ski Club (asst. trip coord. 1991—92). Roman Catholic. Avocations: harp, piano, voice, dance, travel. Home: 1007 Cypress Station Dr #2207 Houston TX 77090 Office Phone: 281-367-8113 ext. 102. Personal E-mail: mlewis3444@aol.com. Business E-Mail: mlewis@trinitywoodlands.org.

LEWIS, MARY JANE, retired elementary school educator; b. Hot Springs, SD, Dec. 11, 1939; d. LeRoy Allen and Mary Jane (Casey) Y.; m. Robert Melroy Lewis; children: Patrick, Christopher, Timothy, Eric. BS, U. Wyo., 1962, MA in Curriculum and Instrn., 1979. Cert. elem. tchr., reading specialist (kindergarten through twelfth grades). Elem. tchr. 2nd and 3rd grade, Medicine Bow, Wyo., 1962-63; elem. tchr. 3rd and 4th grade Shirley Basin, Wyo., 1964—66; jr. high reading, study skills tchr. Laramie, Wyo., 1967—98; reading dept. head, 1967—98; ret., 2003. Adj. prof. undergrad. studies U. Wyo. Coll. Edn., 1998—2003, student tchr. cons.; presenter, spkr. in field. Sect. vice-chair Albany County Reps., Laramie, 1990-92, sect., 1986-90; mem. Albany County United Way; v.p. Little League Baseball; cub scout leader; chpt. vol. Red Cross Mothers, March of Dimes. State Innovative grant State Dept. Wyo., 1989. Mem. IRA Snowy Range Internat. Reading Assn. (pres.), NRA Nat. Reading Assn., U. Wyo. Alumni Assn. (life), Phi Delta Kappa, Alpha Delta Kappa (chaplain, v.p., co-pres.), Delta Kappa Gamma (sect. v.p.), Alpha Kappa PEO(guard). Episcopalian. Avocations: reading, golf, bridge. Home: 203 Arrowhead Rd Torrington WY 82240

LEWIS, MARY MAY SMITH, retired family practice nurse practitioner; b. Curtis, Okla., May 18, 1919; d. James Thomas and Maggie May (Patten) Smith; m. Leo Burch Lewis, July 11, 1993; m. Leslie Wilson Enis, Nov. 8, 1965 (dec. Oct. 11, 1991); 1 child, Mary Corliss Enis. RN, Okla. City Gen. Hosp. Sch. Nursing, 1945. RN, Okla., 1945—50, Okla., 1993—, Calif., 1950—54, Fla., 1958—92, Mass., 1948. Author poetry. Second lt. U.S. Army, 1945—46, South Pacific. Mem.: VFW Ladies Aux. (life), Am. Legion (life). Republican. Christian. Avocations: genealogy, gardening, flower arranging, cooking, research. Mailing: PO Box 932 Perkins OK 74059

LEWIS, MARY-FRANCES, civic volunteer; m. William E. Lewis; children: John, Angela, Mary Sue, Rob, Amie, Clint, Derek. Student, Johns Hopkins U., 1960-61, Ariz. State U., 1966-69. Tech. sec. Johns Hopkins U., Balt., 1959-62; grant sec. Northwestern U., Evanston, Ill., 1962-66. Bd. dirs., chmn., v.p. Ariz. Supreme Ct. Foster Care Rev. Bd., 1979-82; bd. dirs. Tempe Ctr. for Habilitation, 1979-82; mem. governing bd. Tempe Union H.S. Dist., 1978-2003, 04—; foster parent State of Ariz., Phoenix, 1971-94. Named Woman of Distinction, Tempe St. Luke's Hosp., 1992, All Am. Woman, City of Tempe, 1985. Mem. Ariz. Sch. Bd. Assn., Nat. Sch. Bd. Assn., Kiwanis (sec. 1989-91). Republican. Methodist. Avocations: sewing, crocheting.

LEWIS, NANCY L., science educator; b. Houston, July 18, 1949; d. Frank F. and Onoua W. Lewis. BS, Stephen F. Austin State U., Nacogdoches, Tex., 1972; MEd, U. Houston, 1990. Earth sci. tchr. New Caney Mid. Sch., Tex., 1973—78, Kingwood Mid. Sch., Kingwood, Tex., 1978—80; 8th grade sci. tchr. Creekwood Mid. Sch., Kingwood, 1980—. Named Tchr. of the Yr., Creekwood Mid. Sch., 1998—99. Mem.: NESTA, Tex. Regional Collaboration for Sci. Excellence, Nat. Sci. Tchrs. Assn. Home: 357 Irene Deer Park TX

LEWIS, NINA, social worker; b. Cleve., July 21, 1953; d. William Paul and Gloria Louise (Pearch) L. BA in Sociology, Ohio State U., 1976, MSW, 1988. Lic. ind. social worker, Ohio. ACSW, rsch. asst. Disaster Rsch. Ctr. Ohio State U., Columbus, 1974-75; social worker Huckleberry House, Columbus, 1976-78, North Cen. Community Mental Health Ctr., Columbus, 1979-80, CHOICES for Victims Domestic Violence, Columbus, 1980-90; social worker state HIV case, mgmt, cons. AIDS unit Ohio Dept. Health, Columbus, 1990-93; dir. supportive housing dept. Lutheran Social Svcs. Central Ohio, 1992-97; HIV housing coord. Columbus Health Dept., 1997—. Adj. faculty Capital U., Ohio State U., Dominican Coll., Columbus State, Wright State. Coord. operation feed campaign Legal Aid Soc., Columbus, 1987. John H. Smith scholar, 1986-88, Anna Marie Mills scholar, 1986-88; recipient Walter and Marian English award, 1986-88, Social Worker of Yr. award Region V., 1996, Bob Fay award Franklin County ADMH Bd., 2000, Exec. Com. award Columbus Coalition for the Homeless, 2002. Mem. NASW, Ohio State Coll. Social Work Alumni Assn. Office: Columbus Health Dept 240 Parsons Ave Columbus OH 43215-5331 Office Phone: 614-645-7419. Business E-Mail: ninal@columbus.gov.

LEWIS, PATRICIA ANN, music educator; b. Phila., Mar. 17; d. Glenn and Olive Mae Little; m. Floyd Wayne Lewis. BA, Fairmont State Coll., W.Va., 1965; postgrad., U. Md., College Park, 1975—80. Cert. tchr. Md. Tchr. music St. Mary's County Bd. Edn., Leonardtown, Md., 1965—67, Prince Georges County Bd. Edn., Upper Marlboro, Md., 1967—97, Holy Trinity Episcopal Day Sch., Bowie, Md., 1997—. Organist, dir. choir Beltzville Meth. Ch., Md., 1967—71; accompanist Prince Georges Choral Soc., Greenbelt, Md., 1971—83; organist Arlington Forest Meth. Ch., Va., 1975—88; organist, dir. choir St. Matthews Meth. Ch., Bowie, 1988—91, Holy Trinity Episcopal Ch., Bowie, 1997—2005. Named an Outstanding Tchr., City of Bowie, 1985, Outstanding Educator, Prince Georges County Bd. Edn., 1997. Avocation: quilting. Home: 14115 Pleasant View Dr Bowie MD 20720 Office: Holy Trinity Episcopal Day Sch 13106 Annapolis Rd Bowie MD 20720

LEWIS, PATRICIA MOHATT (PATTY), special education educator; children: Christopher Brian, Ginger Louise, Katie Elizabeth Smolen, David Patrick. BS, U. Okla., Norman, 1965. Prin., tchr. Holy Family Cathedral Sch. Diocese Okla., Tulsa, 1995—99; coord. student svcs. Oral Roberts U., Tulsa, 1999—2001; tchr. spl. edn. inclusion Tulsa Pub. Schs., 2001—. Named Tchr. of Yr., Chester W. Nimitz Mid. Sch., 2002—03; recipient Customer Svc. award, Oral Roberts U., 2000, Diligent Svc. Faculty award, 2001. Mem. Rhema Bible Ch. Office: Tulsa Public Schools 3331 E 56th Street Tulsa OK 74105

LEWIS, PRUDENCE FOX, Christian science practitioner; b. Wilkensburg, Pa., Apr. 9, 1943; d. Clarence Cole and Mildred Charlotte Ives. BA, Principia Coll., Elsah, Ill., 1965. Internat. negotiator NOAA, Washington, 1967—99; Christian Sci. practitioner Alexandria, Va., 2004—. Sunday sch. tchr. Christian Sci. Ch., Fairfax, Va., 1978—2006. Recipient Bronze medal, U.S. Dept. of Commerce, 1999. Mem.: Principia Club (sec. 1995—2006). Christian Science. Achievements include aided in concluding agreements on international trade in endangered species, whale conservation through the Internationl Whaling Commission; elimination of foreign fishing in the U.S. 200 mile zone; conservation of fish and marine species and trade measures for conservation objectives. Home: 203 Yoakum Pky #1125 Alexandria VA 22304 Office: Christian Sci Practitioner 1717 K Street NW Washington DC 20036 Office Phone: 703-370-0026.

LEWIS, REBECCA LEE, medical/surgical nurse, educator; b. Waterloo, Iowa, Apr. 21, 1961; d. Raymond M. and Jacqueline (Nerge) Davis; m. Daniel Lewis, Aug. 27, 1983. BSN, Mount Mercy Coll., Cedar Rapids, Iowa, 1983; MS, Tex. Womens U., 1988. Staff nurse Sparks (Nev.) Family Hosp., 1987-88, Presbyn. Hosp. Dallas, 1983-87, 88-92, cardiology rsch. nurse, 1989-90; staff nurse Mercy Med. Ctr., 1993—. Instr. Mt. Mercy Coll., 1994-95, 2004—; home health nurse Gentiva Health Svcs., 1998-2006. Mem. Sigma Theta Tau. Home: 4361 Ridge Rd Cedar Rapids IA 52411-6806 Personal E-mail: christopherjustin@mchsi.com.

LEWIS, RITA HOFFMAN, plastic products manufacturing company executive; b. Phila., Aug. 6, 1947; d. Robert John and Helen Anna (Dugan) Hoffman; 1 child, Stephanie Blake. Student, Jefferson Med. Coll. Sch. Nursing, 1965—67, Gloucester County Coll., 1993—. Gen. mgr. Sheets & Co., Inc. (now Flower World, Inc.), Woodbury, NJ, 1968—72; dir., exec. v.p., treas. Hoffman Precision Plastics, Inc., Blackwood, 1973—. Ptnr. Timber Assocs. Author: The Part of Me I Never Really Meant to Share, 1979, In Retrospect: Caught Between Running and Loving; editor: SPOTLIGHTER; columnist: Innovative Singles Mag., 1989—. Commr. N.J. Expressway Authority, 1990—, sec., 1990—91, treas., 1991—, chmn. pers., 1991—; apptd. mem. N.J. Senate Forum on Budget and Revenue Alternatives, 1991; guest spkr. various civic groups, 1974; active Coun. for Citizens of Glen Oaks, NJ, 1979—, Cloucester Twp. Econ. Devel. Com., 1981—, Cloucester Twp. Day Scholar Com., 1984—; adv. coun. Gloucester Twp. Econ. Adv. Coun., 1985—; chair Gloucester Twp. Day Scholar Found., 1985—96; bd. dirs. Diane Hull Dance Co. Recipient Winning Eagle award, 1982, Mayor's award for Womens' Achievement, 1987, Outstanding Cmty. Svc. award Mayor, Coun. and Com., 1987, Don L. Stackhouse Achievement award, 1996. Mem.: NAFE, Soc. Plastic Engrs., Blackwood Businessmen's Assn., Sales Assn. Chem. Industry, White Horse Rotary Club (sargent-at-arms 2003, sec. 2004, dist. RYLA com. 2004, 2005, pres. 2005—06, dist. gov. 2006—, membership chair, Dist 7640 Presdl. citation 2006). Roman Catholic.

LEWIS, SAMELLA SANDERS, artist, educator; b. New Orleans, Feb. 27, 1924; d. Samuel and Rachel (Taylor) Sanders; m. Paul Gad Lewis, Dec. 22, 1948; children: Alan Stephen, Claude Anthony. Student, Dillard U., 1941-43; BS, Hampton Inst., 1945; MA, Ohio State U., 1947, PhD, 1951; postgrad., U. So. Calif., 1964-66; LHD (hon.), Chapman Coll., 1976, U. Cin., 1993; DHL (hon.), Hampton U., 1990; Doctorate (hon.), Calif. Coll. Arts, 2004. Asst. prof. Hampton (Va.) Inst., 1945-47; asso. prof. art Morgan State Coll., 1950-52; chmn. dept. art, prof. Fla. A&M U., 1953-58; prof. SUNY, Plattsburgh, 1958-67; coordinator edn. Los Angeles County Mus. Art, 1968-69; prof. Asian, African, Afro-Am. Art History Scripps Coll., Claremont, Calif., 1970-84, prof. emerita, 1984—. Author: Art, African American Textbook, 1978, The Art of Elizabeth Catlett, 1984, African American Art for Young People, 1991, African American Art and Artists Textbook, 1993; producer five films on Black Am. artists; founder Mus. African Am. Art, L.A., 1976; founder, dir., The Gallery, L.A., 1969-79, Asanti Gallery, Pomona, Calif., 1980; art editor Internat. Rev. African Am. Art, 1976—; one woman shows include Clark Mus., Claremont, Calif., 1979, Univ. Union Gallery, 1980, Delta Art Ctr., Winston-Salem, N.C., 1989, Bennett Coll., Greensboro, N.C., 1994; group shows include, Huntsville (Ala.) Mus., 1979, Smithsonian Instn. travelling exhbn., 1980-81, Vorpal Gallery, San Francisoc, 1989, Hampton (Va.) U. Mus., 1990, Am. Fedn. Arts, 1993—, Bomani Gallery, San Francisco, 1994; curator Masters Exhbn., Salvador, Bahia, Brazil, 1988, curator Two Sculptures Two Eras-Richmond Barthe and Richard Hunt, travel to mus., 1992—; solo: James E. Kemp Gallery, Dallas, Tex., 1995, Nat. Conf. Artists Gallery, Detroit, 1995; represented in permanent collections, Balt. Mus. Art, Oakland Mus. Art, High Mus., Atlanta, Palm Spring Mus., Va. Mus. Art, also 2 traveling exhibits; editor and curator: (catalog) Caribbean Visions: Contemporary Painting and Sculpture, 1995. Recipient Faculty Recognition award Scripps Coll., 1984, Disting. Alumni award Ohio State U., 1986, Honor award for outstanding achievement in visual arts Women's Caucus for Art, 1989, Legends in Our Time award Essence Mag., 1990, James Van Der Lee Lifetime Svc. to Arts award Brandywine Workshop, Phila., 1992, Lifetime Achievement award Brandywine Workshop, 1992, UNICEF award for visual arts, 1995; Fulbright fellow, 1962, NDEA postdoctoral fellow, 1964-66; Ford Found. grantee, 1965, 81. Mem. Assn. Asian Studies, Nat. Conf. Artists, So. Calif. Art History Assn., Coll. Art Assn. Am. (bd. dirs. 1990—). Home: 1237 Masselin Ave Los Angeles CA 90019-2544 E-mail: samellalewis@yahoo.com.

LEWIS, SANDRA ANN, music educator; b. Dallas, Tex., Oct. 24, 1955; d. Wayne Hitt and Betty Ruth Caldwell; m. Robert Lee Lewis, Jan. 3, 1975; children: Stephen Robert, Jennifer Ann. B of Music Edn., U. of North Tex., Denton, 1977. Tchr. Garland Ind. Sch. Dist., Tex., 1978—79, Spring Ind. Sch. Dist., Houston, 1986—2001, Conroe Ind. Sch. Dist., Tex., 2001—. Concert artist, spkr. Sandi Lewis Ministries, Houston, 1996—2006. Mem.: Tex. Music Educators Assn. (assoc.), Chi Sigma Iota (assoc.). Republican. Baptist. Avocations: gardening, singing, jogging. Home: 1807 Corral Houston TX 77090 Office: Buckalew Elem Sch 4909 W Alden Bridge The Woodlands TX 77382 Office Phone: 281-298-1383. Business E-Mail: salewis@conroeisd.net.

LEWIS, SANDRA B., mathematics educator; BS, U. Va., Charlottesville, 1984; MS, ODU, Norfolk, Va., 1985. Tchr. Northampton H.S., Eastville, Va., 1984—. Methodist. Office: Northampton High School 16042 Courthouse Rd P O Box 38 Eastville VA 23347 Office Phone: 757-678-8040 4017. E-mail: slewis@nhs.ncps.k12.us.va.

LEWIS, SANDRA COMBS, research psychologist, writer; b. Troup County, Ga., Oct. 8, 1939; d. Robert Milton and Imogene (Richardson) Combs; children: Virginia Susan Lewis, Charles James III. AB, Wesleyan Coll., 1961; MEd, Mercer U., 1972, Ga. State U., 1976; PhD, U. Ga., 1980. Personnel asst. Sears Roebuck & Co., Atlanta, 1961—62; rsch. asst. bd. regents U. Sys. Ga., 1962—63; asst. psychol. svcs. Bibb County Bd. Edn., Macon, 1972—73; instr. Macon Jr. Coll., 1973, 1982, Wesleyan Coll., 1973—75, 1981; psychometrist Middle Ga. Psychoednl. Ctr., 1975—76; instr. Mercer U., 1980—82. Presenter at profl. confs. Co-author: Christian Love and Problems of Living, 1992, God and Positive Christianity, 1998, Psychology for Life, 2000, A Revolutionary View of Education and Teaching for the Third Millennium, 2002; assoc. editor Truth Seekers Newsletter, 1998—. Pres. Macon Wesleyan Alumnae Club, 1973-74; bd. dirs. Family Counseling Ctr., Macon, 1975-76; ruling elder, clk. of session Northminster Presbyn. Ch., Macon, 1988-90, 94-96, vice moderator Presbyn. Women, 1989-90, 2002, moderator Presbyn. Women, 1990-91, 2003; v.p. Fore(In)Sight Found., 1991-2006; pres. Fore(In)Sight Found., 2006—. Mem.: APA (life), Mid. Ga. Psychol. Assn., Ga. Psychol. Assn. (life). Avocations: gardening, photography. Home and Office: 4976 Oxford Rd Macon GA 31210-3059 Office Phone: 478-474-3869. Business E-Mail: foreignsight@excite.com.

LEWIS, SHARYN LEE, sculptor; b. Carmel, Calif., July 31, 1946; d. William Albert and Hazel Elisabeth Lewis; m. Robert John Western, Mar. 22, 1986. Asst. art tchr. Benin (Nigeria) Coll., 1974-76; comml. artist KTT Art Svc., Campbell, Calif., 1976-77; graphic artist, illustrator Intersil Corp., Santa Clara, Calif., 1977-80; sr. artist, graphic designer Pro-Log Corp., Monterey, Calif., 1980-83; freelance graphic designer Monterey, 1983-92; sculptor, 1992—. Exhibitions include Mystic Maritime Gallery, Mystic Seaport, Conn., 1995-2006, Big Horn Galleries, Carmel, 1995-96, Fifth Ann. Loveland (Colo.) Sculpture Invitational, 1996, Monterey Peninsula Art Found., 1997, Monterey Mus. Art, 1998-2003, Maritime Gallery, Mystic, Conn., 2004, Pk. Ave. Atrium Gallery, NYC, 2003-04, Brookgreen Gardens, SC, 2003, Monterey Gallery, Calif., 1994-2006, Chirstopher Bell Gallery, 1994-2006; pvt. collections. Mem. Internat. Sculpture Ctr., Washington, Nat. Sculpture Soc. (NYC), Nat. Mus. Women in Art (Washington), Met. Mus. Art (NYC), Monterey Mus. Art.

LEWIS, SYLVIA DAVIDSON, foundation executive; b. Akron, Ohio, Apr. 28, 1927; d. Harry I. and Helen E. (Stein) Davidson; m. Allen D. Lewis, Oct. 12, 1947; children: Pamela Lewis Kanfer, Randy, Daniel, Cynthia Lewis Lagdameo. Student, U. Mich., 1945—47, U. Akron, 1961—62. Editor Akron Jewish News, 1948-50; tchr. Revere Rd. Congregation, Akron, 1964-70; office mgr. Acme Lumber & Fence Co., Akron, 1970-85; nat. pres. NA'AMAT USA (Movement of Working Women & Vols.), N.Y.C., 1993-97. Pres. Planned Parenthood Summit Portage and Medina Counties, 1999-2001; founding mem. Govt. Affairs Com., Columbus, Ohio, 1981—, exec. com., 1988-89; v.p. Akron Jewish Cmty. Fedn., 1988-94, pres. women's divsn., 1987-90; elect mem. Akron Jewish Cmty. Bd., 1999-2006; nat. v.p. Na'amat USA, 2004—. Named Woman of Distinction, YWCA Summit County, 2001; named one of No. Ohio's Top Women Profls., No. Ohio Live mag., 1997; named to Ohio Women's Hall of Fame, 1995; recipient Golden Rule award, J.C. Penney, 1994, Vol. of Yr. award, Lippman Cmty. Day Sch., 1992, Commendation of Honor award, Ohio Gen. Assembly, 1993, Women of Achievement award, YWCA of Summit County, 1999. Democrat. Jewish. Avocations: reading, writing, travel. Home: 4389 Everett Rd Richfield OH 44286 Personal E-mail: syllewis1@aol.com.

LEWIS, TOMMI, magazine editor; Editor-in-chief Disney Adventures Walt Disney Pub. Co.; editl. dir. Radio Guide Magazine; exec. editor Japan. Journal Magazine; exec. editor mag. devel. Petersen Pub.; editor-in-chief Sassy Magazine; exec. editor LIVE! Magazine; editor-at-large Teen Magazine, 1998-2000, editor-in-chief, 2000—02.

LEWIS, VICTORIA ANN, theater educator; d. Hugh Parr and Jane Lewis. BA, Dunbarton Coll. of the Holy Cross, 1967; MA in Lang. and Lit., Columbia U., N.Y.C., 1968; PhD, UCLA, 2000. Editor Ctr. for Ind. Living, Berkeley, Calif., 1977; journalist, editor Vista Vol., Berkeley, Calif., 1977—80; ensemble mem. Lilith: A Woman's Theatre, San Francisco, 1977—81; artist in residence Calif. Arts Coun., Berkely, L.A., 1981—91; dir., founding dir. Other Voices/Mark Taper Forum, L.A., 1981—2002; actress ITP/ Mark Taper Forum, L.A., 1981—84, Lorimar Studios, Culver City, Calif., 1984—91; assoc. prof. theatre arts U. Redlands, Calif., 2000—. Cons. Nat. Endowment for the Arts, Washington, 1997—98, Writers Guild Am./Non-Traditional Casting Project, N.Y.C., 2005—; cons., spkr. President's Coun. on the Arts, Washington, 2000; guest lectr. City Theatre, Pittsburgh, Calif., 2006—; presenter in field. Dir., writer: (plays) Tell Them I'm a Mermaid/ Who Parks in Those Spaces? (Vesta Award for Outstanding Contbn. by a Woman in So. Calif. to the Theatre, 1987); The Greatest Stories

Never Told: Voices form the New American Workplace (The AFL-CIO's Image award, 1990); dir.: (theatre development workshop) Teenage Ninja Moms/Growing Pains (LA County Human Rels. Commn. John Anson Ford Award for the Arts, 1998). Recipient U. Redlands Outstanding Faculty award for Rsch. and Creative Activity, Faculty Rev. Com./ U. Redlands, 2002—03; fellow Aaron Curtis award for Critical Writing, Sch. Theatre, Film and TV, UCLA, 1997; grantee, Durfee Found., 1998—99. Mem.: NOW, AAUW, Am. Soc. for Theatre Rsch., Soc. for Disability Studies (advisor, contbr. 2000—06), Am. Theatre in Higher Edn. (Am. Dissertation Yr. fellowship 1999—2000), Disability Studies Quar. (hon.). Achievements include created the first professional theatre development laboratory in the American Theatre dedicated to the training of disabled playwrights and actors. Office: University of Redlands 1200 East Colton Ave Redlands CA 92373 Office Phone: 909-748-8726. Business E-Mail: victoria_lewis@redlands.edu.

LEWIS, VIRGINIA MARIE, psychologist; b. San Rafael, Calif., June 21, 1942; d. Lyle C. Lewis and Juanita Marie (Nelson) Smith BA, Calif. State U., San Francisco, 1968, MA, 1971; PhD, Pacific Sch. Psychology, Palo Alto, Calif., 1986. Lic. psychologist, ednl. psychologist, marriage and family therapist; cert. sch. psychologist, Calif. Assoc. Mental Rsch. Inst., Palo Alto, 1978—90, sr. rsch. fellow, 1990—; pvt. practice psychologist Palo Alto, 1980—; instr. dept. edn. psychology Calif. State U., Hayward, 1985-87, Western Grad. Sch. of Psychology, Palo Alto, 1987—. Cons., com. mem. doctoral dissertations, 1987; instr. dept. ednl. psychology Calif. State U., Hayward, 1985-87, We. Grad. Sch. Psychology, Palo Alto, 1987—; founder Recovery Forum task force on addiction and recovery issues, 2002—; co-founder, co-dir. Family Recovery Project, 1989—; prin. investigator, author Devel. of Family Goal Attainment Scales, 1980—; co-author grants in field, sr. facilitator, therapist in eye movement desentization and reprocessing, 1990— Author: 2 books; contbr. articles to profl. jours. Recipient Don D. Jackson Meml. award Mental Rsch. Inst., Palo Alto, 1980. Mem. APA, Calif. Psychol. Assn., Calif. Assn. Sch. Psychologists and Psychometrists, Psychologists Assn. San Francisco (exec. sec., editor, 1974-77), EPIC (founder, chair eye movement desentization and reprocessing profl. issues com. 1991-94) Avocation: canine sports. Office: 555 Middlefield Rd Palo Alto CA 94301-2124 Office Phone: 650-326-8752. Business E-Mail: famrec@ix.netcom.com.

LEWIS-BRADSHAW, MAVIS LATISHA, healthcare educator; b. Memphis, Sept. 15, 1960; d. Bessie Lee Neal; children: Cassandra L. Lewis, LaQueta E. Lewis, Nicole U. Lewis, Tommy W. Lewis Jr. Program asst. South Pk. Devel. Ctr., Brownwood, Tex., 1989—90; specialist Ctrl. Tex. MHMR, Brownwood, 1990—98; mhmr specialist Abilene State Sch., Tex., 1998—2004; infant care tchr. Small World of Learning, Abilene, 2004—; health caregiver So. Meadows, Abilene, 2005—. Recipient award, Feed The Children, Oklahoma City, 2006. Home: 5450 Texas Ave Apt 1626 Abilene TX 79605 Personal E-mail: mbradshawa@aol.com.

LEWIS-GILCHRIST, STEPHANIE KAY, primary school educator; d. Bill Wesley and Janet Kay Lewis; m. Elton Carl Gilchrist, Nov. 12, 2005. BS in Interdisciplinary Studies, Tex. A&M U., 2001; postgrad., Our Lady of the Lake U., 2004—. Cert. tchr. Tex. Pre-kindergarten tchr. Floresville (Tex.) Ind. Sch. Dist., 2001—03, kindergarten tchr., 2003—. Campus tech. Floresville Early Childhood Ctr. Baptist. Avocations: scrapbooks, sewing, camping, fishing. Business E-Mail: sgilchrist@fisd.us.

LEWIS-GRIFFITH, DOROTHY ELLEN, music educator, pianist; b. High Point, N.C., July 7, 1932; d. Fleet and Foda Lee (Blakeley) Lewis; m. David Griffith, Dec. 12, 1959 (div. 1967); children: Dorothy Lewis, David Fleet (dec. 1987); m. Adrian Lafayette Shuford, Jr., July 28, 1985 (dec. Dec. 2000). BS, Juilliard Sch., 1954, MS, 1955; D Mus. Arts, Johns Hopkins U., 1978. Grad. asst. Peabody Conservatory, Johns Hopkins U., Balt., 1971-72; assoc. prof. music Valdosta State U., U. Ga. System, 1974-86; artist-in-residence Shuford Sch. Performing Arts, Catawba Coll., Salisbury, NC, 1986—2000. Vis. prof. U. Wis., Superior, summer 1972, Steinway Artists Roster; artist-in-residence Catawba Coll., Salisbury, N.C., 1986-2000. N.Y. debut Town Hall, 1965, recitals at Abraham Goodman House, 1983, Weill Hall at Carnegie Hall, 1992; concerts in Germany, France, Brazil, Peoples Republic of China; soloist with Atlanta Symphony, Brevard Music Festival Orch., N.C. Symphony, Winston-Salem Symphony, Orchestre de la Cité Universitaire, Paris., Kunming, Yunnan (China) Symphony; recs. include Starer Sonata, Ginastera Sonata, 1965, A Christmas Celebration at the Piano, 1978, George Gershwin: A Piano Solo Album, 1994; contbr. to EPTA Music Jour. and New Grove Dictionary Am. Music and Musicians revised edit., New Grove Dictionary of Opera. Bd. dirs. Charlotte (N.C.) Symphony, 1963-65, Lowndes Art Commn., Valdosta, 1975-78, N.C. Symphony, Raleigh, 1988-90, N.C. Sch. Arts, 1994-98; mem. Jr. League Charlotte. Recipient diplôme Geneva Internat. Piano Competition, 1956, winner Brevard (N.C.) Music Festival Concerto Competition, 1965; Fulbright-Hays grantee, 1955, rsch. grantee Valdosta State Coll., 1983. Mem. Music Tchrs. Nat. Assn., Sigma Alpha Iota. Avocations: gardening, swimming.

LEWIS JACKSON, WENDY S., social worker; b. Grand Rapids, Mich., May 9, 1965; d. Thomas James and Karen Susan (Kinard) Lewis BA, U. Mich., 1987, MSW, 1989. Investigator D.C. Pub. Defender Office, Washington, 1985; program asst. Detroit Urban League, 1989; coord. housing Ann Arbor Housing Commn., Mich., 1989—90; sr. assoc. United Way, Grand Rapids, 1990—93; program coord. Grand Rapids Found., 1993—94, program dir., 1994—. Mgr. database Kent County Emergency Needs Task Force, Grand Rapids, 1990—, editor, 1990—; sec. Kent County Emergency Food Subcom., Grand Rapids, 1990—; mem. Kent County Domestic Violence Coordinating Com., Grand Rapids, 1990—; mem. pub. affairs com. Mich. League for Human Svc., Lansing, 1990—; adj. prof. Grand Valley State U. Sch. Social Work, 1994— Contbr. articles to profl. jours Vol. Blodgett Meml. Med. Ctr., Grand Rapids, 1982—; mem. task force Citizen's League, Grand Rapids, 1990—; mem. pub. affairs task force United Way, Lansing, 1990— Recipient Leadership Award Kiwanis Club, 1983; Old Kent Bank and Trust scholar, 1983-87; Am. Marshall Meml. fellow, German Marshall Fund U.S., 2001 Mem. NASW, Nat. Assn. Black Social Workers, U. Mich. Social Work Soc. (bd. mem.), U. Mich. Alumni Assn., Women's Leadership Coun., Urban League Democrat. Episcopalian. Avocations: tennis, racquetball, photography, travel. Home: 16534 Huntington Rd Detroit MI 48219-4072 Office: The Grand Rapids Found 209-C Waters Bldg 161 Ottawa Ave NW Ste 209C Grand Rapids MI 49503-2757 Office Phone: 616-454-1751.

LEWIS RIFFLE, MURIEL ANN, retired secondary school educator; b. Yonkers, NY, Sept. 29, 1936; d. Paul S. and Anne M. (Koyce) Monahan; children: Amy, Scott, Brian, Michael. BS, Coll. Misericordia, 1958; MS, Purdue U., 1977; EdD, Ind. U., 1996. Lic. tchr. Ind. Tchr. Bergenfield (N.J.) H.S., 1958-62; owner, operator Strawberry Barn, Campbellsburg, Ind., 1969-72; tchr. West Washington H.S., Campbellsburg, 1972-97; ret. Bd. dirs. Life Spring, Salem, Ind., 1991-93, Washington County Substance Abuse coun., 1993-99, Washington County Cmty. Found., 1996-99, Project RESPECT, Salem, 1996-99; mem. parish coun. St. Patrick's Ch., Salem, 1990-93; coun. St. Agnes Ch., Nashville, Ind., 2004—. Mem. Am. Assn. Family and Consumer Scis., Ind. Assn. Family and Consumer Scis. (v.p. 1990-93, other offices), Ind. State Tchrs. Assn., West Washington Edn. Assn., U. Notre Dame Alumni Assn.(ct. appt. special adv., 2000—). Roman Catholic. Avocations: travel, reading, interior design, flower arranging, music, water sports.

LEWIS-RYDER, PATRICIA A., medical/surgical and community health nurse; b. N.Y.C., Jan. 17, 1950; d. Barrington E. and Alice B. (MacIsaac) L.; m. Edward G. Ryder, Oct. 15, 1977; children: Victoria, Christopher, Edward, Michael. Grad., Votec BOCES, Port Ewen, N.Y., 1985. LPN; cert. in basic arrythmia, CPR, advanced first aid, respiratory technician aide. With Benedictine Hosp., Kingston, NY; emergency rm. nurse Margaretville (NY) Meml. Hosp.; LPN charge nurse Mountainside RCF, Margaretville. Home: PO Box 85 Shandaken NY 12480-0085 Office: Mountainside RCF Margaretville NY 12455 Personal E-mail: ryderpal@aol.com.

LEWIS-WHITE, LINDA BETH, elementary school educator; b. Fresno, Calif., June 30, 1950; d. Lloyd Ernest and Anne Grace (Barkman) Lewis; m. Francis Everett White, Feb. 15, 1975; children: Anna Justine, Christopher Andrew Arthur. BA in Home Econs., Calif. State U., Sacramento, 1972, MA in Social Scis., 1973; postgrad., Tex. Women's U., 1976-79; PhD in Reading, East Tex. State U., 1994. Cert. bilingual and elem. edn. tchr., Tex. Tchr. bilingual Arlington Sch. Dist., 1977-96; prof. reading Eastern Mich. U., 1996—. Adj. prof. reading Tex. Women's U., Denton, 1989, adj. prof. ESL East Tex. State U., 1993; mem. tchr. trainer cadre, Dallas Ind. Sch. Dist., 1985-92; freelance cons., 1987—; presenter TESOL Internat. Conf., San Antonio, 1989. Cons., writer (book) Ciencias-Silver Burdett, 1988. Troop leader Girl Scouts U.LS., Dallas, 1980-82. Mem. Nat. Reading Conf., Nat. Writing Project, Internat. Reading Assn., Tchrs. of English to Spkrs. of Other Langs. (nominating com. 1990-91), TEXTESOL V (chair elem. edn. com. 1989-91), Tex. Assn. Bilingual Edn., Phi Delta Kappa, Phi Mu. Mem. Christian Ch. Avocations: sewing, knitting, quilting, reading, gourmet cooking. Office: Eastern Mich U 313A Porter Bldg Ypsilanti MI 48197-2210 Business E-Mail: llewiswh@emich.edu.

LEWTER, HELEN CLARK, retired elementary school educator; b. Millis, Mass., Jan. 14, 1936; d. Waldimar Kenville and Ida Mills (Currier) Clark; m. Alvin Council Lewter, June 18, 1966; children: Lois Ida, David Paul, Jonathan Clark. BA, U. Mass., 1958; MS, Old Dominion U., 1978. Tchr. Juniper Hill Sch., Framingham, Mass., 1960—63, Aragona Elem. Sch., Virginia Beach, Va., 1963—65, Park Elem., Chesapeake, Va., 1965—67; edn. specialist Riverview Sch., Portsmouth, Va., 1977—78; reading tchr. Truitt Jr. H.S., Chesapeake, 1979—83; reading resource tchr. Southeastern Elem., Chesapeake, 1983—86; tchr. Deep Creek Elem. Sch., Chesapeake, 1986—99, ret., 1999. Pers. task force, textbook adoption com. Chesapeake Pub. Schs., Va., 1984—85, employee handbook com., Va., 1986—87, K-6 writing curriculum com., Va., 1988—89. Active PTA, 1979—99; mem. mayor's adv. coun. City of Chesapeake, Va., 1988—89; tchr., workshop leader, dir., mem. various coms. Fairview Heights Bapt. Ch., Deep Creek Bapt. Ch., Va. So. Bapt. Retreats, 1968—; mem. summer missionary Va. So. Bapts., 1993. Mem.: NEA, Va. Reading Assn., Internat. Reading Assn., Chesapeake Reading Assn. (v.p., pres., honor and merit coun., chmn. various coms.), Chesapeake Edn. Assn., Va. Edn. Assn., Phi Kappa Phi, Kappa Delta Pi, Delta Kappa Gamma (legis. chmn.). Republican. Avocations: church related activities, reading. Home: 745 Mandarin Ln Chesapeake VA 23323

LEWTON, BETSY, chemistry professor; b. Bklyn., June 10, 1957; d. Karl and Muriel Andersen; m. Richard Lewton, July 5, 1981; children: Trevor, Parker. BS in Biology, L.I. U. CW Post Campus, Brookville, N.Y., 1978; MS in Biology, L.I. U.-CW Post Campus, Brookville, N.Y., 1979. Rsch. asst. SUNY-Stony Brook, 1979—85; adj. prof. Edison C.C., Ft. Myers, Fla., 1986—; tchr. sci. Estero HS, Fla., 1994—97, dir. academy program, 1997—98; tchr. chemistry Canterbury Sch., Ft. Myers, 1998—. Sophomore lead advisor Canterbury Sch., 1999—, chair profl. devel., 2003—, vice chair profl. devel., 2000—03. Nominee AP Tchr. award, Siemen's, 2006; recipient Golden Apple award, Found. Lee County Public Schs., 1996, Head of Sch. award for Ednl. Excellence, Canterbury Sch., 2001, Outstanding Tchr. award, U. Chgo., 2002. Mem.: Nat. Sci. Tchrs. Assn., West Ctrl. Ednl. Leadership Network. Office: Canterbury Sch 8141 College Pkwy Fort Myers FL 33919 Business E-Mail: blewton@canterburyfortmyers.org.

LEWY, HELEN CROSBY, artist, writer, translator, painter; d. Hewitt Crosby and Helen Louise Pratt; m. Hans Lewy (dec.); 1 child, Michael Robert. Studies with Edward Shenton, Swarthmore Coll., 1936—39; AB in Cinematography, U. So. Calif., 1947; studies with Fred Reichman, San Francisco, 1967—69; student, Nat. Art Sch. Analyst strategic svcs. OSS, Wash., N.Y.; polit. cons. Allied Election Mission to Greece; editor Portfolio, Phila., 1937—40; editor polit. intelligence Office Strategic Svcs., London, 1942—44, Naples, Italy, 1944—45; translator German Stories, N.Y.C., 1953—54, Christian Morgenstern Poems, N.Y.C., 1955—60. Exhibited in group shows at U. Calif. Ext., San Francisco, 1969, Richmond Art Ctr., 1972, Brickwall Gallery, Berkeley, 1972, Vacaville Art League Open Competition, 1973 (Blue Ribbon, 1973), ACCI Gallery, Berkeley, 1973, Crown Zellerbach Gallery, San Francisco, 1973, 1st winter ann. art co-op, 1974, Camelia Capital Art Exhbn., Sacramento, 1974; artist (invitational show) Hayward Area Art Festival, 1974; one-woman shows include Mezzanine Gallery, Bank of Calif., Berkeley, 1971, Athena Gallery, Oakland, 1974, Retrospective, Galerie de la cité, Lausanne, Switzerland, 1996, Represented in permanent collections, Italy, Israel, Germany, Switzerland, US (Oreg., Calif., NY); featured in (Italian mag. piece written by Adriano Sofri) Panorama, 2003; author: Amusings From a Life, 2006; contbr. articles to profl. publs. Mem.: Berkeley Art Co-op, Oakland Art Assn., Marin Soc. Artists, Artists Equity Assn., San Francisco Women Artists. Avocations: languages, art, dogs. Personal E-mail: hclewy@speakeasy.net.

LEWYN, ANN SALFELD, retired English as a second language educator; b. N.Y.C., Dec. 1, 1935; d. Henry and Betty (Ahrens) Salfeld; m. Thomas Mark Lewyn, July 15, 1955; children: Alfred Thomas, Mark Henry. BA, Hunter Coll., 1967, MA, 1982. Mem. faculty UN Hospitality Extension Lang. Program, N.Y.C., 1974-86; adj. instr. ESL NYU, 1986-90, adj. asst. prof., 1990-95, adj. assoc. prof., 1995-2000, adj. prof., 2001—02; ret., 2003—. Editor-in-chief (Newsletter) UN Hospitality Com., 1967-86. Mem. exec. bd. Small Press Ctr., N.Y.C., 1990-98; mem. adv. coun. Hospitality Com. for UN Dels. Inc., 1991-98; bd. dirs. Hunter Coll. Scholarship and Welfare Fund, N.Y.C., 1992—, sec., 1998-2000, 3d v.p., 2000-2001, 2d v.p., 2001-06, 1st v.p., 2006—. Mem. Teachers of English as Second Lang. (author in Aug. 1990 newsletter), N.Y. State Tchrs. of English as Second Lang., Pi Sigma Alpha, Kappa Delta Pi. Avocations: travel, tennis, needlepoint, photography, golf. Home: 911 Park Ave New York NY 10021-0337

LEY, CARMEN B., special education educator; d. Manuel and Martha De Brito; m. Ronald Ley, Jan. 16, 1965; 1 child, Jessica Elizabeth. BS, SUNY, Oswego, 1963; MA, SUNY, Albany, 1970. Cert. advanced grad. studies SUNY, 1978. Tchr. West Babylon Sch. Dist., NY, 1963—65; tchr. emotionally disturbed children NYC Schs., 1965—66; jr. guidance program N.Y.C. Schs., 1965—66; tchr. emotionally disturbed children Albany City Schs., 1966—68; tchr. emotionally disturbed, learning disabled Albany High Sch., 1968—99; chief sch. superintendent SUNY, Albany, NY, 1978; docent Albany Inst. Hist. and Art, 2000—. Adj. prof. Coll. St. Rose, Albany, 1998; mentor, educator BOCES, 1998—99, tchr. trainer, 1991—93; cons. Albany Acad. Girls, 1986. Bd. dirs. Families in Need of Assistance, 1999—, YWCA, Albany, 1997. Mem.: Coun. Exceptional Children (pres. 1968—69).

LEYBOURN, CAROL, musician, educator; b. Toledo, Dec. 15, 1933; d. Charles Wilson and Esther Lenore (McCaughey) L.; m. Donald Herbert Kenney, Aug. 21, 1954 (div. 1981); children: James Herbert, Paul McLean, Laura Elizabeth, Matthew McLean; m. Jerry Frederick Janssen, May 26, 1984. MusB, U. Mich., 1955, MusM, 1957. Tchg. asst. U. Mich., Ann Arbor, 1955-57; concert pianist USIA, Kaiserslautern, Germany, 1957-61; dir., instr. Leybourn Studios, Ann Arbor, 1961—90; solo pianist, harpsichordist Ann Arbor, 1961—90; keyboardist, mgr. Sterling Chamber Players, Ann Arbor, 1975-90; keyboardist Ann Arbor Chamber Orch., 1980-90, Ann Arbor Symphony, 1980-90; pianist Leybourn Trio, Janssen Trio, 1986—, Camerata Singers, Lake Forest, Ill., 1990-91; solo pianist, harpsichordist Appleton, Wis., 1998—; pianist, harpsichordist Cappelli Chamber Music Soc., Appleton, Wis., 1998—; pianist Lawrence U. Concert Choir, Appleton, Wis., 2000—01; chamber music specialist Lawrence Univ. Acad. of Music, Appleton, Wis., 1999—. Lectr., cons. various piano tchr. groups, 1975—; dir. Jr. Chamber Players, Ann Arbor, 1978-90, Junior Dixieland Jazz Players, Ann Arbor, 1984-90; dir. vocal music St. Gilbert's Elem. Sch. Grayslake, Ill., 1990-91; performer Nat. Conf. Women in Music, U. Mich., 1981, 83; adj. music instr. Ann Arbor Community Edn., 1984-90; instrumental music dir. Greenhills Sch., Ann Arbor, 1988-90; piano faculty David Adler Cultural Ctr., Libertyville, Ill., 1990-96, dir. chamber music; adj. piano faculty Coll. Lake County, 1993-96. Arranger (Dixieland music book) Combo!, 1987, Intermediated Piano Concerto Reductions "The Frustrated Accompanist", 2005—06, The Frustrated Accompanist, 2005;, musician numerous concert appearances with cellist Laura Kenney. Bd. dirs. Ann Arbor Soc. Mus. Arts, 1962-90; dir. chamber music and jazz workshops David Adler Cultural Ctr., Libertyville, 1991-96; founder, chmn. bd. dirs. Lake County Youth Orch., 1994-96. Regents scholar U. Mich., 1951-55. Mem. Nat. Music Tchrs. Assn., Mich. Music Tchrs. Assn., Ind. Music Tchrs. Assn., Washtenaw Coun. for Arts, Women's City Club (Ann Arbor), Suzuki Assn. of the Ams., Mu Phi Epsilon (pres. Ann Arbor alumnae chpt. 1964-66), Pi Kappa Lambda. Presbyterian. Avocations: gardening, decorating, refinishing furniture, graphic arts. Personal E-mail: carolleybourn@yahoo.com.

LEYDORF, MARY MALCOLM, physician, writer; b. Manila, Philippines; d. Justice George Arthur and Lucille Margaret Malcolm; m. Frederick Leroy Leydorf, 1953; children: Robert, William, Katherine, Thomas, Deborah. MD, UCLA, 1957. Cert. pediatrics, exec. mgmt. Claremont Grad. Sch. Intern Harbor Gen. Hosp., Torrance, Calif., 1957—58, resident pediatrics, 1958—61; fellow devel. medicine Brain Rsch. Inst., UCLA, 1967—68; asst. clin. prof. pediatrics UCI, Irvine, Calif., 1971—73; physician-in-charge L.A. Med. Treatment Unit Calif. Children's Svc., physician-in-charge Glendale Med. Treatment Unit; commr. lic. divsn. Med. Bd. Calif.; physician L.A. County Pub. Health, Calif. State U., L.A.; attending physician child devel. clinic UCI Med. Ctr., Orange, Calif., White Meml. Hosp., L.A.; sch. physician El Monte, San Gabriel, Temple City Sch. Dists. Founder, dir. Leydorf Med. Clinics, Inc., 1969—89. Editor: (quarterly newsletter) Dev. Disability Rsch. Rev., 1987—89; co-author: (articles) Jour. Spl. Edn., Jour. Western Medicine, Pediatrics. Mem. Rotary Internat., 2000, Zonta Internat.; vol. physician YMCA, So. Pasadena, San Marino, Calif., Spastic League, Pasadena. Mem.: Am. Acad. Pediatrics, AMA, Calif. Scholarship Fedn., Palm Springs Writers Guild, Kappa Alpha Theta. Avocations: horseback riding, breeding thoroughbred horses. Home: 75 Majorca Dr Rancho Mirage CA 92270 Personal E-mail: malcolmpub@aol.com.

LEYSE-WALLACE, RUTH LOUISE, dietician, educator; b. Okla. City, Nov. 10, 1939; d. Roy Ray and Clerca (Conley) Newsom; m. David George Wallace, Oct. 8, 2000; m. J. Dee Headley (dec.); children: Dee Anne Headley Thomas, Kent Lawrence Headley; m. Robert Neal Scholl (div.); 1 child, Bryan Neal Scholl. BS, The U. Calif., Davis, Calif., 1968; MS, The U. Kans., Lawrence, Kans., 1971; PhD, The U. Ariz., Tucson, Ariz., 1998. Dietitian Menninger Found., Topeka, 1977—84, Mesa Vista Hosp., San Diego, 1985—89, HCA Willow Pk. Hosp., Plano, Tex., 1989—91; adj. provider nutrition Group Health Med. Assn., Tucson, 1991—98; adj. faculty Pima County C.C., Tucson, 1993—94, Mesa C.C., San Diego, 1999—. Presenter in field. Contbr. articles to profl. jours. Home: 1982 Verbena Ter Alpine CA 91901

LEZAK, CAROL SPIELMAN, communications executive, editor, writer, design consultant, medical librarian; b. NYC, Oct. 24, 1949; d. Murray and Sylvia Zeena (Ruderman) Spielman; m. Jeffrey Mayer Lezak, Mar. 2, 1975; 1 child, Jessica Lilli. BA in Fine Arts and Art History, Boston U., 1971; AMLS, U. Mich., 1972. Cataloguer of books Ryerson and Burnham Librs., Art Inst. Chgo., 1972-76, acting head tech. svcs., 1976-77; head tech. svcs. Gilpin Libr., Chgo. Hist. Soc., 1977-79; asst. editor Gen. Learning Comm., Highland Park, Ill., 1982-83, assoc. editor, 1983-84, mng. editor, 1984-92, sr. editor Northbrook, Ill., 1992-99, editor Eleven mag. for WTTW Chgo., 1995-99; editl. dir. Bounty SCA Worldwide, Chgo., 1999—2001; mgr. corp. comm. Walgreen Co./Walgreens Health Initiatives, Deerfield, Ill., 2001—04; sr. med. writer Walgreens Health Svcs., Deerfield, Ill., 2004—05; health content mgr. Walgreens.com Health Libr., Deerfield, 2005—. Book reviewer Libr. Jour., 1977-2000, Elle mag., 2005; freelance bookbinder, Highland Park, 1980—; owner North Woods Writing, Highland Park, 1994—. Author: Medication Matters Series, 2002—05; author, editor: Clara's Bakery Cookbook, 1995, Chicago Historical Society 5 Year Cumulative Index to Chicago History mag., The Better Health Booklets, 1995—99, Mrs. Applegate's Boarding House Cookbook, 1995; editor: Maturity Matters/Your Healthy Best, 1992—99 (award Soc. Nat. Assn. Publs., 1995), Your Health Report, 1992—99, The Good Health Sourcebook, 1996, Good Health Sourcebook Annual Calendar, Tobacco Free Clinical Care Management, 2005—, Walgreens Health Initiatives Outlook Trend Report, 2005; editor design cons.: mag. Your Health and Fitness, 1984—99; editl. cons. (video) Breast Self-Exam Guide, 1993. Vol., writing lab. tutor Highland Park Pub. Schs., 1994-96. Recipient Ednl. Press Assn. awards, 1988-1995, 1st pl. award logo design Sister Cities Found., 1990, hon. mention awards Gardeners of the North Shore, 1995, Internat. Corp. SMART award for adminstrv. excellence, 6 Mercury 2000 awards of excellence. Avocations: writing, reading, exercise, gardening, bookbinding. Office: Walgreen Co Dept 1458 104 Wilmot Rd Deerfield IL 60015 Business E-Mail: carol.lezak@walgreens.com.

LHUILLIER, MONIQUE (DIANE MONIQUE LHUILLIER), apparel designer; b. Philippines; m. Tom Bugbee. Grad., Fashion Inst. of Design and Merchandising, Los Angeles. Founder, designer Monique Lhuillier & Co., Los Angeles, 1996—; opened Monique Lhuillier Boutique, Beverly Hills, 2001—. Designs featured in numerous magazines including W, In Style, Modern Bride, Elle. Recipient Glamorous Bridal Designer award, 2001, Avant Garde Bridal Designer award, Wedding Dresses Mag., 2002. Mem.: Council of Fashion Designers of Am. Office: Monique Lhuillier & Co 1201 S Grand Ave 3rd Fl Los Angeles CA 90015

LI, LIJUAN, chemistry professor; b. Jilin, China, Mar. 12, 1962; came to U.S., 1998; d. Sheng Li and Shufang; m. Kai Li, May 1, 1987; children: Christopher, Jessica. BSc, Jilin U., 1983, MSc, 1987; PhD, McMaster U., Hamilton, Ont., Can., 1992. Vis. scholar McMaster U., 1987-88, postdoctoral fellow, 1992, asst. prof., 1995-98; rsch. assoc. Nat. Rsch. Coun. Can., Ottawa, Ont., 1993-95; asst. prof. chemistry Calif. State U., Long Beach, 1998-2001, assoc. prof. chemistry, 2001—. Mem. exec. com. Chem. Inst. Can., Hamilton, 1995-98; organizer Ont. Undergrad. Student Conf., Hamilton, 1996; rschr. in inorganic chemistry; guest prof. Jilin U., 1998—. Contbr. numerous articles to profl. jours. J.R. Longstaffe scholar, 1989-90, Yates Fund scholar, 1992, McMaster U. Centennial scholar, 1988-92, Ont. Grad. scholar, 1990-92; recipient Women's Faculty award NSERC, 1995-98, travel award Internat. Union for Pure and Applied Chemistry, 1999-2001; grantee McMaster U., 1995-97, Nat. Scis. and Engring. Rsch. Coun. of Can., 1995-99, Materials Mfg. Ont., 1998-99, Calif. State U., 1998-2000, Nat. Inst. Health, 2001—, Rsch. Corp., 2001—, Am. Chem. Soc.-Petroleum Rsch. Fund, 2001—. Mem. Am. Chem. Soc., Can. Chem. Soc., Internat. Union for Pure and Applied Chemistry. Avocations: travel, reading, swimming, dance, photography. E-mail: lli@csulb.edu.

LI, LINDA (LINDA JIAN-YUH LI), plastic surgeon; b. Morgantown, WV, Sept. 26, 1969; m. Bill Fulcher; 1 child. BA/MD (six yr. program) cum laude, Boston U., 1993. Cert. Am. Bd. Plastic Surgery, 2002. Intern, plastic surgery U. So. Calif., LA, 1993—94, resident, surgery, 1994—98; fellow Cornell Med. Ctr., NYC, 1998—2000; attending physician Hosp. Good Samaritan, LA, 2000; private practice Beverly Hills, Calif., 2000—. Featured on Dr. 90210, 2005—. Fellow: Am. Coll. Surgeons; mem.: Calif. Soc. Plastic Surgeons, Am. Soc. Plastic Surgery, Soc. Grad. Surgeons of LA County/U. So. Calif. Med. Ctr. Avocations: exercise, yoga. Office: 433 N Camden Dr Ste 1190 Beverly Hills CA 90210 Office Phone: 310-273-6252. Office Fax: 310-273-6050.*

LI, MARY J., scientist, educator; b. Jinan, China; came to U.S., 1986; d. Jiawen and Changxian (Liu) Li; m. Liqin Len Wang; 1 child, Stefany C. Wang. BS, Ctrl.-South Inst. Tech., Changsha, China, 1982; MS, U. Md., 1989, PhD, 1992. Engr., instr. Xian (China) Mining Inst., 1982-86; tchg. asst. U. Md., College Park, 1986-92, rsch. scientist, 1992-98, assoc. dir., 1996-98, adj. prof., 1998-2001; prin. scientist Raytheon STX/NASA Goddard Space Flight Ctr., Greenbelt, Md., 1998-2001, chief scientist, 2000—. Panel reviewer NSF, Arlington, Va., 1995, 98. Contbr. chpt. to book, articles to profl. jours. Bd. dirs. Hope Chinese Sch., Md., 1996-98. Recipient Engring. Rsch. award NSF,

1995, Materials Rsch. award Army-DURIP, 1997, others. Mem. IEEE, Soc. Photo-Optical Instrumentation Engrs., Microscopy and Microanalysis Soc., Chinese-Am. Sci. and Tech. Assn. (bd. dirs. 1997—). Avocations: gardening, reading, water-skiing, skiing.

LI, QIN, news anchor, reporter, television director, television producer; came to U.S., 1999;; d. Jinkui and Hong Li. BA in Law, Chinese Youth Coll. Polit. Sc., Beijing, 1992; MS in Econs., Chinese Acad. Social Sci., Beijing, 1998; MS in Journalism, Columbia U., 2000. Cert. in pub. affairs. Reporter People's Daily, Beijing, 1992-94, editor, reporter Shanghai, 1994-99; TV anchor, prodr., news reporter Sino TV, Inc., N.Y.C., 2001—. Dep. editor-in-chief New Asia Culture Found. and Pub. House, Hong Kong, 1999—. Prodr.: (TV news documentary) Blue Sky Station: 8th Avenue-New York's 3d Chinatown, 2000 (Emmy award NATAS, 2000); dir., prodr. (TV documentary) A Hole in Chinatown's Heart-Rebuild Chinatown after 9/11, 2003; contbg. author: First-Hand Experience with China's Hope Project in One Hundred Counties, 1991; co-author: Japan: Another Miracle in the 21st Century?, 1993; contbr. feature stories to internat. publs. Mem. selection com. Internat. Fanzhian Scholarship, Hong Kong, 1998-2001 Recipient Best News award Chinese Nat. Journalists Assn. and Chinese Disability Assn., 1994, Best News award Chinese People's Polit. Consultative Conf., 1993; featured in Selected Works of Outstanding Chinese Editors and Reporters, 1996. Mem. Soc. Profl. Journalists, Nat. Acad. TV Arts and Scis. Office Phone: 212-625-2877. Office Fax: 212-965-8917. Personal E-mail: qlinyc@gmail.com. Business E-Mail: ql20@columbia.edu.

LI, YING, dancer; b. China; Student, Beijing Dance Sch. Prin. dancer Ctrl. Ballet China, BalletMet, Columbus, Ohio, Pitts. Ballet Theatre, 1994—. Dancer Giselle, Romeo and Juliet, Don Quixote, Swan Lake, Sleeping Beauty, The Nutcracker, Rubies. Recipient Prix de Lausanne, Osaka, Varna. Office: Pitts Ballet Theatre 2900 Liberty Ave Pittsburgh PA 15201-1511

LIAO, MEI-JUNE, pharmaceutical executive, researcher; arrived in U.S., 1974; BS, Nat. Tsing-Hua U. Taiwan, 1973; MPh, Yale U., 1977, PhD, 1980. Tchg. asst. Nat. Taiwan U., 1973—74, Temple U., Phila., 1974—75, Yale U., New Haven, 1975—76, rsch. asst., 1976—79; postdoctoral assoc. MIT, Cambridge, 1980—83; sr. scientist Interferon Scis., Inc., New Brunswick, NJ, 1983—84; group leader Interferon Scis., Inc., New Brunswick, NJ, 1984—85, dir. cell biology, 1985—87; dir. R & D Interferon Scis., Inc., New Brunswick, NJ, 1987—94, v.p. R & D, 1995—2003; v.p. regulatory affairs and quality Hemispherx Biopharma, Inc., New Brunswick, 2003—. Contbr. articles to profl. jours.; inventor in field. Mem.: N.Y. Acad. Scis., Soc. Chinese Bioscientists Am., Internat. Cytokine Soc., Internat. Soc. Interferon and Cytokine Rsch., Am. Soc. Biochemistry and Molecular Biology. Office: Hemispherx Biopharma Inc 783 Jersey Ave New Brunswick NJ 08901-3660 E-mail: meijuneliao@yahoo.com.

LIASSON, MARA, news correspondent; BA in Am. History, Brown Univ. Mng. editor, anchor Calif. Edition; journalist The Vineyard Gazette; gen. assignment reporter, newscaster Nat. Public Radio (NPR), 1985, nat. polit. corr., 1985—, White House corr., 1992—2000, congl. corr., 1989—92; political correspondent FOX News Channel, 1997—. Regular contbr., Special Report with Brit Hume FOX News Channel, panelist, FOX News Sunday. Contbr. reports to All Things Considered and Morning Edition. Recipient Merriman Smith award, White House Correspondents' Assn., 1994, 1995, 1997; fellow Bagehot Fellowship in Economics and Business Journalism. Office: FOX News Channel 400 N Capitol St NW Ste 550 Washington DC 20001

LIBBEY, DARLENE HENSLEY, artist, educator; b. La Follettee, Tenn., Jan. 9, 1952; d. Charles Franklin and Geneva (Chitwood) Hensley; children: Michael Damon McLaughlin, Marina Auston. BFA in Painting, San Francisco Art Inst., 1989; MFA in Painting/Drawing, U. Tenn., 1994. Grad. asst. Alliance of Ind. Colls., N.Y.C., 1989; gallery asst. Holley Solomon Gallery, N.Y.C., 1989; teaching assoc., instr. U. Tenn., Knoxville, 1991-94; lectr., instr. U. Tex.-Pan Am., 1994-97, South Tex. Cmty. Coll., 1995-96; instr. Pellissippi Tech. C.C., 1998—, U. Tenn., 1999—. Curator Belleza Salon, Knoxville, 1993-94; invitational rep. San Francisco Art Inst., N.Y. Studio Program, Alliance Ind. Colls., 1989; organizer Multi-Media Group Exhbn., San Francisco; lectr., instr. South Tex. C.C., McAllen; instr. Buck's Rock Camp, New Milford, Conn., summer, 1999. One-woman shows include U. Tex.-Pan Am., 1995, 96; exhibited in group shows at San Francisco Art Inst., 1985, 86, 87, 88, 89, Pacific Ctr., San Francisco, 1988, alliance of Ind. Colls., N.Y.C., 1989, San Francisco Mus. Modern Art, 1990, Bluxom Studios, San Francisco, 1991, Gallery 1010, Knoxville, 1991, 92, Ewing Gallery, U. Tenn., Knoxville, 1991, 92, 93, 94, SUNY, Syracuse, 1992, Printers Mark, Knoxville, 1993, Unitarian Ch., Knoxville, 1993, Tomato Head, Knoxville, 1994, Belleza Salon, Knoxville, 1994, U. Pan Am., 1995, 96; group show Museo Historico de Reynosa, Tamalipus, Mex., 1996. Vol. San Francisco Mus. Modern Art, 1990-91; founding mem. Grad. Student Union, U. Tenn., Knoxville, 1993; vol. instr. Knox County Schs., Knoxville, 1992-93; vis. artist Marin County Schs., San Anselmo, Calif., 1989. Tuition scholar San Francisco Art Inst., 1987; materials grantee U. Tenn., 1993, grantee Buck Found., 1987-89. Mem. Coll. Art Assn. Democrat. Unitarian Universalist. Avocations: cooking, reading.

LIBBIN, ANNE EDNA, lawyer; b. Phila., Aug. 25, 1950; d. Edwin M. and Marianne (Herz) L.; m. Christopher J. Cannon, July 20, 1985; children: Abigail Libbin Cannon, Rebecca Libbin Cannon. AB, Radcliffe Coll., 1971; JD, Harvard U., 1975. Bar: Calif. 1975, U.S. Dist. Ct. (cen. dist.) Calif. 1977, U.S. Dist. Ct. (no. dist.) Calif. 1979, U.S. Dist. Ct. (ea. dist.) Calif. 1985, U.S. Ct. Appeals. (2d cir.) 1977, U.S. Ct. Appeals (5th cir.) 1982, U.S. Ct. Appeals (7th cir.) 1976, U.S. Ct. Appeals (9th cir.) 1976, U.S. Ct. Appeals (D.C. cir.) 1978, U.S. Supreme Ct. 2001. Appellate atty. NLRB, Washington, 1975-78; assoc. Pillsbury Madison & Sutro LLP, San Francisco, 1978-83, ptnr., 1984-99; sr. counsel SBC West Legal Dept., San Francisco, 1999—; dir. Jewish Vocat. Svcs., San Francisco, 2002—. Three Guineas fellow Harvard Law Sch., 1997; dir. Alumnae Resources, San Francisco, 1991-97. Mem. ABA (labor and employment sect.), State Bar Calif. (labor law sect.), Bar Assn. San Francisco (labor law sect.), Radcliffe Club (San Francisco).

LIBBY, WENDY B., academic administrator; m. Richard Libby; children: Glenn, Gregg. BS in Biology, Cornell U., 1972; MBA, Johnson Grad. Sch. of Mgmt. at Cornell U., 1977; PhD in Ednl. Adminstrn., U. Conn., 1994. Dir. adminstrv. ops. Coll. of Architecture, Art and Planning, Ithaca, NY, 1979—84; dir. adminstrn. pub. mgmt. program Johnson Grad. Sch. of Mgmt. at Cornell U., Ithaca, NY, 1979—84; adminstrv. mgr. Coll. Edn. Ohio State U., Columbus, 1984—85, adminstrv. assoc. Office of Fin., 1984—85; asst. dir. U. Conn. Med. Ctr. John Dempsey Hosp., Farmington, Conn., 1985—87, asst. to assoc. exec. dir., 1985—87; spl. asst. to pres. and sr. human resources officer U. Hartford, Conn., 1987—89; chief fin. and bus. officer Westbrook Coll., Portland, Maine, 1989—95; v.p. bus. affairs and CFO Furman U., Greenville, SC, 1995—2003; pres. Stephens Coll., Columbia, Mo., 2003—. Founding bd. mem. Tuition Plan Consortium, Caribbean Inst. of Tech. Bd. mem. Greenville Literacy Assn., mem. fund raising com. Mem.: Soc. Coll. and U. Planning, So. Assn. of Coll. and U. Bus. Officers, Ea. Assn. of Coll. and U. Bus. Officers (bd. dirs.), Nat. Assn. of Coll. and U. Bus. Officers. Office: Stephens Coll 1200 E Broadway Columbia MO 65215

LIBERATI, MARIA THERESA, lifestyle company executive, cooking expert, writer; b. Phila., July 16, 1965; Student, Laval U., Que., Can., 1984; BS in Fgn. Lang. Edn., Temple U., 1986. Pres., bd. dirs. Sierra Ctr., Feasterville, Pa., 1988—; pres. M.T.L. Prodns., Phila., 1989—; exec. pres. Art of Living, Prima Media, 2004—. Spokesperson for Sparkling Cards, 2005—. Author: Fashion, Fun and Fitness, 1989, The Model's Guide, 1998, The Basic Art of Italian Cooking, 2006; editor mag. Better Nutrition for Today's Living, 1990—. Named Miss Pa., 1985, Miss World, 1986; recipient Merit award Actors and Artists Assn., Rome. Mem. AFTRA, NAFE (adv. bd. 1988—). Avocations: reading, cooking. E-mail: marialib@hotmail.com, marialiberati@liberaticorporation.com, lacucinadimaria@yahoo.com.

LIBERATO, LYNNE, lawyer; b. Pensacola, Fla., Dec. 22, 1953; BS in Journalism, Sam Houston State U.; MS in Journalism, Tex. A&M Commerce; JD, South Tex. Coll. Law. Bar: Tex. 1981, admitted to practice: US Ct. Appeals (5th Cir.) 1982, US Dist. Ct. (So. Dist.) Tex. Reporter/photographer Huntsville (Tex.) Item, 1974-75, Commerce Jour., 1975-76, Sta. KHOU-TV, Houston, 1976; with pub. affairs dept. Shell Oil Co., Houston, 1976-81; ptnr., Civil Appeals Haynes and Boone LLP, Houston. Chief staff atty. First Ct. Appeals, Houston, 1981-90; mem. adminstrv. oversign com. State Bar of Tex., 1995-96, gen. counsel oversight com., 1995-96, adv. com. legal svcs. corp., 1995-96, others; examiner Tex. Bd. Legal Specialization, 1989, appellate adv. bd. 1990-92; sec. Com. for Harris County Benchbook, 1993-97; speaker in field. Contbr. articles to numerous profl. jour.; author: Reason for Reversal in Texas Courts of Appeals (Outstanding Law Rev. Article Award, Tex. Bar Found., 2004). Chmn. Bd. United Way of Tex. Gulf Coast, 1996—, chmn. allocations rev. team, fund distbrn. subcom. 1997, chmn. implementation redesign com. 1996-97, steering com. for fund distbrn. redesign adv.com. 1994-95; mem. torch relay judging com. U.S. Olympics, 1996; v.p. Neighborhood Justice Ctr., 1981-85; mem. adv. bd. U. Houston Inst. for Urban Edn., 1997. Named Comml. Prosecutor of yr. Internat. Comml. Litigation mag., 1997, One of Ten Women on the Move, Houston Post, 1992, Woman of Year in Law, YWCA, 1993, Top Notch Appellate Lawyer, Tex. Lawyer, 2002, True Texan Award, Muscular Dystrophy Assn., 2002, Woman of Yr., United Way of Tex. Gulf Coast, 2004, one of top 100 Tex. Super Lawyers, Top 50 Female Lawyers, Top 100 Houston Lawyers, Tex. Montly Mag., 2003, 2004. Fellow Tex. Bar Found., Houston Bar Found.; mem. Am. Law Inst., Fedn. of Houston Profl. Women (Woman of Excellence 1994), Houston Bar Assn. (pres. 1993-94, editor jour. 1990-91, chmn. campaign for homeless 1991-92, legal edn. com. 1989-90, others), State Bar Tex. (chmn. client security fund com. 1995-96, exec. com. 1994-97, chmn. nominations and elections com. 1997-98, chmn. bd. dirs. 1996-97, pres. 2000-2001), Supreme Ct. Hist. Soc., Tex. Assn. Civil Trial and Appellate Specialists (bd. dirs. 1992-93). Office: Haynes and Boone LLP 1 Houston Ctr 1221 McKinney Ste 2100 Houston TX 77010 Office Phone: 713-547-2017. Office Fax: 713-236-5538. Business E-Mail: lynne.liberato@haynesboone.com.

LIBERMAN, GAIL JEANNE, editor; b. Neptune, NJ, Feb. 26, 1951; d. Si and Dorothy (Gold) L.; m. Alan Lavine, Dec. 20, 1991. BA, Rutgers U., 1972. Youth editor AP, NYC, 1972-73; writer United Feature Syndicate, NYC, 1973; reporter, broadcast editor UPI, Phila. and Hartford, Conn., 1973-75; reporter Courier-Post, Camden, NJ, 1976-80, Bank Advt. News, North Palm Beach, Fla., 1981-82; editor Bank Rate Monitor, North Palm Beach, 1982-97. Author: Improving Your Credit and Reducing Your Debt, 1994 (endorsed Inst. CFPs), The Complete Idiot's Guide to Making Money With Mutual Funds, 1996, Love, Marriage and Money, 1998, Rags to Riches: Motivating Stories of How Ordinary People Achieved Extraordinary Wealth, 2000, Short and Simple Guide to Life Insurance, 2000, More Rags to Riches: All New Stories of How Ordinary People Achieved Extraordinary Wealth, 2002, Rags to Retirement, 2003, Quick Steps to Financial Stability, 2006; columnist: Boston Herald, 1994—, America Online, 1996—, Investor Square, 1996—, Mutual Funds Interactive, 1996—, Quicken, 1998—, Palm Beach Daily News, 1998—, CNBC.com, 2000, Fasttrack mag., 2001, Pitts. Post-Gazette, 2001-; contbr. articles to profl. jours. Mem. Soc. Am. Bus. Editors and Writers. Personal E-mail: mwliblav@aol.com.

LIBERT, CLEO PATRICIA, computer scientist, consultant; BS, U. South Fla., 1997; MBA, Regis U., 2002. Analyst LHS Comm., Inc., Miami, 1998—99; cons. Alliance Telecom Solutions, Inc., Deerfield, Ill., 1999—2000; computer software cons. Elite Software Solutions, Inc., Miami, 2000—. Mem.: Assn. Info. Sys. Profls., Quality Assurance Inst. (cert. software tester). Office Phone: 305-812-3825.

LIBERT, NANCY PORTA, retired elementary school educator; b. Bay Shore, N.Y., Nov. 6, 1936; d. Frank and Anna Klenner Porta; m. Calvin Clifford Libert, Sept. 19, 1959; children: Darien Libert Logan, Leslie Libert Cain. Student, Hofstra U., 1954—59; BA Elem. Edn., Stony Brook U., 1973; MA Elem. Edn., Adelphi U., 1977; MA Linguistics, SUNY, Stony Brook, 1985. Cert. TESOL. Tchr. 1st grade Cordello Ave. Sch., Central Islip, NY, 1973—74, tchr. 3d grade, 1974—78, tchr. 5th grade, 1978—79; tchr. ESL Mulligan Sch., Central Islip, 1980—81; tchr. 6th grade Mulligan and O'Neill Schs., Central Islip, 1980—99; ret., 1999. Tchr. English phonology SUNY, Stony Brook, 1984—85; presenter in field. Editor, writer: bi-monthly newsletter Neighborhood News, 1988—2000, monthly newsletter Lamplighter, 1979—; author: (plays) The Western Civ Rap, 1994. Founder, past-pres., editor, com. chmn. Old South Islip Civic Assn., 1980—; tutor, mentor L.I. Youth Mentoring, Deer Park, NY, 2001—; founder, bd. mem., publicity chair Islip Sch.-Age Child Care, 1985—93; co-chmn. annual auction benefit Presbyn. Ch. Islip, 2002—05. Mem.: Hist. Soc. Islip Hamlet (founder 1993, site designation com., edn. liaison, corr. sec. 2004), Central Islip Ret. Tchrs. Assn. (exec. bd. del. 2001—). Democrat. Presbyterian. Avocations: collecting adolescent literature series, local historical research, running. Home: 88 Monell Ave Islip NY 11751

LIBET, ALICE QUANTE, clinical psychologist; b. Savannah, Ga., Feb. 7, 1949; d. Albert Herman and Anita (Mahany) Quante; m. Julian Mayer Libet, Nov. 27, 1976; children: Jared Quante, Ariel Quante. BA cum laude with gen. honors, U. Ga., 1971, MS, 1974, PhD, 1977. Instr. Ga. Retardation Ctr., Athens, 1974-75; research psychologist VA Med. Ctr., Charleston, S.C., 1978-81; clin. psychologist dept. pediatrics Med. U. S.C., Charleston, 1977-83; adminstr. community program S.C. Dept. Mental Retardation, 1983-86; adj. faculty Coll. Charleston, 1985-1991, The Citadel, Charleston, 1988-1991; dir. residential programs Charleston County Mental Retardation Bd., 1987-90; clin. psychologist, asst. prof. dept. physical medicine & rehab. Med. U. S.C., 1990-2000; asst. prof. Med. U. SC Dept. Psychiatry and Behaviorial Scis., 2000—. Contbr. articles to profl. jours. Mem. APA, Psi Chi. Home: 28 Hillcreek Blvd Charleston SC 29412-2521 Office: PO Box 250173 MUSC 30 Bee St Charleston SC 29425

LICARY, CHERYL ANN, retired music educator, church musician; d. Wilbur John and Verna Elise Dietzman; m. Nicholas J. Licary, Mar. 25, 1972 (div. June 15, 1985); children: Nunzio, Chiara. BA, Luther Coll., 1972; MST, U. Wis., Whitewater, 1976. Vocal music instr., dept. chmn. Sch. Dist. Beloit, 1973—2006; ch. musician, 1973—. Clinician, adjudicator, 1975—. Co-author: Beyond Ratings, 2003. Vol. Red Cross, Beloit, 1983—; mem. adv. bd. U. Wis.-Whitewater Sch. Arts and Comms., 2005—; adv. bd. U. Wis. Whitewater Coll. Arts, 2005—; organist, choir dir. Our Savior's Luth. Ch. Recipient Silver Star award, Wis. Dept. Recreation, 1995, Tchr. Recognition award, Beloit Rotary, 2001, Contbr. award, Zonta Commn., 2001, award for Excellence in Tchg. Music, Wis. Music Educators Assn., 2001, Great Minds 21st Century, 2003, 2004, 2005, Woman of Yr., Cambridge Blue Book, 2005, Ecolab Visions for Learning award, 2001, 2005, 2006. Mem.: Wis. Sch. Music Assn., Am. Guild of Organists, Assn. for Supr. and Curriculum Devel., Wis. Alliance for Arts Edn., Beloit Edn. Assn., Wis. Choral Dir.'s Assn., Wis. Music Educator's Assn. (Wis. award 2003), Nat. Edn. Assn., Music Educator's Nat. Conf., Am. Choral Dirs. Assn. Lutheran. Home: 1324 11th St Beloit WI 53511

LICHTENBAUM, GRETA L.H., lawyer; b. Phila., 1965; BA in Religion, with honors, Haverford, 1986; JD, Harvard U., 1990. Bar: Pa. 1990, DC 1991. Atty.-adv. US Internat. Trade Commn., 1995—96; counsel O'Melveny & Myers LLP, Washington. Mng. editor Harvard Human Rights Jour., 1989—90. Mem.: ABA, Phi Beta Kappa. Fluent in French. Office: O'Melveny & Myers LLP 1625 Eye St NW Washington DC 20006 Office Phone: 202-383-5249. Office Fax: 202-383-5414. E-mail: glichtenbaum@omm.com.

LICHTENBERG, MAGGIE KLEE, publishing executive; b. NYC, Nov. 19, 1941; d. Lawrence and Shirley Jane (Wicksman) Klee; m. James Lester Lichtenberg, Mar. 31, 1963 (div. 1982); m. William Shaw Jones, July 2, 2000; children: Gregory Lawrence, Amanda Zoe. BA, U. Mich., 1963; postgrad., Harvard U., 1963. Book rev. editor New Woman mag., 1972-73; assoc. editor children's books Parents Mag. Press, 1974; editor, rights dir. Books for Young People, Frederick Warne & Co., N.Y.C., 1975-78; sr. editor Simon & Schuster, N.Y.C., 1979-80; dir. sales promotion Grosset & Dunlap, N.Y.C., 1980-81; ednl. sales mgr. Bantam Books, N.Y.C., 1982-84; dir. mktg. and sales Grove Press, N.Y.C., 1984-86, dir. of sales, 1986-87; dir. sales Weidenfeld & Nicolson, N.Y.C., 1986-87; mktg. dir. Beacon Press, Boston, 1988-95; bus. and pub. coach, 1995—. Freelance critic, 1961—. Author: The Open Heart Companion: Preparation and Guidance for Open-Heart Surgery Recovery, 2006; contbr. articles, essays, stories, poetry, revs. to mags. newspapers and anthologies. Bd. dirs. Children's Book Council, 1978. Recipient 2 Avery Hopwood awards in drama and fiction, 1962, 2 in drama and poetry, 1963; coll. fiction contest award Mademoiselle mag., 1963; Woodrow Wilson fellow, 1963. Mem. Women's Nat. Book Assn. (past pres. N.Y. chpt.), Internat. Coach Fedn. (cert.), The Coaching Collective, PMA Independent Book Pubs. Assn. (bd. dirs.), N.Mex. Book Assn., PEN N.Mex., Adult Congenital Heart Assn. Home and Office: 4 Cosmos Ct Santa Fe NM 87508-2285 Office Phone: 505-986-8807. Personal E-mail: maggie@openheartcoach.com.

LICHTENSTEIN, ELISSA CHARLENE, legal association executive; b. Oct. 23, 1954; d. Mark and Rita (Field) L. AB cum laude, Smith Coll., Northampton, Mass., 1976; JD, George Washington U., 1979. Bar: D.C. 1980, U.S. Dist. Ct. (D.C. dist.) 1980, U.S. Ct. Appeals (D.C. cir.) 1980. Law clk. U.S. EPA, Washington, 1978-79; staff dir. ABA, Washington, 1979—, assoc. dir. pub. svcs. divsn., 1981-85, dir., 1985—. Editor, contbr.: Common Boundary/Common Problems: The Environmental Consequences of Energy Production, 1982, Exit Polls and Early Election Projections, 1984, The Global Environment: Challenges, Choices and Will, 1986, (newsletter) Environ. Law; co-editor, contbr. The Environ. Network; co-editor: Determining Competency in Guardianship Proceedings, 1990, Due Process Protections for Juveniles in Civil Commitment Proceedings, 1991, Environmental Regulation in Pacific Rim Nations, 1993, The Role of Law in the 1992 UN Conference on Environment and Development, 1992, Trade and the Environment in Pacific Rim Nations, 1994, Public Participation in Environmental Decision-making, 1995, Endangered Species Act Reauthorization: A Biocentric Approach, 1996, Sustainable Development in the Americas: The Emerging Role of the Private Sector, 1996, Environmental Priorities in Southeast Asian Nations, 1997, Law School Public Interest Law Programs, 1995, 99; prodn. contbg. editor American Justice Through Immigrants' Eyes, 2004, A Judge's Guide to Immigration Law in Criminal Proceedings, 2004. Named Outstanding Young Woman of Am., 1982. Mem.: NAFE, ABA, Greater Washington Soc. Assn. Execs., D.C. Bar Assn., Met. Washington Environ. Profls. (pres. 1986—96), Assn. Women in Comms., Am. Soc. Assn. Execs., Environ. Law Inst. (assoc.). Democrat. Jewish. Office: ABA Div Pub Svcs 740 15th St NW 9th Fl Washington DC 20005-1019

LICHTMAN, JUDITH L., lawyer, organization administrator; m. Elliott Lichtman; children: Sarah, Julia. Bachelor's degree, U. Wisconsin, Madison, 1962, LLB, 1965. Worked on sch. desegregation in South US Dept Health, Edn., and Welfare; teacher Jackson State Coll.; with Urban Coalition, US Commn. Civil Rights; worked on George McGovern's presdl. campaign, 1972; legal advisor Commonwealth of Puerto Rico; pres. Women's Legal Def. Fund (National Partnership for Women & Families since 1998), Washington, 1974—. Bd. mem. Women's Law and Pub. Policy Fellowship Program. Recipient Hubert H. Humphrey award, Leadership Conf. on Civil Rights, 2000.

LICK, SUE FAGALDE, writer; b. San Jose, Mar. 9, 1952; d. Clarence Edwin Jr. and Elaine Veronica Fagalde; m. James Brian Barnard, June 22, 1974 (div. May 1981); m. Fred Allan Lick, May 18, 1985; stepchildren: Ted Allan, Gretchen Anne Hedgecock, Michael Douglas. AA in Liberal Arts, West Valley Coll., Saratoga, Calif., 1972; BA in Journalism, San Jose State U., Calif., 1974, postgrad., 1978-80; MFA in Creative Writing, Antioch U., Seattle, 2003. Reporter Meredith Sun Newspapers, Cupertino, Calif., 1973-76, 78-80; editl. asst. Calif. Sch. Employees Assn., San Jose, 1976-78; reporter Pacifica (Calif.) Tribune, 1981-83; copy editor Hayward (Calif.) Daily Rev., 1984-85; editor Adv. Jour., San Jose, 1986-87; freelance writer/editor San Jose, 1987-93, Newport, Oreg., 1996—; reporter, editor Metro Newspapers, San Jose, 1993-96; reporter News-Times Newspaper, Newport, Oreg., 1998-99; instr. Oreg. Coast C.C., 2002—. Asst. dir. contemporary choir Sacred Heart Ch., Newport, Oreg., 2003—. Author: Living in San Jose, 1987, The Iberian Americans, 1990, Stories Grandma Never Told, 1998, Azorean Dreams, 2000. Asst. dir. contemporary choir Sacred Heart Ch., Newport. Named Achiever in Letters, Nat. League Am. Pen Women Santa Clara County Br., 1995. Mem. Oreg. Coast Coun. for the Arts, Portuguese Hist. and Cultural Soc., Willamette Writers (bd. mem., 2006—), Calif. Writer's Club (v.p. 1989-90, pres. 1991). Democrat. Roman Catholic. Avocations: music, photography, history, hiking. Home: 281 SE 97th Ct South Beach OR 97366-9716 E-mail: suelick@casco.net.

LIDDELL, MARY LOUISA, elementary school educator, computers educator; b. Daytona Beach, Fla., Mar. 14, 1931; d. Frank McCloud and Fannie Ruth Harris; m. Julius Woods (div.); m. Edward Liddell, May 28, 1988; children: Anthony, Andrew. BS in Elem. Edn., Bethune-Cookman Coll., 1962; MS in Reading & Sch. Adminstrn., Barry U., 1973; PhD in Ministry, Logos U. Seminary, 2002; specialist degree in ednl. adminstrn., U. Fla., Gainesville, 1976; specialist degree in computer edn., Nova U., 1985. Cert. computer edn. Nova U., 1985. Reading tchr. Dunbar Elem. Sch., Fla., 1962—71, North Beach Elem. Sch., Fla., 1971—74, Myrtle Grove Elem. Sch., Fla., 1974—76; asst. prin. Miami Springs Mid. Sch., Fla., 1977—78; reading tchr. Mae Walters Elem. Sch., Fla., 1977—80; tchr., counselor, asst. prin. COPE (Continuing Opportunities for Progressive Edn.) Ctr. North, Dade County Sch. Sys., Fla., 1980—82; reading tchr. North Twin Lakes Elem. Sch., Fla., 1982—88; instr. reading and computer sci. Bethune-Cookman Coll., Fla., 2000—03; instr. computer sci. Daytona Beach Cmty. Coll., Fla., 2001—02; reading tchr. Miami-Dade County Sch. Sys., Fla. Dir. sch. plays; adv. bd. Bethune-Cookman Coll. Women, 2000—. Sec. YWCA, Miami, 1966—70; voter registration chairperson Dem. Party, Miami, 1980—87, com. woman, 1980—88; hosp. aux. mem. Cancer Rsch. Libr., Daytona Beach, 2002—; mem. Halifax Med. Ctr., Daytona Beach, 2004—; counselor airline stewardesses United Ch. Christ, Miami, 1963—65, counselor U. Miami students, 1963—66; min. Tubman-King Cmty. Ch., UCC, Daytona Beach, 2002—. Named Tchr. of Yr., Mae Walters Elem. Sch., 1989; recipient Gwendolyn Cherry Humanitarian award, Nat. Sigma Gamma Rho, 1981. Mem.: Sigma Gamma Rho (co-sponsor Buds of Spring 1972—75, sponsor The Roses 1975). Democrat. Avocations: painting, knitting, writing poetry. Personal E-mail: mliddell@cfl.rr.com.

LIDEN, HANNA, photographer; b. Stockholm, 1976; BFA in Photog., Parsons Sch. Design, NYC, 2002. Exhibited in group shows at You're Just a Summer Love but I'll Remember You When Winter Comes, 2005, one-man shows include and her shadow Death, Rivington Arms Gallery, NYC, exhibited in group shows at Be In, The Volta Show, 2006, Noctambule, NYC, The Whitney Biennial, Whitney Mus. Art, NYC, 2006. Office: c/o Rivington Arms 102 Rivington St New York NY 10002*

LIDSTROM, ESTHER MARIE, artist, photographer; b. Rockville Centre, N.Y., Aug. 18, 1947; d. Carl John and Helen Marie (Benzie) L. BA, Adelphi U., 1969, MA, 1971. Lic. art educator, N.Y. Tchr. Sayville Pub. Schs., NY, 1972-84; police officer Nassau County Police Dept., Mineola, NY, 1984-86; high sch. art tchr. Sayville HS, 1986—2002. Guest speaker Nat. Audubon Soc., East Islip, N.Y., 1989, Nassau County Visual Arts Ctr., East Norwich, N.Y., 1990, Bryant Libr., Roslyn, N.Y., 1991, KC, Amityville, N.Y., 1991. Group shows include Rochester (N.Y.) Mus. and Sci. Ctr., 1989, Boston Mus. Sci., 1989, Cleve. Mus. Natural History, 1991, Va. Mus. of Natural History,

1992, The Witte Mus., San Antonio, 1992, San Bernardino County Mus., Redlands, Calif., 1992, Anniston (Ala.) Mus. Natural History, 1992, William S. Fairfield Pub. Gallery, 2000, SAA Nat. Georgraphic Headquarters, 2001, Bennington Ctr. Natural and Culteral Arts, 2006; contbr. articles to profl. jours. Recipient Showcase award Visual Art Alliance of L.I. and Nassau County Office Cultural Devel., 1989, Sax award Nat. League Am. Pen Women, Suffolk County, N.Y., 1990. Mem. Soc. Animal Artists (award of excellence 1988), Salmagundi Club, Wildlife Conservation Soc., East African Wildlife Soc., Friends of Conservation. Avocations: gardening, travel, writing, photography. Home: 56 Constantine Way Mount Sinai NY 11766-3005

LIDSTROM, MARY E., chemical engineering professor, microbiology professor; BS in Microbiology, Ore. State Univ., 1973; MS in Bacteriology, Univ. Wis., Madison, 1975; PhD in Bacteriology, Univ. Wis., 1977. Prof., environ. engring. sci. Calif. Tech. Inst.; Frank Jungers Chair, Engring. Univ. Wash., and prof. chem. engring, prof. microbiology, assoc. dean for new initiatives in engring. Rsch. prof. Howard Hughes Med. Inst., 2002—. Editl. bd. Jour. Bacteriology; contbr. articles to profl. journals. Recipient Prather award for Young Women in Sci., CalTech award for Excellence, NSF Faculty award for Women, Howard Hughes Med. Inst. grant, 2002. Fellow: Am. Acad. Microbiology. Office: 263 Benson Univ Wash Box 351750 Seattle WA 98195-1750 Office Phone: 206-616-5282. Office Fax: 206-616-5721. Business E-Mail: lidstrom@u.washington.edu.

LIDTKE, DORIS KEEFE, retired computer science educator; b. Bottineau County, N.D., Dec. 6, 1929; d. Michael J and Josephine (McDaniels) Keefe; m. Vernon L Lidtke, Apr. 21, 1951. BS, U. Oreg., 1952, PhD, 1979; MEd cum laude, Johns Hopkins U., 1974. Programmer analyst Shell Devel. Co., Emeryville, Calif., 1955—59, U. Calif., Berkeley, 1960—62; asst. prof. Lansing (Mich.) C.C., 1963—68; ednl. specialist Johns Hopkins U., Balt., 1968; assoc. program mgr. NSF, Washington, 1984—85, program dir., 1992—93; sr. mem. tech. staff Software Productivity Consortium, Reston, Va., 1987—88; asst. prof. computer sci. Towson U., Balt., 1968—80, assoc. prof., 1980—90, prof., 1990—2002, prof. emerita, 2002—; adj. accreditation dir. computing ABET Inc., 1999—. V.p. Computing Scis. Accreditation Bd., 1993—95, pres., 1995—97. Fellow: Assn. Computing Machinery (edn. bd. 1980—98, coun. 1984—86, spl. interest group bd. 1985—99, chmn. 1994—98, coun. 1994—98, Recognition Svc. award 1978, 1983, 1985, 1986, 1990, 1991, Outstanding Contbn. award 1995); mem.: Assn. Edn. Data Sys. (named Outstanding Educator 1986), Nat. Edn. Computer Conf. (steering com., vice-chmn. 1983—85, chmn. 1985—89, Outstanding Svc. award 1999, Outstanding Leadership award 1999), Computer Soc. of IEEE (Outstanding Contbn. award 1986, 1992, Golden Core). Home: 4806 Wilmslow Rd Baltimore MD 21210-2328 Office: Towson U Computer and Info Scis Baltimore MD 21252-0001 also: ABET Inc 111 Market Pl Baltimore MD 21202 Office Phone: 410-347-7703. Business E-Mail: lidtke@acm.org.

LIEBAU, CATHERINE ANNETTE, cardiac diagnostic nurse; b. Milw., Oct. 10, 1959; d. Donald George and Beverly Annette (Pahule) Bastian; m. William Edward Charles Liebau, Nov. 19, 1988. BSN, Alverno Coll., 1992; MSN, U. Phoenix, 2006. RN, Wis.; cert. BLS instr., ACLS. Nursing asst. St. Joseph's Hosp., Milw., 1977-86, cardiac diagnostic unit tech., 1986-92, critical care nurse, 1992-94, cardiac dianostic unit nurse, 1994—, cardiac diagnostic nurse, 1994—2000, electrophysiology nurse, 2000—01, patient care supr. critical care, 2001—02, patient care supr., house supr., 2002—03, patient care supr. emergency dept., 2003—. Co-author, co-editor computer programs Ataerosclerosis, 1991, Chest Pain, 1992. Avocations: computers, crafts. Home: 6263 N 107th St Milwaukee WI 53225-1302

LIEBELER, SUSAN WITTENBERG, lawyer; b. July 3, 1942; d. Sherman K. and Eleanor (Klivans) Levine; m. Wesley J. Liebeler, Oct. 21, 1971; 1 child, Jennifer. BA, U. Mich., 1963, postgrad., 1963-64; LLB, UCLA, 1966. Bar: Calif. 1967, Vt. 1973, DC 1988. Law clk. Calif. Ct. of Appeals, 1966-67; assoc. Gang, Tyre & Brown, 1967-68, Greenberg, Bernhard, Weiss & Karma, L.A., 1968-70; assoc. gen. counsel Rep. Corp., 1970-72; gen. counsel Verit Industries, 1972-73; prof. Loyola Law Sch., L.A., 1973—85; spl. counsel, chmn. John S. R. Shad, SEC, Washington, 1981-82; commr. U.S. Internat. Trade Commn., Washington, 1984-88, vice-chmn., 1984-86, chmn., 1986-88; ptnr. Irell & Manella, L.A., 1988-94; pres. Lexpert Rsch. Svcs., L.A., 1995—. Vis. prof. U. Tex., summer 1982; cons. Office of Policy Coordination, Office of Pres.-elect, 1981-82; cons. U.S. Ry. Assn., 1975, U.S. EPA, 1974, U.S. Price Commn., 1972; mem. Adminstrv. Conf. U.S., 1986-88. Mem. editl. adv. bd. Regulation mag. CATO Inst.; sr. editor UCLA Law Rev., 1965-66; contbr. articles to profl. jours. Mem. adv. bd. U. Calif. Orientation in USA Law; bd. govs. Century City Hosp., 1992—2002, vice chair, 1997—99, chair, 1999—2001. Stein scholar UCLA, 1966. Mem. State Bar Calif. (treas., vice chair, chair exec. com. internat. law sect.), Practicing Law Inst. (Calif. adv. com.), Washington Legal Found. (acad. adv. bd.), Order of Coif. Jewish. Office Phone: 310-589-5546. Business E-Mail: lexpert@lexpertresearch.com.

LIEBENBERG, ROBERTA D., lawyer; b. Washington, 1949; BA, Univ. Mich., 1970; JD, Cath. Univ., 1975. Bar: Pa. 1980, Va. 1975, DC 1976, U.S. Supreme Ct. 1980. Law clerk U.S Ct. Appeals, Pa., 1975—77; atty. Fine, Kaplan & Black, Phila., 2000—. Bd. dir. Anti-Defamation League, Phila. chpt., Women's Way, Pa. Named one of Top 50 Female Super Lawyers, Philadelphia Magazine, 2004, Top 100 Lawyers in Pa., 2004; recipient Woman of Distinction, Philadelphia Business Journal, 2003. Fellow: Am. Bar Found., Pa. Bar Assn. (bd. govs. 2000—03, Lynette Norton award 2003); mem.: Am. Law Inst., ABA (bd. govs. 2003—05, mem. standing com. fed. judiciary). Office: Fine Kaplan & Black 28th Fl 1835 Market St Philadelphia PA 19103 Office Phone: 215-567-6565. Business E-Mail: rliebenberg@finekaplan.com.

LIEBENSON, GLORIA KRASNOW, interior design executive, freelance writer; b. Chgo., Apr. 6, 1922; d. Henry Randolph and Margaret (Rivkin) Krasnow; m. Herbert Liebenson, Mar. 11, 1944; children: Lauren Ward, Lynn Liebenson Green. Student, Internat. Inst. Interior Design, Washington, 1961; B Am. Studies, Dunbarton Coll., Washington, 1974. Numerous positions Journalism, Advt., editing, 1942-62; interior design exec. Creative Interiors, 1962—. Tchr. interior design YMCA, Washington, 1980-82. Mem. editorial staff Champlin Encyclopedia, 1945-47; journalist Shreveport Jour., 1944; author: Corned Beef on Lies: the Laugh Track From My 83-Year Life Trek, 2005 Bd. dirs. Jewish Social Svc. Agy., Washington, 1983-85, Nat. Coun. Jewish Women. 1982-84; pres. Friends Nat. Museum African Art, 1983-85, D.C. Mental Health Assn., 1986-88. Democrat. Jewish. Avocations: theater, concerts, Scrabble, reading, travel. Home: Ste 615 4200 Massachusetts Ave NW Washington DC 20016-4734 Personal E-mail: glor15@juno.com.

LIEBER, CAROLE MARGUERITE RENEE, human resources specialist, consultant; b. Paris, Feb. 27, 1956; came to U.S., 1957; d. Edward John and Alice Lucie (Barro) L. BSBA, U. Md., 1988; BA in Psychology summa cum laude, Stonehill Coll., 1977; MEd, Boston U., 1978. Lic. cert. social worker, Mass. Program counselor CETA, Chelsea, Mass., 1979-81; asst. dir. Camp Hansen USO, Okinawa, Japan, 1982-84, asst. dir. Camp Foster, 1984-86; pers. mgr. specialist Dept. Navy, Arlington, Va., 1987-91, Dept. Def., Arlington, Va., 1991-98; pers. policy specialist Office Pers. Policy Dept. Treas., Washington, 1998-2001; supr., HR specialist Defense Info. Sys. Agy., 2001—03, chief customer and cmty. rels, 2003—. Tng. officer Human Resources Devel. Coun., Washington, 1985—; mem. Pres.'s taskforcefor Fed. Tng. Tech. Vol. White House, Washington, 1996—, Arlington Dem. Com., 1997—; mem. Arlington Heights Civic Assn., 1998—; del. Dem. Conv., 2004; mem. 8th Congl. Dist. Com.; mem. Va. Dem. State Com. Named Outstanding Young Virginian Virginia Jaycees, 1993, Sec. of the Treasury awd. for Excellence, 2001. Mem. ASTD, Internat. Personnel Mgmt. Assn., Nat. Conf. State Soc.s (sec. 1995-96), Mass. Soc. (pres. 1996-98), Jr. C. of C. (dist. dir., regional dir. Internat. Affairs Commn., program dir. 1992-93, award 1995), Toastmasters Internat. (divsn. gov. 1987-88). Democrat. Avocations: community volunteering, art, photography, travel. Home: 404 S Fenwick St Arlington VA 22204-2082 Office: Defense Information Systems Agency 701 S Courthouse Rd Arlington VA 22204-2199 E-mail: carole.lieber@disa.mil.

LIEBER, CONSTANCE E., medical association administrator; Pres. Nat. Alliance for Rsch. on Schizophrenia & Depression, N.Y.C. Achievements include creation of the Lieber prize for outstanding achievement in schizophrenia research. $50,000 prize is funded annually by the Essel Foundation and awarded by NARSAD Scientific Council members. Office: Natl Alliance Rsch Schizophrenia Dept 60 Cutter Mill Rd Ste 404 Great Neck NY 11021

LIEBER, JOAN SKONBERG, special education educator; b. Osage City, Kans., June 10, 1936; d. John Victor and Hazel Lucille (Lynch) Skonberg; m. William D. Lieber, June 15, 1958; children: David, Cathy. BS, Kans. State U., 1958; MS, Emporia State U., 1989. Nursery sch. tchr. Baumholder Officers Wives Club, Baumholder, Germany, 1959-60; vocat. edn. paraprofessional Three Lakes Spl. Edn. Co-op, Waverly, Kans., 1985-86; tchr. spl. edn. Osage City HS, Osage City, Kans., 1986—2001. Active Kans. Farm Bur., Manhattan, 1958—, mem. resolutions com., 1982-84; pres. div. learning disabled Kans. Coun. Exceptional Children, 1989-90; co-chair IFF Convention, editor IFF Flyer, 2001-. Mem. Internat. Flying Farmers, DAR, (Topeka Chpt. recording sec, 2001-03, chaplain, 2005-), Omicron Nu. Republican. Methodist. Home: 4223 W Hwy K 31 Osage City KS 66523-9057

LIEBERGOTT, JACQUELINE W., academic administrator; b. Balt., Mar. 17, 1942; d. Mendel Stiebel and Jeane (Levin) Weis; m. Harvey Liebergott, June 20, 1965; children: Jessica Liebergott Hamblen, Cory. BA in Hearing and Speech Sci., U. Md., 1963; MS in Speech-Lang. Pathology, U. Pitts., 1966, PhD in Speech-Lang. Pathology, 1973. Lic. in speech-lang. pathology Commonwealth of Mass. Lectr. dept. speech and hearing U. Md., College Park, 1969-70; asst. prof. dept. comm. disorders Emerson Coll., Boston, 1970-73, assoc. prof. divsn. comm. disorders, 1973-79, prof. divsn. comm. disorders, 1979—, dean grad. studies, 1984-87, v.p., acad. dean, 1987-92, interim pres., 1992-93, pres., 1993—. Manuscript reviewer in speech and hearing Grune and Stratton Pub. Co., 1972-73; manuscript reviewer in lang. Little Brown and Co., 1977; vis. assoc. prof. dept. comm. disorders Memphis (Tenn.) State U., summer 1974; co-chairperson conv. program com. Mass. Speech and Hearing Assn., 1978; cons. to ABT Assocs., Evaluating the Health Impact of Head Start, 1978-80; proposal reviewer Boston Univ. Lang. Conf., 1978, 84, 86; cons. on spl. edn. tng. in P.R., U.S. Office of Edn., Bur. Edn. of the Handicapped, 1979, cons. and proposal reviewer divsn. pers. preparation, 1978, 79, 80, 84-88; study sect. reviewer Divsn. Communicative Diseases and Stroke, NIH, 1979, 80, 83, 84, 85; cons. in lang. Brookline Early Edn. Project, 1979-83; project cons. TADS, Chapel Hill, N.C., 1980; program evaluator Pre-Sch. Program, Chepecket, R.I., 1980; editl. advisor in speech and lang. Little Brown and Co., 1980-88; associated sci. staff Children's Hosp. Med. Ctr., Harvard Med. Sch., 1984—; program chairperson and responder Session on Lang. Disabilities, Boston U. Lang. Conf., 1984-85; proposal reviewer minority participation in higher edn. U.S. Dept. Edn., Office of Post-Secondary Edn., 1990-92; accreditation vis. team New Eng. Assn. Schs. and Colls., 1992; presenter and cons. in field. Mem. editl. bd. ACTA Symbolica, 1973-80, Applied Health and Behavioral Scis. Jour., 1977-80, Jour. Speech and Hearing Disorders, 1977-81, Jour. Speech and Hearing Rsch., 1981-85, Am. Speech and Hearing Assn., 1985-90; contbr. articles to profl. jours. Chair staff com. Children's Ctr. Brookline, 1970-75; founding parent, mem. staff com. Newton After-Sch. Program, 1978-81; v.p., trustee Autism Soc., 1984—; trustee, mem. programming com. Boston Cable Access Bd., 1991—; trustee New Eng. Bus. Coun., 1992—, bd. mem., 1993—; bd. mem. Downtown Crossing Assn., 1994—, The Cambridge Partnership for Pub. Edn., 1994—; active Friends of the Pub. Garden and Boston Common, 1994—. Fellow Am. Coun. Edn. (fellowship selection com. 1991-92); mem. Am. Speech-Lang. and Hearing Assn. (com. on lang., subcom. on speech-lang. pathology svc. delivery with infants and toddlers 1987-90), Am. Assn. Higher Edn., Assn. Ind. Colls. and Univs. Mass., Mass. ACE/NIP, New Eng. Assn. Schs. and Coll. Inc. (liaison), New Eng. Coun., Mass. Women's Forum, Boston C. of C. Office: Emerson Coll Office of the Pres 120 Boylston St Boston MA 02116-4624

LIEBERMAN, GAIL FORMAN, investment company executive; b. Phila., May 26, 1943; d. Joseph and Rita Forman. BA in Physics and Math., Temple U., 1964, MBA in Fin., 1977. Dir. internat. fin. Std. Brands Inc., N.Y.C., 1977-79; staff v.p. fin. and capital planning RCA Corp., 1979-82; CFO, exec. v.p. Scali McCabe Sloves, Inc., 1982-93; v.p. fin., CFO, mng. dir. Moody's Investors Svc., N.Y.C., 1994-96; CFO TFPPG Thomson Corp., Boston, 1996-99; CEO Liquid Alternatives Inc., 2000; mng. ptnr. Rudder Capital LLC, 2001—. Bd. dirs. I-TRAX Corp., TriPath Imaging Inc., Trans Technology Corp. Mem. Fin. Execs. Inst. Office Phone: 917-207-4969. Personal E-mail: liebermang@earthlink.net.

LIEBERMAN, JANET ELAINE, academic administrator; b. NYC, Oct. 21, 1921; d. Samuel and Ida (Schubert) Rubensohn; m. Allen L. Chase, July 9, 1940 (div. 1954); children: Gary Andrew, Randolph H.; m. Jerrold S. Lieberman, June 30, 1957. Student, Vassar Coll., 1939-40; BA, Barnard Coll., N.Y.C., 1943; MA, City Coll., N.Y.C., 1946; PhD, NYU, N.Y.C., 1965. Asst. prof. Hunter Coll., NYC, 1965-70; prof. LaGuardia C.C., Long Island City, NY, 1970-72, asst. dean faculty, 1972-74, prof. psychology, 1974-86, asst. to pres., 1986—, prof. emeritus, 2005. Cons. Ford Found., 2004, Woodrow Wilson Found., 2005. Recipient Innovation in Higher Edn. award Charles A. Dana Found., N.Y.C., 1989, Break the Mold award U.S. Dept. Edn., Washington, 1992, LaGuardia medal of honor, 2002, Disting. Alumni award NYU, 2003, McGraw Hill Ednl. Achievement award, 2004. Office: LaGuardia CC 31-10 Thomson Ave Long Island City NY 11101-3071 Office Phone: 718-482-5049.

LIEBERMAN, JOSEFA NINA, psychologist, educator, writer; b. Jaroslaw, Poland, May 16, 1921; came to U.S., 1946; d. David Samuel and Rosa Zerline (Leinwand) Margules; m. Meyer Frank Lieberman, Feb. 12, 1956. BS, Columbia U., 1957, MA, 1959, PhD in Ednl. Psychology, 1964. Lic. psychologist, N.Y. Lectr. Bklyn. Coll., 1964-65, asst. prof., 1965-71, assoc. prof., 1972-79, prof., 1979-83, prof. emerita, 1983—. Spkr. in field. Author: Playfulness: Its Relationship to Imagination and Creativity, 1977, Japanese translation, 1981, He Came to Cambridge, 1982, (chpt.) I Came Alone, 1990, The Salzburg Connection: An Adolescence Remembered, 2004; contbr. articles to profl. jours. and newspapers. Mem., chair Hillel Found., Bklyn., 1964—83; founding mem. Solomon Schechter H.S.I, Bklyn., 1971; mem. Sr. Recreation, Woodstock, NY, 1984—. Recipient fellowships and rsch. grants NIMH, 1958-78. Mem. APA, Phi Beta Kappa, Sigma Xi. Democrat. Avocations: languages, music, chess. Home: 648 Zena Rd Woodstock NY 12498 Personal E-mail: jnina@aol.com.

LIEBERMAN, JUDITH L., retired special education educator; b. Waukegan, Ill., Mar. 31, 1945; d. Norton E. and Esther Landfield; children: Jonathan, Natalie. BS in Speech Correction, U. Ill., 1967; MA in Speech Pathology, 1968. Spl. edn. tchr. Los Angeles Unified Sch. Dist., Sylmar, Calif.; speech pathologist Camarillo State Hosp., Calif., Fullerton Sch. Dist., Calif.; hearing clinician Spl. Sch. Dist., St. Louis. Mem. clinician Calif. Readers, Granada Hills. Mem. Holocaust ednl. bd. mem. Anti Defamation League, Los Angeles; v.p. legal adv. fund Am. Assn. U. Women. Home: 247 Odebolt Dr Thousand Oaks CA 91360

LIEBERMAN, MERYL ROBIN, lawyer; b. Bklyn., Apr. 3, 1958; d. Alan Franklyn and Judith Fiedler; 1 child, Mallory A. BA in Urban Legal Studies, CCNY, 1978; JD magna cum laude, N.Y. Law Sch., N.Y.C., 1981. Bar: N.Y. 1981. Atty. Wilson, Elser, Moskowitz, Edelman & Dicket, N.Y.C., 1982—95; sr. founding ptnr. Traub Eglin Lieberman Straus LLP, N.Y.C., 1996—. Home: 7 Skyline Dr Hawthorne NY 10532

LIEBERMAN, NANCY ANN, lawyer; b. NYC, Dec. 30, 1956; d. Elias and Elayne Hildegarde (Fox) L.; m. Mark Ellman, Sept. 6, 1997. BA summa cum laude, U. Rochester, 1977; JD, U. Chgo., 1979; LLM in Taxation, NYU, 1981. Bar: N.Y. 1980. Intern White House, Washington, 1975; law clk. Hon. Henry A. Politz U.S. Ct. Appeals (5th cir.), Shreveport, La., 1979-80; assoc. Skadden Arps Slate Meagher & Flom LLP, N.Y.C., 1981-87, ptnr., 1987—. Trustee U. Rochester, 1994-2004, sr. trustee, 2004—; bd. dirs. Pacific Coun. Internat. Policy, 2003—. Mem. ABA, Assn. Bar City N.Y., Coun. Fgn. Rels., Phi Beta Kappa. Republican. Jewish. Office: Skadden Arps Slate Meagher & Flom LLP 4 Times Sq New York NY 10036-6595 Home: 435 E 52d St #10D New York NY 10022 Office Phone: 212-735-2050. Business E-Mail: nlieberman@skadden.com.

LIEBERMAN, TRUDY, healthcare journalist; BS with distinction, U. Nebr., LHD (hon.); cert. in economics and bus. journalism, Columbia U. Grad. Sch. Journalism. Consumer writer Detroit Free Press; health policy editor Consumer Reports, Yonkers, NY; dir., ctr. consumer health Consumers Union. Adj. prof. media ethics, sci. and environ. reporting prog. NYU; adj. prof. journalism Columbia U. Grad. Sch. Journalism; bd. dirs. Nat. Com. for Quality Assurance, Medicare Rights Ctr.; contbg. editor Columbia Journalism Review; contbr. The Nation; writer, health and marketplace LA Times; served on Nat. Assn. Insurance Commissioners Adv. Com. on long-term care. Author: Life Insurance: How to Buy the Right Policy from the Right Company at the Right Price, 1988, Family Finance Workbook, 1989, Consumer Reports Complete Guide to Health Services for Seniors, 2000 (named one of the best consumer health books for 2000 by Library Journal), Slanting the Story - The Forces That Shape the News, 2000; co-author: How to Plan for a Secure Retirement, 1992, 1998. Recipient John Bartlow Martin award for public interest mag. journalism, 1991, Nat. Press Club award, 1987, 1991, 1992, 1993, 1994, 1995, 1996, 1998, Society of Professional Journalists Deadline Club awards, 1993, 1994, 1996, Nat. Mag. award, 1987, 1990, James Beard award for Journalistic Excellence, 1993, Deadline Club award, 1994, 1996, National Media award, American Society on Aging, 1997; Knight-Bagehot Fellow, Columbia U. Grad. Sch. Journalism, 1976—77, Fulbright Fellowship to study healthcare in Japan, 1993, John J. McCloy Fellowship to study healthcare in Germany, 1993, The Joan Shorenstein Center Fellow on the Press, Politics and Public Policy, Harvard U., 2001. Mem.: Assn. of Health Care Journalists (v.p. 2000, pres. bd. dir.). Office: Consumers Union 101 Truman Ave Yonkers NY 10703-1057 Office Phone: 914-378-2455. Office Fax: 914-378-2928. Business E-Mail: liebtr@consumer.org.*

LIEBERMAN-CLINE, NANCY, sports commentator, former professional basketball coach, former player; b. July 1, 1958; m. Tim Cline, 1988; 1 child, Timothy Joseph. Grad., Old Dominion U., 1981. Guard WBL's Dallas Diamonds, 1980-86, USBL's L.I. Knights, 1986-87, Washington Generals, 1987-88, Athletes in Action, 1996-97, WNBA - Phoenix Mercury, 1997; head coach, gen. mgr. WNBA - Detroit Shock, 1998—2000; now sports commentator. Women's basketball analyst NBA Broadcasting, ESPN, ABC, ESPN 2, Fox Sports Network, NBC. Recipient Broderick Cup, 1979, 80, Wade Trophy (2), U.S. Olympic Silver medal, 1976; named All- Am., 1978-80, ODU Outstanding Female Athlete of Yr., 1977-80; mem. Women's Am. Basketball Championship team, 1985; Named to Basketball Hall of Fame, 1996. Home: 2636 Creekway Dr Carrollton TX 75010-4227

LIEBERT, LYNN LANGENBACH, psychologist, educator; b. Bayshore, NY, June 1, 1962; d. Herbert John and Joan Charlotte Langenbach; m. Robert Mandel Liebert (dec.); children: Rachel Lynn, Richard Karl. BA in Psychology, State U. NY-Stony Brook, 1987, MA in Psychology, 1990, PhD in Clin. Psychology, 1995. Consulting psychologist neurology SUNY at Stony Brook, 1995—99; psychologist Sagamore Children's Psychiat. Ctr., Dix Hills, 2001—03; psychology instr. Suffolk County C.C., Brentwood, 2003—, asst. acad. chair social scis. dept. Co-author: (book) Personality: Strategies and Issues, 8th ed., 1998, Science and Behavior: An Introduction, 1995; contbr. articles to profl. jours. Elder First Presbyterian Ch. Port Jefferson, 2005—. Mem.: APA, Nat. Parent Tchr. Assn. Avocations: drawing, painting, poetry. Home: 116 Spring St Port Jefferson NY 11777 Office: Suffolk County CC Social Sci Dept Crooked Hill Rd Brentwood NY 11717

LIEBES, RAQUEL, retired import/export company executive; b. San Salvador, El Salvador, Aug. 28, 1938; arrived in U.S., 1952, naturalized, 1964; d. Ernesto Martin and Alice (Philip) Liebes; m. Richard Paisley Kinkade, June 2, 1962 (div. 1977); children: Kathleen Paisley Kinkade, Richard Paisley Kinkade Jr., Scott Philip Kinkade. BA, Sarah Lawrence Coll., 1960; MEd, Harvard U., 1961; MA, Yale U., 1963, postgrad., 1963—65; D (hon.), Oxford U., 1994. Tchg. fellow in Spanish Sarah Lawrence Coll., Bronxville, NY, 1958-60; econ. tchg. fellow Yale U., New Haven, 1964-65, instr. Spanish dept., 1964-66; exec. stockholder Import Export Co., San Salvador, 1968-89, also bd. dirs.; ret., 1989. Adj. prof. Am. U., Washington, 1989—91, Georgetown U., Washington, 1989—93; lectr., conf. participant L.Am. art. Contbr. glossary of Spanish med. terms. Hon. consul Govt. of El Salvador, 1977—80; mem. outreach group L.Am. The White Ho., Washington, 1982—86; vol. Grady Hosp., Atlanta, 1966—71; chmn. Atlanta Coun. Internat. Visitors, 1966—71; docent High Mus. Art, Atlanta, 1972—77; founding mem. John Kennedy Ctr. Peforming Arts, 1980—, Agape, El Salvador, 1981—, Concultura, El Salvador, 1999—, Libr. of Congress, Wahington; mem. Folger/Shakespeare Libr., Smithsonian Inst. Econ. fellow, Yale U., 1964—65, Smithsonian Mus. grantee, 1981—96, Corcoran Mus. Art fellow, 1984—85. Mem.: AAUW, MLA, Rsch. Assn., Am. Biog. Inst., Jr. League of Washington, Concultura El Salvador, Yale Club, Harvard Club. Republican. Avocations: comparative literature, languages, international business, english literature, shakespeare. Office: V I P Sal # 148 PO Box 52-5364 Miami FL 33152-5364

LIEBICH, MARCIA TRATHEN, community volunteer; b. Troy, N.Y., Mar. 10, 1942; d. Roland Henry and Ida Mae (Horsfall) Trathen; m. Donald Herbert Liebich, May 13, 1941; children: Kurt Roland, Mark Christian. BA, Elmira Coll., 1964. With Sunnyview Hosp. and Rehab. Ctr., Schenectady, 1982-96, dir. devel., 1992-94; CEO Sunnyview Hosp. Found., 1994-96. Co-founder Parent Anonymous Lay Therapy, Schenectady, 1974-80; trustee Elmira (N.Y.) Coll., 1978-94; bd. dirs. United Way, Schenctady, 1980-81, pres. 1985, bd. dirs. United Way, N.Y., 1991—, Sunnyview Rehab. Hosp., Schenectady, 1982, pres. 1988-91; social svcs. Women's Legis. Forum, Albany, 1984-91; bd. dirs. Leadership Schenectady, 1987-92, Schenectady C. of C., 1987-90, YMCA Capital Dist., 1991-94, WMHT Pub. Radio and TV, 1991-96; pres. Samaritan Counseling Ctr., Schenectady, 1988-91; bd. dirs., treas. Bridge Ctr. Drug Treatment, Schenectady, 1988-91; bd. dirs. Backstage Theater, 1999-2002; mem. Wood River Med. Ctr. Aux., 2002—, Croy Canyon Ranch Found., Inc., 2004—. Recipient YWCA Community Vol. award, 1986, K.S. Rozendaal award Community Svc. Schenectady, 1987, Liberty Bell award Schenectady Bar Assn., 1990, Women of Vision Betty Bean award YWCA, 1990. Mem. AAUW (pres. 1978), PEO, Jr. League Schenectady (Vol. of Yr. award 1981), Summit Pub. Radio (treas. 1998-2002), Applause (sec. 1998-2002), Breckeridge Resort Chamber (amb. 1998-2002), Phi Beta Kappa. Republican. Lutheran. Avocations: tennis, reading, knitting, skiing, watching hockey. Home: 196 Nez Perce Cir Hailey ID 83333-8573

LIEBMAN, CAROL BENSINGER, lawyer, educator; b. Louisville, Nov. 4, 1940; d. John Marshall and Jean (Lesler) Bensinger; m. Lance M. Leibman, June 28, 1964; children: Jeffrey, Benjamin. BA, Wellesley Coll., 1962; MA, Rutgers U., 1963; JD, Boston U., 1975. Coord. of records and devel. Commonwealth Svc. Corp., Boston, 1964-67; dir. Action for Children's TV, Newton, Mass., 1971-72; with pvt. law firm, Boston, 1975-76; counsel Mass. Dept. Corrections, Boston, 1976-79; clin. prof. and dir./Legal Assistance Bur. Boston Coll. Law Sch., 1979—91; vis. clin. prof. Columbia U., NYC, 1991—92, clin. prof. law, 1992—. Mediator Suffolk and Middlesex County Superior Cts., Boston, Cambridge, Mass., 1989—. Co-author: Mediating Bioethics Disputes: A Guide to Shaping Shared Solutions. Vice-chmn. Dem. Ward Com., Newton, 1984—. Recipient teaching and adv. grant, Boston Coll., 1989. Mem.: Assn. Bar of City of NY (mem. exec. com.), Assn. Am. Law Schs. (exec. com. clin. section 1988—). Home: 322 Central Park W # 6A New York NY 10025-7629 Office: 435 W 116th St New York NY 10027 Office Phone: 212-854-8557. E-mail: cliebman@law.columbia.edu.

LIEBMAN, JUDITH RAE STENZEL, retired operations research specialist; b. Denver, July 2, 1936; d. Raymond Oscar and Mary Madelyn (Galloup) Stenzel; m. Jon Charles Liebman, Dec. 27, 1958; children: Christopher Brian, Rebecca Anne, Michael Jon. BA in Physics, U. Colo., Boulder, 1958; PhD in Ops. Rsch., Johns Hopkins U., 1971. Successively asst. prof., head indsl. systems, assoc. prof. U. Ill., Urbana, 1972-84, prof., 1984-96, prof. emerita, 1996—, acting vice chancellor for rsch., 1986-87, vice chancellor for rsch., 1987-92, acting dean Grad. Coll., 1987-92, dean, 1987-92. Vis. prof. Tianjin (China) U., 1983; charter mem. Ill. Gov.'s Sci. Adv. Com., Ill. Exec. Com., 1989-92; mem. adv. com. for engring. NSF, 1988-92, chmn., 1991-92; mem. NRC Bd. Engring. Edn., 1997-2001, Army Sci. Bd., 1997-99. Author: Modeling and Optimization with GINO, 1986; author numerous articles in field. Bd. dirs. United Way, Champaign, Ill., 1986-91, U. Colo. Found., 1999-2003; bd. dirs. East Cen. Ill. Health Systems Agy., Champaign, 1977-82, pres., 1980-82; trustee U. Colo. Found., 2003—. Mem. Ops. Rsch. Soc. Am. (pres. 1987-88), INFORMS, Nat. Assn. State Univs. and Land Grant Colls. (exec. bd. 1990-92), Rotary, Sigma Xi, Sigma Pi Sigma, Alpha Pi Mu, Phi Kappa Phi. Home: 110 W Whitehall Ct Urbana IL 61801-6664

LIEBMAN, NINA R., economic developer; b. Toledo, Ohio, May 27, 1941; d. Jules Jay and Phyllis Gertrude (Kasle) Roskin; m. Theodore Liebman, Oct. 27, 1968; children: Sophie, Hanna, Tessa. Student, U. Marseilles, Aix-en-Provence, France, 1959-60, Skidmore Coll., 1960-61, NYU, 1961-63; cert. labor negotiator, Cornell U., 1993. Pub. info. officer Young Adult Inst., N.Y.C., 1978-81; U.S.A. dir. Rhone-Alps Econ. Devel. Assn., N.Y.C. and Lyon, France, 1981-85; internat. mktg. specialist N.Y. State Dept. Econ. Devel., N.Y.C., 1985-89, chief internat. programs, 1989-95; cons. Russian Fedn. Housing project The World Bank, 1995, cons. Russian Cmty. Social Infrastructure project, 1997. Exec. dir. Nat. Assn. Export Cos., 1997—99; assoc. dir. Architecture Rsch. Inst., 2000—02; assoc. The Corcoran Group, 2002—. Co-author: Biz Speak: A Dictionary of Business Terms, Slang and Jargon, 1986. Vol., trained mediator Bklyn. Mediation Ctr.; former mem. internat. adv. coun. Eisenhower Found.; mem. internat. adv. bd. Nat. Minority Bus. Coun.; active Murray Hill Neighborhood Assn. Fellow Eisenhower Exch. Fellowship Program, 1993. Mem. UN Assn., Alliance Am. and Russian Women, U.S. Com. for UN, Devel. Fund for Women, Mcpl. Arts Soc., Manhattan C. of C. (bd. dirs.). Democrat. Jewish. Avocation: choral singing. Personal E-mail: nina.liebman@prodigy.net. Business E-Mail: nrl@corcoran.com.

LIEBMAN, PHYLLIS JANICE, volunteer, educator; b. Everett, Mass., July 3, 1938; d. William Ostrovsky and Marriette Steinert; m. Larry J. Liebman, June 16, 1957; children: Steven Philip, Robert Wayne, Kenneth Richard. BA, EdM, Boston U., 1960; post grad. in Holocaust Studies, Yed Vashem, Jerusalem. Israel. Substitute tchr. elem. and spl. needs Newton Pub. Schs., Newton, Mass.; tchr. Hebrew Sch. and Holocaust studies Temple B'Nai Torah, Sudbury; docent Naples Mus. Art, Naples, Fla., 1996—. Tchr. Art Goes to Sch. program Art League of Bonita Springs, Fla.; study group leader Mexican art Naples Mus. Art, Naples, Fla. Conf. co-chmn. Welcome Clubs Internat., 1998; vol. Planned Parenthood, Naples, Fla., 2003—06; guild mem. women's com. Hope Hospice of Bonita Springs; vol. and guild mem. Shelter Abused Women and Children, Naples, 2005—06; past pres. Sisterhood Temple Beth Avudah, Newton, Mass. Recipient Marion Adair Outstanding Svc., Welcome Clubs Internat., 1996. Fellow: AAUW, Royal Soc. Advancement of Arts London; mem.: Frients of Art Naples Mus. Art, Phi Lambda Theta. Avocations: music, tennis, gardening, hobby farmer. Home: 3959 Woodlake Dr Bonita Springs FL 34134-8610 Personal E-mail: frostbrook@aol.com.

LIEBMAN, WILMA B., government agency administrator; b. Phila. BA, Barnard Coll., N.Y.C.; JD, George Washington U., Washington. Staff atty. NLRB, 1974—80; legal counsel Internat. Brotherhood of Teamsters, 1980—89; labor counsel Bricklayers and Allied Craftsmen, 1990—93; asst. to dir. Fed. Mediation and Conciliation Svc., 1994—96, dep. dir.; mem. NLRB, Washington, 1997—. Mem.: Coll. of Labor and Employment Lawyers, Inc. (exec. bd.), Indsl. Rels. Rsch. Assn. (exec. bd.). Office: NLRB 1099 14th St NW Washington DC 20570-0001

LIEF, BETH, educational association administrator; b. Huntington, Ill. married; 2 children. BA in Urban Studies, Barnard Coll.; JD, NYU. Counsel Legal Def. and Ednl. Fund NAACP; spl. asst. to Richard Beattie N.Y. Bd. Edn.; staff counsel Pub. Edn. Assn.; exec. dir. Mayor's Commn. on Spl. Edn., 1984—86; dir. Program for Homeless Families and Spl. Projects Edna McConnell Clark Found.; founding pres. New Visions for Pub. Schs., 1989—2000; sr. v.p. strategic rels. Teachscape, 2000—03; cons. N.Y.C. Dept. Edn. Children First Strategic Planning Initiative; nat. fellow Inst. for Learning, Learning R&D Ctr., Pitts., 2003—. Bd. dirs., sec. Pub. Edn. Network, Washington; bd. dirs. New Visions for Pub. Schs.; sr. fellow edn. New Democracy Project. Bd. dirs. Bank St. Coll. Edn., United Cerebral Palsy N.Y.C.; Parent Resource Ctr. Scholar Root-Tilden scholar 2nd cir.

LIEM, ANNIE, pediatrician; b. Kluang, Johore, Malaysia, May 26, 1941; d. Daniel and Ellen (Phuah) L. BA, Union Coll., 1966; MD, Loma Linda U., 1970. Diplomate Am. Bd. Pediat. Intern Glendale (Calif.) Adventist Hosp., 1970-71; resident in pediatrics Children's Hosp. of Los Angeles, 1971-73; pediatrician Children's Med. Group, Anaheim, Calif., 1973-75, Anaheim Pediatric Med. Group, 1975-79; practice medicine specializing in pediatrics Anaheim, 1979-96, Camas, Wash., 1996—. Fellow Am. Acad. Pediatrics; mem. Los Angeles Pediatric Soc., Orange County Pediatric Soc., Adventist Internat. Med. Soc., Chinese Adventist Physicians' Assn. Avocations: music, reading, gardening. Office: 713 NE 4th Ave Camas WA 98607-2111 Office Phone: 360-833-4519. Personal E-mail: all526@aol.com.

LIEN, JULIE ANN, elementary school educator; b. Hillsdale, Mich., Apr. 10, 1969; d. John Francis and Patricia Gail Bacheldor; m. Matthew Allen Lien, July 9, 1994; 1 child, Joseph Allen. BA in Edn., BA in Ind. Studies, Columbia Coll., Mo., 1993; M in Curriculum and Instrn., Lindenwood U., St. Clarkes, Mo., 2000. Cert. tchr. elem. K-8, tchr. mid. sch. 4-8 langs., tchr. mid. sch. 4-8 social studies. Tchr. 6th grade Valley Park Sch. Dist., Mo., 1993—96; tchr. reading, math., sci. 6th grade Parkway Sch. Dist., Chesterfield, Mo., 1996—. Recipient Vito Maniacj scholarship, Parkway Nat. Edn. Assn., 1999. Mem.: NEA. Roman Catholic.

LIERMANN, KELLY, athletic trainer; BS in Athletic Tng., Duquesne U., Pitts., 2003, MS in Edn., 2003. Lic. profl. rescuer ARC; cert. tchr. Pa., Va. Sports performance enhancement asst. U. Pitts. Med. Ctr. Sports Performance Ctr., 2001—03; athletic trainer Allegheny Gen. Hosp., Pitts., 2003—04; football athletic trainer U. Richmond, Va., 2004—. Intern athletic tnr. Pitts. Steelers, 2002—03. Vol. Winter Spl. Olympics Pa., Blue Knob, 2003; asst. vol., med. staff liason Summer Spl. Olympics Va., Richmond, 2005. Mem.: Va. Athletic Trainer's Assn., Mid Atlantic Athletic Trainer's Assn., Nat. Athletic Trainer's Assn. (cert. athletic trainer, instr.). Office: Univ Richmond The Robins Ctr Rm 163 Richmond VA 23173 Office Phone: 804-289-8001. Business E-Mail: klierman@richmond.edu.

LIES, VALERIE SHARP, foundation administrator; b. Buffalo, Sept. 18, 1948; d. Osborne Kenneth and Norma (Taylor) Sharp; m. Brian P. Lies, July 25, 1970; 1 child, Taylor. BA, Vassar Coll., 1970; MSW, U. Minn., 1974. Human resources planner Minn. State Planning Agy., St. Paul, 1973-74; exec. dir. Otto Bremer Found., St. Paul, 1974-82; v.p. Pub. Edn. Fund, Pitts., 1983-87; pres. Donors Forum Chgo., 1987—. Chmn. bd. Women and Founds., N.Y.C., 1988—, bd. dirs. philanthropy sect., 1985—, 1st Non Profit Risk Pooling Trust, Chgo., 1988—. Chair Nat. Ctr. for Family Philanthropy. Office: Donors Forum Chgo 208 S LaSalle St, Ste 740 Chicago IL 60604 E-mail: vlies@donorsforum.org.*

LIETCH, MARGIE, insurance company administrator; b. Macon, Ga., May 31, 1953; d. James Milton Scarbary and Samantha Lou Mercer; m. Gary Tye Riddle, July 11, 1970 (div. July 1981); children; Gary Kenneth Riddle, Richard Drake Riddle; m. Larry Joe Lietch, Aug. 2, 1991. Student, Ins. Inst. Am., Atlanta, 1989, 98. Cert. profl. ins. woman; cert. assoc. in ins. svcs. Rate and code clk. Ctrl. Mut. Ins. Co., Atlanta, 1972-75; underwriter Byrd & Lancaster Ins. Agy., Atlanta, 1975-77, Vickery & Christopher Ins. Agy., Stone Mountain, Ga., 1978-80; underwriting office mgr. Klepac and Assocs. Ins. Agy., Lilburn, Ga., 1980-92; policy svcs. supr. Atlanta Casualty Ins. Co., Norcross, Ga., 1992-98; underwriting/ops. mgr. Sun States Ins. Group, Decatur, Ga., 1998—2000; ops. mgr. Regulatory Techs., Inc., Roswell, Ga., 2001—. Named Woman of Yr. Gwinnett Assn. Ins. Women, 1983, 87. Mem. Nat. Assn. Ins. Women (pres.N.E. Atlanta chpt. 1990-91, Ga. state dir. 1995-96, Ga. state treas. 1996-97, Woman of Yr. N.E. Atlanta chpt. 1990, 97). Republican. Baptist. Avocations: travel, water sports, flower gardening, arts and crafts. Home: 245 Forest Way Lawrenceville GA 30043-4494 Office: Regulatory Techs Inc 645 Hembree Pkwy S # A Roswell GA 30076-3868 E-mail: Lietch@MCCON.com.

LIEVENS, REBECCA S.A., science educator; b. Marshalltown, Iowa, Jan. 10, 1955; d. Frederick Archibald and Jeanette Bernice Allison; m. Gregory Mark Lievens, July 19, 1980; children: Benjamin, Katherine. BS, Iowa State U., Ames, 1977; MA, Viterbo Coll., LaCrosse, Wis., 2000. Lab. tech. Iowa State U., Ames, 1978; tchr. sci. Dunlap H.S., 1978—83; substitute tchr. Aplington H.S., 1983—86, tchr. science, Aplington-Pakersburg Mid. Sch. Tchr. Summer Enrichment Program, Cedar Falls, Iowa, 2003—05; com. mem. Profl. Devel. Com., Aplington, 2003—; mem. TEAMS-Sci. & Math. Initiative, Cedar Falls, 2002—03; presenter in field. Mem. PEO, Marshalltown, 1976—, Ackley, 1976—. Grantee, McElroy Trust, Cedar Falls, 2002. Mem.: Iowa Edn. Assn. (pres. 1986—), Iowa Acad. Sci., Nat. Sci. Tchrs. Assn. Roman Catholic. Avocations: gardening, kayaking, theater, reading, baseball. Home: 402 8th St Aplington IA 50604 Office: Aplington-Parkersburg Cmty Schs Parkersburg IA 50665

LIFSHUTZ, MELANIE JANET BELL, patient education, medical, and surgical nurse; b. Dallas; d. Trigg Alvin Ralph and Shirley Theo (Templeton) Bell; m. David Martin Lifshutz. BS, Tex. Woman's U., 1971. Cert. Vol., Chaplain in the Chaplaincy Ministry. Nurse practice coord. La. State U., Shreveport; RN intensive care unit Presbyn. Hosp. Dallas; charge RN surgery Parkland Meml. Hosp., Dallas; patient edn. coord. Parker County Surg. Clinic, Weatherford, Tex. Mem. Am. Assn. Critical Care Nurses, Am. Heart Assn., ANA, Am. Soc. for Health Edn. and Tng., Am. Cancer Assn. (pub. edn. chmn.). Home: RR 1 Box 1978 Shelbyville TX 75973-9801

LIGGETT, TWILA C., academic administrator, broadcast executive, educator; b. Pipestone, Minn., Mar. 25, 1944; d. Donald L. Christensen and Irene E. (Zweigle) Christensen Flesher. BS, Union Coll., Lincoln, Nebr., 1966; MA, U. Nebr., Lincoln, 1971, PhD, 1977; DHL (hon.), Marymount Manhattan Coll., 2000. Dir. vocal and instrumental music Sprague (Nebr.)-Martell Pub. Sch., 1966-67; tchr. vocal music pub. schs., Syracuse, Nebr., 1967-69; tchr. Norris Pub. Sch., Firth, Nebr., 1969-71; cons. fed. reading project pub. schs., Lincoln, Nebr., 1971-72; curriculum coord. Westside Cmty. Schs., Omaha, 1972-74; dir. state program Right-to-Read Nebr. Dept. Edn., 1974-76; asst. dir. Nebr. Commn. on Status of Women, 1976-80; asst. dir. project admisntrn./devel. Great Plains Nat. Instructional TV Libr. U. Nebr., Lincoln, 1980-97, 2002—05; sr. v.p. for edn. Lancit Media Ent., Ltd. a Junior Net Co., NY, 1998—2001; exec. prodr. Reading Rainbow/Nebr. ETV Network/GPN, 1980—98, Nebr. ETV Network/6PN, 2001—05; pres. Twila Liggett Media, Inc., 2005—; asst. prof. literacy Marymount Manhattan Coll., 2006—. Cons. U.S. Dept. Edn., 1981; cons. Far West Regional Lab. Nebr. Edn. TV Network, San Francisco, 1978—79; panelist, presenter in field; Blue Ribbon panelist NATAS, 1991—2006; final judge Nat. Cable Ace Awards, 1991—92, 1997. Author: Reading Rainbow's Guide to Children's Books: The 101 Best Titles, 1994, rev. edit., 1996. Bd. dirs. Planned Parenthood, Lincoln, 1979-81. Recipient Grand award, N.Y., 1993, Gold medal, Internat. Film and TV Festival, 1996, 1999, World Gold medal, N.Y. Internat. Film and TV, 1995, Golden Eagle award, Coun. on Non-theatrical Events, 1995, Image award, NAACP, 1994, 1996, 1999, 2002, 24 Nat. Emmy awards, 9 for Outstanding Children's Series, 1985—2006. Mem. NATAS, Internat. Reading Assn. (panelist, presenter, Spl. award Contbns. Worldwide Literacy 1992), Am. Women in Film and TV, Phi Delta Kappa. Presbyterian. Home: 37 Crescent Pl Matawan NJ 07747 Office Phone: 732-583-7481. Business E-Mail: rrainbow1@aol.com.

LIGGIO, JEAN VINCENZA, adult education educator, artist; b. NYC, Nov. 5, 1927; d. Vincenzo and Bernada (Terrusa) Verro; m. John Liggio, June 6, 1948; children: Jean Constance, Joan Bernadette. Student, N.Y. Inst. Photography, 1965, Elizabeth Seton Coll., 1984, Parsons Sch. of Design, 1985. Hairdresser Beauty Shoppe, N.Y.C., 1947-65; instr. watercolor N.Y. Dept. Pks., Recreation and Conservation, Yonkers, 1985-89, Bronxville (N.Y.) Adult Sch., 1989—. Substitute tchr. cosmetology Yonkers Bd. Edn., 1988-89; tchr. watercolor painting J.V.L. Watercolor Workshop of Fine Arts, Jakes Art Ctr., Mt. Vernon, N.Y. Paintings pub. by Donald Art Co., C.R. Gibson Greeting Card Co., Enesco Corp., 1996; paintings for Avon Calendar, Avon Cosmetics Co., 1994, 96, Avon-Can. Publ., 1996-97; greeting cards published by C.R. Gibson Co. Publ., 1996-1997, boxed notecards by C.R. Gibson; painting on cover of C.R. Gibson Jour., 2000, C.R. Gibson Inspirational Jour.; pub. Friends Jour. Mag., Phila.; exhibitor numerous shows, 1981— (more than 256 awards). Mem.: Art Soc. Old Greenwich, Hudson Valley Art Assn., New Rochelle Art Assn., Scarsdale Art Assn. (publicity chmn. 1984—89), Mt. Vernon Art Assn. (pres. membership com. 1983—). Avocation: antiques. Home and Office: 166 Helena Ave Yonkers NY 10710-2524 Office Phone: 914-779-3882.

LIGHT, BETTY JENSEN PRITCHETT, retired dean; b. Omaha, Sept. 14, 1924; d. Lars Peter and Ruth (Norby) Jensen; m. Morgan S. Pritchett, June 27, 1944 (dec. 1982); children: Randall Wayne, Robin Kay Pritchett Church, Royce Marie Pritchett Bishop; m. Kenneth F. Light, Nov. 23, 1985 (dec. 2003). BS, Portland State U., 1965; MBA, U. Oreg., 1966; Ed.D., Oreg. State U., 1973. Buyer Rodgers Stores, Inc., Portland, Oreg., 1947-62; chmn. bus. div. Mt. Hood Community Coll., Gresham, Oreg., 1966-70, dir. evening coll., 1970-71, assoc. dean instn., 1972-77, dean humanities and behavioral scis., 1977-79, dean devel. and spl. programs, 1979-83, dean communication arts, humanities and social scis., 1983-86. State com. for articulation between cmty. colls. and higher edn., 1976-78; mem. Gov.'s Coun. on Career and Vocat. Edn., 1977-86; owner Effective Real Estate Mgmt., 1982-2002. Author: Values and Perceptions of Community College Professional Staff in Oregon, 1973; contbg. author: The Pritchett Study in Retailing, An Economic View, 1969. Mem. Gresham City Council, 1983-86. Mem.: Oreg. Vocat. Assn., Am. Vocat. Assn., Danish Brotherhood, N.W. Danish Found., Danish Heritage Soc. Home: 1635 NE Country Club Ave Gresham OR 97030-4432

LIGHT, JANE ELLEN, librarian; b. Crosby, ND, May 4, 1948; d. Ralph W. and Ethel S. (Cady) Johnson; children: Jessica, David. BA, Calif. State U., Sacramento, 1973; MLS, U. Calif., Berkeley, 1974. Project mgr. Peninsula Libr. Sys., San Mateo, Calif., 1974-78, sys. dir., 1979-83; program mgr. Coop. Libr. Authority, San Jose, Calif., 1978-79; asst. libr. dir. Redwood City (Calif.) Pub. Libr., 1983-84, libr. dir., 1984-97; city libr. San Jose Pub. Libr., 1997—. Del. On-line Computer Libr. Ctr. User's Coun., 1993—2000; chair exec. bd. Urban Librs. Coun., 2005—. Bd. dirs. Child Care Coordinating Coun., San Mateo, 1988-97, pres. 1992-93; bd. dirs. YMCA of Santa Clara Valley, 2001—. Mem. ALA, Calif. Libr. Assn., Pub. Libr. Assn., Rotary Club San Jose. Office: San Jose Pub Libr Sys 150 E San Fernando San Jose CA 95112 Office Phone: 408-808-2150. Business E-Mail: jane.light@sjlibrary.org.

LIGHT, JO KNIGHT, stockbroker; b. DeQueen, Ark., Mar. 15, 1936; d. Donald R. and Auda (Waltrip) Knight; m. Jerry T. Light, June 21, 1958 (dec. 1979); m. Victor E. Menefee Jr., Nov. 18, 1981; 1 child, Jerry T. Jr. BA cum laude, U. Ark., 1958. CFP. Travel cons. Comml. Nat. Bank, Little Rock, 1971-76; dist. mgr. Am. Express Co., N.Y.C., 1976-82; fin. advisor and retirement planning specialist Morgan Stanley, N.Y.C., 1982—, registered investment advisor, 1996—, sr. v.p. investments, 1999—. Mem. Jr. League of Little Rock Sustainers; vol. Happiness Singers. Mem. Fin. Planning Assn., Internat. Assn. Fin. Planners (bd. dirs. 1992-98, pres. bd. 1995-96), U. Ark. Alumni Assn. (bd. dirs. 1974-77), Morgan Stanley Pres.'s Club, Morgan Stanley Dir.'s Club, Phi Beta Kappa, Kappa Kappa Gamma. Avocations: music, tennis, sailing, skiing. Office: Morgan Stanley 425 W Capitol Ave Ste 200 Little Rock AR 72201-3440 E-mail: jo.light@morganstanley.com.

LIGHT, JUDITH ELLEN, actress; b. Trenton, NJ; d. Sidney and Pearl Sue (Hollander) L.; m. Robert Desiderio, 1985. B.F.A., Carnegie-Mellon U., 1970. Actress European USO tour, 1968, Calif. Shakespeare Festival, 1969, Milw. Repertory Theater, 1970-72, 73-74, Seattle Repertory Theater, 1972-73, O'Neill Playwright's Conf., 1977, Streetcar Named Desire, Theatre Plus, Toronto, 1975, Wit, 1999 (off-Broadway and nat. tour), Colder Than Here, 2005 (Off-Broadway); Broadway appearance A Doll's House, 1974, Herzl, 1976, Hedda Gabler, 2001; (playing Karen Woleck) ABC TV show One Life to Live, 1977-82; TV appearances St. Elsewhere, 1983, Family Ties, 1983, (TV movie) Intimate Agony, 1983, The Ryan White Story, 1989, Betrayal of Trust, 1994, Against Their Will: Women in Prison, 1994, Lady Killer, 1995, A Step Toward Tomorrow, 1996, Murder at My Door, 1996, A Husband, a Wife, and a Lover, 1996, (series) Who's the Boss?, 1984-92, The Ryan White Story, 1989, Too Close to Home, 1997, (documentary) Judith Light: An Intimate Portrait, 1998, (radio) The Diary of Anne Frank, 1999, Ugly Betty, 2006. Recipient Emmy award as outstanding actress in a daytime drama, 1979-80, 80-81; recipient Outstanding Actress Soapy award, 1979-80, 80-81, Hall of Fame award Daytime TV Mag., 1981

LIGHT, MARION JESSEL, retired elementary school educator; b. San Antonio, Dec. 5, 1915; d. Marion Jackson and Kate Jessel (Cox) Parr; m. Marion Russell Light, Nov. 8, 1958 (dec. July 1983); children: Russell Jeffers, Paul Love. BA, So. Meth. U., 1936; MA, U. Tex., 1947. Cert. elem. and secondary sch. tchr., Tex. Elem. tchr. Dallas Ind. Sch. Dist., 1936-72. 1st v.p. The Cosmos Rev. Class, 1991—92, 1997—98. Del. to 16th Senatorial Dist. Dem. Conv., 1988; moderator Presbyn. Women, 1st Ch., Dallas, 1989-90, co-moderator, 1994-95. Mem. AAUW (chmn. hobbies and crafts Dallas br. 1970s), Dallas Ret. Tchrs. Assn. (corr. sec. 1984-90), Dallas Women's Forum (rec. sec. Friday study 1987-89), Bay View Century Club (corr. sec. 1988-89, pres. 1993-95), Dallas Symphony Orch. League, Delta Kappa Gamma (pres. Delta Sigma chpt. 1956-58, Chpt. Achievement award 1979, Marion Parr Light Recruitment grantee named in her honor Delta Sigma chpt. 1958). Avocations: photography, reading.

LIGHT, SYBIL ELIZABETH, executive secretary; Student, Berkeley Coll., 1978—79; BA in Comm. and Pub. Rels., Marist Coll., 2006. Cert. pub. rels., profl. sec. Sec. Peale Ctr. for Christian Living, Pawling, NY, 1979—86, exec. sec. to Norman Vincent Peale, 1986—91; exec. sec. to Ruth Stafford Peale Guideposts, Pawling, NY, 1991—2002, outreach comms. assoc., 2002—05; philanthropy coord., asst. editor PLUS mag., 2005—. Editor: My Favorite Bible Passages, 1995. Sec.-treas. 2d Kent Bapt. Ch., Carmel, NY, 1990—2005; organist 2d Kent Bapt.-Faith Bible Fellowship Ch., Holmes, NY, 1976—. Mem.: Internat. Assn. Adminstrv. Profls. (pres. Mid-Hudson chpt. 1997—99). Home: PO Box 439 Pawling NY 12564 Office: Guideposts - Peale Ctr 66 E Main St Pawling NY 12564 Business E-Mail: slight@guideposts.org.

LIGHTBOURNE, ALESA M., writer, educator; b. Carmel, Calif., July 29, 1952; d. Hugh Everett and Gyla M. (Marmont) Smith; m. Michael Lightbourne; children: Marc, Nell, Joel. BA honors, U. Calif., Santa Cruz, 1974; MA, U. Wash., Seattle, 1985, PhD Comm., 1996. Pres. Lightworks Corp. Comm., 1989—. Freelance writer for bus., acad., trade, travel, women's and children's publs.; website writer Microsoft, Weyerhaeuser; prof. English Chapman U., Columbia Coll. Author: numerous books; co-author (with Rafael Colon): The SALSA Solution, 2006. Named Prize winning speechwriter to CEOs. Avocations: anthropology, sailing, travel, harp. Home: 1128 SW Fairhaven Dr Oak Harbor WA 98277 Office Phone: 360-941-3177. Business E-Mail: alesa@lightworks.us.

LIGHTBOURNE, MARVA HENRIETTA, nurse; b. Miami, Dec. 29, 1947; d. Henry Lightbourne and Martil Virginia Lang; 1 child, Ariel Lightbourne-Padron. RN Harlem Hosp., N.Y.C., 1979—80, Jackson Meml. Hosp., Miami, 1981—85, North Shore Hosp., Miami, 1985—. Adv. bd. Hampton Ho. Inc., Miami. Vol. Pulse, Miami, 2006, Dr. Randy Davis, Inc., Miami, 1999—. Recipient Humanity cert., 1981. Mem.: Dade Heritage Trust African-American (sec. 1993—). Avocation: swimming.

LIGHTBURN, CHRISTA PIERPONT, agricultural business manager; b. Marietta, Ohio, July 11, 1947; d. Howard Clemeth and Mary Irene Pierpont; m. John James Thomasson (div.); m. Robert Cole Lightburn, Aug. 20, 1995; children: David, Benjamin, Matthew, Robert, Ashley, Kelby. BS, Radford U., 1969; M in Edn., Curry Sch. Edn./U. Va., 1977. lic. tchr. Tchr. Mercer Co. Schs., Bluefield, W. Va., 1969-71, Fayette Co. Schs., Fayetteville, W. Va., 1971-75, Albemarle Co. Schs., Charlottesville, Va., 1975-97; asst. owner GameBit, Inc., Rochelle, Charlottesville, Va., 1995—; projects coord. Lightburn Farms, Va., 1997—. Assoc. dir. Culpeper Soil and Water Conservation Dist. Recipient Cheatham Leadership award, Thomsa Jefferson Meml. Ch., 1994. Mem. Nat. Edn. Assn., Va. Edn. Assn., Coun. Exceptional Children, Conflict Resolution Ednl. Network, U. Va. Alumni Assn. Avocations: caving, outdoor activities.

LIGHTFORD, KIMBERLY A., state legislator; BA in Pub. Comm., Western Ill. U.; MPA, U. Ill., Springfield. Mem. ins., labor, appropriations, chair edn., vice-chair fin. instns. Ill. Senate, Springfield, 1998—. Elected chair Ill. Senate Black Caucus; former trustee Village of Maywood. Democrat. Address: 1127 S Mannheim Rd Ste 114 Westchester IL 60154 Office Phone: 217-782-8505, 708-343-7444. Business E-Mail: lightford@senatedem.state.il.us.

LIGHTMAN, MARJORIE, historian; b. NYC, Aug. 6, 1940; d. Earl Rivkin and Ida Ola Friedman; m. Benjamin Lightman, Sept. 6, 1959; children: Andrew, Timothy, Suzanne. BA, Hunter Coll., 1961, MA, 1969; PhD, Rutgers U., 1980. Exec. dir. Inst. Rsch. in History, NYC, 1975—88; founding ptnr. QED Assocs., Teaneck, NJ, 1988—; co-founder Women's Working Group Internat. Human Rights, Washington, 1994—95; leader del. Internat. League Human Rights, Vienna, 1994, Beijing, 1995, Geneva, 1996, 2002, rep. to UN commn. on the status of women NYC, 1995—97. Treas. Nat. Coun. Rsch. Women, NYC, 1983—85; commr. Nat. Commn. Women Higher Edn., NYC, 1983—85; cons. Network East/West Women, 1992—94; organizer book exhibit UN Conf. Nairobi, 1985; sr. rsch. fellow Women's Rsch. & Edn. Inst., 2002—; rsch. fellow Soc. Psychol. Study Soc. Issues, Washington, 2006. Co-author: Ellis Island and the Peopling of America, 1997 (Official Guide to the Ellis Island Mus., 1997); co-editor: Outside Academe: New Ways of Working in the Humanities, 1979; co-author: A Biographical Dictionary of Ancient Greek and Roman Women, 1999; co-editor: Without Precedent: The Life and Career of Eleanor Roosevelt, 1985. Exec. dir. Itnernat. League for Human Rights, NY, 1995—98; tester Fair Housing, Bergen County, 1967; co-founder Feminist Action Coalition of Teaneck, NJ, 1973—76; founding bd. advisors Lang Coll., NYC, 1984—86; chair panel scholars Sewall-Belmont House Mus., Washington, 2000—02; bd. dirs. Women's Interart Ctr., NYC, 1985—88, Ctr. Ethics and Action, U. New Eng., Maine, 2001—, Feminist Press, CUNY, NYC, 2003—. Fellow, Soc. for Psychol. Study of Social Issues, Washington, 2006; Ford Found. grantee, Inst. Rsch. History, 1979, 1982, Nat. Endowment Humanities grantee, 1982, Rockefeller Found. grantee, 1985, 2002, Sr. fellow, Women's Rsch. Edn. Inst., 2002—. Home: 2737 Devonshire Pl NW Washington DC 20008 Office: QED Assocs LLC 3509 Connecticut Ave NW Washington DC 20008 E-mail: lightman@QEDassocs.com.

LIGHTNER, CANDY (CANDACE LYNNE LIGHTNER), non-profit management consultant, advocate; b. Pasadena, Calif., May 30, 1946; d. Dykes Charles and Kathryn Josephine Doddridge; children: Serena, Travis. D (hon.), St. Francis Coll., Pa., 1984, Kutztown (Pa.) U., 1987, Marymount U., N.Y., 1987. With various pvt. offices, 1964-70; real estate salesperson Calif., 1972-80; govt. rels. cons. Washington, 1993-94; owner Candace Lightner & Assocs., Alexandria, Va. Spkr., condr. tng. sessions various orgns. Author: Giving Sorrow Words: How to Cope With Grief and Get On With Your Life, 1990; guest nat. talk shows including Good Morning America, Today, 60 Minutes, MacNeil-Lehrer, Phil Donahue, Nightline, Turning Point. Founder MADD, 1980, chief exec. officer, pres., chmn., 1980-85; mem. adv. bd. Mothers Against Sexual Abuse; bd. dirs. Air Crash Support Network; active Sacramento County Task Force on Drunk Driving, Presdl. Commn. on Drunk and Drugged Driving; bd. dirs. Nat. Commn. on Drunk Driving, 1984-86, Nat. Partnership for Drug Free Use, Nat. Hwy. Safety Adv. Com., Love is Feeding Everyone, 1988-89, others; judge Gleitsman Found.; bd. advisors Bhopal Justice Campaign. Recipient Jefferson award Am. Inst. Pub. Svc., Pres. Vol. Action award, Woman of Yr. award YWCA, Woman of Yr. award Women's Internat. Ctr., award for excellence Film Adv. Bd., Testimonial award Civitan Internat., 1984, Epilepsy Found award, 1984, Woman of Year award Mortar Bd. Soc., Baylor U., 1985, Anti-discriminationaward Am. Anti-descrimination Com., 1985, YWCA Woman of Year award, 1986, Commonwealth award U. Del., 1986, Black and Blue award Thomas Jefferson U. Hosp. Emergency Medicine Soc., Human Dignity award Kessler Inst. for Rehab., Woman of Distinction award Third Nat. Congress Coll. Women Student Leaders and Woman of Achievement, 1987, Disting. Leadership award World Congress of Victimology, 1987, Living Legacy award Women's Internat. Ctr., 1988, Friends of Children award Assn. Childhood Edn. Internat., 1988; Named to Good Housekeeping's Most Admired Woman's Poll, 1986; ranked in Top 25 of Am. most influential people World Almanac and Book of Facts, 1986, one of the original thinkers of the eighties, Life mag., 1990; selected by Johns Hopkins U. to participate in Anglo-Am. Successor Generation program, 1985; honored as one of Seven Who Succeeded, Time Mag., 1985; honored by Edquire mag. as mem. Am.'s New Leadership Class, 1985, others. Mem. Nat. Soc. Fund Raising Execs., Women in Arts, Nat. Bd. Realtors. Avocations: gardening, reading, swimming, travel. Office: 1216 Portner Rd Alexandria VA 22314-1317 E-mail: cd_light2003@yahoo.com.

LIGHTWOOD, CAROL WILSON, writer; b. Tacoma, Wash., Oct. 2, 1941; d. Harry Edward and Cora H. Wilson; m. Keith G. Lightwood (div. Dec. 1968); children: Miles Francis, Clive Harry. BA, Smith Coll., 1963. Writer various advt. agencies, 1968-82; v.p. Wakeman & DeForrest, Newport Beach, Calif., 1985-86; owner Lightwood Direct, Las Vegas, Nev., 1986—2003; pres. The Meeting Place, Inc., 2002; owner Pasadena Soaps, 2005—; pub., editor HotGordens.net, 2003—. Author: Malibu, 1984; pub., editor Hotgardens.net, 2003-; contbr. articles to profl. jours. Chair mus. coun. Long Beach Mus. Art, 1989; docent William O. Douglas Outdoor Classroom; bd. dirs. Friends of Channel 10. Mem. Sierra Club, Sisters in Crime. Episcopalian.

LIGOCKI, KATHLEEN A., auto parts company executive; BA, Ind. U., 1978; MBA, U. Penn., 1985; doctorate (hon.), Ind. U., 2002. Dir. bus. strategy Ford Motor Co., 1998—2000; pres., CEO Ford Mex., 2000—01; corp. v.p. Can., Mex. and N.Am. strategy Ford Motor Co., 2001—02; corp. officer, v.p. Ford Customer Svc. Divsn., 2002—03; dir. Tower Automotive, Inc., Haggerty, Mich., 2003—, pres., CEO, 2003—. Office: Tower Automotive Inc 27275 Haggerty Rd Novi MI 48377

LIHS, MARILYN LOUISE, retired accountant; b. Burlington, Iowa, May 5, 1941; d. Omer C. and Geraldine E. (Berges) Wickerham; m. Craig E. Lihs, Mar. 26, 1961; children: Jeffrey A., Michael S. AA, S.E. Iowa C.C., Burlington, 1961; BBA, U. Iowa, 1986, MBA, 1991. Ch. organist Mil. Chapel, Bremerhaven, Germany, 1966-68; accts. payable clk. City of Burlington, 1968-71; accts. recieveable clk. Economy Advt., Iowa City, 1971-74; office mgr. Shay Electric, Iowa City, 1974-76; contr. Midwest Elect. Cont., Iowa City, 1976-82; from adminstrv. asst. to fin. analyst U. Iowa, Iowa City, 1982-86, adminstrv. acct., 1986-98, ret., 1998. Contbr. articles to Iowa Bus. Woman Mag. Pres. Bus. and Profl. Women Iowa Found., Des Moines, 1995—96; program facilitator Iowa City Cable TV, 1997; rep., com. chair U. Iowa Staff Coun., 1991—97; v.p. Village United Meth. Women, 2000—02, pres., 2002—03. Mem. AAUW, Bus. and Profl. Women (Iowa pres. 1995-96, Iowa City pres. 1997-98, newsletter editor 1997-99, Woman of Yr. 1995-96, 98-99, Spa Area Woman of Yr. 2001-2002), U. Iowa Alumni Assn. (life), Village Quilt Guild (pres. 2000-01). Democrat. Methodist. Avocations: travel, quilting, writing, genealogy. Home: 62 Promesa Dr Hot Springs Village AR 71909-7757 E-mail: mllihs@hotmail.com.

LIIMATTA, JANET ANN, mathematics educator; b. Balt., Aug. 25, 1972; d. Peter Erik and Barbara Shipley Liimatta. BA, Case Western Res. U., Cleve., 1994. Std. profl. cert. Md. State Dept. Edn., 2005. Math. tchr. Tunica Pub. Schs., Miss., 1994—96; elem. tchr. Balt. City Pub. Schs., 1996—2003; math. tchr. Old Mill H.S., Millersville, Md., 2003—. Head track and field coach Old Mill H.S., Millersville, 1998—. Trustee, sch. tchr. Pasadena United Meth. Ch., Md., 1996—2005. Named All County Coach of Yr. for outdoor track, Capital Gazette Newspaper, 2002—05, All Metro Outdoor Track and Field Coach, Balt. Sun, 2004, Wash. Post, 2005. Home: 294 Dogwood Rd Millersville MD 21108 Office: Old Mill High School 600 Patriot Ln Millersville MD 21108 Office Phone: 410-969-9010.

LIKINS, ROSE MARIE, federal agency administrator, former ambassador; b. Andrews AFB, Md., Jan. 22, 1959; d. Eugene Aloysius and Merlyn (Houghland) McCartney; m. John Foster Likins, MAy 30, 1981; children: James, Kevin. BA in Internat. Affairs, Mary Washington Coll., Fredericksburg, Va., 1981, BA in Spanish, 1981. Joined Fgn. Svc., U.S. Dept. State, Washington, 1981—, previous fgn. svc. assignments Honduras, Paraguay, Bulgaria, U.S. amb. to El Salvador El Salvador, 2000—03, acting asst. sec. Bur. of Polit.-Military Affairs, 2005—. Rm. mother Tuckahoe Elem. Sch., Arlington, Va., 1993-94. Mem. Am. Fgn. Svc. Assn., Mortar Board (pres. chpt. 1980-81), Phi Beta Kappa. Roman Catholic. Achievements include fluent in Spanish and Bulgarian. Office: Bur Polit-Military Affairs US Dept State 2201 C St NW Washington DC 20520

LIKOVA MINEVA, LORA T., research scientist; d. Tzvetko T. Likov and Angelina B. Tzvetkova; m. Kristyo N. Mineff; 1 child, Zlatko K. Minev. MSc in Computer Sci., Tech. U., Sofia; PhD in Cognitive Neuroscience, Ctrl. and East-European Ctr. Cognitive Scis., New Bulgarian U., Sofia; postgrad., U. Nat. and World Econs., Sofia; fMRI (functional MRI) tng., MIT/HMS/MGH Ctr. for Biomedical Imaging, Boston. Asst. prof. Ctrl. Inst. of Computer Technique, Sofia, Bulgarian Acad. Scis., Sofia, Inst. for Microprocessing Technique, Sofia; rsch. scientist Smith-Kettlewell Eye Rsch. Inst., San Francisco, postdoctoral fellow; vis. scientist U. Warwick, Coventry, England. Hon. prof. Tech. U., Sofia; head Non-Standard Think Group/Computer Inst. Contbr. articles to profl. jours. Recipient award, Nat. Patent Inst.; fellow fellow for European Conf. on Visual Perception, Oxford, Eng., Brit. Coun.; Rachel C. Atkinson fellow, Smith-Kettlewell Eye Rsch. Inst., San Francisco, fellow European Conf. on Visual Perception, Helsinki, Finland, Soros Open Soc. Found. Mem.: Cognitive Neuroscience Soc., Vision Sci. Soc., Orgn. for Human Brain Mapping, Soc. for Neuroscience. Achievements include patents for magnetic head; discovery of new brain areas: first brain imaging studies (fMRI) on dynamic stereovision; discovering a new brain areas for 3D-motion processing; eye disease diagnosis: discovering a fundamental blind-spot related mechanism and inventing a clinical method (Blue Light Papillometry) for early diagnosis of blinding diseases; depth-motion phenomenon: discovering of a new category of perceived 3D-motion in 3D displays (Monopolar Depth Motion); the transient asynchrony/synchrony is a critical organizational factor in visual perception of dynamic world; for the first time in the human brain a figure/ground mechanism based on top-down suppression of the background representation in retinotopic visual areas. Avocations: philosophy, yoga, hiking, drawing, poetry. Office: Smith-Kettlewell Eye Rsch Inst 2318 Fillmore St San Francisco CA 94115 Office Phone: 415-345-2066. Business E-Mail: lora@ski.org.

LI-LAN, artist; b. N.Y.C., Jan. 28, 1943; d. Yun Wing and Helen Charlotte (Zimmer) Gee.; m. Masuo Ikeda, 1969 (div. 1980). One-man shows include Nantenshi Gallery, Tokyo, 1971, 1974, 1977, 1980, 1985, OK Harris Gallery, N.Y.C., 1983, 1985, 1987, Franz Bader Gallery, Washington, D.C., 1989, Asher/Faure Gallery, L.A., 1980, 1982, Robert Miller Gallery, N.Y.C., 1978, James Yu Gallery, 1974, William Benton Mus. Art, Storrs, Conn., 1990, New Arts Program, Kutztown, Pa., 1991, Amelie A. Wallace Gallery SUNY-Old Westbury, 1992, Benton Gallery, Southampton, N.Y., 1992, Southampton, 1993, Art Projects Internat., N.Y.C., 1994, 1996, Lin & Keng Gallery, Taipei, Taiwan, 1995, 1997, 2001, 2006, Rutgers U., New Brunswick, N.J., 2002, DoubleVision Gallery, L.A., 2003, Nabi Gallery, N.Y., 2004, Silent Journey, Jason McCoy Inc., N.Y., 2006, Jason McCoy Inc., N.Y., 2006, exhibited in group shows, East Hampton, 1973, Guild Hall Mus., 1975, 1976,,1978, 1979, 1997, Randolph Macon Women's Coll., Lynchburg, Va., 1974, Philbrook Art Ctr., Tulsa, 1975, Phoenix Art Mus., 1979, Am. Acad. and Inst. Arts and Letters, N.Y.C., 1983, 1987, Sydney and Frances Lewis Found. Collection travelling exhbn., 1978—, Norton Ctr. for Arts, Danville, Ky., 1987, Southampton Campus Fine Arts Gallery, L.I. U., 1988, Parrish Art Mus., Southampton, 1988, 1992, 1993, 2000, Internat. Travelling Exhbn., Mex., S.Am., Spain, Portugal, 1989—90, Travelling Exhbn. including Blum Helman Gallery, N.Y., 1989—90, U. Okla. Mus. Art, Norman, 1989—90, Grand Rapids Art Mus., 1989—90, Mich. U. Art Gallery, 1989—90, U. North Tex., Denton, 1989—90, Hillwood Art Gallery, Brookville, N.Y., 1989—90, Heckscher Mus., Huntington, N.Y., 1992, Huntington, 1995, 1996, PS 1 Mus., Long Island City, N.Y., 1984, Long Island City, 1992, New Mus. Contemporary Art, N.Y.C., 1994, Eretz Israel Mus., Tel Aviv, 1996, Weatherspoon Art Gallery, Greensboro, N.C., 2001, Smithsonian Instn., Washington, 2001, Pace Wildenstein Gallery, N.Y.C., 2003, Represented in permanent collections Sezon Mus. Modern Art, Karuizawa, Japan, Modern Art Mus., Toyama, Sydney and Frances Lewis Found. Collection, Richmond, Vassar Coll. Art Gallery, Poughkeepsie, N.Y., Estee Lauder, Inc., N.Y.C., Security Pacific Nat. Bank, L.A., Atlantic Richfield Co., Dallas, Ohara Mus. Art, Kurashiki, Japan, Guild Hall Mus., East Hampton, Mobil Oil Corp., N.Y.C., Virlane Found., New Orleans, Va. Mus. Fine Arts, Richmond, Visconsi & Jacobs, Cleve., Seattle 1st Nat. Bank, Chermayeff and Geismar Assocs., N.Y., Parrish Art Mus., Southampton, William Benton Mus. Art, Storrs, Westfield State Coll., Mass., Lifetime TV, N.Y.C., Ark. Arts Ctr., Little Rock, Fisher Pharm. Ltd., Tel Aviv, San Diego Mus. Art, Balt. Mus. of Art; author: Canvas with An Unpainted Part: An Autobiography, 1976. Avocations: photography, writing.

LILES, VIRGINIA REMBERT, retired art educator; d. Umsted Samuel and Hazel Hudson Pitts; m. Raeford Bailey Liles, Nov. 27, 1993; m. John Lamar Rembert, Dec. 27, 1944 (dec. 1978). BA in Art and English, U. Montevallo, 1942; MA in Fine Arts Edn., Columbia U., 1944; MA in Art History, U. Wis., 1959; PhD in Art History, Columbia U., 1970. Tchr. art Montevallo Pub. Schs., 1942—43; instr. art Beloit Coll., 1953—55; asst. prof. art Mass. Coll. Art, Boston, 1956—60; from asst. prof. to prof. art, chmn. dept. art Birmingham So. Coll., 1960—73, prof. art, 1970; prof. art, chmn. Dept. Art U. Ala., Birmingham, 1974—75; disting. prof. U. Ark., Little Rock, 1975—81; prof., chmn. Dept. Art U. Ala., Tuscaloosa, Ala., 1981—90, prof. emeritus, 1990—. Chmn. blue ribbon com. U. Ark., Little Rock, 1985—87. Author: Mondrian in the USA, 2002, Bosch, 2004; contbr. articles to profl. jours. Bd. dirs. Birmingham (Ala.) Festival Arts, 1970—73. Recipient Disting. Svc. award, S.E. Coll. Art Conf., 1989, Disting. Career award, Soc. Fine Arts, 1993, Susan B. Riley fellow, AAUA, 1967—68. Mem.: S.E. Coll. Art Conf. (chmn. annual mtgs. 1978, 1986, pres. 1977—78), Coll. Art Assn. (mem. nominating com. 1980). Democrat. Meth. Avocations: travel, drawing, painting, museums.

LIL' KIM, (KIMBERLY DENISE JONES), rap artist, actress; b. Bklyn., July 11, 1975; d. Linwood and Ruby Mae Jones. Singer: (albums) Hard Core, 1996, Notorious K.I.M., 2000, La Bella Mafia, 2003, The Naked Truth, 2005, The Meaning of Family, 2005, (films) Money Talks, 1997, Moulin Rouge!, 2001; composer High School High, 1996, Booty Call, 1997, Nothing to Lose, 1997, Dr. Doolittle 2, 2001; actor: (films) She's All That, 1999, Longshot, 2000, Juwanna Mann, 2002, Gang of Roses, 2003, Nora's Hair Salon, 2004, (guest appearances): (TV series) V.I.P., 1999, DAG, 2001, Moesha, 2001, American Dreams, 2003. Office: c/o Atlantic Records 1290 Avenue of the Americas New York NY 10104-0101

LILLESTOL, JANE BRUSH, educational consultant; b. Jamestown, ND, July 20, 1936; d. Harper J. and Doris (Mikkelson) Brush; m. Harvey Lillestol, Sept. 29, 1956; children: Kim, Kevin, Erik. BS, U. Minn., 1969, MS, 1973, PhD, 1977; grad. Inst. Ednl. Mgmt., Harvard U., 1984. Dir. placement, asst. to dean U. Minn., St. Paul, 1975-77; assoc. dean, dir. student acad. affairs ND State U., Fargo, 1977-80; dean Coll. Human Devel. Syracuse U., NY, 1980-89, v.p. for alumni rels., 1989-95, project dir. IBM Computer Aided Design Lab., 1989—92; prin. Lillestol Assocs.; emeritus faculty Syracuse U., 1995—; faculty U. Phoenix, 2002—, curriculum devel. specialist, 2003. Charter mem. Mayor's Commn. on Women, 1986-90; NAFTA White House Conf. for Women Leaders, 1993. Bd. dirs. Univ. Hill Corp. Syracuse, 1983-93; mem. steering com. Consortium for Cultural Founds. of Medicine, 1980-89; trustee Manlius Pebble Hill Sch., 1990-94, Archbold Theatre, 1990-95, ND State U., 1992—. Recipient award US Consumer Product Safety Commn., 1983, Woman of Yr. award AAUW, 1984, svc. award Syracuse U., 1992; named among 100 Outstanding Alumni Over Past 100 Yrs., U. Minn. Coll. Human Ecology, 2001. Office: 8046 E Via De Los Libros Scottsdale AZ 85258-3056 E-mail: jane@lillestol.com.

LILLEY, MILI DELLA, insurance company executive, entertainment management consultant; b. Valley Forge, Pa., Aug. 29; d. Leon Hanover and Della Beaver (Jones) L. MBA, Tex. Christian U., 1957, PhD, 1959. Various positions G & G Cons. Inc., Ft. Lauderdale, Fla., 1971-75; v.p. AMEX, Inc., Beverly Hills, Calif. and Acapulco, Mex., 1976-80; pres. The Hanover Group, Ft. Lauderdale, 1981—; personal and bus. mgr. entertainers including Ink Spots, Ft. Lauderdale, 1984—, Lanny Poffo, Ft. Lauderdale, 1990—. Dist. agt. ITT Life Ins. Corp., also other leading cos. Named to All Stars Honor Roll Nat. Ins. Sales Mag., 1989. Mem. Fla. Assn. Theatrical Agts., Fla. Guild of Talent Agts., Mgrs., Prodrs. and Orchs. Office: The Hanover Group PO Box 70218 Fort Lauderdale FL 33307-0218 Office Phone: 954-491-1101.

LILLIE, CHARISSE RANIELLE, lawyer, educator; b. Houston, Apr. 7, 1952; d. Richard Lysander and Vernell Audrey (Watson) Lillie; m. Thomas L. McGill Jr., Dec. 4, 1982. BA cum laude, Conn. Wesleyan U., 1973; JD, Temple U., 1976; LLM, Yale U., 1982; LLD (hon.), Seton Hill U., 2005. Bar: Pa. 1976, U.S. Dt. Ct. (ea. dist.) Pa. 1977, U.S. Ct. Appeals (3d cir.) 1980. Law clk. U.S. Dist. Ct. (ea. dist.) Pa., Phila., 1976—78; trial atty., honors program, civil rights divsn. Dept. Justice, Washington, 1978—80; dep. dir. Cmty. Legal Svcs., Phila., 1980—81; asst. prof. law Villanova U. Law Sch., Pa., 1982—83, assoc. prof. Pa., 1983-84, prof. Pa., 1984—85; asst. U.S. atty. U.S. Dist. Ct. (ea. dist.) Pa., Phila., 1985—88; with Redevel. Authority of Phila., 1988—90; city solicitor law dept. City of Phila., 1990—92; ptnr. Ballard, Spahr, Andrews & Ingersoll LLP, Phila., 1992—2005, chair litigation dept., 2002—05; also. bd. dirs. Ballard, Spahr, Andrew & Ingersoll LLP, Phila.; pres. human resources Comcast Corp., 2005—; sr. v.p. human resources Comcast Cable, 2005—. Mem. 3d Cir. Lawyers Adv. Com., 1982—85; legal counsel Pa. Coalition of 100 Black Women, Phila., 1983—88; bd. dirs. Juvenile Law Ctr., Phila., Pa. Intergovtl. Coop. Authority, Fed. Res. Bank Phila., dep. chmn. bd. dirs., 1998—2000, chmn. bd. dirs., 2001—02; commr. Phila. Ind. City Charter Commn., 1991—94; trustee Women's Law Project, Phila., 1984—90; mem. Mayor's Commn. on May 13 MOVE Incident, 1985—86; mem. com. on racial and gender bias in the justice sys. Supreme Ct. Pa., 1999—2003. Mem. adv. com. Women's Way, Phila., 1986—91; chair City of Phila. Bd. Ethics, 2004—; chair bd. trustees The Phila. Award, 2004—; chair bd. dir.s Friends Select Sch., 2003—; bd. dirs. Leadership Inc. Named One of Phila.'s Most Influential African Americans, Phila. Tribune, 2002, 2003, 2004, 2005, One of Top Three Phila. Labor Mgmt. Attys., Phila. Mag., 1994, 1999, One of Phila.'s Most Influential African Americans, Phila. Tribune, 2004; named to the Women's Hall of Fame, Southwest Belmont Cmty. Assn., 2002; recipient Equal Justice award, Cmty. Legal Svcs., Inc., 1991, Outstanding Alumna award, Wesleyan U., 1993, Elizabeth Dole Glass Ceiling award, ARC, Phila. chpt., 1994, Whitney Young Leadership award, Phila. Urban League, 1996, Take the Lead award, U.S. Girl Scouts, 2002, Women of Distinction award, Phila. Bus. Jour., 2002, Penn Towne Links Svc. award, 2002, Image award, Black Women in Sport Found., 2002, J. Michael Brown award, DuPont Minority Counsel Conf., 2002, Bd. Dirs. Hall of Fame award, Teenshop, 2002, Mother of Yr., Mary Mason Cmty. Found., 2002, Women of Achievement award, The Barristers' Assn., 2002, Awards of Excellence, The Thurgood Marshall Scholarship Fund, Inc., 2003, Superlawyer, Top 100, Phila. Mag., 2004, 2005, 2006, Anne X. Alpern award, Pa. Bar Assn., 2003, Inductee to Disting., Daughters of Pa., 2004, Learned Hand award, Am. Jewish Com., Phila. Chpt., 2005, Power award, Profl. Women's Roundtable, 2005; fellow Davenport fellow, 1973, Yale Sch. fellow, 1981. Fellow: Am. Bar Found., Coll. Labor and Employment Lawyers; mem.: ABA (vice chmn. commn. on ethnic diversity in the professio 1997—99, chmn. commn. on ethnic diversity in the professio 1999—2002, mem. standing com. on fed. jud. 2002—05), Hist. Soc. U.S. Dist. Ct. (ea. dist.) Pa. (dir. 1983—87), Phila. Bar Assn. (vice chair bd. govs. 1994, chair bd. govs. 1995—96), Barristers Assn. (J. Austin Norris award 1983—87), Am. Law Inst., Nat. Conf. Black Lawyers (pres. 1970), Fed. Bar Assn. (1st v.p. Phila. chpt. 1982—84, pres. Phila. chpt. 1984—86, 3d cir. rep. 1991—), Nat. Bar Assn. Office: Comcast Corp 1500 Market St Philadelphia PA 19102

LILLY, AIMEE, radio personality; b. Wheaton, Ill., Dec. 09; m. Scott Lilly. Radio host Sta. WMBI, Chgo. Office: WMBI 820 N LaSalle Rd Chicago IL 60610

LILLY, ELIZABETH GILES, small business owner; b. Bozeman, Mont., Aug. 5, 1916; d. Samuel John and Luella Elizabeth (Reed) Abegg; m. William Lilly, July 1, 1976; children: Samuel Colborn Giles, Elizabeth Giles. RN, Good Samaritan Hosp., Portland, Oreg., 1941; student, Walla Walla Coll., Lewis and Clark Coll. Bus., Portland. ARC nurse, tchr. area high schs., Portland; owner Welton Studio Interior Design, Portland; in pub. rels. Chas. Eckelman, Portland, Fairview Farms-Dairy Industry; owner, builder Mobile Park Plaza, Inc., Portland. Del. platform planning com. Rep. Party; mem. Sunnyside Seventh Day Adventist Ch., deaconess. Recipient Svc. award Multnomah County Commrs., 1984. Mem. Soroptimist Internat. (local bd. dirs., bd. dirs. Women in Transition), Rep. Women's Club (pres.), C. of C., World Affairs Coun., Toastmistress (pres.), Oreg. Lodging Assn. (pres. bd. dirs.), Rep. Inner Circle (life).

LILLY, ELIZABETH K., art educator, artist; b. Dayton, Ohio; d. Theodore E. and Elizabeth I. Lilly; children: Seth M. Hardy, Sarah E. Gaut. BA, Oberlin Coll., Ohio, 1959—63; MA, Columbia U., N.Y.C., 1963—64. Lic. Educator Mass. Bd. Edn. Elem. sch. tchr. Dayton Pub. Schools, Ohio, 1964—65, Dayton, Ohio, 1968—70, Internat. Schools Assn., Bangkok, Thailand, 1966—68, US AID, Vientaine, Laos, 1966—68, Brighton, NY; first capital campaign dir. Star Island Corp., Portsmouth, NH, 1986—88; dir., devel. and pub. rels. Boston Higashi Sch. for Autistic Children, Lexington, Mass., 1988—90; art specialist Hingham Pub. Schs., Mass., 1990—. Founding mem. EES Arts. Exhibitions include printmaking, mixed-media. Numerous com. and leadership roles Old Ship Ch., Hingham, Mass., 1986—2006; leadership roles and membership on exec. committees Star Island Corp., Portsmouth, NH, 1978—2006; steering com. Star Island Conf. on the Arts, Portsmouth, NH, 1979—82. Mem.: NEA. Unitarian. Avocations: garden design, scuba diving, rowing.

LILLY, EMILY L., education educator; b. Quincy, Mass., Aug. 18, 1978; d. Fred B. DuFresne and Wilma J. Leinonen; m. Anthony W. Lilly, II, May 20, 2000; 1 child, Lorraine A. AA, Simon's Rock Coll. of Bard, Great Barrington, Mass., 1996; BA, Smith Coll., Northampton, Mass., 1998; PhD, MIT, Cambridge, Mass., 2003. Postdoctoral investigator Harvard U., Cambridge, 2003—05; asst. prof. U. Mass., North Dartmouth, 2005—. Author: (article) Jour. Plankton Rsch., Phycologia, Jour. Phycology, Harmful Algae. Recipient Silver Certificate of Acheivement for Outstanding Presentation, NASA, 2005, Certificate of Distinction in Tchg., Harvard U., 2005; Predoctoral Fellowship, NSF, 1998—2001. Mem.: Phycological Soc. Am., Internat. Symbiosis Soc., Internat. Soc. for the Study of Harmful Algae, Am. Soc. Microbiology, Sigma Xi, Phi Beta Kappa. Office: Univ Mass 285 Old Westport Rd North Dartmouth MA 02747 Office Phone: 508-999-8959.

LILLY, EVANGELINE, actress; b. Fort Saskatchewan, Alberta, Can., Aug. 3, 1979; Attended, U. Brit. Columbia. Actor: (TV series) Judgment Day, 2002, Lost, 2004— (Outstanding Performance by an Ensemble in a Drama Series, Screen Actors Guild award, 2006); (TV miniseries) Kingdom Hospital, 2004; (films) The Long Weekend, 2005; (TV series, guest appearance) Smallville, 2002, Tru Calling, 2003. Address: ABC TV c/o Lost 77 W 66th St New York NY 10023-629*

LILLY, KRISTINE MARIE, professional soccer player; b. Wilton, Conn., July 27, 1971; BA in Comm., U. N.C., 1993. Midfielder U.S. Women's Nat. Soccer Team, Chgo., 1987—; profl. soccer player Boston Breakers, 2001—03. Named Most Valuable Offensive Player, NCAA Championship, 1989, 1991, MVP, U.S. Women's World Cup, 1991, U.S. Soccer's Female Athlete of Yr., 1993, MVP, U.S. Women's World Cup, 1999, U.S. Nat. Team All-Time Appearance Leader (more than 90 games); named to, World Cup Championship Team, 1999; recipient Hemann Trophy, 1991, Gold medal, Centennial Olympic Games, 1996, Athens Olympic Games, 2004, Silver medal, Sydney Olympic Games, 2000. Achievements include member FIFA Women's World Championship Team, 1991; member World Cup Team, 1999; member U. N.C. NCAA National Championship Teams, 1989-92. Office: US Soccer Fedn 1801 S Prairie Ave Chicago IL 60616-1319

LILLY, LUELLA JEAN, retired academic administrator; b. Newberg, Oreg., Aug. 23, 1937; d. David Hardy and Edith (Coleman) Lilly. BS, Lewis and Clark Coll., 1959; postgrad., Portland State U., 1959—61; MS, U. Oreg., 1961; PhD, Tex. Woman's U., 1971; postgrad., various univs., 1959—72. Tchr. phys. edn. and health, dean girls Ctrl. Linn Jr.-Sr. H.S., Halsey, Oreg., 1959—60; tchr. phys. edn. and health, coach swimming, tennis, golf Lake Oswego H.S., Oreg., 1960—63; instr., intramural dir., coach Oreg. State U., Corvallis, 1963—64; instr., intercollegiate coach Am. River Coll., Sacramento, 1964—69; dir. women's phys. edn., athletics U. Nev., Reno, 1969—73, assoc. prof. phys. edn., 1971—76, dir. women's athletics, 1973-75, assoc. dir. athletics, 1975—76; dir. women's intercollegiate athletics U. Calif., Berkeley, 1976—97; ret., 1997. Organizer, coach Lue's Aquatic Club, 1962—64; v.p. PAC-10 Conf., 1990—91. Author: An Overview of Body Mechanics, 1966, 3d rev. edit., 1969. Vol. instr. ARC, 1951; vol. Heart Fund and Easter Seal, 1974—76, Am. Heart Assn., 1991—95, Multiple Sclerosis Soc., 1999—2004; vol. ofcl. Spl. Olympics, 1975; mem. LA Citizens Olympic Com., 1984; bd. dirs. Las Trampas, 1993—98, sec., 1996—98. Named to Athletic Hall of Fame, Lewis and Clark Coll., 1988, First 125 Yrs. Women of Honor, U. Calif., Berkeley, 1995, Athletic Hall of Fame, 2005; recipient Mayor Anne Rudin award, Nat. Girls' and Women's Sports, 1993, Lifetime Sports award, Bay Area Women's Sports Found., 1994, Golden Bear award Vol. of Yr., 1995, Su Stauffer Firend of Edn. award, 2002, Pride of Nev. award, 2006. Mem.: AAUW, AAHPERD (life), No. Calif. Athletic Conf. (pres. 1979—82, sec. 1984—85), Nev. Assn. Health Phys. Edn. and Recreation (state chmn. 1974), No. Calif. Intercollegiate Athletic Conf. (volleyball coord. 1971—72), No. Calif. Women's Intercollegiate Conf. (sec., basketball coord. 1970—71), Nev. Bd. Women Ofcls. (chmn. basketball sect. 1969, chmn. bd. dirs., chmn. volleyball sect.), Calif. Assn. Health, Phys. Edn. and Recreation (chmn.-elect jr. coll. sect. 1970), Ctrl. Calif. Bd. Women Ofcls. (basketball chmn. 1968—69), Oreg. Girls' Swimming Coaches Assn. (pres. 1960, 1963), We. Assn. Intercollegiate Athletics Women (exec. bd. dirs. 1973—75, 1979—82), We. Soc. Phys. Edn. Coll. Women (membership com. 1971—74, program adv. com. 1972, exec. bd. 1972—75), Coun. Collegiate Women Athetics Adminstrs. (membership com. 1989—92), Women's Athletic Caucus, Nat. Assn. Coll. Women Athletic Adminstrs. (divsn. 1-A women's steering com. 1991—92, Lifetime Achievement award 1999),

Women's Sports Found. (awards com. 1994—2004), Nat. Soc. Profs., Soroptomists (bd. dirs., v.p. 1989, 1992—93, sec. 1993—95, 1st v.p. 1996—97, corr. sec. 1997—98, pres. 1998—2000, sec. 2001—02, 1st v.p. 2004—, Women Helping Women award 1991, Women of Distinction award 2002), Theta Kappa, Phi Kappa Phi. Avocation: swimming. Home and Office: 60 Margrave Ct Walnut Creek CA 94597-2511 Office Phone: 925-934-3868.

LILLY, NANCY COBB, civic worker; b. Durham, N.C., Sept. 17, 1930; d. Collier and Emma (Estes) C.; m. Edward Guerrant Lilly, Jr., Nov. 25, 1961; children: Penelope Read, Edward III, Collier Cobb (dec.), Steven Clay. BA, Randolph-Macon Woman's Coll., 1952. Asst. calendar clk. NC State Senate, Raleigh, 1953, 55; sec. to dir. Met. Mus. Art, N.Y.C., 1956-61; tchr. Chapin Sch. for Girls, N.Y.C., 1961. Pres. Women of Ch., White Meml. Presbyn. Ch., Raleigh, 1986-88, bd. deacons 1991-1997, elder 1999-2005; bd. dirs. ARC, Wake County, Raleigh, 1988-92, Chapel Hill, N.C. com. Nat. Mus. Women in Arts; mem. Tyron Palace Commn., New Bern, N.C., 1988-92; regent Gunston Hall Plantation, Lorton, Va., 1988-2003; bd. visitors Peace Coll. Mem. Jr. League, Raleigh Fine Arts Soc., N.C. Soc. (bd. dirs.), Friends of Libr. U. N.C. (bd. dirs.). Republican. Presbyterian. Avocations: tennis, sailing, reading, needlecrafts. Home: 612 Scotland St Raleigh NC 27609-6950

LILLY-HERSLEY, JANE ANNE FEELEY, nursing researcher; b. Palo Alto, Calif., May 31, 1947; d. Daniel Morris Sr. and Suzanne (Agnew) Feeley; children: Cary Jane, Laura Blachree, Claire Foale; m. Dennis C. Hersley, Jan. 16, 1993. BS, U. Oreg., 1968; student, U. Hawaii, 1970; BSN, RN, Sacramento City Coll., 1975. Cert. ACLS, BCLS. Staff and charge nurse, acute rehab. Santa Clara Valley Med. Ctr., San Jose, Calif., staff nurse, surg. ICU and trauma unit; clin. project leader mycophenolate mofetil program team Syntex Rsch., Palo Alto. Pres. Rsch. Consultation Inc., Santa Cruz, Calif, cons. med. rsch. pharmacutical rsch. Featured in: BBC documentary; appearances: nat. TV and radio broadcasts, pub. presentations. Co-founder, CFO, dir. scientific rsch. Citizens United Responsible Environmentalism, Inc., (CURE). Mem. AACN, Nature Conservancy, Nat. Wildlife Fedn., Monterey Bay Aquarium, World Wildlife Fund., Smithsonian Assn., Nature Plant Soc., Nat. Sludge Alliance. Achievements include research and education in mold exposure and human mycotoxicoses. Personal E-mail: jhersley@comcast.net.

LIM, DIANA MAGPAYO, internist; b. Manila, May 25, 1964; came to U.S., 1993; d. Thomas and Pacita King Magpayo; m. Kennedy Kaw, Mar. 18, 1992; children: Nicole Ann, Paul Nathan, Natalie Paige, Neelie Mae. BS in Med. Tech. cum laude, U. Santo Tomas, Manila, 1986, MD, 1990. Diplomate Am. Bd. Internal Medicine. Rotating intern U. Santo Tomas Hosp., Manila, 1990-91; intern, resident, mem. house staff Cath. Med. Ctr. Bklyn. and Queens, Inc., Jamaica, N.Y., 1993-96; mem. staff Christus Schumpert Bossier (formerly Bossier Med. Ctr.), Bossier City, La., 1996—2004, Willis Knighton Bossier Health Ctr., Bossier City, 1999—. Mem. AMA, ACP, La. State Med. Soc., Bossier Parish Med. Soc., Philippine Med. Assn., Manila Med. Assn. Office: Willis Knighton Bossier Internal Medicine Ste 420 2400 Hospital Dr Bossier City LA 71111-2391

LIM, DONNA, music educator; d. Victor and Florence Lim. BA, San Francisco State U., 1971, std. elem. credential, 1973; Suzuki method credential, Talent Edn. Inst., Matsumoto, Japan, 1985. Lic. EMT Calif.; tchr. trainer Suzuki Assn. of the Ams. Tchr. Suzuki violin San Francisco State U., 1972—76; tchr., dir. Round Valley Strings, Covelo, Calif., 1976—93; tchr. kindergarten music Round Valley Sch. Dist., Covelo, 1977—93; tchr. Suzuki violin Dominican U., San Rafael, Calif., 1993—2004; tchr. violin and viola Suzuki Music Studio of San Francisco, 1993—; tchr. music San Francisco Unified Sch. Dist., 1996—2006. Violin clinician various instns., Ariz., Calif., Mont., Idaho, Nebr., Nev., Oreg., Utah, Wash., 1977—; co-founder, co-dir. Music in Round Valley Concert Series, 1977—91, Scholarship Program, 1977—87; asst. condr. Golden Gate Philharm., 2006—. Interim editor: Internat. Suzuki Jour., 2000. With Disaster Med. Asst. Team, 1998—; vol. Asian Art Mus., San Francisco, 1996—2001; EMT, firefighter, pres. Covelo Vol. Fire Dept., 1986—93. Named Fireman of Yr., Covelo Vol. Fire Dept., 1989, 1991. Mem.: Suzuki Assn. of the Ams., Suzuki Music Assn. Calif. (bd. dirs. 1986—89, pres. 1999—2002, bd. dirs. 1994—98), Mu Phi Epsilon. Avocations: chamber music, knitting, gardening. Home: 3518 Santiago San Francisco CA 94116 E-mail: samite@sbcglobal.net.

LIM, JEANETTE J., federal agency administrator; b. July 23, 1940; BS in chem., U. Mich., 1962; MS in med. genetics, U. Wis. Med. Sch., 1965; JD, Temple U. Law Sch., 1978. Spl. asst. to pres. West Chester State U., Pa., 1976—79; spl. asst. Dept. Justice, Washington, 1995—97; acting asst. sec. Office for Civil Rights U.S. Dept. Edn., Washington, 1992—93, atty. Office for Civil Rights, acting asst. sec. Office for Civil Rights, 2000—01, dep. asst. sec. mgmt. and ops, 2002—. Office: US Dept Elem and Secondary Edn 400 Maryland Ave SW FOB-6 Rm 3W314 Washington DC 20202 Office Phone: 202-401-9090. E-mail: jeanette.lim@ed.gov.

LIM, JOALIN PECK-KIAN, biomedical engineer, researcher; b. Singapore, June 19, 1965; AD in Mech. Engring., Ngee Ann Poly., Singapore, 1986; BSEE, Tri-State U., Angola, Ind., 1989; MS in Biomed. Engring., U. Minn., 1994, PhD in Biomed. Engring., 2002. Culture specific bus. cons. Inglingua Internat. Inc. and Window On the World, Inc., Mpls., 1996; computer programmer U. Minn., Mpls., 1993, rsch. asst. dept. surgery, 1991-97, rsch. engr., scientist dept. pediat., 1998-99; biomed engr. Mallinckrodt Inc., 1998-99; clin. rsch. cons. Harvard Med. Sch. Mind and Body Inst., 2000; sr. biomed. engr. Nonin Med., Inc., Plymouth, Minn., 2000—. Contbr. articles to profl. jours. Mem. IEEE (chmn. Twin Cities chpt. Engring. in Meidcine and Biology Soc. 1999-2000, 02-03, Millennium award, Outstanding Chpt. award), Biomed. Engring. Soc., Soc. Women Engrs., Engring. in Medicine and Biology Soc., Focus on Animal Contbn. to Sci., Toastmasters, Tau Beta Pi, Eta Kappa Nu. Achievements include patent for high speed industrial egg sorting machine. Office: 12129 Zealand Ave N Champlin MN 55316-3584 E-mail: joalin@nonin.com.

LIMACHER, MARIAN CECILE, cardiologist; b. Joliet, Ill., May 4, 1952; d. Joseph John and Shirley A. (Smith) L.; m. Timothy C. Flynn, May 17, 1980; children: Mary Katherine Flynn, Brian Patrick Flynn. AB in Chemistry, St. Louis U., 1973, MD, 1977. Diplomate Am. Bd. Internal Medicine, Am. Bd. Cardiovascular Diseases. Resident in internal medicine Baylor Coll. Medicine, Houston, 1977-80, cardiology fellow, 1980-83, instr. medicine, 1983-84; dir. cardiology non-invasive labs. Ben Taub Hosp., Houston, 1983-84; asst. prof. medicine U. Fla., Gainesville, 1984-91, assoc. prof., 1991-97, prof., 1997—; dir. non-invasive labs. Gainesville VA Med. Ctr., 1984-99, chief cardiology, 1995-99. Dir. preventive cardiology program U. Fla., 1987—. Author (with others): Cardiac Transplantation: A Manual for Health Care Professionals, 1990, Geriatric Cardiology, 1992, The Role of Food in Sickness and in Health, 1993, Clinical Anesthesia Practice, 1994, Primary Care, 1994; mem. editl. bd.: Clin. Cardiology, 1990—, Preventive Cardiology, 1997—, assoc. editor: Jour. Watch Women's Health, 2001—, Clin. Jour. Women's Health, 2001; contbr. articles to profl. jours. Mem. bioethics commn. Diocese of St. Augustine, Jacksonville, Fla., 1990-94. Recipient Preventive Cardiology Acad. award NIH, 1987-92; grantee for Women's Health Initiative, NIH, 1994—. Fellow: ACP, Coun. Clin. Cardiology, Soc. Geriatric Cardiology (bd. dirs. 1997—, pres. 2002), Am. Coll. Cardiology (chair com. women cardiology 1998—2002, trustee 1999—2004); mem.: Am. Clin. and Climatological Assn., Am. Heart Assn. (pres. Alachua County divsn. 1986—89), Am. Soc. Preventive Cardiology (pres. 1998). Roman Catholic. Avocations: tennis, jogging, skiing, playing piano. Office: U Fla Coll Medicine PO Box 100277 Gainesville FL 32610-0277

LIMAN, ELLEN, art gallery owner, painter; b. NYC; d. David and Gertrude (Edelman) Fogelson; m. Arthur Liman, Sept. 20, 1959 (dec.); children: Lewis, Emily, Doug. BA, Barnard Coll., 1957; student, N.Y. Sch. Interior Design, 1959. In pub. rels. Tex McCrary, Inc., 1957; interior designer Malanie Kahane Assocs., 1958-60; cons. on grants to the arts The Joe and Emily Lowe Found., 1975-92; pres., trustee Joe and Emily Lowe Found., 1993—2000; pres. Liman Found., 2000—; owner Liman Studio Gallery, Palm Beach, Fla., 2003—. Dir. spl. projects City Gallery for NYC Dept. Cultural Affairs, 1980—84; exec. asst. Adv. Commn. for Cultural Affairs, NYC, 1981—82; chair NYC Adv. Commn. for Cultural Affairs, 1991—93. Author: The Money Savers Guide to Decorating, 1972, Decorating Your Country Place, 1973, Decorating Your Room, 1974, The Spacemaker Book, 1977, The Collecting Book, 1980, Babyspace, 1984, 2000, others; contbr. editor: Kid Smart Mag., 1995-96; contbr. articles to nat. mags. Founding trustee Internat. Ctr. of Photography, 1973-2003; trustee The Jewish Mus., 1974—, hon. trustee, 1993—; trustee The Ctr. for Arts Info., 1985-86, Mus. Am. Indian, 1998—, Westchester Coun. on Arts, 1994-2002; mem. N.Y.C. Commn. for Cultural Affairs, 1986-89; bd. dirs. Art Table, Inc., 1987-90, Trust for Cultural Resources, 1993-96, Am. Fedn. of Arts, 1994-2002; mem. adv. bd. Nat. Acad. Design, 1998—; mem. The Mayor's Fund for N.Y., 2003—. Fax: 646-840-0211.

LIMERICK, DIANNE A., mathematics educator, athletic trainer; b. Yokohama, Japan, Sept. 14, 1954; d. Thomas and Louise Limerick. BA in Elem. Edn., Christopher Newport Coll., Coll. William and Mary, Newport News, Va., 1976; MA in Secondary Edn., Christopher Newport Coll., Coll. William and Mary, Williamsburg, Va., 1981. Lic. athletic trainer Va. Tchr. Williamsburg James City Pub. Sch., 1976—; h.s. athleic trainer Newport News/Hampton Pub. Schs., 1978—2000; nat. team trainer US Swimming Nat. Governing Body, Colorado Springs, Colo., 1985—; athletic trainer, strength coach Williamsburg Aquatic Club, 2000—. Water safety instr., sports safety instr. ARC, Williamsburg, Va., 1970—; sholastic all Am. com. USA Swimming, Colorado Springs, 1999—. Mission dir. King of Glory Luth. Ch., Williamsburg, 2000—06; storybook connection prison ministry coord. King of Glory Luth. Ch. and Va. Peninsula Regional Jail, Williamsburg, 2000—06; safety coord. Va. Swimming Local Swimming Com., Williamsburg. Named to Hall of Fame, ARC, 2005; recipient Glenn Hummer award, USA Swimming, 1988, Phillips 66 Performance award, Va. Swimming, 2004. Mem.: Nat. Athletic Trainers Assn., Va. HS Coaches Assn. (life Dr. Frank McCue award 1988), USA Swimming (life; sec. sports medicine soc., coun. 1979—99). Independent. Lutheran. Avocations: travel, hockey. Personal E-mail: dlime@aol.com.

LIN, ALICE LEE LAN, physicist, researcher, educator; b. Shanghai, Oct. 28, 1937; came to U.S., 1960, naturalized, 1974; m. A. Marcus, Dec. 19, 1962 (div. Feb. 1972); 1 child, Peter A. AB in Physics, U. Calif., Berkeley, 1963; MA in Physics, George Washington U., Washington, 1974. Statis. asst. dept. math. U. Calif., Berkeley, Calif., 1961-63; rsch. asst. in radiation damage Cavendish Lab. Cambridge U., England, 1965-66; info. analysis specialist Nat. Acad. Sci., Washington, 1970-71; tchng. fellow, rsch. asst. George Washington U., Cath. U. Am., Washington, 1971-75; physicist NASA /Goddard Space Flight Ctr., Greenbelt, Md., 1975-80, Army Materials Tech. Lab., Watertown, Mass., 1980—. Contbr. articles to profl. jours. Mencius Ednl. Found. grantee, 1959-60. Mem. AAAS, N.Y. Acad. Scis., Am. Phys. Soc., Am. Ceramics Soc., Am. Acoustical Soc., Am. Men and Women of Sci., Optical Soc. Am. Democrat. Avocations: computers, opera, ballet, gardening, coin collecting/numismatics. Home: 28 Hallett Hill Rd Weston MA 02493-1753 Office Phone: 781-899-6751. Business E-Mail: plinmarcus@alumni.tufts.edu.

LIN, CHIU-TZE, conductor, musician; b. Taipei, Taiwan, Sept. 04; d. Shih-Tsun Lin; m. Robert Kaita, Apr. 19, 2000; children: Courtney Lin Kaita, Constance Lin Kaita. MA, U. Ill. Music dir. Princeton Presbyn. Ch., NJ, 1994—2001, Manalapan Battleground Symphony, NJ, 2001—, condr., 2001—. Officer N. Music Tchrs. Assn., Princeton, 1996—. Musician: (albums) Piano Works of J. S. Bach (Recommended Recording, 2002). Recipient Music Competition award, Artists Internat., 1990, Victor Grossinger award, Parks & Recreations, 2004; scholar, Am. Music Scholarship Assn., 1989; Piano Pedagogy grant, Cecilian Music Club, 2000—05. Mem.: NJ Music Tchrs. Assn. (assoc.; treas. 1996—). Democrat. Home and Office: Chiu-Tze Lin Performing Artist 27 La Valley Dr Manalapan NJ 07726 Home Fax: 732-446-7298. Personal E-mail: chiutze@earthlink.net.

LIN, MARIA C. H., lawyer; b. Kunming, Yunnan, China, Jan. 27, 1942; BSc, Coll. Mount St. Vincent, 1966; MSc, U. Kans., 1970; JD, Fordham U., 1978. Bar: N.Y. 1979, U.S. Dist. Ct. (so. and ea. dists.) N.Y. 1979, U.S. Ct. Appeals (Fed. cir.) 1982, U.S. Patent and Trademark Office, 1979, U.S Supreme Ct. 1985. Ptnr. Morgan & Finnegan LLP, NYC. Internat. Intellectual Propery Soc. (chair 2000—02). Office: Morgan & Finnegan LLP Shanghai Rep Off Aetna Tower Ste 408 107 Zunzi Rd Shanghai 200051 China Office Phone: 86 21 6237 5322. E-mail: mclin@morganfinnegan.com.

LIN, MAYA, architect, sculptor; b. Athens, Ohio, Oct. 5, 1959; d. Henry H. and Julia (Chang) L. m. Daniel Wolf; 2 children. BA, Yale U., 1981, MA, 1986, PhD in Fine Arts, 1987. Architectural designer Peter Forbes & Assocs., N.Y.C., 1986-87; pvt. practice N.Y.C., 1987—. Bd. dir. So. Poverty Law Ctr.'s Teaching Tolerance project, Kennedy Mus. Art at Ohio Univ. Prin. work include Vietnam Veterans Meml., Washington, 1981, Civil Rights Meml., Montgomery, Ala., 1986. Author: Boundaries, 2000. Bd. mem. Yale Corp., Natural Resources Def. Fund. Mem.: AAAL. Achievements include submitting the winning design for the Vietnam Veterans Memorial at the age of 21.*

LIN, SHU-FANG HSIA, librarian; b. Kweiling, China, Jan. 7, 1939; came to U.S., 1962; d. Chien-chen and Yu-chia (Sun) Hsia; m. George Chwen-Chen Lin, Nov. 12, 1966; children: Michael, Lawrence. BA, Tunghai U., 1961; MA, Vanderbilt U., 1963, St. John's U., 1981. Internat. law diplomate. Contbr. articles to profl. jours. Mem. AAUP, ALA, Cath. Libr. Assn., Chinese Am. Librs. Assn., Metro Govt. Docs. Interest Group. Avocations: travel, movies, opera, reading. Office: St John's U Libr 8000 Utopia Pky Jamaica NY 11432-1335

LIN-CEREGHINO, JOAN, science educator; b. Chgo., Feb. 2, 1966; d. Jeong-long and Su-Jen Lin; m. Geoff Paul Cereghino, July 11, 1992; children: Ted, Grace. AB, Princeton U., NJ, 1987; PhD, U. Calif., La Jolla, 1992. Postdoctoral rsch. U. Calif., La Jolla, 1992—95; vis. asst. prof. Haverford Coll., Pa., 1995—96; rsch. assoc. Oreg. Grad. Inst., Beaverton, 1997—2000; asst. prof. U. of the Pacific, Stockton, Calif., 2000—06, assoc. prof., 2006—. Named Outstanding Co-Advisor for a Student Orgn., U. of the Pacific, 2005; AREA grant, NIH, 2002—. Roman Catholic. Office: Univ of the Pacific 3601 Pacific Ave Stockton CA 95211 Office Phone: 209-946-2988. Office Fax: 209-946-3021. Business E-Mail: jlincere@pacific.edu.

LINCOLN, ANNA, publishing executive, language educator; b. Warsaw, Dec. 13, 1932; came to U.S., 1948; d. Wigdor Aron and Genia Szpiro; m. Adrian Courtney Lincoln Jr., Sept. 22, 1951; children: Irene Anne, Sally Linda, Allen, Kirk. Student, U. Calif., Berkeley, 1949-50; BA in French and Russian with honors, NYU, 1965; student, Columbia Tchrs. Coll., 1966-67. Tchr. Waldwick (N.J.) H.S., 1966-69; chmn. Tuxedo Park (N.Y.) Red Cross, 1969-71; pres. Red Cross divsn. Vets. Hosp.; pres. China Pictures U.S.A. Inc., Princeton, NJ, 1994—; prof. fgn. rels. Fudan U., Shanghai, 1994—, prof. English and humanitarian studies, 1996—. Adv. bd. guidance dept. Waldwick (N.J.) H.S., 1966-69; hon. bd. dirs. Shanghai Fgn. Lang. Assn., 1994; hon. prof. Fudan U., Shanghai, 1994; leader seminars, China at top univs., 1996—; pub. spkr., human rels., China, 2003—. Author: Escape to China, 1940-48, 1985, Chinese transl., 1985, The Art of Peace, 1995, Anna Lincoln Views China, 2000; publ.: China Beyond the Year 2000 and the Nature of Love, 1997, Anna Lincoln Views China, 1999; co-dir. (TV docudrama) Escape to China 1941-48, 1998. Hon. U.S. Goodwill amb. for peace and friendship, China, 1984, 85, 86, 88; founder Princeton-Lincoln Found., Inc., 1985—. Named Woman of Yr. Am. Biog. Soc., 1993; recipient Peace Through the Arts prize Assn. Internat. Mujeres en las Artes, Madrid, 1993. Mem. AAUW, Women's Coll. Club (publicity chmn. 1991-96), Lit. Coll. Princeton, Present Day Club. Avocations: reading, swimming, bridge, seminars, ballroom dancing. Home and Office: China Pictures USA Inc 550 Rosedale Rd Princeton NJ 08540-2315

LINCOLN, BLANCHE LAMBERT, senator; b. Helena, Ark., Sept. 30, 1960; m. Stephen R. Lincoln; 2 children. BS in Biology, Randolph-Macon Woman's Coll., 1982. Intern Sotheby's, NYC; sr. assoc. The Pagonis & Donnelly Group, Inc., 1989-91; mem. US Congress from 1st Ark. dist., 1992-96; US Senator from Ark., 1999—. Chair minority outreach team US Senate, mem. com. agr., nutrition, and forestry, com. fin., spl. com. aging. Author (with Catherine Whitney): Nine and Counting: The Women of the Senate, 2000. Bd. dirs. Ark. Delta Coun., U. Ark. Med. Sci. Found.; mem. Lower Miss. Delta Develop. Coun., Am. Red Cross. Named Woman of Yr., Nat. Sportfishing Assn., 1996; named one of Outstanding Young Americans, Jr. C. of C., 1999; recipient Congressional Leadership award, Nat. Telephone Coop. Assn., 2001, Humanitarian of Yr., Ark. Rice Depot, 2002, Humanitarian award, Alzheimer's Assn., 2003, Nat. Energy Leadership award, Nat. Bio-Diesel Bd., 2003, Leg. of Yr. award, Biotechnology Industry Orgn., 2005. Democrat. Episcopalian. Office: US Senate 355 Dirksen Senate Office Bldg Washington DC 20510-0001 also: District Office 912 W Fourth St Little Rock AR 72201 Office Phone: 202-224-4843, 501-375-2993. Office Fax: 202-228-1371, 501-375-7064.*

LINCOLN, JANE L., artist, educator; b. Exeter, N.H., Mar. 17, 1950; d. John Alexander and Jean Manville Lockwood; m. Stanley Ferguson Lincoln, Aug. 7, 1976; children: Elizabeth, Andrea. BA, St. Lawrence U., Canton, N.Y., 1972. Faculty Falmouth Artists Guild. Condr. workshops in field. Contbr. articles to profl. jours.; one-woman shows include Cahoon Mus. Am. Art, 1996, Jacob Fanning Gallery, Wellfleet, Mass., 1997—2006, Cape Cod Mus. Natural History, 1998, Cahoon Mus. Am. Art, Cotuit, Mass., 1999, Cape Gallery, Falmouth, Mass., 2001, Cape Cod Mus. Art, Dennis, Mass., 2005—06, exhibited in group shows at Cape Mus. Fine Arts, 1991—2005, Thornton Burgess Mus., Sandwich, Mass., 1992—, Cahoon Mus. Am. Art, 1994—2004, Market Barn Gallery, Falmouth, 1995—, Richard F. Brush Gallery, Canton, N.Y., 1998—, Juliana Gallery, Wellesley Hills, Mass., 1999—, Ellison Ctr. for the Arts, Duxbury, Mass., 2000—, Marion Craine Gallery, 2001—, Cape Mus. Fine Art, 2004—, Falmouth Artists Guild, 2004—, Attleboro Mus., Mass., 2000—, many others, —. Mem. 21 in Truro, Mass.; mem. arts coun. Stuart Martin County, Fla. Mem.: Vero Beach Mus. Art, Printmakers of Cape Cod, Attleboro Mu. Ctr. for the Arts, Cahoon Mus. Am. Art, Cape Cod Mus. Art, Cape Mus. Fine Arts, Duxbury Art Assn., Falmouth Artists' Guild, Pastel Soc. Am. (signature), Pastel Painters Soc. Cape Cod (signature), Pastel Painters of Maine, Mus. Fine Arts, Boston. Home: 441 Central Ave East Falmouth MA 02536

LINCOLN, MARGARET, library media specialist; b. NYC, May 22, 1949; d. Irving Herman and Ann Ruth (Silver) Goldin; m. Gary Samuel Lincoln, June 5, 1971; children: Geoffrey, Benjamin, Ruth. AB in French, U. Mich., 1970, AMLS, 1973; Edn. Tech. Specialist, Mich. State U., 1996. Libr. media specialist Lakeview HS, Battle Creek, Mich., 1973—. Computer skills, internet rsch. tchr. Battle Creek Area Pub. Schs., 1997—; chair, sec. REMC 12 Media Coun., Marshall, Mich., 1996—. Contbr. articles to profl. jours. Vol. libr. Temple Beth El, Battle Creek, 1984—, Sunday sch. tchr., 1984—. Recipient AASL Sch. Libr. Collaboration award, 2004, Info. Literacy award, Mich. Libr. Assn., 2005; grantee Excellence in Edn., Kellogg Found., 1994, 1999; Am. Memory fellow, Libr. of Congress, 2000, Mandel fellow, US Holocaust Meml. Mus., 2002. Mem.: Phi Beta Kappa, Beta Phi Mu. Home: 13166 11 Mile Rd Ceresco MI 49033-9769 Office: Lakeview HS 15060 S Helmer Rd Battle Creek MI 49015

LINCOLN, ROSAMOND HADLEY, painter, photographer; b. Worcester, Mass., June 27, 1924; d. Ralph Gorham and Grace (Wardwell) Hadley; m. Brayton Lincoln, Jan. 15, 1949; children: Rosamond, Christopher, Daniel, Dorothy. BA, Radcliffe Coll., 1946; postgrad., Assumption Coll., 1975-76. Interior display trainee G. Fox & Co. Dept. Store, Hartford, Conn., 1944; advt. mgr. So. New Eng. Ice and Oil Co., Hartford, Conn., 1945-46; head instr. Worcester (Mass.) Art Mus., 1946-48, 70-76; dir. continuing edn. Swain Sch. Design, New Bedford, Mass., 1980-83; artist self-employed South Dartmouth, Mass., 1983—. Bd. dirs. The Arts Ctr., New Bedford, 1977-80; pres. The Bierstadt Art Soc., New Bedford, 1982-84; chmn. Dartmouth Arts Lottery Coun., 1984-86. Mem. League of Women Voters, New Bedford, 1980-86. Recipient Four First prize awards, Bierstadt Art Gallery, 1989. Mem. AAUW, Westport Art Group, Waterfront Hist. Area League, Rotch-Jones-Duff House and Garden Mus., The Whaling Mus., ARTWORKS! at Dover St., New Bedford Art Mus., Gallery X. Unitarian Universalist.

LINCOLN, SARAH, social worker; b. N.Y.C., July 20, 1954; d. Richard Lee and Sonia (Goldstein) Lincoln; m. Joseph Leland Hester Jr., Aug. 21, 1982; children: Nicole, Cory. MSW, Washington U., St. Louis, 1979; Postgrad. Cert., Menninger Dept. Psychiatry, Denver, 1989. Lic. and bd. cert. social worker, Colo. Social worker/case mgr. Denver Dept. Social Svcs., 1980; social worker Colo. Christian Home, Denver, 1980-83; clin. social worker Boulder (Colo.) Psychiatric Inst., 1983-86; pvt. practice psychiatric social worker Denver, 1984—; therapist Parent Care Ptnrs. in Family Devel., Denver, 1984—. Condr. workshops in field; mem. med. staff Health One-Bethesda, Cleo Wallace Psychiatric Ctr. Bd. dirs. Alliance of Profl. Women of Denver, 1990—; pro bono vol. Pro Bono Mental Health Project, Denver, 1990—. Mem. NASW, Colo. Child and Adolescent Soc., Pre-Perinatal Assn. Democrat. Jewish. Avocations: reading, music, theater, dance. Office: 4900 E Kentucky Ave # 100 Denver CO 80246 Office Phone: 303-691-6140.

LINCOLN, SHARON ANN, retired county official; b. Forsyth, Mont., Oct. 3, 1939; d. Francis Xavier and Catherine Minerva (McRae) Faust; m. Cecil Wilbur Lincoln, Aug. 6, 1957 (dec. May 1992); children: Michael David, Mark Daniel, Teresa Marie. Grad. high sch., Forsyth, Mont. Bookkeeper 1st State Bank, Forsyth, Mont., 1967-69; clk. to county supt. schs. Rosebud County, Forsyth, Mont., 1969-73, deputy county treas., 1973-86, county treas., 1987-98. Chair bd. dirs. Bd. Sch. Trustees, Forsyth, 1982, mem., 1979-82; mem. edn. com. Gov.'s Task Force to Renew Mont. Govt., 1994; apptd. to bd. trustees Mont. Hist. Soc., 2003; bd. dirs. Rosebud Health Care Found., 1998-99. Mem. Mont. County Treas. Assn. (pres. 1989), Forsyth C. of C. (treas. 1989-97, Profl. Person of Yr. 1996), Forsyth Country Club (pres. bd. dirs. 1996-99). Republican. Avocations: stained glass art, painting, gardening, golf, sewing. Home: 2315 Brentwood Ln Billings MT 59102-2105 Office: Rosebud County Courthouse 1200 Main St Forsyth MT 59327

LINCOLN, SHELLEY, elementary school educator; b. Anchorage, Alaska, July 14, 1961; d. Allen and Mary Pat Lincoln; children: Mackenzie Musette Frazier, Joshua Allen Frazier. Degree in Interdisciplinary Studies, U. Tex., El Paso, 1998. Cert. tchg. Tex., 1998. Sr. teller Govt. Employees Credit Union, El Paso, 1987—98; 3rd grade monolingual tchr. North Loop Elem. Sch., El Paso, 1998—2002, Thomas Manor Elem. Sch., El Paso, 2002—05; 5th grade monolingual tchr. Hacienda Heights Elem., El Paso, 2005—. Named Tchr. of Yr., Ysleta Ind. Sch. Dist., 2005—06. Home: 3323 Cork Dr El Paso TX 79925 Office: Hacienda Heights Elem Sch 7530 Acapulco El Paso TX 79915 Personal E-mail: shelleyjlincoln@yahoo.com.

LINDAHL, KATHLEEN ANN, archaeologist; d. Billy Joe and Virginia Mae Dennis. BS, U. Calif., Davis, 1992. Account clk, Alameda County, Oakland, Calif., 1968—73, City of Woodland, Calif., 1987—88; assoc. state archaeologist Calif. Dept. Pks. and Recreation, Sacramento, 1999—. Pres. Whitehead Sch. PTA, Woodland, Calif., 1983—84; cub scout troop den mother Boy Scouts Am., Woodland, 1982—86; vol. Project Linus, Sacramento, 2004—06, Sutter Health Cancer Ctr., Sacramento, 2003—06. Scholar, Heald Bus. Sch., 1968; Sawtell scholar, Yuba CC, 1988. Mem.: Calif. Assn. Profl. Scientists (assoc.), Calif. Coun. for Promotion of History (assoc.), Soc. Calif.

Archaeology (assoc.), Calif. Parent Teachers Assn. (life; pres. 1983—84). Avocations: beading, crocheting. Office: Calif Dept Pks and Recreation 1416 - 9th St Sacramento CA 95814 Office Phone: 916-653-9091.

LINDAHL, SARAH ELIZABETH, theater educator; b. St. Joseph, Mich., Aug. 28, 1976; d. Ken Glenn and Patricia Lee Lindahl. B of Theatre, U. Ga., 2000. Tchr. theatre West Hall H.S., Ga., 2002—. Mem.: Internat. Thespian Soc. (assoc.; dir. 2002—06). Office: West Hall High School 5500 McEver Rd Oakwood GA 30566 Office Phone: 770-967-9826 286.

LINDBERG, JUDITH ANN, retired elementary school educator; b. Vancouver, Wash., Feb. 26, 1944; d. Marvin Julian and Ruth Mary (Miller) Lindberg; children: Shannon Wear, Shebie Karl. BA in Elem. Edn., U. Puget Sound, 1966; EdM in Guidance and Counseling, ESA City U., 1997. Tchr. Portland Sch. Dist., Oreg., 1966-71, Port Angeles Sch. Dist., Wash., 1981—2005, ret., 2004. Part-time counseling Port Angeles (Wash.) Sch. Dist, 2005—. Author: Moonbeams and Mudpuddles, 1986; contbr. to anthologies, poems and articles to ednl. jours. Avocations: writing, reading, crafts. Home: 2515 Columbus Avenue Port Angeles WA 98362-2505 Personal E-mail: judi@olypen.com. Business E-Mail: judi@wavecable.com.

LINDBERGH, JUDITH L., writer, photographer; b. Worcester, Mass., Mar. 30, 1963; d. Paul David and Bernice (Fieldman) L.; m. Chip Davis, 1988. Student, CUNY, 1995. Dancer and actress various employers, 1980-87. Author: The Thrall's Tale, 2006; contbg. writer and photographer: Vikings: The North Atlantic Saga exhbn. Smithsonian Instn., Archaeology mag., other profl. jours.; exhibited photography Cathedral of St. John the Divine, NYC. Mem.: Authors Guild. Avocations: history, archaeology, mythology. E-mail: judith@judithlindbergh.com.

LINDBERGH, REEVE, writer, poet; d. Charles A. Lindbergh and Anne Morrow L.; m. Nathaniel Tripp. Graduate, Radcliffe Coll., 1968. Bd. dir. Charles A. and Anne Morrow Lindbergh Found., 1977—, v.p., 1986—95, pres. 1995—2004, hon. chairwoman, 2004—. Author: (memoirs) Under a Wing, 1998, No More Words: A Journal of My Mother, Anne Morrow Lindbergh, 2001, (novels) Moving to the Country, 1983, The Names of the Mountains, 1992, (book of essays) View from the Kingdom, 1987, (children's books) The Midnight Farm, 1987, Benjamin's Barn, 1990, There's a COW in the Road!, 1993, What Is The Sun?, 1994, Grandfather's Lovesong, 1995, The Day the Goose Got Loose, 1995, If I'd Known Then What I Know Now, 1996, Awful Aardvarks Shop for School, 2000, The Circle of Days, 2002, On Morning Wings, 2002, My Hippie Grandmother, 2003, Our Nest, 2004, The Visit, 2005. Office: Charles A and Ann Morrow Lindbergh Foundation Ste 310 2150 Third Ave N Anoka MN 55303-2200

LINDBLAD-TOH, KERSTIN, medical researcher; PhD, Karolinska Inst., Dept. Molecular Medicine, Sweden, 1998. Postdoctoral fellow Whitehead Inst./MIT Ctr. for Genome Rsch.; co-dir., genome sequencing and analysis program Broad Inst., Cambridge, Mass. Author 40 scientific papers; contbr. articles to profl. jours. Office: Broad Inst 320 Charles St Cambridge MA 02141-2023 Business E-Mail: kersli@broad.mit.edu.*

LINDBLOM, MARJORIE PRESS, lawyer; b. Chgo., Mar. 17, 1950; d. John E. and Betty (Grace) P.; m. Lance E. Lindblom, June 13, 1971; children: Derek, Ian. AB cum laude, Radcliffe Coll., 1971; JD with honors, U. Chgo., 1978. Bar: Ill. 1978, U.S. Dist. Ct. (no. dist.) Ill. 1978, U.S. Ct. Appeals (7th cir.) 1978, U.S. Ct. Appeals (10th cir.) 1983, U.S. Supreme Ct. 1983, U.S. Ct. Appeals (5th cir.) 1984, N.Y. 1995, U.S. Dist. Ct. (so. and ea. dist.) N.Y. 1995, U.S. Ct. Appeals (2d cir.) 1995. Assoc. Kirkland & Ellis, Chgo., 1978-84, ptnr., 1984-94; N.Y.C., 1994—. Asst. dir. fiscal affairs Ill. Bd. Higher Edn., 1973-75; budget analyst Ill. Bur. Budget, Office of Gov., 1972-73; admissions officer Princeton U., 1971-72; adj. prof. Northwestern U., Evanston, Ill., 1994. Comment editor U. Chgo. Law Rev., 1977-78. Bd. dirs. Chgo. Lawyers Com. for Civil Rights Under Law, 1989-94, Pub. Interest Law Initiative, 1989-94. Mem. ABA, Chgo. Coun. Lawyers (bd. govs. 1987-91, legal counsel 1986-87), 7th Cir. Bar Assn., Women's Bar Assn. of Ill., Lawyers Com. for Civil Rights Under Law (co-chair, 2004-2005). Office: Kirkland & Ellis Citicorp Ctr 153 E 53rd St New York NY 10022-4611 Office Phone: 212-446-4868. Office Fax: 212-446-4900. Business E-Mail: mlindblom@kirkland.com.

LINDBOE, BERIT ROBERG, retired language educator, literature educator; b. Stavanger, Norway, July 28, 1944; arrived in U.S., 1947; d. Odd and Ingbjorg Roberg. BA, Wellesley Coll., 1966; MA, Yale U., 1967. English tchr. Daniel Hand H.S., Madison, Conn., 1967—69; tchg. asst. U. Va., Charlottesville, 1971—73; asst. prof. English Humboldt State U., Arcata, Calif., 1973—77; grad. instr. U. Va., 1979—83; English tchr. Barstow Sch., Kansas City, Mo., 1983—2006. Cons. Ednl. Testing Svc., Princeton, NJ, 1991—2004; panelist NEH, Washington, 1991; bd. dirs. Heart of Am. Shakespeare Festival. Contbr. articles to profl. jours. Grantee, NEH, London and Oxford, Eng., English-Speaking Union, Mo. Humanities Coun., Globe Theatre, London, 2004. Mem.: English-Speaking Union (v.p.), Lychnos Honor Soc., Cum Laude Soc., Mensa.

LINDBURG, DAYTHA EILEEN, physician assistant; b. Emporia, Kans., June 24, 1952; d. Kenneth Eugene and Elsie Eileen (Smith) L. BS cum laude, Kans. State U., 1974; BS magna cum laude, Wichita State U., 1976; M in Physician Asst. Studies (summa cum laude), U. Nebr., 2002. Cert. physician asst. Physician asst. in family practice Fredrickson Clinic, Lindsborg, Kans., 1976-93; physician asst. in ob-gyn. Mowery Clinic, Salina, Kans., 1993—. Cons. McPherson County (Kans.) Health Dept., 1983—. Adv. bd. Riverview Estates Nursing Home, 1980—86; women's health advisor Salina YWCA, 2003—04; choir mem. Messiah Luth. Ch., Lindsborg, 1981—2001, liturgist, 1991—, mem. Altar Guild, 1976—, mem. music and worship com., 1981—88, 1999; bd. dirs. McPherson County Humane Soc., 1989—93. Kans. Bd. Regents scholar, 1970-71, Kans. State U. scholar, 1972-73, Smurthwaite scholar, 1970-74. Mem. Assn. Physician Assts. in Ob-Gyn., Kans. Acad. Physician Assts., Am. Acad. Physician Assts., McPherson County-Kans. State U. Alumni Assn. (bd. dirs. 1996-98), Fellowship of Christian Physician Assts. Avocations: crafts, floral arranging, piano, reading, drawing.

LINDE, MAXINE HELEN, lawyer, corporate financial executive, investor; b. Chgo., Sept. 2, 1939; d. Jack and Lottie (Kroll) Stern; m. Ronald K. Linde, June 12, 1960. BA summa cum laude, UCLA, 1961; JD, Stanford U., 1967. Bar: Calif. 1968. Applied mathematician, rsch. engr Jet Propulsion Lab., Pasadena, Calif., 1961—64; law clk. U.S. Dist. Ct. No. Calif., 1967—68; mem. firm Long & Levit, San Francisco, 1968—69, Swerdlow, Glikbarg & Shimer, Beverly Hills, Calif., 1969—72; sec., gen. counsel Envirodyne Industries, Inc., Chgo., 1972—89; pres. The Ronald and Maxine Linde Found., 1989—; vice chmn. bd., gen. counsel Titan Fin. Group, LLC, Chgo., 1994—98. Mem. bd. visitors Stanford Law Sch., 1989—92, law and bus. adv. coun., 1991—94, dean's adv. coun., 1992—94. Mem.: Alpha Lambda Delta, Pi Mu Epsilon, Phi Beta Kappa, Order of Coif.

LINDEMAN, CAROLYNN ANDERSON, music educator; b. Kane, Pa., June 5, 1940; d. David Julius and Aralaine Elizabeth (Wagstaff) Anderson; m. Alfred Lindeman, June 29, 1963; 1 child, David Henry. MusB, Oberlin Coll., 1962; MA in Music, San Francisco State U., 1972; D of Mus. Arts, Stanford U., 1979. Elem. music cons. Commack (N.Y.) Unified Sch. Dist., 1962-67; from lectr. in music to prof. music emerita San Francisco (Calif.) State U., 1973—2005. Mem. nat. bd. examiners Ednl. Testing Svc. NTE-Music, Princeton, N.J., 1990—; mem. Nat. Task Force on Music Standards. Author: PianoLab: An Introduction to Class Piano, 5th edit., 2004, The Piano Advantage, 2006; editor: Strategies for Teaching Series, 1995-98; mem. edit. bd. Intenat. Jour. for Music Edn., 2006—; compiler: Women Composers of Ragtime, 1985. Chair Nat. Women's Polit. Caucus, Marin County. Mem. Music Educators Nat. Conf. (nat. pres. 1996-98, pres.-elect western divsn. 1992-94), Calif. Coalition for Music (chair 1991-94), Calif. Music Educators Assn. (pres. 1990-92), Internat. Soc. Music Edn. (bd. mem. 2000-04).

LINDEMAN, JOYCE IRENE, university administrator; b. Detroit, Jan. 23, 1933; d. Roger and Myrtle Harriet (Esseltine) L. BS, Ea. Mich. U., 1954; postgrad., U. Colo., 1955; MS, U. Mich., 1966. Tchr. South Redford (Mich.) Schs., 1954-65; teaching asst. U. Mich., Ann Arbor, 1965-66; asst. prof. Western Mich. U., 1966-67, U. Mich., 1967-73, assoc. prof., 1973—, coord. tchr. edn., 1983-90, chmn. dept. sports mgmt. and comm., phys. edn., 1989—, assoc. dir. curriculum and instrn. Div. Kinesiology, 1991—. Lectr. in field. Author: Components of Synchronized Swimming, 1975; editor: USSS Inc., 1985-86, Official Rules, 1992-93, others; contbr. articles to profl. jours. Mem. internat. olympic com. USSS, Inc., 1984-90, pers. com./adminstrn., 1984-90, pers. com. internat., 1984-90, v.p. adminstrn., 1984-88; mem. AAU Mich. Bd. Govs., 1978-80, mem. internat. olympic com. for synchronized swimming, 1978-80; v.p. Olympic Internat.-USSSI, 1988-90. Recipient Svc. awards ARC, Disting. Alumni award in phys. edn. Ea. Mich. U., 1989, Disting. Svc. award U. S. Synchronized Swimming, 1990; named to Hall of Fame APHS, 1988. Mem. AAHPERD, Mich. Assn. Health, Phys. Edn., Recreation and Dance, Nat. Acad. Synchronized Swimming (div. of girls and womens sports).

LINDEN, BLANCHE MARIE GEMROSE, history professor; b. Battle Creek, Mich., July 4, 1946; d. George and Lauretta (Cate) Gemrose; m. Thomas Elwood Lindow, Aug. 2, 1968 (div. 1976); children: Julia C. Lindow, Marc T. Lindow; m. Alan Lester Ward, June 26, 1982. BA, U. Mich., 1968; MA, U. Cin., 1976; PhD, Harvard U., 1981. Teaching asst. U. Cin., 1974-76; teaching fellow Harvard U., Cambridge, Mass., 1977-79; instr. Brandeis U., Waltham, Mass., 1979-81; vis. asst. prof. Middlebury (Vt.) Coll., 1981-82; asst. prof. history Brandeis U., Waltham, 1982-85, assoc. prof., 1993-94; asst. prof. history Emerson Coll., Boston, 1985-90, assoc. prof., 1990-93, U. N.H., Durham, 1993—. Hist. cons. Mt. Auburn Cemetery, Cambridge, 1981—, Soc. Preservation of New Eng. Antiquities, African Meetinghouse, Arnold Arboretum, all Boston, 1991-93. Author: Silent City on a Hill: Landscapes of Memory, 1989; co-author: American Women in the 1960's: Changing the Future, 1993; assoc. editor: Encyclopedia New Eng. Culture, 1993—; contbr. articles to profl. jours. Mem. Am. Studies Assn., New Eng. Am. Studies Assn. (pres. 1985-87, sec., newsletter editor 1989—), Am. Hist. Assn., Orgn. Am. Historians, Am. Culture/Popular Culture Assn., New Eng. Hist. Assn. (chair exec. com. 1992-94). Democrat. Avocations: photography, travel in france. Home: 3019 NE 20th Ct Fort Lauderdale FL 33305-1807 Office: U NH Ctr Humanities Murkland Durham NH 03824-3596

LINDEN, CAROL MARIE, special education educator; b. Pitts., Dec. 24, 1953; d. Enio P. and Mary C. (Santillo) Cardone; m. Frank J. Miller Jr., Dec. 21, 1974 (div. 1989); children: Emily, Karl, Richard; m. James Anthony Linden, Dec. 9, 1989; children: Shiloh, Shane, Shasta, Shelby (dec.). BS, California (Pa.) State U., 1974; MS, Youngstown State U., 1981. Cert. moderate, severe, profoundly retarded, educable mentally retarded, learning disabled/behavior disordered, speech and hearing. Tchr. multi-handicapped Youngstown (Ohio) City Schs., 1987—; tchr. multihandicapped Trumbull County Bd. Edn., Lordstown, Ohio, 1986-87; spl. vocat. edn. coord. Trumbull County Joint Vocat. Sch., Warren, Ohio, 1985-86; lang. devel. specialist Fairhaven Sheltered Workshop, Niles and Champion, Ohio, 1976-85. Grantee N.E. Ohio Spl. Edn. Resource Ctr., 1989-92, Ohio Bell and Ameritech Impact II, 1991-92, 95, Consumer/Econ. grantee, 1989-95; Wolves Club Carapolis scholar, 1971. Mem. Ohio Speech and Hearing Assn., Coun. for Exceptional Children, Nat. Soc. for Autistic Citizens (sec. 1986-87). Roman Catholic/Baptist. Avocations: reading, crafts, camping. Home: 432 Hunter Ave Niles OH 44446-1625

LINDEN, MARGARET JOANNE, librarian, foundation administrator; b. Berkeley, Calif., Nov. 20, 1938; d. Arthur William and Johanna Gesina (Zuydhoek) Dickie; m. Roy Joseph Linden, Jan. 6, 1965 (dec. Jan. 1989). BA, Swarthmore Coll., Pa., 1960; MLS, U. Calif., Berkeley, 1962. Librarian Grad. Social Scis. library U. Calif., Berkeley, 1961-65, librarian Giannini Found. for Agrl. Econs., 1965-70; social scis. librarian Idaho State U., Pocatello, 1970-71; head cataloguer Chevron Corp. (formerly Standard Oil Co. of Calif.), San Francisco, 1971-74, asst. chief librarian, 1974-77, chief librarian, 1978-81, mgr. corp. library, 1981—92; ret., 1992. Mem. Calif. Library Assn., Spl. Libraries Assn. (editor chpt. bull. 1972-73). Office: Chevron Credit Union PO Box 2069 Oakland CA 94604-2069

LINDENBERG, ELANNA BETH, communications educator, secondary school educator; b. Colorado Springs, Colo., Mar. 7, 1977; d. Delilah Ann Sanderson. BA in Comm. Edn., U. Ctrl. Okla., Edmond, 2002. Tchr. Putnam City North H.S., Oklahoma City, 2002—. Named Debate Coach of the Yr., Monty Python Norman H.S., 2004, Outstanding Am. Tchrs. Assn., 2006; recipient Da Vinci Scholar award, Da Vinci Inst., 2005. Office: Putnam City North High School 11800 Rockwell Oklahoma City OK 73162 Office Phone: 405-722-4220. Office Fax: 405-721-4946. Business E-Mail: elindenberg@putnamcityschools.org.

LINDENBERGER, KATHLEEN MARIE, literature and language educator; b. Johnson City, NY, Dec. 15, 1967; d. Brian Joseph Pilotti and Maureen Karen Lacatena; m. Herbert Richard Lindenberger, Oct. 19, 1996. BS, Appalachain State U., Boone, NC, 1989. Tchr. English Olympic High Sch., Charlotte, NC, 1991—2000, Ctrl. Concord High Sch., 2000—01; tchr. adult high sch. English Ctrl. Piedmont C.C., Charlotte, 2001; tchr. English Hopewell High Sch., 2001—. Mem. adv. bd. Sch. Leadership Team, Charlotte, 2006. Office: Hopewell High Sch 11530 Beatticsford Rd Cornelius NC 28031

LINDENFELD, NAOMI, ceramic artist; b. Princeton, N.J., May 14, 1958; d. Peter and Lore (Kadden) L. BA, Boston U., 1980. Apprentice Fred Tregaskis, Kent, Conn., 1980, Elizabeth McDonald, Bridgewater, Conn., 1981, Carol Sevick, Westminster W., Vt., 1981; baker Innisfree Farms Bakery, Brattleboro, Vt., 1982; potter Brattleboro Clayworks, 1983; tchr. ceramics The Putney Sch., 1997. Pres. Brattleboro Clayworks, 1988—; ceramics tchr. Putney (Vt.) Sch., 1997—; workshop instr. in field. Bd. dirs. Windham Citizens for Responsible Growth, Brattleboro, 1993-94. Mem. League N.H. Craftmen, Vt. Craftsmen., N.H. Potter's Guild, Am. Crafts Coun. Avocations: dance, hiking, skiing. Office Phone: 802-258-6475.

LINDENMAYER, ELISABETH, international organization administrator; married; 2 children. Degree, U. Paris-Sorbonne, U. Geneva, NYU. Various positions with Office of Human Resources Mgmt., UN, 1977, spl. asst. to the then asst. sec.-gen. for personnel svcs.; provided polit. back-up and support Iraq-Kuwait UN Observation Mission (UNIKOM), UN Hdqs., 1992, UN Ops. in Somalia (UNOSOM I, UNITAF Force and UNOSOM II), UN Hdqs., 1992—94, UN Mission in Rwanda (UNAMIR), UN Hdqs., 1994—96, Great Lakes Region, Burundi and Zaire (now the Dem. Rep. of Congo); budget officer Office of Programme Planning, Budget, and Fin.; spl. asst. to the controller UN Hdqs., exec. asst. to sec.-gen., 1997—2004, asst. sec.-gen. to the post of dep. chef de cabinet in the exec. office of the sec.-gen., 2004—05. Adj. prof. Columbia U., N.Y.C., 2005—. Office Phone: 212-963-1234, 718-625-0597. Office Fax: 212-963-4879, 718-852-5816. Business E-Mail: elindenmayer2@aol.com.

LINDENMUTH, ELISE BELL, psychological consultant, educator; b. Hagerstown, Md., Jan. 22, 1945; d. W. Leigh and Gladys Marilee (Henkel) Bell; m. G. Frank Lindenmuth, Nov. 23, 1968; children: Joshua, Jacob. Student, NYU, 1966; BS, Gettysburg Coll., 1967; MA, MillersvilleU., 1971; PhD, Am. U., 1993. Cert. instrnl. III, Pa. Master tchr. West York (Pa.) Area Schs., 1967-75; dept. chmn. West York (Pa.) Schs., 1970-71; dir. Temple Child Program, York, 1979-80; counselor, speaker Psychol. Cons., York, 1981—; adj. faculty York (Pa.) Coll. of Pa., 1984—; researcher The Am. Univ., Washington, 1989-91. Cons. York (Pa.) City Schs., 1985-91. Author: Economic Education for Elementary School, 1972; co-author: Teachers, Schools and Society: Student Guide, 1991, Instructor's Manual to Accompany Teachers, Schools and Society, 1991, Strategies for Reducing Test Anxiety, 1992. Recipient fellowship The Am. Univ., Washington, 1989. Mem. APA, AAUP, Assn. Mental Health Counselors, Assn. for Adult Devel. and Aging. Avocation: classical piano. Home: 405 Hillcrest Rd York PA 17403-4711 Office: York Coll of Pa Country Club Rd York PA 17404 Office Phone: 717-845-5245. Business E-Mail: elindenm@ycp.edu.

LINDER, BEVERLY L., elementary school educator; b. Kansas City, Mo., Mar. 12, 1951; d. William B. and Una M. (Dishman) Reese; m. John H. Linder, Feb. 24, 1979; 1 child, Elaine M. BSEd, Cen. Mo. State U., 1972; MA in Reading, U. Mo., Kansas City, 1975. Cert. elem. edn., reading. Elem. tchr. Ft. Osage Sch. Dist., Independence, Mo., tchr. 4th grade chpt. I reading. Mem. Internat. Reading Assn., Nat. Coun. Tchrs. Math. Home: 1317 NE Buttonwood Ave Lees Summit MO 64086-8438

LINDER, FANNIE RUTH, psychotherapist, concert soprano; b. Hartwell, Ga., Mar. 14, 1934; d. Marion Taylor and Nobie (Gaines) Barnes; m. Raymond Linder, Jan. 30, 1953; children: Raymond T., Michael C. BA, Empire State Coll., SUNY, 1986; MA, Liberty U., 1990; D in Psychology, Hamilton U., 2002. Tchr. Romulus (N.Y.) Ctrl. Sch., 1969-70; owner, prodr. ISHI Rec. Studio, Apalachin, N.Y., 1981—; pvt. psychologist Apalachin, 1984—. Bd. dirs. The Stewart W. and Willma C. Hoyt Found., Binghamton; bd. mem. So. Tier Inst. for Arts in Edn., Binghamton, 1993—. Eckelberger Towers, Binghamton, 1993—; mem. ethics com. United Health Hosps., Binghamton, 1993—; lectr. in field. Concert soprano worldwide, 1968—. Spokesperson, chair Police/Community Group, Binghamton, 1987-93. Named Outstanding Young Women of Am., 1965; recipient Appreciation award Gen. Commn. on Chaplains and Armed Forces Pers., Romulus, 1970, Lucia Humanitarian award, Cmty. Activism award, Broome County Coun. Churches. Mem. Assn. for Psychol. Type (Merit award), Personality Inst. (bd. chmn., founder, Recognition award). Avocations: reading, research, music. Home: 21 W Glann Rd Apalachin NY 13732-4026

LINDER, IRIS KAY, lawyer; b. Davenport, Iowa, May 3, 1952; d. Forrest Wesley and Josephine Jeanette (Barnett) Shaffer; 1 son, Eric Scott Socolofsky; m. Stephen J. Linder. BS, Mich. State U., 1976; JD, U. Mich., 1980. Bar: Mich. 1980, U.S. Dist. Ct. (we. and ea. dists.) Mich. 1980. Ptnr. Fraser, Trebilcock, Davis & Dunlap, P.C., Lansing., Mich., 1980—. Adj. faculty Cooley Law Sci., 1999-2003; mem. Office Fin. and Ins. Svcs. Securities Coun. Mich., 1991-2004; bd. dirs. Fraser, Trebilcock, Davis & Dunlap, P.C. 1992-96, 2006-. Co-author: Michigan Usury Manual, 1982; contbr. chpt. to Litigation of the Commercial Case, 1992. Mem. planning bd. Ingham County Office for Young Children, 1986—87; mem. Mayor's Parking Adv. Com., 1990—93; chair group com. Shared Vision Sys. and Rsch., 1994—96; bd. dirs. Capitol Area Girl Scouts USA, 1986—88, Capitol Area Polit. Action Com., 1990—96, chair, 1995; bd. dirs. Capitol Enterprise Forum, 1989—95, pres., 1993; bd. dirs. Capitol Area United Way, 1994—2001, Infoguys, Inc., 1996—99, Congregation Kehillet Israel, Venture Ctr., Inc., 1996—2001, chair, 1999—2001. Recipient Book award U. Mich. Law Sch., 1980. Mem. ABA, Ingham County Bar Assn., State Bar Assn. Mich., Lansing Regional C. of C. (bus. women's coun. 1984-87, bd. dirs. 1987-92, dir. govt. affairs 1991-92, Tireless award 1992, Small Bus. Advocate of Yr. award 1993), Lansing Assn. Career Women (bd. dirs. 1985-87), Athena Found. (bd. dirs. 1986-87), Rotary (East Lansing bd. dirs. 2005—). Home: 2550 Dustin Rd Okemos MI 48864-2073 Office: Fraser Trebilcock Davis & Dunlap 1000 Michigan Nat Towers Lansing MI 48933 Office Phone: 517-482-5800.

LINDERMAN, JEANNE HERRON, priest; b. Erie, Pa., Nov. 14, 1931; d. Robert Leslie and Ella Marie (Stearns) Herron; m. James Stephens Linderman; children: Mary Susan, John Randolph, Richard Webster, Craig Stephens, Mark Herron, Elizabeth Stewart. BS in Indsl. and Labor Rels., Cornell U., 1953; MDiv magna cum laude, Lancaster Theol. Sem., 1981; postgrad., clin. pastoral edn., Del. State Hosp., New Castle, 1981. Ordained priest, Episcopal Ch. Mem. pers. staff Hengerer Co., Buffalo, 1953-55; chaplain Cathedral Ch. St. John, Wilmington, Del., 1981-82; priest-in-charge Christ Episcopal Ch., Delaware City, Del., 1982-87, vicar, 1987-91; assoc. rector St. Andrew's Episcopal Ch., Wilmington, 1992—94, priest in charge, 1995-96; assoc. priest for pastoral care The Episc. Ch. of St. Andrew and Matthew, 1998—. Chair human sexuality task force, Diocese of Del., 1981-82, mem. clergy compensation com. and diocesan coun., 1982-86, pres. standing com., 1991—95, com. on constitution and canons, 1989, designer and leader religious/spiritual retreats, chaplain to the ret. clergy, 1999—, bishop's chaplain to the ret. clergy, 2004. Author, editor hist. study papers. Bd. dirs. St. Michael's Day Nursery, Wilmington, 1985-88; mem. secondary schs. com. Cornell U.; bd. dirs., chmn. pers. com. Geriatric Svcs. of Del., 1989-96, sec. bd., 1993-96. Recipient award for excellence in ministry, Lancaster Theol. Sem., 2005. Mem. Episcopal Women's Caucus, Del. Episcopal Clergy Assn., Nat. Assn. Episcopal Clergy, DAR (vice-regent Caesar Rodney chpt. 1996—), Mayflower Soc. (elder Del. chpt. 2000—, surgeon 1983-95, elder gen. 2005—), Nat. Soc. Colonial Dames Am., Dutch Colonial Soc., Stoney Run Questers (pres.), Cornell Women's Club (pres. Del. chpt. 1966), Women of St. James the Less (pres. 1972-73), Women's Witnessing Cmty. at Lambeth, Patriotic Soc. in Del. (sec.-treas. conv. 1965-68), Chi Omega. Republican. Avocations: history, genealogy, travel. Home: 307 Springhouse Ln Hockessin DE 19707-9691 Office: The Episcopal Ch of Sts Andrew and Matthews Eighth And Shipley St Wilmington DE 19801 E-mail: linderjs@bellatlantic.net.

LINDERMAN, LEEANNE B., bank executive; BS in Bus. Admin., Auburn Univ.; graduate, Pacific Coast Banking Sch. Mgmt. Rich's Stores, Atlanta, Broadway Stores, Phoenix, JC Penney Co.; asst. v.p. Zions Bank, Salt Lake City, 1992; exec. v.p., retail branch banking Zion Bank, 2002—. Named one of 25 Most Powerful Women in Banking, USBanker Magazine. Office: Zions First National Bank One So Main St Salt Lake City UT 84111

LINDLAND, MARNETTA, secondary school educator; b. Mich. AAS in Indsl. Chemistry Tech., Ferris State U., Big Rapids, Mich.; BS in Secondary Edn., Saginaw Valley State U., Mich., MEd in Ednl. Leadership. Chem. technician Pacific Environ. Lab., Beaverton, Oreg., 1988—91, Manteq Internat. (subs. Dow Corning), Midland, Mich.; sci. tchr. Buena Vista HS, Saginaw, 1994—. Mem. Buena Vista HS Improvement Team. Grantee, Saginaw Valley State U., Saginaw Ind. Sch. Dist. Mem.: NEA, ASCD. Democrat. Roman Catholic. Avocations: gardening, swimming, aerobics, cooking, interior decorating. Office Phone: 989-754-1492.

LINDLEY, JOLIE BETH, choreographer, educator, actress; b. Louisville, Sept. 23, 1969; d. Robert Benton and Cheryl Ann Lindley. BA, Butler U., Indpls., 1992; M in Liberal Studies, Ind. U. SE, New Albany, 2004. Lic. secondary edn. tchr. Ind. Choreographer Paoli HS Band, Ind., 1988—; journalism and speech tchr. Brownsburg Cmty. Schs., Ind., 1995—97; choreographer Washington County Children's Theatre, Salem, Ind., 1996—; journalism and theatre tchr. Greater Clark County Schs., Jeffersonville, Ind., 1997—. Pres. Miss Ind. Assn. Local Pageants, Zionsville, 2005—; exec. dir. Miss So. Heartland Pageant, Paoli, 1999—; mem. Washington County Actors Cmty. Theatre. Named Tchr. of Month, Jeffersonville HS Renaissance Program, 2004. Mem.: Journalism Edn. Assn., Delta Delta Delta. Democrat. Mem. Soc. Friends. Avocations: travel, skiing, dance, acting, writing. Personal E-mail: joliel@yahoo.com.

LINDLEY, JOYCE E., health facility administrator, consultant, real estate appraiser; b. Clinton, Ind., May 29, 1953; d. Clyde M. and Juanita M. Delp; m. James A. Lindley; children: Brian, Richard Neil; m. William R. Travis, July 22, 1972 (div. 1983). Cosmetologist, Harolds Sch. Beauty, Terre Haute, Ind., 1975; real estate profl., Ind. State U., Terre Haute, 1989; real estate appraiser, Ind. U.-Purdue U., Indpls., 1993; BBA, Am. Intercontinental U., 2006. Cert. assisted living adminstr. Assisted Living Fedn. Am., 2001. Hairstylist, owner, mgr. Hairbarn I, II and You're Special, Wabash Valley area, 1976—89; real estate appraiser Mike Ofsansky and Assoc., Terre Haute, 1993—98; comml. real estate sales dir. Century 21, Terre Haute, 1989—93; mktg. dir. Lakeview Nursing & Rehab., Terre Haute, 1995—99; exec. dir. Morningside Assisted Living, Terre Haute, 1999—2001; pres. Lindley

McVeigh and Assocs., Terre Haute, 2001—; adminstr. Bethesda Gardens, Terre Haute, 2001—. Cons. Lindley Advt., Terre Haute, 1994—99; adv. bd. mem. Vencare Hospice, Terre Haute, 1998—99; chairperson adv. bd. Lakeview Golden Health Unit, Terre Haute, 1997—99; pres., ptnr., CFO, COO Bridle Brook Adult Cmtys. Chairperson United Way, Clark County, Ill., 1999—2000; bd. dirs. ARC, Terre Haute, 2002—, Big Brother / Big Sister, Terre Haute, 1999—. Recipient Above and Beyond award, Bethesda Living Ctrs., 2002. Mem.: C. of C. Greater Terre Haute (amb. 1995—, chairperson 2000—02), Appraisor Assn. (developer mktg. / tng. manuals and classes), Terre Haute Bd. Realtors, Wabash Valley Healthcare Mktg. Group (pres. 1998—99, Outstanding Pres. 1999), Am. Mktg. Assn., Exch. Club Terre Haute (pres. 1999—2001, dist. dir. 2002—03, Outstanding Membership Drive award 2001, Outstanding Pres. 2003). Avocations: professional singing, golf, horticulturist, speaking, songwriting. Home: 7 Lakeview Marshall IL 62441 Office: Bridle Brook Adult Comtys 1002 Commercial Dr Mahomet IL 61853

LINDLEY, SUZANNE EVERS, biology professor, researcher; d. Clifford Leonard and Othelle Polly Creel Evers; m. Stephen Keith Lindley, July 6, 2002; 1 child, Melanie Leah Mitros. BS in Med. Tech., U. Ala., Birmingham, 1974, MS in clin. pathology, 1988, PhD in Exptl. Pathology, 1988. Instr. clin. lab scis. U. Ala., Birmingham, 1978—82; vis. scientist NIH, Bethesda, Md., 1988—89; postdoctoral fellow U. Ala., Birmingham, 1989—92, asst. prof. Huntsville, 1992—98; assoc. prof. Limestone Coll., Gaffney, SC, 2000—. Adj. faculty Post U., Waterbury, Conn., 2005—, Excelsior U., Albany, NY, 2006—, U. S.C., Columbia, SC, 2000—; vis. rsch. scientist Clemson U., SC, 2002—05; mem. strategic planning task force Cherokee County, Gaffney, SC. Contbr. articles to profl. jours. Mem. scenic river commn. Broad River, Columbia, SC, 2001—04. Named Outstanding Biology Instr., Post U., 2006; recipient Fullerton Award for Tchg. Excellence, Limestone Coll., 2005, Excellence in Tchg. award, S.C. Ind. Colls. and Univs.; fellow, U. Ala. Grad. Sch., 1984—88, NIH, 1984—88, RES, 1988—89; grantee, S.C. Biomed. Rsch. Infrastructure Network, 2002—05, others, 1988—2000; scholar, Gen. Mills, 1974—78; Parker B. Francis fellowship, Francis Found., 1989—93. Mem.: AAAS (assoc.), Am. Fedn. Biology Tchrs. (assoc.), Am. Soc. Microbiology (assoc.), Nat. Wildlife Fedn. (assoc.). Achievements include research in biomedical research on processes and regulation of inflammation. Avocations: travel, wildlife habitat restoration, camping, reading. Office Phone: 800-795-7151.

LINDNER, CATHERINE PATRICIA, science educator; b. Easton, Pa., Sept. 10, 1952; d. Carl Louis and Olga Kosek; m. Frank Edward Lindner, Nov. 25, 1978; children: Christina Catherine, Joseph Edward. BS in Edn., Edgecliff Coll., Cin., 1974. Instr. YMCA, Cin., 1970—79; tchr. Immaculate Heart of Mary Cath. Sch., Cin., 1974—80; 2d grade tchr. Orlo Vista Elem., Orlando, Fla., 1980—89, 4th grade tchr., 1990—2001, sci. lab. tchr., 2001—. Mem. writing team, sci. curriculum Orange County Pub. Schs., Orlando, 2001. Parish coun. St. Peter and Paul Ch., Goldenrod, Fla., 1984—87; adv. bd. for CCD St. Peter and Paul Cath. Ch., Goldenrod, 1984; bd. mem. U. S. Fla., Tampa, 2001—06; del. Girl Scouts Am., Orlando, 2002—06; sci. amb. Orlando Sci. Ctr., Orlando, 1993—2004; active Spl. Olympics KC, Orlando, 1986. Named Tchr. of Yr., Orange County Pub. Schs., 1993, 2004; recipient Family of Yr. award, KC, 1992, Elizabeth Seton medal, Girl Scouts Am., 1993. Mem.: Nat. Sci. Tchrs. Assn. (assoc.), Orange County Assn. Sci. Tchrs. (assoc.), Fla. Assn. Sci. Tchrs. (assoc.). Roman Catholic. Avocations: travel, reading, sewing, crafts, volunteer work. Home: 968 Caribbean Pl Casselberry FL 32707-2551 Office: Orlo Vista Elem Sch 3 N Hastings St Orlando FL 32835 Office Phone: 407-296-6490. Personal E-mail: cplteacher@earthlink.net. Business E-Mail: lindnec@ocps.net.

LINDQUIST, SUSAN LEE, biology and microbiology professor; b. June 5, 1949; BA in Microbiology with honors, U. Ill., 1971; PhD in Biology, Harvard U., 1976. Asst. prof. dept. molecular biology U. Chgo., 1978-84, assoc. prof., 1984—99, Albert D. Lasker prof. med. sciences, 1999—2001, investigator Howard Hughes Med. Inst., 1988—2001; dir. Whitehead Inst. Biomedical Rsch., Cambridge, Mass., 2001—04, mem., 2001—; prof. biology MIT, Cambridge, Mass., 2001—; investigator Howard Hughes Med. Inst., 2006—. Mem. com. genetics, com. devel. biology U. Chgo., 1999—; cons. Mus. Sci. & Industry, Chgo., 1983-87; vis. scholar Cambridge U., 1983; cons., prin. in film Lights Breaking, 1985; mem. sci. adv. com. Helen Hay Whitney Found., 1997—; bd. dirs. Johnson & Johnson, 2004-; lectr. in field. Co-editor: The Stress Induced Proteins, 1988, Heat Shock, 1990; assoc. editor The New Biologist, 1991-93; mem. editl. bd. Cell Regulation, 1989—, Molecular and Cell Biology, 1984—, Gene Expression, 1994-95, Cell Stress and Chaperones, 1995—, Current Biology, 1996—, Molecular Biology of the Cell, 1996—; monitoring editor Jour. Cell Biology, 1993—; contbr. articles to profl. jours. Teaching fellow Harvard U., 1973-74, Postdoctoral fellow Am. Cancer Soc., 1976-78; recipient Novartis Drew award, 2000; named one of Top 50 Women Scientists, Discover Mag., 2002. Fellow Am. Acad. Microbiology, AAAS, NAS, Am. Acad. Arts and Sci.; mem. Am. Soc. Cell Biology, Am. Soc. Microbiology, Fedn. Am. Scientists for Exptl. Biology, Genetics Soc. Am. (elected sec. 1998—), Molecular Medicine Soc. Achievements include research in the impact of protein-conformational changes on diverse processes in cellular and organismal biology. Office: Whitehead Inst Nine Cambridge Ctr Cambridge MA 02142-1479 Office Phone: 617-258-5184. E-mail: lindquist_admin@wi.mit.edu.*

LINDROTH, LINDA (LINDA HAMMER), artist, writer, curator; b. Miami, Sept. 4, 1946; d. Mark Roger and Mae Lang Hammer; m. David George Lindroth, May 26, 1968 (div. Mar. 1985); m. Craig David Newick, June 6, 1987; 1 child, Zachary Eran Newick. BA in Art, Douglass Coll., 1968; studied with Gordon Matta-Clark, Rutgers U., 1975; studied with Garry Winogrand, N.Y., 1976; MFA in Art, Rutgers U., 1979; master class in non-fiction writing, Yale U., 1997. Adj. asst. prof. liberal arts Quinnipiac Coll., Hamden, Conn., 1998—. Editor: Co-author, Virtual Vintage: The Insider's Guide to Buyin and Selling Fashion Online. Exhibitions include Aetna Gallery, 1987, 1989, 1991, Franklin Furnace, N.Y.C., 1977, Conn. Commn. Arts, Hartford, 1985, 1996, Aldrich Mus. Contemporary Art, Ridgefield, Conn., 1987, 1987, Downey Mus. Art, Calif., 1989, Zimmerlo Art Mus. Rutgers U., 1989, Wesleyan U. Ctr. for Arts, 1990, Boston Pub. Libr., 1991, John Michael Kohler Art Ctr., Sheboygan, Wis., 1992, Joseloff Gallery U., Hartford, 1994, Artspace, New Haven, 1991, 1992, 1993, 1994, 1995, DeCordova Mus., Lincoln, Mass., 1995, Urban Glass, Bklyn., 1996, U. Conn. Atrium Gallery, 1999, Creative Arts Workship, 1999, New Haven Hist. Soc., 1999, Stedman Gallery, 1999, Rutgers U., 1999, others, Represented in permanent collections The Mus. Modern Art, N.Y.C., The Met. Mus. Art, The Mus. City of N.Y., Internat. Polaroid Collection/Artist Program, N.J. State Mus., Trenton, The Bibliotheque Nationale, Paris, Ctr. Creative Photography, Tucson, The Newark Mus., The Jane Voorhees Zimmerli Art Mus., New Brunswick, N.J., High Mus. Art, Atlanta, Yale U., Mus. d'art et d'histoire, Fribourg, Switzerland; co-author: Out of Bounds, 1994 (1st prize), Virtual Vintage, 2002. Dir. Artspace, Inc., New Haven; mem. Mayor's Task Force on Pub. Art, New Haven. Recipient Ann. Design Rev. award ID Mag., 1990, 91, 93, Honorable Mention, Nat. Peace Garden Design Competition, 1989, Pitts. Corning Archtl. Design Competition, 1988, Individual Artist fellow N.J. State Coun. on Arts, 1974-75, 83-84, Wilmer Shields Rich award Coun. Founds., 1995, Printing Industry Am. award, 1995; grantee Found. Contemporary Performance Arts, Inc., 1989, 90, Fission Fusion NEA InterArts, 1989, New Eng. Found. for Arts, 1992, Fairfield U., 1995, Ruth Chenven Found., NYC, 1997, Ruth Chevnen Found., 1997, fellowship grantee in sculpture Conn. Commn. on the Arts, 2000, Te Found. Grant, 2002, Photography grantee Conn. Commn. on Culture and Tourism, 2006; Conn. Commn. Arts fellow, 1995, New Eng. Found. Arts/NEA Regional Photography fellow, 1995-96; Emerging Voices lectr. Arch. League of NY, 1996. Studio: 219 Livingston St New Haven CT 06511-2209

LINDSAY, ARLENE ROSARIO, federal judge; BA, U. Dayton, 1968; JD, NYU Law Sch., 1975. Bar: N.Y. Asst. D.A. Bronx, 1975—78; asst. U.S. atty. Eastern Dist. N.Y., 1978—83; deputy atty. Suffolk County, 1983—88; town atty. Huntington, 1988—90; chief white collar crime and complex litigation sect., D.A. office Suffolk Country, 1990; chief Long Island div. U.S. Atty. office Eastern Dist. N.Y., 1990—94; magistrate judge for ea. dist. N.Y., U.S. Magistrate Ct., Bklyn., 1994—. Adj. prof. Touro Law Sch. Mem.: ABA. Office: Fed Plaza Long Island Federal Courthouse 814 Central Islip NY 11722

LINDSAY, DIANNA MARIE, educational administrator; b. Boston, Dec. 7, 1948; d. Albert Joseph and June Hazelton Raggi; m. James William Lindsay III, Feb. 14, 1981. BA in Anthropology, Ea. Nazarene Coll., 1971; MEd in Curriculum and Instrn., Wright State U., 1973, MA in Social Studies Edn., 1974, MEd in Edn. Adminstrn., 1977; EdD in Urban History, Ball State U., 1976; MA in Counseling, U. Dayton, 2000. Supr. social edn. Ohio Dept. Edn., Columbus, 1976-77; asst. prin. Orange City Schs., Pepper Pike, Ohio, 1977-79; prin. North Olmsted (Ohio) Jr. High Sch., 1979-81; dir. secondary edn. North Olmsted City Schs., 1981-82; supt. Copley (Ohio)-Fairlawn City Schs., 1982-85; prin. North Olmsted High Sch., 1985-89, New Trier High Sch., Winnetka, Ill., 1989-96, Worthington Kilbourne H.S., Columbus, Ohio, 1996-2001; headmaster Columbus Jewish Day Sch., New Albany, Ohio, 2001—03; prin. Ridgefield H.S., Ridgefield, Conn., 2003—. Bd. dirs. Harvard Prins. Ctr., Cambridge, Mass., adj. prof. ednl. adminstrn., Grad. Sch. Edn., U. Dayton, Bexley, OH Contbr. articles to profl. jours. Bd. dirs. Nat. PTA, Chgo., 1987-89 (Educator of Yr. 1989). Found. Human Potential, Chgo.,; bd. trustee Columbus Jewish Country Day Sch. Named Prin. of Yr. Ohio Art Tchrs., 1989, one of 100 Up and Coming Educators, Exec. Educator Mag., 1988, Milken Educator of the Yr. Ohio, 1999; recipient John Vaughn Achievements in Edn. North Cen. Assn., 1988; named Ohio Prin. of Yr, 2000. Mem. AAUW, Ill. Tchrs. Fgn. Lang., Rotary Internat., Phi Delta Kappa. Methodist. Avocations: stained glass, reading, travel, biking, harpist. Office: Ridgefield HS 700 N Salem Rd Ridgefield CT 06877 E-mail: dlindsay@ridgefield.org.

LINDSAY, JUNE CAMPBELL MCKEE, communications executive; b. Detroit, Nov. 14, 1920; d. Maitland Everett and Josephine Belle (Campbell) McKee; m. Powell Lindsay, Nov. 25, 1967; 1 child, Kristi Costa-McKee. BA in Speech with honors (McGregor Fund Mich. grantee), U. Mich., 1943; cert. in electronics engring., Signal Corps Ground Signal Svc., 1943; postgrad. (Inst. Gen. Semantics grantee), U. Chgo., 1944-45; postgrad. (Armour grantee), NYU, 1945-46; postgrad., Columbia U., 1946-47, Wayne State U., 1960-64, U. Mich., 1964-70, 78—; MA, Specialist-in-Aging Cert., Inst. of Gerontology, 1982. Coord., activator McKee Prodns., Detroit, 1943-56, Being Unltd., Detroit, 1957—, InterBeing Inc., Detroit, 1979—, M.U.T.U.A.L. A.I.D., 1981—. Info. dir. Suitcase Theatre Inc., Lansing and Ann Arbor; cons. Cornelian Corner Detroit Inc., 1957-63, Islamic Ctr. Found. Soc., Detroit, 1959-62, city Ann Arbor Human Rels. Commn., 1966-68, Urban Adult Edn. Inst., Detroit, 1968-69, Mich. Bell Tel. Co., Detroit, 1969, African Art Gallery Founders, Detroit Inst. Arts, 1964, WKAR-TV, Mich. State U., 1971—. Mem. Nat. Caucus, Ctr. for Black Aged; bd. dirs. Mus. Youth Internat., Saline, Mich., Ann Arbor Cmty. Devel. Corp.; chaplain's asst. U. Hosp., Ann Arbor, 1971—72; program dir. People-to-People, Ann Arbor, 1971—72; Suitcase Theatre tour coord. Brit. Empire's Leprosy Relief Assn., 1972—; mem. Baha'i Internat. Health Agy., Inst. for Advancement of Health, Mission Health, Catherine McAuley Health Ctr. Share and Care Support Group; assembly cons. Baha'i Faith, 1960—. Recipient Award for Excellence Mich. Ednl. Assn.,1971, Mich. Assn. Classroom Tchrs., 1972; exec. dir. Powell Lindsay Meml. Program in Theatre and Comm., Louhelen Baha'i Sch. and Residential Coll., U. Mich., Flint, Mott Cmty. Coll., 1988—. Mem.: ACLU, People's Med. Soc., Nat. Assn. Pub. Health Policy, Nat. Coun. Sr. Citizens, Washtenaw County Coun. on Aging, Subarea Adv. Coun., Comprehensive Planning Coun. S.E. Mich., Mich. Soc. Gerontology, Mich. League Human Svcs., Mental Health Assn. Mich., Nat. Inst. Clin. Application of Behavioral Medicine, Internat. Soc. Study of Subtle Energies and Energy Medicine, Assn. Holistic Health, U.S. Assn. Humanistic Psychology, Nat. Coun. on Aging, Mich. Health Coun., Am. Soc. on Aging, Inst. Study Conscious Evolution, Internat. Health Found., Mich. Assn. Holistic Health, Wellness Assocs., Am. Pub. Health Assn., Am. Assn. Adult and Continuing Edn., Am. Women in Radio and TV, Soc. for Individual Responsibility, Age-Groups United Relating On-site Respecting Autonomy (activator, troupe leader, prodr., developer videotape vignettes and revues), UN Assn. of U.S., Orgn. Devel. Inst., Nat. Trust Historic Preservation, World Future Soc., Living Tao Found., Giraffe Soc., Alliance for Democracy and Diversity, Am. Assn. Ret. Persons, Interfaith Coun. Peace and Justice, Assn. Baha'i Studies, Planetary Citizens, Gray Panthers, Internat. Platform Assn. Home: 2339 S Circle Dr Ann Arbor MI 48103-3442

LINDSAY, LESLIE, packaging engineer; b. Amsterdam, N.Y., Oct. 30, 1960; d. R. Gardner and Dorothy (Loucks) Lindsay. BA in Advt., Mich. State U., 1981, BS in Package Engring., 1982. Registered profl. engr. in packaging. Constrn. insp. N.Y. State Dept. Transp., Albany, 1983; sr. package design engr. Wang Labs., Inc., Lowell, Mass., 1983—90; sr. packaging engr. Apple Computer, Inc., Cupertino, Calif., 1990—97, Bose Corp., Framingham, Mass., 1997—2002; dir. packaging Syratech Corp., East Boston, Mass., 2003—05; mgr. tech. bus. Markson Rosenthal & Co., Maynard, Mass., 2005—. Conf. spkr. Internat. Safe Transit Assn., 1994; judge AmeriStar, 1999, 2000. Staff editor: Packaging Horizons Mag. Recipient Silver Ameristar award for Electronics Packaging, 1993, 2000, ID Mag. Packaging award, 1993, Ameristar Judges award for Merit, 1995; N.Y. State Regents scholar, 1977. Mem.: Molded Pulp Environ. Packaging Assn. (seminar spkr. 1997, founding bd. dirs.), Inst. Packaging Profls. (mem. reduction, reuse, and recycling protective packaging task group, cert.), Women in Packaging, Wang Ultimate Frisbee (social chmn. 1986—89), Am. Contract Bridge League, Boston Women's Rugby Club (tour chmn. 1985). Home: 193 Winter St Framingham MA 01702-2435 Personal E-mail: leslie.lindsay@rcn.com.

LINDSAY, LYNDA, research scientist; b. N.Y.C., Nov. 25, 1943; d. Louis and Mildred Greenwald; m. Paul Lindsay. BS, CCNY, 1966. Rsch. technician Rice U., Houston, 1968—69, Max Planck Inst., Heidelberg, Germany, 1969—70, U. Tex., Austin, 1971—89; mgr. Howard Hughes, N.Y.C., 1991—92; rsch. technician Pub. Health Res. Internat., N.Y.C., 1992—96, U. Tex., Austin, 1997—2002. Avocations: dance, photography. Home: 807 W Lynn St Apt 122 Austin TX 78703

LINDSAY, RITA CAROL, mathematics professor; b. Southampton, NY, Feb. 23, 1961; d. Kenneth David Lindsay and Mary Nina Keith; children: Alisa Rita Randolfi, Kenneth Joseph Randolfi, Michael Francis Randolfi. BS in Geology, SUNY, Oneonta, 1983; MS in Math. Edn., C. W. Post U., 1987; PhD in Applied Math., Fla. Tech. U., 2006. Vis. instr. math. Fla. Tech. U., Melbourne, 2002—03; asst. prof. math. Indian River CC, Fort Pierce, Fla., 2003—. Recipient New Your State Math./Sci. Teachers award, NY State, 1985—87; scholar NY State Regents scholar, 1979—83. Mem.: Fla. Coun. Tchrs. Math., Fla. Two Yr. Coll. Math. Assn., Fla. Assn. CCs (assoc.). Achievements include research in achievement in college algebra based on technology and learning style. Office: Indian River CC 3209 Virginia Ave Fort Pierce FL 34981 Personal E-mail: rcr223@comcast.net. Business E-Mail: rlindsay@ircc.edu.

LINDSAY, TWYLA LYNN, music educator; b. Chillicothe, Mo., June 22, 1964; d. Jesse Earl and Linda Louise Dodd; m. Ronald R. Lindsay, Aug. 2, 1986; children: Jesalynn Delores, Ronald Micah. B in Edn. Music, Mo. Western State Coll., 1987; EdM, Lesle Coll., 1998. Music educator Kans. City (Mo.) Sch. Dist., 1987—, program dir., coord. career ladder program, 1999—2003. Sunday sch. tchr., youth worker Concord Bapt. Ch., Kansas City, 1986—2003, dir., musician, 1986—2000. Mem.: Mo. Music Educators Assn. Baptist. Avocations: travel, reading, bowling, singing, piano. Office: Kansas City Mo Sch Dist 1211 McGee Kansas City MO 64109 Office Phone: 816-418-6525.

LINDSEY, BONNIE LOU, minister; b. Chillicothe, Ohio; d. Donald Arthur Sheets and Anna Rowena Nella Seymour; m. Ronald Lee Lindsey, Aug. 30, 1969; children: Katherine Irene Lanch, Ronald Lee Jr. A in Acctg., Southeastern Ohio Bus. Coll., Gallipolis, 1982; Lunbach tutor tng., Franklin Pre-Release, Chillicothe, Ohio, 1996. Ordained min. Ohio, 1998. Pastor Freedom Rd. Holiness Ch., Chillicothe, 1998—2005. Tutor religion classes Franklin Pre-Release, Columbus, 1996. Mem. Harvest Ctr. Ch. of God, Chillicothe, 1994—98. Avocations: reading, cooking, baking. Home: 31700 Dixon Mill Rd Londonderry OH 45647 Office Phone: 740-779-1704.

LINDSEY, JACQUELYN MARIA, editor; b. Buffalo, June 6, 1952; d. George Henry and Patricia Ann (Rott) Bilkey; m. Timothy Paul Murphy, Jan. 29, 1970 (div. May 1981); children: Paul Jeffrey, Jeremy Michael; m. Warren Lee Eckert, Dec. 5, 1987 (div. June 1992); m. Donald J. Lindsey, Nov. 5, 1994. Student, Ind. U., 1984. Adminstrv. asst. Western N.Y. Cath. Visitor, Buffalo, 1979-81; sec. religious edn. Our Sunday Visitor, Huntington, Ind., 1981-84, editl. asst. periodicals dept., 1985, staff editor periodicals and books, editor My Daily Visitor, 1985-91, coord. Diocesan edits., 1986-88, assoc. editor books, 1987-90, editor trade books, 1990-93, acquisitions editor trade books, 1991—, acquisitions editor religious edn., 1991-2001, editl. devel. mgr., 2001—. Co-founder, co-owner Specialty Tool & Engring., LLC, 1995—; pres. J Handles, LLC, 2003; bd. dirs. STE, Inc. Editor, compiler: Photo Directory of U.S. Catholic Hierarchy, 1987, 1990, 1993; editor: Leaves Marianhill Missionaries, 1991—, Catholic Family Prayer Book, 2001, Catholic Pocket Prayer Book, 2002, Catholic Prayer Book, 2003, Prayer Book for Catholics, 2005. Candidate for rep. Ind. Gen. Assembly 21st Dist., 1984; mem. LaFontaine Arts Coun., Huntington County, 1985-88; mem. Huntington County Dems., 1986-88; dep. trustee Polk Twp., 2003-2005. Mem. Cath. Press Assn. Office: Our Sunday Visitor Pub 200 Noll Plz Huntington IN 46750-4304 Personal E-mail: jlindsey@aol.com.

LINDSEY, JERRI KAY, biologist, educator; d. Charles Robert and Joyce Anita Lindsey. BA, McMurry U., Abilene, Tex., 1968; PhD in Biology, U. North Tex., Denton, Tex., 1972. Lab asst. McMurry U., 1966—68; tchg. fellow biology U. North Tex., 1970—71; prof. natural sci. Tarrant County Coll. Dist., Hurst, Tex., 1972—. Instr. All Saints Meml. Hosp., Ft. Worth, 1976; adj. prof. Parker Coll. Chiropractic Medicine, Irving, Tex., 1983—84; cons. Coll. Medicine, Phys. Therapy and Sports Medicine U. North Tex., Ft. Worth, 1979; cons. Arlington (Tex.) Ind. Sch. Dist., 1980—2006, Bedford (Tex.) Ind. Sch. Dist., 1980—92. Author: Human Biology Lab Manual for Dental Assistants, 1978, Human Biology Laboratory Manual for Respiratory Technicians, 1980, (films) Continuing Education Dog Obedience, 1981, Test Bank to Accompany Principles of Anatomy and Physiology 4th Edition by Tortora and Anagnostakos, 1984, Biology Laboratory Manual for the Telecourse Cycles of Life: Exploring Biology, 1987, Biology Laboratory Manual for the Telecourse Introducing Biology, 1997; contbr. articles to mags. Active Citizens on Patrol Ft. Worth (Tex.) Police Dept., 1993—2006; active Citizens on Patrol Urban Search Team Ft. Worth (Tex.) Police Dept. East, 1998—2006; actor tng. scenarios Arlington (Tex.) Police Dept., 1995—2006; judge United Kennel Club, 1983—2006, field rep., 1983—85. Fellow, NDEA, 1968—72; grantee, NSF, 1995—97; scholar, McMurry U., 1964—68. Mem.: Tex. C.C. Tchrs. Assn., Arlington Citizens Fire Acad., Nat. Toy Fox Terrier Assn. (historian 2005—06), Nat. Toy Fox Terrier Assn. (v.p. 1990—91, First Toy Fox Terrier Obedience Title winner 1987), Ft. Worth Citizens Police Acad. (bd. dirs. 2000—02), Gamma Sigma Epsilon, Alpha Chi. Baptist. Avocations: dog shows, horse shows. Office: Tarrant County College-Northeast Campus 828 Harwood Road Hurst TX 76054 Office Phone: 817-515-6506. Business E-Mail: jerri.lindsey@tccd.edu.

LINDSEY, JOANNE M., flight attendant, poet; b. Peoria, Ill., Aug. 27, 1936; d. George Edward and Elsie Rosetta (Mann) Lindsey; AA, El Camino Coll., Torrance, Calif., 1958. Exec. adminstrv. sec. Space Tech. Labs. (formerly Ramo-Woolridge), Hawthorne, Calif., 1958-64; flight attendant Am. Airlines, LA, 1964—, Civil Res. Air Fleet Mil. Missions, 2003. Mem. acad. coun. Diplomatic Acad., London; vice consul Internat. Biog. Ctr.; with Airlift Svcs. Solicitation, 2003—. Contbr. poems to anthologies, including Internat. Libr. Poetry, Noble House. Attended People to People Amb. Program's S. African Tour of Women Writers, 1998; active Civil Res. Air Fleet Mil. Missions, 2003; with Airlift Svcs. Solicitation, 2003—. Named to Internat. Libr. Poetry, 1996, 1997, 1998, 2002, 2004, 2005; recipient 7 Poetry Editor's Choice awards in anthologies. Mem.: Internat. Soc. Poets, Audie Murphy Rsch. Found., Acad. Am. Poets. Avocations: gardening, writing, skiing, mountain biking, home refurbishing. Home: 846 American Oaks Ave Newbury Park CA 91320-5572

LINDSEY, MARGARET A., psychiatrist; children: Jenna, Abigail. BA, Trinity U., San Antonio, 1972; BS, Columbia U., N.Y., 1975; postgrad., Cornell U., Ithaca, N.Y., 1981; MD, Case Western Res. U., Cleve., 1988. Lic. physician N.Y., 1989, diplomate Am. Bd. Psychiatry; RN N.Y., 1975. From resident to sr. instr. child psychiatry U. Rochester, NY, 1988—95, sr. instr. child psychiatry, 1995—; pvt. practice Rochester, 1996—. Cons. in field. Vol. Genessee Valley Women's Found., Rochester, 2000—05. Mem.: APA, Am. Acad. Child and Adolescent Psychiatry. Presbyn. Office: 3700 East Ave Rochester NY 14618

LINDSEY, ROBERTA LEWISE, music researcher, historian; b. Munich, Apr. 23, 1958; d. Fred S. and Elsie E. (White) L. BMus, Butler U., 1980, MMus, 1987; PhD, Ohio State U., 1996. Pres., owner Profl. Typing Svcs., Indpls., 1980-84; mktg. specialist Merchants Mortgage Corp., Indpls., 1985-87; exec. asst. Ind. Arts Commn., Indpls., 1988-90; GTA Ohio State U., Columbus, 1990-94, music libr. asst., 1991-93, student coord. music in Ohio festival, 1993, vol. tutor coord., 1994-95, lectr. Marion, 1995; rsch. editor Ind. High Tech. Directory, 1995-97; lectr. Ind. U. Sch. Music, 1998, vis. asst. prof. Indianapolis, 1999—2001, asst. prof. Indpls., 2001—, advisor music minor program, 2000—, reader IU Press, 2004. Rep. Susan Porter Meml. symposium Ohio State U., Columbus, 1995; program com. AMS Midwest, 2001—02; vis. rsch. fellow Am. Music Rsch. Ctr., 1997; tchr. of record Digital Music Libr. Grant project Ind. U., 2000—05; presenter and spkr. nat. and internat. confs. Book reviewer Ohioana Jour., 1997—2002, contbg. editor Lenten Devotional, 2000—01; contbr. articles to profl. jours. Reader Ctrl. Ind. Radio Reading, Inc., Indpls., 1985-90; co-founder, Grad. Music Students Assn., Ohio State.U., Columbus; multicultural diversity com. Coun. of Grad. Students, Columbus, 1992, orgns. and elections com., 1992, co-chair orientation com., 1993; pre-concert lectr. Carmel Symphony Orch., 1998; active Inst. Rep. for the Arts, 1999—, IUPUI/Eiteljorg; adv. bd. Eiteljorg Mus., 1999—, docent, 2004—. Recipient Grad. Student Alumni Rsch. award, Ohio State U., 1993, Innovative Teaching Recognition award, Ind. U. Sch. Music, 2002, Trustee Tchg. award for tchg. excellence, Ind. U. Purdue U. Indpls., 2006; grantee Dena Epstein grantee, 2001, Ind. U. Purdue U. Indpls., 2001. Mem. Soc. Am. Music, Am. Musicol. Soc. (prof. com. 2001—, program com. midwest chpt. 2001-02), Coll. Music Soc. (Gt. Lakes chpt. conv. 2001-02), Soc. Ethnomusicology, Am. Music Rsch. Ctr. Office Phone: 317-278-7868. Business E-Mail: rlindsey@iupui.edu.

LINDSEY, SUSAN LYNDAKER, zoologist; b. Valley Forge, Pa., Aug. 23, 1956; d. Howard Paul and Lillian Irene (Whitman) Lyndaker; m. Kevin Arthur Lindsey, July 17, 1982; children: Ryan Howard, Shannon Marie. BS in Biology, St. Lawrence U., 1978; MA in Zoology, So. Ill. U., Carbondale, 1980; PhD in Zoology, Colo. State U., 1987. Rschr. St. Lawrence U., Kenya, East Africa, 1978; tchr. Beth Jacob H.S., Denver, 1986-87; rschr. mammal dept. Dallas Zoo, 1988-93; exec. dir. Wild Canid Survival and Rsch. Ctr., Eureka, Mo., 1993—. Adj. prof. Cedar Valley Coll., 1992-93, So. Ill. U., Carbondale, 1996—; mgmt. group mem. Red Wolf Species Survival Plan, Tacoma, Wash., 1994—, Mexican Gray Wolf Species Survival Plan, Albuquerque, 1993—, Maned Wolf Species Survival Plan, Washington, 1999—, African Wild Dog Species Survival Plan, 2005—. Author: (with others) The Okapi: Mysterious Animal of Congo-Zaire, 1999; contbr. articles to profl. jours. Docent Denver Zool. Found., Denver Zoo, 1985-88. Recipient Disting. Alumni citation, St. Lawrence U., 2003. Mem. Acad. Sci. St. Louis, Am. Zoo and Aquarium Assn., Am. Behavior Soc., Am. Soc. of Mammalogists, Beta Beta Beta, Phi Beta Kappa, Psi Chi. Avocations: horseback riding, canoeing, gardening, photography, travel. Office: Wild Canid Survival Rsch Ctr Wash U PO Box 760 Eureka MO 63025-0760 Office Phone: 636-938-5900.

LINDSEY-HICKS, GLENDA, literature and language professor; b. Stillwater, Okla. children: Josh, Jacob. BA in Letters, Okla. U., 1974; MA in English, Okla. State U., 1976, PhD in English, 1979. Prof. English Midland (Tex.) Coll., 1981—. Contbr. numerous poems to lit. publs. Recipient Tchg. Excellence award, Tex. Mem.: MLA, NOW, South Ctrl. MLA. Office: MIdland Coll 3600 N Garfield St Midland TX 79705-6329

LINDSEY-MULLIKIN, JOAN, education educator, researcher; 1 child, Matthew Lindsey-Paek. PhD in Mgmt., U. Ariz., 1999. Contracts adminstr. McDonnell Douglas Corp., St. Louis, 1984—86; assoc. prof. mktg. Babson Coll., Babson Park, Mass., 1999—. Dir. of assessment Babson Coll., 2006—. Contbr. articles to profl. jours. Office: Babson Coll Malloy Hall Babson Park MA 02457 Office Phone: 781-239-5674. E-mail: jmullikin@babson.edu.

LINDSLEY, CATHERINE S., voice educator, director; d. James and Dwan Trimble; m. Kelly Lindsley, Mar. 3, 1990. MusB, U. Mo., 1978; MusM, Tex. A&M U., 1989. Cert. tchg. and AP. Choral dir. Mabank HS, Tex. Soprano Dallas Symphony Chorus. Named Tchr. of Yr., Mabank Jr. HS. Mem.: Am. Choral Dirs. Assn., Tex. Choral Dirs. Assn., Tex. Music Educators Assn. Republican. Avocation: piano. Office: Mabank HS 822 W Mason Mabank TX 75147 Business E-Mail: cslindsl@mabankisd.net.

LINDSLEY, MICHELLE A., theater educator, music educator; MS in Edn., Hofstra U., 1991. Cert. tchr. N.Y. Dir. of drama workshop Valley Stream (N.Y.) Ctrl. H.S., 1990—2003; dir. of choral activities Farmingdale (N.Y.) H.S., 1992—; dir. Playcrafters, 2005—. Vocal coach/tchr. ML Studios, North Babylon, NY, 1986—; mus. dir. Farmingdale H.S., 1993—; drama dir. Weldon E. Howitt Mid. Sch., Farmingdale, 1992—2002. Dir., singer: choral performance Carnegie Hall Debut. Recipient Grammy Signature Sch. grant, Grammy Found., 1997, 2003. Master: Tri M Music Honor Soc. (chpt. sponsor 1992—2003); mem.: Am. Choral Directors Assn. (advocacy chair 2003—05), Nassau Music Educators Assn. (pub. rels. dir. 1995—96, all county vocal jazz chairperson 2005), N.Y. State Sch. Music Assn. (all state vocal jazz chaiperson 2006—), Music Educators Nat. Conf. Liberal. Roman Catholic. Avocations: music, travel, reading, photography. Office: Farmingdale H S 150 Lincoln St Farmingdale NY 11735 Office Phone: 516-752-6761 392. Business E-Mail: mlindsle@fpsmail.k12.ny.us.

LINDSTROM, ROSETTA ARLINE, retired medical technician; b. Fay, Okla., Aug. 30, 1943; d. Paul George and Gladys Arline Prickett; m. Richard Jacobsen, 1962 (div. 1980); children: Richard P. Jacobsen, Ronald J. Jacobsen, Christine Jacobsen Carroll; m. John Lindstrom, 1988 (div. 1996). Degree Med. Assistance, Lawton Coll. Med. Technologies, 1975. Registered Diagnostic Cardiac Sonographer 1988. Sr. technician EKG and Echo Dept. Kaiser-Permanante Hosp., Redwood City, Calif., 1977—87; supr. Echocardiography Lab. VA Med. Ctr. Stanford, Palo Alto, Calif., 1989—2002; ret., 2002. Instr. Echocardiography Stanford U. Fellows Program, 1989—2002; site instr. Dept. Med. Ultrasound Foothill Coll., 1995—2001. Author (editor): El Toro Yearbook, Shovel Bull., 1968. Named Sr. Divsn. Winner, N. Am. Sailing Championship, 1968, Season Champion El Toro Sr. Divsn., Small Boat Racing Assn. No. Calif., 1969; recipient Tchg. award in Echocardiography, Stanford U. Sch. Medicine, Graduating Fellows, 2000. Avocations: writing, childrens literature.

LINEBERRY, LAURIE LAWHORN, urban planner; d. Jarrett Lee and Mary Lou Lawhorn; m. Richard Paul Lineberry, Sept. 2, 2002; children: Caitlin Dale Grimes, Molly Louise Grimes. BS in Urban Planning, Calif. State Poly. U., 1981; MPA, Calif. State U., Northridge, 1990. Asst. dir. advanced planning City of Fontana, Calif., 1985—87; sr. planner City of Chino, Calif., 1987—91; asst. dir. planning and devel. Okanogan County, Wash., 1992—94, dir. planning and devel., 1994—96; asst. dir. Spokane County, Wash., 1996—99; asst. dir. cmty. planning City of Yuma, Ariz., 1999—. Pres. Yuma Fire Dept. Ladies' Aux., 2002—04; sec. Cibola Dance Team Booster Club, 2003—04; mem. handbell choir Trinity United Meth. Ch., 2000—, leader adult Sun. sch. class, 2001—, chair Christian Edn. com., 2002—06, sr. high youth leader, 2003—06. Mem.: Am. Inst. Cert. Planners. Methodist. Office: City of Yuma P O Box 13013 Yuma AZ 85366 Office Phone: 928-373-5177. Business E-Mail: laurie.lineberry@ci.yuma.az.us.

LINEBERRY, REBECCA J., municipal official, treasurer; b. Pulaski, Va., Feb. 12, 1963; d. Leroy Martin Sr. and Virginia Lineberry; div. Jan. 25, 2002. AAS in Acctg., New River C.C., Dublin, Va., 1983. Cert. master govt. treas. U. Va.; notary public Commonwealth of Va. Bookkeeper Bell Realty, Dublin, Va., 1983; clk., sec. Town of Dublin, 1983-87, asst. treas., 1987-90, treas., 1990—. Mem. Va. Govt. Fin. Officers Assn., Treas.' Assn. Va., S.W. Va. Treas.' Assn. (vice chair 1997-99, chmn. 1999-2001), Assn. Govt. Accts. mem. Am. Registry of Outstanding Profl., Pulaski County Humane Soc. (treas. bd. dirs. 2005-). Avocations: archery, tennis, cross-stitch, travel, hot air ballooning. Office: Town of Dublin PO Box 1066 Dublin VA 24084-1066 Office Phone: 540-674-4731. E-mail: rlineberry@dublintown.org.

LINEHAN, LOU ANN, political organization worker; m. Kevin Linehan; 4 children. Student, U. Nebr. Campaign mgr. Congrl. Campaign for Ally Milder, 1990; exec. dir. Douglas County Rep. Party, 1991-93; adminstrv. asst. to Dr. Ron Roskens Action Internat., 1993-95; campaign mgr. U.S. Senate Campaign for Chuck Hagel, 1995-96; chief of staff U.S. Senator Chuck Hagel, 1997—. CCD tchr. Christ the King Ch., 1993-94; chmn. Celebrity Waiter's GOP Fundraiser, 1993; treas. Loveland Parents' Assn., 1994; active Women's Guild-Meyer Children's Rehab. Inst., 1988-95, pres. 1993. Named Vol. of Yr. Douglas County, 1988. Home: 2353 S 87th St Omaha NE 68124-2143 Office: Office of Senator Chuck Hagel 346 Russell Senate Off Bldg Washington DC 20510-0001 also: 294 Federal Bldg 100 Centennial Mall N Lincoln NE 68508 E-mail: louann_linehan@hagel.senate.gov.

LING, CHIEW SING, investment company executive; b. Bintulu, Malaysia, Dec. 5, 1964; came to U.S., 1996; d. Kong Sui L. BS, Monash U., Melbourne, Victoria, Australia, 1986; M of Engring., U. NSW, Sydney, 1990. Mem. tech. staff Info. Tech. Inst., Singapore, 1990-93; asst. v.p. Bank of Am., Singapore, 1994-95; internat. rsch. & portfolio strategist Advanced Investment Tech., Clearwater, Fla., 1996-98; prin. State St. Global Advisors, Boston, 1998—. Mem. Boston Security Analyst Soc. Office: State St Global Advisors 2 Internat Pl Boston MA 02110

LINGLE, LINDA, governor; b. St. Louis, June 4, 1953; BJ, Calif. State U., Northridge, 1975. Mayor County of Maui, Hawaii; chair. Democratic Party of Hawaii; mem. Maui County Coun., 1980—90; mayor Maui County, 1990—98; chmn. Hawaii Republican Party, 1999—2001; gov. State of Hawaii, Honolulu, 2002—. Recipient Evelyn McPhail award, 2000. Republican. Jewish. Office: Off of the Gov State Capitol Executive Chambers Honolulu HI 96813 Address: PO Box 25111 Honolulu HI 96825 Office Phone: 808-586-0034. Office Fax: 808-586-0006.*

LINGLE, MARILYN FELKEL, journalist, columnist; b. Hillsboro, Ill., Aug. 16, 1932; d. Clarence Frederick and Anna Cecelia (Stank) Felkel; m. Ivan L. Lingle, Oct. 4, 1950 (dec. Aug. 2001); children: Ivan Dale, Aimee Lee, Clarence Craig. Sec. Ill. State Police, 1950; with welfare dept. Ill. Pub. Aid, Hillsboro, 1951-52; rschr. Small Homes Coun., Champaign, 1952-53; sec. Hillsboro Schs., 1954; office, payroll clk. Eagle Picher Zinc, Hillsboro, 1955—56; continuity dir. Sta. WSMI, Litchfield, 1966—87. Adv. bd. Am. Savs. Bank/Citizens Savs. Bank, vice chmn., 1986-93; founder Dunsford Books, 2004. Author: Configurations, 2004, numerous poems; columnist: Here's Looking at You, 2006—. Cmty. edn. bridge instr. Lincoln Land C.C.; fin. chmn. Hillsboro Hosp. Aux., 1972; lit. vol. Graham Correctional Ctr., Hillsboro, 1986-97; pres., bd. dirs. Montgomery Players and Encore Play Theatre, 1954-70. Recipient Vol. of Yr. award Graham Correction Ctr., 1995, award of Merit Ill. State Bd. Edn., 1994-95. Mem. Cousteau Soc., Internat. Wildlife Fedn., Nat. Wildlife Fedn., Natural Resources Def. Coun., Phi Theta Kappa Internat., Hillsboro Country Club, Hillsboro Book Club, Red Hat Soc. Democrat. Lutheran. Avocations: bridge, golf, gardening, travel, reading. Personal E-mail: lyn@consolidated.net.

LINGLE, SARAH ELIZABETH, research scientist; b. Woodland, Calif., July 22, 1955; d. John Clayton and Dorothy Adelaide (Dubois) L.; m. Thomas Pratt Washington IV, May 20, 1989. BS, U. Calif., Davis, 1977; MS, U. Nebr., 1978; PhD, Wash. State U., 1982. Lab. asst. U. Calif., Davis, 1975-77; rsch. asst. U. Nebr., Lincoln, 1977-78; rsch., teaching asst. Wash. State U., Pullman, 1979-82; rsch. assoc. Agrl. Rsch. Svc., USDA, Fargo, ND, 1982-84, supr. plant physiologist Weslaco, Tex., 1984-97, acting rsch. leader, 1991-92, plant physiologist New Orleans, 1997—. Assoc. editor Crop Sci., 1991-97; contbr. articles to profl. jours., chpts. to 2 books. Fellow Am. Soc. Agronomy; mem. AAAS, Am. Soc. Plant Physiologists, Crop Sci. Soc. Am., Sigma Xi. Episcopalian. Achievements include research in biochemistry and physiology of sugar deposition in sucrose-storing plant tissues. Office Phone: 504-286-4488. Business E-Mail: slingle@srrc.ars.usda.gov.

LINGO, SHELLEY J., social studies educator; b. Kankakee, Ill., May 27, 1974; d. Dale and Janice Kiedaisch; m. Jason Lingo, June 14, 1997; children: Riley David, Corliss Ann. BS in Social Sci., Ill. State U., Normal, 1997. Social studies tchr. Kankakee H.S., Ill., 1997—. Social studies and fgn. lang. dept. chairperson Kankakee H.S., 2001—, sr. class advisor, 2004—, student coun. sponsor, 1998—2000, bus. acad. tchr., 1997—. Methodist. Avocations: walking, swimming, boating, scrapbooks. Office: Kankakee High School 1200 W Jeffrey Kankakee IL 60901 Office Phone: 815-933-0740.

LINHART, LETTY LEMON, editor; b. Pittsburg, Kans., Sept. 22, 1933; d. Robert Sheldon and Lois (Wise) Lemon; m. Robert Spayde Kennedy, June 8, 1955 (div. 1978); children: Carole Shea, Nancy Schrimpf, Nina Woodward; m. Daniel Julian Linhart, June 9, 1986 (dec. Apr. 2000); m. John M. Calhoun, Jan. 8, 2006. BS, BA in English and Journalism, U.Kans., 1955; MS in Journalism, Boston U., 1975. Reporter Leavenworth (Kans.) Times, 1954; editor Human Resources Rsch. Office George Washington U., Washington, 1955-56; editor Behavior Rsch. Lab. Harvard Med. Sch., Boston, 1956-58; instr. Boston YMCA, 1960-64; freelance writer and columnist, 1975—; editor Somerville (Mass.) Times, 1975-77; pub. rels. dir. Lettermen of Lexington, Mass., 1978; instr. English Rollins Coll., Winter Park, Fla., 1978-79, Valencia Community Coll., Orlando, Fla., 1978-82, U. Cen. Fla., Orlando, 1979-82; tech. writer Kirschman Software, Altamonte Springs, Mass., 1980-81, Dynamic Control Software, Winter Park, Fla., 1981-82; editor Fla. Specifier, Winter Park, 1982-85, Mobile Home News, Maitland, Fla., 1985-86; instr. English Seminole C.C., Sanford, Fla., 1986-94; Elderhostel instr. Canterbury Rsch. Ctr., 1994—98; editor Oviedo (Fla.) Voice, 1994-95, 96, Tuscawilla Today Monthly Mag., 2000—01; columnist Oviedo Voice, Oviedo, Fla., 2001; reporter North County Times, Vista, Calif., 2001—. Resource person Am. on Line, 1996—. Author: Are These Extravagant Promises, 1989, Clues for the Clueless, 1996, Bits and Bytes of Recovery, 1998, Turn Your Eyes, 2002, In The End it's Faith, 2003, The Minister Made Macramé, 2004; editor: The Cascadian Vista, 2004—; author: The Alcoholic Fish, 2005; contbr. articles to profl. jours. Pres. MIT Dames Boston, 1958-59, Boston Alumnae of Delta Delta Delta, 1959-62; dist. pres Delta Delta Delta, Tex., 1962-65; svc. provider, content provider, cmty. leader Am. On Line Careers and Work Forum, 1996—; cmty. leader media & journalism, AOL, 2000-. Named Outstanding Collegiate Delta Delta Delta, 1955. Mem. NAFE, Ctrl. Fla. Jazz Soc. (bd. dirs. 1983-93), Internat. Platform Soc., Soc. Women Execs., Altrusa Club (publicity com. 1980-83), Orlando Press Club (bd. dirs.), Mortar Bd., Phi Beta Kappa (Belmont, Mass. pres. 1965-78), Theta Sigma Phi, Sigma Delta Chi, Delta Sigma Rho. Avocations: swimming, singing, jazz. Home and Office: 1600 E Vista Way # 5 Vista CA 92084-1020 Personal E-mail: vistaletty@sbcglobal.net.

LINK, NINA BETH, publishing executive; b. Bklyn., Sept. 19, 1943; d. Robert R. and Helen (Cohen) Levine; m. William Reyer; children— David Jon, Gregory Adam. BA, Beaver Coll., 1965. Sec. WCBS TV, N.Y.C., 1965-66; ednl. systems analyst edn. div. Xerox, N.Y.C., 1966-68; cons. The Link Group, Inc., N.Y.C., 1968-78; v.p., publisher Children's TV Workshop, Sesame St. mag., Kid City mag., 3.2.1. Contact mag., Creative Classroom mag., N.Y.C., 1978-96; mem. exec. comm. Mag. Publishers of Amer., N.Y.C., 1996—, chair., govt. affairs comm., 1996-99, pres., CEO, 1999—. Cons. publishing, communication cos. Named to YWCA Acad. Women Achievers, 1985 Mem. Direct Mail Mktg. Assn., Writer's Guild, Dramatist's Guild, Internat. Reading Assn., Mag. Pubs. Assn. Office: MPA Fl 24 810 Seventh Ave New York NY 10019 Business E-Mail: president@magazine.org.*

LINK, PHOEBE FORREST, education educator, writer, social worker, poet; b. Palmerton, Pa., Feb. 20, 1926; d. John Nevins and Phoebe Eleanor (Lewis) Forrest; m. Robert H. Link, July 13, 1962; children: David Forrest, Anne Harris. BA in Psychology, Pa. State U., State Coll., 1947, MS in Child Devel. and Family Relationships, 1952; postgrad., U. Rochester, N.Y., 1957—59, Harvard U., 1958. Dir. teen age program YWCA, Lansing, Mich., 1947—50, Rochester, NY, 1952—56; rsch. asst. Pa. State U., State College, 1950—52; tchr. Rochester, 1956—60; demonstration tchr. William Antheil Sch., Trenton, NJ, 1960—63; mem. faculty Trenton State Coll., 1960—63; tchr. State College Area Schs., 1971—93. Lectr. Am. Home Econs. Assn. Conf.; cons. family studies, leader continuing edn. workshops Pa. State U., 1977, others; mem. staff dean women Harvard U., Cambridge, Mass., 1958; dir. Children's Program for Pa. Dist. Attys.; featured author TV series The Writing Life; reader-editor WPSX-TV. Author: Small? Tall? Not At All, 1973, Passionate Realist, 1994; staff writer: Horizon, 1985—87, author, creator: Heartthrob series, 1987; contbr. articles to profl. jours. Trustee Schlow Pub. Libr., State College, 1980—83; founder, 1st chmn. poetry com. Ctrl. Pa. Festival Arts; featured spkr. 50th class reunion Pa. State U.; mentor Women's Leadership Initiative, Pa. State U., 2004; dir. youth choir Univ. Bapt. Ch.; vis. deacon spiritual ministry team State College Presbyn. Ch., 2002; mem. aux. com. Centre Vols. in Medicine, 2004. Recipient Excellence in Edn. award with highest distinction, Pa. State U., 1993, merit award, William Antheil Sch., 1958; AAUW Simmons grantee, 1984. Mem.: NEA, AAUW, State College Area Edn. Assn. (scholarship com.), Peterson Soc., Mortar Bd. Alumni (founder, 1st pres., pres.), Pa. State U. Coll. Human Devel. Alumni (bd. dirs.), Tau Phi Sigma, Omicron Nu Alumni, Phi Delta Kappa. Home: 22 Cricklewood Cir State College PA 16803-2105

LINK, PHYLLIDA KORMAN, artist, educator; b. Bronx, NY, May 2, 1949; d. Charles and Minette Rose (Roschelle) Korman. BA, City Coll., NY, 1970; MA, CUNY, 1987. Cert. Art Sorbonne, Paris, 1980, lic. tchg. NY State Bd. of Edn. Tchr. NYC Bd. Edn., 1971—79; English tchr. Gardiner's Acad., Paris, 1980—85; adj. prof. Hudson County Cmty. Coll., Jersey City, 1988—93, St. Peter's Coll., Jersey City, 1986—. Exhibitions include SI Mus., 1983, Nabisco Gallery, 1988, Milburn Playhouse Gallery, NJ, 1990, Riverdale Gallery, NY, 1997, Internet, 2000—02, Riverdale Gallery, NY, 2005. Grantee Dept. of Comp Lit., Grad. Ctr. CUNY, 1985; scholar found. scholar, Helena Rubinstein Found., 1986—87. Fellow: NOW; mem.: La Maison Française, Columbia U., Pen and Brush Club. Avocations: films, excursions, museums.

LINKLATER, ISABELLE STANISLAWA YAROSH-GALAZKA (LEE LINKLATER), foundation administrator; b. Chgo., Sept. 15, 1939; d. Baron Stanislaw and Isabelle Lydia (Yarosh) Galazka. BE, Chgo. State U., 1959. Cert. tchr., Ill. Pub. rels. coord. Kelling Co., Chgo., 1955-57; tchr. Chg. Bd. Edn., 1957-89, coord. computer lab., 1989—; founder, pres., exec. dir. Assisi Animal Found. Edn. writer, coord. Elsa Internat. Wild Animal Appeal, Ill., 1985—; writer Lakeland Press, 1992. Bd. dirs. Townsquare Players, Woodstock (Ill.) Opera House, 1989-91. Recipient Outstanding Citizen award CBS Broadcasting, 1992. Mem. McHenry County Defenders (bd. dirs. 1989-91), East African Wildlife Soc. (U.S. rep.). Avocations: travel, music, theater. Office: Assisi Animal Found PO Box 143 Crystal Lake IL 60039-0143

LINKONIS, SUZANNE NEWBOLD, retired probation officer, retired counselor; b. Phila., Aug. 24, 1945; d. William Bartram and Kathryn (Taylor) Newbold; m. Bertram Lawrence Linkonis, May 29, 1966; children: Robert William, Deborah Anne, Richard Anthony. AA in Psychology, Albany (Ga.) Jr. Coll., 1979; BA in Psychology, Albany (Ga.) State U., 1981; MS in Indsl. Psychology, Va. Commonwealth U., 1986. Office mgr., media buyer Long Advt. Agy., Richmond, Va., 1981-84; media mgr. Clarke & Assocs., Richmond, 1984-85; human resources asst. Continental Ins., Richmond, 1985; rsch. assoc. Signet Bank, N.A., Richmond, 1986-87; program coord. Med. Coll. Va., Richmond, 1988; personnel mgr. Bur. Microbiology, Richmond, 1988-89; pers. specialist Va. State Dept. Corrections, Richmond, 1989-90; human rights adv. Va. State Dept. Youth and Family Svcs., Richmond, 1990-92, rehab. counselor, 1992-94, sr. rehab. counselor, 1994; pre-trial case mgr./counselor Henrico County Govt., Richmond, 1994-97, cmty. corrections case mgr., counselor, 1997-2000, sr. county probation officer, counselor, 2001—06. Future dir., cons. Mary Kay Cosmetics, Springfield, Va., 1975-77. Republican. Roman Catholic. Avocations: walking, reading, boating, fishing, genealogy. Home: 281 Shore Line Dr New Bern NC 28562 E-mail: slinkonis@cs.com.

LINN, CAROLE ANNE, dietician; b. Portland, Oreg., Mar. 3, 1945; d. James Leslie and Alice Mae (Thorburn) L. BS, Oreg. State U., 1967. Intern U. Minn., 1967—68; nutrition cons. licensing and cert. sect. Oreg. State Bd. Health, Portland, 1968-70; chief clin. dietitian Rogue Valley Med. Ctr., Medford, Oreg., 1970—; clin. faculty, dietetic internship program Oreg. Health Scis. U., Portland, 2000—. Cons. Hillhaven Health Care Ctr., Medford, 1971-83; lectr. Local Spkrs. Bur., Medford. Mem. Am. Soc. Parenteral and Enteral Nutrition, Am. Dietetic Assn., Am. Diabetic Assn., Oreg. Dietetic Assn. (sec. 1973-75, nominating com. 1974-75, Young Dietitian of Yr. 1976), So. Oreg. Dietetic Assn., Alpha Lambda Delta, Omicron Nu. Democrat. Mem. Christ Unity Ch. Avocations: sewing, needlecrafts, cooking, swimming, skiing. Office: Rogue Valley Med Ctr 2825 E Barnett Rd Medford OR 97504-8332

LINN, DIANA PATRICIA, retired elementary school educator; b. Perth, Australia, Dec. 31, 1943; arrived in US, 1948; d. Evan Andrew and Grace Henrietta (Springhall) Jarboe; m. Jim F. Erlandsen, July 9, 1966 (div. Mar. 1989); children: Rebecca Erlandsen, Tim Erlandsen, Jenny Erlandsen; m. Richard George Linn, Mar. 31, 1990; 1 stepchild, Cristal. AA, Olympic Coll., 1963; BA in Elem. Edn., Western Wash. U., 1965; MA, U. Ariz., 1969. Cert. tchr. Wash. Tchr. Neomi B. Willmore Elem., Westminster, Calif., 1965-66; tchr. English and sci. Sunnyside Jr. H.S., Tucson, 1966-70; tchr. kindergarten All Seasons Sch., Tucson, 1972-74; tchr. St. Cyril's Sch., Tucson, 1974-77; elem. tchr. Grace Christian Sch., Tucson, 1977-80; kindergarten and elem. tchr. Ridgeview Christian Ctr., Spokane, Wash., 1983-85, Spokane Christian Schs., 1985-87; dir. Ridgeview Christian Learning Ctr., Spokane, 1987-88; tchr. kindergarten Arlington Elem. Sch., Spokane, 1988-96, Grant Elem. Sch., Spokane, 1996—2005; ret., 2006. Mem. curriculum study com. Sunnyside Sch. Dist., Tucson, 1967—68; chmn. accreditation and sch. bd. St. Cyril's Sch., Tucson, 1976—77; chair faculty involvement group, chair staff devel, chair wellness com. Arlington Elem., Spokane, 1992—93, sch. reporter, 1994—95, chair faculty involvement group, mem. strategic plan equity com., 1995—96; instr. reading readiness Family Learning Fair, Home Schooling Seminar, Spokane Falls CC, Spokane, 1968; chair, coord. pre-sch. coop. Arlington Elem. with Spokane Falls CC, 1992—93; chair faculty involvement group Grant Elem. Sch., 1996—97, wellness chair, 1992—2001, site coun. faculty rep., 2001—05, primary team faculty rep., 2002—03, 2004—05, pres., 2003—04. Brownie troop leader Willmore Elem., Westminster, 1965—66; ednl. restructuring rep. Spokane Sch. Dist. 81 Arlington Elem., 1992—93, mem. equity com., 1996—99, mem. early childhood com., 1996—2004, mem. strategic planning com., 1998—2003, wellness chmn., 1998—2000, mem. instrnl. team, 1999—2003; primary rep. site coun. Grant Elem., 2002; coord. Christian edn. Valley Foursquare Ch., Spokane, 1982—87; coord. children's ch. Victory Faith Fellowship, Spokane, 1993—2003. Scholar, Naval Officer's Wives Club, 1961—62; Eisenhower grantee, 1990, 1994, 1996—97. Mem.: NEA, ASCD, Spokane Edn. Assn. (Arlington Elem. rep. 1991—93), Wash. Edn. Assn., CPA Wives Club (sec., ball chair 1983—84), Alpha Delta Kappa (membership chair 1994—95, corr. sec. 1996—99). Republican. Avocations: doll collecting, plate collecting, swimming, quilting. Home: 1324 S Perry St Spokane WA 99202-3572 E-mail: d2linn@yahoo.com, diane.linn@gmail.com.

LINN, MARCIA CYROG, education educator; b. Milw., May 27, 1943; d. George W. and Frances (Vanderhoof) Cyrog; m. Stuart Michael Linn, 1967 (div. 1979); children: Matthew, Allison; m. Curtis Bruce Tarter, 1987 (div. 2003). BA in Psychology and Stats., Stanford U., 1965, MA in Ednl. Psychology, 1967, PhD in Ednl. Psychology, 1970. Prin. investigator Lawrence Hall Sci. U. Calif., 1970-87, prin. investigator Sch. Edn., 1985—, asst. dean Sch. Edn., 1983-85, prof., 1989—; prin. investigator NSF Funded Ctr.- Tech.-Enhanced Learning in Sci. (TELS), 2003—08; chancellor's prof., 2003—. Fulbright prof. Weizmann Inst., Israel, 1983; exec. dir. seminars U. Calif., 1985-86, dir. instnl. tech. program, 1988-96, chair cognition and devel., 1996—98; cons. Apple Computer, 1983—90; mem. adv. com. on sci. edn. NSF, 1978—85, Ednl. Testing Svc., 1986—90, Smithsonian Instn., 1986—, Fulbright Program, 1983-86, Grad. Record Exam. Bd., 1990-94, adv. com. edn. and human resources directorate, NSF, 2002—; chair Cognitive Studes Bd. McDonell Found., 1994-97; mem. computing svcs. adv. bd. Carnegie Mellon U., 1991-99; mem. steering com. 3d Internat. Math. and Sci. Study, U.S., 1991-2002. Author: Education and the Challenge of Technology, 1987; co-author: The Psychology of Gender--Advances Through Meta Analysis, 1986—, Designing Pascal Solutions, 1992—, Designing Pascal Solutions with Data Structures, 1996, Computers, Teachers, Peers-Science Learning Partners, 2000, Internet Environments for Science Education, 2004; contbr. articles to profl. jours. Sci. advisor Parents Club, Lafayette, Calif., 1984-87; mem. Internat. Women's Forum, Women's Forum West, 1992—, membership com., 1995-98; bd. dirs. Nat. Ctr. for Sci. Edn., 1997—, GIS and edn. com., 2000—; mem. bd. on behavioral, cognitive and sensory scis. Nat. Rsch. Coun., 1997-2005, mem. com. on info. tech. literacy, computer sci. and telecomms., 1997-2000; mem. nat. adv. bd. Nat. Ctr. for Improving Student Learning and Achievement in Math. and Sci., 1997—; mem. com. on info. tech. fluency and H.S. grad. outcomes NRC, 2004-05. Recipient fellow Ctr. for Adv. Study in Behavior. Scis. 1995-96, 2001-02, Excellence Ednl. Rsch. award Coun. Sci. Soc. Pres., 1998. Fellow AAAS (bd. dirs. 1996-2001, chair-elect edn. sect. 2005—), APA, AAUW (mem. commn. tech. and gender 1998-2001), Am. Psychol. Soc.; mem. Nat. Assn. Rsch. in Sci. and Teaching (bd. dirs. 1983-86, assoc. editor jour., Outstanding Paper award 1978, Outstanding Jour. Article award 1975, 83, Disting. Contbns. to Sci. Edn. Through Rsch. award 1994), Am. Ednl. Rsch. Assn. (chmn. rsch. on women and edn. 1983-85, Women Educators Rsch. award 1982, 88, edn. in sci. and tech. 1989-90, ann. mtg. program com. 1996, Willystine Goodsell award 1991), Internat. Soc. Learning Svcs. (bd. dirs. 2005—), Nat. Sci. Tchrs. Assn. (mem. rsch. agenda com. 1987-90, task force 1993-94), Soc. for Rsch. in Child Devel. (editl. bd. 1984-89), Soc. Rsch. Adolescence, Sierra Club. Avocations: skiing, hiking. Office: U Calif Grad Sch Edn 4611 Tolman Hl Berkeley CA 94720-0001

LINNANSALO, VERA, engineer; b. Helsinki, Finland, Oct. 9, 1950; came to U.S., 1960, naturalized, 1969; d. Boris and Vera (Schkurat-Schkuropatsky) L. BS in Computer and Info. Sci., Cleve. State U., 1974, BME, 1974; MBA, U. Akron, 1983. Engring. assoc. B.F. Goodrich Co., Akron, Ohio, 1974-75, assoc. product engr., 1975-77, tire devel. engr., 1977-79, advanced tire devel. engr., 1979-84, quality devel. engr., 1984-85, sr. quality devel. engr., 1985-86; coord. GM-10 Uniroyal Goodrich Tire Co., Akron, 1986-88, sr. tire devel. scientist, 1988-89; mgr. design and product quality Pirelli Armstrong Tire Corp., New Haven, 1989-90; product design engr. truck ops. Ford Motor Co., Dearborn, 1990-93, vehicle quality and process specialist, corp. quality office, 1993-94, supr. econoline quality and reliability comml. truck, 1995-96, supr. ranger quality and reliability light truck vehicle ctr., 1996-98, supr. explorer quality and reliability truck vehicle ctr., 1998-99, supr. tech. strategy, rsch. and advanced tech., 2000—02, mgr. experience and stability of pers. project,

2002—03; in product devel. Six Sigma Black Belt, 2004—. Mem. Am. Soc. Quality (sr., cert. quality engr.), Soc. Automotive Engrs., Mensa. Home: 9234 Mayflower Plymouth MI 48170 Office: PDC 20901 Oakwood Dearborn MI 48121-2053 Business E-Mail: vlinnans@ford.com.

LINNÉA, SHARON, writer, playwright; d. William Diderichsen and Marilynn Joyce Webber; m. Robert Owens Scott; children: Jonathan Brendan Scott, Linnéa Juliet Scott. Student, Wheaton Coll., 1974-76; BA, NYU, 1978. With editl. dept. various titles William Morrow and Co., N.Y.C., 1977-78, Taplinger and Assocs., N.Y.C., 1978-80, Flying Magazine, N.Y.C., 1982-83; features editor Scholastic Voice, N.Y.C., 1983-85; staff writer Guideposts Mag., N.Y.C., 1985-91, contbg. editor, 1991—99, Angels on Earth, 1995—99; prodr. Inspiration Beliefnet.com, 1999—2002; head writer New Morning Show Hallmark Network, 2002. V.p. Imagining Things Enterprises, N.Y.C.; spkr. in field. Producer (film) Knowing Lisa, 1991 (Silver award Worldfest/Houston film festival); author: (study guide) Romeo and Juliet by William Shakespeare, 1984, Hedda Gabbler and A Doll's House by Henrik Ibsen, 1985, (book) Raoul Wallenberg: The Man Who Stopped Death, 1993 (Best Book of 1993 Jewish World, Dayton Jewish Chronicle, The Speaker), Princess Ka'iulani: Hope of A Nation, Heart of A People, 1999 (Carter G. Woodson award), (with Jeff Meyer) America's Famous and Historic Trees, 2001, Chicken Soup from the Soul of Hawaii, 2003, (plays), Clown of God, 1977, The Singer, 1978, A Matter of Time, 1981, Tales from the Vermont Woods, 1982, (screenplays) Missouri, Ma Cheri, Tomorrow Is My Dancing Day; ghostwriter articles in Reader's Digest and Guideposts Mag.; profile biographer World of Heroes Sch. Curriculum; psychology columnist Beliefnet.com; freelancer Marvel Comics, Children's TV Workship, Hallmark Hall of Fame; freelance editor Chicken Soup for the Soul; contbr. to book pubs. including From the Ashes, 2001, Big Book of Angels, 2002; contbr. articles to popular publs. Recipient Storytelling World award, 2004. Mem.: Authors Guild. Avocations: latching rugs, public speaking. Office: Imagining Things Enterprises 36 Crystal Farm Rd Warwick NY 10990-2862

LINNEY, BEVERLY See HALLAM, BEVERLY

LINNEY, LAURA, actress; b. NYC, Feb. 5, 1964; d. Romulus Linney and Ann Leggett Perse; m. David Adkins, Sept. 1995 (div. 2000). BFA, Brown U., 1986; grad., Juilliard Sch., 1989. Motion picture and T.V. actress. Films include Lonrenzo's Oil, 1992, Searching for Bobby Fischer, 1993, Blind Spot, 1993, Dave, 1993, A Simple Twist of Fate, 1994, Congo, 1995, Primal Fear, 1996, The Truman Show, 1998, Absolute Power, 1998, Lush, 1999, You Can Count on Me, 2000, The House of Mirth, 2000, Running Mates, 2000, Maze, 2000, The Laramie Project, 2002, The Mothman Prophecies, 2002, The Life of David Gale, 2003, Mystic River, 2003, Love Actually, 2003, P.S., 2004, Kinsey, 2004, The Squid and the Whale, 2005, The Exorcism of Emily Rose, 2005, Driving Lessons, 2006, Jindabyne, 2006, The Hottest State, 2006, Man of the Year, 2006, (TV films) Tales of the City, 1993, More Tales of the City, 1998, Love Letters, 1999, Wild Iris, 2001; theatre prodn.: The Crucible, 2002 (Tony nominee). Office: c/o Creative Artists Agy 9830 Wilshire Blvd Beverly Hills CA 90212-1804*

LINOFF-THORNTON, MARIAN GOTTLIEB, retired psychologist; b. Mpls., Feb. 17, 1937; d. Jack and Anne (Meirowitz) Gottlieb; m. Alan Lee Linoff, June 17, 1956 (div. 1968); children: Joseph, Deborah, Gordon; m. Thomas Elton Thornton, July 8, 1984. BA cum laude, U. Minn., 1961, MA, 1963; PhD, U. Miami, Fla., 1972. Lic. psychologist, Fla. Psychologist VA Med. Ctr., Miami, 1971-89; cons. Nat. Humanities Faculty, U. Miami Ctr., 1976-79, Nat. Drug Abuse Tng., 1974-78; specialist in geropsychology and aging. Mem. County Employ Handicapped, Miami, 1980-85. NIMH fellow, 1969-71; recipient Outstanding Performance award VA, 1983, 84, 85, Outstanding Handicapped Employee award Dept. Vet. Affairs, 1986. Mem. Am. Psychol. Assn., Gerontol. Soc. Am., Biofeedback Soc. Am., Fla. Psychol. Assn. (Dade County chpt.), Jewish. Research on geropsychological care of the chronically and terminally ill, psychological assessement of the elderly and medically frail. Home: 7450 SW 140th Dr Miami FL 33158-1281

LINS, DEBRA R., bank executive; BA magna cum laude, Lakeland Coll., 1979; MBA, U. Wis., 1984. Loan officer Farm Credit Svcs., Baraboo, Wis., 1979—83; v.p., sr. lender M&I Bank So. Wis., Sauk City, Wis., 1983—90, First Bus. Bank Madison, Wis., 1990—93; pres., CEO, dir. Cmty. Bus. Bank, 1993—. Bd. dir. Sauk Prairie Meml. Hosp., 1992—98, Sauk Prairie United Way, Inc., 1996—2001, benedictine Life Found. Wis., Inc., 2000—02. Named Disting. Woman in Banking, N.W. Fin. Rev., 1994, Outstanding Entrepreneurial Woman in Dane County, Tempo Madgen, Outstanding Woman in Agr., Assn. Women in Agr., 1998, Wis. Woman of Century, Wis. Woman Mag., 2000, One of 25 Most Powerful Women in Banking, U.S. Banker Mag., 2003; recipient, 2004. Mem.: Am. Banker's Assn. (mem. cmty. bankers coun. 2001—). Office: Community Business Bank 1111 Sycamore St PO Box 636 Sauk City WI 53583-0636 Office Phone: 608-643-6300.

LINSENMEIER, CAROL VINCENT, music educator; b. Manchester, Conn., Feb. 5, 1952; d. Donald Scott and Alys (Campbell) Vincent; m. John Andrew Linsenmeier, Dec. 28, 1979; children: Andrew, Thomas. B Music Edn., Coll. of Wooster, Ohio, 1974; M Music Edn., U. Ga., Athens, 1978; PhD in Spl. Edn., Kent State U., Ohio, 2004. Strings specialist Greenville County Schs., SC, 1974—76; Suzuki coord. U. Ga., Athens, 1977—80; violin/viola tchr. Sch. of Fine Arts, Willoughby, Ohio, 1980—, chair music dept., 1988—2005. Violin and viola tchr. Rabbit Run Cmty. Arts Assn., Madison, Ohio, 2005—, Ashtabula Arts Ctr., Ohio. Arranger: children's musical How Big Is Your Circle, 2000. Rschr., bd. trustees No. Ireland Cmty. Cooperation Initiative, Mentor, Ohio, 1999—2003; sec., bd, trustees Svcs. for Ind. Living, Cleve., 1998—; treas., trustee Suzuki Assn. No. Ohio, Stow, Ohio, 2001—. Mem.: Suzuki Assn. of the Americas, Kappa Lambda, Kappa Delta Pi, Phi Kappa Phi. Avocations: Irish fiddling, Traditional Am. fiddling, needlepoint. Office: The Fine Arts Assn 38660 Mentor Ave Willoughby OH 44094 Office Phone: 440-951-7500. Personal E-mail: carollinsenmeier@mac.com.

LINSEY, ELIZABETH ARLLINE, primary school educator; b. Cleve., Ohio, Dec. 27, 1955; d. Martin Louis and Arline Francis Linsey. BA, Hiram Coll., Ohio, 1979. Materials person U.S. Antarctic Program, McMurdo Station, 1985—94; tchr. grade 2 Southern Pines Primary Sch. Moore County Schs., NC, 1997—. Instr. ARC, 1979—. Named Tchr. of Yr., Southern Pines Primary Sch., 2003. Mem.: Moore County Reading Assn. (sec.), Alpha Delta Kappa. Avocations: swimming, hiking, knitting, rollerblading. Office: Southern Pines Primary Sch 1250 W New York Ave Southern Pines NC 28387

LINTNER, ROBERTA POMPILIO, art educator, artist; b. Wahington, June 26, 1937; d. Ermindo Joseph and Hilda Pompilio; m. John Edwin Lintner, May 23, 1959; children: Cynthia, John. BA, George Wahington U., 1959. Watercolor instr. self employed, Springfield, Va., 1973—87, Springfield Art Guild, 1987—. Represented in permanent collections, U.S. Ho. of Reps., Texco Corp. Hdqrs., N.Y. Mem.: Va. Watercolorists Soc. (juried mem. 1980—), Potomac Watercolorists Soc. (juried mem. 1972—), Am. Watercolor Soc. Avocations: swimming, reading, dance.

LINTON, KRISTY ANN, primary school educator; b. Dothan, Ala., Oct. 11, 1975; d. William Kenneth and Peggy Cobb Linton. BS, Troy State U., 1998; post grad., Fla. State U., U. West Fla. Cert. Early Childhood Edn. Ala., Fla., ESOL. From 2nd grade tchr. to kindergarten tchr. Jackson County Sch., Marianna, Fla., 1998—2001, kindergarten tchr., 2001—03, Alachua County Sch., Gainesville, 2003—. Summer kid's coll. tchr. Chipolia Jr. Coll., Marianna, 2000—01. Vol. Am. Heart Assn.; team capt. relay for life Am. Cancer Soc., Marianna, 1999—2002; vol. cheerleader coach Grand Ridge H.S.; cheerleader judge Jackson County H.S.'s; after sch. tutor; vol. Eastside Bapt. Ch., 2001—. Recipient Internat. Educator Yr. award, Who's Who of Am. Educators, 2004. Republican. Baptist. Avocations: teaching cheerleading, volunteering, tennis, reading. Home: #G302 5133 SW 91st Ct Gainesville FL 32608 Office: Kimball Wiles Elem Sch Gainesville FL 32608 Office Phone: 352-955-6955. E-mail: kristylinton594@hotmail.com.

LINTON, PHYLLIS HEFLIN, mathematics educator; children: David Jonathan, Joel Hugh, Rebecca Linton Stone, Rachel Joy. Student, U. N.C., Asheville, 1970; BS, Miss. Coll., Clinton, 1972; BS in Edn., U. North Ala., Florence, 1987, MA, 1990; postgrad., U. Ala., Huntsville, 2003. Nat. bd. cert. EA math. Nat. Bd. for Profl. Tchg. Stds., 2003, Type I state cert.-highly qualified in mathematics, biology State Dept. Edn., 1990. H.s. math. tchr. Florence City Schs., 1987—. Coll. bd. advanced placement grade reader-stats. Coll. Bd., Princeton, NJ, 2006—. Book cover, autobiography of political figure of Taiwan. Mem. mercy com., initiated tutoring at low income sch. site Redeemer Presbyn. Ch., Florence, 2005—06; ind. ESL tutor/advisor Florence, 1995—2006. Named State Dist. 7 Secondary Tchr. of Yr., State Bd. Edn., 2006—; grantee, Florence Found., 2003, Blue Cross/Blue Shield, 2005. Mem.: Assn. Am. Educators, Nat. Coun. Tchrs. Math. Avocations: writing, hiking, travel, singing. Office: Florence High School 1201 Bradshaw Dr Florence AL 35630 Office Phone: 256-768-2200.

LINTULA, MARGARET M., elementary and secondary school educator; b. Duluth, Minn., June 19, 1941; d. Yule Porter Eaton and Catherine Gurine Fleming Eaton Berg; m. John Elias Lintula, Aug. 17, 1963; 1 child, Maija Gurine Lintula Alexandrou. BS, U. Minn., 1963; MS, U. Wis., Superior, 1975. Lic. elem. tchr., K-12 reading specialist, Wis. Tchr. grade 4 Lakeside Elem. Sch., Duluth, 1963-66; tchr. grades 3-4 Boze Elem., Tacoma, 1967-71; tchr. English grades 7-8 Drummond (Wis.) Sch., 1971—2002, K-12 dist. reading specialist, 1976—2002; ret., 2002. Del. Dem. Nat. Conv., N.Y.C., 1992, state convs., 1988—, vice-chmn. Dem. party, Bayfield County, 1986-02. Named Secondary Tchr. of Yr., Wis. Congress Parents & Tchrs. Inc., 1989—90. Mem. NEA (bd. dirs. 1991-98, mem. women's issues com. 1998-02), Wis. Edn. Assn. Coun. (bd. dirs. 1976-82, 88-98), Drummond Edn. Assn. (pres., chief negotiator 1980-01), Wis. State Reading Assn., Internat. Reading Assn., Lions Club (Cable, Wis. chpt.). Democrat. Avocations: poetry, biking, painting, reading, travel. Home: PO Box 136 Drummond WI 54832-0136

LINVILLE, KIMBERLY E., lawyer; d. Joseph F. and Teresa G. Elam; m. Jacob C. Linville, July 12, 1997; children: Logan Grace, Avery Elizabeth. Asst. dist. atty. gen. Office Dist. Atty. Gen., 25th Jud. Cir., Covington, Tenn., 1999—2001; assoc. atty. Law Office of J. Houston Gordon, Covington, 2001—05; atty. Ashe & Wright, P.C., Tuscumbia, Ala., 2005—. Referee Tipton County Juvenile Ct., Covington, 2004—05. Baptist. Office: Ashe & Wright PC 105 W Second St Tuscumbia AL 35674 Office Phone: 256-383-6357.

LINVILLE, SUSAN ELIZABETH, film studies educator; b. Urbana, Ohio, June 17, 1949; d. Avery and Margaret Alexander Linville; m. Kent Casper, Aug. 30, 1982. PhD, U. Colo., Boulder, Colo., 1979; BA in English Lit., Miami U., Oxford, Ohio, 1971. Lectr. humanities divsn. MIT, Cambridge, Mass., 1979—80; lectr. English dept. U. Colo., Boulder, 1980—81, lectr. humanities dept., 1981—92, lectr. film studies program, 1987—92, asst. prof. English and film studies, Denver, 1992—97, assoc. prof. English and film studies, 1998—2005, prof. English and film studies, 2005—. Author: Feminism, Film, Fascism, 1998, History Films, Women, and Freud's Uncanny, 2004; contbr. articles to profl. jours. Mem.: Soc. Cinema and Media Studies. Democrat. Avocations: travel, hiking, gardening, mushroom hunting. Office: University of Colorado at Denver Dept of English C B 175 PO 173364 Denver CO 80217-3364 Office Phone: 303-556-4795. Business E-Mail: susan.linville@cudenver.edu.

LINZEY, JUANITA BIRD, biology professor; d. Ignacio Acosta and Lucy Jennette Bird; m. Donald Wayne Linzey, May 19, 1985; children: Robert Laurence Holton, David Judson Holton. BS, Marymount Coll., Tarrytown, N.Y., 1963; MS, U. N.C., Chapel Hill, 1965, Va. Tech, Blacksburg, 1993. Rsch. asst./assoc. Fla. State U., Tallahassee, 1968—71; lab. specialist Va. Tech, Blacksburg, 1980—85, med. technologist, 1985—89; asst. prof. New River C.C., Dublin, Va., 1989—99, assoc. prof., 1999—. Textbook reviewer West Pub. Co., Amesbury, Mass., Harper Collins Publishers, N.Y.C.; exam. writer for nursing's standardized human anatomy and physiology exam. Nat. League Nursing, N.Y.C., 1991. Author: (sci. rsch.) Jour. Immunology, Biochimica et Biophysica Acta, Jour. of the Elisha Mitchell Sci. Soc., Jour. of the Helminthological Soc. Washington, (abstract) Sixty-third Con. Rsch. Workers on Animal Diseases, (paper presentation) Fourteenth World Congress on Diseases of Cattle, Am. Soc. Immunology. Dir. Blue Ridge Highlands Regional Sci. Fair, Dublin, Va., 1991—2006. Grantee An Evaluation of Declining Amphibian Populations in Bermuda, Va. C.C. Sys., 1995, A Microbiol. Investigation of Declining Amphibian Populations, New River C.C., 1995, A Microbiol. Evaluation of Declining Amphibian Populations, Va. C.C. Sys., 1996, The Incorporation of Multimedia and Interactive Physiology Software into Human Anatomy and Physiology Lab. Courses, 1997, Devel. of Multimedia Presentations for Integration into Human Anatomy and Physiology Lectures, 1998, Devel. of an Asynchronous Distant Learning Course for Human Anatomy and Physiology, 1999, Devel. of an On-line Course: Intro. to Human Systems, 2000, Devel. of Human Anatomy/Physiology Lab. to a Digitally Produced Experience Comparable to On-Campus Lab. Sessions, 2001. Mem.: Va. Assn. Biol. Edn., Va. C.C. Assn., Human Anatomy Physiology Soc., Nature Conservancy, Phi Kappa Phi. Avocations: bicycling, swimming, scuba diving, hiking, photography. Office: New River CC PO Box 1127 Dublin VA 24084 Office Phone: 540-674-3600. Business E-Mail: nrlinzj@nr.edu.

LINZEY, VERNA MAY, minister, writer; b. Coffeyville, Kans., May 17, 1919; d. Carey Franklin Hall Jr. and Alice May (Hart) Hall-Doyle; m. Stanford Eugene Linzey Jr., July 13, 1941; children: Gena May English, Janice Ellen Mathis, Stanford Eugene III, Virginia Darnelle Lemons(dec.), Sharon Faye, George William, Vera Evelyn Clark, Paul Edward, David Leon, James Franklin. Student, Southwestern Assembly of God U., Waxahachie, Tex., 1938—39, Fuller Theol. Sem., Pasadena, Calif., 1980—. Lic. Minister Assembly of God, 1945. Asst. minister First Assembly of God, Baldwin Park, Calif., 1953—54; co-founder Holy Spirit Evangelism, Escondido, Calif., 1976—. Cons. Holy Spirit Evangelism, Escondido, Calif., 1976—; leader Pentecostal Movement Worldwide, 1976; TV interviews/appearances PBS, 2004, Prime Time Christian Broadcasting Network, 2004. Songwriter: O Blessed Jesus, 2004; author: The Baptism with the Holy Spirit, 2004; contbr. articles to religious publs., 2001—02. Mem. adv. bd. Operation Freedom, 2003—; mem. nat. com. Dem. orgn., 1943—45, Republican Orgn., 1946—. Recipient Cert. of Recognition, Mayor of Escondido, Calif., 2001, Congressional Proclamation Rev. Dr. Verna May Linzey Day April 29th, 2001. Avocations: gardening, piano, photography, genealogy, singing. Home: 1641 Kenora Dr Escondido CA 92027 Office: Verna M Linzey 354 E Washington Ave Ste A Escondido CA 92025 Office Phone: 760-735-8961. Personal E-mail: vlinzey@aol.com.

LION, LINDA N., retired federal agency administrator; b. Brookline, Mass., Feb. 18, 1949; m. Donor M. Lion, Sept. 29, 1978; 2 children. BA in Biology, Wheaton Coll., 1970; PhD, MIT, 1975; grad., Nat. Def. U., Ft. Lesley J. McNair, Washington, 1990. Instr. human nutrition MIT, Cambridge, 1975-76; ind. nutrition cons. Haiti, Dominican Republic, Ghana, Bolivia, 1976-77; regional health and nutrition adviser Health & Nutrition Divsn. Office Devel. Resources Bur. Latin Am. and Caribbean USAID, Washington, 1977-78; dir. Office Health, Population & Nutrition USAID, Jamaica, 1978-79; health devel. officer, officer policy devel. & program rev. Bur. Policy and Program Coord. USAID, Washington, 1979; dir. Office Health Population & Nutrition USAID, Guyana, 1979-81, dir. Office Project Devel. & Monitoring Pakistan, 1981-85; chief Mid. East Divsn. Office Project Devel. Bur. Asia and Near East USAID, Washington, 1985-86; chief Capital Devel. Project Divsn. USAID, Peru, 1986-87, dir. Office Human Resources, 1987-89, dep. dir. Office Info. Resources Mgmt. Bur. Mgmt. Washington, 1990-94, mission dir. regional support mission for East Asia Bangkok, 1994-96, dep. asst. adminstr. human resources Bur. Mgmt. Washington, 1996—2000, dep. asst. adminstr. global programs, 2000—02. Avocations: golf, bridge. Office: 6600 Baymeadow Ct Mc Lean VA 22101

LIONE, GAIL ANN, lawyer; b. NYC, Oct. 22, 1949; d. James G. and Dorothy Ann (Marsino) L.; 1 child, Margo A. Peyton. BA in Polit. Sci., magna cum laude, U. Rochester, 1971; JD, U. Pa., 1974. Bar: Pa. 1974, Ga. 1975, D.C. 1990, N.C. 1998. Atty. Morgan, Lewis & Bockius, Phila., 1974-75, Hansell & Post, Atlanta, 1975-80; v.p. 1st Nat. Bank of Atlanta, 1980-86; sr. v.p., corp. sec., gen. counsel Sun Life Group of Am., Inc., Atlanta, 1986-89; v.p. Md. Nat. Bank, Balt., 1989-90; gen. counsel, sec. U.S. News & World Report, L.P., Applied Graphics Technologies, Atlantic Monthly Co., Washington, 1990—97; v.p., gen. counsel, sec. Harley-Davidson, Inc., Milw., 1997—. Bd. mgrs. U. Pa. Law Sch., 1982-85. Sec., dir., com. chair State Bar Ga. (Young Lawyers Sect.), 1976-84; Chmn. bd. Spl. Audiences, Inc., 1983-85, bd. dirs., 1975-89; trustee Client Security Fund State Bar Ga., 1985-89; vice chmn. Metro Atlanta United Way Campaign, 1986-87; chmn. bd. Atlanta Ballet, 1985-86, bd. dirs., 1975-89; mem. Atlanta Legal Aid Soc., 1981-89; bd. mngrs. U. Pa. Law Sch., 1982-85; mem. U. Rochester Trustee Coun., 1994—; bd. dirs. YMCA Balt., 1989-90; past bd. dirs. Metro YMCA, Atlanta, Sudden Infant Death Syndrome Inst., Atlanta Cmty. Food Bank; mem. Leadership Atlanta, 1988; mem. fin. com. Nat. Symphony Ball, 1995; adv. bd. Cardiovascular Ctr. Medical Coll. Wis., 1999-2002; mem., bd. dirs. Bradley Ctr. Sports & Entertainment Corp., 2003-; Milw. Art Mus., 2004-, Outstanding Atlanta award, TOYPA, 1982, outstanding Vol. Golden Rule award, 1984; named Top 40 Under 40 Atlanta Mag., 1984, Top 20 Women in Atlanta by Atlanta Bus. Chronicle, 1987; teaching fellow Salzburg Inst., 1989. Mem. ABA (mem. ho. delegates, 1980-84, chmn. standing com. comm. on assn. comms., 1993-96, co-chair. litig. sect. com. fed. legis. 1994—96, regional co-chair forum on comms. law, 1996—98, standing com. on publishing oversight and strategic comms., 1996-2000), Copywright Soc. USA (trustee 1996-99), Manufacturing Inst., 2002-, Nat. Assn. Manufacturers, Phi Beta Kappa Office: Harley Davidson 3700 W Juneau Ave PO Box 653 Milwaukee WI 53201-0653 Office Phone: 414-343-4044.

LIONE, SUSAN GARRETT, consultant; b. Boston, May 23, 1945; d. Charles Gerard and Josephine (Galgano) Garrett; m. Gerald Frederick Lione, Nov. 9, 1968; children: Mark Garrett, Christina Marie. BA in Econs., Immaculata Coll., 1966. Investment asst. Morgan Guaranty Trust, N.Y.C., 1966-69; portfolio mgr. Union Trust Co., Stamford, Conn., 1969-72; sales coord. Japan Air Lines, Hong Kong, 1977-84; mktg. coord. Hong Kong Tennis Patron Assn., 1982-84; ind. study on schs. Cen. Pk. Task Force, N.Y.C., 1990; sales assoc. Preferred Properties, New Canaan, Conn., 1991-96; assoc. HTG Investment Advisors, Inc., New Canaan, 1997—. Pres. Am. Women's Assn., Hong Kong, 1977-78; sec. New Canaan CARES, 1989-90, v.p., 1990-91, pres., 1991-93, mem. adv. bd., 1998—. Bd. dirs. United Way New Canaan, 1994-2000, bd. sec., 1996-98, mem. allocations com., 1994—, allocations chmn., 1995-96, bd. chmn., 98-2000; bd. dirs. Vol. Ctr. Lower Fairfield County, 1996-99, sec., 1997-98, mem. adv. bd., 1999—; mem. lay adv. bd. St. Aloysius Ch., New Canaan, 1994, 95-98, 2003—. Avocation: tennis. Office: HTG Investment Advisors 50 Locust Ave New Canaan CT 06840 Office Phone: 203-972-8262.

LIOTTA, JEANNE, film director, film instructor; b. NYC, 1960; Film instructor Sch. Mus. Fine Arts, Boston; vis. artist Bard, San Francisco Art Inst. Dir.: (films) Blue Moon, 1988, Soma Sema, 1988, Open Sesame, 1989, Fungus Eroticus, 1990, Dervish Machine, 1992, Cici N'est Pas, 1997, What Makes Day and Night, 1998, Muktikara, 1999, Struck by the Hand, 2001, Window, 2001, L'air du Temps, 2003, One Day This May No Longer Exist, 2005; Exhibited in group shows at Whitney Biennial, Whitney Mus. Art, 2006, Internat. Film Festival, Rotterdam, Pacific Film Archives, Berkeley, Calif., Anthology Film Archives, NYC, Mus. Modern Art, NYC. Fellow MacDowell Colony, 2002; grantee Jerome Found., NY State Coun. Arts, Experimental Television Ctr. Office: SMFA Boston 230 The Fenway Boston MA 02115*

LIOTUS, SANDRA MARY, lighting designer, small business owner, consultant; b. Pitts., Aug. 23, 1959; d. George A. Liotus and Marlene A. Rouse. BFA in Design, Carnegie Mellon U., Pitts., 1984. Designer George Kovacs Lighting, Inc., N.Y.C., 1985-89; lighting designer with LeMar Terry N.Y.C. and Hoboken, N.J., 1993-95; lighting design cons. Sandra Liotus Lighting Design, LLC, N.Y.C., 1995—, Newport, RI, 1995—. Cons. in field. Avocation: lighting design. Office: Sandra Liotus Lighting Design LLC 68 William St Newport RI 02840-3309 Fax: 401-845-8949. Office Phone: 401-845-9236. E-mail: sandraliotus@cox.net.

LIPIEC, SHERRY ANN, art educator; d. John Theodore and Marie Doris Kleinsteiber; m. Edward R. Lipiec, Apr. 6, 1974; children: Karsten, Blase. BS in art edn., Western Mich. U., 1967; EMU in high scope tng. and continuing edn., Eastern Mich. U., 1998, Wayne State U., 1994. Cert. K-12 art tchr. Mich. 7th-9th grade art tchr. Kelly Jr. High, East Detroit, Mich., 1967—68, 1969—75; 9th-12th grade art tchr. San Francisco Unified Schs., 1968—69; pre-school tchr. Chelsea Cmty. Edn., Mich., 1985—89, Sat. program art tchr., 1985, 1988; substitute tchr. K-5th grade Chelsea Sch. Dist., Maine, 1990—93; K-5th grade tchr. Lincoln Consolidated Schs., Ypsilanti, Mich., 1994—2000; elem. art tchr. Grass Lake Schs., Grass Lake, Mich., 2000—. Sch. guide, interpreter Waterloo Farm Mus., Munith, Mich., 1994—98; parent helper Cubscouts/Boy Scouts, Chelsea, Mich., 1986—98; helping parent Chelsea Schs., Mich., 1989—90; mem. PTO program Lincoln Schs., Ypsilanti, Mich., 2000—. Grantee Scholarship, Western Mich. U., 1967. Mem.: Mich. Edn. Assn., Mich. Art Edn. Assn. Avocations: antiques, sewing, mosaic work, ceramics. Home: 2000 McKinley Rd Chelsea MI 48118

LIPINSKI, ANN MARIE, publishing executive; b. Trenton, Mich. m. Steve Kagan; 1 child, Caroline. B in Am. Studies, U. Mich. Joined Chgo. Tribune, 1978, named head investigative team, 1990, assoc. mng. editor met. news., 1991—93, dep. mng. editor, 1994—95, mng. editor, 1995—2000, v.p. & exec. editor, 2000—01, sr. v.p. & exec. editor, 2001—. Juror Pulitzer Prize, 2001, 02; mem. Pulitzer Prize Bd., 2003—. Bd. visitors Poynter Inst., U. Mich. Journalism Fellows program, Stanford U. Journalism Fellows program. Recipient Pulitzer Prize for investigative reporting, 1988; Nieman Fellowship Harvard U., 1989-90. Office: Chgo Tribune 435 N Michigan Ave Chicago IL 60611-4066*

LIPKE, KATHRYN, artist, educator; b. Cooperstown, N.D., Dec. 16, 1939; d. Herluf O. and Ruth E. Vigesaa; children: Tanya, Shannon. BS, N.D. State U., Fargo, 1962; MA, U. Calif., Berkeley, 1969. Prof. faculty fine arts Concordia U., Montreal, 1977—96, founder fibres, dept. sculpture, ceramic and fibres, 1977—96, assoc. dean rsch. faculty fine arts, 1992—96, prof. emeritus, 1997; docent prof. sculpture U. Lapland, Rovaniemi, Finland, 1997—. Vis. artist and prof. Goldsmiths Coll., U. London, Acad. Art and Design, Lodz, Poland, U. Calif., Davis, Emily Carr Coll. Art, Vancouver, B.C., Canada,, Ont. Coll. Art and Harborfront, Toronto, Form Design Ctr., Malmo, Sweden; lectr. textiles Coll. of Marin, Kentfield, Calif., 1972-1974, Ind. U., Bloomington, 1973; lectr. Hartford Arts Sch., U. Hartford, 1977; sculptor, with works in U.S., Cordoba, Argentina, Kemijarvi and Levi Tunturi, Finland, Germany; numerous corp. commns.; solo and group art exhbns. in U.S., Can., Europe; prodr., dir. video Shadows on the Hand, 2005. Vol. art orgns., women's groups, environ. groups, 1969—. Recipient Outstanding Documentary Video Prodn. award Maya Women of Guatemala, 1993, 97, Seagram Fund Acad. Innovation, Re-presenting Women, 1995-97; fellow NEA, 1977-78; grantee Vt. Arts Coun. and NEA, 2004. Mem.: Nat. Mus. Women in the Arts (Vt. state com.), RAVA (Assoc. Visual Arts), Textile Soc. Am., Assoc. Ind. Video and Filmmakers, USA. Home and Office: Laraway Studio LLC 6559 Vt Route 109 Belvidere Center VT 05442-9699 Office Phone: 802-644-2821. E-mail: kathlv@mt-mansfield.com.

LIPKIN, BERNICE SACKS, computer scientist, educator; b. Boston, Dec. 21, 1927; d. Milton and Esther Miriam (Berchuck) Sacks; m. Lewis Edward Lipkin; children: Joel Arthur, Libbe Lipkin Englander. BS in Biology and Chemistry, Northeastern U., 1949; MA in Psychology, Boston U., 1950; PhD in Exptl. Psychology, Columbia U., 1961. Rsch. and devel. scientist Directorate Sci. and Tech., CIA, Washington, 1964-70; scientist dept. computer sci. U. Md., Greenbelt, 1971-72; health sci. adminstr. NIH, Bethesda, Md.,

1972-88; cons. computerized text analysis, data exploration L+B and Co., Bethesda, 1989—. Author: String Processing and Text Manipulation in C, 1994; editor: Picture Processing and Psychopictorics, 1970, Latex for Linux, 1999; contbr. articles on computer-based text searches and data analysis to profl. publs. Cerebral Palsy Soc. fellow in neurophysiology, 1961—62, NIH trainee, 1955—58. Mem. AAAS, IEEE, APA, Optical Soc. Am., Assn. Computing Machinery, Sigma Xi. Jewish. Achievements include design of system for manipulation and analysis of text data files, documentation and instruction manuals; teaching children computer concepts and programming. Office: 9913 Belhaven Rd Bethesda MD 20817-1733 Personal E-mail: bslipkin@erols.com.

LIPMAN, MARILYN LEE, retired elementary school educator; b. St. Louis, July 22, 1938; d. Gustav A. and Gertrude (Berman) Vittert; m. David Lipman, Dec. 10, 1961; children: Gay Ilene, Benjamin Alan. BA, Washington U., St. Louis, 1959; MAT, Webster U., 1985. Cert. tchr., Mo. Tchr. elem. schs. Kirkwood (Mo.) Sch. Dist., 1959-63; tchr. jr. high sch. Parkway Sch. Dist., St. Louis County, Mo., 1977, ret., 1998. Co-author: Jim Hart, Underrated Quarterback, 1977. Bd. dirs. St. Louis chpt. Am. Jewish Com., 1991—, Am. Jewish Congress; trustee United Hebrew Congregation, 1977-79. Mem. NEA, Phi Beta Kappa. Democrat. Jewish. Home: 21 Old Belle Monte Rd Chesterfield MO 63017-6052

LIPMAN-BLUMEN, JEAN, public policy and organizational behavior educator; b. Brookline, Mass., Apr. 28, 1933; AB, Wellesley Coll., 1954, AM, 1956; PhD, Harvard U., 1970; postgrad., Carnegie-Mellon U., 1970-71, Stanford U., 1971-72; LHD (hon.), U. La Verne, 2005. Asst. dir., Nat. Inst. Edn., dir women's rsch. program, 1973-78; spl. asst., mem. domestic policy staff The White House, Office of Asst. Sec. Edn.; pres. LBS Internat., Ltd., 1979-84; prof. orgnl. behavior Claremont (Calif.) Grad. U., Thornton F. Bradshaw prof. pub. policy Peter F. Drucker and Masatoshi Ito Grad. Sch. Mgmt., 1983—. Vis. prof. sociology and orgnl. behavior U. Conn., 1978—80, U. Md., 1980—82; spkr. in field; cons. Exec. Office of Pres., Dept. State, Dept. Labor, Dept. HHS, Dept. Agr., Dept. Edn., Bell Labs., Singapore Airlines, MarketIndex, Finland, various fgn. govts.; tchr. exec. mgmt. and MBA programs. Author, editor (with Jessie Bernard): Sex Roles and Social Policy, 1978; author: The Paradox of Success: The Impact of Priority Setting in Agricultural Research and Extension, 1984, Metaphor for Change: The USDA Competitive Grants Program, 1978-84, 1985, Gender Roles and Power, 1984, Women in Corporate Leadership: Reviewing a Decade's Research, 1996, The Connective Edge: Leading in an Independent World, 1996 (Pulitzer prize nomination); author: (with Harold J. Leavitt) Hot Groups: Seeding, Feeding, and Using Them to Ignite Your Organization, 1999 (Best Book award Assn. Am. Pubs., 1999); author: Connective Leadership: Managing in a Changing World, 2000; author: (with Grace Gabe) Step Wars: Overcoming the Perils and Making Peace in Adult Stepfamilies, 2004, Making Adult Stepfamilies Work-Strategies for the Whole Family When a Parent Marries Later in Life, 2005; author: The Allure of Toxic Leaders: Why We Follow Destructive and Corrupt Politicians-and How We Can Survive Them, 2005. Fellow, Ctr. Advanced Study Behavioral Sci., 1978, 1979. Fellow: AAAS. Office: Claremont Grad U 1021 N Dartmouth Ave Claremont CA 91711 Office Phone: 909-621-8083. Personal E-mail: jeanlipman@earthlink.net.

LIPNICK, ANNE RUTH, advocate; b. Cambridge, Mass., Aug. 9, 1943; d. Henry and Celia Florence (Weinberg) Goldberg; m. Robert Louis Lipnick, June 11, 1967; children: Deborah Ellen Lipnick Bort, David Henry. BA, Brandeis U., 1965; MSW, U. Minn., 1972. Rsch. asst. Brandeis U., Waltham, Mass., 1965—66; social worker Divsn. Child Guardianship, Boston, 1966—68, Jewish Family Svc., St. Paul, 1968—70, Family and Children's Svcs., Stamford, Conn., 1974—78; coord. spl. edn. parent resource ctr. Alexandria (Va.) City Pub. Schs., 1989—. Study group chair Children Together, Alexandria, 1999—; mem. Early Intervention Interagency Coordinating Coun., Alexandria. Exec. com. Brookville-Seminary Valley Civic Assn., Alexandria, 2002—03; v.p. for youth svcs. Agudas Achim Congregation, Alexandria, 1999—2001. Recipient Riggs-ARC Ednl. Leadership award, Assn. for Retarded Citizens No. Va., 1991, John Duty Collins III Outstanding Adv. for Persons with Disabilities award, Alexandria Commn. on Persons with Disabilities, 1996. Mem.: NASW (cert. 2005). Home: 5308 Pender Ct Alexandria VA 22304 Office Phone: 703-706-4552. Business E-Mail: alipnick@acps.k12.va.us.

LIPPA, CAROL FRANCES, neurologist; b. Erie, Pa., Aug. 19, 1955; d. John Winn and Dorothy Marie (Zarembski) Ryan; m. Robert Leo Lippa, July 1982; children: Sara Marie, Alex Mitchell, Adam Lee. BA, McGill U., 1978; MD, U. Mass., 1983. Diplomate Am. Bd. Psychiatry and Neurology, Am. Bd. Neurorehab. Intern St. Vincent Hosp., Worcester, Mass., 1983—84; resident in neurology U. Mass. Med. Ctr., Worcester, 1984—86, chief resident, 1986—87, resident in neuropathology, 1987—88, fellow neurobiology of aging, 1988—89, asst. prof. neurology, 1989—95, dir. brain donation program, 1993—, investigator clin. drug trials, 1992—; physician neurorehab. svc. Fairlawn Rehab. Hosp., 1992—96; prof. neurology Drexel U. Coll. Medicine, Phila., 1996—; chief neurology svc. Med. Coll. Pa.-Hahnemann U., Phila., 2000—03, dir. Memory Disorders Ctr., 1996—. Contbr. more than 150 abstracts and articles to profl. jours. Recipient 2d prize residents and fellows presentation, Boston Soc. Neurology and Psychiatry, 1985. Mem.: Phila. Neurol. Soc. (pres. 2004—05), Am. Neurol. Assn., Am. Soc. Neurorehab., Soc. Neurosci., Am. Acad. Neurology, Alpha Omega Alpha. Home: 16 Radcliff Rd Bala Cynwyd PA 19004-2631 Office: Hahnemann Hosp Mailstop 423 245 N 15th St Philadelphia PA 19102

LIPPARD, LUCY ROWLAND, writer, educator, critic, curator; b. NYC, Apr. 14, 1937; d. Vernon William and Margaret Isham (Cross) L.; m. Robert Tracy Ryman, Aug. 19, 1961 (div. 1968); 1 child, Ethan Isham Ryman. BA, Smith Coll., 1958; MA in Art History, NY Inst. Fine Arts, 1962; DFA (hon.), Moore Coll. Art, 1972, San Francisco Art Inst., 1984, Maine Coll. Art, 1994, Mass. Coll. Art, 1998, Art Institute of Chgo., 2003. Freelance writer, lectr., curator, 1964—; rsch. assoc. Mus. N.Mex., Santa Fe. Prof. Sch. Visual Arts, N.Y.C., Williams Coll., Queensland U., Brisbane, Australia, U. Colo., Boulder; mem. adv. bd. Franklin Furnace, N.Y.C., 1979—; co-founder, bd. dirs. Printed Matter, N.Y.C.; bd. dirs. Ctr. Study Polit. Graphics, L.A., Time & Space Ltd., Hudson, NY, Sustainable Settings, Woody Creek, Colo., Earth Works Inst., Santa Fe, Ctr. Am. Pls., Stanton, Va.; co-founder W.E.B., Ad Hoc Women Artist's Com., Artists Meeting for Cultural Change, Heresies Collective and Jour., Artists Call Against US Intervention in Ctrl. Am., Polit. Art Documentation/Distbn.; lectr. in field. Author: Pop Art, 1966, The Graphic work of Philip Evergood, 1966, Changing: Essays in Art Criticism, 1971, Tony Smith, 1972, Six Years: The Dematerialization of the Art Object, 1973, From the Center: Feminist Essays on Women's Art, 1976, Eva Hesse, 1976, (with Charles Simonds) Cracking (Brüchig Werden), 1979, Issue: Social Strategies by Women Artists, 1980, Ad Reinhardt, 1981, Overlay: Contemporary Art and the Art of Prehistory, 1983, Get the Message? A Decade of Art for Social Change, 1984, Mixed Blessings: New Art in a Multicultural America, 1990, A Different War: Vietnam in Art, 1990, The Pink Glass Swan: Selected Feminist Essays on Art, 1995, The Lure of the Local: Senses of Place in a Multicentered Society, 1997, Florence Pierce: In Touch With Light, 1998, On the Beaten Track: Tourism, Art and Place, 1999, (with Alfred Barr and James Thrall Soby) The School of Paris, 1965, (novel) I See/You Mean, 1979; author, editor: Partial Recall: Photographs of Native North Americans, 1992; editor: Surrealists on Art, 1970, Dadas on Art, 1971; contbg. editor: Art in Am.; founding editor El Puente de Galisteo, 1997—; contbr. monthly columns Village Voice, 1981-85, In These Times, Z Mag., also numerous articles to mag., anthologies, and mus. catalogs, 1964—; curator 50 exhbns.; performer in guerrilla and st. theater. Mem. Santa Fe County Open Lands and Trails Planning and Adv. Com. (COLTPAC), 1999. Recipient Frederick Douglass award North Star Fund, 1994, Frank Jewett Mather award for criticism Coll. Art Assn., 1974, Claude Fuess award for pub. svc. Phillips Andover Acad., 1975, curating award Penny McCall Found., 1989, citation NYC mayor David Dinkins, 1990, Smith Coll. medal, 1992, Athena award RISD, 2004; Guggenheim fellow, 1968, ArtTable award, 1999; grantee Lannan Found., 2000. Avocations: hiking, rock art, local history. Office Phone: 505-466-1276.

LIPPENS, NANCY COBB, music educator; b. Albuquerque, Nov. 15, 1951; d. Ernest Oscar and Mona Faye Hill; m. Larry W. Cobb, July 2, 1977 (div. Mar. 1992); children: Cary Andrew, Allison Elizabeth; m. Stephen Frank, Jan. 8, 2000. BM, Okla. Bapt. U., 1973; MM, Mich. State U., 1975; DMA, U. Okla., 1987. Instr. music Mercer U., Macon, Ga., 1975—76, Okla. Bapt. U., Shawnee, Okla., 1976—2002; prof. music Dallas Bapt. U., 2002—06; founding dir. music Fla. Gulf Coast U., 2006—. Reader and table leader AP music theory ETS, Princeton, NJ, 2000—. Composer: Threnody for chorus and orch., 1998 (ASCAP Spl. Distinction award in Rudolph Nissim competition, 1998), The Seven Last Words. Com. chair Habitat for Humanity, Shawnee, 1999—2000; pres. Shawnee Band Boosters, 1999—2000; bd. dirs. Shawnee Little Theater, 2001—02. Mem.: Am. Choral Dirs. Assn. (Okla. Dir. of Distinction 1995), Pi Kappa Lambda, Sigma Alpha Iota (Nat. Leadership award 1973). Avocations: tennis, reading. Office: Fla Gulf Coast U 10501 FGCU Blvd S Fort Myers FL 33965 Office Phone: 239-590-7374. Business E-Mail: ncobb@fgcu.edu.

LIPPINCOTT, JANET, artist, art educator; b. N.Y.C., May 16, 1918. Student Emil Bisttram, Taos., N.Mex., Colorado Springs Fine Art Ctr., Art Students League N.Y.C., San Francisco Art Inst. Artist in residence, Durango, Colo., 1968; guest artist Tamarind Inst., Albuquerque, 1973; participant TV ednl. programs, Denver, Albuquerque; art instr. Santa Fe Community Coll., N.Mex., 1984—. Participant juried exhbns. including: Denver Mus., 1968, N.Mex. Arts Commn. traveling shows, 1967, Chautauqua Exhbn. Am. Art, N.Y., 1967, High Mus., Atlanta, Butler Inst. Am. Art, Springfield, Ohio, Dallas Mus. Fine Art, Mid Am. Exhbn., Nelson Atkins Mus., Kansas City, Kans., Mus. Fine Arts, Houston, Denver Art Mus., U. N.Mex. Art Gallery, Albuquerque, Ball State Tchrs. Coll., Muncie, Ind., N.Mex. Painting Invitational, 1968, Colorado Springs Fine Art Ctr., 1968, N.Mex. Biennial, Santa Fe, 1969, 72, 73 (award 1962), Tyler Mus. Art, Tex, 1977, Santa Fe Arts Festival, 1978, 79, 80, Enthios Gallery, Santa Fe, 1987; participant invitation exhbns. including: Albuquerque Mus. Art, 1977, Bethune & Moore, Denver, 1969, Yellowstone Art Ctr., Billings, Mont., 1967, Tucson Fine Art Ctr., 1965, Hockaday Sch., Dallas, 1965, Hayden Calhoun Galleries, Dallas, 1966, Leone Kahl Gallery, Dallas, 1965, U. Utah, Salt Lake City, 1966, Roswell Mus. and Art Ctr., N.Mex., 1963, Lucien Labaudt Gallery, San Francisco, 1963, Denver U.S. Nat. Ctr., 1963, Muse d'Art Moderne, Paris, 1962, Instituto Cultural, Mexico City, 1957, Colo. State Coll., Greeley, 1961, Highland U., Las Vegas, N.Mex., 1960-70, St. John's Coll., Santa Fe, 1965, 75, 80, Coll. Santa Fe, 1968, 81, 4748 Galleries, Oklahoma City, 1965, Owen Gallery, Denver, 1970, New West Gallery, Albuquerque, 1970, 71, 72, 73, 74, Columbia Fine Arts Mus., S.C., 1972, Arts and Crafts Mus., Columbus, Ga., 1972, Dubose Gallery, Houston, 1972, Jamison Gallery, Santa Fe, 1972, Tex. Tech U., Lubbock, 1973 (award), Triangle Gallery, Tulsa, 1973, Gallery 26, Tulsa, 1974, West Tex. Mus., Lubbock, 1976, Britton Gallery, Denver, 1975, 77, 78, 79, 80, Osborne Gallery, Winnipeg, Ont., Can., 1979, Blair Gallery, Santa Fe, 1979, 80; works represented in pvt. and mus. collections; represented by Fletcher Gallery, Santa Fe, 1989-90; Day Star Internat. Galleries, Albuquerque, 1990; New Directions Gallery, Taos, N.Mex., 1995—; Laurel Seth Gallery, Santa Fe, N.Mex., 1995—; Tartan Pony Gallery, 1995—; New Directions Gallery, Taos N. Mex., 1996, Karen Ruhen Gallery, Santa Fe, 1996. With WAC, 1943-45, ETO. Purchase awards and prizes include: Southwestern Biennial, Santa Fe, 1966, N.Mex. Mus. Fine Arts, 1957, Roswell Mus., 1958, Okla. Art Ctr., Oklahoma City, 1962, Atwater Kent award, Palm Beach, Fla., 1963, Chautauqua Art Award Assn. prize, 1963, El Paso Mus. prize, 1962, 76. Home and Office: PO Box 52 Riverdale MD 20738-0052

LIPPMAN, DONNA ROBIN, counselor; b. N.Y.C., Jan. 26, 1950; 1 child, Benjamin Aaron Steinberger-Lippman. BA, U. Wis., 1971; MS, CCNY, 1977. Ordained and lic. Interfaith min. 2002; cert. Rubenfeld synergist. Dir., clinician Incest/Rape Recovery Ctr., N.Y.C., 1989—; exec. dir. Incest Awareness Found., N.Y.C.; interfaith minister, 2005. Cons. N.Y.C. Creator To Tell the Truth: Am. Speaks Out Against Incest and Sexual Abuse, N.Y.C., 1993, 1994, 1999—2002. Office: Incest Recovery Ctr 853 Broadway Ste 2022 New York NY 10003-4703 Office Phone: 212-598-4281. E-mail: donnarobin@incestrecovery.org.

LIPPMAN, LAURA, writer; b. Atlanta; BS in Journalism, Northwestern Univ. Reporter Waco Tribune-Herald, Tex., 1981—83, San Antonio Light, 1983—89, Balt. Evening Sun, 1989—91, Balt. Sun, 1991—2001. Author: (novels) Baltimore Blues, 1997, Charm City, 1997 (Edgar award, Shamus award, Anthony award nominee), Butchers Hill, 1998 (Agatha award, Anthony award, Edgar, Shamus, Macavity awards nominee), In Big Trouble, 1999 (Anthony award, Shamus award, Edgar, Agatha awards nominee), The Sugar House, 2000 (Best PI Novel of Yr. nominee, Romantic Times), In a Strange City, 2001 (NY Times Notable Book), The Last Place, 2002, Every Secret Thing, 2003 (Anthony award, Barry award, Nero Wolfe award), By a Spider's Thread, 2004 (Edgar Award nominee for best novel, 2005), To the Power of Three, 2005, No Good Deeds, 2006. Recipient Mayor's award for lit. excellence, Balt. Mailing: c/o Author Mail William Morrow 10 E 53rd St New York NY 10022*

LIPPMAN, SHARON ROCHELLE, art historian, filmmaker, art therapist; b. N.Y.C., Apr. 9, 1950; d. Emanuel and Sara (Goldberg) L. Student, Mills Coll., Columbia U., 1968; BFA, New Sch. Social Rsch., 1970, CCNY, 1972; MA in Cinema Studies, NYU, 1976, postgrad., 1987. Cert. secondary tchr., N.Y.; cert. in nonprofit orgn. mgmt. Instr., dir., founder Sara Sch. of Creative Art, Sayville, NY, 1976-85; founder, exec. dir., tchr. Art Without Walls, Inc., Sayville and N.Y.C., 1985—; curator art exhbn. Mus. Without Walls Heckscher State Park, East Islip, NY, 1985-87; exec. dir., curator Profl. Artist Network for Artists Internationally, 1991—; founder Art Without Walls, Inc., 1985—, Mus. Without Walls, Ctrl. Park, N.Y.C., 2005. Organizer Profl. Artist Network for Nat./Internat. Artists, 1994; curator Pub. Art in Pub. Spaces,Scott Landoll Art Exhbn., West Islip; instr. art therapy sessions Maryhaven Ctr. Pub. Libr., Port Jefferson, N.Y., 2004, Mus. Without Walls - Rhapsody in Art, 2006; head art therapy project Mary Haven Ctr., Port Jefferson, N.Y., 2004; origami zoo art therapist Southside Hosp., Bayshore, N.Y., 2005. Author: Patterns, 1968, College Poetry Press Anthology, 1970, America at the Millennium, 2000; exhibited in group shows at L.I. Children's Mus., Garden City, N.Y., 1995-97, Suffolk County Legislature, Hauppauge, N.Y., 1997, Bayport-Bluepoint Libr., 1997, East Islip Libr., 1997-98, U.S. Dept. Interior, Ft. Wadsworth, N.Y., 2001, Ellis Island Immigration Mus., N.Y., 2002, West Islip Libr., 2000-01, Battery Park, N.Y.C., 2002, Central Park, N.Y.C., 2003, Spirit Walk Gallery, Sayville, N.Y., 2003, Within These Walls, Nassau County Detetion Ctr., Westbury, N.Y., 2003, By Land or By Sea, South St. Seaport, N.Y.C., 2004, Southside Hosp., Bayshore, N.Y., 2005, West Islip (N.Y.) Libr., 2005, South Country Libr., Bellport, N.Y., 2005, Mus. Without Walls-Central Park, N.Y.C., 2005, 06, South County Libr., Bellport, N.Y., 2005, Nassau County Detention Ctr., 2005, Nassau Denention Ctr., Westbury, NY, 2006, others; art exhbn. By Land or By Sea, So. Street Seaport, N.Y.C., 2004; pub. art mural History of L.I. Baymen, 1987, Immigration on the NYS Waterways, 2001, Art Therapy Program and Exhbn. at Leadership Tng. Inst., Hempstead, N.Y., 2003, Nassau County Detention Ctr., 2003, Southside Hosp., Bay Shore, N.Y., 2004, West Islip Pub. Libr., NY, 2006, Mus. Without Walls, NYC, 2006; represented in permanent collection Devel. Disabilities Inst., Suffolk County Legis. Bldg., Polish Consulate, N.Y., West Islip Pub. Libr., East Islip Pub. Libr., Ctrl. Park Zoo, Coll. Art Assn. Bull. Conv. N.Y., Robert Moses State Park, N.Y., Smith Haven Mall Lake Grove, Garden City Mall, N.Y., Southside Hosp., Bayshore, Rhapsody in Art, Mus. Without Walls, N.Y.C., 2006, Nassau Detention Ctr., Westbury, N.Y., 2006; art therapy program and exhbn. Leadership Tng. Inst., 2003, Suffolk Outreach Project, Art Therapy Wellness Program, 2003, Miko Travelling Show, 2006, Mary Haven Ctr., Port Jefferson Station, NY, 2004, Miko Mus. Art Therapy Play Travel Show, 2006. Vol. Good Samaritan Hosp., 1984, Southside Hosp., 1983, U. Stony Brook Hosp., 1985, Schneider Children's Hosp., New Hyde Park, N.Y., 1992, New Light-AIDS Patients, Smithtown, N.Y., 1993, Helen Keller Svcs. for the Blind, Hempstead, N.Y., 1993-94, St. Charles Hosp. and Rehab. Ctr., 1996, Nat. Health Bill Pub. Forum, Sayville Mid. Sch., 1996, Art Puzzles-Art Therapy Geriatrics Ward, Brookhaven (N.Y.) Meml. Hosp., 1990, Art Therapy Program Original Dept. Disabilities, Suffolk County, N.Y., 1988, Din-o-Soar Art Therapy Southside Hosp.-Pediatrics Ward, Bayshore, N.Y., 1999, Art Box-Art Therapy, Pediat. Ward Southside Hosp., Bayshore, 2000, It Takes Two Art Therapy, St. Charles Hosp., Port Jefferson, N.Y., 2000; mem. Whitney Mus., Guggenheim Mus., Mus. Modern Art, Met. Mus. Art, Jewish Mus., Mus. of the City of N.Y., Art in Am., Art News, Am. Artist; trustee Sayville Libr. Bd., 1996; bd. dirs. Friends of the Arts St. Joseph's Coll., N.Y., 1997. Recipient Suffolk County New Inspiration award, 1990, 2006, Am. Artist Art Svc. award Am. Artists mag., 1993, Suffolk County Legis. proclamation, 1993, Newsday Leadership Vol. award Newsday newspaper, 1994, Nat. Women's Month award Town of Islip, 1996, Disting. Women's award Town of Islip, 1996, Nat. Poetry Press award, 1996, Cmty. Action award Suffolk County Ret./Sr. Vol. Program, 2002; named to L.I. Vol. Hall of Fame for Cultural Arts, 2004; Inspiration award Suffolk County News, 2005. Mem. Orgn. Through Rehab. and Tng., Coll. Art Assn., Met. Mus. Art, Mus. Modern Art Univ. Film Assn., Sayville C. of C. Avocations: fine art, books, cinema, political science, inventions. Office: Art Without Walls Inc PO Box 2066 New York NY 10185-2066 also: Art Without Walls Inc PO Box 341 Sayville NY 11782 Office Phone: 631-567-9418. Business E-Mail: artwithoutwalls@webtv.net.

LIPPMAN SALOVESH, DOROTHY, nurse practitioner; b. Long Beach, Calif., Feb. 10, 1950; d. Emile Ferrer and Virginia Frances Lippman; children: Launa, Benjamin, Diana. ADN, Chaffey Coll., 1982; BSN, Calif. State U., Fullerton, 1995; MSN, UCLA, 1999; postgrad., U. Calif., Irvine, 2003. RN, Calif.; family nurse practitioner, gerontological nurse practitioner. Staff nurse St. Jude Med. Ctr., Fullerton, 1982—2002, palliative care nurse practitioner, 2003—; primary care nurse practitioner with Christopher Lundquist, 2002—06. Mem.: Hospice and Palliative Nurses Assn., Am. Acad. Hospice and Palliative Medicine, Am. Coll. Nurse Practioners, Calif. Assn. Nurse Practioners, Nat. Conf. Gerontol. Nurse Practioners, Nat Gerontol. Nurse Assn., Am. Acad. Nurse Practitioners, Sigma Theta Tau. E-mail: dlippman@rocketmail.com.

LIPPOLD, JUDITH ROSENTHAL, retired occupational therapist; b. Chgo., Feb. 27, 1931; d. Irving and Shulamite Hurwitz Rosenthal; m. Henry William Lippold, May 4, 1952; children: Luanne Joy, Laura Beth. BS in occupational therapy, U. Wisc., 1951. Occupational therapist Holladay Park Hosp., Portland, Oreg., 1952-53, Ruth Lodge Residential Tng. Ctr. for C.P. Children, Chgo., 1953-54, The Threshold, Champaign, Ill., 1968-72, Sacred Heart Hosp., Eau Claire, Wis., 1972-96, Next Step, Brotoloc Corp., Eau Claire, 1996-97; facilitator Renewing Life program Sacred Heart Hosp., Eau Claire, 1997—. Leadership roles PTA and Girl Scout Am., Champaign, Ill., 1962-72; newsletter editor Chippewa Valley Ostomy Assn., 1992—. Avocations: reading, drawing, painting, writing. Home: 1304 Bradley Ave Eau Claire WI 54701-6523

LIPS, HILARY MARGARET, psychology educator, writer; b. Ottawa, Ont., Can., June 17, 1949; d. Hilaire John Lips and Justine Mary Dantzer; m. Wayne K. Andrew, May 9, 1986. BA with honors, U. Windsor, 1970; MA, Northwestern U., 1973, PhD, 1974. From asst. prof. to prof. psychology U. Winnipeg, Manitoba, Canada, 1974—89; prof. psychology, dir. Ctr. Gender Studies Radford U., Va., 1989—; dir. women's studies Radford U., 1999—2003, chair, psychology dept., 2003—. Vis. scholar women's studies U. Ariz., Tucson, 1980-81, 88-89, U. Costa Rica, San José, 1994; vis. scholar edn. U. S. Fla., Tampa, 1993; coord. sect. women and psychology Can. Psychol. Assn., 1983-84; mem. adv. bd. Women's Ctr., Va. Tech. U., Blacksburg, 1995-97; adj. prof. psychology U. Winnipeg, 1987-1989. Author: Women, Men and Power, 1991, Sex and Gender: An Introduction, 5th edit., 2005, A New Psychology of Women: Gender, Culture, and Ethnicity, 3rd. edit., 2006. Recipient Jessie Bernard Paper award Nat. Coun. Family Rels., 1998, Disting. Am. Scholar award New Zealand U.S. Ednl. Found., 1998. Fellow APA, Can. Psychol. Assn. (Disting. Mem. award 2006); mem. Assn. Women in Psychology (Disting. Publ. award 1992). Office: Dept Psychology Radford U PO Box 6946 Radford VA 24142-6946 Office Phone: 540-831-5387. Business E-Mail: hlips@radford.edu.

LIPSCOMB, CAROL MATTHEWS, science educator; b. Jackson, Tenn., Sept. 11, 1958; d. George Ross and Joyce Crocker Matthews; 1 child, Matthew Ross. A, Jackson State CC, 1983; BS in Biology, Lambuth U., Jackson, Tenn., 1986; M in Spl. Edn., U. Memphis, 1997. Cert. tchr. Tenn., 1987, secondary edn. Lambuth U., Jackson, Tenn., 1987. Tchr. Tigrett Jr. HS, Jackson, Tenn., 1992—94, West Mid. Sch., Denmark, Tenn., 1994—. Animal keeper Ark Rain Found., Brownsville, Tenn., 1999—. Eisenhower Sci. grant, Eisenhower Found., 1999, Travel grant, People to People, 2005. Mem.: NSTA, NEA, Jackson Madison County Edn. Assn., Tenn. Edn. Assn. Home: 1548 Campbell St Jackson TN 38305 Office: West Mid Sch 317 Denmark Rd Denmark TN 38391 Office Phone: 731-988-3810. Home Fax: 731-988-3810; Office Fax: 731-988-3810. Personal E-mail: cmlips@wmconnect.com.

LIPSCOMB, LAURA, information architect; d. Joe L. and Jane Bivins Lipscomb; 1 child, Sean Baker. BA, Tex. A&M U., Corpus Christi, 1983—86. Cert. e-commerce, So. Meth. U., 2000; chemical pers. reliability program Dept. Def., 1987. Surety analyst SW Rsch. Inst., San Antonio, 1987—96; info. arch. Xceed, Dallas, 2000, i2 Technologies, Dallas, 2001, Imaginuity, Dallas, 2003; bus. analyst Susan G. Komen Breast Cancer Found., Dallas, 2003—04; info. arch. TracyLocke, Dallas, 2004—. Recipient Recognition award for methodology devel., SW Rsch. Inst., 1996. Mem.: Internat. Acad. Visual Arts. Achievements include development of methodology to detect three types of chemical warfare agents simultaneously on one instrument. Avocations: travel, gardening.

LIPSCOMB-BROWN, EDRA EVADEAN, retired childhood educator; b. Marion, Ill., Aug. 3, 1919; d. Edgar and Anna Josephine (Wiesbrodt) Turnage; m. July 5, 1939 (div. Sept. 1950); 1 son, H. Alan; m. Mark S. Brown, 1981. BS, So. Ill. U., 1955; MA, U. Mich., 1955; Ed.D., Ind. U., 1962; postgrad., U. Minn. Tchr. Benton (Ill.) Elem. Schs., 1939-54, DeKalb (Ill.) Consol. Schs., 1955-56; mem. faculty No. Ill. U., DeKalb, 1956-81, prof. elem. edn., 1967-81, chmn. elem. and childhood edn., 1978-81, ret., 1981. Ednl. cons. to various schs., No. Ill.; mem. vis. accreditation com. Nat. Council Accreditation Tchr. Edn., Kent State U., 1974, U. Wis.-Stout, 1975; co-author, director numerous projects sponsored by U.S. Office Spl. Edn., 1979-81 Author: Lipscomb Teacher Attitude Scale; Contbr. articles to profl. jours. Research grantee No. Ill. U., 1965, 73; Research grantee State of Ill., 1972-73 Mem. Internat. Reading Assn., Internat. Assn. Supervision and Curriculum Devel., NEA, Ill. Edn. Assn., Assn. Higher Edn., Am. Ednl. Research Assn., Pi Lambda Theta. Democrat. Home: 2015 S Curson Ave Los Angeles CA 90016-1104

LIPSHUTZ, LAUREL SPRUNG, psychiatrist; b. Easton, Pa., Dec. 11, 1946; d. Joseph A. and Helen A. (Rochlin) S.; m. Robert M. Lipshutz, June 15, 1975; 1 child, Jonathan. BA, U. Pa., 1968; MD, Albany Med. Coll. of Union U., 1972. Diplomate Am. Bd. Psychiatry and Neurology. Resident in psychiatry Johns Hopkins Hosp., Balt., 1972-75; unit chief psychiat. inpatient unit Phila. Gen. Hosp., 1975-77; dir. psychiat. inpatient svc. Pa. Hosp., Phila., 1977-96; assoc. dir. residency tng. Inst. of Pa. Hosp., Phila., 1983-96; coord. psychiat. clerkship for U. Pa. med. students Pa. Hosp., Phila., 1982-95; psychiatrist, 1995—. Sr. examiner Am. Bd. Psychiatry and Neurology, 1979—; sr. attending psychiatrist Inst. Pa. Hosp., Phila., 1989-97, psychiatrist, 1984—; clin. assoc. prof. psychiatry U. Pa. Sch. Medicine, Phila., 1997—, Thomas Jefferson Med. Coll., Phila. 1994-97. Fellow Am. Psychiat. Assn. (disting.); mem. Am. Soc. Psychoanalytic Physicians, Pa. Psychiat.

Assn. (com. on women), Phila. Psychiatry Soc., Assn. Acad. Psychiatry (region III Excellence in Tchg. award 1995). Office: The Curtis Ctr 601 Walnut St Ste 960W Philadelphia PA 19106 Office Phone: 215-923-7851. Office Fax: 215-592-7853.

LIPSKY, LINDA ETHEL, business executive; b. Bklyn., June 2, 1939; d. Irving Julius and Florence (Stern) Ellman; m. Warren Lipsky, June 12, 1960 (div. Sept. 1968); 1 child, Phillip Bruce; m. Jerome Friedman, Jan. 17, 1988. BA in Psychology, Hofstra U., 1960; MPS with hon. in Health Care Adminstrn., Long Island U., 1979. Child welfare social worker Nassau County Dept. Social Svc., NY, 1960-64; adminstr. La Guardia Med. Group of Health Ins. Plan of Greater N.Y., Queens, 1969-72; cons. Neighborhood Svc. Ctr., Bronx, NY, 1973-78; dir. ODA Health Ctr., Bklyn., 1978-82; pres. Millin Assocs., Inc., Nassau, NY, 1982—. Mem. NAFE, Health Care Fin. Mgmt. Assn., Nat. Assn. Cmty. Health Ctrs., Cmty. Health Ctrs., Assoc. of NY, Hofstra U. Alumni Assn. (mem. senate 1984—, chair membership com. 1985—), Pi Alpha Alpha. Republican. Jewish. Avocations: cooking, writing, reading. Office: Millin Assocs Inc 521 Chestnut St Cedarhurst NY 11516-2244 Personal E-mail: llipsky@millinmedical.com.

LIPSKY, PAT, artist; b. NYC, Sept. 21, 1941; d. Bernard G. and Bernice D. (Brown) Sutton; children: David Lipsky, Jonathan Lipsky. BFA, Cornell U., 1963; postgrad., Bklyn. Mus. Art Sch., 1960-61, Art Student's League, 1963; MA, Hunter Coll., 1968. Faculty Fairleigh Dickinson U., 1968-69, Hunter Coll., 1972, San Francisco Art Inst., 1974; assoc. prof. U. Hartford, 1983—2002. Guest lectr. Hirshhorn Mus., 1975, Va. Commonwealth U., Bennington Coll., 1977, U. Pitts., 1974, NYU, 1983, SACI, Florence, 1986, Springfield Mus., 1987-88, U. Miami, 1992, Pollock-Krasner House and Study Ctr., East Hampton, L.I., N.Y., 1995, Am. U., 1997, Muhlenberg Coll., 1999; guest lectr. Parsons Sch. Design, 1990, lectr., 1982-83, 90; instr. SUNY, Purchase, 1980-81; adv. coun. Cornell U. Coll. Art and Architecture, 1988—. One-woman shows include Andre Emmerich Gallery, N.Y.C., 1970, 72, 74, 75, Deichter O'Reilly Gallery, 1976, Medici-Berenson Gallery, 1976, Everson Mus., 1970, Gloria Luria Gallery, Miami, 1988, Slater-Price Gallery, NYC, 1986, Hartell Gallery Cornell U., 1989, Andre Zarre Gallery, 1991, Virginia Miller Gallery, Coral Gables, Fla., 1994, Bookstein Fine Arts, N.Y.C., 1997, The Kitchen, 1999, Elizabeth Harris Gallery, 1999, 2001, 03, 04, Piltzer Gallery, Barbizon, France, 2002, L.I.C.K. Ltd. Fine Art, Long Island City, NY, 2003, Elizabeth Harris Gallery, 2004, New Monotypes, Aurobora Press Gallery, San Francisco, 2005, Cathedral of St. John the Divine, NY, 2006, Elizabeth Harris Gallery, NY, 2006, others; exhibited in group shows at Whitney Mus. Am. Art, 1971, Hirshhorn Mus. and Sculture Garden, 1975, Promenade Gallery, Hartford, 1984, U. Mass. Art Gallery, Amherst, 1987, Gloria Luria Gallery, 1988, 92, Andre Zarre Gallery, 1990, 95, Denise René Gallery, Paris, 1993, Gallery One, Toronto, 1996, Snyder Fine Art, NYC, 1996, Lori Bookstein/Fine Arts, 1997, Am. Acad. Arts & Letters, 2001, DC Moore Gallery, 2004, Am. Embassy, Sarajevo, Bosnia, 2005; represented in permanent collections Herbert Johnson Mus., Ithaca, NY, Witney Mus., Hirshhorn Mus., Walker Art Ctr., Hunter Coll., Fogg Art Mus., Harvard U., San Francisco Mus. Art, Bklyn. Mus., Blanton Mus. Art, U. Tex., Austin, Wadsworth Atheneum, Hartford, Portland Mus. Art, Mus. Fine Arts, Houston, State Dept. U.S.; stage designer (play) Custody, Westbeth Theatre, N.Y.C., 1991; works include silkscreen and poster edit. Lincoln Ctr./List Great Performers Series, 2004. Recipient Childe Hassam Purchase prize AAAL, 2001; grantee N.Y. State Coun., 1972, N.Y. Found. Arts, 1992, Jerome Found., 1999, Adolph & Esther Gottlieb Found., 1999, Pollock-Krasner Found., 2000; sponsorship from Winsor and Newton Paint Co., 1992; fellow Va. Ctr. for Creative Arts, 1986, 93, Tyrone Guthurie Centre, Co., Moneghan, Ireland, 1996. Home: 410 W 24th St New York NY 10011-1303 Studio: 526 W 26th St Rm 1011 New York NY 10001-5541 Personal E-mail: pslipsky@aol.com.

LIPSON, PAMELA, information scientist; m. Pawan Sinha. BA, Harvard U., 1989; MS, MIT, 1993, PhD, 1996. Postdoctoral rschr. Artificial Intelligence Lab., MIT, 1996—97; co-founder, pres., CEO, Imagen, Inc., 1997—. Achievements include development of technology for encoding alphanumeric and graphical information with high density on crystalline substrates. Office: Imagen Inc 955 Massachusetts Ave # 351 Cambridge MA 02139

LIPSTADT, DEBORAH E., Jewish and Holocaust studies professor; BA, CCNY; MA, PhD, Brandeis Univ. Dir., Rabbi Donald A Tam Inst. for Jewish Studies Emory Univ., Atlanta, and Dorot prof. of Modern Jewish and Holocaust Studies, 1993—. Hist. cons. US Holocaust Meml. Mus.; apptd. to US Holocaust Meml. Coun., 1994; appt. to Adv. Com. on Religious Freedom Abroad, 1996. Author: Beyond Belief: The American Press and the Coming of the Holocaust, 1986, 1993 (finalist Nat. Jewish Book award), Denying the Holocaust: The Growing Assault on Truth and Memory, 1993 (NY Times Notable Book, Nat. Jewish Book Honor award, 1994), History on Trial: My Day in Court with David Irving, 2005; contbr. articles to LA Times, Washington Post, Cleve. Plain Dealer, Atlanta Constitution, Balt. Sun, NY Times, Time, Newsweek, NY Newsday, others. Office: Tam Inst Jewish Studies 204C Candler Libr 550 Asbury Cir Atlanta GA 30322 Office Phone: 404-727-2298. Office Fax: 404-727-7597. Business E-Mail: dlipsta@emory.edu.

LIPTON, BRONNA JANE, marketing communications executive; b. Newark, May 10, 1951; d. Julius and Arlene (Davis) L.; m. Sheldon Robert Lipton, Sept. 23, 1984. BA in Spanish, Northwestern U., 1973. Cert. Zumba Instructor. Tchr. Spanish Livingston (N.J.) H.S., 1973-78; profl. dancer Broadway theater, film, TV, N.Y.C., 1978-82; v.p., mgr. Hispanic mktg. svcs. Burson-Marsteller Pub. Rels., N.Y.C., 1982-89; exec. v.p. Lipton Comm. Group, Inc., N.Y.C., 1989-99, Latin Reports, 1996-99; v.p. Bienestar LCG Comm., Inc., 1999—2003; prin. Cmty. Direct, N.Y.C., 2003—. Minority initiatives task force Am. Diabetes Assn., Alexandria, Va., 1987-90, pub. rels. com., 1990-91, visibility and image task force, 1991-92, bd. dirs. NY Downstate affiliate, chmn. visibility and image com., 1992-93. Mem. rev. panel Hispanic Designers, Inc. Recipient Pinnacle award Am. Women in Radio and TV (NY Chpt.), 1984, Value Added award Burson-Marsteller, NYC, 1982-84. Avocations: ballet, jazz dance, tennis, foreign travel, birding. Home: 1402 Chapel Hill Rd Mountainside NJ 07092-1405 Office Phone: 212-966-8222. Business E-Mail: blipton@gocommunitydirect.com.

LIPTON, JACKIE F., artist, educator; b. N.Y.C., Jan. 23, 1950; d. Victor Samuel and Helen Duberstein Lipton; m. John Christopher Bolton, Oct. 17, 1990. BA, Fordham U., 1978; postgrad. in Arts Edn., Sch. Visual Arts, N.Y.C., 1993-94; MFA in Painting, Milton Avery Grad. Sch. Arts, Annandale-on-Hudson, N.Y., 1994. Art educator in spl. edn. P35, N.Y.C., 1994—. One person shows include Art Resources Transfer Gallery, 2001, 02; exhibited in group shows West Chelsea Open Art Studio Festival, 1997, 98, 99, Westbeth Gallery, N.Y.C., 1999, 2004, 05, 06, Art Resources Transfer Gallery, 1999, 2000, 01, Gale-Martin Fine Art, N.Y.C. 2001-02, Gallery Boreas, N.Y.C., 2003, 04, others; peer studio artist Art Resources Ctr. of Whitney Mus. Am. Art, N.Y.C., 1973-75; gallery artist Condeso/Lawler, 1983-88, Gale-Martin Fine Art, N.Y.C. 2001-03. Grantee Pollock-Krasner Found., 1985-86, 86-87, 99-2000; fellow Macdowell Colony, 1988, Cummington Cmty. of the Arts, 1990, Va. Ctr. for Creative Arts, 1991, 93, 95, 97, 99-2000. Home: 55 Bethune St Apt A515 New York NY 10014-2010 Studio: 526 W 26th St Rm 619 New York NY 10001-5523 Office Phone: 212-633-0127. Personal E-mail: jaaris@nyc.rr.com.

LIPTON, JOAN ELAINE, advertising executive; b. NYC, July 12, 1927; 1 child, David Dean. BA, Barnard Coll., 1948. With Young & Rubicam, Inc., NYC, 1948-52, Robert W. Orr & Assocs., NYC, 1952-57, Benton & Bowles, Inc., NYC, 1957-64; asso. dir. Benton & Bowles, Ltd., London, 1964-68; with McCann-Erickson, Inc. (advt. agy.), NYC, 1968-85, v.p., 1970-79, sr. v.p., creative dir., 1979-85; pres. Martin & Lipton Advt. Inc., 1985—. Mem. Bus. Coun. UN Decade Women, 1977-78; bd. vis. PhD program bus. CUNY, 1986—. Recipient Honors award Ohio U. Sch. Journalism, 1976, Matrix award, 1979, YWCA award women achievers, 1979, Clio Classic award; named Woman Yr., Am. Advt. Fedn., 1974, Advt. Woman Yr., 1984; named Matrix Hall Fame, 1998. Mem. Advt. Women NY (1st v.p. 1975-76, v.p. Found. 1977-78), Women's Forum (bd. dirs. 1988-90), Women Comm. (pres. NY chpt. 1974-76, named Nat. Headliner 1976). Office: 163 E 62nd St New York NY 10021-7613 Office Phone: 212-832-3049. Personal E-mail: joanlipton@nyc.rr.com.

LIPTON, NINA ANNE, healthcare executive; b. NYC, Oct. 6, 1959; d. Robert and Rita Kay (Wolfman) L. BA in Econs., Wellesley Coll., Mass., 1981; postgrad., London Sch. Econs., 1981-82. Rsch. asst. Nat. Econ. Rsch. Assocs., White Plains, N.Y., 1983-84; cons. A.T. Hudson and Co., Paramus, N.J., 1984; asst. economist Dean Witter Reynolds, N.Y.C., 1984-89; dir. market rsch. Platinum Guild Internat., N.Y.C., 1989-94; v.p., exec. dir. Ctr. for Alternative Healthcare, Inc., Miami, Fla., 1995-98; exec. dir. Summit Med. Group, Conn., Ga., Ala., Mich., 1995—2001; prin. Lipton Cons., 2003—. Exec. dir., v.p. Aztec Mgmt. Co., 1995-2001; cons. in field Writer This Week in Platinum weekly, 1989-94; contbr. articles to profl. jours. Recruiter, fundraiser, reunion com. chair Wellesley (Mass.) Coll. Alumnae Assn., 1982—, spl. gifts com., 1991, co-chair 20th reunion 2000-01, ann. giving rep. '81, 2001-04, ann. giving com., 2002-04, 25th reunion com., 2004—; dir. Women's Outreach, Erskine Bowles for U.S. Senate, N.C., 2002; annual issues forum Leadership Am., NC, 2005; founder N-Squared Strategic Vision for Non-Profits and Small Bus., 2006; commr. Charlotte-Mecklenburg Planning Commn., 2005—. Office Phone: 704-372-7028. E-mail: Nina_Lipton@alum.wellesley.edu.

LIPTON, SUSAN LYTLE, investment banker, lawyer; b. Ft. Warren, Wyo., Oct. 23, 1945; d. James and Bette Lytle; m. Martin Lipton, Feb. 17, 1982. AB, U. Miami, 1967, JD, 1970; LLM, Harvard U., 1971. Bar: Fla. 1970, N.Y. 1984. From assoc. to ptnr. Greenberg Traurig Askew, Miami, Fla., 1970-77; from assoc. to v.p. Goldman Sachs & Co., N.Y.C., 1988-81; from v.p. to mng. dir. L.F. Rothschild, Unterberg, Towbin, N.Y.C., 1981-86. Trustee Jewish Mus., 1986—, chmn., 2002-04; trustee Brearley Sch., 1991-2005, Wildlife Conservation Soc., 1991-2005; trustee, pres. Jewish Communal Fund, 1992-97.

LISANDRELLI, ELAINE SLIVINSKI, secondary school educator; b. Pittston, Pa., July 11, 1951; d. Leo Joseph and Gabriella Alexandra (Sharek) Slivinski; m. Carl A. Lisandrelli, June 20, 1980. BA, Marywood U., Scranton, Pa., 1973, MS, 1976. Cert. secondary tchr. English and counselor, Pa. Tchr. English North Pocono Mid. Sch., Moscow, Pa., 1973—. Part-time instr. Marywood U., 1986-2000; ednl. cons., Pa., 1988-93. Author: Maya Angelou: More Than a Poet, 1996 (Carter G. Woodson honor), Bob Dole: Legendary Senator, 1997, Ida B. Wells-Barnett: Crusader Against Lynching, 1998, Ignacy Jan Paderewski: Polish Pianist and Patriot, 1999, Jack London: A Writer's Adventurous Life, 1999; co-author: Creating Lifelong Learners: Strategies for Success; contbr. chpt. to book, articles to lit. mags. Named to the Young Adult's Choice List, 1998. Mem. Nat. Coun. Tchrs. English, Soc. Children's Book Writers and Illustrators, Pa. Edn., Assn., Kosciuszko Found., Polish Arts and Cultural Found. Avocations: aerobics, reading, researching, movies. Office: North Pocono Mid Sch Church St Moscow PA 18507 Office Phone: 570-842-4588. Personal E-mail: caleml@aol.com.

LISBOA-FARROW, ELIZABETH OLIVER, public and government relations consultant; b. N.Y.C., Nov. 25, 1947; d. Eleuterio and Esperanza Oliver; m. Jeffrey Lloyd Farrow, Dec. 31, 1980; 1 child, Hamilton Oliver Farrow; 1 stepchild, Maximillian Robbins Farrow. Student pvt. schs., N.Y.C. With Harold Rand & Co. and various other pub. rels. firms, N.Y.C., 1966—75; dir. pub. rels. N.Y. Playboy Club and Playboy Clubs Internat., 1975—79; pres., CEO Lisboa Assocs., Inc., N.Y.C., 1979—. Counselor Am. Woman's Devel. Corp. Sec. Nat. Acad. Concert and Cabaret Arts; mem. nat. adv. coun. SBA, 1980-81, apptd., 1994—; exec. dir. Variety Club of Greater Washington Children's Charity, Inc., 1985-90; bd. dirs. Variety Myoelectric Limb Bank Found., 1990-91, Comcast, 2001, Hispanic Radio Network, 2001, Group Hosp. and Med. Svcs., Inc. d/b/a Carefirst Blue Cross Blue Shield, 2005; co-chmn. Hispanic Coll. Fund, 1995—, vice chair, 1996—, co-chair, 2005—; chair bd. trustees Southeastern U., 1997-2004; mem. adv. bd. Indsl. Bank, N.A., 1996. Named Pub. Rels. Woman of Yr., Women in Pub. Rels., 1992, Empresaria del Milenio, Duodecimo Encuentro Empresarian, P.R., 2001, Hispanic Bus. Woman of Yr., Nat. Hispanic Bus. Coun., 1996, Hispanic of Yr. in Bus., La Nacion Newspaper, 1997, Entrepreneur of Yr., Hispanic Mag., 1999, Bus Woman of Yr., N.Y. State Hispanic Chambers Commerce; recipient Disting. award of Excellence, SBA, 1992, Women Bus. Enterprise award, U.S. Transp. Nat. Hwy. Transp. Safety Adminstrn., 1994, Civic Cmty. Achievement, Black Bus. and Profls. Network, 1999, Excellence in Entrepreneurship award, Dialogue on Diversity, Inc., 1995, Women of Distinction award, Nat. Conf. Coll. Women Student Leaders, 2000, Applause award, Women's Bus. Enterprise Nat. Coun., 2000, Imagen award, San Juan, P.R., 2001, Presdl. medal, Sistema U. Ana G. Mendez, U. Metropolitana, San Juan, 1999, Internat. Leadership award, Mex. Am. C. of C., 2001. Mem. U.S. Hispanic C. of C. (bd. dirs. 1998-2004, Nat. Hispanic Businesswoman of Yr. 1996, vice chair 1999, chair 2000-02), D.C. C. of C. (pres. 2000), Small Bus. Adv. Coun., U.S. C. of C. (Blue Chip Enterprise award 1993), Advt. Coun., Am. Heart Assn., Hispanic Bus. and Profl. Women's Assn., Ibero-Am. C. of C. (bd. dirs. 1993, v.p. 1995, pres. 1997, 1998, adv. chair 1999, Small Bus. award 1993, Corp. of Yr. award 2000), Nat. Edn. Assn. Found. (bd. dirs. 2004). Office: 5335 Wisconsin Ave NW Washington DC 20015 Office Phone: 202-737-2622. E-mail: elisboa@lisboa.com.

LISENBY, DORRECE EDENFIELD, realtor; b. Sneads, Fla., Dec. 2, 1942; d. Neal McLendon and Linnie (McCroan) Edenfield; m. Wallace Lamar Lisenby, Nov. 18, 1961; children: Pamela Ann, Wallace Neal. BS in Tech. Bus. magna cum laude, Athens (Ala.) State Coll., 1991. Stenographer State of Fla., Tallahassee and Miami, Fla., 1960-62, Gulf Oil Corp., Coral Gables, Fla., 1962-64, Gulf Power Co., Pensacola, Fla., 1965-68; loan svc. asst. First Fed. Savs. and Loan Assn., Greenville, SC, 1969-70; various real estate positions Greenville, 1978-85; adminstrv. asst. Charter Retreat Hosp., Decatur, Ala., 1986-91; broker/salesperson Ferrell Realty Plus, Inc., Tallahassee, 1995-2001; broker, owner Lisenby Realty, Inc., 2001—. Mem.: P.E.O. Sisterhood, Tallahassee C. of C., Econ. Club Fla., Tallahassee Symphony Soc., Killearn Ladies Club (pres.), Taylor's Garden Club (prs. Taylor's chpt. 1975—76), Avondale Forest Cmty. Club (pres. Taylors, S.C. chpt. 1969), Am. Legion (Citizenship award 1957). Republican. Baptist. Avocations: reading, music, bridge, gardening. Home: 2925 Shamrock St S Tallahassee FL 32309-3226 Office Phone: 850-383-7567. Business E-Mail: dorrece@lisenbyrealty.com.

LISHAK, LISA ANNE, secondary school educator; b. Berlin, Nov. 27, 1960; (parents Am. citizens); d. Richard Edward Brogdon and Martha (Shuman) Gault; m. Robert Stephen Lishak, Apr. 22, 1989; 1 child, Trent Stephen. BS, Auburn U., 1989, postgrad., 2002—; MEd, Ala. State U., 1998. Cert in early adolescence/generalist category, Ala.; nat. bd. cert. tchr. Nat. Bd. for Profl. Tchg. Stds. Substitute tchr. Lee County, Auburn, Opelika Schs., Ala., 1989; tchr. math. Lanett (Ala.) Jr. High Sch., 1989-91, Opelika (Ala.) Mid. Sch., 1992-95; instr. math. So. Union C.C., Opelika, 1998-2000; tchr. algebra I and pre-algebra Russell County Middle Sch. formerly Jr. High Sch., Ala., 2000—04, Russell County H.S., Ala., 2004—06, Loachapoka H.S., Ala., 2006—. Mem. TEAM-Math. Usher Trinity Luth. Ch., Auburn, Ala., 1989—. Master sgt. USAF, 1978-84, mem. Res., 1978-2000, ret. Recipient Appreciation plaque Math-A-Thon, St. Jude's Children's Hosp., 1991, 2003; named Tchr. of Month, ALFA Ins. Co., 2003; Ala. Power grantee, 1993-94, 2002-03, site-based mgmt. grantee Opelika Mid. Sch., 1994-95, Russell Co. Schs., 2001-02, grantee NIKE, Inc., 2002-03, 2005-06, Best Buy, 2004, SEARCH Found., 2005-06. Mem. NEA, Nat. Coun. Tchrs. Math., Chattahoochee Coun. Tchrs. Math., Ala. Edn. Assn., Columbia Regional Math. Collaborative, Phi Kappa Phi, Kappa Delta Pi, Pi Lambda Theta. Home: 789 Annabrook Dr Auburn AL 36830-7529 Office: Loachapoka HS PO Box 187 Loachapoka AL 36865

LISHER, MARY KATHERINE, lawyer; b. 1950; BA cum laude, Vanderbilt U., 1972; JD summa cum laude, Ind. U., Bloomington, 1975. Ptnr. Baker & Daniels, Indpls. Bd. dirs. Lilly Endowment, Inc., Indpls., 1997—, Indpls. Neighborhood Housing Partnership, 1996—, sec., 1999—2001, vice chmn., 2001—03, chmn., 2003—. Mem.: ABA, Indpls. Bar Assn. Office: Baker & Daniels Ste 2700 300 N Meridian St Indianapolis IN 46204 Office Phone: 317-237-1081. Office Fax: 317-237-1000. E-mail: Mary.Lisher@bakerd.com.

LISI, DEBORAH JEANNE, nurse supervisor; b. Providence, Apr. 10, 1949; d. Henry Joseph and Alice Deborah Brown; m. Robert Guido Lisi, Nov. 6, 1971; 1 child, Sheryl Deborah. BS, Boston U., 1971; MS, U. RI, 1977. Cert. diabetes educator U. RI Coll. Pharmacy, 2005. Asst. prof. nursing Cmty Coll. RI, Lincoln, RI, 1972—81; sales assoc. Uptown Baby, E. Greenwich, RI, 1994—96; mgr., cons. Cinderella's Bridal, E. Greenwich, 1996—2000; staff nurse RI Renal Inst., Warwick, RI, 2000—01, Pawtucket Valley Urgent, Conventry, RI, 2001—04; adj. instr. New England Inst. of Tech., Warwick, RI, 2003—; nurse supervisor CCAP Family Health Svc., Cranston, RI, 2004—. Chmn. infection control CCAP, Cranston, RI, 2004—; mem. med. adv. com. Family Planning Dept. Health, RI. Founder Outreach Quilters, E. Greenwich, RI, 1989—97; mem. Our Lady of Mercy Outreach Steering Com., E. Greenwich, 1992—98. Mem.: Cert. Diabetes Outpatient Educators (bd. mem., mem. credentialing com., fin. officer, bd. dirs.), Boston U. Alumni, R.I. State Nurses Assn., ANA. Cath. Avocations: quilting, embroidery, knitting, reading, exercise. Home: 147 Wunnegin Cir East Greenwich RI 02818 Office: CCAP Family Health Svcs 1090 Cranston St Cranston RI 02920 Office Phone: 401-943-1981. Business E-Mail: dlisi@comcap.org.

LISI, MARY M., federal judge; BA, U. R.I., 1972; JD, Temple U., 1977. Tchr. history Prout Meml. H.S., Wakefield, RI, 1975—76; law clk. U.S. Atty., Providence, 1976, Phila., 1976—77; asst. pub. defender R.I. Office Pub. Defender, 1977—81; asst. child adv. Office Child Adv., 1981—82; also. pvt. practice atty. Providence, 1981—82; dir. office ct. apptd. spl. adv. R.I. Family Ct., 1982—87; dep. disciplinary counsel office disciplinary counsel R.I. Supreme Ct., 1988—90, chief disciplinary counsel, 1990—94; U.S. Dist. judge Dist. Ct., Providence, Dist. R.I. (1st cir.), Providence, 1994—. Mem. Select Com. to Investigate Failure of R.I. Share and Deposit Indemnity Corp., 1991-92. Recipient Providence 350 award, 1986, Meritorious Svc. to Children of Am. award, 1987. Office: Fed Bldg and US Courthouse 1 Exchange Ter Providence RI 02903-1744

LISK, MARTHA ANN, rehabilitation services professional; b. Manchester, Conn., Jan. 20, 1956; d. Burton Roy and Ruth Elizabeth (Coe) L. BA, Colo. State U., 1978; MA, U. No. Colo., 1983. Rehab. counselor State of Colo. Rehab. Ins. Svcs. for Employment, Loveland, 1984-86; owner, mgr. Pro-Three One Wear, Loveland, 1986-89; coord. employment and tng. Epilepsy Found. Am., Denver, 1989-93; vocat. rehab. counselor II Kans. Rehab. Svcs., Garden City, 1993—. Summer youth counselor Colo. Job Svc., Aurora, 1984; adv. Colo. Rehab. Svcs. Adv. Bd., Denver, 1991-93; pres. Job Developers Network, Denver, 1992. Contbr. articles to popular mags. Vol. Friends the Nat. Parks at Gettysburg. Mem. Nat. Trust for Hist. Preservation. Avocations: reading, civil war living history, historical research. Home: 2103 Commanche Dr Garden City KS 67846-3827 E-mail: mlisk0120@aol.com.

LISLE, JANET TAYLOR, writer; b. Englewood, NJ, Feb. 13, 1947; d. Alden Mygatt and Janet Roberton (MacColl) Taylor; m. Richard Waterman Lisle, Oct. 17, 1976; 1 child, Elizabeth. BA, Smith Coll., 1969; cert. in journalism, Ga. State U., 1971. Author: (books) The Dancing Cats of Applesap, 1984, 93, Sirens and Spies, 1985, 90 (Booklist Best of the 80's, SLJ Best Book, ALA Notable Children's Book, ALA Best Book for Young Adults, 1985), The Great Dimpole Oak, 1987 (Golden Kite Honor Book, 1987), Afternoon of the Elves, 1989, 91, (Newbery Honor Book, SLJ Best Book, ALA Notable Children's Book), The Lampfish of Twill, 1991, 92 (SLJ Best Book), Forrest, 1993, 01 (SLJ Best Book), Investigators of the Unknown Quartet: The Gold Dust Letters, 1994, Looking For Juliette, 1994, A Message from the Match Girl, 1995 (SLJ Best Book), Angela's Aliens, 1996, The Lost Flower Children, 1999, 2001 (ALA Notable Children's Book, SLJ Best Book), The Art of Keeping Cool. 2000 (Scott O'Dell award Historical Fiction, 2001, ALA Notable Children's Book), How I Became a Writer and Oggie Learned to Drive, 2002 (Anderson award, Italy), The Crying Rocks, 2003, Black Ducks, 2006; (anthologized short stories) Those in Peril on the Sea, 1992, The Face in the Rafters, 1993, The Beginning of Time, 1999, Delia Broom and the Frog People of Quicksand Pond, 2000. Mem. Author's Guild, Soc. Children's Book Writers and Illustrators Avocations: singing, tennis, gardening.

LISLE, LAURIE, author; b. Providence, R.I., Sept. 11, 1942; d. Laurence Lisle and Adeline Cole Simonds; m. Robert I. Kipniss, Dec. 17, 1994. BA in English, Ohio Wesleyan U., 1965. Rschr. Newsweek mag., N.Y.C., 1970-78; assoc. prof. Southampton Coll. of L.I. U., 1981-82; ind. scholar So. Conn. Libr. Coun., Hamden, 1989—2002; spkr. N.Y. Coun. for the Humanities, N.Y.C., 2000—02. Author: Portrait of an Artist: A Biography of Georgia O'Keeffe, 1980, Louise Nevelson: A Passionate Life, 1990, Without Child: Challenging the Stigma of Childlessness, 1996, Four Tenths of an Acre: Reflections on a Gardening Life, 2005. Mem.: The Authors Guild, The Century Assn., Am. Pen Ctr. Democrat. Unitarian Universalist. Address: c/o Charlotte Sheedy Literary Agy 65 Bleeker St New York NY 10012 Personal E-mail: llisle@ix.netcom.com.

LIST, ILKA KATHERINE, art educator, sculptor, writer, psychotherapist; b. Orange, N.J., Nov. 22, 1935; d. Albert and Phyllis Howells (Carrington) L; children: Lee Maidoff, Jonah Maidoff, Natasha Maidoff. BS, U. Maine, Orono, 1976; MFA, SUNY, 1978; ArtsD, NYU, 1998. Cert. art tchr., N.Y. Adj. prof. SUNY, New Paltz, 1992—2004; pvt. sculpture tchr. Woodstock Sch. of Art, 1993-96; dir. edn. The Mohonk Preserve, New Paltz, 1987-95. Author/illustrator: Let's Explore the Shore, 1962, Grandma's Beach Surprise, 1975, Questions and Answers about Seashore Life (Children's Book Coun. award) 1976, A Walk in the Forest (Children's Book Coun., Nat. Sci. Tchrs. Assn. Joint Com. for best books) 1976; illustrator: (coloring/activity book) What's in the Woods, 1995, Piggy in the Parlor, 1995, Butterflies and Moths of N. Am., 2002; exhibited in group shows at Nat. Arts Club (Grand Ctrl. Galleries award, 1983), Pen and Brush Women Sculptors (Roman Bronze Foundry award, 1983); executed sculpted and painted commns., including natural history mural Mohank Preserve and Moonscape Children's Sci. Discovery Ctr. Santa Ana, Calif., 1998, mural View of Ancient Palestine, 2006; editor, treas. East Coast Sandplay Assn. Jour. Recipient Educator of Yr. award Outdoor Environ. Edn. Assn., 1995; resident fellowships to Yaddo, Saratoga Springs, NY, NY State Assembly (Environ. Disting. Achievement award, 2004, N.Y. State Dist. Achievements award 2005), Mohonk Cons., Inc. (Disting. Acievements, 2006). Avocations: swimming, hiking, music. Home and Office: 428 Springtown Rd New Paltz NY 12561-3027 Studio: 186 Mohonk Rd High Falls NY Business E-Mail: ilist@hrc.rr.com.

LISTER, PATRICIA ANN, elementary school educator; b. Marshalltown, Iowa, Dec. 10, 1949; d. Ernest and Grace Gennevieve Weatherly; m. Marvin Dean Lister, Nov. 15, 1986; children: Bryan Scott Damon, Eric William Damon. BS in Elem. Edn., Iowa State U., Ames, 1976; MA, No. Ariz. U., Flagstaff, 1992. Tchr. Hyder Sch. Dist., Dateland, Ariz., 1987—90, Crane Sch. Dist. #13, Yuma, Ariz., 1990—. Democrat. Avocations: reading, exercise, motorcycling. Office: Crane School District #13 4250 W 16th St Yuma AZ 85364 Office Phone: 928-373-3400.

LISTON, HELEN J., retired minister; b. Joplin, Mo., Nov. 2, 1932; d. Kenneth Harold Latta and Erma Nadine Latta - Pieffer; m. Dan R. Liston, Jan. 2, 1954 (dec. July 31, 1999); children: Diane, Dan, Del, Darin, Darci. BA, Kans. U., Lawrence, 1981; MDiv, St. Paul Sch. Theology, Kans. City, Mo., 1991. Kalaidescope staff Hallmark Cards, Kansas City, Mo., 1987—91; min. Asbury United Meth. Ch., Prairie Village, Kans., 1990—93, Leawood United Meth. Ch., Kans., 1995—2003; chaplain Heartland Hospice, Kansas City,

Mo., 1998—2004. Author: (book) The Dime Store, 2002; presenter Kans. City Hist. Soc., 1998—2004, Women's Wisdom Week, Crete, Greece; contbr. articles to periodicals. Home: 8731 Walmer Overland Park KS 66212 E-mail: hliston@kc.rr.com.

LITMAN, ROSLYN MARGOLIS, lawyer; b. NYC, Sept. 30, 1928; d. Harry and Dorothy (Perlow) Margolis; m. S. David Litman, Nov. 22, 1950; children: Jessica, Hannah, Harry. BA, U. Pitts., 1949, JD, 1952. Bar: Pa. 1952; approved arbitrator for complex comml. litigation and employment law. Practiced in Pitts., 1952—; ptnr. firm Litman Law Firm, 1952—; adj. prof. U. Pitts. Law Sch., 1958—. Permanent del. Conf. U.S. Circuit Ct. Appeals for 3d Circuit; past chair dist. adv. group U.S. Dist. Ct. (we. dist.) Pa., 1991-94, mem. steering com. for dist. adv. group, 1991—; chmn. Pitts. Pub. Parking Authority, 1970-74; mem. curriculum com. Pa. Bar Inst., 1986—, bd. dirs., 1972-82. Bd. dirs. United Jewish Fedn., 1999—, cmty. rels. com., co-chair ch./state com.; bd. dirs. City Theatre, 1999—. Recipient Roscoe Pound Found. award for Excellence in Tchg. Trial Advocacy, 1996, Disting. Alumnus award U. Pitts. Sch. Law, 1996, Disting. Svc. award Acad. Trial Lawyers, 2004; named Fed. Lawyer of Yr., We. Pa. Chpt. FBA, 1999. Mem. ABA (del., litigation sect., anti-trust health care com.), ACLU (nat. bd. dirs., Marjorie H. Matson Civil Libertarian award Greater Pitts. chpt. 1999), Pa. Bar Assn. (bd. govs. 1976-79), Allegheny County Bar Assn. (bd. govs. 1972-74, pres. 1975, Woman of Yr. 2001), Allegheny County Acad. Trial Lawyers (charter), Order of Coif. Home: 5023 Frew St Pittsburgh PA 15213-3829 Office: One Oxford Centre 34th Fl Pittsburgh PA 15219 Office Phone: 412-456-2000. Business E-Mail: rlitamn@Litman-Law.com.

LITOFF, JUDY BARRETT, history professor; b. Atlanta, Dec. 23, 1944; d. John and Dorothy (Woodall) Barrett; children: Nadja Barrett, Alyssa Barrett. BA, Emory U., Atlanta, 1967; MA, Emory U., 1968; PhD, U. Maine, 1975. Asst. prof. history Bryant U., Smithfield, RI, 1975-81, assoc. prof. history, 1981-87, prof. history, 1987—. Scholarly reader U. Ga. Press, Greenwood Press, U. Ill. Press, Prentice Hall, Univ. Press of Ky., Univ. Press of Colo.; project dir. U.S. Info. Agy. Grant, Minsk, Belarus, 1997-2000, higher edn. support program, Grant, Minsk, 1999. Author: American Midwives, 1978, American Midwife Debate, 1986; co-author: Miss You, 1990, Since You Went Away, 1991, Dear Boys, 1991, We're In This War, Too, 1994, European Immigrant Women, 1994, American Women in a World at War, 1997, Dear Poppa, 1997, What Kind of World Do We Want?, 2000, Fighting Fascism in Europe, 2003, An American Heroine in the French Resistance, 2006; contbr. articles to profl. jours.; book reviewer many profl. jours. Bd. dirs. R.I. Hist. Soc.; bd. dirs., chair Goff Inst. for Ingenuity and Enterprise, 1998—2003; bd. dirs. R.I. Com. for Humanities, 1982-86; bd. overseers The Lincoln Sch., Providence, 1982-88, The Moses Brown Sch., Providence, 1984-93; leader Girl Scouts R.I., 1978-87. Recipient Disting. Faculty award Bryant Faculty Fedn., 1988, Bryant Alumni Assn., 1989, James Madison prize Soc. for History in Fed. Govt., 1994, Bryant U. Rsch. and Pub. award, 1997, 2005; Ford Career scholar Emory U., 1965-67. Mem. Orgn. Am. Historians, Am. Hist. Assn., So. Hist. Assn., R.I. Hist. Soc., R.I. Black Heritage Soc. (bd. dirs. 2004—), Humanities Forum R.I. (bd. dirs. 2000—), Coordinating Com. on Women in the Hist. Profession, So. Assn. Women Historians, Phi Kappa Phi, Phi Alpha Theta. Avocations: skiing, hiking. Home: 248 Morris Ave Providence RI 02906-2424 Office: Bryant Univ 1150 Douglas Pike Smithfield RI 02917-1291 Office Phone: 401-232-6248. E-mail: jlitoff@bryant.edu.

LITRENTA, FRANCES MARIE, psychiatrist; b. Balt., June 25, 1928; d. Frank P. and Josephine (DeLuca) L. AB, Coll. Notre Dame Md., 1950; MD, Georgetown U., 1954. Diplomate Am. Bd. Psychiatry and Neurology. Intern St. Agnes Hosp., Balt., 1954-55, asst. resident in psychiatry, 1955-56; fellow psychiatry Univ. Hosp., Balt., 1956-57; fellow child psychiatry Georgetown U. Hosp., Washington, 1957-59; clin. instr. psychiatry Med. Ctr. Georgetown U., Washington, 1959-63, clin. asst. prof. Med. Ctr., 1963-72, clin. assoc. prof. psychiatry Med. Ctr., 1972-87; pvt. practice Balt., 1959—. Cons. St. Vincent's Infant Home, Balt., 1965-75; mem. coun. to dean Georgetown U. Sch. Medicine, 1977-93. Recipient Georgetown U. Alumni Assn. John Carroll award, 1998. Fellow Am. Acad. Child and Adolescent Psychiatry, Am. Orthopsychiat. Assn. (life); mem. Am. Psychiat. Assn. (life), Md. Psychiat. Soc. (life), Georgetown Med. Alumni Assn. (nat. comm. chair 1987-90, class co-chair 1974-87, class comm. chair 1987—, bd. dirs. 1989—, gov. 1989-95, senator 1995—), Georgetown U. Alumni Assn. (Founder's award 1994, John Carroll award 1998). Office: 6110 York Rd Baltimore MD 21212-2697 Office Phone: 410-435-6340.

LITSCHGI, BARBARA NELL, dietician; b. San Pierre, Ind., Oct. 7, 1930; d. Orlyn Jesse Clawson and Kathryn Maurine Maxwell; m. Herman George Litschgi, May 26, 1956 (dec.); children: Mindy Jochem, Ede Boots. BS, N. Ctrl. Coll., Naderville, Ill., 1952; dietetic internship, Mass. Gen. Hosp., Boston, Mass., 1954. Cert. A.D.A. Theraputic dietitian Ill. Masonic Hosp., Chgo., 1952—53; dietitian Ind. Univ., Bloomington, Ind., 1954, St. Mary's Hosp., Evansville, Ind., 1960—63; cons. dietitian Bethel Sanitarium, Evansville, Ind., 1974. Teach nutrition class pvt., Evansville, 2001—03. Author: (nurtrition book) Sprouts & Soy with Prayers & Joy, 2003. Vol. Bethel Manor, Evansville, Ind., 1994—, Vista Care Hospice, Evansville, 2001—, Holiday Home, Evansville, 2004—; clown/mem Rider City Clowns, Evansville, 2002—. Republican. Mem. Unity Ch. Home: 5727 Tribby Ln Evansville IN 47710 E-mail: bblitschgi@sigecom.net.

LITTELL, MARCIA SACHS, Holocaust and genocide studies professor; b. Phila., 1937; d. Leon Harry Sobel and Selma Lipson; children: Jonathan R., Robert L. Jr., Jennifer; m. Franklin H. Littell, Mar. 23, 1980. BS in Edn., Temple U., 1971, MS in Edn., 1975, EdD, 1990. Internat. exec. dir. Anne Frank Inst., Phila., 1981-89; exec. dir. Ann. Scholars' Conf. on the Holocaust & the Chs., Merion, Pa., 1980—; prof. Holocaust and genocide studies, founding dir. MA program Holocaust & genocide studies The Richard Stockton Coll. N.J., 1997—. Adj. prof. Temple U., Phila., 1990-97; vis. prof. Phila. C.C., 1974-76; dir. Phila. Ctr. on the Holocaust, Genocide and Human Rights, 1989—; exec. com. Remembering for the Future, Oxford, Eng. and Berlin, 1986—; mem. edn. com. U.S. Holocaust Meml. Mus., Washington, 1987-89, chmn.'s adv. com., 1985. Mem. editl. bd. Holocaust & Genocide Studies, Oxford U. Press, 1987—, Bridges: An Interdisciplinary Journal of Theology, Philosophy, History and Science, 1995—; editor: Holocaust Education: A Resource for Teachers and Professional Leaders, 1985, Liturgies on the Holocaust: An Interfaith Anthology, 1986, rev. edit., 1996 (Merit of Distinction award), The Holocaust: Forty Years After, 1989, The Netherlands and Nazi Genocide, 1992, From Prejudice to Destruction: Western Civilization in the Shadow of Auschwitz, 1995, Remembrance and Recollection: Essays on the Centennial Year of Martin Niemoeller and Reinhold Niebuhr, 1995, The Uses and Abuses of Knowledge: The Holocaust and the German Church Struggle, 1997, The Holocaust: Lessons For the Third Generation, 1997, Holocaust and Church Struggle: Religion, Power and the Politics of Resistance, 1996, Confronting the Holocaust: A Mandate for the 21st Century, part 1, 1997, part 2, 1998, A Modern Prophet, 1998, Hearing the Voices: Teaching the Holocaust to Future Generations, 1999, Women in the Holocaust, 2001, The Century of Genocide, 2002, The Genocidal Mind, 2005. Exec. com. YM/YWHA Arts Coun., Phila., 1980—; adv. bd. Child Welfare, Montgomery County, 1975-80, Am. Friends the Ghetto Fighters House; bd. govs. Lower Merion Scholarship Fund, 1972-80. Named Woman of the Yr., Brith Sholom Women, Phila., 1993; recipient Eternal Flame award Anne Frank Inst., 1988; named to Hall of Fame Sch. Dist. of Phila., 1988. Fellow Nat. Assn. Holocaust Educators, Assn. of Holocaust Orgns. (founding sec. 1985-88), Nat. Coun. for the Social Studies. Democrat. Jewish. Avocations: walking, travel, reading. Office: PO Box 10 Merion Station PA 19066-0010 Office Phone: 609-652-4418. Business E-Mail: drlittell@comcast.net.

LITTKE, LAEL JENSEN, author; b. Mink Creek, Idaho, Dec. 2, 1929; d. Frank George and Ada Geneva (Petersen) Jensen; m. George Charles Littke, June 29, 1954 (dec. Feb. 1991); 1 child, Lori Sue Littke Silfen. BS, Utah State U., 1952. Sec. Gates Rubber Co., Denver, 1952-54, Life Ins. Assn. of Am., N.Y.C., 1954-63; instr. Pasadena (Calif.) City Coll., 1978-84; tchr. UCLA, 1988. Author: There's A Snake at Girls Camp, 1994, The Bridesmaid's Dress Disaster, 1994, Star of the Show, 1993, The Watcher, 1994, Blue Skye, 1991, Run, Ducky, Run, 1996, The Phantom Fair, 1996, Haunted Sister, 1998, Lake of Secrets, 2002, Stories from the Life of Joseph Smith, 2003, Searching for Selene, 2003, Almost Sister, 2006, also 29 other books. Bd. dirs. PTA, 1976-78, Save the Libr. Com., Pasadena, 1993. Mem.: Children's Lit. Coun. of So. Calif., Soc. of Children's Book Writers and Illustrators. Democrat. Mem. Ch. of LDS. Avocations: animals, travel, hiking, acting. Home: 1345 Daveric Dr Pasadena CA 91107-1645

LITTLE, ANGELA CAPOBIANCO, nutritional science educator; b. San Francisco, Jan. 12, 1920; d. Alfredo Agosto and Elizabeth (Kruse) Capobianco; m. George Gordon Little, Nov. 8, 1947; 1 child, Judith Kristine. BA, U. Calif., Berkeley, 1940, MS, 1954, PhD, 1969. Specialist jr. to asst. to assoc. U. Calif., Berkeley, 1958-69, food scientist, 1969-85, assoc. prof. to prof, 1977-85, prof. emeritus, 1985—, acad. ombudsman, 1985-87, 89-91. Cons. in field; v.p., bd. dirs. Math/Sci. Network, Berkeley; vis. scholar U. Wash., Seattle, 1976-77, Kans. State U., Manhattan, 1972; mem. faculty Fromm Inst., U. San Francisco, 1992-96; pres. bd. dirs. Laguna Heights Co-op Corp., 1999-2001. Author: Color of Foods, 1962. Nutritional adv. bd. Project Open Hand, San Francisco, 1989—91, vol., 1988—91, UNICEF, San Francisco, 1986—89, Saint Francis Hosp., 1992—; bd. dirs. Museo Italo-Am., 2004—; mem. San Francisco Museum of Modern Art, Calif. Palace of the Legion of Honor, Asian Art Museum, Yerba Buena Ctr. of the Arts. Rsch. grantee Robert Woods Johnson Found., 1989-90, others 1960-85. Mem. AAUW, San Francisco Acad. Sci., San Francisco Mus. Soc., U. Calif. Berkeley Emeritii Assn. (pres. 1991-93), Am. Assn. for History of Medicine, Exploratorium, Bay Area History of Medicine Club (pres. 1995-97), Laguna Heights Co-op Corp. (pres., bd. dirs. 1999-2001), Sigma Xi. Avocations: music, books, travel, exercising, walking. Home: 85 Cleary Ct Apt 3 San Francisco CA 94109-6518 Office: U Calif Dept Nutritional Scis Berkeley CA 94720-0001 Business E-Mail: aclittle@uclink.berkeley.edu.

LITTLE, JENIFER RAYE, music educator; b. Greensburg, Pa., Oct. 13, 1972; d. John Robert and Joellyn Little. MusB in Edn., Baldwin Wallace Coll., Berea, Ohio, 1994; MusM in Horn Performance, Carnegie Mellon U., Pitts., 1996. Cert. tchr. Pa., 1996, Ohio, 1994. Music tchr. Plum Borough Sch. Dist., Pitts., 1996—. Dir. West Newton Cmty. Singers, Pa., 2003—06. Com. mem. First United Presbyn. Ch., West Newton, 2002—04. Mem.: Am. Choral Dirs. Assn., Pa. Music Educator's Assn., West Newton Women's Club (bd. dirs. 1994—), Mu Phi Epsilon, Omicron Delta Kappa. Avocations: reading, travel, gourmet cooking. Home: 1920 George Cir North Huntingdon PA 15642

LITTLE, JENNIFER, performing arts educator, director, actress; b. Madison, Wis., Apr. 29, 1961; d. Robert Soutas-Little and Judith Little, Patricia Soutas-Little (Stepmother); m. Scott Jackson, Oct. 11, 1998. BA, San Jose State U., Calif., 1986. Cert. drama tchr. N.J., 2007. Dir. River Dell H.S., Oradell, NJ, 2003—; drama tchr. Franklin H.S., Somerset, NJ, 2005—; guest artist Bergen Acad. Performing Arts, Hackensack, NJ, 2002—06; actress, film Riding in Cars with Boys, East Orange, NJ, 2000—01; Carlotta Phantom of the Opera Broadway, N.Y.C., 1996—97. Dir. Marlboro Players, Marlboro, NJ, 2005—06, Phoenix Players, Red Bank, NJ, 2002—04. Actor: (performance) Phantom of the Opera - Broadway, National Tour, Emma and Company (Backstage Best Book Musical Performance, 2000); singer: (performance) Chess - BC/EFA Charity Performance; actor: (film) Beautiful Mind; author: (musical play) Princess and the Pizza (adaptation), Perfect Plot; dir.: (performance) Man of La Mancha; prodr.: (children's musical theatre performance) Princess and Pizza, Miss Nelson is Missing, Perfect Plot. Educator Literacy Through the Arts, Plainfield, NJ, 2003—05, Making Books Sing, NYC. Mem.: N.J. Edn. Assn. (assoc.), SAG (assoc.), Actors Equity Assn. (assoc.). Democrat-Npl. Avocations: horseback riding, reading, golf, swimming. Office Phone: 732-302-4200 6611.

LITTLE, KAREN J., counselor; b. Santa Fe, N.Mex., Aug. 13, 1960; children: Andrew R., Jenna K. MA in Sociology, N.Mex State U., Las Cruces, 1997; MA in Counseling and Ednl. Psychology, N.Mex State U., Las Cruces, N. Mex., 2004. Lic. Baccalaureate Social Worker N.Mex Regulation and Licensing Dept., 1990; Profl. Mental Health Counselor N.Mex Regulation and Licensing Dept., 1994, cert. Criminal Justice Specialist Nat. Assn. of Forensic Counselors, 2004, Domestic Violence Counselor III Nat. Assn. of Forensic Counselors, 2004, clinical mental health counselor N. Mex. Regulation and Licensing Dept., 2005. Outreach specialist/job developer Alternative Ho., Inc., Las Cruces, N.Mex., 1985—87; case mgmt. supr. SW Counseling Ctr., Inc, Las Cruces, N.Mex., 1987—97; non-resident program coord. La Casa, Inc., Las Cruces, N.Mex., 1997—2002; program mgr. N.Mex Commn. on the Status of Women, Las Cruces, N.Mex., 2002—. Contbr. paper presented to conf. Recipient Counseling Student of the Yr., Counseling Masters Student Assn., 2003. Mem.: ACA (assoc.), Chi Kappa Phi (licentiate). Avocations: reading, bowling. Office: TeamWorks 2205 S Main Suite A Las Cruces NM 88005 Office Phone: 505-524-6290. Business E-Mail: kjlittle2003@yahoo.com.

LITTLE, KATHLEEN C., lawyer; b. Jan. 6, 1953; BS magna cum laude, U. Md., 1977; JD cum laude, George Washington U., 1980. Bar: DC 1980. Ptnr. Vinson & Elkins LLP, Washington. Lectr. in field. Mem.: ABA (pub. contract law sect.). Office: Vinson & Elkins LLP Willard Office Bldg 1455 Pennsylvania Ave NW Ste 600 Washington DC 20004-1008 Office Phone: 202-639-6663. Office Fax: 202-879-8983. E-mail: klittle@velaw.com.

LITTLE, LAURA ANN, elementary school educator, art educator; b. Lincoln Pk., Mich., Feb. 4, 1960; d. John Elliott Little and Patricia Ann Peckham; m. Jeffrey Hart Genthner (div.). Degree in Interior Design, Alma Coll., Mich., 1979; BA in Interior Design, Mich. State U., East Lansing, Mich., 1982. Tchr. elem. art Curriculum Svcs., Elkhart, Ind., 2002—; freelance photographer Detroit (Mich.) News, 2003—. Tchr. art and music Detroit (Mich.) Symphony Orch., 2005. Recipient Best of Photography award, Photographer's Forum, 1996, 1997, 1998, Photo of Day award, Detroit (Mich.) News, 2004; grantee Kodak Camera award for use by 60 children, Nat. Geographic Soc., 1998. Mem.: Mich. Press Photographers Assn., Nat. Press Photographers Assn., Nat. Mus. Women in Arts, Detroit (Mich.) Inst. Arts, The Scarab Club. Republican. Presbyn. Avocations: painting, travel, movies, photography. Home: 100 Riverfront Dr 1010 Detroit MI 48226 Office Phone: 313-610-6837. E-mail: littleimages@comcast.net.

LITTLE, LAURA JANES, educational association administrator; d. Charles Gary and Alice June Saunders Little. BA, W.Va. U., Morgantown, 1991; MA, W.Va. U., 1993, EdD, 2001. Cert. WebCT Trainer WebCT, 2001. Coord. sr. program W.Va. Network, Morgantown, 2000—02; instrnl. technologist Marietta Coll., Ohio, 2002—. Adminstr. title III grant Marietta Coll., 2003—; list moderator Ohio Learning Network, Columbus, 2004—; instr. Women in Scis., Marietta, 2002—05. Swiger Fellowship, W.Va. U., 1998-2000. Mem.: Ea. Ednl. Rsch. Assn., W.Va. TESOL Assn. (pres. 1998—99), Assn. for Advancement of Computing in Edn. (assoc.), Phi Delta Kappa. Business E-Mail: laura.little@marietta.edu.

LITTLE, MARGARET F. DIXON LESNIAK, electrical engineer, educator; b. Albuquerque, Feb. 13, 1951; d. William Lawrence Dixon and Martha Lenoir Stevens; m. Robert Little, Nov. 22, 1995; children: Jessica Marie Martin, Colin Stuart Martin. BS in Elec. Engring., N.Mex. State U., Las Cruces, 1972, MS in Elec. Engring., 1979. Cert. profl. engr., Calif. Assoc. engr. San Diego Gas & Elec. Co., 1972—73; elec. engr. Global Assocs., Kwajalein, Marshall Islands, 1973—77; cons. engr. RW Beck & Assocs., Sacramento, 1979—83, Anchorage, 1987—89; supr., sys. planning Anchorage Mcpl. Dept. Power, 1983—87; adj. prof. Ctrl. Ariz. Coll., Coolidge, 1991—97; tchr. Casa Grande HS, Ariz., 1997—. Mem.: Math. Assn. Am., Nat. Coun. Tchrs. Math. Avocations: scuba diving, needlepoint, swimming, travel. E-mail: mlittle@cguhs.org.

LITTLE, STEPHANIE JEAN, special education educator; b. Pikeville, Ky., Jan. 10, 1970; d. James Garland and Anna Lee Mitchell; m. Shannon Patrick Little, Aug. 11, 1990. BA in Edn., Morehead State U., 1992; MA in Spl. Edn., Ea. Ky. U., 1997. Dir. spl. edn. Carroll County Schs., Carrollton, Ky., 1998—99; dir. spl. edn., preschool Bath County Schs., Owingsville, Ky., 1999—. Sunday sch. tchr. Slaty Point Bapt. Ch., Morehead, Ky., 2000—06. Mem.: Coun. Adminstr. Spl. Edn. (corr.). Democrat-Npl. Bapt. Avocations: boating, reading. Home: 290 Sweetgum Ln Morehead KY 40351 Office: Bath County Schs 405 W Main St Owingsville KY 40360 Office Phone: 606-674-6314. Office Fax: 606-674-2647. Business E-Mail: stephanie.little@bath.kyschools.us.

LITTLE, TESS (TERESA FANNIN), sculptor, fine arts educator; b. Dayton, Ohio, May 8, 1951; d. Robert Earnest and Viola (Bentley) Fannin; m. James R. Little, Oct. 16, 1969; children: Rebbecca, Russell, Alice. BFA in Sculpture, Wright State U., 1975; MFA in Sculpture, Cranbrook Acad. of Art, Bloomfield Hills, Mich., 1980. Instr. fine arts dept. Sinclair C.C., Dayton, 1976-78, 80-90, adj. prof., 1990-93, asst. prof., 1993-97, assoc. prof., 1997—, coord. sculpture in residency program, 1991-92, coord., originator heritage sculpture project, 1995-98, co-chmn. Appalachian out reach program, 1995—, prof., 1997—. Dir./originator Realizing Ethnic Awareness and Cultural Heritage (REACH) Across Dayton Project, 1993—; co-curator art show, LRC Gallery, 1996, others; presenter, confs. in field. One-person shows include: Floating Summer/Sinclair C.C., 1991-93, Summer Daze, 1990-91, Shield for Sinclair, 1989; Noyes Gallery, Antioch Coll., Yellow Springs, Ohio, 1983, Lohrey Ctr. Divsn. of Parks and Recreation, Dayton, 1978, Susan Parke Contemporary Graphics, Monticello, Ill., 1977, Exptl. Gallery, Wright State U., 1974, 75; group exhbns. include Sinclair Fine Arts Dept. Faculty Show, 1987-97, Biltmore Bldg., Dayton, 1991-96, Art Expo, Dayton, 1995, Holistic Women exhibit LRC, 1996, numerous others; film/set designer River City Prodns., 1991, others. Mem. bd. Fairborn City Schs., 2006—; bd. mem. Fairborn City Sch., 2006—. Recipient Hon. Order of Ky. Colonels award Our Common Heritage, 1994, 2005; artist-in-residence grantee, 1994, Challenger grantee, Cambridge, Eng., 1995-96, also others. Mem. Altrusa Internat. of Dayton (pres. 1996-98). Office: Sinclair Comm Coll Fine Arts Dept 444 W 3rd St Dayton OH 45402-1421 Office Phone: 937-512-5318. Personal E-mail: tesslittleart@yahoo.com.

LITTLEJOHN, HEATHER SHERI, music educator; b. Portland, Oreg., Sept. 28, 1979; d. David Ray and Beverly Teruko Marshall; m. F. David Littlejohn, Sept. 17, 2005. BA in Music Edn., Lewis and Clark Coll., 2001, MAT in Music Edn., 2002. Band dir. Sutherlin (Oreg.) Sch. Dist., 2003—; gen. music specialist West Sutherlin Intermediate, 2003—. Fundraiser United Way, Roseburg, Oreg., 2004—. Mem.: NEA (sec. 2004—05, del. to nat. registered assembly 2003, 2004), Oreg. Music Educators Assn. (pres. 2004—05). Republican. Avocations: travel, gardening. Office: Sutherlin Sch Dist 500 E 4th Sutherlin OR 97479 Office Phone: 541-459-9551 ext 236. Office Fax: 541-459-4887. E-mail: heather.littlejohn@sutherlin.k12.or.us.

LITTLETON, GAYE DARLENE, retired nonprofit executive director; b. Parma, Idaho, Nov. 1, 1938; d. Donald Lyle and June E. (Shelton) Graham; m. Jerry M. Littleton, June 11, 1960; children: Leslie, Clark, Laura, Stacey. BS in Edn., U. Idaho, 1960; MS in Ednl. Adminstrn., Utah State U., 1980. Tchr., Seattle, 1960-62; tchr. jr. high sch. Ogden (Utah) Sch. Dist., 1975-76; tchr. Utah State Sch. for the Blind, Ogden, 1976-80; ednl. equity program coord. Weber State Coll., Ogden, 1979-81; councilwoman Ogden City Coun., 1983—; exec. dir. Your Cmty. Connection, 1981-98. Bd. dirs. Zion's State Bank, First Security Bank Housing Com.; rschr. in field; cmty. cons., Sandy City, 1998—. Contbr. articles to profl. jours. Commr. Ogden Redevel. Agy., Ogden Housing Agy., 1993; pub. housing commr. Salt Lake County, 2002; mem. human devel. com. Nat. League of Cities; bd. dirs. Weber County Dept. Aging, City Parks and Recreation, Nature Ctr., Arts Commn., Equal Employment Opportunity; mem. Weber County Social Svcs. Coordinating Coun.; past chair Weber County Title XX Coun.; mem. Weber County Resource Coalition, Weber County Human Rights Coalition, Weber County Homeless Coordinating Com.; mem. ethics com. McKay Dee Hosp., 1990—; bd. dirs. Boys and Girls Club South Valley. Recipient Acad. scholarship for Cmty. Svc., 1956, Thesian award U. Idaho, 1959, LWV Cmty. Svc. award Weber County Mental Health, 1974, Cmty. Svc. award, VIP award Hill AFB, Utah, 1977, Liberty Bell award Utah Bar Assn., 1977, Leadership award Nat. YWCA, 1979, Susa Young Gates award Utah Women's Polit. Caucus for Outstanding Contbn. to Women and Minorities, 1980, Jane Addams award, 1982, Women Helpin Women award, 1983, Utah Women of Achievement award, 1984, Golden Deeds award, 1988, Athena award, Disting. Alumni award WSU, 1994, Outstanding Rotarian Housing Commr., 1990. Mem. LWV, AAUW (Woman of Yr. 1988), Ogden Rotary Club (First Woman Rotarian 1992), Ogden C. of C. (Athenia award 1992). Home: 2217 Karalee Way Sandy UT 84092-4479

LITTLETON, NAN ELIZABETH FELDKAMP, psychologist, educator; b. Covington, Ky., Oct. 23, 1942; d. William Albert and Norma Elizabeth (Smith) Feldkamp; m. O.W. Littleton, Oct. 4, 1969 (div. 1979). AAS, No. Ky. U., Highland Heights, 1976, BS, 1978; MACE, Morehead State U., Ky., 1981; MA, U. Cin., 1986, PhD, 1995. Prof. No. Ky. U., Highland Heights, 1976—, dir. mental health and human svcs. program, 1989—. Officer, pres. Holly Hill Children's Home, Cold Spring, Ky., 1980-86; cons. Attituding Healing Ctr., Cin., 1990-94; treas. ADO Nat. Honor Soc., 2004-. Treas., editor So. Orgn. Human Svcs. Edn. Link, 1997-2002. Bd. dir. Coun. Stds. in Human Svc. Edn., Chgo., 1990-98—, Cancer Family Care, Cin., 1992-96. Mem. APA, Am. Psychol. Soc., Nat. Orgn. Human Svc. Edn., Am. Coun. Assn., So. Orgn. Human Svc. Edn. (state rep. 1991—, treas., 1999-2002), Nat. Women's Studies Assn., Assn. Humanistic Psychologists, Alpha Delta Omega (treas. 2003—). Home: 333 W 17th St Covington KY 41014-1007 Office Phone: 859-572-5188. Business E-Mail: littleton@nku.edu.

LITTMAN, MARLYN KEMPER, information scientist, educator; b. Mar. 26, 1943; d. Louis and Augusta (Jacobs) Janofsky; m. Bennett I. Kemper, Aug. 1, 1965 (dec. June 1987); children: Alex Randall, Gari Hament, Jason Myles; m. Lewis Littman, Apr. 22, 1990. BA, Finch Coll., 1964; MA in Anthropology, Temple U., 1970; MA in Info. Sci., U. South Fla., 1983; PhD in Info. Sci., Nova Southeastern U., 1986. Dir. Hist. Broward County Preservation Bd., Hollywood, Fla., 1979—87; automated systems libr. Broward County Main Libr., Ft. Lauderdale, Fla., 1984—86; assoc. prof. info. sci. Nova U., Ft. Lauderdale, Fla., 1987—94, dir. info. sci. doctoral program, 1987—94; prof. info. sci. Nova Southeastern U., Ft. Lauderdale, Fla., 1995—. Weekly columnist Ft. Lauderdale News, 1975—79; contbg. editor Hyper Nexus-Jour. Hypermedia and Multimedia Studies, 1996—2000; assoc. editor Jour. On-Line Learning, 1997—2002. Author: A Comprehensive Documented History of the City of Pompano Beach, 1982, A Comprehensive History of Dania, 1983, A Comprehensive History of Hallandale, 1984, A Comprehensive History of Deerfield Beach, 1985, A Comprehensive History of Plantation, 1986, A Comprehensive History of Davie, 1987, Networking: Choosing a LAN Path to Interconnection, 1987, Building Broadband Networks, 2002; author: (with others) Mosaics of Meaning, New Ways of Learning, 1996; contbr. articles to profl. jours., chapters to books. Pub. info. officer Broward County Hist. Commn., 1975—79; vice chmn. Broward County Adv. Bd., 1987—92; bd. dirs. Ctrl. Agy. Jewish Edn., 1992—94. Recipient Judge L. Clayton Nance award, 1977, Broward County Hist. Commn. award, 1979. Mem.: IEEE, Assn. Computing Machinery, Info. Resources Mgmt. Assn. Internat., Phi Kappa Phi, Beta Phi Mu, Upsilon Pi Epsilon. Home: 2845 NE 35th St Fort Lauderdale FL 33306-2007 Office: Nova Southeastern U Grad Sch Computer and Info Sci 3301 College Ave Fort Lauderdale FL 33314 Office Phone: 954-262-2078. Business E-Mail: marlyn@nova.edu.

LITTO, JUDITH CHERYL, art educator; b. Amsterdam, NY, June 16, 1945; d. Forrest Whitlock and Gladys Orcelia Van Zandt; m. Leo Litto (div.); 1 child, Teo Matthew. BA, SUNY, Potsdam, 1967; MS, Coll. St. Rose, Albany, 1969. Cert. tchr. NY. Art tchr. Shenendahowa C. Schs., Clifton Park, NY, 1967—70, Schalmont (NY) Ctrl. Schs., 1970—71; art specialist Guilderlund (NY) Ctrl. Schs., 1971—2003; visual arts coord., project arts coord.

Web Dubois HS, Bklyn., 2003—. Visual, performing arts tchr. Rochester (NY) City Schs., 1977—78; owner Litto Design Co., Albany, NY, Parisian Flea, Albany. Editor: Transitions Mag. Pres. NE chpt. NY State Art Tchrs.; v.p. Hudson Mohawk Consortium Coll. and Univ., Albany; pres. Suburban Coun. Art Supervisors Bd., Albany. Grantee, NY State Hist. Assn., 1972, Donors Choose, NYC, 2004—06. Mem.: Am. Mus. Folk Art, Mus. Modern Art. Avocations: antiques, reading, painting, drawing. Home: 378 Greene Ave Brooklyn NY 11216

LITTON, NANCY JOAN, education educator; b. Baton Rouge, Mar. 26, 1952; d. Gilbert Dupre and Mell Baynard Litton. BS in Elem. Edn., La. State U., 1973, MEd in Elem. Edn., 1977, MA in History, 1986. Tchr., various grades various sch., Baton Rouge area, Eng. and Switzerland, 1974—94; tchg. assoc., Learning Assistance Ctr. La. State U., Baton Rouge, 1994—96, instr. for Coll. Edn., 1996—. Evaluator for talented drama students East Baton Rouge Parish Pub. Sch. Actor: over 70 plays. Recipient Best Actress in a Play award, Baton Rouge Little Theater, 1998, Actress of Yr. award, Baker Little Theatre, 1995, Supporting Actress of Yr. award, 1997. Avocations: public speaking, singing, travel, acting. Home: 4900 Claycut Rd Apt 52 Baton Rouge LA 70806 Office: La State U Coll of Edn Baton Rouge LA 70803 E-mail: nlitto@lsu.edu.

LITVIN, INESSA ELIZABETH, piano educator; b. Gorky, Russia, Sept. 13, 1939; came to U.S., 1980; d. Aron J. and Elizabeth I. (Shapiro) Frenkel; m. Edward J. Litvin, Aug. 22, 1975. MA in Piano Performing magna cum laude, Conservatory, Leningrad, Russia, 1965. Prof. music Ctrl. Music Sch., Leningrad, 1965-79; pvt. instr. piano Encinitas, Calif., 1980—. Recipient prize Shostakovich Piano Competition, Leningrad, 1964, recognition for exceptional artistic achievements of students Nat. Found. Advancement in Art, Miami, Fla., 1999. Mem. Calif. Assn. Profl. Music Tchrs., Music Tchrs. Assn. Calif. Home: 1632 Jerrilynn Pl Encinitas CA 92024-4757 E-mail: ielitvin@adelphia.net.

LITWACK, ARLENE DEBRA, psychotherapist, psychoanalyst, educator, consultant; b. Brookline, Mass., July 18, 1945; d. Hyman and Bessie Litwack. BA cum laude, Boston U., 1967; MS, Columbia U., 1969; postgrad., Ctr. for Mental Health, NYC, 1981; psychoanalyst cert., Inst. for Psychoanalytic Tng. and Rsch., 1993. Caseworker Pride Treatment Ctr., Douglaston, NY, 1969—73, supr., 1973—78, sr. worker, 1978—80; pvt. practice psychotherapy and psychoanalysis NYC, 1980—. Mem. faculty Inst. for Mental Health Edn., Englewood, NJ, 1983—89; clin. cons. NY Spaulding for Children, 1989; bd. dirs. child therapy dept. LI Consultation Ctr., Rego Park, NY, 1980—85; faculty workshop leader Human Svcs. Workshops, NYC; adj. faculty Fordham U., 1991—; mem. faculty, supr., chair object rels. Psychoanalytic Study Ctr., 1991—, exec. com.; cons. 9/11 recovery program ARC, 2003—05. Contbr. articles to profl. jours. Mem.: NASW, NY State Soc. Clin. Social Workers (presenter workshops on grief 1999—). Home: 115 4th Ave Apt 3E New York NY 10003-4907 Office Phone: 212-595-3850.

LITWIN, RUTH ANN FORBES, artist; b. Omaha, Apr. 14, 1933; d. Eli Morris and Toby Lena Forbes; m. Martin Louis Litwin, Feb. 10, 1952; children: Brenda, Linda, Bennett, Stuart. Pres. Sculpture Resources, Dallas, 1986; panelist Women in Contemporary Soc., Dallas, 1988; juror Nat. Arts Program, Dallas, 1995; mem. Art in Embassies Program, Washington, Luanda, Angola Exhibited at Dallas Women's Caucus for Art, 1997, Wise Women Speak Exhbn., 1994, Brookhaven Coll., Dallas, 1996, Art in Embassies program, U.S. Embassy, Angola. Recipient Rowena Elkin award, 1997, Soc. Internat. Des Beaux-Arts prize Bern Heim De Villers, Paris, 1998, Purchase award Northlake Coll., Irving, Tex., 2001 Mem. Tex. Fine Arts Assn. (prse. 1982-84), Dallas Women's Caucus for Art (adv. bd. 1994-96), Dallas Visual Art Ctr., Tex. Sculpture Assn. (award for figurative art 2006), Tex. Visual Art Assn. Avocations: reading, travel, crossword puzzles, nature walks, yoga. Home: 6813 Wild Ridge Ct Plano TX 75024-7467 Business E-Mail: rlitwin@litwinco.com.

LITZ, CLAUDIA, science educator; b. Cleve., Aug. 27, 1957; d. Jack Berns and Leah Lewenz; m. Robert Litz, June 25, 1989; 1 child, Megan. BS, Purdue U., West Lafayette, Ind., 1979; MEd, Ashland U., Ohio, 1994. Rsch. asst. parasitology Purdue U., 1979—79, instr. chemistry lab., 1978—79, instr. botany, 1980—80; instr. zoology lab. U. Canterbury, Christchurch, New Zealand, 1981—81; tchr. sci. Laurel Sch., Shaker Heights, Ohio, 1982—85; sci. specialist Lomond Elem. Sch., 1987—87; store mgr. and head cmty. edn. programs Plantscaping, Inc., 1987—88; tchr. sci. Mentor Pub. Schs., 1990—. Mem. restructuring com. Mentor Ridge Jr. H.S., 1993—96, co-leader grade level tchg. team, 1995—96, co-chair tech. assistance team, 2006—, mem. pride com., 2006—; sci. curriculum rev. com. Mentor Pub. Schos., 1993—; project sponsor Northeastern Ohio Sci. and Engring. Fair, 2002—04; participant tchr. assessment field tests Horizon Rsch., Inc., 2004—; judge sci. fair Hathaway Brown Sch., Shaker Heights, 2004—05; participant field test Ohio Dept. Edn., 2004; presenter in field. Vol. Lake Metro Pks, Lake County, Ohio, 2005—. Grantee, NEH, 1985. Mem.: NEA, Mentor Tchrs. Assn., Ohio Edn. Assn. Avocations: running, gardening, travel. Office Phone: 440-974-5400.

LITZENBERGER, LESLEY MARGARET, textiles executive; b. Ramsay, Eng., June 10, 1945; arrived in U.S., 1946; d. Albert Brockney and Margaret Jean Hendricks; m. Robert H. Litzenberger, Jan. 23, 1968 (div. June 18, 1996); children: Kenneth, William. AA, Canal Zone Coll., 1965; postgrad., U. N.C., 1965—66, postgrad., 1967—69. Sec. U.S. Army, Ft. Amador, Canal Zone, 1966—67, U. N.C., Chapel Hill, 1968—69; dancer Ballet Panama, 1961—67, Bay Area Dance Theatre, Oakland, Calif., 1970—72; dance instr. Calif., Pa., 1972—86; CFO Robert Litzenberger Assoc., Stanford, Calif. and Haverford, Pa, 1982—94; textile artist Beaufort, S.C. and California, Pa., 1980—. Bd. dirs. Arts Coun. Beaufort County, 1998—2004; artistic dir. Byrne Miller Dance Theatre, Beaufort, 1999—2002; pub. rels. dir., bd. dirs. Panama Canal Mus., Seminole, Fla., 1999—2004; chairperson City of Beaufort Pub. Arts Commn., 2004—.

LITZENBERGER, RENEE CLAIRE, music educator, elementary school educator; d. Burnie R. and Virgal A. Tiedman; m. Jerry P. Litzenberger, Mar. 20, 1971; children: Brian P., Randy V., Mark D. BS, Dickinson State U., ND, 1968; M in Vocal Arts, Ea. Wash. U., Cheney, 1970. Cert. tchr. Wash., 1982. Choral music tchr. Horace Mann Jr. High, Lakewood, Wash., 1969—70; gen. music instr. Lewis Clark State Coll., Lewiston, Idaho, 1972—79; elem. music specialist Seattle Hill Elem., Snohomish, Wash., 1982—. Soloist Wash./Idaho Symphony, Lewiston, 1978—78, Everett (Wash.) Symphony; choir mem./soloist Seattle Symphony, 1985—90. Scholar, Dickinson State U., 1964—65; Post-graduate fellow music, Ea. Wash. U., 1969—70. Mem.: Snohomish Ed. Assn. (assoc.; sec. 1998—2001, union exec. mem. 1996—2001). Democrat. Avocations: travel, golf, reading, gardening. Office: Snohomish School District 1601 Ave D Snohomish WA 98290 Office Phone: 360-563-7300.

LIU, CAROL, state representative; b. Berkeley, Calif., Sept. 12, 1940; m. Michael Peevey; children: Darcie, Maria, Jared. BA, San Jose State Coll., 1963; student, U. Calif., Berkeley, 1964, student, 1978. Tchr. Richmond Unified Sch. Dist., 1964—77, adminstr., 1978—84; mem. La Cañada Flintridge City Council, 1992—96; mayor La Cañada Flintridge, Calif., 1996—99; mem. Calif. State Assembly, 2000—. Co-chair Asian Pacific Islander Legislative Caucus; mem. Women's Legislative Caucus, Calif. Seismic Safety Commn.; mem. transportation and govt. org. com., higher edu. com., budget com. Calif. State Assembly. Pres. La Canada H.S. PTA; coun. pres. Mus. Contemporary Art; co-chair capital campaign Pasadena City Coll., pres. found. bd., co-chair phys. edn. campaign; trustee U. Calif., Berkeley; bd. dirs. Child Care Info. Svcs., Five Acres; mem. exec. bd. Women's Leadership Network. Democrat. Office: State Capital PO Box 942849 Rm 4112 Sacramento CA 94249

LIU, KATHERINE CHANG, artist, art educator; b. Kiang-si, China; came to U.S., 1963; d. Ming-fan and Ying (Yuan) Chang; m. Yet-zen Liu; children: Alan S., Laura Y. MS, U. Calif., Berkeley, 1965. Instr. U. Va. Ext., Longwood Coll.; mem. tchg. staff Intensive Studies Seminar, Santa Fe, 1995, 96, 97, 98, 99, 2000, 02, 03, 04, 05, 06; invited mem. L.A. Artcore Reviewing and Curatorial Bd., 1993; invited curator Lew Allen Contemporary Gallery 'Contemplation', Santa Fe, 2003, Jenkins Johnson Gallery, San Francisco, 2006, Gail Harvey Gallery, Santa Monica, Calif., 2006; curator Duality, 2004, Lew Allen Contemporary Gallery, Santa Fe; invited juror, lectr. over 75 exhbns. and orgns., Kans., S.C. Watercolor Socs., 1998, Alaska, Ga., Tex. and Okla. Watercolor Soc. Anns., 1997, Adirondacks Nat. Show, N.Y., 1999, Ann. Exhibit Watercolor Ohio, 1999, Watercolor Soc. Oreg., 1999, The Collage Soc. Am., 1999; juror, lectr. Ala. Watercolor Soc. Ann., 1996, Midwest Watercolor Soc. Nat. Exhibit, 1996, Watercolor West Nat. Open, 1996, Charlotte County Open Nat., Fla., 2000; sole juror The Taos (N.Mex.) Exhbn. Am. Watercolor, 2000, Va. Watercolor Soc. Ann., Richmond, 2001, Rocky Mountain Nat. Competition, 2001, Collage/Assemblage/USA I, Ventura (Calif.) Coll. 2001, Collage/Assemblage/USA II, 2002, La. Watercolor Soc.-Internat. Competition, New Orleans, 2003, Aqueous Open Nat. Show, Tubac Art Ctr., Ariz. 2004, Pikes Peak Watercolor Competition, Colo. Springs Coll., Colo., 2005; chmn. jury selection Nat. Watercolor Soc. 80th Annual Competition Exhbn., 2000; curator Jenkin Johnston Galleries, San Francisco, 2006. One-woman shows include Harrison Mus., Utah State U., Riverside (Calif.) Art Mus., Ventura (Calif.) Coll., Fla. A&M U., Gail Harvey Gallery, Santa Monica, 1998, J.J. Brookings Gallery, San Francisco, 1998, Louis Newman Galleries, L.A., L.A. Artcore, Lung-Men Gallery, Taipei, Republic of China, Lew Allen Contemporary, Santa Fe Drawing Exhibit, Golden West Collage Gallery, 1999, Rosaline Koener Gallery, Westhampton, N.Y., 2000, AMA Gallery, Turku, Finland, 2001, Gail Harvey Gallery, Santa Monica, Calif., 2001, Rosaline Koener Gallery, LI, N.Y., 2002, Galerie Egelund, Copenhagen, 2002, Le Cercle Optique, Lyon, France, 2003, Galerie Egelund, Copenhagen, Denmark 2004;, Galerie Parsi Paula, Lyon, France, 2005, Galarie Cour de Louges, Lyon France, 2005; invitational shows include Crossing Cultures, Lewallen Contemporary, 1998, State of the Arts International Biennial, Parkland Coll. Ill., 1989, 91, 97, Treasures for the Community: The Chrysler Mus. Collects, 1989-96, 97, Watercolor U.S.A. Hon. Soc. Invitational, 1989, 91, 93, 95, 97, Hunter Mus. Art, Tenn., 1993, Bakersfield Art Mus., 1994, Sandra Walters Gallery, Hong Kong, 1994, Horwitch-Newman Gallery, Scottsdale, Ariz., 1995, Hong Kong U. Sci. and Tech. Libr. Art Gallery, 1996, J.J. Brookings Gallery, San Francisco, 1996, 97, 98, John N Joe Gallery, L.A., 1996, Bill Armstrong Gallery, Springfield, Mo., 1996, Chrysler Mus. Fine Art, Norfolk, Va., 1997, U. B.C. Art Gallery, 1992, U. Sydney Art Mus., 1992, Ruhr-West Art Mus., Wise, 1992, Macau Art Mus., 1992, Rosenfeld Gallery, Phila., 1994, Mandarin Oriental Fine Arts, Hong Kong, 1994, Hampton U. Mus., 2000, Fukuoka Asian Art Mus., 2001, Lew Allen Contemporary Gallery, N.Mex., 2001, Asian Am. Artists, Calif. State Channel Islands, Calif., 2002, What About Beauty, Invitational Foothills Art Ctr., Golden, Colo., 2002, Inaugural Exhibit Jenkins Johnson Gallery, 2005, Small Works Lew Allen Contemporary Gallery, Santa Fe, N.Mex., 2005, Christel Dahlen Gallery, Copenhagen, 2006, Copenhagen Bienniale, 2006, Jenkins Johnson Gallery, San Francisco, 2006; group exhibits Lew Allen Contemporay, 2003; Europe Campus Art, Travel Exhibit to European coll. campuses, invited guest artist, 2004-05; contbr. chpts. to books, articles to profl. jours. Co-curator Taiwan-USA-Australia Watermedia Survey Exhbn., Nat. Taiwan Art Inst., 1994; sole juror San Diego Watermedia Internat., 1993, Triton Mus. Open Competition, 1994, Northern Nat. Art Competition, 1994, Watercolor West Nat., 1993, Tenn., Utah, Hawaii, N.C. Watercolor Socs., North Am. Open, Midwest Southwest and over 30 state-wide competitions in watermedia or all-media; co-juror Rocky Mountain Nat., San Diego Internat. and West Fedn. Exhibits. Recipient Rex Brandt award San Diego Watercolor Internat., 1985, Purchase Selection award Watercolor USA and Springfield (Mo.) Art Mus., 1981, Gold medal, 1986, Mary Lou Fitzgerald meml. award Allied Arts Am. Nat. Arts Club, N.Y.C., 1987, Achievement award of Artists Painting in Acrylic Am. Artists Mag., 1993; NEA grantee, 1979-80. Mem. Nat. Watercolor Soc. (life, chmn. jury 1985, pres. 1983, Top award 1984, cash awards 1979, 87; chmn. jury selection 80th ann. open competition exhibit 2000), Watercolor U.S.A. Honor Soc., Nat. Soc. Painters in Casein and Acrylic (2nd award 1985), Rocky Mountain Nat. Watermedia Soc. (juror 1984, awards 1978, 80, 86). Personal E-mail: kchangliu@verizon.net.

LIU, LUCY, actress; b. Queens, N.Y., Dec. 2, 1968; Student, NYU; BA in Chinese Lang. and Culture, U. Mich., 1990. Actor: (TV series) Beverly Hills, 90210, 1991, L.A. Law, 1993, Coach, 1994, Home Improvement, 1995, Hercules: The Legendary Journeys, 1995, ER, 1995, The X-Files, 1996, Nash Bridges, 1996, High Incident, 1996, The Real Adventures of Johnny Quest, 1997, NYPD Blue, 1997, Michael Hayes, 1997, Sex and the City, 2001, (voice only) King of the Hill, 2002, Jackie Chan Adventures, 2004, Game Over, 2004, Maya & Miguel, 2004, Pearl, 1996—97, Ally McBeal, 1998—2002; (TV films) Riot, 1997; (films) Ban wo zong heng, 1992, Protozoa, 1993, Bang, 1995, Jerry Maguire, 1996, Gridlock'd, 1997, City of Industry, 1997, Guy, 1997, Flypaper, 1997, Love Kills, 1998, Payback, 1999, True Crime, 1999, Molly, 1999, The Mating Habits of the Earthbound Human, 1999, Play It to the Bone, 1999, Shanghai Noon, 2000, Charlie's Angels, 2001, Hotel, 2001, Ballistics: Ecks vs. Sever, 2002, Cypher, 2002, Chicago, 2002, Charlie's Angels: Full Throttle, 2003, Kill Bill: Vol. 1, 2003, Domino, 2005, Lucky Number Slevin, 2006. Apptd. U.S. Fund for UNICEF amb., 2005. Recipient Visibility award, Asian Excellence Awards, 2006. Office: William Morris Agy One William Morris Pl Beverly Hills CA 90212*

LIU, MARGARET C., music educator; b. Canton, China, Aug. 10, 1947; arrived in U.S., 1972; d. Man-Hymn Wong and Shau-Chung Ng; m. John Pui-Chee, July 28, 1973; children: Amos Tao-Peng, Deborah Tao-En. BA, Hong Kong Bapt. U., 1970; M in Ch. Music, Southwestern Bapt. Theol. Sem., 1975. Freelance vocal and keyboard performer, various cities, 1972—; pvt. music tchr., 1975; music dir. 1st Chinese Bapt. Ch., Atlanta, 1976-80, 85-89, Chinese Bapt. Ch., College Park, Md., 1980-83; pres., CEO Cambridge Acad. Music and Arts, Atlanta, 1999—. Bd. mem. Alliance Theatre Edn. Adv. Coun., Atlanta, 1996-99; pres. North Dekalb Music Tchrs. Assn., Atlanta, 1997-99; Ga. local rep. Associated Bd. of the Royal Schs. Music, London, 1997—. Deacon Hanley Rd. Bapt. Ch., St. Louis, 1984, Briarcliff Bapt. Ch., Atlanta, 2003-. Mem. Music Tchrs. Nat. Assn., Music Educators Nat. Conf., Nat. Guild Piano Tchrs., Kindermusik Educators Assn.

LIU, QINYUE (SHERRY LIU), physician, consultant; d. Tianpei Liu and Manren Rao; m. Yanmin Li, May 3, 1963; children: Lucy Liu Xi Li, Lyndon Luke Li. MD, Nanjing Med. Sch., 1979—84; MS, Chinese Acad. of Med. Sci., Peking Union Med. Coll., 1984—87; PhD, U. of Alta., 1988—92. Bd. Cert. Psychiatrist Am. Bd. of Psychiatry and Neurology, 2002. Asst. prof./attending physician U. of Medicine and Dentistry of NJ, 2001—; rsch. scientist Coll. of Physician and Surgeons of Columbia U., NY, 1994—97; asst. psychiatrist NY Presbyn. Hosp., Weill Cornell Med. Ctr. -Westchester Divsn., White Plains, NY, 1997—2001. Contbr. articles to profl. jours. Recipient Travel awards, Am. Psychiat. Assn. Rsch. Colloquium for Jr. Investigator, 2003, Janssen: Future Leaders in Psychiatry, 2003, Nat. Bd. Exam., Chinese Nat. Bd. Exam., 1984. Mem.: AMA, Soc. for Neuroscience, Am. Heart Assn., Am. Psychiat. Assn. Office: UMDNJ 183 South Orange Ave Newark NJ 07103 Office Phone: 973-972-2977. Office Fax: 973-972-3399. Business E-Mail: liush@umdnj.edu.

LIU, RHONDA LOUISE, librarian; b. Honolulu; d. David Yuk Fong Liu and Shirley May Chong Liu. BA, U. Hawaii at Manoa, Honolulu, 1974, M of Libr. Info. Studies, 1991; grad., FBI Citizens Acad., 1998. Remote regions/homework ctrs. outreach libr. Alu Like Native Hawaiian Libr. Project, Hawaii, 1992; libr. II Hawaii State Libr., Hawaii, 1992; fgn. expert libr. studies in English program Beijing Fgn. Studies U., 1992—93; info. specialist Savs. & Cmty. Bankers of Am., Washington, 1993—94; staff specialist III Md. State Dept. Edn., Md. State Libr. for Blind and Physically Handicapped, Balt., 1995—99; asst. project mgr. Serial Record Holdings Conversion Project/LSSI Libr. of Congress, Washington, 2000; reference libr. George Washington U. at Mt. Vernon Coll., Washington, 2000—01; sr. technician serial record divsn. Libr. of Congress, Washington, 2001—02, serials control specialist, serial record divsn., 2002—03, sr. technician cataloguing in pub. div., 2003—04, cataloguer, history and lit. cataloguing divsn., children's lit. team, 2004—. Libr. asst. State of Hawaii Legis. Reference Bur. Libr., 1989-90; asst. rschr. State of Hawaii Legis. Info. Sys. Office, 1984-85; ESL tutor Keimei Gakuen, Tokyo, 1979; exhibit facilitator Smithsonian Instn., 1999. Active Friends of the Md. State Libr. for Blind and Physically Handicapped, 1994-99, Md. State Dept. Edn. Employees Adv. Coun., 1998-99; sec. Coalition Opposed to Violence and Extremism, State of Md., 1997-99; v.p., sec. U. Hawaii Sch. Libr. and Info. Studies, 1990-91; mem. planning com. Asian Pacific Am. Heritage Month, Libr. Congress, poster coord. Alu Like Native Hawaiian Libr. fellow, 1990-91; Kamehameha Sch./Bishop Estate scholar, 1991. Mem.: Libr. Congress Asian-Am. Assn. (program chmn. 2004—05), Libr. Congress Profl. Assn., Lung Kong Kung Shaw Soc., Kamehameha Schs. Alumni Assn. (East Coast region), U. Hawaii Sch. Lib. and Info. Studies Alumni Assn., U. Hawaii Alumni Assn. Business E-Mail: rliu@loc.gov.

LIU, RUTH WANG, retired academic administrator; b. China, Feb. 25, 1945; d. James D. and Anna H. Wang; m. C.Y. Liu, Feb. 21, 1975; children: Brian, Lora. BS, Union Coll., 1966; MS, U. Calif., San Francisco, 1967; EdD, U. Tenn., 1997. Asst. prof. Sch. of Nursing Loma Linda U., Calif., 1968-72; clin. nurse specialist Cmty. Mental Health, San Francisco, 1972-75; adminstr. Chattanooga Women's Laser Ctr., 1976-95; coord. East Tenn. Consortium for Higher Edn. U. Tenn., 1998—, postdoctoral rsch. assoc. Knoxville, 1998-2000; dir. Institutional Rsch. and Planning, So. Adventist U., Collegedale, Tenn., 2000—04; ret., 2004. Adj. prof. So. Adventist U., Collegedale, Tenn., 1996-2000, cons. 1975; lectr., rschr., cons., 1990—; cons. Taiwan Adventist Hosp., Taipei, Taiwan, 1974, Atlantic Union Coll., South Lancaster, Mass., 1970; adv. bd. Kiddie Kampus, Collegedale, 1994—; bd. dirs. Cmty. Trust & Banking, Ooltewah, Tenn. Contbr. articles to profl. jours. Adv. bd. Seventh-day Adventist Ch., Collegedale, 1999—; trustee Ho. of Grace of Am., Chattanooga, The Bridge to Recovery, Bowling Green, Ky., Samaritan Ctr., Chattanooga, MCR Found., Chattanooga. Mem. Assn. for Instnl. Rschrs., Sigma Theta Tau, Phi Kappa Phi. Seventh-day Adventist. Avocations: music, swimming, hiking.

LIU, TE HUA, neuroradiologist, educator; b. Shanghai, China, Dec. 21, 1924; arrived in U.S., 1978; d. Zila-Chen and Chen Liu; m. Chi-Chien Kao, Apr. 16, 1950; children: Diana K. Chu, William Ceda. MD, Nat. Med. Coll. Shanghai, 1950. Diplomate Am. Bd. Radiology, 1982. Resident Med. Sch. 1st Red Cross Hosp., Shanghai, 1950—54; attending physician radiology Shanghei Med. Sch. Hua-San Hosp., 1954—60, chmn. Dept. Radiology Shanghei Med. Sch., 1960—78; resident radiology Roosevelt and St. Lukes Hosp., N.Y.C., 1980—82; fellow radiology Columbia U., N.Y.C., 1982—83; attending physician neuroradiology Temple U. Hosp., Phila., 1983—86, chief neuroradiology, 1986—94, cons. neuroradiology, 1994—96. Author (co-editor): Diagnostic Radiology, 1978; co-author: MRI & CT of Muscular-Skeletal Systems, 1984; contbr. articles to profl. jours. Mem.: Ea. Neuroradiological Soc., Assn. Program Dirs. Radiology, Radiol. Soc. N.Am., Am. Soc. Neuroradiology (sr.). E-mail: sinocow@comcast.net.

LIVAUDAIS, NOEL ELIZABETH DWYER, special education educator, secondary school educator; b. New Orleans, La., Oct. 2, 1950; d. Noel E. and Antoinette (Massa) Dwyer; m. Jack Charles Livaudais, Jr., Aug. 14, 1971; children: Frank, Michelle. BS, La. State U., New Orleans, 1971; MA, U. N. Mex., Albuquerque, 1979; postgrad., U. No. Colo., Greeley, 1986-87, U. Tex., Arlington, 1991-92; PhD, U. North Tex., Denton, 1995. Cert. math. tchr., emotionally disturbed, learning disabled abd mid-mgmt. adminstrn., Tex. Math. tchr. Orleans Parish Schs., New Orleans, 1972; 6th grade tchr. Sacred Heart Sch., Baton Rouge, La., 1972-73; math. tchr. E. Baton Rouge Parish Schs., 1973-74, Los Lunas (N. Mex.) Consolidated Schs., 1975-76, Albuquerque Pub. Schs., 1976-80; resource tchr. level I Millad Pub. Schs., Omaha, Nebr., 1982-84; resource tchr. Jefferson County Pub. Schs., Golden, Colo., 1984-88; hosp. tchr. Hurst-Euless-Bedford Ind. Sch. Dist., Bedford, Tex., 1988—, mem. strategic planning com., 1990—. Mem. Middle Sch. Com., Littleton (Colo.) Pub. Schs., 1986; hosp. tchr. Hurst-Euless-Bedford Ind. Sch. Dist., 1988-93, spl. edn. coord., 1993-2002. Min. St. John the Apostle Cath. Ch., Fort Worth, 1990—; mem. St. Elizabeth Cath. Ch. Mem.: Coun. Exceptional Children. Republican. Avocations: reading, travel, walking. Home: 4703 Mill Wood Dr Colleyville TX 76034-3691 Personal E-mail: jaynoel@sbcglobal.net.

LIVENGOOD, CAROL ANN, elementary school educator; b. Great Lakes, Ill., June 25, 1948; d. Thomas Joseph and Evelyn Bernadette Pawlowski; m. Paul Frederick Livengood, July 13, 1974; children: Paul Frederick, Jr., Christine Marie, Thomas Michael. BS in elem. edn., George Mason U., 1967—70, MA, 1996—98. Postgraduate Profl. Lic. Richmond, VA, 2004. Tchr. Prince William County Pub. Sch. Sys., Manassas, Va., 1990—2004, Fairfax County Pub. Sch. sys., Fairfax, Va.; lang. arts tchr. Prince William County Pub. Sch. Sys., Manassas, Va., 2004—. Adv. mem. Coles Elem. Adv. Coun., Manassas, Va., 2002—03, J.W. Alvey Elem. Adv. Coun., Haymarket, Va. Grants, Va. Commn. for the Arts., 1995—2004, Skills for Self-Reliance grant, Wash. Post, 1990. Mem.: Prince William Fedn. of Teachers (life). Roman Cath. Achievements include awarded a United States copyright for a Responsibility Chart intended to improve students' work habits and organizational skills. Home: 8052 Stillbrooke Rd Manassas VA 20112 Office: Marsteller Middle Sch 1400 Sudley Manor Dr Bristow VA 20136 Office Phone: 703-393-7608. Personal E-mail: 3kds4me@comcast.net. E-mail: livengoc@pwcs.edu.

LIVENGOOD, CHARLOTTE LOUISE, retired human resources specialist; b. L.A., June 18, 1944; d. James Zollie and Zela (Cogburn) Livengood. BS in Secondary Edn., Tex. A & I U., 1968; MEd in Pers. Guidance and Counseling, North Tex. U., 1971. Cert. secondary tchr. Tex., counselor Tex. Tchr. South Grand Prairie HS, 1969—71, West Springfield HS, Springfield, Va., 1972-73; counselor Gus Grissom HS, Huntsville, Ala., 1971-72; edn. specialist U.S. Dept. Def., El Paso, Tex., 1975-78; instr. El Paso CC, 1977-78; employee devel. specialist U.S. Office Pers. Mgmt., Dallas, 1978-79; pers. mgmt. specialist Dept. Vets. Affairs, Houston, 1979-87, labor rels. specialist VA Med. Ctr., 1987-89, pers. staffing specialist, 1989-90; employee devel. specialist, acad. tng. officer HUD, Ft. Worth, 1990-95; assoc. prof. Ariz. State U., 1995—; Bur. Engraving and Printing Ctr. excellence tng. officer Dept. Treasury, Ft. Worth, 1995—2005, ret., 2005. EEO investigator Dept. Vet. Affairs, 1984—87, fed. women's program mgr., 1984—85; mem. standing panel pers. specialists/fed. suprs./mgrs. Merit Sys. Protection Bd., 1996—; mem. computer design team Dept. Treasury, 2001; spkr. in field. Editor: Pipline, 1980—87; co-author: Plate Printer Apprenticeship Standards Registration with Dept. of Labor, 2002. Mem. Dallas/Ft. Worth Quality Control Coun., Tex. War on Drugs Com., 1990—; hon. mem. Dallas/Ft. Worth Fed. Exec. Bd., 1993—94. Future Secs. Am. scholar, 1962. Mem.: APGA, AAUW, ASTD, Fed. Suprs., Mgrs., Merit Sys. Protection Bd. Standing Panel Pers. Specialists, Fed. Women's Program Mgr., Intergovtl. Tng. Coun. (chairperson 1993—94), Intergovtl. Tng. Assn., Fed. Bus. Assn., Tex. Classroom Tchrs. Assn., Tex. State Tchrs. Assn., Internat. Transactional Analysis Assn., Assn. Quality Participation, AARP, Nat. Assn. Ret. Fed. Employees, VA Employee Assn. Mem. Ch. Of Christ. Avocations: reading, travel, bridge, fishing, theater.

LIVENGOOD, HEATHER JEANNE, coach; d. Michael M. Pistana and Darlene H. Dedrick, Mark C. Dedrick (Stepfather); m. Alan Joseph Livengood, Oct. 10, 1998; 1 child, Katherine Kelly. BA, SUNY, Albany, 2000. Practice coord. Albany Med. Coll., Albany, 1995—2001; auditor process improvement team Fla. Physician's Med. Group, Orlando, 2002—04; educator Lake Co. Schs., Tavares, 2004—. Pres. Livengood's Lawn Care, Belleview, Fla., 2006—; asst. coach Tavares H.S. Swim Team, Fla., 2005—; sponsor - model UN club Tavares H.S., 2004—, sponsor - freshman class,

2004—05. Recipient Rookie Tchr. of Yr., Tavares H.S., Lake Co., 2006. Mem.: Take Stock Children, Nat. Tchrs. Union (assoc.). Office: Tavares High School 603 North New Hamsphire Avenue Tavares FL Office Phone: 352-343-3007.

LIVERIGHT, BETTY FOUCHE, actress, writer; b. La Grange, Ill., Oct. 20, 1913; d. Squire and Edna Amanda (Wright) Fouche; m. Herman Elsas Liveright, Feb. 1, 1936; children: Beth, Timothy. BA, Temple U., 1963. Actress L'Aiglon, N.Y.C., 1934, White Plains (N.Y.) Comty. Theater, 1947-52; coord., actress TV Tulane U., New Orleans, 1953-56; actress TV Commercials, New Orleans, 1954-56; rschr. Friends Libr. Swarthmore (Pa.) Coll., 1956-69; pub. rels. agt. Highlander Rsch. and Edn. Ctr., Knoxville, Tenn., 1969-71; co-dir. Berkshire Forum, Stephentown, N.Y., 1972-90. Editor, co-coord.: (bulletin) This Just In.: A Bulletin for News of Politcal Prisoners and POWs, 1991—. Pres. Yorkville Peace Coun., N.Y.C., 1940-42; bd. dirs. Women's Internat. League for Peace and Freedom, Phila., 1965-85. Home and Office: # 134 2361 E 29th St Oakland CA 94606-3511 Office Phone: 510-261-5408. E-mail: bliveright@aol.com.

LIVERMAN, BETTY JEAN, elementary school educator; b. Murfreesboro, N.C., Sept. 14, 1965; d. Ealone and Minnie Pearl Liverman; 1 child, Grybrielle Micheal. BS, East Carolina U., Greenville, N.C., 1987; MEd, Elon U., N.C., 2006. Cert. tchr. N.C., 1992. Tchr. Wake County Pub. Sch. Sys., Raleigh, NC, 1988—; ptnr. Paper Creations, Durham, NC, 2000—. Co-dir. Saturday Dance Acad., Raleigh, NC, 1990—91; founder/dir. Drama Mama Prodn., Fuquay Varina, NC, 1990—, Team Spirit, Durham, NC, 2000—. (exhibition) A Touch of CL.A.S.S (1st pl. Most Talented award, 2005); dir.: (conducted over 300 dramatic perfomances) Drama Mama Productions, (gospel dramatic performances) Mt. Zion Children Drama and Dance ministry; prodn. dir.: (TV series) Beyond Gifted. Mem. NAACP, Greenville, North Carolina, NC, 1984—85; tchr. Mt. Zion Missionary Bapt. Ch. Children Ministry, Cary, NC, 1996—2006; pres. Head Start Tchr. Parent Student Orgn., Holly Springs, NC, 1995—96. Recipient scholarship, N.C. Bus. Women Orgn., 2004; grantee, Wake Edn. Partnership, 1990, 2005 and 2006. Mem.: N.C. Assn. of Educators (corr.), Apex Arts Coun. (corr.). Avocations: theatre arts, dance, being a mommy, church activities, reading /quiet time. Office Phone: 919-850-8700. Office Fax: 919-850-8709. Personal E-mail: bliverman@wcpss.net.

LIVERMORE, ANN MARTINELLI, computer company executive; b. Greensboro, NC, Aug. 23, 1958; m. Tom Livermore. BA in Econs., U. NC, Chapel Hill, 1980; MBA, Stanford U., 1982. Various mgmt. positions Hewlett-Packard Co., Palo Alto, Calif., 1982-1995, corp. v.p., 1995—2002, pres., CEO enterprise computing divsn., 1998—2003, exec. v.p., 2002—, head tech. solutions grp., 2004—. Bd. dirs. United Parcel Svc., 1997—; bd. advs. Stanford Bus. Sch.; bd. visitors Kenan-Flagler Bus. Sch. Named one of 100 Most Powerful Women in Bus., Forbes mag., 2005—06, 50 Most Powerful Women in Bus., Fortune mag., 2006.*

LIVERMORE, FERN CHRISMAN, retired artist; b. Wooldridge, Mo., May 20, 1921; d. Thomas Oscar and Lulu Ann (Oerly) Chrisman; m. Claude Robert Livermore, Apr. 24, 1941; children: Thomas Robert, Toma Lee, Rosalie Ann. BS, Western N.Mex. U., 1960, MEd, 1965, BA, 1987. Art tchr. Silver City (N.Mex.) Consol. Sch. System, 1960-77. One-woman shows include Frances McCray Gallery Western N.Mex. U., Silver City, 1962, La Azteca Mini-Gallery, Silver City, 1989-90, Home Fed. Savs. and Loan Assn., Silver City, 1990, Miller Libr., Western N.Mex., U., 1990, Sunwest Bank, Silver City, 1989-91, Silver City Pub. Libr., 1991; group exhbns. include N.Mex. Federated Women's Clubs, Silver City, 1962, Pinos Altos (N.Mex.) Ch. Gallery, 1970—, El Paso Ceramic Show, 1977, Eros, Love and Will Gallery, Silver City, 1989, Ea. N.Mex. U., Portales, 1989, Yucca Ford Motor Co., Silver City, 1989, Silver City Women's Club, 1989, Hanover Outpost, Hanover, N.Mex., 1989-90, Hillsboro (N.Mex.) Apple Festival, 1989-91, Branigan Cultural Ctr., Las Cruces, N.Mex., 1990, 13th St. Emporium, Silver City, 1991, West Gallery, El Paso, Yankie Creek Gallery, Silver City, Deming (N.Mex.) Ctr. for arts, 1991. Mem. N.Mex. Ret. Tchrs., Kappa Kappa Iota. Democrat. Methodist. Avocations: snorkeling, travel, hiking, gardening. Home: 151 Roadrunner Pkwy Apt 405 Las Cruces NM 88011

LIVERMORE, JANE, foundation executive; b. Kansas City, Mo., Feb. 21, 1939; d. George P. and Mary Louise (Luccock) L.; children: Jana, Douglas, George. Student, U. Okla. Owner, pres. Mary L. Livermore Enterprises, Lubbock, Tex.; ptnr. Jermac Co., Levelland, Tex.; pres. Mary L. Livermore Found., Lubbock. Mem. chancellor's coun. Tex. Tech. U.; bd. dirs. Lubbock YWCA; mem. Lubbock Symphony Guild. Address: PO Box 12109 Lubbock TX 79452-2109

LIVESAY, JACQUELINE RYDER, elementary school educator, music educator; b. Charlottesville, Va., Feb. 13, 1949; d. Eldridge G. and Elizabeth Row Ryder; m. Charles Jackson Livesay, June 30, 1973; children: Jennifer Livesay Pereira, Jean, Ellen(dec.). MusB, Westminster Choir Coll., Princeton, NJ, 1973; MusM, U. Mich., Ann Arbor, 1977; MA in Edn., Spring Arbor U., Mich., 2001. Organist, min. music Trinity United Meth. Ch., Jackson, Miss., 1977—2003; tchr. elem. music Vandercook Lake Pub. Schs., 1989—98, Jackson Pub. Schs., 1998—; dir. children's music, organist 1st United Meth. Ch., 2003—. Adj. instr. music Albion Coll., Mich., 2003—; planning com. mem. Jackson Symphony Orch. Family Concert, 2003—. Mem. Western High Sch. Acad. Boosters, Jackson, 1995—2004, Tuesday Musical Assn., 1998—, Jackson Symphony Guild, 1999—. Named Outstanding Elem. Educator, Jackson Pub. Schs., 2001. Mem.: Mich. Music Educators Assn. Avocations: reading, travel, walking, gardening. Home: 4897Indian Creek Dr Jackson MI 49201 Office: Frost Elem Sch S Wisner St Jackson MI 49203 Personal E-mail: jlivesay@jpsmail.org.

LIVESAY, TRACIE LYNN, paralegal; b. Martin, Tenn., Jan. 9, 1971; d. Albert Edward and Bonnie Jean Dial; m. Gregory Scott Livesay, Dec. 11, 2005; children: Garrett Scott, Griffin Scott, Grantham Scott. AAS, Pellissippi State Tech. C.C., Knoxville, Tenn., 1995. Cert. paralegal specialist Nat. Assn. Legal Assts. Paralegal O'Neil, Parker & Williamson, Knoxville, 1995—97, The Taylor Law Firm, Knoxville, 1997—2001, Woolf, McClane, Bright, Allen & Carpenter, Knoxville, 2001—05, Costner & Greene, Attys., Maryville, Tenn., 2005—. Recipient Pres.'s award, Pellissippi State Tech. C.C., 1995. Mem.: Smoky Mountain Paralegal Assn. (pres. 2006). Office: Costner & Greene Attys 315 High St Maryville TN 37804

LIVESTON, DENISE ANNE, elementary school educator; d. Joseph Peter and Mary Anne Mozden; m. Thomas William Liveston; 1 child, Thomas Jr. BS in Edn., Kenne State Coll., NH, 1974. Tchr. 1st grade Claremont Sch. Dist., NH, 1974—85; tchr. 1st, 2d & 3d grades Springfield Sch. Dist., Vt., 1985—. Mem. staff devel. Springfield Sch. Dist., 1995—, mem. math. com., 1999—2003; mem. curriculum coun. Claremont Sch. Dist., 2003—, mem. comm. com., 2004—. Leader Boy. Scouts Am., Claremont, 1999—, merit badge counselor, 2004—; pres. PTO, 2002—04. Mem.: Coun. Elem. Sci. Internat., Nat. Sci. Tchrs. Assn. Avocations: crafts, travel, swimming, reading, cross country skiing. Office: Springfield Sch Dist 43 Union St Claremont NH 03743

LIVINGSTON, CAROLYN HARRIS, music educator; b. Cookeville, Tenn., Jan. 7, 1936; d. Frazier and Myrtle (Lee) H.; m. Frank W. Medley, Jr., June 28, 1955 (dec. Dec. 1967); children: Frank, Jane, Jennifer Medley Martin; m. Jesse B. Livingston, Sept. 1, 1969 (dec. Jan. 1993); stepchildren: Jeffrey, Patrick, Laura Livingston Nuttle; m. Burton Zitkin, May 29, 2000. Student, U. Md., 1958—59; BS, Tenn. Tech. U., 1959; MEd, U. Fla., 1981, PhD, 1986. Tchr. music pvt. practice, Bowie, Md., 1960-68; music specialist Prince Georges County Schs., Bowie, Md., 1968—69; tchr. music pvt. practice, Gainesville, Fla., 1970-80; dir. choirs 1st Luth. Ch., Gainesville, Fla., 1976-83; music specialist Putnam County Schs., Cookeville, Tenn., 1984-86, Memphis City Schs., 1986-87; asst. prof. U. R.I., Kingston, 1987-93, coord. music edn., 1989—97, assoc. prof., 1993-99, dir. grad. studies in music, 1997—2006, prof., 1999—. Author: Charles Faulkner Bryan: His Life and Music, 2003; mem. editl. bd. Bulletin Hist. Rsch. Music Edn., 1990—; mem. editl. com. Jour. Hist. Rsch. Music Edn., 2004—; contbr. articles to profl. jours. Founder, dir. U. R.I. Childrens Chorus, 1993-2000. U. RI Humanities fellow, 2004. Mem. Music Educators Nat. Conf., History Spl. Rsch. Interest Group (vice-chair 1997-99, chair 1999-01, Svc. award 2006), Music Tchrs. Nat. Assn., R.I. Music Tchrs. Assn. (pres. 1992-94), Sigma Alpha Iota, Pi Kappa Lambda, Kappa Delta Pi, Phi Kappa Phi. Lutheran. Avocations: gardening, travel. Home: 31 Rosemary St Cranston RI 02920-8157 Office Phone: 401-874-2763. Business E-Mail: musiced@uri.edu.

LIVINGSTON, DEBRA A., law educator; BA, Princeton U., 1980; JD, Harvard U., 1984. Law clk. to Hon. J. Edward Lumbard US Ct. of Appeals (2nd cir.), 1984—85; assoc. Paul, Weiss, Rifkind, Wharton & Garrison, 1985—86, 1991—92; asst. US atty. gen. So. Dist. NY, 1986—91; faculty mem. U. Mich. Law Sch., 1992—94, Columbia Law Sch., NYC, 1994—, Paul J. Kellner prof. law. Legal cons. UN High Commr. for Refugees, Bangkok, 1982—83; commr. NYC Civilian Complaint Review Bd., 1994—2003. Co-author: Comprehensive Criminal Procedure. Office: Columbia Law Sch 435 W 116th St New York NY 10027 Office Phone: 212-854-2527. Office Fax: 212-854-7946. E-mail: sissac@law.columbia.edu.

LIVINGSTON, GWENDELL SHEAWANNA, education educator; b. Phila., Pa., Oct. 3, 1968; d. Wendell Livingston and Elizabeth Tina Walton; children: Andté Wendell, Cyrus Avez, Girish Ricky Zeck Ayir. Diploma, St. Vincent De Paul, Phila., 1980, Immaculate Conception Heart of Mary, 1984, Dobbins AVTS, 1984, John Casablanca's Modeling, Pa., 1989. Lic. Internat. Beauty Sch., Phila., 2002, cert. instr. Pa., 2004. Ballet instr., Phila., 1989—90; comml. video model Krush Video, Phila., 1990—91; haircolor designer Three Brother, Phila., 1996—99; started store Sassy Beauty Outlet, N.J., Conn., Pa., 1998—2000; wig designer Maxx Hair, Phila., 1999—2000; music video model Columbia Records, Phila., 2001—02; started store Hairtown, Phila., 2001—02; instr. cosmetology H. Internat. Beauty Sch., Phila., 2004—. Guest spkr. Mayor City of Phila., 1984. Recipient Phila. Overachievers award, City of Phila. Hon. Soc., 1984. Republican. Avocations: photography, painting, art, antiques, swimming.

LIVINGSTON, JO ELLEN BROOKS, music educator; b. Beckley, W.Va., Dec. 4, 1953; d. Henry Edward and Ramona Ann Brooks; m. James M Livingston, Oct. 3, 1981. BS in music edn., Concord Coll., 1971—77; MusM, U. of So. Miss., 1977—80. Music educator St. Francis de Sales Sch., Beckley, 1980—81; music dir. Theatre W.Va., Beckley, 1981—90, Curtain Callers, Mt. Hope, W.Va., 1981—94; music educator Raleigh County Pub. Schools, Beckley, W.Va., 1981—94, Prince William County Pub. Schools, Manassas, Va., 1995—; music dir. Ctr. for the Arts, Manassas, 1995—, Rooftop Players, Manassas, 2003—. Music curriculum com. Prince William County Pub. Schools, Manassas, 2001; min. of music Meml. Bapt. Ch., Beckley, 1992—94; performer Gary Matheny Trio, Athens, W.Va., 1971—77, Commanders Big Band, Athens, 1972—77; percussionist Hattiesburg Light Opera Co., Hattiesburg, Miss., Opera South, Jackson, Miss., Miss. Ballet Orch., Jackson, Jackson Symphony Orch., Tupelo (Miss.) Symphony Orch., Meridian (Miss.) Symphony Orch., Miss. Opera Co., Jackson; string solo and ensmble chair Prince William County Schools, Manassas, 2002—; percussionist W.Va. Symphony Orch., Charleston; mid. sch. honor choir chair Prince William County, Manassas; Prince William County Mid. Sch. honors orch. chair Prince William County Schools, Manassas; dist. mid. sch. honor choir chair Va. Music Educators Assn., Manassas; dist. 9 honor bands audition chair VBODA, District 9, Va.; region i chair W.Va. Music Educators Assn., Region I, all-state h.s. honors chorus chair, Charleston; auditorium mgr. Woodrow Wilson H.S., Beckley, 1988—90. Mem. Curtain Callers, Mt. Hope, W.Va. Recipient Gilbert award, U. of So. Miss. Theater, Governor's Citation for Musical Contributions, State Of W.Va. Mem.: Nat. Educators Assn. (assoc.; state del. and sch. rep.), Va. Music Educators Assn. (assoc.), Omicron Delta Kappa (assoc.), Mu Phi Epsilon (assoc.; v.p. 1978). Avocation: painting. Home: 9301 Battle St Manassas VA 20110 Office: Parkside Middle School 8602 Mathis Ave Manassas VA 20110 Office Phone: 703-361-3106. Personal E-mail: jbldiva@comcast.net. E-mail: livingjb@pwcs.edu.

LIVINGSTON, KATHRYN E., writer; b. Schenectady, NY, Jan. 11, 1953; d. Abram Fryer Livingston, Virginia Kathryn Swart; m. Mitchell Kriegler, June 5, 1977; 3 children. BA, Kirkland Coll., Clinton, N.Y., 1975; MA, Hunter Coll., N.Y.C., 1979. Freelance writer, 1983—. Text author: Special Effects Photography, 1985, Patrick Demarchelier: Fashion Photographer, 1984, Secrets of Studio Still Life Photography, 1984; co-author: Photographing Your Baby, 1984, Parenting Partners (St. Martins), 1999, All About Motherhood, 2005, The Secret Life of the Dyslexic Child, 2002; contbr. articles to profl. jours. Mailing: 143 Highview Pl Bogota NJ 07603

LIVINGSTON, MARGARET GRESHAM, civic leader; b. Birmingham, Ala., Aug. 16, 1924; d. Owen Garside and Katherine (Morrow) Gresham; m. James Archibald Livingston, Jr., July 16, 1947; children: Mary Margaret, James Archibald, Katherine Wiley, Elizabeth Gresham. Grad., The Baldwin Sch., Phila., 1942; AB, Vassar Coll., 1945; MA, U. Ala., 1946. Acting dir. Birmingham Mus. Art, 1978-79, 81, chmn. bd. dirs., 1978-86, mem. exec. bd., 1978—. Bd. dirs. Birmingham Civic Ctr. Authority, 1988-95; bd. dirs. Altamont Sch., Birmingham, 1963—, chmn. bd., 1986. Named Woman of Yr., Birmingham 1986; named to Ala. Tennis Hall of Fame, 1994. Mem. Am. Assn. Mus., Jr. League, Ala. Tennis Assn. Episcopalian.

LIVINGSTON, PAMELA A., corporate image and marketing management consultant; b. Richmond Hill, N.Y., Nov. 21, 1930; d. Paul Yount and Anna Margaret (Altland) L. BA, Adelphi U., 1951; postgrad., NYU, 1952, Columbia U., 1959, Am. Acad. Dramatic Art, 1954, IBM Sys. and Mktg. Schs., 1967-70, Brandon Sch. Electronic Data, 1973, Pa. State U., 1993. Pers. and pub. rels. depts. Am. Can Co., N.Y.C., 1951-60; exec. sec. to pres. York (Pa.) divsn. Borg-Warner Corp., 1962-65; freelance writer, 1965-67; mktg. ofcl. IBM Corp., 1967-70; rsch. analyst, dir. new EDP bus. Ins. Co. N.Am., 1971-74; asst. to v.p. corp. affairs IU Internat., Phila., 1974-75; comm. and mktg. mgmt. cons. specializing in corp. identity, 1975—. Corp. image cons., 1984—; freelance writer, spkr. on identity, 1994—. Contbr. articles to tech jours. Recipient various journalism awards, award in mktg. and sales IBM, 1969-70, award for innovative product application, 1969. Mem. AAUW, Sales/Mktg. Execs. Internat., Art Alliance, Pub. Rels. Soc. Am., Econs. Club of York C. of C., Phila. Club Advt. Women, Phila. Acad. Fine Arts, World Affairs Coun., English-Speaking Union, Kappa Kappa Gamma. Home and Office: 108 S Rockburn St York PA 17402-3467

LIVINGSTON, SYLVIA JEAN, art appraiser; b. Mexico, Mo., Jan. 13, 1937; d. Lawrence Cecil and Eleanor Elizabeth (Caldwell) Gass; m. Frank Lee Livingston, Jan. 15, 1982; stepchildren: Kimberly Smith, Rachelle Caswell; m. Ivan Leon Boyer (div.); children: Scott Lawrence Boyer, Gregory Lloyd Boyer(dec.). Grad., Durango H.S., Colo., 1954. Clerical State of Wash., 1977—79; personal property appraiser Cowlitz County Assessor, Kelso, Wash., 1979—80, San Juan County Assessor, Aztec, N.Mex., 1981—84, 1988—89, Rogers County Assessor, Claremore, Okla., 1995—2003. Mem.: Mensa. Democrat. Avocations: reading, dance, pool, genealogy. Home: 10651 E Dogwood Ct Claremore OK 74019-0313 Fax: 918-343-8940.

LIVINGSTONE, SUSAN MORRISEY, management consultant, former federal agency administrator; b. Carthage, Mo., Jan. 13, 1946; d. Richard John II and Catherine Newell (Carmean) Morrisey; m. Neil C. Livingstone III, Aug. 30, 1968. AB, Coll. William and Mary, 1968; MA, U. Mont., 1973; postgrad., Tufts U., 1972—73, Fletcher Sch. Law and Diplomacy, 1973—. Rschr. Senator Mark O. Hatfield, Washington, 1969-70; chief legis. and press asst. Congressman Richard H. Ichord, Washington, 1973-75, adminstrv. asst., 1975-81; cons. Congressman Wendell Bailey, Washington, 1981; exec. asst. VA, Washington, 1981-85, assoc. dep. adminstr. logistics and mgmt., 1985-86, sr. procurement exec., 1985-89, assoc. dep. adminstr. logistics, 1985—89; asst. sec. Army U.S. Dept. of Def., Washington, 1989-93; v.p. health and safety svcs. ARC, Washington, 1993-97; cons. mgmt., 1997-2001; under sec. of Navy U.S. Dept. Navy, Washington, 2001—03; mem. return-to-flight task group NASA, 2003—05. Mem interagy. com. on women's bus. enterprise The White House, 1985-89; mem. Pres.'s Coun. on Mgmt. Improvement, 1985-86; cons. Def. Sci. Bd., 1998, 00; mem. adv. bd. Martin Inst. U. Idaho, 2000-01; mem. nat. security studies bd. advs., Maxwell Sch. Syracuse U., 2003—; bd. dirs. The Atlantic Coun., 2004; mem. adv. subcom. on naval history Sec. of Navy, 2004—. Vice chair White House Commn. on Nat. Moment of Remembrance, 2002—03; bd. dirs. The Army Hist. Found. Inc., 2005—. Mem. Procurement Round Table (bd. dirs. 1994-03, 05—), Assn. U.S. Army (bd. dirs. 1994-, coun. trustees 1996-01, CEO, dep. chmn. 2000-01), Women in Internat. Security (mem. adv. bd. 1994-97). Episcopalian.

LIVINGSTON-MACIRELAN, JOAN PERSILLA, artist; b. Wenatchee, Wash., Oct. 9, 1940; d. Herbert Edgar and Maxine Lucina (Irelan) Macy; m. David Warner Livingston, June 15, 1958 (div. Apr. 1981); children: Dolly Jo, Jennifer Lynn. Student in oil painting, Old Town Gallery, Auburn, Calif., 1966; student, Ft. Mason Art Ctr., San Francisco, 1989. Cert. cosmetologist Calif., Wash., N.Mex., massage therapist, med. massage practitioner, 2003. Salon owner TJ's Hair Factory/Hair Today, Auburn, 1969-79; photographer's stylist Ed Young Photography, San Francisco, 1985-86; studio painter Studio Nine, Sausalito, Calif., 1986-90, 94-96; designer sculptor Poupee Millet, San Rafael, Calif., 1990-91; studio painter Studio Nine, San Rafael, 1991-94; wilderness artist Studio Nine Cabin Studio, Stehekin, Wash., 1996-98, Seattle, 1998-99; studio painter, art tchr. Studio Nine, Cashmere, Wash., 1999, studio painter, graphic designer, 2000—03, owner Santa Fe, 2006—, Loyal Pro Bodywork, Albuquerque, 2003—06. Exhibited in one-woman and group exhbns. in Zelos Ventures, San Francisco, 1991, Hanson Art GAlleries, Sausalito, 1992, Royal Palm Gallery, Palm Beach, Fla., 1995, The Black Orchid Gallery, Sanibel Island, Fla., 1997, William Vincent Fine Art Gallery, Santa Fe, 1998, Gallery 76, Wenatchee, Wash., 2000—01; exhibited in one-woman and group exhbns. in, Sunburst Gallery, Chelan, Wash., 2001—03, Dartmouth St. Gallery, Albuquerque, 2003, ABQ Fin., 2004—05, over 30 pvt. collections. Recipient awards for art Placer County Fair, 1957-60, The Artists Mag., 1988, 91, 95, Gallery 76, Wenatchee, 2001. Mem. Nat. Mus. Women in the Arts, Georgia Okeeffe Mus. Avocations: writing children's stories, poetry, flamenco dance, hiking. Office Phone: 505-934-2959. E-mail: josstudio9@msn.com.

LIVNE, NAVA LEVIA, psychologist, researcher; b. Haifa, Israel, Aug. 12, 1952; arrived in U.S., 2002; d. Moshe Yitzchak and Guta Tova Meiri; m. Giora Livne, Jan. 2, 1978; children: Oren, Nilly. Student, U. Ill., Chgo., 1972—73; BA in Advanced Studies in Psychology (disting. scholar), Hebrew U., Jerusalem, 1977; MSc in Social Psychology (disting. scholar), Bar Ilan U., Ramat Gan, Israel, 1996; PhD in Ednl. Psychology (Excellence in Rsch. scholar), Tel Aviv U., 2002. Lic. psychologist Israel. Mentor Hebrew U., Jerusalem, 1974—75; mentor, advisor to highly gifted children Israel, 1978—95; dir. extended learning program City of Kiryat Motzkin, Israel, 1982—89, City of Kiryat Yam, Israel, 1989—91; dir. unit rsch. and assessment Sch. Edn. Bar Ilan U., Ramat Gan, 1996—98; dir. workshops Ctr. Advancement Tchg. Tel Aviv U., 1998—2002; rsch. specialist U. Calif., Irvine, 2002—04; postdoctoral fellow U. N.Mex, Albuquerque, 2004; ednl. rschr. and program dir. U. Utah, Salt Lake City, 2005—06. Contbr. scientific papers to profl. jours.; patent website. Vol. tchr. Jewish Sch. Congregation Kol Ami, Salt Lake City, 2005. With Isreali Def. Force, 1970—72. Recipient Excellence in Rsch. award, Am. Mensa, 1999; Jr. Faculty fellow, NSF, 2004. Mem.: APA, Internat. Soc. Learning Scis., World Coun. Gifted and Talented, Am. Ednl. Rsch. Assn., Alpha Delta Lambda (life). Avocations: hiking, symphonic concert, opera, lectures, reading. Office: U Utah 1901 S Central Campus Dr Rm 3490 Salt Lake City UT 84112 Office Phone: 801-587-5835. Business E-Mail: nlivne@aoce.utah.edu.

LIXEY, ELIZABETH VOULGARAKIS, secondary school educator; b. Erie, Pa., Jan. 28, 1952; d. Paul Thomas Voulgarakis and Irene Elizabeth Gourgonis-Voulgarakis; m. William Henry Lixey, Dec. 16, 1978; children: Heather Elizabeth, Jennifer Laura. AA in Theatre Arts, Am. River Coll., 1971; BA in Drama, Calif. State U., 1973; MEd, Jacksonville State U., Ala., 1991. Cert. tchr. Ala., 1991, Dept. of Def. Dependents Schs., 1992, profl. cert. Pa., 1995, provisional edn. cert. Mich., 1998, cert. profl. educator Mich., 2004. Social Security Adminstrn. benefit authorizer HHS, San Francisco, 1974—79, Social Security Adminstrn. tech. advisor Richmond, Calif., 1979—81, Social Security Adminstrn. svc. rep. Roseville, Mich., 1981—82; mid. and secondary lang. arts educator Taegu Am. H.S., Camp George, Republic of Korea, 1992—93; adj. English prof. Keimyung U., Taegu, Republic of Korea, 1993, Hyosung U., Hayang, Republic of Korea, 1993—94; liturgy and chapel comm. coord. Holy Family Parish, Maxwell AFB, Ala., 1995—96; outreach program coord. U.S. Army Cmty. Svcs., Ft. McClellan, Ala., 1996; secondary lang. arts educator Hale (Mich.) Area H.S., 1998—. Advisor drama club Hale H.S., 1998—, co-advisor English club, 1999—, co-chair sch. improvement team, 2000—, advisor Nat. Honor Soc., 2001—05. Sta. chmn. ARC, Ft. McClellan, 1997—98, teen program dir., 1997; chem. spouses sr. leader Chem. Sch., Ft. McClellan, 1996—98; catechist, lector, eucharistic min. Holy Family Parish, East Tawas, Mich., 1999—. Decorated Outstanding Civilian Svc. medal Dept. of the Army; recipient Comdr.'s award for pub. svc., 1994, 1998; fellow Nat. Writing Project, Jacksonville State U., 1997. Mem.: Nat. Collegiate Players Honorary Dramatic Soc., Hale Fedn. Tchrs. (HS Tchr. of Yr. 2005), Quota Club Internat., Kappa Delta Pi, Delta Kappa Gamma Soc. Internat. (v.p. 2006). Republican. Roman Catholic. Avocations: photography, creating computer media, boating, golf, reading. Home: 2706 Lixey Beach Rd East Tawas MI 48730 Office: Hale Area HS 415 E Main Hale MI 48739 Personal E-mail: eagleteacher98@hotmail.com.

LLORENS, MERNA GEE, elementary school educator, retired music educator; b. Ofahoma, Miss., Oct. 4, 1939; d. Junior McKinley and Birdie Rose Smith; m. Ramon James Llorens Sr., Oct. 1, 1960; children: Regina Llorens Shamburger, Ramon James Llorens Jr. BS, Western Mich. U., 1971. Sec. Follet Pub. Co., Chgo., 1960-62, Mohawk Tablet Co., Chicago Heights, Ill., 1963-65; elem. tchr. St. Basil Cath. Sch., South Haven, Mich., 1965-79, South Haven Pub. Schs., 1979—2004, ret., 2004. Chair Jubilee 100th Ann. St. Basil Ch., Faith and Vision campaign com. Mem.: South Haven Edn. Assn. (chair courtesy com. 1985—2000), Black History Leadership Soc. (charter, treas., publicity/program chair, Spl. Tribute Role Model of Yr. award 2001), St. Basil Altar Rosary Women's Svc. Guild (treas. 2002—, Woman of Yr. 1990, 2005), Lions Club (sgt.-at-arms 2004, dist. 11-B2 Region 1 Zone chmn. 2005—, 1st v.p., region chmn. region 1 2006—, named Lion of Yr. Covert Township Club 2003, pres. Covert Township Club 2004—05), Delta Sigma Theta (pres. 1999—2001, sgt.-at-arms 2002, Benton Harbor/St. Joseph Alumnae chpt.). Democrat. Roman Catholic. Avocations: crafts, camping, gardening, Minnie Pearl impersonation. Home: 67556 County Rd 338 South Haven MI 49090-8372 Personal E-mail: mergee@aol.com.

LLOYD, AMY L., social worker; b. Binghamton, NY, Oct. 24, 1967; d. Ned and Tommie Kendrick; children: Melissa Carter, Douglas, Amani. BS, SUNY, 1989. Educator Discovery Ctr. So. Ivs, Binghampton, NY, 1995—97; asst. social svcs. Crisp Regional Hosp., Cordele, Ga., 1998—99; program mgr. Mid. Flint Behavioral Healthcare, Americus, Ga., 1999—2002; coord. sch. readiness Crisp County Sch. Sys., Cordele, 2002—04, site coord. afterschool, 2004—; family support worker Healthy Families, Cordele, Ga., 2005—. Trainer family support Ga. Gov. Coun. Vol. World Relief, Binghampton, 1993—95, First Steps, Cordele, 2003, Crisp Area Habitat for Humanity, Cordele, 2003; mem. leadership coun. So. Poverty Law Ctr., Montgomery, Ala., 2003—; vol. Big Bros. Big Sisters, Cordele, 2004; adv. bd. Boys and Girls Club, Cordele, 2004. Baptist. Avocation: scrapbooks. Office: Healthy Families 1015 18th Ave E Cordele GA 31015

LLOYD, GWENDOLYN MONICA, mathematics educator; b. Manchester, NH, Aug. 29, 1969; d. Peter and Marie Monica Lloyd; 1 child, Owen. AB, Bryn Mawr Coll., Pa., 1991; MA, U. Calif., Santa Barbara, 1993; PhD, U. Mich., Ann Arbor, 1996. Asst. prof. Dept. Math. Va. Tech., Blacksburg, Va.,

1996—2001, assoc. prof. Dept. Math., 2001—. Contbr. articles to profl. jours. Recipient Alumni Tchg. Excellence award, Va. Tech., 2003; grantee, NSF, 2000—05. Mem.: North Am. Chpt. Internat. Group Psychology Math. Edn. (editor proceedings 2005), Nat. Coun. Tchrs. Math. (editl. panelist jour. 2005—). Office Phone: 540-231-3190. Business E-Mail: lloyd@vt.edu.

LLOYD, JEAN, retired early childhood educator; b. Montgomery, Ala., Mar. 3, 1935; d. James Jack and Dorothy Gladys (Brown) L.; 1 child, Jamie Angelica. BA, Queens Coll., 1957; MA, NYU, 1960, PhD, 1976. Tchr. jr. HS NYC Bd. of Edn., 1961, dir. head start ctr., 1966, 67 summer, tchr. early childhood, 1961-69, tchr. kindergarten, 1984—2004; instr., asst. prof. U. Coll. Rutgers U., Newark, 1969-83; ret., 2004. Cons. Bd. Examiners, N.Y.C., 1982, Dept. of Pers., N.Y.C., 1985; rsch. cons. Seymour Laskow CPA, 1983; chmn. bd. dirs. Your Family Inc., N.Y.C., 1989-2004; prodr. New Ventures cable TV show (Manhattan), 1987-2004. Author: Sociology and Social Life, 1979; contbr. over 10 articles to profl. jours. Recipient Ed Press award Ednl. Press Assn., 1968; Project Synergy fellow Tchrs. Coll., Columbia, 1991-93. Mem. ASCD, United Fedn. of Tchrs., Delta Kappa Gamma. Democrat. Methodist. Avocations: writing poetry and feature articles, singing in church choir. Home: 180 W End Ave New York NY 10023-4902 Personal E-mail: jlpoetry3@verizon.net.

LLOYD, JENNIFER LEIGH, psychology professor; b. Richmond, N.C., May 21, 1970; d. George Wellington and Rebecca Virginia Lloyd; m. Michael Raymond Hawley, Aug. 12, 1995; 1 child, Benson Wellington Hawley. BA, SUNY-Oswego, 1992; MA, Ea. N.Mex U., 1997. Grad. asst. Ea. N.Mex U., Portales, 1993—95; psychology instr. Ctrl. Carolina CC, Sanford, N.C., 1997—. Author: (master's thesis) Audience reactions to the use of specific academic orientations in an academic group setting. Facilitator Human Svc. Club, Sanford, 2002—05. Mem.: N.C. CC Assn. Sociology and Psychology, Nat. Orgn. Human Svc. Edn., So. Orgn. Human Svc. Edn., N.C. CC Leadership Program (life; grad. 2000), Psi Chi (v.p. 1996—97). Office: Ctrl Carolina Community Coll 1105 Kelly Dr Sanford NC 27330 Office Phone: 919-718-7351.

LLOYD, KENITA, museum administrator; b. 1976; BA in Mktg., NYU, 1998. Admin. Mus. for African Art, NYC, 2003—04, dir. ops., 2004—. Recipient Forty under 40, Crain's NY Bus., 2004. Office: Museum for African Art 36-01 43rd Ave at 36th St Long Island City NY 11101 Office Phone: 718-784-7700. Office Fax: 718-784-7718. E-mail: klloyd@africanart.org.

LLOYD, LILA G., business educator; b. Laurens, S.C., Mar. 10, 1937; d. Shellie and Alberta Barksdale Garrett; m. Clifton H. Lloyd Sr.; children: Clifton H. Jr., William P. BS, Benedict Coll., 1957; MEd, U. N.C., Greensboro, 1971; PhD, Columbia Pacific U., 1999. H.S. tchr., Bath, SC, 1958—59, Siler City, NC, 1963—84; tchr. S.E. H.S., Greensboro, NC, 1984—92; instr. bus. edn. A&T State U., Greensboro, NC, 1992—. Mem. sch. leadership team, Greensboro, 1988—91; chmn. recruiting com. N.C. A&T State U., Greensboro, 1986—91, Greensboro, 1992—. Author: Lloyds: Refresher Course in Computer and Office Skills, 2002. Pres. Friends of McGirt-Horton Libr., Greensboro, 1989—94; v.p. precinct 19 Dem. Party, Greensboro, 1986—90; treas. United Meth. Ch., 1996—; bd. dirs. Claremont Housing Project, 1988, vice chmn. edn. program, 1988. Mem.: AAUW (contbr. newsletter 1997—99, pres. 1997—99, Outstanding Leadership award 1999), N.C. Assn. Educators (Human Rels. award 1990), Young Womens Christian Assn. Methodist. Avocations: amateur photography, reading, viewing old classical movies. Home: 1702 Woodbriar Ave Greensboro NC 27405

LLOYD, MARGARET ANN, psychologist, educator; b. Weiser, Idaho, Sept. 14, 1942; d. Laurance Henry and Margaret Jane (Patch) L. BA, U. Denver, 1964; MS in Edn., Ind. U., 1966; MA in Psychology, U. Ariz., 1972, PhD in Psychology, 1973. Asst. prof. psychology Suffolk U., Boston, 1973-76, assoc. prof., 1976-79, prof., 1979-88, chair dept., 1981-88; prof. Ga. So. U., Statesboro, 1988—2004, head dept., 1988—93, prof. emerita and chair, 2004—. Author: Adolescence, 1985; author: (with others) Psychology Applied to Modern Life, 1991, 1994, 1997, 2000, 2003, 2006; contbr. articles to profl. jours. Mem. AAUP, APA (bd. ednl. affairs 2000-2002, sec.-treas. divsn. 2, 1990-93, pres. 1994-95, coun. rep. 2003—), New Eng. Psychol. Assn. (steering com. 1984-86), Mass. Psychol. Assn. (sec. 1979-81, chair bd. acad. and sci. affairs 1981-82), Coun. Undergrad. Psychology Programs (chmn. 1990-91). Home: 805 Shelter Pointe Rd Statesboro GA 30458-9113 Personal E-mail: mlloyd@georgiasouthern.edu.

LLOYD, NANCY G., language educator; m. William Lloyd; 1 child, David. BS in early childhood elem. edn., West Chester U., Pa., 1989, M in English, 2002. Cert. English West Chester U., Pa., 2001. 7th-8th grade lang. arts tchr. Unionville Sch. Dist., Pa., 1989—91; 7th grade reading tchr. Kennett Consolidated Sch. Dist., Lendinberg, Pa., 1991—94, 8th grade lang. arts tchr., 1991—, 8th grade lang. arts for gifted, 1994—. Academic team sponsor; mentor for gifted HS students; sponsor literacy mag. Pena Palilte, 1989—2003. Mem.: Kennett Edn. Assn., NEA, Nat. Council Tchrs. of English. Avocations: embroidery, travel, cooking, reading. Office: Kennett Consolidated Schs 135 Sunny Dell Rd Landenberg PA 15335 Business E-Mail: grmrcrmr@aol.com.

LLOYD, PRISCILLA ANN, finance educator; b. Defuniak Springs, Fla., June 21, 1946; d. Thomas Sherman and Leona Campbell Brown; m. Leroy Lloyd, Aug. 15, 1969; 1 child, Leroy Ericson. BS, U. Okla., 1974, EdM, 1975. Cert. adminstrn. and supervision U. of Ctrl. Fla. Tchr. bus. H.B. Plant H.S., Tampa, Fla., 1975—78, Meadowbrook Jr. H.S., Orlando, Fla., 1978—84, Apopka (Fla.) H.S., 1984—90, Cypress Creek H.S., Orlando, 1990—93; coord. bus. programs Orange County Sch. Dist., Orlando, 1993—96; instr., adminstr. asst. program Mid Fla. Tech, Orlando, 1996—. Pres. Orange County Bus. Edn. Assoc., Orlando, 1991—92, Fla. Bus. Edn. Assn., Orlando, 1992—94; dist. dir. Future Bus. Leaders Am., Orlando, 1992—93. Named Outstanding Tchr., Fla. Bus. Edn. Assn., 1993, Outstanding Educator, Orange County Vocat. Assoc., 1994. Mem.: Fla. Bus. Edn. Assoc. Conf. (chmn. 44th annual conf.), Family Christian Athletic Assn. (bd. mem. 2002—03). Catholic Orthodox. Avocations: reading, writing, photography, travel. Home: 7202 Jonquil Dr Orlando FL 32818 Office Phone: 407-293-6635.

LLOYD, TERRY LEE, retired elementary school educator; b. Abilene, Tex., June 24, 1949; d. Aubrey Thurman and Patricia Ruth Bynum. BS, Abilene Christian Coll., 1972. Tchr. Clyde Elem. Sch., Tex., 1972—81, 2002—06, ret., 2006; tchr. Hamby Elem. Sch., Abilene, 1981—2002. Named Tchr. of Yr., Clyde C. of C., Employee of Month, Clyde Ind. Sch. Dist., 1991; recipient Tchr. Tribute award, Arrow Ford, 1997. Home: 141 Blackburn Rd Abilene TX 79602

LLOYD, TRACY ANN, secondary school educator; b. Evanston, Ill., Apr. 12, 1975; d. Robert E. and Anita N. Lombardi, Debbie Fullerton; m. Duane T. Lloyd, Apr. 22, 1971; 1 child, Wade Austin. BA, No. Ill. U., DeKalb, 1999. Cert. secondary edn. Ga., 2002. Social studies tchr. Fairmont Jr. H.S., Lockport, Ill., 2002—03, Luella H.S., Locust Grove, Ga., 2004—, head social studies dept., 2006—. Office: Luella High School 603 Walker Dr Locust Grove GA 30248 Office Phone: 770-898-9822. Personal E-mail: dtlloyd823@bellsouth.net. Business E-Mail: tracy.lloyd@henry.k12.ga.us.

LLOYD, WANDA SMALLS, newspaper editor; b. Columbus, Ohio, July 12, 1949; d. Gloria Walker; m. Willie Burk Lloyd, May 25, 1975; 1 child, Shelby Renee. BA, Spelman Coll., Atlanta, 1971. Copy editor Providence Evening Bull., 1971-73, Miami Herald, Fla., 1973-74, Atlanta Jour., 1974-75, Washington Post, 1975-76; dep. Washington editor Times-Post News Svc., 1976-86; dpt. mng. editor cover stories USA Today, 1986-87, mng. editor/adminstrn., 1987-88, sr. editor, 1988-96; mng. editor The Greenville News, 1996—2000; exec. dir. Freedom Forum Diversity Inst., 2000—04; exec. editor Montgomery Advertiser, Ala., 2004—. Instr. program for minority journalists Columbia U., N.Y.C., summer 1972; cons. So. Regional Press Inst., Savannah State Coll., Ga., 1973-94; mem. adv. bd. urban journalism workshop Howard U., Washington, 1983-96; trustee Spelman Coll., 1988—; bd. dirs. Dow Jones Newspaper Fund, 1992-99; Accrediting Coun. On Edn. in Journalism and Mass Comm, 2004-2005. Mem., bd. dirs. Nation's Capital coun. Girl Scouts U.S., Washington, 1985; mem. adv. com. Alfred Friendly Found., 1992-96; active Leadership Greenville, 1999—. Journalism fellow Northwestern U., 1987. Mem. Washington Assn. Black Journalists, Nat. Assn. Black Journalists, Washington Spelman Alumnae Assn. (v.p. 1984-86, named Alumna of Yr. 1985), Am. Soc. Newspaper Editors (bd. dirs. 1997—), Delta Sigma Theta. Baptist. Office: The Greenville News PO Box 1688 Greenville SC 29602-1688

LLUMBET, PATSI LYNN, pre-school educator; d. Estell and Sue Jacobs Brewer; m. Joe Llumbet, Oct. 24, 1998; children: Miranda, Brett, Brad, Bridgett, Jacob. AA, Hiwassee Jr. Coll., Madisonville, Tenn., 1974; BA, U. Tenn., Knoxville, 1976; MA, Lincoln Meml. U., Harrigate, Tenn., 1992. Cert. tchr. Tenn. Pre-K - K tchr. Loudon Elem. Sch., Tenn., 1976—, dir. chorus, 1990—2003. Judge, coach Odyssey of the Mind, Loudon, 1992—. Author (and actor): (pre-K Spanish video) My School, 2005—06. Named Loudon County Tchr. of the Yr.; grantee, Loudon Edn. Assn. Mem.: NEA, ASCD, Phi Delta Kappa, Early Childhood Edn. Assn., Tenn. Asssn. for Supervision and Curriculum Devel., Internat. Reading Assn., Tenn. Edn. Assn. Republican. Methodist. Office: Loudon Elementary School 2175 Roberts Rd Loudon TN 37774 Office Phone: 865-458-2001.

LOAR, PEGGY ANN, foundation administrator, museum administrator; b. Cin., May 14, 1948; d. Jerome Vincent and Elizabeth (Ranz) Wahl; m. Bartholomew Voorsanger, 2004. BA in History of Art, U. Cin., 1970, MA in History of Art, 1971; postgrad., Stanford U., 2003. Summer intern Met. Mus. Art, N.Y.C., 1968; curator edn. Indpls. Mus. Art, 1971-76, asst. to the dir., 1974-75, asst. dir., 1975-77; asst. dir. programs and policy Inst. Mus. Svcs., 1977-80; dir. Smithsonian Inst. Traveling Exhbn. Svc., Washington, 1980-87; founding dir. Wolfsonian Found., Miami, Fla., 1987—96, Genoa, Italy, 1987—96; founding dir., pres. Copia: The American Center for Wine, Food and the Arts, Napa, Calif., 1997—2005, pres. emerita; dir. mus. studio Voorsanger Architects, N.Y.C., 1997—2005. Lectr. art history U. Cin., 1970-71; lectr. art appreciation and criticism Ind. U., Purdue U., 1975-77; mem. women's health adv. com. Stanford U., 2002—; guest lectr. in field. Project dir.: The Art of Cameroon Exhibition and Catalog, 1984, Treasures from the Smithsonian Inst. Exhibition and Catalog, 1984, Paris Style 1900: Art Noveau Bing, 1986, Hollywood: Legend & Reality Exhibition Catalog, 1988. Bd. dirs. Jean Louis Palladin Found., 2005—, Aspen Design Summit, 2005—. Travel grantee Japan Found., 1984; Swedish Inst. grantee; Aspen Inst. Humanistic Studies fellow, 1986-87, recipient Smithsonian Gold Medal for Disting. Service, 1987. Mem. Am. Assn. Museums (mus. ethics com. 1980-98), Internat. Coun. Museums (pres. U.S. nat. com., 1996-2002), Com. Internat. Musees d'Art Moderne. Avocations: bicycling, hiking, dogs, gardening, wine. Office: COPIA Am Ctr Wine Food & Arts 500 1st St Napa CA 94559 Address: 845 UN Plaza 11H New York NY 10017 Office Phone: 212-302-6464.

LOAR, SHEILA RAE, small business owner; d. Dennis Paul Leahy and Patricia Mae Cummins; m. Jason Paul Loar, July 10, 1999; children: Austin David children: Abbey Kathryn. MEd, Old Dominion U., Norfolk, Va., 1994. Athletic trainer Trinity Coll., Hartford, Conn., 1995—99, Colo. Coll., Colorado Springs, 1999—2004; head athletic trainer Conn. Coyotes Arena Football, Hartford, 1996; athletic tng. intern US Olympic Tng. Ctr., Lake Placid, NY, 1999; cons. Pampered Chef. Mem.: Nat. Athletic Trainers Assn. (cert.). Home and Office: 9358 Calvary Cir Salisbury MD 21801 Office Phone: 410-896-2275. Personal E-mail: mdloars@comcast.net.

LOBB, CYNTHIA JEAN HOCKING, lawyer; b. San Francisco, June 12, 1962; d. Thomas Messinger and Diane (Knight) Hocking; m. Jerry Mark Lobb, Dec. 1, 1990; children: Sean Thomas, Kevin Joseph, Braden McMillan, William Ryan. BA in Polit. Sci., UCLA, 1984; JD, Golden Gate U. Law Sch., U. San Diego Law Sch., 1993. Bar: Ca., 1993. Asst. Congressman W. Dannemeyer, Washington, 1987-88; legal sec. Fulbright & Jaworski, Washington, 1988; law clerk MCI Internat. Divsn., Rye Brook, NY, 1990, Kern County Counsel, Bakersfield, Calif., 1991; lawyer Lobb & Cliff, Riverside, Calif., 1997-98, Law Office of Cynthia Hocking, Menifee, Calif., 1995—. Spanish tchr. Good Shepard Lutheran Sch., Menifee, Calif., 1996-99. Mem. Riverside Repub. Women's Federated, Temecula Repub. Women's Federated, Lake Menifee Women's Club, 1998—2002; Assoc. mem. Calif. Repub. Party, 1980—; pub. rels. dir. St. Martha's Ch., 1998—2002, Bible sharing leader, 1994—97; bd. dirs. Mothers and Others, 1999—2002. Mem. Alpha Delta Chi (named Most Outstanding mem. 1984, Outstanding Young Women of Am., 1985). Republican. Roman Catholic. Avocations: fitness training, jazzercize, scrapbooking, Spanish and French, travel. Office: Lobb & Cliff 1650 Spruce St Ste 500 Riverside CA 92507-2436 Home: 32938 Avenida Lestonnac Temecula CA 92591-8000

LOBER, IRENE MOSS, educational consultant; b. NYC, Aug. 1, 1927; d. David and Beckie Moss; m. Solomon William Lober, Oct. 25, 1947; children: Clifford Warren, Richard Wayne, Lori Ann. BS in Edn., CCNY, 1948; MA, George Washington U., 1967; EdD, Va. Poly. Inst. and State U., 1974. Registered sch. bus. adminstr. Formerly tchr., libr.; prin. staff devel. Fairfax County Pub. Schs., Va., 1965—77; supt. University City (Mo.) Pub. Schs., 1977—81, Danbury (Conn.) Pub. Schs., 1981—85; prof. SUNY, New Paltz, 1985—98, chmn. dept. ednl. adminstrn., 1990—98, dir. EdD program, 1993—95, coord. distance learning programs, 1995—98, cons. ednl. adminstrn., 1998—. Guest lectr. Washington U., George Washington U., Va. Poly. Inst. and State U., U. Va., Fordham U., C.W. Post Coll., L.I. U.; mem. bus. adv. coun. Datahr, Inc., 1982—85; pres. N.Y. State Coun. for Advancement of Depts. of Ednl. Adminstrn., 1994; cons. in field; founding incorporator Sci. Horizons, Inc., Danbury, 1984—85, COMPUtourney, Inc., 1990—98; designated disting. expert and peer reviewer Asst. Sec. Edn. Chester Finn, 1987—89; spkr./presenter various internat., nat. and state confs. and convs.; book reviewer Tchrs. Coll. Press, Columbia U., 2004. Author: Promoting Your School, 1993; contbr. articles to profl. jours.; book reviewer: Teacher's Coll. Press, 2004. Mem. legal and govt. studies group Nat. Inst. Edn. Dept. HEW; nat. adv. bd. U. Wis. R & D Ctr., 1978—80; chairperson Mo. Instrnl. TV Coun., 1981; lay adv. bd. St. Louis Met. Med. Soc., 1980—81; bd. advisors St. Joseph's Inst. Deaf, 1980—81; apptd. supt. in residence Western Conn. State U., 1984; divsn. chairperson United Way Campaign, 1982—86; mem. bd. edn. Poughkeepsie City Sch. Dist., 1993—96; mem. instl. rev. bd. M.D. Anderson Cancer Ctr., Orlando, 2002—04; pres. Lake Mary chpt. AARP, 2001—03; pres. Rishona-Chavaret group, Orlando chpt. Hadassah, 2005—, co-pres., 2004—05; bd. dirs. Temple Israel, Longwood, Fla., 2005—, v.p. edn., 2006—, adminstrv. v.p., 2005—; pres. adv. cabinet Greater St. Louis coun. Girl Scouts U.S., 1980—81, bd. dirs. Southwestern Conn. Coun., 1981—85; bd. dirs. Fairfield coun. Boy Scouts Am.; bd. dirs. Danbury region Jr. Achievement, 1981—86, Regional Hospice, Danbury, 1984—86, Danbury Coun. Am. Heart Assn., 1985—86; exec. bd., trustee United Way No. Fairfield County; trustee, bd. dirs. United Way, Danbury, 1982—85; bd. dirs. TRIAD Seminole County, Fla., 2001—, Meals on Wheels Inc. Seminole County, Fla., 2000—04. Recipient Townsend Harris medal, CCNY Alumni Assn., Nat. Leadership award, Hadassah, 2005;, IDEA fellow, Ford Found. grantee, 1977—78. Mem.: NEA, ASCD, Authors League, Authors Guild, Nat. Assn. Secondary Sch. Prins. (chair profs. secondary sch. adminstrn. com.), Assn. Sch. Bus. Ofcls. Internat. (nat. chmn. maintenance and ops. rsch. com. 1985—89), N.Y. State Assn. Sch. Bus. Ofcls., N.Y. State Coun. Sch. Supts., Ednl. Rsch. Svc., Sch. Adminstrs. Assn. N.Y. State, Am. Assn. Sch. Adminstrs. (nat. chmn. higher edn. com. 1987—89, chmn. membership svcs. com. 1995—96), Pi Lambda Theta (publs. adv. bd. 1981—84), Phi Kappa Phi, Phi Delta Kappa (pres. New Paltz chpt. 1991—93). Personal E-mail: loberim@bellsouth.net.

LOBIG, JANIE HOWELL, special education educator; b. Peoria, Ill., June 10, 1945; d. Thomas Edwin and Elizabeth Jane (Higdon) Howell; m. James Frederick Lobig, Aug. 16, 1970 (dec. Dec. 2001); 1 child, Jill Christina. BS in Elem. Edn., So. Ill. U., 1969; MA in Spl. Edn. Severely Handicapped, San Jose State U., 1989. Cert. elem. tchr., Calif., Mo., Ill., handicapped edn., Calif., Mo.; ordained to ministry Presbyn. Ch. as deacon, 1984. Tchr. trainable mentally retarded children Spl. Luth. Sch., St. Louis, 1967-68; tchr. trainable mentally retarded and severly handicapped children Spl. Sch. Dist. St. Louis, 1969-80, head tchr., 1980-83; tchr. severly handicapped children San Jose (calif.) Unifed Sch. Dist., 1983-86; tchr. autistic students Santa Clara County Office Edn., San Jose, 1986—; tchr. Suzanne Dancers, 1991-92. Vol. Am. Cancer Soc., San Jose, 1986—89, 1992, Am. Heart Assn., 1985—, Multiple Sclerosis Soc., 1990—, Wildlife Ctr. Silicon Valley, 1998—; moderator bd. deacons Evergreen Presbyn. Ch., 1986—89. Mem. Council for Exceptional Children, Assn. for Severly Handicapped, Nat. Edn. Assn., Calif. Tchrs. Assn. Avocations: golf, motor home travel, bridge, needlecrafts. Office: James Franklin Smith Elem Sch 2220 Woodbury San Jose CA 95121 Home: 3211 Bracciano Ct San Jose CA 95135 Office Phone: 408-270-6368. Personal E-mail: JanieAngel@aol.com.

LOBO, REBECCA, professional basketball player; b. Hartford, Conn., Oct. 6, 1973; BA in Polit. Sci., U. Conn., 1995. Basketball player USA Women's Nat. Team, N.Y. Liberty, 1997—2001, Houston Comets, 2001—02, Conn. Sun, Uncasville, 2003—. Mem. U.S. Olympic Festival East Team, 1992, Jr. World Championship Qualifying Team, 1992, USA Jr. World Championship Team, 1993. Co-author: The Home Team, 1996. Founder Ruth Ann & Rebecca Lobo scholarship in allied health U. Conn., 2001. Named Big East Conf. Player of Yr., Nat. Player of Yr., Naismith, U.S. Basketball Writers Assn., 1995, Big East Tournament Most Outstanding Player, 1994, Big East Conf. Women's Basketball Scholar Athlete of Yr., 1995, Female Athlete of Yr., AP, 1995; named to All-Am. 1st team, Kodak, 1994, 1995; recipient Wade trophy. Office: c/o Conn Sun 1 Mohegan Sun Blvd Uncasville CT 06382

LOBRON, BARBARA L., speech educator, editor, photographer, writer; b. Phila., Mar. 19, 1944; d. Martin Aaron and Elizabeth (Gots) L. Student, Pa. State U., 1962—63; BA cum laude, Temple U., Phila., 1966; student art therapy, Erika Steinberger, N.Y.C., 1994—2003; MS, Coll. Mt. St. Vincent, 2001. Reporter, writer Camden (N.J.) Courier-Post, 1966-68; editl. asst. Med. Insight mag., N.Y.C., 1970-71; mng. editor Camera 35 mag., N.Y.C., 1971-75; also assoc. editor photog. anns. U.S. Camera/Camera 35, 1972, 73; freelance editor as Word Woman N.Y.C., 1975-77, 79-99; acct. exec. Bozell & Jacobs, N.Y.C., 1977-79; copy editor Camera Arts mag., N.Y.C., 1981-83; editl. coord. Ctr. mag. Nat. Ctr. Health Edn., 1985; editl. coord. Popular Photography mag., 1986-95; assoc. editor Sony Style, 1995; tchr. speech improvement N.Y.C. Bd. Edn., 1995—. Contbg. editor: Photograph; participant 3M Editor's Conf. (1st woman), 1972; photography group exhbns. include Internat. Women's Art Festival, N.Y.C., 1975, Rockefeller Ctr., N.Y.C., 1976, Photograph Gallery, N.Y.C., 1981; acrylic painting exhbns. Tchrs. Coll., N.Y.C., 1994, Warwick Hotel, N.Y.C., 1995; represented in collection Libr. Calif Inst. Arts, Valencia; copy editor: The Complete Guide to Cibachrome Printing, 1980, The Popular Photography Question and Answer Book, 1979, The Photography Catalog, 1976, Strand: Sixty Years of Photography, 1976, You and Your Lens, 1975; contbr. articles to comml. publs., chpts. to books. Tchr. Sch. Vol. Program, N.Y.C. Recipient 1st pl. honors Dist. 1, Internat. Assn. Bus. Communicators, 1977. Mem. Soka Gakkai Internat. Buddhist. Avocations: dance, reading, photography, origami, walking. Home: 85 Hicks St Apt 7 Brooklyn NY 11201-6825 E-mail: barbaralobron@hotmail.com.

LOCHANKO, ELIZABETH ALEXANDRA, communications executive; b. Toronto, Ontario, Can., Apr. 30, 1957; came to U.S., 1960; d. Adam and Alexandra Lochanko. BA, Rutgers U., 1979; M of Music, Johns Hopkins U., 1982. Office mgr. Simos C. Dimas Esquire, N.Y.C., 1982-84; pub. rels. mgr. 'K' Lines/Cloud Tours, N.Y.C., 1984-86; sr. acct. exec. Peter Martin Assocs., N.Y.C., 1986-88; sr. v.p. corp. communications Sony Pictures Entertainment, L.A., 1988-96; strategic mktg. and bus. cons., 1996—. Bd. dirs. World Master*Class Collection Ltd. Mem. exec. com. Johns Hopkins Alumni Leadership Coun. Mem. NAFE, Women in Comms. (exec. com.), Douglass Rutgers Alumni Assn., Am. Composers Forum (bd. dirs.), Phi Beta Kappa. Avocations: music, hiking, reading, bicycling, travel. Home: 1509 Washington St Calistoga CA 94515-1501

LOCHEN, LYNNE CAROL, cultural organization administrator; b. N.Y.C., Feb. 13, 1950; d. Maxwell and Juliette Flower Jurmark; m. Thomas John Lochen, Oct. 27, 1973; 1 child, John Maxwell. BA in History and Classics, Fla. State U., 1972. Hist. interpreter The Colonial Williamsburg Found., Williamsburg, Va., 1975—81; tchr., dir. guidance Ryan Acad. Norfolk, Norfolk, Va., 1988—95; conv. and visitor svcs. Norfolk Conv. and Visitors Bur., 1997—. Exec. bd. Va. Civil War Trails, Richmond. Named Norfolks Downtown Person of the Wk., Downtown Norfolk Coun., 1999. Mem.: NAFE, Va. Hospitality and Travel Assn. (officer), Tidewater Area Concierge Assn., Assn. Conv. Ops. Mgmt., Internat. Assn. Conv. and Visitors Burs., Va. Assn. Conv. and Visitors Burs. (exec. bd.). Avocation: travel. Office: Norfolk Conv and Visitors Bur 232 E Main St Norfolk VA 23510

LOCHER, ELIZABETH AIKEN, elementary education educator, reading specialist, library director; b. N.Y.C., Oct. 10, 1943; d. Richard Eustace Jr. and Marjorie Armstrong (Siebers) Aiken; m. Peyton Ring Neal Jr., June 20, 1964 (div.); children: Melissa Davis Neal Reed, Peyton Ring Neal III; m. Baldwin Gerard Locher Jr., Dec. 21, 1979; 1 child, Baldwin Locher III. AA, Peace Coll., 1964; BA, Mary Baldwin Coll., 1980; MEd, U. Va., 1991, PhD, 2002. Cataloger, asst. libr. Georgetown Law Ctr., Washington, 1965-71; asst. libr. Lexington (Va.) High Sch., 1976-79; reading specialist, tchr. Nat. Bridge Elem. Sch. Rockbridge County Pub. Schs., 1989—2003; prof. Mary Baldwin Coll., Staunton, Va., 2003—; libr. dir. Clifton Forge Pub. Libr., 2004—. Presenter in field. Editor: Union List of Legal Periodicals, 1971; contbr. articles to newspapers and jours. Bd. dirs. Rockbridge Regional Libr., Lexington, 1994-98, rec. sec., 1997-98; corr. sec. Colonial Dames XVII Century, Lexington, 1993-94; bd. dirs., sec. Lexington Downtown Devel., 1985-91; bd. dirs. Habitat, 2003-05; libr., docent Stonewall Jackson House, Lexington, 1979-89. U. Va. fellow, Charlottesville, 1991. Mem.: ASCD, Va. Libr. Assn., Shenandoah Valley Reading Coun. (rec. sec. 1994—96, membership chmn. 1997—98, pres. 2005—06, membership chmn. 2003—04, Tchr. of Yr. 1994), Va. State Reading Assn., Internat. Reading Assn., Phi Alpha Theta, Delta Gamma. Episcopalian. Avocations: quilting, needlepoint. Home: 26 Beatty Holw Lexington VA 24450-4040 Office: Clifton Forge Pub Libr 535 Church St Clifton Forge VA 24422-1134 Office Phone: 540-863-2519.

LOCKARD, DIXIE DAVIS, elementary school educator; b. Parkerburg, W.Va., Feb. 9, 1954; d. Harry Edward and Maurine Baker Davis; m. Michael Albert Lockard, Oct. 7, 1983 (div.); children: Chris Cornett, Brandy. BA, Ea. Ky. U., Richmond, 1975, MA, 1979. Cert. elem. tchr. Ky. Tchr. Powell County Bd. Edn., Stanton, Ky., 1979—. Named Ky. Col., Commonwealth of Ky., 1979; recipient Outstanding Tchr. award, Ky. Conservation Dept., 2005. Mem.: PTA (sec. 1991—92). Baptist. Avocations: art, scrapbooks, walking, birdwatching. Home: 526 E College Ave Stanton KY 40380 Office: Stanton Elem Breckenridge St Stanton KY 40380

LOCKCUFF, STACY MARIE, personal trainer, pre-school educator; b. Williamsport, Pa., Jan. 3, 1976; d. Rickey Edward and Sandra Lynn Billman; m. Eric James Lockcuff, Mar. 13, 2004. BS, Elon U., NC, 1998; MS in Edn., Bucknell U., Lewisburg, Pa., 2001. Cert. athletic trainer Nat. Athletic Trainers Assn., 1998. Resident athletic trainer Colgate U., Hamilton, NY, 1998—99; grad. asst. athletic trainer Bucknell U., Lewisburg, 1999—2001; head athletic trainer Elmira (NY) Pioneers, 2000; asst. athletic trainer, adj. instr. Colby-Sawyer Coll., New London, NH; outreach athletic trainer Susquehanna Health Systems, Williamsport, 2002—. Mem. nominating com. Faith Wesleyan Ch., Williamsport, 2006. Named Care Employee of the Month, Susquehanna Health Systems, 2005; recipient Svc. award, South Atlantic Conf., 1997; Grad. Assistantship, Bucknell U., 1999—2001. Mem.: Omicron Delta Kappa (life), Phi Eta Sigma (life), Alpha Xi Delta (life Honor Key 1997). Republican. Wesleyan. Avocations: art, crafts, exercise, reading, researching. Home: 780 Fisher Dr Watsontown PA 17777 Office: Susquehanna Health Systems 1100 Grampian Blvd Williamsport PA 17777 Office Phone: 570-320-7456. Personal E-mail: slockcuff@wrsd.org.

LOCKE, ELIZABETH HUGHES, retired foundation administrator; b. Norfolk, Va., June 30, 1939; d. George Morris and Sallie Epps (Moss) Hughes; m. John Rae Locke, Jr., Sept. 13, 1958 (div. 1981); children: John Rae III, Sallie Curtis. BA magna cum laude, Duke U., 1964, PhD, 1972; MA, U. N.C., 1966; DHum (hon.), Furman U., 2004. Instr. English U. N.C., Chapel Hill, 1970-72; dir. univ. pubs. Duke U., Durham, NC, 1973-79; corp. contbns. officer Bethlehem Steel Corp., Pa., 1979-82; dir. edn. divsn. & comm. Duke Endowment, Charlotte, NC, 1982-96, exec. dir., 1996-97, pres., 1997—2004; ret., 2004. Vis. prof. English Duke U., 1972—73. Editor: Duke Encounters, 1977, prospectus for Change: American Private Higher Education, 1985, (mag) Issues, 1985-96. Pres. Angier B. Duke Meml., Inc., 1997-2005, Duke Endowment, 1997-2005, Nanaline H. Duke Fund, 1997-2005, Doris Duke Trust, 1998, Jr. League, Durham, 1976, Hist. Preservation Soc., Durham, 1977, Charlotte Area Donors Forum; past pres. Comm. Philanthropy, Washington, Sch. of Arts, Charlotte; mem. legis. com. Coun. on Founds., 1997-, Washington, 1995; trustee Southeastern Coun. of Founds., 1997—, Wing Haven Found.; commr. So. Assn. Colls. & Schs., 1998—; bd. vis. Davidson Coll., Charlotte Country Day Sch., Duke U., Johnson C. Smith U.; trustee Winghaven Found. Recipient Leadership award Charlotte C. of C., 1984; Danforth fellow, 1972. Mem. Nat. Task Force, English Speaking Union, The Most Venerable Order of St. John of Jerusalem (officer sister), Colonial Dames Am., Charlotte City Club (bd. govs.), Phi Beta Kappa. Democrat. Epsicopalian. Office: 100 N Tryon St Ste 3500 Charlotte NC 28202-4001 Personal E-mail: betsL@earthlink.net.

LOCKE, EMMA MAE, retired elementary school educator; b. Martinsburg, W.Va., Mar. 24, 1936; d. Clifford Cecil and Mabel Irene (Watson) Starliper; m. James Henry Locke, Mar. 27, 1959; 1 child, James Lester Locke. BA in Elem. Edn., Shepherd Coll., 1958; postgrad., W.Va. U. Elem. sch. tchr. Jefferson County Bd. Edn., Charles Town, W.Va., 1958-89, substitute tchr., 1989-91. Judge social studies fairs Jefferson County Bd. Edn., 1990—. Vol. ARC (Jefferson County chpt.), 1990—. Nominated for Tchr. of Yr., 1987. Mem. AAUW, NEA, W.Va. Edn. Assn., W.Va., Jefferson County Retired Sch. Tchrs. (membership com. 1990—), Delta Kappa Gamma (corr. sec. 1990-92). Methodist. Avocations: reading, antiques, word puzzles, oil and water color painting. Home: 7604 Martinsburg Pike Shepherdstown WV 25443-9801

LOCKE, STEPHANIE FRANCES, anesthesiologist, educator, consultant; b. Washington, July 30, 1961; d. Joseph Wilbert and Goldie Veronica (Queen) Francis; m. James Laron Locke, Dec. 27, 1986; children: Veronica, Erin. BS, Howard U., 1983; MD, U. Pa., 1987. Diplomate Am. Bd. Anesthesiology. Asst. prof. dept. anesthesiology Howard U. Hosp., Washington, 1991—. Cons. Internat. Inst. of Forensic Sci., Phila., 1992—. Mem. Am. Soc. Anesthesiologists, Phi Beta Kappa, Bears, Bulls & Women's Investment Club, The Moles. Avocations: reading, travel, gardening, investing. Home: 7301 Galileo Ct Lanham Seabrook MD 20706-3375 Office: Howard U Hosp Dept Anesthesiology 2041 Georgia Ave NW Dept Washington DC 20060-0001

LOCKE, VIRGINIA OTIS, writer; b. Tiffin, Ohio, Sept. 4, 1930; d. Charles Otis and Frances Virginia (Sherer) L. BA, Barnard Coll., N.Y.C., 1953; MA in Psychology, Duke U., Durham, N.C., 1972, postgrad. Program officer, asst. corp. sec. Agrl. Devel. Coun., N.Y.C., 1954-66; staff psychologist St. Luke's-Roosevelt Med. Ctr., N.Y.C., 1973-75; freelance writer and editor N.Y.C., 1976-85; writer-editor Cornell U. Med. Coll./N.Y. Hosp. Med. Ctr., N.Y.C., 1986-89; sr. editor humanities and social scis. coll. divsn. Prentice Hall, Upper Saddle River, NJ, 1989-96; profl. writer behavioral scis., 1996—. Co-author: (coll. textbook) Introduction to Theories of Personality, 1985, (book) The Agricultural Development Council: A History, 1989, (coll. textbook) Child Psychology: A Contemporary Viewpoint, 6th edit., 2006; co-editor: The Life and Work of Arthur T. Mosher, 2001. Founder Help Our Neighbors Eat Yearround (H.O.N.E.Y.), Inc., N.Y.C., chmn., 1983-87, vol., 1987-99, newsletter editor, 1992-97; reader Recording for the Blind, N.Y.C., 1978-84; vol. Reach to Recovery program Am. Cancer Soc., Bergen County, N.J., 1990-96. Recipient Our Town Thanks You award, N.Y.C., 1984, Mayor's Vol. Svc. award, N.Y.C., 1986, Cert. of Appreciation for Community Svc. Manhattan Borough, 1986, Jefferson award Am. Ins. Pub. Svc., Washington, 1986. Home and Office: 9316 Bocina Ln # G Atascadero CA 93422 Personal E-mail: volwriter@mindspring.com.

LOCKER, CYNTHIA ANN, elementary school educator; b. Gowanda, NY, June 28, 1977; d. Carl Burd Jr. and Eileen Burd; m. David Burd, July 27, 2002. M in Childhood Edn., Elmira Coll., NY, 2006. Cert. elem. tchr. NY, 2006. Mid. sch. math. tchr. Waverly (NY) Sch. Dist., 2002—05, mid. sch. remedial math tchr., 2005—. Math counts coach Waverly Mid. Sch., 2002—05; varsity girls swim aide Waverly Athletics, 2003—04. Home: 498 Marsh Rd Erin NY 14838 Personal E-mail: clocker@gstboces.org.

LOCKETT, BARBARA ANN, librarian; b. Northampton, Mass., Feb. 21, 1936; d. William M. and Anna A. (Vachula) Prabulos; m. Richard W. Rice, June 2, 1957 (div. Feb. 1966); 1 child, Annamarie Louise; m. Benjamin B. Lockett, June 7, 1985. BS, U. Mass., 1957; MLS, U. Calif., Berkeley, 1967. Documents librarian Knolls Atomic Power Lab., Schenectady, N.Y., 1968-74; coordinator bibliog. devel. SUNY, Albany, 1974-81; prin. librarian reference services N.Y. State Library, Albany, 1981-85; dir. libraries Rensselaer Poly. Inst., Troy, N.Y., 1985-94, libr. emeritus, 1994—. Cons. Office Mgmt. Svcs., Assn. Rsch. Librs., Washington, 1981-86. Contbr. articles on collection devel., mgmt. and info. systems to profl. jours. Mem. ALA (cons. collection mgmt. and devel. com., Resources and Tech. Svcs. div. 1983-87), Assn. Coll. and Rsch. Librs. (chmn. standards and accreditation com. 1988-90), N.Y. State Edn. and Rsch. Network (chmn. info. resources com. 1988-89), N.Y. State Libr./NYSERNet (joint planning team 1991-94, del. N.Y. State Gov.'s Conf. on Librs., 1990), Sigma Xi, Phi Kappa Phi, Beta Phi Mu. Mem. Unitarian Ch. Avocations: tennis, master gardener, accordion. Home: 3321 Wessynton Way Alexandria VA 22309-2228

LOCKETT-EGAN, MARIAN WORKMAN, advertising executive; b. Murray, Ky., May 5, 1931; d. Otis H. Workman and Myrtle A. (Jones) Jordan; m. Gene Potts, Jan. 6, 1947 (div. Feb. 1962); children: Reed Nasser, Jennifer Anglin, George M. Potts, Cynthia Klenk; m. Barker Lockett, Oct. 11, 1963 (div. Dec. 1972); 1 child, Stephen R.W.; m. Douglas S. Egan Jr., Feb. 14, 1981 (dec. May 2001). BA, Murray State U., 1962. Asst. media dir. Noble-Dury & Assocs., Nashville, 1963-64; asst. rsch. dir. Triangle Publs., Phila., 1964-66; assoc. media dir. Lewis & Gilman, Phila., 1966-72; v.p. advt. media Scott Paper Co., Phila., 1972-83; pres. DMS Comm. Inc., Ardmore, Pa., 1983—. Exec. dir. The Media Sch., N.Y.C., 1983-85, 87-2003; mem. TV com. Assn. Nat. Advertisers, N.Y.C., 1977-83; guest lectr. Wharton U., Phila., 1981-82, 85, 86, 87; Gannet vis. prof. Sch. Journalism, U. Fla., Gainesville, 1982. Guest editor Media decisions, 1981. Trustee Meth. Hosp. Found., Phila., 1973—87. Mem. Broadcast Pioneers (pres. 1994-96), TV and Radio Advt. Club (pres. 1973). Republican. Episcopalian. Avocation: tennis. Home: 45 Llanfair Cir Ardmore PA 19003-3342 E-mail: dmsmle@aol.com.

LOCKHART, CLAUDIA JO, adult education educator, department chairman; d. Roy Oscar and Helen Mary Eckberg; life ptnr. Charles William Houseman; 1 child, Jennifer Ann Buttram. BFA, U. Long Beach, 1967. Secondary Teaching Degree Dept. Edn. Calif., 1970. Educator, dept. chair Anaheim (Calif.) Sch. Dist., 1968—69, Inglewood (Calif.) Cmty. Adult Sch., 1971—. Grant writing certification L.A. Sch. Grant Writing, 1988—; staff devel. coord. Inglewood Cmty. Adult Sch., 1988—96, mem. chair steering com., 1997—99. Artist, cmty. coord. Art Impacts Day. Recipient Halo awards, Bd. Suprs. L.A., 1982—89. Independent. Achievements include development of principles of alphabet literacy program. Avocations: art, sailing, reading, house design, travel. Office: Inglewood Cmty Adult Sch Ste 350 106 E Manchester Blvd Inglewood CA 90301 Personal E-mail: cjlcwh@aol.com.

LOCKHART, JULIE A., actor, consultant; b. Bloomington, Ind., Apr. 22, 1974; d. David Wayne and Terri Lynn Cross Lockhart, Susan Willing Flinn Lockhart (Stepmother). BS, Northwestern U., Evanston, Ill., 1996. Consulant Aquent, LA, 2001—. Actor: (Operas) Darkling; (films) Death and Taxis, Invocation series; (plays) Romeo and Juliet, (re)main, The Buddha Prince, Cirque Picnique, Hfob-N-Ffos, Strange Beliefs, Valparaiso, The Spanish Cafe, (dance theatre production) The Boy King, (multimedia theatre production) Monster of Happiness. Mem.: Northwestern U. Entertainment Alliance (assoc.), Big Cheap Theatre (assoc.), Theatre Comm. Group (assoc.). Avocations: chocolate making, yoga, music, dance, collaborative art making. Personal E-mail: juliealock@yahoo.com.

LOCKHART, MADGE CLEMENTS, educational organization executive; b. Soddy, Tenn., May 22, 1920; d. James Arlie and Ollie (Sparks) Clements; m. Andre J. Lockhart, Apr. 24, 1942 (div. 1973); children: Jacqueline, Andrew, Janice, Jill. Student, East Tenn. U., 1938-39; BS, U. Tenn., Chattanooga and Knoxville, 1955, MEd, 1962. Elem. tchr. Tenn. and Ga., 1947-60, Brainerd H.S., Chattanooga, 1960-64, Cleveland (Tenn.) City Schs., 1966-88; owner, operator Lockhart's Learning Ctr., Inc., Cleveland and Chattanooga, 1966-2003; co-founder, pres. Hermes, Inc., 1973-79; co-founder Dawn Ctr., Hamilton County, Tenn., 1974; apptd. mem. Tenn. Gov.'s Acad. for Writers. Author numerous poems, short stories; contbr. articles to profl. jours. and newspapers. Pres. Cleveland Assn. Retarded Citizens, 1970, state v.p., 1976; pres. Cherokee Easter Seal Soc., 1973-76, Cleveland Creative Arts Guild, 1980; bd. dirs. Tenn. Easter Seal Soc., 1974-77, 80-83; chair Bradley County Internat. Yr. of Child; mem. panel for grants Coun. Govts. S.E. Tenn. Devel. Dist., 1990-92; mem. Internat. Biog. Centre Adv. Coun., Cambridge, Eng., 1991-92; mayor's com. Mus. for Bradley County, Tenn., 1992—. Recipient Service to Mankind award Sertoma, 1978, Gov.'s award for service to handicapped, 1979; mental health home named in her honor, Tenn., 1987. Mem. NEA (life), Tenn. Edn. Assn., Am. Assn. Rehab. Therapy, S.E. Tenn. Arts Coun., Cleveland Edn. Assn. (Service to Humanity award 1987). Mem. Ch. of Christ. Clubs: Byliners, Fantastiks. Home: 3007 Oakland Dr NW Cleveland TN 37312-5281 Office Phone: 423-476-3066.

LOCKHART, PATRICIA ANN, elementary school educator; b. Bklyn., N.Y., Jan. 7, 1961; d. Grace Copp; 1 child, Dana. AAS, Coll. Staten Island, 1988, BA, 1993, MS in Spl. Edn., 1996. Cert. tchr. N.Y. Life skills specialist Cath. Guardian Soc., N.Y.C., 1980; asst. tchr. Soc. Devel. Disabilities & Autism, Staten Island, NY, 1988—94; elem. sch. tchr. PS 57, Staten Island, 1994—. Vol. coord. Staten Island Tough Love, 1997—2001; outreach spkr. United Fedn. Tchrs., 2000—01. Named woman of achievement, Staten Island Advance, 2001; grantee, HUD, 2002. Home: 50 Dongan Hills Ave 2B Staten Island NY 10306

LOCKHART, PATSY MARIE, secondary school educator, consultant; b. San Francisco, Nov. 7, 1949; d. Alfred Jr. and Georgia Anna (Walker) Lax; m. Terence C. Lockhart, Apr. 23, 1977 (div. Apr. 1984); children: Dana Nolley, Therese C., Mishua. BA, San Jose State U., 1975, MA in Adminstrv. Supervision, 1999; M in Edn.-Integrated Studies, Cambridge (Mass.) Coll., 2003. Cert. Nat. Bd. for Profl. Tchr. Standards. Tchr. Ravenswood City Sch. Dist., East Palo Alto, Calif., 1975-79, edn. specialist, 1979-80, tchr., 1980-84; tchr., curriculum leader, social sci. cons. tchr. Barnard White Middle Sch., New Haven Unified Sch. Dist., Union City, Calif., 1984—. Coord. Urban Sites Writing Network, N.Y.C., 1993-94; cons. Bay Area Writing Project, Berkeley, Calif., 1984—; table leader Calif. Learning Assessment Sys.-State of Calif., Sacramento, 1994; writer curriculum devel Calif. Assessment Program Secondary, Sacramento, 1990-92. Mem. choir and Cantaters Pub. Rels., Allen Temple Bapt. Ch.; curriculum leader Barnard White Mid. Sch., 2000-01. Mem. NAACP, Nat. Coun. for Tchrs. of English, Calif. League of Mid. Schs. (adv. bd. 1992—), Calif. Tchr.'s Assn. Minority Caucus. Democrat. Avocations: swimming, sewing, decorating, singing, writing. Home: 4473 Deep Creek Rd Fremont CA 94555-2059 Office: Barnard White Mid Sch 725 Whipple Rd Union City CA 94587-1300 E-mail: patsy_lockhart@nhusdk12.ca.us.

LOCKHART, SHARON, artist; b. Norwood, Mass., 1964; MFA, Art Ctr. Coll. Design, Pasadena, Calif. One-woman shows include Art Ctr., Pasadena, 1994, Neugerriemschneider, Berlin, 1994, 1996, Friedrich Petzel Gallery, N.Y., 1994, 1996, 1998, Kunstlerhaus Stuttgart, Germany, 1995, Blum and Poe, Santa Monica, 1996, 1998, John Spotten Cinema, Toronto, 1997, S.L. Simpson Gallery, 1997, Cinema Paris, Berlin, 1997, Pacific Film Archive, Berkeley Art Mus., 1997, Wako Works Art, Tokyo, 1998, Brit. Coun. Cinema, Daniel Buckholz Gallery, Cologne, 1998, Mus. Contemporary Art, Tokyo, 1998, L.A., 1998, Galerie Yvon Lambert, Paris, 1998, Kemper Mus. Contemporary Art, Kansas City, Mo., 1998, exhibited in group shows at Bliss House, Pasadena, 1992, Merz Acad., Stuttgart, 1993, Margo Leavin Gallery, L.A., 1994, Galerie Paul Andriesse, Amsterdam, 1995, Studio Guenzani, Milan, Italy, 1996, L.A. County Mus. Art, 1996—97, Armand Hammer Mus. Art, L.A., 1997, Le Magasin, Grenoble, 1998, Inst. Contemporary Arts, London, 1998, Mus. Modern Art and the Film Soc. Lincoln Ctr., N.Y., 1998, Fondazione Sandretto Re Rebaudengo, Torino, Italy, 1998, Torino, 2001, Stedelijk Van Abbemuseum, Eindhoven, 1999, Neugerriemschneider, Berlin, 1999, Galerie für Zeitgenossische Kunst Leipzig, 1999, Art Gallery Ont., Toronto, 2000, Chac Mool Gallery, L.A., 2001, MCA Chgo., 2001, 2003, Galerie Volker Diehl, Berlin, 2001, Mus. für Neue Kunst, Karlsruhe, Germany, 2003, Barbara Gladstone Gallery, N.Y.C., 2003, Vedanta Gallery, Chgo., 2003, Whitney Biennial, Whitney Mus. Am. Art, 2004, ICA Boston, 2004, Represented in permanent collections Boijmans van Beuningen Mus., Rotterdam, Eli Broad Family Found., Santa Monica, Calif., L.A. County Mus., MCA Chgo., Yokohama (Japan) Mus. Art, Henry Art Gallery, Seattle, Fondazione Sandretto Re Rebaudengo, Torino, Italy, Mus. Contemporary Art, San Diego, L.A., Whitney Mus. Am. Art, N.Y., Albright-Knox Gallery, Buffalo, The Israel Mus., Jerusalem, St. Louis Art Mus., Mus. Contemporary Art, Chgo., Walker Art Ctr., Mpls., Worcester (Mass.) Art Mus. Film/Video/Multimedia fellow, Rockefeller Found., 2000, Film Making fellow, John Simon Guggenheim Meml. Found., 2001. Fax: 212-431-6638.

LOCKLEAR, ARLINDA FAYE, lawyer; b. Ft. Bragg, N.C., Sept. 9, 1951; d. Edsel Locklear and Mary Elizabeth (Revels) Joyce; m. Gilbert Leon Hall, June 12, 1983; children, Garret & Rachel. BA, Coll. of Charleston, 1973; JD, Duke U., 1976; DHL (hon.), SUNY, 1990. Bar: N.C. 1976, D.C. 1978, Md., U.S. Supreme Ct. 1982. Staff atty. Native Am. Rights Fund, Boulder, Colo., 1976-77, Washington, 1977—87; atty., private practice Jefferson, Md., 1987—; of counsel, Native Am. Affairs, Public Policy practices Patton Boggs LLP, Washington. Guest lectr. Harvard Inst. Politics, Boston, 1983, NYU Law Sch., 1986, Colgate U., Hamilton, N.Y., 1986. Contbr. articles to profl. jours. Bd. dirs. ACLU, N.Y.C., 1984-88; Inst. for Development of Indian Law; trustee Univ. N.C. Pembroke; mem. bd. adv. Ency. of Native Am. in the 20th Century; mem. adv. panel, Winds of Change (PBS series); mem. Lumbee tribe, Cheraw Indians. Recipient Am. Heroine award Ladies Home Jour., 1984; named one of Young Women of Promise Good Housekeeping Mag., 1985; Outstanding Woman of Color award, Nat. Inst. for Women of Color, 1987; Julian T. Pierce award, Pembroke State Univ. 1994; Carpathian Award for Speaking Out, N.C. Equity, 1995. Democrat. Office: Patton Boggs LLP 2550 M St NW Washington DC 20037-1350 Office Fax: 202-457-6000, 202-457-6315. Business E-Mail: alocklear@pattonboggs.com.

LOCKLEAR, HEATHER, actress; b. Westwood, Calif., Sept. 25, 1961; d. Bill and Diane L.; m. Tommy Lee, May 10, 1986 (div. Aug. 16, 1993); m. Richie Sambora, Dec. 17, 1994 (separated, 2006), 1 child, Eva Elizabeth. Student, UCLA. Appeared in (TV series) Dynasty, 1981-89, T.J. Hooker, 1982-87, Going Places, 1990, Melrose Place, 1993-99, Spin City, 1999-2002, LAX, 2004, Boston Legal, 2005; (films) Firestarter, 1986, Return of the Swamp Thing, 1990, The Big Slice, 1991, Wayne's World 2, 1993, A Dangerous Woman, 1993, The First Wives Club, 1996, Double Tap, 1997, Money Talks, 1997, Uptown Girls, 2003, Looney Toons: Back in Action, 2003, The Perfect Man, 2005; (TV movies) Twil, 1981, City Killer, 1984, Blood Sport, 1986, Rock 'n' Roll Mom, 1988, Rich Men, Single Women, 1990, Her Wicked Ways, 1991, Dynasty: The Reunion, 1991, Highway Heartbreaker, 1992, Body Language, 1992, Fade to Black, 1993, Texas Justice, 1995, Shattered Mind, 1996, Too Many Lovers, 2003, Once Around the Park, 2003.

LOCKLEAR, TINA MICHELLE, science educator; b. Fort Oglethorpe, Ga., Dec. 15, 1970; d. Lizbeth Van Dyke; m. Roy McArthur Locklear III, July 22, 1995. BS in Natural Sci. and Biology, Shorter Coll., Rome, Ga., 1993; MS in Biology, U. West Ga., Carrollton, 1999; Ed Specialist, Instrnl. Supervision, Berry Coll., Rome, 2003. Cert. tchr.(T-6, L-6) Profl. Practices Commn./Ga., 2003. Sci. dept chair / tchr. Rome H.S., Ga., 1995—. Mem.: Ga. Sci. Tchrs. Assn., Kappa Delta Pi, Delta Kappa Gamma, Trout Unlimited (sec. 2001—04, Most active mem. 2001, 2003). Avocations: fishing, cooking, gardening, cycling, backpacking. Office Phone: 706-235-9653 ext. 1244.

LOCKLIN, MURIEL LUCIE, artist; b. Woonsocket, R.I., Oct. 28, 1938; d. Emile Wilfred Henault and Lucie Delia Blondin; m. Francis Gerald Locklin, Jr., July 25, 1959 (div.); children: Diane, Patricia, Cynthia, Kathryn, Nancy, F. Gerald III. AA in Art with hons., Dean Coll., Franklin, Mass., 1985; BA magna cum laude, Framingham State Coll., Mass., 1990. Curator exhibits Bellingham Cultural Coun., 1984—99; visual arts chmn. No. R.I. Coun. Arts, Woonsocket, 1984—94; treas., ways and means com. Blackstone Valley Art Assn., Uxbridge, Mass., 1989—99; artist in residence Coun. on Aging Ctr., Bellingham, Mass., 1991—92; pres. Woonsocket Fine Arts Soc., 1992—94; exhibit com. Monotype Guild N.E., Inc., Boston, 1998, exhibit curator, Worcester, Mass., 2001; asst. curator art Falmouth Hosp. Gallery, 1999—. Mem. fin. com. City of Bellingham, Mass., 1988—93. Named Citizen of Yr., Bellingham Bus. Assn., 1999. Mem.: Cape Cod (Mass.) Art Assn., Blackstone Valley Art Assn., Falmouth Hist. Soc. (vol. asst. textile conservator 2002—), Monotype Guild New Eng., Inc. (treas. 2000—03, v.p. 2003—06), Printmakers Cape Cod, Inc. (treas. 2000—), Duxbury Art Assn., Falmouth Artists Guild, Bourne-Wareham Art Assn. (treas. 2006—). Democrat. Roman Catholic. Avocations: genealogy, travel. E-mail: mhenloc@yahoo.com.

LOCKNER, VERA JOANNE, farmer, rancher, state legislator; b. St. Lawrence, S.D., May 19, 1937; d. Leonard and Zona R. (Ford) Verdugt; m. Frank O. Lockner, Aug. 7, 1955; children: Dean M., Clifford A. Grad., St. Lawrence (S.D.) High Sch., 1955. Bank teller/bookkeeper First Nat. Bank, Miller, SD, 1963-66, Bank of Wessington, SD, 1968-74; farmer/rancher Wessington, 1955-2000. Sunday sch. tchr. Trinity Luth. Ch., Miller, 1968-72; treas. Trinity Luth. Ch. Women, 2005—; treas. PTO, Wessington, 1969-70; treas., vice chmn., chmn., state com. woman Hand County Dems., Miller, 1978-2003, SD state legislator, 1992-2000; mem. S.D. Dem. Exec. Bd., 1997-2000. Named one of Outstanding Young Women of Am., Women's Study Club, Wessington, 1970. Mem. Order of Ea. Star (warder, marshall, chaplain 1970-2002). Democrat. Avocations: painting, crafts, gardening, photography. Home and Office: 301 3rd St NW Saint Lawrence SD 57373-2324

LOCKNEY, JULIANNA COLLEEN, music educator; b. Worcester, Mass., Sept. 27, 1976; d. James Stephan Jr. and Priscilla Mae Lockney. MusB in Music Edn., Moravian Coll., Bethlehem, Pa., 1998; MA in Arts Edn., Fitchburg State Coll., Mass., 2005. Cert. tchr. Mass., Pa. Music tchr. Winchendon Pub. Schs., Mass., 1998—99, Leominster Pub. Schs., Mass., 1999—2001, Auburn Pub. Schs., Mass., 2001—. Drama camp dir. Touchstone Cmty. Sch., Grafton, Mass., 2004—. Singer Greater Auburn Cmty. Chorus, 2004—. Mem.: Music Educators Nat. Conf., Kappa Delta Pi, Alpha Sigma Alpha. Avocations: sewing, quilting, crafts.

LOCKWOOD, DEBORAH JANE, psychotherapist, consultant, educator; b. Buffalo, Mar. 3, 1956; d. Maynard William and Lillian Rose (Boehm) L.; m. Timothy Timon Stepniak, Aug. 26, 1989. BFA minor Psychology, SUNY, Buffalo, 1979; MA in Psychology, Antioch U., 1981. Lic. marriage, family and child counselor. Intern Ctr. Human Problems, Tarzana, Calif., 1980-81, staff clinician, 1981-87; dir./founder Full Life Counseling, Ventura, Calif., 1987-91. Adj. instr. Antioch U., Santa Barbara, Calif., 1988-90; profl. tng. staff Wellness Community, Santa Monica, Calif., 1990, Bernie Siegle, M.D., Buffalo, 1991. Organizer Toys for Tots, Ventura, 1990. Mem. Am. Assn. Marriage Family Therapists (clin.), Calif. Assn. Marriage Family Therapists (clin.). Avocations: lithography, drawing, stained glass, golf, meditation. Home: 6585 Webster Rd Orchard Park NY 14127-1920 Office: Full Life Counseling 6585 Webster Rd Orchard Park NY 14127-1920

LOCKWOOD, RHONDA J., mental health services professional; b. Jacksonville, N.C., Apr. 4, 1960; d. George Barton and Sally Lynn (Hassell) L. BA, Newberry Coll., 1982; MS in Edn., Youngstown State U., 1988. nat. cert. counselor. Corrections/tng. officer Geauga County Sheriff's Dept., Chardon, Ohio, 1982-87; forensic counselor Human Svcs. Ctrs., Inc., New Castle, Pa., 1987-89; dir. children & family svcs. Marion Citrus Mental Health Ctrs., Inc., Ocala, Fla., 1989-96; clin. social worker Fla. Dept. Juvenile Justice, Alachua Halfway House, 1996-97; coord. Family Action, Interface Youth and Ind. Living programs Corner Drug Store, Inc., Gainesville, Fla., 1997—. Co-founder Sexual Abuse Intervention Network, Ocala, 1990-96, chair, 1990-92, Family Svcs. Planning Team, 1992-94; cons. Health & Human Svcs. Bd. Dist. 13, 1993-96; mem. Eckerd Youth Comprehensive Treatment Program adv. bd., 1997-99; adj. fculty Webster U., Ocala campus, 1999—. Polit. vol. state campaigns Dem. Party, Warren, Ohio, 1978-85; mem. Sexual Abuse Prevention Edn. Network, New Castle, 1987-88; cons. to gov.'s task force Sex Offenders and Their Victims; cons. Mad Dads Orgn., Ocala, 1993; mem. Juvenile Justice Coun., Ocala, 1993-94; mem. Hamilton, Lafayette, Suwannee and Columbia Counties Juvenile Justice Couns., 1997-2005; children's svc. rep. Fla. Coun. for Cmty. Mental Health, 1995-96. Recipient Outstanding Teen Vol. award Am. Red Cross, 1977. Fellow N. Eastern Ohio Police Benevolent Assn.; mem. Nat. Mus. for Women in the Arts, Nat. Bd. Cert. Counselors, NGLTF, Ind. Prodr. Womens Music, Am. Counseling Assn., Human Rights Campaign Fund, Chi Sigma Iota, Phi Kappa Phi. Democrat. Avocations: softball, golf, fishing, boating. Home: 1813 SW 86th Ter Gainesville FL 32607 Office Phone: 352-318-9433.

LOCKWOOD, THELMA SHIRLEY, retired social worker; b. Worcester, Mass., Apr. 7, 1923; d. Hyman Meyer and Frances Martha (Josephs) Brodsky; m. Howard Sumner Lockwood, Sept. 8, 1946; children: Gay Ellen, Marsha Frances Cramer, Susan Elaine. AB, Clark U., 1945; M Social Sci., Smith Coll., 1946. Lic. ind. clin. social worker, Mass. Caseworker Family Soc. of Cambridge, Mass., 1946-47, Springfield (Mass.) Family Svc. Assn., 1947-48, Jewish Family Svc. of Worcester, 1959-60, sr. caseworker supr., 1962-92. Mem. team curriculum devel. U. Mass. Med. Sch., Worcester, 1980-90; co-founder Worcester Inst. Sr. Edn., Mass., 1992. Mem. NASW, Clark U. Scholarship Soc., Phi Beta Kappa, Sigma Xi. Avocation: family.

LOCKYER, JUDITH, language educator; d. Charles Roland and Ruth Lutz Lockyer; m. James McCarley, June 24, 1938. BA, U. Ky., Lexington, 1971; MA, U. Ky., 1979; PhD, U. Mich., Ann Arbor, 1984. Tchr. English Frankfort H.S., Kans., 1972—80; lrctr., assoc. dir. composition U. Mich., Ann Arbor, 1984—88; prof. English Albion Coll., Mich., 1985—. Cons. for diversifying coll. curricula Am. Assn. of Colleges & Universities, Washington, 1991—95. Author: (lit. criticism) Language and Narration in the Novels of William Faulkner. Recipient Sr. Tchg. Award, Albion Coll., 2002, Honors Tchg. award, Albion Coll. Honors Program, 1993, Faculty Diversity award, Pres.'s Coun. Intercultural Affairs, 1996, Jr. Tchg. award, Albion Coll. Faculty, 1988. Mem.: MLA (assoc.). Democrat-Npl. Avocations: writing, reading, travel. Office: English Dept Albion College Albion MI 49224 E-mail: jlockyer@albion.edu.

LODGE, PATTI ANNE, state senator; b. Pitts., July 29, 1942; m. Edward J. Lodge; children: Mary Jeanne, Edward, Anne Marie. BA, Maryhurst U., 1964. Edn. media specialist Caldwell Sch. Dist., 1968-99, edn. media coord., 1980-97; pres. Windridge Vineyards, 1987—; mem. Idaho State Senate, Idaho, 2000—. Vice chair health and welfare com., jud. and rules com.; mem. commerce and human resources com., e-commerce interim com., tech.

interim com., drug court coord. interim com.; del. Nat. Rep. Platform Com., 1996; cons. St. Paul's Sch., Our Lady of the Valley, 1999—. Nat. Fedn. GOP Women Resolutions, 1997—99; chair Miss Rodeo Caldwell Com., 1964—80, Canyon County Reps., 1986—88; bd. dirs. Day at the Legislature, 2000; dir. Idaho H.S. Rodeo Dist. 3, 1970—78; precinct chair Canyon County Rep. Com. 22, 1980—2000; pres. Idaho Fedn. Rep. Women, 1991—96; chair Idaho Rep. Gala Celebration, 2000; vol. Latino Voter Registration, 2000; chair bd. dirs. West Valley Med. Ctr., 1986; bd. dirs. Idaho Cath. Found., 1992—. Roman Catholic. Office: Idaho State Senate State Capitol 700 W Jefferson Boise ID 83720-0081 also: PO Box 83720 Boise ID 83720-0003 Fax: 208 459-7199.

LODGE-PETERS, DIANNE SPEED, writer, literature educator, researcher; b. Greenfield, Mass., Nov. 16, 1929; d. Frederick Haigh Speed and Dorris Alice Wood; m. William Riess Peters, Aug. 1, 1953 (div. Sept. 1972); children: Allen Frederick, Benjamin William. BA, U. Mass., 1951; AM, U. Pa., 1953; PhD, U. Mich., 1969. Asst. prof. Tex. Tech. U., Lubbock, 1970—72; assoc. prof. U. Tex., Odessa, 1972—77, dean, 1972—77; assoc. prof. Auburn (Ala.) U., 1977—79; prof. Mont. State U., Bozeman, 1979—89, ret., 1989; writer Evergreen, Ala., 1989—. Mem. editl. bd.: Assn. Study Higher Edn., 1975—77; author: And Pleasantly Ignore My Sex, 1974; contbr. articles to profl. jours. Pres. bd. Globe Theatre, Odessa, 1974—77. Mem.: Magnolia Garden Club (pres. 1991—94). Avocations: reading, travel. Home: Rt 3 Box 620 Evergreen AL 36401

LODOR, MARCI ANN, dietitian; b. Pitts., Pa., Aug. 2, 1965; d. Anthony Nicola Mincucci and Julia Anna Renac; m. John Anthony Lodor Jr., June 1, 2002. BS in Clin. Dietetics, Univ. Pitts., 1988. Registered dietitian Am. Dietetic Assn. Asst. food svc. dir. Morrisons & Wightman, Squirrel Hill, Pa., 1988—91; clin. dietitian Mc Keesport (Pa.) Hosp., 1991—95; cons. dietitian Pvt. Practice, Pitts., 1996—97; food svc. dir. various long term care facilities, Pitts., 1997—2000; regional dietitian Extendicare, We. & Ctrl. Pa., 2000—02; registered dietitian HCR Manorcare, North Hills, Pa., 2003; nutritionist Greater Pitts. Cmty. Food Bank, Duquesne, 2004—05; cmty. connections program coord., nutrition specialist Luth. Svc. Soc., Bellevue, 2005. Dietitian cons. Three Rivers Family Hosp., White Oak, Pa., 1996—. Bd. dir. White Oak Animal Safe Haven, 2002—. Avocations: skating, dance, flea markets, reading, theater. Home: 612 Park St Mc Keesport PA 15132 E-mail: mlodor@aol.com.

LOEB, DEBORA DENISE, music educator, vocalist, conductor; d. Walter Alfred and Barbara Jean Myers; m. David Lee Loeb, June 24, 2001; children: Erin Lynn, Brian David. BA in music, Calif. State U. Stanislaus, 1977—79. Teaching Credential- Music CA, 2005. Music tchr. Modesto City Schs., Calif., 1993—95, William S. Hart Unified Sch. Dist., Valencia, Calif., 1998—2003. Actress, L.A., 1984—93; make up artist, L.A., 1986—93; musical theater -music dir. Canyon Theater Guild, Newhall, Calif., 1998—2003. Com. chmn., edn. outreach Santa Clarita Master Chorale, 1999—2003; mem. Santa Clarita Arts Coun., 2001—03. Recipient Heritage Music Festival of Gold award, Top Vocal Ensemble/Sch. Choirs, 2003; grant for Student performance in Carnegie Hall Mozart Requiem, City of Santa Clarita, 2002. Mem.: AFTRA, SAG, Am. Choral Director's Assn. Avocations: travel, production design. Personal E-mail: dloeb123@aol.com.

LOEB, JANE RUPLEY, academic administrator, educator; b. Chgo., Feb. 22, 1938; d. John Edwards and Virginia Pentland (Marthens) Watkins; m. Peter Albert Loeb, June 14, 1958; children: Eric Peter, Gwendolyn Lisl, Aaron John. BA, Rider Coll., 1961; PhD, U. So. Calif., 1969. Clin. psychology intern Univ. Hosp., Seattle, 1966-67; asst. prof. ednl. psychology U. Ill., Urbana, 1968-69, asst. coord. rsch. and testing, 1968-69, coord. rsch. and testing, 1969-72, asst. to vice chancellor acad. affairs, 1971-72, dir. admissions and records, 1972-81, assoc. prof. ednl. psychology, 1973-82, assoc. vice chancellor acad. affairs, 1981-94, prof. edn. psychology, 1982—. Author: College Board Project: the Future of College Admissions, 1989; co-editor: Academic Couples: Problems and Promises, 1997. Chmn. Coll. Bd. Coun. on Entrance Svcs., 1977-82; bd. govs. Alliance for Undergrad. Edn., 1988-93; active charter com. Coll. Bd. Acad. Assembly, 1992-93. HEW grantee, 1975-76. Mem. APA, Am. Ednl. Rsch. Assn., Nat. Coun. Measurement in Edn., Harvard Inst. Ednl. Mgmt. Avocation: french horn. Home: 1405 N Coler Ave Urbana IL 61801-1625 Office: U Ill 1310 S 6th St Champaign IL 61820-6925

LOEB, LISA, singer, lyricist; b. Bethesda, Md., 1968; BA in Comparative Lit., Brown U., 1990; student, Berklee Sch. Music. Founder Lisa Loeb and Nine Stories, 1990. Singer, musician: (albums) Tails, 1995, Firecracker, 1997 (Grammy nomination), Cake and Pie, 2002, Hello Lisa, 2002; (single): Stay (Reality Bites soundtrack), 1994 (Grammy nomination, 1994, Critic's Choice award, 1995), (children's albums): Catch the Moon (with Elizabeth Mitchell), 2004; co-host: (TV series) Dweezil & Lisa, 2004. Office: Artemis Records 130 5th Ave 7th Fl New York NY 10011

LOEB, SUSANNA, education educator; BSCE, Stanford U., 1988, BA in Polit. sci., 1988; MPP in Pub. Policy studies, U. Mich., 1994, PhD in Econs., 1998. Rsch. asst. U. Mich. Sch. Edn., 1991—93; rsch. asst. dept. econs. U. Mich., 1993—96; rsch. fellow Population Studies Ctr., U. Mich., 1995—; rsch. asst. U. Mich. Sch. Edn., 1996—; asst. prof. U. Calif., Davis, 1998—99; asst. prof. edn. Stanford (Calif.) U., Calif., 1999—. Rsch. cons. Inst. for Rsch. on Women and Gender, U. Mich., 1997—. Office: Stanford U Sch Edn 485 Lasuen Mall Stanford CA 94305-3096

LOEBL, MARAGARET MARGO, corporate financial executive; b. 1960; BA, Wellesley Coll., 1982; MBA, U. Chgo., 1986. Various fin. positions Gen. Motors Corp., 1987—2000; v.p. corp. fin. NIKE, Inc., 2000—01; group v.p. fin. Archer Daniels Midland Co., Decatur, Ill., 2002—. Office: Archer Daniels Midland Co 4666 Farus Pkway Decatur IL 62526

LOEHR, MARLA, chaplain; b. Cleve., Oct. 7, 1937; d. Joseph Richard and Eleanore Edith (Rothschuh) L. BS, Notre Dame Coll., South Euclid, Ohio, 1960; MAT, Ind. U., 1969; PhD, Boston Coll., 1988; Degree (hon.), Notre Dame Coll. Ohio, 1995. Cert. high sch. tchr., counselor, Ohio; cert. spiritual dir., pastoral min. Dean students Notre Dame Coll., South Euclid, Ohio, 1972-85, acting acad. dean, 1988, pres., 1988-95; chaplain Hospice of Western Res., Cleve., 1995—, spiritual dir., 1997—. Author: Mentor Handbook, 1985; co-author: Notre Dame College Model for Student Development, 1980. Hon. mem. Leadership Cleve. Class of 1990; v.p., trustee SJ Wellness Ctr., 1999; mem. leadership coun. Future Ch., Diocese of Cleve. Recipient Career Woman of Achievement award YWCA, 1992; named One of 100 Cleve.'s Most Powerful Women. Mem. Spiritual Dirs. Internat., Nat. Hospice Assn., Alpha Sigma Nu, Kappa Gamma Pi. Avocations: photography, hiking, reading, sports. Office: Hospice Western Res 29101 Health Campus Dr Ste 400 Westlake OH 44145-5268 E-mail: marlajlo@cs.com.

LOEHR, STEPHANIE SCHMAHL, psychotherapist, retired social worker; b. Watertown, N.Y., Dec. 14, 1941; d. John Schmahl and Helene (Mosely) Kay. AB in Elem. Edn., Ripon Coll., 1964; MSW, U. Wis., Milw., 1969, MA in Urban Affairs, 1973; cert. in marriage and family studies, Chgo. Family Inst., 1983. Diplomate Am. Bd. Examiners in Clin. Social Work; lic. clin. social worker, Wis. Case work supr. Milwaukee County Dept. Social Svcs., Milw., 1974—77; clinician Philstan Psychiat. Clinic, Milw., 1977—86; psychotherapist Psychiat. Consultation Assocs., Milw., 1986—89; sch. social worker Milw. Pub. Schs., 1989—2005, ret., 2005; psychotherapist Charter Behavioral Health Svcs., 1990—2000, Renew Counseling Svcs., Milw., 2005—. Field instr. Sch. Social Welfare, U. Wis., Milw.; presenter workshops; pvt. practice psychotherapy. Mem. Nat. Assn. Social Workers (past state and local chpt. officer), Acad. Cert. Social Workers. Democrat. Unitarian-Universalist. Avocations: piano, singing, photography. Office: Renew Counseling Svcs 1225 W Mitchell St Milwaukee WI 53204 Office Phone: 414-383-4455.

LOEPERE, CAROL COLBORN, lawyer; b. Mpls., Oct. 6, 1959; BA in history, Radcliffe Coll., Harvard U., 1981; JD, NYU, 1984. Bar: Md. 1985, DC 1985, US Ct. Appeals 7th Cir. 1986. Assoc. Reed Smith LLP, Washington, 1984—92, ptnr., 1992—, also head health care group. Mem.: Women's Bar Assn. of DC, Am. Health Lawyers Assn., DC Bar Assn. Office: Reed Smith LLP 1301 K St NW, Ste 1100 - East Tower Washington DC 20005 Office Phone: 202-414-9216. Office Fax: 202-414-9299. Business E-Mail: cloepere@reedsmith.com.

LOESCH, KATHARINE TAYLOR, communications educator, theater educator; b. Berkeley, Calif., Apr. 13, 1922; d. Paul Schuster and Katharine (Whiteside) Taylor; m. John George Loesch, Aug. 28, 1948; 1 child, William Ross. Student, Swarthmore Coll., 1939-41, U. Wash., 1942; BS, Columbia U., 1944, MA, 1949; grad., Neighborhood Playhouse Sch., 1946; postgrad., Ind. U., 1953; PhD, Northwestern U., 1961. Instr. speech Wellesley (Mass.) Coll., 1949-52, Loyola U., Chgo., 1956; asst. prof. English and speech Roosevelt U., Chgo., 1957, 62-65; assoc. prof. comm. and theatre U. Ill., Chgo., 1968-87, assoc. prof. emeritus, 1987—. Contbr. articles to profl. jours.; author numerous poems; performer of poetry. Active ERA, Ill., 1975-76. Grantee, Am. Philos. Soc., 1970, U. Ill., Chgo., 1970; Fgn. Travel grantee, 1983, Dylan Thomas scholar. Mem. MLA, Am. Soc. for Aesthetics, Linguistic Soc. Am., Chgo. Linguistic Soc. (co-chmn. 1954-56), Nat. Comm. Assn. (chair interpretation divsn. 1979-80, Golden Ann. award 1969), Celtic Studies Assn. N.Am., Pi Beta Phi. Episcopalian. Office: U Ill Dept Performing Arts M/C 255 1040 W Harrison St Chicago IL 60607-7130 Home: 2400 Lakeview # 1901 Chicago IL 60614 E-mail: william.loesch@goldberg.kuhn.com, dpa@uic.edu.

LOESCH, MABEL LORRAINE, social worker; b. Annandale, Minn., July 1, 1925; d. Rudolph and Hedwig (Zeidler) Treichler; m. Harold Carl Loesch, Oct. 19, 1945; children: Stephen, Gretchen, Jonathan, Frederick. BS, La. State U., 1972, MSW, 1974. Cert. Acad. Cert. Social Worker, bd. cert. diplomate. Tchr. Am. schs., Tegucigalpa, Honduras, 1960-61, Guayaquil, Ecuador, 1962-66, La Ceiba, Honduras, 1966-67; supr. clin. svc. Blundon Home, Baton Rouge, 1974-81; social worker, cons. Dhaka, Bangladesh, 1981-85; social worker Manna Food Bank, Pensacola, Fla., 1986—. Adj. instr. social work dept. Southern U., Baton Rouge, 1976-81. Author: Generations in Germany and America, 1995, 300 Years in the Family, 1998, Family Farms, 2001, revised edit., 2006, Exiled to America, 2001, Scattering Immigrant Families, 2003; editor: Making Do, 1989, Making Do II, 1994. Mem. adv. com. Luth. Ministries of Fla., 1993-97. Mem. NASW, Mensa (local sec. 1986-90, chair scholarships com. 1992—), InterTel, Phi Kappa Phi. Democrat. Lutheran. Avocation: genealogy. Home: 2140 E Scott St Pensacola FL 32503-4957 E-mail: mloesch@bellsouth.net.

LOESCHKE, MARAVENE S., academic administrator, theater educator; m. C. Richard Gillespie. BS, Towson U., 1969, MEd, 1972; PhD, The Union Inst., 1976. Prodn. asst., actress Md. Pub. TV; instr. theatre arts Towson U., 1970—74, asst. prof., 1974—83, assoc. prof., 1983—90, prof., 1990—96, acting dean Coll. Fine Arts and Comm., 1996—97, dean, 1997—2002; provost Wilkes U., 2002—06; pres. Mansfield U. of Pa., 2006—. Contbr. articles to profl. jours. Office: Office of Pres Mansfield Coll 500 North Hall Mansfield PA 16933 Office Phone: 570-662-4046, 570-662-4045.*

LOEVINGER, JANE, psychologist, educator; b. St. Paul, Feb. 6, 1918; d. Gustavus and Millie (Strouse) L.; m. Samuel I. Weissman, July 13, 1943; children: Judith, Michael B. BA in Psychology, U. Minn., 1937, MS in Psychometrics, 1938; PhD. in Psychology, U. Calif., Berkeley, 1944. Instr. psychology and edn. Stanford (Calif.) U., 1941-42; lectr. psychology U. Calif., Berkeley, 1942-43; part-time instr. in stats. and sociology Washington U., St. Louis, 1946-47, research psychologist and cons. air force projects, 1950-53, research assoc. prof. child psychiatry, 1960-64, research assoc. prof., Grad. Inst. Edn., 1964-71, research assoc., Social Sci. Inst., 1964-70, research prof., 1971-74, prof., 1974-88, Stuckenberg prof. human values and moral devel., 1984-88, prof. emeritus dept. psychology, 1988—; rsch. assoc. Jewish Hosp., St. Louis, 1954-60. Mem. personality and cognition research rev. com. NIMH, 1970-74; ad hoc reviewer U. Witwatersrand, Johannesburg, Republic of South Africa, 1985, NSF, NIMH, various other orgns.; mem. various coms. Washington U.; lectr. in field. Author: (with R. Wessler) Measuring Ego Development 1: Construction and Use of a Sentence Completion Test, 1970, (with R. Wessler and C. Redmore) Measuring Ego Development 2: Scoring Manual for Women and Girls, 1970, Ego Development: Conceptions and Theories, 1976, Scientific Ways in the Study of Ego Development, 1979, Paradigms of Personality, 1987; cons. editor: Psychol. Rev., 1983—, Jour. Personality and Social Psychology, 1984—, Jour. Personality Assessment 1987—; contbr. articles to profl. jours., book revs., letters and abstracts. Recipient Research Sci. award NIMH, 1968-73, 74-79; Ednl. Testing Service Disting. Vis. scholar, 1969; Margaret M. Justin fellow, 1955-56, NIMH grantee, 1956-79. Fellow Am. Psychol. Assn. (pres. Div. 5 1962-63, mem. com. on tests, mem. policy and planning bd. 1969-72, mem. policy task force on psychologists in criminal justice system 1976-77, pres. Div. 24 1982-83, com. on early career award in personality 1985), Phi Beta Kappa, Sigma Xi (assoc.). Democrat. Home: 6 Princeton Ave Saint Louis MO 63130-3136 Office: Washington U Dept Of Psychology PO Box 11251 Saint Louis MO 63105-0051 Business E-Mail: jloeving@artsci.wustl.edu.

LOEWENSTEIN, LENORE CECILE, retired school librarian; b. Far Rockaway, N.Y., July 11, 1932; m. Walter Bernard Loewenstein, June 21, 1959; children: Mark, Marcia. BEd, SUNY, Potsdam, 1954; MLS, San Jose State U., 1984. Tchr. East Meadow (N.Y.) Sch. Dist., 1954-57, Plainview (N.Y.)-Old Bethpage Sch. Dist., 1957-59, Downers Grove (Ill.) Sch. Dist., 1960-61; substitute libr. Palo Alto, Menlo Park and Mountain View Sch. Dists., Calif., 1974-78; elem. sch. libr. Palo Alto Sch. Dist., 1978-83, mid. sch. libr., 1984-85; elem. sch. libr. Burlingame (Calif.) Sch. Dist., 1985-90, 2d and 3d grade tchr., 1990-92. Vol. cons. East Palo Alto Sch. Dist., 1985; mem. sch. site coun. Burlingame Sch. Dist., 1986-88. Author curriculum materials for elem. grades. Recipient J. Russell Kent award San Mateo County Bd. Suprs., Redwood City, Calif., 1989. Mem. AAUW. Avocations: writing children's stories, swimming, hiking.

LOEWENTHAL, NESSA PARKER, intercultural communications consultant; b. Chgo., Oct. 13, 1930; d. Abner and Frances (Ness) Parker; m. Martin Moshe Loewenthal, July 7, 1951 (dec. Aug. 1973); children: Dann Marcus, Ronn Carl, Deena Miriam; m. Gerson B. Selk, Apr. 17, 1982 (dec. June 1987). BA in Edn. and Psychology, Stanford U., 1952. Faculty Stanford Inst. for Intercultural Communication, Palo Alto, Calif., 1973-87; dir. Trans Cultural Svcs., San Francisco, 1981-86, Portland, Oreg., 1986—. Dir. dependent svcs. and internat. edn. Bechtel Group, San Francisco, 1973-81, internat. edn. cons., 1981-84; mem. adv. com. dept. internat. studies Lesley Coll., Cambridge, Mass., 1986—; mem. Oreg. Ethics Commns., 1990—; mem. Bay Area Ethics Consortium, Berkeley, 1985-90; chmn. ethics com. Sietar Internat., Washington, 1987—, mem. governing bd., 1992-95; mem. faculty Summer Inst. for Internat. Comms., Portland, Oreg., 1987-97; core faculty Oreg. Gov.'s Sch. Svc. Leadership, Salem, 1995-97. Author: Professional Integration, 1987, Update: Federal Republic of Germany, 1990, Update: Great Britain, 1987; author, editor book series Your International Assignment, 1973-81; contbr. articles to profl. jours. Mem. equal opportunity and social justice task force Nat. Jewish Coun. on Pub. Affairs; bd. dirs. Kids on the Block, Portland, Portland Jewish Acad., 1996—, Portland Ashkalon Sister City Assn., Portland Jewish Fedn., 1999—, Coalition to Eliminate Bias and Hate Crimes in Oreg., 1999—; bd. dirs., co-chair ethics com. Soc. Humanistic Judaism, 1996-99; task force on Racism and Violence, Portland, Oreg.; mem. Lafayette (Calif.) Traffic Commn., 1974-80; bd. dirs. Ctr. for Ethics and Social Policy, 1988-91; mem. exec. bd. and planning com. Temple Isaiah, Lafayette, 1978-82; bd. dirs. Calif. Symphony, Orinda, 1988-90; mem. exec. com. overseas schs. adv. com. U.S. Dept. State, 1976-82; bd. dirs. Jewish Fedn. Oregon; mem. cmty. rels. com. Portland Jewish Fedn.; mem. Nat. Jewish Cmty. Rels.; mem. Task Force on Racism, Ethnicity and Pub. Policy, 1998—. Named Sr. Interculturalist, Sietar Internat., 1986. Mem. ASTD (exec. bd. internat. profl. performance area 1993-97, 99), Soc. for Intercultural Edn. Tng. and Rsch. (chmn. 1986-87, nomination com. 1984-86, co-chmn. 1989-90, chmn. ethics com. 1989-98, governing bd. 1992-95), World Affairs Coun. Democrat. Avocations: photography, swimming.

LOEWY, BECKY WHITE, psychology educator; b. Fountain Inn, S.C., July 24, 1931; d. James Ernest and Agnes (Roberts) White; student Mary Washington Coll., U. Va., 1948-50; B.A., Vanderbilt U., 1952; M.A., Ohio State U., 1953; Ph.D., U. Calif., Berkeley, 1957; m. Frederick Arnold Loewy, Aug. 28, 1962; children— Julia Anne, Caroline Marie. Residence counselor Ohio State U., Columbus, 1953-55; asst. prof. ednl. psychology, sr. counselor Duke U., 1957-59; asst. prof. San Francisco State U., 1959-63, assoc. prof., 1963-69, prof. psychology, 1969—, program dir. gerontology, 1977-82. Danforth assoc., 1979. Mem. Am. Psychol. Assn., Soc. Research in Child Devel., Am. Assn. for Counseling and Devel., Western Gerontol. Soc., Psi Chi, Pi Lambda Theta. Home: 1275 Tuolumne Rd Millbrae CA 94030-1533 Office: Dept Psychology San Francisco State U 1600 Holloway Ave San Francisco CA 94132-1722

LOFARO, NANETTE, information services administrator; b. Bronx, N.Y., Oct. 25, 1948; d. Anthony Martin and Pia (Gentili) Gentili; m. Anthony Philip Lofaro, Nov. 21, 1970; children: Laura, Gina, Tony. BA, Ladycliff Coll., Highland Falls, N.Y., 1970; MS in LS, Cath. U. Am., 1994. Tchr., ednl. cons. various instns., N.Y., 1970-90, libr. cons. Fairfax, Va., 1991-94; libr. Labat Anderson Inc., Washington, 1995-96; asst. supervisory libr. Garcia Cons. Inc., Washington, 1996-97; dir. info. svcs. Head Start Publs. Mgmt. Ctr., Washington, 1997—. Project leader, select excellence and accountability program N.Y. State Bd. Regents, Clifton Park, 1988; fin. dir. Montessori Sch. of Schenectady, N.Y., 1980-83. Author: Distance Learning: A Resource Guide, 1998, Appreciative Inquiry: A Resource Guide, 1998; co-author: Parent Involvement: A Resource Guide, 1998. Recipient Peg award for meritorious svc. LWV, 1988. Mem. ALA, LWV (pres. Clifton Park 1989-91), Knowledge Mgmt. Consortium Internat., Nat. Assn. for Edn. of Young Children, Coun. for Exceptional Children, Cath. Daus Am. (edn. chair). Roman Catholic. E-mail: nanettel@hskids-tmsc.org.

LOFGREN, ZOE, congresswoman; b. Palo Alto, Calif., Dec. 21, 1947; d. Milton R. and Mary Violet Lofgren; m. John Marshall Collins, Oct. 22, 1978; children: Sheila Zoe Lofgren Collins, John Charles Lofgren Collins. BA in Polit. Sci., Stanford U., 1970; JD cum laude, U. Santa Clara, 1975. Bar: Calif. 1975, D.C. Adminstrv. asst. to Congressman Don Edwards, San Jose, Calif., 1970-79; ptnr. Webber and Lofgren, San Jose, 1979-81; mem. Santa Clara County Bd. Suprs., 1981-94, U.S. Congress from 16th Calif. dist., 1995—, Homeland Security com., House Adminstrn. com. and Judiciary com., Joint com. on Libr. Mem. com. on stds. of ofcl. conduct, jud. com., sci. com.; part-time prof. law U. Santa Clara, 1978-80. Exec. dir. Cmty. Housing Developers, Inc., 1979-80; trustee San Jose C.C. Dist., 1979-81; bd. dirs. Cmty. Legal Svcs., 1978-81, San Jose Housing Svc. Ctr., 1978-79; mem. steering com. sr. citizens housing referendum, 1978; del. Calif. State Bar Conv., 1979-82, Dem. Nat. Conv., 1976; active Assn. Immigration and Nationality Lawyers, 1976-82, Calif. State Dem. Ctrl. Com., 1975-78, Santa Clara County Dem. Ctrl. Com., 1974-78, Notre Dame H.S. Blue Ribbon Com., 1981-84, Victim-Witness Adv. Bd., 1981-94. Recipient Bancroft-Whitney award for Excellence in Criminal Procedure, 1973. Mem. Santa Clara County Bar Assn. (trustee 1979—), Santa Clara County Women Lawyers Com. (exec. bd. 1979-80), Santa Clara Law Sch. Alumni Assn. (v.p. 1977, pres. 1978), Nat. Women's Polit. Caucus, Assn. of Bay Area Govts. (exec. bd. 1981-86). Democrat. Office: US Ho Reps 102 Cannon Ho Office Bldg Washington DC 20515-0516 also: Dist Office Ste B 635 N 1st St San Jose CA 95112-5110

LOFLAND, PATRICIA LOIS, secondary school educator, travel company executive; b. New Orleans, Apr. 18, 1937; d. Willie and Philomene (Foster) Seymore; m. Eugene Joseph LeBeauf, Apr. 24, 1954 (div. 1967); children: Valentino, Renee, Merlin, Tammy, Gina; m. Trusten P. Causey Lofland, Jan. 21, 1974. AA, Long Beach City Coll., 1972; BA in Sociology, Calif. State U., Dominguez Hills, 1972; MA Early Childhood Edn., Calif. State U., 1974. Cert. tchr., Calif. Community/liaison tchr. Long Beach (Calif.) Community Improvement League, 1964-70; dep. probation officer Orange County, Orange, Calif., 1972-74; substitute tchr. Compton (Calif.) Unified Sch. Dist., 1974-76; tchr./pers.commr. Long Beach Unified Sch. Dist., 1976—96; customer service rep. Western/Delta Airlines, L.A., 1978-87; travel agt./sales cons., 1986—. Mem. exec. bd. Westside Neighborhood Assn., Long Beach, 1981, Long Beach Fair Housing Found., 1987—; sec. L.A. County Grand Jury, 1982-83; pres. St. Luke Mission Soc., Long Beach, 1978-88; mem. Christian bd. edn. St. Luke Baptist Ch., Long Beach, 1986-88.,mem., State Calif. Sch. Pers. Commn. Assn., 1999; cmty. development advisor, Long Beach, 1993-2002; Relocation Appeals Bd., 1988-1995, Elected Trustee, Long Beach Cmty. Coll. Bd., 1996-2000, Christ Second Bapt. Ch., mem. Youth Worker Missionary Soc., Fin. Comm., New Members Counselor and Dept. sec., 1995- Recipient cert. of appreciation Westside Neighborhood Assn., 1981, cert. of appreciation Lutheran U., 1996; Long Beach City Coll. recognition for commitment and outstanding svc.to the EOPS and CARE program, 1999, cert. of appreciation for outstanding leadership in the Long Beach Cmty., 1996, 1999, recognition as the first african mem. of the Long Beach City Coll. Bd. of Trustees, 1997, cert. of appreciation, Bd. of Trustees, 2000, cert. of appreciation from the Calif. Senate and Assembly, 1999, State of Calif. Senate and Assembly, 1999, Pearl award Alpha Kappa Alpha, 2000, cert. of appreciation L.A. county Bd. Suprs., 2002. Mem. Calif. Tchrs. Assn., Calif. Personnel Commrs. Assn., Nat. Coun. Negro Women, NAACP, Delta Phi Upsilon (v.p. Nu chpt. 1973-77). Democrat. Avocation: world-wide travel. Home: 1281 W Cameron St Long Beach CA 90810-2209

LOFQUIST, VICKI L., journalist; b. Des Moines, Aug. 2, 1949; d. Edgar William and Gwendolyn Marjorie Lofquist; m. Craig Peter Thiesen, May 23, 1997. Student, St. Andrews U., Scotland, 1969—70; BA, Grinnell Coll., 1971; MA, U. Minn., 1976. Cert. fund raising exec. 2004. Prodr. Sta. KUOM Radio U. Minn., Mpls., 1974—85, 1989—91; cons., ind. radio prodr. Mpls., 1992—96; devel. dir. Minn. Internat. Ctr., Mpls., 1997—2000, Books for Africa, St. Paul, 2000—; devel. officer Children's Home Soc. and Family Svcs., St. Paul, 2001—04; alumni rels., ann. fund coord. Metro. State U., St. Paul, 2004—. Prodr.(writer): (radio documentaries) Leading to Beijing: Voices of Global Women (Clarion Award, Women In Communication, 1996, Hon. Mention, Internat. Assn. of Women in Radio & T.V., 1997), Science Lives: Women & Minorities in the Sciences, Sound Studies in Psychology, a CPB/Annenberg Project. Bd. dirs. St. Paul LWV, 2002—. Grantee Bicentennial Swedish-Am. Exch. Fund, Swedish Inst., Stockholm, Sweden, 1991. Office: Metro State Univ 700 E 7th St Saint Paul MN 55106 Office Phone: 651-793-1810. Business E-Mail: vicki.lofquist@metrostate.edu.

LOFSTROM, ARLENE KATHERINE, primary school educator; b. Jersey City, N.J., July 28, 1946; d. Edward and Dorothy Staats McClain; children: Courtney Lynne, Derek Jason. BA, Jersey City State Coll., 1968. Tchr. 4th to 6th grade Jersey City Bd. Edn., 1968—75; tchr. 3d grade Union Beach (N.J.) Bd. Edn., 1989—. Remedial reading tchr. Union Beach Meml. Sch., 1985—89, Latch Key tchr., 1987—88, Gifted and Talented tchr., 1988—89, summer sch. tchr., 1987—; ESL tchr. Union Beach Adult Sch., 2000—01. Mem.: NEA, N.J. Edn. Assn., Highlands Hist. Soc., Highlands Rep. Club. Avocations: golf, travel, book discussion groups. Home: A-12 Oceanview Terr Highlands NJ 07732

LOFTIN, NANCY CAROL, lawyer, utilities executive; b. Phoenix, 1954; BA, Ariz. State U., 1976; JD, U. Ariz. Sch. of Law, 1979. Bar: Ariz. 1979. Special counsel & dir. enforcement Ariz. Corp. Commn.; staff atty. Ariz. Public Service, 1985—87; v.p., gen. counsel, sec. Pinnacle West Capital Corp. & Ariz. Public Service, 1987—. Mem. Edison Electric Inst. Bd. mem. Phoenix Children's Hospital, former bd. chair. Mem.: ABA, Am. Soc. of Corporate Secretaries, Ethics Officer Assn. Office: Pinnacle West Capital Corp PO Box 53999 Phoenix AZ 85072-3999

LOFTON, BRENDA M., middle school educator; b. Alexandria, La., July 10, 1959; d. Bobbie Frank and Bobbiline McLemore; m. Terry Lee Lofton, June 3, 1978; children: Janna Michelle Young, Jennifer Leigh. BA, N.E. La. U., Monroe, 1980; MA, La. Tech U., Ruston, 1986. Cert. early adolescence math. Nat. Bd. Profl. Tchg. Standards, 2002. Tchr. Glen View Elem. Sch., Ruston, 1986—92, A.E. Phillips Lab. Sch., Ruston, 1992—. Children's choir dir. Calvary Bapt. Ch., Ruston, 2003—06, worship leader praise band, keyboard; accompanist Masterworks Young Singers, Ruston, 2000—05. Named Tchr. of Yr., A.E. Phillips Lab. Sch., 2003, 2006, Lincoln Parish Sch. Bd., 2003, 2006, Tchr. of Yr., La. Dept. of Edn., 2006; named one of Finalist Mid. Sch. Tchr. of Yr., 2003. Mem.: Nat. Coun. Tchrs. Math. Baptist. Avocations: piano, hiking, camping, travel, gardening. Home: 5785 Hwy 33 Choudrant LA 71227 Office Phone: 318-257-3469.

LOFTON, SUSAN PRICE, nursing educator, consultant; d. Sidney H. Price; m. Jeffery W. Lofton, Mar. 27, 1982. M in Nursing, U. of So. Miss., Hattiesburg, 1991; PhD, U. of Miss., Oxford, 2001. Clin. nurse specialist, ANA. Prof. nursing U. of Miss., Jackson, 1996—. CEO Lofton Cons., Jackson, 2000—. Author: (nursing jours. and textbooks) Community Health and Geriatric Assessment (Order of Nelson, Tchg. Excellence award U. of Miss., 2004). Mem. Susan Komen Found., Jackson, 2004—06. Recipient U.S. Health Sec. Award for Excellence in Nursing, Dept. Vet. Affairs, 1985. Mem.: Phi Kappa Phi. Home: 505 Westwind Dr Brandon MS 39042 Office: U Miss 2500 N State St Jackson MS 39216 Office Phone: 601-984-6268.

LOFTUS, KAY DOUGLAS COLGAN, social worker; b. Bad Axe, Mich., July 27, 1941; d. James Fletcher and Myrtle Irene (Krueger) Colgan; m. Stephen Deane Loftus, Jan. 2, 1965; children: Amy Loftus Tuitel, Anna. BA, Alma Coll., 1963; MA, Bowling Green State U., 1966; MSW, Western Mich. U., 1983. LCSW; Healthy Families Am. cert. trainer; lic. marriage and family therapist. Clin. social worker Barry County Cmty. Mental Health Svcs., 1983-95; program mgr. Healthy Families Barry County, Hastings, Mich., 1995-98; cons. Children's Charter of the Cts. of Mich., Lansing, 1999—2006. Bd. dirs. Barry County Child Abuse Coun., Hastings, 1977. Bd. dirs. Mich. Assn. for Infant Mental Health, 2006—. E-mail: loftuskay@comcast.net.

LOGA, SANDA, physicist, researcher; b. Bucharest, Romania, June 13, 1932; came to U.S., 1968; d. Stelian and Georgeta (Popescu) L.; m. Karl Heinz Werther, Mar. 1968 (div. 1970); m. Radu Zaciu, 1996. MS in Physics, U. Bucharest, 1955; PhD in Biophysics, U. Pitts., 1978. Asst. prof. faculty medicine and pharmacy, Bucharest, 1963-67; rsch. asst. Presbyn./St. Luke's Hosp., Chgo., 1968-69; assoc. rsch. scientist Miles Labs., Elkhart, Ind., 1969-70; rsch. asst. U. Pitts., 1971-78; rsch. assoc. Carnegie-Mellon U., Pitts., 1978-80; health physicist VA Med. Ctr., Westside, Chgo., 1980; med. physicist, VA Med. Ctr. N. Chgo, 1980-97. Assoc. prof. Chgo. Med. Sch., N. Chgo., 1985-2004. Mem. Am. Assn. Physicists in Medicine, Health Physics Soc. Office: Chgo Med Sch U Health Scis 3333 Green Bay Rd North Chicago IL 60064-3037 Business E-Mail: sanda.loga@rosalindfranklin.edu.

LOGAN, BETTY MULHERIN, human services specialist; b. Augusta, Ga., July 14, 1926; d. James B. and Mayclare (Rice) Mulherin; m. Vance Earle Logan, Jr. June 30, 1951; children: James V., Charles E., Mayclare Scherer, Anne Marie Harvey, Vance E III, E. Carson Johnson. Student, Fontbonne Coll. Tchr. St. Mary's and Aquinas Schs., Augusta, Ga., 1960-76; ret. vol., 1998. Organist St. Mary's Ch., Augusta, 1960-76; treas. parish coun. PCCW, Augusta, 1956-57, chmn. various coms., 1957-70; pres. deanery Coun. Cath. Women, Augusta and Savannah, 1970-72, 76-78; founder, dir. Cmty. Clothing Ctr., Augusta, 1967-76; founder Right to Life, 1969—; founder, treas., bd. dirs., trustee Birthright, Augusta, 1971—; chair Am. Cancer Soc. of Augusta, 1960-66; rep. Savannah Diocese Ga. Legis. Forum, 1978-82; pres. Augusta coun. Cath. Savannah Diocesan Coun. Coun. Cath. Women, 1976-78. Mem. Nat. Hist. Soc., Sacred Heart Cultural Ctr. (aux.). Roman Catholic. Avocations: swimming, learning computers, writing memoirs. Home: 2624 Raymond Ave Augusta GA 30904-5379 Office: Birthright Of Augusta Inc PO Box 15746 Augusta GA 30919-1746

LOGAN, ELIZABETH, middle school educator; d. Robert Joseph and Elizabeth Mary (Ries) Noll; m. Russell Mahlon Logan; 1 child, Jeremy. BS in Edn., Auburn U.; MEd, U. Houston-Victoria. Cert. tchr., Ala., Tex., nat. bd. cert. tchr., EAYA, 2000. Art tchr. Howell Intermediate Sch., Victoria, Tex., 1981-89, Opelika (Ala.) Mid. Sch., 1983—93, Auburn Jr. HS, 1993—. Pres., v.p. treas., sec. Xi Beta Iota, Beta Sigma Phi, Xi Pi Rho, Auburn, Victoria, 1984—. Named Ala. Mid. Level Art Educator of Yr., 1995, Mid. Level Art Educator of Yr., NAEA, 1996; recipient Knowledge Network award, NY Times, 2005—. Mem. NEA, Nat. Art Edn. Assn., Ala. Art Educators Assn., Ala. Edn. Assn., Phi Kappa Phi, Delta Omicron, Tau Beta Sigma, Beta Sigma Phi, Delta Kappa Gamma. Methodist. Avocations: doll collecting, drawing, reading, bowling. Office: Auburn Jr HS 332 Samford Ave Opelika AL 36801-3124 Business E-Mail: blogan@auburnschools.org.

LOGAN, GEORGIANA MARIE, psychotherapist; b. West Palm Beach, Fla., May 6, 1948; d. Georgina Escasena and William D. Logan. MA in sociology, Boston Coll., Chestnut Hill, Mass., 1983, MA in pastoral ministry, 1996; MSW in clin. social work, Boston Coll., Chestnut Hill, Mass., 1996. Tchr. Sacred Heart Sch., San Francisco, 1975—77; ednl. advocate for Hispanic cmty. Alianza Hispana, Inc., Roxbury, Mass., 1977—79; sch. staff Woodlands Acad. Sacred Heart, Lake Forest, Ill., 1984—86; co-dir. Let Nicaragua Live Humanitarian Aid Campaign, Washington, 1986—87; co-coord. Peace Brigades Internat. U.S.A., Cambridge, Nueva Segovia, 1990—91; secretariat staff Soc. Sacred Heart, Casa Generalizia, Rome, 1992—93; psychotherapist Interfaith Counseling Svc. Inc., West Newton, Mass., 1996—; clin. social worker South End Cmty. Health Ctr., Boston, 1997—; clin. fellow Boston Inst. Psychotherapy, 2000—02. Pastoral psychotherapist Franciscan Counseling Ctr., Inc., Boston, 2002—03. Editor: (book) Conferences: Concepción Camacho, RSCJ, 1993, (booklet) REFLECTIONS: Japanese Spirituality Conference, 1999. Fellow: Am. Assn. Pastoral Counselors; mem.: Soc. Sacred Heart U.S. Province, Nat. Assn. Social Workers. Roman Catholic. Avocations: reading, walking, drawing. Office: Interfaith Counseling Svc Inc 60 Highland St West Newton MA 02465 Office Phone: 617-425-2060 x 3049. Business E-Mail: logang8506@yahoo.com. E-mail: glogan@rscj.org.

LOGAN, ISABEALL TALMADGE, psychotherapist, writer; b. NYC, Feb. 27, 1957; d. Walter Wells and Justine Robinson Logan, Jack Bridgman (Stepfather). BA, Marlboro Coll., 1981; MA, Emory U., 1990; PhD, Pacifica Grad. Inst., 2000. Lic. mental health counselor Mass.; cert. domestic abuse counselor Calif. Intern Shelter Svcs. for Women, Santa Barbara, Calif., 1995—96, Vista del Mar Hosp., Ventura, Calif., 1997, Jackson Hole Cmty. Counseling Ctr., Jackson, Wyo., 1999—2000; case mgr. Cottage Hosp. Psychiat. Unit, Santa Barbara, 2000—01; psychotherapist Trauma Ctr., Allston, Mass., 2001—02; affiliate staff psychotherapist Two Brattle Ctr., Inc., Cambridge, Mass., 2002—05; staff psychotherapist Boston Inst. for Psychotherapy, Brookline, Mass., 2002—05; assoc. staff psychotherapist Boston Inst. Psychotherapy, 2005—06; pvt. practice Cambridge, 2002—; asylum program coord. Cmty. Legal Svcs. and Counseling Ctr., Cambridge, Mass., 2005—. Adj. English prof. St. Leo Coll., Key West, Fla., 1991—93, Santa Barbara City Coll., 1996—97. Contbr. articles to local New Eng. newspaper. Founding v.p. Fla. Keys Assn. for Young Children, Key West, 1994—95; vol. Doctors of the World, NYC, 2003—05. Fellow, Two Brattle Ctr., Inc, 2001—02; Working scholar, Breadloaf Writers' Conf., 1984—88, Grad. fellow, Emory U., 1988. Avocations: meditation, yoga, gardening, writing, travel. Office: PO Box 400607 Cambridge MA 02140 Office Phone: 617-532-4531. Personal E-mail: isabealllogan@comcast.net.

LOGAN, JANET ARTISAM, mental health nurse; b. St. Mary, Jamaica, Feb. 24, 1933; arrived in U.S., 1968; d. James Newton and Edith Eliza Watson; m. Gerold George Logan, Nov. 23, 1974; m. Louis Wilberforce Huffstead, 1966 (div. 1970); 1 child, Ruel. Student, St. Francis Coll. Registered mental nurse Saxondale Hosp., Nottinghamshire, England, 1955—59; state RN Sheffield United Hosp., Sheffield, England, 1960—63; registered mental nurse Middlewood Hosp., Sheffield, 1963—64; RN Baycrest Hosp., Toronto, Canada, 1964—68; RN, head nurse Beekman Downtown, N.Y.C., 1970—74; head nurse Interfaith Med. Ctr., Bklyn., 1974—89; RN SUNY Downstate, Bklyn., 1988—2003; ret. Chmn. entertainment St. Pauls United Meth., Bklyn., 1975—, co-chmn. youth coun., 1988—96. Recipient Membership award, St. Pauls United Meth., 1998. Mem.: ANA, Critical Care Nurse Assn., N.Y. State Nurses Assn. (Lifetime award 2000), Black Nurse Assn., Am. Nephrology Nurse (legis. rep. 2000—), Bklyn. Coll. Performing Arts, Lions (first v.p. 1999—), Dem. Club (com. mem., Cmty. Svc. award 2000). Avocations: swimming, reading, travel, dance, theater. Home: 760 E 37th St Brooklyn NY 11210 Office: SUNY Downstate Med Ctr 450 Clarkson Ave Brooklyn NY 11203

LOGAN, JOYCE POLLEY, education educator; b. Providence, Ky., Sept. 18, 1935; d. Vernon and Hattie Alice Polley; m. Jewell Wyatt Logan (dec.), June 4, 1956; 1 child, James Edward. BS, Murray State U., 1956, MA, 1960; EdD, Vanderbilt U., 1988. Cert. bus. tchr., vocat. adminstrn. Student sec. Murray (Ky.) State U., 1954-56; bus. tchr. Hopkins County Schs., Madisonville, Ky., 1956-68; regional coord. Vocational Region 2 Ky. Dept. Edn., Madisonville, 1968-83; prin. Health Occupations Sch., Madisonville, 1983-88; voc., tech. administr. Ky. Dept. Edn., Frankfort, 1988-90; asst. prof. dept. adminstrn. and supervision Coll. Edn. U. Ky., Lexington, 1991—99; state dir. Ky. Com. for Secondary and Middle Schs. So. Assn. Colls. and Schs., 1995-98; assoc. prof. dept. adminstrn. and supervision Coll. Edn. U. Ky., Lexington, 2000—. Evaluator Distance Edn. Training Coun., Washington, 1981—; field coord. military evaluations, Am. Coun. on Edn., Washington, 1984—. Author: (with A.C. Krizan) Basics of Writing, 1993, 2000; contbg. author: Records Management and Business Communication. Mem. alumni bd. Murray (Ky.) State U. Coll. Bus., 1988-2001; fundraiser Ky. Spl. Olympics, Madisonville, 1983, YMCA, Madisonville, 1984; mem. edn. com. Greater Leadership Program Madisonville, Ky. C. of C., 1987-88. Recipient Exceptional Svc. award Coll. Edn., U. Ky., 1999; named FFA Hon. State Farmer, Ky. FFA., 1979, Woman of the Year, Lion's Club, Madisonville, Ky., 1987, Outstanding Tchr. Educator, 1992, Exceptional Achievement award for svc. U. Ky., 1999. Mem. Nat. Bus. Edn. Assn., Am. Vocat. Assn., Ky. Vocat. Assn., Southern Assn. of Colls. and Schs. (trustee 1973, 1976-78, chmn. Commn on Occupational Ednl. Insts. 1973), Ky. Assn. for Sch. Adminstrs., Assn. for Supervision and Curriculum Devel., Phi Delta Kappa, Omicron Delta Kappa (hon.). Avocations: jogging, tennis, reading, piano playing. Office: U Ky 111 Dickey Hall Coll of Edn Lexington KY 40506 Home: 2044 Shadybrook LN Lexington KY 40502-3033 Office Phone: 859-257-5625. E-mail: jploga00@uky.edu.

LOGAN, LYNDA DIANNE, elementary school educator; b. Detroit, June 22, 1952; d. Horatio Bernard and Ruby (Newsom) Graham; m. Keith L. Logan, Aug. 16, 1980 (div); 1 child, Lauren Nicole. BS, Ea. Mich. U., 1974, MA, 1980. Cert. tng. program quality rev., Calif.; cert. tchr., Calif., Miss., Mich.; cert. Lang. Devel. Specialist (CLAD), 1996; lic. guidance counselor basic related edn., Miss.; cert. counselor pupil pers. svc. credential, Mich., Calif. Substitute tchr. Detroit Pub. Schs., 1974-76; mid. sch. tchr., advisor yearbook club, advisor, chair, founder newspaper club Inkster (Mich.) Pub. Schs., 1976-80; CETA vocat. counselor Golden Triangle Vocat.-Tech. Ctr., Mayhew, Miss., 1980-82, basic related educator, 1980-82; elem. tchr. Inglewood (Calif.) Unified Sch. Dist., 1982-93, reading resource specialist, 1993-96; tchr. Crozier Magnet Mid. Sch., Inglewood, Calif., 1996—. Advisor Assn. Student Body, 2000-01; tchr.-mentor The Gear-Up Program, 2000-02, counselor, 2003; mem. forecast adv. bd. COED Mag., N.Y.C., 1979-80; advisor/founder Newspaper Club Fellrath Mid. Sch., Inkster, 1979-80; mem. interviewing com. Golden Triangle Vocat.-Tech. Ctr., Mayhew, 1980-82, evaluation and follow-up com., 1980-82; pronouncer spelling bee Inglewood Unified Sch. Dist., 1991, 94; organizer student study team meetings Worthington Sch., Inglewood, 1993-96, coord. reading program, 1993-96; mem. interviewing com., 1987-95; co-chair yearbook com., 1993-94, prin. adv. bd., 1987-92, ct.-liaison and child welfare attendance rep. L.A. County Edn., 1995-96, sch. leadership team mem., 1991—, supt. adv. coun., 1995-96, reading is fundamental coord., 1993-96, mem. team earthquake preparedness com., 1994-96, coord. after-sch. tutoring program, 1998-99, curriculum coun. rep. 1998-99, mentor tchr.-gear up program, 2000—, grant proposal writer, 2000-01, mem. sch. site coun.; adult edn. tchr. CBET ESL Program, 2001—03; supervising tchr. Calif. State U., Dominguez, 1987, 94, 2002, Nat. U., 1987, 94, 2003, UCLA, 2001-02, dept. chair Highland Elem. Sch., 2003-04; instr. emer. immigrant program Monroe Mid. Sch., 2004-2005. Youth co-chair March of Dimes, Detroit, 1976-80; com. mem. Nat. Coun. Negro Women, L.A. chpt., 1982-84; com. mem. Cmty. Action Program, Eternal Promise Bapt. Ch., L.A., 1991, pres. choir, 1991, v.p. hospitality com., 1987-88; co-chmn. women's com., 1990; mem. parent adv. com. Knox Presbyn. Ch. Nursery Sch., L.A., 1988-89; mem. bldg. fund com. West Angeles Ch. of God in Christ, 2001-03, co-chair higher learning parent com.; v.p., mem. fin. com. Fairview Gardens Homeowner Assn., 2003; mentor, tchr. UCLA. Mem. ASCD, AAUW, NAFE, Radical Fringe Red Hat Soc., Black Women's Forum, Ladies Aux. Knights of St. Peter Claver, Ea. Mich. U. Alumni Assn., Phi Gamma Nu. Avocations: community organizational activities, travel, movies, theater, reading. Office: Crozier Mid Sch 151 N Grevillea Ave Inglewood CA 90301 Office Phone: 310-419-2700. Personal E-mail: lyndalogan2@aol.com.

LOGAN, NANCY ALLEN, media specialist, consultant; b. Rochester, NY, Mar. 27, 1933; d. Warren William and Dorothea Amelia (Pund) Allen; m. Joseph Skinner Logan, Dec. 29, 1952; children: Joseph Skinner Logan Jr., Susan, Annette Logan Miller, Jennifer Logan Haber. Student, Middlebury Coll., 1951-52; BA, Cornell U., 1955; MLS, SUNY, Albany, 1967; cert. legal asst., Marist Coll., 1983. Cert. libr. media specialist, social studies tchr. NY. Libr. media specialist Hyde Park (NY) Sch. Dist., 1971-93. Editor: Dear Friends, 1989; editor: (newsletter) Sch. Libr. Media Specialists, 1984—85, Jamestown Hist. Soc., 1997—2001. Arts chmn. Jr. League, Poughkeepsie, NY, 1967—69; dir. Jr. Arts Ctr., 1967—69, edn. chmn., 1970—71; sec. bd. dirs. Poughkeepsie Tennis Club, 1973—79; indexer periodicals Dutchess County Hist. Soc., Poughkeepsie, 1979—93; county rep. Sch. Libr. Media Specialists, 1982, exhibits chmn. ann. meeting, 1983, 1984; indexer Jamestown (RI) Press, 1993—; bd. dirs. Friends Jamestown Philomenian Libr., 1994—97, trustee, 1999—, v.p, treas. bd. trustees, 2004—, chmn. bd. trustees, 2005—; mem. Jamestown Planning Commn., 1999; stewardship chair Conanicut Island Land Trust, 2002. Mem.: Beavertail Lighthouse Assn. (bd. dirs. 1994—97). Avocations: reading, sailing, travel, bicycling. Home: 149 Seaside Dr Jamestown RI 02835-3117 Personal E-mail: nalogan@cox.net.

LOGAN, PAULA M., entertainment company executive, accountant; b. Bklyn., Nov. 23, 1971; d. Charles L. Price and Vyris Logan; 1 child, Tyrone T. BS in Acctg. and Econs., L.I. U., 1999. Account exec. Blanksteen Cos., N.Y.C., 1990-93, property and casualty ins. broker, 1993; account exec. Rude Boy Internat. Sounds, Bklyn., 1989—, Vy's Bake Shop, Bklyn., 1989—, Lady P's Party Cons. Co., Bklyn., 1989-93, v.p., 1993—; mem. N.Y.C. Special Enforcement Unit, 2002—. Cons. Macy's East Herald Square Bridal Registry, 2002. Vol. income tax assistance program, IRS, Bklyn., 1997—; youth counselor St. Mary's Ch. of Christ, 1993—. Mem. AICPAs, Lions. Democrat. Pentecostal. Avocations: collecting teddy bears and porcelain dolls, stamps and coins, reading, dance. Office: Lady P's Party Cons 166 St Marks Ave Brooklyn NY 11238 E-mail: PLoganGrant@netscape.net, Lady_P_01@hotmail.com.

LOGAN, SANDRA JEAN, retired economics professor, retired business educator; b. Dayton, Ohio, Jan. 3, 1940; d. Max B. and Edna E. (Sanderson) Parrish; m. John E. Logan, Apr. 25, 1964. BA, Drew U., 1962; MBA, Columbia U., N.Y.C., 1964; PhD, U. S.C., 1976. Piano tchr., Whippany, N.J., 1957-64; lab. analyst Bear Creek Mining Co., Morristown, N.J., summer 1957, 58; rsch. asst. Drew U., Madison, N.J., summer 1962; staff asst. N.J. Bell Telephone Co., Newark, summer 1963, 64-67; instr. bus. U. Toledo, 1967-69; asst. prof. econs. and bus. S.C. State Univ., Orangeburg, 1970-76; prof. econs. and bus. Newberry (S.C.) Coll., 1976—2002, emeritus, 2002—, acting v.p. acad. affairs, 1993-95. Cons. econs., Ohio and S.C., 1967—, N.J. Bell Telephone Co., Newark, 1968; lectr. bus. Ea. Mich. U., Ypsilanti, spring 1969. Active Coldstream Home Owners Assn., Columbia, S.C., 1972-80; officer St. Andrews Woman's Club, Columbia, 1969-76. Rsch. grantee, U. SC and SC State U., 1974—75. Mem. Am. Econs. Assn., So. Econs. Assn. Republican. Presbyterian. Home: 112 Smiths Market Ct Columbia SC 29212-1923

LOGAN, SANDRA LA MASTUS, music educator; b. Cleveland, Miss., July 29, 1953; d. James W. and Betty Reynolds La Mastus; m. Hubert H. Logan, July 31, 1999; 1 child, Troy Galtelli. B of Music Edn., Delta State U., Cleveland, Miss., 1976. Cert. tchr. Ark., 1976. Tchr. elem./jr. high music St. Michael's Cath. Sch., West Memphis, Ark., 1976—86; tchr. elem. music West Memphis Sch. Dist., Ark., 1986—99, Marion Sch. Dist., Ark., 1999—. Music dir. Crittenden Arts Coun., West Memphis, Ark. Dir.(muscian, actor, producer, technician): (theater) various prodns. Musician St. Michael's Cath. Ch., West Memphis, Ark., 1976—2006. Home: 224 Roosevelt Ave West Memphis AR 72301 Office: Marion Elem Sch 235 Military Rd Marion AR 72364 Personal E-mail: slogan224@yahoo.com. E-mail: slogan@marion.crsc.k12.ar.us.

LOGAN, SHARON BROOKS, lawyer; b. Nov. 19, 1945; d. Blake Elmer and Esther N. (Statum) Brooks; children: John W. III, Troy Blake. BS Econs., U. Md., 1967, MBA Mktg., 1969; JD, U. Fla., 1979. Bar: Fla. 1979. Prin. Raymond Wilson, Esq., Ormond Beach, Fla., 1980; atty. Landis, Graham & French, Daytona Beach, Fla., 1981, Watson & Assocs., Daytona Beach, 1982—84, Sharon B. Logan, PA, Ormond Beach, 1984—. Legal adv. to paralegal program Daytona Beach CC, 1984—. Sponsor Ea. Surfing Assn., Daytona Beach, 1983—, Nat. Scholastic Surfing Assn., 1987—; bd. dir. Ctr. for Visually Impaired, 1991—. Recipient Citizenship award, Rotary Club, 1962—63; fellow Woodrow Wilson, U. Md., 1967. Mem.: Daytona Beach Area Bd. Realtors, Volusia County Estate Planning Coun., Fla. Supreme Ct. Hist. Soc., Volusia County Real Property Coun., Inc. (sec. 1987—88, bd. dirs., v.p. 1988—89, pres. 1989—90, sec. 1990—91, 1991—97, pres. 1997—98, 1998—), Volusia County Bar Assn. (bd. dir.), Fla. Bar Assn. (cert. real estate atty. 1996, real property and probate sect.), Beech Mountain Country Club, Md. Club, Mus. Arts and Scis., Ducks Unlimited, Gator Club, Sigma Alpha Epsilon, Delta Delta Delta (Scholarship award 1964), Omicron Delta Epsilon, Phi Kappa Phi, Alpha Lamba Delta, Beta Gamma Sigma. Democrat. Episcopalian. Avocations: interior decorating, cooking, sewing, tennis, aerobics. Office: Sharon B Logan PA 180 Vining Ct PO Box 4258 Ormond Beach FL 32175-4258 Office Phone: 386-673-5787. E-mail: sharonbloganpa@clearwire.net.

LOGAN, VICKI, art collector; b. 1947; m. Kent Logan, 1985. BA in Italian, Vassar Coll. With Denver Art Mus., Paine Webber Inc. Trustee San Francisco Mus. Modern Art. Named one of Top 200 Collectors, ARTNews Mag., 2000—. Avocation: art collection. Home: 815 Potato Patch Dr Vail CO 81657-4428

LOGAN-HUDSON, VERYLE, retail executive, realtor; b. St. Louis, Oct. 24; d. Benjamim Bishop and Eddie Mae (Williams) Logan. BS, Mo. U., 1968; postgrad., Wayne State U., 1974, 76, U. Mich., Detroit, 1978, 80. Cert. residential specialist. With Hudson Dept. Store, Detroit, 1968-84, Dayton Hudson, Mpls., 1984-86, divsn. mdse. mgr., 1980-84, retail exec. divsn. mdse. mgr. coats and dresses, 1984-86; pres. Ultimate Connection, Inc., Mpls., 1987—96. Mem. Golden Valley Black History Month Com., 1987—, co-chair, 1991-92. also bd. dirs., 1993-95; trustee Harry Davis Found., 1988-94, mem. exec. bd., 1991, v.p., 1991-92; chair equal opportunity com. Mpls. Bd. Realtors, also bd. dirs., 1993-96. Named Woman of Yr., Am. Bus. Women, 1984. Mem. Grad. Realtors Inst., Am. Bus. Womens Assn. (v.p. 1983-84, named Woman of Yr. 1984), Minn. Black Networking (exec. bd. 1985-90), Delta Sigma Theta (life, Mpls.-St. Paul alumnae chpt., recording sec. 1985-87, chmn. arts and letters, corr. sec. 1987-88, chmn. heritage and archives 1988-89, 1st v.p. 1991-93, pres. 1993-95, named Delta of the Yr. 1988), M.L. King Tennis Buffs Club. Office: Coldwell Banker Burnet Realty Minn Lakes 3033 Excelsior Blvd Ste 100 Minneapolis MN 55416-4678 Office Phone: 612-925-8428. E-mail: vlhudson@cbburnet.com, verylej@aol.com.

LOGEMANN, JERILYN ANN, speech pathologist, educator; b. Berwyn, Ill., May 21, 1942; d. Warren F. and Natalie M. (Killmer) L. BS, Northwestern U., 1963; MA, 1964, PhD, 1968. Grad. asst. dept. communicative disorders Northwestern U., 1963-68; instr. speech and audiology DePaul U., 1964-65; instr. dept. communicative disorders Mundelein Coll., 1967-71; rsch. assoc. dept. neurology and otolaryngology and maxillo, 1970-74; asst. prof., 1974-78; dir. clin. and rsch. activities of speech and lang., 1975—; assoc. prof. depts. neurology, otolaryngology and comm. scis, 1978-83; prof., 1983; chmn. dept. comm. scis. and disorders, 1982-96; Ralph and Jean Sundin Prof. of Comm. Scis. and Disorders, 1995—; mem. assoc. staff Northwestern meml. Hosp., 1976—; Evanston (Ill.) Hosp., 1988—. Cons. in field; assoc. dir. cancer control Ill. Comprehensive Cancer Coun., Chgo., 1980-82; mem. rehab. com. Ill. divsn. Am. CAncer Soc., 1975-79, chmn., 1979—; mem. upper aerodigestive tract organ site com. Nat. Cancer Inst., 1986-89; postdoct. fellow Nat. Inst. Neurologic Disease, Communicative Disorders and Stroke,Northwestern U., 1968-70. Author: The Fisher-Logeman Test of Articulation Competence, 1971, Evaluation and Treatment of Swallowing Disorders, 1983, 2nd edit., 1998, Manual for the Videofluorographic Evaluation of Swallowing, 1985, 93; assoc. editor: Jour. Speech and Hearing Disorders, Dysphagia Jour., 1978—. Fellow Inst. Medicine Chgo., 1981—; grantee Nat Cancer Inst., 1975—, Am. Cancer Soc., 1981-82, Nat. Inst. Dental Rsch., 1996-2000, Nat. Inst. Deafness and Other Comm. Disorders, 1997—; recipient Honors award Com. Speech Lang. Hearing Assn., 1995, Am. Acad. Otolaryngology-Head Neck Surgery, 1997, Appreciation award Coun. Grad. Prgrams in Comms. Scis. and Disorders, 1995, Cellular One award Vanderbilt U., Am. Special Lang. Hearing Assn., 2003. Fellow Speech, Lang. and Hearing Assn. (pres. 1994, 2000, Honors award 2003), Inst. Medicine, Ill. Speech- Lang. Hearing Assn.(honors 2003); mem. Internat. Assn. Logopedics and Phoniatrics, AAUP, Acoustic Soc. Am. (program com. Chgo. regional chpt.), Linguistic Soc. Am., Speech Comm. Assn., Am. Cleft Palate Assn., Ill. Speech and Hearing Assn. (DiCarlo award 1988), Chgo. Heart Assn., Chgo. Speech Therapy and Auditory Soc. Office: Northwestern U Feinberg Sch Medicine 10-205 Galter Pavilion 201 E Huron Chicago IL 60611 also: Northwestern U Dept Comm Sci and Disorder 2240 Campus Dr Evanston IL 60208-0001 Office Phone: 847-491-2490.

LOGGIE, JENNIFER MARY HILDRETH, retired physician, educator; b. Lusaka, Zambia, Feb. 4, 1936; arrived in U.S., 1964, naturalized, 1972; d. John and Jenny (Beattie). M.B., B.Ch., U. Witwatersrand, Johannesburg, South Africa, 1959. Intern Harare Hosp., Salisbury, Rhodesia, 1960-61; gen. practice medicine Lusaka, 1961-62; sr. pediatric house officer Derby Children's Hosp., also St. John's Hosp., Chelmsford, England, 1962-64; resident in pediatrics Children's Hosp., Louisville, 1964, Cin. Children's Hosp., 1964-65; fellow clin. pharmacology Cin. Coll. Medicine, 1965-67; mem. faculty U. Cin. Med. Sch., 1967—, prof. pediatrics, 1975-98, assoc. prof. pharmacology, 1972-77, prof. emeritus pediatrics, 1998—; ret., 1998. Contbr. articles to med. publs.; editor Pediatric and Adolescent Hypertension, 1991. Grantee, Am. Heart Assn., 1970—72, 1989—90. Mem. Am. Pediatric Soc. (Founder's award 1996), Midwest Soc. Pediatric Rsch. Episcopalian. Home: 1133 Herschel Ave Cincinnati OH 45208-3112 Personal E-mail: jennlog@webtv.net.

LOGSDON, CINDY ANN, small business owner; b. Webb City, Mo., Oct. 22, 1960; d. Donald Joseph Dicharry and Rae Marie (Bourgeois) Tuttle; m. Wayne Joseph Logsdon, Dec. 18, 1982; children: Brandy Marie, Ashley Renee, Laura Lynne (dec.). Student, Mo. So. State Coll., 1978-79. Office mgr. Anchala N. Reddy, M.D., Joplin, Mo., 1980-82, Vodur C. Reddy, M.D., Joplin, 1984-85, Joel Dean, D.O., Joplin, 1985-88; co-owner, v.p. Tint 'N More, Inc., Joplin, 1991—; co-owner, operator Profl. Svcs. Plus Med. Transcipiton Svc., Joplin, 1988—; co-owner/operator PM Resource, Joplin,

1999—2001. Bus. cons. Bernard F. Bettasso, M.D., Joplin, 1988-91. Mem. Profl. Assn. of Resume Writers, Joplin C. of C., Nat. Assn. of Resume Writers. Roman Catholic. Avocations: gourmet cooking, volleyball, racquetball. Office: Professional Services Plus 2230 S Main St Ste B Joplin MO 64804-2048 Office Phone: 417-781-8559.

LOGSDON, JUDITH KAY, merchandiser, small business owner, apparel designer; b. Tulia, Tex., Dec. 5, 1947; d. Bill and Audrey Lee (Hendrix) Humphrey; m. Muriel Frazier Bussey, Mar. 19, 1965 (div.); children: Jeffrey Eldon Bussey, Shawn DeWitt Bussey; m. Leon Francis Logsdon, Nov. 28, 1980. Attended, South Plains Coll., 1987-88. Lic. cosmetologist. Cosmetologist K-K Beauty Shop, Dimmitt, Tex., 1966-67, The Blue Room, Dimmitt, 1967-68; reporter, interviewer Tex. Crop & Livestock Reporting Svc., Austin, 1972-74; bookkeeper Kearn Machine Shop, Hereford, Tex., 1975-76, Tex. Sesame divsn. ADM, Muleshoe, Tex., 1978-88; merchandiser, owner J&L Fashions, Muleshoe, 1988—. Sec.-treas. Muleshoe Activities Com., 1992-94; vol. Hospice of the Plains, 1996, The Heart Assn., 1985-86. Avocations: painting, needle work, crafts, cooking. Home and Office: J&L Fashions 1911 W Ave G Ste A Muleshoe TX 79347-3854

LOGSDON, ROSLYN, artist, educator; b. Bklyn., Aug. 13, 1940; d. Aaron and Evelyn Leibson; m. John M. Logsdon, Jan. 20, 1962; children: David, Michael. BA, Bklyn. Coll., 1961, postgrad., 1961-64. One-woman shows include Herkimer C.C., N.Y., 1993, Fed. Courthouse Gallery, Greenbelt, Md., 1997, Greenbelt Libr., 1996, Columbia Art Gallery, Md., 1994, Glenview Mansion Gallery, Rockville, Md., 1999, 2006, Montpelier Cultural Art Ctr., Laurel, Md., 2001, 2003, 2005, Rockville Art Pl., Md., 2002, exhibited in group shows at Mid. Am. Art Coun., 1995—98, Anderson Gallery, Pontiac, Mich., 1996, Lexington Art League, Ky., 1997, 2004, U.S. Embassy, Turkey, Wenham Mus., Mass., 1998, Rochester Art Ctr., Minn., 1998, Spruill Art Ctr., Atlanta, 1999, Textile Ctr., Mpls., 2004, Columbia Art Ctr., 2006, Cahoon Mus., 2006; author: People and Places: Imagery in Fiber, 1998; contbr. articles to profl. jours. Grantee Md. State Arts Coun., 1997-98, Prince George's Art Coun., 1989, 91, 92, 93, 94, 96, 97. Avocations: travel, reading. Office: Montpelier Art Ctr 9652 Muirkirk Rd Laurel MD 20708 Office Phone: 301-807-6261. Personal E-mail: roz.logsdon@verizon.net.

LOGSTROM, BRIDGET A., lawyer; b. 1958; BS magna cum laude, Univ. Minn., 1980; JD magna cum laude, William Mitchell Coll. Law, 1983. Bar: Minn. 1983. Assoc. Dorsey & Whitney LLP, Mpl.s, 1983—90, ptnr, individual, estate & trust svcs. group, 1983. Fellow: Am. Coll. of Trust and Estate Counsel; mem.: Hennepin County Bar Assn., Minn. State Bar Assn.

LOGUE, JUDITH FELTON, psychoanalyst, educator; b. Phila., Aug. 21, 1942; d. Martin and Laura (Goldman) Kirshenbaum; m. Stephen Felton, Feb. 8, 1966 (div. Aug. 1989); 1 child, Jane Jennifer; m. A. Douglas Logue, Feb. 14, 1990. AB in Govt., Wheaton Coll., Mass., 1963; MSW, Rutgers U., 1966, PhD, 1983; grad., NY Ctr. Psychoanalytic Tng., 1978. Diplomate Am. Bd. Psychotherapy, Am. Bd. Forensic Medicine, Am. Bd. Examiners Clin. Social Worker, Am. Bd. Forensic Examiners, Am. Bd. Psychol. Specialties, cert. profl. coach, mentor coach. Clin. social worker VA, Newark, 1967; psychotherapist Santa Barbara (Calif.) Mental Health Svcs., 1967-69; supr. Santa Barbara Counselling Ctr., 1967-69; pvt. practice psychoanalysis, 1969—; pres. Goldilox Co. Inc., 1997—, Shairing Co., 2001—. Psychoanalyst, therapist Fifth Ave. Ctr. for Psychotherapy, NYC, 1969-72; instr. Marymount Manhattan Coll., 1971; psychotherapy supr. clin. faculty, dept. psychiatry Rutgers Med. Sch., New Brunswick, NJ, 1972-75, tchg. asst. Grad. Sch. Social Work, 1974-76; vis. lectr. Bryn Mawr Coll. Sch. Social Work and Social Rsch., 1980; faculty NY Ctr. for Psychoanalytic Tng., 1980—, NJ Inst. Psychoanalysis and Psychotherapy, 1982—; adv. bd. Am. Bd. Forensic Social Workers, 1999—, chair adv. bd., 2000; pres. Goldilox Co., Inc., 1997, ShAIRing, Inc., 2000; faculty So. NJ Psychoanalytic Inst., Brigantine, 2004—, bd. dirs. Mem. editl. bd. jour Current Issues in Psychoanalytic Practice, 1983-93; contbr. articles to profl. jours. Bd. dirs. N.Y. Ctr. for Psychoanalytic Tng., Inst. for Psychoanalysis and Psychotherapy N.J. Faculty, 1982—. Recipient Disting. Faculty award Atlantic County Psychoanalytic Soc., 1987; NIMH fellow, 1965. Fellow N.J. Soc. for Clin. Social Work; mem. AAUP, NASW, APA (pres. divsn. 39 2003-04, bd. dirs. 2005—, com. psychoanalytic psychotherapists, bd. dirs. divsn. 39 2006—), Nat. Assn. for Advancement of Psychoanalysis, Acad. Cert. Social Workers, Soc. for Psychoanalytic Tng. (bd. dirs. 1983-90, dir. social sci. program 1983-86), Am. Coll. Forensic Examiners Internat. (mem. editl. bd. jours. 1999—, Outstanding Svc. award 2000), Internat. Coach Fedn.; mem. APA (pres. div. 39 sec. III, 2003-04), Am. Psychoanalytic Assn. (psychotherapy task force, com. on psychotherapist assocs. 2003—), Am. Coll. Forensic Social Workers (chair 2000-01), Women in Aviation Internat, 99's Internat. Orgn. Women Pilots, Nat. Bus. Aviation Assn, Rutgers U. Alumni Assn. (bd. dirs. 2003-05), So. NJ Psychoanalytic Inst. (faculty mem. 2004-06, bd. dirs. 2004-06). Home and Office: 159 Valley Rd Princeton NJ 08540-3442 Office Phone: 609-921-0828. Personal E-mail: judith@judithlogue.com.

LOGUE-KINDER, JOAN, public relations consultant; b. Richmond, Va., Oct. 26, 1943; d. John T. and Helen (Harvey) Logue; m. Lowell A. Henry Jr., Oct. 6, 1963 (div. Sept. 1981); children: Lowell A. Henry III, Catherine D. Henry, Christopher Logue Henry; m. Randolph S. Kinder, Dec. 13, 1986 (div. Nov. 1995). Student, Wheaton Coll., 1959-62; BA in Sociology, Adelphi U., 1964; cert. in edn., Mercy Coll., Dobbs Ferry, N.Y., 1971; postgrad., NYU, 1973; cert. in edn., St. John's U., 1974. Asst. to dist. mgr. U.S. Census Bur., N.Y.C., 1970; tchr. and adminstr. social studies Yonkers (N.Y.) Bd. Edn., 1971-75; dir. pub. rels. Nat. Black Network, N.Y.C., 1976-83; corp. v.p. NBN Broadcasting (formerly Nat. Black Network), N.Y.C., 1984-90; sr. v.p. The Mingo Group/Plus, N.Y.C., 1990-91; v.p. Edelman Pub. Rels. Worldwide, N.Y.C., 1991-93; dep. asst. sec. pub. affairs U.S. Dept. Treasury, Washington, 1993-94, asst. sec. pub. affairs, 1994-95; dir. corp. comm. programs The Seagram Co., N.Y.C., 1995-96; v.p. Save the Children, Westport, Conn., 1997-98; sr. v.p., dir. mktg. and comm. Lynch, Jones & Ryan, N.Y.C., 1998—99; v.p. investment devel. Overseas Pvt. Investment Corp., Washington, 1999—2001; dir. comm. Office of the Mayor of D.C., 2001; cons. Phila. Acad. Fine Arts, 2001—, Sari Katz for Mayor, 2001—, Greater Jamaica Devel. Corp., 2001—. Mem. alumnae recruitment coun. Wheaton Coll.; mem. Nigerian-Am. Friendship Soc., 1978-81; bd. dirs. Westchester Civil Liberties Union, 1974-77, Greater N.Y. coun. Girl Scouts U.S.A., 1985-93, Operation PUSH, 1985-93; del. White House Conf. on Small Bus.; active polit. campaigns, including Morris Udall for U.S. Pres., Howard Samuels for Gov.; sr. black media advisor Dukakis/Bentsen presdl. campaign, 1988; conv. del. N.Y. State Women's Polit. Caucus, 1975, pres. black caucus, 1976-77. Recipient Excellence in Media award Inst. New Cinema Artists, 1984. Mem. World Inst. Black Comm. (bd. dirs. 1983-91). Address: 5703 Woodcrest Ave Philadelphia PA 19131-2224 Office Phone: 718-291-0282 129. E-mail: jlk45plus@msn.com.

LOHAN, LINDSAY, actress; b. NYC, July 2, 1986; d. Michael and Dina Lohan. Former model. Actor: (TV series) Another World, 1996—97, Bette, 2000; (TV films) Life-Size, 2000, Get A Clue, 2002; (films) The Parent Trap, 1998, Freaky Friday, 2003, Confessions of a Teenage Drama Queen, 2004, Mean Girls, 2004, Herbie: Fully Loaded, 2005, Just My Luck, 2006, A Prairie Home Companion, 2006, Bobby, 2006; singer: (albums) Speak, 2004, A Little More Personal (Raw), 2005. Recipient Breakthrough Actress of the Yr. award, Hollywood Awards, 2006. Office: Creative Artists Agy 9830 Wilshire Blvd Beverly Hills CA 90212*

LOHMAN, LORETTA CECELIA, social scientist, consultant; b. Joliet, Ill., Sept. 25, 1944; d. John Thomas and Marjorie Mary (Brennan) L. BA in Polit. Sci., U. Denver, 1966, PhD in Am. History, 1996; MA in Social Sci., U. No. Colo., Greeley, 1975. Lectr. Ariz. State U., Tempe, 1966-67; survey researcher Merrill-Werthlin Co., Tempe, 1967-68; edn. asst. Am. Humane Assn., Denver, 1969-70; econ. cons. Lohman & Assocs., Littleton, Colo., 1971-75; rsch. assoc. Denver Rsch. Inst., 1976-86; owner, rsch. scientist Lohman & Assocs., Littleton, 1986-99; affiliate Colo. Water Resources Rsch. Inst., Ft. Collins, Colo., 1989-91; Colo. Nonpoint source outreach coord. coop. ext. Colo. State U., 1999—. Tech. adv. com. Denver Potable Wastewater Demo Plant, 1986—90; cons. Constrn. Engring. Rsch. Lab., 1984—; peer reviewer NSF, 1985—86, Univs. Coun. Water Resources, 1989; WERC consortium reviewer N.Mex. Univs.-U.S. Dept. Energy, 1989—, Co-Alliance Environ. Edn. Adv. Bd., 2000—; course cons. Regis Coll., Denver, 1992—. Contbr. articles to profl. jours. Vol. Metro Water Conservation Projects, Denver, 1986-90; co-coord. AWARE Colo., 2003--; vol. handicapped fitness So. Suburban Parks and Recreation. Recipient Huffsmith award Denver Rsch. Inst., 1983; Nat. Ctr. for Edn. in Politics grantee, 1964-65. Mem. ASCE (social and environ. objectives com.), Orgn. Am. Historians, Pub. Hist. Assn., Sigma Xi, Pi Gamma Mu, Phi Alpha Theta. Avocations: vegetable and xeriscape gardening, travel, miniature boxes. Home and Office: 3375 W Aqueduct Ave Littleton CO 80123-2903 Business E-Mail: lorettalohman@npscolorado.com.

LOHMANN, GERRY M., elementary school educator; b. Lorain, Ohio, July 1, 1939; d. John Edwin and Amelia Mae Ontal; m. Frederick John Lohmann, Sr., Apr. 25, 1959; children: Kathleen Ann Bosse, Rebecca Jo Strayer, Frederick John Jr. BS in Elem. Edn., Bowling Green State U., Ohio, 1976. Asst. prin. Crossroads Christian, Cleve., 1982—99; 8th grade lang. arts and sci. tchr. Monroeville (Ohio) Pub. Schs., 1999—. Advisor Key Club, Monroeville, Ohio, 2005—, Power of the Pen, Monroeville, 1999—; 7th and 8th grade class advisor Monroeville Pub. Schs., 2000—. Author short stories and poetry. Sec. Erie County Farm Bur., Oberlin, Ohio, 1991—2004; pres., sec. Home Makers, Milan, Ohio, 1960—2006; Sunday sch. supt. United Ch. of Christ, Milan, 1994—2006; youth advisor St. John's UCC, Milan, 1974—76; hon. chpt. mother FFA, Milan, 1986—87. Grantee, Martha Holding Jennings, 2006. Mem.: Ohio Edn. Assn. (assoc.; bldg. rep 1976—78). Avocations: travel, reading, gardening, stamp collecting/philately. Home: 12118 Livengood Rd Monroeville OH 44847 Office: Monroeville Public Schools 101 West St Monroeville OH 44847 Office Phone: 419-465-2531. Personal E-mail: lohmanncrow@hmcltd.net. Business E-Mail: glohmann@monroeville.k12.oh.us.

LOHMANN, JUDITH LEITH, secondary school educator; b. Bryn Mawr, Pa., Jan. 13, 1940; d. Harvey Bruce and Elizabeth A. (Abernethy) Leith; m. Watson M. Lohmann, July 22, 1960; children: Watson M. Jr., David, Kimberly. BS, Lebanon Valley Coll., Annville, Pa., 1961. Tchr. Pitman (N.J.) Sch. Dist., 1978—98. Cons. State of N.J., 1987—. Mem. coun. Borough of Pitman, 1976-78; trustee McCowan Libr., pres., 1986—; sec. Pitman Edn. Found., 1998—; mem. Pitman Centennial Com., 2003-2005; mem. Friends of McCowan Libr., 2005—. Named Tchr. of Yr., Gov.'s award Pitman Sch. Dist., 1987. Mem. Delta Kappa Gamma (sec.), Broadway Theatre Pitman (adv. bd.). Republican. Episcopalian. Avocations: reading, collecting antiques. Home: 330 Pitman Ave Pitman NJ 08071-1646

LOHMEIER, LYNDA K., secondary school educator; b. Ada, Minn., July 6, 1946; d. Maurice and Ora Jacobson; m. Dean Russell Lohmeier, Apr. 3, 1993; children: Kirsten Marie Jensen, Adam Alan Gilbertson. Student, Concordia Coll., Moorhead, Minn., 1968; M in English Edn., Bemidji State U., Minn., 1992. Cert. secondary English/speech Minn., 1969. Advanced placement English, sr. English, speech tchr. Fosston H.S., Minn., 1969—. Home: 3250 15th Ave S Fargo ND 58103 Office: Fosston High School 301 First St Fosston MN 56542 Office Phone: 218-435-1909. Business E-Mail: lohmeier@fosston.k12.mn.us.

LOHR, LIBERTY ANN, biology educator; b. Columbia, Mo., July 21, 1980; d. Edward J. Lohr and Marsha R. Hansen, Mark A. Hansen (Stepfather) and Marsha L. Lohr (Stepmother). BS in Marine Biology, Ctrl. Meth. U., Fayette, Mo., 2002; MA in Tchg., Columbia Coll., 2005. Cert. tchr. Mo. Dept. Secondary Edn., 2003, Advanced Open Water Scuba cert. NASE, 2005. Student scientist/vol. NOAA, Pascaougla, Miss., 2001—03, shark intern Panama City, Fla., 2003; shark rsch. vol. Bimini Biol. Field Sta., Bimini Island, 2002; claims rep. asst. Cornerstone Nat. Ins. Co., Columbia, 2002—04; biology tchr. Boonville H.S., Mo., 2004—. Mem.: Mo. State Tchr. Assn. Avocations: scuba diving, reading, travel. Office: Boonville High School 1690 West Ashley Rd Boonville MO 65233 Office Phone: 660-882-7426. Personal E-mail: sharkgirl18@hotmail.com.

LOHSE, SUSAN FAYE, county official, educator; b. Fergus Falls, Minn., Dec. 23, 1952; d. Philip Irving and Harriet Elinor Arlene (Hanson) Berg; m. Robert Wayne Lohse, July 7, 1973; children: Trevor Robert, Trisha Sue, Thomas Roger, Tana Ruth. BS, Bemidji State U., 1973; cert. sr. accredited assessor, U. Minn., 1993. Tchr. Kensington Pub. Schs., 1973-75; sub. tchr. Elbow Lake (Minn.)-Wendell Pub. Schs., 1975-80, tchr., 1982-83, Ashby Pub. Schs., 1981, Elbow Lake Cmty. Edn., 1976—82, 1990—; assessor's clk. Grant County Assessor's Office, Elbow Lake, 1983, dep. assessor, office mgr., 1985—94, county assessor, 1994—. Instr. U. Minn. Ext. Svcs., Elbow Lake, 1993—99, Elbow Lake, 2000. Mem.: West Ctrl. and Minn. Assessment Pers. (pres. 1990—92), Minn. Assn. Assessing Officers (sec. region 7 1999, treas. 2000, pres. 2001). Lutheran. Avocations: sewing, crocheting, volleyball, camping. Office: Grant County Assessor 10 2d St NE Elbow Lake MN 56531

LOIACONO, MELISSA ANN, athletic trainer; b. Hackensack, N.J., Dec. 27, 1969; d. Angelo and Joyce Loiacono. BS Athletic Tng., U. N.Mex., Albuquerque, 1992; MS Sports Adminstrn., U. N.Mex., 1997. Cert. CPR. Head athletic trainer, tchr. Rio Rancho H.S., Rio Rancho, N.Mex., 1998—. Instr. CPR ARC, Albuquerque, 1999—. Named H.S. Tchr. of Yr., Rio Rancho H.S., 2004; named to Who's Who Among Am. Tchrs., 2003—04, 2004—05. Mem.: Nat. Athletic Trainers Assn., Rocky Mountain Athletic Trainer Assn., N.Mex. Athletic Trainers Assn. (no. rep. 2000—03), Internat. Automated External Defibrilator. Avocations: needlepoint, kickboxing, volleyball. Office: Rio Rancho HS 301 Loma Colorado Rio Rancho NM 87124

LOIKKANEN, PIRJO TUULIKKI, music educator; b. Helsinki, Finland; d. Aune Kauhanen; m. Matti Loikkanen. M, Sibelius Acad., Helsinki. Cert. tchr. music. Piano tchr. Tampere (Finland) Music Coll., 1974-78, Savonlinna (Finland) Music Coll., 1981-82, Kapyla Music Coll., Helsinki, 1982-89; pvt. piano tchr. Garden Grove, Calif., 1990-98, Bellevue, Wash., 1998—. Mem. Nat. Guild Piano Tchrs., Music Tchrs. Nat. Assn., Wash. State Music Tchrs. Assn.

LOIS, DOLORES CARMEN, literature educator; b. N.Y., Sept. 15, 1973; d. Francisco and Dolores Lois. BA in English, St. John's U., 1995; MA in Tchg. English as Second Lang., Adelphi U., 2000. Cert. tchr. N.Y. State Dept. of Edn., 2002. English tchr. Jr. HS 189, Flushing, NY, 1996—2000, Valley Stream (N.Y.) Ctrl. HS, 2000—. Journalism, newspaper adviser Valley Stream (N.Y.) Ctrl. HS, 2000—. Mem.: L.I. (N.Y.) Lang. Arts Coun., Nat. Coun. Tchrs. English, Kappa Phi Delta. Avocations: travel, reading, theater, music, art. Office: Valley Stream Ctrll HS 135 Fletcher Ave Valley Stream NY 11580 Home: 75 20 113th St 6H Forest Hills NY 11375 Office Phone: 516-561-4400.

LOIS, JENNIFER M., sociologist, educator; b. NY, 1967; PhD in Sociology, U. Colo., Boulder, 2000. Author: Heroic Efforts: The Emotional Culture of Search and Rescue Volunteers, 2006 (Recent Contbn. award Am. Sociol. Assn., 2006). Mem.: Pacific Sociol. Assn. (program com. mem. 2004—05), Am. Sociol. Assn. (sec./treas. sociology of emotions sect. 2001—03, coun. mem. sociology of emotions sect. 2006—), Soc. Study of Symbolic Interaction. Office: Western Wash U Sociology Dept Bellingham WA 98225-9081 Office Phone: 360-650-3007.

LOISELLE, JOAN BRENDA, elementary school educator, art educator; b. Huntington, W.Va., Aug. 22, 1947; d. Irvin Thomas and Anne (Questel) Sowards. BA, U. South Fla., 1969, MA, 1974. Cert. tchr. Fla. Dept. Edn., 1969, assoc. master tchr. cert. Fla. Dept. Edn., 1987, cert. tchr. Fla., 1999. Tchr. Thonatosassa Elem. Sch., Tampa, Fla., 1969—70, Lorah Pk. Elem. Sch., Miami, Fla., 1970—73; head tchr. Day Care Ctr. U. South Fla., Tampa, 1974; tchr. Mabry Elem. Sch., Tampa, 1974—89; specialist art Carrollwood Elem. Sch., Tampa, 1989—92, Hunter's Green Elem. Sch., Tampa, 1992—. Mem. sch. leadership team Hunter's Green Elem. Sch., 1992—; adj. prof. U. Tampa, 2001—; rep. area 1 visual arts Hillsborough County Sch. Dist., Tampa, 1990—, tchr. gifted program, 1993—98; presenter in field. Exhibitions include Teco Plaza Art Gallery, Tampa, Fla., 2000—05. Coord. Neighborhood Involvement Kids Edn. Art Lab., Tampa, 1988; coord. multicultural art box project Tampa Arts Coun., 1989—90; sch. facilitator empty bowls project Second Harvest, Tampa, 1994—2006; rep. area visual arts Friends Offering Children Unlimited Success, Tampa, 1995; tchr. participant Tim Rollins mural project U. South Fla., 1996; facilitator Construction Tampa (Fla.) Archs., 1997; facilitator Tampa Mus. Art Grant: Arts Connect All, Tampa, 2005—06; mem. com. tchr. certification Fla. Dept. Edn., 2002—04, mem. com. Fla. Blueprint 2000 Assessment Design Project, 1994. Finalist County Tchr. of Yr. award, Hillsborough County Sch. Dist., 1994; recipient Tchr. of Yr. award, Hunter's Green Elem. Sch., 1994, Performance Day award, Fla. Dept. Edn., 2003—06, Gold Star Tchr. award, Binnie & Smith, Inc. and Wal-Mart, 2003—05, Maj.'s Outstanding Tchr. award, Tampa Water Conservation Initiative, 2003—06; grantee, Hillsborough Edn. Found., 1993—94, 1996, State of Fla. Artful Truth, 1999. Mem.: Hillsborough Art Edn. Assn. (pres. 2000—01, chmn. profl. devel. com. 2002—05, parliamentarian 2002—05, Disting. Svc. award 2002—05), Fla. Art Edn. Assn., Nat. Art Edn. Assn., Tampa (Fla.) Mus. Art (edn. adv. com. 2000—03), PTA (co-chmn. reflections/cultural arts com. 2000—05), Phi Delta Kappa (chmn. starwalk com. 1994—, parliamentarian 2002—, Fifteen Yr. Member cert. 2003), Phi Kappa Phi (life), Delta Kappa Gamma (internat. chi chpt. pres. 1990—92). Office: Hunters Green Elementary 9202 Highland Oak Dr Tampa FL 33647-2541 Home: 3712 W Santiago St Tampa FL 33629 Office Phone: 813-973-7394. Business E-Mail: joan.loiselle@sdhc.k12.fl.us.

LØJ, ELLEN MARGRETHE, ambassador; b. Gedesby, Denmark, Oct. 17, 1948; Grad. econs., Copenhagen U., 1973. Joined Ministry Fgn. Affairs, 1973; first sec. Permanent Mission to the UN Ministry Fgn. Affairs, N.Y.C., 1977—80, counsellor Permanent Representation of Denmark to the European Cmty. Brussels, 1982—85, head dept., 1986—89; amb. to Israel Ministry Fgn. Affairs, 1989—92; under-sec. multilateral affairs, South Group Ministry Fgn. Affairs, 1992—94, under-sec. bilateral affairs South Group, 1994—96, state sec. South Group, 1996—2001, permanent rep. of Denmark to the UN, amb., 2001—. Mem. supervisory bd. The Investment Fund Ctrl. and Ea. Europe, 1994—96, The Industrialization Fund for Developing Countries, 1994—96, Scandlines AG and Scandlines A/S, 1998—2001; participant Danish dels. to several internat. meetings and U.N. confs. Office: Permanent Rep of Denmark to the UN One Dag Hammarskjöld Plaza 885 Second Ave 18th Fl New York NY 10017-2201 Office Phone: 212-705-4968.

LOK, JOAN MEI-LOK, community affairs specialist, artist; b. Hong Kong, Apr. 2, 1962; d. Chi Hong Stephen Pan and Mui Kan Teresa Chan; m. David Tai-Wai Lok, Jan. 11, 1986; children: Wesley Kevin, Gary Alexander. B in Tourism and Hotel Mgmt., Hong Kong Poly. U., 1983; BBA, Baruch Coll., 1988; MBA, Strayer U., 2005. Commd. compliance examiner FDIC, 1999. Cmty. affairs specialist FDIC, Balt., 1999—, Chinese money smart transl. mgr., 2002—, compliance examiner Holyoke, Mass., 1997—99, affordable housing specialist Hartford, Conn., 1994—97, bank liquidation specialist South Brunswick, NJ, 1988—94. V.p. Lingnam Art Assn. of Am., NYC, 1992—94; nat. pres. Sumi-e Soc. of Am., Inc., Washington, 2002—; mem. Md. Gov.'s Commn. on Asian Pacific Am. Affairs, 2003—, Md. Gov.'s Citation Outstanding Cmty. Svc., 2004. Chairwoman Bus. Fin. and econ, Devel. Com., Md., 2006—, Md. Saves Fin. Svc. Com., Md., 2005—. Recipient Artist's Alternative award, Ea. Arts Connection, 1994, First Pl., Glastonbury Art Guild, 1995, Best in Watercolors award, Audubon Soc. of Conn. in Glastonbury, 1996, Diana Kan award, Sumi-e Soc. of Am., 1997, Grumbacher Gold metal, 1998, Cheng Dia Chien award, 1999, Blue Heron award, 2002, 2004, Benefactors of the Soc. award, 2003, Artist of the Yr. award, Edison Arts Soc., 2000, Gardens of Edison award, 2002, Svc. to Am. medal, Partnership for Pub. Svcs., 2003, Md. Gov. citation for outstanding cmty. svc., 2004, Nat. Cherry Blossom Festival Art contest, 2005; fellow, Walt Disney World, 1983—84; scholar, Hong Kong Hotel Assn., 1982. Mem.: Edison Arts Soc., Glastonbury Art Guild, Internat. Soc. of Lingnam Artists (dir. of pub. rels. 2003—), Assn. of Chinese Calligraphy in Am. Achievements include initiated the first virtual juried exhibition of sumi-e art in the Sumi-e Society of America's 39 years history; first Chinese-American to be elected national President of the Sumi-e Society of America in its 40 years history; first female executive of a Chinese cultural club in New York Chinatown in 1992. Office: FDIC 8850 Stanford Blvd Ste 3000 Columbia MD 21045 Office Phone: 410-872-9024 4032. Business E-Mail: jlok@fdic.gov.

LOKE, JOAN TSO FONG, respiratory therapist; b. Hong Kong, Nov. 29, 1950; d. Choong Shee and Elsie L.C. Loke; m. Fabian Chan, Dec. 2, 1975 (div. July 1993); children: Jeffrey Chan, Jeremy Chan. BS in Biology, U. Puget Sound, 1973, BS in Med. Tech., 1974; AS in Respiratory care, Kapiolani C.C., 1995. Cert. respiratory therapy technician, registered respiratory technologist. Med. technologist Harborview Med. Ctr., Seattle, 1975—76; EKG technologist St. Francis, Honolulu, 1987—94, oxygen technologist, 1994—95, respiratory therapist, 1995, Kapiolani Med. Ctr., Honolulu, 1995—2002, Kaiser Permanent, Honolulu, 1995—, Tripler Med. Ctr., Honolulu, 2002—. Mem.: AARC (pact team mem. 2002—03, pub. rels. chair 2002—03), HSRC (v.p. 2000, bd. dirs. 2000, pres. 2001—03). Avocations: Karate (black belt), swimming, tennis, piano, singing. Home: 965 Prospect St #605 Honolulu HI 96822 Office: Kaiser Permanente 3288 Moanalua Rd Honolulu HI 96819 E-mail: catnap@hawaii.rr.com.

LOKEN, BARBARA, marketing educator, social psychologist; b. Owatonna, Minn., Aug. 22, 1951; d. Gordon Keith and June Rosaline (Iverson) Anderson; 1 child, Elizabeth Loken Diebel. BA in Psychology magna cum laude, U. Minn., 1973; MA, NYU, 1976; PhD in Social Psychology, U. Ill., 1981. Rsch. and statis. asst. Nat. Soc. Prevention Blindness, N.Y.C., 1974-76; rsch. asst. dept. psychology U. Ill., 1976, 78-80, instr., 1977-78; NIMH trainee in measurement, 1979-80; asst. prof. dept. mktg. U. Minn., 1980-86, assoc. prof., 1986-92, prof., 1992—. Co-dir. edn. evaluation Minn. heart health project Sch. Pub. Health, 1982-88, adj. assoc. prof. dept. psychology, 1987-92, adj. prof., 1992—; vis. assoc. prof. mktg. UCLA, 1988. Assoc. editor: Jour. Consumer Rsch., 1996-99; contbr. articles to profl. jours. Rsch. grantee Sch. Mgmt., U. Minn., 1981-84, 86, 88-2005. Mem. Am. Psychol. Assn., Am. Mktg. Assn., Assn. Consumer Rsch., Assn. for Consumer Rsch. 2000 (treas.).

LOKEY, LINDA H., music educator; b. Buffalo, Sept. 1954; m. Charles G. Lokey. BMus in Piano Performance/Piano Pedagogy, U. South Fla.; postgrad., Calif. State U. Nat. cert. tchr. music. Music tchr. Palm Harbor (Fla.) Montessori Sch., 1986—88; coll. staff accompanist Reinhardt Coll., Waleska, Ga., 1993-95; tchr. pvt. and group piano, 1972—. Dir., musical dir., pianist Canton Theatre, 2005. Music com. Cherokee County (Ga.) Arts Coun., 1994-95; adjudicator for music Tchrs. Assn. festivals, Federated Music Clubs; active Cherokee Cmty. Chorale, 1992—, chorale grant com. chair, 2002-2004. U. South Fla. Talent Grant award, 1985-86, Steinway Educator grant, Steinway Piano Galleries, Atlanta, 2002. Mem.: Blue Ridge Mountain Arts Assn., Cherokee County Arts Coun. (program chmn. 2002—04, bd. dirs. 2002—05, exec. bd. 2004—05), Am. Coll. Musicians, Cobb Music Tchrs. Assn., Cherokee Music Tchrs. Assn. (pres. 1993—95, fundraising com. 1993—99, v.p. publicity 1995—98, pres. 2003—05), Ga. Music Tchrs. Assn. (exec. bd. 2000—02, co-chair state conf. 2003, exec. bd. 2003—05), Music Tchrs. Nat. Assn., Golden Key. Home and Office: 866 Valley Dr Canton GA 30114

LOKMER, STEPHANIE ANN, international business development consultant; b. Wheeling, W.Va., Nov. 14, 1957; d. Joseph Steven and Mary Ann (Mozney) Lokmer. BA in Comm., Bethany Coll., 1980; cert., U. Tübingen, Germany, 1980, Sprach Inst., Tübingen, 1980; MGC in Negotiation, Georgetown U., 2003; degree in nat. security telecom., George Washington U., 2003. V.p. Wheeling Coffee and Spice, W.Va., 1981—; pres. Lokmer & Assocs., Inc., McLean, W.Va., 1986-2000; v.p. strategic devel. Telia Internat.

Carrier, Inc., 2000—04; cons. internat. bus. Lokmer & Assocs., 2004—. Bd. dirs. Am. Found. of Ivory Coast. Mem.: Internat. Assn. Tech. of No. Va., Counselors Acad., World Affairs Coun., Pub. Rels. Soc. Am., Fed. City Club, Zeta Tau Alpha. Republican. Avocations: tennis, reading. Office Phone: 202-744-4740. Personal E-mail: slokmer@attglobal.net.

LOMAN, MARY LAVERNE, retired mathematics professor; b. Stratford, Okla., June 10, 1928; d. Thomas D. and Mary Ellen (Goodwin) Glass; m. Coy E. Loman, Dec. 23, 1944; 1 child, Sandra Leigh Loman Easton. BS, U. Okla., 1956, MA, 1957, PhD, 1961. Grad. asst., then instr. U. Okla., Norman, 1956-61; asst. prof. math. U. Ctrl. Okla., Edmond, 1961-62, assoc. prof., 1962-66, prof., 1966-93, prof. emeritus, 1993—. NSF fellow, 1965-67. Mem. Math. Assn. Am., Nat. Coun. Tchrs. Math., Okla. Coun. Tchrs. Math. (v.p. 1972-76), Higher Edn Alumni Coun. Okla., VFW Aux., Delta Kappa Gamma. Home: 2201 Tall Oaks Trl Edmond OK 73003-2325

LOMBARD, MARJORIE ANN, financial officer; b. Stoughton, Mass., Feb. 25, 1956; d. John Joseph and Marie Josephine (Hopkins) Lombard; children: Katie Marie Burt, Elizabeth Ann Burt. BSBA with honors, Northeastern U., Boston, 1979; MBA, Suffolk U., Boston, 2000. Acctg. trainee HEW Audit, Boston, 1976-78; staff acct. Etonic, Inc., Brockton, Mass., 1979-81; ops. acct. Foxboro Co., East Bridgewater, Mass., 1981-82, 86-87; chief acct. New Eng. Structures, Inc., Avon, Mass., 1983-84; bus. mgr. Mutron Corp., Brockton, Mass., 1988-92; contr. Connector Tech. Corp., Warwick, R.I., 1992-94; bus. mgr. Cath. Charities-Laboure Ctr., South Boston, Mass., 1994-97; contr. Cath. Charities, Boston, 1997-98, CFO, 1998-2000; bus. adminstr. Carver (Mass.) Pub. Schs., 2000—05; CFO, Action for Boston Cmty. Devel., 2005—. Tchr. confraternity Christian doctrine program St. Thomas Aquinas Ch., Bridgewater, 1988-94; keyperson Old Colony United Way, Brockton, 1988-91, mem. funds allocation com., 1991—; vol. tchr. You and Me drug prevention program, Bridgewater, 1990-92, Parents for Edn., Bridgewater, 1990-97; vol. Am. Electronics Assn.-Brockton Jr. High Sch. Alliance, 1990-92; mem. Bridgewater Parents Collaborative, 1991-97. Mem. Am. Electronics Assn., Small Bus. Assn. New Eng. Roman Catholic. Avocations: reading, writing, crafts, interior decorating, walking. Office Phone: 617-348-6376.

LOMBARD, REGINA A., elementary school educator; b. Memphis, Jan. 11, 1949; d. Clifton and Geraldine Hester Best; children: Bryan Anthony, Kyle André. BA in Humanities, LeMoyne Coll., Memphis, 1970; MS in Tchg., Drake U., 1972. Cert. tchr. Mo. Adminstrv. asst. Voluntary Action and Info. Ctr., Kansas City, Mo., 1978—80; tchr. pre-sch. U. Mo., Kansas City, 1982—84; tchr. Kansas City Sch. Dist., Kansas City, 1985—. Trainer tchrs. Kansas City Sch. Dist., 1990—2002; profl. devel. com. mem. James Sch., Kansas City, career ladder rep., 2000—03, career ladder mem., 2003—. Democrat. Methodist. Avocations: reading, sewing, travel. Office: James Elem Sch 5810 Scarritt Ave Kansas City MO 64123 Office Phone: 816-418-3700. E-mail: reginalombard@juno.com.

LOMBARDI, MARY LUCIANA, musician, historian; d. John and Maryellen Lombardi, Janice May Lombardi (Stepmother). BA, Occidental Coll., L.A., 1961; MA, Ind. U., Bloomington, 1971; MLS, UCLA, 1965, PhD, 1977. Reference libr. N.Y. Pub. Libr., 1965—66; indexer H. W. Wilson Co., Bronx, 1967—69; bibliographer Ind. U. Librs., Bloomington, Ind., 1969—71, U. Calif., L.A., 1971—74; indexer Lombardi Indexing Svcs., L.A., Davis, Santa Cruz, 1973—92; musician various, Calif. and Ind., 1976—; instr. U. Calif., Santa Cruz, 1977—80, Cabrillo Coll., Aptos, Calif., 2002—03. Classical music DJ Pub. Radio KUSP-FM, Santa Cruz, 1977—2004; founding festival player, concert mgmt. Santa Cruz Baroque Festival, 1977—87; founder/dir./performer, concert mgmt. Santa Cruz Festival Viols, 1978—94; musician, prodr./dir.: performance demonstrations for children Santa Cruz County Schs., Watsonville, Capitola, Santa Cruz, 1984—2001; artistic dir., performer, concert mgmt. Santa Cruz Chamber Players, 1990—97; founder/dir./performer, concert mgmt. Calif. Gamba Consort, Santa Cruz, 1994—98. Editor: (book online) Cantar e Viver/To Sing Is To Live: Music by Lucilia Guimaraes Villa-Lobos, 2002; author: (rev.) The Frontier in Brazilian History; contbr. articles to profl.jour. Mem. planning, ednl. coms. Cultural Coun. Santa Cruz County, 1978—94; area rep., Viola da Gamba Soc. Am., Monterey Bay, Calif., 1984—. Recipient Pataphysician of Yr., Pub. Radio KUSP-FM, 1989; fellow Fgn. Area Fellowship Program, Social Sci. Rsch. Coun./Ford Found., 1970—73; grantee, UCLA, 1972—77; scholar Summer Viol program, Cornell U., 1982, 1983, 1985. Mem.: Early Music Am., Inst. for Hist. Study, Am. Fedn. Musicians (Local 153). Achievements include creation of concerts featuring women composers, 1987, 94-96, 98, 2006; creation of classical music radio broadcasts for 27 yrs., including special programs featuring women composers. Personal E-mail: lombardiml@comcast.net.

LOMBARDO, ANN MARIE, special education educator, writer, artist; b. Melrose, Mass., Jan. 10, 1955; d. James William Pike, II and Mary Ann (Duncan) Pike; m. Steven Edward Lombardo, Sept. 11, 1982; children: Nicholas Michael, Kali Ann. Student, Plymouth State Coll., 1973; BA, Rivier Coll., 1978. Freelance tchr. arts and crafts, Hollis, NH, 1972—73, 1975; art tchr. Hollis (N.H.) Elem. and Secondary Schs., Hollis, NH, 1978; proprietor, asst. Jameson Fine Arts Gallery, La Jolla, Calif., 1978—79; graphic artist, tech. writer J.M. Yurick Assocs., Smersworth, NH, 1980—87; spl. needs educator Winthrop Elem. Sch., Ipswich, Mass., 1995—. Freelance artist, writer, 1983—92; presenter, cons. in field. Author (artist & correspondent): (column) The Portsmouth (N.H.) Herald, 1988—93; Yonder Mountain (A Cherokee Legend), 1999, one-woman shows include Link Art Gallery, Rowley, Mass., 2002; columnist: Annadotes; radio commentary WERZ talk radio. Tchr. arts and crafts Nashua (N.H.) Orphanage, 1970; cook, distributor The Food Kitchen Shelter, San Diego, 1988; rschr., artist Ea. Bank Cherokees, Qualla Bouundary, NC, 1999—2001. Recipient Outstanding Regional Art award, 1973. Mem.: Newburyport Art Assn., San Diego (Calif.) Art Assn. Avocations: painting furniture, cross country skiing, hiking, camping. Home: 101 Leslie Rd Rowley MA 01969 Mailing: PO Box 124 Ipswich MA 01938 Office Phone: 978-376-1856. E-mail: artnannie@yahoo.com.

LOMBARDO APPLEBY, LINDA ROSE, music educator; b. Jamestown, NY, Dec. 6, 1951; d. Philip Patrick and Jacqueline Beatrice Lombardo; children: Venezia Monique Appleby, Zuri Elise Appleby. BS in Music Edn., Daemen Coll., 1974; MA in Student Pers. Adminstrn., SUNY, Buffalo, 1978, postgrad., 2005. Vocal/gen. music tchr. Buffalo Bd. Edn., 1974—. Min. music St. Mary of Sorrows Ch., Buffalo, 1986—; mus. dir. numerous theater groups and orgns., 1974—; home sch. instr., tudor, 2004; facilitator Tchr. Ctr., Buffalo, 2004—, course instr., 2005; performances include Mayor's Inauguration, Buffalo, 1993, Broadway mus., 1995, Supreme Ct. Justice Sandra Day O'Connor, 2000, Gov. of NY, Albany, 2002. Named Tchr. of Yr., Iota Phi Lambda, 2001; recipient Keep the Dream Alive award, City Honors H.S., Buffalo, 2002. Mem.: Nat. Choral Dirs. Assn., NY State Music Educators, Erie County Music Assn., Music Educators Nat. Conf. Democrat. Roman Catholic. Avocations: gardening, bicycling, walking, stained glass, crafts. Home: 60 Winston Rd Buffalo NY 14216 Office Phone: 716-816-3350. E-mail: blusky678@aol.com.

LOMBARDOZZI, DEBRA ANN, music educator; b. Butte, Mont., June 13, 1954; d. Jack Arlington and Ann Jakovac Kearns; m. Kevin Lee Lombardozzi, Dec. 27, 1975; children: Danica, Erika. Bachelor's, Mont. State U., 1976; Master's, Lehigh U., 2004. Tchr. Pampa Ind. Sch. Dist., Tex., 1979—85; pvt. piano tchr. Easton, Pa., 1998—; music tchr. St. Jane Frances, Easton, 2000—03; supr. DeSales U., Ctr. Valley, Pa., 2005. Mem.: Lehigh Valley Chpt. Pa. Music Tchrs. Assn., AAUW, Pa. Music Tchrs. Assn. Home: 2503 Swanson St Easton PA 18045 E-mail: dapis@hotmail.com.

LOMISON, MARIE LUCINDA, mathematics educator; b. Johnstown, Pa., Apr. 12, 1954; d. Nicholas and Margaret Lucinda Hanak; m. Jeffery Lynn Hanak/Parks, May 31, 2003; children: Joelle Lucinda Parks, Travis Wayne Parks. BS in Edn., Lock Haven U., Pa., 1975. Cert. instrnl. II Pa. Dept. Edn., 1975. Math. tchr. Bishop Neuman H.S., Williamsport, Pa., 1981—85, Bald Eagle Area Sch. Dist., Wingate, Pa., 1985—. Mem. Faith Chapel United Meth. Ch., Howard, Pa., 1981—2003. Mem.: NCTM (corr.). Democrat. Avocations: swimming, hiking, gardening, bicycling, yoga. Home: PO Box 362 Howard PA 16841 Office: Bald Eagle Area School Dist 751 South Bald Eagle Valley Rd Wingate PA Office Phone: 814-355-4868. Personal E-mail: mlparks@hotmail.com.

LONA, MARIE A., lawyer; b. St. Louis, June 21, 1966; d. Marco A. and MaryAnn Lona; m. Bradley S. Coolidge, Nov. 6, 1993. BA with distinction, Northwestern U., 1998; JD, Stanford U., 1991. Bar: Ill. 1991, US Dist. Ct. (no. dist.) Ill. 1991, US Ct. Appeals (7th cir.) 1994, US Ct. Appeals (6th cir.) 1996. Ptnr. Winston & Strawn, Chgo., 1991—. Author: Why eBay Heightens Risk for Share-Dealing Directors, 2004; singer: (performance) Christmas Spirits; mng. editor: Stanford Law Rev. Dir. Chgo. Abused Women's Coalition, 2002—, Ravinia Assocs., 2005—, Redmoon Theater, 2006—, Hubbard St. Dance Co., 2006—; dir. women's bd. Goodman Theatre, 2006—. Named to 40 Under 40 Lawyers to Watch in Ill., Chgo. Lawyer Mag., 2005. Mem.: ABA, Profl. Women's Club Chgo., Nat. Assn. Women Execs., Latino Giving Cir., Chgo. Bar Assn. Avocations: performance (singing, dancing, acting), theater, horseback riding, wine, photography. Office: Winston & Strawn 35 W Wacker Chicago IL 60601 Office Phone: 312-558-5692. Business E-Mail: mlona@winston.com.

LONCHYNA-LISOWSKY, MARIA, music educator; b. Munich, Sept. 26, 1945; d. Bohdan Ivan and Irene Lonchyna; m. Bohdan Lisowsky, May 31, 1969; children: Mykola Lisowsky, Danylo Lisowsky, Taras Lisowsky, Petro Lisowsky. Diploma of Artistic Merit, Ukrainian Music Inst. Am., Detroit, 1967; BA, U. Detroit, 1967; MMus, Wayne State U., 1969. Cert. tchr. piano Mich. Music Tchrs. Assn., 2001, nat. cert. tchr. music piano 2005. Piano soloist various venues, 1960—99; piano tchr. Ukrainian Music Inst. Am., Detroit, 1967—, dir., 2001—. Accompanist Suzuki workshops, Troy, Mich., 1984—98, Mich. Sch. Band and Orch. Assn. Solo and Ensemble Festivals, Troy, 1984—98, 2004—06, Trembita Chorus, Detroit, 1975—77, others, 2004—; music dir. Luna Ensemble, Warren, Mich., 1977—83; pianist Ukrainian Music Inst. Trio, Detroit, 1965—67; accompanist Immaculate Conception Ukrainian Cath. H.S. Chorus and Orch., Hamtramck, Mich., 1959—63; accompanist for nat. edn. com. Ukrainian Nat. Women's League Am., Inc. Musician: (recordings) Listen and Sing Along - Ukrainian Christmas Carols, 1981, Ukrainian Stories for Children, 1976, Listen and Sing Along, 1979. Librarian Detroit Symphony Civic Orch., Detroit, 1996—98. Recipient Alumna of Yr. award, Parents Club of Immaculate Conception Ukrainian Cath. H.S., 1991. Mem.: Music Tchrs. Assn., Music Tchrs. Nat. Assn., Ukrainian Arts Soc. (pres. 1996—), Ukrainian Ednl. Assn. (treas. 1985—86, pres. 1986—92, treas. 1992—97), Plast, Inc. (corr. sec. Detroit region 1964—69, subscription chair, sr. divsn. 1984—92, dues, sr. divsn. 1984—92, subscriptions 1992—96, pres. 2005—06, Recognition award 1999), Met. Detroit Musicians League (sec. 2001—04, pres. 2005—, Tchr. of the Yr. 2003—04), Tuesday Musicale of Detroit, Ukrainian Nat. Women's League of Am. (ednl. com. chair chpt. 53 1976—78, rec. sec. chpt. 53 1978—80, corr. sec. 1980—84, pres. chpt. 53 1995—97, corr. sec. regional coun. 1997—99, press sec. Ukranian lang. 2003—05, corr. sec. 2004, corr. sec. regional coun. 2004—05, mem. audit com. 2005—, Recognition award 1998).

LONDON, CHARLOTTE ISABELLA, secondary school educator; b. Guyana, S.Am., June 11, 1946; came to U.S., 1966, naturalized, 1980; d. Samuel Alphonso and Diana Dallett (Daniels) Edwards; m. David Timothy London, May 26, 1968 (div. May 1983); children: David Tshombe, Douglas Tshaka. BS, Fort Hays State U., 1971; MS, Pa. State U., 1974, PhD, 1977. Elem. sch. tchr., Guyana, 1962-66; secondary sch. tchr., 1971-72; instr. lang. arts Pa. State U., University Park, 1973-74; reading specialist/ednl. cons. N.Y.C. C.C., 1975; dir. Skills Acquisition and Devel. Ctr. Stockton (N.J.) State Coll., 1975-77; reading specialist Pleasantville (N.J.) Pub. Schs., 1977—, supr. English dept., supr. gifted and talented program, 1999—, supr. world langs., 2002—. Ind. specialist United Nations Devel. Programme, Guyana, 1988—; v.p. Atlantic County PTA, 1980-82; del. N.J. Gov.'s Conf. Future Edn. N.J., 1981; founder, pres. Guyana Assn. Reading and Lang. Devel., 1987. Sec. Atlantic County Minority Polit. Women's Caucus. Mem. Internat. Reading Assn., Nat. Coun. Tchrs. English, ASCD, AAUW, Pi Lambda Theta, Phi Delta Kappa (sec.). Mem. African Meth. Episcopal Ch. Home: 6319 Crocus St Mays Landing NJ 08330-1107 Office: Pleasantville Pub Schs W Decatur Ave Pleasantville NJ 08232

LONDON, NORA ELEONOR, foundation administrator; arrived in U.S., 1941; d. Jacob Schapiro and Jeanne Begagon; m. George London (dec. 1985); children: Andrew Garvin, Philip Garvin, Marina, Marc. Student, Barnard Coll., NYC, 1941—43. Founder, hon. pres. George London Stiftung, Vienna, 1988—; pres. George London Found. for Singers, NYC, 1991—. Author: Aria for George, 1986, George London, of Gods and Demons, 2005. Home: 1 Lincoln Plz Apt 36P New York NY 10023-7159

LONDON-GIBBON, MARY BETH, elementary school educator; d. Raymond Clair and Jeanne Elizabeth London; m. John David Gibbon, Oct. 7, 1988; 1 child, Meredith London Gibbon. BA, MS, Duquesne U., Pitts., 1976—76. Elem. tchr. Plum (Pa.) Borough Sch. Dist., 1972—90, title I reading specialist, 1990—. Sec. we. region Pa. State Edn. Assn., Pitts., 1986. Mem.: Internat. Reading Assn. Home: 112 Saddlebrook Dr Harrison City PA 15636 Office: Pa State Edn Assn S 19th St Pittsburgh PA Personal E-mail: msmgibbon@msn.com.

LONDRÉ, FELICIA MAE HARDISON, theater educator; b. Ft. Lewis, Wash., Apr. 1, 1941; d. Felix M. and Priscilla Mae (Graham) Hardison; m. Venne-Richard Londré, Dec. 16, 1967; children: Tristan Graham, Georgianna Rose. BA with high honors, U. Mont., Missoula, 1962; MA, U. Wash., Seattle, 1964; PhD, U. Wis., Madison, 1969. Asst. prof. U. Wis. at Rock County, Janesville, 1969-75; asst. prof., head theatre program U. Tex. at Dallas, Richardson, 1975-78; assoc. prof. U. Mo., Kansas City, 1978-82, prof. theatre, 1982-87, curators' prof., 1987—; women's chair in humanistic studies Marquette U., 1995. Dramaturg Mo. Repertory Theatre, Kansas City, 1978-2001, Nebr. Shakespeare Festival, 1990—; guest dramaturg Gt. Lakes Theater Festival, 1988; mem. archives task force Folly Theatre, 1982-83; artistic advisor New Directions Theatre Co., 1983-90; hon. lectr. Mid.-Am. State Univs. Assn., 1986-87; mem. U.S.-U.S.S.R. Joint Commn. on Theatre Historiography, 1989; mem.adv. bd. Contemporary World Writers, 1991—; lectr. univs. Budapest, Pecs, Debrecen, Hungary, 1992; vis. prof. Hosei U., Tokyo, 1993; vis. scholar Wabash Coll., 2003, lectr. U. Rouen, Caen, Paris, 2003; Geske lectr. U. Nebr., Lincoln, 2005. Author: Tennessee Williams, 1979, Tom Stoppard, 1981, Federico Garcia Lorca, 1984, Love's Labour's Lost: Critical Essays, 1997, Words at Play: Creative Writing and Dramaturgy, 2005; (play) Miss Millay Was Right, 1982 (John Gassner Meml. Playwriting award 1982), The History of World Theater: From the English Restoration to the Present, 1991 (Choice Outstanding Acad. Book award 1991), Chow Chow Pizza, 1995 (Kansas City Gorilla Theatre First Prize, winner Stages '95 Competition, Dallas); (opera libretto) Duse and D'Annunzio, 1987; (with Daniel J. Watermeier) The History of North American Theater: The United States, Canada, and Mexico from Pre-Columbian Times to the Present, 1998; co-editor: Shakespeare Companies and Festivals: An International Guide, 1995; book rev. editor: Theatre Jour., 1984-86; assoc. editor: Shakespeare Around the Globe: A Guide to Notable Postwar Revivals, 1986; mem. editl. bd. Theatre History Studies, 1981-87, 89—, Studies in Am. Drama, 1945 to the present, 1984-93, 19th Century Theatre Jour., 1984-95, Bookmark Press, Tennessee Williams Rev., 1985-87, Jour. Dramatic Theory and Criticism, 1986—, On-Stage Studies, The Elizabethan Rev., 1992-99, Theatre Symposium, 1994—, The Oxfordian, 1998—, Estreno Contemporary Spanish Plays, 1998—, So. Ill. U. Press Theater in the Americas series, 2000—, Eugene O'Neill Rev., 2005—; contbr. articles to profl. jours. Hon. co-founder Heart of Am. Shakespeare Festival, bd. dirs., 1991-2004, v.p., 2000-04; bd. dirs. Edgar Snow Meml. Fund, 1993-2002; active UMKC Grad. Coun., 2001-04, acad. stds. com. Coll. Arts and Scis., 2001-04; elected Nat. Theatre Conf., 2001, trustee, 2004-05, sec., 2005—; sec. Coll. Fellows Am. Theatre, 2001-03. Fulbright grantee U. Caen, Normandy, France, 1962-63, NEH grantee, 1971, 80, Faculty Rsch. grantee U. Mo., 1985-86, 90-91, tchr. seminar grantee Mo. Humanities Coun., 1993, 96; recipient Disting. Alumni award U. Mont., 1998, winner Amy and Eric Burger Essay on Theatre Competition, U. Wyo., 2003; grad. fellow U. Wis., 1966-67, Trustees fellow U. Kansas City, 1987-88; inductee Coll. Fellows Am. Theatre. Fellow Mid-Am. Theatre Conf. (chair grad. rsch. paper competition 1985); mem. Am. Soc. Theatre Rsch. (exec. com. 1984-90, program chair 1995), Shakespeare Theatre Assn. Am. (sec. 1991-93), Internat. Fedn. for Theatre Rsch. (del. gen. assembly 1985), Am. Theatre Assn. (commn. on theatre rsch. 1981-87, chmn. 1984-86), Theatre Libr. Assn., Dramatists Guild, Literary Mgrs. and Dramaturgs Am., Shakespeare Oxford Soc., Am. Theatre and Drama Soc. (v.p. 1995-97, pres. 1997-99), Nat. League of Am. PEN Women (v.p. 2002-04, pres. 2004—06, bd. dirs. Kansas City-Westport br.), Assn. for Theatre in Higher Edn. (v.p. for awards 2001-03, Outstanding Tchr. award 2001), Internat. Al Jolson Soc., Lewis and Clark Heritage Found. Roman Catholic. Avocations: travel, theater. Home: 528 E 56th St Kansas City MO 64110-2769 Office: Dept Theatre 4949 Cherry St Kansas City MO 64110-2499 Office Phone: 816-235-2781. Business E-Mail: londref@umkc.edu.

LONG, AMELIA ROSE, psychologist; b. Altus, Okla., Feb. 15, 1944; d. Everett Bailey Holland and Edna Odessa Amelia (Donnohue) Holland Sweetland; adopted by George R. Sweetland; m. Deryl Wayne Long, Aug. 8, 1963 (div. 1976); children: Katherine Kimberley, Kenneth Wayne, Amy Nicole. BA, Ball State U., 1979, MA, 1982, PhD in Counseling Psychology, 1986. Lic. psychologist, N.D. Psychologist N.W. Human Svc. Ctr., Williston, N.D., 1985—; pvt. practice Williston, 1989—. Mem. APA. Unitarian Universalist. Avocations: photography, philosophy, pottery. Home: 1123 7th Ave E Williston ND 58801-4449 Office: NW Human Svc Ctr 316 2d Ave W Williston ND 58801-5218

LONG, AMY E., secondary school educator; d. E. J. Long and Betty Sowers Rogers. BS in Phys. Edn. and Sports Medicine, Meth. Coll., Fayetteville, NC, 1999; MEd in Exercise and Sports Medicine, Tex. State U., San Marcos, 2002. Cert. tchr. NC. Phys. edn. tchr., athletic trainer Cabarrus County Schs., Concord, NC, 2002—. Home: 801 Cloister Ct Apt 21 Concord NC 28027-0808

LONG, BERNEÉ E., academic administrator, educator; b. Kans. City, Kans., Mar. 28, 1960; d. Ira Joe Sr. and Madene (Carter) L. BSBA, Northeast Mo. State U., 1981; JD, Washington U., 1986. Pers. analyst Mo. Dept. Social Svcs., Jefferson City, 1987-88; adminstrv. law judge Iowa Pub. Employment Rels. Bd., Des Moines, 1988-90; dir. admissions Drake U. Law Sch., Des Moines, 1990-92; dir. student svcs. Cumberland Law Sch. Samford U., Birmingham, Ala., 1992-94, asst. dean, 1994—. Dir. So. Region CLEO Inst., summer, 1994; bd. dirs. Sta. KUCB Radio, Des Moines. Former host radio talk show Speak Softly, But Loudly, Des Moines; speaker in field. Vol. Jr. League/Urban Dreams Youth Touch Project, Drake Ctr. Law Related Edn. Mock Trial Competition; mem. planning com. Martin Luther King, Jr. Interfaith Celebration; vol. Ctr. for Urban Missions; mem. exec. com. Des Moines br. NAACP; mem. adv. com. Des Moines Area C.C.; mem. EEO com. Drake U. Recipient 1st annual Black Alumnae Achievement award N.E. Mo. State U.; Outstanding Young Woman of Am., 1984, 91. Mem. ABA (assoc.), Nat. Bar Assn. (assoc. Iowa chpt.), Nat. Network Law Sch. Officers, Magic City Bar Assn., N.E. Mo. State U. Nat. Alumni Assn. (bd. dirs.), Am. Assn. Law Schs. (rsch. com., pubs. com. sect. on student svcs.), Sigma Gamma Rho. Office: U Ala 1530 Third Ave Birmingham AL 35294-0016 Office Phone: 205-934-6355. Office Fax: 205-975-6708.

LONG, CAROLYN EVANS, preschool special education educator; b. Burlington, N.C., Dec. 4, 1951; d. IRvin Ray and Jean (Bouldin) Evans; m. Daniel Alan Long, Nov. 20, 1977. BA in Spl. Edn., U. N.C., 1974, MA in Spl. Edn., 1976; MS in Speech Pathology, Winthrop Coll., 1983. Cert. in learning disabilities, mental retardation, speech and lang. spl. edn., Va. Tchr. educable mentally retarded Winston-Salem (N.C.)-Forsyth County Schs., 1974-75; tchr. autistic children Treatment and Edn. of Autistic and related comm.-handicapped children, Charlotte, N.C., 1976-83; coord. early childhood edn. Human Devel. Ctr., Winthrop Coll., Rock Hill, S.C., 1983-85; infant educator Kluge Children's Rehab. Ctr., U. Va., Charlottesville, 1985—, mem. adv. bd. early intervention agy., 1989—. Mem. adv. bd. TEACCH, Soc. for Autistic Children, 1978-83; mem. steering com. Region 10 Community Svc. Bd., Charlottesville, 1989—. Contbr. articles to profl. jours. Named Tchr. of Yr., Marie G. Davis Sch., Charlotte, 1983; recipient spl. supr.'s awarrd Kluge Children's Rehab. Ctr., 1991. Mem. Coun. for Exceptional Children, Assn. for Care Children's Health, Internat. Soc. on Early Intervention. Home: 14518 Harvey Rd Barboursville VA 22923-8554 Office: U Va Kluge Children's Rehab Ctr 2270 Ivy Rd Charlottesville VA 22903-4977

LONG, DEBORAH JOYCE, lawyer; b. Oct. 26, 1953; d. Thomas C. and Margaret N. (Falks) Long; m. William Daniel Sockwell, May 26, 1979; 1 child, Daniel Long Sockwell. BA, Auburn U., 1975; JD, U. Ala., 1980. Bar: Ala. 1980, U.S. Ct. Appeals (5th cir.) 1980, U.S. Ct. Appeals (11th cir.) 1981, U.S. Dist. Ct. (no. dist.) Ala. 1981. Law clk. U.S. Ct. Appeals for 5th Cir., Montgomery, Ala., 1980-81; assoc. Cabaniss, Johnston, Gardner, Dumas & O'Neal, Birmingham, Ala., 1981-84, Maynard, Cooper & Gale, P.C., Birmingham, 1984—94; mem.; sr. v.p., gen. counsel Protective Life Corp., Birmingham, Ala., 1994—. Recipient Cert. of Appreciation, Ala. Bar Assn., Montgomery. Mem. Farrah Soc., Ala. State Bar (bd. bar examiners 1987-92, bd. editors 1991-94), Birmingham Bar Assn. (bd. editors 1989-90), Assn. Life Ins. Counsel (pres. 2005) Office: Protective Life Corp 2801 Highway 280 S Birmingham AL 35223-2488

LONG, DRUCILLA, special education educator; b. Leesville, S.C., Apr. 20, 1940; d. Horace Tillman and Gerlie Ann (Watson) Fallaw; m. Edward Clyde Long, Aug. 3, 1963; 1 child, Rhonda Ann. BS, Winthrop Coll., 1962. Elem. tchr. West Columbia (S.C.) Schs., 1962-64, Aiken County Schs., North Augusta, S.C., 1964-65; tchr. spl. edn. Lexington County # 3, Batesburg-Leesville, S.C., 1965—. Mem., officer Lexington County Ext. Svc. Women, 1965-90. Mem. Nat. Edn. Assn., S.C. Carolina Edn. Assn., S.C. Cheerleader Coaches Assn. (Outstanding Svc. award 1999), Lexington County Dist.# 3 Edn. Assn., Delta Kappa Gamam, Alpha Tau (pres. 1994, 95). Republican. Baptist. Avocations: antiques, singing, directing weddings, sports, playing with grandson. Home: 739 N Lee St Leesville SC 29070-9584 Office: Batesburg-Leesville Middle Sch 425 Shealy Rd Batesburg SC 29006-8783

LONG, ELAINE, writer, editor; b. Sterling, Colo., Jan. 12, 1935; d. Guy William and Evelyn Irene (Simpson) Mullenax; m. Thomas John O'Rourke, Aug. 17, 1963 (dec. Feb. 1965); 1 child, Mary Kendall; m. Arthur Warren Long, Oct. 4, 1969 (dec. Jan., 2003). BA, U. Colo., 1955. Tchr. Portland (Oreg.) Pub. Schs., 1955-57, Denver Pub. Schs., 1957-58, U.S. Civil Svc., Upper Heyford, Eng., 1958-59; copywriter KBOL Radio, Boulder, Colo., 1959-61; ranch hand Guy Mullenax, Gillette, Wyo., 1961-62; copy and feature writer, traffic mgr. KKAR Radio, Pomona, Calif., 1962-63; freelance writer Denver, 1966—. Editor Boulder, Buena Vista, Colo., 1974—. Author: Jenny's Mountain, 1987, Bittersweet Country, 1991, Bear Ridge-A Novel, 2006; cons. editor: Separate Lives: The Story of Mary Rippon, 1999, Dancing with Principle: Hanya Holm in Colorado, 1941-1983, 2001, A Texas Tragedy: Orphaned by Bootleggers, 2001, Behind the Badge: 125 Years of the Boulder Police Department, 2003, Out of the Shadows, 2004, author short stories; contbr. articles to profl. jours. Mem. Western Writers Am. (Spur awards chmn. 1993, 2005, Svc. award 1994-95, 2005, bd. dirs. 1994-95), Aircraft Owners and Pilots Assn., Women Writing the West, Author's Guild NY, Colo. Authors' League (bd. dirs. 1987-88). Avocations: flying, songwriting, singing, hiking, reading. E-mail: elainelong@chaffee.net.

LONG, JEANINE HUNDLEY, retired state legislator; b. Provo, Utah, Sept. 21, 1928; d. Ralph Conrad and Hazel Laurine (Snow) Hundley; m. McKay W. Christensen, Oct. 28, 1949 (div. 1967); children: Cathy Schuyler, Julie Schulleri, Kelly M. Christensen, C. Brett Christensen, Harold A. Christensen;

m. Kenneth D. Long, Sept. 6, 1968. AA, Shoreline C.C., Seattle, 1975; BA in Psychology, U. Wash., 1977. Mem. Wash. Ho. of Reps., 1983-87, 93-94, mem. Inst. Pub. Policy; mem. Wash. Senate, Dist. 44, Olympia, 1995—2003. Ranking mem. Human Svcs. and Corr. com. Wash. Senate, 1995-96, 99-2002, chair, 1997-98; vice-chair Rep. Caucus, 1997-98; mem. Braam panel to monitor Dept. Social and Health Svcs., 2005—. Mayor protem, mem. city coun. City of Brier, Wash., 1977-80. Republican. Office: PO Box 40482 Olympia WA 98504-0482 E-mail: long_je@leg.wa.gov.

LONG, JO-NELLE DESMOND, editor, consultant, historian; b. Big Stone Gap, Va., Oct. 20, 1930; d. Daniel Joseph and Mary Pearson Desmond; m. Walter Donald Long, June 12, 1954; children: Donna Long La Tourette, Steven William, Robert Lawrence. Student, Transylvania U., 1948—50; cert., Traphagen Sch. Interior Design, N.Y.C., 1951; BA Fine Arts, Ramapo Coll. N.J., 1976; MA Arts Adminstrn., Costume History and Design, NYU, 1983. Adminstrv. asst. Smyth, Urguhart & Marckwald Interior Design, N.Y.C., 1951—54; intern, rsch. asst., vol. Am. Painting & Sculpture Met. Mus. Art, N.Y.C., 1977—; registrar Hermitage Mus., Ho-Ho-Kus, NJ, 1977—80; rsch. cons. Van Cline & Davenport Appraisers, Franklin Lakes, NJ, 1985—90; owner Long Art Rsch. & Cons., Allendale, NJ, 1985—; editor prodn. Ozer Pub., Englewood, NJ, 1991—. Lectr. in field. Treas. Cub Scout Pack 59; co-chmn. Girl Scout Com.; founder Friends of the Libr., v.p.; vol. Archer Ch. Sunday Nursery Sch. Mem.: Victorian Soc., Nat. Trust, Costume Soc. Am. Avocations: reading, tai chi, yoga, crossword puzzles, travel, decorating. Home and Office: Long Art Rsch & Cons 9 Surrey Ln Allendale NJ 07401 E-mail: larc30@aol.com.

LONG, KATHLEEN ANNE, elementary school educator; d. James Long and Eleanor Anne Krimmel. A in Liberal Arts, Lehigh Carbon C.C., Schnecksville, Pa., 1996; B in Elem. Edn., Mansfield U., Pa., 1998; M in Tchg., DeSales U., Center Valley, Pa., 2004. Cert. elem., ednl. tech. tchr. Pa. K-5 computer tchr. Phila. Area Sch. Dist., 1998—99; 5th and 6th grade tchr. Lower Yukon Sch. Dist., Russian Mission, Alaska, 1999—2001; substitute tchr. Lehighton Area Sch. Dist., Pa., 2001—02; 7th and 8th grade tchr. Lehigh Valley Luth. Sch., Whitehall, Pa., 2002—04; 6th to 8th grade computer tchr., 6th grade English tchr. Nazareth Area Sch. Dist., Pa., 2004—05; 6th and 7th grade tchr. Lehigh Valley Luth Sch., Whitehall, Pa., 2005—06; elem. tchr. Lower Yukon Sch. Dist., Eninonak, Alaska, 2006—. After sch. computer tchr. Lehigh Valley Luth. Sch., Whitehall, Pa., 2002—06; clk. Becker's Parent Tchr. Store, Whitehall, Pa., 2002—06. Recipient Future Tchr. award, Lehighton Area H.S., 1994, Inside Track Newspaper Mem. of Yr. award, Lehigh Carbon C.C., 1996, Tchr. award, Mansfield U., 1998. Mem.: ASCD, NSTA, Grange (Middletown). Democrat. Quaker. Avocation: travel. Home: 31 N Sixth St Emmaus PA 18049 E-mail: travelingteacher@hotmail.com.

LONG, KELLY TIDWELL, medical/surgical nurse, director; b. Natchez, Miss., July 20, 1958; d. Clifford Starkes and Lois Wilson (Brister) Tidwell; m. Richard Lynn Brown, Feb. 16, 1980 (div. June 1987); m. Carl Dean Long, Oct. 1, 1988 (dec. May 2002); 1 child, Olivia Sagan. BS, U. So. Miss., 1979; ADN, S.W. Miss. Jr. Coll., Summit, 1986. RN, Miss.; cert. oper. rm. nurse, cert. in inpatient obstetrics; cert. oper. rm. surgery. Staff nurse obstetrics S.W. Miss. Regional Med. Ctr., McComb, 1986-89; staff nurse postpartum/gynecology Hinds Gen. Hosp., Meth. Med. Ctr., Jackson, Miss., 1989-91; staff nurse surgery River Oaks Hosp., Flowood, Miss., 1991—2002, asst. dir. Surgery, 2002—, oper. rm. nurse dir. Mem. Assn. Women's Health, Obstetric and Neonatal Nurses, Assn. Oper. Rm. Nurses. Methodist. Avocations: sewing, reading, baking. Home: 418 Concord Dr Clinton MS 39056-5763 Office: 1030 River Oaks Dr Jackson MS 39232-9553

LONG, LISA VALK, communications company executive; b. Winston-Salem, N.C. Grad., Hollins Coll.; MBA, Harvard Bus. Sch., 1979. Circulation staff Time Mag. TimeInc., N.Y.C., 1979-82, circulation dir. Forbes mag., 1982-84, circulation dir. Sports Illustrated, 1984-85, circulation dir. Time mag., 1985-86, pub. Life mag., 1986-87, v.p., 1987-89, sr. v.p., 1989-95, exec. v.p., 1995—, pub. People mag., 1988-93, pub. Time mag., then pres., 1991-95. Bd. dirs. Hanover Direct, Weehawken, N.J. Bus. com. Mus. Modern Art; bd. dirs. Atlantic Coun.; bd. mgrs. East Side House Settlement, Bronx. Mem. Women in Comms. (Matrix award 1992).

LONG, MAXINE MASTER, lawyer; b. Pensacola, Fla., Oct. 20, 1943; d. Maxwell L. and Claudine E. (Smith) M.; m. Anthony Byrd Long, Aug. 27, 1966; children: Deborah E., David M. AB, Bryn Mawr Coll., 1965; MS, Georgetown U., 1971; JD, U. Miami, 1979. Bar: Fla. 1979, U.S. Ct. Appeals (5th cir.) 1980, U.S. Dist. Ct. (so. dist.) Fla. 1980, U.S. Ct. Appeals (11th cir.) 1981, U.S. Dist. Ct. (mid. and no. dists.) Fla. 1987. Law clk. to U.S. dist. judge U.S. Dist. Ct. (so. dist.) Fla., Miami, 1979-80; assoc. Shutts & Bowen, Miami, 1980-90, of counsel, 1990-92, ptnr., 1992—. Mem. Fla. Bar Assn. (cert. bus. litigator, mem. bus. litigation cert. com. 1995-99, vice chair, 1996-97, past chair bus. litigation com., chair bus. law sect. 2004-05) Dade County Bar Assn. (mem. fed. cts. com., recipient pro bono award/Vol. Lawyers for the Arts 1989). Office: Shutts & Bowen 201 S Biscayne Blvd Ste 1500 Miami FL 33131-4308 Office Phone: 305-358-6300. Business E-Mail: mlong@shutts-law.com.

LONG, NINA P., library director, archivist; d. John Alvin and Pauline (Walter) Packard; children: Edward C., Nora E. BA, Butler U., Indpls., 1969; MLS, Case Western Reserve U., 1983. Cert. Nat. Archives and Records Adminstr., Modern Archl. Inst., 1991. Asst. libr. health sci. libr. Case Western Reserve U., Cleve., 1983—86; asst. tchr. Drexel U., Phila., 1986—87; dir. libr. svcs. Episcopal Hosp., Phila., 1987—92; dir. libr., archivist, mus. curator Wistar Inst., Phila., 1992—. Med. informatics fellow Nat. Libr. Medicine, Woods Hole, Mass., 1995. Contbr. papers to profl. confs. Grantee Local History Grant, Pa. Hist. Mus. Commission, 2001, Preservation grant, Bay Found., N.Y.C., 2001, Mus. Exhibit grant, Wm. Penn Found., 2002, Symposium Support grant, Barra Found., 2003. Mem.: Pa. Libr. Assn. (bd. dirs. Southeast Pa. sect. 2002—04), Med. Libr. Assn. (chair Phila. chpt. 2006, sr. mem.). Office: Wistar Inst 3601 Spruce St Philadelphia PA 19101 Office Phone: 215-898-3826. Office Fax: 215-898-3856.

LONG, PATRICIA N., academic administrator; m. Dennis Long. BA, Southwest Baptist U., 1973; MSE, Ctrl. Mo. State U., 1978; EdD, U. Kans., 1993. Dir. admissions and records Johnson County C. of C., 1987—95, asst. dean student enrollment svcs. and fin. aid, dean student svcs., 1995—2000; vice chancellor student affairs and enrollment mgmt. U. Mo.-Kansas City, 2000—03, dep. chancellor Univ. Comm., 2003—06, acting exec. vice chancellor, 2005—06; pres. Baker U., Baldwin City, Kans., 2006—. Office: Baker U Office of Pres PO Box 65 Baldwin City KS 66006-0065 Office Phone: 816-235-1141. E-mail: longp@umkc.edu.*

LONG, PENNY, mathematics educator; b. Newton, Kans., July 5, 1964; d. Richard and Joan Bell; m. Lester Long, Aug. 2, 1986; children: Emily, Amy. M, Stephen F. Austin State U., Nacogdoches, Tex., 1990. Cert. Tchr. Tex., 1986. Tchr. math. Nacogdoches H.S., 1986—. Edn. coord. First Ch. of God, Nacogdoches, 1990—2006. Home: 10922 N US Hwy 59 Nacogdoches TX 75965 Office: Nacogdoches High School 4310 Appleby Sand Road Nacogdoches TX 75961

LONG, ROBIN JANE ELLINGSWORTH, elementary school educator, special education educator; b. Detroit, Mar. 30, 1961; d. Robert Elmer and Shirley Hope Ellingsworth; m. Patrick Anthony Long, July 26, 1997; 1 child, Patrick Antony II. BS in Edn., Ctrl. Mich. U., 1983; MA in Learning Disabilities, Ea. Mich. U., 1988; cert. specialist leadership and adminstrn., Oakland U., 1994. Tchr. Crestwood Pub. Schs., Dearborn Heights, Mich., 1983—85, St. Linus Schs., Dearborn Heights, 1985—88; tchr. learning disabled, gen. classroom and gifted edn. Northville (Mich.) Pub. Schs., 1988—. Assoc. trainer Ctr. for Tchr. Effectiveness. Mem.: Kids 4 Afghan Kids (bd. dirs. 2000—), Mich. Ednl. Credit Union (bd. dirs. 2000—). Office: Northville Public Schs 847 North Center St Northville MI 48167 Office Phone: 734-216-2383.

LONG, SARAH ANN, librarian; b. Atlanta, May 20, 1943; d. Jones Lloyd and Lelia Maria (Mitchell) Sanders; m. James Allen Long, 1961 (div. 1985); children: Andrew C., James Allen IV; m. Donald J. Sager, May 23, 1987. BA, Oglethorpe U., 1966; M in Librarianship, Emory U., 1969. Asst. libr. Coll. of St. Matthias, Bristol, England, 1970-74; cons. State Libr. Ohio, Columbus, 1975-77; coord. Pub. Libr. of Columbus and Franklin County, Columbus, 1977-79; dir. Fairfield County Dist. Libr., Lancaster, Ohio, 1979-82, Dauphin County Libr. Sys., Harrisburg, Pa., 1982-85, Multnomah County Libr., Portland, Oreg., 1985-89; sys. dir. North Suburban Libr. Sys., Wheeling, Ill., 1989—. Chmn. Portland State U. Libr. Adv. Coun., 1987-89, bd. dirs. Am. Libr., Paris, 2000-02. Contbr. to weekly column in Daily Herald; monthly cable show Whats New in Libraries; contbr. articles to profl. jours. Bd. dirs. Dauphin County Hist. Soc., Harrisburg, 1983-85, ARC, Harrisburg, 1984-85; pres. Lancaster-Fairfield County YWCA, Lancaster, 1981-82; vice chmn. govt. and ednl. divsn. Lancaster-Fairfield County United Way, Lancaster, 1981-82; sec. Fairfield County Arts Coun., 1981-82; adv. bd. Portland State U., 1987-89; mentor Ohio Libr. Leadership Inst., 1993, 95; moderator Congl. Ch., Deerfield Ill., 2006-. Recipient Dir.'s award Ohio Program in Humanities, Columbus, 1982, Emory medal Emory U., 2006; Sarah Long Day established in her honor Fairfield County, Lancaster, Bd. Commrs., 1982. Mem. ALA (pres. 1999-2000, elected coun. 1993-97, chair Spectrum fund raising com. 2001-02), Pub. Libr. Assn. (pres. 1989-90, chair legis. com. 1991-95, chair 1998, nat. conf. com. 1995-98), Ill. Libr. Assn. (pub. policy com. 1991-97, Librarian of Yr. award 1999), Ill. Libr. Sys. Dirs. Orgn. (pres. 2000-05), Libr. Cmty. Found. (bd. dirs. 1995-2005) Office: N Suburban Libr Systems 200 W Dundee Rd Wheeling IL 60090-4750 Business E-Mail: slong@nsls.info.

LONG, SARAH ELIZABETH BRACKNEY, physician; b. Sidney, Ohio, Dec. 5, 1926; d. Robert LeRoy and Caroline Josephine (Shue) Brackney; m. John Frederick Long, June 15, 1948; children: George Lynas, Helen Lucille Corcoran, Harold Roy, Clara Alice Lawrence, Nancy Carol Sieber. BA, Ohio State U., 1948, MD, 1952. Intern Grant Hosp., Columbus, Ohio, 1952—53; resident internal medicine Mt. Carmel Med. Ctr., Columbus, 1966—69, chief resident internal medicine, 1968—69; med. cons. Ohio Bur. Disability Determination, Columbus, 1970—. Physician student health Ohio State U., Columbus, 1970-73; sch. physician Bexley City Schs., Ohio, 1973-83; physician advisor to peer rev. Mt. Carmel East Hosp., Columbus, 1979-86, med. dir. employee health, 1981-96; physician cons. Fed. Black Lung program U.S. Dept. Labor, Columbus, 1979-98. Mem.: AMA, Gerontol. Soc. Am., Columbus Med. Assn., Ohio State Med. Assn., Ohio Hist. Soc., Phi Beta Kappa, Alpha Epsilon Delta. Home: 2765 Bexley Park Rd Columbus OH 43209-2231

LONG, SARAH HOLLEY, lawyer; b. Ft. Worth, Aug. 12, 1977; BS in Corp. Comm., U. Tex., Austin; JD, Baylor U. Bar: Tex. 2002, US Dist. Ct. (no, so. and ea. dists. Tex.). Assoc. atty. Biggers, Beasley, Earle & Hightower, P.C., 2002—03, Touchstone, Bernays, Johnston, Beall, Smith & Stollenwerck, L.L.P., 2003—06; assoc. trial divsn. Walters, Balido & Crain, Dallas. Named a Rising Star, Tex. Super Lawyers mag., 2006. Mem.: ABA (mem. litig. divsn.), Dallas Women Lawyers Assn., Dallas Bar Assn., Dallas Assn. Young Lawyers. Office: Walters Balido & Crain 900 Jackson St Founders Sq Ste 600 Dallas TX 75202 Office Phone: 214-347-8342. E-mail: sarah.long@wbclawfirm.com.*

LONG, SARAH SUNDBORG, pediatrician, educator; b. Portland, Oreg., Oct. 31, 1944; MD, Jefferson Med. Coll., 1970. Diplomate Am. Bd. Pediat. Intern St. Christopher Hosp. for Children, Phila., 1970-71, resident, 1971-73, fellow pediat. and infectious diseases, 1973-75, staff, 1975—2002; prof. pediat. Drexel U. Coll. Medicine, 2002—. Chief editor: Principles and Practice of Pediatric Infectious Diseases, 1997; assoc. editor Jour. Pediatrics, 1997—; contbr. over 100 articles to med. jours. Mem. Am. Acad. Pediat., Soc. for Pediat. Rsch., Am. Pediat. Soc., Pediatric Diseases Soc. (pres. 1999-2001). Office: St Christopher Child Hosp Sect Infectious Diseases Erie Ave at Front St Philadelphia PA 19134 Office Phone: 215-427-5204.

LONG, SHARON RUGEL, dean, molecular biologist, educator; b. Mar. 2, 1951; d. Harold Eugene and Florence Jean (Rugel) Long; m. Harold James McGee, July 7, 1979 (div. 2004); 2 children BS, Calif. Inst. Tech., 1973; PhD, Yale U., 1979. Rsch. fellow Harvard U., Cambridge, Mass., 1979-81; from asst. prof. molecular biology to prof. Stanford U., Palo Alto, Calif., 1982-92, prof. biol. scis., 1992—, William C. Steere, Jr.-Pfizer Inc. prof. biological scis., Vernon R. & Lysbeth Warren Anderson dean Sch. Humanities and Scis., 2001—. Investigator Howard Hughes Med. Inst., 1994—; adv. bd. Jane Coffin Childs Meml. Fund; bd. dirs. Ann. Revs. Inc. Recipient award NSF, 1979, NIH, 1980, Shell Rsch. Found. award 1985, Presdl. Young Investigator award NSF, 1984-89; grantee NIH, Dept. Energy, NSF; MacArthur fellow, 1992-97, Georges Morel fellow I.N.R.A., France, 1998; fellow Noble Found. Fellow Assn. Women in Sci.; mem. NAS, Genetics Soc. Am., Am. Soc. Plant Physiology (Charles Albert Shull award 1989), Am. Soc. Microbiology, Soc. Devel. Biology. Office: Sch of Humanities and Scis Off of Dean Bldg 1 - Main Quad Stanford CA 94305-2070 also: Dept Biol Scis 371 Serra Mall Stanford CA 94305-5020 Office Fax: 650-723-3235. E-mail: srl@stanford.edu.

LONG, SHEILA JOAN, academic administrator; b. Durant, Okla., Sept. 6, 1962; d. Troy E. and Beulah M. Phillips; m. William Donnie Long, May 12, 1984; 1 child, Mitchell R. BA in Edn., Southeastern Okla. U., Durant, 1985; MEd, Southeastern Okla. State U., 1994. Cert. tchr. Okla. Social studies tchr. Bokchito Pub. Schs., Bokchito, Okla., 1986—87; fin. aid svcs. profl. Southeastern Okla. State U., 1988—94; dir. Power I Carl Albert State U., Poteau, Okla., 2001—. Mem. policy coun. Kibois Head Start, 2005—06. Mem.: OKACTE (admntrn. policy coun. 2006—), ACTE (chair profl. devel. 2006—), OKCTEEC (pres.-elect 2004—06, Outstanding Leadership award 2005), CTEEC (conf. co-chair 2004—05). Baptist. Avocations: reading, travel. Home: PO Box 681 Poteau OK 74953 Office: Power I Carl Albert State College 1507 S McKenna St Poteau OK 74953-5207 Office Phone: 918-647-1291.

LONG, SHERI SPAINE, foreign language educator; b. Waterloo, Iowa, Dec. 2, 1958; d. Richard Clifton Jr. and Dorothea Knarr Spaine; m. John A. Long, May 24, 1980; children: Morgan Taylor, John Richard. BA in Spanish, U. Iowa, 1980, MA in Spanish, 1983; PhD in Hispanic Langs. and Lit., UCLA, 1990. Asst. prof. Spanish Samford U., Birmingham, 1991—92, U. Ala., Birmingham, 1993—98, assoc. prof. Spanish, 1998—2002, chair dept. of fgn. lang. and lit., 2002—. Pres. bd. dirs. Children's Dance Found., Birmingham, 1998—2000; acad. dir. Nat. Collegiate Honors Coun. Spain Semester, Alcalá, 2000; assoc. bd. dirs. Nat. Mus. Langs., 2001—06. Co-author: En train d'écrire, 1993, Redacción y revisión, 1993, Hacia la literatura, 1998, Nexos Introductory Spanish, 2005; editor: (jour.) Fgn. Lang. Annals, 2006-. Mem. bd. dirs. Am. Coun. Tchg. Fgn. Langs., 2003—06. Named Outstanding Woman Faculty Mem., U. Ala., Birmingham, 2005. Mem. MLA, So. Conf. on the Tchg. of Fgn. Langs. (bd. dirs. 2002-06) Am. Assn. Tchrs. Spanish and Portuguese (recipient Mead grant 2002), Ala. Assn. Fgn. Lang. Tchrs. (pres. 1998-99, Outstanding Fgn. Lang. Tchr. award 2000), Ala. Assn. Tchrs. Spanish and Portuguese (pres. 1994, Lang. Tchr. award 1999). Democrat. Office: U Ala Birmingham Dept Fgn Langs Birmingham AL 35294-0001 Office Phone: 205-934-4652. Business E-Mail: espanol@uab.edu.

LONG, SUSIE ANN, special education educator, consultant, writer; d. Larue Deffine Manson; children: Christal Deffine, Anthony De, Kandice Latrice, Patricia Marsell. BA, Grambling State U., 1977; MEd, Bowie State U., 1997. Deaf Hard Hearing K-12 Md. State Dept. Edn., 1981, Administration 1 Md. State Dept. Edn., 1997, Special Education Md. State Dept. Edn., 2000. Tchr. asst. Prince George's County Sch. Sys., Fort Washington, Md., 1978—81, tchr. deaf and hard of hearing, 1981—2000, regional spl. edn. specialist Oxon Hill, Md., 2000—. Ednl. cons., workshop presenter Pub. Schools, Univ., Washington, 2004—. Author: (christian book) Healing for the Abandoned Wife. Founder, deaf ministry/interpreter From the Heart Ch. Ministries, Temple Hills, Md., 1986—2005; pres. PGC Alliance Black Sch. Educators, Upper Marlboro, Md., 2003—05. Mem.: NEA (assoc.), Md. State Teachers Assn. (assoc.), Prince George's County Ednl. Assn. (assoc.), Nat. Alliance of Black Sch. Educators (assoc.; pres. of the affiliate 2004—05). Office Phone: 301-749-4118.

LONG, SUZANNE LYNN, silk screening company executive; b. Stockton, Calif., May 27, 1957; d. H. Donald and Nancy J. (Foosaner) L. B.A., Calif. State U.-Sacramento, 1980. Labor relations investigator State of Calif., Sacramento, 1980; ptnr. Pacific Silk Screening, Laguna Beach, Calif., 1980—. Mem. Friends of Sea Lions. Avocations: yachting; languages; scuba diving. Office: Pacific Silk Screening PO Box 722008 Houston TX 77272-2008

LONG, TERESA C., city health department administrator; m. Tom Denune; 1 child, Katherine. MD, U. Calif., San Francisco; MPH, U. Calif., Berkeley. Med. dir., asst. health commr Columbus Health Dept., Ohio, 1986—2002, commr., 2002—; clin. assoc. prof. Ohio State U., Coll. Medicine and Pub. Health. Chair Ctrl. Ohio Med. Dirs. Coalition, Columbus Area Asthma Coalition; co-chair Healthy Columbus Adv. Bd. Recipient Elizabeth Blackwell award for Pioneering Efforts to Improve Women's and Cmty. Health. Mem.: Columbus Med. Assn. (past pres., past pres., bd. trustees found.). Office: Columbus Health Dept 240 Parsons Ave Columbus OH 43215*

LONG, TERESA LOZANO, foundation administrator, educator; BA in Edn., MA in Edn., U. Tex., Austin, PhD in Edn., 1965. Rsch. assoc. Tex. Edn. Agency, cons. Div. Compensatory Edn.; rsch. assoc. Tex. Govs. Com. Pub. Sch. Edn.; cons. Migrant Edn. and Head Start Prog. US Office of Edn.; founder Long Found., Austin, 1999—. Mem. Nat. Coun. Arts, Nat. Endowment for Arts, 2002—. Mem. bd. dirs. Austin Lyric Opera, Umlauf Sculpture Mus., Austin Cmty. Found., Austin Urban League, Laguna Gloria Art Mus., Austin Volunteer Coun., Ballet Austin, Umlauf Sculpture Garden, Tex. Com. for Nat. Mus. of Women in Arts, Interscholastic League Found., U. Tex. Chancellor's Coun., Sherman, Tex. Office: The Long Found 40 N IH 35 Ste 7C2 Austin TX 78701 Office Phone: 512-479-4080.*

LONG, VIRGINIA, state supreme court justice; b. Mar. 1, 1942; m. Jonathan D. Weiner; 3 children. Grad., Dunbarton Coll. of Holy Cross, 1963; JD, Rutgers U., 1966. Dep. atty. gen. State of NJ; assoc. Pitney, Hardin, Kipp and Szuch; dir. NJ Divsn. Consumer Affairs, 1975; commr. NJ Dept. Banking, 1977-78; judge NJ Superior Ct., 1978-84, Appellate Divsn. NJ Superior Ct., 1984-95, presiding judge, 1995-99; assoc. justice NJ Supreme Ct., 1999—. Office: Supreme Ct NJ PO Box 970 Trenton NJ 08625-0970*

LONG, VONDA OLSON, educator, counselor; b. Everett, Wash., Dec. 17, 1947; d. Harold Theodore and Edna Marie (Gabrielson) Olson. Social work diploma, Skara Skifts Folkhögskola, Hjo, Sweden, 1969; BS, Wash. State U., 1971; postgrad., Ea. Wash. State U., 1975; MS, Wash. State U., 1976, PhD, 1979; adminstrv. cert., Ohio State U., 1980. Tchr. Spokane (Wash.) Sch. Dist., 1971, Cheney (Wash.) Sch. Dist., 1972-75; migrant day care dir. Human Svcs. Dept., Wenatchee, Wash., 1976; cons. Instructional Theory Into Practice, Pullman, Wash., 1977-79; therapist Southeast Mental Health Ctr., Columbus, Ohio, 1979-80; asst. prof. U. N.Mex., Albuquerque, 1980-86, assoc. prof., 1986-92, prof., 1992—. Dir. wilderness counseling Passageways, Inc., Albuquerque, 1983—; cons. Albuquerque Pub. Schs., 1980-82. Contbr. articles to profl. jours. Vol. Albuquerque Mountain Rescue, 1984-91, Emergency Med. Disaster Team, Albuquerque, 1985-90; pres. AADA divsn Am. Counseling Assn., 2005-06. Mem. ACA, APA, Am. Edml. Rsch. Assn., N.Mex. Assn. Counselor Edn. and Supervision (pres. 1992-93), Phi Kappa Phi. Avocations: river guide, ski patrol, mountain rescue. Office: Univ NMex Dept Counselor Edn 131 Simpson Hl Albuquerque NM 87131-0001

LONGABERGER, TAMI, home decor accessories company executive; BSBA in Mktg., Ohio State U., 1984. Joined Longaberger Co., Newark, Ohio, 1984, pres., 1994, CEO, 1998. Chair bd. trustees Ohio State U.; mem. 60th commn. human rights United Nation; bd. dirs. Woodrow Wilson Internat. Ctr. Scholars, John Glenn Inst. for Pub. Svc. and Pub. Policy.

LONGAN, SUZANNE M., retired elementary school educator; b. San Francisco, June 8, 1936; d. Walter Emerson Murfee and Ferne Inez Nelson; m. George B. Longan III, Aug. 27, 1958 (div. June 7, 1965); 1 child, Nancy Ann. BA with distinction, U. Ariz., 1958; postgrad., Calif. State U., 1987—89. Elem. sch. tchr. Johnson County Sch. Dist., Leawood, Kans., 1958—60; corp. sec., CEO Villa Chartier-Lanai, Inc., San Mateo, Calif., 1965—84. Dir. San Mateo County Hotel and Restaurant Assn., 1971—79. Treas. Pre-Sch. for the Visually Handicapped, Kans. City, Mo., 1961—62, chmn. advisory bd., 1963—65; div. chmn. Heart of Am. United Campaign, Kans. City, 1962; chair sch. solicitation Johnson County (Kans.) United Funds, 1963; mem. adv. bd. Children's Mercy Hosp., Kans. City, 1963—65; treas. Music in the Mountains, Nev. City, Calif., 1986—90; mem. bd. trustees Foothill Theatre Co., Nev. City, Calif., 1990—92; treas. Nev. County Land Trust, Nev. City, 1995—97; mem. Emmanuel Episc. Ch. Choir, Grass Valley, Calif., 1981—91; treas., CFO Emmanuel Episc. Ch., Grass Valley, Calif., 1988—91; mem. bd. dirs. Twin Cities Concert Assn., Grass Valley, 1984—86. Named Vol. Nurse Aide, Am. Red Cross, 1964, Concessionaire Extraordinaire, Foothill Theatre Co., 1986—87, Master Gardener, U. Calif., 1990; recipient Cmty. Svc. award, United Funds Coun., Inc., 1963. Mem.: Jr. League, Gamma Phi Beta. Republican. Episcopalian. Avocations: gardening, wildlife habitat maintenance. Home: 13350 Wildwood Heights Dr Penn Valley CA 95946

LONGDEN, CLAIRE SUZANNE, retired financial planner, investment advisor; b. Sheffield, Yorkshire, Eng., June 2, 1938; arrived in U.S., 1964; d. John Stewart and Daisy (Heath) L. Diploma in pvt. sec., Coll. Commerce & Tech., Sheffield, 1956; cert. in Fin. Planning, Coll. Fin. Planning, 1979. Sec., Sheffield, 1956-62; G-4 asst. UN/WHO, Geneva, 1962-64; pvt. sec. Arthur Wiesenberger, NYC, 1966-70; v.p. Alex Brown & Sons, NYC, 1970-75; 1st v.p. Butcher & Singer, NYC, 1975-89; pres. Claire Longden Assocs., Rhinebeck, NY, 1989-98. Adj. prof. fin. planning NYU, 1981-82. Conf. spkr. 1980-86; contbr. articles to profl. jours. Bd. dirs. No. Dutchess Hosp., Rhinebeck, 1989-98, pres., 1995-96; bd. dirs. Cross River Healthcare, 1997-98, No. Dutchess Hosp. Found., 1997-99, Wilderstein Preservation, 2000— Named one of Top Planners Nationwide, Money mag., 1987. Mem. Inst. CFPs (nat. bd. dirs. 1984-86, founder, NYC chpt. 1982-86, N.E. regional dir. 1985-86, bd. of ethics 1993-95, CFP of Yr. 1984), Womens Bond Club NY (pres. 1982-84), Inst. Am. Fin. Planners (bd. dirs. 1983-85), Registry Fin. Planning Practitioners, Rotary (pres. Rhinebeck chpt. 1993-94). Avocations: gardening, swimming, walking, riding, skiing.

LONGENECKER, LUANN F., music educator, department chairman; b. Harrisburg, Pa., June 25, 1955; d. Robert B. and Janice C Flickinger; m. Fred E. Longenecker, Nov. 5, 1977; children: Marc R., Eric J. BS in Elem. Edn., Lebanon Valley Coll., 1977; postgrad., Westminster Choir Coll., Princeton, N.J., 2005. Early childhood music tchr. Westminster Conservatory Music Rider U., Princeton, NJ, 1988—, early childhood dept. head, 2003—. Dir.: (handbell choir) Cornwall County (UK) Music Festival (Distinction award received for group, 2001); musician (piano accompanist): Music in the Parks - Disney World, Orlando FL. Organist Middlebush (N.J.) Ref. Ch., 1996—2003, handbell choirs dir., 1997—, Rutgers Cmty. Christian Homeshool Handbells, Somerset, NJ, 2002—05. Mem.: Nat. Assn. Edn. Young Children, Am. Orff Schulwerk Assn. Office: Westminster Choir Coll 101 Walnut Ln Princeton NJ 08540 Office Phone: 609-921-7104. Business E-Mail: llongenecker@rider.edu.

LONGENECKER, MARTHA W., museum director; BA in Art, UCLA; MFA, Claremont Grad. Sch.; studied with Millard Sheets, Shoji Hamada, Tatsuzo Shimaoka. Owner ceramics studio, Claremont, Calif.; prof. art, now prof. emerita San Diego State U.; founder, dir. Mingei Internat. Mus., San Diego. Coord. editing, design and prodn. of exhbn. documentary publs.; condr. tours. Contbr. chpts. to books; developer videotapes; exhibited at

Dalzell Hatfield Galleries. San Diego State U. Found. grantee, 1967, Calif. State U. Rsch. grantee, 1978; recipient Disting. Alumna award Claremont Grad. Sch., 1980, Essence of Life award ElderHelp of San Diego, 1993, Living Legacy award Women's Internat. Ctr., 1994, Women of Distinction award Soroptimist Internat. of La Jolla, 1994, Headliner of Yr. Art, San Diego Press Club, 1998, Disting. Svc. medal, San Diego State U., 1998, Reischauer Internat. Edn. award, Japan Soc. San Diego and Tijuana, 1999, San Diego Women Who Mean Bus. award, Foley Vardner Attys. at Law, San Diego Bus. Jour., 2000, Gold Rays with Rosette, Order of Rising Sun, Emperor of Japan, 2003, Golden Hanger Spl. award, Fashion Careers of Calif. Coll., 2004. Office: Mingei Internat Mus Balboa Park 1439 El Prado San Diego CA 92101-1617 also: Mingei International Museum 1439 El Prado San Diego CA 92101-1617

LONGINO, THERESA CHILDERS, nurse; b. Jacksonville, Fla., Feb. 17, 1959; d. Harold David and Eleanor Theresa (McHarg) Childers; m. Matthew Ray Longino, July 11, 1987 (dec.) Student, Stetson U., 1977—78; ADN, Fla. C.C., Jacksonville, 1981; student, U. North Fla., 1985—86; BSN, U. Phoenix, 2000. RN, Fla. Nurse Meth. Hosp., Jacksonville, 1981, Meml. Med. Ctr., Jacksonville, 1981—86, Good Samaritan Home Health, Jacksonville, 1986, Kimberly Nurses, Jacksonville, 1986, St. Vincents Med. Ctr., Jacksonville, 1986—. Catechist Prince of Peace Cath. Ch., Jacksonville, 1990-91, 97-98, 2006-; lectr. reader, 1991—, youth min., 1996 Mem. Jacksonville Jaguars Booster Club, Sigma Theta Tau (Omicron Delta chpt.) Republican. Roman Catholic. Home: 4135 Hudnall Rd Jacksonville FL 32207-5766 E-mail: tclongino@webtv.net.

LONGLEY, MARJORIE WATTERS, newspaper executive; b. Lockport, N.Y., Nov. 2, 1925; d. J. Randolph and Florence Lucille (Craine) Watters; m. Ralph R. Longley, Oct. 1, 1949 (dec.). BA in English with highest honors cum laude, St. Lawrence U., 1947. Sports editor, feature writer Lockport Union Sun and Jour., 1945; with N.Y. Times, N.Y.C., 1948-88, asst. to v.p. consumer mktg., 1975-78, circulation sales mgr., 1978-79, sales dir., 1979-81, dir. pub. affairs, 1981-88; pres. Gramercy Internat., Inc. (mktg. and pub. rels.), N.Y.C., 1988—; assoc. pub. The Earth Times, N.Y.C., 1996—. Dir. pub. affairs and pub. info., N.Y.C. Off-Track Betting Corp., 1990-94; mem. Nat. Newspapers' Readership Coun., 1979-82; mem. adv. coun. API, 1980-85. Author: America's Taste, 1960. Trustee St. Lawrence U., 1969-75, 77—; chmn. bd. dirs. Am. Forum for Global Edn., 1977-98, chmn. emerita, 1999—; pres. N.Y. City Adult Edn. Coun., 1974-77, Grmercy Pk. Lot Owners Assn., Inc., 1995—; mem. N.Y. State Adv. Coun. for Vocat. Edn, 1976-81, postsecondary edn., 1978-81, Mayor's Coun. Environment of N.Y.C., 1983-96; bd. dirs. Nat. Charities Info. Bur., 1983-96, Literacy Ptnrs., Inc., 1996—; chmn. 42d St. Edn., Theatre, Culture, 1984-88, chmn. emeritus, 1988—. Mem. Nat. Inst. Social Scis., Am. Mgmt. Assn. (nat. mktg. coun. 1972-89, bd. dirs. 1986-88), Nat. Arts Club, Overseas Press Club, Phi Beta Kappa. Democrat. Baptist. Office: Gramercy Internat Inc 34 Gramercy Park E New York NY 10003-1731

LONGMAID, KATE JESSAMYN, psychologist; b. Bryn Mawr, Pa., Oct. 7, 1960; d. Deborah Flint and David Dunlop Longmaid; m. Stephen Christopher Baad, Sept. 1, 1985; children: Olivia Longmaid Baad, Alexander Longmaid Baad. BA in Psychology and Art, U. Mich., 1983; MEd in Clin. Psychology, U. Va., Charlottesville, 1988, PhD in Clin. Psychology, 1994. Lic. psychologist Vt., 1994. Dir. ctr. for psychol. svcs. St. Michael's Coll., Colchester, Vt., 1994—95, adj. lectr. in psychology, 1995—96; pvt. practice Burlington, Vt., 1995—; clin. asst. prof. dept. family practice U. Vt. Coll. Medicine, Burlington, 1999—2003, group therapist, coping together project, dept. psychology, 1999—2002, course co-leader, 1997—2000; predoctoral fellow in psychology Dartmouth Med. Sch., Lebanon, NH, 1992—93, postdoctoral fellow in psychology, 1993—94, adj. asst. prof. psychiatry, 1995—98; group therapist, cancer patient support program Fletcher Allen Health Care, Burlington, 2003—04. Contbr. articles to profl. jours. Bd. dirs. Child Care Resource, Williston, Vt., 1996—97. Mem.: APA, Vt. Psychol. Assn. Office: 166 Battery St Burlington VT 05401 Office Phone: 802-651-7535.

LONGMAN, KAREN A., higher education administrator; b. Washington, Apr. 7, 1952; d. Ernest Retallick Longman and Marion Haefele. BA, Albion Coll., 1974; MA, Trinity Evangelical Divinity Sch., Deerfield, Ill., 1976, U. Mich., 1977, PhD, 1980. With Social Rsch. Ctr. U. Mich., Ann Arbor, 1977-79; dir. Christian edn. St. Andrews United Ch. of Christ, Dexter, Mich., 1977-80; v.p. Coun. Christian Colls. and Univs., Washington, 1980-99; v.p., dean of faculty Greenville (Ill.) Coll., 1999—2005; prof. higher edn. Azusa Pacific U., Calif., 2006—. Project coord. HarperCollins Textbook Series, San Francisco, 1987-99; co-dir. Nat. Assessment Project, Washington, 1994-99; mem. steering com. Exec. Leadership Devel. Inst., Washington, 1996—. Mem. editl. bd.: Rsch. on Christian Higher Edn., 1994—2001. Elder, tchr. 4th Presbyn. Ch., Washington, 1986-92; vol. Folger Shakespeare Theater, 1988-99; bd. mem. Nat. Ctr. Leadership, Washington, 1995-99, English Lang. Inst., China, 1992—, Intervarsity Christian Fellowship, 2002-. Business E-Mail: karen.longman@greenville.edu.

LONGMIRE, VENUS DELOYSE, minister; b. Greenville, Ala., July 21, 1945; d. James Wilbert and Estelle Golson Longmire; m. Melvin Robinson II, July 22, 1966 (div. Nov. 1975); 1 child, Melvin Longmire Robinson III; m. Amon Olugbala Ra, July 28, 2000. BS, Livingstone Coll., 1965; MSW, Ind. U., 1970; M in Theology, Emory U., 1982; D in Theology (hon.), U. Life Ch. Inst., San Fafael, Calif., 1989; PhD, Columbia Pacific U., 1989; D in Divinty (hon.), New Covenant Inst., 1995. Family svcs. supr. City of Atlanta Housing Authority, 1973—76; v.p. contract develop. Longmire Coal Corp., Knoxville, Tenn., 1976—86; dir. religious develop. Ala. State U., Montgomery, 1987—90; med. social worker State of Ala. Dept. Pub. Health, Hayneville, 1991—92; dir. min. The Sisterhood, Inc., Greenville, 1992—. Grant writer cons., 1965—; cons. energy develop. Del Kijaico Inc., Wilmington, Del., 1990—2002. Author: (prose) As We Are, So Is Our World, 1982; author, editor: Mother's Voice: Lost Writings of Mary, 2003. Mem. Hist. Perservation Soc., Montgomery, 1999—2003; advisor, sponsor Saving Our Cmty. & Kids, Greenville High, Ala. Named Cmty. Advocate, City of Atlanta, 1975; named one of Women in Bus., Knoxville Jour., 1983; recipient Ala. Treasure Forestry award, Forestry Commn., USDA, 2003. Mem.: So. Proverty Law Ctr., Coun. on Aging (lobbyist 1995—), Nat. Assn. Social Workers (lobbyist 1983—). Democrat. Methodist. Avocations: running, chess. Office: New Covenant Inst Human Svc Ministries 236 W Commerce St Greenville AL 36037 Office Phone: 334-657-9467. E-mail: venuslongmire@aol.com.

LONGO, PERIE JANE, marriage and family therapist; b. Cin., Ohio, Dec. 7, 1940; d. James Cecil Perry and Nancy Clare Boyce; m. Philip James Longo, June 2001; children: Dana Francis, Cecil Ann. BA, Mt. Mary Coll., Milw., Wis., 1962; MA, U. Calif., Los Angeles, 1967; PhD, Sierra U., Los Angeles, 1986. Tchr. speech commn. U. Calif., Los Angeles, 1967—68; h.s. tchr. Los Angeles Sch. Dist., 1963—67; tchr. speech commn. Brooke Inst., Santa Barbara, 1972—82; pvt. practice Santa Barbara, Calif., 1982—; poetry tchr. Calif. Poets in Sch., Santa Barbara, 1982—; dir. poetry therapy Sanctuary Psychiat. Ctrs., Santa Barbara, 1992—, Hospice of St. Barbara, Santa Barbara, 2002—. Author: (book) Milking the Earth, 1986, The Privacy of Wind, 1997. Chmn. poetry com. Nuc. Age Peace Found., 1996—. Mem.: Calif. Assn. Marriage and Family Therapy, Nat. Assn. for Poetry Therapy (pres. 2005—, exec. dir. 2003—05, v.p. 1996—2000, Outstanding Achievement award 1998). Avocations: hiking, writing. Home: 987 Barcelona Dr Santa Barbara CA 93105 Office: 800 Garden St Ste I Santa Barbara CA 93105

LONGOBARDO, ANNA KAZANJIAN, engineering executive; b. N.Y.C. d. Aram Michael and Zarouhy (Yazejian) Kazanjian; m. Guy S. Longobardo, July 12, 1952; children: Guy A., Alicia. Student, Barnard Coll., 1947; BSME, Columbia U., 1949, MSME, 1952. Sr. systems engr. Am. Bosch Arma Corp., Garden City, NY, 1950-65; rsch. sect. head Sperry Rand Corp., Gt. Neck, NY, 1965-68, rsch. sect. head systems mgmt., 1968-73; mgr. engring. personnel utilization Sperry Corp., Gt. Neck, 1973-77, mgr. systems mgmt. program planning, 1977-81, mgr. planning systems mgmt. group, 1981-82, dir. tech. svc. sys. devel., 1982-89, dir. field engring., 1989-93; dir. strategic initiatives Unysis Corp., Gt. Neck, 1993-95; bd. dirs. Engring. Found. Gateway Engring. Edn. Coalition, 1998—, also bd. dirs.; vice chmn. Engring. Conf. Found. Bd., 2001—04. Chmn. exec. compensation com. Woodward-Clyde Group, Denver, 1989-97. Contbr. articles to profl. publs. Trustee Columbia U., N.Y.C., 1990-96, trustee emerita, 1996—; mem. Columbia Engring. Coun., 1987—, chmn., 1987-91; vice chmn. Bronxville (N.Y.) Planning Bd.; chmn. Bronxville Design Rev. Com., 1993—; pres. Soc. Columbia Grads., 1998-2000. Recipient hon. citation Wilson Coll. Centennial, 1970, Alumni medal for conspicuous svc. Columbia U., 1980, Egleston medal for disting. engring. achievement Columbia U., 1997; named One of 100 N.Y. Women of Influence, New York Woman mag., 1986. Fellow Soc. Women Engrs. (founder, pioneer); mem. AIAA (sr.), ASME (sr.), Columbia U. Engring. Alumni Assn. (pres. 1977-81), Columbia U. Alumni Fedn. (pres. 1981-85), Bronxville Field Club.

LONGORIA, EVA (EVA JACQUELINE LONGORIA, EVA LONGORIA CHRISTOPHER), actress; b. Corpus Christi, Tex., Mar. 15, 1975; m. Tyler Christopher, Jan. 20, 2002 (div. Jan. 19, 2005). BS in Kinesiology, Tex. A&M-Kingsville. Actress (TV series) The Young and the Restless, 2001—03 (ALMA award for Outstanding Actress in a Daytime Drama), L.A. Dragnet, 2003, Desperate Housewives, 2004— (co-recipient, Outstanding Performance by an Ensemble in a Comedy Series, Screen Actors Guild award, 2005, 2006), (video) Snitch'd, 2003, Señorita Justice, 2004, (TV films) The Dead Will tell, 2004, (films) The Sentinel, 2006, actress, co-prodr. Carlita's Secret, 2004, co-prodr., performer (variety show, video) Hot Tamales Live: Spicy, Hot and Hilarious, 2003; performer: (Broadway plays) What the Rabbi Saw; guest appearances Beverly Hills, 90210, 2000, host Nat. Coun. La Raza ALMA awards, 2006. Named Miss Corpus Christi, 1998; named one of Ten New Faces to Watch, Variety, 2004, Fall's TV's Hot 11, USA Today, 2004, New Faces of Fall, TV Guide, 2004, Hot 100 for 2004, Maxim Mag., 2004, 25 Most Beautiful People, People en Espanol's; recipient Person of Yr., Nat. Coun. La Raza ALMA award (Am. Latin Media Arts), 2006. Address: Desperate Housewives Touchstone Televison 100 University City Plaza Bldg 2128 Ste Universal City CA 91608

LONGSTREET, WILMA S., retired education educator; b. NYC, July 3, 1935; d. Hyman Steinberg and Estelle Rosa; widowed; stepchildren: Patricia, Robert, Richard Engle. BA, Hunter Coll., 1956; MS, Ind. U., 1968, PhD, 1970. Cert. tchr., N.Y.C. Asst. prof. U. Ill., Champaign/Urbana, 1970-72; from assoc. prof. to prof. edn. U. Mich., Flint and Ann Arbor, 1972-78; dean, prof. edn. DePaul U., Chgo., 1978-82; dean edn. U. New Orleans, 1982-85, prof. curriculum and instrn., 1982—2004. Mem. Coll. and Univ. Faculty Assembly, 1970—, pres., 1999; with online doctoral program Walden U., 2004—; cons. in field Author: Aspects of Ethnicity, 1978, The Leaders and the Led, 1979; co-author: A Design for Social Education, 1972, (with Shirley H. Engle) Curriculum for a New Millennium, 1993; contbr. over 70 articles to profl. jours. Mem. Profs. of Curriculum (factotum, chair nominating com. 2001), Phi Delta Kappa. Democrat. Unitarian-Universalist. E-mail: wlongstr@walden.edu.

LONGSTRETH-BROWN, KATHRYN, retired museum administrator; b. Denver, Oct. 21, 1934; d. Lawrence Tracy Brown and Esther Longstreth; children: Jennifer G. Gates, Theodore O. Gates. BA, Oberlin Coll., Ohio, 1956; EdM, Harvard U., Cambridge, Mass., 1967. Head registrar Portland (Oreg.) Art Mus., 1973—86; chief registrar Fine Arts Mus. of San Francisco, 1986—90; mus. registrar U. N.Mex. Art Mus., Albuquerque, 1990—99; dir. divsn. collection svcs. and access Colo. Hist. Soc., Denver, 1999—2001; ret. Sect. editor: book The New Registration Methods, 1998. Bd. dirs. ACLU, 1976—86. Recipient Dudley-Wilkinson award, Am. Assn. Mus. Registrars, 1998; fellow, NEA, 1980. Mem.: Mountain Plains Mus. Assn. (mem. registrars com. 1990—2006, bd. dirs. 1993—99, mem. nominating com. 1993—99, Hugo G. Rodek award 2003, Suzanne Cowan and Reba Jones award (Mountain Plains divsn.) 2004), Am. Assn. Mus. (mem. accreditation vis. com. 1993—2006, councilor-at-large 1983—86).

LONGSWORTH, ELLEN LOUISE, art historian, consultant; b. Auburn, Ind., Aug. 21, 1949; d. Robert Smith and Alice Louise (Whitten) L.; m. Frederic Sanderson Stott, Sept. 1, 1973 (div. 1981); m. Joseph Nicholas Teta, June 15, 1991. BA, Mt. Holyoke Coll., 1971; MA, U. Chgo., 1976; PhD, Boston U., 1987. Trainer, designer Polaris Enterprises Corp., Quincy, Mass., 1981-82, asst. v.p., 1982-84, cons., 1989-93; from asst. prof. to assoc. prof. Merrimack Coll., N. Andover, Mass., 1985-95, prof., 1995—, chmn. dept., 1993-2000, 2006—. Adj. instr. art and art history Bradford Coll., Haverhill, Mass., 1975-80; vis. lectr. art history Lowell (Mass.) U., 1981-82, Boston U., 1982-86, 88, 91, Babson Coll., Wellesley, Mass., 1984-85. Active Merrimack Valley Coun. on the Arts and Humanities, Haverhill, 1975-78, Friends of Kimball Tavern, Bradford Coll., Haverhill, 1975-80, Haverhill Arts Commn., 1996-2002; bd. dirs. Winnekenni Found., Haverhill, 1990— Faculty Devel. grantee Merrimack Coll., 1989-90, 92-93, 95-97, 2002; Kress Summer Travel grantee Boston U., 1980, 86;, Ciejek in-house fellow for humanistic rsch., 1998; Boston U. fellow, 1980-82, 85; Isabella Stewart Gardner Mus. intern, Boston, 1979-80. Mem. Coll. Art Assn., South-Ctrl. Renaissance Conf. (exec. com. 1998-2002), Italian Art Soc., Renaissance Soc. Am., Mediterranean Studies Assn. Republican. Methodist. Avocations: reading, playing the piano, painting and drawing, weight training, swimming. Home: 649 Main St Haverhill MA 01830-2647 Office: Merrimack Coll North Andover MA 01845 Business E-Mail: ellen.Longsworth@merrimack.edu.

LONGTON, BRENDA JO, music educator; b. Gold Beach, Oreg., June 26, 1958; adopted d. Edward Joseph and Vernita May Longton, d. June Reed. M in Music Edn., Western Oreg. U., Monmouth, 1989. Std. tchr. cert. music K-12 Tchrs. Stds. and Practices Commn. Oreg., 1989. Tchr. Salem Acad., Oreg., 1981—84, Sonshine Sch., Oreg., 1985—86; substitute tchr. Salem-Keizer Pub. Schs., Oreg., 1986—90; tchr. Yamhill-Carlton Sch. Dist., Oreg., 1991—; ch. choir dir. Zion Luth. Ch., Newberg, Oreg., 2001—. Dir. Carlton Sch. Theatre, 1991—, Yamhill-Carlton HS Drama Dept., 2003—; advisor Yamhill-Carlton HS Playmakers, 2004—. Dir., prodr. (musical theatre). Mem.: Ednl. Theatre Assn. Republican. Avocations: music, drama, travel, history, reading. Office: Yamhill-Carlton School District PO Box 68 Yamhill OR 97148 Office Phone: 503-852-7161 1283. Office Fax: 503-852-7364. Business E-Mail: longtonb@ycsd.k12.or.us.

LONGVAL, GLORIA, artist; b. Tampa, Fla., Feb. 7, 1931; d. Arthur Longval and Beatrice Beiro; m. Dick Ralph (dec.); children: David Longval Ralph(dec.), Rima Renée Ralph. Student, Art Students League, N.Y.C., 1952—53, Nat. Acad. Design, 1955—59. Instr. painting U. Judaism, L.A., 1968—71; guest instr. L.A. Children's Mus., 1987—88. Represented in permanent collections L.A. County Mus. Art, Riverside Art. Mus., Calif., Museo Nacional Palacio Bellas Artes, Havana, Cuba, exhibitions include Paideia Gallery, L.A., London U., England. Recipient 1st prize in multimedia, San Bernardina (Calif.) Mus., 1983, 1st prize, Gannett Billboard Competition, L.A., 1995. Mem.: Brewery Art Assn. (bd. dirs. 1999—2001), Commn. Feminile de Los Angeles. Home and Studio: 638 Moulton Ave Los Angeles CA 90031 Office Phone: 323-441-0241.

LONGWELL, A. KELTON See LONGWELL, KELLY

LONGWELL, KELLY (A. KELTON LONGWELL), lawyer; b. Baton Rouge, La., Oct. 8, 1969; BS, Tulane U., 1991; JD, La. State U., 1994; LLM in Taxation, NYU, 1995. Bar: La. 1994, cert.: La. Bd. Legal Specialization (tax law specialist). With Elkins PLC, New Orleans; assoc. McGlinchey Stafford PLLC, New Orleans, ptnr. Bd. dir. New Orleans Ctr. Creative Arts (NOCCA), 2002; sec., bd. dir. Neighborhood Devel. Found., 2001—02. Mem.: New Orleans Bar Assn., ABA, La. State Bar Assn. Office: McGlinchey Stafford PLLC 643 Magazine St New Orleans LA 70130 Office Phone: 504-596-2757. Office Fax: 504-596-2800. E-mail: klongwell@mcglinchey.com.*

LONSTEIN, SHOSHANNA, fashion designer; b. NYC; BA, UCLA, 1997. Fashion designer, NYC, 1998—; contbr. editor Cosmopolitan, 1999. Fashion cons. E! network and WNBC's Today in NY.

LOO, BEVERLY JANE, publishing executive; b. L.A. d. Richard Y. and Bessie E. Sue Loo. BA, U. Calif., Berkeley. Dir. subs. rights Prentice-Hall, Inc., N.Y.C., 1957—59; fiction editor McCall's mag., 1959—62; exec. editor and dir. subs. rights, gen. books div. McGraw-Hill Book Co., N.Y.C., 1962—82; pres. Beverly Jane Loo Assocs., Inc., N.Y.C., 1982—85; sr. editor, dir. subs. rights World Almanac Pharos Books, N.Y.C., 1985—88; dir. mktg. and subs. rights Paragon House, N.Y.C., 1988—91; dir. mktg. and sales Thomasson-Grant, Charlottesville, Va., 1991—93; dir. pub. and comm. inst. U. Va. Sch. Continuing Edn. and Profl. Studies, Charlottesville, 1993—2004; asst. prof., dir. Masters of Profl. Studies in Pub. George Washington U., Coll. Profl. Studies, Washington, 2005—. Mem.: U. Va. Faculty Club, Va. Writers Club, Overseas Press Club (N.Y.C.), Arts Club (London). Home: Lewis & Clark Sq # 701 250 W Main St Charlottesville VA 22902-5072 Office: George Washington U Coll Profl Studies 805 21st St NW Ste 301 Washington DC 20052 Office Phone: 202-994-3004. Business E-Mail: bevloo@gwu.edu.

LOO, KATHERINE HAUGHEY, nonprofit organization consultant; b. Concordia, Kans., June 24, 1939; d. James M. and Katherine (Hurd) Haughey; m. Lester B. Loo, June 14, 1961; children: Susan Loo Pattee, James O. BA in Polit. Sci., U. Kans., 1961. Pres. Jr. League, Colorado Springs, Colo., 1974-75, Brockhurst Boy's Ranch, Colorado Springs, Colo., 1975-77; dir. Assn. Jr. Leagues, N.Y.C., 1976-78; pres., founder docent aux., chair capital campaign Cheyenne Mt. Zoo, Colorado Springs, 1969-94; dir. UMB Bank Colo., Colorado Springs, 1994-99. Mem. Colorado Springs Urban Renewal Bd., 1979-85; pres. Colo. Women's Forum, 1990-91; founder, bd. dirs. Colo. Women's Found.; hon. trustee Cheyenne Mt. Zoo, 1994—, Colo. Nature Conservancy, 1998—; bd. dirs., v.p. Pikes Peak Cmty. Found., 1998—; co-chmn. Heart of the West Cap. Campaign. Composer, performer piano music. Councilwoman City of Colorado Springs, 1979-85; vice chair Colo. Commn. on Higher Edn., Denver, 1985-87; trustee, chair music dir. search com. Colorado Springs Symphony, 1994-95; mem. Colorado Springs Leadership Inst., 1997—. Recipient Silver Bell award Assistance League, Colorado Springs, 1975. Mem. Broadmoor Garden Club (civic chair 1992-94), Phi Beta Kappa. Avocations: weaving, piano, hiking, biking, composing. Home: 19 Northgate Rd Colorado Springs CO 80906-4331

LOO, LYNN (YUEH-LIN), chemical engineer; BSE in materials sci. and engring., U. Pa., 1996, BSE in chemical engring., 1996; MA in chemical engring., Princeton U., 1998, PhD in chemical engring., 2001. Asst. prof. dept. chemical engring. U. Tex., Austin, Ctr. Nano-and Molecular Sci. and Tech., Tex. Materials Inst. Contbr. articles to profl. jour. Named one of Top 100 Young Innovators, MIT Tech. Review, 2004; recipient Frank J. Padden award for excellence in polymer rsch., APS, 2000, Camille & Henry Dreyfus New Faculty award, 2002, DuPont Young Prof. award, 2003, Career award, NSF, 2004; Porter Ogden Jacobus fellow, Princeton U., 2000. Office: U Tex Dept Chemical Engring CPE 4422 1 University Station C0400 Austin TX 78712-1062 Business E-Mail: lloo@che.utexas.edu.

LOO, NANCY, newscaster; b. Hong Kong; m. Brian Jenkins; 2 children. BA in Broadcast Journalism, U. Oreg. Former journalist English-language news stations, Hong Kong and Japan, NY 1 News, NYC, 1992—94; former news anchor, reporter WABC-TV, NYC, 1994—2001; anchor morning and noon newscasts WFLD-TV (Fox Chicago), 2001—. Named Reporter/Anchor of the Yr., Women in Cable, 1994; recipient Emmy awards, NY Gov.'s award of excellence, 1992. Office: Fox Chicago WFLD-TV 205 N Michigan Ave Chicago IL 60601

LOOK, JANET K., psychologist; b. Bklyn., Mar. 11, 1944; d. Harry and Isabelle (Chernoff) Kaplan; m. Willian Marel; children from previous marriage: Howard, Erika(dec.). AB, NYU, 1964; EdM, Rutgers U., 1967, EdD, 1976. Lic. psychologist; cert. sch. psychologist. Asst. examiner Ednl. Testing Svc., Princeton, NJ, 1964-66; instr. Rutgers U., New Brunswick, NJ, 1968-69; psychologist Seattle Pub. Schs., 1991—; pvt. practice Seattle, 1993—. Lectr. U. Conn., Waterbury, 1973-91; appearances on various TV and radio shows including the Today Show; interviews include Litchfield County Times, 1987, Waterbury Rep.-Am., 1983-87, Manchester Jour. Inquirer, 1986, Danbury News-Times, 1985; presenter APA, San Francisco, 1991, Nation's Concern and Its Response, U. Wis., Milw., 1991, Nat. Assn. Sch. Psychologists, Dallas, 1991, Divorce Issues Inst., So. Conn. State U., New Haven, 1989. Author: (with others) The Troubled Adolescent, 1991; contbr. articles to newspapers, including N.Y. Times, MSNBC. Mem. APA, Wash. State Psychol. Assn., Wash. State Assn. Sch. Psychologists (area rep., bd. dirs. 1991-93). Avocations: sailing, fishing, hiking, motorcycling, travel. Office: 3626 NE 45th St 301 Seattle WA 98105 Personal E-mail: janetklook@aol.com.

LOOMER, MANDEN JANE, elementary school educator; b. Springfield, Mo., Apr. 18, 1977; d. Rodney and Kathleen Loomer. B in Elem. Edn., Drury Coll., Springfield, 1999; EdM, Ga. State U., Atlanta, 2002. 3rd grade tchr. Immaculate Conception Elem. Sch., Springfield, 2000—01; reading tchr. Fordland Elem. Sch., Mo., 2002—06; reading specialist Springfield Pub. Schs., Mo., 2006—. Mem.: Internat. Reading Assn. Home: 1721 E Camino Alto Springfield MO 65804

LOOMIS, CAROL J., journalist; b. Marshfield, Mo., June 25, 1929; d. Harold and Mildred (Case) Junge; m. John R. Loomis, Mar. 19, 1960; children: Barbara, Mark. Student, Drury Coll., 1947-49; B in Journalism, U. Mo., 1951. Editor Maytag News, Maytag Co., Newton, Iowa, 1951-54; rsch. assoc. Fortune Mag., N.Y.C., 1954-58, assoc. editor, 1958-68, mem. bd. editors, 1968—2002, editor-at-large, 2003—. Office: Fortune Mag 1271 Avenue Of The Americas New York NY 10020-1300

LOOMIS, JANICE KASZCZUK, artist; b. New Britain, Conn., June 26, 1952; d. William and Pauline Teresa (Archacki) Kaszczuk; m. Richard Wager Loomis, Oct. 1, 1977 (div. 2000); children: Richard Ward, Brian William. BA cum laude, U. Hartford, 1987. Recipient award for sculpture Acad. Artists Assn., 1994, Honor award for sculpture Acad. Artists Nat. Juried Exhbn., 1996, Gilroy Roberts scholarship Am. Numismatic Assn., 1994, 96. Mem. Conn. Women Artists (bd. dirs. 1997-99), Soc. Conn. Sculptors (founding pres. 1992-93, sec. 1994-95), Am. Medallic Sculpture Assn. (bd. dirs. 1994-97, sec. 1996-97), Canton Artist's Guild. Avocation: people. Office Phone: 860-402-1928. Personal E-mail: janloomis@gmail.com, loomisjan@sbcglobal.net.

LOOMIS, REBECCA C., psychologist; b. New London, Conn., Nov. 9, 1959; d. Aubrey Kingsley and Marillyn Louise (Dirks) Loomis; m. DeWitt Montgomery Smith, Nov. 24, 1984 (div. Sept. 1997); children: Adrienne Kingsley Smith, Walker Loomis Smith; m. Jack G. Gental, July 9, 2005; stepchildren: Alexander Gentul, Robert Gentul. BA in Sociology and Polit. Sci., Vanderbilt U., 1981; MEd, U. Houston, 1990, PhD in Counseling Psychology, 2004. Group rep. Home Life Ins., Houston, 1981—83; sr. account exec. CNA Ins. Co., Houston, 1983—87; rsch. asst. dept. ednl. psychology U. Houston, 1988—90, 1991—93, tchg. asst., 1993, rsch. asst. Clearwater, Tex., 1993; acad. advisor Montclair (N.J.) State U., 2001—02; psychology intern Assn. Help of Retarded Children, NYC, 2002—03; prin. investigator St. Luke's-Roosevelt Hosp. Manhattan Ctr. for Pain Mgmt., 1999—2004; clinician Assn. for Help of Retarded Children, NYC, 2003—. Group facilitator children div. parents, counselor Houston Child Guidance, 1990; counselor learning support svcs. U. Houston, 1990, counselor counseling and testing svcs., 1994—95; facilitator mentorship program Wildwood Elem. Sch., Mountain Lakes, NJ, 1996. Contbr. articles to various profl. jours. Hospice aid Casa de Ninos Hospice, Houston, 1986—87; vol. Houston Area Women's Ctr., 1992—93, 1994—95; cmty. aid Mountain Lakes, 1999—; vol.

organizer grief workshop for September 11, 2001 attacks Cmty. Ch. Mem.: APA, N.J. Psychol. Assn. Democrat. Home and Office: 249 Morris Ave Mountain Lakes NJ 07046 E-mail: beckyloomis@earthlink.net.

LOONEY, CLAUDIA ARLENE, health facility administrator; b. Fullerton, Calif., June 13, 1946; d. Donald F. and Mildred B. Schneider; m. James K. Looney, Oct. 8, 1967; 1 child, Christopher K. BA, Calif. State U., 1969. Dir. youth YWCA No. Orange County, Fullerton, Calif., 1967-70; dir. dist. Camp Fire Girls, San Francisco, 1971-73, asst. exec. dir. L.A., 1973-77; asst. dir. cmty. resources Childrens Hosp., L.A., 1977-80; dir. cmty. devel. Orthopaedic Hosp., L.A., 1980-82; sr. v.p. Saddleback Meml. Found./Saddleback Meml. Med. Ctr., Laguna Hills, Calif., 1982-92; v.p. planning and advancement Calif. Inst. Arts, Santa Clarita, Calif., 1992-96; pres. Northwestern Meml. Found., Chgo., 1996-99; sr. v.p. Childrens Hosp., L.A., 1999—. Instr. U. Calif., Irvine, Univ. Irvine; mem. steering com. U. Irvine. Steering com. United Way, L.A., 1984-86, bd. mem. Woodmark Forum, 2004—. Recipient Orange County Woman of Achievement award, YWCA, 2004. Fellow Assn. Healthcare Philanthropy (nat. chair-elect, chmn. program Nat. Edn. Conf. 1986, regional dir. 1985-89, 98, fin. com. 1988—, pres., com. chn. 1987—, Give To Life com. chmn. 1987-91, mid-west regional conf. chmn. 1998, Orange County Fund Raiser of Yr. 1992, L.A. County fund raiser of yr. 1996); mem. Nat. Soc. Fund Raising Execs. Found. (cert., vice chmn. 1985-90, chair 1993—, mem. Chgo. conf. com. 1997, 98), So. Calif. Assn. Hosp. Devel. (past pres., bd. dirs.), Profl. Ptnrs. (chmn. 1986, instr. 1988—), Philanthropic Ednl. Orgn. (past pres.), Assn. for Healthcare Profls. (regional conf. co-chmn. 2003), Assn. Fundraising Profls. (mem. internat. ethics com. 2003—), Orange County Women of Achievement. Avocations: swimming, sailing, photography. Office: Children's Hosp LA 4650 Sunset Blvd Ste 29 Los Angeles CA 90027 Office Phone: 323-671-3856.

LOOP, CHRISTINE E., elementary school educator; b. Patuxant, Md., Oct. 20, 1970; d. David E. and Jennifer M. Loop; m. Suchip Thitayan; children: Ahmi Dinh Thitayan, Rias Loop Thitayan. BS, James Madison U., Harrisonburg, Va., 1994; MA, George Wash. U., Washington, 2003. Cert. ESL tchr. Tex. Rsch. assoc. Nat. Clearinghouse for English Lang. Acquisition, Washington, 2001—03; tchr. Glasgow Mid. Sch., Alexandria, Va., 2003—. Mentor Glasgow Mid. Sch., Alexandria, Va., 2003—06; active Teach for Am., Roma, Tex., 1995—97; vol. US Peace Corps, Washington, 1998—2000, Nat. History Club, Alexandria, Va., 2004—06. Mem.: Internat. Reading Assn., Kappa Delta Pi (hon.). Democrat. Avocation: travel.

LOOPER, MARCIA LYNN, elementary school educator, consultant; b. Texarkana, Ark., May 6, 1954; d. Charles Benjamin and Nancy Nichols Graves; children: Scott Aaron, Cory Michael, Jonathan Reed. BS in Elem. Edn., U. Tex., Austin, 1976. Cert. tchr. gifted/talented Tex., tchr. Tex. Tchr. Spring Br. Ind. Sch. Dist., Houston, 1992—; trainer, first grade reading acad. Region IV Edn. Ctr., Houston, 1999—2004. Curriculum writer social studies, trainer social studies curriculum overview Spring Br. Ind. Sch. Dist., Houston, 1994—, trainer new tchr. inst., 1998—; adv. bd. Valley Oaks Elem. Sch. PTA, Houston, 1997—; trainer, first grade reading acad. Region IV Edn. Ctr., Houston, 1999—2004; trainer Steven Covey's Seven Habits for Highly Effective People, Houston, 1999—2000; cons., writer, reading specialist Classroom Connect, El Segundo, Calif., 2003—05; sponsor, trip leader to DC WorldStride, Charlottesville, Va., 2004—; presenter in field. Sponsor cmty. svc. projects Valley Oaks Elem. Student Coun., Houston, 2000—06; Houston Ambassador to Saudi Arabia; sunday sch. tchr., bible study leader, choir dir. Houston's First Bapt. Ch., 1981—92. Named Marcia Looper Day in her honor, Robert Eckels County Judge of Harris County, Tex., 2005, Elem. Tchr. of Yr., Spring Br. Ind. Sch. Dist., 2004—05; recipient Christa McAuliffe Excellence in Tchg. award, Houston West C. of C., 2005, Lifetime Mem. award, Valley Oaks PTA, 1999, Tchr. of Yr., Valley Oaks Elem. Sch., 2000—01, 2004—05. Mem.: Spring Br. Social Studies Coun. (corr.; v.p. 2006—), Tex. Gifted and Talented (corr.), Friends of Geography (corr.), Nat. Coun. Social Studies (corr.), Tex. Coun. of Social Studies (corr.). Avocations: reading, travel. Home: 1461 Woodhollow Dr #29203 Houston TX 77057 Office: Valley Oaks Elem Sch 8390 Westview Houston TX 77055 Office Phone: 713-365-4080. Office Fax: 713-365-4086. Personal E-mail: mlooper@aol.com. Business E-Mail: marcia.looper@springbranchisd.com.

LOOS, ROBERTA ALEXIS, advocate, artist, educator; b. Haddonfield, NJ, Dec. 14, 1943; d. John Thompson Loos and Margaret Gladous Browning; children: James Gray Kane, Alexis Browning Kane. B of Design in Art Edn., U. Fla., 1967. Cert. art edn. K-12 Fla. and Md. State Bds. Edn., 1968. Secondary art and English tchr. Montgomery County Pub. Schs., Silver Spring, Md., 1968—71; pres. Kane Corp. Consultants, Inc., 1982—. Mem. Fla. Arts Coun., 1981—85; mem. panel talent bank Nat. Endowment for the Arts, 1983; mem. Fine Arts Coun. Fla., 1981; adv. com. Art in Pub. Places, 1979; bd. dirs. Broward County Art in Pub. Places, 1981—83; chair Broward Arts Coun., 1981—83. Mem. publs. com. Broward County Hist. Commn., 1979; mem. pollutiuon control subcom. Broward County Charter Commn., 1974—75; mem. Broward County Pullution Control Bd., 1974—75, City of Ft. Lauderdale Charter Revision Bd., 1990—94; mem. Internat. Swimming Hall of Fame subcom. City of Ft. Lauderdale Gen. Obligation Bond Project, 1989—90. Mem.: Order of the Daus. of the King (life). Home: 2625 NE 26th Ct Fort Lauderdale FL 33306-1701

LOOSER, VICKIE BEARD, secondary school educator; b. LaGrange, Ga., Mar. 28, 1948; d. Herman Lee and Elsie Mae (Still) Beard; m. Charles Marvin Looser, Dec. 14, 1969; 1 child, Andrew Clinton. BA, West Ga. Coll., Carrollton, 1969; MEd, Auburn U., Ala., 1979, postgrad., 1981, Troy State U. Cert. tchr. Ala. Tchr. LaGrange (Ga.) City Schs., 1969-74, Springwood Sch., Lanett, Ala., 1975-81, Chambers County Schs., Valley, Ala., 1984-85, Southern Union State Coll., Valley, Ala., 1984—, Lanett City Schs., 1989—. Mem. NEA, Ala. Edn. Assn., Ala. Coun. for Social Studies, Ala. Hist. Soc., Lanett Edn. Assn. (v.p. 1993-94). Congregationalist. Avocations: reading, crafts. Office: Lanett High Sch 1301 S 8th Ave Lanett AL 36863-0349 Office Phone: 334-644-5965. Business E-Mail: vlooser@lanettcutyschools.org.

LOPATIN, CAROL KEESLER, artist; b. Spring Valley, N.Y., Oct. 16, 1934; d. Irving Verdin and Jessie Louise Keesler; m. Milton Lopatin, Apr. 5, 1963; 1 child, John David. BS, Skidmore Coll., 1956. Artist mem. Spectrum Gallery, Washington, 1985-93, Touchstone Gallery, Washington, 1996-2000, 2002-05; juried studio artist Arlington (Va.) Art Ctr., 1984-93, Torpedo Factory Art Ctr., Alexandria, Va., 1988—; participating artist Women in Art and Culture, Beijing, 1995. One-woman shows Spectrum Gallery, Washington, 1988, 91, 93, 20th Century Gallery, Williamsburg, Va., 1989, 95, Charles County C.C., La Plata, Md., 1992, Arlington (Va.) Art Ctr., 1993, Holden Gallery, Warren Wilson Coll., Swannanoa, N.C., 1996, Art Assn. Harrisburg, Pa., 1996, Touchstone Gallery, Washington, 1997, 99, 2002, 04, Warm Springs (Va.) Gallery, 1998, 99, Del. Ctr. for Contemporary Arts, Wilmington, 2000; exhibited in group shows Art League Gallery, Alexandria, Va., 1985-2006, Chrysler Mus., Norfolk, Va., 1990, 92, Strathmore Hall Found. Inc., Rockville, Md., 1991, 92, 94, 99, 2002, 04, Assoc. Artists and Milton Rhodes Galleries, Winston-Salem, N.C., 1992, Greater Reston (Va.) Arts Ctr., 1992, 94, 95, 97, Delaplaine Visual Arts Ctr., Frederick, Md., 1994, 95, 97, Adirondacks Art Ctr., Old Forge, N.Y., 1995, 97, 2004, Foothills Art Ctr., Golden, Colo., 1995, 96, 97, 99, Global Focus, Beijing, 1995, Gadsden (Ala.) Ctr. for Cultural Arts, 1995, Olin Fine Arts Gallery, Washington, Pa., 1996, Moss-Thorns Gallery Art, Ft. Hays U., Hays, Kans., 1996, Glenview Mansion, Rockville, Md., 2006, others; represented in permanent collections McGraw-Hill Cos., No. Va. C.C., George Washington U. Med. Coll., also corp. and pvt. collections. Recipient award Watercolor Soc. Ala., 1995, 99, 2003 Mem. Nat. Acrylic Painters Assn. (signature mem.), Nat. Watercolor Soc. (signature mem., 1st Combined award 1995, Past Pres. award 1999, award 2002), Pa. Watercolor Soc. (signature mem.), Watercolor Soc. Ala. (past signature mem.), Artists Equity (1st place award 1992, juror's award 1994), Art League Alexandria (numerous awards), Greater Reston Art Ctr., Rocky Mtn. Nat. Watermedia Soc., Ga. Watercolor Soc., Southern Watercolor Soc., Watercolor U.S.A. Honor Soc. Office: Torpedo Factory Art Ctr 105 N Union St Ste 301 Alexandria VA 22314-3217

LOPATTO, MARY A., lawyer; AB, Princeton U., 1976; JD, Catholic U., 1986. Bar: Pa. 1986, DC 1988. Mng. ptnr. DC office LeBoeuf, Lamb, Greene & MacRae LLP, Washington, chmn. ins. dept., chmn. Life Ins./Health Care Practice Group, co-chmn. Property-Casualty/Arbitration/Litig. Practice Group. Gen. counsel Women in Govt. Relations. Lectr. in field; contbr. Trustee Wyo. Seminary Preparatory Sch., Kingston, Pa. Mem.: Wilkes-Barre Law & Library Assn., AIDA US Reinsurance & Ins. Arbitration Soc. (pres.). Office: LeBoeuf Lamb Green & Mac Rae LLP 1875 Connecticut Ave NW Ste 1200 Washington DC 20009-5715 Office Phone: 202-986-8029. Office Fax: 202-986-8102. Business E-Mail: mxlopatt@llgm.com.

LOPER, LUCIA ANN, retired elementary school educator; b. Albany, Ga., Nov. 11, 1937; d. Andrew and Elizabeth Francis (Bacon) Wurst; m. Leo Gerald Loper (div. Oct. 1984); children: Valecia Ann, Sheri Lee. MusB, Wesleyan Coll., Macon, Ga., 1959. Lic. tchr. music edn. elem., high sch., Fla. Music tchr. Mil. Trail Sch., Palm Beach County Bd., West Palm Beach, Fla., 1959, Cen. Elem. Instrn. Sch., Palm Beach County Bd., West Palm Beach, 1961-65, Jupiter (Fla.) Elem. Sch., Palm Beach County Bd., 1966-70, Eisenhower Elem. Sch., Palm Beach County Bd., Lake Park, Fla., 1970-95, ret., 1995. Gen. chmn. Devel. of Opera for Schs. with Opera Lyrica, West Palm Beach, 1961-62; co-chmn. North County Music in Our Schs. Performance, Lake Worth, Fla., 1984. Active Music Team for Devel Palm Beach County Music Unified Curriculum, 1984, Palm Beach County Arts Council, 1975-76. Recipient Spotlight award Fla. Music Dir. mag., 1986. Mem. Music Educators Nat. Conf., Fla. Elem. Music Educators Assn. (hostess workshop Tampa), Palm Beach County Elem. Music Educators Assn., Am. Orff Schulwerk Assn., Sigma Alpha Iota. Republican. Home: PO Box 571 Jupiter FL 33468-0571

LOPES, LOLA LYNN, psychologist, educator; b. Jackson Heights, N.Y., Mar. 14, 1941; d. Ivan Correa and Elizabeth (Edgemon) L.; m. Gregg Clifford Oden, Apr. 18, 1980. BA, U. Redlands, 1962; MA, Calif. State U., Long Beach, 1971; PhD, U. Calif. San Diego, La Jolla, 1974. Asst. prof. psychology U. Wis., Madison, 1974-81, assoc. prof., 1981-87, prof., 1987-90, chmn. dept., 1988-90; Pomerantz prof. bus. U. Iowa, Iowa City, 1990—, assoc. dean undergrad. programs Coll. Bus., 1995—. Contbr. articles to profl. jours. Sloan Found. fellow, U. Chgo., 1981. Mem. Soc. for Judgement and Decision Making (pres. 1989-90), Psychonomic Soc., Cognitive Sci. Soc., Soc. for Math. Psychology, Am. Psychol. Soc., Sigma Xi. Home: 2021 Laurence Ct NE Iowa City IA 52240-9150 Office: U Iowa Dept Mgmt And Orgns Iowa City IA 52242

LOPES, MARIA FERNANDINA, commissioner; b. Ganda, Angola, Portugal, Dec. 12, 1934; came to U.S., 1963; d. Rodrigo do Carmo and Maria Jose Fernandes (Mendes) Marques; m. Fernandes Esteves Lopes, Aug. 11, 1962; children: Lisa Maria Lopes Moss, Mark Esteves Lopes. Student, Lisbon (Portugal) Comml. Inst., 1953, Massasoit Community Coll., Brockton, Mass., 1988. With archives dept. Portuguese Govt., Lisbon, 1958-62; congl. aide Congresswoman Margaret M. Heckler, Fall River, Taunton, Mass., 1972-74; mem. Taunton (Mass.) Sch. Com., 1976-93; commr., chairperson Bristol County, Mass., 1991—. Founder Day of Portugal, 1974. Avocations: travel, politics, antiques, music. Home: 28 Worcester St Taunton MA 02780-2041 Office: Office County Commissioners Superior Courthouse PO Box 208 Taunton MA 02780-0208

LOPES, MYRA AMELIA, writer; b. Nantucket, Mass., July 9, 1931; d. Leo Joseph and Mary Ellen (Moriarty) Powers; m. Curtis Linwood Lopes, June 25, 1955; children: Dennis, Sherry, Kathy, Curtis, Becky. BS, Bridgewater, 1954; diploma, Inst. Children's Lit., 1982, N.Y. Inst. Journalism, 1984. Cert. elem. educator Mass. Tchr. Fairhaven (Mass.) Sch. Sys., 1954-58; prin. Sheri Ka Kindergarten, Fairhaven, 1960-76; tchr. Oxford Sch., 1977—78, tchr. Title I, 1978—80; writer, 1984—. Author: Look Around You, 1990, Looking Back, 1991, Seeing It All, 1992, But Then There Was More, 1993, Captain Joshua Slocum: A Centennial Tribute, 1994, Captain Slocum's Life Before and After the Spray, 1997, The Rogers Legacy, 1997, The Castle on the Hill, 1998, My Town, 1999, Joshua Slocum: New World Columbus, 2001, Around the Kitchen Table, 2002, Architectural Treasures from the Rogers Mansion: The Michell House, 2002, Pa's Magic Pillow, 2003, Your Poland As Seen Through Our Eyes, 2004, New England Snow Covered Stonewalls, 2004, Fairhaven Improvement Association Updated History, 2005, Causy Goes to Summer Camp, 2005. Bd. dirs. Fairhaven Improvement Assn., 1986—, chair membership, 1986—96, pres., 1990—93; bd. dirs. YWCA, New Bedford, 1982—88, chair cmty. rels., 1982—83, nominating chair, 1983—84, chair pers. bd., 1984—88; trustee Millicent Libr., 1993—; bd. govs. Am. Biog. Instn., 1997—; pres. Heritage Ctr., 2004; v.p. bd. dirs. Millicent Libr., 2004; bd. dirs. Fairhaven HS Hall of Fame, 1999—. Named Woman of the Yr., New Bedford Std.-Times and cmty., 1999; named to Hall of Fame, Fairhaven H.S., 1997, America's Hall of Fame, 2003; recipient BSC Adrian Rondileau award for profl. achievement and comty. svc., 2005. Mem.: Bridgewater State Coll. Alumni Assn., Joshua Slocum Soc. Internat. (historian 1997—, bd. dirs.), Rotary (bd. dirs. 1998—99, v.p. 2000—, pres.-elect 2001, pres. Fairhaven chpt. 2002—03, Paul Harris fellow 2000, Internat. Peace prize 2003, Internat. Pres. citation 2003, Dist. 1090 Significant Achievement award 2003, Gt. Women of the 21st Century). Democrat. Roman Catholic. Avocations: gardening, reading, walking, crafts, music. Home: 71 Fort St Fairhaven MA 02719-2811 Personal E-mail: clopes7081@aol.com.

LOPES, ROSALY MUTEL CROCCE, astronomer, planetary geologist; b. Rio de Janeiro, Jan. 8, 1957; came to U.S., 1989; d. Walmir Crocce and Atir (Mutel) Lopes; m. Thomas Nicholas Gautier, III, Nov. 17, 1990 (div.); 1 child, Thomas N. Gautier. BSc in Astronomy, U. London, 1978, PhD in Physics, 1986. Curator Old Royal Obs., Greenwich, Eng., 1985-88; rsch. assoc. Vesuvius Obs., Naples, Italy, 1989; NRC rsch. assoc. Jet Propulsion Lab., Pasadena, Calif., 1989-91, rsch. scientist Galileo Project, 1990—2002, rsch. scientist Cassini Project, 2002—04, prin. scientist Cassini Project, 2004—. Mem. Volcanic Eruption Surveillance Team, U.K., 1981. Author: Volcanic Worlds, 2004, The Volcano Adventure Guide, 2005, numerous other works in sci. field. Recipient Latinas in Sci. award Commn. Feminil Mexicana Nat., L.A., 1990; named Woman of the Yr. in Sci., Gems TV, 1997. Fellow Explorers Club; mem. Internat. Astron. Union, Am. Astron. Soc. (Carl Sagan medal 2005), Am. Geophys. Union. Office: Jet Propulsion Lab Mail Stop 183-601 4800 Oak Grove Dr Pasadena CA 91109-8001 Office Phone: 818-393-4584. Business E-Mail: rosaly.m.lopes@jpl.nasa.gov.

LOPEZ, ANNIE MARIE, artist; b. Phoenix, Ariz., Dec. 11, 1958; d. Frank Osorio and Juanita Abalos Lopez; m. Jeffrey Neil Falk, Apr. 11, 1986; 1 child, Adam Lopez Falk. Artist Movimiento Artistico del Rio Salado, Phoenix, 1982—99; mem. exec. bd. dirs. Movimento Artistico del Rio Salado, Phoenix, 1984—87, interm dir., 1984. Represented in permanent collections City of Phoenix, Ariz. State Univ., Tucson Mus. of Art., McDonald's Corp., Phoenix Children's Hosp., Nat. Hispanic Cultural Ctr. N.Mex. Vice chair Phoenix Arts and Culture Commn., Phoenix, 2003—05; chair art in pub. pl. com. Arts and Culture Commn., Phoenix, 2001—03; bd. mem. Artlink, Inc., Phoenix, 1999—2001; chair, exec. bd. dirs. Movimiento Artistico del Rio Salado, Phoenix, 1995—98. Grantee Fellowship Grant, Art Renaissance Found., 1998, Ariz. Commn. on the Arts, 1996, Art Matters Found., 1995. Mem.: Arts and Culture Commn., Downtown Artist Coalition, Downtown Voices.

LOPEZ, CAROL SUE, artist; b. McCook, Nebr., Jan. 7, 1945; d. Norma Lee Wessell and Felix M. Rivera; m. Stanley Roland Lopez, May 6, 1962; children: Philip Eugene, Bryan Stanley, Eric Roland, Thea Katharine Hand. Dir. Atsugi Child Care Ctr., Atsugi, Japan, 1978—80; owner/dir. Galeria de Suenos Art Gallery, Mesilla/Las Cruces, N.Mex., 1999—. Display chairperson Mesilla Valley Fine Arts Gallery, 2004—. Encaustic painting (beeswax medium), Stained Glass (Best of Show, Southern N.M. State Fair, 1998), Light Show (Best of Show, Black Range Artists Assn., Deming, N.M., 2005), encaustic (beeswax) miniature painting, Just a Dream (2d pl., Black Mountain Ctr. for Arts, N.C., 2002), Day Dream (2d pl., Miniature Arts Soc. Fla., 2004), Camouflage (award of Merit, Artist's Guild Inc., Casper, Wyo., 2005). Recipient 2d Pl., Miniature Arts Bardean-Albuquerque, N.M., 2003, Hon. Mention, Roswell Fine Arts League, Roswell, N.M., 2003. Mem.: Las Cruces City of Artists Promotional Assn. (v.p., pres. 2005—06), Nat. Mus. Women in Arts, Miniature Art Soc. Fla., Mesilla Valley Fine Arts Gallery (governing bd., display chairperson 2004—06), Black Range Artists, Inc. Independent. Baptist. Avocations: travel, reading, museums & art galleries. Home: 1625 Country Club Cir Las Cruces NM 88001 Office: Galeria de Suenos Gallery and Studio 1625 Country Club Cir Las Cruces NM 88001 Office Phone: 505-523-0731.

LOPEZ, CAROLYN CATHERINE, physician; b. Chgo., Oct. 13, 1951; d. Joseph Compean and Angela (Silva) L. BS, Loyola U., Chgo., 1973; MD, U. Ill., 1978. Diplomate Am. Bd. Family Practice. Intern, resident Rush/Christ Hosp., Chgo., 1978-81; med. dir. Wholistic Health Ctr., Oak Lawn, Ill., 1981-82; clin. dir. Anchor HMO, Oak Brook, Ill., 1982-84, assoc. med. dir., 1984-87; med. dir. Chgo. Pk. Dist., 1987-91; v.p. Rush Access HMO, Chgo., 1992-93; asst. dean Rush Med. Coll., 1990-93; med. dir. Rush Access HMO, Chgo., 1991-93, v.p., 1992-93; v.p. for profl. affairs Rush Anchor HMO, 1993; sr. v.p. and chief med. officer Rush-Prudential Health Plans, 1993-95; chair dept. family practice Cook County Hosp., 1996—. Pres. Inst. Medicine, Chgo., 2006—. Mem. Chgo. Bd. Health, 2004—; bd. govs. Inst. Medicine, Chgo., 2003—. Primary Care Policy fellow USPHS, 1993. Fellow: Inst. Medicine Chgo. (bd. govs. 2003—, pres. 2006—, 2006—); mem.: AMA, Am. Med. Women's Assn., Ill. Acad. Family Physicians (bd. dirs. 1987—89, spkr. 1990—91, bd. chair 1990—91, pres.-elect 1991—92, pres. 1992—93), Am. Acad. Family Physicians (alt. del. 1992—95, del. 1996—99, vice-spkr. 1999—2002, spkr. 2002—04). Roman Catholic. Avocations: swimming, cooking. Office: Cook County Hosp Dept Family Practice 1900 W Polk St Chicago IL 60612-3736

LOPEZ, CLARA M., director; d. Fermin Valencia, Sr. and Mercedes Valencia; m. David Dennis Lopez, Apr. 12, 1975; children: Nicole, Mercy. BA, N. Mex. Highlands U., 1983, MA, 1984. Nurse's aide Four Seasons Nursing Home, Santa Fe, 1972—73; tchr. aide Pecos Schs., N.Mex., 1973—75, tchr., 1984—92, bilingual dir., 1992—97, title I tchr., 1997—99; tchr. Las Vegas City Schs., N.Mex., 1999—2000, prin., 2000—01, bilingual, fed. prgrams dir., 2001—. V.p. bd. dirs. Pecos Med. Ctr., 1989—98; v.p. San Miguel County DWI Bd., Las Vegas, N.Mex., 2003—04. Mem.: ASCD, N Mex. Assn. Bilingual Educators. Office: Las Vegas City Schools 901 Douglas Ave Las Vegas NM 87701 Office Phone: 505-454-5700. Personal E-mail: claralopez@cybercardinal.com.

LOPEZ, JEAN ENGEBRETSEN, neuroscience nurse, researcher; BSN, U. Nebr., 1973; cert. in neuro nursing, Montreal Neurol. Inst., Que., Can., 1978; MSN, Ariz. State U., 1987. RN, Ariz.; cert. clin. rsch. coord. Cert. neuroscience RN U.S. Peace Corps, Kuala Lumpur, Malaysia, 1973-74; staff nurse, charge nurse neuro ICU Barrow Neurolog. Inst. of St. Joseph's Hosp. and Med. Ctr., Phoenix, 1974-89, neuro-oncology and head injury rsch. nurse clinician, 1989-99; clin. rsch. nurse coord. Sun Health Rsch. Inst. Ctr. for Clin. Rsch., Sun City, Ariz., 1999—. Mem. Am. Assn. Neuro Nurses (past. sec. Ariz. chpt., chpt. coun. rep. for S.W.). Office: Sun Health Rsch Inst Ctr for Clin Rsch 10515 W Santa Fe Dr Sun City AZ 85351-3020 Business E-Mail: jean.lopez@sunhealth.org.

LOPEZ, JENNIFER, actress, singer, dancer; b. Bronx, NY, July 24, 1970; d. David and Guadalupe Lopez; m. Ojani Noa, Feb. 22, 1997 (div. Jan. 1, 1998); m. Cris Judd, Sept. 29, 2001 (div. Jan. 26, 2003); m. Marc Anthony, June 5, 2004. Launched clothing line J-Lo by Jennifer Lopez, 2001, lingerie line, 2004; released signature fragrance Glow, 2002, Still, 2004, Miami Glow, 2005, Live Jennifer Lopez, 2005, Love at First Glow, 2006; owner Madre's restaurant, Pasedena, 2002-. Won dance competition and was hired as dancer for TV series In Living Color, 1991-93; actor (TV series) Second Chances, 1993-94, South Central, 1994, Hotel Malibu, 1994; actor (films) Money Train, 1995, Jack, 1996, Blood and Wine, 1996, Anaconda, 1997 (ALMA award 1998), Selena, 1997 (ALMA award 1998), My Family, 1995, U-Turn, 1997, Antz (voice), 1998, Out of Sight, 1998 (ALMA award 1999), Thieves, 1999, Pluto Nash, 1999, The Cell, 2000 (Blockbuster Entertainment award for favorite actress, MTV Movie award for best dressed), The Wedding Planner, 2001, Angel Eyes, 2001, Enough, 2002, Maid in Manhattan, 2002, Gigli, 2003, Jersey Girl, 2004, Shall We Dance?, 2004, Monster-in-Law, 2005, An Unfinished Life, 2005; actor (TV guest appearances) Will & Grace, 2004; singer (albums) On the 6, 1999, J.Lo, 2001, J to Tha L-O!: The Remixes, 2002, This Is Me.Then, 2002, Rebirth, 2005. Recipient ALMA Female Entertainer Yr. award 2000, Lasting Image award 1998, Lone Star Film and TV award 1998; named one of 50 Most Beautiful People in the World, People mag., 1997; voted #1 in 100 Sexiest Women list, FHM, 2000, 2001; named one of 25 Most Influential Hispanics, Time Mag., 2005.

LOPEZ, LINDA CAROL, social sciences educator; b. NYC, Dec. 26, 1949; d. Ralph B. and M. (Taylor) Lopez. BA, U. Wis., Madison, 1972; MA, Ohio State U., Columbus, 1974, PhD, 1976. Vis. asst. prof. U. Wis., Eau Claire, 1976-77; from instr. to asst. prof. SUNY, Oneonta, 1977-83; assoc. prof. Rockford (Ill.) Coll., 1983—89; prof. dept. social scis. Western N.Mex U., Silver City, 1989—, dir. field experience, 1989—91. Contbr. (to profl. jours. articles) including Psychol. Reports, Internat. Jour. Addiction, Hispanic Jour. Behavioral Scis., Jour. Genetic Psychology, Jour. Employment Counseling, Perceptual and Motor Skills, Reading Improvement, Counseling and Values, Social Studies. Recipient Best Paper award, New Eng. Ednl. Rsch. Orgn., 1979; Postdoctoral Faculty fellow, Northeastern U., Boston, 1980—81. Mem.: Ill. Psychol. Assn., Nat. Assn. Hispanic and Latino Studies, Phi Delta Kappa. Avocations: walking, reading, travel. Home: PO Box 1479 Bayard NM 88023 Office: Western NMex U Dept Social Scis 1000 W College Ave Silver City NM 88062 Business E-Mail: lopezl@wnmu.edu.

LOPEZ, NANCY, retired professional golfer; b. Torrance, Calif., Jan. 6, 1957; d. Domingo and Marina (Griego) Lopez; m. Ray Knight, Oct. 25, 1982; children: Ashley Marie Knight, Erinn Shea Knight, Torri Heather Knight. Student, U. Tulsa, 1976-78. Founder, prin. Nancy Lopez Golf Co., 1997—. Player U.S.A. Solheim Cup, 1990. Author: The Education of a Woman Golfer, 1979. Named first victory winner, Bent Tree Classic, Sarasota, Fla., 1978, AP Athlete, 1978, Rolex Rookie of the Yr., 1978, Rolex Player of the Yr., 1978, 1979, 1985, winner, LPGA Championship, 1978, 1985, Mazda LPGA Championship, 1989, others; named to LPGA Hall of Fame, 1987, PGA World Golf Hall of Fame, 1989; recipient Vare Trophy, 1978. Mem.: LPGA (Player and Rookie of the Yr. 1978). Republican. Achievements include winning 48 LPGA Tour events, 3 maj. championships. Office: care Internat Mgmt Group 1360 E 9th St Ste 100 Cleveland OH 44114-1715

LOPEZ, PATRICIA NELL, minister, educator; b. Ft. Myers, Fla., July 20, 1953; d. Margaret Elizabeth Sessions; m. Rodrigo Lopez, July 17, 1984; 1 child, Ruben Rodrigo; m. Wayne Blair (div.); children: Margaret E. Blair, Cynthia D. Blair, Debra L. Blair, Patricia D. Blair. Degree, Tech. Coll., 1972; sec. degree, Lee Vocat. Tech., 1984; degree in Ministry and Counseling, Tomlinson Coll., 1998. Cert. Nursing Assistant, 1994. Mgr. Cir. K., Lakeland, Fla., 1994—98, Lake Wales Care Ctr., Lake Wales, Fla., 1998—2000; treas. clerk Ch. of God of Prophecy, Lake Wales, Fla., 1992—2000, assoc. pastor, 1993—2000, pastor, 2000—05. Cons. Ch. of God of Prophecy, Lake Wales, Fla., 2000—05, dir., 2000—05, clk., 2000—05. Mem.: Ministerial Assn. Avocations: dance, reading, drawing, swimming.

LOPEZ, PLACIDA RAMOS, elementary school educator; b. Stafford, Tex., Oct. 11, 1944; d. Urbano Zapata Ramos and Josefina (Saldaña) Arias; m. Jose Jesus Lopez Sr., Aug. 26, 1969 (dec.); 1 child, Gabriel Elizalde. Student, Victoria Coll., Tex., 1964—66, Our Lady of Lake U., San Antonio, 1967—68; BA Elem. Edn., Dominican Coll., Houston, 1975; postgrad., U. St. Thomas, 1987. Tchr. 3d grade, coach volleyball Our Lady of Guadalupe Parochial Sch., Houston, 1966—73; bilingual tchr. Pasadena Ind. Sch. Dist., Tex., 1972—82; tchr. 1st grade Alvin Ind. Sch. Dist., Tex., 1984—89, tchr. 5th grade, 1989—94, bilingual tchr., 1994—2004; ret., 2004. Bilingual cons. Alvin Ind.

Sch. Dist., 2005—06. Mem. Tex. Bilingual Textbook com. Pasadena Ind. Sch. Dist.; transl. Cmty. and Parish Members; coun. La Raza Southern Poverty Law Ctr. Recipient Tchr. of Year, 1990. Mem.: PTA, NEA, Houston Assn. Bilingual Edn., Alvin Tchrs. Assn., Pasadena Tchrs. Assn., Classroom Tchrs. Assn., Bay Area Reading Coun., Tex. Assn. Bilingual Edn., Tex. State Tchrs. Assn., Nat. Assn. Bilingual Edn., Parent Tchr. Orgn., Tex. Ret. Tchrs. Assn. Avocations: singing, writing. Home: 9540 Ruth Rd Rosharon TX 77583

LOPEZ, PRISCILLA, actress; b. Bronx, NY, Feb. 26, 1948; d. Francisco and Laura (Candelaria) Lopez; m. Vincent Fanuele, Jan. 16, 1972; 2 children. Actress (Broadway plays) Breakfast at Tiffany's, 1996, Henry Sweet Henry, 1967, Her First Roman, 1968, Company, 1970, What's A Nice Country Like You Doing In a State Like This, Pippin, Lysistrata, 1972, A Chorus Line, 1975 (Obie award), A Day in Hollywood/A Night in the Ukraine, 1980 (Tony award best featured actress in a musical, 1980), Nine, 1982, Anna in the Tropics, 2003, Beauty of the Father, 2005, (off Broadway) Key Exchange, 1982, (plays) Buck, 1983, Non Pasquale, 1983, Class Mothers '68, 2002, (films) Cheaper to Keep Her, 1980, Revenge of the Nerds II: Nerds in Paradise, 1987, Simple Justice, 1990, Chutney Popcorn, 1999, Just One Time, 1999, Center Stage, 2000, Maid in Manhattan, 2002, Tony 'n' Tina's Wedding, 2004, (TV films) Doubletake, 1985, The Recovery Room, 1985, Intimate Strangers, 1986, Alone in the Neon Jungle, 1988, Jesse, 1988, For the Love of My Child: The Anissa Ayala Story, 1993, Moment of Truth: Stalking Back, 1993, (TV series) Feeling Good, 1974, In the Beginning, 1978, Kay O'Brien, 1986, guest appearances The Johnny Carson Show, All in the Family, 1977, Law & Order, 1990, LA Law, 1993, As the World Turns, 2003. Office: Sames & Rollnik Assocs Ltd 250 W 57th St New York NY 10107*

LOPEZ, SOLEDAD, actress; d. Primitivo Lopez and Mariana Hernandez; m. Angel Gil Orrios, Feb. 22, 1980; children: Sebastian Gil-Lopez, Mariana Gil-Lopez. Cert. acting The Real Stage, Ny, 1985. Actor: (plays) Jaime Salom's Almost a Goddess (Best Actress award, ACE, 2005), Renaldo Ferradas' La Visionaria, Alegre Cudos' Verde Doncella Asalta Un Cine, Don Juan Por Los Siglos De Los Siglos (Best Actress award, Golden Age Festival, El Paso, 1989), Alegre Cudos' La Madre Que Te Pario, Calderon de la Barca's The Purgatory of Saint Patrick, Garcia Lorca's The Audience & Play Without A Title, Almodovar/Cabal's Dark Habits, Sartre's No Exit, Espriu's Piel de Toro, La Pasion De Cristo, Ramos Perea's We Women Do It Better (Best Actress award, ACE and Hola, 2004), Tiempo Del 98, Santiago Moncada's Caprichos, Carlos Fuentes' The One-eyed Man Is King, Jardiel Poncela's Brake Four Hearts, Picasso's Guernica, Calderon de la Barca's The Great Theatre of the World (Best Actress award, Hola, 2001), Miguel Sierra's Palomas Intrepidas (Best Actress award, ACE, 1996), Santiago Moncada's Entre Mujeres (Best Actress award, ACE, 1995), Martin Descalzo's Las Prostitutas Os Precederan en el Reino de los Cielos (Best Actress award, ACE, 1994). Recipient Vermeil medal, French Acad. Arts, Scis. and Letters, Paris, 2005. Mem.: Hispanic Orgn. Latin Actors (Best Actress award 2001, 2003). Personal E-mail: soledad@thaliatheatre.org.

LOPEZ LYSNE, ROBIN, counselor, writer, artist; b. Rockford, Ill., Jan. 3, 1953; d. Robert Edward and Martha Virginia (Lysne) Heerens; m. Carter Blocksma, Nov. 1, 1976 (div. Jan. 18, 1985); m. Ernesto Lopez-Molina, July 26, 1998; children: Chris Lopez, Matt Lopez, Mari Luna del Sol(dec.). BFA cum laude, U. Wis., Milw., 1975; MA in Spirituality and Psychology, Holy Names Coll., 1988. Art tchr. Battle Creek (Mich.) Art Ctr., 1979—85, Detroit Art House Lectrs., 1979—85, Ella Sharp Mus., Jackson, Mich., 1979—85, curator exhibits and edn., 1980—; pvt. practice Santa Cruz, Calif., 1985—; founding practioner Energy Medicine, 1996—; founding dir. Ctr. for the Soul, Santa Cruz, 2002—. Mem. Somatics Group, Marin County, Calif., 1989—95; presenter in field; lectr. in field; owner Blue Bone Books, Santa Cruz, Calif., 2006—. Author: (non-fiction and poetry) Dancing Up the Moon, 1995, Living a Sacred Life, 1997, 1999. Exec. bd. Together for Youth-United Way, Santa Cruz, Calif., 1999—2002; cmty. organizer Mountain Cmty. Resources, Ben Lomond, Calif., 1999—2002. Grantee, Friends of Creation, Oakland, 1988, Flow Fund, N.Y., Calif., 1992, Rockford (Ill.) Arts Coun., 1996, 1997, Santa Cruz Mountain Art Ctr., Ben Lomond, 2000. Mem.: Valley Unity Action Group (dir. 1999—2002).

LÓPEZ-MORILLAS, FRANCES (MAPES), translator; b. Fulton, Mo., Sept. 3, 1918; d. Erwin Kempton and Laura (Hinkhouse) Mapes; m. Juan López-Morillas, Aug. 12, 1937; children: Martin Morell, Consuelo, Julian. BA, U. Iowa, 1939, MA, 1940. Translator Collins Radio Co., Cedar Rapids, Iowa, 1940-43; tchr. Spanish Lincoln Sch., Providence, 1943-44; tchr. French and Spanish Mary C. Wheeler Sch., Providence, 1951-64; tchr. ESL Internat. Inst., Madrid, 1957-58; freelance translator, 1964—. Editor (with E. K. Mapes): J. J. Fernandez de Lizardi, El Periquillo Samiento, 1952; translator: 25 books and numerous articles, Journey to the Alcarria: Travels through the Spanish Countryside, 1964, Miguel de Unamuno, 1966, An Economic History of Spain, 1969, Spain in the Fifteenth Century, 1971, Tales of Potosi, 1975, The Krausist Movement and Ideological Change in Spain, 1981, Torquemada, 1986, Understanding Spain, 1990, The Medieval Heritage of Mexico, 1992, Castaways: The Narrative of Álvar Núñez Cabeza de Vaca, 1993, Selected Writings of Andrés Bello, 1997, Natural and Moral History of the Indies, 2002. Recipient Transl. prize, Tex. Inst. Letters, 1991; grantee, NEH, 1984, NEA, 1986. Mem.: Am. Lit. Translators Assn., Internat. Assn. Hispanists, Phi Beta Kappa. Home: 355 Blackstone Blvd Providence RI 02906-4946 Personal E-mail: fmorillas@aol.com.

LOPEZ-MUNOZ, MARIA ROSA P., real estate development company executive; b. Havana, Cuba, Jan. 28, 1938; came to U.S., 1960; d. Eleuterio Perfecto and Bertha (Carmenati Colon) Perez Rodriguez; m. Gustavo Lopez-Munoz, Sept. 9, 1973. Student, Phillips & Candler Coll., Havana, 1951—53, Sch. Langs., U. Jose Marti, 1954-55. Lic. interior designer, real estate broker. Pres. Fantasy World Acres, Inc., Coral Gables, Fla., 1970-84, pres., dir., 1984—; sec. Sandhills Corp., Coral Gables, 1978-85, dir., 1978—. Treas., Am. Cancer Soc., Miami, Fla., 1981, sec. Hispanic bd., 1987, pres. Hispanic divsn., 1989, bd. dirs., aux. treas.; bd. dirs Am. Heart Assn., Miami, 1985, chmn. Hispanic divsn.; 1992; bd. dirs. YMCA, Young Patronesses of Opera, Miami, 1985, Lowe Mus. of U. Miami, 1986—, Linda Ray Infant Ctr.; former pres. Ladies Aux. Little Havana Child Care Ctr.; trustee Ronald McDonald House, sec. exec. bd., 1992; mem. exec. bd., rec. sec. Young Patronesses of the Opera; mem. Fla. Grand Opera; mem. cabinet Children's Cardiac Found., New Horizons Cmty. Devel., Transplant Ctr. Sch., Medicine, U. Miami-Jackson Meml. Hosp., 1992; bd. dirs. Cultura Italiana, Inc.; pres. Messengers of Peace, 2002; amb. 1999 Alpine Ski Championships, Vail, Colo. Recipient Merit award Am. Cancer Soc., 1980, 81, 82, 83, 84, Dynamic Woman award, 1992; Woman with Heart award Am. Heart Assn., 1985, Merit awards, 1980-84, Woman of Yr., 1986, Outstanding Lady award Greater Miami Opera, 1992, Cultural Star of the Millennium award Vizcaya Mus., 1999; named Woman of Yr., Children's Hosp., 1993; named to Great Order José Marti, 1988; named Leading Miami's Beautiful Couples for ACS, 1995. Mem. Real Estate Bd. Realtors, Coral Gables Real Estate Assn., Vail 50 Club, Ocean Reef Club (Key Largo, Fla.), Opera Guild Miami, YPO, Key Biscayle Yacht Club, Regine's Interna. Bath Club (Miami Beach), Villar Ctr. Guild. Republican. Roman Catholic. Avocations: yachting, skiing, scuba diving, guitar, piano. Office Phone: 305-299-5179.

LOPO, DIANA M., lawyer; b. Havana, Cuba, 1957; BS cum laude, U. Miami, 1978; JD, U. Mich., 1981; LLM, NYU, 1982. Bar: N.Y. 1984. Ptnr. Skadden, Arps, Slate, Meagher & Flom, N.Y.C.

LORAINE, SANDRA F., secondary school educator; d. Thomas E. and Carolyn F. Loraine. BA in History, Edn., St. Louis U., 2001. Cert. social studies educator. Secondary tchr. Hazelwood Sch. Dist., Florissant, Mo., 2001—. Scholar Leadership, St. Louis U., 1996-2001. Mem.: Orgn. Am. Historians, Nat. Coun. Social Studies. Avocation: travel. Home: 1595 Yearling Dr Florissant MO 63033

LORBER, BARBARA HEYMAN, communications executive, event producer; b. NYC; d. David Benjamin and Gertrude (Meyer) Heyman. AB in Polit. Sci., Skidmore Coll.; MA, postgrad., Columbia U. Asst. dir. young citizens divsn. Dem. Party; exec. asst. to dean Albert Einstein Coll. Medicine, Bronx, NY; exec. asst. to v.p. devel. Vanderbilt U., Nashville; spl. projects dir. Am. Acad. in Rome, NYC, Met. Opera, NYC; sr. v.p. Hill and Knowlton, NYC; pres. Lorber Group, Ltd., NYC; v.p. comms. and planning NYC Partnership and C. of C.; sr. v.p. major events and promotions NYC & Company. Guest lectr. Arts and Bus. Coun., NYC, Internat. Soc. Performing Arts Admisntrs., Columbia U. Tchrs. Coll., NYC, 1988; event prodr. Broadway Under the Stars, 2002—; team leader Salt Lake Olympic Torch Relay NYC, 2002, 2004 Athens Olympic Torch Relay in NYC, 2004; spl. projects cons. NYC 2012 Olympic Games Bid Com. Contbr. chapters to books, articles to profl. jours. Office: NYC & Company/Major Events 810 7th Ave 3d Fl New York NY 10019-5818

LORBER, CHARLOTTE LAURA, publisher; b. Bklyn, Apr. 11, 1952; d. Morris and Libby (Slatsky) L. BBA in Fin., U. Miami, 1975. Dir. special events Third Century U.S.A. Dade County Bicentenial Orgn., Miami, Fla., 1975-76; promotion dir. Donato Advt. Co., Coral Gables, Fla., 1977-78; pres. Towne Pub. & Advt. Co., Inc., Coral Gables, Fla., 1979—. Publisher: (directories) View of our City, 1985-86 (Excellence award), Greater Miami Chamber, 1986-87 (Merit award), (brochure) Big Does Mean Better, 1986-87 (Merit award). Recipient Merit award City of Hialeah, 1977. Mem. Am. C. of C. Execs., Greater Miami C. of C. (trustee), Coral Gables C. of C., Miami Beach C. of C. (trustee), South Miami C. of C., North Dade C. of C., World Trade Ctr. Lodges: Rotary. Avocations: lic. pilot, cert. race car driver, cooking. Address: PO Box 1440010 Coral Gables FL 33114 Office Phone: 305-444-6000.

LORCH, MARISTELLA DE PANIZZA, writer, educator; b. Bolzano, Italy, Dec. 8, 1919; came to U.S., 1947, naturalized, 1951; d. Gino and Giuseppina (Cristoforetti) de Panizza Inama von Brunnenwald; m. Claude Bové, Feb. 10, 1944 (div. 1955); 1 child, Claudia; m. Edgar R. Lorch, Mar. 25, 1956; children: Lavinia Edgarda, Donatella Livia. Student, Liceo Classico, Merano, 1929-37; Dott. in Lettere e Filosofia, U. Rome, 1942; DHL (hon.), Lehman Coll., CUNY, 1993. Prof. Latin and Greek Liceo Virgilio, Rome, 1941-44; assoc. prof. Italian and German Coll. St. Elizabeth, Convent Station, NJ, 1947-51; faculty Barnard Coll. and Columbia U., 1951-90; prof. Barnard Coll., 1967—, chmn. dept., 1951-90, co-founder, chmn. medieval and renaissance program, 1972-90; vice chmn. emeritus prof. Columbia U., 2005—, v.p. ERIC emeritus, 2006—. Founder, dir. Ctr. for Internat. Scholarly Exch., Barnard Coll., 1980-90; dir. Casa Italiana, Columbia U., 1969-76, chmn. exec. com. Italian studies, 1980-90, founding dir. Italian Acad. Advanced Studies in Am., 1991-96, founding dir. emerita and dir. external rels., 1996—. Author: Critical edit. L. Valla, De vero falsoque bono, Bari, 1970, (critical edit.) Michaelida (with W. Ludwig), 1976, On Pleasure (with A. K. Hieatt), 1981, A Defense of Life: L. Valla's Theory of Pleasure, 1985, Folly and Insanity in Renaissance Literature, 1986, (with E. Grassi) All' America, 1990, Italy at the Millennium, 2001, (novel) Mamma in Her Village, 2005; editor: Il Teatro Italiano del Renascimento, 1981, Humanism in Rome, 1983, La Scuola, New York, 1987; mem. editorial bd. Italian jour. Romanic Review; also articles on Renaissance lit., philosophy and theater. Chmn. Am. Ariosto Centennial Celebration, 1974; trustee Lyceé Française NY, 1986—2004, mem. adv. bd., 2004—; adv. bd. Marconi Found., 1998; chmn. bd. trustees La Scuola NY, 1986—92. Decorated cavaliere della Repubblica Italiana, commendatore della Repubblica Italiana, grande ufficiale della Repubblica Italiana; recipient AMITA award for Woman of Yr. in Italian Lit., 1973, Columbus '92 Countdown prize of excellence in humanities, 1990, Elen Cornaro award Sons of Italy Woman of Yr., 1990, Father Ford award, 1994, hon. mem. Legendary Women, 1997, founding dir. emeritus Italian Acad. in Advance Studies in Am., Columbia U. Mem. Medieval Acad. Am., Renaissance Soc. Am., Am. Assn. Tchrs. Italian, Am. Assn. Italian Studies (hon. pres. 1990-91), Internat. Assn. for Study of Italian Lit. (Am. rep., assoc. pres. 8th Congress 1973), Acad. Polit. Sci. (life), Pirandello Soc. (pres. 1972-78), Arcadia Acad. (Asteria Aretusa 1976). Home: 445 Riverside Dr New York NY 10027-6801 Office: Columbia Univ Italian Acad Adv Study Casa Italiana New York NY 10027 Office Phone: 212-854-8649. Business E-Mail: ML48@columbia.edu.

LORD, EVELYN MARLIN, mayor; b. Melrose, Mass., Dec. 8, 1926; d. John Joseph and Mary Janette (Nourse) Marlin; m. Samuel Smith Lord Jr., Feb. 28, 1948; children: Steven Arthur, Jonathan Peter, Nathaniel Edward, Victoria Marlin, William Kenneth. BA, Boston U., 1948; MA, U. Del., 1956; JD, U. Louisville, 1969. Bar: Ky. 1969, U.S. Supreme Ct. 1973. Exec. dir. Block Blight Inc., Wilmington, Del., 1956—60; mem. Del. Senate, Dover, 1960—62; administrv. asst. county judge Jefferson County, Louisville, 1968—71; corr. No. Ireland News Jour. Co., Wilmington, 1972—74; legal adminstr. Orgain, Bell & Tucker, Beaumont, Tex., 1978—83; v.p. Tex. Commerce Bank, Beaumont, 1983—84; councilman City of Beaumont, 1980—82, mayor pro tem, 1982—84, mayor, 1990—94, 2002—05. Tourism chmn. U.S. Conf. Mayors, 1994, adv. bd., chmn. arts, culture and recreation, 1992—94, 2002—05; sr. counselor Ky. Bar, 2002—; adv. bd. U.S. Com. Mayors, 2002—05. Pres. United Way, 1994, 1997; adv. bd. Boy Scouts Am., Three Rivers, 1978—84, 1989—94, exec. bd., 2000—05; life mem. Girl Scouts U.S.A., pres. Kentuckiana coun., 1966—70, governing bd. San Jacinto coun., 2006—; trustee Lamar U. Found., 1999—2003; pres. Tex. Energy Mus., 1995—2001; trustee United Way, Beaumont, 1990—; bd. dirs. Evelyn M. Lord Teen Ct., 1993—, Found. S.E. Tex., 1990—, Lincoln Inst., 1994—2001, Beaumont Pub. Schs. Found., 1993—99, 2006—. Ptnrs. for Children, Child Protective Svcs.; chmn. Spindletop 2001 Com. Named Citizen of Yr., Sales and Mktg. Assn., 1990, Beaumont Man of the Yr., 1993, Woman with Heart, Am. Heart Assn., 2000, Free Ent. Person of the Yr., Assn. Bldg. Contrs., 2000, Newsmaker of the Yr., Press Club Jefferson County, 2001, Hurricane Evelyn, ARC, 2001, Disting. Law Alumni, U. Louisville, 2002, Woman of Yr., Quota Club Internat., 2002; recipient Silver Beaver award, Boy Scouts Am., Beaumont, 1979, Disting. Alumni award, Boston U., 1983, Disting. Leadership award, Nat. Assn. Leadership Orgns., Indpls., 1991, Labor-Mgmt. Pub. Sector award, 1991, Cmty. Builder award, Grand Masonic Lodge of Tex., 1991, 2003, Disting. Grad. award, Leadership Beaumont, 1993, Rotary Svc. Above Self award, 1994, Excellency award, Tex. State Hist. Commn., 2001, Athena award, Beaumont C of C, 2003, Mrs. S.E. Tex. award, Dogwood Festival, 2004, Regional Leadership award, S.E. Tex. Regional Planning Commn., 2005. Mem.: DAR, LWV (Del. state pres. 1960—62, bd. dirs. Tex. 1978—80), Bus. and Profl. Women Assns. (Woman of Yr. 1983), Colonial Dames (Citizenship award 2004), Symphony Soc. S.E. Tex. (hon.; bd. dirs. 1990—98, 2002—), Soc. Mayflower Descs., Rotary, 100 Club (pres. 1995—97). Avocations: writing, reading, african violets, genealogy. Home: 1240 Nottingham Ln Beaumont TX 77706-4316 Personal E-mail: evelynlord@aol.com.

LORD, JACQUELINE WARD, accountant, photographer, artist; b. Andalusia, Ala., May 16, 1936; d. Marron J. and Minnie V. (Owen) Ward; m. Curtis Gaynor, Nov. 23, 1968. Student U. Ala., 1966, Auburn U., Ala., 1977, Huntingdon Coll., Montgomery, Ala., 1980, Troy State U., Ala., 1980; BA in Bus. Adminstrn., Dallas Bapt. U., 1985. News photographer corr. Andalusia (Ala.) Star-News, 1954-59, Sta. WSFA-TV, Montgomery, Ala., 1954-60; acct., bus. mgr. Reihardt Motors, Inc., Montgomery, 1962-69; office mgr., acct. Cen. Ala. Supply, Montgomery, 1969-71; acct. Chambers Constrn. Co., Montgomery, 1972-75; pres. Foxy Lady Apparel, Inc., Montgomery, 1973-76; acct. Rushton, Stakely, Johnston & Garrett, attys., Montgomery, 1975-81; acctg. supr. Arthur Andersen & Co., Dallas, 1981-82; staff acct. Burgess Co., CPAs, Dallas, 1983; owner Lord & Assocs. Acctg. Svc., Dallas, 1983—; tax acct. John Hasse, CPA, Dallas, 1984-86; Dallas Bapt. Assn., 1986—. Vol. election law commr. Sec. of State of Ala. Don Siegelman, Montgomery, 1979-80; active Montgomery Art Guild, 1964-65, Ala. Art League, 1964-65, Montgomery Little Theatre, 1963-65, Montgomery Choral Soc., 1965. Recipient Outstanding Achievement Bus. Mgmt. award Am. Motors, 1968. Mem. Am. Soc. Women Accts. (del. ann. meeting 1975-78, pres. Montgomery chpt. 1976-77, area day chmn. 1978), Soroptimists Internat. (pres. elect Montgomery chpt. 1975-76), Nat. Assn. Ch. Bus. Adminstrn. Home: 5209 Meadowside Dr Garland TX 75043-2731

LORD, M. G., writer; b. La Jolla, Calif., Nov. 18; d. Charles Carroll and Mary (Pfister) L.; m. Glenn Horowitz, May 19, 1985 BA, Yale U. Editl. cartoonist, columnist Newsday, N.Y.C., 1979-94. Cartoons syndicated L.A. Times Syndicate, 1984-89; column syndicated Copley News Svc., 1989-94; resident humanities fellow U. Mich., 1986-87. Author: Mean Sheets, 1982, Prig Tales, 1990, Forever Barbie: The Unauthorized Biography of a Real Doll, 1994, Astro Turf, The Private Life of Rocket Science, 2005. Knight-Wallace fellow U. Mich., 1986-87. Office: care Eric Simonoff Janklow & Nesbit Assoc 445 Park Ave New York NY 10022-2606

LORD, MARJORIE, actress; b. San Francisco, July 26; d. George Charles and Lillian Rosalie (Edgar) Wollenberg; m. John Archer, Dec. 30, 1941 (div. 1954); children: Gregg, Anne; m. Randolph M. Hale, May 26, 1958 (dec. Aug. 1974); m. Harry Joseph Volk, Aug. 14, 1976 (dec. 2000). Student high sch., San Francisco. Bd. dirs. The Joffrey Ballet, The Friends of the Library, U. So. Calif. Appeared in theater prodns. including The Old Maid, Anniversary Waltz on Broadway, Springtime for Henry; more than 30 feature films including Johnny Come Lately; starred in Make Room for Daddy, 1957-64; countless TV shows including Love American Style, Sweet Surrender, 1987; TV film Side by Side, 1987; dir. and actress theater prodns.; dir. Sunday in New York, Black Comedy, The Tiger at Claremont College, Ginger in the Morning; author (memoir) A Dance & Hug, 2005. Bd. dirs. Hollywood Entertainment Mus., Friends of Libr. Home: 1110 Maytor Pl Beverly Hills CA 90210-2600 Office Phone: 310-273-0273. Personal E-mail: maggielord@adelphia.net.

LORD, MIA W., advocate; b. N.Y.C., Dec. 2, 1911; m. Robert P. Lord (dec. Nov. 1977); children: Marcia Louise, Alison Jane. BA in Liberal Arts cum laude, Bklyn. Coll., 1935; postgrad., San Francisco State U., 1984—99. Hon. sec. Commonwealth of World Citizens, London; membership sec. Brit. Assn. for World Govt., London; sec. Ams. in Brit. for U.S. Withdrawal from S.E. Asia, Eng.; organizer Vietnam Vigil to End the War, London; pres. Let's Abolish War chpt. World Federalist Assn., San Francisco State U. Appointed hon. sec. Commonwealth of World Citizens, London; officially invited to Vietnam, 1973; organizer Vietnam Vigil to End the War, London. Author: The Practical Way to End Wars and Other World Crises: the case for World Federal Government: listed in World Peace through World Law, 1984, and in Strengthening the United Nations, 1987, War: The Biggest Con Game in the World, 1980. Hon. sec., nat. exec. mem. Assn. of World Federalists-U.K.; founder, bd. dirs. Crusade to Abolish War and Armaments by World Law. Nominated for the Nobel Peace Prize, 1975, 92, 93; recipient four Merit awards Pres. San Francisco State U. Mem. Secretariat of World Citizens USA (life), Assn. of World Federalists USA, Brit. Assn. for World Govt. (membership sec.), Crusade to Abolish War and Armaments by World Law (founder, dir.), World Govt. Orgn. Coord. Com., World Fed. Authority Com., Campaign for UN Reform, Citizens Global Action, World Constitution and Parliament Assn., World Pub. Forum, Internat. Registry of World Citizens. Home: 174 Majestic Ave San Francisco CA 94112-3022

LORD, RUTH, retired researcher, philanthropist, writer; b. NYC, Jan. 14, 1922; d. Henry Francis duPont and Ruth Wales; m. George deForest Lord (div.); children: Pauline, George de Forest Jr., Edith S.(dec.), Henry; m. John Grier Holmes, Mar. 3, 1990 (dec. 1997). BA, Vassar Coll., 1943; MA, Yale U., 1950. Rsch. affiliate Yale Child Study Ctr., New Haven, 1967—85, rsch. assoc., 1986—98; ret., 1998. Spkr. in field. Co-author: When Home is No Haven, 1992; author: Henry F. duPont and Winterthur, 1999; contbr. numerous articles to psychol. jours. Vol. Pub. Edn. Assn., NYC, 1943—47; intermittent team capt. United Fund, New Haven, 1948—53; trustee Winterthur Mus., 1952—74; pres. Long Wharf Theatre, New Haven, 1967—90, bd. dirs., 1980—, Vassar Coll., 1956—57, Austen Riggs Found., Stockbridge, Mass., 1975—; dir. Cornerstone Inc., New Haven, 1968—75. Recipient Foxcroft Disting. Alumna award, 1994, Nat. Arts Club award, 1989; fellow, Saybrook Coll., 1980—. Mem.: Family Svc. Assn. Am. (bd. dirs. 1954—57), Public Edn. Assn. (trustee 1947—51), Colonial Dams Am., Century Assn., Colony Club, Phi Beta Kappa. Democrat. Avocations: bridge, gardening, bicycling, theater, writing. Home: 19 St Ronan St New Haven CT 06511

LORD, VICTORIA LYNN, artist; b. Danville, Ill., May 29, 1956; d. Delno and Merlyn LaDonna (Gillis) Gilliland; m. Maurice Powers Lord II, Dec. 1, 1987. Student, Purdue U., 1974-77. Host, instr. painting series PBS, Learning Channel, U.S., Can., Mexico, 1990—; instr. various orgns. Author: Techniques in Acrylics, Alkyds, Oils, 1987, Painting with Alkyds and Oils, 1989, First Steps in Acrylics, 1996. Named one of Top 100 Wildlife Artists, Artist Mag., 1990, Sponsor Artist, Ducks Unltd., Ind., 1991, Featured Ad Artist, Winsor & Newton, 1990-91. Mem. Soc. of Layerists in Multimedia, Soc. Exptl. Artists, Soc. Decorative Painters, Am. Craft Coun., Soc. of Painters in Casein and Acrylic, Tippecanoe Arts Fedn. (bd. dirs. 1992-95). Office: PO Box 2195 West Lafayette IN 47996-2195 Office Phone: 765-463-6425.

LOREDO, DORISELDA, elementary school educator; b. Baytown, Tex., Oct. 2, 1975; d. Jose Trinidad and Ninfa Ramirez; m. Agustin Loredo III, Mar. 4, 2000; children: Agustin Daniel, Antonia Leonila, Diego Guadalupe. Student, U. Houston, Clear Lake, 2004—. Paraprofl. Lamar Elem., Baytown, 2003—04; bilingual elem. tchr. Williams Elem., Pasadena, Tex., 2004—. Mem. West Baytown Civic Assn., 2001—06. Office Phone: 713-920-8080. Personal E-mail: greenmokis@yahoo.com.

LOREDO, LINDA S., marketing executive; b. Newark, Mar. 30, 1959; d. Charles Frances and Mary Josephine Loredo. With Dolls by Consolidated Enterprise, Roselle Park, N.J. Office: Dolls by Consolidated 440 E Westfield Ave Roselle Park NJ 07204-2432

LORELL, BEVERLY H., medical products executive; BA with distinction, Stanford U., 1971; MD, Stanford Sch. Medicine, 1975. Intern to resident physician Stanford U. Hosp.; clin. rsch. fellowship, cardiology Mass. Gen. Hosp., Harvard Med. Sch.; dir., program in heart failure, also mem. interventional cardiology team Besth Israel Deaconess Med. Ctr.; prof., medicine Harvard U. Med. Sch.; v.p., chief med. tech. officer Guidant Corp., Indpls., 2003—. Served as an advisor to the fed. govt., including svc. on study sect. of the NIH and Cardiovascular and Renal Drugs Adv. Com. of the FDA; lectr. at various heart conf. and symposiums around the world. Contbr. articles to profl. jours. Mem.: Besth Israel Intervention Cardiology Team, Am. Coll. Cardiology, Heart Failure Soc. of Am., Am. Heart Assn., Guidant Compass Bd. Office: Guidant Corp 111 Monument Cl 2900 Indianapolis IN 46204-5129 Mailing: Guidant Corp PO Box 44906 Indianapolis IN 46244*

LORELLE, LINDA, journalist; b. Chgo., Aug. 11, 1955; d. Clay Henry and Anita Clarice (Steele) Jones; m. Louis Wesley Gregory, June 23, 1990; 1 child, Lindsey Lorelle Gregory. BA in Devel. Psychology and Italian, Stanford U., 1977; MJ, U. Mo., Columbia, 1987. Weekend anchor, reporter Sta. KOMU-TV, Columbia, Mo., 1986-87; gen. assignment reporter Sta. KMOV-TV, St. Louis, 1987-89; weekend anchor, reporter Sta. KPRC-TV, Houston, 1989-90, anchor 6 and 10 p.m., 1990—. Mem. adv. bd. Houston Zoo, 1994—. Recipient Sch. Bell award Tex. State Tchrs. Assn., 1990, 91, Media award Tex. Assn. for Yr.-Round Edn., 1992, Sampson award Houston Tennis Assn., 1992, Matrix award Women in Commn., 1993, Makeda award Nat. Coalitino of 100 Black Women, 1994, Commendation award Am. Women in Radio and TV, 1995, Media Cmty. Svc. award Cancer League, 1995, Media Excellence award Cancer Counseling, 1995. Mem. Soc. Profl. Journalists (mem. adv. bd. 1993—). Avocations: tennis, dance. Office: Sta KPRC-TV 8181 Southwest Fwy Houston TX 77074-1705

LORELLI, ELVIRA MAE, artist, art educator; d. Clement Vladimir Svoboda and Sylvia Georgiana Nikl; m. Pasqualino Geovani Lorelli, Nov. 22, 1955 (dec.); children: Patrick Eugene, Rhonda Mae Gilbert, Nancy Diane

Yomogida. BA, Pomona Coll., 1950; MA in Art Edn., Claremont Grad. U., 1961, MA in Edn., 1969. Cert. elem. edn. Calif., 1960, secondary edn. Calif., 1960, tchg., jr. coll. specialiation Calif., 1968. Art tchr. Trona Jr.-Sr. HS, Calif., 1952—54; art tchr., art coord. Barstow Unified Sch. Dist., Calif., 1954—59; art tchr. Barstow HS, 1959—62; art dept. head Barstow CC, 1962—82; art instr. U. Calif., Riverside, 1978—87, Chapman Coll., Barstow, 1979—84, Calif. Veteran's Home, Barstow, 1996—; artist, art instr. Elmae Studio, Barstow, 1976—. Coord. instructor's guide Stamp & Stencil, 1965; organizer faculty art workshops Barstow Sch. Dist., 1960—64. Author: (book) Art With And Without Music, 1960; murals, Barstow Bapt. Ch., 1969, Barstow Meth. Ch., 1984, sculptures, Centennial Park, Barstow, Calif., 1990, sculpture, St. Philip Neri Ch., Lenwood, Calif., 1996, exhibitions include, Lorain's Coffee Shop, Barstow, 2004—. Judge Ann. Art Exhibition Newberry Art Guild, Newberry Springs, Calif., 1985; judge Ann. Art Show Officer's Wives, Fort Irwin, Calif., 1987; judge, parade floats Kiwanis Club, Barstow, 1989, 1995; designer parade float Veteran's Home, Barstow, 1997; literacy tutor Barstow Libr., 1999—; bd. mem. Projects for Achieving Creativity in Edn. in San Bernadino, 1976—84. Recipient Cert. Appreciation, Skyline North Sch. PTA, 1984, Kederka award, Barstow Veteran's Home Calif., 2004. Mem.: Calif. Retired Tchrs. Assn., Barstow Artists' Guild (pres. 1966—68), Barstow Emblem Club (trustee 2003—, historian 1994—96, 1998—99, Sister of Yr. 1998—99). Republican. Roman Catholic. Avocations: photography, camping, swimming, bowling, golf, line dancing. Office Phone: 760-256-6636.

LOREN, PAMELA, telecommunications executive; b. Paris, Jan. 11, 1944; d. Theodore and Mattie (Ephron) Loren; m. Morton P. Levy, June 2, 1963; children: Cristopher Aram, Stirling Brett, Cristina Sahula. BS in Sociology, Columbia U., 1964; MS in Sociology, U. Madrid, 1968, MS in Langs., 1970. Pres. Pamela Loren, Ltd., N.Y.C., 1969—74, Loren Comm. Internat., Ltd., N.Y.C., 1972—74; chmn. bd. Loren Comm. Internat., Caracas, Venezuela, London, Milan, Italy and N.Y.C., 1974; exec. v.p. Cinnamon World Trade Corp., 1974; pres., CEO LorenAire Aviation, N.Y. and Brazil, 1988. Dir. Panda Internat. Export Corp., Durable Housing Internat., Loren Group, Danbury, Conn., Crespi, Rosann & Ponti; speaker on interdependence of medicine and comm. Author: The Generation In-Between, 1977, Looking Ahead to Thirty-Five, 1978, Slowing Down in the Fast Lane, 1987, When Having It All Isn't Enough, 1988, New Patterns of Power: Women and Influence, 1989. Bd. dirs. Burden Ctr. for Aging. Named Young Woman of Achievement YWCA, 1983, Woman of Vision, Caracas, 1986, Woman of the Future, Madrid, 1998; recipient Humanitarian award Community Svc. Soc., 1972, Burden Ctr. for Aging, 1977, Soc. Order Helpers, 1978, 1982, 1986, 1988, 1992, Otty award, 1986. Mem.: Am. Soc. Prevention Cruelty to Animals (bd. dirs., media adv. bd.), World Trade Coun., Women's Econ. Round Table, N.Y. Assn. Women Bus. Owners, Soc. Latin-Am. Bus. Owners, Am. Mgmt. Assn., Am. Arbitration Assn., Columbia Univ. Home: 7425 E 58th St New York NY 10022 Office: Loren Communications Internat 155 E 55th St New York NY 10022-4038

LORENSEN, GUNNHILDUR S., librarian; b. Flateyri, Iceland, Aug. 1922; arrived in U.S., 1943; d. Snorri Sigfusson and Gudrun Johannesdottir; m. Lyman E. Lorensen, 1950; children: Gudrun, Ingrid, Gilda. BS, Am. U., 1946; MS, Cornell U., 1949; MLS, U. Calif., Berkeley, 1968. Rsch. asst. Icelandic Dept. Edn., Reyjavik, 1949—50; sch. libr. Martinez (Calif.) Sch. Sys.; hon. consul of Iceland Icelandic Govt., Orinda, Calif., 1989—97. Libr. Orinda Cmty. Ch., 1989—99; mem. San Francisco Consular Corps, 1989—97. Mem.: AAUW, Icelandic Soc. No. Calif. (co-founder 1956, pres. 1956—66, v.p. 1999). Democrat. Avocations: gardening, reading, singing. Home: 9 Broadview Terr Orinda CA 94563-3101

LORENZ, KATHERINE MARY, bank executive; b. Barrington, Ill., May 1, 1946; d. David George and Mary (Hogan) L. BA cum laude, Trinity Coll., 1968; MBA, Northwestern U., 1971; grad., Grad. Sch. for Bank Adminstrn., 1977. Ops. analyst Continental Bank, Chgo., 1968, supr. ops. analysis, 1969—71, asst. mgr. customer profitability analysis, 1971—73, acctg. officer, mgr. customer profitability analysis, 1973—77, 2d v.p., 1976, asst. gen. mgr. contr.'s dept., 1977—80, v.p., 1980, contr. ops. and mgmt. svcs. dept., 1981—84, v.p., sector contr. retail banking, corp. staff and ops. depts., 1984—88, v.p., sr. sector contr. pvt. banking, centralized ops. and corp. staff, 1988—90, v.p., sr. sector contr. bus. analysis group/mgmt. acctg., 1990—94, mgr. contrs. dept. adminstrn. and tng., 1990—94; v.p., chief of staff to chief adminstrv. officer Bank Am. Ill., Chgo., 1994—96, sr. v.p., mgr. adminstrv. svcs., 1996—97, mng. dir., mgr. adminstrv. svcs., 1998—99; sr. v.p., Chgo. adminstrn. exec. Bank Am., 1999—. Mem.: Execs. Club Chgo. Office: Bank of Am ILI-231-13-20 231 S La Salle St Chicago IL 60697 Office Phone: 312-828-4756.

LORENZ, NANCY, artist; BFA in Painting and Printmaking, U. Mich., 1985; MFA in Painting, Tyler Sch. Art, Phila. and Rome, 1988. Instr. R.I. Sch. Design, 1996; lectr. in field. One-woman shows include Temple U., Rome, 1988, Willoughby Sharp Gallery, NY, 1990, Genovese Gallery, Boston, 1990, 1991, 1994, others, exhibited in group shows at Helander Gallery, NY, 1989—93, JG Contemporary, NYC, 2006, Helander Gallery, Palm Beach, 1989—91, NY Pub. Libr., 1994, Austin Ackles Studio, NY, 1995, PDX, Portland, 1996, 1998, 2000, Galerie Verneil des Saints-Péres, Paris, Galerie Xippas, numerous others, Represented in permanent collections Senayan Hotel, Jakarta, Yokahama Hotel, Japan, Soho Grand Hotel, NY, MIA Ins., Pan Am. Bldg., San Francisco, Muscat Hilton, Oman, David Barton Gym, NY Pub. Libr., Champion Paper, Ohio, Shinwa Med. Inc., Nagoya, Japan, Aero Studios, NY, The Boston Co., numerous others. Guggenheim fellow, 1998. Office: Pdx Gallery 925 NW Flanders St Portland OR 97209-3123 E-mail: pdxgallery@aol.com.*

LORFANO, PAULINE DAVIS, artist; b. Westbrook, Maine; d. Paul A. and Nellie R. (Robinson) Davis; m. Joseph James Lorfano, Apr. 18, 1952; children: Mary-Jo, Paula, Julie-Ann, Joseph III. Student, Westbrook Coll., 1946-48; Assoc. degree, Maine Coll. Art, 1950; BS, U. Maine, 1951; degree (hon.), Maine Coll. Art, 2000. Tchr. Riggs Sch., Gloucester, Mass., 1951-52; art tchr. Westbriar Elem., Vienna, Va., 1969-76, George Mason U., Fairfax, Va., 1976-80; art tchr., workshop instr. Va., 1980—; juror, lectr. art Va., 1980—. Illustrator: (book) Visiting Historic Vienna.A Child's Book to Color, 1995; one person shows include Summer Sch. Mus., 1988, Nat. Wildlife Fedn., 1989, Fisher Gallery, Schlesinger Art Ctr., No. Va. C.C., 2002, Dyn Corp. Gallery, Reston, Va., 2003, Result Gallery, Washington, 2005; group shows include Hilton Head Island Exhbn., Va. Watercolor Exhbn., Result Gallery, Wash., DC, 2005, alt. Watercolor Soc. Mid-Atlantic Regional, Maritime Mus. Concord, Calif., 2006, Result Gallery, Washington, 2006, Ventura Maritime Mus., Oxnard, Calif., 2006; works featured for mag. covers. Recipient Heritage Preservation award Historic Vienna, Inc., also awards for art. Mem. Vienna Arts Soc. Inc. (permanent, bd. dirs. 1990-98, pres. 1979-81, 88-90, 2004-05, Gold medal 1987, Stillwell award 1988, Treasury of Art 2004), Nat. League Am. PEN Women (juried-in mem., cons. art bd. 1994-96, chmn. art bd. 1982-84, art adv. 2004-06, 2d Pl. award Biennial Art Exhibit 1992), Va. Watercolor Soc. (co-pres. 2004, Richmond Region Watercolor award 2002), Internat. Soc. Marine Painters, Potomac Valley Watercolorists (juried, bd. dirs. 1990-98, pres. 1989-90, exec. bd. 2000—), Washington Watercolor Assn. (juried, exec. bd. chair 1996-97, newsletter editor 1997-2003, Am. Artist award), Arts Coun. Fairfax County, McLean Art Soc. Home: 402 Old Courthouse Rd NE Vienna VA 22180-3603 E-mail: pdl4art@aol.com.

LORIMER, LINDA KOCH, university educator; children: Katharine Elizabeth, Peter Brailler. AB, Hollins Coll., 1974; JD, Yale U., 1977; DHL (hon.), Green Mountain Coll., 1991, Washington Coll., 1992, Randolph-Macon Coll., 1992. Bar: N.Y. 1978, Conn. 1982. Assoc. Davis Polk and Wardwell, N.Y.C., 1977-78; asst. gen. counsel Yale U., New Haven, 1978-79, assoc. gen. counsel, 1979-84, assoc. provost, 1983-87, acting assoc. v.p. human resources, 1984-85; prof. law, pres. Randolph-Macon Woman's Coll., Lynchburg, Va., 1987-93; v.p., sec. Yale Univ., New Haven, 1993—. Lectr. Yale Coll. Undergrad. Seminars, 1980, 83; bd. dirs. Sprint, McGraw Hill, Yale-New Haven Hosp.; mem. corp. Yale U., 1990-93, chair Virginia Rhodes scholarship com., 1991-93; trustee HollinsU., Berkeley Divinity Sch. Chair editorial bd. Jour. Coll. and Univ. Law, 1983-87. Former trustee Hollins Coll., Berkeley Div. Sch.; mem. com. on responsible conduct rsch. Inst. Medicine, NAS, 1988; bd. dirs. Norfolk Acad.; cabinet mem. United Way of Greater New Haven. Mem. Nat. Assn. Coll. and Univ. Attys. (exec. bd. 1981-84), Nat. Assn. Schs. and Colls. United Meth. Ch. (1st v.p.), Am. Assn. Colls. and Univs. (pres. bd.), Assn. Am. Colls.,(pres. bd. dirs., chmn. bd.), Am. Assn. Theol. Schs. (bd. dirs.), Mory's Assn., Phi Beta Kappa. Episcopalian. Office: Woodbridge Hall PO Box 208230 Yale Univ New Haven CT 06520-8230

LORING, GLORIA JEAN, vocalist; b. N.Y.C., Dec. 10, 1946; d. Gerald Louis and Dorothy Ann (Tobin) Goff; m. Alan Willis Thicke, Aug. 22, 1970 (div. 1986); children: Brennan Todd, Robin Alan; m. Christopher Beaumont, June 18, 1988 (div. 1993); m. René Lagler, Dec. 20, 1994. Grad. high sch. Owner Glitz Records, L.A., 1984—; pres. Only Silk Prodns., L.A., 1985-90; owner Silk Purse Prodns., 1992—. Began profl. singing, Miami Beach, 1965; appeared in numerous TV shows; featured singer: Bob Hope's Ann. Armed Forces Christmas Tour, 1970; featured several record albums; featured actress: Days of Our Lives, 1980-86; composer: TV themes Facts of Life, 1979, Diff'rent Strokes, 1978; author: Days of Our Lives Celebrity Cookbook, 1981, Vol. II, 1983, Living the Days of Our Lives, 1984, Kids, Food and Diabetes, 1986, Parenting a Diabetic Child, 1991, The Kids Food and Diabetes Family Cookbook, 1991, Parenting a Child with Diabetes, 1999. Celebrity chmn. Juvenile Diabetes Rsch. Found. Recipient Humanitarian of Yr. award Juvenile Diabetes Rsch. Found., 1982, 88, Lifetime Commitment award Juvenile Diabetes Rsch. Found., 1999, Woman of Achievement award Miss Am. Orgn., 1999. E-mail: gloria@glorialoring.com.

LORING, HONEY, small business owner; b. Phila. BA in Psychology, U. Md., 1970; MEd, Washington U., St. Louis, 1971. Lic. psychologist-master Vt.; directress cert. Assn. Montessori Internat. Counselor Gardenville Diagnostic Ctr., St. Louis, 1971-72; tchr. Early Learning Pre-Sch., St. Louis, 1972-74; music dir., cabin counselor Follow Through Day Camp, Brattleboro, Vt., 1972-74; tchr. Montessori Sch., Dublin, 1974-75; ednl. cons. children's books Left Bank Books, St. Louis, 1975-76; program dir. day camp Brattleboro Child Devel., 1975-79; behavioral therapist Behavioral Medicine Unit, Dartmouth Med. Sch., 1979-84; pvt. therapist Brattleboro, Vt., 1984-85; founder, pres. Gone to the Dogs, Inc., Putney, Vt., 1984—. Dog groomer, 1979—92; founder Camp Gone to the Dogs, 1990—2004, Tails Up Inn, 1995—98; mfr. dog collars, 1984—; took wolves around U.S. to do ednl. environ. programs with the Clem and Jethro Lectr. Svc., 1974—76. Author: (with Jeremy Birch) You're On.Teaching Communication Skills, 1984, The Big Good Wolf, Horsin' Around, Custom Leads and Reins, 2006; contbr. articles to profl. jours. Leader 4-H Dog Club; helper Riding for the Physically Handicapped, St. Louis, 1974; founder, dir. Women in Arts, 2005—. Home and Office: PO Box 600 Putney VT 05346-0600 Office Phone: 802-387-5673.

LORKOVIC, TATJANA, librarian; b. Beograd, Yugoslavia, Jan. 17, 1933; d. Krunoslav and Antonija (Benišek) Bujas; m. Hrvoje Lorkovic, Sept. 8, 1956 (div. 1980); children: Maja, Radoslav, Ivan. Diploma, Music Acad. Zagreb, Yugoslavia, 1953, U. Croatia, Zagreb, 1957; student, U. London, 1963-64; MLS, U. Minn., 1968; MA in Russian Lang. and Lit., U. Iowa, 1972. Instr. in Serbo-Croatian lang. Workers U. of Zagreb, Yugoslavia, 1957-59; staff mem. State Ctr. for Edn. of Mgrs., Zagreb, 1959-63; Slavic libr. U. Iowa Librs., Des Moines, 1968-89, head cataloging dept., 1973-85, 86-89, libr. III, 1974, libr. IV, 1981, adminstr. serials, binding and marking ops., 1984; curator Slavic and East European collections Sterling Meml. Libr., Yale U., New Haven, 1989—; fellow Pierson Coll., Yale U., 1989—. Chair East Coast Consortium for Slavic Collections, 1993—; lectr., presenter in field. Editor, transl.: The University of the Future (Miroslav Pecujlic), 1987, (with Tomas J. Whitby) Introduction to Soviet National Bibliography, 1979; contbr. articles to profl. jours. U.S. Inst. of Peace grantee, 1991; Fulbright scholar, 1982. Mem. ALA (mem. nominating com. for cataloging and classification sect. of resources and tech. svcs. divsn. 1983-84, 89-90), Am. Assn. Advancement Slavic Studies. Office: Yale U Libr Slavic & E European Collection PO Box 208240 New Haven CT 06520-8240

LORMAN, BARBARA K., retired state senator; b. Madison, Wis., July 31, 1932; 3 children. Student, U. Wis., Whitewater and Madison. Pres. Lorman Iron and Metal Recycling Co., Ft. Atkinson, Wis., 1979—87; mem. Wis. Senate, Madison, 1980—94. Formerly chair edn. com.; mem. health, human svc. and aging com., mem. fin. insts. and cultural affairs com., mem. select com. on healthcare reform; sec. Legis. Coun., also chmn. spl. com. on farm safety, mem. spl. com. on women offenders in correctional system; mem. spl. com. study sch. aid formula; commr. Edn. Commn. of States. bd. mem. Ft Atkinson Health Svcs., Auril; bd. mem. Ft. Healthcare Ptnrs. Bd. dirs. Rainbow Hospice Care, Inc., Ft. Atkinson (Wis.) Devel. Coun., Ft. Atkinson Meml. Hosp., Madison Area Tech. Coll., Wis. Pub. Radio Assn., past pres.; bd. dirs., past pres. Ft. Atkinson Hist. Soc., Ft. Atkinson Cmty. Found.; mem. exec. bd. Sinissippi coun. Boy Scouts Am.; mem. Wis. Gov.'s Commn. USS Wisconsin; mem. bd. visitors U. Wis. Extension; active Wis. Rep. Com.; chmn. spl. projects com. City of Ft. Atkinson. Mem.: Rotary. Address: 1245 Janette St Fort Atkinson WI 53538-1526

LO RUSSO, DIANE, radiologist; b. N.Y.C., NY, Apr. 22, 1946; MD, SUNY, 1969. Cert. diagnostic radiology 1974. Intern Brookdale Hosp. Med. Ctr., Bklyn., 1969—70; resident Montefiore Med. Ctr., Bronx, 1971—74; radiologist Rye Radiology Assoc., Rye Brook, NY, 1974—. Office: Rye Radiology Assoc 30 Rye Ridge Plz Rye Brook NY 10573-2830

LOSADA-ZARATE, GLORIA, psychologist; b. Havana, Cuba, Apr. 20, 1957; came to U.S., 1962; m. Juan Zarate. BA, Fla. Internat. U., 1980; D Psychology, Nova U., 1984. Lic. psychologist, Conn. Pre-doctoral psychology fellow Yale U., New Haven, 1983-84; dir. treatment program for mentally retarded offenders Southbury Tng. Sch., Stat of Conn., 1984—86; clin. psychologist State of Conn. Dept. Mental Retardation New Haven Ctr., New Haven, 1986-88; dir. psychol. svcs. State of Conn. Dept. Mental Retardation Region 6, Waterford, Conn., 1988-92; clin. psychologist State of Conn. Dept. of Mental Health and Addiction Svcs., Middletown, 1997—2002; supervising psychologist Conn. Dept. Children and Families, Middletown, 2002—. Pvt. practice psychology, 1986—. Mem. APA. Democrat. Roman Catholic. Avocations: ballet, classical music, jazz, contemporary dance. Office: 95 E Main St Ste B-15 Meriden CT 06450

LOSASSO, VICKI RAE, political organization worker, artist; b. Kearney, Nebr., Nov. 3, 1948; d. Murl Ray Watson and Thelma Irene Fagan; m. James Raymond Brauner (dec. Oct. 21, 1998); m. Jerry Thomas LoSasso (div.); 1 child, Lynette Adelle. BA English and Women's Studies summa cum laude, Met. State Coll., 1982. Registered Am. Bd. Electroencephalographic and Evoked Potential Tech. Technician cardiology St. Anthony Hosp. Sys., Denver, 1969—85; technician Mercy Med. Ctr., Denver, 1985—90, dir. neurodiagnostic testing, 1985—90; crisis counselor Com. Aid Abused Women, Reno, 1990—92, coord. transitional housing, 1992—94; coord. edn. and outreach Nev. Network Against Domestic Violence, Nev., 1994—96; info. specialist family violence project Nat. Coun. Juvenile and Family Ct. Judges, Reno, 1996—. Attaché Sen. Bob Coffin State Nev., Carson City, Nev., 2001—02; state chmn., region chmn. Nev. Women's Lobby, Nev., 2001—06; expert in field of domestic violence; freelance leader art workshops, Reno, 2006—. Art exhbns. in various galleries, Reno, 1997—. Tnr. Crisis Call Ctr., Reno, 1991—92, Com. Aid Abused Women, Reno, 1998—; bd. dirs. Nev. Network Against Domestic Violence, Nev., 1991—94, Progressive Leadership Alliance Nev., 2001—; state aide svcs. com. Nev. Women's Lobby, 1995—; bd. dirs. Nev. Women's Agenda, 1999—. Colo. scholar, Met. State Coll., 1980—82. Democrat. Home and Office: 1785 Chaska Pl Reno NV 89502

LOSCHIAVO, FRANCESCA, set designer; Set decorator (films) E la nave va, 1983, Der Name der Rose, 1986, (TV miniseries) The Secret of the Sahara, 1987, (films) The Adventures of Baron Munchausen, 1988, La Voce della luna, 1990, Hamlet, 1990, Interview with the Vampire: The Vampire Chronicles, 1994, Kundun, 1997, Gangs of NY, 2002, Cold Mountain, 2003, The Aviator, 2004 (Academy award for best art direction, 2005).

LOSCHIAVO, LINDA BOSCO, library director; b. Rockville Ctr., N.Y., Aug. 31, 1950; d. Joseph and Jennie (DelRegno) Bosco; m. Joseph A. LoSchiavo, Sept. 7, 1974. BA, Fordham U., 1972, MA, 1990; MLS, Pratt Inst., 1974. Picture cataloguer Frick Art Reference Libr., N.Y.C., 1972-75; sr. cataloguer Fordham U. Libr., Bronx, NY, 1975-87, head of retrospective conversion, 1987-90, systems libr., 1990-91, dir. libr. at Lincoln Ctr., 1991—. Libr. cons. Mus. Am. Folk Art Libr., N.Y.C., 1985-90; indexer Arco Books, N.Y.C., 1974. Editor: Macbeth, 1990, Julius Caesar, 1990, Romeo and Juliet, 1990. Mng. producer Vineyard Opera, N.Y.C., 1981-88. Mem. ALA, N.Y. Tech. Svcs. Librs., Beta Phi Mu, Alpha Sigma Nu. Home: 317 Collins Ave Mount Vernon NY 10552-1601 Office: Fordham Univ Library 113 W 60th St New York NY 10023-7404

LOSE, CYNTHIA A., psychologist, educator; b. New Britain, Conn., Feb. 19, 1950; d. Russell D and Agnes B Lose; m. Bill Shott, Sept. 5, 1998; stepchildren: Ross V. Shott, Mark A. Shott, Timothy Shott. BS in spl. edn., So. CT. State U., 1968—72; MS in spl. edn. for emotionally disturbed, U. of Wis., 1978—81; D of psychology, Chgo. Sch. of Profl. Psychology, 1987—95. Licensed Psychologist Calf. Bd. of Psychology, 2005, N. Mex Bd. of Exam. Psychology, 2001, Certified Correctional Health Professional Nat. Commn. on Correctional Health Care, 2004, Professional Lecturer NM Dept. Pulic Safety Tng. and Recruiting Divsn., 2002. Learning disability tchr. Windsor Locks Bd. of Edn., Conn., 1972—74; tchr. of emotionally disturbed Unified Sch. Dist., Lisbon, Wis., 1974—79; tchr. pre-school hearing impaired Easter Seals Rehab. Ctr., Gary, Ind., 1979—80; tchr. emotionally disturbed Kankakee Spl. Edn. Dist., Ill., 1980—82, Arlyn Sch., Wheeling, Ill., 1982—83, Evanston Dist. 65, Ill., 1983—93; psychology intern Fed. Med. Ctr., Rochester, Minn., 1993—94; substitute tchr., halfway ho. case worker Windsor Locks Bd of Ed, Halway Ho., Inc, Windsor Locks, Hartford, Conn., 1994—95; mental health provider N. Mex Dept. Corrections, Grants, N.Mex., 1995—97; dir. of mental health New Mex. Dept Corrections, Grants, N.Mex., 1997—99; clin. supr. GEO Group, Lea County Correctional Facility, Hobbs, N.Mex., 1999—2001; dir. of mental health (acting) GEO Group, Guadalupe County Correctional Facility, Santa Rosa, N.Mex., 2001—02; clin. supr. GEO Group, Lea County Correctional Facility, Hobbs, N.Mex., 2002—03; psychologist GEO Group-Taft Correcitonal Instn., Taft, Calif., 2003—. Psychol. evaluations Zia Consulting, Inc., Hobbs, N.Mex., 2002—03; adj. prof. Coll. of the SW, Hobbs, 2001—02; instr. GEO Group-Correctional Acad., Hobbs, 2000—02. Lay eucharistic min. St. Andrew's Episcopal Ch., Taft, Calif., 2004. Mem.: APA, Nat. Commn. on Correctional Healthcare, Am. Assn. for Correctional Psychology, Honor Soc. of Phi Kappa Phi. Episcopal. Avocation: crafts. Home: P O Box 1071 Taft CA 93268 Office: Taft Correctional Inst 1500 Cadet Rd Taft CA 93268

LOSEY, LORI, media specialist; b. Lancaster, Calif. BA in Broadcasting, Pepperdine U., 1987. Freelance Jones Intercable Channel 3; sr. prodr., dir. NASA Dryden Flight Rsch. Ctr., Edwards, Calif., 1988—. Office: NASA Dryden Flight Rsch Ctr PO Box 273 MS 4851 Edwards CA 93523-0273 Business E-Mail: lori.losey@mail.dfrc.nasa.gov.

LOSIER-COOL, ROSE-MARIE, Canadian senator; b. Tracadie-Sheila, NB, Can., June 18, 1937; 2 children. BEd, U. Moncton; tchg. cert., École Normale, Fredericton. Tchr. Népisiguit H.S., Bathurst, 1972—93; senator The Senate of Can., Ottawa, 1995—, spkr. pro tempore, 1999—2002, chair ofcl. langs. com., 2002—03, govt. whip, 2004—06. Chair Can. Assn. Parliamentarians on Population and Devel. Mem.: Can. Tchrs. Fedn. (Status of Women com., Ednl. Dev. com.). Liberal. Office: 456-S Centre Block The Senate of Canada Ottawa ON Canada K1A 0A4

LOSS, LYNNE FRANKLIN, artist, volunteer; b. Vinita, Okla., July 28, 1943; d. Henry Franklin Davis and Elizabeth Viranda Franklin; m. David Martin Loss, Sept. 3, 1961; children: Scott Martin, Mark Gregory. Degree in Bus. Edn., Draughons Bus. Coll., Albuquerque, 1964. Mem.: DAR (registrar Zia chpt., past vice regent Zia chpt., Cert. of Award for various donations 2001), U.S. Daus. 1812 (organizer and state registrar N.Mex. state chpt.). Baptist. Home: 216 E Clairidge Dr Queen Creek AZ 85243-3842

LOSS, MARGARET RUTH, lawyer; b. Phila., June 17, 1946; d. Louis and Bernice Rose (Segaloff) L.; 1 child, Elizabeth Loss Johnson. BA, Radcliffe Coll., 1967; LLB, Yale U., 1970. Bar: Conn. 1970, N.Y. 1973. Assoc. Sullivan & Cromwell, N.Y.C., 1971-77; with Equitable Life Assurance Soc. U.S., N.Y.C., 1977-88, asst. gen. counsel, 1979-85, v.p. and counsel, 1985-88; counsel LeBoeuf, Lamb, Greene & MacRae, N.Y.C., 1988-98. Mem. com. Yale Law Sch. Fund. Mem. ABA, Am. Law Inst., Conn. Bar Assn., Assn. of Bar of City N.Y. Home and Office: 201 E 80th St # 12A New York NY 10021-0516 Office Phone: 212-717-6132. E-mail: margaretloss@cs.com.

LOSSE, CATHERINE ANN, pediatrics nurse, critical care nurse, educator, family practice nurse practitioner; b. Mount Holly, N.J., Mar. 12, 1959; d. David C. and Bernice (Lewis) Losse; children: Kaitlyn, Sarah. Diploma, Helene Fuld Sch. Nursing, 1980; BSN magna cum laude, Thomas Jefferson U., 1986; MSN, U. Pa., 1989; Family Nurse Practitioner Cert., Widener U., 1997. RN N.J., Pa. Staff nurse adult med.-surg. Meml. Hosp. Burlington County, Mount Holly, N.J., 1980-81; staff nurse pediatric home care Newborn Nurses, Moorestown, N.J., 1986-87; clin. nurse II surg. intensive care Deborah Heart & Lung Ctr., Browns Mills, N.J., 1986-87, clin. nurse III pediatric cardiology, 1981-86, 87-97; ednl. nurse specialist critical care The Children's Hosp., Phila., 1992-94; instr. nursing of families, maternal-child health, pediat., geriatrics Burlington County Coll., 1994-96; staff nurse pediatric home care Bayada Nurses, Burlington, N.J., 1995; family nurse practitioner Alliance Family Medicine Ctr. Fam. Med. Res. Prog., Mt. Holly, N.J., 1997-99; nurse practitioner long term care The Masonic Home of N.J., Burlington, 1999—. Clin. instr. pediat. Thomas Jefferson U., 1990; clin. instr. adult med. surg. Burlington County coll., 1991. Rep. Congress on Policy and Practice: Gerongol. Health rep., 2001—03. Mem.: ANA, Am. Acad. Nurse Practitioners, Congress on Policy and Practice (rep. gerontologic health 2001—03), Am. Geriatrics Soc., N.J. State Nurses Assn. (cabinet on continuing edn. rev. team III 1992—96, advanced practice forum 1994—). Home: 253 Spout Spring Ave Lumberton NJ 08048-2041 Office Phone: 609-239-3954. Business E-Mail: cal@njmasonic.org.

LOTAN, RACHEL, education educator; BA in English Lit. and French Lang., Lit. and Civilization, Tel Aviv U., 1971; MA in Edn., Stanford U., 1981, MA in Sociology, 1983, PhD in Edn., 1985. Tchr. jr. and sr. h.s., 1969—80; rsch. asst. Ctr. for Ednl. Rsch., Stanford U., Calif., 1982—85; assoc. prof. edn. Stanford (Calif.) U., 1999—, and dir., tchr. edn. program. Vis. asst./assoc. prof. Inst. for Advancement of Social Integration in Schs., Bar-Ilan U., Israel, 1986—91. Mem. editl. bd.: European Jour. for Intercultural Edn. Office: Stanford U Sch Edn 485 Lasuen Mall Stanford CA 94305-3096

LOTANO, DENISE ARLENE, mathematician, educator; b. Oswego, NY, May 17, 1953; d. Henry Thomas and Loretta Miriam Buske; m. Richard Arthur Lotano, Nov. 28, 1987; children: Kimberly Jennifer Boutwell, Bryan Michael. BS, SUNY, Oswego, 1975, MS, 1982. Tchr. math. Baldwinsville Ctrl. Sch. Dist., NY, 1975—. Coord. sch. contest NY State Math League, Baldwinsville, 1998—; mem. Baldwinsville Sch. Dist. Mentoring Com., 1995—. Tchr. religion St. Michael's Ch., Camillus, NY, 1990—2000. Mem.: Nat. Coun. Tchrs. Math., Assn. Math. Tchrs. NY State, Onondaga County Math. Tchrs. Assn. (judge 1980—92, coord. sch. contest 1998—). Lutheran. Avocations: travel, gardening, walking, reading, sewing. Home: 121 Coachman's Whip Drive Baldwinsville NY 13027 Office: Donald S Ray Middle School 7650 Van Buren Road Baldwinsville NY 13027 Office Phone: 315-638-6106. Personal E-mail: dlotano@bville.org.

LOTAS, JUDITH PATTON, advertising executive; b. Iowa City, Apr. 23, 1942; d. John Henry and Jane (Vandike) Patton; children: Amanda Bell, Alexandra Vandike. BA, Fla. State U., 1964. Copywriter Liller, Neal, Battle and Lindsey Advt., Atlanta, 1964-67, Grey Advt., N.Y.C., 1967-72; creative group head SSC&B Advt., N.Y.C., 1972-74, assoc. creative dir., 1974-79, v.p., 1975-79, sr. v.p., 1979-82, exec. creative dir., 1982-86; founding ptnr. Lotas Minard Patton McIver, Inc., N.Y.C., 1986—. Fundraiser Nat. Coalition Homeless, N.Y.C., 1986—; mem. creative rev. bd. Partnership Drug-Free Am.; rep. Afghan Am. Peace Corp., Kabul and Talalabad; bd. dirs. Samuel Wasman Cancer Rsch. Found., N.Y.C., 1981—88, Women's Venture Fund, 1995—; active scholarship fund raising, 2004. Named Woman of Achievement, YWCA; named one of Advt.'s 100 Best Women, Ad Age, 1989; recipient Clio award, Venice Film Festival award, Graphics award, Am. Inst. Graphic Artists, 1970, Effie award, Grad. of Distinction award, Fla. State U., 1993. Mem.: Ad. Coun. (mem. creative rev. bd. 1994—, bd. dirs. 1995—), Advt. Women N.Y. (bd. dirs. 1981—87, 1st v.p. 1984—87, Advt. Woman of the Yr. 1993), Kappa Alpha Theta. Democrat. Office Phone: 212-288-5676. E-mail: jlotas@earthlink.net, jlotas@lpny.com.

LOTCHIN, PHYLLIS MORRIS, English language educator; b. Springfield, Ill., July 12, 1936; d. E. L. and Vera Pelletier Morris; m. Roger Williams Lotchin, June 1, 1958; 1 child, Theodore R. BA, Millikin U., Decatur, Ill., 1958; MA, U. N.C., Chapel Hill, 1966, PhD, 1977; postgrad., Duke U., Durham, N.C. Tchr. h.s. English, Ill. and Calif., 1958—65; tchr. English N.C. Cen. U., Durham, 1967—; tchr. continuing edn. Meredith Coll., Raleigh, NC. Chmn. restoration of founder's home N.C. Cen. U.; chair Arts Downtown Com.; mem. sch. bd. Chapel Hill, NC; chair Com. to Assess Effect of Nuclear Power Plant on Chapel Hill. Recipient Alumni award, Millikin U. Mem.: LWV (pres. Chapel Hill), AAUP (pres. local chpt.).

LOTEMPIO, JULIA MATILD, retired accountant; b. Budapest, Hungary, Oct. 14, 1934; came to U.S., 1958, naturalized 1962; d. Istvan and Irma (Sandor) Fejos; m. Anthony Joseph LoTempio, Mar. 11, 1958. AAS in Lab. Tech. summa cum laude, Niagara County C.C., Sanborn, N.Y., 1967; BS in Tech. and Vocat. Edn. summa cum laude, SUNY, Buffalo, 1970; MEd in Guidance and Counseling, Niagara U., 1973, BBA in Acctg. summa cum laude, 1983, MBA in Mgmt., 1998. Sr. analyst, rschr. Gt. Lakes Carbon Co., Niagara Falls, N.Y., 1967-71; tchr. sci. Niagara Falls Schs., 1973-75; tchr. sci. and English Starpoint Sch. System, Lockport, N.Y., 1975-77; club adminstr., acct. Twinlo Racquetball, Inc., Niagara Falls, 1979-81; bus. cons. Twinlo Beverage, Inc., Niagara Falls, 1981-85; staff acct. J.D. Elliott & Co. PC, CPAs, Buffalo, 1986-87; acct. Lewiston, NY, 1988—2001; instr. applied chemistry Niagara County C.C., Sanborn, NY, 1979, instr. acctg. principles, 1989—2001; ret., 2001. Bd. dirs. Niagara Frontier Meth. Home Inc., Niagara Frontier Nursing Home Inc., The Blocher Homes Inc., Buffalo. Mem. faculty continuing edn., speaker, chairperson fin. and community rels. coms. United Meth. Ch., Dickersonville, N.Y., 1985-90; guest speaker, counselor, tchr. Beechwood Svc. Guild, Buffalo, 1987-91; bd. dirs. Niagara Frontier Meth. Home, Inc., Getzville, N.Y., 1988-2001; bd. dirs., mem. fin., investment, pension, ins., and community rels. coms. Niagara Frontier Nursing Home Co., Inc., Getzville, 1988-2001, Blocher Homes, Inc., Williamsville, N.Y., 1988-2001; asst. sec., bd. dirs., mem. exec., quality and assurance coms., chmn. community rels. com. Beechwood/Blocher Community, Buffalo, 1990-2001; mem. Coop. Parish Coun., Sanborn, N.Y., 1991-94; mem. adminstrv. bd., chmn. outreach com. Pekin (N.Y.) United Meth. Ch., 1992-2000; sec. to bd. dirs. Beechwood/Blocher Found., Amherst, N.Y., 1992-93, asst. treas., 1993-94, treas., 1994, vice chmn., 1994-2001. Mem. NAFE, Nat. Soc. Pub. Accts., Nat. Assn. Accts., Nat. Fedn. Bus. and Profl. Women's Club, Internat. Platform Assn., Niagara U. Alumni Assn., SUNY Coll. Buffalo Alumni Assn., Niagara County C.C. Alumni Assn. Avocations: public speaking, walking, travel, reading, computers. Home and Office: 1026 Ridge Rd Lewiston NY 14092-9704 Personal E-mail: ajlotempio@juno.com.

LOTEYRO, CORAZON BIGATA, physician; b. Manila, Apr. 9, 1951; arrived in U.S., 1979; d. Victor G. Loteyro and Emilia Bigata; 1 child, Elizabeth. BS, Mindanao State U., Marawi City, Philippines, 1972; MD, U. East Med. Ctr., Manila, 1976. Bd. cert. Am. Bd. Family Physicians, Diplomate Fellow Am. Acad. Family Physicians. Physician Humana Medfirst, Peoria, Ill., 1984-85, Family Health Plan, Elm Grove, Wis., 1985-96, Covenant Health, Pewaukee, Wis., 1996—. Vol. Salvation Army, Milw., 1993. Fellow Am. Acad. Family Physicians; mem. Filipino-Am. Med. Assn. (pres. 1994-95), U. of East Alumni Assn. Midwest (treas. 1990-94). Republican. Roman Catholic. Avocations: skiing, travel, movies, reading, music. Home: 4285 Windsong Pl Plover WI 54467 Office: 2401 Plover Rd Plover WI 54467 Office Phone: 715-295-3800. Personal E-mail: cbloteyromd@yahoo.com.

LOTRINGER, SYLVERE, writer; b. Paris, Oct. 15, 1938; came to U.S., 1969; s. Cudek and Doba (Borenstein) L.; 1 child, Mia-Laure. B.A., Sorbonne U., Paris, 1962, M.A., 1963; Ph.D., Ecole Pratique Hautes Etudes, Paris, 1967. Lectr., U. New South Wales, Sidney, Australia, 1968-69; asst. prof. Swarthmore Coll. (Pa.), 1969-70; assoc. prof. Case Western Res. U., Cleve., 1970-72; prof. French, Columbia U., N.Y.C., 1972—. Author: Pure War, 1983, New York Scene, 1983, Forget Baudrillard, 1987, Overexposed, 1988, Antonin Artaud, 1990; editor fgn. agts. series of books, 1982—; editor Semiotext(e), 1974—. Office: Columbia U Dept of Philadelphia Autonomedia 55 S 11th St Brooklyn NY 11211-7036

LOTT, BRENDA LOUISE, insurance company executive; b. Clinton, Ind., July 29, 1955; d. John and Thelma Louise (Anderson) Pastore; m. Robert Ralph Rundle, June 16, 1974 (div. July 1985); children: Danielle Marie Rundle, John Robert Rundle; m. Mark Lee Lott, July 4, 1985. BA in Polit. Sci., Colo. Women's Coll., Denver, 1976; student, Ins. Inst. of Am. Claim adjuster Allstate Ins. Co., Englewood, Colo., 1973-83; field claim adjuster Transamerica Ins. Co., Englewood, 1983-86; claim examiner Colonial Ins. Co., Denver, 1986-87, examiner/supr., 1987-89, regional claim mgr., 1990-92; dir. financial and insurance svcs. Innovative Svcs. Am., Golden, Colo., 1992—. Staff speaker Western Ins. Info. Svc., Denver, 1983-85; participant, invited faculty mem. 5-day lecture series Colonial Univ., Anaheim, Calif., 1990. Sponsor Plan Internat. foster parents program, 1989—. Mem. NAFE, LWV, NAACP (mem.-at-large), Ins. Women of Denver, Internat. Customer Svc. Assn., Colo. Claims Assn. (bd. dirs. 1986-88), Claim Mgrs. Coun., Denver Claims Assn., PGA Tours Ptnrs. Avocations: raquetball, co-ed flag football, basketball, tennis, golf. Office: Innovative Svcs of Am 13922 Denver West Pkwy Ste 200 Golden CO 80401-3142

LOTT, CINDY M., lawyer; m. Kris Grube; 2 children. BA, Ind. U., 1989; JD, Yale U., 1993. Clk. 1st U.S. Cir. Ct. Appeals, 1993; sect. chief adminstrv. and regulatory litigation Atty. Gen. Jeff Modisett; dep. counsel 2000 Dem. Conv., 2000; former ptnr. Cadwalader, Wickersham & Taft; chief counsel 2004 Dem. Conv., 2004—. Mem.: Phi Beta Kappa. Office: Dem Nat Com 430 S Capitol St SE Washington DC 20003

LOTT, DAWN ALISHA, mathematics professor; b. Phila., Aug. 27, 1965; d. Robert Delon and Carolyn Edwina Lott; m. Kenneth Frederick Green, Mar. 19, 2005; children: Samuel Darius Crumpler, Carilyn Anmarie Kenedie Green. BS in Math., Bucknell U., 1987; MS in Applied Math., Mich. State U., 1989; PhD in Engring. Scis., Applied Math., Northwestern U., 1994. Postdoctoral rsch. assoc. U. Md., Coll. Park, 1994—97; asst. prof. NJ. Inst. Tech., Newark, 1997—2003; assoc. prof. Del. State U., Dover, 2004—. Contbr. articles various profl. jours. Recipient Cert. Recognition, NJIT Ronald E. McNair Post baccalaureate Achieve. Program, 2002, Appreciation award, Greater Phila. Region Louis Stokes Alliance for Minority Participation, 2004, Cert. Recognition, Girls Exploration Math. and Sci., 2004; grantee Applied Math. Rsch. Ctr., Dept. Def., 2005-2008. Mem.: Soc. Indsl., Applied Math. (assoc.), Math. Assn. Am. (assoc.; vice-chair speakers, nj sect. 2000—03, Cert. Appreciation 2003), Biomedical Engring. Soc. (assoc.), Assn. Women Math. (assoc.; exec. com. mem. 2006—06, Internat. Travel award 2005), Am. Math. Soc. (assoc.), Nat. Assn. Mathematicians (life; v.p. 2005—06, Appreciation award 2004), Delta Sigma Theta (life). African Meth. Avocations: sewing, swimming. Office: Del State U 1200 N DuPont Hwy Dover DE 19901 Office Phone: 302-857-7059. Home Fax: 302-857-7054; Office Fax: 302-857-7054. Personal E-mail: dawnalott@aol.com. Business E-Mail: dlott@desu.edu.

LOTT, JOHNNYE JO, elementary school educator, writer; b. Natchitoches, LA, Dec. 6, 1935; d. John Adams and Mildred (Slaughter) Foshee; m. Stanley George Lott, Sept. 2, 1956; children: Philip, Jo Lynn Chesser, Brantley. B of Music Edn., Northwestern State U., 1957. Cert. Tchg. La. Tchr. music Orleans Parish Bd. Edn., New Orleans, 1958—59; tchr. first grade Ferncrest Pvt. Sch., 1962; tchr. lang. arts, gifted cirriculum Monroe County Schs., Forsyth, Ga., 1969—80; tchr. gifted curriculum Rapides Parish Schs., Alexandria, La., 1980—85; dir., bus. owner Sylvan Learning Ctr., 1987—96; freelance writer Murfreesboro, NC, 1996—. Author: In The Cold Of The Sun: Children In Crisis, 2002. Vol. Habitat Humanity, Murfreesboro, NC, 2002; bd. dirs. Hist. Assn.; leader Dulcimer Ensemble sponsored by Emmanuel Bapt. Ch., Alexandria, La., 2005—; vol. tchr. Mountain Dulcimer, Alexandria, La., 2005. Mem.: Friends Whitaker Libr. (bd. dirs. 2000—02), La. Coll. Faculty Women (pres. 1994—95), Phi Kappa Phi, Sigma Alpha Iota. Democrat. Baptist. Avocations: piano, reading, travel, gardening, writing. Home: 157 Adams Path Pineville LA 71360-7905

LOTT, KATHY L., language educator; b. Hinsdale, Ill., July 22, 1964; d. James E. and Connie Lott. BA in Spanish Lang., Elmhurst Coll., Ill., 1991; MA in Spanish Lang. and Lit., St. Louis U., 2004. Cert. tchr. Ill., 1998. Ins. claims rep. Ohio Casualty Group Ins. Co., Lombard, Ill., 1992—98; translator self-employed Ill., 1992—2000; dept. coord./tchr. Spanish Westmont H.S., Ill., 1998—; tchg. asst./adj. prof. St. Louis U., 2002—03. Sponsor World Lang. Clubs, Westmont, Ill., 1998—; freshman class sponsor Westmont H.S., 1998—2002, yearbook advisor, 1998—2002, tchrs.' asst. team mem., 2000—. Sponsor (high sch. yearbook) Sentinel 2000 (Waslworth Pub. Gallery of Excellence, 2001). Mem.: Am. Assn. Tchrs. Spanish & Portuguese (assoc.), Ill. Coalition Tchrs. Fgn. Lang. (assoc.), Assn. for Curriculum & Devel. (assoc.), Alpha Mu Gamma, Alpha Sigma Chi (assoc.), Kappa Delta Pi (assoc.). Office: Westmont HS 909 North Oakwood Dr Westmont IL 60559

LOTT, VERA NAOMI, artist, educator; b. Allentown, Pa., Oct. 26, 1923; d. Russell Edgar and Tivilia Landis (Gerhart) Kemmerer; m. Jack Edward Lott (dec. Nov. 1998); children: Dennis Michael, Jack Andrew(dec.), Gary Randall, Timothy Blair, Bruce Edward. Grad. h.s., Phila. Art tchr., 1960—, YWCA, Ohio, Westerville, Ohio. Judge Ohio State Fair for Childrens Art Show; art tchr., Westerville, Ohio; pvt. dance instr. Singer for 3 ch. choirs; singer for 2 sr. ctrs. With U.S. Coast Guard, 1940—42. Recipient 1st place for pencil portraits of children, Graceland. Mem.: Westerville Art League (past pres., sec.). Lutheran. Home: 7000 Lee Rd Apt3R Westerville OH 43081-9557

LOTZE, BARBARA, retired physicist; b. Jan. 4, 1924; came to U.S., 1961, naturalized, 1967. d. Matyas and Borbala (Toth) Kalo; m. Dieter P. Lotze, Oct. 6, 1958 (dec. Dec. 1987); m. Herbert L. Retcofsky, July 1998. Applied Math. Diploma with honors, Eotvos Lorand U. Scis., Budapest, Hungary, 1956; PhD, Innsbruck U., Austria, 1961. Mathematician Hungarian Cen. Statis. Bur., Budapest, 1955-56; tchr. math. Iselsberg, Austria, 1959-60; from asst. prof. physics to assoc. prof. to prof. Allegheny Coll., 1963-90, prof. emeritus, 1990—, chmn. dept., 1981-84. Lectr. in history of physics; spkr. to civic groups. Editor: Making Contributions: An Historical Overview of Women's Role in Physics, 1984; co-editor: The First War Between Socialist States: The Hungarian Revolution of 1956 and Its Impact, 1984; contbr. articles to profl. jours. Mem. AAUW, Am. Phys. Soc. (mem. com. internat. freedom of scientists 1993-95), Am. Inst. Physics (mem. adv. com. history of physics 1994-97), Am. Assn. Physics Tchrs. (coun., sect. rep. Western Pa. 1978-86, chmn. com. on women in physics 1983-84, com. internat. physics edn. 1991-93, com. history and philosophy of physics 1996-98, Disting. Svc. award 1986, cert. of appreciation 1988), Am. Hungarian Educators Assn. (pres. 1980-82). Home: 2269 Watchfield Dr South Park PA 15129-8977

LOTZE, EVIE DANIEL, psychodramatist; b. Roswell, N.Mex., Mar. 6, 1943; d. Wadsworth Richard and Lee Ora (Norrell) Daniel; m. Christian Dieter Lotze, June 9, 1963; children: Conrad, Monica. BA cum laude, La. State U., 1964; MA, Goddard Coll., 1975; PhD, Union Inst., Cin., 1990. Dir. Casa Alegre, Hogares, Albuquerque, 1979-80; pvt. practice Riyadh, Saudi Arabia, 1980-83, Silver Spring, Md., 1983-85; dir. Gulf States Psychodrama Tng., Houston, 1986-88; founder, dir. Innerstages Psychodrama Tng., Houston and Washington, 1988-99; program devel. cons. in tng. Children's Nat. Med. Ctr., Washington, 1994-96; pvt. practice Paris, 1996-97; mem. sr. profl. staff Pretrial Svcs. Resource Ctr., Washington, 1998-2001; mem. Work Culture Transformation Bd., USAF, 2001; cons. Work Transformation Group, 2001—03. Supr. Houston Area psychodramatists, 1988—98; tng. cons. Assn. Applied Psychologists, Moscow, 1992—97; cons. in field. Author: Work Culture Transformation: From Straw to Gold, A Modern Hero's Journey, 2004; (tng. manual) Clinical Psychodrama Training Manual, 3 vols., 1990, Pretrial Services Reference Book, 1999. Bd. dirs. Interact Theater, Houston, 1992, Arts and Humanities Alliance, Jefferson County; mentor First in Your Family, 2005-. Recipient Fulbright sr. scholars award for Russia. Democrat. Lutheran. Avocations: cross country skiing, biking, hiking, camping, reading. Home: 2231 Old Leetown Pike Kearneysville WV 25430 Office Phone: 304-728-7928. Personal E-mail: evielotze@citlink.net, roxleyfarms@citlink.net.

LOUCKS, KATHLEEN MARGARET, lawyer; b. Milw., 1971; Student, Bethel Coll., 1989—92; BA, U. Minn., Mpls., 1995; JD, William Mitchell Coll. Law, 1999. Bar: Minn. 1999, US Dist. Ct. (dist. Minn.), Iowa 2005. Assoc. Gislason & Hunter, L.L.P., Minnetonka. Named a Rising Star, Minn. Super Lawyers mag., 2006. Mem.: Minn. Trial Lawyers Assn., Minn. State Bar Assn., ABA, Minn. Women Lawyers, Hennepin County Bar Assn., Minn. Def. Lawyers Assn. Office: Gislason & Hunter LLP 701 Xenia Ave S Ste 500 Minneapolis MN 55416 Office Phone: 763-225-6000. E-mail: kloucks@gislason.com.*

LOUD, PATRICIA CUMMINGS, curator; b. Beaumont, Tex., Feb. 20, 1930; d. Patrick A. and Gaynelle Guinn Cummings; m. John Fiske Loud, June 8, 1958 (dec.); children: Sarah, John Timothy, Alexander Guinn. BFA, U. Tex., Austin, 1951; MA, Radcliffe Coll., Cambridge, Mass., 1954, Harvard U., 1954, PhD in Fine Arts, 1990. Ford fellow history art Brown U., Providence, 1956—60; sr. resident Cabot Hall Radcliffe Coll., 1964—68; lectr. U. Conn., Groton, Conn., 1971—72; instr. Tex. Christian U., Ft. Worth, 1972—76; exec. asst. Van Cliburn Found., Ft. Worth, 1980—81; curator Kimbell Art Mus., Ft. Worth, 1981—. Cons. in field. Author: In Pursuit of Quality: The Kimbell, 1987, The Art Museums of Louis L. Kahn, 1989; contbr. chapters to books. Mem.: AIA (hon.), Dallas (Tex.) Arch. Assn., Soc. Arch. Historians, Coll. Art Assn., Tex. Soc. Archs. (hon. John G. Flowers award 1998). Office: Kimbell Art Museum 3333 Camp Bowie Blvd Fort Worth TX 76107 Business E-Mail: ploud@kimballmuseum.org.

LOUDON, KAREN LEE, physical therapist; b. Kansas City, Mo., July 25, 1958; d. Walter Raymond and Clarice Frances (Washburn) L. BS in Edn., U. Kans., 1980; BS in Phys. Therapy, U. Kans. Med. Ctr., 1985; MS in Edn., U. Kans., 1987; MS in Orthop. Manual Phys. Therapy, Ola Grimsby Inst. Consortium, 1997. Registered phys. therapist, Kans., Mo.; cert. clin. specialist in orthop. phys. therapy. Phys. therapist Watkins Ctr. U. Kans., Lawrence, 1985—. Athletic trainer, Sunflower State Games, Lawrence, 1990-92; clin. instr. U. Kans. Med. Ctr., Lawrence, 1987—; presenter in field. Contbr. articles to profl. jours. Mem. Am. Phys. Therapy Assn. (mem. Kans. legis. com. 1983-84, Kans. Disting. Clin. Svc. award 1995), Nat. Athletic Trainer Assn., Am. Coll. Sports Medicine, Phi Kappa Phi. Avocations: golf, biking, softball, hiking. Office: Watkins Health Ctr U Kans Lawrence KS 66045-0001

LOUGEAY, DENRUTH COLLEEN, clinical psychologist, educator; b. Chicago, Il., Nov. 7, 1943; d. Denzil Gordon Barre and Ruth Marian (Bergstrom) Larsen; m. Denis Howard Lougeay, Aug. 14, 1965; children: Stace Michael, Gregg Christopher. BS, U. Ill., Urbana, 1965; MEd, U. Ill., 1968; PhD, U.S. Internat. U., San Diego, 1986. Lic. clin. psychologist, Calif. Tchr. spl. edn. Urbana (Ill.) Pub. Schs., 1965-68; ednl. diagnostician Clin. Classroom Joliet (Ill.) Pub. Schs., 1968-69; counselor Women's Resource Ctr., San Luis Rey, Calif., 1980-82; psychologist Delmont Prt. Hosp., Victoria, Australia, 1982-83; group therapist Parents United East and North San Diego County, 1982-84; psychologist Palomar Coll., San Marcos, Calif., 1984-87; pvt. practice, Encinitas, Calif., 1988—. Disaster mental health officer ARC, San Diego, 1994—. Recipient State ARC award, 1991—97. Fellow San Diego Psychol. Assn. (pres. 1998); mem. APA (Calif. state coord. disaster response 1995—, nat. adv. bd. disaster response 1998-2001, Presdl. Citation 2000), Calif. Psychol. Assn. (state chair disaster response 1995—, Silver Psi award, 1998, Disting. Humanitarian award, 2006), Soc. Mental Health Profls. (pres. 1989-90, bd. dirs.), Assn. Psychol. Type (sec. San Diego chpt. 1988-90, bd. dirs.), Mensa, Illini Club San Diego County (bd. dirs. 1987—). Avocations: hot air ballooning, genealogy, travel. Office: Arrow Psychol Svc 404 Alviso Way Encinitas CA 92024-2616

LOUGEE, WENDY PRADT, library director, educator; b. Rhinelander, Wis., Aug. 9, 1950; d. Alan Emmons Pradt and Marie Elizabeth Wendland; m. Michael Durand Lougee, Aug. 25, 1973; 1 child, Mariel. BA, Lawrence U., 1972; MS, U. Wis., 1973; MA, U. Minn., 1977. Head grad. libr. U. Mich. Libr., Ann Arbor, Mich., 1984—93, assoc. dir., 1993—2002; univ. libr., McKnight presdl. prof. U. Minn., Mpls., 2002—. Contbr. articles to profl. jours. JSTOR Project grantee Mellon Found., 1996. Mem. ALA (life), Am. Soc. Info. Sci. Office: U Minn 499 O Meredith Wilson Libr 309 19th Ave S Minneapolis MN 55455 Fax: 612-626-9353. Office Phone: 612-624-1807. E-mail: wlougee@umn.edu.*

LOUGHLIN, ANN URSULA, professional golfer, educator; d. John Dominic and Joanne Loughlin. BS, U. Iowa, 1974, MA, 1976. Cert. class A membership PGA, LPGA. Writer, coach Iowa Western CC, Council Bluffs, 1978—80; athletic coord. Mary Crest Coll., Davenport, Iowa, 1980—82; sports writer Quad City Times, Davenport, 1983—85; rules offcl. WPGA, Palo Alto, 1985; asst. golf profl. Lakeway, Austin, 1986—88; golf tchg. profl. Bay Area Calif. Driving Ranges, San Jose, 1988—93; tchg. profl., owner Loughlin Golf, U. Mont. Golf Course, Missoula, Mont., 2000—. Coach student svcs. North Iowa Area Coll., Mason City, 1976; retail sales Franklin Covey, San Francisco, 1996; sales Sun Mountain Specialties, Missoula, Mont., 2000. Author: (book) Signs of Their Times, Iowa Hometown Slogans, Photos and Stories, 2006. Instr., participant Susan B. Komen Events, 1998—, Poetry Ctr.; vol. U. Ariz., Tucson, 2005—06. Named one of Golf for Women Top 50 Tchrs., Consumer Rsch. Council Top Profl.; named to Top 50 Tchrs., 2001; recipient Consumer Rsch. award, 2001; Rural Golf Grant, USGA, 2001. Mem.: U. Iowa Alumni Assn., Women's Sports Found., Noetic Scis., Kappa Kappa Gamma. Avocations: walking, writing, reading, golf. Personal E-mail: annloughlin@hotmail.com.

LOUIE, PEGGY C., secondary school educator; b. Danbury, Conn., Apr. 19, 1971; d. S. Y. and S. J. Chuang; m. Wai D. Louie, July 11, 1998; children: Jessica, Samantha. BA, U. Tex., Austin, 1993. Cert. tchr. Tex. Tchr. Newman Smith HS, Carrollton, Tex., 1995—. Named Educator of Yr., Greater Dallas Asian Am. C. of C., 2003. Office: Newman Smith High Sch 2335 N Josey Ln Carrollton TX 75006 Office Phone: 972-968-5200.

LOUIS-DREYFUS, JULIA, actress; b. N.Y.C., Jan. 13, 1961; d. William and Judith Louis-Dreyfus; m. Brad Hall, 1987; children: Henry, Charles. Attended, Northwestern U. Former mem. Second City and the Practical Theatre Company, Chicago, Ill. Actor (TV series) Saturday Night Live, 1982-85, Day by Day, 1986-89, The Art of Being Nick, 1986, Seinfeld, 1989-98 (Emmy award supp. actress, 1996, Emmy nom., 1992, 93, 94, 95, 97, 98, Amer. Comedy award best supp. actress, 1993, 94, 95, 97, 98, Golden Globe award supp. actress, 1994, SAG award, 1997, 98), The New Adventures of Old Christine, 2006-(Emmy award for outstanding lead actress in a comedy series, 2006); actor, prodr. Watching Ellie, 2002-2003; (TV appearances) Family Ties, 1988, Dinosaurs, 1991, The Single Guy, 1995, Hey Arnold, 1997, Curb Your Enthusiasm, 2000, 01, The Simpsons (voice), 2001, Arrested Development, 2002, 04, 05; (films) Soul Man, 1986, Troll, 1986, Hannah and Her Sisters, 1986, National Lampoon's Christmas Vacation, 1989, Jack the Bear, 1993, North, 1994, Father's Day, 1997, Deconstructing Harry, 1997, A Bug's Life (voice) 1998, Gilligan's Island, 1999, Speak Truth to Power, 2000; (TV movies) London Suite, 1996, Animal Farm (voice), 1999, Gepetto, 2000 Office: Jonas PR 240 26th St Ste 3 Santa Monica CA 90402 also: Hofflund/Polone 9465 Wilshire Blvd Beverly Hills CA 90212*

LOUISELL, LINDA KAY, elementary education educator, musician; b. Mt. Pleasant, Mich., July 17, 1955; d. Ernest and Betty L. Wolters; m. Robert S. Louisell, May 21, 1976; children: David, Daniel. B Music Edn., Cen. Mich. U., 1977, MA, 1985. Cert. K-12 music tchr., Mich. Tchr. vocal music, asst. band dir. Beal City Pub. Sch., Mt. Pleasant, 1977-79; elem. tchr. music Mt. Pleasant Pub. Schs., 1979—. Dir. carol choir 1st Presbyn. Ch., Mt. Pleasant, 1977-80; dir. jr. choir 1st United Meth. Ch., Mt. Pleasant, 1980— Mem. Genesis Bell Choir, Mt. Pleasant, 1981—; leader clarinet sect., treas. Cen. Mich. Area Concert Band, Shepherd, 1973—; pres. Winn (Mich.) Parents' Club, 1989-91; musician Back Porch Pickers Assn., Midland, Mich., 1992-2000. Grantee Eisenhower Found., 1991. Mem. NEA, Mich. Edn. Assn., Mt. Pleasant Edn. Assn., Mich. Assn. for Computer Users in Learning, Delta Omicron (chpt. advisor 1981-91, Advisor of Yr. award 1987), Mich. Music Educator's Assn. (data coord., membership chairperson, Tchr. of Yr., 2005), Art Reach of Mid Mich., (bd. mem.). Avocations: telecommunications, computers, bicycling, cross country skiing, astronomy. Office: Mt Pleasant Public Schools 720 N Kinney Ave Mount Pleasant MI 48858-1757

LOUISON, DEBORAH FINLEY, global public affairs consultant; b. Aberdeen, S.D., Sept. 20, 1951; d. Donald S. and Barbara F. (Lowenstein) Finley; 1 child, Stacey Renee. BA, Nat. Coll. Edn., 1987. Asst. to sec. Dept. Edn. & Cultural Affairs State of S.D., Pierre, 1973-77; program dir. forestry div. State of S.D., Pierre, 1978-81; legisl. dir. Congressman Clint Roberts, Washington, 1981-83, Congresswoman Barbara Vucanovich, Washington, 1983-84; assoc. dir. fed. affairs Nat. Conf. State Legisl., Washington, 1984-89, dir. govt. affairs, 1989; dept. asst. sec. U.S. Dept. of Energy, 1989-93; sr. v.p., dir. global svcs. APCO Assocs. Worldwide, Washington, 1993—2003; v.p. govt. relations Cadbury Schweppes Am. Region, 2004—. Contbr. articles to profl. jours. Planning and devel. com. Pierre C. of C., 1974-76; campaign asst. Clint Roberts for Congress, 1979-80; coordinator for state legisl. Bush/Quayle Campaign, Washington, 1988. Mem.: NAFE, Women Govt. Rels. (com. chair). Republican. Roman Catholic. Avocation: golf. Office: Cadbury Schweppes 1225 I St NW Ste 300 Washington DC 20005 Office Phone: 202-661-6188. E-mail: deborah.louison@am.csplc.com.

LOUIZOS, ANNA ALEXANDRA, set designer; b. Marysville, Calif., June 24, 1957; d. Evangelos and Dianna (Marenakis) L.; m. Andrew Brian Farber, Sept. 21, 1984 (div. Apr. 1989). Student, Mills Coll., 1975-77; BFA, NYU, 1980, MFA, 1989. Assoc. designer Regional Theatre/Off Broadway, 1983-93; art dir. The Tony Awards, N.Y.C., 1990-93; asst. designer The Cosby Show, N.Y.C., 1989-90, Broadway plays My Fair Lady, 1993, The Red Shoes, 1993, Birdie Blue, 2005; assoc. designer A Christmas Carol, N.Y.C., 1994, (game show) Snakes and Ladders, 1996, Whistle Down the Wind, 1996, The Scarlet Pimpernel, 1997; interior designer Passport Mex. Restaurant, 1991, Sharaku Japanese Restaurant, 1993. Recipient The Irving Goldman award The Friars

Club, 1988. Mem. Acad. TV Arts and Scis. (Emmy award nominee 1993, Tony award for art direction 1992), United Scenic Artists. Democrat. Avocations: music writing, singing. Home: 207 E 5th St Apt 12 New York NY 10003-8540

LOUK, DONNA PAT, elementary school educator, music educator; b. Phoenix, Mar. 26, 1954; d. Donald Duane and Patsy Lea Louk. BA in Christian Edn. and Church Music, Pacific Christian Coll., 1978; MusM, Ariz. State U., 1985, PhD in Curriculum and Instrn., 2002. Elem. edn. cert. with music endorsement, Grand Canyon U., Phoenix, 1982; Kodaly Cert., Holy Names Coll., Oakland, Calif., 1987-89; Dalcroze cert. Ariz. State U., 1986, Orff Level III, 1996. Elem. music tchr. Alhambra Elem. Sch. Dist., Pendergast Sch. Dist., Kyrene Sch. Dist., Washington Elem. Sch. Dist.; music coord., 5th grade tchr. Alhambra Elem. Sch. Dist.; grad. tchg. asst. U. Ariz., 1993-94, Ariz. State U., 1998—2000; adj. faculty Ariz. State U. W, 2002—03. Presenter in field of music edn., rsch., various confs. and workshops in U.S., U. S. Ala., 2004-; children's choir dir., HS choir pianist, Sunnyslope Christian Ch., Phoenix, 1972-74; pvt. piano tchr. Fullerton, 1977-78, Phoenix, 1984-86; pianist Santa Ana (Calif.) Christian Ch., 1978; ch. musician, Peoria (Ariz.) Christian Ch., 1995. Newsletter editor Alhambra Dist. Assn. Classroom Tchrs., 1989-90 (Sch. Bell award for outstanding publ.). Adjudicator All-State Solo & Ensemble, Choral Dirs. Assn., 1992-99. Mem. Orgn. Am. Kodaly Educators (hospitality chair/steering com. nat. conf. Provo, Utah 1996), Am. Orff Schulwerk Assn., Music Educators Nat. Conf., Ariz. Music Educators Assn., Ariz. Soc. Gen. Music (regional rep. 1987-93), Ariz. Kodaly Tchrs. Soc. (pres. 1991, 94, 2000-02, newsletter editor 1990-97), Phi Kappa Phi. Republican. Home: 4617 W Solano Dr S Glendale AZ 85301-6243 E-mail: dlouk@aol.com.

LOVE, APRIL GAYE MCLEAN, librarian; b. San Jose, Calif., Apr. 28, 1947; d. Frederick F. and Geneva A. (Gmelin) McL.; m. Glen Bolinger, 1974 (div. 1984). B.A., U. Oreg., 1969, M.L.S., 1970, M.A. in Biology, 1976, BA in Dance, U. Calif., Irvine, 1989. Rsch. asst. Oreg. State U., Corvallis, 1972-74; sci. illustrator Smithsonian Inst., La Jolla, Calif., 1974; sci. bibliographer U. Calif.-Irvine, 1975-94; phys. scis. reference librarian, phys. sci. bibliographer dept. collection and devel., also mem. percussion ensemble, Sch. Fine Arts, U. Calif.-Irvine Symphony Orch., 1986-94; libr. phys. sci. Univ. Calif., Irvine, Calif., 1994-2004; libr. sci. and engring. libr. U. Utah, Salt Lake City, Utah, 2004—. Co-dir. classical music Sta. KUCI-radio, 1983-2000. Mem. ALA (conf. attendant, 1981, 87), Calif. Acad. Research Librarians, Sci. and Engring. Academic Librarians (chair program com., sec. so. br., 1988—), So. Calif. Botanists, Orange County Library Assn; attended confs. in field. Choreographer: Everyone Gets the Blues, 1980; contbr. article to popular mag. Office: Univ Utah J Willard Marriott Libr Sci and Engring 295 South 1500 East Salt Lake City UT 84112-0860 Office Phone: 801-581-7533. Business E-Mail: april.love@utah.edu.

LOVE, BEVERLY ANNE, retired elementary school educator; b. Newton, Kans., Feb. 20, 1947; d. Charles E. Jr. and Maeanna (Seedle) Rudicel; m. Stephen W. Love, Aug. 24, 1968; children: Stephanie Anne, Kristina Dianne. AA, Hutchinson Jr. Coll., Kans., 1967; BA in Edn., Ft. Hays State Coll., 1969; MEd, Wichita State U., 1980. Tchr. Graber Sch., Hutchinson, Kans., 1969-71, McCandless Sch., Hutchinson, 1975-77, Rosalia Grade Sch., Rosalia, Kans., 1977-79, Grandview Elem. Sch., El Dorado, Kans., 1979—2004, ret., 2004. TESA trainer, mem. bldg. level improvement team, chair profl. devel. com., summer sch. coord. Grandview Elem. Sch. Mem. NEA, Alpha Delta Kappa. Methodist. E-mail: blove@eldoradoschools.org.

LOVE, BRENDA ZEJDL, writer; b. Temple, Tex., Dec. 13, 1950; d. Johnnie James Billings and Robbie Erlene (Frazier) Welch; m. Lee James Harwell (div.); 1 child, Clinton Dee; m. Frank Lincoln Leary III, Feb. 14, 1982 (div. 1987); m. Mark K. Zejdl, Oct. 16, 1996. Student, Austin C.C., 1978-80, Foothill Coll., 1984-93; BA, Trinity Coll. and U., 1990; PhD, Hamilton U., 1992—; postgrad., Inst. Advanced Study, San Francisco, 1993—. Emergency med. tech.; lic. pilot. Emergency med. tech. Breckenridge Hosp., Austin, Tex., 1979, Santa Clara Valley (Calif.) Med. Ctr., 1980; outside sales rep. Bus. Equipment Co., San Francisco, 1981-82; counselor Nat. Sexually Transmitted Disease Hotline, Palo Alto, Calif., 1984-86, Nat. AIDS Hotline, Palo Alto, 1986-87, San Francisco Sex Information Switchboard, San Francisco, 1987-88; adminstrv. asst. ALZA Corp., Palo Alto, 1983—2001; adminstr. Alexza MDC, Palo Alto, Calif., 2002—05. Lectr., rschr. Inst. for Advanced Study of Human Sexuality; bus. mgr. Frank Leary Racing, 1981-83. Author: Encyclopedia of Unusual Sex Practices, 1992; co-producer: (video) 500 Unusual Sex Practices, 1992; contbr. articles to profl. jours. Mem. Author's Guild, Inst. for Advanced Study of Human Sexuality, Am. Assn. Sex Educators, Counselors and Therapists, Soc. for Sic. Study of Sex, Calif. Writers Club, Mystery Writers Am. Jewish. Avocations: flying, photography, travel, writing, bridge. Home and Office: 2 Orebitzka Prague 3 Czech Republic E-mail: zejdl@hotmail.com.

LOVE, COURTNEY, singer, actress; b. San Francisco, July 9, 1964; d. Hank Harrison and Linda Carroll; m. James Moreland, 1989 (div. 1989), m. Kurt Cobain, Feb. 24, 1992 (dec. April 5, 1994); 1 child, Frances Bean. Singer, writer, musician Hole, 1989—2002. Albums (with Hole) Pretty on the Inside, 1991, Live Through This, 1994, Celebrity Skin, 1998; (Solo albums) America's Sweeteart, 2004; actress (films) Sid and Nancy, 1986, Straight to Hell, 1987, Tapeheads, 1988, Basquiat, 1996, Feeling Minnesota, 1996, The People vs. Larry Flynt (Best Supporting Actress award, NY Film Critics Cir., Boston Soc. of Film Critics), 1996, Not Bad For a Girl, 1996 (also co-prodr.), Man on the Moon, 1999, 200 Cigarettes, 1999, Beat, 2000, Julie Johnson, 2001, Trapped, 2002; author (books) Dirty Blonde, 2006.*

LOVE, LISA A., lawyer; b. 1959; BS, U. Tenn., Knoxville; JD, Salmon P. Chase Coll. of Law. Assoc. counsel, mgr. insurance ops. Cincinnati Insurance Co., 2000—03, sr. counsel, 2003—. Office: Cincinnati Insurance Co PO Box 145496 6200 S Gilmore Rd Cincinnati OH 45250

LOVE, MARGARET MARKS, business owner; b. Ft. Benning, Ga., June 27, 1948; d. Edwin Hall and Mildred (Ashmore) Marks; m. James Fulford Love, July 18, 1970; children: Halley Margaret, Julia Marks, Benjamin Ashmore. AA, Stephens Coll., 1968; BA, U. S.C., 1970; MA, George Mason U., 1985. Kindergarten tchr. Ft. Benning Children's Schs., 1970-71, West Point (N.Y.) Elem. Sch., 1971-72, Dept. of Def. Schs., Munster, Fed. Republic Germany, 1980-81; pre-sch. tchr. Accotink Acad., Springfield, Va., 1983-84; community liaison officer U.S. Consolate, Hamburg, Germany, 1990-91; owner, founder, CEO, pres. Full Circle Internat. Relocations, Inc., 1994—. Bd. dirs. St. Andrew's Episcopal Day Sch., Burke, Va., 1982-85. Co-chmn. Adopt-A-Sch. program, Killeen, 1985-87; vestry mem., St. Christopher's Episcopalian Ch. Mem. Jr. League Hampton Roads, Officers Wives Club (bd. dirs. 1986—), Jr. League Northern Va. (bd. dirs. 1996-99), Tex. State Tchrs. Assn. (named Friend of Edn. 1986), DAR, Daughters of U.S. Army, Greater Killeen C. of C. (co-chmn. com. 1986-87).

LOVE, MARGARET WYNN, physical education educator; b. Greensboro, N.C., June 19, 1960; d. Edmund Robert and Doris Whitley Wynn; m. Timothy John Love, Nov. 9, 1985; 1 child, Ryan Wynn. BA, U. N.C. - Wilmington, 1982; MS in Curriculum Design and Instrn., Western Md. Coll., Westminster, 2001; MS in Phys. Edn., W.Va. U., Morgantown, 2004. Cert. phys. education educator Md., 2004. Elec. quality control insp. Brunswick Power & Light Co., Southport, NC, 1980—85; field engr. - hatch nuc. power plant Onsite Engring., Vidalia, Ga., 1985—91; title i asst. for reading and math St. Leonard Elem. Sch., St. Leonard, Md., 1995—2001; phys. edn. tchr. Calvert Elem. Sch., Prince Frederick, Md., 2001—. Jump rope for heart coord. Am. Heart Assn., Prince Frederick, Md., 1992—. Pres. Pk. Chesapeake Homeowners Assn., Lusby, Md., 1993—99. Grantee Nickelodeon Let's Just Play World-wide Day of Play, Viacom, 2005. Mem.: Md. Assn. for Health, Phys. Edn., Recreation and Dance. R-Liberal. Avocations: reading, swimming, surfing, running, distance bicycling. Home: 2340 Park Chesapeake Dr Lusby MD 20657 Office: Calvert Elementary School 1450 Dares Beach Rd Prince Frederick MD 20678 Office Phone: 410-535-5719.

LOVE, SHARON REDHAWK, education educator; 1 child, Daniel W. Parker. PhD, U. of Okla., 2001. Prof. Pa. State U., Altoona, 2001—. Mem.: Acad. of Criminal Justice Scis., Am. Soc. of Criminologists. Avocation: golf. Office: Pa State U 3000 Ivyside Pk 103 Cypress Bldg Altoona PA 16601 E-mail: srl11@psu.edu.

LOVE, SHIRLEY BELLE, psychotherapist; b. N.Y.C. d. Morris and Rachel Greenstein; m. Sidney I. Love; children: Carolyn Beth Love Bersak, Jeanine Deborah Love Dropkin. BA, Bklyn. Coll., 1944; MSW, Columbia U., N.Y., 1948; PhD, Heed U., 1980. Cert. psychoanalyst, Nat. Assn. Advancement Psychoanalysis, 1974; diplomate Clin. Social Worker, Nat. Assn. Social Workers. Founder, faculty supr. Manhattan Ctr. Psychoanalytic Studies, N.Y.C., 1970—; faculty Phila. Sch. Psychoanalysis, 1976—; faculty supr. Internat. Sch. Social Services, N.Y.C., 1977—. Co-founder, co-dir., faculty, supr. Riverdale Seminars, 1981—. Co-founder, v.p. Riverdale YM-YWHA, 1967-73. Recipient Disting. Alumni awared, Heed Sch. Psychoanalysis, 2001, Honorable plaque, Ctr. Modern Psychoanalytic Studies, 2005. Fellow Clin. Social Work Psychotherapist, Inc., Am. Orthopsychiat. Assn. (life); mem. NASW, Assn. Modern Psychoanalysis.

LOVE, SUSAN DENISE, accountant, consultant, small business owner; b. Portland, Oreg., Aug. 5, 1954; d. Charles Richard and Betty Lou (Reynolds) Beck; m. Daniel G. Oliveros, Dec. 21, 1979 (div. Nov. 1983); m. Michael Dean Love, Aug. 24, 1984 (div. Mar. 1989); m. Michael Eugene Watson, July 28, 1990 (div. Dec. 1994); m. David Phillip Dulaney, Aug. 22, 1998. BA in Graphic Design, Portland State U., 1976. Office mgr. Rogers Machinery Co., Portland, 1972-77; exec. sec. Creighton Shirtmakers, N.Y.C., 1977-80; dir. adminstrn. Henry Grethel div. Manhattan Industries, N.Y.C., 1980-81; exec. asst. S.B. Tanger and Assocs., N.Y.C., 1981-83; exec. asst., bookkeeper M Fin. Corp., Portland, 1983-84; acct. cons., owner Office Assistance, Portland, 1984—; owner WE LOVE KIDS Clothing Store, Portland, 1985—; owner, pres. Oreg. Music and Entertainment, 1989—99; v.p. Coral Sales Co., 2002—. Sec./treas. Designers' Roundtable, Portland, 1985-88; co-owner, The Tuxedo Club, 1992-95. Mem. Oreg. State Pub. Interest Rsch. Group, Portland, 1985-90, Oreg. Fair Share,Salem, 1987, mem. adv. bd. career and life options program Clackamas Community Coll., 1989-91. Mem. Women Entrepreneurs Oreg. (bd. dirs. 1988-98, pres. 1992-95, Mem. of Yr. award 1991, 95), Brentwood-Darlington Neighborhood Assn. (treas. 1993-2000), Parkside Homeowners Assn. (treas. 2002-2003), North Clackamas County C. of C., Nat. Fedn. Ind. Bus., Outer S.E. Coalition. Democrat. Avocations: bicycling, aerobics, sewing, hiking, music. Office: Office Assistance PO Box 1784 Clackamas OR 97015-1784

LOVE, SUSAN L., music educator; m. Zermeno Love, Aug. 1988. Undergraduate studies in Music Bus., West Tex. State U. (now West Tex. A&M), Canyon; Kodaly Studies, U. North Tex., Denton; MusB Edn., Tex. Tech U., Lubbock, 1996. Cert. Level IV Kodaly Orgn. Am. Kodaly Educators, 1999, Tchr. All-Level Music State Tex., 1996. Tchr. music Odessa Ind. Sch. Dist., Tex., 1996—99; music specialist-kodaly Kerrville Ind. Sch. Dist., Tex., 1996—, dir. choir Blue Notes Honor Choir, 2000—. Flute instr. Schriener U., Kerrville, 2003—05; flutist Symphony of the Hills, Kerrville, 2000—; faculty/music camp Schriener U., 2004—05; tutor Schriener U. Student Svcs., Kerrville, 2004—05; flutist Andante Group, Kerrville. Planner music camp pedagogy Schriener U., Kerrville. Grantee, Kerrville Pub. Sch. Found., 2004—05. Mem.: Tex. Music Educators Assn., Kodaly Educators Tex., Orgn. Am. Kodaly Educators, Omichron Delta Kappa. Avocation: fly fishing. Office: Tom Daniels Elementary 2002 Singing Wind Kerrville TX 78028 Office Phone: 830-257-2208. Personal E-mail: lovemusic@omniglobal.net. E-mail: susan.love@kerrvilleisd.net.

LOVE, SUSAN MARGARET, surgeon, educator, writer; b. NJ, Feb. 9, 1948; d. James Arthur and Margaret Connick (Schwab) L.; life ptnr. Helen Sperry Cooksey, Sept. 8, 1982; 1 child, Katherine Mary Love-Cooksey. BS, Fordham U., 1970; MD, SUNY, NYC, 1974, DSc (hon.), 1998; MBA, UCLA, 1998; DSc (hon.), Northeastern U., 1991, Trinity Coll., 1999; D of Humane Sci. (hon.), Simmons Coll., 1992; LHD (hon.), U. R.I., 1997. Surgery intern Beth Israel Hosp., Boston, 1974—75, surgical resident, 1975—79, chief resident, 1979, clin. fellow in pathology, 1980, asst. in surgery, 1980—87, dir. breast clinic, 1980-88, assoc. surgeon, 1987—92; clin. fellow in surgery Harvard Med. Sch., Boston, 1977-78, clin. instr. in surgery, 1980-87, asst. clin. prof. surgery, 1987-92; clin. assoc. in surg. oncology Dana Farber Cancer Inst., Boston, 1981-92; dir. Faulkner Breast Ctr. Faulkner Hosp., Boston, 1988-92; assoc. prof. clin. surgery UCLA Med. Sch., 1992-96, adj. prof. divsn. gen. surgery, 1996—2002; dir. Revlon/UCLA Breast Ctr., 1992-96; clin. prof. divsn. gen. surgery David Geffen Sch. Medicine, UCLA, 2002—; founder, chief med. officer Windy Hill Med., 2006—. Prin. investigator Nat. Surg. Adjuvant Breast and Bowel Project, 1985—96; adv. com. Women's Health Initiative Program, Washington, 1993—95; adv. coun. Breast and Cervical Cancer Program and Breast Cancer Early Detection Program, State of Calif. DHS, 1994—98; mem. Pres.'s Nat. Action Plan on Breast Cancer, DHHS, 1994—2000; co-chair Biol. Resources Working Group, 1994—98; mem. Nat. Cancer Adv. Bd., 1998—2004; nat. adv. environ. health sci. coun. NIH, 2003—04; med. dir. Dr. Susan Love Rsch. Found. (formerly Santa Barbara Breast Cancer Inst., 1983-2000, The Susan Love MD Breast Cancer Research Foundation, 2000-04), 1995—; pres. bd. dirs. Dr. Susan Love Rsch. Found.; founder, sr. ptnr., dir. LLuminari, Inc., 2000—; bd. dirs. Sanarus Med.; cons. Cytyc Health Corp., 2002. Author: Dr. Susan Love's Breast Book, 1990, 4th edit., 2005, Dr. Susan Love's Menopause and Hormone Book, 1997, 2nd edit., 2003; Atlas of Techniques in Breast Surgery, 1996; contbr. chpts. to books, articles to profl. jours. Founder, bd. dirs. Nat. Breast Cancer Coalition, 1991—; bd. dirs. Lesbian Health Found., 1992—. Soc. Menstrual Cycle Rsch., 2000—, Y-ME Nat. Breast Cancer Orgn., 2001—. Recipient Rose Kushner award, Am. Med. Writers Assn., 1991, Achievement award, Am. Assn. Physicians for Human Rights, 1992, Women Making History award, U.S. Senator Barbara Boxer, 1993, Woman of Yr. award, YWCA, 1994, Frontrunner award, Sara Lee Corp., 1994, Spirit of Achievement award, Albert Einstein Coll. of Yeshiva U., 1995, Abram L. Sachar medallion, Brandeis U., 1996, Bicentennial honoree, U. Louisville, 1997, Walker prize, Boston Mus. Sci., 1998, Radcliffe medal, 2000, Humanitarian of Yr. award, Western U. Health Sci., Pomona, Calif., 2001, Excellence in Cancer Awareness award, Cancer Rsch. Found. Am., 2002, Dir.'s award, Nat. Cancer Inst., 2004;, Dept. Def. grantee, 1994, 1996, others. Mem. Am. Med. Women's Assn. (pres. br. 39 1987, Lila Wallis Women's Health award 2004), Soc. for Study of Breast Disease, Am. Soc. Preventive Oncology, Southwestern Oncology Group (women's health and breast com. 1992-96, surg. rep. 1992-96), L.A. Med. Soc., Boston Surg. Soc., N.Am. Menopause Soc., Am. Assn. Cancer Rsch., Am. Coll. Women's Health Physicians, Assn. Women Surgeons. Office: Dr Susan Love Rsch Found PO Box 846 Pacific Palisades CA 90272-0846 Office Phone: 310-230-1712. Business E-Mail: slove@earthlink.net.

LOVE-HASSELL, ESTHER BOYER, special education educator, consultant; b. Raleigh, N.C., July 18, 1950; d. James Alexander and Emma Perry Boyer; m. Cedric Ricardo Hassell, Aug. 9, 1991; children: Jaimye Love Hassell, Sheryl Love Hassell, Emily Skinner, Elizabeth Camille Hassell. BA in English Edn., St. Augustine's Coll., Raleigh, N.C., 1972; MA in Edn. English, U. Rochester, N.Y., 1974; cert. in spl. edn., LI U., Bklyn., 1991. Substitute tchr. Peekskill and Rockland County, NY, 1980—81, N.Y.C. Schs., 1981—83; tchr. choral music Schimer Jr. HS, Queens, NY, 1983; reading & critical thinking instr. Malcolm/King Coll., N.Y.C., 1983—87; spl. edn. tchr. Pub. Sch. 76, N.Y.C., 1984—88, Jr. HS 88 Wadleigh, N.Y.C., 1988—89; resource rm. tchr. Pub. Sch. 180, N.Y.C., 1989—. Reading specialist Rochester City Schs., 1974—78; head reading dept. Culbreth Jr. HS, Chapel Hill, NY, 1979—80; tutorial instr. Mercy Coll., Peekskill, NY, 1980—81. Dir. ARC, Rochester, 1972. Recipient Humanitarian award, Harlem Cmty. Harlem Week, 1989. Mem.: Sigma Tau Delta (pres. 1974), Delta Sigma Theta. Democrat. Episcopalian. Avocations: singing, travel, running, reading, writing. Home: 350 W 115th St Apt 2B New York NY 10026 Office: PS 180 Hugo Newman Coll Prep 370 W 120th St New York NY 10026

LOVEJOY, JEAN HASTINGS, social services counselor; b. Battle Creek, Mich, July 1, 1913; d. William Walter and Elizabeth (Fairbank) H.; m. Allen Perry (dec. 2003); children: Isabel L. Best, Linda L. Ewald, Elizabeth L. Fulton, Margaret L. Baldwin, Helen L. Battad. BA, Mt. Holyoke Coll., So. Hadley, Mass., 1935. Traveling sec. Student Vol. Movement, NYC, 1935; bookkeeper Hartford Consumers Co-op, Conn., 1944; tchr. Pre-School, Congl. Ch., West Hartford, Conn., 1944-45; instr. St. John's U., Shanghai, 1946—49; tchr. Edn., 1st Congl. Ch., Berkeley, Calif., 1958-59; instr. Tunghai U., Taiwan, 1960-63; sec. Pres. Tunghai U., Taichung, Taiwan, 1960-63. Pres. Ecumenical Assn. for Housing, San Rafael, 1971, 78-80; founding mem. Hospice of Havasu, 1982, pres. bd. dir., 1985-87, vol. trainer, 1987-92; bereavement vol. Cmty. Hospice, Tucson, 1993-96; vol. friendly visitor N.W. Interfaith Ctr., Tucson, 1995-98; vol. libr. La Rosa Health Ctr., Tucson, 1998—. Recipient OACC Sr. Achievement award, 1991; named Vol. of Yr., Marin County, Calif., 1970, 79; street named Lovejoy Way in her honor Novato (Calif.) City Coun., 1980. Mem. LWV (program v.p. Pierce County, Wash.chpt. 1967, pres. cen. Marin County chpt. 1973-75, legis. analyst land use 1979-80, Calif. chpt.). Mem. United Ch. of Christ (Stephen min.) Home: Apt 8208 7500 N Calle Sin Envidia Tucson AZ 85718-7363

LOVEJOY, KRISTIN GALLINA, information technology executive; BA in English, Lafayette Coll. Cons. New Horizons; v.p. security assurance services TruSecure Corp.; joined Consul Corp., 2003, chief tech. officer, v.p. tech. & services Herndon, Va. Named one of top 25 CTOs, InfoWorld Media Group, 2005. Achievements include patent for object oriented risk mgmt. model and methodology. Office: Consul Corp Ste 250 2121 Cooperative Way Herndon VA 20171*

LOVELACE, GAIL T., human resources specialist; married. Various positions Gen. Svcs. Adminstrn., Washington, 1979—98, chief people officer, 1998—. Chief Human Capital Officers Coun. Recipient Presdl. Rank award, 2002, Sr. Exec. Svc. Disting. Exec. award, 2001. Mem.: Internat. Personnel Mgmt. Assn. Office: 1800 F St NW Washington DC 20405

LOVELACE, JULIANNE, former library director; b. Jackson, Miss., July 30, 1941; d. Benjamin Travis and Julia Elizabeth (Knight) Robinson; m. William Frank Lovelace, July 6, 1963 (div. Mar. 17, 1972); 1 child, Julie Lynn. BA in History, So. Meth. U., 1963; MLS, U. North Tex., 1970. Clk. Dallas Pub. Libr., 1963-64, children's libr. asst., 1964-66, children's libr., 1966-69; libr. Richardson (Tex.) Pub. Libr., 1971-72, supr. pub. svcs., 1972-87, dir., 1987-2001; CFO 4womenShopping, Inc., 2000—. Active Richardson Adult Literacy Ctr., Altrusa Internat., Inc. Richardson, Leadership Richardson Alumni Assn., Friends of the Richardson Pub. Libr., Richardson Regional Med. Ctr., Women's Adv. Coun.; mem. exec. steering com. Wildflower Arts & Music Festival. Named one of 21 for the 21st Century, Collin County Bus., 2000. Mem.: Rotary. Avocation: blackjack. Personal E-mail: jl3430@swbell.net.

LOVELACE, ROSE MARIE SNIEGON, federal space agency administrator; b. Sweet Hall, Va., Feb. 19, 1937; d. Adolph and Annie (Mickel) Sniegon; m. William Wayne Lovelace, Aug. 11, 1962. Degree in bus., Longwood Coll., 1957. Adminstrv. aide Dept. of Navy, Washington, 1957-60; adminstrv. asst. Joint Blood Coun.-Pvt., Washington, 1960-63; exec. staff NASA, Washington, 1963-73, program analyst-specialist, 1973-80, chief adminstrv. ops. and Congl. affairs br., 1980-92; ret., 1992. Cons. NASA, 1992—. Editor, author: (pamphlet) Space Operations, 1989, (video) Space Communications, 1991. Pres. Jr. Achievement Co., 1953-55, Kettering Recreation Coun., Largo, Md., 1974-76; league coord. U.S. Tennis Assn., Anne Arundel County, Md., 1989-91, team capt., 1984-99, 2001, 04-06; active Hospice Cup Regatta, sponsor 2000-, Hospice Beacon Hope Gala Com. Fundraiser, 2004-06, Hospice Circle of Care Soc., 2005-, LWV, Hospice Planned Giving Coun. Recipient Jr. Achievement Exec. award and Nat. Speakers award, 1954, Gold medal Parks and Planning, Prince Georges County, Md., 1976, Exceptional Svc. award NASA, 1983, Exceptional Svc. medal NASA, 1992. Mem.: Nat. Women's Hist. Mus. (charter mem.), Hospice Cir. of Care Soc., Heritage Soc. Anne Arundel Med. Ctr., Historic Annapolis Found., Anne Arundel County Tennis Assn., Am. Heart Assn. (Heart Ball com. fundraiser 2000), Annapolis Opera, Inc., Sportfit Racquet and Fitness Club, Severn Town Club (pres. 1996—98, chair Holly Ball fundraiser 1998—99). Republican. Methodist. Avocations: tennis, gardening, flower arranging, organizing social and tennis events, designing and painting wearable art.

LOVELAND, CHRISTINE FRANCES, psychologist; b. Chester, Pa., Jan. 27, 1953; d. Frank Preston and Elizabeth Theresa (Meehan) L.; 1 child, Catherine Elizabeth Loveland-Jones. BS, Ind. U. of Pa., 1974; MA, West Chester U., 1986; PhD, Temple U., 1993. Lic. psychologist, 1998; cert. elem. and secondary prin.; cert. sch. psychologist. Educator, ESL-Bilingual program dir. Avon Grove Sch. Dist., West Grove, Pa., 1978—; family therapist Counseling Network SCCMC, West Grove, 1989-92; support group facilitator Epilepsy Found. of Phila., 1986-92; pres., psychologist Brandywine Psychol. Svcs., West Grove, 1999—. Adj. prof. Immaculata (Pa.) Coll., 1999; LA curriculum com. Avon Grove Sch. Dist., West Grove, 1998—. Councilwoman Dem. Polit. Party, West Grove, 1998—. Named Outstanding Young Woman of Yr. Avon Grove Jaycees, 1980. Fellow Pa. Psychol. Assn.; mem. APA, NEA, West Grove Avondale Rotary (pres. 1999—, bd. dirs. 1998), Pa. Edn. Assn., Avon Grove Edn. Assn. Avocations: reading, hiking, piano, spanish, travel. Home: 416 Dartmouth Ln West Grove PA 19390-8828 E-mail: clovel7778@aol.com.

LOVELESS, KATHY LYNNE, client services executive; b. Corsicana, Tex., Mar. 7, 1961; d. Vernon Ray and Barbara Alice (Brown) L. BA, Baylor U., 1983. Cert. project mgmt. profl., master six sigma. Adminstrv. asst. InterFirst Bank, Dallas, 1983-85, Chaparral Steel Co., Midlothian, Tex., 1985-89, audio/visual coord., 1989-93; freelance computer instr. Duncanville, Tex., 1993-94; tng. specialist U. Tex. Southwestern Med. Ctr., Dallas, 1994-95, supr. client svcs. ctr., 1995-97, database coord., 1997-98; tester, trainer Sabre Holdings, Southlake, Tex., 1998-2000, product mgr., 2000—04; group mgr. Verizon Info. Svcs., DFW Airport, Tex., 2004—. Bd. dirs. Richardson Theatre Ctr., 1999—; pres., v.p. Midlothian Cmty. Theatre, 1990-93, mem., 1987-94; v.p. Lovers Ln. United Meth. Ch. Choir, Dallas, 1994, 95, adminstrv. bd., 1995-96, 1999—, chmn. broadcast com., 2001; chmn. worship and mem. care com. Elmwood United Meth. Ch., 1990, 91; bd. dirs. Trinity River Mission, Dallas, 1994, 95, 96. Mem.: Soc for Theatrical Artists Guidance and Enhancement. Avocations: films, music, reading, sports, theater. Home: 9947 Knoll Krest Dr Dallas TX 75238 Personal E-mail: ilvmovies@aol.com.

LOVELESS, PATTY (PATTY RAMEY), country music singer; b. Pikeville, Ky., Jan. 4, 1957; m. Terry Lovelace (div.); m. Emory Gordy, Jr., Feb. 1989. Recording artist MCA, 1985-93, Sony Music, 1993—. Albums: Patty Loveless, 1987, If My Heart Had Windows, 1988, Honky Tonk Angel, 1988 (gold), On Down the Line, 1990, Up Against My Heart, 1991, Only What I Feel, 1993, Greatest Hits, 1993, When Fallen Angels Fly, 1994, The Trouble With the Truth, Sings Songs of Love, 1996, Long Stretch of Lonesome, 1997, Classics, 1999, Strong Heart, 2000, 20th Century masters: The Millenium Collection, 2000, Mountain Soul, 2001, Bluegrass & White Snow, 2002, On Your Way Home, 2003; # 1 hit singles Timber, I'm Falling in Love, Chains. Named Favorite New Country Artist by Am. Music Awards, 1989, Album of Yr. Country Music Awards, 1995, Top Female Vocalist Acad. Country Music, 1996, Female Vocalist of Yr. Country Music awards, 1996, Vocal Event of Yr., Country Music awards, 1993, 98, 99; recipient TNN Music City News Country Award, Female Artist, 1990, Country Music Awards' Album of the Yr.; co-recipient Grammy award for Best Country Collaboration with Vocals, 1998; inductee Grand Ole Opry, 1988.

LOVELL, EMILY KALLED, retired journalist; b. Grand Rapids, Mich., Feb. 25, 1920; d. Abdo Rham and Louise (Claussen) Kalled; m. Robert Edmund Lovell, July 4, 1947. Student, Grand Rapids Jr. Coll., 1937-39; BA, Mich. State U., 1944; MA, U. Ariz., 1971. Copywriter, asst. traffic mgr. Sta. WOOD, Grand Rapids, 1944-46; traffic mgr. KOPO, Tucson, 1946-47; reporter, city editor Alamogordo (N.Mex.) News, 1948-51; Alamogordo corr., feature writer Internat. News Svc., Denver, 1950-54, El Paso Herald-Post, 1954-65; Alamogordo news dir., feature writer Tularosa (N.Mex.) Basin Times, 1957-59; co-founder, editor, pub. Otero County Star, Alamogordo, 1961-65; newscaster KALG, Alamogordo, 1964-65; freelance feature writer Denver Post, N.Mex. Mag., 1949-69; corr. Electronic News, N.Y.C., 1959-63, 65-69; Sierra Vista (Ariz.) corr. Ariz. Republic, 1966; freelance editor N.Mex. Pioneer Interviews, 1967-69; asst. dir. English skills program Ariz. State U., 1976; free-lance editor, writer, 1977—2003; ret., 2003. Part-time tchr., lectr. U. Pacific, 1981-86; part-time interpreter Calif., 1983-91, Interpreters Unlimited, Oakland, 1985-91; sec., dir. Star Pub. Co., Inc., 1961-64, pres., 1964-65, 3d v.p., publicity chmn. Otero County Cmty. Concert Assn., 1950-65; mem. Alamogordo Zoning Commn., 1955-57; mem. founding com. Alamogordo Ctrl. Youth Activities Com., 1957; vice chmn. Otero County chpt. Nat. Found. Infantile Paralysis, 1958-61; charter mem. N.Mex. Citizens Coun. for Traffic Safety, 1959-61; pres. Sierra Vista Hosp. Aux., 1966; pub. rels. chmn. Ft. Huachuca chpt. ARC, 1966; mem. nat. bd. Hospitalized Vets. Writing Project, 1972-99; vol. instr. autobiography and creative writing, 1991-2002. Author: A Personalized History of Otero County, New Mexico, 1963, Weekend Away, 1964, Lebanese Cooking, Streamlined, 1972, A Reference Handbook for Arabic Grammar, 1974, 77; contbg. author: The Muslim Community in North America, 1983. Recipient 1st Pl. awards N.Mex. Press Assn., 1961, 62, Pub. Interest award Nat. Safety Coun., 1962, 1st Pl. award Nat. Fedn. Press Women, 1960, 62; named Woman of Yr. Alamogordo, 1960, Editor of Week Pubs. Aux., 1962, adm. N.Mex. Navy, 1962, col. A.D.C. Staff Gov. N.Mex., 1963, Woman of Yr., Ariz. Press Women, 1973. Mem. N.Mex. Press Women (past sec.), Ariz. Press Women (past pres.), N.Mex. Fedn. Womens Clubs (past dist. pub. rels. chmn., hon. life Alamogordo), N.Mex. Hist. Soc. (life), N.Mex. Fedn. Bus. and Profl. Womens Clubs (past pres., hon. life Alamogordo), Pan Am. Round Table Alamogordo, Theta Sigma Phi (past nat. 3d v.p.), Phi Kappa Phi. Democrat. Moslem. Home: 1925 Possum Hollow Rd Apt 623 Slidell LA 70458-8321

LOVELL, JOAN ELLEN, mental health professional; b. Alton, Ill., Oct. 24, 1955; d. Lee Roy and Arlou (Brown) Waller; 1 child, Frank. AS, RN, Monticello Coll., Godfrey, Ill., 1974; BA in Social Work, Calif. State U., Northridge, 1977; MA in Psychology, Calif. Grad. Inst., Westwood, 1988, PhD in Psychology, 1996. RN, Calif.; registered psychologist Calif. Nurse, asst. head nurse St. Francis Med. Ctr., 1977-80; crisis resolution unit nurse Dept. Mental Health L.A. County, L.A., 1983-85, homeless coord., 1985-87, patient rights advocate, 1987-92, children and youth svc. coord., 1993—; mental health cons. Fed. Project 90044, L.A., 1992-93; owner Medi Fact Rsch., Huntington Beach, Calif., 1992-97. Cons. Philippine-Am. Orgn., Long Beach, Calif., 1985-87. Ct. advocate for victims of rape L.A. Commn. Against Assaults on Women, L.A., 1977, rape hotline counselor, 1976-77. Mem. APA (affiliate), Calif. Psychol. Assn. Office: 3938 Foothill Ave Carlsbad CA 92008-7000

LOVELL, LISA INEZ, special education educator; b. Hobbs, N.Mex., June 13, 1968; d. Earnest Clay and Betty Dell Cox; m. Stacy Monroe Lovell, Feb. 24, 1995; children: Kyle, John. AA, Ranger Jr. Coll., Tex., 1994; BS, Midwestern State U., Wichita Falls, Tex., 1996, studied. Spl. edn. tchr. Graham Ind. Sch. Dist., Tex., 1996—. Mem.: Assn. Tex. Profl. Educators, Coun. for Exceptional Children, Delta Kappa Gamma. Baptist. Avocations: reading, water-skiing, cooking, travel. Office: Graham Ind Sch Dist 1317 Old Jacksboro Rd Graham TX 76450 Business E-Mail: lisa.lovell@grahamisd.com.

LOVELL, MARGARETTA M., art history educator, museum curator; b. Pitts., Oct. 30, 1944; m. Jonathan H. Lovell, June 19, 1967; children: Stephanie, Helen. BA, Smith Coll., 1966; MA in Early Am. Culture, U. Del., 1975; PhD in Am. Studies, Yale U., 1980. Curatorial asst. Yale Art Gallery, New Haven, 1972—75; acting instr. Dept. Art History Yale U., 1978—80, asst. prof. Dept. Art History, 1980—81; Duane and Virginia S. Dittman prof. Am. studies Coll. William and Mary, 1990—92; asst. prof. Dept. Art History U. Calif., Berkeley, 1981—90, assoc. prof. art history, 1992, prof. art history; curator Am. paintings collection Fine Arts Mus., San Francisco, 1981—85; co-dir. Am. studies program Fine Arts Mus., U. Berkeley, San Francisco, 1995—2000, dir. Am. studies program, 2003—04; R. Stanton Avery vis. chair Huntington Libr., 1994—95. Adv. com. Archives Am. Art-Western Divsn. Smithsonian Instn., Washington; exec. com. Yale Ctr. for Study Am. Art and Material Culture, New Haven, 1978—81. Author: (book) A Visitable Past: Views of Venice by American Artists, 1860-1925, 1989, Art in a Season of Revolution: Painters, Artisans and Patrons in Early America, 2005, (catalogues) American Paintings 1730-1960: A Selection from the Collection of Mr. and Mrs. John D. Rockefeller 3rd., 1982, William Morris: The Sanford and Helen Berger Collection, 1984, Venice: The American View, 1860-1920, 1984—85. Recipient Ralph Henry Gabriel prize, Am. Studies Assn., 1981, Charles C. Eldridge prize disting. scholarship in Am. art, Smithsonian Am. Art Mus., 2006; grantee Gladys Krieble Delmas Found., 1978, ACLS, 1988; Nat. Endowment for Arts Mus. Profl. fellow, 1973, Danforth Found. Women's fellow, 1975—78, rsch. fellow, Henry E. Huntington Libr. and Art Gallery, 1987, 1989, 1993. Office: Dept History of Art Univ Calif Berkeley 416 Doe Library #6020 Berkeley CA 94720-6020

LOVELL, MICHELLE PAULETTE, physician's associate; b. Fresno, Calif., May 3, 1961; d. Eddie J. Sr. and Joan Ilean (Barbour) Johnson; m. Jim W. Lovell, July 31, 1986 (div.); children: Dallis Frie, Miriah Grace, Jeremy Wayne, Joseph Lee, Joshua Wayne; m. Randolph H. Covey, Oct. 1, 1982. BS in Mgmt., Northeastern State U., 1990; BS in Phys. Assoc., U. Okla., Oklahoma City, 1993. Cert. phys. asst., Nat. Commn. on Cert. of Physician's Assts.; lic. physician assoc., Okla. Owner/operator J&M Enterprises/Am. Med. Svc., Wagoner, Okla., 1987-90; physician's assoc. Hagglund Clinic, Inc., Norman, Okla., 1993; physician's asst./patient liason Dr. John Porter, Phoenix, 1994; physician's asst. wound care mgmt. Transitional Hosp. Corp., Albuquerque, 1995-96; physician's asst. primary care provider Jackson County Meml. Hosp. Clinics, Frederick, Okla., 1996—. Tribal mem. Citizen Band Potawotomie Tribe Okla., Shawnee, 1961—. Recipient Cert. of Excellence Native Am. Student Assn., U. Okla., 1993. Fellow Am. Acad. Physician Assts., Am. Assn. Surgeon Assts., Am. Assn. Surg. Physician Assts., Okla. Acad. Physician Assts., N.Mex. Acad. Physician Assts.; mem. First Nations Coun. Physician Assts. Avocations: cattle breeding, operating a working ranch.

LOVEMAN, AURELIA LEFFLER, psychologist, writer; b. N.Y.C., Oct. 31, 1916; d. Louis and Anna (Bush) Leffler; m. Howard Levi, Oct. 5, 1935; m. 2d Joseph Heller Loveman, Nov. 9, 1972; 1 child, Jonathan Levi. PhD, Columbia U., 1961. Diplomate William Glanson White Inst. Psychiatry and Psychoanalysis, 1971. Chief psychologist Child Devel. Ctr., N.Y.C., 1961-63, Jewish Bd. of Guardians, N.Y.C., 1963-70; pvt. practice Balt., 1970-86; textile designer, 1980—. Editor Internat. Old Lace Inc., 1985-87, Chesapeake Region Lace Guild, Balt., 1986-88; cons. in field. Author: The Good Wife, 1959; contbr. articles to profl. and med. jours. Postdoctoral fellow Albert Einstein Coll. Medicine, 1961-63. Mem. Internat. Old Lace, Embroiderers Guild Am. (editl. bd., tchr. lace corr. course, editor newsletter 1992-2000), Chesapeake Lace Guild (pres. 1984-86), Fan Soc. N.Am., Pioneer Camellia Soc. (v.p.). Avocations: music, gardening, lacemaking.

LOVERIDGE-SANBONMATSU, JOAN MEREDITH, communication studies and women's studies educator, poet; b. Hartford, Conn., July 5, 1938; d. Gilbert Thomas and Rosabel Frances (Nowry) Loveridge; m. Akira Sanbonmatsu, Aug. 29, 1964; children: James Michael, Kevin Yosh. BA, U. Vt., 1960; MA, Ohio U., 1963; PhD, Pa. State U., 1971. Writer, programming radio/tv WRUV, WCAX, Burlington, Vt., 1956-60, WOUB, Athens, Ohio, 1962-63, AFKN, Korea, 1960-61; unit head ARC, Japan, Korea, 1960-61; asst. prof. SUNY, Brockport, 1963-77, prof. comm. studies and women's studies Oswego, 1977-98, prof. emerita, 1999—, instr. intensive English summer program, 1993—2001, co-coord. women's studies program, 1978-80, 82, instr. internat. studies infusion program, 1985-91. Vis. prof. Rochester (N.Y.) Inst. Tech., 1971; assoc. adj. prof. Monroe C.C., Rochester, 1972-76; instr. Pa. State, State College, 1966-67; cons. for oral history project ARC Overseas Assn., 1994—; cons. Cazenovia Coll., N.Y., 1988-89; pres. bd. dirs. Woman's Career Ctr. Inc., Rochester, 1975-76; invited Japan Lecture Tour, 1997. Author: Winged Odyssey: Poems and Stories, 2002, Imperial Valley Nisei Women: Transcending Poston, 2006; co-author: Feminism and Woman's Life, 1995; contbg. author: Women Public Speakers in the US, 1925-1993, Vol. 2, 1994, Life in a Fishbowl: A Call to Serve, 2003; author numerous poems; poetry editor/edit. bd. Lake Effect, 1985-92; contbr. articles to profl. jours. Religious edn. team tchr. May Meml. Unitarian Universalist Soc., Syracuse, 1979-81; mem. adv. parent com., Oswego H.S., 1986-87. Recipient Unsung Heroine award Ctrl. NY NOW, Syracuse, 1987; presdl. citation for social change ARC Overseas Assn., 1998, Creative Contbn. award, 2005; Rsch. grantee Pa. State U., 1970, SUNY, Oswego, 1978, 91-92, 94-96, NY State United Univ. Professions Profl. Devel. and Quality of Working Life grantee, 1985, 87, 93-94, 98, SUNY Oswego Women's Ctr. award, 1996, 98, SEED award for outstanding work with disabled students, 1998, Internat. Awareness and Peace award Coalition for Peace Edn., 2000, Student award ESL, 1995-96, 98, Syracuse Poster Project Haiku award, 2005; fellow U. Ill., Chgo., 1983. Mem. NY Asian Studies Assn., Nat. Comm. Assn. (women's caucus job placement dir., exec. bd. 1977-78), Ea. Comm. Assn., NY Nat. Comm. Assn., Soc. for Intercultural Edn., Tng. and Rsch., Nat. Women's Studies Assn., Speech Comm. Assn. P.R., NY State Women's Studies Assn., ARC Overseas Assn. (v.p. 1999-2001), Nat. Assn. Poet and Writers, Inc., Nat. Japanese Am. Citizens League, Imperial Valley Japanese Am. Citizens Leaue, Imperial County Hist. Soc. Avocations: Spanish, walking. Home: 23 McCracken Dr Oswego NY 13126-6011

LOVERING, EMMA, secondary school educator; b. Laredo, Tex., Mar. 11, 1947; d. Samuel Jordan and Janet Lucy Leyendecker; children: Andrew, Jimmy, Greg, Anna. BSc, U. Houston, 1970; MSc, Tex. Tech. U., Lubbock, 2003. Cert. med. technologist Am. Soc. Clin. Pathologists; tchg. Tex. Tech. U., 1990. Med. technologist Yakohama Naval Dispensary, Japan, 1970—71, Meml. Bapt. SE Br. Hosp., Houston, 1973—79, St. Mary's Hosp., Lubbock, 1989—91; tchr. Irons Jr. H.S., Lubbock, 1991—. Presenter NSTA Conv., Atlanta, 2004, Dallas, 05. Author: (article) Sci. Scope, 2006. Hon. life mem. PTO, Lubbock, 1989—, tchr. rep., 1991—. Grantee, SBC/1420 Found., Lubbock, 2001, 2002, NASA, 2006. Mem.: NSTA, Assn. Tex. Profl. Educators, Audubon Soc. (edn. chair 2004—), Tex. Master Naturalist, Sierra Club. Democrat. Roman Catholic. Avocations: cooking, gardening, camping, bicycling, birdwatching. Home: 7008 Utica Pl Lubbock TX 79424 Office: Irons Jr HS 5214 79th St Lubbock TX 79424 Business E-Mail: ehintze@lubbockisd.org.

LOVETT, CLARA MARIA, retired academic administrator, retired historian; b. Trieste, Italy, Aug. 4, 1939; came to U.S., 1962; m. Benjamin F. Brown. BA equivalent, U. Trieste, 1962; MA, U. Tex., Austin, 1967; PhD, U. Tex., 1970. Prof. history Baruch Coll. CUNY, N.Y.C., 1971-82, asst. provost, 1980-82; chief European divsn. Libr. of Congress, Washington, 1982-84; provost, v.p. acad. affairs George Mason U., Fairfax, Va., 1988-93; on leave, dir. Forum on Faculty Roles and Rewards Am. Assn. for Higher Edn., 1993-94; pres. No. Ariz. U., Flagstaff, 1994-2001, pres. emerita, 2001—; sr. fellow, dir. Ctr. for Competency-Measured Edn. The Oquirrh Inst., 2002—03; pres., CEO Am. Assn. for Higher Ed., 2003—05; ret., 2005. Vis. lectr. Fgn. Svc. Inst., Washington, 1979-85. Author: Democratic Movement in Italy 1830-1876, 1982 (H.R. Marraro prize, Soc. Italian Hist. Studies); Giuseppe Ferrari and the Italian Revolution, 1979 (Phi Alpha Theta book award); Carlo Cattaneo and the Politics of Risorgimento, 1972 (Soc. for Italian Hist. Studies Dissertation award), (bibliography) Contemporary Italy, 1985; co-editor: Women, War, and Revolution, 1980, (essays) State of Western European Studies, 1984; contbr. sects. to publs., U.S., Italy. Organizer Dem. clubs Bklyn., 1972-76; mem. exec. com. Palisades Citizens Assn., Washington, 1985-87; vestry mem. St. David's Episc. Ch., Washington, 1986-89; bd. dirs. Blue Cross Blue Shield Ariz., 1995-2004, Nat. Coun. Tchr. Quality, 2005-, Ariz. Women's Edn. Employment Inc., 2001-; trustee Western Govs. U., 1996—, Thunderbird, The Grad. Sch. of Internat. Mgmt., 2006—; mem. Ariz. State Bd. Edn., 1999-2001; advisory bd. Project Ariz. Future, 2005-, Channel 8 PBS Station, 2005-. Fellow Guggenheim Found., 1978-79, Woodrow Wilson Internat. Ctr. for Scholars, 1979 (adv. bd. West European program), Am. Coun. Learned Socs., 1976, Bunting Inst. of Radcliffe Coll., 1975-76, others; named Educator of Yr. Va. Fedn. of Bus. and Profl. Women, 1992. Mem. Am. Assn. Higher Edn. (cons. 1979—), Soc. for Italian Hist. Studies, Assn. Am. Coll. and Univs. (bd. dirs. 1990-93). Avocations: choral singing, swimming. Office Phone: 602-728-9505. Business E-Mail: clara.lovett@nau.edu.

LOVETT, JUANITA PELLETIER, clinical psychologist; b. Youngstown, Ohio, Mar. 9, 1937; d. Joseph Arcadia and Alice Beatrice (Davis) Pelletier; children: Laura Ann, James Emmett. BA summa cum laude with honors in Psychology, Fairleigh Dickinson U., 1975; MPhil, Columbia U., 1978, MA, 1979, PhD, 1980. Freelance fashion cons., 1958-70; psychology fellow Westchester divsn. NY Hosp.-Cornell Med. Ctr., White Plains, 1977-80; program dir. inpatient svc. Fair Oaks Hosp., Summit, NJ, 1980-82; pvt. practice Summit, 1980—; asst. dir. med. rsch. CIBA-GEIGY Pharms., Summit, 1982-83; cons. AT&T Bell Labs., Murray Hill, NJ, 1983, Lucent Techs., 1996—. Adj. asst. prof. psychology and edn., Dept. Psychology, Tchrs. Coll., Columbia U., NYC, 1980-84; field supr. grad. sch. applied profession psychology Rutgers U., 1981-83; assoc. prof. Polytechnic, NY, 1988—. Union County Mental Health Bd. mem., 1974-76; bd. dirs. Wye River Group on Healthcare, Am. Found. for Healthcare Policy. Author: (book) Solutions for Adults With Aspergers Syndrome; contbr. articles to profl. jours. Recipient Laurie Shavel award, 1975; Mennen scholar, 1975. Mem. APA, NY Acad. Scis., NJ Psychol. Assn., Sigma Xi, Phi Omega Epsilon. Office: 86 Summit Ave Summit NJ 07901-3647 Office Phone: 908-273-5147. E-mail: jplovett@comcast.net.

LOVETT, KRISTI SUMMER, art educator; b. Kingfisher, Okla., July 11, 1975; d. Larry and Delores Horn; m. John Michael Lovett, Oct. 14, 1995; children: Josiah Michael, Faith Mariah, Micah Grace. BSc, Okla. Bapt. U., 1997. Design asst. Diana Coffman Interiors, Shawnee, Okla., 1995—96; educator Crescent Pub. Sch., Okla., 1998—, Cashion H.S., Okla., 1998—99. Sec. Crescent Edn. Found., Okla., 2004—06; gifted and talented svc. coord. Crescent Pub. Sch., 1999—. Vol./drama tchr. First Bapt. Ch., Crescent, 1997—; vol. Found. for the Disabled, Edmond, 2004—06. Mem.: NEA, Okla. Edn. Assn., Okla. Art Edn. Assn., Nat. Art Edn. Assn. Republican. Southern Bapt. Home: P O Box 202 Crescent OK 73028 Office: Crescent Pub Sch 106 N Magnolia Crescent OK 73028

LOVETT, MELENDY, semiconductor company executive; BS in mgmt. and mgmt. info. systems, Tex. A&M; MS in acctg., U. Tex., Dallas. CPA. Sr. mgr. Coopers & Lybrand; v.p. human resources Tex. Instruments Inc., sr. v.p. Dallas, 2004—, pres. ednl. and productivity solutions bus., 2004—. Named to Hall of Fame, Women in Tech. Internat., 2005. Office: Tex Instruments Inc 12500 TI Blvd Dallas TX 75243 Office Phone: 972-995-2011. Office Fax: 972-995-4360.*

LOVICK, NORMA MCGINNIS, social studies educator; b. Norfolk, Va., June 20, 1964; d. Harry Ralph McGinnis and Jenny Cavender Michel; children: Sarah Louise, Allen James. MEd, Cambridge Coll., Chesapeake, Va., 2004; BS in secondary edn., social studies, Old Dominion U., 1985. Cert. advanced grad. studies Cambridge Coll., 2005. Tchr. social sci. St. Matthews Sch., Virginia Beach, Va., 1985—86, Norfolk Pub. Sch., Va., 1987—. Master tchr. WHRO-Pub. TV, Norfolk, Va., 1998—2001. Eucharistic min. St. Pius X Ch., Norfolk, Va., 2003—05; mem. PTA - St. Pius X Sch., Norfolk, Va., 1998—, Va. Living Mus., Newport News, Va., 1998—, Va. Marine Aquarium, Virginia Beach, Va., 1999—, PTA- Norview Mid. Sch., Norfolk, Va., 2001—; supporter Sta. WHRO-Pub. TV, Norfolk, Va., 1988—. Recipient Nat. Tchr. Tng. Inst. Tchr. of the Yr., Sta. WHRO-Pub. TV, 2000, Sch. Bell award, Norfolk Pub. Schs., 2001, 2004, 2005. Mem.: ASCD, Nat. Wildlife Fedn., Am. Fedn. Tchrs., Nat. Coun. for the Social Studies, Mil. Order of World Wars (life; historian 1989—90). Independent. Roman Catholic. Avocations: historical reenacting, garden design/landscaping, reading, genealogy. Office Phone: 757-852-4600. Personal E-mail: normalovick@aol.com. E-mail: nlovick@nps.k12.va.us.

LOVING, SUSAN BRIMER, lawyer, former state official; m. Dan Loving; children: Lindsay, Andrew, Kendall. BA with distinction, U. Okla., 1972, JD, 1979. Asst. atty. gen. Office of Atty. Gen., 1983-87, 1st asst. atty. gen., 1987-91; atty. gen. State of Okla., Oklahoma City, 1991-94; ptnr. Lester, Loving & Davies, Edmond, Okla., 1995—. Master Ruth Bader Ginsburg Inn of Ct., 1995-97. Mem. Pardon and Parole Bd., 1995—96, 2003—, vice-chmn., 1995, chmn., 2004; mem. Gov.'s Commn. on Tobacco and Youth, 1995—97; mem. med. steering com. Partnership for Drug Free Okla., Inst. for Child Advocacy, 1996—97; bd. dirs. Bd. for Freedom of Info., Okla. Inc., 1995—2001, Legal Aid Svcs. of Okla., 2002—03, Legal Aid of West Okla., 1995—2001. Recipient Nat. Red Ribbon Leadership award Nat. Fedn. Parents, Headliner award, By-liner award Okla. City and Tulsa Women in Comm., First Friend of Freedom award, Freedom of Info., Okla., Dir. award Okla. Dist. Attys. Assn. Mem.: Oklahoma County Bar Assn. (bd. dirs. 2001—), Okla. Bar Assn. (mem. ho. dels. 1996—97, 2001—04, past chmn. adminstrv. law sect., chmn. adminstrn. of justice com., chmn. profl. responsibility commn., Spotlight award 1997), Phi Beta Kappa. Office: Lester Loving & Davis PC 1701 S Kelly Ave Edmond OK 73013-3623 Office Phone: 405-844-9900. Business E-Mail: sloving@lldlaw.com.

LOVINGER, SOPHIE LEHNER, child psychologist; b. N.Y.C., Jan. 15, 1932; d. Nathaniel Harris and Anne (Rosen) Lehner; m. Robert Jay Lovinger, June 18, 1957; children: David Fredrick, Mark Andrew. BA, Bklyn. Coll., 1954; MS, City Coll., N.Y.C., 1959; PhD, NYU, 1967. Diplomate in clin child psychology Am. Bd. Profl. Pschology. Sr. clin. psychologist Bklyn. State Hosp., 1960-61; grad. fellow NYU, N.Y.C., 1964—67; psychotherapy trainee Jamaica (N.Y.) Ctr., 1964-67; asst. prof. Hofstra U., Hempstead, N.Y., 1967-70; prof. Cen. Mich. U., Mt. Pleasant, 1970-98; psychotherapist, psychoanalyst Mt. Pleasant, Mich., 1970—98, Charleston, S.C., 1999—. Author: Learning Disabilities and Games, 1978, Language-Learning Disabilities, 1991, Child Treatment from Intake Interview to Termination, 1998; contbr. articles to profl. jours. Fellow: APA, Am. Acad. Clin. Psychology; mem.: Nat. Register Health Svc. Providers. Office: Ste A3 1744 Sam Rittenberg Blvd Charleston SC 29407 Office Phone: 843-556-0997. Personal E-mail: sllov@earthlink.net.

LOVINS, L. HUNTER, public policy institute executive, consultant, educator; b. Middlebury, Vt., Feb. 26, 1950; d. Paul Millard and Farley (Hunter) Sheldon; m. Amory Bloch Lovins, Sept. 6, 1979 (div. 1999). BA in Sociology, Pitzer Coll., 1972, BA in Polit. Sci., 1972; JD, Loyola U., L.A., 1975; LHD, U. Maine, 1982. Bar: Calif. 1975. Asst. dir. Calif. Conservation Project, L.A., 1973-79; policy advisor Friends of the Earth, 1979—81; co-CEO, co-founder Rocky Mountain Inst., Snowmass, Colo., 1982—2002; co-chair Natural Capitalism Group, Snowmass, 2000—; pres. Natural Capitalism Solutions, 2004—. Vis. prof. U. Colo., Boulder, 1982; Henry R. Luce vis. prof. Dartmouth Coll., Hanover, N.H., 1982; prof. sustainable mgmt. Presidio World Coll., 2003—; pres. Nighthawk Horse Co., 1993; bd. dirs. EcoStructure Fin. Co-author: Brittle Power, 1982, Energy Unbound, 1986, Least-Cost Energy Solving the CO2 Problem, 2d edit., 1989, Factor Four, 1997, Green Development, 1998, Natural Capitalism, 1999, The Natural Advantage of Nations, 2005. Bd. dirs. Basalt and Rural Fire Protection Dist., 1987-2000, Nighthawk Horse Co., Rocky Mountain Inst., 1982-2002, Windstar Land Conservancy, 1996-2002, Internat. Ctr. Sustainable Devel., 2004-; vol. EMT and firefighter, Engrs. Without Borders, 2003, bd. dirs., 2003-; advisor Energy Ministry Afghanistan, 2004—. Recipient Mitchell prize Woodlands Inst., 1982, Right Livelihood Found. award, 1983, Best of the New Generation award Esquire Mag., 1984, Nissan prize, 1995, Lindbergh award, 1999, Bd. Govs.' award Loyola Law Sch., 2000, LOHAS award for svc. to bus., 2001, Shingo Prize for Excellence in Mfg. Rsch., 2001, Leadership in Bus. award, 2001; named Hero of Planet, Time Mag., 2000. Mem. Calif. Bar Assn., Am. Quarter Horse Assn., Am. Polocrosse Assn. Avocations: rodeo, fire rescue, polocrosse. Office: Natural Capitalism Solutions PO Box 3125 Eldorado Springs CO 80025 Office Phone: 303-554-6550.

LOVISONE, SYLVIA RUTH, lawyer; d. Robert Hickman Smellage and Ruth Manion Siddons; m. Harry Carter Lovisone, Dec. 8, 1990. BA with honors, Ind. U., Bloomington, 1971; JD class rank 2d, U. Denver, 2001. Bar: Colo., US Dist. Ct. Colo., US Bankruptcy Ct. Pres. Recreational Ventures, Inc., Boulder, Colo., 1984—91; developer Green Scene Family Ctr., 1984, mgr., 1984—94; developer Gateway Pk., 1997; clk. Colo. Supreme Ct., Denver, 2001—02; atty. pvt. practice, Longmont, 2002—. Vol. Longmont Humane Soc., 1996—98, Meals on Wheels, Arvada, 1982—84, Colo. Therapeutic Riding Program, Boulder, 1984—85; bd. dors. Monroe County Humane Soc., Bloomington, Ind., 1968. Scholar, U. Denver, 2001. Mem.: Colo. Bar Assn., Phi Delta Phi. Avocation: ballroom dancing. Business E-Mail: slovisone@msn.com.

LOVITCH, JOAN, science educator, coach; b. N.Y.C., Oct. 14, 1950; d. Isidore and Bella Weider; m. Jeffrey D. Lovitch, Mar. 25, 1972; children: Scott Benjamin, Gina Jennifer. BA, MA, CCNY, N.Y.C. Cert. tchr. sci. N.Y. and N.J., 1973. Tchr. sci. No. Valley Regional H.S., Old Tappan, NJ, 1996—; coach US Academic Decathlon, 1993—. Regional dir. Academic Decathlon NJ, 2005—. Recipient Decade of Championships, Academic Decathlon, 2004; grantee, Bergen County Sch. Boards Assn., 1999, No. Valley Edn. Found., 1999. Mem.: Phi Beta Kappa (life). Achievements include 12 consecutive Academic Decathlon state championships. Home: 27 Amelia Dr Old Tappan NJ 07675 Office: Northern Valley Regional HS Central Ave Old Tappan NJ 07675 Office Phone: 201-666-7655. Business E-Mail: lovitch@nvnet.org.

LOVVORN, AUDREY MARIE, mental health therapist; b. Chandler, Ariz., Nov. 29, 1961; d. Raymond Wesley and Frankie Elouise Davis; 1 child, Cecil Kessinger. BRE, Tenn. Temple U., Chattanooga, 1985; AAS in Criminal Justice, George Wallace Cmty. Coll., Clanton, Ala., 1998; MEd, U. Montevallo, Ala., 2003. Shift leader, care worker Three Springs, Inc., Jemison, Ala., 1996—99; shift leader, treatment aid The Bridge, Inc., Jemison, 1999—2000, child counselor C.A.R.E. unit Gadsden, Ala., 2000—01; home mgr. Chilton/Shelby Mental Health, Ala., 2001—02; residential youth worker, crisis counselor Oak Mountain Youth Svcs., Pelham, Ala., 2002—03; CRS residential mgr. Glenwood, Inc., Birmingham, Ala., 2003—06. Substance abuse counselor Montgomery CAPS Program, Ala., 2002, Ala. Dept. Corrections, 2006; substance abuse counselor intern Firehouse Shelter, Birmingham, 2003; child counselor intern Oak Mountain Youth Svcs., Pelham, 2003. Medicaid eligible therapist, Birmingham, 2004. Mem.: ACA. Republican. Avocations: crocheting, hiking, swimming, travel, writing. Office Phone: 205-467-2755.

LOW, ANNE DOUGLAS, nurse; b. Balt., Feb. 21, 1947; m. Thomais Aiken Low, 1966; children: Matthew Aiken, Corey Canan. BSN cum laude, U. N.C., Greensboro, 1978; MS, Hood Coll., Frederick, Md., 1988. Utilization rev. evaluator U.S. Dept. Vets. Affaris, Martinsburg, W.Va., 1986-97, quality mgmt. specialist, 1981—. Maj., flight nurse USAF, W.Va. Air N.G. Decorated Air Force Commendation medal and Aerial Achievement medal for hazardous flying duty over Bosnia, 1996-97; recipient nat. fed. award for role in developing a cost recovery program U.S. Dept. Treasury, 1992. Mem. AAUW. Home: 176 Harbor Pointe Dr Brunswick GA 31523-8982

LOW, LOUISE ANDERSON, consulting company executive; b. Saline, Mich., May 1, 1944; d. Harry Linné and Rose Josephine (Chvala) Anderson; m. James Thomas Low, Dec. 30, 1967; children: James William, Eric Linné, Kari Louise, Antony Anderson. BA in Biology, U. Mich., 1966. Permanent teaching cert., Mich.; cert. master gardener Coop. Ext. Svc. Tchr. secondary sci. Novi (Mich.) Community Schs., 1966-67; rsch. asst. U. Mich. Med. Sch., Ann Arbor, 1967-68; tchr. secondary sci. Livonia (Mich.) Pub. Schs., 1968-72; tax preparer H&R Block, Saline, 1991; sr. exec. asst. Low & Assocs., Saline, 1991—. Mem. Saline H.S. PTO, 1995—2003, Saline Mid. Sch. PTO, 1996; mem. ball com. St. Joseph Hosp., 1994; active Friends of Saline Dist. Libr.; mem. Saline Area Schs. Project, 1997, also mem. bldg. com.; parent advisor; com. mem. Saline H.S. Alumni Assn., 2001—; mem. youth bd. Zion Luth. Ch., Ann Arbor, 1993—98; mem. long-range planning com. Saline Area Schs., 1990—94, mem. gifted and talented com., 1996—2003. Mem. AAUW (life, bd. dirs., com. chairperson), Washtenaw County Alliance for Gifted Edn. (v.p., bd. dirs. 1988-97), U. Mich. Conger Alumnae Group (bd. dirs., mem. exec. bd.), Alumni Assn. U. Mich. (life), Interlochen Ctr. for Arts Alumni Orgn. (life), Ann Arbor Area Panhellenic Alumnae (pres. 1976-77), Saline H.S. Alumni Assn. (bd. dirs.), Wayne State U. Faculty Wives, Jenny Lind Swedish Cultural Club of Mich. (bd. dirs., program chair 2000-2002), U. Mich. Waterman Alumnae Group (bd. dirs., mem. exec. bd.), Travis Pointe Country Club, Huron Valley Swim Club, Sigma Kappa (alumnae pres. 1970-72), Alpha Mu Sigma Kappa (mem. corp. bd., mem. found.). Lutheran. Home and Office: Low & Assocs 3431 Surrey Dr Saline MI 48176-9571 Business E-Mail: james_low@wayne.edu.

LOW, LOUISE O., volunteer; b. Monroe, Mich., July 6, 1926; d. Peter Orth and Dora M. Grundman; m. Raymond Low, Aug. 16, 1952 (div. Feb. 1986); children: John D., Scott D. (dec.) Student, Southeastern Univ., Washington D.C. Grants specialist fed. govt., 1946-80. Apptd. Fayette County bd. Care and Treatment of Mentally Deficient Persons, 1991—; bd. dirs FayCo Enterprises workshop for devel. disabled adults, 1998-2002; bd. dirs., vol. Operation OUTING, 1987-94; bd. dirs., meml. gift officer Friends and Families of Fayette County Hosp., 1988-99; vol. Fayette County Hosp. Aux., 1995—, scholarship com., 1995—, corr. sec., 1998—, v.p., pres. 2000—; mem. So. Ill. Constituency of Vols. Recipient Abe award, Jan. 1997. Mem. Vandalia Women's Club (exec. bd. 1996—, 2d v.p. 1996-98, pres. 1998-2000, del. state convs. 1998, 99, 2000).

LOW, MARY LOUISE (MOLLY LOW), documentary photographer; b. Quakertown, Pa., Jan. 3, 1926; d. James Harry and Dorothy Collyer (Krewson) Thomas; m. Antoine Francois Gagné, Nov. 3, 1945 (div.); children: James L., David W., Stephen J., Jeannie Wolff-Gagné; m. Paul Low, July 11, 1969 (dec. July 1991). Student, Oberlin Conservatory of Music, 1943-44, Oberlin Coll., 1944; cert., Katharine Gibbs Sec. Sch., 1945; degree in psychiat. rehab. work, Einstein Coll. Medicine, 1968-70. Sec. Dept. Store, N.Y.C., 1945; sec., treas. Gagné Assocs., Consulting Engrs., Binghamton, NY, 1951-66; psychiat. rsch. asst. Jacobi Hosp., Bronx, 1969-70; asst. to head of sch. Brearley Sch., N.Y.C., 1976-78; pvt. practice San Diego, 1984—. Contbr. articles to profl. jours. Pres., bd. trustees Unitarian-Universalist Ch., 2005—. Recipient Dir.'s award for excellence Area Agy. on Aging, San Diego, 1993, Citizen Recognition award County of San Diego, Calif., 1993. Avocations: singing, documentary photography, writing, travel. Office: Molly Low Photography 5576 Caminito Herminia La Jolla CA 92037-7222 Personal E-mail: molly@mollylow.com.

LOW, MERRY COOK, civic worker; b. Uniontown, Pa., Sept. 3, 1925; d. Howard Vance and Eleanora (Lynch) Mullan; m. William R. Cook, 1947 (div. 1979); m. John Wayland Low, July 8, 1979; children: Karen, Cindy, Bob, Jan. Diploma in nursing, Allegheny Gen. Hosp., Pitts., 1946; BS summa cum laude, Colo. Women's Coll., 1976. RN Colo. Dir. patient edn. Med. Care and Rsch. Found., Denver, 1976-78. Contbr. chpt. to Pattern for Distribution of Patient Education, 1981. DuArt bd. dirs. U. Denver, 1998—2004; docent Denver Art Mus., 1979—99, vol. exec. bd., 1988—94, nat. docent symposium com., 1991, chair collectors' choice benefits, 1988, pres. vols., 1988—90; co-chair art auction Colo. Alliance Bus., 1992—93, com., 1994—97; founding chair Rocky Mountain Conservation Ctr., 1989; trustee ch. coun., chair invitational art show 1st Plymouth Congl. Ch., Englewood, Colo., 1981—84; bd. dirs. women's libr. assn. U. Denver, 1982—, vice chmn., 1985—86, chair, 1986—87, co-chair spl. event, 1992; bd. dirs. Humanities Inst., 1993—, pres., 1999; bd. dirs. Rocky Mountain Conservation Ctr., 1999—2000, co-chair Founder's Day com., 1994—, chair Culturefest, 1995—96; bd. dirs. Lamont Sch. Music Assocs., 1990—96. Recipient Disting. Svc. award U. Denver Coll. Law, 1988, King Soopers Vol. of Week award, 1989, Citizen of Arts award Fine Arts Found., 1993, Outstanding Vol. Colo. Alliance of Bus., 1994, U. Denver Cmty. Svc. award, 1996. Mem. Am. Assn. Mus. (vol. meeting coord. 1990-91), P.E.O. (pres. Colo. chpt. DX 1982-84), U. Denver Alumni Assn. (bd. dirs. 1994-2000, sec. 1996-98), Welcome to Colo. (sec. 2004-06), Women for Profit Investment Club (sec. 1999-2002, co-presiding ptnr. 2003-05). Republican. Congregationalist. Home: 2552 E Alameda Ave Apt 11 Denver CO 80209-3324 Personal E-mail: merrylow@aol.com.

LOWE, CAROL HILL, social services director, management consultant; b. Washington, Sept. 12, 1943; d. Lawrence Alexander and Corinne (Thorne) Hill; m. John W. Lowe, Nov., 1968 (div. 1981); 1 child, Paul Alejandro. BA cum laude, Albright Coll., 1965; MSW summa cum laude, Howard U., 1967; cert., John F. Kennedy Sch. of Govt., 1986. Caseworker Child Welfare Dept., City of Washington, 1966-67; caseworker welfare U.S. Dept. Pub. Welfare, Washington, 1967-68, Child Welfare Dept., City of Washington, 1968-70; sr. worker, supr. Social Rehab. Agy., 1970-78; assoc. chief Office of Maternal and Child Health, 1978-82; spl. asst. Office of City Adminstr., 1982-85; exec. dir. DC Commn. for Women, 1986—92; dir. DC Dept. of Recreation and Parks, 1992—95; dir. office of extragovernment and affairs Office Parks Mgmt., 1995—98; mgr. DC Asthma Coalition, 1999—2002; ret., 1998, 2003. Adj. prof. Howard U. Sch. Social Work, 2004—. Mem. Task Force on Pay Equity, Older Adult Learning Com., Child Devel. Coordinating Coun., Employment and Tng. Coalition, Washington, 1985—, D.C. Child Support Advocacy Coalition and Adv. Com., Instl. Appeals Bd., Domestic Ptnrship. Commn.; bd. dirs. Washington Urban League, 1968—1985, chairperson, 1983-85; bd. dirs. DC United Way, 1984—1986, Nat. Assn. Commns. for Women, Women in Mcpl. Govt.; mem. Leadership Washington Bd. Trade, 1987. Fellow Nat. Assn. Social Workers (cert.); mem. NOW, Black Women's Agenda, Nat. Coun. Negro Women, Assn. Black Women Attys., D.C. Urban Mgmt. Assn., Nat. Assn. Black Pub. Adminstrs., Bus. Profl. Women U.S.A. Democrat. Episcopalian.

LOWE, DANIELLE FRANCES, elementary school educator; b. N.Y., Mar. 1, 1977; d. Clifford Edward and Diane Marie Lowe. Student, SUNY, Delhi, N.Y., 1995—96; BS in Elem. Edn., SUNY, New Paltz, N.Y., 2000, MS with hons. in Elem. Edn., 2003. Vet. asst. Lefferts Animal Hosp., Richmond Hills, NY, 1993—97, New Paltz (N.Y.) Animal Hosp., 1997—2000; tchr. Middletown (N.Y.) Bd. Edn., 2000—. Asst. Dr. Molly Caugill, Highland, NY, 2000—04; vet. asst. Luv My Pet, Paugh, NY, 2001—; adj. prof. SUNY, New Paltz, 2004—; case mgr. inst. support team, Middletown, 2002—; facilitator Starlab Truman Moon Sch., Middletown, 2002—. Organizer ground zero notes and funds Truman Moon Sch., 2001, fundraiser eyeglasses for 3d world countries, 2003—04, fundraiser Tsunami Relief Fund, 2005; police dispatcher City of Middletown, 2004—; fundraiser eyeglasses for 3d world countries ASPCA, Middletown, 2002—03. Avocations: reading, hiking, travel, swimming. Office: Truman Moon School 53 Bedford Ave Middletown NY 10940

LOWE, FLORA LESTER, librarian; b. Richmond, Va., Feb. 22, 1948; d. Gerald Kennedy and Mary Opal (Booth) Stith; m. William Curtis Lowe, June 14, 1969; 1 child, Elizabeth Nell. AB, Coll. William & Mary, 1969; M.Libr., Emory U., 1977. Libr. paraprofl. Emory U., Atlanta, 1969-77; libr. asst. Marshall U. Med. Sch. Libr., Huntington, W.Va., 1978-79; retrospective conversion cataloger Deere & Co., Moline, Ill., 1979-80; libr. dir. Mt. St. Clare Coll., Clinton, Iowa, 1980—, instr. ESL, 1980-91. Chairperson, co-founder River Cities Libr. consortium, Clinton, 1988-90, 95—. Mem. ALA, AAUW (scholarship chairperson 1990-91), Iowa Libr. Assn., Iowa Pvt. Acad. Librs., Assn. Coll. and Rsch. Librs., Assn. Coll. and Libr. Rsch., Beatrix Potter Soc., Arnold Bennett Soc., Midwest Archives Conf., Jr. C. of C. (Outstanding Young Woman Am. 1979), Brontë Soc., Kappa Delta Pi, Pi Delta Phi, Beta Phi Mu. Episcopalian. Home: 717 S 15th St Clinton IA 52732-5311 Office: Mt St Clare Coll Coll Libr 400 N Bluff Blvd Clinton IA 52732-3997

LOWE, JENNIFER RUTH, mental health services professional; b. Jackson, Miss., Mar. 20, 1978; d. R. Gregory and Nancy Ellen Watson Presnall; m. Will Lowe, July 3, 2005. BA in Psycholog, BA in Modern Langs., Winthrop U., 2000; postgrad., U. Ky., 2005—. Counselor, cert. nursing asst. Park Ridge Hosp., Fletcher, NC, 2000—02; mental health technician Mental Health and Rehab. Svcs. of Warren and Clinton Counties, Lebanon, Ohio, 2003—05. Recipient Winthrop Scholars award, Winthrop U., 1996—2000; Daniel R. Reedy Quality Achievement fellow, U. Ky., 2005—, Ky. Opportunity fellow, 2005—06. Mem.: Mensa. Avocation: running. Office: U Ky 111-E Kastle Hall Lexington KY 40506-0044

LOWE, KATHLENE WINN, lawyer; b. San Diego, Dec. 1, 1949; d. Ralph and Grace (Rodes) Winn; m. Russell Howells Lowe, Oct. 3, 1977; 1 child, Taylor Rhodes. BA in English magna cum laude, U. Utah, 1971, MA in English, 1973, JD, 1976. Bar: Utah 1976, U.S. Dist. Ct. Utah 1976, U.S. Ct. Appeals (10th cir.) 1980, Calif. 1989, U.S. Dist. Ct. (ctrl. dist.) Calif. 1990. Assoc. Parsons, Behle & Latimer, Salt Lake City, 1976-80, ptnr., 1980-84; v.p. law, asst. gen. counsel Am. Stores Co., Salt Lake City, 1984—89; office mng. ptnr. Brobeck, Phleger & Harrison, Newport Beach, Calif., 1999—2003; ptnr.-in-charge, So. Calif. Dorsey & Whitney LLP, Irvine, Calif. Comment editor Utah Law Rev., 1975-76. Mem. ABA, Calif. Bar Assn., Utah Bar Assn.,Phi Kappa Phi. Avocations: fly fishing, reading, skiing, golf, travel. Office: Dorsey & Whitney LLP 38 Technology Dr Irvine CA 92618-5310 Office Phone: 949-932-3600. Office Fax: 949-932-3601. Business E-Mail: lowe.kathlene@dorsey.com.

LOWE, LISA, education educator, department chairman; BA in history, Stanford U., 1977; PhD in lit., U. of Calif., Santa Cruz, 1986. Prof. comparative lit. U. Calif. at San Diego, 1986—, chmn., lit. dept., 1998—2001. Exec. com. Divsn. on Sociol. Approaches to Lit. of the Modern Lang. Assn., 2001—; adv. bd. U. of Calif. Humanities Rsch. Inst., U. of Calif. President's Humanities Commn.; disting. faculty vis. Ctr. for Ideas and Soc. at U. of Calif., Riverside. Author: (book) Critical Terrains: French and British Orientalisms, 1991, Immigrant Acts: On Asian American Cultural Politics, 1996 (Book award in Cultural Studies from the Assn. for Asian Am. Studies, 1997); co-editor: The Politics of Culture in the Shadow of Capital, 1997. Fellowship, John Simon Guggenheim Meml. Found., 2003. Mem.: Nat. Coun. of the Am. Studies Assn. Office: U of Calif, San Diego Lit Dept 9500 Gilman Dr La Jolla CA 92093

LOWE, MARY FRANCES, federal official; b. Ft. Meade, Md., Apr. 15, 1952; d. Benno Powers and Peggy Catherine (Moore) L. BA, Coll. William and Mary, 1972; MA, Fletcher Sch. Law and Diplomacy, 1974, MA Law and Diplomacy in, 1975; diplome, Grad. Inst. Internat. Studies U. Geneva, Switzerland, 1975; M.P.H. in epidemiology, Johns Hopkins Sch. Hygiene and Pub. Health, 1986. External collaborator ILO, Geneva, 1974; legis. asst. to U.S. Senator Richard S. Schweiker Washington, 1975-76; profl. staff mem. health and sci. rsch. subcom. U.S. Senate Com. Labor and Human Resources, Washington, 1976-81; exec. sec. U.S. Dept. HHS, Washington, 1981-85; sr. asst. to commr. program policy FDA, 1985-89; sr. asst. pesticide programs EPA, 1989-96; asst. Office Environ. Policy U.S. Dept. State, Washington, 1997-99; program advisor pesticide program govt. and internat. svcs. EPA, Washington, 1999—. Rep. U.S. delegations World Health Assemblies, Geneva, NAFTA and WTO Coms., 1995-98, Codex Alimentarius, UN Sub-Com. Experts on the Globally Harmonized System of Classification and Labelling Chems.; alt. trustee Woodrow Wilson Internat. Ctr. Scholars. Mem. Soc. for Epidemiologic Rsch., Am. Assn. World Health, Exec. Women in Govt., Soc. for Chem. Hazard Comm., Soc. Risk Analysis, Washington World Affairs Coun., Delta Omega. Home: 7920 Spotswood Dr Alexandria VA 22308-1125 Office: US EPA 1200 Pennsylvania Ave NW Washington DC 20460-0001 Office Phone: 703-305-5689. Business E-Mail: lowe.maryfrances@epa.gov.

LOWE, PATRICIA A., psychologist, educator; b. Landstuhl, Germany, July 31, 1957; (parents Am. citizens); d. Gerald H. and Hazel C. Lowe. BS magna cum laude, Boise State U., 1980; PhD, Tex. A&M U., 2000. Lic. psychologist Idaho, cert. sch. psychologist Idaho, Kans. Grad. rsch./tchg. asst. Tex. A&M U., College Station, 1995—99; psychology intern Warm Springs Counseling Ctr. and Tng. Inst., Boise, Idaho, 1999—2000, post-doctoral resident, 2000—01; prof. U. Kans., Lawrence, 2001—. Cons. for tech. initiative grant The Ind. Sch. Dist. of Boise City, 1999—2000; cons./tech. advisor to Nat. Ctr. on Learning Disabilities U. Kans., Lawrence, 2002—, clin. supr. Assoc. editor: book Encyclopedia of School Psychology; co-author: (test manual) Adult Manifest Anxiety Scale, (test) Adult Manifest Anxiety Scale-Elderly Version, Adult Manifest Anxiety Scale-Adult Version, Adult Manifest Anxiety Scale-College Version, (book) Clinical Applications of Continuous Performance Tests: Measuring Attention and Impulsive Responding in Children and Adults, Encyclopedia of School Psychology, (test) Test Anxiety Inventory for Children and Adolescents; contbr. chapters to books, articles to profl. jours.; mem. editl. bd. profl. jours. Faculty rep. U. Kans. Cir. K Svc. Orgn., Lawrence, 2001—03; univ. trainer Kans. Assn. Sch. Psychologists, 2001—02. Recipient Alumni award, Boise State U., 1980, cert. of achievement, Kans. Assn. Sch. Psychologists; Lechner Grad. Merit fellow, Tex. A&M U., 1995—96, Rsch. grantee, U. Kans., 2002, 2003. Mem.: APA, NASP, Psi Chi, Kappa Delta Phi, Phi Kappa Phi. Achievements include test development. Avocations: skiing, tennis, racquetball, swimming, running. E-mail: tlowe@ku.edu.

LOWE, PATRICIA MCLAUGHLIN, real estate company executive; b. Little Rock, Aug. 12, 1930; d. William Heber McLaughlin and Jessie May Walker; m. Robert McKinley Lowe, Sr., Jan. 31, 1951 (div.); children: Patricia Ann, Robert McKinley Jr., John McLaughlin, Jessica Jean. BS, U. Ark., Fayetteville, 1952, MS, 1972, EdD, 1977. Home econ. tchr. US Dept. Edn., St. Thomas, V.I., 1983—84; counselor Coll. V.I., St. Thomas, 1984—85; real estate sales Realty World, Fayettevillea, 1986—90; tchr. Peace Corps, Sierra Leone, 1991—93; social worker Cath. Social Svc., Roseau Dominica, 1994—95; office mgr. Red Cross, Roseau Dominica, 1995—96; dir. Real Estate Renovations, Fayetteville, 1996—. Ednl. examiner Spl. Sch. Dist., Ft. Smith, Ark., 1982—83. Vol. Peace Corps, Brazil, 1977—81, Kenya, 1981—82, 1982—83; bd. dirs. Wall of Tolerance Poverty Law Ctr., Montgomery, Ala., 2005; bd. dirs. Hispanic devel. Ark. Presbytery, 2000—06. Mem.: Human Svc. Profls., Phi Upsilon Omicron. Democrat. Avocations: gardening, knitting.

LOWE, SANDRA ELVETA, psychologist; b. Petersburg, Va., Sept. 27, 1946; d. James Elwood and Senora Stith Lowe. BA, Davis and Elkins Coll., Elkins, W. Va., 1968; MS, Ill. Inst. Tech., Chgo., 1970; MA, PhD, Loyola U. Chgo., 1980. Lic. Clin. Psychologist Ill., 1982. Rehab. counselor J.J. Madden Mental Health Ctr., Hines, Ill., 1970—72; instr. psychology Luther Coll., Decorah, Iowa, 1972—74; resident in clin. psychology Northwestern Meml. Hosp., Inst. Psychiatry, Chgo., 1976—77; clin. psychology intern Ravenswood Hosp. Med. Ctr., Chgo., 1977—78; counselor Ctrl. Austin Counseling Ctr., Chgo., 1979—80; staff psychologist Loyola U. Chgo., 1980—2002; clin. psychologist Sandra E. Lowe, Ph.D., Chgo., 1981—. Bd. dirs. Cathedral Counseling Ctr., Chgo., 1994—2000. Voter registrant City of Chgo., 49th Ward, 1992—96; mem., co-chair Peace and Social Justice Commn., St. James Cathedral, Chgo., 1994—2002; presbyterate discernment weekend listening team mem. Episcopal Diocese of Chgo., 1999—; mem. Commn. on Ordained Ministry, Episcopal Diocese of Chgo., 2002—06; vol. Deborah's Pl., Chgo., 1992—. Mem.: APA, Assn. Black Psychologists (pres. 1997—98, co-chair, social action com. 1992—96, bd. dirs. 1988—99, treas. 1989—96), Episcopal Peace Fellowship, Nat. Alliance against Racist and Polit. Repression (life). Episcopal. Avocations: reading, travel, photography, politics. Office: Sandra E Lowe PhD 737 N Mich Ave Chicago IL 60611 Office Phone: 312-440-1709, 312-771-5090. Personal E-mail: elveta@aol.com.

LOWELL, JANET ANN, nurse; b. Greenfield, Mass., Dec. 12, 1946; d. Edward Franklin and Helen Elizabeth (Walker) A; m. Brian Theodore Lowell, Oct. 22, 1965 (div. 1982); children: David Earle, Jennifer Lee. AS, Greenfield Community Coll., 1984; BSN summa cum laude, Norwich U., 1991. RN, Mass.; cert. breast self-exam instr., advanced continuing care nurse (ACCC), oncology nurse, advanced continuity of care, Nat. Bd. Certification in Continuity of Care, Oncology Nursing Certification Corp. Sec. U. Md., Far East Div., Tokyo, 1966-68; receptionist, sec., prodn. supr. Greenfield (Mass.) Paper Box Co., Inc., 1975-81; staff nurse Franklin Med. Ctr., Greenfield, 1984-85, Farren Meml. Hosp., Turners Falls, Mass., 1985-88; nursing supr. Hospice in Franklin County, Greenfield, 1988-90; staff ednl. coord. Farren Care Ctr., Turners Falls, Mass., 1990-91; staff nurse oncology, hematology Dartmouth Hitchcock Med. Ctr., Lebanon, N.H., 1991-94, clin. rev. case facilitator, 1994-95, continuing care nurse patient and family svcs., 1995—96; patient care coord. Cheshire Med. Ctr., Keene, NH, 1996—2001; clin. care coord. Concord Hosp., 2001—. Mem. Am. Cancer Soc. Profl. Edn. Com., Greenfield, 1986-89; mem. mission com., rep. mission coun. Farren Care Ctr., Turners Falls, 1990-91; rep. to nursing profl. practice coun. Dartmouth Hitchcock Med. Ctr., Lebanon, 1991-94, mem. bereavement support group, 1995—. Vol. Big Bros./Bis Sisters, 1992—. Recipient Hap Adams scholarship, 1983, Ethel Dow Wells scholarship, 1982-84, Fred B. Wells scholarship, 1982-84, Greenfield Community Coll., Franklin Med. Ctr. scholarship, Franklin Med. Ctr., 1983. Mem. Case Mgmt. Soc. Am. (cert. case mgr.), Oncology Nursing Soc. (cert. oncology nurse, Vt./N.H. chpt.), Mohawk Woman's Club (chpt. treas. 1979-80, pres. 1980-81), Nat. Oncology Nursing Soc. (advanced continuity of care cert.), Nat. Alliance Mentally Ill. Avocations: cross country skiing, gardening, hiking. Office: Concord Hosp 250 Pleasant St Concord NH 03301 Office Phone: 603-227-7000 ext. 3953. Business E-Mail: jlowell@crhc.org.

LOWELL, VIRGINIA LEE, retired librarian; b. San Jose, Calif., Nov. 21, 1940; d. Earnest S. and Dorothy (Givens) Greene; children: Michael Edward, Christopher Scott. Student, Reed Coll, 1958-61; BA, U. Calif., Berkeley, 1963; MSLS, Western Res. U., 1964. Cataloger Wittenberg U., Springfield, Ohio, 1965-66, John Carroll U., Cleve., 1966-68, Cuyahoga Community Coll., Cleve., 1968-70, cons., instr., 1970; head catalog dept. Cuyahoga County Pub. Library, Cleve., 1976-78; dir. tech. svcs. Cuyahoga County Pub. Libr., Cleve., 1979-89; dir. Jackson (Mich.) Dist. Libr., 1989—98; state libr. State of Hawaii, 1998—2003. Chmn. bd. trustees Ohionet, Columbus, 1987-89. Mem. ALA, Ohio Libr. Assn. (coord. automation and tech. div. 1988—), No. Ohio Tech. Svc. Librs. (chmn. 1988-89), Ohio Women Librs. (treas. 1987-89), Am. Mgmt. Assn., Mich. Libr. Assn. Democrat. Roman Catholic. Avocation: choral singing.

LOWENBERG, GEORGINA GRACE, retired elementary school educator; b. El Paso, Tex., Feb. 15, 1944; d. Eduardo Antonio and Grace Elizabeth (Fletcher) Orellana; m. Edward Daniel Lowenberg, June 14, 1968, (div. 1985); 1 child, Jennifer Anne. BSEd, U. Tex., El Paso, 1965, postgrad., 1965-66, U. St. Thomas, 1983. Permanent profl. teaching cert., Tex. Tchr. 5th grade El Paso Pub. Sch. Dist., 1965-70; tchr. 3d grade gifted, talented Ysleta Ind. Sch. Dist., El Paso, 1980—2002. Mem. com. Tex. State Textbook Selection Com., Austin, 1984-85, Tex. State TEAMS Math Adv. Com., Austin, 1986-87; sci. presentor Silver Burdett, Albuquerque, 1985-86; critic reader Scott-Foresman, Dallas, 1986; pres., v.p. Scotsdale Elem. Sch. PTA, El Paso, 1976-83; v.p. Eastwood Middle Sch. PTA, El Paso, 1984-85; mem. Eastwood Heights Elem. Sch. PTA, 1980-2002; sec. Eastwood High Sch. Band Boosters, El Paso, 1985-89, Speech Boosters, 1986-88; life mem. Tex. State PTA, 1981—. Troop leader Brownie and Jr. Girl Scouts Am., El Paso, 1977-82; dir. Eaglette Dance Team, 1994-95; libr. asst. Eastwood Heights Libr., 2004—. Named Tchr. of Yr., Eastwood Heights Elem., 1983, Top Ten Dist. Tchr. of Yr., 1983. Mem. Assn. Tex. Profl. Educators (regional treas. 1987-88), Yseta and Tex. Ret. Tchrs. Assn. (chmn. Hall of Fame 2002—). Roman Catholic.

LOWENSTEIN, ARLENE JANE, nursing educator, health facility administrator; b. Phila., Oct. 10, 1936; d. Nathan Morris and Rae (Greenburg) Needleman; m. Manfred Lowenstein, June 9, 1957; children: Jay David, Russell Scott. Diploma in nursing, Hosp. of U. Pa., Phila., 1957; BSN, Fairleigh Dickinson U., 1969; MA, NYU, 1974; PhD, U. Pitts., 1985. Staff and tchg. nurse Albert Einstein Med. Ctr., Hosp. U. Pa., 1957-59; instr. Middlesex County Coll., Edison, NJ, 1969-71; staff nurse Vis. Nurse Svc., N.Y.C., 1970-72; supr. obstet. and pediat. Middlesex Gen. Hosp., New Brunswick, NJ, 1972-74; dir. ambulatory & cmty. health Peter Bent Brigham Hosp., 1974-79, dir. nurse practitioner program, 1974-81; dir. surg. nursing Brigham and Women's Hosp., Boston, 1980—81; acting dir. nursing Peter Bent Brigham Hosp., Boston, 1978-80; assoc hosp. dir., dir nursing svc. U. Ky. Med. Ctr., Lexington, 1981-83; asst. prof. U. Pitts., 1983-85; prof. nursing, dept. chair. Med. Coll. Ga., Augusta, 1985-95; prof., dir. grad. program in nursing Mass. Gen. Hosp. Inst. of Health Professions, Boston, 1995—2003, prof. emeritus, 2003—. Lectr. Simmons Coll., 2005-. Author textbooks; contbr. articles to profl. jours. Bd. dirs. Sr. Citizens Coun. of Ctrl. Savannah River Area, Augusta, 1982-95; coord. vols. Opera Boston. Mem. ANA, Coun. Grad. Edn. for Nursing Adminstrs. (chair 1990-92), Sigma Xi, Sigma Theta Tau. Avocations: opera, music, art. Home: 312 Lewis Wharf Boston MA 02110-3905 Business E-Mail: alowenstein@mghihp.edu.

LOWENTHAL, CONSTANCE, art historian, consultant; b. NYC, Aug. 29, 1945; d. Jesse and Helen (Oberstein) L. BA cum laude, Brandeis U., 1967; AM, Inst. Fine Arts, NYU, 1969; PhD, Inst. Fine Arts, NYU, N.Y.C., 1976. Mem. faculty Sarah Lawrence Coll., Bronxville, NY, 1975-78; asst. mus. educator Met. Mus. Art, N.Y.C., 1978-85; exec. dir. Internat. Found. Art Research, N.Y.C., 1985-98; dir. Commn. for Art Recovery World Jewish Congress, N.Y.C., 1998-2001; cons. art ownership disputes N.Y.C., 2001—. Bd. dirs. Ctr. for Edn. Studies, Inc. Regular contbr. Art Crime Update column Wall Street Jour., 1988-97; mem. editl. bd.: The Spoils of War, World War II and Its Aftermath: The Loss, Reappearance and Recovery of Cultural Property, 1997; contbr. articles to Mus. News and other profl. publs. Office Phone: 212-876-3140. Business E-Mail: cl@lowenthal-inc.com.

LOWER, WENDY MORGAN, historian, educator; b. Hanover, N.H., Apr. 7, 1965; d. James Morgan Lower and Mary Suzanne Liljequist; m. Christof Ulrich Mauch, June 3, 1995; children: Ian Maxwell Mauch, Alexander Morgan Mauch. BA, Hamilton Coll., Clinton, N.Y., 1987; PhD, Am. U., Washington, 1999. Dir. vis. scholars program U.S. Holocaust Meml. Mus., Washington, 2000—04; asst. prof. Towson U., Md., 2004—. Mem. internat. adv. bd. Jour. of Genocide Rsch., 2005—. Author: (book) Nazi Empire Building and the Holocaust in Ukraine. Mem., activist savedarfur.org, 2005; com. mem. fundraising and planning activities Chevy Chase Playground, Washington, 1998—99. Recipient rsch. fellowship, U.S. Holocaust Meml. Mus., 1999, dissertation rsch. grant, German Hist. Inst., 1997, 1998, Nat. Paper prize, Phi Alpha Theta, 1995; scholar, Am. U., 1993—97. Mem.: German Studies Assn. Democrat. Achievements include research in Oral History Collection, OSS Veterans. Avocations: piano, travel, tennis.

LOWERY, DEBORAH GARRISON, freelance writer, editor; b. Johnson City, Tenn., Oct. 2, 1957; d. Clyde Mack and Joyce Dean (Stout) Garrison; m. David Ryan Lowery, Nov. 5, 1983; children: Caroline Nicole, Benjamin David. BS in Home Econs., U. Ga., 1979, MA in Journalism, 1981. Asst. editor So. Living Mag., Birmingham, 1981-87, assoc. editor, 1987-88; sr. editor Progressive Farmer Mag., Birmingham, 1988-92; mng. editor Cooking Light Mag., Birmingham, 1992-94, exec. editor, 1994; foods editor Oxmoor House Pub. Co., Birmingham, 1994-98. Charter mem. bd. advisors Coll. Family & Consumer Svcs. U. Ga., Athens, 1995-98; charter mem. work & family com. So. Progress Corp, Birmingham, 1991-97; media con. mem. Childhood Agrl. Injury Prevention Symposium Nat. Farm Medicine Ctr., 1992; owner, instr. Kids Can Cook! (children's cooking sch.), 1998—; adj.

instr. Samford U., 2001-2004. Editor: (cookbook) Low Fat High Flavor Cookbook, 1995, Cooking Light Five-Star Recipes, 1996, Weight Watchers Light & Easy Cookbook, 1997, Weight Watchers Cook Quick Cook Healthy, 1997; coord. editor Countryplace Mag., 1991-97; freelance journalist, 1998—; contbr. articles to profl. jours. Sunday sch. tchr. Valleydale Bapt. Ch., Birmingham, 1997-98; parent coll. com. mem. Oak Mountain Elem. Sch., Birmingham, 1997-2004; leader Girl Scouts Am., 2004—. Recipient Writer of Yr., 1991, master writer award Am. Agrl. Editors Assn., 1992, Nat. Bus. Home Economist Yr. Home Economists Bus., 1993, Ala. Home Economist Yr. Ala. Home Economists Bus., Birmingham, 1993, Samford U. Journalism Found. Dept. award, 2002. Mem. Am. Assn. Family and Consumer Scis. (food and nutrition com. 1981-98, chmn. Birmingham group bus. sect. 1984-85), Ala. Assn. Family and Consumer Sci. (v.p. program devel. 1986-88). Avocations: herb gardening, inspirational writing. Home and Office: 3004 Stonehill Cir Birmingham AL 35244-3438 Fax: 205-980-5062. E-mail: writer1118@bellsouth.net.

LOWERY, DIANNE ARMOUR, music educator; b. Fort Worth, Tex., Dec. 7, 1954; d. Warren G. Armour and Lala Elizabeth Cathey; m. Gary Vern Lowery, Aug. 22, 1956; 1 child, Brian Reid. BA, Union U., Jackson, Tenn., 1980. Cert. music specialist Tenn., 1980. Counselor Jackson Counseling Ctr., Jackson, Tenn., 1984—88; music specialist Henry Elem. Sch., Henry, Tenn., 1989—, Milan Elem. Sch., Milan, Tenn., 1996—99. R-Consevative. Southern Baptist. Avocation: gardening. Home: 5022 West Main St Milan TN 38358 Office: Henry Elementary School 937 Pioneer Rd Henry TN 38358 Office Phone: 731-243-7114. Office Fax: 731-243-2951. Personal E-mail: loweryd54@aol.com. E-mail: loweryd@k12tn.net.

LOWERY, LAURIE BLOUNT, elementary school educator; b. Jacksonville, Fla., Aug. 21, 1966; d. Walter Isaac and Jeanette Leaptrot Blount; m. Paul Ellis Lowery, July 13, 1964; children: Katie Leigh, Patrick Ellis. B, Ga. Southwestern Coll., Americus, 1988. Tchr. Fullington Acad., Pinehurst, Ga., 1989—2000, Unadilla Elem. Sch., 2000—02, Dooly County Elem. Sch., Pinehurst, 2002—06. Tchr. Sunday sch. Mt. Pleasant Bapt. Ch., Vienna, Ga., 1994—2006. Home: PO Box 260 Pinehurst GA 31070 Office: Dooly County Elementary Schoo Highway 41 Pinehurst GA 31070 Office Phone: 229-645-3421.

LOWERY, WILLA DEAN, obstetrician, gynecologist; b. Caryville, Fla., Apr. 16, 1927; d. Ernest and Nadine (Fowler) L. BS in Chemistry, Stetson U., 1948; MS in Microbiology, U. Fla., 1952; MD, U. Miami, 1959; MPH, U. Pitts., 1963; MDiv in Theology, Pitt. Theol. Sem., 1995. Diplomate Am. Bd. Ob-Gyn.; ordained to ministry Presbyn. Ch. Microbiologist Fla. Dept. Pub. Health, Jacksonville, 1948-52, pub. health officer, 1959-65; microbiologist U. S. Operation Mission to Brazil, Belém, 1952-55; rotating intern Jackson Meml. Hosp., Miami, Fla., 1959-60; resident in ob-gyn. Magee Women's Hosp., Pitts., 1965-68; asst. prof. ob-gyn. Sch. Medicine, U. Pitts., 1968-69; pvt. practice Pitts., 1970-88; pastor Presbyn. Ch. So. Ind. County Parish, 1995—. Cons. Med. Mission in Brazil, Teresina, 1986-89; mem. Ethics Bd. of Chldns. Hosp U. Pittsburgh, 1998. Contbr. articles to profl. jours. Recipient Disting. Alumni award, Stetson U., 2003. Mem. AMA, ACOG, Pa. State Med. Soc., Allegheny County Med. Soc. Home: 119 Sunnyhill Dr Pittsburgh PA 15237-3666

LOWERY-O'CONNELL, SUSAN ELLEN, psychologist; d. William Rockne and Rosemary Lowery; m. Michael Patrick O'Connell, Aug. 17, 1999; 1 child, Jeffrey Andrew Schultz. B in Music Edn., Ashland U., Ohio, 1978; MA, Ohio State U., 1985, PhD, 1989. Lic. psychologist Ohio. Psychologist Children's Hosp. Med. Ctr. of Akron, Ohio, 1989—92; asst. prof. psychology in psychiatry N.E. Ohio Univs. Coll. Medicine, Rootstown, 1991—2003; psychologist, dir. Susan E. Lowery, Ph.D. & Assocs., Tallmadge, Ohio, 1991—96; assoc. prof. Walsh U., North Canton, Ohio, 1992—2001; CEO, psychologist Personal Solutions, Inc., Tallmadge, 1996—2000; project supr. Ashland U., Massillon, Ohio, 2001—03; program dir. Stark County Family Coun., Canton, Ohio, 2003—. Consulting staff Children's Hosp. Med. Ctr. of Akron, 1993—2003, Akron Gen. Med. Ctr., 1993—95; mem. Kellogg's leadership team Sisters of Charity Found., Canton, 2002—03; mem. Help Me Grow adv. bd. Stark County Family Coun., Canton, 2004—; mem. profl. devel. adv. com. Cmty. Svcs. of Stark County, Inc., Canton, 2004—; mem. early childhood mental health consultation leadership coun. Ohio Dept. Mental Health, Columbus, 2003—; local program mentor DECA, 2003—; adj. prof. Ashland U., Massillon, Ohio, 2003—; program mentor Incredible Years Tng. Series, Ohio, 2006—. Recipient Faculty Recognition award, NEOUCOM, 1990—91; grantee Delta Theta Tau, Hoover Found., 2004, Sisters of Charity Found., 2004—05. Mem.: APA, Ohio Assn. for Infant Mental Health, Phi Kappa Phi. Achievements include development of The Childhood Resiliency Project, a childcare-based early childhood consultation program, building social, emotional and behavioral skills for young children ages 2 to 6. Office: Stark County Family Coun 800 Market Ave N Ste 1500 Canton OH 44702 Office Phone: 330-455-1225. Office Fax: 330-455-2026. E-mail: Susan_L@starkfamilycouncil.org.

LOWEY, NITA MELNIKOFF, congresswoman; b. NYC, July 5, 1937; m. Stephen Lowey, 1961; children: Dona, Jacqueline, Douglas. BA in Mktg., Mt. Holyoke Coll., Mass., 1959. Cmty. activist, prior to 1975; asst. to NY sec. state for econ. devel. and neighborhood preservation, dir. divsn. econ. oppurtunity NY State, 1975—85, asst. sec. state, 1985—87; mem. US Congress from 20th NY dist., 1989-92, US Congress from 18th NY dist., 1993—. Mem. homeland security com. US Congress, mem. appropriations com., ranking minority mem. fgn. ops., export financing and related progs. subcommittee, co-chair Congl. anti-terrorism financing task force, co-founder Hudson River Caucus. Bd. dirs. Close-Up Found., Effective Parenting Info. for Children, Windward Sch. Named Legislator of Yr., MADD; named one of 10 Women's Health Heroes, Reader's Digest, 1999; recipient Herbert Tenzer award, Pub. Svc., Five Towns Jewish Coun., 1999, Excellence in Nat. Pub. Leadership award, Nat. Assembly Health and Human Svc. Orgns., 1999, Congl. Leadership award, Coalition to Stop Gun Violence, 2001, Responsible Choices award, Planned Parenthood Fedn. Am. Mem.: Women's Network of YWCA. Democrat. Jewish. Office: US House Reps 2329 Rayburn House Office Bldg Washington DC 20515-0001 Office Phone: 202-225-6506.*

LOWRANCE, MURIEL EDWARDS, retired educational specialist; b. Ada, Okla., Dec. 28, 1922; d. Warren E. and Mayme E. (Barrick) Edwards; B.S. in Edn., E. Ctrl. State U., Ada, 1954; 1 child: Kathy Lynn Lowrance Gutierrez. Acct., adminstrv. asst. to bus. mgr. E. Ctrl. State U., 1950-68; grants and contracts specialist U. N.Mex. Sch. Medicine, Albuquerque, 1968-72, program specialist IV, dept. orthopaedics, 1975-86; asst. adminstrv. officer N.Mex. Regional Med. Program, 1972-75. Bd. dirs. Vocat. Rehab. Center, 1980-84. Cert. profl. contract mgr. Nat. Contract Assn. Mem. Am. Bus. Women's Assn. (past pres. El Segundo chpt., Woman of Yr. 1974), AAUW, Amigos de las Americas (dir.). Democrat. Methodist. Club: Pilot (Albuquerque) (pres. 1979-80, dir. 1983-84, dist. treas. 1984-86, treas. S.W. dist., 1984-86, gov.-elect S.W. dist. 1986-87, gov. S.W. dist. 1987-88). Home: 4333 Berwick Dr Wichita Falls TX 76309

LOWRANCE, RITA GALE HAMRICK, elementary school educator; b. Chattanooga, Sept. 27, 1951; d. Thomas Austin and Alma Lucille (Horne) Hamrick; m. Bill R. Hilliard, Jan. 11, 1974 (div. Aug. 1980); stepchildren: Terri Feraghat, Renee Beaumont; m. James Kamenik, June 27, 1981 (div. Feb. 1994); m. Charles L. Lowrance, Jr., Mar. 30, 2000. BS in Band and Choral Music Edn., U. Tenn., Chattanooga, 1975, elem. and spl. edn. endorsement, 1981, MEd in Spl. Edn., 1984; postgrad., W. Ga. Coll., 1986-87; cert. edn. specialist, U. Ala., 1996; postgrad., Walker Tech. C.C., 1996—. Cert. tchr. spl. edn., Ga., band and choral music, spl. edn., Tenn. Tchr. spl. edn. Chattanooga City Schs., 1981-83, Walker County Schs., Lafayette, Ga., 1983-93; dir., owner Sterling Learning Ct., Ft. Oglethorpe, Ga., 1991-93; tchr. partial hospitalization program for children Cumberland Hall Psychiat. Hosp., 1993-94; music tchr. Daisy Elem. Sch., Chattanooga, 1994-2000; tchr. Birchwood (Tenn.) Elem. Sch., 2000—. Founder, dir. Sterling Learning Found., Ft. Oglethorpe, 1992-93. Singer Rita G. Hamrick Southern Belle album, 1995. Pres. Bradley County Rep. Women, Cleveland, Tenn., 1975; leader Girl Scouts U.S.A., Chattanooga, 1981-82; mem., choir soloist, dir. youth handbells St. Timothy's Episcopal Ch., Christian Motorcyclists Assn., Am. Motocyclists Assn., Signal Mountain, Tenn. Named Hon. Sgt. at Arms Tenn. Ho. of Reps., Nashville, 1975. Mem. NEA, Nat. Story League, Tenn. Edn. Assn., Hamilton County Edn. Assn., Tenn. Aquarium, Ladies Oriental Shrine N.Am., Order of Amaranth (life, royal matron 1978-79, grand musician 1992-93), Kappa Delta Pi. Baptist. Avocations: scuba diving, underwater photography, writing, music, riding motorcycles. Home: 910 Irongate Ct NE Cleveland TN 37312-4703 Office: Birchwood Elem Sch Hwy 60 Birchwood TN 37408

LOWREY, BARBARA R., educator, former federal official; BA, Mich. State U., 1963; MS, U. Wis., 1964; PhD, Mich. State U., 1970. Former assoc. sec., ombudsman of bd. Bd. Govs. of Fed. Res. Sys., Washington; adj. prof. Univ. Md., 2001—. Chief staff support to Gov. Yellen on interagy. com. Women's Bus. Enterprises; bd. rep. NWBC, 1992-93. Mem. Fairfax Partnership for Youth. Office: Dept Econ Univ Md 3105 Tydings Hall College Park MD 20742*

LOWREY, LIDA MILLER, artist; b. Jellico, Tenn., Nov. 24, 1934; d. Elbert Kyle and Louise Austin Miller; m. Austin Sheridan Lowrey, Oct. 25, 1958; children: Elizabeth Lowrey Clapp, Sheridan Miller. BA in Applied Art, Auburn U., Ala., 1956; MA in Visual Design, N.C. State U., Raleigh, N.C., 1982. Graphic designer Hal Zamboni Assocs., N.Y.C., 1958—60, Jack Beck Design, N.Y.C., 1960—63; head graphic designer N.C. Mus. Art, Raleigh, 1979—82, chief designer, 1985—89; dir. visual and literary arts N.C. Arts Coun., Raleigh, 1982—85; chief design cons. Royal Ontario Mus., Toronto, Canada, 1989—91; sr. design cons. Mpls. (Minn.) Inst. Arts, 1991—92; freelance artist L.A., 1992—. One-woman shows include Fine Arts Gallery Reed Whipple Cultural Ctr., City Las Vegas (Nev.) Cultural and Cmty. Affairs, 2001, exhibitions include Los Angeles County Mus. Art, Calif., 2000, Irvine (Calif.) Fine Arts Ctr., 2000, 2002, Angles Gate Cultural Ctr., San Pedro, Calif., 2002, Am. Inst. Graphic Arts, L.A., Calif., 2003. Home: 1419 S Pacific Ave San Pedro CA 90731

LOWRIE, KATHRYN YANACEK, special education educator; b. Midland, Mich., Nov. 23, 1958; d. Frank Joseph and Jacqueline Ann (Sipko) Yanacek; m. David Bruce Lowrie, Mar. 14, 1987; 1 child, Alexandra Yanacek. BA in Psychology, Northea. U., 1980. Psychology technician Rsch. Inst. of Environ. Medicine, U.S. Army, Natick, Mass., 1980-81, computer programmer, 1981-83; assoc. recruiter Mgmt. Adv. Svcs., Burlington, Mass., 1983-85, v.p. mgmt. info. sys., 1985-86, exec. v.p., 1986-89; CEO Computer Careers, Raynham, Mass., 1989-90; v.p. G.R.S.I. Corp., Middleboro, Mass., 1990-94; owner S.B. Industries, Taunton, Mass., 1994-96; pres. Enviro-Screen, Inc., Taunton, 1996-97; sr. assoc. Franklin (Mass.) Key Assocs., 1997—99; contract recruiter, 1999—2001; spl. edn. tchr. J.E. Richards Mid. Sch., Lawrenceville, Ga., 2001—05, Graham A. Barden Elem. Sch., Havelock, NC, 2005—. Avocations: reading, physical fitness, travel, motivational training, environmental issues. Office Phone: 252-444-5100. Personal E-mail: kylowrie@hotmail.com.

LOWRY, ALAIRE HOWARD, psychologist; b. Phila., June 4, 1943; d. Lorn Lambier and Etha Johannaber Howard; m. Thomas Wells Lowry, Apr. 20, 1963; children: Michael Andrew, Thomas Ethan. BA in Music with high honors, So. Meth. U., Dallas, 1965; MusM in Conducting, U. Tex., Austin, 1969, Dr.Mus.Arts, 1972, PhD in Psychology, 1988. Diplomate in group psychology Am. Bd. Profl. Psychology; lic. psychologist Tex., 1990. Harpist Dallas Symphony Orch., 1962—65, 1967; tchr. 2d grade St. Mary's Cathedral Sch., Austin, 1965—66; tchr. Ursuline Acad., Dallas, 1966—67; tchg. asst. U. Tex., Austin, 1967—72; instr. Southwestern U., Georgetown, Tex., 1972—79; from asst. to assoc. prof. U. Tex., Austin, 1973—82; psychologist in pvt. practice Austin, 1988—. Asst. scoutmaster, Philmont Trek leader Boy Scouts Am., Austin, 1988—90; chair Psy-Pac, Tex., 1993—94; adminstrv. bd. chair Univ. United. Meth. Ch., Austin, 2001—03; v.p. bd. dirs. Capital Area Mental Health Ctr., Austin, 1992—94; bd. dirs. Am. Group Psychotherapy Found., 2000—01. Mem.: Am. Group Psychotherapy Assn. (membership chair, ann. meeting mktg. chair 2006), Southwestern Group Psychotherapy Soc. (sec., inst. chair, tng. chair, newsletter editor), Austin Mental Health Ind. Practice Assn. (sec. bd. dirs. 1996—97), Tex. Psychol. Assn. (bd. trustees 1998—2001), Phi Beta Kappa. Democrat. Methodist. Avocations: travel, reading, photography, hiking, skiing. Office: 8140 N Mopac Bldg 2 Ste 200 Austin TX 78759 Office Phone: 512-346-2332. Business E-Mail: dr_lowry@mac.com.

LOWRY, KAREN M., biomedical research scientist, pharmacist; b. Stamford, Conn., July 8, 1945; d. Joseph John and Helen Elizabeth (Wykowski) Markovich; m. Atherton Clark Lowry Aug. 17, 1968; children: Atherton Clark Matthew, Suzanne Marie. BS summa cum laude, Fordham U., 1968; MS in Pharmacology, Cornell U., 1971; MA, St. Charles Sem., Wynnewood, Pa., 1983. Registered pharmacist, Pa. Rsch. asst. in biochemistry/molecular biology Thomas Jefferson Med. Sch., Phila., 1971-74; adj. prof. chemistry Holy Family Coll., Phila., 1975-76, Arcadia U., Glenside, Pa., 1984-87; sr. biochemist, lab. mgr. Beacon Rsch. Inc., Glenside, 1987-95; pharmacist Abington (Pa.) Meml. Hosp., 2000—; staff U. Pa. Health System/Presbyn. Med. Ctr., 2000. Asst. sec. Biocoat Inc., Ft. Washington, Pa., 1991-95; mem. sci. adv. bd. UHT, Dobbs Ferry, N.Y., 1987-95. Contbr. articles to profl. jours.; patentee in field. Libr. dir. Immaculate Conception Sch., Jenkintown, Pa., 1980-86; Am. sponsor Vietnamese refugees Cath. Social Svcs., Phila., 1975—. NSF rsch. participant, 1964-68; USPHS grantee, 1968-71 Mem. Am. Chem. Soc., GFWC Everywoman's Club of Glenside (publicity chair 1995-96, pres. 1996-99). Roman Catholic. Avocations: philosophy, growing roses, reading, social justice and peace issues. Home: 631 Baeder Rd Jenkintown PA 19046-1555 Personal E-mail: karenmarkovich@yahoo.com.

LOWRY, LINDA ELEANOR, artist, educator; b. Lubbock, Tex., June 30, 1956; d. David Auld and Stella (West) L. BA, Colo. Coll., 1978; postgrad., Sch. Visual Arts, 1978-79, Tyler Sch. Art, 1979-80; MFA, U. Colo., 1983. Instr. U. Colo., Boulder, 1982-91, Colo. State U., Ft. Collins, 1983-84, Rocky Mountain Coll. Art and Design, Denver, 1984-85, Colo. Coll., Colorado Springs, 1989-90, U. Colo., Denver, 1990; chair art dept. Arapahoe Cmty. Coll., Littleton, Colo., 1990-95, coord. painting and drawing, 1990-97. Instr. Artreach, Denver, 1983-90; vis. artist Denver Art Mus., 1985, 1999; chair exhibition com. Colo. Gallery of Arts, Littleton, 1993-97; juror The Eleventh Congl. Art Competition, Denver, 1993, Congressman Shaeffer's Nat Scholarship Award, Denver, 1994, U. No. Colo. Student Show, Greeley, 1994. Author, illustrator: (book) Inside Colorado: An Artist's View of Colorado Interiors, 1993; one-person shows include Gallery 44, Boulder, 1993, Martin County Arts Mus., Stuart, Fla., 1994; exhibited in group shows at Indpls. Mus. Art, 1984, Viridian Gallery, N.Y.C., 1988, Denver Art Mus., 1983, David Uhl Gallery, Denver, 1999, Dairy Ctr.For Arts, Boulder, 2006. Mem. arts adv. bd. Paul Mellon Arts Ctr., Wallingford, Conn., 1997—. Recipient Merit award Henry Hopkins, Artreach '88, Salt Lake City, 1988, Excellence award Artists of Colo., Denver, 1996; artist-in-residence Rocky Mountain Nat. Park, 1990; adj. faculty U. Colo., Boulder, 2004-2005, Metro. State Coll. Art, Denver, 2005—. Mem. Coll. Art Assn., Arapahoe Cmty. Coll. Art Club (advisor 1990-97, Appreciation award 1990-95). Avocations: equestrian skiier, gardener.

LOWRY, LOIS (LOIS HAMMERSBERG), writer; b. 1937; Author: A Summer to Die, 1977, Find A Stranger, Say Goodbye, 1978, Anastasia Krupnik, 1979, Autumn Street, 1980, Anastasia Again, 1981, Anastasia at Your Service, 1982, The One Hundredth Thing About Caroline, 1983, Taking Care of Terrific, 1983, Anastasia, Ask Your Analyst, 1984, Us and Uncle Fraud, 1984, Anastasia on Her Own, 1985, Switcharound, 1985, Anastasia Has the Answers, 1986, Anastasia's Chosen Career, 1987, Rabbie Starkey, 1987, All About Sam, 1988, Number the Stars, 1989 (John Newbery medal 1990), Your Move, J.P.!, 1990, Anastasia at This Address, 1991, Attaboy, Sam!, 1992, The Giver, 1993 (John Newbery medal 1994), Anastasia Absolutely, 1995, See You Around, Sam!, 1996, Stay! Keeper's Story, 1997, Looking Back, 1998, Zooman Sam, 1999, Gathering Blue, 2000, Gooney Bird Greene, 2002, The Silent Boy, 2003, Messenger, 2004, Gooney Bird and the Room Mother, 2005, Gossamer, 2006. Recipient Chgo. Tribune Young Adult Book prize, 2003. Address: 205 Brattle St Cambridge MA 02138-3345 Office: care Houghton Mifflin 222 Berkeley St Boston MA 02116-3748

LOWRY, MARCIA ROBINSON, legal association administrator; b. Bklyn., N.Y., May 24, 1941; d. Sophie and Arthur Robinson; m. Frederic Adams Mosher, Apr. 27, 1980; 1 child, Avram Lev Robinson-Mosher. JD, NYU Sch. of Law, N.Y.C., 1966—69. Bar: NY 1969. Dir., children's rights project N.Y. Civil Liberties Union, N.Y.C., 1973—79, ACLU, N.Y.C., 1979—95; exec. dir., founder Children's Rights, N.Y.C., 1995—. Office: Children's Rights 330 Seventh Ave New York NY 10001 Office Phone: 212-683-2210. Office Fax: 212-683-4015.

LOWRY, MARILYN JEAN, horticultural retail company executive; b. Greensburg, Pa., Oct. 19, 1932; d. Clifford Henry and Martha McCune (Whitehead) Bushyager; m. John Cathcart Lowry, June 14, 1958; children: Martha Kim Hultberg, John Ryan, Nancy Lynn. BS, Ind. U. of Pa., 1954; MEd, Pa. State U., 1958. Tchr. Jeannette (Pa.) pub. schs., 1954-57; grad. asst. Pa. State U., University Park, 1957-58; demonstration sch. tchr. Towson (Md.) U., 1958-59; sec.-treas. Lowry & Co., Inc., Phoenix, Md., 1964—, 1987—. Master flower show judge Nat. Council State Garden Clubs, Inc., St. Louis, 1987—, landscape design critic, 1985—; master gardener U. Md. Extension Svc., 1984—. Mem. Lutherville Garden Club (pres. 1979—), Am. Assn. Nurserymen Aux. (pres. 1972), Federated Garden Clubs Md. (dir. dist. III 1981-83), Am. Nursery and Landscape Assn. (chmn. wholesale plant sales profls. 1999—). Republican. Presbyterian.

LOWTHIAN, PETRENA, academic administrator; b. Feb. 10, 1931; d. Leslie Irton and Petrena Lowthian; m. Clyde Hennies (div.); children: David L. Hennies, Geoffrey L. Hennies; m. Nisson Mandel. Grad., Royal Acad. Dramatic Art, London, 1952. Retail career with various orgns., London and Paris, 1949-57; founder, pres. Lowthian Coll. divsn. Lowthian Inc., Mpls., 1964-97. Mem. adv. coun. Minn. State Dept. Edn., St. Paul 1974-82; mem. adv. bd. Mpls. Comty. Devel. Agy., Mpls., 1983-85; mem. Downtown Coun. St. Paul, 1972, chmn. retail bd., 1984-92; mem. Bd. Buss. Indsl. Advisors U. Wis.-Stout, Menomonie, 1983-89. Mem. Fashion Group, Inc. (regional bd. dirs. 1980), Rotary (mem. career and econ. edn. 1988—). Address: 10 Creekside Dr Long Lake MN 55356-9431

LOXLEY, ALICE A., writer, educator; b. Cleve., Apr. 7, 1948; d. Daniel Robert Keating and Josephine Louise Greeson; m. Colin John Loxley, May 20, 1972 (div. Aug. 2002); children: Katharine Anne, Christopher John. BA, Case Western Reserve U., Cleve., 1971, BS, 1972; MS, U. Pa., Phila., 1978; MFA, Sarah Lawrence Coll., 2002. Clin. nurse I & II U. Hosps., Cleve., 1972—76; psychotherapist Human Svcs., Inc., Westchester, Pa., 1978—81; pvt. practice Bryn Mawr, Pa., 1982—86; adj. faculty mem. Fordham U., Tarrytown, NY, 2002—. Contbr. articles to profl. jours. Mem.: Nat. Assn. Ind. Scholars, Acad. Am. Poets, Sigma Theta Tau. Office: Fordham Univ Marymount Ave Tarrytown NY 10591 Home: PO Box 516 Chesapeake City MD 21915-0516 E-mail: aliceloxley@atlanticbb.net.

LOXLEY, KATHRYN, retired elementary school educator; b. Darke County, Ohio, Mar. 25, 1918; d. Fred and Henrietta (Hosier) Harleman; m. Orval B. Loxley, Mar. 15, 1935; children: Connie K. Wharton, Ted, Cheryl E., Carolyn L. Loxley. BS in Edn., Miami U., Oxford, Ohio, 1962; postgrad., Ohio U., 1980. Lic. minister 1993. Elem. tchr. Milton-Union Dist., West Milton, Ohio, Jackson (Ohio) City Dist.; ret., 1995—. Councilor and pastor Christian ch., Gallia County, Ohio. Named State Tchr. of Yr. nominee, 1984-85, Regional Conservation Tchr., State Social Studies Tchr. of Yr., State Econs. Tchr., Ohio Alliance Environ. Tchr. of Yr.; recipient Gov. Arbor Day award, Community Svc. award; Martha Holden Jennings grantee. Mem. NEA, Ohio Edn. Assn. (human rels.), Jackson City Edn. Assn. (pres., del. to conv.). Home: State Route 788 Wellston OH 45692

LOYD, BETSY FRANKLIN, primary school educator; d. Ralph Albert and Libby Shoffner Franklin; m. Troy Mylon Loyd, June 11, 1994. AA in visual arts, Northeast State, Ala., 1992; B in elem. edn., Athens State U., Ala., 1994; M in elem edn., U. Ala., 2005. 2d grade tchr. Madison County, New Hope, Ala., 1997—2005. Mem.: Friends of the Libr., MCEA, NEA, AEA, Internat. Reading Assn., Ala. Reading Assn., Christian Women's Club, Kappa Delta Pi. Methodist. Office: New Hope Elem 5300 Main Dr New Hope AL 35760

LOYD, MARTHA ROSE, forester; b. Sanford, Fla., Oct. 24, 1951; d. Charles W. and Geraldine (Greer) Rose; m. Randall Allen Loyd, Oct. 1, 1983 (div. Oct. 1998); children: Erin Leslie, Matthew Allen. BS in Forestry, U. Fla., 1978. Unit mgr. Scott Paper Co., Monroeville, Ala., 1978—86, regional mgr., 1986—93; mgr. silvicultural ops. Kimberly-Clark, Monroeville, 1993—99; divsn. forester Molpus Timberlands Mgmt., Huxford, Ala., 1999—2002; pres. Southeast Timberlands Mgmt., Monroeville, 2003—. Founder Monroeville Bus. Women, 1985; bd. dirs. YMCA, Monroeville, 1998—99. Mem.: Ala. Forestry Assn. (com. chairperson 1991—93). Avocations: gardening, travel, yoga, home improvement projects. Home: 456 Overlook Dr Monroeville AL 36460 Office: Southeast Timberlands Mgmt PO Box 477 Monroeville AL 36461

LOYD, PAMELA ANN, academic administrator, educator; b. Detroit, June 18, 1968; d. David Jr. and Deborah Ann (Young) Dail; m. Keith Lamar Loyd, Jan. 19, 1996; children: Keith Lamar, Kristopher Levon. AS, Hawaii Pacific U., 1992; BBA, Detroit Coll. Bus., 1994; MSA, Ctrl. Mich. U., 1995; PhD, Capella U., 2001. Cert. in credit mgmt. Mfg. supr. Ford Motor Co., Livonia, Mich., 1996-97; adj. faculty Baker Coll., Auburn Hills, Mich., 1998—, U. Detroit-Mercy, 1998—2001; mem. faculty dept. bus. and corp. svcs., instr. Monroe County C.C., Monroe, Mich., 1998—2002; dir. grad. admissions and student svcs. Marygrove Coll., Detroit, 2002—05. Adj. faculty Davenport U. Online, Grand Rapids, Mich., 2002-; cons., mem. Southfield 2020 Project, City of Southfield, Mich., 1998—. Author: Success.Old Testament Truths: A 30-Day Guide to Reaching Your Goals and Objectives, 1998, Newness of Life, Poetry for the Soul, 1998; contbr. articles and poetry to publs. Participant, Sportfishing Facility, Del Mar Beach, Calif., 1987. Sgt. USMC, 1986-95. Decorated Navy Commendation medal; recipient Cert. of Appreciation, Christian Broadcasting Network, 1998. Mem. AAUP, Women Marine Assn., Am. Legion, Nat. Black MBA Assn., Sigma Iota Epsilon. Christian. Avocations: reading, writing, exercise, listening to christian music. E-mail: ployd53787@hotmail.com.

LOZANO, ARACELI E., foundation administrator, consultant; b. Laredo, Tex., Dec. 30, 1967; d. Juan Ovidio Jr. and Rosa F. Bautista; m. Romeo Lozano II, May 5, 1995. Student, Laredo C.C., 1986-87, 98-99. Human resource specialist, tng. coord. Sears Roebuck & Co., Laredo, 1986-91; office mgr. Santos & Assocs., Laredo, 1991-92; payroll mgr. Gonzalez, Farias, Guerra & Flores, Laredo, 1992-97; bus. devel. specialist Small Bus. Devel. Ctr., Laredo, 1997; dir. Laredo Devel. Found. Small Bus. Devel. Ctr., Laredo, 1997—. Mem. adv. bd. RCCI, Laredo, 1998—, Welfare to Work, Laredo, 1999—. Mem. Fin. Women's Assn., Laredo C. of C. (chair small bus. com. 1998-99), Laredo Bus. and Profl. Women's Assn. (sec. 1998-99, v.p. 1999-2000, pres. 2000—). Office: Laredo Devel Found 616 Leal St Laredo TX 78041

LOZANO, MONICA CECILIA, publishing executive; b. LA, July 21, 1956; d. Ignacio Eugenio and Marta Eloisa (Navarro) Lozano; m. Marcelo Centanino, Sept. 27, 1987 (div.); c. Santiago Alberto and Gabriela. Student, U. Oreg., 1974—76; student San Francisco City Coll.; LHD (hon.), Occidental Coll., 1999. Mgr. Copy-Copia, Inc., San Francisco, 1980—85; mng. editor La Opinion, L.A., 1985—89, assoc. pub., 1989—91, assoc. pub., exec. editor, 1991—2000, pres., COO, 2000—04, pub., CEO, 2004—; pub. El Eco del Valle, San Fernando, Calif., 1990—91; v.p. Lozano Comm., 2000—04; sr. v.p. ImpreMedia LLC, 2004—. Bd. dirs. The Walt Disney Co., Union Bank

Calif., Calif. Health Care Found., Tenet Healthcare Corp., Nat. Coun. La Raza; trustee SunAm. Asset Mgmt. Corp. Trustee U. So. Calif.; mem. bd. regents U. Calif., 2000—; bd. dirs. L.A. County Mus. Art, Venice Family Clinic, Ctrl. Am. Resource Ctr. Co-recipient José Ortega y Gasset award, Madrid, 2006; recipient Humanitarian award, Cen. Am. Refugee Ctr., L.A., 1989, Outstanding Achievement, Mex. Am. Opportunities Found., L.A., 1989. Mem. Nat. Assn. Hispanic Pubs., Nat. Assn. Hispanic Journalists, Calif. Hispanic Pubs., Am. Soc. Newspaper Editors, Calif. Chicano News Assn., Nat. Network Hispanic Women. Avocations: photography, reading, water sports. Office: La Opinion 411 W Fifth St Los Angeles CA 90013*

LOZITO, LISA CAROL, music educator, church musician; b. St. James, Minn., Mar. 5, 1960; d. Floyd and Grace Wilkening; m. William Lozito, Apr. 28, 1995. BA in Music Edn., St. Olaf Coll., 1982; MA in Music Edn., U. St. Thomas, 2004. Cert. tchr. Minn. Dept. Edn., 1982. Music tchr. Little Falls Pub. Schs., Minn., 1982—94; pvt. music instr. Chaska, Minn., 1995—2001; children's choral camp coord. U. St. Thomas, St. Paul, 2000—02; music tchr. Waconia Pub. Schs., Minn., 1994—. Ch. musician First Luth. Ch., Little Falls, 1982—94, Trinity Luth. Ch., Carver, Minn., 1997—, Sunday sch. music. dir., 2003—. Mem.: Orgn. Am. Kodaly Educators (on-site mgr. nat. children's choral camp 1999, nat. honor choir coord. 2003), Minn. Music Educators Assn. (region rep. 1998—2000, classroom music v.p. 2005—, Music Educator of Yr. 2001), Nat. Educators Assn., Music Educators Nat. Conf., Am. Choral Dirs. Assn. (repertoire and stds. chair children's choirs 1995—97, North Ctrl. regional children's honor choir co-chair 1998, all state elem. honor choir co-chair 1996—97). Lutheran. Avocations: piano, singing, playing the organ, hiking, gardening. Office Phone: 952-442-0620.

LOZOFF, BETSY, pediatrician, educator; b. Milw., Dec. 19, 1943; d. Milton and Marjorie (Morse) L.; 1 child, Claudia Brittenham. BA, Radcliffe Coll., 1965; MD, Case Western Res. U., 1971, MS, 1981. Diplomate Am. Bd. Pediat. From asst. prof. to prof. pediatrics Case Western Res. U., Cleve., 1974-93; prof. pediat. U. Mich., Ann Arbor, 1993—, dir. Ctr. Human Growth and Devel., 1993—2004, rsch. prof. Ctr. Human Growth and Devel., 2004—. Recipient Rsch. Career Devel. award Nat. Inst. Child Health and Human Devel., 1984-88. Fellow Am. Acad. Pediatrics; mem. Soc. for Pediatric Rsch., Soc. Rsch. in Child Devel. (program com. 1991-97), Soc. Behavioral Pediatrics (exec. com. 1985-88), Ambulatory Pediatric Soc. Office: Univ Mich Ctr Human Growth and Devel 300 N Ingalls St Ann Arbor MI 48109-2007 Office Phone: 734-764-2443. E-mail: blozoff@umich.edu.

LOZOSKY, LISA LYNN, music educator, elementary school educator; b. Fort Riley, Kans., June 4, 1965; d. Dwight Burnell and Charlotte Ann Cavender; m. Albert Francis Lozosky III, June 26, 1993; children: Sergey, Irina. BS, SW Mo. State U., Springfield, 1987. Tchg. credential Calif., 1990. Elem. tchr. Nicolas Valley Elem. Sch., Temecula, Calif., 1990—99, music specialist, 1999—. Choral dir. Nicolas Valley Chorus, Temecula, 1999—2006; coord. Dist. Elem. Choir Showcase. Composer: (school song) March of the Knights. Women's ministry leader Cmty. Ch. of the Valley, Temecula, 1990—2006, Sunday sch. coord., 2002—05, bible study leader, 2005—06, keyboardist, vocalist, 1991—2006. Avocations: crafts, travel, baking, cooking. Office: Nicolas Valley Elementary School 39600 N General Kearny Rd Temecula CA 92591 Office Phone: 951-695-7180. Business E-Mail: llozosky@tvusd.k12.ca.us.

LU, CAIXIA, television director, language educator; b. Wuhe, Anhui, China, Nov. 3, 1956; arrived in U.S., 1998; B, Changsha Railway Inst., China, 1983; cert. English Lang. and Lit., S.W. Normal U., China, 1994; MA, postgrad., U. Hawaii, 2001. Translator, editor Tunnel and Tunneling Mag., China, 1983—86; lectr. English S.W. Jiaotong U., China, 1987—94, dir. internat. culture exch. ctr., 1994—95; assoc. prof. English Wuhan U., China, 1996—98; assoc. editor Ctr. Chinese Studies, U. Hawaii, Manoa, 2000—. Translator, broadcast, editor MiracleNet TV Network, 2000—02, asst. mgr., translator, broadcaster, editor, 2002, gen. mgr. translator, broadcaster, editor, 2002—. Assoc. editor: An English-Chinses Usage Dictionary, 1994; translator (English into Chinese): Rambo-The First Blood Part II, 1986, Rambo-The First Blood Part I, 1990, The Voice of Night, 1995, Moonstone, 1996, How to Be Entertaining, 1998, The Adventure of Huckleberry Finn, 1998, The Wonderful Adventure of Nils, 1999, The Turn of the Screw, 1999, Daisy Miller, 1999, The Demon and The Princess, 1999. Recipient Harry Friedman award, U. Hawaii, 2004. Office: Univ Hawaii at Manoa Porteus 640, 2424 Maile Way Honolulu HI 96822

LU, MAY, psychologist, counselor, writer, watercolorist; b. China, Aug. 8, 1945; came to U.S., 1966; d. Conrad and Yvonne (Shaw) Cho; m. Tzu C. Lu, July 12, 1967; children: Tina, Tammy. MS, UCLA, 1969; PhD, U. Tex., Houston, 1979; MA, Norwich U., Burlington, Vt., 1990. Lic. marriage and family therapist. Counseling psychologist in pvt. practice, Houston, 1997—. Guest lectr. Family Inst., Houston, 1994, U. Houston, 1995, Chinese Cmty. Ctr., L.A., 1996, Chgo., 1998, Miami, Fla., 1999; spkr. and moderator in field. Author: Mental Health of the New Chinese American Elders, 1993, How Men and Women Communicate, 1994, How to Raise New Immigrant Chilren, 1999; watercolorist. English sec. Tex. Buddhist Assn., Houston, 1979—; trustee Inst. Chinese Culture, Houston, 1980-83; vol. counselor Chinese Sr. Assn., Houston, 1985-91, Chinese Health Ctr., Houston, 1980—. Recipient award as Best Informative Writer Overseas, Taiwan Edn. Ministry, 1997. Mem. Watercolor Art Soc. Buddhist.

LU, MI, computer engineer, educator; b. Chongqing, Sichuan, China, July 22, 1949; d. Chong Pu Lu and Shu Sheng Fan. MS, Rice U., 1984, PhD, 1987. Registered profl. engr. From asst. prof. to assoc. prof. Tex. A&M U., Coll. Sta., 1987-98, prof., 1998—. Stream chmn. 7th Internat. Conf. Computing and Info., Peterborough, Ont., Can., 1995; conf. chmn. 5th Internat. Conf. Computer Sci. and Informatics, 2000, 6th Internat. Conf., 2002. Assoc. editor Jour. Computing and Info., 1995—, Info. Sci., 1996-97, 2002--; contbr. articles to profl. jours. Mem. Computer Soc. of IEEE (sr.). Office: Tex A&M U Dept Elec Engring College Station TX 77843

LU, NINGPING, environmental chemist; b. Sichuan, China, June 18, 1941; d. Yiungdi and Jinghua (Liu) L.; m. Li Pin-Fun, July 23, 1964 (div. 1990); children: Ying, Nin. BS in Biophysics, Sichuan U., 1964; MS of Soil Chemistry, Auburn U., 1990, PhD in Environtl. Soil Chemistry, 1993. Dir. Atomic Agrl. Ins., Sichuan, 1983; rsch. assoc. Fertilizer Ins., Sichuan, 1985-86; postdoctoral rsch. assoc. Auburn U., 1993-94, Los Alamos Nat. Lab., 1994-97, tech. staff mem., 1997—. Vis. scientist Purdue U., West Lafayette, Ind., 1983-84, Auburn U., 1984-85; cons. UN Devel. Program in China, Beijing, 1997—. Contbr. over 70 articles to profl. pubs. Mem. Agronomy Soc. of Am., Soil Sci. Soc. of Am., Am. Chem. Soc., N.Y. Acad. of Sci., Phi Kappa Phi. Achievements include development of remedial processes of radionuclide contaminated soils, surface water, and ground water; utilization of municipal solid wastes on agricultural land; actinide interactions with colloids of metal oxides, clays, and silica; transport of radio-colloids in groundwater; stability, solubility, and speciation of actinides at nuclear waste repository sites. Office: E-ET Los Alamos Nat Lab Ms J514 Los Alamos NM 87545-0001 E-mail: ningping@lanl.gov.

LUARK, LILLIAN, retired city clerk; b. Hoquiam, Wash., Dec. 25, 1925; d. William B. and Hazel Howard Purvis; m. Gerald Monroe Luark, Mar. 1, 1947; children: Steven, Douglas(dec.), Shirley, Gary. Attended, Ctrl. Wash. U. Bookkeeper to teller Peoples Nat. Bank, Hoquiam, Seattle, Renton, Wash., 1947—52; teller Rainier Nat. Bank, Cosmopolis, Wash.; dep. clerk City of Cosmopolis, 1976—81, city clerk, treas., 1981—95, chmn. city centennial celebration, chmn. city parades, chmn. city festival in pk.; ret., 1995. Dist. pres. PTA, Wash., state area v.p.; treas. LWV Gray Harbor. Mem.: Cosmopolis PTA (life), Beta Sigma Phi (treas., Girl of Yr. award). Methodist. Avocation: painting. Home: 215 H St PO Box 257 Cosmopolis WA 98537-0257 Personal E-mail: lillianluark@hotmail.com.

LUBAN, NAOMI L. C., hematologist; Degree., Conn. Coll., 1968; MD, Mt Sinai Sch. Medicine, NY, 1972. Pediatric hematologist Children's Nat. Med. Ctr., Washington, 1972—. Fellow, Rockefeller U.; grantee, Meml. Sloan Kettering Inst., NYC;, Cornell U. Office Phone: 202-884-5292. Business E-Mail: nluban@cnmc.org.

LUBBOCK, MILDRED MARCELLE (MIDGE LUBBOCK), former small business owner; b. Clebourne, Tex., Apr. 9, 1920; d. Richard Talmadge and Nell Bouregarde (Boykin) Hardin; m. Wilson Neibuhr Munz; children: Pamela Ann Sanders, Timothy Ray Munz, Phyllis Gail Glasscock; m. Charles William Lubbock, Aug. 12, 1990. Grad. high sch. and bus. sch., Houston. Asst. photographer Robinson Portraits, Houston; clk.-typist U.S. Naval Lighter-Than-Air Base, Houma, La., U.S. Naval Air Sta., Norfolk, Va.; sales distbr. Nina Ross Cosmetiques, Brenham, Tex., Midge's Health Food Store, Brenham, 1992-95. Contbr. poetry to various anthologies. Mem. libr. bd. Fortnightly Club, Brenham, 1970—, pres. arts dept., TFWC, GFWC; pres. Brenham Fine Arts League, 1985. Recipient Golden Poet award, 1987-90, medal of honor World of Poetry, 1990, Outstanding Acheivement in Poetry award Internat. Soc. Poetry; Vol. Woman of Yr., Fortnightly Club, 2004. Mem. UDC (past pres.), Am. Legion Aux. (past pres.). Baptist. Avocations: painting, travel, poetry, reading. Home: 1501 E Stone St Brenham TX 77833-5050

LUBELL, ELLEN, writer; b. Bklyn., Apr. 7, 1950; d. Edward and Sonia Lubell. BA in Fine Arts, SUNY, Stony Brook, 1971. Contbg. editor Arts Mag., N.Y.C., 1972-79; founder, editor Womanart Mag., Bklyn., 1976-78; columnist Soho Weekly News, N.Y.C., 1977-79; contbr. Art in Am., N.Y.C., 1981-85; dir. pub. rels. Gerstman & Meyers Inc., N.Y.C., 1984-89; freelancer, columnist, publicist The Village Voice, N.Y.C., 1984-91; columnist, freelancer N.Y. Newsday, 1988—89; dir. comm. Inform, Inc., N.Y.C., 1991-95; comm. dir. Child Care Action Campaign, N.Y.C., 1995-99; freelance writer Star-Ledger, Newark, 1996-97; dir. pub. rels. The Childrens Aid Soc., N.Y.C., 1999—. Art Critics fellow, Nat. Endowment for the Arts, 1978.

LUBETSKI, EDITH ESTHER, librarian; b. Bklyn., July 16, 1940; m. Meir Lubetski, Dec. 23, 1968; children: Shaul, Uriel, Leah. BA, Bklyn. Coll., 1962; MLS, Columbia U., 1965; MA in Jewish Studies, Yeshiva U., 1968. Judaica libr. Stern Coll. Yeshiva U., N.Y.C., 1965-66, acquisitions libr., 1966-69, head libr., 1969—. Author (with Meir Lubetski): (book) Building a Judaica Library Collection, 1983; author: The Jewish Woman: Recent Books, 1995; contbr. articles to profl. jours. Mem. exec. bd. Jewish Book Coun., 1998—. Mem.: ACRL, ALA, N.Y. Libr. Assn., Assn. Jewish Librs. (corr. sec. 1980—84, pres. N.Y. chpt. 1984—86, nat. v.p. 1984—86, nat. pres. 1986—88, Fanny Goldstein Merit award 1993, Life Membership award 2003). Office: Yeshiva U Hedi Steinberg Libr 245 Lexington Ave New York NY 10016-4605 Office Phone: 212-340-7720. E-mail: Lubetski@ymail.yu.edu.

LUBIC, BENITA JOAN ALK, travel company executive; b. Green Bay, Wis., May 18, 1936; d. Isadore George and Marion (Segal) Alk; m. Robert Bennett Lubic, May 31, 1959; children: Wendy Alison, Bret David, Robin Kimberly Lubic Bliss. BBA, U. Wis., 1958. Cert. travel cons. Pres., owner Transeair Travel, LLC, Washington, 1959—. Instr. Internat. Travel Tng. Sch., 1982-91; lic. Cuba Travel Svc. Provider, 2000—. Contbr. articles on incentive travel to mags. Mem. SKAL, Washington; mem. adv. bd. Braniff Airlines, Republic Airlines, Sonesta Hotel Corp. Mem. Am. Soc. Travel Agts. (pres. Washington sub chpt. 1985-88, bd. dirs. 1979-96), Prost Exec. Women in Travel (v.p. 1982-83, treas. 1984-85, bd. dirs., 1985-2005), Internat. Fedn. Women's Travel Orgns. (dir. 1993-94, 1999-2005). Democrat. Jewish. Avocations: golf, tennis, swimming, bicycling, travel. Home: 2813 McKinley Pl NW Washington DC 20015-1104 Office: Transeair Travel LLC 2813 McKinley Pl NW Washington DC 20015-1104 Office Phone: 202-362-6100. Personal E-mail: blubic@aol.com.

LUBIC, RUTH WATSON, health facility administrator, nurse midwife; b. Bucks County, Pa., Jan. 18, 1927; d. John Russell and Lillian (Kraft) Watson; m. William James Lubic, May 28, 1955; 1 child, Douglas Watson. Diploma, Sch. Nursing Hosp. U. Pa., 1955; BS, Columbia U., 1959, MA, 1961, EdD in Applied Anthropology, 1979; cert. in nurse midwifery, SUNY, Bklyn., 1962, DSc (hon.), 1993; LLD (hon.), U. Pa., 1985; DSc (hon.), U. Medicine and Dentistry, NJ, 1986; LHD (hon.), Coll. New Rochelle, 1992, Pace U., 1994. Staff nurse through head nurse Meml. Hosp. for Cancer and Allied Disease, NYC, 1955-58; clin. assoc. Grad. Sch. Nursing NY Med. Coll., NYC, 1962-63; parent educator, cons. Maternity Ctr. Assn., NYC, 1963-67, gen. dir., 1970-95, dir. clin. projects, 1995-97; project dir. Nat. Assn. of Childbearing Ctrs., Washington, 1997-99; pres., CEO DC Developing Families Ctr., 1998—2002, founder, pres. emeritus, 2003—, also bd. dirs.; pres., CEO, bd. dirs. DC Birth Ctr., 1998—. Cons. in midwifery, nursing and maternal and child health Office Pub. Health and Sci. HHS, 1995—97; adj. prof. divsn. nursing NYU, 1995—; bd. dirs., v.p. Am. Assn. World Health U.S. Com. WHO, 1975—94, pres. Am. Assn. World Health U.S. Com., 1980—81; mem. bd. maternal child and family health NRC, 1974—80; mem. Commn. Grads. Fgn. Nursing Schs., 1979—83, v.p., 1980—81, treas., 1982—83; bd. govs. Frontier Nursing Svc., 1982—92; bd. dirs. Pan Am. Health Edn. Found., pres., 1987—88; vis. prof. King Edward Meml. Hosp., Perth, Australia, 1991; Kate Hanna Harvey vis. prof. cmty. health nursing Frances Payne Bolton Sch. Nursing Case Western Res., 1991; Lansdowne lectr. U. Victoria, B.C., Canada, 1992; adj. prof. Sch. Nursing, Georgetown U., 1997—; Therese Dondero lectr. Am. Coll. Nurse-Midwives Found., 1995; Andrea Printy Meml. lectr. U. Minn., 1998; Kemble lectr. Sch. Nursing, U. NC, Chapel Hill, 2000; Hugh P. Davis lectr. Emory U. Sch. Nursing, 2004. Author (with Gene Hawes): (book) childbearing: A Book of Choices, 1987; contbr. articles to profl. jours. Named Maternal-Child Health Nurse of the Yr., ANA, 1985, Disting. Alumna, U. Pa., 1992; named to Nursing Hall of Fame, 1999; recipient Letitia White award, Florence Nightingale medal, 1955, Nursing Practice award, U. Pa., 1980, Rockefeller Pub. Svc. award, 1981, Hattie Hemschemeyer award, 1983, Alumnae award, Sch. Nursing U. Pa., 1986, McManus medal, Tchrs. Coll. Columbia U., 1992, Disting. Svc. award, Francis Payne Bolton Sch. Nursing, 1993, Hon. Recognition, NY State Nurses Assn., 1993, Nurse-Midwifery Faculty award, Columbia U., 1993, Spirit of Nursing award, Vis. Nurses Svc. NY, 1994, Maes-Macinnes award, Divsn. Nursing NYU, 1994, Hon. Recognition, ANA, 1994, Carola Warburg Rothschild award, Maternity Ctr. Assn., 1997, Healthy Babies Project award, 1998, Woman of Distinction award, Nat. Assn. Women in Edn., 1999, Never Say Die award, DC Primary Care Assn., 2001; Irving Harris vis. scholar, Coll. Nursing U. Ill., 1999, MacArthur fellow, 1993. Fellow: AAAS, Soc. for Applied Anthropology, Am. Acad. Nursing (Living Legend award 2001); mem.: APHA (mem. com. on internat. health, sec. maternal and child health coun. 1982, mem. governing coun. 1986—89, mem. nominating com. 1987, mem. action bd. 1988—90), Vis. Nurse Svc. of NY (Lillian Wald award 2003), Herman Biggs Soc. (sec.-treas. 1989—90), Am. Assn. Colls. Nursing (McGovern lectr. 1997), Nat. Assn. Childbearing Ctrs. (pres. 1983—91, Lifetime Achievement award 2005), Inst. of Medicine of NAS (Lienhard award 2001), Am. Coll. Nurse Midwives (v.p. 1964—66, pres.-elect 1969—70), NY Acad. Medicine, Alpha Omega Alpha (hon.). Office Phone: 202-484-6289. Personal E-mail: Rlubic@aol.com.

LUBKIN, GLORIA BECKER, physicist; b. Phila., May 16, 1933; d. Samuel Albert and Anne (Gorrin) B.; m. Yale Jay Lubkin, June 14, 1953 (div. Apr. 1968); children: David Craig, Sharon Rebecca. AB, Temple U., 1953; MA, Boston U., 1957; postgrad., Harvard U., 1974—75. Mathematician Fairchild Stratos Co., Hagerstown, Md., 1954, Letterkenny Ordnance Depot, Chambersburg, Pa., 1955-56; physicist TRG Inc., N.Y.C., 1956-58; acting chmn. dept. physics Sarah Lawrence Coll., Bronxville, NY, 1961-62; v.p. Lubkin Assocs., electronic cons., Port Washington, NY, 1962-68; assoc. editor Physics Today Am. Inst. Physics, N.Y.C., 1963-69, sr. editor, 1970-84, editor, 1985-94, editl. dir., 1994-00, editor-at-large, 2001—03, editor emerita, 2004—. Cons. in field; mem. Nieman adv. com. Harvard U., 1978-82; co-chmn. search/adv. com. Theoretical Physics Inst., U. Minn., 1987-89, co-chmn. oversight com. 1989—; mem. mng. com. Westinghouse Sci. Writing Prizes, 1988-91; mem. selection com. Knight Fellowships, 1990. Contbr. articles to profl. publs. Gloria Becker Lubkin Professorship of Theoretical Physics established in her honor U. Minn., 1990; Nieman fellow, 1974-75. Fellow: AAAS (chmn. nominating com. for sect. B physics 1989, nominating com. sect. B physics 2003—06, chmn. 2005, 2006), Am. Phys. Soc. (founding mem. com. status of women in physics 1971—72, exec. com. forum physics and soc. 1977—78, exec. com. history physics divsn. 1983—86, 1992—95, 1998—2005, coun. mem. 1998—2005, mem. Lilienfeld prize com. 1999—2002, exec. bd. 2000—01, com. on coms. 2000—02, chmn. Lilienfeld prize com. 2002, com. on coms. 2002—06, audit com. 2004, com. on coms. 2004—); mem.: Com. Concerned Journalists, DC Sci. Writers Assn., Nat. Assn. Sci. Writers, NY Acad. Scis. (mem. The Scis. pub. com. 1992—93), Sigma Pi Sigma. Jewish. Office: Am Inst Physics One Physics Ellipse College Park MD 20740 Office Phone: 301-209-3050. Business E-Mail: glubkin@aip.org.

LUCAS, BARBARA B., electrical equipment manufacturing executive; b. 1945; BA magna cum laude, U. Md., 1967; MA, Johns Hopkins U., 1968. V.p., sec. Equitable Bancorp, 1977-85; sr. v.p. pub. affairs, corp. sec. Black & Decker Corp., Balt., 1985—96, sr. v.p., pub. affairs, 1996—, corp. sec., 1996—. Bd. dirs. Provident Bankshares; chair bd. dirs. Greater Balt. Med. Ctr., Balt. Named one of The 100 Women to Watch in Corp. Am., Bus. Month. Mem.: Am. Soc. Corp. Secretaries (pres. Mid-Atlantic Regional chpt., nat. dir.). Office: Black & Decker Corp 701 E Joppa Rd Baltimore MD 21286-5502

LUCAS, CAROL LEE, biomedical engineer; b. Aberdeen, S.D., Feb. 13, 1940; d. Howard Cleveland and Sarah Ivy (Easterby) Nogle; m. Richard Albert Lucas, Feb. 26, 1961; children: Wendy Lee, Sean Richard. BA, Dakota Wesleyan U., 1961; MS, U. Ariz., 1967; PhD, U. N.C., 1973. Tchr. Spanish, Mitchell (S.D.) H.S., 1960-61; tchr. math., English and sci. U.S. Army, Furth, Germany, 1961-62; sys. analyst Cargill Inc., Mpls., 1962-65; rsch. assoc. U. N.C., Chapel Hill, 1973-76, lectr., 1976-77, asst. prof. curriculum in biomed. engring. and math., 1977-84, assoc. prof. dept. surgery, 1984-89, prof., 1989—, acting chmn. curriculum biomed. engring. and math., 1990-92, chmn. biomed. engring., 1992—2001; program dir. NSF, 2001—04. NIH trainee, 1968-73. Contbr. articles to profl. jours. Mem. IEEE, Am. Heart Assn., N.C. Heart Assn., Biomed. Engring. Soc., Cardiovasc. Sys. Dynamics Soc., Am. Inst. Biol. and Med. Engrs. Democrat. Methodist. Home: 2421 Sedgefield Dr Chapel Hill NC 27514-6810 Office: U NC Sch Medicine Dept Biomed Engring 152 Macnider Hall Chapel Hill NC 27599-7575 Business E-Mail: clucas@bme.unc.edu.

LUCAS, CATHERINE, biotechnology company executive; b. Casablanca, Morrocco, Apr. 28, 1954; came to US 1978; d. Igor Vinner and Denise Marguerite Eugenie Pichenot; m. Jody Leopold Lucas, Aug. 10, 1977 (div. Sept. 1987); 1 child, Joelle. BS in Chemistry-Biology, U. Scis., Paris, 1972; MS in Biochemistry, U. Scis., 1974, PhD in Neurochemistry, 1978. NIH postdoctoral fellow Stanford U., Palo Alto, Calif., 1978-80; sr. rsch. scientist Tago Inc., Burlingame, Calif., 1981-84; mgr. R&D Daryl Labs., Santa Clara, 1984-85; scientist Genentech Inc., South San Francisco, 1985-89, sr. scientist, 1989-93; dir. quality control and assay devel. Cell Genesys Inc., Foster City, Calif., 1993-95; dir. analytical sci. Alza Corp., Palo Alto, 1995-96, sr. dir. analytical, 1996-99, exec. dir. analytical, 1999-2000, v.p. implant R&D, 2000—. Fellow French Nat. League Cancer, Paris, 1976-78, Philippe Found. and UNESCO, 1978-79. Mem. Am. Soc. Neurochemistry, Am. Assn. Clin. Chemistry, Calif. Tissue Culture Assn., N.Y. Acad. Scis., Calif. Separations Soc. Avocations: Tae Kwon Do, bicycling, skiing, knitting, painting. Office: Alza Corp 1900 Charleston Rd Mountain View CA 94043-1218 E-mail: catherine.lucas@alza.com.

LUCAS, ELOISA B., tax consultant, management consultant; b. Manila, Philippines, Apr. 11, 1938; came to U.S., 1973; d. Florentino Olazabal Bonicacio and Amalia Granados Alvarez; m. Pablo Matias Lucas, Dec. 26, 1960; children: Judy Marie, Mary-Anne, Michaelangelo (dec.), Robert, Christine, Heidi Marie. BBA in Acctg., U. of the East, Manila, 1959. CPA, Philippines; cert. govt. fin. mgr., Va.; lic. life ins. agt., Calif. Gen. acct. Cal-Island Devel. Co., Tamuning, Guam, 1973-76, San Diego State U., 1980-84; acctg. mgr. EBL Assocs., San Diego, 1985-87; fed. auditor Def. Contract Audit Agy., San Diego, 1987-90; field auditor FEMA, Office of Insp.Gen., San Francisco, 1990-92; tax/fin. mgmt. cons. EBL & Assocs., San Diego, 1992—; life ins. agt. San Diego, 1984—. Fin. cons. Ukraine Fedn. Profl. Accts. and Auditors; advisor Citizen Democracy Corps, Washington. Bd. dirs., CFO, treas. Lucas Arts and Voices, Inc., San Diego, 1999—; mem. ch. choral group Santa Sophia Cath. Ch., Spring Valley, Calif., 1999—; sec. Filipino-Am. Cmty. of St. John of the Cross, Lemon Grove, Calif., 1984-86; vol. advisor Citizens Democracy Corps, Inc., Washington, 1997—. Recipient Leadership award U. of the East, 1958. Mem. Assn. Govt. Accts., Inst. Mgmt. Accts., Assn. Cert. Fraud Examiners. Avocations: music, concerts, art work, stamp collections. Office: EBL & Assocs 636 Broadway Ste 319 San Diego CA 92101-5410 E-mail: eblandassociates@yahoo.com.

LUCAS, GEORGETTA MARIE SNELL, retired educator, artist; b. Harmony, Ind., July 25, 1920; d. Ernest Clermont and Sarah Ann (McIntyre) Snell; m. Joseph William Lucas, Jan. 29, 1943; children: Carleen Anita Lucas Underwood, Thomas Joseph, Joetta Jeanne Lucas Allgood. BS, Ind. State U., 1942; MS in Edn., Butler U., 1964; postgrad., Herron Sch. of Art, 1961-65, Ind. U., Indpls. and Bloomington, 1960-62, 65. Music, art tchr. Jasonville City Schs., Ind., 1942-43, Van Buren H.S., Brazil, Ind., 1943-46, Plainfield City Schs., Ind., 1946-52, Met. Sch. Dist. Wayne Twp., Indpls., 1952-56, 59-68; art tchr. Met. Sch. Dist. Perry Twp., Indpls., 1968-81. Lectr. Art Educators Assn. Ind., Ind. U.-Bloomington, 1976. Illustrator: (book) Why So Sad, Little Rag Doll, 1963; artist (painting) Ethereal Season, 1966, (lithograph) Bird of Time, 1965-66; exhibited in group shows at Hoosier Salon, 1954-56, 60, 62-65, 67-68, 70, 72, 87, 94, NY Lincoln Ctr., NYC, 1994; represented in permanent collections Ind. State U., Ind.-Purdue U.-Indpls. Jane Voorhees Zimmerli Art Mus., Rutgers U., NJ, Indpls. Pub. Sch. Collection; drummer with Hendricks County Ramblers, 1986—. Mem. NEA (life), Nat. Assn. Women Artist, Ind. Artist Craftsmen, Inc. (hon., pres. 1979-85, 87, 88, scholarship chmn. 1986—, bd. dirs. 1986—), Ind. Fedn. Art Clubs (hon., pres. 1986-87, counselor 1988-91, bd. dirs. 1991—, parliamentarian 1992-94, conv. mgr. 1999, Best of Show 1997), Hoosier Salon, Ind. State U. Mortar Bd., Art Edn. Assn. Ind. (life), Nat. League Am. Pen Women (Ind. state art chmn. 1984-96, Best of Show award 1983, 97, pres. Indpls. br. 1994-96, Ind. State Assn. pres. 1998-2000, front cover drawing Pen Women Nat. Mag. 1994), Fine Art for State Ind. (Internat. Women's Yr. fine art chmn. 1977), Ctrl. Ind. Artists (hon.), Alpha Delta Kappa (life, Ind. state chmn. of art 1973-77, pres. 1972-74, represented by painting in nat. hdqrs.-Kansas City, Mo., Fidelis Delta first v.p.), Retired Educators Sorority (1st v.p., pres. 1997-99), Order of Eastern Star. Republican. Methodist. Avocations: genealogy, travel, coin collecting/numismatics. Home: 6990 E County Road 100 N Apt 223 Avon IN 46123-9714

LUCAS, KAREN, music educator; d. Clemon Willis and Celina Lucas. BS, Nazareth Coll., 1984; M in Music Edn., Mansfield U., 1986. Cert. music tchr. K-12 N.Y., 1990. Dir. bands Olinville Jr. H.S., Bronx, 1987—87, Kensington H.S., Buffalo, 1987—94; tchr. dist. wide music Geneva Mid. Sch., 1994—2001; dir. band Geneva H.S., 2001—03; tchr. dist. wide music Geneva Mid. Sch., 2003—. Playground supr. Geneva Recreation Dept., 1998—2001; unit supr. Nassau County AHRC, Hunter, 1989—90, athletic dir., 1987—89, camp counselor, Hunter, 1985—87. Guest conductor Rochester All City Elem. Band, Finger Lakes Concert Band. Bd. mem. Boys & Girls Club of Geneva, 2001—; commr. Geneva Human Rights Commn., 2003—. Mem.: N.Y. State Music Adminstrs., N.Y. State Music Educators Assn., Finger Lakes Music Educators Assn., Music Educators Nat. Conf., N.Y. State Band Dirs. Assn. Baptist. Avocations: music, softball, bicycling, camping, golf. Home: 188 High St Geneva NY 14456 Office: Geneva Middle School 101 Carter Rd # 200 Geneva NY 14456-1053 Office Phone: 315-781-2093. Personal E-mail: lucask@usadatanet.net.

LUCAS, KAREN WILLIAMS, controller; b. Ottawa, Can., Nov. 22, 1960; came to U.S., 1981; d. Lloyd George and Irene Katherine Williams; m. Ken W. Lucas, Apr. 18, 1981 (div. Apr. 1999); children: Kennith, James, Nicholas. AA with high honors, Broward C.C., 1990; BBA cum laude, Fla. Atlantic U., 1996, post grad. Cert. mgmt. acct., fin. mgmt., 2000. Asst. contr. EHP/Carico, Ft. Lauderdale, Fla., 1981-84; staff acct. MAP Builders, Coral Springs, Fla., 1984-86; contr. Conviber Co. Inc., Ft. Lauderdale, 1986-89, Commerce Group, Deerfield Beach, Fla., 1991-96, Purosys., Inc., Tamarac, Fla., 1996—2005; mgr. store acctg. Nations Rent, 2005—. Mem. Inst. Mgmt. Acct. (bd. 2000-2001), Beta Gamma Sigma. E-mail: lucas59205@bellsouth.net.

LUCAS, M. FRANCES, university administrator; b. Jackson, Miss., Oct. 24, 1956; d. Aubrey and Ella Lucas; children: Michael, Anna Catherine. BA in Comms., Miss. State U., 1978; MA in Higher Edn. Adminstrn., U. Ala., 1980, PhD in Higher Edn. Adminstrn., 1985; postgrad., Harvard U., 1989. Resident life coord. U. Ala., Tuscaloosa, 1979-83; asst. dean for student life Miss. State U., Starkville, 1983-86; v.p. for student affairs Baldwin-Wallace Coll., Berea, Ohio, 1986-92; v.p., sr. v.p. for campus life Emory U., Atlanta, 1992—. Faculty mem. Nat. Housing Tng. Inst., Gainesville, 1993, Mid-Mgrs. Inst., 1991-93, 94-95. Author: NASPA Journal, 1990, 91, College Student Affairs Journal, 1994, About Campus Journal, 1996. Mem. Nat. Assn. of Student Pers. (Greek rels. chair 1985—), The Nat. V.P.'s Group, So. Assn. of Coll. Student Affairs, Nat. Interfraternity Conf., Am. Coll. Pers. Assn., Assn. of Fraternity Advisors, Nat. Assn. of Student Pers. Adminstrs. (assoc. dir. Mid-Mgrs. Inst. 1993-94), Omicron Delta Kappa. Office: Emory U Campus Life 605 Asbury Cir Atlanta GA 30322-1006

LUCAS, MICHELE ANGELYN, learning consultant, special education educator; d. Robert Stephen Burrows and Mary Elizabeth Carvin-Burrows; m. Joseph William Lucas, Oct. 17, 1970; 1 child, Danielle Angelyn. BA, Ricker Coll., 1969; MS in Edn., Monmouth U., 1979, MSEd, 1988. Cert. learning disability tchr. cons., reading specialist, tchr. of handicapped, elem. tchr. Learning cons., reading specialist, 1st and 2d grade tchr. Freehold Twp. (NJ) Bd. Edn., 1973—; learning cons. Jersey Shore U. Med. Ctr., Neptune, NJ, 1994—. Sec. Manasquan (NJ) PTA, 1983; mem. Manasquan Tchr. Advisory, 1991, Manasquan Hist. Assn., 1997. Fellow: Learning Disability Assn., Coun. Exceptional Children (Edn. Diagnosis Spl. Education recognition 2004—); mem.: NEA, NJ Edn. Assn. Avocations: collecting vintage jewelry, walking, theater, reading, antiques.

LUCAS, MICHELLE DENISE, information technology manager; b. Richmond, Va., Apr. 3, 1970; d. Michael T. and Carolyn S. Lucas; 1 child, Morrigan Paige. BS, U. Fla., Gainesville, 2000; AS in Computer Programming and Sys. Analysis, Santa Fe C.C., Gainesville, 2001; M of Computer Info. Sci., U. Phoenix, 2004. Programmer analyst Fla. Farm Bur. Ins. Co., Gainesville, 2002—05; info. tech. mgr. Safeway Property Ins. Co., 2005—. Mem.: Math. Assn. Am., U. Fla. Alumni Assn., Mensa. Conservative. Roman Catholic. Avocation: renaissance history. Home: 25577 SW 22nd Place Newberry FL 32669 Office: Safeway Property Insurance Company 132 NW 76th Drive Suite A Gainesville FL 32607 Office Phone: 352-333-0160. Personal E-mail: smilinshel@yahoo.com.

LUCAS, NANCY JEAN, elementary school educator; d. William Howard and June Allison Floyd; m. Wayne Lee Lucas, Aug. 23, 1969; children: Jeffrey Warren, Keri Ann Lucas Dillingham. BA, U. Mo., Kansas City, 1987; MAT, Webster U., Kansas City, 1993. Elem. tchr. Park Hill Sch. Dist., Kansas City, 1987—. Math.-sci. facilitator Park Hill Sch. Dist., 1989—96; sci. instr. Success Link-MESC, Jefferson City, Mo., 1997—2003. Mem.: Sci. Tchrs. Mo., Nat. Sci. Tchrs. Assn., Alpha Delta Kappa. Avocations: folk art painting, cooking, travel. Home: 218 NW 53d St Gladstone MO 64118 Office Phone: 816-741-1531.

LUCAS, PATRICIA WHITTLINGER, small business owner; b. Madison, Wis., Mar. 17, 1925; d. Charles Edward and Jennie G. (Crowley) Whittlinger; m. Thomas Joseph Lucas, Oct. 29, 1946; children: Trisha Ruth, Kathryn Jean. Student, U. Wis., 1942—46, Edgewood Coll. Asst. dept. mgr. Manchesters Dept. Store, Madison, 1946-48; library asst. LaFollette High Sch., Madison, 1969-74; co-owner Artisan Gift Shoppe, Madison, 1974—. Vol. Girl Scouts Am., Madison, 1951-62, City Health Nichols Sch., Madison, 1953, Red Cross, 1955; facilitator Anorexia/Bulimia Support Group, 1985—. Mem. Madison Rotary Club. Lodges: Zonta (local bd. dirs., fellowship com., attendance and reservations com.). Avocations: golf, painting, music. Home: 300 Ela Ter Madison WI 53716-3106 Office: Artisan Gift Shoppe 4116 Monona Dr Madison WI 53716-1698

LUCAS, TAMMI MICHELLE, music educator; b. Tifton, Ga., Nov. 27, 1971; d. Louis Elvin Lucas and Faye Wynema Allmond. B of Music Edn., Troy State U., 1995. Tchr. music W. Bainbridge Elem., Ga., 1995—96, Potter St. Elem., Bainbridge, 1996—97; dir. band Hutto Mid. Sch., Bainbridge, 1997—. Active ch. choir. Mem.: Profl. Assn. Ga. Educators, Ga. Music Educators Assn. (sec. 1999—). Republican. Baptist. Home: 1505 Lakewood Dr Bainbridge GA 39819

LUCAS, TERI KATHLEEN, elementary school educator; d. Donald Paul and Joan McKee; m. Martin Vince Lucas, Dec. 23, 1970; children: Shawn Martin, Brian Donald, Kevin Michael, Heather Kathleen. BA, Francis Marion U., S.C., 1987. Cert. Edn. in English, Speech, Drama, Health Tex. Edn. Agy., 1988. Tchr. Pflugerville Mid. Sch., Tex., 1989—. Author: (non-fiction novel) Spontaneous Beats (Second Pl.- Golden Triangle Writer's Guild, 1997). Vol. EMT Pflugerville Vol. Fire Dept., Tex., 1997—2006; pres. Unity Ctr., Austin, 2006; spkr. Am. Heart Assn., Austin, 2003—06. Decorated USARELUR Helping Hand award VII Army; recipient Cert. of Appreciation, ARC, 1981, Honored Hero award, 2004, Pres.'s award, Pflugerville Vol. Fire Dept., 1999, Humanitarian of Yr., Pflugerville Mid. Sch., 2002; scholar, Women of Francis Marion U., 1986. Avocations: sign language classes, swimming, reading, travel, needlepoint. Office Phone: 512-594-2000.

LUCCHETTI, LYNN L., career officer; b. San Francisco, Aug. 21, 1939; d. Dante and Lillian (Bergeron) L. AB, San Jose State U., 1961; MS, San Francisco State U., 1967; grad., U.S. Army Basic Officer Course, 1971, U.S. Army Advanced Officer Course, 1976, U.S. Air Force War Coll., 1983, Sr. Pub. Affairs Officer Course, 1984. Media buyer Batten, Barton, Durstine & Osborn, Inc., San Francisco, 1961-67; producer-dir. Sta. KTVA-TV, Anchorage, 1967-68; media supr. Bennett, Luke and Teawell Advt., Phoenix, 1968-71; commd. 1st lt. U.S. Army, 1971, advanced through grades to lt. col., 1985, col., 1989, brig. gen. nom., 1993, officer, 1971-74, D.C. N.G., 1974-78, U.S. Air Force Res., 1978-99; program advt. mgr. U.S. Navy Recruiting Command, 1974-76; exec. coordinator Joint Advt. Dirs. of Recruiting (JADOR), 1976-79; dir. U.S. Armed Forces Joint Recruiting Advt. Program (JRAP) Dept. Def., Washington, 1979-91, resources mgr. Exec. Leadership Devel. Program, 1991-94. Author: Broadcasting in Alaska, 1942-1966. Active Vols. of ARC. Decorated U.S. Army Meritorious Svc. medal, Nat. Def. medal, U.S. Air Force Longevity Ribbon, U.S. Navy Meritorious Unit Commentation, Dept. Def. Joint Achievement medal, 1984, N.Mex. Legion of Merit, 1999; Sigma Delta Chi journalism scholar, 1960. Mem. Women's Affairs Asn., AF Pub. Affairs Alumni Assn. Home: 16775 W Cathedral Rock Ct Surprise AZ 85387 Personal E-mail: lynn_lucchetti@excite.com.

LUCCI, SUSAN, actress; b. Scarsdale, N.Y., Dec. 23, 1946; d. Victor and Jeanette L.; m. Helmut Huber, 1969; children: Liza Victoria, Andreas Martin. BA, Marymount Coll., 1968. Portrays Erica in TV series All My Children, 1970—; appearances in other series include: Fantasy Island, The Love Boat, The Fall Guy; TV films: Invitation to Hell, 1985, Mafia Princess, 1985, Ebbie, 1995, Seduced and Betrayed, 1995, (mini-series) Anastasia: The Mystery of Anna Anderson, 1986, Haunted by Her Past, 1988, Lady Mobster, 1988, The Bride in Black, 1990, The Women Who Sinned, 1991, Double Edge, 1992, Between Love and Hate, 1993, French Silk, 1994, Blood on Her Hands, 1998; host of spl. with Tony Danza 99 Ways to Attract the Right Man. Recipient 20 Emmy nominations and 1 Emmy award for best actress in daytime drama series, numerous other awards. Office: All My Children 320 W 66th St New York NY 10023-6397

LUCE, Mrs. HENRY See HADLEY, LEILA

LUCE, PRISCILLA MARK, public relations executive; b. N.Y.C., Feb. 4, 1947; d. S. Carl and Patricia (Greenfield) Mark; m. Robert Warren Luce, July 19, 1969; children: James Warren, David Mark. BA, U. Pa., 1968. Adminstrv. asst. Phila. Mus. Art, 1968-69; asst. dir. pub. info. Mt. Holyoke Coll., South Hadley, Mass., 1969-71; v.p. Barnes & Roche, Inc., Phila., 1971-82; mgr. civic programs TRW Inc., Cleve., 1982-85, mgr. cmty. rels., 1985-88, mgr. external comm., 1988-90, dir., pub. affairs and advt., 1990-92, v.p. TRW info. sys. and svcs. comms., 1992-94, v.p. mktg. and orgn. comm., 1994—2001, v.p. corp. comm., 2001—03. Trustee New Orgn. Visual Arts, Cleve., 1983—97, pres., 1984—86; trustee Cmty. Info. Vol. Action Ctr., Cleve., 1984—86, Albert M. Greenfield Found., Phila., 1989—, pres., 1999—; trustee Cleve. State U. Found., 1996—, chmn. devel. com., 1998—, vice-chmn., 1999—2004, chmn., 2004—; trustee Bus. Vols. Unltd., Cleve., 1998—2003, WVIZ/PBS, WCPN Radio, 1997—2005, chmn. pub. rels. com., 1998—2001; chmn. media and mktg. com. Cleve. Today, 1999—2001; trustee Ohio Chamber Orch., Cleve., 1986—92, chmn. devel. com., 1987—88, chmn., trustee, 1991—92, exec. v.p., 1990—91; mem. steering com. Cleve. Art Festival, 1983—84, Mayor's Cultural Arts Planning Task Force, 1985—87; trustee Ret. Sr. Vol. Prog., 1991, Western Res. Hist. Soc., 1999—2002; leadership devel. prog. participant United Way Svcs., Cleve., 1983, cons., 1983—85; steering com. Bus. Volunteerism Coun. of Cleve., 1984—92; comm. adv. com. Work in NE Ohio Coun., 1991—94. Recipient Woman of Profl. Excellence award, YWCA of Cleve., 1990.

LUCERO, ANNE, critical care nurse; b. Lynwwod, Calif., Aug. 21, 1954; d. Kenneth and Dorothy Irene (Berkland) Boulter; m. Emmett Ronald Lucero, Jan. 15, 1977 (div. June 1993); children: Christina Marie, Kathleen Anne. BSN, Calif. State U., Chico, 1976; MSN in Nursing Edn., Calif. State U., San Jose, 2001. RN, 1976, CCRN 1983, ACLS. Staff nurse Watsonville Cmty. Hosp., Calif., 1977-78, staff nurse/relief charge critical care, 1979-2000, 2005—; part-time faculty Sch. Nursing, Cabrillo Coll., Aptos, Calif., 1992-2000, full-time faculty, 2000—. Leader Campfire Boys and Girls, Santa Cruz Co., 1984-90, Bethel Guardian Internat. Order Jobs Daughters, 1993-98. Mem. Calif. Nurses Assn. (nurse rep. 1979-83, bd. dirs. 1980-91, political action com. 1989-91, legis. laison congressman, 1982-92), Am. Nurses Assn. (delegate 1990-92), Calif. Tchrs. Assn., Sigma Theta Tau. Avocations: golf, walking, bike riding, reading. E-mail: anlucero@cabrillo.edu.

LUCIA, MARILYN REED, physician; b. Boston; m. Salvatore P. Lucia, 1959, (dec. 1984); m. C. Robert Russell, (dec. 2000); children: Elizabeth, Walter, Salvatore, Darryl. AB with highest honors, U. Calif., Berkeley, 1951; MD, U. Calif., San Francisco, 1956. Cert. in psychiatry and child psychiatry Am. Bd. Psychiatry and Neurology. Intern Stanford U. Hosp., 1956-57; NIMH fellow, resident in psychiatry Langley Porter, U. Calif., San Francisco, 1957-60; NIMH fellow, resident in child psychiatry Mt. Zion Hosp., San Francisco, 1964-66; NIMH fellow, in cmty. psychiatry U. Calif., San Francisco, 1966—68, clin. prof. psychiatry, 1982—. Founder, cons. Marilyn Reed Lucia Child Care Study Ctr., U. Calif., San Francisco; cons. Craniofacial Ctr., U. Calif., San Francisco; No. Calif. Diagnostic Sch. for Neurologically Handicapped Children; dir. children's psychiat. svc. Contra Costa County Hosp., Martinez. Fellow Am. Psychiat. Assn. (disting. life), Am. Acad. Child Psychiatry; mem. Am. Cleft Palate Assn., San Francisco Med. Soc., Phi Beta Kappa. Office: 350 Parnassus Ave Ste 602 San Francisco CA 94117-3608

LUCIA, MARY ANN, elementary school educator; b. NYC, May 19, 1942; d. John Daniel and Anne Catherine Cleary; m. William Peter Lucia, June 27, 1964; children: Timothy Joseph, Jeffrey Joseph, Christopher Joseph. BA, Elms Coll., 1963, MA, 1992. English tchr. Holy Cross Sch., Springfield, Mass., 1980—, Wilbraham Jr. H.S., Wilbraham, 1980, Kiley Jr. H.S., Springfield. Lector Holy Cross Ch., Springfield, Mass., 1980—. Mem.: Nat. Coun. of Teachers of English, Nat. Cath. Edn. Assn. Office: Holy Cross Sch 153 Eddywood St Springfield MA 01118 Office Phone: 413-782-5246.

LUCIANO, CARA, mental health services professional; b. Phila., Feb. 8, 1979; d. Kim Palmieri and Robert Luciano, Sr. BA in Psychology, U. Del., 2001; MS in Mental Health Counseling, Capella U., Mpls., 2005. Intake coord./counselor Horizon Behavioral Healthcare, Prospect Park, NJ, 2001—04; group facilitator Mental Health Clinic of Passaic, Clifton, NJ, 2004—05, clin. counselor, 2005—. Mem.: ACA, Am. Mental Health Counselors Assn. Avocations: traveling, advocacy. Office Phone: 973-473-2775 131.

LUCIANO, ROSELLE PATRICIA, advertising executive, editor; b. Bklyn., Feb. 10, 1921; d. Giacomo Roberto and Francesca Rosa (Ruvolo) Rubino; m. Anthony Vincenzo Luciano, Nov. 24, 1946; 1 child, Nino Vincenzo Luciano. Attended, NYU. College shop mgr. Abraham & Straus, Bklyn., 1939-41, advtg. copywriter, 1941-44; fashion editor Syndicated MB Reports, N.Y.C., 1945-48; advtg. mgr., fashions copywriter Macy's 34th St., N.Y.C., 1949-54; publicist, adminstr. Fun With Prodns., N.Y.C., 1959-69; chair, adminstr. U.U. Plandome Forum, Manhasset, N.Y., 1970-78, UU Veatch Found., Manhasset, N.Y., 1979-84; dir. devel. IALRW Literacy For Women Program, Great Britain and India, 1984—. Coord. numerous workshops in field for various orgns.; served as spkr., editor, writer, publicist, 1984—. Operator political booth Democratic Party, Garden City, 1984, 88, 92; founder R.P.L. Literacy Fund for Women, 1996—. Recipient Best Advtg. Ad of the Yr. award Women's Wear Daily, 1954, Citizen of the Yr. award Carle Place Schs., 1965, award for outstanding leadership and encouragement for working women Women-On-the-Job, Inc., N.Y., 1987, Susan B. Anthony award U. U. Women;s Fedn., 1997. Unitarian Universalist. Avocations: environmental activism, opera, ballet, theater, travel.

LUCID, SHANNON W., biochemist, astronaut; b. Shanghai, Jan. 14, 1943; d. Joseph Oscar and Mary Wells; m. Michael F. Lucid, 1968; children: Kawai Dawn, Shandara Michelle, Michael Kermit. BS in Chemistry, U. Okla., 1963, MS in Biochemistry, 1970, PhD in Biochemistry, 1973. Sr. lab. technician Okla. Med. Rsch. Found., 1964-66, rsch. assoc., from 1974; chemist Kerr-McGee, Oklahoma City, 1966-68; astronaut NASA Lyndon B. Johnson Space Ctr., Houston, 1979—, mission specialist flights STS-51G and STS-34, mission specialist on Shuttle Atlantis Flight, 1991, mission specialist flight STS-58, 1993, mission specialist flight STS 76 & 79, 1996, mgmt., astronaut office Houston, 2003—; mission specialist stationed on Space Station Mir, 1996; chief scientist NASA Hdqs., Washington, 2003—03. Recipient Space award Aviation Week and Space Tech., 1997; first woman to fly on the shuttle three times; remained aloft 188 days in shuttle Mir. Address: NASA Johnson Space Ctr CB-Astronaut Office Houston TX 77058

LUCKERT, MARLA JO, state supreme court justice; b. Goodland, Kans., July 20, 1955; d. William Gottleib and Gladys Iona (Rohr) L.; m. Steven. K. Morse, May 25, 1980; children: Sarah, Alisa. BA, Washburn U., 1977, JD, 1980. Bar: Kans. 1980, U.S. Dist. Ct. Kans. 1980, U.S. Ct. Appeals (10th cir.) 1980. Assoc. Goodell, Stratoon, Edmond & Palmer, Topeka, 1980—92; judge Third Jud. Dist., Kans. Supreme Ct., Kans., 1992—2000, chief judge Kans., 2000—03; justice Kans. Supreme Ct., Kans., 2003—. Adj. prof. Washburn Univ. Sch. Law, Topeka, 1980-81, 1990—. Author: Kansas Consent Manual, 1988, Record Relations Guide, 1988, Kansas Law for Physicians, 1989. Pres. Mobile Meals of Topeka (Kans.), Inc., 1987-89, Mobile Meals of Topeka (Kans.) Found., 1989—; co-chair YWCA Nominating Com., Topeka, 1988-89. Recipient Woman of Excellence Award, YWCA, Topeka, Kans. Mem. ABA (co-chair young lawyers health law com. 1988-90), Am. Acad. Hosp. Attys., Kans. Assn. Hosp. Attys., Kans. Assn. Def. Counsel (bd. dirs. 1988—, disting. svc. award 1990), Kans. Bar Assn. (pres. young lawyers 1989-90, outstanding svc. award 1990), Topeka Bar Assn. (chair law day pubs. com.), Women Attys. Assn. Kans., Topeka (pres. 1988-89), Sam A. Crow Inn of Ct., Am. Judges Assn., Nat. Assn. Women Judges, Nat. Ctr. State Courts, Supreme Ct. Historical Soc., Am. Judicature Soc.; fellow Am. Bar Found., Kans. Bar Found. Office: Kansas Judicial Ctr 301 SW 10th Ave Topeka KS 66612-1507*

LUCKEY, DORIS WARING, civic volunteer; b. Union City, NJ, Sept. 17, 1929; d. Jay Deloss and Edna May (Ware) Waring; m. George William Luckey, Mar. 29, 1958; children: G. Robert, Jana Elizabeth, John Andrew. AB, U. Rochester, 1950; CLU, Am. Coll., Bryn Mawr, Pa., 1957. With pers. dept., supr. life dept. Travelers Ins. Co., Rochester, NY, 1952-58; agt. asst. life underwriting Mass. Mut. Ins. Co., Rochester, NY, 1958. Chair, various past offices Bd. Coop. Ednl. Svc. and State Edn. Dept. Vocat. Tech. Adv. Com., Rochester and Albany, NY, 1975—2003, pres. Rochester, 1975—85, Monroe County Sch. Bd. Assn., Rochester, 1980—81; v.p. Penfield (N.Y.) Sch., 1978—81; mem., past pres. William Warfield Scholarship Fund Bd.; coord. Young Artist Competition Penfield Symphony Orch; former adv. to bd. St. John's Home for Aging Bd., former mem. fin., pension and pers. com., former bd. dir., former exec. com.; pres. Leslie Norwood Carter Music Scholarship Fund; vol. numerous other civic, cultural, ch. and artistic orgn.; former pres. new investments United Ch. Christ, Genesee Valley, trustee ch. coun., former pres. ch. coun., former chair ch. and min. com.; property trustee Brighton United Ch. Christ, chair pastoral search com., 2001—02, co-chair investment com., co-chair long-range planning com; mem. program and mission com. Genesee Valley Assn. United Ch. Christ. Mem.: LWV (co-chm. nominating com. Rochester Metro chpt., chair spkrs. bur. Rochester Metro chpt.), AAUW (past pres. Greater Rochester br., past bd. dirs., dist. 1 state rep.). Republican.

LUCKEY, NORMA JEAN, music educator; b. Grove City, Pa., Mar. 4, 1949; d. Norman Butler and Mildred (Thompson) Humphrey; m. Robert August Luckey, May 22, 1971; children: Michelle Jean, Robert Jennings. BS Music Edn., Indiana U. Pa., 1971; M Music Edn., Duquesne U., 1974. Tchr. choral music, band state sch. sys., Pa., 1971—78; dir. Christian edn. chs., Ill., Iowa, N.C., 1978—84; tchr. music Durham City Schs., NC, 1985—86; dir. band & chorus Episcopal Sch. Acadian, Cade, La., 1986—96, Vermilion Parish Schs., Maurice, La., 1996—2000; dir. chorus Acadian Mid. Sch., Lafayette, La., 2000—03; tchr. music, band St. Pius Sch., Lafayette, 2003—05; tchr. St. Thomas More H.S., 2005—. Singer, instrumentalist Bob Luckey Jazz Combo, 1978—; dir. children's chorus U. La., Lafayette, 1988—. Elder 1st Presbyn. Ch., Lafayette, 1989—; condr. CD Toys to Recovery, Lafayette, 2001. Mem.: Orgn. Am. Kodaly Educators (former pres.), La. Assn. Kodaly Educators (bd. dirs. 1986—99).

LUCKMAN, SHARON GERSTEN, arts administrator; b. Sioux City, Iowa, Oct. 10, 1945; d. Robert S. and Libbie (Izen) Gersten; m. Peter Luckman, Nov. 22, 1968 (div. 1979); children: Melissa, Gregory; m. Paul Shapiro, Dec. 13, 1981. BS, U. Wis., 1967; cert. Inst. Not-For-Profit Mgmt., Columbia U., 1982. Dir. 92d St YM/YHA Dance Ctr., NYC, 1978-86; dir. devel. & new ventures Twyla Tharp Dance Found., NYC, 1986-87, exec. dir., 1988; dir. Vol. Lawyers for Arts, NYC, 1988-92; dir. devel. Alvin Ailey Dance Found., NYC, 1992—95, exec. dir., 1995—. Dance tchr. 92nd St. Y, N.Y.C., 1963-78, Nassau C.C., Garden City, N.Y., 1963-78, Long Beach (N.Y.) Pub. Schs., 1963-78; dir. Brant Lake (N.Y.) Dance and Sports Ctr., 1980-86; bd. dirs. Dance USA. Chairperson Laban/Bartenieff Inst. Movement Studies, N.Y.C., 1984-87. Democrat. Jewish. Office: Alvin Ailey Dance Foundation 405 W 55th St New York NY 10019-4402

LUCKTENBERG, JERRIE ČADEK, music educator; b. July 19, 1930; d. Ottokar Theodore and Sara (Hitchcock) Č; m. George Lucktenberg, 1953 (div. 1984); children: Judith, Kathryn, Ted. MusB, Curtis Inst., 1952; MusM, U. Ill., 1953; D of Mus. Arts, U. S.C., 1983. Concertizing as soloist and in chamber groups, Europe, Korea, Australia, U.S., 1954—96; assoc. prof. music Converse Coll., Spartanburg, SC, 1960—84; artist tchr., chmn. string dept. S.C. Gov.'s Sch. of Arts, Greenville, 1983—97; prof. music, chmn. string dept. U. So. Miss., Hattiesburg, 1984—96; concertmaster Pensacola (Fla.) Symphony, Meridian (Miss.) Symphony, 1986—96, Greater Spartanburg (S.C.) Philharm., 1996—2003. Author: The Joy of Shifting and Double Stops, a Violinist's Guide to Ease and Artistry, 1991; contbr. articles to profl. jours.; leader numerous workshops and clinics. Fulbright grantee State Acad. Music, Vienna, 1956-57; Ford Found. grantee, 1966-67; recipient Heart of Gold award The Arlington Assisted Living Facility, Hattiesburg, Miss., 1994, Tchr. Recognition award nat. winner Music Tchrs. Nat. Assn., 1974, Excellence in tchg. award, U. Southern Miss., 1990, Alumni Citation Outstanding Achievement as a performer and educator, U.S.C., 1991; citation for Exceptional Leadership and Merit award, 1992. Mem.: Suzuki Assn. of Ams., Music Educators Nat. Conf., Music Tchrs. Nat. Assn. (chmn. S.C. chpt. 1979—82, strings chmn. Miss. chpg. 1987—90), Am. String Tchrs. Assn. (life; founding pres. Miss. chpt. 1985, jour. reviewer 1987—97), Pi Kappa Lambda. Home: 311 Saranac Dr Spartanburg SC 29307-1141

LUCOFF, KATHY ANN, art advisor; b. L.A., Jan. 28, 1953; d. Marvin and JoAnn Ruth (Blaugrund) Miller Lucoff; m. Martin Gary Godin, Apr. 26, 1992. BFA, Calif. Coll. of Arts, Oakland, 1974. Asst. dir. L.A. Louver Gallery, Venice, Calif., 1976-78; instr. Santa Monica (Calif.) Coll., 1977; prin. Kathy Lucoff Arts Adv. Svcs., 1978—; instr. Dept. of Continuing Edn. Rice U., Houston, 1987-88. Bd. dirs. Univ. Art Mus., Long Beach, Calif.; art critic KABC Talk Radio, 1980-85. Art advisor: Poets Walk, Pub. Art Program, CBS Med. Art Ctr., L.A. C. of C. Pub. Art Programs, Burbank (Calif.) Empire Ctr. Avocations: travel, cooking, horseback riding. Office: 10520 Wilshire Blvd Ste 604 Los Angeles CA 90024-4595 Office Phone: 310-441-1040.

LUDDINGTON, BETTY WALLES, school library media specialist; b. Tampa, Fla., May 11, 1936; d. Edward Alvin and Ruby Mae (Hiott) L.; m. Robert Morris Schmidt, Sept. 20, 1957 (div. Dec. 1981); children: Irene Schmidt-Losat, Daniel Carl Schmidt. AA, U. South Fla., 1979, BA in Am. Studies and History, 1980, MA in Libr., Media and Info. Studies, 1982, EdS in Gifted Edn., 1986. Cert. tchr. media and gifted edn., Fla. Media intern Witter Elem. Sch., spring 1982; media specialist Twin Lakes Elem. Sch., 1982-84, Just Elem. Sch., 1984-87, Blake Jr. H.S., 1987-88, Dowdell Jr. H.S. (now Dowdell Mid. Sch.), 1988—. Educator Saturday enrichment program for gifted children U. South Fla., springs 1980, 84, 85; participant pilot summer program in reading and visual arts Just Elem. Sch., 1987; educator gifted edn. program in visual and performing arts Kingswood Elem. Sch., summers 1985, 86, gifted edn. program in video camera Apollo Beach Elem. Sch., summer 1989, Gifted Enrichment Prog. Imagi-lympics 2012, Maniscalco Elem. Sch., 1998, others. Author: (book of poetry) Aaron Tippin: A Hillbilly Knight, 1993; composer Luddington Cottage, 2004; contbr. articles and poems to various books and periodical publs., 1986—. Parent vol. media ctr. Witter Elem. Sch., 1976-78; tchr. sponsor Storytelling Club, Dowdell Jr. H.S., 1994-95; news media liaison, tchr. vol. Dowdell Jr. H.S., 1993-96. Recipient Student Affairs Golden Signet award U. South Fla., 1980, Parent award for continuing support of Fla. chpt. # 39 Am. Indsl. Arts Student Assn., 1987-88, Editor's Choice awards for outstanding achievement in poetry Nat. Libr. of Poetry, 1996; nominee Tchr. of Month, Sta. WTSP-TV, 1994; recognized for contbn. of motivational activity for Sunshine State Young Reader's Award program Fla. Assn. for Media in Edn., Inc., 1985; named to Internat. Poetry Hall of Fame, 1996. Mem. Internat. Soc. Poets (Disting. mem. 1995), Hillsborough Classrm. Tchrs. Assn. (grantee 1988, 90), Hillsborough Assn. Sch. Libr. Media Specialists, Clan Wallace Soc. (life), Phi Kappa Phi, Kappa Delta Pi, Phi Alpha Theta (pres., v.p., rep. to honors coun. 1980, 81, Outstanding Student award), Omicron Delta Kappa (treas., chairperson, del., mem. selection com. 1981, Leslie Lynn Walbolt book award), Pi Gamma Mu. Episcopalian. Avocations: poetry, books, cats, country music. Home: 1032 E Robson St Tampa FL 33604-4344

LUDDY, PAULA SCOTT, nursing educator; b. Plymouth, Mass., May 29, 1945; d. James Bernard Scott and Margaret Elizabeth Legge Scott; m. Robert Thomas Luddy, May 20, 1944; children: Scott, Shawn. BSN, Bowie State U., 1993, MSN, 1996. RN Mass., 1966, Md., 1970. Educator Group Health Assn., Washington, 1983—87; ob/lactation cons. Dr. Rafiq Mian, Cheverly, Md.,

1984—94; childbirth educator Childbirth Edn. Assn., Washington, 1971—95; staff nurse Prince George Hosp. Ctr., Cheverly, Md., 1981—87, patient educator, 1987—2002; coord./home interviewer Prince George Med. Soc., Prince George County, 1994—2002. Mem. adj. faculty dept. nursing Prince George's C.C., 1997—. Recipient Award of Excellence in Health Care, Assn. Women's Health Obstetric Neonatal Nurses, 2000, Hero for Babies, March of Dimes, 2002, Excellence in Edn. award, Prince George's C. of C. Bd. Edn., 2001. E-mail: lastnerbob@aol.com.

LUDERITZ, PAMELA ANN, secondary school educator; b. Apr. 6, 1943; d. William Neil and Mary Alice (Dean) Salter; m. Kurt Paul Luderitz, Aug. 9, 1981. BS, Boston U., 1964; MEd, U. San. Francisco, 1981. Cert. tchr. secondary edn., adminstrn. Calif. Tchr. Fanning Trade Sch., Worcester, Mass., 1964—66, Watsonville (Calif.) H.S., 1966—91, mem. sch. improvement plan, 1980—90, mem. dist. curriculum coun., 1984—90; owner P.S.L. Enterprises, 1991—. Vol. Make A Wish Found.; mem. Ben Lomond Fire Dept. Aux., Calif., Christmas Sharing Program. Mem.: AAHPER, Calif. Assn. Health, Phys. Edn., Recreation & Dance (task force substance abuse 1985), Make A Wish Found., Sports Car Club Am. (scorer, timer 1968—95, Regional Exec. award 1981, 1982, Race Chmn. award 1981, Worker of Yr. award 1981), Internat. Motor Sports Assn. (scorer, timer, Regional Exec. award 1984), Moose, Emblem Club. Avocations: tennis, swimming, sports cars.

LUDINGTON, JANICE FAY, speech pathology/audiology services professional; b. Fulton, N.Y., Sept. 18, 1920; d. Elon Kellogg Rowlee and Gertrude Frances Candee; m. Ramsey G. Ludington, Feb. 26, 2000; m. Wilbur Forrest Fay, July 24, 1944 (dec. Feb. 19, 1998); children: Trudy F. Duisenberg, Lynne F. Suljic, Faith F. Timerson, Gene F. Fay. BS, Syracuse U., N.Y., 1941. Itinerate pathologist Oswego County BOCES, NY, 1962; speech pathologist City Schs., Fulton, 1963—85. ESL tchr. N.Y. State Migrant Commn., Wolcott, 1967; mem. Head Start Bd., Fulton, 1985—86. Author (newspaper column): That Reminds Me, 1996—. Pres. Friends of Libr., Fulton, 1990—2000; vol. Lee Meml. Hosp. Aus., Fulton, Friends of History Fulton. Recipient Fundraising award, Oswego County Heritage Soc., 2004, Lifetime Member award, Friends of Libr., Fulton, 2005. Mem.: Delta Kappa Gamma. Unitarian-Universalist. Avocations: gardening, hiking, writing, reading, observing. Home: 217 Oneida St Fulton NY 13069

LUDOLF, MARILYN MARIE KEATON, lay worker; b. Morganton, NC, July 19, 1932; d. Charles Jefferson and Dora Esther (Whitener) Keaton; m. Edwin Forrest Ludolf, Dec. 22, 1957; children: David Forrest, Jonathan Charles. BA, Lenoir Rhyne, 1954. Youth worker Cen. Bapt. Ch., Greenville, SC, 1964-71, Park Bapt. Ch., Rock Hill, SC, 1958-64; with coll. students Becks Bapt. Ch., Winston Salem, NC, 1971-89; lay worker singles Calvary Bapt. Ch., Winston Salem, 1989—. Youth seminar leader youth activities Park Bapt., Rock Hill, S.C.; youth-Sunday sch. Tng. Union-All areas of Ch. Work, Greenville, S.C. and Winston Salem, N.C.; pub. spkr., sem. leader, Women's Conf. Keynoter. Author: Freed by Faith, 1995; contbr. articles to profl. jours. Chmn. Christian Women's Club Luncheon, Winston Salem, 2000-2002. Mem. Old Town Woman's Club (pres. 1975-77, Woman of Yr. 1977). Republican. Home: 3745 Whitehaven Rd Winston Salem NC 27106-2530 Personal E-mail: eludolf@prodigy.net.

LUDWIG, LAURA LONSHEIN, poet; b. Bklyn., July 26, 1955; d. Howard Lonshein, Gloria Lonshein; m. Ray Ludwig. Student, Franconia Coll., 1975—77. Writer Self-Employed, New York, NY, 1991—. Resident poet Joe Franklin Memory Lane Radio Show, WOR-AM, New York City, 1999—; screenwriter Joe Franklin Prodns., Inc., New York City, 1999—. Author (poetry, satires): Robo-Sapiens, 2001; author: (screenplays) Sounds Like a Plot, 2001, (novels) Reflections for the Renaissance, 2004, The Haunted House and the Stolen Gold, Gulliver of New York, 2006, (plays) The Stolen Gold, 2006; co-author (with Richard Ornstein): Of the Desk; prodr.(actress): classical concerts, ballet, opera, stage, short screenplays and T.V. programs,: (TV series) Earth is not on Tape. Recipient Guardian Angel award, Hope for Children Found., 1999; grantee, N.Y. State Coun. for the Arts. Home: 71 Joel M Austin Rd N Cairo NY 12413 Office Phone: 518-622-9747.

LUDWIG, MARTHA, biochemist, educator; BA, PhD, Cornell U.; MA, U. Calif., Berkeley. Postdoctoral fellow Harvard U., MIT; prof. dept. biol. chemistry U. Mich., Ann Arbor, 1967—. Mem.: NAS. Office: Dept Biological Chemistry Univ Mich Ann Arbor MI 48109

LUEBBEHUSEN, TINA MARIE, secondary school educator; b. Evansville, Ind., Nov. 28, 1973; d. David Wayne and Leona Agnes Zuelly; m. Cory Alan Luebbehusen, Oct. 10, 1998; children: Noah Scott, Jobe David. MS, Ind. U., Bloomington. Tchr. Jasper H.S., Ind., 1996—. Home: 2015 W Skyview Dr Jasper IN 47546 Office: Jasper High School 1600 St Charles St Jasper IN 47546 Office Phone: 812-482-6050. Office Fax: 812-634-1301. Personal E-mail: luebbeh@msn.com. Business E-Mail: tluebbeh@gjcs.k12.in.us.

LUEBBE-KEMEN, KATHY, music educator; b. Cin. d. Leo Bernard and Mary Lousie Luebbe; m. Frederick W. Kemen (dissolved); children: Susan, John. BA, Coll. Mt. St. Joseph, Cinn., 1974; MEd, Ind. Wesleyan Coll., Marion, 2005. Music tchr. Franklin (Ohio) City Sch., 1976—77, Wintonwood Sch., Cin., 1977—84, Norwell (Mass.) Sch., 1987—88, St. Therese Sch., Kansas City, 1988—89, Archdiocese of Cin., 1994—99, Mt. Healtim City Sch., Cin., 1999—2003, Princeton City Sch., Cin., 2003—06. Vocal dir. Thespis Theater, Cin., 1990—98, Lawrenceburg Cmty. Theater, 2003. Democrat. Avocations: walking, boating, travel, reading, theater.

LUEBKE, ELIZABETH ANNE SILVA, elementary school educator; b. El Paso, Tex., Nov. 5, 1961; d. Antonio T. and Ascencion Vega Silva; m. Jerry A. Luebke, Jan. 20, 1990; children: Ryan C., Caitlyn V. BS in Mgmt. and CIS cum laude, Park U., 2003. Cert. tchr. Tex. Computer edn. tchr. St. Clement's Episcopal Sch., El Paso, Tex., 2002—05; 4th grade tchr. H. D. Hilley Elem. Sch., El Paso, 2005—. Asst. leader Girl Scouts USA, El Paso, 1999—2000; tchr. San Antonio Cath. Ch., El Paso, 1998—2006; active Bel Air Highland Clan, El Paso, 2005—. Mem.: NEA, ASCD, Internat. Soc. for Tech. Educators, Tex. Computer Educators Assn., Socorro Edn. Assn., Tex. State Tchrs. Assn., Internat. Reading Assn. Roman Catholic. Avocations: reading, crocheting, cake decorating.

LUECHTEFELD, MONICA, retail executive; b. LA, Jan. 23, 1949; 1 child. BS, Mount St. Mary's Coll., LA, 1971. With recruiting office Mount St. Mary's Coll., LA; sales rep. Maloney's office supply, LA, 1979—93; from gen. mgr. So. Calif. Region to exec. v.p. E-Commerce Office Depot, Inc., Delray Beach, Fla., 1993—2000, exec. v.p. E-Commerce, 2000—. Office: Office Depot Inc 2200 Old Germantown Rd Delray Beach FL 33445

LUECKE, ELEANOR VIRGINIA ROHRBACHER, civic volunteer; b. St. Paul, Mar. 10, 1918; d. Adolph and Bertha (Lehman) Rohrbacher; m. Richard William Luecke, Nov. 1, 1941; children: Glenn Richard, Joan Eleanor Ratliff, Ruth Ann (dec.). Student, Macalester Coll., St. Paul, 1936-38, St. Paul Bus. U., 1938-40. Author lit. candidate and ballot issues, 1970-2003; producer TV local issues, 1981—; contbr. articles to profl. jours. Founder, officer, dir., pres. Liaison for Inter-Neighborhood Coop., Okemos, Mich., 1972—; chair countrywide special edn. millage proposals, 1958, 1969; trustee, v.p., pres. Ingham Intermediate Bd. Edn., 1959-83; sec., dir. Tri-County Cmty. Mental Health Bd., Lansing, 1964-72; founder, treas., pres. Concerned Citizens for Meridian Twp., Okemos, 1970-86; mental health rep. Partners of the Americas, Belize, Brit. Honduras, 1971; trustee Capital Area Comprehensive Health Planning, 1973-76; v.p., dir. Assn. Retarded Citizens Greater Lansing, 1973-83; chair, mem. Cmty. Svcs. for Developmentally Disabled Adv. Coun., 1973-87; dir., founder, treas. Tacoma Hills Homeowners Assn. Bd., 1985-97; facilitator of mergers Lansing Child Guidance Clinic, Clinton and Eaton counties Tri-County Cmty. Mental Health Bd., Lansing Adult Mental Health Clinic, founder; founder, treas., officer Mid-Mich. Land Conservancy, 2002—. Recipient Greater Lansing Cmty. Svcs. Coun. "Oscar," United Way, 1955, state grant Mich. Devel. Disabilities Coun., Lansing, 1983, Disting. award Mich. Assn. Sch. Bds., Lansing, 1983, Pub. Svc. award C.A.R.E.ing, Okemos, 1988, Earth Angel award WKAR-TV 23, Mich. State U., East Lansing, 1990, Cert. for Cmty. Betterment People for Meridian, Okemos, 1990, 2nd pl. video competition East Lansing/Meridian Twp. Cable Comm. Commn., 1990, 1st pl. award video competition, 1992, Outstanding Sr. Citizen award Charter Twp. of Meridian, Okemos, Mich., 2001; Ingham Med. Hosp. Commons Area named in her honor, Lansing, 1971. Mem. Advocacy Orgn. for Patients and Providers (dir. 1994-99). Avocations: reading, interior design, landscaping, gardening. Home: 2700 Burcham Dr Rm 230 East Lansing MI 48823-3891

LUENZ, PAMELA MARIE, educator; b. Dec. 16, 1947; d. August S. and Ethel A. (Franklin) Weisler; m. John V. Grabel (div. 1974); m. Michael F. Luenz. BA, Bradley U., Peoria, Ill., 1973, MS, 1974. Cert. spl. edn. tchr., Ill., Ind. Tchr. Loucks Sch., Peoria, 1974-77, W. Wilson Sch., Peoria, 1977, C. Lindbergh Sch., Peoria, 1978-80; staff devel. specialist Peoria Dist. 150, 1980; tchr. Glen Acres Sch., Lafayette, Ind., 1980-81, 81-87, Sunnyside Mid. Sch., Lafayette, 1987-89, 92—. Vol. Indpls. Zoo, 1988-89, Glen Oak Zoo, Peoria, 1976-80; sec. Friends of The Lafayette Zoo, 1981-84; grad. Leadership Lafayette, 1982; treas. Greater Lafayette Reading Coun., 1988-89; vol. in spl. edn. classes Bethany High Sch., 1989-90, Aditi Sch., Bangalore, India, 1989-92; bd. dirs. DIVA, Indpls., 1992—; devel. dir. Greater Lafayette Children's Choir, 1992-93. Recipient Sagamore of the Wabash award, Ind. Gov., 1999. Mem. Overseas Women's Club (sec. 1989-91), Lafayette Ind Historic Auto Club (treas. 1998—, bd. dirs.). Avocations: music, antiques, computers, reading, animals. Home: 4550 S 175 W Lafayette IN 47909-8905

LUESCHOW, SARAH LYNNE, biology educator; b. Champaign, Ill., July 21, 1962; d. Marvin John and Ruth Ellen Espenscheid; m. Kevin Jay Lueschow, June 9, 1990; children: Shiloh, Jesse, Andrew. BS in Animal Sci., SD State U., Brookings, 1984; MS in Edn., U. Wis., Platteville, 1988. County coord. Cmty. Action Program, Dodgeville, Wis., 1985; customer svc. profl. Swiss Colony, Monroe, Wis., 1985—86; supr. student libr. U. Wis., Platteville, 1986—88; tchr. jr. high sci. Peoria (Ill.) Sch. Dist., 1993—94; tchr. biology Dunlap (Ill.) H.S., 1994—; land sales assoc. Famous Barr, Peoria, 1998—2001; prof. biology Ill. Ctrl. Coll., East Peoria, Ill., 2001—. Mem. curriculum com. Dunlap H.S., 1997—99; judge state and regional sci. fairs, Macomb and Champaign, Ill., 2001—; judge pub. spkg. Future Farmers Am., Elmwood, 2002—. Asst. leader 4-H, Elmwood, Ill., 2004—; pre-K helper Elmwood (Ill.) Presbyn. Ch., 2004—. Mem.: Am. Hampshire Sheep Assn., Nat. Assn. Biology Tchrs., Nat. Assn. Sci. Tchrs. Avocations: youth activities, livestock, reading, music, painting. Home: 19520 Southport Elmwood IL 61529 Office: Dunlap H S Legion Hall Rd Dunlap IL 61525 Business E-Mail: slueschow@dunlapcusd.net.

LUETSCHWAGER, MARY SUSAN, educational consultant; b. Bloomingdale, Ind., Nov. 19, 1937; d. William Blaine Shade and Goldina VandaVeer (Newlin) Brown; children: Roger, Tisa, Julia, Angela, Robert, William; m. Bruce E. Luetschwager, Sept. 9, 2000. Grad. high sch., Rockville, Ind. Sec., treas. Tri-State Transport, Inc., 1968-73; road driver Roadway Express, Chicago Heights, Ill., 1977—, safety team capt., 1991-92, 94; program mgr., instr. Rider's Edge New Rider Tng., Calumet Harley-Davidson, Munster, Ind., 2006—. Completed Passport Tour (Abate), 1990, 94, 2000; mem. Roadway Express Dist. Road Team Dist. 12, 1995-97, Roadway Express, Chicago Heights, Ill., 1977-2006 Past mem. newsletter com. focus group Roadway Express; mem. focus group Kenworth Driver's Bd., 1992—; active Motorcycle Safety Found., Basic Rider Course; Rider coach 1999-, ABATE of Ind., Ind. Dept. of Edn. Recipient truck driving competition awards and motorcycle rally trophies, 3d place 8/48 rally Motorcycle Endurance Rider's Assn., 1996; 1st woman to finish on a Harley-Davidson motorcycle World Famous Iron Butt Rally, 1995, finished 6th place out of 78 starts and 61 finishers in 8th Iron Butt Rally, 1997, placed 3d in twin-trailer truck driving championships in Ill., 2000; placed 2nd in competition at Delta Nu Alpha truck driving fraternity in Rockford Ill, 2001, 1st pl. award (grand champion overall) in twin-trailer divsn. of truck driving championships, Ill., 2001; named Ill. TDC Sportsman of the Yr., 1995. Mem.: Ladies of Harley, Harley Owners Group (newsletter editor Calumet region chpt. 1994—96, Munster, Ind. asst. dir. Calumet region chpt. 1996—99, historian 2000—, sec. 2004, newsletter editor Calumet region chpt. 2005), Am. Radio Relay League, Am. Bikers Aim Toward Edn., Am. Motorcycle Assn. Avocations: motorcycling, amateur radio. Home and Office: PO Box 316 Griffith IN 46319-0316

LUFKIN, MARTHA B.G., lawyer, legal writer, art law correspondent; b. Boston, May 7, 1954; d. Nathaniel C. and Sareen R. (Epstein) Gerson. Grad., Phillips Exeter Acad., 1972; BA in Polit. Sci. magna cum laude, Yale U., 1976; MLitt in Politics, Oxford (Eng.) U., 1979; JD, Columbia U., 1982. Bar: N.Y. 1983, Mass. 1987. Collaborateur juridique Law Offices of S.G. Archibald, Paris, summer 1981, 82; assoc. Shearman & Sterling, N.Y.C., 1982-87, Bingham, Dana & Gould, Boston, 1987-92; legal writer, 1997—; pvt. practice, probate, estate settlement, wills and trusts Lincoln, Mass., 1999—. Lectr. in field. Author humor column Lincoln Jour., 1992— (Humor prize New Eng. Press Assn. 1996, 97), Alfred Hitchcock Mystery Mag., 1995, 97; U.S. legal corr. The Art Newspaper, 1997—; contbr. Art Antiquity and Law, Jour. Cultural Property; written about antitrust investigations of the auction houses Sotheby's and Christie's; claims by Italy and Egypt to recover antiquities looted from their soil; and lawsuits related to Nazi-looted art. Sr. Scholar Hertford Coll., Oxford U., 1978-79; Harlan Fiske Stone Scholar Columbia Law Sch., 1982.

LUFT, CECILE E., music educator; b. Brooklyn, NY, May 14, 1925; d. Jacob and Sophie Burrows; m. Morris Luft; children: Tamara, Leslie Noymer. Diploma in piano, Juilliard School of Music, N.Y.C., 1946; MA, C.W. Post U., Brookville, N.Y., 1985—87. Choir dir. Temple Beth El, Bellmore, NY, 1953—56; music dir. Reform Jewish Congregation, Westbury, NY, 1960—68; music tchr. Pvt. Lessons, Merrick, NY, 1950—2001; music dir. Camp Rosemont & Roselake, Honesdale, Pa., 1967—68. Choir dir. Evangelical Covenant Ch., Floral Park, NY, 1986—2001. Mem.: Assn. Piano Tchrs. Long Island Inc. Avocations: travel, swimming.

LUFTY, JOYBETH, minister; d. Pat Apple. BSc, Steven F. Austin State U., 1975; MSW, Western Mich. U., 1979; Dr. of Ministry, U. Creation Spirituality (now Wisdom U.), 2003. Head counselor, asst. dir. Otero Jr. Coll., LaJunto, Colo., 1976—77, instr. psychology, 1977; adolescent and family specialist Cmty. Health Counseling Svcs., Bangor, Maine, 1979—81; cons.-in-charge Crawford Health Rehab. Svcs., Bangor, 1983—85; counselor/educator Med. Care Devel., Bucksport, Maine, 1985—88; counselor Mystic Pines, East Orland, Maine, 1981—99; dir./internat. presenter Soul Integrators, East Orland, 1999—. Cons./sys. analyst WERU Cmty. Radio, East Orland, 1990—2000; vis. faculty Sch. of Holistic Spirituality, Buenos Aires, 2004—. Author: (book) Beyond Belief Into Knowing, 2001, A Soul's Delight, 2001, The We That Is Me, 2004. Vol. The Grand Theatre, Ellsworth, Maine; mem. campaign mgmt., trails com. Great Pond Mountain Conservation Trust, 2005—. Mem.: Sacred Dance Guild (ea. regional dir. 2005—). Avocations: singing, painting, hiking, swimming, dance. Personal E-mail: souldelite@aol.com.

LUGO-PAOLI, LUZ MINERVA, counselor, educator; b. Mayaguez, Puerto Rico, Aug. 7, 1976; d. Julio Cesar Lugo and Luz Minerva Rivera; m. Omar Ismael Paoli Breban, July 29, 2001. BSN, U. P.R., 2000; MA in Edn. with honors, U. Interamericana, 2005. Asst. social and cultural activities dept. U. P.R., Mayaguez, PR, 1994—99; assoc. prof. Sistema U. Ana G. Mendez- U. del Este, Santa Isabel, PR, 2003—04, profl. counselor, 2002—. Activities bd. Sistema U. Ana G. Mendez, 2005—; mem. adv. bd. U. del Este Santa Isabel, Santa Isabel, PR, 2006—. Vol. Lance Armstrong Found., 2005; mem. Livestrong Survivor Found., 2006; dir. Sabbath sch. Seventh Day Adventist Ch., Salinas, PR, 2004—. Recipient Gonzalez Excellence award, U. Interamericana at Aguadilla Campus, 1998, P.R. Youth medal, Gov. P.R., Anibal Acevedo Vila, 2005. Fellow: Am. Cancer Assn. (corr.); mem.: Nat. Acad. Advising Assn. (assoc.), Assn. Puertorriquena de Consejeros Profls. (assoc.), Am. Counselor Assn. (assoc.), Student Nurses Assn. (nat. constituent, nat. pres. 1999—2000, cons. 1999—2004, del pres. P.R. chpt. 1998—99, nominee Isabbel Hampton Robb Leadership award 2000), U. Students Assn. (activities planner 2003—), P.R. Epilepsy Soc. (assoc.). Mormon. Achievements include design of. Avocations: travel, scrapbooks, wedding planner, interior decorating, cultivate orchids. Office: Sistema Universitario Ana G Mendez-UNE PO Box 756 Santa Isabel PR 00757-9998 Office Phone: 787-845-3080. Office Fax: 787-845-3660. Personal E-mail: luz_lugo@hotmail.com. Business E-Mail: llugo@mail.suagm.edu.

LUHRS, CARO ELISE, internal medicine physician, administrator, educator; b. Dover, N.J., Jan. 21, 1935; d. Albert Weigand and Ethel Adelaide (Voss) L. BA, Swarthmore Coll., 1956; MD, Harvard U., 1960. Diplomate Am. Bd. Internal Medicine; cert. personal fitness trainer, fitness instr., strength and conditioning specialist. Instr., asst. prof. medicine, dir. hematology labs. Georgetown Univ. Hosp., Washington, 1964-68; White House fellow USDA, Washington, 1968-69, spl. asst. to Sec. of Agr., 1969-73; dir. health and med. divsn. Booz, Allen & Hamilton, Washington, 1973-77; v.p., med. dir. EHE/Nat. Health Svcs., Washington, 1977-78; physician Washington, 1978—; med. dir. Hummer Cos., Washington, 1989-99; clin. prof. family medicine Georgetown U., Washington, 1991-99. Trustee Swarthmore (Pa.) Coll., 1975-79; bd. dirs. USDA Grad. Sch., Washington, 1970-74, The Pillsbury Co., 1973-89, White House Fellow Found., Washington, 1979; bd. regents Uniformed Svcs. U. of Health Scis., Bethesda, Md., 1980-85; cons. Office Sci. and Tech. Policy, The White House, 1977-80; with D.C. Mayor's Adv. Com. on Emergency Med. Svcs., 1980-84; mem. adv. com. hazardous materials EPA, 1970-76. Recipient Disting. Svc. award Uniformed Svcs. U. Health Scis., 1985. Fellow ACP, Royal Soc. Medicine; mem. AMA, Am. Coll. Sports Medicine, Med. Soc. D.C., Cosmos Club.

LUHRS, CAROL, physician; b. N.Y.C., Dec. 29, 1951; d. Eugene Frederick and Jane Elsie Luhrs; m. David Robert Blumenthal, Apr. 12, 1981; children: Alex Michael, Kelly Anne. BA, Hunter Coll., 1973; MD, SUNY, Bklyn., 1977. Diplomate Am. Bd. Internal Medicine, Am. Bd. Hematology and Med. Oncology, Am. Bd. Palliative Medicine. Intern, resident in internal medicine Kings County Hosp.-Downstate Med. Ctr., Bklyn., 1977-80; fellow in hematology/oncology Bklyn. VA Med. Ctr., 1980-83, staff physician, 1983-84, NIH postdoctoral trainee in hematology, 1984-86, staff physician, 1986-94, chief hematology/oncology sect., 1995—; asst. prof. SUNY Hlth. Scis. Ctr., Bklyn., 1986-94, assoc prof. clin. medicine, 1996—. Contbr. articles to profl. jours. NIH grantee, 1986-91, VA grantee, 1992-95. Mem. Am. Soc. Hematology, Am. Fedn. Clin. Rsch., Am. Soc. Clin. Oncology. Office: Bklyn VA Med Ctr 800 Poly Pl Brooklyn NY 11209-7104

LUHRS, JOYCE ANN, business owner, consultant, communications and management consultant, writer; b. Toledo, Ohio; d. Carl Edward and Gladys Isabel Hormigo (Fajardo) L.; m. David Miller, Aug. 27, 1989. BA with honors in Soc. and Anthropology, Oberlin (Ohio) Coll., 1983; Cert. in Public Policy, SUNY, Albany, 1986; MA, Columbia U., N.Y.C., 1987. Cert. in tng. Legis. fellow N.Y.S. Assembly Com. Edn., Albany, 1986; coord., rsch. assoc. Project Minority Women FORWARD, Columbia U., N.Y.C., 1986-88; assoc. N.Y.C. Office of Bus. Devel., N.Y.C., 1987-88; cons., pres., owner Luhrs & Assocs., Leonia, N.J., 1987—. Del. UN Sponsored Children's Banner of Peace Assembly, Sofia, Bulgaria, 1982; legis. fellow women & public policy SUNY, Albany, 1986, Edn. Policy fellow Inst. Ednl. Leadership, Washington D.C., 1988-89; leadership N.J. fellow Partnership for N.J., New Brunswick, N.J., 1993; presenter in field. Columnist Dancing USA, 1996-2003, Amateur Dancers Mag., 2001—; Contbr. articles to profl. jours. Reviewer nat. selection com. Nat. Hispanic Scholarship Fund, Calif., 1987-94; founder, trustee Resource Reutilization Network, Leonia, N.J., 1990—, mem., vice chair, publicist Leonia Hist. Preservation Commn., 1990-95; mem. state edn. com. LWV, 1991-93; mem. bd. dirs. Leonia LWV, 1991-94; vol. Shelter Our Sisters, Bergen County, NJ, 2005, Bergen Family Ctr., Englewood, NJ, 2006. Scholar Nat. Hispanic Scholar Fund, 1983-87, Columbia U., 1983-1985; Urban fellow, NYC, 1987, Gilchrist-Potter Grad. fellow, Oberlin Coll., 1985; recipient: Cmty. Svc. award The Bergen Record, 1995, Good Neighbor award Cable TV Network of N.J., 1995, N.J. Women of Achievement award Douglass Coll. Rutgers U., 1996, Adult Vol. Group award Vol. Ctr. of Bergen County, 1996, Vol. Recognition award, Leonia Centennial Writers Fest, 1994, Teal Heart award, NJ Assn. Women Bus. Owners, 2004, Vol. award NY Metro. Chpt. A. Soc. Training and Devel., 1992. Mem. NAFE, Nat. Assn. Women Bus. Owners, N.J. Assn. Women Bus. Owners (v.p. mktg. on bd. trustess, 2003-2004, editor chpt. newsletter, 1995-1995, Teal Heart award 1996, honoree Salute to Women Leaders 1996). Avocation: ballroom dancing. Office: Luhrs & Assocs PO Box 413 Leonia NJ 07605-0413

LUHTA, CAROLINE NAUMANN, airport manager, flight educator; b. Cleve., Mar. 26, 1930; d. Karl Henry and Fannie Arletta (Harlan) Naumann; m. Fred Harlan Jones, July 2, 1955 (div. 1961); m. Adolph Jalmer Luhta, Dec. 12, 1968 (dec. 1993); 1 child, Katherine Louise. BA, Ohio Wesleyan U., Delaware, 1952; BS magna cum laude, Lake Erie Coll., Painesville, Ohio, 1977. Rsch. chemist Standard Oil Co. Ohio, Cleve., 1952-68; office mgr. Adolph J. Luhta Constrn. Co., Painesville, 1968-83; acct. Thomas Y. Ellis, CPA, Painesville, 1978; bd. dirs. Painesville Flying Svc., Inc., 1968—, flight instr., 1970—, pres., 1993—. Bd. dirs. Concord Air Park, Inc., Painesville, 1968—, pres. 1993—; accident prevention counselor FAA, Cleve., 1975-85. Contbr. articles to profl. jours. Trustee Northeastern Ohio Gen. Hosp., Madison, 1973-83, chmn. bd. 1980-82; trustee Internat. Women's Air and Space Mus., Cleve., 1989—, treas. 1991-95, pres., 1997—; trustee Concord Twp., 1992—. Recipient Aerospace award Cleve. Squadron, Air Force Assn., 1966, Woman of Achievement award Lakeland C.C., 1999, Harvey High Sch. Alumni Assn. Hall Fame, 2001. Mem. Nat. Assn. Flight Instrs., Exptl. Aircraft Assn., Aircraft Owners and Pilots Assn., Ninety-Nines (life, chmn. All-Ohio chpt. 1969-70, Achievement award 1965, Amelia Earhart Meml. scholar 1970), Silver Wings (life), Order Ea. Star, Alpha Delta Pi (life). Avocation: air racing. Office: Painesville Flying Svc Inc 12253 Concord Hambden Rd Painesville OH 44077-9566 Office Phone: 216-623-1111. E-mail: cluhta@iwasm.org.

LUIS, BELINDA, graphic designer; b. Luanda, Angola, June 15, 1967; came to U.S., 1979; Crispiniano and M. CArmo (Antunes) L. BA in Liberal Arts, Seton Hall U., 1990. Art dir. Luso Americano Newspaper, Newark, 1990-95; pres., owner On Design Graphics, Matawan, N.J., 1995—. Home: 18 Sonoma Ct Old Bridge NJ 08857-2573 E-mail: ondesign@aol.com.

LUISI, LOUISA, secondary school educator; b. Hackensack, NJ, Nov. 19, 1982; d. Francesco Luisi and Anna Marino. BS in English Edn., Bloomsburg U., 2003. Cert. tchr. NJ. History and English tchr. Saddle Brook (NJ) HS, 2004; English tchr. Ridgewood (NJ) HS, 2004—. Home: 10 Woodward St Saddle Brook NJ 07663

LUKACIK, DENISE MARIE, dance studio owner, choreographer; b. Syracuse, Ny, Mar. 12, 1957; d. Richard Lyle Meshurle and Patricia June Weiand Meshurle Coffey; m. Mark Dunlap Lukacik, Sept. 9, 1989; children: Sarah Elizabeth, Abigail Lee. Student, SUNY, Brockport, 1975—76. Lic. 220 Fla., 1987, life and variable annuities Fla., 1992. Ins. agt., asst. State Farm Ins., Tampa Bay, Fla., 1979—2003; dance instr. Contempo Sch. Dance, Lutz, Fla., 1999—2005; owner, dance instr. DancExperience, Land O Lakes, Fla., 1999—2006; studio owner Dancexperience I Inc, Dade City, Fla., 2006—. V.p. planning and devel. Arts in Motion Cmty. Youth Theatre/Arts Edn. Inc, Dade City, 2005—. Dir.: Arts in Motion Cmty. Youth Theatre productions, 2004—. Asst. children's and youth performance activities Harvester United Meth. Ch., Land O Lakes, 2002—06. Recipient Cmty. Svc. award, Zephyrhills Jaycees, 2006. Mem.: Profl. Dance Tchrs. Assn., Fla. Dance Edn. Orgn., Nat. Dance Edn. Orgn. R-Conservative. Methodist. Avocations: praise and liturgical dance, reading, children's groups and activities, volunteering. Office: Dancexperience I Inc 36813 Sr 52 Dade City FL 33525 Office Phone: 813-453-4325. Personal E-mail: dancexperience01@hotmail.com.

LUKENS, SUSAN ACKLEY, school system administrator; d. James Ackley and Barbara DeSousa; m. Jay Phelps Lukens, May 21, 1977; children: Clinton, Ashley, Walker. BBA, Tex. A&M U., 1980; BS cum laude, U. Houston, 1995, EdM, 2002. Cert. tchr. history/music K-8th grade Tex. With Tex. Commerce Bank Investments, Houston, 1985—86; dir. Mother's Day Out Program Meml. Luth. Ch., Houston, 1987—90; tchr. Grace Middle Sch., Houston, 1996—2002; dean Middle Sch. St. Francis Episcopal Day Sch., Houston, 2002—. Pool advisor Briar Meadow Bd., Houston, 1987—89; active United Way Houston Women's Initiative Alexis de Tocqueville Soc., Houston, 2004—. Recipient Crystal award for tchg., Spring Br. Edn. Found., 2005; fellow, Woolrich Found., 2005. Mem.: ASCD, Nat. Social Studies Supr. Assn., Nat. Assn. for Gifted Students. Presbyterian. Avocations: bicycling, ornithology. Home: 11752 Cawdor Way Houston TX 77024 Office: St Francis Episcopal Day Sch 335 Piney Point Dr Houston TX 77024

LUKER, KRISTIN, sociology educator; b. San Francisco, Aug. 15, 1946; d. James Wester and Bess (Littlefield) L. BA, U. Calif., Berkeley, 1968; PhD, Yale U., 1974. Postdoctoral fellow U. Calif., Berkeley, 1974-75, asst. prof. sociology San Diego, 1975-81, assoc. prof., 1981-85, prof., 1985-86, co-dir. women's studies program, 1984-85, prof. jurisprudence and social policy and sociology Berkeley, 1986—. Doris Stevens prof. women's studies, prof. sociology Princeton (N.J.) U., 1993-95. Author: Taking Chances: Abortion and the Decision Not To Contracept, 1976 (hon. mention Jessie Bernard award), Abortion and the Politics of Motherhood, 1984 (Charles Horton Dooley award, 1985). Bd. dirs. Ctr. for Women's Studies and Svcs., San Diego, Ctr. Population Options, Washington. Grantee Guggenheim Found., 1985. Mem. Am. Sociol. Assn., Sociologists for Women in Society. Office: U Calif Jurisprudence and Social Policy 2240 Piedmont Ave Berkeley CA 94720-2150

LUKERT-DEVOE, LINDA PAULINE, elementary school educator; b. Holton, Kans., Dec. 5, 1958; d. Ernest Oscar and Esther Fidelia (Gilbert) L.; m. Richard Devoe, Nov. 19, 1993; 1 child, Michael Benjamin. BS, Kans. State U., Manhattan, 1980; MEd, Washburn U., Topeka, Kans., 1989. Cert. learning disabilities and elem. edn. tchr., Kans. Tchr. elem. Unified Sch. Dist. 501, Topeka, 1980—, tchr. learning disabilities, 1988—, tchr., 1996—. Cons. social studies curriculum Unified Sch. Dist. 501, 1983, cons. math. curriculum, 1991, mem. student resource team, 1988-90, 91-94, cons. math. textbook com., 1990-91, cons. social studies textbook com., 1992-93, mem. norm-referenced test selection subcom., 1992. Adv. Battered Women Task Force, Topeka, 1984-87. Den leader Cub Scouts, 2003—. Vol. of the Yr., Battered Women Task Force, 1986. Mem. Phi Kappa Phi. Avocations: photography, sewing, dragon collector. Office: Meadows Elem Sch 201 SW Clay St Topeka KS 66606-1194 Home: 620 NW 35th St Topeka KS 66617-1706 Business E-Mail: llukert-@topeka.k12.ks.us.

LUKEY, JOAN A., lawyer; b. Malden, Mass., Dec. 28, 1949; d. Philip Edward and Ada Joan (Roberti) L.; m. Philip Davis Stevenson. BA magna cum laude, Smith Coll., 1971; JD cum laude, Boston Coll., 1974. Bar: Mass. 1974, U.S. Dist. Ct. Mass. 1975, U.S. Ct. Appeals (1st cir.) 1976, U.S. Supreme Ct. 1985. Assoc. Hale & Dorr, Boston, 1974-79, jr. ptnr., 1979-83, sr. ptnr., 1983—. Mem. Joint Bar Com. on Judicial Appointments, Mass., 1985-87, steering com. Lawyers' Com. for Civil Rights Under the Law, Boston, 1987-90. Fellow: Internat. Acad. Trial Lawyers, Am. Coll. Trial Lawyers (state com. 1993—2000, chair 1997—99, regent 2002—); mem.: ABA, Boston Bar Assn. (mem. coun. 1987—90, chair litigation sect. 1990—92, v.p. 1998—99, pres.-elect 1999—2000, pres. 2000—01), Mass. Bar Assn., Boston Club. Office: Wilmer Cutler Pickering Hale & Dorr 60 State St Boston MA 02109-1816 Office Phone: 617-526-6000. E-mail: joan.lukey@haledorr.com.

LUKOMSKY, VERA, musicologist, music educator, pianist; b. St. Petersburg, Russia, May 30, 1947; came to U.S., 1990; d. Eugene and Sofia (Levin) L.; m. Alexander Lukomsky, Sept. 21, 1966; children: Eva Jane, Daniel. BA in Music, Rimsky-Korsakov Coll. Music, St. Petersburg, 1968; MA in Music, St. Petersburg Conservatory, 1973; postgrad., U. Calif. San Diego, 1992-98. Instr. music State Coll. Music, Novgorod, Russia, 1972-73; instr. Inst. Culture, St. Petersburg, 1972-75, Rachmaninov Sch. Music, St. Petersburg, 1975-89; instr., owner Allegro Piano Studio, Encinitas, Calif., 1990—; lectr., asst. condr. U. Calif. San Diego, 1997-98; choral dir. San Diego H.S. and Meml. Jr. H.S., 1999-2000. Adj. prof. Nat. U., San Diego, 1999—. Author: The Analysis of Harmony in the Course of Solfeggio and Ear Training, 1985; contbr. articles to profl. jours. Recipient 1st pl. award Third Russian Republic Methodology Competition for Instrs. of Music and Art, 1983, Hendrikson fellowship U. Calif. San Diego, 1994-95. Mem. Am. Musicological Soc., Music Tchrs. Nat. Assn., Music Tchrs. Assn. Calif. (cert. of excellence 1999, 2000, 01, 02). Avocations: reading, travel, playing chamber music, theater, movies. Business E-Mail: vlukomsk@ucsd.edu.

LUM, JEAN LOUI JIN, nursing educator; b. Honolulu, Sept. 5, 1938; d. Yee Nung and Pui Ki (Young) L. BS, U. Hawaii, Manoa, 1960; MS in Nursing, U. Calif., San Francisco, 1961; MA, U. Wash., 1969, PhD in Sociology, 1972. Registered nurse, Hawaii. From instr. to prof. Sch. Nursing U. Hawaii Manoa, Honolulu, 1961-95, acting dean, 1982, dean, 1982-89, prof. emeritus, 1995—. Project coordinator Analysis and Planning Personnel Svcs., Western Interstate Commn. Higher Edn., 1977; extramural assoc. div. Rsch. Grants NIH, 1978-79; mem. mgmt. adv. com. Honolulu County Hosp., 1982-96; mem. exec. bd. Pacific Health Rsch. Inst., 1980-88; mem. health planning com. East Honolulu, 1978-81; mem. rsch. grants adv. coun. Hawaii Med. Svcs. Assn. Found., Nat. Adv. Coun. for Nursing Rsch., 1990-93. Contbr. articles to profl. jours. Trustee Straub Pacific Health Found., Honolulu; bd. dirs. Friends of the Nat. Inst. of Nursing Rsch., 1994-97. Recipient Nurse of Yr. award Hawaii Nurses Assn., 1982; named Disting. Practitioner in Nursing, Nat. Acads. of Practice, 1986; USPHS grantee, 1967-72. Fellow Am. Acad. Nursing; mem. Am. Nurses Assn., Am. Pacific Nursing Leaders Conf. (pres. 1983-87), Council Nurse Researchers, Nat. League for Nursing (bd. rev. 1981-87), Western Council Higher Edn. for Nurses (chmn. 1984-85), Western Soc. for Research in Nursing, Am. Sociol. Assn., Pacific Sociol. Assn., Assn. for Women in Sci., Hawaii Pub. Health Assn., Hawaii Med. Services Assn. (bd. dirs. 1985-92), Western Inst. Nursing, Mortar Bd., Phi Kappa Phi, Sigma Theta Tau (Kupuna award 2003), Alpha Kappa Delta, Delta Kappa Gamma. Episcopalian. Office: U Hawaii Manoa Sch Nursing Webster Hall 2528 The Mall Honolulu HI 96822

LUM, MARY, artist, art educator; BFA, U Mich.; MFA, Rochester Inst. Tech. Mem. faculty Sch. Art & Design, Albert U., NY, 1984—2004, prof. painting NY, co-chair MFA program in electronic integrated arts NY; mem. faculty painting and drawing Bennington Coll., Vt., 2005—. Work exhibited at, Hallwalls, Buffalo, NY, INTAR Gallery, NYC, Washington Project for the Arts, Washington, DC, So. Exposure, San Francisco, Art in General, NYC, Burchfield Art Ctr. and State Mus. of NY, Buffalo, Kean Coll., Union, NJ, Printed Matter, NYC, Ernest Rubenstein Gallery, U. Wis., Bernard Toale Gallery, Boston, Paris Project Room, 2002, Aldrich Contemporary Mus. Art, Ridgefield, CT, 2004. Grantee, Nat. Endowment for the Arts, NY Found. for the Arts, Constance Saltonstall Found. for the Arts, NY State Coun. on the Arts; Radcliffe Inst. Fellow, Harvard U., 2004—05, residency, Cite Internationale des Arts, Paris, Internat. Studio/Curatorial Program, NY, MacDowell Colony, Petersborough, NH, 2003. Office: Bennington Coll 1 Coll Dr Bennington VT 05201-6003

LUM, VIOLA DORIS, music educator, personal financial analyst; b. San Benito, Tex., Apr. 3, 1928; d. Ernest Lee and Jewell Avis (Hughes) Marley; m. S.E. Lum, Dec. 25, 1949; children: Donald Gene, Karen Ann Lum Boer. Tchg. cert., St. Louis Inst. Music, 1947, advanced tchg. cert., 1959. Lic. ins. and securities dealer, Tex. and Okla.; cert. PFA. Instr. music Tarkington Sch., Cleveland, Tex., 1947-53; tchr. piano Cleveland, Pasadena and Conroe, Tex., 1953—, Lifestyle Christian Sch., Conroe, 1986-96; newspaper editor Southwestern Gospel Music Assn., Pasadena, 1975-85; fin. analyst Primerica Fin. Svc., Conroe, 1987—. Newspaper pub. Southwestern Gospel Music Assn., Pasadena, 1975-85; beauty cons. Mary Kay Cosmetics, 1982-90; traveled nationwide with Kingdom Seekers, Inc., gospel music ministry, 1970-87. Treas. East Side Assembly of God Ch., Conroe, 1987-94, pianist, Riverside, 1987—. Mem. NASD, Nat. Piano Guild (chmn., hon. tchr. 1993-2001), Music Tchrs. Nat. Assn., Tex. Music Tchrs. Assn. (bd. dirs. 2004-2006, chmn. Divsn. I, student affiliate coun. 1994—), Conroe Music Tchrs. (pres. 1991-94, 2004-2006, Tchr. of Yr. 1994, 2003), Cypress Creek Music Tchrs. Assn. (v.p. 1998-2000, Selected Tchr. of the Yr. 1998). Avocations: photography, coin collecting/numismatics, computers.

LUMBY, BETTY LOUISE, music educator, organist, composer; b. Detroit; d. Avery Lewellyn and Besse Alena (Baker) L. MusB, Detroit Inst. Mus. Art; MusB summa cum laude, U. Detroit, 1947; MusM, U. Mich., 1949; D of Sacred Music, Union Theol. Sem., 1956. Instr. Detroit Inst. Mus. Art, Detroit; asst. prof. Music Howard Coll., Brimingham, Ala.; prof. music, univ. organist U. Montevallo, Ala., 1956—. Titular organist St. Bernard Abbey, Cullman; concert organist, lectr. Composer: To Play the Organ—From Spinette to Full-sized Console, vol. I/II, 1993, rev. 2d edit., 1994; mus. compositions: Metaphors on Mystery for Corpus Christi, 1990, Music for the Hallowing of a Church, 1990, The Wise Men, 1990, Lullaby for a Winged Church Mouse, 1990, To Play the Organ—A Method, 1989-90, Greetings for a Cathedral, 1991, Mass of St. Mary Magdalene, 1991, Vesper Hymn on Ar Hyd y Nos, 1991, Translucences on the Holy, 1991, Cecilian Allegories for the Feast of a Martyr, 1991, Questing Paradigms, 1992, Exsultet for Easter Vigil for Flute and Organ, 1995, Luminary on The Green Blade Riseth for Organ, 1996, Durations: 7 Studies on Time for Organ, 1996, 3 Songs of Theophilus (Baritone & Organ), 1996, Leaves of Revelation, (for organ), 1997, Paean for a Jubilee (Baritone and Organ solo), 1997, The Christ Child's Crown (2-pt. treble children's anthem 1997), Four Sonic Reliquaries for Millenium III, 2001, Glimpses on the Nativity of the Lord, 2001, St. Malachy, 1998, Cortége, 2003, Exultet Christus Victor, 2006. Fulbright scholar West Germany, 1956. Fellow The Am. Guild of Organists; mem. Ala. Music Tchrs. Assn. Music Tchrs. Nat. Assn., Soc. of Composers Inc., Southeastern Composers' League, Southeastern Hist. Keyboard Soc., Delta Omicron, Pi Kappa Lambda, Phi Kappa Phi. Avocations: stamp collecting/philately, music, painting. Home: PO Box 357 Montevallo AL 35115-0357

LUMBYE, BETSY, editor; BA in English, U. Va., 1977. Reporter Colo. Springs Sunday, Knoxville Jour., Tenn., asst. city editor Tenn., city editor Tenn.; metro editor The Record, Stockton; mng. editor The Herald, Rock Hill, SC, 1994—97; asst. mng. editor Fresno (Calif.) Bee, 1997, mng. editor, 1998—. Office: Fresno Bee 1626 E St Fresno CA 93706-2098

LUMMIS, CYNTHIA MARIE, state official, lawyer; b. Cheyenne, Wyo., Sept. 10, 1954; d. Doran Arp and Enid (Bennett) L.; m. Alvin L. Wiederspahn, May 28, 1983; children: Annaliese Alex. BS, U. Wyo., 1976, BS, 1978, JD, 1985. Bar: Wyo. 1985, U.S. Dist Ct. of Wyo. 1985, U.S. Ct. of Appeals (10th cir.) 1986. Rancher Lummis Livestock Co., Cheyenne, 1972—; law clk. Wyo. Supreme Ct., Cheyenne, 1985-86; assoc. Wiederspahn, Lummis & Liepas, Cheyenne, 1986—; treas. State of Wyo., 1999—. Mem. Wyo. Ho. Judiciary Com., 1979-86, Ho. Agriculture, Pub. Lands & Water Resources Com., 1985-86, Wyo. State Senate, 1993-94, Senate Judiciary Com., 1993-94, Senate Mines, Minerals, Econ. Devel. Com., 1993-94, U. Wyo. Inst. for Environment and Natural Resource Policy and Rsch.; chmn. County Ct. Planning Com., Wyo., 1986-88, Ho. Rev. Com., 1987-92, Joint Revenue Interim Com., 1988-89, 91-92; mem. adv. bd. U. Mont. Ctr. for the Rocky Mountain West, 1998—. Sec. Meals on Wheels, Cheyenne, 1985-87; mem. Agrl. Crisis Support Group, Laramie County, Wyo., 1985-87; mem. adv. com. U. Wyo. Sch. Nursing, 1988-90; mem. steering com. Wyo. Heritage Soc., 1986-89. Mem.: Rep. Women's (Cheyenne) (legis. chmn. 1982). Republican. Lutheran. Office: State Treasurer 200 W 24th St Cheyenne WY 82002-0001

LUMMUS, CAROL TRAVERS, artist, printmaker; b. Hyannis, Mass., Nov. 2, 1937; d. Frank and Doris (Brown) Travers; m. Bertrand W. Lummus, Jan. 27, 1962; children: Sarah Travers, Jonathan Ames. Student, Walnut Hill Sch., Natick, Mass., 1952-55; AA, Colby-Sawyer Coll., New London, N.H., 1957; student, U. Geneva, 1960-62. Artist, printmaker. Mem. art adv. panel N.H. Commn. on Arts, 1980. One-woman shows include Hammerquist, N.Y.C., 1979, La Galeria, San Mateo, Calif., 1980, Alice Bingham, Memphis, 1980, P.S. Gallery, Ogunquit, Maine, 1980, 927 Gallery, New Orleans, Saint Gaudens Nat. Hist. Site, Cornish, N.H., Gallery Z, Providence, R.I., 2005, Artique Ltd., Anchorage, Barn Gallery, Ogunquit, Maine, 2006, exhibited in group shows at All New Eng. Show, 1975—76, Currier Mus., Manchester, N.H., 1976, 1980, Fitchburg (Mass.) Mus., 1975—76, Inst. Brasil-Estados Unidos, Brazil, 1978, Hobe Sound (Fla.) Gallery, 1976—, Payson-Waldron, Portland, Maine, 1982, Nat. Assn. Women Artists, 1994, 1999, Royal Miniature Art Soc., London, 1995, C.C.C.C. Gallery, Phila., 1999, Inspires Gallery, Oxford, Eng., 2000, Franklin Pierce Law Sch., Concord, NH, 2000—, Cove Gallery, Wellfleet, Mass., 2002, Barn Gallery, Ogunquit, Maine, 2006, Sharon (N.H.) Arts Ctr., 2004, Nat. Assn. Women Artists, NYC, 2006, Three Graces Gallery, Portsmouth, N.H., Represented in permanent collections Springfield (Utah) Mus., Snow Coll., Ephraim, Utah, Georgetown U., Washington, Ogunquit Mus. Art; illustrator Cin. mag., Yankee mag.; two-person show, Barn Gallery, Maine, 2006. Recipient Rosmond de Kalb award Currier Mus., 1975, 1st prize Fitchburg Mus. Art, 1973, award Miniature Painters and Gravers Soc., Washington, 1996. Mem. Cape Cod Performing Arts Assn. (bd. dirs.), Mass. League N.H. Craftsmen, Nat. Assn. Women Artists N.Y., Barnstable (Mass.) Yacht Club. Episcopalian. Home (Winter): Box 525 Barnstable MA 02630 Home (Summer): 7 Railroad Ave Barnstable MA 02630 Business E-Mail: prints@carollummus.com.

LUMPKIN, VICKI G., minister; b. Denver, Sept. 4, 1950; d. Lester S. and L. Faye (Felton) Gapen; m. Charles D. Lumpkin, Feb. 12, 1971; children: L. David, Michael A., Andrew C. BA, George Mason U., 1973, MA, 1976; MDiv, Bapt. Theol. Seminary, Richmond, Va., 1993; PhD, Union Theol. Sem. in Va., Richmond, 1999. Ordained to ministry Am. Bapt. Ch. Protestant religious edn. coord. U.S. Army, Ft. Dix, N.J., 1984-85; minister of edn. and youth Haymarket (Va.) Bapt. Ch., 1991-95; group facilitator, homiletics Union Theol. Seminary, Richmond, 1995; interim co-pastor Ravensworth Bapt. Ch., Annandale, Va., 1997-98; pastor CityCh., Dallas, 2000—03, Bapt. Seminary Ky., 2004—05; chaplain, bereavement coord. Hospice, Rockingham County, NC, 2006—. Adj. prof. Bapt. Theol. Sem., Richmond, 2000, John Leland Ctr. for Theol. Studies, Falls Church, Va., Mid. Tenn. State U., 2004-2005; guest lectr. Bapt. heritage Bapt. Theol. Sem., Richmond, 1996; mem. Leadership Coun., Va. Alliance of Bapts., Richmond, 1995-98. Bd. dirs. Prince William Interfaith Vol. Caregivers, Manassas, Va., 1991-93, Greater Dallas Coun. Chs., 2003—; co-founder Interdenominal Support Group for Women in Ministry, Bristow, Va., 1992; tchr. of English YMCA, Panama City, 1976-77. Recipient Smyth and Helwys Seminarian award Bapt. Theol. Sem., Richmond, 1993. Mem. N.Am. Acad. of Liturgy, Am. Acad. Religion, Soc. Bibl. Lit., Baptist. Avocation: photography. Office: 2150 NC 65 Wentworth NC 27375 Home: 7680 Oak Level Rd Bassett VA 24055-4742 E-mail: vglumpkin@comcast.net.

LUMSDEN, LYNNE ANN, publishing executive; b. Battle Creek, Mich., July 30, 1947; d. Arthur James and Ruth Julia (Pandy) L.; m. Jon B. Harden, May 3, 1986; 1 child, Heather Lynne. Student, U. Paris, 1967-69; BA, Sarah Lawrence Coll., Bronxville, N.Y., 1969; postgrad., NYU, 1970-71, City Grad. Ctr., 1979-81; cert. of mgmt., Am. Mgmt. Assn., 1982. Copy editor Harcourt, Brace, Jovanovich, N.Y.C., 1970-71; editor Appleton-Century Crofts, N.Y.C., 1971-73, Coll. div. Prentice-Hall, Englewood Cliffs, N.J., 1974-78, sr. editor, 1978-81; asst. v.p., editor-in chief Spectrum Books, 1981-82, v.p., editl. dir. gen. pub. divsn., 1982-85; exec. v.p., publ., co-owner Dodd, Mead & Co., Inc., N.Y.C., 1985-89; owner, chmn. Gamut Pub. Co., Hartford, Conn., 1989—; pub. Hartford News and Greater Hartford Mag., 1989—. Pres., trustee, treas. Friends of Mark Twain House; v.p. Women of St. James's; buyer Mark Twain Mus. Store. Mem.: Jr. League of Hartford, Pub. Lunch Club, Hartford Golf Club. Episcopalian. Office: 99A Hanmer St Hartford CT 06114-2617 Office Phone: 860-296-6128.

LUNA, BERNADETTE, mechanical engineer; 3 children. B in Bioengineering, U. Pa.; M in Mech. Engring., Stanford U., postgrad. Rsch. engr. NASA Ames Rsch. Ctr. Avocations: knitting, jogging. Office: NASA Ames Rsch Ctr Bldg 200 Rm 116 Moffett Field CA 94035 Business E-Mail: bluna@mail.arc.nasa.gov.

LUNA, ELIZABETH (JEAN), cell biologist, educator, researcher; b. Poplar Bluff, Mo., Oct. 18, 1951; d. William Marion and Frieda L (Phillis) Luna; m. Alonzo H. Ross, June 24, 1974. BA with highest honors, So. Ill. U., 1972; PhD in Phys. Chemistry, Stanford U., 1977. Postdoctoral fellow dept. cell and molecular biology Harvard U., Cambridge, Mass., 1977-81; asst. prof. dept. biology Princeton (N.J.) U., 1981-88; sr. scientist Cell Biology group Worcester Found. for Biomed. Rsch., Shrewsbury, Mass., 1988-93; prin. scientist, 1993-97; assoc. prof. dept. cell biology U. Mass. Med. Sch., Worcester, 1989-94; prof. dept. cell biology, 1994—. Mem. adv. com. on personnel for rsch.-B, Am. Cancer Soc., Atlanta, 1989-93; mem. NIH Cell Biol. Physiol. I Study Sect., 1996-99. Mem. editl. bd. Jour. Cell Biology, 1990-93, Cell Motility and Cytoskeleton, 1994—; assoc. editor Jour. Cellular Biochemistry, 1994—. Mem. profl. adv. com. March of Dimes Birth Defects Found., Cen. N.J. chpt., 1983-88. Recipient Borden award, Merck award So. Ill. U., 1971; grantee Am. Cancer Soc., NIH, Robert R. Bensley award Am. Assn. Anatomists, 1993, Muscular Dystrophy Assn., Dept. Def Mem. AAAS, Am. Chem. Soc., Am. Soc. for Cell Biology, Am. Women in Sci., Biophys. Soc., Protein Soc., Sigma Xi. Achievements include research on cytoskeleton-membrane interactions. Office: U Mass Med Sch Biotech 4 Rm 306 377 Plantation St Worcester MA 01605-2300 Office Phone: 508-856-8661. Business E-Mail: Elizabeth.Luna@umassmed.edu.

LUNA, PATRICIA ADELE, marketing executive; b. Charleston, SC, July 22, 1956; d. Benjamin Curtis and Clara Elizabeth (McCrory) L. BS in History, Auburn U., 1978, MEd in History, 1980; MA in Adminstrn., U. Ala., 1981, EdS in Adminstrn., 1984, postgrad. in Adminstrn. Cert. tchr., Ga., Ala. History tchr. Harris County Mid. Sch., Ga., 1978-79, head dept. Ga., 1979-81; residence hall dir. univ. housing U. Ala., 1981-83, asst. dir. residence life, 1983-85; intern Cornell U., Ithaca, NY, 1983; dir. mktg. Golden Flake Snack Foods, Inc., Birmingham, Ala., 1985-89; sr. v.p. Quest U.S.A., Inc., Atlanta, 1989-90; pres. Promotion Mgmt. Group, Inc., Montgomery, Ala., 1990—. Cons. Capital Campaigns; lectr. in field. Author: Specialization: A Learning Module, 1979, Grantsmanship, 1981, Alcohol Awareness Programs, 1984, University Programming, 1984, Marketing Residential Life, 1985, The History of Golden Flake Snack Foods, 1986, Golden Flake Snack Foods, Inc., A Case Study, 1987, Cases in Strategic Marketing, 1989, Cases in Strategic Management, 1990, Frequency Marketing, 1992. Fundraiser U. Ala. Alumni Scholarship Fund, Tuscaloosa, 1983, Am. Diabetes Assn., Tuscaloosa, 1984, Urban Ministries, Birmingham, 1985-88; fundraiser, com. chmn. Spl. Olympics, Tuscaloosa, 1985; chmn. Greene County Relief Project, 1982-89; bd. dirs. Cerebral Palsy Found., Tuscaloosa, 1985-86; lay rector and com. chmn. Kairos Prison Ministry, Tutwiler State Prison, Ala., 1986-92; lobbyist, com. chmn. task force Justice Fellowship, 1988-91; bd. dirs. Internat. Found. Ewha U., Seoul, Korea, 1988-91; chmn. bd. dirs. Epiphany Ministries, 1991-98; bd. dirs. Hunting Coll. Fine Arts, chair Coll. Ministries, Whitfield Meml. United Meth. Ch., 1999-2000, chmn. capital fund campaign, 2000, chmn. stewardship bd. discipleship, 2000-02; chair Ala.-West. Fla. conf. United Meth. Ch., 2002; chair bd. discipleship Ala. UMC Conf., 2002—; retreat leader Upper Room, Acad. for Spiritual Formation, 2005—; com. chmn. Emmaus Ministry, 1985—; chmn. Chrysalis steering com., 1995-97; mem. bd. devel. Upper Rm. Ministries. Recipient Nat. award Joint Coun. Econ. Edn., 1979, Rsch. award NSF, 1979, Harry Denman Evangelism award, 2001; named to Hon. Order Ky. Cols. Commonwealth of Ky., 1985. Mem. Sales and Mktg. Execs. (chmn. com. 1985-86), Leadership Ala. (pres. 1982-83), Am. Mktg. Assn. (Disting. Leadership award 1987, Commemorative Medal of Honor 1988), Assn. Coll. and Univ. Housing Officers (com. chmn. 1983-85), Nat. Assn. Student Pers. Officers, Snack Food Assn. (mem. mktg. com. and conf. presenter), Internat. Coun. Shopping Ctrs. (Merit award 1991, program com.), Commerce Exec. Soc., Omega Rho Sigma (pres. 1983-84), Omicron Delta Kappa, Phi Delta Kappa, Kappa Delta Pi, Phi Alpha Theta. Mem. United Methodist Ch. Avocations: skiing, tennis, kayaking, community/church work, public speaking. Home and Office: 1327 Woodward AVE Montgomery AL 36106-2023 Office Phone: 334-262-9440. E-mail: patluna@charter.net.

LUNABURG, DIANE GAYLE, chemistry educator; b. Arlington Heights, Ill., Nov. 30, 1966; MS in Edn., Kennesaw State U., Ga., 2004; Specialist in Sci. Edn., U. West Ga., Carrollton, 2006. Tchr. sci. Nequa Valley H.S., Naperville, Ill., 1998—99. Mem.: Am. Chem. Soc. (assoc.). Home: 45 Evanston Ct Dallas GA 30157 Office: South Cobb HS 1920 Clay Rd Austell GA 30106

LUNA PADILLA, NITZA ENID, photography educator; b. San Juan, P.R., Mar. 13, 1959; d. Luis and Carmen Iris (Padilla) Luna. BFA, Pratt Inst., 1981; MS, Brooks Inst., 1985. Instr. U. P.R., Carolina, 1981-82, Cultural Inst., San Juan, 1988; prof. photography U. Sacred Heart, Santurce, P.R., 1987—; assoc. dir. communication ctr. U. Sagrado Corazon, Santurce, P.R., 1989-90. Contbr. articles to profl. publs.; one-woman shows P.R. Inst. Culture, 1988, Art and History Mus., San Juan, 1989, 94, 96, U. P.R., 1989, 90, Brooks Inst. Photography, Santa Barbara, Calif., 1990, Miriam Walsh Gallery, Glenwood Springs, Colo., 1991, Mus. Ponce, 1991, Spokane (Wash.) C.C., 1994, Centro Europa, San Juan, 1996, Galería de Arte, P.R., 1996; exhibited in group shows Santa Barbara Mus. Art, 1987, Coll. of Santa Fe, N.Mex., 1988, Durango (Colo.) Arts Ctr., 1988, 90, Laband Art Gallery, L.A., 1989, Cultural Ctr., Vercelli, Italy, 1989, Univ. Union Gallery Calif. Poly. State U., 1990, Coconino Ctr. Arts, Flagstaff, Ariz., 1990, Centro Cultural Washington Irving, Madrid, 1991, L.A. County Fair, 1991, Museo del Grabado Latinoamericano, San Juan, 1992, 93, 94, P.R. Inst. Culture, 1994, Hostos Art Gallery, N.Y.C., 1996, The Platinum Gallery, Sante Fe, 1996, Gallería Botello, San Juan, 1996, The Queens Mus., N.Y.C., 1997, The Platinum Gallery, N.Y.C., 1997, Arsenal, San Juan, 1997, Wis. Union Art Gallery, U. Wis., 1998; in permanent collections; juror Fotografía de prensa "Mandín," 1991-92. MacDowell Colony grantee, Instituto de Cultural Puertorriqueña grantee, 1993, 94, 96. Mem.: Soc. Photog. Edn., Friends of Photography. Roman Catholic. Avocations: painting, aerobics. Office: U Sagrado Corazón PO Box 192182 San Juan PR 00919-2182 E-mail: nitzaluna@prtc.net.

LUNARDINI, CHRISTINE ANNE, writer, historian, school administrator; b. Holyoke, Mass., Jan. 27, 1941; d. Virgil Joseph and Christine Hildegarde (Cavanaugh) L. AA, Holyoke C.C., 1973; BA, Mt. Holyoke Coll., 1975; MA, Princeton U., 1979, PhD, 1981. Instr. history Princeton (N.J.) U., 1981-85; adminstrv. asst. Refco Inc., N.Y.C., 1985-87; assoc. prof. Pace U., N.Y.C., 1987-91; freelance writer, N.Y.C., 1991—; exec. asst. to pres. Lynn Chase Designs, Inc., N.Y.C., 1999-2000; dir. devel. St. Michael Acad., N.Y.C., 2000—. Vis. assoc. prof., Barnard Coll., Columbia U., N.Y.C., 1984-85; project mgr., sr. editor Carlson Pub., Bklyn., 1992-93. Author: From Equal Suffrage to Equal Rights: Alice Paul and the National Woman's Party 1910-1928, 1986, The American Peace Movement in the 20th Century, 1994, What Every American Should Know About Women's History, 1996, Women's Rights, 1996; editor, project mgr.: Black Women in America, An Historical Encyclopedia, 2 vols., 1993 (Dartmouth medal 1994), Columbia Guide to American Women: The Nineteenth Century, 1999; mem. editl. adv. bd. Am. Heritage Multi Media, Am. Heritage: Women in Am., 1994—. Princeton U. fellow, 1975—79, Woodrow Wilson nat. fellow, 1980, AAUW nat. fellow, 1980—81. Mem. NOW, Women's Bond Club N.Y., Phi Beta Kappa. Democrat. Episcopalian. Home: 26 Beaver St New York NY 10004-2311 Office: 425 W 33rd St New York NY 10001

LUND, RITA POLLARD, aerospace engineer, consultant; b. Vallscreek, W.Va., Aug. 28, 1950; d. Willard Garfield and Faye Ethel (Perry) Pollard. Student, Alexandria Hosp. Sch. Nursing, 1969-70, Columbia Pacific U., 1989-91. Notary pub. Va. Confidential asst. U.S. Ho. of Reps., Washington, 1975-76; exec. asst. White Ho. Domestic Policy Staff, Washington, 1977-82; exec. asst. to dep. sci. advisor to pres. White Ho. Sci. Office, Washington, 1982-83; asst. to pres. Telecom Futures Inc., Washington, 1983-84, v.p. for adminstrn., 1985-86; internat. accounts mgr. TFI Ltd., McLean, Va., 1987-89; ind. cons. telecom. Washington, 1989-90; aerospace cons., 1990—98; rep. Scott Sci. & Tech., Washington, 1992—2000; cons. Vanguard Space Corp., Washington, 1992—2000. Exec. dir. Puckett Bros. Corp., 1995—. Marriage commr. State of Va., 2000—; pres. Fairvew Beach Residents Assn., 1997—2001. Mem.: AIAA, Competitive Alliance Space Enterprise, Am. Space Transp. Assn., Women in Aerospace, NAFE. Republican. Methodist. Avocations: travel, genealogy, reading.

LUNDE, DOLORES BENITEZ, retired secondary school educator; b. Honolulu, Apr. 12, 1929; d. Frank Molero and Matilda (Francisco) Benitez; m. Nuell Carlton Lunde, July 6, 1957; 1 child, Laurelle. BA, U. Oreg., 1951, postgrad., 1951-52, U. So. Calif., L.A., 1953-54, Colo. State U., 1957-58, Calif. State U., Fullerton, 1967-68. Cert. gen. secondary tchr., Calif.; cert. lang. devel. specialist. Tchr. Brawley (Calif.) Union High Sch., 1952-55; tchr. Fullerton (Calif.) Union High Sch. Dist., 1955-73; tchrs. aide Placentia (Calif.) Unified Sch. Dist., 1983-85; tchr. continuing edn. Fullerton Union High Sch. Dist., 1985-91; tchr. Fullerton Sch. Dist., 1988, Fullerton Union H.S. Dist., 1989-94. Presenter regional and state convs., so. Calif., 1986-88. Innovator tests, teaching tools, audio-visual aids. Vol. Luth. Social Svcs., Fullerton, 1981-82, Messiah Luth., Yorba Linda, Calif., 1981-88, 91-2001. Recipient Tchr. of Yr. award Fullerton Union High Sch. Dist., 1989. Mem. NEA, AAUW (life, bull. editor 1979-80, corr. sec. 1981-83, program v.p. 1983-84, gift honoree Fullerton br. 1985), Calif. State Tchrs. Assn., Fullerton Secondary Tchrs. Assn., Internat. Club/Spanish Club (advisor La Habra, Calif. 1965-72), Tchrs. English to Speakers Other Langs., Calif. Assn. Tchrs. English to Speakers Other Langs. Avocations: singing, folk and interpretive dance, guitar, reading, travel. Home: 4872 Ohio St Yorba Linda CA 92886-2713

LUNDEEN, MARGA LAIRD, art educator; b. Mpls., July 16, 1927; d. John Pierce and Gertrude Laird; m. Lyle August Lundeen; children: Richard, Cathrine, John, David. Student, U. Minn., Mpls. Sch. Art (now Mpls. Coll. Art and Design. Tchr. drawing and art history Stephens Sch. for Girls, Mpls. Portraits, Botanicals, Murals and Decorative Works. Avocations: walking, writing, naturalist.

LUNDEN, JOAN, television personality; b. Fair Oaks, CA, Sept. 19, 1950; d. Erle Murray and Gladyce Lorraine (Somervill) Blunden; m. Michael Krauss, 1978 (div. 1992); children: Jamie Beryl, Lindsay Leigh, Sarah Emily; m. Jeff Konigsberg, 2000; children: Kate Elizabeth, Max Aaron, Kimberly, Jack. Student, Universidad de Las Americas, Mexico City, U. Calif., Calif. State U., Am. River Coll., Sacramento, Calif. Began broadcasting career as co-anchor and prodr. at Sta. KCRA-TV and Radio, Sacramento, 1973-75; with Sta. WABC-TV, N.Y.C., 1975—97, co-anchor, 1976-80; co-host Good Morning America, ABC-TV, 1980-97; host spl. report TV for Whittle Comm.; host Everyday with Joan Lunden, 1989, Behind Closed Doors With Joan Lunden, 1994-2000 (ABC), 2000- (A&E); pres., host Women's Supermarket Network; film appearances include: Macho Callahan, 1970, What About Bob?, 1991, Free Willy 2, 1995, Conspiracy Theory, 1997; film appearances include Thank You for Smoking, 2006; spl. appearances: (TV series) Murphy Brown, 1992, 93, LateLine, 1998; Author: Good Morning, I'm Joan Lunden, 1986, Joan Lunden's Mother's Minutes, 1986, Your Newborn Baby: Everything You Need to Know, 1988, Joan Lunden's Healthy Cooking, 1996, Joan Lunden's Healthy Living, 1997, Joan Lunden's A Bend in the Road Is Not the End of the Road, 1998, Wake-Up Calls: Making the Most Out of Every Day, 2000; syndicated columnist: Parent's Notes. Recipient Outstanding Mother of Yr. award, Nat. Mother's Day Com., 1982; Albert Einstein Coll. of Yeshiva U. Spirit of Achievement award; Nat. Women's Polit. Caucus award; NJ Divsn. of Civil Rights award; Baylor U. Outstanding Woman of the Year award; Decoration for Disting. Civilian Svc., US Army. Office: LMNO Prodns PO Box 4361 Los Angeles CA 90028 also: Creative Artists Agy c/o Debra Goldfarb 9830 Wilshire Blvd Beverly Hills CA 90212-1825 also: Rm 4332 1271 Avenue Of The Americas New York NY 10020-1401

LUNDERGAN, BARBARA KEOUGH, lawyer; b. Chgo., Nov. 6, 1938; d. Edward E. and Eleanor A. (Erickson) Keough; children: Matthew K., Mary Alice. BA, U. Ill., Urbana, 1960; JD, Loyola U., Chgo., 1964. Bar: Ill. 1964, Ga. 1997, Minn. 2004, U.S. Dist. Ct. (no. dist.) Ill. 1964, U.S. Tax Ct. 1974. Ptnr. Seyfarth Shaw LLP, Chgo., 1971—98, of counsel, 1998—2004, Hristendahl Moersch and Dorsey PA, Northfield, Minn., 2004—. Fellow Am. Coll. Trust and Estate Counsel; mem. ABA (com. on fed. taxation), Ill. Bar Assn. (coun. sect. on fed. taxation 1983-91, chair 1989, coun. sect. on trusts and estates sect. coun. 1992-97, sec. 1996-97, editl. bd. Ill. Bar Jour. 1993-96), Chgo. Bar Assn. (chmn. trust law com. 1982-83, com. on fed. taxation). Office: Hristendahl Moersch and Dorsey PA 311 Water St Northfield MN 55057 Office Phone: 507-645-9358. Business E-Mail: bkl@hvmd.com.

LUNDGREN, COLLEEN BOWLING, elementary school educator, consultant; b. Frankfort, Mich., Sept. 25, 1949; d. Steven Bowling and Vera Opal Grossnickle; m. Dennis David Lundgren, Dec. 18, 1971; 1 child, David Steven. BA, Western Mich. U., 1971, MA, 1976. Cert. tchr. K-8 Mich., 1976. Tchr. Seely-McCord Elem. Sch., Benton Harbor, Mich., 1971—80; adult reading tchr. Lakeshore Pub. Schs., Stevensville, 1978—78; reading curriculum specialist Benton Harbor Area Schs., 1979, English lang. arts presenter, 1991—, Mich. literacy progress profile trainer, 2001—, title I reading tchr., 1980—2006; Reading First facilitator Mich. Dept. Edn., 2006—. Grantee AT&T. Mem.: Internat. Reading Assn., Mich. Reading Assn., Phi Delta Kappa. Lutheran. Avocations: reading, singing, gardening. Office: MLK Elem Sch 750 E Britain Ave Benton Harbor MI 49022 Personal E-mail: colleen.lundgren@bhas.org. Business E-Mail: clundgre@remc11.k12.mi.us.

LUNDGREN, KAREN MARIE, disabilities professional; b. Oakland, Calif., Nov. 28, 1951; d. Karl Albert and Verna Marie (Baeta) L.; children: Simone M. Wren, Alison J. Wren. BS in Child Devel., Calif. State U., 1973. Cert. elem. tchr., Calif.; cert. spl. edn. tchr., Calif., Oreg. Diagnostic tchr. Vacaville Unified Schs., Calif., 1977-83; resource specialist Grenada Schs., Calif., 1983-85; ABA tchr. Jackson Edn. Svc. Dist., Medford, Oreg., 1986—2004; disabilities svcs. and mental health svcs. coord. So. Oreg. Head Start/Early Head Start, Central Point, 1994—2001, Jackson City Sch. Dist. 9, 2004—. Instr. Rogue CC, 2006—. Mem. Jackson County Early Intervention Coun., Medford, Oreg., 1994-2001, Josephine County Early Intervention Coun., Grants Pass, Oreg., 1994-2001, Oreg. Head Start Coord. Coun., 1998-2001; pres. Oreg. Divsn. for Early Childhood, 2000-2003; vol. Oreg. Shakespeare Festival, Ashland, Oreg., 1983—, Schneider Mus. Art, Ashland, 1991—; mem. Ashland Sch. Bd. Com., 1996-2001. Recipient Mentor Tchr. award Calif. Dept. Edn., 1982; exch. tchr. So. Australia Dept. Edn., 1988, Innovator award S. Oregon Edn. Svc. Edn., 2003. Mem. World Assn. for Infant Mental Health, Coun. for Exceptional Children. Avocations: travel, skiing, hiking, reading, genealogy. Home: 2261 Siskiyou Blvd Ashland OR 97520-3033 Office: Jackson County Dist 9 PO Box 549 Eagle Point OR 97524 Office Phone: 541-830-6116.

LUNDGREN, RUTH WILLIAMSON WOOD (RUTH LUNDGREN WILLIAMSON WOOD), public relations executive, writer; b. Bklyn. d. John William and Hanna (Carlson) L.; m. W. F. Williamson, Dec. 17, 1949 (dec.); children: John Ross (dec.), Mark Ward; m. John Earle Wood, Aug. 27, 1988 (dec.). Student, Bklyn. Coll., 1936-41, Columbia U., 1942. Assoc. editor Everywoman's mag., 1940-42; pub. relations staff exec. J.M. Mathes Advt. Agy., 1942-45; dir. pub. relations Pan-Am. Coffee Bur., 1945-48; pres. Ruth Lundgren Ltd., N.Y.C., 1948-92. Pub. Ruth Lundgren Newsletter, 1950-58; writer daily column St. Petersburg (Fla.) Times, 1956-60; contbg. editor, writer monthly column Motor Boating and Sailing mag., 1962-80; contbr. to popular profl. publs. Home: PO Box 267 Sterling MA 01564-0267

LUNDSAGER, MARGRETHE (MEG LUNDSAGER), federal official; b. Dec. 27, 1951; married; two children. Grad., Am. U., U. Md. With U.S. Exec. Dirs. Office, Internat. Monetary Fund; spl. asst. to under sec. for internat. affairs US Dept. Treasury, Washington, 1987-90; dir. Nat. Security Coun. staff Internat. Econ. Affairs Directorate, 1990-91; dir. Office Asian and Near East Nations US Dept. Treasury, Washington, 1991-95, dep. asst. sec. for trade & investment policy, 1996—2000, adv. to exec. dir., IMF, 2000, US alt. exec. dir. IMF, 2001—. Atlantic fellow in pub. policy London Sch. Econs., 1995-96. Office: IMF 700 19th St NW Washington DC 20431*

LUNDSTROM, MARJIE, editor; Grad., U. Nebr. Columnist, editor, nat. corr. The Denver Post, 1981-89; with The Sacramento Bee, 1989-90, 91—; nat. corr. Gannett News Svc., Washington, 1990-91. Recipient Pulitzer Prize for nat. reporting, 1991. Office: The Sacramento Bee PO Box 15779 Sacramento CA 95852-0779 Business E-Mail: mlundstrom@sacbee.com.

LUNDY, BARBARA JEAN, training services executive; b. Chgo., Feb. 2, 1950; Cert. hynotherapist 2003. Tchr., facilitator Red Rocks C.C., Golden, Colo., 1986—90, AMI, St. Luke's Hosp., Denver, 1986—90; tchr. Arapaho C.C., Denver, 1991—95; tng. mgr. Denver Options, 1995. Mediator U. Denver; dir. Am. Poets and Fiction Writing, Denver. Author, poet, editor Market Mountain Writer's, 1978-81 (Pushcart Prize nominee 2006); co-author: You Can Collect Child Support, 1989; contbg. author Directory of Am. Poets and Fiction Writer's. Profl. vol. VIDA Vol., Pueblo, Colo., 1971-73; vol. dir. Legal Aid Soc., Denver, 1980-85; bd. mem., editl. bd. Colo. Women's Polit. Caucus, Denver, 1980-81; state commn. mem. Colo. Child Support Commn., Denver, 1984-85; co-founder Kids in Need Support (KINS), Denver, 1986-87; com. mem. Denver Dist. Ct., Bench, Bar, Cmty. Rels. Com., Denver, 1987-89. Mem. Assn. Persons Supported Employment (spkr. nat. conv. 1998), Hayna Writer's. Avocations: science, history and philosophy reading, piano, writing. Office: Denver Options Inc 9900 E Iliff Ave Denver CO 80231-3462 Business E-Mail: blundy@denveroptions.org.

LUNDY, JACKELYN RUTH, financial consultant, economist, researcher; b. Palo Alto, Calif., Nov. 8, 1951; d. Jack E. and Ruthe A. (Rose) L.; 1 child, Maia Rose. BA, U. Calif., Davis, 1973, MS, 1976, PhD, 1987. Staff rsch. assoc. U. Calif., Davis, 1976-80; tech. assistance officer Nat. Consumer Coop. Bank, Washington, 1980-82; assoc. analyst Calif. Office Econ. Opportunity, Sacramento, 1982-87; assoc. dir. agroecology program U. Calif., Santa Cruz, 1987-93, acting dir. Ctr. for Agroecology, 1993-97; owner Lundy and Assocs., Palo Alto, Calif., 1997—. Contbr. numerous articles to profl. jours. Bd. dirs. Internat. Tree Crops Inst., Davis, 1983—, Assoc. Coops., Richmond, Calif., 1994-96; mem. supervisory com. Santa Cruz Cmty. Credit Union, 1987-97. Fellow Resources for Future, 1988, leadership fellow Kellogg Found., 1991-94. Avocations: breeding and training golden retrievers, storytelling, tennis, piano. Home: 2055Bowdoin Palo Alto CA 94306

LUNDY, SADIE ALLEN, small business owner; b. Milton, Fla., Mar. 29, 1918; d. Stephen Grover and Martha Ellen (Harter) Allen; m. Wilson Tate Lundy, May 17, 1939 (div. 1962); children: Wilson Tate Jr., Houston Allen, Micheal David, Robert Douglas, Martha Jo-Ellen. Degree in acctg., Graceland Coll., 1938. Acct. Powers Furniture Co., Milton, 1939-40; acct., v.p. Lundy Oil Co., Milton, 1941-52; controller First Fed. Savs. & Loan, Kansas City, Mo., 1953-55, Herald Pub. Co., Indepenence, Mo., 1956-58; mgr. Baird & Son Toy Co., Kansas City, 1959-62; regional mgr. Emmons Jewelers NY, Kansas City, 1963-65; owner, pres. Lundy Tax Svc., Independence, 1965-85; corp. sec., treas., purchasing mgr. Optimation, Inc., Independence, 1974-85, mgr., 1985—, corp. sec., treas., 2006—; COO Wasber Industries LLC, Independence, 2001—; dir. ops., corp. sec., treas. ReEngineer Profit LLC, Independence, 2003—06. Contbr. articles to profl. jours. Mem. com. Neighborhood Coun., Independence, 1985. Mem.: Am. Bus. Women's Assn., Independence C. of C. (mem. com. 1965—85), Independence Women's Club. Republican. Cmty. Of Christ Ch. Avocations: counseling, swimming, bicycling. Home: PO Box 520238 Independence MO 64052-0238 Office: ReEngineer Profit LLC PO Box 520238 Independence MO 64052 Office Phone: 816-228-2100. Business E-Mail: slundy@optinest.com. E-mail: slundy@comcast.net.

LUNDY, SHEILA EDWARDS, lawyer; b. Balt., Nov. 29, 1954; d. James Morris and Christine Anne E.; children: Tiffany D., Christopher R. BA, U. Balt., 1978, JD, 1991. Bar: U.S. Ct. Appeals Md. 1992, U.S. Dist. Ct. Md. 1994. Adminstrv. specialist BWI Airport, Md. Aviation Adminstrn., Balt., 1988-91, risk mgmt. specialist, 1991-92; staff atty. Md. Office Atty. Gen., Glen Burnie, 1992-94, asst. atty. gen., 1994—. Faculty The Md. Inst. for Continuing Profl. Edn. of Lawyers, 1999. Mem. Mt. St. Josephs H.S. Mother's Club, Balt., 1997—. Mem. Am. Inns of Ct., Md. Bar Assn. (mem. lawyer counseling com. 1998—), Paca-Brent Joint Inn of Ct., Anne Arundel County Bar Assn. (mem. com. 1994—, bd. trustees 1999), U. Balt. Alumni Assn., Paca-Brent Inn of Ct. (bd. dirs. 1999), Monumental Bar Assn. Democrat. Roman Catholic. Avocations: gardening, reading, old movies. Home: 2009 Sentry Cir Apt 203 Odenton MD 21113-3235

LUNG, AURISTELA R., music educator; b. Barranquilla, Colombia, Jan. 14, 1955; arrived in U.S., 1958; d. Julio Rodríguez Buelvas and Estela Merlano Rodríguez. Grad., Watchtower Bible Sch. of Gilead, 1982; BA in Music Edn., U. Tex.-Pan Am. U., 1996; MA in Spanish Lit., U. Tex.-Pan. Am., 2000. Cert. bilingual educator, all-level music tchr. Missionary Jehovah's Witnesses, Colombia, 1982—85; piano tchr., owner Starr County Piano Studio, Rio Grande City, Tex., 1990—; 4th grade bilingual tchr. Rio Grande City Ctrl. Ind. Sch. Dist., 1997—99; instr. South Tex. Coll., Rio Grande City, 1999—. Vol. educator Jehovah's Witnesses, Roma, Tex., 1986—, regular pioneer Hebronville, Tex., 2005—. Mem.: Magic Valley Music Tchrs. (sec. 1998—2005), Tex. Faculty Assocs., Tex. Music Tchrs. Assn., Phi Kappa Phi. Jehovah'S Witness. Avocations: reading, crocheting, travel, cat. Home: PO Box 804 Rio Grande City TX 78582 Office Phone: 956-488-5857. Business E-Mail: alung@southtexascollege.edu.

LUNGARO CID, LISA, educational association administrator; b. Baton Rouge; children: Carina, Eddie. BA, San Francisco Coll. for Women; MA, U. Chgo.; cert. in non-profit mgmt., Case Western Res. U.; postgrad., Yale U., Columbia U. Educator pvt. schs., New Orleans, San Francisco; dir. comm. Girl Scouts, New Orleans, 1978—80, assoc. CEO, 1980—83; CEO Girl Scouts Ctrl. Md., 1993—. Mem. United Way Agy. Exec. Steering Com., 1995—2000, chair, 1998. Mem. Md. Assn. of Non-Profit Orgn., 1993—2000; active Jr. League Adv. Bd., 1997—99, Coppin State, Am. Humanics Adv. Bd., 1999—, Md. Student Svc. Alliance Adv. Bd., 2000; mem. edn. com. Greater Balt. Com., 2000; active Gov.'s Coun. on the Status of Girls, 2000. Named to Md. Top 100 Women, 1991, 2001; recipient Cert. of Honor for Svc. to San Diego County, 1991. Mem.: Network 2000 (sec. 1997—99). Office: Girl Scouts Ctrl Md 4806 Seton Dr Baltimore MD 21215

LUPARDUS, S. CAROL, education educator; b. London, Feb. 21, 1953; d. Tom Brooks-Pilling and Sue (Hampton) Lackey; m. James R. Lupardus, May 20, 1978; children: Nancy, Michael, Hannah. BS in Edn., U. Mo., 1975; MA in Edn., St. Louis U., 1999, PhD in Edn., 2005. Elem. sch. tchr. Meramec Valley Sch. Dist., Pacific, Mo., 1975—83; cons. Mo. Sch. Bd. Assn., Columbia, 1990—; assoc. prof. St. Louis CC, 2001—. Mem. sch. bd. Washington (Mo.) Sch. Dist., 1990—2005. Mem.: ASCD, Mo. Sch. Bd. Assn. (pres. 2003—04), Phi Delta Kappa. Office: St Lous CC 3400 Pershall Rd Saint Louis MO 63135

LUPEI, CYNTHIA THERESE, music educator; d. Kenneth Leroy and Mary Jean Petersen; m. Donald Eugene Lupei, Aug. 14, 1971; children: Michelle Renee, Nichole Suzanne. AA, Waubonsie C.C., Sugar Grove, Ill., 1989; MusB, No. Ill. U., 1992; MusM in Edn., VanderCook Sch. of Music, Chgo., 1999. Type 9 Specialist Ill. Bd. of Edn., 1993, Type 10 Music Vocal Secondary Ill. Bd. of Edn., 1994. Gen. music tchr. Cowherd Mid. Sch. Dist. 131, Aurora, Ill., 1993—94; vocal/gen. music tchr. J. W. Gates Elem. Dist. 131, Aurora, 1994—. Music dir. Fourth St. Meth. Ch., Aurora, 1993—97. ACT 1/Twentieth Century Drama grant, Cmty. in Schools Aurora, Ill., 2002—, Wireless Tech., Aurora East Edn. Found., 2005, Keyboard Lab, 2000. Mem.: Music Educators Nat. Conf. Home: 62 Kingmoor Lane Yorkville IL 60560-9466 Office: J W Gates Elem Dist 131 800 Seventh Ave Aurora IL 60505 Office Fax: 630-299-5601. E-mail: clupei.gates@d131.org.

LUPIANI, JENNIFER LYNNE, school psychologist; b. Bronx, NY, Mar. 24, 1975; d. Donald Anthony and Linda Lupiani. BA, Boston Coll., 1993—97; MS in edn., Fordham U., 1997—2001, profl. diploma, 1997—2001, PhD, 1997—2004. Cert. school psychologist NY, 2001. Sch. psychologist Astor Child Guidance Ctr., Bronx, NY, 2001—02, Croton Harmon Sch. Dist., Croton-on-Hudson, NY, 2002—04; asst. psychologist Ind. Practice, Yonkers, NY, 1999—; sch. psychologist Putnam No. Westchester BOCES, Yorktown Heights, NY, 2002—, Hendrick Hudson Sch. Dist., Cortlandt Manor, NY, 2004—. Field specialist for applied behavior analysis Fordham U., New York, NY, 2001—02. Recipient Ted Bernstein award, NY Assn. of Sch. Psychologists, 2004, Lambda Xi Chpt. of Kappa Delta Pi, Fordham U., 2000, Golden Key Nat. Honor Soc., Boston Coll., 1995, Psi Chi, 1996. Mem.: NASP, NY Assn. of Sch. Psychologists, APA. Avocations: sewing, knitting, painting, swimming, travel. Home: 227 Mile Square Rd Yonkers NY 10701 Office: Furnace Woods Elementary Sch 239 Watch Hill Rd Cortlandt Manor NY 10567 Office Phone: 914-736-5416. Personal E-mail: jlupiani@aol.com.

LUPONE, PATTI, actress; b. Northport, L.I., NY, Apr. 21, 1949; d. Orlando Joseph and Angela Louise (Patti) LuP.; m. Matt Johnston, 1988; 1 child, Joshua Luke. BFA, The Juilliard Sch., 1972. Off-Broadway prodns. include: The Woods, School for Scandal, The Lower Depths, Stage Directions; regional prodns. include: The Lady With The Torch, 2004, The Little Foxes, 2005, Anyone Can Whistle, 2005; Broadway prodns. include: Next Time I'll Sing to You, The Time of Your Life, The Three Sisters, The Robber Bridegroom, 1976 (Tony award nominee), The Water Engine, The Beggar's Opera, Edward II, The Baker's Wife, 1976, The Woods, 1977, Working, 1978, Catchpenny Twist, 1978, As You Like It, 1982, The Cradle Will Rock, 1983, Stars of Broadway, 1983, Edmond, 1982, Oliver, 1984; star Broadway musicals Evita, 1979 (Best Actress in Musical Tony award, 1980), Anything Goes, 1987, Pal Joey, 1995, Sweeney Todd, 2005, Gypsy, 2006; London prodns. Les Miserables, 1985, Sunset Boulevard, 1993; films include: King of the Gypsies, 1978, 1941, 1979, Fighting Back, 1982, Witness, 1985, Wise Guys, 1986, Driving Miss Daisy, 1989, Family Prayers, 1993, State and Maine, 1999, Just Looking, 1999, Bad Faith, 1999, The 24 Hour Woman, 1999, Summer of Sam, 1999, Bad Faith, 2000, State and Main, 2000, The Victim, 2001, Heist, 2001, City By the City, 2002; TV appearances include: Kitty, The Time of Your Life, Lady Bird in LBJ, 1987, The Water Engine, 1992, Family Prayers, 1993, The Song Spinner, 1995, Her Last Chance, 1996; TV series, Life Goes On, 1989-93, Falcone, 2000; TV guest appearances Law & Order, 1990, Frasier, 1993, Remember WENN, 1996, Saturday Night Live, 1998, Touched by an Angel, 2001, Oz, 2003, The Tony Danza Show, 2004, Will & Grace, 2005. Volunteer Craft and Folk Art Mus., 1999—2000. Recipient John Houseman award, 2006. First Am. actress to win an Olivier award in England, 1985. Office: ICM 40 W 57th St Fl 16 New York NY 10019-4098*

LUQUE, NANCY, lawyer; BA, San Diego St. Univ., Calif., 1973; JD, Univ. San Diego, 1976. Bar: Calif. 1976, DC 1989. Trial atty. Dept. Justice Antitrust Div., Washington, 1979—82; asst. US atty. US Dept. Justice, Washington, 1983—89; assoc. Washington Perito & Dubuc, 1989—91; ptnr. Katten Muchin Zavis, 1989—91, Reed Smith, Washington, 1995—2002, Luque Sheinbach, Washington, 2002—04, DLA Piper Rudnick Gray Cary US, LLP, Washington, 2004—. Chmn. ABA, Criminal Justice Section, White Collar Crime Com., Washington; past pres. Asst. US Atty. Assn. Editor: (Newsletter) White Collar Crime Com.; co-author: (Criminal Justice Magazine) Joint Defense Agreements: Protecting the Privilege and the Future, 1990, (Nat. Inst. HJealthcare Fraud, ABA) Grand Jury: Conflicts and Document Production, 1993, (Nat. Inst. Healthcare Fraud, ABA) Sentencing Guidelines, 1994. Office: DLA Piper Rudnick Gray Cary US LLP 1200 Nineteenth St NW Washington DC 20036-2412 E-mail: nancy.luque@dlapiper.com.

LURENSKY, MARCIA ADELE, lawyer; b. Newton, Mass., May 4, 1948; BA magna cum laude, Wheaton Coll., 1970; JD, Boston Coll. Law Sch., 1973. Bar: Mass. 1973, D.C. 1990, U.S. Dist. Ct. (we. dist.) Wis. 1978, U.S. Dist. Ct. Mass. 1974, U.S. Ct. Appeals (1st cir.) 1974, U.S. Ct. Appeals (3d cir.) 1982, U.S. Ct. Appeals (4th cir.) 1984, U.S. Ct. Appeals (5th cir.) 1995, U.S. Ct. Appeals (8th cir.) 1985, U.S. Ct. Appeals (9th cir.) 1976, U.S. Ct. Appeals (10th cir.) 1995, U.S. Ct. Appeals (11th cir.) 1982, U.S. Ct. Appeals (fed. cir.) 1989, U.S. Claims Ct. 1989, U.S. Supreme Ct. 1979. Atty. U.S. Dept. Labor, Washington, 1974-90, Fed. Energy Regulatory Commn., U.S. Dept. Energy, Washington, 1990—. Mem. Phi Beta Kappa. Office: Fed Energy Regulatory Commn 888 1st St NE Washington DC 20426-0002

LURIA, MARY MERCER, lawyer; b. Boston, Dec. 29, 1942; d. Albert and Mabel (Jacomb) Mercer; m. Nelson J. Luria, June 19, 1967. AB, Radcliffe Coll., 1964; LLB, Yale U., 1967. Bar: N.Y. 1968. Assoc. Simpson, Thacher & Bartlett, N.Y.C., 1967-68, Hale & Dorr, Boston, 1968-69, Satterlee & Stephens, N.Y.C., 1969-74, ptnr., 1974-86, Patterson, Belknap, Webb & Tyler, N.Y.C., 1986-97, Davis & Gilbert, N.Y.C., 1997—. Mem. ABA, N.Y. State Bar Assn., Assn. Bar City N.Y. Avocations: gardening, photography. Office: Davis & Gilbert 1740 Broadway Fl 20 New York NY 10019-4379 Office Phone: 212-468-4813. E-mail: mluria@dglaw.com.

LURIE, ALISON, writer; b. Chgo., Sept. 3, 1926; children: John, Jeremy, Joshua. AB, Radcliffe Coll., 1947. Lectr. English Cornell U., 1968-73, adj. assoc. prof. English Ithaca, NY, 1973-76, assoc. prof., 1976-79, prof., 1979—. Author: V.R. Lang: A Memoir, 1959, Love and Friendship, 1962, The Nowhere City, 1965, Imaginary Friends, 1967, Real People, 1969, The War Between the Tates, 1974, Only Children, 1979, The Language of Clothes, 1981, Foreign Affairs, 1984 (Pulitzer prize in fiction, 1985), The Truth About Lorin Jones, 1988, Don't Tell the Grownups, 1990, Women and Ghosts, 1994, The Last Resort, 1998, Familiar Spirits, 2001, Boys and Girls Forever, 2003, Truth and Consequences, 2005. Recipient award in lit. Am. Acad. Arts and Letters, 1978; fellow Yaddo Found., 1963-64, 66, Guggenheim Found., 1965, Rockefeller Found., 1967, Prix Femina Etranger, 1989. Mem.: Am. Acad. Arts and Letters (v.p. 2006—). Mailing: Am Acad Arts and Letters 633 West 155th St New York NY 10032 Business E-Mail: al28@cornell.edu.*

LURIE, ANN LASALLE, investment company executive, foundation administrator; b. Fla. m. Robert H. Lurie (dec. 1990); 6 children. BS in Nursing, Univ. Fla. Former pub. health, pediatric intensive care nurse; pres. Lurie Investments, Chgo., 1990—; pres., treas. Ann and Robert H. Lurie Foundation, Chgo., 1992—; founding pres. Africa Infectious Disease (AID) Village Clinic, Kenya, 2002—. Bd. trustees Northwestern Univ. Named one of Top 10 Women in Philanthropy, Chgo. Sun-Times, 100 Most Influential Women, Crain's Chicago Bus., 2004; recipient Jane Addams History Maker award for distinction in social services. Office: Ann and Robert H Lurie Found Ste 1500 2 N Riverside Plz Chicago IL 60606

LURIE, NICOLE, former health science association administrator; BA, U. Pa., 1975, MD, 1979; MSPH, UCLA, 1982. Resident UCLA, 1982; cons. RAND Corp., Santa Monica, Calif.; asst. prof. medicine UCLA; asst. to assoc. prof. U. Minn., prof. medicine and pub. health, 1985-98, dir. primary care rsch. and edn., dir. divsn. gen. and internal medicine; prin. dep. asst. sec. for health Office Pub. Health and Science, Washington, 1998—2001; senior researcher Rand Corp., 2002—. Former sr. assoc. editor Health Svcs. Rsch. Recipient Henry J. Kaiser Found. Faculty Scholar award, 1987, Nellie Westerman Prize for Rsch. in Ethics, 1987, Young Investigator award Assn. Health Svcs., 1990, Heroine in Health Care award Minn. Women's Consortium, 1994, award Am. Soc. Clin. Investigation, 1995, Article of Yr. Assn. Health Svcs., 1996, spl. recognition for Physical-Led Rsch. Minn. Physicians, 1997. Mem.: Soc. Gen. Internal Medicine (coun., treas., pres.), Inst. of Medicine. Office: Rand Corp 1200 South Hayes St Arlington VA 22202-5050

LUSHER, JEANNE MARIE, pediatric hematologist, educator; b. Toledo, June 9, 1935; d. Arnold Christian and Violet Cecilia (French) L. BS summa cum laude, U. Cin., 1956, MD, 1960. Resident in pediat. Tulane divsn. Charity Hosp. La., New Orleans, 1961-64; fellow in pediat. hematology-oncology Child Rsch. Ctr. Mich., Detroit, 1964-65, St. Louis Children's Hosp./Washington U., 1965-66; instr. pediat. Washington U., St. Louis, 1965-66; from instr. to prof. Sch. Medicine Wayne State U., Detroit, 1966—97, disting. prof., 1997—; dir. divsn. hematology-oncology Children's Hosp. Mich., Detroit, 1976—. Marion I. Barnhart prof. hemostasis rsch. Sch. Medicine Wayne State U., Detroit, 1989—; med. dir. Nat. Hemophilia Found., N.Y.C., 1987—94, chmn. med. and sci. adv. coun., 1994—2001, bd. dirs., 1997—2001, co-chmn. gene therapy working group, 2000—; pres. Wayne State U. Acad. of Scholars, 2004—05. Author, editor: Treatment of Bleeding Disorders with Blood Components, 1980, Sickle Cell, 1974, 76, 81, Hemophilia and von Willebrand Disease in the 1990's, 1991, Acquired Bleeding Disorders in Children, 1981, F VIII/von Willebrand Factor and Platelets in Health and Disease, 1987, Inhibitors to Factor VIII, 1994, Blood Coagulation Innhibitors, 1996. Mem. Citizens Info. Com., Pontiac Township, Mich., 1980-82; apptd. mem. Hazardous Waste Incinerator Commn., Oakland County, Mich., 1981. Recipient Disting. Alumnus award U. Cin. Alumni Assn., 1990, Lawrence Weiner award Wayne State U. Sch. Medicine Alumni Assn., 1991, Disting. Career award Am. Soc. Pediat. Hematology-Oncology, 2000, Disting. Career award Nat. Hemophilia Found., 2003. Mem. Am. Bd. Pediat. (chmn. sub-bd. on hematology-oncology 1988-90), Am. Soc. Hematology (chmn. sci. com. pediat. 1991-92, sci. com. hemostasis 1998—), Am. Pediat. Soc., Soc. Pediat. Rsch., Internat. Soc. Thrombosis-Hemostasis (chmn. factor VIII/IX subcom. 1985-90, chmn. sci. and standardization com. 1996-98), Mich. Humane Soc., Humane Soc. U.S., Wayne State U. Acad. Scholars (pres. 2004-05). Avocations: nature, wildlife. Office: Children's Hosp Mich 3901 Beaubien Blvd Detroit MI 48201-2119 E-mail: jlusher@med.wayne.edu.

LUSK, DELLA S., psychologist; d. Lee Washburn Lusk. BA, Smith Coll., 1988; PhD, Calif. Sch. Profl. Psychology, San Diego, 1996. Lic. psychologist, Ariz.; cert. sch. psychologist, Ariz. Bilingual sch. psychologist Flagstaff (Ariz.) Unified Sch. Dist., 1993—98; clin. psychologist Ariz. Behavioral Health, Flagstaff, 1996—, clin. dir., 1996—. Mem. APA. Office: Ariz Behavioral Health Assocs PC 710 N Beaver St Flagstaff AZ 86001-3145 E-mail: info@psychotherapy.com.

LUSK, GLENNA RAE KNIGHT (MRS. EDWIN BRUCE LUSK), librarian; b. Aug. 16, 1935; d. Otis Harvey and Lou Zelle Knight; m. Bruce 2d Edwin Lusk, Nov. 28, 1970; m. John Earle Uhler, May 26, 1956; children: Anne Knight, Camille Allana. BS, La. State U., 1956, MS, 1963. Asst. libr. Iberville Parish Libr., Plaquemine, La., 1956—57, 1962—68; tchr. Iberville Parish Pub. Schs., Plaquemine, 1957—59, Plaquemines Parish Pub. Schs., Buras, La., 1959—61; dir. Iberville Parish Libr., Plaquemine, 1969—89. Chmn. La. State Bd. Libr. Examiners, 1979—89; pres. Camille Navarre Gallery, Ltd., Zachary, La., 1989—94. Author (with John E. Uhler Jr.): Cajun Country Cookin', 1966, Rochester Clarke Bibliography of Louisiana Cookery, 1966, Royal Recipes from the Cajun Country, 1969, Iberville Parish, 1970. Mem. Iberville Parish Econ. Devel. Coun., Plaquemine, 1970—71; sec. Iberville Parish Bicentennial Commn., 1973—; mem. La. Bicentennial Commn., 1974; bd. dirs. McHugh House Mus., 1991—92. Named Outstanding Young Woman Plaquemine, La. Jr. C. of C., 1970. Mem.: Capital Area Libr. (chmn. com. 1972—74), Riverland Libr. Assn. (sec. 1973—74), La. Libr. Assn. (sect. chmn. 1967—68). Republican. Episcopalian. Home: 13291 Legacy Ct Baton Rouge LA 70816-7936

LUSK, MARY MARGARET, music educator; b. Athens County, Ohio, Mar. 17, 1936; d. Raymond Edward and Clara Grace (Johnston) Sanborn; m. Harold Waldo Mowery, Jan. 3, 1953 (div. Apr. 1961); children: Margaret Maria Barnhill, Harold Waldo 2nd; m. Ned Eugene Lusk, June 22, 1961; children: Bonita Jean Denig, Amy Beth Noykos, Melissa Kae Pfenning. Student, Ashland Jr. Coll., Russell, Ky., 1955—56, Ohio No. U., 1957. Apprentice music tchr., Nelsonville, Ohio, 1951—53; pvt. music tchr., 1951—. Traveling pianist Princeton Sem. Summer Mission Tour, 1949-52; ch. and youth camp music instr., 1953-60; adjudicator Teen Talent Contests, Ctrl. and Northwestern Ohio, 1968—; organist Patrick Heinl Funeral Home, 1976-88, Bayliff and Eley Funeral Home, 1988—. Columnist Wapakoneta Daily News, 1987—90; author: poetry. Dir., leader Singing Lusk Family, 1975—; active Ohio Alliance for Arts Edn., 2002—; min. music Ch. of the Nazarene, Wapakoneta, Ohio, 1968—76, Cridersville, Ohio, 1976—83, First Presbyn. Ch., St. Marys, Ohio, 1984—85, United Meth. Ch., Botkins, Ohio, 1986—88, Salem United Meth. Ch., Wapakoneta, 1988—99; organist Byron Ch., Fairborn, Ohio, 2000—06, Botkins United Meth., 2006—, Uniopolis United Methodist, 2006—. Mem.: Pub. Employee's Retirement Sys., Northwestern Ohio Music Tchrs. Assn., Ohio Music Tchrs. Assn., Music Tchrs. Nat. Assn. Republican. Avocations: reading, writing, travel, collecting miniature pianos, collecting precious moments figurines. Home: 920 Springwood Ln Wapakoneta OH 45895-9236 Office Phone: 419-738-6940. E-mail: mlusk@bright.net.

LUSK, PEGGY JUNE, retired counseling administrator; b. Springfield, Mo., Aug. 31, 1925; d. James G. and Cecile C. (Slagle) L. BA magna cum laude, Drury U., Springfield, 1947; MA, Syracuse U., NY, 1950; postgrad., U. Chgo., 1958-61. Field dir., camp dir. Girl Scouts U.S.A., Springfield, 1946-48; student dean Syracuse (N.Y.) U., 1948-50; resident counselor Winthrop Coll., Rock Hill, S.C., 1950-52; asst. dean women, instr. Ohio Wesleyan U., Delaware, 1952-58; asst. dean students U. Chgo., 1958-61; counselor, asst. prof. Rush Presbyn. St. Luke's Med. Ctr., Chgo., 1961-96, ret., 1996. Recipient Friend of Nursing award Rush U., Chgo., 1993; Danforth faculty fellow, 1956. Mem. AAUP, Nat. League for Nurisng, Am. Counseling and Pers. Assn., Am. Assn. Mental Health Workers, Nat. Assn. for Women in Edn., Am. Assn. for Higher Edn., Ill. Assn. for Women in Edn. (exec. bd., pres. 1977-79), Alumni Assn. Drury Coll. (pres. Chgo. chpt. 1961-63), Mortar Board. Avocations: classical music, gardening, bird study, camping. Office: Rush Presbyn St Lukes Med 1743 W Harrison St # 840 Chicago IL 60612-3823

LUSTED, DONA SANDERS, music educator, consultant, organist; b. Washington, Oct. 2, 1951; d. Troy Harry and Rosemarie (Klemann) Sanders; m. Barry Emile Lusted, Nov. 7, 1982; children: Lori Marie, Luke Alan. Degree in ch. music, Evang. Landeskirchen Musik., Dusseldorf, Germany, 1969; BS in Music Edn. and German, Jacksonville State U., 1973; MM in Piano Performance, La. State U., 1975, PhD in Music, 1984. Instr. Northeastern Okla. State U., Tahlequah, 1975-76, Baker (La.) Mid. Sch., 1976-77; organist First United Meth Ch., Tahlequah, 1975-76; assoc. dir. music, organist Broadmoor United Meth. Ch., Baton Rouge, 1977—; pvt. music instr. Okla., Ala., La., 1969—; instr. La. State U., Baton Rouge, 1978-79. Dir. Summer Music and Arts/Theater Camp, Baton Rouge, 1987—; adjudicator Okla. Fedn. Music Clubs, Muskogee, 1976, Bayouland Choral Festival, Nichols State U., Thibadoux, 1994, 2000, Baton Rouge Choral Soc., 1978-79; co-founder/co-dir. South La. chpt. Choristers Guild, 1994-2000. Mem. Am. Guild Organists, Music Tchrs. Nat. Assn., La. Fedn. Music Clubs, Baton Rouge Piano Tchrs. Methodist. Avocations: swimming, reading, travel. Home: 10709 Waverland Dr Baton Rouge LA 70815-5056 Office: Broadmoor United Meth Ch 10230 Mollylea Dr Baton Rouge LA 70815-4698 Office Phone: 225-924-6269. E-mail: dllb@juno.com.

LUSTENADER, BARBARA DIANE, human resources specialist; b. Albany, NY, Nov. 26, 1953; d. Charles Elmer and Janet Barbara (Bergh) Setzer; m. Robert Alan Lustenader, May 20, 1972. BA in English, Coll. St. Rose, Albany, 1974; MA in English, SUNY, Oswego, 1979; postgrad., Northwestern U. Cert. sr. profl. human resources, global profl. in human resources, compensation profl., global remuneration profl., tng. generalist, instrnl. designer, tng.facilitator, master trainer. Tchr. English Port Byron (N.Y.) Ctrl. Schs., 1974-79; sales exec. Miller/Hahn, Auburn, NY, 1979—80; exec. asst. to v.p. devel. Wells Coll., Aurora, 1980-83, adminstrv. asst. to pres., 1983-85, assoc. dir. admissions, 1985-87; asst. div. mgr. human resources Yaskawa Electric Am., Inc., Northbrook, Ill., 1987-89, divsn. mgr. corp. adminstrn. and human resources, 1989-90, dir. adminstrn. and human resources, br. mgr., 1990-94; pres. Lake Assocs., Inc., Albany, 1994—. Adj. instr. Coll. St. Rose, 2002—. Columbia Greene CC, 2006—; spkr. in field. Mem. Lake County Youth Conservation Corps, Ill., 1993—96, chmn. 501(3)(c) com. Ill., 1993—94; bd. dirs., vol., co-chmn. Friends Schweinfurth Meml. Art Ctr., Auburn, 1983; bd. dirs., sec., chmn. human resource com., mem. nominating com. YWCA Lake and McHenry Counties, 1995—97; bd. dirs., co-chair student chpts. Capital Region Human Resources Assn., 2001—02, v.p., 2002—03, chair website mgmt. com., 2002—03, pres., 2003—04, chair salary survey com., 2002—, co-chair human resources exec. briefing series, 2004—, co-chair human resources leadership program, 2006—, chair nominating com., 2004—05. Mem.: LWV (fin. chmn. Cayuga County, N.Y. chpt. 1984—86, bd. dirs.), Human Resource Exec. Roundtable (chair salary survey com. 2003—, co-chair 2004—), N.Y. State Soc. for Human Resource Mgmt., Inc. (certification dir. 2001—06, chair white paper com. 2004—06), Bus. Coun. N.Y. State, Lake County Women in Mgmt. (awards com. 1991, 1994, chair program com. 1994—96, awards com. 1995, chair 1996, Women of Achievement award 1996), Am. Soc. Healthcare Human Resource Adminstrs., WorldatWork, MRA/The Mgmt. Assn. (co-chmn. pers. generalists roundtable 1987—97, compensation com. 1989—2000, human resources policies and practices com. 1989—2000, Outstanding Individual Contbr. award 1995), No. Ill. Soc. Human Resource Mgmt. (fin. com. 1990, cert. com. 1995—96, program com. 1996—97, Profl. Excellence award 1995), Nat. Women in Mgmt. Orgn. (Charlotte Danstrom award 1996), Basically Bach (devel. com. 1991). Office: Lake Assocs Inc 18 Thatcher St Albany NY 12207-3009 Office Phone: 518-732-0526.

LUSTENBERG, MICHELLE WILLIAMSON, gifted and talented educator; b. Rabbit Hash, Ky., Mar. 22, 1968; d. Rita Ryle and Kenny Dean Williamson; m. Jeffrey Alan Lustenberg, Aug. 5, 1989; children: Michayla Jullaine, Madison Marta, Maya Victoria, Mikinley Grace. B, M, No. Ky. U. Cert. Teacher Nat. Bd. for Profl. Tchg. Standards Bd., 2002. Elem. art tchr. No. Elem., Butler, Ky., 1992—95; mid. sch. art tchr. Phillip A. Sharp Mid. Sch., Butler, Ky., 1995—2001; gifted and talented tchr. Pendleton County Schools, Falmouth, Ky., 2001—. Arts & humanities lead tchr. Phillip A. Sharp Mid. Sch., Butler, Ky., 2002—; Ky. cac com. for arts & humanities Ky. Dept. of Edn., Frankfort, 1999—2002; artfest coord. Ky. Art Edn. Assn., Richmond, 2000—, v.p., 1998—2001; southeastern region mid. level dir. Nat. Art Edn. Assn., Reston, Va., 2002—03; evening of the arts coord. Pendleton County Schools, Falmouth, Ky., 1997—, summer enrichment tchr., 1995—. Contbr. monotypes Licking Valley Review. Coord. of Pendleton county's walk for a cure Am. Diabetes Assn.; team capt. for sharp mid. sch. relay for life team Am. Cancer Soc.; bible sch. tchr. East Bend Bapt. Ch., Rabbit Hash, Ky. Grant, Very Spl. Arts Ky., 1996, Ky. Sch. to Work, 1997, Pendleton County 109 Environ. Bd., 1996, Ky. Art Edn. Assn., 1998, Pendleton County 109 Environ. Bd., 1997, 1998, 1998, grant, 1999, 2000. Mem.: Ky. Art Edn. Assn. (artfest coord. 1999—2003, Mid. Sch. Art Educator of the Yr. 2000, 2001), Ky. Assn. for Gifted Edn., East Bend Bapt. Ch. Independent-Republican. Bapt. Achievements include 2000 & 2001 Kentucky Middle School Art Educator of the Year; 2000-01 Pendleton County Chamber of Commerce Teacher of the Year; 1998-99 & 2000-01 Phillip A. Sharp Middle School Teacher of the Year; 1997 & 2001 Who's Who Among American Teachers; 1996-97 Pendleton County Conservation District Teacher of the Year; 2001 Esteemed Educator Citations from Kentucky House Representative Tom McKee and Senator Katie Stine. Avocations: parenting, digital photography, printmaking, sewing, learning. Home: 1245 Baker Williams Rd Corinth KY 41010 Office: Pendleton County Schools 35 Wright Rd Butler KY 41006 Personal E-mail: mlustenberg@aol.com. E-mail: mlustenber@pendleton.k12.ky.us.

LUSTGARTEN, CELIA SOPHIE, freelance consultant, writer; b. N.Y.C., Oct. 24, 1941; d. Benjamin and Sarah Goldie (Marcus) L. Author numerous poems, short stories. Recipient 1st prize for short story Alt. Realities Soc. and Imaginative Fiction Soc., Victoria, B.C., Can., 1986. Avocation: travel. Home: c/o Carol Goldstein 130-30 68th Ave #2C Forest Hills NY 11375 E-mail: cgarten_1@netzero.com.

LUSTIG, SUSAN GARDNER, occupational therapist; b. Beloit, Wis., Apr. 27, 1942; d. James and Sally Howell; m. Karl Lustig, Aug. 16, 1969 (div. 1997); children: Kurt, Daniel, Benjamin, David, Amy, Richard, Lauren. BS with distinction, U. Minn., 1965. Lic. occupl. therapist. Occupl. therapist Minn. State Hosp., Hastings, 1965—66; occupl. therapy cons. Hawaii Divsn. Vocat. Rehab., Honolulu, 1966—67; occupl. therapist Kaneohe State Hosp., Kaneohe, Hawaii, 1967, Minn. VA Hosp., Mpls., 1967—68, unit supr., 1968—70; chief occupl. therapist, mgr. occupl. therapy dept. Avery Health Care Sys., Newland, NC, 1997—2000; established occupl. therapy depts. Autumn Care Marion.Autumn Care, Drexel, NC, 2000—01, occupl. therapist, 2001—05, Yancey County Schs., 2005—, Evergreen Rehab and Carolina Therapy Svcs., 2005—. Mem Nat. Bd. Cert. Occupl. Therapy, 1997—; del. to Russia, People to People Amb. Program. Pres. LaSalle County Med. Aux., Ill., 1976—78; tutor, mentor Burke County Elem. Sch. Students; organist New Life Bapt. Ch., Newland, NC, 2003—, Crossmore 1st Bapt. Ch., NC, 1999—2001; organist, pianist, dir. of music Linville River Bapt. Ch., NC; organist, Sunday sch. tchr. Long Ridge Bapt. Ch., 2001—03; bd. dirs. Harrison County Sheltered Workshop, 1971—72, Ottawa Pub. Health Nursing, Ill., 1976—78, Cooking for Christ, 1998—2002, Heartland Christian Acad. Sch., 1986—88, Diversified Industries, Port Angeles, Wash., 1980—82. Mem.: N.C. Occupl. Therapy Assn., Nat. Bd. for Cert. of Occupl. Therapists, Am. Occupl. Therapy Assn. Republican. Baptist. Avocations: organ, antiques, woodcarving, ice skating, reading. Home: 15 Little Cow Camp Rd Newland NC 28657-8704

LUSTYK, MARY KATHLEEN, neuroscientist, educator; d. Vincent de Paul and Patricia Ann Burkhart; m. Michael John Lustyk, Dec. 12, 1993; children: Zachery Michael, Luke Vincent. BS in Psychology, U. Wash., 1988, PhD, 1992. Asst. prof. Seattle Pacific U., 1996—2000, assoc. prof. psychology, 2000—, adj. faculty, 1995. Affiliate assoc. prof. U. Wash. Sch. Nursing, Seattle; affiliate prof. U. Wash., 1996—; presenter in field. Contbr. articles and abstracts to profl. jours. Mem.: Stress and Anxiety Rsch. Sco., We. Psychol. Assn., Am. Psychol. Soc., APA, Psi Chi.

LUTCHMAN, EVA, elementary school educator; arrived in U.S., 1989; children: Liane, Lola Siewdass. BA in Math., York U., Toronto, Can., 1976; EdB in Math., Ont. Tchr. Edn. Coll., Toronto, 1977. Cert. flight attendant Air Can., profl. tchr. Fla. Flight attendant Air Can., Toronto, 1972—77; math tchr. grades 6-12 Pleasantville Sr. Compr. Sch., Trinidad, West Indies, 1977—89, Alt. Edn.-King H.S., Tampa, Fla., 1989—2001; math. tchr. Pierce Middle Sch., Tampa, 2001—03, Perry Middle Sch., Miramar, Fla., 2003—, math dept. head, 2004—. Adj. instr. math. Hillsborough C.C., Tampa, 1993—2003, Broward C.C., Pines/Hollywood, Fla., 2003—; mem. Discipline Com., 2003—, Faculty Coun., 2003—; math. competition coord. Title 1 Math. Challenge, 2003—. Named Tchr. of Yr., Alt. Edn. Hillsborough County, 1998—99. Mem.: Broward County Coun. Tchrs. Math. (math competition coord. 2003—). Home: Apt 203 10777 S Preserve Way Miramar FL 33025 Office: Broward Cmty Coll 7200 Pines/Hollywood Blvd Hollywood FL 33024

LUTES, CHARLENE ANN, academic administrator, director, consultant; d. Charles Frederick Tonagel and Anne Mae Tonagel (maiden, Miskovitch); m. Dennis L. Lutes, Sept. 18, 1993; children: Annie Mae Kelly, Andrew Steven. B of Journalism & Bus. Adminstrn., Ball State U., 1967; M of Ednl. Adminstrn., Ctrl. Mich. U., 1991; PhD, Mich. State U., 2005. Cert. tchr. grades 6-12 Ball State U., Muncie, Ind., 1967, provisional tchr. grades 7-12 State of Mich., 1991. Columnist, film writer Lafayette Jour. & Courier and Sojourn Prodns., Ind., 1970—74; dir. pub. affairs Interlochen Ctr. Arts, Interlochen, Mich., 1975—78; cmty. program designer Northwestern Mich. Coll., Traverse City, 1979—87; coord., writer TV 7 film Sojourn Productions, Cedar, 1980—89; trainer, instr. Northwestern Mich. Coll., Traverse City, 1989—94, transition coord., bridge program, 1994—. Nat. adv. bd. Nontraditional Student Report, Palm Beach Gardens, Fla., 2004—; mich. family independence agy. edn. & tng. com. State Mich. Governor's Office, Lansing, 1994—2000; pathways from poverty action team North Ctrl. Regional Ctr. Rural Devel., Des Moines, 1996—98; women's resource ctr. founder Zonta Internat., Traverse City, 1994—. Vol. Women's Resource Ctr., Traverse City, 1994—2004. Named Outstanding Educator Yr., Traverse City Area C. of C., 2003; recipient Nat. Coun. Workforce Edn. award, 2003. Mem.: Mich. Assn. Adult and Continuing Edn., Mich. Assn. Cmty. and Adult Edn., Nat. Nontraditional Students Network, Zonta Club Traverse City (founder, scholar 1994—2005, Traverse City Zonta Internat. 2003, Woman of Yr.). Independent. Achievements include development of creation of a community college program to allow nontraditional learners to access higher education; first American woman in northernmost Greenlandic village of Kulusuik in 1971. Avocations: licensed glider pilot, columnist, motivational speaker and trainer. Office: Northwestern Mich Coll 1701 East Front St Traverse City MI 49686 Office Phone: 231-995-1971. Home Fax: 231-995-1972; Office Fax: 231-995-1972. E-mail: clutes@nmc.edu.

LUTHER, SIGRID, music educator; b. Milw., July 27, 1948; d. Norman Cyrus and Marilyn Joyce (Carlson) Skogstad; m. David Alan Luther, Dec. 30, 1969; children: Kelly Lynn, Tara Joy. BA, Bob Jones U., 1970; MusM, La. State U., 1978, D in Musical Arts, 1986. Instr. music Pillsbury Bapt. Bible Coll., Owatonna, Tenn., 1970—73; staff accompanist New Orleans Bapt. Theol. Sem., 1974—76; tchg. asst. La. State U., Baton Rouge, 1976—78, 1983—84; prof. music Bryan Coll., Dayton, Tenn., 1978—, humanities chair, 1998—2002. Area chair Nat. Guild Piano Tchrs., Dayton, 1979—2001; founder, liaison Bryan Cmty. Music Sch., Dayton, 1985—. Named Hon. Alumna, Bryan Coll., 1995, Outstanding Tchr., Govs. Sch. for Arts, 1994; Boeppler scholar, Wis. Conservatory, 1966. Fellow: Music Tchrs. Nat. Assn. (pres. so. divsn. 2000—02, bd. dirs. 2002—04, chair code of ethics revision 2004—, nat. cert. tchr. music, chair divsn. pres. adv. coun., founder, advisor collegiate chpt.); mem.: Chattanooga Music Tchrs. Assn. (pres. 1981—83, Tchr. of Yr. 1983), Rhea Arts Coun. (music festival founder and chair 2002—), Tenn. Music Tchrs. Assn. (pres. 1995—97, found. fellow, Tchr. of the Yr. 1995), Pi Kappa Lambda, Phi Kappa Phi. Republican. Presbyterian. Avocation: interior decorating. Office: Bryan Coll PO Box 7818 Dayton TN 37321 Business E-Mail: luthersi@bryan.edu.

LUTHER-LEMMON, CAROL LEN, elementary school educator; b. Waverly, N.Y., May 8, 1955; d. Carl Rose and Mary Edith (Auge) Luther; m. Mark Kevin Lemmon, June 21, 1986; children: Mattew C. Lemmon, Cathryn M. Lemmon. BS, Ithaca Coll., 1976; MS in Edn., Elmira Coll., 1982. Cert. elem. and secondary tchr. Pa., N.Y. Reading aide Waverly Ctrl.l Schs., 1978-80; tchr. reading N.Y. State Divsn. Youth, Lansing, 1981-82; tchr. title I reading, mem. student assistance program and instrnl. support team Rowe Mid. Sch., Athens (Pa.) Area Sch. Dist., 1982-94; tchr. Title I reading Lynch Elem. Sch., 1995—. Robotics team advisor Waverly HS, 2003. Basketball coach Youth Activities Dept., Athens, 1982—85, asst. softball coach, 1990—91; mem. ad hoc com. Waverly Sch. Dist., 1990—91; mem. Goal G parents & edn. mid sch. implementation team WINGS-Waverly in Global Soc., Waverly Ctr. Sch. Dist. Strategic Plan; active Girls' Softball League, Waverly, 1978—80, commr., 1980; mem. Valley Chorus, Pa. and N.Y., 1983—86, 1998—2002, Village of Waverly Recreation Commn., 1999—; robotics advisor Waverly H.S., 2003—04; bd. dirs. Waverly Cmty. Ch., 1976—78; choir mem. Meth. Ch., Waverly, 1976—90, 1997—, adminstrv. bd., 1995, trustee, 1996, chmn. bd. trustees, 2001—03; bd. dirs. SACC, 1995—96. With USAR, 1977—83. Mem.: AAUW (v.p. Waverly br. 1982—83, pres. 1992—97), ASCD, N.Y. State Reading Assn., Chemung Area Reading Coun., Am. Legion Aux. (girl's state rep. 1972, girl's state chmn. 1976—80, Waverly post counselor 1977). Republican. Home: 490 Waverly St Waverly NY 14892-1102 Office: Athens Area Sch Dist Pennsylvania Ave Athens PA 18810-1440 Personal E-mail: c_lutherlemmon@yahoo.com.

LUTKENHOUSE, ANNE, non-profit executive; b. S.I., N.Y., Feb. 18, 1957; d. Emile Anthony and Jane Anne Lutkenhouse. BA magna cum laude, Wagner Coll., 1979; cert. Goethe Inst., N.Y.C., 1981, Emergency Med. Tech., State of N.Y., CPR Instr. Supr. Credit Suisse, N.Y.C., 1979-85; dist. office adminstr. N.Y. City Council, 1985-86; asst. dir., Appalachian Trail Field asst., N.Y.-N.J. Trail Conf., N.Y.C., 1986-01, asst. dir. Office of Grants and Rsch., Coll. S.I./CUNY, 2002—; mem. City U. of N.Y. Coun. of Grants Officers, 2002-; scholarship fundraising co-chmn., Wagner Coll.;dir. N.J. Appalachian Trail Ridge Runner Program; contbg. cons. Wagner Coll. Study Program, Bregenz, Austria, 1978-92. Photographer, producer photography show, 1984. instr. safety program ARC, S.I., 1977; campaign aide council member Fossella, N.Y. City Council, S.I., 1985; sec., bd. dirs. South Shore Swimming Club, Inc.; pres., bd. dirs. S.I. Chamber Music Players, 1984-86; co-chmn. Flag Day Parade, Tottenville Improvement Council, Inc., 1986; vol. Am.-Scandinavian Found.; producer Appalachian Trail 50th Anniversary Celebration, N.Y., 1987; alumni agt. telefund/ann. fund Wagner Coll., 1992. Recipient EMT Student Yr. award, St. Vincent's Cath. Med. Ctr./S.I. U. Hosp. Reg. Coun., 2003. Contbr. travel articles to mags; contbg. writer Appalachian Trailway News, 1987-2001, Appalachian Trail Guide to N.Y., N.J., 11th and 12th edts. Mem. NAFE, Am.-Scandinavian Found., Protectors of Pine Oak Woods, Norwegian-Am. C. of C. Democrat. Avocations: needlecrafts, ballet, skiing, travel. Home: 1100 Clove Rd Apt 9J Staten Island NY 10301-3633 Office: Coll of Staten Island/CUNY 1A-302 2800 Victory Blvd Staten Island NY 10314

LUTSYSHYN, OKSANA, concert pianist, organist; b. Sokal, Ukraine, July 22, 1964; d. Yaroslav and Lubov Lutsyshyn; m. Andrey Rafailovich Kasparov, Nov. 1, 1991. MusM, Moscow State Conservatory, 1987, MusD, 1991. Soloist and accompanist Chernovtsy State Philharmony, Chernovtsy, Ukraine, 1987—89; dir. ARK Mgmt., Bloomington, Ind., 1995—98; music dir., organist Prince Peace Luth. Ch., Virginia Beach, Va., 1999—; dir. Prince Peace Concert Series, 2000—. Pianist (concertizing) Concert Tours of Europe, Japan, Latin America, South Africa, South America and the United States, (recording) Andrey Kasparov's Toccata (Second prize Internat. Vienna Modern Masters Rec. Competition, 1997), (Grammy nomination, 1999), Recordings on VMM and CRS labels, (competition) William Kapell International Piano Competition (Prince George Coun. County Art prize, 1990), (recording) Appeared with violinist Joshua Bell and Josef Gingold in the BBC documentary, organist (organ recitals) Organ recitals throughout the United States and Ukraine. Bd. mem. Feldman Chamber Soc., Norfolk, Va., 2004—05; founding mem. Old Dominion U. Contemporary Musc. Ensemble, 1998—, Invencia Piano Duo, 2003—. Mem.: Coll. Music Soc. Home: 1460 Harmott Ave Norfolk VA 23509 Office: Prince Peace Luth Ch 424 Kings Grant Rd Virginia Beach VA 23452 Office Phone: 757-340-8420. Personal E-mail: oksana_lutsyshyn@yahoo.com.

LUTTRELL, GEORGIA BENA, musician; b. Carbondale, Ill., Oct. 24, 1927; d. George Newton and Phyllis Bena (Gent) Gher; m. Claude Edward Luttrell, Mar. 25, 1964 (dec. Aug. 1987). BA, So. Ill. U., 1947; MusM, Northwestern U., Evanston, Ill., 1948; postgrad., various univs. Asst. prof. music Huntingdon Coll., Montgomery, Ala., 1948-50; music supr. Community Unit Dist. 2 Williamson County, Marion, Ill., 1950-53; music tchr. Dubois Grade Sch., Springfield, Ill., 1953-55; dir. choral music Feitshas High Sch., Springfield, 1955-67; chairperson music dept. Springfield S.E. High Sch., 1967-83; ind. music coord./pianist Springfield, 1983—. Accompanist various soloists and choirs, 1944—; accompanist Ill. Music Educators Assn., 1956-66; talent adjudicator Ill. High Sch. Assn., 1957-89, Ill. Elem. Sch. Assn., 1957-89. Pianist Springfield Symphony Orch., 1954-55; author (poet): American Poetry Anthology, 1988, Love's Greatest Treasures, 1989. Dir. choirs Douglas United Meth. Ch., Springfield, 1964-72; choir dir. Unity Ch., Springfield, 1981-85; vol. vocalist Ill. Symphony Chorus, formerly Springfield Symphony Chorus, 1986—. Grantee Carnegie Rsch. Found., 1949, State of Ill., Evanston Twp. High Sch., 1968. Mem. Internat. Platform Assn. (gov., music dir., pianist), Ill. Ret. Tchrs. Assn. Avocations: swimming, writing, sewing, dance, crafts, travel.

LUTTRELL, MARY LOU, elementary school educator; b. Monroe County, Iowa, June 22, 1929; d. Forrest Charles and Catherine Cecilia (Stone) Sutcliffe; m. John Joseph, June 24, 1950; children: John S. (dec.), William A., Mary Elizabeth. AA, Ottumwa Heights Coll., 1949; BS in Elem. Edn., No. Ariz. U., 1969. Cert. tchr., N.Mex. 5th grade tchr. Albia (Iowa) Pub. Schs., 1949-51; 6th grade tchr. Chariton (Iowa) Pub. Schs., 1953-59, Cortez (Colo.) Pub. Schs., 1959-61, Cathedral Elem. Sch., Gallup, N.Mex., 1962-69; 5th grade tchr. Farmington (N.Mex.) Pub. Schs., 1969-90, sci.-math. advisor, 1994—; prin. Sacred Heart Sch., Farmington, 1990-92. Mem. N.Mex. history curriculum writing com. Farmington Pub. Schs., 1978-79. Pres. Lucas County Iowa Edn. Assn., 1957-58. Recipient Robert H. Taft Inst. Govt. award Robert H. Taft Found., 1976. Mem. N.Mex. Assn. Edn. Retirees, San Juan County Assn. Edn. Retirees (v.p. 1997, pres. 1998). Roman Catholic. Avocations: travel, reading, bridge. Home: 600 W 20th St Farmington NM 87401-3994 Personal E-mail: marylouluttrell@hotmail.com.

LUTZ, BETSY ANN, elementary school educator; b. Morris, Ill., Apr. 1, 1960; d. Louis Michael and Jean Ann Naretto; m. Kurt Allen Lutz, June 22, 1985; children: Michael Allen, Daniel Matthew, Kelsey Ann. BE, Ill. State U., 1982; EdM, Olivet Nazarene U., Kankakee, Ill., 1989. Cert. tchr. grades K-8 Ill., 1982. Tchr. Ford Ctrl., Thawville, Ill., 1982—85, Morris Dist. #54, Ill., 1985—. Home: 508 N Center St Gardner IL 60424 Office Phone: 815-942-0047.

LUTZ, DANIELLE RENEE, academic administrator; b. Dayton, Ohio, Dec. 18, 1957; d. Charles Ora and Nadina Kay Lutz. BA, U. So. Miss., Hattiesburg, 1981; MEd, U. Houston, Tex., 1988; EdD, Sam Houston State U., Huntsville, Tex., 2006. Cert. English tchr. Tex. Edn. Agy., 1988, journalism Tex. Edn. Agy., 1988, mid-mgmt. Tex. Edn. Agy., 1996, skills for adolesence Quest Internat., Nat., 1991. Tchr. Houston ISD, Houston, Tex., 1986—90, Cypress-Fairbanks ISD, Houston, Tex., 1990—93, asst. prin., 1993—98, grant coord., 1998—. Mem. adv. bd. adult edn. Harris County Dept. Edn., Houston, 2004—. Mem.: Tex. Assn. Secondary Adminstrn. (assoc.), ASCD (assoc.), Am. Assn. Grant Profls. (assoc.; treas. 2005—, mem. profl. growtha nd devel. nat. com. 2005—), SE Tex. After Sch. Assn. (assoc.; treas. 2005—, v.p. 2003—05, bd. mem. 2002—), After Sch. Initiative (assoc.; chairperson standards com. 2003—05, mem. adv. bd. 2003—05). Avocations: horse owner and competitor, travel, reading. Office: Cypress-Fairbanks ISD 10300 Jones Road Houston TX 77065 Office Phone: 281-517-6007. Office Fax: 281-517-2126. Business E-Mail: danielle.lutz@cfisd.net.

LUTZ, HEATHER, information scientist, researcher; m. Christopher Lutz. BS - Math. in Math., Pa. State U., University Park, 1996; MBA, George Wash. U., Washington, 1996—98. Program mgr. Agilent Technologies, Loveland, Colo., 1998—2003; instr. Syracuse U., Syracuse, NY, 2003—. Instr. Ednl. Soc. Resource Mgmt., Syracuse, NY, 2004—. Tchg. fellow, Syracuse U., 2005—. Office: Syracuse Univ Ste 311 721 Univ Ave Syracuse NY 13224 Office Phone: 315-443-3498. Office Fax: 315-443-5457.

LUTZ, LAURA ELISE, science educator; b. Kans. City, Mo., Aug. 15, 1961; d. Murrel Frances Bruce and Marilyn Mae Johnson; m. Gregory Vincent Lutz, Dec. 21, 1985; children: Patrick Joseph, Heather Nicole. BS, Eastern Ky. U., Richmond, Ky., 1984; MEd, U. S.C., Columbia, 1997. Cert. Nat. Bd. Profl. Tchg. Standards. Sci. educator Woodford County High, Versailles, Ky., 1986—88, Greenwood High, Greenwood, SC, 1988—94, Emerald High, Greenwood, SC, 1994—. Leader Boy Scouts, 1992—95, Girl Scouts, 1995—2003. Recipient Tchr. of the Yr., Emerald High, 2002, Outstanding H.S. Chemistry Tchr., Western Carolina ACS Section, 1993—94. Mem.: Palmetto Tchrs. Assn., S.C. Sci. Coun., S.C. Assn. Chemistry Tchrs. Republican. Christian. Office: Emerald HS 150 By Pass 225 Greenwood SC 29646

LUTZ, MARIE BURNS, retired secondary school educator; b. Tuscaloosa, Ala., Jan. 18, 1954; d. Alan Clifford and Ella Marie Burns; m. Richard Paul Lutz, Apr. 6, 1954. BEd., Auburn U., 1976, MEd., 1977, degree in Edn. Specialist, 1989. Cert. tchng. Okla., Ala. Music tchr. Montgomery (Ala.) Bd. Edn., 1976—2002; ch. choir dir. Ch. Holy Comforter, Montgomery, 1988—2002; mid. sch. tchr. McAlester (okla.) Pub. Schs., 2004—. Mem.: Am. Choral Dirs. Assn., Okla. Edn. Assn. (life), Delta Omicron (life), Tri-M Music Honor Soc. (life), Sigma Beta Phi. Avocations: travel, gourmet cooking. Home: PO Box 3823 Mcalester OK 74501-3823 Office: McAlester HS 1 Buffalo Dr Mcalester OK 74501 Office Phone: 918-423-4776. Business E-Mail: m.lutz@mcalester.k12.ok.us.

LUTZ, NANCY COLE, educational consultant; b. Rockford, Ill., Sept. 23, 1936; d. Sanford and Mildred Cole; m. Raymond P. Lutz. BA in English Edn., U. N.Mex., 1958, MA in English Lit., 1964; EdD in Curriculum and Instrn., N.Mex. State U., 1969. English tchr. John Adams Jr. H.S., Albuquerque, 1958—61, Ames (Iowa) Sr. H.S., 1961—64; asst. prof. edn./reading U. Okla., Norman, 1969; clin. practical reading Cleveland County Mental Health, Norman, 1970—73; curriculum cons., dir. Learning Ctr. U. Tex., Dallas, 1973—80; pvt. ednl. cons. Dallas, 1979—. Mng. editor: Engring. Economist, 1974—77; editor: Tech. Impact Assessment, 1974. Curriculum cons. U. Houston, 1973—75; mem. edn. com. annual fund com. Santa Fe Opera Bd., 2001—; mem. stewardship com. First Presbyn. Ch., Santa Fe, 2004—; bd. mem. United Cerebral Palsy Am., N.Y.C., 1984, United Cerebral Palsy, Dallas, 1973—80, pres., 1983—84. Grantee, State of Tex. Health and Edn. Adolescents, 1973—75. Mem.: Nat. Coun. Tchrs. Math., Coun. for Exceptional Children, Internat. Reading Assn., Sigma Alpha Iota, Pi Lambda Theta. Democrat. Avocations: opera, music, reading, gardening, hiking. Home and Office: 1230 Turquoise Trail Cerrillos NM 87010 Office Phone: 505-471-6709. Personal E-mail: nclutz@att.net.

LUXTON, JANE CHARLOTTE, lawyer; b. Phila., June 25, 1951; d. Elvin L. and Charoltte M. (Herring) Luxton; m. Charles Matz Horn, May 29, 1976; children: Andrew Luxton Horn, Caroline Charlotte Horn. BA, Harvard U., 1973; JD, Cornell U., 1976. Bar: D.C. 1976. Atty. advisor Commr. FTC, Washington, 1976-78; trial atty. US Dept. Justice, Washington, 1978-81; assoc. Steptoe & Johnson, Washington, 1981-86, Bell Atlantic, Washington, 1986-89; assoc., then ptnr. Prather Seeger Doolittle & Farmer, Washington, 1989-94; ptnr. Vedder Price, Kammholz PC, Washington, 1994-95, Seeger Potter Richardson Luxton Joselow & Brooks LLP, Washington, 1995-99, King & Spalding LLP, Washington, 1999—. Mem. ABA, D.C. Bar Assn. Republican. Office: King & Spalding LLP 1700 Pennsylvania Ave NW Washington DC 20006 Office Phone: 202-626-2627. Business E-Mail: jluxton@kslaw.com.

LY, VI KIM, artist, educator; b. Saigon, Vietnam, Jan. 10, 1967; came to U.S., 1980; d. Tai and Muoi (Huynh) L. BFA, U. Cin., 1990; MFA, San Francisco Art Inst., 1992. Asst. art dir. Euphrat Mus. Art, Cupertino, Calif., 1992-94; prof. art Monterey (Calif.) Peninsula Coll., 1994-96, Cabrillo (Calif.) Coll., 1994-95, San Jose (Calif.) City Coll., 1993-96; chair visual arts dept. Learning Tree U., Chatsworth, Calif., 1998; dept. chair media arts & animation, game art & design programs Art Inst. Calif. LA, Santa Monica, Calif., 1998—2004, asst. dean academic affairs, 2004—05, dean academic affairs, 2005—. Represented in permanent collections San Jose Mus. Art, 1996. Recipient Silver award Art of Calif. Mag., 1993, Crocker-Kingsley Merit award Crocker Art Mus., 1993. Mem. Women in Animation, L.S. Siggraph, Coll. Art Assn. Office: Art Inst Calif LA 2900 31st St Santa Monica CA 90405

LYALL, KATHARINE CULBERT, former academic administrator, economist, educator; b. Lancaster, Pa., Apr. 26, 1941; d. John D. and Eleanor G. Lyall. BA in Econs., Cornell U., 1963, PhD in Econs., 1969; MBA, NYU, 1965. Economist Chase Manhattan Bank, N.Y.C., 1963-65; asst. prof. econs. Syracuse U., 1969-72; prof. econs. Johns Hopkins U., Balt., 1972-77, dir. grad. program in pub. policy, 1979-81; dep. asst. sec. for econs. Office Econ. Affairs, HUD, Washington, 1977-79; v.p. acad. affairs U. Wis. Sys., 1981-85; prof. of econ. U. Wis., Madison, 1982—; acting pres. U. Wis. Sys., Madison, 1985-86, 91-92, exec. v.p., 1986-91, pres., 1992—2004, pres. emeritus, 2005—. Bd. dirs. Marshall & Ilsley Bank, Alliant, Carnegie Found. for Advancement of Tchg. Author: Reforming Public Welfare, 1976, Microeconomic Issues of the 70s, 1978, True Genius of America At Risk, 2005. Mem. Mcpl. Securities Rulemaking Bd., Washington, 1990-93. Mem. Am. Econ. Assn., Phi Beta Kappa. Business E-Mail: klyall@wisc.edu.

LYBARGER, MARJORIE KATHRYN, nurse; b. Holland, Mich., Apr. 23, 1956; d. Richard Simon and Mary Kathryn (Homan) Den Uyl; m. John Steven Lybarger, Aug. 22, 1981; children: Ashley Ann, Ryan Christopher. BA in Psychology, Biola U., Calif., 1979, BS in Nursing, 1984. RN, Calif. Staff nurse Presbyn. Intercommunity Hosp., Whittier, Calif, 1985-86, Healthcare Med. Ctr., Tustin, Calif., 1986-88; staff nurse med.-telemetry unit Friendly Hills Regional Med. Ctr., La Habra, Calif., 1988-90; staff nurse telemetry unit Riverside (Calif.) Community Hosp., 1990-93; staff nurse med. telemetry unit St. Anthony's Ctrl. Hosp., Denver, 1993-94; clin. RN 1 cardiovascular intermediate care unit St. Anthony's Ctr., Denver, 1994-98, staff RN, 1998—, case mgr., 1999—2002; staff RN float pool, case mgr. Luth. Med. Ctr., Wheatridge, Colo., 2002—05, RN case mgr. transitional care unit and CCU, 2005—. Mem. Gamma Phi Beta. Republican. Avocations: snowskiing, swimming, tennis. Home: 8489 W 95th Dr Broomfield CO 80021-5330 Personal E-mail: mklyb@aol.com.

LYCARDI, JOAN C., artist; b. Chgo., June 6, 1946; d. Tony P. Wojciechowski and Clara M Botwinski; children: Christopher Melnyk, Gregory Melnyk, Kerry Melnyk. Student, Am. Acad. Art, Chgo., 1979—81. Art dir. Rauch & Assocs., Orland Park, Ill., 1980—81; advt. asst. Vondrak Publs., Chgo., 1981—83; small bus. owner Cleaning Cruise, Chgo., 1984—2003. Pub. rels. Vondrak Publs., Chgo., 1982. Encyclopedia of Living Artists, 1988, The Chicago Art Review, 1989, Midway Review, 1981—82, exhibitions include Ft. Wayne Mus. Art, 1987—88, Lincoln Cultural Arts Found., 1988, Mamaroneck artists Guild, 1988, Dell Arte' Players, Ink People, 1988, Amos Eno Gallery, Soho, N.Y., 1987, Greeley Nat. Art Mart, 1987, one-woman shows include Monroe Gallery, Chgo., 1986, Am. Artists Gallery, 1986, SW Women Working Together, 1986, Chgo. Pub. Libr., Clearing br., 1986—87, West Lawn br., 1987, Talman Fed. Savs., Chgo., 1987, Marquette Fed. Savs., 1987, Matrix Gallery, Sacramento, Calif., 1988, Arc Gallery, Chgo., 1989, New Dimensions, Inc., 1990, exhibited in group shows at Riverbend Studios, Blue Island, Ill., 2003, Robert F. DeCaprio Art Gallery, Palos Hills, Ill., 2004—05, Blake-Lamb Art Show, Chgo., 2004, Mcpl. Art League Chgo., 2004, Manhattan Arts Internat. HERSTORY, N.Y.C., 2004 (Artist Profile award), Alice and Arthur Baer Art Competition, Chgo., 2004, Catharine Lorillard Wolf Art Club, N.Y.C., 2004, NW Cultural Coun., Rolling Meadows, Ill., 2004, Northbrook (Ill.) Pub. Libr., 2004, SW Art League, Inc., Indpls., 2004 (3d pl. award, 05), Tranzart-Art in Alternative Spaces, Chgo., 2004, 8th Annual Chgo. Art Open, 2005, Human Pixel Project traveling exhbn., Somerville, Mass., 2005, 8th Annual Chgo. Art Open, 2005, exhibited in group shows at Mcpl. Art League of Chgo., 2006, Robert F. DeCaprio Art Gallery, Palos Hills, Ill., 2006, Catharine Lorillard Wolf Art Club, N.Y.C., 2006, Pen & Brush, Inc., 2006, 9th Chgo. Art Open, 2006. Artist for newsletter and logo design SW Women Working Together, Chgo., 1981—82; mem. selection com. for pub. art Chgo. Pub. Libr., 1994; bd. mem. SW Women Working Together, Chgo., 1981. Recipient 1st pl., Chgo. Ridge Art Ctr., 1982, 2d pl. watercolor, S.W. Cultural Arts League, 1981—82, 3d pl. graphics, Fine Arts League, La Junta, Colo., 1987, 2d pl. drawing, Emerald City Classic Internat. Competition, Wichita, Kans., 1988. Mem.: Mcpl. Art League Chgo., Chgo. Artists' Coalition. Avocations: random acts of kindness, study of natural history, writing, fishing, gardening. Home and Studio: 10406 S 73rd Ct Palos Hills IL 60465 Office Phone: 773-450-3088. Personal E-mail: inki46@sbcglobal.net.

LYCETT, SARA F. See FINNEGAN, SARA

LYDDANE, ANNE ALEXANDRA, retired writer; b. Washington, Nov. 24, 1917; d. John Clarence and Mildred Katherine (Linder) L. Student, Fla. State U., 1936-38. Staff writer Llewellyn Publs., St. Paul, 1976-96, ret., 1996. Tchr., lectr. Asheville (N.C.) C.C., 1986-96, Charlottesville (Va.) C.C., 1986-96; freelance spkr., lectr. throughout U.S., 1986-96. Author: Kaleidoscope, 1985, Astrological Color Magic and You, 1985, Travellers' Rest, 1991, Angels, Incorporated, 1995, Love Is An Energy That Never Dies, 2000. Avocations: swimming, travel, historical research, gardening, tutoring. Home: Apt 114 12105 Ambassador Dr Colorado Springs CO 80921-3647

LYDICK, NANCY M., psychologist; b. Belville, Tex., June 18, 1942; d. John Samuel Jr. and Dale (Crawford) McCelvey; m. Larry Stuart Lydick (div.); children: L. Drew, Todd W.; m. M'Baye Fara Gaye, Sept. 23, 1999. BA in Psychology, Antioch U., West L.A., 1980; MA in Marriage, Family and Child counseling, Asuza Pacific U., L.A., 1982; PhD in Gen. Psychology, U.S. Internat. U., San Diego, 1994. Lic. Marriage and Family Therapist Calif., Pa. Intern Calif. Family Study Ctr., 1982, L.A. Psychiat. Ctr., 1993—94; drug counselor, dual diagnosis Parkside Recovery/ Dept Human Svcs., Phila., 1999—, dir. family program, 2002—; pres., CEO For Love of the Family, Inc., 2004—. Presenter confs. and workshops Various Assns. and Groups, in U.S. and Can.; dir. workshops Dream, Sex Edn., Adolescents, Eating Disorders; interat. spkr. Women, Youth and Family (an Islamic perspective). Author (producer and dir.): (TV series) Women in Islam, 1996; author: (producer and host) Healing from the Heart, 1998; columnist (monthly mag. article) Ask Nasiha. Nat. Fellowship Ahmadu Bamba Internat. Sufi Sch.; presenter Development in Literacy; pres. Khidmatul Khadim Internat. Sufi Sch.; mem. Greater Phila. Healthy Marriage Coalition; Vol. thrift shop, Big Sisters program, fund raiser Fort Worth Jr. League, Tex., 1965—73; vol. book mobile Nat. Coun. Jewish Women, Fort Worth, 1964. Mem.: Pa. Commn. for Health and Families, Phila. Assn. Marriage and Family Therapy, Acad. Family Mediators, Assn. Family and Conciliation Cts., Assn. Play Therapy, Internat. Assn. Eating Disorders Specialists, Am. Psychol. Assn., Calif. Assn. Marriage and Family Therapy (clin. mem.), Am. Assn. Marriage and Family Therapy (clin. mem.), Kappa Kappa Gamma (Epsilon Alpha chpt.). Islam. Office: Parkside Recovery 5000 Parkside Ave Philadelphia PA 19131 E-mail: nm.lydick@verizon.net.

LYERLA, KAREN DALE, special education educator; b. Kansas City, Kans., Aug. 2, 1948; d. Dale Donelly Lyerla, Alberta Pauline Cromer-Lyerla. BS, U. Kans., 1970, MS Honors, 1972, postgrad., U. Tex. Cert. Tchg. Tex., Kans. Tchr. learning disabled, homebound tchr. Round Rock H.S., Tex., 1973—75; tchr. learning disabled Lawrence H.S., Lawrence Alternative H.S., Kans., 1975—77, 1995—96, Lawrence H.S., Kans., 1977—95, 1996—, chair, spl. edn. dept., 2002—. Cons., ctr. rsch. in learning U. Kans., Lawrence, 1980—, tchr. strategy girl's basketball team, 1989—90; mem., faculty adv. commn. Lawrence H.S., Kans.; mem. Lawrence Leadership Coun., Kans.; mem., moderator Scholar's Bowl; dist. USD 497; trainer inspiration software, read and write gold software; assessment coord.; edn. plan revision team mem. U. SD, 2004; trainer inspiration software Read and Write Gold Program. Author: The Paragraph Writing Strategy, 1990, Pre-Writing Organizers, 2001, Thesis Statement, 2001, Themewriting: Format, Steps, Structure and Introductions, 2002, Themewriting: Body and Conclusions, 2002. Grantee Kans. Child Svc. Demostration Ctr.-Project STILE, 1984-1988. Mem.: Assn. Children with Learning Disabilities, Coun. on Exceptional Children (presenter Kans. Fedn. 1986, presenter 65th ann. conf. 1987), One Hundred Good Women, River City Women's Club (historian 1975—), Phi Delta Kappa. Avocations: exercise, reading, sports, music, travel. Home: 746 Alabama Lawrence KS 66044 Office: Lawrence High Sch USD 497 1901 Louisiana Lawrence KS 66046

LYERLY, CYNTHIA LYNN, history professor; b. Hickory, NC, May 14, 1960; d. David Mark and Sarah Anne Lyerly; m. Michael Sol Pollens, Aug. 0, 2003; 1 child, Michael Alexander Pollens. PhD, Rice U., Houston, 1995. Assoc. prof. Boston Coll., Chestnut Hill, Mass., 2001—. Author: (book) Methodism and the Southern Mind. Staff sgt. U.S. Army, 1982—89. Fellow, NEH, 1993—94, Women's Studies Religion Program, Harvard Div. Sch., 1998—99. Office: Boston College Department of History Chestnut Hill MA 02467 Office Phone: 617-552-3783.

LYERLY, ELAINE MYRICK, advertising executive; b. Charlotte, NC, Nov. 26, 1951; d. J.M. and Annie Mary (Myrick) L. AA in Advt. and Comml. Design, Cen. Piedmont Community Coll., 1972. Freelance designer Sta. WBTV, Charlotte, NC, 1972; fashion illustrator Matthews Belk, Gastonia, NC, 1972-73; designer Monte Curry Mktg. and Communication Svcs., Charlotte, 1973-74, exec. v.p., 1974-77; pres. Repro/Graphics, Charlotte, 1975-77, Lyerly Agy. Inc., Charlotte, 1977—. Organizing dir. First Trust Bank. Illustrator: Mister Cookie Breakfast Cookbook, 1985. Former chmn. regional blood com. Greater Carolinas chpt. ARC, 1990-93, mem. nat. implementation com., 1991, chair nat. conv., 2001, mem. nat. bd. govs., 2002-, Red Cross, nat. exec. com. and chair pub. support, nat. co-chair task force non-episodic fundraising, vice chmn. nat. bd. govs., 2006; bd. dirs. United Way, 1996, YMCA, Women's Impact Fund, 2003-, Levine Mus. of New South; bd. dirs., chair Child Care Resources, Inc., 2003-, Women's Impact Fund, 2002-; mem. bd. advisors Belmont Abbey Coll. Named Bus. Woman of Yr., Shearson Lehman Hutton/Queens Coll., 1989, N.C. Young Careerist Bus. and Profl. Women's Club, 1981; recipient ACE award Women in Comms., 1993, CPCC Hagemeyer award, 1996, Schley Lyons Leadership Charlotte award, 1999, Bus. Jour. Top 25 Women of Achievement award 2001. Mem. Women Execs., Women Bus. Owners (adv. coun., Leadership award 1990, Woman Bus. Owner of Yr. award 1994), Pub. Rels. Soc. Am. (Counselors Acad. 1985—), Charlotte C. of C. (bd. dirs., diversity coun., long-range planning com., Bus. Woman of Yr. award 1985), Hadassah. Republican. Jewish. Office: Lyerly Agy Inc 4819 Park Rd Charlotte NC 28209-3274 E-mail: elyerly@lyerly.com.

LYJAK CHORAZY, ANNA JULIA, pediatrician, educator, retired health facility administrator; d. Walter and Cecilia (Swiatkowski) Lyjak; m. Chester John Chorazy, May 6, 1961; children: Paula Ann Chorazy Peters, Mary Ellen Chorazy-Cuccaro, Mark Edward Chorazy. BS, Waynesburg Coll., 1958; MD, Women's Med. Coll. Pa., 1960. Diplomate Am. Bd. Pediat. Intern St. Francis Gen. Hosp., Pitts., 1960-61; resident in pediat., tchg. fellow Children's Hosp. Pitts., 1961-63, pediatrician, devel. clinic, 1966-75; pediat. house physician Western Pa. Hosp., Pitts., 1963-66; med. dir. Rehab. Instn. Pitts., 1975-98, Children's Inst., Pitts., 1998—2001, interim med. dir., 2002—03. Clin. asst. prof. pediat. Children's Hosp. Pitts. and U. Pitts. Sch. Medicine, 1971—94, clin. assoc. prof. pediat., 1994—2001; pediat. cons. Children's Home Pitts., 1985—2001. Author chpts. to books. Co-chmn. EACH Joint Planning and Assessment, Pitts., 1980-85; mem. adv. com. 10th Nat. Conf. on Child Abuse, Pitts., 1993. Recipient Miracle Maker award, Children's Miracle Network, 1995, Disting. Alumni award, Waynesburg Coll., 2002. Fellow Am. Acad. Pediat.; mem. Pitts. Pediat. Soc. Avocations: reading, comedy, theater, music, opera. Home: 131 Washington Rd Pittsburgh PA 15221-4437

LYKKEN, CATHERINE TOWNLEY, social worker; b. Norman, Okla., Mar. 21, 1936; d. Thomas Lee and Marie Winnie (Nemecek) Townley; m. Jerry Don Farren, June 8, 1963 (div. Feb. 1970); m. Gary Lee Lykken, Nov. 28, 1974. BA, U. Okla., 1959. Lic. real estate agt. Children's worker Wesley Community House, Louisville, 1959-63; caseworker Weld County Dept. Social Services, Greeley, Colo., 1965-68; asst. dir. Weld County Svcs. for Aging, Greeley, 1968-69; caseworker Routt County Social Svcs., Steamboat Springs, Colo., 1969-77, dir., 1977-85; instr. Colo. Mountain Coll., Steamboat Springs, 1985—93. Sec. Colo. County Dirs. Social Services Assn., 1982-84, Routt County Council Aging, Inc., 1975-78, bd. dirs. 1985-2000; sales assoc. Morrison & Assocs., Steamboat Springs, 1986-94; broker, owner Catherine Lykken Real Estate, Inc., 1995-; broker assoc. Coldwell Banker-Silver Oak Ltd., 2004-; pres.Routt County LWV, 2003-. Mem. Am. Soc. on Aging, Colo. Gerontol. Soc., LWV (pres. Routt County chpt. 1976-78, bd. dirs. 1985-86). Democrat. Avocations: gardening, skiing, cooking. Home: PO Box 770399 Steamboat Springs CO 80477-9998

LYLE, KATIE LETCHER, writer, educator; b. Peking, China, May 12, 1938; d. John Seymour and Elizabeth Marston Letcher; m. Royster Lyle Jr., Mar. 16, 1963; children: Royster Cochran, Virginia Letcher. BA, Hollins (Va.) Coll., 1959; MA, Johns Hopkins U., 1960. English prof. Southern Seminary, Buena Vista, Va., 1962-87. Adj. prof. Hollins Coll., 1987-93. Author: Lyrics of Three Women, 1964, I Will Go Barefoot All Summer for You, 1973, Fair Day, and Another Step Begun, 1974, The Golden Shores of Heaven, 1976, Dark But Full of Diamonds, 1981, Finders Weepers, 1982, Scalded to Death by the Steam, 1984, The Man Who Wanted Seven Wives, 1986, The Wild Berry Book, 1994, The Foraging Gourmet, 1997, When the Fighting is All Over, 1997, Goodbye to Old Peking 1936-1939, 1998, My Dearest Angel (letters of Katie Paul Letcher and Greenlee Davidson Letcher, 1895-1947), 2002, All Time is Now: Adventures with Jennie, 2004, The Complete Guide to Edible Wild Plants, Mushrooms, Fruits and Nuts, 2004; contbr. articles to profl. publs. Chmn. bd. New Hope Day Care, Lexington, Va., 1993; bd. dirs. Rockbridge Area Hospice, Lexington, 1996—, ARC Rockbridge, Lexington, 1980-93; adv. bd. Rockbridge Regional Libr., 1992-96. Bread Loaf fellow, 1973, Bread Loaf Tchg. fellow, 1974. Avocations: travel, reading, cooking, music, folklore. Home: 110 W Mcdowell St Lexington VA 24450 Personal E-mail: katieletcherlyle@rockbridge.net.

LYLE, VIRGINIA REAVIS, retired archivist, genealogist; b. Nashville, Apr. 19, 1926; d. Damon Ashley and Nellie Alice (Vaughan) R.; m. John Reid Lyle, Sept. 25, 1943; 1 child, Judith L. Haggard. BA, Vanderbilt U., 1974, MLS, 1975. Cert. genealogist, archivist. Administrv. officer Commerce Union Bank, Nashville, 1961-70, 75-78; rsch. asst. R.C.H. Mathews, Jr., Nashville, 1970-75, 78-79; genealogist Nashville, 1980; archivist Metro Nashville-Davidson County Archives, Nashville, 1981-93; ret., 1993; organizing sec. Friends of Metro Archives, 1994-95. Sec. Homecoming '86 Metro Steering Com. for Tenn., 1986; mem. Pub. Libr. Bd., 1978-81; historian, archivist Dalewood United Meth. Ch., 1995—. Mem. Tenn. Archivists, Nat. Geneal. Soc., DAR, Ladies Hermitage Assn., Soc. Am. Archivists, Acad. Cert. Archivists, Woman's Club of Nashville (adv. bd.), Historical Soc. Hopkins Co., Nat. Trust Historical Preservation, Middle Tenn. Genealogical Soc., Century Soc. Geo. Peabody Coll., Vanderbilt Univ. Methodist. Home: 36 Asbury Ln Hermitage TN 37076-2166

LYLES, BARBARA DIGGS, retired human development educator; b. Sewickley, Pa., Aug. 12, 1930; d. Lucien M. Diggs and Ruselle (Turner) Bembry; children: Jocelyn J., Russell B. III (dec.), Lauri C. BS, Marietta Coll., 1951; MA, Howard U., 1954; PhD, U. Md., 1971. Assoc. prof. human devel. Howard U., Washington, 1964-96, prof. emeritas, 1996—. AIDS lectr. Contbr. Strategies, Rhetoric and Reader, 1991, Powerful Reading, 1994; contbr. to Newsweek, 1989. Vol. Pub. Defenders Office, Balt., Clks. Office, 2001—; vol. lawyers at bail project U. Md. Law Sch., clks. office Borgerding Ct. House Dist., Balt., 2001. Named Tchr. of Yr., Howard U., 1978, 79, 80; grantee NSF, 1961, Ford Found., 1970-71; scholar Howard U., 1981. Democrat. Avocations: reading, flowers, writing. Home: Mt Washington Hills Condo 1703 Mt Washington Ct Baltimore MD 21209-4573

LYLES, TRACEE, art association administrator, actress; Grad. degree, Drake Coll., Jersey City, 1961. Founder, pres. Women in Focus, Inc., L.A.; actress Am. Acad. Dramatic Art, Negro Ensemble Co. Lectr. in field; founder, treas. Media Forum, L.A., 1975—83; co-founder, prodr. Wel Co., L.A., 1985—87. Poetry editor: Essence Mag., 1975—83; actor: (films) Lady Sings the Blues (Best Supporting Actress award Golden Globes), (TV series, movies-of-the-week, feature films); prodr.: The Book of the Crazy African (Drama-Logue Prodr. award); writer, prodr.: Downpayments (5 Drama-Logue awards, NAACP Best Prodr. award); writer: TV programs Gimmie a Break, What's Happening, Sugar and Spice; asst. to prodr.: (theatrical prodn.) My One Good Nerve, 1999. Mistress of ceremony New Frontier Dem. Club, L.A., 1985; cons., prodr. Pacific Bell Telephone Co., L.A., 1986—90; L.A. County commr. Motion Picture and Teleprodn. Task Force, 1996—98. Recipient Newsmaker award, Nat. Assn. Media Women, Inc., 1989, Disting. Heroine award, L.A. chpt. Top Ladies of Distinction, 1994, award, Creative Excellence in Bus. Advt., 1982, award for Best Supporting Actress, Hollywood Fgn. Press, Golden Globe awards, 1984. Mem.: ASCAP, AFTRA, SAG, Actors Equity, Writers Guild Am., Dramatists Guild. Achievements include KCET-TV TV spl. Voices of Our People produced by Media Forum won 10 Emmy awards. Avocations: exercise, bicycling, singing. Office: Women in Focus Inc PO Box 480436 Los Angeles CA 90048 Office Phone: 323-665-5385.

LYMAN, PEGGY, artistic director, dancer, choreographer, educator; b. Cin., June 28, 1950; d. James Louis and Anne Earlene (Weeks) Morner; m. David Stanley Lyman, Aug. 29, 1970 (div. 1979); m. Timothy Scott Lynch, June 21, 1982 (div. 1997); 1 child, Kevin Lynch; m. Richard R. Hayes, Feb. 26, 2005. BFA in Dance, U. Hartford, 2006. Solo dancer Cin. Ballet Co., 1964-68, Contemporary Dance Theater, 1970-71; chorus dancer N.Y.C. Opera, 1969-70; Radio City Music Hall Ballet Co., 1970; chorus singer, dancer Sugar, Broadway musical, N.Y.C., 1971-73; prin. dancer Martha Graham Dance Co., N.Y.C., 1973-88, rehearsal dir., 1989-90, assoc. rehearsal dir., 2005—; artistic dir. Martha Graham Ensemble, N.Y.C., 1990-91; faculty Martha Graham Sch., 1975—; co-artistic dir. Dance Conn., Hartford, 1998-2000. Head dance divns. No. Ky. U., 1977—78; artistic dir. Peggy Lyman Dance Co., N.Y.C., 1978—89; asst. prof. dance, guest choreographer Fla. State U., Tallahassee, 1982—89; guest choreographer So. Meth. U., Dallas, 1986; adjudicator Nat. Coll. Dance Festival Assn., 1983—; co-host To Make a Dance, QUBE cable TV, 1979; mem. guest faculty Am. Dance Festival, Durham, NC, 1984; site adjudicator NEA, 1982—84; tchr. Sch. Dance Conn., 1992—2004, East Conn. Concert Ballet, 1992—94; guest faculty Wesleyan U., Middletown, Conn., 1992; guest artist Conn. Coll., 1993; chair dance divsn. Hartt Sch., U. Hartford, Conn., 1994—2001, dir. dance divsn., Conn., 2002—04; freelance master tchr. internat. univs. Prin. dancer (TV spls.) Dance in America, 1976, 79, 84; guest with Rudolph Nureyev (CBS-TV) Invitation to the Dance, 1980; guest artist Theatre Choreographique Rennes, Paris, 1981, Rennes, France, 1983; Adelaide U., 1991; site dir. Martha Graham's Diversion of Angels for student concert U. Mich., 1992, Martha Graham's Panorama, U. Ill., Champaign-Urbana, 1993, Towson State U., 1997, Martha Graham's Diversion of Angels for Dutch Nat. Ballet, 1995, Diversion of Angels and Acts of Light for Dance Conn., 1998, Ballet Argentino, 1999, Lamentation For Ballet de Lorraine, 2004; choreographer: Conundrum (solo), 1982, Mantid (group), 1984, Roll, Spin, Draw, or Fold (group), 1984, Chope Dance (solo), 1985, Mirror's Edge (group), 1986, No Gavotte Bach (group), 1995, Interior Landscapes (group), 1997, Family Portrait (group), 1999, Yes, Is A World (group), 2002; co-creator (with John Feierabend) Move It (CD/DVD), 2003. Founding mem. Cin. Arts Coun., 1976-78. Mem. Am. Guild Mus. Artists. Office: care Martha Graham Sch Contemporary Dance 316 E 63d St New York NY 10021 Office Phone: 212-838-5886. Personal E-mail: peggylhayes@comcast.net.

LYNAM, BETH, elementary school educator; b. Lima, Pa., Aug. 15, 1979; d. Robert and Glenys Zigmont; m. James Keller Lynam, Apr. 12, 2003. BE, Drexel U., 2001; postgrad., Pa. State U. Cert. tchr. Pa. 4th grade tchr. Garnet Valley Sch. Dist., Glen Mills, Pa., 2001—05; 8th grade lang. arts and sci. tchr. Radnor Mid. Sch., Wayne, Pa., 2005—. Tchr. cons. Sci. in the Summer program GlaxoSmithKline, 2003; presenter in field. Recipient Keystone Tech. Innovator award, Pa. Dept. Edn., 2004. Mem.: ASCD, NSTA, Internat. Reading Assn., Discovery Educator's Network, Pi Lambda Theta. Avocations: traveling, reading, boating, playing the flute. Office: Radnor Mid Sch 131 South Wayne Avenue Wayne PA 19087 Office Phone: 610-688-8100. Personal E-mail: bzigmont@hotmail.com.

LYNAUGH, BARBARA, judge; d. Robert and Angelina Lynaugh; 1 child, Charles Robert Treadwell. JD with honors, Hofstra U., Hempstead, N.Y., 1984. RN N.Y. Staff atty. Suffolk County Legal Aid Soc., Central Islip, NY, 1985—93; family ct. hearing examiner Suffolk County Family Ct., Central Islip, 1993—2000, family ct. judge Riverhead, NY, 2001—. Mem.: Suffolk County Matrimonial Bar Assn., Suffolk County Women's Bar Assn., Suffolk County Bar Assn. Office Phone: 631-852-3845. Office Fax: 631-852-2986. Business E-Mail: blynaugh@courts.state.ny.us.

LYNCH, ALESSANDRA JACQUELINE, literature educator, poet; b. N.Y.C., Aug. 22, 1965; d. James F. Lynch and Jacqueline F. Oliva. BA, Sarah Lawrence Coll., Bronxville, N.Y., 1986; MFA, Iowa Writers' Workshop, Iowa City, Iowa, 1988; cert. in Tchg. Secondary Sch. English, Pace U., NY, 1997. Tchr. English Horace Greeley H.S., Chappaqua, NY, 1997—2003; vis. asst. prof. U. Pitts., Johnstown, Pa., 2003—. Author: Sails the Wind Left Behind, 2002 (award Alice James Books, 2002). Fellow, MacDowell Colony for Arts, 2003, The Corp. of Yaddo, 2005. Avocations: reading, running, gardening, travel, daydreaming. Home: 1937 Minno Drive Johnstown PA 15905 Office: University of Pittsburgh at Johnstown Johnstown PA 15905 Office Phone: 814-269-7166. Personal E-mail: awakadoodl@aol.com. Business E-Mail: alynch@pitt.edu.

LYNCH, BEVERLY PFEIFER, education and information studies educator; b. Moorhead, Minn. d. Joseph B. and Nellie K. (Bailey) Pfeifer; m. John A. Lynch, Aug. 24, 1968. BS, N.D. State U., 1957, L.H.D. (hon.); MS, U. Ill., 1959; PhD, U. Wis., 1972. Librarian Marquette U., 1959-60, 62-63; exchange librarian Plymouth (Eng.) Pub. Library, 1960-61; asst. head serials div. Yale U. Library, 1963-65, head, 1965-68; vis. lectr. U. Wis., Madison, 1970-71, U. Chgo., 1975; exec. sec. Assn. Coll. and Research Libraries, 1972-76; univ. librarian U. Ill.-Chgo., 1977-89; dean, prof. Grad. Sch. Libr. and Info. Sci. UCLA, 1989-94, prof. Grad. Sch. Edn. and Info. Studies, 1989—, dir. sr. fellows program, 1990—; interim pres. Ctr. for Rsch. Librs., Chgo., 2000-01; founding dir. Calif. Rare Book Sch., 2004—. Sr. fellow, vis. scholar UCLA, 1982. Author: (with Thomas J. Galvin) Priorities for Academic Libraries, 1982, Management Strategies for Libraries, 1985, Academic Library in Transition, 1989, Information Technology and the Remaking of the University Library, 1995. Recipient Cert. of Appreciation, Chinese Am. Librs. Assn., 2001; named Acad. Libr. of Yr., 1982, one of top sixteen libr. leaders in Am., 1990; fellow Indo-U.S. Subcommn. on Edn. and Culture, 1992-93; vis. scholar U. Nebr., 1981. Mem. ALA (pres. 1985-86, coun. 1998-2004, com. on accreditation 1999-2002, chair 1999-2000, co-chair joint com. ALA, Soc. Am. Archivist and Am. Assn. Museums 2005—), Nat. Info. Stds. Orgn. (bd. dirs. 1996-2005, vice chair 1999-2001, chair 2001-03), Acad. Mgmt., Am. Sociol. Assn., Assn. for the Study of Higher Edn., Bibliog. Soc. Am., Scottish Libr. Assn. (hon.), Caxton Club, Grolier Club, Book Club Calif., Phi Kappa Phi. Office: UCLA Grad Sch Edn Info Mailbox 951520 Los Angeles CA 90095-1520 Office Phone: 310-206-4294. Business E-Mail: bplynch@ucla.edu.

LYNCH, CAROL, special services director, psychologist; d. Joseph Louis and Ellen (Birish) Dobkowski; 1 child, Eric Alexander. BA, William Paterson Coll., 1966; MA, NYU, 1970, PsyD, 1984. Lic. psychologist, N.J., N.Y. Tchr. Bloomfield (N.J.) Pub. Schs., 1966-68, psychologist, 1970-87; dir. spl. svcs. Waldwick (N.J.) Pub. Schs., 1987—, acting supt. schs., 1995-96, 98. Adj. clin. prof. NYU, N.Y.C., 1983-86 adj. prof. Montclair (N.J.) State Coll., 1984-85. Mem. prof. alumni coun. Sch. Edn., Health and Nursing, NYU, 1989—91; alumni coun. chair Sch. Edn., NYU, 1991—93, sec., 2002—03; trustee First Church of Religious Sci., 2001—, bd. trustees, 2002—, lic. practitioner, 2005, v.p., 2006—. NYU fellow, 1981-82; recipient Best Practice award N.J. State Dept. Edn. for Fast Families Program, 1995, Disting. Grad. Brian E. Tomlinson Meml. award NYU, 1995, Exemplary Practice award N.J. Adminstrs. Assn./N.J. Sch. Bds. "Crisis Response Initiative," 2002. Mem. APA (sch. psychology task force 1989-90), N.J. Psychol. Assn. (treas. 1985-86, Sch. Psychologist of Yr. 2003), Nat. Assn. Sch. Psychologists (del. 1984-88), N.J. Assn. Sch. Psychologists (pres. 1982-83, Sch. Psychologist of Yr. 2003), Ea. Ednl. Rsch. Assn. (pres. 1993-95), Bergen County Assn. Lic. Psychologists (bd. dirs. 1991-93), NYU Sch. Psychology Alumni Assn. (founder 1988-92), Ramapo Valley Adminstrs. (v.p. 1996-98, pres. 1998—). Avocations: skiing, antiques, tennis, gourmet cooking. Home: 124 Frank Ct Mahwah NJ 07430-2963 Office: Waldwick Pub Schs 155 Summit Ave Waldwick NJ 07463-2133 Office Phone: 201-652-5052. Personal E-mail: drcarollynch@msn.com. Business E-Mail: carol.lynch@waldwick.k12.nj.us.

LYNCH, CATHERINE GORES, social services administrator; b. Waynesboro, Pa., Nov. 23, 1943; d. Landis and Pamela (Whitmarsh) Gores; m. Joseph C. Keefe, Nov. 29, 1981; children: Shannon Maria, Lisa Alison, Gregory T. Keefe, Michael D. Keefe. BA magna cum laude with honors, Bryn Mawr Coll., 1965; postgrad., Cornell U., 1966-67. Cert. police instr. Mayor's intern Human Resources Adminstrn., N.Y.C., 1967; rsch. asst. Orgn. for Social and Tech. Innovation, Cambridge, Mass., 1967-69; cons. Ford Found., Bogota, Columbia, 1970; staff Nat. Housing Census, Nat. Bur. Statistics, Bogota, 1971; evaluator Foster Parent Plan, Bogota, 1972; rsch. staff FEDESARROLLO, Bogota, 1973-74; dir. Dade County Advocates for Victims, Miami, Fla., 1974-86; asst. to dep. dir. Dept. Human Resouces, Miami, 1986-87, computer liaison, 1987-88, asst. adminstr. placement svcs. program, 1988-89; exec. dir. Health Crisis Network, Miami, 1989-96; liaison HIV cmty. svc. State of Fla. Health and Rehab. Svcs., 1996-97; program ops. adminstr. adult protective svcs. Fla. Dept. Children and Families, 1997-2000; dir. grants mgmt. U. Miami Sch. Nursing, 2000—03; ann. giving and grants mgr. Audubon of Fla., 2003—05; dir. devel. svcs. Miami Children's Hosp. Found., 2005—. Guest lectr. local univs. Participant, co-chmn. various task forces rape, child abuse, incest, family violence, elderly victims of crime, nat. state, local levels, 1974-86, 1999-2000; developer workshops in field; participant, chair, co-chair task forces on HIV/AIDS impact; long term care, children and AIDS, AIDS orgnl. issues, 1991-96; mem. gov.'s task force on victims and witnesses, gov.'s task force on sex offenders and their victims, gov.'s Red Ribbon panel on AIDS, 1992-93, gov.'s interdepartmental work group, 1993-96; mem. ednl. rev. com. Am. Found AIDS Rsch., 1991-96; vice chair Metro-Dade HIV Svcs. Planning Coun., 1991-93; active Fla. HIV Svcs. Adv. Coun., 1991-96; rev. panel Fed. Spl. Projects of Nat. Significance, 1994, 96; adv. coun. Metro Dade Social Svcs., 1995-96; bd. dirs., v.p. Dade County Healthy Start Coalition, 2002—04; cert. expert witness on battered women syndrome in civil and criminal cts. Contbr. writings to field to publs. Recipient various pub. svcs. awards including WINZ Citizen of Day, 1979, Outstanding Achievement award Fla. Network Victim Witness Svcs., 1982, Pioneer award Metro-Dade Women's Assn., 1989; Fulbright scholar U. Central de Venezuela, Caracas, 1965-66; Lehman fellow Cornell U. Mem. Nat. Orgn. of Victim Assistance Programs (bd. dirs. 1977-83, Outstanding Program award 1984), Fla. Network of Victim/Witness Programs (bd. dirs., treas. 1980-81), Am. Soc. Pub. Adminstrs., Dade County Fedn. Health and Welfare Workers, Fla. Assn. Health and Social Svcs. (chpt. treas. 1979-80), LWV (bd. dirs. Dade County chpt. 1988-92, 2005—), Fla. Consortium Sch.-Based Health Ctrs. (sec. 2001-03). Office: Miami Children's Hosp Found 3000 SW 62d Ave Miami FL 33155 Office Phone: 786-268-1841. Business E-Mail: clynch@mchf.org.

LYNCH, CHARLOTTE ANDREWS, retired communications executive, consultant; b. Fall River, Mass., Mar. 25, 1928; d. Alan Hall and Florence (Worthen) Andrews; m. Francis Bradley Lynch, June 7, 1952; children: Sarah Faldetta, Richard, Stephen, William. AB in Philosophy, Radcliffe Coll., 1950; postgrad., U. Bridgeport, 1969-71. Adminstrv. asst. Mass. Congl. Confs. and Missionary Soc., Boston, 1951-52; journalist Town Crier newspaper, Westport, Conn., 1968; asst. dir. devel. Cape Cod Hosp., Hyannis, Mass., 1975-76; parish adminstr. S. Congl. Ch., Centerville, Mass., 1976-83; cons. to ethnic advt. agy. Loiminchay, Inc., N.Y.C., 1992-98; ret. Mem. Radcliffe Club Cape Cod (v.p. 1990-97, pres. 1997-2000, exec. com. 1990-2000), Harvard Club of Boston. Republican. Roman Catholic. Avocation: travel.

LYNCH, CHERYL STELLY, psychology educator; b. Abbeville, La., Dec. 21, 1954; d. Velton Joseph and Hilda Marie (Duhon) Stelly; children: Tabby Anne Luquette, Mindy Desiree Menard; m. David C. Lynch; 1 child, Adelai J. BA, Nicholls State U., 1985; MS, U. Southwestern La., 1987; PhD, Tulane U., New Orleans, 1991. Tchg. asst. Tulane U., New Orleans, 1987-90, instr., 1990-91; postdoctoral fellow Tulane Med. Sch., New Orleans, 1991-94; assoc. prof. U. La., Lafayette, 1994—. Curriculum com. mem. psychology dept., U. La., 1994—. Contbr. articles to profl. jours. Recipient Outstanding Tchr. award Beacon Club U. La., Lafayette, 1995, 97, Nat. Rsch. Svc. award Nat. Inst. Drug Abuse, 1992-94; enhancement grantee La. Ednl. Quality Support Fund, 1994-95, 97-98. Mem. Soc. for Neurosci., Soc. for Behaviorial Neuroendocrinology, Psi Chi. Achievements include work with estrogen-dependent cholinergic regulation of female sexual behavior, androgenicanabolic steroid regulation of cen. nervous system mechanisms. Home: 5500 Cheryl Dr New Iberia LA 70560-9784 Office: U La Dept Psychology PO Box 43131 Lafayette LA 70504-0001 E-mail: csm5689@louisiana.edu.

LYNCH, CONSTANCE, reading specialist; Guest spkr. WNYE, Bklyn., 1965, Bd. Edn., Bklyn., 1965, promotional policy adv. coun., 68; guest lectr., reading cons. Branch Coll., N.Y.C., NY, 1970. Author: Reflections, 1988, It Takes a Kitongoji, 1999, In Other Words, 2005, Reflections of the Day, 2005. Mem. MADD; vol. Charlotte County Retired Educator Assn., Port Charlotte, Fla., 1994—, v.p., 1995—99; vol. Unity Ch. of Peace, Port Charlotte, 1994—; mem. Christopher Reeves Found., Nat. Com. to Preserve Social Security and Medicare, Operation Smile. Recipient Life Mem. plaque, NAACP, 1994, Voice of Civil Rights cert., 2005. Mem.: Peace River Ctr. for Writers, Nat. Women's Hist. Mus., Charlotte County Retired Educators Assn., Am. Assn. U. Women, Nat. Fed. for the Blind, Girls' HS Alumni Assn. Democrat. Avocations: sewing, music, poetry, dance. Home: 26287 Copiapo Cir Punta Gorda FL 33983

LYNCH, DIANE, volunteer; d. Gerald Charles and Karen L. Lynch; 1 child, Thomas. Diploma, Diesel Inst. of Am., Md., 1998. Firefighter Md. Inst. Fire Rescue Inst., cert. tree care Md., 1994. Forest and pks. employee Md. Conservation Corps., Anapolis, 1993—94; firefighter Bowmans Addition Vol. Fire Dept., Cumberland, Md., 1993—95; environ. coord. AmeriCorps Frostburg (Md.) St. U., 1995; cook Penn Alps Restaurant, Grantsville, Md., 2001. Coun. mem. Md. Conservation Corps, 1994. Vol. Boy Scouts of Am., 2002. Avocations: fishing, camping, cooking. Home: 110 W College Ave Frostburg MD 21532-1620

LYNCH, EMILY, elementary school educator; d. Jim and Kris Lynch. Degree in Math. Edn., U. No. Iowa, Cedar Falls, 2002. Tchr. math. John Adams Mid. Sch., Rochester, Minn., 2002—. Mem.: Rochester Edn. Assn., Minn. Edn. Assn., NEA, Nat. Coun. Tchrs. of Math. Office: John Adams Mid Sch 1525 31st St NW Rochester MN 55901 Office Phone: 507-285-8840.

LYNCH, FLORENCE, art gallery director; BS, MA in Art Adminstrn. With Salvatore Ala Gallery; independent curator Japan, Germany, France, Netherlands, Italy; founder, curator Florence Lynch Gallery, NYC. Named one of Seven Emerging Young Dealers in Chelsea, NY Arts Mag., 1999. Office: 531-539 W 25th St New York NY 10001 Office Phone: 212-924-3290. Office Fax: 212-924-2775. Business E-Mail: flynch@florencelynchgallery.com.

LYNCH, JESSICA, military officer; b. Palestine, W. Va., Apr. 26, 1983; d. Gregory O. and Deadra Lynch. Army Pvt. First Class, Hon. Med. Disability Discharge, 2003. Spokesperson Operation Purple. Decorated Purple Heart, Bronze Star, POW Medal; named West Virginian of Yr., 2003, Glamour Woman of Yr., 2003; recipient Heroes of Health award, 2003. Achievements include first POW/MIA recovered from Operation: Iraqi Freedom; subject of songs, poems, tributes, TV movies and reports; subject of Rick Bragg biography: I Am A Soldier Too: The Jessica Lynch Story, 2003; created the Jessica Lynch Found. to educate children of veterans.

LYNCH, KIRSTEN, food products executive; b. Chgo., 1968; BA, Ill. State U., 1990; MA, Washington U., St. Louis, 1990. With Kraft Foods, Chgo., 1996—; mktg. dir., Macaroni & Cheese Kraft Foods, Inc., 2005—. Avocation: snowboarding. Office: Kraft Foods Inc 3 Lakes Dr Northfield IL 60093 Office Phone: 847-646-2000, 847-646-0372. Office Fax: 847-646-6005. E-mail: klynch@kraft.com.*

LYNCH, LORETTA E., lawyer, former prosecutor; b. Durham, N.C., May 21, 1959; d. Lorenzo Lynch. Grad., Harvard Coll., 1981; JD, Harvard U., 1984. Bar: N.Y., U.S. Dist. Ct. (ea. dist. NY), U.S. Dist. Ct. (so. dist. NY), U.S. Ct. Appeals (2nd cir.). Litigation assoc. Cahill, Gordon & Reindel, 1984-90; with Office of U.S. Atty. for Ea. Dist. of N.Y., 1990—2001; chief L.I. offices, 1994-98; chief asst. U.S. States Atty., 1998—99; U.S. atty. ea. dist. N.Y. U.S. Dept. Justice, Bklyn., 2000—01; ptnr. Hogan & Hartson LLP, NYC, 2002—. Instr. Dept. Justice Criminal Trial Advocacy Prog.; adj. prof. St. John's Univ. Sch. Law; bd. dir. Fed. Reserve Bank N.Y., Office of the Appellate Defender; trustee Nat. Inst. Trial Advocacy; mem. Magistrate Judge Selection Panel Ea. Dist. N.Y., Judicial Screening Panel of Sen. Charles Schumer, NYC Charter Revision Commn., NY State Commn. on Jury, 2003—04; bd. advs. Brennan Ctr. for Justice, NYU Sch. Law. Author: White-Collar Crime: Counseling Corporate Clients Under Investigation, 2003. Bd. dirs. Nat. Inst. Law and Equity. Named one of Am.'s Top Black Lawyers, Black Enterprise Mag., 2003. Mem.: ABA (mem. sec. on litig.), Ea. Dist Com. on Civil Litigation, Fed. Bar. Coun., Assn. Bar N.Y.C. (chair Criminal Law Com.). Avocations: reading, tennis. Office: Hogan & Hartson 875 Third Ave New York NY 10022

LYNCH, MONIQUE CHRISTINE, mathematics educator; b. Washington, Feb. 20, 1970; d. Verel Willard and Carol Sue Benson; m. John Patrick Lynch, July 17, 1999. BA, U. No. Colo., 1992; MA, U. Colo., 1996; PhD, George Mason U., 2003. Cert. Math Tchr. Va., 2000, Colo., 1992. Math. tchr. Englewood Pub. Schs., Colo., 1992—96; rsch. assn. CORD, Waco, Tex., 1996—97; math. curriculum specialist Ingenius, Englewood, 1997—98; math. tchr. Jefferson County Pub. Schs., Lakewood, Colo., 1998—99; continuing edn. mgr. Coun. for Exceptional Children, Reston, Va., 1999—2000; faculty, project mgr. George Mason U., Fairfax, Va., 2000—03; asst. prof. Salisbury U., Md., 2003—05; dir. of profl. devel. programs and svcs. Nat. Coun. of Tchrs. of Math., Reston, Va., 2005—. Freelance author, 1992—2003. Vol. Habitat for Humanity, Leesburg, Va., 2004. Doctoral Rsch. fellow, George Mason U., 2002-2003, PT3 grant, Tex. Instruments, 2003-2004. Mem.: Mathematics Assn. Am., Assn. Advancement Computers in Edn., Internat. Soc. Tech. in Edn., Nat. Coun. Tchrs. Math., Am. Ednl. Rsch. Assn. Avocations: rubber stamping cards, pottery painting, walking, scrapbooks. Home: 400 Salyor Way SW Leesburg VA 20175 Office: Nctm 1906 Association Dr Reston VA 20191 Office Phone: 703-620-9840 2150. Personal E-mail: drmlynch@yahoo.com. E-mail: mlynch@nctm.org.

LYNCH, NANCY ANN, computer scientist, educator; b. Bklyn., Jan. 19, 1948; d. Roland David and Marie Catherine (Adinolfi) Evraets; m. Dennis Christopher Lynch, June 14, 1969; children: Patrick, Kathleen (dec.), Mary. BS, Bklyn. Coll., 1968; PhD, MIT, 1972. Asst. prof. math. Tufts U., Medford, Mass., 1972-73, U. So. Calif., Los Angeles, 1973-76, Fla. Internat. U., Miami, 1976-77; assoc. prof. computer sci. Ga. Tech. U., Atlanta, 1977-82, MIT, Cambridge, 1982-86, prof. computer sci., 1986—, NEC prof. software sci. and engring., 1996—. Ellen Swallow Richards chair MIT, 1982-87, Cecil H. Green chair, 1994-96. Contbr. numerous articles to profl. jours. Recipient Adriaan van Wijngarden Achievement award for excellence in math. and computer sci., 2006. Fellow: Assn. Computing Machinery; mem.: NAE. Roman Catholic. Office: MIT 32-G668 Comp Sci & Artificial Intelligence Lab 32 Vassar St Cambridge MA 02139

LYNCH, PATRICIA GATES, broadcast executive, consultant, ambassador; b. Newark, Apr. 20, 1926; d. William Charles and Mary Frances Lawrence; m. Mahlon Eugene Gates, Dec. 19, 1942 (div. 1972); children: Pamela Townley Gates, Lawrence Alan Gates; m. William Dennis Lynch (dec. 1997); m. Julian Johnson Ewell, June 30, 2005. Student, Dartmouth Inst., Dartmouth Coll., Hanover, NH, 1975. Broadcaster Sta. WFAX-Radio, Falls Ch., Va., 1958—68; pub. TV host Sta. WETA, Washington, 1967—68; broadcaster NBC-Radio, Europe, Iran, USSR, 1960—61; internat. broadcaster, producer Voice of Am., Washington, 1962—69; staff asst. to First Lady The White House, Washington, 1969—70; host Voice of Am. Breakfast Show, Morning show, 1970—86; U.S. amb. to Madagascar and the Comoros, 1986—89; dir. corp. affairs Radio Free Europe/Radio Liberty, Washington, 1989—94; chmn. bd. Assn. Diplomatic Studies & Tng. Fgn. Svc. Inst., Arlington, Va., 1998—2005. Worldwide lectr., 1968—86; adv. com. Ind. Fed. Savs. and Loan Assn., Washington, 1970—86; bd. dirs. Assn. Diplomatic Studies and Tng. Author stories on Am. for English teaching dept. Radio Sweden, 1967—68, others on internat. broadcasting. Chair internat. svc. com. Washington chpt. ARC, 1979—86; bd. visitors Duke U. Primate Ctr., Durham, NC. Recipient Pub. Svc. award, U.S. Army, 1960; grantee AMPART grant, USIA, 1983. Mem.: Washington Inst. Fgn. Affairs (bd. dirs.), Am. News Women's Club, Am. Women in Radio and TV (Washington chpt. pres. 1966—67), Coun. Am. Ambs. (v.p., bd. dirs.), Am. Acad. Diplomacy (bd. dirs. 2003—). Republican. Episcopalian. Avocations: reading, volunteer work, wildlife conservation.

LYNCH, PRISCILLA A., nursing educator, psychotherapist; b. Joliet, Ill., Jan. 8, 1949; d. LaVerne L. and Ann M. (Zamkovitz) L. BS, U. Wyo., 1973; MS, St. Xavier Coll., Coll., 1981. RN, Ill. Staff nurse Rush-Presbyn.-St. Luke's Med. Ctr., Chgo., 1977-81, psychiat.-liaison cons., 1981-83, asst. prof. nursing, unit dir., 1985—. Mgr. and therapist Oakside Clinic, Kankakee, Ill., 1987—; mem. adv. bd. Depressive and Manic Depression Assn., Chgo., 1986—; mem. consultation and mental health unit Riverside Med. Ctr., Kankakee, 1987—; speaker numerous nat. orgns. Contbr. numerous abstracts to profl. jours., chpts. to books. Bd. dirs. Cornerstone Svcs., ARC of Ill. Recipient total quality mgmt. award Rush-Presbyn.-St. Luke's Med. Ctr., 1991, named mgr. of the quarter, 1997, Wayne Lerner Leadership award, 1998. Mem. APNA, ISPN, Ill. Nurses Assn. (coms.), Coun. Clin. Nurse Specialists, Profl. Nursing Staff (sec. 1985-87, mem. coms.). Presbyterian. Home: 606 Darcy Ave Joliet IL 60436-1673 Office Phone: 312-942-5100. Business E-Mail: priscilla_lynch@rush.edu.

LYNCH, SANDRA LEA, federal judge; b. Oak Park, Ill., July 31, 1946; d. Bernard Francis and Eugenia Tyus Lynch; married; 1 child. AB in Philosophy, Wellesley Coll., 1968; JD cum laude, Boston U., 1971. Bar: Mass. 1971, U.S. Supreme Ct. 1974. Law clk. to Hon. Raymond J. Pettine U.S. Dist. Ct., Providence; asst. atty. gen. Commonwealth of Mass., Boston, 1974; gen. counsel Mass. Dept. Edn., Boston, 1974—78; ptnr. Foley, Hoag & Eliot, Boston, 1978—95; judge 1st cir. U.S. Ct. Appeals, Boston, 1995—. Instr. Boston Univ. Law Sch., 1973—74. Contbr. articles to profl. jours. Past co-chair leading industries com. Greater Boston C. of C. Recipient Disting. Alumnae award, Boston U. Law Sch., 1993, Wellesley Coll., 1997, Disting. Svc. award, Planned Parenthood, 1991. Mem.: ABA, Boston Bar Assn. (pres. 1992—93, Jud. Excellence award 2001), Mass. Bar Assn., Nat. Assn. Women Judges, Women's Forum. Office: US Ct Appeals One Courthouse Way Ste 8710 Boston MA 02210-3010*

LYNCH-STEMPFER, TARA KATHLEEN, physical therapist; b. Latrobe, Pa., Dec. 30, 1978; d. Bernard J. and Constance Grace Lynch; m. Garret Frank Stempfer, Aug. 13, 2005. BS in Sports Medicine, Mercyhurst Coll., Erie, Pa., 2001; PhD in Physical Therapy, Drexel U., Phila., 2006. Cert. athletic trainer. Athletic trainer Laurel Highlands Health Ctr., Latrobe, Pa., 2001—03; physical therapist Ctr. Sports Medicine, Pitts., 2006—. Mem.: Am. Physical Therapy Assn., Nat. Athletic Trainer's Assn. Avocations: golf, running, boxing, knitting, singing.

LYNDRUP, PEGGY B., lawyer; b. Winnipeg, Can., Mar. 27, 1949; BS in Edn. magna cum laude, U. N.D., 1969; MEd, Kent State U., 1971; JD summa cum laude, U. Louisville, 1979. Bar: Ky. 1979, U.S. Dist. Ct. (we. dist.) Ky. 1979, U.S. Dist. Ct. (ea. dist.) Ky. 1981. Atty. Greenebaum Doll & McDonald, PLLC, Louisville, 1979—. Recipient Disting. Alumnus award, U. Louisville Sch. Law, 1989; Brandeis scholar. Mem. ABA, Louisville Bar Assn. (pres. 1989). Office: Greenbaum Doll & McDonald PLLC 3500 National City Tower Louisville KY 40202 Office Phone: 502-587-3626. Business E-Mail: pbl@gdm.com.

LYNDS, GAYLE HALLENBECK, writer; b. Omaha, June 23; d. Paul Duane and Marian Lucille (Tice) Hallenbeck; m. Thomas F. Stone, Aug. 14, 1966 (div. 1984); children: Paul F. Stone, Julia L. Stone; m. Dennis Lynds, Feb. 14, 1986. BA in Journalism, U. Iowa, Iowa City, 1967. Reporter Ariz. Rep., Phoenix, 1967; editor, rsch. asst. Iowa Ctr. for Edn. in Politics, Iowa City, 1968; editor GE-Tempo, Santa Barbara, Calif., 1968—71, Santa Barbara Mag., 1983—86, Prime Mag., Santa Barbara, 1986—89. Tchr. creative writing courses U. Calif., Santa Barbara, Pima Coll., Tucson, Asilomar Writing Conf., Monterey, Calif., So. Calif. Writers Conf., San Diego, others. Author: Masquerade, 1996, Mosaic, 1998; author: (with Robert Ludlum) The Hades Factor, 2000, The Paris Option, 2002, The Altman Code, 2003; author: The Coil, 2004, The Last Spymaster, 2006, Mesmerized, 2001; author: (contbr. first chpt., edited by Mardla Talley) I'd Kill For That, 2004. Mem. Authors Guild, Mystery Writers Am., Internat. Crime Writers, Internat. Thriller Writers, Inc. (co-founder and co-pres.)

LYNDS, LUCINDA, music educator; b. Taunton, Mass., Sept. 12, 1953; d. Charles Francis and Wilma Ruth MacDonald; m. Warren Eugene Lynds, Oct. 7, 1978 (div.); children: Matthew Warren, Victoria Leigh. MusB, Lowell State Coll., 1975; MEd, Lesley Coll., 1989; cert. in Advanced Grad. Study, Fitchburg State Coll., 1997. Cert. music tchr., Mass., supr./dir. Elem. music specialist Fall River (Mass.) Pub. Sch., 1975—. Co-founder, co-dir. Fall River Elem. Select Chorus, 1994-96. Choir, soloist, asst. organist Memorial United Meth., Taunton, Mass., organ restoration com., music com., scholarship com., Christian edn. com., trustee. Mem. Am. Fedn. Musicians (bd. dirs. 1981-91), Music Educators Nat. Conf., Mass. Music Educators Assn., Mass. Tchrs. Assn., Fall River Educators Assn. Avocations: sewing, crafts, organ playing, gardening, private music lessons. Office: Fall River Music Dept 615 Tucker St Fall River MA 02721-3348

LYNE, DOROTHY-ARDEN, secondary school educator; b. Orangeburg, N.Y., Mar. 9, 1928; d. William Henry and Janet More (Freston) Dean; m. Thomas Delmar Lyne, Aug. 16, 1952 (div. June 1982); children: James Delmar, Peter Freston, Jennifer Dean. BA, Ursinus Coll., 1949; MA, Fletcher Sch. Law and Diplomacy, 1950. Assoc. editor World Peace Found., Boston, 1950-51; editorial assoc. Carnegie Endowment Internat. Peace, N.Y.C., 1951-52; dir. Assoc. of Internat. Rels. Clubs, N.Y.C., 1952-53; editor The Town Crier, Westport, Conn., 1966-68; editorial assoc. Machinery Allied Products Inst., Wash., 1959-63; tchr. Helen Keller Mid. Sch., Easton, Conn., 1967-89. Vice chmn. Cooperative Ednl. Svcs., Fairfield, 1983-85. Editor: Documents in American Foreign Rels., 1950, Current Rsch. in Internat. Affairs, 1951. Chmn. Westport Zoning Bd. of Appeals, 1976-80, Westport Bd. of Edn., 1985-87; vice chmn. Westport Bd. of Edn., 1980-85; mem. Westport Charter Revision Commn., 1966-67. Democrat. Episcopalian.

LYNE, JANET KAY, music educator, director; b. Bryan, Ohio, May 26, 1958; d. Alpheus Albert and Gwendolyn Norine (Snyder) McCord; m. Larry Bruce Lyne, June 23, 1984; 1 child, Zachary Lawrence; 1 stepchild, Chadwick Neal. MusB, Bowling Green State U., Ohio, 1980, MusM, 2004. Cert. tchr. Ohio. Vocal music dir. Mt. Gilead HS, Ohio, 1980—81, North Baltimore HS, Ohio, 1981—82, Liberty Ctr. HS, Ohio, 1982—92, Waite HS, Toledo, 1992—, Detiamine Coll., Ohio, 2006. Dept. chair fine arts Waite HS, Toledo, 1996—; rehersal section leader U. Choral Soc., Bowling Green, Ohio, 2002—06; vocal music dir. Maunue Valley Civic Theatre, Napolean, Ohio, 1996, Napolean, 97, Napolean, 98. Recipient Blade (newspaper) Tchr. of Month, Toledo, 2003. Mem.: Am. Choral Dirs. Assn., Ohio Choral Dirs. Assn., Music Educators Nat. Conf., Ohio Music Edn. Assn. (rehersal asst. dist. I hon. chair 2003—). Republican. Lutheran. Avocation: antiques. Home: 620 Sheffield Ave Napoleon OH 43545 Office: Waite HS 501 Morrison Dr Toledo OH 43605 Personal E-mail: lyne@adlephia.net.

LYNE, SUSAN MARKHAM, multi-media company executive, former broadcast executive; b. Boston, Apr. 30, 1950; d. Eugene and Ruth (Lally) L.; m. George Crile III; children: Susan Markham, Jane Halle; stepchildren: Katherine Murphy, Elizabeth McCook. Assoc. editor City Mag., San Francisco, 1975-76; west coast editor New Times, San Francisco, 1976-77, mng. editor NYC, 1978, The Village Voice, NYC, 1978-82; v.p. creative devel. IPC Films, NYC, 1982-85; ptnr. Lazar/Lyne Films, NYC, 1985-86; founder Premiere mag., NYC, 1987-96, editor-in-chief, publication dir., 1987—96; exec. v.p. acquisitions, development, and new bus. Walt Disney Motion Picture Group, 1996—98; exec. v.p. movies and miniseries ABC Entertainment, 1998—2002, pres., 2002—04; pres., CEO Martha Stewart Living Omnimedia, Inc., 2004—. Bd. dirs. Lifetime Network, 1996—, Martha Stewart Living Omnimedia, Inc., 2004—, CIT, 2006—. Bd. dirs. Pub. Theater. Mem. Am. Soc. Mag. Editors (bd. dirs. 1993-96). Oversaw the development of recent hits including "Desperate Housewives", "Lost" and "Extreme Makeover, Home Edition". Also guided other programs, including "8 Simple Rules for Dating My Teenage Daughter", "The Bachelor" and "Hope and Faith". Office: Martha Stewart Living Omnimedia Inc 11 W 42nd St New York NY 10036*

LYNES, BONNIEJEANE, mathematics educator, sales executive; b. Mesa, Ariz., Aug. 30, 1976; d. Robert Dinsmore and Namoe Spencer Lynes. Math. Edn., Brigham Young U., Provo, Utah, 2000. Lic. level IV math tchr. Utah, 2000. Math tchr. Murray (Utah) H.S., 2003—; sales rep. Eclipse Mktg./Ind., Salt Lake City, 2005—. Co-author benchmark tests Pk. City/Murray Coalition, 2005—06; presenter in field. Relief soc. pres. LDS Ch., Salt Lake City, 2004—05. Mem.: Nat. Coun. Tchrs. Math. Home: 2125 S 2100 E Salt Lake City UT 84109 Office: Murray High School 5440 S State Murray UT 84107 Office Phone: 801-264-7460 5225. Personal E-mail: bonniejeane@hotmail.com.

LYNN, BARBARA HOFFMAN, music educator; b. Alexandria, Va., Aug. 11, 1961; d. Donald Lee and Mary Lucille Hoffman; m. James Albert Lynn, Aug. 6, 1988; children: Melisa Anne, Benjamin James. BMED, James Madison U., Harrisonburg, Va., 1984. Cert. Orff Schwerk Pedagogy George Mason U., 1994, tchr. Va. Music tchr. Fairfax County Pub. Schs., Alexandria, 1992—. Music dir., choir dir. Pohick Ch., Lorton, Va., 1996—; choral dir. Cameron Caveliers Chorus, Kings Dominion Music Festival. Mem.: Fedn. Edn. Assn., Fairfax Gen. Music Edn. Assn. Office: Cameron Elementary 3434 Campbell Dr Alexandria VA 22303 Office Phone: 703-329-2100.

LYNN, BRENDA, physical education educator; b. San Gabriel, Calif., Feb. 3, 1964; d. Richard Joseph and Charlene Sue Lynn. BS in Edn., Mo. We. State Coll., St. Joseph, 1987. Tchr. phys. edn. and coach Savannah R-III Sch. Dist., Mo., 1991—96; customer svc. and sales Pickup Palace, St. Joseph, 1996—2001; tchr. phys. edn. and health South Holt R-I Sch. Dist., Oregon, 2001—. Volleyball coach South Holt R-I Sch. Dist., Oregon, Mo., 2001—, coach Jr. H.S. basketball, 2001—05, mem. profl. devel. com., 2003—, chair profl. devel. com., 2005—06, mem. Character Plus leadership com., 2005—, sponsor smokebuster, 2004—, coach Jr. H.S. track, 2001—, sponosr jr. class, 2001—, mem. welfare com., 2005—. Mem.: AAHPERD, Mo. State Tchrs. Assn., Cmty. Tchrs. Assn. (v.p. 2006—), Mo. Alliance Health, Phys. Edn., Recreation and Dance. Office: S Holt RI Sch Dist 201 S Barbour St Oregon MO 64473

LYNN, D. JOANNE, physician, researcher; b. Oakland, Md., July 2, 1951; d. John B. and Mary Dorcas (Clark) Harley; m. Barry W. Lynn; children: Christina, Nicholas. BS summa cum laude, Dickinson Coll., 1970; MD cum laude, Boston U., 1974; MA in Philosophy and Social Policy, George Washington U., 1981; MS Clin. Evaluative Scis., Dartmouth Coll., 1995. Diplomate Am. Bd. Internal Medicine. Resident internal medicine The George Washington U. Med. Ctr., 1974-77; emergency rm. physician, triage physician Washington VA Hosp., 1977-78; faculty assoc. for medicine and humanities divsn. experimental programs George Washington U., Washington, 1978-81, dir. divsn. aging studies, 1988-92, prof. health care scis. and medicine, 1991-92, assoc. chairperson dept. health care scis., 1990-92, dir of the Ctr. to Improve the Care of the Dying, 1995-2000; prof. medicine, cmty. and family medicine, sr. assoc. Ctr. Evaluative Clin. Scis. Dartmouth-Hitchcock Med. Ctr., Hanover, NH, 1992-95, assoc. dir. Ctr. for Aging, 1992-95; dir. RAND Ctr. to Improve Care of the Dying, Arlington, Va., 2000—02; pres. Ams. for Better Care of the Dying, 1995—2005; dir. The Washington Home Ctr. for Palliative Care Studies, 2002—05; sr. natural scientist RAND, 2005—06; med. officer Ctr. Medicine and Med. Svcs., 2006—. Robert Wood Johnson clin. scholar George Washington U., 1977-78, sr. fellow Ctr. Health Policy Rsch., 1991-92; asst. dir. med. studies The Pres. Commn. for Study of Ethical Problems in Medicine and Biomed. and Behavioral Rsch., 1981-83; med. dir. The Washington Home, 1983-89, Hospice of Washington, 1979-91, George Washington Cancer Home Care Program and Home Health Svcs. of The Washington Home, 1990-92, staff physician, 1979-92; fellow Hastings Ctr., 1984—; mem. working group on guidelines for care of terminally ill, 1985-87, rsch. project on ethical issues in care and treatment of chronically ill, 1985-87, working group on new physician-patient relationship, 1991-94, v.p., 1987, chair fellows nominating com., 1991; mem. coordinating coun. on life-sustaining med. treatment decision making by cts. Nat. Ctr. State Cts., 1989-93; fellow Kennedy Inst., 1991; mem. geriat. and gerontology adv. com. Dept. Vet. Affairs, 1991-97; mem. bioethics com. Vets. Health Adminstrn., 1991-93; active Washington Area Seminar on Sci., Tech., and Ethics, 1982-92, Nat. Clin. Panel on High-Cost Hospice Care, Washington, 1991; presenter in field. Author: (with J. Harrold) Handbook for Mortals: Guidance for People Facing Serious Illness, 1999, (with A. Kabenell and J. Lynch Schuster) Improving Care for the End of Life: A Sourcebook for Health Care Managers and Clinicians, 2000, Sick to Death and Not Going to Take It Any More, 2004; author chpts. to books; mem. editl. bd. The Ency. of Bioethics, 1994-95; mem. adv. editl. bd. Biolaw, 1983, The Hospice Jour., 1984—, Med. Ethics for the Physician, 1985-92, Med. Humanities Rev., 1986—, Cambridge Quar., 1991-95; contbr. articles, revs. to profl. jours. Peter Jeffries and Jeanne Arnold scholar, 1973; recipient Wellington Parlin Sci. Scholarship award, 1979, Dr. Bertha Curtis prize Boston U. Med. Sch., 1974, Nat. Bd. award Med. Coll. Pa., 1992. Master ACP (mem. subcom. on aging 1986-91), Am. Geriatrics Soc. (mem. com. public policy 1983-98, mem. ethics com. 1988, chair subcom. on ethics and policy 1986, chair ethics com. 1991-98, bd. dirs. 1991-97); mem. AAAS, APHA, Am. Fedn. Clin. Rsch., Am. Health Care Assn. (mem. task force on AIDS 1987-89), Am. Hosp. Assn. (mem. spl. com. on biomedical ethics 1983-85, 89-94), Am. Med. Dirs. Assn., Am. Soc. Law and Medicine, Am. Coll. Health Care Adminstrs. (mem. nat. adv. com. wandering patients 1987-88), Nat. Inst. on Aging (mem. senile dementia of Alzheimer's type, mem. rsch. ethics task force 1981-82, Am. Geriatrics Soc. rep. 1984-86), Soc. Health and Human Values (mem. gov. coun. 1981-84), Inst. Medicine (mem. com. on future issues in med. tech. devel. 1992-94), N.H. Med. Soc., Soc. Health and Human Values (mem. gov. coun. 1981-84), Internat. Hospice Inst. (mem. physician's adv. com. 1984-86), Med. Soc. D.C. (mem. legis. affairs com. 1985-92, vice chairperson 1991-92), Soc. Gen. Internal Medicine (mem. editl. adv. bd. Jour. 1988-91), Inst. of Medicine, Americans for Better Care of the Dying (pres. 1994-2005) Home: 2318 Ashboro Dr Chevy Chase MD 20815-3055 Business E-Mail: JLynn@medicaring.org.

LYNN, EVELYN JOAN, state senator, consultant; b. NY, Feb. 2, 1930; d. Leo A. and Helen (Shep) Hoes. BA in Psychology, Queens Coll., N.Y., 1950; MA English and Edn., Stetson U., 1969; EdD, U. Fla., 1979. Cons. for bus., edn. and govt., 1979—; rep. Fla. House, 1994—2002, Fla. Senate Dist. 7, Fla., 2002—. Bd. dirs. Edn. Commn. States; mem. So. Regional Edn. Bd. Mem. Nat. Coun. State Legislators (com. vice chair, mem. Blue Ribbon com.). Home: PO Box 4236 Ormond Beach FL 32175-4236 Office Phone: 386-667-4000. Business E-Mail: lynn.evelyn.web@FLsenate.gov.

LYNN, JUDITH, opera singer, artist, voice educator; b. Chgo. d. Louis Leo and Mollie (Rudman) Cogan; m. Filippo Joseph DeStefano, Dec. 26, 1965. Student, LA Conservatory Music & Art, 1959—62, U. Vienna, 1964; degree in Tchg. (hon.), Conservatorio de Musica, Maracay, Venezuela, 1987; student, Fashion Inst. Tech., 1987-91; pvt. student music and voice, Filippo De Stefano; coaching, Giuseppe Pais, Lina Pagliughi, Felix Popper, Ruth and Mario Chamlee, Richard Hageman; student art, Albert & Yolanda Pels. V.p. and musical adminstr. Opera Linca De Stefano, Caracas, Venezuela, 1983—87; sec.-treas. De Stefano Presents, N.Y.C., 1991—. Art represented by Met. Opera Gallery at Lincoln Ctr., N.Y.C. Singer (lead roles): Don Giovanni (Elvira & Zerlina), Rigoletto (Gilda), La Bohème (Mimi & Musetta), Magic Flute (Queen of the Night), La Traviata (Violetta), Les Pêcheurs de Perles (Leila), Lucia di Lammermoor (Lucia), Die Entführung aus dem Serail (Konstanze), Showboat (Magnolia), Lakmé (Laame), Carmen (Micaela), Il Barbiere Di Siviglia (Rosina); performer: Phila. Grand Opera Co., N.Y.C. Opera, Israel Nat. Opera, Stichting Haagse Volsopera, Teatro alla pergola, Teatro de la Opera de Maracay, Riverside Opera Assn., Redlands Bowl Assn., Conn. Grand Opera, Group Opera; TV appearances include Opera at the Cloisters and La Traviata, Teleprompter Cable TV, (solo concert) Juventud Musical Venezolana, Caracas; singer: (recordings) Madama Butterfly, 2003, The Messiah, G.F. Handel; exhibitions include Galeria EuroAmericano, Caracas, Venezuela Casa de la Cultura, Maracay, Ateneo de los Teques, Venezuela, Landmark Edn. Corp., N.Y., Bayside Hist. Soc., N.Y. Hilton and Towers, Pen and Brush Club, N.Y.C., poster, Gt. Am. Children's Theatre, 1995, children's books, By the Way, My Name is José, 1991, Just Try It Once Mother, 1991, carpet design. Recipient 1st prize voice Ebell of L.A., 1960, winner Am. Opera Auditions, 1963 (debut Milan, Italy), 3d prize painting Salon Imagen and Grumbacher, Venezuela, 1984. Mem.: Am. Watercolor Soc. (assoc.). Office: The Ansonia Studio 14-40 2109 Broadway New York NY 10023-2106 E-mail: jlynnart@mindspring.com, destefanopresent@mindspring.com.

LYNN, JULIA CAROLYN, school nurse practitioner; b. Marshall, Tex., Feb. 8, 1945; d. Alva Jenkins and Delphia May Brazzeal Irvin; m. John Franklin Lynn, Mar. 21, 1965 (dec.); children: John Franklin Jr., Vaughan Alva, Roseann Denise Lynn Morris. Diploma, Tex. Eastern Sch. Nursing, 1966. With Marshall Hosp. ER, Tex., 1966—67; sch. nurse Beckville I.S.D., Tex., 1969—; nursing supr. Longview Regional Hosp., Tex., 1988—90, Henderson Meml. Hosp., Tex., 1988—99. Mem.: Nat. Assn. Sch. Nurses, Tex. Sch. Nurse Assn.

LYNN, KRISTINA, journalist, actress, writer, producer; b. Dayton, Ohio, Apr. 18, 1954; d. Donald Louis Craddock and Carol Rose (Righthouse) Guthrie; m. Gerald Lee Diez, Oct. 19, 1985 (div. Aug. 1988). BA with honors in Speech, English and Theatre, U. West Ga., 1976; postgrad. in Psychology, Ga. State U., Atlanta, 1978. Tchr., drama dir. Redan H.S., Stone Mountain, Ga., 1976-78; co-hostess Am. Radio Network, Balt., 1988-90; co-host, interviewer WNTR Radio, Washington, 1988—91; pres., owner Lynn Prodns., L.A., Atlanta, N.Y.C., 1985—. Spkr., tchr., coord. Learning Annex, Washington, 1987-91; corr. Joan Rivers Show, N.Y.C., 1992, Geraldo Show; corr., reporter Paramount TV, L.A., 1993-99; corr. celebrity reporter E Entertainment TV, L.A., 1995-96; corr., reporter, anchor Backstage Prodns., Nashville, 1994-97; host Dishin' Up Country T.V., Dishin' Up In the Country Kitchen, Vital Force Entertainment; mem., film festival asst. chair Women in Film, Washington, N.Y.C., 1988-92; talent coord. One Light Project, Dream Castle Prodns., 1999, exec. asst., european dir., The Alpha Omega Colelction of Gary Koenig. Dir. (theatre) Plaza Suite, 1977 (1st place region competition award 1977), Sorry Wrong Number, 1978 (2d place region competition award 1978), host, prodr. The Kristina Lynn Show, The Alpha-Omega Colection for Gary Koenig, CEO-Exec. Asst. Bd. dirs. Child Savers, Inc., Rockville, Md., 1991-96, fund raiser, 1991-96. Mem. AFTRA (mem. outreach program 1996, press dir. world music awards, Monaco), N.Am. Rec. Industry and Songwriters Assn., Talk Radio Assn. (bd. dirs. 1996), Nashville Songwriters Assn., Screen Actors Guild (vol. womens com. 1985), Women in Music Bus. Assn. (chmn. com. 1994-95), Phi Kappa Phi, Phi Alpha Gamma. Democrat. Roman Catholic. Avocations: singing, songwriting, dance, filmmaking, swimming. Home: 8750 Mount Rushmore Dr Alpharetta GA 30022-6888 Office Phone: 678-548-5099. Personal E-mail: lynn_kristina@yahoo.com. E-mail: klyn30022@yahoo.com.

LYNN, NAOMI B., academic administrator; b. NYC, Apr. 16, 1933; d. Carmelo Burgos and Maria (Lebron) Berly; m. Robert A. Lynn, Aug. 28, 1954; children: Mary Louise, Nancy Lynn Francis, Judy Lynn Chance, Jo-An Lynn Cooper. BA, Maryville Coll., Tenn., 1954; MA, U. Ill., 1958; PhD, U. Kans., 1970. Instr. polit. sci. Cen. Mo. State Coll., Warrensburg, Mo., 1966-68; asst. prof. Kans. State U., Manhattan, 1970-75, assoc. prof., 1975-80, acting dept. head, prof., 1980-81, head polit. sci. dept., prof., 1982-84; dean Coll. Pub. and Urban Affairs, prof. Ga. State U., Atlanta, 1984-91; chancellor U. Ill., Springfield, 1991-2001, chancellor emerita, 2001—. Cons. fed., state and local govts., Manhattan, Topeka, Altanta, 1981-91; bd. dirs. Bank One Springfield; bd. trustees Maryville Coll., 1997—. Author: The Fulbright Premise, 1973; editor: Public Administration, The State of Discipline, 1990, Women, Politics and the Constitution, 1990; contbr. articles and textbook chpts. to profl. pubs. Bd. dirs. United Way of Sangamon County, 1991-98, Ill. Symphony Orch., 1992-95, Urban League, 1993-99, Ill. State Mus. Soc., 2002-05. Recipient Disting. Alumni award Maryville Coll., 1986; fellow Nat. Acad. Pub. Adminstrn. Mem. Nat. Assn. Schs. Pub. Affairs and Adminstrn. (nat. pres.), Am. Soc. Pub. Adminstrn. Endowment Bd. (nat. pres. 1985-86, pres. 2005-), Am. Polit. Sci. Assn. (mem. exec. coun. 1981-83, trustee 1993—96, Am. Assn. State Colls. and Univs. (bd. dirs.), Midwest Polit. Sci. Assn. (mem. exec. coun. 1976-79), Women's Caucus Polit. Sci. (pres. 1975-76), Greater Springfield C. of C. (bd. dirs. 1991-99, mem. U.S. Senate jud. nominations commn. State Ill. 1999-01), Pi Sigma Alpha (nat. pres.). Presbyterian. Personal E-mail: nlynn416@aol.com.

LYNN, VALERIE ROEMER, psychotherapist; b. Pitts., Jan. 31, 1927; d. Carl and Sylvia (Huot) Roemer; m. Kenneth Schuyler Lynn, Sept. 23, 1948; children: Andrew S., Elisabeth, Sophia. BA, Wellesley Coll., 1948; MS, Simmons Sch. Social Work, 1968. Diplomate Acad. Cert. Social Workers. Caseworker Robert Breck Brigham Hosp., Boston, 1959; social worker Chestnut Lodge, Rockville, Md., 1969-80; pvt. practice psychotherapy, 1980—. Mem. NASW. Home and Office: 1709 Hoban Rd NW Washington DC 20007-2036

LYNNE, SHELBY (SHELBY LYNN MOORER), country singer; b. Quantico, Va., Oct. 22, 1968; Singer: (albums) Sunrise, 1989, Tough All Over, 1990, Soft Talk, 1991, Temptation, 1993, Restless, 1995, I Am Shelby Lynne, 2000 (Grammy award best new artist, 2000), Love, Shelby, 2001, Identity Crisis, 2003, Suit Yourself, 2005, (singles) I'll Lie Myself to Sleep, 1990, Things Are Tough All Over, 1990, Feelin Kind of Lonely Tonight, 1993, (duet with George Jones) If I Could Bottle This Up, 1988; actor: (films) Walk the Line, 2005; (TV films) Another Pair of Aces: Three of a Kind, 1991; appearances (TV special) Willie Nelson and Friends, Outlaws and Angles, (TV series) Nashville Now. Named best new female artist, ACM, 1991; recipient Horizon award, CMA, 1991. Office: Capital Records 1750 N Vine St Hollywood CA 90028*

LYNTON, SANDRA M., psychologist; b. London, Eng., Nov. 17, 1957; came to U.S., 1983; d. Paul Stefan and Lya Lynton. BA with honors, U. Keele, Eng., 1982; MA, U. Colo., 1985; PsyD, Calif. Sch. Profl. Psychology, Berkeley, 1998. Women's counselor Women in Crisis Battered Women's Shelter, Jefferson County, Colo., 1985-87; social worker Ctr. for People with Disabilities, Boulder, Colo., 1988-93; program coord. OMI Children's Psychodiagnostic Assessments, San Francisco, 1993-95; pvt. practice Boulder, 1999—; clin. psychologist Childre's Specialized Svcs., Imperial County Behavial Svcs., El Centro, Calif., 2002—. Bd. dirs. Domestic Violence Initiative for Women with Disabilities, Denver, 1990-93; mem. Disability Task Force, City of Boulder, 1989-92, participant Task Force on Childhood Abuse, 1991-92; bd. dirs. Mental Health Ombuds Program Colo., Denver, 2004— Mem. APA. Avocations: art, music, outdoor wilderness. Personal E-mail: slynton@yahoo.com.

LYON, BARBARA KENNEDY, retired editor; b. Albion, Mich., Feb. 16, 1918; d. Walter Scott Kennedy and Agnes Eleanor Chambers; m. Richard Norton Lyon, Sept. 24, 1939 (dec.); children: Kennedy Lyon, Payson Lyon. AB, U. Chgo., Ill., 1939. Rap reporter, humanity seminars Oak Ridge Industry Nuc. Studies, Tenn., 1960—65; editor Oak Ridge Nat. Lab., Tenn., 1966—82; ret. Contbr. articles to profl. jour. Past bd. mem., sec. Oak Ridge Art Ctr.; mem. Oak Ridge Civic Ballet Assn., Recording for the Blind; past bd. mem. Oak Ridge Playhouse, Friends Oak Ridge Pub. Libr., Tri-County Literacy Coun. Mem.: Internat. Assn. Bus. Comm., Soc. for Tech. Comm. (past pres. East Tenn. chptr.).

LYON, DIANA, counselor, art educator, psychotherapist; b. Paragould, Ark., June 21, 1935; d. Wakeman Richard and Frances Jane Bell; m. Joseph Edward Dornbusch, Dec. 24, 1956 (div. 1974); children: Jeff Dornbusch, Dan K. Dornbusch. BA, U. No. Colo., 1958, MA, 1967, PhD, 2004. Lic. profl. counselor, N.Mex., 1994. Art instr. Island of Guam Edn. Dept., Agana, 1958-60; spl. edn. tchr. of the deaf Cedar Rapids (Iowa) Pub. Sch., 1967-69; dean, dir. Shapley Internat. House, Florence, Italy, 1974-79; chief classification officer N.Mex. Dept. Corrections, Radium Springs, 1979-83; pvt. practice D. Lyon Enteprises, Hillsboro, N.Mex., 1979-83; dir., counselor Domestic Abuse Intervention Ctr., Truth or Consequences, N.Mex., 1990-91; project dir. Cmty. Partnership for a Healthy Environment, Truth or Consequences, 1991-94; VISTA Vol. Corp. for Nat. and Cmty. Svc., Truth or Consequences, 1994-95; profl. counselor Domestic Abuse Intervention Ctr., Truth or Consequences, 1995-96, bd. dirs., 1998—. Bus. owner D. Lyon Enterprises, Las Cruces and Truth or Consequences, N.Mex., 1983-2004; organizer/facilitator Female and Fully Alive Workshop Series, Sierra County, N.Mex., 1986-88, Youth Leadership Tng., Truth or Consequences, 1988-90; facilitator/advisor Mayor's Drug and Alcohol Prevention Task Force, Truth or Consequences, 1989-90; adj. prof. Western N.Mex. U., Truth or Consequences, 1997—; pres. Ancient Waters Preservation Corp., 1996—. Contbr. art to Present Time Jour., 1975—; art works on exhbn. in U.S., Italy, Guam, 1975-96. Bd. dirs. Hillsboro (N.Mex.) Cmty. Ctr., 1986-89; county co-chair Dem. Party of Sierra County, Hillsboro, 1985-86; pres., charter mem. Sierra County Kiwanis, Truth or Consequences, 1986-91. Recipient Exemplary Svc. award N.Mex. Dept. Corrections, 1983, Resourceful Women award, Resourceful Women, San Francisco, 1994; mem. 4th World Conf. on Women, UN, Beijing, China, 1995. Mem. Women's Caucus for the Arts (charter, chpt. pres. 1984-86, 96-98), Black Range Artists, Inc., Sierra Art Soc., Optimist Club of Sierra County, Sierra County Arts Coun. (grant writer 1995-96). Avocations: drawing, water sports, travel, gardening, music. Home: 915 Grape St Truth Or Consequences NM 87901-1731

LYON, JOANNE B., psychologist; b. Little Rock, June 2, 1943; d. F. Ike and Marie (Graham) Beyer; m. James S. Lyon, Dec. 1971 (div. Sept. 1975), m. John M. Lofton, May 22, 1983 (dec. Feb. 1990). BA, Webster U., 1966; MEd, U. Mo., St. Louis, 1976, PhD, 1986. Lic. psychologist, Kans. Reading specialist Rockwood Sch. Dist., St. Louis, 1976-79; psychology cons. handicapped component St. Louis Head Start, 1982-83; intern Topeka State Hosp., 1983-84; dir. partial hosp. programs Family Svc. & Guidance Ctr., Topeka, 1985-89; pvt. practitioner and joint owner Shadow Wood Clin. Assocs., Topeka, 1989—2006, adminstr., 1999-2000. Clin. supr. Family Svc. and Guidance Ctr., Topeka, 1989-93; psychology adv. bd. Behavioral Scis. Regulatory Bd., 1996-98. Mem. exec. bd. Interfaith of Topeka, 1995-99, I Have a Dream Coalition, 1994-98; bd. dirs. Temple Beth Sholom Sisterhood, 1997-2000, Temple Beth Sholom, 1997-2000, Torah Learning Ctr., 2000—. Sherman scholar U. Mo., St. Louis, 1982. Mem. APA, Kans. Psychol. Assn., Am. Orthopsychiat. Assn., Soc. for Personality Assessment. Jewish. Home: 10027 Mackey Cir Overland Park KS 66212 Office: 8340 Mission Rd Prairie Village KS 66206 Office Phone: 913-381-1690. Personal E-mail: drjoannelyon@aol.com.

LYON, LINDA M., biology professor; b. Batavia, NY, Dec. 20, 1970; d. Joseph and Janet Lyon; m. Diresh Badawaly, Nov. 11, 1998. BA in Biology, Hartwich Coll., Oneonta, NY, 1993; MS, Wash. State U., Pullman, 1999, PhD in Environ. and Natural Resource Scis., 2003. Asst. prof. Frostburg State U., Md., 2002—. Avocations: dog training, hiking, travel. Home: 3562 Greenville Rd Meyersdale PA 15552 Office: Frostburg State U 101 Braddock Rd Frostburg MD 21532

LYON, MARTHA SUE, research engineer, retired military officer; b. Oct. 3, 1935; d. Harry Bowman and Erma Louise (Moreland) Lyon. BA in Chemistry, U. Louisville, 1959; MEd in Math., Northeastern Ill. U., 1974; postgrad., McGeorge Sch. Law, 1981-82, Northwestern Calif. U., 1999—, George Washington U., 1995—96. Cert. tchr. Ill., Ky. Rsch. assoc. U. Louisville Med. Sch., 1959-61, 62-63; commd. ensign USNR, 1965; advanced through grades to commr. USN, 1983; instr. instrumentation chemistry Northwestern U., Evanston, Ill., 1968-70; tchr. sci., chemistry, gifted math. Waukegan (Ill.) pub. schs., 1970-75; phys. scientist Libr. of Congress, Washington, 1975-76; rsch. engr. Lockheed Missiles & Space Co., Sunnyvale, Calif., 1976-77; instr., assoc. chmn. dept. physics U.S. Naval Acad., Annapolis, Md., 1977-80; analyst sys. analysis divsn. Office of Chief of Naval Ops. Staff, Washington, 1980-81; comdg. officer Naval Rsch. Ctr., Stockton, Calif., 1981-83; mem. faculty Def. Intelligence Coll., 1983-85; program mgr. Space and Naval Warfare Sys. Command, 1985-86; commdg. officer PERSUPPACT Memphis, 1986-88; program mgr. Space and Naval Warfare Sys. Command, 1988-91; sect. chief Def. Intelligence Agy., 1991-95. Chief marching divsn. Nat. Homecoming Parade and N.Y.C. Regional Parade Task Force Desert Storm, 1991; contractor mgr. supporting spl. asst. to Sec. of Def. for Gulf War Illnesses Investigations, 1997—98; pro bono work for Class Act Group; Fla. chpt. svc. officer, comdr. dist. 4 DAV. Mem. citizen rev. panel Fla. Foster Care Project Marion County, 1999; vet.'s advocate; mem. exec. com. Marion County Dem. Grantee, Am. Heart Assn., 1960—62, 1997—98, NSF, 1971, 1982. Mem.: Nat. Assn. Parliamentarians, Pvt. Investigators Assn. Va., Evidence Photographers' Internat. Coun., Internat. Soc. Bassists, Internat. Conf. Women in Sci. Engring. (protocol chair), Am. Soc. Photogrammetry, Am. Statis. Assn., Am. Fedn. Musicians, Soc. Women Engrs., Am. Chem. Soc., Mensa, Order Eastern Star, Delta Phi Alpha, Zeta Tau Alpha. Achievements include development of processes used in archival photography. E-mail: mslyon@att.net.

LYON, MARY LOU, retired secondary school educator; b. Wichita, Kans., Sept. 18, 1926; d. Theodore Joseph and Hazel Pearl (Johnson) Cochran; m. William Madison Lyon, Mar. 15, 1944 (div. July 1970); children: William Madison, Jr., Theodore Richard. AA, Coll. San Mateo, Calif., 1958; BA with distinction and honors, San Jose (Calif.) State U., 1960, lifetime secondary credential, 1961, MA, 1967. Cert. secondary edn. tchr., Calif. Tchr. Los Gatos (Calif.) HS, 1961, Blach Jr. HS Los Altos (Calif.) Elem. Dist., 1961-62, Homestead High, Fremont Union HS Dist., Cupertino, Calif., 1962—93, Metropolitan Adult Edn. Program, San Jose, 1986—. Tchr. San Jose State U. Extension, Cupertino, 1974-76, Fremont Union High Sch. Adult Edn., 1977; various offices Calif. Coun. for Social Studies, Sacramento, 1962-80; historian, photographer Anza Trek Observance Bicentennial, Santa Clara County (Calif.) Bicentennial Commn., 1975-76; cons. Calif. map Hearne Bros. Map Co., 1981; speaker Genealogical Soc., San Jose Hist. Mus., Calif. Hist. Soc., others. Author, editor (pamphlet) Social Sci. Rev., 1975-76; author numerous books on Santa Clara County, 2006, photographer (one-woman show) Cupertino Hist. Soc., 1975; photographer: (textbook) Addison Wesley, 1980; author: Some Women in Santa Clara County, 1996, Some More Women in Santa Clara County, 2001, Elisha Stephens of the Stephens-Murphy Party of 1844, 2005, Some Men in Santa Clara History, Cupertino by Arcadia, 2006. Chair of site & times Conf. Calif. hist. soc., 1985—; commr. Santa Clara County Hist. Heritage, 1994—2003; delegate Calif. State Sesquicentennial commn. for CCHS, 1998—2000; deacon Union Ch. of Cupertino. Recipient history honor, Phi Alpha Theta, 1959—60, Award of excellence for tchng. Calif. history, Conf. of Calif. Hist. Soc., 1973, Honored as an Achiever, Santa Clara County Penwomen, 1976, Coke Wood award, Conf. of Calif. Hist. Soc., 1994, 1997, award of merit, Calif. Pioneers of Santa Clara County, 1999, Pres. award, Conf. of Calif. Hist. Soc., 1999, 2002. Mem.: San Francisco Hist. Soc., Menlo Park Hist. Soc., Santa Clara County Pioneers (editor Trailblazer), San Jose Hist. Soc. (cons.), Cupertino Hist. Soc., Nat. Oreg.-Calif. Trail. Assn., Oreg.-Calif. Trail. Assn. (publicity com. Calif.-Nev. Hawaii br. 1985—), Conf. Calif. Hist. Soc. (various offices 1973—, pres. 1983—84, organizer confs. 2005, co-chair no. symposium 2005), San Francisco Corral of Westerners (sheriff 1995, editor Signals from Telegraph Hill), San Jose Hist. Mus. Assn., Nat. Parks and Conservation Assn., Lewis & Clark Hist. Assn., Westerners Internat. (bd. dirs.). Democrat. Avocations: photography, travel, lecturing, western history. Home: 879 Lily Ave Cupertino CA 95014-4261 Personal E-mail: malyon_1999@yahoo.com.

LYON, NORMA DUFFIELD, sculptor, agriculturist; b. Nashville, July 29, 1929; d. Benton J. and Elsa (Walburn) Stong; m. Gaylord Joe Lyon, July 22, 1950; children: Emily, Mark, Eric, Michelle, Gregory, Valerie, Lori, Kurt, Douglas. BS, Iowa State U., 1951. AnSci sculptor Iowa State Fair, Des Moines, Ill. State Fair, Springfield, Kans. State Fair, Hutcheson, Mo. State Fair, Nat. Cattle Congress, Waterloo, 1960; cattle judge, 1960—; art tchr. gifted and talented, South Tama (Iowa) Sch., 1986—, elem. nutrition tchr., 1986—, Toldeo, Iowa, 1986—; mem. Iowa Vet. Medicine Bd., 1992-97. Prin. works include numerous temporary and permanent sculptures in Iowa, Calif., Wis., Ariz., Kans., Tex., Ill., NY, Mo., Can.; illustrator pen and ink drawings for books. Mem. County Dem. Cen. Com., Tama, Friends of Extension ISU '91. Named Disting. Grad. Dairy Sci. Club, 1990, World Dairy Expo Woman of Yr., 1990, Iowa Master Farm Homemaker, 2004; recipient Pioneer award Nat. Dairy Shrine, 2000, Ralph Keeling award Iowa Dairy Industry, 2002. Mem. AAUW (treas. 1987-91), Iowa 4-H Found. (trustee 1986-91), Arts Coun. Tama-Toledo Area, Iowa Jersey Cattle Assn., Am. Jersey Cattle Club, Nat. Dairy Shrine (state membership chmn.), 4-H (hon.), Alpha Delta Pi. Roman Catholic. Avocations: music, knitting, reading, social concerns, religious edn. Home: 2621 K Ave Toledo IA 52342-9446

LYONS, BERYL BARTON ANFINDSEN, advertising executive; b. Jersey City, Dec. 12, 1925; d. Edward I. and Beatrice (Means) Anfindsen; m. Robert Lyons, Dec. 18, 1954; children: Susan E.L. Paglia, Robert Jr., Christopher B. Student, Traphagen Sch. Fashion Illustration, summer 1943-44, St. Elizabeth Coll., N.J., 1945-46; BA, Coll. N.Y.U., 1949. With Lord & Taylor, N.Y.C., 1949-52; jr. exec. Hahne & Co., Newark, 1952; hostess Statler Hotel, L.A., 1952; model Powers Modeling Agency, N.Y.C., 1952; mdse. demonstration REH, Wayne, N.J., 1978-94, Prestige Promotion, Wayne, 1978-94, McKenzie Assoc., Cape Cod, Mass., 1994-97, Wal-mart - Shaws Food; with promotional advt. dept. Checkers Product Servicing, Hopkinton, Mass., 1997—, Promotional Advt., Saco, Maine, 1997—2005, Fraser & Wagner, Scituate, Mass., 1997—2005, Suray Promotions, 2000—04. With Avon, 1971-2005, team leader, asst. mgr., 1971-78. Author numerous poems. Election worker Livingston, N.J., 1991, 92, 93. Scholar Phoenix Art Sch., 1944. Mem.: AAUW (life). Republican. Presbyterian. Avocations: art illustration, poetry, aerobic and aqua exercies, reading. Home: 500 Pennsylvania Ave Apt 208 Leominster MA 01453-7413

LYONS, BRIDGET GELLERT, language educator; b. Prague, Czechoslovakia, Aug. 28, 1932; came to U.S., 1940; d. Leopold and Marianne (Petschek) Gellert; m. Robert B. Lyons, Feb. 6, 1971. BA, Radcliffe Coll., 1954; MA, Oxford U., 1956; PhD, Columbia U., 1967. Instr. Rutgers U., New Brunswick, NJ, 1965-67, 1967-71, assoc. prof., 1971-78, chmn. dept. English, 1979-81, dir. grad. program in English, 1981-90, prof., 1978—2003, prof. emeritus, 2003—. Author: Voices of Melancholy, 1971; co-editor: Renaissance Quar., 1978-92; editor: Reading in an Age of Theory, 1997. Mem. Renaissance Soc. Am. (exec. bd. 1978—2000) Home: 30 W 60th St New York NY 10023-7902 E-mail: robridge@rcn.com.

LYONS, CATHY, computer company executive; BS in Bus. Adminstrn. and Mktg., U. Colo. Gen. mgr. LaserJet Solutions Grp. European Operation Hewlett-Packard Co., Bergamo, Italy, v.p., gen. mgr. Supplies Bus. Palo Alto, Calif., 1999—2001, v.p., gen. mgr. Inkjet Supplies Divsn., 2001—03, sr. v.p. bus. and imaging printing Imaging and Personal Systems Grp., 2003—05, exec. v.p., chief mktg. officer, 2005—. Office: Hewlett Packard Co 3000 Hanover St Palo Alto CA 94304-1185*

LYONS, GLORIA ROGERS, medical/surgical nurse, nursing educator; b. Durham, NC, Sept. 2, 1940; d. Roy Lee Rogers and Annie Bullock; m. James Lyons, Dec. 26, 1965; children: Jamesia, Anthony. BSN, Winston-Salem State U., N.C., 1962; MS, Tex. Woman's U., 1979. Cert. clin. nurse specialist. Charge nurse obstetrics Duke U. Med. Ctr., Durham, NC, 1962—65; charge nurse ob-gyn. John Hopkins Hosp., Balt., 1966; pub. health nurse Long Branch Pub. Health Agency, Long Branch, NJ, 1968; clin. rsch. nurse Clin. Rsch. Labs, Edgewood Arsenal, Md., 1966—68; charge nurse surgery Long Branch Med. Ctr., Long Branch, NJ, 1968—69; instr. LVN program Marlboro (N.J.) State Hosp., 1969—70; house supr. R.E. Thomason Gen. Hosp., El Paso, Tex., 1970—73; staff nurse emergency Darnall Army Cmty. Hosp., Fort Hood, Tex., 1974; prof. nursing, coord. med.-surg. I Ctrl. Tex. Coll., Killeen, 1975—97, prof. emeritus, 2003—. Mem.: Ctrl. Tex. Coll. Ret. Tchrs. Assn., Delta Sigma Theta.

LYONS, GRACE JEAN, librarian, educator; b. N.Y.C., June 22, 1932; d. Edward Joseph and Grace Emma (Dreeland) L. B.S. in Chemistry, Univ. Coll. St. John's U., 1954; M.L.S., Columbia U., 1960. Cert. prof. librarian N.Y. Sr. librarian Kings Park Psychiat. Ctr. (N.Y.), 1960-72; librarian D.C. Regional Library for Blind and Physically Handicapped, 1973—; assoc. prof. Sch. Library and Info. Scis., Kent State U. (Ohio), summers 1980, 81, 83. Contbr. articles in field to jours. Chmn. com. on libraries and info. services Pres.'s Com. on Employment of Handicapped, 1983—; bd. dirs. Washington Vol. Readers for Blind, 1978—. Recipient Exceptional Service award, ALA, 1977. Mem. Am. Mgmt. Assn., D.C. Commn. on Arts and Humanities (spl. constituencies sect.), Am. Council of Blind (Friends of the Arts Affiliate). Home: 1530 Moorings Dr # 12B Reston VA 20190-4209 Office: D C Regional Library for Blind and Physically Handicap Ped 901 G St NW Washington DC 20001

LYONS, MARY E., academic administrator; b. Calif. BA, Sonoma St. Univ., 1971; MA, San Diego St. Univ., 1976; PhD, Sonoma St. Univ., 1983. Prof. Franciscan School of Theology, Berkeley, Calif., 1984—90; pres. Calif. Maritime Acad., Vallejo, 1990-96, Coll. of St. Benedict, St. Joseph, Minn., 1996—2003, U. San Diego, 2003—. Office: Office of Pres U San Diego 5998 Alcala Pk San Diego CA 92110-2492 Office Phone: 619-260-4520. Office Fax: 619-260-6833. E-mail: president@sandiego.edu.*

LYONS, MONA, lawyer; b. NYC, Jan. 10, 1950; BA, Coll. Potomac, 1972; JD, Catholic Univ. Am., 1975. Bar: DC 1975. Private practice, Washington. Named one of 75 Best Lawyers in Washington, Washingtonian Mag., 2002. Mem.: DC Bar. Office: Law Office of Mona Lyons 1666 Connecticut Ave NW Ste 500 Washington DC 20009 Office Phone: 202-387-7000. Office Fax: 202-387-7116.

LYONS, NATALIE BELLER, family counselor; b. Havana, Cuba, Apr. 3, 1926; d. Herman Lawrence and Jennie (Engler) B.; widowed, Apr. 18, 1986; children: Anne, Sara. Degree in Surveying and Land Appraising, Inst. Vedado, Havana, 1943, BS, 1943; BA, U. Mich., 1946; MEd, U. Miami, Fla., 1967. Family counselor, mem. staff furniture design and mfg. co. George B. Bent Co., Gardner, Mass., 1953-58; tchr. H.S., Winchendon, Mass., Hollywood, Fla., 1962, parochial sch., Ft. Lauderdale, Fla., 1963-64; family counselor Miami, 1967—; project dir. Cen. Am. fisheries program Peace Corps, 1972-74. Bd. dirs. mem. Com. for Accuracy in Mid-East Reporting in Am. Pres. Miami region Hadassah, 1989—91; mem. cmty. rels. coun. Greater Miami Jewish Fedn., 1985—; nat. women's divsn. Am. Soc. for Technion, 1991—, pres., 2000—; co-chmn. Pro-Israel Rally, Tri County, 1991; co-chmn Joint Action Com., Miami, 1989—91; founder, dir. Cmty. Inst. Jewish Studies, Hollywood, Fla., 1962—64; tng. dir. Los Amigos de las Ams., 1975—2002. Recipient Leadership award Hadassah, 1987, honoree Am. Soc. for Technion Scholarship Fund, 1991; named Woman of Yr., Hadassah, 1991. Mem.: Am. Inst. Tech. (nat. pres. women's divsn.), Israel Inst. Tech. (pres. so. region 1996—2000), Am. Soc. for Technion (nat. pres. 2001—04, nat. chmn. bd. dirs. 2004—). Democrat. Avocations: travel, reading, antiques, performing arts.

LYSHAK-STELZER, FRANCES, artist; b. Detroit, June 3, 1948; d. Peter Paul and Frances Ellen (Harrington) Lyshak; m. Stephen Stelzer, Oct. 10, 1994 BFA, Wayne State U., 1970; MPS, Pratt Inst., 1978. Art therapist Creative Women's Collective, N.Y.C., 1978—79; creative arts therapy coord./dir. art therapy internship tng. Bronx Children's Psychiat. Ctr., 1979—. One-woman shows include La Mama La Galleria, N.Y.C., 1993, 96, 98, 2004, Claire Dunphy's Studio, N.Y.C., 1985, Wow Theatre/Gallery, N.Y.C., 1983, Bill Rice Studio, N.Y.C., 1984, 88; group shows include Provincetown (Mass.) Art Assn. and Mus., 1983, Art Quest 86, L.A., Mus. of Hudson Highlands, N.Y., 1985, Interart de St. Armand Gallery, 1983, Park Ave. Atrium, 1984, Cash/Newhouse Gallery, 1985, Marymount Manhattan Coll. Gallery, 1989, La Mama La Galleria, N.Y.C., 1985, 86, 92, Denise Bibro Fine Art, N.Y.C., 1996, RC Fine Art, N.J., 1999, Barbara Ann Levy Gallery, N.Y.C., 1999; author: The Secret: Art and Healing from Sexual Abuse, 1999 Mem. Am. Art Therapy Assn. (bd. cert. art therapist registered), Nat. Registry Cert. Group Psychotherapists (cert. group psychotherapist), cert. alcohol and substance abuse counselor) Office Phone: 718-239-3790. Personal E-mail: flyshak@msn.com. Business E-Mail: bcrtfel@omh.state.ny.us.

LYSTAD, MARY HANEMANN (MRS. ROBERT LYSTAD), sociologist, writer; b. New Orleans, Apr. 11, 1928; d. James and Mary (Douglass) Hanemann; m. Robert Lystad, June 20, 1953; children: Lisa Douglass, Anne Hanemann, Mary Lunde, Robert Douglass, James Hanemann. AB cum laude, Newcomb Coll., 1949; MA, Columbia U., 1951; PhD, Tulane U., 1955. Postdoctoral fellow social psychology S.E. La. Hosp., Mandeville, 1955-57; field rsch. social psychology Ghana, 1957-58, South Africa and Swaziland, 1968, China, 1986; chief sociologist Collaborative Child Devel. Project, Charity Hosp. La., New Orleans, 1958-61; feature writer African div. Voice Am., Washington, 1964-73; program analyst NIMH, Washington, 1968-78, asso. dir. for planning and coordination div. spl. mental health programs, 1978-80; chief Nat. Ctr. for Prevention and Control of Rape, 1980-83, Ctr. Mental Health Studies of Emergencies, 1983-89; pvt. cons. specializing on mental health implications social and econ. problems Bethesda, Md., 1990—. Cons. on youth Nat. Goals Research Staff, White House, Washington, 1969-70. Author: (nonfiction) Social Aspects of Alienation, 1969, As They See It: Changing Values of College Youth, 1972, Violence at Home, 1974, A Child's World As Seen in His Stories and Drawings, 1974, From Dr. Mather to Dr. Seuss: 200 Years of American Books for Children, 1980, At Home in America, 1983; (fiction for children) Millicent the Monster, 1968, James the Jaguar, 1972, Jennifer Takes Over P.S. 94, 1972, Halloween Parade, 1973, That New Boy, 1973, Play Ball, 1997; editor: Innovations in Mental Health Services to Disaster Victims, 1985, Violence in the Home: Interdisciplinary Perspectives, 1986, Mental Health Response to Mass Emergencies: Theory and Practice, 1988. Recipient Spl. Recognition award USPHS, 1983, Alumna Centennial award Newcomb Coll., 1986. Home and Office: 4900 Scarsdale Rd Bethesda MD 20816-2440

LYTTON, LINDA ROUNTREE, marriage and family therapist, consultant; b. Suffolk, Va., Mar. 30, 1951; d. John Thomas and Anne Carolyn (Edwards) Rountree; m. Daniel Michael Lytton, June 23, 1973; 1 child, Seth Daniel. BS, Radford U., 1973; MS, Va. Poly. Inst. and State U., 1992. Collegiate profl. cert.; lic. profl. counselor, Va.; lic. marriage and family therapist. Tchr., cons. Fauquier County Pub. Schs., Warrenton, Va., 1973-74, Chesterfield County Pub. Schs., Richmond, Va., 1974-78, Williamsburg (Va.)-James City Pub. Schs., 1979-83, Prince William County Pub. Schs., Manassas, Va., 1983-89; hist. area interpreter Colonial Williamsburg Found., 1978-79; outpatient therapist Prince William County Community Svcs. Bd., 1989-91, emergency svcs. therapist, therapist cons., 1991-93; marriage and family therapist Menninger Care Sys., Inc., Manassas, 1993-99; pvt. practice Sudley Park Profl. Ctr., Manassas, Va., 1995—. Cons. Horizons for Learning, Inc., Richmond, 1989—. Great Books Leader, 1993—. Mem. Am. Assn. Marriage and Family Therapy, Va. Assn. Marriage and Family Therapy, Internat. Assn., Marriage and Family Counselors, Sigma Kappa (life). Avocations: tennis, biking, boating, water-skiing. Home: 12046 Market Square Ct Manassas VA 20112-3214 also: Fairfield Office Pk 12890 Harbor Dr Woodbridge VA 22192-2921 Office: Sudley Park Profl Ctr 8421 Dorsey Cir Manassas VA 20110 Office Phone: 703-330-5633. Personal E-mail: llyttonlmft@verizon.net.

LYUBOMIRSKY, SONJA, psychology professor; d. Anatoly and Tina Lyubomirsky; m. Peter Frank Del Greco; children: Gabriella Arpege Del Greco, Alexander Armand Del Greco. AB, Harvard U., Cambride, Mass., 1989; PhD, Stanford U., Calif., 1994. Prof. U. Calif., Riverside, Calif., 1994—. Editor: Jour. Positive Psychology, 2005—; contbr. articles to profl. jours. Grantee, NIMH, 2004—. Mem.: APA (Templeton Found. Positive Psychology prize 2002). Office: University of California Riverside Department of Psychology Riverside CA 92521 Office Phone: 951-827-5041. Office Fax: 951-827-3985. Business E-Mail: sonja.lyubomirsky@ucr.edu.

MA, JING-HENG SHENG, language educator; b. Beijing, Mar. 15, 1932; arrived in U.S., 1963; d. Xue Shu and Guo Ying (Yin) Sheng; m. Wei-Yi Ma, Sept. 28, 1958; children: Lyou-fu, Syau-fu. BEd, Taiwan Normal U., 1958; MA, Philippine Women's U., 1963; MA in Applied Linguistics, U. Mich., 1971, PhD in Linguistics, 1983. Instr. Chinese Cornell U. Extension Program, Taipei, Taiwan, 1959-62; lectr. Chinese U. Mich., Ann Arbor, 1963-84; assoc. prof., chairperson dept. East Asian langs. Williams Coll., Williamstown, Mass., 1984-88. Vis. prof. Chinese dept. Wellesley Coll., 1988-89, prof., chair dept., 1989-92, 95-98, Mayling Soong prof. Chinese studies, 1997, chair dept., 2000—. Author: Chinese Language Patterns, 1985, A Study of the Mandaring Chinese Verb Suffix Zhe, 1986, At Middle Age: A Learning Guide for Students of Chinese, 1988, 2nd edit. 1991, Strange Friends: A Learning Guide for Students of Chinese, 1989, 2nd edit. 1991, Great Wall: A Learning Guide for Students of Chinese, 1990, 2d edit., 1993, The True Story of Ah Q: A Learning Guide for Students of Chinese, 1992, Difficult Points in Chinese Grammar, 1992, others; co-author: HyperChinese: The Grammar Modules (CD), 1993, Chinese Unmasked: Grammatical Principles and Applications, 1994, HyperChinese: The Pronunciation Modules, 1995, Drills and Quizzes in Mandarin Chinese Pronunciation, 1999, Keys to Chinese Character Writing, 2000, (book and CD) Learning Through Listening: An Introduction to Chinese Proverbs and Their Origins, 2002. Mem. Chinese Lang. Tchrs. Assn. (exec. bd. 1990-93), Assn. for Asian Studies, Internat. Soc. for Chinese Lang. Tchg. (bd. dirs. 1997—). Home: 10 Nonesuch Dr Natick MA 01760-1041

MA, VIVIENNE, dancer, educator; d. May Mee (Choo) Ng. BSBA, Hawaii Pacific U., Honolulu, 1996, MBA, 1998. Cert. higher edn. U. Surrey. Tchr. Royal Acad. Dance, London, 2004—06, Dance Studio No. 1, L.A., 2006—. Recipient Acad. Achievement Pres. award, Dept. Treasury N.Y., 1995. Mem.: Am. Acad. Ballet, Internat. Assn. Dance Medicine. Avocations: weightlifting, ballet, yoga, kickboxing, pilates. Office: Dance Studio # 1 2037 Granville Ave Los Angeles CA 90025

MA, XING, optical engineer; b. Jianjin, People's Republic of China, Dec. 15, 1954; d. Tai and Suwen (Yu) M.; m. Tianxiang Liu, Sept. 28, 1984; children: Patrick, Alex. BS in Physics, Normal U. Tianjin, China, 1980; PhD in Elec. Engring., U. New South Wales, Sydney, Australia, 1995. Optical engr. Electronic Material Co., Tianjin, China, 1981-86; rsch. asst. U. New South Wales, Sydney, Australia, 1987-94; rsch. engr. Dept. Comm. RMIT, Melbourne, Australia, 1994-97; sr. fiber optics engr. E-TEK Dynamics, San Jose, Calif., 1998—. Chief tech leader for design of new products: CADM and 5-part WDM device. Mem. IEEE. Avocations: coin collecting/numismatics, shell collecting, swimming, volleyball. Office: Etek Dynamics Inc 1768 Automation Pkwy San Jose CA 95131-1873 E-mail: xing.ma@etek.com.

MAACK, JEAN ELIZABETH, retired elementary school educator; b. Ossian, Iowa, June 5, 1920; d. Cyrus Rodney and Elizabeth Bertha (Plagman) Nicholson; m. Arthur Charles Maack, Aug. 16, 1939 (dec. Dec. 1989); children: David John, Stephen Charles, Christopher Arthur, Rodney Alan. BS, U. Ill., 1940, MS, 1941. Cert. tchr., Ill. Sales Montgomery Ward, St. Paul, 1941-42; rsch. Econ. Lab., St. Paul, 1942-43, U. Minn. Soils Dept., St. Paul, 1943; nutrition rsch. U. Minn. Hormel Found., 1943-45; tchr. Sch. Dist. 58, Downers Grove, Ill., 1956-78. Bd. dirs. Ill. Edn. Assn., Springfield, 1970-77. Contbr. articles to profl. jours. Pres. ERA Ill., 1977-82, West Suburban Rep. Women, 1983, Rogue Valley Womens Pol. Caucus, 1988-91; pres. Oreg. Womens Pol. Caucus, 1999—; founder, mem. Pro-Choice Coalition, 1989—. Mem. AAUW, LWV, Rogue Valley Geneal. Soc. Democrat. Presbyterian. Avocations: genealogy, camping, travel. Home: 2983 Siskiyou Blvd Medford OR 97504-1918

MAARBJERG, MARY PENZOLD, retired office equipment company executive; b. Oct. 2, 1943; d. Edmund Theodore and Lucy Adelaide (Singleton) Penzold; m. John Peder Maarbjerg, Oct. 20, 1966; 1 child, Martin Peder. AB, Hollins Coll., 1965; MBA, Wharton Sch., Pa., 1969. Cons. bus. and fin., Stamford, Conn., 1977-78; corp. staff analyst Pitney Bowes, Inc., Stamford, 1978-80, mgr. pension and benefit fin., 1980-81, dir. investor rels., 1981-85; v.p. planning and devel. Pitney Bowes Credit Corp., Norwalk, Conn., 1985-86, treas., v.p. planning, 1986-94; v.p. mktg. devel. and mng. dir. Asia Pacific Bowes Fin. Svcs., 1994-95, v.p. ops. and mng. dir., 1995-97; v.p. corp. svcs. Pitney Bowes, Inc., Stamford, 1997-99, v.p. real estate and adminstrn., 1999-2001, v.p. adminstrn. and process integration, 2001—05. Bd. dirs. Stamford Dental Ctr., 2003—; mem. cmty. bd. U. Conn., Stamford, 2003—; bd. dirs. Person-to-Person, 2004—, treas., 2005—. Mem. adv. com. City of Stamford Mcpl. Employees Retirement Fund, 1980-85; mem. fin. adv. com. YWCA, Stamford, 1982-86; bd. dirs. Stamford Symphony, 1985-95, Vis. Nurses Assn., 1984-86, Am. Recorder Soc., 1986-98, Am. Classical Orch., 1999-2002; bd. dirs. Stamford Partnership, chmn., 1998—2004; bd. dirs., treas. Amherst Early Music, 2000—. Fellow Royal Statis. Soc.; mem. Fin. Execs. Inst., Phi Beta Kappa. E-mail: mmaar@optonline.net.

MAAS, JANE BROWN, advertising executive; b. Jersey City; d. Charles E and Margaret (Beck) Brown; m. Michael Maas, Aug. 30, 1957; children: Katherine, Jennifer. BA, Bucknell U., 1953; postgrad., U. Dijon, France, 1954; MA, Cornell U., 1955; LittD, Ramapo Coll., 1986, St. John's U., 1988. Assoc. producer Name That Tune TV Program, N.Y.C., 1957—64; v.p. Ogilvy and Mather Inc., N.Y.C., 1964—76; sr. v.p. Wells, Rich, Greene, Inc., N.Y.C., 1976—82; pres. Muller Jordan Weiss Inc., N.Y.C., 1982—89, Earle Palmer Brown Cos., N.Y.C., 1989—92, chmn., 1992—94, chmn. emeritus, 1994—. Co-author: (book) How to Advertise, 1975, Better Brochures, 1981, Adventures of a Advertising Woman, 1986, The New How to Advertise, 1992, Christmas in Wales: A Homecoming, 1994. Bd govs comt Scholastic Achievement, 1985—92; active Girl Scouts US, NY, 1970—76; mem adv bd William E Simon Grad Sch Bus, Univ Rochester, 1989—2005; pub dir AIA, 1993—95; trustee Bucknell Univ, Lewisburg, 1976—86, Fordham Univ, NY, 1983—91. Named Woman of the Yr, NY Advert, 1986; recipient Matrix Award, Women in Communications, 1980. Mem.: AIA (hon.), Am Assn. Advt. Agys. (bd govs), Am Archtl. Found (regent 1993—2000), Phi Beta Kappa. Avocations: creative writing, jogging. Home: 3 Meadow Way Westhampton Beach NY 11978 Office Phone: 631-288-5881. Personal E-mail: janemaas@att.net.

MAAS, MAXINE ANNA ADELAIDE SCHUMANN, retired juvenile justice administrator; b. San Diego, July 23, 1925; d. James Maximilian Schumann and Johanna Catherine Meyer; m. Albert L. Maas, Sept. 26, 1944 (dec.); children: Albert L. III, Marilynn Maxine Maas Jones. Degree in drama, U. Calif., Berkeley, 1946; degree, Calif. U., Hayward, 1978; MA in edn., U. San Francisco, 1978. Actress, model Austin Studios, San Francisco, 1939—44, Powers, N.Y.C., 1944—50; counselor Contra Costa County Probation Dept., Martinez, Calif., 1950—69, supt. girls ctr., 1969—80, juvenile instn. adminstr., 1980—89; ret. Contbr. articles to profl. jours. Founding mem. Juvenile Justice Network Napa County, 1990—; mem. San Francisco Opera Found., 1990—2005, di Rosa Preserve, Napa, Calif., 1996—2005; vol. Jarvis Conservatary Music, Napa, 1998—2005, numerous orgns.; sponsor Internat. Ball, NY. Mem.: Napa Valley Yacht Club (bd. dirs. 1991—2005), Delta Zeta. Lutheran. Home: 19 S Newport Dr Napa CA 94559 Address: PO Box 595 Poulsbo WA 98370

MAATSCH, DEBORAH JOAN, manufacturing executive; b. Lincoln, Nebr., Mar. 26, 1950; d. Leon F. Forst and Jarolyn J. Hoffman Forst Conrad; m. Gordon F. Maatsch, Mar. 14, 1969; children: Jason, Diana. BS, U. Nebr., Lincoln, 1976; MBA, U. Phoenix, 1997. Accredited tax advisor; IRS enrolled agt. Acct., supr. US Civil Svc., Heidelberg, Germany, 1971—73; paralegal Mattson Rickets Davies et al, Lincoln, Nebr., 1976—87; tax cons., 1981—; paralegal Wade Ash Woods & Hill, P.C., 1986—94; sr. trust adminstr. Investment Trust Co., 1994—96; compliance officer Nelson, Benson and Zellmer, Inc., 1995—96; pres. DGJD Inc., 1993—; contr. Arena Devel., Inc., 1996—2000; pres. Boyd Industries, Inc., 2001—. Mem. Park County Sr. Wellness Team, 1999—; mem. bus. adv. bd. Ponderosa HS, 1994-98. Contbr. articles to profl. jour. Event chmn., vol. Jefferson Cmty. Ctr., 1999—; bd. dirs. JCCA, 2001-03, pres., 2002-03; bd. dirs. Kids Roundup, 2002—; coord. Jefferson Hist. Preservation Fund; mem. Women's C. of C. Mem. Doane Coll. Alumni Assn. (dir. 1989-93), Nebr. Alumni Assn. Avocations: travel, outdoor activities, horses. Office: DGJD Inc PO Box 267 Jefferson CO 80456-0267 also: Boyd Industries Inc PO Box 315 Boyd TX 76023 E-mail: dgjdine@wildblue.net.

MABB, KAREN TERRI, ornithologist; d. Norman P. and Song Tae Mabb. BS in Biology, Calif. State Poly. U., Pomona, 2001, MS in Biol. Scis., 2003. Rschr./ornithologist Calif. Parrot Project, L.A., 1995—; grad. tchg. assoc. Rutgers U., New Brunswick, NJ, 2004—. Author: (jour. article) Western Birds (Ralph Schreiber Meml. Ornithology Rsch. award, 2002), (rsch.) Roosting bevavior of naturalized parrots (McNair Scholar's Program, 2000), Seasonal roosting behavior of naturalized parrots (NSF Grad. Rsch. Fellowship Hon. Mention, 2002), Flock composition of naturalized parrots in California (NSF Grad. Rsch. Fellowship Hon. Mention, 2003), Native origins of Australia's avian imports (Calif. Pre-doctoral Scholar Program, 2003). Recipient Student Membership award, Am. Ornithologists Union, 2001, Eva MacKenzie scholarship, Calif. State Poly. U., 2000, Grad. Equity scholarship, 2001, Grad. Sch. of NB Spl. Study award, Rutgers U., 2005; Grad. Presdl. Fellowship, Calif. State Poly. U., 2002. Mem.: Am. Ornithologists Union, Western Field Ornithologists (life), Am. Mensa Soc., Pasadena Audubon Soc. Office: Rutgers Univ Ecology & Evolution 14 College Farm Rd New Brunswick NJ 08901 Office Phone: 732-932-1050. Personal E-mail: kmabb@hotmail.com.

MABEE, SANDRA IVONNE NORIEGA, musician, educator, clergy member; b. Hato Rey, P.R., Jan. 13, 1955; d. Nelson Custudio Noriega and Norma Ruth (Eiseman) Lee; m. Carl Mabee, 1980 (div. 2000); 1 child, Rebecca Lee. BA in Bibl. Studies summa cum laude, Patten Coll., 1977; BM magna cum laude, San Francisco Conservatory, 1983; MA in Music cum laude, Calif. State U., Hayward, 1985; PhD in Religion, Christian Bible Coll., N.C., 2000. Ordained min. Evang. Ch. Alliance, 1991; cert. Evangelical Tchr.'s Tng. Assn. Prin. timpanist Bay Area Women's Philharm., San Francisco, 1980—2004; prof. music Patten Coll., Oakland, Calif., 1980—89, chairperson profl. studies divsn., 1986-88; min. of music El Cerrito (Calif.) Christian Ctr., 1988-91; prof. music Hayward Christian Sch., 1988-91; intern pastor, dir. music ministry Trinity Ch., Oakland, Calif., 1991-92; pastor, dir. music ministries Unveiled Christ Ministries, Calif., 1992—2003; prof. music Las Positas Coll., 1998—; founder, pastor Up to Zion Ministries, 2003; music tchr. Contra Costa Christian Sch., 2003—04, Valley Christian H.S., 2004—05, Hacker Sch., San Jose, Calif., 2005—. Tympanist, percussionist various orchs., Bay Area, Calif., 1977—; pvt. tchr. music lessons, Bay Area, 1977—; percussion ensemble Patten Coll., Oakland, 1983-84; prodr. sing-it-yourself Messiah Patten Coll., Oakland, 1986; guest dir. choral Landmark Ministries, Oakland, 1990; seminar instr., Landmark Sch. Ministries, Oakland, 1990, Internat. Radio Broadcast, 1998; founder, condr., artistic dir. Bay Area Women's Percussion Troupe, 2005; drum set instr. Day Jams Rock Music Corp., Palo Alto, Calif. Prison ministry vol. Alameda County Jail, Oakland, 1990, Vacaville Fed. Prison, Follow-up Ministries; vol. Assn. of Christian Schs. Inc./Song Shop; founder Tracy Percussion Ensemble, 1999—. San Francisco Conservatory scholar, 1980-83; named Outstanding Young Woman of Am., 1986, 87, winner concerto soloist Redwood Symphony, 1988, for Outstanding Svc. to Teaching Profession A.B.I. Mem. Percussive Arts Soc., ASCAP, Internat. Alliance of Woman Musicians, Nat. Women's History Mus. (charter). Home: PO Box 2948 Castro Valley CA 94546 Office Phone: 925-577-7443. E-mail: drsm1@sbcglobal.net.

MABRY, J. BETH, sociologist, educator; b. Washington; PhD, Va. Poly. Inst. and State U., Blacksburg, 1999. Postdoctoral fellow U. So. Calif., L.A., 1999—2002; assoc. prof. sociology Indiana U. of Pa., 2002—, coord. doctoral program adminstrn. and leadership studies. Fellow, Nat. Inst. Aging, 1999—2002. Mem.: AAUW, Gerontology Soc. Am., Am. Sociol. Assn. Achievements include research in identifying that stress coping processes in regard to anger vary by race. Office: Indiana U Pa Dept Sociology 102 McElhaney Hall Indiana PA 15705-1087 Office Phone: 724-357-1289.

MABRY, LINDA S., education educator; d. Thurlow B. Weed Jr. and Betty A. Bailey; children: Laura S Song, Lisa N. Eichler, Frank J. III. BS magna cum laude, U. Houston, 1972; MEd, U. Ill., Urbana-Champaign, 1986, PhD, 1995. Lic. tchr. Ill. Spencer fellow Spencer Found.-Nat. Acad. Edn., Chgo., 1991—92, 1999—2000; mem. performance assessment rev. bd. NY Performance Stds. Consortium, NYC, 1999—; prof. edn. Wash. State U., Vancouver, 2000—. Evaluator programs in edn. Wash. State U., Vancouver, 2000—03, coord. secondary edn. program, 2004—05, coord. MEd program, 2001—04, chair rsch. com. Author: Conducting Evaluation in the Real World (nominee Book of Yr., Am. Evaluation Assn.), Custom and Cherishing: The Arts in Elementary Schools; editor: Evaluation and the Postmodern Dilemma; contbr. articles to profl. jours. Named Outstanding Graduating Sr. in Coll. of Edn., Phi Kappa Phi, U. Houston, 1972, Edmund J. James scholar, Coll. of Edn., U. Ill., 1984, maj. contbr. to field of evaluation, Am. Evaluation Assn., Ency. of Evaluation, 2004; recipient Outstanding Conf. Presentation award, Am. Ednl. Rsch. Assn., 1991, Outstanding Doctoral Dissertation award, Phi Delta Kappa, U. Ill., 1994, Tchg. Excellence Recognition award, Dept. Counseling and Ednl. Psychology, Ind. U., 1997; William Chandler Bagley scholar, Coll. of Edn., U. Ill., 1990—91, 1991—92, rsch. fellow, Proffitt Endowment, Ind. U., 1997. Mem.: Wash. Ednl. Rsch. Assn. (Evaluation grantee 2000), Oreg. Program Evaluators Network (program com. 2003—04), Am. Evaluation Assn. (bd. dirs. 2002—04, pub. affairs com. 2002—05, chair Theories of Evaluation Topical Interest Group 2002, Early Career award 2000). Office: Wash State U 14204 NE Salmon Creek Avenue VLIB 210P Vancouver WA 98686-9600 Office Phone: 360-546-9428.

MACALISTER, KIM PORTER, advertising executive; b. Providence, Oct. 25, 1954; d. Bruce Barnes and Jeanne Marie (Cahill) Macalister; m. Bruce Phillip Person, Dec. 29, 1979 (div. June 1984); m. Arthur Gene Quinby, Feb. 19, 1988. BS, Skidmore Coll., Saratoga Springs, NY, 1976. Media planner, acctt. exec. J.H. Dietz Advt., Providence, 1976—79; media planner Della Femina, Travisano, LA, 1979—80; from media planner to v.p. media dir. J. Walter Thompson, LA, 1980—85; v.p., media dir. Thompson Recruitment Advt. subs. J. Walter Thompson, 1985—86, mgr., v.p., 1986—89, pres., COO, 1989—90, pres., CEO, 1990—. Former faculty AAAA Inst. Advanced Advt. Studies. Trustee Skidmore Coll. Mem.: Young Pres.' Orgn., LA Advt. Club. Republican. Office: Jwt Specialized Comm 5200 W Century Blvd Ste 310 Los Angeles CA 90045-5923

MACARIN-MARA, LYNN, psychotherapist, consultant; b. Queens, N.Y., Feb. 27, 1948; d. David and Grace Macarin; m. Marvin Weingast, Sept. 2, 2000; 1 child, Leah Mara. MA, NYU, 1972; MSW, Hunter Sch. Social Work, 1980. Cert. psychoanalytic psychotherapy, hypnotherapy and hypnoanalysis. With Greenwich Inst. Psychotherapy and Psychoanalysis, 1984-87; pvt. practice, 1987—; pres. Face to Face Psychotherapy Svcs., Metuchen, N.J., 1987—; dir. family and children svcs. Ednl. Alliance, Inc., N.Y.C., 1990-95. Adj. prof. SUNY, Staten Island, N.Y., 1972-73, New Sch. for Social Rsch., N.Y.C., 1980-81. Contbr. articles to profl. jours. Chairperson membership com. Temple Emanu-El, Edison, N.J., 1998-2001. Mem. N.J. Soc. for Clin. Social Work (newsletter editor 1997-99). Democrat. Jewish. Avocations: travel, dance, writing, painting. Office: Face to Face Psychotherapy Svcs 2 Blair Ave Metuchen NJ 08840

MACARTHUR, DIANA TAYLOR, advanced technology executive; b. Santa Fe, July 7, 1933; widowed; children: Elizabeth Tschursin, Alexander Tschursin. BA, Vassar Coll., 1955. Cons. economist Checchi & Co., 1957-61; v.p., dir. Thomas J. Deegan Co., 1961-62; dep. chief West Africa Peace Corps, 1963, reg. program officer for North Africa, Near East, South Asia, 1964, dir. divsn. pvt. and internat. orgns., 1965-66; pvt. cons., 1966-74; program mgr. Aerospace Divsn. Gen Elec. Co., 1974-76; pres. Consumer Dynamics, 1977-80; v.p., dir. Dynamac Internat. Inc., 1980-88, chmn., pres., CEO, 1988—; chmn., CEO Rsch. Analysis and Mgmt. Corp., 1988-92. Pres. Fgn. Traders, Inc., 1980—86. Trustee Menninger Found., Topeka, 1972-04, Santa Fe Inst., 2005-; bd. dirs. Sci. and Tech. Corp. U. N.Mex.; bd. visitors Menninger-Baylor Coll. Medicine, Meth. Hosp. Found., 2004-06; Lady Bird Johnson Wildflower Ctr., 1985-; mem. Pres.'s Com. of Adv. on Sci. and Tech., 1994-01; citizens adv. bd. to the Pres. Coun. on Youth Opportunity, 1966-70; served on CSIS Strengthening of Amer. Com., 1992, Nat. Benefits from Nat. Lab. Com., 1993, Sr. Policy on Nat. Challenges, 1996, Geopolitics of Energy Com., 2000; mem. The Chancellor's Adv. Coun. U. Sys. of Md.; bd. visitors U. Md. Biotech. Inst.; adv. com. Ctr. Strategic & Internat. Studies; bd. dirs. Atlantic Coun. USA; bus. adv. coun. Ctr. for China-U.S. Coop., U. Denver. Mem. Coun. on Competitiveness, Business-Higher Edn. Forum (mem. exec. com.), Tech. Coun. Md. (mem. exec. com.), Los Alamos Nat. Lab. Found. (mem. exec. com.), Nat. Hispanic Cultural Ctr. Found., The Santa Fe Opera, Phi Beta Kappa. Office: Dynamac Internat Inc 2275 Research Blvd Rockville MD 20850-3268 E-mail: dmacarthur@dynamac.com.

MACARTHUR, MARJORIE ELLEN HOTTLEY, secondary school educator; b. Los Angeles, Calif., Mar. 16, 1946; d. David Cecil and Ethel Marjorie Holtby; m. James Sterling MacArthur, Sept. 9, 1970; 1 child, Heather Anne MacArthr. BA, Calif. State U., 1968. English tchr. Chatsworth H.S., 1969—2006. Rep. Sch. Site Coun., Chatsworth, Calif., 2000—06. Mem.: Nat. Endowment for Humanities, Delta Kappa Gamma Soc. Republican. United Meth. Avocations: writing, travel, baking. Home: 242 Cay Ct Newbury Park CA 91320

MACARTNEY, LISA LANI, science educator, consultant; b. Honolulu, Hawaii, Sept. 15, 1960; d. Ronald and Sandra Lind MacArtney; life ptnr. Bird S. Ramirez, Nov. 1, 1991; 1 child, Lani Ashton. MSEd, Nat. Louis U., Lisle, Ill., 1998. Cert. tchr. sci. Ill., 1992. Zoo keeper Roosevelt Pk. Zoo, Minot, ND, 1990—92; sci. tchr. and energy mgr. Cmty. H.S. Dist. 99, Downers Grove, Ill., 1992—. Able facilitator Cmty. H.S. Dist. 99, Downers Grove, Ill., care team success group mem. With USAF, 1983. Mem.: NEA. Libertarian. Home: 2943 Gypsum Cir Naperville IL 60564 Office: Comty HS Dist 99 6301 Springside Downers Grove IL 60516 Office Phone: 630-795-8822. Office Fax: 630-795-8599. E-mail: lmacartney@csd99.org.

MACAULAY, SUSAN JANE, lawyer, law educator; b. Oceanport, NJ, Feb. 18, 1952; d. Gordon Livingston and Mary Forrest Macaulay; children: Lauren Mei, Anna Haiqiong. MusB, Oberlin Conservatory Music, 1974; JD, Loyola U., Chgo., 1984; LLM, Chgo.-Kent Coll. Law, 1990; M in Liberal Arts, U. Chgo., 1995. Bar: Ill. 1984, U.S. Dist. Ct. (no. dist.) Ill. 1984. Regional counsel Burroughs Corp., Lombard, Ill., 1984—86; atty. Borg-Warner Acceptance Corp., Chgo., 1986—86; assoc. gen. counsel Heller Fin., Inc., Chgo., 1986—94; gen. counsel ArcVentures, Inc., Chgo., 1994—95; v.p., corp. counsel Caremark Internat., Inc., Northbrook, Ill., 1995—96; sr. assoc. Skadden Arps Slate Meagher & Flom, Chgo., 1996—2001; ptnr. Gardner Carton & Douglas LLP, Chgo., 2001—06; gen. counsel Lamb Ptnrs., 2006—. Adj. prof. law Chgo.-Kent Coll. Law, 1992—. Contbr. chapters to books, articles to profl. jours. Bd. dirs. The Thereplay Inst., Skokie, Ill., 2004—. Named Ill. Leading Lawyer, The Law Bull. Ill. Superlawyers Chgo. Mag., 2004—06, Ill. Superlawyer, Chgo. Mag., 2004—06. Mem.: ABA, Chgo. Bar Assn., Families with Children from China. Avocations: classical music, local symphony orchestra member, writing. Office: Lamb Ptnrs 900 N Michigan Ste 1900 Chicago IL 60606 Office Fax: 312-915-3053. Business E-Mail: macaulay@lambllc.com.

MACAVINTA-TENAZAS, GEMORSITA, physician; b. Numancia, Aklan, Phillippines, Dec. 18, 1938; arrived in U.S., 1967; d. Dominador Zalazar and Georgina Estrada (Tabanera) Macavinta; m. Salvador Torrefiel Tenazas Jr., Apr. 18, 1963; children: Alan, Alex, Albert, Alfred. BA, Far Ea. U., Manila, 1959, MD, 1964. Diplomate Am. Bd. Family Practice. Intern North Gen. Hosp., Manila, 1963-64; pvt. practice Manila, 1965-67; extern Chinese Gen. Hosp., Manila, 1965-67; with St. Joseph Med. Ctr., Burbank, Calif., 1967-69; chief cytotechnologist Cancer Screening Svcs., North Hollywood, Calif., 1969-73; resident in family practice medicine Health Scis. Ctr., Tex. Tech. U., Lubbock, 1974-75; staff physician VA Outpatient Clinic, L.A., 1975—. Recipient physician recognition awards AMA, 1973-85, 92-94; named Mrs. Aklan, 1986, Disting. Alumna, Aklan Acad., Philippines, 1991, Most Outstanding Parent award Builders Lions Club, 1995, Citizen of Yr. Builders Lions Club, 1996, Outstanding Physician Club Filipino, 1996, one of 10 Outstanding Women of Nation, Uliran, 1997. Fellow Am. Acad. Family Physicians (bd. govs. 2003-05); mem. Philippine-Am. Assn. Family Physicians (bd. govs. 1996, 2003—, sec. 1998, outstanding leader award 2000, sec. 1998-2002, Mrs. Philippine Am. 2000), Am. Assn. Family Physicians, Calif. Acad. Family Physicians, Filipino Asian-Pacific VA Employees Soc. (pres. L.A. chpt. 1988—), Assn. Philippine Physicians in Am. (bd. govs. 2004—, named Mrs. Mindanao 2002), Aklanons of Am. (pres. 1988—, bd. govs. 1998-2000, 04-06, bd. dirs. 2004-06, 1st Mrs. Aklan 1986-89), Far Ea. U. Med. Alumni Assn. (life mem., asst. sec. 1988—). Roman Catholic. Avocations: dance, singing, sewing, piano playing, gardening. Office: VA Outpatient Clinic 425 S Hill St Los Angeles CA 90013-1110 Office Phone: 213-253-2677. Business E-Mail: tenazas@med.va.gov.

MACBAIN, LOUISE T. BLOUIN, publishing executive; b. Can., 1958; m. David Stewart (div.); m. John H. McBain (div.); 3 children. Grad., Harvard U. With various investment banking firms, 1977—87; co-founder, CEO ops. Hebdo Mag Group (now Trader Classified Media), Montreal, Canada, 1987—2000; CEO Phillips, de Pury & Luxembourg, 2002; chmn. LTB Holdings, 2003—; owner Art & Auction Mag., 2003—, Art Knowledge Corp., 2004—, Spoon mag., Paris, 2004—. Chmn. Louise T Blouin Found.; bd. trustees Solomon R. Guggenheim Found.; bd. dir. Bard Ctr., NYC; hon. mem. Chmn's Coun., Whitney Mus.; mem., internat. coun. Tate Mus., London; mem., internat. com. Les Arts Decoratifs, Paris; internat. chmn. Byrd Hoffman Watermill Ctr. Office: Art & Auction Mag 9th Fl 11 E 36th St New York NY 10016 also: LTB USA Inc Ste 302 111 Eighth Ave New York NY 10011

MACCALLUM, LORENE (EDYTHE MACCALLUM), pharmacist; b. Monte Vista, Colo., Nov. 29, 1928; d. Francis Whittier and Berniece Viola (Martin) Scott; m. David Robertson MacCallum, June 12, 1952; children: Suzanne Rae MacCallum Barslund and Roxanne Kay MacCallum Batezel (twins), Tracy Scott, Tamara Lee MacCallum Johnson, Shauna Marie MacCallum Bost. BS in Pharmacy U. Colo., 1950. Registered pharmacist, Colo. Pharmacist Presbyn. Hosp., Denver, 1950, Corner Pharmacy, Lamar, Colo., 1950-53; rsch. pharmacist Nat. Chlorophyll Co., Lamar, 1953; relief pharmacist, various stores, Delta, Colo., 1957-59, Farmington, N.Mex., 1960-62, 71-79, Aztec, N.Mex., 1971-79; mgr. Med. Arts Pharmacy, Farmington, 1966-67; cons. pharmacist Navajo Hosp., Brethren in Christ Mission, Farmington, 1967-77; sales agt. Norris Realty, Farmington, 1977-78; pharmacist, owner, mgr. Lorene's Pharmacy, Farmington, 1979-88; tax cons. H&R Block, Farmington, 1968; cons. Pub. Svc. Co., N.Mex. Intermediate Clinic, Planned Parenthood, Farmington; first woman registered pharmacist apptd. N.Mex. Bd. Pharm., 1982-92. Author numerous poems for mag. Advisor Order Rainbow for Girls, Farmington, 1975-78. Mem. Nat. Assn. Bds. Pharmacy (com. on internship tng., com. edn., sec., treas. dist. 8, mem. impaired pharmacists adv. com., chmn. impaired pharmacists program N.Mex., 1987—, mem. law enforcement legis. com., chmn. nominating com. 1992), Nat. Assn. Retail Druggists, N.Mex. Pharm. Assn. (mem. exec. coun. 1977-81), Order Eastern Star (Farmington). Methodist.

MACCARTHY, TALBOT LELAND, civic volunteer; b. St. Louis, Jan. 28, 1936; d. Austin Porter Leland and Dorothy (Lund) Follansbee; m. John Peters MacCarthy, June 21, 1958; children: John Leland MacCarthy, Talbot MacCarthy Payne. BA, Vassar Coll., 1958. Sec., treas. Station List Pub. Co., St. Louis, 1975-85, pres., 1985-90. Hon. trustee Robert E. Lee Meml. Assn., Arts and Edn. Coun. Greater St. Louis, pres., 1978-80, emerita; past vestry mem. St. Michael and St. George Ch., 1997-00; past trustee St. Louis Art Mus., St. Louis Merc. Libr. Assn., Family & Children's Svc. Greater St. Louis, Health and Welfare Coun., Greater St. Louis, Jr. Kindergarten St. Louis Page Park YMCA, Scholarship Found. St. Louis, Friends St. Louis Art Mus. Bd., Ch. St. Michael and St. George Sch. Bd., Mid-Am. Arts Alliance; chmn. Mo. Arts Coun., 1980-85; past chmn. Vol. Action Ctr. Greater St. Louis; past vice chmn. bd. dirs. Mary Inst.; past pres. Jr. League St. Louis; mem. Nat. Coun. Arts, 1985-91; past mem. nat. coun. for Sch. of Art Washington U.; bd. dirs. Sheldon Art Galleries; trustee, sec. bd. Seabury-Western Theol. Sem. Recipient Woman of Achievement citation St. Louis Globe Democrat, 1979, Mo. Citizens for Arts/Arts Advocacy award, 1987, Mo. Arts Award, 1993, Honor medal, Mary Inst. and Country Day Sch., 2005. Mem. Vassar Club St. Louis (past pres.), Mary Inst. Alumnae Assn. (past pres.), Colonial Dames Am., Garden Club St. Louis, Belvedere Club (Charlevoix, Mich.; former mem. bd. dirs.). Republican. Episcopalian. Avocations: tennis, visual arts, performing arts.

MACCOBY, ELEANOR EMMONS, psychology professor; b. Tacoma, May 15, 1917; d. Harry Eugene and Viva May (Johnson) Emmons; m. Nathan Maccoby, Sept. 16, 1938 (dec. Apr. 1992); children: Janice Carmichael, Sarah Maccoby Blunt, Mark. BS, U. Wash., 1939; MA, U. Mich., 1949, PhD, 1950. Study dir. div. program surveys USDA, Washington, 1942-46; study dir. Survey Rsch. Ctr. U. Mich., Ann Arbor, 1946-48; lectr., rsch. assoc. dept. social rels. Harvard U., Cambridge, Mass., 1950-58; from assoc. to full prof. Stanford (Calif.) U., 1958-87, Barbara Kimball Browning prof., 1979, chmn. dept. psychology, 1973-76, prof. emeritus, 1987—. Author: (with R. Sears and H. Levin) Patterns of Child-Rearing, 1957, (with Carol Jacklin) Psychology of Sex Differences, 1974, Social Development, 1980, (with R.H. Mnookin) Dividing the Child: Social and Legal Dilemmas of Custody, 1992, (with Buchanan and Dombusch) Adolescents after Divorce, 1996, The Two Sexes: Growing Up Apart, Coming Together, 1998; editor: (with Newcomb and Hartley) Readings in Social Psychology, 1957, The Development of Sex Differences, 1966. Recipient Gores award for Excellence in Tchg., Stanford U., 1981, Disting. Contbn. to Ednl. Research award Am. Ednl. Rsch. Assn., 1984, Lectureship award Soc. for Devel. and Behavioral Pediats., 2002. Fellow APA (pres. Divsn. 7, 1971-72, G. Stanley Hall award 1982), Soc. for Rsch. in Child Devel. (pres. 1981-83, mem. governing coun. 1963-66, Disting. Sci. Contbn. award 1987), Am. Psychol. Soc. (Disting. Sci. Contbns. award 1988); mem. NAS, Am. Acad. Arts and Scis., Inst. Medicine, Western Psychol. Assn. (pres. 1974-75, Lifetime Achievement award 2004), Inst. for Rsch. on Women and Gender, Social Sci. Rsch. Coun. (chmn. 1984-85), Consortium of Social Sci. Assns. (pres. 1997-98), Am. Psychol. Found. (Life Achievement award 1996). Democrat. Office: Stanford U Dept Psychology Stanford CA 94305-2130 Personal E-mail: Maccoby@psych.stanford.edu.

MACCONNELL-DAVINROY, IRENE J.H., secondary education educator, consultant; b. Trenton, N.J., Nov. 26, 1936; d. Irving John and Frances Emily (Bentley) MacConnell; m. Thomas Bernard Davinroy, Sept. 17, 1955 (div. 1990); children: Ellise, Thomas C., E. Timothy. BA with honors, Pa. State U., 1974, postgrad., 1977-79. Cert. secondary edn. tchr., Pa. Tchr. social studies Mt. Nittany Mid. Sch., State College, Pa., 1994—. Cons. N.J. Geographic Alliance, Rutgers U., 1986-87, Pa. Geographic Alliance, Indiana U. of Pa., 1987—; tchr. cons. Nat. Geographic Soc., Washington, 1986. Attendant, emergency med. technician Alpha Cmty. Ambulance Svc., State Coll., 1984-92. Fulbright fellow U.S. Dept. Edn., 1983; PGS Disting. Teaching award, 1993. Mem. Nat. Coun. for Geog. Edn. (Disting. Tchg. award 1989), Pa. Geog. Soc. (bd. dirs. 1988—, pres. 1994-96, Tchg. award 1993). Avocation: reading. Home: 246 Mccormick Ave State College PA 16801-6121

MACCORMACK, JEAN F., academic administrator; d. George and Helen MacCormack. BA, Emmanuel Coll., Boston, 1969; MEd, U. Mass., Amherst, 1978, EdD, 1979. Assoc. dean Coll. of Edn. U. Mass, Boston, 1984—87, acting dean Coll. of Edn., 1984—85, assoc. chancellor, 1987—88, vice chancellor arts and fin., 1988—95, interim chancellor, 1995—96, dep. chancellor and vice chancellor arts and fin., 1996—99, chancellor Dartmouth, 1999—. Mem. South Coast Econ. Devel. Partnership, 1999, Joint CEO Group, 2000, Racial and Ethnic Access and Fairness Adv. Bd., 2001; chair South Coast Edn. Compact, 2000; mem. vis. com. U. So. Maine New Eng. Assoc. of Sch. and Coll., 2000—01; ex-officio mem. U. Mass. Dartmouth Libr. Archive Campaign, 2001; bd. mem. South Coast Health Sys., Inc., 2002; mem. marine sci. com. Fall River CEO Group, 2003, mem. med. device com., 03, mem. south coast edn. com., 03; mem. Regional Competitiveness Coun., 2003. Vice chair bd. govs. New Bedford Oceanariun, 1999, chair edn and rsch. com., 1999, trustee, chair edn. com., 2000; trustee Artworks! at Dover St., 2000, mem. edn. com, 2000, mem. pers. com., 2000; trustee Global Learning Charter Sch., 2000; bd. mem. Greater New Bedford Workforce Investment Bd., 2000, mem. legis. affairs and pub. info. com., 2000, mem. youth coun., 2000; mem. New Bedford Econ. Devel. Coun., 2000; corporator Child and Family Svcs., Inc., 2002; incorporator Home Aged People in Fall river, 2003; corporator Narragansett Fin. Corp. Citizens - Union Savs. Bank, 2003; mem. pres.'s coun. New Bedford Symphony Orch., 2003; mem. leadership coun. New Bedford Whaling Mus. Mem.: YMCA of Southeastern Mass., WHALE, Am. Assn. of State Coll. and U., U. Mass. Dartmouth Libr. Assoc. E-mail: jmaccormack@umassd.edu.

MACDONALD, ANDARA, secondary school educator; d. Neil John and Bernadine Dutra Macdonald. BA, Ea. Wash. U., Cheney, 1970; MA, San Diego State U., 1976. Life tchr. cert. Calif., 1976. Tchr. Holtville H.S., Calif., 1971—, forensic coach, 1971—. Grantee, Borderlinks, 2003—04. Mem.: Calif. Assn. Tchrs. English, Calif. H.S. Speech Assn. (area 4 chair 2000—06, past pres. 1995—99, named to Hall of Fame), Holtville Tchrs. Assn. (v.p. 1998—2006). Democrat. Roman Catholic. Avocations: travel, reading. Office: Holtville HS 755 Olive Ave Holtville CA 92250 Office Phone: 760-356-2926 ext. 156. Personal E-mail: andaram@hotmail.com. Business E-Mail: andy@holtville.k12.ca.us.

MACDONALD, CHRISTINE, social worker; b. Lowell, Mass., Sept. 13, 1952; d. Robert Francis and Ruth Olive (Breed) MacD.; children: Jessica Eireanne MacDonald, Braea Walters. BGS in Behavioral Sci., Sch. of Life Long Learning, Conway, N.H., 1987; postgrad., N.H. Tech. Coll., Berlin, 1994-95. Family strength counselor Familystrength, Concord, NH, 1987-90; resident mgr., family support consumer liaison, agy. trainer The Ctr. of Hope, Conway, 1990—; dir. family support The Ctr. of Hope Inc., 2000—02, dir. of adult and family svcs., 2002—04; social worker White Mt. Com. Health Ctr., 2004—, infant mental health coord., 2005—, supr. Ptnrs. in Health Program, 2006—. Intern, trainer, vol. Carroll County Against Domestic Violence and Rape (now Starting Point), Conway, 1983—; bd. alt. Carroll County Transport Alliance, 1994—2000; co-chair, group facilitator Outright/North, 1996; mem. NH chpt. Am. Assn. Mental Retardation, bd. dirs., 1990—, Big Bros./Big Sisters, Carroll County, NH, 1988—89, 1994, Friends of Families, 2003—. Mem. NOW, Mt. Washington Valley Bus. and Profl. Women. Avocations: gardening, reading, writing, basket weaving, camping. Office: WMCHC 2800 White Mt Hwy Conway NH 03818

MACDONALD, DUNCAN, broadcaster, writer, communications consultant; b. Beaumont, Tex. d. William Whyte MacDonald and Martha (Schalies) Hammond. Grad. high sch., Houston. Supr. women's and religious programming DuMont TV Network, N.Y.C., 1950-53; prodr. Home show NBC-TV, N.Y.C., 1954; broadcaster Yankee Network, Boston, 1955-59, Sta. WQXR, N.Y.C., 1962-67; monthly article writer House Beautiful, N.Y.C., 1966-67, exec. asst. to editor, 1967-70; pres. The Media Group, Edgartown, Mass., 1967—; exec. dir. Nat. Friends Pub. Broadcasting, N.Y.C., 1970-72; adminstrv. aide Dukes County Commrs., Edgartown, 1976-82; features editor Martha's Vineyard (Mass.) Times, 1983-88. Mem. White House Conf. Nutrition, Washington, 1969. Author: Rain, Hail & Baked Beans, 1958; home editor Yankee Mag., 1956-63; food editor Old Farmer's Almanac, 1957-65. Founder, pres. Com. for the Ams., N.Y.C., 1963-67; trustee Nat. Coun. Women, N.Y.C., 1962-72, Am. Youth Hostels, N.Y.C., 1968-73, Am. Friends Scottish Opera, N.Y.C., 1982-87, pres., 1986-87; trustee Caledonian Found., Inc., Sarasota, Fla., 1987—, pres., treas. Recipient UN Children's Fund award UNICEF, 1957, citation Pres.'s Com. on Aid to Physically Handicapped, 1957, citation OAS, 1970; recordings and writings in Duncan MacDonald Collection U. Wyo., Coun. Scottish Clans & Assns. nat. award, 2001. Fellow Soc. Antiquaries of Scotland; mem. Am. Women in Radio and TV (pres. N.Y.C. chpt.), Overseas Press Club, Clan Donald USA, Broadcast Pioneers, Sarasota Opera Guild, Caledonian Found. Inc. (trustee Sarasota, Fla. 1987-, pres., treas. 2000, exec. v.p., treas. 2001-), Scottish Soc. Martha's Vineyard (co-founder 1986), Scottish Coalition (co-founder 1997-). Baptist. Achievements include Called a key figure in the establishment of Tartan Day as a national observance. Address: PO Box 1242 Edgartown MA 02539-1242

MACDONALD, KAREN CRANE, occupational therapist, geriatrics services professional; b. Denville, N.J., Feb. 24, 1955; d. Robert William and Jeanette Wilcox (Crane) M.; m. Geno Piacentini, Oct. 22, 1993. BS, Quinnipiac U., 1977; MS, U. Bridgeport, 1982; PhD, NYU, 1998. Cert. occupl. therapist. Occupational therapist, coord. of spl. care unit Jewish Home for the Elderly, Conn., 1987-92, N.Y. Inst., N.Y.C., 1984-86; pvt. practice Fairfield County, Conn., 1977-88; occupl. therapist Rehab. Assocs., Fairfield, Conn., 1993-96; instr. Housatonic Cmty. Coll., Conn. Instr. NYU, 1985—89, Quinnipiac Coll., 1986—92, Housatonic CC, Bridgeport, Conn., 2002; lectr., cons. in field. Contbr. articles to profl. jours. Youth leader, deacon Union Meml. Ch., Stamford, Conn., 1980-88; deacon Southport Congl. Ch., 1992-94; chair consumer com. Alzheimer's Coalition of Conn., 1991-92. Teaching fellow NYU, 1983-86. Mem. AAAS, P.E.O., World Fedn. Occupl. Therapy, Am. Occupl. Therapy Assn. (scholar 1985, coun. edn.), Conn. Occupl. Therapy Assn. (gerontology liaison 1980-83), Am. Bd. Disability Analysts, NY Acad. Scis., Grange, Pi Lambda Theta. Avocations: poetry writing, quilting. Home: 198 Glenbrook Rd Bridgeport CT 06610-1149

MACDONALD, LAURIE, film company executive; m. Walter Parkes, 1983; 2 children. BA in English Lit., Sonoma State U., Calif. Documentary and news prodr. K-RON, NBC affiliate, San Francisco; creative exec. Columbia Pictures, 1984—85, v.p. prodn., 1985—88; head Aerial Pictures, 1988—94; exec. prodr. Amblin Entertainment, 1994; co-head motion pictures divsn. DreamWorks Pictures, 1994—. Prodr.: (films) Hayseed, 1997, Men in Black, 1997 (nominated Golden Globe best musical or comedy), Men in Black II, 2002, The Ring, 2002, The Terminal, 2004, Lemony Snicket's A Series of Unfortunate Events, 2004, The Ring Two, 2005, The Island, 2005, Just Like Heaven, 2005, The Legend of Zorro, 2005; (TV series) SFO; exec. prodr.: (films) How to Make an American Quilt, 1995, The Trigger Effect, 1996, Twister, 1996, The Mask of Zorro, 1998, Gladiator, 2000, The Time Machine, 2002, The Tuxedo, 2002, Catch Me If You Can, 2002. Named one of 100 Most Powerful Women in Hollywood, Hollywood Reporter, 2003, 2005, 50 Most Powerful People in Hollywood, Premiere mag., 2004—05; recipient Women in Hollywood Icon award, Premiere Mag., 1999. Office: DreamWorks SKG 100 Flower St Glendale CA 91201 Office Phone: 818-733-7000. Office Fax: 818-695-7574.*

MAC DONALD, MARIAN LOUISE, psychologist, educator; b. Jackson, Tenn., June 1, 1947; d. John D. and Dona (Skinner) MacD; 1 child Lisa Qiao Louise. BA, Auburn U., 1969; MA, U. Ill., 1972, PhD, 1974. Clin. counselor with rank of instr. dept. psychology Univ. Ill., Champaign-Urbana, 1973-74; asst. prof. clin. psychology SUNY, Stony Brook, 1974-78; vis. assoc. prof. Univ. Hawaii, Honolulu, 1978; assoc. prof. psychology Univ. Mass., Amherst, 1979-85, prof. psychology, 1985—; vis. prof. social work Smith Coll., Northampton, Mass., 1985—94. Chair merit rev. bd., rehab. and R & D, VA dept. vets. affairs, Washington, 1989-1996; pvt. practice in clin. psychology Northampton, 1980—. Author: Behavioral Approaches to Community Psychology, 1977, Research Design for Social Work and the Human Services, 1994; contbr. articles to profl. jours. Pro bono work as a clin. psychologist, Northampton, 1974—; mem. John's Epsic. Ch., Northampton, Mass., 1996—. Fellow APA; mem. Am. Psychol. Soc., Assn. for Advancement Behavior Therapy, Assn. for the Advancement Applied and Profl. Psychology (founding mem.), Midwestern Psychol. Assn. Democrat. Avocations: home decorating, pets. Office: Univ Mass Tobin Hall Amherst MA 01003 Home: 141 Crescent St Northampton MA 01060

MACDONALD, SALLY POLK BOWERS, retired addictions therapist; b. Memphis, Tenn., Feb. 23, 1930; d. Joel Polk and Sara Louise (Nee Zearing) Bowers; m. Lemuel Coover Shattuck, Jr. (div.); children: L. C. Shattuck III, Mark Bowers Shattuck, Melissa Polk Shattuck; m. Robert Donald Macdonald, Mar. 1, 1960; 1 child, Heather Stuart Macdonald LaMarre. BA, U. Ariz., Tucson, 1950. Lic. Alcohol and Drug Abuse Counselor State of Tenn. Adminstr. Clare Found., Santa Monica, Calif., 1978—88; counselor Wilder Youth Devel. Ctr., Somerville, Tenn., 1981—90; alcohol and drug abuse therapist Profl. Care Svcs., Inc., Somerville, 1983—2006; ret., 2006. Contbr. articles various profl. jours. Founding mem. Memphis Alcohol and Drug Coun., Memphis, 1984—86, Fayette County Animal Rescue, Somerville, Tenn., 1996—98; thriftshop chmn. Women's Symphony Assn., Ojai, Calif., 1967—69; precinct com. GOP, Tucson, 1952. Mem.: AOPA, Clare Found. (bd. mem. 1977—80), Assn. Preservation Tenn. Antiquities, Fayette County Hist. Soc. Republican. Episcopal. Avocations: birdwatching, painting, interior decorating, dog rescue. Home and Office: 612 S Somerville St Somerville TN 38068-1837

MACDONALD, SHARON ETHEL, dancer, educator, choreographer, administrator; b. Pittsfield, Mass., Mar. 24, 1952; d. Harry and Angeline (Saracco) MacD. BA, Skidmore Coll., 1974; MA, Smith Coll., 1992. Faculty Smith Coll., Northampton, Mass., 1974-76; dancer and tchr. Berkshire Ballet, Pittsfield, 1968—77; dance dir. Becket (Mass.) Arts Ctr., 1977-80; faculty mem. Williams Coll., Williamstown, Mass., 1979-80; co-artistic dir., owner N.E. Am. Ballet, Northampton, 1980-85; devel. dir., tchr. Berkshire Ballet, Pittsfield, 1984-85; adminstr., tchr. Hartford (Conn.) Ballet, Inc., 1985-90; artistic dir., exec. dir. Am. Dance Inst., 1995—; freelance dir., choreographer, master tchr. Asst. choreographer Easthampton Mass. Cmty. Theatre Assn., 1981—83, Project Opera, 1982; bd. dirs. Jacob's Pillow Dance Festival, Becket, 1978—81; bd. trustees Becket Arts Ctr., 1979—80; tchr. Trinity Coll., Hartford, 1990—96, Hartford Conservatory, 1996—2005; dance specialist Pittsfield Pub. Schs., 1996—99; dir. mktg., bus. cons. Limelight Prodns., Inc., 1990—2002; guest artist numerous pub. schs., pvt. studios, colls. and univs.; bd. overseers Sch. Hartford Ballet. Pres. Friends of Jacob's Pillow, Becket, 1978-81, Friends of The Hartford Ballet, 1988-91, Jacob's Pillow Alumnae/Archives Com., 1988-96, Dance History Scholars, 1976-78, 91—; chmn. Lee (Mass.) Cultural Coun., 1995—. Mass. Arts Lottery grantee Mass. Arts Coun., 1984, Arts Lottery grantee Northampton Arts Coun., 1984; Smith Coll. fellow. Mem.: Smith Coll. Club. Democrat. Baptist. Avocations: writing, antiques, collecting dance and theatre memorabilia. Home: PO Box 697 Stockbridge MA 01262-0697

MACDOUGALL, FRANCES KAY, marketing consultant; b. Saginaw, Mich., Mar. 25, 1937; d. Frank King and Emily Runke Beck; m. Kenneth Jacobus, 1958 (div. 1969); m. Robert Louis Gilmore, 1972 (div. 1979); children: Peter Gilmore (dec.), Christoper Gilmore; m. Colin Kennedy MacDougall, 1981 (div. 1993). BA, Northwestern U., 1958; MBA, Loyola U., 1974; postgrad., Northwestern U. Sr. corp. analyst Am. Hosp. Supply, Inc., Evanston, Ill., 1969-71; rsch. assoc. Am. Hosp. Assn., Chgo., 1971-72; product mgr. Litton Med. Products, Elk Grove, Ill., 1972-74; cons. Technomic Cons., Chgo., 1974-79; mktg. dir. Just Jobs, Inc., Chgo., 1980-81; sr. cons. The Chgo. Group, Inc., Chgo., 1981-88; sr. assoc. SWF Cons. Group, Ft. Myers, Fla., 1988—. Dir. Lee Mental Health, Inc., Ft. Myers, 1988—; com. chmn. Lee County Infrastructure Task Force, 1988. Hon. scholar Nat. High Sch. Inst. Northwestern U., Evanston, 1954. Mem. Forest Country Club, Southwest Fla. Jazz Soc. Avocations: adventure travel, golf, bridge, poetry, music. Home: 20490 Foxworth Cir Estero FL 33928

MACDOWELL, ANDIE (ROSE ANDERSON MACDOWELL), actress; b. Gaffney, S.C., Apr. 21, 1958; m. Paul Qualley, 1986 (div. 1999); children: Justin, Rainey, Sarah Margaret; m. Rhett DeCamp Hartzog, Nov. 10, 2001 (div. Oct. 2004). LittD (hon.), Lander U., Greenwood, 2001. Spokesmodel L'Oreal cosmetics and haircare. Films include: Greystoke, 1984, St. Elmo's Fire, 1985, Sex, Lies and Videotape, 1989, Green Card, 1990, Hudson Hawk, 1991, The Object of Beauty, 1991, The Player, 1992, Ruby, 1992, Groundhog Day, 1993, Luck, Trust and Ketchup, 1994, Short Cuts, 1993, Four Weddings and a Funeral, 1994, Bad Girls, 1994, Unstrung Heroes, 1995, Michael, 1996, Multiplicity, 1996, The End of Violence, 1997, Town and Country, 1998, Shadrack, 1998, The Scalper, 1998, The Muse, 1999, Muppets From Space, 1999, Just the Ticket, 1999, Harrison's Flowers, 2000, Town & Country, 2001, Crush, 2001, Ginostra, 2002, The Last Sign, 2005, Beauty Shop, 2005, Tara Road, 2005, (voice) Barnyard: The Original Party Animals, 2006; TV movies include The Secret of the Sahara, 1987, Women and Men: Stories of Seduction, 1990, Women and Men 2: In Love There Are No Rules, 1991, On the Edge, 2000, Dinner With Friends, 2001, Jo, 2002, Riding the Bus with My Sister, 2005; prodr. Just the Ticket, 1999; TV guest appearances include Spenser: For Hire, 1985, Clive Anderson All Talk, 1996, Muppets Tonight!, 1997, The Practice, 2003.*

MACDUFF, ILONE MARGARET, music educator; b. Berwyn, Ill., Jan. 30, 1938; d. Albert Kenneth Hinckle and Dorothy Lydia Ardina Lange; m. James Donald Macduff, Jr., Apr. 2, 1959; children: Gordon Scott, James Alexander, Charles Colin. MusB, U. Idaho, 1976. Internat. rep. Boy Scouts Am., 1983—93; mem. Thurston County (Wash.) Hist. Commrs., 1984—98; active Boy Scouts Am., Tumwater, Wash., 1968—93, dist. Cub Scout program chmn., 1973—75, mem. coun. Pow Wow staff, 1973—76; founder Cub Scout Day Camp, Tumwater Area Coun., 1973; chmn. Coun. Scout-O-Rama, 1979, 1980, 1981; mem. coun. Eagle bd. Boy Scouts Am., 1985—90; dir. monthly musicales State Captial Mus., 1970—74. Recipient Single and Double awards, Nat. Fedn. Music Clubs, 1969, 1977, Silver Beaver award, Boy Scouts Am., 1981, Disting. Commr. award, 1981, Lamb award, 1987. Mem.: Am. Coll. Musicians, Olympia Music Tchrs. Assn. (pres. 2003—04, student recitals chair 2005), Music Tchrs. Nat. Assn. (Olympia chpt. voice auditions chair 2001, 2004), Gordon Setter Club Am. (chmn. nat. dog show 2003), Puget Sound Gordon Setter Club (treas. 1998—2000, show chmn. 2003—04). Lutheran. Avocation: photography. Home: 8524 Delphi Rd SW Olympia WA 98512 Personal E-mail: delphimuse@msn.com.

MACE, JERILEE MARIE, performing arts association administrator; BA in Speech Comm. and Mgmt. magna cum l, Simpson Coll., 1991. Mem. adminstrv. staff Des Moines Metro Opera, 1976, dir. mktg., exec. dir., 1988—. Developer OPERA Iowa, Des Moines Metro Opera; cons. various opera cos. On-site evaluator NEA; grad., bd. dirs. Greater Des Moines Leadership Inst.; founding mem. Warren County Leadership Com. Named Iowa Arts Orgn. of Yr., 2000, Employee of Yr., Indianola C. of C., 2004; recipient Outstanding Achiever award, Ft. Dodge C. of C., 1994, Best Kept Secret award for bus. excellence, Greater Des Moines Partnership 2001, Women of Influence award, Des Moines Bus. Record, 2001; fellow exec., OPERA Am., 1993. Office: Des Moines Metro Opera 106 W Boston Ave Indianola IA 50125-1836 E-mail: jerimace@aol.com.

MACEK, PAMELA KAY, tax specialist, business executive; b. Mt. Plesant, Mich., Nov. 20, 1951; d. Harold D. and Betty Mae (Merrifield) Reynolds; m. Robert M. Macek, Jr., May 3, 1969; children: Kerry, Kristene, Robert. Student, Calif. Coast U., Calif. State U., San Bernardino, N.Am. Sch. Acctg., Newport Beach, Calif. Cert. tax preparer, Calif. Pvt. practice tax preparation; CFO Arrow Industries, Anaheim, Calif.; ret., 2002. Mem. Inland Soc. Tax Preparers, NAFE, Employer Adv. Coun. (award for Treas. and V.P., cert. appreciation). Home: 1585 Crevasse Ct Riverside CA 92506-4807

MACERO, JEANETTE DIRUSSO, academic administrator; b. Somerville, Mass., Feb. 21, 1931; d. Pietro and Alessandria (Pennacchio) DiRusso; m. Daniel J. Macero, June 14, 1952; children: Diana, Peter. BA, Barnard Coll., N.Y.C., 1952; MA, Columbia U., N.Y.C., 1955; student, U. Mich., Ann Arbor, 1957. Asst. prof. Syracuse U., 1970-76, assoc. prof., 1977—. Cons. Laubach Lit. Internat., Syracuse, 1980—. Author: Laubach Way to English, 1977-86. Mem. N.Y. State Tchrs. to Speakers of other Languages (chairperson, pres., chair publs. com. 1989—), Internat. TESOL, Nat. Assn. Fgn. Student Advisors, Nat. Coun. Tchrs. of English. Office: Syracuse U Dept Fgn Langs Lit Syracuse NY 13244-0001

MACER-STORY, EUGENIA ANN, writer; b. Mpls., Jan. 20, 1945; d. Dan Johnstone and Eugenia Loretta (Andrews) Macer; divorced; 1 child, Ezra Arthur Story. BS in Comms., Northwestern U., Evanston, Ill., 1965; MFA, Columbia U., N.Y.C., 1968. Writing instr. Polyarts, Boston, 1970-72; theater instr. Joy of Movement, Boston, 1972-75; artistic dir. Magik Mirror, Salem, Mass., 1975-76, Magick Mirror Comm., 1977—. Author: Congratulations: The UFO Reality, 1978, Angels of Time, 1982, Project Midas, 1986, 2d edit., 2004, Dr. Fu Man Chu Meets the Lonesome Cowboy: Sorcery and the UFO Experience, 1991, 3d edit., 1994, Gypsy Fair, 1991, The Strawberry Man, 1991, Sea Condor/Dusty Sun, 1994, Awakening to the Light-After the Longest Night, 1995, Battles with Dragons: Certain Tales of Political Yoga, 1993, 2d edit., 1994, Legacy of Daedulus, 1995, The Dark Frontier, 1997, Troll and Other Interdimensional Invasions, 1999, Congratulations: The UFO Reality, 2000, Vanishing Questions, 2000, Carrying Thunder, 2002, Crossing Jungle River, 1998, Doing Business in the Adirondacks; True Tales of the Bizarre and Supernatural, 2003, The Merry Piper's Hollow Hills, 2003, Struck By Green Lightning aka Project Midas, 2004, reissued 2006; (poetry) Theatre Cosmos, 2005; (novels) The Sin of Love, 2006, OM/NADA, 2006; (plays) Fetching the Tree, Archaeological Politics, 1986, Strange Inquiries, Divine Appliance, 1989, The Zig Zag Wall, 1990, The Only Qualified Huntress, 1990, Telephone Taps Written Up for Tabloids, 1991, Wars with Pigeons, 1992, Conquest of the Asteroids, 1993, Commander Galacticon, 1993, Meister Hemmelin, 1994, Six Way Time Play, 1994, Radish, 1996, Setting Up for the World Trade Centaur, 1996, Mister Shooting Star, 1998, Wild Dog Casino, 1999, Magic Mirror Space Installation at 515 Greenwich Street, 1999-2001, The Old Gaffer From Boise (at Gallery 113), 2000, The Redecoration According to Currier (at Gallery 113), 2001; (plays) Ars Chronicon Sylvestre, 2002, Swords of the Equinox, 2003, New Life Expo, New Yorker Hotel, NYC, 2003, Sayeed/Sayeeda, NYC, 2003, New Day, 2004, New Life Expo, 2005, Theatre For The New City, NYC, 2005, Honky Tonk Tornado Warnings, 2005, The Liberation of Little Lulu, Martin Luther King Detained in Limbo, 2006, Eternal Flowers of Ghost Mountain, Lower East Side Festival of Arts, 2006 others; editor Yankee Oracle Gazette, 1999; personal appearance as profl. clairvoyant (TV documentary) Haunted Houses, 1996, UFO Desk, Sta. WBAI radio shows, 1996-2001, Star People Confs., 1998—; exhbn. paintings Barcelona, Spain, 1999, 2000, 02, Magick Mirror Comm. Installation, 1999-2001, 515 Greenwich Gallery, So-Ho, N.Y., 1999, City Art Gallery, Stockholm, 2000, 04, Gam'Art Diffusion, Port Frejus, France, 2003, Kelikian Gallery, Beirut, 2002-03, Holland Art Fair, The Hague, 2003, BCN Art-Directe Gallery, Barcelona, Spain, 2003, Times Square Fashion Dist., Magick Mirror Space Fashion Ctr., 2003-06, Europ'art Expo, Geneva, 2006; author numerous poems; contbr. articles to profl. jours. and mags. Shubert fellow, 1968. Mem. Am. Soc. Dowsers, Dramatists Guild (spkr., interviewer on radio shows and internet confs.), Theosophical Soc. Democrat. Avocations: swimming, outdoor activities, hiking. Office: Magick Mirror Comm PO Box 741 New York NY 10116-0741 Office Phone: 212-727-0002. Personal E-mail: e.macer-story@att.net. E-mail: magickmirr@aol.com.

MACEWAN, BONNIE, librarian, dean; b. Memphis, Sept. 10, 1950; m. Thomas Manig. BA, Whitter Coll., 1972; M, U. Denver, 1978. Humanities libr. Ctl. Mo. State Coll., Warrensburg, 1978—84; art, archaeology and music libr. U. Mo., Columbia, 1984—91; asst. dean scholarly comm. Pa. State U., University Park, 1991—98, dean collections and scholarly comm., co-dir. digital scholarly pub., 1998—2003; dean librs. Auburn U., Ala., 2006—. Mem.: ALA (vice chair, chair-elect collection mgmt. and develop. sect. 2001—02). Office: Auburn U Librs 231 Mell St Auburn University AL 36849 Office Phone: 334-844-1715. E-mail: macewbj@auburn.edu.*

MACEWAN, ELIZABETH MARIE, pianist, vocalist; b. Palm Beach Gardens, Fla., Dec. 29, 1979; d. John Hamish and Barbara Marie MacEwan. MusB in Music Edn., Palm Beach Atlantic U., West Palm Beach, Fla., 2003. Musician: (composer, singer, pianist) various performances/works. Ch. mem., small groups coach Christ Fellowship, Royal Palm Beach, Fla., 2004—06. R-Consevative. Christian. Avocations: travel, music. Home: 1196 Grandview Cir Royal Palm Beach FL 33411 Office Phone: 561-330-8860.

MACEY-CALOCA, PATRICIA ANN, secondary school educator; d. George Herbert and Virginia Dare Macey; m. Frank Michael Caloca, Dec. 19, 1992; 1 child, Frank Dean Caloca. BA, Brigham Young U., Provo, Utah, 1968. Cert. tchr. Idaho, 1970. Tchr. english Ft. Lupton (Colo.) H.S., 1968—70; tchr. theater Coeur d' Alene (Idaho) H.S., 1970—. Stage mgr. N.W. Summer Playhouse, Coeur d' Alene, 1990—93. Recipient Drama Tchr. of Yr., Idaho State Activities Assn., 1988. Mem.: Internat. Thespians (life; idaho state dir.). Mem. Lds Ch. Avocations: travel, theater. Office: Coeur d' Alene HS N 5530 4th St Coeur D' Alene ID 83815 Office Phone: 208-769-2999. Personal E-mail: calocateacher@aol.com. Business E-Mail: pcaloca@sd271.k12.id.us.

MACFARLANE, BARBARA ANN, secondary school educator; b. Bronx, N.Y., May 16, 1947; d. James H. and Mary F. Roche; m. Douglas George MacFarlane, Nov. 22, 1969; children: Brian, Scott. BA, Caldwell Coll., N.J., 1965—69; grad., SUNY, New Paltz, 1970. English tchr. Arlington Sch. Dist., Poughkeepsie, NY, 1969—73; English/history tchr. Regina Coeli Sch., Hyde Pk., 1986—96; history tchr. Sahuaro HS, Tucson, 1996—. Adv. Nat. Honor Soc., Tucson, 1997—2003. Nominee Tchr. of Yr., U. Ariz. & Circle K Corp., Tucson, 2000.

MACFARLANE, CATHY M., federal agency administrator; BS, Manhattanville Coll.; MA, Georgetown U. Counter-intelligence specialist FBI, 1980; with Nat. Inst. Justice U.S. Dept. Justice; dir. bus. devel. Jones Day, Dallas and Washington; assoc. Cassidy & Assocs.; v.p. Devillier Comm.; founder Marcom 21; exec. v.p. Direct Impact Co.; dir. pub. rels. FTC, 2001—04; asst. sec. pub. affairs U.S. Dept. Housing and Urban Devel., Washington, 2004—. Vis. scholar East China Inst. Politics and Law, Shanghai, 1987—88. Office: Dept Housing and Urban Devel Mail Code W 451 Seventh St SW Rm 10130 Washington DC 20410 Office Phone: 202-708-0980. Office Fax: 202-708-3106. E-mail: cathy_macfarlane@hud.gov.

MACGOWAN, EUGENIA, lawyer; b. Turlock, Calif., Aug. 4, 1928; d. William Ray and Mary Bolling (Gilbert) Kern; m. Gordon Scott Millar, Jan. 2, 1970 (dec. Jan. 1997); 1 dau., Heather Mary. AB, U. Calif., Berkeley, 1950; JD, U. Calif., San Francisco, 1953. Bar: Calif. 1953; cert. family law specialist Calif. State Bar Bd. Legal Specialization. Research atty. Supreme Ct. Calif., 1954, Calif. Ct. Appeals, 1955; partner firm MacGowan & MacGowan, Calif., 1956-68; pvt. practice, San Francisco, 1968-99. Bd. dirs. San Francisco Speech and Hearing Center, San Francisco Legal Aid Soc., J.A.C.K.I.E. Mem. Am., Calif., San Francisco bar assns., Queen's Bench. Clubs: San Francisco Lawyers, Forest Hill Garden. Office: 236 W Portal Ave San Francisco CA 94127-1423

MACGOWAN, SANDRA FIRELLI, publishing executive, consultant; b. Phila., Nov. 9, 1951; d. William Firelli and Barbara (Gimbel) Kapalcik. BS in Biology, BA in English, Pa. State U., 1973, MA in English Lit., 1978. Cert. supervisory analyst N.Y. Stock Exch. Editor McGraw-Hill Pub. Co., N.Y.C., 1979-81; sr. acquisitions editor Harcourt Brace Jovanovich, Inc., N.Y.C., 1981-82; sr. editor The Coll. Bd., N.Y.C., 1982-88; v.p., head editorial CS First Boston Corp., N.Y.C., 1988-94; v.p. supervisory analyst internat. rsch. SBC Warburg, N.Y.C., 1994-96; v.p., supervisory analyst internat. rsch. Arnhold and S. Bleichroeder, N.Y.C., 1996—2003; sr. v.p. Natexis Bleichroeder Inc. (formerly Arnhold and S. Bleichroeder), N.Y.C., 2003—, mgr. Rsch. Dept., 2003—. Part time assoc. prof. pub. NYU Sch. Continuing Edn., N.Y.C., 1985—. Author: 50 College Admission Directors Speak to Parents, 1988. Democrat. Avocations: art, reading, travel. Office: Natexis Bleichroeder Fl 44 1345 Avenue Of The Americas New York NY 10105-4300 Office Phone: 212-698-3219. Business E-Mail: sandra.macgowan@natexisblr.us.

MACGRAW, ALI, actress; b. Pound Ridge, N.Y., Apr. 1, 1939; m. Robert Evans, 1970 (div.); 1 child, Joshua; m. Steve McQueen, 1973 (div.). Student, Wellesley Coll. Former editorial asst. Harper's Bazaar Mag.; former asst. to photographer Melvin Sokolsky. Actress in films including Goodbye, Columbus, 1969, Love Story, 1971, The Getaway, 1973, Convoy, 1978, Players, 1979, Just Tell Me What You Want, 1979, Natural Causes, 1994, Glam, 2001; TV mini-series The Winds of War, 1983, China Rose, 1983, Dynasty, 1985, Falcon Crest; TV movies Survive the Savage Sea, 1992, Gunsmoke, The Hollywood Fashion Machine, 1995: the Long Ride, 1993; Broadway plays Festen, 2006; author: (autobiography) Moving Pictures, 1991. Address: PO Box 284 Tesuque NM 87574-0284*

MACGREGOR, MARILYN ELNA, director; b. Portland, Aug. 1, 1926; d. Dade and Alta Mae Russell; m. Neil John MacGregor, Sept. 18, 1949 (dec.). BA, Oreg. State U., 1949. Sec. dept. animal husbandry Oreg. State U., 1949—50; sec. dept. German U. Calif., Berkeley, 1951—57, adminstr. asst. dept. psychology, 1957—59, adminstr. officer dept. sociology, 1959—76, coord. employee devel., acting mgr., employee devel. unit, 1973—76, coord. sr. employee devel. unit, 1976—89; ret., 1989. Cons. US Office Personnel Mgmt., 1972—80; dir. Inst. for Natural Resources, 2001; pres. Scowrers and Molly Maguires, San Francisco, 1998—. Mem.: Adventuresses of Sherlock Holmes, Baker St. Irregulars, P.G. Wodehouse Soc., Sherlock Holmes Soc. London, Sherlock Holmes Soc. Czech Republic (hon.). Avocations: Japanese art, reading. Home: 1515 Shasta Dr #4210 Davis CA 95616-6692

MACGUIRE, NINA LITTLE, social worker; b. Greenville, Ala., Oct. 13, 1925; d. John Goodwin and Louise (Hobbs) Little; m. Colin Herbert MacGuire, Aug. 27, 1949 (dec. Nov. 2003); children: Colin Philip, Caroline. BA, Judson Coll., Marion, Ala., 1947. Jr. high tchr. Handley H.S., Roanoke, Ala., 1947—48; field dir. Montgomery Girl Scouts U.S., Montgomery, Ala., 1948—50; caseworker Butter County Welfare Dept., Greenville, Ala., 1951—56, Crenshaw County Welfare, LuVerne, Ala., 1962—63, Butter County Welfare, Greenville, 1963—91, child welfare supr., 1963—91; social worker Butler County Human Resources, 1991—. Pres. Women in the Ch. First Presbyn. Ch., Greenville, 1995—98. Mem.: DAR (registrar 1995—), United Daus. of Confederacy (pres., sec.). Home: 323 Hickory St Greenville AL 36037

MACH, ELYSE, music educator, author, pianist; b. Chgo., Jan. 12, 1942; d. Theodore August and Minna Louise (Holz) M.; children: Sean, Aaron, Andrew. B in Music Edn., Valparaiso U., 1962; MusM, Northwestern U., 1963, PhD in Music, 1965. Mem. faculty Northeastern Ill. U., Chgo., 1964—, prof. music, 1974—, assoc. chairperson dept. music, 1983-86; concert tours of Netherlands, Germany, Switzerland; recitalist, guest soloist; guest lectr. Northwestern U., Yale U., Juilliard Sch. Music, St. Catherine's Coll. of Oxford U.; cons., book reviewer Harcourt Brace Jovanovich and Macmillan;

writer monthly column Practice Notes for Clavier music mag.; disting. prof. of bd. govs. state colls. and univs. in Ill., 1990-91. Author: The Liszt Studies, 1973, Contemporary Class Piano, 1976, rev. 6th edit., 1993, 88, 6th edit., 2003, Great Pianists Speak for Themselves, 1980, (London) 81, (Tokyo) 86, The Rare and the Familiar: Twenty-eight Piano Pieces by Franz Liszt, 1982, Great Pianists Speak for Themselves, Vol. 2, 1988, Vols. 1 and 2, 1991, Great Contemporary Pianists Speak for Themselves, 1991, (with others) The Well-Tempered Keyboard Teacher, 1991, 2d edit., 2001, Contemporary Class Piano, Vol. 2, 1994, Learning Piano: Piece by Piece, 2005; contbg. music critic Chgo. Sun-Times. Mem. Edgebrook Community Assn., Chgo., 1975—. Recipient Presdl. Merit award Northeastern Ill. U., 1978, 81, 89, 92, 95, 96, 98, 2000, 02, Bd. Govs. Disting. Prof. award, 1990-91; Northeastern Ill. U. Found. grantee, 1980. Mem. Am. Liszt Soc. (bd. dirs.), Music Educators Nat. Conf., Ill. Music Tchrs. Assn., Midland Soc. Authors. Avocations: traveling, film, reading, theater. Home: 6551 N Waukesha Ave Chicago IL 60646-2726 Office: Northeastern Ill U 5500 N Saint Louis Ave Chicago IL 60625-4679 Office Phone: 773-442-5913.

MACH, JAN ELLEN WALKENHORST, literature educator, editor; b. Madison, Nebr. d. Dale Edward and Mary Moyer Walkenhorst; m. Daniel Blount (div.); 1 child, Byron K. Rupp; m. Robert Mach, 2006. BS in English Edn., U. Nebr., 1974. Cert. tchr. Tex., 1982, Nebr., 2001, cdl. bd. cert. 1995. Pres. Papillion (Nebr.) Edn. Assn., 1976—79; tchr. english Papillion (Nebr.) Pub. Schs., 1974—80, Richardson (Tex.) Ind. Sch. Dist., 1982—2000, Lincoln (Nebr.) Pub. Schs., 2001—04; instr. writing, asst. acad. counselor, tchr. theory of knowledge U. Nebr., Lincoln, 2004—. Mem. core team successful strategies, English Dept. chair, site-based facilitator, tchr. cadre; mem. project to convert curriculum to software Baylor U., 1994; rater statewide writing assessment Nebr., 2003. Editor: McGraw-Hill, 2000—, DC Health. Mem.: Nat. Assn. Acad. Advisors for Athletics. Avocations: reading, politics, travel. Office: Univ Nebr Athletic Dept 1 Memorial Stadium Lincoln NE 68588 Home: 1561 Rokeby Rd Pleasant Dale NE 68423 Office Phone: 402-472-9985. Personal E-mail: janwalk1952@aol.com. Business E-Mail: jwalkenhorst@huskers.com.

MACH, MICHELE R., special education educator; b. E. Chgo., Ind., Aug. 25, 1949; d. Chester J. and Irene M. Franciski; m. Daniel W. Mach, Apr. 18, 1975; 1 child, William B. BA, Purdue U., 1972, MS in Edn., 1975; reading specialist, Ind. U., 1978. Endorsement in learning disabilities and mildly mentally handicapped Ind. Least Restrictive Environ. facilitator and spl. edn. tchr. N.W. Ind. Spl. Edn. Coop., Crown Point, 1975—, tchr. learning disabilities Griffith, 1975—78, tchr. mildly mentally handicapped Highland, 1978—, tchr. autistic spectrum, 1978—; tchr. gifted and talented Highland Pub. Schs., 1980—84; tchr. St. John Sch., Ind., 1972—75; Least Restrictive Environ. facilitator Southridge Sch., Highland, 1975—. Mentor first year tchrs. N.W. Ind. Spl. Edn. Cooperative, Crown Point, 1985—. Remedial reading tutor Tradewinds, Merrillville and Hammond, Ind., 1977—82; tchr./leader St. Thomas More Ch., Munster, Ind., 1996. Named one of Outstanding Elem. Tchrs. Am., Diocese of Gary, 1975. Mem.: Coun. Exceptional Children, Hammond Area Reading Coun. Avocations: knitting, writing, reading. Home: 25 Beverly Pl Munster IN 46321 Office: Southridge Sch 9221 Johnston St Highland IN 46322

MACHADO-ECHEZURIA, MARIANELLA PERPETUA, composer, writer, educator; b. Caracas, Venezuala, Aug. 4, 1959; arrived in U.S., 1981; d. German Machado and Isabel C. Echezuria de Ruiz. MusB, Ind. U., 1984, MusM, 1986; MusD, U. Cin., 1993, MMA, 1996, PhD in Hispanic Lit., 1998. Rsch. asst. Romulo Coll., Caracas, Venezuela, 1987—88, Biblioteca Nacionel, Caracas, 1988—89; grad. tchg. asst. U. Cin., 1989—97; asst. prof. arts U. Catolica Andres Bello, Caracas, 1998—2003; asst. prof. Spanish Ea. Ky. U., Richmond, Ky., 2003—. Libr. music Cin. (Ohio) Symphony Orch., 1993—94; spkr. in field. Composer: (works) Obertura, 1987, Distonia, 1988, Las Semanas Tienen Sabados, 1988, Parafernalia, 1988, Psalm 32:10, 1990, Finneytown Suite, 1995; contbr. articles to profl. jours. Fellow, Taft Found., 1997—98; scholar, Ministry Edn., Caracas, Venezuela, 1974—80, Found. Gran Mariscal de Ayacucho, 1981—85, U. Cin., 1989—93, 1994—97; U. Rsch. Coun. fellow, 1991. Mem.: ASCAP (scholar 1993), Nat. Capital Lang. Resource Ctr., Multimedia Ednl. Resource Learning and On-line Tchg., Opera Am., Am. Composers Forum, Am. Music Ctr. Office: Eastern Ky Univ Lancaster Ave Richmond KY 40475 Home: 303 Timothy Way Apt 4 Richmond KY 40475-2724

MACHANIC, MINDY ROBIN, artist, photographer, educator, consultant, writer; b. NYC, June 21, 1950; d. Harmon Jack Machanic and Helen Jewel (Wolf) Mamolen; m. Bradley K. Shearer, Mar. 18, 1990 (div., 2005). BFA, San Francisco Art Inst., 1973; BS, U. State N.Y., 1983; M Planning, U. So. Calif., 1980; MA, Calif. State U., L.A., 1984; PhD, The Union Insts., 1995. Exec. dir. YWCA of U. So. Calif., L.A., 1980-81; instr. UCLA Extension, 1980, Calif. State U., Northridge, 1982, Otis Art Inst. of Parsons Sch., L.A., 1979-82, Maricopa Co. C.C., 1993-95; prof. Walden U., 1990—2005; adj. prof. U. Md., 2004—, Excelsior Coll., SUNY, 2006—. Facility planner-analyst Steinmann, Grayson, Smylie, L.A., 1981-82; asst. prof., program coord. environ. design program Sch. of Art, E. Carolina U., Greenville, N.C., 1984-86, psychology intern TASC Inc., Phoenix, Ariz., 1994-95, assoc. faculty Goddard Coll., 1995-97; mem. faculty Union Inst. Ctr. for Distant Learning, 1993-99; project mgr. ednl. tech. and learning Tech. U. BC, 1998; psychologist Napa (Calif.) State Hosp., 1997-98; writer Fannie Mae, Washington, 1988; field editor Area Devel. mag., 1989-92; rsch. asst. HUD, San Francisco, 1975; pres., prin. City Arts, L.A., 1978-84, Greenville, N.C., 1984-86, Washington, 1986-90, Machanic & Co., Phoenix, 1992-95, mindymac.com/Embracing Change, Portland, Oreg., 1998-2003, Growing Places/growing-places.com, Newberg, Oreg., 2000-2002; computer software trainer Forhan & Wakefield Group, Vienna, Va., 1989-90; instrnl. writer, project mgr. ComputerPrep, Phoenix, 1990-91; quality cons., instrnl. developer AG Comm. Systems, 1992; mental health therapist Salt River Indian Cmty. Mental Health Svc., 1993-94; instructional designer/developer U. Phoenix, 1993-95; mental health investigator Washington County, Oreg., 2001-2002. Movie reviewer Daily Reflector, Greenville, N.C., 1985, Dissertation: Waiting for Cancer Test Results: Impacts on the Patient & Family, 1996; contbr. articles and book revs. to profl. jours.; one-man shows include Lycoming Coll., Pa., 1974; exhibited in group shows So. Exposure Gallery, San Francisco, 1974, 75, Barnsdall Park Mcpl. Gallery, L.A., 1981, Gray Gallery, East Carolina U., 1984, 85, 86, Cmty. Coun. for Arts, Kinston, N.C., 1985, Art League Gallery, Alexandria, Va., 1986, Gallerie Triangle, Washington, 1987, Western Eye, Phoenix Coll., 1991; contbr. chpts. to books and articles to publs.; patentee Hover Seat The tay-Dry Toilet Seat; contract dissertation and thesis devel. editor and advisor internat. clients, 2004-05; freelance writer, author multiple articles trade jours. and newspapers and trade book chpts.; interviewer documentary Women in Black, Progressive Women of Prescott/Yarapai County, Ariz., 2005. Mem. hist. properties selection com. City of Greenville Planning and Zoning Commn., NC, 1985-86; peer counselor Bosom Buddies Breast Cancer Hotline, 1993-95; mem. Maricopa County South Area Behavioral Health Adv. Coun., Phoenix, 1993-94; spkr., facilitator Parents Anonymous, Phoenix, 1992; vol. zookeeper Heritage Pk. Zoo, Prescott, Ariz., 2005; edn. and curation vol. Mus. of Am. Quilt Soc., Paducah, 2006-; mem., facilitator, session presenter Interracial Women's Group, Paducah, 2006-. Democrat. Jewish. Avocations: science, gardening, travel, drawing, photography. Home: 217 Fountain Ave Paducah KY 42001 Personal E-mail: mindy@mindymac.com.

MACHI, RITA MAE, retired medical/surgical nurse, retired healthcare educator; b. Riverside, Calif., May 7, 1927; d. Lambert Joseph Sr. and Helen Ann Ninteman; m. Rocco Alfred Machi (dec.); m. Salvatore Alfred Machi, Dec. 27, 1957 (dec.); children: Rosemary Machi Gunsett, Terrie Machi Faust, Judith Machi Daviau. Attended, Riverside Jr. Coll., Calif., 1944, attended, 1947, U. Calif., Berkeley, 1944—46; diploma in nursing, Mercy Coll. Nursing, San Diego, 1951; BA summa cum laude, San Jose State Coll., Calif., 1955; postgrad., St. Anselm's Coll., Manchester, NH, 1958, U. Calif., San Diego, 1965—70, San Diego State U., 1968—70. RN Calif.; cert. tchr. Calif. Entomoloyg lab. asst. U. Calif., Riverside and Berkeley, 1944—46; charge nurse Golden Hill Convalescent Hosp., San Diego, 1955—56; staff nurse Elliott Hosp., Manchester, NH, 1957—60; staff/charge nurse Dr.'s Hosp., San Diego, 1960—64, Salvation Army Door of Hope, San Diego, 1964—70, asst. dir., 1970—75, dir. nursing, 1975—80; instr. childbirth preparation, child devel. CC Dist., San Diego, 1990; ret., 1990. Asst. editor: various sch. newspapers, newsletters; contbr. articles to profl. publs. Treas., reference dir. Parenthood Coun., San Diego, 1971—75; pres., sec., co-author bylaws Profl. Tchg. Prepared Childbirth, San Diego, 1970—80; mem., co-author bylaws Perinatal Coalition, San Diego, 1970—74; mem. Child Abuse Coun., San Diego, 1972—73; fundraiser Italian-Cath. Fedn., San Diego, 1970—80. Scholar, Panhellenic Soc., 1944—45. Roman Cath. Avocations: reading, history, science fiction, cooking, music. Home: 8837 Revelstoke Way San Diego CA 92126

MACHOWSKI, LIISA ERVIN SHARPES, science educator; b. New Brunswick, N.J., Feb. 9, 1953; d. William and Gladys Ervin Sharpes; m. Daniel John Machowski, Oct. 6, 1979; children: Anne Marie, Michael Joseph. M in Curriculum & Instrn., The Citadel, Charleston, S.C., 1992—96. Nat. Bd. cert. chemistry tchr. 2002. J.v. varsity girls basketball coach Titusville HS, Fla., 1975—76; jv girls basketball coach Palm Bay HS, 1977—78; head, sci. dept. Bishop Eng. HS, Charleston, SC, 1983—84; sponsor nat. honor soc. chpt. James Island Charter HS, Charleston, 1990—, sailing team sponsor, 2005—, sci. tchr. Contbr. for devel. of curriculum tchg. units for phys. sci. Charleston County Schs., 1999—2002; presenter of phys. sci. curriculum unit on chem. reactions S.C. Sci. Coun., Charleston, 2002—03. Mem.: Fla. Fedn. Tchrs., S.C. Sci. Coun., Charleston Ocean Racing Assn. (scorer 2005—06). Roman Catholic. Avocations: sailing, bicycling, collector. Office: James Island Charter HS 1000 Fort Johnson Rd Charleston SC

MACIEL, PATRICIA ANN, not-for-profit developer, consultant; b. Providence, Jan. 13, 1940; d. Raymond Wallace Sr. and Elizabeth Josephine (Kelly) Ross; m. John Maciel Jr., July 24, 1963; children: Kelly Patricia, Christopher John. EdB, R.I. Coll., 1961, MA in Tchg., 1976. Cert. tchr., R.I. Tchr. 3rd tchr. Pawtucket (R.I.) Pub. Schs., 1961-62; tchr. 5th and 6th grades Providence Pub. Schs., 1962-63; tchr. Pawtucket and Providence Pub. Schs., 1963-72; tchr., curriculum coord. Holy Name Sch., Providence, 1972-80; dir. ednl. programming Basic Skills, Inc., Providence, 1980-83; dir. devel./pub. rels. IN-SIGHT, Warwick, R.I., 1983-88; coord. ann. giving and spl. events St. Joseph Health Svcs. R.I., North Providence, 1988-2000; pvt. fundraising cons., 2000—; job skills specialist R.I. Coll. Outreach Programs, 2004—. Editor, author newsletter IN-SIGHT News, 1980-83. Sec. exec. bd. Holy Name Sch., 1972-80; pres. employee activities com. St. Joseph Health Svcs. R.I., 1991-93; founding mem., pres. Friends of the Pawtucket Pub. Libr., 1966; pres. Pawtucket Jr. Woman's Club, 1965; publicity chair Middlebridge Assn., South Kingstown, R.I., 1989-90; mem. Narrow River Preservation Assn., South Kingstown, 1976—; mem. Save the Bay, State of R.I., 1987—; ex officio mem. R.I. Coll. Found., 1992-94, corporate bd. dirs., 1996-97, sec., 1997-99, v.p., 1999-2001, pres., 2001-03, immediate past pres., 2003—2005, chair ad hoc com. capital campaign, 2000-01, vice chair alumni capital campaign, 2001—; rev. com. United Way S.E. New England, 1999, 2002, 03; mem. adv. bd. Villa at St. Antoine, 2002—; job skills specialist RI Coll. Outreach Program, 2004-. Recipient Alumna of Yr award Rhode Island Coll., 1992. Mem. R.I. Coll. Alumni Assn. (treas. exec. bd. 1990-92, chair ann. fund dr. 1990-92, chair class reunion 1981, 86, 91, class news sec. 1972-78, pres. 1992-94). Roman Catholic. Avocations: swimming, boating, walking, bicycling. Home: 3 Hunters Run North Providence RI 02904 E-mail: jmjpam@cox.net.

MACILWAINE, MARY JARRATT, public relations executive; b. Clifton Forge, Va., Oct. 29, 1942; d. Robert Bell and Mary Louise (Wood) J. BA, Mary Baldwin Coll., Staunton, Va., 1964; cert. bus., Katharine Gibbs Sch., Boston, 1965. Staff asst. com. on agr. U.S. Ho. of Reps., 1975-81; asst. sec. food and consumer services Dept. Agr., 1981-85; v.p. Wampler & Assocs. Inc., Washington, 1985-86; pres. Jarratt & Assocs., Inc., Washington, 1986-90; asst. to pres and CEO Va. Nat. Bank, Charlottesville, 2000—. Editor various legis. reports. Republican. Episcopalian. Home: 1149 Marion Dr Charlottesville VA 22903-4649 E-mail: mmacilwaine@virginianb.com.

MACIUSZKO, KATHLEEN LYNN, librarian, educator; b. Nogales, Ariz., Apr. 8, 1947; d. Thomas and Stephanie (Horowski) Mart; m. Jerzy Janusz Maciuszko, Dec. 11, 1976; 1 child, Christina Aleksandra. BA, Ea. Mich. U., 1969; MLS, Kent State U., 1974; PhD, Case Western Res. U., 1987. Reference libr. Baldwin-Wallace Coll. Libr., Berea, Ohio, 1974-77, dir. Conservatory of Music Libr., 1977-85; dir. bus. info. svcs. Harcourt Brace Jovanovich, Inc., Cleve., 1985-89; staff asst. to exec. dir. Cuyahoga County Pub. Libr., Cleve., 1989-90; dir. Cleve. Area Met. Library System, Beachwood, Ohio, 1990; media specialist Cleve. Pub. Schs., 1991-93, Berea (Ohio) City Sch. Dist., 1993—. Author: OCLC: A Decade of Development, 1967-77, 1984; contbr. articles to profl. jours. Named Plenum Pub. scholar, 1986. Mem. Spl. Librs. Assn. (pres. Cleve. chpt. 1989-90, v.p. 1988-89, editor newsletter 1988-89), Baldwin-Wallace Coll. Faculty Women's Club (pres. 1975), Avocation: music. Office: Midpark HS 7000 Paula Dr Middleburg Heights OH 44130

MACK, CAROLE, financial consultant; b. N.Y.C., Feb. 28, 1943; d. August and Anne Cahier; m. Arthur R. Mack II, Aug. 21, 1965; children: Arthur R. Mack III, Alan R., John Wendell Howard. Student, Zion U. Customer svc. Blue Cross-Blue Shield, Rochester, NY; instr. baton twirling The Wine Country Club, Naples; owner Carriage House Christian Bookstore; real estate broker, owner Carole Mack Realty; consumer loan officer Citifinancial, Asheville, NC. Sec. Finger Lakes Bd. Realty, Penn Yan; real estate appraiser bd. assessors Town of Milo; bd. dirs. Keuka Housing Coun. Author: (songbook) Ascending the Holy Hill, 1993. Treas. Mt. Zion Christian Assembly, Penn Yan, 1990—98. Republican. Avocations: gardening, music, omnichord. Home: 219 Adams Hill Rd Asheville NC 28806

MACK, CHERYL A., principal; b. Hannibal, Mo., Feb. 4, 1956; d. Jonathan G. and Belva J. Wisdom; m. David G. Mack, Oct. 25, 1980; children: Erin B., Jonathan D., Daniel J., Ethan G. MEd in Adminstrn., SW Bapt. U., Bolivar, Mo., 2004, specialist degree, 2006. Tchr. 1st Assembly Christian Sch., Hannibal, Mo., 1981—85; tutor West Orange Cove Ind. Sch. Dist., Orange, Tex., 1991—94; tchr./substitute tchr./aide Ralls County R-II Sch. Dist., Center, Mo., 1994—2003, prin. jr. H.S., 2003—.

MACK, INA LEAH, secondary school educator, pre-school administrator; b. Macon, Mo., Jan. 10, 1959; d. David Neil and Ina Bernadine Milburn; m. Gary Ray Mack, Sept. 3, 1988; children: Brittany, Cameron, Delaney. BA in Edn., Ariz. State U., 1982; MA in Edn., No. Ariz. U., 2005. Tchr. Antelope High Sch., Wellton, Ariz., 1983—86, Mt. View High Sch., Tucson, 1987—90, Snowflake High Sch., 1990—95, Northland Pioneer Coll., Holbrook, 1991—, Blue Ridge High Sch., Lakeside, 1995—. Advisor Family, Career, Cmty. Leaders Am., Lakeside, 1990—; coach various schs., 1983—93. Vol. Hope Ho., Show Low, Ariz., 2003—05. Mem.: Ariz. Family and Consumer Scis. Edn. Assn., Nat. Assn. Edn. Young Children, Ariz. Career & Tech. Edn. Assn. Republican. Baptist. Avocations: camping, motorcycling, water-skiing, scrapbooks. Office: Blue Ridge High Sch 1200 W White Mountain Rd Lakeside AZ 85929 Home: 4837 Oakwood St Lakeside AZ 85929-5537

MACK, JEANNETTE ANA, medical technician; b. Jacksonville, Fla., July 14, 1951; d. Willie Lee and Dorothea Scott Mack; m. Luther Baker Jr. (div.); children: Luther Baker III, Calecia Baker Fowlers, Christopher Baker. AS in Bus. Sci., Fla. Tech. Coll., Jacksonville, Fla., 1987, AS in Electronics Tech. with honors, 1986. Nurse's aide St. Lukes Hosp., 1974—79; monitor tech. and patient care Meml. Hosp., 1978—86, Riverside Hosp., 1987—89; neurodiagnostic tech. Meml. Hosp., 1986—88, U. Med. Ctr., 1989—96; supr. neurodiagnostic Meml. Hosp., 1996—. Baptist. Home: 98 Lake Run Blvd Jacksonville FL 32218-0806 Office: 3625 Univ Blvd S Jacksonville FL 32216

MACK, JUDITH COLE SCHRIM, retired political scientist; b. Cin., Aug. 9, 1938; d. James Douglass and Cathleen (Cole) Schrim; m. Thomas H. Mack, Jan. 3, 1968; children: Robert Michael, Cathleen Cole. AB with high distinction, U. Ky., Lexington, 1960; AM, Radcliffe Grad. Sch., 1962; MPhil, Columbia U., N.Y.C., 1988, postgrad., 1986—. Tchr. Lexington Sch., Ky., 1962-63; instr. Russian Emory U., Atlanta, 1963-64, Kent State U., Ohio, 1964-65; instr. Hunter Coll., N.Y.C., 1988-90; adj. lectr. Barnard Coll., N.Y.C., 1991—92; instr. Douglass Coll. Rutgers U., New Brunswick, NJ, 1992—93; ret., 1993. Rsch. asst. sociology dept. U. Ky., 1961; rsch. asst. Russian and E. European Studies Ctr. UCLA, 1965—67, rsch. asst. Security Studies Ctr., 1967—68; adj. lectr. Hunter Coll., N.Y.C., 1988; presenter in field. Chmn. state pub. affairs com. N.J. Jr. Leagues, 1979—80; bd. dirs. Children's Aide Adoption Soc., Hackensack, NJ, 1979—90, v.p., 1985—90; bd. dirs. Assn. Children N.J., Newark, 1982—2003, v.p., 1983—88, chair spl. events, 1999; trustee Divsn. Youth and Family Svcs., Trenton, NJ, 1982—91, v.p., 1983—88; others; trustee Dumbarton Ho., Washington; mem. vis. bd. Music Acad. of the West, Women's Aux.; active Millburn-ShortHills County Rep. Com., 1994—2003, corr. sec., 1994—96, chmn., 1996—98. Woodrow Wilson fellow, Radcliffe Coll., 1960—61, Nat. Def. fellow, 1961—62. Mem.: Am. Bd. Music Acad. West (treas.), Mortar Bd., Nat. Soc. Colonial Dames Am. (N.J. treas. 1995—2001), Phi Sigma Iota, Phi Beta Kappa. Episcopalian. Avocations: bridge, cooking, ballet, theater, movies. Home: 657 Del Parque Dr Unit C Santa Barbara CA 93103 E-mail: jsmack22@att.net.

MACK, JULIA COOPER, retired judge; b. Fayetteville, NC, July 17, 1920; d. Dallas L. and Emily (McKay) Perry; m. Jerry S. Cooper, July 30, 1943; 1 dau., Cheryl; m. Clifford S. Mack, Nov. 21, 1957. BS, Hampton Inst., 1940; LLB, Howard U., 1951; JD (hon.), U. DC, 1999. Bar: DC 1952. Legal cons. OPS, Washington, 1952-53; atty.-advisor office gen. counsel Gen. Svcs. Adminstrn., Washington, 1953-54; trial appellate atty. criminal div. Dept. Justice, Washington, 1954-68; civil rights atty. Office Gen. Counsel, Equal Employment Opportunity Commn., Washington, 1968-75; assoc. judge Ct. Appeals, Washington, 1975-89; sr. judge DC Ct. of Appeals, Washington, 1989—2001. Mem. Am., Fed., Washington, Nat. Bar Assns., Nat. Assn. Women Judges. Home: 1610 Varnum St NW Washington DC 20011-4206

MACK, PHYLLIS GREEN, retired librarian; b. Charleston, W.Va., July 1, 1941; d. Leroy Stanley and Gladys (Webster) Green; m. Arnold Rudolph Mack (dec. 1989); children: Stephanie Michele, Nicole Renee. BS in Edn., W.Va. State Coll. Inst., 1963; MLS, Pratt Inst., 1967; advanced cert., Columbia U., N.Y.C., 1985. Jr. libr. asst. Hunter Coll. Libr., N.Y.C., 1965; clk. N.Y. Pub. Libr., N.Y.C., 1963-64, libr. trainee, then libr., 1966-68, sr. libr., 1968-73, supervisory libr., 1973-84, regional libr., 1984—2002; ret., 2002. Mem. Cmty. Bd. 10, Manhattan, N.Y., 1987-91, chairperson, 1989-90; trustee Sch. Bd. Dist. # 5, N.Y.C., 1997-99; pres. Maple Ct. Housing Devel., 2000-2003. Doctoral fellow Columbia U., 1983-84; recipient citation for community svc. N.Y.C. Coun., 1990. Mem. ALA (mem. black caucus 1980—), Rotary (Upper Manhattan club), Delta Sigma Theta, Inc. (1st v.p. North Manhattan alumnae chpt. 1980-83, 89-93, 2004—). Home: 1901 Madison Ave Apt 521 New York NY 10035-2732

MACK, VALERIE LIPPOLDT, music educator, performing arts educator, freelance/self-employed choreographer; b. Wichita, Kans., Aug. 30; d. Vaughn Lippoldt and Velma Miller; m. Tom M. Mack, Aug. 7, 1987; children: Stevie, Zane. BA, Bethany Coll., Lindsborg, Kan., 1983; BME, Wichita State Univ., Wichita, Kan., 1987, MME, 1993. Dance instr. Bethany Coll., Lindsberg, Kans., 1981—83; aerobics instr. Mary Mayt Fitness, Wichita, Kans., 1984—86; ballet, tap instr. Kans. Dance Acad., Wichita, Kans., 1986—87; choreographer Wichita State Univ., Wichita, Kans., 1987—95; vocal music H.S. instr. Maize H.S., Maize, Kans., 1986—87; lead vocal and dance instr. Butler C.C., El Dorado, Kans., 1987—, master tchr., 1998—2006. Clinician Emporia State Univ., Emporia, Kans., 1998—2003; prodr., bd. dir. Miss Wichita, Wichita, Kans., 1983—2003; prodr. Miss Butler, 1983—2003; artistic dir. Butler Showchair Showcase, El Dorado, Kans., 1993—2003. Choreographer (plays) 100 Years Of Broadway, Carnegie Hall, 2000, (video) Mary Mayta Fitness for Life, 1986; performer: (video) Mary Mayta Fitness for Life, 1986; contbr.: chpt. Warm-Ups for Choral Directors, 2003. Praise choir, praise team dir. Risen Savior Luth. Ch., Wichita, Kans., 1994—, bells, chimes, Sunday sch., 1994—; prod., bd. mem. Miss Wichita, Wichita, Kans., 1988—2002; bd. mem. Alzheimer Assn., Wichita, Kans., 1995. Mem.: Music Educators Nat. Conf. Republican. Luth. Avocations: dance, travel, Broadway shows. Home: 4104 Plum Tree St Wichita KS 67226 Office: Butler Cmty Coll 901 S Haverhill Rd El Dorado KS 67042

MACKALL, CRYSTAL L., medical researcher; BS/MD, Northeastern Ohio Universities Coll. Medicine, 1984. Medicine/pediatrics resident, Akron, Ohio; clin. assoc. Pediatric Oncology Br. Nat. Cancer Inst., 1989—92, postdoctoral sci. training Expt. Immunology Br., 1990—96, rschr. Pediatric Oncology Br., 1996—, now also chief Pediatrics Oncoolgy Br., chief Immunology Sect. Office: Pediatric Oncology Br Ctr Cancer Rsch 10 CRC 1W 3940 Bethesda MD 20892-1104 Office Fax: 301-451-7052. Business E-Mail: cm35c@nih.gov.

MACKAY, GAIL, librarian; b. New Castle, Ind., Nov. 13, 1948; d. Frederick Earl and Rosemary (Garvey) Brown; children: Heather E., Douglas F. BA in English, Purdue U., 1971; MLS, Ball State U., 1973. Cert. tchr., libr., Ind. English tchr. Taylor H.S., Kokomo, Ind., 1977-84; libr. Ind. U., Kokomo, 1992—. Author and presenter. Pres., Tribal Trails coun. Girl Scouts U.S.A., 1995—, nat. cert. instr. of trainers, 1992—. Thank Badge, Girl Scouts, 1989. Mem. ALA, Ind. U. Librs. Assn. (chair profl. devel. 1994), Ind. Libr. Fedn. (co-chair instrn. sect. 1994—). Roman Catholic. Office: Ind U Kokomo PO Box 9003 Kokomo IN 46904-9003 E-mail: gmackay@iuk.edu.

MACKAY, GLADYS GODFREY, retired adult education educator; b. Buffalo, N.Y., Sept. 17, 1915; d. Joseph Edwin and Hazel Winifred (Brown) Godfrey; m. James Albert MacKay, July 11, 1944 (wid. June 1997); children: Michael Paul, Cynthia Louise. BS, Cornell U., Ithaca, N.Y., 1936; MA, Columbia U., N.Y.C., 1940; postgrad., Case Western Res. U., Cleve., 1948—50. Cert. tchr. N.Y. Asst. home demonstration agt. Cornell U., N.Y., 1936-38; tchr. rural vocat. home econs. Consolidated Schs., Gilbertsville, N.Y., 1938-39; jr./sr. h.s. home econs. tchr. City Pub. Sch., Peekskill, N.Y., 1940-42; home econs. instr. Mather Coll./Cleve. Coll., Western Res. U., Cleve., 1946-48; marriage counselor/probation officer Lucas County Ct of Domestic Rels., Toledo, 1950-51; tchr./psychologist, spkr.'s bur. Family Health Assn. and Cen. Sch. of Practical Nursing, Cleve., 1951-54; ret. Rep. to nat. consumer-retailer coun. for AAUW, Am. Stds. Assn., N.Y.C., 1940-42; mem. com. setting textile color-fastness stds. for FTC, Am. Stds. Assn., 1941; mem. task force to develop health edn. curriculum, Cleve. Heights Bd. of Edn., Ohio, 1967-69; mem. adv. bd. Children's Svcs., Cleve., 1963-65; mem. mental health com. Fedn. for Cmty. Planning, Cleve., 1977-78, others. Active Coun. on World Affairs, Cleve., 1960-76, in chg. fgn. doctors at Univ. Hosp., VA Hosp.; presenter Cleve. Growth Assn., 1964, Ohio Citizen's Coun., Columbus, 1974-77, others; presenter Met. Health Planning Corp., Cleve., 1978, chair Health Edn. Conf., 1978. Lt. USNR, 1942-46, WWII. Recipient Navy Commendation; named to Nat. Inst. of Pub. Affairs Conf. on Met. Problems, Washington, 1968. Mem. AAUW (life, honoree Ohio Wall of Fame 2000), Case Western Res. Univ. Women's Club (bd. mem. Sch. Medicine), Cleve. Acad. of Medicine Aux., Pi Lambda Theta, Alpha Xi Delta. Presbyterian. Achievements include being one of first 2 women to fly Navy antisubmarine Patrol NAS, Norfolk, Va., 1943. Home: 162 Kendal Dr Oberlin OH 44074-1907

MACKAY, PATRICIA MCINTOSH, psychotherapist; b. San Francisco, Sept. 12, 1922; d. William Carroll and Louise Edgerton (Keen) McIntosh; m. Alden Thorndike Mackay, Dec. 15, 1945 (dec. June 2002); children: Patricia Louise, James McIntosh, Donald Sage; m. Richard John Rihn, July 26, 2003. AB in Psychology, U. Calif., Berkeley, 1944, elem. tchg. credential, 1951; MA in Psychology, John F. Kennedy U., Orinda, Calif., 1979; PhD in Nutrition, Donsbach U., Huntington Beach, Calif., 1981. Cert. marriage, family and child counselor. Elem. tchr. Mt. Diablo Unified Sch. Dist.,

Concord, Calif., 1950-60; exec. supr. No. Calif. Welcome Wagon Internat., 1960-67; wedding cons. Mackay Creative Svcs., Walnut Creek, Calif., 1969-70; co-owner Courtesy Calls, Greeters and Concord Welcoming Svcs., Walnut Creek, 1971-94; marriage, family and child counselor, nutrition cons., Walnut Creek, 1979—. Coord. Alameda and Contra Costa County chpts. Parents United Internat., 1985—, pres. region 2, bd. dirs., 1992; bd. dirs. New Directions Counseling Ctr., Inc., 1975-81, founder, pres. aux., 1977-79. Bd. dirs. Ministry in Marketplace, Inc.; founder, dir. Turning Point Counseling; active Walnut Creek Presbyn. Ch.; bd. dirs., counseling dir. Shepherd's Gate, shelter for homeless women and children, 1985-92, Contra Costa County Child Care Coun., 1993-95. Recipient award New Directions Counseling Ctr., 1978, yearly awards Neo-Life Co. Am. Prestige Club, 1977-856, Cmty. Svc. award Child Abuse Prevention Coun., 1990, 92, 94. Mem. AAUW, Am. Assn. Marriage and Family Therapists, U. Calif.-Berkeley Alunni Assn. (sec. 1979-94), Walnut Creek C. of C., Prytanean Alumnae, Soroptomists (bd. dirs. Walnut Creek 1976, 86), Delta Gamma. Republican. Home: 1101 Scots Ln Walnut Creek CA 94596-5432

MACKENZIE, CLARA CHILDS, writer, editor; b. Asheville, N.C., May 28, 1931; d. William Wallace and Mildred (Stevens) Childs; m. Allen H. Mackenzie, June 15, 1957; children: David, Sarah, Clara, William. BA, Converse Coll., 1951; MA, Duke U., 1954; PhD, Case Western Reserve U., 1971. Instr. English Cleve. State U., 1959-63, asst. dir. Ctr. for Effective Learning, 1974-76; head English, communications Bratenahl (Ohio) High Sch., 1971-74; writer, editor Seaforth Publs., Cleve., 1976—. Asst. prof. English, dir. pub. relations James Madison U., Harrisonburg, Va., 1954-57; instr. Kent State U., 1960-61. Author: (biographies) Wolfsmeller (Zhoh Gwatson), 1985, Sarah Barnwell Elliott, 1980, (with others) Edisto, A Sea Island Principality, 1978; editor (short story collection) Some Data and Other Stories of Southern Life, 1981. Co-pres. Bratenahl Community Found., 1985-87; v.p. Bratenahl Bd. Edn., 1965-70; sr. warden Trinity Cathedral, 1986, mem. Village Coun., 1989-93. Fellow NDEA, 1966-67; grantee So. Fellowships Fund, 1956; Spartanburg County Found. scholar, 1948-51, Fulbright scholar, 1951-52. Democrat. Episcopalian. Avocations: photography, gardening, travel. Home: PO Box 186 Roebuck SC 29376-0186

MACKENZIE, DORIS LAYTON, psychologist, educator, researcher, criminologist; b. Riverton, N.J., June 20, 1943; d. H. Grandon and Ellen S. Layton; m. David Robert MacKenzie, June 29, 1963; children: Wendy, Scott, Todd. BS in Psychology, Pa. State U., 1976, MS in Psychology, 1978, PhD, 1983. Asst. prof. La. State U., Baton Rouge, 1983-89, assoc. prof., 1989-90, U. Md., College Park, 1990-93, rsch. scholar, 1993—. Vis. sci. Nat. Inst. Justice, Washington, 1988-92; co-chair conf. The Am. Prison, Nags Head, N.C., 1987; prin. investigator U. Md., College Park, 1990—; cons. Nat. Inst. Corrections, Washington, 1993. Co-editor: The American Prison, 1989, Measuring Crime, 1990, Drugs and Crime, 1994, Correctional Boot Camps, 2004, What Works In Corrections, 2006. Mem. Am. Soc. Criminology, Am. Correctional Assn. (mem. rsch. coun.), Acad. Criminal Justice Scis. Avocations: scuba diving, swimming, biking. Office: U Md Dept Criminal Justice 2220 Lefrak Hall College Park MD 20742-8235

MACKENZIE, LINDA ALICE, media company executive, radio personality, writer, hypnotherapist; b. Bronx, N.Y., June 24, 1949; d. Gino Joseph and Mary J. (Damon) Arale; m. John Michael Lassourreille, Aug. 7, 1968 (div. 1975); 1 child, Lisa Marie Lassourreille; m. Donald John Mackenzie, July 2, 1978 (div. 1982). Student, Richmond Coll., 1967-68, West L.A. C.C., 1978-81. Spl. rep. N.Y. Telephone Co., White Plains, 1968-71; asst. mgr. Paul Holmes Real Estate Inc., Richmond, N.Y., 1974-77; telcom applications specialist engring. Continental Airlines, L.A., 1977-83; data transmission specialist Western Airlines, L.A., 1983-87; owner Computers on Consignment, El Segundo, Calif., 1984-94. Cons. Caleb Feb. Credit Union, Las Vegas, Nev., 1985, Nat. Dissemenators, Las Vegas, Nev., 1985, Vega & Assocs. Prodn. Divsn., 1987, Uptech/Downtech, 1986, Dollar Rent-a-Car, 1987, Advanced Digital Networks, 1987, Pomona Sch. Dist., 1987, State Senate, 1988, Nordstroms, 1988, Flying Tigers, 1988, Fed. Express, 1989, Sita/ITS, 1990—92, Neutrogena, 1991, B & B Computers, 1992; mktg. cons. AT&T, L.A., Calif., 1984—85, Radio KPSL, 1995—97, Carter Broadcasting Talk Am., 1995—97, WDRC, 1995, WXLW, 1995, CRN, Pax, 1995—2002, CHSR Healthylife.net, 2002—; radio host Creative Health & Spirit Show, 1995—; owner Creative Health & Spirit, Manhattan Beach, Calif., 1995—; spkr. in field. Author: The World Within, 1983, Inner Insights-The Book of Charts, 1997, The Total Mind-Body-Spirit Weight Loss Program Audiovisualization Tapes, 1998, How to Self-Publish Your Personal Growth Book, 1999; (audio tape) Help Yourself Heal-Menopause 1999, Help Yourself Health With Self-Hypnosis, 2000; author numerous poems. Recipient Alexander award, Met. Mus. Art, N.Y.C., 1967, Covr Best Metaphys. Book, 2nd place, 1998, Covr Best Spoken World Audio, 2nd place, 1999. Mem. Am. Bd. Hypnotherapists, Am. Inst. Hypnotherapy, Nat. Assn. Alt. Health Care Providers. Republican. Avocations: painting, creative writing, golf, skiing, travel. Home: 2514 Graham Ave #3 Redondo Beach CA 90278-2124 Office Phone: 800-555-5453. E-mail: info@healthylife.net.

MACKENZIE, SUE, music educator, theater director; MusB in Edn., Cen. Mich. U., Mt. Pleasant, 1974. Elem. music tchr. Indian Hill Elem. Sch., Grand Blanc, Mich., 1999—. Dir., singer, actor: (dinner theater) New Vic Supper Theater; dir., music dir.: Quilters (Best Musical Dir. of Regional Theater, 2000); singer: (choral music) Carolyn Mawby Chorale. Office Phone: 810-591-4165.

MACKERT, RITA MARIE, elementary school educator; b. Lakewood, Ohio, Nov. 1, 1934; d. Albert William and Pearl Matilda (Leonard) Mackert. BE, MEd, St. Johns Coll., Cleve., 1967. Tchr. St. Vincent de Paul Sch., Cleve., 1955—58, St. Mary's Berea, Berea, Ohio, 1958—62, St. Thomas Aquinas, Cleve., 1962—67, St. Colman, Cleve., 1967—68, St. Joseph John, Strongsville, Ohio, 1968—. Facilitator Adventures in Attitudes St. Joseph Parish, 1978—88. Named Outstanding Tchr. of Yr., St. Joseph and John Sch., 2005.

MACKEY, PAMELA ROBILLARD, lawyer; b. Harlingen, Tex., July 16, 1956; d. Gregory Leo and Rosanne Elizabeth (Niland) Robillard; m. Craig W. Mackey, Dec. 30, 1983. BS in Journalism, U. Colo., 1981; JD, George Wash. U., 1985. Bar: Colo. 1985, U.S. Dist. Ct. Colo. 1985. Assoc. Davis, Graham & Stubbs, Denver, 1985-87, Haddon, Morgan & Foreman, P.C., Denver, 1987—, shareholder, 1997—. Pub. defender Colo., 1989-94. Exec. editor George Wash. Law Review, 1984-85. Mem. ABA, Colo. Bar Assn., Denver Bar Assn., Colo. Women's Bar Assn. (bd. dirs. 1988-96; pres. 1995-96), Colo. Criminal Def. Bar (newsletter editor 1988—). Democrat. Roman Catholic. Avocations: skiing, golf. Office: Haddon Morgan Mueller Jordan Mackey & Foreman PC 150 E Tenth Ave Denver CO 80203 Office Phone: 303-831-7364. E-mail: pmackey@hmflaw.com.

MACKEY, PATRICIA ELAINE, university librarian; b. Balt., July 29, 1941; d. Timothy and Hazel Mozelle (Davis) M. BA in Anthropology, CUNY, 1978; MLS, Columbia U., 1981. Asst. libr. I, European Exch. Sys., Mainz-Kastel, Germany, 1966-68; interlibr. loan asst. Poly. U., Bklyn., 1968-72, Rockefeller U., N.Y.C., 1972-73, sr. libr. asst., 1974-80, libr., 1981-91, univ. libr., 1991—. Mem. various libr. coms., N.Y.C., 1991—. Chair pub. svc. scholars program Hunter Coll. CUNY, 1992—; trustee Met. N.Y. Libr. Coun., 2000—, also 1st v.p. Named to, Hunter Coll. Hall of Fame, 2002. Mem.: ALA, Assn. Coll. and Rsch. Librs., N.Y. State Libr. Assn., Hunter Coll. Alumni Assn. (bd. dirs. 1998—, 2d v.p. 1998—2002). Democrat. Roman Catholic. Avocations: reading, chess, gardening. Office: Rockefeller U Libr RU Box 263 1230 York Ave New York NY 10021-6307 Office Phone: 212-327-8909. Business E-Mail: rmackey@mail.rockefeller.edu.

MACK-HARVIN, DIONNE, library director; MA in Africana Studies, SUNY, Albany, 1995, MLS in Info. Sci., 1996. Libr. Queens Coll., NY, 1996; libr. Crown Heights Libr. Bklyn. Pub. Libr., NY, 1996, asst. branch libr. NY, branch mgr. NY, regional libr. NY, dir. Ctrl. Libr. NY, chief of staff NY, 2005—06, interim dir. NY, 2006—. Office: Bklyn Pub Libr Ctrl Libr Grand Army Plaza Brooklyn NY 11238 E-mail: d.mack@brooklynpubliclibrary.org.*

MACKICHAN, MARGARET ANNA, artist, art educator; b. Charleston, W.Va., Feb. 27, 1948; d. Kenneth Allen and Lois Alma (Deyton) MacK.; 1 child, Jemma Moccasin. BFA, U. Nebr., 1970; MA, U. N.Mex., 1974, MFA, 1977. Assoc. VISTA, Ky., 1966-67; photographer Ky., 1968—87, Rosebud (S.D.) Reservation, 1987-92; founding dir. Great Plains Art Inst., Sinte Gleska U., Rosebud Reservation, SD, 1987. Curatorial intern Internat. Mus. of Photography, George Eastman House, Rochester, N.Y., 1971-72; artist-in-community Western Nebr. Art Ctr., Scottsbluff, 1978-79; instr. Nebr. Western Coll., Scottsbluff, 1978-79; vis. prof. Nebr. Wesleyan U., Lincoln, 1980-87; participant Annual Plains Indian Seminar, 1987-98. Co-author: In the Kingdom of Grass, 1992. Recipient 1st prize photography Mademoiselle Mag., 1970, Vreeland award U. Nebr., 1970, Artist grant Nebr. Arts Coun./Nebr. Com. on Humanities, 1978, Artist fellowship Mid-Am. Arts Alliance, 1983, Outstanding Svc. in Art Edn. award S.D. Gov., 2003. Fellow Ctr. for Great Plains Study; mem. Soc. for Photographic Edn., Nat. Am. Art Studies Assn., Scottish Soc. Artists. Presbyterian. Avocations: walker horses, Lakota arts, Scottish dancing, banjo, bagpipes. Home: PO Box 6 Mission SD 57555-0006 Office: Sinte Gleska University PO Box 105 Mission SD 57555-0105

MACKINNON, ANN LAURIE, retired elementary school educator; 1 child, Brian John Stempel. BS, St. John's U., Jamaica, 1967, JD, 1996; MEd, Hafetra U., NY, 1971. Elem. sch. tchr. Babylon Union Free Sch. Dist., NY, 1967, Connetquot Ctrl. Sch. Dist. of Islip, LI, NY, 1969—2000; ret., 2000. Colored pencil, oil portraits, clay and sculptures. Union bd. mem. Connetquot Tchrs. Assn., Bohemia, NY, 1968—89; v.p. S. Corp. Laureu-Curtis Assocs., d.b.a. Anne Lauren, Setauket, NJ, 1980. Lt. col. USMC, 1967—. Mem.: Suffolk County Bar Assn. Avocations: quilting, reading, walking, swimming, gardening. Home: 12 Harbor Hills Dr Port Jefferson NY 11777

MACKINNON, CATHARINE ALICE, lawyer, educator, writer; d. George E. and Elizabeth V. (Davis) MacKinnon. BA in Govt. magna cum laude with distinction, Smith Coll., 1969; JD, Yale U., 1977, PhD in Polit. Sci., 1987. Vis. prof. Harvard U., Stanford U., Yale U., others, Osgoode Hall, York U., Canada, U. Basel, Switzerland; prof. law U. Mich., Ann Arbor, 1990—, Elizabeth A. Long Prof. Law. Long term vis. prof. U. Chgo., 1997—; co-dir. LAW Project Equality Now, 2001—; fellow Ctr. for Advanced Study, 2005-06. Author: Sexual Harassment of Working Women, 1979, Feminism Unmodified, 1987, Toward a Feminist Theory of the State, 1989, Only Words, 1993, Sex Equality, 2001, Women's Lives, Men's Laws, 2005, Are Women Human? and other international dialogues, 2006; co-author: In Harm's Way, 1997, Directions in Sexual Harassment Law, 2003. Mem.: AAAS (assoc.). Office: U Mich Law Sch 625 S State St Ann Arbor MI 48109-1215 Office Phone: 734-647-3595. Office Fax: 734-764-8309. E-mail: camtwo@umich.edu.

MACKINNON, NANCY WILLIAMS, retired educator, state legislator; b. Boston, July 18, 1925; d. Nathaniel White and Rose Francis (Bates) Williams; m. Gerald Langtry MacKinnon Jr., Apr. 3, 1948 (dec. 1967); children: Marcia MacKinnon Calabro, Geoffrey W. BS in Edn., Boston U., 1947; M in Edn. and Human Resources, New Eng. Coll., 1982. Cert. tchr., N.H. Sec. Boston Navy Yard, Charlston, Mass., 1944-45; tchr. Derry (N.H.) Sch. Dist., 1967-88; mem. N.H. Ho. of Reps., Concord, 1988—. Mem. Derry Budget Com., 1978-82; mem. fin. com. Derry Sch. Dist., 1986-88. Mem. N.H. Retired Tchrs. Assn., Orgn. Women Legislators, P.E.O. (chaplain Derry chpt. 1988—). Avocations: swimming, gardening, reading, travel.

MACKINNON, REBECCA, media consultant, researcher; Grad. magna cum laude, Harvard U. Taiwan stringer Newsweek mag., 1991—92; bur. asst. CNN, Beijing, 1992—93, assoc. prodr., 1993—96, prodr., correspondent, 1997—98, bur. chief, 1998—2001, Tokyo, 2001—03; media cons., 2004—; fellow Shorenstein Ctr. on the Press Harvard U., 2004; rsch. fellow Berkman Ctr. for Internet and Society Harvard Law Sch., 2004—; co-founder Global Voices Online. Office: Harvard Law Sch Baker House 1587 Massachusetts Ave Cambridge MA 02138 Office Phone: 617-495-7547. Office Fax: 617-812-7950. E-mail: rmackinnon@cyber.law.harvard.edu.*

MACKINNON, SALLY ANNE, retired fast food company executive; b. Chgo., Apr. 20, 1938; d. Eugene and Anne Elizabeth (Jones) MacK. BA, Smith Coll., 1960; postgrad., U. Ark., 1961-62. Brand mgr. Speidel div. of Textron, Providence, 1967-70; mktg. mgr. Candy Corp. Am., Bklyn., 1970-72; v.p. account service William Esty Advt., N.Y.C., 1972-76; mktg. mgr. R.J. Reynolds Tobacco, Winston-Salem, N.C., 1976-84, v.p. new brands, 1984-86; v.p. new products mktg. Ky. Fried Chicken, Louisville, 1986-88; ret., 1988. Democrat. Episcopalian. Avocations: photography, travel. Home: 7500 E Boulders Pkwy # 20 Scottsdale AZ 85262

MACKLER, TINA, artist; b. London; d. Leon and Ethel Mackler. Student, Arts Students League, N.Y.C., Indsl. Sch. Design, New Sch. Tchr. art Nat. Acad. Ballet, N.Y.C., 1966-69; tchr. adults West Side YMCA, N.Y.C. Asst. studio instr. Met. Mus. Art, N.Y.C., vol. program, 1990—. Illustrator: Informal Dictionary of Ballet, 1966; co-author, illustrator: To Dance, To Live; pub. Dance Horizons, 1977; one-persons shows include Alfred Valente Gallery, N.Y.C., 1967, Mus. Performing Arts, N.Y.C., 1973, Adelphi U., L.I., 1975, Phila. Art Alliance, 1976, Jackson (Miss.) Mus. Art, 1978, Northeastern U., Boston, 1980; exhibited in group and solo shows Alfredo Gallery, N.Y.C., 1964, 66, Dutchess Hall Gallery, Poughkeepsie, N.Y., 1969, Wright/Hepburn/Webster Gallery, N.Y.C., 1960, 70, N.Y. Pub. Libr., 1973, O'Keefe Ctr., Ont., Can., 1974, Ball State U., 1974, N.A.D. annual, 1974, Audubon Artists Annual, 1975, Nat. Pastel Show, 1975, Commedia Dell Art Adelphi U., 1974, Guild Gallery, N.Y.C., 1978, Met. Mus. of Art, 1987-88; works represented in permanent collections Nat. Coll. Fine Prints, Smithsonian Instn., Washington, Israel Mus., Jerusalem, La Jolla (Calif.) Mus., U. Wis. Mus., Circus World Mus., Baraboo, Wis., Fairleigh Dickinson U., Circus Hall of Fame Mus., Sarasota, Fla., Adelphi U., Creative Dance Found. for Negro Arts, Tuskegee, Ala., Mus. Performing Arts Lincoln Ctr., N.Y.C., Jackson (Miss.) Mus. Art, Original Print Collectors Group Ltd., Northeastern U., also pvt. collections. Home: 25 Central Park W New York NY 10023-7253

MACKLIN, ELIZABETH JEAN, poet, editor; b. Poughkeepsie, N.Y., Oct. 28, 1952; d. Edward Carlyle and Margaret Jean (Herkenratt) Wood; m. Francis Gerald Macklin, Jr., Jan. 12, 1974 (div. Mar. 1979). BA, SUNY, Potsdam, 1973. Poetry editor Wigwag Mag., N.Y.C., 1989-91; query editor The New Yorker, N.Y.C., 1978-99. Author: (poetry collections) A Woman Kneeling in the Big City, 1992, You've Just Been Told, 2000; co-translator (book) In a Paper Boat, 1989, An Anthology of Basque Short Stories, 2004; translator: (CD-book) Too Old, Too Small, Maybe; contbr. poems and essays to popular mags., including The New Yorker, The Nation, The New Republic, Paris Review, others. Fellow in poetry Guggenheim Found., N.Y.C., 1994; recipient Poetry award Ingram Merrill Found., N.Y.C., 1990, Amy Lowell Poetry Traveling scholarship, 1998-99; grantee PEN Translation Fund, 2005 Mem. Author's Guild, PEN Am. Ctr. (exec. bd. 1995-96). Home: 207 W 14th St Apt 5F New York NY 10011-7140 E-mail: elizabethmacklin@writersartists.net.

MACKLIN, RUTH, bioethics educator; b. Newark, Mar. 27, 1938; d. Hyman and Frieda (Yaruss) Chimacoff; m. Martin Macklin, Sept. 1, 1957 (div. June 1969); children: Meryl, Shelley Macklin Taylor. BA with distinction, Cornell U., 1958; MA in Philosophy, Case Western Res. U., 1966, PhD in Philosophy, 1968. Instr. in philosophy Case Western Res. U., Cleve., 1967—68, asst. prof., 1968—71, assoc. prof., 1971—76; assoc. for behavioral studies The Hastings Ctr., Hastings-on-Hudson, NY, 1976—80; vis. assoc. prof. Albert Einstein Coll. Medicine, Bronx, NY, 1977—78, assoc. prof., 1978—84, prof. dept. epidemiology and social medicine, 1984—. Cons. NIH, 1986—; advisor WHO, Geneva, 1989—; mem. White House Adv. Com. on Human Radiation Experiments, Washington1994; chair ethical rev. com. UNAIDS, Geneva, 1996—2001. Author: Man, Mind and Morality, 1982, Mortal Choices, 1987, Enemies of Patients, 1993, Surrogates and Other Mothers, 1994, Against Relativism, 1999, Double Standards in Medical Research, 2004; contbr. articles to ethics, law and med. jours. Fellow: APHA, Am. Soc. Law, Medicine and Ethics, Inst. Medicine NAS, The Hastings Ctr., Am. Philosophys. Assn. (life); mem.: Am. Soc. Bioethics and Humanities (bd. dirs. 1997—99), Internat. Assn. Bioethics (bd. dirs., pres. 1999—2001). Democrat. Office: A Einstein Coll Medicine Dept Epidemiology Population Health 1300 Morris Park Ave Bronx NY 10461-1926 E-mail: macklin@aecom.yu.edu.

MACKNIGHT, CAROL BERNIER, educational association administrator; b. Quincy, Mass., Apr. 12, 1938; d. Harold Nelson and Marguerite (Norris) Bernier; m. William J. MacKnight, Aug. 19, 1967. BS, Ithaca Coll., N.Y., 1960; MM, Manhattan Sch. Mus., N.Y.C., 1961; Dipl., Fontainebleau Sch. Music/Art, France, 1968; EdD, U. Mass., 1973. Asst. to supt. Falmouth (Mass.) pub. schs., 1975-76; dir. bus., mgmt., engring. prog. Sch. Bus. Adminstrn. U. Mass., Amherst, 1976-79, assoc. dir. continuing edn., 1979-82, dir. Office Instructional Tech., 1982—93. Trustee New Eng. Regional Computer Program, Inc., 1986—92; bd. dirs. Info. Sys. and Bus. Exch., 1992—93; keynote spkr. Australian Soc. for Computers in Learning In Tertiary Edn. Conf., Adelaide, 1996; conf. chair Transforming Practice with Tech., 2002. Editor: Jour. Computing in Higher Edn., 1988—, Jour. Info. Sys. for Mgrs., 1992—93; mem. editl. rev. bd.: Jour. of Computer-Based Instrn., 1988—2002, author/editor: computer progs.; contbr. articles to profl. jours. Grantee, CDC, 1986, Regents of Boston, 1988; Lilly Fellow Mentor, 1991—92. Mem. ACM, Assn. for Computing Machinery, Educom, Soc. Applied Learning Techs. (bd. dirs. 2003-05), New England Regional Computer Program. Avocations: music, photography, tennis, hiking, skiing. Office: Norris Consulting and Pub PO Box 2593 Amherst MA 01004 Business E-Mail: cmacknight@oit.umass.edu.

MACKOWSKI, PAMELA ANNE, science educator; b. Erie, Pa., Sept. 5, 1960; d. David E. and Patricia A. Mackowski. BS, Pa. State U., Behrend Coll., Erie, Pa., 1990—93; MS, Ohio State U., Columbus, 1994—97. Cert. Tchr., Biology Pa. Dept. Edn., 2000, Tchr., Chemistry Pa. Dept. Edn., 2002, Tchr., Environ. Sci. Pa. Dept. Edn., 2003, Sch. Admnstrn. Pa. Dept. Edn. Rsch. asst. Cleve. Clinic, Ohio, 1997—98. Mem.: NSTA, Pa. State Edn. Assn., Nat. Assn. Biology Tchrs., ASCD. Democrat. Roman Catholic. Avocations: golf, softball, travel, photography, bicycling. Office: East HS 1001 Atkins St Erie PA 16503 Office Phone: 814-874-6437. Personal E-mail: pmackowsi@eriesd.iu5.org. Business E-Mail: pmackowski@eriesd.iu5.org.

MACLACHLAN, PATRICIA, author; b. Cheyenne, Wyo., Mar. 3, 1938; d. Philo and Madonna (Moss) Pritzkau; m. Robert MacLachlan, Apr. 14, 1962; children: John, Jamie, Emily. BA, U. Conn., 1962. Tchr. English Bennett Jr. High Sch., Manchester, Conn., 1963-79. Vis. lectr. Smith Coll., Northampton, Mass., 1986. Author: The Sick Day, 1979, Arthur, for the Very First Time, 1980 (Golden Kite award Soc. Children's Book Writers 1980), Moon, Stars, Frogs, and Friends, 1980, Through Grandpa's Eyes, 1980, Cassie Binegar, 1982, Mama One, Mama Two, 1982, Tomorrow's Wizard, 1982, Seven Kisses in a Row, 1983, Unclaimed Treasures, 1984 (Boston Globe/Horn Book award 1984), Sarah, Plain and Tall, 1985 (Golden Kite award 1985, Scott O'Dell Historical Fiction award 1985, John Newbery medal 1986, Jefferson Cup award Va. Libr. Assn. 1986, Christopher award 1986, Garden State Children's Book award N.J. Libr. Assn. 1988), The Facts and Fictions of Minna Pratt, 1988 (Parent's Choice award Parent's Choice Found. 1988), Three Names, 1991, Journey, 1991, All the Places to Love, 1993, Baby, 1993, Skylark, 1994, What You Know First, 1995, Caleb's Story, 2001, More Perfect Than The Moon, 2004, Who Loves Me?, 2005; author (screenplays): Sarah Plain and Tall, 1988, Skylark, 1992, Journey, 1992. Bd. dirs. Children's Aid Family Svc. Agency, 1970-80. Recipient numerous awards for children's fiction. Office: Curts Brown Ltd c/o Marilyn Marlow 10 Astor Pl Fl 3D New York NY 10003-6935

MACLACHLAN, PATRICIA LYNN, political science professor; b. Vancouver, BC, Canada, Jan. 24, 1964; arrived in U.S., 1988; d. James V. and Mae I. MacLachlan; m. Zoltan D. Barany; 1 child, Catherine E. Barany. BA in Polit. Sci. with honors, U. B.C., Vancouver, 1986; MA in Polit. Sci., Columbia U., N.Y.C., 1991, cert. in Japanese Studies, 1991, PhD in Polit. Sci., 1996. Post doctoral rsch. assoc. Program on U.S.-Japanese Rels. Harvard U., Cambridge, Mass., 1995—96; asst. prof. polit. sci. U. Calgary, Canada, 1996—97; asst. to assoc. prof. Asian studies and govt. U. Tex., Austin, 1997—. Author: Consumer Politics in Postwar Japan, 2002; contbr. articles to profl. jours. Abe Fellows grant, Social Sci. Rsch. Coun. and Japan Found. Ctr. Global Partnership, 2001. Mem.: Assn. Asian Studies. Office: Dept Asian Studies U Tex 1 Univ Sta 9300 WCH 4 134 Austin TX 78712 Office Phone: 512-475-6047.

MACLAINE, SHIRLEY, actress; b. Richmond, Va., Apr. 24, 1934; d. Ira O. and Kathlyn (MacLean) Beatty; m. Steve Parker, Sept. 17, 1954 (div. 1982); 1 child, Stephanie Sachiko. Broadway appearances include Me and Juliet, 1953, Pajama Game, 1954, films appearances The Trouble With Harry, 1954, Artists and Models, 1954, Around the World in 80 Days, 1955-56, Hot Spell, 1957, The Matchmaker, 1957, The Sheepman, 1957, Some Came Running, 1958 (Fgn. Press award 1959), Ask Any Girl, 1959 (Silver Bear award as best actress Internat. Berlin Film Festival), Career, 1959, Can-Can, 1959, The Apartment, 1959 (Best Actress prize Venice Film Festival), Children's Hour, 1960, The Apartment, 1960, Two for the Seesaw, 1962, Irma La Douce, 1963, What A Way to Go, The Yellow Rolls Royce, 1964, John Goldfarb Please Come Home, 1965, Gambit and Woman Times Seven, 1967, The Bliss of Mrs. Blossom, Sweet Charity, 1969, Two Mules for Sister Sara, 1969, Desperate Characters, 1971, The Possession of Joel Delaney, 1972, The Other Half of the Sky: A China Memoir, 1975, The Turning Point, 1977, Being There, 1979, A Change of Seasons, 1980, Loving Couples, 1980, Terms of Endearment, 1983 (Acad. award 1984, Golden Globe-Best Actress), Cannonball Run II, 1984, Madame Sousatzka, 1988 (Best Actress Venice Film Festival, Golden Globe-Best Actress), Steel Magnolias, 1989, Waiting For the Light, 1990, Postcards From the Edge, 1990, Defending Your Life, 1991, Used People, 1992, Wrestling Ernest Hemingway, 1993, Guarding Tess, 1994, Evening Star, 1995, Mrs. Winterbourne, 1996, Carolina, 2003, Bewitched, 2005, In Her Shoes, 2005, Rumor Has It., 2005; TV appearances Shirley's World, 1971-72, Shirley MacLaine: If They Could See Me Now, 1974-75, Gypsy in My Soul, 1975-76, Where Do We Go From Here?, 1976-77, Shirley MacLaine at the Lido, 1979, Shirley MacLaine.Every Little Movement, 1980 (Emmy award 1980), TV movie appearances Out On A Limb, 1987, The West Side Waltz, 1995, Joan of Arc, 1999, These Old Broads, 2001, Hell on Heels: The Battle of Mary Kay, 2002, TV mini-series Salem Witch Trials, 2002; (directorial debut) Bruno, 2000; co-dir. documentary: China The Other Half of the Sky; star U.S. tour stage musical Out There Tonight, 1990; author: Don't Fall Off the Mountain, 1970, The New Celebrity Cookbook, 1973, You Can Get There From Here, 1975, Out on a Limb, 1983, Dancing in the Light, 1985, It's All in the Playing, 1987, Going Within: A Guide for Inner Transformation, 1989, Dance While You Can, 1991; editor: McGovern: The Man and His Beliefs, 1972, My Lucky Stars, 1995, The Camino, 2000, Out On A Leash: Exploring The Nature of Reality and Love, 2003. Address: C/O ICM 8942 Wilshire Blvd Beverly Hills CA 90211-1934*

MACLEAN, RHONDA, information technology executive; m. Lynn Maclean. Various positions to sr. mgr. computer and comm. security The Boeing Co., 1982—96; dir. corp. info. security Nations Bank (now Bank of Am.), 1996; sr. v.p. Bank of Am., 1998—. Tech. adv. Pres. Nat. Security Telecom. Adv. Com. Fin. Services Risk Assessing, 1997; private sector coord. for fin. services industry public/private partnership on critical infostructure protection and homeland security Dept. of Treasury, 2002—. Mem. bd. adv. U. NC, Charlotte Coll. of Info. Tech. Named Women of Vision, Information Security mag., 2003, one of the 50 Most Powerful People in Networking, Networking

World mag., 2003. Mem.: Fin. Services Info. Security Analysis Ctr. (FS/ISAC) (adv. to bd. dirs.), Internat. Inst. Info. Integrity (vice chmn. mem. Adv. Com.), Banking Industry Tech. Secretariat (elected mem. of Security Laboratory Governance Bd.).

MACLENNAN, BERYCE WINIFRED, psychologist; b. Aberdeen, Scotland, Mar. 14, 1920; came to U.S., 1949, naturalized, 1965; d. William and Beatrice (MacRae) Mellis; m. John Duncan MacLennan, Nov. 29, 1944. BSc with honors, London Sch. Econs., 1947; PhD, London U., 1960. Diplomate Am. Bd. Clin. Psychology, cert. group therapist, trauma specialist. Group psychotherapist, youth specialist cons., N.Y.C. and Washington, 1949-63; dir. Ctr. for Prevention Juvenile Delinquency and New Careers, Washington, 1963-66; sect. chief NIMH, Mental Health Study Ctr., Adelphi, Md., 1967-70, chief, 1971-74; regional adminstr. Mass. Dept. Mental Health, Springfield, 1974-75; sr. mental health adv. GAO, Washington, 1976-90; pvt. practice, specialist psychotherapy Bethesda, Md., 1990—. Clin. prof. George Washington U., 1970—; group therapy cons. D.C. Mental Health Svcs., 1993-2002, Washington Assessement and Therapy Svcs., 1992-2006; lectr. Montgomery C.C., 1988-91, Washington Sch. Psychiatry Geropsychiatric Program, 1997—; mem. tech. adv. com. Prince George's County Mental Health Assn., 1968-84; cons. Washington Bus. Group on Health, 1990-91, KOBA, 1991; leader Trauma Psychotherapy Groups, 2002-03, Hebrew Home Rsch. Inst. Elder Housing Socialization and Memory Improvement Groups, 2000-02. Mem. NIMH Prevention Intervention Rsch. Task Force, 1990-91, Montgomery County Victims Assistance Programs, 1990-95; v.p. Compliance, Federally Employed Women, 1979-81; pres. Glenecho chpt. Older Women's League, 1993-94; mem. Montgomery County Disaster Outreach Team, 2004—. Fellow APA, Am. Orthopsychiat. Assn.; disting. fellow Am. Group Psychotherapy Assn.; mem. Washington Mushroom Club. Democrat. Office Phone: 301-320-4151.

MACLENNAN, FAITH ALICE, physical therapist, educator; b. Three Rivers, Mich., Nov. 7, 1914; d. Henry Etherington McLennan and Dimies Camille Knaggs. AB, Western Mich. U., Kalamazoo, 1935; postgrad., Fitzsimons Army Hosp., Denver, 1944. Tchr. Comstock Pub. Schs., Mich., 1936—42; phys. therapist Ftizsimons Army Hosp., Denver, 1943—45; phys. therapist med. dept. US Army, Manila, Philippines, 1945—46; phys. therapist Vets. Hosp., Dearborn, Mich., 1947—74; ret., 1974. Mem.: LWV, Fairlane Club. Avocations: tennis, golf, reading, music. Home: 3132 Lindenwood Dr Dearborn MI 48120

MACLEOD, JOAN ANN, medical/surgical nurse, administrator; b. Clinton, Mass., Jan. 30, 1950; d. Joseph C. and Eva R. (Chapman) Kosinski; m. Neil MacLeod, June 20, 1970; children: Sheryl, Neil, Rebecca, Bryan, Daniel. BSN, U. Mass., 1971; MSN, U. Conn., 1982. Clin. nurse mgr. Day Kimball Hosp., Putnam, Conn., 1982-84; dir. nursing edn. HRS Pediatric Cluster, Gainesville, Fla., 1985-87; instr. U. Fla. Coll. Nursing, Gainesville, 1987-88; head nurse, case mgr. Gainesville VA Med. Ctr., 1988—. Contbr. articles to profl. jours. Mem. ANA, Fla. Nurses Assn., Sigma Theta Tau. Home: 4411 NW 15th Pl Gainesville FL 32605-4509 Office: VA Med Ctr 1601 SW Archer Rd Gainesville FL 32608-1135

MACLEOD, NORMAJEAN, writer; b. Logansport, Ind., Feb. 27, 1929; d. Norman and Mabel (Clark) Ulery; m. John Charles MacLeod, Sept. 13, 1947; 1 child, Ian. Asst. mgr. Village Theatre, Bloomington, Ind., 1969-71; mgr. Motel 6 Corp., Santa Barbara, Calif., 1972-73; data sys. coord. Ind. U., Bloomington, 1973-90, editor edn. comm., 1990-95. Lectr., workshop dir., 1981-. Author: Womanclature: The Queen Bee Syndrome, 1984, Poetica Erotica, 1988; pub. in anthologies. Mem. Internat. Women's Writing Guild, United Poets Laureate Internat., Internat. Lawrence Durrell Soc. E-mail: redshedstudio@hotmail.com.

MACMANUS, SUSAN ANN, political science professor, researcher; b. Tampa, Fla., Aug. 22, 1947; d. Harold Cameron and Elizabeth (Riegler) MacM. BA cum laude, Fla. State U., 1968, PhD, 1975; MA, U. Mich., 1969. Instr. Valencia C.C., Orlando, Fla., 1969-73; rsch. asst. Fla. State U., 1973-75; asst. prof. U. Houston, 1975-79, assoc. prof., 1979-85, dir. MPA program, 1983-85; rsch. assoc. Ctr. Pub. Policy, 1982-85; prof., dir. PhD progam Cleve. State U., 1985-87; prof. pub. adminstrn. and polit. sci. U. South Fla., Tampa, 1987—, chair dept. govt. and internat. affairs, 1987-93, disting. univ. prof., 1999. Vis. prof. U. Okla., Norman, 1981—; field rsch. assoc. Brookings Inst., Washington, 1977—82, Princeton (N.J.) U., 1979—, Cleve. State U., 1982—83, Westat, Inc., Washington, 1983—; summer field rsch. assoc. Columbia U., N.Y.C., 1979, Nat. Acad. Pub. Adminstrn., Washington, 1980. Author: Revenue Patterns in U.S. Cities and Suburbs: A Comparative Analysis, 1978, Reapportionment and Representation in Florida: A Historical Collection, 1991, Doing Business with Government: Federal, State, Local and Foreign Government Purchasing Practices for Every Business and Public Institution, 1992, Federal Aid to Houston, 1993, Young v. Old: Generational Combat in the 21st Century, 1996, Targeting Senior Voters, 2000; co-author (with others): Governing A Changing America, 1984; co-author: (with Francis T. Borkowski) Visions for the Future: Creating New Institutional Relationships Among Academia, Business, Government, and Community, 1989; co-author: (with Elizabeth R. MacManus) Citrus, Sawmills, Critters & Crackers: Life in Early Lutz and Central Pasco County, 1998, The Lutz Depot, 2000; editor: Mapping Florida's Political Landscape: The Changing Art and Politics of Reapportionment and Redistricting, 2002; co-editor (with Thomas R. Dye): Politics in States and Communities, 11th edit., 2003; co-editor: (with Dano Moreno and Kevin Hill) Florida's Politics: Ten Media Markets, One Powerful State, 2004; writer: manuals in field, mem. editl. bd.: various jours; contbr. articles to profl. jours., chapters to books. Bd. dirs. Houston Area Women's Ctr., 1977, past pres., v.p. fin., treas.; mem. LWV, Gov.'s Coun. Econ. Advisers, 1988-90, Harris County (Tex.) Women's Polit. Caucus, Houston; bd. dirs. USF Rsch. Found., Inc.; chair Fla. Elections Commn., 1999-2003; mem. Fla. Gov.'s Coun. Econ. Advisers, 2000—. Recipient U. Houston Coll. Social Scis. Tchg. Excellence award, 1977, Herbert J. Simon award for best article in 3d vol., Internat. Jour. Pub. Adminstrn., 1981, Theodore & Venette Askounes-Ashford Disting Scholar award U. South Fla., 1991, Disting. Rsch. Scholar award, 1991, Tchg. Excellence award, 1999; Ford Found. fellow, 1967-68; grantee Valencia C. C. Faculty, 1972, U. Houston, 1976-77, 79, 83; Fulbright Rsch. scholar, Korea, 1989; Choice mag. award, 1996; named Disting. Univ. Prof., 1999; rsch. fellow Fla. Inst. of Govt., 2000—. Mem. Am. Polit. Sci. Assn. (program com. 1983-84, chair sect. intergovtl. rels., award 1989, mem. exec. coun. 1994—, pres.-elect sec. urban politics 1994-95, pres. sect. urban politics 1995-96), So. Polit. Sci. Assn. (v.p. 1990-91, pres.-elect 1992-93, pres. 1993-94, V.O. key award com. 1983-84, best paper on women and politics 1988, Diane Blair award 2001), Midwest Polit. Sci. Assn., Western Polit. Sci. Assn., Southwestern Polit. Sci. Assn. (local arrangements com. 1982-83, profession com. 1977-80), ASPA (nominating com. Houston chpt. 1983, bd. mem. Suncoast chpt., pres.-elect 1991, Lilly award 1992), Policy Studies Orgn. (mem. editl. bd. jour. 1981—, exec. coun. 1983-85), Women's Caucus Polit. Sci. (portfolio pre-decision rev. com. 1982-83, projects and programs com. 1981, fin.-budget com. 1980-81), Fla. Polit. Sci. Assn. (pres. 1997-98, Manning Dauer Disting. Fla. Polit. Sci. award 2001), Acad. Polit. Sci., Mcpl. Fin. Officers Assn., Phi Kappa Phi (Artist/Scholar award U. South Fla. 1997), Phi Beta Kappa, Pi Sigma Alpha (mem. exec. coun. 1994-96, pres. 2000-02), Pi Alpha Alpha. Methodist. Home: 2506 Collier Pky Land O Lakes FL 34639-5228 Office: U South Fla Dept Polit Sci Tampa FL 33620 E-mail: samacmanus@aol.com.

MAC MASTER, HARRIETT SCHUYLER, retired elementary school educator; b. Maxbass, ND, Nov. 5, 1916; d. Hugh Riley and Christine (Park) Schuyler; m. Jay Myron Mac Master, May 27, 1944 (dec.); children: Jay Walter (dec.), Robert Hugh, Anne Schuyler BS, postgrad., Coll. N.J., 1971; grad., Inst. for Children's Lit., 1993. With staff spl. govt. WWII project Office Sci. R & D, 1943-44; tchr. Woodfern Elem. Sch., Neshanic, N.J., 1972-87; ret., 1987. Freelance writer elem. sci. program Silver Burdett Co., 1983. Elite mem. Nat. Rep. Congl. Com.; active Grace United Meth. Ch. Named Republican of Yr. from Fla., 2001. Fellow: LWV, AAUW. Republican. Home: 230 NE 22nd Ave Cape Coral FL 33909-2820

MACMILLAN, SHANNON ANN, professional soccer player; b. Syosset, N.Y., Oct. 7, 1974; Student in social work, U. Portland. Profl. soccer player San Diego Spirit, 2001—03. Mem. U.S. Nat. Women's Soccer Team, 1993—, including silver medal World Univ. Games team, 1993, gold medal U.S. Olympic Team, 96; mem. U.S. Women's Under-20 Nat. Team, 1993—94, including championship Internat. Women's Tournament, France, 1993; mem. LaJolla (Calif.) Nomads club soccer team, winning state club championship, 1991, 92, Japanese Women's Profl. League, 1996, 97. Named 1995 Soccer Am. Player of Yr., Female Athlete of Yr., 1993, 1995, U. Portland, World Cup Champion, 1999; named to San Diego Union Tribune All-Acad. team; recipient Mo. Athletic Club award, 1995, Hermann award, U. Portland, 1995, Bill Hayward award, 1995, Silver medal, Sydney Olympic Games, 2000. Office: US Soccer Fedn 1801-1811 S Prairie Ave Chicago IL 60616

MACMULLEN, PATRICIA ELLEN, theater educator, theater director; b. Jasper, Tex., Oct. 21, 1959; d. Legran Jason and Mildred Elizabeth Bradshaw; m. John Michael Bradshaw-Cox, June 23, 2000; children: Megan Louise, Cassandra Mae, Kevin Christopher Cox, Kayla Jayne, Jordan Michael. BA in Theatre, Sam Houston State U., Huntsville, Tex., 1981. Theatre dir. Beverly Hills Mid. Sch., Houston, 1982—86, C. E. King Mid. Sch., Houston, 1986—88; English, lang. arts, gifted and talented tchr. Jasper (Tex.) Mid. Sch., 1988—92; theatre dir. Jasper H.S., 1992—2000, Taylor (Tex.) H.S., 2000—04, John B. Connally H.S., Austin, Tex., 2004—. Play dir. John B. Connally H.S., Austin, 2004—. Dir.: (one act play) A Company of Wayward Saints, Assassins, The Voice of the Prairie. Dir. actor Jasper Cmty. Theatre, Jasper, Tex., 1988—2000. Named Outstanding Dir., Tex. State Thespian Festival, 1995. Mem.: Tex. Ednl. Theatre Assn. (assoc.). Office: John B Connally HS 13212 N Lamar Linn TX 78563 Office Phone: 512-594-0800.

MACMURREN, MARGARET PATRICIA, secondary school educator, consultant; b. Newark, Nov. 4, 1947; d. Kenneth F. and Doris E. (Lounsberry) Bartro; m. Harold MacMurren, Nov. 21, 1970. BA, Paterson State U., 1969; MA, William Paterson Coll., 1976; postgrad., Jersey City State Coll., 1976—. Tchr. Byram (N.J.) Twp. Schs., 1969-77; learning cons., child study team coord. Andover Regional Schs., Newton, N.J., 1977—. Mem.: NEA, Andover Regional Edn. Assn. (pres. 1986—87), Sussex County Assn. Learning Cons. (pres. 1982—83, 1993—94, sec.-treas. 1991—92, v.p. 1992—93), N.J. Learning Assn., N.J. Edn. Assn. Avocations: skiing, dance, weightlifting, travel, reading. Home: 4 Systema Pl Sussex NJ 07461-2833 Office: Andover Regional Schs 707 Limecrest Rd Newton NJ 07860-8801 Office Phone: 973-940-1234 246. Business E-Mail: haroldm@nac.net.

MACO, TERI REGAN, accountant, engineer; b. Allentown, Pa., Nov. 4, 1953; d. Francis M. and Jacqueline K. (Becker) Regan; m. Bruce F. Maco, Oct. 1, 1983; children: Adam S., Alex M. BSChemE with honors, Lehigh U., 1975; MBA with distinction, U. New Haven, 1979; cert. in sci., West Chester U., 1994. Supr. Ivory, Procter & Gamble Mfg. Co., S.I., N.Y., 1975-77; asst. mgr. processing Chesebrough-Ponds, Inc., Clinton, Conn., 1977-81, sec. and bd. dirs. credit union, 1980; group supr. McNeil Consumer Products, Ft. Washington, Pa., 1981-83; mgr. processing Johnson & Johnson, Ft. Washington, Pa., 1983-84, mgr. nat. planning, 1984-87, group mgr. acctg., 1987-93; pres. Child Placement Network, Inc., Norristown, Pa., 1989-93; tchr. Phoenixville (Pa.) H.S., 1993-94; treas. Borough of Collegeville, 1995-97; pres. T. Maco & Assocs. LLC, Collegeville, 1996—. Treas. United Fund Collegeville-Trappe, Inc., 1996—2000; developer computer-based tng. program. Author: Capital Asset Pricing Model: Capital Budgeting Applications (NAA Manuscript award, 1979). Recipient Achievement award, Johnson & Johnson, 1989, 1992. Democrat. Roman Catholic. Home and Office: T Maco & Assoc 4183 Ironbridge Dr Collegeville PA 19426-1189 Office Phone: 610-489-7215. E-mail: tmaco@tmaco.net.

MACOMBER, DEBBIE, writer; m. Wayne Macomber. Author: Morning Comes Softly, 1993 (Waldenbooks Bestselling Non-Series Debut Romance, finalist, Romance Writers of Am. Member's Golden Choice award, Colo. Romance WRiters Keeper award, 1996), Trouble With Angels, 1994 (Waldenbooks Trend Book award), One Night, 1994, Someday Soon, 1995, Sooner or Later, 1996, Mrs. Miracle, 1996, This Matter of Marriage, 1997, Three Brides, No Groom, 1997, Lonesome Cowboy, 1998, Texas Two-Step, 1998, Caroline's Child, 1998, Dr. Texas, 1998, Nell's Cowboy, 1998, Lone Star Baby, 1998, Montana, 1998, Can This Be Christmas, 1998, Shirley, Goodness & Mercy, 1999, Moon Over Water, 1999, Promise Texas, 1999, A Season of Angels, 1999, The Touched by Angels, 1999, Dakota Born, 2000, Return to Promise, 2000, Thursdays at Eight, 2001 (one of Amazon.com's Top 10 Women's Fiction titles of 2001), Buffalo Valley, 2001, Always Dakota, 2001, 16 Lighthouse Road, 2001 (finalist, Dorothy Parker award of excellence for best contemporary romance novel), 204 Rosewood Lane, 2002, Between Friends, 2002, The Christmas Basket, 2002 (RITA award, Romance Writers of America), 311 Pelican Court, 2003, Those Christmas Angels, 2003, Changing Habits, 2003, The Snow Bride, 2003, 44 Cranberry Point, 2004 (Quills award for romance, 2005), The Shop on Blossom Street, 2004 (Named one of best romances of 2004, Oakland Press, Publishers Weekly paperback bestseller, 2005), When Christmas Comes, 2004, A Good Yarn, 2005, 50 Harbor Street, 2005 (Publishers Weekly paperback bestseller), There's Something About Christmas, 2005, Savannah's Garden, 2006, numerous others. Named a Tennessee Colonel for humanitarian svc., Gov. State of Tenn., 1994; named Favorite Top 10 Author, Affaire de Coeur Mag., 1995; recipient Regional Svc. award, Romance Writers of Am., 1989, Career Achievement award for contemporary romance, Romantic Times, 1992—93, Woman of Distinction award, Soroptimist Internat., 1996—97. Avocation: knitting. Mailing: c/o Author Mail Mira Books eHarlequin PO Box 5190 Buffalo NY 14240-5190*

MACPHERSON, ELLE, model; b. Sydney, Australia, Mar. 29, 1964; m. Gilles Bensimon, May 24, 1986 (div.) Appeared on covers of Sports Illustrated swimsuit edit., 1986, 87, 88, 94, Elle, Cosmopolitan, Self; film appearences include Husbands and Wives, 1992, Sirens, 1994, If Lucy Fell, 1996, Jane Eyre, 1996, The Mirror Has Two Faces, 1996, The Edge, 1997, Batman and Robin, 1997, Beautopia, 1998, With Friends Like These, 1998, South Kensington, 2001; TV mini-series, A Girl Thing, 2001; TV appearance in Friends, 1999-2000.

MACPHERSON, SHIRLEY, clinical therapist; b. Bayonne, N.J., June 16, 1934; d. Alexander Phillip and Milldred (Gurstelle) Gottlieb; m. Duncan MacPherson, Jan. 2, 1981; children from previous marriage: Suzanne Pugsley, Brett Barber. BS, Columbia U., NYU, 1951; MS, Juilliard Sch. Music, 1955; MEd, Calif. State U., Northridge, 1967; MA in Psychology, Pepperdine U., 1992; PhD in Psychology, Pacific Western U., 1998. Concert pianist Norman Seman Prodns., N.Y.C., 1952-61; indsl. health educator Am. Med. Internat., L.A., 1968-70; cons., lectr. Hosp. Mgmt. Corp., L.A., 1970-80; regional dir. Control Data Corp., L.A., 1980-86; outplacement specialist Ind. Cons., L.A., 1986-90; psychologist, intern Airport Marina Counseling Svcs., L.A., 1990-93; staff psychologist Forensic Psychology Assocs., Sherman Oaks, Calif., 1993-94; staff clin. psychologist Pacific Psychologist Assocs., L.A., 1992-94; clin. therapist employee profiling and crisis intervention MacPherson Relationship Counseling, L.A., 1993—. Author: Rx for Brides, 1990, Understanding Your Man, 1998. Vol. Cmty. Alliance to Support and Empower, L.A., 1994-96, South Bay Free Clinic, L.A., 1995-97; mem. Town and Gown Scholarship program, U. So. Calif., L.A. Mem. AAUW, APA, Calif. Psychol. Assn., L.A. Psychol. Assn., L.A. World Affairs Coun., Am. Bd. Hypnotherapy, Am. Assn. Humanistic Psychology, Am. Assn. Suidiology, Juilliard Alumni Assn., Pepperdine Allumni Assn., Internat. Wound Ballistics Assn. Avocations: studying French and Italian, piano, studies. Office Phone: 310-322-9959. Personal E-mail: Shirlmac@ix.netcom.com.

MACQUEEN, CHERIE K., interior designer, retired newscaster, sportscaster; b. Kansas City, Mo., Mar. 20, 1952; d. Ira Raymond and Peggy Estelle (Turner) Milks. AA in Liberal Arts, L.A. Valley Coll., 1982; BS in Liberal Studies, Excelsior Coll., Albany, N.Y., 1993; grad., Barbizon Sch. Modeling, 1996; postgrad., Calif. State U., San Bernardino, 1998—; cert. in Interior Design, U. Calif., Riverside, 2002. Lic. radio-TV operator. Personnel specialist U.S. Army, Honolulu, 1973-75, adminstrv. specialist San Francisco, 1975-77, broadcast journalist Vicenza, Italy, 1977-80; radio traffic specialist Armed Forces Radio and TV, L.A., 1980-84, radio prodn. specialist, 1984-86, supr. broadcast support specialist Sun Valley, 1986-90, broadcast support mgr, 1990-91, internal info. mgr., 1991-94, news and sports specialist, 1994-99; owner The Keilani Co., Highland, 2003—, Ladysmythe Handcrafts, Highland, 2003—. Mem.: DAV (life), Am. Soc. Interior Designers (bd. dirs. Inland/Palm Springs chpt. 2003—04, allied mem. Pasadena chpt. 2004—), Pacific Pioneer Broadcasters, Women in Mil. Svc. for Am. (charter), Armed Forces Broadcasters Assn. (v.p. L.A. chpt. 1991—93). Avocations: crafts, crocheting. Home: PO Box 276 Highland CA 92346-0276

MACRAE, ELIZABETH (ELIZABETH MACRAE HALSEY), counselor, actor; b. Columbia, SC, Feb. 22, 1936; d. James and Dorothy (Hendon) MacRae; m. Charles Day Halsey, Jr., 1969; m. Nedrick Young, 1965 (dec. 1968); children: Benjamin Young(dec.), Beryl MacRae Young(dec.). Student, Herbert Berghof Studio, N.Y.C., 1956—58, Arts Students League, 1958, U. So. Calif., L.A., 1965, Marymount Manhattan Coll., N.Y.C., 1989—91, Breakthrough at Gracie Sq. Hosp., 1990—91. Cert. Alcoholism and Alcohol Abuse, Credentialed Alcoholism Counselor 1992. Intern Arms Acres, Carmel, NY, 1990; counselor chem. dependency Breakthrough at Gracie Sq. Hosp., 1990; adult counselor Manhattan Bowery Corp., 1991—93; program dir., counselor alcoholism outpatient clinic Freedom Inst., 1993—98. Actor: (plays) off Broadway, 1956, New. Eng. Stock, 1957, 1963, (as Elizabeth MacRae): (films) Everything's Ducky, 1961, Love in a Goldfish Bowl, 1961, The Incredible Mr. Limpet, 1964, The Wild Westerners, 1962, For Love or Money, 1963; (TV series) Route 66, 1969, 1972, 1974; (films) The Conversation, 1974; (TV series) Naked City, 1960, 77 Sunset Strip, 1961, Harrigan and Son, 1961, Surfside 6, 1961, Maverick, 1961, Asphalt Jungle, 1961, Dr. Kildare, 1962, Hawaiian Eye, 1962, Stoney Burke, 1962, Death Valley Days, 1962, Sam Benedict, 1962, Gunsmoke, 1961—64, The Untouchables, 1962, Burke's Law, 1963, Rawhide, 1963, The Virginian, 1964, The Fugitive, 1964, I Dream of Jeannie, 1965, Gomer Pyle, USMC, 1966—68, Andy Griffith, 1967, Bonanza, 1968, Judd for the Defense, 1969, Rheingold Theatre - England, 1969, Kojak, 1974, Petrocelli, 1974, Mannix, 1974, Rhoda, 1976, Barnaby Jones, 1976, General Hospital, 1969, 1971; (TV films), 1974); (TV series) Days Of Our Lives, 1976—77, All My Children, 1978, Guiding Light, 1980, Another World, 1980, 1989, Search for Tomorrow,: (live TV) The Verdict is Yours, 1958—59, Ellery Queen, 1960, Ninotshka, 1960. Vol. Help Line, NYC, 1982. Recipient Disting. Counselor award, Freedom Inst., 2003. Mem.: AFTRA, SAG, Nat. Assn. Alcoholism and Drug Abuse Counselors, Actors Equity, Acad. Motion Picture Arts and Scis., Nat. Soc. Colonial Dames Am. (N.C. chpt.). Home: 1405 Raeford Rd Fayetteville NC 28305 Office Phone: 910-485-5061. E-mail: chalsey@nc.rr.com.

MACRAE HALSEY, ELIZABETH See MACRAE, ELIZABETH

MACRAKIS, A. LILY, academic administrator; b. Athens, Greece; arrived in U.S., 1953; d. Chryss and Irene (Carabini) Chryssanthacopoulos; m. Michael S. Macrakis, Oct. 1, 1953; children: Stavros M., Michele A., I. Kristie. Professorat, Inst. Français, Athens, 1946; diploma, U. Athens, 1951; MA, Radcliffe Coll., 1955; PhD, Harvard U., 1983. Fellow Bunting Inst. Radcliffe Coll., Cambridge, Mass., 1961-63; assoc. prof. history, chmn. dept. Regis Coll., Weston, Mass., 1962-83, prof., dir. internat. rels., 1983—2002, dir. Greek programs, 1971—2002; dean Hellenic Coll., Boston, 2002—. Co-founder, moderator Greek group Ctr. European Studies Harvard U., Cambridge, 1975—77, vis. prof., George Seferis chair classics dept., 1982—84; vis. prof. U. Crete, Greece, 1987—88, U. Aegean, Mytiline, Rhodes, Greece, 1988—89, Boston Coll., 1990, 91; bd. dirs. Aegean Inst., Poros, Greece, 1971—91. Author: Cretan Rebel: E. Venizelos in Crete, 1983, E. Venizelos: The Formation of a Leader, 1992; editor, contbr.: Modern Greek Historiography, Women and Men in Greece, Modern Greek Bibliography, 1999; contbr. articles to profl. jours. Recipient Biography prize, Acad. Athens, 1988; Fulbright Sr. Rsch. grantee, Coun. Internat. Exch. Scholars, Athens, 1987—88. Mem.: AAUP (pres. Regis Coll. chpt. 1990—92), Bunting Inst. Fellows, Modern Greek Studies Assn. (pres. 1977—79, chmn. Endowment Fund 1980—), Friends of Gennadeion, Pi Gamma Mu. Avocations: travel, reading. Home: 61 Ellery St Cambridge MA 02138-4230 also: 17 Loukianou St Athens 10675 Greece Office Phone: 617-850-1253. Business E-Mail: lmacrakis@hchc.edu.

MACSAI, MARIAN SUE, ophthalmologist; d. John and Geraldine Macsai; m. Jack S. Kaplan; children: Ezra Samuel Kaplan, Max Sidney Kaplan, Emma Rose Kaplan. BSD, U. Mich., 1979; MD, Rush Med. Coll., Chgo., 1984. Diplomate Am. Bd. Ophthalmology, 1990. Med. dir. Med. Eye Bank W.Va., Inc., South Charleston, 1989—99; prof., dir. cornea & external disease svc. W.Va. U., Morgantown, 1989—99; chief divsn. ophthalmology Evanston (Ill.) Northwestern Healthcare, 1999—; prof., vice chair dept. ophthalmology Northwestern U. Med. Sch., Evanston, 1999—2005. Examiner Am. Bd. Ophthalmology, 2000—. Author: Eye and Skin Disease; co-author: Surgical Reconstruction of the Anterior, Surgical Management of Anterior Segment Trauma; contbr. chapters to books, articles to profl. jours. Mem.: Castroveijo Cornea Soc. (bd. dirs.), Cornea Soc. (chairperson), Eye Bank Assn. Am. (med. adv. bd. and cert. bd., Paton award 2003), Am. Acad. Ophthalmology (com. on eye banking 2002—, Sr. Achievement award 2005). Office: Evanston Northwestern Healthcare Ste 220 2050 Pfingsten Rd Glenview IL 60026 Office Phone: 847-657-1860.

MACTIER, ANN DICKINSON, state agency administrator; b. Ravenna, Nebr., June 29, 1922; d. Robert Smith and Carrie (Clark) Dickinson; m. James Allan Mactier, Feb. 26, 1944; children: James Allan II, Judith Ann, Robert Dickinson. BS, Northwestern U., 1944; BA, U. Nebr., Omaha, 1963, MA, 1969; EdD (hon.), U. Nebr., 2005. Owner, mgr. Ponca Hills Riding Acad., Omaha, 1966-73; cmty. coord. Coll. Fine Arts, U. Nebr., Omaha, 1974-75; mem. Nebr. State Bd. Edn., 1996—, v.p., 2001—. Mem. Omaha Jr. League, 1944—57; mem. exec. com. Riverfront Devel. Corp., Omaha, 1973—79; founder, pres. Florence Arts Coun., Omaha, 1975—79; mem. Omaha Pub. Schs. Bd. Edn., 1983—98; mem. steering com. Coun. Urban Bds. Edn., 1996—98; bd. dirs. Coun. Great City Schs., 1984—89. Home: 3811 N Post Rd Omaha NE 68112-1209 Office Phone: 402-453-4580. E-mail: mactier@starband.net.

MACVICAR, LISA, music educator; d. Nick and Rose Ciccarone; m. Theodore Michael MacVicar; children: Casey Lynn, Emily Rose, Sarah Elizabeth. MusB, William Paterson U., Wayne, N.J., 1992. Cert. tchr. music N.J., 1992. Gen. music tchr. South River Bd. Ed., NJ, 1993—94; dir. bands Hackensack H.S., NJ, 1994—. Faculty advisor Tri-M Nat. Music Honor Soc., Hackensack, NJ, 2001; faculty rep. Tchrs. and Administrator's Liason Com., 2005, Hackensack Edn. Assn., 2006. Participating mem. Mar. of Dimes. Mem.: N.J. Edn. Assn., Music Educators Bergen County, Inc., Music Educators Nat. Conf., Bergen County Educator's Assn., N.J. Music Educator's Assn. Office: Hackensack HS 135 First St Hackensack NJ 07601 Office Phone: 201-646-7938. Office Fax: 201-646-7922. E-mail: l.macvicar@hackensackschools.org.

MACWILLIAM, BARB, science educator; b. Portland, Oreg., Jan. 26, 1969; d. Ron and Jill MacWilliam. BS, Oreg. State U., Corvallis, 1991, MAT, 1995. Math tchr., sci. tchr. Orcas Island Mid. Sch., Eastsound, Wash., 1995—97; earth sci. tchr. Cal Young Mid. Sch., Eugene, Oreg., 1998—. Outdoor/environ. edn. instr. YMCA Camp Orkila, Orcas Island, Wash., 1989—94; effective behavior support com. chair Jefferson and Cal Young Mid. Schs., Eugene, Oreg., 2001—03; discrimination free zone com. chair Cal Young Mid. Sch., Eugene, Oreg., 2004—. Mem.: Nat. Sci. Tchr. Assn. Business E-Mail: macwilliam@4j.lane.edu.

MACYS, SONJA, science association director; b. 1971; Exec. dir. Tucson Audubon Soc. Mem., Found. Bd. Rsch. Ranch Found.; mem., environ. adv. com. Racel Grijalva; mem., exec. com. Sonoran Joint Venture, US Fish &

Wildlife Svc. Named an 40 Under 40, Tucson Bus. Edge, 2006. Office: Tucson Audubon Society 300 E University Blvd 120 Tucson AZ 85705 Office Phone: 520-622-5622. Office Fax: 520-623-3476.*

MADAGAN, BETTY KATHERINE See ORNDOFF, BETTY

MADARIAGA, LOURDES MERCEDES, accountant; b. Sagua La Grande, Cuba, July 10, 1959; came to U.s., 1967; d. Jose I. and Mercedes (Estrada) M. AA with honors, Miami Dade C.C., 1978; BBA, Fla. Internat. U., 1981. Staff/audit mgr. Pub. Svc. Commn., Miami, Fla., 1981-89; sr. acct. Price Waterhouse, Miami, 1990-92; staff analyst Regulated Industries, Miami, 1992; CFO, YWCA, Miami, 1992-93; chief fiscal dir. Little Havana Activities and Nutrition Ctrs. of Dade County, Miami, 1993-96; CFO, N.W. Dade Ctr., Miami, 1996-97; cons., sole practitioner acctg. and tax svcs., Miami, 1997-99; pres. Madariaga & Assocs., Inc., acctg. and tax svcs., Miami, 1999—. Vol. League Against Cancer, Miami, 1991—; co-chair GESU Centennial Alumni Reunion, Miami, 1996; treas., mem. host com. Willy Chirino Found., 1999-2000. Mem. Am. Soc. Woman Accts. Democrat. Roman Catholic. E-mail: lmmadariaga@aol.com.

MADAWICK, PAULA CHRISTIAN, artist, educator; b. Ft. Worth, Feb. 14, 1945; d. Tucker Paul Madawick and Lois (Percy) Long; m. Thomas J. Huggins III, Jan. 23, 1965 (div. Jan. 1981); children: Jonathan, James; m. John R. Burger, Oct., 2006. Student, Sch. Visual Arts, N.Y.C., 1962-92, SUNY, Purchase, 1989-90; B in Visual Studies, Empire State Coll., 1992. Artist asst. Jasper Johns, A. Warhol, Robert Rauschenberg, N.Y.C., 1962-65; asst. art dir. Flair Display Co., Bronx, N.Y., 1980-83; real estate broker Jan Connor, Realtor, N.Y.C., 1983-92; instr. drawing Rockland Ctr. for Art, West Nyack, 1993, 1994, 1999—; gallery dir. Edward Hopper House Art Ctr., Nyack, N.Y., 1993-98, exec. dir., 1996-99; gallery dir. O.C.C. Art Ctr., Demarest, N.J., 2000—. Adj. prof. SUNY Empire Coll. and Rockland Coll., Hartsdale, N.Y., 1994-2001; mem. panel Snug Harbor Cultural Ctr., S.I., 1997; artist-in-residence Blue Hill Cultural Ctr., Pearl River, N.Y., 1994. Contbr. Creative Colored Pencil Landscape, 1996, Realist Painting After Edward Hooper, 1996, The Best of Colored Pencil #2 and #3, 1993, 94; represented in collections at Snake Island Rsch., Toronto, Chase Manhattan Bank, N.A., Bergen Mus. Art and Sci. Mem. Arts Coun. Rockland County, 1990—, Rockland Ctr. for the Arts, 1977—. Recipient Ted and Carol Shen drawing award Silvermine Guild Arts Ctr., 1999, Rockland County Exec. award for visual art, 2002; grant Vt. Studio Ctr., 1998. Mem. Colored Pencil Soc. Am. (signature mem., nat. workshop instr. 1999). Avocations: bicycling, hiking. Studio: 159 Piermont Ave Piermont NY 10968-1259

MADDALENA, LUCILLE ANN, management consultant; b. Plainfield, N.J., Nov. 8, 1948; d. Mario Anthony and Josephine Dorothy (Longo) M.; m. James Samonte Hohn, Sept. 7, 1975; children: Vincent, Nicholas, Mitchell. AA, Rider U., 1968; BS, Monmouth U., 1971; EdD, Rutgers U., 1978. Newscaster, dir. pub. rels. Sta. WBRW, Bridgewater, N.J., 1971-73; editor-in-chief Commerce mag., New Brunswick, N.J., 1973-74; dir. pub. rels. Raritan Valley Regional C. of C., New Brunswick, N.J., 1973-74; aide pub. relations to mayor City of New Brunswick, 1974; dir. comm. United Way Cen. Jersey, New Brunswick, 1974-77; mgmt. cons. United Way Am., Alexandria, Va., 1977-78; pres., owner Maddalena Assocs., Chester, N.J., 1978—; sr. cons. United Rsch. Co., Morristown, N.J., 1980-81; sr. ptnr., dir. OCD Group, Parsippany, N.J., 1984-87; chmn. bd. dirs. OCD Group (subs. Xicom Inc.), Morristown, N.J., 1988; pres. Morris Bus. Group, Chester, 1989—; prin. Maddalena Transitions Mgmt., Belmar, 2006. Adj. faculty Somerset County Coll., Bridgewater, NJ, 1970, Fairleigh Dickinson U., 1980; guest lectr. Rutgers U., New Brunswick, NJ, 1975—80; designer publicly offered seminars for Bell Atlantic, 1992—98; cons. change Howmet, Alloy, Dover, NJ, 1993—98; consortium trainer Johnson & Johnson, 1982—, condr. transition to mgmt. tng. for new hires, 1988—; developer redesign program Howmet Alloy Divsn., 1994; instr. on-line worldwide grad. mgmt. program Seton Hall U., 1999—2001; profl. mentor to execs. in maj. firms, 1990—; chair energy, mfg., utilities study team Global Orgn. Devel. Network, 2004—05, chair bus. strategies action team. Author: A Communications Manual for Non-Profit Organizations, 1980, (online program) Position Yourself, 2005; editor: New Directions for Instl. Advancement, 1980—81; author: Transition Advice from IRS Managers, 2006. Chmn. pers. com., police com. Chester Borough Coun., 1984-87; pres. Chester Consolidation Study Commn., 1990; chair Energy, Mfg., Utility Industroes, N.J. OD Network, 2005. Recipient Mayor's Commendation City of New Brunswick, 1973, Chester Borough, N.J., 1988. Mem. AAUW, LWV, Nat. Assn. Press Women, N.J. Elected Women Officials, Kappa Delta Pi. Clubs: N.J. Sled Dog Assn. Republican. Roman Catholic. Avocations: writing, working with non-profits. Office: Morris Bus Group PO Box 641 Chester NJ 07930-2920 Home: 414 12th Ave Belmar NJ 07719-2420 Office Phone: 732-280-6885. Business E-Mail: lucille@mtmanagement.net.

MADDALENA, ROSALIE ANNE, retired educator; b. Grove City, Pa., Sept. 15, 1946; d. Albert Michael Maddalena and Maria Sepe. BS, Grove City (Pa.) Coll., 1968; MS, Ea. Mich. U., 1972. Bus. edn. tchr. Riverside H.S., Dearborn Heights, Mich., 1968-85; office tech. tchr. Henry Ford C.C., Dearborn, 1972-84; bus., social studies tchr. Crestwood H.S., Dearborn Heights, 1985-98, ret., 1998. Instr. CPS exam reviewer Schoolcraft Coll., Livonia, Mich., 1982-87; bus., social studies dept. head Crestwood H.S., 1987-95, advisor nat. honor soc., 1985-92, curriculum coun., 1986-95, class sponsor, 1992-96. Co-author: (textbook/workbook) Microcomputer Applications, 1989. Recipient Spl. Tribute State of Mich. Legislature, 1998. Mem. Delta Pi Epsilon. Roman Catholic. Avocations: historic preservation, films, party planning.

MADDEN, GLENDA GAIL, sales professional; b. Norman, Okla., Aug. 30, 1949; d. John Samuel Jr. and Z. June (Pence) M. BA in Polit. Sci., Okla. Coll. Liberal Arts, U. Arts & Scis., 1970. Account clk. U. Okla. Press, Norman, 1977-78, advt. asst., 1978-80, asst. supr., 1980-81, sales mgr., 1981-98, asst. dir. mktg., 1998—. Avocations: home renovation, antiques, reading, genealogy.

MADDEN, TERESA DARLEEN, insurance agency owner; b. Dallas, Aug. 4, 1960; d. Tommy Joe Frederick Dodd and Mary Helen (Sterner) Smith; m. Kim Ashley Madden, June 2, 1989. Student, Tex. Tech U., 1978-81. Cert. ins. counselor, 1985, risk mgr., 2006. With personal lines svc. Charles R. Ervin Ins., Midland, Tex., 1981, Bryant Scalf Ins., Richardson, Tex., 1981-82; with comml. ins. svc. Street & Assocs. Inc., Dallas, 1982-84; with comml. ins. sales/svc. Hotchkiss Ins., Dallas, 1984-85; mgr. sales Abbott-Rose Ins. Agy., Dallas, 1985-89; owner Glenn-Madden & Assocs. Ins., Dallas, 1990—. Bd. dirs. Ind. Ins. Agents of Dallas, 2004—06, exec. bd., 2006. Methodist. Office: Glenn Madden & Assocs Inc 13601 Preston Rd Ste 106E Dallas TX 75240-4906 Business E-Mail: dmadden@glenn-maddeninsurance.com.

MADDEN, THERESA MARIE, elementary school educator; b. Phila., Feb. 12, 1950; d. James Anthony and Marie Margaret (Clark) Madden. BA in Social Sci., Neumann Coll., 1977; postgrad., Beaver Coll., Immaculata Coll. Cert. tchr. Pa., prin. Pa. Tchr. elem. grades St. Anthony Sch., Balt., 1971-73, St. Mary-St. Patrick Sch., Wilmington, Del., 1973-74, Queen of Heaven Sch., Cherry Hill, N.J., 1974-77, St. Bonaventure Sch., Phila., 1977-78, 79-83, St. Stanislaus Sch., Lansdale, Pa., 1978-79; substitute tchr. various schs. Phila., 1983-84; tchr. 8th grade math. St. Cecilia Sch., Phila., 1984-94; tchr. math., vice prin. Corpus Christi Sch., Lansdale, Pa., 1994-99; tchr. grades 6-8 St. Maria Goretti Sch., Hatfield, Pa., 1999—2004, prin., 2004—. Mem. vis. team Mid. States Assn., Phila., 1992, Phila., 97, Phila., 99, Phila., 2000, Phila., 02, chair, 03; presenter workshops. Mem.: Assn. Tchrs. Math. Phila. and Vicinity, Pa. Coun. Tchrs. Math., Nat. Coun. Tchrs. Math. Roman Catholic. Avocations: crocheting, cross stitch, baking, horseback riding, walking. Office: St Maria Goretti Sch Cowpath Rd Hatfield PA 19440 Office Phone: 215-721-9098. Personal E-mail: tghee@aol.com. Business E-Mail: smg2980@yahoo.com.

MADDEN-LUNSFORD, KERRY ELIZABETH, writer; b. Daytona Beach, Fla., Nov. 22, 1961; d. Joseph Anthony Madden and Mary Janis Baker; m. Alfred Kiffen Lunsford, Sept. 22, 1986; children: Flannery, Lucy, Norah. Student, U. Manchester, Eng., 1983; BA, U. Tenn., 1984, MFA, 1986. Voice and diction tchr. U. Tenn., Knox, 1984-86; English and drama tchr. Ningbo (China) U., 1986-87; ESL, speech and writing tchr. L.A. Unified Sch. Dist./Garfield Adult Sch., East Los Angeles, Calif., 1989-95; creative writing tchr. Vol.-Teen Moms, East Los Angeles, 1992—; guest playwright-in-schs. Audrey Skarball-Kenis, L.A., 1998—. Tchr. Sewanee (Tenn.) Young Writers Conf., summers 1997—. Author:(play) Blood and Marriage, 1993, (novel) Offsides, 1996, (children's book)Gentle's Holler, 2005, also essays and short stories. Vol. TeenMoms, 1992—; vol. creative writing tchr. L.A. elem. schs., 1994—. Mem. Am. PEN West, Authors Guild. Mailing: c/o Viking Publicity 375 Hudson St New York NY 10014 E-mail: kiffnkerry@aol.com.

MADDING, CLAUDIA, agricultural products executive; b. Detroit, Dec. 27, 1950; d. Clarence Irving and Theresa Flemming; m. John Eldon Madding, Apr. 4, 1979; children: Jonathan, Bryan, Collin. Student, Millikin U., 1969, Richland C.C., Decatur, Ill., 1979-80. Stenographer State of Ill., Springfield, 1968-74; adminstrv. asst. Archer Daniels Midland Co., Decatur, 1979-93, asst. sec., 1993—2001, exec. asst. to chmn. bd., 1994—2001, pres. ADM found., asst. sec., 1997—, exec. asst. to chmn. emeritus, exec. asst. to chmn. bd., 1999—, sec. to exec. com., 1999—2001. Bd. dirs. Hickory Point Bank, Decatur, Ill. Bd. dirs. United Way of Decatur, Decatur Club; past bd. dirs. Jr. Achievement Decatur, Holy Family Sch.; adv. bd. The Parent Project for Duchenne, Muscular Dystrophy Rsch., Inc., Middletown, Ohio; bd. St. Teresa H.S. Mem.: Country Decatur. Roman Catholic. Avocations: reading biographies, watching 1930-40's movies, foreign stamp collecting. Home: 16 Oakridge Dr Decatur IL 62521-4600 Office: Archer Daniels Midland Co 4666 E Faries Pkwy Decatur IL 62526-5666

MADDOCK, DIANA GAIL, visual artist, educator; b. Chgo., Nov. 5, 1938; d. Clark Edward and Kathleen (Maston) M. AA with honors, Lorain County C.C., Elyria, Ohio, 1988; BA magna cum laude, Baldwin-Wallace Coll., 1995. Office asst. G.D. Searle Pharms., Skokie, Ill., 1960—61; chemical analyst Micro-Tech Labs., Inc., Skokie, Ill., 1961—65; personnel sec. Northrop Corp., Rolling Meadows, Ill., 1969—71; sales sec. Vickers, Bensenville, Ill., 1971—72; office mgr. Elmhurst (Ill.) Meml. Hosp., 1972—74; pers. mgr. Glen Ellyn (Ill.) Clinic, 1976—79; adminstrv. sec. Guardian Angel Home Child Welfare Agy., Joliet, Ill., 1980—82; developer visual arts programs, instr. Asbury's Save Our Children, Elyria, Ohio, 1995-96; developer visual arts program, instr. art urban youth-at-risk, Elyria, Ohio, 1996-97; tchr. nat. summer inst. for gifted teens Oberlin (Ohio) Coll., 1997. Adj. faculty art Lorain County C.C., Elyria, 1996-2000; art instr. Firelands Assn. for Visual Arts, Oberlin, 1996. Works exhibited Very Spl. Arts Gallery, Washington, 1991—, Beverly Hills, Calif., 1997—; work reproduced in Very Spl. Arts calendar, 1998. Founder, chmn., Share Christmas, Inc., 1991-96; founder, adminstr. Red Roses in Snow Bereavement Support Group. Recipient 1st Place in painting, 1989, Artists award Ohio Arts Coun., 1991, Drahos award for best painting, 1994; winner Seasons of Ohio notecard competition Very Spl. Arts Ohio, 1997. Achievements include development of graduate program in African and African-American art. Avocations: music, writing, reading. E-mail: artistdgm@cox.net.

MADDOUX, BARBARA TILY, critical care nurse; b. Phila., Sept. 27, 1947; d. H. Coleman and Betty Tily; m. Kent Caldes, Dec. 19, 1970 (div. May. 23, 1977); 1 child, Joshua Coleman Caldes; m. Gerry L. Maddoux, Apr. 15, 1979 (div. Apr. 1993); 1 child, Morgan Lindsay. Diploma in nursing, Albert Einstein Med. Ctr., 1972; BSN, U. N.Mex., 1970; M in Oriental Medicine, Internat. Inst. Chinese Med., Albuquerque, 1999. RN. Staff nurse ICU Presbyn. Hosp., Alburquerque, 1972-74; cardiovasc. nurse specialist Surg. Assocs., Alburquerque, 1974-80, Puget Sound Cardiology Cons., Everett, Wash., 1980-82; med. office mgmt. cons. Albuquerque, 1982-84; CEO Maddoux Way Arabian Farm, Albuquerque, 1984-93; nurse ICU St. Joseph Med. Ctr., Albuquerque, 1993—. Mem. Am. Assn. Critical Care Nurses, Nat. Acupuncture & Oriental Medicine Alliance, Oriental Medicine Assn. N.Mex., Nat. Assn. Oriental Medicine & Acupuncture, Am. Heart Assn. Avocations: skiing, yoga, hiking, gardening, horseback riding. Office: Ste 202 7510 Montgomery Blvd NE Albuquerque NM 87109-1500 Home: 8747 Eagle Springs Dr NE Albuquerque NM 87113-1258 E-mail: btyoga@aol.com.

MADDOW, RACHEL, radio personality, political activist; BA, Stanford U., 1994; PhD in Politics, Oxford U. Host The Big Breakfast, WRSI, Northhampton, Mass., 2002—04; co-host (with Chuck D. & Liz Winstead) Unfiltered, Air Am. Radio, NYC, host The Rachel Maddow Show, 2005—. Fellow AIDS Legal Referral Panel, San Francisco; grantee John Gardner Pub. Svc. Fellowship, Ludlam Health Policy Fellowship; Rhodes Scholar, 1995. Office: Air America Radio 641 Avenue Of The Americas Fl 4 New York NY 10011-2038

MADDOX, AMY B., statistician, educator; b. Tex. m. Jodi Maddox; children: Ana, Ava, Ali. PhD, Baylor U., 2003; BS in Math., SW Tex. State U., 1994. Lectr. Dept. Stats. Baylor U., Waco, Tex., 1996—. Baptist. Avocations: weightlifting, reading, scrapbooks, arbonne. Office: Baylor University One Bear Place # 97140 Waco TX 76708 Business E-Mail: amy_maddox@baylor.edu.

MADDOX, LAUREN M., federal agency administrator; B, Creighton U.; M, Northwestern U. Sr. v.p. Comm. Fedn. Am. Hospitals; sr. Comm. adv. US Rep. Newt Gingrich, US Rep. J.C. Watts, Jr.; sr. comm. adv. to US Rep. Joel Hefley US Congress; comm. dir. Ho. Rep. Conf.; prin. PodestaMattoon; asst. sec. for comm. & outreach US Dept. Edn., Washington, 2006—. Office: 400 Maryland Ave SW Rm 7C115 Washington DC 20202-1510 Office Phone: 202-401-0404. Office Fax: 202-401-8607.*

MADDOX, MARTHA LACEY GARDNER, artist; b. Birmingham, Ala., Jan. 5, 1926; d. Searcy Preston and Willard Morris Gardner; m. Steve Wilson Maddox, Mar. 3, 1946; children: Steve Wilson Jr., James Wayne, David Worthington. B in Applied Art, Ala. Poly. Inst. (now Auburn U.), 1947. Cert. tchr. Ala., Fla. Art prof. U. Ala., Tuscaloosa, 1947, 1948; H.S. and elem. sch. tchr. Ala. Sch. Bd., Flomaton, 1949—51; tchr. Byrneville (Fla.) Elem., 1951—52. Exhibitions include Vincent Price Touring Exhbn., Golden Heritage Exhbn., Cheaha Exhbn., Old Mobile Exhbn., Dauphin Island Exhbn., Art for Art's Sake, Wiregrass Mus. Art, Outstanding Artists S.E., Met. Mus. Art, High Mus. Art, Fine Arts Mus. of the South, Birmingham Mus. Art, Ea. Shore Art Ctr., Alpha Omicron Pi scholar, 1947. Mem.: Exptl. Artists Ala., Pastel Soc. Am., United Pastelists Am., Oil Pastel Soc., Watercolor Soc. Ala., Ea. Shore Art Assn., Mobile Art Assn., Nat. Women in the Arts, Malone Painters, Panama Art Assn., Hoover Art Assn., Dothan-Wiregrass Art League. Methodist. Home and Office: 2724 Southview Terr Birmingham AL 35216 Office Phone: 205-824-6426.

MADDUX, SANDRA O'KELLY, retired language educator; b. Gallipolis, Ohio, Feb. 14, 1943; d. Guy Ritch O'Kelly and Gayle Clarke Woodward; m. Terry Wayne Maddux, Dec. 13, 1979 (dec.); 1 child, Joseph Woodward. BA in English and French, Winthrop Coll., Rock Hill, SC, 1965; MA in Tchg. English, The Citadel, Charleston, SC, 1974. Cert. tchr. SC, Tenn. English tchr., Orange Park, Fla., 1965—68, Charleston, SC, 1968—79, Hendersonville, Tenn., 1980—81, Gallatin, Tenn., 1985—87, Springfield, Tenn., 1987—2000; ret., 2000. Author: (poetry chapbook) Memories, 1995. Mus. docent Robertson County Hist. Soc., Springfield, 2001—; hosp. vol. North Crest Aux., Springfield, 2001—; driver Rd. to Recovery, Springfield, 2001—. Named My Favorite Tchr., Channel 5 TV, Nashville, 1992; recipient Cert. of Merit, Springfield HS, 1989. Mem.: Tenn. Ret. Tchrs. Assn., Robertson County Ret. Tchrs. Assn. Avocations: needlecrafts, crocheting, reading, piano, bridge. Home: 5150 Conrad Dr Springfield TN 37172

MADDY, PENELOPE JO, philosopher, educator; b. Tulsa, Okla., July 4, 1950; d. Richard and Suzanne (Lorimer) Parsons. BA in Math., U. Calif., Berkeley, 1972; PhD in Philosophy, Princeton U., N.J., 1979. Asst. prof. U. Notre Dame (Ind.), 1978-83; assoc. prof. U. Ill., Chgo., 1983-87, U. Calif., Irvine, 1987-89, prof., 1989—, chair philosophy dept., 1991-95, chair logic and philosophy of sci., 1998-2001. Author: Realism in Mathematics, 1990, Naturalism in Mathematics, 1997 (Lakatos award 2002); editor Notre Dame Jour. Formal Logic, 1979-84, editl. bd., 1984—; editl. bd. Jour. Philos. Logic, 1985-2004, Jour. Symbolic Logic, 1995-2000, Philosophia Mathematica, 1993—, Bull. Symbolic Logic, 2004-. Fellow AAUW, 1982-83, U. Calif., 1988-89; NSF grantee, 1986, 88-89, 90-91, 94-95, Marshall scholar, 1982-83, Westinghouse Sci. scholar, 1968-72. Mem. Assn. Symbolic Logic (mem. exec. com. 1993-96, v.p. 2001-04), Am. Philos. Assn. (mem. exec. com. 1993-95), Philosophy of Sci. Assn. (mem. governing bd. 1993-95), Am. Acad. Arts and Scis. Office: U Calif at Irvine Dept Logic and Philosophy of Sci Irvine CA 92697-5100 Business E-Mail: pjmaddy@uci.edu.

MADEJSKI, ROSE MARY, pharmacist, educator; b. May 1, 1937; BS cum laude, U. Buffalo, 1959. Lic. pharmacist, N.Y. Staff pharmacist VA Hosp., Buffalo, 1959-60, Pritchard Pharmacy, Buffalo, N.Y., 1967-69, Niagara Falls (N.Y.) Meml. Ctr., 1969-70, Columbus Hosp., Buffalo, N.Y., 1970-73; enterostomal therapist, orthopedic fitter, pharmacist Stalls Health Svcs., Buffalo, N.Y., 1973-90; cons. enterostomal therapist Kenmore (N.Y.) Mercy Hosp., 1988-90; pres. M&R Pharmacy Cons., Grand Island, N.Y., 1975-90; v.p. Stalls Pharmacy and Health Svcs., Buffalo, N.Y., 1980-90; clin. asst. prof. pharmacy SUNY, Buffalo, 1990—. Contbr. articles to profl. jours. including Am. Pharmacist, U.S. Pharmacist, N.Y. State Pharmacist, among others. Grantee Marion Merrell Dow, Merck, Sharp & Dohme, and the Upjohn Co.; recipient Leadership award Bristol Myers Squibb, Inc., 1990, award Am. Cancer Soc., 1978, Outstanding Pharmacist award Indo-Am. Pharm. Soc., 1991, Bowl of Hygeia, 1995, Susan B. Anthony award, 1996, Pharmacist of Yr. award, 2001; named Outstanding Alumnus U. Buffalo, 1992; named to Pharmacy Hall of Fame, 2001. Mem. Pharmacists Soc. State N.Y. (pres. 1989-90, chmn. 1990-91), Pharmacists Assn. Western N.Y. (bd. dirs. 1975-78, 94-99, Hall of Fame 2002), Health Sys. Agy. Erie County (vice chair 1975). Business E-Mail: madejski@acsu.buffalo.edu.

MADELEINE, ELIZABETH LEIGH, science educator; b. Detroit, Mich., Dec. 27, 1979; d. Kenneth and Deborah Lynn Madeleine; life ptnr. Bryon Richard Burkel. BS, Western Mich. U., 2003. Personal trainer Bally Total Fitness, Sterling Heights, Mich., 2003—04; tchr. HEART Acad., Harper Woods, Mich., 2003—. Coach, mentor HEART Acad., 2003—. Donator WWF, Humane Soc., IFAW, COTS - Coalition on Temp. Shelter, Easter Seals, Mar. of Dimes, Detroit Mission Ministries, Detroit, 2003—06. Named Tchr. of Yr., HEART Acad. Students, 2004. Mem.: AAHPERD (assoc.). D-Liberal. Luth. Avocations: scuba diving, travel, sports, reading, exercise. Office: HEART Acad 19800 Anita Harper Woods MI 48225 Office Phone: 313-882-4631. Office Fax: 313-882-4761. Business E-Mail: bmadeleine@heartacademyhs.com.

MADGETT, NAOMI LONG, poet, editor, publisher, educator; b. Norfolk, Va., July 5, 1923; d. Clarence Marcellus and Maude Selena (Hilton) Long; m. Julian F. Witherspoon, Mar. 31, 1946 (div. Apr. 1949); 1 child, Jill Witherspoon Boyer; m. William H. Madgett, July 29, 1954 (div. Dec. 1960); m. Leonard P. Andrews, Mar. 31, 1972 (dec. May 1996). BA, Va. State Coll., 1945; MEd, Wayne State U., 1955; PhD, Internat. Inst. for Advanced Studies, 1980; LHD (hon.), Siena Heights Coll., 1991, Loyola U., 1993; DFA (hon.), Mich. State U., 1994. Reporter, copyreader Mich. Chronicle, Detroit, 1946; svc. rep. Mich. Bell Telephone Co., Detroit, 1948-54; tchr. English pub. high schs. Detroit, 1955-65, 66-68; rsch. assoc. Oakland U., Rochester, Mich., 1965-66; mem. staff Detroit Women Writers Conf. Ann. Writers Conf., 1968—; lectr. English U. Mich., 1970-71; assoc. prof. English Eastern Mich. U., Ypsilanti, 1968-73, prof., 1973-84, prof. emeritus, 1984—; editor-pub. Lotus Press, 1974—. Editor Lotus Poetry Series, Mich. State U. Press, 1993-98. Author: (poetry) Songs to a Phantom Nightingale (under name Naomi Cornelia Long), 1941, One and the Many, 1956, Star by Star, 1965, 2d edit., 70, (with Ethel Tincher and Henry B. Maloney) Success in Language and Literature B, 1967, Pink Ladies in the Afternoon, 1972, 2d edit., 90, Exits and Entrances, 1978, A Student's Guide to Creative Writing, 1980, Phantom Nightingale: Juvenilia, 1981, Octavia and other Poems (Creative Achievement award Coll. Lang. Assn.), 1988, Remembrances of Spring: Collected Early Poems, 1993, Octavia: Guthrie and Beyond, 2002, Connected Islands, 2004, (autobiography) Pilgrim Journey, 2006; editor: (anthology) A Milestone Sampler: 15th Anniversary Anthology, 1988, Adam of Ife: Black Women in Praise of Black Men, 1992; In Her Lifetime tribute Afrikan Poets Theatre, 1989 Participant Creative Writers in Schs. program. Recipient Esther R. Beer Poetry award Nat. Writers Club, 1957, Disting. English Tchr. of Yr. award, 1967; Josephine Nevins Keal award, 1979; Mott fellow in English, 1965, Robert Hayden Runagate award, 1985, Creative Artist award Mich. Coun. for the Arts, 1987, award Nat. Coalition 100 Black Women, 1984, award Nat. Coun. Tchrs. English Black Caucus, 1984, award Chesapeake/Virginia Beach chpt. Links, Inc., 1981, Arts Found. Mich. award, 1990, Creative Achievement award Coll. Lang. Assn., 1988; Arts Achievement award Wayne State U., 1985, The Black Scholar Award of Excellence, 1992; Am. Book award, 1993, Mich. Artist award, 1993; Creative Contbrs. award Gwendolyn Brooks Ctr. Black Lit. and Creative Writing Chgo. State U., 1993, Lifetime Achievement award Furious Flower, 1994, George Kent award, 1995, Lifetime Achievement award Gwendolyn Brooks Ctr., 2003; Naomi Long Madgett Poetry award named for her, 1993—, Alain Locke award Detroit Inst. Arts, Friends of African and African Am. Art, 2003; inducted Sumner H.S. Hall of Fame, St. Louis, 1997, Nat. Lit. Hall Fame for Writers of African Descent, Chgo. State U., 1999, Mich. Women's Hall of Fame, 2002; named Poet Laureate, City of Detroit, 2001—, Mayor's award Literary Excellence, 2005; named one of 23 Enterprising Women, Detroit Hist. Soc., 2004; Bronze Bust created by Artis Lane unveiled at Charles H. Wright Mus. African Am. History, 2005. Mem. NAACP, Coll. Lang. Assn., So. Poetry Law Ctr., Langston Hughes Soc., Charles H. Wright Mus. of African Am. History, Detroit Working Writers, Detroit Inst. Arts, Fred Hart Williams Geneal. Soc., Alpha Kappa Alpha. Congregationalist. Home: 18080 Santa Barbara Dr Detroit MI 48221-2531 Office: PO Box 21607 Detroit MI 48221-0607 Office Phone: 313-861-1280. Personal E-mail: nlmadgett@aol.com.

MADIGAN, AMY, actress; b. Chgo., Sept. 11, 1950; m. Ed Harris, 1983; one child, Lily Dolores With rock music group, 10 yrs. Appeared in films Love Child, 1982, Love Letters, 1984, Streets of Fire, 1984, Places in the Heart, 1984, Alamo Bay, 1985, Twice in a Lifetime, 1985, Zeisters, 1986, Nowhere to Hide, 1987, The Prince of Pennsylvania, 1988, Uncle Buck, 1989, Field of Dreams, 1989, The Dark Half, 1993, Female Perversions, 1996, Loved, 1997, With Friends Like These., 1998, A Time for Dancing, 2000, Pollock, 2000, The Sleepy Time Gal, 2001, The Laramie Project, 2002, Just a Dream, 2002, In the Land of Milk and Money, 2004, The Discontents, 2004, Admissions, 2004, Winte Passing, 2005; prodr., After the Past, 2004; (TV films) Crazy Times, 1981, The Ambush Murders, 1982, Victims, 1982, Travis McGee, 1983, The Day After, 1983,Eureka Stockade, 1984, The Laundromat, 1985, The Revolt of Mother, 1986, Roe vs. Wade, 1989 (Golden Globe award, Best Supporting Actress in a Series, Mini-Series, Motion Picture for TV), Lucky Day, 1991, And There THere Was One, 1994, Crocodile Shoes, 1994, A Bright Shining Lie, 1998, Having Our Say: The Delany Sisters' First 10 Years, 1999, In the Name of the People, 2000, Shot in the Heart, 2001, The Ranch, 2004;(TV series) Carnivale, 2003-05 exec. prodr., actor, Riders of the Purple Sage, 1996; (TV appearances), Hart to Hart, 1981, CHiPs, 1981, Frasier, 1994; appeared in Broadway revival A Streetcar Named Desire, 1992 Office: William Morris Agency 151 S El Camino Dr Beverly Hills CA 90212-2775

MADIGAN, LISA, state attorney general; m. Pat Byrnes; 1 child, Rebecca. BA, Georgetown U., 1988; attended, Loyola U. Asst. dean adult, continuing edn., dir. Sr. Acad. Lifelong Learning Wrights Family Coll. Wilbur Wright Coll., with positive alts. project; litigator Sachnoff & Weaver, Ltd., Chgo.; mem. Ill. Senate, Springfield, 1998—2002, mem. senate appropriations com., edn. com., joint com. adminstrv. rules; atty. gen. State of Ill., 2002—. Former vol. tchr., South Africa. Bd. dirs. AIDS Living Rememberance Com. Named one of Top 40 Lawyers Under 40, Nat. Law Jour., 2005. Mem. Ill. Bar Assn., Women's Bar Assn. Ill., Chgo. Bar Assn. Republican. Office: Office of Atty General James R Thompson Ctr 100 W Randolph St Chicago IL 60601 Office Phone: 312-814-3000.*

MADIGAN, RITA DUFFY, career planning administrator; b. N.Y.C., Jan. 22, 1919; d. Anthony E. and Mary (Feichter) Duffy; m. John Callanan Madigan, May 1, 1943; children: John C., James A., Paul F. BA in English History, Our Lady of Good Counsel Coll., 1940; M of Adminstrn., U. Bridgeport, 1963, postgrad., 1970. Tchr. English City of Bridgeport (Conn.), 1961-63, Birkshire Jr. High Sch., Birmingham, Mich., 1963-66; career counselor East Side Mid. Sch., Bridgeport, 1969-71; coord. career edn. Ctrl. HS, Bridgeport, 1972—99, ret., 1999. Recipient State SCOVE award, 1986, CCCA Meritorious award, 1993, Meritorious award Teikyo Post Univ, 1993, Meritorious award for svc. to cmty. Girl Scouts of Am., 1996. Mem. AAUW, NEA, Conn. Edn. Assn., Conn. Career Counselors Assn., Bridgeport Edn. Assn., St. Joseph's Ladies League (bd. dirs. 1992-94), Bridgeport U. Alumnae Assn. Republican. Roman Catholic. Avocations: skiing, golf, tennis, sailing, travel. Home: 119 Lantern Ln Wethersfield CT 06109-4049

MADISON, ANNE CONWAY, marketing professional, public relations professional; b. Balt., Mar. 13, 1963; d. Earl Cranston Jr. and Nancy C.; 1 child, Ryan Douglas. BS in Comm., Wittenberg U., 1985. Pub. rels. specialist Springfield (Ohio) Met. Housing Authority, 1984-85; account rep. CT Corp. Sys., Washington, 1985-86; pub. rels. asst. Ryland, Columbia, Md., 1986-88, comm. coord., 1988-90, mgr. mktg. comm., 1990-92, dir. mktg. comm., 1992-94, v.p. comm., 1994—2003; v.p. mktg. and comm. ESIC, Inc., Columbia, 2003—05; v.p. corp. comm. Choice Hotels Internat., Silver Spring, Md. Bd. dirs., officer Domestic Violence Cr. of Howard County, Columbia, 1987-96; bd. dirs. Norbel Sch., Nat. Family Resiliency Ctr. Named Vol. of Yr. Domestic Violence Ctr., 1988, recipient Spirit award, 1992; named one of Top 100 Women in Md., The Daily Record, 1996. Mem. Pub. Rels. Soc. Am., Nat. Investor Rels. Inst. Republican. Roman Catholic. Office Phone: 301-592-6723. Personal E-mail: acmadison@comcast.net. Business E-Mail: anne_madison@choicehotels.com.

MADISON, DEBORAH LEAFY, writer, chef; b. West Hartford, Conn., June 21, 1945; d. John Herbert and Winifred (Law) Madison; m. Dan Welch, Mar. 17, 1979 (div. Nov. 1986); m. J. Patrick McFarlin, May 29, 1991. BA, U. Calif., Santa Cruz, 1968. Founding chef The Greens Restaurant, San Francisco, 1978-83, Cafe Escalera, Santa Fe, N.Mex., 1990-93; menu cons. Rancho San Miguel, Baja Sur, Mex., 1996. Cons. to various restaurants, 1986—. Author: The Greens Cookbook, 1986 (Andre Simon award 1987), The Savory Way, 1990 (Best Cookbook of Yr. Julia Childs award 1991), The Vegetarian Table: America, 1996, Vegetarian Cooking for Everyone, 1997 (James Beard Award), This Can't be Tofu, 2000, Local Flavors: Cooking and Eating from America's Farmers' Markets, 2002, Vegetarian Suppers from Deborah Madison's Kitchen, 2005; adv. editor Saveor, 1994—; contbg. author books; contbr. articles to profl. jours. Bd. dirs. Santa Fe Area Farmers Mkt., 1990—; mem. Student Nutrition Action Com., Santa Fe, 1995—. Named to Honor Roll of Am. Chefs, Food and Wine Mag., 1983; recipient Contessa Premium Foods Whos Who of Food and Beverage in Am. award, James Beard Found., 2005. Mem. Internat. Assn. Culinary Professions, The Chef's Collaborative (founder), Les Dames D'Escoffier (MFK Fisher Mid-Career award 1994). Avocations: gardening, reading.*

MADISON, PAULA, broadcast executive; b. NYC, 1952; m. Roosevelt Madison; 1 child, Imani. Grad., Vassar Coll., 1974. Reporter Syracuse Herald Jour., 1974—80; investigative bur. reporter Ft. Worth Star - Telegram, 1980—82; asst. city editor Dallas Times Herald, 1982; cmty. affairs dir. WFAA-TV, Dallas, 1982—84, news mgr., 1984—86; news dir. KOTV-TV, Tulsa, 1986—87; exec. news dir. KHOU-TV, Houston, 1987—89; asst. news dir. WNBC, N.Y.C., 1989—96, v.p., news dir., 1996—2000; v.p., sr. v.p. diversity NBC, N.Y.C., 2000—02; pres., gen. mgr. KNBC, L.A., 2000—; regional gen. mgr. KNBC, KVEA, KWHY, 2002—. Bd. trustees Vassar Coll. Named Disting. African-Am. New Yorker, N.Y.C. Comptroller Alan Hevesi, Citizen of Yr., City of LA Marathon, 2004; recipient Ida B. Wells award, Nat. Assn. Black Journalists', 1998, Ellis Island medal of honor, Nat. Ethnic Coalition of Orgns., 1999, President's award, NAACP, 2001, Frederick C. Patterson award, United Negro College Fund, 2001, Diversity award, Nat. Assoc. Minority Media Execs., 2002, Woman of the Year, Los Angeles County Commn. for Women, 2002, Excellence in Media Award, Calif. NOW Chap., 2003, TRISCCORT award, Tri-State Catholic Com. on Radio and TV, Asian-Pacific Am. Corp. Impact award, Org. Chinese Americans Greater Los Angeles Chap. Image award Corp. Achievement., Deborah award, Anti-Defamation League, 2003. Mem.: N.Y. Assn. Black Journalists, Nat. Assn. Black Journalists. Office: NBC 4 3000 West Alameda Ave Burbank CA 91523*

MADISON, RACHEL CHRISTINE, science educator; b. Farmington, Maine, Apr. 24, 1976; d. Dennis Roger and Sylvia Bearor Desjardins; m. Marco Michael Madison, July 24, 1999; children: Zachary Dennis, Mayla Lucille. BS in Secondary Edn., U. Maine, Bangor, 1999; MS in Edn., U. So. Maine, Portland, 2004. Cert. tchr. life sci. Maine, 1999, tchr. gifted and talented Maine, 2006. Sci. tchr. Poland Regional H.S., Poland, Maine, 1999—2004, gifted and talented tchr., 2004—. E-mail: rmadison57@netzero.net.

MADLOCK, YVONNE, city health department administrator; m. Lawrence Madlock; 3 children. BS, Wellesley Coll.; MAT, Wesleyan U., Middletown, Conn.; studied, U. Tex. Sch. Pub. Health. Adminstr., bur. personal health svcs. Shelby Co. Divsn. Health Svcs., Memphis, dir., 1995—. Bd. pres. Cmty. Inst. for Early Childhood; bd. dirs. W. Tenn. Area Health Edn. Ctr., Memphis Leadership Inst., Cmty. Found. of Greater Memphis, Shelby Co. Ground Water Quality Control Bd. Mem.: Nat. Assn. City and County Health Officials (bd. dirs.). Office: Shelby Co Divsn Health Svcs 814 Jefferson Ave Memphis TN 38103 Business E-Mail: HealthDirector@co.shelby.tn.us.*

MADONNA, (MADONNA LOUISE VERONICA CICCONE), singer, actress, producer; b. Bay City, Mich., Aug. 16, 1958; d. Sylvio and Madonna Ciccone; m. Sean Penn, Aug. 16, 1985 (div. Sept. 14, 1989); m. Guy Ritchie, Dec. 22, 2000; 2 children: Lourdes, Rocco, 1 adopted child, David Student, U. Mich., 1976-78. Dancer Alvin Ailey Dance Co., N.Y.C., 1979; CEO Maverick Records, L.A., 1992—. Singer: (albums) Madonna, 1983, Like a Virgin, 1985, True Blue, 1986, You Can Dance, 1987, Like a Prayer, 1989, I'm Breathless: Music From and Inspired by the Film Dick Tracy, 1990, The Immaculate Collection, 1990, Erotica, 1992, Bedtime Stories, 1994, Something to Remember, 1995, Ray of Light, 1998 (Grammy award for Best Pop Album 1999), Music, 2000, GHV2: Greatest Hits Volume II, 2002, American Life, 2003, Confessions on a Dancefloor, 2005, I'm Going to Tell You a Secret, 2006; (soundtracks) Who's That Girl, 1987, Evita, 1996; actor (films) A Certain Sacrifice, 1980, Vision Quest, 1985, Desperately Seeking Susan, 1985, Shanghai Surprise, 1986, Who's That Girl, 1987, Bloodhounds of Broadway, 1989, Dick Tracy, 1990, Shadows and Fog, 1992, Body of Evidence, 1992, A League of Their Own, 1992, Dangerous Game, 1993, Blue in the Face, 1995, Four Rooms, 1996, Girl 6, 1996, Evita, 1996 (Golden Globe, 1997), The Next Best Thing, 2000, Swept Away, 2002; (documentaries) Truth or Dare, 1991, I'm Going to Tell You a Secret, 2005; Broadway theater debut in Speed-the-Plow, 1987, stage appearance in Up for Grabs, 2002; (TV appearances) Happy Birthday Elizabeth: A Celebration of a Life, 1997, Will & Grace, 2003; author: Sex, 1992, (children's books) The English Roses, 2003, Mr. Peabody's Apples, 2003, Yakov and the Seven Thieves, 2004, Adventures of Abdi, 2004, Lotsa de Casha, 2005.*

MADORE, TERESA SHARON, secondary school educator; d. Wilfred and Anne Doucette; m. Mark James Madore, July 25, 1986; children: Jonathan E., Olivia Lottie Anne. BS in Elem. Edn., McMurry U., Abilene, Tex., 1990. Cert. tchr. Tex., Maine, 1992. 5th grade tchr. Snyder Ind. Sch. Dist., Tex., 1993—94; elem. tchr. Madawaska Sch. Dept., Maine, 1994—96, French immersion tchr., 1996—99, H.S. English tchr., 1999—. Support sys. mem. Madawaska Sch. Dept., Maine, 2002—03; v.p. Delta Kappa Gamma, Madawaska, Maine, 1999—2001. Author poetry; digital collage card, Ice Cream Therapy, artists trading cards, Altered Arts Mag. Mem.: Nat. Coun. Tchrs. English.

MADRAS, BERTHA KALIFON, federal official, neuroscientist; b. Montreal, Quebec, Canada, Dec. 9, 1942; m. Peter Madras, June 21, 1964; children: Cynthia Gumbert, Claudine D. BSc, McGill U., 1963, PhD, 1967. Postdoctoral fellow Tufts U., Boston, 1966-67; postdoctoral fellow rsch. assoc. MIT, Cambridge, 1967-69, 72-74; asst. prof. U. Toronto, 1979—80, Harvard Med. Sch., Boston, 1986-90, assoc. prof., 1990-99, prof., 1999—2006, assoc. dir. pub. edn. divsn. addictions, 1998—2006; dep. dir. for demand reduction Office Nat. Drug Control Policy, Washington, 2006—. Sci. adv. com. Brookhaven Nat. Lab., Upton, N.Y., 1998—; rev. com., cons. Nat. Inst. Drug Abuse, chair B study sect., 1998-99; MDCN-5 MNPS rev. com.; cons. Ont. Mental Health Found., 1984-90, chmn. fellowships and awards com., 1988-90; chmn. radiation safety Harvard U., 1995-99, acting dir. Primate Ctr., 1998-99; chmn. faculty affairs Harvard Med. Sch.; mem. Dana Alliance for Brain Initiatives. Author: (book chpt.) Dopamine, 1984; editor: Neurosci.; mem. editl. bd. Synapse, 1991-2004; contbr. articles to profl. jours. Sci. fair judge. Recipient Rsch. grants Nat. Inst. Drug Abuse, 1992—, 94—, Sci. Edn. Partnership award grant, 1992-94, Parkinson's Disease Found., 1990-91, Nat. Inst. Neurol. Disease and Stroke, 1994, 99—, NIMH, Dana Alliance for Brain Initiatives, Merit award NIH, Sr. Scientist award. Mem. Soc. for Neuroscience, Coll. Probs. Drug Dependence. Achievements include development of a marker for Parkinson's disease and attention deficit hyperactivity disorder, a probe for cocaine binding sites in brain; developed a PET imaging SPECT for living brain; developed a PET and SPECT imaging drug to monitor Parkinsonism in brain; rsch. in how drugs work in brain; co-developer of CD-ROM on how drugs affect brain. Office: Office Nat Drug Control Policy 750 17th St NW Rm 609 Washington DC 20503*

MADRID, NANCY ELIZABETH, counselor, consultant, small business owner; d. Poly Carpio and Mary Katherine Madrid. AS, Paris Jr. Coll., Tex., 1981; BA, Southeastern State U., Durant, Okla., 1983, MA in Counseling Psychology, 1984. Lic. profl. counselor Tex., 1992, N.Mex., 1995, nat. cert. master level psychologist Profl. Psychologist Cert. Bd., 2000. Mental health counselor Moriarty Pub. Schs., N.Mex., 2000—02, Charter Schs., Albuquerque, 2002—04; mental health counselor and owner Nancy Madrid's Counseling, 2004—. Recipient cert. Appreciation, Minority Bus. Devel. Agy. Mem.: ACA, N.Mex. Counseling Assn., Native Am. Bus. Owners. Avocations: music, animals, movies, football, pow-wows. Office: Nancy Madrids Counseling Sch and Home Based Counseling PO Box 11876 Albuquerque NM 87192 Office Phone: 505-362-5169.

MADRID, OLGA HILDA GONZALEZ, retired elementary school educator, school system administrator; b. San Antonio, May 4, 1928; d. Victor A. and Elvira Ardilla Gonzalez; m. Sam Madrid, Jr., June 29, 1952; children: Ninette Marie, Samuel James. Student, U. Mex., San Antonio, St. Mary's U.; BA, Our Lady of Lake U., 1956, MEd, 1963. Cert. bilingual tchr., adminstr., Tex. Sec. Lanier HS San Antonio Ind. Sch. Dist., San Antonio, 1945-52; tchr. Collins Garden Elem. Sch., Storm Elem. Sch., San Antonio Ind. Sch. Dist., San Antonio, 1963-92; tutor Dayton, Ohio, 1952-54. Bd. dir., sch. rep. San Antonio Tchr. Coun., 1970-90; chair various coms. Collins Garden Elem., 1970-92. Elected dep. precinct, senatorial and state Dem. Conv., San Antonio, 1968—; apptd. commr. Keep San Antonio Beautiful, 1985; life mem., past pres. San Antonio YWCA; bd. dir. Luth. Gen. Hosp., Nat. Conf. Christians and Jews, Cath. Family and Children's Svc., St. Luke's Luth. Hosp.; nat. bd. dir. YWCA, 1985-96, also mem. exec. com.; mem. edn. commn. Holy Rosary Parish, 1994—; mem. bus. assoc. com. Our Lady of the Lake U., 1995—. Recipient Outstanding Our Lady Lake Alumni award Our Lady Lake U., 1975, Guadalupana medal San Antonio Cath. Archdiocese, 1975, Yellow Rose Tex. citation Gov. Briscoe, 1977; Olga H. Madrid Ctr. named in her honor, YWCA San Antonio and San Antonio City Coun., 1983; Lo Mejor De Lo Nuestro honoree San Antonio Light, 1991, honoree San Antonio Women's History Month Coalition, 1996; named Our Lady of Lake Outstanding Alumna, 1999, one of five women honored for promoting literacy and cultural hertiage with a sch. wall mural titled "Mis Palabras, Mi Poder", 2002. Mem. San Antonio Bus. and Profl. Women, Inc. (mem. exec. com.), Salute Quality Edn. (honoree 1993), Delta Kappa Gamma (Theta Beta chpt., mem. exec. com.). Avocations: reading, gardening. Home: 2726 Benrus Blvd San Antonio TX 78228-2319

MADRID, PATRICIA A., state attorney general; BA in English and Philosophy, U. N.Mex., 1969, JD, 1973; cert., Nat. Jud. Coll., U. Nev., 1978. Bar: N.Mex. Dist. judge State of N.Mex., 1978—84, atty. gen., 1999—. Chmn. Western Conf. of Attys. Gen. Named Latina Atty. of Yr., Nat. Hispanic Bar Assn., 2001, N.Mex. Power Broker, N.Mex. Bus. Weekly; recipient Mary V. Orozco Abriendo Caminos award, Latina Lawyers Bar Assn., 2003, Trailblazer award, N.Mex. Commn. on the Status of Women, Las Primeras award, MANA, 2004, Woman of the Yr. in Govt. award, Capital Bus. and Professional Women of Santa Fe, 2004, Exec. Dir. award, Animal Protection of N.Mex., 2004. Democrat. Office: Atty Gens Office PO Drawer 1508 Santa Fe NM 87504-1508

MADRY-TAYLOR, JACQUELYN YVONNE, educational association administrator; d. Arthur Chester and Janie (Cowart) Madry; 1 child, Jana LeMadry. BA, Fisk U., 1966; MA, Ohio State U., 1969; EdD, U. Fla., 1975. Cert. Inst. for Ednl. Mgmt., Harvard U., 1981. Tchr. Spanish Terry Parker Sr. High Sch., Jacksonville, 1967-72; instr. U. Fla., Gainesville, 1972-75; asst. to v.p. for acad. affairs. Morris Brown Coll., Atlanta, 1975-76; dean for instructional svcs. No. Va. Community Coll., Annandale, Va., 1976-83; dean undergrad. studies Bridgewater (Mass.) State Coll., 1983-92, exec. asst. to acting pres., 1988, acting v.p. acad. affairs, 1988-90; dir. Acad. Leadership Acad. Am. Assn. State Coll. and Univs., Washington, 1992-94; dir. ednl. programs and svcs. United Negro Coll. Fund Hdqs., 1994-97; pres. JYM Assocs., 1999—; sr. advisor Nat. Assn. for Equal Opportunity in Higher Edn., 1997—2003. Cons. to colls., univs. and orgns., 1997-99; cons. W.K. Kellog Found., 1993-97; bd. dirs. Bridgewater State Coll. Early Learning Ctr., 1984-88; evaluator U.S. Dept. State/Fgn. Svc., Washington, 1982—, U.S. Dept. Edn., 1989—; pres. JYM Assocs., 1999—. Vice chmn. No. Va. Manpower Planning Coun., Fairfax County, Va., 1981. Recipient Cert. Achievement Bridgewater State Coll. Black Alumni, 1988, Women Helping Women award Soroptimist Internat., 1983, Outstanding Young Women Am. award, 1976, 78; named Personalities of South, 1977; recipient Outstanding Tchr./Student Rels. Humanitarian award B'nai B'rith, 1972. Mem. Pub. Mem. Assn. U.S. Fgn. Svc., Soroptimist Internat., Boston Club (v.p. 1986-88), Jack and Jill of Am., Inc., Am. Assn. of Univ. Women, Phi Delta Kappa, Alpha Kappa Alpha, Links Inc. (Reston, Va. chpt.). Methodist. Avocations: playing piano, bike riding. Home and Office: 12274 Angel Wing Ct Reston VA 20191-1119 Fax: 703-716-4364. E-mail: jkemt@aol.com.

MADSEN, BARBARA A., state supreme court justice; b. Renton; BA, U. Wash., 1974; JD, Gonzaga U., 1977. Pub. defender King and Snohomish Counties, 1977—82; staff atty. Seattle City Atty.'s Office, 1982—84, spl. prosecutor, 1984—88; judge Seattle Mcpl. Ct., 1988—92; justice Wash. Supreme Ct., Olympia, 1993—. Chair Wash. State Gender and Justice Commn., Supreme Ct. Circulation Com., Ct. Personnel Com.; co-chair Internal Rules Com., Death Penalty Rules Com.; mem. Ct. Budget Com., Administrative Com., Reporter of Decisions Com. Active in Judges in the Classroom prog., Tacoma Public Sch. Recipient Wash. Women Lawyers Vanguard award, 1998, Wash. Women Lawyers Found. award, 2001, Presidents award, Nat. Assn. of Women Judges, 2002, Equal Justice Coalition Judicial award, 2004, Access to Justice award of distinction for public svc., 2006. Mem.: Judicature Soc., Nat. Assn. of Women Judges, Am. Judges Assn. Office: Wash Supreme Ct PO Box 40929 Olympia WA 98504-0929*

MADSEN, DOROTHY LOUISE (MEG MADSEN), writer; b. Rochester, N.Y. d. Charles Robert and Louise Anna Agnes Meyer; m. Frederick George Madsen, Feb. 17, 1945 (dec.) BA, Mundelein Coll., Chgo., 1978; grad., U.S. Army Command and Gen. Staff Coll., 1960. Feature writer Gannett Newspapers, Rochester Democrat & Chronicle, NY, 1937—41; pub. rels. rep. Rochester Tel. Corp., 1941—42; exec. dir. LaPorte chpt. ARC, Ind., 1964; dir. adminstrv. svcs. Bank Mktg. Assn., Chgo., 1971—74; exec. dir. Eleanor Women's Found., Chgo., 1974—84; founder Meg Madsen Assocs., Chgo., 1984—88, women's career counselor; founder Eleanor Women's Forum, Clearinghouse Internat., Eleanor Intern Program Coll. Students and Returning Women. Chief global radiotelephone and radioteletype top secret encrypted conf. ctr. war dept. gen. staff Pentagon, Washington, 1944—46; conf. aide to Pres. Harry S Truman, Washington, 1945. Lt. col. WAC, 1942-47, 67-70 Decorated Legion of Merit, Meritorious Svc. award Mem.: Res. Officers Assn. (life), Mundelein Alumnae Assn., Ret. Officers Assn. (life), Phi Sigma Tau (charter mem. Ill. Kappa chpt.). Achievements include Aide to Pres. Truman during Sigsaly encoded phone conf. with Prime Min. Winston Churchill and U.S. Joint Chiefs Staff concerning terms of German surrender, WWII, Apr. 25, 1945. Home and Office: 1030 N State St Apt 25H Chicago IL 60610-2831 E-mail: megmadsenchgo@aol.com.

MADSEN, KAREN F., retired elementary school educator; b. Lincoln, Nebr., July 25, 1941; d. Carl William and Marjorie (Brandt) Friendt; m. James E. Madsen, June 25, 1961; children: Deborah L., Michael C. AA, Pasadena (Calif.) City Coll., 1961; BA, Calif. State U., L.A., 1979. Cert. tchr., Calif. Elem. tchr. South Pasadena Unified Sch. Dist., Calif., 1980—2003, part-time tchr. gifted and talented, 1988—2003; ret., 2003. Producer News team, cable TV. Vol. Acad. Internat. Elem. Sch., Colorado Springs, 2003—. Recipient Hon. Svc. award, PTA, Disting Svc. award, 2003, Monterey Hills Sch. Tchr. of the Yr., (2). Mem. Internat. Reading Assn., Calif. Reading Assn., Santa Anita Reading Coun., So. Calif. Coun. Lit. Young People, East San Gabriel Valley Reading Coun., Tchrs. Assn. South Pasadena, Delta Kappa Gamma. Home: 2047 Wildwood Dr Colorado Springs CO 80918-1120

MADSEN, VIRGINIA, actress; b. Chgo., Sept. 11, 1963; m. Danny Huston, 1989 (div. 1992); 1 child. Represented by Creative Artists Agy., Beverly Hills, Calif. Actor: (films) Class, 1983, Dune, 1984, Electric Dreams, 1984, Creator, 1985, Fire with Fire, 1986, Modern Girls, 1986, Slam Dance, 1987, Zombie High, 1987, Mr. North, 1988, Hot to Trot, 1988, Heart of Dixie, 1989, The Hot Spot, 1990, Highlander II—The Quickening, 1991, Becoming Colette, 1992, Candyman, 1992, Blue Tiger, 1994, Caroline at Midnight, 1994, The Prophecy, 1995, Ghosts of Mississippi, 1996, The Rainmaker, 1997, Ambushed, 1998, Ballad of the Nightingale, 1998, The Florentine, 1998, The Haunting, 1999, After Sex, 2000, Lying in Wait, 2000, Almost Salinas, 2001, American Gun, 2002, Artworks, 2003, Tempted, 2003, Nobody Knows Anything!, 2003, Sideways, 2004 (Screen Actors Guild Award, outstanding performance by cast in motion picture, 2005), Firewall, 2006, A Prairie Home Companion, 2006; (TV films) A Matter of Principle, 1984, The Hearst and Davies Affair, 1985, Long Gone, 1987, Gotham, 1988, Third Degree Burn, 1989, Ironclads, 1991, Victim of Love, 1991, Love Kills, 1991, A Murderous Affair: The Carolyn Warmus Story, 1992, Linda, 1993, Bitter Vengeance, 1994, The Apocalypse Watch, 1997, Children of Fortune, 2000, The Inspector General, 2000, Crossfire Trail, 2001, Just Ask My Children, 2001, Tempted, 2003, Brave New Girl, 2004; (TV miniseries) Mussolini: The Untold Story, 1985; (TV series) American Dreams, 2002-03, Smith, 2006-; TV appearances include The Hitchhiker, 1987, Moonlighting, 1989, Earth 2, 1994, Star Trek: Voyager, 1998, Frasier, 1999, The Practice, 2001, (voice) Justice League, 2002, Dawson's Creek, 2003, CSI: Miami, 2003, Boomtown, 2003. Democrat.*

MADY, BEATRICE M., artist; d. Raymond J. and Beatrice A. Mady; m. David W. Cummings. Student, Bklyn. Mus. Art Sch.; BFA, U. Dayton; MFA, Pratt Inst. Asst. prof. graphic arts St. Peter's Coll., Jersey City. One-woman shows include Rockville Centre Pub. Gallery, N.Y., 1976, Jersey City Visual Art Gallery, 1988, Caldwell Coll., N.J., 1991, Johnson & Johnson Consumer Products divsn., Skillman, N.J., 1993, Rabbet Gallery, New Brunswick, N.J., 1996, Maurice M. Pine Gallery, Fair Lawn, N.J., 1997, exhibited in group shows at Newark Mus., 1982, Summit Art Ctr., N.J., 1985, Gallery Jupiter, Little Silver, N.J., 1986, Morris Mus., Morristown, N.J., 1987, Yuma Art Ctr., Ariz., 1989, Van Vorst Gallery, Jersey City, 1990, City Without Walls Gallery, Newark, 1993, 1998, Rabbet Gallery, New Brunswick, 1995, Watchung Arts Ctr., N.J., 1996, Seton Hall U. Law Sch., Newark, 1996, 2000, Merck Corp. Hdqs., White House, N.J., 1997, Ben Shahn Gallery, Wayne, N.J., 1998, Represented in permanent collections Dayton Art Inst., Ohio, Pfizer, Morris Plains, N.J., Ortho Dermatol., Skillman, Janssen Pharmaceutia, Titusville, N.J., Bristol-Meyers Squibb, Plainsboro, Lawrenceville, N.J., Johnson & Johnson, New Brunswick, Sydney & Francis Lewis Found., Richmond, Va., Drew U. Mus., Madison, N.J., Arenol Chem. Corp., N.Y.C., Goetz and Mady-Grove, Jericho, N.Y. Grantee, Ford Found., 1978; Painting fellow, Pratt Inst., Bklyn., 1977—78, N.J. State Coun. Arts, 1985, Kenny fellowship, 2004, 2006. Mem.: Coll. Art Assn., Kappa Pi.

MADZIK, ELIZABETH MAY, hospital administrator; b. St. Louis, Mo., Sept. 21, 1965; d. William J. and Nadine Madzik; children: Derek Embry, Nathaniel Embry. Student, St. Leo U., 2003—. Client liaison Receivables Mgmt., Arlington, Tex., 1996—99; denials mgmt. mgr. Presbyn. Hosp. Dallas, 1999—2005, privacy and compliance officer, 2005—. Dir. bd. dirs. HM Caps, Inc., 2004—. Author: Dark Passion Deef Reflections, Book of Poetry, 2006. Exec. bd. mem. Parkway Elem. Sch. PTA, Ft. Worth, 2000—03; mem. Am. Ex-Prisoners of War, Ft. Worth, 2001. Mem.: Health Care Compliance Assn., Healthcare Fin. Mgmt. Assn., Phi Theta Kappa. Mem. Lds Ch. Avocations: reading, exercise, poetry, dance, music. Home: 1728 Wild Willow Trail Fort Worth TX 76134 Office: THR - Presbyn Hosp Dallas 8200 Walnut Hill Ln Dallas TX 75231 Personal E-mail: madzik@sbcglobal.net. Business E-Mail: elizabethmadzik@texashealth.org.

MAEDA, J. A., data processing executive, consultant; b. Mansfield, Ohio, Aug. 24, 1940; d. James Shunso and Doris Lucille Maeda; m. Robert Lee Hayes; 1 child, Brian Sentaro Hayes. BS in Math., Purdue U., 1962, postgrad., 1962—63, Calif. State U., Northridge, 1968—75; cert. profl. designation in tech. of computer operating systems and tech. of info. processing, UCLA, 1971. Cons., rsch. asst. computer ctr. Purdue U., West Lafayette, Ind., 1962-63; computer operator, sr. tab operator, mem. faculty Calif. State U., Northridge, 1969, programmer cons., tech. asst. II, 1969-70, supr. acad. applicatons, EDP supr. II, 1970-72, project tech. support coord. programmer II, office of the chancellor, 1972-73, tech. support coord. statewide timesharing tech. support, programmer II, 1973-74, acad. coord., tech. support coord. instrn., computer cons. III, 1974-83; coord. user svcs. info. ctr., mem. tech. staff IV CADAM INC subs. Lockheed Corp., Burbank, Calif., 1983-86, coord. user svcs., tech. specialist computing dept., 1986-87; v.p., bd. dirs. Rainbow Computing, Inc., Northridge, 1976-85; dir. Aki Tech/Design, Northridge, 1976—. Mgr. mktg. thaumaturge Taro Quipu Cons., Northridge, 1987—; tech. cons. Digital Computer Cons., Chatsworth, Calif., 1988; computer tech., fin. and bus. mgmt., sys. integration, 1988—90; tech. customer software support Collection Data Sys., Westlake, Calif., 1991; sr. tech. writer info mgmt. divsn. Sterling Software, 1992—2000; sr. tech. writer, quality analyst Computer Assocs. Internat., Inc., 2000—. Author, editor more than 460 user publs., tutorials, reference manuals, user guides, CD graphics/packaging; contbr. articles and photos to profl. jours. Mem.: DECUS (ednl. spl. interest group 1977—83, ednl. steering com. RSTS/E 1979—82), SHARE, IEEE, Soc. for Tech. Comm. Avocations: photography, photojournalism, vintage automobiles.

MAEDER-CHIEN, REBECCA L., music educator; b. Warren, Pa., Feb. 17, 1964; d. Richard and Nancy Maeder; m. Dan Chien, Aug. 18, 2001. AA Humanities, Jamestown C.C., 1984; BMus. Music Edn., SUNY, Fredonia, 1989; MS Edn., Coll. of St. Rose, Albany, N.Y., 1991. Vocal music tchr K-12 South Kartright Ctrl. Sch., NY, 1988—. Mem.: N.Y. State Sch. Music Assn., Del. County Sch. Music Assn. Democrat. Presbyterian. Avocation: acting.

Home: 31 Clinton St Delhi NY 13753 Office: S Kortright Ctrl Sch 58200 State Hwy 10 South Kortright NY 13842 Office Phone: 607-538-9111. Office Fax: 607-530-9205. E-mail: rebeccamaeder@chienworks.com, rmaederchien@southkortrightcs.org.

MAEHARA, PAULETTE V., fundraising executive; b. Happy, Tex. married; 2 children. BA, U. Hawaii. Cert. Fund Raising Exec. (CFRE), Assn. Exec. (CAE). Exec. U. Hawaii Found., March of Dimes Birth Defects Found., Hawaii Chap.; v.p. devel. Project HOPE; exec. Am. Red Cross; CEO Epilepsy Found.; pres., CEO Assn. of Fundraising Profls. (AFP). Exec. com. Internat. Bur. for Epilepsy, Internat. Svc. Agencies, chair membership com.; bd. dirs. Nat. Health Coun.; mem. Assn. Com. of 100, US C. of C. Recipient Best Direct Mail Program award, Direct Mktg. Assn. of Am., 1994. Mem.: Am. Soc. of Assn. Execs. (bd. dirs. 2000—02, vice chair exec. bd. dirs. 2001, sec., treas. 2003, past chair Exec. Mgmt. Coun., bd. chair 2005—). Office: Assn of Fundraising Profls 1101 King St, Ste 700 Alexandria VA 22314 Office Phone: 703-684-0410. Office Fax: 703-684-0540.*

MAEHR, KATE, social services organization executive; m. Sam Maehr; 2 children. B, Macalester Coll.; M in Pub. Policy and Adminstrn., U. Wis. Mng. editor nonprofit lit. pub. house, Mpls.; dir., individual giving Greater Chgo. Food Depository, dir. devel., 1999—2006, exec. dir., 2006—. Named one of Chgo.'s 40 under 40 to watch, Crain's Chgo. Bus. Fellow: Leadership Greater Chgo. Office: Greater Chicago Food Depository 4100 W Ann Lurie Pl Chicago IL 60632 Office Phone: 773-247-3663.*

MAES, PETRA JIMENEZ, state supreme court justice; widowed; 4 children. BA, U. N.Mex., 1970, JD, 1973. Bar: N.Mex. 1973. Pvt. pratice law, Albuquerque, 1973-75; rep., then office mgr. No. N.Mex. Legal Svcs., 1975-81; dist. judge 1st Jud. Dist. Ct., Santa Fe, Los Alamos, 1981-98; chief judge, 1984-87, 92-95; assoc. justice N.Mex. Supreme Ct., 1998—, chief justice, 2003—04. Mem. N.Mex. Commn. on Access to Justice; mem. nat. rev. bd. U.S. Conf. Cath. Bishops. Mem.: Nat. Hispanic Bar Assn., N. Mex. Hispanic Bar Assn., N. Mex. Women's Bar Assn., N. Mex. Bar Assn. Office: Supreme Court NMex PO Box 848 Santa Fe NM 87504-0848 Office Phone: 505-827-4883.

MAFFEI, SUSAN MARTIN, artist, educator; b. Havre de Grace, Md., Apr. 7, 1947; d. Ebner Roger Martin and Alvia Mae Disbrow; m. John Maffei, Dec. 24, 1974 (dec. Nov. 27, 2000); life ptnr. Archibald O. Brennan. Commn. tapestry weaver Scheuer Tapestry Studio, NYC, 1985—87; conservator of textiles Artweave, NYC, 1988—89. Woven tapestry exhibitions, Tapestries by Susan Martin Maffei. Hancock fellow, Victorian Tapestry Workshop, Australia, 2000, Empire State Crafts Alliance grantee, NY Found. Arts, 1989. Mem.: Am. Tapestry Alliance. Independent. Office: Brennan Maffei Tapestry 77 Cooper St 3G New York NY 10034 Office Phone: 646-796-9798.

MAFFIA, ROMA, actress; b. Brooklyn, May 31, 1958; Actress: (films) Smithereens, 1982, Stuck on You!, 1984, Married to the Mob, 1988, American Blue Note, 1989, The Paper, 1994, Disclosure, 1994, Nick Of Time, 1995, Eraser, 1996, Kiss the Girls, 1997, Double Jeopardy, 1999, Things You Can Tell Just By Looking at Her, 2000, The New Women, 2001, I Am Sam, 2001, Treading Water, 2002, Holes, 2003; (TV movies) Internal Affairs, 1988, Her Deadly Rival, 1995, The Heidi Chronicles, 1995, Her Costly Affair, 1996, Mistrial, 1996, The Defenders: Payback, 1997, Route 9, 1998, The David Cassidy Story, 2000; (TV series) Chicago Hope, 1994-95, Profiler, 1996, Nip/Tuck, 2003-.

MAGANA, MELANIE G, psychologist, consultant; b. New York, NY, Feb. 21, 1954; d. Anthony Dominic Thomas Guggenheimer; m. John R Magana, Oct. 4, 2003; children: Justin Anthony Moss, Timothy Andrew Moss. MS in Sch. Psychology, Nat. U., San Diego, Calif., 1995. Lic. Psychologist Calif., 2000. Sch. psychologist Oceanside Unified Sch. Dist., Oceanside, Calif., 1996, Chino Valley Unified Sch. Dist., Chino, Calif., 1996—. Parenting instr. Chino Human Services, Chino, Calif., 2000—; cons. in trauma and loss in children. Mem.: APA (assoc.), Calif. Assn. Sch. Psychologists, Nat. Assn. Sch. Psychologists. Roman Catholic. Personal E-mail: ottermgm@sbcglobal.net.

MAGANN, JOYCE L., music educator; d. Harry Eastwood and Elsie Virginia Magann. MusB Edn. magna cum laude, Temple U., Phila., 1985; MusM Edn., VanderCook Coll. Music, Chgo., 2003. Cert. K-12 music tchr. NJ, 1985, Pa., 1985, K-12 music tchr. level 2 Pa., 2001. Music tchr. stringed instruments Atlantic City Pub. Schs., 1985—97; pvt. violin tchr. Somers Point, NJ, 1985—97; asst. musical dir. Methacton H.S., Norristown, Pa., 1997—2005, music tchr., orch. dir., 1997—. Adminstr., dir. summer music program Atlantic City Schs., 1985—97; cmty. edn. guitar instr. Methacton Sch. Dist., 2000—. Art show performer Phoenixville Soroptomists, Pa., 1999—2005. Recipient Nat. Sch. Orch. award, Wyalusing Valley Jr./Sr. H.S. Orch., 1981; Outstanding Achievement scholar, AAUW, 1981. Mem.: NEA, Pa. and Del. String Teachers Assn. (sec. 2002—06, Orch. Dir. of Yr. 2006), Am. String Teachers Assn., PA Music Educators Assn. (sec., dist. 11 2003, host, mgr. All State Orch. 2005—06, host, mgr. Dist. 11 Orch. 2005—06, host/mgr. instrumental auditions), Music Educators Nat. Conf., Sigma Alpha Iota. Avocations: biking, reading, music, travel. Office: Methacton HS 1001 Kriebel Mill Rd Norristown PA 19403 Office Phone: 610-489-5088. Personal E-mail: jlmagann@iglide.net. Business E-Mail: jmagann@methacton.org.

MAGDOSKO, PAULA, school psychologist; b. Weehawken, NJ, Mar. 21, 1958; d. Paul and Linda Magdosko. BA in Psychology, Fairleigh Dickinson U., 1981, MA in Tchg., 1994, MA in Sch. Psychology, 2002. Cert. elem. tchr. NY, NJ, sch. psychologist NJ. V.p. F.G. Distributors Inc., Teaneck, NJ, 1984—92; tchr. Paramus (NJ) Pub. Schs., 1994—2003; sch. psychologist Ridgefield Park (NJ) Pub. Schs., 2003—. Athletic scholar, Fairleigh Dickinson U., 1976—78. Mem.: NEA, APA, Ridgefield Park Edn. Assn., NJ Assn. Sch. Psychologists, NJ Edn. Assn., Nat. Assn. Sch. Psychologists. Avocations: gardening, refinishing furniture, antiques. Office: Ridgefield Park Pub Schs Office Spl Svcs 98 Central Ave Ridgefield Park NJ 07660

MAGEE, ELIZABETH SHERRARD, civic organization volunteer; b. Rock Island, Ill., Sept. 11, 1922; d. Benjamin Harrison and Helen Lucile (Williams) Sherrard; m. Harber Homer Hall, June 15, 1944 (div. 1949); 1 child, John Sherrard Hall; m. Curtis Lyness Johnson, Dec. 18, 1951 (dec. July 1957); children: Peter Hays Johnson, Julie Jaye Johnson Kimball; m. Robert Milton Magee, Sept. 21, 1963 (dec. 1988); 1 child, Robert Decker (dec. 1983). Student, Augustana Coll., Rock Island, 1940-42. Office mgr., sec. Chgo. Motor Club, Rock Island, 1942-44; personal shopper M.L. Parker Co., Davenport, Iowa, 1945-46. Mem. Jr. Bd. Rock Island, 1944—65, ARC nursing duties, Rock Island, 1971—75, Presbyn. Women Rock Island, 1960—99; clerk of session Broadway Presbyn. Ch., 1990—93, 1995—98, 2002. Recipient Disting. Alumni award, Rock Island H.S., 2005. Mem. DAR (state rec. sec. 1995-97, divsn. I dir. 1997-99, editor Biennial Procs. Ill. State Orgn. 1995-97, state vice regent 2000-02, pres. state officers club, 2002-03), Internat. Order Kings Daus. and Sons, P.E.O. Sisterhood (past pres., sec., treas.). Republican. Presbyterian. Avocations: computers, stamps, coins. Home: 17575 Warner Castle Rd Orion IL 61273-9181

MAGEE, MEGAN, elementary school educator; b. Pitts., Pa., Apr. 9, 1981; d. Robert and Geri Magee. BS in Psychology, U. Pitts., Pitts., Pa., 2002. Cert. tchr. social scis. Ga., 2003. Tchr. social studies Duluth (Ga.) Mid. Sch., 2004—. Coach 8th grade cheerleading Duluth (Ga.) Mid. Sch. Mem.: NCSS, U. Pitts. Alumni Assn., Phi Eta Sigma, Golden Key Honor Soc., Nat. Soc. Collegiate Scholars. Personal E-mail: magee_megan@hotmail.com.

MAGEE-EGAN, PAULINE CECILIA, psychology professor, management educator; b. NYC, Feb. 27, 1934; d. John Joseph and Rosina (Sweeney) Magee; m. Patrick Joseph Egan, Aug. 5, 1967; children: Anne, Patrick, Deirdre, John. BS, Fordham U., 1956, MS, 1957, PhD, 1963. Cert. psychologist, N.Y. Rsch. asst. Fordham U., N.Y.C., 1956-58; asst. dir. Bur. Testing and Guidance St. John's U., Jamaica, N.Y., 1958-62, asst. prof. psychology, 1962-78, assoc. prof. mgmt., 1978-98, prof., 1998—, assoc. dean external rels. Coll. Bus. Adminstrn., 1997-2000, pres. faculty assn., 2001—. Cons. in field, 1962—. Contbr. articles to profl. publs. Bd. dirs. Winston Pres. Sch., N.Y.C., 1989—, St. Vincent's Hosp., Harrison, N.Y. Mem. APA, N.Y. State Psychol. Assn. (past pres. pers., indsl. and orgnl. div.). Avocations: gourmet cooking, trap shooting, tennis. Home: 321 Avenue C New York NY 10009-1628 Personal E-mail: eganpm@pipeline.com. Business E-Mail: mageeep@stjohns.edu.

MAGERKO, MARGARET HARDY (MAGGIE MAGERKO), lumber company executive; b. Pitts., Dec. 7, 1965; d. Joseph Hardy; m. Peter Magerko. Student, W.Va. U. Pres. Nemacolin Woodlands Resort & Spa, 1987—, 84 Lumber Co., Eighty Four, Pa., 1994—. Named one of 400 Richest Ams., Forbes mag., 2006. Office: 84 Lumber Co 1019 Route 519 Eighty Four PA 15330 Business E-Mail: magerkom@84lumber.com.

MAGGIOLO, PAULETTE BLANCHE, writer; b. Ballon, France, Mar. 2, 1922; d. Fernand Epinal and Blanche Audineau; m. Anthony Maggiolo, Dec. 29, 1946 (dec. Sept. 1982); children: Denise, Daniel, Annette. MA Columbia U., 1966; D Fgn. Lang.s, Middlebury U., 1972. Tchr. French lit. Lycee of Le Mans, France, 1942—45; head fgn. lang. dept. Leonia H.S., NJ, 1955—88; tchr. French Lord Fairfax C.C., Middletown, Va., 1990—97. Author: The Guilty Teacher, 1999. Home: 207 S Church St Woodstock VA 22664

MAGGIONI, ANDREA, pediatrician; b. Rome, Jan. 9, 1965; came to U.S., 1992; d. Giorgio Maggioni and Luisa Guarneri; m. Gallarello Francesca; children: Luisa, Alessandra. MD, U. La Sapienza, Rome, 1989, PhD in Pediatric Nutrition, 1994. Diplomate Am. Bd. Pediatrics. Resident in pediats. U. Rome, 1989-92, Maimonides Med. Ctr., Bklyn., 1994-96, chief inpatient svcs., 1996-97; dir. inpatient svcs. Miami (Fla.) Children's Hosp., 1997—; asst. prof. pediatrics SUNY Health Sci. Ctr., Bklyn. Assoc. editor jour. Internat. Pediats., 1997—; contbr. articles to profl. jours. Fellow Am. Coll. Nutrition, Am. Acad. Pediatrics; mem. AMA. Office: Miami Children's Hosp 3100 SW 62d Ave Miami FL 33155 Home: 11100 Paradela St Coral Gables FL 33156-4257 E-mail: andrea.maggioni@mch.com.

MAGILL, M(ARY) ELIZABETH, law educator; b. Fargo, ND; m. Leon Francis Szeptycki; children: Alexander Magill Szeptycki, Claire Magill Szeptycki. BA in History, Yale Coll., New Haven, 1988; JD, U. Va. Sch. Law, Charlottesville, 1995. Bar: Md. 1997. Legis. asst. for energy & natural resources US Senator Kent Conrad, Washington, 1988—92; summer assoc. Covington & Burling, Washington, 1994; law clk. to Hon. J. Harvie Wilkinson III US Ct. Appeals 4th Cir., 1995—96; law clk. to Hon. Ruth Bader Ginsburg US Supreme Ct., Washington, 1996—97; assoc. prof. U. Va. Sch. Law, Charlottesville, 1997—2002, prof., 2002—, John V. Ray rsch. prof., 2003—. Mem.: ABA (vice-chair jud. rev. subcom., assoc. reporter Adminstrv. Procedure Act Project). Office: U Va Sch Law 580 Massie Rd Charlottesville VA 22903-1789 Office Phone: 434-924-3898. E-mail: mem2a@virginia.edu.

MAGLIO, GESOMINA V., clinical social worker; MSW, Fordham U., 1982, PhD in Social Welfare, 1995. Diplomate Am. Bd. Examiners in Clin. Social Work. Clin. social worker, psychotherapist, N.J., 1984—; pvt. practice, Peapack, NJ, 1984—; pres. Soft Sci. Inc., Far Hill, NJ, 2000. Adj. prof. Coll. of St. Elizabeth, Convent Station, N.J., 1996; pres. G.V. Mgmt. Cons., LLC, 2005— Fellow Am. Orthopsychiat. Assn.; mem. NASW, Acad. Cert. Social Works, N.Y. State Soc. Clin. Social Workers, Nat. Registry Health Care Providers in Clin. Social Work. Office Phone: 908-781-0864.

MAGLIONE, LILI, artist, consultant; b. Manhasset, N.Y., Jan. 30, 1929; d. Angelo and Mary (Marciano) M.; m. Bernhart H. Rumphorst, June 1, 1957; children: Catherine, Douglas. AD, Traphagen Sch., N.Y.C., 1950; student, Art Students League, N.Y.C., 1950-52. Fashion artist Butterick Pattern Co., N.Y.C., 1952-53; fashion art cons. Miss. America Inc., N.Y.C., 1953-54; dept. head fashion art office Simplicity Pattern Co., N.Y.C., 1953-58, fashion art cons., 1958-62; art dept. cons. Nassau County Mus., Roslyn, N.Y., 1984-86; dir. decorative affairs Harbor Acres Assn., Port Washington, N.Y., 1987-89, Sands Point (N.Y.) Mus., 1989-91; art cons. Horst Design Assocs., Huntington, N.Y., 1992—. One-woman shows include Palm Gallery, Southampton, N.Y., 1980, Art Internat., Chgo., 1985, Isis Gallery, Port Washington, 1987, Gallery 84, N.Y.C., 1989, 1991, 1993; artist (one-woman retrospective shows include) Harkness Gallery, 1978, James Hunt Barker Gallery, 1984, Sands Point Mus., 1988, Fairfield U., 1995; exhibitions include Nat. Arts Club, N.Y.C., 1997; contbr. poetry Nat. Libr. Poets, 1997, Artists Mag., 1998, Am. Artist Mag., 1999, Internat. Artist Mag., 2002 (Master Painters of the World, 2002). Hon. trustee Parents TV Coun., 2000—. Recipient Winner Art Expo 98, B.J. Spoke Gallery, N.Y.C., 1998, Manhattan Arts Internat. Critics Choice award, 1998, Artists Mag. Ann. Competition finalist, 2001, Liquetex Purchase award, 1998, Amsterdam award of excellence, 1998, award for acrylic painting, Nat. Arts Club, N.Y.C., 1998, Art Calendar Centerfold award, 1998, award of merit, Allied Artists of Am., 1999, cert. of merit, Art Calendar mag., 1999, Award of Excellence, Manhattan Arts Internat., 2000, award, Nat. Assn. Women Artists, 2000, Meml. award, Pen and Brush N.Y.C., 2003, Am. Artists Profl. League award, 2004, Ann. award, Artists Mag., 2005, Meml. award, Nat. Arts Club N.Y.C., 2005. Mem.: Nat. Soc. Painters in Acrylic and Casein (Meml. award 2001, best in show award Pen and Brush 2001, finalist Artists Mag. ann. competition 2001, award 2004), Portrait Soc. Am. Inc. (Artists Mag. Annual award 2005), Internat. Soc. Poets, Nat. Mus. Women in the Arts (Nat. City Club NYC Meml. award 2005), Nat. Assn. Women Artists (Meml. award 2001, Salmagundi Meml. award 2001). Roman Catholic. Avocations: horticulture, flower arrangement, nutrition, music, child care. Home: 8 Saw Mill Ln Cold Spring Harbor NY 11724 Office Phone: 631-692-9363. Personal E-mail: maglione@optonline.net.

MAGNABOSCO-BOWER, JENNIFER LYNN, mental health services professional; b. Champaign, Ill., Aug. 14, 1963; d. Peter Thomas and Gail Gwendolyn Magnabosco; m. Anthony G. Bower, July 12, 1997. BA, MA, U. Chgo., 1985; MPhil, Columbia U., 1995, PhD, 2001. Staff therapist Postgrad. Ctr. for Mental Health, N.Y.C., 1988-90; rsch. assoc. Grad. Sch. Bus. Decision Rsch. Lab., U. Chgo., 1985—86, 1993—94, Ctr. for Psychiat. Rehab., U. Chgo., 1994; adminstr., rsch. assoc. Ctr. for the Study of Social Work Practice, N.Y.C., 1991-92, project mgr., 1995-96, dir. adminstrn. and ops., 1994-97; mental health cons. Wayne, Pa., Redwood City and L.A., Calif., 1998—2000; assoc. policy rschr. RAND, Santa Monica, Calif., 2001—. Ad hoc tech. rev. com. Dept. of Health and Human Svcs., Substance Abuse and Mental Health Svcs. Adminstrn., Ctr. for Mental Health Svcs., Rockville, 1997-99. Author, co-editor: Outcomes Measurement in the Human Services: Cross Cutting Issues and Methods (NASW Press Best Seller 1997-98); co-author: Cultural Contingencies: Behavior Analytic Perspectives, 1997; manuscript reviewer Jour. Behavioral Health Svcs. and Rsch., 2001—; book reviewer Adminstn. in Social Work, 2001—. Mem. AAAS, Am. Psychol. Assn., Am. Pub. Health Assn., U. Chgo. Alumni Assn. (bd. govs., v.p., Young Alumni Citation 1997, Vol. Leadership All Univ. award). Democrat. Avocations: tennis, piano playing, doll and fan collecting, fund-raising, history ancient civilizations. Office: 1700 Main St PO Box 2138 Santa Monica CA 90407-2138 Home: 807 18th St Apt 4 Santa Monica CA 90403-1950

MAGNAN, RUTHANN, nurse, social worker; b. Camden, N.J., July 6, 1953; d. Kenneth Clifford and Mary (Gilbert) Hall; m. Frank W. Magnan, Dec. 21, 1974; children: Robert, Michele, Johnathan. LPN, Cumberland County Vocat.-Tech.; AAS in Nursing, Regents U., 1997. Cert. social worker, N.J. Nurse Newcomb Hosp., Vineland, N.J., 1982-89, Bridgeton (N.J.) Nursing Ctr., 1989-95, 98—, asst. adminstr., 1993-95; nurse So. State Prison, Delmont, N.J., 1996-98. Avocations: bowling, gardening. Home: 319 Buck Rd Glassboro NJ 08028-3307

MAGNAN, SARAH E., court reporter; d. Henry Joseph and Loretta Agnes Magnan; m. Tommy Bentley. AS, Champion Coll., Burlington, Vt., 1986. Court reporter State of N.H., Manchester, 1987—93, Lyon Reporting, Inc., Atlanta, 1993—. Mem.: Nat. Ct. Reporters Assn. Home: 4515 Otha Way Lilburn GA 30047 Office Phone: 770-458-5500. E-mail: slmagnan@aol.com.

MAGNER, MARJORIE, former bank executive; b. Bklyn. BS in Psychology, Brooklyn Coll., NY, 1968; MS, Purdue U., 1974; D of Mgmt. (hon.), Purdue University, 2004. Mng. dir. Chem. Tech. Divsn. Chemical Bank; from mem. staff Commercial Credit to chmn., CEO Citigroup, NYC, 1987—2003, chmn., CEO Global Consumer Group, 2003—05. Bd. dirs. Gannett Co., 2006—, The Charles Schwab Corp., 2006—, Accenture, 2006—; chmn. bd. trustees Bklyn. Coll. Found.; mem. dean's adv. coun. Krannert Sch. Mgmt. Purdue U. Bd. dirs. Welfare to Work Partnership, Dress for Success Worldwide, Port Discovery Children's Mus., Balt., Md. Bus. Roundtable Edn. Named One of 50 Most Powerful Women in Am. Bus., Fortune mag., 2001, 2002, 2003, 2004, One of 25 Most Power Women in Banking, US Banker mag., 2003, 2004, 2005; named one of Most Powerful women, Forbes mag., 2005; recipient Am. Found. for the Blind Helen Keller Achievement award, 2001.*

MAGNESS, RHONDA ANN, retired microbiologist; b. Stockton, Calif., Jan. 30, 1946; d. John Pershing and Dorothy Waneta (Kelley) Wetter; m. Barney LeRoy Bender, Aug. 26, 1965 (div. Jan. 1977); m. Gary D. Magness, Mar. 5, 1977; children: Jay D.(dec.), Troy D. BS, Calif. State U., Sacramento, 1977. Med. asst. C. Fred Wilcox, MD, Stockton, 1965-66; clk. typist Dept. of U.S. Army, Ft. Eustis, Va., 1967, Def. Supply Agy., New Orleans, 1967-68; med. asst. James G. Cross, MD, Lodi, Calif., 1969, Arthur A. Kemalyan, MD, Lodi, 1969-71, 72-77; med. sec. Lodi Meml. Hosp., 1972; lab. aide Calif. State U., Sacramento, 1977; phlebotomist St. Joseph's Hosp., Stockton, 1978-79; microbiologist Dameron Hosp. Assn., Stockton, 1980—2004. Active Concerned Women Am., Washington, 1987—. Mem.: San Joaquin County Med. Assts. Assn., Calif. Assn. Clin. Lab. Technologists, Nat. Audubon Soc., Nat. Geog. Soc., Jobs Daus. (chaplain 1962—63). Baptist. Avocations: birdwatching, sewing, reading. Home: 9627 Knight Ln Stockton CA 95209-1961

MAGNUSON, KAREN M., editor; m. Tod Myers. City editor Sturgis (Mich.) Daily News; writer, bur. mgr. UP Internat., Ill., Iowa, Utah and Calif.; various mgmt. positions Daily News, L.A.; editor Oxnard (Calif.) Press-Courier, Calif.; mng. editor Valley Times, Pleasanton, Calif., 1994—97, Wichita (Kans.) Eagle, 1997—99, Rochester (NY) Dem. and Chronicle, 1999—2001, editor, v.p. news, 2001—. Mem.: AP Mng. Editors (vice chmn. journalism studies 2002—). Office: Rochester Dem and Chronicle 55 Exchange Blvd Rochester NY 14614-2001

MAGNUSON, NANCY, librarian; b. Seattle, Aug. 15, 1944; d. James Leslie and Jeanette (Thomas) M.; 2 sons, Daniel Johnson, Erik Johnson. BA in History, 1977; MLS, U. Wash., 1978. With. King County Libr. System, Seattle, 1973-80; rsch. asst. Free Libr. Phila., 1980-81; asst. libr. Haverford (Pa.) Coll., 1981-87; libr. dir. Goucher Coll., Balt., Md., 1987—. Contbr. to profl. publs. Mem. ALA (com. on status of women in librarianship, various others), Online Computer Libr. Ctr. Users Coun., Md. Libr. Assn., Congress Acad. Libr. Dirs., NOW, Women's Internat. League for Peace and Freedom, Balt. Bibliophiles, Jane Austen Soc. N.Am. Democrat. Office: Goucher Coll Julia Rogers Libr 1021 Dulaney Valley Rd Baltimore MD 21204-2753

MAGOON, NANCY AMELIA, art association administrator; b. N.Y.C., Apr. 19, 1941; d. Jack and Norma Harriet (Hirschl) Parker; m. Robert Cornelius Magoon, Mar. 16, 1978; children: Adam Glick, Peri Curnin. Student, Cornell U., 1958-59. Gallerist Hokin Gallery, Miami, 1986-89; sec. Nat. Found. Advancement in Arts, 1989-94; nat. coun. mem. Aspen Art Mus., 1985—, Aspen Ballet, 1985—. V.p. Ctr. for Fine Arts, Miami, 1984-94, Miami City Ballet, 1990-94. Bd. dirs. Cmty. Alliance Against AIDS, 1990-92; coun. mem. Susan Komen Breast Cancer, Aspen, 1994—; hon. trustee Ctr. for Fine Arts, Miami Beach, 1996; trustee Site Santa Fe, 1996; mem. nat. coun. Jazz Aspen, 1999—; mem. collectors com. Nat. Gallery, Washington, 2000; bd. dirs. Aspen Cmty. Found., 2000; nat. coun Whitney Mus, 2003-, Fulbright Knox Mus., 2005-. Named one of Outstanding Women in Miami, 1992; NEA grantee, 1995. Avocations: skiing, golf, fly fishing, skeet and clay target shooting.

MAGOULICK, MARY, literature and language professor; b. Livonia, Mich., May 25, 1961; d. John David and Pauline Mary Magoulick. BA, U. Mich., Dearborn, 1983; MA, U. Va., Charlottesville, 1986; PhD, Ind. U., Bloomington, 2000. Assoc. prof. Ga. Coll. & State U., Milledgeville, 2000—. Vis. prof. Semester at Sea, 2005, Fulbright, Rijeka, Croatia, 2006. Contbr. articles to profl. jours. Peace corps vol. US Peace Corps, Senegal, 1986—88. Fulbright grantee, State Dept., 2006. Mem.: AAUW (membership v.p. 2005—06), S. Atlantic MLA (sect. chair 2003—04), Soc. Study Indigenous Langs. Am., Assn. Study Am. Indian Lit., Am. Folklore Soc. (assoc.; ann. meeting com. 2004—05). Democrat. Avocations: yoga, travel, reading, cooking. Office: Ga Coll Engish Dept CBX 044 Milledgeville GA 31061 Office Phone: 478-445-3177. Office Fax: 478-445-5961. Personal E-mail: magoulick@yahoo.com.

MAGRATH, JANE, music educator; b. Conway, S.C., Dec. 27, 1949; MusB, Wesleyan Coll., 1972; MusM, U. N.C., 1974; MusD, Northwestern U., 1982. Prof. U. Okla., Norman, 1981—; author, editor Alfred Pub., Inc., Van Nuys, Calif., 1985—. Lectr. in field. Author: Pianist's Guide to Standard Literature, 1995; editor (music series) Masterwork Classics, 1988, 89, 92, 2000, Encore, 1990; editl. bd. Piano Forum; Technical Skills, 1992, Masterpieces with Flair, 1993, Melodious Masterpieces, 1993, Modern Masterworks, 1999, Classics Alive, 2003. Office: Univ Okla Sch Music 500 W Boyd St Norman OK 73019-2070 Business E-Mail: jmagrath@ou.edu.

MAGRATH, KATHLEEN BARRY, retired municipal official; b. Raymond, Neb., Aug. 10, 1930; d. Leo D. Barry and Eileen K. Larkin; m. Frank J. Magrath, June 6, 1953 (dec. Dec. 13, 1992); children: Maureen, Teresa, Patricia, Timothy, Cecilia, Mary Kathleen. BS in Chemistry, Mt. Marty Coll., Yankton, S.D., 1952; MPA, Nova Southeastern U., Ft. Lauderdale, Fla., 1978, D in Pub. Adminstrn., 1979. Cert. med. technologist S.D., 1952. Med. technologist St. Catherine Hosp., McCook, Nebr., 1952—53, St. Joseph's Hosp., South Bend, Ind., 1953—54; adminstrv. asst. Dade County Sch. Bd., Miami, Fla., 1974—84; dir. child care ctr. Riviera Presbyn. Ch., Miami, 1980—82; mem. and vice chair Dade County Sch. Bd., Miami, 1984—86; coord. portfolio program Barry U., Miami, 1987—92, adj. prof. orgnl. comms., 1987—89. Founding mem. Greater Miami Urban League Fair Housing Group, 1966—70; mem. Dade County Cmty. Rels. Bd., Miami, 1983—90; dir. Fla. Sch. Bds. Assn., Talahassee, 1985—86; mem. Dade County Property Adjustment Bd., Miami, 1986. Contbr. book reviews to Miami Herald, 1966—68; poet:. Mem. Archdiocese of Miami Synod, 1986—89; mem. local and state bds. PTA, 1970—74; vol. Fairchild Tropical Bot. Gardens, 1998—. Recipient Svc. award, Music Edn. Dade County Schs., 1985, Outstanding Svc. to Edn., Kappa Delta Pi, 1985, Recognition cert., Fla. Women's Hall of Fame, 1986, Women Helping Women cert. of Appreciation, Soroptimist Internat. of the Ams., 1991, Vol. of Yr., Homestead Mid. Sch., 2002—03. Democrat. Roman Catholic. Avocations: watercolor, drawing, volunteering, reading. Home: 7730 SW 134th St Miami FL 33156 E-mail: KBM810@aol.com.

MAGRILL, ROSE MARY, library director; b. Marshall, Tex., June 8, 1939; d. Joe Richard and Mary Belle (Chadwick) M. BS, East Tex. State U., 1960, MA, 1961; MS, U. Ill., 1964, PhD, 1969. Asst. to dean women E. Tex. State U., Commerce, 1960-61, librarian II, 1961-63; teaching asst. U. Ill., Urbana, 1963-64; instr. to asst. prof. E. Tex. State U., Commerce, 1964-67; asst. prof. Ball State U., Muncie, 1969-70; asst. prof. to prof. U. Mich., Ann Arbor, 1970-81; prof. U. N. Tex., Denton, 1981-99; dir. libr. E. Tex. Bapt. U., Marshall, 1987-2001. Accreditation site visitor ALA, Chgo., 1975—; cons. in field. Co-author: Building Library Collections, 4th edit. 1974, Library Technical Services, 1977, Building Library Collections, 5th edit. 1979, Acquisition Management and Collection Development in Libraries, 2d edit. 1989; author: Family of Faith, 1998. Trustee Memphis Theol. Sem., 1988-98; treas. Mission Synod of Cumberland Presbyn. Ch., 1989—; mem. bd. fin. Trinity Presbytery, 1989—98; sec.-treas. Harrison County Hist. Commn., 1995—; trustee Hist. Found., 1999—; sec. Nat. Conv. Cumberland Presbyn. Women, 2000-02, chmn. bd., 2003—05, sec., 2005—. Recipient award Cumberland Presbyn. History, 1995. Mem. ALA (RTSD Resources Sect. pub. award 1978), Tex. Libr. Assn., Presbyn. Hist. Soc. of S.W. (bd. dirs. 2000—, sec. 2005—), Marshall (Tex.) Regional Med. Ctr. Aux. (treas. 2004—). Home: 203 Pitts ave Marshall TX 75672-4719

MAGSIG, JUDITH ANNE, retired primary school educator; b. Saginaw, Mich., Nov. 9, 1939; d. Harold Howard and Catherine Louise (Barstow) Gay; m. George Arthur Magsig, June 22, 1963; children: Amy Catherine, Karl Joseph. BA, Alma Coll., 1961. Cert. tchr., early childhood tchr., Mich. 1st grade tchr. Gaylord (Mich.) Schs., 1961-64, spl. edn. tchr., 1965-67, kindergarten tchr., 1968-99; violin tchr. Concord Acad. Antrim, Mancelona, Mich., 2003—04. Instr. Suzuki violin method; second violinist Traverse (Mich.) Symphony Orch., 1985-92, Cadillac (Mich.) Symphony Orch., 1999-2000, Gaylord Chamber Orch., 2001—, Great Lakes Chamber Orch., 2001—. Mem.: NEA, ASCD, Music Tchrs. Nat. Assn., Am. String Tchrs. Assn., Suzuki Assn. Am., Assn. for Childhood Edn. Internat., Assn. for Edn. of Young Children, Gaylord Edn. Assn. (historian 1997—99), Spirits of the North, Order Ea. Star (chaplain 1997—98, warder 1999—2000, electa 2000—), Alpha Delta Kappa (pres. Beta Rho chpt. 1980—82, 1984—86, treas. 1996—2000, music chmn. Mich., v.p. Beta Rho chpt. 2000—02, pres. 2002—04). Methodist. Avocations: cross-stitch, camping, canoeing, sewing. Home: 2130 Evergreen Dr Gaylord MI 49735-9165 Office: Musik Haus 2300 S Otsego Ave Gaylord MI 49735-1869 Office Phone: 989-731-2842. Business E-Mail: gjmagsig@avci.net.

MAGSINO, MARISSA ESTIVA, internist, pediatrician; b. San Pablo, Laguna, The Philippines, Oct. 5, 1961; came to U.S., 1990; d. Rodelo Estiva and Mercy Balandan; m. Winston Q. Magsino, July 27, 1990; children: Ryan, Eryn. BS in Zoology, U. Philippines, Quezon City, 1982; MD, U. of East Ramon Magsaysay, Quezon City, 1986. Diplomate Am. Bd. Internal Medicine, bd. eligible Am. Bd. Pediat. Resident in medicine and pediat. U. Medicine and Dentistry N.J., Newark, 1992-97; pvt. practice, Orlando, Fla., 1997—. Internist, mem. active staff Orlando Regional Hosp., 1997—, Fla. Hosp., Orlando, 1997—; pediatrician, mem. active staff Health Ctrl. Hosp., Orlando, 1997—; med. dir. Bestchoice. Mem.: Am. Home Care Physicians, Philippine-Am. Med. Soc. Ctrl. Fla. Achievements include research in geriatric medicine and women's health. Office: Ste 7425 Conroy-Windermere Rd Orlando FL 32835 Home: 9073 Heritage Bay Cir Orlando FL 32836-5063

MAGUIRE, CHARLOTTE EDWARDS, retired pediatrician; b. Richmond, Ind., Sept. 1, 1918; d. Joel Blaine and Lydia (Betscher) Edwards; m. Raymer Francis Maguire, Sept. 1, 1948 (dec.); children: Barbara, Thomas Clair II (dec.). Student, Stetson U., 1936—38, U. Wichita, 1938—39; BS, Memphis Tchrs. Coll., 1940; MD, U. Ark., 1944; LHD (hon.), Fla. State U., 2002. Intern, resident Orange Meml. Hosp., Orlando, Fla., 1944—46, med. staff., 1944—69, instr. nurses, 1947—57; resident Bellevue Hosp. and Med. Ctr., NYU, NYC, 1954—55; staff mem. Fla. Santarium and Hosp., Orlando, 1946—56, Holiday House and Hosp., Orlando, 1950—62; mem. courtesy and cons. staff West Orange Meml. Hosp., Winter Garden, Fla., 1952—67; active staff, chief dept. pediat. Mercy Hosp., Orlando, 1965—68; med. dir. childrens med. svcs., asst. sec. Fla. Dept. Health and Rehab. Svcs., 1969—71, med. dir. med. svcs. and basic care, 1975—84; med. exec. dir., med. svcs. divsn. worker's compensation Fla. Dept. Labor, Tallahassee, 1984—87; chief of staff physicians and dentists Ctrl. Fla. divsn. Children's Home Soc. Fla., 1947—56; dir. Orlando Child Health Clinic, 1949—58; pvt. practice Orlando, 1946—68; asst. regional dir. HEW, 1970—72; ret., 1987. Asst. dir. health and sci. affairs Dept. Health Edn. & Welfare, Atlanta, 1971-72, Washington, 1972-75; pediat. cons. Fla. Crippled Children's Commn., 1952-70, dir., 1968-70; med. dir. Office Med. Svcs. and Basic Care, sr. physician Office of Asst. Sec. Ops., Fla. Dept. Health and Rehab. Svcs.; clin. prof. dept. pediat. U. Fla. Coll. Medicine, Gainesville, 1980-87; mem. Fla. Drug Utilization Rev., 1983-87; real estate salesperson Investors Realty, 1982-2003; bd. dirs. Stavros Econ. Ctr. Fla. State U., Tallahassee; pres.'s coun. Fla. State U., U. Fla., Gainesville; Charlotte Edwards Maguire eminent scholar chair and scholarships for qualified students, 1999. Mem. profl. adv. com. Fla. Ctr. for Clin. Svcs. at U. Fla., 1952-60; del. to Mid-century White House Conf. on Children and Youth, 1950; U.S. del from Nat. Soc. for Crippled Children to World Congress for Welfare of Cripples, Inc., London, 1957; pres. of corp. Eccleston-Callahan Hosp. for Colored Crippled Children, 1956-58; sec. Fla. chpt. Nat. Doctor's Com. for Improved Med. Svcs., 1951-52; med. adv. com. Gateway Sch. for Mentally Retarded, 1959-62; bd. dirs. Forest Park Sch. for Spl. Edn. Crippled Children, 1949-54, mem. med. adv. com., 1955-68, chmn., 1957-68; mem. Fla. Adv. Coun. for Mentally Retarded, 1965-70; dir. ctrl. Fla. poison control Orange Meml. Hosp.; mem. orgn. com., chmn. com. for admissions and selection policies Camp Challenge; participant 12th session Fed. Exec. Inst., 1971; del. White House Conf. on Aging, 1980; dir. Stavros Econ. Ctr. Fla. State U.; trustee Fla. State U. Found., 1998—, mem. campaign com. Charlotte Edwards Maguire Eminent Scholarship named in her honor Fla. State U., Charlotte Edwards Maguire MLS Med. Libr., Fla. State U. Coll. Medicine named in her honor, 2005; named Outstanding Woman in Our Cmty. AAUW, Tallahassee, 2002; recipient David M. Solomon Disting. Pub. Svc. award Am. Geriatric Soc., 2005, Torch award Fla. State U., 2005. Mem. AMA (life), Nat. Rehab. Assn., Am. Congress Phys. Medicine and Rehab., Fla. Soc. Crippled Children and Adults, Ctrl. Fla. Soc. Crippled Children and Adults (dir. 1949-58, pres. 1956-57), Am. Assn. Cleft Palate, Fla. Soc. Crippled Children (trustee 1951-57, v.p. 1956-57, profl. adv. com. 1957-68), Mental Health Assn. Orange County (charter mem.; pres. 1949-50, dir. 1947-52, chmn. exec. com. 1950-52, dir. 1963-65), Fla. Orange County Heart Assn., Am. Med. Women's Assn., Am. Acad. Med. Dirs., Fla. Med. Assn. (life, chmn. com. on mental retardation), Orange County Med. Assn., Orange Med. Soc. (life), Fla. Pediat. Soc. (pres. 1952-53), Fla. Cleft Palate Assn. (counselor-at-large, sec.), Nat. Inst. Geneal. Rsch., Nat. Geneal. Soc., Assn. Profl. Genealogists, Tallahassee Geneal. Soc., Fla. State U. Found. Inc. (bd. dirs. Stavoris Ctr. for Econ. Edn.), Capital City Tiger Bay Club, Fla. Econs. Club, Francis Eppes Soc. Fla. State U., Econ. Club Fla., Governors Club. Home: 4158 Covenant Ln Tallahassee FL 32308-5765

MAGUIRE, DEIRDRE, federal community development management analyst; b. Bklyn., Oct. 21, 1954; d. James Michael and Dorothy Ursula (Gronske) Maguire; m. Nicholas A. Zinni, Aug. 27, 1977, now div.; 1 child, Miles Angelo. BA with honors, SUNY, Stony Brook, 1976; MSP, Fla. State U., 1981. Housing specialist Suffolk Community Devel. Corp., Coram, N.Y., 1977-78; planner Palm Beach County Housing and Community Devel., West Palm Beach, Fla., 1980-83, sr. planner, 1983-84, mgr. adminstrn. and ops., 1984-87; fed. community planning and devel. rep. HUD, Jacksonville, Fla., 1987-88, community planning and devel. specialist, Entitlement Cmtys. Divsn. Washington, 1988-91, asst. dir. entitlement communities, 1991-94, dir. entitlement communities divsn., 1994-99, mgmt. analyst office of CFO, 1999—2001; sr. mgmt. analyst Office of Cmty. Planning and Devel. Dep. Asst. Sec. for Ops., 2001—. Staff liaison Affordable Housing Task Force, West Palm Beach, 1985-86, Fla. Community Devel. Assn., 1985-87; agy. rep. task force fed. gov. e-grants initiative, 2006-. Democrat. Roman Catholic. Avocations: reading, sewing. Office Phone: 202-708-0614 4529. Business E-Mail: Deirdre_Maguire@hud.gov.

MAGUIRE, JOANNE M., aerospace transportation executive; BS, Mich. State Univ.; MS, UCLA. Positions with TRW Space & Electronics, 1975—2003, prog. mgr. Defense Support, dep. gen. mgr. Defense Systems div., v.p., gen. mgr. Space & Tech. div., v.p., gen. mgr. Space & Laser Programs div., v.p., dep. bus. develop.; v.p., deputy Space Systems Co. Lockheed Martin Corp., Bethesda, Md., 2003—06, exec. v.p. Space Systems Co., 2006—. Bd. dir. Space Found., INROADS Inc. Named one of Most Powerful Women in Bus., Fortune mag., 2006; recipient Outstanding Leadership award, Women in Aerospace, 1999. Mem.: AIAA, Soc. Women Engineers. Office: Lockheed Martin Corp 6801 Rockledge Dr Bethesda MD 20817*

MAGUIRE, MARGARET LOUISE, lawyer; b. Bklyn., Oct. 31, 1944; d. William L. and Elizabeth L. (Steinbugler) M.; 1 child, William Egginton. BA, Marymount Coll., 1965; MA, Colgate U., 1969; JD, U. Louisville, 1977. Bar: Ky. 1977, D.C. 1987. Counsel 1st Ky. Nat. Corp., Louisville, 1977-79; atty. Fed. Res. Bd., Washington, 1979-80; dep. to chmn. FDIC, Washington, 1980-86; atty., cons. The Secura Group, Washington, 1986—. Co-author: Bank Holding Companies: A Practical Guide to Bank Acquisitions and Mergers, 1978-79. Office: The Secura Group Ste 950 1921 Gallows Rd Vienna VA 22182

MAGUIRE, MARTIE (MARTHA ELENOR ERWIN MAGUIRE), musician; b. York, Pa., Oct. 12, 1969; d. Paul and Barbara Erwin; m. Ted Seidel, 1995 (div.); m. Gareth MacGuire, Aug. 10, 2001. Student, So. Meth. U. Performer Blue Night Express, 1984—89; fiddle player, violinist, vocalist Dixie Chicks, 1989—. Musician: (albums) Thank Heavens for Dale Evans, 1990, LIttle Ol' Cowgirl, 1992, Shouldn't a Told You That, 1993, Wide Open Spaces, 1998 (Album of Yr., Acad. Country Music, 1998, Best Country Album, Grammy Awards, 1998, Best Country Artist Clip of Yr., Billboard Awards, 1998, Maximum Vision Clif of Yr., Billboard Awards, 1998, Best Selling Album, Can. Country Music Award, 1999, Song of Yr. (Country), WB Radio Music Awards, 1999, Album of Yr., Acad. Country Music, 1999), Fly, 1999 (Best Country Album, Grammy Awards, 1999, Best Selling Album, Can. Country Music Awards, 2000, Internat. Album, British Country Music Awards, 2000, Country Album of Yr., Billboard Awards, 2000, Album of Yr., Acad. Country Music, 2000, Album of Yr., CMA, 2000), Home, 2002 (Favorite Country Album, Am. Music Awards, 2002, Best Recording Package, Grammy Awards, 2002, Best Country Album, Grammy Awards, 2002), Top of the World Tour: Live, 2003 (Grammy award for Best Country Group Vocal Performance, 2005), Taking the Long Way, 2006; performer: (documentary) Dixie Chicks: Shut Up and Sing, 2006. Named Top New Country Artist, Billboard, 1998, Most Significant New Country Act, Country Monitor, 1998, Group of Yr., CMA, 1998, Top Vocal Group, Acad. Country Music, 1998, Internat. Rising Star, British Country Music Awards, 1999, Country Artist of Yr., Rolling Stone, 1999, Artist of Yr. (Country), WB Radio Music Awards, 1999, Favorite New Artist (Country), AMA, 1999, Vocal Group of Yr., CMA, 1999, Country Artist of Yr., Billboard, 1999, 2000, Vocal Group of Yr., CMA, 2000, Entertainer of Yr., 2000, ACM, 2000, 2001, Vocal Group of Yr., 2001, Favorite Musical Group or Band, People's Choice Awards, 2001, Favorite Country Band, Am. Music Award, 2002, Vocal Group of Yr., Country Music Assn. Award, 2002, Country Duo/Group of Yr., Billboard, 2002; named one of 100 Most Influential People, Time Mag., 2006; recipient Horizon award, CMA, 1998, others. Office: Monument Sony Nashville 34 Music Sq East Nashville TN 37203*

MAGUIRE, MILDRED MAY, chemistry professor, researcher; b. Leetsdale, Pa., May 7, 1933; d. John and Mildred (Sklarsky) Magura. BS in Chemistry, Carnegie-Mellon U., 1955; MS in Phys. Chemistry, U. Wis., 1960; PhD in Phys. Chemistry, Pa. State U., 1967. Devel. chemist Koppers Co., Monaca, Pa., 1955-58; rsch. chemist Am. Cyanamid Co., Stamford, Conn., 1960-63; asst. prof. chemistry Waynesburg (Pa.) Coll., 1967-70, assoc. prof., 1970-74, prof., 1974—. Leverhulme vis. prof. U. Leicester, Eng., 1980-81, 1989; cons. Pitts. Energy Tech. Ctr., summers 1978-86; faculty rsch. participant Oak Ridge Assoc. Univs., 1978-80, 82-85; U.S. del. Internat. Conf. Phys. Chemists, China, 1996, Sci. and Tech. Conf., India, 1997; vis. prof. chemistry U. Wis., Madison, 2004. Contbr. articles to sci. jours., chpt. to book. Sec. Waynesburg Women's Club, 1981-82; citizen amb. People to People Program, 1996, 97. Recipient Woman of the Yr. award AAUW, Waynesburg, 1983; Cottrell grantee Rsch. Corp. N.Y., 1970-71; Leverhulme vis. fellow U.K., 1980-81; Curie Internat. fellow AAUW, U.K., 1980-81; Robert West Superconductor Rsch. Grantee, Univ. Wis., 2001-05. Mem. AAUP, AAAS, Am. Chem. Soc.; Spectroscopy Soc. of Pitts.; Pitts. Soc. of Analytical Chemists. Avocations: gardening, painting, swimming, classical music, reading. Home: 1550 Crescent Hills Waynesburg PA 15370-1654 Office: Waynesburg Coll College St Waynesburg PA 15370 Office Phone: 724-852-3265. Business E-Mail: mmaguire@waynesburg.edu.

MAGUIRE, ROBERTA JOAN, elementary school educator, writer; b. N.Y.C., Mar. 21, 1946; d. Benjamin Solomon and Sophia Ellen Gulkis; children: Thomas Cornwall, Gabriela Marie, Paul Kaputa, Camilla Sophia, David Keith. BA, CCNY, 1967; Phil. Cand., U. Stockholm, Sweden, 1971. Cert. Bilingual crosscultural educator Calif., 1996. Caseworker Dept. Social Svcs., N.Y.C., 1967—70; social worker Cath. Relief Svcs., Andhra Pradesh, India, 1971—75, Caritas, Guatemala, 1975—77; freelance writer, editor San Francisco, 1977—; tchr. West Contra Costa Unified Schs., San Pablo, Calif., 1987—. Editor: (jour.) New Oxford Review. PTA leader Fairmont Sch., El Cerrito, Calif., 1987—97; parent leader Boy Scouts of Am., Albany, Calif., 1988—98. Recipient Creative Tchg. award, Disney Corp., 2002. Mem.: Mensa (life). Roman Catholic. Avocations: mountain climbing, travel, dance, reading, writing. Home: 2926 San Luis St Richmond CA 94804 Office: Bayview Elem Sch 3001 16 St San Pablo CA 94806 Office Phone: 510-292-6370. Personal E-mail: robertamaguire@hotmail.com.

MAGYAR, TINA MICHELLE, physical education educator; d. Jeff and Linda Magyar. BA, U. of Calif., Berkeley, 1994; MS, Purdue U., West Lafayette, Ind., 1998; PhD, Mich. State U., East Lansing, 2002. Postdoctoral fellow UCLA, Calif., 2002—05; asst. prof. Calif. State U., Long Beach, 2005—. Author (rschr.): (sport and exercise psychology) Psychology of Athletic Injury, Psychology of Leadership in Sport, Psychology of Excellence in Women. Named Outstanding Grad. Student, Mich. State U. Dept. of Kinesiology, 2002; recipient Emerging Profl., Western Soc. for the Phys. Edn. of Coll. Women, 2005; fellow, UCLA, 2002—06; grantee Rsch. Tng. grantee, Spencer Found., 2000—02; scholar Young scholar, Nat. Assn. for Kinesiology and Phys. Edn. in Higher Edn., 2006. Mem.: Nat. Assn. for Sport and Phys. Edn. (chair, sport and exercise psychology acad. 2005—), Assn. for the Advancement of Applied Sport Psychology (nat. student rep. 2000—01), Alpha Phi. Office: California State University 1250 Bellflower Blvd Long Beach CA 90803 Office Phone: 562-985-4116.

MAGYARY, CYNTHIA MARIE, retired elementary school educator, music educator; b. New Brighton, Pa., June 3, 1956; d. Nicholas (m) Magyary and Mary Helen Bedo-Magyary. BS in Music Edn., Geneva Coll., 1978, BS in Elem. Edn., 1978; MMus in Music Edn., Youngstown State U., 2006. Elem. music tchr. Wilmington Area Sch. Dist., New Wilmington, Pa., 1983—. Youth choir dir. Neshannock Presbyn. Ch., New Wilmington, Pa., 2001—. Mem.: Wilmington Area Educators Assn. (sec.), Pa. State Educators Assn., Pa. Music Educators Assn. Avocations: piano, golf, swimming, sewing, reading. Office: New Wilmington Elem 450 Wood St New Wilmington PA 16142 Home: 40 Wynfield Ln New Wilmington PA 16142

MAHALEY-JOHNSON, HOSANNA, school system administrator; b. 1968; BA, Marquette U., Milw., 1991; MEd, U. Ill., Chgo. Chief of staff Chgo. Pub. Schools, 2001—, dir. New Schools Devel., dir. Renaissance 2010 initiative, 2006—. Bd. dirs. City Yr. Chgo.; bd. advisors Chgo. Comty. Trust. Named one of 40 Under 40, Crain's Chgo. Bus., 2006. Office: Chgo Pub Schools 5th Fl 125 S Clark St Chicago IL 60603 Office Phone: 773-553-1530. Office Fax: 773-553-2199.*

MAHAN, MARY HOYLE, retired physical educator; b. Boston, July 19, 1939; d. Frederick John and Mary Dwyer Hoyle; m. J. Roger Mahan Jr., Mar. 21, 1970 (dec. June 1999). BS in Phys. Edn., Bridgewater State Coll., 1960; MS in Phys. Edn., U. N.C., 1963; EdD, Nova U., 1975. Tchr. phys. edn. Stoughton Jr. High Sch., Mass., 1960—62; tchr. phys. edn., coach Locust Valley Jr./Sr. High Sch., NY, 1963—65; prof. phys. edn., coach Ctrl. Conn. State U., New Britain, 1965—71, Miami-Dade C.C. North, 1971—2001, assoc. athletic dir., dept. chair, prof., 1980—2001, ret., 2001. CEO, pres. The Teaching Well, Ftr. Lauderdale, Fla., 2000—. Bd. trustees Cheshire Acad., Conn., 2000—, Bridgewater State Coll. Found., 2002—, Lake Isle Woods, Centerville, 2004—; edn. found. Villanova U., Pa., 2003—. Named Weymouth High Sch. Hall Fame, Bridgewter State Coll. Hall Fame, Fla. C.C. Activities Assn. Hall Fame; named to Hall of Fame, Nat. Assn. Coll. Dirs. Athletics; recipient 3 Outstanding Faculty awards, Miami-Dade C.C., 1985, Case Prof. of Yr., U. Tex., 1996, Endowed Tchg. Chair, Bowden award, Cheshle Acad. Mem.: Nat. Assn. Coll. Directors of Athletics, Am. Alliance Health, Phys. Edn., Recreation and Dance, Am. Coll. Sports Medicine, Delta Psi Kappa. Independent. Roman Catholic. Avocations: golf, interior decorating, travel. Home (Winter): 3750 Galt Ocean Dr #2007 Fort Lauderdale FL 33308 Home (Summer): 30 Crestview Cir Centerville MA 02632

MAHAR, CAROL, psychologist, consultant; b. Lubec, Maine, Sept. 19, 1949; d. Philip Martin and Margaret Gertrude Mahar; children: Maura, Taylor. BS, U. Maine, Farmington, 1971; MEd, U. Maine, Orono, 1972; PhD, U. Mich., Ann Arbor, 1979. Pvt. practice spl. edn. cons., Kittery, Maine, 1973—; pvt. practice sch. psychologist various schs., NH, 1999—. Cons., tutor various schs., NH, 1996—. Scholar, Internat. Rotary, 1976—77. Mem.: NH Assn. for Sch. Psychologists (region 6 coord.). Avocations: gardening, kayaking, tennis, sailing. Home: 48 Ambush Rock Rd Eliot ME 03903-1202

MAHDAVIANI, MIRIAM, choreographer, educator; Student, Sch. Am. Ballet, 1968. Past mem., instr. Balanchine Co. Choreographer Jacob's Pillow Dance Festival, 1986, 87, Am. Music Festival N.Y.C. Ballet, 1988. Choreographer (ballets) N.Y.C. Ballet's Am. Music Festival, 1988, Dance Preludes Dancer's Emergency Fund Benefit, N.Y.C., 1991, Images, N.Y.C., 1992, Images Maggio Danza Festival, Florence, Italy, 1994, Correlazione N.Y.C. Ballet, 1994; dancer over 40 ballets including Ballo Della Regina, Coppelia, Donizetti Variations, Jewels, Raymonda Variations, La Valse. Office: Pacific Northwest Ballet 301 Mercer St Seattle WA 98109-4600

MAHER, FRANCESCA MARCINIAK, lawyer, former air transportation executive; b. Chgo., Oct. 27, 1957; BA, Loyola U., 1978, JD, 1981. Ptnr. Mayer, Brown & Platt, Chgo., 1981—84, 1987—93; v.p. law, corp. sec. UAL Corp., Elk Grove Village, Ill., 1993-97, v.p., gen. counsel, sec., 1997-98, sr. v.p., gen. counsel, sec., 1998—2003; spl. counsel Mayer, Brown, Rowe & Maw, Chgo., 2003—. Bd. dirs. YMCA Met. Chgo., Lincoln Park Zool. Soc. Mem. Ill. Humane Soc. (pres. 1996-98).

MAHER, JAN COLLEEN, writer, educator; b. Huntington, Ind., Feb. 10, 1946; BA, New Sch. Social Rsch., N.Y.C., 1969; MA in English Lit., Millersville (Pa.) U., 1988; PhD, The Union Inst., 1997. Cert. 4-12 tchr. Artist in residence Seattle Arts Commn., Seattle Pub. Schs., 1980—. Pres., project dir. Local Access, Seattle, 1990-. Author: (novel) Heaven, Indiana, 2000, History in the Present Tense: Engaging Students through Inquiring and Action, 2003, Most Dangerous Women: Bringing History to Life Through Readers Theater, 2006, (plays) Intruders, 1992 (Best of Festival), Ismene, 1992, Solitaire, 1993, Widow's Walk, 1995Most Dangerous Women: Bringing History to Life Through Readers' Theater; co-author: Southeast Asian Americans, African Americans, Irish Americans, Mexican Americans, Japanese Americans, Inhabiting History, 1990. Mem. bd. dirs. New City Theater, Seattle, 1988-91; mem. adv. bd. Seattle Fringe Theater Festival, 1993-95. Mem. Nat. Writers Union, N.W. Playwrights Guild, Dramatists Guild.

MAHER, JEAN ELIZABETH, counseling administrator; b. Cortland, N.Y., Aug. 13, 1953; d. Russell Edgar and Frances Mae (MacGregor) Owen; m. Kevin John Maher, Aug. 6, 1983; children: Zachary Kevin, Megan Jean. BA, Houghton Coll., 1975; MS, SUNY, Oneonta, 1979, cert. of advanced study, 1980. Cert. profl. counselor, N.J. Tchr. English Monticello (N.Y.) High Sch., 1975-80, dir. gifted program, Sr. Hon. Soc. advisor, 1978-79; sch. counselor Lounsberry Hollow Mid. Sch., Vernon, NJ, 1980—94, coord. spl. svcs., 1982-94; sch. counselor Glen Meadow Middle Sch., Vernon, 1997—. Tchr. Gen. Equivalency Diploma program Port Jervis (N.Y.) High Sch., 1985-86. Leader Youth Group, Port Jervis, 1982; editor ch. newsletter Port Jervis, 1986-89; jr. ch. leader, Milford, Pa., 2000—, mem. ch. Christian edn. com., 2001—. Named Vernon Twp. Tchr. of Yr., 1989-90, Sussex County Counselor of Yr., 1993. Mem. NEA, Am. Assn. Counseling and Devel., N.J. Edn. Assn., Sussex County Sch. Counselors Assn. (sec. 1983-85, treas. 1985-87, pres. 1987-88), N.J. Profl. Counselors Assn. (ethics com. 1988-91). Avocations: music, photography. Home: 104 Tomahawk Ter Montague NJ 07827-3100 Office: Glen Meadow Mid Sch PO Box 516 Vernon NJ 07462-0516 Office Phone: 973-764-4534.

MAHER, LISA KRUG, editor; b. N.Y.C., Nov. 11, 1952; d. George William and Rita (Earle) Krug; m. Barney Rosset, Nov. 5, 1980 (div. Dec. 1990); 1 child, Chantal; m. Richard Maher, July 29, 2000. BA magna cum laude, Smith Coll., 1974; MA, Columbia U., 1976. Editor Latin Am. Series, N.Y.C., 1976-86; gen. editor Grove Press, N.Y.C., 1987-89; mng. editor Aperture, N.Y.C., 1987-90; pvt. practice N.Y.C., 1990—. Writer and editor UNICEF, N.Y.C., 1995—. Author: James Baldwin, 1989, Thurgood Marshall, 1993 (Outstanding Book For Teenagers award 1994). Mem. Phi Beta Kappa

MAHER, VIRGINIA JONES, art historian, educator; b. Milw., Oct. 11, 1941; d. Frederick Thomas Murphy and Virginia June Harmon; m. William H. Jones, Aug. 22, 1964 (dec. Nov. 23, 1982); children: William H. Jones Jr., Michael J. Jones, Megan Jones Townsend; m. J. Thomas Maher, III, May 14, 1994. BS, U. Wis., Milw., 1964, MA in Art History, 1994, cert. art mus. studies, 1994. Tchr. French and English Custer HS, Milw., 1964; curatorial asst. Kohler Art Ctr., Sheboygan, Wis., 1993; curator fine arts commn. Cathedral of St. John, Milw., 1995—2003; instr. art history Cardinal Stritch U., Milw., 1997—99, Peninsula Art Sch., Fish Creek, Wis., 2001—; lectr. art history Milw. Art Mus., 2004—. Guest art curator Miller Art Mus., Sturgeon Bay, Wis., 2000—; bd. dirs. Peninsula Art Sch., chmn. acquisitions com., 2002—; lectr. in field. Organizer Friends of Art History, Milw., 2000—03; hist. preservation Jr. League Evanston, Ill., 1980—81, lectr. art in the sch., 1978—80; mem. dean's adv. com. Inst. Visual Arts U. Wis. Milw., 2004; bd. dirs. Wis. Heritages Inc., Milw., 1996—99, Am. Heritage Soc. Milw. Art Mus., 1994—98. Named Writer of Yr. award, Metalsmith Mag., 1998; recipient Grad. of Last Decade (G.O.L.D.) award, U. Wis., Milw., 2000. Mem.: Nat. Mus. Women in Arts, Collectors' Corner Milw. Art Mus., Contemporary Art Soc. Milw. Art Mus., Womans Club Wis., Alpha Phi. Roman Catholic. Avocations: art collecting, painting, gardening. Home: 5611 Schauer Rd Sturgeon Bay WI 54235 Personal E-mail: vmaher@itol.com.

MAHEU, MARLENE MURIEL, psychologist; b. Hartford, Conn., June 1, 1954; d. Robert Joseph and Claire M. BA summa cum laude, U. Hartford, 1977; MA, PhD in Clin. Psychology, Calif. Sch. Profl. Psychology, 1985. Psychol. intern Mid-City Community Clinic, San Diego, 1982-83, Cath. Community Services, San Diego, 1983-84, San Diego Police Dept., 1984-85; pvt. practice psychology San Diego, 1984—. Dir. Nicotine Recovery Inst. Author health maintenance program Ex-Smokers for LIfe, 1986; contbr. articles to profl. jours. Researcher health maintenance program, stop smoking program. Mem. Am. Psychol. Assn., Am. Acad. Psychotherapists, Am. Assn. Marriage and Family Therapists, Acad. San Diego Psychologists, NOW, Sigma Xi, Psy Chi, Alpha Chi. Avocations: travel, reading, gardening. Office: 5173 Waring Rd #124 San Diego CA 92120

MAHLENDORF, URSULA RENATE, literature educator; b. Strehlen, Silesia, Germany, Oct. 24, 1929; arrived in US, 1953; Student, Oberschule an der Hamburgerstraße, Bremen, Fed. Republic Germany, 1950, U. Tübingen, Fed. Republic Germany, 1950-52, Brown U., 1953-57, MA in English Lit., 1956, PhD in German Lit., 1958; student, Bonn U., Fed. Republic Germany, 1953, London U.; grad., New Directions in Psychoanalysis, Washington, 2002. Teaching asst. Brown U., Providence, 1953-57; from acting instr. to prof. German U. Calif., Santa Barbara, 1957—93, prof. women's studies, 1988—93, assoc. dir., campus coord. edn. abroad program, 1967—69, chmn. dept. Germanic and Slavic langs. and lits., 1980-83, assoc. dean Coll. Letters and Sci., 1986-89, emeritus, 1993—. Chmn. symposium in honor of Harry Slochower, 1977; campus coord. edn. abroad program U. Calif., 1967-69, assoc. dir., 1969-72; co-chair Nietzsche symposium Dept. Germanic and Slavic Langs. and Lits., U. Calif., Santa Barbara, 1981. Author: The Wellsprings of Literary Creation, 1985; editor: (with John L. Carleton) Man for Man: A Multi-Disciplinary Workshop on Affecting Man's Social and Psychological Nature through Community Action (Charles C. Thomas), 1973, Dimensions of Social Psychiatry, 1979, (with Arthur Lerner) Life Guidance through Literature, 1992, (in German) Surviving Childhood; assoc. editor Am. Imago, Am. Jour. Social Psychiatry, Jour. Evolutionary Psychology; contbr. more than 90 articles to profl. jours. Recipient Alumni Tchg. award, 1981; rsch. grantee, U. Calif., 1974—, Fulbright fellow, 1951—52, Festschrift named in her honor, 2004. Mem. MLA, Am. Assn. for Aesthetics and Art Criticism (past pres. Calif. div.), Assn. for applied Psychoanalysis (profl. mem.), Am. Assn. Social Psychiatry (councillor 1977-81), Internat. Assn. Social Psychiatry (treas. 1978-83). Avocations: sculpting, woodcarving. Home: 1505 Portesuello Ave Santa Barbara CA 93105-4626 Office: U Calif Dept Germanic Semitic Slavic Studies Santa Barbara CA 93106 E-mail: mahlendo@gss.ucsb.edu.

MAHMOOD, SAMAR, psychiatrist; b. Lahore, Punjab, Pakistan, May 23, 1967; arrived in U.S., 1995; d. Altaf Mahmood and Shakila Nuzhat; m. Kamran Syed Sabir, Feb. 10, 1996; children: Aadil Kamran, Aliyah Kamran. MB BChir, Allama Iqbal Med. Coll., Lahore, 1991. Psychiatry resident Harvard Med. Sch., Boston, 2001—02, U. Chgo., 2002—05; staff psychiatrist Ben Gordon Mental Health Ctr., Dekalb, Ill., 2005; staff mem. Hinsdale (Ill.) Psychiatry, 2005—; staff psychiatrist Dupage County Health Dept., Wheaton, Ill., 2005—. Group therapist Winfield (Ill.) Woods. Recipient Nat. Merit scholarship for acad. excellence, Punjab U., 1983, 1985. Mem.: Am. Psychiat. Assn. Avocations: painting, music, cooking. Office: Hinsdale Psychiatry SC Ste 102 911 N Elm St Hinsdale IL 60521

MAHMOOD, TALLAT, oncologist, hematologist; b. Lahore, Pakistan, Apr. 9, 1968; arrived in U.S.A., 1994; d. Mahmood Ali and Furrukh Begum Khan; m. Shahid H. Khan, Jan. 29, 1993; children: Aquila, Nadir, Mohsin. MD, Aga Khan U., 1991. Diplomate Am. Bd. Internal Medicine, Oncology, and Hematology. Clin. fellow Tulane U. Med. Ctr., New Orleans, 1997—99, rsch. fellow, 1999—2000; staff physician Marquette (Mich.) Gen. Hosp., 2000—. Contbr. articles to profl. jours. Mem.: AMA, Am. Soc. Hematology, Am. Soc. Oncology. Avocations: skiing, golf. Office: Marquette General Hospital 1414 W Fair Ave Ste 332 Marquette MI 49855

MAHMOUDI, HOMA, clinical psychologist; b. Tehran, Iran, Apr. 24, 1941; came to U.S., 1959, naturalized, 1977; d. Jalil and Badri M.; grad. certificate Middle Eastern studies, U. Utah, 1967; Ph.D. in Clin. Psychology, 1970; 1 child, Jason. Tng. officer Peace Corps, 1962-68; dir. police selection research project County of Los Angeles, 1970-73; asst. clin. prof. med. psychology Sch. Medicine UCLA, 1973-77; chief psychologist Occupational Health Service, 1977-85; psychologist Cedar-Sinai Med. Ctr., 1986—; pvt. practice, Los Angeles. Mem. Am. Psychol. Assn., Western Psychol. Assn., Soc. for Intercultural Edn. Tng. and Research, Am. Soc. Tng. and Devel. Baha'i. Author: The Urban Policeman in Transition: A Psychological and Sociological Review, 1973; co-author: Persian Phrasebook & Dictionary, 1977; contbr. articles in field to publs. Home: 909 Stonehill Ln Los Angeles CA 90049-1412 Office Phone: 310-780-5757. Personal E-mail: homamahmoudi@gmail.com.

MAHMUD, SHIREEN DIANNE, photographer; b. Chittagong, Pakistan, Oct. 4, 1949; came to U.S., 1974; d. Mohammed Mazhurul Qudus and Mumtaz Mahal Begum; m. Abdul Wazed Mahmud, Apr. 10, 1966 (div. 1996); children: Sharmin, Anita. BA in Mass Comm., U. Hartford, 1982. Part-time med. sec., Middletown, Conn., 1979—82; freelance photographer, 1985—; typist Aetna Ins. Co., Middletown, 1991. Prodr. feature program Storer Cable Comm., Clinton, Conn., 1991-95; mem. Bridgeport Regional Bus. Coun., 1997; realtor Buyer's Capital. Literacy vol. Russell Libr., Middletown, Conn. Mem. AAUW, Nat. League Am. Pen Women, Internat. Soc. Poets (Hall of Fame award 1997), Conn. Soc. Poets, Conn. Songwriter's Assn., Internat. Platform Assn. Office Phone: 860-306-9090. E-mail: sdshireen@optonline.net.

MAHON, ANNA NORGREN, literature and language educator, coach; b. Stamford, Conn., Dec. 19, 1974; d. Jane F. and Philip E. Norgren; m. Sean R. Mahon, July 7, 2001; 1 child, Grace Neala. BA English and Psychology, U. Vt., Burlington, 1996; MAT English, Boston U., 1997; 6th Yr. Edn. Leadership, So. Conn. State U., New Haven, 2004. Coach track and field Yale U. Professional athlete (track and field) Hammer Thrower. Mem.: Pi Lambda Theta (assoc.). Achievements include 2004 Olympian; 2001 and 2003 World Championship Team Member; 2002 and 2003 National Champion; National Record Holder 2002 through 2004. Office: Amity Regional School District 25 Newton Road Woodbridge CT 06525

MAHON, JULIA, speech pathology/audiology services professional, educator; d. James F. and Mary Rosalind Weiss; m. John Francis Mahon, Oct. 18, 1969; 1 child, Elizabeth. BA, Temple U., 1970; MS, U. R.I., 1980; EdD, Boston U., 1994. Tchg. asst. Temple U., Phila., 1970; adminstrv. asst. Jamos Rozes, DMD, Middletown, RI; tchg. asst. U. R.I., Kingston; speech and lang. pathologist Newport (R.I.) Sch. Dist.; pvt. practice Tiverton and Portsmouth, RI; asst. prof. Salve Regina U., 1989—95; assoc. prof. Endicott Coll., 1996—2000, Maine Sch. Adminstn. Dist., Hampton, Maine, 2002—. Mem.: Assn. Supervision and Curriculum Devel., Am. Speech Lang. Hearing Assn., R.I. Speech Hearing Lang. Assn. (MBR 1988—96, sec. 1993—95). Avocations: hiking, cross country skiing, singing. Office: Maine Sch Adminstr Dist 22 Main St Hampden ME 04444

MAHONE, BARBARA JEAN, automotive executive; BS, Ohio State U., 1968; MBA, U. Mich., 1972; program for mgmt. devel., Harvard U., 1981. Sys. analyst GM, Detroit, 1968-71, sr. staff asst., 1972-74, mgr. career planning, 1975-78, dir. pers. adminstrn. Rochester, NY, 1979-81, mgr. indsl. rels. Warren, Ohio, 1982-83, dir. human resources mgmt. Chevrolet-Pontiac-Can. group, 1984-86, dir. gen. pers. and pub. affairs Inland divsn. Dayton, Ohio, 1986-88, gen. dir. pers. Indland Fisher Guide divsn. Detroit, 1989-91, gen. dir. employee benefits, 1991-93, dir. human resources truck group Pontiac, Mich., 1994—2000, exec. dir. human resources, 2001—. Chmn. Fed. Labor Rels. Authority, Washington, 1983-84, Spl. Panel on Appeals; dir. Metro Youth; mem. bd. govs. U. Mich. Alumni. Bd. dirs. ARC, Rochester, 1979-82, Urban League Rochester, 1979-82, Rochester Aea Multiple Sclerosis; mem. human resources com. YMCA, Rochester, 1980-82; mem. exec. bd. Nat. Coun. Negro Women; mem. allocations com. United Way Greater Rochester. Recipient Pub. Rels. award Nat. Assn. Bus. and Profl. Women, 1976, Mary McLeod Bethune award Nat. Coun. Negro Women, 1977, Senate resolution Mich. State Legislature, 1980; named Outstanding Woman, Mich. Chronicle, 1975, Woman of Yr., Nat. Assn. Bus. and Profl. Women, 1978, Disting. Bus. Person, U. Mich., 1978, one of 11 Mich. Women, Redbook mag., 1978. Mem. Nat. Black MBA Assn. (bd. dirs., nat. pres. Disting. Svc. award, bd. dirs., nat. pres. Outstanding MBA), Women Econ. Club (bd. dirs.), Indsl. Rels. Rsch. Assn., Internat. Assn. for Pers. Women, Engring. Soc. Detroit. Republican. Home: 2697 Melcombe Cir Unit 402 Troy MI 48084

MAHONEY, CAROLYN RAY, academic administrator; b. Memphis, Dec. 22, 1946; d. Stephen and Myrtle (Gray) Boone; m. Charles Augustus Mahoney, May 20, 1972; children: Cindy Rae, Megan Ruth, Carolyn Bernadette. BS, Sienna Coll., 1970; MS in Math., Ohio State U., 1972, PhD in Math., 1983. Asst. prof. math. Denison U., Granville, Ohio, 1984-87; founding faculty prof. math. Calif. State U., San Marcos, 1989—2000; dean sch. math. sci. and tech. Eiizabeth City State, Elizabeth City, NC, provost, vice chancellor academic affairs; pres. Lincoln U., Jefferson City, Mo., 2005—. Mem. Coll. Bd. Test Devel. Com., Princeton, N.J., 1986-89; advisory com. Coll. Bd. Math. Scis., 1992—; vis. asst. prof. math. Ohio State U., Columbus, 1987-89; instr. South African Program Denison U., Granville, 1987; math. campus coord. Young Scholars Program, Columbus, 1987—; cons., researcher regarding increasing the numbers and achievement of minorities and women in math. at all levels; dir. Middle Sch. Math. and Sci. San Marcos, 1992—. Contbr. articles to Jour. Combinatorial Theory, Soc. Indsl. and Applied Math. Newsletter. Active Edn. Commn. of States Task Force on Improving Achievement of Minorities in Higher Edn., 1990. Grantee NSF, 1987, 90, 92, Math. Assn. Am., 1992, Charles A. Dana Found, 1989, Ohio Bd. Regents, 1989, Math. Scis. Edn. Bd., 1989; named to State of Ohio Women's Hall of Fame, 1989. Mem. Am. Math. Soc., Assn. for Women in Math., Math. Assn. Am., Nat. Assn. Mathematicians, Phi Kappa Phi. Office: Lincoln Univ 820 Chestnut St Jefferson City MO 65102-0029 E-mail: president@lincolnu.edu.

MAHONEY, CATHERINE ANN, artist, educator; b. Macon, Mo., Nov. 18, 1948; d. Joe H. and Berniece Joyce (Garnett) Dickson; m. Michael W. Mahoney, July 19, 1969; children: Karin Lynn Mahoney Broeker, Ryan Michael. BS in Edn. with honors, Truman U., Kirksville, 1969. Mo. state life cert. for tchg. art. Elem./secondary art instr. Bucklin (Mo.) R-I Schs., 1970-74; pvt. art instr. Groom (Tex.) Artist's Assn., 1974-75; substitute tchr. Gasconade R-I Schs., Hermann, Mo., 1977-89; pvt. art instr. Colorful Brushes Studio, Hermann, Mo., 1987—; elem./secondary art instr. Crosspoint Christian Schs., Union, Mo., 1994-98. Pres. City of Hermann Arts Coun., 1983-87, membership chmn., 1980-82; dir. Summertime Children's Watercolor Workshops, Colorful Brushes, Hermann, 1987—; artist-in-residence Mo. State Fair, 2005. One-woman shows at Truman U., Kirksville, 1969, Capitol City Art Guild, Jefferson City, Mo., 1983, Kolbe Gallery of Art, Hermann, 1984, Colorful Brushes Studio, Hermann, 1987-94; designer Sister Cities Emblem City of Hermann/Arolsen, Germany, 1989, 20 ft. histl. mural, Gasconade County; works published in: Best of Watercolor: Texture, 1998, The Artful Home II, 2004, Art Resource Book IV, Mo. Life Mag, 2005, Guild's Source Book of Residenital Art 4, 2006. Pres. Hermann Parent-Tchr. Orgn., 1985—87; leader 4-H, Girl and Boy Scouts, Hermann, 1982—95; organist, pianist, tchr. Hermann Cath. and Bapt. Chs., 1977—97, E. Free Ch., 1997—. Named Outstanding Young Woman of Yr., Hermann Jaycees, 1984, 1st place award Mo. Artists Collection, Mo. Pub. Svc., Sedalia, Mo., 1992, 3d place award and purchase prize Watercolor USA, Springfield (Mo.) Art Mus., 1995, 1st place award Arts Rolla Art Show, 1999, 2004, 1st pl. watercolor Top 50 Exhbn., Sedalia Excellence award, Tex. Watercolor Soc. and Traveling Exhbn., 2005. Mem.: Mo. Watercolor Soc. (signature mem., bd. dirs. 1998—2006, M. Graham Mdse. award 2003, Daniel Smith award 2006), Oil Painters Am., St. Louis Artist Guild (mem. art sect., Hon. Mention 1993, 1998, 2002), Watercolor USA Honor Soc. (hon. Art Show award 1995), Okla. Watercolor Assn. (assoc. included Art Show 1989), Nat. Watercolor Soc. (assoc. included Nat. Art Show 1995). Avocations: piano, reading, embroidery, sewing, knitting. Home: 1058 Old Stonehill Hermann MO 65041 Office: Colorful Brushes Studio 126 E 4th St Hermann MO 65041-1130 Office Phone: 573-486-2444. E-mail: camahoney@ktis.net.

MAHONEY, JILL ELIZABETH, music educator; b. Phoenix, Oct. 2, 1961; d. John Richard and Janet Louise Mahoney. Student, Grand Canyon Coll., 1979—80; MusB, Ariz. State U., 1984, postgrad., 1984—89. Secondary tchg. cert. grades K-12 with music endorsement. Music tchr. Avondale (Ariz.) Elem. Sch. Dist., Ariz., 1984—85; band/instrumental music tchr. Peoria Unified Sch. Dist., Glendale, Ariz., 1985—. Honor band condr. Isaac Mid. Sch., Phoenix, 1997; honor orch. condr. Paradise Valley (Ariz.) Unified Dist., 1998. Editor: (newsletter) PEA Educator, 1989—91 (Sch. Bell award, 1991). Recipient Pride in Peoria award, 1994, Raymond S. Kellis Leadership in Tchg. award, 2002. Mem.: Ariz. Music Educators Assn. (v.p. 1997—99, condr. Elem. All State Band 2000, George C. Wilson Leadership award 1999, OM Harsell Excellence in Tchg. Music award 2006), Am. String Tchrs. Assn., Internat. Assn. Jazz Educators. Avocations: gardening, music, reading. Home: 2154 W Earll Dr Phoenix AZ 85015 Office: Marshall Ranch Elem Sch 12995 N Marshall Ranch Glendale AZ 85304

MAHONEY, JULIA DELONG, law educator; b. Boston; BA, Barnard Coll., Columbia U., 1984; JD, Yale U., 1987. Bar: NY 1988. Mem. faculty U. So. Calif. Law Sch., U. Chgo. Law Sch.; named assoc. prof. U. Va. Sch. Law, 1999, now prof., also David H. Ibbeken rsch. prof. Office: U Va Sch Law 580 Massie Rd Charlottesville VA 22903-1789 Office Phone: 434-924-3942. E-mail: jdm8t@virginia.edu.

MAHONEY, KELLEY K., language educator; d. Wayne Jackson and Myra Jean Kinney; m. Mike James Mahoney, Dec. 13, 1986; children: Caleb Michael, Hannah Elizabeth. AA, Truett-McConnell U., Cleve., Ga., 1982; BA, Carson-Newman U., Jefferson City, Tenn., 1984; MA, U. Ga., Athens, 1986. Tchr. English, French, Brewer H.S., Ft. Worth, 1987—90; instr. English, Tarrant Co. Jr. Coll., Ft. Worth, 1987—90, Tex. Christian U., Ft. Worth, 1987—90; assoc. prof. English, Dalton State Coll., Ga., 1990—. Cons. to numerous H.S. English classes, Ga., 1995—2005. Editor: Expressions of Culture Reader, 2004; planner, dir. (conf.) Connections Conf., 1998, Collaborative Conf. of Writing, 2000. Bible study tchr., leader Friendship Bapt. Ch., Roclay Face, Ga., 1990—. Recipient grant, Ga. Humanities Coun., 1998, 2000. Mem.: Southeastern Conf. on English, So. Assn. of MLA, Nat. Coun. Tchrs. of English. Avocations: reading, walking, movies. Office: Dalton State Coll 650 College Dr Dalton GA 30720 Office Phone: 706-272-2593. Office Fax: 706-272-2610. E-mail: kmahoney@daltonstate.edu.

MAHONEY, MARGARET ELLERBE, foundation executive; d. Charles Hallam and Leslie Nelson (Savage) M. BS magna cum laude, Vanderbilt U., 1946; LHD (hon.), Meharry Med. Coll., 1977, U. Fla., 1980, Med. Coll. Pa., 1982, Williams Coll., 1983, Smith Coll., 1985, Beaver Coll., 1985, Brandeis U., 1989, Marymount Coll., 1990, Mt. Sinai Sch. Medicine, 1992, Rush U., 1993, SUNY, Bklyn., 1994, N.Y. Med. Coll., 1995. Fgn. affairs officer State Dept., Washington, 1946-53; exec. assoc., assoc. sec. Carnegie Corp., N.Y.C., 1953-72; v.p. Robert Wood Johnson Found., Princeton, NJ, 1972-80; pres. Commonwealth Fund, N.Y.C., 1980-94, MEM Assocs., Inc., N.Y.C., 1995—. Spkr. in field. Contbr. articles to profl. jours. Trustee Carnegie Found. Advancement of Tchg., 1963—2001, John D. and Catherine T. MacArthur Found., 1985—2002, Smith Coll., 1988—93, Columbia U., 1991—96, Arthur Ashe Found., 1997—2005; vis. fellow Sch. Archtl. and Urban Planning, Princeton U., 1973—80; bd. dirs. Coun. on Found., 1982—88, Skillbuilders Fund, 1993—99, adv. dir., 1999—; bd. dirs. Alliance for Aging Rsch., 1986—99, Overseas Devel. Coun., 1988—2001, Nat. Found. Ctrs. for Disease Control and Prevention, Inc., 1994—2004; mem. MIT Corp., 1984—89, N.Y.C. Commn. on the Yr. 2000, 1985—87; chmn. Nat. Found. Ctrs. for Disease Control and Prevention, Inc., 1996—98; bd. govs. Am. Stock Exch., 1987—92, Am. Skin Assn., 1994—, Classroom Inc., 1996—2005, Buckminster Fuller Inst., 2005; mem. adv. bd. Office of Med. Examiner, N.Y.C., 1987—; vice chmn. N.Y.C. Mayor's Com. for Pub./Pvt. Partnerships, 1990—93; mem. vestry Parish of Trinity Ch., 1982—89, 1991—95. Recipient Frank H. Lahey Meml. award, 1984, Women's Forum award, 1989, Walsh McDermott award, 1992, Disting. Grantmaker award Coun. Founds., 1993, Edward R. Loveland award ACP, 1994, Spl. Recognition award AAMC, 1994, Merit medal Lotos Club, 1994, Terrance Keenan Leadership award in health philanthropy Grantmakers in health, 1995, Distinction award Am. Skin Assn., 1998, Rsch. Am. award, 1999, Hon. Classmate Class of 1976 award Princeton U., 2001, Picker Inst. award, 2003. Mem. AAAS, Inst. Medicine of NAS, Am. Acad. Arts and Scis., Am. Philos. Soc., Coun. Fgn. Rels., Fin. Women's Assn. N.Y., N.Y. Acad. Medicine, N.Y. Acad. Scis., Alpha Omega Alpha. Office: MEM Assocs Inc 521 5th Ave 29th Fl New York NY 10175-0088 Office Phone: 212-297-0500.

MAHONEY, MARGARET ELLIS, accountant; b. Detroit, Mar. 17, 1929; d. Seth Wiley and Mildred Elizabeth (Hill) Ellis; m. Stephen Bedell Smith, Mar. 15, 1956 (div. Oct. 1962); 1 child, Laura Elizabeth; m. Patrick John Mahoney, Sept. 1, 1972 (dec.). BA, Butler U., 1953. Copywriter Hook Drugs Inc., Indpls., 1953; continuity dir. Sta. WXLW, Indpls., 1954-57; ptnr. Steve Smith and Assocs. Advt., Indpls., 1956-62; account mgr. Sive Advt., Cin., 1963-64, Associated Advt., Cin., 1964-65; copywriter SupeRX Drugs Inc., Cin., 1965-72; promotion writer U.S. News and World Report, Washington, 1974; asst. mgr. advt. Drug Fair, Alexandria, Va., 1975-82; dir. advt. Cosmetic and Fragrance Concepts Inc./DBA Cosmetic Ctrs., Beltsville, Md., 1982-89; advt., prodn. cons. Nat. Red Cross, Galladet U., Washington, 1989-94; asst. to real estate agt. Carmel, Ind., 1994-96; editl. cons., mem. svc. rep., acct. clk. Angie's List, Carmel, Ind., 1996—. Vestrywoman St. Matthews Episcopal Ch., Cin., 1969-71; vol. jr. achievement hosp. chmn. Sleepy Hollow Citizens Assn., Falls Church, Va., 1973; vol. resident assoc. program Smithsonian Instn., Washington, 1989-94; chmn. membership and pub. rels. Friends Chinn Park Regional Libr., Woodbridge, Va., 1991-94; vol. Indpls. Art Ctr. Gift Shop, 1997—, Prince William Symphony Orch., Prince William County Voter Registration Bd. Mem. Potomac Valley Aquarium Soc. (past treas., past sec., editor jour.), Am. Cichlid Assn. (nat. pub. rels. chair 1985-90), Delta Delta Delta. Avocations: swimming, reading, needlecrafts, travel, computers. Home: 9850 Greentree Dr Carmel IN 46032-9099 Office Phone: 317-803-3961. Personal E-mail: mmah317@aol.com.

MAHONEY, MARGARET H., history professor; d. William John and Lillian Elizabeth Mahoney. BA, U. Great Falls, Mont., 1953; MA, U. Minn., 1965; PhD, U. Minn., Mpls., 1965. Prof. history/political sci. Bellarmine U., Louisville, 1958—. Chair of history/polit. sci. dept. Bellarmine U., Louisville, 1992—. Author: St. Francis Church 1886-1986. Centennial historian com. Cathedral of the Assumption, Louisville, 1999—2000. Democrat. Roman Catholic. Avocation: travel. Home: 112 St Francis Court #75 Louisville KY 40205 Office: Bellarmine Univ 2001 Newburg Rd Louisville KY 40205 Office Phone: 502-452-8171. Business E-Mail: mmahoney@bellarmine.edu.

MAHONEY, MAUREEN A., academic administrator; PhD in Human Devel. and Family Studies, Cornell U., 1977. Prof. psychology Hampshire Coll., Amherst, Mass.; dean Smith Coll., Northampton, Mass., 1996—. Office: Smith Coll Dean of the College College Hall 21 Northampton MA 01063

MAHONY, SHEILA ANNE, retired communications executive; b. Yonkers, N.Y., Jan. 30, 1942; d. Paul Ambrose and Grace (Sullivan) M.; m. Charles A. Riggs, July 7, 1983; stepchildren: Charles Riggs, Julia Riggs Shultis. BA, Newton Coll. Sacred Heart, Mass., 1963; JD, Fordham U., 1967. Asst. corp. counsel Law Dept. City of N.Y., N.Y.C., 1967—72; regional dir. Cable TV Info. Ctr., The Urban Inst., Washington, 1972—74, gen. counsel, 1974-75, exec. dir., 1976-77, Carnegie Commn. on Future of Pub. Broadcasting, N.Y.C., 1977-79, Cablevision Systems Corp., Woodbury, NY, 1980—95, sr. v.p. comm. and pub. affairs, 1995—99, exec. v.p. comm., govt. and pub. affairs, 1999—2004, dir., 1988—2005. Mem. exec. com. CSPAN, 2000—04. Author: Keeping PACE With the New Television, 1979. Dir. C-SPAN, Washington, 1990-2004, Found. for Minority Interests in Media, N.Y.C., 1992-2003; bd. dirs. Lustgarten Found., 2000—, Legal Aid Soc. of N.Y., 2000-2004. Office: Cablevision Systems Corp 1111 Stewart Ave Bethpage NY 11714-3581

MAHOOD, MARIE I., counselor, educator; b. Hackensack, NJ, Aug. 25, 1961; d. James George Mamood and Marie Josephine (Karlovsky) Mahood. BA in English, Montclair State U., 1983, MA in Counseling and Sch. Social Work, 1991. Lic. profl. counselor NJ; cert. secondary tchr. NJ. English tchr. Marylawn of the Oranges HS, South Orange, NJ, 1983—87; grad. asst., counselor Montclair State Coll., Upper Montclair, NJ, 1989—90, asst. to dir. Women's Ctr., 1990—91; counselor, tchr. Hudson County CC, Jersey City, 1992—. Mem.: ACA, NEA, NJ Counseling Assn., NJ Edn. Assn., Nat. Acad. Adv. Assn., Psi Chi, Kappa Delta Pi, Phi Kappa Phi. Democrat. Roman Catholic. Avocations: reading, writing, pets. Office: Hudson County CC 162 Sip Ave Jersey City NJ 07306

MAHURIN HADAWAY, MELANIE L., secondary school educator; b. Anchorage, Feb. 18, 1969; d. Marshall and Karen Mahurin; m. William R. Hadaway, Aug. 5, 2000; children: Hannah Hadaway, Aileen Hadaway, Jedidiah Hadaway. BA in English, U. Alaska, Fairbanks, 1995. Tchr. FA Degnan H.S., Unalakleet, Alaska, 1995—98; English tchr. Austin E. Lathrop H.S., Fairbanks, 1998—. Mem.: Fairbanks Edn. Assn. (dir. 2000—06), Delta Kappa Gamma. Office: Lathrop High School 901 Airport Way Fairbanks AK 99701 Office Phone: 907-456-7794. Personal E-mail: mhadaway@northstar.k12.ak.us. Business E-Mail: mhadaway@northstar.k12.a.us.

MAIER, PAULINE, historian, educator; b. Apr. 27, 1938; d. Irvin Louis and Charlotte (Winterer) Rubbelke; m. Charles Steven Maier, June 17, 1961; children: Andrea Nicole, Nicholas Winterer, Jessica Elizabeth Heine. AB, Radcliffe Coll., 1960; postgrad., London Sch. Econs., 1960-61; PhD in History, Harvard U., 1968; LLD (hon.), Regis Coll., 1987; DHL (hon.), Williams Coll., 1993. Asst. prof. then assoc. prof. history U. Mass., Boston, 1968-77; Robinson-Edwards prof. history U. Wis., Madison, 1977-78; prof. history MIT, Cambridge, Mass., 1978—, William R. Kenan Jr. prof. history, 1990—. Dept. head, MIT, 1979-88, mem. coun. Inst. Early Am. History, 1982-84; trustee Regis Coll., 1988-93; trustee Commonwealth Sch., 1991-96; bd. mgrs. Old South Meeting House, 1987-97, bd. advisors Internat. Ctr. Jefferson Studies, 2000-. Author: From Resistance to Revolution: Colonial Radicals and the Development of American Opposition to Britain, 1765-1766, 1972, The Old Revolutionaries: Political Lives in the Age of Samuel Adams, 1980, The American People: A History, 1986, American Scripture: Making the Declaration of Independence, 1997; co-author: Inventing America, 2002, 2d edit. 2006. Recipient Douglass Adair award Claremont Grad. Sch.-Inst. Early Am. History, 1976, Kidger award New Eng. History Tchrs. Assn., 1981; fellow Nat. Endowment Humanities, 1974-75, 88-89, Charles Warren fellow, 1974-75, Guggenheim fellow, 1990. Mem. Orgn. Am. Historians (mem. exec. bd. 1978-82), Am. Hist. Assn. (mem. nominations com. 1983-85, chmn. 1985), Soc. Am. Historians, Am. Antiquarian Soc. (mem. exec. coun. 1984-89), Colonial Soc. Mass. (mem. exec. coun. 1990-93), Mass. Hist. Soc., Am. Acad. Arts and Scis., The Hist. Soc. (bd. govs. 1998—). Home: 60 Larchwood Dr Cambridge MA 02138-4639 Office: MIT E51-279 77 Massachusetts Ave Cambridge MA 02139-4307 Office Phone: 617-253-2646. Business E-Mail: pmaier@mit.edu.

MAIERLE, BETTE JEAN, director; b. Greenville, Mich., Sept. 8, 1933; d. Clinton and Bonnie (Briggs) Peckham; m. Ronald Matthew Maierle, Aug. 27, 1960; children: Steven, Suzanne Maierle-Liesé, Peter, AnneMarie Maierle Krepela, Laura. AD in Secretarial Sci., Davenport Univ., 1952; BA in Speech Pathology, Mich. State U., 1956; MA in Human Devel. and Resources, Wayne State U., 1976. Speech pathologist Ferndale (Mich.) Schs., 1956-60; tchr. of deaf Walled Lake (Mich.) Schs., 1960-61; tchr. spl. edn. Troy (Mich.) Schs., 1961-69; part time theme reader Detroit Pub. Schs., 1964—65; speech pathologist Birmingham (Mich.) Schs., 1967—89; tchr. spl. edn. Avondale Schs., Auburn Hills, Mich., 1965—; owner, dir. Meadowbrook Preschool, Troy, 1968—; speech pathologist Mich. Sch. for Deaf and Blind, Flint, Mich., 1991-97. Fruit and vegetable insp. USDA, Traverse City, Mich., summers 1990-95. Vol. St. Daniel's Cath. Ch., Clarkston; vol. Rep. Party, Clarkston. Republican. Roman Catholic. Avocations: travel, antiques. Home: 8220 Reese Rd Clarkston MI 48348-2742 Office: Meadowbrook Preschool 6995 Livernois Rd Troy MI 48098-1572 Office Phone: 248-879-0473.

MAILLET, LUCIENNE, humanities educator; b. Lewiston, Maine, Apr. 16, 1934; d. Leon J. and Alice (Lizotte) Thibault; m. Daniel J. Maillet, July 14, 1956; 1 child, Daniel Jr. BA in Chemistry, Bates Coll., 1956; MA in Edn., George Washington U., 1963; MLS, Cath. U., 1969; cert. of profl. devel. and library and info. scis., CUNY, 1975; DLS, Columbia U., 1982; MBA, L.I. U., 1999. Librarian Conn. Park Elem. Sch., 1965-69, Southwoods Jr. High Sch., 1969-70; head curriculum materials and audiovisual ctr. CUNY, York Coll., Jamaica, NY, 1970-75; asst. prof. Palmer Sch., Long Island U., Brookville, NY, 1975-84, dean, 1984-89, prof., 1975—. Mem. Am. Library Assn., Am. Soc. Info. Sci., Assn. Colls. and Rsch. Libraries, Spl. Libraries Assn., Assn.

Library and Info. Sci. Edn., Beta Phi Mu. Home: 71 Andrew St Manhasset NY 11030-2309 Office: Long Island Univ Palmer Sch Libr & Info Sci CW Post Campus Greenvale NY 11548 Office Phone: 516-299-2175. Business E-Mail: lmaillet@liu.edu.

MAIMON, ELAINE PLASKOW, university chancellor; b. Phila., July 28, 1944; d. Louis J. and Gertrude (Canter) Plaskow; m. Morton A. Maimon, Sept. 30, 1967; children: Gillian Blanche, Alan Marcus. AB, U. Pa., 1966, MA, 1967, PhD, 1970. Asst. prof. Haverford (Pa.) Coll., 1971-73; lectr. Arcadia U., Glenside, Pa., 1973-75, asst. prof., dir. writing, 1975-77, assoc. prof., 1977-83, assoc. dean, 1980-84, assoc. v.p., prof. English, 1984-86; adj. assoc. prof. U. Pa., Phila., 1982-83; assoc. dean of coll. Brown U., Providence, 1986-88; dean, prof. English Queens Coll. CUNY, Flushing, NY, 1988-96; campus CEO, provost Ariz. State U. West, Phoenix, 1996—2004; v.p. Ariz. State U., 1996—2004; chancellor U. Alaska, Anchorage, 2004—. Nat. bd. cons. NEH, 1977-81; mem. adv. bd. Cox Comm., 1997-2001; bd. dirs. Arrowhed Cmty. Bank. Co-author: Writing in the Arts and Sciences, 1981, A Writer's Resource, 2003; co-editor: Readings in the Arts and Sciences, 1984, Thinking, Reasoning and Writing, 1989, A Writer's Resource, 2003, 2d edit., 2007, The New McGraw Hill Handbook, 2007, Writing Intensive, 2007. Trustee Heard Mus., Phoenix, 1999—2005. Recipient Golden Heart award, Today's Ariz. Woman, 2000, Women of Distinction award, YMCA, Maricopa County, 2001, YWCA award in Edn., 2002, World award, Girl Scouts Am., Ariz. Cactus-Pine Coun., 2002, Woman of Vision award, Phoenix Bus. Jour.; Elaine Maimon award for Excellence in Writing named in her honor, Arcadia U., 1994. Mem.: MLA (exec. com., tchg. of writing divsn.), Am. Assn. Colls. and Univs. (exec. bd. 2002—), Conf. on Coll. Composition Comm. (exec. com. 1985—87), ACE Nat. Commn. Women, Nat. Coun. Tchrs. English (nominating com. 1986—87, teaching of writing divsn. 1991), Phi Beta Kappa. Office: U Alaska Anchorage 3211 Providence Dr Anchorage AK 99508-8060 Home: 2831 UAA Dr Unit B Anchorage AK 99508 Office Phone: 907-786-1437. Business E-Mail: elaine.maimon@uaa.alaska.edu.

MAIN, EDNA DEWEY (JUNE MAIN), education educator; b. Hyannis, Mass., Sept. 1, 1940; d. Seth Bradford and Edna Wilhelmina (Wright) Dewey; m. Donald John Main, Sept. 9, 1961 (div. Dec. 1989); children: Alison Teresa Main Ronzon, Susan Christine Main Leddy, Steven Donald. Degree in merchandising, Tobe-Coburn Sch., N.Y., 1960; BA in Edn., U. North Fla., Jacksonville, 1974, MA in Edn., 1979, M in Adminstrn. and Supervision, 1983; PhD in Curriculum and Instrn., U. Fla., Gainsville, 1990. Asst. buyer Abraham & Straus, Bklyn., 1960-61; asst. mdse. mgr. Interstate Dept. Stores, NYC, 1962-63; tchr. Holiday Hill Elem. Sch., Jacksonville, Fla., 1974-86; instr. summer sci. inst., 1984-92; prof. edn. Jacksonville U., 1992—, dir. masters program in integrated learning and ednl. tech. Instr. U. Fla., 1987—90, U. North Fla., 1990—92; cons. Assn. Internat. Schs. Africa, 1994—97. Co-author: (book) Developing Critical Thinking Through Science, Book I, 2001, Developing Critical Thinking Through Science, Book II, 2002. Rep. United Way, 1981—86; tchr. rep., chpt. leader White Ho. Young Astronaut Program, 1984—85; team leader NSF Shells Elem. Sci. Project. Named Fla. Prof. of the Yr., Carnegie Found., 2002, Prof. of Yr., Jacksonville U., 2003; recipient Innovative Excellence in Tchg., Learning and Tech. award, Internat. Coll. Conf., 1999, Outstanding Alumni award, U. North Fla., 1999, Eve award for Edn., 2001, Apple Disting. Educator award, 2003—05. Mem.: Internat. Soc. Tech. Edn., Soc. Info. Tech. and Tchr. Edn., ASCD, NSTA (Sci. Tchrs. Achievement Recognition award 1983), Kappa Delta Pi, Phi Delta Kappa, Phi Kappa Phi. Episcopalian. Office: Jacksonville U 2800 University Blvd N Jacksonville FL 32211-3394 Personal E-mail: main750@bellsouth.net.

MAINE, KATHRYN LEW, social studies educator; d. David Gabriel and Marilyn Ann LaGrange; m. Bradley Matthew Maine; 1 child, Grace Kathryn. BS, Ball State U., Muncie, 2003. Social studies tchr. Daleville Jr./Sr. HS, Ind., 2003—05, Delta HS, Muncie, Ind., 2005—. Avocations: reading, travel. Office: Delta HS 3400 E State Rd 28 Muncie IN 47303 Office Phone: 765-288-5597.

MAINELLA, CINDY L., artist, researcher; b. Duluth, Minn., June 4, 1945; d. Frank P. and Arline D. Mainella; m. J. Kent Riley, Feb. 21, 1982. Student, Mpls. Coll. Art and Design, 1965—67. Guest juror Sister Kenny Invitational Art Show for Artists with Disabilities, Mpls., 1999. Represented in permanent collections Minn. Mining and Mfg. 3M, St. Paul, First Bank, Fort Dodge, Iowa, exhibitions include No. Minn. Juried Art Show, Duluth, 1974, 1975, Arrowhead Art Show, Duluth Art Inst., 1975, 1976, Third Annual Bus. and the Professions Corp. Art Show, Mpls., 1977, Jury Show for Minn. Artists, Minn. Ctr. for Arts and Edn., Mpls., 1979, 1983, Jewish Cmty. Ctr., Mpls., 1979, Groveland Gallery, 1981, Pillsbury Co., Pillsbury Ctr., Mpls., 1981, Twenty Duluth Grads. Exhbn., 1986, 3M Concourse Gallery, 3M Ctr., St. Paul, 1999. Mem.: Minn. Art Pottery Assn. Avocations: baking, art. Office Phone: 612-824-2444.

MAINELLA, FRAN (FRANCES P. MAINELLA), former federal agency administrator; b. Groton, Conn., 1947; BS cum laude, U. Conn.; MS cum laude in Counseling, Ctrl. Conn. State Coll.; PhD in Pub. Svc. (hon.), Ctrl. Conn. State U., 2002. H.S. phys. edn. tchr. Vernon Pub. Sch., Rockville, Conn., 1969—77; asst. ctr. dir. Tallahassee Parks and Recreation Dept., 1977—78; dir. recreation Town of Lake Park, Fla., 1978—83; exec. dir. Fla. Recreation and Park Assn., Tallahassee, 1983—89; dir. divsn. Recreation and Parks Fla. Dept. Environ. Protection, Tallahassee, 1989—2001; dir. Nat. Park Svc. US Dept. Interior, Washington, 2001—06. Spkr. in field. Contbr. numerous articles to profl. publs. Co-chair Com. for Preservation of the White House, mem. adv. coun. on hist. preservation; bd. trustees John F. Kennedy Ctr. for Performing Arts; liaison White House Hist. Soc.; sec., treas. Nat. Park Found.; mem. Am. Folklife Bd.; past pres. Nat. Assn. State Park Dirs.; past bd. mem. Am. Acad. Park and Recreation Adminstr.; past mem. Fla. Commn. Ttourism; past officio bd. mem. Fla. Recreation and Park Assn.; past mem. Gov.'s Mansion adv. com.; past bd. mem. Fla. Gov.'s Coun. on Phys. Fitness and Sports; past sec., bd. dirs. Spl. Olympics; past pres. Tallahassee Soc. Assn. Execs.; past chair United Way Drive for Tallahassee Soc. Assn. Execs.; past bd. dirs. Tallahassee Leon County Convention and Visitors Bur.; bd. dirs. Ford's Theatre Soc., Wolf Trap Found. for Performing Arts. Recipient Disting. Svc. award, Nat. Assn. Recreation Resource Planners, 1996, Woman of Distinction award, Girl Scout Coun. of Apalachee Bend, 1998, Pugsley medal, Am. Acad. Park and Recreation Adminstrn., 1998, Disting. Svc. award, Nat. Assn. State Park Dirs., 1999, Senator Bob Williams award, State of Fla., 2001, Sheldon Coleman Outdoors award, 2002, Walter T. Cox Pub. Svc. Achievement award, Clemson U., 2002. Mem.: Nat. Recreation and Park Assn. (congress planning com. 1984, 1987, past chair coun. exec. dirs., pres. 1997—, Harold D. Meyer Profl. award 2000).

MAINES, NATALIE LOUISE, musician; b. Lubbock, Tex., Oct. 14, 1974; d. Lloyd and Tina M.; m. Michael Tarabay, May 9, 1997 (div. Jan. 1999); m. Adrian Pasdar, June 24, 2000; children: Jack Slade, Beckett Finn. Student, Tex. Tech.; grad., Berklee Coll. Music, Boston, 1995. Performer Dixie Chicks, 1995—. Singer: (albums) Wide Open Spaces, 1998 (Maximum Vision Clip of Yr., Billboard, 1998, Best New Country Artist Clip of Yr., Billboard, 1998, Best Country Album, Grammy Awards, 1998, Album of Yr., Acad. Country Music, 1998, Best Selling Album, Can. Country Music Awards, 1999, Song of Yr. (Country), WB Radio Music Awards, 1999, Album of Yr., ACM, 1999), Fly, 1999 (Best Country Album, Grammy Awards, 1999, Best Selling Album, Can. Country Music Awards, 2000, Internat. Album, British Country Music Awards, 2000, Country Album of Yr., Billboard, 2000, Album of Yr., CMA, 2000), Home, 2002 (Favorite Country Album, Am. Music Awards, 2002, Best Recording Package, Grammy Awards, 2002, Best Country Album, Grammy Awards, 2002), Top of the World Tour: Live, 2003 (Grammy award for Best Country Group Vocal Performance, 2005), Taking the Long Way, 2006; performer: (documentary) Dixie Chicks: Shut Up and Sing, 2006. Named Most Significant New Country Act, Country Monitor, 1998, Top New Country Artist, Billboard, 1998, Group of Yr., CMA, 1998, Top Vocal Group, Acad. Country Music, 1998, Country Artist of Yr., Rolling Stone, 1999, Top Country Artist, Billboard, 1999, Internat. Rising Star, British Country Music Awards, 1999, Artist of Yr., WB Radio Music Awards, 1999, Favorite New Artist (Country), AMA, 1999, Vocal Group of Yr., CMA, 1999, Country Artist of Yr., Billboard, 1999, Entertainer of Yr., CMA, 2000, ACM, 2000, 2001, Vocal Group of Yr., 2001, Favorite Musical Group or Band, People's Choice Award, 2002, Vocal Group of Yr., Country Music Assn. Awards, 2002, others; named one of 100 Most Influential People, Time Mag., 2006; recipient Horizon award, CMA, 1998. Office: Monument Sony Nashville 34 Music Sq East Nashville TN 37203*

MAINOR, DEBRA L., elementary school educator; b. Cleve., Tenn., May 18, 1953; d. Edward Mital and Orena Ford; m. Thomas R. Mainor, May 7, 1977; children: Jenny Raye, Benjamin Thomas. BS in Elem. Edn., Lee U., Cleve., Tenn., 1975. Tchr. Bradley County, Cleve., Tenn., Dayton City Sch., Tenn. Choral tchr. Dayton City Sch., Tenn. Pianist Grace Bible Ch., Dayton, Tenn. Avocations: music, gardening, camping.

MAINS, SUSAN JANE, mathematics educator; b. Greensburg, Pa., Oct. 13, 1953; d. Malcolm Franklin and Hazel Rose Sias; m. Dale Thomas Mains, Apr. 19, 1973; children: Thomas Matthew, Jonathan Douglas, Laura Elizabeth, David Robert. BA in Math., Seton Hill Coll., Greensburg, Pa., 1977. Cert. tchr. math. Pa., 1977. Math. tchr. Diocese of Greensburg, Greensburg, Pa., 1977—79, Hempfield Area Sch. Dist., Greensburg, 2003—. Mem. Latrobe Unity Parks and Recreation Commn., 1996—. pres. Latrobe, Pa., 2006—; sch. bd. v.p. Greater Latrobe Sch. Bd., Latrobe, Pa., 1991—; pres. Latrobe Unity Parks and Recreation Commn., Latrobe, Pa., 1996—2006, v.p., 1997—. Democrat-Npl. Evangelical Lutheran. Avocations: walking, gardening, tutoring, reading. Office Phone: 724-834-9000.

MAINWARING, SUSAN ADAMS, recreational facility executive; b. Detroit, Apr. 30, 1948; BA in Elem. Edn., Elmira Coll., 1970. Elem. tchr. The Am. Sch., Mexico City, 1971—73; travel cons. Columbus, Ohio, 1973—80; dist. sales mgr. Top Brands, Inc., Columbus, 1980—85, v.p., CEO Cleve., 1985—89; exec. dir. Classic Chamber Concerts, Naples, Fla., 1998—2000. Office Phone: 941-434-8505. Business E-Mail: info@classicchamberconcerts.org.

MAIO, ELSIE REGINA, communications consultant; b. Bklyn., Dec. 20, 1951; d. Ralph Joseph and Joan Anne (McNally) M. BA summa cum laude, CUNY, 1977. Editor Smith Barney Co., N.Y.C., 1977-78; sr. editor Dean Witter, N.Y.C., 1978-79, Instl. Investor mag., N.Y.C., 1979-80; comm. cons. McKinsey & Co., N.Y.C., 1980-83; founding prin. Maio Assocs., Guttenberg, N.J., 1986-89; sr. v.p. Lippincott & Margulies, N.Y.C., 1989-94; sr. ptnr. Diefenback Elkins, N.Y.C., 1994-96; pres. Maio and Co., Inc., 1996—. Spkr. in field. Bd. dirs. Sisters of Mercy of Ams. Mem. Soc. Profl. Journalists. Avocations: human potential movement, watercolor painting.

MAIOCCHI, CHRISTINE, lawyer; b. N.Y.C., Dec. 24, 1949; d. George and Andreina (Toneatto) M.; m. John Charles Kerecz, Aug. 16, 1980; children: Charles George, Joan Christine. BA in Polit. Sci., MA in Polit. Sci., Fordham U., 1971, JD, 1974; postgrad., NYU, 1977—. Bar: N.Y. 1975, U.S. Dist. Ct. (so. and ea. dists.), N.Y. 1975, U.S. Ct. Appeals (2nd cir) 1975. Law clk. to magistrate U.S. Dist. Ct. (so. dist.) N.Y., N.Y.C., 1973-74; atty. corp. legal dept. The Home Ins. Co., N.Y.C., 1974-76; asst. house counsel corp. legal dept. Allied Maintenance Corp., N.Y.C., 1976; atty. corp. legal dept. Getty Oil Co., N.Y.C., 1976-77; v.p., mgr. real estate Paine, Webber, Jackson & Curtis, Inc., N.Y.C., 1977-81; real estate mgr. GK Techs., Inc., Greenwich, Conn., 1981-85; real estate mgr., sr. atty. MCI Telecom. Corp., Rye Brook, N.Y., 1985-93; real estate and legal cons. Wallace Law Registry, 1994-96; sr. assoc. counsel Met. Transp. Authority, 1996-99, dep. gen. counsel, 1999—2005, gen. counsel, 2005—. Lectr. Practicing Law Inst., N.Y.C., NY, 1999—. Mem.: ABA, CoreNet Global, Indsl. Devel. Rsch. Coun. (program v.p. 1985, Profl. award 1987), Nat. Assn. Corp. Real Estate Execs. (pres. 1983—84, treas. 1984—86, bd. dirs. 1995—, exec. v.p. N.Y. chpt. 2000—01), The Corp. Bar (sec. real estate divsn. 1987—89, chmn. 1990—92), Women's Bar Assn. Manhattan, NY. Bar Assn., Dobbs Ferry Women's Club (program dir. 1981—92, 1994—96, publicity dir. 1992—94), Jr. League Club. Avocations: sports, theater, gardening. Home: 84 Clinton Ave Dobbs Ferry NY 10522-3004 E-mail: cmaiocch@mtahq.org.

MAISNER, SUZANNE, technology consultant, educator; BA in Econs., U. Calif., Santa Cruz, 1977; MPhil in Urban and Regional Planning, The London Sch. Econs., 1983. Cert. profl. Microsoft Corp., Wash., 1996; in secondary edn. tchg. Dept. Edn., Calif., 2000, in adult edn. tchg. Dept. Edn., Calif., 2004. Pres. Zanne and Assocs., Inc., Portland, 1988—96, Share Comm., Inc., Seattle, 1989—90; quality assurance cons. 20th Century Fox Studios, Prudential Real Estate Assocs., The Getty Inst., LA, 1996—97; software devel. cons. Reuters, El Segundo, Calif., 1998; bus. continuity cons. TRW Space and Electronics Group, Manhattan Beach, Calif., 1999; tchr. LA Unified Sch. Dist., 2001—05. Author: Adult Children of Aging Parents: A Primer. Bd. dirs. Substitute Unit United Teachers LA, 2004—05; dir. A Step Up, LA, 2005. Edward Reuben Leadership scholar, Santa Monica Coll., 1975. Mem.: Women in Tech. Internat.

MAITOZA, COLLEEN, professional sports team executive; Gen. mgr., co-owner Sacramento (Calif.) Sirens, 2001—. Achievements include an undefeated 2003 season in the Independent Women's Football League; the Sacramento Sirens won the 2003 Independent Women's Football League Championship against the New York Sharks.

MAIZE, LINDA LOU, elementary school educator; b. Hazen, ND, Aug. 30, 1952; d. F. Robert and Mary (Keller) Oestreich; m. Kirk Edward Maize, Aug. 10, 1974; 1 child, Allen Edward. BS in Elem. and Spl. Edn., U. Nebr., 1974; MS, Minot State U., 1998. Nat. bd. cert. tchr., 2002. Tchr. Naughton Sch., Bismarck, N.D., 1974-75; elem. tchr. Golden Valley (N.D.) Pub. Sch., 1975-78, Beulah (N.D.) Pub. Schs., 1978—. Tchr. Bible sch. Concordia Luth. Ch., Beulah, 1976-77, Wednesday sch. tchr., 1994-98; vol. campaign for U.S. senator, Beulah, 1982, 84; past sec. Dist. 33 Dem. Com., Beulah; leader Boy Scouts Am.; leader 4-H, 1999; sec. Beulah Area Dollars for Scholars, Mercer County 4-H Coun.; foster parent, 1986-87. Mem. ASCD, Internat. Reading Assn., Nat. Coun. Tchrs. Math., Nat. Coun. Tchrs. English, ND Edn. Assn. (Dist. 33 govt. rels. contact 1982-88, 93-, bd. dirs. 2006-), Beulah Edn. Assn. (treas. 1979-80, v.p. 1981-82, pres. 1982-83), Am. Quarter Horse Assn., Delta Kappa Gamma. Avocations: reading, riding, stamp art, photo albums, quarter horses. Office: Beulah Elem Sch 200 7th St NW Beulah ND 58523

MAJERS, ELIZABETH LOUISE, lawyer; b. Chgo., Sept. 25, 1958; children: Katelyn Christine Majers Bonds, Kellyanne Louise Majers Bonds. BS, U. Ill., 1979; JD, Ind. U., 1982. Bar: Tex. 1982, Ill. 1983; CPA, Ill. Tax atty. Exxon Co., U.S.A., Houston, 1982-83; assoc. Chapman and Cutler, Chgo., 1983-90, ptnr., 1990-92, capital ptnr., 1992-97, McDermott, Will & Emery, Chgo., 1998—, ptnr. in charge client rels., 2003—. Spkr. in field, 1983—. Fellow Am. Coll. Investment Counsel (past pres. 1995-97, pres., v.p. 1993-95, trustee 1991—). Avocations: golf, cooking, photography, travel. Office: McDermott Will & Emery 227 W Monroe St Ste 4400 Chicago IL 60606-5096 E-mail: emajers@mwe.com.

MAJESKE, PENELOPE KANTGIAS, education educator, educator; b. Detroit, Sept. 21, 1937; d. George and Amelia (Malevitou) Kantgias; m. Francis Thomas Majeske, July 26, 1958; children: Matthew, Amelia, Nicholas. PhD, Wayne State U., 1979. V.p. Human resources Wayne State U., Detroit, 1981-84, spl. asst. to pres., 1984-85, asst. provost and dean grad. sch., 1985-86, asst. prof. weekend coll., 1976—. Cons. CSC, Lansing. Mich, 1985-86; dir. Delta Dental Plan of Mich., Okemos, 1985—. Contbr. articles to profl. jours. Democrat. Greek Orthodox. Avocation: gardening. Home: 4238 Greensboro Dr Troy MI 48085-3675

MAJETTE, DENISE, former congresswoman; b. Bklyn., May 18, 1955; d. Voyd and Olivia Majette; m. Rogers Mitchell Majette; 2 children. BA, Yale U., 1976; JD, Duke U., 1979. Atty. Legal Aid Soc. Winston-Salem, NC, 1981—83; law asst. Ga. Ct. Appeals, 1984—89; ptnr. Jenkins Nelson & Welch, 1989—92; spl. asst. atty. gen. State of Ga., 1991—92; adminstrv. law juste Ga. State Bd. Workers' Compensation, 1992; judge State Ct. of DeKalb County, 1993—2002; congresswoman 4th Dist. Ga. U.S. Ho. Reps., 2003—05; mem. budget, edn. and workforce, and small bus. ho. coms. Grad. Leadership DeKalb, 1992; mem. Kidney Caucus; former com. mem. Miller Grove PTA; past mem. vestry Episcopal Ch. of Holy Cross; former pres. DeKalb Lawyers Assn.; mem. Childcare Com. YMCA, Decatur; mem. adv. bd. Jr. League DeKalb County; mem. Congl. Black Caucus, Congl. Caucus on India and Indian Ams.; mem. steward bd. Antioch AME Ch. Recipient Judge's Cmty. Recognition award, Black Law Students' Assn., Ga. State U. Coll. Law, 2001, You Go Girl award, Ga. Assn. Black Women Attys., 2003. Democrat. Home: PO Box 33678 Decatur GA 30033-0678

MAJOR, MARY JO, dance school artistic director; b. Joliet, Illinois, Dec. 5, 1955; d. George Francis and Lucille Mae (Ballun) Schmidberger; m. Perry Rex Major, June 9, 1979. AA, Joliet Jr. Coll., 1976; BA, Lewis U., 1978; MS, Ill. State U., 1983; postgrad., No. Ill. U., Nat. Louis U., Governor's State U., Olivet Nazarene U., Aurora U. Cert. tchr. in Ill. Tchr., softball coach St. Rose Grade Sch., Wilmington, Ill., 1977-78; tchr., coach volleyball, basketball, softball Reed Custer High Sch., Braidwood, Ill., 1978-79; pvt. tutor, 1979; tchr. Coal City (Ill.) Middle Sch., 1980—, basketball coach, 1980-84; owner, dir., choreographer Major Sch. Dance, Inc., Coal City, 1984—; owner Technique Boutique, 1991—. Aerobics instr. Wilmington Pk. Dist., 1977-82, Coal City Shape Shoppe, 1980-82; cheerleading sponsor Joliet Jr. Coll., 1976-77, aerobics instr., 1980-81; pvt. dance instr., Coal City, 1981; dancer, choreographer Coal City Bi-Centennial Celebration, 1981, Coal City Cmty. Celebration, 1982; founder Major Motion Dancers, 1984—; tchr., Russia, 1990; dancer, choreographer various performances for ch. and civic orgaizations; televised half time performance and tour Citrus Bowl. Commd. to choreograph and appear in video prodn.: Jacinta, Not an Ordinary Love, The Patty Waszak Show A Bit of Branson, 1995-2000; performer Easter Seals Telethon from the Empress Casino, Joliet. Mem. Arts Coun. Coop. Recipient Proclamation of Achievement Award Dance Olympus, Chgo., 1986-2005, Best Choreographer Award 1990, Merit Award Tremaine Dance Conv., 1991-92; named Best Actress, Joliet Kiwanis, 1989, Best Musician, 1990. Mem. NEA, Ill. Edn. Assn., Coal City Cmty. Unit Edn. Assn. Office: Major Sch Dance 545 E 1st St Coal City IL 60416-1643 Office Phone: 815-634-3003. E-mail: mmajor55@sbcglobal.net.

MAJORAS, DEBORAH PLATT, commissioner; m. John Majoras. BA summa cum laude, Westminster Coll.; JD, U. Va., 1989. Law clk. to Hon. Stanley S. Harris US Dist. Ct., DC; dep. asst. atty. gen. US Dept. Justice, Antitrust Div., 2000—01, prin. dep. asst. atty. gen., 2002—03; ptnr. antitrust sec., mem. tech. issues practice Jones Day, Washington, DC, 2004; chmn. FTC, Washington, DC, 2004—. Chair Internat. Competition Network's (ICN) Merger Working Group; mem. Antitrust Modernization Commn. Mem.: ABA (mem. Antitrust Law Sec.). Avocations: golf, shopping. Office: FTC 600 Pennsylvania Ave, NW Washington DC 20580 Office Phone: 202-326-2100.

MAJORS, BETTY-JOYCE MOORE, genealogist, writer; b. Tullahoma, Tenn., Nov. 22, 1930; d. Frank Russell and Willie Eveline (Cope) Moore; m. Charles Anderton Majors, June 19, 1953; children: Robert Cope Majors, Carolyn Lynn (Majors) Diehl. Student, Israel Conservatory of Music, Jerusalem, 1951; BS, Mid. Tenn. State U., 1952. Pub. sch. music tchr., Lynchburg, Tenn., 1953-54; computer programmer AEDC, Arnold Air Force Station, Tenn., 1954-86; genealogist, author, lectr., 1986—. Author: DeKalb County, Tennessee Genealogy from Settlement Books, 1992, Warren County, Tennessee Deed Book A, 1992, Warren County, Tennessee Will Books, 3 vols., 1992-95; co-author: Warren County, Tennessee Annotated Cemetery Books, 4 vols., 1994-99. Chmn. Coffee County Tenn. Records Commn., Manchester, Tenn., 1990—, also archivist, Coffee County Tenn., 1997—. Mem.: DAR (state chmn. 1980—82), Plantagenet Soc., Soc. Descs. Knights Most Noble Order of Garter, Colonial Order of Crown, Ams. of Royal Descent, Magna Charta Dames (state chmn. 1972—73), Sons and Daus. of Pilgrims (state officer 1981—82), USD1812 (chpt. officer 2000—01), Colonial Dames XVII Century (nat. officer 1979—83). Avocations: reading, painting. Home: 111 Oak Park Dr Tullahoma TN 37388-4677

MAKEPEACE, MARY LOU, foundation administrator, former mayor; 2 children. BA in Journalism, U. ND, 1962; MPA, U. Colo., Colorado Springs, 1980. Tchr. Am. Sch., Tananarive, Madagascar; asst. to Def. Attaché Am. Embassy, Prague, Czechoslavakia; adult edn. officer Ramstein AFB, Germany; case worker, adminstr. El Paso County Dept. Social Svcs., 1974-82; exec. dir. Cmty. Coun. Pikes Peak Region, 1982-84; dist. 1 rep. City Colorado Springs, 1985-97, vice mayor, 1997, mayor, 1997—2003; exec. dir. Leadership Pike's Peak, Colo. Springs, 2003—04, Gill Found. Gay and Lesbian Fund, Colo., 2004—. Exofficio mem. Econ. Devel. Coun. Bd. Dirs.; chair Econ. Devel. Com., Task Force City Svcs. to Srs., urban affairs com. Pikes Peak Area Coun. Govts.; apptd. Colo. Space Adv. Coun.; adj. prof. U. Colo.; ex-dir. leadership Pikes Peak mem. steering com. Imagination Celebration; sr. advisor Palmer Found., Pikes Peak Partnership; mem. Nat. League Cities Leadership Tng. Coun.; past mem. Colo. Mcpl. League Exec. Bd., 1st United Meth. Ch. Gates Found. fellow, 1992; recipient Svc. Mankind award Centennial Sertoma Club, 1985, Mary Jean Larson Cmty. Svc. award Girl Scouts Wagon Wheel Coun., 2002, Spence Vanderlin Pub. Ofcl. award Am. Pub. Power Assn., 2002, Outstanding Cmty. award Econ. Devel. Corp., 2003; named Super Woman Women's Health Ctr., 1988, Best City Councilmem. Springs Mag., 1991; honored Women in Your Life dinner Women's Found. Colo., 2002. Mem. Am. Soc. Pub. Adminstrn., Pi Alpha Alpha. Personal E-mail: maryloum@gillfoundation.org.

MAKER, JANET ANNE, writer, retired literature educator; b. Woburn, Mass., Feb. 13, 1942; d. George Walter and Margaret Anna (Kopasz); children: Thomas Walter, Jane McKinley. BA, UCLA, 1963; MS, Columbia U., 1967; PhD, U. So. Calif., 1978. Prof. L.A. Trade Tech. Coll., 1991—2003, ret., 2003. Author: Get It All Together, 1979, Interpretive Reading Comprehension, 1984, Keys to a Powerful Vocabulary, Level I, 1981, 88, 94, Level II, 1983, 90, 94, Keys to College Success, 1980, 85, 90, 98, College Reading, Book 1, 1984, 88, 91, 96, 00, Book 2, 1982, 86, 89, 92, 96, 00, Book 3, 1985, Academic Reading with Active Critical Thinking, 1995. Avocation: blues music. Home and Office: 925 Malcolm Ave Los Angeles CA 90024-3113 Personal E-mail: jamaker2001@hotmail.com.

MAKI, HOPE MARIE, art educator; b. St. Joseph, Mo., Jan. 14, 1938; 3 children. Host TV art show Channel 6, Fort Walton Beach, Fla.; owner art sch., gallery; tchr. art, 1957—. Exhibited in shows at Arts-Inter-Salon Int des Sekneurs de L'Art, Chateauneuf du Pape, France, 1994, Salon Int des Seigneurs de L'Art, Palais des Congres Marseille, 1994, Mountserrat Gallery, N.Y.; represented in permanent pvt. and pub. collections; created art for the blind, 1963—; author, illustrator: Trader Jon His Life, 2001 Named One of Best New Poets Am. Poetry Assn., 1987, 88, 89; recipient Award of Poetic Achievement, Amherst Soc., recognition of outstanding achievements in art edn. Cox Comm., 2000; poem placed in spl. collection Statue of Liberty Nat. Monument, 1992 Mem. Nat. Mus. Women in Arts Avocation: poetry. Home: 3985 Langley Ave Pensacola FL 32504-8371 Office Phone: 850-478-4673.

MAKKAY, MAUREEN ANN, broadcast executive; b. Chgo. d. John Paul and Bernice Ann (Williams) Monaghan; m. Albert Makkay, Oct. 20, 1962; children: Allison, Albert Jr., Colleen. BA, U. R.I., 1974. Cert. secondary sch. tchr., Mass. Adminstr. Ednl. Records Bur., Wellesley, Mass., 1979-81; local sales mgr. Sta. WKZE, Orleans, Mass., 1981-83; nat. sales mgr. Sta. WKFM, Syracuse, NY, 1983-85; pres. Sta. WPXC-FM, Hyannis, Mass., 1987—; v.p. Sta. WRZE, Nantucket, Mass., Sta. WCIB-FM, Falmouth, Mass. Corporator Cape Code Five Cents Savings Bank, 1998—. Pres. Cape and Islands unit Am. Cancer Soc., 1988-91, bd. dirs., 1989-95; mem. pers. bd. Town of Barnstable, Mass., 1989-94, chmn., 1990-91; bd. dirs. Cape Cod Alcoholism

Intervention and Rehab., Inc., 1995—. Mem. Bus. and Profl. Women Cape Cod (bd. dirs. 1989—), Am. Women in Radio and TV, Nat. Assn. Broadcasters. Office: Sta WPXC-FM Radio 154 Barnstable Rd Hyannis MA 02601-2930 Home: 15 Meadow Farm Rd Centerville MA 02632-3161 Personal E-mail: capemo@aol.com.

MAKOWIECKA, MARIA HANNA, literature educator, educator; b. Warsaw, May 4, 1960; came to U.S., 1988; d. Stefan and Leokadia Marta (Cibor) M. MA, Warsaw U., 1984; DEA, Paris U., 1986; postgrad., CUNY. EFL instr. Meth. Coll. English, Warsaw, 1984-85, Soc. for Popularization of Culture & Sci., Warsaw, 1986-87, Sch. of British & Am. English, Warsaw, 1987-88; office dir. Office of Linguistic Svcs., Warsaw, 1986-88; ESL/ABE instr. N.Y. City Tech. Coll., N.Y.C., 1989-92; adj. lectr. Borough of Manhattan C.C., N.Y.C., 1990-94, Bronx C.C., 1992-94, asst. prof., 1994—. Mem. colloquium com. Grad. Ctr., CUNY, 1988-90. Contbr. articles to profl. jours. Elected student rep. Grad. Coun. Grad. Ctr. CUNY, 1990-92, elected mem. exec. com. in comparative lit., 1988-90. Helena Rubinstein scholar Grad. Ctr. CUNY, 1988-92. Mem. MLA, Am. Comparative Lit. Assn., Am. Assn. Tchrs. Slavic & Eastern European Lits. Avocations: hiking, african dance, in-line skating, skiing. Office: Bronx Cmty Coll Co 408a 181 University Pl New York NY 10003-4509 Office Phone: 201-447-9281. Business E-Mail: mmakowiecka@bergen.edu.

MAKRI, NANCY, chemistry professor; b. Athens, Greece, Sept. 5, 1962; came to the U.S., 1985; d. John and Vallie (Tsakona) M.; m. Martin Gruebele, July 9, 1992; children: Alexander Makris Gruebele, Valerie Gruebele Makri. BS, U. Athens, 1985; PhD, U. Calif., Berkeley, 1989. Jr. fellow Harvard U., Cambridge, Mass., 1989-91; from asst. prof. to assoc. prof. U. Ill., Urbana, 1992-99, prof., 1999—. Recipient Beckman Young Investigator award Arnold & Mabel Beckman Found., 1993, Ann. medal Internat. Acad. Quantum Molecular Sci., 1995, Camille Dreyfus Tchr.-Scholar award The Camille and Henry Dreyfus Found., 1997, Agnes Fay Morgan award Iota Sigma Pi, 1999, physics prize Bodossaki Found., 1999; named NSF Young Investigator, 1993; Packard fellow for sci. and engring. David and Lucile Packard Found., 1993, Sloan Rsch. fellow Alfred Sloan Found., 1994, Cottrell scholar Rsch. Corp., 1994; univ. scholar U. Ill., 1999. Fellow: AAAS, Am. Phys. Soc. Home: 2722 Valley Brook Dr Champaign IL 61822-7634 Office: U Ill Urbana Dept Chem 601 S Goodwin Ave Urbana IL 61801-3709 E-mail: nancy@makri.scs.uiuc.edu.

MAKRIS, MARGARET LUBBE, elementary school educator; b. Everett, Wash., July 17, 1930; d. Fred Roy and Edna (McFarland) Lubbe; m. Andreas Makris, June 12, 1959 (dec. Feb. 2005); children: Christos, Myron. BA, San Francisco State U., 1956; MEd, U. Md., College Park, 1970. Tchr. San Francisco Pub. Schs., 1954—56; recreation dir. U.S. Army Spl. Svcs. Staff, Germany, 1956—58; tchr. St. Louis Pub. Schs., 1959—61, Montgomery County Pub. Schs., Rockville, Md., 1961—86; ret., 1986. Republican. Achievements include established Andreas Makris Music Endowment-Nat. Philharm. at Music Ctr. Strathmore Hall, Bethesda, Md., 2005; created Andreas and Margaret Makris Music Scholarship Fund at Colo. State U., Coll. Liberal Arts, Ft. Collins, 2006; donated Andreas Makris violin crafted by Nicolaus Gagliano, Italy 1732 to Heritage Found., Washington, 2006. Home: 11204 Oak Leaf Dr Silver Spring MD 20901

MAKSYMOWICZ, VIRGINIA, art educator, writer, artist; b. Blyn., Feb. 19, 1952; BA, CUNY, Bklyn. Coll., 1973; postgrad., Bklyn. Mus. Art Sch., 1973-74; MFA, U. Calif., San Diego, 1977. Artist-in-residence Cultural Coun. Found. Artist Project, N.Y.C., 1978-79; asst. prof. dept. art Oberlin Coll., Ohio, 1980-81; vis. sculptor art, art history depts. Wayne State U., Detroit, 1981-82; exec. dir. Amos Eno Gallery, N.Y.C., 1983-86; articles editor Art&Artists Found. for the Cmty. of Artists, N.Y.C., 1986-89; vis. artist Mpls. Coll. Art & Design, 1990; adj. prof. art Moore Coll. of Art and Design, Phila., 1996—99; asst. prof. art Franklin & Marshall Coll., Lancaster, 2000—06, assoc. prof. art, 2006—. Adj. asst. prof. Drexel U., Phila., 1988. One-woman shows include Phoenix Gallery Project Room, NY, 2000, Silicon Gallery, Phila., 2001, Phillip's Mus., Lancaster, Pa., 2002, Ceres Project Room, NY, 2002, Richard E. Peeler Art Ctr., Greencastle, Ind., 2003, Penelec Gallery, Meadville, Pa., 2005, Ctr. Art Gallery, Grand Rapids, Mich., 2006, exhibited in group shows at Westby Gallery, Glassboro, N.J., 1998, Laband Gallery, L.A., 1998, Borowsky Gallery, Phila., 1998, Balt. Artscape, Md., 2003, one-woman shows include U. Mich., Ann Arbor, 2003, Mus. Contemporary Art, Ft. Collins., Colo., 2003, Williams Art Ctr. Gallery, Easton, Pa., 2005, Brookfield Craft Ctr., Brookfield, Conn., 2005; contbr. articles to profl. jour. NEA fellow, 1984; N.Y. State Coun. on Humanities grantee, 1991. Mem. Coll. Art Assn., Women's Caucus for Art. Home: 3719 Lancaster Ave Philadelphia PA 19104-2334 Office: TandM Arts 3719 Lancaster Ave Philadelphia PA 19104-2334

MAKUPSON, AMYRE PORTER, broadcast executive; b. River Rouge, Mich., Sept. 30, 1947; d. Rudolph Hannibal and Amyre Ann (Porche) Porter; m. Walter H. Makupson, Nov. 1, 1975; children: Rudolph Porter, Amyre Nisi. BA, Fisk U., 1970; MA, Am. U., Washington, 1972. Asst. dir. news Sta. WGPR-TV, Detroit, 1975-76; dir. pub. rels. Mich. Health Maintenance Orgn., Detroit, 1976-77; mgr. pub. affairs, news anchor Sta. WKBD-TV, Southfield, Mich., 1977—2004, Children's Miracle Network Telethon, 1989—. Mem. Co-Ette Club, Inc., Met. Detroit Teen Conf. Coalition; mem. adv. com., bd. dirs. Alzheimers Assn.; bd. dirs. com. March of Dimes; bd. dirs. Providence Hosp. Found., Sickle Cell Assn., Covenant House Mich., AAA, Home Fed. Savs. Bank, Skillman Found. Recipient 6 Emmy awards 4 Best Commentary/Best Anchor, Best Interview/Discussion Show, 26 Emmy nominations NATAS, Editl. Best Feature award AP, Media award UPI, Oakland County Bar Assn., TV Documentary award, Detroit Press Club, Bishop Gallagher award Mental Illness Rsch. Assn., Svc. award Arthritis Found. Mich., Mich. Mchts. Assn., DAV, Jr. Achievement, City of Detroit, Salvation Army, Spirit award City of Detroit, Spirit award City of Pontiac, Golden Heritage award Little Rock Bapt. Ch., 1993, Neal Shine award outstanding contbn. Nat. Soc. Fundraising Execs., Virginia Merrick award outstanding contbn. Christ Child Soc., Outstanding Achievement award Tuskegee Airmen, Best Feature Story award Mich. Assn. Broadcasters; named Media Person of the Yr., So. Christian Leadership Conf., 1994, Humanitarian of the Yr., March of Dimes, 1995, Michiganian of the Yr., Detroit News, Outstanding Woman of the Yr., GM Women's Club. Mem. Pub. Rels. Soc. Am., Am. Women in Radio and TV (Outstanding Achievement award 1981, Outstanding Woman in TV Top Mgmt. 1993, Mentor award 1993), Women in Comm., Nat. Acad. TV Arts and Scis., Detroit Press Club, Ad-Craft, Howard U. Nat. Gold Key Honor Soc. (hon.). Roman Catholic. Office: 26955 W 11 Mile Rd Southfield MI 48034-2292

MALACHOWSKI, NICOLE, pilot; b. 1974; Grad., Air Force Acad., 1996. F-15E (Strike Eagle fighter jet) pilot Royal Air Force, Lakenheath, Eng., 494th Fighter Squadron; No. 3 right wing pilot Thunderbirds, US Air Force Air Demonstration Squadron, 2005—. Served in Operation Iraqi Freedom, 2005. Achievements include being the first female demonstration pilot in the 52 year history of the Thunderbirds, US military high performance jet team. Office: USAFADS 4445 Tyndall Ave Nellis Afb NV 89191

MALAMUD, DEBORAH C., law educator; b. 1955; BA in Religion, magna cum laude, Wesleyan U., 1976; grad. work in Anthropology, U. Chgo., 1978—81, JD cum laude, 1986. Bar: Pa. 1987, DC 1988. Law clk. to Hon. Louis H. Pollack US Dist. Ct. Ea. Dist. Pa., Phila., 1986—87; law clk. to Hon. Harry A. Blackman US Supreme Ct., Washington, 1988—89; assoc. Bredhoff & Kaiser, DC, 1987—88, 1989—92; asst. prof. law U. Mich. Law Sch., 1992—97, prof., 1997—2003, James E. and Sarah A. Degan prof. law; prof. NYU Sch. Law, 2003—, An-Bryce prof. law. Vis. prof. NYU, 2002, Yale U., 2002—03. Mem.: Am. Soc. Legal History, Law and Soc. Assn. Office: NYU Sch Law Vanderbilt Hall Rm 310 40 Washington Sq S New York NY 10012-1099 Office Phone: 212-992-8902. E-mail: deborah.malamud@nyu.edu.

MALANEY, STEPHANIE J., reading specialist; b. Lafayette, Ind., Feb. 7, 1949; d. George Walter Joseph and Audrey (Fisher) Schneider; m. Michael J. Malaney; children: Amanda Lynn, Kyle Patrick, Ryan Elliot. BS Elem. Edn., U. Wis., Oshkosh, 1990, MS Elem. Edn., 1992; MSE Reading, U.Wis., Oshkosh, 1997; MS Ednl. Adminstrn., U.Wis., Madison, 2004. Tchr. grades 1-3 Appleton Area Sch. Dist., Wis., 1990—92, instrnl. lead tchr. and dist. leader social studies program, 1992—95, tchr. 6th grade, 1995—98, reading specialist, 1998—. Docent Ontagami Hist. Soc. Grigmon Mansion, Appleton, 2002—, Hearthstone (Hist. Site), Appleton, 2005—. Mem.: NEA, AAUW (pres. Appleton chpt. 2004—06), Wis. Edn. Assn. (bd. dirs.), Mid East Reading Coun. (pres. 2004—06). Avocations: reading, gardening, walking, travel, history research. Home: 307 E McArthur St Appleton WI 54911 Office: Appleton Area Sch Dist 2505 W Capitol Dr Appleton WI 54914 Office Phone: 920-832-4608. Office Fax: 920-993-7078. Business E-Mail: malaneystephan@aasd.k12.wi.us.

MALBERG, MELISSA DAWN, music educator, dancer; b. Lakenhearth, UK, Mar. 11, 1979; arrived in U.S., 1979; d. Eugene Austin and Mianne Sue Malberg. BA in Music Edn. and Music Performance, Ft. Lewis Coll., Durango, Colo., 2002. Music instr. Denver Pub. Sch., Denver, 2002—05, Jeffco Pub. Schs., Golden, Colo., 2005—06.

MALBON, LOUISE, nursing educator, hypnotherapist; b. Fayetteville, N.C., Feb. 13, 1956; d. Margaret Bess and John Bullard, Fletcher Bess (Stepfather); children: Lessel Malbon, III, Lawrence A., Leslie. Assoc. Applied Scis., Excelsior Coll., 1987. Cert. CPR instr., ACLS instr.; RN; cert. clin. hypnotherapist. Clin. resource nurse educator DC Gen. Hosp., Washington, 2001—02; ambulatory svs. coord. Wash. Hosp. Ctr., Washington, 2002. ACLS instr. Wash. Adventist Hosp. Tng. Ctr., Takoma Park, 2002—. Author: Caring Enough to Change, 2002. Cmty. activist 8th Precinct Civic Assn., Chillum, 1987—2002. Named 100 Extra Ordinary Nurses, Sigma Theta Tau Internat. Honor Soc. Nursing, 2001. Mem.: Emergency Nurses Assn. Democrat. Baptist. Home and Office: Fresh Start Hypnotherapy and Pub 5405 13th Avenue Chillum MD 20783 Personal E-mail: LSMLB@AOL.COM. Business E-Mail: Freshstarthypnotherapy.com.

MALCOLM, CHRISTINE ANNE, university hospital administrator; b. St. Paul, Jan. 25, 1950; d. Harold Thomas and Velma Lucille (Kuefler) Lehto; m. Mark Justin Malcolm, Sept. 18, 1971; children: Justine Emily, Benjamin Alexander. AB with hons., U. Chgo., 1972, MBA in Hosp. Adminstrn., 1978. Clinic mgr. Hennepin County Med. Ctr., Mpls., 1972-76; adminstrv. resident Ingalls Meml. Hosp., Harvey, Ill., 1977-78; cons. A.T. Kearney, Chgo., 1977, Coopers & Lybrand, Chgo., 1978-80; mgr. Amherst Assocs., Chgo., 1980-81; dir. Coopers & Lybrand, Chgo., 1981-86; v.p. planning and corp. devel. U. Chgo. Hosps., 1986—93; v.p. managed care and network devel. U. Health-System Consortium, Chgo.; v.p. provider solutions Global Health Solutions Group Computer Sci. Corp.; sr. v.p. strategic planning, mktg. and program devel. Rush U. Med. Ctr., Chgo., 2002—. V.p. Q.V., Inc., Chgo., 1987—. Author: (Digital Perspectives column) Healthcare Fin. Mgmt. mag. Sec., treas. and bd. dirs. Chgo. Child Care Soc., 1978—. Recipient Am. Mktg. Assn. Innovator award, 1988; named one of Chicago's 100 Most Influential Women, Crain's Chgo. Bus., 2004; NSF grantee, 1971. Mem. U. Hosp. Consortium, Am. Coll. Healthcare Execs., Am. Mktg. Assn. Lutheran. Avocations: gardening, canoeing, cooking. Office: Rush Univ Med Ctr 1653 W Congress Pkwy Chicago IL 60612

MALCOLM, ELLEN REIGHLEY, small business owner; b. Hackensack, N.J., Feb. 2, 1947; d. William Ford Reighley and Barbara (Hamilton) Malcolm. BA, Hollins Coll., 1969; MBA, George Washington U., 1984. Regional mgr. Common Cause, Washington, 1971-74, nat. issues coord., 1974-75, so. states coord., 1975-76; pub. info. coord. Nat. Women's Polit. Caucus, Washington, 1978-79, project dir., 1979; media coord. Cambodia Crisis Ctr., Washington, 1980; press sec. to spl. asst. to pres. for consumer affairs White House, Washington, 1980-81; pres. Windom Fund, Washington, 1980—, EMILY's List, Washington, 1985—. Bd. dirs. Ctr. for Policy Alternatives, Washington, 1989—; chair Women's Legal Def. Fund, Washington, 1984—. Mem. Washington Ednl. Telecomms. Assn. (bd. dirs. 1996—). Democrat. Office: Emilys List 1120 Connecticut Ave NW Ste 1100 Washington DC 20036-3949

MALCOLM, GLORIA J., small business owner; b. Atlanta, Apr. 16, 1956; d. George and Norella Camp; m. Ericka Monique Malcolm. B in Bus. Mgmt., DeKalb Coll., Atlanta; PhD in Edn. Leadership, Nova Southeastern U. Cert. notary pub. Team leader MS Soc., Atlanta; cons., advisor Home Testing Inst., NYCq; rep., organizer Nielsen TV, Dunedin, Fla.; mem. Alliance Orgn., Memphis; assoc., advisor Joyner Hutcheson Rsch., Atlanta; owner, pres. GJM Profl. Cleaning Svc., Inc., East Point, Ga., 1988—2004; floor supr., U-scan coord. Kroger Co., Atlanta, 2005—. Bd. dirs. Atlanta FCU. Active United Food Comml. Unions, Home Inst., MS Walk Soc., Am. Stroke Assn.; mem. svcs. Mt. Carmel Bapt. Ch., Atlanta; bd. dirs. St. Matthew's Ch. Mem.: NAFE, Bldg. Trader Assn., Piedmont Conservancy Com., Am. Stroke Assn., Rep. Senate Leadership, Nat. Home Garden Club. Avocations: travel, reading, volleyball, tennis, bicycling. Home: PO Box 490365 Atlanta GA 30349

MALCOLM, MOLLY BETH, political organization worker, counselor; BAS in Elem. Edn. with high honors, So. Meth. U., 1976; MS in Counseling and Guidance, Tex. A&M U.-Texarkana, 1988. Lic. profl. counselor, lic. chem. dependency counselor, Tex. Tchr. pub. schs., Ark., Tex., Okla., 1977-87; elem. counselor Texarkana (Ark.) Schs., 1987-89; drug. abuse prevention and counseling specialist Region VII Edn. Svc. Ctr., Kilgore, Tex., 1989-90; drug free schs. student assistance coord. Longview (Tex.) Ind. Sch. Dist., 1990-92; counseling and student svcs. coord. Texarkana (Tex.) Ind. Schs., 1992-93; owner, counselor Malcolm Cons., 1993—; field dir. Max Sandlin for Congress Campaign, 1996; dist. cmty. outreach coord. Congress Max Sandlin, Tex. 1st Dist., 1997-98; state chair Tex. Dem. Party, 1998—2003. V.p. nominations exec. com. Lyceum, 2005—. Contbr. publs. and curricula. Active Dem. Nat. Com., 1998-2003, exec. com., 2000-2003; active Presbytery of the Pines, Synod of the Sun Presbyn. Ch. USA, Pine Street Middle Sch. PTA; pres. Texarkana Ind. Sch. Dist., 1993-94, mem. adv. bd.; active Main Street Texarkana Bd.; bd.d irs. Texarkana People's Clinic; chair cmty. awareness com. Women for A&M Texarkana Bd.; deacon First Presbyn. Ch., Texarkana; advisor career devel. U. Tex. Chi Omega, 1999-2001; v.p. Lyceum Nominations Exec. Com., 2005- Named one of Rising Stars in Politics, Campaigns and Elections Mag., 2000, Pres.' award Ark. Counseling Assn., 1989, Hon. Bill Clinton Gov. Ark. Traveler award, 1989, Texarkana Alumni Achievement award Tex. A&M U., 1989, Winnsboro ISD Disting. Alumni award, 2003, Tex. Women's Polit. Caucus Blazing New Trails award, 2004. Mem. NAACP (life), Tex. Counseling Assn. (Disting. Svc. award 1993, 96), Tex. Mental Health Counselors Assn., Tex. Sch. Counselors Assn., Tex. Assn. for Multicultural Counseling and Devel. (chair awards com. 1994), N.E. Tex. Counseling Assn., Assn. State Dem. Chairs (co-chair resolution com. 1999-2001, exec. com., treas. exec. com. 2001-2004), Tex. Rural Cmtys. Bd., Clinton Birthplace Found. Bd., Assn. State Dem. Chairs Alumni Assn. (pres. 2005), Texarkana Mus. Sys. Bd., Texarkana Hist. Landmark Preservation Commn., Texarkana Regional Arts and Humanities Coun., Inc.(mem. AMAX adv. bd. 2004-), Tex. Dem. Women (pres. 1997-99, Mem. of Yr. 1998), Leadership Texarkana Alumi Assn. (adv. bd. 1996-99), Jr. League Texarkana, Leadership Tex. Alumnae Assn. (life, adv. bd. 1996-99), Ark. PTA (life), DAR, Tex. A&M U. at Texarkana Alumni Assn. (life, Achievement award 1989), So. Meth. U. Alumni Assn. (life), Assn. State Dem. Chairs Alumni Assn. (pres. 2005), Rotary Internat., Psi Chi (v.p. 1987-89), Delta Kappa Gamma (pres. chpt. 1988-89), Chi Omega (pres. chpt. alumni assn. 1998-99), Texarkana C. of C. (mil. affairs com.), Am. Legion. Office: Malcolm Consulting PO Box 6282 Texarkana TX 75505

MALCOM, SHIRLEY MAHALEY, science association executive; b. Birmingham, Ala., Sept. 6, 1946; m. Horace Malcom, 1975; children: Kelly A., Lindsey E. BS in Zoology, U. Wash., 1967; MA in Zoology, UCLA, 1968; PhD in Ecology, Pa. State U., 1974; LHD, Coll. St. Catherine, 1990, Knox Coll., 1993; DSc, N.J. Inst. Tech., 1991, Coll. St. Joseph, 1992, Hood Coll., 1994, Ball State U., 1996. Asst. prof. biology U. N.C., Wilmington, 1974-75; rsch. asst., staff assoc. and project dir. Office of Opportunities in Sci., AAAS, 1975-77, program head, 1979-89; program mgr. Minority Inst. Sci. Improvement Program NSF, 1977-79, mem. equal opportunities sci. and technol. com., 1983-86, chair equal opportunities sci. and technol. com., 1984-86; head directorate edn. and human resource programs AAAS, 1989—. Mem. technol. and women's employment panel, Commn. on Behavioral and Social Sci. and Edn., NRC, 1984-86, panel to evaluate Nat. Ctr. for Edn. Statistics, com. on nat. statistics, 1984-86; mem. adv. coun. Carnegie Forum on Edn. and Econs., 1984-88, task force tchg. profession, 1985-87; bd. dirs. Carnegie Corp., N.Y. Hon. trustee, Am. Museum Natural History; bd. dir. Howard Heinz Endowment, H. John Heinz III Ctr. for Sci., Econ. and Environment; adv. bd., Nat. Park Sys.; mem. adv. coun. Smithsonian Inst., 1990—; mem. Nat. Sci. Bd., 1994-98; mem. Pres.'s Com. for Advancement of Sci. and Tech., 1994-2001; regent, Morgan State Univ.; trustee, Calif. Inst. Tech. Named to Top 50 Black Scientists, Career Comm. Group, 2004; recipient Alumna Summa Laude Dignata award, Univ. Wash. and UW Alumni Assn., 1998, Public Welfare medal, NAS, 2003. Fellow AAAS, Am. Acad. Arts and Sci.; mem. Sci. Rsch. Soc., Sigma Xi. Office: AAAS 1200 New York Ave NW Ste 640 Washington DC 20005-3928

MALDONADO, JUDITH ANN BATORSKI, art association administrator; b. Eden, N.Y., Oct. 8, 1949; d. John Michael and Ethel (Owens) B.; m. Michael J. Rocco (div. Oct. 1980); 1 child, Flora; m. Maximino Maldonado Jr., Oct. 13, 1997. Student, Colo. Springs Coll. Bus., 1981; AS in Fine Arts, Suffolk C.C., 1983; BA, SUNY, Stonybrook, 1985, MA, 1987; postgrad., Columbia Coll. Chgo. Film Sch., 1985. Caretaker, asst. mgr. Farmer's Shared Home, Danbury, N.H., 1979-80; cert. educator Assn. for Childbirth at Home, Internat., L.A., 1980; accts. payable clk. Pikes Peak C.C., Colorado Springs, Colo., 1981-82; office mgr. Three Village Meals-on-Wheels, Stonybrook, 1984; grad. sec. art dept. SUNY, 1986-87, art gallery intern Fine Arts Ctr., 1987; dir. ops., dir. master classes and free concerts Islip Arts Coun., East Islip, N.Y., 1987-89; cons. N.Y. State Coun. on the Arts, N.Y.C., 1989—; co-owner, cons. Fire and Earth Designers and Feng Shui Consultants, Patchogue, N.Y., 1999—. Participant Arts in Bus. Mgmt. seminar Citibank/ABC, N.Y.C., 1987, cmty. leaders luncheon Fox Channel 5, N.Y.C., 1987; asst. to dir. Newsday's L.I. Summer Arts Festival Cmty. Affairs Dept., 1989, Suffolk County Motion Picture and TV Commn., Hauppauge, N.Y., 1988—, Summer Film Festival, 1988-90; cons. N.Y. State Coun. Arts, 1989-90, cons., 1990-91; interior decorator Trans-Designs, 1992; ind. contractor KM-Matol Corp, Que., Can., 1993; intern Nat. Inst. Inner Healing, Rich in Mercy Inst.; Feng Shui cons., 1998; interior design cons. Black Hat Sect. Tibetan Buddhism Feng Shui, 1999. Photographs included in Photography Forum's Coll. Photography Ann., 1985. Campaign dir. Food for Poland, Colorado Springs, 1982; organizer Granite State Alliance, Portsmouth, N.H., 1979, Safe 'n' Sound anti-nuclear campaign, Shoreham, N.Y., 1979; grad. rep. Sch. Continuing Edn. SUNY Stonybrook, judicial com. on acad. standing, SUNY Stonybrook, 1986-87; vol. Vietnam Vets. Theatre Ensemble, 1988, New Community Cinema, Huntington, N.Y., 1988; active exec. com. Dowling Coll. Spring Tribute Concert, Oakdale, N.Y., 1989; asst. to dir. Newsday Community Rels. Dept. L.I. Arts 89, 1989; founding mem. com. corr. L.I. Green Party, Brookhaven Twp., 1990—; participant Life in the Spirit seminar Cath. Charismatic Renewal, N.Y., 1992; tchr. Our Lady of Mt. Carmel Ch., N.Y., 1991—; active Pastoral Coun., 1992—. Mem. Internat. Platform Soc., Contemporary Hispanic Artists of L.I. (advisor to bd. dirs. Ctrl. Islip 1988-89). Roman Catholic. Avocations: screen-writing, poetry, photography, interior design and decoration, therapeutic touch healing. Home: 3275 Byron St # 24 Wantagh NY 11793-4213

MALDONADO-BEAR, RITA MARINITA, economist, educator; b. Vega Alta, P.R., June 14, 1938; d. Victor and Marina (Davila) Maldonado; m. Larry Alan Bear, Mar. 29, 1975. BA, Auburn U., 1960; PhD, NYU, 1969. With Min. Wage Bd. & Econ. Devel. Adminstr., Govt. of P.R., 1969-70; asst. prof. econs. Manhattan Coll., 1970-72; assoc. prof. econs. Bklyn. Coll., 1972-75; assoc. prof. fin. & econs., undergrad./grad. divsn. Stern Sch. Bus. NYU, 1975-81, prof., 1981—2004, prof. emerita, 2004—. Vis. assoc. prof. fin. Stanford (Calif.) Grad. Bus. Sch., 1973-74; acting dir. markets, ethics & law, NYU, 1993-94; cons. Morgan Guaranty Trust Co., N.Y.C., 1972-77, Bank of Am., N.Y.C., 1982-84, Res. City Bankers, N.Y.C., 1978-87, Swedish Inst. Mgmt., Stockholm, 1982-91, Empresas Master of P.R., 1985-90. Author: Role of the Financial Sector in the Economic Development of Puerto Rico, 1970; co-author: Free Markets, Finance, Ethics and Law, 1994, The Economy of Puerto Rico: Restoring Growth, 2006; contbr. articles to profl. jours. Bd. dirs. Medallion Funding Corp., 1985-87; mem. NYU Senate and Faculty Coun., 1995-2003, chair fin. com., 1996-2000; apptd. adv. bd. dirs. equity & diversity in ednl. environs. Mid. States Commn. Higher Edn., 1991—; trustee Securities Industry Assn., N.Y. Dist. Econ. Edn. Found., 1994—; chair NSF, Nat. Vis. Com. Curriculum Devel. Project Networked Fin. Simulation, 1995—; econ. cons. Inst. Women of Color, Nat. Coun. Black Women Cmty. Svcs. Fund, 2000—; trustee Bd. Edn., Twp. Mahwah, N.J., 1991-92. P.R. Econ. Devel. Adminstrn. fellow, 1960-65, Marcus Nadler fellow, NYU, 1966-67, Phillips Lods Dissertation fellow, 1967-68. Mem. Am. Econs. Assn., Am. Fin. Assn., Metro. Econ. Assn. N.Y., Assn. Social Econs. (trustee exec. coun. 1994-96). Home: 95 Tam O Shanter Dr Mahwah NJ 07430-1526 Office: Mgmt Edn Ctr 44 W 4th St Ste 9-190 New York NY 10012-1106 Business E-Mail: rmaldona@stern-nyu.edu.

MALEKIAN, FATEMEH, nursing educator; d. Davood Malekian and Zahra Olfat; children: Elizeh Gomez, Elahe Russell, Julie Perkins, Crystal Ramezanzadeh. PhD, La. State U., Baton Rouge, 1192—1998. Cert. instr. La. Dept. Health, Hosps. & Nat. Restaurant A, 2000. Rsch. assoc. Pennington Biomed., Baton Rouge, 1992—2004; faculty U. Pheonix, Baton Rouge, 2002—; assoc. prof. So. U. Agrl. Ctr., Baton Rouge, 2004—; adj. faculty La. State U., Baton Rouge, 2004—, So. U. Sch. Nursing, Baton Rouge. Contbr. articles to profl. jours. Pres., lt. gov. Kiwanis Internat., Baton Rouge, 1991; chair, co-chair, moderator, facilitator Inst. Food Technologists, Baton Rouge, 1995. Mem.: IFT (assoc.). Achievements include research in nutritional benefits of food components on health. Office: So Univ Agricultural Ctr PO Box 10010 Baton Rouge LA 70813 Office Fax: 225-771-4464. Business E-Mail: fatemeh_malekian@suagcenter.com.

MALENFANT, SUZANNE MARIE, science educator; b. Gladstone, Mich., Feb. 10, 1949; d. Delbert George and ethel Marie Nelson; m. James Edward Malenfant, Mar. 31, 1979; children: Heather Van Brocklin, Danilyn Lewis, Mindy. AA, Baydenol C.C., Escanaba, Mich., 1985; BS, No. Mich. U., Marquette, 1987, MEd, 1992. Cert. R.T. Sch. Radiologic Tech., Am. Registry Radiologic Technologists. X-ray tech. St. Mary's Hosp., Greenbay, Wis., 1969—70; x-ray lab tech., nurse Dr. Dehin, Gladstone, Mich., 1970—78; x-ray nuc. medicine OSF Hosp., Escanaba, Mich., 1978—87; sci. tchr. Escanaba HS, Escanaba, Mich., 1987—. Instr. CPR Am. Heart Assn., 1981—; adv. bd. Substance Abuse Pathways, Marquette, Mich., 1987—. Contbr. scientific papers to profl. jour. Mem.: NSTA, Mich Sci. Tchrs. Assn. Avocations: camping, gardening, walking, hiking, bicycling. Office: Escanaba HS 500 S Lincoln Rd Escanaba MI 49829

MALESKI, CYNTHIA MARIA, lawyer; b. July 4, 1951; d. Richard Anthony and Helen Elizabeth (Palovcak) Maleski; m. Andrzej G. Groch, Aug. 7, 1982; 1 child, Elizabeth Maria. Student, U. Rouen, France, 1970; BA summa cum laude, U. Pitts., 1973; JD, Duquesne U., 1976. Bar: Pa. 1976, U.S. Dist. Ct. (we. dist.) Pa. 1976, U.S. Supreme Ct. 1980, U.S. Ct. Appeals (3d cir.) 1984. Indsl. rels. adminstr. Allegheny Ludlum Industries, Inc., Brackenridge, Pa., 1972—74; law clk. Conte, Courtney, Tarasi & Price, Pitts., 1974, Paul Hammer, Pitts., 1974—76; solo practice Natrona Heights, Pa., 1978—92, 1995—. Adj. prof. law Sch. Law Duquesne U., Pitts., 1998—; ins. commnr. Penna, 1992—; mem. Gov.'s cabinet, 1992—95; v.p., regulatory coun. Highmark Blue Cross/Blue Shield, 1995—99; assoc. dir. pers. Mercy Hosp., Pitts., 1976—77, dir. legal affairs, 1977—81, gen. counsel, 1981—92; spl. master Allegheny County Ct. Common Pleas, 1989; bd. dirs. legal adv. bd. Cath. Health Assn., 1980—82; gen. counsel, vice chmn. nat. assembly of reps. Nat. Confedn. Am. Ethnic Groups, 1980—; health law cons. and lectr.

Co-author: The Legal Dimensions of Nursing Practice, 1982 (Nurses' Book of Month Club award, 1982); contbr. articles to publs. Mem. Allegheny-Kiski Hist. Soc., 1995—; mem. exec. bd. Pa. Fedn. Women, 2003—; elected mem. Allegheny County Dem. Com., 1986—89; corp. sec., pres. Duquesne U. Tamburitzans, Pitts., 1985—92; vice chmn. Czechoslovak room com. Nationality Rooms Program, U. Pitts., Pitts., 1983; v.p. Slovak League Am., 1990—; mem. adv. bd. Children's and Youth Svcs., Allegheny County, 1984—92; soloist, spkr. various groups Pitts. Slovakians. Named Disting. Alumnus, 1993; recipient Acad. Excellence award, Duquesne U., 1976; scholar, U. Rouen, 1970; Allegheny Ludlum Industries scholar, 1969—73, Andrew Mellon scholar, 1969—73, tuition scholar, U. Pitts., 1969—73, tuition remission grantee, Duquesne U., 1975, 1976. Mem.: ABA, St. Thomas More Soc. (bd. govs. 1980—), Slavic Edn. Assn. (nat. treas. 1981—86), Allegheny County Bar Assn., Pa. Bar Assn. (commn. on women 1996—, exec. women's coun.), Soc. Hosp. Attys. We. Pa., Soc. Hosp. Attys. of Hosp. Assn. Pa. (v.p.), Women Execs. in State Govt. (mem. nat. bd. 1994), Nat. Health Lawyers Assn., Am. Soc. Hosp. Attys., Nat. Slovak Soc., 1st Cath. Slovak Ladies' Assn. (nat. trustee), First Cath. Slovak Union, Slovak Cath. Sokols, Polish Falcons, Phi Beta Kappa. Roman Catholic. Home: 137 Oak Manor Dr Natrona Heights PA 15065-1949 Office: 2413B Freeport Rd Box 263 Natrona Heights PA 15065-0046 Office Phone: 724-224-6800.

MALETTA, ROSE HELEN, anesthesiologist; b. NYC, Apr. 25, 1916; d. Frank Maletta and Carmela Ponterio; m. Vincent Conti, Mar. 4, 1943 (dec.); children: Vincent, Gloria Griffin. Pre-med, Hunter Coll., NY, 1936; MD, U. Naples, 1941. Intern Met. Hosp., NYC, 1941—42; resident Flower Fifth Ave. Hosp., NYC, 1942—44; dir. anesthesia St. John's Hosp., NYC, 1945—50, Luth. Hosp., Bklyn., 1950—56, anesthesia cons., 1956—71; asst. prof. NY Med. Coll., 1967—71; anesthesiologist Broward Gen., Ft. Lauderdale, Fla., 1971—81, Holy Cross Hosp., Ft. Lauderdale, 1971—81. Mem.: Brookfield Golf Country Club. Avocations: golf, painting. Home: 975 Brooksglen Dr Roswell GA 30075

MALEWITZ, JOAN, elementary school educator, multi-media specialist; b. Dec. 15, 1947; d. Benjamin and Minnie Malewitz. B in Elem. Edn., Queens Coll., 1968, M in Elem. Edn., 1972, MLS, 1992. Cert. tchr. N-6 N.Y. Tchr., sch. libr. media specialist Pub. Sch. 160Q, Jamaica, NY, 1968—. Children's book reviewer Kirkus Revs., N.Y.C., 2000—. Recipient Success award, Citibank, N.Y.C., 1994. Mem.: ALA, Beta Phi Mu. Avocations: reading, travel, New York City history. Office: PS 160Q 109-59 Inwood St Jamaica NY 11435

MALEY, JEAN CAROL, foreign language educator; b. Jacksonville, Fla., Apr. 23, 1944; d. Charles D. and Esther L. Hosfield; m. Austin Quinn Maley, June 8, 1968; children: Lynn May, Mark Austin. BS, U. Minn., 1967; MA, U. Ariz., 1981. Tchr. Goddard High Sch., Roswell, N.Mex., 1967-69, 72, N.Mex. Mil. Inst., Roswell, 1974—2005; ret., 2005. Mem. Am. Assn. Tchrs. of German (sec.-treas. N.Mex. chpt. 1989-91, v.p. 1991-93, pres. 1993-95), Delta Kappa Gamma (chpt. pres. 2004-06). Avocations: bicycling, reading. Home: 2008 Brazos St Roswell NM 88201-3374 Personal E-mail: jeanmaley@msn.com.

MALEY, PATRICIA ANN, preservation planner; b. Wilmington, Del., Dec. 25, 1955; d. James Alfred and Frances Louise (Fenimore) M.; m. Scott A. Stone, Dec. 7, 1991 (div. June 1994). AA, Cecil C.C., 1973; BA, U. Del., 1975, MA, 1981. Cert. secondary tchr., Del. Analyst econ. devel. City of Wilmington, 1977-78, evaluation specialist, 1978-80, planner II mayor's office, 1980-86, cons. preservation, 1986-87; dir. Belle Meade Mansion, Nashville, 1987-88; dir. planning, devel. Children's Bur. of Del., Wilmington, 1988; prin. preservation planner Environ. Mgmt. Ctr., Brandywine Conservancy, Chadds Ford, Pa., 1988-92; planning cons., 1992-95; design review and preservation commn. coord. Wilmington Dept. Planning, 1995—, code enforcement constable, 1997—. Cons. cultural resources M.A.A.R. Inc., Newark, Del., 1987, ITC Cons., Wilmington, 1985-86; mem. Planned Approach to Comty. Health, Wilmington, task force for Wilmington Enterprise Comty. Health Benchmarking Project. Contbg. photographer America's City Halls, 1984; author numerous Nat. Register nominations, 1980-86; 88—. Pres., founder Haynes Park Civic Assn., Wilmington, 1977-80; photographer Biden U.S. Senate Campaign, New Castle County, Del., 1984; sec. parish coun. Our Lady Fatima Roman Cath. Ch., 1985-86, choir dir., 1983-87; mem. com. on design & renovation of worship spaces Diocese of Wilmington, also mem. Diocesan com. on music; bd. dirs. Del. Children's Theatre; music dir. St. Elizabeth Ann Seton parish, Bear, Del., 1988—, mem. long range planning com./demographics. U. Del. fellow, 1976-77. Mem.: Del. Inst. for Planning and Design (bd. dirs. 2002—, v.p. 2004), New Castle County (Del.) Bd. Realtors, Am. Planning Assn. (exec. com. Del. chpt. 1997, elected state chpt. treas. 1997—2005, elected v.p. 2005, chpt./regional conf. organizer 2006), Am. Inst. Cert. Planners (cert. planner), Nat. Trust Hist. Preservation, Del. Hist. Soc., Nat. Pastoral Musicians Assn., Pi Sigma Alpha. Democrat. Avocations: photography, singing, piano, cello. Office: City of Wilmington Dept Planning 800 N French St Fl 7 Wilmington DE 19801-3590 Office Phone: 302-576-3113. Personal E-mail: trish1225@aol.com. Business E-Mail: pmaley@ci.wilmington.de.us.

MALFA, FRANCES, lawyer; b. Bklyn., Dec. 16, 1969; BA, Baruch Coll., 1991; JD, Touro Coll., 1994. Bar: NJ 1994, NY 1995, US Dist. Ct. Ea. Dist. NY, NY Dist. Ct. So. Dist. NY. Ptnr. Wilson, Elser, Moskowitz, Edelman & Dicker LLP, NYC. Office: Wilson Elser Moskowitz Edelman & Dicker LLP 23rd Fl 150 E 42nd St New York NY 10017-5639 Office Phone: 212-490-3000 ext. 2296. Office Fax: 212-490-3038. Business E-Mail: malfaf@wemed.com.

MALHOTRA, MADHU BALA, psychiatrist; b. New Delhi, June 10, 1951; arrived in U.S., 1974; d. Faqir Chand and Krishna Khandpur; m. Amjed Hussain; 1 child, Saira H. Amjed. MBBS, India. Unit chief inpatient psychiatry Jamaica Hosp., Richmond Hill, NY. Mem.: Am. Assn. Psychiatrists from India, Am. Psychiat. Assn. Office: Jamaica Hosp 8900 Van Wyck Expressway Richmond Hill NY 11418

MALIFF, LORI CHRISTINE, elementary school educator; b. Long Branch, N.J., Aug. 31, 1971; d. John and Joyce Fielder; m. Thomas Maliff, July 26, 2002; 1 child, Ronan. BS in pub. health, Stockton State Coll., 1993; MA in Tchg., Monmouth U., 1996. Cert. tchr. ele.. edn. N.J., 1996. Tchr. Wall (N.J.) Twp., 1997—. Instr., supr. Silton Swim Sch., Manasquan, NJ, 1985—2002. EMT Wall (N.J.) Twp. First Aid & Rescue, 1991—99.

MALIHAN, AMIE A., physician; b. Kalibo, Aklan, Philippines, Nov. 19, 1950; came to U.S., 1974; d. Guadencio Rabe and Anastacia (Alvarez) M. BS in Pre-Med., U. Philippines, Manila, 1971; MD, U. of the East RMMC, Manila, 1976. Cert. Am. Bd. Plastic Surgery. Gen. surgery residency tng. Morristown (N.J.) Meml. Hosp., Columbia-Presbyn. Med. Ctr., N.Y., 1979-83; chief residency tng., gen. surgery Meml.-Sloane Kettering Cancer Ctr., 1983-84; plastic and reconstructive surgery N.Y. Hosp.-Cornell Med. Ctr., 1984-86; pvt. practice N.Y.C., 1986—. Fellow AMA, ACS, Med. Soc. State of N.Y., Richmond County Med. Soc.; mem. Am. Soc. Plastic Surgery. Roman Catholic. Avocation: golf. Office: 161 Madison Ave Ste 9sw New York NY 10016-5405 also: 5046 Amboy Rd Staten Island NY 10312-4834

MALIK, JOSIE M. MEZA, psychologist; b. Brawley, Calif., Nov. 29, 1947; d. Johnnie Villegas and Elvera (Ramirez) Meza; m. Sherkhan Malik, Aug. 12, 1976; children: Tarig Joshua, Shaunna Yasmin. AA, San Joaquin Delta Coll., 1968; BS, U. The Pacific, 1973, MA, 1975. Cert. sch. psychologist, Calif. Psychologist Lincoln Unified Sch. Dist., Stockton, Calif. Learning disability specialist, sch. psychologist San Joaquin Delta Coll., Stockton, Calif., 1990. Mem. Calif. Assn. Sch. Psychologists.

MALIN, JO, college administrator; b. St. Louis, Sept. 25, 1942; d. Louis and Bernice (Lasky) M.; children: David Roodman, Sarah Malin-Roodman. BA, Washington U., St. Louis, 1964; MA, Ind. U., 1968; PhD, SUNY, Binghamton, 1995. Asst. to vice provost for undergrad. studies SUNY, Binghamton, 1996—2000, project dir. ednl. talent search Sch. Edn. and Human Devel., 1987—. Field reader Upward Bound Proposal Competition, U.S. Dept. Edn., 1995; presenter in field. Author: HERSPACE: Women, Writing and Solitude, 2003, The Voice of the Mother: Embedded Maternal Narratives in Twentieth Century Women's Autobiographies, 2000; contbr. book reviews, articles to profl. jours. Recipient Woman of Achievement award Broome County Status of Women Coun., 1995, Mary McLeod Bethune Edn. award Broome County Urban League, 1992. Mem. N.Y. State Fin. Aid Adminstrs. Assn. Avocation: dance. Office: Binghamton U PO Box 6000 Binghamton NY 13902-6000

MALINOWSKI, MARYELLEN, photographer, artist; b. Oak Park, Ill., Oct. 10, 1961; d. Richard A. and Mary Jo (Curran) Lamz; m. Preston Malinowski; children: Nicole, Brielle, Demi. Student, Internat. Acad. Merch./Design, Chgo., 1985, Maine Photog. Workshops, Rockport, 1996, Elgin (Ill.) C.C., 1993-94. Owner Visual Elements, Dundee, Ill., 1992-94; owner, dir. The Infrared Light Gallery, St. Charles, Ill., 1994—; prin., owner Enlighten Pub., St. Charles, 2004—. Spkr. in field. Author: The Sacred Light, 1999; exhibited infrared photography in shows. Founder, bd. dirs. The Sacred Light Found. Recipient awards for photography; People's Choice award Women's Work Exhbn., Woodstock, 1995, 1st place Georgetown Internat. Fine Art Exhbn., Washington, 1997; recipient Ill. Women's Works Scholarship, 1996. Mem. Kodak Profl. Network, Luminos Printmakers Guild, Theosophical Soc., Nat. Mus. Women in Arts. Home: 6N779 IL RT 31 Saint Charles IL 60175 Office: Infrared Light Gallery PO Box 1281 Saint Charles IL 60175 Office Phone: 800-571-2730, 630-584-8068. Business E-Mail: maryellen@infraredlight.com.

MALINSKY, MARCI ANN, education educator; b. New Orleans, July 10, 1950; d. Walter Henry Tekippe and Mary Margaret Martin; m. Robert A. Malinsky, July 13, 1991; stepchildren: Matthew, Craig, Jennifer. BA in Edn., U. New Orleans, 1972; MA in Adminstrn., Coll. St. Thomas, St. Paul, 1983; PhD in Curriculum and Instrn., U. New Orleans, 2001. Tchr. Orleans Parish Sch., New Orleans, 1972—2001; asst. prof. Ark. State U., Jonesboro, Ark., 2001—05. Mem.: Nat. Sci. Tchrs. Assn., Internat. Reading Assn., Kappa Delta Pi. Roman Catholic. Avocations: reading, bridge. Home: 1607 Roleson Ln Jonesboro AR 72404 Office Phone: 870-972-3059. Personal E-mail: mmalinsky@cox-internet.com.

MALKIEL, NANCY WEISS, dean, historian, educator; b. Newark, Feb. 14, 1944; d. William and Ruth Sylvia (Puder) Weiss; m. Burton G. Malkiel, July 31, 1988. BA summa cum laude, Smith Coll., 1965; MA, Harvard U., 1966, PhD, 1970. From asst. to assoc. prof. history Princeton (N.J.) U., 1969-82, prof., 1982—, master Dean Mathey Coll., 1982-86, dean coll., 1987—. Author (as Nancy J. Weiss): (book) Charles Francis Murphy, 1858-1924: Respectability and Responsibility in Tammany Politics, 1968; author: (with others) Blacks in America: Bibliographical Essays, 1971, The National Urban League, 1910-1940, 1974, Farewell to the Party of Lincoln: Black Politics in the Age of FDR, 1983 (Berkshire Conf. of Women Historians prize, 1984), Whitney M. Young Jr., and the Struggle for Civil Rights, 1989. Trustee Woodrow Wilson Nat. Fellowship Found., 1975—, chmn. bd. trustees, 1999—; trustee Smith Coll., Northampton, Mass., 1984—94. Fellow, Woodrow Wilson Found., 1965, Charles Warren Ctr. Studies in Am. History, 1976—77, Radcliffe Inst., 1976—77, Ctr. Advanced Study Behavioral Scis., 1986—87. Mem.: So. Hist. Assn., Orgn. Am. Historians (chmn. status women hist. profession 1972—75), Am. Hist. Assn., Phi Beta Kappa. Democrat. Jewish. Office: Princeton U Office Dean Of College Princeton NJ 08544-0001

MALKIN, MICHELLE, syndicated columnist; b. Phila. married; 2 children. B, Oberlin Coll., Ohio. Editorial writer, columnist LA Daily News, 1992—94; editorial bd. Seattle Times, 1996—99. Author: Invasion: How America Still Welcomes Terrorists, Criminals and Other Foreign Menaces to Our Shores, 2002 (NY Times bestseller), In Defense of Internment: The Case for Racial Profiling in World War II and the War on Terror, 2004 (NY Times bestseller), Unhinged: Exposing Liberals Gone Wild, 2005; syndicated columnist, commentator Fox News Channel, polit. blogger michellemalkin.com, 2004— (rated as one of the best polit. blogs in 2005, Forbes Mag. and The Week Mag.). Warren Brookes Fellow, Competitive Enterprise Inst., 1995. Avocations: fishing, piano, crocheting. Mailing: Creators Syndicate Ste 700 5777 W Century Blvd Los Angeles CA 90045 E-mail: writemalkin@gmail.com.*

MALLARD, CARRIE CHARLENE, science educator; b. Canton, Ill., Apr. 12, 1976; d. Robert Darwin and Barbara Charlene Mallard. BS, U. Ill., 1998, MS, 2001. Grad. tchg. asst. dept. agrl. and consumer econ. U. Ill., Champaign/Urbana, 1998—99, grad. rsch. asst. dept. animal scis., 1998—2001, vis. vet. rsch. asst. dept. clin. medicine, 2001—03; life sciences instr. Lincoln Trail Coll., Robinson, Ill., 2003—. Contbr. articles to profl. jours. Mem.: Nat. Mastitis Coun., Am. Dairy Assn. Avocations: travel, scrapbooking, reading. Office: Lincoln Trail Coll 11220 State Hwy 1 Robinson IL 62454 Office Phone: 618-544-8657.

MALLEIN, DARLA J., social studies educator; BS in Secondary Edn., Emporia State U., 1980, MS, 1994; PhD in Curriculum and Instrn., Kans. State U., 2003. Tchr. Americus Elem. Sch., 1981-83; 8-12th grade lang. arts, yearbook LeRoy H.S., 1983-87; 9-11th grade lang. arts Emporia H.S., 1987-88; 8th grade social studies Emporia Mid. Sch., 1988—2001; social studies edn. specialist Emporia State U., 2001—, asst. prof. social scis. edn., 2003. Adj. faculty Emporia State U. Coll. Liberal Arts and Scis., 1998. Contbr. articles to profl. jours. Named Outstanding Young Educator Kans. Jaycees, 1996, Wal-Mar Tchr. of Yr. 1998, Kans. Tchr. of Yr. 1998, Outstanding Grad. Student in Edn., Kans. State U., 2003; grantee Emporia Middle Sch. PTO, 1992, Southeastern Kans. Edn. Found., 1995, 7 grants Southwestern Bell Execellence in Edn., 1991-95, Emporia Schs. Found., 1998, 99, Michael Jordan Found. grant, 2000. Mem. NEA (chair comms. com. 1997-99, bd. edn. liaison 1995-99, others), Kans. Coun. for the Social Studies (state bd. dirs. 1994—, pres. 2003-04, others), Nat. Coun. for the Social Studies, Phi Kappa Phi, Phi Delta Kappa. Home: 1901 Meadowlark Ln Emporia KS 66801-6125 Office Phone: 620-341-5567. E-mail: malleind@emporia.edu.

MALLET, KATHLEEN W., elementary school educator; b. Cleve., Aug. 13, 1943; d. William Easton and Kathleen (Riley) Wilson; children: Matthew G., Maureen K. BS in Edn., Wheelock Coll., Boston, 1965; MEd, Boston U., 1968. Cert. tchr. Mass. 2d grade tchr. Norwood Pub. Schs., Mass., 1965—68, substitute tchr., 2001—; primary tchr., literacy support staff Cambridge Pub. Schs., Mass., 1968—2001. Bldg. rep. Cambridge Tchrs. Union, 1990—2000; treas. Norwood Mothers Club, 1987—91; vol. driver Meals on Wheels, Norwood, 1996—; vol. Charwell Nursing Home, Norwood, 2000—. Mem.: Ret. Educators Mass. (treas. Norfolk West chpt. 2002—05), Norwood Woman's Club (bd. dirs. 2003—). Avocations: golf, reading, knitting, hiking. Home: 147 Ridgewood Dr Norwood MA 02062

MALLETTE, JENNIFER DENISE, mathematics educator; b. Sparta, Ill., Aug. 9, 1981; d. Gary and Denise Ebers; m. Clayton E. Mallette, July 26, 2003. BS magna cum laude, So. Ill. U., Carbondale, 2002; postgrad., So. Ill. U., Edwardsville, 2002—. Tchr. secondary math Belleville West HS, Ill., 2003—. Coach cheerleading Belleville West H.S., 2004—, coach math. team, 2003—, sponsor sophomore class, 2005—. Mem.: Ill. Coun. Tchrs. Math. Office: Belleville West High School 4063 Frank Scott Parkway Belleville IL 62223 Office Phone: 618-222-7500. Business E-Mail: jmallette@bths201.org.

MALLIA, MARIANNE, medical writer; b. Davenport, Iowa, Feb. 14, 1948; d. Norman Bramblett and Mary Jane (Hilkemeyer) Hagar; 1 child from previous marriage, Lindsay Sharyn. BA in English, U. Iowa, 1970. Cert. tchr. Tchr. tech. writing Houston Ind. Sch. Dist., 1970—76; med. writer Tex. Heart Inst., Houston, 1976—; editl. cons. Tex. Heart Inst. Jour., Houston, 1977—87, head sci. publ., 1986—, sr. med. writer, 1994—. Instr. Sch. Allied Health Sci. and Sch. Pub. Health U. Tex., 1990—94. Editor: Techniques in Cardiac Surgery, 1984; editor: (with Denton A. Cooley) Surg. Treatment of Aortic Aneurysms, 1985; editor: (essays) Reflections and Observation, Denton A. Cooley, MD, 1985; author: (handbook) Heart Owner's Handbook, 1995; bd. editors: Life Sci., 2002. Fellow: Am. Med. Writers Assn. (core curriculum cert. 1984, instr. 1985—, advanced curriculum cert. 1989, honor roll workshop leader 1992—, bd. dir., exec. com. 1996—2005, pres. 2002—03, writer advanced core curriculum, Award Tchg. Excellence 1998); mem.: Women in Comm. (cert. editor in life sci., Matrix award 1996—2000), Coun. Biology Editors, Pi Beta Phi. Avocation: classic cars. Office: Tex Heart Inst PO Box 20345 Houston TX 77225-0345 Home: 3779 Tangley St Houston TX 77005-2031 Office Phone: 832-355-6776. Business E-Mail: mmallia@heart.thi.tmc.edu.

MALLIN, JENNIFER, Internet company executive, writer; b. N.Y.C., Nov. 28, 1961; d. Joel and Judith (Young) Mallin; m. Henry S. Edelson, May 25, 1991; 1 child, Alexandria Elizabeth. BA cum laude, Brandeis U., 1983. Fashion model print and TV, N.Y.C., 1979-86; art dealer, dir. Foxworth Gallery, N.Y.C., 1983-84; writer fiction and poetry, N.Y.C., 1983—; pres., chmn. JM Ageless.com., N.Y.C., 1999—. Author: (novel) The Bamboo Heart, 1999; author poetry and art revs. Recipient award for Poem of Yr., Am. Libr. of Poetry, 1985. Avocations: equestrian show jumping, collecting contemporary art, travel. Home: 55 Cedar Cliff Rd Riverside CT 06878-2603

MALLING, MARTHA HALE SHACKFORD, social worker, educator; b. Atlanta, Aug. 20, 1944; d. James Atkins and Ada Vernon (Morrow) Shackford; m. Heinrich Valdemar Malling, July 18, 1969; children: Richard, Kevin, Kirsten. Student, U. Tenn., 1968-70; BA in Psychology, U. N.C., 1978, MSW, 1983; postgrad., Tavistock Clinic, London, 1987-88. Cert. clin. social worker NC, 1991, LCSW NC, 2000. Lab. technician in genetics NC State U., Raleigh, 1964-66, Oak Ridge (Tenn.) Nat. Lab., 1966-67; spl. edn. tchr. Hill Learning Ctr. Durham (NC) Acad., 1978-81; social worker II IDTU Children's Inst. John Umstead Hosp., Butner, NC, 1983-84; clin. social worker Duke U. Med. Ctr., Durham, NC, 1985-87, U. N.C. Hosps., Chapel Hill, 1989-90; social work clin. specialist Child-Outpatient Clinic Dorothea Dix Hosp., Raleigh, NC, 1990—; pvt. practice Chapel Hill and Durham, 1990—. Peer counselor Office Continuing Edn. Duke U., Durham, 1976—77; crisis counselor and tng. team mem. Orange-Person-Chatham Mental Health Ctr., Chapel Hill, 1979—82; workshop leader N.C. State Tchrs. Duke U. Med. Ctr., Durham, 1986, diabetes day workshop leader, 87; adj. instr. U. N.C. Sch. Social Work, 1996—2001, mem. adv. com. on field edn., 1999—, adj. field asst. prof., 2001—, adj. field prof., 2006—. Co-chair PTA Carolina Friends Sch., Durham, 1978—79, chmn. children's sect. art festival, 1978—81. Recipient Lineburger award, 2004; scholar VA, State of NC, 1964. Mem.: C. G. Jung Soc. (mem.-at-large 1989—90), Assn. Cert. Social Workers, NC Soc. Clin. Social Work (exec. bd. dirs., treas. 1990—94, co-chair com. psychoanalysis 1995—97). Democrat. Presbyterian. Avocations: hiking, design, music, reading. Home: 3200 Winged Elm Ln Chapel Hill NC 27514-9530 Office: Dix Hosp Child Outpatient Clinic 820 S Boylan Ave Raleigh NC 27603-2246 Office Phone: 919-733-5344.

MALLO-GARRIDO, JOSEPHINE ANN, advertising executive; b. Agana, Guam, Mar. 20, 1955; d. Benjamin Corneja and Salvacion (Lacuesta) Mallo; m. John Marco Haniu Garrido, Feb. 16, 1980; children: Josiah Michael (dec.), Jordan Thaddeus. Student, U. Guam, Agana, 1972-74; BA in Journalism, Seattle U., 1976; MBA, Pepperdine U., 1982. Reporter Pacific Daily News, Agana, 1976, features editor, 1977-78, asst. city editor, 1978-79; copy editor features Honolulu Star-Bull., 1979-81; advt. copywriter Advt. Factors, Honolulu, 1981-83; communications specialist Liberty House, Honolulu, 1983-84; editor, advt. copywriter Safeway Stores Inc., Oakland, Calif., 1984-88; features writer Tracy (Calif.) Press, 1988-91; mktg. mgr. ComputerLand of Guam, Maite, 1992-93; mktg. officer Citibank, Agana, 1993-94; owner JMG Advt., 1994—. Newspaper graphics cons. Pacific Daily News, 1984. Editor/writer Foods Unltd., 1984-88, Tracy Community Hosp. Health Beat and Update, 1988-91; editor Pacific Voice, 1977-78; contbr. articles to profl. jours. Vol. Engaged Encounter, Honolulu, 1989, Trans-Pacific Yacht Race, Honolulu, 1983, United Way, Oakland, 1986; advt. coord. Easter Seals, Oakland, 1987; organist St. Patrick's Ch., Honolulu, 1980—84, Immaculate Heart of Mary Ch., Toto, Guam, 1994—; mem. adv. bd. Cath. Social Svcs., Agana, Guam, 1993—97, bd. dirs., 1997—, bd. trustees, 2002—. Recipient Cert. Achievement award Advt. Age Mag., 1985, Cert Appreciation award Am. Heart Food Festival, 1985, Best in the West award Am. Advt. Fedn., 1986, Retail Nutrition award Nat. Potato Promotion Bd., 1986, Spl. Achievement award Newspaper Spl. Sect. Mother's Day/Father's Day Coun., 1989, 90, Best Feature Story 2d place Calif. Newspaper Pubs. Assn., 1989, 1st place Classified Advt. Assn., 1989, 1st place appetizer Spam Food Festival, 1991. Mem. Guam C. of C. (media coord. 1993-95), Citiclub (exec. sec. 1994-95). Roman Catholic. Avocations: piano, travel, Karate (black belt).

MALLON, KELLIE JANE, special education educator; b. Silver Spring, Md., Apr. 18, 1969; d. James A. and Barbara E. Mallon. B, St. Leo Coll., Fla., 1994; Master's degree, Nova Southeastern U., 1997. Cert. profl. tchr. Fla. Specific learning disabilities and spl. edn. tchr. Pasco County Sch. Bd., New Port Richey, Fla., 1996—. Sec. Schwettman Alternative Sch. Adv. Bd., New Port Richey, 1997—2004. Recipient After Sch. Activities grant, Pasco County Sch. Bd., 1997—98, Svc. Learning grant, Fla. Dept. of Edn. Mem.: CEC (assoc.; specific learning disability divsn. 2001—02). Roman Catholic. Avocations: reading, rescue animal advocate. Home: 6618 Crosbow Ln New Port Richey FL 34653 Office: Pasco County Sch Bd 7227 Land O' Lakes Blvd Land O Lakes FL 34638 Office Phone: 727-774-2000. Personal E-mail: kmallon@ij.net. E-mail: kmallon@pasco.k12.fl.us.

MALLORY, JOAN MATEY, music educator, composer; b. Bridgeport, Conn., Mar. 25, 1937; d. Andrew and Anna Matey; m. Daniel Payne Oppenheim, Aug. 2, 1958 (div.); 1 child, Vicki Oppenheim Michalica; m. Franklin Bernard Mallory, Feb. 14, 1982 (dec. June 2004); stepchildren: Frank B. Mallory Jr, Jennifer E. Mallory McBee. MusB, Yale U., New Haven, Conn., 1959. Pvt. piano tchr., 1972—82; piano performance, 1990—. Composer: (CD) Joan Plays.#1 Piano, 1999, Joan Plays.#2 Piano, 2001. Avocations: interior decorating, feeding wildlife, making jewel boxes.

MALLORY, PATRICIA JODY, museum curator; b. De Ridder, La., Sept. 22, 1951; d. William Buford and Gwendolyn (singletary) M. BBA, La. State U., 1979. Mgr. Harpers Records, De Ridder, 1979-83; dir. pub. rels. Goldband Records, Lake Charles, La., 1983-89; mgr. Bargain Time, Baton Rouge, 1989-91, Hills Music, De Ridder, 1991-96; sales and mktg. exec. Krok Radio, De Ridder, 1996-97; mus. curator Beauregard Parish, De Ridder, 1997—. Leader blues band Blues Horizon. Drummer Goldband Studios, 1971-83, Lake Charles; drummer recs. include Blessed Rain (Blue Rain), 1987, Drenched (Blue Rain), 1989, Saturday Nights and Sunday Mornings (OFB), 1987. Active Beauregard Econ. Devel., De Ridder; mem. main street promotions com.; mem. bd. dirs. Downtown Mchts. Assn., Beauregard Assn. Retarded Citizens. Named one of Best Unsigned Drummers, Promark, 1995. Mem. Percussive Arts Soc., Daus. of Confederacy, Humane Soc., People for Ethical Treatment Animals, Nat. Geog. Soc., World Wildlife Fund, Beauregard Woman's Orgn. Avocations: music, travel. Home: 501 S Stewart St Deridder LA 70634-4955 Office Phone: 337-463-8148. E-mail: museum@beau.org.

MALLOW, KATHLEEN KELLY, accountant; b. Chgo., Dec. 27, 1946; d. Robert Henry Kelly and Irene Alice Smith Kelly; m. Kenneth R. Mallow, July 9, 1983; children: Heather K. Peet, Christopher C. Mallow, Daniel S. Peet. BSc in Acctg., De Paul U., 1971; MBA, Keller Grad. Sch., 1986. Asst. supr. Dept. Fin. Instns. State of Ill., Chgo., 1994—, review examiner, 1994—. Mem. working group of edn. and tng. Commn. of Status of Women, Ill. Mem. AAUW (bd. dirs., past pres. 1971—), Home of the Sparrow. Home: 1219 E Plate Dr Palatine IL 60074-7260 Office: State of Ill Dept Fin Instns 100 W Randolph St Ste 15-700 Chicago IL 60601-3234

MALLOY, ELLEN ANN, athletic trainer; d. William Francis Thomas and Janet Day Malloy. BS in Health and Phys. Edn., Bridgewater State Coll., Mass., 1977; MEd in Sports Medicine and Athletic Tng., U. Va., Charlottesville, 1979. Cert. EMT Mass., 1981; health and phys. edn. tchr. Mass., 1977, lic. athletic trainer Mass., 1984, cert. instr. ARC, 2003, Am. Heart Assn., 2000. Head women's athletic trainer, head baseball athletic trainer Duke U., Durham, NC, 1979—81; head athletic trainer Regis Coll., Weston, Mass., 1981—83, Sports Innovation and Diagostic Ctr., Charlottesville, 1984—86, Noble and Greenough Sch., Dedham, Mass., 1988—2003, Thayer Acad., Braintree, Mass., 2003—. Dir. sports medicine Europa Cup Hockey, Wellesley, Mass., 2001—. Vol. Spl. Olympics, Charlottesville, 1978—79; vol. athletic trainer Bay State Games, Boston, 1981—2000, Boston Marathon, Boston, 1981—2004, Jimmy Fund Walk, Boston, 2000—06; participant Doug Flutie Walk for Autism, Natick, Mass., 2004; vol. Meals on Wheels, Cohasset, Mass., 2000—06. Recipient Robert J. Agostini award, Noble & Greenough Sch., 1990, 1997. Mem.: Ind. Sch. Athletic Trainer's Assn. (pres. 1990—97), Ea. Athletic Trainer's Assn., Nat. Athletic Trainer's Assn. (cert.), State of Mass. - Allied Health (licentiate), Cohasset Golf Club (Mother-Daughter Champion 1975—79), Cohasset Golf Club (Father-Daughter Champion 1975—79), Cohasset Golf Club (Lincoln Bowl Champion 1975), Cohasset Golf Club (Women's Club Champion 1990—92), Cohasset Golf Club (Mixed Scotch Club Champion 1984), Cohasset Sailing Club (Lincoln Bowl Champion 1985, Father-Daughter Champion 1988—92, Mother-Daughter Champaion 1988—92, Mixed Scotch Club Champion 1989), Hatherly Country Club (Women's Tennis Club Champion 1969), South Shore Women's Golf League (Mother-Daughter Champion 1988), U. of Va. Alumni Assn. (life). Independent. Roman Catholic. Avocations: golf, tennis, hockey, sailing, sewing. Office: Thayer Acad 745 Washington St Braintree MA 02184 Office Phone: 781-843-3580. Office Fax: 781-848-1027. Business E-Mail: emalloy@thayer.org.

MALLRICH, SHANNON MARIE, secondary school educator; d. Wesley and Beverly Stueber; m. J.J. Mallrich, May 30, 1998; 1 child, MariEva Roselyn. BA, McKendree Coll., Lebanon, Ill., 1998. Mid. sch. lang. arts and h.s. journalism tchr. Marissa Jr./Sr. H.S., Ill., 1998—99; mid. sch. lang. arts and math tchr. Triad Mid. Sch., Troy, Ill., 1999—2000; English, speech and drama tchr. Triad H.S., Troy, Ill., 2000—. Thespian sponsor Triad H.S., Troy, 2000—. Stephen min. Trenton First United Meth. Ch., Ill., 2005—06. Mem.: Ednl. Theater Assn., Kappa Delta Pi, Sigma Tau Delta, Alpha Psi Omega (pres. 1996—98). Avocations: reading, memory book making, photography, travel, films. Office: Triad High School 703 East Highway 40 Troy IL 62294 Office Phone: 618-667-8851.

MALM, MIA, actress; b. Ann Arbor, Mich., Oct. 18, 1962; d. William P. and Joyce A. (Rutherford) M. Student, San Francisco Sch. of the Arts, Herbert Berghof Studios, N.Y.C.; studied with Maria Vegh. Dance instr. Marin Ballet Sch., 1978-79. Appeared in (stage prodns.) Make Mine Disco, 1979, Dancin', 1981-83, 42nd Street, The Showgirl Musical, 1986, (films) Moscow on the Hudson, Curtain Call, 1984, Joan-Lui, A Chorus Line, 1985, Ishtar, (TV) Dance Through Time, 1978. Mem. Actors' Equity Assn., Screen Actors Guild, AFTRA, NOW, Planned Parenthood. Avocations: drawing, watercoloring, reading.

MALMAN, LAURIE L., law educator; b. 1946; BA, Vassar Coll., 1968; JD, NYU, 1971. Bar: NY 1972. Assoc. Sullivan & Cromwell, NYC, 1971-79; instr. NYU Sch. Law, 1979-80, asst. prof. law, 1980-83, assoc. prof., 1983-86, prof., 1986—. Co-author: Federal Income Tax Problems, Cases, and Materials, 1994. Mem.: ABA, NY State Bar Assn. Office: NYU Sch Law Vanderbilt Hall Rm 430I 40 Washington Sq S New York NY 10012-1099 Office Phone: 212-998-6166. E-mail: malmanl@juris.law.nyu.edu.

MALMSTADT, MARY JANE, music educator; b. Milw., Apr. 12, 1923; d. Daniel Monte and Angela Marie LaFata; m. Robert Guy, June 25, 1949 (dec. Mar. 1998); children: Keith Robert, Deborah Jean. BS in Music Edn., U. Wis., 1945; postgrad., U. Wis., Marinette and Madison, 1950—83. Music tchr. K-12 NeKoosa (Wis.) Pub. Schs., 1945—46; music tchr. 9-12 Marinette (Wis.) H.S., 1946—51; music tchr. K-6 Elem. Schs., Marinette, 1965—2006; organist, pianist Pioneer Presbyn. Ch., Marinette, 1970—2006; pvt. piano tchr. Marinette, 1955—. Bd. dirs. Tri-City Cmty. Concerts, Wis. Mem.: Golden Soc. of Alumni/U. Wis. Milw., Gen. Fedn. of Women's Club (pres. 1988). Presbyterian. Avocation: oil painting, gardening, reading, travel, floral arrangements. Home: 1303 Elizabeth Ave Marinette WI 54143

MALMSTROM LAKEMAN, DOROTHY E., psychologist; b. Guatemala City, Guatemala, Apr. 4, 1945; d. Carl Olof and Esther Butler Malmstrom; m. C David Lakeman, June 1, 2002; children: Spencer Van Hoof Lakeman, Leslie Anne Lakeman. BA in sociology, U. of Calif., 1969; MA in marriage, family and child counseling, Azusa Pacific U., 1980; PhD in clin. psychology, Union Inst. and U., 1992. Licensed Psychologist Bd. of Psychology, Calif., 1998. Mktg. exec. Good Stuff Nat. Bakery, Los Angeles, Calif., 1974—81; founder Health Network Inst., Santa Monica, 1981—82; co-founder Fin. Services, Inc., Santa Monica, 1982—88; psychology intern Profl. Consultation Services, Inc., Los Angeles, 1988—92; sch. dir. Progress Preschool, Santa Monica, 1992—93; post-doctoral asst. Geriatric Organizations, Santa Monica, 1993—98; geriatric psychologist Self Employed, Santa Monica, 1998—; rsch. sociologist U. of Calif., Riverside, 1969—70; exec. asst. Yamaha of Indio, Indio, Calif., 1971—73. Mem.: APA, Am. Psychotherapy Assn., LA County Psychol. Assn. (assoc.), Amnesty Internat. Avocations: hiking, gardening, music, art. Home: 2727 Sixth St #301 Santa Monica CA 90405 Office Phone: 310-399-7823. Personal E-mail: drdorothym@msn.com.

MALO, MICHELE LEE, marketing professional; b. Chgo., Dec. 21, 1972; d. William Reining and Candyce Lee Collins; m. James John Malo, Oct. 4, 2003. B of Advt., U. Nebr., 1996; MBA with honors, Lake Forest Grad. Sch. Mgmt., 2003; postgrad., Lake Forest Grad. Sch. Mgmt. Internat. Bus. Specialization, 2005. Mktg. asst. Allied Domecq, Chgo., 1996—98, field mktg. specialist, 1998—2000; asst. promotions mgr. Kraft Foods, Glenview, 2000—02, assoc. promotions mgr., 2002—03; assoc. bus. mgr. Oscar Mayer, 2003—04; customer mktg. mgr. Kellogg's, Elmhurst, 2004—06, bus. unit mgr. biscuit, 2006—. Breast cancer fundraising com. Women in POP. Mem.: Women's Food Svc. Forum, Am. Mktg. Assn., Alpha Sigma Alpha. Avocation: softball. Office: Kellogg 545 Lamont Rd Elmhurst IL 60126 E-mail: esmalo@yahoo.com.

MALONE, CLAUDINE BERKELEY, financial and management consultant; b. Louisville, May 9, 1936; d. Claude McDowell and Mary Katharine (Smith) M.; BA, Wellesley Coll., 1963; MBA, Harvard U., 1972. CPA, Md. Systems engr. IBM Corp., Washington, 1964; sr. systems analyst Crane Co., Chgo., 1966; contr., mgr. data processing Raleigh Stores, Washington, 1967-70; asst. prof. Harvard U., 1972-76, assoc. prof., 1977-81; pres., CEO, Fin. and Mgmt. Consulting Inc., Bethesda, Md., 1981-; vis. prof., Georgetown U., 1982-84, U. Va., 1984-87; dir. Scott Paper Co., Houghton Mifflin Co., Campbell Soup Co., Boston Co., Dart Group Inc., Hasbro Inc., 1994-, Novell Inc., 2003-; trustee Penn Mut. Life Ins. Co. Chmn. Bus. for Reagan-Bush Com. Mass., 1980; trustee Wellesley Coll., 1982-. Recipient Candace award, 1982. Mem. Assn. Women CPA's, UN Assn., Wellesley Coll. Alumnae Assn., Washington Wellesley Club. Episcopalian. Office Phone: 703-821-8861.

MALONE, JEAN HAMBIDGE, educational consultant; b. South Bend, Ind., Nov. 23, 1954; d. Craig Ellis and Dorothy Jane (Piechorowski) Hambidge; m. James Kevill Malone, July 8, 1978; children: Julia Mae, James Kevill III, John Thomas. BS in Edn., Butler U., 1976, MS in Edn., 1977. Tchr. Indpls. Pub. Schs., 1977-78; dir. student center and activities Butler U., Indpls., 1978-87. Trustee Eisenhower Meml. scholarship, 1977-80; bd. dirs. Heritage Place of Indpls., 1983-88, Ind. Office Campus Ministries, 1985-87, 89—91, Campfire of Cen. Ind., 1980-84, 86-87, Intercollegiate YMCA, Indpls., 1985-87, 89-90, Indpls. Jr. League, 1989—, Indpls. Urban Parish Coop, 1987-90, v.p., pres., 1991, 92; bd. dirs. Gennesaret Free Clinic of Indy, 1992-94; mem. overseers coun. Camp Delafield Children with Dyslexia, 1993-95, bd. pres., 1997-2000; bd. dirs. Dyslexia Inst. Ind., 1996—, bd. pres., 1997-2000; mem. Commn. Youth Archdiocec. 2000-01; community adv. for the homeless of Indpls. Recipient Outstanding Faculty award, Butler U., 1980. Mem. Ind. Assn. Women Deans (v.p. bd. dirs. 1987-88), Adminstrs. and Counselors (bd. dirs. 1982-83), Internat. Dyslexia Assn. (mem. Ind. br. 1992—), Kappa Delta Pi, Phi Kappa Phi, Alpha Lambda Delta, Kappa Kappa Gamma. Roman Catholic. Office: 5256 N Illinois St Indianapolis IN 46208-2636 Personal E-mail: jhmalone2@aol.com.

MALONE, JENA, actress; b. Lake Tahoe, Nev., Nov. 21, 1984; d. Debbie. Actress (films) Contact, 1997, Stepmom, 1998, The Book of Stars, 1999, For Love of the Game, 1999, Donnie Darko, 2001, Life as a House, 2001, Corn, 2002, The Dangerous Lives of Altar Boys, 2002, The Badge, 2002, American Girl, 2002, The United States of Leland, 2003, Cold Mountain, 2003, Saved!, 2004, Howl's Moving Castle, 2004, Bickford Shmeckler's Cool Ideas, 2005, The Ballad of Jack and Rose, 2005, Pride & Prejudice, 2005, (TV films) Hidden in America, 1996, Hope, 1997, Ellen Foster, 1997, Cheaters, 2000, The Ballad of Lucy Whipple, 2001, Hitler: The Rise of Evil, 2003, guest appearances Punk'd, 2004, On-Air with Ryan Seacrest, 2004, Dennis Miller, 2004, Tonight Show with Jay Leno, 2004, actress (Broadway plays) Doubt, 2006. Mailing: c/o UTA 9560 Wilshire Blvd Beverly Hills CA 90212*

MALONE, NANCY J., librarian; b. Council Grove, Kans., Feb. 26, 1951; d. William O. and Elsie M. Newell; m. Jerry A. Malone, Nov. 1, 1948; children: Michael S., Rodney S., Brett S. MLS, Emporia State U., 1992. Libr. dir. Ctrl. Christian Coll. of Kans., McPherson, 1989—2002; continuing edn. coord. South Ctrl. Kans. Libr. Sys., South Hutchinson, 2002—. Chair youth and program com. McPherson Light Capitol Kiwanis, Kans., 2001—; H.S. small group leader McPherson Free Meth. Ch., Kans., 1998—2005, bd. trustees, 2005—; mem. Ctrl. Christian Coll. of Kans. Alumni Bd., McPherson, 2003—. Mem.: Kan-ed Adv. Coun. (rep. of coll. 2000—02), Kans. Rsch. Edn. Network (coll. rep. 1999—2002), Pvt. Acad. Librs. (pres., sec., membership com. 1990—2002), Kans. Libr. Assn. Office Phone: 620-663-3211 ext. 149.

MALONEK, JENNIE SUE, science educator; b. Phoenix, Ariz., June 3, 1959; d. Robert Nelse and Jaqueline Anne Malonek. BA, BS, UCLA, 1981; MA in Secondary Edn., Calif. State U. Northridge, LA, 1991; postgrad., Fuller Sem., Pasadena, Calif., 1993, Pepperdine U., LA, 1998. Single subject credential Calif., cert. language devel. specialist Calif., 1995. Bear Wear mail order supr. ASUCLA, LA, 1981—83, Bear Wear gift buyer, 1983—84; sci. tchr. Bret Harte Intermediate Prep./ Jefferson H.S., LA, 1985—91, Alhambra H.S., Calif., 1991—. Calif. writing project Calif. State U. Northridge, 1986; target sci. region C lead tchr. LA Ednl. Partnership, 1987—89; sci. project participant and presenter UCLA, 1987—2001; project VISM participant James Madison U. and NSF, Harrisonburg, Va., 2000; STEER/RET participant and NSF Calif. State U., LA, 2003—05; sci. edn. amb. Eisenhower Person to Person Ambassadors Program, St. Petersberg, Russia, 2006—. Academic decathlon coach Alhambra High, 1992—2006, sci. olympiad coach, 1993—2006, catalyst co-chair, 1999—2002, sch. site coun. rep., 2003—05, vol. softball coach, 2006; network N co-coord. Calif. League High Schs., LA, 1993—94. Recipient Alhambra Golden Apple, Talbot Ednl. Found., 2002. Mem.: NSTA (life), Nat. Assn. Biology Tchrs., Computer Using Educators, Calif. Sci. Tchrs. Assn. Independent. Avocations: computers, reading, music, movies, woodworking. Office: Alhambra High School 101 S 2nd St Alhambra CA 91801 Office Phone: 626-308-2342. Personal E-mail: eagleswings59@yahoo.com.

MALONEY, CAROLYN BOSHER, congresswoman; b. Greensboro, NC, Feb. 19, 1948; d. R.G. and Christine (Clegg) Bosher; m. Clifton H.W. Maloney, 1976; children: Christina, Virginia. BA, Greensboro Coll., 1968. Cmty. affairs coord. welfare edn. prog. Bd. Edn., NYC, 1972—75, spl. asst. ctr. career and occupl. edn., 1975—76; legis. aide housing com. NY State Assembly, 1977, sr. prog. analyst cities com., 1977—79; exec. dir. adv. coun. Office of NY State Senate Minority Leader Manfred Ohrenstein, 1979—82, dir. spl. projects, 1980—82; mem. City Coun. from Dist. 8, NYC, 1983-93, US Congress from 14th NY dist., 1993—, chair Ho. Dem. Caucus Task Force on Homeland Security, 2003—, ranking Ho. Dem. joint econ. com., 2005—, mem. fin. svcs. com., ranking minority mem. domestic and internat. monetary policy, trade and tech. subcommittee, 2003—, mem. govt. reform com., ranking minority mem. census subcommittee, 1999—. Mem. US del. Fourth World Conf. on Women, Beijing, Internat. Conf. on Population and Devel., The Hague, Netherlands. Active Assn. for a Better NY, Manhattan Women's Polit. Caucus. Decorated Mil. Order of the Purple Heart; recipient Spl. Impact award, Healthy Mothers, Healthy Babies, 2000, Women's Leadership award, UN Family Planning, 2002, Disting. Pub. Svc. award, Nat. Family Planning and Reproductive Health Assn., Ellis Island Medal of Honor, Global Peace award, Peace Action, Queens Women of Distinction award, Queen's Women's Polit. Caucus. Mem.: Hadassah (Myrtle Wreath award), NOW, NAACP. Democrat. Presbyterian. Office: US Ho Reps 2331 Rayburn Ho Office Bldg Washington DC 20515-3214 Office Phone: 202-225-7944.*

MALONEY, CHERYL ANN, not-for-profit administrator, consultant; b. Mpls., Aug. 30, 1949; d. Arlie Chester and Mary Dawn (Holm) M. AA, U. Minn., 1969, BA in Speech and Theatre, 1972; MA in Theology/Spirituality, Coll. St. Catherine, St. Paul, 1989, MA cert. in Pastoral Ministry, 1990; postgrad., Calif. Inst. Integral Studies, 1994—95; DMin, U. Creation Spirituality, 2001. Cert. grantsmanship, Calif., financial mgmt. Assn. Gov. Accts. Bus. adminstr. Al's Auto Crushing, Inc., Mpls., 1980-81; rsch. assoc. St. Paul Ramsey Med. Ctr., 1981-83; cons. Autowoman Consulting, Mpls., 1982—; adjustor Dependable Auto Appraisal, Inc., Bloomington, 1983; dir. mktg. and devel. Health Recovery Center, Mpls., 1983-85; dir. sales and mktg. Dashe and Thomson, Mpls., 1987-89, Fredrickson Comm., Mpls., 1989-91; chaplain U. St. Thomas, St. Paul, 1989-90; ind. cons. Mpls., 1991-94; dir. devel. Sisters of Holy Family, Fremont, Calif., 1994-98; co-owner, co-founder Bras for Body and Soul, Fremont, 1995—2004; dir. Fremont Festival Arts, 1998; co-founder, exec. dir. HERS Breast Cancer Found., Fremont, 1999—2004. Dir. Women's Network, Mpls., 1974—77; dir. cultural arts City of Bloomington, Minn., 1977—78; spkr. U. Bethlehem, Israel, 1993; tchr. Holy Childhood High Sch., Jamaica, 1992; prodr. Keep Abreast-Walking Together for HER 5K Run/Walk; dir. devel. Sisters Holy Family, editor Family of Friends Newsletter, co-coord. Women's Spirituality Workshop series, 1996—97; cons. Sisters of St. Joseph of Carondelet, St. Paul, 1992—94; assoc. v.p. devel. San Mateo Cmty. Colls. Found., 2000; ofcl. photographer Internat. Women's Ecumenical Decade Chs. Solidarity Women, 1993; interim fin. dir. Hellic Q. Brown Cmty. Ctr., St. Paul, 2006; exec. dir. Women's Cancer Resource Ctr., Mpls., 2006—; quality cons.; presenter in field. Goodwill Designer Showcase Mag., 1975, Mpls., 1971—94; contbr. Women's Network Directory, 1976, Streams from the Sacred River, 1998. Coord. Internat. Youth Leadership Conf., Caux, Switzerland, 1996; cmty. organizer Mpls. Crime Prevention Program, 1979—80; mem. Gov.'s Com. Women in Econ. Concern, St. Paul, 1972—77; state Dem. del. St. Paul, 1976; coach, youth leader Unity South Ch., Bloomington, 1967—93; coach Ind. Ch., Mpls., 1984—92; chaplain U. St. Thomas, St. Paul, 1989—92, chair women and religion com.; outreach min. Unity of Valley, Minn., 1990—93; lay consociate Sisters St. Joseph, 1992, apptd. peace and justice commn. and comm. adv. bd., 1993—95; chair 125th Anniversary Celebration Sisters of the Holy Family, 1997. Recipient Celtic Studies award Coll. St. Catherine, St. Paul, 1988; honoree Hamnline U., St. Paul, 1993; Great Lakes Region scholar, 1986. Mem.: Am. Assn. Breast Care Specialists (pres. 2002—04), Nat. Assn. Self-Employed (women's nat. adv. coun. 2003), M.R.A. Internat. (nat. team planners for M.R.A. N.Am. and S.Am. activities), Sales and Mktg. Execs. Am., Mission San Jose C. of C. (pres. 1999—2000, sec. 2000—01, co-founder olive festival 2001—), Minn. Coun. Quality (editor newsletter 1993—94), Le Group (founding mem.), Self-Employed Women's Rotary (co-dir. 1982—94), Mpls. Women's Rotary (parliamentarian 1980—, bd. dirs. 1990—94), Commonwealth Club Calif. (dir. devel. and cmty. rels. 2005). Independent. Avocations: integrating spirituality and work, cultural arts, sports, international relations. Home: 5501 Queen Ave S Minneapolis MN 55410 Office: HERS Breast Cancer Found Inc No Place Like Home Communities 2005 4101A W Broadway Robbinsdale MN 55422 Office Phone: 612-746-4890 206. E-mail: camaloney@aol.com.

MALONEY, ELIZABETH MARY, mental health nurse, psychiatric health nurse; b. Eaton, NY, Sept. 5, 1922; d. Edward Farrell and Gena (Bagley) M. Diploma, St. Elizabeth Hosp., Utica, N.Y., 1943; BS, Columbia U., 1951, MA, 1952, EdD, 1966. Head and staff nurse Greystone Park (N.J.) State Hosp., asst. dir. nursing; assoc. prof. nursing edn. Tchrs. Coll., Columbia U., N.Y.C.; chmn. dept. nursing edn. Tchr.'s Coll. Columbia U., 1970-76; chair Tchr.'s Coll. Columbia U., 1991-93. Cons. mental health-psychiat. nursing VA Outpatient Clinic, Bklyn. Editor: Jour. Psychiatric Nursing, 1964-66. 1st Lt. Army Nurse Corps, 1944-46, ETO. Recipient R. Louise McManus medal, 1988, 93; named to Hall of Fame, Nursing Programs, Tchrs. Coll. Columbia U., 1999. Mem. Sigma Theta Tau.

MALONEY, ELLEN CLAIRE, elementary school educator; b. Buffalo, Jan. 12, 1946; d. Eugene Michael and Norma Ann Gooley; m. John Charles Maloney, Aug. 9, 1986; children: Matthew Donovan Lennert, Elizabeth Anne Lennert, Patrick O'Neal Johnson. MEd, U. San Diego, Calif., 1978. Elem. tchr. San Diego Unified Sch. Dist., 1978—. Reader, sodality mem. St. Rita's Cath. Ch., San Diego, 1986—2006; mem. Whispering Winds Aux., San Diego, 2001—06. Named Tchr. of Yr., Encanto Elem., 1995, 1997, Zamorano Elem., 2002, 2004, 2005. Office: San Diego Unified Sch Dist 4100 Normal Ave San Diego CA 92105 Office Phone: 619-725-8000.

MALONEY, KRISTEN, gymnast; b. Hacketstown, NJ, Mar. 10, 1981; d. Richard and Linda. Mem. U.S. Gymnastics Team, 1994—2001, UCLA Gymnastics Team, 2000—. Mem. U.S. World Championships Team, 1997, 99, U.S. Gymnastics Team Sydney Olympics, 2000. Recipient numerous awards, 1st pl. Am. Classic, 1997, 98, 1st pl. (3) Foxsport Challenge, Sydney, 1997, 1st team, 1st balance beam, 1st floor exercise 1st AA, Internat. Team Championships, 1998, 1st team, 1st AA, Pacific Alliance Champaionships, Winnipeg, Can., 1998, 1st balance beam Goodwill Games, 1998, others. Mem. Parketts Club. Avocations: reading, music, movies, shopping. Office: UCLA Women's Gymnastics PO Box 24044 Los Angeles CA 90024

MALONEY, MARILYN C., lawyer; b. New Orleans, Nov. 24, 1950; BA, La. State U., 1972, JD, 1975. Bar: La. 1975, Tex. 2005, U.S. Dist. Ct. (ea. dist.) La. Ptnr. Liskow & Lewis, New Orleans, 1975—, Houston, 2005—. Contbr. articles to profl. jours. Fellow: Am. Coll. Real Estate Lawyers; mem.: La. State Law Inst. (pres.), Order of Coif, Omicron Delta Kappa. Office: Liskow & Lewis Ste 3485 Three Allen Center 333 Clay St Houston TX 77002 Office Phone: 713-651-2938. Business E-Mail: mcmaloney@liskow.com.

MALONEY, MARY D., lawyer; BA, U. Akron, 1984; JD summa cum laude, Cleve. State U., 1987; LLM, Case Wester Res. U., 1995. Bar: Ohio 1987. With Jones Day, Cleve., 1987—, ptnr., 2001—. Mem.: Ohio State Bar Assn. Office: Jones Day North Point 901 Lakeside Ave Cleveland OH 44114-1190

MALONEY, PATRICIA DIANA, artist, educator; b. Louisville, Oct. 15, 1948; d. Bernard Joseph and Dorothy (Schoo) M. BFA, Louisville Sch. Art, 1972; MA, Murray State U., 1974; MFA, Okla. U., 1976. Cert. tchr. K-12, Ky., 1974. Artist-in-residence Allied Arts & Humanities Council, Bartlesville, Okla., 1976-77; prof. art Washington and Jefferson Coll., Washington, Pa., 1977—. Vis. researcher Smithsonian Instn. Dept. of Anthropology, Nat. Mus. Natural. History, Washington, summer 1987; instr. studio arts program, resident assoc. program, Smithsonian Instn., summer 1987; research assoc. in ceramics Harvard Semitic Mus., 1988-89. Contbr. to Ceramics Monthly. Merit badge counselor The Boy Scouts of Am., Washington, Pa., 1978—; lectr. Am. Assn. Univ. Women, washington, Pa., 1982. Recipient 1st place visual arts award Wm. Penn Meml. Mus., Harrisburg, Pa., 1981, ceramic cons. grant NEH. 1985, vis. fellow grant The Smithsonian Instn., Nat. Mus. Natural History, 1987, presdl. discretionary fund grant Washington and Jefferson Coll., 1987; named one of outstanding and prominent women of Washington County, Jay Stock, Photographer, 1988; Fulbright scholar, Ghana, Africa, 1993-95. Mem. Fulbright Assn., Carnegie Instn.-Mus. of Art & Natural History Mus., Pitts. Ctr. for the Arts, Washington County Hist. Soc. Roman Catholic. Avocations: ice skating, walking, gardening. Office: Washington and Jefferson Coll S Lincoln St Washington PA 15301 E-mail: pmaloney@washjeff.edu.

MALONEY, STEPHANIE JERNIGAN, art history educator, archaeologist; b. Jackson, Miss., Mar. 31, 1945; d. Stephen Alphonse Baginski and Lois (Matthews) Jernigan; m. Thomas Stephen Maloney, Mar. 25, 1977. AB, Mount Holyoke Coll., 1967; MA, U. Mo., 1971, PhD, 1974. Instr. Mt. Holyoke Coll., South Hadley, Mass., 1971; asst. prof. U. Louisville, 1974—80, assoc. prof. art history, 1980—; dir. Allen R. Hite Art Inst., U. Louisville, 1981—86. Vol. Peace Corps, Piracanjuba, Brazil, 1967—69; Mem. Jefferson County Hist. Landmark and Preservation Dists. Commn., Louisville, 1979—88. Recipient Rsch. Field Trip award, Smithsonian Instn., Poland, 1975—76; grantee archaeol., Poland, 1977—79, NEH, Portugal, 1983—84, 1983—84, Samuel H. Kress Found., 1983—84, CE&S Found., 1986—91. Mem.: Am. Assn. Field Archaeologists, Am. Soc. Hispanic Art Hist. Studies, Coll. Art Assn., Medieval Acad. Am., Ky. Soc. Archeol. Inst. Am. Democrat. Presbyn. Home: 7406 Woodhill Valley Rd Louisville KY 40241-5836 Office: U Louisville Allen R Hite Art Inst Louisville KY 40292-0001

MALONEY, THERESE ADELE, insurance company executive; b. Sept. 15, 1929; d. James Henry and F. Adele (Powers) M. BA in Econs., Coll. St. Elizabeth, Convent Station, N.J., 1951; AMP, Harvard U., 1981. CPCU. With Liberty Mut. Ins. Co., Boston, 1951-94, asst. v.p., asst. mgr. nat risks, 1974-77, v.p., asst. mgr. nat. risks, 1977-79, v.p., mgr. nat. risks, 1979-86, sr. v.p. underwriting mktg. and adminstrn., 1986-87, exec. v.p. underwriting, policy decision, 1987-94, also bd. dirs.; pres. and bd. dirs. subs. Liberty Mus. (Bermuda) Ltd., 1981-94, LEXCO Ltd.; cons. Exec. Svc. Corp., 1994—2002. Bd. dirs., dep. chmn. Liberty Mut. (U.K.) Ltd., London; bd. dirs. Liberty Mut. Ins. Co., Liberty Mut. Fire Ins. Co., Liberty Mut. Life Assurance Co., Liberty Fin. Cos.; mem. faculty Inst. Northeastern U., Boston, 1969—74; mem. adv. bd., risk mgmt. studies Ins. Inst. Am., 1977—83; mem. adv. coun. Suffolk U. Sch. Mgmt., 1984—96; mem. adv. coun. to program in internat. bus. rels. Fletcher Sch. Law and Diplomacy, 1985—94; cons. Exec. Svc. Corp., Boston, 1994—2002. Trustee Coll. St. Elizabeth, N.J., 1993-02. Mem. Soc. CPCUs (past pres. Boston chpt.), Univ. Club, Boston Club, Neighborhood Club of Quincy. Personal E-mail: therese.maloney@verizon.net.

MALOUF, PAMELA BONNIE, film editor, video editor; b. Reseda, Calif., July 9, 1956; d. Jubert George and Marguerite I. (Llido) Malouf. AA in Cinema with honors, Valley CC, 1976. Asst. film editor various film studios including Paramount, 20th Fox, CBS/MTM, and others, 1976-80; post prodn. coordinator, supr. David Gerber Co., Culver City, Calif., 1981-82; post prodn. coord. Paramount TV, L.A., 1982-84; sole proprietor Trailers, Etc., North Hollywood, Calif., 1984-85; film and video editor Paramount Pictures, L.A., 1985-86; film editor Universal Studios, Universal City, 1987-89; film, video editor New World TV, L.A., 1991-92; associate dir. Tri-Star TV, Studio City, Calif., 1992-93; film and video editor various studios, Studio City, 1993—. Owner, mgr. Choice Editing Sys., Northridge, Calif., 1993—. Editor: (TV series) Casino, The Apprentice, Rude Awakening, Strong Medicine, Anna Says, Magnificent 7, A Year in the Life, MacGyver, Call to Gloray, The Making of Shogun, Nightingales, Mission Impossible, Muder C.O.D., I'll Take Romance, Get a Life, A Fire in the Dark, The Fifth Corner, Stong Medicine, Casino, (TV films) Search for Grace, Eyes of Terror, Then There Was One, Sweet Bird of Youth, Without You I'm Nothing, All in the Family, Rockford Files, Is There Life Out There?, Thrill, Breaking Free, Something Borrowed.Something Blue, A Time to Stay Goodbye?, An Unexpected Life, A Father For Brittany, Love Song, Custody of the Heart, 2000, Snap Decision, The Familiar Stranger, Taking Back Our Town, 2001; asst. editor: (films) King of Gypsies, Star Wars, others. Mem.: Dirs. Guild Am., Acad. TV Arts and Scis., Am. Cinema Editors, Acad. Magical Arts, Inc., Tri-Network (pres. 1979—80), Internat. Alliance Theatrical Stage Employees and Moving Picture Machine Operators U.S. and Can. Democrat. Roman Catholic. Avocations: water-skiing, skiing, sand castle building, script writing.

MALTIN, MARJORIE SOLOMON, psychologist, psychoanalyst; b. Hartford, Conn., Nov. 15, 1943; d. Joseph and Sylvia Muriel (Clark) S.; m. Lawrence J. Maltin, July 29, 1973; children: Samantha, Marla. BS in Psychology & Elem. Edn. cum laude, Tufts U., 1965; MA in Developmental Psychology, Columbia U., 1966, EdD, 1978; postdoctoral diploma, Adelphi U., 1987. Cert. psychologist, N.Y., early childhood and elem. tchr., N.Y., sch. psychologist, N.Y. Rsch. asst. Tufts U., Boston, 1964; social caseworker Conn. State Social Svcs., 1965; headstart tchr. East Harlem Schs., NYC, 1966; rsch. bd. higher edn. CUNY, 1966-67; rsch. asst. Tchrs. Coll. Columbia U., 1966-69; sch. psychologist intern Hewlitt-Woodmere Pub. Schs., 1969-70; staff psychologist forensic divsn. Nassau County Family Ct., 1970-75; pvt. practice psychologist Woodbury, NY, 1979—. Faculty Suffolk Inst. for Psychotherapy and Psychoanalysis, 1995, dir., 1999-2002. Vol. psychologist acute psychiat. unit Northport VA Hosp., 1981-82; supr. Denver Inst., Adelphi U., 1989—. Mem. APA (co-chair profl. issues com. divsn. 39 1992-95), N.Y. State Psychol. Assn., Nassau County Psychol. Assn., Adelphi Soc. Psychoanalysis and Psychotherapy (sec. 1986-89, pres.-elect 1989-90, pres. 1990-92), Soffok Soc. Psychoanal and Psycho Therapy. Avocations: skiing, biking, travel, reading. Home and Office: 102 Cypress Dr Woodbury NY 11797-1522

MALVRE, MAILI, artist, educator, secondary school educator; b. Tallinn, Estonia, Jan. 24, 1936; arrived in U.S., 1950; d. Peter Megler and Elfriede Helene Reinveldt; m. Olavi Malvre, Aug. 6, 1955; children: Kersti Anne, Astrid Merike, Erich Olavi. BA, Calif. State U., 1969; student, U. Calif., Berkeley, Calif., 1972; student in Art and Art History, Saint Mary's Coll., 1972—77. Tchr. English Pleasanton Unified Sch. Dist., Calif., 1970—96; freelance artist Danville, Calif., 1996—. Mem. com. English lang. State of Calif., San Francisco, 1981—84; specialist curriculum resource Dept. Edn., Estonia, 1990—94; spkr. in field. Vol. docent Tao Ho. Nat. Pk. Svc., Danville, 1986—89; art therapist Guardian Rehab. Hosp., San Ramon, Calif., 1996—2001. Recipient Excellence in Tchg. award, Dublin (Calif.) H.S., 1985, Vol. Svc. award, Guardian Rehab. Hosp., 2001. Mem.: Alamo-Danville (Calif.) Artist Soc., Friends Filoli. Lutheran. Avocations: history, writing, travel, photography, reading.

MAMLOK, URSULA, composer, educator; b. Berlin, Feb. 1, 1928; d. John and Dorothy Lewis; m. Dwight G. Mamlok, Nov. 27, 1947. Student, Mannes Coll. Music, 1942-45; MusB, Manhattan Sch. Music, 1955, MusM, 1958. Faculty dept. music NYU, 1967-74, CUNY, 1971-74; prof. composition Manhattan Sch. Music, N.Y.C., 1968—2003. Composer numerous works including Variations and Interludes for 4 percussionists, 1973, Sextet, 1977, Festive Sounds, 1978, When Summer Sang, 1980, piano trio Panta rhei, 1981, 5 recital pieces for young pianists, 1983, From My Garden for solo viola or solo violin, 1983, Concertino for wind quintet, strings and percussion, 1984, Der Andreas Garten for voice, flute and harp, 1986, Alariana for recorder, clarinet, bassoon, violin and cello, 1986, 3 Bagatelles for harpsichord, 1987, 5 Bagatelles for clarinet, violin, cello, 1988, Rhapsody for clarinet, viola, piano Inward Journey for Piano, 1989, Sonata for violin and piano, 1989, Music for flute, violin, cello, 1990, Girasol, a sextet for flute, violin, viola, cello and piano, 1991, Constellations for orch., 1993, Polarities for flute, violin, cello, piano, 1995, Festive Sounds for Organ, String Quartet II, 1996-97, Two Thousan Notes for Piano, 2000-01, Confluencies for Clarinet, Violin, Cello, Piano, 2002, Rückblick for Saxophone and Piano, 2002, piano pieces for 25th anniversary archive Woman and Music, 2004, 2 Bagatelles for String Quartet, rev., 2004. Recipient Opus One Rec. award Am. Composers Alliance, 1987, Serge Koussevitzky Found. commn., 1988, Walter Hinrichsen award Acad. Inst. Arts and Letters, 1989, commn. San Francisco Symphony, 1990; Nat. Endowment Arts grantee, 1974, Am. Inst. Acad. Arts and Letters grantee, 1981, 89, Martha Baird Rockefeller grantee, 1982; John Simon Gugenheim fellow, 1995. Mem. Am. Soc. Univ. Composers, Am. Women Composers, N.Y. Women Composers, Internat. League Women Composers, Am. Music Ctr., Internat. Soc Contemporary Music (bd. dirs.), Fromm Found. Commn., Am. Guild Organists Continuum Commn. Address: 315 E 86th St New York NY 10028-4714

MAMMEN, MARY A., elementary school educator; b. Springfield, Ill., Oct. 14, 1955; d. James Dominic and Martha Louise (Hawkins) Sullivan; m. Steven James Mammen, July 12, 1975; children: Heather, Carey, Jason. AA, Springfield Coll., Ill., 1975; BA in Child Family Cmty. Svcs., U. Ill., Springfield, 1976; postgrad., U. South Fla., Ft. Myers, 1982—86. Tchr. emotionally handicapped Clewiston Primary Sch., Fla., 1982—89; tchr. 5th grade Clewiston Intermediate Sch., 1989—90, Eastside Elem. Sch., 1990—2003; tchr. work geography Clewiston Mid. Sch., 2003—. Coach cheerleading Clewiston H.S., 1992—2005. Chair United Daus. Confederacy, Ft. Myers, 2004—06. Mem.: NEA, Am. Assn. Cheerleading Counselors and Advisors, Hendrik County Educators Assn. Roman Catholic. Avocations: boating, snorkeling. Office: Clewiston Mid Sch 601 W Pasadena Ave Clewiston FL 33440

MAMPRE, VIRGINIA ELIZABETH, communications executive; b. Chgo., Sept. 12, 1949; d. Albert Leon and Virginia S. (Joboul) M. BA with honors, U. Iowa, 1971; Masters degree, Ind. U., 1972; spl. cert., Harvard U., 1981, Purdue U., 1999. Cert. tchr. Harris Intern WTTW-TV Sta., Chgo., 1972, asst. dir., 1972-73; prod. and dir. WSIU/WUSI-TV Sta., Carbondale, Ill., 1973-74; instr. So. Ill. U., Carbondale, 1972-77; prog. and prod. mgr. WSIU/WUSI-TV, Carbondale, 1974-77; prog. dir. KUHT-TV Sta., Houston, 1977-83; pres. Victory Media, Inc., Houston, 1984-89, Mampre Media Internat., Houston, 1984—. Cons. Corp. Pub. Broadcasting, Washington, 1981—83; bd. dirs. TVPC; program bd. Ea. Ednl. Network; spkr., presenter in field Europe, Asia, Australia, S. Am. Contbg. author/editor to mags. including Focus, 1989, News & Views, 1987-88, In the Black, 1984-93, Festivals; creator: (report card campaign) Multi-media, U.S., 1985—; exec. prodr. TV spls., pub. affairs and info., 1977-83 (awards 1978-91). Pres. Child Abuse Prevention Coun., Houston, 1984—97; chmn. exhbns. Mayor's 1st Hearing, Children and Youth, Houston, 1985—88; rep. Houston 2nd World Conf. on Mayors, Japan, 1989; bd. govs. Houston Read Commn., pres., 1995—2001, chair adv. bd., 1993—2001; mem. nat. faculty Ctr. Children's Issues, 1995—97; pres. Episcopal Ch. Women, 2002—, 2006; pres. bd. dirs. Houston Fin. Coun., 1983—; bd. dirs. Child Abuse Prevention Network, 1990—97; chmn. bd. dirs., gala chair Crime Stoppers Houston, 1984—99; founder, bd. dirs. Friends of WSIU-TV, 1974—77; chmn. St. Kevork/ACYO Nat. Sports Fair, St. John the Divine, 1990; mem. exec. bd. Nat. Com. To Prevent Child Abuse, 1990—97; pres., bd. dirs. Fedn. Houston Profl. Women Found., 1996; bd. dirs. Humanities Tex., 1998—, Tex. Coun. Humanities, Operation Rainbow, 1997—, pres. bd. gala chair; bd. dirs. Kellogg Fellows Leadership Alliance; adv. bd. Southwest Area Media Project. Fellow W.K. Kellogg Found., Battle Creek, Mich., 1987-90; recipient award for Excellence Pres. Pvt. Sector, White House, Washington, 1987, Ohio State U., Columbus, 1983, Feddersen award for excellence in Pub. TV Ind. U., Bloomington, 1981, Heritage award Child Abuse Prevention Coun., 1990, Dona J. Stone Founders award Nat. Assn. for Prevention of Child Abuse, 1990; named among Outstanding Women Vols. for community, civic and profl. contbns., Fedn. Houston Profl. Women, 1989; honoree Woman on Move, 1997. Mem.: Houston Culinary Guild (pres. 2006—), Internat. Festivals Events. Assn. (officer 1994—2003, sec. 1994—, bd. dirs. 1995—2002, creator Mampre Media Internat. Leadership Devel.), Profls. in Culinary Arts (pres. 2002—), TV Program Conf. (sec. bd. 1990—), Ctr. Bus. Women's Devel., Nat. Assn. Programming TV Execs., Nat. Assn. Ednl. Broadcasters (presenter nat. conv. 1975—76), Houston Fed. Profl. Women (del. 1986—93, chmn. 1994—, pres.), Am. Women in Radio and TV (bd. dirs. 1985—, nat. v.p. 1986—90, award 1987, pres. Houston chpt. 1990), Kellogg Fellows Leadership Alliance (bd. trustees), Dau. of the King, Christ in the Arts (chair), Dephians, Tex. Lyceum (v.p., bd. dirs. 1990—96). Republican. Episcopalian. Avocations: photography, swimming, sailing, languages, travel. Office: Mampre Media Internat 5123 Del Monte Dr Houston TX 77056-4391 Office Phone: 713-960-9849. Personal E-mail: mampremedi@aol.com.

MAMUT, MARY CATHERINE, retired entrepreneur; b. Calabria, Italy, Oct. 17, 1923; came to U.S., 1928; d. Carmelo Charles and Caterina (Tripodi) Cogliandro; m. Michael Matthew Mamut, May 15, 1954; children: Anthony Carl, Charles Terrance. Student, Stenotype Comml. Coll., 1946-50. Sec. to pres. Thomas Goodfellow, Inc., Detroit, 1942-50; asst. to v.p. R.G. Moeller Co., Detroit, 1951-52; sec. to pres. United Steel Supply Co., Detroit, 1952-54; sec. to libr. Farmington (Mich.) Schs., 1962-68; real estate agt., 1969; owner, mgr. Crystal Fair, Birmingham, Mich., 1969-88, ret. Mich. Tchr. Stenotype Comml. Coll., Detroit, 1952-54. Vol. Henry Ford Mus., Dearborn, Mich., 1989-90, Greenfield Village, 1989-90, West Bloomfield Libr., 1993-95. Recipient World Lifetime Achievement award Am. Biog. Inst. U.S.A., 1993. Mem. Am. Bus. Women's Assn., Birmingham-Bloomfield C. of C., Profl. Secs. Internat, NAFE. Roman Catholic. Avocations: reading, music, art, theater. Home: 7423 Coach Ln West Bloomfield MI 48322-4022

MANAHAN, VANDA GALEN, social work educator, columnist; b. Frenchburg, Ky., Sept. 7, 1946; d. Bruce and Irene (Mynhier) Botts; children: Valerie, Don, Christopher Hedges; m. James Hinchon Manahan, Jan. 30, 1989. AB, Morehead (Ky.) State U., 1970, MA, 1977; MSW, Va. Commonwealth U., 1975; PhD, U. Minn., 1991. Social worker, team leader, supr. Ky. Dept. Human Resources, Frankfort, 1970-77; asst. prof. social work Morehead State U., 1977-79; assoc. prof., then prof. Mankato (Minn.) State U., 1979—2001. Mem. Fin. Assistance Task Force, Mankato, 1983, Area Agy. on Aging Adv. Coun., Mankato, 1983, Community Svcs. Adv. Coun., Mankato, 1984, Blue Earth County Social Svcs. Task Force, Mankato, 1990; v.p. Minn. Valley Action Coun., 1997-98; former mem. exec. bd. Minn. Gerontol. Soc.; bd. dirs. Minn. Area Geriatric Edn. Ctr.-South. Home: 1200 W River Dr Mankato MN 56001-1735

MANASC, VIVIAN, architect, consultant; b. Bucharest, Romania, May 19, 1956; d. Bercu and Bianca (Smetterling) M.; m. William A. Dushenski, Feb. 25, 1984; children: Peter Gabriel, Lawrence Alexander. BS in Architecture, McGill U., Montreal, Que., Can., 1977, BArch, 1979; MBA, U. Alta., Edmonton, 1982. Architectural insp. Transport Can., Edmonton, 1977-79; project architect Bell Spotowski Architects, Edmonton, 1980-82; asst. dir. design constrn. Edmonton Pub. Schs., 1982-84; mgr., prin. Ferguson, Simek, Clark Architects Ltd., Edmonton, 1985-88; mng. dir. FSC Groves Hodgson Manasc Architects Ltd., Edmonton, 1988-97; pres. Manasc Isaac Archs., Edmonton, 1997—. Adj. asst. prof. of architecture, U. Calgary; bd. dirs. Can. Archtl. Accreditation Bd. Contbr. articles to profl. jours. Co-chair innovative practice group in arch. United Way Edmonton, sect. chair, cabinet mem., Edmonton, 1980-82; mentor RAIC Syllabus Program, Edmonton, 1982-88; bd. dirs. Econ. Devel. Edmonton. Scholar McGill U., 1974. Fellow Royal Archtl. Inst. Can. (bd. dirs.); mem. Alta. Assn. Archs., Manitoba Assn. Archs., B.C. Assn. Archs., Saskatchewan Assn. Archs., Coun. Edn. Facility Planners, Nat. Coun. Jewish Women (past pres. Edmonton sect.), Jewish Fedn. Edmonton (v.p. planning). Avocations: travel, photography, writing. Fax: (780) 426-3 70. E-mail: vivian@miarch.com.

MANASSE, ARLYNN H., pediatric nurse practitioner; b. Aurora, Ill., Apr. 10, 1947; d. Oliver J. and Arlene M. (Lehman) Hem; m. Henri R. Manasse Jr., Aug. 9, 1969; children: Bryan, Sheralynn. BSN, U. Ill., Chgo., 1969, MPH, 1989; pediatric nurse practitioner cert., Rush-Presbyn.-St. Luke's Ctr., 1971. Pub. health nurse, pediatric nurse practitioner, acting dir. Infant Welfare Soc., Chgo., 1969-72; pediatric nurse practitioner Mpls. Health Dept., 1972-74; pub. health nurse, pediatric nurse practitioner LaGrange (Ill.) Cmty. Nurse and Svc. Assn., 1978-88; pediatric nurse practitioner Bethel Wholistic Health Ctr., Chgo., 1991-93, Circle Family Care, Chgo., 1994—; adj. nursing faculty U. Ill., Chgo., 1994—. Regional health adv. bd. Cmty. and Econ. Devel. Assn., Head Start, Chgo., 1978-88. Active, mem. of choir Western Springs (Ill.) Bapt. Ch., 1976—; bd. dirs., officer Westside Holistic Family Svcs., Chgo., 1990—. Fellow Nat. Assn. Pediatric Nurse Assocs. and Practitioners; mem. ANA, Ill. Nurses Assn., APHA, Ill. Pub. Health Assn. Avocations: professional sports, travel.

MANATT, KATHLEEN GORDON, publishing company executive; b. Boone, Iowa, June 3, 1948; d. Richard Condon and Lewise Ryan (Gordon) M.; BA, Coll. Wooster, 1970. Prodn. coord. Scott, Foresman & Co., Glenview, Ill., 1970-73, editor, 1973-81, product mgr., 1981-87; exec. editor McDougal, Littell & Co., Evanston, Ill., 1987-90; developer ednl. text and video projects Soviet and Am. authors and orgns., 1990—. Mem. Am. Ednl. Rsch. Assn., Assn. for Supervision and Curriculum Devel., Nat. Coun. Social Studies, Ill. Coun. Social Studies, N.E. Conf. for the Teaching of Fgn. Langs. Presbyterian. Home: 680 N Lake Shore Dr Fl 19 Chicago IL 60611-3495

MANCALL, JACQUELINE COOPER, library and information scientist, educator; b. Phila., Mar. 31, 1932; d. Morris and Bertha Cooper; m. Elliott Lee Mancall, Dec. 27, 1953; children: Andrew Cooper, Peter Cooper. BA, U. Pa., 1954; MS, Drexel U. Sch. Libr. and Info. Sci., 1970, PhD, 1979. Adminstr. Miquon Sch., Pa., 1966—67, libr., 1967—76; tchg. asst. Drexel U., Phila., 1976—78, rsch. assoc., 1978, asst. prof., assoc. prof., 1979—89, prof., 1989—. Chair Phila. Children's Reading Round Table, 1982—84, mem. steering com., 1979—89; mem. faculty coun. Drexel U., 1984—89, chair faculty coun., 1987—89, mem. senate, 2000—05, chair senate, 2001—02; mem. sch. libr. survey com. State Libr. Pa., 1993; cons. Author (with M.C. Drott): Measuring Student Information Use: A Guide for School Library Media Specialists, 1963; author: (with E.S. Aversa) Management of Online Search Services in Schools, 1989; author: (with Sandra Hughes-Hassell) Collection for Management Youth, 2005; rsch. editor: Sch. Libr. Media quar., 1982—88, mem. editl. bd.: Jour. Libr. and Info. Sci. Edn., 1981—86, mem. editl. adv. bd.: Multimedia Schs.; contbg. editor: Cath. Libr. World, 1981—85; contbr. chapters to books, articles to profl. jours. Bd. dirs. Friends of William Jeannes Meml. Libr., Plymouth Meeting, Pa., 1976—79; pres. bd. dirs. Miquon Sch., 1964—66. Recipient Ann. award, Phila. Sch. Libr., 1994. Mem.: ALA (adv. com. office info. tech. 1995—97, continuing edn. task force 1995—98, co-chair ICONect evaluation com. 1996—2000, libr. congress nat. digital libr. adv. com. 1997, pub. awareness com. 1997—99, dir. KidsConnect 2000—02), Am. Assn. Sch. Libr. (chmn. continuing edn. com. 1985—87, rsch. stats. com. 1988—92, v.p./pres.-elect 1993, pres. 1994, Disting. Svc. award 1999), Pa. Sch. Librs. Assn. (chmn. profl. std. com. 1980—82, bd. dirs. 1984—87, chmn. profl. std. com. 1991—, Outstanding Contbr. award 1997), Phi Delta Kappa, Beta Phi Mu, Pi Gamma Mu. Democrat. Jewish. Office: Drexel U Coll Info Sci & Tech Philadelphia PA 19104 Office Phone: 215-895-2473. Business E-Mail: jackie.mancall@drexel.edu.

MANCHER, RHODA ROSS, federal agency administrator, financial planner; b. N.Y.C., Sept. 28, 1935; d. Joseph and Hannah (Karpf) Ross; m. Melvin Mancher, May 27, 1962 (dec.); children: Amy Backus, James Marc. BS in Physics, Columbia U., 1960; MS in Ops. Research, George Washington U., 1978. Staff FEA, Washington, 1974-77; dir. info. systems devel. div. The White House, Washington, 1977-79; dir. office systems devel. Social Security Adminstrn., Balt., 1979-80; dep. asst. atty. gen. Office Info. Tech., Dept. Justice, Washington, 1980-84; assoc. dir. info. resources mgmt. Dept. Navy, Washington, 1985-87; dir. Office Info. Tech. VA, Washington, 1987-94; pres. H.W.& W., Inc., 1994—. Mem. ad hoc com. on recommendations to merge chem. and biol. info. systems Nat. Cancer Inst., Washington; chmn. permanent com. on info. tech. Iternat. Criminal Police Orgn. (INTERPOL); mem. curriculum com. USDA, adv. bd. computer system security and privacy U.S. Govt.; internat. tech. com. AFCEA. Contbr. articles to profl. publs. Recipient Assoc. Commr.'s citation Social Security Adminstrn., 1980, managerial excellence award Interagy. Com. on ADP, 1983; Meritorious award Sr. Exec. Svc., 1982, 83, 85, 87, 88, 91-93, Presdl. Rank of Meritorious Exec., 1990. Mem. Am. Fedn. Info. Processing Socs. (nat. info. issues panel) Office: 7900 Wisconsin Ave Ste 201 Bethesda MD 20814

MANCHESTER, KATHLEEN A., music educator; b. Iola, Wis., June 25, 1957; d. Arden Sellin and Elaine Harrington; m. John Manchester, Aug. 1, 1987. MusB, Lawrence U., 1975—80; MusM in edn., U. of Ill., 1995—99. Music tchr. Wis. Dells Schools, 1980—82, Dodgeland Schools, Juneau, Wis., 1982—86, Hawthorn Aspen Sch., Vernon Hills, Ill., 1988—. Adj. instr. U. of Ill., 2003—04. Contbr. presentation, clinic, articles to jours. Tech. MiniGrant, Hawthorn Dist. 73, 2000. Mem.: Am. Orff-Schulwerk Assn., Orgn. of Am. Kodaly Educators, Ill. Music Educators Assn., Music Educators Nat. Conf. Avocations: cooking, reading, astronomy, gardening. Home: 3107 Eastway Dr Island Lake IL 60042 Office: Hawthorn Aspen Sch 500 Aspen Dr Vernon Hills IL 60061 Office Phone: 847-990-4337.

MANCILLA, FAUSTINA RAMIREZ, retired psychologist; b. Tijuana, Mexico, Feb. 15, 1943; d. Domingo Gomez and Carmen Castillo Ramirez; m. Armando Hernandez Mancilla, Nov. 30, 1957; children: Irene M. Torres, Alice M. Kincaid, Edward, Sergio Armando, Jaime. BA in Liberal Studies, Loyola Marymount U., LA, 1980, MA in Counseling and Guidance, 1986, MA in Counseling Psychology, Marriage and Family, 1986, MA in Ednl. Psychology, 1987, MA in Sch. Adminstrn., 1993; MA in Profl. Adminstrv. Svcs., Azusa Pacific U., Azusa, Calif., 1999; PhD in Behavioral Studies, Azusa Pacific U., 2000. Guidance tech. Culver City Unified Sch. Dist., Calif., 1980—84; tchr. k-5, bilingual Lennox Sch. Dist., 1984—85, tchr. spl. edn., 1985—86; bilingual sch. psychologist Santa Monica/Malibu Unified Sch. Dist., 1986—90; asst. prin. Lennox Sch. Dist., 1990—91, sr. psychologist, 1991—93, dir. pupil pers. svcs., 1993—97; dist. psychologist Murrieta Valley Unified Sch. Dist., 1997—99; coord., prin., infant cir., presch. grasp Riverside County Office Edn., 1999—2003; interim dir. pupil svcs. Murrieta Valley Unified Sch. Dist., 1999—99; coord., site adminstr., interagency assessment and tng. ctr. Riverside County Office Edn., 2003—05. Early childhood devel. cons. Riverside County Office Edn., 2003—06. Cert. parent trainer instr. Ctr. Improvement Children, LA, 1986—90; trainer trainer Los Padres Richstone Family Ctr., Lawndale, 1987—90; cert. interpreter/translator trainer Loyola Marymount U., LA, 1990—2006; cert. trainer spl. projects bilingual edn. San Diego County Dept. Edn., 1995—96; trainer trainers tchg. strategies young children Dept. Edn. -Nat. Project, 1993—96. Recipient Outstanding Bilingual Psychologist award, Santa Monica/Malibu Unified Sch. Dist., 1989, Outstanding Svc. award, Supr. and Trainer, Loyola Marymount U., 1994, 1996, Outstanding Svc. award, Dist. Adv. Coun., Lennox Sch. Dist., 1997. Mem.: Calif. Assn. Sch. Psychologists, Assn. Calif. Sch. Adminstrs. (assoc.), Nat. Assn. Sch. Psychologists (assoc.), Kappa Delta Phi (hon.). Avocations: travel, dance, painting. Home: 31597 Vignes Court Winchester CA 92596 Office: Riverside County Office of Education 3939 Thirteenth Street Riverside CA 92502-0868 Office Phone: 951-826-4600.

MANCINELLI, JUDITH, piano teacher, recitalist, chamber music performer; b. Johnstown, Pa., Sept. 23, 1948; m. Aldo L. Mancinelli, June 1, 1971; children: Michelle, Brian. BA, Maryville (Tenn.) Coll., 1970; MMusic, U. Tulsa, 1971. Piano tchr. U. Tulsa, 1971-80, staff accompanist, 1978-80; piano tchr. Millikin U., Decatur, Ill., 1980—, supr. student accompanying, 1998—. Pianist with Kirkland Trio, Decatur, 1988—; violinist Millikin-Decatur Symphony, 1980—, Lee Pondel Quartet, Decatur, 1985—. Mem. Music Tchrs. Nat. Assn., Nat. Guild Piano Tchrs. (judge), Ill. Music Tchrs. Assn. (chair dist. competition 1994-99), Pi Kappa Lambda, Tau Kappa Chi. Avocations: stained glass, gardening, fish. Office: Millikin U Dept Music 1184 W Main St Decatur IL 62522-2084

MANCINI, JOYCE KATHERINE, family practice nurse practitioner; b. Woburn, Mass., Dec. 5, 1968; d. George Russell and Roberta Katherine (Miles) B. Diploma, Tewksbury Hosp. Sch. Nursing, 1989; ADN, Rivier Coll., 1995; BSN, Framingham State Coll., 1998; MSN, Regis Coll., Weston, Mass., 2004. RN Mass., FNP, Mass. LPN Hogan Regional Ctr. North Reading (Mass.) ICF, 1989—95; staff nurse subacute unit Sunbridge Care & Rehab. of Milford, Mass., 1998—; nurse practitioner Beth Israel Deaconess Family Practice, Medfield, 2006—. Class sec. Rivier Coll.-St. Josephs Sch. Nursing, Nashua, NH, 1993—95; vis. nurse Am. Health Care, 1995—96; charge nurse Westridge Healthcare Ctr., Marlboro, Mass., 1996—98. Sch. coun. mem. PTO; co-founder George R. Brazee Meml. Fund Mesothelioma Rsch. Mem.: Sigma Theta Tau (Rho Phi chpt.). Avocations: boating, snowmobiling, shopping, jet skiing. Home: 55 Maple St Milford MA 01757-3650

MANCINI, LORRAINE, science educator; b. Bridgeport, Conn., Feb. 11, 1952; d. George and Claire Venables; children: Allan Guglielmoni, Sara Lynn Guglielmone, Jessica Eve, David Richard. MEd, U. Bridgeport, Conn., 1999. Cert. sci. tchr. Conn. Dept. Edn., 2000. Social worker Nerological Assocs., Stratoford, Conn., 1989—92; sci. tchr. CIE Alternative Edn., Bridgeport, 1992—99. Cons. Girl Scouts Housatonic Coun., Bridgeport, 1990—2006.

MANCINI, MARY CATHERINE, cardiothoracic surgeon, researcher; b. Scranton, Pa., Dec. 15, 1953; d. Peter Louis and Ferminia Teresa (Massi) M. BS Chemistry, U. Pitts., 1974, MD, 1978; PhD Anatomy and Cellular Biology, La. State U. Med. Ctr., New Orleans, 2000; M Med. Mgmt., U. Tex. Southwestern, Dallas, 2005. Diplomate Am. Bd. Surgery (speciality cert. critical care medicine), Am. Bd. Thoracic Surgery, cert. Med. Mgmt. U. Tex. Southwestern, 2000. Intern surgery U. Pitts., 1978—79, resident surgery, 1979—87; fellow pediat. cardiac surgery Mayo Clinic, 1987—88; asst. prof. surgery, dir. cardio-thoracic transplantation Med. Coll. Ohio, Toledo, 1988—91; assoc. prof. surgery, dir. cardio-thoracic transplantation La. State U. Health Scis. Ctr., Shreveport, 1991—98, prof. surgery, chief cardiothoracic surgery, 1999—2002; dir. cardiovasc. rsch. Willis Knighton Med. Ctr., 1991—2004. Med. advisor Total Artificial Heart Devel., ABIOMED Corp. Author: Operative Techniques for Medical Students, 1983; editor-in-chief: Cardiothoracic Surgery and Transplantation EMedicine Textbooks; contbr. articles to profl. jours. Mem. physicians adv. bd. Rep. Com. Named one of Am.'s Top Thoracic Surgeons, Consumer's Rsch. Coun. Am., 2006; recipient Pres. award, Internat. Soc. Heart Transplantation, 1983, Charles C. Moore Tchg. award, U. Pitts., 1985, Internat. Order of Merit award, 1995, Nina S. Braunwald Career Devel. award, Thoracic Surgery Found., 1996—98, Nat. Leadership award, Rep. Com., 2000, Disting. Alumni award, U. Pitts. Dept. Chemistry, 2002, Tchg. award, dept. surgery La. State U. Health Sci. Ctr., 2005; grantee Am. Heart Assn., 1988, Whittaker, 1998, NIH, 2000. Fellow ACS, AHA, Am. Coll. Chest Physicians, Internat. Coll. Surgeons (councillor 1991—); mem. Assn. Women Surgeons, Am. Surg. Assn., Am. Assn. Thoracic Surgery, Am. Physiol. Soc., So. Surg. Assn., Rotary (gift of life program 1991), Beta Gamma Sigma, Gamma Sigma Gamma. Roman Catholic. Achievements include first multiple organ transplant in La; first pediatric heart transplant in La., 1993. Office: La State U Med Ctr 1501 Kings Hwy Shreveport LA 71103-4228 Office Phone: 318-675-6154. Personal E-mail: mcmmd@hotmail.com. Business E-Mail: mmanci@lsuhsc.edu.

MANCINO, ANNE ROCHELLE, surgeon; b. Little Rock, June 9, 1958; d. Ronald Greer and Patricia Joyce (Glass) Thompson; m. Michael John Mancino, Nov. 26, 1994; 1 child, Parker Kathleen. BA in Molecular Biology, Vanderbilt U., 1980; MD, U. Ark., 1984. Intern U. Louisville, 1984-87, resident in surgery, 1989-92; fellow in endocrine rsch. Mass. Gen. Hosp./Harvard Med. Sch., Boston, 1988-89; asst. prof. surgery U. Miss., Jackson, 1992-98; fellow diseases of the breast U. Ark., Little Rock, 1998—2000, asst. prof. surgery, 1998—2002, assoc. prof. surgery, 2002—, dir. student edn. dept. surgery, 2002—. Dir. student edn. dept. surgery U. Miss., 1992-98. Contbr. articles to profl. jours. Lt. col. U.S. Army, 1991. Fellow ACS; mem. Am. Assn. Endocrine Surgeons, Assn. for Surg. Edn., Assn. Acad. Surgeons, Alpha Omega Alpha. Democrat. Roman Catholic. Avocations: singing, boating. Office: U Ark Medical Sciences 4301 W Markham St # 725 Little Rock AR 72205-7101

MANCUSO, JULIA, skier, Olympic athlete; b. Reno, Nev., Mar. 9, 1984; d. Ciro and Andrea Mancuso. Mem. U.S. Winter Olympics Team, 2006; designer Super Jules Underwear. Mem.: U.S. Ski Team. Achievements include Am. record for medals and gold medals, Jr. World Championships Downhill Skiing; bronze medal in Super-G and Giant Slalom, World

Championships, 2005; gold medal in Giant Slalom, Olympic Winter Games, Torino, 2006. Avocations: surfing, water-skiing, mountain biking, kite-boarding. Office: US Ski and Snowboard Assn 1500 Kearns Blvd Park City UT 84060*

MANDARINO, CANDIDA ANN, education educator, consultant; b. Buffalo, N.Y., July 26, 1944; d. Amerigo and Adelaide (Alfieri) Mandarino. BS in Edn., SUNY, Buffalo, 1966; MA in Ednl. Psychology, Calif. State U., Long Beach, 1974; postgrad. in interior and environ. design, 1980—85; PhD in Psychology, Berne U., Wolfboro Falls, N.H., 2000. Tchr. on spl. assignment Norwalk (Calif.)-La Mirada Unified Sch. Dist. Office, 1990—99; mentor/master tchr.; literacy and resource specialist Los Alisos Middle Sch., Norwalk, 1999—2000; prin. Escalona Elem. Sch., La Mirada, 2000; ednl. trainer, cons. K-12 and univs. Heuer Corp., N.Y.C., 2001. Spkr., presenter in field. Mem.: Tchrs. Assn. Norwalk-LaMirada Area, Calif. Tchrs. Assn., Assn. Supervision and Curriculum Devel., Pi Lambda Theta. Home: 178 Roycroft Ave Long Beach CA 90803

MANDEL, ADRIENNE ABRAMSON, state legislator; b. Irvington, N.J., Sept. 30, 1936; d. Nathaniel and Florence (Lebovitz) Abramson; m. Emanuel Mandel, 1958; children: Lisa Mandel-Trupp, David. BA, Rutgers U., 1958; MA, George Washington U., 1984. Exec. program cert.: Harvard U., JF Kennedy Sch. Govt. 2003. Chairwoman, vice chairwoman Precinct 13-56, 1979-94; parole officer, social svc. case worker N.J. Dept. Inst. & Agencies, 1958-60; survey interviewer U.S. Census Bur., 1973-77; monitoring and evaluation specialist Divsn. Labor Svc., Montgomery County Govt., 1979-81; asst. dir. Sr. Ctr. Divsn. Elder Affairs, Dept. Family Resources, 1981-84; staff asst. Office Chief Adminstr., 1984-85; legis. rep. Office Intergovt. Rels., 1985-94; mem. Md. State Legislature, 1995—, mem. commerce govt. matters com., 1995—2002, mem. health and govt. ops. com., 2003—, dep. majority whip, 2003—. Pres. Women's Caucus, 2002-03; bi-county chair Montgomery County Del., 1999—; health issues chair Nat. Order Women Legislators, 1999—; mem. exec. bd. Nat. Found. Women Legislators, 2004—. Named one of Md. Top 100 Women, The Daily Record, 2002, 2004; recipient Woman of Valor award, B'nai B'rith Women, 1972, MD Profl. Driver Educators Legis. of Year, 1998, MD League Conservation Voters Environ. Leadership award, Nat. Capitol Homecare Assn. Pres. award, 2001, MD Nurses Assn. Legislator of Yr., 2002, Montgomery County NOW Legislator of Yr., 2003, Significant Contribution to Med. Cmty. award, Montgomery County Med. Soc., 2005. Mem. Women's Polit. Caucus, Mothers Against Drunk Driving, Md. Govt. Rels. Assn., Montgomery County Ethnic Heritage Festival, LWV, Alpha Psi Omega, Delta Phi Delta.

MANDEL, CAROL, librarian; b. Bklyn., Dec. 18, 1946; d. Irwin Daniel and Charlotte Mandel; m. Vincent T. Covello. BA magna cum laude, U. Mass., 1968; MSLS with honors, Columbia U., 1970, MA in Art History, 1975. Reference libr. Northeastern U. Libr., Boston, 1970; architecture and fine arts cataloger Columbia U. Librs., NYC, 1971-75, asst. to head original monographs cataloging dept., 1975-77, head original monographs cataloging dept., 1977-79, dir. tech. svcs., 1986-91, dir. tech. and networked info. svcs., 1991-93, dep. univ. libr., 1993—99; assoc. exec. dir. Assn. Rsch. Librs., Washington, 1979-83; asst., assoc. univ. libr. assess svcs. U. Calif., San Diego Librs., 1983-86; dean libr. NYU, 1999—. Mem. coop. cataloging coun. Libr. Congress, 1993-95, mem. seminar on copy cataloging, 1992, cons., 1985; reviewer, panelist, site visitor NEH, 1978-94; panelist NEA Title II-C grant program Dept. Edn., 1982, 84, 86, 89; mem. pres.'s commn. on tech. processing Rsch. Librs. Group, 1991, mem. bibtech steering com., 1988-90; presenter in field. Contbr. articles to profl. publs. Grantee NEH, 1980-83, 83-86, 89-93, 93—, Dept. Edn., 1989-95. Mem. ALA (vice chair tech. svcs. dirs. of large rsch. librs. discussion group 1992, editorial bd. 1993—, chair various coms., Margaret Mann citation for outstanding profl. achievement in cataloging or classification 1994), Assn. Rsch. Librs. (cons. 1983-86, project dir. microform project, CONSER A&I coverage project), Coun. on Libr. Resources (chair bibliographic svcs. study com. 1987-93, cons.), Ctr. for Rsch. Librs. (mem. access adv. panel 1992—). Office: Columbua U Librs 535 W 114th St New York NY 10027-7035 also: Bost Libr Rm 1134 NYU 70 Washington Sq S New York NY 10012 Office Phone: 212-998-2444. Office Fax: 212-995-4070. E-mail: carol.mandel@nyu.edu.*

MANDEL, JUDITH LYNN, primary school educator; b. Mpls., June 20, 1936; d. Lloyd L. and Gussie Miller Elzas; m. Seymour L. Mandel (div.); children: Lloyd J., Paula J. Cert. of X-Ray Tech., U. Minn., Mpls., 1958; BEd, Nat. Lewis U., Evanston, Ill., 1979. Substitute tchr. pub. schs., Wilmette and Winnetka, Ill., 1979—83; tchr. 2d grade Solomon Schechter Sch., Skokie, Ill., 1984—85; tchr. Haugan Sch., Chgo., 1986—90, Patrick Henry Sch., Chgo., 1991—. Vol. in pediatrics dept. Evanston Hosp., Ill.; den mother cub scouts Boy Scouts Am., Wilmette; leader brownie troop Girl Scouts U.S., Wilmette. Mem.: Chgo. Tchrs. Union, North Shore Sr. Ctr., Chgo. Bot. Gardens, Kappa Delta Pi, Alpha Epsilon Phi. Jewish. Avocations: rug hooking, exercise, reading, antiques, gardening. Home: 245 Essex Pl Wilmette IL 60091 Personal E-mail: judylyn2@aol.com.

MANDEL, KARYL LYNN, accountant; b. Chgo., Dec. 14, 1935; d. Isador J. and Eve (Gellar) Karzen; m. Fredric H. Mandel, Sept. 29, 1956; children: David Scott, Douglas Jay, Jennifer Ann. *Son, David Scott Mandel, graduated magna cum laude, Brown University, 1982, JD from Cornell Law School in 1986 and opened his own practice in 1997. He is the Managing Partner of Mandel & Mandel, LLP, Miami. Currently resides in Florida with his wife Nina Stillman Mandel and three children, Aaron, Jessica, and Noah. Son, Douglas Jay Mandel, resides in Florida with two daughters, Rachael and Sheridan. Daughter, Jennifer Ann Mandel, graduated National Louis University in 1999 and is currently working in the information technology and accounting fields. She lives in the Northern suburbs of Chicago.* Student, U. Mich., 1954-56, Roosevelt U., 1956-57; AA summa cum laude, Oakton Community Coll., 1979. CPA, Ill; registered investment advisor; lic. life ins. provider. Pres. Excel Transp. Service Co., Elk Grove, Ill., 1958-78; tax mgr. CTB, Ltd., CPAs, Northbrook, Ill., 1981-83; tax ptnr. Chunowitz, Teitelbaum & Baerson, CPA's, Northbrook, Ill., 1984—. Sec-treas. Lednam, Inc., Coffee Break, Inc.; mem. acctg. curriculum adv. bd. Oakton C.C., Des Plaines, Ill., 1987—; pres. Lednam Enterprises, LLC, 2001—. Contbg. author: Ill. CPA's News Jour., Acctg. Today. Recipient State of Israel Solidarity award, 1976. Mem. AICPA, Am. Soc. Women CPA, Women's Am. ORT (pres. Chgo. region 1972-74, v.p. midwest dist. 1975-76, nat. endowment com., nat investment adv. com.), Ill. CPA Soc. (chmn. estate and gift tax com. 1987-89, legis. contact com. 1981-82, pres. North Shore chpt., award for Excellence in Acctg. Edn., Bd. dirs. 1989-91), Chgo. Soc. Women CPA, Chgo. Estate Planning Coun., Nat. Assn. Women Bus. Owners, Lake County Estate Planning Coun., Greater North Shore Estate Planning Coun. Office: 401 Huehl Rd Northbrook IL 60062-2300 Business E-Mail: klm@ctbltd.com.

MANDEL, LESLIE ANN, investment advisor, writer; b. Washington, July 29, 1945; d. Seymour and Marjorie (Syble) Mandel; m. Arthur Herzog III, Oct. 27, 1999. BA in Art History, U. Minn., 1967; cert., N.Y. Sch. Interior Design, 1969. Cert. Brailled Libr. Congress. Pres. Leslie Mandel Enterprises, Inc., N.Y.C., 1968—; sr. v.p. Maximum Entertainment Network, L.A. and N.Y.C., 1988-90; pres. Rich List Co., 1968—; pres., CEO Mandel Airplane Funding and Leasing Corp., N.Y.C., Hong Kong, China and Mongolia, 1990—; CEO Mandel-Khan Inc., Ulaanbaatar, Mongolia, 1994—. Travel Safe: keep hers, keep his, 2002—. Fin. advisor Osmed, Inc., Mpls., 1986—, Devine Comm./Allen & Co., NY, Del., Utah, N.Mex., NY, N.Y. WUWV, Utah KBER, WKTC-AM-FM, 1984—89, Am. Kefir Corp., N.Y.C., 1983—89, Shore Group (Internat., Guyana), Flight Internat., 1991—; owner The Rich List Co., 150 internat. catalogs, mags. and fundraising lists; joint venture Mongolian Ind. Broadcasting Channel, Ulaanbaatar, 1995; pres., owner Mandel Airplane Funding and Leasing Corp.; rep. Israeli Govt. IAI Satellite, China, Romania, Costa Rica, Mongolia, Amos Satellite Network, China, 1992—; advisor rep. Gt. Wall Corp., Long March Corp., China, 1992—, Chinese Silk, 1993—, Am. Oil Refinery, 1993—; bd. dirs. Coastal Equipment Co., Bristol Airlines; cons. Exclusive Miat Airlines, Mongolia; purchasing agt. People's Republic of China-Aircraft; advisor Aeropostalis, Mexico, 1994—95; photographer; lectr. UN Internat. Direct Mail; advisor Aruba Airlines, Mexicana Airlines; aircraft agt., bd. dirs. Lazorlines Landing Equipment, 1997—; lease Estafada Airlines 757-200-C, 2000—, Chile Airlines 757-200C, 2002; advisor Guyana 2000 Airlines; ptnr. Laserline/Vulcan Power Plant, Greece, 2005—, China, 2005. Photographer: Vogue, 1978, New Earth Times, 1995, Fortune mag.; Braille transcriber: The Prophet (Kalil Gibran), 1967, Getting Ready for Battle (R. Prawe Jhabuala), 1967; exec. prodr. film: Hospital Audiences, 1975 (Cannes award 1976); author: Hungry at the Watering Hole, Gardiners Island, 1636-1990, 1989, Expedition: In the Steps of Ghengis Kahn, 1994; advisor Port Libertè Ptnrs., 1988-94; contbr. articles to profl. jours. Fin. advisor Correctional Assn., Osborn Soc., 1977—; founder, treas. Prisoners Family Transportation and Assistance Fund, N.Y., 1972-77; judge Emmy awards of Acad. TV Arts and Scis., N.Y.C., 1970; bd. dirs. Prisoners Assn., 1990; chmn. U.S.A. com. Violeta B. de Chamarro for Pres. of Nicaragua Campaign. Recipient Inst. for the Creative and Performing Arts fellowship, N.Y.C., 1966, Appreciation cert. Presdl. Inaugural Com., Washington, 1981. Fellow N.Y. Women in Real Estate, Explorers Club (lectr. on Mongolia, fin. com., housing, student, hospitality and Lowell Thomas coms., reciprocity com.); mem. Com. on Am. and Internat. Fgn. Affairs, Lawyers Com. on Internat. Human Rels., Bus. Exec. Nat. Security, Venture Capital Breakfast Club, The Coffee Club House, Sigma Delta Tau, Sigma Epsilon Sigma. Democrat. Avocations: painting, writing, fishing, canoeing, horseback riding, breeding cockatiels. Home: 4 E 81st St New York NY 10028-0235 Office: Mandel-Khan Inc PO Box 97 care Boldbaatar Mandel Kahn Ulaanbaatar 210648 Mongolia also: Leslie Mandel Enterprises PO Box 294 Wainscott NY 11975-0294 also: PO Box 294 Wainscott NY 11975-0029 Office Phone: 212-737-8917. Personal E-mail: mandelair@aol.com. E-mail: richlistco@aol.com, leslie_mandel@yahoo.com.

MANDELL, GAIL PATRICIA, language educator; b. St. Louis, Apr. 15, 1940; d. Howard David Porter and Genevieve Catherine (Foley) Henneman; m. Patrick Anthony Lucas, Jan. 23, 1964 (dec. 1968); m. Daniel Neil Mandell, Oct. 17, 1970. BA, Maryville Coll., St. Louis, 1962; MA, U. Mich., 1965; PhD, U. Notre Dame, 1980. Tchr. Austin High Sch., Stann Creek, Honduras, 1962—63, Villa Duchesne Acad., St. Louis, 1967—69; tenant mgr. King-Bison Co., Boston, 1969—70; tchr. Ind. U., South Bend, Ind., 1970—72; asst. dean St. Mary's Coll., Notre Dame, 1972—78, prof. humanities, 1978—2005, Schlesinger endowed chair in humanities, 2005—. Author: Phoenix Paradox, 1983 (Chgo. Women in Pub. award 1984), Life into Art, 1991, Madeleva: One Woman's Life, 1995, Madeleva: A Biography, 1997; contbr. articles to profl. jours. Lilly Endowment fellow, 1987-88, grantee, 1984, 91; recipient Maria Pieta award for teaching St. Mary's Coll., 1982, Spes Unica award for svc., 1991. Mem. MLA. Democrat. Roman Catholic. Avocations: running, piano, gardening, music, reading. Office Phone: 574-284-4465. E-mail: gmandell@saintmarys.edu.

MANDERNACH, BERYL JEAN, psychologist, educator; d. Myron and Barbara Mason; m. Eric Mandernach, July 28, 2001; children: Savannah, Mason, Aibrey. BS, U. Nebr., Kearney, 1995; MS, Western Ill. U., Macomb, 1997; PhD, U. Nebr., Lincoln, 2001. Assoc. prof. psychology and online learning Pk. U., Parkville, Mo., 2001—. Mem.: APA, Rocky Mountain Psychol. Assn., Sigma Xi. Office: Park University 8700 NW River Park Drive Parkville MO 64152 Office Phone: 308-236-5828.

MANDERNACH, DIANNE, state agency administrator; married; 4 children. Attended, Coll. St. Theresa; BA, Univ. Minn. Cert. Nursing Home Adminstrn. Jr. high sch. teacher, 1976—87; positions through dir. human resources & assoc. adminstr. Mercy Hosp. & Health Care Ctr., Moose Lake, Minn., 1987—94, CEO, 1994—2003; commr. Minn. Dept. Health, Saint Paul, 2003—. Bd. dir. Minn. Hosp. & Healthcare Partnership. Fellow: Am. Coll. Health Care Executives. Office: Dept Health 625 N Robert St Saint Paul MN 55155 Mailing: Dept Health PO Box 64975 Saint Paul MN 55164-0975*

MANDERS, SUSAN KAY, artist; b. Burbank, Calif., Dec. 29, 1948; d. Gus H. and Erika (Stadelbauer) M.; m. Allan D. Yasnyi, Dec. 18, 1992; children: Brian Mallut. Attended, U. Guadalajara, 1969; BA, Calif. State U., 1971; postgrad., UCLA, Otis Parsons, LA, 1985, Royal Coll. of the Arts, London, 1987; grad., Silicon Digital Arts. Owner, dir., tchr. The Art Experience Sch. and Gallery, Studio City, Calif., 1978—. Cons. in field. U.S. artist Athens (Greece) Summer Olympic Games, 2004; exhibitions include UN World Conf. on Women, Beijing, 1996, LA, NY, Chgo., Beverly Hills, Irvine, San Francisco, New Orleans, 1990—, prin. works include Steel Sculpture, Harry Ross Industries, 2003, Represented in permanent collections Nat. Mus. Women in the Arts, Smithsonian, Washington. Docent UCLA; active Tuesday's Child, Pillars of Hope Project San Fernando Valley County Fair, 1995. Mem. AAUW, LA Art Assn., Beverley Hills Art Assn., Nat. Mus. Women in the Arts, Nat. Assn. Univ. Women, LA County Mus. of Art, Dada, LA, Mus. Contemporary Art Coun., Women in Animation, Nat. Assn. Univ. Women, Vidamation Assn. (bd. dirs.). Office: The Art Experience 11830 Ventura Blvd Studio City CA 91604-2617 Office Phone: 818-506-7806. Personal E-mail: susanmanders@aol.com.

MANDLER, JEAN MATTER, psychologist, educator; b. Oak Park, Ill., Nov. 6, 1929; d. Joseph Allen and May Roberts (Finch) Matter; m. George Mandler, Jan. 19, 1957; children: Peter Clark, Michael Allen. Student, Carleton Coll., 1947-49; BA with highest honors, Swarthmore Coll., 1951; PhD, Harvard U., 1956. Rsch. assoc. lab. social rels. Harvard U., 1957-60; rsch. assoc. dept. psychology U. Toronto, Ont., Canada, 1961-65; assoc. rsch. psychologist, lectr. U. Calif. at San Diego, La Jolla, 1965-73, assoc. prof., 1973-77, prof. psychology, 1977-88, prof. cognitive sci., 1988—96, disting. prof., 1996—2000, disting. rsch. prof., 2000—; mem. adv. com. memory and cognitive processes NSF, 1978-81. Hon. rsch. fellow U. Coll., London, 1978-89, vis. prof., 1990—; hon. mem. Med. Rsch. Coun. Cognitive Devel. Unit, 1982-98. Author: (G. Mandler) Thinking: From Association to Gestalt, 1964, Stories, Scripts and Scenes, 1984, The Foundations of Mind: Origins of Conceptual Thought, 2004 (APA Divsn. 7 Eleanor Maccoby Book award 2005); assoc. editor Psychol. rev., 1970-76; mem. editl. bd. Child Devel., 1976-89, Discourse Processes, 1977-94, Jour. Exptl. Psychology, 1977-85, Text, 1979-97, Jour. Verbal Learning and Verbal Behavior, 1980-88, Lang. and Cognitive Processes, 1985—, Cognitive Devel., 1990-99, Jour. Cognition and Devel., 1999—; contbr. articles to profl. jours Pres. San Diego Assn. Gifted Children, 1968-71; v.p. Calif. Parents for Gifted, 1970-71; mem. alumni council Swarthmore Coll., 1975-78. NIMH research grantee, 1968—81, NSF research grantee, 1981—99. Fellow: APA (mem. exec. com. divsn. 3 1983—85), Am. Acad. Arts and Scis.; mem.: Soc. Exptl. Psychologists, Cognitive Devel. Soc., Cognitive Sci. Soc., Psychonomic Soc. (mem. governing bd. 1982—87, chmn. 1985—86), Phi Beta Kappa. Office: U Calif San Diego Dept Cognitive Sci 9500 Gilman Dr La Jolla CA 92093-0515 Business E-Mail: jmandler@ucsd.edu.

MANDRACCHIA, VIOLET ANN PALERMO, psychotherapist, educator; b. NYC; d. Anthony and Anna (Yetto) Palermo; m. John J. Mandracchia (dec. 1979); children: Dona Williams, Anne Marino, Marisa, John, Matthew, Lisa Williams. Student, Coll. Mt. St. Vincent; BA, St. John's U.; MA, Bklyn. Coll.; cert. in ednl. adminstrn. & supervision, Hofstra U.; MSW, SUNY, Stony Brook, 1990; advanced study in psychotherapy, L.I. Gestalt Ctr., 1988-92. LCSW, registered RCSW N.Y.; cert. secondary sch. adminstr., supr., practitioner Eye Movement Desensitization and Restructuring. Tchr. English Bay Ridge H.S., Bklyn., Ctrl. Islip (N.Y.) H.S., Smithtown (N.Y.) H.S.; asst. prin. Shoreham-Wading River (N.Y.) H.S., 1977-81; prin. West Islip (N.Y.) H.S., 1981-83; pvt. practice as psychotherapist Stony Brook and Manhattan, 1990—. Satellite psychotherapist Health House, Islandia, N.Y., 1988-97, supr., 1990-97. Active Suffolk County (N.Y.) Human Rights Commn., 1979-84, 88-92; chair adv. bd. Office for Women, Suffolk County, 1986-89; treas. bd. dirs. Women's Ctr., SUNY, Farmingdale, N.Y., 1985-87; chair Women's Equal Rights Coalition, Suffolk County, 1979-84, 88-92; chair North Fork Task Force in Arts, Suffolk County, 1977-79. Recipient Woman of Yr. award Suffolk County Exec. Office for Women, 1989; named Citizen of Yr., Smithtown LWV, 1984, Educator of Yr., Suffolk County Exec. & Women's Equal Rights Coalition, 1982; practitioner writing grantee Harvard U. Grad. Sch. Edn., 1981. Mem. NASW, NOW, Nat. Assn. Secondary Sch. Prins. Avocations: writing, films, theater, travel, painting. Home: Apt 3L 15 Shore Oaks Dr Stony Brook NY 11790-1417 Office: 211 Thompson St New York NY 10012-1365 Office Phone: 212-979-5656, 631-689-3116. Personal E-mail: mandracchia55@optimumonline.net.

MANDRAVELIS, PATRICIA JEAN, retired healthcare administrator; b. Hanover, NH, May 7, 1938; d. William J. and Ruth E. (Darling) Bartis; m. Anthony M. Mandravelis, Nov. 8, 1959; children: Michael A., Tracy J. Diploma in nursing, Nashua Meml. Hosp. Sch. Nursing, NH; BS in Psychology, Sociology, New Eng. Coll.; MBA, So. NH Coll., 1989. Cert. nursing adminstr., advanced nursing adminstr. Staff nurse Nashua Meml. Hosp. (name now So. N.H. Regional Med. Ctr.), 1959-60, obstet. nurse, 1962-65, charge nurse, 1969-71, supr., 1971-76, assoc. dir. nursing, 1976-81, dir. nursing, 1981-83, asst. exec. dir. nursing, 1983-87, v.p. nursing, 1987-91; v.p. ops., chief operating officer Nashua Meml. Hosp., 1991-95; v.p. cmty. health and wellness S. N.H. Regional Med. Ctr., Nashua, 1995—2000. Mem. healthcare transition fund State of NH, 1996—2002, Nashua Bd. for Continuum Care, 1997—2000. Contbr. articles to profl. jours. V.p. Nashua chpt. ARC, 1985—87; mem. citizens adv. bd. W.R. Grace, 1989—95; mem. Bd. Neighborhood Health Ctr. Greater Nashua, 1996—2000, pres., 2000; mem. allocations com. United Way Greater Nashua, 1997—; mem. Bridges, 1996—, bd. pres., 2000—02; loaned exec. United Way of Greater Nashua, 1996—; bd. dirs. deNicola Women's Ctr., Nashua, NH, 1987—95, Nashua Vis. Nurse Program, 1986—88, Home Health Hosp., 1988—94, chmn. bd., 1991—93, vice chmn. bd., 1993—94. Mem. Am. Coll. Healthcare Execs., Nat. League of Nursing, Am. Nurses Assn., Am. Orgn. Nurse Execs., N.H. Assn. Pub. Health, N.H. Nurses Assn., N.H. Orgn. Nurse Execs., Sigma Theta Tau. Avocation: antiques.

MANEKER, ROBERTA S(UE), public relations executive; b. N.Y.C., July 9, 1937; d. Maxwell Roy and Esther (Gerson) Scheff; m. Hannan Wexler, June 4, 1961 (div. 1983); children: Daniel, Joanna Bayer; m. Morton M. Maneker, June 1, 1985. BA, Oberlin Coll., 1957. Mng. editor True Love mag., N.Y.C., 1960-62; publicity dir. Capt. Kangaroo, CBS, N.Y.C., 1962-66; syndicated columnist Oleg Cassini, N.Y.C., 1967-69; freelance writer, N.Y.C., 1967-70; dir. pub. rels. Direct Mktg. Assn., N.Y.C., 1983-85, v.p. pub. rels., 1985-87; v.p. pub. rels. Christie's, N.Y.C., 1987-91, sr. v.p. corp. comm./mktg., 1991-94; freelance cons. mktg. and pub. rels., 1995—; mktg. dir. Phillips Auctioneers, 2000-01; mktg. cons. Lechters, Inc., 2000, dir. 1991-2001. Contbr. articles to publs. Ford Found. scholar, 1953-57. Trustee Jewish Home and Hosp., 1996-04, chmn. Manhattan Divsn., 2000-03; trustee Oberlin Coll., 1997-2006, mem. exec. com., 2004-2006, hon. trustee, 2006—; chmn. vis. com. Allen Meml. Art Mus., 2002—. Mem. Oberlin Coll. Alumni Assn. (pres. 1989-91), Phi Beta Kappa

MANELLA, NORA MARGARET, judge; BA with high hons. in Italian, Wellesley Coll., Mass., 1972; JD, U. So. Calif., 1975. Bar: Calif. 1976, U.S. Ct. Appeals (5th cir.) 1976, D.C. Ct. Appeals 1978, U.S. Dist. Ct. (ctrl., so., no. and ea. dists.) 1980-81, U.S. Ct. Appeals (9th cir.) 1982. Law clk. to Hon. John Minor Wisdom U.S. Ct. Appeals (5th cir.), New Orleans, 1975-76; legal counsel Subcom. on Constn., Senate Com. on Judiciary, Washington, 1976-78; assoc. O'Melveny & Myers, Washington and L.A., 1978-82; asst. U.S. atty. U.S. Dept. Justice, L.A., 1982—90, trial asst. major crimes, 1982-85, dep. chief, criminal complaints, 1986-87, chief criminal appeals, 1988-90; judge L.A. Mcpl. Ct., 1990—93, L.A. Superior Ct., 1992-93, U.S. Dist. Ct. (ctrl. dist.) Calif., LA, 1998—2006; justice pro tem Calif. Ct. of Appeal 2d appellate dist. LA, 1992, assoc. justice, 2006—; U.S. Atty. (ctrl. dist.) Calif. U.S. Dept. Justice, LA, 1994—98. Instr. U.S. Atty. Gen. Advocacy Inst., 1984-86, Calif. Jud. Coll., 1992-93; mem. Atty. Gen.'s Adv. Com., 1994-95. Mem. editl. bd. State Bar Criminal Law Newsletter, 1991-92. Mem. adv. bd. Monroe H.S. and Govt. Magnet, 1991-94; acad. specialist USAID Delegation, 1993; judge L.A. Times Cmty. Partnership Awards, 1993; bd. councilors Law Sch. U. So. Calif., 1996—. Mem. Am. Law Inst., Calif. Judges Assn., Nat. Assn. Women Judges, Calif. Women Lawyers, Women Lawyers L.A., Phi Beta Kappa, Order of the Coif. Office: Calif Ct of Appeal 2d Appellate Dist LA 300 South Spring St Los Angeles CA 90013 Office Phone: 213-830-7443. Business E-Mail: arlene.chavez@jud.ca.gov.

MANES, ANDREA M., science educator; b. Cleve., Dec. 18, 1962; d. Andrew J. and Lucia R. Dulik; m. Michael A. Manes, Dec. 23, 1999; 1 child, Sarah Marion. BS, Ill. Coll., Jacksonville, 1985; MEd in Secondary Sci. Edn., Kent State U., Ohio, 1992. Permanent tchg. cert. in biology and gen. sci. grades 7-12 Ohio, 1998. Biology tchr. Parma City Schs., Ohio, 1985—87; sci. tchr. Richmond Heights Local Schs., Ohio, 1987—, coach volleyball, 1987—95, lead mentor, 2002—. State Praxis III assessor Ohio Dept. Edn., Valley View, 2002—. Contbr. articles and presentations. Recipient Tandy Tech. Scholar award outstanding tchr., Tandy Corp., 1991-1992, Jennings Tech. Co-Leader award, Martha Holden Jennings Found., 1995, Nat. Mid. Sch. Conf. Presenter award, 1999; Jennings scholar, Martha Holden Jennings Found., 1993-1994. Mem.: Ohio Mid. Sch. Assn., Sci. Edn. Coun. Ohio, Local Profl. Devel. Com. (chmn. 2000—), Phi Delta Kappa. Avocations: crafts, boating, fishing, camping. Home: 9473 Deer Ridge Mentor OH 44060 Office: Richmond Heights Local Schs 447 Richmond Rd Cleveland OH 44143 Home Fax: 440-358-9167; Office Fax: 216-692-8487. Personal E-mail: mmanes2626@aol.com. Business E-Mail: andrea.manes@lnoca.org.

MANESS, ELEANOR PALMER, researcher; b. Raleigh, N.C., June 24, 1935; d. Oren Alston and Lillian Way Palmer; m. Charles B. Maness, Feb. 1, 1955 (dec. July 1989); children: Reid, Brian, Teresa. BA, Meredith Coll., 1958. Tchr. St. Timoth Sch., Raleigh, 1958—64; rsch. analyst N.C. State U., Raleigh, 1966—99; cons., 1999—. Contbr. articles to sci. jours. Recipient L.M. Ware Rsch. award, Am. Soc. for Hort. Sci., 1974, Excellence in Environment Rsch. award, Fed. Hwy. Adminstrn., 1997. Presbyterian. Avocations: hiking, swimming, gardening, rock hunting, fishing. Home: 2104 Gray Walsh Dr Wilmington NC 28405

MANETTA, AMEDA AVRILL, social sciences educator; d. Malcolm James and Mabel Manetta; children: Lola P Sutherland, Morgan J. J. Sutherland. BA in Sociology, The U. of Western Ont., London, Ont., Can., 1988; BSW, The U. of Western Ont., 1989; MSW, U. of Windsor, Ont., 1990; PhD, Va. Commonwealth U., 1997. Faculty Stephen F. Austin State U., Nacogdoches, Tex., 1997—98; assoc. prof. Winthrop U., Rock Hill, SC, 1998—. Bd. dirs. Safe Passage, Inc, Rock Hill, SC, 2003—. Contbr. articles to profl. jours., chapters to books. Mem. profl. adv. bd. Home Care Connections, Richmond. Grantee, Winthrop Faculty grantee, 1999, Stephen F. Austin Faculty grantee, 1998. Mem.: NASW (bd. dirs. 2001), Coun. on Social Work Edn., Am. Assn. of Suicidology. Office: Winthrop University 128 Bancroft Bldg Rock Hill SC 29733 Business E-Mail: manettaa@winthrop.edu.

MANEY, LOIS JEAN, postmaster; b. Marion, N.C., May 1, 1945; d. Frank Shannon and Virginia Mae (Helton) M.; m. Arthur Edison Walker, Sept. 21, 1963 (div. June 1982); 1 child, Linda Jean Walker; m. Anthony Joseph Paterno, July 7, 1984 (div. Apr. 1988). Grad. h.s., Nebo, N.C. Lace trimmer Shadowline Inc., Morganton, N.C., 1965-77; distbn. window clk. U.S. Postal Svc., Glen Alpine, N.C., 1977-79, Morganton, N.C., 1979-88, supr. mails and delivery, 1988-90, supt. postal ops., 1990-93, postmaster, 1993—2002, Jefferson, NC, 2002—. Postal co-chair Western Piedmont Postal Customer Coun., Western N.C., 1996—. Pres. Burke County Stamp Club, Morganton, 1996. Mem.: Burke County C. of C., Quaker Meadows Golf Club. Avocations: golf, scuba diving, exercise-walking. Office: US Postal Svc 410 E Main Street Jefferson NC 28640

MANGLONA, RAMONA V., judge, former attorney general; b. 1967; BA, U. Calif., 1990; JD, U. N.Mex., 1996. Bar: New Mex. Bar Assn. 1997, No. Mariana Islands Bar Assn. 1997. Asst. atty. gen., 1997—2002; atty. gen. No. Mariana Islands, Saipan, 2002—03; assoc. judge Commonwealth Superior Ct., 2003—. Office Phone: 670-236-9751.*

MANGO, CHRISTINA ROSE, psychiatric art therapist; b. Garden City, NY, May 13, 1962; d. Camillo Andrew and Dorothy Mae (Harrison) Mango; m. Keith Hurdman, Sept. 11, 1993 (div. 2001); children: Clarissa Rose Hurdman, Andrew James Hurdman. BFA summa cum laude, Coll. of New Rochelle, 1984; MA, NYU, 1987. Registered art therapist; bd. cert. structural family therapy tng.; cert. psycho-edn. multi family therapy tng. Art therapist Bronx Mcpl. Hosp. Ctr., 1984-88; clin. supr. Fordham-Tremont Cmty. Mental Health Ctr., Bronx, 1988-98, unit dir., 1998—. Art therapy fieldworker Bronx State Hosp., 1984, art therapy intern Bronx Children's Hosp., 1985, Saint Lukes Hosp., N.Y.C., 1986. Contbr. articles to profl. jours. Mem. N.Y. Art Therapy Assn., No. N.J. Art Therapists Assn., Am. Art Therapy Assn. Home: 234 Garfield St Haworth NJ 07641-1420 Office Phone: 718-960-0469. E-mail: crm07641@aol.com.

MANGOLD, SYLVIA PLIMACK, artist; b. NYC, Sept. 18, 1938; d. Maurice and Ethel (Rein) Plimack; m. Robert Mangold. Student, Cooper Union, 1956-59; BFA, Yale U., 1961. Exhibited one-person shows Daniel Weinberg Gallery, San Francisco, 1974, 75, Fischbach Gallery, N.Y.C., 1974, 76, Fischbach, 1974, 76, Annemarie Verna Gallery, Zurich, 1978, 91, 97, Droll-Kolbert Gallery, N.Y.C., 1978, 80, Young Hoffman Gallery, Chgo., 1980, Ohio State U., Columbus, 1980, Pa. Acad., 1981, Contemporary Arts Mus., Houston, 1981, Madison Art Ctr., (Wis.), 1982, Brooke Alexander, Inc., 1982, 83, 84, 85, 86, 89, 92, 95, Duke Art Mus., N.C., 1982, Rhona Hoffman Gallery, Chgo., 1982, 85, Tex. Gallery, 1986, Fuller Goldeen Gallery, San Francisco, 1987, U. Mich, Ann Arbor, 1992, Minn. Inst. Arts, 1992, Grunwald Ctr. for Graphic Arts, UCLA, 1992, Neuberger Mus. Art, SUNY, Purchase, 1993, Davison Art Ctr., Wesleyan U., Middletown, Conn., 1993, Albright-Knox Art Gallery, Buffalo, 1994, Wadsworth Atheneum, Hartford, Conn., 1994, Blaffer Gallery U. Houston, 1994, Mus. Fine Arts, Boston, 1994, Herbert F. Johnson Museum, 1998, Cornell U., Ithaca, N.Y., 1998, Alexander and Bonin, N.Y., 2000, 2003; group shows at Young Hoffman Gallery, Chgo., 1979, Walker Art Ctr., Mpls., 1979, Droll-Kolbert Gallery, 1979, Denver Art Mus., 1979, U. So. Calif., 1979, Honolulu Acad. Art, 1979, Oakland Mus., (Calif.), 1979, Univ. Art Mus. of U. Tex.-Austin, 1979, Cornell U., Ithaca, N.Y., 1979, The New Museum of Contemporary Art, N.Y.C., 1979, Nat. Museum, Belgrade, Yugoslavia, 1979, Internat. Biennial Ljibljana, Yugoslavia, Phoenix Art Mus., 1979, Art Latitute Gallery, N.Y.C., 1980, Thorpe Intermedia Gallery, Sparkhill, N.Y., 1980, U. Colo. Art Galleries, Boulder, 1980, Nina Freudenheim Gallery, Buffalo, 1980, U.S. Pavillion of Venice Biennial, 1980-81, Indianapolis Museum of Art, 1980, Civici Musei e Gallerie di Storia e Arte, Sala Ajace, Udine, Italy, 1980, Young Hoffman, Chicago, 1980-81, Delahurty, Dallas, 1980, Museum of Modern Art, 1981, Wesleyan U. Art Gallery, 1981, Davison Art Ctr., Middleton, Conn., 1981, Virginia Museum of Fine Arts, Richmond, 1981, Oakland Museum, Calif., 1981, Inst. Contemporary Art of U. Pa., Phila, 1980-81, Yale U. Art Gallery, 1981, San Antonio Mus. Art, 1981, Indpls. Mus. Art, 1981, Tucson Mus. Art, 1981, Pa. Acad., 1981, Mus. Art of Carnegie Inst., Pitts., 1981, Brooke Alexander, Inc., N.Y.C., 1982, Ben Shahn Ctr. Visual Arts, 1982, Castle Gallery, Coll. of New Rochelle, N.Y., 1983, Thomas Segal Gallery, Boston, 1982-83, Siegel Contemporary Art, N.Y., 1983, Freedman Gallery, Albright Coll., Reading, Pa., 1983, Fuller Goldeen, San Francisco, 1983, Yale U. Art Gallery, New Haven, 1983-84, 86, Wilcox Gallery, Swarthmore, Pa., 1984, The Hudson River Mus., Yonkers, N.Y., 1984, Sardonia Art Gallery, Wilkes Coll., Wilkes-Barre, Pa., 1985, Kent State U. Gallery, Ohio, 1985, Brooke Alexander, N.Y., 1985, John C. Stoller Co., Minn., 1985, Knight Gallery, Spirit Sq. Arts Ctr., Charlotte, N.C., 1986, Mus. Art, R.I. Sch. Design, Providence, 1986, Yale U. Gallery, 1986, CUNY, 1986-87, Lorence Monk Gallery, N.Y.C., Vanquard Gallery, Phila., 1986-87, Aldrich Mus., Ridgefield, 1986-87. Flander's Contemporary Art, Mpls., 1987, Annemarie Verna Galerie, Zurich, 1988, U. N.C., 1988, R.I. Sch. Design, 1988, Grace Borgenicht Gallery, N.Y.C., 1988, Fay Gold Gallery, Atlanta, 1988, U. N.C., Greensboro, Three Rivers Arts Festival, Pitts., 1989, Cin. Art Mus., New Orleans Mus. Art, Denver Art Mus., Pa. Acad. Fine Arts, 1989, U. Mich., 1992, Mpls. Inst. Arts, 1992, Grunwald Ctr. Graphic Arts, UCLA, L.A., Neuberger Mus. Art, SUNY Purchase, 1993, Davison Art Ctr., 1993, Montgomery Glasoe Fine Art, Mpls., 1993, Yale U. Art Gallery, New Haven, 1993, Daniel Weinberg Gallery, Santa Monica, Calif., 1993, Museum of Fine Arts, Boston, 1993, Barbara Mathes Gallery, N.Y.C., 1993, Nina Freudenheim Gallery, Buffalo, 1993, Kansas City Gallery of Art, U. Mo., 1994, Midtown Payson, N.Y.C., 1994, Katonah Museum of Art, N.Y., 1994, Rhona Hoffman Gallery, Chgo., 1994, Feigen Inc., Chgo., 1994, Brooke Alexander, N.Y.C., 1994, Elga Wimmer Gallery, N.Y.C., 1995, Aargauer Kunsthaus Aarau, Austria, 1995, The Am. Acad. of Arts and Letters, N.Y.C., 1995, Andre Zarre Gallery, N.Y.C., 1996, Aspen Art Museum, Colo., 1996, The Am. Acad. of Arts and Letters, N.Y.C., 1996, Anne Marie Verna Gallery, Zurich, Switzerland, 1997, Queens Museum of Art, 1997, Aspen Art Museum, 1997, U. Gallery, Fine Arts Ctr., U. Mass., Amherst James Graham & Sons, N.Y.C., 1997, The Museum of Modern Art, 1997, Seattle Art Museum, 1997, State U. N.Y., 1998, N.Y.C. Dowd Fine Arts Gallery, 1998, The Am. Acad. of Fine Arts and Letters, 1998, Karen McCready Fine Art, 1999, Alexander and Bonin, N.Y.C., 1999, Henry Art Gallery, Seattle, 2000, Small Work, Nina Freudenheim Inc., Buffalo, Whitney Mus., 2006, and numberous others; exhibited in permanent collections, Albright-Knox Art Gallery, Buffalo, Allen Meml. Art Mus., Oberlin, Ohio, Bklyn. Mus., Dallas Mus. Fine Arts, Detroit Inst. Art, Mus. Fine Arts, Houston, Indpls. Mus. Art, Madison (Wis.) Art Ctr., Milw. Art Mus., Yale U. Art Gallery, Mus. Modern Art, N.Y.C., Mus. Fine Arts, U. Utah, Tampa (Fla.) Mus., Walker Art Mus., Mpls., Whitney Mus. Am. Art, N.Y., Weatherspoon Art Gallery, Greensboro, N.C., Wadsworth Athenaeum, Hartford, U. Mich., Utah Mus. Fine Art, Museum of Fine Arts, Boston, N.Y.C. Public Library, Smith Coll. Museum, Northampton, Mass., Achenbach Found. for Graphic Arts, San Francisco, St. Louis Art Museum, The Tampa Museum, Art Inst. Chgo., Modern Art Mus. Fort Worth Tex., Indpls. Mus. Art, Telfair Mus. Art, Savannah Ga. Achievements include work reviewed in newspapers and mags. Office Phone: 212-367-7474. Business E-Mail: gallery@alexanderandbonin.com.

MANGONE, JOELLEN L., retired hospital administrator; b. Tulsa, Okla., July 20, 1933; d. Albert Lloyd Latta and Myrtle Irene Lay; m. William K. Sellars (div.); children: Steven Albert Sellars, Tracy Sellars; m. Robert Patrick Mangone, July 8, 1980 (dec.). BA, Okla. Bapt. U., Stillwater; MD, Okla. U. Fed. physician; chief ambulatory care Evans Army Hosp., Colorado Springs. Decorated Order Mil. Med. Merit, Superior Civilian Svc. medal. Avocation: golf. Home: 4106 Tumbleweed Dr Colorado Springs CO 80918 E-mail: jomangone@adelphia.net.

MANGUM, MYLLE BELL, information technology executive; b. Thomas, Ga. BA, Emory U., 1970. Tchr. N. Syracuse Sch. Sys., NY; computer programmer and systems analyst Gen. Electric Corp., 1972, gen. mgr. systems ops.; pres. BellSouth Internat., 1990; bd. dirs., exec. v.p. strategic mgmt. Holiday Inn Worldwide, 1992, exec. v.p. mktg.; pres. global systems and sr. v.p. strategic planning and expense mgmt. Carlson Wagonlit Travel; CEO MMS Incentives, 1999, True Mktg. Services, Internat. Banking Technologies, 2003—. Bd. dirs. Scientific Atlanta, Payless ShoeSource, Inc., Haverty Furniture Companies, The Barnes Group, Inc., Respironics, Inc., Emageon, Inc. Bd. trustees Piedmont Coll., Boys & Girls Club; adv. bd. Emory Bus. Sch.; mem. bd. Ga. Ctr. Advanced Telecommunications Tech. Named Decision Maker of Yr., Bus. to Bus. mag., Marketer of Yr., Am. Mktg. Assn.-Atlanta chpt.; named one of Divas 2000, Bus. to Bus. mag., 100 Most Influential Atlantans, Atlanta Bus. Chronicle; recipient Woman of Yr. Tech., (WIT) Women in Tech., 2004. Mem.: Soc. Internat. Bus. Fellows, Committee of 200 (former pres.). Office: Internat Banking Tech Ste 300 1770 Indian Trail Norcross GA 30093 Office Phone: 770-381-2023. Office Fax: 770-381-2123.*

MANHART, MARCIA Y(OCKEY), art museum director; b. Wichita, Kans., Jan. 14, 1943; d. Everett W. and Ruth C. (Correll) Yockey; children: Caroline Manhart Sanderson, Emily Alexandrea Morrison. BA in Art, U. Tulsa, 1965, MA in Ceramics, 1971. Dir. edn. Philbrook Art Ctr., Tulsa, 1972-77, exec. v.p., asst. dir., 1977-83, acting dir., 1983-84; exec. dir. Philbrook Mus. Art (formerly Philbrook Art Ctr.), Tulsa, 1984—2003; exec. dir., trustee The Judith and Jean Pape Charitable Foun., 2004—. Instr. Philbrook Art Ctr. Mus. Sch., Tulsa, 1963-72; gallery dir. Alexandre Hogue Gallery, Tulsa U., 1967-69; NEH Challenge Grant panelist, 1991, presenter to AAM Conv., 1991; MAAA Craft Fellowship panelist, 1988, 93, NEA Craft Fellowship panelist, 1990; NEA spl. exhbn. panelist, 1996; curator nat. touring exhibit Nature's Forms/Nature's Forces: The Art of Alexandre Hogue, 1984-85; co-curator internat. exhbn.: The Eloquent Object, 1987-90; curator Sanford and Diane Besser Collection exhbn., 1992. Author essays in field. Vis. com. Smithsonian Instn./Renwick Gallery, Washington, 1986; cultural negotiator Gov. George Nigh's World Trade Mission (Okla.), China., 1985; com. mem. State Art Coll. of Okla., 1985—; mem. Assocs. of Hillcrest Med. Ctr., 1983-88, exec. com., 1985-88; com. mem. Neighborhood Housing Services, 1985-87; mem. City of Tulsa Arts Commn., 1996-2003; steering com. Harwelden Isnt. for Aesthetic Edn., 1983; com. mem. River Parks Authority, 1976; mem. Jr. League of Tulsa Inc., 1974-78; adv. panel mem. Nat. Craft Planning Project, NEA, Washington, 1978-81; craft adv. panel mem. Okla. Arts and Humanities Council, 1974-76; juror numerous art festivals, competitions, programs; reviewer Inst. Mus. Services, Washington, 1985, 88, 92, 95, 98; auditor Symposium on Language & Scholarship of Modern Crafts, NEA and NEH, Washington, 1981; nominator MacArthur Fellows Program, 1988; panelist Lila Wallace Reader's Digest Internat. Artists Fellowship, 1992, panelist Pew Charitable Trust, 1996. Recipient Harwelden award for Individual Contbrn. in the Arts, 1989, Gov.'s award State of Okla., 1992. Mem. Gillespie County Hist. Soc. (bd. dirs. 2005—), Phi Beta Kappa. Home: 105 S Cherry St Fredericksburg TX 78624 Office Phone: 830-997-7347. E-mail: mmanhart@austin.rr.com.

MANHEIM, CAMRYN, television and film actress; b. Caldwell, NJ, Mar. 8, 1961; d. Jerry and Sylvia Manheim; 1 child, Milo Jacob. BFA, UC Santa Cruz, 1984; MFA, NYU, 1987. Actor: (TV series) The Practice, 1997—2004 (Emmy award for Outstanding Supporting Actress in a Drama Series, 1998, Golden Globe award for Best Performance by an Actress in a Supporting Role, 1999); (TV films) Jackie's Back!, 1999, The Loretta Claiborne Story, 2000, Jenifer, 2001; (TV miniseries) The 10th Kingdom, 2000, A Girl Thing, 2001, Elvis, 2005; actor, prodr. (TV films) Kiss My Act, 2000; actor: (films) Bonfire of the Vanities, 1990, The Road to Wellville, 1994, Jeffrey, 1995, Eraser, 1996, Romy and Michele's High School Reunion, 1997, David Searching, 1998, Wide Awake, 1998, Mercury Rising, 1998, Happiness, 1998 (Nat. Bd. Rev. award, 1998), Fool's Gold, 1998, Joe the King, 1999, What Planet are You From?, 2000, East of A, 2000, The Laramie Project, 2002, Just Like Mona, 2003, Scary Movie 3, 2003, Twisted, 2004, Marilyn Hotchkiss' Ballroom Dancing and Charm School, 2005, Dark Water, 2005, An Unfinished Life, 2005; guest appearances Law and Order, Touched By an Angel, New York Undercover, Ally McBeal, Oh Baby, Chicago Hope, Will and Grace; writer: (off-Broadway play) Wake Up, I'm Fat, 1995; theater appearances include N.Y. Shakespeare Festival, Lincoln Ctr., Yale Repertory, N.Y. Theatre Workshop, Classic Stage Co., Home for Contemporary Theater. Office: Creative Artists Agy 9830 Wilshire Blvd Beverly Hills CA 90212

MANHEIMER, HEIDI, cosmetics company executive; Diploma in Bus. Mgmt., Ithaca Coll., 1985. Various buying and mgmt. positions Bloomingdales; v.p. cosmetics Barneys NY; with Bluemercury.com, 1999; gen. mgr. Beauty.com; exec. v.p. Shiseido Cosmetics (Am.) Ltd., pres., 2002—06, CEO, 2006—. Bd. dirs. Fragrance Found. Recipient Skin Sense award, Skin Cancer Found., 2005. Office: Shiseido Cosmetics Am Ltd 178 Bauer Dr Oakland NJ 07436-3131*

MANION, BONNIE J., volunteer, poet, composer; b. South Bend, Ind., Apr. 13, 1942; d. Serge A. and Inez (Reed) Rivard; m. Paul T. Manion, Aug. 12, 1961; children: Christine, Sheila, Stephanie, Michael, Daniel, John Brian. BS in Elem. Edn., DePaul U., 1965; grad. lay ministry leadership program, Cath. Diocese, Peoria, Ill., 1988. Cert. elem. tchr. Ill. Author: Soul Search, 2002; contbr. poetry to mags. and books. Host family Rotary Internat., Hoopeston, Ill., 1985, 1995, 1996, 2002; vol. Hosp. Auxillary, Little League, United Way, Lions Club, local libr.; Hoopeston Music Boosters; vol. Dem. Party, Danville, Ill., 1972—2004; tchr. CCD programs St. Anthony's, Hoopeston, 1969—89, lay pastoral care min., 1985—2006; presenter diocesan programs Cath. Diocese, Peoria, Ill., 1980—2005. Recipient Pere Marquette Medal, Cath. Diocese, Peoria, 2001. Mem.: St. Davids' Christian Writers' Assn., Mary Hartwell Catherwood Book Club. Avocations: painting, poetry, hiking.

MANION, KAY DAUREEN, financial and office manager; b. St. Francis, Kans., Feb. 7, 1943; d. Edward William and Martha Dankenbring; children: Todd, Jon, Bandel. AS in Mktg. and Art, Western Nebr. C.C., 1990; postgrad., Colby (Kans.) C.C., 1992-95, Ft. Hays (Kans.) State Coll., 1997—. Various banking positions, Kans. and Nebr., 1960-73; mgr. Alliance (Nebr.) Area C. of C., 1974-79; bridal cons., dept. mgr. Hatch Drug, Alliance, 1980-85; bridal cons. Herbergers, Scotts Bluff, 1986-88; salesperson, script writer Sta. KIMB, Kimball, 1989-90; med. records analyst Dunn Med. Equipment and Svcs., Inc., Colby, 1990-93; graphic designer Quad County Star, Oakley, Kans., 1993-95; news asst., advt. sales rep. Sherman County Star, Goodland, Kans., 1995-97; fin. and office mgr. Steinke Farm Svcs., Holdredge, Nebr., 2000—. Freelance creative designer, 1988—; dir. tng. H.S. Distributive Edn. Clubs Am., Alliance, 1980-85, CETA, Alliance, 1976-79; advt. mgr. Russell Daily News, Russell Record, 1997-99. Bd. dirs., sec. Alliance Cmty. Improvement Com., Alliance, 1974-79; mem. Oakley Tourism Com., 1994-96. Named Businesswoman of Yr. Alliance Area C. of C., 1978, One of the Oustanding Young Women in Am., 1976, 78; recipient Disting. Svc. award Jaycees, Alliance, 1979. Mem. Am. Legion Aux., Eagles Ladies' Aux., Phi Theta Kappa. Republican. Methodist. Avocations: art, drawing, photography, nature, music. Home: P O Box 193 Logan KS 67646-0193

MANIS, LAURA GLANCE, retired psychology educator; b. Chgo., May 25, 1924; d. Nathan Glance and Minnie Walters; m. Jerome G. Manis, May 31, 1949; children: Robert, Lisa Neela. BEd, Chgo. State U., 1945; MA, Western Mich. U., 1965. Elem. sch. tchr. City Chgo., 1945-47; aptitude, personality assessor Johnson O'Conner Human Engring. Co., Chgo., 1947-49; pers. dir. Dr.'s Hosp., N.Y.C., 1949-52; counselor Climax (Mich.) H.S., 1965-66; psychol. counseling assoc. prof. Western Mich. U., Kalamazoo, 1966-83, assoc. prof. emerita, 1983—. Co-founder, dir. Women's Ctr., Western Mich. U., 1975-83, developer of women's studies, chair, 1979-73; dir. Mock Silver Legis. Project, 2005 Author: (manual) Woman Power, 1977, Assertion Training, 1983, revised edit., 1998, Training for Alzheimer's Group Leaders, 1984, Finding Your Voice, With Lisa N. Manis, 2001; contbr. articles to profl. jours. Pres. League Women Voters, Kalamazoo, 1964-66; v.p. ACLU, Kalamazoo, 1978-82; chair Hawaii State Legis. Co. AARP, Honolulu, 1994-95; pres. bd. dirs. Alzheimer's Assn. Hawaii, Honolulu, 1988-90; apptd. to State Health Planning Commn., Honolulu, 1995-01; bd. mem. Planned Parenthood, 1978-82; chair Coalition for Affordable Long Term Care, Honolulu, 1998-04; chair edn. fund Kokua Coun., Honolulu, 2005—; chair Kokua Coun. Legis. Com., 1998—, v.p., 1998—; bd. mem. Hawaii Alliance Ret. Am. Bd. Mems., 2003—; bd. Kokua Coun. Advocacy Sr. Citizens, 1998—. Recipient Women Pioneer award Mich. Women Lawyer's Assn., Detroit, 1978, Women of Yr. award Commn. on Status of Women, Kalamazoo, 1980, Outstanding Sr. Vol. award Gov. First Lady Awards, Honolulu, 1993, Outstanding Alumna of Yr. Western Mich. U., 1995, Honoree Hawaii State Legislature, 2003, Honoree Hawaii House of Rep., 2006. Mem. Hawaiian Women in Sci. (bd. dirs. 1982-97), AARP (state legis. com. chair 1995), Honolulu Acad. Art. Avocations: swimming, snorkeling, painting, travel, reading. Personal E-mail: manis@lava.net.

MANLEY, AUDREY FORBES, retired academic administrator, pediatrician, retired military officer; b. Jackson, Miss., Mar. 25, 1934; d. Jesse Lee and Ora Lee (Buckhalter) Forbes; m. Albert Edward Manley, Apr. 3, 1970. AB with honors (tuition scholar), Spelman Coll., Atlanta, 1955; MD (Jesse Smith Noyes Found. scholar), Meharry Med. Coll., 1959; MPH, Johns Hopkins U.-USPHS traineeship, 1987; LHD (hon.), Tougaloo Coll., Miss., 1990, Meharry Med. Coll., Nashville, 1991; LLD (hon.), Spelman Coll., 1991, Tskegee U., 1998; DSc (hon.), Coll. New Rochelle, 1998, Morehouse Coll., 2002, U. Del., 2002. Diplomate: Am. Bd. Pediatrics. Intern St. Mary Mercy Hosp., Gary, Ind., 1960; from jr. to chief resident in pediatrics Cook County Children's Hosp., Chgo., 1960—62; NIH fellow neonatology U. Ill. Rsch. and Ednl. Hosp., Chgo., 1963—65; staff pediatrician Chgo. Bd. Health, 1963—66; practice medicine specializing in pediatrics Chgo., 1963—66; assoc. Lawndale Neighborhood Health Ctr. North, 1966—67; asst. med. dir., 1967—69; asst. prof. Chgo. Med. Coll., 1966—67; instr. Pritzker Sch. Medicine, U. Chgo., 1967—69; asst. dir. ambulatory pediatrics, asst. dir. pediatrics Mt. Zion Hosp. and Med. Center, San Francisco, 1969—70; med. cons. Spelman Coll., 1970—71, med. dir. family planning program, chmn. health careers adv. com., 1972—76; med. dir. Grady Meml. Hosp. Family Planning Clinic, 1972—76; commd. officer, advanced though grades to rear adm. USPHS, 1976—97; chief genetic diseases services br. Office Maternal and Child Health, Bur. Community Health Services, Rockville, Md., 1976—81; acting assoc. adminstr. clin. affairs Office of Adminstr. Health Resources and Services Adminstrn., 1981—83, chief med. officer, dep. assoc. adminstr. planning, evaluation and legis., 1983—85; sabbatical leave USPHS Johns Hopkins Sch. Hygiene and Pub. Health, 1986—87; dir. Nat. Health Service Corps.; asst. surgeon gen. US Dept. Health & Human Services, 1988, dep. asst. sec. for health, 1989—93, acting asst. sec. health, 1993, dep. asst. sec. health & intergovtl. affairs, 1993—94, dep. surgeon gen., acting dep. asst. sec. for minority health, 1994—95, acting surgeon gen., 1995—97; pres. Spelman Coll., 1997—2002, pres. emerita, 2003—04; pres. History Makers, 2003. Mem. U.S. del. UNICEF, 1990-94, Am. Acad. Family Physicians (pub. adv. bd.), Am. Coun. Learned Socs., Am. Med. Assn. Minority Affairs Consortium (sr. advisor), Ctrs. for Disease Control Found. (bd. visitors), Morehouse Sch. Medicine (clin. Prof. Pediats., Pub. Health Lectr.), Rollins Sch. Pub. Health Emory U (Commrs., Adv. Coun., Ga. Leadership Commn. Organ, Tissue, Blood Marrow donation amont African Ams. Author numerous articles, reports in field; artist permanent collections Nat. Acads. Sci., Spelman Coll. Alumnae Hall of Fame, 2005. Trustee Spelman Coll., 1966-70; The Coll. Fund (UNCF com. Archives, Hist. Govtl. Affairs Com.), Coun. Fgn. Rels., bd. dirs. coun. Ind. Colls.; bd. dirs. March of Dimes, 1998, Nat. Merit Scholarship Corp., Nat. Minority Mil. Mus. Found. Edl. Adv. Coun., Am. Cancer Soc. Found., CDC Found., Compas Compact, Downtown Atlanta Chpt. Rotary, Atlanta 2000 Adv. Com., Quality Edn. for Minorities; adv. bd. Atlanta Regional Health Summit, Commerce Club, Ga. Found. Ind., Food and Drug Adv. Com., publ. advisory bd. Am. Acad. Family Physicians, sr. advisor AMA Minority Affairs Consortium, bd. visitors CDC Found., hon. advisor coun., charter mem. The Children's Inn at NIH, mem. Coun. on Fgn. Rels., Adv. Com., vaccine and biologics com. Food and Drug Adminstrn., mem. Health Careers Exploring Advisory Com., Tribal Colls.; chair, advisory group Univ. S.Carolina Rural Health Initiative. Rear adm. USPHS, ret. USPHS. Recipient Meritorious Svc. award USPHS, 1981, Mary McLeod Bethune award Nat Coun. Negro Women, 1979, Dr. John P. McGovern Ann. Lectureship award Am. Sch. Health Assn., Disting. Alumni award Meharry Med. Coll., 1989, Spelman Coll. 108 Founder's Day Convocation, 1989, Disting. Svc. medal USPHS, 1992, Hildrus A. Poindexter award OSG/PHS, 1993, numerous other svc. and achievement awards; named to African Americans in Sci., Engring., and Medicine Portrait Collection, Nat. Acads., 2005. Fellow Am. Acad. Pediatrics; mem. Nat. Inst. Medicine of Nat. Acad. Sci., Nat. Med. Assn., APHA, AAUW, AAAS, Coun. Fgn. Rels., Spelman Coll. Alumnae Assn. (Hall of Fame 2005), Meharry Alumni Assn., African Am. Collection Portraits of NAS, Operation Crossroads Africa Alumni Assn., Atlanta C. of C., Rotary, Delta Sigma Theta (hon.), Phi Beta Kappa. Address: 2807 18th St NW Washington DC 20009 Office Phone: 202-462-5214. Personal E-mail: amanley009@aol.com, amanley007@netaccess.com.

MANLEY, CATHEY NERACKER, interior design executive; b. Rochester, N.Y., Feb. 10, 1951; d. Albert John and Eleanor (Roberts) Neracker; m. Keith Howard Manley, Dec. 2, 1972 (div. Sept. 1977). AS, Endicott Jr. Coll., Beverly, Mass., 1971. Interior designer Bayles Furniture Co., Rochester, 1971-78, dir. mktg. and design, 1978-81; pres. Fabric PRO-TECTION Rochester, 1982—; bus. cons. Susanne Wiener & Assocs., Stamford, Conn., 1981—; owner Cathey Manley Assocs., Rochester and Clearwater, Fla., 1981—. Cons. Womens' Career Ctr., Rochester, 1976—. Contbr. to book: What Do You Say To A Naked Room, 1981; designer TV show Great American Home; writer, hostess video How to Sell Accessories. Mem. bldg. com. Rochester Health Assn., 1978-83; dir. Family Service of Rochester at Greece (N.Y.), 1973-76, Town of Greece Youth Bd., 1973-77; founder "The Point", Greece, 1971. Fellow Interior Design Soc. (pres. Rochester chpt. 1977-78, nat. bd. dirs. 1977—, nat. pres. at Chgo. 1983-85). Home: 1154 Edgemere Dr Rochester NY 14612-1506

MANLEY, JOAN A(DELE) DANIELS, retired publishing executive; b. San Luis Obispo, Calif., Sept. 23, 1932; d. Carl and Della (Weinmann) Daniels; m. Jeremy C. Lanning, Mar. 17, 1956 (div. Sept. 1963); m. Donald H. Manley, Sept. 12, 1964 (div. 1985); m. William G. Houlton, May 31, 1991. BA, U. Calif., Berkeley, 1954; DBA (hon.), U. New Haven, 1974; LLD (hon.), Babson Coll., 1978. Sec. Doubleday & Co., Inc., N.Y.C., 1954-60; sales exec. Time Inc., 1960-66, v.p., 1971-75, group v.p., 1975-84, also bd. dir.; circulation dir. Time-Life Books, 1966-68, dir. sales, 1968-70, pub., 1970-76; chmn. bd. Time-Life Books Inc., 1976-80. Vice chmn. bd. Book-of-the-Month Club, Inc., N.Y.C., until 1984; supervising dir. Time-Life Internat. (Nederland) B.V., Amsterdam, until 1984; mem. exec. bd. Coll. Letters and Sci. U. Calif., Berkeley, Calif., 2005— Past trustee Mayo Found., Rochester, Minn., Nat. Repertory Orch., William Benton Found.; former mem. adv. coun. Stanford U. Bus. Sch., Haas Sch. Bus. U. Calif. Named to Direct Mktg. Hall of Fame, 1993; U. Calif.-Berkeley fellow, 1989. Mem. Assn. Am. Pubs. (past chmn.).

MANLEY, JUDITH L., director; b. Columbus, Ohio; B in Bus., Ohio State U., 1970; MEd, Xavier U., 1986. Copy writer advt. agy., Columbus, 1970—74; program asst. Ohio State U., Columbus, 1974—. Advisor, counselor, tchr. dept. Spanish and Portuguese Ohio State U., Columbus, 1991—. Author poems. Commr. Greater Hilltop Area Commn., Columbus, 1989—; bd. dirs. Greater Hilltop Cmty. Devel. Corp., Columbus, 1989—; alumnae Leadership Columbus, Columbus, 1993; mem. citizens' adv. coun. Columbus Devel. Ctr. Named Vol. of the Month, Children's Hosp., Columbus, 2002; recipient Pres.'s Vol. Svc. award, 2003, 2004, 2005, Va. Denman Vol. award, 2004. Mem.: ACA, Am. Assn. Tchrs. Spanish and Portuguese. Avocations: writing, photography, music, theater.

MANLEY, MICHELLE S., social worker, educator; b. Norwich, N.Y., Dec. 15, 1965; d. Thomas Frederick Jr. and Joann (Castaldy) M. BS in Psychology, Syracuse U., 1987, MSW, 1990. Cert. social worker, N.Y. Preventive social worker sch. based program Salvation Army, Syracuse, N.Y., 1990-93, social worker teen violence intervention program, 1993-94, dir. sch. based adolescent pregnancy and parenting svcs., 1994-98, interim dir. daycare, 1999, dir. women's shelter, 1999—. Adj. prof. Cazenovia Coll., N.Y., 1997—. Bernard B. Given scholar Syracuse U., 1984-87, Univ. scholar, 1989-90. Mem. NASW (chmn. women's issues com. Ctrl. N.Y. chpt. 1995-98), Acad. Cert. Social Workers. Democrat. Avocations: reading, sewing, various crafts. Office: 703 Scarboro Dr Syracuse NY 13209-2246

MANLEY, NANCY JANE, environmental engineer; b. Ft. Smith, Ark., Sept. 13, 1951; d. Eugene Hailey and Mary Adele (Chave) M. BSE, Purdue U., 1974; MSE, U. Wash., 1976; postgrad., U. Minn., 1976-77; grad., Air Command and Staff Coll., 1984, Exec. Leadership Devel. Program Dept. Def., 1988. Lic. profl. engr., Ga.; registered environ. mgr.; bd. cert. environ. engr. Am. Acad. Environ. Engrs. Sanitary engr. Minn. Dept. Health, Mpls., 1976-77; sanitary engr. water supply EPA, Chgo., 1977, leader primacy unit water supply Atlanta, 1977-79, leader tech. assistance team, 1979-82; chief environ. and contract planning, project mgr. Grand Bay Range design USAF, Moody AFB, Ga., 1982-84, dep. base civil engr. Carswell AFB, Tex., 1984-86, Scott AFB, Ill., 1986-89, mem. tech. adv. com. Scott AFB master plan study Belleville, Ill., 1986-89, dep. base civil engr. Robins AFB, Ga., 1989-91, acting chief engr., 1990-91, chief pollution prevention divsn., dir. environ. mgmt., 1991-93; chief engr. divsn. 78 Civil Engr. Group, Robins AFB, Ga., 1993—. Mem. Fla. Tech. Adv. Com. for Injection Wells, Tallahassee, 1980-82, Nat. Implementation Team for Underground Injection Control Program, Washington, 1979-82, tech. panel Nat. Groundwater Protection Strategy Hearings, 1981; judge Internat. Sci. and Engring. Fair, 1986. Active various ch. activities, 1969-74, St. Louis Math. and Sci. Network Day, 1989, Adopt-a-Sch. Program, Lebanon, Ill., 1987-89; sec. Perry Area Hist. Soc., 1991-93; vol. Meals-on-Wheels, Girl Scouts U.S., Ga. Voluntary Tech. Assistance Group, others, various locations, 1982—; founder, crisis intervention counselor Midwest Alliance, West Lafayette, Ind., 1970-74; scientist by mail Boston Mus. Sci., 1989-99, Mathcounts, 1991—; mentor Purdue U., U. Washington, others, 1986—. Named Engr. of Yr., Robins AFB, 1997, 2000, 2003, Air Force Material Command, 1998, 2000, Ga. Engr. of Yr., Ga. Soc. Profl. Engrs., 2001, USAF Civilian Engr. of Yr., 2003, Fed. Engr. of Yr., 2004; named to Gallery Women Engrs., NAE, 2006; recipient Recipient Presdl. Point of Light award, USAF, 1991, Disting. Govt. Svc. award, Dallas/Ft. Worth Fed. Exec. Bd., 1986, Lady of the Black Knights award, 19th Air Refueling Wing, 1991, Celebration of Women in Engring. award, Nat. Acad. Engring., 2000. Fellow ASCE (vol. Ga. sect., Govt. Civil Engr. of Yr. 2005), NSPE (chpt. bd. dirs. 1991-94, 97—, v.p. local chpt. 1994-95, pres.-elect local chpt. 1995-96, pres. 1996-97, 2001, nat. govt. and legis. affairs com. 1999—, state dir. 2000—, Govt. Civil Engr. of Yr. 2005), Soc. Am. Mil. Engrs. (local membership and contingency coms., local bd. dirs., profl. soc. liaison, 1998, sec. 1999-2001, exec. bd. 2003—); mem. Soc. Women Engrs. (sr., regional mem.-at-large rep. 1990-93, local officer 1979-82, 84-86), Am. Women in Sci. Achievements include assignment as 1st woman dep. base civil engr. USAF, Carswell AFB; first woman engineer hired by U.S. Environmental Protection Agency. Office: 778 CES/CEC 775 Macon St Robins Afb GA 31098 Office Phone: 478-926-3533 ext. 28100. Personal E-mail: nanjmanley@cs.com. Business E-Mail: nancy.manley@robins.af.mil.

MANLY, SARAH LETITIA, retired state legislator, ophthalmic photographer, angiographer; b. Greenville, S.C., Feb. 1, 1927; d. Victor Harris and Elsie Clippard (Burnett) Gillespie; m. Basil Manly IV, Sept. 11, 1947; children: Sarah Manly Cornish, Basil V, Jean Manly McDowell, Mary Manly Mounce. BS cum laude, Furman U., 1947; postgrad., MIT, 1972; MEd, Clemson U., 1974; postgrad., Cambridge (Eng.) U., 1981. Cert. physics tchr., Pa., S.C.; cert. retinal angiographer. Ward sec. Roper Hosp., Charleston, S.C., 1947; analytical chemist Parker Labs., Charleston, 1948; tchr. sci. Upper Darby (Pa.) Sch. Dist., 1961-63; tchr. physics Sch. Dist. Greenville (S.C.) County, 1963-64, 70-76; ophthalmic photographer Basil Manly IV, MD, Greenville, 1976-96; lectr. physics Clemson (S.C.) U., 1979-81. Cons. MIT, Cambridge, 1972-75, Georgetown U., Washington, 1974-76, NASA, Houston, 1974-76. Editor, cons. physics study guides MIT, 1972-75; editor lab. materials NASA, 1974-76; contbr. articles to profl. jours. Trustee Sch. Dist. Greenville County, 1976-88. Named S.C. Legislator of Yr., S.C. Sch. Bds. Assn., 1991, Hon. Alumnus of Phi Beta Kappa, 1994. Mem. Greenville County Med. Aux. (sec. 1953-54), Delta Kappa Gamma. Democrat. Baptist. Avocations: travel, reading, volunteering. Home: 201 Robin Ln Greenville SC 29605

MANN, AIMEE, singer, songwriter; b. Richmond, Va., Aug. 9, 1960; m. Michael Penn. Vocals, bass 'Til Tuesday, 1983—89; solo artist, 1993—. Singer: (albums) (with 'Til Tuesday) Voices Carry, 1985, Welcome Home, 1986, Everything's Different Now, 1988, (solo) Whatever, 1993, I'm With Stupid, 1995, Bachelor No. 2, 2000, Lost in Space, 2002, (songs) Save Me, 1999 (nom. for Acad. Award for Original Song, 1999). Office: SuperEgo Records 511 Ave of the Americas #197 New York NY 10011

MANN, EMILY BETSY, writer, artistic director, theater director; b. Boston, Apr. 12, 1952; d. Arthur and Sylvia (Blut) M.; m. Gary Mailman; 1 child, Nicholas Isaac Bamman. BA, Harvard U., 1974; MFA, U. Minn., 1976; D of Fine Arts (hon.), Princeton U., 2002. Resident dir. Guthrie Theater, Mpls., 1976-79; dir. BAM Theater Co., Bklyn., 1980-81; freelance writer, dir. N.Y.C., 1981-90; artistic dir. McCarter Theater Ctr. for the Performing Arts, Princeton, N.J., 1990—. Author: (plays) Annulla, An Autobiography, Still Life (6 Obie awards 1981, Fringe First award 1985), Execution of Justice (Helen Hayes award, Bay Area Theatre Critics Circle award, HBO/USA award, Playwriting award Women's Com. Dramtists Guild for Dramatizing Issues of Conscience 1986), Greensboro: A Requiem, Having Our Say (L.A. NAACP award for Best Play), Meshugah; co-author: (with Ntozake Shange) (musical) Betsey Brown; (screenplays) Fanny Kelly, The Winnie Mandela Story, Having Our Say (Christopher award, Peabody award), Having Our Say (Peabody award); dir. Hedda Gabbler, A Doll House, Annulla, Still Life (Obie award), Execution of Justice (Guthrie and Broadway), Betsey Brown, The Glass Menagerie, Three Sisters, Cat on a Hot Tin Roof, Twilight: L.A., 1992 (L.A. NAACP award for best dir.), The Perfectionist, The Matchmaker, Safe as Houses, The Mai, Betrayal, Fool for Love, The Cherry Orchard, Because He Can, Romeo and Juliet, All Over, The Tempest, Uncle Vanya (McCarter and Lo Jolla Playjpise); adaptor, dir. Miss Julie, Having Our Say (Tony nomination-direction of a play 1995, Dramatist Guild's Hull Warriner award, L.A. NAACP award), Greensboro, A Requiem, The House of Bernarda Alba, Meshugah, The Cherry Orchard, Because He Can, Romeo and Juliet, Uncle Vanya; translator: Nights and Days (Pierre Laville), 1985; pub. in New Plays U.S.A. 1, New Plays 3, American Plays and the Vietnam War, The Ten Best Plays of 1986, Out Front, Testimony: 4 Plays by Emily Mann, 1997; co-editor: Political Stages, 2002. Recipient BUSH fellowship, 1975-76, Rosamond Gilder award New Drama Forum Assn., 1983, NEA Assocs. grant, 1984, Guggenheim fellowship, 1985, McKnight fellowship, 1985, CAPS award, 1985, NEA Playwrights fellowship, 1986. Mem. Soc. Stage Dirs. and Choreographers, Theatre Comms. Group (v.p.), New Dramatists, PEN, Writers' Guild, Dramatists' Guild (exec. bd. mem.), Phi Beta Kappa.

MANN, JACINTA, academic administrator, mathematician, educator; b. Pinckneyville, Ill., May 13, 1925; d. Bernard Albert and Magdalen Elizabeth (Ruppert) M. BS, So. Ill. U., 1946; MS, U. Wis., 1947, PhD, 1958. Statistician U. Wis., Madison, 1948-50; novitiate Sisters of Charity, Greensburg, Pa., 1950-53; tchr. secondary math. Altoona (Pa.) Cath. High Sch., 1953-56; with Seton Hill Coll., 1958—, dir. admissions, 1960-67, acad. dean, 1968-71, prof., 1971—; adminstrv. intern Scripps Coll., Claremont, Calif., 1967-68. Contbr. articles to profl. jours. Mem. Pa. Gov.'s Commn. on Women, 1979-89. Recipient faculty award Seton Hill Coll., 1971, Prof. of Yr. award, 1988; Medal of Honor, Inst. for Women Today, 1977, teaching award Freedoms Found., 1987, State Continuing Educator of Yr. award Continuing Edn. Assn. Pa., 1991; Kemper K. Knapp fellow U. Wis., 1957-58, fellow Am. Coun. on Edn., 1967-68. Democrat. Roman Catholic. Avocations: potter, tailor. Office: Seton Hill Coll Greensburg PA 15601 Home: Apt 243 2100 NE 38th St Lighthouse Point FL 33064-3925

MANN, JOAN ELLONA, artist, editor; b. Seattle, Aug. 21, 1931; d. Henry Hughes and Jeanetta Maurine (Baker)) Jacobsen; m. Hugh Mann, Sept. 2, 1955 (div. Aug. 1981); children: Susan, Kristi, Steven, Nancy, Roy. BA in Journalism, U. Wash., 1953, BFA in Sculpture, 1970, MFA in Sculpture, 1985. Reporter East Side Jour., Kirkland, Wash., 1953-55; med. editor Virginia Mason Med. Ctr., Seattle, 1965-69; info. specialist Continuing Edn. News Svc. U. Wash., Seattle, 1969-73; editor Seattle Arts Commn., 1973-77; pub. info. officer King County Arts Commn., Seattle, 1973-90; owner, mgr. Joan Mann, Editor, Seattle. Sculptures include multi-media floor sculpture Trident, Ship of Fools, 1988 (award); shows include U. Wash. Henry Gallery, 1971; group shows include Roscoe Louie Gallery, Seattle, 1975, Univ. Unitarian Gallery, 1978, U. Wash. Henry Gallery, 1987, U. Wash. Meany Hall, 1987, SJW Studios, Seattle, 1988, Seattle Ctr. Opera House, 1988, PNAC, Bellevue, 1988, Ctr. for Contemporary Art, Seattle, 1989. Precinct del. Wash. Dem. Com., Seattle, 1992. Recipient 2d and 3d place ann. awards Wash. Press Women, 1971, 1st prize Ctr. for Contemporary Art, 1989; travel grantee Goethe Inst., Berlin, 1988. Mem. Women in Comm. (Nat. Clarion award 1974), Allied Arts Seattle (adv. bd. 1990—), Seattle Art Mus. Roman Catholic. Avocations: photography, skiing, hiking on beaches, travel.

MANN, KAREN, consultant, educator; b. Kansas City, Mo., Oct. 9, 1942; d. Charles and Letha (Anderson) M. BA, U. Calif., Santa Barbara, 1964; MPA, Golden Gate U., 1975, PhD, 1994. Mem., tchr. Sisters of Immaculate Heart, L.A., 1964-68; group counselor San Francisco and Marin County Probation Depts., 1968—70; parole agt. Calif. Dept. Corrections, Sacramento, San Francisco, 1970-86; rschr. and cons. Non-profit Orgnl. Devel., 1986—, Computer Applications for Persons with Disabilities, 1986—. Adj. faculty Grad. Theol. Uion, Berkeley, 1984—; Compuserve Disabilities Forum, 1985-2000; forum adminstr., 1988-2000; mem. faculty Golden Gate U., 1990; ind. cons. to numerous non-profit orgns. Co-author: Prison Overcrowding, 1979, Community Corrections: A Plan for California, 1980. Sec., bd. dirs. Spirit Rock Mediation Ctr., 1989-93; co-founder Network Ctr. for Study of Ministry, San Francisco, 1982; pres. San Francisco Network Ministries, 1980-82; mem. Disabled Children's Computer Resource Group, 1988-90, Spingwater Ctr. for Mediative Inquiry and Retreats, 1986-88; emotional support counselor Marin AIDS Project, 1992-97; bd. dirs. Siskiyou Humane Soc., pres., 2003—. Fellowship of Reconciliation, N.Y., 1970—, Buddhist Peace fellowship, 2000—. Mem.: St. Vincent de Paul Soc. (pres. 2005—). Address: 8535 Aspen Dr Weed CA 96094 Personal E-mail: ldveroof1@gmail.com. Business E-Mail: karenmail@nctv.com.

MANN, LAURA SUSAN, editor; b. Houston, Sept. 20, 1958; d. Manfred Walter and Sally Mae (Hennels) Schaefer; m. Richard Drew Mann, Aug. 1, 1987; children: W. Cole, Devon S. BS in Physics cum laude, U. Houston, 1986. Mktg. sec. Vector Cable/Schlumberger, Sugar Land, Tex., 1981-83; adminstrv. asst. Bekaert Internat. Trade, Inc., Houston, 1983-84; polit. pollster, rsch. and teaching asst. U. Houston, 1984-86; flight contr. Johnson Space Ctr., NASA, Houston, 1986-91, mgr. grapple fixture subsystem, 1991-92, mgr. space sta. engring. configuration, 1992-93; part time beauty cons. Mary Kay cosmetics, 1992; contract editor R.G. Landes Co., Georgetown, Tex. Mem. tech. adv. com. flight telerobotic servicer Goddard Space Flight Ctr., NASA, Greenbelt, Md., 1989; mission ops. directorate rep. hand contr. commonality study, leader space shuttle payload and deployment system tech. team/space sta. flight compatability rev. Johnson Space Ctr., NASA, 1990; rsch. asst. medium energy physics expt. U. Houston at Brookhaven Nat. Lab., Upton, N.Y., 1985, 86; mem. configuration mgmt. process improvement team for Space Sta. Freedom Program, 1992-93. Pres. Durham Pk. Homeowners Assn., Houston, 1990-92; vol. Tex. Water Commn. Testing Program, 1994-95. Mem. Am. Horse Shows Assn., U.S. Combined Tng. Assn. (adult team co-coord. 1998), Greater Houston Hunter Jumper Assn. (bd. dirs. 1991-92, contbg. newsletter columnist 1991-92, Jr./Adult Jumper Champion 1990, 4th in open jumper ann. awards 1992), Third Coast Eventers (newsletter columnist 1995—, sec.-treas. 1996—), U. Houston Alumni Orgn., MENSA, Phi Theta Kappa. Avocations: horse showing, camping, walking, gardening. Home: 691 Meadow Bend Rd Bellville TX 77418-9625

MANN, MARY ANNEETA, author; b. Rockhampton, Queensland, Australia; came to U.S., 1965; d. Willie Augustus and Dorothy Louisa M.; 1 child, Attica Andrew. BA, Sydney U., Australia, 1964; MA, U. Calif., Berkeley, 1970; PhD, U. So. Calif., 1982. Author: Los Angeles Theatre Book, 1978, Los Angeles Theatre Book, 1984, The Construction of Tragedy, 1985, ThuGun and Natasha, 2003, Two Family Plays: Maria and the Comet The Round Table, 2004, Hubris, The Construction of Tragedy, rev., 2004; author, editor: Science and Spirituality, 2004; playwrite: Tortoise Shell, Diana Devereaux, The Senator's Daughter, The Tongue-Cut Sparrow, Maria and the Comet, 1983, Anzac I and II, 1984, Thugun and Natasha, 1993 (Artistic Dir. achievement award Valley Theatre League 1994), The Round Table, 1995, The Right of the Womb-post 911, 2003. Mem. Australian Soc. Accts.

MANN, REBECCA ANN, science educator, secondary school educator; d. Helen Louise and James Irvin Mann (Stepfather); m. Jack Irvin Mann, Mar. 19, 1988. BS, Wright State U., 1991; MS in Edn., U. Dayton, 1998; MS in Tchg., Wright State U., 2000. Cert. tchr. sci. Ohio. Tchr. sci. mid. sch. Xenia (Ohio) Cmty. Schs., 1991—2003; sci. tchr. Bellbrook (Ohio) H.S. Sugarcreek Local Schs., 2003—. Jennings scholar, Martha Holden Jennings Found., 2005. Mem.: NSTA. Home: PO Box 102 Bowersville OH 45307 Office: Bellbrook High School 3737 Upper Bellbrook Road Bellbrook OH 45305 Office Phone: 937-848-3737.

MANN, ROANNE L., federal judge; b. 1951; BA, Yale U., 1972; JD, Stanford U., 1975. Bar: N.Y. 1975. Asst. dist. atty. Manhattan Dist. Atty.'s Office, N.Y.C., 1975-76; law clk. U.S. Ct. Appeals for D.C. Circuit, Washington, 1976-77; spl. asst. to asst. atty. gen. civil divsn. U.S. Dept. Justice, Washington, 1977-78; asst. U.S. atty., chief appeals, sr. litigation counsel U.S. Atty.'s Office for So. Dist. N.Y., N.Y.C., then dept. chief criminal divsn., 1978-86; ptnr. Stein, Zauderer, Ellenhorn, Frischer & Sharp, N.Y.C., 1986-94; magistrate judge for ea. dist. N.Y., U.S. Magistrate Ct., Bklyn., 1994—. Mem.: Fed. Bar Coun. Office: US Magistrate Ct 225 Cadman Plz E Brooklyn NY 11201-1818 Office Phone: 718-260-2350.

MANN, SALLY, photographer; b. Lexington, Va., 1951; married; children: Emmett, Jessie, Virginia. Student, Putney Sch., 1966-69, Bennington Coll., 1969-71, Praestegaard Film Sch., Denmark, 1971-72, Aegean Sch. Fine Arts, Greece, 1971-72; BA summa cum laude, Hollins Coll., 1974, MA, 1975; DFA (hon.), Corcoran Coll., 2006. Guest lectr. Honolulu Acad. Arts, 1989, Women Photog. Conf., 1989, Md. Inst. Art, 1989, Bard Coll., 1989, San Francisco Cameraworks, 1990, Photog.-Retrospect/Prospect Conf., 1990, others; instr. Maine Photog. Workshops, 1985-89, Palm Beach Photog. Workshops, 1987-89, Ctr. Photog. Woodstock, 1988, 90, Internat. Ctr. Photog., N.Y., 1989, Image Found., Honolulu, 1989, Okla. Arts Found., 1989, Friends Photog. Workshops, 1990. One-woman shows include Cleve. Ctr. Contemporary Art, 1990, Edwynn Houk Gallery, Chgo., 1990, 92, Tartt Gallery, Washington, 1990, Md. Art Pl., Balt., 1991, Houk Friedman, N.Y., 1992-94, Mus. Contemporary Photog., Chgo., 1993-94, Mus. Modern Art, N.Y., 1991, Milw. Mus. Art, 1991, Whitney Mus. Am. Art, N.Y., 1991, Met. Mus. Art, N.Y., 1991, Frumpkin Adams Gallery, N.Y., 1994, Elizabeth Leach Gallery, Portland, Oreg., 1994, Bard Coll., Mass., 1994, Wellesley Coll., Mass., 1995, Edwynn Houk Gallery, N.Y., 1997, Gagosian Gallery, Calif., 1997; exhibited in group shows Corcoran Gallery Art, Washington, 1977, Va. Mus. Fine Arts, Richmond, 1988, New Orleans Mus. Art, 1990; represented in permanent collections Addison Gallery Am. Art, Andover, Mass., Balt. Mus. Art, Birmingham (Ala.) Mus. Art, Boston Mus. Fine Art, In Response to Place: Photographs from The Nature Conservancy's Last Great Places, Corcoran Gallery Art, 2001, Hirshhorn Mus. and Sculpture Garden, Nat. Mus. Am. Art, Smithsonian Inst., Washington, Met. Mus. Art, N.Y., Mus. Modern Art, N.Y., Whitney Mus. Am. Art, N.Y., San Francisco Mus. Art, Va. Mus. Fine Arts, Richmond, Gagosian Gallery, NYC, 2006, others; author/photographer: (with Ann Beattie) Second Sight: The Photographs of Sally Mann, 1984, (with Reynolds Price) At Twelve: Portraits of Young Women, 1988, Imediate Family, 1992, Still Time, 1994, What Remains, 2003. Fellow Nat. Endowment Arts, 1982, 88, 92, Guggenheim Found., 1987, Southeastern Ctr. Contemporary Arts, 1989, Artists Visual Arts, 1989; named Best Photographer in Am., Time Mag., 2001.*

MANN, TORI, secondary school educator; b. Barnesboro, Pa., Oct. 14, 1944; d. William and Anne Victoria Todhunter; m. Weldon Mann, Sr., Jan. 28, 1968; chilren: Weldon, Todd Hunter. BA in Psychology, Sterling (Kans.) Coll., 1966; MS in Spl. Edn., Calif. State U., Hayward, 1993. Cert. tchr., Calif. Tchr. Oakland (Calif.) Pub. Schs., 1990-92; tchr. social studies Stockton (Calif.) Unified Schs., 1992—. Mem. Coun. for Exceptional Children, Calif. Assn. for Resource Specialists. Avocations: reading, theater, travel. Office: Hamilton Mid Sch 2245 E 11th St Stockton CA 95206-3697

MANN-BONDAT, LYDIA RACHEL, writer, researcher; d. Jonathan Max Mann and Marie-Paule Therese Bondat; m. Michael Stafford Masland, Mar. 25, 2000; 1 child, Dayton Jonathan Mann Bondat-Masland. MS in Fgn. Svc., Georgetown U., 2002; BA, Harvard U., 1995. Admissions and fin. aid officer Grad. Sch. of Arts and Scis. Harvard U., Boston, 1996—98; program assoc. Partners in Health, Boston, 1998—2000; writer, rschr. Inst. for the Study of Internat. Migration, Washington, 2001—. Adv. bd. mem. Robert F. Kennedy Meml. Health and Human Rights Fellowship, 2002—03. Recipient Citizen Appreciation award, Harvard U. Police Dept., 1995; fellow, Georgetown U., 2000—02. Mem.: Youth Against AIDS (advisor 2002).

MANNE, DEBORAH SUE, dental hygienist, educator, oncological nurse; b. Vincennes, Ind., Nov. 20, 1954; d. Charles Kenneth and Susan Jane (Fox) Thornberry; m. Marshall Stanley Manne, Dec. 21, 1985. AA, Maplewoods C.C., Kansas City, Mo., 1973; BS in Dental Hygiene, U. Mo., 1975; BSN, St. Louis U., 1991, MSN in Oncology Nursing, 1998. RN, reg. dental hygienist, Mo.; cert. oncology nurse, Oncology Nurse Soc. Dental hygienist Dr. Marshall S. Manne, St. Louis, 1978—2001, office nurse, 1991—2001; oncology nurse CIRCLE Barnes-Jewish Hosp., St. Louis, 1993—98; staff nurse Radiation Oncology Ctr. Barnes-Jewish Hosp. North, 1997; nurse educator Cancer Family Care, St. Louis, 1998; clin. asst. prof. divsn. dental hygiene Sch. Dentistry U. Mo., Kansas City, 1999—; clin. nurse John Krey Cancer Info. Ctr., St. John's Mercy David C. Pratt Cancer Ctr., St. Louis, 2001—04; staff dental hygienist, dept. grad. periodontics Ctr. for Advanced Dental Edn., St. Louis U., 2005—; ind. contractor, oral health sect. Mo. Dept. Health and Human Svcs., 2005; dental hygienist dept. otorhinolaryngology-head-neck surgery Cancer Ctr., St. Louis U., 2005—; clin. instr. dept. adult and older adult nursing St. Louis U., 2006—, adj. instr. divsn. geriatric medicine, 2006—. Instr. dental hygiene dept. St. Louis C.C., Forest Park, 1999—2000; clin. instr. So. Ill. U., Carbondale, 2000; coord., cons. Oncology Dental Support Svcs., St. Louis, 1992—; mem. curriculum rev. com. dental hygiene program St. Louis C.C., 1993; mem. adv. bd. ACCESS Dental Hygiene Jour., 1994—2003; editl. bd. Jour. of Dental Hygiene, 2003—; reviewer Oncology Nursing Forum, 2003—; pilot reviewer Clin. Jour. of Oncology Nursing, 2003—. Contbr. articles to profl. jours. Chair Gt. Am. Smokeout, 1992; mem. Breast Cancer task force, 1994—98; bd. dirs, v.p. Am. Cancer Soc., St. Louis, 1992—93; mem. profl. adv. com. Wellness Cmty., St. Louis, 1994—; chmn. Tobacco-Free Mo. Super Coalition, St. Louis, 2000. Recipient Vol. Recognition award, Am. Cancer Soc., 1995, Irene Newman award, 1997, Susan Brockman-Bell Humanitarian award, U. Mo. Kans. City Dental Hygiene Alumni Assn., 2000, Rhinehart Medallion, Rhinehart Found., U. Mo. Kans. City Sch. Dentistry, 2005, Rhinehart medallion, Roy J. Rhinehart Found., U. Mo.-Kansas City Sch. Dentistry, 2005. Mem. Am. Dental Hygienists Assn. (council on pub. rels., coun. on edn., coun. on rsch., 2004-), Oncology Nursing Soc. (chair oral care focus group, pres.-elect St. Louis chpt. 1998, pres. 1999, editor patient edn. sig newsletter 1999-2000), Mo. Dental Hygienists' Assn. (pres.), Greater St. Louis Hygienists' Assn. (pres.), Sigma Phi Alpha, Sigma Theta Tau. Avocations: walking, raising golden retrievers. Home: 11617 Larkmont Dr Creve Coeur MO 63141-6907 E-mail: mannedt@slu.edu.

MANNER, JENNIFER FOUSE, social worker; b. Balt., June 15, 1964; d. Richard Erb and Patricia Ann (Matthews) Fouse; m. David Bruce Manner, Aug. 16, 1986; 1 child, Jessica Lynn. BA in Psychology, Hope Coll., 1986; MS in Social Adminstrn., Case Western Reserve U., 1988. Lic. ind. social worker, Ohio, Vt; lic. alcohol and drug abuse counselor, Vt.; cert. chem. dependency counselor. Adolescent continuing care coord. Lakeland Inst., Lorain (Ohio) Cmty. Hosp., 1988-90; dir. Laurelwood Counseling Ctr., Mayfield Heights, Ohio, 1990-93; field instr. Mandel Sch. Applied Social Scis., Case Western Res. U., Cleve., 1991-95; ind. social worker, chem. dependency counselor Elyria, Ohio, 1993—2005; social worker Rutland Mental Health, Vt., 2005—06; asst. prof. Coll. St. Joseph, Rutherland, Vt., 2006—. Adj. instr. Lorain County C.C., 1998-2005, Baldwin Wallace Coll., 2004-05, Coll. St. Joseph; lectr. in field. Mem. NASW, Psi Chi. Democrat. Avocations: canoing, writing children's books, skiing.

MANNERS, PAMELA JEANNE, secondary school educator; b. Holyoke, Mass., Mar. 20, 1951; d. Francis Edward and Helen Mary (Kurtyka) Herbert; div. 1985; children: Tracy, Kristen. BA, U. So. Miss., 1986, MEd, 1993. Cert. elem. edn. K-3, 4-8, secondary Eng., Social Studies; cert. elem. prin., secondary prin., elem. and secondary adminstrn. Registrar Michel Mid. Sch., Biloxi, Miss., 1987-88, tchr. Eng. and Social Studies, 1988-90, tchr. reading/law related edn., 1990-95; curriculum coord. Biloxi Pub. Schs., 1995-98; administrator Fernwood Jr. High Sch., Biloxi Pub. Schs., 1998-2000; dir. ABA Reading Curriculum Program, 1989-95; prin. Michel Jr. H.S., Biloxi Pub. Schs., 2000—04, Biloxi H.S., 2004—. Law-related edn. trainer Miss. Law-Related Edn. Ctr., Jackson, 1990-2002; law-related trainer Ctr. Civic Edn., Calabasas, Calif., 1993; law-related trainer Constitutional Right Found., 1994-2002. Participant program Lawyer in Every Class Miss. Bar Assn., Jackson, 1990-93 On-site target grantee Miss. Bar/Dept. Justice, 1992; A+ Site recognition U.S. Dept. Edn. Mem. Leadership Gulf Coast C. of C. (edn. com. 1996—). Roman Catholic. Office: Biloxi Pub Schs 1845 Richard Dr Biloxi MS 39532 Business E-Mail: pamela.manners@biloxischools.net.

MANNES, ELENA SABIN, film and television producer, television director; b. NYC, Dec. 3, 1943; d. Leopold Damrosch and Evelyn (Sabin) M. BA, Smith Coll., 1965; MA, Johns Hopkins U., 1967. Rschr. Pub. Broadcast Lab. Nat. Edn1. TV, N.Y.C., 1968-70; writer Sta. WPIX-TV, N.Y.C., 1970-73; assignment editor Sta. ABC-TV, N.Y.C., 1973-76; prodr., writer Sta. WCBS-TV, N.Y.C., 1976-80; prodr. CBS News, N.Y.C., 1980-87, Pub. Affairs TV/Bill Moyers PBS Documentaries, N.Y.C., 1987-90. Ind. documentary dir. and prodr., 1987—. Recipient Emmy award NATAS, 1984, 85, 87, 90, 94, 96, 2002, Peabody award, 1985, Cine Golden Eagle award, 1988, 90, 93, 94, 95, 99, Robert F. Kennedy Journalism award, 1989, DGA awards, 1987, 90. Mem. Writers Guild Am., Dirs. Guild Am., Am. Film Inst. (dir. Workshop for Women). Avocations: tennis, still photography.

MANNING, BRENDA ARGOSY, painter; b. New Britain, Conn., Mar. 29, 1940; d. Henry Joseph and Ann Shebed Argosy; m. John Schultz Manning, Sept. 4, 1961; children: Gregory, Allyson Manning Jaye. Grad., Art Inst. Pitts., 1960; attended, Art Students League, NYC, 1987—88. Freelance illustrator, 1960—; portrait painter Conn., 1988—. Docent, lectr. chair New Britain Mus. Am. Art, New Britain, Conn., 1974—92, mem. acquisition & loan commn., 1996—; chmn., bd. mem.Art for the Cure Komen Conn. Race for the Cure, 1995—99; trustee New Britain Mus. Am. Art, 2004—06. One-woman shows include Sec. of State's Office, Hartford, Conn., 1991, Seabury Cmty., Bloomfield, Conn., 1998, Mooreland Hill Sch., Kensington, Conn., 1999, Jerome Cmty., New Britain, Conn., 2005, exhibitions include Town & Country Club Hartford, Conn., 1989, Lily Pad Gallery, Charelston, RI, 1995, Hartford Fine Art & Framing, East Hartford, Conn., 1998, U. Conn. Med. Ctr., Farmington, Conn., 2000, New Britain Mus. Am. Art, 2001. Mem.: New Britain Art League, Meriden Arts & Crafts Assn., West Hartford Art League, Conn. Pastel Soc., Conn. Acad. Fine Arts. Avocations: golf, travel, reading. Home: 118 Mooreland Rd Kensington CT 06037

MANNING, DEBORAH COTHRAN, art educator; b. Easley, SC, July 5, 1948; d. Ernest Weston and Purdie McCall Cothran; m. James McCotter Manning, May 30, 1969; 1 child, James McCotter Jr. AA, Brevard Coll., 1968; BA, Meth. Coll., 1970; MA, Campbell U., 1999. Lic. tchr. NC-, 1970. Tchr. Hoke County Bd. Edn., Raeford, NC, 1970—72, Harnett County Bd. Edn., Lillington, NC, 1972—75; tchr. social studies and English Cen. Tex. Coll., Hanau, Germany, 1976—79; instr., coord. Fayetteville (N.C.) Tech. C.C., Fayetteville and Ft. Bragg, NC, 1980—. Mem. Fayetteville (NC) Area Habitat for Humanity, 2001—05, mem. family selection com., 1995—2005, chmn. family selection com., 2002—05, mem. exec. com., 2004—05. Mem.: NC C.C. Adult Educators Assn. Baptist. Avocations: reading, travel, cooking. Home: 7509 Marie Dr Fayetteville NC 28311 Office: Soldier Devel Ct Fort Bragg NC 28310 Office Phone: 910-396-6982. Office Fax: 910-396-8331.

MANNING, JANICE, editor, writer; d. Edna Joan and Robert Franklin Lohnes; children: Betty-Faye Michelle, Bobby Ray Jr. AA in English, Crafton Hills Coll., Yucaipa, Calif., 2004. Editor Your Own World Books, Scotts Valley, Calif., 2004—. Writer, editor www.yowusa.com, Scotts Valley, Calif., 2000—. Editor (contbr.): (ancient anthology) The Kolbrin, Your Own World Books First Edition, The Kolbrin Bible, Your Own World Books 21st Century Master Edition, Egyptian Texts of the Bronzebook, Celtic Texts of the Coelbook. With U.S. Army WAC, 1971—72. Libertarian. Messianic Jew. Achievements include historical research for the introduction to The Kolbrin Bible, 21st Century Master Edition; historical research for the Introduction to Egyptian Texts of the Bronzebook; historical research for the Introduction to

Celtic Texts of the Coelbook. Avocation: rock collecting, crystals, fishing, swimming. Office Phone: 775-546-1472. Personal E-mail: ms_sith.lady@yahoo.com. E-mail: janice@yowbooks.com.

MANNING, JOAN ELIZABETH, health association administrator; b. Davenport, Iowa, July 7, 1953; d. George John and Eugenie Joan (Thomas) Stolze; m. Michael Anthony Manning, July 30, 1977. BA, U. No. Iowa, 1975; MPH, U. Minn., 1990. Traveling collegiate sec. Alpha Delta Pi Nat. Sorority, Atlanta, 1975—76; recreational therapist Americana Healthcare Ctr., Mason City, Iowa, 1976—81; communication coord. Area Agy. on Aging, Mason City, 1981—83; exec. dir. United Way Cerro Gordo County, Mason City, 1983—85, Health Fair of the Midlands, Omaha, 1985—87; dir. health services ARC, Omaha, 1987—90, COO, 1990—95, CEO, Pacific Northwest region, 1995—. Vis. rsch. prof. Niels Bohr Inst., Denmark, 1995-96. Bd. dirs. YMCA of U.S.A., Chgo., 1981-83, Mason City YMCA, 1980-84, Mason City Parks and Recreation Bd., 1983-85, Camp Fire Coun., 1989—, Potters Therapy House, 1989—; mem. spl. adv. bd. Cerro Gordo County Human Svcs. Bd., 1983-85; mem. spl. activities com. Omaha Wellness Coun. of Midlands, 1986-89; chmn. wider opportunity task force Great Plains (Nebr.) Girl Scouts U.S., 1986-89; bd. dirs. Omaha South YMCA, Cath. Charities; mem. Jr. League of Omaha. Mem. U. Minn. Alumnae Assn., Suburban Rotary, Alpha Delta Pi. Republican. Roman Catholic.

MANNING, NANCY CHRISTINE, retired elementary school educator; d. Alexander Anthony and Millie (Burczak) Pawlikowski; m. Richard Wayne Manning. BS in Elem. Edn. cum laude, East Stroudsburg U., 1971. Cert. Family Math. instr. Rutgers U., 1994. Tchr. Green Twp. Bd. Edn., Greendell, NJ, 1971—2003; ret. Treas. Green Twp. Edn. Assn., Greendell, 1978—2002. Recipient Tchr. Recognition award, NJ Dept. Edn., 1993. Avocations: reading, gardening, cooking, baking, quilting.

MANNING, PATRICIA ANNE, small business owner; b. East Liverpool, Ohio, Jan. 22, 1939; d. Theodore James and Irene Ivy (Adamson) Lessel; m. Richard Edwin Manning, Mar. 30, 1957; children: Lisa Ann, Richard James. BS in Edn. summa cum laude, Kent State U., 1973, postgrad., 1973-79. Cert. elem. sch. educator, N.J. Tchr. math. Daw Jr. High Sch., Wellsville, Ohio, 1974-81; substitute tchr. East Liverpool, Ohio, 1982-83; tchr. supplemental math., reading Middletown (N.J.) High Sch., 1984-85; tchr. basic skills Highlands (N.J.) Elem. Sch., 1985-86; pvt. tutor Atlantic Highlands, N.J., 1986-91; owner, operator Tutors Unltd., Atlantic Highlands, N.J., 1990-94. Mem., Lector, communion asst., coun. mem., chmn. Evangelism Com., pre-school com. Our Saviour Luth. Ch., Whispering Pines, N.C., 1994-2006. Named Woman of Yr., Bus. & Profl. Women, 1986. Mem. Whispers Women's Philanthropic Orgn., Whispering Pines Thrift Shop, Coll. Club. Lutheran. Avocations: travel, reading, art. Home: 23 Winding Trl Carthage NC 28327-6729

MANNING, SANDRA CHAPMAN, psychologist, consultant; b. Ft. Oglethorpe, Ga., Aug. 7, 1955; d. David Lee and Marlene Craig Chapman; m. Jim S. Manning, Dec. 31, 1982; children: Jim, Luke. BA, U. Ga., 1977, MEd, 1978; PhD, U. S.C., 1987. Sch. psychologist III cert. S.C., nat. cert. sch. psychologist NASP. With Walker County Bd. Edn., Rossville, Ga., 1978—81; rsch. asst. S.C. House of Reps., Columbia, 1983—84; sch. psychologist Lexington Sch. Dist. 3, Batesburg-Leesville, SC, 1984—89; bd. dirs. Richland Sch. Dist. 1, Columbia, 1992—2004; adj. faculty Midlands Tech. Coll., Columbia, 1997—99; sch. psychologist Richland Sch. Dist. 2, Columbia, 2002—. Named Pub. Citizen of the Yr., NASW Ctrl. Unit, 2004; named to All-State Sch. Bd., S.C. Sch. Bds. Assn., 1999. Mem.: S.C. Assn. Sch. Psychologists (exec. dir. 1991—). Home and Office: 4531 Briarfield Rd Columbia SC 29206 Office Phone: 803-790-6895.

MANNING, SHERRY FISCHER, retired academic administrator, telecommunications industry executive; b. Washington, Apr. 28, 1943; d. Fred W. and Eleanor A. (Mertz) Fischer; m. Charles W. Manning, Dec. 23, 1966; children: Shannon Marie, Charles Fischer, Kelly Eleanor. BA cum laude in Math., McDaniel Coll., 1965, LHD, 1979; MS in Math., William and Mary Coll., 1967; PhD in Mgmt. Sci., U. Colo., 1973. Mktg. rep., systems engr. IBM, 1967-71; staff assoc. Nat. Ctr. for Higher Edn. Mgmt. Sys., 1971-72; exec. asst. to exec. dir. Nat. Commn. of the Financing of Postsecondary Edn., 1972-73; adj. prof. U. Colo., 1973-74; asst. prof. ops. rsch. U. Kans., 1975—77; cons. to v.p. acad. planning Universidade Fed. de Ceara, 1976-77; exec. v.p. Colo. Women's Coll., 1977-78, pres., 1977—82, pres. emerita, 1982—; CEO John Madden Co., Englewood, Colo., 1983—88, bd. dirs., 1983—88; founder, chmn., and CEO ECCI, 1988—2004; interim pres. Teikyo Marycrest U., 1994; pres. Netwolved EECI Corp. Bd. dirs. Solar Energy Rsch. Inst., 1987-90, Regis Coll., 1987-91, Univ. So. Colo. Found., 1987-91, United Bank Svcs. Co., 1978-81, Imperial Am. Energy Inc., Adopt-A-School, 1979-82, Denver Symphony, 1979-82, Colo. Council on Econ. Edn., 1984-87, Colo. Assn. Commerce and Industry, 1985-89, Meyers Land and Cattle Co., 1989-94, 96-2001, 2004—; chmn. bd. ECCI, 1988—; spkr. in field Host community affairs program KHOW Radio, 1979-80; contbr. articles in field; columnist Campus Communique, 1990-2000; author: (books) Telecommunications and Higher Education: Leadership Perspectives, Telecommunications and Higher Education: Issues, Opportunities, and Applications Trustee Fountain Valley Sch., Colorado Springs; co-chmn. Armstrong Campaign for U.S. Senate, Colo., 1986, Kramer Campaign for U.S. Senate, Colo., 1988. Recipient DAR Outstanding Citizen award, 1961, Faculty Devel. award U. Kans., 1976, Soroptimists Women Helping Women award, 1980, Nat. Conf. Christians and Jews Brotherhood-Sisterhood award, 1990, Extrapreneur award Chivas Regal, 1990, Sports Hall of Fame, 1992, U.S. Small Bus. Adminstrn. Entrepreneur of Yr., 2000, NRC Businesswoman of Yr., 2003, Disting. Alumna award McDaniel Coll., 2004, Ronald Reagan Gold medal 2004 Mem. Nat. Assn. Christians & Jews, Nat. Women's Coalition, Women's Forum, Zonta, Altrusa., Com. of 200 Club, Newcomen Soc. of U.S., Sports Hall of Fame Western Md. Coll., Phi Beta Kappa, Denver Met. Club. Republican. Presbyterian. Office: The Tech Bldg 511 Central Ave Charleston WV 25302-1909 Office Phone: 719-330-9900. Business E-Mail: sherry@campusecci.com.

MANNING, SYLVIA, language educator; b. Montreal, Que., Can., Dec. 2, 1943; came to U.S., 1967; d. Bruno and Lea Bank; m. Peter J. Manning, Aug. 20, 1967; children— Bruce David, Jason Maurice BA, McGill U., 1963; MA, Yale U., 1964, PhD in English, 1967. Asst. prof. English Calif. State U.-Hayward, 1967-71, assoc. prof., 1971-75, assoc. dean, 1972-75; assoc. prof. U. So. Calif., 1975-94, prof., assoc. dir. Ctr. for Humanities, 1975-77, assoc. dir. Ctr. for Humanities, 1975-77, chmn. freshman writing, 1977-80, chmn. dept. English, 1980-83, vice provost, exec. v.p., 1984-94; prof. English U. Ill., Champaign, 1994—, v.p. for acad. affairs, prof. English, 1994—, interim chancellor Chgo., 1999-2000, chancellor, 2000—. Author: Dickens as Satirist, 1971; Hard Times: An Annotated Bibliography, 1984. Contbr. essays to mags. Woodrow Wilson fellow, 1963-64, 66-67 Mem. MLA, Dickens Soc. Office: U of Ill Office of Chancellor 2833 University Hall 601 S Morgan St Chicago IL 60607-7100 Office Phone: 312-413-3350.

MANNO, RITA, state agency administrator; b. Buffalo, Sept. 11, 1946; d. Anthony Joseph and Irene Pawlowski; m. Donald F. Manno, July 11, 1970; children: Kimberly, Rebecca. Student, Exetr (Eng.) U., 1965-66; BA, Canisius Coll., Buffalo, 1967; MA, U. Wis., 1968. State polit. editor Courier-Post, Cherry Hill, N.J., 1980-93; press sec. Gov. Christine Whitman, N.J., 1994-95; dir. comms. N.J. Dept. Health and Sr. Svcs., 1996—. Mem. exec. bd. Nat. Pub. Health Info. Coalition, 1996—. Recipient Best of Gannett award Gannett Corp., 1990-93; Knight scholar, 1993. Mem. N.J. C. of C. (N.J. 300 Women 1998-99). Avocations: hiking, weight training, movies, motorcycles.

MANNS, ESSIE JEANETTE DELANEY, advocate; b. Roanoke, Va., June 20, 1946; d. Walter Leon Delaney and Nanny Rebecca Minor Delaney Volley; divorced; children: Christa Manns Hall, Robert Marcellus Jr. AAS, Va. Western C.C., Roanoke, 1979; BA in Psychology/Sociology, Mary Baldwin Coll., Staunton, Va., 1987; MA in Psychology, PhD in Psychology, Am. State U., Honolulu, 1998. Self-employed seamstress, Columbus, Ohio, 1968—73, Roanoke, 1973—76; daycare provider Social Svcs., Roanoke, 1973—76; pub. rels. coord. Roanoke Valley Outreach Assn., 1976—77; parent coord. counselor Opportunity Industrialization Ctr., Roanoke, 1977—78; peer counselor Va. Western C.C., Roanoke, 1978—79; GS-4 nursing asst. Salem (Va.) Vets. Med. Ctr., 1980—85; outreach worker 23d Dist. Juvenile Ct., Roanoke, 1983—85; project fundraiser, alcohol and drug abuse counselor, battered women's counselor Total Action Against Poverty, Roanoke, 1987—89; project image counselor Social Svcs. 5th Planning Dist., Roanoke, 1989. 3d v.p. labor and industry So. Christian Leadership Conf., 1992—97; co-pres. Washington Pk. Alliance for Neighborhoods, Roanoke, 1998—; co-founder, pres. STRIVE Econ. Empowerment, Inc., Roanoke, 1998—; bd. dirs. Cmty. Orgn. for Rsch. and Devel., Roanoke, 1976—, S.W. Va. Cmty. Devel. Fund, Roanoke, 1979—. Recipient Outstanding Svcs. award, S.W. Va. Cmty. Devel. Fund, 1980—85, Vol. of Yr. award, Total Action Against Poverty, 1994, Svc. Learning Program award, Roanoke Coll., 2001, Dr. Martin Luther King Jr.'s Drum Major for Justice award, So. Christian Leadership Conf., 2002, Timeless Enthusiasm Dedication Hard Work award, Inner City for Selective Devel., Roanoke, 2003. Baptist. Achievements include Roanoke Gladiators Wrestling Team joining STRIVE, a chartered community service organization, 2004. Avocation: human and civil rights. Home: 1826 10th St NW Roanoke VA 24012 Office: Economic Empowerment Inc 1826 10th St NW Roanoke VA 24012 E-mail: ejdmanns@aim.com.

MANNS, HELEN MARGARET, vice principal; d. Marcellus Edward Johnson, Sr. and Margaret Griffin Johnson; m. Terry Lee Manns, Aug. 31, 1985; 1 child, Jordyn Nicole. BS, Hampton U., 1987; MA, George Wash. U., 2003. Cert. Nat. Bd. Profl. Tchng. Standards, Tex. Sr. office asst., typist Newport News (Va.) Waterworks, 1987—89; data tech. Newport News Police Dept., 1990—96; bus. tchr. Franklin (Va.) City Pub. Schs., 1996—97, Hampton (Va.) City Schs., 1997—2004; asst. prin. New Horizons Regional Edn. Ctr., Hampton, Va., 2004—. Network rep. Southeastern Va. Nat. Bd. Cert. Tchrs., Hampton, Va. Recipient Tchr. of Yr., Franklin HS, Va., 1996-1997, Nat. Bd. Cert. Tchr. award, Nat. Bd. Profl. Tchg. Standards, 2002, Tchr. of Yr., Bethel HS, VA, 2003-2004. Mem.: Assn. Curriculum and Devel., Southeastern Va. Nat. Bd. Cert. Tchrs. Regional Network (assoc.), Va. Assn. Career & Tech. Edn. Adminstr. (assoc.). Achievements include first black bus. tchr. in Franklin City Public Schs., Va. 1996; first black tchr. to achieve Nat. Bd. Cert. in Hampton City Schools, VA 2002. Office: New Horizons Regional Edn Ctr 520 Butler Farm Rd Hampton VA 23666 Office Phone: 757-766-1100 306. Office Fax: 757-766-3591. Personal E-mail: hmanns@verizon.net. Business E-Mail: hmanns@nhgs.tec.va.us.

MANNWEILER, MARY-ELIZABETH, painter; b. Norwood, Ohio, June 23, 1916; d. Wilbur Lawrence Young Davis and Augusta Minnis (Newman) Davis; m. Robert Mays Lang, Sr., May 25, 1940 (dec. July 1981); children: Robert Mays Lang, Jr., Gary Davis Lang, Julianna Elizabeth Lang Crawford; m. Gordon Bannatyne Mannweiler, Apr. 17, 1982 (dec. Aug. 2001). Student, Miami U., Oxford, Ohio, 1935-37. Portrait painter; permanent collections; donated (with husband) stained glass window to Congl. Ch., Naugatuck, Conn. Past pres. Athena Club, Freeport, N.Y., Woodbury (Conn.) Women's Club, 1977-78, Watertown (Conn.) Art League; past dir. Waterbury (Conn.) Symphony Orch.; pres. Mary Elizabeth and Gordon Mannweiler Found., Naugatuck, Conn.; trustee YMCA, Naugatuck; mem. scholarship com. Naugatuck H.S., 2003. Recipient blue ribbons for artwork; Paul Harris fellow Rotary, 2001; music room named in honor of Mr. and Mrs. Mannweiler Conn. Jr. Republic, Litchfield, 1997m Meml. Vol. award Naugatuck YMCA, 2005. Mem. DAR (regent Ruth Floyd Woodhull chpt. 1966-67, pres.). Home: 435 Hillside Ave Naugatuck CT 06770-2727

MANOGUE, CAROLINE B., lawyer; b. 1968; m. Christopher Manogue; 1 child. BA cum laude, Middlebury Coll., 1990; JD, Fordham U., 1995. Paralegal Skadden Arps, 1990—92, assoc., 1995—2000; sr. v.p., gen. counsel, sec. Endo Pharmaceuticals, Inc., Chadds Ford, Pa., 2000—04, exec. v.p., chief legal officer, sec., 2004—. Office: Endo Pharmaceuticals 100 Endo Blvd Chadds Ford PA 19317 Office Phone: 610-558-9800. Office Fax: 610-558-7699.

MANROSS, MARY, mayor; m. Larry; 4 children. BS in Polit. Sci. Mayor City of Scottsdale, Ariz., 2000—. Mem. Scottsdale (Ariz.) City Coun., 1992—. Chmn. Scottsdale (Ariz.) Parks and Recreation Commn., Maricopa Assn. Govts. Youth Policy Adv. Com.; bd. dirs. Ariz. Women in Mcpl. Govt.; mem. Planning Commn.; vice chmn. Scottsdale Bond Com.; mem. Sub-com. TPC-Westworld, City Ct., C. of C./Econ. Devel.; mem. Govs. Task Force on Urban Planning, Ariz. Town Hall, Nat. League of Cities Energy, Environment and Nat. Resource Policy Com.; mem. steering com. NLC Transp., Infrastructure and Svcs. Address: 3939 N Drinkwater Blvd Scottsdale AZ 85251-4433 Office: City Hall 3939 N Drinkwater Blvd Scottsdale AZ 85251-4433

MANSBRIDGE, JANE JEBB, political scientist, educator; b. N.Y.C., Nov. 19, 1939; d. Ronald and Georgia St. Claire (Mullen) Mansbridge; m. Christopher Jencks; 1 child, Nathaniel Mansbridge Jencks. BA, Wellesley Coll., 1961; MA, Harvard U., 1966, PhD, 1971. Asst. prof. polit. sci. U. Chgo., 1973-80; assoc. prof. Northwestern U., Evanston, Ill., 1980-86, prof. polit. sci., 1986-91, Jane W. Long prof. arts and scis., 1991-96; prof. J.F. Kennedy Sch. Govt. Harvard U., 1996-98, Adams prof. polit. leadership and democratic values, 1998—. Author: Beyond Adversary Democracy, 1980, Why We Lost the ERA, 1986; editor: Beyond Self-Interest, 1990; editor: (with Susan M. Okin) Feminism 2 vols., 1994; editor: (with Aidon Morris) Oppositional Consciousness, 2001; mem. editorial bd. Signs, Jour. Polit. Philosophy. Russell Sage Found. scholar, 1991-92; fellow Inst. for Advanced Study, 1985-86, Rockefeller Humanities, 1982-83, NSF, 1971-72, Ctr. Advanced Study in the Behavioral Scis., 1997-98, 2001-02, Radcliffe medal Radcliffe Grad. Soc., 2004; fellowship Radcliffe Inst. Advanced Study, 2004-05. Mem. Am. Acad. Arts and Scis., Am. Polit. Sci. Assn. (v.p. 1992-93, program chair 1990, exec. com. 1987-89, coun. 1987-89, pres. Women's Caucus 1996, Schuck award 1988, Kammerer award 1987), Soc. Advancement of Socio-Econs. (pres. 1992-93), Internat. Polit. Psychology Assn. (governing coun. 1993-94). Office: JF Kennedy Sch Govt 79 JFK St Cambridge MA 02138-5801 Office Phone: 617-495-9343.

MANSFIELD, KAREN LEE, lawyer; b. Chgo., Mar. 17, 1942; d. Ralph and Hilda (Blum) Mansfield; children: Nicole Rafaela, Lori Michele. BA in Polit. Sci., Roosevelt U., 1963; JD, DePaul U., 1971; student U. Chgo., 1959-60. Bar: Ill. 1972, U.S. Dist. Ct. (no. dist.) Ill. 1972. Legis. intern Ill. State Senate, Springfield, 1966-67; tchr. Chgo. Pub. Schs., 1967-70; atty. CNA Ins., Chgo., 1971-73; law clk. Ill. Apellate Ct., Chgo., 1973-75; sr. trial atty. U.S. Dept. Labor, Chgo., 1975—, mentor Adopt-a-Sch. Program, 1992-95. bd. dirs. Chgo. lawyer chpt. Am. Constn. Soc., 2006-. Contbr. articles to profl. jours. Vol. Big Sister, 1975-81; bd. dirs. Altgeld Nursery Sch., 1963-66, Ill. div. UN Assn., 1966-72, Hull House Jane Addams Ctr., 1977-82, Broadway Children's Ctr., 1986-90, Acorn Family Entertainment, 1993-95; active Oak Park Farmers' Market Commn., 1996-02; rsch. asst. Citizens for Gov. Otto Kerner, Chgo., 1964; com. mem. Ill. Commn. on Status of Women, Chgo., 1964-70; del. Nat. Conf. on Status of Women, 1968; candidate for del. Ill. Constl. Conv., 1969. Mem. Chgo. Coun. Lawyers, Women's Bar Assn. Ill., Lawyer Pilots Bar Assn., Fed. Bar Assn. Unitarian. Clubs: Friends of Gamelan (performer), 99's Internat. Orgn. Women Pilots (legis. chmn. Chgo. area chpt. 1983-86, legis. chmn. North Ctrl. sect. 1986-88, Legis. award 1983, 85). Home: 204 S Taylor Ave Oak Park IL 60302-3307 Office: US Dept Labor Office Solicitor 230 S Dearborn St Fl 8 Chicago IL 60604-1505

MANSFIELD, LOIS EDNA, mathematics professor, researcher; b. Portland, Maine, Jan. 2, 1941; d. R. Carleton and Mary Bowdish) M. BS, U. Mich., 1962; MS, U. Utah, 1966, PhD, 1969. Asst. prof. computer sci. U. Kans., Lawrence, 1970-74, assoc. prof., 1974-78; assoc. prof. math. N.C. State U., Raleigh, 1978-79; assoc. prof. applied math. U. Va., Charlottesville, 1979-83, prof., 1983—. Vis. asst. prof. computer sci. Purdue U., 1969-70; mem. adv. panel computer sci. NSF, 1975-78; cons., vis. scientist Inst. Computer Applications in Sci. & Engring., Hampton, Va., 1976-78. Consbr. articles to profl. jours. Grantee NSF and DOE, 1976-91. Mem. Am. Math. Soc., Soc. Indsl. and Applied Math. (mem. editl. bd. Jour. Sci. Statis. Computing 1979-88), Assn. Computing Mathinery (bd. dirs. SIGNUM 1980-83).

MANSON, JOANN ELISABETH, endocrinologist; b. Cleve., Apr. 14, 1953; d. S. Stanford and Therese (Palay) M.; m. Christopher N. Ames, June 12, 1979; children: Jennifer, Jeffrey, Joshua Simon. AB magna cum laude, Harvard U., 1975; MD, Case Western Res. U., 1979; MPH, Harvard Sch. Pub. Health, 1984, DPH, 1987. Bd. cert. internal medicine; bd. cert. in subspecialty of endocrinology and metabolism. Intern and resident internal medicine NEDH, Harvard Med. Sch., Boston, 1979-82; fellowship in endocrinology U. Hosp. Boston, Mass., 1982-84; rsch fellow in medicine Brigham and Women's Hosp., Boston, 1984-87, Andrew W. Mellon Found. fellow, 1987-89, dir. endocrinology, co-dir. women's health divsn. preventive medicine, 1993—, chief divsn. preventive medicine, 1999—; staff physician, consulting endocrinologist Harvard Vanguard Med. Assocs., Peabody, Mass., 1986—2003; prof. medicine Harvard Med. Sch., Boston, 1999—, Elizabeth Brigham prof. women's health, 2003—. Mem. editl. bd.: Jour. Women's Health, 1996—, Menopause, 2004—; contbr. chapters to books, more than 600 articles to profl. jours.; author, editor: several books and textbooks. Vol. physician Lynn (Mass.) Shelter for the Homeless, 1989-93; med. adv. bd. Harvard Health Letter, Boston, 1992—, Greater Boston (Mass.) Diabetes Soc., 1993—, Harvard Women's Health Watch, Boston, 1993—; vol. Am. Heart Assn., 1992—. Named Hero in Women's Health, Am. Health for Women Mag., 1997, one of Top 10 Champions of Women's Health, Ladies Home Jour., 2000, one of Top Docs for Women, Boston mag., 2001; recipient Connors award for outstanding leadership in women's health, 1999-, Woman in Sci. award, Am. Med. Women's Assoc., 2003, Henry I. Bowditch award for excellence in pub. health Mass. Med. Soc., 2002. Fellow ACP, ACE; mem. AMA, Am. Med. Women's Assn., Am. Heart Assn., Am. Diabetes Assn., Women's Health Initiative (mem. steering com.), Assn. Am. Physicians, Alpha Omega Alpha. Avocations: reading, hiking, music, travel. Home: 14 Washington St Beverly MA 01915-5820 Office: Brigham and Women's Hosp 900 Commonwealth Ave E Fl 3 Boston MA 02215-1204 Office Phone: 617-278-0871. Business E-Mail: jmanson@rics.bwh.harvard.edu.

MANSON, ZYNORA DAVIS, music educator, minister; b. Richmond, Va., Sept. 9, 1954; d. Henry and Ada Ellis Davis; m. Isaiah Jacob Manson, Aug. 8, 1993; children: Elizabeth Nicole, Chenaniah Jacob, Lateisha Rene', Isaiah Jacob Jr. BS in Music Edn., Norfolk State U., 1979. Profl. collegiate cert. Va., 1979. Sec. Henrico County Govt., Richmond, Va., 1972—73; tchr. music Fairfax County Pub. Schs., 1979—86, Henrico County Pub. Schs., Richmond, 1986—. Composer: (music book and music cd's) Catch Zynora's SOL Songs. Pastor Bethany Bapt. Ch., Sandston, Va., 1996—2005. Finalist Tchr. award of Excellence, REB, 2005; named Jacob L. Adams Tchr. of Yr., 1991, 1992, Henrico Music Educator of Yr., 2002; recipient Telly award, Henrico County Pub. Schs., Channel 36, 2001, Disting. Communicator award, Channel 36, Henrico County, 2001. Mem.: Va. Music Educators Assn. (assoc.). Democrat. Baptist. Avocations: walking, travel, skating. Home: 1070 Nash Rd Sandston VA 23150 Office: Prophetic Full Tone Praise Ministries In 1070 Nash Rd Sandston VA 23150 Office Phone: 804-737-7042. Office Fax: 804-737-7042. Personal E-mail: pftpm@aol.com.

MANSOOR, LORETTA JULIA, retired medical and surgical nurse; b. Walnut Grove, Minn., Oct. 28, 1924; d. Oscar Ramie and Irma Mary (Verlinde) Callewart; m. Raja Audi Mansoor, (div.); 1 child, Mary Ann. Grad., Presentation Sch. of Nursing-McKennan Unit, Sioux Falls, S.D., 1946. RN, Minn. Head nurse Veteran's Hosp., Hot Springs, S.D., 1946-48; pvt. duty nurse various pvt. hosps., Mpls., 1949-50; asst. head nurse St. Mary's Hosp., Mpls., 1951-59; charge nurse Tracy (Minn.) Hosp., 1953-54, Renville County Hosp., Olivia, Minn.; charge nurse, team leader, staff nurse med. and surgical Redwood Mcpl. Hosp., Redwood Falls, Minn., 1962-94; ret., 1994. Hospice vol.; active in cmty. orgns. Cadet nurse, U.S. Army, 1943-46. Democrat. Roman Catholic. Avocations: reading, music, aerobics. Home: 407 E Wyoming St Redwood Falls MN 56283-2123

MANSSON, JOAN, librarian, consultant; b. Sacramento, June 9, 1950; d. Gunnar Emanuel Mansson and Signe Evy Johansson. BA in Fine Arts, N.J. City U., 1982, MA in Studio Art, 1983, postgrad., 1983-84; MLS, Rutgers U., 1985. Grad. asst. art dept. N.J. City U., Jersey City, 1982-84; tchg. asst. Rutgers Art Libr., 1984-85; pub. svcs. libr. Maitland (Fla.) Pub. Libr., 1986—; rsch. cons. Tradingwise, Casselberry, Fla., 1989—; ind. rsch. cons., 1995—; freelance illustrator, 2002—. One-woman shows include Maitland Pub. Libr., 1999, W.T. Bland Pub. Libr., 2000, Maitland Pub. Libr., 2001, 2003, Sunshine State Libr. Leadership Inst., 2004—05; illus., designed Patio Escapes: A Guide, 2003; illustrator: Patio Escapes II, 2006. Mem.: ALA, Maitland C. of C., Ctrl. Fla. Reads (steering com. 2003—06), Ctrl. Fla. Libr. Consortium (continuing edn. com.), Fla. Pub. Libr. Assn. (spkr. conf. 1988), Fla. Libr. Assn. (chair young adult network 1988—92, steering com. 1994—96, chair YA caucus 1996—97, Transformers Honor Roll 1996). Lutheran. Avocations: pastel artist, writing, digital photography, animated films, graphic novels. Office: Maitland Pub Libr 501 S Maitland Ave Maitland FL 32751-5672 E-mail: jmansson@maitlandpubliclibrary.org.

MANTEI, LORRAINE E., school system administrator; b. Albuquerque, Feb. 27, 1961; d. Chester T. and Ella Strange Mantei; m. Richard E. Tuck, July 6, 2001; m. Donald G. Keene (div.); children: Cassandra D. Keene, Pamela Preston, Kendall Keene, Daniel Keene. BS, U. So. Ind., Evansville, 1986; MEd, Tex. A&M U., Commerce, 1999. Tchr. Duncanville Ind. Sch. Dist., Tex., 1994—2000, Arlington Ind. Sch. Dist., Grand Prairie, 2000—02; asst. prin. Dallas Ind. Sch. Dist., 2002—05; supr., prin. La Academia de Estrellas Charter Sch., 2006—. Mem. arts commn. bd. City of DeSoto, 2004—; precinct chair Dallas Dem. Party, 2004—; v.p. DeSoto Dining & Dialogue, Tex., 2005—. Mem.: ASCD, Hispanic Woman's Network, Tex. Elem. Prins. and Suprs. Assn. Democrat. Avocations: reading, walking, travel.

MANTELL, SUZANNE RUTH, editor; b. West Orange, N.J., Nov. 26, 1944; d. Milton A. and Florence B. M.; m. Peter Gray Friedman, 1985; 1 child, Erica Mantell Friedman Student, U. Chgo., 1962; B.F.A., Pratt Inst., 1967. Formerly assoc. editor Harper's mag., N.Y.C., exec. editor, 1977-80; editor Harper's Bookletter, 1974-77, Learning Mag., 1980-81, Family Learning Mag., 1983-84; reader Book of the Month Club, 1985-87, 91-99; editor Travel Bookstore Catalogue, Banana Republic, 1985-87; assoc. editor The N.Y. Observer, N.Y.C., 1987-91; acting Book News editor Pubs. Weekly, 1992-93, contbg. editor, 1993—. Also lectr. mag. writing Stanford U., U. Calif. at Santa Cruz. Consulting editor Spelman Coll. Messenger, 1994-98; columnist L.A. Times Book Review, 1998-99; arts editor New Times L.A., 1999-2001; author Art of the State: Vermont, 1998. Mem. PEN, PEN West USA, Nat. Book Critics Circle. Home: 101 Warwick Pl South Pasadena CA 91030-4062

MANTON, LINDA MARIE, academic administrator; b. Hanford, Calif., Nov. 17, 1949; d. John Batista and Evelina Garcia (Miranda) Nunes; m. Frank P. Manton, Apr. 14, 1971. AA, Coll. of Sequoias, Visalia, Calif., 1970; BA, Calif. State U., Fresno, 1972; MS, U. Ill., 1983. Cert. home economist. County extension advisor U. Ill. Cooperative Extension, Urbana, 1973-85; county dir. U. Calif. Cooperative Extension, Oakland, 1985. Author: Factors Contributing to Job Turnover, 1982; contbr. articles to profl. jours. Bd. dirs. health com. County Head Start, Merced County, Calif., 1986-88. Named one of Outstanding Young Women of Am., 1981. Mem. Calif. Assn. of Extension Home Economists, Nat. Assn. Extension Home Economists, Am. Home Economists Assn., Nat. Assn. Extension 4-H Agents (bd. dirs. 1984, Disting. Svc. award 1982), Ill. Assn. Youth Advisors (pres. 1980, Disting. Svc. award 1982), Calif Assn. Youth Advisors (pres. 1992), Calif. Assn. for the Edn. of Young Children, AAAW, Calif. Women for Agr. (v.p.), Toastmasters (v.p.), Epsilon Sigma Phi, Phi Kappa Phi. Democrat. Roman Catholic. Avocations: race car driving, three wheeling, walking. Office: U Calif Ctrl Valley Regional Office 9240 South Riverbend Ave Parlier CA 93648

MANTYLA, KAREN, distance learning consultant; b. Bronx, N.Y., Dec. 31, 1944; d. Milton and Sylvia (Diamond) Fischer; 1 child, Michael Alan. Student, Rockland C.C., Suffern, N.Y., 1962, NYU, 1967, Mercer U., 1981. Coord. mktg. Credit Bur., Inc., Miami, Fla., 1973—79; dist. mgr. Rsch. Inst. Am., N.Y.C., 1979—80, regional dir., 1980—85, mgr. field sales, 1985—86, mgr. nat. sales, 1986—87, mgr. nat. accounts, 1989; v.p. sales Bur. Bus. Practice/Paramount Comm., Inc., Waterford, Conn., 1989—93; pres. Quiet Power, Inc., Washington, 1993—. Author: Consultative Sales Power, 1995, Interactive Distance Learning Exercises That Really Work, 1999, The 2000/2001 ASTD Distance Learning Yearbook, 2000, Blending e-Learning: The Power is in the Mix, 2001; co-editor The 2001/2002 ASTD Distance Learning Yearbook; co-author: Distance Learning: A Step-By-Step Guide for Trainers, 1997, Blending E-Learning: The Power is in the Mix, 2001. Bd. dirs. Federal Govt. Distance Learning Assn. Named to Distance Learning Hall of Fame, Fed. Govt. Distance Learning Assn., 2003. Mem. ASTD, Sales and Mktg. Execs. (past bd. dirs. N.Y. chpt., v.p. Ft. Lauderdale chpt. 1979), U.S. Distance Learning Assn. (editor Distance Learning News, mem. tech. and comm. com. Fla. chpt.), Nat. Assn. Women Bus. Owners, U.S. C. of C., Women Entrepreneurs. Avocations: antiques, tennis, writing, swimming. Office: Quiet Power Inc 1201 Pennsylvania Ave NW Washington DC 20004-2401 Office Phone: 202-661-4646. Personal E-mail: quietpower@aol.com.

MANTZELL, BETTY LOU, school nurse practitioner, consultant; b. Brookville, Pa., Oct. 16, 1938; d. Elmer William and Wilda Mae (Enterline) M. Diploma, Ind. (Pa.) Hosp. Sch. Nursing, 1959; BSN, Case Western Res. U., 1969, MA, 1978; cert. supr. edn.l. adminstrn., Cleve. State U., 1983; cert. supr., John Carroll U., 1989. RN Ohio, Pa.; cert. supr. Ohio Dept. Edn., basic life support Am. Heart Assn., 2002. Oper. room nurse Univ. Hosps. of Cleve., 1963—69; sch. nurse various locations Cleve. Pub. Schs., 1969—85, coord. sch. nurses, 1976—85, acting asst. supr. health svcs., 1985—86, supr. health svcs., 1986—98, sch. nurse, 1998—. Mem. adv. com. to baccalaureate nursing program Cleve. State U.; prevention of blindness adv. com. Cleve. Sight Ctr.; active All Kids Count Consortium Cleve. Dept. Pub. Health; mem. sch. health com. Acad. Medicine Cleve.; Frances Payne Bolton Sch. Nursing, mem. alumni assn.; clin. instr. cmty. health nursing Case We. Res. U., Cleve., 1988-90, women's connection; mem. coun. econ. opportunities Greater Cleve.; mem. adv. com. Headstart Health Svcs.; ind. cons. health svc. adminstrn.; ind. health care provider Met. Life Ins. Co., 2004-; clin. instr. cmty. health nursing, Case Western Res. U., Cleve., 2005-. Mem. eye care profl. adv. com. Cleve. Sight Ctr. Mem. Am. Sch. Health Assn., Nat. Assn. Sch. Nurses, Ohio Assn. Sch. Nurses, Northeastern Ohio Assn. Sch. Nurses, Ohio Assn. Secondary Sch. Adminstrs., Cleve. Coun. Adminstrs. and Suprs., Cleve. Med. Libr. Assn., Cleve. Tchrs. Union Local 279, Order Ea. Star. Avocations: swimming, water-skiing, reading. Office: Buhrer Elem Sch 1600 Buhrer Ave Cleveland OH 44109 Office Phone: 216-631-2036.

MANUEL, JENNY LYNN, elementary school educator; b. Pomeroy, Ohio, Jan. 17, 1964; d. Charles Raymond and Osie Evelyn (Snyder) M. BS in Elem. Edn. magna cum laude, Rio Grande Coll., 1986; MA in Tcrh. Edn., U. Dayton, 1989. Cert. elem. tcrh., Ohio. Chpt. 1 reading tchr. So. Local Schs., Letart and Syracuse, Ohio, 1986-88; substitute tchr. Meigs County Schs., Pomeroy, Ohio, 1988-91, Mason County Schs., Point Pleasant, W.Va., 1988-91; tchr. 6th grade So. Local Schs., Racine, Ohio, 1991—2001, So. Elem., 2001—. Active So. Elem. Sch. PTO. Mem. NEA, U. Dayton Alumni Assn., Phi Alpha Theta, Alpha Lambda Delta. Avocations: reading, shopping, outdoor activities, community involvment. Home: 49115 Manuel Rd Racine OH 45771-9725 Office: Letart Elem Sch SR 338 Racine OH 45771-0407

MANUEL, VIVIAN, public relations executive; b. Queens County, NY, May 6, 1941; d. George Thomas and Vivian (Anderson) M. BA, Wells Coll., 1963; MA, U. Wyo., Laramie, 1965. Mgmt. analyst Dept. Navy, 1966-68; account supr. GE Co., N.Y.C., 1968-72, corp. rep. bus. and fin., 1972-76; dir. corp. comm. Standard Brands Co., N.Y.C., 1976-78; pvt. cons. N.Y.C., 1978-80; pres. V M Comm. Inc., N.Y.C., 1980-97; pub. info. officer Mont. Dept. Commerce, Helena, 1997—2002; adminstr. Gough, Shanahan, Johnson & Waterman, Helena, 2003—04. Mem. com. Girls Club N.Y., 1983—84; mem. adv. bd. Glenholme Sch., 1991—92; mem. allocation com. United Way Mont., 1998—; bd. dirs. Am. Lung Assn. of No. Rockies, 1999—2002; trustee Wells Coll., 1983—90. Mem. AAUW, N.Y. Women in Comms. (bd. v.p. 1983-85, chair Matrix awards 1985), Women Execs. in Pub. Rels. (bd. dirs. 1985-88), Women's Econ. Roundtable. Address: 109 Oakwood Ln Helena MT 59601-6024

MANUELIAN, LUCY DER, art historian, architecture educator; b. Arlington, Mass. AB in English lit., Radcliffe Coll.; MA in Art History, Boston U., 1975, PhD in Art History, 1980. Head tchg. fellow Boston U., 1975-76; vis. lectr. Framingham State Coll., 1979-80; archivist Armenian Archtl. Archives Project, 1979—84; holder lectureship in Armenian Art and Architecture Tufts U., 1984—89, Arthur H. Dadian and Ara Oztemel prof. Armenian Art and Architecture Medford, 1989—. Mus. cons. Dartmouth Coll.; author, narrator 4 TV documentaries on Armenian art; holder lectureship in Armenian art and architecture Tufts U., 1984; lectr. Harvard U., 1984—89, McGill U., 1984—89, Boston U., 1984—89, Boston Coll., 1984—89, U. Mass., 1984—89, Northeastern U., 1984—89. Author: Armenian Architecture, 4 vols., 1981—88, Dictionary of Middle Ages, 1982—89, Dictionary of Art, The Gregorian Collection-Armenian Rugs, 1983, Weavers, Merchants and Kings: The Inscribed Rugs of Armenia, 1984; author, prodr. Lost Treasure of Christianity: The Ancient Monuments of Armenia; contbr. chapters to books, articles to profl. jours. Fellow to USSR, 1977-78, fellow Bunting Inst., Radcliffe Coll., 1971-73; Samuel H. Kress grantee Boston U., 1975, 78, Rsch. grantee Nat. Assn. for Armenian Studies and Rsch. to USSR, 1972, 78; sr. scholar grantee Am. Coun. Learned Socs./Soviet Acad. Scis., 1983; recipient Jack H. Kolligian award Nat. Assn. Armenian Studies and Rsch., 1981, Boyan award Armenian Students Assn., Woman of Achievement award Armenian Internat. Women's Assn., 1994, Kohar award Armenian Rugs Soc.; named to Boston U. Acad. Disting. Alumni, 1986, Armenian of Yr., Masons, 1990. Mem. Armenian Acad. Sci. (cons. Art Inst. symposium 1990—), Nat. Assn. Armenian Studies and Rsch. (adv. bd. 1991—), Soc. Armenian Studies, Aga Khan Program Islamic Architecture (affiliate), Middle East Studies Assn., Coll. Art Assn., Medieval Acad. Accademia Tiberina Rome (assoc.), Assn. Internat. Etudes Armeniennes, Nat. Assn. Armenian Studies and Rsch. (hon. life), Phi Beta Kappa (hon. Radcliffe Coll.). Achievements include research in archaeology with ground penetrating radar technology; medieval American Armenian architecture sculpture and illuminated manuscripts, the crusades; restoration of 5 medieval Armenian churches. Avocations: music, piano, tennis. Office Phone: 617-484-0668. Business E-Mail: lucy.manuelian@tufts.edu.

MANVILLE, GRETA CRAIG, writer; b. Clarinda, Iowa, June 12, 1932; d. William Donald Craig and Eunice Catherine Nolan; m. Wallace Carruthers Manville, Jr., Feb. 1, 1953. BA, San Jose State U., 1975, MA, 1978. Asst. treas. Argonaut Ins. Co., Menlo Park, Calif., 1962-75; exec. mgr. quality control Consol. Freightways, Menlo Park, 1977-91; freelance writer Sun City West, Ariz., 1991—. Bd. dirs., lit. contest coord. Ariz. Authors Assn., 2006—. Author: The Man on the Train, 1994 (3rd prize S.W. Writers Workshop 1994), Murder On-Line, 1998, Death Key, 2000; co-author: The Purgatory Trail, 1993 (1st prize S.W. Writers Workshop 1993), Death Key, 2000 (1st place mystery/suspense category Authorlink.com New Authors Awards Competition, 2000); author (poetry) Passage, 1999 (Grand prize Sparrowgrass Poetry Forum, 1999). SteinbeckFellowship, San Jose State U., 2002—03. Mem. AAUW (newsletter editor Sun City West br. 1999-2000). Republican. Methodist. Avocations: duplicate bridge, golf. Personal E-mail: GManville@aol.com.

MANZI, ALICE M., artist, educator; b. Bklyn., June 16, 1951; d. Frank J. and Anna M. (Reeves) M. BA, Bklyn. Coll., 1973; MA, NYU, 1976. Dir. art programs Hamilton Hill Art Ctr., Schenectady, NY, 1980-82; scenic designer N.E. Ballet Co., Schenectady, 1987—; artist, owner Manzi Studios, Porter Corners, NY, 1994—. Adj. prof. Russell Sage/Jr. Coll. Albany, N.Y., 1986-94, Skidmore Coll., Saratoga, N.Y., 1988—. Exhibited in one-woman and group shows at Albany Inst. of History and Art, 1985, N.Y. State Women Artists, Schenectady, N.Y., 1986, Cooperstown (N.Y.) Ann. Nat. Show, 1987-91, Chasen Galleries, Sarasota, Fla., 1988, Nat. Mus. of Dance, Saratoga Springs, N.Y., 1991, Sculpture '91 Internat. Exhibit, Rochester, N.Y., 1991, Ellen Harris Gallery, Provincetown, Mass., 1988-94, Design Toscano, Arlington Hts., Ill., 1992, Skidmore Coll., Saratoga Springs, 1994; numerous sculpture commns. for chs. throughout the U.S, 1996—. CETA grantee Schenectady Employment and Tng. Act, 1978, Spl. Opportunity Stipends grantee N.Y. Found. for the Arts, N.Y., 1991, NYSCA, 2003. Mem. Saratoga Arts Coun., Nat. Alliance of Lit. Artists, Guild of Adirondack Artists (dir. at large). Home and Office: Manzi Studios 1112 N Creek Rd Porter Corners NY 12859-1906 Personal E-mail: Manzisculpture@aol.com.

MAO, DORA, lawyer; b. Taipei, Taiwan, 1962; AB magna cum laude, Harvard U., 1984; JD, U. Calif. Berkeley, Boalt Hall, 1987. Bar: Calif. 1987. Ptnr. Orrick, Herrington & Sutcliffe LLP, San Francisco, profl. devel. ptnr., ptnr. in charge of San Francisco office, 2001—03. Bd. dirs. Girl Scouts San Francisco Bay Area. Mem.: State Bar Calif. Office: Orrick Herrrington & Sutcliffe LLP The Orrick Building 405 Howard St San Francisco CA 94105 Office Phone: 415-773-5628. Office Fax: 415-773-5759. Business E-Mail: dmao@orrick.com.

MAPES, GWENYTH B., humanities educator, writer; b. Bad Canstatt, Germany, Nov. 28, 1962; BA, Hollins U., Va., 1984; MFA, U. Mont., Missoula, 1989. English instr. U. Mont., Missoula, 1987—89, humanities instr., 1989—99, Grossmonto Coll., El Cajon, Calif., 1999—. Mem.: Phi Beta Kappa (sec. Epsilon chpt. 2005—). Office: Grossmont College 8800 Grossmont College Dr El Cajon CA 92020 Office Phone: 619-644-7525. Business E-Mail: gwenyth.mapes@gcccd.edu.

MAPLE, MARILYN JEAN, educational media coordinator; b. Turtle Creek, Pa., Jan. 16, 1931; d. Harry Chester and Agnes (Dobbie) Kelley; 1 child, Sandra Maple. BA, U. Fla., 1972, MA, 1975, PhD, 1985. Journalist various newspaper including Mountain Eagle, Jasper, Ala., Boise (Idaho) Statesman, Daytona Beach (Fla.) Jour., Lorain (Ohio) Jour.; account exec. Frederides & Co., N.Y.C.; prodr. hist. films Fla. State Mus., Gainesville, 1967-69; writer, dir., prodr. med. and sci. films and TV prodns. for 6 medically related colls. U. Fla., Gainesville, 1969—. Pres. Media Modes, Inc., Gainesville. Author: On the Wings of a Butterfly; columnist Health Care Edn. mag.; contbr. Fla. Hist. Quar. Recipient Blakslee award, 1969, spl. award, 1979; Monsour lectr., 1979. Mem. Health Edn. Media Assn. (bd. dirs., awards 1977, 79), Phi Delta Kappa, Kappa Tau Alpha. Office: U Fla PO Box 16J Gainesville FL 32602-0016 Home: 125 Deep Lake Tr Melrose FL 32666 Personal E-mail: mmaple@atlantic.net.

MAPLES, CAROL J., director; d. Ishmael Worth Maples and Imogene Carroll. MS in Edn., Mo. State U., Springfield, Mo., 1993; student in Edn., U. Mo., Columbia, Mo., 2005—. Cert. speech and theatre edn. Mo., 1980, tchr. math. Mo., 1980, thoughtful curriculum and assessment sys. Thoughtful Edn., 1995, choice theory, reality therapy, and lead mgmt. William Glasser Inst., 1997. Educator, dir. theatre, speech, math., computers Marshfield (Mo.) Schs., 1984—98; educator, dir. theater Springfield (Mo.) Schs., 1998—2000; coord. BS in Edn., Speech and Theatre Program Mo. State U., Springfield, 2002—. Prodn. mgr. Tent Theatre, Springfield, Mo., 1987. Prodr.(dir.): Freelance-A-Lat Prodns., 1992—2001; contbr. articles to profl. jours. Recipient Tchg. Excellence award, Mo. State U. Coll. Arts and Letters, 2004, Svc. Excellence award, 2006. Mem.: Profl. Edn. Unit (chmn. BS in edn. secondary oversight com. 2006—), Speech and Theatre Assn. Mo. (bd. govs. 2004, dir.), Ednl. Theatre Assn., Assn. Theatre in Higher Edn., Am. Alliance Theatre and Edn. Office: Missouri State University 901 S National Ave Springfield MO 65897 Office Phone: 417-836-6389. Business E-Mail: cjmaples@missouristate.edu.

MAPLES, MARY LOU, elementary school educator; Tchr. kindergarten Lessie Moore Elem. Sch., Pineville, La., 1974-97; early childhood Title I supr. Media Ctr., Pineville, 1997—. Recipient La. Tchr. of Yr. award La. Dept. Edn., 1992. Office: Media Ctr PO Box 1230 Alexandria LA 71309-1230 E-mail: maplesml@cox-internet.com.

MAPLESDEN, CAROL HARPER, marriage and family therapist, music educator; b. Phila., Aug. 27, 1947; d. Emmitt Dewain and Helen Esther (Davison) Harper; m. James Paul Maplesden, May 27, 1967; children: Andrew James, Elizabeth Elvira. BA, Holy Family Coll., Phila., 1979; MA, La Salle U., Phila., 1984. Cert. counselor Nat. Bd. Cert. Counselors, lic. profl. counselor of mental health Del., Pa. Child, youth and family therapist People Acting To Help (PATH), Phila., 1983-86, Benjamin Rush Cmty. Mental Health, Phila., 1987-88; clin. dir. N.E. Treatment, Phila., 1988-89; outpatient supr. Interact Com. Mental Health, Phila., 1989; program supr. Cath. Charities Christopher House, Trenton, N.J., 1989-90; dir. Carden Family Inst., Phila., 1984—, CEO, 1984—, instr. keyboard, organist, vocal performer, vocal choir and handbell choir dir. Carden music div., 1993—. Seminar lectr. in Phila. area. Author: (piano course and audio tape) Young Beginnings Piano Course, Part I, 1993. Mem.: APA, NRC (hon. bus. chmn. 2004), ACA, Internat. Assn. Marriage and Family Counselors, Daus. Am. Colonists (chpt. vice regent 2006—), Daughters Union Vets. Civil War (Pa. state pres. 2001—02). Republican. Methodist. Avocations: history studies, genealogy, crafts. Office Phone: 215-741-4234.

MAQUAT, LYNNE E., biomedical researcher; Grad., U. Conn.; PhD in Biochemistry, U. Wis., Madison. Postdoctoral rschr. McArdle Lab. Cancer Rsch. U. Wis., Madison; rsch. scientist Roswell Pk. Cancer Inst.; mem. faculty to prof. biochemistry and biophysics James P. Wilmot Cancer Ctr. U. Rochester Med. Ctr., NY, 2000—. Contbr. articles to profl. jours.; mem. editl. bd.: RNA, Molecular and Cellular Biology, RNA Biology. Recipient Davey Meml. award, Outstanding Cancer Rsch., 2002. Fellow: Am. Acad. Arts & Scis.; mem.: Am. Soc. Cell Biology (mem. pub. info. com. 1992—), RNA Soc. (dir. 2000—02, pres. 2006—). Office: Dept Biochemistry and Biophysics U Rochester Sch Medicine and Dentistry 601 Elmwood Ave Box 712 Rochester NY 14642 E-mail: Lynne_Maquat@urmc.rochester.edu.*

MARAFIOTI, KAYALYN A., lawyer; b. Rochester, N.Y., 1954; AB cum laude, Harvard U., 1976; JD, NYU, 1979. Bar: N.Y. 1980. Ptnr. Skadden, Arps, Slate, Meagher & Flom, N.Y.C. Note and comment editor NYU Jour. Internat. Law and Politics, 1978-79. Office: Skadden Arps Slate Meagher & Flom 4 Times Sq Fl 24 New York NY 10036-6595

MARANO, DONNA INEZ, academic administrator; b. Bklyn., July 7, 1954; d. Carlo Frederick Marano and Marjorie Ann Caudill; m. John Paul Fillo, June 22, 1975 (div. Jan. 1992); children: Matthew Paul Fillo, Alexander Paul Fillo, Jennifer Ann Fillo; m. Anthony E. Ricci, May 8, 2004. Student, Carnegie Mellon U., 1977—81, U. Phoenix, 2005—. Cert. rsch. adminstr. Sec. Carnegie Mellon U., Pitts., 1975-78, adminstrv. asst., 1978-86, prin. adminstrv. assoc., 1989-98, dir. fin. and adminstrn., 1998—. Bd. dirs. Rsch. Adminstrs. Cert. Coun. Mem. Dem. Com., Moon Twp., Pa., 1988-94, vice-chmn., 1989-90, chmn., 1992-94. Mem. Soc. Rsch. Adminstrs. (pres. Allegheny chpt. 2000-01, treas. N.E. sect. 2001-03, internat. treas. 2003-05), Nat. Coun. Univ. Rsch. Adminstrs., Order of the Rainbow for Girls (grand charity 1974-75, worthy advisor 1973, 74; scholar 1973; recipient Grand Cross of Color 1975). Roman Catholic. Avocations: strength training, volleyball, bicycle riding, country music. Office: Carnegie Mellon U 119 Porter Hall Pittsburgh PA 15213 Office Phone: 412-268-2942.

MARASCO, ROSE C., artist, educator; b. Utica, N.Y., Dec. 25, 1948; d. Ernest Salvatore Marasco and Concetta Regina (Faga) Massa. BFA, Syracuse U., 1971; MA, Goddard Coll., 1981; MFA, Visual Studies Workshop, 1991. Instr. photography Munson-Williams-Proctor-Inst. Sch. of Art, Utica, 1974-79; prof. dept. art U. So. Maine, Portland, 1979—, chair dept. art, 1992-94; instr. photography Maine Coll. of Art, Portland, 1981-87. Exhibitions include Photokina, 1988, Portland Mus. Art, 1989, Farnsworth Mus., Rockland, Maine, 1992—93, Davis Mus. and Cultural Ctr., Wellesley, Mass., 1995, 2002, Sarah Morthland Gallery, 1998, 2000, 2003, Bowdith Coll. Mus. of Art, Portland Mus. of Art, Smithsonian Nat. Mus. of Am. Hist., Fogg Art Mus. At Harvard U. Residency fellow MacDowell Colony, 1985, Artists fellow Maine Arts Commn., Women's Studio Workshop, 1994; Percent for Art grantee Maine Arts Commn., 1983, Major grantee Maine Humanities Coun., 1990-92, Excellence in Photographic Tchg. award, Santa Fe Ctr. Photography, 2005—. Mem. Soc. Photographic Edn. Office: U So Maine Dept of Art 37 College Ave Gorham ME 04038-1032 Office Phone: 207-780-5277. Business E-Mail: marasco@usm.mahe.edu.

MARATTA SNYDER, GRACE ELVIRA, volunteer; b. Jackson, Ohio, July 22, 1922; d. John William and Mary Ann (Lewis) Matthews; m. James Edward Maratta, Oct. 14, 1957 (div. May 1971); m. Price Knapp Snyder, Sept. 19, 1998. Student, Rio Grande Coll., 1940-41, Columbus Bus. U., 1941-42. Clk.-typist Ohio State Dept. Trans., Columbus, 1942-44; adminstrv. office mgr. Div of Police City of Columbus, 1944-77, ret., 1977; legis. agt. Police and Fire Retirees of Ohio, Reynoldsburg, 1978—. Trustee Columbus Police Sub-Relief Fund, 1967—, Adult Life Care Ctr., Reynoldsburg, Ohio, 1990—; lobbyist Police and Fire Retirees of Ohio, Columbus, 1978—. Past pres. Reynoldsburg Womens Civic Club, 1979-81, Reynoldsburg Womens Rep. Club, 1982-84; pres. Reynoldsburg Sr. Citizens Ctr., 1988—; trustee Wesley Ridge Retirement and Health Complex, 1996—. Recipient Disting. Svc. award Ohio Gen. Assembly, 1970, Cmty. Builders award Masonic Lodge 340, 1996; named Outstanding Svc. Sr. Citizen Reynoldsburg Jaycees, 1987, Outstanding Eldercare Work, Ohio State Dept. Aging, 1989; inducted into Ohio Sr. Citizens Hall of Fame, 1994. Mem. Columbus Police Retirees Assn. (Outstanding Svc. 1981). Republican. Methodist. Avocations: musical theatre, reading, tv watching, shopping, eating out. Office: Police & Fire Retirees 7335 E Livingston Ave Reynoldsburg OH 43068 E-mail: pfro@iwaynet.net.

MARAZITA, ELEANOR MARIE HARMON, retired secondary school educator; b. Madison County, Ind., Oct. 25, 1933; d. William Houston Harmon and Martha Belle (Savage) Hinds; m. Philip Marazita; children: Mary Louise, Frank, Dominic, Vincent, Elizabeth Faye, Candice Marie, Daniel William. BS in Home Econs., Ctrl. Mich. U., 1955; MA in Human Ecology, Mich. State U., 1971. Cert. vocat. home econs. tchr., K-Jr. Coll., cert. speech correction tchr. Tchr. adult edn., Mt. Pleasant, Mich., 1956; substitute tchr. North Branch (Mich.) Schs., 1961-64; tchr. Pied Piper Coop. Nursery Sch., Lansing, Mich., 1964-69, Lansing C.C., 1971-81, Grand Ledge (Mich.) H.S., 1969-98; ret., 1998. Mich. tchr. del. World Conf. Tchg. Profls., 1985, 98; adv. mem. Mich. Tchr. Competency Testing Program, 1992. Bd. dirs. Greater Lansing chpt. U.N., 1995-98; vol. St. Lawrence Mental Health Hosp., 1972-73, Listening Ear Crisis Intervention Ctr., 1973-77, Capital City Convalescent Home, 1969-73; chmn. study com. Delta Twp. Libr., 1969-73, Jr. League, 1969—; interviewer Youth for Understanding, 1978-83; active exch. student orientation program Mich. State U., 1977, exch. trips, 1979-82; mem. adv. bd. Mich. League Human Svcs., 1988-91, Eaton County Extension Svcs., 1988-91, Mich. Women's Assembly, 1986-91; mem. Friends of Waverly Libr., 1963—; participant 3rd Congress Educators Caucus, 1986-92; 4-H leader, 1950-65. Recipient State Tchr. Multicultural award, 1989, UN Global Educator award, 1991, State Tchr. Maureen Wyatt feminist award, 1996. Mem. AAUW, LWV, NEA (del. 1998, observer 2d ann. Ednl. Internat. Congress 1998), DAR (co-chair State Good Citizen 1999-2003, v.p. Cameo Club 2002-05, pres. 2006—), PEO (state bd. dirs. 2003—, Mich. Edn. Assn. (polit. action exec. bd. 1986-98, v.p. women's caucus 1986-93, Liz Siddell State Internat. Cultures award 1992), Circumnavigators Club (travel around world in one trip 1993), Century Club (travel in 100 countries outside U.S. 1994, tread 24 Time Zones 2002, Seven Continent award 2003, Globetrotter award 2003), Delta Kappa Gamma (co-chair State World Fellowship 1993-95, chair state legislation com. 1997-99, chpt. Women of Distinction award 1993), Phi Delta Kappa (Tchr. of Yr. Mich. State U. 1992). Avocation: travel. Home: 214 Farmstead Ln Lansing MI 48917-3015

MARAZITA, MARY LOUISE, genetics researcher; b. Cheboygan, Mich., June 13, 1954; m. Richard T. McCoy, 1984; 5 children. BS, Mich. State U., East Lansing, 1976; PhD in Genetics, U. NC, Chapel Hill, 1980. Fellow U. So. Calif., 1980-82; statistician, instr. UCLA, 1982-86; asst. prof. human genetics Med. Coll. Va., 1986-93; dir. Cleft Palate-craniofacial Ctr. U. Pitts., 1993-00, dept. chair oral biology, 1999—, asst. dean for rsch. Sch. Dental Medicine, 2000-2001, assoc. dean rsch., 2001—, dept. chair, 2006—. Instr. biomath. U. Calif., 1984-86; asst. prof. dentistry Med. Coll. Va., 1992-93; assoc. prof. human genetics and oral biology U. Pitts., 1993-97, prof. human genetics and oral and maxillofacial surgery, 1997—, prof. psychiatry, 2003—. Fellow Am. Coll. Med. Genetics, Am. Cleft Palate Assn., Am. Soc. Human Genetics, Internat. Genetic Epidemiol. Soc., Internat. Assn. Dental Rsch. Achievements include research in genetics of cleft lip, cleft palate and other craniofacial anomalies, including statistical genetic analysis and gene mapping studies. Office: U Pitts Divsn Oral Biology/Genetics Ste 500 Cellomics Bldg/100 Technology Dr Pittsburgh PA 15219 Business E-Mail: marazita@sdmgenetics.pitt.edu.

MARBACH, DONNA MAUREEN, writer; b. King City, Calif., Dec. 9, 1948; d. William Edward and Elfriede Hendrika (Maurer) M.; m. John Andrew Feldmann, Sept. 14, 1969 (div. Aug. 1977); m. Joseph Patrick Brennan, Sept. 6, 1980; children: Brian Timothy, Erin Coleen, Shannon Margaret, Kevin Michael, Colin Riley. BA in Lit., U. Calif., Santa Cruz, 1971; MSEd, U. Pa., 1975. V.p. asst. for cmty. program and others U. Pa., Phila., 1971-75; program dir. Am. Lung Assn. of Phila., 1975-78; rehab. counselor Horizon House, Phila., 1978-79; employment and tng. mgr. City of Phila., 1979-84; v.p. adminstrn. Vols. of America, Rochester, N.Y., 1984-93; pres. Easter Seal Soc. of Monroe County, Rochester, 1993-94; bus. mgr. Scholars Choice, Rochester, 1995-97, mktg. specialist, exhibitor, 1997—; art tchr. Am. Sch. of GDL, Guadalajara, Mexico, 1999; freelance writer, artist Guadalajara, 1997—. Mem. PTA (treas.), Rochester, 1996-97, Browncroft Neighborhood Assn., 1984-97, Monroe Co. Foster Parents Assn., 1985-89, Del. Regional Planning Commn., Rochester, 1985-93, U. Calif. Alumni Assn.; pres. Rochester Interfaith Jail Ministry, 1988-92. Mem. Am. Craft Coun., Art and Cultural Coun. Rochester, Internat. Soc. Poets (disting. mem.), Poetry Soc. Am., Acad. Am. Poets, Internat. Womens Writing Guild, Nat. Mus. Women In Arts. Democrat. Roman Catholic. Avocations: fundraising, painting, teaching. Home: 1935 Penfield Rd Penfield NY 14526-1434

MARBURY, VIRGINIA LOMAX, insurance and investment executive; b. Ruston, La., June 25, 1918; d. Dallas Daniel and Della (Southern) Lomax; m. William A. Marbury Jr., Sept. 5, 1943; children: Rebekah, Caroline. BA, La. Tech. U., 1936, LLD (hon.), 1987; MusB, La. State U., 1938. Exec. v.p. Marbury Corp., Ruston, La., 1944—; sec.-treas. Bankers Life La., Ruston, 1959—. 1st v.p., membership chmn. Lincoln Parish Mus. and Hist. Soc., Ruston, La., 1992—. Recipient Tower Medallion award La. Tech. U., 1991. Mem. Shreveport Symphony Soc. Republican. Episcopalian. Office: Marbury Corp 601 N Trenton St Ruston LA 71270-3840

MARCALI, JEAN GREGORY, retired chemist; b. Jermyn, Pa., May 29, 1926; d. John Robert and Anna Marie Gregory; m. Kalman Marcali, Oct. 6, 1956; children: Coleman, Frederick. Student, U. Pa., 1948—52, U. Del., 1971—72. Microanalyst E.I. du Pont de Nemours & Co., Deepwater, NJ, 1943-60, tech. info. analyst, organic chems. dept., 1960-64, tech. info. analyst info. systems dept. Wilmington, Del., 1964-67, sr. adviser tech. info., 1967-70, supr. tech. info., 1970-82, 85-89, supr. adminstrv. svcs. Ctrl. Rsch. Dept., 1982-85, cons., 1989-92, ret., 1992. Sec. Alfred I. Dupont Elem. PTA, 1971, pres. 1972; pres. PTA Brandywine Sch. Dist., 1973; mem. Wilmington Dist. Rep. Com., 1976—, Winterthur Mus., 1996—. Mem. Am. Chem. Soc. (treas. divsn. chem. info. 1976-81, chmn.-elect 1981, chmn. 1982, 83, divsn. councilor 1983-90), Am. Chem. Soc. (com. on chem. abstracts svc. 1983-85, 87-93, mem. joint bd. coun. com. on chem. abstracts svc. 1994-96, 98, 99, 2000, Del. sec. chem. lit. topical group, chmn. 1979-80, chem. vets. chmn.-elect 1999), Order Ea. Star, Du Pont Country Club, Winterthur Mus. Guild. Lutheran. Home: 312 Waycross Rd Wilmington DE 19803-2950

MARCDANTE, KAREN JEAN, medical educator; b. Milw., Sept. 15, 1955; d. Willard Karl and Beth Elaine (Maule) Kohn; m. Mark Wendelberger, Aug. 5, 1978 (div. Sept. 1985); m. Anthony Marcdante, Oct. 17, 1998. Student, Marquette U., 1973-76; MD, Med. Coll. Wis., 1980. Diplomate Am. Bd. Pediat. & Pediat. Crit. Care. Resident in pediat. Med. Coll. Wis. affiliated hosps., Milw., 1980-83; instr. pediat. Med. Coll. Wis., Milw., 1983-85, asst. prof. pediat., 1987-94, assoc. prof. pediat., 1994-2000, prof. pediat., 2000—, assoc. dean curriculum, 1997—2003, vice-chair edn. dept. pediat., 1994—; fellow in pediatric critical care U. Calif., San Francisco, 1985-87; vice chief staff Children's Hosp. Wis., Milw., 1995-97. Dir. Respiratory Care Svcs., 1992-98, Transport Program, 1998—; chief dept. pediat. Children's Hosp. Wis., 1991-95, dept. critical care 1993-95, mem. numerous coms., including care mgmt. steering com., 1994-, critical care com., 1991—, pres.-elect, 2003-05; pres. med. dental staff, 2005-. Contbr. numerous articles to profl. jours. Recipient New Investigator award Assn. Am. Med. Colls., 1992, Cert. Leadership award YWCA and Marquette Electronics Found., 1992, Laureate award Ctrl. Group Ednl. Affairs, 2004; grantee Dept. HHS, 1996—. Mem. Am. Acad. Pediat. (pub. rels. chair Wis. chpt. 1988-91, sec.-treas. 1990-95, v.p. 1995-96, chair careers and opportunities 1996-2001), Soc. Critical Care Medicine (chair task force on quality improvement pediat. 1994-96, quality indicator devel. work group 1997-98, Presdl. citation 1996, 97), Coun. on Med. Student Edn. in Pediat. (co-chair task force on tchg. methods 1991-96, nominating com. 1993-95, exec. com. 1996-99, sec.-treas. 1997-99). Business E-Mail: kwendel@mcw.edu.

MARCEAU, JUDITH MARIE, retired elementary school educator, small business owner; b. Gardner, Mass., Aug. 10, 1946; d. George Joseph and Bernice Victoria (Johnson) Babineau; m. James Victor Krymowski, Aug. 20, 1976 (div. Mar. 1985); children: Kathryn Victoria, Kenneth James; m. Glenn Francis Marceau, Aug. 30, 1989. Grad., Sch. Worcester Art Mus., 1967; BFA, Clark U., 1971. Tchr. elem. art Quabbin Regional Pub. Schs., Barre, Mass., 1967-70, Gardner (Mass.) Pub. Schs., 1970—2003, ret., 2003; propr. Babineau's Corner Antiques Shop, Hubbardston, 2003—. Author, editor: Fascinating Facts of Gardner, 1977, 2d edit., 1999, Hubbardston as Seen Through the Eyes of its Children, 1987; author numerous poems. Active Hubbarston Hist. Commn.; vol. Hubbarston Recycling Initiative; bd. dirs. Gardner Edn. Assn., 1975-86; bd. dirs. Youth Advocacy and Counseling Ctr., Gardner, 1979-82. Recipient Citation of Outstanding Edn. City of Gardner, 1994, 2000, Cert. of Commendation, Mayor of City of Gardner, Cert. of Achievement Gardner Pub. Sch. Com., 2004. Mem. Mass. Tchrs. Assn., Nat. Tchrs. Assn. Achievements include my third grade class 2000-01 petitioned for a bill to declare offical state colors to be cranberry, green and blue for Mass. This became a law signed by Gov. Mitt Romney in Dec. 2004 (students in 7th). Avocations: writing history, poetry, antiques, watercolor painting, sketching. Home: 221 Gardner Rd Hubbardston MA 01452-1655 Office: Babineau's Corner Antiques 221 Gardner Rd Hubbardston MA 01452 Office Phone: 978-632-2840.

MARCEAU, YVONNE, ballroom dancer, educator; b. Chgo., July 13, 1950; BFA, U. Utah, 1972; AA, Imperial Soc. Ballroom Dance. Ballet dancer Ballet West; ptnr. with Pierre Dulaine, 1976; founder, artistic dir. Am. Ballroom Theatre, N.Y.C., 1984-93; educator dance divsn. Julliard Sch., N.Y.C., 1993—. Guest tchr. Sch. Am. Ballet, N.Y.C.; tchr. ballroom dancing Juilliard Sch. Appearances include The Smithsonian Inst., JFK Ctr. for Performing Arts, N.Y. State Theater, N.Y.C., Sadlers Wells, London, (Broadway and London show) Grand Hotel, 1989-92, toured with Pierre Dulaine and Am. Ballroom Theatre worldwide. Recipient Recipient Brit. Theatrical Arts Championships 4 times, Spl. Astaire award, Dance Educator awards, Outstanding Achievement in Dance award Nat. Coun. Dance Am., 1992, Dance Mag. award, 1993.

MARCEAUX, LINDA D'AUGEREAU, elementary school educator; b. Abbeville, La., Sept. 27, 1947; d. Charles d'Augereau, Jr. and Hazel Marie Bellot d'Augereau; m. Alex John Marceaux, Aug. 31, 1968; 1 child, Jana Nichole. BA, U. Southwestern La., 1988. Cert. elem. edn. grades 1-8, spl. edn. mild/moderate grades 1-12 generic Dept. Edn. State La. Spl. edn. grades 4th-6th behavior disorder/resource Lafayette Parish Sch. Bd., La., 1988—91, educator 4th grade, 1991—2000, educator 6th grade math, 2000—01, educator 8th grade math, 2001—03, educator 7th -8th grade math. honors, 2003—. Mem. Student La. Assn. Educators U. Southwestern La., Lafayette, 1983—88; membership chair Coun. for Exceptional Children, 2001—02; mem. Lafayette Parish Assn. Educators, 1988—; pres. Student Coun. for Exceptional Children, U. SW La., 1986—88. Sponsor Jr. Nat. Young Leaders Conf., 2004—; v.p. KC Aux., Abbeville, La., 1983—85; pres. Parents for Progress, Meaux, La., 1983—85; coach/advisor Vermilion Boys Football League Cheerleaders, Abbeville, 1983—86; coach/asst. Vermilion Girls Basketball, Abbeville, 1985—87; cheerleader coach Milton Mid. Sch., 1992—2000; co-organizer, co-chair Wives of Workers, Tex. City, Tex., 1972—74; mem. Sch. Crisis Team, 2004. Nominee Outstanding Inclusion Tchr., Coun. for Exceptional Children, 1998—99, Tchr. award, Lafayette Edn. Found., 1999; recipient Coach's award, Universal Cheerleading Assn., 1999. Mem.: La. Tchrs. Math. (math tournament com., Prin.'s award com., sch. crisis team 2001), La. Fedn. Coun. Exceptional Children (state membership chair 2002—05, state exec. bd. 2001—04), Lafayette Paris Assn. Classroom Tchrs., La. Assn. Educators. Roman Catholic. Avocations: woodworking, motorcycling, travel. Home: 410 Quail Dr Lafayette LA 70508 Office: Paul Breaux Mid Sch Lafayette LA 70508

MARCEL-CALDERON, LINDA, music educator; m. Gene Calderon. MusB, Brigham Young U.; MusM, SUNY, Potsdam; EdD, Columbia U. Assoc. prof. music Bergen C.C., Paramus, NJ, 1987—. Author: Discover the Power of Music Listening, 2001. Recipient award, NISOD, 2005; Princeton U. fellow, 2005—. Mem.: Coll. Music Soc. Office: Bergen CC 400 Paramus Rd Paramus NJ 07652-1508 Office Phone: 201-447-7143. Business E-Mail: lmarcel@bergen.edu.

MARCH, KATHLEEN PATRICIA, judge; b. May 18, 1949; married; 2 children. BA, Colo. Coll., 1971; JD, Yale U., 1974. Bar: N.Y. 1975, Calif. 1978. Law clk. to hon. judge Thomas J. Griesa U.S. Dist. Ct. (so. dist.) N.Y., 1974-75; assoc. Cahill, Gordon & Reindel, N.Y.C., 1975-77; asst. U.S. atty. criminal div. Office of U.S. Atty. Cen. Dist. Calif., L.A., 1978-82; assoc. Adams, Duque & Hazeltine, L.A., 1982-85; ptnr. Demetriou, Del Guercio & Lovejoy, L.A., 1985-88; judge U.S. Bankruptcy Ct. Cen. Dist. Calif., L.A., Calif., 1988—. Bd. editors Yale U. Law Jour. Mem.: ABA, Fin. Lawyers Assn., L.A. Bankruptcy Forum (bd. dirs.), Nat. Assn. Women Judges, Women Lawyers Assn., L.A. County Bar Assn., Fed. Bar Assn., Phi Beta Kappa. Avocations: horseback riding, scuba diving, photography.

MARCHAK, MAUREEN PATRICIA, anthropology and sociology educator, academic administrator; b. Lethbridge, Alta., Can., June 22, 1936; d. Adrian Ebenezer and Wilhelmina Rankin (Hamilton) Russell; m. William Marchak, Dec. 31, 1956; children: Geordon Eric, Lauren Craig. BA, U. B.C., Vancouver, Can., 1958, PhD, 1970. Asst. prof. U. B.C., Vancouver, 1972-75, assoc. prof., 1975-80, prof., 1980—, head dept. anthropology and sociology, 1987-90, dean faculty arts, 1990-96, disting. scholar in residence Peter Wall Inst., 2000—, prof., dean emerita of arts, 2001—; sr. rsch. fellow Ctr. Internat. Rels. Liu Inst. for Study of Global Issues, 2002—, interim dir., 2005—06. Author: Ideological Perspectives on Canada, 1975, 2d edit., 1981, 3d edit., 1988, In Whose Interests, 1979, Green Gold, 1983 (John Porter award 1985), The Integrated Circus, The New Right and The Restructuring of Global Markets, 1991, Logging the Globe, 1995, Falldown, Forest Policy in British Columbia, 1999, Racism, Sexism and the University, the Political Science Affair at UBC, 1996, God's Assassins. State Terrorism in Argentina in the 1970's, 1999 (Wallace J. Ferguson prize, Hon. Mention), Reigns of Terror, 2003, Global Pieces, 2006; author, co-editor: Uncommon Property, 1987; mem. editl. bd. Can. Rev. Sociology and Anthropology, Montreal, 1971-74, Studies in Polit. Economy, Ottawa, Ont., Can., 1980-87, Current Sociology, 1980-86, Can. Jour. Sociology, 1986-90, B.C. Studies, 1988-90, 2000-04. Bd. dir., chair ethics com. Univ. Hosp., 1992-93; trustee Cedar Lodge Trust Soc., 1989-92; mem. adv. coun. Ecotrust, 1991-93, bd. dir., 1993-97, Eco-trust Can., 1995-99; chmn. bd. dir. B.C. Bldgs. Corp., 1992-95; mem. B.C. Forest Appeals Commn., 1992-2002; bd. govs. U. B.C., 1999-2001; bd. dir. Pub. Svc. Employees for Environ. Ethics, 2002-04; mem. sector study steering com. Can. Coun. Profl. Fish Harvesters, 2002—05. Named Woman of Distinction, YWCA, 1999. Fellow Royal Soc. Can. (v.p. Acad. II 1994-98, pres. Acad. II 1998-2000); mem. Can. Sociology and Anthropology Assn. (pres. 1979-80, other offices), Internat. Sociol. Assn., Can. Polit. Sci. Assn., Assn. for Can. Studies, Forest History Soc. (mem. exec. com. 1991-92). Avocations: hiking, swimming, travel, listening to music. Home: 4455 W 1st Ave Vancouver BC Canada V6R 4H9 E-mail: patricia.marchak@gmail.com.

MARCHESE, LISA MARIE, lawyer, educator; b. Seattle, Sept. 13, 1962; d. John Sebastian and Joanne Spino Marchese. BA, Cath. U. Am., 1984; JD, Georgetown U. Law Ctr., Washington, D.C., 1987. Bar: Wash. 1988, Oreg. 2003, U.S. Supreme Ct. 1998, U.S. Dist. Ct. (ea. and we. dists.) Wash. 1998, U.S. Ct. Appeals (9th cir.) 2003. Legis. counsel Hon. Daniel J. Evans, Washington, 1983—88; sr. dep. pros. atty. King County Prosecutor's Office, Seattle, 1989—98; ptnr. Stafford Frey Cooper, 1998—2006, Dorsey & Whitney LLP, Seattle, 2006—. Adj. law prof. U. Wash. Law Sch., 1999—, Seattle U. Sch. Law, 2000—; faculty mem. Nat. Inst. Trial Advocacy, 1999—; bd. mem. Wash. Women Lawyers, 2000—02; spkr. in field. Contbr. articles to various law jours. Mem.: Washington Women Lawyers, Phi Beta Kappa. Roman Cath. Avocations: sports, opera, reading, golf. Office: Dorsey & Whitney LLP 45 Bank Centre 1420 Fifth Ave 3400 Seattle WA 98101 Office Phone: 206-903-2379. Business E-Mail: marchese.lisa@dorsey.com.

MARCHESSEAULT, ANITA, music educator; b. Moosup, Conn., June 15, 1917; d. Henry Marchesseault and Rose Brault; ptnr. Anita. MusB, Laval U., 1950; MusM, Boston U., 1957, D Mus. Arts, 1970. Cert. music tchr. Music tchr. Schs. of Mt. Royal, Montreal, Que., Canada, 1935-52; prof. music, piano and organ tchr., band dir. Notre Dame Coll., Manchester, NH, 1952—. Ch. organist, pvt. piano tchr., Manchester, 1952—. Recipient Key to City. Mem. Music Tchrs. Nat. Assn. (cert. chair 1968—), N.H. Music Tchrs. Assn. (Music Tchr. of Yr. 1970). Home: 357 Island Pond Rd #1 Manchester NH 03109

MARCHETTI-PONTE, KARIN, lawyer, land conservation consultant; b. Devens, Mass., Nov. 3, 1951; d. Robert Joseph and Patricia (Morico) M.; children: Haley Warden, Henry Warden, Chrisopher W. Kaiser. BA summa cum laude, U. Maine, 1975, JD, 1978. Bar: Maine, 1979, Maine, 1979. Reporter Sta. WGBH-TV, Portland, Maine, 1978-79; news anchorperson Sta. WMTW-TV, Poland Spring, Maine, 1977-78; atty., founder Advocates, Inc., Portland, 1979-80; assoc. corp. counsel City of Portland, 1980-83; vol. Peace Corps, Tunisia, 1983-84; gen. counsel, clk. Maine Coast Heritage Trust, Topsham, Maine, 1985—; prin. Land Conservation Legal Svcs., Bernard, Maine, 1992—. Spkr. Land Trust Alliance, 1988—, Lincoln Inst., 1992, Nat. Land Conservation Leadership Program, Washington, 1997—, Georgetown U. Law Taxings Conf. Co-author: Conserving Land with Conservation Easements, 1999, Conservation Easement Handbook, Easement Drafting Guide, 2005. Office: Land Conservation Legal Svcs PO Box 100 Bernard ME 04612-0100 also: Maine Coast Heritage Trust Topsham ME 04086 also: PO Box 100 Bernard ME 04612-0100 Office Phone: 207-244-5100.

MARCHUK, PAMELA ANN, retired elementary school educator; d. Chester Joseph and Rose Felicia Marchuk. BS, Cen. Mich. U., Mt. Pleasant, 1973, MA, 1982. Provisional cert. State Dept., Mich., continuing cert. State Dept., Mich., 30-hr. continuing cert. State Dept., Mich. Substitute tchr. pub. schs., Clio, Montrose, Birch Run, Chesaning, Mich., 1973—77; elem. tchr. Montrose (Mich.) Cmty. Schs., 1977—2002; ret. Coord. asst. to prin. - integrated visual learning Carter Elem. Sch., Montrose, 1995—97. Active Montrose United Meth. Ch.; chaperone Spl. Olympics, Mt. Pleasant, 1982; judge Genesee County Sr. Winter Olympics Spelling Bee, Flushing, 2002—05; local coord. Grand Rapids Acad. Summer Program, Montrose, 1993—98. Mem.: Nat. Coun. Tchrs. of Math., Mich. Coun. Tchrs. of Math., Internat. Reading Assn. (Celebrate Literacy award 1995), Mich. Reading Assn. (spkr., check-in asst. to chair conf. 1997—, presenter 2002, bd. mem. 2003—), Flint Area Reading Coun. (sch. rep. 1988—2002, planning and registration of young authors' conf. 1992—2004, treas. 1996—), Mich. Assn. Ret. Sch. Pers. (life), Flint Geneal. Soc., Delta Kappa Gamma Soc. Internat. (treas. 2005—, Alpha Iota state, Alpha Omega chpt.). Avocations: reading, needlecrafts, travel, genealogy.

MARCIL, VANESSA, actress; b. Indio, Calif., Oct. 15, 1969; 1 child, Kassius Lijah Marcil-Green. Actor: (TV series) General Hospital, 1992—98, 2000, 2002—03, Beverly Hills, 90210, 1998—2000, Las Vegas, 2003—; (films) The Undertaker, 1995, The Rock, 1996, 976-WISH, 1997, Nice Guys Sleep Alone, 1999, This Space Between Us, 2000, Storm Watch, 2002, Fish Without a Bicycle, 2003; (TV films) To Love, Honor, and Deceive, 1996, The Superstars, 1998; host ABC in Concert, 1991. Office: c/o Innovative Artists 1505 Tenth St Santa Monica CA 90401

MARCINEK, MARGARET ANN, nursing education administrator; b. Uniontown, Pa., Sept. 29, 1948; d. Joseph Hugh and Evelyn (Bailey) Boyle; m. Bernard Francis Marcinek, Aug. 11, 1973; 1 child, Cara Ann. RN, Uniontown Hosp., 1969; BSN, Pa. State U., 1970; MSN, U. Md., 1973; EdD, W.Va. U., 1983. Staff nurse Presbyn. U., Pitts., 1970-71; instr. nursing W.Va. U., Morgantown, 1973-77, asst. prof., 1977-80, assoc. prof., 1980-83, California U. Pa., 1983-87, prof., 1987—2004, dept. chmn., 1985—2004, assoc. provost, 2004—. Program evaluator Commn. on Collegiate Nursing Edn.; mem. adv. coun. In Home Health, Inc.; mem. adv. coun. Albert Gallatin VNA. Contbg. author: Critical Care Nursing; contbr. articles to profl. jours. Mem.: ANA, Commn. on Collegiate Nursing Edn. (site evaluator), Oncology Nursing Soc., Sigma Theta Tau. Business E-Mail: marcinek@cup.edu.

MARCO, PATRICIA LOUISE, music educator; b. New Kensington, PA, July 23, 1947; d. Adam Paul and Mary Louise Chovanes; m. Donald Anthony Marco; children: Maria, Christina, Adam. BS, Ind. U. of Pa., 1969. Tchr., band dir. Kiski Area Sch. Dist., Vandergrift, Pa., 1969—. Founder Kiski Valley Cmty. Band, dir. Founding dir. Kiski Valley Cmty. Band. Recipient Disting. Citizen award, Leechburg Elks, 2002, Citation of Execellence award, Music Educators Assn., 2005. Mem.: Pa. State Edn. Assn., Music Educators Nat. Conf., Assn. Concert Bands, Women Band Dirs. Internat., Delta Kappa Gamma.

MARCOLINA, KATHRYN WATKINS, personal and professional success coach; b. West Chester, Pa., Jan. 17, 1959; d. Dwain Joseph and Kathryn Gertrude (Wood) W.; m. Peter Jerome Marcolina, Feb. 11, 1984. BS in Edn., U. Del., Newark, 1981; MSW, Bryn Mawr (Pa.) Coll., 1985. Cert clin. social worker, N.C. Family therapist Family Svc. Burlington County, Mt. Holly, N.J., 1985-89, Family Svc. Lower Cape Fear, Wilmington, N.C., 1989-90, The Parkside Clinic, Wilmington, 1990-96, Cape Fear Pschol. and Psychiat. Svcs., Wilmington, 1996-97; student counselor U. N.C., Wilmington, 1997-98; personal and profl. success coach Wrightsville Beach, NC, 2000—. Mem. NASW (chairperson local chpt. 1992), Acad. Cert. Social Workers, N.C. Cert. Bd. Social Work. Avocations: protection of sea turtles and wetlands, environmental awareness, study of nutrition, health and healing. Home: 2301-F Cordgrass Bay Wrightsville Beach NC 28480

MARCOULLIS, ERATO KOZAKOU, ambassador; b. Limassol, Cyprus, Aug. 3, 1949; m. George Marcoullis; 1 child, Panos. Degree in law, U. Athens, Greece, 1972; degree in pub. law and polit. scis., Dept. Pub. Law and Polit. Scis., 1975; PhD Social Scis., U. Helsinki, Finland, 1979. Practice law, 1973—74; advisor Permanent Mission of Cyprus UN, 1980—83, attaché Permanent Mission of Cyprus, 1983—88; consulate gen. Cyprus, 1982—83; amb. extraordinary and plenipotentiary with concurrent accreditation to Finland, Lithuania, Latvia, Sweden, Iceland, Norway, Denmark, and Estonia, 1996—98; mem. 1st polit. divsn. Cyprus question Ministry Fgn. Affairs, 1989—93, dir. office of permanent sec., 1993—96, amb. extraordinary and plenipontentiary to U.S. with concurrent accreditation to Can., Brazil, Guyana, Jamaica Washington, 1998—2003. Office: Embassy of Cyprus 2211 R St NW Washington DC 20008

MARCOUX, JULIA A., midwife; b. St. Helens, Eng., Aug. 7, 1928; d. Robert Patrick and Margaret Mary Theresa (White) Ashall; m. Albert Marcoux, Apr. 23, 1955; children: Stephen, Ann Marie, Richard, Michael, Maureen, Patrick, Margaret, Julie. Diploma, Withington Hosp., Manchester, England, 1950; grad., Cowley Hill Hosp., St. Helens, England, 1952; BS in Pub. Adminstrn., St. Joseph's Coll. RN, Conn.; lic. midwife, Conn. Nurse, labor, delivery rm. and nursery Day Kimbal Hosp., Putnam, Conn.; sch. nurse Marianapolis Prep. Sch., Thompson, Conn.; occupational nurse U.S. Post Office, Hartford, Conn.; pvt. duty and gerontology nurse Conn. Cons. in field. Contbr. articles to profl. jours. Named Internat. Cath. Family of Yr., 1982.

MARCUCCIO, PHYLLIS ROSE, retired educational association administrator, editor; b. Hackensack, N.J., Aug. 25, 1933; d. Filippo and Rose (Henry) Marcuccio. AB, Bucknell U., 1955; MA, George Washington U., 1976. Trainee Time, Inc., 1956—57; art prodn. for mags. of Med. Econs., Inc., 1958—60; mem. staff Nat. Sci. Tchrs. Assn., Washington, 1961—99; assoc. editor Sci. and Children, 1963, editor, 1964—93, dir. divsn. elem. edn., 1974—78, dir. divsn. program devel. and continuing edn., 1978—83, pub., 1993—99; dir. publs. Nat. Sci. Tchrs. Assn., 1983—99, assoc. exec. dir., 1990—99; pub. Dragonfly, 1996—99. Lectr., cons. in field. Author (photographer, illustrator numerous articles); co-author: Investigation in Ecology, 1972; editor: Science Fun, 1977, Science Fun, 2d edit., 1994; Selected Readings for Students of English as a Second Language, 1966; compiler: Opportunities for Summer Studies in Elementary Science, 1968, Opportunities for Summer Studies in Elementary Science, 2d edit., 1969, pub.: Sci. and Children, 1993—99, Dragonfly Mag., 1997—99. Apptd. commr. Rockville (Md.) Housing Authority, 1981—91, chairperson, 1984—86; bd. dirs. Nat. Sci. Resource Ctr., NAS, 1986—96, Hands on Sci. Outreach, Inc., 1991—2001; pres. East Rockville Civic Assn., 2000—; elected mem. City Coun. of Rockville, 2005—. Recipient Citizenship medal, DAR, 1951, Golden Lamp award, Edpress, 1998. Mem.: AAAS, NSTA (life), Pocono Environ. Edn. Ctr. (bd. dirs. 1989—98), Sci. Tchg. Assn. N.Y. (Outstanding Svc. to Sci. Edn. award 1987), Ednl. Press Assn. Am. (regional dir. 1969—71, sec. 1979—, Disting. Achievement award 1969, 1971—74, 1976, 1977, Eleanor Fishburn award 1978, Disting. Achievement award 1980, 1988, 1993, 1995), The Washington Forum, Washington edn. Press Assn. (treas. 1966—67, pres. 1975—76), Ohio Coun. Elem. Sch. Sci. (life), Nat. Assn. Industry Edn. Coop. (bd. dirs. 1980—86), Nat. Press Club (Silver Owl), Am. Nature Study Soc., Coun. Elem. Sci. Internat. (Internat. award for outstanding contbns. sci. edn. 1971, 1972, 1986, 1994), Kiwanis Internat., Sigma Delta Chi, Phi Delta Kappa, Phi Delta gamma, Theta Alpha Phi. Home: 406 S Horners Ln Rockville MD 20850-1556 E-mail: marcu@erols.com.

MARCUM, DEANNA BOWLING, library administrator; b. Salem, Ind., Aug. 5, 1946; d. Anderson and Ruby (Mobley) Bowling; m. Thomas P. Marcum, June 13, 1974; 1 child, Ursula. BA, U. Ill., 1967; MA, So. Ill. U., 1969; MLS, U. Ky., 1971; PhD, U. Md., 1991. Tchr. Deland-Weldon (Ill.) High Sch., 1967-68; instr. English U. Ky., Lexington, 1969-70, cataloging librarian, 1970-73, asst. to dir., 1973-74; asst. dir. pub. svcs. Joint U. Librs., Nashville, 1974-77; mgmt. tng. specialist Assn. Rsch. Librs., Washington, 1977-80; sr. cons. Info. Systems Cons., Inc., Washington, 1980-81; v.p. Coun. on Libr. Resources, Washington, 1981-89; dean Sch. Libr. and Info. Sch. Cath. U., Washington, 1989-92; dir. pub. svcs. and collections mgmt. Libr. of Congress, Washington, 1993-95, assoc. libr., 2003—; pres. Coun. on Libr. Resources and Info., Washington, 1995—2003. Adv. bd. So. Edn. Found., Atlanta, 1986-91; chmn. grants com. Coun. on Libr. resources, Washington, 1990-94. Author: Good Books in a Country Home, 1993, Development of Digital Libaries, An American Perspective, 2001, Digital Library Development: View from Kanazawa, 2005; co-author: (with Richard Boss) The Library Catalog, 1980, On-Line Acquisitions Systems, 1981; contbr. articles to profl. jours. Pres., Commn. on Preservation and Access, 1995—. Mem. ALA, Am. Studies Assn., Orgn. Am. Historians, Am. Antiquarian Soc. (adv. bd. 1989—), Beta Phi Mu, Phi Kappa Phi. Home: 3315 Wake Dr Kensington MD 20895-3218 Office: Coun on Libr and Info Resources Ste 500 1755 Massachusetts Ave NW Washington DC 20036-2124 Office Phone: 202-707-6240. E-mail: dmarcum@loc.gov.

MARCUS, ABIR A., psychiatrist; arrived in US, 1995; d. Assaad Aziz Abdel-Sayed and Nadra Nassry Soriall; divorced; 1 child, Gina Marie. MD with honors, Ain Shams U., Cairo, 1991. Diplomate Am. Bd. Psychiatry and Neurology, Am. Bd. Med. Specialties, lic. psychiatrist NJ, NY. Intern Ain Shams Med. Sch., Cairo, 1992—93, instr. forensic medicine and toxicology, 1994—95; resident in psychiatry NJ Med. Sch., Newark, 1996—2000; fellow, asst. prof. Robert Wood Johnson, Piscataway, NJ, 2000—01; pvt. practice Hazlet, NJ, 1999—. Adj. asst. prof. Robert Wood Johnson Med. Sch., Piscataway, 2001—; task force com. for curriculum devel. in psychotherapy tng. for residents U. Medicine and Dentistry NJ Med. Sch., Newark, 1999—2000; cons. CPC Behavioral Health Care, Red Bank, NJ, 2001—; cons. in field. Contbr. articles to profl. jours. Recipient Physician's Recognition award, AMA, 1999, 2005; scholar, Nat. Inst. Drug Abuse. Mem.: Am. Psychiatric Assn. (assoc. mem.), Neurosci. Edn. Inst., Am. Soc. Clin. Psychopharmacology, NJ Psychiat. Assn. (pres. resident chpt. 1999, pres. 2000, early career psychiatry com., pub. edn. com., disaster preparedness com., resident and med. student com.), Am. Psychiat. Assn., Am. Acad. Addiction Psychiatry, Am. Soc. Addiction Medicine. Avocations: reading, travel, ballroom dancing, salsa dancing. Office: Unit 2C 34 Sycamore Ave Little Silver NJ 07739 Office Phone: 917-204-5960. Personal E-mail: abirmarcus@aol.com.

MARCUS, ADRIANNE STUHL, writer; b. Everett, Mass., Mar. 7, 1935; d. George Zachariah and Edith Delores (Cohen) Stuhl; m. Warren M. Marcus (div. 1981); children: Stacey Ann, Shelby Alice, Sarah Naomi; m. Ian Holroyde Wilson. AB, San Francisco State U., 1955, MA, 1961. Poet, 1955—; tchr. Coll. of Marin, 1965-79; food columnist San Francisco Chronicle, 1985-87; writer, 1968—. Author: The Moon is a Marrying Eye, 1969, The Chocolate Bible, 1975, Magritte's Stones, 2001, The Resurrection of Trotsky, 2004; co-author: Carrion House World of Gifts, 1980 Fellow Ossabaw, 1982, Yaddo Corp., 1985, Va. Ctr. for Creative Arts, 1993-95-97. Mem. PEN, Acad. Am. Poets, Assn. Food Journalists, Overseas Press Club. Democrat. Jewish. Home and Office: 79 Twin Oaks Ave San Rafael CA 94901-1915 Office Phone: 415-454-6062. Personal E-mail: medea999@aol.com.

MARCUS, BECCA NIMMER, psychotherapist; b. LA, Aug. 6, 1948; d. Melville Bernard and Gloria Dee (Madoff) Nimmer; m. Paul Marcus, Dec. 22, 1968; children: Emily, Beth, Daniel. Cert. de Français, École Internat. de Genève, 1966; BA summa cum laude, UCLA, 1970; MSW, U. Ill., 1982. Tchr. Los Angeles City Schs., 1970-73; intern therapist Champaign (Ill.) County Mental Health Ctr., 1982; adj. faculty mem., counselor San Diego State U., 1983; family therapist Adlerian Family Counseling, Tucson, 1983-86; pvt. practice psychotherapy Tucson, 1986-91; therapist Coll. William and Mary Counseling Ctr., Williamsburg, Va., 1991—. Mem. adv. com. sex. edn. Catalina Foothills Sch. Dist., 1984; bd. dirs. Champaign County Mental Health Ctr., 1979-82; interviewer Adult Diversion Program, Champaign, 1976-77. Mem. Nat. Assn. Social Workers, Ariz. Assn. Social Workers, Adlerian Soc. Ariz., Alpha Delta Mu. Avocation: travel. Home: 109 Sheriffs Pl Williamsburg VA 23185-4921 Office: Coll William and Mary Counseling Ctr Blow Hall Williamsburg VA 23185-4921

MARCUS, CAROL A., information technology manager; b. Chgo., Ill. AA, Coll of Du Page, 1978; BS, Elmhurst Coll., 1992; MBA, Dominican U., 1998. From merchandising application devel. to info. tech. project mgr. Ace Hardware Corp., Oak Brook, Ill., 1979—2001, info. tech. project mgr., 2001—. Cons. in hist. preservation. Chmn. Villa Pk. Hist. Preservation Commn., Villa Park, Ill., 1985—. Mem.: Microsoft Project User Group,

Project Mgmt. Inst., Nat. Trust, Chgo. Architecture Found., Ill. Assn. Historic Preservation Commn. (chmn. 1998—), Villa Park His. Soc. (v.p. 1986—). Republican. Roman Catholic. Avocations: history, gardening, travel, photography, architecture. Office: Ace Hardware Corp 2200 Kensington Ct Oak Brook IL 60523-2100

MARCUS, CYNTHIA ANN, lawyer; b. Corona, Calif., Apr. 15, 1954; d. Paul A. and Marye A. Newcombe; m. Edward S. Marcus, July 27, 1986; children: Tamara, Benjamin. At, U. Mich., Ann Arbor, 1972—74; AS in Nursing, Grand Rapids Jr. Coll., Mich., 1981; BSN, Ball State U., Muncie, Ind., 1991; JD, Ind. U., Indpls., 1994. RN, 1981—94; assoc. York, Schrager, Baxter, Indpls., 1995—2002; sole practitioner Marcus Law Firm, Fishers, 2002—. Guardian Ad Litem Hamilton County, Ind., 2003—; bd. mem. Hoosier H.S. Hockey Assn., Fishers, 2004—, Ind. State Hockey Assn., Indpls., 2004—. Capt. USAR, 1976—91. Mem.: Ind. Trial Lawyers Assn., Am. Trial Lawyers Assn., Indpls. State Bar Assn. (mem. legal svc. adv. com. 2005—), Ind. State Bar Assn. (mem. ethics com. 2005—). Office: Marcus Law Firm 11978 Fishers Crossing Dr Fishers IN 46038-2702

MARCUS, DEVRA JOY COHEN, internist; b. Bronx, N.Y., Sept. 5, 1940; d. Benjamin and Gertrude (Siegel) Cohen; m. Robert A. Marcus, Apr. 1963 (div. 1974); children: Rachel, Adam; m. Michael J. Horowitz, Mar. 2, 1975; 1 child, Naomi. BA, Brandeis U., 1961; MD, Stanford U., 1966. Diplomate Am. Bd. Internal Medicine. Intern Stanford U., 1966-67, resident in internal medicine, 1967-68; gen. internist D.C. Dept. Pub. Health, 1968-69, Cardozo Neighborhood Health Ctr., Washington, 1969-73; med. dir. East of the River Health Assn., Washington, 1973-75; fellow in infectious disease Washington Hosp. Ctr., 1975-77; gen. internist Police and Fire Clinic, Washington, 1977-78; pvt. practice Washington, 1977—; assoc. clin. prof. medicine George Washington U. Med Ctr., Washington, 1978—; gen. internist World Bank, Washington, 1978-81; ptnr. Traveller's Med. Svc. D.C., 1980-82; gen. internist Community of Good Hope Med. Clinic, Washington, 1984-85; assoc. clin. prof. medicine Georgetown U. Med. Ctr., Washington, 1987—. Preceptor Georgetown U. Hosp., 1986—; med. missions to Honduras, 2001, Romania, 2002, Dominican Republic, 2004, 05, 06, China, 2005. Contbr. articles to profl. jours. Exec. com. Woodley Park Citizen's Assn., 1979-80; chair mayor's adv. com. on prevention, 1982-83; bd. dirs. Exodus Youth Svcs., 1987-89. Named Best Physicians of Washington, Washingtonian Mag., 1999, 2005 Fellow: ACP; mem.: AMA (Physicians Recognition award 1981, 1984, 1987, 1990, 1993, 1996, 1999, 2002, 2005), Physicians for Human Rights (asylum applications), Med. Soc. D.C. (founder com. on women 1983, pres. com. on women 1985—87, med. ethics and judiciary com. 1987—91, judiciary coun. 1992—96, credentials com., communicable disease com.). Home: 1205 Crest Ln Mc Lean VA 22101-1837 Office: 1145 19th St NW Ste 510 Washington DC 20036-

MARCUS, JOYCE (JOYCE MARCUS FLANNERY), anthropology educator; Student, U. Calif., Berkeley; MS, PhD, Harvard U. Prof. of anthropology, mus. anthropology U. Mich., Ann Arbor, curator, Latin American Archaeology. Serves on Smithsonian Coun. Contbr. articles to profl. jours. Mem.: Am. Acad. Arts and Sciences, NAS (mem. gov. coun. 2005—). Office: U Mich 101 West Hall 1092 Ann Arbor MI 48109 Office Phone: 734-763-5164. Business E-Mail: joymar@umich.edu.

MARCUS, KAREN MELISSA, language educator; b. Vancouver, BC, Can., Feb. 28, 1956; arrived in U.S., 1962; d. Marvin Marcus and Arlen Ingrid (Sahlman) Bishop; m. Jorge Esteban Mezei, Jan. 7, 1984 (div. Mar. 1987). BA in French, BA in Polit. Sci., U. Calif., Santa Barbara, 1978, MA in Polit. Sci., 1981; MA in French, Stanford (Calif.) U., 1984, PhD in French, 1990. Lectr. French Stanford U., 1989—90; asst. prof. No. Ariz. U., Flagstaff, 1990—96, assoc. prof., 1996—2004, prof., 2004—. Cons. Houghton Mifflin, 1993, Grand Canyon (Ariz.) Natural History Soc., 1994. Vol., letter writer Amnesty Internat. Urgent Action Network, 1991—95; vol. No. Ariz. AIDS Outreach Orgn., Flagstaff, 1994—95. Named Scholarship Exch. Student, U. Geneva, 1979—80; recipient medal for Outstanding Achievement in French, Alliance Française, Santa Barbara, 1978; Doctoral fellow, Stanford U., 1981—85. Mem.: MLA, Coordination Internat. des Chercheurs sur les Litteratures Maghrebines, Women in French, Am. Lit. Translators Assn., Am. Coun. Tchg. Fgn. Langs., Am. Assn. Tchrs. French, Phi Beta Kappa, Alpha Lambda Delta, Pi Delta Phi. Democrat. Jewish. Avocations: walking, yoga, reading, writing short stories. Office: No Ariz Univ Modern Lang Dept PO Box 6004 Flagstaff AZ 86011-6004 Office Phone: 928-523-6781. Business E-Mail: melissa.marcus@nau.edu.

MARCUS, KELLY STEIN, psychologist, health science association administrator; b. Baltimore, Md., July 11, 1968; d. Anthony Alan and Barbara Marlene Stein; m. Matthew Alexander Marcus, May 23, 1999; 1 child, Samantha Haleigh. MA, MEd, Columbia U., 1991—93; PhD, Yeshiva U./Ferkauf Grad. Sch. Psychology, Bronx, NY, 1993—98. Cert. psychologist NY, 1999, Pa., 2000. Med. sci. mgr., neuroscience divsn. Bristol-Myers Squibb, Co., Philadelphia, Pa., 2001—; assoc. rsch. scientist Yale U. Sch. Medicine, New Haven, 1999—2003; attending psychologist Thomas Jefferson U. Hosp. Dept. Psychiatry, Philadelphia, Pa., 2000—01; attending psychologist, dept. anesthesiology Thomas Jefferson U. Sch. Medicine, Jefferson Pain Ctr., Philadelphia, Pa., 2000—01; post doctoral fellow Yale Sch. Medicine, Dept. Psychiatry, New Haven, 1998—99; psychologist Assn. for the Help of Retarded Children, New York, NY, 1994—2000; med. dir. Healthcare Mktg. Sys. Cardinal Health, 2000—. Prin. investigator Young Investigator Grant, Yale Sch. Medicine, New Haven, 1999—2003; ad hoc reviewer Annals of Internal Medicine, 2000—03. Contbr. articles to medical jours. Recipient Young Investigator Award, Nat. Alliance for Rsch. in Schizophrenia and Depression, 1999, Leadership Award, Bristol-Myers Squibb, Co. Neuroscience Med. Sci. Divsn., 2002; fellow Pre-Doctoral Fellowship, Meml. Sloan Kettering Cancer Ctr., Nat. Inst. Mental Health, 1994-1997. Mem.: APA. Democrat-Npl. Jewish. Avocations: running, creative arts.

MARCUS, LINDA SUSAN, dermatologist; b. Bklyn. d. Nathaniel and Eugenia (Portnay) Marcus; m. Ronald Carlin, July 5, 1976; children: Robert Adam, Neal Marc. BS, Adelphi U., Garden City, N.J., 1970; MD, Downstate Med. Sch., Bklyn., 1975. Diplomate Am. Bd. Dermatology. Intern Long Island (N.Y.) Jewish Med. Ctr., 1975-76; resident in dermatology Columbia-St. Luke's, N.Y.C., 1976-77, Boston U.-Tufts U., 1977-79; pvt. practice Wyckoff, NJ, 1980—. Dir. dermatology Valley Hosp., Ridgewood. Contbr. articles to profl. jours. Mem. Am. Acad. Dermatology (editor pamphlet editl. bd.), Am. Soc. Dermatol. Surgeons, Internat. Soc. Dermatol. Surgeons, N.J. Dermatol. Soc. (program dir.), N.J. North Dermatol. Soc. (co-chair), Dermatol. Soc. of NJ (pres.). Avocations: swimming, ice skating. Office: 271 Godwin Ave Wyckoff NJ 07481-2057 Office Phone: 201-891-4373. Personal E-mail: sexyderm@earthlink.com.

MARCUS, MARIA LENHOFF, lawyer, educator; b. Vienna, June 23, 1933; came to U.S., 1938, naturalized, 1944; d. Arthur and Clara (Gruber) Lenhoff; m. Norman Marcus, Dec. 23, 1956; children: Valerie, Nicole, Eric. BA, Oberlin Coll., 1954; JD, Yale Law Sch., 1957. Bar: N.Y. 1961, U.S. Dist. Ct. (so. and ea. dists.) N.Y. 1962, U.S. Ct. Appeals (2d cir.) 1962, U.S. Supreme Ct. 1964. Assoc. counsel NAACP, N.Y.C., 1961-67; asst. atty. gen. N.Y. State, N.Y.C., 1967-78; chief litigation bur. Atty. Gen. N.Y. State, 1976-78; adj. assoc. prof. NYU Law Sch., 1976-78; assoc. prof. Fordham U. Law Sch., N.Y.C., 1978-86, prof., 1986—, Joseph M. McLaughlin prof., 1997—. Arbitrator Nat. Assn. Securities Dealers; chair subcom. interrogatories U.S. Dist. Ct. (so. dist.) N.Y., 1983-85. Contbr. articles to profl. jours. Named Tchr. of Yr., Fordham Law School Students, 2001. Fellow N.Y. Bar Found.; mem. Assn. Bar City of N.Y. (v.p. 1995-96, long range planning com. 1996-2000, exec. com. 1976-80, com. audit 1988-95, labor com. 1981-84, judiciary com. 1975-76, chmn. civil rights com. 1972-75), N.Y. State Bar Assn. (exec. com. 1979-81, ho. dels. 1978-81, com. constitution and by-laws 1984-93), N.Y. Women's Bar Assn. (Pres.'s award 1999). Office: Fordham U Law Sch 140 W 62nd St New York NY 10023-7485

MARCUS, RUTH BARCAN, philosopher, educator, writer, lecturer; b. NYC; d. Samuel and Rose (Post) Barcan; divorced; children: James Spencer, Peter Webb, Katherine Hollister, Elizabeth Post. BA, NYU, 1941; MA, Yale U., 1942, PhD, 1946; DLH (hon.), U. Ill., 1995. Rsch. assoc. in anthropology Inst. for Human Relations, Yale U., New Haven, Conn., 1945-47; AAUW fellow U. Chgo., 1947-48; vis. prof. (intermittently) Northwestern U., 1950-57, Guggenheim fellow, 1953-54; asst. prof., assoc. prof. Roosevelt U., Chgo., 1957-63; NSF fellow, 1963-64; prof. philosophy U. Ill. at Chgo., 1963-70, head philosophy dept., 1963-69; fellow U. Ill. Center for Advanced Study, 1968-69; prof. philosophy Northwestern U., 1970-73; Reuben Post Halleck prof. philosophy Yale U., 1973-93; sr. rsch. scholar, 1994—. Fellow Ctr. Advanced Study in Behavioral Sci., Stanford, Calif., 1979; vis. fellow Inst. Advanced Study, U. Edinburgh, 1983, Wolfson Coll., Oxford U., 1985, 86; vis. fellow Clare Hall, Cambridge U., 1988, lifetime mem. coll. room, 1989—; past or present mem. adv. coms. Princeton U., MIT, Calif. Inst. Tech., Cornell U. Humanities Ctr., Columbia U., UCLA, Ohio State U., U. Calif. Santa Barbara, Carnegie Mellon, Brown U., U. Va., U. Tex., others; disting. vis. prof. U. Calif., Irvine, 1995—. Author: Modalities, 1993; editor: The Logical Enterprise, 1975, Logic Methodology and Philosophy of Science VII, 1986; mem. editorial bd. Past or Present Metaphilosophy, Monist, Philos. Studies, Signs, Jour. Symbolic Logic, The Philosophers Annual; editor, contbr. to profl. jours. and books. Recipient Machette prize for contbn. to profession; Medal, College de France, 1986, Wilbur Cross medal Yale U., 2000; Mellon sr. fellow Nat. Humanities Ctr., 1992-93; vis. disting. prof. U. Calif., Irvine, 1994, 96, 97, 98, 99, 2000; fellow Conn. Acad. Arts and Scis. Fellow Am. Acad. Arts and Scis.; mem. Coun. on Philos. Studies (pres. 1988-90), Assn. for Symbolic Logic (past exec. coun., exec. com. 1973-83, v.p. 1980-82, coun. 1980-85, pres. 1982-84), Am. Philos. Assn. (past sec., treas., nat. bd. dirs. 1977-83, pres. ctrl. divsn. 1975-78, chmn. nat. bd. officers 1977-85), Philosophy of Sci. Assn., Inst. Internat. Philosophie (past exec. com., v.p. 1983-86, pres. 1990-93, hon. pres. 1994—), Fedn. Internat. Philosophy (exec. com., steering com. 1985-99), Elizabethan Club (v.p. 1989, pres. 1989-90), Phi Beta Kappa. Office: Yale U Dept Philosophy PO Box 208306 New Haven CT 06520-8306 E-mail: ruth.marcus@yale.edu.

MARCUSS, ROSEMARY DALY, economist; b. Stamford, Conn., Aug. 27, 1945; d. Eugene Lawrence and Margaret Mary (Murphy) Daly; B.A. in Econs. cum laude, Newton (Mass.) Coll., 1967; M.S., U. Md., 1973, Ph.D., 1979; m. Stanley J. Marcuss, July 6, 1968; children— Elena Daly, Aidan Stanley. Jr. staff economist President's Council of Econ. Advisers, 1968-70; economist, asst. to pres. Am. Fedn. State, County and Mcpl. Employees, Washington, 1973; economist, mgmt. cons. Data Resources, Inc., Washington, 1974-78; dep. asst. dir. tax analysis Congressional Budget Office, Washington, 1980-83, asst. dir. tax analysis, 1983-98; dep. dir. Bur. Econ. Analysis, Washington, 1998—; pres. Nat. Assn Bus. Econ., 2005-. NSF fellow, 1970-73. Mem. Am. Econ. Assn., Nat. Tax Assn., Tax Inst. Am., So. Econ. Assn., Soc. Govt. Economists, Nat. Economists Club, Nat. Assn. Business Economists (v.p. 2003-), Washington Women Economists. Home: 4616 29th Pl NW Washington DC 20008-2105 Office: Congressional Budget Office 2nd & D Sts SW Washington DC 20515-0001

MARCUSSEN, CARIN LEIGH, lawyer; b. Millington, Tex., Oct. 31, 1977; d. Raymond Erling and Reda Jo Marcussen. BSc, Okla. State U., Stillwater, 2000; JD with honors, U. Okla., Norman, 2003. Bar: Okla. 2003. Intern Whitten, Nelson, McGuire, Terry & Roselius, Okla. City, 2001—03, assoc. atty., 2003—. Coord. Queen Pagent Okla. H.S. Rodeo Assn., Woodward, 2004. Cadet Acad. USAF, 1996—97, Colo. Named Miss Okla., H.S. Rodeo, 1994, 1995. Mem.: Okla. Bar Assn., Assn. Trial Lawyers Am., Phi Alpha Delta. Avocations: horseback riding, sewing, painting, travel. Office: Whitten Neslon McGuire Terry & Roselius 211 N Robinson Ste 400N Oklahoma City OK 73102 Office Phone: 405-239-2522. Office Fax: 405-239-2573. Business E-Mail: cmarcussen@whitten-nelson.com.

MARCZINSKI, CECILE ANNE, psychologist, researcher; b. Barrie, Ont., Can., Aug. 23, 1973; arrived in US, 2002; d. Charles August Edward Marczinski and Hilde Edith Lorenz; m. Christopher Scott Horn, Nov. 3, 2001. BSc. U. We. Ont., 1996; PhD, McMaster U., 2001. Post doctoral fellow U. Ky., 2002, St. Joseph Hosp., London, Canada, 2003, U. Ky., 2004, Nat. Inst. Drug Abuse, U. Ky., 2005—. Cons. editor Exptl. and Clin. Psychopharmacology Jour., 2004—; contbr. articles to profl. jours. Recipient Age Plus prize, Can. Inst. for Health Rsch. Initiative on Aging, 2004. Mem.: Psychonomic Soc., Am. Psychol. Soc., Rsch. Soc. on Alcoholism. Lutheran. Home: 7190 Highpoint Dr Florence KY 41042 Office: U Ky Kastle Hall Lexington KY 40506 Office Phone: 859-257-4977. Business E-Mail: cecile.marczinski@uky.edu.

MARDER, CAROL, advertising specialist and premium firm executive; b. Bklyn., Sept. 20, 1941; d. Simon and Sylvia (Rothstein) Cohen; m. Edwin Marder, Apr. 15, 1961; children: Elisa, Steven Alan, Susan. Prin. owner Boys Ego Retail Clothing, Englishtown, NJ, 1974-76; pres. Motivators, Inc., Old Bridge, NJ, 1976-83, Inkwell Promotions Corp., Morganville, NJ, 1983—. Cons. Specialty Advt. of N.Y., 1988—. Recipient citation Monmouth County Bd. Recreation Commrs., Lincroft, N.J., 1987. Mem. East Flatbush League Retarded Children (bd. dirs. 1965-69), Marlboro Chpt. Retarded Children (founder, pres. 1969-71, 73-74, bd. dirs. 1971-76), Marlboro Jewish Ctr. Sisterhood (bd. dirs. 1971-73), N.J. Women in Bus., Middlesex County C. of C., Western Monmouth C. of C. Democrat. Jewish. Avocations: golf, cooking, travel. Office: Inkwell Promotions 1020 Campus Dr W Morganville NJ 07751-1260 Office Phone: 732-536-2822. E-mail: carolm@inkwellusa.com.

MARDER, EVE ESTHER, neuroscientist, educator; b. NYC, May 30, 1948; d. Eric Marder and Dorothy Silverman. AB, Brandeis U., 1969; PhD, U. Calif., San Diego, 1974. Postdoctoral fellow U. Oreg., Eugene, 1975, Ecole Normale Superieure, Paris, 1976-78; from asst. prof. to assoc. prof. Brandeis U., Waltham, Mass., 1978-90, prof., 1990—; program dir. Sloan Ctr. for Theoretical Neuroscience; chief editor Jour. of Neurophysiology, 2002—. Forbes lectr., 2000. Founding editor: Jour. Computational Neurosci.; mem. editorial bd., Jour. Exptl. Biology, Jour. Neurobiology, curr. biol; jour. comp. physiol A; curr. opinion in Neurobiology; jour. of comp. neurology; contbr. papers and chpt. to sci. jour. Trustee Grass Found. Coun., 1999—2002. Recipient Javits award in neurosci. NINDS, 1987, Investigators award McKnight Found., 1994, NIMH Merit award, 1995; Alfred P. Sloan Found. fellow, 1978; McKnight scholar, 1978. Fellow AAAS, Am. Acad. of Arts and Sci., Women in Neuroscience, Biophysical Soc. (trustee). Office: Brandeis U Volen Ctr Waltham MA 02454

MARDIS, ELMA HUBBARD, county administrator, consultant; b. Memphis, July 16, 1932; d. Walter Lee Sr. and Edith (Scott) Hubbard; m. William Columbus Mardis, Dec. 22, 1957; 1 child, Marlah Mardis-Phillips. BS, LeMoyne-Owen U., 1952; MEd, U. Ill., 1960; EdD, U. Tenn., 1974. Tchr. Memphis City Schs., 1952-75; asst. prof., coord. Bur. Ednl. Rsch., U. Tenn., Knoxville, 1975-80; instr. Shelby State C.C., Memphis, 1977-78; nat. dir. edn. PUSH Excel Program, Chgo., 1980-82; tchr. Memphis City Schs., 1982-84; dir. computer ctr. Memphis Urban League, 1984-94; exec. dir. Pvt. Industry Coun., Memphis, Shelby, Fayette Counties, Tenn., 1994—. Dir. Am. Tutoring Ctr., Memphis, 1982—; cons. Josten's Learning Corp., San Diego, 1997—. Editor: PUSH for EXCELLENCE, 1981; author instrnl. curriculum; contbr. articles to profl. jours. Mem., alumnus Leadership Memphis, 1980—; organizer/charter pres. River City chpt. The Links, Inc., Memphis, 1987-95; commr./vice chair Memphis Housing Authority, 1992—; mem. Tenn. Commn. on Children and Youth, Nashville, 1995—; bd. trustees Memphis Urban League, sec.; mem. NAACP, Memphis, 1997; sec. Second Congl. United Ch. of Christ, 1989-97. Recipient Disting. Grad. award LeMoyne-Owen Coll., 1988. Mem. Nat. Assn. Pvt. Industry Couns., Tenn. Assn. Pvt. Industry Couns., Southeastern Employment and Tng. Assn., So. Assn. Colls. and Schs. (cons., facilitator review team 1977—), Phi Delta Kappa, Kappa Delta Pi, Pi Lambda Theta, Alpha Kappa Alpha. Avocations: reading, travel, working with children, community projects, basketball. Home: 2324 Bridgeport Dr Memphis TN 38114-5714 Office: 100 N Main St Ste 2810 Memphis TN 38103-0528

MARDIS, LINDA KEISER, music educator, writer; b. New Haven, Jan. 9, 1937; d. Donald Eskil and Elizabeth Marie Hallsten; m. Gordon Delbert Craig, June 29, 1957 (dec. Jan. 1963); m. Harry Robert Keiser, June 11, 1964 (div.); children: Harry Rudolph, Robert Hungerford; m. Arthur Lowell Mardis, Dec. 29, 1990. BA, Mount Holyoke Coll., 1957; MA, Yale U., 1958. Chmn. dept. fgn. langs. Walter Johnson H.S., Bethesda, Md., 1960-65; music dir. Geneva United Presbyn. Ch., Rockville, Md., 1966-79; assoc. dir. ICM Tng. Seminars, Balt., 1979-85; facilitator, trainer Bonny Method of Guided Imagery and Music, 1980—; master Usui Sys. Reiki Healing, 1982—; pres., founder Archedigm, Inc., Olney, Md., 1985—; v.p. Archedigm Pubs., 1985—. Founder, dir. The Archedigm Collection, 1990—; workshop, retreat leader, 1959—; bd. dirs. Well-Springs Found., Madison, Wis., 1980—88; cons. LIND Inst., San Francisco, 1988—2001. Author: Conscious Listening, 1986, Light Search, 1987, Teaching Guided Imagery & Music, 1989, Program 33: A New Guided Imagery & Music Program and a New Programming Concept, 1996, Creativity I, II and III, Grieving, Expanded Awareness, Changing Patterns, 1984—88, Mythic Experience, 1989, Program 34: Labyrinth, 2000, Program 35: Peace, 2003, Program 36: Quest, 2006, Creativity IV, V, VI, 2005, Creative Music Resources for Facilitators of the Bonny Method of GIM, 2005, (music program series) Relax with the Classics series, Classical Spirit, Classical Harmonies, Classical Impressions, 1998. Deacon Christ Congl. Ch., Silver Spring, Md., 1981-84. Fellow Inst. Music and Imagery (bd. dirs. 1981-88, assoc. exec.-dir. 1986-89); mem. Soc. Noetic Scis., Assn. for Rsch. and Enlightenment, Assn. Music and Imagery, Associated Bodywork and Massage Profls., Mt. Holyoke Coll. Alumnae Assn. (bd. dirs. 1978-83). Democrat. Home: 17247 Sandy Knoll Dr Olney MD 20832-2036 Office: Archedigm Inc PO Box 1109 Olney MD 20830-1109 Personal E-mail: linda@archedigm.com.

MARDUEL, ALIX, venture capitalist; MD, U. Paris. Med. residency, Paris; postdoctoral fellowship U. Calif., San Francisco, Stanford U.; assoc. med. dir. ICI Pharma (now AstraZeneca), France, England; gen. ptnr. Sofinnova Ventures, 1990—97; mng. dir. Alta Partners, San Francisco, 1997—. Bd. dir. Cytos Biotechnology, 2000—, Corcept Therapeutics, 2001—, Syntonix, 2002—, NeurogesX, Metabolex, Inc., Genteric, Memory Pharm.; actively involved with the creation of several life sci. co. in the US and Europe, including Millennium Pharm., CV Therapeutics, Medicine Co., Genset & Aviaron. Office: Alta Partners One Embarcadero Ctr Ste 4050 San Francisco CA 94111

MARECEK, JEANNE, psychologist, educator; b. Berwyn, Ill., May 28, 1946; d. Frank J. and Josephine (Serio) M. BS, Loyola U., Chgo., 1968; MS, Yale U., 1971, PhD, 1973. From asst. prof. to prof. psychology Swarthmore (Pa.) Coll., 1972—, chmn. dept., 1986—91, 1994—95, 1998—99, head women's studies program, 1996—99. Fulbright sr. lectr., Sri Lanka, 1988. Co-author: Making a Difference: Psychology and the Construction of Gender; contbr. numerous articles to profl. jours. and chpts. to books. Bd. dirs. Women in Transition, Phila., 1980-86; vice patron Nest, Hendala, Sri Lanka, 1995—; bd. dirs. Women's Therapy Ctr., Phila., 1996-2004, CHOICE, Phila., 2006—. Fellow Swedish Collegium for Advanced Study in Social Scis., 1997; various fed. research grants. Mem. APA, Assn. for Asian Studies, Am. Inst. Sri Lanka Studies (sec. 1995-2000, pres. 2001—), Am. Overseas Rsch. Ctrs. (mem. exec. coun.). Office: Swarthmore Coll Dept Psychology 500 College Ave Swarthmore PA 19081-1306 Business E-Mail: jmarece1@swarthmore.edu.

MARÉE, KATHLEEN NANCY, retired language educator; b. Belleville, NJ, Nov. 8, 1942; d. Jacobus and Marie Theresa (Lilore) Marée. BA, Rutgers U., Newark, N.J., 1965; MA in Tchg. magna cum laude, Fairleigh Dickinson U., Rutherford, N.J., 1970. Elem. French tchr. Freehold (N.J.) Elem. Schs., 1965—66, River Edge (N.J.) Elem. Schs., 1966—71, dept. head and fgn. langs. in elem. sch. rep.; elem. French tchr. Hanahouli Elem. Sch., Honolulu, 1971—73; pub. rels. coord. Oceanic Cablevision, Honolulu, 1974—75; pub. rels. rep., adminstrv. asst. Hawaii State Legis., Honolulu, 1975; ESL instr., head tchr., asst. coord. New Intensive Course in English program U. Hawaii at Manoa, Honolulu, 1976—79; founder, pres., dir. Lang. Inst. Hawaii, Honolulu, 1979—86; advisor, coord. study cultural tours Internat. Pacific Asian Consortium, Honolulu, 1979—86; ESL instr. Fairleigh Dickinson U., Seton Hall U., Rutgers U., NJ, 1987—89; ESL lectr. and adj. Bergen CC, Paramus, NJ, 1989—2000. Pub. rels. Fgn. Lang. Elem. Sch., 1966—71; chairperson N.J. Assn. Tchrs. Fgn. Langs. Elem. Sch., 1970—71. ESL tchr., coord. employment Vietnamese Immigrant Vol. Assistance, Honolulu, 1975; mem., ESL sponsor CIVITAN, Honolulu, 1980—86. Grantee, East-West Ctr.-Culture Learning Inst., 1975—76. Avocations: reading, oil painting.

MAREK, JOYCELYN, publishing executive; m. Andrew Marek; children: Allison, Matthew. BBA, U. Houston, 1978; postgrad., Northwestern U., 1996, Hearst Mgmt. Inst., 1997-98. Rsch. analyst Houston Chronicle, 1978, chief analyst, 1978-84, asst. rsch. mgr., 1984-85, rsch. mgr., 1985-88, display advt. dir., 1988-90, mktg. dir., 1990-95, v.p. mktg. and electronic products, 1995—. Bd. dirs., exec. com. Sheltering Arms; mem. mktg. com. Houston Symphony; former bd. dirs. Houston Advt. Fedn. Mem. Am. Mktg. Assn. (edn./intern chair, past pres. Houston chpt.), Newspaper Assn. Am. (former chair market devel. and promotion coun.). Avocations: tennis, reading, golf. Office: Houston Chronicle PO Box 4260 Houston TX 77210-4260

MARENOFF, SUSAN, professional athletics manager; NY/NJ venue dir. FIFA Women's World Cup soccer tournament, 1999; gen. mgr. New York Power, NYC, 2000—03; chief mktg. officer Intrepid Sea Air Space Mus., NYC, interim exec. dir., 2005.

MARESSO-NEWELL, DEE, arbitrator, educator; b. Chgo., Dec. 26, 1953; d. Michael Joseph Maresso and Theresa Messina; m. Donald Lee Newell, Nov. 1992; 1 child, Milinda Lowe. BS, Northwestern U., Evanston, Ill., 1976; JD, Kent Coll. Law Ill. Inst. Tech., Chgo., 1986; grad. Program on Negotiations and Dispute Resolution, Harvard Law Sch., Cambridge, Mass., 2000. Congressional aide U.S. Ho. Reps., Washington, 1977—81; account exec. Merrill Corp., Chgo., 1985—89; solo practice arbitrator Las Vegas, Nev., 1990—2003; pres. and sr. arbitrator Arbitrations & Mediations Solutions, Inc., 2003—. Instr. U. Nev., Las Vegas, 2003—; mem. instl. rev. bd. Sunrise Mountain View Hosps., Las Vegas, Nev., 2004—; arbitrator Nev. Supreme Ct., U.S. Dist. Ct. (8th dist.) Nev., N.Y. Stock Exchange, Nat. Assn. Securities Dealers, Dept. Bus. and Industrey State of Nev., State Bar of Nevada, Nat. Arbitration Forums, Auto Line, Nat. Bus. Burs. Vol. mediator Mediators of Southern Nev., Las Vegas, Nev., 2000—06, Justice Ct., 2003—05; vol. Neighborhood Justice Ctr., 2003—05. Named Exec. on Move, State of Ill., 1985—86, Recognized Arbitrator, Las Vegas Dept. of Bus. and Industry, 2006. Mem.: Assn. Confict Resolution, Bassette Hound Rescue Orgn. Avocations: travel, tennis, swimming. Office: Pres Arbitration and Mediation Solutions Inc 5736 Willowcreek North Las Vegas NV 89031 Office Phone: 702-399-4440.

MAREZ, REBECCA ANN, literature and language educator; b. Corpus Christi, Tex., Jan. 13, 1955; d. Anthony Botello Zepeda and Amelia Zepeda (Garcia); children: Philip Michael, Kathryn Marie Marez Clements. A, Del Mar Coll., Corpus Christi, 1982; BA, Corpus Christi State U., 1984; MS, Tex. A&I U., Kingsville, 1990. Cert. tchg. Tex., 1984. English instr. Tex. A&I U., Kingsville, 1989—91, Del Mar Coll., Corpus Christi, Tex., 1991—96, asst. prof., 1996—2001, assoc. prof., prof., 2006—. Named Master Tchr., Outstanding Educator, Del Mar Coll., Koch Refinery, 2001. Home: 2301 Nautical Wind Corpus Christi TX 78414 Office: Del Mar College 101 Baldwin Blvd Corpus Christi TX 78404 Office Phone: 361-698-1234. Business E-Mail: rmarez@delmar.edu.

MAREZ, TRINNIE MARIE, marketing professional; b. Marietta, Ga., July 29, 1958; d. Felix Martin Marez and Linda Joan Higgins; m. Thomas Ian MacDougall Christopher (dec.). BA in Comm. cum laude, Ga. State U., 1987. Corp. comm. The Coca-Cola Co., Atlanta, 1987—94; dir. guest relations Olympic Games Day Tripper Program, Atlanta, 1995—96; meteorology programming & prodn. The Weather Channel, 1997—98; dir. mktg. Wild

Oats Mkts., Inc., Nashville, 2001—. Prodr.: (films) Charlie's War, 2003, Heike and the Mermaid, 2004, Dodge City, 2004, Daltry Calhoun, 2005; (TV series) Lorianne Crook's Celebrity Kitchen, 2003, Great American Country, 2003—04. 1st lt., dir. pub. affairs Ga. Wing Hdqs. USAF, 1987—94, Dobbins ARB, Marietta, Ga. Decorated Award of Excellent Svc. The Ga. Wing, CAP, Search & Rescue award, Lifesaving award, Comdr.'s commendations, Unit Citation awards, Brewer Aerospace Edn. award. Republican. Roman Catholic. Avocations: literature, painting, writing, skiing, films.

MARGALITH, HELEN MARGARET, retired librarian; b. N.Y.C., Nov. 19, 1914; d. Louis and Caroline (Stern) Fleischer; m. Aaron Margalith, Jan. 26, 1947 (dec.); children: Carol Lenore, Joan Louise. BA, Hunter Coll., 1936, MA, 1944; MLS, Columbia U., 1958. Editl. corr. Book of the Month Club, 1936-47; rschr. libr. N.Y.C. Bd. Edn., 1955-80; prof. pibr. Touro Coll., N.Y.C., 1980-90; mentor in libr. Empire State Coll., SUNY, 1991—. Cons. in field. Fellow Royal Soc. Medicine (libr. com., gerontology com., history of medicine com.); mem. Ch. and Synagogue Libr. Assn. (book reviewer), Internat. Honor Soc. Women in Edn., Am. Geolinguistic Assn. (bd. dirs. 2003—), Am. Soc. Geolinguistics, Delta Kappa Gamma Democrat. Avocations: reading, travel, research. Home: 205 W End Ave Apt 25S New York NY 10023-4804

MARGED, JUDITH MICHELE, network technician, educator; b. Phila., Nov. 27, 1954; d. Bernard A. and Norma Marged. Student, Drexel U., 1972-73; AA in Biology, Broward CC, Ft. Lauderdale, Fla., 1975; BA in Biology, Fla. Atlantic U., 1977, BA in Exceptional Edn., 1980, MEd in Counseling, 1984; EdD in Early and Middle Childhood, Nova U., 1991; postgrad., Capella U., 2002—03. Cert. tech. trainer Microsoft, MCSE, MCP, cert. Microsoft Office specialist & master instr. 2003; tchr. Fla. Tchr. Coral Springs (Fla.) Mid. Sch., 1979-80, Am. Acad., Wilton Manors, Fla., 1980-83, Ramblewood Mid. Sch., Coral Springs, 1984-96; info. tech. prof. Am. InterContinental U., Plantation, Fla., 1999—2002; adj. prof. Baker Coll., Flint, Mich., 2006—. Adj. online prof. Baker Coll., Flint, Mich., 2006—; creator programs mid. sch. students and coll. curriculum. Author: A Program to Increase the Knowledge of Middle School Students in Sexual Education and Substance Abuse Prevention, An Alternative Education Program to Create Successful Learning for Middle School Children At-Risk. Mem.: IEEE, Assn. Career and Tech. Edn., Phi Delta Kappa. Home: 9107 NW 83d St Tamarac FL 33321-1509 E-mail: margedj@ieee.org.

MARGIOTTA, MARY-LOU ANN, application developer; b. Waterbury, Conn., June 14, 1956; d. Rocco Donato and Louise Antoinette (Carosella) M. AS Gen. Edn., Mattatuck C.C., Waterbury, 1982; BSBA, Teikyo Post U., 1983; MS Computer Sci., Rensselaer Polytech. Inst., 1989. Programmer analyst Travelers Ins. Co., Hartford, Conn., 1985-87; sr. programmer analyst Conn. Bank and Trust Co., East Hartford, Conn., 1987-88; programmer analyst Ingersoll-Rand Corp., Torrington, Conn., 1990-91; sr. programmer analyst Orion Capital Cos. Inc., Farmington, Conn., 1991-92; pres., prin., software engr. A.M. Consultants, New Britain, Conn., 1992—. Pres. C++ Spl. Interest Group, 1995-96; bd. dirs. Conn. Object Oriented Users Group, 1995-96; tech. team leader Computer Scis. Corp., East Hartford, Conn., 1998-, Asnuntuck C. C., Enfield, Conn., 2003; adj. prof. Ctrl. Conn. State U., New Britain, 2000, New Eng. Tech. Inst., New Britain, Conn., 2002. Mem. social action com. St. Helena's Parish, West Hartford, Conn., 1988-95; advisor Jr. Achievement, Waterbury, 1981-83; tutor Traveler's Ins. Co. Tutorial Program, West Hartford, 1986-87; trainer CPR, ARC, Hartford, 1986-87; mem. Lang. and Cultural Adoptation Programs, Conn. and Mass., 1998— Clayborn Pell grantee Post Coll., 1982-83, State of Conn. grantee, 1982-83; recipient Citation, Jr. Achievement, 1982; Bd. Trustees scholar Post Coll., 1982-83. Mem. IEEE (chairwoman membership devel., Conn. chpt.), Am. Aculturation Assocs. (bd. dirs.), Toastmasters Internat., Tau Alpha, Beta Gamma. Roman Catholic. Avocations: european travel, gourmet cooking, reading, tennis, golf. Home: 210 Brittany Farms Rd Ste E New Britain CT 06053-1282 Office Phone: 860-229-3496. E-mail: raebedet@aol.com.

MARGO, KATHERINE LANE, family physician, educator; d. Warren Wilson and Virginia (Penney) Lane; m. Geoffrey Myles Margo, Apr. 20, 1980; 1 child, Benjamin stepchildren: Jenny, Judy. BA, Swarthmore Coll., 1974; MD, SUNY Health Sci. Ctr., Syracuse, 1978. Cert. in family medicine. Resident physician St. Joseph's Hosp., Syracuse, 1979-82; attending physician Health Svcs. Assn., Syracuse, 1982-90, asst. med. dir. for quality assurance, 1985-90; asst. prof. family medicine SUNY-HSC at Syracuse, 1990-94; mem. residency faculty Harrisburg (Pa.) Hosp., 1994-2000; med. dir. Harrisburg Kline Family Practice Ctr., 1996-2000; assoc. residency dir. Harrisburg Family Practice Residency, 1997-2000; predoctoral dir. Dept. Family Practice Cmty. Medicine U. Pa., 2000—, asst. prof., assoc. dir. family practice residency, 2000—. Clin. assoc. prof. Allegheny Med. Sch., 1997—2000. Contbr. articles to profl. jours. Bd. trustees Pt. Choice, Syracuse, 1993—94; chair med. com. Planned Parenthood, Syracuse, 1984—94; bd. dirs. Planned Parenthood Susquehanna Valley, 1996—2000; active Friends of Chamber Music, Syracuse, 1985—94; keyboard player Old World folk Band. Recipient Exemplary Tchg. award, Pa. Acad. of Family Practice, 2003, Penn Pearls Tchg. award, U. Pa. Sch. Medicine, 2004. Mem.: Am. Acad. Family Practitioners (v.p. Syracuse chpt.), Soc. Tchrs. of Family Medicine (chair group on predoctoral edn. 2003—04). Democrat. Avocations: music, theater, gardening, birdwatching. Home: 426 Carpenter Ln Philadelphia PA 19119-3040 Office: Univ Pa Dept Family Practice Community Medicine 2 Gates 3400 Spruce St Philadelphia PA 19104 Office Phone: 215-662-8941. E-mail: margok@uphs.upenn.edu.

MARGOLIES, ALLISON, clinical psychologist; b. N.Y.C., Feb. 11, 1953; d. Sol and Bunny (Wertans) M.; MA, Hofstra U., 1976, PhD, 1979. Psychologist, Bernard Fineson Developmental Ctr., Queens Village, N.Y., 1979-82; cons. psychologist Aurora Concept, Flushing, N.Y., 1981-84; assoc. psychologist Queens Children's Psychiat. Hosp., Bellerose, N.Y., 1982-85; lic. psychologist Creedmoor Psychiat. Ctr., Queens Village, 1985—; pvt. practice clin. psychology, Valley Stream, N.Y., 1982. Lic. psychologist N.Y. State; cert. sch. psychologist N.Y. State. Mem. Am. Psychol. Assn., N.Y. State Psychol. Assn., Nassau County Psychol. Assn., Phi Beta Kappa. Qualified expert witness, N.Y. Supreme Ct. Home: 232 Cedarhurst Ave Cedarhurst NY 11516-1601 Office: 210 East Sunrise Hwy Ste 101 Valley Stream NY 11581-1330 Office Phone: 516-872-2005.

MARGOLIN, FRANCES MONGIN, clinical psychologist, educator; b. Montgomery County, Pa.; d. Harry and Dorothy (Blanc) Mongin; m. Elias L. Margolin, Mar. 12, 1944; children— Janice, John, Carol, Paul. B.A., Temple U., 1948; M.A., Ohio U., 1955; Ph.D., U.S. Internat. U., 1973. Lic. psychologist, lic. marriage and family therapist, Calif.; diplomate Am. Bd. Clin. Psychology. Clin. psychologist Dayton State Hosp., Ohio, 1948-53; pvt. practice clin. psychology, Dayton, 1953-55, La Jolla, Calif., 1974—; marriage counselor San Diego County Superior Ct., San Diego, 1955-74; asst. prof. psychology San Diego State U., 1975-76; prof. LaVerne Coll., San Diego, 1976-78; prof. Chapman Coll., San Diego, 1978-88. vice pres. AAUW, Dayton, 1954; chair psychology com., Harbor View Hosp., S.D., 1985-88. Mem. Am. Psychol. Assn., Calif. Psychol. Assn., Assn. Psychologists in Pvt. Practice, Am. Women in Psychology (San Diego rep. 1982-90), S.D. Nurses Council (Woman of Wisdom Leader, 2004), San Diego Acad. Psychology, Psi Chi. Home and Office: PO Box 3056 La Jolla CA 92038-3056

MARGOLIN, JEAN SPIELBERG, artist; b. NYC, Oct. 12, 1926; d. Jack and Ida (Grossman) Spielberg and Bess Liebowitz Spielberg (stepmother); m. Paul Margolin, May 19, 1946 (dec. Mar. 1989). Student, Ind. U., 1951-55, Skowhegan Sch. Painting/Sculp., 1954. Tchr. painting and drawing Ind. U., Bloomington, 1954-55; curator group show Pace U. Gallery, N.Y.C., 1984. Paintings exhibited John Herron Art Mus., Indpls., 1952-55, J.B. Speed Art Mus., Louisville, 1953, Cin. Mus. Art, 1955, L.A. County Mus. Art, 1956, A.C.A. Gallery, N.Y.C., 1959-60, Pa. Acad. Fine Arts, Phila., 1962, Heckscher Mus., Huntington, N.Y., 1964, Skowhegan Benefit Exbhn., Nat. Arts Club, N.Y.C., 1974, Arthouse, Storrs, Conn., 1979, Landmark Gallery, N.Y.C., 1980-82, Pace U. Gallery, N.Y.C., 1980, 84, The Artists Choice Mus., Alex Rosenberg Gallery, N.Y.C., 1983; paintings exhibited by appointment only, N.Y.C., 1985—. Recipient 1st prize purchase award for painting Skowhegan Sch. Painting and Sculpture, 1954, scholar, 1954. Home: 4 Washington Square Vlg Apt 12S New York NY 10012-1908

MARGOLIS, NADIA, language educator, translator, medievalist; b. Neuilly-sur-Seine, France, Apr. 27, 1949; came to U.S., 1950; d. Morton Margolis and Diane Seyfort-Ruegg Kensler; m. Peter Kenneth Marshall, May 23, 1984. BA, U. N.H., 1971; PhD, Stanford U., 1977. Lectr. in French Stanford (Calif.) U., 1976-77; editorial asst. Medieval Acad. of Am., Cambridge, Mass., 1977-78; asst. prof. in French Amherst (Mass.) Coll., 1978-85; assoc. prof. French U. Utah, Salt Lake City, 1985-89; rsch. assoc. Inst. Advanced Study in Humanities/U. Mass., Amherst, 1993—. Asst. coord. Jr. World Cycling Championships, Trexlertown, Pa., 1978; adj. instr. French, U. Mass., 1992-93, vis. lectr. in comparative lit., 1993; panelist NEH, Washington, 1984, 86-87; cons. Garland Medieval Series, N.Y.C., 1992—, for composer Richard Einhorn, 1994, for Capella Films, 1994; rsch. profl. Ctr. Nat. Sci. Rsch., Paris, 1973—; vis. assoc. prof. French U. Calif., Santa Barbara, 2002, UCLA, 2003, U. Mass., 2005, Mt. Holyoke Coll., 2006; vis. prof French Mt. Holyoke Coll., 2006. Author: Joan of Arc in History, Literature and Film; co-author, co-editor: Christine de Pizan, 2000, Women in the Middle Ages: An Encyclopedia, 2004, co-translator: Book of the Duke of True Lovers, 1991. Author, panel mem. Bicycle Safety/Bike Path com., Amherst, 1984. Miner Crary fellow Amherst Coll., 1979, NEH Ind. fellow, 1981; Rsch. grant Am. Philos. Soc., 1982. Mem. Modern Lang. Assn., Soc. Rencesvals, Medieval Acad. of Am., Christine de Pizan Soc. (sec. 1991—, editor newsletter 1991-96), Internat. Courtly Lit. Soc. Democrat. Jewish. Avocations: bicycling, gardening, drawing, painting. Home: 75 Amherst Rd Leverett MA 01054-5402 Office Phone: 413-548-9721. Personal E-mail: margolis@rcn.com.

MARGOLIS, SUSAN ELLEN, psychiatric clinical nurse specialist, artist; b. Cleve., May 11, 1955; d. William Nathan and Sarah Aranow Zuckerman; m. Larry S. Margolis; children: William Zuckerman, Jacob Nathan, Sarah Rebekah. BSN, U. Tex., 1981, MSN, 1989; PhD, Tex. Woman's U., 2000. RN, Tex.; cert. clin. nurse specialist-psychiat./mental health. Charge/staff nurse NurseFinders, Arlington, Tex., 1984-88; clin. asst. Post Oak Psychiatry Assocs., Waxahachie, Tex., 1988-89; team leader Ft. Worth (Tex.) Vet.'s Ctr., 1989-90; nursing instr. Tarleton State U., Stephenville, Tex., 1990; pvt. practice cons., educator, lectr., therapist Benbrook, Tex., 1991-92; geri-psychiat. nurse therapist Ft. Worth Family Inst., 1992-93; dir. geriatric svcs. Psychiat. Ctr. of North Tex., DeSoto, 1993—2002; corp. psychiat. cons. VeriCare Inc., 2002—. Spkr. many profl. and cmty. burs., 1989-. Vol. Arlington (Tex.) Night Shelter, 1988-96, Presbyn. Night Shelter, Ft. Worth, 1997—; del. to China, Am. Del. Psychol. Nurses, 1990; foster parent; active local Orthodox synagogue. With U.S. Army, 1973-75; lt. USAF, 1982-83. Full chemistry scholar Stephen F. Austin State U., 1972; selected for individual study Royal Acad. Nursing, Edinburgh, Scotland, 1973. Mem. ANA, Tex. Nurse's Assn., Disabled Vet.'s Assn., U. Tex. at Arlington Alumni Assn., Tex. Woman's U. Alumni Assn., Sigma Theta Tau. Jewish. Avocation: stained glass art. Office Phone: 800-257-8715 ext. 280. Personal E-mail: margolis7@hotmail.com.

MARGOSEIN, CAROL MARIE, secondary school educator; b. Chgo., Apr. 12, 1951; d. Morris Phillip and Dolores Marie Vanderhack; m. Kim John Margosein, Aug. 4, 1973; children: Holland Peter, Marie Annabelle. EdM, U. Ill., Chgo., 1981, postgrad., 1999—. Cert. elem. edn. grades K-9 Ill., 1973, reading specialist grades K-12 Ill., 1981, secondary edn. grades 6-12 Ill., 1990. Tchr. St. Procopius Sch., Chgo., 1978—81, Rosa Parks Mid. Sch., Harvey, Ill., 1984—85, Thornwood H.S., South Holland, Ill., 1985—. Instr. Pearson Skylight Orgn., Glenview, Ill., 2005—. Mem.: NEA (assoc.; bldg. rep. 2003), Ill. Edn. Assn. (assoc.), Internat. Reading Assn. (assoc.). Democrat. Roman Catholic. Achievements include research in teaching vocabulary. Avocation: reading. Home: 2813 192nd St Lansing IL 60438 Office: Thornwood HS 17101 South Park Ave South Holland IL 60473 Office Phone: 708-205-4959. Personal E-mail: teach2813@aol.com. Business E-Mail: margosein.carol@dist205.net.

MARGRAVE, KATHY CHRISTINE, nurse anesthetist; b. Pittsburg, Kans., Oct. 23, 1957; d. James Raymond and Nancy Jeanne (Evans) M.; 1 child, Erica. BSN, Marymount Coll., Salina, Kans., 1980; MS, U. Kans., 1996. Med. surgery staff nurse St. Mary's Hosp., Manhattan, Kans., 1980; med./surg. staff nurse S.W. Jefferson Community Hosp., Louisville, 1980-81; commd. U.S. Army, 1981-93, advanced through grades to maj., 1991; operating rm. staff nurse Frankfurt Army Reg. Med. Ctr., W. Ger., 1981-85, Brooke Army Med. Ctr., San Antonio, 1985-88; sr. clin. staff nurse Dwight D. Eisenhower Army Med. Ctr., Fort Gordon, Ga., 1989-90, 91-94; 86th Evacuation Hosp., Saudi Arabia, 1990-91; neuro ICU staff nurse U. Hosp., Augusta, Ga., 1993-94; CRNA Anesthesia Assoc. of Savannah, 1997—2003, locmtenens CRNA, 2003—. Faculty Acad. Health Scis., U.S. Army, Ft. Sam Houston, Tex.; pres. Empty Nest Anesthesia P.C., 2004—. Mem.: Am. Assn. Nurse Anesthetists.

MARGULES, CECELIA, composer, poet; b. Stockholm, Apr. 11, 1947; d. Morris Berkowitz; m. Rubin Margules, June 5, 1971; children: Julie, Rachyl, Adam. BA, Bklyn. Coll., 1970; Interior Design Degree, N.Y. Sch. Interior Design. Design cons. ARM Mgmt. Co., Bklyn., 1985—. Composer N.Y.C. Parks Dept., Emma Lazarus tribute, 2004, Celebration '350'. Contbr. articles and poetry to profl. jours.; contbg. editor: Harmony, 1987; composer: (songs) Guiliani, 1987, New Sinai Sound, 2005. Chmn. Yossi Berger Holocaust Study Ctr., 1990—; cultural chmn. Jewish Heritage, N.Y.C.; bd. dirs. Jewish Cmty. Rels. Coun., N.Y.C, 2000—. Recipient State of Israel Bonds award, 1996, Woman of Valor award, Coun. Jewish Orgns., 2003, 1st prize Zionist nat. song contest, Am. Zionist Movement, 1998. Mem.: Emunah of Am. (v.p., Woman of the Yr. 1991). Jewish. E-mail: ceceliaproductions@yahoo.com.

MARGULIES, JULIANNA, actress; b. Spring Valley, NY, June 8, 1966; BA, Sarah Lawrence Coll., 1989. Actor (films) Out for Justice, 1991, Traveller, 1997, Paradise Road, 1997, A Price Above Rubies, 1997, The Newton Boys, 1998, The Big Day, 1999, What's Cooking, 2000, (voice only) Dinosaur, 2000, Ten Unknowns, 2001 (Lucille Lortel Award for outstanding featured actress, 2001), The Man From Elysian Fields, 2001, (voice only) Love Gets You Twisted, 2002, Ghost Ship, 2002, Evelyn, 2002, Slingshot, 2005, The Darwin Awrds, 2006, Snakes on a Plane, 2006; (TV series) Philly Heat, 1994, ER, 1994-2000 (Emmy award for supporting actress Drama, 1995, Golden Globe award winner, 1998, SAG award winner 1997, 98, 99); (TV mini-series) The Grid, 2004; (TV movies) The Mists of Avalon, 2001, Jenifer, 2001, Hitler: The Rise of Evil, 2003; (TV appearances) Law & Order, 1993, Murder, She Wrote, 1993, Homicide: Life on the Street, 1994, Scrubs, 2004, The Sopranos, 2006; (theater appearances) The Substance of Fire, At Home, Fefu and Her Friends, The Substance of Fire, Living Expenses, Dan Drift, Book of Names, Balm in Gilead, In the Boom Boom Room, The Vagina Monologues, 2000, Festen, 2006. Office: c/o William Morris Agency 151 S El Camino Dr Beverly Hills CA 90212*

MARGULIS, HEIDI, health products executive; Licensure analyst Humana, Inc., 1985—95, v.p. govt. affairs, 1995—2000, sr. v.p. govt. affairs, 2000—. Mem. fed. adv. com. to streamline regulations to ensure quality health care svcs., 2002; mem. com. on Medicare edn. HFCA. Mem.: Women's Polit. Forum (bd. dirs.), Bus. and Profl. Women (pres. 1978—79), Bus. Roundtable, Health Care Leadership Coun., Am. Assn. Health Plans (policy, legis., advocacy and strategic planning coms.). Office: Humana Inc 500 W Main St Louisville KY 40202

MARGULIS, LYNN (LYNN ALEXANDER), evolutionist, educator; b. Chgo., Mar. 5, 1938; d. Morris and Leone Alexander; m. Carl Sagan, June 16, 1957; children: Dorion Sagan, Jeremy Sagan; m. Thomas N. Margulis, Jan. 18, 1967; children: Zachary Margulis-Ohnuma, Jennifer Margulis di Properzio. AB, U. Chgo., 1957; AM, U. Wis., 1960; PhD, U. Calif., Berkeley, 1965; Doctorate (hon.), U. Montreal, Can., 1987, U. Valencia, Spain, 2001; DSc (hon.), Southeastern Mass. U., North Dartmouth, 1989, Westfield State Coll., Mass., 1989, Plymouth State Coll., NH, 1991, Tulane U., New Orleans, 1996, U. Montreal, 1997, Autonomous U. Madrid, 1998, Union Coll., Schenectady, NY, 2001, San Francisco U., Quito, Ecuador, 2001, Rutgers U., New Brunswick, 2004, Bates Coll., Lewiston, Maine, 2005, Tufts U., Medford, Mass., 2006, NC State U., Raleigh, 2006; Dr.rer.nat (hon.), U. Oldenburg, Germany, 1999. Mem. faculty Boston U., 1966—68, asst. prof. biology, 1967—71, assoc. prof., 1971—77, prof., 1977—88, Univ. prof., 1986—88; Disting. Univ. prof. U. Mass., Amherst, 1988—. Sherman Fairchild Disting. scholar Calif. Inst. Tech., 1976—77; vis. prof. dept. microbiology U. Autónoma de Barcelona, Spain, 1986, Spain, 88; Disting. univ. prof. U. Mass. Author: Origin of Eukaryotic Cells, 1970, Symbiosis in Cell Evolution, 1981, Early Life, 1982, 2d edit., 2002, Symbiosis in Cell Evolution, 2d edit., 1993, Microcosmos Videos, 1999; editor (with Mitchell Rambler and René Fester): Global Ecology, 1989; editor: (with others) Handbook of Protoctista, 1990; co-editor (with René Fester): Symbiosis as a Source of Evolutionary Innovation: Speciation and Morphogenesis, 1991; co-editor: Concepts of Symbiogenesis: A Historical and Critical Study of the Research of Russian Botanists, 1992, Environmental Evolution: Effects of the Origin and Evolution of Life on Planet Earth, 1992, Environmental Evolution: Effects of the Origin and Evolution of Life on Planet Earth, 2d edit., 2000, Glossary of Protoctista, 1993; co-editor: (with Dorion Sagan) What Is Sex?, 1998; co-editor: Slanted Truths: Essays on Gaia, Evolution and Symbiosis, 1997, What is Life?, 1995, Diversity of Life: The Illustrated Guide to the Five Kingdoms, 2d edit., 1999; co-author: Five Kingdoms, 1982, 3d edit., 1998, Microcosmos, 1986; co-author: (with Dorion Sagan) Origins of Sex, 1986; co-author: Garden of Microbial Delights, 1988, 2d edit., 1998, Biospheres From Earth To Space, 1988, Mystery Dance: On the Evolution of Human Sexuality, 1991, What Happens to Trash and Garbage: An Introduction to the Carbon Cycle, 1993, Living Sands: Mapping Time and Space with Forams, 2000, Early Life, 2d edit., 2002, Acquiring Genomes: A Theory of the Origins of Species, 2002, Peces Luminosos: Historias de Ciencia y Amor, 2002, Una Revolucion en la Evolucion, 2002; co-author: (with Andrew Wier) Vol. I Cells and Reproduction, Vol. II Evolution and Diversity; co-author: (with Lorraine Olendzenski) (videos) Looking at Microbes, An Introduction to the Microbiology Laboratory for Students, Symbiotic Planet. A New Look at Evolution, 1997; contbr. chapters to books, articles to profl. jours. Recipient Nat. Medal Sci., 1999, Humboldt Prize, 2002, Commonwealth of Mass. award; Guggenheim fellow, 1979. Fellow: AAAS; mem.: NAS, Soc. Sci. Rsch., Soc. Evolutionary Protistology (co-founder), Sigma Xi (pres. 2005—06). Office: U Mass Dept Geosci 611 No Pleasant St Amherst MA 01003-9297 Mailing: PO Box 671 Amherst MA 01004-0671 Office Phone: 413-545-3244.

MARI, DAWN, composer, artist; b. Cooperstown, NY, Apr. 16, 1954; Sales rep., acct. exec. WBZ Boston, 1978—82, KABC Los Angeles, 1982—83; fine mural artist Self-Employed, 1983—, composer, writer, prodr. Los Angeles, 1988—. Chmn. of bd. Renegade Repertory Co., Los Angeles, 1994—2001; v.p. himalayan coun. Pacific Asia Mus., 2004—. State grant, NY State, 1972, grant, Syracuse U., 1972, Pvt. grant, Clark Fund, 1972. Mem.: MENSA. Avocations: hiking, dance.

MARIANI, THERESA LYNN, sociologist, educator; d. Norman E. and Aurelia M. Mariani; children: Jennifer E. Chandler, Michael D. Chandler II. BS in Sociology, Ill. State U., Normal, 1989, MS in Sociology, 1991. Mem. faculty Spoon River Coll., Canton, Ill., 1991—99; family therapist, case mgr. Cath. Charities, Canton, 2000—03; mem. faculty Bradley U., Peoria, Ill., 2003—. Mem. faculty Maricope C.C., Phoenix, 1992—2000. Sr. dog trainer Pet Smart, Peoria, 1992—2000. Named Best Coll. Instr., Canton Daily Ledger, 1995, Most Inspirational Tchr., Western Ill. U., 1997. Mem.: Midwest Sociol. Soc. (mem. com. 1991—2000), Am. Sociol. Soc., Ill. Sociol. Assn. (pres.-elect 1991—2000, bd. dirs. 1991—2000). Avocation: dog training. Office: Bradley U 109 Bradley Hall Peoria IL 61625

MARIANO, ANA VIRGINIA, retired pathologist; b. Baguio City, The Philippines, Nov. 20, 1938; came to US, 1963; d. Celestino Chuongco and Ana (Tanseco) Juan; m. Gregorio Torres Mariano, June 4, 1966; children: Joel, Eric, Greg, Anita. AA, U. St. Tomas, Manila, 1957, MD, 1962. Bd. cert. in anatomic pathology and clin. pathology Am. Bd. Pathology; lic. physician, NY, Pa. Med. intern Youngstown Hosp., Ohio, 1963; pathology resident I RI Hosp., Providence, 1964; pathology resident II-IV Wayne State U. Med. Sch., Detroit, 1965-68; assoc. pathologist Newark-Wayne Cmty. Hosp., Newark, NY, 1979-83; interim pathologist Clifton Springs Hosp., NY, 1983; lab. dir. and acting lab. dir. VA Med. Ctr., Altoona, Pa., 1995—97, staff pathologist, 1997-99. Locum tenens Altoona Hosp., Pa., 1999-2001; mem. courtesy med. staff Newark-Wayne Cmty. Hosp., 1983-92, Clifton Springs Hosp., NY, 1983-89; mem. adv. bd. Cath. Physicians Guild, Rochester, NY, 1991-92; cons. in pathology VA Med. Ctr., Altoona, 1993-96. Tchr. religious edn. St. Michael's Ch., Newark, 1978-80, 82-84. Fellow Am. Soc. Clin. Pathologists, Coll. Am. Pathologists. Roman Catholic. Avocations: swimming, aerobics, gardening. Home and Office: 320 Bristol Ln Hollidaysburg PA 16648-2901

MARICHAL, MARIA P., physical education educator, soccer coach; b. Ponce, P.R., Aug. 12, 1960; d. Carlos Marichal and Flavia Lugo; children: Carlos Paniagua, Francisco Paniagua. Ba in Phys. Edn., U. P.R., San Juan, 1982; MA in Instrnl. Sys., U. Sagrado Corazón, San Juan, P.R., 1990; MA in Sch. Adminstrn., U. P.R., San Juan, 2001. Asst. prof. U. Costa Rica, San José, 1984; phys. edn. tchr. and coach Colegio Lourdes, San Juan, PR, 1986—96, St. John's Sch., 1996—2006. Cooperating tchr. U. P.R., San Juan, PR, 1992—97; soccer coach Conquistadoras de Guaynabo, Guaynabo, PR, 2003—; spkr. Dept. Edn., San Juan, 1995, Interamerican U., 1996, Vocational Inst. San Juan, 1998. Author: Desarrollo Integral Comunitario Estudiantes Maestros, 2001. Mem.: AAPHERD, Alpha Delta Kappa. Achievements include first to establish soccer camp for girls in Puerto Rico. Avocations: soccer, basketball, reading, music, beach. Mailing: PO Box 21411 Station San Juan PR 00931-1411 Home: Bo Jayveyes Aguas Buenas PR 00703

MARICLE, ROBYN LUANN (FORD), band director; b. Waco, Tex., Dec. 29, 1959; d. Robert Charles and Peggy Lou (Brown) Ford; m. Dale Louis Maricle; children: Alan Louis, Aaron Lee. AA, McLennan C.C., 1981; MusB Edn., Baylor U., 1984. Cert. all-level music. Asst. dir. of music First United Meth. Ch., Waco, Tex., 1977—95, music sec., 1982—84; music tchr. Waco I.S.D. (Mountainview Elem.), Waco, Tex., 1984—85, Waco I.S.D. (Parkdale Elem.), Waco, Tex., 1990—99; dir. music Florence United Meth. Ch., Florence, Tex., 1995—98; choral dir. middle sch. and h.s. Lorena I.S.D., Tex., 1999—. Cub scout/boy scout leader Pack 308/Troop 308, Waco, 1991—2001; chmn. worship com. Mooreville United Meth. Ch., 2000—02, leader children's time, 1999—2002; asst. leader for youth Mooreville United Methodist Ch., 2000—02; youth Sunday sch. tchr. Mooreville United Meth. Ch., 2001—. Recipient Harry Hosier award, Ctrl. Tex. Conf. of the United Meth. Ch., 2000. Mem.: Ctrl. Tex. Conf. Music Edn., Music Educators Nat. Conf., Tex. Music Educator Assn. Methodist. Avocations: outdoors, crafts. Home: 1029 FM 1239 Eddy TX 76524-2442 Office: Lorena ISD PO Box 97 Lorena TX 76655 Business E-Mail: RobynMaricle@lorena-isd.net.

MARIE, SHANTI, artist; b. Fresno, Calif., Aug. 29, 1954; life ptnr. Art Goddard, June 13, 1996; 1 child, Amy Woody. BFA, Fresno State U., 1977. Mem.: Charlotte Art League. Personal E-mail: shantmarie@aol.com.

MARIETTA, ELIZABETH ANN, real estate broker; b. Oshkosh, Wis., Feb. 28, 1954; d. Frederick Damler and Connie Steiger Dempsey; children: Hunter H. Student, U. Autonima, Guadalajara, Mex., 1974; BA in Architecture, U. N.Mex., 1979. Lic. Oreg. Real Estate Compass Realty. Project mgr. drafting Hutchinson, Brown & Ptnrs., Architects, Albuquerque, 1978-80; engr. facilities constrn. mgmt. divsn. Albuquerque Ops. Office, 1982-90, engr. quality engring. divsn., 1982-90, engr. budget and resources mgmt., 1982-90, site mgr. uranium mill tailings remedial action project, 1982-90, environ. engr. performance assessment divsn., 1995—98; sect. chief indsl. tech. Bonneville Power Adminstrn., Portland, Oreg., 1990—. Employee support sounding bd. Bonneville Power Adminstrn., Portland, 1990-91, women's resource group,

1990-93. Author: Ricochet Stepparenting. Mem. City Club Portland, 1990-91. Mem.: Coun. Women Realtors, Le-Tip Coalition of Women, Ind. Real Estate Brokers Assn., Network Orgn. Avocations: reading, sailing, travel, scuba diving. Home: 580 First St Lake Oswego OR 97034-3115 Office Phone: 503-675-2995, 503-753-5558.

MARINACCIO, BRIDGET C., social sciences educator; d. Sandra A. Kennedy; m. Carmen Marinaccio, Aug. 14, 1993; children: Ashley A., Carmen, Andre F., Dominic, Julian A, Benjamin. PhD, SUNY, Buffalo, 2001. Rape crisis cousnelor NY, 1995. Chair social scis. Medaille Coll., Buffalo, 2003—, program dir., 2003—06. Clin. counselor Amherst Family Counseling, NY, 1995—. Author: (text book) Counseling Children and Adolescents. Scholar, Buffalo's Bus. First, 2006. Mem.: Am. Couseling Assn. (profl. standards com. 2004—06), NY Mental Health Counseling (assoc.; dir. buffalo/niagara region 2002—06). Office: Medaille Coll 18 Agassiz Cir Buffalo NY 14214 Office Phone: 716-880-2193. Personal E-mail: drbmarin@aol.com.

MARINE, SUSAN SONCHIK, analytical chemist, educator; b. Maple Heights, Ohio, Mar. 10, 1954; d. Stephen Robert and Gloria Ann (Hach) Sonchik; m. Michael David Marine; 1 child, Matthew Robert Marine. BS in Chemistry magna cum laude, John Carroll U., Cleve., 1975; MS in Analytical Chemistry, Case Western Res. U., Cleve., 1978; PhD in Phys. Chemistry, Case Western Res. U., 1980. Asst. chemist Horizons Research Inc., Beachwood, Ohio, 1974-75; chemist specialist Standard Oil of Ohio, Warrensville Heights, Ohio, 1975-79; organic chemistry br. mgr. Versar, Inc., Springfield, Va., 1980-83; mgr. gas chromatography program IBM Instruments Inc., Danbury, Conn., 1983-87, radiation safety officer, 1985-87; expert witness, cons. Martin, Craig, Chester & Sonnenschein, Chgo., 1981-83; adv. engr. in advanced lithography IBM Corp., Essex Junction, Vt., 1987-95; vis. assoc. prof. chemistry Centre Coll., Danville, Ky., 1995-98; asst. prof. chemistry and biochemistry, coord. tech. program Miami U., Middletown, Ohio, 1998—2004; spl. term appointment energy sys. divsn. Argonne Nat. Lab., Ill., 2003—05; assoc. prof. chemistry and biochemistry, coord. tech. program Miami U., Middletown, Ohio, 2004—. Vis. asst. prof. chemistry and math. Heritage Coll., 1991—92; spkr. in field. Author: African Walking Safari, 1985; editl. adv. bd. Jour. Chromatographic Sci., 1977-93, guest editor, 1987. Mem. Danbury Conservation Commn., 1986-87, tchr. and tutor chemistry, 1985-89, 91-92, 94; troop leader Lake Erie coun. Girl Scouts U.S.A., 1971-80, Southwestern Conn., 1983-87; leader explorer post Cleve. coun. Boy Scouts Am., 1977-78; managerial advisor Jr. Achievement, Warrensville Heights, Ohio, 1977-78; judge State or Regional Sci. Fair, 1977, 80, 89-91, 99, 2000, Odyssey of the Mind, 1994; asst. leader Internat. Folk Dancers, Newtown, Conn., 1985-87; tchr. religion, 1981-84, 87-90, 93-94; mem. sch. bd. John XXIII Elem. Sch., 2004—. Recipient Overall Best Paper award Eastern Analytical Symposium, 1984, First Gas Chromatograph award IBM Instruments Inc., 1985, contbn. award (tech. paper) 10th Internat. Congress of Essential Oils, Flavors, Fragrances, Washington, 1986. Mem. ASTM (exec. com. E-19 1985-2000, chmn. subcom. 1986-2000, vice chmn. arrangements 1994-98), Am. Chem. Soc. (chmn. membership com. Green Mountain sect. 1988-89, chmn. 1990-91, local coord. Nat. Chemistry Week 1991, 93-98, 2002-04, mem. nat. com. on technician affairs 2005, 2006, nat. com. on cmty. activities 2005, Phoenix award 1994, 97, Salute to Excellence award 2004), Iota Sigma Pi (pres. N.E. Ohio chpt. 1978-79, mem.-at-large fin. mgr. 1993-97, nat. v.p. 1996-99, nat. pres. 1999-2002, immediate past pres. 2002-05), No. Vt. Canoe Cruisers (treas. 1990-92), Green Mountain Steppers (sec. 1993-95), Centre Coll. Outdoors Club (faculty advisor 1996-98), Miami U. Middletown Chemistry Club (faculty advisor 2003-04), Miami U. Middletown Ski and Snowboard Club (faculty advisor 2004—), Phi Theta Kappa (faculty advisor Miami U. Middletown 2004—). Roman Catholic. Avocations: camping, dance, travel. Home: 4667 Sebald Dr Franklin OH 45005-5328 Office: Miami U Middletown 4200 E University Blvd Middletown OH 45042-3458 Business E-Mail: mariness@muohio.edu.

MARINEAU, MICHELLE LYNN, nursing educator; b. Detroit, May 28, 1955; d. Edward Wilton and Mary Elizabeth Marineau; m. Richard A. Briggs, Apr. 1, 1961; children: Amanda Leigh Williams, Thomas Michael Williams. PhD, U. Hawaii, 2005. Assoc. prof. nursing Hawaii Pacific U., Honolulu, 1999—; clinician, rschr. Kaiser Permanente, 1999—. Recipient Excellence Nursing Edn. award, Blodgett Meml. Med. Ctr., 1991. Mem.: Mich. Nurses Assn. (legis. liaison Grand Traverse dist. 1994—95), Sigma Theta Tau (hon. 2005). Home: 55-247 Kamehameha Hwy Laie HI 96762 Office: Hawaii Pacific University 45-045 Kamehameha Hwy Kaneohe HI 96744-5297 Office Phone: 808-236-5589. Home Fax: 808-432-7796; Office Fax: 808-432-7796. Personal E-mail: 808 432-7793. E-mail: mmarineau@hpu.edu.

MARINELLI, JANICE, broadcast executive; b. N.Y., 1958; m. Thomas Mazza; 3 children. BS in Comm., St. John's U., NY. Rsch. analyst TeleRep; sr. rschr. Lorimar TV, Katz TV Group; acct. exec. Buena Vista TV, 1985, dir. sales western divsn., exec. v.p., 1996—99, pres. Burbank, Calif., 1999—. Office: Buena Vista TV 500 S Buena Vista St Burbank CA 91521*

MARINELLO, KATHRYN V., information technology executive; married; 3 children. BS, SUNY, Albany; MBA, Hofstra Univ. Mgmt. positions with Barclay's, Citibank, Chemical Bank; pres. U.S. Bank Card Services; pres. electronic payments group First Data Corp.; mgmt. positions with Gen. Electric, 1997—2006, exec. v.p. GE card services, pres. GE Capital cons. fin. services, pres., CEO GE Fin. Assurance Mktg. group, pres., CEO GE Fleet Services, 2002—06; pres., CEO Ceridian Corp., Mpls., 2006—. Bd. dir. Greater Twin Cities United Way, Minn. Bus. Partnership. Named an Industry Leader, Mpls./St. Paul Bus. Journal, 2006. Office: Ceridian Corp 3311 E Old Shakopee Rd Minneapolis MN 55425*

MARINER, LINDA KETTERMAN, minister; d. Charles Albert and Margaret Jane Hearn; m. Howard Paul Ketterman, Sept. 20, 1957 (dec. Oct. 14, 1990); children: Howard Paul Ketterman Jr., Jane Elizabeth Ruark; m. William Bentley Mariner, Feb. 24, 1994 (dec. July 2000). AA in Chem. Dependency Counseling, Wor-Wic C.C., 2000. Course of Study Wesley Theol. Sem., Wash., DC, 2001, License to Preach Drew Theol. Sem., Madison, NJ., 1992, Ordained Deacon United Meth. Ch., 2001. Cert. nursing asst. McCready Meml. Hosp., Crisfield, Md., 1978—85; adminstr. day care ctr. Little Lambs, Ocean Pines, Md., 1991—93. Pastor Sharptown-Asbury Charge, Md., 1993—99, Nanticoke-West Side Parish, Md., 1999—2002. Named Mother of Yr., Asbury United Meth. Ch., Crisfield, Md., 1978, Rookie of Yr., Am. Cancer Soc., 1991, Vol. of Yr., Kent County C. of C., 2005; recipient Gov's award for Voluntarism, State of Md., 2004, Martin Luther King, Jr. Humanitarian award, Chester Valley Mins. Assn., 2005. Mem.: Lion's Club (dist. chaplian 1999—2000, dist. chaplain 2004—05), Phi Theta Kappa. Home: 6190 Rock Hall Rd Rock Hall MD 21661 Office: Rock Hall United Meth Charge PO Box 66 Rock Hall MD 21661 Office Phone: 410-639-2144.

MARING, MARY MUEHLEN, state supreme court justice; b. Devils Lake, ND, July 27, 1951; d. Joseph Edward and Charlotte Rose (Schorr) Muehlen: m. David Scott Maring, Aug. 30, 1975; children: Christopher David, Andrew Joseph. BA in Polit. Sci. summa cum laude, Moorhead State U., 1972; JD, U. N.D., 1975. Bar: Minn., N.D. Law clk. Hon. Bruce Stone, Mpls., 1975—76; assoc. Stefanson, Landberg & Alm, Ltd., Moorhead, Minn., 1976—82, Ohnstad, Twichell, Breitling, Rosenvold, Wanner, Nelson, Neugebauer & Maring, West Fargo, ND, 1982—88, Lee Hagan Law Office, Fargo, ND, 1988—91; pvt. practice Maring Law Office, Fargo, 1991—96; justice ND Supreme Ct., Bismarck, ND, 1996—. Women's bd. mem. 1st Nat. Bank, Fargo, 1977-82; career day speaker Moorhead Rotarians, 1980-83; mem. Court Svcs. Com., 1996-, Jud. Compensation, subcom. of Jud. Conf., 1998-, Five-State Jud. Conf. Planning Com., 1997-98, 99-2000; chmn. Gender Fairness Implementation Com., 1997-, Jud. Conf. Exec. Bd., 1998-, chair-elect, 2004-05, chair, 2005, Juvenile Drug Ct. Study, planning and Implementation Com., 1998-2000, Juvenile Drug Ct. Adv. Com., 2000-, Personnel Policy bd., 1999-2004, Govs. Drug and Alcohol Policy Adv. Bd., 1999-2001, N.Dak. Commn. on Drug and Alcohol Abuse, 2002-, No. Plains Ethics Inst., 2000-, Juvenile Policy Bd., 2001-, Jud. Edn. Com., 2005-, Jud. Planning Com., 2001-, Harold Schafer Leadership Ctr. Com. Contbr. note to legal rev.; note editor N.D. Law Rev., 1975. Mem. ABA (del. ann. conv. young lawyers sect. 1981-82, bd. govs. 1982-83), Minn. Women Lawyers, N.D. State Bar Assn. (bd. govs. 1991-93), Clay County Bar Assn. (v.p. 1983-84), N.D. Trial Lawyers Assn. (pres. 1992-93), Internat. Soc. of Barristers, Nat. Assn. of Women Judges (dist. 10 dir. 2001-03). Roman Catholic. Office: ND Supreme Ct 600 E Boulevard Ave Dept 180 Bismarck ND 58505-0530*

MARINO, DEIRDRE J., science educator; d. Corrado A. and Nancy Marino; 1 child, Daniella N. BA, Columbia U., N.Y.C., 1988; MS, NYU, 1993, MPhil, 1991; MEd, Queens Coll., N.Y., 2006. Sr. editor Plenum Sci. Pub., N.Y.C., 1993—98; supervising editor Lippincott Williams & Wilkins, N.Y.C., 1998—2003; educator sci. Steinway Ind. Sch. 141, Astoria, NY, 2003—. Patricia Harris Fellowship, NYU Grad. Sch. Arts & Scis., 1990—93. Mem.: NSTA, Kappa Delta Pi. Personal E-mail: deem345@aol.com.

MARINO, GENA, speech educator; b. Ridgewood, NY, Apr. 4, 1975; d. John Joseph and Angela Marie Marino. BA, St. John's U., 1997, MS, 2000. Tchr. speech improvement NYC Dept. Edn., Bklyn., 1997—; pvt. practice spl. edn. provider Queens, NY, 2000—. Mem.: Coun. for Exceptional Children. Roman Catholic. Avocations: reading, exercise. Home: 6487 84th St Middle Village NY 11379 Office: 141K0380 370 Maicy Ave Brooklyn NY 11206

MARINO, MARION LILLIAN, health service administrator; b. Newark, Dec. 9, 1942; d. Thomas Inard and Marie Viola (Favata) Reed; m. Thomas John Marino, Oct. 27, 1962 (dec. Dec. 1990); children: Deborah, June, Patricia, Jillian; m. John Stephen Meyash, May 18, 1996. RN, The Bklyn. Hosp., 1963; student, Western Conn. State U., 1976-83, Gulf Coast C.C., 1986-90. Staff nurse, asst. head nurse Nassau County Med. Ctr., East Meadow, N.Y., 1963-66; staff nurse ICU Ctrl. Gen. Hosp., Plainview, N.Y., 1966-72, Danbury (Conn.) Hosp., 1972-84; nurse mgr. Bay Med. Ctr., Panama City, Fla., 1984-88; house supr. Jackson County Hosp., Marianna, Fla., 1988-90, Gulf Coast HCA Hosp., Panama City, Fla., 1990-96; med. supr. Corrections Corp. Am., Panama City, 1993—. Mem. TB Task Force, Panama City, 1995—; mem., sec. Fla. Nurse Commn., Tallahassee, 1986-87. Rep. com. Bethel Chpt., 1980; Apple Blossom com. Apple Blossom Festival, Bethel, 1976. Roman Catholic. Avocations: reading, crafts, gardening, family. Office: Corrections Corp Am 5600 Nehi Rd Panama City FL 32404-2049

MARINO, MARISSA A., language educator; b. New Haven, June 17, 1982; d. Anthony Joseph and Mary Ellen Marino. Student, Ctr. Cross Cultural Study, Seville, Spain; degree in spanish cum laude, Assumption Coll., 2004; postgrad., Quinnipaic U., 2004—. Spanish tchr. Amity Mid. Sch., Bethany, Conn., 2004—05, Amity HS, Woodbridge, Conn., 2005—. Spanish tchr. Conn. Orgn. Spanish Tchrs.; ESL tchr., Spanish tutor. Dir. Little Buddies program, vol. Spl. Olympics Assumption Coll. Reach Out Ctr., Worcester, Mass., 2000—04. Scholar, Americorps, 2003; Wepawaug Flagg Cmty. Svc. scholar, 2000, Lyceum achievement scholar, 2000—04. Mem.: Am. Assn. Tchrs. Spanish and Portuguese, Nat. Dance Assn., Psi Chi. Home: 1500 Dunbar Hill Rd Hamden CT 06514

MARINO, SHEILA BURRIS, education educator; b. Knoxville, Nov. 24, 1947; d. David Paul and Lucille Cora (Maupin) Burris; m. Louis John Marino, Dec. 19, 1969; children: Sheila Noelle, Heather Michelle. BS, U. Tenn., 1969, MS, 1971, EdD, 1976; postgrad., W.Va. U., Europe, Clemson U. Elem./early childhood tchr. Knoxville City Schs., 1969-71; cooperating tchr. U. Tenn., Knoxville, 1969-71; dir. early childhood edn./tchr. Glenville (W.Va.) State Coll., 1971-72, Colo. Women's Coll., Denver, 1972-73; asst. prof. edn. Lander U., Greenwood, SC, 1973-75; instr., spl. asst. to coord. elem./early childhood edn. U. Tenn., 1975-76; prof. edn., dir. clin. experiences, asst. dean Lander U. Sch. Edn., 1976—93, dean, 1993-94, dir. sci. discovery program, 1995—, prof. edn., dir. tchg. fellows program, 1995—. Cons. in field; dir. Creative Activities Prog. for Children, Lander U., 1979—; mem. W.Va. Gov.'s Early Childhood Adv. Bd., 1971-72, Gov.'s Team of Higher Edn. Profls. on Comprehensive Plan for S.C. Early Childhood Edn., 1982. Contbr. articles to profl. jours. and books; author: International Children's Literature, 1989. Bd. dirs. Greenwood Lit. Coun., v.p., 1990, pres., 1991; bd. dirs. St. Nicholas Speech and Hearing Ctr., Greenwood, pres., 1992; bd. dirs. Old Ninety-Six coun. Girl Scouts U.S.A., 1987-92; vol. March of Dimes Program, Greenwood, 1987; vice chair Greenwood County First Steps, 2004—. Mem. AAUW (pres. 1990-92), AAUP, SNEA (state advisor 1981-88, 98-99), S.C. Student Edn. Assn., Piedmont Assn. Children and Adults with Learning Disabilities (pres. 1986-93, exec. bd.), Learning Disabilities Assn. S.C. (pres. 1990-94), S.C. Edn. Assn., S. C. Assn. for Children Under Six, So. Assn. for Children under Six, S.C. Assn. Tchr. Educators, Piedmont Reading Coun. (v.p. 1985-86, 90-91, pres. 1986-88, 91-92, 96-97), S.C. Coun. Internat. Reading Assn. (exec. bd. 1986-88, 91-96), Delta Kappa Gamma (pres. Epsilon chpt. 1984-88, 92-94, mem. exec. bd.), Pi Lambda Theta, Kappa Delta Pi (pres. U. Tenn. chpt. 1974-75), Phi Delta Kappa (v.p. 1988-90, pres. Lander U. chpt. 1990-91, 94-96, 2005—). Democrat. Presbyterian. Avocations: reading, gardening, swimming, music, arts and crafts. Home: 103 Essex Ct Greenwood SC 29649-9561 Office: Lander U Stanley Avenue Greenwood SC 29649

MARINOFF, ELAINE, artist; b. LA, Sept. 24, 1934; d. George Lawrence and Lena (Brown) M.; m. Robert Glen Good, June 9, 1957 (div. 1980); children: Cynthia Ellen Good Reiman, Glendon Robert, Bradley Lawrence Good. Student, Chinouard Art Inst., 1950, U. Calif., Berkley, 1953-55, Ecole Guerre Lavigene, Paris, 1955-56; BA, UCLA, 1957; postgrad., Sch. Visual Arts, N.Y.C., 1989. Pres. Elaine Good Interiors, L.A., 1960-72; instr. The Serigraphic Process UCLA, 1986-88. Author, illustrator: (books) Windows, 1988, Power Sources, 1989; exhibited in group shows and one-woman shows at Laguna Mus. Art, Calif., 1974, Brand Mcpl. Mus. Gallery, Glendale, Calif., 1979, LA County Mus. Art, 1979, 80, 81, Calif. Mus. Sci. and Industry, 1980, Sateria Galeria fur Erotisch Kusnt, Kronberg, Germany, 1981, Downey Mus. Art, Calif., 1981, Heritage Gallery, LA, 1982, Galerie Das Bilderhaus, Frankfurt, Germany, 1983, Cabrillo Marine Mus., San Pedro, Calif., 1984, Galerie Woeller Paquet, Frankfurt, 1984, Criteria Gallery, Denver, 1985, Artworks Gallery, LA, 1988, Eva Cohon Gallery, Chgo., 1992, Kouros Gallery, NYC, 1993, Claudia Chapline Gallery Stinson Beach, Calif., 1993, 95, Andre Zarre Gallery, NYC, 1994, NYU, 1995, Noyes Mus., Oceanville, NJ, 1995, Bedford Hist. Soc., NY, 1996, Korean Cultural Ctr., LA, 1998, U. Judaism, LA, 1999, Sampson Fine Arts, NYC, 2001-2003, Guild Hall, East Hampton, NY, 2003-04, Allen Sheppard Gallery, NYC, 2004, Cooperman Gallery, Newhope, Pa., 2006, Bluehill Cultural Ctr., Piermont, NY, 2006. Cmty. Bd. # 1, N.Y.C., 1998—. Mem. Fine Arts Fedn. N.Y.C.(bd. dir. 2003—), Artists Talk on Art (bd. dir. 1990-2000), Artists Equity (bd. dir. L.A. chpt. 1980), Women's Caucus Arts, Bus. and Profl. Women, Artists Econ. Action. Democrat. Jewish. Avocation: writing. Studio: 214 N Sea Rd Southampton NY 11968

MARION, ANN, retired elementary school educator, psychologist; b. Mobile, Ala., Apr. 30, 1936; d. Edmund Charles and Lela Marie (Franklin) Guidroz; m. Donald Orrin Marion, June 25, 1965; children: Janet Marie, Kathryn Elizabeth. BA, Millsaps Coll., Jackson, Miss., 1963; MEd, U. So. Miss., Hattiesburg, 1972. Cert. tchr., cert. sch. psychologist, Miss. Classrm. tchr. Natchez-Adams Sch. Dist., Natchez, Miss., 1963-72, tchr. Title III ESEA, 1967-69, psychometrist, 1969-72, sch. psychologist, 1977-94; ret. Past pres. Mental Health Assn., Adams County Assn. for Child Protection; mem. Gov.'s Criminal Justice Task Force, 1991; bd. dirs. Natchez Child Protection Assn.; mem. craft com. Natchez Career and Tech. Ctr. Mem. Pilgrimage Garden Club, Nat. Rep. Assn., Phi Delta Kappa. Avocations: reading, study groups, bridge, collecting antiques, dollhouses. Home: 105 Mansfield Dr Natchez MS 39120-4930 E-mail: agmarion@netscape.net.

MARION, BERNICE ALEXANDER, elementary school educator; b. Winnsboro, S.C., Aug. 20, 1956; m. Samuel Marion, Apr. 3, 1983; children: Samuel Rashad, Brittany Alexis. MEd, Ga. State U., Atlanta. Cert. tchr. Ga. Tchr./dept. chair Dekalb County Sch. Sys., Clarkston, Ga., 1978—. Named Tchr. of the Yr., Salem Mid. Sch., 1999. Office: Martin Luther King Jr High School 3991 Snapfinger Rd Lithonia GA 30083 Office Phone: 678-874-5402.

MARION, ELENA MENDES, secondary school educator; b. Ludlow, Mass., Apr. 8, 1955; d. Antonio Nunes and Elena Pereira Mendes; m. Paul Richard Marion, Apr. 12, 1980; 1 child, Ryan Paul. BA in Math. & Spanish, Coll. of Our Lady of the Elms, Chicopee, Mass., 1973—77; MA in Ednl. Adminstrn., Westfield State Coll., Mass., 1987—90, Cert. of Advanced Grad. Studies, 1990—93. Cert. Tchr. Mass. Dept. Edn., 2009. Tchr. Cathedral HS, Springfield, 1977—80, Ludlow Pub. Schs., 1980—. Home: 157 Cedar St Ludlow MA 01056 Office: Baird Mid Sch 1 Rooney Rd Ludlow MA 01056 Office Phone: 413-583-5685. Personal E-mail: e_marion@ludlowps.org. Business E-Mail: e_marion@lulowps.org.

MARION, MARJORIE ANNE, English language educator, educational consultant; b. Winterset, Iowa, May 6, 1935; d. Virgil Arthur and Marilyn Ruth (Sandy) Hammon; m. Robert H. Marion, Dec. 20, 1964; 1 child, Kathryn Ruth BA, Colo. Coll., 1958; MA, Purdue U., 1969; postgrad., Inst. Mgmt. Lifelong Edn. Harvard U., 1981. Chairperson English dept. Lincoln-Way H.S., New Lenox, Ill., 1964—68; dir. pub. rels. U. St. Francis, Joliet, Ill., 1968—70, chairperson English dept., 1971—75, chairperson humanities and fine arts divsn., 1975—79, coord. instrnl. devel., 1979—80, dir. continuing edn., 1980—84, acting v.p. acad. affairs, 1984—85, dean faculty, 1985—89, assoc. prof. English, 1989—97, dir. Freshman Core Program, 1993—95, dir. Writing Ctr., 1996, prof. emeritus, 1997—. Cons. to presdl. search U. St. Francis, 2001—02; mem. vis. team North Ctrl. Assn., Joliet and Lockport, Ill., 1975—79; lectr. at ednl. workshops and instns.; condr. writing workshops for adults returning to coll., 1995—; TV and radio appearances regarding lifelong edn., Chgo., St. Louis, Albuquerque, Phoenix, 1982—85; lectr. writing workshops. Author: A Guide to Writing for the Faint at Heart, 1996; author monograph; drama critic Joliet Herald News, 1970-82 Chmn. Cath. Franciscan Charisma Coun., 2005—06. Recipient Pres.'s award Coll. St. Francis, 1975 Mem. Am. Assn. Higher Edn., Nat. Coun. Tchrs. English, Nat. Acad. Advising Assn. Roman Catholic. E-mail: mamarion1@msn.com.

MARION, SARAH ELIZABETH, elementary school educator; b. Livingston, N.J., Sept. 24, 1982; d. Kenneth Eugene and Nancy Michele Marion. BS in Elem. Edn., St. Joseph's U., Phila., 2004; postgrad., Kean U., Union, N.J., 2005—. Cert. tchr. N.J. 2d grade tchr. Scotch Plains Bd. of Edn., NJ, 2004—. N.J. ASK test prep adminstr. Scotch Plains Bd. Edn., 2006, piloted new sci. curriculum, 2005—06. Grantee JVC grantee, Scotch Plains Bd. Edn., 2005. Mem.: NEA, Internat. Reading Assn., Kappa Delta Pi. Roman Catholic. Home: 67 Irving Ave Livingston NJ 07039 Office: Brunner Elementary School 721 Westfield Rd Scotch Plains NJ 07076

MARION, SARAH KATHLEEN, music educator; b. Wenatchee, Wash., Mar. 31, 1974; d. John Alfred Braden and Diana Lee Black; m. Jim Johan Marion; children: Christina, Daniel. AAS, Wenatchee Valley Coll., Wenatchee, Wash., 1995. Pvt. piano instr., Wenatchee, 1990—; part-time instr. Wenatchee Valley Coll., Wenatchee, 2001. Sec. Family Issues and Awareness Team, Wenatchee, 2000—; at-large bd. mem. Wenatchee Free Meth. Ch., 2001. Mem.: Wenatchee Chpt. Wash. State Music Tchrs. Assn. (publicity chmn. 1997—99), Music Tchrs. Nat. Assn., Wash. State Music Tchrs. Assn., Phi Theta Kappa. Avocations: travel, languages, running, outdoor recreation. Home: PO Box 5063 Wenatchee WA 98807-5063

MARIOTTI, MARGARET, executive secretary; b. Derby, Conn., Nov. 1, 1956; d. Peter J. and Matrona (Iannotti) M. Student, Stone Sch. Bus., New Haven, 1975-76. Sec. Sikorsky Aircraft, Stratford, Conn., 1977—. Mem. Alpha Iota. Home: 411 Coram Ave Shelton CT 06484-3134 E-mail: mmmariotti@aol.com.

MARIS, BETH, clinical social worker, sex therapist; b. Bklyn., Nov. 18, 1949; d. Bernard Troy and Lillan Rochelle Cohen-Troy; m. Ronald William Maris, Aug. 15, 1976; children: Elizabeth, Catherine, Amanda Leigh, Gabriella Eliese. BS, Syracuse U., 1971; MSW, Cath. U., 1974. Lic. social worker; cert. group therapist; cert. sex therapist; cert. suicidologist; cert. EMDR therapist. Fellow in suicidology NIMH, Washington, 1971; clin. social worker S.C. State Hosp., Columbia, 1974, clin. social work supr., 1975-78; pvt. practice clin. social work, Columbia, 1978—; dir. psychiat. hosp. Blanding House, Columbia, 1983-86; clin. dir. sex trauma unit S.C. State Hosp., Columbia, 1986-88; clin. social work supr. Bryan Psychiat. Hosp., Columbia, 1991—2002. Cons., trauma expert. Hebrew tchr. Tree of Life Congregation, Columbia, 1996-98, bd. dirs., 1993—. Recipient Tchg. award Tree of Life Congregation, 1997. Mem. AASECT, AGPA, NASW. Office Phone: 803-736-7133.

MARISCOTTI, JANINE M., psychotherapist, educator; MSW, Rutgers U., N.J., 1984. LCSW Pa. Psychotherapy pvt. practice, Glenside, Pa., 1984—; asst. prof. La Salle U., Phila., 1989—, chair dept. sociology, social work and criminal justice, 2004—. Office: La Salle University 1900 West Olney Ave Philadelphia PA 19141 Office Phone: 215-951-1000.

MARISOL, (MARISOL ESCOBAR), sculptor; b. Paris; Student, Ecole des Beaux-Arts, Paris, 1949, Art Students League, NYC, 1950, New Sch. Social Research, 1951-54, Hans Hofmann Sch., NYC, 1951-54; DFA (hon.), Moore Coll. Arts, Phila., 1969, R.I. Sch. Design, 1986, SUNY, Buffalo, 1992. One-woman shows include Leo Castelli Gallery, 1958, Stable Gallery, 1962, 64, Sidney Janis Gallery, N.Y.C., 1966, 67, 73, 75, 81, 84, 89, Hanover Gallery, London, 1967, Moore Coll. Art, Phila., 1970, Worcester (Mass.) Art Mus., 1971, N.Y. Cultural Center, 1973, Columbus (Ohio) Gallery of Fine Arts, 1974, Makler Gallery, Phila., 1982, Boca Raton Mus. Art, Fla., 1988, Galerie Tokoro, Tokyo, 1989, Hasagawa Gallery, Tokyo, 1989, Nat. Portrait Gallery, Washington, 1991, Marlborough Gallery, 1995, Hakone Open Air Mus., Kanagawa, Japan, 1995, Mus. Modern Art, Shiga, Japan, 1995, Iwai City Art Mus., Fukushima, Japan, 1995, Kagoshima City (Japan) Mus. Art, 1995, Malborough, 1995, 98, Museo de Arte Contempo Ranio, Caracas, Venezuela, 1996, numerous others; exhibited in group shows including Painting of a Decade, Tate Gallery, London, 1964, New Realism, Municipal Mus., The Hague, 1964, Carnegie Internat., Pitts., 1964, Art of the U.S.A. 1670-1966, Whitney Mus. Am. Art, N.Y.C., 1966, American Sculpture of the Sixties, Mus. of Art, Los Angeles, 1967, Biennale, Venice, 1968, Art Inst. Chgo., 1968, Boymans-van Beuningen Mus., Rotterdam, The Netherlands, 1968, Inst. Contemporary Art, London, 1968, Fondation Maeght, Paris, 1970, Hirshhorn Mus. and Sculpture Garden, 1984, Nat. Portrait Gallery, Washington, 1987, Heckscher Mus., Huntington, N.Y., 1987, Whitney Mus. at Philip Morris, N.Y.C., 1988, Rose Art Mus., Waltham, Mass., 1990, Nat. Portrait Gallery, London, 1993; represented in permanent collections at Mus. Modern Art, N.Y.C., Whitney Mus. Am. Art, Albright-Knox Gallery, Buffalo, Hakone Open Air Mus., Tokyo, Nat. Portrait Gallery, Washington, Harry N. Abrams Collection, N.Y.C., Yale U. Art Gallery, Art Inst. Chgo., Met. Mus., N.Y.C., numerous others; pub. installation Am. Mcht. Mariner's Meml., Promenade Battery Pk. Pier A., Port of N.Y., N.Y.C. Mem. Am. Acad. and Inst. Arts and Letters (v.p. art 1984-87), NAD (academician).

MARJORIE, REED L., science educator; b. Spangler, Pa., Sept. 12, 1964; d. William L. and Grace Schilling; m. George L. Reed, Sept. 16, 1989; children: Alison M. Reed, George W. Reed. BS, U. Pitts., Johnstown, Pa, 1997; MSc, Miss. State U., Starkville, 2004. Cert. earth and space sci. Pa. Dept. Edn., 1997, environ. sci. edn. Pa. Dept. Edn., 2006. Earth, space and environ. sci. tchr. Elizabethtown Area Sch. Dist., Eliabethtown, Pa., 1997—. Recipient Instrnl. Excellence award, Elizabethtown Area Sch. Bd., 2003. Mem.: Conoy Creek Watershed Assn. (life; treas. 2005—06). Independent. Avocations: travel, hiking. Office: Elizabethtown Area HS 600 East High St Elizabethtown PA 17022 Office Phone: 717-367-1533. E-mail: margie_reed@etown.k12.pa.us.

MARK, HON FONG LOUIE, cytogeneticist; m. Roger Mark; children: Yvonne, Roger Jr., Seamus. PhD, Brown U. Diplomate Am. Bd. Med. Genetics. Postdoctoral fellow in med. genetics R.I. Hosp., Providence, asst., assoc. dir. cytogenetics, fellow molecular biology, dir. cytogenetics, 1990-99, clin. cytogeneticist Cancer & Leukemia Group B, 1990—99; pres., CEO KRAM Corp., 1994—; dir. human genetics RIDOH, 1999—2001; exec. dir. RIACA, 2001—02; dir. cytogenetics dept. Presbyn. Lab. Svcs., Charlotte, NC, 2002—04; dir. cytogenetics Boston U. Sch. Medicine, 2004—, clin. prof., 2004—. Instr. pathology Brown U., Providence, asst. prof. pathology; clin. prof. Brown Med. Sch., 1998—; assoc. mem. Maine Toxicology Inst., 1993—; chair grants rev. com. mem., prenatal diagnosis com., chair cancer genetics com., steering com.; grant reviewer NIH, U.S. Army Breast Cancer Rsch. Program, U.S. Army Prostate Cancer Rsch. Program; reviewer numerous other panels. Author: Medical Cytogenetics, 2000; mem. editl. rev. bd. Applied Cytogenetics, Pathobiology, Exptl. and Molecular Pathology, Cancer Genetics and Cytogenetics; contbr. 200 articles to profl. jours. Recipient award Time Mag. Essay Writing Contest, Balfour award, Award R.I. Found.; NSF rsch. grantee Brown U., co-grantee Dept. Energy; Florence Seibert postdoctoral fellowship AAUW Ednl. Found.; North Providence Citizens scholar, Fruithill Jr. Women's Club scholar; others. Fellow Am. Coll. Med. Genetics; mem. AAAS, Am. Soc. Human Genetics, Assn. Genetic Technologists, Sigma Xi.

MARK, JUDI, actress, choreographer; b. Chgo., Mar. 20; d. Leonard and Dorothy March. BS in Edn., So. Ill. U.; postgrad., San Diego State U., U.S. Internat. U. Performing Arts. Dancer U.S. Internat. Dance Theatre, Balboa Park Theatre, San Diego. Founder, choreographer Judi Mark & Co.; dance instr. P.S. 190, N.Y.C., 1986—; elem. tchr. Dade County Schs., 1970-74. Appeared in (stage prodns.) West Side Story, The Rose Tattoo, The Rainmaker, Time and Involvement, (films) Deathtrap, 1982, Turk 182!, 1985, Private Resorts, 1986, (TV) Miami Vice. Mem. AFTRA. Jewish. Avocation: travel.

MARK, LOIS NORA, psychotherapist, consultant; b. Honolulu, Oct. 2, 1937; d. Yin O. Mark and Katherine Kim (Moy) Mark Shim. BA, Wheaton Coll., Ill., 1959; MSW, Mich. State U., East Lansing, 1961. LCSW Calif. Case worker Liliokani Trust Child Welfare Agy., Honolulu, 1961—63; clin. social worker Child Guidance Clinic, San Mateo, Calif., 1964—65; psychiat. social worker Peninsula Hosp., Burkingame, 1965—71; psychotherapist pvt. practice, San Mateo, Calif., 1966—. Fellow, Mt. Zion Hosp. & Med. Ctr., San Francisco, 1964. Fellow: Soc. Clin. Social Work; mem.: NASW, Calif. Assn. Marriage & Family Therapists, Pi Gamma Mu. Avocations: photography, sailing, flying. Office: 327 N San Mateo Dr Ste 10 San Mateo CA 94401

MARK, MARSHA YVONNE ISMAILOFF, artistic director; b. Bridgeport, Conn., Mar. 15, 1938; d. Nicholas and Louba (Foullon) Ismailoff; m. Robert Louis Mark, June 25, 1960; children: Robert, William, Staci. Ballet tng. with, George Balanchine, 1956-57, George Volodine, 1945-60, 65-69; student, Skidmore Coll., 1978-80, Vaganova Method Sch., Minsk, USSR, 1983, U. of the Arts, 1990. Founder Marsha Imailoff Mark Sch. of Ballet, Newtown, Conn., 1969—; artistic dir. Conn. Com. for Ballet Miniatures, Newtown, Conn., 1974—, Malenkee Ballet Repertoire Co., Newtown, Conn., 1980—. V.p. Cmty. Arts Project Ext., Newtown, 1987-91; artistic dir. Danbury (Conn.) Music Ctr., 1989; instr. for neurologically impaired Ripton Sch., Shelton, Conn., 1992; choreographed section of Nutcracker Ballet for Special Children; toured Russia with Malenkee Ballet Repertoire Co. Choreographer including original works: Mademoiselle Angot, 1974, Circus, 1975, Haydn Concerto, 1976, Evening at the Zoo, 1977, Match Girl, 1978, The Four Seasons, 1979, Malenkee Waltz, 1980, Magic Key, 1981, Midsummer Night's Dream, 1982, Macbeth A Witches Haunt, 1983, Etudes, 1984, Toy Boutique, Etudes, 1985, Under the Sea, 1986, Nutcracker, 1987, 88, 89, 90, 91, 92, 93, 94, 95, 96, 97, Mere, Mere, Mere, 1988, Ellis Island Memoirs, 1991, Moonlight Etudes, 1992, Echoes of Soft Thunder, 1995, Coppelia, 1998; premiered in Baku USSR. Hostess for artists from Russia, translator UN Hostess Com., N.Y.C., 1988; Russian translator Friends of Music, Newtown, 1990, Sacred Heart U., Fairfield, Conn., 1994; founding pres. Seabranch Art League, Hobe Sound, Fla., 2006-; pres. Questors #1153, Treasure Coast, Fla., 2006-. Home: 9221 SE Eldorado Way Hobe Sound FL 33455 Office Phone: 203-240-1967. Personal E-mail: marshamashkh@adelphia.net.

MARK, MARY ELLEN, photographer; b. Phila., Mar. 20, 1940; d. A. DeRoy and Beatrice (Silverman) M.; m. Frank Anthony Macaoge, 1963 (div. 1964); m. Martin Bell. BA, U. Pa., 1962; MA, Annenberg Sch. Communication, 1964. Lectr., presenter workshops in field. One-woman shows include Photographers Gallery, London, 1976, Castelli Graphics, NYC, 1978, Olympus Gallery, London, 1981, Seson Art Gallery, U. Calif-Santa Cruz, Calif. Mus. Photography, Riverside, Drew U., NJ, 1982, Gallery of Fine Arts, Daytona Beach Community Coll., Fla., Friends of Photography, Carmel, Calif., 1983, Allen Street Gallery, Dallas, 1985, Birmingham (Ala.) Mus. of Art, 1989, numerous others; exhibited in group shows at Photokina, Cologne, 1973, Sidney Janis Gallery, NYC, 1976, Internat. Ctr. of Photography, NYC, 1979, Bibliotheque Nationale, Paris, 1979, Corcoran Gallery of Art and George Eastman House, NY, U. Colo., 1982, Eaton Shoen Gallery, San Francisco, 1983, Barbican Art Gallery, London, 1985, Munich Stadt Mus., 1985, Walker Art Ctr., Mpls., 1986, Portland (Maine) Mus. Art, 1986, Castle Gallery, New Rochelle, NY, Hillwood Art Gallery, Greenvale, NY, UN 40th Anniversary Photography Exhibit, 1985, Paris Opera, 1988, Zeitgenossischen Photography, Frankfurt, 1989, numerous others; author: Passport, 1974, Ward 81, 1979, Falkland Road: Prostitutes of Bombay, 1981, Streetwise, 1988, Mary Ellen Mark: Indian Circus, 1993, A Cry for Help: Stories of Homelessness and Hope, 1996, Mary Ellen Mark: American Odyssey, 1999, Twins, 2003, Exposure, 2005, others; contbr. articles, photographs to profl. publs., mags. Fulbright scholar, 1965-66; grantee USIA, 1975, NEA, 1977, 80, NY State Coun. for Arts, 1977, NEA, 1979-80; recipient Page One award The Newspaper Guild of NY, 1979, First Pl. Feature Picture Stroy U. Mo., 1980, Canon Photo Essayist award Life Mag., 1983, 1st prize Robert F. Kennedy Journalism, 1985, Philippe Halsman award ASMP, Photojournalism award George W. Polk, 1988. Mem. Assn. Soc. Mag. Photographers.

MARK, SUSAN A., music educator; b. Millville, N.J., Oct. 13, 1965; d. George J. and Barbara J. Chopek; m. James D. Mark, June 25, 1988; children: Douglas James, Bryan Christopher. BS in Music Edn., West Chester U., Pa., 1987. Cert. tchr. music instrnl. I Pa., elem. tchr. K-8 N.J., tchr. music K-12 N.J. Mgr. MaryAnn Shop, Vineland, NJ, 1984—87, The Corner House, Vineland, 1987—91; tchr. of music Bridgeton Pub. Schs., NJ, 1987—89; dir. of music Upper Pittsgrove Twp. Schs., Monroeville, NJ, 1989—98; dir. of instrumental music Rosa Internat. Mid. Sch., Cherry Hill, NJ, 1998—. Marching band judge Marching Band Festivals, 1987—99; guest condr. South Jersey Band and Orch. Dirs. Assn., NJ, 2002; asst. marching band dir. Bridgeton Pub. Schs., 1987—93, Haddonfield Pub. Schs., NJ, 1986—95; marching band drill designer Cherry Hill Marching Band, NJ, 1996—99; pvt. vocal, piano, and woodwind instr., Millville and Sewell, NJ, 1983—. Musician, lector St. John Bosco Roman Cath. Ch., Millville, 1981—2002. Recipient N.J. Gov.'s award - Tchr. of Yr., Upper Pittsgrove Schs., 1993. Mem.: Music Educators Nat. Conf., N.J. Music Educators Assn. (guest presenter conv. 2005), Kappa Delta Pi, Sigma Alpha Iota. Roman Catholic. Avocations: softball, reading. Office: Rosa Internat Mid Sch 485 Browning Ln Cherry Hill NJ 08034 Office Phone: 856-616-8787. Business E-Mail: smark@chclc.org.

MARKARIAN, ALEXIA MITRUS, artist; b. Binghamton, N.Y. m. Raymond Markarian. Studied with Robert Beverly Hale, Art Students League, N.Y.C. Artist, 1985—. Juror 10th Ann. Congressional Arts Caucus, 41st Dist., 1991, Scott Watson Meml. Salon, Soc. Calif. Assn. Camera Clubs, 1991, North County Artist's Coop., Excondido, Calif., 1993, San Diego Art Inst., 1992, lectr. isomata master class, Idyllwild, Calif., 1992, Art Mus. of Greater Victoria, Can., 1993, San Diego Art Inst., Calif., 1989, 1990; originator Photropolis 95 Internat. Photo/Art Exhbn., San Diego, 1995. Solo shows include Fla. So. State Coll. Melvin Art Gallery, Lakeland, 1988, U. Mo. Gallery 210, St. Louis, 1988, Witter Gallery, Storm Lake, Iowa, 1988, Mira Costa Coll. James Crumley Gallery, Oceanside, Calif., 1988, Dietrich Jenny Gallery, San Diego, 1989, Cazenovia (N.Y.) Coll. Chapman Cultural Ctr., 1989, Rogue C.C. Wiseman Gallery, Grants Pass, Oreg., 1989, U. No. Colo. Miriani Gallery, Greeley, Colo., 1989, Memphis State U., 1989, Butte Coll. Coyote Gallery, Oroville, Calif., 1990, Oneiros Gallery, San Diego, 1991, Visual Arts Ctr. Alaska, Ancorage, 1991, Wichita Falls Mus. and Art Ctr., 1991, Edmonton Art Gallery, Alta., Can., 1992, Roberson Ctr. Arts and Scis., Binghamton, N.Y., 1992, Washington and Jefferson Coll., Washington, Pa., 1992, Art Gallery Greater Victoria, B.C., Can., 1993, Kelowna (Can.) Mus., 1993, Red Venus Gallery, San Diego, 1994, Simay Space, San Diego, 2001; exhibited in group shows at Orange County Art Assn. Nat., Brea, Calif., 1985, Internat. Soc. for Airbrush Arts, 1985, Pitts. Ctr. for Arts, 1985, Chautauqua Nat. Exhibit of Am. Art, N.Y., 1985, Touring Group Exhibit "Five Women Artists, 1986, Small Works Nat., N.Y., 1986, San Diego Art Inst. Ann. Nat., 1986, San Diego Mus. Art, 1986, Riverside Art Mus., Calif., 1986, Butler Inst. Am. Art, Youngstown, Ohio, 1985, Calif. Watercolor and Drawing Survery, 1986, Butler Inst. Am. Art, Youngstown, Ohio, 1987, San Diego Art Inst., 1987 (Mid Winter award), Fresno Arts Ctr., 1987, Mus. No. B.C., Prince Rupert, Can., 1987, Elvehjem Mus. Art, Madison, Wis., 1987, Minot (N.D.) Art Gallery, 1987, Coll. Ea. Utah, Price, 1987, Mt. Mercy Coll., Cedar Rapids, Iowa, 1987, Masur Mus. Art, Monroe, La., 1988, Fla. Nat./Fla. State U., Tallahassee, 1988, LaGrange (Ga.) Nat. XIII, 1988 (Purchase award), Tex. A&M U., College Station, 1988, John Thomas Gallery, Fullerton, Calif., 1989, Dietrich Jenny Gallery, San Diego, 1989, San Diego Art Inst., 1990 (award), Artists Union Gallery, Moscow, 1990, San Diego Mus. Art, 1991, Calif. Ctr. for Arts, Escondido, 1993, Centro Cultural, X Festival Internacional, Tijuana, Mex., 1994, Mcpl. Art Gallery, L.A., 1995, Galeria Dos Damas, San Diego, 1996, Miracosta Coll., Oceanside, Calif., 1996, Oakland Mus. of Art, Calif., 1997, Facere Jewelry Art Gallery, Seattle, 1997, L.A. Mcpl. Gallery, 1997, McAllen Internat. Mus., Tex., 1998, Vancouver Mus., B.C., 1998, University Art Gallery, Calexico, Calif., 1998, Big Lots the Exhibit, San Diego, 2003, Cassius King Gallery, San Diego, 2004-, Simay Space, 2000, 2001, 2003, Schneider Mus. Art, Oreg., 2000, Oceanside Mus. Art, Calif., 2000, Evansville Mus. Art, Ind., 1999, others; represented in pvt. and public collections; contb. articles to profl. jours.; set designer San Diego, public collections; contb. articles to profl. jours.; set designer San Diego, 1991-93. Recipient Visual Arts fellowship Calif. Arts Coun., 1989-90, Pub. Art grant Calif. Transp./City Heights Community Devel. Corp., 1993. Home: 1702 Primrose Dr El Cajon CA 92020-5649

MARKEE, KATHERINE MADIGAN, librarian, educator; b. Cleve., Feb. 24, 1931; d. Arthur Alexis and Margaret Elizabeth (Madigan) M. AB, Trinity Coll., Washington, 1953; MA, Columbia U., 1962; MLS, Case Western Res. U., 1968. Employment mgr., br. store tng. supr. The May Co., Cleve., 1965-67; assoc. prof. libr. sci., data bases libr. Purdue U. Libr., West Lafayette, Ind., 1968—96, libr. spl. collections, 1996—2006, oral history libr., 2006—. Contbr. articles to profl. jours. Mem. ALA, AAUP, Spl. Librs. Assn., Ind. Online Users Group, Sigma Xi (Rsch. Support award 1986). Avocations: photography, sailing, gardening. Office: Purdue U Libr 504 W State St West Lafayette IN 47907-2058 Office Phone: 765-496-1323. Business E-Mail: kmarkee@purdue.edu.

MARKEL, GERALDINE, educational psychologist, consultant; b. N.Y.C., Jan. 4, 1939; d. Charles and Anne (Handelman) Ponte; m. Sheldon Foster Markel, July 5, 1958; children: Laura, David, Stephen BA Social Scis., U. Mich., 1959, MA Ednl. Psychology, 1964; EdS Spl. Edn., George Washington U., 1968, PhD Ednl. Psychology, 1974. With exec. edn. ctr. Grad. Sch. Bus. U. Mich., Ann Arbor, 1972—, assoc. dir. reading and learning skills ctr., asst. prof. dept. spl. edn. Sch. of Edn., 1974—82, sr. rsch. assoc. reading and learning skills ctr., 1982—94, lectr. dept. prevention and health care Sch. Dentistry, 1987—; prin. Mng. Your Mind Coaching and Seminars, 1984—. Mgmt. cons. Ford Motor Co., Price Waterhouse, N.Y.C., Readers Digest, Pleasantville, N.Y., Time Warner, Viacom, Schlumberger, Ann Arbor, Pitney-Bowes, Atlanta, Mfrs. Hanover Bank, N.Y.C., U.S. Customs Dept. Law Enforcement Tng. Ctr., Sea Isle, Ga., Fin. Mgmt. Svcs., L.A, Domino's Pizza, Ann Arbor, Catherine McAuley Health Ctr., Ann Arbor Co-author: Performance Breakthroughs for Adolescents with LD and ADD, 1996, Finding Your Focus: Practical Strategies, For the Everyday Challenge Facing Adults with ADD, 2006, Peterson's Parent's Guide to the SAT and ACT, 2005; contbr. numerous articles to profl. jours Mem. Assn. for Behavior Therapy (pres. Mich. affiliate 1989-92), Nat. Spkrs. Assn Democrat. Jewish. Avocations: skiing, golf. Home: 3975 Waldenwood Dr Ann Arbor MI 48105-3008 Office Phone: 734-761-6498.

MARKER, RHONDA JOYCE, librarian; b. Ft. Meade, Md., Sept. 25, 1956; d. James W. and Virginia Mae (Conaway) Marker; m. William F. Pittock, Oct. 1, 1983; children: Alexandra Mae Marker Pittock, Olivia Joy Marker Pittock. BA, Greenville (Ill.) Coll., 1978; MS in Libr. and Info. Sci., Pratt Inst., Bklyn., 1985. Catalog libr. Port Authority of N.Y. and N.J., N.Y.C., 1981-85, assoc. chief libr., cataloging svcs., 1985-89; head, original monographic cataloging Rutgers U. Librs., New Brunswick, N.J., 1989-96, head cataloging dept., 1996—2004, metadata libr., 2004—. Contbr. articles to profl. jours. Mem.: Recipient Wilson R. King Sr. Religion award Greenville Coll., 1978. Mem.: NOW, ALA, NY Tech. Svcs. Libr. (pres. 2002—03), NJ Libr. Assn. (edn. com. 1991—93, sec. tech. svcs. sect. 1992, pres. tech. svcs. sect. 1993—94), Documents Assn. NJ (chmn. state documents task force 1990—, pres. 1992, travel grantee 1991), Govt. Documents Round Table (cataloging com. 1991—95, chair 1992—93), Assn. Libr. Collections and Tech. Svcs. (membership com. 2004—, support staff travel grant jury 2004—, chair 2006—), Beta Phi Mu, Alpha Kappa Sigma.

MARKERT, CYNTHIA ALLIN, artist; b. Oak Ridge, Tenn., Apr. 7, 1954; d. George Wilbur and Barbara Anderson Allin. BFA, U. Tenn., 1977. Exhibitions include So. Living Mag. Dream House, Atlanta, Bennett Gallery, Alexis Georges, New Orleans, Circa Gallery, Setting the Stage Artspace, Alexandria, Va., DC Space, Washington, Veni Vidi Vici, Zenith Gallery, Fla. Design Mag., Susan Key Gallery, Knoxville, Tenn., Vetrum Gallery, Asheville, NC, Michael B. Tusing Gallery, Staunton, Va., Impeccable Art, Winston Salem, NC, Kress Emporium, Asheville, Hanson Gallery, Knoxville, Studio E Gallery, Jupiter, Fla., Raiford Gallery, Roswell, Ga., C.J. Varnum Gallery, Palm Beach, Fla., Louis Aronow Gallery, San Francisco, Through the Lens Gallery, Knoxville, Tenn., World Grotto Marketplace, Vagabondia, archives, Nat. Mus. Women in the Arts, Washington, commns. include, Stanford U. Dept. Lively Arts, No. Ky. U. Dept. Dance, U. Tenn. Dept. Theatre, Pandora's Books, Knoxville, Tenn. Festival Ballet, Tressa'a Jazz Club, Asheville, New Millennium Writings, Image Conscious of San Francisco, Spiral Licensing of Cherre, France. Office: Markert Du Jour PO box 724 Knoxville TN 37901 Business E-Mail: cynthia@cynthiamarkert.com.

MARKESSINI, JOAN, research scientist, psychologist; b. N.Y.C., Aug. 14, 1942; d. John Demetrios and Diana (Vlahos) M.; m. Peter John Georges, Jan. 28, 1981. BA in English and French, U. Del., 1964, PhD in Cognitive Psychology, 1979; MA in Linguistics, U. Wash., 1966. Tng. analyst U.S. Dept. State, Washington, 1967-70; writer, editor-in-chief Edcom Systems, Inc., Princeton, N.J., 1970-72; ednl. psychologist U. Del., Newark, 1972-78; dir. corp. and found. rels. Cath. U. Am., Washington, 1978-84; asst. dir. resources devel. Nat. Trust for Hist. Preservation, Washington, 1984-85; sr. staff psychologist BDM Internat., Inc., McLean, Va., 1985-87; dir. publs. and communications Maxwell Communication Corp., McLean, 1987-90; psychologist Allen Corp., Alexandria, Va., 1990—95; dir. R&D, dep. dir. med. systems and distance learning L-3 Comm., Inc.: LINK Simulation and Tng., NYC, 1995—2002; founder, pres. WELLTrek Internat., LLC, 1995—. Author: The First Year of Life (13 vols.), 1971, The First Twelve Months of Life, 1973, Effects of Listener Familiarity and Topic Knowledge on Speech Communication, 1979, TeleMedicine Art and Practice: An Instructional Program Series, 1995, A Taxonomy of Cognitive Capabilities for Executives, (film) Meeting the Challenge, 2000; editor: Perspectives on Leadership, Vols. 1-5, 1993; contb. articles to profl. jours.; prodr. (film) Death of a Giant, 1967; numerous reports. U. Wash. grad. fellow, 1965-66, U. Mich. fellow, 1965, U. Del. fellow, 1977-79. Mem. Am. Psychol. Assn., Assn. Psychol. Type (gen.), N.Y. Acad. Scis., Nat. Mus. Women in Arts (charter), Am. Film Inst. Club. Avocations: theater, opera, interior decorating, gardening. Home: PO Box 4218 Arlington VA 22204-0218

MARKEY, JUDY, radio personality, writer; b. Calif., Feb. 18, 1944; BS in Journalism, Northwestern Univ., 1965. Reporter Chgo. Sun-Times; radio talk show host with Kathy O'Malley WGN-AM, Chgo., 1989—. Author: How to Survive Your High School Reunion and Other Mid-Life Crises, 1984, You Only Get Married for the First Time Once, 1988, The Daddy Clock, 1998, Just Trust Me, 2004. Named one of 100 Most Influential Women, Crain's Chicago Bus., 2004, 100 Most Important Talk Show Hosts in Am., Talkers Mag., 2005; named to Medill Sch. Hall of Achievement, Northwestern Univ., 2005. Office: WGN Radio 435 N Michigan Ave Chicago IL 60611 Office Phone: 312-222-4700. Office Fax: 312-222-5165. Business E-Mail: judymarkey@wgnradio.com.

MARKEY, LEAH GENE, elementary school educator; b. Saginaw, Mich., Apr. 21, 1974; d. Ivan Claude and Della Juanita Wilder; m. Matthew John Markey, Oct. 4, 1997; children: Eva Eileen, Abigail Leah. Bachelors, Kalamazoo Coll., Mich., 1996; Grad., Ctrl. Mich. U., 2005. Cert. Profl. Tchr. Mich., 1996. Tchr. Orchard View Cmty. Schs., Muskegon, Mich., 1997—98, Coleman Cmty. Schs., Mich., 1998—99, Saginaw Twp. Cmty. Schs., Mich., 1999—. Mem. Freeland United Meth. Ch., Mich., 1988—2006. Mem.: Mich. Coun. for Social Studies. Office: Heritage HS 3465 N Center Saginaw MI 48603 Office Phone: 989-799-5790. Personal E-mail: lmmm0904@aol.com.

MARKGRAF, ROSEMARIE, real estate broker; b. Grantsburg, Wis., Oct. 31, 1934; d. Helen Elizabeth Pribil. BS, U. Wis., 1957, MS, 1958. Cert. tchr. Tchr. H.S., Wis., Conn, 1958-61; office mgr. Robert S. Palmer, Middletown, Conn., 1962-64; edn. adv. Girl Scouts U.S.A., N.Y.C., 1964-66; cmty. rels. assoc. Motion Picture Assn. Am., N.Y., 1967-69; mgr. The Chateau Inn, Stamford, N.Y., 1970-78; real estate salesperson Atkins Realty, Ltd., Bklyn., 1979—80; real estate broker, prin. Markgraf Group, Ltd., Bklyn., 1980—. Cons. Real Estate Counseling Group Conn., Storrs, 1963-91; pres. Tuff Transport, Inc., 1977-2000; adj. prof. Real Estate Inst. and Real Estate Edn. Ctrs., 1995—. Hunter Coll., 2005. Past pres. Brownstone Rep. Club; candidate 12th Congl. Dist., Bklyn., 1998, 2000; exec. com. Kings County Rep. Com.; conservative candidate 52d State Assembly Dist., 2002, dist. leader; mem. Rep. State Com., 2002—. Mem. Real Estate Bd. NY, Steuben Soc. (past pres.), Yeats Soc. NY. Roman Catholic. Avocations: water aerobics, crossword puzzles, oenology. Home and Office: The Markgraf Group Ltd 60 Remsen St Brooklyn NY 11201-3453 Office Phone: 718-625-0808. Personal E-mail: rmarkgraf@att.net.

MARKLE, CHERI VIRGINIA CUMMINS, nurse; b. N.Y.C., Nov. 22, 1936; d. Brainard Lyle and Mildred (Schwab) Cummins; m. John Markle, Aug. 26, 1961 (dec. 1962); 1 child, Kellianne. RN, Ind. State U. and Union Hosp., 1959; BS in Rehab. Edn., Wright State U., 1975; BSN, Capital U., 1987; postgrad. in nursing adminstrn., Wright State U., 1987-89; MS, Calif. Coll. Health Sci. Administration, 1994; postgrad., Columbia Pacific U., 1996-2000. Cert. clin. hypnotherapist Nat. Guild Hypnotherapists. Coordinator Dayton (Ohio) Children's Psychiat. Hosp., 1962-75; dir. nursing Stillwater Health Ctr., Dayton, 1975-76; rehab. cons. Fairborn, Ohio, 1976-91, N.Y.C.; sr. supr. VA, Dayton, 1977-85, nurse coord. alcohol rehab., 1985-86; DON Odd Fellows, Springfield, Ohio, 1987-88, Miami Christel Manor, Miamisburg, Ohio, 1988-99; DON, rehab. cons. NMS Tng. Sys., Dayton, 1989-91. Psychiat. nurse VA Med. Ctr., N.Y. Rehab., 1991, mem. com. women vets., 1991-93; advisor Calif. Coll. Health Sci. Newspaper columnist Golden Times, Clark County. Bd. dirs. Temple Universal Judaism, 1992, 97; mem. Town and Village Synagogue, 1999—. 1st lt. USAF, 1959-61. Mem. ANA (cert. adminstrn. 1983, cert. gerontology 1984), AAUW, Nurse Mgrs. Assembly, Gerontol. Nurse Assembly, Rehab. Soc., Nat. Guild Hypnotherapists, Internat. Assn. Counselors and Therapists, Nat. Coun. Jewish Women, Jewish War Vets. (sr. vice comdr. Post 1), Wright State U. Alumni Assn., Am. Legion (life), Hadassah, Women's City Club N.Y., Gilbert and Sullivan Soc., Internat. Consortium Parse Scholars, Alpha Sigma Alpha, Sigma Theta Tau. Democrat. Jewish. Avocations: cats, reading, music, needlecrafts, swimming, grandchildren. E-mail: cherimarklern@yahoo.com.

MARKLEY, KATE, social worker, consultant; b. Jacksonville, Fla., Dec. 1, 1948; d. Elizabeth Kalt Tongue M. AA, Polk C.C., Winter Haven, Fla., 1969; BA, U. So. Fla., 1975; MSW, Fla. State U., 1982. Lic. clin. social worker; Diplomate in clin. social work; ACSW. Caseworker Polk County Social Svcs., Bartow, Fla., 1975-83; clin. social worker Children's Home Soc., Lakeland, Fla., 1983-98; pvt. practice Lakeland, Fla., 1998—. Adj. instr. Fla. So. Coll., Lakeland, Fla., 1984-87, Polk C.C., Winterhaven, Fla., 1988-89, Hillsborough C.C., Plant City, Fla., 1990—; social work cons. Winter Haven Physical Therapy, Fla. 1985-92, Gessler Clinic, Winter Haven, Fla., 2000—; bd. mem., sec., treas. Mental Health Assn. Polk County, Fla.; bd. mem. Polk C.C. (social svcs. tech. adv. bd.). Named Outstanding Young Careerist Bus. and Profl. Women, Lakeland, Fla., 1977. Mem. NASW (unit chair 1999-2001, former program chair). Avocations: travel, reading. Office: PO Box 2659 Lakeland FL 33806

MARKO, MARLENE, psychiatrist; b. N.Y.C., July 3, 1945; m. Loren R. Skeist; children: Marc, David, Sarah. BA, Sarah Lawrence Coll., 1967; MD, Mt. Sinai Sch. Medicine, 1972. Diplomate Am. Bd. Psychiatry. Intern Lenox Hill Hosp., 1973; resident Mt. Sinai Hosp., 1976; clin. instr. Mt. Sinai Sch. Medicine.

MARKOVICH, ALEXANDRIA, assistant principal; b. N.Y.C., Jan. 18, 1954; d. Alexander and Mary Markovich; m. Robert Steven Young, Nov. 15, 1987; children: Anastasia Nicole Young, Christopher Robert Alexander Young. BA, SUNY, Stony Brook, N.Y., 1976; MPS, Pratt Inst., Bklyn., 1978; MSE, Coll. New Rochelle, N.Y., 2002. Cert. art tchr. N.Y. State Bd. Edn., 1979, tchr. nursery, kindergarten, grades 1-6 N.Y. State Bd. Edn., 1979, spl. edn. tchr. N.Y. State Bd. Edn., 1982, specialization in staff devel. N.Y. State Bd. Edn., 2001, asst. prin. spl. edn. day H.S. N.Y. State Bd. Edn., 2003, health conservation tchr. N.Y.C. Bd. Edn., 1982, fine arts jr. H.S. tchr. N.Y.C. Bd. Edn., 1982, fine arts Day H.S. tchr. N.Y.C. Bd. Edn., 1982, spl. edn. tchr. N.Y.C. Bd. Edn., 1996, asst. prin. spl. edn. schs. N.Y.C. Bd. Edn., 2003, asst. prin. elem., intermediate, and jr. H.S. N.Y.C. Bd. Edn., 2003, asst. prin. in Fine Arts Day H.S. N.Y.C. Bd. Edn., 2003, supr. spl. edn. N.Y.C. Bd. Edn., 2003, SDA N.Y. State Dept. Edn., 2002. Spl. edn. tchr., art therapist P.S. 177 Queens, Fresh Meadows, NY, 1982—2003; asst. prin. P.S. 4 @ 179 Queens, Fresh Meadows, 2003—; asst. to prin. Saw Mill Elem. Sch., Bellmore, NY, 2000—01. Actor: (plays) Little Shop of Horrors, Bye, Bye Birdie. Nominee N.Y. State Tchr. of Yr. award, N.Y. State Dept. Edn., 1985, 1986, 1987; named Tchr. of Yr., Coun. Exceptional Children, 1985, 1986; recipient Outstanding Spl. Educators award, 1982, Outstanding Performance as an Art Educator award, N.Y.C. Bd. Edn., 1984, Superior Art Instrn. award, A.A.A., Nat. Traffic Safety Program, 1986. Mem.: ASCD, NYC Art Tchrs. Assn. (fin. sec. 1988—89, sec. 1987—88), NY State Alliance for Arts Edn., NY State Art Tchrs. Assn. (ad hoc com. mem. 1986—87), Girl Scouts Nassau County (del. 2001—05), Girl Scouts Merrick Assn. (treas. 2000—06, recruiter registrar 1995—2000). Office Phone: 718-264-0916. Personal E-mail: alexandria11566@yahoo.com.

MARKOWITZ, DEBORAH LYNN, state official; b. Tarrytown, N.Y., Sept. 14, 1961; d. Gerald Harvey and Sandra Lee (Schulner) M.; m. Paul William Markowitz, June 19, 1988; children: Aviva Lee, Sandra Rose, Ari David. BA with honors, U. Vt., 1982; JD magna cum laude, Georgetown U., 1987. Bar: Vt. 1988, U.S. Dist. Ct. Vt. 1989. Assoc. Covington & Burling, Washington, summer 1986; jud. law clk. Justice Peck-Vt. Supreme Ct., Montpelier, 1987-88; assoc. Langrock, Sperry & Wool, Burlington, Vt., 1988-90; dir. Law Ctr. Vt. League of Cities and Towns, Montpelier, Vt., 1990—97; devel. cons. Vt. Law Sch., South Royalton, 1997—; sec. of state State of Vt., 1998—. Adj. faculty Vt. Law Sch., South Royalton, 1992; examiner Vt. Bd. Bar Examiners, Montpelier, 1994-98. Contbr. articles to profl. jours. Bd. dirs. Ctrl. Vt. Cmty. Action Agy., Vt. Hist. Soc.; trustee Woodbury Coll. Mem. ABA (state and local govt. sect.), Vt. Bar Assn. (mcpl. com.), Internat. Mcpl. Lawyers Assn. (chair pers. sect. 1993—), Nat. Assn. Secs. of State (pres.), Nat. Mus. of Women in the Arts (bd. dirs. Vt. chpt.), Order of Coif. Democrat. Avocations: cross country skiing, singing, sketching, gardening. Office: Office Sec of State Redstone Bldg 26 Terrace Street, PO Box 9 Montpelier VT 05609-0001 Office Phone: 802-828-2148. Office Fax: 802-828-2496. E-mail: dmarkowitz@sec.state.vt.us.*

MARKOWITZ, PHYLLIS FRANCES, retired mental health services professional, retired psychologist; b. Malden, Mass., Sept. 2, 1931; d. Abraham and Rose (Kaplan) Kalishman; children: Gary Keith, Carol Diane Donnelly. AB, Harvard U., 1972, EdM, 1974; EdD, Boston U., 1987. Lic. psychologist Health Svc. Provider; LCSW Mass. Rsch. asst. Boston Coll., Newton, Mass., 1971-73; social worker Combined Jewish Philanthropies, Boston, 1973-74; instr. Harvard U., Cambridge, Mass., 1974-75, sr. counselor, 1974-79; supr. Dept. Social Svcs., Newton and Marlborough, Mass., 1979-88; area dir. case mgmt. and tng. Dept. Mental Health, Boston, 1988-94, area coord. medically-mentally ill, 1988—, chair consumer/family empowerment project, 1992-96. Area dir. Svcs. Integration, 1994—95, Clin. Affairs and Rehab., 1995—2000; project dir. Supported Employment Svcs., 1994—95; area Am. with Disabilities coord. Dept. of Mental Health, Boston, 1995—2000; instr. human devel. U. Mass., Boston, 1990—97. Grantee, Radcliffe Inst., 1972; Rsch. scholar, Boston U., 1981—82. Mem.: Mass. Psychol. Assn. Avocations: music, opera, writing.

MARKS, DEBRA JANE, special education educator; b. Rockville Centre, NY, Aug. 22, 1948; d. Warren Godfrey and Beth Hyman; m. Michael Joel Marks, Aug. 23, 1969; children: Melissa, Stephanie, Karen. BS in Elem. Edn., U. Cin., 1970; M in Elem. Edn., LI U., 1973; cert. in spl. edn., Hofstra U., 1998. Tchr. 6th grade Hillside Grade Sch., New Hyde Park, NY, 1970—74; HS tchr. Jericho (NY) Jewish Ctr., 1978—80; owner Happily Ever After, Plainview, NY, 1985—89; from spl. edn. tchr. asst. to spl. edn. tchr. Nassau BOCES, Wantagh, NY, 1994—2000; spl. edn. tchr. W.T. Clarke Mid. Sch., East Meadow, NY, 2000—. Presenter in field; participant Nat. Svcs. Learning Conf., Phila., 2006; facilitator parallel report card devel. for spl. edn. W.T. Clarke Mid. Sch., 2005; coord., pres. Penny Harvest Exec. Svc. Learning Club, 2000—06. Contbr. chpts. to sch. dist. curriculum books. Named Founder's Day Honoree, East Meadow Sch. Dist., 2004—06; recipient, Nat. Wall of Tolerance Recognition, 2006; grantee, Common Cents NY, 2001—06, Future Corps, Newsday, 2004—06. Mem.: Spl. Edn. PTA (tchr. rep. 2004—06), Penny Harvest Exec. Svc. Learning Club, Martin Luther King Racial/Cultural Awareness Club (awareness com. 2004—05), Kappa Delta Pi. Avocations: travel, reading, golf. Office: WT Clarke Mid Sch 740 Edgewood Dr Westbury NY 11590

MARKS, LAURA B., psychologist; b. L.A., Feb. 9, 1967; d. Stuart and Marsha Marks. RN, BSN, U. So. Calif., L.A., 1990; MA, Calif. Sch. Profl. Psychology, Alhambra, 1994, PhD, 1996. RN, Calif.; diplomate Am. Acad. Pain Mgmt. Pain mgmt. fellow Brotman Med. Ctr., Culver City, Calif., 1996-97; dir. pain mgmt. Psychol. Svcs., L.A., Calif., 1997-99; pvt. practice Santa Monica, Calif., 1997—. Guest spkr. UCLA; dir. psychol. svcs. and pain mgmt. Pain Mgmt. Ctr., Beverly Hills, Calif., 1999; clin. dir. pain mgmt. unit, pain mgmt. psychologist Centinela Med. Hosp., Inglewood, Calif. Contbr. articles to profl. jours. Mem. APA, Am. Pain Soc., Am. Acad. Pain Mgmt., Internat. Assn. for the Study of Pain, Calif. Psychol. Assn., U. So. Calif. Alumni Assn. Office: Centinela Med Hosp 935 S Flower St Inglewood CA 90301-4110

MARKS, LEAH RUTH, judge; b. Greenwich, Conn., Apr. 30, 1931; d. Irving and Frieda Israel Marks; children: Dorothy Ellen, Marian Paula. BA, U. Mich., 1952, JD, 1955; MA in Edn., Columbia Tchrs. Coll., 1959. Bar: NY 1959, US Supreme Ct. 1960. Legis. asst. Conn. State Legislature, Hartford, 1956—57; pvt. practice N.Y.C., 1959—61, 1975—78, 1997—99; staff atty. Sol Charles Levine, N.Y.C., 1959—61; dep. exec. officer Family Ct. NY State for N.Y.C., 1972—75; judge Family Ct. State NY, N.Y.C., 1978—97; jud. hearing officer Office Ct. Adminstrn., N.Y.C., 1999—. Atty. citizen's com. Children NY, 1961—72. Address: 39 Gramercy Park Apt 15A New York NY 10010-6302

MARKS, LILLIAN SHAPIRO, retired secretarial studies educator, writer, editor; b. Bklyn., Mar. 16, 1907; d. Hayman and Celia (Merowitz) Shapiro; m. Joseph Marks, Feb. 21, 1932; children: Daniel, Sheila Blake, Jonathan. BS, NYU, 1928. High sch. tchr., N.Y.C., 1929-30; tchr. Evalina de Rothschild Sch., Jerusalem, 1930-31; social worker United Jewish Aid Bklyn., 1931-32; tchr. Richmond Hill High Sch., 1932-40, Andrew Jackson High Sch., Cambria Heights, NY, 1940-71; staff Vassar Summer Inst., 1946; mem. faculty New Sch. Social Rsch., N.Y.C., 1977-87; ret., 2006. Vol. tchr. English Israel schs., 1987—2000. Am. editor: Teeline, A System of Fast Writing, 1970; author: College Teeline, 1977, College Teeline Self Taught, 1988, Touch Typing Made Simple, 1985; contbr. articles to profl. lit. jours. Mem. Am. Fedn. Tchrs. Democrat. Home and Office: 300 E46 St 17J New York NY 10017

MARKS, MARTHA ALFORD, writer; b. Oxford, Miss., July 27, 1946; d. Truman and Margaret Alford; m. Bernard L. Marks, Jan. 27, 1968. BA, Centenary Coll., 1968; MA, Northwestern U., 1972, PhD, 1978. Tchr. Notre Dame High Sch. for Boys, Niles, Ill., 1969-74; teaching asst. Northwestern U., Evanston, Ill., 1974-78, lectr., lang. coord., 1978-83; asst. prof. Kalamazoo (Mich.) Coll., 1983-85; writer Riverwoods, Ill., 1985—2002. Cons. WGBH Edn. Found., Boston, 1988-91, Am. Coun. on the Tchg. of Fgn. Langs., 1981-92, Ednl. Testing Svcs., 1988-90, Peace Corps., 1993. Co-author: Destinos: An Introduction to Spanish, 1991, 96, Al corriente, 1989, 93, 97, Que tal?, 1986, 90; author: (workbook) Al corriente, 1989, 93; contbr. articles to profl. jours. Mem. Lake County (Ill.) Bd., Forest Preserve Commn., 1992-2002; co-founder Lake County Conservation Alliance; co-founder Reps. for Environ. Protection, 1995, pres. Reps. for Environ. Protection. Office Phone: 505-889-4544.

MARKS, NORA MARALEA, retired secondary school educator; b. Tarentum, Pa., Aug. 17, 1939; d. Chauncey Holmes and Mary Hettie (Bartmas) Elliott; m. Donald Richard Jacobs, July 8, 1961 (div. June 1979); children: Matthew John Jacobs, Donna Marie Gentz; m. Carr Bishop Marks, June 24, 1989; 1 stepchild, Michele Binkley. BS in Edn., Temple U., 1961, MS in Music Edn., 1981, postgrad., Hofstra U., Westminster Choir Coll., Trenton, N.J. Choral dir. Upper Perkiomen Schs., East Greenville, Pa., 1961—67; music tchr. Valley Stream Schs., NY, 1973—79; choral dir. Gettysburg H.S., Gettysburg, Pa., 1979—2000. State sec. Pa. Rural Letter Carriers Assn., 1993—; handbell choir dir. Uriah United Meth. Ch., Gardners, Pa., 1984—, dir. instrumental ensemble, adult choir dir., asst. organist; music dir. Uriah United Meth. Ch. Daycare, Gardners, 2003—. Scholar, Berkshire Music Ctr., Mass., 1963. Mem.: NEA, Adams County Music Educators Assn., Am. Choral Dirs. Assn. Home: 1971 Shippensburg Rd Biglerville PA 17307

MARKS, ROBERTA BARBARA, artist, educator; b. Savannah, Ga.; d. Philip W. and Eleanore (Margolis) Dilner; children: Jeffery Allen, Steven Craig. BFA, U. Miami, Coral Gables, Fla., 1980; MFA, U. South Fla., 1981. Instr., lectr. multi-media, lectr., vis. artist to numerous art schs., including U. South Fla., Tampa, 1998-05, Custom House Mus., Armory Art Ctr., Palm Beach, Fla., 2002, Key West, Fla., 2003, Galerie Jonas, Neuchatel, Switzerland, 2003, Chgo. Anderson Ranch Art Sch., Colo., 2004, U. South (Tampa) Fla., U. Miami Lowe Art Mus., Fla., Armory Art Ctr., Palm Beach, Fla., Valparaiso U., Ind., Rochester Inst. Tech. Am. Sch. of Crafts, N.Y., Galerie de Koull, Murten, Switzerland, Santa Fe Community Coll., Gainesville, Brookfield Craft Ctr., Conn., Fla. Keys Community Coll., U. Wis.-Milw., Parson Sch. Design, Key West (Fla.) C.C., 1991, Am. Embassy, Bern, Switzerland, 1993; juror Riverside Avondale Preservation Art Festival, Jacksonville, Fla., 1981, Ybor Square Art Festival, Tampa, 1980, Miami Lakes Art Festival, Fla., 1975. One woman shows include Brevard Community Coll., Melbourne, Fla., 1982, Cocoa, Fla., 1982, Coventry Galleries, Ltd., Tampa, 1983, Barbara Gillman Gallery, Miami, 1984, 87, Tennessee Williams Fine Arts Ctr., Key West, 1985, Garth Clark Gallery, NYC, 1985, Fred Gros Gallery, Key West, 1985, Key West Art and Historical Soc. East Martello Mus. and Gallery, 1985, U. Miami New Gallery, Fla., 1987, Katie Gingrass Gallery, Milw., 1987, Zimmerman Saturn Gallery, Nashville, 1987, Bern, Zurich Switzerland, 1988, Galerie Alte Krone, Altstadt, Biel, Switzerland, 1990, Helander Gallery, NYC, 1990, Gump's Gallery, San Francisco, 1990, Helander Gallery, NYC, 1991, LeMieux Gallery, New Orleans, 1991, Helander Gallery, Palm Beach, 1992, Galerie Etc., Bern, 1992, Galerie Bel Arte, Lengnau, Switzerland, 1992, Lucky Street Gallery, Key West, 1994-05, Barbara Gillman Gallery, Miami, 1994-05, Galerie Vinelz, Switzerland, 1994, Galerie Quattro, Zurich, 1994, many others; exhibited in group shows at Netsky Gallery, Miami, 1982, The Craftsman's Gallery, Scarsdale, N.Y., 1982, Garth Clark Gallery, Los Angeles, 1983, Nelson-Atkins Mus. Art, Kansas City, Mo., 1983, Am. Craft Mus., NYC, 1984, N. Miami Mus. and Art Ctr., 1985, Joanne Lyon Gallery, Aspen, Colo., 1984, Key West Art and Hist. Soc. East Martello Mus. and Gallery, 1985, Garth Clark Gallery, NYC and Los Angeles, 1985, 24X24, Ruth Siegel Ltd., NYC, 1987, Artforms Gallery, Louisville, 1986, The Pvt. Collection Women Artists, Ohio, 1987, East Martello Mus., Key West, Fla., 1990, East Martello Mus., Key West, Fla., 1990, Philharmonic Ctr. for Arts, Naples, Fla., 1993, Ctr. for Arts, Vero Beach, Fla., 1993, Helander Gallery, Palm Beach, 1993, Gingrass Gallery, Milw., 1993, many others; represented in permanent collections Mint Mus., Charlotte, NC, N.Mex Mus. Fine Arts, Sante Fe, Smithsonian Instn., Renwick Gallery, Rochester Inst. Tech. Fine Arts Dept., U. Utah Mus., U. South Fla. Fine Arts Dept., Galerie du Manoir, La Chaux-de-Fonds, Switzerland, Valencia Community Coll., Okum Gallery, Victoria and Albert Mus., London, IBM, Jacksonville, Fla., AT&T, NYC, Custom Ho. Mus., Key West, Fla., 2002, U. South Fla., Galerie Jonas, Neuchatel, Switzerland, 2003, Lucky St. Gallery, 2005, Mint Mus., Charlotte, NMex. Mus. Fine Arts, Sante Fe, others. Recipient Regional Visual Artist fellow, Miami, Fla., 1990, also numerous awards. Mem. World Craft Council, Artists Equity Assn., Internat. Sculpture Ctr.

MARKS, STEPHANIE I., secondary school educator, biologist; d. Arnold I. Marks and Mary Edwin, Dennis R. Edwin (Stepfather) and Dennette Marks (Stepmother); 1 child, Angelica J. Firmin. BS in Biol. Scis., U. Alaska, Fairbanks, 2003. Cert. tchr. Alaska Dept. Edn., 2004. Youth supr. Rampart Village Coun., Alaska, 1998—98; wildland fire fighter North Star Fire Crew (Alaska Fire Svc.), Fairbanks, 1999—2000; acad. tutor U. Alaska, 2000—00; rsch. asst. U. Alaska, Neuroscience Program, 2001—02, tchg. asst., 2003—03; tchr. h.s. math & sci. Tanana City Sch. Dist., 2004—. Coach h.s. girls basketball Maudrey J. Sommer Sch., Tanana, 2004—06, athletic dir., 2004—06, coach cross country running, 2005—05. Home: PO Box 132 Tanana AK 99777 Office Phone: 907-366-7203.

MARKS, VERONIQUE, art educator; b. San Francisco, Sept. 14, 1974; d. Jerome and Monique Marks; m. Paul Anastasopoulos. BA in Fine Art, U. Calif., Santa Cruz, 1996; multiple subject tchg. credential, Calif. State U., Monterey Bay, 1998; single subject tchg. credential in Art, San Jose State U., Calif., 2004. Tchr. grade 4 Structured English Immersion Ohlone Elem., Watsonville, Calif., 1999—2002; tchr. art Aptos HS, Calif., 2002—. Named one of 2006 Educators of Distinction, Nat. Soc. HS Scholars, 2006. Office Phone: 831-688-6565 611.

MARKUS, MAURA, bank executive; BA summa cum laude, Boston Coll., Mass.; MBA, Harvard U. Joined Citibank, N.Y.C., 1987, pres. North Am. Retail Distbr. Group, 2000—. Office: CBNA One Court Sq 49th Fl Long Island City NY 11120

MARLAR, JANET CUMMINGS, retired public relations officer; b. Burnsville, Miss., Dec. 22, 1942; d. James E. and Juanita (Hale) Cummings; m. David C. Linton, May 21, 1961 (div. 1984); 1 child, Jeffory Mark; m. Thomas Gilbert Cupples, Mar. 5, 1984 (div. 1990); m. Fredrick Marlar, Nov. 19, 1994. Student, N.E. Miss. Jr. Coll., 1960—61, Memphis State U., 1975—76, Sheffield Tech. Ctr., Memphis, 1984—85. Property owner, Burnsville, 1974—, Glen, Miss., 1994—2003. Mem. bus. adv. com. Sheffield Tech. Ctr., 1997—; docent Curlee House, Corinth, Miss., 1989—; exec. bd. Internat. Heritage Commn., Memphis, 1987-92; pub. rels. officer Internat. Heritage Ethnic Festival, Memphis Co-editor: Internat. Heritage Bull./Newsletter; contbr. articles to Tishomingo County Newspaper. Vol. Memphis Brooks Mus. Art, 1980—; mem. exec. com., pub. info. officer Bldg. Bridges for Better Memphis, 1985—; pres. Eagle Watch Assn.; founder Janet C. Cupples Citizenship awards, Memphis City Inter-City Sch., 1975; founder, chair women's com. on crime City of Memphis, 1985—, hon. mem. city coun., 1987; donor, exec. com. Women Achievement, Inc., Memphis, 1986; mem. spkrs. bur. United Way Greater Memphis, Friends Shelby County Libr., 1986—, YMCA; chair ethnic outreach com. Neighborfest, Memphis, 1987, chairperson exec. com., 1988, internat. coord. Neighborfest '88; amb. Memphis Internat. Heritage Commn., 1988; youth mentor Memphis Youth Leadership Devel. Inst.; chairperson Internat. Heritage City of Memphis, 1987; mem. cmty. coun. Memphis City Schs., Memphis Cablevision Edn. Task Force; apptd. col. aide de camp to Gov. Ned McWherter of Tenn., 1988; apptd. hon. mem. Tenn. State Senator Steve Cohen's staff, 1989; sec. safety com. St. Francis Hosp., 1992; sec., pub. rels. officer Burnsville H.S. com., 1960, exec. com., 1994-2004, chair book donation com., 2000-04; participant Vol. Miss. Food Network Distbn. for Disabled Persons, 1996; active Dem. Nat. Com., 1994—; founder Inter City Sch. Citizenship award, 1986, Art award Bernsville Sch., 2006; founder Burnsville Sch. Accelerated Reader awards, 2000, Libr. award, Citizenship Essay award, 2001—, founder book donation program, Mr. Jim Cummings Citizenship essay awards, 2000; sec., founding mem. Tchg. Tolerance, 1994 Recipient 11 certs. of recognition Memphis City Coun., 1986-89, Outstanding Svc. to Pub. Edn. award 1986, Merit award City of Memphis, 1987, Royal award HRH Prince Kevin, 1996; named Outstanding Female Participant, Neighborhood, Inc., 1987; honored by Pres. George Bush as Outstanding Vol., 1989; featured as one of top 1000 Vols. in Mid-South, 1989; Svc. award Cummings Sch., 1993; apptd. Hon. Memphis City Councilwoman, 1995-96; recognized by Gen. Colin Powell, 1997; Burnsville Libr. Project commended by First Lady, Laura Bush, 2002; recipient Outstanding Svc. award Memphis City Schs., 2002, 03 Mem. NAFE, NOW (2d v.p. Memphis chpt. 1987, del. nat. conf. 1987, 2d v.p.), Network Profl. Women's Orgn., NCCJ, Rep. Career Women, Memphis Peace and Justice Ctr., Women's Polit. Caucus Tenn., Nat. Children's Cancer Soc. (friend 1995-96) Methodist. Avocations: community service, writing, teaching.

MARLATT, PATRICIA ANNE, secondary school educator; b. Balt., Mar. 3, 1951; d. Robert H. and Marie M. Wiedefeld; m. F. Patrick Marlatt, Feb. 12, 1972; children: Michael P., Colleen P.(dec.), Eric P.(dec.). BA, Towson U., Balt., Md., 1972; MA, U. Md., Balt., 1997; Doctorate (hon.), Mt. St. Mary's Coll., Emmittsburg, Pa., 2002. Svc. counselor C&P Telephone Co. Md. and DC, Balt., 1969—74; tchr. trainer Union of Md. Fire and Rescue Inst., College Park, Md., 1980—2000; childbirth educator, Lamaze tchr. CEA of Balt., 1980—2000. Office: Mt De Sales Acad 700 Academy Rd Catonsville MD 21228-1899

MARLER, JOAN, writer, educator; b. Chico, Calif., June 6, 1947; d. William Thomas Marler and Grace Elizabeth Paddock; m. Dan Dimitrov Smith, Jan. 1, 1975; 1 child, Sorrel Smith. BA in Dance, Mills Coll., Oakland, CA, 1969; MA in Archaeomythology, Sonoma State U., Rohnert Park, Calif., 1998. Instr. folk and ethnic dance Santa Rosa (Calif.) Jr. Coll., 1975—; prof. archaeomythology Calif. Inst. Integral Studies, San Francisco, 1996—. Radio prodr. KPFA, Berkeley, 1982—96; vis. prof. art history Sonoma State U., Rohnert Park, 1998; adj. faculty New Coll. Calif., San Francisco, 1998—2001; founder, dir. Inst. Archaeomythology. Editor: From the Realm of the Ancestors: An Anthology in Honor of Marija Gimbutas, 1997; author: (article in anthology) Treasures: Studies in Honor of Ivan Marazov, 1998, In Le radici prime dell'Europa: Gli intrecci genetici, linguistici, storici, 2002, In Women in Transition: Voices, 2001, Il Mito e il Cueto della grande Dea, 2003, Die Diskriminierung der Matriarchatsforschung, 2003, Notable American Women, 2003; editor: (jour.) ReVision Jour., (by Marija Gimbutas) Civilization of the Goddess, 1991, Jour. of Archaeomythology. Founding mem. Monastery Project. Grantee, Calif. Inst. Integral Studies, 2000. Mem.: Anthrop. Assn. Am. (assoc.). Office: Institute of Archaeomythology PO Box 1902 Sebastopol CA 95473 Office Phone: 707-823-7727. Business E-Mail: jmarler@archaeomythology.org.

MARLETT, JUDITH ANN, nutritional sciences educator, researcher; b. Toledo; BS, Miami U., Oxford, Ohio, 1965; PhD, U. Minn., 1972; postgrad., Harvard U., 1973-74. Registered dietitian. Therapeutic and metabolic unit dietitian VA Hosp., Mpls., 1966-67; spl. instr. in nutrition Simmons Coll., Boston, 1973-74; asst. prof. U. Wis., Madison, 1975-80, assoc. prof. dept. nutritional scis., 1981-84, prof. dept. nutritional scis., 1984—. Cons. U.S. AID, Leyte, Philippines, 1983, Makerere U., Kampala, Uganda, 2005; acting dir. dietetic program dept. Nutritional Scis. U. Wis., 1977-78, dir., 1985-89; cons. grain, drug and food cos., 1985—, adv. bd. U. Ariz. Clin. Cancer Ctr., 1987-95; sci. bd. advisors Am. Health Found., 1988—; reviewer NIH, 1982-2004; vis. prof. Makerere U., Kampala, Uganada, 2005; spkr. in field. Mem. editl. bd. Jour. Sci. of Food and Agrl., 1989—, Jour. Food Composition and Analysis, 1994-2000, Jour. of Nutrition, 2002—; contbr. articles to profl. jours. Mem. NIH (Diabetes amd Digestive and Kidney Disease spl. grant rev. com. 1992-96), Am. Soc. Nutrition, Am. Dietetic Assn. Achievements include research on human nutrition and disease, dietary fiber and gastrointestinal function. Office: U Wis Dept Nutritional Sci 1415 Linden Dr Madison WI 53706-1527 Office Phone: 623-972-5221. Business E-Mail: jmarlett@nutrisci.wisc.edu.

MARLETTE, CYNTHIA, lawyer; Joined Fed. Energy Regulatory Commn., Washington, 1979—, dep. gen. counsel, 1979, assoc. gen. counsel, hydro-electric and electric, acting gen. counsel, 2001, gen. counsel, 2001—. Office: Fed Energy Regulatory Commn Rm 10A01 888 First St NE Washington DC 20426-0001 Office Phone: 202-502-6000. Office Fax: 202-208-2115.

MARLIN, ELMEREE MCGOON, mathematics educator; b. Springfield, Mo., Feb. 5, 1958; d. David E. and Nina Faye (Hyde) McGoon; m. Rolland Keith Marlin, Oct. 20, 1979; children: Eimee Mariah, Ethan Keith, Evangeline Marie. BS in Edn., Mo. State U., Springfield, 1976—79; MS in Edn., Missouri State U., Springfield, 1979—86. Math. tchr. Greenfield HS, Mo., 1980—2000, Marshfield HS, Mo., 2000—; adj. instr. Ozarks Tech. CC, Springfield, Mo., 2002—. Treas. S.W. Mo. Dist. Assn. Math. Tchrs., Springfield, 2004—. Mem.: Mo. State Tchrs. Assn., Delta Kappa Gamma (pres., beta lambda chpt. 1994—2006). Methodist. Avocations: reading, needlecrafts. Office: Marshfield HS 370 State Highway DD Marshfield MO 65706 Office Phone: 417-859-2120 2187.

MARLING, KARAL ANN, art history educator, social sciences educator, curator; b. Rochester, NY, Nov. 5, 1943; d. Raymond J. and Marjorie (Karal) M. PhD, Bryn Mawr Coll., 1971. Prof. art history and Am. studies U. Minn., Mpls., 1977—. Author: Federal Art in Cleveland, 1933-1943: An Exhibition, 1974, Wall-to-Wall America: America: A Cultural History of Post-Office Murals in the Great Depression, 1982, 2d edit., 2001, The Colossus of the Roads: Myth and Symbol Along the American Highway, 1984, 2d edit., 2000, Tom Benton and His Drawings: A Biographical Essay and a Collection of His Sketches, Studies and Mural Cartoons, 1985, Frederick C. Knight (1898-1797), 1987, George Washington Slept Here: Colonial Revivals and American Culture, 1876-1986, 1988, Looking Back: A Perspective on the 1913 Inaugural Exhibition, 1988, Blue Ribbon: A Social and Pictorial History of the Minnesota State Fair, 1990; author: (with John Wetenhall) Iwo Jima: Monuments, Memories, and the American Hero, 1991; author: Edward Hopper, 1992, As Seen on T.V.: The Visual Culture of Everyday Life in the 1950's, 1994, Graceland: Going Home with Elvis, 1995; editor (with Jessica H. Foy): The Arts and the American Home, 1890-1930, 1994; editor: Norman Rockwell, 1997, Designing the Disney Theme Parks: The Architecture of Reassurance, 1997, Merry Christmas! Celebrating America's Greatest Holiday, 2000, Looking North, 2003, Debutante, 2004, Old Glory Unfurled, 2004, Norman Rockwell: America's Favorite Painter, 2005, Behind The Magic: 50 Years of Disneyland, 2005, Designs on The Heart: The Homemade Art of Grandma Moses, 2006; contbr. essays to catalogs. Recipient award Minn. Humanities Commn., 1986, Book History award Minn., 1994, Robert C. Smith award Decorative Arts Soc., 1994, award Internat. Assn. Art Critics, 1998; Woodrow Wilson fellow, fellow Luce Found. Office: 1920 S 1st St Ste 1301 Minneapolis MN 55454-1190 Office Phone: 612-339-6172. Business E-Mail: marli001@umn.edu. E-mail: kmarling@mn.rr.com.

MARLOW, LYDIA LOU, retired elementary school educator; b. Aledo, Ill., Aug. 21, 1954; d. Dwayne Elwood Irwin and Phyllis Jean (McKeown) Graff; m. Sidney G. Marlow Jr.; children: Erika Lynn, John Andrew. BA in Edn. with honors, Stephens Coll., 1976; MA in Reading, U. Mo., Kansas City, 1983. Cert. elem. tchr., Mo. Tchr. 2d grade Atlanta C-3 Sch. Dist., Mo., 1976—81; from tchr. headstart to tchr. 2d grade Independence Sch. Dist., Mo., 1982—92; reading clinician Santa Fe Trail & Procter Elem. Sch., Independence, 1993—99; tchr. Title 1 reading George Caleb Bingham 7th Grade Ctr., Independence, 1999—2000; tchr. gifted and talented Christian Ott Elem. Sch., Independence, 2001—05, Procter Elem. Sch., Independence, 2005—06; ret., 2006. Adj. prof. children's lit. Webster U., Kansas City, Mo., 1994; developer program Focus on Reading, Independence, Mo., 1996; dept. chair, contbr. Missouri Reader, 1998—; presenter in field. Author: (novels) The Master Teacher: Memorable Moments, 2001; contbr. articles. Facilitator attention deficit hyperactivity disorder support group Caring Cmty. Santa Fe Trail Sch., Independence, 1996—97; rschr., author Truman Whistlestop Project, Independence, 1996—97; reading clinician Literacy Learning Ctr., Independence, 1997—2001. Recipient True Friend award Friends United Ednl. Support, Independence, 1994, Excellence in Tchg. award Govt. Employees Hosp. Assn., 1997, 2002. Mem.: Cmty. Assn. for the Arts, Children and Adults with Attention Deficit Disorder, Internat. Reading Assn. (local pres., publicity com. 1989—90, publicity co-chmn., editor Indep. IRA local 1991—93, editor Mo. state IRA 1992—95, Pres. award 1989), AAUW (publicity chair 1982—83), NEA (MNEA/Reliant grantee 1997), ASCD, Writers Club (coord. 1993—99, Editor's Choice 2001). Avocations: writing, gardening, reading, collecting antiques and elephant figurines. Home: 14609 E 44th St S Independence MO 64055-4810 Office Phone: 816-686-5874. Personal E-mail: lydz14609@yahoo.com.

MARLOW, MARCIA MARIE, secondary school educator, publishing executive; b. Maywood, Calif., Jan. 24; d. George Murf Chandler and Zelda Marie Chandler; m. L. K. Higginbotham (dec. Dec. 23, 1998); children: Kevin Darrell Smith, Trisha Nicole Ailey Abbott, Shannon Marie Ailey Alexander, Bryan Chandler Ailey. A in Bus., No. Okla. Coll., 1980; BS in Edn., Mo. So. State Coll., 1984, cert. reading specialist, 1985, degree in art edn., 1993. Tchr. McDonald County Sch., Jane, Mo., 1984—88; owner Southwestern Steel, Inc., Grove, Okla., 1988—99, New Horizons Steel, Grove, Okla.; pub. Chandler Day Pub., Inc., Fairland, Okla., 1999—. Educator Wyandotte Pub. Sch., Okla., 2001—. Editor: (book) Murphy, The Littlest Elf, 2000; author: Love Verses, 2001; acrylic and oil paintings. Recipient Tchr. of the Yr., McDonald County Sch., Jane, Mo., 1988. Mem.: Brush and Palette Club, Phi Theta Kappa (life). Baptist. Avocations: art, singing, reading, horseback riding, gardening.

MARLOW, PATRICIA BAIR BOND, realtor; b. Altoona, Pa., Dec. 3, 1932; d. John Lesley and Gladys Marie Bair; m. Neal Nelson Jensen Bond, Aug. 7, 1953 (dec. July 1963); children: John Scott Bond, Lisa Suzanne Moody, Lesley Ann Stephen; m. Laurin Purcell Marlow, Apr. 4, 1967. Student, Mary Washington Coll., 1950-52. Realtor Everitt/Luby, Dallas, 1971-80; with Merrill Lynch, Dallas, 1980-89; realtor Adleta Fine Properties, 1989—. Contbr. poetry to anthologies. Recipient Diamond Summit. Mem. Dallas Mus. Art, Dallas Arboretum, Les Femmes du Monde, Dallas Mus. Art League, Tex. Kidney Found., Salvation Army (women's aux.). Avocation: watercolor painting. Home: 5336 Nashwood Ln Granbury TX 76049 Office: Adleta Fine Properties 5950 Berkshire Ln Dallas TX 75225 Personal E-mail: patti@pattimarlow.com.

MARLOWE, WILLIE, artist, fine arts educator; b. Whiteville, NC, Jan. 17, 1943; d. John David and Tessie Ernestine (McLawhorn) M.; m. Thomas Blakeslee Speight, July 11, 1980. Student, Pa. Acad. Fine Arts, Phila., 1964; BS, East Carolina U., 1965; MFA, U. Idaho, 1969; postgrad., Peace Coll., 1993. Instr. dept. art Skidmore Coll., Saratoga Springs, NY, 1970-74, mentor univ. without walls, 1972-74; instr. dept. art Columbia-Greene C.C., Hudson, NY, 1973-74; instr. Empire State Coll. SUNY, Albany, 1974; prof. Dept. Visual Arts Sage Coll., Albany, 1977—; chmn. The Sage Colls., Albany, 1979-81. Co-founder, tchr. Saratoga Arts Workshop, Saratoga Springs, N.Y., 1970-74; watercolor tchr. abroad Sage Colls., Scotland, Ireland, 2001; tchr. Somerville Coll., Oxford U., Eng., 1992; vis. artist U. Ga. studies abroad program, Cortona, Italy, 1989; vis. artist, Wexford Arts Ctr., Ireland, 1998, artist-in-residence for Ptnrs. of the Americas, Barbados, W.I., 1986, The Millay Colony for the Arts, Austerlitz, N.Y., 1999; artist selection com. Albany Ctr. Gallery, 1998; internat. artists' residency Cill Rialaig Project, Ballinskelligs, Ireland, 2005, Emily Harvey Found., Venice, 2006; lectr. in field. One-woman shows include The Mint Mus. Art, Charlotte, NC, 1971, Schenectady Mus., NY, 1975, Marist Coll., Poughkeepsie, NY, 1976, Stockton State Coll., Pomono, NJ, 1977, Greenville Mus. Art, NC, 1982, 97, Ann Grey Gallery The Casino, Saratoga Springs, NY, 1985, The Barrett Art Gallery Utica Coll. Syracuse U., NY, 1986, The Atrium Gen. Electric Corp. R&D Ctr., Schenectady, 1988, Forum Gallery, Gütersloh, Germany, 1992, Albany Ctr. Gallery, 1992, 97, McHenry County Coll., Crystal Lake, Ill., Main St. Gallery, Dobbs Ferry, 1995, The Wexford Arts Ctr., Ireland, 1998, The Saratoga Arts Ctr., Saratoga Springs, NY, 2000, Fondo del Sol Gallery and Visual Arts Ctr., Washington, 2002, Barrett Arts Ctr., Poughkeepsie, NY, 2002, Gallery C, Raleigh, 2003, Color and Space traveling solo show, NC, 2006; exhibited in group shows at Fulton St. Gallery, Troy, NY, 2003, Adirondack CC, Queensbury, NY, 2006, Gallery Neptune, Bethesda, Md., 2005, Wexford (Ireland) Arts Ctr., 2004, Art Ctr. for the Capital Region, Troy, NY, 2002, Reprize Internat. Invitational Show, Wexford Arts Ctr., Ireland, 2002, Martinez Gallery, Troy, NY, 2002, Artemisia Gallery, Chgo., 2000, 03, Nexus Gallery, NYC, 1997-99, Gang Gallery, NYC, Eng. & Co., London, 1993, Steinbaum-Krauss Gallery, NYC, 1990, Stux Gallery, Boston, 1987, Nat. Mus. Women Arts, Washington, 1987, Westbeth Gallery, NYC, 1994, Clocktower, NYC, 1986, Rice Gallery The Albany Inst. History & Art, 1986, Deborah Davis Fine Arts, Hudson, 2003-04, 06, Firlefanz Gallery, Albany, 2004, Gallery 100, Saratoga Springs, 2004, U. West Eng., Bristol, 2004, Nat. Coll. Art and Design, Dublin, Ireland, 2004; represented in pvt. collections; represented in permanent collections Legis. Offices Empire State Plz., Albany, First Albany Corp., Md. Dept. Econ. & Cmty. Devel., Balt., Quad Graphics, Boston, SUNY Albany, NC Nat. Bank, Charlotte, Greenville Mus. Art, East Carolina U., Greenville, NC, Boston Pub. Libr., Budapest Gallery, Russell Sage Coll., Troy, Mint Mus. Art, Charlotte, NC, Four Winds Ctr., Saratoga Springs, U. Mus. SUNY Albany, Bullard and McLeod & Assocs., Inc., Albany, NY, Rocky Mount Art Ctr., NC, Adirondack CC, NY; co-curator and curator for mail art shows. Recipient Purchase award in painting Hudson Mohawk Regional Ann., SUNY Albany, 1977, 95, 97, medal Internat. Art Competition Metro Arts, Inc., Scarsdale, N.Y., 1986, honorable mention in painting Third Ann. Nat. C.C. Miniature Painting Show, Lexington, 1987, Sywer award, 1995, and numerous others; N.Y. State Coun. on the Arts grantee Barrett Art Gallery Syracuse U., 1986, grantee Artists' Space, 1988, Spl. Opportunity grant N.Y. Found. Arts. Mem.: Nat. Assn. Women Artists, Albany Inst. History and Art, Fulton St. Gallery, Albany Ctr. Gallery, Woman's Caucus For Art. Avocations: painting, visual poetry, mail art. Personal E-mail: info@williemarlowe.com.

MARMER, ELLEN LUCILLE, pediatrician, cardiologist; b. Bronx, N.Y., June 29, 1939; d. Benjamin and Diane (Goldstein) M.; m. Harold O. Shapiro, June 5, 1960; children: Cheri, Brenda. BS in Chemistry, U. Ala., 1960; MD, U. Ala., Birmingham, 1964. Cert. Nat. Bd. Med. Examiners; diplomate Am. Bd. Sports Medicine, Bd. Pediat., Bd. Qualified and Eligible Pediatric Cardiology, Bd. cert. sports medicine. Intern Upstate Med. Ctr., Syracuse, NY, 1964-65, resident, 1965-66; fellow in pediatric cardiology Columbia Presbyn. Med. Ctr.-Babies Hosp., N.Y.C., 1967-69; pvt. practice Hartford, Vernon, Conn., 1969—. Examining pediatrician child devel. program Columbia Presbyn. Med. Ctr.-Babies Hosp., N.Y.C., 1967, instr. pediat., 1967-69; dir. pediatric cardiology clinic St. Francis Hosp., Hartford, 1970-80; asst. state med. examiner, Tolland County, Conn., 1974-79; sports physician Rockville (Conn.) High Sch., 1976—; advisor Cardiac Rehab. com., Rockville, 1984-90; mem. bd. examiners Am. Bd. Sports Medicine, 1991—, chmn. credentials com., 1991-93. Mem. Vernon Town Coun., 1985-89; bd. dirs. Child Guidance Clinic, Manchester, Conn., 1970—; life mem. Tolland County chpt. Hadassah, v.p., 1969-70, pres., 1970-72, bd. dirs., 1973-74; mem. B'nai Israel Congregation and Sisterhood, Vernon, 1969—, chmn. youth commn., 1970-72; mayor Town of Vernon, 2003-05, 05-. Recipient Outstanding Svc. award Indian Valley YMCA, 1985. Fellow Am. Acad. Pediat., Am. Coll. Cardiology, Am. Coll. Sports Medicine; mem. Conn. Med. Soc., Am. Heart Assn. (mem. coun. cardiovasc. disease in young 1969—, chmn. elect New Eng. regional heart com. 1990-91, mem. Heritage affiliate 1998—), Conn. Heart Assn. (bd. dirs. 1974-75, 83-84, pres. 1986-88), Heart Assn. Greater Hartford (bd. dirs. 1970-89, mem. exec. com. 1972-73, 79-84, pres. 1982-84), Tolland County Med. Assn. (sec. 1971-72), Vis. Nurse and Cmty. Care Tolland County, LWV (state program chairperson Vernon chpt. 1971-73). Democrat. Jewish. Avocation: sports. Office: 520 Hartford Tpke Vernon Rockville CT 06066 Office Phone: 860-870-9366.

MARMER, NANCY, editor; b. N.Y.C., Nov. 19, 1932; d. Carl and Frances Marmer; m. Gerald Jay Goldberg, Jan. 23, 1954; 1 child, Robert. BA magna cum laude, Queens Coll., 1954; postgrad., U. Minn., 1954-57, UCLA, 1968-71. L.A. corr. Art Internat., 1965-67; West Coast editor Artforum, 1976-77; sr. editor Art in America, N.Y.C., 1979-81, exec. editor, 1981-83, book rev. editor, 1983-97, mng. editor, 1983-97, editor-at-large, 1997-98, contbg. editor, 1998—. Lectr. Mellon seminar R.I. Sch. Design, 1983; lectr. art criticism Visual Arts dept. U. Calif., San Diego, 1978; faculty expository writing Dept. English, U. Minn., 1954-57. Author: The Modern Critical Spectrum, 1962; contbr. numerous articles to profl. jours.; art critic/reviewer for Art in America, Art Internat., Artforum, L.A. Times. Recipient Samuel Kress Found. Award in Art History; Nat. endowment for the Arts fellow in art criticism. Mem. Phi Beta Kappa. E-mail: 102424.711@compuserve.com.

MARMORSTEIN, VICTORIA E., lawyer; BA with distinction, Univ. Okla., 1973; JD, Am. Univ., 1977; LLM, Univ. Va., 1978. Bar: DC 1977, NY 1980, Calif. 1989. Ptnr., global chair, fin. and real estate dept. Latham & Watkins, LA. Adj. prof., UCLA Sch. of Law. Editor: Va. Jour. of Internat. Law; author: numerous articles in profl. publications. Named in Chambers & Partners Guide to America's Leading Lawyers for Bus., 2004, in Euromoney's Legal Group Guide to the World's Leading Securitization Lawyers; named one of Top Women Lawyers in LA, LA mag., 2004. Mem.: Phi Beta Kappa. Fluent in Spanish. Office: Latham & Watkins Ste 4000 633 W Fifth St Los Angeles CA 90071-2007

MARNEY, BRENDA JOYCE, minister, computer programmer; b. Welch, W. Va., Sept. 15, 1952; d. Franklin Garfield Brown and Anna Sarah Toler; m. Barry Lynn Marney, Oct. 3, 1970; children: Joecina Lynn Dasher, Brian Paul. Computer programmer, Topeka Tech., 1982. Ordained Licensed Minister. Pres., spkr. Women's Aglow, Topeka, 1983—95; pastor/founder Good Shepherd Family Ch., Topeka, 1995—; partnership The Diamond House, Topeka, 1999—; radio show Good Shepherd Min., Topeka, 1994. Area dir. World Harvest Fellowship, Columbus, Ohio, 2003—. Avocation: water-skiing. Office: Good Shepherd Family Ch 7630 SW 21st Topeka KS 66615

MARNEY, SHEILA K., science educator; d. Harlan and Norma Grafel; m. Greg Marney, May 25, 1989; children: Jayson Wylie, Jennifer. BA in Edn., Wichita State U., Kans., 1975. Cert. tchr. Kans. State Dept. Edn., 1975. Tchr. sci. grades 7, 8 Rossville Jr. and Sr. H.S., Kans., 1982—. Vol. tchr. Summer Acad., Rossville, Kans., 2005—06. Recipient 25 Yrs. Svc. as Tchr. award, U. Kans., 2005. Mem.: Kans. Nat. Edn. Assn. Home: 7113 NW Arn Rd Rossville KS 66533 Office: Rossville Jr and Sr HS 800 S Main Rossville KS 66533 Personal E-mail: sheila227k@earthlink.net.

MAROLD, JUDY L., secondary school educator; d. F. Addison and Pauline Elizabeth Harvey; m. R. G. Marold, June 6, 1970; children: Eleana Maria Merriam, Aaron Carl. BS, Tex. Woman's U., Denton, 1967, MA, 1968. Instr. Ft. Lewis Coll., Durango, Colo., 1969—71; agr. specialist Peace Corps, Candarave, Peru, 1971—73; tchr. Mountain Valley Sch., Saguache, Colo., 1978—. Fellow Nat. History Day Seminar, Nat. History Day and Libr. of Congress, 1991. Mem.: NEA. Avocations: travel, gardening, crafts. Office: Mountain Valley Sch P O Box 127 Saguache CO 81149 Office Phone: 719-655-2578.

MARONEY, JANE PERKINS, former state legislator, consultant; b. Boston, July 29, 1923; d. John Henry and Mary (Boland) Perkins; m. John Walker Maroney, July 7, 1956; children: Jane Maroney El Dahr, John Walker Jr. Student, Radcliffe Coll., 1940—41, Katharine Gibbs Sch., 1941—42; LHD (hon.), Golden Beacom Coll., 1995. Elected ofcl. Del. Gen. Assembly, Dover, 1978-98; former project mgr. Milbank Meml. Fund, N.Y.C. Del. Family Law Commn., 1990—99, Health and Human Devel. Com., 1984—99; moderator, panelist Pub. Policy Conf., annually; past mem. Jr. League Wilmington (Del.); vice chair Creative Grandparenting, Inc., 1999—; pres. Lincoln Club of Del., 2002—03; trustee Christiana Care Health Sys., 2000—; mem. bd. Health and Nursing Scis. U. Del., 1998—; bd. dirs. YWCA, New Castle County, Family and Workplace Connection, Coord. Coun. Children with Disabilities, chmn., 1990—91; pres. adv. coun. Girl Scouts Del.; mem. adv. bd. Del. Internat. Yr. of Family, March of Dimes, Inst. Human Behavior; bd. dirs. Afghanistan-Del. Cmtys. Together, 2001—, St. Michaels Sch. and Nursery, 2000—. Named 1 of 10 Best Rep. Legislators of Yr., Pres. Reagan, 1985; named to, Women's Hall of Fame, Del., 1996, Outstanding Legislator of Yr., Easter Seals of Del., 1998; recipient Outstanding Svc. to Children award, Acad. Pediat., Disting. Svc. award, Del. Bar Assn., Alfred R. Shands Disting. Svc. award, 1992, Order of Merit award, U. Del., 1993, J. Donaldson Brown Disting. Svcs. award, Children and Family Svcs. Del. to Dr. & Rep. Maroney, 1992, Nathan Davis award, AMA, 1996, Order of the First State award, Gov. of Del., 1998, Advocacy and Leadership in Children's Issues award, Epilepsy Found. Del., 2000, Outstanding Lifetime Contbn. award, Health Edn. Network Del., 2001, Cmty. Builder award, Nat. Conf. for Cmty. and Justice, 2001, Woman Pioneer award, Boy Scouts Am., 2001, Liberty Bell award, Del. State Bar Assn. Law Day, 2003, Carrie Chapman Catt award, Wilmington LWV, 2004. Roman Catholic. Avocations: public policy, continuing education. Fax: 302-478-2677. Personal E-mail: jpmaroney@aol.com.

MARONI, DONNA FAROLINO, biologist, researcher; b. Buffalo, Feb. 27, 1938; d. Enrico Victor and Eleanor (Redlinska) Farolino; m. Gustavo Primo Maroni, Dec. 16, 1974. BS, U. Wis., 1960, PhD, 1969. Project assoc. U. Wis., Madison, 1960-63, 68-74; Alexander von Humboldt fellow Inst. Genetics U. Cologne, Fed. Republic Germany, 1974-75; Hargitt fellow Duke U., Durham, NC, 1975-76, rsch. assoc., 1976-83, rsch. assoc. prof., 1983-87; sr. program specialist N.C. Biotech. Ctr., Research Triangle Park, 1987-88, dir. sci. programs div., 1988-92, v.p. for sci. programs, 1992-94, ret., 1995. Mem. adv. com. MICROMED at Bowman Gray Sch. Medicine, Winston-Salem, NC, 1988—94; mem. sci. adv. bd. NC Biosci. Fund, LLC, 1998—99, Minority Sci. Improvement Alliance for Instrn. and Rsch. in Biotech, Ala. A&M U., Normal, 1990—91. Contbr. over 20 articles and revs. to profl. jours. Grantee NSF, 1977-79, NIH, 1979-82, 79-83, 82-87. Mem. Genetics Soc. Am., N.C. Acad. Sci., Inc. (bd. dirs. 1983-86), Sigma Xi (mem. exec. com. Duke U. chpt. 1989-90). Achievements include research in electron microscopy, evolution of chromosomes, chromosome structure, evolution of mitosis, and mitosis and fungal phylogeny. Personal E-mail: dmaroni@email.unc.du.

MAROTTA, GINA, athletic trainer; b. Newburgh, NY, Apr. 18, 1976; d. Joseph Marotta Sr. and Debra Marotta. BS, SUNY, New Paltz, 1999; MS, Bloomsburg U., Pa., 2003. Cert. athletic trainer Nat. Athletic Trainers Assn., 2000, strength and conditioning specialist Nat. Strength and Conditioning Assn., 2002. Grad. asst. athletic trainer Bloomsburg U., 2002—03; athletic trainer Geisinger-Healthsouth Sports Medicine, Danville, 2003—. Grad. asst. athletic trainer, outreach program Bloomsburg U., 2001—02; asst. softball coach SUNY, Cortland, 1999—2001, summer sports camp chief med. personel, 2003; dir. recreation camp Town of Shawangunk, Wallkill, 1998—99; assoc. head softball coach SUNY, New Paltz, 1998—99, asst. basketball coach, 1998—99. Mem.: Pa. Athletic Trainers Soc. (licentiate), Nat. Strength and Conditioning Assn. (licentiate), Nat. Athletic Trainer's Assn. (licentiate). Roman Catholic. Achievements include tried out for the women's professional softball team and played semi-professional softball in Albany, NY for the Adirondack ice in 1999-2001. Avocations: mountain biking, weightlifting, softball, hiking, travel. Personal E-mail: everlast4u22@yahoo.com.

MARPLE, DOROTHY JANE, retired church executive; b. Abington, Pa., Nov. 24, 1926; d. John Stanley and Jennie (Stetler) M. AB, Ursinus Coll., 1948; MA, Syracuse U., 1950; Ed.D., Columbia U. Tchrs. Coll., 1969; L.H.D., Thiel Coll., 1965, Gettysburg Coll., 1979, Ursinus Coll., 1981; D. Humanitarian Services, Newberry Coll., 1977; DD, Trinity Luth. Sem., 1987. Counselor, asst., office dean undergrad. women Women's Coll., Duke, 1950-53; dean women, fgn. student adv. Thiel Coll., 1953-61; asst. social dir. Whittier Hall, Columbia Tchrs. Coll., 1961-62; exec. dir. Luth. Ch. Women, Luth. Ch. Am., Phila., 1962-75; asst. to bishop Luth. Ch. Am., 1975-85; coord. Transition Office Evang. Luth. Ch. Am., 1986-87; asst. gen. sec. ops. Nat. Coun. Chs. of Christ in U.S., N.Y.C., 1987-89. Coord. Luth. Ch. in Am. commn. on function and structure, 1970-72; chairperson Luth. World Fedn. Commn. Ch. Cooperation, 1983-90; mem. bd. dirs. Luth. Theol. Sem., Gettysburg, 1989-98; bd. trustees United Bd. Christian Higher Edn. in Asia, 1989-98. Home: 8018 Anderson St Philadelphia PA 19118-2936

MARQUAND, BARBARA K., freelance writer; b. Denver, May 13, 1962; d. Kenneth Earl and Betty H. (Farley) M.; m. John Marvin Seelmeyer, May 19, 1990; 1 child, Sara Day Seelmeyer. BA, Colo. State U., Ft. Collins, 1984. Reporter The Sentinel Newspapers, Arvada, Lakewood, Wheat Ridge, Colo., 1984-87, The Greeley (Colo.) Tribune, 1987-89; contbg. editor Chico (Calif.) News and Rev., 1990-92; freelance writer, Grass Valley, Calif., 1992—. Contbr. articles to regional and nat. trade and consumer mags. Vol. tutor Hennessy Sch., Grass Valley, 1992, Girl Scout Leader, 1999-2002, The Friendship Club, Nevada County Schs., Grass Valley, 1997-98; vol. crisis counselor Catalyst, Chico, 1991. Recipient 2d place award feature writing Calif. Newspaper Pubs. Assn., 1991, 1st place series awrd Colo. Assoc. Editors and Reporters, 1987, numerous others. Mem. Soc. Children's Book Writers & Illustrators (mem. regional conf. com.), LWV (sec. Western Nevada County 1996), Sierra Trailblazers (sec. 1998-2000). Episcopalian. Avocations: running, reading, camping, hiking, painting.

MARQUAND, JEAN MACMURTRY, educational association administrator; b. Schenectady, N.Y., Feb. 1, 1947; d. Louis Frederick, Jr. and Eleanore Jean (Noyes) MacMurtry. BA in Edn. with honors, Simmons Coll., 1969; MEd, U. Vt., 1975; cert. advanced studies in mgmt., Harvard U., Cambridge, Mass., 1993. Elem. tchr., Pittsford, 1969-70; reading specialist Lincoln, Vt., 1971-73, Pembroke, Mass., 1976; grad. teaching asst U. Vt., 1975; elem tchr. Chatham, Mass., 1977-80; with Arthur D. Little, Cambridge, Mass., 1981-82; exec. sec. Meredith & Grew, Inc., Boston, 1982—2003; prin. On Holiday, LLC, 2003—. Bd. mgrs. Jr. League, Boston, 1990—92, v.p., 1993—94, mem. sustaining com., 1997—, dir. sustainer mem., 2006—; mem. Orleans chpt. Philanthropic Ednl. Orgn., 1983—, treas., 2005—, chair Mass. state bylaws com., 1998. Recipient Vol. Recognition award, Jr. League Boston, 1989, 2006. Mem.: Internat. Alliance, PEO, Chowder Soc., Coll. Club (pres. 1994—98, chair bylaws com. 1998—2003, parliamentarian 2001—03). Personal E-mail: jean@onholidaydresswear.com.

MARQUARDT, CHRISTEL ELISABETH, judge; b. Chgo., Aug. 26, 1935; d. Herman Albert and Christine Marie (Geringer) Trolenberg; children: Eric, Philip, Andrew, Joel. BS in Edn., Mo. Western Coll., 1970; JD with honors, Washburn U., 1974. Bar: Kans. 1974, Mo. 1992. Tchr. St. John's Ch., Tigerton, Wis., 1955-56; pers. asst. Columbia Records, L.A., 1958-59; ptnr. Cosgrove, Webb & Oman, Topeka, 1974-86, Palmer & Marquardt, Topeka, 1986-91, Levy and Craig P.C., Overland Park, Kans., 1991-94; sr. ptnr. Marquardt and Assocs., L.L.C., Fairway, Kans., 1994-95; judge Kans. Ct. Appeals, 1995—. Mem. atty. bd. discipline Kans. Supreme Ct., 1984—86; mem. Kans. Sentencing Commn., 2004—, Kans. Criminal Justice Recodification, Rehab. and Restoration Com., 2004—. Mem. editorial adv. bd. Kans. Lawyers Weekly, 1992-96; contbr. articles to legal jours. Bd. dirs. Topeka Symphony, 1983-92, 95-2002, Arts and Humanities Assn. Johnson County, 1992-95, Brown Found., 1988-90; hearing examiner Human Rels. Com., Topeka, 1974-76; local advisor Boy Scouts Am., 1973-74; bd. dirs., mem. nominating com. YWCA, Topeka, 1979-81; bd. govs. Washburn U. Law Sch., 1987-2002, v.p., 1996-98, pres., 1998-2000, disting. alumni, 2004; mem. dist. bd. adjudication Mo. Synod Luth. Ch., Kans., 1982-88. Named Woman of Yr., Mayor, City of Topeka, 1982; Obee scholar Washburn U., 1972-74; recipient Jennie Mitchell Kellogg Atty. of Achievement award, 1999, Phil Lewis medal of Distinction, 2000, Atty. of Achievement award Kans. Women Attys. Assn., Disting. Svc. award Washburn U. Law Sch., 2002, 04; named Disting. Alumni, Washburn U. Fellow: Kans. Bar Found. (trustee 1987—89), Am. Bar Found.; mem.: ABA (mem. ho. dels. 1988—, chmn. specialization com. 1991—93, lawyer referral com. 1993—95, state del. 1995—99, bar svcs. and activities 1995—99, bd. govs., program and planning com. 1999—2002, bd. govs. 1999—2002, ctrl. and ea. European law initiative 2001—02, African law coun. 2002—04, del-at-large ho. of dels. 2002—, standing com. on jud. independence 2004—, 2004—), Scape and Correlation of Work (chair 2006—), Law and Organizational Econ. Ctr. (bd. dirs. 2000—02), Am. Bus. Women's Assn. (lectr., corr. sec. 1983—84, pres. career chpt. 1986—87, named one of Top 10 Bus. Women of Yr. 1985), Topeka Bar Assn., Kans. Trial Lawyers Assn. (bd. govs. 1982—86, lectr.), Kans. Bar Assn. (sec., treas. 1981—85, bd. dirs. 1983—, v.p. 1985—86, pres. 1987—88, mem., lawyer referral com. 1999—). Home: 3408 SW Alameda Dr Topeka KS 66614-5108 Office: 301 SW 10th Ave Topeka KS 66612-1502 Business E-Mail: marquardtc@kscourts.org.

MARQUARDT, SHIRLEY MARIE, retired management consultant; b. Orlando, Okla., Aug. 20, 1941; d. Arthur Theodore Jack and Eleanor Lou Hurst; m. Donald Lee Marquardt, June 7, 1960; 1 child, Shirley Marie. Diploma, Army Mgmt. Staff Coll., 1994; A in Gen. Studies, Ctrl. Tex. Coll., 1983; BS in Gen. Studies, Am. Technol. U., 1987; MS in Human Resource Develop., U. Ctrl. Tex., 1988; diploma in Orgnl. Effectiveness, US Army Orgnl. Effectiveness Ctr. and Sch., 1985. Cert. Journeyman Mgmt. Analyst Civilian Career Intern Program, Dept. Army, Info. Mapping Course Instr. Info. Mapping, Inc., Prevention Sexual Harassment Course Instr. III Corps, Ft. Hood, Number Skills Course Instr. Mc-Graw Hill Book Co., Investment in Excellence Course Facilitator Pacific Inst. Mil. personnel clerk III Corps., Ft. Hood, Tex., 1968—70, sec. computer sys. command, 1970—72, adminstrv. specialist, sec. stenographer, 1978, pers. clk., Civilian Pers. Dir., 1980—81, mgmt. analyst, Directorate of Resource Mgmt., 1981—84, asst. dir., Dir. Program Integration, Leadership, 1984—94, divsn. chief, Dir. Info. Mgmt., 1994—98; sec. First Meth. Ch., Perry, Okla., 1959—60; exec. sec. YMCA, El Paso, Tex., 1960—62; clk. typist Hdqs., US Army Ryukyu Islands, Okinawa, Japan, 1963—66; mil. pers. clk., adj. gen. office, hdqrs. Berlin Brigade, 1966—68; sec. U.S. Army Corps Engrs., Frankfurt, Germany, 1976—78; clk. stenographer VII Corps Arty., Aschafffenburg, Germany, 1975; pers. clk. Test, Evaluation Command Civilian Pers. Office, Aberdeen Proving Ground, Md., 1978—79; supr. mgmt. asst. U.S. Army Toxic, Hazardous Materials Agy., Aberdeen Proving Ground, 1979—80; office svcs. supr. Facilities Engring. Divsn., Aberdeen Proving Ground, 1979; ret., 1998. Prodr.: (30 minute TV film) Waverley Historic District; editor: Enid Oklahoma Waverley Wind. Mem. City Spl. Tax Oversight Com., Enid, 1999—2005, City Enid Comprehensive Planning Com., 2000—05, City Enid Cmty. Rels. Bd., 2003—06, Enid A.M. Too Am. Bus. Club, 2004—06, City Enid Hist. Preservation Commn., 2005—06, Garfield County Rep. Women's Club, Enid, 2004—06; pres. Waverley Hist. Neighborhood Assn., Enid, Okla., 1999—2005; bd. mem. Horn of Plenty, Enid, 2004—06; bd. mem., adm. chair Sons and Daughters Cherokee Strip, Enid, 2005—06; mem. Am. Bus. Club. Decorated Achievement medal for Civilian Svc. US Army, III Corps, Ft. Hood, Army Individual Superior Civilian Svc. award, Army Comdr. award with two oak leaf clusters United States Army, III Corps, Ft. Hood; recipient Employee of Yr., III Corps, Ft. Hood, 1987. Mem.: Nat. Trust Hist. Preservation, Okla. Hist. Soc. Conservative-R. Avocations: historic preservation, cmty. volunteerism. Home: 1323 W Broadway Ave Enid OK 73703-5720

MARQUART, PETRA A., training consultant; b. Fairmont, Minn., July 16, 1948; d. Walter H. and Mavis I. Marquart. BA in Comms., Metropolitan State U., Mpls., 1998. Cert. trainer 1993, achieve global 1991, resident mgr. 1984, lic. realtor Minn., 1982. Prin. Petra Marquart and Assocs., Minnetonka, Minn., 1998—; tng. coord. Customized Tng. Svcs./Hennepin Tech. Coll., Plymouth, Minn., 1990—. Adj. instr./CRM cert. Minn. Multi Housing Assn., Bloomington, 1987—98; bd. dirs. edn. Minn. Multi Ho. Asssn., Bloomington, Minn., 1992—97; bd. dirs. ACE, Honeywell, Minn., 1994—98; cons. Mayo Clinic, Rochester, 1999—2001. Singer: (singer with ensemble) The 10th Story Window, 1973; author: (novels) The Power of Service: Keeping Customers for Life, 1998, (customer svc. tng. program) Mall of America's Guest Service Training, 1995, Svc. at the Ctr. - Fairview Hosps., 1997, First Bank Sys. - Customers First, 1996, Capri Svc.-Casinos Am., 1998, (Property Mgmt. Course Series) Introduction to Property Management, 1987; actor: (films, supporting role) The Crucible, 1965 (Best Actress, 1965). Stephen Minister Gethsemane Luth. Ch., Hopkins, Minn.; pres. NOW, Jackson, Minn., 1975—76. Lutheran. Avocations: fishing, golf, music. Office: Petra Marquart and Assocs PO Box 55 Hackensack MN 56452 Business E-Mail: info@petramarquart.com.

MÁRQUEZ-MAGAÑA, LETICIA MARIA, biology professor; b. Sacramento, Aug. 15, 1963; d. Jesús José and Guadalupe María Márquez; married; children: Joaquín, Elías. BS,MS in Biol. Scis., Stanford U., 1986; PhD in Biochemistry, U. Calif., Berkeley, 1991. Postdoctoral fellow Stanford (Calif.) U., 1991—94; asst. prof. biology San Francisco State U., 1994—99, assoc. prof. biology, 1999—2004, prof. biology, 2004—, microbial geneticist, 1994—. Contbr. articles to profl. jours., including Jour. Bacteriology and Jour. Biol. Chemistry. Motivational spkr. to minority students, No. Calif., 1994—; mem. task force Hispanic-Serving Inst. Hispanic Assn. Colls. and Univs.; mentor to UC San Franisco Tchg. postdoctoral fellows, 2002—. Named Hispanic Powerhitter, Hispanic Engr. mag., 2003; named one of 100 Most Influential Hispanics, Hispanic Bus. mag., 1998. Mem.: AAAS (Mentor award 2001), Soc. Advancement of Chicanos and Native Americans in Sci. (e-mentor for K-12 educators 2001—, bd. dirs. 1989—91), Am. Soc. Microbiology. Office: San Francisco State U Dept Biology 1600 Holloway Ave San Francisco CA 94132 E-mail: marquez@sfsu.edu.

MÁRQUEZ-PETERSON, LEA, business broker; b. 1970; m. Daniel Harold Peterson. B in Mktg. and Entrepreneurship, U. Ariz., 1992; MBA, Pepperdine, 1996. Franchise and bus. devel. Shell Oil Co., LA; founder Am. Retail Corp., Am. Fuel, Marquez-Peterson Grp., Marquez-Peterson II, Valle Verde Partners; exec. dir. Greater Tucson Leadership; owner TucsonBizForSale-.com; bus. broker Bus. Source. Founder, former chairperson Pima County Small Bus. Commn.; former chairperson City of Tucson Small Bus. Commn. Mem., Dean of Students adv. bd. U. Ariz., mem., Pres. Bus. Adv. Coun.; mem. YWCA, Regional Transportation Authority Com., Tucson Convention Ctr. Commn. Named Tucson Small Bus. of Yr., Small Bus. Devel. Coun., 2000, Tucson Minority Small Bus. Retailer of Yr., 2002, Small Bus. Leader of Yr., Tucson Metro. Chamber of Commerce, Wells Fargo Bank, 2003; named one of 40 Under 40, Tucson Bus. Edge, 2006. Mem.: Nat. Fedn. Ind. Bus., Nat. Assn. Women Bus. Owners (former pres., Woman Bus. Owner of Yr. 2001). Office: Greater Tucson Leadership 5151 E Broadway Blvd Ste 1600 Tucson AZ 85711 Office Phone: 520-512-5485. Office Fax: 520-512-5401.*

MARQUIS, HARRIET HILL, social worker; b. Rocky Mount, N.C., Sept. 4, 1938; d. Robert Foster and Anne Ruth (Daughtry) Hill; m. James Ralph Marquis, Apr. 23, 1967; children: Margaret Anne, Karen Lee. BA in English, Meredith Coll., 1960; MA in English, Seton Hall U., 1971; PhD in English,

Drew U., 1984; MSW, NYU, 1987; cert., N.Y. Sch. Psychoanalytic Psychotherapy, 1991, Inst. Study Psychotherapy & Psychoanalysis N.J., 1998. Tchr. English S.C. Pub. Schs., 1960-62, Peace Corps, Sierra Leone, West Africa, 1963-65; adj. prof. English Farleigh Dickinson U., Madison, 1983-85; psychotherapist Child Guidance & Family Svc. Ctr., Orange, N.J., 1987; staff clinician Esther Dutton Counseling Ctr., Morristown, N.J., 1987-90; psychotherapist Ctr. Evaluation & Psychotherapy, Morristown, N.J., 1990-93; pvt. practice Madison, N.J., 1990-98, Brevard, N.C., 1998—. Mem. Internat. Conf. Advancement of Pvt. Practice Clin. Social Work; speaker in field. Fellow N.C. Soc. Clin. Social Workers; mem. NASW (bd. cert. diplomate in social work), Nat. Fedn. of Socs. for Clin. Social Work (nat. membership com. psychoanalysis in clin. social work). Democrat. Methodist. Avocations: reading, walking, writing, travel. E-mail: harrieth@brinet.com.

MARR, CARMEL CARRINGTON, retired state official; b. Bklyn., June 23, 1921; d. William Preston and Gertrude Clementine (Lewis) Carrington; m. Warren Marr II, Apr. 11, 1948; children: Charles Carrington, Warren Quincy III. BA, Hunter Coll., 1945; JD, Columbia U., 1948. Bar: N.Y. 1948, U.S. Dist. Ct. (ea. dist.) N.Y. 1950, U.S. Dist. Ct. (so. dist.) N.Y. 1951. Clk. Dyer & Stevens, N.Y.C., 1948-49; pvt. practice N.Y.C., 1949-53; adviser legal affairs U.S. mission to UN, N.Y.C., 1953-67; sr. legal officer Office Legal Affairs UN Secretariat, 1967-68; mem. N.Y. State Human Rights Appeal Bd., 1968-71, N.Y. State Pub. Svc. Commn., 1971-86; cons. Gas. Rsch. Inst., 1987-91. Lectr. N.Y. Police Acad., 1963-67. Contbr. articles to profl. jours. Mem. N.Y. Gov.'s Com. Edn. and Employment of Women, 1963-64; mem. Nat. Gen. Svcs. Pub. Adv. Council, 1969-71; mem., former chmn. adv. coun. Gas. Rsch. Inst.; mem. chmn. tech. pipeline safety standards com. Dept. Transp., 1979-85; former mem. task force Fed. Energy Regulatory Commn. and EPA to examine PCBs in gas supply system; past chmn. gas com. Nat. Assn. Regulatory Utility Commrs.; past pres. Great Lakes Conf. Pub. Utilities Commrs., mem. exec. com.; mem. UN Devel. Corp., 1969-72; bd. dirs. Amistad Rsch. Ctr., New Orleans, 1970—, chmn. bd. dirs., 1981-94; bd. dirs. Bklyn. Soc. Prevention Cruelty to Children, Nat. Arts Stblzn. Fund, 1984-93, hon. bd. mem., 1998, Prospect Park Alliance, 1987-98; bd. visitors N.Y. State Sch. Girls, Hudson, 1964-71; mem. exec. bd. Plays for Living, N.Y.C., 1968-75; pres. bd. dirs. Billie Holiday Theatre, 1972-80; mem. nat. adv. coun. Hampshire Coll.; pres.'s coun. Tulane U., 1988-95. Mem. Phi Beta Kappa, Alpha Chi Alpha, Alpha Kappa Alpha. Republican. Episcopalian.

MARR, CATHERINE MARY, physical education educator; d. Ernest George and Mary Harris; m. Brian Edward Marr, July 19, 1997. BS in Edn., George Mason U., Fairfax, Va., 1992. Cert. athletic tng. NATA BOC/ Tex., 1995, lic. athletic trainer Med. Adv. Bd. Tex., 1996, athletic tng. lic. Tex. Dept. Health, 1996; lic. tchr. phys. edn./health Tex. Dept. Edn., 1992. Phys. edn. tchr. Rosa Guerrero Elem. Sch., El Paso, Tex., 1992—93; asst. athletic trainer Coronado H.S., El Paso, Tex., 1992—93; grad. asst. athletic trainer/ clin. Ga. State U., Atlanta, 1993—96; asst. athletic trainer Cypress Falls H.S., Tex., 1996—2000; athletic trainer Peachtree Orthopaedic Clinic, Atlanta, 1993—2006; phys. edn. tchr. Farney Elem. Sch., Cypress, Tex., 2000—03; athletic trainer The Woodlands H.S. McCullough Campus, Tex., 2003—06; head athletic trainer The Woodlands Coll. Pk. H.S., Tex., 2006—. Mem.: SWATA (licentiate), ATPE (licentiate), Greater Houston Athletic Trainers Soc. (licentiate), NATA (licentiate), Chi Omega Nat. Frat. (life). R-Consevative. Greek Orthodox. Avocations: travel, sports. Office: Cavalier Sports Medicine Department 3701 College Park Dr The Woodlands TX 77387 Office Phone: 936-709-3160. Office Fax: 936-709-3044. Personal E-mail: turbocatm@yahoo.com. E-mail: cmarr@conroeisd.net.

MARR, PHEBE ANN, retired historian, educator; b. Mt. Vernon, NY, Sept. 21, 1931; d. John Joseph and Lillian Victoria (Henningsen) Marr. BA, Barnard Coll., N.Y.C., 1953; PhD, Harvard U., Cambridge, Mass., 1967. Rsch. assoc. ARAMCO, Dhahran, Saudi Arabia, 1960-62; dir. mid. east program Fgn. Svc. Inst., 1963-66; asst. prof. Stanislaus State Coll., Turlock, Calif., 1970-71, assoc. prof., 1971-74; assoc. prof. history U. Tenn., Knoxville, 1974-85, chmn. Asian studies program, 1977-79. Cons. ARAMCO, 1979-83. Author: The Modern History of Iraq, 1985, 2d edit., 2003; co-editor: Riding the Tiger: Middle East Challenge After the Cold War, 1993; contbr. articles to profl. jours. Bd. dirs. Mid. East Policy Coun., 2004. Rsch. fellow Mid. East Ctr., Harvard U., Cambridge, Mass., 1968-70, sr. fellow Nat. Def. U., Washington, 1985-97, Woodrow Wilson Ctr. fellow, 1998-99, Coun. on Fgn. Rels., U.S. Inst. Peace fellow, 2004-06. Mem. Mid. East Inst., Mid. East Studies Assn. Home and Office: 2902 18th St NW Washington DC 20009-2954 Office Phone: 202-462-3580. Personal E-mail: marrphebe@aol.com.

MARRACK, PHILIPPA CHARLOTTE, immunologist, researcher; b. Ewell, Eng., June 28, 1945; m. John Kappler, 1974; children: Kate, Jim. BA, U. Cambridge, 1967, PhD in Biology, 1970. Post-doctoral fellow, lab. rschr. U. Calif., San Diego, 1971-73; post-doctoral rschr. fellow U. Rochester, NY, 1973-79, assoc. rschr. NY, 1974-75, asst. prof. immunology NY, 1975-79, assoc. prof. NY, 1980-85; prof. dept. microbiology and immunology U. Colo. Health Scis. Ctr., Denver, 1988—94, prof. integrated dept. of Immunology, 1994—, prof., dept. biochemistry and molecular biology, prof. medicine; head, div. of basic immunology Nat. Jewish Ctr. for Immunology and Respiratory Medicine, Denver, 1988—90; prof. dept. biophysics, biochemistry and genetics U. Colo. Health Scis. Ctr., Denver, 1985-88; head, div. of Basic Immunology Nat. Jewish Medical and Rsch. Ctr., Denver, 1998—99, sr. faculty mem., Integrated Dept. of Immunology; investigator Kappler and Marrack Rsch. Lab. Howard Hughes Med. Inst., Chevy Chase, Md., 1986—. Mem. dept. medicine Nat. Jewish Hosp. and Rsch. Ctr., Denver, 1979—. Contbr. articles to profl. jours.; mem. editl. bds. Cell, Science, and Journal of Immunology. Served on panels for Am. Cancer Soc., US NIH, Burroughs Wellcome Fund. Recipient Feodor Lynen medal, 1990, William B. Coley award Cancer Rsch. Inst., 1991, Wellcome Found. lecturer Royal Soc., 1990, Paul Ehrlich and Ludwig Darmstädter prize, 1993, Louisa Gross Horwitz prize, 1994, Women's Excellence Scis. award Fedn. Am. Socs. Exptl. Biology, 1995, Women in Sci. award, L'Oreal-UNESCO, 2004. Mem. NAS, Royal Soc., Am. Assn. Immunologists (pres. 2000-2001, Lifetime Achievement award, 2003), Brit. Soc. Immunology, Internat. Union of Immunological Societies (past pres.). Office: Howard Hughes Med Inst Natl Jewish Med and Rsch Ctr 1400 Jackson St 5th fl Goodman Bldg Denver CO 80206*

MARRAM, ELLEN R., investment company executive; BS, Wellesley Coll., 1968; MBA, Harvard U., 1970. Pres. grocery divsn. Nabisco, 1987—88; pres., CEO Nabisco Biscuit Co., 1988—93, Tropicana & Tropicana Beverage Corp., 1993—98; exec. v.p. Segram Ltd., 1998—99; pres., CEO EfDex, Stamford, Conn., 1999; mng. dir. N. Castle Partners, 2000—. Bd. dirs. Ford Motor Co., N.Y. Times Co., Eli Lilly and Co. Bd. dirs. N.Y. Presbyn. Hosp., Lincoln Ctr. Theater, Families and Work Inst., City Meals on Wheels. Office: N Castle Partners 138 E Putnam Ave Greenwich CT 06830

MARRERO, TERESA, lawyer; b. N.Y.C. d. Miquel Angel and Jovita (Otero) Marrero. BA in Bus., Marymount Manhattan Coll., 1988; JD, N.Y. Law Sch., 1991. Bar: N.Y. 1992. Lawyer FCC, Washington, 1991-93; lawyer firm Akin, Gump, Washington, 1993-94; lawyer Teleport Comms. Group, N.Y.C., 1994-98, AT&T, Basking Ridge, N.J., 1998—. Mem. ABA. N.Y.C. Bar Assn., N.Y. State Bar Assn., P.R. Bar Assn., Adirondack Hiking Club, Audubon. Avocations: ornithology, birdwatching, bicycling, hiking. Office: At T 900 US Highway 202 206 Bedminster NJ 07921-2662

MARRETT, CORA B., science educator; b. Richmond, Va., June 15, 1942; d. Horace Sterling and Clora Ann (Boswell) Bagley; m. Louis Everard Marrett, Dec. 24, 1968. BA, Va. Union U., 1963; MS, U. Wis., 1965, PhD, 1968. Asst. prof. U. N.C., Chapel Hill, 1968-69; from asst. to assoc. prof. Western Mich. U., Kalamazoo, 1969-73; from assoc. prof. to full prof. U. Wis., Madison, 1973-97; asst. dir. NSF, Arlington, Va., 1992-96; provost, vice chancellor for acad. affairs U. Mass., Amherst, 1997—2001; sr. v.p. for acad. affairs U. Wis. System, 2001—. Mem. sci. adv. panel U.S. Army, Washington, 1976-77; mem. Naval Rsch. Adv. Com., Washington, 1978-81, Pres. Commn. on the Accident at Three Mile Island, 1979; bd. govs. Argonne (Ill.) Nat. Lab., 1983-90, 96-99. Editor: Research in Race and Ethnic Relations, 1988, Gender and Classroom Interaction, 1990. Resident fellow NAS, 1973-74; fellow Ctr. for Advanced Study in Behavioral Scis., 1976-77. Mem. AAAS, ASA, Phi Kappa Phi. Avocations: reading, travel, film appreciation. Home: 7517 Farmington Way Madison WI 53717 Office: Office Acad Affairs U of Wisconsin System 1620 Van Hise Hall Madison WI 53706 Office Phone: 608-262-3826. E-mail: cmarrett@uwsa.edu.

MARRINAN, SUSAN FAYE, lawyer; b. Vermillion, SD, May 29, 1948; BA, U. Minn., 1969, JD, 1973. Bar: Minn. 1973, Wis. 1973. Atty. Carlson Cos., Plymouth, Minn., 1973-74, Prudential Ins. Co., Mpls., 1974-75; v.p., gen. counsel, corp. sec. H.B. Fuller Co., St. Paul, 1977—90; gen. counsel, sec. Snap-On, Inc., Kenosha, Wis., 1990—92, v.p., gen. counsel, sec., 1992—2004, v.p., sec., chief legal officer, 2004—. Fundraiser Am. Cancer Soc.; bd. dirs. Family Svcs. St. Paul, Childrens Theatre Co. Mem. Am. Assn. Corp. Counsel (bd. dirs. Minn. chpt. 1986—), Am. Corp. Counsel Assn. (bd. dirs. 1997-02). Republican. Avocation: running. Office: Snap-On Inc 2801 80th St Kenosha WI 53141

MARRIOTT, KARLA-SUE CAMILLE, forensic specialist; b. Kingston, Jamaica, Sept. 1974; d. Herman Carlton DaCosta and Claire Yvonne Marriott. BS in Biochemistry (hon.), U. W.I., Jamaica, 1996; PhD in Synthetic Organic Chemistry, U. W.I., 2001. Forensic officer/ crime scene investigator Govt. of Jamaica Forensic Lab., Kingston, 1996; organic chemistry lectr. U. W.I., Kingston, 2001—02; rsch. fellow Clemson U., SC, 2002—06; asst. prof. of forensic sci. Savannah State U., Ga., 2006—. Contbr. articles to profl. jours. Mem.: Internat. Cannabinoid Rsch. Soc., Am. Chem. Soc. Achievements include research in synthesis and pharmacology of 11-nor-1-methoxy-9-hydroxyhexahydrocannabinols & 11-nor-1-deoxy-9-hydroxyhexahydrocannabinols: New selective ligands for cannabinoid CB(2) receptor, Bioorg Med Chem, 20; a photochemical route to dibenzonaphthyrones, Heterocycles, 2002; synthesis of 2, 3-dimethoxy-7-methyl-7, 12-dihydro-6H--benzofuro---benzaz-epin-6, 12-dione, Molecules, 2002; synthesis of a 2, 3-Dimethoxyrotenonoid, Heterocycles, 2001; development of recent advances in the development of selective ligands for the Cannabinoid CB2 Receptor. Office: Savannah State University 3219 College St Hubert D212 Savannah GA 31404 Business E-Mail: marriottk@savstate.edu.

MARRIOTT, MARCIA ANN, business educator, economics professor, health facility administrator; b. Rochester, N.Y., Mar. 21, 1947; d. Coyne and Alice (Schleper) M.; children: Brian, Jonathan. AA, Monroe C.C., Rochester, 1967; BS, SUNY, Brockport, 1970, MA, 1975; PhD, S.W. U. La., 1985. Program adminstr. N.Y. Dept. of Labor, N.Y.C., 1970-75; employment mgr. Rochester Gen. Hosp., 1975-77, salary adminstr., 1982-98, compensation mgr., 1996—; corp. dir. wage and salary dept. Gannett Newspapers, Rochester, 1977-80; compensation and benefits adminstr. Sybron Corp., Rochester, 1980-82; compensation mgr. Rochester Gen. Hosp., 1996—; dir. compensation Via Health, Rochester, 1995-98; pres. Compensation Link, 1997—; prof. Grad. Sch. Bus. Rochester Inst. Tech., 1998—2003, SUNY, Brockport, 1998—2003. Instr. N.Y. State Sch. Indsl. Rels., Cornell U., N.Y.C., 1976-79; assoc. prof. Rochester Inst. Tech., 1978—, Monroe C.C., 1981—, dir. career adv. coun., 1989—; assoc. prof. SUNY, Brockport; assoc. prof. Nazareth Coll., 1998; dir. Rochester Presbyn. Home, 1987-91, 96—, v.p. bd. dirs., 1997-98, pres. bd. dirs., 1998—; dir. area hosp. coun. Kidney Svc. Ctrs., Rochester, 1988-91; cons. in field. Author: (pamphlets) Guideline for Writing Job Descriptions, 1983, (manual) Career Planning Manual, 1985, (booklet) Guideline for Writing Criteria-Based Job Descriptions, 1988, Skill-based Job Descriptions: A Quality Approach, 1994, Redesigning the Performance Appraisal Process, 1996. Campaign mgr. Carter Campaign Commn., Rochester, 1975; mem. coun. Messiah Luth. Ch., Rochester, 1991-94. Davenport-Hatch Found. grantee, 1973, Wegman Found. grantee, 1975. Mem. Am. Compensation Assn., Single Adopted Parents Group (pres. 1988-93). Avocations: tennis, hiking, reading, swimming, skiing. Office: Rochester Gen Hosp 1425 Portland Ave Rochester NY 14621-3095

MARROLLI, KAREN LYN, conductor; b. Mount Holly, NJ, May 4, 1975; d. Paul and Ursula Marrolli. BMus in Music Theory and Composition, Westminster Choir Coll., Princeton, NJ, 1997, MusM in Choral Conducting/Sacred Music, 2000. Asst. condr. Grace Episcopal Ch., Charleston, SC, 2000—; dir. chorus and orch. James Island Charter HS, Charleston, 2004—. Founding artistic dir. Lux Aeterna, Charleston, 2003—; asst. condr. Charleston Symphony Orch. Chorus, 2004—. Composer: (choral music) Set Me As A Seal; artistic dir., condr. Annual Concert for Child Abuse Awareness Month; musician: (opera/choral) Spoleto Festival USA. Recipient Hoke Ch. Music award in Composition, Westminster Choir Coll., 1997. Mem.: Music Educators Nat. Conf. Avocations: making jewelry, kayaking, travel, writing poetry.

MARRON, PAMELA ANNE, artist; b. Hackensack, N.J., Nov. 16, 1945; d. Chester Charles and Edith Anne Marron. AA, Parsons Sch. Design, N.Y.C., 1968; postgrad., Stanford U., Calif., 1970. Mem. art com. Stratton Art Festival, Stratton Mountain, Vt.; founder, art com. Elm St. Arts, Manchester, Vt. Archtl. Digest, 1998, Women Artists Calendar, 1999, one-woman shows include Stratton Arts Festival, 1974—94, Park McCullough House, Bennington, Vt., 1976, The Hoosac Sch., N.Y., 1978, Garden Gallery, Londonderry, Vt., 1980, AVA Gallery, Hanover, N.H., 1984, Castleton State Coll., Vt., 1986, Pindar Gallery, N.Y.C., 1987, Northstar Gallery Show, Stratton Mountain, 1989—2002, Avanti Gallery, Lambertville, N.J., 1990, Nicholas Roerich Mus., N.Y.C., 1990, Lotus Gallery, Cambridge, Mass., 1990, Vt. State House, Montpelier, 1992, Chaffee Art Ctr., Rutland, Vt., 1994, Elm St. Arts, Manchester Center, Vt., 1994, 95, 1994, 1995, Gallery Two, Woodstock, Vt., 1995, Olde Moon Gallery, Breckenridge, Colo., 1998, Grayson Gallery, Woodstock, 1999, Gardner Colby Gallery, Naples, Fla., 2001, Schenectady Mus., 2004, Haddad Lascano Gallery, Greater Barrington, Mass., 2005, Redux Gallery, Dorset, Vt., 2005, Nancy Price Gallery, Jamaica, Vt., 2005, Doreset Theater Festival, 2005, So. Vt. Art Ctr., 2006, So. Vt. Coll., Manchester Center, 1975, 79, 2006, Beside Myself Gallery, Arlington, Vt., 1982, 86, 90, Cove Gallery, Wellfleet, Mass., 1991, 97, Represented in permanent collections Lotus Corp., Omni Corp., N.Y.C., Yoder Brothers Internat., Barherton, Ohio, numerous group exhbns. Recipient Max Beckman scholarship, 1967, 1968, Jurors award, Berkshire Mus., 1978, Stratton Art Festival, 1983, 1988, Jay Conaway award, 1987, 1990. Mem.: Vt. Coun. on Arts, So. Vt. Art Ctr. (art com., numerous art exhbns., Jurors award 1998). Avocations: singing, swimming, walking. Home: Box 563 Dorset VT 05251 Office Phone: 802-867-2246.

MARRS, CAROL FAYE, performing arts educator, writer; b. Fairbanks, Alaska, Sept. 22, 1955; d. Morris Elton Robinson and Mary Emogene Hall; m. Gregory Evan Marrs; children: Matthew, Haley. BSc, West Tex. State U., Canyon, 1977. Tchr. English/Speech Hereford Ind. Sch. Dist., Tex., 1979—81; tchr. speech/drama/English River Rd. Ind. Sch. Dist., Amarillo, Tex., 1981—82, Canyon Ind. Sch. Dist., Tex., 1982—90; tchr. grade 1 Lewisville Ind. Sch. Dist., Carrollton, Tex., 1996—98, tchr. creative dramatics, 1998—2005, Flower Mound, 2005—. Workshop presenter Tex. Educators Theatre Assn., Austin, 2005; author, pub. spkr. Tex. Panhandle Penwomen, Amarillo, 1988—; dir. summer music theatre camp for children; tchr. music class for toddlers. Author: (children's poetry) Pet Cobwebs, 1988, (speech textbook) The Complete Book of Speech Communication, 1991. Mem. Grace Cmty. Assembly of God, Flower Mound, 2005—. Finalist Tchr. of Yr., LISD, 2003, 2004; named Elem. Tchr. of Yr., Indian Creek Ind. Elem. Sch., Lewisville Ind. Sch. Dist., 2003—04; grantee, Lewisville Edn. Found., 2003—04; 3 nominations Tchr. of Yr., Disney. Mem.: PTA, Tex. Educators Theatre Assn., Mothers In Touch (campus coord. 2005—06). Home: 420 Moran Dr Highland Village TX 79070 Office: Wellington Elem Flower Mound TX Office Phone: 469-713-5989.

MARS, CHERI HIGDON, science educator; b. Chattanooga, Sept. 18, 1960; d. Harold G. and Mary S. Higdon; m. Steve Ausmus Mars, Apr. 28, 1984; children: Alexander Higdon, Anderson Ausmus. BA, U. Tenn., Knoxville, 1983; MEd, Lincoln Meml. U., Harrogate, Tenn., 1993. Instr. sci. J. Frank White Acad., Harrogate, 1993—99, Middlesboro H.S., Middlesboro, Ky., 2002—. Coach Sci. Olympiad, Middlesboro, 2003—06. Named Vol. of the Yr., Coop. Christian Ministry, Middlesboro, 1986. Mem.: Nat. Sci. Tchrs. Assn. Methodist. Avocations: walking, golf.

MARS, JACQUELINE BADGER, food products executive; m. David Badger, 1961 (div.); 3 children; m. Harold Vogel, 1986 (div.). Degree in anthropology, Bryn Mawr Coll., 1961. Co-owner Mars, Inc., McLean, Va., 1973—, corp. v.p., 1990—. Trustee Bryn Mawr Coll.; bd. trustee mem.-at-large Washington Nat. Opera. Named one of World's Richest People, Forbes, 2000—, Forbes Richest Americans, 2006. Office: Mars Inc 6885 Elm St Mc Lean VA 22101

MARS, VIRGINIA CRETELLA, civic volunteer; b. New Haven; d. Albert William and Josephine Vera (Nutile) Cretella; m. Forrest E. Mars Jr., Oct. 20, 1955 (div. Jan. 1990); children: Victoria B., Valerie A., Pamela D., Marijke E. BA, Vassar Coll., 1951. Cert. tchr. Mem. Nat. Symphony Orch. Bd., Washington, chmn. exec. com., 1980-83, pres., 1983-87; mem. Smithsonian Women's Com., Washington, 1988—; past trustee The Potomac Sch. Bd., McLean, Va., The Langley Sch., McLean, Vassar Coll. Bd., Poughkeepsie, N.Y., 1987-99, adv. coun., 2001—; bd. dirs. Wildlife Trust, 1990-2004, v.p., 1996, pres., 2001-04, coun. 2004—, chmn. 2006-; chmn. Campaign for Vassar; mem. Cathedral chpt. bd. dirs. Washington Nat. Cathedral, 1993-2001; bd. dirs. Cathedral Choral Soc., 1998-2004; trustee Forcroft Sch., 2003—, Am. Symphony Orch. League, 2005— Mem.: Chevy Chase Club, Cosmos Club, Vassar Club Washington. Episcopalian. Avocations: skiing, fly fishing, needlepoint, golf, cooking. Home: 702 Belgrove Rd Mc Lean VA 22101-1836

MARSALA-CERVASIO, KATHLEEN ANN, medical/surgical nurse; b. Mar. 22, 1955; d. James Patrick and Kathleen (McLoughlin) Waters. AAS with honors, S.I. Coll., 1974, BS in Nursing with honors, 1984; MSN with honors, CUNY, 1986; PhD in Pub. Adminstrn., Kensington U., 1997. RN, N.Y.; cert. CS, CCRN, CNAA. Staff nurse USPHS Hosp., S.I., 1974-80; head nurse MICU-critical care unit-surg. ICU Bayley Seton Hosp., N.Y., 1980-82; staff nurse surg. ICU, MICU, critical care unit East Orange (N.J.) VA Med. Ctr., 1982-86, critical care nurse specialist; clin. specialist, cons. Med. Ctr. Bklyn. VA Med. Ctr., 1989-95; dir. nursing svcs., asst. prof. nursing U. Hosp./SUNY Health Sci. Ctr., Bklyn., 1990-2000; mem. faculty L.I. U., 2001—. Asst. clin. prof. Met. Jewish Healthcare Sys.; adj. prof. Touro Coll., 2006. Mem. AACN, Sigma Theta Tau. Home: 8898 16th Ave Brooklyn NY 11214-5804

MARSALISI, PATRICIA DIANNE, nurse anesthetist; d. Charles Patrick and Florence Josephine (Meehan) Marsalisi. BA, Fordham U., 1978; M of Nursing, Columbia U., 1982. RN N.Y., cert. CRNA. Staff RN med.-surg. unit Roosevelt Hosp., N.Y.C., 1967-68, staff nurse emergency rm., 1968-74, oper. rm. nurse, 1974-82; nurse anesthetist St. Luke's-Roosevelt Hosp., N.Y.C., 1982-94; cert. RN anesthetist Good Samaritan Hosp., Suffern, N.Y., 1994—; instr. Columbia U. Sch. Nursing, 1999—. Mem.: N.Y. State Nurses Assn., Am. Assn. Nurse Anesthesists. Avocation: reading, needleworking, skiing, playing bridge, dancing. Office: 255 Lafayette Ave Suffern NY 10901-4817

MARSDEN, HERCI IVANA, classical ballet artistic director; b. Omis-Split, Croatia, Dec. 2, 1937; d. Ante and Magda (Smith) Munitic; m. Myles Marsden, Aug. 10, 1957 (div. 1976); children: Ana, Richard, Mark.; m. Dujko Radovnikovic, Aug. 27, 1977; 1 child, Dujko. Student, Internat. Ballet Sch., 1955. Mem. corps de ballet Nat. Theatre, Split, 1954-58; founder Braecrest Sch. Ballet, Lincoln, RI, 1958—, State Ballet of R.I., Lincoln, 1960—, artistic dir., 1976—. Artistic dir. U. R.I. Classical Ballet, Kingston, 1966—, lectr., 1966—. Office: Brae Crest School of Ballet 52 Sherman Ave Lincoln RI 02865-3809 Office Phone: 401-334-2560. Business E-Mail: hmarsden@stateballet.com.

MARSEE, SUSANNE IRENE, vocalist; b. San Diego, Nov. 26, 1941; d. Warren Jefferson and Irene Rose (Wills) Dowell; m. Mark J. Weinstein, May, 1987; 1 child, Zachary. Student, Santa Monica City Coll., 1961; BA in History, UCLA, 1964; postgrad., Juilliard, 1969, La. State U., 1991—92. Mem. voice faculty Am. Mus. and Dramatic Acad., N.Y.C., 1994-97, Pitts. Civic Light Opera Acad., 1997—2000, Duquesne U., 1998-2000; artist's lectr. Carnegie Mellon U., 2000—. Appeared with numerous U.S. opera cos., 1970—, including N.Y.C. Opera, San Francisco Opera, Boston Opera, Houston Grand Opera; appeared with fgn. cos., festivals, Mexico City Bellas Artes, 1973, 78, Canary Islands Co., 1976, Opera Metropolitana, Caracas, Venezuela, 1977, Spoleto (Italy) Festival, 1977, Aix en Provence Festival, France, 1977, Calgary, Alta., Can., 1986; recorded Tales of Hoffmann, ABC/Dunhill Records; TV appearances include Live from Lincoln Center, Turk in Italy, Cenerentola, 1989, Live from Wolftrap Roberto Devereux, 1975, Rigoletto, 1988, A Little Night Music, 1990, Marriage of Figaro, 1991, (PBS TV) Rachel, La Cubana; recs. and CDs Anna Bolena with Ramey, Scotto, Roberto Devereux with Beverly Sills, Roberto Devereux with Monserat Caballé Carreras, Tales of Hoffmann with Beverly Sills, Rigoletto with Quilico and Carreras; videotape Roberto Devereux with Beverly Sills. Recipient 2d place award Met. Opera Regional Auditions, 1968, San Francisco Opera Regional Auditions 1968; named winner Liederkranz Club Contest, 1970; Gladys Turk Found. grantee, 1968-69; Corbett Found. grantee, 1970-73; Martha Baird Rockefeller grantee, 1969-70, 71-72 Mem. AFTRA, Am. Guild Mus. Artists (past bd. dirs.), Nat. Assn. Tchrs. of Singing (past bd. dirs. for N.Y.). Democrat.

MARSELLA, JULIA, music educator; b. Cedarville, N.J., July 29, 1929; d. Joseph and Marion Marie (Sanza) Nardelli; m. Anthony Joseph Marsella, Apr. 4, 1971. Student of Percy Ross, Phila. Conservatory of Music; Phila. Mus. Acad.; student of Joseph Arcaro, Phila. Conservatory of Music. Ptnr. Nardelli Hardware, Cedarville, 1946—90; pvt. piano tchr. Cedarville, 1962—. Organist, choir dir. St. Michael's Ch., Cedarville. Mem. Cumberland County Hist. Soc., Cedarville Hist. Soc.; trustee Cedarville Libr., 2000. Roman Catholic. Avocations: painting, reading, travel, cooking. Home: 329 Main St Cedarville NJ 08311

MARSH, ALMA FERN, retired music educator, director, organist; b. Kincaid, Kans., Dec. 30, 1921; d. George William Marsh and Adora Verle Hummiston Marsh. BSE, Emporia State Tchrs. Coll., Kans., 1952; MS, Pitts. State Coll., Kans., 1969. Cert. tchg. Music tchr. 3 rural schs., Hepler, Bronson, Kincaid, Kans., 1940—43; music tchr. 1-8 Elmdale, Kans., 1943—45; music tchr. 1-6 Horton, Kans., 1945—47, Ellsworth, Kans., 1948—51, Pitts., Kans., 1952—71, Iola, Kans., 1971—87; music dir. and organist First Presbyn. Ch., Iola, Kans., 1971—. Viola 1st chair Iola area Symphony Orch., Kans., 1971—; percussion Iola City Band, Kans., 2000—. Mem. Iola Cmty. Theatre, Kans., 1971—. Named Woman of Yr., First Presbyn. Ch., 2006, fine arts scholarship in her name, Allen County C.C., 2006. Mem.: NEA, Kans. Music Educators Assn., Music Educators Nat. Conf., Allen County Ret. Personnel Assn., Delta Kappa Gamma. Republican. Presbyn. Achievements include mentoring children in piano and string instruments. Avocations: painting, sewing, crocheting, music, cultral attractions. Home: 220 W Jackson Ave Iola KS 66749 Office Phone: 620-365-2976.

MARSH, BARBARA LYNN, elementary school educator; b. L.A., Nov. 7, 1945; d. Jacob John Schillinger and Charlyne Alice Brewster; m. Terrell Marsh, Dec. 14, 1968; children: Michael Edward, Timothy Lawrence. BA, Pepperdine Coll., L.A., 1968. Cert. tchr. life lic. Tchr. 3d grade Gardena Elem. Sch. L.A. City Schs., 1968—88; tchr. 5th grade Peninsula Heritage Sch., Rolling Hills Estate, Calif., 1988—97; tchr. 3d grade Rolling Hills Country Day Sch., 1997—. Coord. Mentally Gifted Minors Gardena Elem. Sch., 1974—80; instr. Master Tchr. Program Pepperdine Coll., 1970—88. Vol. Rolling Hills Covenant Ch., 2000—. Named to Who's Who Among Tchrs., 1998; recipient Outstanding Tchr. award, Pepperdine Coll., 1975. Mem.: PTA (Hon. Lifetime award 1975). Avocations: reading, sports, gardening. Home: 27613 Conestoga Dr Rolling Hills Estates CA 90274 Office: Rolling Hills Country Day Sch 26444 Crenshaw Blvd Rolling Hills Estates CA 90274

MARSH, BETTY JUNE, retired education educator; d. Harrison Scaman and Jessie Lucille Marsh; children: Manda Beckett, Denise Bradlyn. BS, UCLA, 1956, MS, 1965. Tchr. LA City Schs., 1956—58, war on poverty, 1965—67; tchr. Claremont City Schs., 1960—61, Newport Beach Schs., 1961—62, Santa Monica City Schs., 1964—65, Peace Corps Jamaica, 1967—68; tchg. asst. UCLA, 1958—60; social work coord. Parent Child Svcs., Portland, Oreg., 1968—69; Peace Corps trainer, 1969—70; asst. prof. Cornell U., 1971—72, N.W. Ednl. Lab, Portland, 1973—75; title 9 specialist Portland State U., 1975—76; small bus. owner Vintage Furniture, 1977—80; sch. counselor Alaska, 1980—82; curator Alaska State Mus., 1982—87, ret., 1987. Participant legis. lobbying of discrimination training for sch. pers., Oreg., 1977—78. Cons. we. states War on Poverty, 1970; bd. mem., v.p. ACLU, 1962—; mem. NAACP, 1962—; vol. Peace Corps., Jamaica, 1967—68. Mem.: Women's Internat. League Peace and Freedom, Amnesty Internat. Democrat. Avocations: politics, travel. Home: 37-800 De Vall Dr 28 Rancho Mirage CA 92270

MARSH, CARYL AMSTERDAM, retired curator, retired psychologist; b. N.Y.C., Mar. 9, 1923; d. Louis and Kitty (Weitz) Amsterdam; m. Michael Marsh, Sept. 3, 1942 (dec. 1993); children: Susan E., Anna L. BA, Bklyn. Coll., 1942; MA, Columbia U., N.Y.C., 1946; PhD, George Washington U., 1978. Lic. psychologist, D.C. Asst. cultural attache Am. Embassy, Paris, 1946-48; psychologist D.C. Recreation Dept., 1957-69; spl. asst. Smithsonian Instn., Washington, 1966-73; curator exhbns. Nat. Archives, Washington, 1978-85, sr. exhbns. specialist 1985-86; dir. traveling psychology exhbn. Am. Psychol. Assn., 1986-93, sr. advisor, 1993-95; chair humanities seminars in sci. mus. Assn. Sci. Tech. Ctrs., 1994—2001; ret., 2003. Rsch. fellow exptl. gallery Smithsonian Instn., 1992; rsch. cons. Nat. Zoo, 1981-92, Smithsonian Folk Life Festival, Nat. Mus. Am. History, 1977-78; organizer Discovery Room Nat. Mus. Natural History, 1969-73; cons. Meyer Found., 1964-66; advisor Lemelson Ctr. for Study of Invention and Innovation, Nat. Mus. Am. History, 1999-2000. Editor: Exhibition: The American Image, 1979. Organizer Anacostia Neighborhood Mus., Washington, 1967, bd. dirs., 1974—, v.p. 1993—; sec. D.C. Commn. on Arts and Humanities, 1969-72; pres. Pre-Sch. Parents Coun., Washington, 1956-57; adv. bd. Youth Alive, 1997-99. Fellow Nat. Mus. Am. Art, 1975-77; vis. scholar Nat. Mus. Am. Art, 1978—; grad. fellow CUNY, 1945-46; scholar George Washington U.; noted for Disting. Contbn. to Pub. Understanding of Psychology, APA, 1993. Mem. AAAS, APA (Outstanding Svc. award 1992, Disting. Contbn. to Pub. Understanding of Psychology award 1993), D.C. Psychol. Assn., Am. Assn. Mus., Mus. Edn. Roundtable (bd. dirs. 1983-87). Home and Office: 10450 Lottsford Rd # 3011 Mitchellville MD 20721-2734

MARSH, CLARE TEITGEN, retired school psychologist; b. Manitowoc, Wis., July 7, 1934; d. Clarence Emil and Dorothy (Napiezinski) Teitgen; m. Robert Irving Marsh, Jan. 30, 1955; children: David, Wendy Marsh Tootle, Julie Marsh Domino, Laura Marsh Beltrame. MS in Sch. Psychology, U. Wis., Milw., 1968. Sch. psychologist Milw. Pub. Schs., 1975-76; lead psychologist West Allis (Wis.)-West Milw. Pub. Schs., 1968-95; sch. psychologist Wauwatosa (Wis.) Pub. Schs., 1987; instr. Milw. Sch. Engring., 1989-90, Alverno Coll., 1990-91, ret., 1995. NDEA fellow, 1966-68. Mem. Nat. Assn. Sch. Psychologists (del.), Suburban Assn. Sch. Psychologists (pres. 1976-77, 86-87), Wis. Assn. Sch. Psychologists (pres. 1990-91, chmn. membership com. 1980-84, sec. 1985-89, chmn. conv. 1987), Wis. Fedn. Pupil Svcs., Menomee Falls Symphony Orch., Our Lord's United Meth. Ch., United Meth. Women (pres. 2003—), Phi Kappa Phi, Pi Lambda Theta (past pres. 1992), Kappa Delta Pi, Phi Delta Kappa, Sigma Tau Delta, Alpha Chi Omega. Home: 14140 W Honey Ln New Berlin WI 53151-2442 Personal E-mail: claremarsh@wi.rr.

MARSH, FRANCES EMILY FRANCIS, state agency administrator, set designer; b. Mt. Tamalpais, Calif., June 4, 1973; d. Frank Emery Marsh and Ruth Alice Stoddard; life ptnr. Dana L. Denning. BFA, Tarleton State U., Stephenville, Tex., 1999; MFA, Humboldt State U., Arcata, Calif., 2001. Mem. profl. tech. edn. quality assurance com. Edn. Dept. for State of Oreg., Phoenix, 2005—. Scenic designer: (theatrical prodn.) Ismene, 2000; Killing Oscar Wilde, 2001; tech. dir. Arcadia, 1999. Head gay pride com. Abdill-Ellis Lambda Cmty. Ctr. Assn., Ashland, Oreg., 2003—06, treas., 2003—05. Mem.: Theater Communication Group, US Inst. Theatre Tech., Alpha Phi Omega.

MARSH, JOAN KNIGHT, educational film company executive, video company executive, computer company executive, publishing executive; b. Apr. 8, 1934; d. E. Lyle and Ruth (Hopkins) Knight; m. Alan Reid Marsh, Sept. 27, 1958; children: Alan Reid, Clayton Knight. BA, Tex. Tech U., 1956. Owner, pres. MarshMedia, Kansas City, Mo., 1969—. Tchr. evaluation guides. Mem. ctrl. governing bd. Children's Mercy Hosp., 1996-05; mem. coun. Family Study Ctr., U. Mo., Kansas City, 1983-89, Children's Relief Assn. Mercy Hosp., Kansas City, 1984—, pres., 1989-91; chmn., hon. co-chmn. Rose Brooks Ctr. Cabaret, 1995, 2000; pres. Friends of Children's Mercy Hosp., 1996-98; chmn. The Jewel Ball, 1997, Great Ball of China II, 1999, Genevieve Byrne Spkr. Series ARC Kansas City chpt., 2004. Mem. Jr. League (sustaining chmn. 1982-84, Cmty. Svc. award 1999), Gamma Phi Beta. Republican. Presbyterian. Avocations: egyptology, filmology. Office Phone: 816-523-1059.

MARSH, LYNN, elementary school educator; Tchr. Meridian (Idaho) Alternative Sch. Recipient Tchr. Excellence award Internat. Tech. Edn. Assn., Idaho, 1992.

MARSH, MARIAN E., voice educator; b. San Mateo, Calif., Apr. 5, 1936; d. Richard Harding and Helen McGregor (Grant) Marsh; m. David Wade, Sept. 18, 1955. Voice tchr. Sonoma State U., Rohnert Park, Calif., 1965—70, U. Calif., Santa Cruz, 1974—88, Dominican U., San Rafael, Calif., 1975—; pvt. practice Calif., 1962—. Cruise ship entertainer, 1970—82, 1993, 95. Singer: San Francisco Symphony, LA Philharmonic, Oakland Symphony, Sinfonia Nat.; singer: (soloist) Schola Cantorum, De Anza Coll., San Francisco Civic Chorale, Winifred Baker Chorale, Coll. Marin, Diablo Valley Coll., San Mateo Masterworks Chorale, Contra Costa Chorale, Peninsula Singers, Coll. Marin Cmty. Chorus. Organist various chs., Calif., 1950—60, soloist San Francisco, 1964—97, Temple Emanuel, San Francisco, 1960—96; organist dir. Ch. of Nativity, San Rafael, Calif., 2002—. Recipient Met. Opera award, 1963, 1965, East Bay Opera League award, 1964. Mem.: Music Tchrs. Assn. (scholarship chair), Nat. Assn. Tchrs. Singing, Womens Musicians Club (pres., v.p., recital chair). Episcopalian. Home: 91 Grande Paseo San Rafael CA 94903 Office: Dominican Univ 50 Acacia San Rafael CA 94901 Personal E-mail: davidmarionsong@aol.com.

MARSH, MARTHA H., hospital administrator; BS, U. Rochester; MPH, MBA, Columbia U. Pres. and CEO Matthew Thornton Health Plan, Dartmouth-Hitchcock Med. Ctr., 1986—94; sr. v.p., profl. svcs. and managed care and v.p. managed care U. Pa. Health Sys., 1994—98; COO U. Calif.-Davis Health Care Sys., 1999—2002; dir., Hosp. and Clinics U. Calif.-Davis Medical Ctr., 1999—2002; pres. and CEO Stanford (Conn.) Hosp. and Clinics, 2002—. Apptd. by Pres. Bush Nat. Infrastructure Adv. Coun., 2003; bd. dirs. Calif. Healthcare Assoc., Integrated Healthcare Assoc., Blue Cross of Calif. Hosp. Relations Com. Office: Stanford Hosp 300 Pasteur Dr Ste H3200 Stanford CA 94305 Office Phone: 650-723-4000.*

MARSH, MERRILYN DELANO, sculptor, artist, painter; b. Larchmont, NY, Dec. 26, 1923; d. Merrill Potter and Hazel (Holmes) Delano; m. George Estabrook Marsh, Sept. 18, 1954; children: Merrill Delano, George Estabrook Jr., Robert Houston. Diploma, Sch. of Mus. of Fine Arts, Boston, 1946, cert., 1947; postgrad., Acad. Grande Chaumière, Paris, 1947-48. Art tchr. Choate Sch., Brookline, Mass., 1948, 49, Brookline Cmty. Ctr., 1948, 49; pvt. art tchr. Newton, Mass., 1948-49; comml. sculptor for display and mfg. cos., 1948-55; sculpture tchr. De Cordova Mus., Lincoln, Mass., 1950-54. Juror for numerous art exhbns., New Eng. area, 1954-55, 72-74. One-woman show at Copley Soc. of Boston, 1996, Wellesley Libr., Mass., 2006; commd. 7 reliefs for Sch. for Environ., Levine Sci. Ctr., Duke U., Durham, N.C., 1994, bronze statue for cloister garden St. Andrew's Episcopal Ch., Wellesley, Mass., 1995, bronze portrait reliefs for Houston and Sargent Athletic awards Tufts U., Medford, Mass., 1997, 2 bronze reliefs, Ellis Oval Athletic Field Tufts U., 2001, bronze portrait relief of Clarence P. "Pop" Houston, Houston Hall, Tufts U., 1965, bronze portrait relief for Rocco J. Carzo Cage, Cousens Gymnasium, Tufts U., 2002, others; profiled in Wellesley Weston Mag., 2006. Mrs. David Hunt Sculpture scholar Mus. Fine Arts, 1947; recipient Katherine Thayer Hobson award Pen and Brush Soc., 1991, Best in Show award Juliani Gallery, 1991, Pres.'s Cup award for golf Wellesley (Mass.) Country Club, 1998, 2d Pl. award Wellesley Soc. Artists, 2003, Hon. mention Wellesley Soc. Artists Spring Show, 2004, Margaret E. Fearnside Meml. award Wellesley Soc. Artists Fall Show, 2004. Mem. Copley Soc. Boston (Copley master, Maria Maravigna award 1988, 1st prize in sculpture and large works 1994, other awards, 1983, 89), New Eng. Sculptors Assn. (bd. dirs. 1986, award 1988), Wellesley Soc. Artists (awards 1985, 87, 89, 91-92, 95, 2001-02, 2d pl. award 2003, bd. dirs. 1970, 88—, Hon. Mention award 2004, Margaret E. Fearnside Meml. award 2004), Cambridge Art Assn. (Jack Schultz award, 2000, other awards 1993-94). Republican. Episcopalian.

MARSH, SARA MARIA, music educator; b. Glen Ellyn, Ill., Sept. 2, 1980; d. James Richard Marsh and Mary Elizabeth Miller. BA in Music Edn., U. Ill., Urbana-Champaign, 2003. Piano tchr. Pvt., 2003—06; choir dir. St. John's Ch., Urbana-Champaign, Ill., 2002—03, St. Petronille Ch., GlenEllyn, Ill., 2003—05; tchr. music Chgo. Pub. Schs., 2004—05, Miami-Dade Pub. Schs., 2005—. Named Rookie Tchr. of Yr., Miami Lakes Elem. Sch., 2005—06; grant, Chgo. Found. for Edn., 2005. Mem.: Fla. Edn. Assn., Music Educators Nat. Conf. Avocations: piano, ballet. Home: 2825 SW 6th St Miami FL 33135

MARSH, TIFFANY NICHELLE, music educator; b. New Albany, Ind. m. Ryan Marsh. B in Music Edn., U. Louisville, 2002, MusM, 2004. Choral dir., tchr. Franklin County Pub. Schs., Frankfort, Ky., 2004—. Mem.: Internat. Fedn. Choral Music, Ky. Educators Assn., Ky. Music Educators Assn., Am. Choral Dirs. Assn. Avocations: travel, cooking, gardening. Office: Western Hills HS 100 Doctors Dr Frankfort KY 40601 Office Phone: 502-875-8400.

MARSH, VIRGINIA JEAN, art educator; b. Sherman, Tex., Aug. 13, 1945; d. Elmer Leonard Nelson and Marilynn (Griffith) Stein; m. E. Thomas Marsh, Dec. 27, 1968 (dec. 1991); children: Rebekah, Nathan; m. Thomas A. Van, Sept. 6, 1997. AB, DePauw U., 1967; MFA, Ohio State U., 1969. Assoc. prof. fine arts U. Louisville, 1975—. Artist in residence Banff (Canada) Centre Sch. of Fine Arts, 1984; workshop instr. Arrowmont Sch. Arts and Crafts, Gatlinburg, Tenn., 1984, 86; editl. advisor Chilton Book Co., Radnor, Pa. Exhibited pottery in numerous group shows including Bendigo Pottery Internat. Award, Melbourne, Australia, 1977, Concorso Internazionale del Arte Ceramica, Faenza, Italy, 1979, Internat. Cone Box Show, 1995, Virtual Ceramics, 1995, 21st Century Ceramics, 2003; one-woman shows include Greenwich HousePottery, NYC, 1978, Earlham Coll., Images Friedman Gallery, Louisville, 1994; work represented in a permanent collection include Smithsonian Inst., Wash.; archtl. commns. include Interfaith Chapel and Our Lord Woods New Harmony Inn, Ind., First Unitarian Ch., Louisville, Mt. St. Francis Conventual Friary, Ind., Douglass Blvd. Christian Ch., Louisville. Univ. fellow Ohio State U., 1967. Mem. Nat. Coun. on Edn. for Ceramic Arts, Am. Gravestones Assn., Phi Beta Kappa. Episcopalian. Office: U Louisville Fine Arts Dept Louisville KY 40292-0001 Home: 5915 Vol Pl Rockwall TX 75032

MARSHAK, HILARY WALLACH, psychotherapist, small business owner; b. N.Y.C., May 27, 1950; d. Irving Isaac and Suni (Fox) Wallach; m. Harvey Marshak, Jan. 1, 1981; children: Emily Fox, Jacob Randall. BA, U. Conn., Storrs, 1973; MSW, N.Y.U., 1992; cert., Inst. for Study of Culture, and Ethnicity, N.Y.C., 1994. Lic. clin. social worker, N.Y.; qualified clin. social worker; cert. secondary English tchr., N.Y. Tchr. English. Glastonbury (Conn.) H.S., 1973; instr. English, U. Autonoma de Guerrero, Acapulco, Mexico, 1974; administrv. asst. 4M Pub. Svcs. Corp., N.Y.C., 1975, bus. mgr.; exec. v.p. Vitalmedia Enterprises Inc., N.Y.C., 1977-87, pres., CEO, 1987-2001; psychotherapist Fifth Avenue Ctr. Counseling and Psychotherapy, N.Y.C., 1992-95; pvt. practice, N.Y.C., 1992—; co-dir. Inst. for Advanced Thinking, N.Y.C., 2000—; asst. dir. adult undergrad. admissions Pace U., N.Y.C., 2003—. Mktg. cons. Frana Ltd., London, 1988-89; infertility counselor; v.p. Think Impossible, 2000—; adj. faculty Pace U., 2005—. Editor: Before the Bar, 1978-80, Guide to Higher Edn., 1980; reviewer vol 32, The Jour. of Sex Rsch. Founder Women's Radical Caucus, U. Conn., 1970; broadcaster Sta. WHUS; bd. dirs. N.Y. Theater Ballet, 1990—, Am. AIDS Assn., 1992-97; mem. writers coun. Writers in Performance series Manhattan Theater Club. Recipient 2nd Place Flowers Ulster County Agrl. Fair, New Paltz, N.Y., 1987, 1st Place Herbs, 1988. Mem. NASW (qualified clin. social worker), Soc. for Sci. Study of Sex, Sex Edn. and Info. Coun. of U.S., Nat. Coun. Family Rels., Am. Infertility Assn., Am. Soc. for Reproductive Medicine, Resolve. Jewish. Avocations: gardening, birdwatching, cooking, reading. Home: 75 Montgomery St H 7C New York NY 10002 Office: 817 Broadway 9th Fl 4 New York NY 10003 Office Phone: 212-349-0011. Office Fax: 212-349-0011. E-mail: hilarymarshak@hotmail.com.

MARSHALL, BEVERLY FORREST, writer; d. Ernest Belo and Ouida Whittington Forrest; m. Francis Chester Marshall, Aug. 22, 1965; 1 child, Angela Beth. BA in English, U. Miss., Oxford, 1968; MA in English, S.E. La. U., Hammond, 1993. Writer in residence S.E. La. U., Hammond. Author: (novel) Walking Through Shadows, 2002, Right As Rain, 2004 (Fiction of Yr. award Miss. Libr. Assn., 2004), Hot Fudge Sundae Blues, 2005. Named Outstanding Faculty Advisor, S.E. La. U., 1997; recipient Regional Arts award for Exellence in Lit., Hammond Regional Arts, 2005, Best Novels of 2005 Book for the Teen Age, N.Y. Pub. Libr., 2006. Mem.: New Orleans Lit. Inst., S.E. La. U. Alumni Assn., Hammond Regional Arts Ctr., Tenn. Williams Lit. Festival, Miss. Inst. Arts and Letters.

MARSHALL, CAK (CATHERINE ELAINE MARSHALL), music educator, composer; b. Nashville, Nov. 24, 1943; d. Dean Byron and Petula Iris (Bodie) M. BS in Music Edn., Ind. U. Pa., 1965; cert., Hamline U., 1981, cert., 1982, cert., 1983, Memphis State U., 1985; MME, Duquesne U., 1992. Nat. registered music educator, 1993; vocal music tchr., Pa. Tchr. music Mars Area Sch. Dist., Pa., 1965—66; music specialist Fox Chapel Area Sch. Dist., Pa., 1966—, Duquesne U. City Music Ctr., Pitts., 1994—98; ednl. dir. Peripole-Bergerault, Inc., Salem, Oreg., 2001—; performer Figs and Thistles Recorder Consort, Willamette Master Chorus. Orff specialist Chatham Coll. Fine Arts Camp, Pitts., 1977-91; instrn. rep. elem. curriculum Dist. I, Pitts., 1986-92; arts curriculum project Pa. Dept. Edn., 1988; level one basic Orff tchr. U. Wis.-Milw., 2002, U. South Fla., 2002, U. Fla., Gainesville, 2003. Author: (plays) The Rainbow Recorder, 1988, The Gift Disk Dilemma, 1989; composer, (play) Pittsburgh-The City with a Smile on Her Face, 1986, (holiday musical) The Dove That Could Not Fly, 1986, (book) Seasons in Song, 1987, (play) The Search for Happiness, 1990; composer: What Color Was the Baby, 1990, Kaia, 1990, Sing Praises To His Name, 1990, Go In Peace, 1990, Sing Unto The Lord, 1990, Simple Gift, 1991, I Love America, 1992, The Cost Is Correct Caper, 1993, The Adventures of Arffie, 1997, The Greatest Snow on Earth, 1997, A Second Grade "Informance", 1998, Stopping by Woods, 1999, A Play-Party Play-in, 1999, Give Thanks, 1999, Star of the Universe, 2000, Tootles: A Book of Original Recorder Trios, 2006. Actor North Star Players, Pitts., 1975-80; soloist Landmark Bapt. Ch., Penn Hills, Pa., 1981-86, Bible Bapt. Ch., 1987; performer Pitts. Camerata, 1977-89; group leader Pitts Recorder Soc., 1985-86; soloist Grace Bapt. Ch., Monroeville, 1991— Willamette Master Chorus, 2002—, Figs and Thistle Mixed Consort, 2004—. Recipient Citation of Excellence award Pa. Dept. Edn., 1996. Mem. NEA, Am. ORFF-Schulwerk Assn., Pitts. Golden Triangle Chpt. (pres. 1985—), Music Educators Nat. Conf., Pa. Music Educators Assn. (elem. jour. 1986—), Am. Recorder Assn., Pi Kappa Lambda. Baptist. Avocations: cake decorating, needlepoint, swimming, folk dancing. Office: Peripole-Bergerault Inc PO Box 12909 Salem OR 97309 Home: 997 Burley Hill Dr NW Salem OR 97304 Personal E-mail: cakmarshall@aol.com.

MARSHALL, CAROL JOYCE, science administrator; b. Mt. Holly, NJ, July 29, 1967; d. Oliver and Ruby Jean (Bennefield-Smith) Marshall. BA in Biol. Scis., Rutgers U., 1985-89. Transplant-procurement coord. Nat. Disease Rsch. Interchange, Phila., 1989-90, supr. procurement dept., 1990-91, rsch. mgr., 1991-92; clin. rsch. data coord. U.S. Biosci., West Conshohocken, Pa., 1992-93; clin. rsch. project mgr. Covance, Inc., Princeton, N.J., 1993—. Avocations: piano, flute, calligraphy, swimming. Home: 54 Chapel Hill Rd Mount Laurel NJ 08054 Office: Covance Inc 210 Carnegie Ctr Princeton NJ 08540-6233 Office Phone: 609-452-4134. Personal E-mail: cmarsh729@aol.com.

MARSHALL, CINDY LOU, science educator, social studies educator; b. Elkhart, Ind., Sept. 7, 1956; d. James Allen (Stepfather) and Georgiane Pearl Mitchell; m. Thomas James Marshall, July 16, 1977; children: Jennifer Lillian Emerson, Christy Leigh, Lori Anne. A in Animal Health, Abraham Baldwin Agrl. Coll., Tifton, Ga., 1976; B in Mid. Sch. Edn., Ga. Southwestern, Americus, 1991, M in Edn., 1992. Gifted cert. Ga. Southwestern U., 1999. Animal health technician Cutler Ridge Vet. Clinic, Miami, 1972—79; tchr. remedial math grade 9-12 Terrell HS, Dawson, Ga., 1991—92; tchr. sci. grade 7 Lee County Mid. Sch., Leesburg, Ga., 1992—2003; tchr. sci./social studies grade 8 Merry Acres Mid. Sch., Albany, Ga., 2003—04; tchr. sci./social studies grade 6 Robert Cross Mid. Magnet Sch., Albany, 2004—. Sci. dept. chairperson Lee County Mid. Sch., 1991—2003, sci. fair organizer, 1992—98, club advisor, 1992—94, sci. fair advisor (regional/state/internat.), 1992—98, sci. olympiad coach, 1995—2000, sci. club advisor, 1995—2000; sci. olympiad coach Robert Cross Mid. Magnet Sch., 2004—, beta club advisor, 2004—, chairperson Honors Day, 2005—; organizer sci. curriculum grade 6 Dougherty County Sch. Sys., Albany, 2005—. Vol. Dawson Manor Nursing Home, Ga., 1987—91; Secret Santa for foster children First Bapt. Ch., Dawson, 1987—92, tchr. Bible sch., 1988—2001, tchr. Sunday sch., 1995—99, tchr. Girls in Action, 1992—98, dir. summer youth camp, 1997—2000. Named Tchr. of Yr., Lee County Mid. Sch., 2001—02; named to Wall of Fame, 2003. Mem.: Delta Kappa Gamma (life; 2d v.p. 2002—03, corr. sec. 2006). Baptist. Office: Robert Cross Middle Magnet Sch 324 Lockett Station Rd Albany GA 31721-4005 Office Phone: 229-431-1212. Business E-Mail: cindy.marshall@dougherty.k12.ga.us.

MARSHALL, COLLEEN, newscaster; m. Gary Marshall; children: Garret, Shannon. BA, Point Park Coll.; postgrad., Capital U.; D (hon.), Roi Grande U., 2000, Park Point Coll, 2001. Writer, prodr., editor Sta. KQV, Pitts.; news dir., anchor, reporter Sta. WEIR, Weirton, W.Va.; anchor, reporter Sta. WWVA, Wheeling; reporter Sta.WTRF-TV, Sta. WCMH-TV, Columbus, Ohio, 1984—87, anchor, 1987—. Bd. dirs. Columbus AIDS Task Force, Cirrenton Family Svcs. Recipient Capital Area Humane Soc. Consumer Reporter award, 1988, Best Newscast and Best Spot News Coverage, The Associated Press, 1998, Emmy award, 1999, Stonewall Media award, 1999. Office: WCMH-TV 3165 Olentangy River Rd PO Box 4 Columbus OH 43202

MARSHALL, CONSUELO BLAND, federal judge; b. Knoxville, Tenn., Sept. 28, 1936; d. Clyde Theodore and Annie (Brown) Arnold; m. George Edward Marshall, Aug. 30, 1959; children: Michael Edward, Laurie Ann. AA, L.A. City Coll., 1956; BA, Howard U., 1958, LLB, 1961. Bar: Calif. 1962. Dep. atty., City of LA, 1962-67; assoc. Cochran & Atkins, LA, 1968-70; commr. LA Superior Ct., 1971-76; judge Inglewood Mcpl. Ct., 1976-77, LA Superior Ct., 1977-80, US Dist. Ct. (ctrl dist.) Calif., LA, 1980—, chief judge, 2001—. Lectr. U.S. Information Agy. in Yugoslavia, Greece and Italy, 1984, in Nigeria and Ghana, 1991, in Ghana, 1992. Contbr. articles to profl. jours.; notes editor Law Jour. Howard U. Mem. adv. bd. Richstone Child Abuse Center. Recipient Judicial Excellence award Criminal Cts. Bar Assn., 1992, Ernestine Stalhut award; named Criminal Ct. Judge of Yr., U.S. Dist. Ct., 1997; inducted into Langston Hall of Fame, 2000, Outstanding Jurist Award, LA County Bar Assn., 2005; rsch. fellow Howard U. Law Sch., 1959-60. Mem. State Bar Calif., Century City Bar Assn., Calif. Women Lawyers Assn., Calif. Assn. Black Lawyers, Calif. Judges Assn., Black Women Lawyers Assn., Los Angeles County Bar Assn., Nat. Assn. Women Judges, NAACP, Urban League, Beta Phi Sigma. Office: US Dist Ct 312 N Spring St Los Angeles CA 90012-4701

MARSHALL, CYNTHIA LOUISE, language educator; b. Ellwood City, Pa., Aug. 16, 1956; d. Luther Harold and Elizabeth (Prescott) Marshall; m. William H. Smith, Dec. 30, 1985. BS in English summa cum laude, Slippery Rock (Pa.) U., 1978, MA in English, 1980; PhD in Edn., U. Pitts., 1987. Cert. yoga instr. 2005. Grad. asst. Slippery Rock U., 1978—80; owner, mgr. Whistler Enterprises, Butler, Pa., 1980—; adj. instr. English, Butler County C.C., Butler, 1988-90; instr. English C.C. Beaver County, 1990—, asst. prof., 1990-97, prof., 1997—. Grant evaluator Pa. Humanities Coun., 2006; presenter, lectr. in field. Contbr. articles, book revs. and poems to publs. Appraiser, vol. United Cerebral Palsy, Butler, 1987—; mem. Pa. Gov.'s Conf. Librs., 1990—; writer Internat. Diversity Conf. UCLA, 2004; bd. dirs. C.C. Beaver County Found., 1993; mem. Stratford Festival Friends. Named scholarship in her name, Butler County C.C., 1990; recipient Excellence award, NISOD, 2005; grantee, Pa. Humanities Coun., 1990, NEA, 1999—2001. Mem.: NCTE, AAUW, MLA, Am. Assn. Endigenous Profs., Native Am. Coll. & Univ. Profs., Am. Assn. Am. Indian, Pa. Coll. English Assn., Smithsonian Assocs., Nat. Trust Hist. Preservation, Wintherthur Mus., Slippery Rock U. Alumni Assn. (life). Democrat. Presbyterian. Avocations: antiques, movies, collecting quilts, yoga. Home: 115 Shanor Heights Butler PA 16001 Office: Community Coll Beaver County College Dr Monaca PA 15061 Office Phone: 800-335-0222 ext. 134. Personal E-mail: cynthia.marshall@ccbc.edu.

MARSHALL, DEBORAH KAY, instructional technology resource specialist; b. Charlottesville, Va., July 13, 1964; d. David Edward and Maude Ward Marshall. EdS, The George Wash. U., 2002—03. Postgrad. Profl. Lic. State of Va., 1992. Facilitator for summer tech prep camp Rappahannock C.C., Glenns, Va., 2000—04; bus. & info. tech. tchr. Peasley Mid. Sch., Gloucester, 1990—2005; tech. specialist Granby H.S., Norfolk, Va., 2005—. Prin. mid. sch. summer sch. Gloucester County, 2003—04. Team capt. for walkamerica March of Dimes, Newport News, Va., 2003—05. Mem.: ASCD, Va. Mid. Sch. Assn., Va. Bus. Edn. Assn., Va. Soc. Tech. in Edn. (assoc.), Iota Lambda Sigma. Methodist. Avocations: reading, puzzles, cross stitch. Home: 803 Grand Bay Cove Newport News VA 23602 Office: Granby HS 7101 Granby St Norfolk VA 23515 Personal E-mail: lichen7@aol.com. Business E-Mail: dmarshall@nps.k12.va.us.

MARSHALL, DEBRA LYNN, secondary school educator; b. Charleston, W.Va., July 7, 1956; d. James L. Marshall and Lena B. Bailey. BA in English cum laude, Ohio State U., Columbus, 1998; MEd in English, Ohio State U., 1999. Tchr. H.S. English Piqua (Ohio) City Sch., 1999—2003, Moreno Valley (Calif.) Unified Schs., 2003—. Adj. faculty Edison C.C., Piqua, 2001—03; coord. Ohio Writing Project, Piqua, 2000—02. Author: (short stories) Super Boy, 2003 (Hon. Mention award Sinclair C.C., 2003). Mem. pub. rels. team Spring Arts Show The Piqua (Ohio) Arts Coun., 2003. Mem.: NEA, Nat. Coun. Tchrs. English, Calif. Assn. Tchrs. English, Calif. Tchrs. Assn. Avocations: dog training, painting, cello. Office: CanyonSprings High School 23100 Cougar Canyon Dr Moreno Valley CA 92557 Office Phone: 951-571-4760. E-mail: marshalld4@adelphia.net.

MARSHALL, ELAINE FOLK, state official; b. Lineboro, Md., Nov. 18, 1945; d. Donald and Pauline Folk; m. Bill Holdford; 5 stepchildren. BS in Textiles and Clothing, U. Md., 1968; JD, Campbell U., 1981; D (hon.), Meredith Coll., 2004, Lees McRae Coll., 2004. Bar: N.C., U.S. Dist. Ct. (ea. and mid. dists.), U.S. Ct. Appeals (4th cir.), U.S. Supreme Ct. Tchr., 1968—75; owner retail bus., 1968-79; assoc. Bain Law Firm, Lillington, NC, 1981-84; ptnr. Bain & Marshall, Lillington, 1985-92, Marshall & Marshall, Lillington, 1993-96; sec. of state State of N.C., 1997—. Legal advisor Bus. and Profl. Women, N.C., 1982-90; mem. 15th dist. N.C. Senate, 1993-94, N.C. Capital Planning Commn., 1993-94, 1997-, N.C. Cts. Commn., 1993-94, bd. mem. Nat. Electronic Commerce Coord. Coun., 2001-03, 2005—, v.p., 2005-06, bd. mem. Nat. Assn. Secretaries of State, 2001-04. Bd. dirs. Harnett

County United Way, 1987-97, N.C. 4-H Devel. Fund, Inc., 1990—, N.C. Rural Econ. Devel. Fund, 1993-95, N.C. Bd. Econ. Devel., 1993-94, 97—, N.C. Ctr. Pub. Policy Rsch., 1994-99, N.C. Justice Acad. Found., 1994-98; mem. Divine St. United Meth. Ch.; founding chmn., hon. chmn. Harnett HelpNet Children, 1992—; trustee Meredith Coll., 1997-2002. Recipient N.C. Friends Ext. award, 1992, Spl. Achievement award, N.C. Acad. Trial Lawyers, 2000, Alumni of Yr. award, N.C. 4-H Found., Lifetime Achievement award, 2003, Best of Breed, In the Arena awards, Ctr. Digital Govt., 2002, Top 25 award, Govt. Tech. Mag., 2003, Atty. of Yr. award, N.C. Assn. Women Attorneys, 2004, Women in Bus. award RBC Centura Bank and Triangle Bus. Jour., 2005, Hon. Gold Record award Recording Industry Am., 2005, U.L. Lab. award, 2005, Get Real award Internat. Anti Counterfeit Coalition, 2005. Fellow N.C. Inst. Polit. Leadership (bd. dirs. 1996—); mem. Women's Forum N.C., Gamma Sigma Delta, Delta Kappa Gamma. Democrat. Office: 2 S Salisbury St Raleigh NC 27601 Office Phone: 919-807-2005. Business E-Mail: emarshall@sosnc.com.

MARSHALL, ELIZABETH ANNETTE, auditor; b. Ft. Worth, Dec. 22, 1962; d. Joe Donald and Gail Annette Marshall. B of Bus. Adminstrn., Stetson U., 1986. CPA, Fla. Sr. pub. accts. auditor Auditor Gen., Tallahassee, Fla., 1987—. Mem. G.F.W.C. Tallahassee Jr. Woman's Club, 1988—, custodian of files, 1992, treas., 1993; mem. Tallahassee Winds Cmty. Band. Mem.: St. Andrews Soc., Daus. Am. Colonists, U.S. Daus. of 1812, Nat. Huguenot Soc., Fla. Inst. CPAs, DAR (chpt. regent 1997—99, Fla. rec. sec. 1999—2001), AICPA, UDC, Scottish Gaines Coun., Alpha Kappa Psi. Democrat. Presbyterian. Avocations: genealogy, cooking, travel, music (flute). Office: Auditor Gen 111 W Madison St Tallahassee FL 32399-1450 Home: 2413 McWest St Tallahassee FL 32303-7119

MARSHALL, ELLEN RUTH, lawyer; b. NYC, Apr. 23, 1949; d. Louis and Faith (Gladstone) M. AB, Yale U., 1971; JD, Harvard U., 1974. Bar: Calif. 1975, D.C. 1981, N.Y. 1989. Assoc. McKenna & Fitting, LA, 1975-80; ptnr. McKenna, Conner & Cuneo, LA and Orange County, Calif., 1980-88, Morrison & Foerster, LLP, Orange County, 1988—2003, Manatt, Phelps & Phillips LLP, Orange County, 2003—. Mem. ABA (bus. law sect., mem. savs. inst. com., mem. asset securitization com., tax sect., mem. employee benefits com.), Orange County Bar Assn., Center Club (Costa Mesa, Calif.), Yale Club (N.Y.C.). Office: Manatt Phelps & Phillips LLP 695 Town Ctr Dr Costa Mesa CA 92626

MARSHALL, HELEN M., city manager; m. Donald E. Marshall; children: Donald Jr., Agnes Marie. BA, Queens Coll.; student, L.I. U. Dir. Langston Hughes Libr., 1969, Elmcor Testing Assessment and Placement Program; mem. NY State Assembly, Dist. 35, 1983—91; city councilwoman Dist. 21, NYC, 1992—2001; borough pres. Queens, 2001—. Chmn. stds. and ethics com., mem. edn., housing and bldg. and environ. protection coms. Dem. nat. committeewoman, N.Y., 1975; del. Dem. Nat. Conv., 1980; mem. Nat. Dem. Exec. Com., N.Y. State assemblywoman, Dist. 35, 1983-91, past mem. cities, election law, higher edn., labor and transp. coms., chairwoman airport devel. subcom., 1985; vice chairwoman Women's Legis. Caucus, 1985, past chairwoman standing com. on state-fed. rels. Office: 120-55 Queens Blvd Kew Gardens NY 11424 Office Phone: 718-286-3000. E-mail: Marshall4Queens@aol.com.*

MARSHALL, JILL GALLEY, social studies educator; d. Joseph Edward Galley and Vivian Lee Potter; m. Lorne David Marshall, Dec. 18, 1998; 1 child, Luke Benjamin. BS in Sociology, Buffalo State Coll., N.Y., 1989; MS in Edn. and Elem. Reading, Canisius Coll., Buffalo, 1996; PhD in Elem. Edn., U. Buffalo, 2004. Tchr. grade 6 Hamburg Ctrl. Sch. Dist., NY, 1994—2001; staff devel. instr. Southtowns' Tchrs. Ctr., Hamburg, 1998—2000; instr. NYSUT Edn. and Learning Trust, Albany, 1998—2001; asst. prof. edn. Fredonia State Coll., NY, 2003—. Mem. ministry involvement leadership team Hamburg Wesleyan Ch., 2004—, mem., leader consultation team, 2004—. Mem.: Internat. Reading Assn., Nat. Coun. Social Studies. Avocations: travel, singing. Office: Fredonia State College E246 Thompson Hall Fredonia NY 14063 Office Phone: 716-673-3370. Business E-Mail: jill.marshall@fredonia.edu.

MARSHALL, JO TAYLOR, social worker; b. N.Y.C. BA, Sarah Lawrence Coll., 1957; MSW, Columbia U., 1959. Cert. clin. social worker, NY, NJ; bd. cert. diplomate. Caseworker Youth Cons. Svcs., 1960-62; program cons. Social Work Recruiting Ctr., 1962-63; casework supr. Louise Wise Svcs., 1963-68; faculty field instr. sch. social work Columbia U., N.Y.C., 1968-70; coord. social work vol. and student tng. programs St. Lukes/Roosevelt Hosp. Ctr., 1970-75; asst. dir. fieldwork, faculty lectr. in health care Columbia U., N.Y.C., 1975-78; dir. social work and psychiat. emergency svcs. Morristown Meml. Hosp., 1978—95; social worker pvt. practice, 1995—2002; ret., 2002. Adj. prof. Columbia U.; adv. bd., faculty Nat. Discharge Planning Inst. SUNY, Buffalo; prin. speaker, cons. Hosp. Assn. Pa., 1983, Mid-Atlantic Health Congress, 1985, VA, East Orange, N.J., 1986, Hosp. Assn. Tenn., 1987; adv. com. Rutgers GGrad. Sch. Social Work; mem. multidisciplinary state rev. com. for discharge planning standards in N.J. Contbr. articles to profl. jours.; produced and cons. on numerous film and TV prodns. Named Dir. of Yr., N.J. Hosp. Social Work, 1989-90. Mem.: NASW, Acad. Cert. Social Workers, Soc. Hosp. Social Work Dirs. (exec. bd., pres. N.J. chpt. 1988—89, chmn. nat. media task force). Achievements include The New Welcome Terrace at Columbia Grad. Sch. of Social Work named in her honor. Home (Winter): 1230 Hillsboro Mile Hillsboro Beach FL 33062-1344 Home (Summer): PO Box 40 Far Hills NJ 07931-0040 Office Phone: 908-553-5444. Personal E-mail: jomase@msn.com.

MARSHALL, JOYCE RAMSEY, secondary school educator; b. Morton, Tex., Oct. 22, 1934; d. Stevenson Adlia and Cora Almeda (Lisenbee) Ramsey; m. Wayman Dare Marshall, Aug. 27, 1955; children: Lea Ann Wilson, Tracy Glen, Dan Edward. BS in Home Econ., S.W. Tex. State U., 1972. Sec. 1st Bapt. Ch., Vernon, Tex., 1959-60, Wichita Falls, Tex., 1960-62; tchr. N.E. Sch. Dist., San Antonio, 1972-93. Creator home econ. curriculum Tex. Tech. U., 1978. Co-author: Parenting: Rewards and Responsibilities, 1994. Adv. com. career tech. N.E. Sch. Dist., San Antonio, 1993-. Mem.: Home Econ. Profl. Orgn. (v.p. 1995—). Baptist. Home: 4085 Jung Rd San Antonio TX 78247-2710

MARSHALL, JULI WILSON, lawyer; BA magna cum laude, Mich. State U., 1981; JD, U. Mich., 1984. Bar: Calif. 1984, Ill. 1995. Assoc. Latham & Watkins LLP, LA, 1984—91, named ptnr., 1991, now ptnr. Chgo., co-chair firm product liability and mass torts practice group. Office: Latham & Watkins LLP Sears Tower Ste 5800 233 S Wacker Dr Chicago IL 60606 Office Phone: 312-876-7700. Office Fax: 312-993-9767. E-mail: juli.marshall@lw.com.

MARSHALL, JULIE W. GREGOVICH, investor relations executive; b. Pasadena, Calif., Mar. 3, 1953; d. Gibson Marr and Anna Grace (Peterson) Wolfe; m. Michael Roy Gregovich Dec. 18, 1976 (div. June 1994); children: Christianna, Kerry Leigh; m. Robert Brandon Marshall, Aug. 6, 1994. BA magna cum laude, Randolph-Macon Woman's Coll., 1975; MBA, Pepperdine U., 1983. cert. tchr. K-12, Calif. Test engr. Westinghouse Hanford, Richland, Wash., 1975-76; startup engr. Bechtel Power Corp., Norwalk, Calif., 1976-77; test engr. Wash. Pub. Power, Richland, 1978-80; from mgr. to v.p. Sun Tech. Svcs., Mission Viejo, Calif., 1983-93; cons. Mission Energy Co., Irvine, Calif., 1993-94; owner, CEO, pres. Key Employee Svcs., Inc., Key Largo, Fla., 1994-97; from assoc. to pres. Hawk Assocs., Inc. Investor Rels., Key Largo, Fla., 1996—. Contbr. article to jour. Named Young Career Woman of the Yr. Wash. Pub. Power Supply System, 1979. Mem. Phi Beta Kappa. E-mail: jmarshall@hawkassociates.com.

MARSHALL, KATHLEEN, choreographer, theater director; Mem. exec. bd. Soc. Stage Dirs. and Choreographers. Asst. choreographer (Broadway plays) Kiss of the Spider Woman, 1993—95, She Loves Me, 1993—94, Damn Yankees, 1994—95, choreographer Swinging on a Star, 1996 (Drama Desk nomination), 1776, 1997—98, Ring Round the Moon, 1999, Kiss Me, Kate, 1999—2001 (Tony nom. best choreography, 2001, Laurence Olivier nom. best choreography, 2002, Drama Desk nomination, Outer Critics Circle nomination, Astaire Award nomination), Seussical, 2000—01, Follies, 2001 (Outer Critics Circle award nomination), Little Shop of Horrors, 2003; dir.: (Broadway plays) Wonderful Town, 2003 (Tony nom. best dir. musical, 2004, Drama Desk award best choreography, 2004); choreographer (Broadway plays) Wonderful Town, 2003 (Tony award best choreography, 2004), The Pajama Game, 2005 (Outer Critics' Cir. award, outstanding choreography, 2006, Drama Desk award outstanding choreography, 2006, Tony award, best choreography, 2006), (TV films) The Music Man, 2003. Recipient Mr. Abbott Award, Stage Directors & Choreographers Found., 2005. Office: Ste 702 311 W 43rd St New York NY 10036*

MARSHALL, KATHRYN SUE, lawyer; b. Decatur, Ill., Sept. 12, 1942; d. Edward Elda and Frances M. (Minor) Lahniers; m. Robert S. Marshall, Sept. 5, 1964 (div. Apr. 1984); children: Stephen Edward, Christine Elizabeth; m. Robert J. Arndt, June 25, 1988 (dec. 1999). BA, Lake Forest Coll., 1964; JD, John Marshall Law Sch., Chgo., 1976. Intern U.S. Atty.'s Office, Chgo., 1974—76; mng. ptnr. Marshall and Marshall Ltd., Waukegan, Ill., 1976—84; pvt. practice Waukegan, 1984—93, Preemptive Solutions, Wash. Contbr. articles to profl. jours. Bd. dirs., v.p. Lake Forest (Ill.) Fine Arts Ensemble; bd. dirs. Island Hosp. Health Found.; mem. steering com. Equal Justice Coalition; cert. jud. Dem. candidate Lake County, Ill.; bd. dirs. Camerata Soc., Lake Forest. Fellow: ABA (gov. 1993—96), Coll. Law Practice Mgmt., Ill. Bar Assn.; mem.: Navy League (life). Avocations: boating, reading, travel.

MARSHALL, LINDA LANTOW, pediatrics nurse; b. Tulsa, Dec. 13, 1949; d. Lawrence Lee and Lena Mae (Ross) Lantow; m. David Panke Hartson, Aug. 25, 1970 (div. 1982); children: Michael David, Jonathan Lee; m. Roger Nathan Marshall, Dec. 11, 1985; 1 child, Sarabeth Megan. A, U. Okla., 1970; BSN, U. Tulsa, 1983. Cert. pediatric nurse, 1995. Pediats. nurse Youthcare, Claremore, Okla., 1983-85, 87-98; staff nurse ICU Doctors Hosp., Tulsa, 1985-87; sch. nurse Wilson Tulsa Pub. Schs., 1998—. Bd. dirs. PTA Barnard, Tulsa, 1993-95; leader Brownie troop Girl Scouts U.S., Tulsa, 1994-95, leader jr. scouts, 1995—. Mem. Sigma Theta Tau. Avocation: gardening. Home: 2628 E 22nd St Tulsa OK 74114-3123 Office: Wilson Middle Sch 1127 S Columbia Ave Tulsa OK 74104-3928

MARSHALL, LUCILLE RUTH, retired mathematics professor; b. Waukegan, Ill., Mar. 20, 1941; d. James Arthur and Emily Ruth Cunnington; AA, Santa Rosa Jr. Coll., 1990; BA, Sonoma State U., 1994; MS, Mo. State U., 2000; post grad. in math., U. Mo., 2003. Tchg. asst. Mo. State U., Springfield, Mo., 1998—2000; grad. tchg. asst. U. Mo., Rolla, 2000—03; ret., 2004. Adj. faculty Ozarks Tech. Coll., Springfield. Vol. Family Violence Ctr., Springfield, 2005. Mem.: Order Eastern Star. Home: PO Box 8 Winona MO 65588

MARSHALL, MARGARET HILARY, state supreme court chief justice; b. Newcastle, Natal, South Africa, Sept. 1, 1944; came to U.S., 1968; d. Bernard Charles and Hilary A.D. (Anderton) M; m. Samuel Shapiro, Dec. 14, 1968 (div. Apr. 1982); m. Anthony Lewis, Sept. 23, 1984. BA, Witwatersrand U., Johannesburg, 1966; MEd, Harvard U., 1969; JD, Yale U., 1976; LHD (hon.), Regis Coll., 1993. Bar: Mass. 1977, U.S. Dist. Ct. Mass., U.S. Dist. Ct. N.H., U.S. Dist. Ct. D.C., U.S. Dist. Ct. (ea. dist.) Mich., U.S. Tax Ct., U.S. Ct. Appeals (1st, 11th and D.C. cirs.), U.S. Supreme Ct. Assoc. Csaplar & Bok, Boston, 1976-83, ptnr., 1983-89, Choate, Hall & Stewart, Boston, 1989-92; v.p., gen. counsel Harvard U., Cambridge, Mass., 1992-96; justice Mass. Supreme Jud. Ct., 1996-99, chief justice, 1999—. Mem. jud. nominating coun., 1987-90, 92; chairperson ct. rules subcom. Alternative Dispute Resolution Working Group, 1985-87; mem. fed. appts. commn., 1993; mem. adv. com. Supreme Judicial Ct., 1989-92, mem. gender equality com., 1989-94; mem. civil justice adv. group U.S. Dist. Ct. Mass., 1991-93; spl. counsel Jud. Conduct Commn., 1988-92; trustee Mass. Continuing Legal Edn., Inc., 1990-92. Trustee Regis Coll., 1993-95; bd. dirs. Internat. Design Conf., Aspen, 1986-92, Boston Mcpl. Res. Bur., 1990-94, Supreme Judicial Ct. Hist. Soc., 1990-94, sec., 1990-94. Fellow Am. Bar Found. (Mass. state chair); mem. Boston Bar Assn. (treas. 1988-89, v.p. 1989-90, pres.-elect 1990-91, pres. 1991-92), Internat. Women's Forum, Mass. Women's Forum, Boston Club, Phi Beta Kappa (hon.). Office: Supreme Judicial Court 1 Pemberton Sq Ste 2-500 Boston MA 02108-1717*

MARSHALL, MARY JONES, civic worker; b. Billings, Mont.; d. Leroy Nathaniel and Janet (Currie) Dailey; m. Harvey Bradley Jones, Nov. 15, 1952 (dec. 1989); children: Dailey, Janet Currie, Ellis Bradley; m. Boyd T. Marshall, June 27, 1990. Student, Carleton Coll., 1943-44, U. Mont., 1944-46, UCLA, 1959. Owner Mary Jones Interiors. Founder, treas. Jr. Art Coun., LA County Mus., 1953-55, v.p., 1955-56; mem. costume coun. Pasadena (Calif.) Philharm.; co-founder Art Rental Gallery, 1953, chmn. art and architecture tour, 1955; founding mem., sec. Art Alliance, Pasadena Art Mus., 1955-56; benefit chmn. Pasadena Girls Club, 1959, bd. dirs., 1958-60; chmn. LA Tennis Patron's Assn. Benefit, 1965; sustaining Jr. League Pasadena; mem. docent coun. LA County Mus.; mem. costume coun. LA County Mus. Art, program chmn. 20th Century Greatest Designers; mem. blue ribbon com. LA Music Ctr.; benefit chmn. Venice com. Internat. Fund for Monuments, 1971; bd. dirs. Art Ctr. 100, Pasadena, 1988—; pres. The Pres.'s LA Children's Bur., 1989; co-chmn. benefit Harvard Coll. Scholarship Fund, 1974, steering com. benefit, 1987, Otis Art Inst., 1975, 90th Anniversary of Children's Bur. of LA, 1994; mem. Harvard-Radcliffe scholarship dinner com., 1985; mem. adv. bd. Estelle Doheny Eye Found., 1976, chmn. benefit, 1980; adv. bd. Loyola U. Sch. Fine Arts, LA, Art Ctr. Sch. Design, Pasadena, 1987—; patron chmn. Benefit Achievement Rewards for Coll. Scientists, 1988; chmn. com. Sch. Am. Ballet Benefit, 1988, NYC; bd. dirs. Founders Music Ctr., LA, 1977-81; mem. nat. adv. coun. Sch. Am. Ballet, NYC, nat. co-chmn. gala, 1980; adv. coun. on fine arts Loyola-Marymount U.; mem. LA Olympic Com., 1984, The Colleagues; founding mem. Mus. Contemporary Art, 1986; chmn. The Pres.'s Benefit LA Children's Bur., 1990; exec. com. LA Alive for LA Music Ctr., 1992; mem. exec. com. Children's Bur. of LA Found., 1992; chmn. award dinner Phoenix House, 1994, 96; bd. dirs. Andrews Sch. Gerontology, U. So. Calif., 1996—, Leakey Found., 1996—; bd. regents Children's Hosp. LA, 1996—. Mem. Am. Parkinson Disease Assn. (steering com. 1991), Valley Hunt Club (Pasadena), Calif. Club (LA), Kappa Alpha Theta. Home: 10375 Wilshire Blvd Ste 8B Los Angeles CA 90024-4712

MARSHALL, MARYANN CHORBA, executive secretary; b. Scranton, Pa., Apr. 18, 1952; d. Edward M. and Mildred (Polc) Chorba; m. Daniel V. Marshall III. BA, Emmanuel Coll., 1974. Personal, social sec. Jordan Embassy Mil. Office, Washington, 1974-76; exec. asst, office mgr. Jordan Embassy Info. Bur., Washington, 1976-81; asst. to pres. Nat. Press Club, Washington, 1982-91; adminstr. Harvard Bus. Sch. Club, Washington, 1995-96; co-coord. frontiers in clin. genetics lecture series George Washington U. Med. Ctr., Washington, 1999-2000; exec. sec. The Gridiron Club, Washington, 2001—. Mem. League Rep. Women. Republican. Roman Catholic. Office: The Gridiron Club Capital Hilton Hotel 1001 16th St NW Washington DC 20036

MARSHALL, NATALIE JUNEMANN, economics professor; b. Milw., June 13, 1929; d. Harold E. and Myrtle (Findlay) Junemann; m. Howard D. Marshall, Aug. 7, 1954 (dec. 1972); children: Frederick S., Alison B.; m. Phillip Shatz, May 27, 1988. AB, Vassar Coll., 1951; MA, Columbia U., 1952, PhD, 1963, JD, 1994. Instr. Vassar Coll., Poughkeepsie, NY, 1952-54, 59, 59-60, 63, dean studies, prof. econs., 1973-75, v.p. for student affairs, 1975-80, v.p. for adminstrn. and student services and prof. econs., 1980-91, prof. econs., 1991-94; teaching fellow Wesleyan U., Middletown, Conn., 1955-56; from asst. prof. to prof. SUNY, New Paltz, 1964-73; prof. econs. Vassar Coll., Poughkeepsie, NY, 1973-94; of counsel Donoghue, Thomas, Auslander & Drohan, Hopewell Junction, NY, 1997—. Editor (with Howard Marshall): The History of Economic Thought, 1968; editor: Keynes, Updated or Outdated, 1970; author (with Howard Marshall): Collective Bargaining, 1971. Trustee St. Francis Hosp., 1979-88, Area Fund Dutchess County, 1981-87, Coll. New Rochelle, 1994-2000, Hudson Valley Philharm., 1985-92, pres., 1989-91. Mem. AAUP, Am. Assn. Higher Edn., Am. Econ. Assn., AAUW (v.p. N.Y. State div. 1964-66), Poughkeepsie Vassar Club (pres. 1965-67). Home: 157 Skidmore Rd Pleasant Valley NY 12569-5001

MARSHALL, PENNY (C. MARSHALL, CAROLE PENNY MARSHALL), director, actress; b. NYC, Oct. 15, 1943; d. Anthony W. and Marjorie Irene (Ward) M.; m. Michael Henry (div.); 1 child, Tracy Lee; m. Robert Reiner, Apr. 10, 1971 (div. 1979). Student, U. N.Mex., 1961-64. Appeared on numerous television shows, including The Odd Couple, 1972-74, Friends and Lovers (co-star), 1974, Let's Switch, 1974, Wives (pilot), 1975, Chico and the Man, 1975, Mary Tyler Moore, 1975, Heaven Help Us, 1975, Saturday Night Live, 1975-77, Happy Days, 1975, Battle of Network Stars (ABC special), 1976, Barry Manilow special, 1976, The Tonight Show, 1976-77, Dinah, 1976-77, Mike Douglas Show, 1975-77, Merv Griffin Show, 1976-77, Blansky's Beauties, 1977, Network Battle of the Sexes, 1977, Laverne and Shirley (co-star), 1976-83, Entertainment Tonight's Presents: Laverne and Shirley Together Again, 2002; TV films More Than Friends, 1978, Love Thy Neighbor, 1984, Challenge of a Lifetime, 1985, The Odd Couple: Together Again, 1993; guest appearances include Mary Tyler Moore, 1975, Happy Days, 1975, Chico and the Man, 1975, Mork & Mindy, 1978, Bosom Buddies, 1982, Taxi, 1983, The Simpsons (voice), 1990, Frasier, 2004, I'm With Her, 2004; appeared in motion pictures How Sweet It Is, 1967, The Savage Seven, 1968, The Grasshopper, 1970, 1941, 1979, Movers and Shakers, 1985, She's Having a Baby, 1988, The Hard Way, 1991, Hocus Pocus, 1993, Get Shorty, 1995, Stateside, 2004; dir. films: Jumpin' Jack Flash, 1986, Big, 1988, Awakenings, 1990 (exec. prodr.), A League of Their Own, 1992 (exec. prodr.), Renaissance Man, 1994 (exec. prodr.), The Preacher's Wife, 1996, The Time Tunnel: The Movie, 1999, Special Delivery, 1999, Riding in Cars with Boys, 2001 appeared in TV movie Jackie's Back, 1999; prodr. TV series A League of Their Own, 1993 (also dir. pilot), Dynasties, 2003, Crossover, 2004; dir. (TV Series) Working Stiffs, 1979; prodr. films Getting Away With Murder, 1996, With Friends Like These, 1998, Risk, 2003; exec. prodr. Calender Girl, 1993. Avocations: needlepoint, jigsaw puzzles, antique shopping. Office: c/o William Morris Agy 151 El Camino Dr Beverly Hills CA 90212

MARSHALL, PRISCILLA JACKSON, elementary school educator; d. Clyde and Corine Jackson; m. John Davis Marshall, July 8, 1978; children: Terrence LaVelle Whitsitt, Marrkus Anthonious, Jondreia AnnLesheia, Johnathan Matthew. BS in Edn., Freed Hardeman U., Henderson, Tenn., 1993; MS in Edn., Walden U., Mpls., Minn., 2003; Cert. Ednl. Specialist, Lincoln Meml. U., Harrogate, Tenn., 2005. Tchr. Avondale Elem. Sch., Avondale Estates, Ga., 1993—2002, DESA@Hooper Alexander, Decatur, Ga., 2002—. Paraprofessional Howard Hall Elem. Sch., Fayetteville, NC, 1988—90. Mem.: NEA, Ga. Assn. of Educators. Office: Dekalb County Sch Sys 3414 Memorial Dr Decatur GA 30032 Personal E-mail: marshall722@aol.com.

MARSHALL, SHEILA HERMES, lawyer; b. NYC, Jan. 17, 1934; d. Paul Milton and Julia Angela (Meagher) Hermes; m. James Josiah Marshall, Sept. 30, 1967; 1 child, James J.H. BA, St. John's U., N.Y.C., 1959; JD, NYU, 1963. Bar: N.Y. 1964, U.S. Ct. Appeals (2d, 3d, 5th and D.C. cirs.), U.S. Supreme Ct. 1970. Assoc. LeBoeuf, Lamb, Greene & MacRae, N.Y.C., 1963-72, ptnr., 1973—95, of counsel, 1996—. Specialist in field. Mem. ABA, N.Y. State Bar Assn., Assn. of Bar of City of N.Y. Republican. Home: 325 E 72nd St New York NY 10021 Office: LeBoeuf Lamb Greene & MacRae 125 W 55th St New York NY 10019-5369 Office Phone: 212-424-8624. Business E-Mail: shmarsha@llgm.com.

MARSHALL, SIMONE VERNIERE, psychologist, psychoanalyst; b. Paris; came to U.S., 1951; d. Urbain and Gabrielle (Cadiergues) Verniere; m. Robert J. Marshall, Sept. 13, 1953; childrren: Gabrielle, Annette. Lic. psychology, Sorbonne U., 1948; MA in Devel. Psychology, Columbia U., 1951, PhD in Clin. Psychology, 1959. Cert. in psychoanalysis, White Inst., N.Y.C., 1970. Rsch. sch. psychologist Nat. Bd. of Edn., Paris, 1948-51; child clin. psychologist Children's Hosp., Buffalo, N.Y., 1953-54; clin. psychologist N.J. Dept. of Instns., Trenton, N.J., 1956-58; clin. instr. Rutgers Univ. Psychology Clinic, New Brunswick, N.J., 1958-59; part-time cons. Bd. of Edn., Ossining, N.Y., 1960-64; child therapist Rockland Mental Health Ctr., Monsey, N.Y., 1961-65; pvt. practice psychologist, psychoanalyst Westchester, N.Y., 1960-90, N.Y.C., 1966—. Tng. analyst Blanton Peale Inst. Religion & Health, N.Y.C., 1984—; supr. Inst. for Contemporary Psychotherapy, N.Y.C., 1974-97; faculty Nassau County Med. Ctr., L.I. Inst. for Psychoanalysis, 1980-94; lectr. Union Theol. Sem., N.Y.C., 1983-8 6. Co-authnor: (with R.J. Marshall) The Transference-Countertransference Matrix, 1988. Coord., founder Croton-Cortlandt Women's Ctr., Croton-on-Hudson, N.Y., 1976-81. Recipient Fullbright scholarship Columbia Univ., 1951-52. Mem. Am. Psychol. Assn., Am. Group Psychotherapy Assn., White Psychoanalytic Soc., Westchester County Psychol. Assn. Avocations: photography, painting. Home and Office: 300 E 74th St Apt 33D New York NY 10021-3746 Office Phone: 212-988-0634.

MARSHALL, SIRI SWENSON, lawyer; BA, Harvard U., 1970; JD, Yale U., 1974. Bar: NY 1975. Assoc. Debevoise & Plimpton, 1974-79; atty., sr. atty., asst. gen. counsel Avon Products, Inc., NYC, 1979-85, v.p. legal affairs, 1985-89, sr. v.p., gen. counsel, 1990-94, Gen. Mills, Inc., Mpls., 1994—. Bd. dirs. CPR Internat. Inst. Dispute Resolution, Internat. Inst. for Conflict Prevention and Resolution, Ameriprise Fin., Equifax. Trustee Mpls. Inst. Arts. Office: Gen Mills Inc Number One Gen Mills Blvd Minneapolis MN 55426

MARSHALL-BEASLEY, ELIZABETH, landscape architect; b. Wilton, Conn., Mar. 14, 1959; d. Hamilton West Marshall, Jr. and Mary Barno Marshall; m. James W. Beasley, Jr., Nov. 28, 1986. BA, Princeton U., 1981; M in Landscape Arch., Fla. Internat. U., 1998. Policy analyst N.J. Legislature, 1981; field devel. dir. The Rouse Co., 1984; devel. mgr. Disney Devel. Co., Orlando, Fla., 1988; devel. dir. Norton Mus. Art, West Palm Beach, Fla., 1995; state orgn. dir. Jeb Bush for Gov., Tallahassee, 1996; project mgr., apprentice Morgan Wheelock Inc., West Palm Beach, 1999—2001; cons. Elizabeth Marshall-Beasley, West Palm Beach, 2001—02; pres. Elizabeth Marshall-Beasley, MLA, West Palm Beach, 2003—. Pres. coun. Nat. Pub. Radio, Washington, 2001—; gov. apptd. Bd. Landscape Arch., Tallahassee, 2002—; bd. dirs. Habitat for Humanity, West Palm Beach, New Horizon Svc. Dogs, Orlando. Sponsor Nantucket Conservation Found.; mem. curriculum com. Fla. A&M U. Grad. Sch. Arch.; active US VA Task Force Health and Rehab. Gardens; apptd. mem. City West Palm Beach Art in Pub. Places Commn.; mayor Art in Pub. Places Commn., 2006—. Recipient, ADDY, 1987, Comml. Project of 1989, Architecture Record, 1989; Fairchild Tropical Gardens: Off Site Collection Grad. scholar, 1997. Mem.: Am. Soc. Landscape Arch. (cert.), Sigma Alpha Lambda, Phi Kappa Phi. Episcopalian. Avocations: travel, theater. Office: Ste 1500 505 S Flagler Dr West Palm Beach FL 33401 E-mail: em-b@landplandesign.com.

MARSHALL-CHAPMAN, PAULA, food products executive; d. Paul Marshall. BS in Bus., Okla. City U., 1983, PhD in commercial sci., 1993. CEO Bama Companies, Tulsa, Okla., 1984—. Adv. bd. Fed. Reserve Bank, Kans. City; bd. dirs. Am. Fidelity Corp., Bank of Oklahoma, Helmerich and Payne. Pres. Okla. Quality Found. Bd.; trustee Tulsa Community Found.; mem. Ronald McDonald Advisory Bd.; chmn. Salvation Army Advisory Bd.; bd. mem. U. Tulsa. Named Advocate of the Year, Domestic Violence Intervention Services, 2000; named to Bus. Hall of Fame, Okla. Dept. of Commerce, 1998, Hall of Fame, Sales and Mktg. Executives Internat. Academy of Achievements, 1999; recipient Entrepreneur of Yr. award, Ernst & Young LLP, 1997, Pinnacle award, Sales and Mktg. Executives Internat. Academy of Achievements, 1999, Outstanding Philanthropist award, 2001, Amigo of the Year, Tulsa Hispanic C. of C., 2001. Mem.: Women's Foodservice Forum (bd. mem), Tulsa C. of C. (past chair). Office: Bama Companies 2745 E 11th St Tulsa OK 74104

MARSHALL-DANIELS, MERYL, mediator, executive coach; b. LA, Oct. 16, 1949; d. Jack and Nita Corinblit; m. Raymond Daniels, Aug. 19, 2000. BA, UCLA, 1971; JD, Loyola Marymount U., L.A., 1974. Bar: Calif. 1974. Dep. pub. defender County of L.A., 1975—77; sole practice L.A., 1977—78; ptnr. Markman and Marshall, L.A., 1978—79; sr. atty. NBC, Burbank, Calif., 1979—80, dir. programs, talent contracts bus. affairs, 1980, asst. gen. atty. N.Y.C., 1980—82, v.p., compliance and practices Burbank, 1982; v.p. program affairs Group W Prodns., 1987—89, sr. v.p. future images, 1989—91, TV prodr., Meryl Marshall Prodns., 1991—93; pres. Mediation Ptnrs. and Two Oceans Entertainment Group, 1991—. Chmn., Nat. Women's Polit. Caucus, Westside, Calif., 1978-80; mem. Calif. Dem. Ctrl. Com., 1978-79; mem. Hollywood Women's Polit. Com., 1988; bd. mem. George Foster Peabody Awards. Mem.: Women in Film, Acad. TV Arts and Scis. (treas. 1985, bd. govs. 1989—2001, treas. 1993—97, chmn. bd., CEO 1997—2001). Democrat. Jewish. Office: Two Oceans Consulting Group 2017 Lemoyne St Los Angeles CA 90026 E-mail: merylmarsh@aol.com.

MARSHALL-HARDIN, FLOY JEANNE, art educator; b. Clinton, Okla., July 30, 1949; d. James Edward and Mary Josephine (Mangold) Marshall; m. John Thomas Hardin Jr., June 2, 1992; m. Daniel Paul Ahern; 1 child, Jeanne Danielle Ahern; m. Randall Lee Martin; 1 child, Mackenzie Jin Martin. BFA, U. Ariz. 1978, MA, 1982. Dir. Fenster Ranch Camp, Tucson, 1988—92, Yuma Sch. Dist., Yuma, Ariz., 1986—88, elem. art edn., 1986—88; art educator Sunnyside HS, Tucson, 1994—95, Oracle (Ariz.) Mid. Sch., Oracle, Ariz., 1996—98; elem. art edn. grades K-12 Knox County Schools, Knoxville, Tenn., 2002—. Exhibtor (fibers) Art Educators Exhibit, 2002—03. Mem. Colonial Williamsburg Found., Williamsburg, Va., 2003—. Mem.: Tenn. Art Educators Assn., Nat. Art Educators Assn., Tenn. Educators Assn., Nat. Educators Assn., Knoxville Mus. of Art, U. Ariz. Alumni Assn. Democrat. Methodist. Avocations: travel, fibers. Home: 109 Sanwood Rd Knoxville TN 37923-5549 Office: Knox County Sch Knoxville TN Office Phone: 865-386-3156. Personal E-mail: MADDIEROSE74@hotmail.com.

MARSTON-SCOTT, MARY VESTA, nurse, educator; b. St. Stephen, N.B., Can., Apr. 5, 1924; d. George Frank and Betsey Mildred (Babb) M.; m. John Paul Scott, June 30, 1979. BA, U. Maine, 1946; M.N., Yale U., 1951; M.P.H., Harvard U., 1957; MA, Boston U., 1964, PhD, 1969. Research asst. Roscoe B. Jackson Meml. Lab., Bar Harbor, Maine, 1946-48; nurse, 1952-54; instr. Yale U. Sch. Nursing, 1955-56; nurse cons. Div. Nursing, Washington, 1957-62; asso. prof. Frances Payne Bolton Sch. Nursing, Case-Western Res. U., Cleve., 1969-74; prof. grad. program community health nursing Boston U., 1974-86; assoc. prof. Coll. Nursing U. Ill., Chgo., 1986-94, assoc. prof. emerita, 1994—. Cons. in field. Contbr. articles to profl. jours. Served with USPHS, 1957-62. Fellow Am. Acad. Nursing; mem. Am. Psychol. Assn., Am. Public Health Assn., Am. Nurses Assn., Sigma Theta Tau. Home: Dirigo Pines 2 Hawthorn Ct Orono ME 04473

MARSZALEK, ELIZABETH A., computer graphics designer, educator; b. Davenport, Iowa; BS, Marycrest Coll., Davenport, Iowa, 1985; MS, No. Ill. U., DeKalb, Ill., 1987. Dir. mail computer programmer Gen. Bus. Forms, Skokie, Ill., 1987—89; sys. operator ProData, Des Plaines, Ill., 1989—90; sr. sys. operator Techtron Studio, Chgo., 1990—91; sr. trainer Linotype-Hell Co., Chgo., 1991—93; prof. Coll. DuPage, Glen Ellyn, Ill., 1993—. Mem.: Graphic Arts Tchrs. Ill., Soc. Am. Artists, Graphic Arts Tech. Found. Office: College of DuPage 425 Fawell Blvd Glen Ellyn IL 60137 Office Phone: 630-942-2045. Home Fax: 630-942-4472. Personal E-mail: marszale@cod.edu.

MART, JOANN, social sciences educator; d. Robert Weisenfluh and Ann Verna Weiss; m. Robert T. Mart, July 3, 1993; children: Paul Smit, Jamie Smit Blair. BA in Polit. Sci., U. Wash., Seattle, 1991; MEd, Azusa Pacific U., Calif., 2001. Single subject social sci. tchg. credential Calif., cross-cultural lang. and devel. credential Calif. Tchr. social sci. Covina Unified Sch. Dist., Calif., 1993—2001, Rocklin Unified Sch. Dist., Calif., 2004—. Pub. rels. chair Calif. Scholarship Fedn., 1999—2002; mem. govt. rels. com. Calif. Coun. for Social Studies, 2005—06; mem. bd. dir. Calif. Coun. Soc. Studies, 2006—. Co-author: (lesson plan CD) Comparison of Samurai and Knights, 1996; author: (lesson plan book) German Immigration, 2005. City commr. comty. svcs. City of West Covina, Calif., 1998—2001; mem. City of Citrus Heights Leadership, Calif., 2003—04. Named one of Tchrs. Who Make a Difference, Placer County Dept. Edn., 2006; fellow, Goethe Inst. Atlanta-Tchrs. Promoting Modern Germany, Williamsburg Tchr.'s Inst., Japan-U.S. Tchrs. Program. Mem.: Calif. Tchr.'s Assn., Nat. Coun. Social Studies, Calif. Coun. for Social Studies. Avocation: travel. Home: 7647 Brookover Ct Citrus Heights CA 95610

MARTA, DAWN RENEÉ, psychologist; b. Ottawa, Ill., Sept. 10, 1963; d. Bruce Roger Rooks and Marsha Ann (Meade) Monroe; m. David Lee LeBeau (div. Oct. 1987); 1 child, Nicholas Scott LeBeau; m. Scott Kennedy Echols (dec. Feb. 1996); m. Anthony John Marta, Dec. 21, 2001. Student, Fla. C.C., Jacksonville, 1990—93; AA in Medicine, Ctrl. Fla. C.C., Ocala, Fla., 1994; student, Santa Fe C.C., Gainesville, 1994; BA in Philosophy with high honors, U. Fla., 1997; MDiv in Theology, Duke U., 2000; postgrad., George Fox U., 2000; D in Psychology, Argosy U., 2004. Cert. personal trainer Am. Coun. Exercise. Membership dir. Duval County Med. Soc., Jacksonville, Fla., 1987—93; emergency rm. admissions rep. Munroe Regional Med. Ctr., Ocala, Fla., 1993—94; admissions rep. Shands Hosp. U. Fla., Gainesville, 1994; adminstr. Covenant Presbyn. Ch., Gainesville, 1994—95; chaplain Duke U. Med. Ctr., Durham, NC, 1998—2000; personal trainer Ottawa, Elgin, 2000—04; resident Meridian Behavioral Health Svcs., 2004—05; clin. psychologist, owner, operator Ctr. Human Flourishing, Andrews, 2005—. Part-time pvt. practice forensic psychologist, Cherokee County, NC, 2004—. Usher First United Meth. Ch., Chgo., 2002, Elgin, 2003—04, trustee edn. com., 2003—04; mem. Andrews Methodist Ch, Andrews, NC. Mem.: APA, NC Psychology Assn. Avocations: bodybuilding, bicycling, hiking, kayaking, travel. Office: Ctr Human Flourshing Box 2462 34 First St Andrews NC 28901 Office Phone: 828-321-9900. E-mail: drmarta11@verizon.net.

MARTE-BAUTISTA, HELEN I., retired performing arts educator; d. Diosdado and Modesta Inocencio Marte; 1 child, Andreliz Marte Bautista. MA, San Francisco State U., 1970. Cert. Calif. State credential. Educator, staff devel. San Francisco Unified Sch. Dist., 1968—98. Commr. San Francisco Pub. Libr., 2000—; trustee Am. Libr. Trustee Assn., Chgo., 2002—. Choreographer (prodn.) dance drama, Santa Cruzan (Dance-in-Residence award, 1968). Pres. City Celebration, Inc. Ethnic Dance Festival, San Francisco, 1984—88; sec., bd. mem. Kearny St. Housing Corp., Inc., San Francisco, 1986; pres. Friends of the San Francisco Commn. and Status of Women, 1986—88; treas. YWCA - San Francisco, Marin and San Mateo County, 1990—96; treas. Mayor's Protocol Office San Francisco/Manila Sister City Com., 1996; citizen adv. mem. Presidio Redevel. U.S. Dept. of Interior, San Francisco, 1997—99; sec., mem. bd. Internat. Hotel Sr. Housing Corp., Inc., San Francisco, 1998. Recipient Summer/Residence Citizenship award, Ethical Union Soc., Philippine Scouts Assn., U. Calif., Berkeley, 1961, Merit award outstanding pub. svc., San Francisco Mayor's Office Diane Feinstein, 1984, Human Rights award, San Francisco, Human Rights Commn., 1985; grantee Spl. Edn. program bilingual tchrs., U. San Francisco, 1979; Melvin Jones fellow, Lion's Found., 2005. Mem.: Delta Kappa Gamma (assoc.; pres. 1982—84, Beta Chi chpt.), Am. Fedn. of Teachers (assoc.; mem. of the bd. 1971—76), Fil-Am. Lions Club San Francisco (pres.), Am. Lions Club San Francisco (assoc.; mem. of the bd. 1988, Presdl. award 1996). Avocations: travel, art, music, literature, dance. Office Phone: 415-557-4233.

MARTEL, EVA LEONA, accountant; b. Bristol, Conn., Feb. 14, 1945; d. Samuel L. and Irene A. (Beaulieu) Martel. BS in Acctg., N.H. Coll., 1986; MBA, Plymouth State U., 1990. Cert. mgmt. acct.; cert. continuing edn. educator. Accts. payable Elliot Hosp., Manchester, N.H., 1971-79, bookkeeper, 1979-84, dir. acctg., 1984-94; portfolio mgr. Optima Health Inc., Manchester, N.H., 1994-97, mgr. managed care contracting, 1997-98, dir. managed care, 1998-2000; exec. dir. managed care Elliot Hosp., 2000—. Adj. faculty N.H. Coll., 1991—; speaker Daniel Webster coun. Boy Scouts Am., Manchester, 1988, Med. Assts. Workshop, 1997; mem. supervisory com. of bd. Telephone Credit Union, 2004—; panel mem. ednl. seminar, 1993. Treas. N.H. Indian Coun., 1980-84; vol. United Way, Manchester, 1988—, accountexec., 1990, 91; mem. adv. coun. health care adminstrn. N.H. Coll., 1990, faculty advisor weekend program, 1990-91; vol. N.H. Heart Assn., 1990-92; bd. dirs. N.H. chpt. Am. Cancer Soc., 1991—; road race com. Elliot Hosp.; mem. scholarship com. Jewett Sch. Recipient Excellence in Tchg. award N.H. Coll., 2000. Mem. NAFE, Hosp. Fin. Mgmt. Assn., Speaker's Bur. (smoke free com., recycling com. 1991), IMA, Healthcare Fin. Mgmt. Assn, Telephone Credit Union, (supr. com., 2004—). Roman Catholic. Avocations: physical fitness, reading, music, writing, teaching, coin collecting/numismatics. Home: 129 Riverledge Dr Goffstown NH 03045-6203 Office Phone: 603-663-6181. Business E-Mail: emartel@elliot-hs.org.

MARTELL, MAXINE A., artist; b. Muskogee, Okla., Aug. 23, 1937; d. Carroll Leo and Anna Mae (Corr) M.; m. Richard DiBene, Feb. 4, 1955 (div. Feb. 1970); 1 child, Deanna; m. James Douglas Burns, Nov. 25, 1971. BA, Holy Names Coll., 1960; MFA, U. Wash., 1962. Curator of art N.W. Mus. Arts and Culture, Spokane, Wash., 1970-73; dir. Spokane Art Sch., 1970-74; mem. staff and/or, Seattle, 1978-79; represented by Grover, Thurston Gallery, 1991—2003. Resident Western Wash. U., Bellingham, 1973, Centrum, Port Townsend, Wash., 1984, Pilchuck Glass Ctr., Stanwood, Wash., 1987; represented by Lorinda Knight Gallery, Spokane, Wash. Prin. works include glass installations at St. Joseph Children's Home, Spokane, Temple Beth Shalom, Spokane, Clover Park H.S., Tacoma, U.S. Customs Sta., Lynden, Wash., paintings at Sea-Tac Internat. Airport, 1992, Bienale Internat. Dell' Arte Contemporanea Di Firenze, 1999 (Life Time Achievement Silver medal); solo show Jundt Art Mus., Gonzaga U., Spokane, 1998; creator film Elle, 1978 (1st prize Women's Film Festival, Seattle); curator Suspended Animation Exhbn., 1979. Trustee Pratt Fine Art Ctr., Seattle, 1988-92, v.p., 1989-91; mem. art adv. com. Expo '74, 1973-74; trustee Western Assn. Art Mus., 1971-72. Home: 841 S Blockhouse Rd Coupeville WA 98239-3508 E-mail: maxine@maxinemartell.com.

MARTH, MARY ELLEN (KIM MARTIN), entertainer; b. Atkinson, Minn., July 15, 1936; d. Sigvard B. Kanikkeberg and Beatrice M. (Lundberg) Wangen; m. T.A. Martinez (div.); m. Luther H. Marth (div.); children: Mitzie, Leslie, Tina, Allen. Entertainer The Kim Martin Show, 1960—. Band leader Kim Martin Show, 1960—; real estate owner Marth Properties, Mpls., 1972—. Author of poems, songs, articles, short stories, childrens books, historian, humanitarian. Sec. Hennepin County Adult Foster Care, Mpls, 1983—; mem. Summit Ministries, Colo, 1995, Columbia Heights Owners Assn., 1990—, Multi-Housing Assn., Mpls, 1993—, Vesterheim Geneal. Mus., 1990, Norwegian Am. Mus., 1988—. Named Queen of Country Music, Country Entertainers Assn., Mpls., 1977, Entertainer of Yr. 1978, Female Vocalist of Yr., 1978, Best Band of Yr., 1979, Songwriter of Yr., 1980. Mem. Winnesheik Geneal. Soc., Filmore County Hist. Soc., Vesterheim Geneal. Soc., Minn. Historical Soc. Lutheran.

MARTIKAINEN, A(UNE) HELEN, retired health specialist educator; b. Harrison, Maine, May 11, 1916; d. Sylvester and Emma (Heikkinen) M. AB, Bates Coll., 1939, DSc (hon.), 1957; MPH, Yale U., 1941; DSc, Harvard U., 1964; DSc (hon.), Smith Coll., 1969. Health edn. sec. Hartford (Conn.) Tb and Pub. Health Assn., 1941; cons. USPHS, 1942—49; chief health edn. WHO, Geneva, 1949—74; chair internat. affairs AAUW-NC, 1986—94, rep. to NC Coalition on Aging, 2001—, bd. dirs., 2001—; mem. NC Health Adv. Bd. for Aging, 2001—. Hon. trustee Bridgton Acad., North Bridgton, Maine; mem. NC Women's Forum, 1984—; bd. dirs. NC Ctr. of Laws Affecting Women, Inc.; bd. dirs. West Triangle chpt. UNA-USA; chair residents health and social svcs. com., residents coun., residents com. for cmty. rels. Carol Woods. Recipient Delta Omega award Yale U., Nat. Adminstrv. award Am. Acad. Phys. Edn., Key award Bates Coll., Internat. Svc. award, France, 1953, Prentiss medal, 1956, Spl. medal, cert. for internat. health edn. svc. Nat. Acad. Medicine for France, 1959, Profl. award Soc. Pub. Health Educators, 1963, Benjamin Elijah Mays award Bates Coll. Alumni Assn., 1989, Legacy of Leadership honoree Pines of Carolina coun. Girl Scouts U.S., 2002; named to Bridgeton Acad. Hall of Fame, Maine, 2003. Fellow APHA (chmn. health edn. sect., Excellence award 1969); mem. AAUW, LWV, Women's Internat. League for Peace and Freedom, U.S. Soc. Pub. Health Educators, Internat. Union Health Edn. (Parisot medal, tech. adviser), Acad. Phys. Edn. (assoc.), NC Coun. Women's Orgns. (mem. coun. assembly 1988-92, Women of Distinction award 1989), Phi Beta Kappa. Home: 3113 Carol Woods 750 Weaver Dairy Rd Chapel Hill NC 27514-1443 Personal E-mail: ahm3113@hotmail.com.

MARTIN, ALICE HOWZE, prosecutor; b. Memphis, Apr. 25, 1956; married; 3 children. BSN, Vanderbilt U., 1978; JD, U. Miss., 1981. Bar: Tenn. 1981, Miss. 1981, Ala. 1989. Asst. U.S. atty. U.S. Attys. Office, Memphis, 1983-89; ptnr. Harris Harris & Martin, Florence, Ala., 1992—94; dist. mcpl. judge City of Florence, Ala., 1993—97; judge Cir. Ct. State of Ala., 1997—99; U.S. Atty. (no. dist.) Ala. US Dept. Justice, 2001—. Avocations: travel, skeet shooting. Office Phone: 205-244-2001. E-mail: Alice.Martin@usdoj.gov.*

MARTIN, ALISON CADY, interior designer; b. N.Y.C., May 12, 1949; d. Everett Ware Jr. and Ruth Anne (Payan) Cady; m. Robin Bradley Martin, Jan. 29, 1972 (div. 1979); m. Frederic Bradley Underwood, Oct. 8, 1988 (div. 1999). BA, Middlebury Coll., Vt., 1971. Pres. Alison Martin Interiors, Ltd., Washington, 1976—. Sec. Great Falls (Va.) Concert Series, 1983-88, treas., 1988-96. Named to Washington Design Hall Fame, 2004. Mem. Colony Club (N.Y.C.). Democrat. Episcopalian. Avocation: singing. Office: PO Box 949 Berryville VA 22611 Personal E-mail: amartinu@aol.com.

MARTIN, AMY H., science educator; b. Westfield, N.Y., May 25, 1974; d. Kipling and Constance Olson; m. Sean A. Martin, May 27, 2000; children: Lauren Elisabeth, Andrew Kipling. BS in Recombinant Gene Tech., SUNY, Fredonia, 1996; MS in Secondary Sci. Edn., Niagara U., Niagara Falls, N.Y., 1998. Cert. secondary sci. edn. State of N.Y., 2000. 8th grade sci. tchr. Cassadaga Valley Mid./High Sch., Sinclairville, NY, 1999—. Office: Cassadaga Valley Mid/High Sch PO Box 540 Sinclairville NY 14782 Office Phone: 716-962-8581. Personal E-mail: amymartin424@hotmail.com.

MARTIN, ANDREA LOUISE, actress, comedienne, writer; b. Portland, Maine, Jan. 15, 1947; m. Bob Dolman, 1980 (div.); children: Joe, Jack. Grad., Emerson Coll. Appearances include (plays) Hard Shell, 1980 (off-Broadway debut), Sorrows of Stephen, 1980, What's a Nice Country Like You Doing in a State Like This?, 1974, She Loves Me, My Favorite Year, 1993 (Tony award, Featured Actress in a Musical), (films) Cannibal Girls, 1973, Black Christmas, 1974, Wholly Moses!, 1980, Soup for One, 1982, Club Paradise, 1986, Innerspace, 1987, Martha Ruth and Eddie, 1988, Worth Winning, 1989, Boris and Natasha, 1989, Rude Awakening, 1989, Too Much Sun, 1991, Stepping Out, 1991, All I Want for Christmas, 1991, (voice) The Itsy Bitsy Spider, 1992, Striking Distance, 1993, Bogus, 1996, (voice) Anastasia, 1997, Wag the Dog, 1997, The Rugrats Movie (voice), 1998, Bartok the Magnificent, 1999, Believe, 2000, Loser, 2000, Recess: Schools Out (voice), 2001, All Over the Guy, 2000, Jimmy Neutron: Boy Genius, 2001, My Big Fat Greek Wedding, 2002, New York Minute, 2004, The Producers, 2005, The TV Set, 2006, How to Eat Fried Worms, 2006, (TV) Second City TV, 1977-81, That Thing on ABC, 1978, Torn Between Two Lovers, 1979, The Robert Klein Show, 1981, Kate and Allie, 1982, The Comedy Zone, 1984, Late Night Film Festival, 1985, Second City Twenty-Fifth Anniversary, 1985, Martin Short Concert for the North Americas, 1985, The Smothers Brothers Comedy Hour, 1988, Poison, 1988, The Martin Short Show, 1994, Earthworm Jim, 1995, Life.and Stuff, 1997, Damon, 1998, Committed, 2001, My Big Fat Greek Life, 2003, others; (TV movie) Charles Dickens' David Copperfield, 1993, Gypsy, 1993, In Search of Dr. Seuss, 1994, Harrison Bergeron, 1995, My Funny Valentine, 2000, The Kid, 2001, Sick in the Head, 2003, Kim Possible: A Sitch in Time, 2003, (voice) Jimmy Neutron: Attack of the Twonkies, 2005; TV host Women of the Night II, 1988, Second City Fifteen Anniversary Special, 1988, Andrea Martin: Together Again, 1989; actress/writer: TV series SCTV Network 90, 1981-83 (2 Emmy awards 1982, 83), SCTV Channel, 1983-84, TV pilot From Cleveland, 1980; also The Completely Mental Misadventures of Ed Grimley, 1988-90 (voice of Mrs. Freebus).*

MARTIN, ANGELA DENISE, educator; b. Beaumont, Tex., Dec. 27, 1967; m. Steven Lorne Martin, Nov. 26, 2003; m. Hillman Webb Madison, Dec. 30, 1989 (div. Feb. 1, 2000); children: Sydney Ellis Madison, Jaxson Wyndham, Sheridan Elizabeth. BS in Exceptional Edn., U. Ctrl. Fla., Orlando, 1995. Tchr. Volusia County Sch., Daytona Beach, Fla., 1995—2000, bus. ptnr. coord., 1996—2000; tchr. Nederland Ind. Sch. Dist., Tex., 2001—. Vol. Jr. League of Beaumont, Tex., 2005—06. Home: 3675 Augusta Dr Beaumont TX 77707 Office: Nederland Ind Sch Dist 220 17th St Nederland TX 77627 Office Phone: 409-727-5765. Personal E-mail: amartin@nederland.k12.tx.us.

MARTIN, ANN MCCARTHY, library-media specialist; b. Bklyn., Nov. 26, 1948; d. John G. and Cornelia (Dinneen) McCarthy; m. Charles S. Martin Jr., Aug. 23, 1969; children: Elizabeth Ann, Andrew Charles BS, Radford U., 1969; MA, George Washington U., 1995. Tchr. history, media specialist, Orono, Maine; libr.-media specialist Chesterfield County, Va.; ednl. specialist, Libr. Info. Svcs. Henrico County Schs., Richmond, Va. Mem. ALA, Am. Assn. Sch. Libraries, Va. Ednl. Media Assn Home: 5039 Bonnie Brae Rd Richmond VA 23234-3765 Office: PO Box 23120 3820 Nine Mile Rd Richmond VA 23222

MARTIN, BARBARA LYNNE, retired elementary school educator; b. Lynn, Mass., May 21, 1943; d. Edward M. and Margaret (Deacon) Kehoe; m. Gerald W. Weber (div. Dec. 1978); 1 child, Karen Michelle; m. E. Dale Martin, Dec. 26, 1983. BA, U. N.H., 1965. Tchr. Norwalk (Conn.) Sch. Dist., 1965-67, Fremont (Calif.) Unified Sch. Dist., 1967-68, Los Altos (Calif.) Sch. Dist., 1972—2002; ret., 2002. Home: 22954 Longdown Rd Cupertino CA 95014-2652

MARTIN, BRENDA J., science educator; b. Plentywood, Mont., Mar. 4, 1968; d. David E. and Jane C. Williams; m. Douglas Martin. BS in Edn., U. Wyo., Laramie, 1991. Lic. tchr. State of Mont., 1991. Tchr. Dutton Sch., Mont., 1991—96, Custer County Dist. H.S., Miles City, Mont., 1996—, dept. chair, 1996—. Mem.: Miles City Womens Club. Home: 63 Prima Vista Dr Miles City MT 59301 Office: Custer County District High Sch 20 S Center Miles City MT 59930 Office Phone: 406-234-4217. E-mail: bmartin@milescity.k12.mt.us.

MARTIN, CARMEN GUINN, literature and language educator; d. Ewing Elbert and Minnie Hamilton Guinn; m. Terry Lyn Martin, Aug. 6, 1977; 1 child, Lynlea Cameron. BA, Western Ky. U., Bowling Green, 1978, MA, 1980, Reading Specialist, 1982. Mid. sch. tchr. Hart County Bd. Edn., Munfordville, Ky., 1978—87; mid. and h.s. tchr. Caverna Bd. Edn., Horse Cave/Cave City, Ky., 1987—2006. Club sponsor Beta Club, Speech Club, Horse Cave, Cave City, Munfordville, 1978—2006; cheerleader coach Hart County Mid. and High Schs., Munfordville, 1978—87; academic team coach Caverna & Cub Run Mid. Sch., 1983—89; homecoming sponsor Caverna H.S., 1987—2006; writing portfolio cluster leader Ky. Writing/Lang. Arts Tchrs., 1992—2000; intern tchr. mentor Ky. Tchr. Internship Program, 1995—2000. Recipient Tchr. of the Yr. award, Hart County C. of C., 2002, Sr. Class Appreciation Recognition, Caverna HS Seniors, 2000, Cmty. Svc. Recognition award, Caverna Bd. Edn., 2000, Outstanding Tchr. of Yr. recognition, 2006. Mem.: NEA (assoc.), Ky. Edn. Assn. (assoc.), Caverna Edn. Assn. (assoc.; com. mem., chair 1987—). Avocations: travel, reading, decorating. Office: Caverna High School 2276 S Dixie St Horse Cave KY 42749 Office Phone: 270-773-2828. Business E-Mail: carmen.martin@caverna.kyschools.us.

MARTIN, CAROL JACQUELYN, artist, educator; b. Ft. Worth, Tex., Oct. 6, 1943; d. John Warren and Dorothy Lorene (Coffman) Edwards; m. Boe Willis Martin, Oct. 6, 1940; children: Stephanie Diane, Scott Andrew. BA summa cum laude, U. North Tex., 1965; MA, U. Tex., El Paso, 1967. Tchr. Edgemere Elem. Sch., El Paso, 1965—66, Fulmore Jr. H.S., Austin, Tex., 1966—67, Monnig Jr. H.S., Ft. Worth, 1967—68, Paschal H.S., Ft. Worth, 1968—69; instr. Tarrant County Jr. Coll., Ft. Worth, 1968—69, 1971—72; instr. English Eastfield C.C., Dallas, 1981; instr. Richland C.C. Dist., 1982; instr. art Meml. Student Ctr. UPlus Tex. A&M U., 2002—03; instr. art Brenham Fine Arts League, 2006. Artist Vt. Studio Ctr., 1998; press sec. Senator Gaylord Nelson, Washington, 1969—71. Editor The Avesta Mag., 1964-65; various art exhbns Mem. Nat. Mus. Women in Arts; mem. Brenham Fine Arts League, Friends of Meml. Student Ctr.-Opera and Performing Arts Soc., The Woman's Club. Mem. Lone Star Art Guild, Brazos Valley Art League, Brazos Valley Symphony Soc., Mortar Board, Alpha Chi, Sigma Tau Delta, Kappa Delta Pi, Delta Gamma Democrat. Methodist. Avocations: travel, photography, skiing, painting. Address: 4055 Sweetwater Dr College Station TX 77845-9650

MARTIN, CAROL JAYE, retired elementary school educator; b. Bellaire, Ohio, Jan. 12, 1944; d. Foster Charles and Beatrice Elizabeth (Watters) M. BS in Elem. Edn., Ohio U., 1965, MS in Elem. Edn., 1970. Cert. elem. tchr., Ohio, W.Va. Tchr. Bellaire City Schs., 1963-73, Wetzel County Schs., New Martinsville, W.Va., 1973-76, Switzerland of Ohio Schs., Woodsfield, 1978—98; area mgr. World Book Ency., Chgo., 1976—83; ret., 1998. Mem. NEA (life), Ohio Edn. Assn. Democrat. Methodist. Avocations: travel, reading, piano, plants. Home: PO Box 7 Shadyside OH 43947-0007

MARTIN, CAROLYN A. (BIDDY MARTIN), provost; BA in English, Coll. of William and Mary, 1973; PhD in German Lit., U. Wis., 1985. Mem. faculty Cornell U., Ithaca, NY, 1983—, sr. assoc. dean Coll. Arts and Scis., 1977—2000, univ. provost, 2000—. Grad. field rep. for German studies Cornell U., 1991—96, grad. field rep., co-founder lesbian and gay studies, 1992—96, assoc. dir. program women's studies, 1993—94, chair dept. German studies, 1994—97. Author: numerous books; contbr. articles to profl. jours.; mem. edtl. bd.: Studies in Gender and Sexuality, New German Critique, Gay and Lesbian Quar., Diacritics, Signs, Women in German. Mem.: Phi Beta Kappa. Office: Office of the Provost Cornell U Ithaca NY 14853

MARTIN, CAROLYN STEWART, retired school system administrator; b. Pitts., May 16, 1951; d. Robert Thomas and Mary (Schoenecker) Stewart; m. Bradley W. Ritter, Feb. 14, 1973 (div. 1979); m. Scott Harwood Martin, July 29, 1983; 1 child, Carrie Lee. BS, Calif. State U., 1972; MA, Ohio State U., 1978; postgrad., Stetson Univ., DeLand, Fla., 1985-87. Tchr. Garrett County Schs., Oakland, Md., 1972-74, Little Darlings Sch., Columbus, Ohio, 1974-75, Colegio Nueva Granada, Bogota, Colombia, 1978-80; bilingual tchr. Othello (Wash.) Sch. Dist., adminstr. title VII, 1981-82; primary specialist, counselor Lake County Sch. Dist., Fla., 1982-84; tchr. Volusia County Sch. Dist., Deltona, Fla., 1984-85; guidance counselor Volusia County Schs., Deltona, Fla., 1989—2005, ret., 2005. Ind. parenting instr., DeLand, 1988; chair Volusia Mental Health Assn., Daytona, 1987; mem. Fla. State Dept. Edn. Task Force, Orlando, 1989; presenter at profl. confs.; guest speaker Women Volusia Conf., 1989. Co-author: Survival Spanish for Teachers, 1982; presenter, guest speaker in field. Bd. dirs. S.W. Volusia YMCA, 1988-93, House Next Door I-CARE Counseling Ctr., 1991-96; chpt. coord. C.H.A.D.D., West Volusia, 1993-95. Named Elem. Counselor of Yr., Volusia/Flagler Counties, 1995-96. Mem. ASCD, AAUW, Fla. Assn. for Counseling and Devel., Volusia Assn. for Counseling and Devel.

MARTIN, CHRISTY, communications executive; BS in Computer and Info. Sci., UC, Santa Cruz, 1988. Prin. engr. Divicom, 1995; video-on-demand contractor Canal+Technologies, 1999—2001, mgr., voice-on-demand integration, 2001—. Spkr. in field. Vol. Habitat for Humanity, Santa Cruz, Calif. Mem.: Soc. Cable Telecom. Engrs. (Women in Tech. award 2002), Women in Cable TV.*

MARTIN, CLAIR, academic administrator; BSN, Goshen Coll., 1966; MN in Psychiatric-Mental Health Nursing, U. Fla., 1967, MA in Sociology, 1971, PhD in Sociology, 1975; Cert. Inst. Ednl. Mgmt., Harvard U., 1991. Instr. Coll. Nursing U. Fla., Gainesville, 1967-69; assoc. prof. and head dept. nursing Western Carolina U., Cullowhee, N.C., 1975-76; assoc. prof., Sch. Nursing U. N.C., Greensboro, 1975-76; DON and assoc. prof. dept. nursing Anchorage (Alaska) C.C., 1976-77; dean and assoc. prof., Coll. Nursing and Health Scis. U. Alaska, Anchorage, 1977-81, dean and prof., Coll. Nursing and Health Scis., 1981-86; dean and prof., Sch. Nursing Emory U., Atlanta, 1986-92, U. Colo. Health Scis. Ctr., Denver, 1992-95; pres. Cumberland U., Lebanon, Tenn., 1995. Mem. bd. dirs. Ga. League for Nursing, 1988-92; vis. com. mem. Sch. Nursing U. Miami, 1988-95; spl. project grant review bd. mem. divsn. of nursing Dept. Health & Human Svcs. USPHS, 1988-95; mem. nat. adv. com. Cmty. Health Leadership Program Robert Wood Johnson Found., 1993-95; mem. adv. com. Fuld Inst. for Technology in Nursing Edn., Helene Fuld Health Trust, 1993-95; mental health care providers in rural areas wrok groups U.S. Dept. Health & Human Svcs., 1994-95, numerous others. Contbr. to numerous profl. jours. Awarded numerous grants and scholarships. Mem. ANA, Am. Acad. Nursing, Am. Assn. Colls. Nursing (chair interest group "collaboration between nursing education and practice" 1986-92, planning com. for master's edn. for the 21st century conf. 1990, chair govtl. affairs com. 1990-93, bd. dirs. 1990-93), Nat. League Nurses (chair resolutions com. 1978-80, bd. of review 1979-84, chair baccalaureate and higher degree coun. 1982-83, planning com. 6th nat. conf. on nursing edn. 1989, network of cons. 1989-95, chair long term care com. 1991-93, coun. of nurse execs. 1989-91, chair exec. com. 1991-93, bd. govs. 1991-93, pub. policy com. 1993-94, ad-hoc com. for mem. review NLN/NLHC relationship, fact finding com. 1994-95), Colo. Nurses Assn., Colo. Assn. Colls. Nursing, Colo. Soc. Nurse Execs., Sigma Theta Tau, Western Inst. for Nursing, Western Soc. for Rsch. in Nursing. Office: Cumberland U S Greenwood St Lebanon TN 37087

MARTIN, COLEEN MARIE, elementary school educator; b. Peoria, Ill., Jan. 2, 1952; d. James Marshal and Shirley Jane Belcher; m. James L. Martin, June 23, 1973. BS in Elem. Edn., Ill. State U., Normal, 1974; MA in Elem. Edn., Bradley U., Peoria, Ill., 1983. Cert. tchr. Ill. Tchr. Dunlap Sch. Dist., Dunlap, Ill., 1974—. Bd. dirs. Ill. Valley Striders, Peoria, 1986—, pres., 1997—2001. Recipient Presdl. Award for Excellence in Math and Sci. Tchg., NSF, 2001. Mem.: Ill. Sci. Tchrs. Assn. (bd. dirs. 2005—). Avocation: running. Home: 719 Taylor Dr Chillicothe IL 61523 Office: Dunlap School District 10021 Pacific Ave Peoria IL 61615 Office Phone: 309-243-7728. Business E-Mail: cmartin@dunlapcusd.net.

MARTIN, COLLEEN E., nurse; b. Oklahoma City, July 10, 1955; d. Wm. D. and Dona Jean (O'Day) M. Student, Oklahoma State U., Stillwater, 1973-75, Rose State Coll., Midwest City, Okla., 1988; BSN, U. Okla., 1979. Cert. in med.-surg. nursing. Charge nurse Okla. Meml. Hosp., Oklahoma City; staff and charge nurse Midwest City Regional Hosp., head ambulatory surgery unit; Assoc. Med. Profls., 1994—. Mem. ANA, Am. Soc. Post Anesthesia Nurses, Okla. Soc. Post Anesthesia Nurses.

MARTIN, DALE, health facility administrator; b. N.Y.C., May 10, 1935; d. Byron Pink Molter and Ruth Nobel; m. Robert A. Wishart, Dec. 13, 1985; children from previous marriage: Elizabeth, Devon. BS, U. Conn., 1957. RN, cert. case mgr., disability mgmt. specialist, lic. rehab. counsellor, Mass. Dental asst., Hempstead, NY, 1951; with Wesson Maternity Hosp., Springfield, Mass., 1957—58, Huntington Hartford Meml. Hosp., Pasadena, Calif., 1958—59; mgr. office Indsl. By Products Inc., Kalamazoo, 1969—72, contr. Chgo., 1970—74; cons. Mgmt. Resources Inc., Broomall, Pa., 1978—81; cons., owner Martin-Collard Assocs., Inc., Monmouth Beach, NJ, 1980—84; cons., owner, chmn. bd. dirs. MCA, Inc., St. Helena Island, SC, 1984—. Bd. dirs. Consortium Advantage, Inc., St. Helena Island, Silvers Assocs., Plymouth, Mass., Low Country Human Devel. Ctr., Beaufort, SC, mentor program dir., 2001—04, exec. com., steering com., chmn. vol. program, 2001—04; cons. Viewfinder, Old Chatham, NY, 1987—99, Phoenix Inc., Global Explorations, Inc., 1987—99, Fallon Inc., Dr. Martens Shoe Distbr., 1998—2000, Retail Swap.com, 2000—02, shoespot.com, 2001—02; chmn. Okatie Acad. Tennis Benefit. Contbr. articles to profl. jours., 2001. Bd. govs. Rumson-Fair Haven HS, NJ, 1976—78; mem. corp. fundraising com. Beaufort Orch., SC, 2003—04; mem. Beaufort Orch. League, 2004; benefit tennis co-chair Jordan Hosp.-White Cliffs County Club. Mem.: Case Mgmt. Soc. Am., Mass. Nurses Assn. (chmn. image com. 1984—85, pub. info. com. 1986—89), Individual Case Mgmt. Assn., Internat. Assn. Psychosocial Rehab. Specialists, Nat. Rehab. Assn. (pvt. sector group), Nat. Assn. Rehab. Profls. in Pvt. Sector (forensic sect., past rep. region 1 to bd. dirs.), Beaufort Orch. League, Jr. League, Visual Arts Assn. Dataw Isle (pres. 2005—, bd. dir. 2006—, found. collaborator), Dataw Island Club (bd. dir. and tennis assn. social chmn. 2001—04, chmn. visual arts 2003—04, bd. dirs. visual arts club 2004—, tennis ctr. fundraising com. 2005—, chmn. clubhouse pub. art 2006—, rec. com. 2003—, pres. 2003—06), Miles Grant Country Club (bd. dirs. Tennis Assn. 1997—2001, pres. 1998—2000), Jr. Women's Club, Mountain Lakes Ski Club (founder), Town Club (v.p.), Alpha Delta Pi, Sigma Theta Tau. Avocations: painting, tennis, croquet, N.J. state girls gymnastic judge, kayaking.

MARTIN, DEBRA JANE, assistant principal, basketball coach; d. Charles Preston and Janie Crawford; m. Rick Dean Martin, May 6, 1989. B in Elem. Edn., B in Spl. Edn., Ind. U. South Bend, 1995, M in Spl. Edn., 2002; Adminstrv. Lic., Ind. Wesleyan, Marion, 2006. Cert. emotional disabilities Ind. U. South Bend, 2000. Tchr. South Bend Cmty. Sch. Corp., Ind., 1995—2005; asst. women's basketball coach Ind. U. South Bend, 1995—; asst. prin. Harrison Primary Ctr., South Bend, 2005—. Recipient Tchr. of Yr., Harrison Primary Ctr., 2004. Methodist. Home: 23133 Arbor Pointe Dr South Bend IN 46628 Office: Harrison Primary Ctr 3302 W Western Ave South Bend IN 46619 Office Phone: 574-283-7300.

MARTIN, DONNA LEE, retired publishing company executive; b. Detroit, Aug. 7, 1935; d. David M. Paul and Lillian (Paul); m. Rex Martin, June 5, 1956; children: Justin, Andrew. BA, Rice U., 1957. Mng. editor trade dept. Appleton-Century-Crofts Co., N.Y.C., 1961-62; dir. publs. Lycoming Coll., Williamsport, Pa., 1966-68; editor Univ. Press of Kans., Lawrence, 1971-74; mng. editor Andrews McMeel Publ., Kansas City, Mo., 1974-80, v.p., editorial dir., 1980-95, v.p., editor-at-large, 1995-98; v.p. Universal Press Syndicate, Kansas City, 1980-98. Lectr. U. Mo., Kansas City, Johnson County Cmty. Coll., Kans.; free-lance writer, editor; cons. editor Kans. City Star Books. Author: (adaptation) Charles Dickens' A Christmas Carol: Adapted for Theatre; co-author (with Melissa Hayden) The Nutcracker Ballet; contbr. articles to profl. jours. Named Disting. Alumna Rice U., 1990. Mem. Ctrl. Exchange (Kansas City), The Groucho Club (London), Phi Beta Kappa. Home: 6810 W 66th Ter Shawnee Mission KS 66202-4147 Business E-Mail: donnamartin@kc.rr.com.

MARTIN, DOROTHY SUE, secondary education educator, counselor; b. Hearne, Tex., Aug. 27, 1945; d. John Bud and Jimmie (Stroud) M. BS, Sam Houston State U., 1967; MEd, U. Alaska, 1988. Lic. tchr., counselor, Tex., Alaska. Tchr. Wharton (Tex.) Ind. Sch. Dist., 1967-69; tchr., coach Taylor Jr. High Sch., Fairbanks, Alaska, 1969-79; tchr., counselor Eielson High Sch. Fairbanks North Star Borough, 1980—, coach, 1980-85. Mem. com. on curriculum Fairbanks North Star Sch. Dist., 1969—, com. on phys. plant usage, com. student handbook, 1991—; Natural Helper coord. State of Alaska, Eielson High Sch., Fairbanks, 1988—, dist. coord. Sch. to Work, 1998-2000. Author: (pamphlet) Eielson Physical Education, 1980. Commr. Timberlane Rd. Svc. Area, North Pole, Alaska, 1988—. Grantee Fairbanks Sch. Dist., 1991. Mem. NEA, AAHPER, Phys. Edn. Assn. Tchrs. (v.p. 1990). Office: Eielson Jr/Sr High Sch Industrial Ave North Pole AK 99705

MARTIN, DUY-THU PHAN-DINH, obstetrician, gynecologist; b. Can Tho, Vietnam, Dec. 20, 1972; arrived in US, 1982; d. Phu Tan and Nhan Tp Dinh; m. Anthony Andrew Martin, May 6, 2006. BS, Coll. William & Mary, Williamsburg, Va., 1995; MD, Ea. Va. Med. Sch., Norfolk, 1999. FACOG Am. Coll. Ob/Gyn, 2005. Pvt. practice, Knoxville, Tenn., 2005—. Recipient Benjamin Stoddert Ewell award, Coll. William & Mary, 1995, Outstanding Tchg. award, Berlex, 2001, Outstanding Manuscript, York Hosp., 2002, Donald Richardson Meml. Prize, Am. Coll. Ob/Gyn, 2002. Fellow: Am. Coll. Ob/Gyn (life), Phi Beta Kappa (life); mem.: Mortar Bd. (life). Office: Dr Martin's Ob/Gyn 939 E Emerald Ave Ste 801 Knoxville TN 37917 Office Phone: 865-546-6721. Office Fax: 865-546-6724.

MARTIN, EVELYN G., small business owner; b. Flemington, W.Va., July 19, 1928; d. William Bee Smith and Olga Estella Reed; m. James Eugene Martin, Feb. 18, 1956 (dec.); children: William V., Robert E. BS, Salem Coll., W.Va., 1950; MS, W.Va. U., Morgantown, 1956. Cons. dietitian various hosps. and nursing homes, W.Va., 1960—72; Title VII nutrition dir. North Ctrl. Cmty. Action, Fairmont, W.Va., 1967—72; adminstrv. dietitian W.Va. U., 1972—79; dietitian Marion Health Care Hosp., Fairmont, 1979—94; co-owner S&M Glass Inc., Fairmont, 1984—. Sec. W.Va. Dietetic Assn., Charleston, 1974. Mem.: AAUW (pres. Fairmont br. 2001—), Lions (sec./treas., pres.), Soroptomist (pres. 1998—2000). Democrat. Methodist. Avocations: walking, quilting, crossword puzzles, travel, volunteer work. Home: 1208 Parkside Dr Fairmont WV 26554 Office: SUM Glass Inc 204 Mortantown Ave Fairmont WV 26554

MARTIN, FELICIA DOTTORE, mental health services professional, marriage and family therapist; b. Cleve., July 7, 1956; d. Vincent James and Roseanne Dottore; m. William Arthur Martin, Mar. 26, 1983; children: Trevor Matthew, Trent Michael. BA in Psychology, Calif. State U., 1983; MA in Marriage Family Therapy, Pacific Oaks Coll., 1995. Lic. marriage family therapist Calif., 1999. Therapist Florence Crittenton Svcs., Fullerton, Calif., 1995—99, clin. dir., 1999—2001; dir. mental health South Coast Children's Soc., Costa Mesa, 2001—. 1st v.p. Oxford Acad. Instrumental Music Program, Cypress, Calif., 2000—03; mem. of com. Team for Bldg. com. Partnerships, 2003—. Mem.: Am. Assn. Marriage and Family Therapists. Home: 5023 Cherrywood Dr Oceanside CA 92056-2017 Office: South Coast Childrens Society 3100 S Harbor Blvd Ste 200 Santa Ana CA 92704-6810 Personal E-mail: fdm777@aol.com. E-mail: fmartin@sccskids.org.

MARTIN, FRANCES LEE, nursing educator; b. Filbert, Pa., Sept. 17; d. Mack and Nellie (Allen0 Marshall; 1 child, Tanya. Diploma in nursing, Fordham Hosp., 1951; BSN, Hunter Coll., 1957, MSN, 1964; MS in Edn., Bklyn. Coll., 1974. Instr. nursing Cumberland Hosp., Bklyn., 1959-61; substitute tchr. Sara Hale Vocat. HS, Bklyn., 1963-64; instr. Meth. Sch. Nursing, Bklyn., 1964-70; asst. prof., then assoc. prof. Coll. S.I., NY, 1970—; instr. Coney Island Hosp., Bklyn., 1989. Mem. adv. bd. CRTS South Beach Psychiat. Ctr., S.I., NY, 1981—; mem. adv. bd. NY Urban League, S.I., 1988—, vice chairperson, 1990—; clin. cons. Regents Coll., Mineola, NY, 1988—; presenter in field. Author: Nurse Test Medical-Surgical Nursing, 1992; contbg. author: Nursing Decision, 1982; contbr. articles to profl. publs. Vol. tutor First Ctrl. Bapt. Ch., S.I., NY, 2005. Mem. ANA (cert.), AAUP, NAACP, Assoc. Degree Orgn. Nursing Edn., Nat. League Nursing, NY Urban League, Sigma Theta Tau. Democrat. Avocations: theater, tennis, reading, sewing. Home: 27 Kathy Pl Apt 3A Staten Island NY 10314-5920 Office: Coll SI 715 Ocean Ter Staten Island NY 10301-4542

MARTIN, GRACE BURKETT, psychologist; b. Sumter, S.C., Aug. 27, 1939; d. John Hazel and Grace Thomasine (Briggs) Burkett; BA magna cum laude, Armstrong State Coll., 1976; MS, Fla. State U., 1979, PhD, 1980; m. H. Russell Martin, Jr., Oct. 9, 1957; children— H. Russell, Carolyne, Melinda. Lic. psychologist. Hist. preservationist, 1962—; dir. Christian edn. St. Thomas Parish, Savannah, Ga., 1970-74; prof. psychology Armstrong State Coll., Savannah, 1980-2001, prof. emeritus, 2002-, dept. head psychology, dir. gen. studies degree program; head. divsn. social and behavioral scis., interim dean arts and scis.; pres. Orgn. Cons.; lectr.; radio and TV appearances. Author, collaborator nat. and cross-nat. studies of women and work; co-author UNESCO manual for nat. leaders and policy makers; cons. editor Jour. Supplementary Abstract Svc., 1980, 81. Bd. dirs. Coastal Empire YMCA, 1972-75; mem. Savannah Symphony Soc.; mem. commn. on mission Episcopal Diocese of Ga., 1972-74, mem. liturg. commn., 1972-74, also lic. lay reader; pres. Operation Return, 1972-76. Named Mrs. Ga., 1962. Mem. Am. Psychol. Assn., Am. Psychol. Soc. (charter), Southeastern Psychol. Assn., Soc. Indsl. Organizational Psychology, Am. Mgmt. Assn., Nat. Assn. Women Deans and Administrators, Ga. Assn. Women Deans and Adminstrators, Commerce Club Savannah (charter), Ga. Ednl. Research Assn. Home: 50 Shipwatch Rd Savannah GA 31410-2950 Personal E-mail: martingrace@comcast.net.

MARTIN, HELEN ELIZABETH, educational consultant; b. West Chester, Pa., Feb. 19, 1945; d. Thomas Edwin and Elizabeth Temple (Walker) M. BA, The King's Coll., NYC, 1967; MEd, West Chester U., 1970; postgrad., Goethe Inst., Freiberg, Fed. Republic Germany, 1979, Oxford U., Eng., 1979. Nat. bd. cert. tchr. adolescent/young adult sci., 2000. Tchr. math. and sci. Unionville (Pa.) H.S., 1967-99; ret., 1999; ednl. cons. Adj. prof. West Chester U., 1989—; mem. Carnegie Forum on Edn. and the Economy. Mem. Pa. Rep. State Com., 1982-90, Rep. Com. of Chester County, 1984-94. Named Alumna of Yr., The King's Coll., 1987; recipient State Presdl. award, 1989, Frank G. Brewer Civil Air Patrol Meml. Aerospace award, 1989, Outstanding Achievement award U.S. Dept. Commerce, 1993; Bus. Week/Challenger Seven fellow, 1991. Fellow Am. Sci. Affiliation; mem. AAAS, Nat. Bd. Profl. Tchg. Stds. (founding dir., 1987-94), Satellite Educators Assn. (pres. 1990-2000), Nat. Sci. Tchrs. Assn., Nat. Coun. Tchrs. Math., Nat. Sci. Tchrs. Assn. (internat. lectr. 1987), Assn. for Sci. Edn. in U.K. (internat. lectr. 1987). Home: PO Box 605 Unionville PA 19375-0605 E-mail: SatTeacher@aol.com.

MARTIN, HELEN LOENE, minister; b. Muleshoe, Tex., Dec. 27, 1941; d. Benjamin Franklin and Vella Dean Hays; m. K. Ray Martin, Feb. 2, 1960; children: David (Deceased) Ray, Daniel Dean. Pastoral Counsel, Inst. of Pastoral Counseling, Akron, Ohio, 1994; Assoc. of Bibl. Sci., Harvest Conf. (IPHC), Wichita, Kans., 1994. Ordained minister Pentecostal Ch., 1993. Care pastor Abundant Life Ch., Hutchinson, Kans., 1988—93; evangelist Internat. Pentecostal Holiness Ch., Okla., 1994—98; asst. conf. supt. Harvest Conf., Wichita, Kans., 1996—2000, evangelism dir., 2006—, bd. dirs., 2005; care pastor Eagles Nest Ch., Wichita, Kans., 1997—99; ch. planter, pastor New Beginnings Christian Fellowship Ch., Minneapolis, Kans., 2001—. Ch. planter (Russia) IPHC, Okla., 1994; missionary to Mex. Abundant Life Ch., Hutchinson, Kans., 1987—91; missionary to Nicaragua Internat. Pentecostal Holiness Ch., Okla., 1998. Editor: (ch.newspaper) A Conversation with God. Bd. dirs. Love Inc., Minneapolis, Kans., 2004—. Recipient Svc. and Outstanding Acad. award, Harvest Conf., 2000, Servant's award, 2006, Appreciation award, 2006. International Pentecostal Holiness Church. Avocation: piano.

MARTIN, IRIS WEBER, retired minister; b. Yakima, Wash., Nov. 23, 1922; d. Walter Herman and Ada Clerice (Canfield) Weber; life ptnr. Adrian Ellis Martin, Sept. 10, 1954 (dec.); children: Joyce Emily Martin Emery, Paul Walter, Noel Stephen. BS, U. Wash., Seattle, 1945; BD with hons., San Francisco Theol. Sem., San Anselmo, Calif., 1954, MA Christian Edn. with hons., 1955. Ordained Minister Presby. Ch., 1975. Parish worker Bd. Nat. Missions Presbyn. Ch., Tacoma, 1945—50; dir. Christian Edn. Trinity Reformed Ch., Kent, Wash., 1967—73, Fife Presbyn. Ch., Tacoma, 1973—75, asst. pastor, 1975—77; pastor Ch. of The Indian Fellowship, Tacoma, 1978—90, Dupont Cmty. Presbyn. Ch., Dupont, Wash., 1992—2001. Mem. com. on ministry Olympia Presbytery, S.W. Wash., camp dir., Woodland, Wash.; garden cons. fairs, flower shows, 1975—. Master Gardener, Wash. State U., Pyallup, 2002—. Mem.: Tacoma Orchid Soc., Pierce County Iris Soc. (pres., v.p. 1979—). Achievements include planting and supervision of a garden of bible plants, Olympia Presbytery Offices, Tillicum, Wash. Avocations: gardening, photography. Home: 9925 18th St Ct E Edgewood WA 98371

MARTIN, JACQUELINE BRIGGS, writer; b. Maine; m. Rich Martin; children: Sarah, Justin. Author: Bizzy Bones and Moosemouse, 1986, Bizzy Bones and the Lost Quilt, 1988, Bizzy Bones and Uncle Ezra, 1984, Button, Bucket, Sky, 1998, The Finest Horse in Town, 1992, Grandmother Bryant's Pocket, 1996 (Lupine award 1996), The Green Truck Garden Giveaway: A Neighborhood Story and Almanac, 1997, Good Times on Grandfather Mountain, 1992, Higgins Bend Song and Dance, 1997, Snowflake Bentley, 1998 (Caldecott Award 1999, Lupine Award 1998), Washing the Willow Tree Loon, 1995, The Lamp, The Ice and The Boat Called Fish, 2001, The Water Gift and the Pig of the Pig (Lupine award 2003), 2003, On Sand Island, 2003. Office: Houghton Mifflin Co Juvenile Dept Boston MA 02116

MARTIN, JANET LYNN, health facility administrator; b. Spokane, Wash., Aug. 9, 1957; d. Donald Melvin Reynolds and Judith Marie (Gorman) Daly; m. Steven Arnold Martin, June 26, 1976; children: Joseph, Randall, Richard. ADN, Spokane C.C., 1979; BSN, SUNY, Albany, 1989. Cert. emergency nurse. Staff RN critical coronary intensive care unit (CICU) Sacred Heart Med. Ctr., Spokane, 1979-83, staff RN emergency, 1983-89, asst. nurse mgr., 1989-95, dir., 1995—. Mem. Emergency Nurses' Assn. (trauma nurse core course instr. 1985—). Avocations: waterskiing, gardening, reading. Home: 23924 N Westlake Dr Nine Mile Falls WA 99026-8711 Office: Sacred Heart Med Ctr PO Box 2555 101 W 8th Ave Spokane WA 99204-2307

MARTIN, JEAN H., retired interior designer; d. Irving William and Doris Gaffield Howland; m. Raymond Ray Martin, Feb. 28, 1976; children from previous marriage: Darron G. Spalty, Maren Jane Spalty Halliday. At, Rider Coll., Trenton, N.J., Rochester Inst. Tech., N.Y. Lic. interior designer State of Fla. Interior designer Lauer Furniture, Rochester, NY, 1962—67; sr. interior designer Sibley's, 1967—79, Burderes, Boca Raton, Fla., 1979—92; owner Jean H. Martin Interiors, Boca Raton and Weeki Wachee, 1992—; ret., 1995. Design advisor Schlegel Mfg., Rochester, NY, Gioia Mfg., Case Hoyt Printing, George Ballard, Inc., Norman Matthews, Loxahatchie Club, CEO Federated Dept. Stores. Prin. works include NY Lab. Supply, NYC, Ian Calder Nat. Enquirer, Hypaloso, Fla., Mr. and Mrs. John Graeme residence, 1985, Johnson-Higgens de Venezuela. Sec. and v.p. Rochester C. of C., 1962—79; pres. and charter mem. Satin Wood Twig Rochester North Side Hosp., 1962—79; charter mem. Opus Soc. Boca Raton Symphony, Boca Raton and Ft. Lauderdale, 1979—, Boca Mus. Art, 1979—. Named Most Outstanding Designer, Burdines, 1985; named to Rochester Jr. League Showcase, 1980. Mem.: Am. Soc. Interior Designers, Philanthropic Ednl. Orgn., Glen Lakes Country Club, Stafford Country Club. Avocations: golf, skiing, bowling, big game fishing.

MARTIN, JEANINE KAY, retired elementary school educator; d. John Albert and Virginia Grace (Smith) Hawthorne; m. Earl John Martin, June 20, 1962; children: Gregory, Christine. BA, Marycrest Coll., Davenport, Iowa, 1965. Cert. early childhood educator Iowa, reading endorsement Iowa. Kindergarten tchr. Bettendorf Schs., Iowa, 1958—60; 1st grade tchr. DeWitt Cmty. Schs., 1960—68; presch. tchr. Sugar Plum Presch., 1st Congl. Ch., DeWitt, 1971—78; Title I reading tchr., reading recovery tchr. West Liberty Cmty. Sch., Iowa, 1984—2003; ret., 2003. Pres. West Liberty Edn. Assn., 1990; coord. bus./sch. book giveaway West Liberty Schs., 1998—2005; activities coord. West Liberty Children's Festival, 2004—06; pres. ladies bd. West Liberty Country Club, 1981; pres. West Liberty Choral Aux., 1987; chmn. West Liberty After Prom, 1987; organizer, coord. Treats for Troops, West Liberty, 2003; Sunday sch. tchr. De Witt and West Liberty, 1976—81; bd. dirs. Iowa Assn. Edn. of Young Children, Des Moines, 1973—75, Louis and Ida Rich Day Care Ctr., West Liberty, 1990—95, West Liberty Cmty. Ctr., West Liberty, 1995—. Named Reading Tchr. of Yr., Old Capitol Reading Assn., 2003, Rotary Citizen of Month, West Liberty Rotary Club, 2004; recipient award, Carver Trust, 1998, Comdr.'s award for pub. svc., Dept. of Army, Camp Dodge, Johnston, Iowa, 2005, Cmty. Svc. award, West Liberty C. of C., 2005; grantee, West Liberty Schs. Found., 1997—2002. Mem.: Nat. Reading Recovery Assn., Nat. TTT Soc. (pres. 1977, 1995, 2000). Avocations: golf, reading, travel.

MARTIN, JERRI WHAN, public relations executive; b. Aurora, Ill., Oct. 21, 1931; d. Forest Livings and Geraldeane Jeanette (Cutler) Whan; m. Charles L. Martin (div.); children: Vicki, Bill, Erica, Kevin. BMus, Wichita State U., 1952. Co-owner Sta. KCNY, San Marcos, Tex., 1957-70; correspondent Austin Am.-Statesman, 1959-85; co-owner Sta. KWFT, Wichita Falls, Kans., 1965-96. Cons. U.S. Office Econ. Opportunity, Austin, 1966-68, Tex. Ednl. Found., Inc., San Marcos, 1975—. Pres. Hays County Women's Polit. Caucus, Tex., 1985-89; officer Tex. Women's Polit. Caucus, 1990; del. State Dem. Convs., Dallas, Houston, 1982, 84, 96; bd. dirs. Ctrl. Tex. Higher Edn. Authority, San Marcos, 1982-87, Scheib Opportunity Ctr., San Marcos, 1983-90; bd. dirs., chm. Edwards Underground Water Dist., San Antonio, 1985-96; trustee Tex. Ednl. Found., Inc., 1991—; chair Citizen Rev. Commn., 2000—. Named Outstanding Reporter in Tex., Tex. Legis., 1960; inducted into San Marcos Hall of Fame, 1993; recipient Extraordinary Svc. award Trust for Pub. Land, 1994. Mem. San Marcos C. of C., LWV, Hays Women's Ctr. Office: Tex Ednl Found Inc PO Box 1108 San Marcos TX 78667-1108 Home: 504 Goodwin Dr Richardson TX 75081-5601

MARTIN, JOAN CALLAHAM, psychologist, educator; b. N.Y.C., June 9, 1930; d. Jack Alfred and Mary Louise (Williams) Callaham; m. Donald Charles Martin, Aug. 15, 1959; children: Walter Michael, Steven Raymond. BA, U. Fla., 1959; MS, Fla. State U., 1962, PhD, 1965. Postdoctoral trainee Duke U. Med. Center, Durham, N.C., 1965-67; postdoctoral fellow Duke U. Med. Center (Center for Aging and Human Devel.), 1967-69, asst. prof. psychiatry and research asso. anatomy, 1969-71; adminstrv. fellow NIH, Bethesda, Md., 1971-72; asso. prof. psychiatry and behavioral sci. U. Wash., Seattle, 1972-79; asso. dean U. Wash. (Grad. Sch.), 1977-80, prof./research coordinator psychiatry and behavioral scis., 1979—; clinical psychologist, 1990—. Mem. gen. research support review com., div. research resources NIH, 1980—; cons. Nat. Cancer Inst., NIH, 1971-79; lectr. Mem. editorial bd. Neurobehavioral Toxicology and Teratology; contbr. articles to profl. jours.; referee: Sci., Physiology and Behavior, Pharm. Biochem. and Behavioral Psychopharmacology. Mem. Am. Psychol. Assn., N.Y. Acad. Sci., Teratology Soc., Psychonomic Soc., Assn. Women in Sci., Am. Assn. Univ. Profs. (pres. 1993-95), Sigma Xi. Office: U Wash Dept Psychiatry & Behavioral Seattle WA 98195-0001

MARTIN, JOANNE, social sciences educator; b. Salem, Mass., Sept. 25, 1946; d. Richard Drake and Nathalie (Ashton) M.; m. Beaumont A. Sheil, July 9, 1977; 1 child, Beaumont Martin Sheil. BA, Smith Coll., 1968; PhD in Social Psychology, Harvard U., 1977; PhD in Econs. and Bus. Adminstrn. (hon.), Copenhagen Bus. Sch., 2001; PhD (hon.), Vrije U., Amsterdam, 2005. Assoc. cons. McBer & Co. (formerly Behavior Sci. Ctr. of Sterling Inst.), 1968-70, dir. govt. mktg., 1970-72; asst. prof. orgnl. behavior Grad. Sch. Bus., Stanford (Calif.) U., 1977-80; assoc. prof. grad. sch. bus. Stanford U., 1980-91, prof. grad. sch. bus., 1991—, dir. doctoral programs, grad. sch. bus., 1991-95, Fred H. Merrill prof. orgn. behavior and, by courtesy, sociology, 1996—. Sec. faculty adv. bd. Stanford U., 1995—96, vice chair adv. bd., 1996—97; vis. scholar Australian Grad. Sch. Mgmt. U. N.S.W., 1989—90, Copenhagen Bus. Sch., 1998, 2004; vis. scholar dept. psychology Sydney (Australia) U., 1989—90; Ruffin fellow bus. ethics Darden Grad. Sch. Bus. Adminstrn. U. Va., 1990; mem. bd. advisors iMahal, 1990—; bd. dirs. C.P.P., Inc., 1993—2003; mem. internat. adv. bd. Internat. Ctr. for Rsch. in Orgnl. Discourse, Strategy and Change; Bus. Sch. rep. Stanford U., 1995—; vis. scholar U. Tech. Sydney, 2004—05. Mem. editl. bd. Adminstrv. Sci. Qtrly., 1984—88, Jour. Social Issues, 1981—83, Acad. Mgmt. Jour., 1984—85, Social Justice Rsch., 1985—90, Jour. Mgmt. Inquiry, 1991—, Orgn., 1994—, Jour. Mgmt. Studies, 1996—2004, Gender, Work and Organization, 1998—, Orgn. Studies, 2003—, Scandinavian Jour. Mgmt., 2003—, consulting editor Internat. Jour. Mgmt. Reviews, 1998—; co-author: five books; contbr. over 60 articles to profl. jours. and edited books. Recipient Centennial medal for contbns. to soc. Harvard U. Grad. Sch. Arts and Scis., 2002; Lena Lake Forrest Rsch. fellowship Bus. and Profl. Women's Found., 1978, James and Doris McNamara Faculty fellowship Grad. Sch. of Bus., Stanford U.,

1990-91, Grad. Sch. Bus. Trust Faculty fellow, 2005-06. Fellow: APA, Am. Psychol. Soc., Acad. Mgmt. (nat. rep.-at-large 1983—85, divsn. program chair 1985—87, divsn. chair 1987—89, nat. bd. govs. 1992—95, we. divsn. Promising Young Scholar award 1982, Nat. Disting. Educator award 2000, We. Divsn. Disting. Scholar award 2003, Nat. Orgn. and Mgmt. Divsn. Disting. Scholar career achievement award 2005); mem.: Nat. Assn. Corp. Dirs. (adv. bd. 2000—04). Office: Stanford U Grad Sch Bus Littlefield Ctr 353 Stanford CA 94305 Office Phone: 650-723-4791.

MARTIN, JUDITH SYLVIA, journalist; b. Washington, Sept. 13, 1938; d. Jacob and Helen (Aronson) Perlman; m. Robert Martin, Jan. 30, 1960; children: Nicholas Ivor, Jacobina Helen. BA, Wellesley Coll., 1959; DHL (hon.), York Coll., 1985, Adelphi U., 1991. Reporter-critic, columnist Washington Post, 1960—83; syndicated columnist United Feature Syndicate, N.Y.C., 1978—; columnist Microsoft, 1996—. Critic-at-large Vanity Fair, 1983—84. Author: The Name on the White House Floor, 1972, Miss Manners' Guide to Excruciatingly Correct Behavior, 1982, Gilbert, 1982, Miss Manners' Guide to Rearing Perfect Children, 1984, Common Courtesy, 1985, Style and Substance, 1986, Miss Manners' Guide for the Turn-of-the-Millennium, 1989, Miss Manners on (Painfully Proper) Weddings, 1996, Miss Manners Rescues Civilization, 1996, Miss Manners' Basic Training: Communications, 1997, Miss Manners' Basic Training: Eating, 1997, Miss Manners' Basic Training: The Right Thing to Say, 1998, Miss Manners' Guide to Domestic Tranquility, 1999, Star-Spangled Manners, 2002, Miss Manners Guide to Excruciatingly Correct Behavior (Freshly Updated), 2005, No Vulgar Hotel, The Desire and Pursuit of Venice, 2007. Bd. dirs. Friends of Scuola San Rocco. Recipient Nat. Humanities medal, 2005. Mem. Cosmos Club, Literary Soc. Office: United Feature Syndicate 200 Madison Ave Fl 4 New York NY 10016-3911 Business E-Mail: MissManners@unitedmedia.com.

MARTIN, JUNE JOHNSON CALDWELL, journalist; b. Toledo, Oct. 06; d. John Franklin and Eunice Imogene (Fish) Johnson; m. Erskine Caldwell, Dec. 21, 1942 (div. Dec. 1955); 1 child, Jay Erskine; m. Keith Martin, May 5, 1966. AA, Phoenix Jr. Coll., 1941; BA, U. Ariz., 1943, 59; postgrad., Ariz. State U., 1939, 40. Freelance writer, 1944—; columnist Ariz. Daily Star, Tucson, 1956-59, 70-94, book reviewer, 1970-94, co-founder Ann. Book and Author Event; editor Ariz. Alumnus mag., Tucson, 1959-70; ind. book reviewer, audio tape columnist Tucson, 1994—; coord. S.W. Books of Yr. sponsored by Tucson Pima Pub. Libr., Ariz., 2000—. Panelist, co-producer TV news show Tucson Press Club, 1954-55, pres., 1958. Contbg. author: Rocky Mountain Cities, 1949; contbr. articles to World Book Ency., and various mags. Mem. Tucson CD Com., 1961; vol. campaigns of Samuel Goddard, U.S. Rep. Morris Udall, U.S. amb. and Ariz. gov. Raul. Castro. Recipient award Nat. Headliners Club, 1959, Ariz. Press Club award, 1957-59, 96, Am. Alumni Coun., 1966, 70. Mem. Nat. Book Critics Circle, Ariz. Press Women, Jr. League of Tucson, Tucson Urban League, PEN U.S.A. West, Planned Parenthood So. Ariz., Tucson Press, Pi Beta Phi. Democrat. Methodist. Home: Desert Foothills Sta PO Box 65388 Tucson AZ 85728-5388

MARTIN, KATHLEEN SUZANNE, librarian; b. San Diego, Nov. 9, 1950; d. Theodore Finley and Betty (Balton) M.; m. William Scherr Renninger; children: Elizabeth Martin, Theodore Renninger, Margaret Renninger. AB, San Diego State U., 1973; MLS, UCLA, 1978. Libr. Ginsburg, Feldman & Bress, Washington, 1980-84, Cohen & Uretz, Washington, 1984-85, Davis, Polk & Wardwell, Washington, 1985-94; head libr. Morgan, Lewis & Bockius LLP, Washington, 1994—2000; dir. librs. McKenna Long & Aldridge LLP, Washington, 2005—. Editor: (newsletter) Law Library Lights, 1985-86; contbr. articles to jours. Mem. Spl. Librs. Assn., Am. Assn. Law Librs. (bd. dirs.), Law Librs. Soc. Washington (rec. sec. 1987-89, pres. 1990-91). Office: McKenna Long & Aldridge LLP 1900 K St NW Washington DC 20006 E-mail: kmartin@mckennalong.com.

MARTIN, KATHRYN A., academic administrator; Dean Sch. Fine and Performing Arts Wayne State U., Detroit; chancellor U Minn, Duluth, 1995—. Office: Univ Minnesota-Duluth Office of Chancellor Admin Bldng 1049 University Dr Duluth MN 55812-3011

MARTIN, KELLI LYNNE, education educator; b. Auburn, Wash., May 31, 1972; d. Judy Kay and Stephen Vincent Johnson; m. Jeffrey Rober Martin, June 22, 2002; children: Sierra McKenzie, Logan Jeffrey. B in Math., Oreg. State U., Corvallis, OR, 1995. Tchr. Mapleton H.S., Mapleton, Oreg., 1997—2003, Pleasant Hill H.S., Pleasant Hill, Oreg., 2003—. Recipient Tchr. of Yr., Mapleton H.S., 1998. Home: 85217 Winding Way Pleasant Hill OR 97455 Office: Pleasant Hill HS 36386 Hwy 58 Pleasant Hill OR 97455 Office Phone: 541-736-0719. Business E-Mail: kmartin@lane.k12.or.us.

MARTIN, KELLIE (NOELLE), actress; b. Riverside, Calif., Oct. 16, 1975; Movie and motion picture actress. Actress T.V. series Life Goes On, 1989, (voice) Taz-Mania, 1992, Christy, 1994-1995, Crisis Ctr., 1997, ER, 1998-2000, Fiona, 2002, others; movies and TV movies include Jumpin' Jack Flash, 1986, Secret Witness, 1988, Troop Beverly Hills, 1989, Matinee, 1993, If Someone Had Known, 1995, Her Last Chance, 1996, On The Edge of Innocence, 1997, About Sarah, 1999, All You Need, 2001, Malibus Most Wanted, 2003, Open House, 2003; voice characterization A Goofy Movie, 1995, also T.V. guest appearances. Office: c/o The Gersh Agy 232 N Canon Dr Beverly Hills CA 90210-5302

MARTIN, KIM See MARTH, MARY

MARTIN, KRISTEN LACEY, secondary school educator; b. Rome, Ga., Feb. 12, 1982; m. Matt Martin, Aug. 2, 2003; children: Tyler, Andrew. BS, Shorter Coll., Rome, Ga., 2004. Tchr. Adairsville H.S., Ga., 2004—. Mem.: Ga. Assn. Educators. Office: Adairsville HS 519 Old Hwy 41 Adairsville GA 30103 Office Phone: 770-606-5841. E-mail: kristen.martin@bartow.k12.ga.us.

MARTIN, KRYSSI WYCKOFF, playwright, educator; b. San Pedro, Calif., Oct. 10, 1965; d. Gary Leroy and Judy Ann Wyckoff; m. James Lyndon Martin, May 27, 1989; children: Genoa Pauline, Harper Jaime. BA, Colo. U., Denver. Cert. tchr. Colo., 2006. Artistic dir. Genoa's Mother Presents, Denver, 1996—2000. Author: (play) Paul's Place (nominee Denver Drama Critics Cir. award, 1999), Legalize Wisdom (produced by Edward Albee, 1991). Office Phone: 303-347-7700. Personal E-mail: kwmartin@comcast.net.

MARTIN, LAURA KEIDAN, lawyer; b. Detroit, Oct. 8, 1964; BA, U. Mich., 1986; JD, Harvard U., 1989. Bar: Ill. 1989. Ptnr. Katten Muchin Rosenman LLP, Chgo. Mem.: ABA, Nat. Health Lawyers Assn., Ill. Assn. Healthcare Attys. (bd. dirs., pres.), Chgo. Bar Assn. (chair antitrust law com. 2004—05). Office: Katten Muchin Rosenman LLP 525 W Monroe St Chicago IL 60661 Office Fax: 312-902-5487, 312-577-8951. E-mail: laura.martin@kattenlaw.com.

MARTIN, LAURABELLE, property manager; b. Jackson County, Minn., Nov. 3, 1915; d. Eugene Wellington and Mary Christina (Hansen) M. BS, Mankato State U., 1968. Tchr. rural schs., Renville County, Minn., 1936-41, 45-50, Wabasso (Minn.) Pub. Sch., 1963-81; pres. Renville Farms and Feed Lots, 1982-86. Author: Hist. Biography of Joseph Renville, 1996; poet: Nat. Libr. Poetry (Silver Cup award, 2003). Pres. Wabasso (Minn.) Edn. Assn., 1974-75, publicity chmn., 1968-74; sec. and publicity agt. Hist. Renville Preservation Com., 1978-86; publicity chmn., sec. Town and Country Boosters, Renville, 1982-83. Recipient Outstanding Achievement in Poetry Award, Internat. Soc. Poets. Mem. Genealogy Soc. Renville County, Am. Legion Aux. Democrat. Lutheran. Avocations: antique furniture, travel, sewing, poetry. Home and Office: 334 NW 1201st Rd Holden MO 64040-9378

MARTIN, LESLIE, performing arts association administrator; 3d v.p. Am. Dance Guild, N.Y.C. Office: American Dance Guild Inc PO Box 2006 Lenox Hill Station New York NY 10021

MARTIN, LINDA GAYE, demographer, economist; b. Paris, Ark., Dec. 17, 1947; d. Leslie Paul and Margie La Verne (Thomas) Martin. BA in Math., Harvard U., 1970; MPA, Princeton U., 1972, PhD in Econs., 1978; DHL (hon.), Marlboro Coll., 2002; D in Pub. Policy (hon.), Rand Grad. Sch., 2006. Dir. mgmt. info. sr. ctrs. bur. purchased social svcs. for adults City of N.Y., 1972—74; rsch. assoc., rsch. dir. U.S. Ho. of Reps. Select Com. on Population, Washington, 1977—79; rsch. assoc. East-West Population Inst., Honolulu, 1979—89, asst. dir., 1982—84; asst. prof. econs. U. Hawaii, Honolulu, 1979—81, assoc. prof., 1981—89, prof., 1989; dir. com. on population Nat. Acad. Scis., Washington, 1989—93; dir. domestic rsch. divsn., v.p. RAND, Santa Monica, Calif., 1993—95, v.p. for rsch. devel., 1995—99; pres. Population Coun., N.Y.C., 1999—2004; scholar in residence Inst. Medicine, 2004—. Neurosci. behavior and sociology of aging rev. com. Nat. Inst. on Aging, Bethesda, 1991—95; chair panel on aging in developing countries NAS, Washington, 1987, com. on population, 1993—99, panel on internat. aging data, 1999—2001; peer rev. oversight group NIH, 1998—2004. Editor: The ASEAN Success Story, 1987; co-editor: Demographic Change in Sub-Saharan Africa, 1993, The Demography of Aging, 1994, Racial and Ethnic Differences in the Health of Older Americans, 1997; contbr. articles to profl. jours. Mem. adv. coun. Woodrow Wilson Sch. Pub. and Internat. Affairs, Princeton U., NJ, 2000—. Recipient Fulbright Faculty Rsch. award, Coun. for Internat. Exch. of Scholars, 1988. Mem.: AAAS (adv. coun. 2003—06, chair elect social, econ. and polit. scis. sect. 2006—), Population Assn. Am. (bd. dir. 1991—93), Internat. Union for Sci. Study Population, Gerontol. Soc. Am. Democrat. Office: Inst of Medicine 500 5th St NW Rm 863 Washington DC 20001 Home: 3419 Mansfield Rd Falls Church VA 22041

MARTIN, LISA DEMET, lawyer; b. Pa., 1959; BA with honors, Wellesley Coll., 1980; JD, U. Pa., 1984. Bar: Mo. 1984. Ptnr., mem. exec. com. Bryan Cave LLP, St. Louis. Durant scholar Wellesley Coll. Mem. Phi Beta Kappa. Office: Bryan Cave LLP One Metropolitan Sq, Ste 3600 211 N Broadway Saint Louis MO 63102 Office Phone: 314-259-2125. E-mail: lmartin@bryancave.com.

MARTIN, LISA MARLENE, language educator; b. Syracuse, NY, Aug. 18, 1969; d. James Patterson and Evelyn Marlene (Pendleton) Kirk; m. John Costa Martin Jr., Oct. 7, 2000. Diploma in Spanish Lang., U. Internat. Melendecy Pelayo, Spain, 1998; BA in English, Hood Coll., 1993; BEd in Lang., Fairfield U., 2000. Bilingual tchr. Windham Pub. Schs., Willimantic, Conn., 2000—03; dual lang. tchr. New London (Conn.) Pub. Schs., 2003—. Vice chair St. Mary's Parish Coun., New London, 2006; bd. mem. Covenant Shelter, New London, 2006; bone marrow donor, 2005. Mem.: Nat. Assn. Bilingual Educators. Roman Cath. Home: 94 Riverview Ave New London CT 06320 Office: New London Pub Schs 134 Williams St New London CT 06320 Personal E-mail: lisamarlene@sbcglobal.net.

MARTIN, LORRAINE B., humanities educator; b. Utica, N.Y., Aug. 18, 1940; d. Walter G. and Laura Bolanowski; m. Charles A. Martin; children: Denise M. Stringer, Tracy M. Weinrich. Student, SUNY, Albany, 1958-60, postgrad., 1992—; BA in English and Edn. magna cum laude, Utica Coll. of Syracuse U., 1977; MS in Edn. and Reading, SUNY, Cortland, 1979, CAS in Edn. Adminstrn., 1984; postgrad., Syracuse U., 1990—. Cert. nursery, elem. tchr., secondary tchr., sch. adminstr. and supr., sch. dist. adminstr., reading specialist, N.Y. From tchr. to reading specialist, adminstrv. intern Poland (N.Y.) Cen. Sch., 1972-84; instr. reading Utica Coll. of Syracuse U., summer 1982-84; adminstr. spl. edn. and chpt. 1 remedial program Little Falls (N.Y.) City Sch. Dist., 1984-85; adminstr. adult and continuing edn. Madison-Oneida Bd. Coop. Ednl. Svcs., Verona, N.Y., 1985-86; dir. gen. programs Herkimer (N.Y.) Bd. Coop. Ednl. Svcs., 1986-88. Prof. emeritus English, SUNY SLN Internet English 1, children's lit., intro. edn., and honors program Herkimer County C.C. of SUNY, 1988—, participant brainstorming session on underprepared students SUNY, 1993, trainer tchr. performance evaluation program N.Y. State Dept. Edn., Herkimer, 1984, facilitator effective schs. program, 1986-88; co-developer edn. degree program Herkimer County C.C., developed summer reading, writing and study skills course for Bridge program; cons. Two-Yr. Coll. Devel. Ctr. SUNY, 1985-89; tchr. trainer for the Writing Process; tchr. asst. cert. program; cons. in field. Author: The Bridge Program-Easing the Transition from High School to College, 1990; editorial bd. Research and Teaching in Developmental Education; contbr. to Teaching Writing to Adults Tips for Teachers: An Idea Swap, 1989; textbook reviewer for pubs., 1993—. Vol. arts and crafts fair HCCC Found.; advisor Network for Coll. Re-Entry Adults; mem. Coun. of Profs., Parents Weekend Com. Recipient Leader Silver award for volunteerism 4-H Coop. Extension, Utica, 1980; HCCC Found. grantee, Writing grantee Readers's Digest. Mem. Internat. Reading Assn., Assn. Supervision and Curriculum Devel., Nat. Coun. Tchrs. English, Phi Kappa Phi. Avocations: English, current events, travel, public, cable and satellite television, computers. Home: 7099 Crooked Brook Rd Utica NY 13502-7203 Office: Herkimer County CC Internet Acad SUNY Reservoir Rd Herkimer NY 13350-1545

MARTIN, LYNN MORLEY, former secretary of labor; b. Evanston, Ill., Dec. 26, 1939; d. Lawrence William and Helen Catherine (Hall) Morley; children from a previous marriage: Julia Catherine, Caroline; m. Harry D. Leinenweber, Jan. 1987; stepchildren: Jane, John, Stephen, Justin, Thomas Leinenweber. BA, U. Ill., 1960. Former tchr. pub. schs.; mem. Ill. Ho. of Reps., 1977-79, Ill. Senate, 1979-81, 97th-101st Congresses from 16th Ill. Dist., 1981-91; sec. Dept. of Labor, Washington, 1991-93; faculty Northwestern U., 1993—2000. Bd. dirs. Dreyfus Funds, Procter & Gamble Co., Constellation Energy Group; mem. Coun. Fgn. Relations, Chgo. Network. Co-chmn. Bush-Quayle Presdl. campaign, 1988. Named one of Outstanding Young Women in Am., U.S. Jaycees; named Rep. Woman of the Yr., 1989; named a Mother of the Yr., Nat. Mother's Day Com., 1992; 1st woman elected to leadership post in House of Reps., 1982. Mem. AAUW, Jr. League, Phi Beta Kappa (hon. doctorate). Republican.

MARTIN, MARCELLA EDRIC, retired community health nurse; b. Rosedale, Miss., Jan. 25, 1930; d. Amos and Alma Allen; m. Reuben Clifton Martin, Jan. 25, 1969; children: Brunetta, Jacqueline, Cornell, Constance. Student, Marygrove Coll., Detroit, 1971; ADN, Highland Park Sch. Nursing, Mich., 1979; ThB, Cmty. Bible Coll., Detroit, 1968. Lic. LPN. Nurse VA Hosp., Ann Arbor, Mich., Crittendon Hosp., Detroit, Vis. Nurses Assn., Detroit. Instr. Charles H. Mason Bible Sch., Detroit, 1991—95; mem. C.O.G.I.C. Bus. owners Assn., 1982—. Author: Women Who Struggle, 2001; prodr.: (plays) And Didn't Those Knees Bow, 2004. Founder Prime of Life Adult Foster Care Home, 1979, Somebody's Got To Care Min., 2003; mem. Nat. Campaign Tolerance-The Wall of Tolerance, 2003; missionary over women Chs. of God in Christ, 1986—2002; vol. Redford Geriatric Home, Mich., 1999—. Named to Wall of Tolerance, New Civil Rights Meml. Ctr., Montgomery, Ala., 2003; recipient Spirit of Detroit award, City of Detroit, 1978, 2000, 2002, Disting. Citizen of Detroit award, 1980, Testimonial Resolution award, 1985. Mem.: Detroit Writers Guild. Democrat. Pentecostal Ch. Avocations: reading, writing. Home: 25332 Shiawassee Cir Apt 106 Southfield MI 48034 Personal E-mail: reumarone@comcast.net.

MARTIN, MARCIA D., science educator; d. James David Davis and Mary Louise Merriman; m. Francis P. Martin (div.); children: Marc Jon, Scott Anthony. Grad., U. So. Miss., Hattiesburg, 1986. Cert. tchr. Miss., Ark. Tchr. asst. remedial reading Pascagoula Sch. Dist., Miss., 1983—85; tchr. remedial reading Moss Point H.S., Miss., 1986—88; tchr. TLC program Pulaski County Sch. Dist., Little Rock, 1989—92, tchr. math., sci., 1992—95, 1995—97, tchr. 6th grade sci., 1997—. Sci. fair sponsor Daisy Bates Elem., Little Rock, 1989—93; tchr., curriculum writer MAST Program, Daisy Bates Elem., Little Rock, 1992—94; mem. West Nile Virus study County Sch. Dist., 2003. Recipient Disting. Leadership award, Ark. Leadership Acad., 1986; grantee, Pulaski County Sch. Dist., 2003. Mem.: Pulaski Assn. Classroom Tchrs. Avocations: classical piano, needlecrafts. E-mail: marcia_martin2002@yahoo.com.

MARTIN, MARCIA GRAY, retired architecture educator, artist, designer; b. Chgo., May 18, 1932; d. Harry Gray and Emma Bernstein; children: Elizabeth Anne, Charles Brandon. BArch, Ill. Inst. Tech., 1956; attended, De Paul Law Sch., 1957—58, U. Chgo., 1948—50; MA in Liberal Studies, North Ctrl. Coll., 1997. Freelance architect designer, Chgo., 1956—79; instr. architecture Coll. Dupage, Glen Ellyn, Ill., 1980—88, prof. architecture, 1989—2004, coord. architectural programs, 2000—04, prof. emeritis, 2004—; asst. art gallery Inspire Fine Art, Chgo., 2004—. Head traveling exhibition Coll. Dupage, 2001—; illustrator, artist Wheaton History Ctr., Ill., 1985—. Author: (books) Wheaton, USA, 1991, Architectural Drafting, 1997. Sec. Wheaton Historic Preservation Coun.; mem. City Wheaton Historic Com., Ill., 1992—93, Landmark Preservation Coun., Wheaton, 1990—2004; pres. Waterford Condominium Assn., Wheaton, 2005—; mem., bd. dirs. Dupage Art League, Wheaton, 1980—85; pres. bd. dirs. Wheaton Historic Preservation Coun.; bd. dirs. Waterford Condominium Assn., Wheaton. Recipient Wisdom & Coun. award, Wheaton Youth Outreach, 1990. Achievements include created one of the few undergraduate historic preservation education programs. Home: 455 W Front St #302 Wheaton IL 60187 E-mail: marciagraymartin@yahoo.com.

MARTIN, MARGARET GATELY, elementary school educator; b. Teaneck, N.J., July 24, 1928; d. Martin F. and Grace (Hammell) Gately; m. Phillips H. Martin, June 27, 1953 (div. 1977); children: Paul H., Patrick W., Thomas P. BA, Hunter Coll., 1950, MA, 1953. Cert. elem. tchr. N.Y. Tchr. Pub. Sch. # 5, Queens, N.Y., 1950-53, Wappingers Cen. Sch., Wappingers Falls, N.Y., 1953-55, Jamestown Pub. Schs., 1968—95; ret., 1996; tchr. Rainbow Child Devel. Ctr., Centerville, Ohio, 2006. Tchr. Wenzler Day Care and Learning Ctr., 2000—04; tchr. religious edn. St. Francis of Assissi, Centerville, Ohio, 2001; tchr. Mulberry Bush Day Care and Learning Ctr., 2004—, World of Young Learners Day Care and Learning Ctr., Centerville, Ohio, 2005. Citizen amb. to Pargue and Russia People to People, 1995; tchr. Sunday sch. Sts. Peter and Paul Ch., Jamestown, 1977—95. Mem.: AAUW (pres. 1980—82, 1992—94, Edn. Found. Program award 1985), NEA, Jamestown Tchrs. Assn. (membership chair 1976—78, sec. 1982—84), Green Thumb Garden Club (pres. 1986—88, 1996—, v.p. 1991—93, 1995—96), Jamestown Inter Club Coun. (pres. 1984—86, v.p. 1995—96, Woman of the Yr. 1991), Delta Kappa Gamma (corr. sec. 1988—90, membership chair 1991—94, v.p. 1994—96, pres. 1998—2000). Republican. Roman Catholic. Avocations: gardening, needlepoint, travel, theater, genealogy. Home: 3708 Wenzler Dr Kettering OH 45429-3366

MARTIN, MARIELA, secondary school educator; b. Tulare, Calif., Jan. 14, 1975; d. Jose Jesus and Delfina Ruiz; m. Alvaro Martin, July 1, 2006; 1 child, Yvette Nicole Munoz. BA in Liberal Arts, Calif. State U., Monterey Bay, 1999; MA in Marriage, Family Therapy, Pacific Oaks Coll., Pasadena, Calif., 2006. Cert. clear CLAD Calif. Tchr. Credential, 2000. Tchr. Lindsay Unified Sch. Dist., Calif., 2001—. Summer team leader Calif. Mini-Corps, Visalia, 2003; trainee Visalia Youth Svcs., Calif., 2005—. Recipient Outstanding Achievement award, Calif. Mini-Corps, 1996—97. Mem.: Calif. Assn. Marriage and Family Therapist (assoc.), Calif. Tchr.'s Assn. (assoc.). Democrat-Npl. Roman Catholic. Avocations: reading, travel, music, dance. Office Phone: 559-562-1311. E-mail: mruiz@lindsay.k12.ca.us, varosmija@sbcglobal.net.

MARTIN, MARILYN MANN, retired media specialist; b. Greencastle, Ind., July 14, 1939; d. Emil Albert and Edith Costa Mann; m. Max Lee Martin; children: Michael Lee, Melanie Sue Martin Boesen. BS, Ind. State U., 1960, MS, 1970, MS, 1988. Tchr. Latin, sch. libr. Danville H.S., Ind., 1960; libr., media specialist Greencastle H.S., 1971—2002, ret., 2002. Mem. tech. connections com. Greencastle H.S., 1997-98; mem. exec. bd. Stone Hills Libr. Svcs., Bloomington, Ind., 1990-96. Mem.: NEA, ASCD, Greencastle Classroom Tchrs. (scholarship chmn. 1985—2002), Assn. Ind. Media Educators (dist. advocacy chmn. 1998), Ind. Coop. Libr. Svcs., Ind. Libr. Found., Ind. Ret. Tchrs. Assn., Ret. Sr. Vol. Program, Nat. Home Gardening Club, Down-to-Earth Garden Club, Phi Kappa Phi. Avocations: gardening, reading, volunteering.

MARTIN, MARY WOLF, newspaper editor; b. Corwith, Iowa, Nov. 6, 1930; d. Henry Herbert and Mabel M. (Keeney) Wolf; m. Charles William Martin, Oct. 16, 1950; children: Stephen C., Neal J., Sally Martin Kindell. Grad. high sch., Weyauwega, Wis. Corr. Britt (Iowa) News Tribune, 1946-47; staff writer Wheaton (Ill.) Daily Jour., 1963-65; reporter, photographer Rhinelander (Wis.) Daily News, 1967-69, news editor, 1969-74, mng. editor, 1974-76, Neenah-Menasha Northwestern, Neenah, 1976-80; editor Oshkosh Northwestern, 1980-94. Pres. Fox Valley Press Club, Oshkosh, 1982; bd. dirs. Goodwill Industries N.E. Wis., Menasha, 1978-86, Rape Crisis Ctr., Oshkosh, 1981-85, Fox Valley Arts Alliance, Appleton, Wis., 1980-85, Fox Valley Cmty. Tech. Coll., Oshkosh, 1986-92; trustee Paine Art Ctr. Arboretum, Oshkosh, 1990-93. Named Woman of Yr., Bus. and Profl. Women, Rhinelander, 1975, Vol. of Yr., Sexual Abuse Svcs., Oshkosh, 1989. Mem. Wis. Assoc. Press Mng. Editors (pres. Milw. 1985-86), Nat. Assoc. Press Mng. Editors, Am. Soc. Newspaper Editors, Media-Law Com. Wis. Bar Assn. Roman Catholic. Avocations: reading, travel, photography, golf. Home: 898 County Road Q Pelican Lake WI 54463-9409

MARTIN, MARY-ANNE, art gallery owner; b. Hoboken, NJ, Apr. 26, 1943; d. Thomas Philipp and Ruth (Kelley) Martin; m. Henry S. Berman, June 9, 1963 (div. 1976); 1 child, Julia Coyote. Student, Smith Coll., 1961—63; BA, Barnard Coll., 1965. Head dept. painting Sotheby Parke Bernet, N.Y.C., 1971-78; founder Latin Am. dept. Sotheby's, N.Y.C., 1977, sr. v.p., 1978-82; pres. Mary Anne Martin, Fine Art, N.Y.C., 1982—. Mem.: Art Dealers Assn. Am. (sr. v.p.). Avocations: art collecting, scuba diving. Office: 23 E 73rd St New York NY 10021-3522 Business E-Mail: mail@mamfa.com.

MARTIN, MAUREEN FRANCES, medical educator; b. Montreal, Can., Feb. 12, 1950; d. George Alguire and Frances Dorothy May (Brenner) M. BS, Concordia U., 1978; MD, McGill U., 1982. Fellowship in hepatobiliary surgery Lahey Clinic, Boston, 1988; fellowship in transplantation New England Deaconess Hosp., Boston, 1989; lectr. in anatomy McGill U., Montreal, 1984-88; instr. in surgery Harvard U., Boston, 1988-89; asst. prof. surgery U. Pitts., 1989-92; assoc. prof. surgery U. Iowa, Iowa City, 1992-99, dir. organ transplant, 1992-99; assoc. prof. surgery Harvard U., Boston, 1999—; chief divsn. liver surgery/transplantation, dir. Liver Ctr., Beth Israel Deaconess Med. Ctr., Boston, 1999—2002; chmn. surgery Kern Med. Ctr., Bakersfield, Calif., 2002—. Reviewer NIH, 1995, scientific advisor, 1994; principle investigator Cooperative Clin. Trials, Iowa City, 1994. Author: (with others) Current Trends in New Development, 1995; contbr. articles to profl. jours. Spkr. Rotary Club, Cedar Rapids, 1996, U. Iowa Alumni, Des Moines, 1996, Johns Hopkins, 1995; del. Citizen Amb. Program, Russia, 1995. Scholar Sandoz, 1990, McGill U., 1978-82, Concordia U., 1974-77. Mem. ACS, Midwest Surg. Assn., Am. Soc. of Transplant Surgeons, Am. Assn. for the Study of Liver Disease, Internat. Transplant Soc., United Network for Organ Sharing. Roman Catholic. Avocations: skiing, golf. Home: 2502 Twickenham Ct Bakersfield CA 93311- Office: 1830 Flower St Ste 3000 Bakersfield CA 93305-

MARTIN, MELANIE, music educator; b. Pikeville, Ky., July 7, 1978; d. Douglas Grant and Loretta Newsome Martin; m. Jason Garrett Potter, July 24, 2004. BA in Music Edn., Ea. Ky. U., 2000, MusM, 2004. Tchr. Pike County Bd. Edn., 2000—. Choir dir. Elem. Choir, Robinson, Ky., 2002—; camp counselor Camp Begomi, Pound, Va., 2005. Judge Miss Southwest Va. sect. Miss Teen USA Pageant, Abingdon, Va., 2005. Mem.: Music Educators Nat. Conf. Democrat. Office: George F Johnson Elem 2172 Long Fork Rd Virgie KY 41572

MARTIN, MELISSA CAROL, radiological physicist; b. Muskogee, Okla., Feb. 7, 1951; d. Carl Leroy and Helen Shirley (Hicks) Paden; m. Donald Ray Martin, Feb. 14, 1970; 1 child, Christina Gail. BS, Okla. State U., 1971; MS, UCLA, 1975. Cert. radiol. physicist Am. Bd. Radiology, radiation oncology Am. Bd. Med. Physics. Asst. radiation physicist Hosp. of the Good Samaritan, L.A., 1975-80; radiol. physicist Meml. Med. Ctr., Long Beach, Calif., 1980-83, St. Joseph Hosp., Orange, Calif., 1983-92, Therapy Physics, Inc., Bellflower, Calif., 1993—. Cons. in field. Editor: (book) Current Regulatory Issues in Medical Physics, 1992. Fund raising campaign divsn. mgr. YMCA, Torrance, Calif., 1988-92; dir. AWANA Youth Club-Guards Group, Manhattan Beach, Calif., 1984—. Named Dir. of Symposium, Am. Coll. Med. Physics, 1992. Fellow Am. Coll. Med. Physics (chancellor western region 1992-95, treas. 2004-05), Am. Assn. Physicists in Medicine (profl. coun. 1990-95, treas. 1998-2003, bd. dirs. 1994-2003), Am. Coll. Radiology (econs. com. 1992-95, govt. rels. com. 1998—, councilor at large 2001-, commn. on med. physics 2002-); mem. Calif. Med. Physics Soc. (treas. 1991-98), Am. Soc. for Therapeutic Radiology and Oncology, Health Physics Soc. (pres. So. Calif. chpt. 1992-93), Am. Brachytherapy Soc. Baptist. Avocation: christian youth group dir. Home: 507 Susana Ave Redondo Beach CA 90277-3953 Office Phone: 310-612-8127. Personal E-mail: melissamartin@compuserve.com. Business E-Mail: melissa@therapyphysics.com.

MARTIN, OLIVIA JEAN, social studies educator; b. L.A., Nov. 08; d. Henry and Stella Martin. BA in Clin./Physiol. Psychology, U. So. Calif., 1990; MA in Edn. Adminstrn., Azusa Pacific U., 2005. Mgr. Eastman West, Montebello/Buena Park, Calif.; asst. mgr. Hortman Jewelers; peer coll. tutor East LA Coll., Monterey Park, Calif., 1985—86; facilitator U. So. Calif.-Biomed. Rsch. Program, L.A., 1987—91; behavioral counselor, nutritional specialist Nutri Sys., West Covina, Calif.; tchr. asst. Franklin Adult H.S., L.A.; elem. tchr. L.A. Unified Sch. Dist., 1994—2001; asst. dir. curriculum L.A. Archdiocese/San Gabriel Mission H.S., 2001—02, sci. tchr., 2000—01; mid. sch. social studies and sci. tchr. Azusa (Calif.) Unified Sch. Dist., 2002—06, dist. mgmt. trainee, 2004—06. Participant Olive Crest Cruise for Kids, L.A., 2004; hon. mem. exec. bd. Azusa PTA Coun., 2004—06; fundraiser Corvettes United Spl. Wish Found., L.A., 1999—2005. Recipient Merit award, Gov. of Calif., 1998—2000, Congl. award, Rep. Edward Roybal, L.A., 1986, Best Facilitator AP Biology award, U. So. Calif., 1989. Mem.: ASCD, NEA, Calif. Assn. Bilingual Edn. (v.p. Azusa Canyon chpt.), Nat. Coun. Social Studies, Assn. Calif. Supts. and Adminstrs., Corvettes Ltd. Club, Phi Lambda Theta. Republican. Roman Catholic. Avocations: racquetball, auto shows, auto racing. Home: PO Box 80892 San Marino CA 91118-9982

MARTIN, PAULA S., principal; b. Rumford, Maine, May 31, 1951; d. Gerard Joseph and Eleanor Helen Martin; m. Gary Michael Fishbeck. BS in Edn., U. Maine, Gorham, 1973; MA in Edn., Framingham State Coll., Mass., 1980; Edn. Specialist, U. Minn., Mpls., 2001. Lic. print. K-12 Minn. Tchr. Cape Elizabeth Pub. Schs., Maine, 1973—76, Wellesley Pub. Schs., Mass., 1976—93, Orono Pub. Schs., Minn., 1993—95, curriculum dir., 1995—2000, prin., 2003—, Wayzata Pub. Schs., Wayzata, Minn., 2000—03. Author: Giants: A Study in Geometry/Measurement, 1992, Elementary Number Sense Explorations, 1991. Recipient Presdl. Award for Math., PAMST, 1992. Mem.: ASCD, Minn. Elem. Sch. Prins. Assn. (bd. dirs. 2003—05, divsn. pres. 2004—05, P-16 partnership com. 2004—), Phi Delta Kappa (bd. dirs. 2000—03). Avocations: sailing, fitness activities, bicycling, snorkeling.

MARTIN, REBECCA REIST, librarian; b. Princeton, N.J., Mar. 2, 1952; d. Benjamin A. and Harriet (Nold) Reist; 1 child, Benjamin R. BA, U. Calif., Santa Cruz, 1973; MA, San Jose State U., 1975; DPA, U. So. Calif., 1992. Med. libr. VA Med. Ctr., San Francisco, 1975-77, chief libr. svc., 1977-81; head biology libr. U. Calif., Berkeley, 1981-85; assoc. libr. dir. San Jose (Calif.) State U., 1985-90; dean of librs. U. Vt., Burlington, 1990—. Author: Libraries and the Changing Face of Academia, 1994; contbr. articles to profl. jours., chpts. in books. Mem. Libr. Commn. San Jose, 1989-90. Mem. ALA (coun. 1996—), New England Libr. Assn., Am. Soc. Pub. Adminstrn., Am. Assn. Coll. and Rsch. Librs., Libr. Adminstrn. and Mgmt. Assn. (bd. dirs. 1987-89), NELINET (bd. dirs. 1995—). Office: U Vt Bailey/Howe Libr Burlington VT 05405

MARTIN, RENEE COHEN, forensic document examiner, author, expert witness; b. Bklyn., Feb. 26, 1928; d. Aref Max and Eleanora (Cofino) Cohen; m. Howard Martin Kessler, Dec. 24, 1950 (div. 1978); children: Kenneth S., Laurel R. Van Blarcum, Elena A. Covert (dec.), Julia M. Diplomate Nat. Assn. Document Examiners, 2000, cert. Nat. Assn. Document Examiners, 1979. Pres. Handwriting Cons., Inc., Princeton, N.J., 1950-90, chief exec. officer, 1965-85; pres., chief exec. officer Questioned Documents, Inc., 1985—, exec. dir. forgery forensics (c) a Div-f, 1995—. Coord. Metamorphosis II, Princeton, 1984-86; frequent lectr., presenter workshops; adj. prof. Mercer County CC, NJ, 1985-87. Author: Your Script is Showing, 1969, Secrets of Handwriting, 1970, Scriptease, 1976, Experts in Court, 1986, Handwriting Analysis, 1971, Mensa Cooks Book, 1989, (videotape, handbook, workbook) Personalysis Dynamics, 1990, Forgery Protection Tips, 1989; contbr. articles to profl. jours. Com. mem. East Windsor Democratic Club, 1983-84, sgt.-at-arms, 1984, sec., 1986-87; mem. Mercer County Commn. on Women, 1989-91; mem. Ea. Windsor (N.J.) Local Assistance Bd., 1995-98. Recipient Woman of Yr. award Hightstown Bus. and Profl. Women Club, 1974, Honor from Chapel of the Four Chapels. Mem. Nat. Assn. Document Examiners (co-founder, life, chmn. diplomate com., Examiner of Yr. 1984, past pres. 1979-83, diplomate 1993), Evidence Photographers Internat. Coun., Nat. Forensic Soc. (co-founder), Friends of N.J. Librs. (pres. 1980-85), Mensa (Ctrl. N.J. program chmn. 1984, local sec. 1984-86, bd. dirs. 1986-88, author Compiled Mensa Cooks' Book 1987, mem. local scholarship com. 1994—), Princeton Area (N.J.) C. of C. (chair small bus. coun. 1996), Nat. Assn. Document Examiners. Office Phone: 609-452-7030. Personal E-mail: forgerynet@aol.com.

MARTIN, RUTH C. (RUTH MARTIN STAFF), actress; d. Paul James Constantine, Sr. and Josephine Statler Constantine; m. Michael T. Staff, Sept. 21, 1986; children: Bryan A. Staff, Seth B., Courtney R., Lauren M. Staff. AS in Early Childhood Edn., Jr. Coll. Albany, 1966; BS in Elem. Edn., Russell Sage Coll., 1969; MS in Developmental Reading, SUNY, Albany, 1973; student in Acting and Voice, Russell Sage Coll., 1998—; studied with Margaret Danner and Steve Fletcher, currently studying voice with Nancy Wozny. NYS Permanent Tchr. Cert. 1973, professionally trained comml. and narrative voice talent 2001. Tchr. Montessori Sch. Albany, NY, 1966—69, North Colonie Ctrl. Sch. Dist., Newtonville, NY, 1969—74; actress, 1986—; profl. actress, 2004. Performer in several local venues, Broadway, Beacon Theater, Powers Auditorium, Whitting Auditorium, Detroit Music Hall, Landmark Theater, Shea's Performing Arts Ctr.; appeared in several independent films, cabaret musicals, and TV commercials. Pres., sec., treas. Southern Saratoga City Coun., 1992—2005; bd. mem. Roustabout Players, Troy, NY, 2000—, Albany Civic Theater, 2003—04. Mem.: Actors Equity Assn., Theater Assn. N.Y. (Excellence in Acting award 2001, 2002), Xi Delta Lamba of Beta Sigma Phi (pres., v.p., sec., treas.). Avocations: travel, reading, higher education. Home: 1282 Ruffner Rd Niskayuna NY 12309

MARTIN, SANDRA ANN, special education educator, writer; b. Sewickley, Pa., Feb. 9, 1954; d. Antoni S. and Marian M. Jankiewicz; m. Stephen Patrick Martin, June 26, 1976; children: Caitlin Lauren, Alyssa Ann. BS in Edn., Bloomsburg U., Pa., 1976; M in Edn., Shippensburg U., Pa., 1979. Learning disabilities and emotional support resource rm. tchr. southwestern sch. dist. Lincoln Intermediate Unit # 12 Emory Markle Intermediate Sch., Hanover, Pa., 1976—77; learning disabilities and emotional support tchr. grades 6-12 math, reading, and lang. arts resource rm. settings Lincoln Intermediate Unit # 12 New Oxford (Pa.) Jr. HS, 1977—79, learning disabilities tchr. grades 7-9 math, reading, and lang. arts resource rm. settings, 1979—83; learning disabilities tchr. grades 6-8 math, reading, and lang. arts resource rm. settings New Oxford Mid. Sch., 1983—88, learning support tchr. grades 7-8 math, reading, and lang. arts resource rm. and inclusion settings Lincoln Intermediate Unit, 1988—96, learning support tchr. grades 7-8 math, reading, and lang. arts resource rm. and inclusion settings Conewago Valley Sch. Dist., 1996—. Spkr. in field, 2000—; supr. spl. edn. tchrs. Western Md. Coll., Shippensburg U., 1997—98. Author: Breaking the Sound Barrier to Fluent Reading, Level 1, 2002, Mathopedia, Level 1, Level 2, 2003. Chaperone, dance instr. New Oxford Mid. Sch., 1990—2003, drama coach, 1977—85; chaperone, dance instr. Girl Scouts, New Oxford, 1993—99; fundraiser Immaculate Conception Ch., New Oxford. Finalist Pa. Tchr. of Yr., 2004; named one of Outstanding Educators of Adams County. Mem.: NEA, Pa. State Edn. Assn., Coun. Exceptional Children (divsn. learning disabilities), New Oxford Area C. of C. Avocations: travel, concerts, Broadway plays and musicals, antiques, spectator sports. Home: 316 Lincoln Way W New Oxford PA 17350 Office: Conewago Valley Sch Dist 130 Berlin Rd New Oxford PA 17350 Office Phone: 717-624-4513. Business E-Mail: specialtypublishers@hotmail.com.

MARTIN, SUSAN JANE, secondary school educator; b. Houlton, Maine, Nov. 4, 1955; d. Charles Edward Johnston and Rae Marie Johnston; m. Chris Martin, June 10, 1989; children: Jeremy, Jay, Matt, Stormy. BA in English and Journalism, U. N.H., Durham, 1977; cert. in tchg., Boise State U., 1988; cert. in vocat. and tech., U. Idaho, Moscow, 1999. Reporter Foster's Daily Dem., Dover, NH, 1977—79; tchr. Mountain Home (Idaho) H.S., 1988—. Owner Photo Express Portraits and Graphic Arts, Mountain Home, 2005—. Recipient Idaho Journalism Tchr. of Yr., 1993. Mem.: NEA, Columbia Scholastic Press Assn., Idaho Journalism Adv. Assn. (sec. 1998—), Mountain Home C. of C. Avocations: reading, walking, photography. Home: 1177 NW Dardelion Ln Mountain Home ID 83647 Office: Photo Express Portraits and Graphic Arts 590 N 2d E Mountain Home ID 83647 Office Phone: 208-587-2570. Office Fax: 208-587-2579. Business E-Mail: martin-sj@sd193.k12.id.us.

MARTIN, SUSAN KATHERINE, librarian; b. Cambridge, Eng., Nov. 14, 1942; came to U.S., 1950, naturalized, 1961; d. Egon and Jolan (Schonfeld) Orowan; m. David S. Martin, June 30, 1962. BA with honors, Tufts U., 1963; MS, Simmons Coll., 1965; PhD, U. Calif., Berkeley, 1983. Intern libr. Harvard U., Cambridge, Mass., 1963-65, systems libr., 1965-73; head systems office gen. libr. U. Calif., Berkeley, 1973-79; dir. Milton S. Eisenhower Libr. Johns Hopkins U., Balt., 1979-88, exec. dir. Nat. Commn. on Libraries and Info. Sci., 1988-90; univ. libr. Georgetown U., Washington, 1990-2001, tchr., cons., 2001—; pres. SKM Assocs., 2001—; cons. dir. Marstons Mills Pub. Libr., 2003—05, dir., 2005—. Mem. libr. com. Princeton (N.J.) U., 1987—95; mem. vis. com. Harvard U. Libr., 1987—93, 1994—2000; bd. overseers for univ. libr. Tufts U., 1986—2001, Tufts U. Sch. Arts and Scis., 2001—06; cons. various librs. and info. cos., 1975—; mem. libr. adv. com. Hong Kong U. Sci. Tech., 1988—95; mem. acad. libr. adv. group U. Md. Sch. Librs. and Info. Scis., 1994—96; mem. adv. bd. ERIC, 1990—92; mem. Chadwyck-Healey N.Am. Adv. Com. on Lit. Online, 1997—99; vice chair, chair Chesapeake Info. and Rsch. Libr. Alliance, 1996—98; cons. libr. devel. & fundraising, 1998—; spkr. in field; mem. adv. bd. Georgetown U. Libr., 2001—. Author: Library Networks: Libraries in Partnership, 1986—87; editor: Jour. Libr. Automation, 1972—77; co-editor: Portal: Libraries and the Academy, 2000—04; mem. editl. bd. Portal: Libraries and the Academy, 2005—; mem. editl. bd.: Advanced Tech./Librs., 1973—93, Jour. Libr. Adminstrn., 1986—2000, Libr. Hi-Tech., 1989—93, Jour. Acad. Librarianship, 1994—99; contbr. articles to profl. jours. Trustee Phila. Area Libr. Network, 1980—81; bd. dirs. Universal Serials and Book Exch., 1981—82, v.p., 1983, pres., 1984; trustee Capital Consortium, 1992—95; mem. bd. Potomac Internet, 1995—96; pres., trustee Marstons Mills Pub. Libr., 2002—03. Named Samuel Lazerow disting. lectr., Drexel U., 1984, L.I. U., 2002; recipient Simmons Coll. Disting. Alumni award, 1977; Coun. on Libr. Resources fellow, 1973. Mem.: ALA (coun. 1988—92, structure revision TF 1995—97, chair task force on external accrediting body 1999—2002), Assn. Coll. and Rsch. Librs. (pres. 1994—95, vis. program officer for scholarly com. 2002—03), Coalition for Networked Info. (leader working group 1990—92), Assn. Jesuit Colls. and Univ. Librs. (chair 1997—98), Libr. of Congress (optical disk pilot project adv. com. 1985—89), Assn. Rsch. Librs. (info. policy com. 1995—97, stats. com. 1998—2000), Libr. and Info. Tech. Assn. (pres. 1978—79), Rsch. Librs. Group (bd. govs. 1981—88, exec. com. 1985—87), Internat. Fedn. Libr. Assns. Commn. on Access to Info. and Freedom of Expression, Cranberry Shores Chorus (publicity coord. 2002—05, pres. 2005—, webmaster 2004—), Sweet Adelines Internat. (region 1 mgmt. team 2005—), Cosmos Club (libr. com. 1988—2005), Phi Beta Kappa (chair Georgetown U. chpt. 2000—01). Home: 10 Colonial Farm Cir Marstons Mills MA 02648 Office: Marston Mills Pub Library PO Box 9 2160 Main St Marstons Mills MA 02648 Office Phone: 508-428-5175. Business E-Mail: martin@skmassociates.net.

MARTIN, TRISA, education and human development educator; d. Heber and Edna Jensen; m. Keith Martin, Sept. 4, 1970; children: David, Jonathan, Michelle, Steven, Deborah, Joseph. BS in Elem. Edn., Brigham Young U., 1970; MEd, U. Utah, 1973. Elem. tchr. Davis Sch. Dist., Farmington, Utah, 1970—73, substitute tchr. k-12, 1989—98; adj. prof. edn. and human devel. Salt Lake C.C., Salt Lake City, 1998—. Contbr. articles to mags. Edn. leader Women's Orgn., Bountiful (Utah) 30th Ward, 2000—03. Mem.: League of Utah Writers (pres. Bountiful chpt. 1995—96).

MARTIN, VALERIE GAIL, dean, music educator; b. Fayetteville, NC, Aug. 3, 1963; d. Howard Vining and June Williams Martin; m. Kevin Dale Henry, Nov. 27, 1998. MusB in Edn., Murray State U., 1985; MusM, U. Ala., 1988, D of Musical Arts, 1994. Dir. bands, asst. prof. music Centenary Coll. La., Shreveport, 1988—92, Susquehanna U., Selinsgrove, Pa., 1994—2004, dean sch. arts, humanities and comm., 2004—. Scholar, Rotary Internat., Mozarteum Conversatory in Salzburg, Austria, 1985—86. Mem.: Pa. Collegiate Bandmasters Assn. (pres. 2005—), Sigma Alpha Iota. Office: Susquehanna U 514 Univ Ave Selinsgrove PA 17870 Office Phone: 570-372-4268.

MARTIN, VIVIAN, soprano; b. Detroit, May 09; d. George W. and Lillie (Champion) M.; m. Clement A. McDowell. Student, Detroit Conservatory Music; BS in Edn., Wayne State U.; studied with, Nadia Boulanger, Germaine Martinelli, France, Samuel Margolis, N.Y.C., Paul Daubner, Munich, Elsa Verena, Berlin, Celeste Cole, Detroit. Educator Bd. of Edn., Detroit, N.Y.C. Vocal coach and tchr. private, 1996—. Soloist with Robert DeCormier Singers, Munich Philharm., Neurnberg Symphony and Philharm. Chorus, 1970, Gävleborgs Symfoniorkester, Gavle, Sweden, 1978, Symphony Radio Concert, Paris, 1978, Warsaw Symphony Orch.; operatic debut as Leonora in La Forza del Destino, 1971; appeared in Antigone and Carmina Burana with Munich Philharm. Orch. and Chorus, Das ewige Evangelium with Nürnberg Symphony Orch. and Philharm. Chorus, L'Africaine in Ghent, Belgium, Oberon in Wexford (Ireland) Opera Festival, 1972, Bess from Porgy and Bess, Bratislava, 1979, Il Travatore, Constantza, 1980; performed with Royal Opera Ghent, Stadt Opera Essen, Badische Opera Karlsruhe, Stadt Opera Bonn, Mainz Opera, Royal Opera Lisbon, Portugal, Stadtheatre Bremen; TV broadcasts include BBC, BRT Belgium, Bratislava (Czechoslovakia) Philharm. Orch. and Opera, Bavarian Radio; rec. artist RCA, Command Records, Concord Records, Halo Records; tour India, Iran, Afghanistan, U.S. State Dept., 1976; toured with Gävleborgs Symphony Orch., Sweden, 1981-84; appeared in opera concert on radio and TV, Bucharest, 1979; sang Leonora in Il Travatore in opera festival, Constantza, Rumania, 1979; concerts in Belgrade, Tivoli Gardens, Copenhagen, Zagreb, Yugoslavia, 1979; opera concert tour of Sweden with Gävle Symphony Orch., 1979; soloist Belgium TV Flanders Expo, Gent, Belgium, 1990, concert tour Czechoslovakia, 1991, performed New Opera House, Maastricht, Holland with Limburgs Symphony Orchestra, 1992, Concert Koor, 1992, Olavshallen, Trondheim, Norway with Trondheim Symfoniorkester and Trondheim Kammerkor, 1993, concert tours U.S.A., 1994-96, soprano soloist Gershwin Gala Porgy and Bess, 1989-96, (with Philharm. Orch.)concerts and performances in U.S.A. and abroad. World of Gershwin, 1998; concert tours Belgium, Germany, (with St. Petersburg (Russia) Phil. Orch.) Shostakovich, 1998, (with Russian Nat. Symphony Orch.), Moscow, 1998; solo recitals festival St. Petersburg, 1998, Moscow, 1998. Recipient Jean Paul Alaux award Conservatoire de Fontainebleau, 18 singing scholarships and awards. Mem. AFTRA, Am. Guild Mus. Artists, Actors Equity Assn., New Initiatives for the Arts, Wayne State U. Alumni Assn., Alpha Kappa Alpha. Office: Dr Gosta Schwarck Intl Ltd 18 Groennegade 1st Fl DK-1007 Copenhagen K Denmark

MARTIN-BOWEN, LINDSEY, freelance writer; b. Kansas City, Kans., Aug. 4, 1959; d. Lawrence Richard and V. Marie Pickett; m. Frederick E. Nicholson (div.); 1 child, Aaron Frederick; m. Edwin L. Martin (div.); 1 child, Ki Elise; m. Michael L. Bowen (div.). BA in English Lit., U. Mo., Kansas City, 1972, MA in English and Creative Writing, 1988, postgrad., 1991-94; JD, U. Mo. Kansas City Sch. Law, Kansas City, 2000. Bar: Mo. 2001. Tech. editor Office Hearings and Appeals, U.S. Dept. Interior, Washington, 1976-77; reporter, photographer Louisville Times, 1982-83; reporter, features editor Sun Newspapers, Overland Park, Kans., 1983-84; assoc. editor Modern Jeweler, Overland Park and N.Y.C., 1984-85; writer Coll. Blvd. News, Overland Park, 1985-89, KC View, Kansas City, Mo., 1988-89; editor Number One, Kansas City, Mo., 1986-88, cons., 1988-89; copywriter Sta KXEO/KWWR Radio, Mexico, Mo., 1989; editorial asst. New Letters, 1985—; features writer, columnist The Squire, Prairie Village, Kans., 1990-95. Instr. lit., fiction writing, intro. to journalism, reporting, English, cultural studies, tech. writing, acad. writing and lit. U. Mo., Kansas City, 1986-88, 97-, Johnson County CC, 1988-95; fiction writer, 2002—; instr. world lit., writing Rockhurst U., 2002-03; tchr. English and fiction Longview CC, 1988-95, 97-98, 2004—; instr. writing and mass comm. Webster U., 1990; instr. world lit., Am. lit., women in lit., creative writing Penn Valley CC, 1993-97, faculty sponsor The Penn; owner, writer Paladin Freelance Writing Svc., Kansas City, 1988—; prodn. editor Nat. Paralegal Reporter, 1992-95, editor 1994-97, columnist; staff writer, columnist NPR, 1992-2005; writing contest judge New Letters, 1987-; judge poetry contest BkMk Press, U. Mo., Kansas City, 1998—; coord. written English proficiency test, U. Mo., Kans. City, 2005- Author: (novel) The Dark Horse Waits in Boulder, 1985, Deep City, 2005, Harvest, 2002, Denvie USA, 2003, Deep City, 2005, (poetry book) Second Touch, 1990, Standing on the Edge of the World, 2006, (fiction) Cicada Grove and Other Stories, 1992; author numerous poems; contbr. articles to profl. jours.; lead actress prodns. Coach House Players, 1969-70; extra HBO film Truman, 1995; staff mem., contbr. UMKC Law Rev., 1997-99. Campaigner McGovern for Pres. Campaign, Kansas City, 1971-72. Regents scholar, 1967; GAF fellow, 1986. Mem. U. Mo.-Kansas City Alumni Assn. (media com. 1983-84), Phi Kappa Phi. Roman Catholic. Avocations: acrylic and oil painting, downhill skiing, music, Greek cooking, paralegal work. Office: U Mo Kansas City English Dept Cockefair Hall Rm 111 5100 Rockhill Rd Kansas City MO 64110-2481 Home: 1129 SE 7th St Lees Summit MO 64063-6442

MARTINE, ANDREA SCHULTZ, secondary school educator; b. Washington, Aug. 24, 1945; d. George Norman and Grace Lois (DiBetetto) S.; m. Leonard Francis Martine, June 10, 1967 (div. Apr. 1978) BS, Duquesne U., Pitts., 1967, MA, 1970; postgrad., U. Pitts., 1970. Cert. English tchr., prin., Pa. Tchr. English Allderdice H.S., Pitts., 1967—98; acad. coach English Beaver Area Sch. Dist., 1998—2000; ednl. assessment specialist Pa. Dept. Edn., Harrisburg, 2000—04; dir. curriculum and instrn. Warrior Run Sch. Dist., Turbotbville, 2004—. Dir. Tot Town Day Care Ctr., Pitts., 1978-82; instr. English dept. Allegheny C.C., Pitts., 1982—94; chair English dept. Alderdice H.S., 1970-90, facilitator Ctrs. for Advanced Studies, 1990-95, coord. advanced placement, 1995-98; advanced placement English cons. Coll. Bd., Phila., 1986—. Contbr. chpts. to books; author curriculum in field Vol. Mercy Hosp., Pitts., 1985-87; vol. various elections Rep. Com., Pitts., 1980—Howard Heinz fellow, 1990-94, Harper Collins fellow, 1991; finalist Pa. Tchr. of Yr., 1992 Mem. AAUW, Conf. Coll. Composition and Comm., Nat. Coun. Tchrs. English, Pa. Coun. Tchrs. English, Duquesne U. Alumni Assn. (bd. dirs. 1970-78, v.p. 1972-76), Tchr. of Yr. Orgn., Internat. Poetry Forum (adv. bd. 1978—), Nat. Assn. Gifted Children, Alpha Delta Kappa (pres. Pa. Iota chpt. 1994-96), Delta Kappa Gamma Roman Catholic. Avocations: photography, embroidery, writing. Home: 316 Fairmont Dr Watsontown PA 17777 Office: Warrior Run Sch Dist 4800 Susquenanna Trail Turbotville PA 17772 Office Phone: 570-649-5138 226. Business E-Mail: amartine@wrsd.org.

MARTINE, CATHY, telecommunications industry executive; BA in Econ., Coll. Mt. St. Vincent; MS, MIT; MBA, NYU Stern Sch. Branch mgr. AT&T Bus. Svcs., NYC; hired into mgmt. tng. prog. and had assignments in Network Ops., Fin., and Mktg. AT&T, gen. mgr., internat. consumer long distance bus., 1994—97, mktg. v.p., consumer svcs., 1997—99, v.p. internat. traffic mgmt., pres., internat. carrier svcs., 1999, led consumer long distance svcs., sr. v.p., Voice over Internet Protocol (VoIP), 2003, sr. v.p., Internet Telephony, Consumer Marketing and Sales Morristown, NJ, 2004—. Bd. dir. MIT Sloan Sch. Bd. of Gov., 1998—2001, US Telecommunications Tng. Inst., Washington, 1998—2001, Jersey Battered Women's Shelter, Brooklyn Acad. of Music, NYC, mem. fin. com.; bd. advisors Rutgers Sch. Bus.; co-lead Women of AT&T org. Sloan Fellow, 1993. Office: AT&T 412 Mount Kemble Ave Morristown NJ 07960-6654

MARTINES, EUGENIA BELLE, elementary school educator, special education educator; b. Marion, Va., Feb. 28, 1939; d. Howard Kelly Gullion and Mary Enias Edwards-Gullion; m. Frank Fuentes Martines, May 23, 1959 (dec. Oct. 25, 1991). Student, Marion Jr. Coll., 1958; AA, Coll. of Sequoias, 1960; BEd, Calif. State U., Fresno, 1966; cert. in bilingual edn., Calif., 1996. Kindergarten tchr. Five Points (Calif.) Sch., 1962—63; 3d grade spl. edn. tchr., 6th grade and 1st grade tchr. Corcoran (Calif.) Joint Unified Schs., 1963—97. Tutoring spl. children. Mem. Kings County Citizens Adv. Bd. on Alcohol and Other Drugs, Hanford, Calif., 1986—2001, chmn., 1992; mem. Red Ribbon Com. on Kings County and Corcoran, 1989—2001, Kings County Health Adv. Bd., Hanford, 1997—2001, Kings County Master Plan on Alcohol and Other Drugs, Hanford, 1991—2001; tutoring students with dyslexia; credentials person region 6 Reform Party of Calif., 1997—. Recipient Poet Merit Silver Bowl award, Internat. Poet Soc., 2002, Shakespeare trophy, Famous Poets Soc., 2004, Poet's Merit award, Internat. Poets Soc., 2005. Mem.: NEA, PTA (life), Corcoran Faculty Assn., Calif. Tchrs. Assn., Internat. Soc. Poets, Fiction Writers' Connection, Valley Writer's Network (pres. 1991—92), Romance Writers of Am., Soc. Children's Writers, Kings County Critiquing (cofounder), Photographers Assn., Nat. Writers' Club. Reform. Roman Catholic. Avocations: poetry, reading, writing, dog breeding, politics. Address: PO Box 458 Corcoran CA 93212-0458 Personal E-mail: poet-jbel@savypro.com.

MARTINEZ, ADRIANA, political organization worker, photographer; Student, U. Nev., Las Vegas; BA, Brooks Inst. Photography. Photography instr. C.C. So. Nev.; wedding photographer So. Nev. News Bur.; chair Nev. State Dem. Party, Las Vegas, 2003—. Mem.: PTA. Office: 1325 Vegas Valley Dr Ste C Las Vegas NV 89109-6219

MARTINEZ, ALMA R., actress, theater director, educator; b. Monclova, Coahuila, Mex. Student, U. Guadalajara-Artes Plasticas, Mex., 1972-73, Ibero-Am. U., 1976, UNAM, Mexico City, 1976-77; BA in Theatre, Whittier Coll., 1984; MFA in Acting, U. So. Calif., 1995; postgrad., Stanford U., 1994—; student, Jerzy Grotowski Para Theatre, Berkeley, Calif., 1977, Lee Strasberg Theatre Inst., Hollywood, Calif., 1982, Royal Acad. Dramatic Arts, London, Eng., 1987, Mnouchkine/Theatre du Soleil, Paris, 1993. Asst. prof. theatre arts U. Calif., Santa Cruz, 2001—. Appeared in plays including In the Summer House, Lincoln Ctr., N.Y.C., Greencard, Joyce Theatre, N.Y.C., Zoot Suit, Mark Taper Forum, L.A., Bocon, Mark Taper Forum, L.A., Macbeth, Oreg. Shakespeare Festival, The Skin of Our Teeth, Oreg. Shakespeare Festival, Hello Dolly, Long Beach Civic Light Opera, A Christmas Carol, South Coast Repertory, House of Blue Leaves, Pasadena Playhouse, Sundance Inst., Sundance, Utah, Fuente Ovejuna, Berkeley Repertory Theatre, Burning Patience, San Diego Repertory Theatre, Marriage of Figaro, Ariz. Theatre Co., Sons of Don Juan, Asolo Theatre, Fla., Wait Until Dark, Pa. Stage Co., La Carpa de los Rasquachis, Teatro Campesino; TV appearances include Gen. Hosp., Twilight Zone, Sequin, Corridos (Peabody award), Tough Love, Dress Gray, The Boys, In a Child's Name, The Gambler Returns, Quiet Killer, The New Adam 12 (series regular), 500 Nations, Nash Bridges (guest star); film appearances include Ballad of a Soldier, Jacaranda, The Novice,

Trial by Terror, Dollie Dearest, Maria's Story, For A Loves One, Soldado Razo, Shattered Image, Zoot Suit, Barbarosa, Born in East L.A., Under Fire, among others; dir. (plays) Bed of Stone, 1996, La Gran Carpa de los Rasquachis, 1997, Heroes & Saints, 2001. Active Assistance with Alcohol and Sobriety Uniting Latinas, United L.Am. Youth, Med. Aid for El Salvador, Save the Children, the Christian Children's Fund; vol. and charity work in refugee camps in Ethiopia, India, Thailand, Sri Lanka, and The Philippines; bd. dirs. Mexican Mus., El Teatro Compresing. Recipient Cert. of Appreciation El Teatro Campesino, 1978, Recognition award Barrio Sta., 1980, Alumni Hall of Fame, El Rancho H.S., 1982, Outstanding Hispanic Alumni award Whittier Coll., 1984; co-recipient with Anthony Quinn and Edward James Olmos Hispanic Entertainer of Yr., The Equitable Co., 1987; Escobedo fellow Stanford U., 1996, Dorothy Danforth Compton Rsch. fellow, 1996. Mem. NATAS, AFTRA, SAG (John Dales scholar 1995-96, 98), TCG, Modern Lang. Assn., Assn. for Theatre in Higher Edn., Nat. Theatre Conf., Nat. Assn. Chicas and Chicano Studies, Actors Equity Assn. Address: JE Talent 323 Geary St #302 San Francisco CA 94102 Office: Univ Calif J-14 Theatre Arts Ctr Santa Cruz CA 95064 Business E-Mail: almamar@ucsc.edu.

MARTINEZ, BELINDA, health insurance company executive; MBA, U. So. Calif.; MPH, Loma Linda U. With Delta Ins.Co., 1988—, dir. acct. svcs. Delta Dental; v.p. profl. svcs. PMI Dental Health Plan Delta Ins.Co., v.p. underwriting and fin., 1999—2001, sr. v.p., COO, 2001—; COO Delta Ins.Co., 2003—. Named one of Top 10 Latinos in Healthcare, LatinoLeaders mag., 2004. Office: Delta Dental Calif 100 1st St San Francisco CA 94105*

MARTINEZ, CARMEN MARIA, ambassador; b. Pensacola, Fla., July 1950; married; 1 child. MA in Medieval Hist., MS in Nat. Security and Strategic Resources. Various positions US Fgn. Svc., Sao Paulo, Brazil, 1981; chief of the consular sect. Quito, Ecuador, 1989—93; prin. officer US consulate, Barranquilla, Colombia, 1993—94; dep. chief of mission US Dept. State, Maputo, Mozambique, 1997—99; prin. officer US consulate, San Paolo, Brazil, 1999—2000; charge d'affaires to Burma US Dept. State, Rangoon, 2002—05, US amb. to Zambia Lusaka, 2005—. Office: US Dept State 2310 Lusaka Pl Washington DC 20521*

MARTINEZ, CHERYL A., mathematics professor; d. Tommy Everett and Carrol Joan Dow; m. Ernesto B. Martinez, Aug. 20, 1983; children: Carrie Maria, Teresa Lynne, Grace Caroline, Catherine Elizabeth, Steven Gilbert, Jacqueline Nicole, Michaela Rose. MS, N.Mex Inst. Mining and Tech., Socorro, 1989. Tchr. Denver Acad., 1982—83, Albuquerque Pub. Schs., 1983—84, Las Cruces Pub. Schs., N.Mex., 1984—86; prof. N.Mex Mil. Inst., Roswell, 1986—. Leader Girl Scouts USA, Roswell, 1994—2006. Mem.: Delta Kappa Gamma (pres. 2006—). Roman Catholic. Avocations: swimming, silversmithing. Home: 3303 W McGaffey Roswell NM 88203 Office: NMex Mil Inst 101 W College Blvd Roswell NM 88201 Office Phone: 505-624-8151.

MARTINEZ, DEBBIE, electronics engineer; BS, Embry-Riddle Aero. U.; postgrad. Electronics engr., aerospace technologist NASA Langley Rsch. Ctr., 1990—. Mem. Fed. Women's Program Com., 1993—; chair Hispanic Adv. Group, 1996—. Recipient Latina of the Yr. award in Sci. and Tech., Latina Mag., 1999. Office: NASA Langley Rsch Ctr Bldg 1268A Rm 2124 Hampton VA 23681-2199 Business E-Mail: d.martinez@larc.nasa.gov.

MARTINEZ, DIANNA, secondary school educator; d. James Cumberland and Gayle Spackman, Henry Spackman (Stepfather); children: Heather McBride, Eric, Nicole. B, Grand Canyon U.; M. D, Ashwood U. Tchr. Liberty Elem. Sch. Dist., Buckeye, Ariz., 1996—98, Buckeye Union H.S., 1998—. Sponsor BUHS Marine Sci. Club, Buckeye, 1999—. With U.S. Army, 1982—86. Grantee, APS, 2001, West Side Impact, 2002, Wells Fargo, 2002—03, Michael Jordan Found., 2003. Mem.: DAV, Nat. Sci. Tchrs. Assn., Nat. Assn. Gifted, Nat. Biology Tchrs. Assn., Nat. Marine Educators Assn. Office: Buckeye Union High School 902 Eason Ave Buckeye AZ 85326 Office Phone: 623-327-2259.

MARTINEZ, DONNA F., federal judge; BA, U. Conn., 1973, MSW, 1975, JD, 1978. Bar: Conn. 1979. Corp. counsel City of Hartford, Conn., 1979-80; asst. U.S. atty. Office U.S. Atty., Hartford and New Haven, 1980-94; chief organized crime drug enforcement task force Dist. of Conn., New Haven, 1989-94; magistrate judge U.S. Magistrate Ct., Hartford, 1994—. Instr. trial practice Yale U. Law Sch., New Haven, 1996-2001. Mem. Conn. Bar Assn., Fed. Bar Assn., Hispanic Bar Assn., Fed. Magistrate Judges Assn., Am. Inns of Ct. (past. v.p., past pres.), Am. Leadership Forum (past bd. dirs.). Office: US Magistrate Ct 450 Main St Rm 262 Hartford CT 06103-3002 Office Phone: 860-240-3605.

MARTINEZ, GLORIA ELENA, elementary school educator; b. Scottsbluff, Nebr., Apr. 20, 1970; d. Guillermo Martinez and Gloria Berumen. BS, U. Tex. at El Paso, 1996. Cert. tchr. Tex., 1997. 8th grade math and algebra tchr. Ysleta Ind. Sch. Dist., El Paso, Tex., 1998—2004, 7th grade math tchr., 2004—. Dance coach Hawkette Dance Team - Indian Ridge, El Paso, 2001—02; u. interscholastic league number sense coach Indian Ridge Mid. Sch., El Paso, 2001—, spelling bee coord. and coach, 2002—. Mem. Ctrl. Seventh Day Adventist Ch., El Paso, 2004—06. Office: Indian Ridge Middle School 11201 Pebble Hills Blvd El Paso TX 79936 Office Phone: 915-434-5400.

MARTINEZ, HERMINIA S., economist, banker; b. Havana, Cuba; came to U.S., 1960, naturalized, 1972; d. Carlos and Amelia (Santana) Martinez Sanchez; m. Mario Aguilar, 1982; children: Mario Aguilar, Carlos Aguilar. BA in Econs. cum laude, Am. U., 1965; MS in Fgn. Svc. (Univ. fellow); MS in Econs., Georgetown U., 1967, PhD in Econs., 1969; postgrad., Nat. U. Mex. Instr. econs. George Mason Coll., U. Va., Fairfax, 1967-68; researcher World Bank, 1967-69, indsl. economist, devel. econs. dept., 1969-71; economist World Bank Latin Am. (Ctrl. Am., Mex., Venezuela, Equador, Panama and Dominican Republic, Washington, 1971-79; sr. loan officer for Middle East and North Africa World Bank, 1977—84, sr. loan officer, sr. economist Africa Region, 1988-91, prin. ops. officer pvt. sector fin. group Africa region, 1992-96, lead specialist, regional mgr., 1996-2000; pvt. practice fin., econ. devel., 2000—. Contbg. author: The Economic Growth of Colombia: Problems and Prospects, 1973, Central American Financial Integration, 1975. Mid-Career fellow Princeton U., 1988-89. Mem. Am. Econ. Assn., Soc. Internat. Devel., Brookings Inst. Latin Am. Study Group. Roman Catholic. Home: 5145 Yuma St NW Washington DC 20016-4336 Office: World Bank 1818 H St NW Washington DC 20433-0001

MARTINEZ, IRIS, state senator; b. Chgo. 1 child. Grad., Northeastern U., U. Ill., Chgo. Mem. Ill. State Senate, Springfield, 2003—, mem. appropritions II com., health and human svcs. com. and sbucom. on health care, vice chhair com. on ins. and pensions, mem. subcom. on mandates. Liaison to Hispanic Ministry. Committeewoman Ill. Dem. State Com.; mem. Dem. Nat. Com. Democrat. Catholic. Office: Capitol M-106 Capitol Bldg Springfield IL 62706 also: District 3024 N Pulaski Rd Chicago IL 60641 Home: 3154 W Grace St # 1 Chicago IL 60618-4529

MARTINEZ, JENNY S., lawyer; BA cum laude, Yale U., 1993; JD magna cum laude, Harvard Law Sch., 1997. Bar: Va., DC. Law clk. to Honorable Guido Calabresi, US Ct. Appeals Second Circuit, 1997—98, Chambers of Justice Stephen Breyer, US Supreme Ct., 1998—99; assoc. legal officer to Judge Patricia Walk, UN Internat. Criminal Tribunal for Former Yugoslavia, 1999—2000; assoc. Jenner & Block LLC, 2000—03; sr. rsch. fellow, vis. lectr. Yale U., 2002—03; asst. prof. law Stanford Law Sch., 2003—. Mng. editor Harvard Law Review; cons. Internat. Ctr. Transitional Justice, 2003—. Contbr. articles to profl. jours. Vol. tutor Thurgood Marshall Acad. Charter HS, Washington, 2001; vol. atty. DC Bar Law Firm Pro Bono Project, 2001; vol. cons. atty. Human Rights First, 2003—. Named one of Top 40 Lawyers Under 40, Nat. Law Jour., 2005; recipient Sears prize, Harvard Law, Temple Bar Scholar, Am. Inns Ct., 1999. Mem.: Hispanic Bar Assn. DC (v.p. internal affairs 2003—). Office: Stanford Law Sch 559 Nathan Abbott Way Stanford CA 94305-8610 Office Phone: 650-725-2749. Business E-Mail: jmartinez@law.stanford.edu.

MARTINEZ, JOANNE O., corporate executive; b. Phila., Jan. 19, 1950; d. Joseph F. and Nina Duvgoluk Olekszyk; m. Ernest J. Martinez; children: Kristin C., Erik J. BA, U. Pa., 1970; MBA, Adelphi U., 1973. Various positions Internat. Paper and Singer Co., NYC, 1977-82; v.p. Ambase Corp., NYC, 1982-92, ADP, Roseland, NJ, 1992-94, Am. Banknote, NYC, 1995-96; pres. Martinez Cons. Enterprises, Bklyn., 1996—2002; sr. v.p. Marquis Who's Who LLC, New Providence, NJ, 2003—06, News Communications, Inc., NYC; chief adminstrv. officer B2X Corp., Jersey City, 2006—. Bd. mem. ARC-Bklyn. chpt., 1989—. Achievements include placing in the Top 10 in the Veteran Women's Indoor Rowing Championship. E-mail: jmartinez@pipeline.com.

MARTINEZ, MARIA DOLORES, pediatrician; b. Cifuentes, Cuba, Mar. 16, 1959; d. Demetrio and Alba Silvia (Perez) M.; m. James David Marple, Apr. 25, 1992 (div.). MD, U. Navarra, Pamplona, Spain, 1984. Med. diplomate. Resident in pediatrics Moses Cone Hosp., Greensboro, NC, 1986-89; pvt. practice Charlotte, NC, 1989-93, Mooresville, NC, 1993-96; pediat. pulmonary fellow Univ. Med. Hosp., Tucson, 1996-99; pediatric pulmonologist, also in sleep medicine/transplants Duke U., Durham, NC, 1999—, dir. pediat. lung transplant svcs., assoc. dir. sleep medicine lab., 2000—, St. Joseph's Hosp., Phoenix, 2004. Mem. AMA, Am. Acad. Pediatrics, N.C. Med. Soc., Mecklenburg County Med. Soc. Republican. Roman Catholic. Avocations: horseback riding, travel. Office: St Joseph s Hosp and Med Ctr 3600 N 3d Ave Phoenix AZ 85013 Office Phone: 602-406-4645. Personal E-mail: maria.martinez2@chw.edu.

MARTINEZ, NATALIE, newscaster; b. Buffalo; Degree, SUNY, Buffalo. Anchor, reporter, prodr. at upstate N.Y. radio and TV stations; reporter and weekend anchor WXAA-TV, Albany, NY, primary anchor; co-anchor weekend morning news and reporter WMAQ-TV, Chgo., 2001—. Mem.: Nat. League Female Execs., Nat. Assn. of Hispanic Journalists, One Voice. Office: WMAQ-TV NBC Tower 454 N Columbus Dr Chicago IL 60611-5555 Office Phone: 312-836-5830.

MARTINEZ, ROSE MARIE, health science association administrator; PhD, Johns Hopkins Sch. Hygiene and Pub. Health. Former asst. dir. health fin. and policy U.S. Gen. Acctg. Office; sr. health rschr. Mathematica Policy Rsch.; dir. IOM Bd. Health Promotion and Disease Prevention, 1999—. Office: Inst of Med 500 Fifth St NW Washington DC 20001

MARTINEZ, VERONICA, special education educator; b. Ft. Worth, June 21, 1959; d. Joe and Helen (Guereca) M.; divorced. BS, Tex. Wesleyan U., 1981; MEd, U. North Tex., 1986. Cert. elem. tchr., Tex. Spl. Edn. resource tchr. Ft. Worth Ind. Sch. Dist., 1981—. Active Learning Disabilities Assn. Ft. Worth Coun. Reading. Mem. NEA, Internat. Reading Assn., Nat. Coun. Tchrs. English, Tex. State Tchrs. Assn., Delta Kappa Gamma.

MARTÍNEZ, YOLANDA R., social services administrator; b. Feb. 11, 1936; d. Eduardo R. and Consuelo (Rincon) Martínez; m. William Edward Hawkins, Mar. 27, 1963 (dec. May 11, 1996); children: Ricardo, Eduardo, William T. AA, San Bernardino Valley Coll., 1959; BA, U. Wash., 1974. Tchr. pub. schs., Calif., 1958—59; parole adviser, project dir., counselor Active Mexicanos, Seattle, 1972—76; instr. Everett (Wash.) C.C., 1975—76; rschr., translator Wash. State Coun. Crime and Delinquency, Seattle, 1977; program asst., minority affairs Seattle Ctrl. C.C.; cons. to cmty. offenders programs, 1977—81; sr. cmty. svc. rep. Seattle Dept. Human Resources, 1981—, ret., 2003; bus. owner Neighborhood Solutions, 2003—. Cons. in field. Author: Usted y La Ley, 1977. Translator ARC Lang. Bank, 1975—; chmn. Region 10 Chicago Task Force on Drug Abuse, 1977—79; mem. Seattle Cable Citizens Adv. Bd., 1988—90; v.p. Concilio for Spanish Speaking; state dir., mem. nat. exec. bd. League United L.Am. Citizens, 1980—82; chmn. Hispanic adv. bd. Seattle Cmty. Coll. Dist. 6, 1981—83; chmn. Seattle/Mazatlan Sister City Assn., 1981—83; v.p. Neighborhoods U.S.A., 1987—92, 1995—, bd. dirs., 1986. United Way of King County; dist. adv. com. group health Northgate Clinic; del. White House Conf. on Families, L.A., 1980; bd. dirs. N.W. Kidney Ctr. Regional Coun., 2002; bd. mem. Northgate Chamber, 2002; Dem. precinct committeeman, 1968, 1970, 1988—2002; vol. worker various local and state polit. campaigns. Named One of 100 Women Role Models for Pub. Schs., State Office Pub. Instrn., Lake City Citizen of Yr., 2000; recipient Gov.'s citation, 1974, award for committment to higher edn., Seattle C.C. Dist., 1983, One of 10 Unsung Heroes in Seattle, Radical Women, 1983, Cmty. Svc. award, Am. G.I. Forum, 1984, Golden Maple Leaf award, Maple Leaf Cmty. Coun., 1991, Commn. award, Seattle Commn. on Children and Youth, 1991, 1993, assoc. mem., Eastern Washington U. Found., Seattle Works award, Cmty. Ambassador, 2001, Seattle Works Award, 2002. Mem.: Northgate C. of C. (founding mem.), Rotary. Home: 12018 17th Ave NE Seattle WA 98125-5116 E-mail: ymart@earthlink.net.

MARTINEZ BLAND, VERONICA KAY, elementary school educator; b. Chillecothe, Ohio, Apr. 7, 1953; d. Robert Charles and Martha Josephine Fannin; m. Ralph Edward Bland, Oct. 4, 2003; 1 stepchild, Sarah Rachel Bland;children from previous marriage: Amadeo Enrico Martinez, Miguel Domingo Martinez. Student, Urbana U., Ohio, 1971—72; BS in Elem. Edn. summa cum laude, Cumberland U., Lebanon, Tenn., 1991. Tchr. 6th grade reading/lang. Rosebank Elem. Sch., Nashville, 1991—98, 1999—2000, 2d grade tchr., 1998—99, 4th grade tchr., 2000—02, reading specialist, 2002—. Sponsor Student Writers' Club, Nashville, 1991—2001; mentor intern program Belmont U., 1995—2000, mem. com., chair faculty adv. com., 1999—2000, 2003—, chmn. faculty adv. com., 2001—02; curriculum developer Metro Nashville Pub. Schs., 1997, Time to Rise YMCA program, 2003. Author: (reading material for ednl. software) Bredex Corp., 2002. Rosebank chair United Way Giving Campaign, Nashville, 1993—2004; faculty rep. PTA, 1999—2000, 2004—; mem. Tying Nashville Together, 2005. Named Rosebank Tchr. of Yr., Metro Nashville Pub. Schs., 1996—97, 2005—06; recipient Disting. Classroom Tchr. award, Metro Nashville Edn. Assn., 1994—95, Elem. Edn. award, Mayor's Coun. for Disabilities, Nashville, 1996—97; grantee, Met. Nashville Pub. Edn. Found., 1996—97, 1997—98. Mem.: Mid. Tenn. Reading Assn., Internat. Reading Assn., Tenn. State PTA (hon. life), Kappa Delta Pi, Delta Kappa Gamma. Disciples Of Christ. Avocations: reading, gardening, pottery. Office: Rosebank Elem Sch 1012 Preston Dr Nashville TN 37206 Office Phone: 615-262-6720 ext 1303. Office Fax: 615-262-6717. E-mail: veronica50@msn.com.

MARTÍNEZ-LÓPEZ, CARMEN LEONOR, management consultant, educator; b. Aracataca, Magdalena, Colombia, Oct. 13, 1956; d. Domingo Ramón Martínez and Alicia Esther Acosta de Martínez; m. Iván R. López, May 26, 2000. Licenciate in Ednl. Adminstrn., U. San Buenaventura, Medellín, Colombia, 1980; M in Ednl. Adminstrn., U. Antioquia, Medellín, 1989; specialist in Pub. Adminstrn., U. Escuela de Adminstrn. Publica, Medellín, 1995; specialist in Indsl. Rels., U. Escuela de Adminstrn. and Fin., Medellín, 1983, MBA, 2003; PhD in Internat. Bus., U. Tex.-Pan Am., Edinburg, 2003. Bd. dirs. Inst. Polictectico Jaime Isaza Cadavid, Medellín, 1980—82; dep. and bd. dirs. budget commn. Dept. de Antioquia, Medellín, 1982—84; regional mgr. Nat. Agy. Social Security, Medellín, 1983—86; pres. External Orgnl. Cons., Medellín, 1987—93; prof., rsch. and cons. U. Escuela de Adminstrn. and Fin., Medellín, 1989—92; adminstrv. mgr. Am. Med. Holding, Medellín, 1992—93; dept. chair Inst. Colombiano de Edn. Superior de Incolda, Cali, Colombia, 1993—96; rschr. and tchr. asst. U. Tex.-Pan Am., Edinburg, 1998—2003; asst. prof. CUNY, 2004—. Strategic planning cons. Am. Med. Holding, Medellín, 1989—92; strategic mgmt. cons. U. ICESI, Cali, 1995—96; strategic planning cons. Ednl. Cooperative Uraba, Apartadó, Antioquia, Colombia, 1999—2001; vis. prof. U. Monterrey, Mexico, 1999—2000. Dep. Dept. of Antioquia, Medellín, 1982—84; v.p. Colombian Conservative Party, Medellín, 1981—83; active Poly. Inst. Jaime Isaza, Medellín, 1980—82. Fellow: Ptnrs. of the Ams. (assoc.); mem.: Acad. Internat. Bus., Bus. Assn. L.Am. Studies, Acad. Mgmt. Conservative. Roman Catholic. Avocations: golf, soccer, travel. Office: CUNY S661 199 Chambers St New York NY 10007-1097 Home: Apt 3A 450 Pelham Rd New Rochelle NY 10805 Office Phone: 212-220-8389. Home Fax: 914-637-9305. Personal E-mail: carleo13@aol.com.

MARTINEZ-NEMNICH, MARICELA, realtor; b. Acapulco, Mex., June 24, 1949; arrived in U.S., 1995; d. Gilberto Martinez and Elena Errasquin; m. Guillermo Duran, Nov. 19, 1969 (div. Oct. 1983); children: Marisela, Veronica, Ana; m. Larry L. Nemnich, July 13, 1996. Lic. realtor. Mem.: Nat. Notary Assn. (pub. notary), Aurora Assn. Realtors, Nat. Assn. Realtors. Avocations: gardening, tennis, cooking. Home: 5617 S Winnipeg St Aurora CO 80015

MARTINEZ TUCKER, SARA, educational association administrator; b. Laredo, Tex. BA, Univ. Tex., Austin, MBA with high honors. Reporter San Antonio Express-News; various positions through regional v.p. AT&T, 1981—97; pres., CEO Hispanic Scholarship Fund, San Francisco, 1997—. Bd. dir. Student Loan Mktg. Assn. (Sallie Mae), 2001—; mem. No. Am. diversity adv. bd. Toyota Motor Corp.; founding mem. Nat. Ctr. for Edn. Accountability; mem. steering com. Council for Aid to Edn., RAND Corp.; mem. Sec. of Edn.'s Commn. on Future of Edn., 2005. Mem. Chancellor's Council Univ. Tex., Austin, mem. adv. council, Coll. of Nat. Sci.; mem. adv. bd. Oxygen Media / Markle Found. Named Hispanic of the Year, Hispanic mag., 2000; named one of 80 Elite Hispanic Women, Hispanic Bus. mag., 2003, 25 Most Influential Hispanics, Time Mag., 2005. Office: Hispanic Scholarship Fund Ste 1500 55 Second St San Francisco CA 94105

MARTIN-LOWRY, BEVERLY ANNE, writer, columnist; b. Washington, Oct. 25, 1948; d. James Aubrey and Gertha Mae Martin; m. Courtland Alan Milner, Apr. 20, 1968 (div. Oct. 17, 1989); children: Jennifer Anne Litton, Martin Alan Milner; m. Peter Hans Lowry, Dec. 29, 1999. CEO Pen 2 Paper, Ink, Live Oak, Tex., 2003—. Author: In October, I Turn Fifty! A Satirical Look Back on Life, 2000, Memoirs and Confessions: From Europe to the USA, 2001, (novels) Strong Appetites, 2004, Can't Cook Anonymous, 2004, The Most Unlikely Angel: A Trilogy of Love, Life, and Laughter, 2005; columnist: Sounding Off; contbr. articles to local newspapers. Mem.: Am. Legion (life). Republican. Presbyterian. Avocations: swimming, reading, travel. Office Phone: 210-646-9877. Personal E-mail: n2books@satx.rr.com.

MARTINO, CHERYL DERBY, insurance company executive; b. Paterson, N.J., Jan. 19, 1946; d. Elles Mayo and Sarah Emma (Steele) D.; m. Leonard D. Martino, Nov. 4, 1995. BA, Elmira Coll., 1967; MBA, NYU, 1982. Tchr. Ramsey (N.J.) High Sch., 1967-70; contbns. analyst Met. Life Ins. Co., N.Y.C., 1970-83, fin. writer investments dept., 1983-93, asst. sec., 1994—. Bd. trustees United Meth. Ch. of Waldwick, N.J., v.p., 1989-91, pres., 1992-93, fin. sec., 2000—. Fellow Life Mgmt. Inst. (bd. dirs. Greater N.Y. chpt. 1984-91, pres. 1986, edn. coun. 1990-93), Life Mgmt. Inst. Edn. Coun. (nat. adminstrv. com. chmn. 1990-92, mktg. subcom. 1985-93), Nat. Orchestral Assn. (bd. dirs. 1990-92); mem. Elmira Coll. Alumni Club N.J. (exec. bd. 1982-87); mem. alumni bd. dirs. Elmira Coll.,1992—. Methodist.

MARTINO, ROBIN LEIGH, elementary school educator; b. Phila., Nov. 3, 1962; d. Daniel Harold Cooper and Joan Margaret Reading; m. Albert Robert Martino, Dec. 29, 1998; 1 child, Joseph; m. Troy Allen Rushing, Sept. 21, 1985 (div. 1997); children: Beth Rushing, Leah Rushing. BS, Coll. of N.J., Trenton, 1985; MEd, Holy Family Coll., Phila., Pa., 1998. Cert. health, phys. edn. tchr. Pa., 1989, elem. edn. tchr. Pa., 1998. Substitute tchr. Coun. Rock Sch., Richboro, Pa., 1989—91; aquatics dir. Breezy Point, Langhorne, Pa., 1994—2000; substitute tchr. Neshaminy Schs., Pa., 1994—95, Pennsbury Sch. Dist., Fallsington, Pa., 1995—97; tchr. instrnl. support Coun. Rock Sch. Dist., Richboro, Pa., 1997—98; substitute tchr. Ctrl. Bucks Sch. Dist., Doylestown, Pa., 1998—99; tchr. health, phys. edn. Wissahickon Sch. Dist., Ambler, Pa., 1999—. Lifeguard tng. and cmty. first aid and safety Am. Heart Assn., Langhorne, Pa., 1994—2001, instr. candidate trainer Doylestown, Pa., 1998—99; water safety instr. ARC, Langhorne, Pa., 1994—2001, adult CPR/AED instr. Ambler, Pa., 2006—. Home: 114 Kings Ct Chalfont PA 18914 Office: Blue Bell Elem Sch 801 Symphony Ln Blue Bell PA 19422

MARTINO MAZE, CLAIRE DENISE, nursing educator; d. Samuel Joseph and Clara Fusco Martino; 1 child, Elizabeth Raye Maze Hileman. AS, Broward C.C., Coconut Creek, Fla., 1975; BSN, Fla. Atlantic U., 1994; MSN, Barry U., 2000, PhD in Nursing, 2004. RN Fla. Staff nurse Vanderbilt U. Hosp., Nashville, 1975—77; charge nurse Wilford Hall Med. Ctr., San Antonio, 1977—79; charge and staff nurse Dial-Rent-A-Nurse, Hialeah, Fla., 1980—82, Holy Cross Hosp., Ft. Lauderdale, Fla., 1982—85; office nurse Gyn. Office, Ft. Lauderdale, 1985—88; sch. and camp nurse Pine Crest Prep. Sch., Inc, Boca Raton, Fla., 1988—95; dir. nursing Venture Ambulatory Surgery Ctr., North Miami Beach, Fla., 1995—97; nurse educator Atlantic Tech. Ctr., Coconut Creek, Fla., 1997—2000; assoc. prof. nursing Palm Beach C.C., Lake Worth, Fla., 2000—02; asst. prof., nursing, dir. nursing resource ctr. Barry U., Miami Shores, Fla., 2002—. Nominating com. Sigma Theta Tau Internat., Iota XI Chpt., 1997—98; newsletter editor Sigma Theta Tau Internat., Lambda Chi Chpt., 2002—; presenter in field. Author: Nursing Care of Patients with Gastrointestinal Cancer: A Staff Development Approach, 2002. Mem. Nat. Org. for Women, Ft. Lauderdale, Fla., 1983—; bd. dirs. FNA Del., Fla. Nurses Assn., Ft. Lauderdale, Fla., 2001—. Decorated Army Svc. Ribbon 324 Combat Support Hosp., Nat. Def. Svc. medal 324th Combat Support Hosp., Army Res. Components Achievement medal 10/108 (PN/HS) Bn.; recipient faculty recognition, 10th Bn. PN Detachment, 1999; Fla. Nurses Found. grantee, 2000, Barry U. Mini Rsch. grantee, 2003. Mem.: NOW, ANA, Fla. Nurses Assn. (del. 2001), Nat. League Nurses, Sigma Theta Tau Internat. (nominating com. Iota Xi chpt. 1997—98, newsletter editor Lambda Chi chpt. 2002—, pres. elect). Office: Barry U 11300 NE 2nd Ave Miami Shores FL 66161-6695 E-mail: cmaze@mail.barry.edu.

MARTIN-O'NEILL, MARY EVELYN, advertising executive, management consultant, marketing professional, consultant, educator; b. Lexington, Ky. d. George Clarke and Georgann Elizabeth (Bovis) M.; m. John Michael O'Neill, May 24, 1998. BA magna cum laude, Lindenwood Coll.; MA with honors, U. Ky. Asst. to pres. The Hamlets, Ltd/Park Place Country Homes, Louisville, 1984-85; advt. designer, copywriter Park Place Country Homes, Anchorage, Ky., 1985-86; creative dir. of advt., mktg., v.p., treas. Park Place Country Homes/Park Place Properties, Anchorage, Ky., 1986—; mktg. comm. specialist Mayfield Publ., Mountain View, Calif., 1998; curriculum developer Oracle Corp., Redwood Shores, Calif., 1998-2000; sr. info. designer/tech. writer BenefitPoint, Inc., San Francisco, 2000—02; sales tng. and mktg. comms. mgr. Applied Underwriters, San Francisco, 2002—04; learning strategist Convergys Corp., San Francisco, 2004—05; faculty devel. mgr. DeVry U. Online, 2005—. Founder, pres. Good Help Cons. Svcs., Louisville and Lexington, Maison Marche Advt. & Promotions, Louisville, 1989; instr. dept. English U. Ky., 1989—91; adj. prof. composition U. Louisville, 1991—97; vis. lectr. lit. Bellarmine Coll., Louisville, 1992; adj. prof. humanities Ind. U. S.E., 1991—95; prof. DeVry U., 2002—, Keller Grad. Sch. Mgmt., 2006—; instr. Am. Intercontinental U., 2003—, City Coll. San Francisco, 2003—; prof. arts and humanities McKendree Coll., Louisville, 1993—97; lectr. San Francisco State U. Coll. Bus., 2000—; writer, historian Home Builders Assn. Louisville, 1996; instr. Keller Grad Sch. Mgmt., 2006—. Editor: The Griffin, 1979-80, Bus. Wire, 1997; contbr. series to mag., 1996. Mem. People for the Am. Way, Greenpeace. Recipient Spahmer creative writing award, 1979; Haggin fellow U. Ky., 1987; grantee U. Louisville, 1992-95. Mem. Am. Film Inst., Nat. Assn. Home Builders (affiliate), Ky. Film Artists Coalition, Women in Tech. Internat. Democrat. Avocations: weaving, screenwriting. Office: 912 Cole St 300 San Francisco CA 94117 Personal E-mail: mem_oneill@yahoo.com.

MARTINSON, CONSTANCE FRYE, television personality, television producer; b. Boston, Apr. 11, 1932; d. Edward and Rosalind Helen (Sperber) Frye; m. Leslie Herbert Martinson, Sept. 24, 1955; 1 child, Julianna Martinson Carner. BA in English Lit., Wellesley Coll., 1953. Dir. pub. rels.

Coro Found., LA, 1974-79; prodr., host KHJ Dimensions, LA, 1979-81, Connie Martinson Talks Books, LA, 1981—. Instr. dept. humanities UCLA, 1981—, bd. dirs. Friends of English; moderator, instr. U. Judaism; celebrity advisor Book Fair-Music Ctr., LA, 1986; advisor, moderator LA Times Festival Books, 1996; TV rep. LA Pub. Libr. LA Cityview, Sta. WNYE-TV. Author: Dramatization of Wellesley After Images, 1974; book editor, columnist: Calif. Press Bur. Syndicate, 1986—, columnist: Beverly Hills Courier, 1997—. Pres. Mayor's Adv. Coun. Volunteerism, LA, 1981—82; chmn. cmty. affairs dept. Town Hall of Calif., LA, 1981—85; bd. dirs. legal def. fund NAACP, LA, 1981—84. Mem.: Nat. Book Critics Assn., PEN, Am. Film Inst., Women in Cable, Jewish TV Network (bd. dirs. 1985—87), Mulholland Tennis Club, Wellesley Coll. Club (pres. 1979—81). Democrat. Jewish. Avocations: tennis, theater, reading. Home and Office: 2288 Coldwater Canyon Dr Beverly Hills CA 90210-1756 Personal E-mail: conniemartinson@qmail.com. Business E-Mail: talksbooks@lycos.com.

MARTINSON, DEBORAH ANN, education educator, writer; b. Ventura, Calif., May 20, 1946; d. Sidney Wayne and Mary Martha Stewart; m. Barry Allan Martinson, June 27, 1970; children: Jay Stewart, Hope Elizabeth Mendez. PhD, U. So. Calif., LA, 1991. Tchr. Crescenta Valley HS, La Crescenta, Calif., 1971—90; assoc. prof. Occidental Coll., LA, 1991—. Author: In the Presence of Audience: The Self in Diaries and Fiction, 2003, Lillian Hellman: A Life with Foxes and Scoundrels, 2005. Founder Occidental Writers Network, LA, 1991—2006. Fellow, NEH, 1997; Sophie Newcomb Collection Travel grant, Sophie Newcomb Coll. for Women, Tulane, 1999. Mem.: MLA, Coll. Composition and Comm. Democrat. Avocations: gardening, travel, walking dogs, theater. Home: 1046 N Avon St Burbank CA 91505 Office: Occidental Coll 1600 Campus Rd Los Angeles CA 91505 Office Phone: 323-259-2801. Home Fax: 503-905-1136. Personal E-mail: dmartin@oxy.edu.

MARTINSON, IDA MARIE, medical/surgical nurse, educator, physiologist; b. Mentor, Minn., Nov. 8, 1936; d. Oscar and Marvel (Nelson) Sather; m. Paul Varo Martinson, Mar. 31, 1962; children: Anna Marie, Peter. Diploma, St. Luke's Hosp. Sch. Nursing, 1957; BS, U. Minn., 1960, M.N.A., 1962; PhD, U. Ill., Chgo., 1972. Instr. Coll. St. Scholastica and St. Luke's Sch. Nursing, 1957—58, Thornton Jr. Coll., 1967—69; lab. asst. U. Ill. at Med. Ctr., 1970—72; lectr. dept. physiology U. Minn., St. Paul, 1972—82, asst. prof. Sch. Nursing, 1972—74, assoc. prof. rsch., 1974—77, prof., dir. rsch., 1977—82; prof. dept. family health care U. Calif., San Francisco, 1982—2003, chmn. dept., 1982—90. Vis. rsch. prof. Nat. Taiwan U., Def. Med. Ctr., 1981; vis. prof. nursing Sun Yat-Sen U. Med. Scis., Guang Zhou, China, Ewha Women's U., Seoul, Republic of Korea, Frances Payne Bolton Sch. Nursing, Case Western Res. U., Cleve., 1994—96; chair, prof. dept. health scis. Hong Kong Poly. U., 1996—2000. Author: Mathematics for the Health Science Student, 1977; editor: Home Care for the Dying Child, 1976, Women in Stress, 1979, Women in Health and Illness, 1986, The Child and Family Facing Life Threatening Illness, 1987, Family Nursing, 1989, Home Health Care Nursing, 1989, Home Health Care Nursing, 2d edit., 2002; contbr. chapters to books, articles to profl. jours. Active Am. Cancer Soc. Recipient Book of Yr. award, Am. Jour. Nursing, 1977, 1980, 1987, 1990, Humanitarian award for pediat. nursing, 1993; fellow, Fulbright Found., 1991. Mem.: ANA, Inst. Medicine, Am. Acad. Nursing, Coun. Nurse Rschrs., Sigma Theta Tau, Sigma Xi. Lutheran. Address: 12149 E Movil Lake Rd NE Bemidji MN 56601

MARTONE, JEANETTE RACHELE, artist; b. Mineola, N.Y., June 5, 1956; d. John and Mildred Cecilia (Loehr) M. BFA, SUNY, Purchase, 1978. One woman shows include Ariel Gallery, N.Y.C., 1990, La Mantia Gallery, Northport, N.Y., 1994-96, Inter-Media Arts Ctr., Huntington, N.Y., 1996, St. Xavier U. SXU Gallery, Chgo., 2003; exhibited in group shows including Harbor Gallery, Cold Spring Harbor, 1980, Huntington Coun. Arts, 1986, Pindar Gallery, N.Y.C., 1987, Mills Pond House, Smithtown, N.Y., 1987, Suffolk County Exec. Offices, Hauppage, N.Y., 1988, La Mantia Gallery, Northport, N.Y., 1990, Nassau County Office Cultural Affairs, 1991, Ward-Nasse. Gallery, N.Y.C., 1991, Monsterrat Gallery, N.Y.C., 1991, Priscilla Redfield Roe Gallery, Bellport, N.Y., 1991, L.I. U., Brookville, 1992, Northport B.J. Spoke Gallery, Huntington, N.Y., 1992, Fischetti Gallery, N.Y., 1992, Artists Space, N.Y.C., 1992, N.Y. Botanical Gardens, Bronx, N.Y., 1993, Visions Gallery, Albany, L.I. U., Brookville, N.Y., 1994, Goodman Gallery, Southampton, N.Y., 1994, B.J. Spoke Gallery, Huntington, N.Y., 1994-95, 2003, Islip Art Mus., East Islip, N.Y., 1994, 2003, L.I. MacArthur Airport, Ronkonkoma, N.Y., 1995, The Stage Gallery, N.Y., 1997, Lightworks Gallery, Glen Cove, N.Y., 1997, Showcase 98, Smithtown Twp. Arts Coun., St. James, N.Y., 1998, Nat. League Am. Pen Women, Inc., 1999, N.Y. Open Ctr., N.Y.C., 1999, Cork Gallery, Lincoln Ctr., N.Y.C., 1999, Omni Gallery, Uniondale, N.Y., 1999, Nat. League Am. Pen Woman Inc., Belmont, Calif., 2002, Smithtown, N.Y., 2001, NYC, 2005, St. John's U., Jamaica, N.Y., 2001, Huntington Arts Coun., 2001, 03, Smithtown Twp. Arts Coun., 2001, Marymount Manhattan Coll., N.Y.C., 2002, 03, St. Xavier U. Gallery, Chgo., 2003, Ai Gallery Ill. Inst. Art, 2004, Olin Fine Arts Ctr., Washington and Jefferson U., Washington, Pa., 2004, Nat. League Am. Pen Women, Inc. Arts Ventures, Venezuelan Consulate, N.Y., 2005; publs. include The Other Side Mag., 1997, 1999, 2000-03, The Artist's Mag., 1999, Art Calendar, 1995, 2000, 2004, Portrait Inspirations, 1997, The Best of Oil Painting, 1996, American Artist Drawing mag., 2005; artwork published in profl. publs. Recipient Award of Excellence Gold medal Art League of Nassau County, 1993, Best in Show award Nat. League Am. PEN Women Artists, 1990, 92, Windsor and Newton award for oil Arts Coun. East Islip, N.Y., 1989, award of excellence Art League of Nassau County, 1987, 88, many best in shows including 1st Ann. Juried Art Exhibit, Brookhaven Arts and Humanities Coun., Farmingville, N.Y., 1996, Supervisor's award Babylon Citizens Coun. Arts Juried Exhbn., 1994, Bob Jones Glad Hand Press award Stamford Art Assn., 1995, Faber Biren Nat. Color award Stamford Art Assn., 1995, Ann. Mem. Art Forum award of Excellence, Smithtown, N.Y., 1999, Excellence award Smithtown Twp. Arts Coun. Mem. Show, St. James, N.Y., 1997, 1999, Excellence award Nat. League of Am. Pen Woman, Inc. Belmont, Calif., 2002, Catharine Lorillard Wolfe Art Club Inc. Portrait award, 2002, Anna Hyatt Huntington Horse's Head award for best painting, 2003, Art League of L.I., Huntington, N.Y., Excellence award Pall Corp., 2003, Best in Show award Nat. League Am. Pen Women, Inc., Denver, Colo., 2006, Best Graphics in Show award Catharine Lorillard Wolfe Art Club, N.Y., 2006. Mem. Nat. League Am. Pen Women (Biennial Best in Show 2006), Catherine Lorillard Wolfe Art Club (Frank B. and Mary Anderson Cassidy Meml. award 1992, Award for Oil 1987, Margaret Dole Portrait award 2002), Allied Artists of Am. (John Young Hunter Meml. award 1993, Antonio Cerino Meml. award 1990, award of Excellence 1997), Hudson Valley Art Assn., Knickerbock Artists of Am., Nat. Art League. Avocations: travel, reading, volunteer work. Home: 47 Summerfield Ct Deer Park NY 11729-5642

MARTONE, PATRICIA ANN, lawyer; b. Bklyn., Apr. 28, 1947; d. David Andrew and Rita Mary (Dullmeyer) Martone; m. Barbara Ann Rosen, Sept. 2, 2006. BA in Chemistry, NYU, 1968, JD, 1973; MA in Phys. Chemistry, Johns Hopkins U., 1969. Bar: N.Y. 1974, U.S. Dist. Ct. (so. and ea. dists.) N.Y. 1975, U.S. Ct. Appeals (2d cir.) 1975, U.S. Ct. Appeals (1st cir.) 1981, U.S. Patent and Trademark Office 1983, U.S. Ct. Appeals (fed. cir.) 1984, U.S. Supreme Ct. 1984, U.S. Dist. Ct. (ea. dist.) Mich. 1985, U.S. Dist. Ct. (no. dist.) Calif. 1995. Tech. rep. computer timesharing On-Line Sys., Inc., NYC, 1969-70; assoc. Kelley Drye & Warren, NYC, 1973-77, Fish & Neave, NYC, 1977-82, ptnr., 1983—2004, Fish & Neave Intellectual Property Group at Ropes & Gray LLP, NYC, 2005—. Adj. prof. NYU Sch. Law, 1990—; mem. adv. coun. Engelberg Ctr. Innovation Law & Policy, 1996—; participating atty. Cmty. Law Offices, N.Y.C., 1974—78; atty. Pro Bono Panel U.S. Dist. Ct. (so. dist.) N.Y., 1982—84; lectr. Practising Law Inst., N.Y.C., 1995—, Aspen Law & Bus., 1990—95, Franklin Pierce Law Sch., 1992—97, Lic. Exec. Soc.; chair, bd. dirs. N.Y. Lawyers for the Pub. Interest, 1996—98, vice chair, 1998—2000, 2002—05, emeritus bd., 2006—; vice chair Legal Svcs., N.Y.C., 1991—95. Mng. editor NYU Law Sch. Rev. Law and Social Change, 1972-73; contbr. articles to profl. jours. Recipient Founder's Day award NYU Sch. Law, 1973; NSF grad. trainee Johns Hopkins U., 1968-69; NYU scholar, 1964-68. Mem. ABA, Assn. Bar City N.Y. (mem. environ. law com. 1978-83, trademarks, unfair competition com. 1983-86), Fed. Bar Coun., Fed. Cir. Bar Assn., Copyright Soc., Am. Chem. Soc., Licensing Execs. Soc., N.Y. Intellectual Property Law Assn., Univ. Club. Office: Fish & Neave Intellectual Property Group at Ropes & Gray LLP 1251 Ave of the Americas Fl 49 New York NY 10020-1105 Office Phone: 212-596-9021. Business E-Mail: patricia.martone@ropesgray.com.

MARTORANA, BARBARA JOAN, secondary school educator; b. N.Y.C., Oct. 18, 1942; d. Samuel and Joan Renee (Costello) M. BA, St. John's U., Jamaica, N.Y., 1970; MS in English Edn., St. John's U., 1972; advanced cert. computers in edn., L.I. U., 1988, profl. diploma in edn. adminstrn., 1990. Cert. sch. dist. adminstr., sch. adminstr. and supr., tchr. English grades 7-12, NY, Ed.D, Lit. Studies, Hofstra U., Hempstead, NY, 2003. Exec. sec. Am. Petroleum Inst., N.Y.C., 1960-65; exec. asst. to v.p. Goldring, Inc., 1965-67; exec. asst. Rsch. Inst. for Cath. Edn., 1967-69; English tchr. St. Martin of Tours Sch., Amityville, 1970-77, Oceanside Jr. HS, 1977-78, Freeport HS, 1979—. Rec. sec. Freeport (N.Y.) Tchr. Ctr. Policy Bd., 1986-89; co-chair Middle States Steering Com., Freeport, 1988-90; chair Freeport H.S. Shared Decision Team, 1992-93; adv. bd. L.I. Writing Project, Garden City, N.Y., 1993—, co-leader Summer Insts.; adj. prof. literacy studies dept. Hofstra U., N.Y., 1999—. Co-author: (textbooks) Writing Competency Practice, 1980, Writing Competency Practice-Revised and Expanded, 1989. With Seaford (NY) Rep. Club, 1975—. Mem. Nat. Coun. Tchrs. English (conf. on English edn.), N.Y. State English Coun., L.I. Writing Project. Avocations: reading, writing, travel. Office: Freeport HS 50 S Brookside Ave Freeport NY 11520-3144 Office Phone: 516-867-5300. Personal E-mail: engteech@aol.com.

MARTORE, GRACIA, publishing company executive; b. 1951; m. Joseph Martore; 2 children. BA, Wellesley Coll. Asst. treas. Gannett Co., Inc., Mc Lean, Va., 1985—93, v.p. Treasury Svcs., 1993, head Investor Rels., 1996—98, treas., v.p. Investor Rels., 1998—2001, sr. v.p., 2001—06, CFO, 2003—06, exec. v.p., CFO, 2006—. Office: Gannett Co Inc 7950 Jones Branch Dr Mc Lean VA 22107-0910*

MARTORELL, CLAUDIA, infectious diseases physician; b. San Juan, Puerto Rico, May 25, 1972; d. Edgar and Maria (Berrios) Martorell. BS in Gen. Sci., U. P.R., 1994, MD magna cum laude, 1998; MPH, Harvard U., 2004. Diplomate in internal medicine and infectious diseases Am. Bd. Internal Medicine. Trainee in internal medicine Baystate Med. Ctr. Tufts U., Springfield, Mass., 1998—2001, fellow in infectious diseases, 2001—02; rsch. fellow in social medicine, Commonwealth Fund/Harvard U. Fellowship in Minority Pub. Health Harvard Med. Sch., 2003—04; cons./clinical investigator Cmty. Rsch. Initiative of New England, Springfield, Mass., 2004—05, assoc. dir. rsch.-west, 2005—. Coord. Mass. Legis. Oversight Hearings on Health Disparities, 2004. Vol. HIV Awareness and Support Group Mochilas Salvavidas, 1997—98, Primary Health Care Clinics for Medically Underserved People., Lares, PR, 1996, Primary Health Care Clinics for the Underserved and Geriatric Population, Loiza, PR, 1993, Jarabacoba, Dominican Republic, 1993. Recipient Bristol Myers Squibb scholarship, 1997, NHMA resident leadership program, 2000, AMA Found. Leadership award, 2004. Mem.: ACP, AMA (governing coun. rep. Minority Affairs Consortium 2004—), Mass. Med. Soc., Mass. Infectious Diseases Soc., Nat. Hispanic Med. Assn. (Resident Leadership Program award 2001), Infectious Diseases Soc. Am., Alpha Omega Alpha. Avocations: Tae Kwon Do, piano, sports. Office: Cmty Rsch Initiative of New England Ste 30 780 Chestnut St Springfield MA 01107-1610 Office Phone: 617-534-2646.*

MARTYL, (MRS. ALEXANDER LANGSDORF JR.), artist; b. St. Louis, Mar. 16, 1917; d. Martin and Aimee (Goldstone) Schweig; m. Alexander Langsdorf, Jr., Dec. 31, 1941; children: Suzanne, Alexandra. AB, Washington U., St. Louis, 1938. Instr. art dept. U. Chgo.; artist in residence Tamarind Inst., U. N.Mex., Albuquerque, 1974 Solo shows include, Calif. Palace of Legion of Honor, 1956, Chgo. Art Inst., 1949, 76, Feingarten Galleries, N.Y.C., Beverly Hills and Chgo., 1961, 62, 63, St. Louis, 1962, Feingarten Gallery, N.Y.C., 1963, L.A., 1964, Kovler Gallery, Chgo., 1967, Washington U., St. Louis, 1967, U. Chgo. Oriental Inst. Mus., 1970, Deson&Zaks Gallery, 1973, Fairweather-Hardin Gallery, 1977, 81, 83, Ill. State Mus., 1978, Fermilab, 1985, 91, Bklyn. Mus., 1986, Oriental Inst. Mus., 1987, Gibbes Art Mus., Charleston, S.C., 1988, Fairweather-Hardin Gallery, 1988, Tokyo Internat. Art Expo, 1990, State of Ill. Art Gallery, Chgo., 1990, Expo Navy Pier, Chgo., 1993, Printworks Gallery Ltd., Chgo., 1995, 97, 99, 2002, 04, Navy Pier, Chgo., 2003, 04, Oriental Inst. Mus., Chgo., Martyl: Nature/Artifice Ft. Wayne Mus. Art, 2000; represented in permanent collections, Met. Mus. Art, Chgo. Art Inst., Pa. Acad. Fine Arts, Ill. State Mus., Bklyn. Mus., DuSable Mus., Chgo., Los Angeles County Mus., Whitney Mus. Am. Art, Davenport (Iowa) Municipal Mus., St. Louis Art Mus., Washington U., U. Ariz., Arnot Gallery, Elmira, N.Y., Greenville (S.C.) Mus., Nat. Coll. Fine Arts, Hirshhorn Mus. and Sculpture Gallery, Rockford (Ill.) Mus. Recipient 1st prize City Art Mus., St. Louis, 1943, 44, Armstrong prize Chgo. Art Inst., 1947, William H. Bartels award, 1953, Frank Logan medal and prize, 1950, Walt Disney Purchase award L.A. (Calif.) Mus., Portrait of America Competition Purchase prize Colo. Springs Fine Arts Ctr., 1961, Hon. award AIA, 1962, Outstanding Achievement award YWCA, 1986, Artistic Contbn. to Cmty. award Schaumburg, Ill., 2005, Artistic Vision award Atomic Scientist, 2005, Artful Life award, 2005; grantee The Art Inst. Chgo., 2005; named Artist of Year Am. Fedn. Arts, 1958. Mem. Chgo. Network, Arts Club (Chgo.). Unitarian Universalist.

MARTYN, EVI, music educator, musician; b. Athens, Greece, Nov. 12, 1941; arrived in U.S., 1965; d. Anastasios and Sophia (Alivizatos) Giannatos; BA, Royal Conservatory Athens, 1959; MA, Royal Conservatory Athens, Greece, 1959; PhD Music, Hochschule fur Musik, Munich, Germany, 1963. Owner, founder Martyn Sch. Music, Los Alamitos, Calif., 1973—, chair keyboard dept., 1973—. Lectr., adjudicator, demonstrator numerous competitions, seminars, workshops etc. Author: Art of Piano Playing, 1988, The Root of Evil, 2005; contbg. author: Hellenic Voice; contbr. articles to profl. mags.; internat. performances include Wigmore Hall, London, Playel Hall, Paris, Merkin Hall, NYC, soloist SW Symphony of Utah, St. George, 2006. Performer at numerous benefit concerts including: D.C. Performing Arts Ctr., 1983, KLON Pub. Radio, Long Beach, Calif., Rotary Club Benefit for Needy, Huntington Beach, Calif., 1985, Hellenic U. Club, Loyola Marymount U., Calif., 1996. Recipient Excellent Artistic Evaluation, Internat. Comm. Agy., Washington, 1980, Award of Merit, Rotary Club of So. Calif., 1986, Knights of Pythias, 1993, The Andreas Sygros Gold medal, Greece Minister of Culture, First prize with gold medal, Royal Conservatory, Athens, 1959. Mem.: Internat. Assn. Music Competitions, Nat. Assn. Music Tchrs., Nat. Guild Piano Tchrs. (Named to Hall of Fame 1989). Avocation: swimming. Home Fax: 714-995-5699. E-mail: evimartyn@aol.com.

MARTYSKA, BARBARA, composer, performer, educator; b. Phila., Nov. 16, 1936; d. Alexander Thomas and Sophia Victoria (Romanek) M.; m. Gerald Bernard Buckley, Dec. 29, 1956 (div. 1972); children: Regina Buckley-Fried, Sandra Buckley-Rusnov, Gerald Thomas Buckley, Paul David Buckley, Mary Elizabeth Buckley; m. James William Lieberman, Sept. 17, 1978. Freelance composer home studio, Allentown, Pa., 1980—; pvt. studio tchr. Allentown, 1971—, Cmty. Music Sch., Allentown, 1986-96; music for handicapped Good Shepherd Home, Allentown, 1986-91. Founder Second Sunday Salon performance series, 2001—; adjudicator various piano/composition competitions. Composer Cloud Watching, 1994, Two Minuets, 1995, In the Silence, 1996, Russian Legend, 1997, In the Still Hours, 1998, (CD) Alaskan Spring, 2005; author (piano books) From Canyons to Highlands, 1995, Ancient Echoes, 1995, Adventures and Amusements, 1998, Ordinary and Extraordinary Animals, 1998. Recipient ASCAP spl. award, 1996-2006. Mem. ASCAP, Internat. Alliance Women in Music, Music Tchrs. Nat. Assn. (composition chair 1998-2000, pres. local chpt. 1995-97, v.p. local chpt. 1993-95), Nat. Fedn. Music Clubs (composers award merit 1993, 98), Am. Music Ctr. Avocations: reading, gardening. Home: 1716 Saratoga Ct Allentown PA 18104-1716 E-mail: BMmusic@fast.net.

MARTZ, JUDY HELEN, former governor; b. Big Timber, Mont., July 28, 1943; m. Harry Martz, June 23, 1965; children: Justin, Stacey. Owner, operator Martz Disposal Svc., Butte, Mont., 1971—; skater U.S. World Speed Skating Team, Japan, 1963, U.S. Olympic Team, Innsbruck, Austria, 1964; exec. dir. U.S. High Altitude Speed Skating Ctr., Butte, Mont., 1985-89; field rep. Senator Conrad Burns, 1989—95; lt. gov. State of Mont., Helena, 1997-2001, gov., 2001—05. Coach Mont. Amateur Speed Skating Assn.; bd. dirs. Youth Hockey Assn.; pres. adv. bd. U.S. Internat. Speed Skating Assn.; chair, Montanans for Judge Roberts (chief justice nominee), 2006. Bd dirs. St. James Cmty. Hosp., Legion Oasis HUD Housing Project. Named Miss Rodeo Mont., 1963; inducted Butte Sports Hall of Fame, 1987. Republican.*

MARUCA, RITA, real estate company executive, real estate broker; b. Italy, Sept. 15, 1957; came to the U.S., 1974; d. Italo Talarico and Rosa Rotundo; m. Luigi Maruca, Oct. 27, 1973; children: Concetta, Italo, Anthony. Student, Italy. Mgr. FNY, Jackson Heights, N.Y., 1988-90, Era Vision, Corona, N.Y., 1990-91; salesperson Century 21 Sam & Raj, Corona, 1991-95, Era Today, Floral Park, N.Y., 1995-97; broker, owner Parkview Realty LLC, Corona, 1997—. Mem. Lions Internat. Office: Parkview Realty LLC 50-07 108th St Corona NY 11368

MARUOKA, JO ANN ELIZABETH, retired information systems manager; b. Monrovia, Calif., Jan. 1, 1945; d. John Constantine and Pearl (Macovei) Gotsinas; m. Lester Hideo Maruoka, Nov. 8, 1973 (div. Aug. 1992); 1 child, John Nicholas Reyes-Burke; stepchildren: Les Scott Kaleohano, Lee Stuart Keola. BA with honors, UCLA, 1966; MBA, U. Hawaii, 1971. Office mgr. and asst. R. Wenkam, Photographer, Honolulu, 1966-69; computer mgmt. intern and sys. analyst Army Computer Sys. Command, Honolulu, 1969-78; reservations mgr. Hale Koa Hotel, Honolulu, 1978-79; equal employment opportunity specialist U.S. Army Pacific Hdqs., Honolulu, 1979-80, computer specialist, 1980-87, supervisory info. sys. mgr., chief info. tech. plans and programs, 1987-2001; ret., 2001. Bd. dirs. High Performance Computing and Comm. Coun., Tiverton, R.I.; Pacific v.p. Fedn. Govt. Info. Processing Couns., Washington, 1992-95. Active Nat. and Hawaii Women's Polit. Caucus, Honolulu, 1987—; pres. Fed. Women's Coun. Hawaii, Honolulu, 1976-77, advisor, 1977—. Recipient Svc. award Fed. Women's Coun. Hawaii, 1986, EEO Excellence award Sec. of Army, 1989, Pacific Fed. Mgr. award Honolulu-Pacific Fed. Exec. Bd., 1990, Info. Resources Mgmt. award Interagy. Com. on Info. Resources Mgmt., 1991, Lead Dog Leadership award Fedn. Govt. Info. Processing Couns., 1993; named One of Fed. 100 (Execs.) of Yr., Fed. Computer Week, 1996. Mem. AAUW, LWV (sec. Hawaii State Bd. 2003-05, dir. 2005—), Hawaii State League Women Voters (bd. dirs.), NAFE, Nat. Women's Polit. Caucus, Armed Forces Comm.-Electronics Assn. (Hawaii chpt., Internat. award for Info. Resources Mgmt. Excellence 1992), Assn. U.S. Army (Pacific Fed. Mgr. award 1990), Federally Employed Women (advisor Aloha and Rainbow chpts. 1977—), Army Signal Corps Regtl. Assn. (Bronze Order of Mercury 1997, Silver Order of Mercury, 2001), Hawaii Intergovt. Info. Processing Coun. (pres. 1988-89, svc. award 1989), Beta Gamma Sigma. Avocations: travel, reading, tai chi, theater. Personal E-mail: maruokaj@hawaii.rr.com.

MARVEL, L. PAIGE, federal judge; b. Easton, Md., Dec. 6, 1949; d. E. Warner Marvel and Louise H. Harrison; m. Robert H. Dyer, Jr., Aug. 9, 1975; children: Alex W. Dyer, Kelly E. Dyer. BA magna cum laude, Notre Dame Coll., 1971; JD with honors, U. Md., 1974. Bar: Md. 1974, U.S. Dist. Ct. Md. 1974, U.S. Tax Ct. 1975, U.S. Ct. Appeals (4th cir.) 1977, U.S. Supreme Ct. 1980, U.S. Ct. Claims 1981, D.C. 1985. Assoc. Garbis & Schwait, P.A., Balt., 1974-76, shareholder, 1976-85, Garbis, Marvel & Junghans, P.A., Balt., 1985-86; mem. Melnicove, Kaufman, Weiner, Smouse & Garbis, P.A., Balt., 1986-88; ptnr. Venable, Baetjer and Howard LLP, Balt., 1988-98; judge U.S. Tax Ct., Washington, 1998—. Mem. U. Md. Law Sch. Bd. Vis., 1995—2001; mem. adv. com. U.S. Dist. Ct. Md., 1991—93; mem. Commr.'s Rev. Panel on IRS Integrity, 1989—91. Co-editor procedure dept. Jour. Taxation, 1989-98; contbr. chpts. to books, articles to profl. jours. Active Women's Law Ctr., 1974-85, Md. Dept. Econ. and Cmty. Devel. Adv. Com., 1978-80; trustee Loyola-Notre Dame Libr., Inc., 1996-2003. Recipient Recognition award Balt. Is Best Program, 1981; named One of Md.'s Top 100 Women, The Daily Record, 1998; recipient MSBA Taxation section's Tax Excellence award, 2002. Fellow Am. Bar Found., Md. Bar Found., Am. Coll. Tax Counsel (regent 1995-98); mem. ABA (sect. taxation coun. dir. 1989-92, vice-chair com. ops. 1993-95, Disting. Svc. award, Jules Ritholz award 2004), Am. Law Inst. (advisor restatement of law third, law governing lawyers), Md. Bar Assn. (chmn. taxation sect. 1982-83, bd. dirs. 1988-90, 96-98, Disting. Svc. award), Balt. Bar Assn. (at-large exec. coun.), Am. Tax Policy Inst. (trustee 1997-98), Serjeant's Inn. Avocations: golf, music, travel. Office: US Tax Ct 400 Second St NW Washington DC 20217-0001 Office Phone: 202-521-0740.

MARVIN, BARBARA JOYCE, writer; b. Garden City, N.Y., July 31, 1954; d. Roland Reed Jr. and Ruth Doris (Henze) Hummel; m. Lewis Beach Marvin III, July 5, 1977; children: Lewis Beach Marvin IV, Henze Louise, Maximilian Gardner. BA in English Lit., Finch Coll., 1975; postgrad., Marymouht Manhattan, 1975, Adelphi U., 1975. Ballerina Malibu Ballet by the Sea, 1980-98; owner animal sanctuary Moonfire Ranch, Malibu, 1957—. Author: Tales from Moonfire, 4 vols., 1995-98; author short stories, hist. love tales. Mem. Pacific Asian Mus., Malibu Libr. Mem. Met. Club (N.Y.), Malibu Ballet Soc. Republican. Avocations: ballet, exotic animals, vegetarianism, poetry and prose, fashion modeling, private investor. Home and Office: 23852 Pacific Coast Hwy # 349 Malibu CA 90265-4879

MARVIN, CATHERINE A., financial consultant; b. Asheville, N.C., Aug. 16, 1966; d. Robert L Morrison and Anne C. Veitch, Thomas H Veitch (Stepfather), Kay Morrison (Stepmother). BBA, S.W. Tex. State U., 1988. Cert. Series 7, 63, 65. Asst. v.p./trust officer Bank of Am., Dallas, 1994—99; fin. cons. Salomon Smith Barney, San Antonio, 1999—2002. Mem. Bexar County Young Republicans, San Antonio, 2001—02. Mem.: Southwest Tex. State U. Alumnae Assn., Humane Soc. U.S., Zeta Tau Alpha Alumnae Assn. (coord. collegiate/alumnae rels. 2000—02). Baptist. Avocations: travel, reading, cooking. Office: Smith Barney 300 Convent St 28th Fl San Antonio TX 78205 Business E-Mail: catherine.a.marvin@rssmb.com.

MARVIN, D. JANE, consumer products company executive; B in Econs., U. Sussex, Eng.; MBA, U. Mich. V.p. human resources Ameritech, Gen. Bus. Svcs., 1997—99; exec. v.p. human resources Covad Com. Group, Inc., 1999—2001, AT&T Wireless Svcs., Inc., Redmond, Wash., 2001—.

MARVIN, FREDA MARY, art educator, nurse; b. Everett, Wash., July 3, 1930; d. Robert Laffayette and Georgeina (Mahlstedt) Pressey; m. Donald Conrad Lawrence, 1950 (div. 1966); children: Linda, Karen, Donna, Betty; m. William Hammond Marvin, July 30, 1971. AA, San Jose City Coll., 1964; BS, Calif. State U., Fresno, 1974; cert., Beartooth Sch. Wildlife, 1995, 96. RN, Calif.; cert. sch. audiometrist Calif. Head nurse II Agnew State Hosp., San Jose, Calif., 1964-71; head nurse I Med. Ctr. Fresno (Calif.), 1971-72; intern nurse St. Agnes Hosp., Fresno, 1974-75; sch. nurse Teague Sch. Dist., Fresno, 1976-78; intensive care pvt. duty nurse Fresno, 1980-94; relief dir. nursing Sierra View Convescent Hosp., Fresno, 1995; art tchr. Marvin Art Studio, Prather, Calif., 1995—. Numerous two-women and group shows including Timberline Gallery, Oakhurst, Calif., Marvin Art Gallery, Prather, Calif. Fresno State Coll. scholar, 1973, 74; recipient Art award Clovis Art Guild, Soc. Western Artists Signature Show award, 1999. Mem. Soc. Western Artists (pres. 1994, 95, degree of honor 1993), Yosemite Western Artists (exec. bd. dirs. 1980-90, exec. bd. 1995, awards). Republican. Avocations: gardening, painting, reading, computer. Fax: 209-322-0904. E-mail: Bilfrema@msn.com.

MARVIN, LAURA LYNN, art educator; b. Balt., Jan. 30, 1975; d. Donald Elbert and Esther Mae Head; m. Brian Marvin, July 6, 2002 (div. Mar. 4, 2006); 1 child, Kyle Everett. Assoc., Balt. County C.C., 1996; Bachelors, Towson U., 2002; Masters, Goucher Coll., Balt., 2002. Cert. elem., reading tchr. Md. Art/tech. tchr. Colgate Elem. Sch., Balt. County Pub. Schs., 2002—.

Mentor tchr. Balt. County Pub. Schs., 2005—06. Meml. scholarship, Vietnam Vets. of Am. Chpt. 451, 1997. Mem.: NEA (life), Tchrs. Assn. of Balt. County (life), Md. State Tchrs. Assn. (life). Avocations: painting, drawing, decorating, sculpting. Office Phone: 410-887-7010.

MARVIN, URSULA BAILEY, retired geologist; b. Bradford, Vt., Aug. 20, 1921; d. Harold Leslie and Alice Miranda (Bartlett) Bailey; m. Lloyd Burton Chaisson, June 28, 1944 (div. 1951); m. Thomas Crockett Marvin, Apr. 1, 1952. BA, Tufts Coll., 1943; MA, Harvard/Radcliffe Coll., 1946; PhD, Harvard U., 1969. Rsch. asst. dept. geology U. Chgo., 1947-50; mineralogist Union Carbide Corp., N.Y.C., 1952-58; instr. dept. geology Tufts U., Medford, Mass., 1958-61; geologist Smithsonian Astrophysics Obs., Cambridge, Mass., 1961-98; lectr. geology Harvard U., Cambridge, 1974-92; sr. geologist emeritus Harvard-Smithsonian Ctr. for Astrophysics, Cambridge, 1998. Vis. prof. dept. geology Ariz. State U., Tempe, 1978; trustee Tufts U., 1975-85, trustee emeritus, 1988—; trustee U. Space Rsch. Assn., Columbia Md., 1979-84, chmn., 1982-83; sec.-gen. Internat. Commn. on History Geol. Scis., 1989-96, v.p. for N.Am., 1996-2004. Author: Continental Drift, 1973; contbr. chpt.: Astronomy from Space, 1983, The Planets, 1985, Les Météorites, 1996, James Hutton-Present and Future, 1999, The Earth Inside and Out: Some Major Contributions to Geology in the Twentieth Century, 2002; assoc. editor Earth in Space, Am. Geophys. Union, 1988-90; contbr. articles to profl. jours. Chair profl. accomplishments evaluation com. Smithsonian Astro-Phys. Obs., 1986-92, 2001-04; mem. Lunar and Planetary Sci. Coun., Houston, 1987-91; chair Antarctic Meteorite Working Group NSF-NASA-Smithsonian Instn., 1993-99. Recipient Antarctic Svc. medal NSF, 1983, Sustained Superior Achievement award SAO, 1988, 93, 96, Lifetime Achievement award Women in Sci. and Engring., 1997, Lifetime Achievement award Harvard-Smithsonian Ctr. for Astrophysics, 1997, Sue Tyler Friedman award for history of geology The Geol. Soc. London, 2005; Asteroid Marvin named in her honor Minor Planet Bur. of Internat. Astron. Union, 1991, Marvin Nunatak (mountain peak rising through the Antarctic ice sheet) named in her honor U.S. Bd. on Geog. Names, 1992. Fellow AAAS, Meteoritical Soc. (pres. 1975-76), Geol. Soc. Am. (chmn. history of geology divsn. 1982-83, History of Geology award 1986, Sue Tyler Friedman award, Geol. Soc. London); mem. Assn. Women in Sci., Am. Geophys. Union, History of Earth Scis. Soc. (pres. 1991), Sigma Xi (pres. Harvard-Radcliffe chpt. 1971-72). Avocation: worldwide birding. Office: Harvard-Smithsonian Ctr for Astrophysics 60 Garden St Cambridge MA 02138-1516 Office Phone: 617-495-7270. Business E-Mail: umarvin@cfa.harvard.edu.

MARX, NICKI DIANE, sculptor, painter; b. LA, Oct. 3, 1943; d. Donald F. and Ruth H. (Ungar) M. Student, U. Calif., Riverside, 1965, U. Calif., Santa Cruz, 1973. Represented by Nicki Marx Studio, Taos, N.Mex., Fred Kline Gallery, Santa Fe, N.Mex. One-woman shows include Palm Springs Desert Mus., 1977, Julie Artisans Gallery, NYC, 1975, Phoenix Art Mus., 1975, Weston Gallery, Carmel, Calif, 1981, Kirk de Gooyer Gallery, LA, 1982, Rocklands Gallery, Monterey, Calif., 1983, Fetish Gallery, Taos, 1988, Fenix Gallery, Taos, 1991, Earthworks, 1993, Lamberts, 1994, Stables Gallery, Taos, 1995, Fred Kline, 1995, Sun Cities Mus. Art, Ariz., 1996, Harwood Mus. Art, Taos, 1999, others; group exhbns. include E.P. Smith Gallery, Santa Cruz, 1994, Lumina Gallery, Taos, 1994, Cafe Gallery, Albuquerque, 1991, Bareiss Gallery, Taos, 1990, Ctr. for Contemporary Art, Santa Fe, 1989, Jordan Gallery, Taos, 1988-89, Stables Art Gallery, Taos, 1988, 94, Albuquerque State Fair Grounds, 1986, San Francisco Mus. Modern Art, 1977-78, Elements Gallery, Greenwich, Conn., 1977, Pacific Design Ctr., LA, 1976, Lester Gallery, Inverness, Calif., 1976, others; represented in pub. collections IBM, Milford, Conn., NYC, San Jose, Calif., Bank of Am., San Francisco, The Continental Group, Inc., Stamford, Conn., Cedars-Sinai Hosp., LA, Farm Bur. Fedn., Sacramento, Calif., Sherman Fairchild Sci. Ctr., Stanford, Calif., Palm Springs Desert Mus., Calif., U. Mus., Ariz. State U. at Tempe, Mills Coll. Art Gallery, Berkeley, Calif.; exhibited in pvt. collections of Estate of Eugene Klein, Estate of Louise Nevelson, Estate of Georgia O'Keeffe, Fritz Scholder, Ray Graham, Bunny Horowitz, Sue and Otto Meyer, Burt Sugarman, Craig Moody, Paul Pletka, others; subject of numerous articles in jours. and mags. MacDowell Colony fellow, 1975; recipient Adolph and Esther Gottleib Found. grant, 1985. Studio: PO Box 128 Penasco NM 87553 Office Phone: 505-587-2383.

MARY, DIANE BRADLEY, elementary school educator, secondary school educator; d. William Joseph and Mary Ann Bradley; children: William Bradley, James Corbett, Megan Shannon Mary. Degree, Stanford U., Calif.; MA in Edn., U. Calif., Berkeley, 1965. Cert. counselor U. Calif. Berkley; tchr. San Francisco State U. Tchr. 7th grade sci., biology Sullivan Mid. Sch., Fairfield, 1989—, counselor. Mentor tchr. U. Calif., Davis. Recipient Tchr. Yr., Sullivan Middle Sch., Disting. Alumni award, Stanford U. Home: 2889 St Andrews Rd Fairfield CA 94534 Office: Sullivan Middle Sch 2195 Union Ave Fairfield CA 94533 Office Phone: 707-421-4115. Office Fax: 707-421-3964. Personal E-mail: dmscience@aol.com. Business E-Mail: dianem@fsusd.12.ca.us.

MARYLES, DAISY, editor; B, City Coll. NY. Joined Publishers Weekly, NYC, 1965—, dept. editor, News, Bookselling, Mktg., exec. editor, 1986—. Author: (columns) Behind the Booksellers, Publishers Weekly. Recipient Harry Scherman Lifetime Svc. award, UJA-Fedn. NY pub. divsn., 2005. Office: Publishers Weekly 13th Fl 360 Park Ave S New York NY 10010-1710 Office Phone: 646-746-6767. Office Fax: 646-746-6631. Business E-Mail: dmaryles@reedbusiness.com.

MARYSCHUK, OLGA YAROSLAVA, artist, executive secretary; b. Greenwich, Conn., July 21, 1928; d. George and Rose Greshchyshyn M. BFA, Cooper Union Sch. Art/Arch., 1979. Exec. asst. I.M. Pei & Ptnrs., N.Y.C., 1966—92. One-woman shows include I.M. Pei & Ptnrs., Archs. & Planners, N.Y.C., 1984, Fifth Street Gallery, N.Y., 1980, Ukrainian Can. Art Found., Toronto, 1980, Ukrainian Artists Assn. in USA, N.Y.C., 1979, Ukrainian Friendship Soc., Kyiv, 1971, Peter Cooper Gallery, N.Y., 1968, exhibited in group shows at Old N.Y. Gallery, 1998, 2000, Tenement Mus., N.Y., 1999, Ukrainian Inst., 1999, Richmond Art Ctr., Calif., 1997, Chgo. Ctr. for Book and Arts, 1996, Michael Ingbar Gallery, N.Y.C., 1993—94, others, Represented in permanent collections AT&T, Atlanta, C&S/Sovran Bank, Carter Wallace, N.Y., Kohn Pedersen Fox, Archs., N.Y.C., Mortgage Bankers Assn., Washington, Ternopil Regional Mus., Ukraine, Ukrainian Mus. of Fine Art, Kyiv, United Way, Atlanta, West Allis Meml. Hosp., Milw., Consul Gen. Ukraine in N.Y., Amos Eno Gallery, N.Y.C., exhibitions include paintingsdirect.com. Founding mem. Fulton Art Fair, Bklyn., 1957; vol. Sta. WNYC, N.Y.C., 1992-99, UNICEF, N.Y.C., 1999— Fellow Ragdale Found., 1984, 1986, Va. Ctr. for Creative Arts, 1982, 1983; scholar Kyiv State Art Inst., 1970—71. Mem.: Artist Equity. Unitarian Universalist. Avocations: tai chi, travel, writing, curatorial work. Home: 170 Avenue C Apt 2C New York NY 10009

MARZIGLIANO, TAMMY, lawyer; b. N.Y., Aug. 29, 1971; d. Nicholas Joseph and Carolyn Marzigliano. BA, Hofstra U., Hempstead, N.Y., 1995; JD magna cum laude, Quinnipiac U., Hamden, Conn., 2001. Atty. Klebanoff & Phelan, West Hartford, Conn., Dutten & Golden, LLP, N.Y.C., 2004—. Home: 3 Park Ave Fl 29 New York NY 10016-5902

MASAOKA, JAN, not-for-profit executive; BA, San Francisco State U. Regional dir. US.-China Friendship Assn., 1978—80; bus. mgr. Cognos Assocs., 1982—83; fin. dir. Advocates for Women, 1983—85; dir. cons. svcs. Support Ctr. for Nonprofit Mgmt., 1988—90; exec. dir. CompassPoint Nonprofit Svcs., San Francisco, 1993—. Lectr. Grad. Sch. of Pub. Adminstrn. Golden Gate U., 1987—96. Writer, editor Board Café, 1999—, mem. nat. editl. adv. com. BoardSource, 1999—; contbr. articles to profl. jours. Chair bd. dirs. Asian & Pacific Islander Wellness Ctr.; founding pres., mem. bd. dirs. San Francisco Found. Cmty. Initiative Funds. Named Nonprofit Exec. of Yr., NonProfit Times, 2002; recipient Robert E. Kantor Medal, Pacific Grad. Sch. Psychology, 2000, Woman Warrior, Pacific Asian Am. Women's Bay Area Coalition, 2002; grantee Gerbode Fellowship, Sch. of Social Work, U. Calif., Berkeley, 2001. Office: CompassPoint Nonprofit Svcs Ste 200 731 Market St San Francisco CA 94103 Office Phone: 415-541-9000. Office Fax: 415-541-7780.*

MASCHERONI, ELEANOR EARLE, marketing communications executive; b. Boston, June 6, 1955; d. Ralph II and Eleanor Forbes (Owens) Earle; m. Mark Mascheroni, May 30, 1981; children: Olivia Forbes, Isabella Starbuck, Rex Owens. AB, Brown U., 1977. Dept. adminstr. Sotheby Parke Bernet, N.Y.C., 1978-79; asst. dir. devel. Inst. Architecture and Urban Studies, N.Y.C., 1979-81; assoc. in pub. rels. Prudential Securities Inc., N.Y.C., 1981-84, asst. v.p., 1984-86, assoc. v.p., 1986-87, v.p., mgr., 1987—89, 1st v.p., dir. corp. commns., 1989—91; v.p. corp. comms. Zurich Scudder Investments, Inc., N.Y.C., 1991-95, prin., sr. v.p., dir. corp. comms., 1996-99, mng. dir., 1999—2001; CMO Ogilvy & Mather, 2001—. N.Y. Alumnae bd. govs. St. Timothy's Sch., Stevenson, Md., 1994—; trustee Hartley House, 2000—. Avocations: running, yoga, photography. Office Phone: 212-237-7239. Business E-Mail: eleanor.mascheroni@ogilvy.com.

MASEKELA, BARBARA JOYCE MOSIMA, ambassador; 2 children. B, U. Ohio. Chief of staff to Nelson Mandela, 1990—94; exec. dir. for pub. and corp. affairs De Beers Consol. Mines (ret. 2003); South African amb. to France and UNESCO, 1995—99; South African amb. to the US Washington, 2003—. Asst. prof. English lit. Staten Island CC, NY, Rutgers U., NJ; trustee Nelson Mandela Children's Fund, Nelson Mandela Found.; various exec. and non-exec. directorships including Standard Bank of South Africa, South African Broadcasting Corp., and Internat. Mktg. Coun., 1999—2003. Achievements include founding African Nat. Congress Office of Arts and Culture. Office: Embassy of South Africa 3051 Mass Ave NW Washington DC 20008

MASHIN, JACQUELINE ANN COOK, health facility administrator, consultant; b. Chgo., May 11, 1941; d. William Hermann and Ann (Smidt) Cook; m. Fredric John Mashin, June 7, 1970; children: Joseph Glenn, Alison Robin. BS, U. Md., 1984; BSN, Cath. U. Am., Washington, 1993. Cert. realtor. Adminstrv. asst. CIA, Washington, 1963-66; asst. to mng. dir. Aerospace Edn. Found., Washington, 1966-74; exec. asst. to asst exec. dir. Air Force Assn., Washington, 1974-79; v.p., ptnrship. owner Discount Linen Store, Silver Spring, Md., 1979-81; asst. regional polit. dir. Office of Pres.-elect, Washington, 1980-81; confidential asst. to dir. Office of Personnel Mgmt. (US), Washington, 1981-83; spl. asst. to dep. dir. Office of Mgmt. and Budget, Washington, 1983-86; dir. internat. communications and spl. asst. to commr. Dept. of the Interior, Washington, 1986-89, cons., 1989-93; with Washington Hosp. Ctr., 1993—. Chmn., vol. coord. Mo. County Rep. Party, 1999; chmn. Bayclub, Mo. County Fedn. Rep. Women, 1999, 2000. Pres. Layhill Civic Assn., Silver Spring, Md., 1980; state chmn. Md.'s Reagan Youth Delegation, Annapolis, Md., 1980; state treas., office mgr. Reagan-Bush State Hdqrs. of Md., Silver Spring, 1980; mem. Women's Com. Nat. Symphony Orch.; pres. Rock Creek Women's Rep. Club, 1998, Montgomery County Rep. Party, 1999, Montgomery County Fedn. Rep. Women, 1999—; steering com. Wheaton Redevel. Program, 2001—; gov.'s adv. bd. Md. Bd. Health and Mental Hygiene Balt., 2003- Mem.: Air Force Assn. (life), U.S. Capital Hist. Soc., Aux. Salvation Army (life), Indian Spring Country Club. Republican. Avocations: golf, horseback riding, collecting wine glasses, hibel plates, lithos and lalique crystal. Home and Office: 2429 White Horse Ln Silver Spring MD 20906-2243 Personal E-mail: Jaguar041@aol.com.

MASI, DALE A., project director, social sciences educator, research and development company executive; b. NYC; d. Alphonse E. and Vera Avella; children: Eric, Renee, Robin. BS, Coll. Mt. St. Vincent; MSW, U. Ill.; PhD Social Work, Cath. U. Lectr. Sch. Social Svcs., Ipswitch, Eng., 1970-72; project dir. occupational substance abuse program, asso. prof. Boston Coll. Grad. Sch. Social Work, 1972-79; dir. Office Employee Counseling Svc., Dept. Health/Human Svcs., Washington, 1979-84; pres. Masi Research Cons., Inc., 1984—2005; prof. emeritus U. Md. Grad. Sch. Social Work, 1980—2004; adj. prof. U. Md. Coll. Bus. and Mgmt., 1980—2004, prof. emeritus, 2004—; lectr. Bacconi U., Milan, 2004—; project dir. NIH Rsch. grantee coll. bingo drinking Northeastern U., 2005—. Mem. IBM Mental Health Adv. Bd., 1990-95; cons. IBM, Toyota, Mobil Chm., The Washington Post, U.S. Ho. Reps., U.S. Postal Svc., White House, WHO, Bechtel Corp., other orgns. in pub. and pvt. sector; bd. advisors Nat. Security Inst., Wayside Youth and Family Support Network; USIA Ampart lectr. on alcohol, drugs and AIDS in the workplace; chair CMHS Joint Industry Alliance, 2002—; acad. advisor Northwestern U. Author: Human Services in Industry, Organizing for Women, Designing Employee Assistance Programs, Drug Free Workplace, AIDS Issues in the Workplace: A Response Model for Human Resource Management, The AMA Handbook for Developing Employee Assistance and Counseling Programs, Evaluating Your Employee Assistance and Managed Behavioral Care Program, Internat. Employee Assistance Anthology, I, II and III edits., Productivity Lost: Alcohol and Drugs in the Workplace; co-author: Shrink to Fit: Answers to Your Questions About Therapy; also over 40 articles. Named Disting. Scholar, Nat. Acad. Practice, 2001—; named to Employee Assistance Program Hall of Fame; recipient award, Employee Assistance Program Digest; fellow Fulbright fellow, 1969—70, 1994, AAUW postdoctoral fellow, NIMH, 1962—64; Fulbright Sr. Specialist Canidate, 2002. Mem. AAUW, NASW (Internat. Rhoda G. Sarnat award 1993), Acad. Cert. Social Workers, Employee Assistance Profls. Assn. (nat. individual achievement award 1983), Fulbright Assn. (nat. bd.). Democrat. Roman Catholic. Office: 4 Copley Pl Suite 145 Boston MA 02116 Office Phone: 202-223-2399, 617-536-1930.

MASI, JULIA A., elementary school educator; d. Ralph Michel and Frances Marie Masi. MS, Adelphi U., 1987; MA, Adlephi U., 1991; cert. in Chinese, NYU, 1994; cert. in non-profit mgmt., U. Ill., Chgo., 2005. Cert. diamond appraiser Gemological Inst. Am. Tchr. Pub. Sch. 169, NYC Dept. Edn., Bklyn., 1988—97; sci. tchr. Pub. Sch. 24, NYC Dept. Edn., Bklyn., 1997—. Mng. editor: Fanzeen Mag., contbr.: Dance Pages; exhibitions include Brooklyn Hist. Soc., 2002. Vol. editor newsletter, website Magic Hosp.; vol. www.GourmetSoupKitchens.org; mem. Jane Godall Inst.; bd. dirs. Children of the City, Bklyn., 2005—; jr. assoc. Mus. of Modern Art, NYC, 1996—; mem. young collectors coun., aquisitons com. Guggenheim Mus., NYC, 1993—; vol. NY Cares, NYC, 2005—. Mem.: APA (assoc.). Democrat. Roman Catholic. Avocations: writing, ballet, mentoring, drawing, languages.

MASIELLO, LISA ANNE, elementary school educator; b. Bradford, Pa., May 17, 1979; d. Sharon Anne Panasiewicz and Robert John Crone; m. Samuel Michael Masiello, July 19, 2003. BS Elem. Edn., Social Studies Edn., Buffalo State Coll., N.Y., 2001. Cert. elem., secondary social studies tchr. Colo., 2005. Tchr. social studies St. Edmund's Sch., Tonawanda, NY, 2001—03; tchr. 2nd grade Pinnacle Charter Sch., Federal Heights, Colo., 2003—04; tchr. 6th grade literacy Columbia Mid. Sch., Aurora, Colo., 2004—. Sunday sch. tchr. LDS Ch., Brighton, Colo., 2004—06.

MASINI, ELEONORA BARBIERI, futurist; b. Quirigua, Los Amates, Guatemala, Nov. 19, 1928; d. Vincenzo and Edith Frances (Fullerton) Barbieri; m. Francesco Maria Masini, Jan. 31, 1953; children: Alessandro, Andrea, Federico. LLD, U. Rome, 1952, D in Sociology, 1964; D (hon.), Budapest U., 1998. Dir. Ctr. of Forecasting Instituto Richerche Applicate Documentazione E Studi, Rome, 1972—75; rsch. dir. UNESCO, 1972—78, Centro Italiano Femminile, 1972—78; coord. projects UN Univ., 1978, 1984—90; chmn. social forecasting Pontifical Gregorian U., Rome, 1977—, prof. emeritus, 2004. Sec. gen. World Future Studies Fedn., Rome, 1975—80, pres., 1980—, Women's Internat. Network Emergency and Solidarity. Author: Space for Man, 1972, Social and Human Forecasting, 1973, Social Indicators and Forecasting, 1977, Visions of Desirable Societies, 1983, Why Futures Studies?, 1993; actor: Directory of Women's Groups in Emergency Situations, 1999; editor: Women, Households and Change, 1991, The Future of Asian Cultures, 1993, Penser Le Futur, 2000. Named Fulbright fellow, 1951, Fulbright prof., U.S.A., 1986; recipient Fulbright fellow, 1985. Mem.: Club of Rome. Home and Office: Via Bertoloni 23 00197 Rome Italy E-mail: e.masini@mclink.it.

MASKALA, KRISTEN LUCY, orthopedic surgeon; b. Blue Island, Ill., May 24, 1971; d. Joseph Arnold and Christine Carolyn Maskala; m. Monte Gene Smith, May 31, 2003. BA, Marquette U., Milw., Wis., 1991—94; MD, Rush Med. Coll., Chgo., 1994—98. Lic. MD Wis., Fla. Orthop. resident/physician Med. Coll. Wis., Milw., 1998—2003; sports medicine fellow Fla. Orthop. Inst., Tampa, 2003—04; orthop. surgeon W. Bend Clin., Wis., 2004—. Sports medicine dir. W. Bend Clin., 2004—; team physician Hartford HS, 2005—. Vol. basketball coach W. Bend HS, 2006. Named Woman of Yr.-Wis., NCAA, 1994, Student of Yr., Marquette U., 1994; recipient GTE All Am. Player of Yr., Women's Basketball, 1994, Academic All Am. Div., I Basketall, 1992, 1993, 1994, Inducted; grantee Grad. scholarship, NCAA, 1994, Resident Rsch. award, Med. Coll. Wis., 2003. Mem.: Alpha Omega Alpha. Office: West Bend Clinic 1700 W Paradise Dr West Bend WI 53095

MASKELL, KATHLEEN MARY, English and reading educator; b. Balt., Md., Aug. 25, 1962; d. Francis E. and M. Dolores Maskell. BS in Comms., Towson U., Md., 1984, MEd, 1993; postgrad., Johns Hopkins U., 2004—. Dept. chair Holy Rosary Sch., Balt., 1987—95; Anthony coord. Archbishop Curley, Balt., 1995—. Vol. Franciscan Youth Ministry, Balt., 1995—. Recipient Archbishop's Tchg. award, 1989, 1997, 2001. Home: 7925 35th St Rosedale MD 21237

MASKER, DEBERA ANN, middle school educator; d. Elmer Harvey and Barbara Grace King; m. R. John Masker, July 2, 1977; children: Ellen, Claire, Amanda, TJ., Zachary. BS in Elem./Secondary Edn., N.W. Mo. State U., Maryville, 1977; MS in Elem. Adminstrn., Creighton U., Omaha, 1988. Master tchr. lic. Iowa Dept. Edn. Tchr. Treynor Cmty. Sch., Iowa, 1977—83, OPS Bryan Jr. High, Omaha, 1984—89; elem. prin. Shelby County Cath. Schs., Harlan, Iowa, 1989—94; asst. HS prin. Roncalli Cath. Sch., Omaha, 1995—99; tchr. Council Bluffs-Kirn Jr. High, Council Bluffs, Iowa, 1999—. Staff devel. presenter Council Bluffs Schs., 1999—; dir. Leadership Acad., 2004—. Contbr. articles to profl. pubs. Leader NBM 4-H Club, Neola, Iowa, 1999—; cantor St. Patrick's Ch., Neola, 1982—. Recipient Tchr. of Yr. award, Kirn Jr. High, 2004, 4-H Alumni award, W. Pott Ext., Council Bluffs, Iowa, 2005, Iowa History Day Tchr. of Yr. award, State Hist. Soc., Des Moines, 2006. Mem.: Iowa State Edn. Assn., Council Bluffs Edn. Assn., Phi Delta Kappa. Avocations: reading, crafts. Office: Kirn Jr High 100 North Ave Council Bluffs IA 51503

MASLACH, CHRISTINA, psychology professor; b. San Francisco, Jan. 21, 1946; d. George James and Doris Ann (Cuneo) M.; m. Philip George Zimbardo, Aug. 10, 1972; children: Zara, Tanya. BA, Harvard-Radcliffe Coll., 1967; PhD, Stanford U., 1971. Prof. psychology U. Calif.-Berkeley, 1971—, vice provost for undergrad. edn., 2001—. Author: Burnout: The Cost of Caring, 1982; co-author: Influencing Attitudes and Changing Behavior, 1977, Maslach Burnout Inventory (rsch. scale), 1981, 2d edit., 1986, 3d edit., 1996, Experiencing Social Psychology, 1979, 4th edit., 2001, Professional Burnout, 1993, The Truth About Burnout, 1997, Preventing Burnout and Building Engagement, 2000, Banishing Burnout, 2005. Recipient Disting. Teaching award, 1987, Best Paper award Jour. Orgnl. Behavior, 1994, Prof. of Yr. award Carnegie/CASE, 1997. Fellow AAAS, APA, Am. Psychol. Soc., Soc. Clin. and Exptl. Hypnosis (Henry Guze rsch. award 1980), We. Psychol. Assn. (pres. 1989); mem. Soc. Exptl. Social Psychology. Democrat. Office: U Calif Office of Chancellor 200 California Hall # 1500 Berkeley CA 94720-1500 Office Phone: 510-642-9594. Business E-Mail: maslach@berkeley.edu.

MASLIN, JANET, critic; b. NYC, Aug. 12, 1949; d. Paul and Lucille (Becker) M.; m. Benjamin Cheever; children: John, Andrew. BA in Math., U. Rochester, 1970. Film and music critic The Boston Phoenix, 1972-76; film critic Newsweek, NYC, 1976-77; dep. film critic NY Times, NYC, 1977-93, chief film critic, 1993-99, now book critic. Office: NY Times 229 W 43rd St New York NY 10036-3959 Office Phone: 212-556-5801. Office Fax: 212-556-1516.*

MASLOW, PHYLLIS F., retired educator; b. Cleve., May 6, 1927; d. Joseph C. and Avis Ethel (Leggett) Findley; m. William C. Maslow (dec. Mar. 1987); children: Mark J., Carolyn J., Leslie A PhB, U. Chgo., 1946, MA, 1951; PhD, U. So. Calif., 1975. Adminstrv. sec. Ctr. for Study Am.-Fgn. and Mil. Power U. Chgo., 1951—52; rsch. coord. Marianne Frostig Ctr. Ednl. Therapy, L.A., 1961—69, 1970—74, asst. to dir., 1969—70; dir. spl. edn. programs Mt. St. Mary's Coll. and Frostig Ctr., L.A., 1974; asst. prof. ednl. psychology Calif. State U., Long Beach, 1977—81, assoc. prof. ednl. psychology, 1981—86, prof. ednl. psychology, 1986—90, acting assoc. dean, 1988—90, prof. emerita, 1990—. Sec. exec. bd. Multidisciplinary Acad. Clin. Educators, 1988-91 Author: (with others) Learning Problems in the Classroom, 1973; cons. mem. editl. bd. Jour. Learning Disabilities, 1979-98 Calif. State U. Disting. scholar, 1982 Fellow Assn. Ednl. Therapists; mem. Assn. Ednl. Therapy, Coun. for Exceptional Children, Learning Disabilities Assn., Phi Beta Kappa. Avocation: hiking. Home: 900 E Harrison Ave Apt A26 Pomona CA 91767-2080 Office Phone: 909-626-6315. Personal E-mail: pmaslow@earthlink.net.

MASON, ANNE R. HARDIN, municipal official; b. Hamlet, N.C., Dec. 19, 1931; d. William Herbert and Catherine Holder Robertson; m. C. Dwight Hardin, Jr., June 18, 1955 (dec. June 1972); 1 child, Charles David Hardin; m. Robert L. Mason, Mar. 29, 1975 (dec. Mar. 1989); children: Shelly Mason Ivey, Jennifer Mason Fanjoy. BA, U. N.C., Greensboro, 1954. Tchr. North Sch., Gastonia, NC, 1954—55, Oakwood Sch., Hickory, NC, 1955—59, College Park Jr. H.S., Hickory, NC, 1972—77, Southwest Elem. Sch., Hickory, NC, 1977—81, College Park Mid. Sch., Hickory, NC, 1981—92. Chief judge Bd. Elections, Newton, NC, 1992—2003. Mem.: NEA, N.C. Assn. Educators. Democrat. Presbyterian. Avocations: bridge, garden club. Home: 771 9th St NW Hickory NC 28601

MASON, BOBBIE ANN, writer; b. Mayfield, Ky., May 1, 1940; d. Wilburn A. and Christianna (Lee) M.; m. Roger B. Rawlings, Apr. 12, 1969. BA, U. Ky., 1962; MA, SUNY, Binghamton, 1966; PhD, U. Conn., 1972. Asst. prof. English Mansfield (Pa.) State Coll., 1972-79. Writer-in-residence, U. Ky., Lexington, 2001—. Author: Nabokov's Garden, 1974, The Girl Sleuth: A Feminist Guide to the Bobbsey Twins, Nancy Drew and Their Sisters, 1975, 2d edit., 1995, Shiloh and Other Stories, 1982 (PEN Hemingway award, Nat. Book Critics Circle award nominee, Am. Book award nominee, PEN Faulkner award nominee), 2d edit., 2001, In Country, 1985, 2d edit., 2005, Spence + Lila, 1988, 2d edit., 1998, Love Life, 1989, Feather Crowns, 1993 (Nat. Book Critic's Circle award nominee, So. Book award), Midnight Magic, 1998, Clear Springs, 1999 (Pulitzer prize finalist), Zigzagging Down a Wild Trail, 2001 (So. Book award), Elvis Presley, 2003 (Ky. Literary award), An Atomic Romance, 2005; editor: Missing Mountains, 2005, Nancy Culpepper, 2006; contbr. regularly to the New Yorker, 1980—; contbr. fiction to The Atlantic, Redbook, Paris Rev., Mother Jones, Harpers, N.Am. Rev., Va. Quar. Rev., Story, Ploughshares, So. Rev., Crazyhorse, DoubleTake; contbr. works Best American Short Stories, 1981, 83, The Pushcart Prize, Best of the Small Presses, 1983, 86, 97. Recipient O. Henry Anthology awards, 1986, 88, Hillsdale prize, 1999; grantee Pa. Arts Coun., 1983, 89, Nat. Endowment Arts, 1983, Am. Acad. and Inst. Arts and Letters, 1984; Guggenheim fellow, 1984. Mem.: PEN, Author's Guild, Fellowship of So. Writers. Office: Internat Creative Mgmt care Amanda Urban Agt 40 W 57th St New York NY 10019-4001 Business E-Mail: aurban@icmtalent.com.

MASON, BRENDA KAY, elementary school educator; b. Hot Springs, Ark., Dec. 3, 1945; d. Lottie Ester Johnson Tolleson; m. Loy Eugene Tuner (div.); children: Clinton Eugene Turner, Brent Thomas Turner; m. Joe Milburn

Mason, Aug. 22, 2003. BS in Elem. Edn., Henderson State U., Arkadelphia, Ark., 1979, MS in Ednl. Adminstrn., 1986. Math. and sci. tchr. Caddo Hills Elem., Norman, Ark., Kirby Elem. Sch., Ark. V.p., pres. pers. policy com. Kirby Sch. Space program tchr. Rocket Launch; basketball coach Pee Wee Basket; active Pikes County Libr. Bd., 2005—. Named Tchr. of Yr., Kirby Sch.; Christa McCauliff grantee. Republican. Mem. Ch. Of Christ. Avocations: reading, travel, swimming. Home: 70 Mason Rd Amity AR 71921 Office: Kirby Sch PO Box 9 Kirby AR 71950

MASON, CAROL ANN, medical educator; Prof. anatomy and cell biology Columbia U., N.Y.C. Editor: Jour. of Neurosci.; contbr. articles to profl. jours. Mem.: Soc. for Neurosci. Achievements include research in on the cellular interactions among neurons and betweenneurons and glia during axonal outgrowth and formation of synaptic connections in mammalian (rodent) brain. Office: Columbia Univ Dept Pathology 630 W 168th St New York NY 10032-3702

MASON, CHRISTINE CHAPMAN, psychotherapist; b. El Paso, Tex., Sept. 17, 1948; d. Wilson A. and Mary (McGovern) Chapman; m. Gary R. Mason, Nov. 3, 1973; children: Ryan, Alison, Amanda, Sean. BA in Journalism, Tex. Tech. U., 1970; certificate, Am. U., 1973; MA, Marymount U., 1995, George Washington U., 1997, MA, 1998; PsyD, So. Calif. U., 2003. Cert. Paralegal 1985, Counselor, lic. Profl. Counselor. Flight attendant supr. Eastern Airlines, Washington, 1971—84; pres. Stratford Properties, Charles County, Md., 1980—; psychotherapist Charles County Mental Health Ctr., Loplata, Md., 1995—98, Eva Turner Elem. Sch., Waldorf, Md., 1999—. Dir. rehab. svc. Edgemeade, Waldorf, Md., 1999—2000; emergency psychiat. clinician St. Mary's Hosp., Leonardtown, Md., 1998—; psychotherapist Calvert Psychiat. Assn., Leonardtown, 1998—. Bd. dir. On Our Own of Charles County, Waldorf, Md., 1998—2000, Charles County Mental Health Authority, Waldorf, 1993—96. Mem.: Md. Assn. Counseling-Devel., Am. Counselors Assn. Republican. Roman Catholic. Home: 13535 Waverly Point Road Newburg MD 20664-2821

MASON, CONNIE JEANNE, writer; b. Niles, Mich., Apr. 22, 1930; d. Frank G. and Frances (Coda) Roti; m. Lewis Gerald Mason, July 1, 1950; children: Jeri A. Vlasicak, Michelle A. Osborn, Mark. Grad. high sch., Buchanan, Mich. Author: Promise Me Forever, 1990, Brave Land, Brave Love, 1990, Surrender to The Fury, 1990, Ice @ Rapture, 1991, A Promise of Thunder, 1991, Lord Of The Night, 1991, Treasures Of The Heart, 1992, Tears Like Rain, 1993, Wind Rider, 1993, Sierra, 1994, The Lion's Bride, 1994, Taken By You, 1995, pure Temptation, 1995, Flame, 1996, A Love To Cherish, 1996, Shadow Walker, 1997, To Love A Stranger, 1997, Sheik, 1997, Viking!, 1998, The Black Knight, 1999 (N.Y. Times Extended Bestseller List), Pirate, 1998, Gunslinger, 1999, To Tempt a Rogue, 1999, The Black Knight, 1999 (N.Y. Times Extended List 1999), The Outlaws: Rafe, 2000, A Taste of Sin, 2000, The Outlaws: Jess, 2000, A Breath of Scandal, 2001, The Outlaws: Sam, 2001, The Dragon Lord, 2001, The Rogue and the Bastion, 2002, Lionheart, 2002, Seduced by a Rogue, 2003, The Laird of Stonehaven, 2003, The Last Rogue, 2004, The Pirate Prince, 2004, Gypsy Lover, 2005, A Knight's Honor, 2005, A Taste of Paradise, 2006, also novellas. Named Story Teller of Yr., Romantic Times, 1990; recipient Career Achievement award, 1994. Mem. Romance Writers Am., Novelists, Inc. Avocations: reading, travel.

MASON, EILEEN B., federal arts administrator; b. Bklyn., 1943; m. Arthur Mason; children: Elizabeth, Laura. BA, Cornell U.; MPA, Am. U. Tchr. math. and reading Hephzibah High Sch., Ga.; editor Little Brown, Boston; music adv. panelist Md. State Arts Coun.; v.p. grants Arts and Humanities Coun., Montgomery County, Md.; mgr. and adminstr. U.S. NRC, FERC; sr. dep. chmn. NEA, Washington, 2001—, acting chmn., 2002—03. Performer: (violinist) Cornell U. Symphony, MIT Symphony, Augusta Symphony, Am. U. Symphony Orchestra. Mem.: Phi Alpha Alpha. Office: NEA 1100 Pennsylvania Ave NW Washington DC 20506

MASON, EMILY, painter; b. NYC, 1932; d. Alice Trumbull Mason; m. Wolf Kahn. Attended, Bennington Coll., 1950—52; BFA, Cooper Union, NYC; DFA (hon.), Wheaton Coll., Mass., 2000. Tchr. Hunter Coll., NYC. Exhibitions include Grace Borgenicht Gallery NYC, Landmark Gallery NYC, Walker-Kornbluth Gallery Fairlawn NJ, Thomas Babeor Gallery San Diego, MB Modern NYC, Virginia Lynch Gallery Tiverton R.I., Brattleboro Mus. Art, Mugar Art Gallery Colby-Sawyer Coll., David Findlay Jr. Fine Arts, NYC; represented in collections Springfield (Mass.) Mus., Rockefeller Group NYC, Ciba-Geigy Chemical Group Ohio Hon. trustee Brattleboro Mus. & Art Ctr., Vt. Grantee Fulbright Fellowship, Accademia delle Belle Arti, Venice, 1956. Mem.: NAD (academician).

MASON, JOAN ELLEN, nurse; b. Reading, Pa., June 29, 1947; d. Richard Lenhart and Mary Jane (Miller) Fritz; m. W. Davis Mason, Feb. 12, 1977 (dec. Jan. 2002). RN, Temple U. Hosp. Sch. Nursing, 1968; BS in Nursing Edn., Temple U., 1971, EdM in Health Edn., 1981; postgrad., U. Pa. Staff nurse Temple U. Hosp., Phila., 1968-71; nursing instr. Phila. Gen. Hosp. Sch. Nursing, 1971-76; coord. staff devel. Meml. Hosp., Roxborough, Pa., 1976-84; clin. editor Springhouse Corp., Pa., 1984-94; nurse cons. Kelly Sci. Resources, 1995-98; adminstrn., profl. nurse Bed and Breakfast Inn, Cape May, NJ, 1982—2003; nurse cons. Reading, 1999—2003, Orwigsburg, 2003—. Mem. exhibit com. Mus. Nursing History, Inc., 1988-2001. Editor Congl. Free Ch. of Chirst newsletter; contbr. articles to profl. jours. Vol. Reading Mus., Berks Arts Coun., Am. Diabetes Assn. Mem. Mid-Atlantic Ctr. for Arts, Orwigsburg Women's Libr. Soc. Republican. Home: 225 Eisenhower Dr Orwigsburg PA 17961-1605

MASON, JOHANNA HENDRIKA ANNEKE, retired secondary school educator; b. Indramajoe, Indonesia, Feb. 17, 1932; came to U.S., 1957; d. Johannes Simon and Hendrika Jacoba (De Vroedt) Vermeulen; m. Alfred Bob Markholt, Feb., 1958 (div. Dec. 1966); children: Bob, Anneke, Joe Ralph, Lee Markholt; m. Rollin Mason, 1968 (div. 1978). French lang. diploma with top honors, Paris Alliance Française, 1952; BA in Philosophy summa cum laude, U. Puget Sound, 1976, MA in Comparative Lit., 1979, BA in Edn., 1988. Cert. tchr. 4-12. Adminstrv. asst. to pres. N.V. Nutricia, Zoetermeer, The Netherlands, 1953-57; pvt. sec. Grad. Sch. Bus. Harvard U., Cambridge, Mass., 1957; adminstrv. asst., lectr. humanities divsn. U. Puget Sound, Tacoma, 1966-88; tchr. English and French h.s. and mid. sch. Tacoma, 1988-94. Pres. staff orgn. U. Puget Sound, Tacoma, 1978-80, budget task force, 1981-86. Author: (poetry compilation) Journey, 1981, A Handfull of Bubbles, 1981, Echoes, Mirrors, Reflections, 1983, Glimpses, 2006; contbr. poetry to lit. mags. Mem. city's task force on hate crimes, Tacoma, 1992, translator, 1974-90; bd. dirs. Unitarian Universalist Assn. of Tacoma, 2003-05. Selected to literary pub. art registry, City of Tacoma, 1999. Mem. So. Poverty Law Ctr., Amnesty Internat., Phi Kappa Phi (nat. com. on comms. 1991-94, pres. chpt. 1973-77). Avocations: reading, hiking, theater, needlecrafts, poetry.

MASON, JOYCE J., lawyer, telecommunications industry executive; BA, CUNY; JD, NY Law Sch., 1983. Bar: NY 1984, DC 1990, NJ 1996. Gen. counsel, sec. IDT Corp., Newark, 1995—, sr. v.p., 1998—; dir. IDT Telecom, Inc., 1999—2001, Net2Phone, Inc., 2001—04. Office: IDT Corp 520 Broad St Newark NJ 07102 Office Phone: 973-439-1000. E-mail: jmason@mail.corp.idt.net.

MASON, KAROL V., lawyer; b. Amityville, NY, Aug. 20, 1957; AB, Univ. NC, Chapel Hill, 1979; JD, Univ. Mich., 1982. Bar: Ga. 1983. Ptnr., chair, pub. fin. group Alston & Bird LLP, Atlanta. Notes editor Univ. Mich. Jour. Law Reform. Named Distinguished Young Alumna, Univ. NC, Chapel Hill, 1991. Mem.: Ga. Assn. Black Women Attys., Nat. Assn. Bond Lawyers. Office: Alston & Bird LLP One Atlantic Ctr 1201 W Peachtree St NW Atlanta GA 30309-3424 Office Phone: 404-881-7494. Office Fax: 404-881-7777. Business E-Mail: kmason@alston.com.

MASON, LINDA, broadcast executive; b. Middletown, NY; m. Cary Aminoff; 2 children. BA in Internat. Rels., Brown U., 1964; MS in Filmmaking, Syracuse U., 1965. Fellow Syracuse U.; reporter Providence Jour., RI; radio desk asst. CBS News, NY, 1966; news writer WCBS-TV, NY; writer, assoc. prodr. CBS Morning News, 1968—70, field prodr., 1971, sr. prodr., 1980—86; exec. prodr. CBS News (Weekend Broadcasts), 1986—92, CBS News Sunday Morning, 1987—92; exec.-in-charge Eye to Eye, CBS Mag., 1993—95, 60 Minutes.25 Years, 1993, 60 Minutes at 30, 1998; v.p. pub. affairs CBS News, 1992—, sr. v.p. standards and spl. projects NY, 2004—. Oversaw partnership between CBS News and the Smithsonian Institution, "Smithsonian Minutes", 1996; CBS News rep. working with other member networks to reform Voter News Svc. Helped develop "Before Your Eyes", CBS News, headed panel, author 87 page report examining the mistakes of Election Night 2000, CBS News; exec. prodr.: "The Class of 2000", CBS Reports, CBS News/Time 100 Project. Recipient William Rogers award, 1991, Peabody award (Three), Edward R. Murrow awrd, RTNDA, Alfred I. duPont-Columbia U. award, Grand Prize of Robert F. Kennedy Journalism awards, Emmy awards (Thirteen), Honorable Mention, Overseas Press Club. Office: CBS News 524 N 57th St New York NY 10019-2924

MASON, LINDA ANNE, daycare administrator; m. Roger Brown; 3 children. BA, Cornell U., 1976; DLCF, Sorbonne U., Paris, 1977; MBA, Yale U., 1980. Relief worker, Cambodian refugee camp CARE, Thailand, 1980; cons. Booz, Allen & Hamilton, N.Y.C., Paris, 1981-82; co-dir. Save the Children, Sudan, 1984-1986; co-founder Horizons Initiative; chmn., co-founder Bright Horizons Family Solutions, 1986—. Bd. dirs. Horizon Initiative, Whole Foods Market, Inc., Boston Globe. Co-author: (book) Rice, Rivalry, and Politics, 1983; author: Working Mother's Guide to Life, 2002. Mem. adv. bd. Sch. Mgmt. Yale U., trustee. Named Entrepreneur of the Yr., Ernst & Young/USA Today, 1996, Cornell U., 1997; named one of Best Entrepreneurs, Bus. Week, 1997; recipient Ten Outstnding Young Leaders award, Boston Jaycees, 1987, Mothers and Shakers award, Redbook, 1998. Office: Bright Horizons Family Solutions 200 Talcott Ave South Watertown MA 02472 Fax: 617-673-8650.

MASON, LOIS E. (J. DAY MASON), painter, poet, actress, educator; b. Boston, May 4, 1919; d. Harold Monroe and Orpah Cecil (Smith) Scheibe; m. Lucien Bunce Day, June 21, 1941 (div. 1954); children: Felicity, Christopher, Sarah; m. Frederick Dike Mason, Apr. 27, 1964 (dec.); children: Frederick Dike III, Victoria, Johanna. Student, U. Leiden, Netherlands, 1939; BA, Oberlin (Ohio) U., 1940; postgrad., Cranbrook Acad. Art, Bloomfield Hills, Mich., 1941. Set-up and tchr. art dept. Pingree Sch., Hamilton Mass.; TV, lectr. creative arts and writing, Mass. and Conn., 1949-58. Actress appearing in Alien Corn, Twelfth Night, Crucible, George Washington Slept Here, Philadelphia Story, Auntie Mame, Skin of our Teeth, Spoon River, Anything Goes, Call Me Madame, Seven Keys to Baldpate, Other People's Money, Quilters, Golden Pond, Cat on a Hot Tin Roof, Little Foxes, Lettice and Lovage, Close Ties, Grace and Glorie, others; set designer, decorator Auntie Mame, See How They Run, Tea House of the August Moon, Spoon River, Archie and Mehitable; author: Speaking to Strangers, 1987-88; one-woman shows include New Britain (Conn.) Mus., Am. Ballet, N.Y., Green Mountain Gallery, N.Y.C., Essex (Mass.) Inst., Marblehead Arts, Quadrom, Mast Cove, 6 Deering, Miles Hosp., Atty. Gen.'s Office, Kennebec Valley Art Assn., Chocolate Ch. Art Ctr., Maine Gallery, Kristina's, Oliver's, Islesboro Historic Soc., West Island Gallery, Bath, Maine. Ch. ladies com. Hamilton Hall, Salem, Mass., 1975—78; set designer Cty. Theater, Swampscott, Mass., 1973—78. Recipient C. Law/Watkins fellowship Phillips Gallery, Mus., Washington, 1944-46. Mem. Nat. Assn. Women Painters, Conn. Acad., Silvermine, Maine Gallery, Kennebec Valley Arts, Chocolate Ch. Art Ctr., Marblehead Arts, Conn. Acad., Maine Writers and Publs. Avocations: cooking, sailing, gardening.

MASON, LOIS RUTH, retired elementary school educator; b. Monroe, Wis., Oct. 8, 1929; d. Roy Abraham Speich and Ada Verona Benkert; m. David Eugene Mason, Aug. 20, 1953; children: James, Mary, Thomas, Julie, Nancy, Holly. BS, U. Wis., LaCrosse, 1951. Tchr. elem. edn. Lincoln Sch., Beaver Dam, Wis., 1951—53, Green Bay, Wis., 1953—54, Cuba City Elem., Wis., 1954—55, Prospect Elem., Lake Mills, Wis., 1958—59, Lincoln Sch., Waupun, Wis., 1959—64, Hiawatha Sch., Monroe, Wis., 1975—76, Morrisonville Elem., Wis., 1977—92; ret. Mem.: NEA, Wis. Edn. Assn. Avocations: reading, golf, bicycling, walking, card playing. Home: 9679 Troon Ct Lakeland FL 33810

MASON, LUCILE GERTRUDE, not-for-profit fundraiser, consultant; b. Montclair, N.J., Aug. 1, 1925; d. Mayne Seguine and Rachel (Entorf) Mason. AB, Smith Coll., Northampton, Mass., 1947; MA, NYU, 1968, MA, 1976. Editor ABC, N.Y.C., 1947—51; asst. dir. casting Compton Advt., Inc., N.Y.C., 1951—55, dir. and head casting, 1955—65; conf. mgr. Camp Fire Girls, Inc., N.Y.C., 1965—66; exec. dir. Assn. of Jr. Leagues of Am. Inc., N.Y.C., 1966—68; dir. divsn. pub. affairs Girl Scouts U.S.A., N.Y.C., 1969—71; dir. pub. rels. YWCA of City of N.Y., 1971—73; dir. cmty. rels. and devel. Girl Scout Coun. of Greater N.Y., N.Y.C., 1973—76; dir. devel. Montclair Kimberley Acad., 1976—78, Ethical Culture Schs., N.Y.C. and Riverdale, N.Y., 1978—80; pres. Lucile Mason & Assocs., Montclair, 1980—83; devel. officer founds. Fairleigh Dickinson U., Rutherford, NJ, 1983—85; dir. devel. Whole Theatre, Inc., Montclair, 1985—86, YMWCA of Newark & Vicinity, 1986—88; v.p. adminstrn. and fin. devel. Inst. Religion and Health, N.Y.C., 1988—90; dir. corp. and found. rels. Upsala Coll., East Orange, NJ, 1990—91; pres. Lucile Mason & Assocs., Montclair, 1991—. Vol. bd. counselors Smith Coll., 1964—74, chmn. theatre com., mem. exec. com., 1969—74; trustee Citizens Com. Presby. Meml. Iris Gardens of Montclair, 1992—98, Friends of Barnet, 1994—95; v.p. Neighborhood Coun., Inc., Montclair, 1987—95, 1997—98, bd. dirs., 2000—01; mem. fund devel. com. Girl Scout coun. Greater Essex and Hudson Counties, 1986—92. Mem.: Pub. Rels. Soc. Am., Assn. Fundraising Profls. (bd. dirs. N.J. chpt. 1983—86, mem. awards com. 1994, co-chair awards com. N.J. Conf. on Philanthropy 1995), Cmty. Agys. Pub. Rels. Assn. (membership chmn. 1973—76), Am. Women in Radio and TV (pres. N.Y.C. chpt. 1955—56), Smith Coll. Club Montclair (bd.dirs. 1986—90). Avocations: collecting pewter, gardening, concerts, plays. Home and Office: 142 N Mountain Ave Montclair NJ 07042-2350 Office Phone: 973-744-9143. Personal E-mail: janm142@aol.com.

MASON, MARGARET CRATHER, elementary school educator; b. Wilmington, Del, Aug. 15, 1945; d. William F. and Regina (Mays) Crather; children: Donna Lynn, R. Brian. BA, U. Del., 1968; postgrad., Loyola Coll. Balt., Del. State Coll.; M in Ednl. Leadership, Wilmington Coll. Cert. English, secondary and elem. tchr., elem. prin., Del. Secondary tchr. English, Podua Acad., Wilmington; elem. tchr. St. John the Beloved Sch., Wilmington; elem. tchr. sci. Christina Sch. Dist., Wilmington, asst. prin. elem. sch. Active numerous community orgns. and local ch. Recipient Fire Safety Edn. award New Castle County Vol. Firefighters. Mem. Del. Assn. Sch. Adminstrs.

MASON, MARILYN GELL, library administrator, writer, consultant; b. Chickasha, Okla., Aug. 23, 1944; d. Emmett D. and Dorothy (O'Bar) Killebrew; m. Carl L. Gell, Dec. 29 1965 (div. Oct. 1978); 1 son, Charles E.; m. Robert M. Mason, July 17, 1981. BA, U. Dallas, 1966; M.L.S., N. Tex. State U., Denton, 1968; M.P.A., Harvard U., 1978. Libr. N.J. State Libr., Trenton, 1968-69; head dept. Arlington County Pub. Libr., Va., 1969-73; chief libr. program Metro Washington Coun. Govts., 1973-77; dir. White House Conf. on Librs. and Info. Svcs., Washington, 1979-80; exec. v.p. Metrics Rsch. Corp., Atlanta, 1981-82; dir. Atlanta-Fulton Pub. Libr., Atlanta, 1982-86, Cleve. Pub. Libr., 1986-99; writer, cons., 1999—. Trustee Online Computer Library Ctr., 1984-97; Evalene Parsons Jackson lectr. divsn. librarianship Emory U., 1981; commr. Nat. Commn. Libr. Info. Svcs., 2001-02; book project dir. Information for the 1980's, 1980 Author: The Federal Role in Library and Information Services, 1983, Strategic Management for Today's Libraries, 1999; editor: Survey of Library Automation in the Washington Area, 1977 Bd. visitors Sch. Info. Studies, Syracuse U., 1981-85, Sch. of Libr. and Info. Sci., U. Tenn.-Knoxville, 1983-85; trustee Coun. on Libr. Resources, Washington, 1992-2000. Recipient Disting. Alumna award, N. Tex. State U., 1979, Herbert and Virginia White award, ALA, 1999; inducted into Ohio Libr. Coun. Hall of Fame, 1999. Mem. ALA (mem. council 1986—90), Am. Assn. Info. Sci., Ohio Library Assn., D.C. Library Assn. (pres. 1976-77) Home and Office: 2929 First Ave 1122 Seattle WA 98121 Office Phone: 206-714-3009. Personal E-mail: marilyngmason@earthlink.net. Business E-Mail: mgmason@oclc.org.

MASON, MARSHA, actress, theater director, writer; b. St. Louis, Apr. 3, 1942; d. James and Jacqueline M.; m. Gary Campbell, 1965 (div.); m. Neil Simon, Oct. 25, 1973 (div.). Grad., Webster Coll., Mo. Performances include cast broadway and nat. tour Cactus Flower, 1968; other stage appearances include The Deer Park, 1967, The Indian Wants the Bronx, 1968, Happy Birthday, Wanda June, 1970, Private Lives, 1971, You Can't Take It With You, 1972, Cyrano de Bergerac, 1972, A Doll's House, 1972, The Crucible, 1972, The Good Doctor, 1973, King Richard III, 1974, The Heiress, 1975, Mary Stuart, 1982, Amazing Grace, 1995, Night of the Iguana, 1996; one-woman show off-Broadway, The Big Love, Perry St. Theatre, 1988, Lake No Bottom, Second Stage, 1990, Escape From Happiness, With Naked Angels, 1994, Amazing Grace, 1998, House, 1998, (London) Prisoner of Second Avenue, 1999, Steel Magnolias, 2005; film appearances include Hot Rod Hullabaloo, 1966, Beyond the Law, 1968, Blume in Love, 1973, Cinderella Liberty, 1973 (recipient Golden Globe award 1974, Acad. award nominee), Audrey Rose, 1977, The Goodbye Girl, 1977 (recipient Golden Globe award 1978, Acad. award nominee), The Cheap Detective, 1978, Promises in the Dark, 1979, Chapter Two, 1979 (Acad. award nominee), Only When I Laugh, 1981 (Acad. award nominee), Max Dugan Returns, 1982, Heartbreak Ridge, 1986, Stella, 1988, Drop Dead Fred, 1990, I Love Trouble, 1994, Nick of Time, 1995, Two Days in the Valley, 1996, Bride & Prejudice, 2004, Bereft, 2004; (TV films) PBS series Cyrano de Bergerac, 1972, The Good Doctor, 1978, Lois Gibbs and the Love Canal, 1981, Surviving, 1985, Trapped in Silence, 1986, The Clinic, 1987, Dinner at Eight, 1989, The Image, 1990, Broken Trust, 1994, Dead Aviators, 1999, Life with Judy Garland:Me and My Shadows, 2001, The Long Shot: Believe in Courage, 2004; (TV series) Where the Heart Is, 1971, Love of Life, 1971-72, Young Dr. Kildare, 1972, Sibs, 1991; dir. (plays) Juno's Swans, 1987, Heaven Can Wait; dir. ABC Afternoon Spl. Little Miss Perfect, 1988; guest appearances include One Life to Live, 1993, Frasier, 1997, 1998 (Emmy Nom.), The Education of Max Bickford, 2002; author: Journey: A Personal Odyssey (Simon & Schuster), 2000. E-mail: douhlem@newmexico.com.

MASON, NANCY TOLMAN, retired state agency administrator; b. Buxton, Maine, Mar. 14, 1933; d. Ansel Robert and Kate Douglas (Libby) M. Grad., Bryant Coll., Providence, R.I., 1952; BA, U. Mass., Boston, 1977; postgrad., Inst. Governmental Services, Boston, 1985, The Auditor's Inst., 1988. Asst. to chief justice Mass. Superior Ct., Boston, 1964-68; cmty. liaison Action for Boston Cmty. Devel., Boston, 1968-73; mgmt. cons. East Boston Cmty. Devel. Assn., Boston, 1973-78; asst. dir. Mass. Office of Deafness, Boston, 1978-86; dir. of contracts Mass. Rehab. Commn., Boston, 1986-98; ret., 1998. Cons. Jos. A Ryan Assocs., Boston and Orleans, Mass., 1981-86, Radio Sta. WFCC, Chatham, Mass., 1987-91, Networks, Inc., 2003-05. Author: Bromley-Heath Security Patrols, 1974, Reorganization of East Boston Community Development Corporation, 1976, How to Start Your Own Small Business, 1981. Bd. dirs. Deaf-Blind Contact Ctr., Boston, 1988-91; vol. Am. Cancer Soc., Winchester, Mass., 1986-93, Tax Equity Alliance Mass., 1994; treas. Sunset Bay Condo Assn., 1998-99, bd. dirs. 1998-2001, Highland Cemetery Assn., 2002-; mem. vestry Trinity Episc. Ch., Saco, Maine, 2005—. Recipient Good Citizen award DAR, 1950, Community Svc. award Northeastern U., 1986, Gov.'s citation for outstanding performance, 1993; named to Outstanding Young Women of Am., 1965. Mem. NOW, NAFE, Mass. State Assn. Deaf, Mass. Rehab. Commn. Statewide Cen. Office Dirs. (chair 1995-98, MRC procurement mgmt. team 1997-98, co-chair Take Your Daughters to Work Day 1998-99), Red Hat Soc. Democrat. Episcopalian. Avocations: reading, music, swimming, sign language. Address: 5 Elmwood Dr Saco ME 04072-2103

MASON, RACHEL J., lawyer; b. Cin., Dec. 8, 1977; BA, Lehigh U., 2000; JD, Dickinson Sch. of Law, Pa. State U., 2003. Bar: Ohio 2003. Named one of Ohio's Rising Stars, Super Lawyers, 2006. Mem.: Assn. Credit and Collection Professionals, Nat. Assn. Retail Collection Attorneys, Comml. Law League Am. (award of Excellence), ABA, Ohio State Bar Assn., Cin. Bar Assn. Office: Mason Schilling & Mason Co LPA 11340 Cincinnati OH 45249-2313 Office Phone: 513-489-0829. Office Fax: 513-489-0834.*

MASON, REBECCA SUSSA, retired secondary school educator; b. Knoxville, Tenn., Sept. 21, 1945; d. Max and Greta (Hans) M. BA, SUNY, Fredonia, 1967; MA, Columbia U., 1977. Cert. permanent tchr., N.Y. Tchr. music Kakiat Jr. High Sch., East Ramapo Ctrl. Sch. Dist., Spring Valley, N.Y., 1967-95, head dept., 1985—, condr. All Dist. Band, 1980, 97—, asst. condr., 1989-96; tchr. music Ramapo Sr. H.S., 1995-2001; ret., 2001. Musician South Orange (N.J.) Symphony, 1986-87, Rockland Cmty. Band, Pearl River, N.Y., 1988—. Recipient various plaques, awards and letters of commendation East Ramapo Sch. Dist., 1968—, letter of commendation SUNY, 1990. Mem. Music Educators Nat. Conf., N.Y. State Sch. Music Assn., East Ramapo PTA (life). Avocations: travel, pottery, collecting autographs and baseball cards, quilting, counted cross-stitch. Home: 116 Hillcrest Ln Peekskill NY 10566

MASON, ROSANNA MARIE, lawyer; b. Arlington, Va., Feb. 22, 1959; d. James Waverly and Elizabeth Anne Mason; life ptnr. Deborah Sheftz, Dec. 19, 1987. BA, U. Va., 1981; JD, Antioch Sch. Law, 1984. Bar: Mass. 1985, Md. 1985, Washington 1986. Staff atty. Legal Aid Bur., Salisbury, Md., 1984—86; supervisory staff atty. Univ. Legal Svcs., Washington, 1986—92; staff atty. U.S. Ct. Appeals (D.C. cir.), Washington, 1992—98, sr. staff atty., 1998—2002, staff counsel, 2002—. Rules com. mem. Sceintist Cliffs Assn., Port Republic, Md., 2005—06. Recipient Performance award, U.S. Ct. Appeals (D.C. cir.), 2002—05. Mem.: So. Poverty Ctr. Home: 4018 Elder Rd Port Republic MD 20676 Office: DC Ct Appeals 500 Indiana Ave NW 6th Floor Washington DC 20001 Office Phone: 202-879-2718. Business E-Mail: rmason@dcca.state.dc.us.

MASON, SALLY KAY FROST, biology professor, academic administrator; b. N.Y.C., May 29, 1950; d. Michael and Alberta Viparina; m. John S. Frost, Aug. 1975 (div. Feb. 1982); m. Kenneth Andrew Mason, Mar. 17, 1990. BA in Zoology, U. Ky., 1972; MS in Cell/Devel. Biology, Purdue U., 1974; PhD in Cell/Devel. Biology, U. Ariz., 1978. Rsch. assoc. Ind. U., Bloomington, 1978-80; asst. prof. biology U. Kans., Lawrence, 1981-86, assoc. prof. biology, 1986-91, prof. biology, 1991-2001, chair dept. physiology and cell biology, 1986-89, assoc. dean scis., 1990-95, dean arts and scis., 1995-2001; provost, prof. biology Purdue U., West Lafayette, Ind., 2001—. Chmn. bd. Inproteo, 2003—; chmn. EHR adv. bd. NSF, 2005—; mem. exec. com. Nat. Assn. State U. and Land Grant Colls., 2002—; mem. Pres.'s Nat. Medal of Sci. Selection Com., 2006—. Mem. editl. bd. Pigment Cell Rsch., 1988-99; contbr. chpts. to books and articles to profl. jours. Dissertation fellow AAUW, 1977-78, Kemper Tchg. fellow U. Kans., Lawrence, 1997; grantee NSF, NIH, Washington, 1981—; Wesley Found. grantee Welsey Health Found., Wichita, Kans., 1991-93. Mem. Internat. Fedn. Pigment Cell Scis. (coun. mem. 1997-2000), Pan Am. Soc. for Pigment Cell Rsch. (coun. mem. 1988-98, pres. 1996-98), Coun. Colls. Arts and Scis. (bd. mem. 1997-99, pres. elect 1999-2000, pres. 2000-2001). Avocations: travel, reading, writing. Office: Purdue U Office of Provost Hovde Hall West Lafayette IN 47905 Office Phone: 765-494-9709. E-mail: sfmason@purdue.edu.

MASON, SARA SMITH, healthcare consultant; b. Rochester, N.Y. d. Harry F. and Louise S. (Sullivan) Smith; m. Larry S. Mason. BA, Lewis and Clark Coll., Portland, Oreg., MA in Tchg.; MBA, U. Oreg., 1987. Dir. N.W. area Intracorp., Portland, 1979-90; dir. ops. Western region Ptnrs. In Exec. Solutions, Irvine, Calif., 1990-91; asst. v.p. group and casualty svcs. ETHIX Nat., Portland, Oreg., 1992-94; managed care product mgr. Fireman's Fund Ins. Cos., Portland, 1994-95; exec. v.p. Cyber Metrix, Beaverton, Oreg., 1995-99; exec. dir. One Health Plan of Oreg., Inc., Portland, 1999—2002; dir.

health care delivery svcs. Life Wise Health Plan of Oregon, 2003—05. Bd. dirs. Vision N.W.; prin. Healthcare Cons. Northwest LLC., 2003—. Mem. med. subcom. Worker's Compensation, Salem, Oreg., 1987; vice chair healthcom., bd. dirs. Oregon Bus. Assn., 2002-05, chair health policy com., 2003—. Mem. Oreg. Exec. MBA Alumni Bd. (bd. dirs.), Nat. Assn. Rehab. Profl. in Pvt. Sector, Portland City Club (bus. labor com. 1990-91).

MASON, SONJA, secondary school educator; b. Woodruff, S.C., Aug. 23, 1963; d. William Robert and Edith Smith Jenkins; m. Don Mason, Apr. 13, 2001; children: Nathan, Jesse, Kimberly. BS, Western Carolina U., Cullowhee, NC, 1985; MEd, Western Carolina U., 1995. Cert. Tchr. Nat. Bd. Cert. Tchrs., 2004. HS math tchr. Robbinsville HS, Robbinsville, NC, 1990—98; 7th grade math tchr. Swain Mid. Sch., Bryson City, NC, 1998—. Tchr., youth dir. Mt. Carmel Missionary Bapt. Ch., Bryson City, NC, 2001—06. Mem.: NEA. Office: Swain Mid Sch 135 Arlington Ave Bryson City NC 28713 Office Phone: 828-488-3480.

MASON, SUSAN HELEN, mathematics educator; b. Waynesboro, Pa., Jan. 28, 1961; d. Donald and Helen Elizabeth Wolfe; m. Gregory Eugene Mason, Nov. 6, 1998. BS in Edn., Shippensburg U., Pa., 1983. Math tchr. Waynesboro Area Sch. Dist., Pa., 1985—. Democrat. Lutheran. Avocations: travel, baseball, camping, hiking. Office: Waynesboro Area Mid Sch 702 E 2d St Waynesboro PA 17268 Office Phone: 1-717-762-1191 ext.13100. Personal E-mail: gsmason@yellowbananas.com. Business E-Mail: susan_mason@wasd.k12.pa.us.

MASON FOSTER, ANGELA MARIE, biology professor; b. Washington, NC, Nov. 23, 1966; d. Charles Raymond and Marie Daw Mason; m. Andrew James Foster, Mar. 16, 2002. MS in Biology, East Carolina U., 1993, M in speech, lang. and Auditory Pathology, 1993; PhD in Biol. Anthropology, Anatomy, Duke U., 1995; EdD in Higher Ednl. Adminstrn., NC State U., 1998. Cert. environ. trainer. Asst. prof. biology East Carolina U., Greenville, NC, 1987—91; chmn. environ. sci. dept. Beaufort County CC, Washington, NC, 1991—2001; assoc. prof. biology NC Wesleyan Coll., Rocky Mount, 2002—04; prof. biology, chmn. honors program Mount Olive (NC) Coll., 2004—. Natural photographer Nat. Geog., Natural History, Life mag.; tchr. Sch. for Field Studies, Boston U., LaSuerte Field Sch., Nicaragua and Costa Rica. Author: Environmental Science, 2000, 4th edit., 2005. Loaned exec. United Way, Wayne County, NC, 2004—. Capt. USAR, 1985—91, Kuwait. Mem.: NC Acad. Sci., Brit. Mycological Soc., Am. Fern Soc., Bot. Soc. Am., Bot. Soc. Am. (chmn. mycological sect. 2005—), Rotary (local pres. 2001), Tri-Beta Biol. Honor Soc., Phi Kappa Phi, Sigma Xi. Avocations: stained glass restoration, wildlife photography, travel. Home: Po Box 128 Mount Olive NC 28365 Office: Mt Olive Coll 654 Henderson St Mount Olive NC 28365 Office Phone: 919-658-7854. Business E-Mail: afoster@moc.edu.

MASON-HIPKINS, PATRICIA, minister; b. Pitts., Pa. d. Oliver Ellwood and Clarice Jane Hipkins; widowed; children: Rodney Williams Jr., Rhonda Haynes, Gregory Williams. MDiv, Interdenominational Theol. Sem., 1984, D in Ministry, 1990. Assoc. minister Ch. of God in Christ, Atlanta, 1981—90; dir. enlistment Interdenominational Theol. Sem., Atlanta, 1990—93; ch. devel. pastor Presbyn. of Atlanta, 1994—2000; pastor Hazelwood Presbyn., Pitts., 2001—. Grief counselor Arlington Cemetery, Atlanta, 1998—2000; therapist Auberle Ctr. Dep. and Delinquent Youth, 2000; grief counselor Anegheny Cemetery, Pitts., 2000—01. Commr. Gen. Assembly PC USA, Louisville, 2004—; mem. Com. Racial and Social Justice, Pitts., 2001—05, Com. on Ministry; commr. New Ch. Devel. Mem.: Nat. Black Presbyn. Caucus, Theta Phi. Presbyterian. Avocation: interior decorating. Home: 1870 Graham Rd Pittsburgh PA 15235 Office: Hazelwood Presbyn Ch 5000 2nd Ave Pittsburgh PA 15207 Office Phone: 412-421-0947. Personal E-mail: drpatmason@aol.com.

MASS, SHARON, social worker; b. Bklyn., Jan. 29, 1945; d. Jack and Rose Mass; m. Samuel Achs, June 16, 1976. BA, Bklyn. Coll., 1968; MSW, Hunter Sch. Social Work, 1975; PhD, U. So. Calif. Sch. Social Work, 1985. Lic. clin. social worker. Reference librarian Donaldson, Lufkin & Jenrette, Inc., N.Y.C., 1968-73; clin. social worker Jewish Hosp. and Med. Ctr., N.Y.C., 1975-79; dir. social services United Western Med. Ctr., Santa Ana, Calif., 1979—; mem. faculty sch. of social work U. So. Calif., Los Angeles, 1985—. Cons. Western Med. Ctr., 1982—; adv. bd. U. So. Calif. Tri County Branch Sch. Social Work, 1985—; dir. case mgmt. Palliative Care/Hospice, Cedars-Sinai Med. Ctr., L.A., 1991—. Contbr. articles to profl. jours. Named Hosp. Social Work Dir. of Yr., 1992; recipient Disting. Alumna award, U. So. Calif., 1991, CSMC Pres. award for outstanding performance, 1995. Fellow: Soc. Clin. Social Workers, Nat. Assn. Social Workers; mem. Soc. Hosp. Social Workers, Am. Case Mgmt. Assn. (bd. mem. 1999—). Democrat. Jewish. Avocations: swimming, fishing, cooking, piano. Home: 395 S Old Bridge Rd Anaheim CA 92808-1361 Office: Western Med Ctr 1001 N Tustin Ave Santa Ana CA 92705-3502

MASSA, MARTHA JOANN, retired elementary school educator; b. East St. Louis, Ill., Oct. 16, 1939; d. Joseph Edgar and Martha Eugenia Massa. BS in Elem. Edn., So. Ill. U., Carbondale, 1961, MS in Elem. Edn., 1964. 2d grade tchr. Collinsville Cmty. Unit Sch. Dist., Ill., 1961—64, 1965—94, reading cons., 1964—65, Head Start tchr., 1965; ret. Pvt. tutor; field experience student supr. So. Ill. U., Edwardsville; presenter in field. Pronouncer spelling bee, judge Collinsville Coun. PTA; guide 1st Madison County Young Authors Conf; primary ch. dir. 1st Bapt. Ch., Collinsville. Named Outstanding Young Educator, Collinsville Jaycees; past honored queen, Job's Daus, Collinsville. Mem.: Madison County Ret. Tchrs. Assn., Ill. Congress Parents and Tchrs. (hon.; life), Madison County Geneal. Soc. (membership chmn.), Delta Kappa Gamma (1st v.p., chmn. program com. Beta Eta chpt.), Pi Lambda Theta. Democrat. Avocations: reading, travel. Home: 107 Ashwood Ct Collinsville IL 62234 Personal E-mail: marthamassa@aol.com.

MASSA, NANCY G., columnist; b. Huntingdon Co., Pa., Mar. 27, 1942; d. Harry Franklin Geissinger and Marian Romain Clark; m. James E. Massa (dec.); children: John C., Jennie C. Ishler. Student, Pa. State U. Clerk, supr. U.S. Postal Svc., Lewistown, Pa., 1967, superintendent postal operations Carlise, Pa., 1984, postmaster Mill Hall, Pa., 1990; columnist The County Observer, Yeagertown, Pa., 1994. Home: 125 Broad St Milroy PA 17063-0342

MASSAGLI, JENNIFER ANN, science educator; BA in Environ. Sci. & Policy, Hood Coll., Frederick, Md., 1998; MEd in Curriculum Devel., U. Md., College Park, 2004, MS in Biology, 2006. Cert. tchr. Md., 2003. Tchr. biology Eleanor Roosevelt H.S., Greenbelt, Md., 2002—. Recipient Sci. & Tech. Tchr. of Yr., Eleanor Roosevelt Class of 2006.

MASSAH, CHERILYN, auditor; b. Dallas, Jan. 31, 1951; d. Herman Hiram and Mary Charlene (Thomas) Hill; m. Fathollah Massah, June 30, 1979. AA with highest honors, Tarrant County Jr. Coll., Hurst, Tex., 1982; BBA, U. Tex., Arlington, 1987. CPA, Tex. Sr. auditor Def. Contract Audit Agy., Dallas, 1987—2006. Spl. Interest grantee Tarrant County Jr. Coll., 1982; nominated to Nat. Dean's List U. Tex.-Arlington, 1986-87. Mem. Assn. Govt. Accts., Beta Alpha Psi. Avocation: stamp collecting/philately. Home: 4708 Michelle Dr Arlington TX 76016-5339 Office: Def Contract Audit Agy 6321 Campus Circle Dr E Irving TX 75063 Personal E-mail: chmassah@comcast.net.

MASSARO, TRACI LYNN, special education educator; b. Gadsden, Ala., Jan. 16, 1969; d. James Michael Cushing and Sheltie Anna Griffin; m. Thomas Christopher Massaro, Aug. 18, 1992; children: Lorren Elizabeth, Ryan Thomas, Andrew Michael. BS in Spl. Edn., Jacksonville State U., 1992; M, Kennesaw State U., 2000. Tchr. Bartow County Schs., Cartersville, Ga., 1992-93, Douglas County Schs., Douglasville, Ga., 1993-99, Etowah County Schs., Gadsden, Ala., 1999—. Recipient Mamie Jo Jones scholarship, 1995, Hope Tchr. scholarship, 1996-98, Outstanding Grad. Student Special Edn. award, 1999, Pledge of Yr. award Gadsden City Coun., 2002. Mem. Coun. Exceptional Children (v.p. 1996-97, pres. 1997—), Kiwanis (Circle K, v.p. 1989-90, pres. 1990-91), Anchor Club (v.p. 1985-86, pres. 1986-87), Beta Sigma Phi (v.p. 2003-04, pres. 2004—, Gadsden City Coun. Pledge of Yr. 2002, Woman of Yr. 2003). Republican. Baptist. Avocations: crafting, sewing. Home: 505 Cosby St Gadsden AL 35903-6911

MASSÉ, MICHELLE A., language educator; b. Woonsocket, R.I. d. Annette and Lucien Massé. PhD, Brown U., Providence, R.I. Prof. La. State U., Baton Rouge. Author: (critical study) In the Name of Love: Women, Masochism, and the Gothic. Fellow, NEH, Newberry Libr., Nat. Humanities Ctr., Rutgers Ctr. for Hist. Analysis, 1985, 1989, 2000, 2005. Mem.: MLA (chair del. assembly organizing com. on status of women 1999—2006).

MASSEE, JUDITH TYLE, editor, educator; b. Portland, June 26, 1937; d. Axel Buch Tyle and Annette Dorothy Brown; m. Richard S. Tron, Aug. 15, 1970; m. Michael David Massee, Aug. 22, 1959 (div. Mar. 1968). BS, Portland State U., 1959; postgrad., U. Oreg., 1970. Recreational dir., dance specialist Bur. Pks. and Recreation, Portland, 1958—60; profl. dancer Broadway, Off-Broadway, N.Y.C., 1960—68; dir. dance dept. Reed Coll., Portland, 1968—98; ptnr., poetry editor Media Weavers LLC, Portland, 1998—. Adv. com. Portland Ctr. for Performing Arts, 1982—86. Choreographer (profl. production) New Savoy Opera Co., 1959—62; author: (poetry, anthology) Blooming in the Shade, 1997, (poetry book revs.) Writers NW Newspaper, 1997—. Design com. Performing Arts Ctr., Portland, 1980—86; mem. Multnomah County Arts Commn., Portland, 1982—86. Recipient Tchr. of Yr., Oreg. Dance Assn., 1992, Pacific NW Am. Assn. for Phys., Edn., Health, Recreation and Dance, 1993. Mem.: Oreg. Writers Colony (bd. mem. 1997—). Avocations: mentoring begining writers/poets, reading. Home: 3415 SE Steele St Portland OR 97202

MASSELINK, NORALYN, literature educator; b. Whitinsville, Mass., Apr. 27, 1959; d. Dewey James and Kathryn Mae Hoitenga; m. Oscar Davis; children: Emmalon Mika Davis, Eena Mae Davis, Endira Madre Davis. BA, Calvin Coll., Grand Rapids, Mich., 1981; PhD, U. Ill., Urbana-Champaign, 1987. Lectr. Interboro Inst., NYC, 1987; prof. SUNY, Cortland, 1988—. Vis. asst. prof. Hofstra U., Hempstead, NY, 1987—88; profl. writing instr. TC3.Biz, Dryden, NY, 1990—2006. Contbr. articles to profl. jours. Recipient Chancellor's award for Excellence in Tchg., SUNY, 2005. Mem.: MLA, Assembly for Tchrs. English Grammar, Nat. Coun. Tchrs. English, John Donne Jour. (exec. com. 1998—2000). Home: 3745 Lyncort Dr Cortland NY 13045 Office: SUNY - College at Cortland PO Box 2000 Cortland NY 13045 Office Phone: 607-753-2068. Business E-Mail: masselinkn@cortland.edu.

MASSENBURG, JOHNNYE SMITH, speech pathology/audiology services professional, minister; b. Durham, N.C., July 4, 1954; d. John Franklin and Florence Rowland Smith; m. C. Warren Massenburg, Aug. 4, 1990 (dec. June 2005). BS in Speech Pathology and Audiology, Hampton U., Va., 1975; MS in Speech Pathology and Audiology, Towson State U., Md., 1978; PhD in Theology, Piedmont Theol. Sem., 2000. Lic. ordained minister Va. Speech pathologist and audiologist Balt. City Schs., 1975—78, Durham City Schs., NC, 1978—89; speech pathologist Richmond City Schs., Va., 1989—; pres. and CEO Massenburg & Massenburg Inc., Midlothian, 1990—; minister First Bapt. Ch., 1998—2006, Fifth Bapt. Ch., Richmond, 2006—. Named Woman of Yr., First Bapt. Ch., 1992, 2005; recipient Svc. award, Vets. Assn., 1993, 1994, 1998, Achievement award, Bus. Women Assn., 1994. Mem.: Am. Speech and Hearing Assn., Ministers Wives and Widows (treas. 1991—93). Democrat. Bapt. Avocations: singing, reading. Home: 13302 Farm Crest Ct Midlothian VA 23112 Office: Fifth Bapt Ch 1415 West Cary St Richmond VA 23220 Office Phone: 804-780-5078. E-mail: j_mass_midlo@att.net.

MASSENGILL, BARBARA DAVES, artist; d. Raleigh Whitson Daves and Laura Hermena Cox; m. Thomas Allan Rudisill, Dec. 19, 1954 (div. Sept. 1986); children: Carol Marie Rudisill, Allan Daves Rudisill, Sandra Lynn Rudisill Porter; m. James Robert Massengill, Mar. 19, 1989. Student, U. N.C., 1952—55. Substitute tchr. Raleigh (N.C.) Pub. Schs., 1968—69; co-owner Tinker's Dam, Ltd., Raleigh, 1970's; asst. DP coord. N.C. Dept. NRCD, Raleigh, 1982—87; DP coord. N.C. Dept. Human Resources, Raleigh, 1987—90; ret., 1990; v.p. Del-Mar Enterprises, Inc., Raleigh, 1996—; owner, artist Studio # 12 Hwy. 152, Hillsboro, N.Mex., 2003. Author: (tng. manual) A Function Oriented Guide for the Client, 1990; one-woman shows include First Savings Bank, Truth or Consequences, N.Mex., 2003, Elephant Butte (N.Mex.) C. of C., 2003, Bank of the Southwest, Elephant Butte, 2003, Truth or Consequences, 2003, exhibited in group shows at Apple Festival, Hillsboro, 2003, Sierra County Fair, Truth or Consequences, 2003, Quality Inn, Elephant Butte, 2003 (1st Pl. award Balloon Regatta Logo Design Contest), Geronimo Springs Mus., Truth or Consequences, 2003, Truth or Consequences C. of C., 2003 (1st Pl. award Fiesta Poster Contest), Represented in permanent collections Alaska, Calif., NC, N.Mex., Tex. Mem.: Sierra Arts Coun., Nat. Mus. of Am. Indian, N.Mex. Watercolor Soc., Black Range Artists (v.p. 2004), Nat. Mus. Women in the Arts, Sierra Art Soc. (treas. 2003), Sierra County Hist. Soc., DAV Aux., Nat. League Am. Pen Women, Inc. (treas. 2004—05, Rio Grande br., N.Mex.). Democrat. Avocations: gardening, cake decorating, photography, geological study and collection, wildlife study and preservation. Home: HCR 31 Box 97A Caballo NM 87931 E-mail: bmassen@zianet.com.

MASSEY, ALLYN FRANCIS, artist, educator; b. Norwood, Mass., Aug. 3, 1949; d. Gordon J. and Gwendolyn M. BFA, Corcoran Sch. Art, 1986; MFA, Md. Inst. Coll. Art, 1989. Prof. U. Md., Coll. Park, 1990-91, Corcoran Sch. Art, Washington, 1992-97; prof. and chmn. art and art history dept. Goucher Coll., Balt., 1997—. Bd. dir. Md. Art Pl., Balt., chair program adv. com., 1998—2000; adv. bd. Clipper Artists Fire Fund, 1996; resident Goya Girls Press, 2000; artist in residence Jentel Found., Banner, Wyo., 2001, Bemis Ctr. for Contemporary Art, Omaha, 2002; Jesse DuPont Nat. Humanities Ctr., Raleigh, NC, 2000. Illustrator: Second Person Rural, 1980; sculptor, printmaker, installation artist. Artist, panelist Balt. Mus. Art, 1993, BWI airport commn. Md. Aviation Bd., Linthicum, 1995, 1% for art commn. GSA, Balt./Washington, 1996; mem. pres.'s coun. Md. Inst., Coll. Art, 1998-. Recipient awards for individual artist, new genre Md. State Arts Coun., 1992, 95, 97, 2001; Henry A. Walters fellow Md. Inst. Coll. Art, 1989. Mem. Internat. Scuplture Ctr., Balt. Mus. Art, School 33 Art Ctr., Sculptors Inc. (sec. 1991-93, editor newsletter 1995-97), Creative Alliance, Contemporary Mus. Avocations: astronomy, geology. Office: Goucher Coll 1021 Dulaney Valley Rd Baltimore MD 21204-2753 Business E-Mail: amassey@goucher.edu.

MASSEY, GARNETTA D., bank executive; Sr. v.p., head of bus. develop. and mktg. Harbor Bank of Md., Balt. Trustee Caroline Ctr.; mem. Greater Balt. Com. Named one of 25 Women to Watch, US Banker mag., 2005. Mem.: Balt. Mktg. Assoc. (mem. fin. com.). Office: Harbor Bank of Md 25 W Fayette St Baltimore MD 21201*

MASSIE, ANNE ADAMS ROBERTSON, artist; b. Lynchburg, Va., May 30, 1931; d. Douglas Alexander and Annie Scott (Harris) Robertson; m. William McKinnon Massie, Apr. 30, 1960; children: Anne Harris Massie-Apperson, William McKinnon, Jr. Grad., St. Mary's Coll., Raleigh, NC, 1950; BA in English, Randolph Macon Woman's Coll., 1952. Tchr. English E.C. Glass H.S., Lynchburg, 1955-60. Juror Am. Watercolor Soc. Ann. Exhbn., 1998, Ctrl. Va. Watercolor Guild, 1996. Represented in permanent collections at Hotel de Ville, Rueil-Malmaison, France, L'Association des Amis de la Grande Vigne, Dinan, France, Randolph Macon Woman's Coll., Lynchburg Coll., Va. Episcopal Sch., Va. Sch. of Arts, Va. State Bar Assn., Richmond, St. John's Episcopal Ch. Bd. dirs. Lynchburg Hist. Found., 1968-81, 91-95, pres., 1978-81; bd. dirs. Lynchburg Fine Arts Ctr., 1992-98, Point of Honor Mus., 1988-99, collections com., 1970-, chmn. 1989-99; bd. dirs. Amazement Sq. Children's Mus., 1996-2004; trustee Va. Episcopal Sch., Lynchburg, 1983-89, Va. Ctr. for Creative Arts, 1999-2005; mem. Friends of Rivermont, 2000-05, pres. 2000-02. Fellow, Va. Ctr. Creative Arts, 1997. Mem. Am. Watercolor Soc. (signature, Dolphin fellow 1993, Gold medal of Honor 1993), Nat. Watercolor Soc. (signature, Artist's Mag. award), Nat. League Am. Pen Women (pres. 1987, Best in Show 1994), Knickerbocker Artists (signature, Silver medal Watercolor 1993), Watercolor USA Honor Soc., Watercolor West (signature), Catharine Lorillard Wolfe Art Club (signature, medal of honor for water media, 2003), Allied Artists Am., Inc. (signature), Southern Watercolor Soc. (signature), Va. Watercolor Soc. (artist mem., Best in Show 1992, 97, chmn. exhbns. 1986, pres. 1995-96), Nat. Arts Club (exhibiting artist mem.), Artists' Fellowship, Colonial Dames Am. (chmn. 1987-90), Hillside Garden Club (pres. 1974-76), Jr. League (editor 1953-72), Lynchburg Art Club (bd. dirs. 1995-96, chmn. 1981-4), R.M.W.C. Maier Mus. Art (adv. bd. 2004-), Antiquarian Club. Episcopalian. Avocations: book club, gardening, tennis, historic preservation. Home: 3204 Rivermont Ave Lynchburg VA 24503-2028

MASSIE, BETSY MCPHERSON, clergywoman; b. Oakland, Calif., Feb. 18, 1949; d. Andrew Harper and Elizabeth (Wright) M.; m. James Carl Bauder, June 12, 1976; children: Carl Bauder, Simon Massie. AB, Goucher Coll., 1971; MDiv, McCormick Sem., Chgo., 1975. Ordained to ministry Presbyn. Ch., 1975. Asst. pastor 1st Presbyn. Ch., Sioux City, Iowa, 1975-77; pastor Portalhurst Presbyn. Ch., San Francisco, 1977-95; stated clk. San Francisco Presbytery, Berkeley, Calif., 1992—. Adj. prof. San Francisco Theol. Sem., San Anselmo, Calif., 1980-86; lectr. com., San Francisco State U., 1983-85; mem. U.S. Racquetball Team, 1981. Pres. Laguna Salada Parent Coun., Pacifica and San Bruno, Calif., 1993-95, Pacifica Dems., 1995; mem. sch. bd. Laguna Salada Union Sch. Dist., Pacifica and San Bruno, 1994—; rep. Calif. Sch. Bd. Del. Assembly, 1995. Recipient Elena Flynn vol. award Laguna Salada Parent Coun., 1994, vol. award City of Pacifica, 1995. Mem. Stated Clk. Assn. (exec. com. 1994—). Avocation: racquetball (nat. champion 1981). Office: San Francisco Presbytery 2024 Durant Ave Berkeley CA 94704-1513

MASSIE, TAMMY JEANNE PARLIMENT, statistician; b. Suffern, N.Y., Jan. 4, 1972; d. Thomas Holden and Marjorie Eleanor (Wood) Parliment; m. Tristan Shaw Massie, Dec. 28, 1969. BS in Math., Stockton State Coll., 1994; MS in Stats., U. Ctrl. Fla., 1998; PhD in Biostatistics, Med. Coll. Va., Va. Commonwealth U., 2002. Grad. tchg. asst. U. Ctrl. Fla., Orlando, 1995—98; lfeguard, cast mem. Walt Disney World, Lake Buena Vista, Fla., 1996—98; statistician Whitehall Robins, Richmond, Va., 1999—2000; grad. rsch. asst. Med. Coll. Va., Va. Commonwealth U., 1998—2002; math. statistician Ctr. Vet. Medicine, FDA, Rockville, Md., 2002—04, Ctr. Drug Evaluation and Rsch., FDA, Rockville, 2004—. Statis. cons. U. Ctrl. Fla., 1995—98; statis. cons., biostatistical consulting lab student leader Med. Coll. Va., Va. Commonwealth U., 1998—2002. Contbr. to roundtable discussions, posters to sci. forums. Recipient Karl E. Peace award of Excellence, Med. Coll. Va., 2000—01; scholar Youth for Understanding Exch. Student award, Kraft Foods, 1990, Philip Morris Academic award, Philip Morris, 1992—94. Mem.: FDA Stats. Assn., Drug Info. Assn. (poster ann. meeting 2005), Soc. Clin. Trials (presenter ann. meeting 2005), Am. Statis. Assn., Assn. Women in Sci. Home: 171 Sharpstead Lane Gaithersburg MD 20878 Office: Food and Drug Administration-CDER 2901 Corporate Blvd Rockville MD 20850 Office Phone: 301-827-2549. Office Fax: 301-827-2577. Business E-Mail: tammy.massie@fda.gov.

MASSIE-BURRELL, TERRI L., educational association administrator; b. Balt., Mar. 29, 1964; d. Edward Forest and Eleanor Dease Massie; m. Robinson Burrell, Jr., Feb. 14, 1990; 1 child, Robinson Burrell III. BA, Howard U., 1986; MA, Johns Hopkins U., 1990; student, U. MD, 1990—. Substitue tchr. Balt., Md., 1990—92; special educator Balt. City Pub. Schs., 1996—98; spl. educator Montgomery County Pub. Schs., Rockville, Md., 1998—2000; counselor Howard Cmty., Columbia, Md., 1999—2003; learning specialist Towson (Md.) U., 2000—02, faculty, 2001—, sr. dir., 2002—. Bd. mem. Md. State Rehab., Balt., 2001—; lectr. Towson (Md.) U., 1995—; co-chair Jack & Jill of Am., Balt., 2002—; pres. Howard U. Alumni, 1996—2001; adv. Delta Sigma Theta, Inc., Morgan State U., 1993—95. Recipient Presenters award, Balt. Tchrs. Union, 2001. Mem.: Learning Ctr. Coll. Reade and Learn. Assoc., Am. Coll. Personnel Assoc. Democrat. Roman Catholic. Avocation: singing. Office: Towson U Academic Achievement Ctr 8000 York Rd Baltimore MD 21252 E-mail: tmassieburrell@towson.edu.

MASSINGALE, FAITH L., bank executive; Grad., Ind. U., U. So. Calif. Joined Citibank, Ind., 1974, state mgr. Ind.; chief credit officer, asset portfolio mgr. Citigroup, Inc., Singapore, bus. mgr. Credit Cards bus. Athens, Greece, mng. dir. Consumer Value and Growth Markets Bus. Unit N.Am. Cards, head Internat. Cards NYC, 2004—. Bd. mem. VISA Internat., Europay. Trustee Children's Aid Soc. Office: Citigroup Inc 399 Park Avenue New York NY 10043

MASSINO, LAURA ANGELA, small business owner; b. Huntington, N.Y., June 18, 1960; d. William and Phyllis Massino; m. Andrew John Smith, Dec. 12, 1996. AAS in Interior Design, Fashion Inst. Tech., N.Y.C., 1984, BFA in Interior Design, 1986; MA in Art History, Calif. State U., L.A., 1995. Adminstr. Met. Fine Art Assoc., L.A., 1993—99; dir. ops. and registrar Ace Gallery, 1999—2000; owner and tour guide Architecture Tours L.A., 2000—. Spkr. Beverly Hills Forum, Calif., 2004. Author: (guidebooks) Architecture Tours L.A.: Silver Lake, 2004, Architecture Tours L.A.: Hollywood, 2004, Architecture Tours L.A.: Downtown, 2004, Architecture Tours L.A.: West Hollywood/Beverly Hills, 2004, Architecture Tours L.A.: Hancock Park/Miracle Mile, 2005, Architecture Tours L.A.: Pasadena, 2006, Architecture Tours L.A.: Frank Gehry, 2006. Mem.: Soc. Archtl. Historians, L.A. Conservancy, Nat. Trust Hist. Preservation. Avocation: travel. Office: Architecture Tours LA PO Box 93134 Los Angeles CA 90093 Office Phone: 323-464-7868.

MAST, BERNADETTE MIHALIC, lawyer; BS, Ohio State U., 1982; JD magna cum laude, Case Western Res. U., 1988. CPA; bar: Ohio 1988; cert. prodn. and inventory mgr., systems profl. 1985. With Jones Day, Cleve., 1988—, ptnr., 2000—. Mem.: Cleve. Bar Assn. (real estate sect.), Ohio State Bar Assn. Office: Jones Day North Point 901 Lakeside Ave Cleveland OH 44114-1190

MAST, KANDE WHITE, artist; b. St. Louis, Mar. 10, 1950; d. Elliott Maxwell and Mary (Barritt) W. Student, U. Mo., 1968-70, Longview C.C., Kansas City, Mo., 1970-71. Portrait painter, free-lance artist, Albany, N.Y., 1973-74, Kansas City, 1974—; dir., tchr. Studio Kande, Sch. Fine Arts, Kansas City, 1983-86; founder, exec. dir. Art Ctr. Kansas City, 1986-90; behavioral foster parent, 1989—; master foster parent, 1992—. Mem. psychiat. diversion team, mental health rev. team Jackson County Divsn. Family Svcs., 1992-95. Portrait painter and free-lance artist. Pres., bd. dirs. Advocates for Children, Inc., 1996—; vol. Ozanam Home for Boys, Kansas City, 1987—, mem. adv. bd., 1991—; mem. Cmty. Response Team, Jackson County, Divsn. Family Svcs.; founding mem. Nat. Campaign for Tolerance. Named Therapeutic Foster Parent of Yr., 1992. Mem.: Code Pink: Women for Peace, Nat. Mus. of Women in Arts (charter). Home and Studio: 12406 Baltimore Ct Kansas City MO 64145

MASTEN, JACQUELINE GWENDOLYN, small business owner; b. Brunswick, Maine, Oct. 24, 1941; d. Ralph Henry Bennet and Phyllis Estelle Crooker; children from previous marriage: Geraldine Frances Bullwinkel, Jennifer Lynn. Diploma in Bus., Pluss Sch. of Business, Portland, Maine, 1966. Shop owner Hudson Chair Caning Svcs., Hudson, NH, 1982; data entry operator Digital Corp., Nashua, NH, 1980; real estate landlady Hudson, NH, 1996—. Author: A Shaker Poetry Poetic History Book: A Tribute to My Aunt Eldress Gertrude Soule Shaker, 2003; contbr. poems to books. Named 1999 Poet of the Year, Famous Poets Soc., Nev., 1999, World Champion Amature, Internat. Soc. of Poets, 2001; recipient Shakespear medallion of Excellence, 2002. Mem.: New Eng. Saddlebred and Pony Assn., Quartzsite Roadrunner Gem and Mineral Club. Avocation: Shaker poetry writing, shaker tape chair seating, silversmith, gem faceting, lapidary. Personal E-mail: JGMas1025@aol.com.

MASTERS, ANN BROWNING, education educator, poet; d. Shirley A. and William T. Browning; m. Jeremy A. Masters; 1 child, Forrest J. BA, U. Fla., 1973, MEd, 1976, PhD, 1992, EdS, 1976. Exec. dir. Jan House Drug Abuse Prevention and Edn. Ctr., St. Augustine, Fla., 1976—77; consultation edn. coord. Tri-County Mental Health Svcs., St. Augustine, 1979—80; sr. case mgr., staff coord. St. Johns County Coun. Aging, 1981—85; academic advisor St. Johns River C.C., St. Augustine, 1985—96, prof. edn. program coord., 1996—. Author of poems; contbr. articles to profl. jours. Founding bd. dirs. Los Floridanos Soc., St. Augustine, Fla., 2000—03. Recipient Tchg. Excellence award, Nat. Inst. for Staff and Orgnl. Devel., 1998. Mem.: AAUW, Edn. Law Assn., Fla. Assn. of C.Cs. (chpt. pres. 1993), Los Floridanos Soc., Menorcan Cultural Soc., St. Augustine Hist. Soc. (bd. dirs. 2004—).

MASTERS, BETTIE SUE SILER, biochemist, educator; b. Lexington, Va., June 13, 1937; d. Wendell Hamilton and Mildred Virginia (Cromer) Siler; m. Robert Sherman Masters, Aug. 6, 1960; children: Diane Elizabeth, Deborah Ann. BS in Chemistry, Roanoke Coll., 1959, D.Sc. (hon.), 1983; PhD in Biochemistry, Duke U., 1963. Postdoctoral fellow Duke U., 1963-66, advanced research fellow, 1966-68, assoc. on faculty, 1967-68; mem. faculty U. Tex. Health Sci. Ctr. (Southwestern Med. Sch.), Dallas, 1968-82, assoc. prof. biochemistry, 1972-76, prof., 1976-82, research prof. surgery, dir. biochem. burn research, 1979-82; prof. biochemistry, chmn. dept. Med. Coll. Wis., Milw., 1982-90; Robert A. Welch disting. prof. chemistry, dept. biochemistry U. Tex. Health Sci. Ctr., San Antonio, 1190—. Mem. pharmacology-toxicology rsch. rev. com. Nat. Inst. Gen. Med. Scis., NIH, 1975-79; mem. bd. sci. counselors Nat. Inst. Environ. Health Scis., 1982-86, chmn., 1984-86; mem. adv. com. on biochemistry and endocrinology Am. Cancer Soc., 1989-92, chmn., 1991-92, mem. coun. for extramural grants, 1998—; mem. phys. biochemistry study sect. NIH, 1989-90; mem. adv. com. to the dir. of NIH, 2001-04; chair nat. rsch. coun. study com. on identifying and assessimg inintended effects of genetically engineered foods on human health NAS/Inst. of Medicine, 2002-04; vis. scientist Japan Soc. for Promotion Sci., 1978. Mem. editl. bd. Jour. Biol. Chemistry, 1976-81, 96-2001, Archives Biochemistry and Biophysics, 1991-94, Drug Metabolism and Disposition, 1993-, Nitric Oxide, Biology and Chemistry, 1996-, Internat. Union Biochemistry and Molecular Biology Life, 1999-; contbr. chpts. to books and articles, revs. and abstracts to profl. publs. Mem. coun. extramural grants Am. Cancer Soc., 1998-2000. Recipient Merit award Nat. Heart, Lung and Blood Inst., 1988-97, grantee, 1970—; recipient Excellence in Sci. award Fedn. Am. Socs. for Exptl. Biology, 1992; postdoctoral fellow Am. Cancer Soc., 1963-65, advanced rsch. fellow Am. Heart Assn., 1966-68, established investigator, 1968-73; rsch. grantee NIH, 1970—, Nat. Heart Lung Blood Inst., 1970—, Nat. Inst. Gen. Med. Scis., 1980—, Robert A. Welch Found., 1971-82, 90—; elected to Inst. Medicine of NAS, 1996. Fellow AAAS; mem. Am. Soc. Biochemistry and Molecular Biology (nominating com. 1983, coun. 1985-86, awards com. 1992-96, fin. com. 1993-98, publs. com. 1994-97, pres.-elect 2001, pres. 2002-04), Am. Soc. Pharmacology and Exptl. Therapeutics (exec. com. drug metabolism divsn. 1979-81, chmn. exec. com. 1993-94, bd. publs. trustees 1982-87, Bernard B. Brodie award 2000), Am. Chem. Soc., Assn. Am. Med. Colls. (adv. bd. biomed. rsch. 1995-98), Fedn. Am. Socs. for Exptl. Biology (bd. dirs. 1998—2002, v.p. 2001-02), Internat. Union Biochemistry and Molecular Biology (nominating com. 1994-97, chair U.S. nat.com. 1997—), Phi Beta Kappa, Sigma Xi, Alpha Omega Alpha. Office: U Tex Health Sci Ctr Dept Biochemistry 7703 Floyd Curl Dr MSC 7760 San Antonio TX 78229-3900 Office Phone: 210-567-6627. E-mail: masters@uthscsa.edu.

MASTERSON, CARLIN See GLYNN, CARLIN

MASTERSON, ELLEN HORNBERGER, accountant; b. Ft. Smith, Ark., Feb. 19, 1951; d. Evans Zacharias and Nancy Cravens (Eads) H.; m. Conrad J. Masterson, Jr., Sept. 26, 1987. BA, Emory U., 1973; MBA, So. Meth. U., 1978. CPA, Mass. Staff acct. Coopers & Lybrand, Boston, 1973, gen. practice ptnr. Dallas, 1985—97; CFO Am. Gen. Corp., Houston, 1997—99; ptnr. PricewaterhouseCoopers, N.Y.C., 1999—. Instr. Sch. Mgmt. and Adminstrv. Scis., U. Tex., Dallas, 1980-81. Bd. dirs. Shakespeare Festival Dallas, 1983-86, Leadership Dallas, 1985-86, USA Film Festival, 1986-88, Dental Health Program, Inc., 1986-88; mem. Jr. League, The 500, Inc.; workshop leader, vol. Cmty. Bd. Inst.; cons. Ctr. for Non Profit Mgmt. Mem. AICPA, Mass. Soc. CPAs, Tex. CPAs, So. Meth. U. MBA Alumni Assn., Kappa Kappa Gamma, Alpha Iota Delta, Beta Gamma Sigma. Presbyterian. Office: PricewaterhouseCoopers 300 Madison Ave 24th fl New York NY 10017

MASTERSON, MARY STUART, actress; b. N.Y.C., June 28, 1966; d. Peter and Carlin Glynn Masterson. Theatre appearances include Alice in Wonderland, 1982, Been Taken, 1985, The Lucky Spot, 1987, Lily Dale, 1987, Three Sisters, 1991; TV movies include Love Lives On, 1985, City in Fear, 1980, Lily Dale, 1996, On the 2nd Day of Christmas, 1997; films: The Stepford Wives, 1975, Heaven Help Us, 1984, At Close Range, 1985, My Little Girl, 1986, Gardens of Stone, 1987, Some Kind of Wonderful, 1987, Mr. North, 1988, Chances Are, 1989, Immediate Family, 1989, Funny About Love, 1990, Married To It, 1990, Fried Green Tomatoes, 1991, Benny and Joon, 1993, Bad Girls, 1994, Radioland Murders, 1994, Heaven's Prisoners, 1996, Bed of Roses, 1996, Digging to China, 1997, Dogtown, 1997, The Postman, 1997, The Florentine, 1998, The Book of Stars, 1999, Black and Blue, 1999, The Book of Stars, 2000, Leo, 2002, West of Here, 2002; dir., writer for Showtime 2000; TV guest appearances include Amazing Stories, 1985, Inside the Actors Studio, 1994. Office: Creative Artists Agency 9830 Wilshire Blvd Beverly Hills CA 90212-1825

MASTRIAN BELL, SAMANTHA, music educator, vocalist; b. Cumberland, Md., July 3, 1980; d. Samuel Eugene and Cynthia Ann Mastrian. BA in Music Performance and Edn., Edinboro U. of Pa., 2001; Mus M in conducting, Ohio U., Athens, 2003. Cert. tchr. music k-12 Ohio. Vocal artist Opera Columbus, 2004—; tchr. choir and drama Zanesville (Ohio) H.S., 2003—05; tchr. elem. music Granville Exempted Village Schs., 2005—. Pvt. music tchr. Mem.: Music Educators Nat. Conf., Ohio Music Educators Assn. Democrat. Roman Catholic.

MASTRONY, SARA ELIZABETH, music educator, director; b. Bridgeport, Conn., June 3, 1981; d. Donald and Alice Mastrony. BA in Music History, Bucknell U., 2003; MA in Tchg., Sacred Heart U., Fairfield, Conn., 2004. Choral dir. Tomlinson Mid. Sch., Fairfield, Conn., 2003—. Chamber choir dir. Tomlinson Mid. Sch., 2003—, musical dir., drama, 2003—; A capella adv. Fairfield HS, 2004—. Mem.: Music Educator's Nat. Conf., Am. Choral Dir.'s Assn. Avocation: performing/arranging A capella music. Home: 107 Wilson St Bridgeport CT 06605 Office: Tomlinson Mid Sch 200 Unquowa Rd Fairfield CT 06824 Business E-Mail: smastrony@fairfield.k12.ct.us.

MATA, LINDA SUE PROCTOR, writer, consultant; b. Topeka, Oct. 22, 1950; d. Frank Robert and Anabelle Simpson Proctor; m. Robert William Mata, Aug. 29, 1980; children: Adrian Robert-Proctor, Christiana Nicole. BA in Sociology, U. Ctrl. Okla., 1973; BA in Edn., Pacific Luth. U., 1983; MBA, City U., Renton, Wash., 1999; postgrad., Capella U. Tchr. North Thurston Sch. Dist., Olympia, Wash., 1986—88; cons. Dept. Social and Health Svcs., Olympia, 1988—. Tchr. Kid's Outreach, Olympia, 2001—. Author: Roads and Reminiscences, 2002; co-author (with Christiana Mata): Upon the Stars, 2004, Flowers in Bloom, 2005, Evening Shadows, 2006. Mem. Blacks in Govt., Olympia, 2001—03. With U.S. Army, 1977—81. Recipient Diversity award, Dept. Soc. and Health Svcs., Diversity award for state employees, Washington State, 2004, Cert., South Sound Poets, 2004, Toastmaster Speakers award, 2005. Mem.: U. Okla. Alumni Assn. (assoc.), Toastmasters Internat. (sec.). Avocations: travel, doll collecting, reading, camping, poetry. Personal E-mail: mata@comcast.net. E-mail: matals@dshs.wa.gov.

MATALAMAKI, MARGARET MARIE, educator, consultant; b. Hampton, Iowa, May 10, 1921; d. Byron Jacob and Vera Margaret (Wheaton) Myers; m. William Matalamaki, Sept. 11, 1942 (dec. 1978); children: Judith Marie Gerlinger-Thiem, William Micheal. A.A., Itasca Community Coll., 1941. High sch. instr. Sch. Dist. 1, Bigfork, Minn., 1942-45, U. Minn. Sch. Agr., Grand Rapids, Minn., 1955-58; high sch. substitute Sch. Dist. 318, Grand Rapids, 1967-69; vocat. instr. Itasca Community Coll., Grand Rapids, 1970-78. bd. dirs. Blandin Found., Grand Rapids, trustee, 1981-92, v.p., 1985-87, chmn. 1988-92; bd. dirs. Christus Home, Grand Rapids; cons. to Keewatin Community Devel. Corp., Grand Rapids, 1985; mem. consumer adv. bd. Land of Lakes Inc., St. Paul, 1984-87, chmn. 1986-87; pres. Kooch-Itasca Action Council, Grand Rapids, 1981-84; adv. council mem. Women's Econ. Devel. Corp., Mpls., 1984-87; bd. dirs. Itasca Meml. Hosp., 1975-85, Itasca County Nursing Home, 1975-85, No. Itasca Nursing Home, 1982-85, Itasca County Social Services, 1975-85; county commr. Itasca County, 1981-85; legis. coord. Luth. Ch. Am., 1983-86, staff, advocacy coord. Minn. Synod, 1983-86; mem. adv. council Inst. Agr., Forestry and Home Econ. U. Minn., 1981-90; 4-H club leader, Esko, Minn., 1945-49, Grand Rapids, Minn., 1949-63; home extension leader, Esko, 1945-49, Grand Rapids, 1949-63; county fair judge No. Minn., 1950-84; bd. dirs. United Way Grand Rapids, 1980-84; commr. Itasca County, 1980-84; dir. Grand Rapids Citizen's League, 1980—98, pres., 95-97, Minn. Women for Agr., 1982-88, Joint Religious Legis. Coalition, Mpls., 1977-78, U. Minn. Nat. Alumni bd. dirs., 1987-91, U. Minn. 4H Found. bd. dirs., 1987-91, U. Minn. North Cen. Research Station Found./Fund, 1987-97; bd. dirs., chair Luth. Social Svcs. Minn., 1986-94, Soc. Svcs. Found., 1995-2003; past vice chair, mem. adv. bd. Luth. Social Services North Eastern Minn., 1986-87; mem. Minn. Child Abuse Team, 1986-87; pres. Luth. Ch. Women, 1959-62, Minn. synodical bd., 1972-76, dist. chmn., 1964-65; mem. Minn. Med. Found., 1991-93, bd. trustees, 1992—; com. mem. Commn. for a New Luth. Ch., 1985, chmn. transition team, 1986-87, mem. exec. com. Synod Council, 1976-79; trustee Gustavus Adolphus Coll. Bd., 1988-95; dir., bd. govs. U. Minn. Hosp. and Clinic, 1990-92. Recipient Good Govt. award Grand Rapids Jr. C. of C., 1977, Good Neighbor award WCCO Radio, 1976, Outstanding Achievement award U. Minn., 1989; named Citizen of Yr., Grand Rapids Herald Rev., 1999, day in her honor Minn. Gov. Carlson, 1999. Mem. LWV, U. Minn. Women's Club (pres. 2001-02), Grand Rapids C. of C. (life), PEO Club (pres., sec. 1964-97). Avocations: cross country skiing, canoeing, traveling. Home and Office: 910 Old Town Dr New Brighton MN 55112-2766

MATALIN, MARY, political consultant; b. Chgo., Aug. 19, 1953; d. Steven and Eileen Matalin; m. Artie Arnold (div.); m. James Carville, Nov. 25, 1993; 2 children. BA in Political Sci., Western Ill. Univ.; student, Hofstra Law Sch. With RNC, since the early 80's; voter contact dir. Reagan-Bush re-election campaign, 1984; chief staff to co-chmn. RNC, 1985; Midwest regional political dir. primary elections Bush-Quayle election campaign, 1988, dir. nat. victory '88 gen. election, 1988; polit. dir. George Bush's 1992 re-election campaign; co-host CNBC talk show, Equal Time, 1993—96; host radio show, CBS Talk Radio Network The Mary Matalin Show, 1996—98; co-host Crossfire, 1999—2001; asst. to the Pres. and Counselor to the V.P., 2001—02. Author (with James Carville): All's Fair: Love, War and Running for President, 1992; author: Letters to My Daughters, 2004; appearance: (TV political series) K-Street. Office: The Office of Mary Matalin 424 S Wash St Lower Level Alexandria VA 22314 Office Phone: 703-739-6006. E-mail: mary@matalin.info.

MATALLANA, LYNNE, medical association administrator; m. Richard Matallana. Former ptnr. advt. agy., Calif.; co-founder, pres. Nat. Fibromyalgia Assn., Calif., 1997—. Mem. FDA Ctr. for Drug Evaluation Rsch., Arthritis Adv. Com., Nat. Inst. Arthritis & Musculoskeletal & Skin Diseases Coalition. Pub., editor-in-chief Fibromyalgia AWARE mag, 2002—; co-author: The Complete Idiot's Guide: Fibromyalgia, 2005. Office: Nat Fibromyalgia Assn Ste A 2200 Glassell St Orange CA 92865 Office Phone: 714-321-0150. Office Fax: 714-921-6920.

MATAN, LILLIAN KATHLEEN, secondary school educator, consultant, interior designer; b. Boston, Aug. 18, 1937; d. George Francis and Lillian May (Herbert) Archambault; m. Joseph A. Matan, Aug. 6, 1960; children: Maria, Meg, Tony, Elizabeth, Joan, Molly. BS, Seton Hall Coll., 1960; MA, San Francisco State U., 1984; EdD, U. San Francisco, 1999. Tchr. St. Jane de Chantal, Bethesda, Md., 1956-60; tchr. home econs. Surrottsville (Md.) H.S., 1960-61; tchr., head home econs. dept. Bruswick (Md.) H.S., 1972-73; designer Dudley Kelley and Assocs., San Francisco, Calif., 1976-84; designer (prin.) K. Matan Antiques and Interiors, Ross, Calif., 1985-87; designer Charles Lester Assocs., San Francisco, 1987-88; dean of students St. Rose Acad., San Francisco, 1988-90; dir., asst. devel. The Branson Sch., Ross, Calif., 1990-92; prin. St. Anselm Sch., San Anselmo, Calif., 1993-94; adminstrv. head Ring Mt. Day Sch., Tiburon, Calif., 1995-96; sabbatical, 1997-98. Ednl. cons. Head Start, Frederick County, Md., 1972-73. Pres. Cath. Charities, Marin County, Calif.; mem. Ecumenical Assn. for Housing, Marin County. Mem. KM (dame), Am. Soc. of Interior Designers, Am. Assn. Family and Consumer Scis., Serra Club, Phi Delta Kappa. Democrat. Home: PO Box 1140 Ross CA 94957-1140 E-mail: lmatan6561@aol.com.

MATARAZZO, MARIA C., finance educator, department chairman; b. Somerville, Mass., Nov. 9, 1945; d. Anthony Samuel and Rose Matarazzo. BS in Bus. Edn. cum laude, So. NH U., Manchester, 1974, MBA, 1983; postgrad., Nova Southeastern U., 1993—94. Instr. So. NH U., Manchester, 1980—84; prof. NH Cmty. Tech. Coll., Manchester, 1984—88; divsn. chair, assoc. prof. Rivier Coll., Nashua, NH, 1988—. Presenter in field. Named Bus. Tchr. of Yr., Dept. Edn., 2005. Mem.: Acad. Mgmt., Bus. and Profl. Women (bd. dirs. 2001—, legis. chair 2002—), Ea. Bus. Edn. Assn., Nat. Bus. Edn. Assn., NH Bus. Edn. Assn. (pres., v.p., bd. dirs., Achievement award 2004), Alpha Delta Kappa, Alpha Sigma Lambda, Pi Omega Pi. Office: Rivier Coll 420 Main St Nashua NH 03060

MATARAZZO, RUTH GADBOIS, retired psychologist, educator; b. New London, Conn., Nov. 9, 1926; d. John Stuart and Elizabeth (Wood) Gadbois; m. Joseph D. Matarazzo, Mar. 26, 1949; children: Harris, Elizabeth, Sara. AB, Brown U., 1948; MA, Washington U., St. Louis, 1952, PhD, 1955. Diplomate in clin. psychology and clin. neuropsychology Am. Bd. Examiners Profl. Psychology. Rsch. fellow pediat. Washington U. Med. Sch., 1954-55; rsch. fellow psychology Harvard U. Med. Sch., 1955-57; asst. prof. med. psychology Oreg. Health Scis. U., Portland, 1957-63, assoc. prof., 1963-68, prof. dept. behavioral neurosci., 1968—, prof. emerita, 1997. Woman liaison officer Assn. Am. Med. Coll.s, 1979—90; cons. Tillamook Job Corps, Oreg. Bd. Med. Examiners, Social Security Adminstrn., Portland Ctr. Hearing and Speech. Author (E. Greif): (book) Behavioral Approaches to Rehabilitation: Coping with Change, 1982; contbr. chapters to books, articles to profl. jours., book reviews to jours. Bd. dirs. Portland Opera Assn., Morrison Child Guidance Clinic, Portland Chamber Orch., Neskowin Valley Sch., Hoover-Minthorn Mus. Fellow: APA (policy and planning bd., edn. and tng. bd., vice-chair accreditation bd., chair accreditation task force, accreditation bd., site visitor APA accreditation of grad. programs, coun. of reps.), Oreg. Psychol. Assn. (past pres.); mem.: AAAS, Portland Psychol. Assn. (past pres.), We. Psychol. Assn. (bd. dirs.), Sigma Xi. Home: 1934 SW Vista Ave Portland OR 97201-2455 Office Phone: 503-494-0279. Business E-Mail: matarazr@ohsu.edu.

MATARIC, MAJA J., engineering educator; BS with honors in Computer Sci., U. Kans., 1987; SM in Computer Sci., MIT, Cambridge, 1990, PhD in Computer Sci. and Artificial Intelligence, 1994. Mem. tech. staff NASA Jet Propulsion Lab., Pasadena, Calif., 1988; cons. Advanced Rsch. and Devel. Grp. LEGO Futura, Cambridge, Mass., 1989—90; rsch. scientist Free U. Brussels, 1990, GTE Labs., Waltham, Mass., 1991; postdoctoral fellow MIT Artificial Intelligence Lab., 1994; asst. prof. computer sci. dept. and Volen Nat. Ctr. Complex Systems Brandeis U., Waltham, Mass., 1995—97; asst. prof. computer sci. dept. and neuroscience prog. U. So. Calif., LA, 1997—2001, assoc. prof., 2001—06, prof., 2006—. Vis. prof. Fed. Poly. Sch. Lausanne, Switzerland, 1994, Swedish Inst. Computer Sci., Stockholm, 1994; founding dir. Interaction Lab., 1995—; vis. rschr. ATR Human Info. Processing Rsch. Lab., Kyoto, 1996; dir. Robotics Rsch. Lab. U. So. Calif., LA, 1998—, assoc. dir. Inst. Robotics and Intelligent Systems, 1998—, founding dir. Ctr. Robotics and Embedded Systems, 2002—, sr. assoc. dean rsch. Viterbi Sch. Engring., 2006—; mem. sci. adv. bd. Evolution Robotics, Pasadena, Calif., 2002—; mem. academic adv. bd. Ctr. Neuromorphic Sys. Engring. Calif. Inst. Tech., 2002—05. Contbr. articles to profl. jours., chapters to books; assoc. editor: Adaptive Behavior Jour., 1995—, IEEE Transactions on Robotics and Automation, 2001—03, Internat. Jour. Humanoid Robotics, 2003—, mem. editl. bd.: Jour. Artificial Intelligence Rsch., 1999—2001, Internat. Jour. Autonomous Agents and Multi-Agent Systems, 2000—, mem. editl. adv. bd.: Internat. Jour. Advanced Robotic Systems, 2004—. Recipient Career award, NSF, 1996-2001, Paper award, Assn. Computing Machinery, 1999, TR100 Innovation award, MIT Tech. Rev., 1999, Early Career award, IEEE Robotics and Automation Soc., 2000, Best Paper award, Hawaii Internat. Conf. Sys. Scis., 2003, Okawa Found. award, 2004. Mem.: IEEE Robotics and Automation Soc., Sigma Xi, Internat. Soc. Adaptive Behavior, Am. Assn. Artificial Intelligence (exec. com.), IEEE (sr.), Phi Kappa Phi. Office: Computer Sci Dept U So Calif 941 W 37th Pl MC 0781 Los Angeles CA 90089-0781 E-mail: mataric@usc.edu.*

MATASAR, ANN B., retired dean, finance educator; b. NYC, June 27, 1940; d. Harry and Tillie (Simon) Bergman; m. Robert Matasar, June 9, 1962; children— Seth Gideon, Toby Rachel AB, Vassar Coll., 1962; MA, Columbia U., 1964, PhD, 1968; M of Mgmt. in Fin., Northwestern U., 1977. Assoc. prof. Mundelein Coll., Chgo., 1965-78; prof., dir. Ctr. for Bus. and Econ. Elmhurst Coll., Elmhurst, Ill., 1978-84; dean Roosevelt U., Chgo., 1984-92; prof. Internat. Bus. and Fin. Walter E. Heller Coll. Bus. Adminstrn. Roosevelt U., 1992—2005, prof. bus. emerita, 2005—. Dir. Corp. Responsibility Group, Chgo., 1978-84; chmn. long range planning Ill. Bar Assn., 1982-83; mem. edn. com. Ill. Commn. on the Status of Women, 1978-81 Author: Corporate PACS and Federal Campaign Financing Laws: Use or Abuse of Power?, 1986; (with others) Research Guide to Women's Studies, 1974, (with others) The Impact of Geographic Deregulation on the American Banking Industry, 2002, Women of Wine: The Rise of Women in the Global Wine Industry, 2006; contbr. articles to profl. jours. Dem. candidate 1st legis. dist. Ill. State Senate, no. suburbs Chgo., 1972; mem. Dem. exec. com. New Trier Twp., Ill., 1972-76; rsch. dir., acad. advisor Congressman Abner Mikva, Ill., 1974-76; bd. dirs. Ctr. Ethics and Corp. Policy, 1985-90. Named Chgo. Woman of Achievement, Mayor of Chgo., 1978. Fellow AAUW (trustee ednl. found. 1992-97, v.p. fin. 1993-97); mem. Am. Polit. Sci. Assn., Midwest Bus. Adminstrn. Assn., Acad. Mgmt., Women's Caucus for Polit. Sci. (pres. 1980-81), John Howard Assn. (bd. dirs. 1986-90), Am. Assembly of Coll. Schs. of Bus. (bd. dirs. 1989-92, chair com. on diversity in mgmt. edn. 1991-92), North Ctrl. Assn. (commr. 1994-97), Beta Gamma Sigma. Democrat. Jewish. Avocations: walking, biking, opera, crosswords. E-mail: amatasar@roosevelt.edu.

MATASEJE, VERONICA JULIA, sales executive; b. St. Ann's, Ontario, Can., Apr. 5, 1949; came to U.S., 1985; d. John and Anna Veronica M. Grad. H.S., Smithville, Can. Clk. typist, typesetter Crown Life Ins. Co., Toronto, 1966-70; typesetter Toronto Life/Calendar Mag., 1970-71; typesetter, exec. sec. Cerebrus Prodns. Ltd., Toronto, 1971-74; pres. Veron Prodns. Ltd., Toronto, 1975-81, Acclaim Records Inc., Toronto, 1981-88; pvt. health care provider Las Vegas, 1989-94; retail sales mgr. Top Cats, Las Vegas, 1994-00; pres. Abracadabra Music Corp., 2000—. Campaign vol. Dist. Atty., Las Vegas, 1994; vol. pilot Angel Planes, Las Vegas, 1989. Avocations: gardening, interior decorating, travel, music. Home: 4326 Caliente St Las Vegas NV 89119-5801 Office: Top Cats PO Box 61173 Las Vegas NV 89160-1173 E-mail: vm@abracadabramusic.com.

MATCHETTE, PHYLLIS LEE, editor; b. Dodge City, Kans., Dec. 24, 1921; d. James Edward and Rose Mae (McMillan) Collier; m. Robert Clarke Matchette, Dec. 4, 1943; children: Marta Susan, James Michael. AB in Journalism, U. Kans., 1943. Reporter Dodge City Daily Globe, 1944; tchr. English Dodge City Jr. H.S., 1944-45; asst. instr. U. Kans. Coll. Liberal Arts, Lawrence, 1945-47; dir. Christian edn. Southminster United Presbyn. Ch., Prairie Village, Kans., 1963-65; editor, publs., dir. comm., supr. in-plant printing Village United Presbyn. Ch., Prairie Village, Kans., 1965-86; freelance journalist, 1987-91. Author: The Village Church Story, 1996. Hon. mem. Commn. Ecumenical Mission and Rels., Program Agy., Presbyn. Ch., U.S.A.; ordained elder Village Presbyn. Ch., 1964, elected elder, 1988-90. Recipient Woman of Faith award, Village Ch., 2006. Mem. DAR, Women in Comm., Kans. U. Dames (pres. 1946), Kansas City Young Matrons, P.E.O., Order of Eastern Star, Alpha Chi Omega (pres. Edn. Found. Phi chpt. 1951). Republican.

MATEJKA, TINA SOCHIA, music educator; b. Fulton, NY, Jan. 5, 1960; d. Marlene Lois Sochia; m. Dennis James Morris (div.); m. Steven Reid Matejka, Aug. 1, 1998. BS in music edn., West Chester State Coll., 1982; MusM, U. Mass., 1984. Jr. high music educator John Jay Sch. Dist., Katonah, NY, 1984—86; HS music educator Union-Endicott Sch. Dist.; jr., sr high music educator Dundee Ctrl. Schs., Dundee, NY, 1989—2003; HS music educator Horseheads Ctrl. Sch., Horseheads, NY, 2003—. Mem.: Am. Horse Shows Assn., NY State Sch. Music Assn., Music Educators Nat. Conf., NY Fed. of Contest Judges. Democrat. Episcopalian. Office: Horseheads HS 401 Fletcher St Horseheads NY 14845 E-mail: tmatejka@horseheadsdistrict.com.

MATELIC, CANDACE TANGORRA, museum director, educator; b. Detroit, Aug. 21, 1952; d. Paul Eugene and Madeline Marie (Tangora) M.; m. Steven Joseph Mrozek, Sept. 17, 1983 (div. Sept. 1987); 1 child, Madeline Rose. BA, U. Mich., 1974; MA, SUNY, Oneonta, 1977; postgrad. doctoral studies, SUNY, Albany. Interpretive specialist Living History Farms, Des Moines, 1978-80; mgr. adult edn. Henry Ford Mus./Greenfield Village, Dearborn, Mich., 1981-82, mgr. interpretive tng., 1982-84; dir., prof. mus. studies Cooperstown grad. program SUNY, Oneonta, 1985-94; exec. dir. Mission Houses Mus., Honolulu, 1994-96, Historic St. Mary's City, Md., 1997-98; pres./CEO CTM Profl. Svcs., Inc., 1999—, working leader, 2004—; founder, prin. The Cherry Valley Group, 2002—04. Cons. history mus., 1979—; lectr., tchr. nat. and regional confs., workshops, seminars, 1979—; frequent keynote spkr.; grant reviewer NEH and Inst. for Mus. Svc., Washington, 1982—, PEW Charitable Trusts, 2003; mem. guest faculty U. Victoria, BC, 1993, 2000, 02, 03, 04, 06; faculty Distance Cruise, 2004, 05. Author: (with others) Exhibition Reader, 1992, Distance Learning Course, 2002-, Strategic Interpretation and Program Plan for the Mill and Anselma, 2005; co-author: A Pictorical History of Food in Iowa, 1980, Survey of 1200-Plus Museum Studies Graduates, 1988; contbr. articles and videos on mus. interpretation, tng., orgnl. change and mentoring in mus., 1979—; author conf. procs. Trustee Motown Hist. Mus., 1985—2004; bd. dirs. Hawaii Youth Opera Chorus, 1996; project mgr. program plan for the Richard and Sarah Allen Ctr. for Faith, Freedom and Cmty, Mother Bethel Found., 2004-05. Mem. Am. Assn. State and Local History (sec., bd. dirs. 1988-93, program chmn. ann meeting 1988, mem. edn. com. 1996-99, co-chair task force on edn. and tng. 1994-96, faculty nat. workshop series 2001-04, Historic House Initiative), designed profl. tng. workshop series, 1999-00, Assn. Living Hist. Farms and Agrl. Mus. (bd. dirs. 1980-88, pres. 1985, John T. Schlebecker award Lifetime Disting. Svc. 1996), Midwest Open Air Mus. Coordinating Coun. (founder, bd. dirs., pres. 1978-80, Candace Tangorra Matelic essay award competition established by MOMCC 2002), Am. Assn. Museums (mus. studies com. 1986-94), Internat. Coun. Museums, Nat. Trust for Hist. Preservation, Hawaii Museums Assn. (bd. dirs. 1994-96), So. Md. Mus. Assn. (bd. dirs. 1997-98). Democrat. Roman Catholic. Home and Office: 338 Navigators Dr Pawleys Island SC 29585-7068 Office Phone: 843-237-5078. Personal E-mail: ctmatelic@sc.rr.com.

MATENAER, TEGWIN A., retired artist, educator, consultant; BS in Art, Calif. State U., Fresno, 1982. Cert. tchg. Calif. Dept. Edn. Art tchr., grant participant Fresno City Elem. Dist., 1980; tchr. Fresno County Office of Edn., 1980—82, Shasta County Office of Edn., Redding, Calif., 1982—89; art tchr. Sequoia Mid. Sch., Redding Elem. Sch. Dist., 1989—95; art and photography tchr. Shasa Coll. Cmty. Edn., 1996—98; art. coord., artist in residence Redding Sch. of the Arts, K8 Visual and Performing Arts Charter Sch., 1999—2006. Mentor tchr. Shasta County Office of Edn., Redding, 1986—88;

art grant coord. Calif. arts project Sequoia Mid. Sch., Redding Elem Sch. Dist., 1994—95; selected artist exhibitor, art in pub. places Redding City Hall Civic Ctr., 1998, 2001—05; juror fine art, photgraphy numerous organizations. Exhibited in group shows at Funnel Follies (Category award pastel, 2006), River Run (Best of Show, 2005), Summer Rains (Category award pastel, 2002), Center Stage, Plein Air Beauty, Ahjumawi Reeds, Lassen Rains', Fajada Songs, Acad. Scis., Moscow, 2001; contbr. Calif. Art Rev., Best of Photography Annual. Artist participant Cornucopia Fall Fundraiser, Women's Refuge, Redding. Mem.: AAUW (past cultural coord., artist participant annual home tour scholarship fundraiser 1998—), Sierra Pastel Soc., Pastel Soc. of the West Coast, Pastel Soc. of the SW, Pastel Soc. of N.Mex, Pastel Soc. of Colo., NW Pastel Soc. Office: Tegwin Matenaer Fine Arts PO Box 992538 Redding CA 96099-2538 Office Phone: 530-243-7694. E-mail: tegsmail@tegwinart.com.

MATER, MAUD, lawyer; b. Portland, Oreg., May 12, 1947; BA in English, Case Western Reserve U., 1969, JD, 1972. Asst. gen. counsel Freddie Mac, McLean, Va., 1976-78, assoc. gen. counsel, 1978-79, v.p., dep. gen. counsel, 1979-82, v.p., gen. counsel, 1982-84, sr. v.p., gen. counsel, sec., 1984-98, exec. v.p., gen. counsel, sec., 1998—2003. Mem.: FBA, ABA (com. corp. gen. counsel), Washington Met. Corp. Counsel Assn., Conf. Bd. Coun. of Chief Legal Officers, DC Bar, Ohio Bar, Am. Arbitration Assn. (dir.), Am. Corp. Counsel Assn.

MATERA, CRISTINA, gynecologist, educator; b. Englewood, N.J., Sept. 29, 1960; MD, NYU, 1986. Cert. in ob-gyn. and reproductive endocrinology and infertility. Resident ob-gyn. Columbia Presbyn. Med. Ctr./Presbyn. Hosp., N.Y.C., 1986—90, fellow, 1990—92; asst. prof. Columbia P&S, 1990—. Office: 50 E 77th St New York NY 10021-5856 Office Phone: 212-639-9122. E-mail: cmateramd@hotmail.com.

MATERA, FRANCES LORINE, elementary school educator; b. Eustis, Nebr., June 28, 1926; d. Frank Daniel and Marie Mathilda (Hess) Daiss; m. Daniel Matera, Dec. 27, 1973. Luth. tchrs. diploma, Concordia U., Seward, Nebr., 1947, BS in Edn., 1956; MEd, U. Oreg., Eugene, 1963. Elem. tchr. Our Savior's Luth. Ch., Colorado Springs, Colo., 1954—57; tchr. 5th grade Monterey (Calif.) Pub. Schs., 1957—59; tchr. 1st grade Roseburg (Oreg.) Schs., 1959—60; tchr. several schs. Palm Springs (Calif.) Unified Sch. Dist., 1960—93; tchr. 3rd grade Vista del Monte Sch., Palm Springs, Calif., 1973—93; ret., 1993. Named Tchr. of the Yr., Palm Springs Unified Schs. Mem. Kappa Kappa Iota (chpt. and state pres.). Personal E-mail: Franmatera7@aol.com.

MATERIA, KATHLEEN PATRICIA AYLING, nurse; b. Jersey City, Nov. 7, 1954; d. Donald Anthony and Muriel Cecilia (Joyce) Ayling; m. Francis Peter Materia, June 5, 1983; children: Christopher Michael, Donna Nicole. BSN, Fairleigh Dickinson U., 1976. RN, N.J. Critical care nurse Palisades Gen. Hosp., North Bergen, N.J., 1976-87; grad. nurse, 1976-77; nurse critical care unit North Hudson Hosp., Weehawken, NJ, 1977-78. Mem. Alpha Sigma Tau. Democrat. Avocations: bowling, dance.

MATES, SUSAN ONTHANK, physician, educator, musician, writer; b. Oakland, Calif., Aug. 8, 1950; d. Benson and Lois (Onthank) M.; m. Joseph Harold Friedman, Dec. 10, 1978; children: Rebecca, Deborah, William. Student, Juilliard Sch. Music, 1967-69; BA magna cum laude with distinction, Yale Coll., 1972; MD, Albert Einstein Coll. Medicine, 1976. Cert. Am. Bd. Internal Medicine, Nat. Bd. Med. Examiners. Intern Boston City Hosp., 1976-77; fellow in gen. medicine Coll. of Physicians and Surgeons-Columbia U., N.Y.C., 1977-78; resident/fellow in infectious diseases Montefiore Hosp., Bronx, 1978-82; asst. prof. medicine Brown U., Providence, 1982-85, asst. prof. biochemistry, 1985-86, clin. assoc. prof. medicine, 1993-98; staff mem., former dir. R.I. State Tb Clinic, R.I. Dept. Health, Providence, 1986-96, cons. Tb program, 1987-96. Judge short story contest Providence Jour., 1994, 98; mem. jury R.I. Coun. Arts Fellowship; contbg. editor Pushcart Prize, Pushcart Press, 1995, 96, 97, 98, 99. Author: (fiction) The Good Doctor, 1994 (John Simmons Short Fiction Award, U. Iowa Press, 1994); contbr. sci. articles to profl. jours., stories to revs. and jours. and anthologies. Recipient Recognition award for young scholars AAUW, 1985, Clin. Investigator award NIH, 1984, R.I. Found. award, 1983; McDowell Colony fellow, 1995, Yaddo fellow, 1996; Symposium scholar in lit. and medicine for 21st Century, Brown U., 1997. Mem. Am. Med. Women's Assn., Poets and Writers, Alpha Omega Alpha.

MATESKY, NANCY LEE, music educator; b. West Point, Mo., Nov. 30, 1941; d. Enoch Ivy and Layla Nixon Miller; m. Michael Paul Matesky, Aug. 10, 1973; children: Angela Lynn, Michael Paul II. BS in Edn., U Ark., 1963, MS in Edn., 1971. Piano tchr. self employed, Tex., Ark., Wash., 1960—90; music tchr. Rogers Ark. Sch., 1963—64, Fayetteville Sch., Ark., 1964—65, Springdale Sch., Ark., 1965—70; instr. U Ark., Fayetteville, 1971—72; asst. prof. West Tex. State U, Canyon, 1972—75; prof. Shoreline CC, Seattle, 1976—. Founder, first pres. Ark. Elem. Music Educators Assn., 1965—67. Performer: Shoreline CC, 1981—98, Seattle Art Mus., 2000, 2002, Matesky-Swisher Two Piano Duo. Named one of Outstanding Young Women in Am., 1968; recipient Outstanding Young Educator award, Jaycees, 1967. Mem.: Music Educators Nat. Conf., Music Tchr. Nat. Assn. (assoc.), Seattle Ladies Musical Club, Sigma Alpha Iota (Nat. Coll. Leadership award 1963, Nat. Alumnae Leadership award 2001). United Meth. Home: 23004 35th Ave S E Bothell WA 98021-8913 Office: Shoreline CC 16101 Greenwood Ave N Shoreline WA 98133 Office Phone: 206-546-4618. Personal E-mail: opus.four@gte.net.

MATHANS, SHARRON HITT, retired librarian; b. Chico, Calif., Sept. 3, 1930; d. Cecil Perkins and Miriam Leola Hitt; m. Eugene Louis Kessler, Feb. 4, 1951 (div. June 0, 1974); m. Mitchell Patrick Mathans, Feb. 19, 1977 (div. Nov. 0, 2003); children: Frederik Louis Kessler, Therese Cecile Stefanson, Miriam Melinda Riley. BA, U. of Calif., Berkeley, 1953, MLS, 1974; Calif. Lifetime Tchg. Credential, Calif. State U., Sacramento, 1970. Cert. tchr. Calif., 1974. Tchr. Rio Americano H.S., San Juan Unified Sch. Dist., Sacramento, 1970—71; libr. clk. Am. River C.C., Los Rios Sch. Dist., Sacramento, 1972—73; libr. Vista H.S., Vista Unified Sch. Dist., Vista, Calif., 1974—93; ret. sch. libr. Vista H.S., 1993. Pres. Chico Newcomers Club - Encore Divsn., Chico, Calif., 2002—03; chmn. Chico Newcomers Club Book Group, 2004—06; vol. Enloe Med. Ctr., Chico, 2006; mem. Bidwell Presbyn. Ch., Chico, 2003—06. Mem.: Osher Lifelong Learning Inst., Phi Beta Kappa. R-Consevative. Presbyterian. Avocations: strength conditioning, travel, bridge, reading. Home: 311 W Frances Willard Ave Chico CA 95926

MATHEIS, CHERYL, not-for-profit developer; b. Buffalo, N.Y., May 15, 1951; d. Charles Wililam and Mary Aileen Matheis; m. Thomas Gillett Goodwin, Sept. 22, 1984; children: John Thomas Mary Claire. BA, Manhattanville Coll., 1973; JD, Cath. U. Am., 1978. Bar: D.C. 1978. Rsch. analyst Civil Rights Divsn. Dept. Justice, Washington, 1973-77; pvt. practice Washington, 1978-86; legis. rep. AARP, Washington, 1986-99, dir. state legis., 1999—. Mem. Am. Health Lawyers Assn., Women in Govt. Rels. Office: AARP 601 E St NW Washington DC 20049-0003

MATHEIS, VICKIE LYNNE, nurse; b. Ft. Campbell, Ky., Oct. 15, 1954; children: Alison Corinne, Craig Richard. AAS, Queensborough Community Coll., Bayside, N.Y., 1980; student, Adelphia U., 2000—. Staff nurse surg. floor Booth Meml. Med. Ctr., Flushing, N.Y., 1981-82, per diem nurse, 1988-90, staff nurse respiratory step-down, 1990—, asst. nurse mgr., 2002—03, case mgr., 2003. Recipient Ruth S. Blumenthal award. Mem. Phi Theta Kappa. Office: NY Hosp Med Ctr of Queens 56-45 Main St Flushing NY 11355-5000

MATHENY, RUTH ANN, editor; b. Fargo, N.D., Jan. 17, 1918; d. Jasper Gordon and Mary Elizabeth (Carey) Wheelock; m. Charles Edward Matheny, Oct. 24, 1960. BE, Mankato State Coll., 1938; MA, U. Minn., 1955; postgrad., Universidad Autonoma de Guadalajara, Mex., 1956, Georgetown U., 1960. Tchr., U.S. and S.Am., 1938-61; assoc. editor Charles E. Merrill Pub. Co., Columbus, Ohio, 1963-66; tchr. Confraternity Christian Doctrine, Washington Court House, Ohio, 1969-70; assoc. editor Jr. Cath. Messenger, Dayton, Ohio, 1966-68; editor Witness Intermediate, Dayton, 1968-70; editor in chief, assoc. pub. Today's Cath. Tchr., Dayton, 1970—2002, editor-in-chief emeritus, 2002—; editor in chief Catechist, Dayton, 1976-89, Ednl. Dealer, Dayton, 1976-80; v.p. Peter Li, Inc., Dayton, 1980—. Editl. collaborator: Dimensions of Personality series, 1969—; co-author: At Ease in the Classroom; author: Why a Catholic School?, Scripture Stories for Today: Why Religious Education?; freelance writer, 1943— Bd. dirs. Friends Ormond Beach Libr. Mem.: 3d Order St. Francis (eucharistic min. 1990—2006), Nat. Coun. Cath. Women. Home: 26 Reynolds Ave Ormond Beach FL 32174-7043 Office: Peter Li Ednl Group 2621 Dryden Rd Ste 300 Dayton OH 45439 Personal E-mail: chilermat@aol.com.

MATHER, ELIZABETH VIVIAN, healthcare executive; b. Richmond, Ind., Sept. 19, 1941; d. Willie Samuel and Lillie Mae (Harper) Fuqua; m. Roland Donald Mather, Dec. 26, 1966. BS, Maryville (Tenn.) Coll., 1963; postgrad., Columbia U., 1965-66. Tchr. Richmond Cmty. Schs., 1963-67, Indpls. Pub. Schs., 1967-68; systems analyst Ind. Blue Cross Blue Shield, Indpls., 1968-71, Ind. Nat. Bank, Indpls., 1971; med. cons. Ind. State Dept. Pub. Welfare, Indpls., 1971-78, cons. supr., 1978-86; systems analyst Ky. Blue Cross Blue Shield, Louisville, 1988-89; contracts specialist Humana Corp., Louisville, 1989—. Active Rep. Cen. Com. Montgomery County, Crawfordsville, 1976-86, Centenary Meth. Ch., adminstrv. bd., 1990. Mem. DAR (treas. 1963-66, sec. 1978-86). Avocation: designing and sewing clothes. Home: 6106 Partridge Pl Floyds Knobs IN 47119-9427 Office: 500 W Main St Fl 6 Louisville KY 40202-2946 Office Phone: 502-580-2519. Business E-Mail: emather@humana.com.

MATHER, LYNN, law educator, political science professor; BA, Univ. Calif. Los Angeles; postgraduate, Univ. Wis., Univ. Calif., Berkeley; PhD, Univ. Calif., Irvine. Nelson A. Rockefeller prof. govt. Dartmouth Coll.; acting dir. Rockefeller Ctr. Social Sci., Dartmouth Coll.; prof. Law & Polit. Sci. SUNY Buffalo, 2002—; dir. Baldy Ctr. for Law & Social Policy, Buffalo, 2002—. Author: Plea Bargaining or Trial? The Process of Criminal Case Disposition; co-author: Divorce Lawyers at Work: Varieties of Professionalism in Practice (C. Herman Pritchett award, Am. Polit. Sci. Assn.); contbr. articles to prof. jour. Mem.: Am. Polit. Sci. Assn. (chair, Law & Ct. sect. 1993—94), Law & Soc. Assn. (pres. 2001—02). Office: University at Buffalo Law School 418 O'Brien Hall Buffalo NY 14260

MATHER, MILDRED EUNICE, retired archivist; b. Washington, Iowa, July 25, 1922; d. Hollis John and Delpha Irene (Cummings) Whiting; m. Stewart Elbert Mather, Aug. 7, 1955; children: Julie Marie, Thomas Stewart(dec.). Cert., Burlington and Des Moines, 1941, 1947, Stenotype Inst., 1948. Typist Burlington Willow-Weave, 1941-42, Burlington Basket Co., 1942; clk. typist U.S. Dept. War, Washington, 1942-43; supr. internat. conf. U.S. Dept. State, Washington, 1949-52; bookkeeper Iowa Wesleyan Coll., Mt. Pleasant, 1952-55; clk. typist Herbert Hoover Presdl. Libr., West Branch, Iowa, 1964-69, archives technician, 1964-72, archivist, libr., 1972-92, ret., 1992. With WAC U.S. Army, 1943—46. Mem.: Am. Legion, Order Ea. Star. Republican. Home: 1794 Garfield Ave West Branch IA 52358-9403

MATHER, STEPHANIE JUNE, lawyer; b. Kansas City, Mo., Dec. 5, 1952; d. Edward Wayne and H. June (Kunkel) M.; m. Miles Christopher Zimmerman, Sept. 23, 1988. BA magna cum laude, Okla. City U., 1975, JD with honors, 1980. Lawyer Pierce, Couch, Hendrickson, Johnston & Baysinger, Okla. City, Okla., 1980—88, Manchester, Hiltgen & Healy, P.C., Okla. City, 1989—90; sr. staff counsel Nat. Am. Ins. Co., Chandler, Okla., 1990—98; atty. Ctr. for Edn. Law, Oklahoma City, 1998—, v.p., shareholder, 2003—. Asst. v.p. Lagere & Walkingstick Ins. Agy., Inc., Chandler, Okla., 1993-98. Co-chair Lincoln County Dem. Party, 1991-92, 95-97; v.p. Lincoln County Dem. Women, 1992-95, pres., 1995-97; bd. dirs. Lincoln County Partnership for Children, 1994—, Gateway to Prevention and Recovery, 1996-97. Mem. Okla. Bar Assn. (editor, bd. editors, 1992-99), Lincoln County Bar Assn. (mem. libr. bd. 1990—), Nat. Sch. Bds. Assn. (coun. of sch. attys. 1998—), Okla. State Sch. Bds. Assn. (coun. of sch. attys. 1998—, bd. dirs. 2002-05, pres. 2005-), Lincoln County Profl. Women, Alpha Phi (treas. Ctrl. Okla. Alumnae 1997-99, Outstanding Okla. City Alumnae, 2005, Panhellenic Woman of Yr. Okla. City, 2005). Democrat. Avocations: reading, genealogy, ranching, cooking. Office: Center For Education Law 900 N Broadway Ave #300 Oklahoma City OK 73102-5828 Home: 808 Manvel Ave Chandler OK 74834-3858 also: 808 Manvel Ave Chandler OK 74834 Office Phone: 405-528-2800. E-mail: smather@cfel.com.

MATHERLY, VIRGINIA WILLIAMS, music educator; b. Elizabethtown, Ky., Mar. 3, 1955; d. Ivan Taylor and Virginia Brown Williams; m. David Coleman Matherly, July 16, 1977; children: Laurel Elizabeth, Kathryn Taylor. BS in Music Edn., Campbellsville Coll., Ky., 1977; M of Music Edn., U. Tenn., Chattanooga, 1982. Tchr. music Wallace Mid. Sch., Charleston, SC, 1978—81; tchr. music, choral dir. Sale Creek Sch., Chattanooga, 1982—84; tchr. piano pvt. practice, Decatur, Ala., 1990—2003; dir. fine arts sch. 1st Bapt. Ch., 1997—; choral asst. Decatur H.S., 2003—. Mem. Decatur City Schs. PTA, 1994—2003; dir. childrens choir 1st Bapt. Ch., Decatur, 1988—. Mem.: Am. Orff-Schwartz Assn., Early Childhood Music and Movement Assn., Music Educators Nat. Conf. Democrat. Avocations: travel, reading. Home: 1242 Branddywine Ln SE Decatur AL 35601 Office: Sch Fine Arts 123 Ch St NE Decatur AL 35602

MATHERS, PAULA JANECEK, lawyer; b. Zlin, Czech Republic, June 12, 1972; BA, Prairie View A&M U., 1994; JD, South Tex. Coll. Law, 1997. Bar: Tex. 1997, US Dist. Ct. (no., ea. and so. dists. Tex.) 1998. Atty. Hagans, Burdine, Montgomery, Rustay & Winchester, P.C., Houston, 1997—. Named a Rising Star, Tex. Super Lawyers mag., 2006. Mem.: Assn. Trial Lawyers of Am., Houston Young Lawyers Assn., Tex. Trial Lawyers Assn., Tex. Young Lawyers Assn., ABA, Houston Bar Assn. Office: Hagans Burdine Montgomery Rustay Winchester PC 3200 Travis 4th Fl Houston TX 77006 Office Phone: 713-222-2700. E-mail: pjmathers@hbb-law.com.*

MATHERSON, RACHAEL AKERS, secondary school educator, dancer; b. Anniston, Ala., June 28, 1978; d. Ronnie Thomas and Katrina Lloyd Akers; m. Jason Matherson. BA, The U. Ala., Tuscaloosa, Ala., 2000. Cert. tchr. Ala., 2003. Tchr. Spain Pk. H.S., Hoover, Ala. Dir. dance Spain Pk. Dance, Hoover, Ala., 2002—. Recipient Best Choreographer award, 2005. Home: 1433 Secretariat Dr Helena AL 35080 Office: Spain Park High School 4700 Jaguar Dr Hoover AL 35242 Office Phone: 205-439-1400. Business E-Mail: rmatherson@hoover.k12.al.us.

MATHES, DOROTHY JEAN HOLDEN, occupational therapist; b. Paterson, N.J., Mar. 13, 1953; d. Cornelius Fred and Dorothy Johanna (Ferguson) Holden; m. Clayton Derald Mathes, May 26, 1973 (div. Dec. 1984); children: Christy, Carl, Chuck, Chad; m. Elie Youssef Hajjar, Oct. 4, 1989 (dec. Dec. 1996). BS in Occupational Therapy, Tex. Woman's U., Denton, Tex., 1988; MA in Occupational Therapy, Tex. Woman's U., 1995. Lic. occupational therapist, Tex. Occupational therapy cons. Lakes Regional-SOCS Early Childhood Intervention, 1988-97, Denton (Tex.) State Sch., 1997—, Rehab. Svcs. Unlimited, 2003—05, Rehab Works, 2005—. Mem. Am. Occupational Therapy Assn., Tex. Occupational Therapy Assn. Avocations: gardening, reading, swimming. Home: 2608 Woodhaven St Denton TX 76209-1340 Office: Denton State Sch PO Box 368 Denton TX 76202-0368 Office Phone: 940-591-3654. E-mail: djmathes@peoplepc.com.

MATHESON, LINDA, retired social worker; b. Martna, Estonia, Mar. 29, 1918; came to U.S., 1962, naturalized, 1969; d. Endrek and Leena Endrekson; m. Charles McLaren Matheson, Feb. 5, 1955. Diploma, Inst. Social Scis., Tallinn, Estonia, 1944; MS, Columbia U., 1966, D in Social Work, 1974. Diplomate clin. social work. Social work officer UN Rehab. and Resettlement Assn., Germany, 1946-48; social worker Victorian Mental Hygiene, Australia, 1955-62; rsch. assoc., social work project dir. Arthritis Midway House, N.Y.C., 1966-68; rsch. Columbia Presbyn. Med. Ctr., N.Y.C., 1971-75; field instr. Columbia U. Sch. Social Work, 1977-79, Columbia Presbyn. Med. Ctr., NYU Sch. Social Work, 1989-90; ret., 1992. Family Found. fellow, 1966, 89-90; grantee NIMH, 1969-72. Mem. Nat. Assn. Social Workers, Nat. Wildlife Fedn., Ctr. for Study of Presidency, Internat. Platform Assn., United Leaders, BATUN, Baltic-Am. Freedom League, Smithsonian Assn., English Spkg. Union, Alliance Francaise, Columbia U. Alumni Assn., Met. Mus. N.Y. Lutheran. Home: 30-95 29th St Astoria NY 11102-2735

MATHEWS, BARBARA EDITH, gynecologist; b. Oct. 5, 1946; d. Joseph Chesley and Pearl (Cieri) Mathews. AB, U. Calif., 1969; MD, Tufts U., 1972. Diplomate Am. Bd. Ob-Gyn. Intern Cottage Hosp., Santa Barbara, Calif., 1972-73, Santa Barbara Gen. Hosp., 1972-73; resident in ob-gyn Beth Israel Hosp., Boston, 1973-77; clin. fellow in ob-gyn Harvard U., Boston, 1973-76, instr., 1976-77; gynecologist Sansum Med. Clin., Santa Barbara, 1977-98; sr. scientist Sansum Med. Rsch. Inst., 1998—; med. dir., gynecologist Women's Health Svcs., Santa Barbara, 1998—. Faculty mem. ann. postgrad. course Harvard Med. Sch.; bd. dirs. Sansum Med. Clinic, 1989-96, vice chmn. bd. dirs., 1994-96; dir. ann. postgrad course UCLA Med. Sch. Bd. dirs. Meml. Rehab. Found., Santa Barbara, Channel City Club, Santa Barbara, Music Acad. of the West, Santa Barbara, St. Francis Med. Ctr., Santa Barbara; mem. citizen's contg. edn. adv. coun. Santa Barbara C.C.; moderator Santa Barbara Cottage Hosp. Cmty. Health Forum. Author: (with L. Burke) Colposcopy in Clinical Practice, 1977; contbg. author Manual of Ambulatory Surgery, 1982. Bd trustees Furman U., Greenville, SC, 2005—, bd. dirs., 2005—. Fellow ACOG, ACS; mem. AMA, Am. Soc. Colposcopy and Cervical Pathology (dir. 1982-84), Harvard U. Alumni Assn., Tri-counties Obstet. and Gynecol. Soc. (pres. 1981-82), Birnam Wood Golf Club (Santa Barbara), Phi Beta Kappa. Home: 2105 Anacapa St Santa Barbara CA 93105-3503 Office: 2235 De La Vina St Santa Barbara CA 93105-3815 Office Phone: 805-687-7778. Office Fax: 805-687-0012.

MATHEWS, DONNA MAE, special education educator; b. Riverside, Calif., Dec. 3, 1968; m. Ronny Lynn Mathews, July 22, 1989; children: George Franklin Bemis, Jamie Lee, Russell Jay. BS, Ball State U., 2003. Cert. spl. edn. tchr. Idaho, 2004. Spl. edn. tchr. Twin Falls Sch. Districk, Twin Falls, Idaho, 2003—. Mem.: Coun. for Exceptional Children. Office: Twin Falls Sch Dist 411 Lincoln Elem 238 Buhl St N Twin Falls ID 83301 Office Phone: 208-733-6900. Personal E-mail: mathewsdo2@tfsd.k12.id.us.

MATHEWS, E. ANNE JONES, retired library educator, academic administrator; b. Phila. d. Edmond Fulton and Anne Ruth (Reichner) Jones; m. Frank Samuel Mathews, June 16, 1951; children: Lisa Anne Mathews-Bingham, David Morgan, Lynne Elizabeth Bietenhader-Mathews, Alison Fulton Sawyer. AB, Wheaton Coll., 1949; MA, U. Denver, 1965, PhD, 1977. Field staff Intervarsity Christian Fellowship, Chgo., 1949-51; interviewer supr. Colo. Market Rsch. Svcs., Denver, 1952-64; reference libr. Oreg. State U., Corvallis, 1965-67; program dir. Ctrl. Colo. Libr. Sys., Denver, 1969-70; inst. dir. U.S. Office of Edn., Inst. Grant, 1979; dir. pub. rels., prof. Grad. Sch. Librarianship and Info. Mgmt. U. Denver, 1970-76, prof., dir. continuing edn., 1977-80; dir. office libr. programs, office ednl. rsch., improvement US Dept. Edn., Washington, 1986-91; dir. Nat. Libr. Edn., Washington, 1992-94; cons. Acad. Ednl. Devel., Washington, 1994—; cons. mil. installation vol. edn. rev. Am. Coun. on Edn., 1990—; from asst. prof. to prof., 1977—85; ret., 2004. Mem. adv. com. Golden H.S., 1973—77; faculty assoc. Danforth Found., 1974—84; mem. secondary sch. curriculum com. Jefferson County Pub. Schs., Colo., 1976—78; vis. lectr. Simmons Coll. Sch. L.S., Boston, 1977; mem. book and libr. adv. com. USIA, 1981—91; spkr. in field; cons. USIA, 1984—85; del. Internat. Fedn. Libr. Assns., 1984—93; mem. adv. coun. White House Conf. on Librs. and Info. Svcs., 1991; cons. Walden U., Mpls., 2001. Author, editor 6 books; contbr. articles to profl. jours., numerous chpts. to books. Mem. rural librs. and humanities program Colo. planning and resource bd. NEH, 1982—83; bd. mgrs. Friends Found. of Denver Pub. Libr., 1976—82; pres. Faculty Women's Club, Colo. Sch. Mines, 1963—64; bd. dirs. Jefferson County Libr. Found., 1996—, v.p., 1997—2000. Mem.: ALA (visionary leaders com. 1987—89, mem. coun. 1979—83, com. on accreditation 1984—85, orientation com. 1974—77, 1983—84, pub. rels. com.), English Speaking Union, Assn. Libr. and Info. Sci. Edn. (comm. com. 1978—80, program com. 1977—78), Colo. Libr. Assn. (pres. 1974, bd. dirs. 1973—75, continuing edn. com. 1976—80), Mountain Plains Libr. Assn. (profl. devel. com. 1979—80, pub. rels. and publs. com. 1973—75, continuing edn. com. 1973—76), Am. Soc. Info. Sci. (chmn. pub. rels. 1971), Naples Philharm. League, Pelican Bay Women's League Fla., Mountain Rep. Women's Club (v.p. 1997—2000), Mt. Vernon (Colo.) Country Club, Cosmos Club (Washington). Avocations: travel, reading, museum and gallery activities, volunteer work. E-mail: afmathews2@earthlink.net.

MATHEWS, JEAN ANN H., political science educator; b. Ogden, Utah, Oct. 17, 1941; d. Walter H. and Connie Laverne (Jorgenson) Holbrook; m. John Phillip Mathews, Sept. 8, 1960; children: Michael, Mark, Nanette. Student, Weber Coll., Ogden, Utah, 1959-61; AA, Florissant Community Coll., 1973; BS in Edn. magna cum laude, U. Mo.-St. Louis, 1980; MPA, U. Mo.-Columbia, 1988. Cert. tchr., Mo. Tchr., Mathews Vocal Studio, Florissant, 1964-80; profl. sales evaluator Edison Bros., Inc., St. Louis, 1971-73; mem. Mo. Ho. of Reps., 1981-90; instr. polit. sci. U. Mo., St. Louis, 1991—; mem. Mo. State Bd. Registration for Healing Arts, 1991—, pres., 1993. Author: Letting Go Is the Hardest, 1972; Repeat Drunken Driver Slips Through the System, 1982. Vice chmn. Florissant Bd. Appeals, 1976-80; committeewoman Florissant Twp., 1979—; sec. Mo. State Rep.Party, Jefferson City, 1981-88; mem. Gov.'s Commn. on Crime, 1984-92.Recipient Golden Gleaner award Ch. Jesus Christ Latter-day Saints, 1969; Rookie Legislator of Yr. award Capitol City Press Corp., Jefferson City, 1981; Eagle award Eagle Forum, 1982; Leadership in Mo. State Govt. award AAUW, 1982; Americanism award VFW, 1983; YWCA Women in Govt. award, 1988; inducted Alumni Hall of Fame, St. Louis Community Coll., Florissant Valley, 1987, Community Svc. award North County, 1991; named one of Outstanding Young Women of Am., 1974. Mem. Nat. Order Women Legislators, Am. Legis. Exch. Coun. (state chmn. 1982-88, nat. dir. 1988-91, Outstanding State Legislator 1984), Nat. Fedn. Republican Women, Kappa Delta Pi. Club: Rep. Women North St. Louis County (pres. 1978-82).

MATHEWS, JESSICA TUCHMAN, research executive, federal official, newswriter; b. NYC, July 4, 1946; d. Lester Reginald and Barbara (Wertheim) Tuchman; m. Colin D. Mathews, Feb. 25, 1978 (div.); children: Oliver Max Tuchman, Jordan Henry Morgenthau; m. Charles G. Boyd, Dec 31, 2005. AB magna cum laude, Radcliffe Coll., 1967; PhD, Calif. Inst. Tech., 1973. Congrl. sci. fellow AAAS, 1973-74; profl. staff mem. Energy and Environment subcom. House Com. on Interior and Insular Affairs, Washington, 1974-75; dir. issues and rsch. Udall Presdl. campaign, 1975-76; dir. Office of Global Issues NSC staff, Washington, 1977-79; mem. editorial bd. The Washington Post, 1980-82; v.p., dir. rsch. The World Resources Inst., Washington, 1982-92; dep. to undersec. for global affairs U.S. Dept. State, Washington, 1993; sr. fellow Coun. on Fgn. Rels., Washington, 1993-97; columnist Washington Post, 1991-97; pres. Carnegie Endowment Internat. Peace, Washington, 1997—. Mem. numerous adv. panels Office Tech. Assessment, NAS, AAAS, EPA; adv. com. Air Products Corp., 1995—99; bd. dirs. Somalogic Inc. Trustee Rockefeller Found., Century Found., Nuc. Threat Initiative; mem. Coun. Fgn. Rels.; bd. dirs. Joyce Found., Chgo., 1984—91, Inter-Am. Dialogue, 1991—2000, Surface Transp. Policy Project, 1991—2003, Radcliffe Coll., 1992—96, Carnegie Endowment for Internat. Peace, Washington, 1992—, Rockefeller Bros. Fund, N.Y.C., NY, 1992—96, Brookings Instn., Washington, 1995—2001. Mem.: Inst. Internat. Econs. (adv. com.), Fedn. Am. Scientists (bd. dirs. 1985—87, 1988—92), Trilateral Commn. Democrat. Jewish. Office: Carnegie Endowment Internat Peace 1779 Massachusetts Ave NW Washington DC 20036-2109 Office Phone: 202-939-2210.

MATHEWS, JOAN HELENE, pediatrician; b. Manchester, N.H., Feb. 3, 1940; d. John Barnaby and Helen A. Wlodkoski; m. Ernest Stephen Mathews, June 1, 1965; 3 children. BS, U. N.H., 1961; MD, Columbia U., 1965. Diplomate Am. Bd. Pediatrics. Med. intern Roosevelt Hosp., N.Y.C., 1965-66; pediatric resident Babies Hosp. Columbia Presbyn. Med. Ctr., N.Y.C., 1966-68, pediatric endocrine fellow Babies Hosp., 1968-70; instr. clin. pediat. Columbia U. Coll. Physicians and Surgeons, N.Y.C., 1973-77; asst. prof. pediat. Cornell U. Med. Coll., N.Y.C., 1977-81; clin. instr. pediat. Harvard Med. Sch., Boston, 1985—2003, clin. asst. prof. pediat., 2003—; clin. assoc. children's svc. Mass. Gen. Hosp., Boston, 1985—. Fellow: Am. Acad. Pediat.; mem.: Phi Beta Kappa. Office: 777 Concord Ave Cambridge MA 02138-1053 Office Phone: 617-876-6800. Office Fax: 617-876-5713.

MATHEWS, KATHLEEN ANN, social worker, psychotherapist; b. Minneapolis, Minn., Feb. 1, 1958; d. Lois Elaine Mathews, Wallace Edward Mathews; m. Bradley Scott Turner; children: Carsen Turner, Frances Turner. MSW, Columbia U., 1990; BS in Family Relationships, U. Minn., 1981. Lic. ind. clin. social work 1993. Supr. Home Front program Washburn Child Guidance Ctr., Mpls., 1993—, psychotherapist, 1998—, supr. Vision Program, 1997—2000; contract psychotherapist Chrysalis, A Center for Women, Mpls., 1994—98; program coord. Allendale Assn., Lake Villa, Ill., 1992—93; social worker Jewish Home and Hosp. for Aged, New York City, 1990—92. Mem.: NASW. Avocations: sewing, reading. Office: Washburn Child Guidance Ctr 2430 Nicollet Ave S Minneapolis MN 55404

MATHEWS, LINDA MCVEIGH, newspaper editor; b. Redlands, Calif., Mar. 14, 1946; d. Glenard Ralph and Edith Lorene (Humphrey) McVeigh; m. Thomas Jay Mathews, June 15, 1967; children: Joseph, Peter, Katherine. BA, Radcliffe Coll., 1967; JD, Harvard U., 1972. Gen. assignment reporter L.A. Times, 1967-69, Supreme Ct. corr., 1972-76, corr. Hong Kong, 1977-79, China corr. Beijing, 1979-80, editor op-ed page, 1980-81, dep. nat. editor, 1981-84, dep. fgn. editor, 1985-88, editl. writer, 1988-89, editor L.A. Times Mag., 1989-92; corr. Wall Street Jour., Hong Kong, 1976-77; sr. prodr. ABC News, N.Y.C., 1992-93; nat. editor N.Y. Times, N.Y.C., 1993-96; editor USA Today, McLean, Va., 1997—. Lectr.; freelance writer. Author (with others): Journey into China, 1982, One Billion: A China Chronicle, 1983. Mem. Women's Legal Def. Fund, 1972-76; co-founder, pres. Hong Kong Montessori Sch., 1977-79; bd. dirs. Ctr. for Childhood. Mem.: Fgn. Corrs. Club Hong Kong. Office: USA Today 7950 Jones Branch Dr Mc Lean VA 22108 Office Phone: 703-854-5581. Personal E-mail: LiMathews@aol.com. Business E-Mail: lmathews@usatoday.com.

MATHEWS, LINNEA KOONS, science educator, librarian; b. Waterville, Maine, Jan. 27, 1957; d. Edwin Donaldson and Elizabeth (Ortquist) Koons; m. Thomas Joseph Mathews, Oct. 11, 1986. BA, Colby Coll., 1979. Cert. phys. sci. and life sci. Dept. of Edn., Maine, 1988. Science tchr. SAD 39, Buckfield, Maine, 1987—2002, Mt Blue HS, Farmington, Maine, 2002—. Digital libr. Math. and Sci. Tchg. Excellence Collaborative, Portland, Maine, 2001—. Educator (devel. assessment tasks) Maine Assessment Portfolio, Local Assessment Development (Maine Math. and Sci. Alliance Tchr. Leader, 2004). Grantee MMSTEC Digital Libr., Nat. Science Found. Mem.: NSTA, Nat. Coun. Tchrs. Math., US Eventing Assn., Am. Connemara Pony Soc. Democrat. Achievements include development of MMSTEC Digital Library. Avocations: horseback riding, cooking, gardening. Home: 230 Lovejoy Pond Rd Fayette ME 04349 Office: Mt Blue HS 129 Seamon Rd Farmington ME 04938 Office Phone: 207-778-3561. Home Fax: 207-685-4465. Personal E-mail: tayfarm@aol.com. Business E-Mail: lmathews@mbhs.msad9.k12.me.us, lkoons@msad9.org.

MATHEWS, MARY KATHRYN, retired government official; b. Washington, Apr. 20, 1948; d. T. Odon and Kathryn (Augustine) M. Student, Pa. State U., 1966-68; BBA, Am. U., 1970, MBA, 1975. Personnel mgmt. specialist, coordinator coll. recruitment program, GSA, Washington, 1971-75, adminstrv. officer, 1975-78; personnel mgmt. specialist Office of Personnel Mgmt., Washington, 1978; employee devel. specialist Office Sec. Transp., Washington, 1978-80, dep. chief departmental services and spl. programs div., 1980-81; asst. dir. adminstrv. div. Farm Credit Adminstrn., Washington, 1981-84, dir. adminstrv. div. McLean, Va., 1984-86, chief adminstrv. services div., 1987-88; dep. staff dir. for mgmt. U.S. Commn. Civil Rights, Washington, 1988-90, asst. staff dir. for mgmt., 1990-91, asst. staff dir. for congl. affairs, 1991-94, staff dir., 1994-97; ret., 1997. Chief spl. programs staff and homebound handicapped employment program GSA, Washington, 1973-74; mem. task force Presdl. mgmt. intern program U.S. Office Pers. Mgmt., Washington, 1977-78; coord. mgmt. devel. program for women Office Sec. Transp., Washington, 1979-81. Vol. mentor, speaker Alexandria Commn. on Women, 1991-93. Mem. Exec. Women in Govt. (treas. 1993-94, v.p. 1994-95, pres. 1995-96, bd. dirs.), Small Agy. Coun. (exec. com. 1990-91, 94-96, chmn. micro agy. group 1990-91), Internat. Alliance (bd. dirs. 1996-97), Nat. Trust Hist. Preservation, Nat. Assn. Mus. Women in Arts (charter), Delta Gamma (rush advisor 1971-73, pres. bd. dirs. local chpt. house corp. 1972-73).

MATHEWS, PEGGY ANNE, nurse, consultant; b. Oakdale, La., Sept. 10, 1941; d. Howard Douglas and Huldah Mary (Hicks) Tyler; children: Joseph, Mark, Debra. A.Nursing, La. State U., Alexandria, 1975; BSN Northwestern State U., La. Cert. legal nurse cons., Legal Nurse Cons. Inst., Houston. R.N., La. Nurse intensive care unit St. Frances Cabrini Hosp., Alexandria, 1975-78, 78-80, staff educator nurse edn. dept, 1978-80, dir. noninvasive cardiology dept, 1980-85, nurse edn. dept., 1979-80, dir. cardiology, 1980—, established cardiac rehab. program, 1982, dir. Cardiac Catheterization Lab.; med. dir. TRACE Detection Svcs. Mem. Am. Assn. Critical Care Nurses, Am. Heart Assn. Democrat. Roman Catholic. Avocations: dancing, fishing, horse back riding, gardening, hunting. Home: 122 Cedar Point Ln Boyce LA 71409-8798 Office: St Frances Cabrini Hosp 3330 Masonic Dr Alexandria LA 71301-3899 Personal E-mail: pmrn41@yahoo.com.

MATHEWS, SHARON WALKER, performing company executive, secondary school educator; b. Shreveport, La., Feb. 1, 1947; d. Arthur Delmar and Nona (Frye) Walker; m. John William (Bill) Mathews, Aug. 14, 1971; children: Rebecca, Elizabeth, Anna. BS, La. State U., 1969, MS, 1971. Dance grad. asst. La. State U., Baton Rouge, 1969-71, choreographer, 1975-76; 6th grade tchr. East Baton Rouge Parish, 1971-72, health phys. edn. tchr., 1972-74; dance instr. Magnet High Sch., Baton Rouge, 1975—; artistic dir. Baton Rouge Ballet Theatre, 1975—; dance dir. Dancers' Workshop, Baton Rouge, 1971—; choreographer Baton Rouge Opera, 1989-94, Univ. H.S. Musical Theatre, 1998—; choreographer Baton Rouge Gilbert and Sullivan Soc. summer musical La. State U., 2000, 2001; choreographer Baton Rouge Little Theater, 2000, 2002. Author: East Baton Rouge Parish Dance Curriculum. Mem. La. Supts. Task Force Arts in Edn., 1999—2001, La. Content Stds. Com. Dance, 2001, East Baton Rouge Parish Curriculum Com. Dance, 1997, La. Arts Consortium, 2000—, La. Arts Content Stds. Com., 2002—, La. Arts Content Revision Com., 2002—03. Named Dance Educator of the Yr., La. Alliance Health, Phys. Edn., Recreation and Dance; named to Univ. HS Hall of Distinction, 2003, Baton Rouge Magnet HS Hall of Fame, 2003; recipient Stream award for Artistic Excellence, S.W. Regional Ballet Assn., 1991, Mayor's Pres.'s award for Excellence in the Arts, 1999, Creative Ticket award for excellence in the arts, Kennedy Ctr., 2005. Mem.: La. Assn. Health, Phys. Edn., Recreation and Dance (dance chairperson 1995), Southwestern Regional Ballet Assn. (bd. dirs. 1981—, treas., exec. bd. dirs. 1989—92). Republican. Baptist. Office: Baton Rouge Ballet Theater 11017 Perkins Rd Baton Rouge LA 70884 Office Phone: 225-767-5814.

MATHEWS, SYLVIA MARY, foundation administrator; b. Hinton, W.Va., June 23, 1965; d. William Peter and Cleo P. M. AB, Harvard Coll., 1987; BA, Oxford U., 1990. Assoc. McKinsey & Co., N.Y.C., 1990-92; dep. dir. econ. policy Clinton/Gore '92, Little Rock, 1992; staff dir. Nat. Econ. Coun., Washington, 1993-94; chief of staff to Sec. Robert Rubin U.S. Dept. Treasury, Washington, 1995-96; dep. chief of staff to Pres. The White House, Washington, 1997-98; dep. dir. Office of Mgmt. & Budget, Washington, 1998—2001; COO, exec. dir., The Bill and Melinda Gates Found., Seattle, 2001—. Rhodes scholar, 1987. Mem. Coun. Fgn. Rels.; bd. dirs. MetLife, Inc., 2004- Democrat. Office: The Bill & Melinda Gates Found PO Box 23350 Seattle WA 98102*

MATHEWS-MATHENA, JENNIFER KAY, elementary school educator; d. Daryl Wayne Mathews and Laura Lynn Haugen; m. James Kenneth Mathena, Jan. 17, 1968. MA, San Diego State U., 2002. Cert. tchr. Tex. Bd. Edn., 1995. Tchr. Alief Ind. Sch. Dist., Houston, 1995—96, Bonita Country Day Sch., Calif., 1996—97, Chula Vista Elem. Sch. Dist., 1998—. Master tchr. Chula Vista Elem. Sch. Dist., 2000—05. Mem.: NEA, Calif. Tchrs. Assn. (assoc.), Internat. Reading Assn. (assoc.), Pi Lamda Theta (assoc.), Kappa Delta Pi (life), Zeta Tau Alpha (life; corr. sec. 2004—06). Conservative. Roman Catholic. Avocations: reading, travel, camping.

MATHIAS, ALICE IRENE, business management consultant; b. N.Y.C., Mar. 2, 1949; d. Murray and Charlotte (Kottle) Mathias. BS in Math., Western New Eng. Coll., 1972. Programmer Carnation Co., L.A., 1973-78; programmer/analyst Cedars-Sinai Med. Ctr., L.A., 1978-79, Union Bank, L.A., 1979-81; group leader Kaiser Found. Health Plan, Pasadena, Calif., 1981-98; sr. cons. KPMG LLP, L.A., 1998—99; prin. Info. Tech. Mgmt., L.A., 1999—. Mem. NAFE, Am. Mgmt. Assn., L.A. County Mus. Art (sponsor), Smithsonian Inst., KCET Pub. TV, Choice In Dying, U.S. Holocaust Meml. Mus. (charter mem.), Caithness Collectors Club, Statue of Liberty Ellis Island Found. Home: 2031 Dracena Drive Apt 320 Los Angeles CA 90027 Office: Info Tech Mgmt 2031 Dracena Dr Ste 320 Los Angeles CA 90027

MATHIAS, BETTY JANE, communications and community affairs consultant, editor, educator, writer; b. Ely, Nev., Oct. 22, 1923; d. Royal F. and Dollie B. (Bowman) M.; 1 child, Dena. Student, Merritt Bus. Sch., 1941—42, San Francisco State U., 1941—42. Asst. publicity dir. Oakland (Calif.) Area War Chest and Comty. Chest, 1943-46; pub. rels. Am. Legion, Oakland, 1946-47; asst. to pub. rels. dir. Cen. Bank of Oakland, 1947-49; pub. rels. dir. East Bay chpt. Nat. Safety Coun., 1949-51; propr., mgr. Mathias Pub. Rels. Agy., Oakland, 1951-60; publicity dir. U.S. Nat. Figure Skating Championships, Berkeley, Calif., 1957; gen. assignment reporter, teen news editor Daily Rev., Hayward, Calif., 1960-62; freelance pub. rels. and writing Oakland, 1962-66, 67-69; dir. corp. comms. Systech Fin. Corp., Walnut Creek, Calif., 1969-71; v.p. corp. comms. Consol. Capital cos., Oakland, 1972-79, v.p. comty. affairs Emeryville, Calif., 1981-84, v.p. spl. projects, 1984-85; v.p., dir. Consol. Capital Realty Svcs., Inc., Oakland, 1973-77, Centennial Adv. Corp., Oakland, 1976-77; comms. cons., 1979—. Cons. Mountainair Realty, Cameron Park, Calif., 1986-87; pub. rels. coord. Tuolumne County Visitors Bur., 1989-90; lectr. in field. Editor: East Bay Mag., 1966-67, TIA Traveler, 1969, Concepts, 1979-83; editor, writer souvenir program: Little House on the Prairie Reunion, 1998. Bd. dirs. Oakland YWCA, 1944-45, ARC, Oakland, So. Alameda County chpt., 1967-69, Family Ctr., Children's Hosp. Med. Ctr. No. Calif., 1982-85, March of Dimes, 1983-85, Equestrian Ctr. of Walnut Creek, Calif., 1983-84, also sec.; mem. Women's Ambulance and Transport Corps of Calif., Oakland, 1942-46; active USO and Shrine Hospitality Ctrs., Oakland, USO-Travelers Aid Soc., Oakland, 1942-46; publicist Oakland Area War Bond Com., 1943-46; adult and pubs. adv. Internat. Order of the Rainbow for Girls, 1953-78; comms. arts adv. com. Ohlone (Calif.) Coll., 1979-85, chmn., 1982-84; mem. adv. bd. dept. mass comms. Calif. State U.-Hayward, 1985; pres. San Francisco Bay Area chpt. Nat. Reyes Syndrome Found., 1981-86; vol. staff Columbia Actors' Repertory, Columbia, Calif., 1986-87, 89; mem. exec. bd., editor newsletter Tuolumne County Dem. Club, 1987; publicity chmn. 4th of July celebration Tuolumne County C. of C., 1988; vol. children's dept. Tuolumne County Pub. Libr., 1993-97; vol. Ann. Comty. Christmas Eve Dinner, Sonora, Calif., 1988-96; mem. adv. com. Ride Away Ctr. for Therapeutic Riding for the Handicapped, 1995-96, vol. Hold Your Horses Therapeutic Riding Acad., 1997; vol. Tuolumne County Visitors Bur. and Film Commn., 1996-99. Recipient Grand Cross of Color award Internat. Order of Rainbow for Girls, 1955. Mem. Order Ea. Star (life, worthy matron 1952, publicity chmn. Calif. state 1955), East Bay Women's Press Club (pres. 1960, 84). Home: 20575 Gopher Dr Sonora CA 95370-9034

MATHIAS, DENISE SUSANNE, music educator, music minister; b. Bradford, Pa., Apr. 19, 1957; d. Millard Benjamin and Margaret Thelma (Hess) Niver; m. Mark Steven Mathias, Dec. 15, 1979; children: Erin Ruth, Rachel Elizabeth, Breanne Elyse. BS, Malone Coll., 1979; M in Ch. Music, So. Bapt. Theol. Sem., 1995. Cert. tchr., Iowa. Piano tchr., 1979—; pianist Watkins United Meth. Ch., Louisville, 1990-95; music tchr. Ottumwa Cmty. Schs., 1995-98; co-min. music First Presbyn. Ch., Ottumwa, Iowa, 1995—2002, dir. music New Phila., Ohio, 2002—. Freelance pianist, accompanist, 1979—. Local v.p. publicity S.E. Iowa Symphony Bd., Ottumwa, 1996-97. Mem. Nat. Guild Piano Tchrs., Music Tchrs. Nat. Assn. (profl. cert.), Presbyn. Assn. Musician. Republican. Avocations: gardening, walking, sewing. Home: 119 W 22nd St Dover OH 44622-2414 Office: First Presbyn Ch 217 E High Ave New Philadelphia OH 44663

MATHIAS, LYNDA ROWELL, secondary school educator; b. Orangeburg, S.C., Aug. 31, 1943; d. Harold Deland and Edna (Hancock) Rowell; m. Ervin McDonald Mathias Jr., June 26, 1965; children: Ervin M. III, Michael K BA, Newberry Coll., 1984; MEd, U. S.C., 1985. Cert. tchr., S.C. Tchr. bus. edn. Orangeburg H.S., 1964—65; tchr. English Saluda Mid. Sch., SC, 1965—67; tchr. econs. St. Andrews H.S., Charleston, SC, 1968; tchr. bus. edn. Allendale Vocat. Edn. Ctr., SC, 1970—73; tchr. English, guidance counselor Allendale Acad., 1976—88; instr. continuing edn., adj. prof. Trident Tech. Coll., Charleston, 1989, 1990; tchr. gifted and talented Charleston County Schs., 1989—92; guidance counselor Montrie Mid. Sch., Mt. Pleasant, SC, 1992—93; counselor Sullivan's Island Elem. Sch., SC, 1993—95; guidance counselor Myrtle Beach Mid. Sch., 1995—98. Solo vocalist, various local church, sch. and civic functions Active Am. Cancer Soc., Am. Heart Assn Mem. NEA, S.C. Edn. Assn., Charleston County Edn. Assn., S.C. Ind. Sch. Assn. (workshop presenter, tchr. improvement com., advanced accreditation evaluator, judge 1989 tchr. of yr. award, named Tchr. of Yr. 1988) Republican. Avocations: tennis, aerobics, needlecrafts, reading. Home: 1633 Wells Branch Rd Ulmer SC 29849

MATHIAS, SHARON A, secondary school educator; b. Dayton, Ohio, Oct. 28, 1943; d. Neville Dean Anders and Edna Pauline Mountjoy; m. David Grant Mathias, July 11, 1964; children: Todd Andrew, Tobin Grant. BSEd, Ohio U., 1966; MA, Coll. Mt. St. Joseph, 1995. Social dir. Miami Valley Hosp. Sch. Nursing, Dayton, 1964-67; tchr. Trotwood-Madison Schs., Ohio, 1967-75, Peoria (Ariz.) Unified Dist., 1976-79; owner Kachina Uniforms, Phoenix, 1977-79; dep. dir. Greene Co. Bd. of Elections, Xenia, Ohio, 1980-84; owner Creative Resources, Beavercreek, Ohio, 1991-93; tchr. Xenia (Ohio) City Schs., 1984—. Mem. adv. bd. Today Ctr. for Adults, Xenia. Precinct chair Greene County Dem. Party, Xenia, 1981-83. Mem. AAHPERD, AAUW (pres. 1994-95), NEA, Ohio Edn. Assn., Xenia Edn. Assn., Kiwanis Internat. Found. (Hixson fellow 1996, lt. gov.-elect 1999, lt. gov. (divsn. 4) 2000, Tablet of Honor 1998), Kiwanis Club (Disting. pres. 1997-98). Democrat. United Methodist. Presbyn. Avocations: golf, camping, gardening, bridge. E-mail: dmath45857@aol.com.

MATHIEU, GAIL DENNISE, ambassador; b. N.J. m. Erick Mathieu; 1 child, Yuri. BA in Spanish and Latin Am. studies, Antioch Coll., 1973; JD, Rutgers U., 1976. Bar: N.J. 1976, D.C. 1977. Dep. chief of mission in Accra; U.S. observer UNESCO, 1991—95; dep. office dir. Pacific Island affairs US Dept. State, 1995—97, dep. office dir. of West African affairs, 1997—99, dep. chief of mission Accra, 1999—2002, U.S. amb. to Niger, 2002—. Asst. prosecutor City of Newark, NJ. Home: 2420 Niamey Pl Dulles VA 20189-2420

MATHIEU, MICHELE SUZANNE, grant writer, computer scientist, consultant; b. Chgo., Mar. 24, 1950; d. Joseph Edward Mathieu and Mary Ellen Fisher; m. Robert Steven Harris, May 1, 1988 (dec. Sept. 2000); life ptnr. Kathryn Ruth Huff, Aug. 16, 2002. BS in Mktg., Regents Coll., Albany, N.Y., 1998; cert. web site design, Columbia Coll., Chgo., 2000; cert. in Perl and CGI Scripting, San Diego C.C., 2003. Microsoft cert. profl. Broadcast coord. Grey-North Advt., Chgo., 1967-71; head drama dept. Patricia Stevens Coll., Chgo., 1972; instr. beginning acting Ted Liss Sch. Performing Arts, Chgo., 1973-75; project coord. grants and contracts Am. Dietetic Assn., Chgo., 1974-81, adminstr. govt. affairs, 1981-86, mgr. licensure comm., 1986-90, adminstr. nutrition svcs. payment systems, 1990-94, team leader, health care fin. team, 1994-97, dir. health care fin. team, 1998—2000, dir. mem. web, 2000—01, dir. applications devel., 2001—02; technician Networks Plus Tech. Group, San Diego, 2003—04; pc imaging technician Knowledge Info. Solutions, San Diego, 2004; dir. grants and contracts Virtual Reality Med. Ctr., San Diego, 2004—. Grant proposal cons. various performance arts, Chgo., 1978-2000; med. reporter, writer various internat. clients, 1994-; PC cons., Chgo., 1994-2002, San Diego, 2002—. Editor Legis. Newsletter, 1981-86; contbg. editor Nutrition Forum, 1986, Courier, 1987—2002; contbr. articles to profl. jours., mags., newspapers. Website project mgr. DigitalEve, Chgo., 2001. Ill. Arts Coun. grantee, 1981. Mem. Am. Med. Writers Assn., Am. Soc. Assn. Execs. (Excellence in Govt. award 1989), WebSanDiego. Avocations: reading, fitness walking, sailing.

MATHIEU, SUSAN LEIFER, recreational therapist, educator; b. Long Beach, Calif., Nov. 13, 1952; d. Sally and Oscar Solomon Leifer; m. Jeff Mathieu, Mar. 20, 1976; children: Joseph Gabriel Mathieu 18, Daniel Jacob Mathieu 16. BA, Calif. State U., Long Beach, 1975, MS, 1992; EdD, U. La Verne, 1999. Cert. therapeutic recreation specialist Nat. Coun. Therapeutic Recreation, 1984. Lectr. Calif. State U., Dominquez Hills, 1990—2002, asst. prof. Long Beach, 2002—. Therapeutic recreation tng., cons. ChildNet, Long Beach, 1989—. Contbr. articles to profl. jours. Recreation commr. City of Long Beach, Parks, Recreation and Harbor Recreation Commn., 1981—85; bd. dirs. Jr. League, Long Beach, 1983—2005, PTA, Rancho Palos Verdes, Calif., 1994—99; sisterhood bd. dirs. Congregation Ner Tamid, Rancho Palos Verdes, Calif., 2000—04. Recipient Spl. Recognition award, Cath. Charities Family Shelter for Homeless, 1996, Golden Rule award, JC Penny, 1998. Mem.: Nat. Recreation and Pk. Assn. (assoc.; spkr. 1996—2005, Profl. award Pacific S.W. region 1984, 1994), Long Beach Area Child and Domestic Violence Coun. (assoc.; spkr.), Calif. Pk. and Recreation Soc. (assoc.; com. chair 1998—99, Outstanding Therapeutic Recreation Educator award 1996), Calif. State U. Long Beach Alumni Assn. (bd. dirs. 2004—05), Guild for Infant Survival (assoc.; parent support 1990—95), Chi Kappa Rho Gamma (assoc.; scholarship com. 2002—04, mem. women in leisure svcs.). Jewish. Achievements include first to introduced reading to former gang members in a residential treatment facility. Avocations: kayaking, drums, international folk dancing, developing comedy routines as a teaching tool, guitar. Office: Calif State Univ Long Beach 1250 Bellflower Blvd Long Beach CA 90840 Office Phone: 562-985-8075. Office Fax: 562-985-8154. Business E-Mail: smathieu@csulb.edu.

MATHIEU BYERS, DEBORAH ANNE, performing company executive; d. Edward F. and Marjorie V. Mathieu; m. Stephen Paul Byers, June 29, 1996. Studied with, Nafe Katter, Jerry Rojo, 1976—77; BFA, U. Conn., 1978; studied at, A.C.T., San Francisco, 1978; studied with, Ray Burke, 1978, Charles Hampton and Stuart Chenoweth, 1979; MA, San Francisco State U., 1979; studied with, Michael Graves, N.Y.C., 1984; master classes, Kate Collins, N.Y.C., 1987; studied at, Video Assoc., 1990, Three of Us Studios, N.Y.C., 1994, HB Studios, 1994. Exec. asst. to pres. and owner prodn. coord. Silver Blue Prodn., Ltd., N.Y.C., 1982—86; freelance promoter and pub. rels. coord. Deborah Mathieu Consulting, Inc., 1984—90, designer makeup, hair and costume, 1987—90; assoc. casting dir. Stark Naked Prodn. Elsie Stark Casting, 1994—97; exec. asst. to owner R & V Internat. Inc., 1986—2002; chairperson acting technique dept. Sch. for Film and TV, 1995—2000; founder, president and producing artistic dir. Streetlight Prodn., Inc., 2000—. Pvt. acting coach, N.Y.C., 1995—. Dir.: (plays) Chamber Music, 1979, Ghost Sonata, 1978, Your Carolyn Skiddoo Period, 1995, Communion, 2002, Cityscapes, 2002, Yearning for the Fourth Grade, 2002, Leavin' the Life & Hangin' at Joe's, 2003, Faith, Hope and Charity, 2004, The American Dream and Other Fractured Fairy Tales, 2005; actor: Bus Stop, 1978, A Midsummer's Night Dream, 1978, West Side Story, 1978, Anne of a Thousand Days, 1979, Macbeth, 1979, Chamber Music, 1980, A Faded Rose, 1980, Comedy Tonite!, 1982, All Ye Faithful, 1982, Reasonable Circulation, 1983, Lullaby Eve, 1986, Law School Suicide, 1990, Mary Tudor, 1993, Mary Stuart, 1994, The Knickerbockers, 1995, Nicola Sacco & Bartolomeo Vanezetti, 1999, Hamlet, 2001; dir., actor: (plays) Leaving My Apartment & Other Urban Adventures, 2003; (films) The Deadliest Season, 1976, U.H.F., 1988, Guess Who?, 1989, Dreamstreets, 1989, Funny About Love, 1989, State of Grace, 1989, Quiet on the Set!, 1990, Heidi Loves Missy, 1993, Annie, 1995; (TV series) The Days and Nights of Molly Dodd, 1988—90, Saturday Night Live, 1994, (commercials and industrial films); choreographer Jumpers, San Francisco, 1977, The Darkening of the Light, 1978; costumer: The Tempest, 1978. Mem.: AFTRA, SAG, Theatre Comm. Guild, Actors Equity Assn., The Drama League. Democrat. Office: Streetlight Prodns 110-64 Queens Blvd PMB 175 Forest Hills NY 11375

MATHIS, DIANE, cell biologist, educator; BSc in Biology, Wake Forest U., 1971; MSc in Cell Biology, U. Rochester, 1976, PhD in Cell Biology, 1978. Postdoctoral fellow Lab. Génétique Moléculaire des Eucaryotes, Strasbourg, France, 1977—81; postdoctoral fellow Dept. Med. Microbiology Stanford (Calif.) U. Med. Ctr., 1981—83; sr. investigator Dept. Immunology Inst. Génétique et de Biologie Moléculaire et Cellulaire, Strasbourg, 1983—99; sr. investigator immunology and immunogenetics Joslin Diabetes Ctr. Harvard Med. Sch., Boston, 1999—, prof. medicine, 1999—. Vis. prof. Walter and Elisa Hall Inst., Melbourne, 1997—98; mem. adv. bd. Deutsches Rheuma-Forschungszentrum, Berlin, 1997—, Max Planck Inst. Immunology, Freiburg, Germany, 1997—, Walter and Eliza Hall Inst., Melbourne, 1998—, Peptimmune, 2000—, Inst. Pasteur, Paris, 2001—, Jackson Lab., Bar Harbor, Maine, 2001—, Riken Inst., Yokohama, Japan, 2001—, NIH Study Sect., 2001—. Mem. editl. bd.: European Jour. Immunology, 1988—2001, EMBO Jour., 1992—95, 1999—, Internat. Immunology, 1992—96, Immunology Today, 1992—2000, Sci., 1993—, Cell, 1994—; translator: Current Biology, 1994—2001; Jour. Exptl. Medicine, 1996—, Immunity, 1997—, Diabetes, 1999—, Modern Rheumatism, 2000—, EMBO Reports, 2000—, Current Sci. Faculty of 1000, 2001—; contbr. over 120 articles to profl. jours. Fellow, Damon Runyon-Walter Winchell Cancer Fund, 1977—81, Leukemia Soc. Am., 1981—83. Office: Joslin Diabetes Center One Joslin Place Boston MA 02215

MATHIS, KAREN J., lawyer, legal association administrator; b. Providence, Nov. 7, 1950; d. Charles H. Young and Elizabeth L. (Kriegal) Ballard; m. Stan A. Mathis, Sept. 7, 1970 (div. 1978). BA, U. Denver, 1972; JD, U. Colo., 1975; postgrad., U. Colo., Denver, 1975-76; LLD, Sienna Coll., 2003, Sturm Law Sch., U. Denver, 2005. Bar: Colo. Supreme Ct. 1975, U.S. Dist. Ct. 1975, U.S. Ct. Appeals (10th cir.) 1978, U.S. Tax Ct. 1980. Tax acct. Peat Marwick Mitchell, Denver, 1975-76; ptnr. Rothenberg & Mathis, Denver, 1976-79; sole practitioner Denver, 1979-80; assoc. Sterling & Simon PC, Denver, 1980-83; ptnr. Hughes & Dorsey, Denver, 1983-84; shareholder, dir. Sterling & Miller, Denver, 1984-86; pres. The Mathis Law Firm, Denver, 1986—2004; pres., CEO Mathis Asset Mgmt., Inc., Denver, 1989—2004; ptnr. McElroy, Deutsch, Mulvaney & Carpenter LLP, Denver, 2004—. Contbr. articles to profl. jours. Bd. dirs. CORRA, Denver, Planned Parenthood Rocky Mountains, Denver; bd. dirs., v.p. Rocky Mountain Meml. Soc., Denver; mem. adv. com. Colo. Dept. Social Svcs., Denver. Named Disting. Alumni U. Colo., 1992; recipient Order of the Coif (hon.) U. Colo., 2002 Mem. ABA (ho. of dels. 1982-, interim Colo. state del. 1992-2000, chair standing com. on mem., 1994-97, chair commn. on women in the profession, 1997-2000, chair ho. dels., 2000-02, chair gen. practice, solo & small firm section, 2002-03, pres-elect, 2005-06, pres., 2006-), Colo. Bar Assn. (1st v.p. 1992-93, bd. govts. 1983-, outstanding young lawyer in Colo.), Denver Bar Assn. Office: McElroy Deutsch Mulvaney & Carpenter LLP Mile High Ctr 1700 Broadway Ste 1900 Denver CO 80290

MATHIS, MARSHA DEBRA, customer service administrator; b. Detroit, Dec. 22, 1953; d. Marshall, Jr. and Anita Willene (Biggers) Mathis. BS, Fla. State U., 1978; MBA, Miss. Coll., 1982. With telecom. dept. Fla. State Dept. Safety, Tallahassee, 1973-76; asst. to chmn. Tallahassee Savs. and Loan Assn., 1976-78; sales engr. Prehler, Inc., Jackson, Miss., 1978-82; mktg. mgr. Norand Corp., Arlington, Tex., 1982-87; v.p. mktg. and sales Profl. Datasolutions, Inc., Irving, Tex., 1987-88; v.p. mktg. and sales, ptnr. Target Systems, Inc., Irving, 1988-89, also bd. dirs.; v.p. mktg. Profl. Datasolutions, Inc., Irving, 1990—2002, Onvance, Atlanta, 2002; v.p. bus. devel. Performance Retail, Austin, Tex., 2004—. Contbr. articles to profl. jours. Advisor Am. Diabetes Assn., Jackson, 1983—, Diabetes Found. Miss., Jackson, 1983—. Mem.: Network Exec. Women, Nat. Assn. Convenience Stores (mem. industry task force 1987—88), Nat. Adv. Group, Internat. Platform Assn. Republican. Roman Catholic. Avocations: scuba diving, sailing, reading, coin collecting/numismatics. Home: 1615 Purple Sage Dr Cedar Park TX 78613 Office: Dresser Wayne Bldg 2 Ste 101 6500 River Place Blvd Austin TX 78730 Office Phone: 512-527-6623. Personal E-mail: marshamathis@austin.rr.com. Business E-Mail: marsha_mathis@performanceretail.com.

MATHIS, PRUDENCE MARCHMAN, realtor; b. Throckmorton, Tex., Aug. 21, 1956; adopted d. Jack Robert and Grace Alma Hurst Brockman; m. Leonard Renfro Marchman, June 8, 1974 (div. May 4, 1990); children: Jeremy Robert Marchman, Caitlin Breanne Marchman; m. Jimmy Dale Mathis, June 9, 1990 (div. May 24, 1999). Student, Mountain View Coll., Dallas, 1985—90. Comml. ins. & workers compensation clk. Lovett-Meredith Clinic, Olney, Tex., 1977—79; credit corr., accounts receivable clk., fin. inventory control analyst, accounts payable clk., bid clk. Am. Hosp. Supply Co., Grand Prairie, Tex., 1979—85; credit analyst/adjuster Gifford-Hill & Co., Inc., Dallas, 1985—88; acctg. clk. - part-time Roy Rabenaldt, CPA, Farmers Branch, Tex., 1988—89; office mgr. Evelyn Cannon Showroom of Women's Apparel, Dallas, 1989—90; asst. office mgr./payroll coord. Site Concrete, Inc., Grand Prairie, 1990—94; customer svc. rep./accounts receivable collector Occupl. Health Centers, Dallas, 1994—95; human resources mgr., benefits specialist Site Concrete, Inc., Grand Prairie, 1995—98; exec. adminstrv. asst. Kelly Services for Johnson & Johnson Med., Arlington, Tex., 1998—2000; travel coord. Galactic Mktg., Arlington, Tex., 2000—01; human resources mgr. Site Concrete, Inc., Grand Prairie, 2001—02; ptnr. and co-owner Quest Residential & Comml. Properties, Ltd, Grand Prairie, Tex., 2002—, REALTOR, 2005—. Trainer Site Concrete, Inc., Grand Prairie, 2001—02. Vol. Habitat for Humanity, Grand Prairie, Tex., 2001—05; vol. adult leader and facilitator Boy Scouts Am., Grand Prairie, 1999—; mem. Grand Prairie C. of C.; mem. chancel choir First United Meth. Ch., Grand Prairie, 2001—02. Mem.: NAFE (assoc.), Women's Coun. of Realtors, Grand Prairie Bd. Realtors (mem. hospitality com., edn. com.), Metro Tex. Assn. Realtors, Tex. Assn. Realtors, Nat. Assn. Realtors, Am. Bus. Women's Assn. (assoc.; sec. 1999—2000), Phi Theta Kappa. Methodist. Avocations: reading, singing, photography, crocheting, travel. Office: 4116 S Carrier Pkwy Ste 280-827 Grand Prairie TX 75052 Personal E-mail: prudencemathis@comcast.net.

MATHIS, SAMANTHA, actress; b. N.Y.C., May 12, 1970; d. Bibi Besch. Actress: (films) Forbidden Sun, 1989, Pump Up the Volume, 1990, This is My Life, 1992, FernGully: The Last Rainforest (voice), 1992, Super Mario Bros., 1993, The Music of Chance, 1993, The Thing Called Love, 1993, Little Women, 1994, Jack and Sarah, 1995, How to Make an American Quilt, 1995, The American President, 1995, Broken Arrow, 1996, Museum of Love, 1996, Sweet Jane, 1998, Waiting for Woody, 1998, Freak City, 1999, The Simian Line, 2000, American Psycho, 2000, Attraction, 2000, The Punisher, 2004; (TV movies) Aaron's Way: The Harvest, 1988, Cold Sassy Tree, 1989, American Nuclear, 1989, Extreme Close-Up, 1990, 83 Hours 'Til Dawn, 1990, To My Daughter, 1990, Harsh Realm, 1999, Mermaid, 2000, Collected Stories, 2002; (TV series) Knightwatch, 1988-89, Aaron's Way, 1988, Harsh Realm, 1999, First Years, 2001; (TV miniseries) The Mists of Avalon, 2001. Office: Creative Artists Agy care Rick Kurtzman 9830 Wilshire Blvd Beverly Hills CA 90212-1804

MATHIS-THORTON, DIANNA DAWN, protective services official, writer, publishing executive, not-for-profit developer; b. Dallas, Tex., Nov. 16, 1967; d. Jimmie Lee and Billie Jo Mathis; m. Ryan Lee Thorton, Dec. 22, 2002. BS Home security, Fla. Met. Univ., 1989—. Cert. crime prevention inspector Tex., domestic violence counselor. Exec. sec. Sears logistic Svcs., Dallas, 1986—90; police officer Dallas police Depart., Dallas, 1991—; owner, pres. Mathis Pub. Co., Dallas, 1991—; founder, pres. Domestic Awareness, Dallas, 2003—. Instr. safety first Dallas after sch. program, 2004—, future writers of Am., 2005—. Author: Dianna's poetry of Life, 2001, Safety First Children's Guide, 2004, Future Writers of Am., 2005. Mem. counselor Victim relief Ministries, Dallas, 2004—; mentor, counselor Speak Life Ministries, Dallas, 1999—. Recipient Officer of the Yr, Woman of Dallas Inc., 1998, Nat. Assn. ins. Woman of Dallas Inc., 1998, Life Saving award, Dallas police dept., 1997. Mem.: Intenat. Code Coun. Christian. Avocations: reading, writing, poetry, movie scripts. Office: Dallas Police Dept 725 N Jim Miller Dallas TX 75217

MATILE, MADELON ELIZABETH, secondary school educator; b. Youngstown, Ohio, Feb. 9, 1940; d. Oscar William and Alice Elizabeth (Laflin) Mitchell; m. Robert William Matile, July 13, 1963; children: David Robert, Elizabeth Ann, Michael William. BS in Edn., Bowling Green (Ohio) State U., 1962; MEd, U. Toledo, Ohio, 1987; postgrad, U. Toledo, 1988—. Tchr. Youngstown (Ohio) City Schs., 1962-63, Sylvania (Ohio) City Schs., 1963-69, LD tutor, 1978-82, tchr., 1982—, GRADS coord., 1991-97, elem. counselor, 1997—. Facilitator Sylvania City Schs., 1985-90. Mem. Jr. League, Toledo, 1972—, sec. exec. com., 1978-80; v.p. exec. com. Crittenton Svcs., Toledo, 1978-84, 88-94; mem. bd. dirs., v.p., sec. Parents Helping Parents, Toledo, 1989—. Mem. AAUW (exec. com. 1969-74), Toledo Home Econs. Assn., Phi Upsilon Omicron. Avocations: reading, gardening, travel. Home: 26 Sundance Ln Okatie SC 29909-5065

MATJASKO, M. JANE, anesthesiologist, educator; b. Harrison Twp., Pa., 1942; MD, Med. Coll. Pa., 1968. Diplomate Am. Bd. Anesthesiology. Resident in anesthesiology Md. Hosp., Balt., 1968-72; prof., chmn. anesthesiology U. Md., Balt., 1990—. Bd. dirs. Am. Bd. Anesthesiology. Mem. Am. Soc. Anesthesiologists, Assn. Univ. Anesthesiologists. Office: U Md Hosp Dept Anesthesiology 22 S Greene St Baltimore MD 21201-1544

MATKIN, JUDITH CONWAY, product designer; b. Ontario, Oreg., Jan. 26, 1943; d. Edward Owen and Lois Lorraine Conway; m. Eltjo Emile Witkop, Feb. 23, 1963 (div. Jan. 1970); children: Gregory Lyn, Joella Monique, Bradley Michael; m. Reuel P. Matkin, Mar. 20, 1995; stepchildren: Chris, Marcie, Ryan. Designer, sales rep. Jerome I. Silverman, Inc., N.Y.C., 1970-86, Gem East Corp., Seattle, 1986-87; designer Nova Stylings, Van Nuys, Calif., 1987-91, Bagley & Hotchkiss, Santa Rosa, Calif., 1991-94; designer, owner Judith Conway, Windsor, Calif., 1994—. Design cons. Jade and Gem Corp., Hong Kong, 1986; career fair advisor Gemol. Inst. Am., L.A., N.Y.C., 1990-99. Designer Diamond Internat. Awards, 1990, Jewelers of Am. Awards, 1991, Platinum Guild Internat., 1998. Lobbiest Parents of Blind Children, Oreg., 1978-79; pres. Lambda Chi Alpha Parents Orgn., Oreg. State U., Corvallis, 1983, 84, Lakeridge Parents Music Orgn., Lake Oswego, Oreg., 1984-85; mem. adv. coun. Couture Internat. Jewelry Collections and Cong. Mem. Calif. Jewelers Assn., Womans Jewelers Assn. (chairperson annual dinner 1990, Designer of the Yr. 1998), Jewelry Info. Ctr., Contemporary Design Group, Chaine Des Rotisseurs (dame de la chaine). Avocations: art collecting, wine and food, musical instruments and listening, boating. Office: Judith Conway Inc PO Box 956 Windsor CA 95492-0956 E-mail: judith@judithconway.com.

MATLIN, MARLEE, actress; b. Morton Grove, Ill., Aug. 24, 1965; m. Kevin Grandalski, Aug. 29, 1993; 3 children Attended William Rainey Harper Coll. Appeared in films Children of a Lesser God, 1986 (Acad. award for best actress, Golden Globe award), Walker, 1987, Linguini Incident, 1990, The Player, 1992, Hear No Evil, 1993, It's My Party, 1996, When Justice Fails, 1998, Freak City, 1999; TV films: Bridge to Silence, 1989, Against Her Will: The Carrie Buck Story, 1994, When Justice Fails, 1997, Dead Silence, 1997, Where the Truth Lies, 1999; TV series: Reasonable Doubts, 1991-93; guest star: Picket Fences, 1993, 94-96 (Emmy nomination, Guest Actress-Drama Series, 1994), Seinfeld, 1993 (Emmy nomination Guest Actress-Comedy Series, 1994), The Larry Sanders Show, 1992, Spin City, 1996, ER, 1999, Judging Amy, 1999, The West Wing, 2000—; author: Deaf Child Crossing, 2002

MATLIN, SUSANNE SUMMER, lawyer; b. Chgo., July 3, 1949; d. Leroy and Annette Summer. BS, So. Ill. U., 1971; MA, Northwestern U., 1972; JD, Loyola U., 1982. Bar: Ill., Ill. (No. Dist.), Wash. DC (U.S. Supreme Ct.), Ill. (U.S. Dist. Ct.). Tchr. of deaf No. Suburban Spl. Edn. Assoc., Arlington Heights, Ill., 1972—77, Chgo. Pub. Schs., 1977—86; sr. atty. Fed. Labor Rels. Authority, Chgo., 1986—. Mem. Nat. Multiple Sclerosis Soc., Chgo., 1986—2006, U.S. Holocaust Meml. Mus., Washington, 1995—2006, Jewish United Fund, Chgo., 1990—2006; donor Goodman Theatre, Chgo., 2002—06. Recipient Performance awards, Fed. Labor Rels. Authority, 1987-2006, Employee of Quarter, 1997, Employee of Yr., 1997. Mem.: ABA (assoc.), Chgo. Bar Assn. (assoc.). Office: Fed Labor Relations Authority 55 W Monroe St 1150 Chicago IL 60603 Office Phone: 312-886-3465.

MATLOCK, ANITA KAY, family nurse practitioner; b. Kingsport, Tenn., Aug. 25, 1948; d. James Leonard and Frances Anita Pearl (Liddle) Gibson; m. Ronald Wayne Martin, Nov. 9, 1964 (div. Mar., 1986) children: Lisa Kay Martin McLaughlin, Rhonda Suzanne Martin Ford; m. Neal C. Matlock Jr., May 1, 1987. AS in Nursing cum laude, E. Tenn. State U., 1977; BS in Profl. Arts, St. Joseph's Coll., 1989; MS in Nursing, U. Tenn., 1991. RN, Tenn., Va.; nurse practitioner Va.; cert. family nurse practitioner ANCC. Critical care nurse Holston Valley Comty. Hosp., Kingsport, Tenn., 1977-80, sr. dialysis nurse, 1980-82; head nurse Bristol (Tenn.) Meml. Hosp., 1982-83; head nurse, supr. Mountain Empire Dialysis Ctr., Big Stone Gap, Va., 1983-88; nursing supr. Lee County Comty. Hosp., Pennington Gap, Va., 1988-90; family nurse practitioner Pennington Med. Group, Pennington Gap, 1991-93, Stone Mountain Health Svc., St. Charles, Va., 1993—. Mem. disaster com. Kingsport chpt. ARC, 1985, Lee County Coalition for Health, Pennington Gap, Va., 1991-97; nurse practitioner student preceptor U. Tenn., Knoxville, 1992-97; adj. nursing faculty East Tenn. State U., Johnson City, 1995-97, Mountain Empire C.C., Big Stone Gap, Va., 1995-97, Old Dominion U., Norfolk, Va., 1997. CPR instr. and instr. trainer ARC, Kingsport, Tenn., 1974-90; v.p. Women's Auxiliary to Tnn. Assn. Rescue Squads, 1984; pres., life-time mem. Kingsport Life Saving Crewettes, 1986; mem. adv. bd. Am. Cancer Soc. Lee County, Pennington Gap, Va., 1993-97, Lee County Hosp. Hospice, Pennington Gap, 1997. Recipient scholarship Ky. Coalition Nurse Practitioners and Nurse Midwives, 1991. Mem. ANA, Va. Nurses' Assn., Nurse Practitioner Physicians' Assts. E. Tenn., Order Eastern Star (Worthy Matron 1982), Women of the Moose, Sigma Theta Tau, Phi Kappa Phi. Democrat. Avocations: reading, crafts, computer skills, piano, swimming. Home: RR 4 Box 899 Jonesville VA 24263-9277 Office: Stone Mountain Health Svcs Drawer S Main St Saint Charles VA 24282

MATLOCK, B. JANE, science educator; b. Kankakee, Ill., Jan. 31, 1953; d. Richard Lea Mann and Edith Lucille Joy-Mann; m. Michael Dean Matlock, July 15, 1972; 1 child, Leslie Joy Matlock-Starling. BS in Psychology and Elem. Ed., Olivet Nazarene U., 1989. Cert. K-9 Ill. State Bd. Edn., 1989, mid. sch. endorsements Ill. State Bd. Edn., 1991. Tchr. 3rd grade Bruning Elem. Sch., Wilmington, Ill., 1989—90; edn. coord. Ideal Computer Systems, Kankakee, Ill., 1990—91; social studies methods tchr. Olivet Nazarene U., Kankakee, 1991; sci. tchr. 7th grade L.J. Mid. Sch., Wilmington, 1991—92; sci. tchr. 7th gr. Oster-Oakview Jr. High, New Lenox, Ill., 1992—94, L.J. Stevens Mid. Sch., Wilmington, 1994—2005; tchr. 5th gr. Plainfield (Ill.) Sch. Dist. 202, 2005—. Sch. improvement team Oster-Oakview Jr. High, New Lenox, Ill., 1992—94; sch. leadership team Wilmington SD# 209-U, 1995—2002; Jjr. Beta Club sponsor L.J. Stevens Mid. Sch., 1997—2000, head volleyball coach, 1998—99, sci. club sponsor, 1999—2005; Challenger team trainer Will County Aerospace Team, 2000—; tchr. Jason Expdn., 2004—; MAD sci. tchr. River View Elem. Sch., 2006—; sponsor Astronomy Resources Connection Schs., 2005—. Chancel choir and worship com. First United Meth. Ch., Wilmington, 1986—2006. Recipient Bright Idea award, Oster-Oakview PTO, 1993, Extra Mile award, L.J. Stevens Mid. Sch., 2005. Mem.: AAUW, NSTA, Space Exploration Educators Conf., Ill. Sci. Tchrs. Am., Kappa Delta Pi, Mensa (assoc.). Methodist. Home: 817 Mae St Wilmington IL 60481 Office: River View Elem Sch 2097 Bronk Rd Plainfield IL 60586 Office Phone: 815-439-4840. Personal E-mail: matlock817@msn.com. Business E-Mail: jmatlock@learningcommunity202.org.

MATNEY, JUDY MCCALEB, secondary school educator; b. Dumas, Tex., Jan. 31, 1944; d. Alex Truman McCaleb and Minnie May Curley; m. Roy Matney II, Dec. 21, 1963 (div. Jan. 1999); 1 child, Roy Matney III. BS in Chemistry, U. Tex., 1965; MEd in Math., Southwestern U., San Marcos, Tex., 1967. Cert. tchr. math., tchr. biology, tchr. chemistry, tchr. physics. Tchr. Taylor Ind. Sch. Dist., Tex., 1965—66, Austin Ind. Sch. Dist., Tex., 1967—69, Fort Bend Ind. Sch. Dist., Sugar Land, Tex., 1975—, head dept. sci. Active state textbook rev. panel Tex. Edn. Agy., Austin, 2001; active gov.'s block grants State Tex., Austin, 1983. Named Tex. State Tchr., Tex. Edn. Agy., 1981; recipient Termann Engring. award, Stanford U., 1997, Southwestern Region U.S. AP Physics Tchr. award, Coll. Bd., 1997, Excellence in Sci. award, Exxon. Mem.: Nat. Sci. Tchrs. (Excellence in Sci. Tchg. award). Avocation: computer technology. Home: 2911 Blue Lakes Missouri City TX 77459 Office: FBISD PO Box 1004 Sugar Land TX 77487-1004 Office Phone: 281-634-5600. Business E-Mail: 001JM318@fortbend.k12.tx.us.

MATORIN, SUSAN, social work administrator, educator; b. Boston, Jan. 9, 1943; d. Mervyn Donald and Eleanor (Marinoff) M.; m. Richard Charles Friedman, Nov. 24, 1978; 1 child, Jeremiah Simon. AB, Vassar Coll., 1964; postgrad., Columbia Sch. Social Work, 1966. Cert. social worker, N.Y. Chief social work Washington Heights Cmty. Svc., N.Y. State Psychiat. Inst., 1966-78; chief ambulatory social work in psychiatry Presbyn. Hosp., Columbia Med. Ctr., N.Y., 1978-81; dir. social work Payne Whitney Clinic of N.Y. Hosp., Cornell, 1981-97; program dir. Cornell Psychiatry Intensive Outpatient Program, 1997—2000, treatment coord., affective disorder team, 2000—. Mem. adv. coun., 2d vice chair Columbia U. Sch. of Social Work, 1994—; adj. assoc. prof. Columbia Sch. Social Work, 1977—; bd. trustees Selig Ednl. Inst. Jewish Bd. Family Svcs., N.Y.; mem. pastoral edn. & rsch. com. Healthcare Chaplancy; spkr. in field. Contbr. articles to profl. jours. and books. Recipient Disting. Svc. medal Columbia U., 1989, Centennial award, 1998, Hyman J. Weiner award, Soc. Social Work Leaders In Health Care, 2006. Fellow Am. Orthopsychiatry Assn.; mem. NASW (Met. chpt. licensing task force, bd. dirs.), Acad. Cert. Social Workers, Soc. for Social Work Leaders in Health Care (N.Y. chpt. program co-chair 1994—, nominated Social Work Dir. of Yr. 1995). Democrat. Jewish. Avocations: family, playing piano, reading, walking, ballet and art. Home: 27 W 86th St Apt 9C New York NY 10024-3615 Office: Payne Whitney Clinic 525 E 68th St # 140 New York NY 10021-4870 Office Phone: 212-746-5772.

MATSA, LOULA ZACHAROULA, social services administrator, educator; b. Piraeus, Greece, Apr. 16, 1935; came to U.S., 1952, naturalized 1962; d. Eleftherios Georgiou and Ourania E. (Fraguiskopoulou) Papoulias; m. Ilco S. Matsa, Nov. 27, 1953; 1 child, Aristotle Ricky. Student, Pierce Coll., Athens, 1948-52; BA, Rockford Coll., 1953; MA, U. Chgo., 1955. Diplomate clin. social worker; bd. cert. clin. social workers, N.Y. cert. social orkers, pub. employees fedn. Marital counselor Family Soc., Cambridge, Mass., 1955-56; chief unit II social svc. Queen's (N.Y.) Children's Psychiat. Ctr., 1961-74; dir. social svcs., supr.-coord. family care program Hudson River Psychiat. Ctr., Poughkeepsie, N.Y., 1974-91; supr. social work Harlem Valley Psychiat. Ctr., Wingdale, N.Y., 1991-93, Hudson River Psychiat. Ctr., 1993—. Field instr. Adelphi, Albany and Fordham univs., 1969—. Contbr. articles to profl. jours.; instrumental in state policy changes in treatment and court representation of emotionally disturbed and mentally ill. Fulbright Exch. student, 1952-53; Talcott scholar, 1953-55. Mem. NASW, Internat. Platform Assn., Internat. Coun. on Social Welfare, Acad. Cert. Social Workers, Assn. Cert. Social Workers, Pierce Coll. Alumni Assn. Democrat. Greek Orthodox.

MATSON, FRANCES SHOBER, retired social worker; b. Cin., Mar. 21, 1921; d. Frank Lyford and Florence Leone (Bridgeford) Shober; student U. Cin., 1939-41, B.A., 1951, postgrad., 1951-52; M.S.W., U. Calif., 1956; Nat. Registry of Clin. Social Work; m. John Alan Matson, Dec. 2, 1942 (dec.). Diplomate Am. Bd. Examiners in Clin. Social Work. Councillor, County of San Mateo, 1956-57; therapist, supr. Center for Treatment and Edn. on Alcoholism, Oakland, Calif., 1957-63; pvt. practice social worker, Berkeley, Calif., 1960-64; supr. dept. social service County of Marin, Calif., 1966; psychotherapist Marin Inst., 1966-70, Oaknoll Naval Hosp., 1969; public health social worker Dept. Health County of Contra Costa (Calif.), 1972; psychotherapist Day Care Center for Schizophrenics, Contra Costa County Med. Services, 1972-74; dir. Martinez Mental Health Clinic, Contra Costa County Med. Services, 1974-81; coordinator adult outpatient services, edn., group therapy Contra Costa County Mental Health Center, 1981-88, ret., 1988. Amem. Nat. Assn. Social Workers, Acad. Cert. Social Workers, Internat. Transactional Analysis Assn., Marin Assn. Mental Health, Contra Costa County Mental Health Assn., Soc. Clin. Social Work.

MATSON, PAMELA ANNE, environmental scientist, science educator; b. Eau Claire, Wis., Aug. 3, 1953; BS, U. Wis., 1975; MS, Ind. U., 1980; PhD, Oreg. State U., 1983. Prof. U. Calif., Berkeley, 1993—97; Goldman prof. environ. studies Stanford U., Calif., 1997—, Naramore dean sch. earth sci., 2002—. Contbr. articles to profl. jours.; editor: Annual Rev. of Environment & Resources. Fellow MacArthur fellow, 1995. Fellow: Am. Acad. Arts & Scis.; mem.: Nat. Acad. Sci. Achievements include research in interactions between the biosphere and the atmosphere; land-use changes on atmospheric change, analyzing the effects of greenhouse gas emissions resulting from tropical deforestization; intensive agriculture on the atmosphere, especially the effects of tropical agriculture and cattle ranching; development of agricultural productivity can be expanded without causing off-site environmental consequences. Office: Stanford U Sch Earth Scis Stanford CA 94305-2210

MATSUI, CONNIE L., pharmaceutical executive; b. Piedmont, Calif. m. William Beckman; 2 children. BA, Stanford U., MBA, 1977. Various positions Wells Fargo Bank, 1977—91; sr. dir., planning and resource devel. IDEC Pharm., 1992—94, v.p., planning and resource devel., 1994—2000, sr. v.p., planning and resource devel., 2000—03; exec. v.p. corp. strategy and communication Biogen Idec Inc., 2003—. Bd. dirs. Halozyme Therapeutics, Inc., 2006—. Nat. pres. Girl Scouts Am., 1999—2002. Office: Biogen Inc 14 Cambridge Ctr Cambridge MA 02142

MATSUI, DORIS OKADA, congresswoman; b. Poston, Ariz., Sept. 25, 1944; m. Robert Takeo Matsui (dec. Jan. 1, 2005), Sept. 17, 1966; 1 child. BA in Psychology, U. Calif., Berkeley, 1966. Dep. dir. pub. liaison The White House, Washington, 1993—94, 1996—99, dep. asst. to the Pres. for pub. liaison, 1994—96; dir. govt. rels. Collier, Shannon & Scott PLLC, Washington, 1999—2005; mem. US Congress from 5th Calif. dist., 2005—. Mem. Clinton-Gore Transition Team, 1992—93; bd. trustees Woodrow Wilson Internat. Ctr. Scholars, Meridian Internat. Ctr., Calif. Inst. Bd., Arena Stage. Recipient Action for Breast Cancer Awareness award, Advocates award, Nat. Assn. Mental Health, Mentor award, U. So. Calif. -Sacramento Sch. Pub. Adminstrn., Newmyer award, Sidwell Friends Sch., Rosalie Stern award, U. Calif. Alumni Assn. Democrat. Methodist. Office: US Ho Reps 2310 Ho Office Bldg Washington DC 20515-0505 also: Robert T Matsui Fed Courthouse Ste 12-600 501 I St Sacramento CA 95814*

MATSUMOTO, CAROLEE SETSUKO, researcher, education developer and administrator; b. Denver, Feb. 13, 1943; d. Harry Katsumi and Pearl Shizuho (Nakamura) M.; m. David Luther Gilbertson, Oct. 20, 1990. BA, Ea. Mich. U., 1965; MEd, Wayne State U., 1968; EdD, Harvard Univ., 1991. Cert. biology, sci. tchr., adminstr., Mass. Sci. tchr. Greenburgh Sch. Dist. #8, Hartsdale, NY, 1965-67; sci. dept., head tchr. Nagoya Internat. Sch., Japan, 1968-70; tchr. sci. grades 7-8 Brookline HS, Mass., 1970—73, tchr. biology, 1976—79, sci. supr., 1979-81; sci. dept. head Graded Am. Sch., Sao Paulo, Brazil, 1973-76; asst. supt. curriculum, instrn. Concord and Concord/Carlisle Pub. Schs., Mass., 1981-87; teaching fellow Harvard U., Cambridge, Mass., 1984-85; curriculum dir., prin. investigator Edn. Devel. Ctr., Newton, Mass., 1987-93, sr. project dir., sr. scientist, 1993—. Bd. dirs. New Eng. & Islands Reg. Lab., Andover, Mass., 1985-96, Lloyd Environ. Ctr., S. Dartmouth, Mass., 1990-97; mem. adv. coun. Collaboration for Equity, Am. Assn. for Advancement Sci., Washington, 1994-96; mem. Mass Dept. Edn. Cultural Proficiency Steering Com., 2006-; vis. scholar Stanford U., Palo Alto, 1993; rep. Carpe Vitam Found., Sweden; co-dir. U. Mass., Dartmouth, K-12 Rsch. Devel. Dissemination Ctr. Bd. dirs. Tchrs. 21, Wellesley, Mass.; bd. trustees New Bedford Oceanarium. Mem. ASCD, NSDC, Nat. Sci. Tchrs. Assn. Avocations: travel, photography. Home: 17 Arnold Pl New Bedford MA 02740-3634

MATSUMOTO, KIYO A., federal judge; Grad., U. Calif., Berkeley; JD, Georgetown U. Law Sch. Litigation assoc. MacDonald, Hoague and Bayless, Seattle; asst. US atty. US Dist Ct. (Eastern Dist NY), deputy chief, first deputy chief, chief civil div., chief financial litigation unit, civil health care fraud coord., sr. trial counsel, magistrate judge, 2004—. Instr. civil litigation, financial litigation and trial advocacy Atty. General's Advocacy Inst., Nat. Advocacy Ctr., Office Legal Education US Dept. Justice; adj. prof. legal rsch. and writing Brooklyn Law Sch.; adj. prof. govt. civil litigation clinic and seminar NYU Law Sch. Mem.: Nat. Asian Pacific American Bar Assn., Asian American Bar Assn. NY, Eastern Dist. New York's Com. Civil Litigation, Assn. Bar of the City NY, Fed. Bar Coun. Office: 225 Cadman Plaza E Brooklyn NY 11201 Business E-Mail: kiyo_matsumoto@nyed.uscourts.gov.

MATSUMURA, VERA YOSHI, pianist; b. Oakland, Calif. d. Naojiro and Aguri Tanaka; m. Jiro Matsumura, Aug. 8, 1942; 1 son, Kenneth N. BA in Piano Pedagogy, Coll. Holy Names, Oakland, 1938; pvt. studies with F. Moss, M. Shapiro, L. Kreutzer, P. Jarrett. Mem. staff, pianist Radio Sta. KROW, Oakland, 1938-39. Numerous concert performances in Far East (Japan, Thailand), 1940—; numerous tchg. appointments, 1940—; dir. Internat. Music Coun., Berkeley, Calif., 1969—. Named to Hall of Fame, Piano Guild, 1968. Mem. Nat. Music Tchrs. Nat. Assn., Music Tchrs. Assn. Calif., Internat. Platform Assn., Alpha Phi Mu. Methodist. Home: 2 Claremont Cres Berkeley CA 94705-2324

MATTEO, CHRISTINE E., librarian; b. Jersey City, May 26, 1952; d. Peter J. G. and Doris Ella (Stoffel) Dirschauer; m. Joseph A. Matteo, Sept. 9, 1978. BA in Psychology, Washington Coll., Chestertown, Md., 1974; MLS, Rutgers U., 1977. Cert. libr. N.J. Sr. libr., br. mgr. Ocean County Libr., Beachwood, NJ, 1976-78, prin. libr., br. mgr. Jackson, NJ, 1978-86, automation implementation mgr. Toms River, NJ, 1986-89, supervising libr. ctrl. svcs., 1989-91, chief libr. pub. svcs., 1991-95, chief libr. tech., 1995—2003, chief libr. adminstrn., 2003—. Mem. exec. bd., treas. Customers Dynix, Inc., Provo, Utah, 1989—91, Ctrl. Jersey Regional Libr., Freehold, 1994—96; editor, mem. steering com. Ocean County Libr. Master Plan, Toms River, 1984—85, 1991—92, 1997—98; mem. exec. bd. One Ease-E-Link, Toms River, 1998—2002; presenter in field, 2005—06. Mem.: ASPCA, ALA, N.J. Libr. Assn. (info. techs. sect., mem. LGBT Roundtable), World Future Soc., Animal Birth Control Inc., Monmouth County SPCa, Toms River Seaport Soc., Greenpeace, Humane Soc. U.S., Earthwatch, Tuckerton Seaport Soc. (charter), Environ. Def. Fund, World Wildlife Fund, Associated Humane Socs., Humane Soc. U.S., Toms River Yacht Club. Avocations: sailing, gardening, dog obedience, kayaking, science fiction. Office: Ocean County Libr 101 Washington St Toms River NJ 08753-7688 Office Phone: 732-349-6200. Business E-Mail: matteo_c@oceancounty.lib.nj.us.

MATTERSON, JOAN MCDEVITT, physical therapist; b. Bryn Mawr, Pa., Feb. 24, 1949; d. William J. and Wanda Jean (Edwards) McD.; children: Brian, Jennie, Kira. BS in Biology, St. Joseph's U., Phila., 1973; cert. in Phys. Therapy, U. Pa., 1974. Assoc. pharmacologist, rschr. immunology and arthritis Prog. Phys. Therapy, P.A., Wilmington, Del., 1976-93, pediatric phys. therapist, 1974-81, pres., 1976-95; rehab. dir. Achievement Rehab.; phys. therapist Liberty Home Health, 1995—; rehab. dir. Office of Joan Matterson, 1995—, Integrated Health Svcs.- Kent, Smyrna, Del., 1996—; dir. rehab. Keystone Care Therapies, Media, Pa., 1997—, with Pain Mgmt. Ctr. Chester, Pa., 1999; with Hands on Health, Wilmington, 1999—2000; phys. therapist Hickory House Nursing and Rehab. Ctr., Honeybrook, Pa., 2000—; pvt. practice Wilmington, 2000—. Lectr. in field of low level laser therapy. Dep. gov. Am. Biog. Rsch. Inst.; mem. adv. bd. Internat. Biog. Rsch. Inst., Cambridge, Eng. Mem. NAFE, Am. Soc. Laser Medicine and Surgery, Internat. Platform Assn., Am. Acad. Pain (assoc.), Inst. Noetic Sci., Am. Bd. Forensic Examiners, N.Am. Assn. Laser Therapy, Internat. Exec. Service Corp. Avocations: dance, skiing, cooking. Office Phone: 610-457-9158. Personal E-mail: jnmttrsn711@aol.com.

MATTESON, CAROL J., academic administrator; BS in Health Edn., Slippery Rock U. of Pa.; MS in Psychomotor Learning, U. Oreg.; PhD in Bus. Adminstrn., U. Pitts. Faculty Sturt Coll. of Edn., South Australia, Slippery Rock U., U. Maine, Augusta, Rowan U., NJ; asst. to pres. Slippery Rock U. of Pa.; dean coll. of bus. Bloomsburg U., Pa., provost and v.p. academic affairs Pa., 1992—95; exec. v.p. and provost Rowan U., NJ, 1995—2000; pres. Mt. Ida Coll., Newton, Mass., 2000—. Office: Mt Ida Coll 777 Dedham St Newton MA 02459

MATTESON, CLARICE CHRIS, artist, educator; b. Winnipeg, Man., Can., Sept. 2, 1918; came to U.S., 1922; d. Sergis and Nina (Balter) Alberts; m. D.C. Matteson, 1956 (dec. 1976); children: Kemmer, Gretchen. BA, Met. State U., 1976; MA in Liberal Studies, Hamline U., 1986; PhD in Humanities, LaSalle U., 1995. Mem. Orson Welles' staff, Hollywood, Calif., 1945-46; owner Hilde-Gardes Co., L.A., 1952—56; instr. art North Hennepin C.C., Brooklyn Park, Minn., 1975-81; instr. continuing edn. for women U. Minn., 1980. Prodr., host TV program Accent on Art, St. Paul, 1979—; instr. art Lakewood C.C., 1979, U. Minn., Bloomington (Minn.) Sch. Dist., 1980-2004, Mpls. Sch. Dist., St. Paul Sch. Dist., 1981-2002, 03-04; guest artist Montserrat Gallery, Soho, N.Y.C., 1999; appeared as guest artist WCCO-TV, 1998; spkr. on TV, Am. Pen Women Spirituality and Creativity in Art, 2003. (one-woman shows) Decathlon Club, 1998, State Capital Rotunda, 1986, Lindbergh Home, 1988, Hamline U., 2002, exhibited (group shows) Mpls. Inst. Art, 1994—98, Art in Bloom, 1999—2002, St. Paul, 2000, Landmark Ctr., Hamline U., St. Paul, 2002, U. Minn. Womens Club Art Show, 2003, Fairmount Hotel, 2002; Exhibited in group shows at Art in Bloom, 1999—2003; (represented by) Gov. Ventura's Ofcl. Residence and now by Gov. Jim Pawlenty, 2003—04, Montserrat Art Gallery, N.Y.C., Gallery 416, Mpls., Jean Stephen Art Gallery, 1999—2002, Premier Gallery, 2001—02, (corr.) Schaumburg (Ill) Newspapers, 1962—68; prodr.: (TV series, host) Kids Art, 1995—, (series program) Internat. Cafe Internet Arts, 1996—; patentee plastic products; prodr.: Men Aware TV, 2001—02, Punt, Pass, or Pie TV, 2001—02; composer: I Want You Near; Exhibited in group shows at Women's Club, 2002—03, exhibited in group shows, Gov. Ventura's and Gov. Tim Pawlenty's, 2001—05; composer: You Make a Difference, God is in my Heart. Active Minn. Orch. (WAMSO), Mpls., 1972—, vol. Recipient award for creative leadership Minn. Assn. for Continuing Adult Edn., 1977, Gold Cup award Bloomington Cable, 1989, Gov.'s Letter of Commendation, 1994; named Outstanding Grad. for past 25 yrs. Met. State U., 1997, Disting. Alumna John Marshall H.S., L.A., 2002, Outstanding Nominee of Grad. Students Met. State U., 2002; Park Cable TV grantee, 1982, Minn. Humanities Commn. grantee, 1985. Qem. ASCAP (award 1997-2003, award for popular music, 2003-04), AAUW (dir. arts com. 1989-90, bd. dirs. 1990-92), Am. Pen Women (Minn. chpt. 1994—, v.p. 1998), Internat. Biog. Assn. (dep. dir. Cambridge, Eng. 2001, participate art and comm. congress, 2001), Am. Composers Forum, Minn. Artists Assn., Minn. Territorial Pioneers (bd. dirs. 1995—, v.p. 1997-99, 1st v.p. 1999-2003, elected Minnesotan of Yr., 1999-2002, elected 1st v.p. 2003-04), Internat. Alliance for Women in Music, St. Paul Neighborhood Network (elected bd. dirs. TV station SPNN, 2002), N.Y. Neighborhood Network, Internat. Platform Speakers (award 1998), Mpls. Telecom. Network, Metro Cable Network, Adelphi Cable, Manhattan Cable, Duluth-Superior Cable, NDT, Eagan. Avocations: tennis, dance, writing children's books, composing liturgical music. Home and Office: 2119 Sargent Ave Saint Paul MN 55105-1126

MATTESON, KARLA J., health science association administrator; BS in Chemistry, Beloit Coll., Wis., 1969; MS in Chemistry, Marquette U., 1976; PhD, Med. Coll. Wis., 1981. Postdoctoral fellow Baylor Coll. Medicine, Houston, 1981—83; former asst. dir. U. Tenn Devel. and Genetic Ctr., Knoxville; assoc. prof. med. genetics and pathology U. Tenn., Knoxville, 1986—, dir. biochem. and molecular genetics lab., 1986—; bd. dirs. Am. Bd. Med. Genetics, 1998—2001, exec. dir., 2001—. Fellow: Am. Coll. Med. Genetics; mem.: AAAS, Soc. for Inborn Metabolic Disorders. Office: U Tenn Grad Sch Medicine Ste 435 1924 Alcoa Hwy Knoxville TN 37920-6999 also: Am Bd Med Genetics 9650 Rockville Pike Bethesda MD 20814-3998*

MATTHEW, LYN, sales executive, consultant, marketing professional; b. Long Beach, Calif., Dec. 15, 1936; d. Harold G. and Beatrice (Hunt) Matthew; m. Wayne Thomas Castleberry, Aug. 12, 1961 (div. Jan. 1976); children: Melanie Castleberry, Cheryl Castleberry, Nicole Castleberry, Mathew Castleberry. BS, U. Calif., Davis, 1958; MA, Ariz. State U., 1979. Cert. hotel sales exec., meeting profl., hospitality mktg. exec., hospitality mgmt. exec. Pres. Davlyn Cons. Found., Scottsdale, Ariz., 1979-82; cons., vis. prof. Art Bus., Scottsdale, 1982—; pres., dir. sales and mktg. Embassy Stes., Scottsdale, 1987-98; pres. Matthew Enterprises, Inc., Scottsdale, 1998—. Vis. prof. Maricopa CC, Phoenix, 1979—, Ariz. State U., Tempe, 1980—83; cons. Women's Caucus Art, Phoenix, 1983—88; coun. adminstr. Lynn Andrews Prodns., 2001—. Author: The Business Aspects of Art, Book I, 1979, Book II, 1989, Marketing Strategies for the Creative Artist, 1985, Moxibustion Manual, 1999. Bd. dirs. Rossom Ho. and Heritage Sq. Found., Phoenix, 1987—88; trustee Hotel Sales and Mktg. Assn. Internat. Found., 1988—90, chmn., 1991—93, mem. exec. com., 1993—95. Recipient Cmty. Bldg. award, 2000. Mem.: Am. Orgn. Bodywork Therapies Asia (pres., state dir. 1999—2003), Ariz. Acad. Performing Arts (v.p. bd. dir. 1987—88, pres. 1988—89), Soc. Govt. Meeting Planners (charter bd. dir. 1987, nat. conf. co-chair 1993—94, Sam Gilmer award 1992), Meeting Planners Internat. (v.p. Ariz. Sunbelt chpt. 1989—91, pres. 1991—92, CMP cert. trainer 1995—, Supplier of the Yr. award 1988), Cert. Hospitality Mktg. Execs. (profl. designation tng. chair 1995), Hotels Sales and Mktg. Assn. Internat. (bd. dir. 1985—90, pres. Great Phoenix chpt. 1988—89, regional dir. 1989—90, mktg. exec. 1998—), Ariz. Vocat. Edn. Assn. (sec. 1978—80), Ariz. Women's Caucus Art (pres. 1980—82, hon. advisor 1986—87), Nat. Women's Caucus Art (v.p. 1981—83), Women in Higher Edn., Ariz. Visionary Artists (treas. 1987—88), Women Image Now (Achievement and Contbn. in Visual Arts award 1983), Coun. Whistling Elk (worldwide coun. adminstr. 2001—06).

MATTHEWS, BARBARA CARIDAD, lawyer; d. Frederick Lawrence and Caridad Ofelia Matthews; m. Andrew Michael Danas, Nov. 6, 1999; 1 child, Lydia Marguerite Danas. B.Sc.F.S., Georgetown U., 1986; JD, LLM, Duke U., 1991. Bar: N.Y. 1992. Assoc. banking advisor Inst. Internat. Fin., Washington, 1992—94, banking advisor, regulatory counsel, 1996—2003; assoc. Morrison & Foerster, Washington, 1994—96; sr. coun., Fin. Svc. Com. House of Rep., 2003—06; sr. advisor to the asst. sec. internat. affiars and fin. attaché U.S. Mission to the European Union U.S. Dept. Treasury, Brussels, 2006—. Mem. editl. bd. Jour. Derivatives Use, Trading and Regulation, 1997—2003; contbr. articles to profl. jours., chapters to books. Pres. Friends Assisting the Nat. Symphony, Washington, 1998—99; bd. dirs. Young Audiences, Washington, 2000—04; mem. exec. com. women's leadership group Boys & Girls Clubs Greater Washington, 2000. Fellow internat. law, Ford Found., 1991—92. Mem.: ABA, Coun. Fgn. Rels., N.Y. State Bar Assn., Internat. Assn. Fin. Engrs., Coun. Fgn. Rels., Pi Sigma Alpha, Alpha Sigma Nu. Avocations: photography, tennis, travel. Office Phone: 202-225-7502. Business E-Mail: barbara.matthews@mail.house.gov, barbara.matthews@do.treas.gov.

MATTHEWS, EVELYN J., nurse; b. Franklin, La., Nov. 9, 1929; d. Charlie and Mary Foster; m. Lucien Bourgeois Matthews, June 8, 1947 (dec. Jan. 5, 2001); 1 child, Dewana Patrice Matthews Jackson. LUN, U. Tex., 1949. Lic. nurse Nursing Career, Galveston, Tex., 1949—85; bus. owner LED Mat Plumbing, La Marque, Tex., 1957—2000. Lioness tamer Tex. City Mainland Lioness Club, 1984—85, pres., 1985—86, 1991—93, 2006—, sec., 2002—06. Mem.: Lions Club Internat. Home: 2539 Jackson St La Marque TX 77568

MATTHEWS, JANICE C., financial consultant; b. Livingston, Mont., Apr. 7, 1955; d. Frank L. and A. Kathryn Hocevar; children: Amanda, Andrew. BS in Econs., Mont. State U., 1977. Sales rep. IBM, Boise; fin. cons. Merrill Lynch, Idaho Falls. Avocations: fishing, theater, biking. Home: 152 W Stone Run Ln Idaho Falls ID 83404 Office: 560 S Woodruff Ave Idaho Falls ID 83401-5298 E-mail: Janice_Matthews@ml.com.

MATTHEWS, KAREN SUE, music educator; d. Billy Charles and Jean Alice Matthews; m. Donald B. Mohler Jr., Mar. 28, 1999. BA in Instrumental Music, U. New Orleans, 1988, MEd in Adminstrn., 1990. Music tchr. Jefferson Parish Pub. Sch., Marrero, La., 1991—. Musician: New Orleans Concert Band, 1988—. Mem.: Music Educators Nat. Assn., La. Music Educators, La. Flute Soc.

MATTHEWS, KATHLEEN SHIVE, biochemistry educator; b. Austin, Tex., Aug. 30, 1945; d. William and Gwyn Shive; m. Randall Matthews. BS in Chemistry, U. Tex., 1966; PhD in Biochemistry, U. Calif., Berkeley, 1970. Post doctoral fellow Stanford (Calif.) U., 1970-72; mem. faculty Rice U., Houston, 1972—, chair dept., 1987-95, Wiess prof., 1989-96, Stewart Meml. chair, 1996—, dean natural scis., 1998—. Mem. BBCB study sect. NIH, Bethesda, Md., 1980-84, 86-88, BRSG adv. com., 1992-94; mem. adv. com. on rsch. programs Tex. Higher Edn. Coord. Bd., Austin, 1987-92; mem. undergrad. edn. initiative rev. panel Howard Hughes Rsch. Inst., Bethesda, 1991, mem. rsch. resources rev. panel, 1995, mem. predoctoral fellowships rev. panel, 2001, trustee S.W. Rsch. Inst., 2003—, steering com. adv. bd. Vinson & Elkins Women's Initiative, 2001-06. Mem. editl. bd. Jour. Biol. Chemistry, 1988-93, assoc. editor, 1994-99; contbr. 140 reviewed papers. Fellow AAAS; mem. Am. Soc. Biochemistry and Molecular Biology (nominating com. 1993-94, 96-97, fin. com. 2001-2002), Protein Soc., Biophys. Soc. (pub. affairs com. 2002-05), Am. Chem. Soc., Phi Beta Kappa. Office: Rice Univ PO Box 1892 6100 Main St MS102 Houston TX 77005-1892 E-mail: ksm@rice.edu.

MATTHEWS, LINDA NELL, secondary school educator; b. Decatur, Ala., May 12, 1948; d. Clinton Van and Lela Magdalene (Pressnell) Bowers; m. David Latrell Matthews, Sept. 4, 1971; children: Amy Leanne, Lorrie Suzanne. BS in Edn., Athens State Coll., 1991; postgrad., U. North Ala., 1991—, MA in Secondary Edn., 1997. Cert. tchr. elem. edn., early childhood, mid. sch. lang. arts, social sci., 7-12 English, Ala., Tenn. Sales assoc. Longaberger Baskets, Athens, Ala., 1988-92; substitute tchr. Giles County and Limestone County, Ala. and Tenn., 1991-92; tchr. English Elkton (Tenn.) Elem. Sch., 1992-93; tchr. English Limestone County Bd. Edn. West Limestone H.S., Athens, 1993—. Beauty cons. Mary Kay Cosmetics, Athens, 1984—. Vol. tutor Laubach Literacy Action, 1991-93; participant Ptnrs. for Drug-Free Edn. Orgn., Athens, 1991-93; pres. West Limestone PTO, Lester, Ala., 1991-93. Recipient Tchr. of the Yr., Limestone County, 2006—; grantee NEH grantee, 1993, Ala. Humanities Found. grantee, 1996. Mme. Phi Theta Kappa, Kappa Delta Pi (pres. 1992-93). Mem. Ch. of Christ. Avocations: volunteer tutor, reading. Home: 15283 Hobbs Rd Athens AL 35614-4929 Office: West Limestone HS 10945 W School House Rd Lester AL 35647-3635

MATTHEWS, LOIS MARR, musician, music educator; b. Washington, July 10, 1928; d. Ralph Dorian and Ruth Hayes Marr; m. Richard Matthews, June 23, 1956; children: Julia Louise Pagio, Christine Dorian Trout, Melanie Marr Doss. BA, Wilson Tchrs. Coll., 1950; MA in Music, Columbia U., 1953. Organist Calvary Meth. Ch., Arlington, Va., Cmty. Meth. Ch., Meml. Bapt. Ch. Mem.: DAR, Am. Guild Organists. Methodist. Avocations: piano, organ, painting. Home: 6329 Arbor Way Elkridge MD 21075

MATTHEWS, MILDRED SHAPLEY, freelance/self-employed editor; b. Pasadena, Calif., Feb. 15, 1915; d. Harlow and Martha (Betz) Shapley; m. Ralph Vernon Matthews, Sept. 25, 1937; children: June Lorrain, Bruce Shapley, Melvin Lloyd, Martha Alys. AB, U. Mich., 1936. Rsch. asst. Calif. Inst. Tech., Pasadena, 1950—61; bilingual editor, rsch. asst. Astron. Obs. Merate-Milan and Trieste, Italy, 1960—70; rsch. asst. Lunar-Planetary Lab., editor space sci. series U. Ariz., Tucson, 1970—96; ret., 1996. Contbr. articles to Sky and Telescope, Astronomia. Recipient Masursky Meritorious Svc. award div. planetary sci. Am. Astron. Soc., 1993. Avocations: classical music concerts, especially opera, travel. Home: 3154 Del Vina St Pasadena CA 91107

MATTHEWS, RONDRA J., publishing executive; b. Inglewood, Calif., July 13, 1955; d. Nedra Plummer; m. Keith Matthews. BS in Behavioral Sci., High Point U.; MBA, Rollins Coll. Former pres. Better Bus. Bur, Ctrl. Fla.; various mgmt. positions Orlando (Fla.) Sentinel Comms., 1980—99, v.p., gen. mgr., 1999—2000; pres., pub., CEO Daily Press, Newport News, Va., 2000—06; publisher, CEO Baltimore Sun Co., 2006—. Bd. dirs. Peninsula Alliance for Econ. Devel., Hampton Roads Partnership, Greater Peninsula NOW; bd. advisors Christopher Newport U. Sch. Bus.; chair-elect bd. dirs. United Way of the Va. Peninsula. Office: Baltimore Sun Co 501 N Calvert St PO Box 137 Baltimore MD 21278-0001*

MATTHEWS, ROWENA GREEN, biological chemistry educator; b. Cambridge, Eng., Aug. 20, 1938; (father Am. citizen); d. David E. and Doris (Cribb) Green; m. Larry Stanford Matthews, June 18, 1960; children: Brian Stanford, Keith David. BA, Radcliffe Coll., 1960; PhD, U. Mich., 1969. Instr. U. S.C., Columbia, 1964-65; postdoctoral fellow U. Mich., Ann Arbor, 1970-75, asst. prof., 1975-81, assoc. prof. biol. chemistry, 1981-86, prof., 1986—, assoc. chmn., 1988-92, G. Robert Greenberg disting. univ. prof., 1995—, chair biophysics rsch. divsn., 1996—2001. Mem. phys. biochemistry study sect. NIH, 1982-86; mem. adv. coun. Nat. Inst. Gen. Med. Scis., NIH, 1991-94; adv. bd. NATO, 1994-96; mem. Commn. on Advancement of Women and Minorities in Sci., Engring. and Tech. Devel., 1999; mem. faculty Life Scis. Inst., 2002—. Mem. editl. adv. bd. Biochem. Jour., 1984-92, Arch. Biochemistry, Biophysics, 1992-97, Biochemistry, 1993—, Jour. Bacteriology, 1995-2003; contbr. articles to profl. jours. Recipient Merit award Nat. Inst. Gen. Med. Scis., 1991-2001; NIH grantee, 1978—, NSF grantee, 1992-2003. Fellow AAAS, NAS, Am. Acad. Arts & Scis, Inst. Medicine; mem. Am. Soc. Biochem. and Molecular Biology (program chair 1995, chair human resources 1996-98, William C. Rose award 2000), Am. Chem. Soc. (program chair biochemistry divsn. 1985, sec. biochemistry divsn. 1990-92, chair 1994-96, Repligen award 2001), Inst. Medicine (2004), Phi Beta Kappa, Sigma Xi. Office: Life Sci Inst U Mich 210 Washtenaw Ave Ann Arbor MI 48109-2216 Home: 1609 S University Ann Arbor MI 48104 Business E-Mail: rmatthew@umich.edu.

MATTHEWS, WYHOMME S., retired music educator, academic administrator; b. Battle Creek, Mich., July 22, 1948; d. Woodrow R. and LouLease (Graham) Sellers; m. Edward L. Matthews, Apr. 29, 1972; children: Channing DuVall, Triston Curran, Landon Edward, Brandon Graham. AA, Kellogg C.C., 1968; MusB, Mich. State U., 1970, MA, MusM, Mich. State U., 1972. Cert. elem. and secondary tchr., Mich. Tchr., vocal music dir. Benton Harbor (Mich.) Pub. Schs., 1971-72, dir. vocal music, 1972; dir. edn. head start program Burlington (N.J.) County, 1972-73; pvt. music tchr., 1973-89; tchr. Southeastern Jr. H.S., 1986-87, W.K. Kellogg Jr. H.S., 1987-89; chair visual and performing arts dept. Kellogg C.C., Battle Creek, Mich., 1989-99, dir. Eastern acad. Ctr., 1999—2003, ret., 2003. Part-time instr. Kellogg C.C., 1973—, dir. Eclectic Chorale, 1973-2005, dir., organizer Kellogg C.C. Eclectic Chorale Sacred Cultural Festival, 1979—, judge various contests; artistic dir. Battle Creek Sojourner Truth Monument Presentation Day, 1999; presenter in field. Pres. Dudley Elem. Sch., 1981-85; active Battle Creek Pub. Schs. PTA, Pennfield Pub. Schs. PTA, Mt. Zion African Meth. Episc. Ch.; v.p. Life Care Amb. Bd., 1990-2003; bd. dirs. Leila Aboretum Soc.; mem. Battle Creek Cmty. Found., Glen Cross Arts and Infrasture Fund; founder Echoes of Grace, 2005. Recipient Outstanding Cmty. Svc. award, 1975, Sojourner Truth award, 2000, George award, City of Battle Creek, 2000; fellow, Mich. State U., 1971. Mem. Mich. Music Tchr. Assn., Nat. Music Tchrs. Assn., Battle Creek Music Tchrs. Assn., Battle Creek Morning Music Club (bd. dirs.), Nat. Leadership Acad., Battle Creek Cmty. Concert Assn. Home: 466 Alton Ave Battle Creek MI 49017-3212 Personal E-mail: wmatth5278@aol.com.

MATTHEWS ELLIS, BONNIE, management consultant; b. Fostoria, Ohio, Nov. 14, 1942; d. Blaine Garfield and Mildred Mae (Reed) Hummel; m. Gary Matthews, May 20, 1961 (div. Mar. 1978); children: Christopher, Jennifer, Jonathan; m. William C. Ellis, Sept. 20, 1998. BS, Bowling Green State U., 1965; MA, Ohio State U., 1973, PhD, 1978; postgrad., Franklin U., 1978. Accredited pub. rels. Coord. supplementary tng. Bowling Green (Ohio) State U., 1965-68; supervising tchr. Head Start, Rising Sun, Ohio, 1965-68; assoc. dir. Ohio Community Mental Health & Mental Retardation Assn., Columbus, 1974-77; dir. community programs Ohio Mental Health & Mental Retardation Adv. and Rev. Commn., Columbus, 1977-78; dir. pub. rels. Columbus Mus. Art, 1978-81; chmn., pres. Mgmt. Dimensions, Inc. dba MD Staffing, 1981—; pres. Matthews/Colburn Inc., 1984-86; mng. ptnr., chmn. Fund Raising Dimensions, 1990-92. Adj. prof. Franklin U., Columbus, 1974-85, Otterbein Coll., Westerville, Ohio, 1988-94; therapist, Columbus, 1989-94. Therapist, Columbus, 1989—. Mem. Pub. Rels. Soc. Am. (pres. 1986-87), Nat. Soc. Performance and Instrn., Ohio Bd. Realtors, Ohio State U. Pres. Club, Ohio State U. Alumni (life),Pres of Bd. All The World's A Stage; Bd. mem. The Macomb Symphony. Lutheran. Avocation: tennis. Home: 70901 Carnegie Ln Romeo MI 48065

MATTHIS, EVA MILDRED BONEY, retired academic administrator; b. Magnolia (Waycross), NC, Aug. 18, 1927; d. James Horace and Eva Alice (Merritt) Boney; m. George Clifton Matthis, Aug. 31, 1949; 1 child, George Clifton Jr. AA, Louisburg Coll., 1946; BS, East Carolina U., 1969, MLS, 1971. Advt. mgr. Efirds, Wilmington, N.C., 1946-49; advt. acct. Lenoir Co. News, 1950; syn. aviation instrument instr. Serv-Air Aviation, Kinston, N.C., 1951-57; advt. account exec. Kinston Free Press, 1959-64; libr. Caswell Ctr., 1965-66; history tchr. North Lenoir High Sch., 1969-70; libr. Sampson Elem. Sch., 1970-72; head libr. media program Lenoir C.C., Kinston, 1972-76, dean, learning resources, 1976-89, dean, mktg. instl. devel., learning resources, 1989—90, dean, instl. advancement, 1990, v.p. instrnl. svcs., 1990—92; ret., 1992. Alumni rep. East Carolina U. LS SACS Self-study, Greenville, 1987-89. Family editor: Heritage of Lenoir County, 1981. Developer Heritage Place, local history mus., 1988; pres. Jr. Women's Club, Kinston, 1960; dist. dir. N.C. Jr. Women's Club, 1961; mem. Kinston Mayor's All-Am. City Com., 1988, co-chair, 1996-97; rep. Lenoir County Bicentennial Com., Kinston, 1987; staff-parish chmn. Queen Street United Meth. Ch., 1988-90, mem. bishop's coun., 1988-90, com. chmn., 1988-90, chmn. fin. com., 1992-94, bldg. com., 1992-94, Sunday Sch. tchr., mem. adminstrv. bd., 1984—, v.p., 2000-02, dist. chair nominations, 2003-05; mem. Kinston Mus. com., Fireman Mus. com., 1992-93; chair archtl. survey, Lenoir county, 1993; mem. SACS vis. team, Lereland, Tex., 1990; chair Louisburg Coll. Class of '46 Golden Anniversary. Named Scouting Family of Yr., 1970; recipient merit award N.C. Hist. Soc., 1989, Excellence award Kinston C. of C., 1985, Educators Office Pers. Lenoir C.C., Adminstr. of Yr. award, 1990, Pease History award, N.C. Hist. Soc., 1995. Mem. N.C. C.C. Learning Resources Assn. (life, pub. info. officer 1989-92, exec. bd., dir. dist. II 1986-89, Achievement award 1992, Hon. Mention Libr. Jour. LIbr. of Yr. 1991), Librs. of Lenoir County (pres. 1985, 92), Lenoir County Hist. Assn. (v.p., exec. bd.), Coun. on Resource Devel., Hist. Lenoir County-Kinston Celebration, East Carolina U. Alumni Assn., Phi Beta Kappa, Delta Kappa Gamma (yearbook editor). Avocations: basketmaking, reading, gardening. Home: PO Box 6340 Kinston NC 28501-0340 also: 6532 English Oak Dr Raleigh NC 27615 Personal E-mail: gmatthis@ipass.net.

MATTIAS, MONA CAROL, elementary education educator, consultant; b. Oroville, Calif., Aug. 17, 1944; d. Harvey Dean and Helen Margaret (Post) Northcutt; m. Victor LeRoy Lasley, June 10, 1967; 1 child, Robert; m. Marc M. Mathias Oct. 18, 2003. BA, Chico (Calif.) State Coll., 1966. Cert. tchr., Calif. Tchr. Thermalito Sch. Dist., Oroville, 1967-68, Pierce Joint Unified Sch. Dist., Arbuckle, Calif., 1969-88, Natomas Unified Sch. Dist., Sacramento, 1988—. Math. cons. No. Calif. Math. Project, Davis, 1986—, tchr., rschr., 1989—, mentor tchr., 1987-90, 91-92, 98-99, also co-dir. and coord. for profl. devel.; math. coach demonstration Bay Area Math. Project, Berkeley, Calif., 1990-91; cons. D-Q U. Math. and Sci. Acad. Tchrs. and Am. Indian Students, 1992-94; del. U.S.-Russia 1st Joint Conf. Math. Edn., 1993. Mem charter Grandes Dames Ctr, for the Arts, Grass Valley, 2005—; mem. Nev. County Dem. Ctrl. Com., 2005—. Grantee Calif. Math. Projects, 1990—, Calif. Math. Tech., 1992. Mem. ASCD, Nat. Coun. Tchrs. of Math., No. Calif. Math. Project, Calif. Math. Coun., Calif. Tchr.'s Assn., Northern Mines Bus. and Profl. Women. Avocations: reading, crocheting, quilting, puzzles, book and card making. Office: Jefferson Elem Sch 2001 Pebblewood Dr Sacramento CA 95833-1400 Home: 15887 Rattlesnake Rd Grass Valley CA 95945-8713

MATTICE, DEBORA J., special education educator, consultant; b. Concord, Calif., June 21, 1959; d. Fred Alexander and Sarah Elizabeth Elder; m. Galen Donald Mattice, July 24, 1993; 1 child, Paul Daniel Reininger. AS, Monroe C.C., 1990; BS, SUNY, Brockport, 1990; MS, Nazareth Coll., 1995; postgrad., Cumberland U., 2002. Cert. profl. tchg. State Dept. Edn., Tenn., permanent tchg. State of N.Y. Tchr. Rochester City Sch., 1993—94, spl. edn. tchr., 1995—96, Dede Wallace Sch., Nashville, 1996, Stones River Acad., Murfreesboro, Tenn., 1996—97, Metro Nashville Sch., 1997—. Notary pub., Tenn. Foster parent Dept. Children's Svcs., Davidson County. Mem.: Assn. Supr. and Curriculum Design, Christian Educators Assn., Nat. Geographic, Smithsonian Instn., Davison County Foster and Adoptive Care Assn. (sec. 2000—06), Am. Civil Liberties Union, Kappa Delta Epsilon Phi, Kappi Delta Pi. Democrat. Presbyterian. Avocations: reading, crafts, writing. Home: 5020 Sunshine Dr Antioch TN 37013 Office: John F Kennedy Mid Sch 5832 Pettus Rd Antioch TN 37013 Office Phone: 615-941-7515 ext. 1216.

MATTILA, MARY JO KALSEM, elementary school educator, special education educator, art educator; b. Canton, Ill., Oct. 26, 1944; d. Joseph Nelson and Bernice Nora (Milbauer) Kalsem; m. John Peter Mattila, Jan. 27, 1968. BS in Art, U. Wis., Madison, 1966; student, Ohio State U., Columbus, 1972, Drake U., Des Moines, Iowa, 1981; MS in Ednl. Adminstrn., Iowa State U., Ames, 1988. Cert. tchr., prin., supr., adminstr., art tchr., secondary tchr., Iowa. Tchr. 2d grade McHenry Pub. Schs., Ill., 1966-67, Wisconsin Hts. Schs., Black Earth, Wis., 1967-69; substitute tchr. Columbus City Schs., Ohio, 1969-70; elem. art tchr. Southwestern City Schs., Columbus, 1972-73; adminstrv. intern Ames, Iowa, 1984-86; lead tchr. at Roosevelt Sch. Ames Cmty. Schs., 1986-87, art vertical curriculum chair, 1983-89, art educator, elem. and spl. edn., 1973—2003. Contbr. articles to profl. jours. Mem. human rels. commn. City of Ames, prevention policy bd. youth and shelter svcs., Breaking Down Barriers, Ames, Iowa, 2004—. Recipient Very Spl. Svc. award for Disting. Svc. in Very Spl. Arts, Gov. of Iowa, 1984. Mem.: LWV, Ctrl. Iowa Orchid Soc., Questers, Am. Orchid Soc. Avocations: collecting old stoneware jugs, growing orchids, reading. Home: 2822 Duff Ave Ames IA 50010-4710 Office: Ames Cmty Schs 415 Stanton Ave Ames IA 50014-7331

MATTIS, CONSTANCE MARIE, controller; b. Buffalo, Aug. 28, 1960; d. William James Pierce and Welma Rebecca Armstrong; m. Mark Eugene Mattis, Aug. 27, 1983; 1 child, Colleen. BS in Acctg., Plattsburgh State U.,

1982; MBA, Gannon U., 2000. Acct. Appletree & Kern PC, CPAs, Erie, Pa., 1984-88, Zurn Industries, Inc., Erie, 1988-96; contr. Uniflow Mfg. Co., Erie, 1996—. Fin. advisor, rev. com. United Way of Erie County, 1998—. Bd. dirs. Our Lady of Mt. Carmel Sch., 1999-01. Mem. Inst. Mgmt. Accts. (dir. meetings/mem. attendance 1997—). Democrat. Roman Catholic. Avocations: golf, reading, boating, swimming. Office: Uniflow Mfg Co 1525 E Lake Rd Erie PA 16511-1088 Fax: (814) 455-6336. E-mail: cmmattis@hotmail.com.

MATTISON, KATHLENE, secondary school educator; m. Raymond Mattison. Tchr. English & Spanish Beecher-Dunbar-Pembine Sch., Pembine, Wis., 1979—. Office: Beecher-Dunbar-Pembine Sch Box 247 Sauld St Pembine WI 54156 Office Phone: 715-324-5314 102.

MATTOS GRELL, ELIZABETH, artist; b. N.Y.C., Oct. 22, 1929; d. Percy Peter Allwork and Dorothy Edna Albers; m. Martin Grell, Feb. 14, 1981; children: Shelley(dec.), Debra, Lill. One-woman shows include Kipness Gallery, Westport, Conn., 1955, Bruce Mus., Greenwich, 1968—69, Rye N.Y. Libr., 1988, exhibited in group shows at Nat. Acad. Design, Manahattan, 1951, Greenwich Village Out Door Art Fair, 1951, Contempories, N.Y.C., 1960, White Barn, Greenwich, Conn., 1961, Somers Gallery, N.Y., 1983.

MATTOX, SHARON M., lawyer; b. Wichita Falls, Tex., Oct. 4, 1952; BA, Emporia State U., 1974; JD, U. Tex., 1974, PhD, 1978. Ptnr., co-head Adminstrv. / Environ. Law Sect. Vinson & Elkins LLP, Houston. Fellow: Tex. Bar Found. Office: Vinson & Elkins LLP First City Tower 1001 Fannin St, Ste 2300 Houston TX 77002 Office Phone: 713-758-4598. E-mail: smattox@velaw.com.

MATTRELLA, ANNE LAURA, secondary school educator; b. Waterbury, Conn., Aug. 30, 1954; d. Jack and Victoria (Tomasiello) M. Student, U. Salamanca (Spain), 1975, U. Dijon (France), 1976; BA, U. Conn., 1976, MA, 1979; PhD, Cath. U., Washington, 1985, cert. in adminstrn. and supervision, 1991. Cert. adminstr./supr. Supr. Project Promesa, Waterbury, 1979; translator Embassy of Ecuador, Washington, 1980-81; editor, transcriber Internat. Monetary Fund, Washington, 1982; press analyst Embassy of Japan, Washington, 1982-85; coord. English as a second lang. dept. Southeastern U., Washington, 1985-88; prof. So. Conn. State U., New Haven, 1988—91; fgn. lang. instr. Roberto Clemente Mid. Sch., New Haven, 1988—91; prof. U. Conn., Conn., 1993—97; assoc. prof. foreign languages Naugatuck Valley CC, 1997—. Lectr. for various convs. including Tchrs. of English to Speakers of Other Langs. Nat. Conv., Miami, Fla., 1987, San Juan, 1987-88, Georgetown U., Washington, 1988. Author: An ESL Approach to Hemingway, 1989; contbr. articles to various jours. Mem. exec. bd. Hispanic Cultural Soc. Mem. AAUP, N.E. MLA, S.E. MLA, Nat. Italian Am. Found., Tchrs. of English to Speakers of Other Langs., Conn. Assn. Adult and Continuing Edn., Columbus Day, Inc. Phi Beta Kappa, Phi Kappa Phi, Kappa Kappa Gamma. Republican. Roman Catholic.

MATTSON, CAROL LINNETTE, social services administrator; b. Frederic, Wis., Oct. 3, 1946; d. Clarence Waldemar and Lucille Anna Mathilda (Bengtson) Hedlund; m. Wesley Harlan Mattson, June 24, 1967; 1 child, Aaron Ray. BS, U. Wis., Menomonie, 1968. Home econs. tchr. Luck (Wis.) High Sch., 1968-72; clk. Daniels Twp., Siren, Wis., 1973-75; family living instr. Wis. Indianhead Tech. Inst., New Richmond, 1974-77; aging program dir. Polk County, Balsam Lake, Wis., 1977—. Treas., bd. dirs. Polk County Transp. for the Disabled and Elderly, Inc., Balsam Lake, 1978—; mem. com. Long Term Support Com., Balsam Lake, 1985—. Mem. Wis. Assn. Nutrition Dirs., Wis. Assn. Aging Unit Dirs. Lutheran. Avocations: reading, needlecraft. Office: Polk County Aging Programs 300 Polk County Plz Ste 20 Balsam Lake WI 54810-9096

MATTSSON, LISA MILLER, lawyer, social worker; b. Duluth, Minn., June 11, 1954; d. Charlene Peura Miller; m. Donald Marvin Mattsson, Jr., Oct. 23, 1986; children: Nicole Hope Walter, Ryan Roy Walter. BS, U. Minn., 1985, MSW, 1987; JD, Drake U., 2003. Bar: Iowa 2004, U.S. Dist. Ct. (so. dist.) Iowa 2004, U.S. Ct. Appeals (eighth cir.) 2004. Mgr. purchasing and traffic Diamond Tool & Horseshoe Co., Duluth, Minn., 1981—83; adminstr. group therapy Mt. Sinai Optifast Program, Mpls., 1987—90; clin. social worker, orgnl. cons. Consulting Practice, Mpls., 1990—99; mortgage loan officer Conseco Fin., Des Moines, 1999—2001; assoc. Benzoni Law Office, P.L.C., Des Moines, 2004—06. Adj. prof. social work U. St. Thomas, St. Paul, 1996—97. Mem. women's leadership com. Soka Gakkai Internat.-USA, Des Moines, 1998—2005. Recipient Pub. Svc. scholarship; scholar, Drake U. Law Sch., 2001—03. Mem.: Iowa Bar Assn. Dfl. Avocations: travel, making jewelry, scrapbooks. Office: Benzoni Law Office PLC 2912 Beaver Ave Des Moines IA 50310 Home: 91 Stoneyside Ln Olivette MO 63132 Business E-Mail: lmattsson@sbcglobal.net.

MATULICH, ERIKA, marketing educator; b. Sacramento, Sept. 14, 1963; d. Serge and Margarete (Manderscheid) M.; m. John H. Porter, 1995. BBA, Tex. Christian U., 1984, MBA, 1986; PhD, U. Wis., 1994. Profl. cert. marketer. Ops. officer M Bank Dallas, 1986-87; ops. analyst Bell Helicopter, Textron, Ft. Worth, 1987-89; teaching asst. U. Wis., Madison, 1989-92; instr. Tex. Christian U., Ft. Worth, 1986-89, asst. prof. mktg., 1993-98; assoc. prof. mktg. U. Tampa, Fla., 1998—. Market researcher All Saints Epis. Hosp., Ft. Worth, 1984, Shakespeare in the Park, Ft. Worth, 1985, Informart, Dallas, 1985; strategic planner Williamson-Dickie, Ft. Worth, 1985; presenter at confs. Editor: Pets.com, 1999—2000. Mem. Am. Mktg. Assn. (bd. dirs.), Soc. Mktg. Advances (Tchg. Champion 2001), Acad. Mktg. Sci., Ferret Lovers' Club Tex. (pres. 1996-98), Beta Gamma Sigma. Avocations: carriage driving, computers, ferrets, drawing. Office: U Tampa Box 105F 401 W Kennedy Blvd Tampa FL 33606-1450 Office Phone: 813-253-6221 3187. Business E-Mail: ematulich@ut.edu.

MATUS-MENDOZA, MARIADELALUZ, language educator, sociologist; b. Mexico City, Apr. 10, 1961; arrived in U.S., 1991; d. MariadelaPaz Matus-Mendoza; m. Geoffrey Fitch, Sept. 3, 1993. BA in English Lit. and Applied Lang., Mex. Autonoman U., Mexico City, 1984; MA, Temple U., 1993, PhD, 1999. Tchr. Mex. Autonomon U., 1984—91; tchg. asst. Temple U., Phila., 1991—94, adj. instr., 1994—95, LuSulle U., Phila., 1995—98, U. Pa., Phila., 1996—99; asst. prof. Spanish U. Ctrl. Fla., Orlando, 1999—2001, Drexel U., Phila., 2001—. Cons. ETS, Princeton, NJ, 2001—. Mem.: MLA, Am. Assn. Tchrs. of Spanish and Portugese, Nat. Assn. Hispanic and Latino Studies. Roman Catholic. Office: Drexel Univ 229 N 33rd St Philadelphia PA 19104

MATUSZAK, ALICE JEAN BOYER, pharmacy educator; b. Newark, Ohio, June 22, 1935; d. James Emery and Elizabeth Hawthorne (Irvine) Boyer; m. Charles Alan Matuszak, Aug. 27, 1955; children: Matthew, James. BS summa cum laude, Ohio State U., 1958, MS, 1959; postgrad., U. Wis., 1959-60; PhD, U. Kans., 1963. Registered pharmacist, Ohio, Calif. Apprentice pharmacist Arensberg Pharmacy, Newark, 1953-58; rsch. asst. Ohio State U., Columbus, 1958, lab. asst., 1958-59; rsch. asst. U. Wis., Madison, 1959-60, U. Kans., Lawrence, 1960-63; asst. prof. U. of the Pacific, Stockton, Calif., 1963-67, assoc. prof., 1971-78, prof., 1978—2000, prof. emerita, 2000—; order of Pacific, 2000. Vis. fgn. prof. Kobe-Gakuin U., Japan, 1992. Contbr. articles to profl. jours. Mem. rev. bd. U.S. Adopted Names Commn. Recipient Disting. Alumna award Ohio State U. Coll. Pharmacy, 1994, Profl. Frat. Assn. Career Achievement award, 2000, Order of Pacific award U. of Pacific, 2000; NIH grantee, 1965-66. Fellow Am. Pharm. Assn. (chmn. basic scis. 1990); mem. Am. Assn. Colls. of Pharmacy (chmn. chemistry sect. 1979-80, bd. dirs. 1993-95), Am. Inst. History of Pharmacy (exec. coun. 1984-88, 90-92, 92-95, chmn. contributed papers 1990-92, pres.-elect 1995-97, pres. 1997—99, cert. of commendation 1990), Am. Chem. Soc., Internat. Fedn. Pharmacy, Acad. Pharm. Rsch. Sci. (pres. 1993-94), Coun. Sci. Soc. Pres., U.S. Adopted Names Coun. Review Bd., U.S. Pharmacopeial Conv., Clan Irwin Assn., Donald Salvatori Calif. Pharmacy Mus., Sigma Xi, Rho Chi, Phi Lambda Sigma, Phi Kappa Phi, Kappa Epsilon (Unicorn award, award of merit 1995, Merck Vanguard leadership award 2000), Lambda Kappa Sigma, Delta Zeta. Democrat. Episcopalian. Avocation: collecting pharmacy artifacts. Home: 1130 W Mariposa Ave Stockton CA 95204-3021 Office: U Pacific Sch Pharmacy Stockton CA 95211-0001 E-mail: amatuszak@pacific.edu.

MATYAS, CINDY SUSANNE, psychologist, educator; b. Pasadena, Calif., Jan. 4, 1971; d. John Robert and Louise Natalie Matyas. AA, Pasadena City Coll., Calif., 1992; BS in Psychology, UCLA, 1994; MS in Ednl. Psychology and Counseling (hon.), Calif. State U., Northridge, 1999. Sch. psychologist LA Unified Sch. Dist., Sun Valley, Calif., 1999—; prof. Calif. State U., Northrdige, 2002—. Vol. crisis response team LA County Mayor's Office, LA, 2006—. Mem.: NASP, LA Assn. Sch. Psychologists, Calif. Assn. Sch. Psychologists. Personal E-mail: matyascs@yahoo.com.

MATYI, CINDY LOU, psychology professor, consultant; b. Toledo, Ohio, Feb. 22, 1955; d. Carol Ann and Robert Morris Patterson (Stepfather); 1 child, Tanya Nicole. PhD, Ohio U., Athens, Ohio, 1989. Lic. clin. psychologist Ohio, 1990. Asst. prof. psychology Ohio U., Chillicothe, Ohio, 1990—. Referring travel agent Your Travel Bus., Edwardsville, Ill., 2006—; cons. in field. Named Faculty Mem. of Yr., Ohio U., Chillicothe, 1998, Cons. of Yr., Ohio Assn. Disability Examiners, 2006. Democrat. Avocations: travel, creative writing, crafts, gardening. Office: Ohio University-Chillicothe 101 University Drive Chillicothe OH 45601 Personal E-mail: matyi@ohio.edu.

MATYSKIELA, KRISTINA L., director; b. Wheeling, W.Va., Nov. 7, 1972; d. Robert W. and Edith A. (Letzelter) Milvet; m. Eric Matyskiela, June 4, 1994. Cert. in surg. tech., W.Va. No. CC, Wheeling, 2000, AS, 2002; BA, W.Va. U., Morgantown, 2004. Cert. sci. tutor W.Va. No. CC, 2006. Program coord., part time faculty W.Va. No. CC, 2005—. Adj. faculty West Liberty State Coll., W.Va., 2005. Artist Holocaust Memls., 1990—. Vol. W.Va. No. CC, 2006—; mem. String of Pearls/Ladies of Grace, Wheeling, 2006. Daniel B. Purinton, Jr. scholar in philosophy, W.Va. U. Dept. Philosophy, 2004. Mem.: NRA (assoc.), Am. Philos. Assn. (assoc.). American Independent. Reformed Baptist. Avocations: outdoors, camping, bass fishing, hunting, hiking. Office: WV No CC 1704 Market St Wheeling WV 26003 Personal E-mail: matyskiela@fastmail.fm. Business E-Mail: klmatyskiela@northern.wvnet.edu.

MATZKIN, ELIZABETH, orthopedic sports medicine surgeon; d. Michael and Sara Matzkin; m. Eric Smith, Apr. 24, 1999; children: Abigail Smith, Samantha Smith. MD, Tulane U., 1998. Diplomate Am. Bd. Orthopedic Surgery. Orthopaedic resident U. Hawaii, Honolulu, 1998—2003; sports medicine fellow Duke U., Durham, NC, 2003—04; sports medicine physician Foundry Sports Medicine, Providence, 2004—. Team physician US Women's Soccer. Contbr. articles to profl. publs. Recipient 1st Pl. Resident Rsch. award, AAP, 2003, 1st Pl. Richardson award, HOA, 2000, 2003; fellow, OO-OREF, 2003. Mem.: AANA (assoc.), AOSSM (assoc.), AAOS (assoc.), Alpha Omega Alpha.

MAU, C. S. See SALERNO, CHERIE

MAU, LISA ANNE, special education educator; b. Niskayuna, NY, Jan. 13, 1966; d. Joanne Elizabeth and William DiCaprio; m. Matthew Walter Mau, July 1, 1989; 1 child, Joshua Matthew. AA in Early Childhood Edn. with high honors, SUNY, Cobleskill, 1986; BS in Spl. Edn. magna cum laude, Coll. St. Rose, Albany, 1988, M with honors, 1993. Cert. Tchr. NY Dept. Edn., 1993. Spl. edn. tchr. grades 3-5 Middleburgh Elem., NY, 1988—. Wilson reading tchr. Middleburgh Elem., 2002—. Home: 405 Glen Ave Scotia NY 12302 Office: Middleburgh Elem Sch 245 Main St Middleburgh NY 12122 Office Phone: 518-827-3600.

MAUCH, DIANE FARRELL, music educator; b. Flushing, NY, Jan. 15, 1934; d. Edward Joseph Farrell and Adelaide Mary Hopkins; m. Robert Kurt Mauch, Aug. 24, 1963; children: Anneliese Farrell, Bronwen Adele. MusB, Manhattanville Coll., 1955; MusM, U. Mich., 1971; postgrad., Juilliard Sch. Music, Manhattan Sch. Music, Aspen Music Sch. Cert. tchr. Fla. Bd. Edn., ministry formation cert. Nat. Assn. Pastoral Musicians. Asst. prof. music Trevecca Coll., Nashville, 1973—77; music tchr. St. Bernard Acad., Nashville, 1976—82; music specialist Carrollton Sch., Coconut Grove, Fla., 1983—99; assoc. faculty vocal performance U. Miami, Coral Gables, Fla., 1994—. Music rep. Sch. Arts Planning, Ann Arbor, Mich., 1969—72; dir. Liturgy Com., Nashville, 1975—83; adj. prof. music Scarritt Coll., Nashville, 1976—80, Miami-Dade C.C., 1983—90; dir. edn. Fla. Grand Opera, Miami, 1990—93; del. Children Cultural Coalition, Miami, 1990—93; music rep. Visual and Performing Arts Steering Com., Miami, 1991—94; opera cons. Opera Am., Washington, 1992—94; choir dir. St. Mary's, Manchester, Mich., 1966—69, St. Lawrence Ch., North Miami Beach, Fla., 1984—86; soloist St. Henry, Nashville, 1975—82, Ch. by the Sea, Bal Harbour, Mich., 1991—2001. Contbr. chapters to books;, performer (radio, concert, opera, oratorios). Chairperson Cmty. Concerts, Nashville, 1976—78; active Dade County Cultural Coalition, Miami, 1998—. Recipient Leadership award, Nat. Assn. Pastoral Musicians, Washington, 1980; grantee, NEA, 1977, NEH, 1991; scholar, Cambridge U., 2004. Mem.: Miami Music Tchrs. Assn., Music Tchrs. Nat. Assn. (permanent nat. profl. cert., honors chair, v.p., scholarship chair), Nat. Assn. Tchrs. Singing (past officer, v.p., pres., auditions chair). Roman Catholic. Avocations: travel, linguistics and languages, choral singing. Home: 10645-C SW 113 Pl Miami FL 33176 Office: U Miami Foster Bldg San Amaro Dr Miami FL 33124

MAUCK, ELAINE CAROLE, retired secondary education educator; b. Martinsburg, W.Va., Dec. 25, 1946; d. Ace William and June Elaine Gray; m. Jess Willard Mauck Jr., May 26, 1972. BA in Secondary Edn., Shepherd Coll., 1968; MS in Phys. Edn., W.Va. U., 1977. Cert. tchr., W.Va., appraiser Inst. of Appraisal of Personal Property, 2000. Libr. asst. Shepherd (W.Va.) Coll., 1964-68; libr., rschr. King Daus. Nursing Sch., Martinsburg, W.Va., 1967-68; tchr. Washington Co. Schs., Hagerstown, Md., 1968-69, Berkele County Schs., Martinsburg, 1969-99; ret., 1999; owner E&J Enterprizes, 1985—, Silver Age Svcs., 1996—, Crim de la Crim, 2000—. Mem. phys. edn. Mountain Top Summit W.Va. Bd. Edn., Charleston, 1993-95, Health Schs. com., 1990-93, Nutrition Cadre com., 1987-99; spkr. U. N.C., 1990. Mem. Calvary Meth. Ch., Martinsburg. Recipient Excellence award Berkeley County Sch. Bus., 1987-94, W.Va. Fitness award Pres.'s Challenge, 1992; grantee Women's Found., 1992. Mem. W.Va. Edn. Assn. (polit. action com. 1983-92), AAHPERD (Secondary Tchr. award 1993), W.Va. Alliance Health, Phys. Edn., Recreation, and Dance (Secondary Tchr. award 1992), Wash. County Hist. Soc., Berkely County Hist. Soc., Easton Panhandle Assn. Ins. and Fin. Advs. (v.p. 2005-06) Home: 263 Nameless Way Martinsburg WV 25401-9803 Office Phone: 304-260-9394.

MAUE, LETA JO, instructional support teacher; b. York, Pa., Dec. 7, 1951; d. Wilford Thomas and Helen Louise Myers; m. Frederick Robert Maue, Sept. 24, 1994; children: Frederick C., Patrick P. BS in Elem. Edn., Mansfield U., 1973; MA in Spl. Edn., Shippensburg U., 1979; Cert. in Supervision of Spl. Edn., Bloomsburg U., 1998. Cert. in reality therapy. Elem. tchr. Shikellamy Sch. Dist., Sunbury, Pa., 1973-76, spl. edn. tchr., 1986-90, instrnl. support diagnostician, 1990-97, spl. edn. supr., 1997—; tchr. of gifted York (Pa.) Suburban Sch. Dist., 1976-83. Dir. Camp Pennwood, York County Arc, 1982-83; staff devel. trainer Shikellamy Sch. Dist., 1991—, supt. leadership adv. coun., 1997—. Mem. Local Right to Edn. task force, Danville, Pa., 1997—, Susquehanna Valley Chorale, 2001—06; mem. coun. Zion Luth. Ch., 1990—94, pres. coun., 1993—94, mem. choir, 1984—; bd. dirs. Northumberland County ARC; mem. adv. bd. McCann Bus. Sch. Mem. Coun. for Exceptional Children awarded profl. spl. edn. adminstrn. (CEC, 2001), William Glasser Inst., SAI Hon. Music Frat. Avocations: playing piano, singing, opera, travel, camping. Home: 168 N 11th St Sunbury PA 17801-2444 Office: Shikellamy Sch Dist 200 Island Blvd Sunbury PA 17801-1028

MAUGANS, STACY, music educator, musician; b. Kokomo, Ind., Feb. 20, 1969; d. John Conrad and Judith Marie Maugans. BA, MusB, Ind. U., 1992, MusD, 2000; MusM, Ariz. State U., 1994. Pvt. music tchr., Ariz., Tex. and Ind., 1985—; musician Tex. Wind Symphony, Ft. Worth, 1997—2001; asst. prof. music Valparaiso (Ind.) U., 2002—, asst. dean Coll. Arts and Scis., 2004—. Contest judge Ind. State Sch. Music Assn., 2002—. Editor: (jour.) Saxophone Symposium, 2005. Vol. pet ptnr. team Delta Soc., Valparaiso, 2002—; mem. choir, instrumentalist Immanuel Luth. Ch., Valparaiso, 2001—. Recipient award for woodwinds or brass, Coleman Chamber Music Competition, Pasadena, Calif., 1994; grantee, Social Sci. Rsch. Coun., 1996; fgn. lang. area studies fellow, US Dept. Edn., 1997. Mem.: Math. Assn. Am., N.Am. Saxophone Alliance, Mensa. Avocations: dog training, reading, running, bicycling. Office: Valparaiso U 1709 Chapel Dr Valparaiso IN 46383 Office Phone: 219-464-5469.

MAUKE, LEAH RACHEL, retired counselor; b. Newport, R.I., Aug. 29, 1924; d. Louis and Annie (Price) Louison; m. Otto Russell Mauke, June 18, 1950. BSBA, Boston U., 1946, MBA, 1948. Teaching fellow Boston U., 1946-48; head advt. dept. Endicott Coll., Beverly, Mass., 1948-66; guidance counselor Vineland (N.J.) Sr. High Sch., 1966-69, Black Horse Pike Regional Sch. Dist., Blackwood, N.J., 1969-86, ret., 1986. Vol. ARC, Vero Beach, Fla., 1988—. Boston U. fellow 1946. Mem. AAUW (life, pres. North Shore br. 1955-59, state fellowship chmn. 1957-58), NEA, N.J. Edn. Assn., Camden County Pers. and Guidance Assn. (sec. 1972). Avocations: reading, travel, crossword puzzles. Home: 2119 E Lakeview Dr Sebastian FL 32958-8519

MAUL, CAROL ELAINE, small business owner; b. Joliet, Ill., Feb. 28, 1953; d. Donald James and Virginia Olive (Wilson) Johnson; m. Richard Kester Maul, June 16, 1979. Student, Met. State Coll., 1971-76. Mgr. So-Fro Fabrics, Elgin, 1976-79; owner, operator Port Arthur Pie Co., Denver, 1985-87; freelance musician Denver, 1987—; owner CAMA Creative Mktg. Bus. Promotion, Profl. Voice Work. Prin. flutist Elgin Symphony Orch., 1976-79; mem. Denver Botanic Gardens. Mem. Colo. Rail Passenger Assn., Nat. Trust Hist. Preservation, Citizens for Classical FM Radio (bd. dirs.), Colo. Water Garden Soc., Denver Garden Railway Soc., Rocky Mtn. Koi Club. Independent. Episcopalian. Lodge: Job's Daughters (Honored Queen 1970-71). Avocations: needlepoint, calligraphy. Home and Office: 387 S Pontiac Way Denver CO 80224-1335

MAUMENEE, IRENE H., ophthalmology educator; b. Bad Pyrmont, Germany, Apr. 30, 1940; MD, U. Gottingen, 1964. Cert. Am. Bd. Ophthalmology, Am. Bd. Med. Genetics. Rsch. asst. U. Hawaii, 1968; vis. geneticist Population Genetics Lab., 1968-69; fellow dept. medicine Johns Hopkins U., 1969-71; ophthalmology preceptorship Wilmer Inst. Johns Hopkins Hosp., 1969-71, from asst. prof. to assoc. prof. Wilmer Ophthalmology Inst., 1972-87; prof. ophthalmology and pediatrics Wilmer Ophthalmology Inst., 1972—; dir. Johns Hopkins Ctr. Hereditary Eye Disease, Wilmer Inst., 1979—. Cons. John F. Kennedy Inst. Visually & Mentally Handicapped Children, 1974—; dir. Low Vision Clinic, Wilmer Inst., 1977-88; vis. prof. French Ophthalmology Soc., Paris & French Acad. Medicine, 1988; advisor Nat. Eye Inst. Task Forces, 1976, 81. Mem. AMA, Am. Soc. Human Genetics, Am. Acad. Ophthalmology, Assn. Rsch. Vision & Ophthalmology, Internat. Soc. Genetic Eye Disease, Am. Ophthal. Soc., Pan Am. Assn. Ophthalmology. Achievements include research in nosology and management of ophthalmic and general medical genetics; population genetics; computer application to genetic analysis; molecular genetics; over 200 publications on human genetics and eye diseases. Office: Johns Hopkins Ctr Hereditary Eye Diseases 600 N Wolfe St # 517 Baltimore MD 21287-0005 E-mail: jhched@jhmi.edu.

MAUN, MARY ELLEN, computer consultant; b. NYC, Dec. 18, 1951; d. Emmet Joseph and Mary Alice (McMahon) M. BA, CUNY, 1977, MBA, 1988. Sales rep. N.Y. Telephone Co., N.Y.C., 1970-76, comml. rep., 1977-83, programmer, 1984-86; systems analyst Telesector Resources Group, N.Y.C., 1987-89, sr. systems analyst, 1990-95; pres. Sleepy Hollow (N.Y.) Techs., Inc., N.Y., 1995—. Corp. chmn. United Way of Tri-State Area, N.Y.C., 1985; recreation activities vol. Pioneers Am., N.Y.C., 1982—; active Sleepy Hollow Hist. Soc.; founder Mary Ellen Maun Philanthropic Found., 1998; dist. leader for Dem. Party Tarrytown Recipient Outstanding Community Service award, Calvary Hosp., Bronx, N.Y., 1984. Mem. N.Y. Health and Racquet Club, Road Runners. Avocations: antique restoration, classical music, skiing, running. Office: Sleepy Hollow Techs Inc 539 Martling Ave Tarrytown NY 10591-4719 E-mail: mauningnews@msn.com.

MAUNEY, BRANDI SAVAGE, special education diagnostician; b. Miami, Mar. 5, 1976; d. Victor Martin and Yvonne Marie Savage; m. John David Mauney, Mar. 30, 1975. B in Psychology, Ga. Coll. and State U., 1999, M in Spl. Edn., 2004; student in Child, Youth and Human Svcs., Nova Southeastern U., 2005—. Cert. tchr. Profl. Stds. Commn. in Ga. Spl. edn. tchr. Henry County Bd. of Edn., McDonough, Ga., 2002—04, spl. edn. liason/diagnostician, 2004—. Spl. edn. homebound tchr. for medically fragile Henry Count Bd. of Edn., McDonough, 2004—. Mem.: Collaboration Team: Direct On-going Tng. of Adminstrn. and Staff, State Monitoring Com. (assoc.), Continuous Improvement Monitoring Com. (assoc.), Interagency Child Coun. (assoc.; com. chair 2005—05), Sigma Alpha Iota (life; v.p. 1995—97). Republican. Baptist. Achievements include research in effects of Child-Find and Early Intervention. Avocations: music, swimming, yoga, travel, bicycling. Home: 70 Mountain Ct Covington GA 30016 Office: Henry County Bd Edn 33 N Zack Hinton Pkwy Mcdonough GA 30253 Office Phone: 770-316-5830. Personal E-mail: brandisavage@yahoo.com. E-mail: bmauney@henry.k12.ga.us.

MAUPIN, ELIZABETH THATCHER, theater critic; b. Cleve., Oct. 21, 1951; d. Addison and Margaret (Thatcher) M.; m. Jay Yellen, Dec. 29, 1995. BA in English, Wellesley (Mass.) Coll., 1973; M in Journalism, U. Calif., Berkeley, 1976. Editorial asst. Houghton Mifflin Co., Boston, 1973-74; reporter, movie critic Times-Standard, Eureka, Calif., 1976-78; theater and movie critic Chronicle-Telegram, Elyria, Ohio, 1978-79; movie critic Ledger-Star, Norfolk, Va., 1979-82; feature writer Va.-Pilot and Ledger-Star, Norfolk, 1982-83; sr. theater critic Orlando (Fla.) Sentinel, 1983—. Fellow Nat. Arts Journalism program Columbia U., 1995-96. Fellow Nat. Critics Inst.; mem. Am. Theatre Critics Assn. (exec. com. 1993-99, 05-06, chair 1996-99). Office: Orlando Sentinel 633 N Orange Ave Orlando FL 32801-1349

MAUPIN, KARIN LOUISE, secondary school educator; d. Alfred Bertil and Kathryn Louise (Snapp) Swanson; m. Bernard Kent Fredrick Maupin, Aug. 11, 1973; children: Kristin Louise, Kevin Alfred. BA in Anthropology, Northwestern U., 1970, tchg. cert., 1972; postgrad., U. Ill., 1972—73, Aquinas Coll., 1994—95; M in Spl. Edn. and Learning Disabilities, Calvin Coll., 1998. Commodities trading asst. E.F. Hutton & Co., Chgo., 1972—73; comml. paper trader Montgomery Ward Credit Corp., Chgo., 1973—77; tchr. Creative Learning Ctr., Grand Rapids, Mich., 1982—83; program dir. Alternative Methods for Internat. Stability/Trees Corps., 1989—; tutor SLD Ctr., Grand Rapids, 1995—98; substitute tchr. Forest Hills Pub. Schs., Grand Rapids, 1996—97, tchr., 1997—. Odyssey of the Mind coach Forest Hills No. Middle Sch., Grand Rapids, 1995; adult sponsor F.O.M.E. Environ. Club Forest Hills No. H.S., 1995—98. Contbg. editor: mag. Our Children, 1991—93. Tutor Head Start Program, Grand Rapids, Mich., 1966, James Taylor Sch., Chgo., 1971, Cabrini Green Housing Project, 1976—77; vol. curator Field Mus. Natural History, Chgo., 1978—80; vol. curator, docent Grand Rapids Pub. Mus., 1981—83; bd. mem. Summerfest Ballet Sch., 1983—85; pres. Kent County Med. Soc. Aux., 1984—85; coord. Citizens Liability Action Com., 1984—87; legis. chmn. Mich. State Med. Soc. Aux., 1985—87; pres. Coffinberry Archaeol. Soc., 1988; bd. mem. Children's Inter-active Sci. Ctr., 1995—99, SLD Learning Ctr. Western Mich., 1995—99; rep. Northwestern U. Alumni, 1996—; mem. edn. com. Frederik Meijer Gardens, 1997—2001. Recipient Cert. Appreciation, Mich. State Med. Soc., 1987, AMA, 1987, Letter Appreciation for environ. stewardship, Former Pres. Gerald R. Ford, 1989, Achievement award, Global Releaf, 1990, Letter Appreciation for environ. stewardship, Pres. George Bush, 1992, Cert. Appreciation, Gov. Engler, Mich. Office of Governor, 1992, Cmty. Svc.

award, Mich. Forestry & Park Assn., 1992, State Winner, Pres. Bush's Take Pride in Am., 1992, Nongovtl. Agy. award for environ. stewardship, Mich. Audubon Soc., 1993, Letter Appreciation, Kent County Commrs., 1994, Cert. Appreciation, Grand Rapids Pub. Schs., 1994, Pres. Clinton's Coun. on Sustainable Development, 1997. Avocations: travel, gardening, tennis, bicycling, golf. Office: Forest Hills Pub Schs 6590 Cascade Rd SE Grand Rapids MI 49506 E-mail: amistrees@aol.com.

MAURAS, NELLY, pediatrics professor, department chairman, researcher; b. PR, Nov. 4, 1956; m. Gerardo Colon-Otero; 3 children. BS in Chemistry magna cum laude, U. PR, San Juan, 1977, MD, 1981. Diplomate Am. Bd. Endocrinology, Am. Bd. Pediatrics, Nat. Bd. Med. Examiners. Intern in pediat. Mayo Grad. Sch. Medicine, Rochester, Minn., 1981—84; fellow in pediatric endocrinology U. Va. Med. Ctr., Charlottesville, 1984—86; chief divsn. endocrinology The Nemours Children's Clinic, 1987—; med. dir. CRC Wolfson Children's Hosp., Jacksonville, 1997—; asst. prof. pediat. Mayo Med. Sch., 1996—2002, prof. pediat., 2002. Tchr. vis. med. students and pediat. residents Mayo Clinic; tchr. pediatric residency program U. Fla./Mayo Clinic-Jacksonville Family Practice Program; rschr., invited nat. and internat. spkr., presenter in field. Mem. editl. bd. Metabolism, 1996—; contbr. chapters to books, articles to profl. jours. Named Most Outstanding Attending U. Fla., Jacksonville Program, 1992; recipient Pediatric Travel award, Mayo Clinic, John A. Beals award med. rsch., Duval County Med. Soc., 1990, 1999, Nemours Excellence Acad. Achievement award, 2004. Mem.: Soc. Pediatric Rsch., Lawson Wilkins Pediatric Endocrine Soc., Internat. Soc. Insulin-Like Growth Factor Rsch., Growth Hormone Rsch. Soc., Fla. Med. Assn., Duval County Med. Soc. (assoc. editor bulletin 1987—89, chmn. Beals Awards com. 1989), Am. Diabetes Assn. Home: 5844 Clifton Ave Jacksonville FL 32211 Office: The Nemours Children's Clinic 807 Children's Way Jacksonville FL 32207 Office Phone: 904-390-3674. Business E-Mail: nmauras@nemours.org.

MAURER, KAREN ANN, special education educator; b. New Kensington, Pa., Apr. 5, 1954; d. James Clair and Carrie Carmella (Siciliano) Blissell; m. Kevin Michael Maurer, June 25, 1983; children: Kevin Shawn, Kari Ann, Katelyn Elisabeth. BS in Elem. Edn./Spl. Edn., Edinboro U. of Pa., 1976, MEd in Mental Retardation, 1979, behavior mgmt. specialist cert., 1979. Cert. Pa. Instructional II; cert. emotional support tchr. Tchr. of mental/phys. handicapped preschs. Dr. Gertrude A Barber Ctr., Erie, Pa., 1976-80; tchr. of primary socially/emotionally disturbed students N.W. Tri County Intermediate Unit, Edinboro, Pa., 1980-83; tchr. h.s. emotionally disturbed students Allegheny Intermediate Unit, Pitts., 1983-91, South Fayette Twp. Sch. Dist., McDonald, Pa., 1991—. Lead tchr. elem. spl. edn. dept. South Fayette Elem. Sch., McDonald, 1992-93; master tchr. elem spl. edn. dept. N.W. Tri-County Intermediate Unit, Edinboro, 1981-83; presenter staff devel. South Fayette Twp. Schs., McDonald, 1993. Life mem. Girl Scouts of Am., N.Y.C., 1998—; sponsor Multicultural Club of South Fayette H.S., McDonald, 1995—. Mem. Coun. for Exceptional Children, Pa. State Edn. Assn. (rep.), Pa. Assn. of Supervision and Curriculum Devel. (western region), Pa. Middle Sch. Assn. Democrat. Roman Catholic. Avocations: singing, sewing, church work. Home: 42 W Manilla Ave Pittsburgh PA 15220-2838 Office: South Fayette Twp Sch Dist 3700 Old Oakdale Rd Mc Donald PA 15057-2580 E-mail: maurer@southfayette.org.

MAURER, MARSHA KURS, art educator; d. Bernard Kurs and Anne Buchman; m. Richard William Maurer, Apr. 27, 1982; children: Parris Brandon Wood, Richard William III, Anne Kathryn. BA magna cum laude, Christopher Newport U., 2001; MFA, Old Dominion, Norfolk State U., 2005. RN, Va., 2005. Intensive care and emergency RN Norfolk (Va.) Gen. Hosp., 1973—76; charge nurse Tidewater Psychiat. Inst., Norfolk, 1976—80; artist Am. Craft Coun., Norfolk, 1990—91; artist, educator Old Dominion U., Norfolk, 2001—; artist, educator Christopher Newport U., Newport News, Va., 2004—. Faculty adv. Hillel, Newport News, 2005—. Stain glass installation, Women of the Old Testament, painting, Vardner, 3-D sculpture, creche, 3-D sculptures, Angels Of The Creche, 10 painting installation with video, 10 Prinzhorn Patients: A Study in Isolation. Lectr. So. Jewish Hist. Soc., Atlanta, 2002—05. Recipient Mayor's award, City of Newport News, 2001. Mem.: Collage Arts Assn. (assoc.), Alpha Chi (assoc. membership 2001). Personal E-mail: m.maurer@gmail.com.

MAURER, VIRGINIA GALLAHER, law educator; b. Shawnee, Okla., Nov. 7, 1946; d. Paul Clark Gallaher and Virginia Ruth (Watson) Abernathy; m. Ralph Gerald Maurer, July 31, 1971; children: Ralph Emmett, William Edward. BA, Northwestern U., 1968; MA, Stanford U., 1969, JD, 1975. Bar: Iowa 1976. Tchr. social studies San Mateo H.S. Dist., Calif., 1969—71; spl. asst. to pres. U. Iowa, Iowa City, 1976—80, adj. asst. prof. law, 1979—80; affiliate asst. prof. law U. Fla., Gainesville, 1981, asst. prof. bus. law, 1980—85, assoc. prof., 1985—93, prof., 1993—, Huber Hurst prof., 1997—. Dir. Poe Bus. Ethics Ctr., 1998—, MBA program U. Fla., 1987, chair dept. mgmt., 1994-2003; vis. scholar Wolfson Coll., Cambridge, 1994; vis. prof. SDA Bocconi U., Milan, 1994-96, Helsinki Sch. Econs. and Bus., 1998, U. Catania, Sicily, 1999, 2002-03; cons. Gov.'s Com. on Iowa 2000, Iowa City, 1976-77, Fla. Banker's Assn., Gainesville, 1982, various law firms, 1995—; bd. dirs. Water & Air Rsch., Inc Contbr. articles to profl. jours.; jr. editor Am. Bus. Law Jour., 1989-90, mng. editor, 1990-91, editor-in-chief, 1992-94 Bd. dirs. Gainesville Chamber Orch., 1990-93; fundraising com. Pro Arte Musica, Gainesville, 1980-84; sr. warden, vestry Holy Trinity Episc. Ch., 1991-93, 99—, jr. warden, 2000-02; bd. dirs. Holy Trinity Found., Gainesville, 1991-93; com. charter and canon law Episc. Diocese Fla., 1994-96; bd. dirs. Samaritan Ctrs. of North Ctrl. Fla., Inc., 1995-97 Named Fla. Bluekey Disting. Faculty mem., 2004, Woman of Distinction, Alachua County, 2005. Fellow Soc. Advanced Legal Studies (UK); mem. ABA, AAUW, Acad. Legal Studies in Bus. (ho. of dels. 1989-90, exec. com. 1992, 98—, sec.-treas. 1998-99, v.p. 1999-2000, pres-elect 2000-01, pres. 2001-02, exec. com. 2002-), Southeastern Bus. Law Assn. (proc. editor 1984-87, treas. 1985-86, v.p. 1986-87, pres.-elect 1987-88, pres. 1988-89), Iowa Bar Assn., LWV, U. Fla. Athletic Assn. (bd. dirs., v.p. chmn. fin. com.), Gainesville Womens' Forum (bd. dirs. 1988-91), Fla. Women' Network (bd. dirs. 1995-99), Univ. Woman's Club (Gainesville, Fla.), Rotary (bd. dirs. 1989-91, dist. scholarship com. 1997-99, regional scholarship com. 2000, chair 2001), Beta Gamma Sigma, Kappa Alpha Theta, Delta Sigma Pi Home: 2210 NW 6th Pl Gainesville FL 32603-1409 Office: U Fla Grad Sch Bus Gainesville FL 32611 Office Phone: 352-392-1048. Business E-Mail: virginia.maurer@cba.ufl.edu.

MAURESMO, AMELIE, professional tennis player; b. Laye, France, July 5, 1979; d. Francis and Francoise Mauresmo. Mem. French Olympic Team, 2000; profl. tennis player WTA, 1996—; winner (singles) Bratislava, 1999, Sydney, 2000, Paris Indoors, Nice, Amelia Island, German Open, 2000, Dubai, Canadian Open, 2001; finalist (singles) German Open, 1998, Paris Indoors, Australian Open, 1999, Bol, Italian Open, 2000, Italian Open, 2001, 2003; winner (singles) Warsaw, 2003, Canadian Open, 2002, Antwerp, 2005, Rome, 2005, Paris Indoors, 2006, Australia Open, 2006, Sony Ericsson WTA Tour Championship, 2006, 17 career WTA Titles. Nominee Sanex WTA Tour Most Impressive Newcomer award, 1998; named Nasdaq Player of Month for Feb., 2001. Achievements include winner grand slam singles, Austalian Open, 2006, Open Gaz de France, 2006, Proximus Diamond Games, 2006, Wimbledon, 2006. Office: WTA Tour 1 Progress Plz Ste 1500 Saint Petersburg FL 33701-4335*

MAURICE, PATRICIA ANN, geochemist, educator; b. Manchester, Conn., Sept. 3, 1960; d. Robert Aime and Helen (Kennedy) M.; m. Gregory Richard Madey; 1 child, Alexander Gregory. BA, Johns Hopkins U., Balt., 1982; MS, Dartmouth Coll., 1985; PhD, Stanford U., 1994. Project chief hydrogeochemistry U.S. Geol. Survey, 1985-89; asst. prof. geochemistry Kent (Ohio) State U., 1994-99, assoc. prof., 1999-2000, U. Notre Dame, Ind., 2000—. Assoc. editor Geochimica et cosmochimica Acta, 2000—; mem. editl. bd. Chem. Geology, 1999—; contbr. numerous articles to profl. jours. Mem. Am. Geophys. Union, Am. Chem. Soc., Clay Minerals Soc. Office: Univ of Notre Dame Dept Civil Eng/Geol Sci Notre Dame IN 46556

MAURIDES, ELAINE, retired mental health services professional, retired social worker; b. Akron, Ohio, July 24, 1936; d. Paul A. and Clara Regas Maurides; children: Kimberly Ann Morgan, Patty Blower, Denise M. Riegler. BA, U. Akron, Ohio, 1970, MEd, 1980. Elem. tchr. Cath. Diocese Cleve., 1966—76; psychiat. social worker Western Res. Human Svcs., Stow, Ohio, 1976—88; counselor, case mgr. Cmty. Support Svcs., Akron, 1988—2003; psychiat. screener Psychiat. ER Svcs., 1988—98; ret., 2003. Family therapist Barberton Citizens Hosp., Ohio, 1988; adv. bd. Summit County Homeless, 1989—90; organizer First Family Support Group for Families of Emotionally Ill of Summit County, 1980—88. Citizens adv. bd. Summit County Bd. Mental Retardation, Akron, 1990; treas., pres. Ohio Mental Health Counselors, Columbus, 1990—91. Recipient Excellence cert., Ohio Dept. Mental Health, 1988. Mem.: Nat. Health and Wellness Club, Sigma Phi Omega. Democrat. Avocations: reading, walking, bicycling, movies. Home: 76 Emerald Woods Dr #L9 Naples FL 34108

MAURINO, PAULA SAN MILLAN, business educator, computer professor; b. Elmhurst, N.Y. m. Robert L. Maurino; children: Robert Louis, Keith Joseph, Cynthia Paula, Stacey Jean. BBA, Hofstra U., Hempstead, N.Y., 1979; MS, N.Y. Inst. Tech., Old Westbury, N.Y., 1992; PhD, L.I. U., Old Brookville, N.Y., 2006. Prof. Five Towns Coll., Dix Hills, NY, 1988—2001, dep. chmn. Dept. Bus. and Tech., 1988—2001; prof. Farmingdale State U., NY, 2001—. Mem. fact com. SUNY. Contbr. columns in newspapers, articles to profl. jours. Scholar, L.I. U., 2003—04. Mem.: Phi Sigma. Achievements include research in online education. Office: Farmingdale State University Route 110 Farmingdale NY 11735 Office Phone: 631-420-2304. Personal E-mail: pmaurino@optonline.net. Business E-Mail: maurinpl@farmingdale.edu.

MAUS, MARY ANN DILLMAN, elementary school educator; b. Jersey City, Jan. 18, 1947; d. James William and Joan (Minnix) Dillman; m. Vincent Kevin Maus, Nov. 20, 1971; children: F. Adam, Margaret, Elizabeth. BA, Coll. Mt. St. Vincent, Bronx, N.Y., 1968; MS, L.I. U., 1973; Specialist diploma in Adminstrn. and Supervision, Queens Coll., 2001. Cert. permanent tchr. elem. edn., N.Y., sch. adminstr. and supr., NY, shc. dist. adminstr., NY; lic. common br. tchr., NYC. Adj. instr. Borough of Manhattan (N.Y.) C.C., 1990-91; tchr. The John Harvard Sch., PS34, Queens Village, NY, 1968—2003; adj. instr. edn & cmty programs ednl. leadership Queens Coll., 2001—. Workshop presenter profl. devel. PS34, Queens Village, sch. leadership team, 1999-2003, liaison multicultural initiative, 2000-03; grant writer, coord. REA, 2002-03 V.p. West Hempstead (N.Y.) Basketball Assn., 1990-93; coord. Cath. Youth Orgn., St. Thomas the Apostle, West Hempstead, 1991-93; mem. St. Thomas Sch. Bd., 1994-2003 Home: 43 Stratford Rd West Hempstead NY 11552-1721

MAU-SHIMIZU, PATRICIA ANN, lawyer; b. Jan. 17, 1953; d. Herbert G. K. and Leilani (Yuen) Mau; 1 child, Melissa Rose. BS, U. San Francisco, 1975; JD, Golden Gate U., 1979. Bar: Hawaii 1979. Law clk. State Supreme Ct., Honolulu, 1979-80; atty. Bendet, Fidell & Sakai, Honolulu, 1980-81; legis. atty. Honolulu City Coun., 1981-83, House Majority Staff Office, Honolulu, 1983-84, dir., 1984-93; chief clk. Hawaii Ho. of Reps., 1993—. Mem. Hawaii Bar Assn., Hawaii Women Lawyers, Jr. League Hawaii. Democrat. Roman Catholic. Home: 7187 Hawaii Kai Dr Honolulu HI 96825-3115 Office: State House Reps 415 S Beretania St Rm 027 Honolulu HI 96813-2407 Office Phone: 808-586-6127. Business E-Mail: pat@capital.hawaii.gov.

MAUSKOPF, ROSLYNN R., prosecutor; b. Washington, 1957; d. Barry and Regina Mauskopf. BA, Brandeis U., 1979; JD, Georgetown U., 1982. Asst. dist. atty. N.Y. County Dist. Atty.'s Office, 1982—95, dep. chief spl. prosecution bur., 1992, chief frauds bur., 1993; insp. gen. State of N.Y., 1995—2002; U.S. atty. U.S. Dept. Justice, (ea. dist.) N.Y., Bklyn., 2002—. Chair Moreland Commn. N.Y.C. Schs., 1999. Office: US Attys Office 147 Pierrepont St Brooklyn NY 11201*

MAUTNER, GABRIELLA, writer, educator; b. Chemnitz, Germany, Jan. 8, 1922; arrived in U.S., 1946; d. Norbert and Charlotte Regina (Cohn) Kramer; m. Fred Solinger, Mar. 1942 (div. Nov. 1951); 1 child, Tom David Solinger; m. Ervin Mautner, July 24, 1954 (dec.); children: Daria Cohen, Eva. BA, San Francisco State U., 1972, MA, 1975. Tchr. creative writing San Francisco State U., 1975—77; tchr. comparative lit. Coll. of Marin, Kentfield, Calif., 1977—78; lectr. creative writing The Fromm Inst. U. San Francisco, 1982—2005. Author: (novels) Out of a Season, 1968, Lovers and Fugitives, 1986; translator (and author) The Good Place (in German), 2004 (Book of August, 2004), The Good Place (in English), 2006. Democrat. Avocations: swimming, yoga, literature, theater, music. Home: 7 Keats Dr Mill Valley CA 94941

MAUZY, MARTHA ANNE, retired deaf educator, audiologist; b. Birmingham, Ala., June 1, 1929; d. Huell Olon and Verna Eleanor (Evans) Rogers; m. Billy Burton Rister, Mar. 30, 1951 (div. 1973); children: Melanie Kofnovec, Jennifer Tyson, Randy Rister; m. Oscar Holcombe Mauzy, Feb. 14, 1976 (dec. Oct. 2000); stepchildren: Catherine, Charles, James. BA, U. Tex., 1948; MEd, U. Houston, 1954. Cert. elem. tchr., tchr. of deaf, Tex.; lic. audiologist, Tex. Tchr. Aldine Schs., Houston, 1948-49, Spring Br. Schs., Houston, 1949-50, Victoria (Tex.) Schs., 1950-51, Pasadena (Tex.) Schs., 1951-55, Corpus Christi Schs., 1955-58; supr., dir. children's programs Speech and Hearing Inst., Houston, 1958-73; asst. prof. Speech and Hearing Inst. U. Tex., Houston, 1973—75, ret. Co-author (2 chpts. in book) Language and Learning of the Preacademic Child, 1985. Mem. Gov.'s Commn. for Women, Austin, 1983-86; mem. adv. coun. Coll. Edn., U. Tex., 1988—, chmn. centennial celebration, 1991; treas. Tex. Dem. Women (Outstanding Mem. 1992, chair fedn. conv. nat. Fedn. Dem. Women 1993); mem. U. Tex. Nursing Sch. Coun., 1999—, U. Tex. Adv. Coun. Athletics Found., 2002—. Recipient Disting. Alumni award Coll. of Edn. Univ. Tex., 1991. Mem. AAUW, Am. Speech and Hearing Assn., Tex. Speech and Hearing Assn. (sec. 1957-58, hon. award 1985), Tex. Speech-Lang.-Hearing Found. (pres. 1992-94), Senate Ladies Club (pres. 1983). Unitarian Universalist. Avocations: politics, educational opportunities through travel. Home: Apt 131 4100 Jackson Ave Austin TX 78731-6033

MAVROUDI, MARIA, philologist, educator; BA, U. Thessaloniki, 1990; MA, Harvard U., 1992, PhD, 1998. Postdoctoral fellow Byzantine studies Dumbarton Oaks, 2000—01; postdoctoral tchg. fellow Hellenic studies Princeton U., 2001—02; asst. prof. U. Calif., Berkeley, 2002—05, assoc. prof., 2005. Author: A Bzyantine Book on Dream Interpretation: The Oneirocriticon of Achmet and its Arabic Sources, 2002. MacArthur fellow, 2004. Office: U Calif Berkeley 2223 Dwinelle Hall Berkeley CA 94720 Office Phone: 510-643-4413. E-mail: mavroudi@berkeley.edu.

MAX, CLAIRE ELLEN, physicist; b. Boston, Sept. 29, 1946; d. Louis William and Pearl (Bernstein) M.; m. Jonathan Arons, Dec. 22, 1974; 1 child, Samuel. AB, Harvard U., 1968; PhD, Princeton U., 1972. Postdoctoral rschr. U. Calif., Berkeley, 1972-74; physicist Lawrence Livermore (Calif.) Nat. Lab., 1974—; dir. Livermore br. Inst. Geophysics and Planetary Physics, 1984-93, dir. univ. rels., 1993-2000; prof., astronomer U. Calif., Santa Cruz, dir. Ctr. for Adaptive Optics, 2005—. Mem. Math.-Sci. Network Mills Coll., Oakland, Calif.; mem. com. on fusion hybrid reactors NRC, 1986, mem. com. on internat. security and arms control NAS, 1986-89, mem. com. on phys. sci., math. and applications NRC, 1991-94, mem. policy and computational astrophys. panels, astron. and astgrophys. survey NRC, 1989-91; mem. sci. steering com. W.M. Keck Obs., 1992-96, mem. adaptive optics sci. team, 1994—; mem. vis. com. Space Telescope Sci. Inst., 1996-2000, Hubble Space Telescope Second Decade Com., 1998-2000. Editor: Particle Acceleration Mechanisms in Astrophysics, 1979; contbr. numerous articles to sci. jours. Recipient E.O. Lawrence award, US Dept. Energy, 2004. Fellow AAAS (coun. rep. physics sect. 2001—), Am. Phys. Soc. (exec. com. divsn. plasma physics 1977, 81-82) Am. Acad Arts and Scis.; mem. Am. Astron. Soc. (exec. com. divsn. high energy astrophysics 1975-76), Am. Geophys. Union, Internat. Astron. Union, Phi Beta Kappa, Sigma Xi. Achievements include rsch. on adaptive optics and laser guide stars for astronomy; astrophys. plasmas. Office: U Calif Santa Cruz Ctr for Adaptive Optics 1156 High St Santa Cruz CA 95064 Business E-Mail: max@ucolick.org.

MAXEY, DIANE MEADOWS, artist; b. Lufkin, Tex., Feb. 26, 1943; d. Warren Gaston and Jackie Meadows; m. William Brant Maxey, Sept. 5, 1964; children: Dananne, Robert Warren. BA in Art and Edn., U. North Tex., 1965; postgrad., U. Tex., Arlington, Tex. Tech U., Lubbock; studied with Al Brouilette, Bud Biggs, Edgar Whitney, Dick Phillips, Robert E. Wood, Rex. Brandt, Milford Zornes. Art tchr. Dallas Pub. Schs., 1965-66; substitute tchr. Arlington Pub. Schs., 1969-72; pvt. classes San Angelo, Tex., 1973-77; owner Maxi Watercolor Studio, Paradise Valley, 1978—, Bandanna Tours, Scottsdale, 1988-91. Mem. staff Scottsdale Artist Sch., The Shemer Art Ctr.; tchr. numerous watercolor workshops for different local schs. and internat. tours cos. Exhibited at Gold Nuggett Art Gallery, Wickenburg, Ariz., Long Gallery, Scottsdale, Ariz.; featured artist in Freshening Your Paintings with New Techniques, Fresh Flowers The Best of Flower Painting, The Best of Watercolor 2, The Best of Watercolor Composition, Splash 5, 2002, Splash 7, 2004, Splash 9, 2006, Watercolor Artists Color Mixing Book, 2006, How to Paint Watercolor Landscapes, 2006; featured in Internat. Artist Mag., 1998; cover artist Watercolor Magic, spring 2000, Scottsdale Life mag., 2002—, A Valley Virtuoso, Five Outstanding Artist. Dir. visual ministry First So. Bapt. Ch., Scottsdale, 1988-95. Recipient numerous awards including Outstanding Artist Scottsdale Mag., 2002. Mem. Western Fedn. Watercolor Soc. (gen. chmn. 1981-82), Southwestern Watercolor Assn. (signature), Ariz. Artist Guild (hon. life; pres. 1982-83), Ariz. Watercolor Assn., Tex. Watercolor Assn. (signature), 22 x 30 Profl. Critique Group. Avocations: gardening, travel. Home and Office: Maxi Watercolor Studio 7540 N Lakeside Ln Paradise Valley AZ 85253-2857 Office Phone: 480-951-2723. Personal E-mail: dmaxey.watercolor@worldnet.att.net.

MAXFIELD, BROOKE DAVIS, mathematics educator; b. Washington, D.C., Aug. 13, 1978; d. Kent Alvah and Betty Davis Maxfield. BSc, James Madison U., Harrisonburg, Va., 2002; ME, Old Dominion U., Satellite Campus in No. Va., 2006. Cert. mid. sch. edn. Va., 2002, algebra 1 Va., 2005. Dance coach Langely H.S., McLean, Va., 2002—04; math. tchr. Poe Mid. Sch., Annandale, Va., 2002—03, Kilmer Mid. Sch., Vienna, Va., 2003—. Tutor, Va., 2003—; del. leader People to People Student Ambassadors, Spokane, Wash., 2005—; mentor Kilmer Mid. Sch., 2005—, Poe Mid. Sch., 2002—04; mentor to new tchrs. Kilmer Mid. Sch., 2004—05, step/dance team sponsor, 2003—, team leader, 2004—, field day com. head, 2004—. Recipient Achievement in Mentoring and Tchg., Nat. Youth Leadership Coun., 2006. Mem.: Optimist Club (life), Alpha Phi Omega Nat. Svc. Frat. (life; pledge class pres. 2000—01, Overall Brother award, Svc. award, Disting. Key of Svc. Award 2002), Alpha Chi Omega Sorority (life). Avocations: travel, mentoring, coaching, dance, deejaying. Office Phone: 703-846-8800. Business E-Mail: brooke.maxfield@fcps.edu.

MAXFIELD, LOUISA FONDA GRIBBLE, executive secretary; b. Waco, TX, Sept. 27, 1924; d. Theodore Miles and Louise Irwin Gribble; m. Jack G.S. Maxfield, July 21, 1951 (dec.); children: Martha Woodson Maxfield Cottingham, Elizabeth Fonda. BA, Randolph-Macon Woman's Coll., Lynchburg,Va., 1945; M Liberal Arts, So. Meth. U., Dallas, 1982. Editor, indsl. house organ Gen. Tire & Rubber Co., Waco, Tex., 1945—51; bus. mgr. Maxfield Clin./Hosp., Dallas, 1976—84, Covenant Presbyn. ch., Carrollton, Tex., 1984—99. Named Woman of Yr., Carrollton, Tex., 2004; Paul Harris fellow, Rotary Internat.

MAXFIELD, ROSE MARY, retired government official; b. Shelbyville, Ill., Mar. 23, 1918; d. Claude Fielding Stiarwalt and Nina Eugenia Whitlock; m. Orville Eldred Maxfield, June 6, 1941; children: Mary Patricia, Mary Constance, Marilyn Joan. BS, U. Ill., Champaign-Urbana, 1939. Adminstrv. asst. U.S. Treasury Dept., Washington, 1942—73; ret., 1973. Author: (chpt.) Amy White of the Old 300, 1986, Biography for New Texas Handbook, 1996. Mem. Sam Houston Regional Libr. and Rsch. Ctr., Va. Tech. Ctr. Civil War Studies. Recipient Meritorious Svc. award, U.S. Treasury Dept., 1967, Sec.'s Cert., 1969, Albert Gallatin award, 1973, Spl. Achievement award, 1973. Mem.: Nat. Soc. DAR, Wharton County Hist. Mus., Glover Park Citizens Assn., Swiss Club Washington, Nat. Mus. Women in Arts (charter mem.), Nat. Soc. Daus. of Colonial Wars, Daus. of Republic of Tex., United Daus. Confederacy, Nat. Soc. U.S. Daus. of 1812, Flagon and Trencher (life), Assn. for Preservation of Va. Antiquities (life), Soc. Descs. of Colonial Clergy (life), U. Ill. Alumni Assn. (life), Treasury Hist. Assn. (charter mem. 1968), Nat. Soc. Col. Dames 17th Century, Soc. Descs. of Austin's Old 300, Nat. Soc. Sons and Daus. of the Pilgrims, So. Relief Soc. D.C., Friends of Folger Libr., Shelby County Hist. and Geneal. Soc., Delta Zeta. Avocations: reading, genealogy, needlecrafts, travel, musical performances. Home: 218 Mayfair Cir Wharton TX 77488 Personal E-mail: msmaxfield@sbcglobal.net.

MAXIMCIUC, DEBORAH JEAN, special education educator; b. Rochester, N.Y., Feb. 13, 1957; d. William Joseph and Jean Ann Dietrich; m. Vladimir Maximciuc, Nov. 22, 1996; children: Patrick A. Coleman, Nicholas A. Coleman, Casey M. Coleman. BS, SUNY, Geneseo, N.Y., 1979; MS, SUNY, Buffalo, N.Y., 1983. Tchr. special edn. Attica Ctrl. Sch., Attica, NY, 1979—81, Lake SHore Ctrl. Sch., Angola, NY, 1981—. Mem.: Coun. for Execptional Children (treas. N.Y. divsn. 1992—96), Phi Delta Kappa. Avocations: reading, crafts, cross country skiing.

MAXMAN, SUSAN ABEL, architect; b. Columbus, Ohio, Dec. 30, 1938; d. Richard Jack Abel and Gussie (Brenner) Seiden; m. Rolf Sauer; children: Andrew Frankel, Thomas Frankel, Elizabeth Frankel, Melissa, Abby, William Jr., Madeleine Sauer. Student, Smith Coll., 1960; MArch., U. Pa., 1977; HHD, Ball State U., 1993, U. Detroit Mercy, 1997. Registered profl. arch. Pa., Mich., NH, Nat. Coun. Archtl. Registration Bds. Project designer Kopple Sheward & Day, Phila., 1978-80; ptnr. Maxman & Sutphin, Phila., 1980-83; prin. Susan Maxman & Ptnrs., Phila., 1984—. Mem. bd. overseers Grad. Sch. Fine Arts U. Pa., mem. corp. vis. com. MIT; mem. Planning and Design Commn., Ga. Inst. Tech. Works include design of Women's Humane Soc. Animal Shelter, Bensalem, Pa. (Northeastern Sustainable Energy Assn.'s Comml. Bldg. award, 1994, Metal Constrn. Assn. award 1995, Gov.'s Award for Environ. Excellence 1997, AIA Pa. Hon. award 1997), Camp Tweedale-Freedom Valley Girl Scouts USA (AIA Honor award, 1991), Cusano Environ. Edn. Ctr. at John Heinz Nat. Wildlife Refuge at Tinicum, Phila. (US Dept. Energy Fed. Energy Saver Showcase award, US Dept. Interior Environ. Achievement award, Top Ten Green Bldg. award AIA 2003, AIA Cote Top Ten Green Buildings award, 2003), Robert Lewis House (McArthur award 1985), Phila., Restoration Pennock Farmstead (Grand Prize Nat. Trust Hist. Preservation 1995), Canaan Valley Inst. Hdqs., Renovation of Second Bank of US, Phila., Navy Yard Bldg. 10 (Honor award, AIA, Phila. chpt., 2004, citation of merit, PA Historic Presercation award), Natural Lands Trust Hdqs. Expansion, Media, Pa. (N.E. Sustainable Energy Assn. Bldg. award 2004, Exemplary Sustainable Bldgs. Industry Coun. award 2005), Kutztown U., Pa. Sisters Servants of the Immaculate Heart of Mary Renovation of the Motherhouse (Mich. Hist. Preservation Network Bldg. award 2003, Top Ten Green Bldg. award AIA 2006), Renovation of U. Pa. Nursing Edn. Bldg., Phila., Barbara C. Harris Camp and Conf. Ctr., Greenfield, NH, Chestnut Hill Nat. Bank, Phila., Somerset (Pa.) Hist. Ctr., Seneca Rocks Visitor Ctr., Seneca Rocks, W.Va., Fort Necessity/Nat. Rd. Interpretive Edn. Ctr., Farmington, Pa., The Woods Residence Hall at Pa. State-Berks, Reading, Roberts Hall Renovation and Addition U. Pa. Law Sch., Phila. Navy Yard Bldg. 10 Restoration (Merit citation Phila. chpt. AIA 2004), others. Mem. Eco-Efficiency Task Force Pres. Coun. Sustainable Devel.; past chair Environ. Coun., Urban Land Inst.; mem. trustee's coun. for Pa. Women, U. Pa. Recipient Disting. Dau. Pa. award Gov. Tom Ridge, 1995, Excellence citation Engrng. News Record, Shattering the Glass Ceiling award Women's Nat. Dem. Club, Mayor's commendation City Phila., citation Pa. Ho. Reps., Gov.'s award Environ. Excellence, 1997, Pa. Hist. and Mus. Commn. Preservation Achievement award Preservation Alliance Greater Phila.; named to Pa. Honor Roll of Women, Pa. Commn. for Women, 1996, named 1 of Pa.'s

Best 50 Women in Bus. 1996. Mem. AIA (nat. pres. 1993), Pa. Women's Forum, Forum Exec. Women, Carpenter's Co. Phila. Avocation: sailing. Office: 1600 Walnut St Fl 2D Philadelphia PA 19103-5405 Office Phone: 215-985-4410. Business E-Mail: sam@maxmanpartners.com.

MAXMIN, JODY LEWIS, art educator; b. Phila. d. Henry Wertheimer and Louise Olga (Strousse) M. BA, Oberlin (Ohio) Coll., 1971; diploma with distinction, Oxford (Eng.) U., 1973, PhD, 1979. Acting asst. prof. Stanford (Calif.) U., 1979-80, asst. prof., 1980-88, assoc. prof., 1988—. Undergrad. advisor, chair honors com. art dept. Stanford U., 1989—. Author poems; contbr. articles to profl. jours. Woodrow Wilson Found. fellow, 1971; Danforth Found. fellow, 1971; Leonard and Katherine Woolley fellow Somerville Coll, Oxford U., 1973; Jr. Rsch. fellow Wolfson Coll., Oxford U., 1975-79; recipient Hoagland award for undergrad. tchg., 1989, ASSU Stanford U. Tchg. award, 1997, Gores award for excellence in tchg., 2004, Excellence in Tchg. asard Phi Beta Kappa, No. Calif. Assn., 2004. Mem. Archaeol. Inst. Am., Coll. Art Assn. (Millard Meiss award 1982), Soc. for Promotion Hellenic Studies, Soc. for Preservation of Greek Heritage, Phi Beta Kappa (Excellence in Teaching award 1991, Excellence in Undergrad. Teaching award 1992). Jewish. Avocations: painting, guitar, tennis, football. Office: Stanford U Dept Art Stanford CA 94305 Business E-Mail: jmaxmin@stanford.edu.

MAXSON, BARBARA JEANETTE, social worker, educator; b. Whittier, Calif. BA, Westmont Coll., 1970; MSW, Ariz. State U., 1987. cert. social worker. Family therapist Family Svc. Agy., Phoenix, 1987-89; dir. counseling ctr. Grand Canyon U., Phoenix, 1987; pvt. practice, 1991—. Adj. prof. Grand Canyon U., Phoenix, 1987—. Tchr., trainer Am. Bapt. Conv., Phoenix, 1988—. Mem. NASW, Am. Assn. Marriage and Family Therapy, Am. Assn. Christian Counselors. Office: 14001 N 7th St Ste B104 Phoenix AZ 85022 Office Phone: 623-780-0866, 602-993-2959.

MAXSON, CAROL S., health facility administrator; b. LA, Sept. 22, 1942; d. Walter Henry and Marjory Frazier Maxson. BFA in Drama and Speech, Drake U., Des Moines, Iowa, 1963—64; MA in Comms., SUNY, NYC, 1976; MA in Psychology, Beacon Coll., Washington, 1986. Cert. med. asst. Am. Med. Technologists; massage therapist N.Mex., Trager bodywork USA Trager Assn., Rubenfeld synergist RSM Assn. Editl. asst., prodn. asst. Travel and Leisure Mag., NYC, 1972—80; art asst., writer Am. Express Pub.; script coord., asst. Good Morning Am. ABC-TV, NYC, 1980—81, asst. literary rights, 1981—86; case mgr. Girls Residential Facility, Albuquerque, 1994—96, Counseling Ctr., Domestic Violence Shelter, Albuquerque, 1998—2000; hosp. svcs. asst. U. N.Mex. Hosp., Albuquerque, 2003—. Scholar, Michiana Area Sch. Bd., 1960, OLOC, Athens, Ohio, 2004, 2006; scholar in Gestalt therapy, Esalen Inst. Big Sur, Calif., 1988. Religious Scientist. Avocations: theater, QiGong, dance, writing, tantric meditation. Home: 10804 Towner Ave NE # D Albuquerque NM 87112

MAXSON, LINDA ELLEN, biologist, educator; b. N.Y.C., Apr. 24, 1943; d. Albert and Ruth (Rosenfeld) Resnick; m. Richard Dey Maxson, June 13, 1964; 1 child, Kevin. BS in Zoology, San Diego State U., 1964, MA in Biology, 1966; PhD in Genetics, San Diego State U./U. Calif., Berkeley, 1973. Instr. biology San Diego State U., 1966-68; tchr. gen. sci. San Diego Unified Sch. Dist., 1968-69; instr. biochemistry U. Calif., Berkeley, 1974; asst. prof. zoology, dept. genetics and devel. U. Ill., Urbana-Champaign, 1974-76, asst. prof. dept. genetics, devel. and ecology, ethology & evolution, 1976-79, assoc. prof., 1979-84, prof., 1984-87, prof. ecology, ethology and evolution, 1987-88; prof., head dept. biology Pa. State U., State College, 1988-94; assoc. vice-chancellor acad. affairs/dean undergrad. acad. affairs, prof. ecology and evolutionary biology U. Tenn., Knoxville, 1995-97; dean Coll. Liberal Arts & Scis., prof. biol. scis. U. Iowa, Iowa City, 1997—. Exec. officer biology programs Sch. Life Scis., U. Ill., 1981-86, assoc. dir. acad. affairs, 1984-86, dir. campus honors program, 1985-88; vis. prof. ecology and evolutionary biology U. Calif., Irvine, 1988; mem. adv. panel rsch. tng. groups behavioral biol. scis. NSF, 1990-94; rsch. assoc. Smithsonian Instn. Author: Genetics: A Human Perspective, 3d edit., 1992; mem. editl. bd. Molecular Biology Evolution; exec. editor Biochem. Sys. & Ecology, 1993-2001; contbr. numerous articles to scientific jours. Recipient Disting. Alumni award, San Diego State U., 1989, Disting. Herpetologist award, Herpetologists' League, 1993. Fellow: AAAS; mem.: Soc. Molecular Biology and Evolution (treas. 1992—94, sec. 1992—95), Soc. Study Evolution, Soc. for Study of Amphibians and Reptiles (pres. 1991), Am. Men and Women in Sci., Phi Beta Kappa. Office: U Iowa 240 Schaeffer Hall Iowa City IA 52242-1409 Business E-Mail: linda-maxson@uiowa.edu.

MAXWELL, CARLA LENA, dancer, choreographer, educator; b. Glendale, Calif., Oct. 25, 1945; d. Robert and Victoria (Carbone) Maxwell. Student, Bennington Coll., 1963-64; BS, Juilliard Sch. Music, 1967. Mem. Jose Limón Dance Co., N.Y.C., 1965, prin. dancer, 1969—, acting artistic dir., 1977-78, artistic dir., 1978—. Lectr., tchr. in field. Dancer soloist Louis Falco Dance Co., 1967—71, Harkness Festival at Delacorte Theater, N.Y.C., 1964—, artist-in-residence Gettysburg Coll., 1970—, Luther Coll., Decorah, Iowa, 1971—, U. Idaho, 1973—; guest tchr., performer Centre Internat. de la Danse, Vichy, France, 1976—; choreographer Function, 1970—, Improvisations on a Dream, 1970—, A Suite of Psalms, 1973—, Homage to José Linón, Place Spirit, 1975, Aadvark Brothers: Schwartz and Columbo Present Please Don't Stone the Clowns, 1975, Blue Warrior, 1975, Sonata, 1980, Keeping Still Mountain, 1987; featured Carlota, Dances for Isadora, La Malinche, Comedy, The Moor's Pavane, The Winged, There is a Time, The Shakers, Brandenburg Concerto No. 4, Translucence, Caviar, Missa Brevis, Day on Earth, Two Ecstatic Themes, A Choreographic Offering, The Exiles, Sacred Conversations; dancer toured East and West Africa, 1969. Recipient Dance Mag. award, 1995; N.Y. State Cultural Coun. grantee, 1971. Home: 7 Great Jones St New York NY 10012-1135 Office: Jose Limon Dance Fedn 611 Broadway Fl 9 New York NY 10012-2608

MAXWELL, CAROLE ANN, director; b. Phila., Sept. 10, 1944; d. Frank J. Coyne and Ruth M. (Steck) Steck-Coyne; m. Richard A. Nuzzo, Jan. 10, 1998; 1 child, Courtney Ruth. BA, Immaculata Coll., Pa., 1967; M of Music Edn., Temple U., Phila., 1972; D of Sacred Music, Grad. Theol. Inst., South Bend, Ind., 2003. Dir. choral and liturgical music Fairfield U., Conn., 1980—; artistic dir., conductor Mendelssohn Choir of Conn., Fairfield, 1984—. Guest conductor Westchester County HS All State Choir, 1999, So. Conn. Region HS All State Choir, 2005. Chorusmaster Conn. Grand Opera and Orch., Stamford, 1990—, Yale Opera Co., New Haven, 1997—2002, Bridgeport Symphony, Conn., 1999—, Norwalk Symphony, Conn., 2002—; guest conductor Gregg Smith Singers/Adirondack Music Festival, 1989; prin. conductor Nat. Pastoral Musicians Conv., 1997, 2006; guest conductor Messiah Sing-in Lincoln Ctr., NYC, 2004—05; hunger clean-up Fairfield U., 1987—; bd. dirs. Mendelysohn Choir Conn., Fairfield, 1984—, Fairfield County Children's Choir, 1996—. Named Disting. Music Alumnae, Immaculata Coll., 1992, Woman of the Yr., Fairfield U. Women's Study, 2000. Mem.: Music Educators Nat. Conf., Am. Choral Dirs. Assn., Phi Kappa Lambda. Avocations: reading, travel. Home: 39 Regency Cir Trumbull CT 06611 Office: Fairfield Univ North Benson Rd Fairfield CT 06824

MAXWELL, JUDITH, think-tank executive, economist; b. Kingston, Ont., Can., July 21, 1943; d. James Ruffee and Marguerite Jane (Spanner) McMahon; m. Anthony Stirling Maxwell, May 8, 1970; 2 children. B in Commerce, Dalhousie U., 1963, LLD, 1991; postgrad., London Sch. Econs., 1965-66; LLD, Queen's U., 1992. Researcher Combines Investigation Br. Consumer and Corp. Affairs, Ottawa, Can., 1963-65; econs. writer, mem. editorial bd. Fin. Times, Montreal, Que., Can., 1966-72; dir. policy studies C.D. Howe Inst., Montreal, 1972-80; cons. Esso Europe Inc., London, Eng., 1980-82, Coopers & Lybrand, Montreal, Que., 1982-85; chmn. Econ. Council Can., Ottawa, Ont., 1985-92; exec. dir. Queen's-U. Ottawa Econ. Projects, 1992—. Dir. Can. Found. for Econ. Edn., 1985-88, Inst. for Rsch. on Pub. Policy, 1987-88. Author: Energy From the Arctic, 1973; (with C. Pestieau) Economic Realities of Contemporary Confederation, 1980; (with S. Currie) Partnership for Growth: Corporate University Education in Canada, 1984. Active Ont. Premier's Coun., 1988-90, Nfld. and Labrador Sci. and Tech. Adv. Coun., 1988-90. Mem. Can. Assn. Bus. Econs. (pres. 1976-77), Montreal Econs. Assn. (pres. 1975-76). Office: Canadian Policy Rsch Networks 600-250 Albert St Ottawa ON Canada K1P 6M1 Office Phone: 613-567-7500. E-mail: jmaxwell@cprn.org.

MAXWELL, MAUREEN KAY, media specialist, educator; d. William J. and Sylvia A. Maxwell. BA in History, Colo. State U., MS Agr. and Resources Econs. Legislative aide and press sec. U.S. Rep. Patricia Schroeder, Washington, 1982—90; asst. dir., population program The Wilderness Soc., 1993—96; mgr. pub. rels., govt. affairs Am. Acad. Family Physicians, 1998—2005. Instr. DC Self Def. Karate Assn., 1998—2005; bd. dirs. DC Impact, 2000—03, chair, 2003—05. Recipient Pillar of the School award, D.C. Self Def. Karate Assn., 2002. Mem.: Nat. Press Club. Avocations: writing, reading, martial arts. Office Phone: 303-946-2949. E-mail: arethamax42@hotmail.com.

MAXWELL, RUTH ELAINE, artist, interior designer, painter; b. Cleve., Oct. 7, 1934; d. Norman Lee and Katherine Ellen (Hamilton) Brown; m. Clarence L. Maxwell, June 25, 1955; children: Lisa Maxwell Callahan, Lynne Maxwell Quinn, Laura Maxwell Jochem, James. BFA, Ohio State U., 1956. Cert. elem. sch. tchr. Ohio. Tchr. Hilliard Elem. Sch., Ohio, 1956—58; comptr. Callahan Family Golf Ctr., Hilliard, 1989—99. Vol. Columbus Assn. Performing Arts Colleagues, 1981—, pres., 1986—87; mem. Hilliard Arts Coun., 1989—91; vocalist Damenchor of Columbus Maennerchor, 1975—, treas., 1979—81, fin. sec., 1991—94, recording sec., bd. dirs.; mem. Canterbury Unit Columbus Symphony Orch. Women's Assn., 1992—2002, pres., 1995—96; mem. Women's Guild Opera, Columbus, 1994—2001, sec., 2000—01, v.p., 2004—06, pres., 2006—, Damenchor of Columbus Maennerchor, 2003—06; buyer Ohio Theatre Shop, 1995—, pres. gov. bd., 2003—04. Mem.: Gamma Phi Beta, Gamma Alpha Chi (hon.; sec. Ohio State U. chpt. 1954). Republican. Avocations: reading, gardening, travel. E-mail: maxdarbyoaks@aol.com.

MAXWELL, SONIA L., social worker; b. Kokomo, Ind., Dec. 15, 1947; d. Charles Clayton and Bernice Louise (Tyrrell) M.; m. Roger E. Armstrong, July 14, 1984. BA, Washburn U., 1970; MSW, U. Kans., 1974. Diplomate lic. clin. social work. Probation officer Pima County Juvenile Ct., Tucson, 1974-75; clin. social worker St. Mary's Hosp., Tucson, 1975-79, dir. social work, 1979-83; prin. Counseling, Therapy, and Mediation Assocs., Tucson, 1984—90; pvt. practice, 1990—2006; developer, owner A Room With A View, Lake Patagonia, Ariz., 1997—2006; ret., 2006. Service and rehab. vol. Am. Cancer Soc., Tucson, 1980—, bd. dirs. 1981-84; chmn. Pima Unit Rehab. and Service Com., Tucson, 1982-83; conf. participant Ariz.-Sonora Commn., 1982; mem. allocations com. Tucson United Way, 1984-85. Mem. Nat. Assn. Social Workers, Acad. Cert. Social Workers (cert.). Avocations: swimming, reading, tennis, weightlifting. Home and Office: HC 2 Box 282 Nogales AZ 85621-9794

MAXWELL-BROGDON, FLORENCE MORENCY, school system administrator, educational consultant; b. Spring Park, Minn., Nov. 11, 1929; d. William Frederick and Florence Ruth (LaBrie) Maxwell; m. John Carl Brogdon, Mar. 13, 1957; children: Carole Alexandra, Cecily Ann, Daphne Diana. BA, Calif. State U., L.A., 1955; MS, U. So. Calif., 1957; postgrad., Columbia Pacific U., San Rafael, Calif., 1982-86. Cert. tchr., Calif. Dir. Rodeo Sch., L.A., 1961-64; lectr. Media Features, Culver City, Calif., 1964—; dir. La Playa Sch., Culver City, Calif., 1968-75; founding dir. Venture Sch., Culver City, Calif., 1974—, also chmn. bd. dirs. Bd. dirs., v.p. Parent Coop. Preschools, Baie d'Urfe Que., Can., 1964—; del. to Ednl. Symposium, Moscow-St. Petersburg, 1992, U.S./China Joint Conf. on Edn., Beijing, 1992, Internat. Confedn. of Prins., Geneva, 1993, Internat. Conf., Berlin, 1994, Internat. Confedn. of Sch. Prins., Helsinki, Finland, 2000, Edinburgh, Scotland, 2003. Author: Let Me Tell You, 1973, Wet'n Squishy, 1973, Balancing Act, 1977, (as Morency Maxwell) Framed in Silver, 1985; (column) What Parents Want to Know, 1961—; editor: Calif. Preschooler, 1961-74; contbr. articles to profl. jours. Treas. Dem. Congl. Primary, Culver City, 1972. Mem. NASSP, Calif. Coun. Parent Schs. (bd. dirs. 1961-74), Parent Coop. Preschs. Internat. (advisor 1975—), Pen Ctr. USA West, Mystery Writers of Am. (affiliate), Internat. Platform Assn. Liberatarian. Home: 10814 Molony Rd Culver City CA 90230-5451 Office: Venture Sch 11477 Jefferson Blvd Culver City CA 90230-6115 Office Phone: 310-559-2678. Personal E-mail: morencee@aol.com. Business E-Mail: vntrschl@comcast.net.

MAXWELL DIAL, ELEANORE, foreign language educator; b. Norwich, Connecticut, Feb. 21, 1929; d. Joseph Walter and Irene (Beetham) Maxwell; m. John E. Dial, Aug. 27, 1959. BA, U. Bridgeport, Conn., 1951; MA in Spanish, Mexico City Coll., 1955; PhD, U. Mo., 1968. Mem. faculty U. Wis., Milw., 1968—75, Ind. State U., Terre Haute, 1975—78, Bowling Green State U., Ohio, 1978—79; asst. prof. dept. fgn. lang. and lit. Iowa State U., Ames, 1979—85, assoc. prof., 1985—96, emerita assoc. prof., 1996—. Cons. pub. companies; participant workshops; del. First World Congress Women Journalists and Writers, Mex., 1975, mem. edn. commn. Contbr. articles, anthologies, and reviews to scholarly journals. Active governor's commn. on fgn. lang. and internat. studies, 1988-95. NDEA grantee, 1967, Ctr. Latin Am. grantee, 1972, NEH summer seminar UCLA, 1981, U. Calif., Santa Barbara, 1984. Mem. MLA, Am. Assn. Teachers Spanish and Portuguese, Midwest MLA, N. Ctrl. Coun. Latin Americanists, Midwest Assn. Latin Am. Studies, Clermont County Geneal. Soc., Ohio Geneal. Soc., Story County Iowa Geneal. Soc., Caribbean Studies Assn., P.G. Wodehouse Soc., Phi Beta Delta, Phi Sigma Iota, Sigma Delta Pi. Home: 190 North St Batavia OH 45103-2911 Office: Iowa State U Ames IA 50011-0001

MAY, AVIVA RABINOWITZ, music educator, musician, linguist; b. Tel Aviv; naturalized, 1958; d. Samuel and Paula Pessia (Gordon) Rabinowitz; children: Chelley Mosoff, Alan May, Risa McPherson, Ellanna May/Gassman. AA, Oakton C.C., 1977; BA in Piano Pedagogy, Northeastern Ill. U., 1978. Folksinger, educator, musican Aviva May Studio/Piano and Guitar, 1948—; Sunday sch. dir. Canton (Ohio) Synagogue, 1952-54; nursery sch. tchr. Allentown (Pa.) Jewish Cmty. Ctr., 1954-56; Hebrew music tchr. Brith Shalom Cmty. Ctr., Bethlehem, Pa., 1954-62; Hebrew tchr. Beth Hillel Congregation, Wilmette, Ill., 1964-83; tchr. B'nai Mitzva, 1978; music dir. McCormick Health Ctrs., Chgo., 1978-79, Cove Sch. Perceptually Handicapped Children, Evanston, 1978-79; prof. Hebrew and Yiddish, Spertus Coll. Judaica, Chgo., 1980-89; Hebrew tchr. Anshe Emet Day Sch., 1989—, West Suburban Temple Har Zion, Oak Park, Ill., 1993—; music studio tchr. Cosmopolitan Sch., Chgo., 1992—. Tchr. continuing edn. Northeastern Ill. U., 1978-84, Niles Twp. Jewish Congregation, 1993—97, also Jewish Cmty. Ctrs., 1977-78; with Office Spl. Investigations, Dept. Justice, Washington; music dir. Temple Emanuel Rosenwald Sch. Composer classical music for piano, choral work, folk songs; developer 8-hour system for learning piano or guitar; contbr. articles to profl. jours. Recipient Magen David Adom Pub. Svc. award 1973; grantee Ill. State, 1975-79, Ill. Congressman Woody Bowman, 1978-79. Mem. Music Tchrs. Nat. Assn., Ill. Music Tchrs. Assn., Organ and Piano Tchrs. Assn., Am. Coll. Musicians, Ill. Assn. Learning Disabilities, North Shore Music Tchrs. Assn. (charter mem., co-founder), Sherwood Sch. Music, Friends of Holocaust Survivers, Nat. Yiddish Book Exch., Nat. Ctr. for Jewish Films, Chgo. Jewish Hist. Soc., Oakton C.C. Alumni Assn., Northeastern Ill. U. Alumni Assn. Office: Aviva May Studio 410 S Michigan Ave Ste 920 Chicago IL 60605-1471 Office Phone: 773-348-8700.

MAY, CATHY JUNE, elementary school educator; b. Johnson, Tenn., Mar. 26, 1960; d. Joe Fayette and Joyce Marie Nichols; children: Preston, Bristol, Jordan. BS in Music Edn., David Lipscomb U., 1982; MA in Music, Mid. Tenn. U., 1997. Tchr. Midland (Tex.) Christian Sch., 1982—84, Killeen (Tex.) Ind. Sch. Dist., 1984—85, Hamilton County Schs., Chattanooga, 1987—, Coastal Caroline U., Myrtle Beach, SC, 2002. Choral dir. Soddy Daisy (Tenn.) HS, 2004—. Bd. dirs., edn. dir. Choral Epiphany, Chattanooga, 2004—; vocal tchr. missions music and singing schs. Ch. of Christ, U.S. and Russia, 1993. Recipient Character Edn. award, Hamilton Dep. Edn., 2004, 2005. Mem.: East Tenn. Vocal Assn., Tenn. Music Educators Assn., Orgn. Am. Kodaly Educators (v.p. 2001—03). Avocations: gardening, photography. Home: 7302 Meacham Ln Hixson TN 37343 Office: Soddy Daisy HS 618 Sequoyah Access Rd Soddy Daisy TN 37379

MAY, ELAINE, actress, film director, theater director; b. Phila., Apr. 21, 1932; d. Jack Berlin; m. Marvin May (div.); 1 child, Jeannie Berlin; m. Sheldon Harnick, Mar. 25, 1962 (div. May 1963). Studied Stanislavsky method of acting withMarie Ouspenskaya. Stage and radio appearances as child actor; performed with Playwright's Theatre, in student performance Miss Julie, U. Chgo.; appeared with improvisational theatre group in night club The Compass, Chgo., 1954-1957, (with Mike Nichols) appeared N.Y. supper clubs, Village Vanguard, Blue Angel, also night clubs other cities; TV debut on Jack Paar Show, 1957; also appeared in Omnibus, 1958, Dinah Shore Show, Perry Como Show, Laugh Line, Laugh-In, TV spls.; comedy albums include Improvisations to Music, An Evening with Mike Nichols and Elaine May, Mike Nichols and Elaine May Examine Doctors; weekly appearance NBC radio show Nightline; appeared (with Mike Nichols) NBC radio show, N.Y. Town Hall, 1959, An Evening with Mike Nichols and Elaine May, Golden Theatre, N.Y.C., 1960-61; theater appearances include The Office, N.Y.C., 1966, Who's Afraid of Virginia Woolf?, Long Wharf Theatre, New Haven, Conn., 1980; dir. plays The Third Ear, N.Y.C., 1964, The Goodbye People, Berkshire Theater Festival, Stockbridge, Mass., 1971, various plays at Goodman Theatre, Chgo., 1983; dir., author screenplay, actress film A New Leaf, 1972; dir. films The Heartbreak Kid, 1973, Mikey and Nicky, 1976 (writer, dir. remake 1985), Ishtar, 1987 (also writer); appeared in films Luv, 1967, California Suite, 1978 (Acad. award Best Supporting Actress 1978), In The Spirit, 1990; co-author screenplay Heaven Can Wait, 1978, Birdcage, 1996, Primary Colors, 1998; author plays A Matter of Position, 1962, Not Enough Rope, 1962, Adaptation, 1969, Hot Line, 1983, Better Part of Valor, 1983, Mr. Gogol and Mr. Preen, 1991, (one act) Death Defying Acts, 1995, After the Night and the Music, 2005; stage revue: (with Mike Nichols) Telephone, 1984; co-recipient (with Mike Nichols) Grammy award for comedy performance, Nat. Acad. Recording Arts & Scis., 1961; actress (film) Small Time Crooks, 2000.

MAY, ELAINE TYLER, social sciences educator, history professor; b. L.A., Calif., Sept. 17, 1947; d. Edward Teitelbaum and Lillian Bass Tyler; m. Lary Linden May, Mar. 7, 1970; children: Michael Edward, Daniel David, Sarah Lillian. PhD, UCLA, 1975. Prof. Am. studies and history U. Minn., Mpls., 1978—. Author: Homeward Bound: American Families in the Cold War Era, Great Expectations: Marriage and Divorce in Post-Victorian America, Barren in the Promised Land: Childless Americans and the Pursuit of Happiness. Office: U Minn Am Studies Dept 104 Scott Hall 72 Pleasant St Minneapolis MN 55455 Office Phone: 612-624-4190.

MAY, GITA, literature educator; b. Brussels, Sept. 16, 1929; came to U.S., 1947, naturalized, 1950; d. Albert and Blima (Sieradska) Jochimek; m. Irving May, Dec. 21, 1947. BA magna cum laude, CUNY-Hunter Coll., 1953; MA, Columbia U., 1954, PhD, 1957. Lectr. French CUNY-Hunter Coll., 1953—56; from instr. to assoc. prof. Columbia U., N.Y.C., 1956—68, prof., 1968—, chmn., 1983—93, mem. senate, 1979—83, 1986—88, chmn. Seminar on 18th Century Culture, 1986—89. Lecture tour English univs., 1965. Author: Diderot et Baudelaire, critiques d'art, 1957, De Jean-Jacques Rousseau à Madame Roland: essai sur la sensibilité préromantique et révolutionnaire, 1964, Madame Roland and the Age of Revolution, 1970 (Van Amringe Disting. Book award), Stendhal and the Age of Napoleon, 1977, French Women Writers, 1991, Encyclopedia of Aesthetics, 1998, Dictionnaire de Diderot, 1999, The Feminist Encyclopedia of French Literature, 1999, Elisabeth Vigée Le Brun: The Odyssey of an Artist in an Age of Revolution, 2005; co-editor: Diderot Studies III, 1961; mem. editl. bd. Romanic Rev., 1959—, 18th Century Studies, 1975—78, French Rev., 1975—86, 1998—, Women in French Studies, 2000—; contbg. editor: Oeuvres complètes de Diderot, 1984—, 1995—; gen. editor The Age of Revolution and Romanticism: Interdisciplinary Studies, 1990—, extensive essays on Diderot and George Sand in European Writers, 1984, 1985, and on Rebecca West, Anita Brookner and Graham Swift in British Writers, 1996, 1997, 1999, Bayle, Fontenelle and Fénelon in Dictionary of Literary Biography, 2003, Voltaire's Candide (in Barnes and Noble Classics), 2003; contbr. articles and revs. to profl. jours. Decorated chevalier and officier Ordre des Palmes Acad.; recipient award Am. Coun. Learned Socs., 1961, award for outstanding achievement CUNY-Hunter Coll., 1963; Fulbright rsch. grantee, 1964-65; Guggenheim fellow, 1964-65, NEH fellow, 1971-72. Mem. AAUP, MLA (del. assembly 1973-75, com. rsch. activities 1975-78, exec. coun. 1980-83), Am. Assn. Tchrs. French, Am. Soc. 18th Century Studies (pres. 1985-86, 2d v.p. 1983-84, 1st v.p. 1984-85, One of Gt. Tchrs. award 1999), Soc. Française d'Etude du Dix-Huitième Siècle, Soc. Diderot, Am. Soc. French Acad. Palms, Soc. des Etudes Staëliennes, N.Am. Soc. for Study of Jean-Jacques Rousseau, Soc. des Professeurs Français et Francophones d'Amérique, Phi Beta Kappa. Office: Columbia U Dept French/Romance Philol 516 Philosophy Hall MC4918 New York NY 10027 Business E-Mail: gm9@columbia.edu.

MAY, JANET SUE, playwright, lyricist; b. Bloomington, Ill., Dec. 24, 1946; d. James Woolston and Josephine Elisabeth (Ferguson) Grubb; children: John, Darbi, Heather, Brandy. Student, Lincoln Coll., 1965, Wabash Coll., 1965, St. Joseph's Hosp., 1966, Indian River C.C., 1983, Bloomington Sch. Practical Nursing, 1984; cert. in food svc. sanitation, Ill. State U., 1988. Chem. lab. tech. Eureka Williams, Bloomington, 1966; histology tech. St. Joseph's Hosp., Bloomington, 1966—67; activity dir. McLean County Nursing Home, Normal, Ill., 1968—70; rsch. asst. U. Fla. Med. Entomology Lab., Vero Beach, Fla., 1984—85; asst. libr. condemned unit Pontiac Prison, Ill., 1974—75; activity dir., meal supr. Bloomington Housing Authority, 1987—89; pub. rels. mgr. Miracle Ear, Peoria, Ill., 1990—92. Author: (children's poetry books) Winston-Smythe Worm, Prissy Penelope Grasshopper Presents, (children's books) Four Little Creatures; co-author (with James Kitzmiller): Patronymics of Mosquitoes, 2d edit., 1986; playwright: More Than Just A Man, 2001; playwright: Abrahams House, 2005, songwriter: Ice Age; author: (musical) Abraham's House, 2005. Achievements include co-inventor, tissue vacuum pump; invention of jeweled perfumed hair tie; blinking hair tie. Avocations: art, poetry, singing.

MAY, KATHERINE ELEANOR, art educator, photographer; d. Charles Harold May, II and Mary Virginia May; children: Cynthia Sue Baine, Kandace Ann Constantine. BA, Rocky Mountain Coll., Billings, Mont., 1992; MA, Temple U., Phila., 1996; MFA, Acad. of Art U., San Francisco, 1998. Dept. asst. Rocky Mountain Coll., Billings, Mont.; archaeology lab. technician Temple U., Phila.; photography asst. Morton Beebee, San Francisco; photographer INSTAP, Crete, Greece; tutor K-12 Kumon Learning Ctr., Hesperia, Calif.; realtor Coll. Realty, Hesperia; art tchr. Crosswalk Learning Pathways, Hesperia. Author: Imaging the Ancient, 1998; Mochos, 2003, book, Pseina, 2004. Recipient Dept. award, Rocky Mountain Coll., 1990, 1992. Mem.: Nat. Assn. Realtors. Avocations: painting, photography, Yorkies, redecorationg, gardening. Home: 19265 Westlawn St Hesperia CA 92345

MAY, LINDA KAREN CARDIFF, occupational health nurse, safety engineer, consultant; b. San Mateo, Calif., Oct. 26, 1948; d. Leon Davis and Jane Vivian (Gallow) Cardiff; m. Donald William May, Dec. 7, 1969 (div. Feb. 1988); children: Charles David, Andrew William. At, So. Ill. U., 1969; post grad., Ill. Wesleyan U., 1989; AAS, Parkland Coll., 1977; BS in Pub. Health and Safety Engring. with honors, U. Ill., Urbana, 1987; BSN, Lakeview Coll., 1990. RN Ill., Ind., Mo., N.Mex., Tex., Wis., registered profl. nurse; nat. registered EMT Ill., accredited instr. constrn. safety and health OSHA. Indsl. nurse C.S. Johnson Co., Champaign, Ill., 1979—84; safety engr. Clinton Nuclear Power Plant Ill. Power Co., 1984—86; occupl. safety and health specialist Danville Vet.'s Med. Ctr., 1986—. With LKM Health and Safety Cons., Inc., Champaign, Ill. Active Mercy Hosp. Aux., Covenant Hosp Aux., 1977—, Champaign County Task Force on Arson, 1981—; alumni assn. liason Parkland Coll. Found. Bd., 1993; mem. Champaign County Crime Prevention Coun., 1978—83, bd. dir., 1980—82. Ill. State Gen. Assembly scholar, 1967. Mem.: APHA (occpl. health and safety sect.), AACN, Lakeview Coll. Nursing Alumni Assn., N.Y. Acad. Sci., Ill. EMTs Assn., Pre-Hosp. Care Providers Ill., Associated Ill. Milk, Food and Environ. Sanitarians, Ill. Soc. Pub. Health Educators, Ill. Environ. Health Assn., Nat. Registry EMT, Am. Assn. Occupational Health Nurses, Am. Nuc. Assn. (mem. biology and medicine divsn., mem. radiopharm. and isotope product stds. com.), Am. Soc. Safety Engrs. (vice chair Ctrl. Ill. sect. 1985—86), Ill. Wesleyan U. Alumni Assn., U. Ill. Alumni Assn. (life), Parkland Coll. Alumni Assn. (life; bd. dir. 1987—, v.p. 1992—), Eta Sigma Gamma. Methodist. Home: PO Box 3954 Champaign IL 61826-3954 Personal E-mail: lmay4111@aol.com.

MAY, MARGRETHE, healthcare educator; b. Tucson, Oct. 6, 1943; d. Robert A. and Margrethe (Holm) M. BS in Human Biology, U. Mich., 1970, MS in Anatomy, 1986. Cert. surg. technologist. Surg. technologist Hartford (Conn.) Hosp., 1965-68, U. Mich. Hosps., Ann Arbor, 1968-70; asst. operating room supr. U. Ariz. Med. Ctr., Tucson, 1971-72; coord. operating room tech. program Pima Coll., Tucson, 1971-76; prof., coord. surg. tech. and surg. first asst. programs Delta Coll., University Center, Mich., 1978—99, coord., surg. first asst. distance edn. program, 1999—2003, coord. surg. tech. program, 2003—. Commr. Commn. on Accreditation of Allied Health Ednl. Programs, Chgo., 1994-97, Coun. Accreditation and Unit Recognition, 1994-96. Editor: Core Curriculum for Surgical Technology, 3d edit., 1990, Core Curriculum for Surgical First Assisting, 1993; contbr. articles to profl. jours. Mem. Assn. Surg. Technologists (bd. dirs. 1987-89, pres.-elect 1989-90, pres. 1990-91, on-site visitor program accreditation 1974—, chmn. exam writing com. 1981, liaison coun. on cert. co-chmn. 1977, chmn. 1978, sec.-treas. 1979, chmn. accreditation review com for edn. in surg. tech. 1994-97, Mich. state assembly AST bd. dirs. 2000-04), Am. Soc. Law, Medicine and Ethics, Mich. Assn. Allied Health Professions (sec. 1994-97), Nat. Network Health Career Programs in Two-Year Colls. Avocation: international health care issues and allied health education. Home: 2506 Abbott Rd Apt P-2 Midland MI 48642-4876 Office: Delta Coll Health and Wellness Divsn 1961 Delta Rd University Center MI 48710-0001 Office Phone: 989-686-9505. Business E-Mail: mmay@delta.edu.

MAY, MISTY, Olympic athlete; b. July 30, 1977; Majored in Kinesiology & Physical Ed., Long Beach State U. Mem. U.S. National Indoor Team, 1998, 1999; beach volleyball player Team USA, Sydney Olympic Games, 2000, Team USA, Athens Olympic Games, 2004. Named BVA Rookie of the Yr., 2000, AVP Team of the Yr. (with Kerri Walsh), 2003. Achievements include member of NCAA national championship team, 1998; one of only three players to be named a two-time AVCA National Player of the year, 1997, 1998; winning FIVB Tour with teammate Kerri Walsh, 2002, 2003; winning a gold medal at Athens Olympic Games, beach volleyball, 2004. Office: c/o USOC One Olympic Plz Colorado Springs CO 80909

MAY, PHYLLIS JEAN, financial executive; b. Flint, Mich., May 31, 1932; d. Bert A. and Alice C. (Rushton) Irvine; m. John May, Apr. 24, 1971 (dec. 1997). Grad., Dorsey Sch. Bus., 1957; cert., Internat. Corr. Schs., 1959; MBA, Mich. U., 1970; cert., Nat. Tax Inst., 1978. Registered real estate agt; lic. life, auto and home ins. agt. Office mgr. Comml. Constrn. Co., Flint, 1962-68; bus. mgr. new and used car dealership Flint, 1968-70; contr. various corps., 1970-75; fiscal dir. Rubicon Odyssey Inc., Detroit, 1976-87, Wayne County Treas.'s Office, 1987-93; exec. fin. office Grosse Pointe Meml. Ch., Mich., 1993—. Acad. cons. acctg. Detroit Inst. Commerce, 1980-81; pres. small bus. specializing in adminstrv. cons. and acctg., 1982—; supr. mobile svc. stat., upholstery and home improvement businesses; owner retail bus. Pieces and Things. Pres. PTA Westwood Heights Schs., 1972; vol. Fedn. of Blind, 1974-76, Probate Ct., 1974-76; mem. citizens adv. bd. Northville Regional Psychiat. Hosp., 1988, sec., 1989-90; pres. La Renaissance Condominium Assn., Atlantic City, 1996-2000, sec., 2000-02, treas., 2004—. Recipient Meritorious Svc. award Genesee County for Youth, 1976, Excellent Performance and High Achievement award Odyssey Inc., 1981. Mem. NAFE (bd. dirs.), Am. Bus. Women's Assn. (treas. 1981, rec. sec. 1982, v.p. 1982-83, Woman of Yr. 1982), Womens Assn. Dearborn Orch. Soc., Dearborn Cmty. Art Ctr., Mich. Mental Health Assn., Internat. Platform Assn., Guild of Carillonneurs in N.Am., Pi Omicron (officer 1984-85, treas. 2002-05, state treas. 2004, dist. treas. 2005-06, nat. treas. 2006). Presbyterian. Office Phone: 313-882-5330. Business E-Mail: pmay@gpmchurch.org.

MAYAK, JEANNETTE M., speech pathology/audiology services professional, educator; b. Boswell, Pa., Feb. 12, 1952; d. Glenn A. Lintz and Josephine A. Bazyk-Lintz; m. James G. Mayak, June 1, 1974; children: Jaime, Jeffrey. BS in Edn., Calif. State Coll., Pa., 1973; MEd, Ind. U. Pa., 1979. Speech lang. pathologist Intermediate Unit 08, Ebensburg, Pa., 1973—92, Crossroads Speech & Hearing, McMurray, Pa., 1991—92, Somerset Area Sch. Dist., Somerset, Pa., 1992—2006. Vol., day camps Somerset Welfare League, Pa., 2000—03; dir., religious edn. All Saints Parish, Boswell, Pa., 1983—95, 1998—2006, pastoral coun. mem., 2002—05. Mem.: PTA, Pa. State Edn. Assn., Pa. Speech Lang. Hearing Assn. Roman Catholic. Avocations: reading, walking, volunteer work. Home: 180 Ralphton Rd Stoystown PA 15563 Office: Maple Ridge Elem Sch 105 New Centerville Rd Somerset PA 15501 Personal E-mail: jmayak00@netzero.net.

MAYBIN, JEANNETTE ERGLER, elementary school educator, art educator; d. Paul Charles Ergler, Sr. and Dorothy Pollard Ergler; m. Arthur H. Maybin, III, June 5, 1976; children: Lindsay, Caitlin. BA, Western Md. Coll., Westminster, Md., 1972; MA in Edn., U. Ga., Athens, 1975. Nat. bd. cert. tchr. Nat. Bd. for Profl. Tchg. Stds. Art tchr. Balt. County Schs., 1972—74, Duval County Schs., Jacksonville, Fla., 1976—78, Richland Sch. Dist. 1, Columbia, SC, 1978—80, Sch. Dist. 5 Lexington and Richland Counties, Ballentine, SC, 1981—. Arts and crafts dir. Crooked Creek Riding Acad. Summer Camp, Lexington, SC, 1993—. Active Shady Grove United Meth. Ch., Irmo, SC. Mem.: SC Art Edn. Assn. (Elem. Art Educator of Yr. 1998), Nat. Art Edn. Assn. Avocations: horseback riding, painting. Office: HE Corley Elem Sch 1500 Chadford Rd Irmo SC 29063

MAYDEN, BARBARA MENDEL, lawyer; b. Chattanooga, Sept. 18, 1951; d. Eugene Lester Mendel and Blanche (Krugman) Rosenberg; m. Martin Ted Mayden, Sept. 14, 1986. AB, Ind. U., 1973; JD, U. Ga., 1976. Bar: Ga. 1976, N.Y. 1980. Assoc. King & Spalding, Atlanta, 1976-79, Willkie Farr & Gallagher, N.Y.C., 1980, Morgan Lewis & Bockius, N.Y.C., 1980-82, White & Case, N.Y.C., 1982-89; spl. counsel Skadden, Arps, Slate, Meagher & Flom, N.Y.C., 1989-95; mem. Bass, Berry & Sims PLC, Nashville, 1996—; lectr. Vanderbilt U. Sch. Law, Nashville, 1995-97. Mem. editl. bd.: mag. Business Law Today; editor: Business Lawyer; chair sect. bus. law:, 2004—05. Mem. bd. visitors U. Ga. Sch. Law, Athens, 1986—89; mem. Leadership Nashville, 1999—2000; mem. adv. bd. Women's Fund of the Cmty. Found. of Mid. Tenn., 2001—; bd. dirs. YWCA, 2001—, Jewish Cmty. Ctr., 2001—02. Fellow Am. Bar Found. (life); mem. ABA (chair young lawyers divsn. 1985-86, ho. of dels. 1986—2004, commn. on women 1987-91, commn. opportunities for minorities in profession 1986-87, select com. of the house 1989-91, chmn. assembly resolutions com. 1990-91, membership com. of the house 1991-92, bd. govs. 1991-94, chair com. on rules and calendar 1996-98, chair bd. govs. ops. com., exec. com. 1993-94, task force long range fin. planning 1993-94, com. scope correlation of work 1998-2003, chair 2001-02, sec. bus. law sect. 2001-02, vice-chair 2002-03, chair-elect 2003-04, chair 2004—05), Nat. Assn. Bond Lawyers (bd. dirs. 1985-86), Bond Attys.' Workshop (chmn. 1986), N.Y. State Bar Assn. (ho. of dels. 1993-95), Assn. Bar City N.Y. (internat. human rights com. 1986-89, 2d century com. 1986-90, com. women in the profession, 1989-92), N.Y. County Lawyers Assn. (com. spl. projects, chair com. rels with other bars), Am. Law Inst., Tenn. Bar Assn. (com. chair), Am. Bar Ins. Plans Cons., Inc. (bd. dirs., treas.). Democrat. Jewish. Home: 4414 Herbert Pl Nashville TN 37215-4544 Office: Bass Berry & Sims PLC AmSouth Center 315 Deaderick St Ste 2700 Nashville TN 37238-3001 Office Phone: 615-742-6208. Business E-Mail: bmayden@bassberry.com.

MAYEAUX, ANNE RUSSELL, education educator; b. Meridian, Miss., Aug. 27, 1943; d. Constant Hyacinth and Laura Archer Mayeaux. BA, St. Xavier U., 1961—65; PhD, Emory U., 1968—75. Dir. World Peace Ctr., Chgo., 1967—68; postdoctoral fellow and adj. faculty Candler Sch. of Theology, Atlanta, 1975—81. Exec. dir. Ga. Endowment for the Humanities, 1979—81; faculty and pres. Aquinas Ctr. of Theology at Emory U., Atlanta, 1983—90; vis. scholar in ethics and soc. Harvard Div. Sch., Cambridge, Mass., 1990—91; assoc. prof. Siena Heights U., Adrian, Mich., 1991—96; rschr. Inst. for Social Rsch., U. of Mich., 1996—99; chair, theology dept., and faculty St. Joseph, Madison, Miss., 1999—; adj. faculty Hinds C.C., Jackson, Miss., 2000—. Contbr. articles to jours. Pres. Las Casas, Nat. Ministry among the Native Americans, Clinton, Okla., 1989—93; bd. dirs. Nat. Assembly of Religious Women, Chgo., 1991—94; sec./treas. Internat. Found. for Scholarly Exch., Atlanta, 1988—94. Recipient Human Rights Citation, Dominican Justice Promoters of N.Am., 1991, Outstanding Tchg. of the Yr., Siena Heights U., 1992—93, Internat. Del. of Scholars to Russia and the Ukraine, People to People and Am. Acad. of Religion, 1993, Outstanding Tchg., Archdiocese of Atlanta, 1983—84, Catharine of Siena award, St. Catharine's Dominican Congregation, 1990, Citation for Courage for Human Rights Work in Gulf War, U.S. Dominican Leadership Conf., 1991; Catherine McAuley scholar, St. Xavier U., 1965, Raskob Found. grant, Raskob Found., 1992—94, N.E.H. Landmarks of Am. History: Summer Inst., Nat. Endowment for the Humanities, 2004, grant, 2002, Fulbright Scholar, U. of Tuebingen, German, Fulbright Commn., 1966—67. Mem.: AAUP (v.p., siena heights u. chpt. 1995), Am. Acad. of Religion (chair, program sect., s.e. region 1975—91). Democrat-Npl. Roman Catholic. Home: 217 Melrose Dr Jackson MS 39211

MAYEK, HELEN CECILIA, executive secretary; arrived in U.S., 1923; d. Sigmund and Felicia Mayek. AA, NYU, 1974, BA, 1976, MA in adminstrn., 1984. Sec. expediting sales asst. Indsl. Sales Corp., N.Y.C.; mktg. sales asst. Dean Witter Inter Capital, Wall Street; sec. Julius Klein Pub. Rels., Washington, ITT Corp., N.Y.C., Raymeon Corp., Washington. Cons. The Kosciuszko Found., 1983—84. Conductor (cultural events) The Kosciuszko Found., 1976—80, Washington Square East Gallery, 1981. Sec., vol. Hospice of Lake Co., 1987—88. Mem.: Found. Cmty. Artists, Am. Assn. Mus. Democrat. Roman Catholic. Home: 3000 Brook Field Ave Mount Dora FL 32757

MAYER, ANNE BRESTEL, music educator; b. Cleve., Nov. 25, 1935; d. Theodore Clinton and Martha Elizabeth (Hazzard) M. BA in Music, Coll. Wooster, 1957; M Music in Piano and Music Literature, Eastman Sch. Music, Rochester, N.Y., 1959. Instr., prof. Carleton Coll., Northfield, Minn., 1959—99, Dye prof. music, 1983—, co-chmn. music dept., 1973-86, 89-90. Profl. accompanist Columbia Artists, 1965; test writer Coll. Bds. Advanced Placemnt Test in Music Theory, 1975; recording accompanist Orion Records, 1979. Chair adminstrv. bd. Meth. Ch., Northfield, 1985—88. Recipient Fulbright award, 1962-63, Pi Kappa Lambda prize in music. Mem. Coll. Music Soc., Music Tchrs. Nat. Assn., Fulbright Alumni Orgn., Matthay Soc., Thursday Musical Club. Democrat.

MAYER, BEATRICE CUMMINGS, civic worker; b. Montreal, P.Q., Can., Aug. 15, 1921; came to U.S., 1939, naturalized, 1944; d. Nathan and Ruth (Kellert) Cummings; BA in Chemistry, U. N.C., 1943; postgrad. U. Chgo., 1946; LHD (hon.)1991, Spertus Coll. Judaica, 1983, Kenyon Coll., 1987; m. Robert Bloom Mayer, Dec. 11, 1947 (dec.); children: Robert N., Mrs. Ruth M. Durchslag. Mem. vis. com. Sch. Social Svc. Adminstrn. U. Chgo., 1964—, dept. art, 1972—; dir. women's bd., 1973—, Art Inst. Chgo. (life trustee) 1984—; bd. dirs. Michael Reese Hosp. Corp., Chgo., 1974-1982—, bd. dirs. Spoleto Festival, 1980—1989; trustee Kenyon Coll., Gambier, Ohio, 1976-89, trustee emritus, 1989—; bd. fellows Brandeis U., Waltham, Mass., 1977—;trustee Anshe Emet Synagogue, Chgo., 1974—1990, (life trustee 1990-); trustee Mus. Contemporary Art, Chgo., 1974—1990, (life trustee 1990-); mem. adv. com. U.N.C. Ackland Mus. visiting com.1985-, Recipient Brandeis U. Disting. Community Service award, 1972, medallion Am. Jewish Com. Human Rights, 1976, Outstanding Achievement award in the Arts, YWCA Met. Chgo., 1979, Centennial Gold Medal for Disting. Community Service Jewish Theol. Sem., 1986, Alumni Laureate award Loyola Coll. Balt., 1984; named to Hall of Fame, Jewish Community Ctrs. Adult Services, 1987, Rosary Coll. Bravo award in Art, 1994, U. Chic. Alumni Nation award, 2001, Jewish Council on Urban Affairs Cmty. Svc. award, 2002.; Clubs: Tavern, Standard (Chgo.); Lake Shore Country (Glencoe, Ill.). Home: 160 E Pearson St # 3103 Chicago IL 60611-2148

MAYER, EVE ORLANS, marketing professional, writer; b. Bklyn., Apr. 26, 1930; d. Abraham Salem Orlans and Rose V. Wissotsky; m. Sidney A. Mayer, Jun. 8, 1952; children: Marc Orlans Mayer and Jonathan Orlans Mayer. BA cum laude, Hunter Coll., 1951; MS, Columbia Univ., 1952. Asst. editor Human Interest Mag., N.Y.C., 1952-53; asst. prodr. Channel 5, N.Y.C., 1953-54; publicity writer NYU, N.Y.C., 1954-57; freelance writer N.Y.C., 1957—; publ. rels. dir. Parsons Sch. of Design, N.Y.C., 1970-74, 1979-84; owner, prin. Eve Orlans Mayer, Inc., N.Y.C., 1984-92. Contbr. articles to newspapers and mags.; ghost writer, speech writer:, interviewer: Steven Spielberg's Survivors of the Shoah Visual History Found., 1993—2000. Bd. dirs. CARING at Columbia, Columbia U. Coll. Phys. and Surg., 1991—2000; mem. alumni exec. com. Sch. Journalism, 1995—2006; mem. ann. fund com. Columbia U. Grad. Sch. Journalism, 2006—; mem. Dem. Congl. Campaign Com., 1995—. Recipient Columbia U. Alumni medal, 2002. Mem. Hadassah Women's Zionist Orgn. Am., World Jewish Congress, Anti-Defamation League, Am. Jewish Congress, NARAL, NOW, Planned Parenthood, Compassion and Choice, Hemlock Soc., Mother's Voices, Emily's List, Phi Beta Kappa, Sigma Tau Delta. Democrat. Jewish. Avocations: theater, travel, reading, music, movies. Home: 15 W 81st St Apt 8A New York NY 10024-6022 Personal E-mail: eveomayer@aol.com.

MAYER, HEIDI MARIE, primary school educator; d. Roy B. and Hertha R. Mayer. AAS, Westchester Bus. Inst., White Plains, NY, 1986; BS in Bus. Edn., Concordia Coll., Bronxville, NY, 1993; MEd, Fordham U., Tarrytown, NY, 2000. Cert. tchr. NY. 3d and 4th grade tchr. St. Marks Luth. Sch., Yonkers, NY, 1993—97, kindergarten tchr., 1997—. Cons. in field; liaison St. Marks PTL, Yonkers, 2001—06. Mem.: Alpha Chi. Avocations: singing, piano, reading, painting, crafts. Home: 4216 Oneida Ave Bronx NY 10470 Office: St Marks Luth Sch St Marks Pl and Kimball Ave Yonkers NY 10704

MAYER, JOYCE HARRIS, artist; b. N.Y.C., May 7, 1935; d. Harold and Dorothy Harris; m. Bernard Charles Mayer, Mar. 15, 1969; 1 child, Robert Charles. AAS, Inst. of Applied Art and Sci., N.Y.C., 1957. Sketcher Merrylen Cartooning Studio, 1952. Client contact, layout artist, Haire Publ., N.Y.C., 1957-59; art dir., Real Estate Forum, N.Y.C., 1959-60; Denhard and Stewart, N.Y.C., 1960-67; Herb Lubalin Graphic Art Award, 1964; self employed N.Y.C., 1967-71; co curator, New Orleans Mus. of Art, 1985. Among first women to have work pub. in Art Direction, 1964, exhibitions include N.Y. Inst. of Applied Arts and Sci., New Orleans Mus. of Art, 2003, Horizon Gallery, Royal Typographers, N.Y., Nat. Arts Club, Tulane Univ., Dominican Coll., Robinson Gallery, Mario Villa and Arthur Roger, New Orleans, TWEED Gallery, Plainfield, N.J., Barbara Gillman Gallery, Miami, Contemporary Art Ctr., New Orleans, Bruce Mus., Conn., Historic New Orleans Collection, N.C. Mus. Art, LBI Found. Arts and Sci. N.J., Cheltenham Art Ctr., Pa., Long Beach Island Nat. Exhbn., 2004, NJ Print Coun. Traveling Internat. Competition, 2005, AIR Gallery, Chelsea, N.Y., 2006, Spring Bull Gallery, Newport, R.I., 2006, Represented in permanent collections paintings, mono prints, and digital art in numerous collections in Europe and. U.S., Digital La., Contemporary Art Ctr., New Orleans, 2002, Biennale Internazionale dell Arte Contemporanea, Florence, Italy, 2003, N.C. Mus. Art, numerous others. Mem. Bd. Edn., Greenwich, Conn., 1978; art advisor Freeport McMoRan Art Collection, New Orleans, 1985; curator Mario Villa Gallery, New Orleans, 1989; juror Arts Coun., New Orleans, 1990. Recipient Chiam Gross sculpture award, 1967, N.Y. Graphic Soc. award, 1976, medal in photography, Florence Biennale, 2003, Otis B. Morse Meml. award, Am. Coll., Pa., 2005. Mem. Medici Coll. Art Assn., Am. Color Print Soc., The Print Ctr. Avocations: reading, theater, ballet, birdwatching. Studio: 8 Golfview Dr Medford NJ 08055 Office Phone: 609-953-2390. E-mail: joycehmayer@aol.com.

MAYER, KAY MAGNOR, writer; b. 1943; d. Frank J. and Harriet (Schnell) Magnor; m. Kenneth W. Mayer, May 2, 1943; children: Michael J., Patricia A., Mark T. Student, Northwestern U., 1938-43. News reporter Tampa Times, 1943; advt. copywriter Marshall Field & Co., Chgo., Earle Ludgin & Co., Chgo.; Henri, Hurst & McDonald Chgo., 1944-58; spl. editor, writer Scott, Foresman & Co., Glenview, Ill., 1966-71; freelance writer Columbia, 1971—. Recipient Press Women's awards, 1983, 84, 85, 89, 92, 93, 98. Mem. Nat. Fedn. Press Women, Ill. Press Women, Western History Assn., Soc. Southwestern Authors (dir. 1981-83), The Writers (hon. mem.), Glencoe, Ill.

MAYER, KRISTINE I., psychotherapist, writer; b. Tulsa, Okla., Dec. 11, 1969; d. Harry W. and Eleanor M. (Westphal) Meeker; m. Heinz C. Mayer, Jan. 18, 1986 (div. 1995); children: Justin, Forrest. BA in journalism, Okla. State Univ., 1987; MS in counseling psych., Northeastern State Univ., 1991. Lic. profl. counselor Okla. Mental health counselor Mayer Counseling Svcs., Inc., Tulsa, 1991-96; child welfare specialist State of Okla. Dept. Human Svc., 1996—2000; profl. gun seller Broken Arrow, Okla., 2000—. Mem. Am. Counseling Assn., Okla. Scholar Leadership, Psi Chi. Avocations: travel, equestrian sports, history, music, theater.

MAYER, LYNNE SUPOVITZ, academic administrator; b. Steubenville, Ohio, Apr. 30, 1946; d. Paul and Sylvia Supovitz; m. Paul Jay Mayer, June 1, 1969; children: Rachel Elaine, Deborah Joyce. BA in Edn., U. Mich., 1968; MA, Columbia U., 1969; MBA, Marshall U., 1982; EdD, W.Va. U., 1991. Summer rsch. asst. U.S. Office Edn., Washington, 1968; rsch. specialist info. svcs. W.Va. Rsch. Coord. Unit for Vocat. Edn., Huntington, 1970-72; asst. dir. Bur. Voc-Tec. & Adult Edn. W.Va. State Dept. Edn., Charleston, 1974; adminstrv. asst. Marshall U., Huntington, W.Va., 1976-84, dir. planning, asst. to pres., 1984-87, spl. asst. to pres., 1987-91, asst. v.p. instnl. advancement, 1991—2001, assoc. v.p. devel., 2002—. Contbr. articles and revs. to profl. jours. Active Huntington Mus. Art, B'nai Sholom Congregation, past pres., Huntington. Named one of Outstanding Young Women Am., 1981. Mem. LWV, Nat. Coun. Jewish Women. Nat. Soc. Fund Raising Execs., Coun. for Advancement and Support of Edn., Hadassah, Phi Delta Kappa, Huntington Rotary club. Democrat. Avocations: reading, travel, weightlifting, bicycling. Home: 219 12th Ave Huntington WV 25701-3126

MAYER, MARGARET ELLEN, medical coding specialist; d. Theodore Robert and Doris Jane Mayer; children: J. Bradford Bellamy, Christian D. Bellamy, Stephen J. Bellamy. Student, Towson U., Md.; AA, Essex CC, Balt., 1990. Coding and data mgr. Union Hosp. Cecil County, Elkton, Md.; coding specialist Johns Hopkins Bayview Med. Ctr., Balt., Greater Balt. Med. Ctr., Towson. Cons. Receivables OutSourcing, Inc., Tominium, Md., FMAS Corp., Columbia, Md., Quadra Med. Corp., Bethlehem, Pa. Docent Md. Zoo, Balt., 2005; mem. gov.'s team Md. Rep. Party, 2006. Mem.: Am. Health Info. Mgmt. Assn. (cert. coding specialist), Phi Theta Kappa. Republican. Methodist. Avocations: equestrian events, painting, history, wildlife conservation, beekeeping. Office: Union Hosp Cecil County 106 Bow St Elkton MD 21921

MAYER, MARILYN GOODER, steel company executive; b. Chgo. d. Seth MacDonald and Jean (McMullen) Gooder; m. William Anthony Mayer, Nov. 14, 1959; children: William Anthony Jr., Robert MacDonald. Grad., Career Inst., Chgo., 1941; student, Lake Forest Coll., Ill., 1942. Adminstrv. asst. Needham, Louis & Brorby, Chgo., 1949-53; v.p. RMB Corp., Chgo., 1963-71, Mayer Motors, Ft. Lauderdale, Fla., 1965-74, Gooder-Henrichsen, Chicago Heights, Ill., 1975—. Dir. Barnett Bank, West Palm Beach, Fla. Trustee Gulf Stream (Fla.) Sch.; trustee emerita St. Andrew's Sch., Boca Raton, Fla.; bd. dirs. Bethesda Hosp. Assn., Boynton Beach, Fla., pres. 1981-82; bd. dirs. Gulf Stream Civic Assn. Mem. Soc. Four Arts, Little Club, Gulf Stream Bath and Tennis Club (gov.). Avocation: travel. Home: 2925 Polo Dr Delray Beach FL 33483-7331

MAYER, MARISSA ANN, information technology executive; b. Wausau, Wis., May 30, 1975; BS with honors in Symbolic Sys., Stanford U., MS in Computer Sci. With UBS rsch. lab. Zurich, Switzerland, SRI Internat., Menlo Park, Calif.; programmer, software engr. Google Inc., 1999, dir. consumer web products Mountain View, v.p. search products & user experience. Tchr. computer programming Stanford U. Named one of 25 Masters of Innovation, BusinessWeek, 2006; recipient Centennial Tchg. award, Stanford U., Forsythe award. Office: Google Inc 1600 Amphitheatre Pky Mountain View CA 94043 Office Phone: 650-253-0000. Office Fax: 650-253-0001. E-mail: marissa@google.com.*

MAYER, PATRICIA E., SR., elementary school educator; b. Union City, NJ, Dec. 20, 1929; d. Joseph Victor and Johanna Bruns Mayer. BA, Coll. St. Elizabeth, Convent Station, NJ, 1964. Joined Sisters of Charity Roman Cath. Ch.; cert. tchr. Alaska. Tchr. 1st grade St. Aloysius Sch., Jersey City, 1949—50, St. Andrew's Sch., Westwood, NJ, 1950—51; tchr. 4th grade St. Rose of Lima Sch., Short Hills, NJ, 1951—53; tchr. 5-6th grade St. Michael's Sch., Union City, NJ, 1953—59; tchr. 4th grade St. Nicholas Sch., Passaic, NJ, 1959—60; tchr. 3rd, 6-7th grades St. Bridget Sch., Jersey City, 1960—70; tchr. 7-8th grade St. Paul of the Cross Sch., Jersey City, 1970—83, Immaculate Conception/Monroe Cath. HS, 1983—. Spkr. in field. Bd. dirs. Monroe Found., 2004—. Recipient Appreciation cert., Alaska Interagy. Coord. Ctr., 2004, Dir. Cath. Schs. Fairbanks. Avocations: bowling, tennis, cooking, baking, sewing. Office: Monroe Cath Jr/Sr High Sch 615 Monroe St Fairbanks AK 99701

MAYER, ROSEMARY, artist; b. Ridgewood, N.Y., Feb. 27, 1943; d. Theodore Albert and Marie Anne (Stumpf) M. AB magna cum laude, U. Iowa, 1964; postgrad., Bklyn. Mus. Art Sch., 1964—65, Sch. Visual Arts, N.Y.C., 1967—69. Model Raphael Soyer, N.Y.C., 1968—74; writer Arts Mag., N.Y.C., 1972—75, Art in Am., N.Y.C., 1974—75. Vis. artist many schs. including Hartwick Coll., Oneonta, N.Y., 1976, Art Inst., Chgo., 1974; guest artist Nat. Endowment Workshop, Tyler Sch. Art, Phila., Mpls. Acad. Art and Design, 1981; adj. lectr. La Guardia C.C., CUNY, 1992—; adj. prof. L.I. U., 1988—; writer, speaker A.I.R. Gallery, N.Y.C., 1972-74. Translator: Pontormo's Diary 1983; author: Swatches, 1969, Surroundings, 1977. Grantee numerous orgns. including NEA, CAPS, 1976—. Democrat. Home: 55 Leonard St New York NY 10013-2928

MAYER, SONDRA, printmaker, art dealer; b. N.Y.C., July 12, 1933; d. Irving and Grace (Eil) Elster; B.A., Syracuse (N.Y.) U., 1954; M.A., Columbia U., 1955; postgrad. Pratt Inst., 1967-68, Art Students League, 1972-73; divorced; children— Howard Jeffrey, Jessica Beth. Pvt. art dealer Sondra Mayer Fine Art Gallery, Great Neck, NY, 1986-2006, Tchr. adult edn., art collecting Great Neck Schs., 2006-. One-woman shows: Everson Mus., Syracuse, N.Y., 1980; one-woman exhibit: Bryant Library, Roslyn, N.Y., 1984; two-person show: New Rochelle (N.Y.) Pub. Library, 1982; group exhbns. include Artists Equity, 1972, 76, 77, Nat. Arts Club, 1977, Nat. Print Exhbn., 1977, Davidson Galleries, Seattle, 1976, Phila. Print Club, 1978, Hunterdon Art Center, Clinton, N.J., 1978, Dreyfuss Gallery, Ann Arbor, Mich., 1978, Heckscher Mus., Huntington, N.Y., 1979, 80, 82, DeCordova Mus., Lincoln, Mass., 1979, Nat. Assn. Women Artists, 1979, 80 (Leila Sawyer Meml. prize for graphics 1979), Queens Mus., Flushing, N.Y., 1981, Great Neck (N.Y.) Library, 1981, Mini-Print Internat., Barcelona, Spain, 1981, Burnside Gallery, Greenport, N.Y., 1982, Mini Print Exhibit, Seoul, Korea, 1982, Invitational, Viridian Gallery, N.Y.C., 1983, Art Expo, N.Y.C., 1985; instr. Ruth Leaf Studio, Douglaston, N.Y., 1976—; assoc. dir. Gallery 169, Great Neck, N.Y.; art editor Great Neck Record; represented in permanent collections Albright-Knox Gallery, Buffalo, Los Angeles County Mus. Art, Syracuse U., Lowe Gallery, Bus. Com. for Arts, N.Y., Crocker Nat. Bank, San Francisco, MacDowell Colony, Portland (Oreg.) Art Mus., Inter First Bank, Dallas; works reproduced on greeting cards by Met. Mus. Art, Mus. Modern Art, UNICEF, Cartiers. MacDowell Colony fellow, 1978. Mem. Artists Equity, Phila. Print Club. Address: 6 Wooleys Ln Great Neck NY 11023-2137

MAYER, SUSAN LEE, nurse, educator; b. N.Y.C., Feb. 10, 1946; d. Hans and Frieda (Schein) Abramson; m. Steven Mayer, June 24, 1973; children: Jason, Stuart, Richard, Deborah. BSN, Hunter Coll., 1968; MA, NYU, 1974; EdD, Columbia U., 1996; postgrad., Yeshiva U., 1986, Adelphi U., 1987. RN, N.Y.; cert. in gerontology; cert. tchr., N.Y. Staff nurse ICU-CCU Montefiore Hosp., Bronx, N.Y., 1968; organizer CCU Jewish Meml. Hosp., N.Y.C., 1968; supr., adminstr. Morrisania City Hosp., N.Y.C., 1969-76; instr. Adelphi U., Garden City, N.Y., 1977-78; substitute nurse Great Neck (N.Y.) Pub. Schs., 1980-90; rsch. asst. to dean Adelphi U. Sch. Nursing, 1987-88; network dir. nursing ambulatory North Bronx Healthcare Network, 2001—. Staff nurse Winthrop U. Hosp., Mineola, NY, 1987—90, per diem nurse, 1987—90; instr. dept. nursing edn. Bronx Mcpl. Hosp. Ctr. (now Jacobi Med. Ctr.), 1990—96; asst. prof. Helene Fuld Coll. Nursing, 1996—2001; adj. instr. Bronx C.C., 1992, Queensborough C.C., 1987—89; adj. asst. prof. Iona Coll. Sch. Nursing; adj. assoc. prof. Tchrs. Coll./Columbia U., 1997—; field nurse coord. RN Home Care Winthrop U. Hosp., Mineola, 1996—2001; lectr. and presenter in field. Contbr. articles to profl. jours. including Nursing and Health Care. Bd. dirs. Great Neck Synagogue, 1981-91, v.p. Sisterhood, 1978-79, pres., 1979-81; former bd. dirs. Russell Gardens Assn.; founder Work for Share Zedek Hosp., 1977—; pres., past fin. sec. L'Chaim chpt. Hadassah Nurse Coun. N.Y. State Regents scholar, 1963. Mem. ANA, Assn. Orthodox Jewish Scientists, Am. Assn. Ambulatory Care Nurses, N.Y. Counties Registered Nurses Assn., N.Y. State Nurses Assn. (dist. 13 bd. dirs., past chmn. nurse practice com., past treas., past chair coun. ethical practice), N.Y. Assn. Ambulatory Care, Am. Assn. for History of Nursing, Nurses Edn. Alumni Assn. (past historian), Sigma Theta Tau, Kappa Delta Pi. Democrat. Office Phone: 718-515-1438. Business E-Mail: susan.mayer@nbhn.net.

MAYER, SUSAN MARTIN, art educator; b. Atlanta, Oct. 25, 1931; d. Paul McKeen and Ione (Garrett) Martin; m. Arthur James Mayer, Aug. 9, 1953; 1 child, Melinda Marilyn. Student, Am. U., 1949-50; BA, U. N.C., Greensboro, 1953; postgrad., U. Del., 1956-58; MA, Ariz. State U., 1966. Artist-in-residence Armed Forces Staff Coll., Norfolk, Va., 1968-69; mem. art faculty U. Tex., Austin, 1971—2003. Co-editor: Museum Education: History, Theory and Practice, 1989; author various mus. publs.; contbr. articles to profl. jours. Recipient award Austin Ind. Sch. Dist., 1985. Mem. Nat. Art Edn. Assn. (bd. dirs. 1983-87, award 1987, 91), Tex. Art Edn. Assn. (mus. edn. chair 1982-83, Mus. Educator of Yr. 1986), Tex. Assn. Mus. (mus. edn. chair), Austin Visual Arts Assn., Am. Assn. Mus. Personal E-mail: susanm@mail.utexas.edu.

MAYERSON, SANDRA ELAINE, lawyer; b. Dayton, Ohio, Feb. 8, 1952; d. Manuel David and Florence Louise (Tepper) M.; m. Scott Burns, May 29, 1977 (div. Oct. 1978); 1 child, Katy Joy. BA cum laude, Yale U., 1973; JD, Northwestern U., 1976. Bar: Ill. 1976, N.Y. 1997, U.S. Ct. Appeals (7th cir.) 1976, U.S. Dist. Ct. (no. dist.) Ill. 1977, U.S. Dist. Ct. Md. 1989, U.S. Ct. Appeals (5th cir.) 1994, U.S. Dist. Ct. (so. and ea. dists.) N.Y. 1997, U.S. Ct. Appeals (2nd Cir.) 1997, U.S. Dist. Ct. (ea. dist.) Mich. 2000. Assoc. gen. counsel JMB Realty Corp., Chgo., 1979-80; assoc. Chatz, Sugarman, Abrams et al, Chgo., 1980-81; ptnr. Pollack, Mayerson & Berman, Chgo., 1981-83; dep. gen. counsel AM Internat., Inc., Chgo., 1983-85; ptnr. Kirkland & Ellis, Chgo., 1985-87; ptnr., chmn. bankruptcy group Kelley Drye & Warren, N.Y.C., 1987-93; ptnr., chmn. N.Y. bankruptcy group McDermott, Will & Emery, N.Y.C., 1993-99; ptnr., bankruptcy nat. practice group leader Holland and Knight, N.Y.C., 1999—. Examiner Interco chpt. 11, 1991. Contbr. articles to profl. jours. Bd. dirs. Jr. Med. Rsch. Inst. coun. Michael Reese Hosp., Chgo., 1981-86, Self Help Inc., 2000-; met. divsn. Jewish Guild for Blind, 1990-92; nat. legal affairs com. Anti-Defamation League, 1990-91; lawyers' exec. com. United Jewish Appeal; chair Holland & Knight Nat. Bankruptcy & Creditors Rights Group, 2001-. Named one of Top 50 Women Litigators, Nat. Law Jour., 2001; assoc. fellow, Branford Coll., Yale U., 1993—. Mem. ABA (bus. bankruptcy com. 1976—, sec. 1990-93, chair avoiding powers subcom. 1993-96, chair claims trading subcom. 1997-2000, chair strategic planning subcom., 2000-), Ill. State Bar Assn. (governing council corp. and securities sect. 1983-86), Chgo. Bar Assn. (current events chmn. corp. sect. 1980-81), 7th Cir. Bar Assn., Yale Club (N.Y.C.). Democrat. Jewish. Office: Holland and Knight 195 Broadway Fl 24 New York NY 10007-3100 Business E-Mail: sandy.mayerson@hklaw.com.

MAYES, ELAINE, photographer, educator; b. Berkeley, Calif., Oct. 1, 1938; d. Don Cooper and Helen Theresa (Sweet) M.; m. Bill Arnold (div.). BA, Stanford (Calif.) U., 1958; postgrad., San Francisco Art Inst., 1958-61. Freelance photographer, San Francisco, 1961-68; asst. prof. U. Minn., Mpls., 1968-70; assoc. prof. Hampshire Coll., Amherst, Mass., 1971-81, Bard Coll., Annandale, N.Y., 1982-84, NYU, N.Y.C., 1984—. Photographer, editor: When I Dance, 1967; author, photographer: chpt. Darkroom, 1977; photographer 50 Years of Color Photography, 1986, San Francisco Viewed, 1987. Nat. Endowment for the Arts fellow, 1971, 78, 78-79; N.Y. Creative Arts Pub. Svc. fellow, 1983. Mem. Soc. for Photographic Edn. Office: NYU Tisch Sch Arts 721 Broadway New York NY 10003-6862

MAYES, ILA LAVERNE, minister; b. Eldorado, Okla., Dec. 23, 1934; d. Thomas Floyd and Irene Elizabeth (Buchanan) Jordan; m. Forrest Clay Mayes, July 2, 1954; children: Barbara, Marian, Cynthia, Janice. BA, U. Tex., El Paso, 1973; MSW, U. Mich., 1976; MDiv, Austin Presbyn. Sem., 1986. Ordained to ministry Presbyn. Ch. (U.S.A.), 1986; cert. social worker. Pastor First Presbyn. Ch., Childress, Tex., 1986-97; interim pastor Trinity Presbyn. Ch., Iowa Port, Tex., 1999—, First Presbyn. Ch., Iowa Port, 1999—; med./social worker Childress Regional Med. Ctr., 1996-97; parish assoc. Westminster Presbyn. Ch., Ann Arbor, Mich., 2004—; pastor Covenant Presbyn. Ch., Amarillo, Tex., 2005—. Mem. Austin Sem. Alumni Bd., 1991-94, Synod of the Sun Evangelism Com., Denton, 1990-93, Transition Coordinating Agy., 1991-97 Chmn. ARC, Childress, 1990; bd. dirs. Am. Cancer Soc., Childress, 1988-89; vice moderator, Palo Duro Presbytery, 1996-98. Mem. AAUW, Mortarboard, Rotary Internat., Alpha Chi, Alpha Lambda Delta. Office Phone: 806-376-5244. E-mail: ilamaz@comcast.net.

MAYES, MICHELE COLEMAN, lawyer; b. LA, July 9, 1949; BA, U. Mich., 1971, JD, 1974. Bar: Mich. 1974, U.S. Dist. Ct. 1974, Ea. Dist. of Mich. 1976, Ill. 1980, U.S. Supreme Ct. 1988, Pa. 1988. Adj. prof. Wayne State U., 1981—87; in-house counsel Colgate-Palmolive, 1992—2003; sr. v.p., gen. counsel Pitney Bowes Inc., 2003—. Mem.: ABA (mem. commn. on women in the profession 1992, co-chair, arbitration com. 1990—92). Office: Pitney Bowes Inc World Hdqs 1 Elmcroft Rd, Mail Stop MSC 6411 Stamford CT 06926-0700

MAYFIELD, KATIE SMITH, music educator; b. Valdosta, Ga., Aug. 31, 1978; d. Marcus Lee and Lyndia Johnson Smith; m. Lyndon Earl Mayfield, Nov. 27, 2004. B in Music Edn., Brewton Parker Coll., Mt. Vernon, Ga., 2000; M in Spl. Edn., Kennesaw State U., Ga., 2004. Music tchr. Ellijay Primary Sch., Ga., 2000—. Home: 279 Burgess Rd Ellijay GA 30540 Personal E-mail: ksmith@gilmerschools.com.

MAYFIELD, PEGGY JORDAN, psychologist, minister; b. Atlanta, Aug. 4, 1934; d. Claude Emmett and Ruby Earnestine (Hutchison) Jordan; children: Steven Jay, David Lee. BA with high honors, Agnes Scott Coll., 1956; MEd, Ga. State U., 1971, SEd, 1976, PhD, 1978. Diplomate Am. Bd. Adminstrv. Psychology; lic. psychologist, Ga., cons. indsl. & orgnl. psychology; ordained minister. Tchr. music, Atlanta, 1956-70; exec. dir. Hi Hope Ctr., Lawrenceville, Ga., 1971-74; devel. svc. chief program dir. Gwinnett Rockdale Newton Mental Health & Mental Retardation, Lawrenceville, Ga., 1974-78; owner, dir. Gwinnett Mental Health Assocs., Lilburn, Ga., 1978-85; pres. So. Clinic Inc.; pvt. practice clin. psychologist and counselor in assessment Lawrenceville, 1982-94; pres. Child Train, Inc., 1993—; owner Jay Lee Enterprises; pres. Mayfield Cons. Svcs., Child Train, Inc. Cons. Creative Enterprises, Lawrenceville, 1978-82; children's min. New Hope Christian Ch., 1996-98; adjudicator Nat. Guild Piano Tchrs., Austin, Tex., 1979-; min. Gordon Christian Ch., 2002; dir. Peachtree Childtown, Peachtree Christian Ch., 2002—. Author community project reports, ednl. materials, workbooks, seminars; workshop presenter depression in children and adolescents You Can Do It Parents!. Named to Hall of Fame, Nat. Guild Piano Tchrs., 1962-63; HEW fellow, 1969-71; recipient Community Program award Ga. Assn. Retarded Citizens, 1973, Nat. Tng. award, Nat. Assn. Retarded Citizens. Mem. APA, Am. Assn. Marriage and Family Therapists, Ga. Psychol. Assn., Am. Psychological Assn. (life), Phi Beta Kappa. Avocations: music, writing, reading, fishing, travel. Office: # 100 223 Scenic Hwy Lawrenceville GA 30045-5621 Office Phone: 770-995-1846. E-mail: childtrain@aol.com.

MAYFIELD, PEGGY LEE, counselor; d. Ralph Russel Horn and Dorothy Fae Roll; m. Jack Lynn Mayfield. AS in Biology, Richland C.C., Decatur, Ill., 1988; BA in Psychology, U. Ill., Springfield, 1993, MA in Counseling, 1996. Cert. nat. counselor Nat. Bd. Cert. Counselors. Child and adolescent therapist Decatur Mental Health Ctr., Ill., 1994—95, intensive family therapist, 1995—96; foster care supr., therapist Cath. Social Svcs., Bloomington, Ill., 1996—97, foster care supr., 1997—2000; lic. clin. profl. counselor Decatur, 2000—; adj. human devel. instr. U. Ill., Springfield, 1988—, accredition exhibit rm. coord., 2002—. Compassion fatigue trainer, Decatur, 1996—; comm. skills trainer, Decatur, 1998—2000. Mem.: U. Ill. Alumni Assn. (Loyalty award 2005), U. Ill. Coll. of Edn. Human Svcs. Alumni (chair 2004—, Alumnist of Yr. 1998). Home: 2155 W Center St Decatur IL 62526 E-mail: mayfield.peggy@uis.edu.

MAYHAR, ARDATH FRANCES (FRANK CANNON, JOHN KILLDEER, FRANCES HURST), writer; b. 1930; Ind. book cons., 1979—; dairyman, 1947—57; prin. East Tex. Bookstore, Nacogdoches, 1958—62; proofreader Capital Jour., Salem, Oreg., 1968—75; chicken farmer, 1976—78; proofreader Daily Sentinel, Nacogdoches, 1979—82; writer, 1982—; co-mgr. View From Orbit Bookstore, Nacogdoches, 1984—99; writing instr. Writer's Digest, 1982—2005. Author: How the Gods Wove in Kyrannon, 1979, The Seekers of Shar Nuhn, 1980, Soul Singer of Tyrnos, 1981, Warlock's Gift, 1982, Khi to Freedom, 1982, Runes of the Lyre, 1982, Golden Dream, 1983, Lords of the Triple Moons, 1983, Exile on Vlahil, 1984, The Saga of Grittel Sundotha, 1985, The World Ends in Hickory Hollow, 1985, Medicine Walk, 1985, Carrots and Miggle, 1986, The Wall, 1987, Makra Choria, 1987, Feud at Sweetwater Creek (as Frank Cannon), 1988, A Place of Silver Silence, 1988; (collaboration with Marylois Dunn) The Absolutely Perfect Horse, 1983; (collaboration with Ron Fortier) Trail of the Seahawks, 1987, Monkey Station, TSR, 1989; (as John Killdeer) Wild Country, The Untamed, Wilderness Rendezvous, Blood Kin, People of the Mesa, 1992, Island in the Lake, 1993, Towers of the Earth, 1994, Passage West, 1994, Far Horizons, 1994, Hunters of the Plains, 1995, (as Frances Hurst) High Mountain Winter, 1996, Riddles and Dreams, 2003, elec. edits., 2004-05. Mem.: Sci. Fiction/Fantasy Writers Am. Home: 533 CR 486 Chireno TX 75937 Office Phone: 936-362-2913. E-mail: ardathm@netdot.com.

MAYHUGH, TIFFANY, science educator; b. Nashville, Oct. 16, 1973; d. Terry and Joyce Mayhugh. BS in Biology, Mid. Tenn. State U., Murfreesboro, 1996. Cert. tchr. Fla. Tchr. OCPS, Orlando, 1998—. Personal E-mail: tmayhugh@cfl.rr.com.

MAYHUGH, WANDA E., language educator; d. Edwin Bryant and Ollie Mae (Terry) Ellis; children: Melissa Mayhugh Sweetman, Terra Mayhugh Futch, Justin Lewis. BA, U. Miss., Oxford, 1970. Cert. secondary English SC. English tchr. Chester (SC) Mid. Sch., 1972—77, Chester Sr. HS, 1982—. Recipient C.P.Q. award for Excellence in Job Performance, Chester Sr. HS, 2002. Presbyterian. Avocations: travel, music, reading. Home: 1672 Oak View Way Rock Hill SC 29730 Office: Chester Sr HS 1330 JA Cochran Bypass Chester SC 29706 Office Phone: 803-377-3161. Personal E-mail: wandam@cetlink.net.

MAYLEAS, RUTH ROTHSCHILD, foundation administrator; d. Alfred Rothschild and Anna Cohen; 1 child, Alexandra Mayleas Heth. BA, Cornell U., 1946. Dir., nat. theatre svc. ANTA, NYC, 1955—65; dir., US ctr. Internat. Theatre Inst., NYC, 1955—65; program dir., theatre Nat. Endowment for Arts; program officer edn. and culture Ford Found., NYC, 1983—91, adv. overseas countries program, 1991—95. Cons. on performing arts ctr. Cornell U., Ithaca, NY, 1980—86; bd. dirs. Grantmakers in the Arts, NYC, 1985—92; v.p. bd. dirs. Theatre Comm. Group, NYC, 1992—2000; cons. on cultural fund in st. petersburg World Bank, Washington, 1997. Author: Theater Artist's Resource, 1998, (essay for Libr. Congress exhbn.) Roger L Stevens, The Arts Endowment Years, 2002; prodr.: (TV series) Women in Theatre on CUNY-TV. V.p. Theatre Comm. Group, NYC, 1992—2000; trustee Nat. Theatre Conf., 1980—91. Recipient Disting. Svc. to Theatre award, Nat. Theatre Conf., 1973, League Resident Theatres, 1978, Dance and Performance award, Dance Theatre Workshop, 1985, Disting. Contbn. to Theatre award, Women's Project and Prodns., 1986; Travel and Study grantee, Ford Found., 1963. Mem.: League Profl. Theatre Women (v.p. 2000—05, editor ann. newsletter Roundup, Lee Reynolds award 2002), Century Assn. Liberal. Avocations: travel, reading - literary fiction, films. Home: 320 Ctrl Pk W New York NY 10025 Office Phone: 212-580-7797. Personal E-mail: rmayleas@verizon.net.

MAYNARD, JOAN LAW, elementary school educator; b. Putnam, Conn., Jan. 13, 1972; d. Walter Roy Law, Jr. and Mary Margaret McCormick; children: Daniella Mae, Nadine Eve, Maggie Ann, Trent Randall. BS, R.I. Coll., Providence, 1994; MEd, Providence Coll., 2004. Cert. tchr. elem. edn. R.I., 1994, tchr. spl. edn. R.I., 1994, tchr. mid. sch. R.I., 2000, in spl. edn. adminstr. R.I., 2004. Specialist student employment Career Devel. Ctr. R.I. Coll., Providence, 1990—94; spl. educator Ctr. Individualized Tng. and Edn., Providence, 1994—95, No. R.I. Collaborative, Cumberland, RI, 1995—98; tchr. Foster-Glocester Regional Sch. Dist., No. Scituate, RI, 1998—. Author: Internat. Libr. Poetry, 2006. Tchr. Sunday sch. East Putnam Cmty. Ch., Conn., 2001—03, tchr. vacation bible sch., 2002—04. Mem.: NEA (mem. exec. bd. 2005—), Internat. Reading Assn., Am. Fedn. Tchrs., Nat. Coun. Tchrs. English. Avocations: gardening, walking, reading, writing. Home: 1289 Reynolds Rd Chepachet RI 02814 Office: Ponaganset Mid Sch 91 Anan Wade Rd North Scituate RI 02857 Personal E-mail: jmaynard@fg.k12.ri.us.

MAYNARD, MENDY J., secondary school educator; d. Billy J. and Nancy H. Jordan; m. Fred G. Maynard, July 20, 1996; children: Jordan G., William J. BM, Columbus State U., 1995. Tchr. cert. Profl. Stds. Commn. Ga. Tchr. Muscogee County Sch. Dist., Columbus, 1997—. Mem.: Prof. Assn. Ga. Educators. Avocations: embroidery, reading, travel. Office Phone: 706-748-2744.

MAYNARD, NANCY GRAY, biological oceanographer; b. Middleboro, Mass., Apr. 18, 1941; d. Thomas LaSalle and Clara (Gray) M.; m. Conrad Dennis Gebelein, Jan., 1969 (div. 1977); 1 child, Jennifer Lynn. BS, Mary Washington Coll., 1963; MS, U. Miami (Fla.), 1968, PhD, 1974. Rsch. assoc. Bermuda Biol. Sta., Ferry Reach, 1972-75; rsch. fellow Lamont-Doherty Geol. Obs. Columbia U. (CLIMAP), 1972-75; post-doctoral fellow Div. Engring., Applied Physics Harvard U., Cambridge, Mass., 1975-76; field coord. environ. studies Alaska Outer Continental Shelf Office U.S. Dept. Interior, Anchorage, 1976-78; with oil spills sci. support Nat. Oceanic and Atmospheric Adminstrn., Alaska and S.E. U.S., 1978-81; policy analyst Exec. Office Pres. U.S. Office Sci. and Technology Policy, Washington, 1982-83; fellow Dept. of Commerce Sci. and Tech., 1982-83; staff dir. Bd. Ocean Sci. and Policy NAS, Washington, 1983-85; resident rsch. assoc. Nat. Rsch. Coun. Scripps Instn. Oceanography and Jet Propulsion Lab NASA, 1985-87; br. head Oceans and Ice Br. Goddard Space Flight Ctr. NASA, Greenbelt, Md., 1987-88, assoc. chief rsch. Lab. for Oceans, 1988-89; asst. dir. for environment Exec. Office of Pres. Office Sci. and Tech. Policy, Washington, 1989-93; dep. dir. sci. divsn. NASA Mission to Planet Earth HQ, Washington, 1993-98; dir. divsn. applications, commercialization, and edn. NASA Office of Earth Sci. Hdqrs., Washington, 1998—2000; assoc. dir., Environment and Health NASA Goddard Space Flight Ctr., Greenbelt, Md., 2000—. Contbr. numerous articles profl. jours. Recipient Pub. Svc. Commendation USCG, 1979. Mem. AAAS, Assn. Women in Sci., Am. Geophys. Union, Women's Aquatic Network, Corp. Bermuda Biol. Sta. Rsch., Explorers Club. Office: NASA Goddard Space Flight Ctr 610 Greenbelt MD 00771-0001 Office Phone: 301-614-6572. Business E-Mail: nancy.g.maynard@nasa.gov.

MAYNARD, NATALIE RYSHNA, pianist, educator; b. Phila., Aug. 21, 1930; d. George Thomas Hook and Helen Agatha Reese; m. Harry Edgar Maynard, Jan. 30, 1960; children: Melanie Dawn, Amie Anne. Degree in piano performance, Juilliard Graduate Sch. Music, N.Y.C., 1952. Concert pianist Columbia Artists Mgmt., tours in U.S. and Europe, 1963-94; rec. artist Contemporary Records and Ambiphon Records, 1957-75; pvt. piano instr., 1985—; project dir. Title III and State Urban Edn. program N.Y.C. schs. Founder, chmn. edn. com. Sta. WNET/13-TV, N.Y.C., 1973—77; pres. Performers Conn., Westport, 1985—91, bd. dirs., 1982—; exec. dir. R. B. Fisher Found. Composer Awards, 1986—96; v.p. ednl. outreach Friends of Music Fairfield County, 1995—99. Bd. dirs. Friends of Channel 13, Nat. Friends of Pub. Broadcasting, 1971—82; apptd. to arts adv. com. Town of Westport, 1998—2000, 2000—, co-chair town millenium edn. com., 1998; mem. adv. bd. Stamford Symphony Orch. Recipient Outstanding Women Conn. award, Lt. Gov. Conn., 2003. Mem.: Conn. State Music Tchrs. Assn., Nat. Music Tchrs. Assn., Schubert Club.

MAYNARD, VIRGINIA MADDEN, foundation administrator; b. New London, Conn., Jan. 29, 1924; d. Raymond and Edna Sarah (Madden) Maynard. BS, U. Conn., 1945; postgrad., Am. Inst. Banking, 1964—66, Cornell U., 1975. With Nat. City Bank (now Citibank), N.Y.C., 1954—79, asst. cashier, 1965—69, asst. v.p., 1969-74, v.p. internat. banking group, 1974-76, comptroller's div., 1976-79; v.p. First Women's Bank, N.Y.C., 1979-80; rep. Internat. Fedn. Univ. Women UN, 1982—2003. Trustee fellowships endowment fund AAUW Ednl. Found., Washington, 1977—80, Va. Gildersleeve Internat. Fund Univ. Women, Inc., pres., 1987—93, bd. dirs., 1994—2000, rep. UN, 1997—; bd. dirs. Conf. Nongovtl. Orgns. Found., Inc., 1997—, treas., 1999—. Mem.: AAUW (fin. chmn. N.Y.C. br. 1976—79, bylaws chmn. 1979—83, adminstr. Meml. Fund 1983—92, 2000—, bd. dirs. 1992—94, 1996—99, Woman of Achievement 1976). Republican. Congregationalist. Home: 601 E 20th St New York NY 10010-7622

MAYNE, LUCILLE STRINGER, finance educator; b. Washington, June 6, 1924; d. Henry Edmond and Hattie Benham (Benson) Stringer; children: Pat A., Christine Gail, Barbara Marie. BS, U. Md., College Park, 1946; MBA, Ohio State U., Columbus, 1949; PhD, Northwestern U., Evanston, Ill., 1966. Instr. fin. Utica Coll., 1949-50; lectr. fin. Roosevelt U., 1961-64, Pa. State U., 1965-66, asst. prof., 1966-69, assoc. prof., 1969-70; assoc. prof. banking and fin. Case-Western Res. U., 1971-76, prof., 1976-94, prof. emerita, 1994—, grad. dean Sch. Grad. Studies, 1980-84. Sr. economist, cons. FDIC, 1977-78; cons. Nat. Commn. Electronic Fund Transfer Sys., 1976; rsch. cons. Am. Bankers Assn., 1975, Fed. Res. Bank of Cleve., 1968-70, 73; cons. Pres.'s Commn. Fin. Structure and Regulation, 1971, staff economist, 1970-71; analytical statistician Air Materiel Command, Dayton, Ohio, 1950-52; asst. to promotion mgr. NBC, Washington, 1946-48; expert witness cases involving fin. instns. Assoc. editor: Jour. Money, Credit and Banking, 1980-83, Bus. Econs., 1980-85; contbr. articles to profl. jours. Vol. Cleve. Soc. for Blind, 1979-2004, Benjamin Rose Inst., 1995-2005; mem. policyholders nominating com. Tchrs. Ins. and Annuity Assn./Coll. Retirement Equities Fund, 1982-84, chair com., 1984; bd. dirs. Women's Cmty. Found., 1994-96. Grad. scholar, Ohio State U., 1949, doctoral fellow, Northwestern U., 1963—65. Mem. LWV (bd. dirs. Shaker Heights chpt. 1999--), Midwest Fin. Assn. (pres. 1991-92, bd. dirs. 1975-79, officer 1988-93), Phi Kappa Phi, Beta Gamma Sigma. Episcopalian. Home: 3723 Normandy Rd Cleveland OH 44120-5246 Office: Case Western Res U Weatherhead Sch Mgmt U Circle Cleveland OH 44106-7235 Business E-Mail: lucille.mayne@case.edu.

MAYO, CORA LOUISE, educator; b. Chgo., Oct. 31, 1925; d. Charles Amos and Mary (Elder) Scott; m. Marion Wesley Mayo, July 21, 1948; children: Lynne, Charles (dec.), Janice (dec.), Jo Ann, Thomas. BS, U. Ill.-Urbana, 1949, advanced degree in adminstrn. and supervision, 1973; MA, U. Chgo., 1961; PhD, Heed U., Fla., 1981. Program facilitator Chgo. Bd. Edn., 1955—; owner/pres. From the Black Experience, Inc., Chgo., 1979—; dir. pub. relations Afro-Am. Pub. Co., Chgo., 1972-73; ednl. cons. Ednl. Leadership Inst., Chgo., 1976-78; cmty. prof. Govs. State U., Park Forest, Ill., 1975—83. Author: Developmental Skills Activities Guide, 1982; columnist Teaching Black Positively; editor Human Relations Digest; author/pub.: (early childhood learning kit) Mwenzi Compañeros, 1982. Bd. dirs. Woodson Delany Ednl. Fund, Chgo., 1975—77, House of the Black Madonna, Chgo., 1978—80; cons. Head Start, St. Stephen's Ch., Chgo., 1982-83; organizer Women for Washington, 1982-83, Women for Jackson, 1984; vol. instr. parenting House of the Black Madonna; proposals cons. Du Sable Mus. Afro-Am. History, Chgo. Recipient Leadership award Boy Scouts Am., 1971; named Outstanding Educator of Yr., Woodson-Delany Ednl. Fund, 1976, Sr. Citizen of Yr, Chgo. Dist., 1994; others. Mem. Assn. for Study of Ancient Classical African Civilizations (bd., elder), Nat. Assn. Media Women (pres., fin. sec. 1983—, sec. chpt. 1982—, v.p. 1973), Nat. Hook Up of Black Women, Women in Comm., Friends of Amistad (bd. dirs.), Alpha Gamma Pi (v.p., corres. sec.), Delta Sigma Theta, Phi Delta Kappa. Democrat. Congregationalist. Club: Debonnettes (pres. 1984) (Chgo.). Home: 1618 E 85th Pl Chicago IL 60617-2235 Fax: 773-374-6749.

MAYO, MARTI, museum director, curator; b. Bluefield, W.Va., Oct. 17, 1945; d. Robert J. and Kathryn Ann (Kearns) Kirkwood; m. Edward K. Mayo, May 13, 1974 (div. 1983); 1 child, Nesta. BA, Am. U., 1970, MFA, 1974. Asst. dir. Jefferson Place Gallery, Washington, 1973-74; coord. exhbns. Corcoran Gallery Art, Washington, 1974-80; curator Contemporary Arts Mus., Houston, 1980-86; dir. Blaffer Gallery U., Houston, 1986—94; dir., chief curator Contemporary Arts Museum, Houston, 1994—. Mem. review panel, Inst. of Museum & Library Services; panelist Nat. Endowment for Arts, Texas Commn. on Arts. Author: Robert Morris Selected Works; 1970-80, 1981, Other Realities: Installations for Performance, 1981, Arbitrary from Four Series: A Sesquicentennial Exhibition, 1985, Joseph Glasco 1948-86: A Sesquicentennial Exhibition, 1986, Six Artists/Six Idioms, 1988. V.p. Cultural Arts Council of Houston/Harris County. Mem. Am. Assn. Mus., Coll. Art Assn.; bd. dirs. Houston Museum District Assn. (vice pres. 1998-99, pres. 2001-02), bd. trustees Am. Federation of Arts, Assn. of Art Museum Directors. Office: Contemporary Arts Museum 5216 Montrose Blvd Houston TX 77006-6598

MAYO-JOHNSTON, JULIA A., psychiatry professor, psychotherapist; b. Phila., Aug. 16, 1926; d. Henry Mayo and Mamie Clark; 1 child, Wilvena Gordon. BA in Sociology with honors, U. Pa., Phila., 1947, PhD in Social Rsch., Social Work and Adminstrn., 1958; MS in Social Rsch., Bryn Mawr Coll., Pa., 1949. ACSW NY State Dept. Edn., bd. cert. diplomate clin. social work Am. Acad. Experts in Traumatic Stress, diplomate, master therapist Am. Psychotherapy Assn.; cert. in individual and group psychotherapy, supervision and adminstrn. Wash. Sch. Psychiatry, 1963. Probation officer Family Ct., Wilmington, Del., 1949—52; psychiatric social worker intern Embreeville State Hosp., Pa., 1952—53; psychiatric social worker Vets. Adminstrn. Hosp., Lyons, NJ, 1953—54, asst. chief, outpatient clinic Wilmington, 1954—61, chief social worker, dept. psychiatry, 1954—61; chief clin. social worker and psychosocial rsch. clin. studies CNRC, NIMH, NIH, Washington, 1961—66; chief clin. sociologist, rsch. divsn., dept. psychiatry St. Vincent's Hosp., NYC, 1966—72, chief evaluation unit/preventive treatment program, dept. psychiatry, 1972—75, chief clin. studies, dept. psychiatry, 1975—96, clin. supr. group and individual psychotherapy, chmn. clin. studies group, 1980—96, mem. various committees; assoc. prof. clin. psychiatry and behavioral sci. NY Med. Coll., Valhalla, 1978—92, clin. prof. psychiatry, 1993, clin. prof. psychiatry emeritus, 1996. Field work supr. for grad. students various schs., 1958—88; rsch. com. I.R.B. St. Vincent's Hosp. and Med. Ctr., 1974—76; adj. prof. med. anthropology New Sch. Social Rsch., 1978; mem. editl. bd. Comprehensive Psychiatry, 1975—, Group Psychotherapy Glossary, Clin. Sociology Review; cons. in field; pvt. practice, 1958—; alumni secondary sch. com. U. Pa. Undergraduate Admissions, 1981; bd. mem. Nat.

Assn. D.M.D.A., 1992; lectr. and presenter in field. Contbr. articles to jour., chapters to books. Recipient Outstanding Performance award, Vets. Adminstrn. Hosp., Wilmington, 1959, Commendation/Meritorious Svc., 1961, Outstanding Tchr. of Yr. award, Dept. Psychiatry, St. Vincent's Hosp. and Med. Ctr., NY, 1989, 1992, Cert. of Commendation, John Templeton Spirituality and Medicine award, Award for Excellent Contbn., 2003; grantee, Karp Found., 1987, 1989; John F. Creed grant for rsch., 1985. Fellow: APPA, Am. Assn. Family and Marriage Counselors, Am. Group Psychotherapy Assn., Am. Psychopathological Assn. (life); mem.: APGA, AAAS, Nat. Inst. Healthcare Rsch., Am. Assn. Social Work and Rsch., Am. Assn. Profl. Hypnotherapists, Am. Assn. Behavioral Therapists, Internat. Soc. Psychologists, Internat. Acad. Counseling and Psychotheraphy, NY Acad. Scis., Internat. Coun. Sex Edn. and Parenthood, Assn. Profl. Responsibility in Medicine and Rsch., Am. Acad. Psychotherapists, Met. Med. Anthropology Assn., Soc. Study Social Biology, Am. Assn. Clin. Psychosocial Rsch., Acad. Cert. Social Workers, Ea. Sociol. Assn., Clin. Sociology Assn. (bd. mem. at large, Disting. Career in Clin. Sociology award 1986), Am. Sociol. Assn. Democrat. Episcopalian. Avocations: travel, music, theater, dance. Home and Office: 205 W End Ave 24J New York NY 10023 Office Phone: 212-787-6524.

MAYS, GLENDA SUE, retired education educator; b. Freer, Tex., July 18, 1938; d. Archie Richard and Helen Hildred (Morgan) Cox; m. Dewey William Mays, Sept. 7, 1963; children: Rose Marie, Teresa Sue, Frank Dewey. BS, Tex. Tech. U., 1959, MA, 1961; PhD, North Tex. State U., 1969. Cert. tchr., supr., prin. Tchr. Lubbock (Tex.) Pub. Schs., 1959-61, Amarillo (Tex.) Pub. Schs., 1961-62, Austin (Tex.) Pub. Schs., 1962-63; curriculum intern/rsch. asst., elem. coord. U. Tex. at Austin, Hurst, Tex., 1963-65; asst. prof. McMurry U., Abilene, Tex., 1965-67; assoc. prof. Dallas Bapt. U., 1968-71; reading resource tchr., dept. chair Ft. Worth (Tex.) Ind. Sch. Dist., 1971-74, reading specialist, 1974-82, instructional specialist, 1982-95, ret., 1995; owner Cornucopia Antiques, Jewelry and Collectibles, Ft. Worth, 1969—, Cornucopia Estate and Appraisal Svcs., Ft. Worth, 1998—. Spkr. lang. acquisition and reading 7th World Congress in Reading, Hamburg, Germany, 1978. Advisor/writer (English textbook): McDouglas Littel Language, 1985-86; writer: Bilingual Stories for Ft. Worth Ind. Sch. Dist., 1979-80; contbr. poems to anthologies. Patron Kimbell Mus. Art, Ft. Worth, 1994—; mem. Nat. Cancer Soc., Ft. Worth, 1980—. Fulbright-Hays scholar, Kenya, Africa, 1970; grantee in fgn. langs. Nat. Endowment Arts U. Ark., 1987, Ft. Worth Ind. Sch. Dist. Study grantee U. London, 1978. Fellow ASCD, NEA, Tex. State Tchrs. Assn., Ft. Worth Edn. Assn., Internat. Reading Assn. (hostess 1st Tex. breakfast 1969), Nat. Geog. Soc., Smithsonian Instn., Libr. of Congress, Ft. Worth Reading Assn., Nat. Coun. for Social Studies spkr. social studies symposium N.Y.C. 1970, Tex. Elem. Prins. and Suprs. Assn. (sec. 1971-72). Avocations: travel, reading, music, writing, antique collecting. Home: 1225 Clara St Fort Worth TX 76110-1009

MAYS, JANICE ANN, lawyer; b. Waycross, Ga., Nov. 21, 1951; d. William H. and Jean (Bagley) M. AB (hon.), Wesleyan Coll., Macon, Ga., 1973; JD, U. Ga., 1975; LLM in Taxation, U. Georgetown, 1980. Bar: Ga. 1976. Tax counsel com. on ways and means U.S. Ho. Reps., Washington, 1975-88, chief tax counsel com. on ways and means, staff dir. subcom. select revenue measures, 1988-93, chief counsel, staff dir. com. on ways and means, 1993-95, minority chief counsel, staff dir. com. on ways and means, 1995—. Recipient Disting. Achievement in Profession Alumnae award Wesleyan Coll., 1998. Mem. Tax Coalition (past chair). Office: Ways & Means Com 1106 Longworth Office Bldg Washington DC 20515-0001

MAYS, LINDA, performing arts association administrator; Pres. Am. Guild Musical Artists, N.Y.C. Office: Am Guild Musical Artists 14th Fl 1430 Broadway New York NY 10018

MAYSILLES, ELIZABETH, speech communication professional, educator; b. Sleepy Creek, W.Va. d. Evers and Rose (Scott) M. AB, W.Va. U., Morgantown; MA, Hunter Coll., NYC, 1963; PhD, NYU, 1980. Announcer Radio Sta. WAJR, Morgantown, W.Va.; broadcaster Radio Sta. WGHF-FM, Rural Radio Network, N.Y.C.; group leader GMAC, N.Y.C.; instr. NYU, N.Y.C.; adj. prof. speech comm. Pace U., N.Y.C., 1978—2002; exec. adminstr. Am.-Scottish Found., N.Y.C., 1980-90; adminstrv. asst. Brit. Schs. and Univs. Found., Inc. Personal investment portfolio mgmt.; numerous radio and television appearances; lectr. in field; cons. Vol. counselor Help Line, N.Y.C., 1971-75. Recipient Disting. Svc. award NYU Grad. Orgn., 1970-71. Mem. Internat. Platform Assn. (bd. govs. 1980—), N.Y. Acad. Scis., Caledonian Club N.Y. (bd. dirs. 1994-96, 04-06, chieftain 2001-02). Avocations: reading, swimming, gardening, travel in England and Scotland. Home: 155 E 77th St Apt 6F New York NY 10021

MAZAK, ARLENE PATRICIA, marriage and family therapist; d. John Andrew Mazak and Irene Kraszewski. AA in Liberal Arts, Sarah Lawrence Coll., Bronxville, N.Y., 1967; BA in Counseling, U. San Francisco, Calif., 1992; PhD in South Asian Langs. and Civilization, U. Chgo., Ill., 1994. Cert. orgnl. devel. and transformation specialist Calif. Inst. Integral Studies, 1993, spiritual direction specialist Loyola Marymount U., 2006, lic. marriage and family therapist Calif. Core faculty Calif. Inst. Integral Studies, San Francisco, 1986—93; tng. dir. Spiritual Emergency Network, Menlo Park, Calif., 1990—91; core faculty Inst. Transpersonal Psychology, Palo Alto, Calif., 1993—2000; adj. faculty gerontology Coastline C.C., Fountain Valley, Calif., 2001—; marriage and family therapist Innercall: Transpersonal Healing and Devel. Svcs., Fountain Valley and Encinitas, Calif., 2001—. Home: 8816 Yuba Cir Unit 1111A Huntington Beach CA 92646-8711

MAZANY, TERRY, foundation administrator; BA in Anthropology, MA in Anthropology, MBA, U. Ariz. Positions in public sch. adminstrn. Mich. Sch. Dist.; former assoc. superintendent for curriculum and instruction Oakland Unified Sch. Dist., Calif.; former dir. orgnl. learning and devel. Calif. Sch. Leadership Acad.; dir., sr. prog. officer for ed. initiative Chgo. Cmty. Trust, 2001—03, COO, 2003—04, pres., CEO, 2004—. Office: Chgo Cmty Trust 111 E Wacker Dr Ste 1400 Chicago IL 60601*

MAZAR, DEBI, actress; b. Queens, NY, Aug. 15, 1964; m. Gabriele Corcos, Mar. 16, 2002; children: Evelina Maria Mazar Corcos, Giulia Isabel Mazar Corcos. Actor: (films) Goodfellas, 1990, The Doors, 1991, Jungle Fever, 1991, Little Man Tate, 1991, In the Soup, 1992, Inside Monkey Zetterland, 1992, Singles, 1992, Malcolm X, 1992, Toys, 1992, So I Married an Axe Murderer, 1993, Love Is Like That, 1993, Money for Nothing, 1993, Beethoven's 2nd, 1993, Bullets Over Broadway, 1994, Batman Forever, 1995, Empire Records, 1995, Girl 6, 1996, Trees Lounge, 1996, Red Ribbon Blues, 1996, Things I Never Told You, 1996, Space Truckers, 1996, Meet Wally Sparks, 1997, Nowhere, 1997, She's So Lovely, 1997, Trouble on the Corner, 1997, The Deli, 1997, Frogs for Snakes, 1998, Hush, 1998, There's No Fish Food in Heaven, 1998, The Insider, 1999, More Dogs Than Bones, 2000, Held for Ransom, 2000, Ten Tiny Love Stories, 2001, Deception, 2001, The Tuxedo, 2002, Who Killed the Idea?, 2003, Return to Babylon, 2004, Goodnight, Joseph Parker, 2004, Collateral, 2004, My Tiny Universe, 2004, Be Cool, 2005, Edmond, 2005, Wait, 2005, The Alibi, 2006; (TV series) Civil Wars, 1991—93, L.A. Law, 1993—94, Temporarily Yours, 1997, Working, 1998—99, That's Life, 2000, Entourage, 2004—; (TV films) Witch Hunt, 1994, Musical Shorts, 1996, Casper: A Spirited Beginning, 1997, Witness to the Mob, 1998, David and Lisa, 1998, The Sissy Duckling (voice), 1999, The Groovenians (voice), 2002; guest appearances (TV series) Burke's Law, 1995, Providence, 1999, Get Real, 2000, Wanda at Large, 2002, Friends, 2002, 7th Heaven, 2003—04, All of Us, 2004, The Practice, 2004, CSI: Miami, 2004, NYPD Blue, 2005, Living with Fran, 2005—06. Office: c/o Creative Artists Agy 9830 Wilshire Blvd Beverly Hills CA 90212

MAZES-ROQUE, JANET MARIA, physician assistant; b. L.A., Dec. 19, 1964; d. Ruben and Inez Lamour Mazes; m. Loren James Fletcher, June 19, 1985 (div. Apr. 1987); children: Janette Lauren, Alisha Nicole-Lamour; m. Charles therdore Roque, June 1, 1996. AA in Liberal Arts, L.A. S.W. Coll., 1989; BS in Health Sci., Charles Drew U. Medicine/Sci., 1991. Cert. physician asst., Calif. Instr. Ctr. Ednl. Achievement Sat. Sci. Acad. Charles Drew U. Medicine and Sci., L.A., 1991-93; physician asst. VA Med. Ctr. West L.A., Calif., 1993-94, Manchester Med. Group, L.A., 1994-96, Your Family Med. Ctr., Inglewood, Calif., 1996-98, L.A. County/King Drew Med. Ctr./S.W. Health Cluster, 1998—. Health screener ARC, L.A., 1995, 99. Mem. Charles Drew Physician Asst. Assn. (sec. 1994-95, scholar 1991). Democrat. Avocations: drawing, music, decorating, program organization, travel. Address: 2204 E 92d St Los Angeles CA 90002-2601 E-mail: JanetMazesRoque@MSN.Net.

MAZIAR, CHRISTINE M., academic administrator; BSEE, MSEE, Purdue U., PhD in Elec. Engring. Mem. faculty U. Tex., 1987—98, vice provost, 1995—98; faculty mem. U. Minn., Mpls., 1998—, v.p. for rsch., dean Grad. Sch., 1998—2002, exec. v.p., provost, 2002—04; mem. faculty U. Notre Dame, Ind., 2004—. Contbr. articles to profl. jours. Recipient Presdl. Young Investigator award, NSF, 1990, Tech. Excellence award, Semiconductor Rsch. Corp., 1992. Home: Office of Provost 800 Main Blvd Notre Dame IN 46556

MAZUR, RHODA HIMMEL, community volunteer; b. Bklyn., July 4, 1929; d. Morris and Gussie (Nadler) Himmel; m. Marvin Irwin Mazur, June 7, 1952; children: Jody, Amy, Leslie, Eric. Student, CCNY, CUNY. Bd. dirs. Newport News Social Svcs. Adv. Bd., 1979-84, Gov.'s Commn. Status Women, Richmond, 1981-84, Coun. Jewish Fedns., NYC, 1985-87, Nat. Coun. Christians and Jews, 1985-89, Rodef Sholom Endowment Com., 1996—, Peninsula Jewish Hist. Soc., 1998—; v.p. Anti-Defamation League Regional Bd., Richmond, 1983-85, bd. dirs., 1985-98; pres. Newport News Hadassah, 1984-85, United Jewish Cmty. Va. Peninsula Inc., Newport News, 1985-88, Rodef Sholom Sisterhood, 1997-98; active Newport News Task Force on Emergency Housing, 1984-85; chair fin. com. Peninsula Peace Edn. Ctr., Newport News, 1984-85; adv. bd. Friends of the Homeless, Inc., 1987-00, pres., 1993-98, v.p., 1998-99; adv. bd. Associated Marine Inst., 1988-92; mem. social svcs. com. United Jewish Cmty. Va. Peninsula, 1995—, mem. campaign coun., 1999-, Jewish Hist. Soc. Va. Peninsula, 1995-; chair social action com. Rodef Sholom Temple, 1993-96, endowment com., 1998—; cmty. activist; bd. dirs., Peninsula Camp Fund, 2001—, Fed. Emergency Mgmt. Agy., 2001. Recipient Young Leadership award Jewish Fedn. Newport News, 1968, Brotherhood citation Nat. Conf. Christians and Jews, 1984, Anti-Defamation Leadership award, 1997. Democrat. Avocations: hand crafts, reading, music, photography. Home: 114 James River Dr Newport News VA 23601-3604

MAZZA, MARALYN J., director; b. June 14, 1927; d. Donald Walter and Laura (Mansfield) Davis; m. Serafino Paul Mazza; children: Laura, Thomas, David, Virginia, Susan, Paul III. BA in Sociology, Bates Coll., Lewiston, Maine, 1949. Dir. teenagers YWCA, Manchester, NH, 1950—52, Oakland, Calif., 1952—53; exec. dir. Girl Scouts Am., Natick, Mass., 1953—57; dir. South Hills Sch. Bus. and Tech., State Coll., Pa., 1975—. Home: 1906 Park Forest Ave State College PA 16803

MAZZAFERRI, KATHERINE AQUINO, lawyer, bar association executive; b. Phila., May 14, 1947; d. Joseph William and Rose (Aquino) M.; m. William Fox Bryan, May 5, 1984 (div.); 1 child, Josefa Mazzaferri Bryan. BA, NYU, 1969; JD, George Washington U., 1972. Bar: D.C., 1972. Trial atty. EEOC, Washington, 1972-75; dir. litigation LWV Edn. Fund, Washington, 1975-78; dep. asst. dir. for advt. practices FTC, Washington, 1978-80, asst. dir. for product liability, 1980-82, asst. dir. for advt. practices, 1982; exec. dir., v.p. pub. svcs. activities corp. D.C. Bar, Washington, 1982—. Bd. dir. regulatory analysis project U.S. Regulatory Coun.; mediator D.C. Mediation Svc., 1982; vis. instr. Antioch Law Sch., Washington, 1985; mem. Bd. of Women's Bar Assn. Found., 1990-93; mem. FBA Meml. Found., 1991-96. Bd. dirs. River Rd. Unitarian Ch., 2001—, bd. dir., 2001—. Recipient Superior Service award FTC, 1979 Mem. ABA (rep. of the homeless project steering com. 1988-90), D.C. Bar, Womens Legal Def. (pres. 1972-73, bd. dirs. 1971-75, 76-79), FBA Meml. Found. Home: 5832 Lenox Rd Bethesda MD 20817-6070 Office: DC Bar 1250 H St NW Lbby 6 Washington DC 20005-5906

MAZZARELLI, DEBRA JEAN, real estate broker; b. Suffolk County, N.Y. d. Edward and Jean Werner; m. Gary Mazzarelli; children: Jessica, Kristy, Tori. Student, Boston U.; BA, St. Joseph's Coll., Patchoque, N.Y. Intern County Legislator Ed Romaine, N.Y.; staff mem. Assemblyman John Cochrane, Albany, N.Y.; coord. Regional Fair Housing Conf.; writer Main Street Express, Patchoque, N.Y.; real estate broker Patchoque; assemblywoman N.Y. State Assembly, Albany, 1995—2001. Mem. edn., tourism, small bus., environ. conservation coms.; mem. legis. task force on women's issues; mem. vol. firefighter subcom. Mem. N.Y. State Bd. Realtors, South Ocean PTA, Concerned Taxpayers of Patchoque, Patchoque C. of C., Bus. and Profl. Women (pres. Brookhaven chpt.), Nat. Women's Polit. Caucus. Democrat.

MAZZENGA, CAROLYN, accountant; Former pvt. practice; with Marcum & Kliegman LLP, Woodbury, NY, 1991—97, tax ptnr., 1997—. Vol. counselor Small Bus. Develop. Ctr., Stony Brook; mem. women reentering the workforce task force Ctr. for Bus. & Profl. Women, Long Island, exec. v.p. bd. dirs.; bd. dirs. Girl Scouts Am., Nassau County. Named One of Long Island's Top 50 Women, Long Island Bus. News, 2000; recipient Achiever's award in acct., Ctr. for Bus. and Profl. Women, Long Island, 1998. Mem.: AICPA, Long Island Women's Agenda, Nat. Assn. Mothers' Ctrs. (corp. resource develop. com.). Office: Marcum & Kliegman 655 3rd Ave 16th Flr New York NY 10017 also: Marcum Kliegman Llp 10 Melville Park Rd Melville NY 11747-3146

MAZZEO, BETTY TERESA, music educator; b. Ahosky, N.C., Apr. 14, 1964; d. Charles Hamilton and Betty Helene Armstrong; 1 child, Madelyn Elise. BS, U. Md., College Park, 1987, MusM, 1997. Vocal music tchr. Matthew Henson Mid. Sch., Bryans Road, Md., 1988—2000, McDonough H.S., Pomfret, Md., 2000—. Recipient Outstanding Tchr., Charles County Pub. Schs., 1994, Agnus Meyer Outstanding Tchr., Wash. Post, 1997. Mem.: Md. Music Educators Assn. (assoc.; pres. so. region 1996—97), Am. Choral Dirs. Assn. (assoc.; chair show and jazz choir 2005—06). Avocation: scrap booking. Office: McDonough HS 7165 Marshall Corner Rd La Plata MD 20646 Office Phone: 301-934-2944. Business E-Mail: bmazzeo@ccboe.com.

MAZZIO-MOORE, JOAN L., retired radiology educator, physician; b. Belmont, Mass., Oct. 26, 1935; d. Frank Joseph and Maria L. Mazzio; children: James Thomas Moore, Edwin Stuart Moore. BA in Chemistry and Theology, Emmanuel Coll., 1957; MA in Genetics and Physiology, Mass. Wellesley Coll., 1961; PhD in Genetics, Bryn Mawr (Pa.) Coll., 1964; MD, Phila. Coll. of Medicine, 1977, MSc in Radiology, 1981. Instr. in biochemistry Gwynedd Mercy Coll., Springhouse, Pa., 1963—65; instr. in genetics Holy Family Coll., Phila., 1965—66; instr. in anatomy Phila. Coll. of Medicine, 1971—77, instr., 1973—77, asst. prof., 1977—84; prof. W.Va. Sch. of Medicine, 1984—2003, ret.; rotating intern Phila. Coll. of Medicine Hosp., 1977—78, resident in radiology and radiation therapy, 1978—81; advanced through grades to lt. col. USAR, 1984—2002; med. dir. 91W transition program U.S. Army Med. Corps Reserves, divsn. surgeon, 80th divsn. (IT) Richmond, Va., ret., 2004. Author (with Dr. DiVirgilito): Essentials of Neuropathology, 1974. Treas. Hist. Soc. of Frankford, Phila., 1968—75, Sch. Mother's Assn., Devon, Pa., 1980—81; vol. mem. Ct. Appts. Spl. Adv. for Children; parlamentarian Greenbrier Com. on Aging; bd. trustees Lake Erie Coll. Medicine and Pharmacy, Erie, Pa.; organist Ch. of Incarnation, W.Va., St. Charles Borromeo Ch., White Sulphur Springs, W.Va., 2001—; lector St. Ann's Cath. Ch., Phoenixville, Pa., 1981—84. Lt. col. M.C. U.S. Army, 1992—2003. Mem. AAUP, Am. Acad. Family Physicians, Am. Assn. Women Radiologists, Am. Med. Women's Assn., Am. Osteo. Coll. of Radiology (life), Am. Soc. Clin. Oncology, Am. Soc. Therapeutic Readiologists, Hist. Soc. of Lewisburg (life), Pa. Osteo. Med. Assn., Pa. Osteo. Gen. Practitioner's Soc., Radiol. Soc. N.Am., Radiation Rsch. Soc., Res. Officers Assn. (life), W.Va. Soc. Osteo. Medicine, Greenbrier River Hike and Bike Trail. Home: PO Box 97 Frankford WV 24938 Home Fax: 304-497-2752. Personal E-mail: drjoanlmoore@frontiernet.net.

MAZZO, KAY, ballet dancer, educator; b. Evanston, Ill., Jan. 17, 1946; d. Frank Alfred and Catherine M. (Hengel) M.; m. Albert C. Bellas, 1978; children: Andrew, Kathryn. Student, Sch. Am. Ballet, 1959-61. Co-chair faculty Sch. Am. Ballet. Profl. debut in ballets U.S.A. 1961, touring Europe with co., performing for Pres. Kennedy at White House, 1961, joined N.Y.C. Ballet, 1962-80, soloist, 1965-69, prin. ballerina, 1969-80, prin. roles in world premiere of ballets including Tschaikowsky Suite No. #3, 1970, PAMTGG, 1971, Stravinsky Violin Concerto, 1972, Scherzo A La Russe, 1972, Duo Concertant, 1972, Sheherazade, 1975, Union Jack, 1976, Vienna Waltzes, 1977, Davidsbundlertanze, 1980; ballet tchr. Sch. Am. Ballet, 1980—; appeared as guest artist in leading roles with numerous cos. including Boston Ballet, Washington Ballet, Berlin Ballet, Geneva Ballet; appeared on TV in U.S., Can., Fed. Republic Germany. Recipient Mademoiselle Merit award 1970 Office: Sch Am Ballet 70 Lincoln Center Plz New York NY 10023-6548

MAZZOLI, LINDA FABRIZIO, personal trainer, consultant, marketing professional; BS in Student Design, Athletic Tng., West Chester U., Pa., 1990; AS in Phys. Therapy Asst., Harcum Coll., Bryn Mawr, Pa., 1994; MS, Calif. U. Pa., 2004. Mgr. clin. NovaCare, Breemall, Pa., 1993—94, regional dir. athletic tng. cert. svcs. Exton, Pa., 1994—97, nat. dir. King of Prussia, Pa., 1997—2000, dir. program devel., 1998—2000; pres. QuinTech Health Svcs., LLC, Essington, Pa., 2000—02; v.p. clin. svcs. Benchmark Med. Inc., Malvern, Pa., 2002—04; dir. mktg. & profl. devel. Cooper Univ. Hosp., Camden, NJ, 2004—. Cons., 2004—06; adj. prof. Eastern U., Wayne, Pa., 2005—06; bus. adv. bd. Harcum Coll., Bryn Mawr, 2005—06. Mem.: Am. Phys. Therapy Assn., Athletic Trainers Soc. NJ (bd. dirs. 2006), Nat. Athletic Trainers Assn. (Dist. II liaison to COR 2001—06, BOC), Pa. Athletic Trainers Soc. (bd. dirs. 1997—2001, athletic trainer cert., Svc. award 2005). Republican. Roman Cath. Avocations: gardening, reading, golf. Home: 3828 Marsh Rd Boothwyn PA 19061 Office: Cooper Bone and Joint Inst 3 Cooper Plz Ste 411 Camden NJ 08103

MAZZUCELLI, COLETTE GRACE CELIA, author, educator; b. Bklyn., Nov. 26, 1962; d. Silvio Anthony and Adeline Marie De Ponte. BA, U. Scranton, 1983; MALD in Law and Diplomacy, Fletcher Sch., Tufts U., 1987; PhD, Georgetown U., 1996; post grad., Columbia U., 2003—. Asst. ratification process Treaty European Union German Fgn. Ministry, 1992—93; lectr. U.S. Info. Svc. Spkrs. Program, Europe, 1994; dir. internat. programs and lectr. Budapest Inst. Grad. Internat. and Diplomatic Studies, 1995—97; instr. in-ho. tng. negotiations Hungarian Fgn. Ministry, 1996—97; del. to NATO accession talks Hungarian Ministry Def., 1997; advisor to bd. dirs. Transatlantic Info. Exch. Svc., 1997—98; founding dir., internat. peace and conflict resolution grad. program, asst. prof. polit. sci. Arcadia U., 1998—2000; chair Transatlantic internet multimedia seminar S.E. Europe (TIMSSE) ScPo, Paris, 2000—03; fellow EastWest Inst., 2001; program officer, edn. NGO rep. UN Carnegie Coun. Ethics and Internat. Affairs, 2001—02; program devel. assoc. Tchrs. Coll. Columbia U., 2002—04; faculty John C. Whitehead Sch. Diplomacy and Internat. Rels. Seton Hall U., 2005—06; asst. prof. dept. history and polit. sci. Molloy Coll., Rockville Centre, 2006—. Rsch. fellow Inst. Europaeische Politik, Deutsche Gesellschaft Auswaertige Politk, Bonn, Deutsch-Franzoesisches Inst., Ludwigsburg; instr. Georgetown U., Washington, 1990, 96; adj. asst. prof. MS program global affairs Sch. Continuing and Profl. Studies NYU, 2005—; rsch. fellow Inst. Europaeische Politik Deutsche Gesellschaft Auswaertige Politik. Author: France and Germany at Maastricht Politics and Negotiations to Create the European Union, 1997, paperback 2d edit., 1999; asst. editor: The Evolution of an International Actor: Western Europe's New Assertiveness, 1990; author: Monnet Case Studies in European Affairs, 1995; co-editor: Ethics and Global Politics: The Active Learning Sourcebook, 2004, Leadership in the Big Bangs of European Integration, 2006; contbr.: Dimensions of German Unification, 1994, Redefining European Security, 1999, United Nations Chronicle, 2001, 40th Anniversary vol. commemorating Treaty of Friendship between France and Germany, 2005; contbr. articles to profl. jours. Mem. founding cabinet World Peace and Diplomacy Forum, 2003—. Grantee Swiss U., 1984-85, Profl. Devel. grant NYU, 2006; scholar Pi Gamma Mu, 1985, Rotary grad. scholar, 1987-88, Fulbright scholar, 1991; fellow Jean Monnet Coun., 1991, European Commn., 1992, Robert Bosch Found., 1992-93, Salzburg Seminar, 1997, 21st Century Trust fellow Merton Coll., Oxford (Eng.) U., 2001, Bosch Pub. Policy fellow Am. Acad., Berlin, Aspen Inst., Berlin, 2001; Da Vinci Laureate, 2004; named Internat. Educator of Yr., 2003, Pirate of Yr., 2006; recipient citation Nat. Women's Conf., 2006. Mem.: AAUW, Phi Alpha Theta, Fgn. Policy Assn., Robert Bosch Found. Alumni Assn. (mem. exec. com. 1994—96, 1997—98, co-pres. 1999—2000), European Union Studies Assn., Am. Coun. Germany, Am. Assn. Advancement Slavic Studies, Am. Polit. Sci. Assn., Rotary Club Metro N.Y., The Fletcher Club of N.Y. (v.p. 1998), Delta Tau Kappa, Alpha Mu Gamma, Pi Sigma Alpha, Phi Sigma Tau (founder Scranton chpt.), Pi Gamma Mu (chpt. sec. 1982—84, Frank C. Brown scholarship medal 1984), Alpha Sigma Nu (student pres. 1984). Avocations: chess, swimming, creative writing, astrology, Tae Kwon Do. Home: 1864 74th St Brooklyn NY 11204-5752 Office: Molloy Coll PO Box 5002 1000 Hempstead Ave Rockville Centre NY 11571 Office Phone: 646-372-4396. Business E-Mail: cgm7@nyu.edu, cmazzucelli@molloy.edu.

MBADUGHA, LORETTA NKEIRUKA AKOSA, social services administrator, consultant; b. Onitsha, Anambara, Nigeria, Dec. 10, 1957; d. James and Sylvia O. (Asika) Akosa; m. Christian Mbadugha; children: Kristen Ogechi, Kyle Kelechi, Kelsey Odinaka. Assoc., Langham Secretarial Coll., London, 1978; BS, Tex. So. U., Houston, 1981, MS, 1982; PhD, U. New Orleans, 2000, PhD in Higher Edn. Adminstrn., 2001. Program analyst Tex. So. U., Houston, 1982-84; sanitarian City of Houston Health Dept., 1984-85; adj. faculty So. U., New Orleans, 1981-90; asst. to exec. dir. YWCA, New Orleans, 1984-93; family rep. Jefferson Parish Human Svcs. Authority, New Orleans, 1993—2001; CEO Profl. Family Support Svcs., New Orleans, 1994—. Cons., founder, bd. mem. Camelot Providers, New Orleans, 1987—; bd. mem. United Svcs. AIDS Found., 1990-92; trainer Coun. for Early Childhood Profl. Recognition, 1987—; cons., trainer on child devel. State of La., 1987-89; exec. dir. Gilbert Acad.; asst. prof. edn. Dillard U. Sec. Chapel of Praise, 1997. Recipient Mayoral Cert. of Merit, New Orleans, 1991; Grace Hodge fellow YWCA, 1992. Mem. ACA, Nigeria Ebony Club for Women (pres. 1995).

MCADAMS, RACHEL, actress; b. London, Ont., Can., Oct. 7, 1976; d. Lance and Sandy McAdams. BFA with honors, NYU. Actor: (films) My Name is Tanino, 2002, Perfect Pie, 2002, The Hot Chick, 2002, Mean Girls, 2004, The Notebook, 2004, Wedding Crashers, 2005, Red-Eye, 2005, The Family Stone, 2005; (TV films) Guilt by Association, 2002; (TV series) Shotgun Love Dolls, 2001, Slings and Arrows, 2003. Named Choice Movie Actress: Comedy, Teen Choice awards, 2006. Office: The Gersh Agy 232 N Canon Dr Beverly Hills CA 90210 Office Phone: 310-274-6611.

MC AFEE, MARGARET ANNE, retired art educator; b. Denver, May 14, 1929; d. Abe I. and Anne M. Blomquist; m. George Lafayette Finn McAfee, July 22, 1972. AA, UCLA, 1947, BA, 1951; MA in Edn., Calif. State Coll., 1967. Cert. tchr. Calif. State Bd. Of Edn., 1955. Tng. tchr. UCLA, USC & Mt. St. Mary's Coll., 1955—66; art tchr. and dept. chmn. Hamilton Sr. HS, LA, 1952—69; tchr. and prof. of art emeritus LA (Calif.) C.C. Dist., 1969—89; assoc. tchr. art Saddleback C.C., Mission Viejo, Calif., 1990—2003. Cons. in field. Dir.: (TV series) How to Design, Make and Use Mosaic Projects In and Around the Home, 1961—66; contbr. articles to newspapers. Troop leader Girl Scouts Am., LA, 1949—50. Mem.: AAUW, Assn. Ret. Tchrs., The Enamelist Soc., Am. Fedn. Tchrs. Emeritus, Nat. Art Edn. Assn., Calif. Art Edn. Assn., Calif. Tchr.'s Assn., Phi Kappa Phi (hon.), Pi Lambda Theta (hon.). Avocations: gardening, drawing, cooking, reading, travel. Home: 27826 Torroba Mission Viejo CA 92692-2131 Personal E-mail: mgmcafee@cox.net.

MCAFEE, NOELLE CLAIRE, philosopher, educator; b. Tagiura, Libya, Nov. 25, 1960; d. Horatio Paul and Marika Chaniotakis McAfee; m. David G Armstrong, Aug. 8, 1992; children: Guthrie McAfee Armstrong, Eliza Dorothy Armstrong. BA in hist., U. of Tex. at Austin, 1986; MA in pub. policy, Duke U., 1987; MA in Philosophy, U. of Wis. at Madison, 1990; PhD, U. of Tex. at Austin, 1998. Lectr. in polit. theory U. Tex., Dept. of Govt., 1998—99; asst. prof. philosophy U. Mass., 1999—2003, assoc. prof. philosophy, 2003—. Dir. honors program U. Mass., 2004—; vis. prof. philosophy Brandeis U., Waltham, Mass., 2004. Assoc. editor Kettering Review, 1991—; author: Julia Kristeva, 2003, Habermas, Kristeva and Citizenship, 2000; editor: Standing with the Public, 1997; contbr. chapters to books, articles to profl. jours. Office: Dept of Philosophy, U Mass Lowell One University Ave Lowell MA 01854 Office Phone: 978-934-3912.

MCALEER, RUTH BRESNAHAN, priest; b. Newbury Port, Mass., Aug. 18, 1931; d. Thomas Lawrence Bresnahan and Catharine Elizabeth Donahue; m. John Joseph McAleer, Oct. 25, 1958 (dec.); children: Mary Catharine, John Sheridan; 1 child, Thomas. BA, Barat Coll., 1976; MA, Webster U., 1978; cert., Seabury Western Theol. Seminary, 1991. Ordained priest Episcopal Ch., 1992. RN head nurse Peter Bent Brigham Hosp. Sch. Nursing, Boston, 1954—56; RN Nat. Inst. Health, Bethesda, Md., 1956—57, Lake Forest Hosp., Ill., 1969—90, hospice dir., 1984—91; resident chaplain St. Luke's Med. Ctr., 1991—92; hospice dir. Vis. Nurse Assn., Detroit, 1993—95; rector Grace Ch., Ottawa, Canada, 1996—99; clergy mem. pastoral care Christ Ch., Overland Pk., Kans., 1999—2004; asst. rector pastoral care St. Michael and All Angels, Mission, Kans., 2004—. Mem. ethics com. Lake Forest Hosp., Ill., 1985—91, Vis. Nurse Assn. of Southeast Mich., 1994—95, Nat. Hospice Org., Wash., 1993—95, St. Luke's South Hosp., Overland Park, Kans., 1998—. Democrat. Home: 8700 Metcalf Ave #102 Overland Park KS 66212 Office: St Michael and All Angels Ch 6630 Nall Ave Mission KS 66202 Office Phone: 913-236-8600.

MCALINDEN, LAURA A., humanities educator; b. East Orange, N.J., Sept. 18, 1964; d. Joseph J. McAlinden and Rosemarie Sardo; m. Kevin T. Pearson, Feb. 19, 1958; children: Jared G. Pearson, Kate R. Pearson. BA, Mount Holyoke, South Hadley, Mass., 1986; PhD, U. Wis., Madison, 2004. Asst. prof. Bridgewater State Coll., Mass., 2004—. Mem.: Am. Philos. Assn. Office: Philosophy Dept Bridgewater State Coll Bridgewater MA 02325

MCALINDON, MARY NAOMI, retired nursing consultant; b. Ebensburg, Pa., Oct. 16, 1935; d. S. David and Genevieve (Little) Solomon; m. James Daniel McAlindon, Nov. 25, 1961; children: Robert, Donald, James, Peter, M. Catherine. BSN, Georgetown U., 1957; MA, U. Mich., 1979; EdD, Wayne State U., 1992. RN, Mich. Staff nurse Georgetown U. Hosp., Washington, 1957-59; instr. St. Joseph Hosp., Flint, 1959-62; clin. instr. Mott. C.C., Flint, 1980-81; asst. DON McLaren Hosp., Flint, 1980-89, adminstrv. asst., 1989-92, asst. v.p., 1992-95; clin. informatics mgr. McLaren Health Care Corp., Flint, 1995-97; pres. McAlindon Assocs., 1997-99, ret., 1999. Asst. prof. U. Mich., Flint, Mich., 1992—2001. Trustee United Way Genesee County, Flint, Mich., 1988—95, Cmty. Found. Greater Flint, 1997—2001, chmn. personnel com., 2000—01; trustee Mclaren Home Health, 1996—2001. Mem.: Nursing Honor Soc. U. Mich. (pres. 1996—98), ANA (exec. com. 1991—93), Dist. Nurses Assn. (pres. 1993—96), Vis. Nurses Assn. (pres. 1988—90, bd. dir. 1984—96), Mich. Nursing Informatics Network, Am. Med. Informatics Assn. (chmn. nursing group 1993—94), Sigma Theta (pres. Pi Delta chpt. 1998—2001). Home and Office: 8230 Sawgrass Trl Grand Blanc MI 48439-1874 Personal E-mail: mmcalind@comcast.net.

MCALISTER, CHRIS, elementary school educator; d. Marvin and Catherine Weast; m. Scott McAlister, July 21, 1984; children: Ryan, Sean. BS, U. So. Calif., L.A., 1975. Cert. tchr. Calif. Tchr. Marine View Mid. Sch., Huntington Beach, Calif., 1976—. Parent vol. Marina H.S., Huntingotn Beach. Home: 17102 Tiffany Cir Huntington Beach CA 92649 Office: Marine View Mid Sch 5682 Tilburg Dr Huntington Beach CA 92649 Office Phone: 714-846-0624.

MCALISTER, MICHELLE NICOLE, mathematics educator; b. Houston, May 31, 1981; d. Douglas James and Diana Lynn McAlister. Degree Math., Graceland U., Lamoni, Iowa, 1999; MBA, Tex. Womans U., Dallas, 2006. Tchr. Math. Coppell H.S., Tex., 2003—. Office: Coppell High School 185 W Parkway Coppell TX 75019 Office Phone: 214-496-6100. Personal E-mail: mmcalister@coppellisd.com.

MCALLEN, REGINA K., voice educator; b. Saskatoon, Saskatchewan, Canada, Jan. 3, 1969; d. Paul and Sheila Rosemary Freeman; m. John McAllen, July 19, 1997; children: Parker Anne, Lincoln. Attended, Vienna Conservatory of Music, Austria, 1986—87, Italian Inst. Fgn. Studies, Florence, 1993; Music Edn., Piano Pedagogy and Performance, Westminster Choir Coll., 1993; attended, The Juilliard Sch. of Music, 2003. Musical dir. The Guild Hall, Whitehorse, Yukon Territory, Canada, 1986, Diamond Tooth Gerties Saloon Hall Casino, Dawson City, Yukon Territory, 1986, Premier Theatre Co., Lincroft, N.J., 1994—2000; vocal dir. Pt. Pleasant Borough HS, N.J., 1997—; musical dir. Phoenix Prodns., Red Bank, N.J., 2003—. Pres., sec. and accompanist All Shore Chorus Orgn., Manasquan, N.J., 1997—2003. Recipient Can. Advanced Artists grant, Can. Arts Bd., 1990, 1991, Outstanding Choral Excellence, MENC, ACDA, Teen Arts Festival, 1997—2005; grantee Can. Advanced Artists grant, Can. Arts Bd., 1988. Mem.: The Coll. Bd. (faculty advisor 2001—), Drama League, Music Educators Nat. Assn., Piano Guild, Nat. Assn. Tchrs. Singing. Home: 203 Chatham Lane Point Pleasant Beach NJ 08742 Office: Pt Pleasant Borough HS Laura Herbert Dr Point Pleasant Beach NJ 08742 Office Phone: 732-701-1900 ext. 2239.

MCALLISTER, LYNETTE J., financial consultant; b. Salt Lake City, July 17, 1961; d. Robert E. Cheney Sr. and Marie Jane Thurman; m. Robert Dale McAllister, May 16, 1986; children: Cherise Lynne, Ethan Trevor. Grad., Salt Lake City Coll. Med. and Dental Careers, 1986. Credit proof operator First Security Bank, Salt Lake City, 1979-81; dental asst. FHP of Utah (HMO), Midvale, 1981-84, Dr. Mark Blaisdell DDS, Bountiful, Utah, 1984-86; ops. mgr. First Security Investor Svcs., Salt Lake City, 1986-90, brokerage trader, 1990-96; fin. cons. Zions Investment Securities, Salt Lake City, 1996—. Mem. Fin. Women Internat. (edn. chair, sec. 1997—, Woman of Yr. 1997, com. festival of trees 1998). Avocations: camping, sports, crocheting, painting. Office: Zions Investment Securities One South Main St 3d Fl Salt Lake City UT 84111

MCALLISTER, SINGLETON BERYL, lawyer; b. Balt., Mar. 25, 1952; d. James Winfred and Ann (Hughes) McAllister. BA, U. Md., 1975; JD, Howard U., 1984. Bar: Pa., 1985, DC, 1986, US Supreme Ct. Legis. asst. Congressman Parren J. Mitchell, Washington, 1975-78; asst. dir. Trans-Africa, Washington, 1978-79; legis. dir. Congressman William H. Gray III, Washington, 1979-81; spl. asst. Congressman Mickey Leland, Washington, 1981-83; law clk. to Judge Jack E. Tanner US Dist. Ct. We. Dist. Wash., Tacoma, 1984-86; sr. counsel US Ho. of Reps. Com. on the Budget, Washington, 1986-88; ptnr. Reed, Smith, Shaw & McClay, Washington, 1988—92; counsel Shaw Pittman Potts & Trowbridge, Washington, 1992—96; gen. counsel US Agy. for Internat. Devel., 1996—2001; ptnr. Patton Boggs LLP, 2001—03; ptnr., pub. law & policy strategies group Sonnenschein Nath & Rosenthal LLP, Washington, 2003, chair firm Corp. Diversity Counseling Group, 2003—05; ptnr. Mintz Lewin, 2005—. Past mem. adv. bd. African Devel. Found., Washington; counsel to Nat. Dem. Platform Drafting Com., 1988. Bd. dirs. Nat. Women's Bus. Ctr., Washington. Mem. ABA, Nat. Bar Assn., Delta Theta Phi. Avocations: aerobics, horseback riding.

MCALPINE, LISA K., science educator; b. Laredo AFB, Tex., Dec. 22, 1967; BS, Baylor U., Waco, Tex., 1990; MEd, Tex. A&M U., College Station, 1994. Sci. educator College Station Ind. Sch. Dist., 1992—2004; dir. magnet programs Spring Valley HS, Columbia, SC, 2004—. Biotechnology edn. resource agt. Tex. A&M U., College Station, 1993—98; co-instr. profl. devel. sch. College Station Ind. Sch. Dist./ Tex. A&M U., 1999—2003. Named Outstanding New Tchr., College Station Edn. Assn., 1994, Tchr. of Yr., A&M Consol. HS/College Station Ind. Sch. Dist., 1997, Class 5A Sci. Coach of Yr., Tex. Math and Sci. Coaches Assn., 2003—04; recipient Tchr. of Yr., A&M Consol. HS/College Station Ind. Sch. Dist., 2003; grantee, College Station Edn. Found., 2001—02. Mem.: ASCD, NSTA. Office: Spring Valley High Sch 120 Sparkleberry Ln Columbia SC 29229 Office Phone: 803-699-3500 5513. Personal E-mail: lmcalpine@worldnet.att.net. Business E-Mail: lmcalpin@svh.richland2.org.

MCAMIS, ANGIE M., elementary school educator; d. Keith A. McAmis and Donna D. Urban. BS in Edn., U. Tenn.-Chattanooga; EdnM, Lincoln Meml. U., Herrogate, Tenn., 2003. Cert. elem. edn. K-8 Tenn., 1998. Tchr. Bradley County Schs., Cleveland, Tenn., 1998—. Cons. Mailbox Mag., Greensboro, NC; presenter in field. Office Phone: 423-478-8821.

MCANARNEY, ELIZABETH R., pediatrician, educator; b. NYC, May 7, 1940; d. Henry Kellers and Kathryn (Blaney) McA. AB, Vassar Coll., 1962; MD, SUNY, Syracuse, 1966. Diplomate Am. Bd. Pediatrics in pediatrics and adolescent medicine. Intern, resident SUNY Upstate Med. Ctr., Syracuse, NY, 1966-68; fellow in behavioral pediatrics U. Rochester (N.Y.) Med. Ctr., 1968-70, sr. instr. pediatrics, 1969-71, asst. prof. pediatrics, 1971-77, assoc. prof. pediatrics, 1977-85, prof. pediatrics, 1985—, chair pediatrics dept., 1993—. Adv. com. Fertility and Maternal Health FDA, Bethesda, Md, 1987-92; mem. program adv. bd. Robert Wood Johnson Clin. Scholars Program, Princeton, N.J., 1995—. Editor: (books) Premature Adolescent Pregnancy, 1983, Identifying Social/ Psychological Antecedents of Adolescent Pregnancy, 1984, Textbook of Adolescent Medicine, 1992; co-author of nearly 200 papers, chpts., and comm. Recipient McNeil Outstanding Achievement award Soc. for Adolescent Medicine, 1989, Job Lewis Smith award Cmty. Pediat., Am. Acad. Pediat., 1990; named to Alumni Honor Roll, SUNY, 1998. Fellow AAAS; mem. Soc. for Pediatric Rsch., Am. Pediatric Soc. (mem. exec. coun. 1998—, pres. 2004-2005), Assn. for Med. Sch. Pediatric Chairs (pres. 1999), Inst. Medicine, Nat. Acad. Sci. Achievements include determination of relationship between young maternal age and maternal/neonatal outcomes. Office: U Rochester Med Ctr Dept Pediatrics 601 Elmwood Ave Box 777 Rochester NY 14642-0001 E-mail: carole_berger@urmc.rochester.edu.*

MCANDREWS, SHANNON MARIE, elementary school educator; b. Kailua, Hawaii, Mar. 23, 1969; d. James Edward and Marie Louise Sniffen; m. Kenneth Lloyd McAndrews, Aug. 21, 1993; children: Logan Marie, Jordan Elizabeth. BS, San Diego State U., 1991; MS in Spl. Edn., U. San Diego, 1993. Tchr. San Diego Unified, 1992—93, Poway Unified, 1993—94, Ramona Unified, Ramona, Calif., 1995—. Mem.: Calif. Coun. Social Studies. Achievements include recognition as the first of 2 PATH program educators in Calif. Avocation: dance. Office: James Dukes Elem Sch 24908 Abalar Way Ramona CA 92065 Office Phone: 760-788-5060. Personal E-mail: mcandrewsjd@aol.com.

MCANIFF, NORA P., publishing executive; b. NY, 1958; BA, Baruch Coll. From mktg. info. mgr. to pres. People Mag. Time Inc., NYC, 1982—98, pres. People Mag., 1998—2002, pub. Life Mag., 1992—93, pub. Teen People, 1997—98, exec. v.p., women's entertainment & luxury group, 2002—, and co-COO, 2005—. Dir. Saks Inc., 2002—; bd. dir. Michael J. Fox Found. for Parkinson's Rsch. Office: Time Inc 1271 Avenue of the Americas New York NY 10020-1300*

MCARDLE, BARBARA VIRGINIA, elementary school educator; b. Worcester, Mass., Sept. 4, 1925; d. Patrick Michael Brosnan and Nora Catherine Ferriter; m. William Henry McARdle, June 20, 1956. BS in Edn., Worcester State Tchrs. Coll., 1947, MEd, 1953. Elem. grade tchr. Grove St. Sch., Spencer, Mass., 1947—48, Allen L. Joslin Sch., Oxford, Mass., 1948—56, Euclid Sch., St. Petersburg, Fla., 1957—63, Wood Lawn Sch., St. Petersburg, 1963—91. Sch. rep. Pinellas County Tchrs. Assn., St. Petersburg, 1957—91; active Boys and Girls Club of Am.; vol. Dem. Orgn., St. Petersburg. Named to Kindergarten Playground at Wood Lawn Sch. Mem.: St. Jude's Guild, St. Anthony's Guild. Roman Catholic. Home: 5266 26th Ave N Saint Petersburg FL 33710

MCARDLE, PATRICIA ANNE, security company executive; b. Freeport, N.Y., Oct. 8, 1963; d. John Fergerson and Dorothy Patricia (Williamson) McA.; m. Robert Tyszkowski, Dec. 30, 1995. BBA, Pace U., 1985; MBA, N.Y. Inst. Tech., 1990; postgrad., John Jay Coll., 1993-94. Lic. pvt. detective, Mass., N.Y. Mfg. planner Grumman Aerospace, Milledgeville, Ga., 1981-82, Hazeltine Corp., Commack, N.Y., 1987-89; contracts analyst N.Y.C. Transit Authority, Bklyn., 1989-90, contracts mgr., 1991-92, acting dir. procurement, 1992-93; spl. investigator City of N.Y., 1993-96; prin., CEO, chmn. bd. dirs. P.M.T. Assocs. Inc., Boston, 1996—; CEO, pres., chmn. bd. dirs. Evidaunt Investigations, Inc., Boston, 1997—. Author: Handbook of Investigations, 1995. Event vol. U.S. Special Olympics, Hempstead, N.Y., 1992; mem. Redwood Libr. and Athenaeum, Newport, R.I. Recipient Silver Leader award DAV, 1997, 98, 99. Mem. Athenaeum (Boston, Newport, R.I.), Nat. Assn. Investigative Specialists, Tennis and Racquet Club (Boston), Redwood Libr. Republican. Avocations: reading, international travel. Office: Evidaunt Investigations Inc Prudential Ctr PO Box 990067 Boston MA 02199-0067 E-mail: evidaunt@aol.com.

MCARTHUR, BETH GOLDEN, elementary school educator; b. Panama City, Fla., Nov. 30, 1947; d. Loyce Harvey Golden; m. James(Sonny) Newton McArthur, Sept. 29, 1972; children: Scott Allen, Bobbi Lynn. AA, Gulf Coast C.C., 1967; BS in Early Childhood Edn., U. West Fla., 1969; Gifted Endorsement Courses, Fla. State U. Cert. profl. educator Fla., Nat. Bd. Tchr. Early childhood, elem. k-6 tchr. Bay Dist. Schs., Panama City, Fla., 1969—2005, mentoring, tchr., 2005—. Nat. cert. growing healthy trainer Bay Dist. Schs., 1986—97. Grantee, Bay Edn. Found., 1998-2005, St. Joe Paper Co., 1998—2005, Lynn Haven Parent Tchr. Assn, 1998—2005. Mem.: NEA (assoc.), Fla. Edn. Assn. (assoc.), Bay County Reading Assn. (assoc.), Fla. Reading Assn. (assoc.), Internat. Reading Assn. (assoc.). Meth. Home: 499 Candlewick Dr Panama City FL 32405 Office: Bay Dist Schs 1311 Balboa Ave Panama City FL 32401 Office Phone: 850-872-7524. Office Fax: 850-873-7126. Personal E-mail: mac32405@knology.net. Business E-Mail: mcartbg@bay.k12.fl.us.

MCARTHUR, LISA R., music educator, musician; d. Tremaine James and Judith Hammon McArthur. PhD in Music Theory, U. of Ky., Lexington, Kentucky, 1995—99; MA in Music Theory, Kent State U., Kent, Ohio, 1990—94, MusM in performance, 1990—93; MusB in Music Edn., SUNY Potsdam Coll., Crane Sch. of Music, Potsdam, New York, 1986—90. Grad. asst. Kent State U., Kent, Ohio, 1990—92; orch. dir., grades 4-12 Akron Pub. Schools, Akron, Ohio, 1993—95; grad. tchg. asst. U. of Ky., Lexington, Ky., 1995—98; assoc. prof. Campbellsville U., Campbellsville, Ky., 1998—. Clinician Emerson Flutes, Elkhart, Ind., 2000—; dir. flute ensemble Campbellsville (Ky.) U., 1998—; presenter in field. Musician: (albums) Something Old, Something New, Something Borrowed, Something Blue, 2004; arranger: for flute ensemble Symphony No. 1, for flute solo and flute ensemble accompaniment Scherzino by Andersen and Concerto in D Maj. by Mozart. Named Coll./U. Educator of the Yr., Ky. Music Educators Assn., 2001; recipient Performer's cert., Crane Sch. of Music, 1990. Mem.: Nat. Assn. of Coll. Wind and Percussion Instructors, Nat. Flute Assn., Soc. for Music Theory, Coll. Music Soc., Music Educators Nat. Conf. (coll. chpt. advisor 1998—, state chpt. advisor 2003—05), Ky. Music Educators Assn., Flute Soc. of Ky. (pres. 2000—), Pi Kappa Lambda, Sigma Alpha Iota (life). Office: Campbellsville University UPO 922 Campbellsville KY 42718 E-mail: lrmcarthur@campbellsville.edu.

MCATEER, DEBORAH GRACE, travel company executive; b. NYC, Nov. 3, 1950; d. Edward John and Ann Marie (Cassidy) McA.; m. William A. Helms, Feb. 5, 1948 (div. 1993); children: Elizabeth Grace, Kathleen Marie, Margaret Ann; m. M. Lees Sherwood, Mar. 8, 1949 (div. 2002). Student, Montgomery Coll., 1969, Am. U., 1972. Sec. Polinger Co., Chevy Chase, Md., 1969-72, Loews Hotels, Washington, 1972-73; adminstr. asst. Am. Gas Assn., Arlington, Va., 1973-75; mgr. Birch Jermain Horton Bittner, Washington, 1975-77; asst. mgr. Travel Services, McLean, Va., 1977-79; founder, pres. Travel Temps, Washington, Atlanta, Phila., Miami and Ft. Lauderdale, Fla., 1979—; pres. Diversified Communications, Atlanta, 1990—; tchr. Ga. State U., Atlanta, 1996; pres. The Internet Employment Source, Atlanta, 1987—. Tchr. Montgomery Coll., Rockville, Md., 1980-84, Ga. State U., 1996. Mem. Christ Child Soc., Washington, 1975—; bd. dirs. Atlanta Ballet, 1995—. Mem. Internat. Travel Soc. (pres. 1983-84), Am. Soc. Travel Agts., Pacific Area Travel Assn., Inst. Cert. Travel Cons. (cert., life mem.), Nat. Assn. Women Bus. Owners (chair membership com. 1983-84), Women Bus. Owners Atlanta (bd. dirs. 1991—, pres. 1994), Women's Commerce Club, PROST (v.p. 1991), Atlanta Women in Travel. Republican. Roman Catholic.

MCAULIFFE, CATHERINE A., counselor, psychology educator, retired psychotherapist; b. Northampton, Mass., July 31, 1952; d. Francis G. and Emliy R. (Hanley) Ciarfella; m. Francis J. McAuliffe, Aug. 14, 1999; children: Richard Jr. DiPersio, Edward DiPersio, Mary Catherine DiPersio. BS in Elem. Edn., U. Conn., 1974; MS in Counseling, So. Conn. State U., 1988; postmaster's sch. counseling cert., Cen. Conn. State U., 1992. Cert. K-12 counselor, K-8 tchr. Conn., adult edn. tchr. 1st grade tchr. Granby (Conn.) Pub. Schs., 1974-75; pvt. psychotherapist Meriden, Conn., 1988—97; dir. counseling Paier Coll. Art, Hamden, Conn., 1988—91; h.s. counselor Sacred Heart H.S., Waterbury, Conn., 1990-91; sch. counselor Meriden Pub. Schs., Cheshire (Conn.) Pub. Schs., 1997—2000, Bridgeport (Conn.) Pub. Schs., 2001—. Pers. devel. counselor U. Conn., Waterbury, 1991—97; psychology instr. Paier Coll. Art, 1991—97. Scout leader Cub Scouts Am., Meriden, 1984-86, Girl Scouts Am., 1986-87; hospitality chairperson PTA, Meriden, 1984-85; vol. Rep. Party, Meriden, 1988. Mem.: Am. Assn. Christian Counselors, Conn. Sch. Counseling Assn., Conn. Sch. Counseling Assn., ACA, Phi Kappa Phi. Roman Catholic. Avocations: singing, directing choirs, playing keyboard, guitar, composing lyrics and music. Home: 15 Spring Glen Dr Meriden CT 06451-2720 Office: 265 George St Bridgeport CT 06604-3320

MCAULIFFE, MAUREEN, science educator; d. Jerry and Jane McAuliffe. MEd, Worcester State Coll., Mass., 2003. Tchr. St. Peter Marian Jr-Sr. HS, Worcester, 1998—2001; secondary h.s. tchr. Ashland (Mass.) Pub. Schs., 2001—02; h.s. secondary sci. tchr. Nashoba Regional Sch. Dist., Bolton, Mass., 2002—. Office Phone: 978-779-2257.

MCAULIFFE-CURNIAS, SUSAN EILEEN, secondary school educator; b. Hartford, Conn., June 28, 1951; d. Daniel Joseph and Shirley Anne (Pierce) McAuliffe; m. James Michael Curnias, Aug. 16, 1985; 1 child, Christina McAuliffe Curnias. BS in health and physical edn., Southern Conn. State U., 1973; MS, Ctrl. Conn. State U., 1976. Cert. tchr./coach. Tchr./coach West Hartford Bd. Edn., Conn., 1973—. Roman Catholic. Avocation: cooking. Home: 37 Summerfielde Dr Wethersfield CT 06109 Office: William Hall HS West Hartford 975 W Main St West Hartford CT 06117 Personal E-mail: macurn@sbcglobal.net.

MCAVENEY, MARY SUSAN, marketing executive; b. Perth Amboy, N.J., Jan. 1, 1965; d. Catherine Geraldine and Charles Joseph McAveney; m. David Clifford Briggs, Sept. 27, 1997; children: Alexander Patrick Briggs, Colin Andrew Briggs. BA, Coll. of NJ., 1989. Writer The Herald, Wall Township, NJ, 1984—88; mktg. assoc. Graphis US, Inc., N.Y.C., 1989—92; mktg. mgr. Harry N. Abrams, Inc., N.Y.C., 1992—98; mktg. dir. HarperCollins Children's Books, N.Y.C., 1998—. Spkr. Internat. Quality and Productivity Ctr. Kid Power XChange, Fla., 2003, Internat. Quality and Productivity Coun.; Kid Power XChange, Fla., 2005—. Contbr. poetry. Sec. Sch. Leadership Team Pub. Sch. 58, Bklyn., 2004—05; mem. Curriculum Com., Pub. Sch. 58, Bklyn., 2004—05, Women's Dem. Com., Washington, 2004—05; mem., fundraiser Nat. Dem. Com., Washington, 2004—05; mem. Families First, Family Ctr., Bklyn., 2000—03. Garden State scholarship, State of N.J., 1983. Mem.: Promotion, Advt., and Mktg. Assn., Children's Book Coun. Democrat-Npl. Avocations: travel, photography, writing, cooking. Office: HarperCollins Children's Books 1350 Avenue of Americas New York NY 10019 Office Phone: 212-307-3623. Office Fax: 212-261-6785. Business E-Mail: mary.mcaveney@harpercollins.com.

MCAVOY, KATHLEEN FLEMING, mathematics educator; b. Bronx, N.Y., May 9, 1959; d. Peter Joseph and Frances Beisner Fleming; m. John Joseph Mcavoy, May 30, 1981; children: Kelly Frances, Maureen Nicole, Siobhan Mary, Jacqueline Marie. BA in Math., Coll. Mt. St. Vincent, Bronx, 1981; MS in computer sci., Pace U., N.Y., 1984. Cert. Tchr. Nat. Bd. for Profl. Tchrs., 2004. Aquatics dir. Bronx Devel. Ctr., NY, 1979—81; math and computer sci. tchr. Acad. of the Resurrection, Rye, NY, 1981—82; math and computer tchr. Cardinal Spellman HS, Bronx, 1982—84; math and computer sci. tchr. Hendrick Hudson Sch., Buchanan, NY, 1984—85; math tchr. Fox Lane HS, Bedford, NY, 2000—01, Mahopac HS, NY, 2001—. Basketball coach Mahopac Sports Assn., NY, 1996—2003; drama coach St. John the Evangelist, Mahopac, NY, 1997—2005; swim coach Kennedy Cath. HS, Somers, NY, 2005. Leader Girl Scouts of Am., Mahopac, NY, 1990—2006. Liberal. Roman Catholic. Avocations: swimming, basketball, travel. Office: Mahopac HS 472 Baldwin Place Rd Mahopac NY 10541 Office Phone: 845-628-3256. Personal E-mail: mcavoyk@mahopac.k12.org.

MCBAY, IDA LAVERNE, special education educator; b. Dallas, May 3, 1949; d. Russell and Edna Marie Green; 1 child, Mshindi Jamal. AA, Alameda Coll., 1971. Instrnl. asst. Berkeley Unified Sch. Dist., 1981—, tchr. child devel. program, 2000—. Resource asst. Berkeley Unified Sch., 1995—2000. Mem.: Nat. Trust, Smithsonian. Democrat. Baptist. Avocations: tennis, sewing, art, knitting, growing plants. Home: 1933 Stuart St B Berkeley CA 94703 Personal E-mail: mcbari@sbcglobal.net. E-mail: i.mcbay@sbcglobal.net.

MCBEE, CHRISTY DAWN, art educator, pre-school educator; b. Tullahomo, Tenn., Nov. 15, 1974; d. Larry Wayne and Dorothy Jean McInturff; m. Michael Scott McBee, June 26, 2004; children: Stacy Carol, Mitchell Larry. BSc, Mid. Tenn. State U., Murfreesboro, 1997. Art endorsement Arrowmont Sch. Arts & Crafts, 2002, registered visual arts tchr. Tenn., 2002. Tchr. 3rd grade Broadview Elem. Sch., Winchester, Tenn., 1997—98; Sparks grant tchr. Warren County Schs., McMinnville, Tenn., 1998—2000; tchr. art Woodland Elem. Sch., Woodbury, Tenn., 2000—03, Cascade H.S., Shelbyville, Tenn., 2003—04, Crab Orchard & Pineview Elem. Schs., Crossville, Tenn., 2004—. Head fine arts dept., mem. spl. concerns com. Cascade H.S., Crab Orchard, Pineview, Shelbyville, Crossville, 2003—06; chmn. flower com. Crab Orchard Elem. Sch., Crossville, 2006—. Author: (poem) Anthology of Am. Poetry, 1997. Sponsor Awana Internat. Worldwide Missions, 2005—06, Habitat for Humanity, Warren County, 1997—2006, Jesus Film Project Worldwide Missions, 2005—06. Nominee 10 Yr. Svc. award, Cumberland County Schs., Crossville, 2006; recipient Awana Achievement award, Morrison 1st Bapt. Ch., 2005; grantee Sparks grant, Warren County Schs., 1998—2000. Mem.: Tenn. Edn. Assn., Nat. Tchrs. Edn. Assn. Democrat. Southern Bapt. Achievements include leading a student to receive statewide recognition for winning My Home Is Tenessee Art Contest in Nashville. Avocations: reading, poetry, painting, music, birdwatching. Office: Crab Orchard Elem Sch 240 School Rd Crab Orchard TN 37723 Business E-Mail: mcbee@cumberlandcountyk-12.com.

MCBEE, MARY LOUISE, retired state legislator, retired academic administrator; b. Strawberry Plains, Tenn., June 15, 1924; d. John Wallace and Nina Aileen (Umbarger) McB. BS, East Tenn. State U., 1946; MA, Columbia U., 1951; PhD, Ohio State U., 1961. Tchr. East Tenn. State U., Johnson City, 1947-51; asst. dean of women, 1952-56, 57-60; dean of women, 1961-63, U. Ga., Athens, 1963-67; world campus afloat adminstr., 1966-67; assoc. dean of students, 1967-72; dean of students, 1972-74; asst. v.p. acad. affairs, 1974-76;

assoc. v.p. acad. affairs, 1976-86; v.p. acad. affairs, 1986-88; ret., 1988; state rep. Clarke County Ga. Gen. Assembly, 1991—2004. Author: College Responsibility for Values, 1980; co-author: The American Woman: Who Will She Be?, 1974, Essays, 1979, 2d edit. 1981. Bd. dirs. Salvation Army, Athens, 1978—, United Way, Athens. Fulbright scholar, The Netherlands, 1956-57. Mem. Athens C. of C. (bd. dirs.). Democrat. Methodist. Avocations: gardening, tennis, hiking. Home: 145 Pine Valley Pl Athens GA 30606-4031 Personal E-mail: louisemcbee@charter.com. Business E-Mail: lmcbee@legis.state.ga.us.

MCBEE, SUSANNA BARNES, retired journalist; b. Santa Fe, N.Mex., Mar. 28, 1935; d. Jess Stephen and Sybil Elizabeth (Barnes) McBee; m. Paul H. Recer, July 2, 1983. AB, U. So. Calif., 1956; MA, U. Chgo., 1962. Staff writer Washington Post, 1957-65, 73-74, 77-79, asst. nat. editor, 1974-77; asst. sec. pub. affairs HEW, 1979; articles editor Washingtonian mag., 1980-81; assoc. editor U.S. News & World Report, 1981-86; news editor Washington Bur., Hearst Newspapers, 1987-89, asst. bur. chief, 1990—2003, ret., 2003; Washington corr. Life mag., 1965—69; Washington editor McCall's mag., 1970—72. Bd. dirs. Washington Press Club Found., 1992-95. Recipient Penney-Missouri mag. award, 1969, Hall of Fame award, Soc. Profl. Journalists, 1996, Sigma Delta Chi Pub. Svc. award, 1969, Hearst Eagle award, 1994. Mem. Nat. Press Club, Cosmos Club. Home: 5190 Watson St NW Washington DC 20016-5329

MCBREEN, MAURA ANN, lawyer; b. N.Y.C., Aug. 18, 1953; d. Peter J. and Frances S. (McVeigh) McB. AB, Smith Coll., 1975; JD, Harvard U., 1978. Bar: Ill. 1978. Ptnr. Kirkland & Ellis, Chgo., 1978-86, Isham, Lincoln & Beale (merged with Reuben & Proctor), Chgo., 1986-88, Baker & McKenzie, Chgo., 1988—. Mem. bd. dir. Juvenile Protective Assn.; mem. Econ. Club Chgo., 2004—. Auth. several articles profl. jours. Mem. bd. dir. Lyric Opera Chgo. Mem. ABA, Chgo. Bar Assn., Ill. St. Bar Assn., Midwest Pension Conf. Office: Baker & McKenzie 1 Prudential Pla 130 E Randolph Dr Ste 3700 Chicago IL 60601-6342

MCBRIDE, ANGELA BARRON, nursing educator; b. Balt., Jan. 16, 1941; d. John Stanley and Mary C. (Szczepanska) Barron; m. William Leon McBride, June 12, 1965; children: Catherine, Kara. BS in Nursing, Georgetown U., Washington, 1962; MS in Nursing, Yale U., New Haven, Conn., 1964; PhD, Purdue U., West Lafayette, Ind., 1978; doctorate of Pub. Svc. (hon.), U. Cin., 1983; LittD (hon.), Purdue U., 1998; LLD (hon.), Ea. Ky. U., 1991; LHD (hon.), Georgetown U., 1993; DSc (hon.), Med. Coll. Ohio, 1995; LHD (hon.), U. Akron, 1997. Asst. prof., rsch. asst. inst. Yale U., New Haven, 1964-73; assoc. prof., chairperson Ind. U. Sch. Nursing, Indpls., 1978-81, 80-84, prof., 1981-92, assoc. dean rsch., 1985—91, interim dean, 1991—92, univ. dean, 1992—2003, disting. prof., 1992—2005, disting. prof., univ. dean emerita, 2006—; sr. v.p. acad. affairs, nursing Clarian Health Ptnrs., 1997—2003; Am. Acad. Nursing, Am. Nurses Found. scholar-in-residence Inst. Medicine, 2003—04; Helene Denne Schulte vis. prof. U. Wis., Madison, 2006. Mem. Nat. Adv. Mental Health Coun., 1987—91; adv. com. NIH Office of Women's Health Rsch., 1997—2001, NIH Office of Women's Health Rsch. Specialized Ctrs. Rsch. on Sex and Gender Factors, 2003—; coun. mem. Yale U., 1999—2005; ext. acad. advisor Sch. Nursing, Hong Kong Polytechnic U., 2000—; adv. bd. Meth. Health Found., 2000—; advisor U. Hong Kong, 2004—, Hong Kong Acad. Nursing, 2004—; Helen Denn Schulte vis. prof. U. Wis. Madison, 2006. Author: The Growth and Development of Mothers, 1973 (Best Book award 1973), Living with Contradictions, A Married Feminist, 1976, How to Enjoy A Good Life With Your Teenager, 1987; editor: Psychiatric-Mental Health Nursing: Integrating the Behavioral and Biological Sciences, 1996 (Best Book award 1996); compiler: Nursing and Philanthropy, 2000. Adv. bd. Women's Fund Indpls., 2000—05; bd. dirs. United Way of Ctrl. Ind., 2002—06, Clarian Health Ptnrs., 2004—, chair quality and patient care com. Recipient Disting. Alumna award Yale U., Disting. Alumna award Purdue U., Univ. Medallion, U. San Francisco, 1993, Hoosier Heritage award, 2000, Disting. Nurse Educator award Coll. Mt. St. Joseph, Cin., 2000, Ross Pioneering Spirit award Am. Assn. Critical-Care Nurses, 2004, Lifetime Achievement award Assn. Fundraising Profls., Ind., 2005, Woman of Achievement award, Ball State U., 2005 Torchbearer award Ind. Commn. for Women, 2005, Melva Jo Hendrix Leadership award Internat. Soc. Psychiat. Nursing, 2006; named Influential Woman in Indpls., Indpls. Bus. Jour./Ind. Lawyer, 1999, HealthCare Hero Indpls. Bus. Jour., 2003, Adele Herwitz Disting. scholar Commn. Fgn. Nursing Schs., 2005; Kellogg nat. fellow; Am. Nurses Found. scholar, Salute to Women award Indpls. YMCA, 1999, Sagamore of Wabash, 1999. Fellow: Nat. Acads. Practice, Am. Acad. Nursing (dir. leadership devel. bldg. acad. geriatric nursing capacity program 2000—, past pres., Living Legend 2006), APA (Nursing and Health Psychology award divsn. 38 1995); mem.: Nat. Acad. Scis., Inst. of Medicine (mem. bd. health policy ednl. programs and fellowships 2006—), Soc. for Rsch. in Child Devel., Midwest Nursing Rsch. Soc. (Disting. Rsch. award 1985), Sigma Theta Tau (past pres., Mentor award 1993, disting. lectr 1995—99, Melanie Dreher award for contbns. as a dean 2001), Chi Eta Phi (hon.). Home: 744 Cherokee Ave Lafayette IN 47905-1872 Office Phone: 317-278-9076. Business E-Mail: amcbride@iupui.edu.

MCBRIDE, BEVERLY JEAN, lawyer; b. Greenville, Ohio, Apr. 5, 1941; d. Kenneth Birt and Glenna Louise (Ashman) Whited; m. Benjamin Gary McBride, Nov. 28, 1964; children: John David, Elizabeth Ann. BA magna cum laude, Wittenberg U., 1963; JD cum laude, U. Toledo, 1966. Bar: Ohio 1966. Intern Ohio Gov.'s Office, Columbus, 1962; asst. dean women U. Toledo, 1963-65; assoc. Title Guarantee and Trust Co., Toledo, 1966-69; spl. counsel Ohio Atty. Gen.'s Office, Toledo, 1975; assoc. Cobourn, Smith, Rohrbacher and Gibson, Toledo, 1969-76; v.p., gen. counsel, sec. The Andersons Inc., Maumee, Ohio, 1976—2005, of counsel, 2005—. Exec. trustee, bd. dirs. Wittenberg U., Springfield, Ohio, 1980-83; trustee Anderson Found., Maumee, 1981-93, Toledo Cmty. Found., 2006-; mem. Ohio Supreme Ct. Task Force on Gender Fairness, 1991-94, Regional Growth Partnership, 1994—; chmn. Sylvania Twp. Zoning Commn., Ohio, 1970-80; candidate for judge Sylvania Mcpl. Ct., 1975; trustee Goodwill Industries, Toledo, 1976-82, Sylvania Cmty. Svcs. Ctr., 1976-78, Toledo-Lucas County Port Authority, 1992-99; chair St. Vincent Med. Ctr., 1992-99; founder Sylvania YWCA Program, 1973; active membership drives Toledo Mus. Art, 1977-87. Recipient Toledo Women in Industry award YWCA, 1979, Outstanding Alumnus award Wittenberg U., 1981. Fellow Am. Bar Found.; mem. ABA, AAUW, Ohio Bar Assn., Toledo Bar Assn. (pres., treas., chmn., sec. various coms.), Toledo Women Attys. Forum (exec. com. 1978-82), Pres. Club (U. Toledo exec. com.). Home: 5274 Cambrian Rd Toledo OH 43623-2626 Office: The Andersons Inc PO Box 119 Maumee OH 43537

MCBRIDE, JANET MARIE, small business owner; b. Ft. Wayne, Ind., Nov. 21, 1948; d. Robert W and Helen F Plasterer; m. Joey W McBride, July 26, 1976; children: Kenneth Schortgen, Jr., Christian Schortgen, Dawna McBride Ross, Brand. Grad., Phoenix Coll., 1995. Feng Shui practitioner Western Sch. of Feng Shui, Calif., 2000. Dod ednl. exec asst DOD Schools-Europe, Madrid, 1979—82; engring. project adminstr. Honeywell, Inc., Tempe, 1987—95; cons., coach Young Living, Salt Lake City, 2000—. Singer (songwriter/producer): (spiritual songs) Irish Girl with the Heart of a Jew; singer: (musician/producer) (messianic hymns) Irish Girl with Heart of a Jew; author: Scriptural Essence; Radio Health Talk Personality. Office: Essential Opportunities Inc 500 N Estrella Pky Ste B-2 #124 Goodyear AZ 85338 Address: 5388 Mountain Gate Cir Lakeside AZ 85929 Office Phone: 623-925-8994. E-mail: essentialvitality@cox.net.

MCBRIDE, JUDITH, elementary school educator; BFA in Interior Design, Utah State U., 1963; MFA, U. Wyo., 1980. Art tchr. Beitel Elem. Sch., Laramie, Wyo., Spring Creek Elem. Sch., Laramie, Centennial Valley Elem. Sch., Laramie. Named Wyo. State Tchr. of Yr., 1993. Office: Spring Creek Elem Sch 1203 Russell St Laramie WY 82070-4682

MCBRIDE, MARTINA, vocalist; b. Medicine Lodge, Kans., July 29, 1966; d. Daryl and Jeanne Schiff; m. John McBride, May 15, 1988; children: Delaney Katherine, Emma Justine, Ava Rose Kathleen. Vocalist Schiffters, 1975-86, assorted bands, Wichita, Kans.; represented by RCA Records, 1991—; backup singer Garth Brooks, 1992—93, European tour, 1994. Singer: (albums) The Time Has Come, 1992, The Way That I Am, 1993 (Platinum), Wild Angels, 1995 (Platinum), Evolution, 1997 (Triple Platinum), Martina McBride Christmas, 1998, Emotion, 1999 (Platinum), White Christmas, 1999 (Platinum), (various artists) Girls Night Out, 1999, (Group recording) Safe In The Arms Of Love, 2000, Greatest Hits, 2001 (Dounble Platinum), Martina, 2003 (Gold), (songs) (Runaway Bride soundtrack) I Love You, 1999, (Backstage at the Grand Ole Opry) Wrong Again, 2000, (Where The Heart Is soundtrack) There You Are, 2000, (The Mercy Project) You'll Get Through This, 2000; performer: (tv appearances co-star Pat Benatar) CMT Crossraods, 2003, (tv appearances) Stand By You Man, 2003, (tv appearance) Nat. Anthem, NBA All Star Game, 2003, (presenter of award) CMT Flameworthy Awards, 2003, (tv biography) Lifetime Intimate portrait, 2002. Nominee Best Country Song for "Independence Day", Grammy, 1994, Video Yr. for "Independence Day", Acad. Country Music, 1994, Best Country Collaboration with Vocals for "Own My Own" with Reba McEntire, Linda Davis, and Trisha Yearwood, Grammy, 1995, Vocal Event Yr. for "On My Own" with Reba McEntire, Linda Davis, and Trisha Yearwood., Country Music Assn., 1996, Album Yr. for "Wild Angels", 1996, Best Country Female Vocal Performance for "Safe In The Arms of Love", Grammy, 1995, Vocal Event Yr. for "Still Holding On" with Clint Black, Country Music Assn., 1997, Best Country Collaboration with Vocals for "Still Holding You" with Clint Black, Grammy, 1997, Video Yr. for "A Broken Wing", Country Music Assn., 1998, Single Yr. for "A Broken Wing", 1998, Acad. Country Music, 1999, Song Yr. for "A Broken Wing", 1999, Video Yr. for "A Broken Wing", 1999, Best Country Female Vocal Performance for "I Love You", Grammy, 1999, Single Yr. for "Blessed", Country Music Assn., 2002, Best Female Country Vocal Performance for "Blessed", Grammy, 2002, Video Yr. for "Concrete Angel", Country Music Assn., 2003, Top Female Vocalist, Acad. Country Music, 1993, 1998, 2000, 2001, Horizon award, Country Music Assn., 1994, Female Vocalist Yr., 1996, 1998, 1999, 2001, Am. Music Awards, 2003; recipient Breakthrough Artist Video for "My Baby Loves Me", Music Row Ind. Summit Award, 1994, Music Video Yr. for "Independence Day", Country Music Assn. Awards, 1994, Best Video Yr. for "Independence Day", Gt. Brit. Music Awards, 1994, Video Yr. for "Independence Day", Nashville Music Awards, 1995, TNN Music City News Award, 1995, Gold Clio for Country Music Video Yr. for "Independence Day", Clio Awards, 1995, Best Southern Gospel, Country Gospel or Bluegrass Gospel for "Amazing Grace - A Country Salute To Gospel", Grammy Awards, 1995, Country Album Yr. for "Wild Angels", Nashville Music Awards, 1996, Video Yr. for "Safe In The Arms of Love", 1996, Female Video Yr. for "Blessed", CMT Flameworthy Awards, 2002, Female Video Yr. for "Concrete Angel", CMT Flameworthy Awards, 2003, Top Female Vocalist, Acad. Country Music, 2002, Acad. Country Music award, 2003, 2004, Female Vocalist Yr., Country Music Assn. Award, 2002, Female Vocalist Yr. award, Country Music Assn., 2003, 2004, Country Female Artist Yr., Billboard Music Award, 2002, Best Female Artist, Country Radio Music Awards, 1996, Favorite Female Artist, Country, Am. Music Awards, 2003, Favorite Female Artist, Country Weekly, 2003. Address: RCA Records 1400 18th Ave S Nashville TN 37212-2809*

MCBRIDE, MELANIE GRACE, lawyer; d. Bruce and Betty McBride. BA in Elem. Edn., Ariz. State U., 2001; JD, Suffolk U., Boston, 2004. Bar: Ariz. 2005, US Ct. Appeals (9th cir.). Assoc. Plattner Verderame, Phoenix, 2004—05, Gust Rosenfeld, Phoenix, 2005—. Vol. lawyer Ariz. Vol. Lawyers, Phoenix, 2005—; sustaining mem. Lorna Lockwood Inn of Ct., Phoenix, 2006—. Mem.: ABA, Ariz. Assn. Def. Counsel, Ariz. Trial Lawyers Assn., State Bar Ariz., Fed. Bar Assn., Ariz. Women Lawyers Assn., Maricopa Bar Assn., Phi Delta Phi. Democrat. Avocations: golf, travel. Office: Gust Rosenfeld 201 E Washington St Ste 800 Phoenix AZ 85004 Office Phone: 602-257-7675.

MCBRIDE, MILDRED MAYLEA, retired elementary school educator; b. Bowerston, Ohio, Oct. 7, 1922; d. Harry Scott and Mary McGary (Mowl) McB.; 1 adopted child, Marjorie Mi Sang McBride. BS in Music, Baldwin-Wallace Coll., 1944; MA, Columbia U., N.Y.C., 1949. Cert. tchr., Ohio, Hawaii. Traveling music tchr. Tuscarawas County Sch., 1944-45; tchr. elem. music Parma (Ohio) Schs., 1945-48, tchr. jr. h.s. music, 1946-48; tchr. h.s. gen. music, chorus Kamehameha Sch. for Girls, Honolulu, 1949-59; tchr. elem. music Tempe (Ariz.) Schs., 1959-60, Hawaii Pub. Sch. Sys., 1960-86, ret., 1986. Co-founder Elem., Intermediate, Gen. Music Interest Group, Honolulu, 1969-79. Author, editor: (biography) Meg!, 1996, Three Women of Kintail, 2001, (hist. novels) Lady Janet, Genny MacKenzie and Her Bairns, The Troubled Child, Angus and Margaret Meira, Two Brothers, Travels with MiSang, Trouble in Paradise, Alexander and Margaret; writer mus. plays. Helper Bowerston Pub. Libr., 1939, 48, 97—; bd. dirs.; mem. Honolulu Symphony Chorus; soup kitchen, vol. Harris United Meth. Ch., Honolulu, 1990-96, mem. choir, 1975-96. Avocations: golf, travel, singing, cooking, enjoying daughter.

MCBRIDE, PAULA BREWER, chemistry educator, dean; d. Paul Leonard and Quinta Nahrendorf Brewer; m. Chester Warren McBride, Sept. 9, 1969; children: Kimberly McBride Claxton, Stuart Blayre, Kirk Dunn. BS, Tex. Luth. U., Seguin, 1966; MEd, U. Incarnate Word, San Antonio, 1986. Cert. med. technologist Am. Soc. Clin. Pathology. Med. technologist VA Hosp., Durham, NC, 1967—68, Bexar County Hosp., San Antonio, 1968—70; spl. edn. aide Stahl Elem. Sch., San Antonio, 1980—81, James Madison HS, San Antonio, 1981—83, sci. tchr., 1989—, sci. instrnl. dean, 2002—; spl. edn. sci. tchr. Ctr. Sch., San Antonio, 1983—89. Mem.: Mole Day Found., Assn. Chemistry Tchrs. Tex., Sci. Teachers Assn. Tex., Tex. Classroom Tchrs. Assn. Office Phone: 210-637-4400. Office Fax: 210-637-4435. Business E-Mail: pmcbr005@neisd.net.

MCBRIDE, SANDRA, secondary school educator; b. St. Louis, Dec. 15, 1948; d. Henry and Doris Emily (Kessler) Hartmann; m. Joseph McBride, Jan. 24, 1970; children: Ed, Lori, Kevin, John, Jaime. BS, U. Mo., Rolla, 1970; MEd, Coll. Mt. St. Joseph, 1986; postgrad., Xavier U., No. Ill. U., Rockford Coll., Nat. Louis U., U. Cin., North Ctrl. U., U. Ill. Cert. secondary math., computer and sci. tchr., Ill. Computer edn. tchr. St. Bartholomew Cath. Sch., Cin.; 5th and 6th grade math. tchr. St. Ann Sch., Cin.; math and computer sci. tchr. Waubonsie Valley High Sch., Aurora, Ill. Active various profl., community and ch. orgns. Mem. ASCD, NEA, IPEA, GCCM, OCM, Internat. Soc. Tech. Edn., Nat. Coun. Tchrs. Math., Ill. Edn. Assn. Ill. Coun. Tchrs. Math., Math. Assn. Am., Tau Beta Pi, Phi Kappa Phi, Kappa Mu Epsilon. Home: 422 Arboretum Way Oswego IL 60543-8384 Office Phone: 630-375-3581. Business E-Mail: sandra_mcbride@ipsd.org.

MCBRIDE, SANDRA TEAGUE, psychiatric nurse; b. Corinth, Miss., Sept. 13, 1958; d. Clarence R. and Alice (Ingram) T. AAS, Shelby State Community Coll., 1983; BSN, U. North Ala., 1987; MSN, Union U., 2001. RN, Miss., Tenn. Nurse supr. Alcorn County Care, Inc., Corinth, Miss., 1985-87; staff nurse Bolivar (Tenn.) Cmty. Hosp., 1988-90; shift supr. Tenn. Dept. of Corrections, West Tenn. High Security Facility, Ripley, 1990-91; staff nurse U.S. Med. Ctr. for Fed. Prisoners, Springfield, Mo., 1991-92, Western Mental Health Inst., Bolivar, 1992—.

MCBRIDE, SUSAN ALYSE, interior designer, consultant; b. Watsonville, Calif., Sept. 24, 1948; d. Allan Edwin and Jeanne Marie Petersen; life ptnr. James R. Dutra. BA, Ariz. State U., 1970. Prin. designer Susan Alyse Enterprises, Watsonville, Calif., 1980—. Sales mgr. Andrew Morgan Collection, Bklyn., 2001—. Mem.: NEWH (assoc.). Roman Catholic. Avocations: travel, art history, architecture, swimming. Home: 100 Via Del Sol Watsonville CA 95076 Office: Susan Alyse Enterprises 100 Via Del Sol Watsonville CA 95076 Office Phone: 831-768-1868. Home Fax: 831-768-1878; Office Fax: 831-768-1878. E-mail: susanalyse@aol.com.

MCBRIDE, TAMERA SHAWN DEW, geologist; d. Lawrence Bernard Dew, Jr. and Daris Virginia Hutchinson Dew; m. William Scott McBride, June 6, 1998; children: Roger, Rastus. BA cum laude, Rollins Coll., 1993; MS, U. So. Fla., 1995. Cert. radon measurement technician Fla. Dept. Health, Divsn. Environ. Health, 1997, profl. geologist Fla. Dept. Bus. and Profl. Regulation, 2002. Phys. sci. technician U.S. Geol. Survey, Ocala, Fla., 1991—94; scientist Environ. Resources Mgmt., Inc., Tampa, Fla., 1995—2000; planner S.W. Fla. Water Mgmt. Dist., Brooksville, Fla., 2000—04, profl. geologist, 2004—. Acting ex-officio mem. Ctrl. Fla. Regional Planning Coun., Bartow, Fla., 2000—04. Soloist St. Catherine (Fla.) United Meth. Ch., 1975—, mem. choir, 2001—, vice chair com. lay leadership, 2005; asst. sec. S.W. Fla. Water Mgmt. Dist. Employee Com., 2003—04, vice-chair, 2004—. Mem.: U. South Fla. Geology Alumni Soc. (bd. dirs. 1998—2000), Fla. Assn. Profl. Geologists, Chronic Fatigue and Immune Dysfunction Syndrome Assn. of Am., Phi Eta Sigma. Avocations: fishing, travel, dance. Home: PO Box 1223 Bushnell FL 33513 Office: Southwest Florida Water Mgmt Dist 2379 Broad St Brooksville FL 34604 Office Phone: 352-796-7211. Personal E-mail: dewfish@aol.com. E-mail: tamera.mcbride@swfwmd.state.fl.us.

MCBURNEY, CHRISTINE, performing arts educator, actress, director; b. Brooklyn Heights, Ohio, Aug. 04; d. Carole Lynn McBurney; m. Paul Desmond Coen (div.); 1 child, Ciaran A Coen. BA, Columbia U., N.Y.C., 1991; MFA, Kent State U., Ohio, 1996. Cert. tchr. Ohio, 2002. Dept. chair, theatre arts Shaker Heights H.S., Shaker Heights, Ohio, 2004—. Writer (reviews, essays, interviews). Grantee, NEH grantee, 2006. Home: 2127 Coventry Rd Cleveland Heights OH 44118 Office: Shaker Heights High School 15911 Aldersyde Dr Shaker Heights OH 44120 Office Phone: 216-295-4200.

MCBURNEY, ELIZABETH INNES, dermatologist, physician, educator; b. Lake Charles, La., Dec. 24, 1944; d. Theodore John and Martha (Caldwell) Innes; divorced, 1980; children: Leanne Marie, Susan Eleanor. BS, U. Southwestern La., 1965; MD, La. State U., 1969. Diplomate Am. Bd. Internal Medicine, Am. Bd. Dermatology. Intern Pensacola (Fla.) Edn. Program, 1969-70; resident in internal medicine Boston U. and Carney Hosps., 1970-72; resident in dermatology Charity Hosp., New Orleans, 1972-74; staff physician Ochsner Hosp., New Orleans, 1974-80; assoc. head of dermatology Ochsner Clinic, New Orleans, 1974-80; clin. asst. prof. La. Health Scis., New Orleans, 1976-79, clin. assoc. prof., 1979-90, clin. prof., 1990—; clin. asst. prof. Tulane Health Scis., New Orleans, 1976-88, clin. assoc. prof., 1988-91, clin. prof., 1991—. Courtesy staff Northshore Regional Med. Ctr., Slidell, La., 1985—; staff Slidell Meml. Hosp., 1988—, chmn. CME courses, 1988—, pres.-elect med. staff, 2000-01, pres., 2001—02; regional dir. Mycosis Fungoides Study Group, Balt., 1974-94. Contbr. articles to profl. jours. Bd. dirs. Slidell Art Coun., 1988—, Camp Fire, New Orleans, 1979-83, Cancer Assn. New Orleans, 1978-83; juror Art in Pub. Places, Slidell, 1989; councilman St. Tammany Art Coun., 2003-06. Recipient Disting. Woman Physician award AMA, 1999, Thomas Pearson edn. meml. award, 2004. Fellow ACP; mem. Am. Soc. Dermatologic Surgery (treas. 1991-94, bd. dirs. 1988-91, pres. elect 1995-96, pres. 1996-97), Women's Dermatol. Soc. (pres. 2006—, Samuel Stegman award 2000, Pub. Svc. award, 2001), Am. Acad. Dermatology (bd. dirs. 1994-98), Am. Bd. Laser Medicine and Surgery (bd. dirs. 1991-96), La. Dermatologic Soc. (pres. 1989-90), St. Tammany Med. Soc. (pres. 1988), Phi Kappa Phi, Alpha Omega Alpha. Avocations: reading, gardening, fine art, music, films. Office: 1051 Gause Blvd Ste 460 Slidell LA 70458-2985 Office Phone: 985-649-5880.

MCCABE, LINDA JEAN, elementary school educator; d. Francis E. and Virginia M. Brazes; m. Robert D. McCabe. BA, U. No. Colo., Greeley, 1969. Lic. profl. tchr. State of Colo., 1969, cert. tchr. Tex. Edn. Agy., 1981, profl. edn. State of Wash., 2000. Tchr. Pub. Schs., Colo., 1969—76, tchr., coach k-12 phys. edn., 1971—79, tchr. elem. sch. Tex., 1980—97, Colo., 1997—2001, Wash., 2001—. Com. mem. Develop Comprehensive Math Model OSPI, Wash., 2004—05; trainer and facilitator cert. Project Wild, PLT, WET, FLP, Colo.; math modules trainer Tex. Edn. Agy., Tex. Amateur radio operator lic.; fire fighter US Forest Svc.; vol. fire fighter Maybell Fire Dept., Colo., 1999—2001. Recipient Outstanding Rural Educator, Moffat County Edn. Assn., 1998, John Irwin award, Colo. Dept. Edn. Mem.: Nat. Sci. Tchr. Assn., Nat. Coun. Tchrs. Math., Internat. Reading Assn. Avocations: outdoor activities, travel, music.

MCCABE, MARY F., marketing professional; d. Frank Camarda and Inez Cunningham; children: Vincent Joseph Papile, Kristin Julia Papile. BA, Smith Coll., 1982, MA, 1983; MFA, Yale U., 1994. Co-founder, mng. dir. Children's Theatre of Mass., Springfield, 1980—91; assoc. mng. dir. Yale Repertory Theatre; mng. dir. Nat. Playwrights Conf., O'Neill Ctr., 1994—2001; assoc. mktg. solution Lehman Bros., 2001—. Strategic planning com. O'Neill Theater Ctr., 1997—2000, transition com. to identify exec. dir., 1999—2000. Edn. task force Springfield Schs., 1987—99; liaison for Yale Repertory Theatre Spl. Olympic World Games, 1993; mem. Coast Guard Auxiliary, 1997—; bd. advisors Seven Devils Playwrights Festival, Boise, Idaho, 2000—. Recipient regional award for artistic achievement, New England Theater Conf. (NETC), 1990. Democrat. Roman Catholic. Home: 95 Cabrini Blvd Apt 3-L New York NY 10033 Office: Lehman Bros 745 7th Ave 30th Fl New York NY 10033 Office Phone: 212-526-8272. Personal E-mail: acthuman@aol.com. Business E-Mail: mmccabe@lehman.com.

MCCABE, MARY OTILLIA SORG, secondary school educator; b. Caldwell, Ohio, Feb. 26, 1934; d. Ben Peter and Clara Amelia (Crum) Sorg; m. Leo James McCabe, Aug. 17, 1957; children: Patricia Ann Kaufman, Mary Elizabeth Reeves, Thomas Michael. BSc, Ohio State U., 1955. Tchr. Bd. Edn., Columbus, Ohio, 1955-58; substitute tchr. English and social studies Glassboro (N.J.) Bd. Edn., 1965—. Advisor Cities Sch. of Excellence. Mem. World Affairs Orgn., Glassboro State Coll., 1979; mem. Friends of the Libr. Bd., Glassboro, 1975-89; mem. adult. edn. adv. com. Glassboro Pub. Schs.; mem. Glassboro Child Devel. Ctr., 1970-78; mem. Glassboro Main St. Promotions Com., Bd. Gloucester County Boys and Girls Club, 2002-. Mem. AAUW (program chmn., pres. 1978-80, Outstanding Svc. award 1979), Heritage Glass Mus. (life), Glassboroa Arts Alliance. Roman Catholic. Avocations: travel, reading, bridge. Home: 1204 Glen Ridge Dr Glassboro NJ 08028-1313

MCCABE, MELISSA CHRISTINE, music educator, researcher; b. Kansas City, Mo., Feb. 19, 1975; d. Deborah Louise and Thomas Michael McCabe. MusB, Simpson Coll., 1996; MusM in Edn., U. Mo., 2004, student in Music Edn., 2004—. Cert. K-12 music educator Iowa State Bd. Edn., Kans. State Bd. Edn. Band and choir tchr. Ind. Sch. Dist. of West Burlington, Iowa, 1997—2000; band and orch. tchr. Coronado Mid. Sch., Kansas City, Kans., 2000—04. Pvt. music instr. Studio Saxophone Lessons, Olathe, Kans., 2001—; rschr. in field. Mem. Ch. of the Resurrection Adult Orch., Leawood, Kans., 2001—; dir. Ch. of the Resurrection Mid. Sch. Orch., Leawood, 2001—; mem. Midwest Winds, Stanley, Kans., 2002—, Midwest Sax Quartet, Kansas City, Mo., 2002—. Recipient Outstanding Voluntary Svc. award, Ch. of the Resurrection, 2002. Mem.: Tech. Inst. for Music Educators, Kans. Music Educators Assn., Music Educators Nat. Conf., Women Band Dirs. Internat., Pi Kappa Lambda. Avocations: travel, scrapbooking, playing in music ensembles, reading. Home: 14212 S Brougham Dr Olathe KS 66062 Personal E-mail: melissamccabe@comcast.net.

MCCABE, MONICA JANE, oncological nurse; b. Anaheim, Calif. d. Thurman Huston and Marcia Diane (Gandy) Walker; m. Roger Alan McCabe, July 27, 1985; children: Justin Robert, Sarah Jane. Assoc. Nursing, N.Mex. State U., Alamogordo, 1993. RN N.Mex., Ariz., cert. oncology nurse. Med.-surg. nurse Meml. Med. Ctr., Las Cruces, N.Mex., 1993-94; oncology nurse Dr. Bishnu Rauth, Las Cruces, 1994-95; oncology and bone marrow transplant nurse Univ. Med. Ctr., Tucson, 1995-98, mem. reengring. core team, 1996; nurse clinician Nat. Med. Care Homecare, Tucson, 1995-96; oncology nurse specialist Ariz. Oncology Assocs. divsn. U.S. Oncology, Tucson, 1998-2000; sr. rsch. nurse Ariz. Cancer Ctr., U. Ariz., Tucson, 2000—02; clin. rsch. monitor Protein Therapeutics, Inc., Tucson, 2001—03; rsch. nurse sr. clin. coord. U. Az., Tucson, 2003; clin. rsch. assoc. Genzyme Therapeutics, Inc., Tucson, 2002—03, PPD, Inc., 2003—06; clin. team mgr. CRA III, Tucson, 2003—05, sr. clin. rsch. assoc., 2005—06, clin. team mgr., 2006—. Unit asst. liaison Univ. Med. Ctr., 1996—98, clin. practice com. cost containment com., 1997, Keystone computer trainer, 97, lectr. in oncology,

1997—98; computer cons. Meml. Med. Ctr., Las Cruces, 1994; mem. Caring Environ. Patient Edn. Team U. Med. Ctr., 1996; mem. Spkrs. Bur. for Better Bone Health for Breast Cancer Survivors, 1999—2003; mem. spkrs. bur. Omni Network, 2001—03, Better Bone Health for Prostate Cancer Survivors; clin. rsch. assoc., registry coord. Gaucher Registry, Boston, 1998—2003; lectr. in field; spkr. in field. Mem.: ANA, Assn. Clin. Rsch. Profls., So. Ariz. Oncology Nursing Soc. (pres.-elect 1999, pres. 2000, nominating chair 2001), N.Mex. Nurses Assn., Ariz. Nursing Assn., Oncology Nursing Soc. (cert. Oncology Nursing Cert. Corp. subs.). Avocations: ceramics, outdoor activities, computers. Home: 1018 W Placita Camillia Tucson AZ 85704-

MCCAFFERTY, BARBARA JEAN (BJ MCCAFFERTY), sales executive; b. Lincoln, Nebr., Dec. 6, 1940; d. Russell Rowley and Ruth Alice (Williams) Wightman; m. Eriks Zeltins, Dec. 29, 1962 (div. Oct. 1976); 1 child, Brian K. Zeltins; m. Charles F. McCafferty Jr., Oct. 3, 1981 (div. July 1986). Student, Drexel U., 1958—61; BS magna cum laude, Del. Valley Coll. Sci. and Agri., Doylestown, Pa., 1984; MBA in Mktg., LaSalle U., 1998, MBA in Fin., 2002. Dept. mgr. Strawbridge & Clothier, Neshaminy, Pa., 1968-73, asst. buyer Phila., 1973-76; office adminstr. Am. Protein Products, Croydon, Pa., 1976-78; tech. librarian Honeywell Power Sources Ctr., Horsham, Pa., 1978-85; sales dir. Colonial Life and Accident Ins., Wayne, Pa., 1985-86; adminstrn. mgr. Mobi Systems, Inc., Ft. Washington, Pa., 1986-88; spl. rep. Universal Mktg. Corp., Southampton, Pa., 1988-89; ind. contractor McCafferty Ins. Svcs., Doylestown, Pa., 1989—; bus. rsch. asst. Merck & Co., Inc., West Point, Pa., 1993—. Alumni recruitment connection Delaware Valley Coll. Sci. and Agr Mem. NAFE, Nat. Assn. Profl. Saleswomen, Options, Inc., Franklin Mint Collectors Soc., Optomists, Lenox Collections Republican. Presbyterian. Avocations: aerobics, walking, reading, yoga, bicycling. Home: 224 Hastings Ct Doylestown PA 18901-2506 Business E-Mail: barbara_mccafferty@merck.com.

MCCAFFREY, CARLYN SUNDBERG, lawyer; b. NYC, Jan. 7, 1942; d. Carl Andrew Lawrence and Evelyn (Back) Sundberg; m. John P. McCaffrey, May 24, 1967; children: John C., Patrick, Jennifer, Kathleen. Student, Barnard Coll., 1963; AB in Econs., George Washington U., 1963; LLB cum laude, NYU, 1967, LLM in Taxation, 1970. Bar: NY 1974, US Tax Ct. 1975. Law clk. to C. J. Traynor Calif. Supreme Ct., 1967-68; teaching fellow law NYU, NYC, 1968-70, asst. prof. law, 1970-74; assoc. Weil, Gotshal & Manges LLP, NYC, 1974-80, ptnr., 1980—, co-head trust and estate dept. Prof. in residence Rubin Hall NYU, 1971-75; asst. prof. law 1970-74, adj. assoc. prof. law 1975-79, adj. prof. law 1979-, NYU Sch. Law; adj. prof. law U. Miami, 1979-81; lectr. in field; mem. adv. bd. Tax Analysts, mem. adv. com. Philip E. Heckerling Inst. on Estate Planning, U. Miami, 1978-. Co-author Structuring the Tax Consequences of Marriage and Divorce; Contbr. articles to profl. jours. Mem. bd. trustee Blythedale; bd. dir. Breast Cancer Rsch. Fund, Children's Hosp.; mem. NY Archdiocese Planned Gifts Bequests Com.; mem., sec. bd. dirs. Catholic Communal Fund; chair Central Park Profl. Adv. Com.; mem. planning giving adv. com. Mus. Modern Art; mem. profl. advisors coun. com. Lincoln Ctr. for the Performing Arts, Inc. Mem. ABA (chmn. and vice-chmn. com. on generation-skipping transfer tax com. 1979-81, 93—, mem. coun. real property probate and trust law sect.), NY State Bar Assn. (exec. com. tax sect. 1979-80, co-chmn. estate and gift taxation com. 1976-78, 85—88, chmn. life ins. com. trusts and estates and tax sects. 1983-85, former co-chair com. income taxation of trusts and estates 1988-89, co-chmn. estates and trusts com. 1995-), Assn. of Bar of City of NY (matrimonial law com., chmn. tax subcom. 1984-86, Am. College Trusts & Estates Counsel (fellow, bd. regents 1992-97, mem. exec. com. 1995-97, past pres. 2002), Internat. Acad. Trust & Estate Counsel (mem., v.p.); fellow Am. Coll. Tax Counsel. Home: PO Box 232 Waccabuc NY 10597-0232 Office: Weil Gotshal & Manges LLP 767 5th Ave New York NY 10153 Office Phone: 212-310-8136. Office Fax: 212-310-8007. E-mail: carlyn.mccaffrey@weil.com.

MCCAFFREY, CINDY, information technology executive; BA in journalism, U. Nebr. Former reporter, editor publ. including Omaha World-Herald, Springfield (Mo.) Leader & Press, Kansas City Bus. Jour., Contra Costa Times, Macintosh Today; former comm. dir./mgr. co. including Apple Computer, E*TRADE, 3DO Co., and Smart Force; current v.p. corp. mktg. Google Inc., Mountain View, Calif.

MCCAFFREY, JUDITH ELIZABETH, lawyer; b. Providence, Apr. 26, 1944; d. Charles V. and Isadore Frances (Langford) McC.; m. Martin D. Minsker, Dec. 31, 1969 (div. May 1981); children: Ethan Hart Minsker, Natasha Langford Minsker. BA, Tufts U., 1966; JD, Boston U., 1970. Bar: Mass. 1970, D.C. 1972, Fla. 1991. Assoc. Sullivan & Worcester, Washington, 1970-76; atty. FDIC, Washington, 1976-78; assoc. Dechert, Price & Rhoads, Washington, 1978-82, McKenna, Conner & Cuneo, Washington, 1982-83; gen. counsel, corp. sec. Perpetual Savs. Bank, FSB, Alexandria, Va., 1983-91; ptnr. Powell, Goldstein, Frazer & Murphy, Washington, 1991-92, McCaffrey P.A., 1992—. Contbr. articles to profl. jours. Mem. Leadership Collier, 1998. Mem. ABA (chair subcom. thrift instns. 1985-90), D.C. Bar Assn. (bd. govs. 1981-85), Fla. Bar Assn. (chmn. fin. svcs. com. 1999-2000, exec. coun. bus. law sect. 1998-), Women's Bar Assn. D.C. (pres. 1980-81), Collier County Women's Bar Assn. (pres. 1997-98), Gulf Coast Venture Forum (pres. 2001-03). Episcopalian. Avocations: travel, reading, martial arts, Spanish. Office: McCaffrey PA 568 9th St S Ste 255 Naples FL 34102-6620 Home: 3801 Portar SP NW Washington DC 20016

MCCAIN, BETTY LANDON RAY (MRS. JOHN LEWIS MCCAIN), political party official, state official; b. Feb. 23, 1931; d. Horace Truman and Mary Howell (Perrett) Ray; m. John Lewis McCain, Nov. 19, 1955; children: Paul Pressly III, Mary Eloise. Student, St. Mary's Jr. Coll., Raleigh, N.C., 1948—50; AB in Music, U. N.C., Chapel Hill, 1952, LLD (hon.), 1998; MA, Columbia U., N.Y.C., 1953; LittD (hon.), U. N.C., Wilmington, 1997; HHD (hon.), Wake Forest U., Winston-Salem, N.C., 1999; LLD (hon.), Barton Coll., Wilson, N.C., 1999. Courier, European tour guide Ednl. Travel Assocs., Plainfield, NJ, 1952-54; asst. dir. YWCA, U. N.C., Chapel Hill, 1953-55; chmn. N.C. Dem. Exec. Com., 1976-79; mem. Dem. Nat. Com., 1971-72, 76-79, 80-85, chmn. sustaining fund NC, 1981, 88-91, mem. com. on presdl. nominations (Hunt Commn.), 1981-82, mem. rules com., 1982-85, mem. cabinet Gov. James B. Hunt, Jr., 1993-2001, sec. dept. cultural resources, 1993-2001; mem. State Dem. Exec. Com., 1971—99, 2001—. Mem. Winograd Commn., 1977-78; pres. Dem. Women of N.C., 1971-72, dist. dir., 1969-72; pres. Wilson County Dem. Women, 1966-67; precinct chmn., 1972-76; del. Dem. Nat. Conv., 1972, 88; mem. Dem. Mid-Term Confs., 1974, 78, mem. jud. coun. Dem. Nat. Com., 1985-89; dir. Carolina Tel. & Tel. Co. (now Embarq), 1981-97 (1st woman); bd. trustees U. N.C.-TV, 2002—, vice chmn., 2006—; interim chair McCain Internat. Empowerment Project, 2001—. Contbg. editor: History of N.C. Med. Soc. Treas. Wilson on the Move, 1990—92; mem. Coun. on State Goals and Policy, 1970—72, Gov.'s Task Force on Child Advocacy, 1975—78; chmn. Wilson-Greene Morehead scholarship com., 1986—89; mem. career and personal counseling svc. adv. bd. St. Andrews Coll.; charter mem. Wilson Edn. Devel. Coun.; active Arts Coun. of Wilson, Inc.; pres. Wilson County Mental Health Assn., bd. dirs., legis. chmn.; bd. govs. U. N.C., 1975—81, 1985—93, pers. and tenure com., 1985—91, chmn. budget and fin. com., 1991—93; bd. regents Barium Springs Home for Children, chair Founds. com. Capital Campaign, 2003—; bd. dirs. N.C. Mus. History Assocs., 1982—83, pres., 1982—83, membership chair, 1987—88; co-chmn. Com. to Elect Jim Hunt Gov., 1976, 1980, co-chmn. senatorial campaign, 1984; mem. N.C. Adv. Budget Com. (1st woman), 1981—85; chmn. State Employees Combined Campaign N.C., 1993; bd. visitors Peace Coll., Wake Forest U. Sch. Law, 1980—83, U. N.C., Chapel Hill; co-chmn. fund dr. Wilson Cmty. Theater; v.p. Wilson County Hist. Assn., 2004—; chmn. devel. com., bd. visitors Lineberger Comprehensive Cancer Clinic, 2006—; chmn. centennial Am. Lung Assn., NC, hon. chmn. hist. observance centennial N.C.; Sunday sch. tchr. 1st Presbyn. Ch., Wilson, 1970—71, 1986—88, 1990—92, mem. chancel choir, 1985—, deacon, 1986—92, chmn. fin. com., 1990—91, chair, 1992—93, elder, 1992—98, 2006—; N.C. state bd. dirs. Am. Lung Assn., state bd. dirs., 1985—88; bd. dirs. Roanoke Island Commn.; mem. battleship commn. USS/NC, 1993—2001; bd. dirs. Wilson Rose Garden, 2002—. Recipient state awards N.C. Heart Assn., 1967, Easter Seal Soc., 1967, Cmty. Svc. award Wilson Downtown Bus. Assocs., 1977, award N.C. Jaycees, 1979, 85, Women in Govt. award N.C. and U.S. Jaycettes, 1985, Alumni Disting. Svc. award U. N.C., Chapel Hill, 1993, Flora Mac Donald Scottish Heritage award, 1995, Carpathian award N.C. Equity, 1995, Pinnacle award, 1997, 1st winner Holderness-Weaver award U. N.C., Greensboro, 1999, Citizen of Yr. award Wilson C. of C., 2001, Ruth Coltrane Cannon award for hist. preservation Preservation N.C., 2000, N.C. State U. Sch. of Design award, 2000, The North Caroliniana award, 2006; named to Order of Old Well and Valkyries, U. N.C., 1952; named Dem. Woman of Yr., N.C., 1976, Internat. Founders award Eta State Delta Kappa Gamma Soc., 2005; named Outstanding Wilson Citizen of Yr., Wilson Red Cross, 2004. Mem.: DAR, UDC (historian John W. Dunham chpt.), Rotary Internat. (Paul Harris fellow 2003), N.C. Inst. Medicine (bd. dirs. 1993—2005), N.C. Sch. Arts (trustee 1993—2001), N.C. Equity (bd. dirs.), N.C. Soc. Internal Medicine Aux. (pres.), N.C. Symphony (trustee 1993—2001, 2002—05), Info. Resources Mgmt. Commn. N.C. (bd. dirs. 1993—2001), N.C. Agy. Pub. Telecom. (bd. dirs. 1993—2001), N.C. Found. for Nursing (bd. dirs. 1989—92), St. Mary's Alumni Assn. (regional v.p., Most Disting. Alumna 2005), U. N.C. Chapel Hill Alumni Assn. (chmn. 2001—02, dir.), Nat. Soc. Colonial Dames Am. NC (sec. local com., program co-chmn.), AMA Alliance (dir., nat. vol. health svcs. chmn., aux. liaison rep. AMA Coun. on Mental Health, aux. rep. Coun. on Vol. Health Orgns.), N.C. Art Soc., N.C. Lit. and Hist. Assn., Wilson Country Club, Little Book Club, The Book Club (pres.), Pi Beta Phi. Home: 1134 Woodland Dr NW Wilson NC 27893-2122

MCCAIN, DEBBIE M., elementary school educator; b. Edgefield, SC, Aug. 9, 1961; m. John Thomas McCain, Oct. 11, 1980; children: Leslie, Ernest Ronale. BE, U. SC, Aiken, 1991—95; MEd, Lesley U., Cambridge, Mass., 2004—05. Tchr. Saluda Sch. Dist., SC, 1996—2001, Edgefield County Sch. Dist., SC, 2001—. Mem.: Mt. Canann Bapt. Assn. (dean 2005—), Plametto Tchrs. Assn., SC Sci. Coun.

MC CAIN, ELIZABETH JEAN, elementary school educator; b. Alexandria, Va., Mar. 21, 1962; d. Joseph Manley and Clara-Jean (Foote) L. BA in Edn., Ea. Wash. U., 1984. Elem. tchr. Sierra Sands Unified Sch. Dist., Ridgecrest, Calif., 1984—. SAT coord. Sch. Site Cell trained. Scottish Rite scholar. Mem. Internat. Reading Assn., Kappa Delta Pi. Personal E-mail: wwaw@tmccain.com.

MCCAIN, LENDA HAYNES, librarian; b. Roanoke, Ala., Oct. 19, 1929; d. Crawford Clift and Gulema (Harrod) Haynes; m. Marvin Enloe McCain, May 19, 1949; children— Eleanor, Allen Haynes. B.A., Peabody Coll., 1949, M.A., 1951; Ed.S., Fla. State U., 1975. Librarian Cheatham County Schs., Ashland City, Tenn., 1949-53; librarian Bay County Schs., Panama City, Fla., 1953-69, county media specialist, 1969-86; supr. interns Fla. State U., Panama City, 1990—. Mem. DAR, Phi Delta Kappa, Delta Kappa Gamma. Democrat. Presbyterian. Avocation: genealogy. Office: Fla State U 4750 Collegiate Dr Panama City FL 32405-1000 Home: 712 West Pierson Dr Lynn Haven FL 32444

MCCAIRNS, REGINA CARFAGNO, pharmaceutical executive; b. Phila., Dec. 23, 1951; d. Carmen Augustus and Regina Mary (Yost) Carfagno; m. Robert Gray McCairns Jr., Nov. 6, 1982. BS, Marymount Manhattan Coll., 1973; MS, Villanova U., 1976; cert. in bus., U. Pa., 1982; MS, Temple U., 2001. Rsch. asst. Temple U. Med. Coll., Phila., 1975-77; mfg. supr. William H. Rorer, Ft. Washington, Pa., 1977-79; from mgmt. trainee, tech. asst. to validation coord. SmithKline & French Labs., Phila., 1979-87; mgr. validation svcs. SmithKline Beecham, Phila., 1987-96; quality assurance investigator pharm. tech. Glaxo Smith Kline, Upper Providence, Pa., 1996—99. Trustee Country Day Sch. of the Sacred Heart, 1993-99, PDA Sci. Found., 1997-2003. Mem. Parenteral Drug Assn. (bd. dirs. 1985-92, chmn. spring program 1988, 90, chmn. tng. com. 1986-88, chmn. nat. program com. 1990-93), Jefferson Med. Coll. Faculty Wives Club (v.p. 1988-90, program chmn., 1988-90, pres.-elect 1990-92, pres. 1992-94). Democrat. Roman Catholic. Avocations: golf, books. Office: Glaxo Smith Kline UW 2909 709 Swedeland Rd PO Box 5089 King Of Prussia PA 19406 Office Phone: 610-270-6619. Business E-Mail: regina_c_mccairns@gsk.com.

MCCALEB, ANNETTE WATTS, executive secretary; b. Darbfork, Ky., Dec. 11, 1931; d. Benjamin Taylor and Suzanna Elizabeth (White) Watts; m. John Henry McCaleb, Oct. 23, 1962; children: Jonathan Jeffrey, Suzanna Elizabeth McCaleb Woodhead, Sarah Leslie McCaleb Kaza. BS, U. Ky., 1954. Med. technologist Good Samaritan, Lexington, Ky., 1953-54; lab. supr. Charleston (W.Va.) Meml., 1954-58; chief med. technologist Meml. Hosp., Indpls., 1958-63; assoc. prof. UAMC, Little Rock, 1963-66; sec., treas., co-owner John H. McCaleb Constrn., Inc., Little Rock, 1966—. Justice of the peace Pulaski County Quorum Ct., Ark., 1989—; state bd. dirs. F.L.A.G., 1989-. Mem. S.W. Kiwanis (pres. 1997-99), Pulaski County Property Owners Assn. (pres. 1990-2000). Democrat. Baptist. Avocations: reading, crossword puzzles, gardening, sewing, swimming. Home and Office: 3900 Annette Ln Little Rock AR 72206-5357 Office Phone: 501-888-4253. Personal E-mail: annmccaleb@sbcglobal.net.

MCCALEB, MARGARET ANNE SHEEHAN, application developer; b. Washington, Jan. 15, 1956; d. Rourke Joseph and Anne Marie (Fahy) Sheehan; m. Michael Ray McCaleb, May 2, 1987. Bachelors cum laude, Rosemont Coll., 1978; Masters, Cath. U., 1980. Co-dir. Media Analysis Project, Washington, 1980—81; dir., litigation support staff Morgan Assocs., Washington, 1981—90; software devel. mgr. Adminstrv. Office of U.S. Cts., Washington, 1990—. Co-author: Over the Wire and On TV, 1983; contbr. articles to mags. and newspapers. Recipient scholarship, Cath. U., 1978—79, grant, Russell Sage Found., 1980—81. Roman Catholic. Office: Adminstrv Office US Cts 1 Columbus Cir NE Washington DC 20544

MCCALL, DOROTHY KAY, social worker, psychotherapist; b. Houston, July 18, 1948; d. Sherwood Pelton Jr. and Kathryn Rose (Gassen) McC. BA, Calif. State U., Fullerton, 1973; MS in Edn., U. Kans., 1978; PhD, U. Pitts., 1989; cert. in Aroma Therapy, Australasian Coll. Health Scis., 2002. LCSW Pa., 1991. Counselor/intern Ctr. for Behavioral Devel., Overland Park, Kans., 1976-77; rehab. counselor Niagra Frontier Voc. Rehab. Ctr., Buffalo, 1978-79; counselor/instr. dept. motor vehicles Driving While Impaired Program N.Y. State, 1979-80; alcoholism counselor Bry Lin Hosp., Buffalo, 1979-81; instr. sch. social work U. Pitts., 1984, 91; alcohol drug counselor The Whale's Tale, Pitts., 1984-86; sole practice drug and alcohol therapy Pitts., 1986—; faculty Chem. People Inst., Pitts., 1987-89; CEO Kingsbury Fragrances, Inc., 2004—. Guest lectr. sch. social work U. Pitts., 1982-87, 89; educator, trainer Community Mental Health Ctr., W.Va., 1986-87, Tenn., 1986; trainer Tri-Cmty. Sch. Sys., Western Pa., 1984-87; cons. Battered Women's Shelter, Buffalo, 1980, Buffalo Youth and Alcoholism Abuse program, 1980; lectr. in field. Mem. Spl. Adv. Com. on Addiction, 1981-83; bd. dirs. Chem. People, Task Force Adv. Com., 1984-86, Drug Connection Hot Line, 1984-86; co-founder Greater Pitts. Adult Children of Alcoholics Network, 1984; mem. adv. bd. Chem. Awareness Referral and Evaluation System Duquesne U., 1988-93; hon. bd. dirs. Pa. Assn. for Children of Alcoholics, 2000. Recipient Outstanding Achievement award Greater Pitts. Adult Children of Alcoholics Network, 1987, Disting. Svc. award Pa. Assn. for Children of Alcoholics, 1993; Nat. Inst. Alcohol Abuse tng. grantee, 1981; U. Pitts. fellow, 1983. Mem. Am. Acad. Experts in Traumatic Stress, NASW, Pa. Assn. for Children of Alcoholics (bd. dirs. 1987-99, v.p. 1990-94, hon. bd. dirs. 2000, Disting. Svc. award 1993), Employee Assistance Profls. Assn., Am. Soc. for Clin. Hypnosis, Nat. Assn. for Children of Alcoholics, Internat. Soc. for Study of Subtle Energies and Energy Medicine, Am. Recorder Soc. (Pitts. chpt.), Soc. Creative Anachronism. Democrat. Avocations: perfumery, films, reading, drawing, playing the recorder. Office: 673 Washington Rd Pittsburgh PA 15228-1917 Office Phone: 412-687-2720, 412-343-4066.

MCCALL, JENNIFER JORDAN, lawyer; b. NYC, Feb. 15, 1956; m. James W. McCall; children: Caroline, Hillary. BA cum laude in English Lit., Princeton U., 1978; JD, U. Va. Sch. Law, 1982; LLM in Taxation, NYU, 1988. Bar: N.Y. 1983, Calif. 2002. Assoc. Lord Day & Lord, NYC, 1982-92; ptnr. Lord Day & Lord, Barrett Smith, NYC, 1992-94; ptnr. Pvt. Client Group Cadwalader, Wickersham & Taft, NYC, 1994—2003; ptnr. Pillsbury Winthrop, LLP, NYC & Palo Alto, Calif., 2003—05; ptnr., co-chmn. Wealth Mgmt. & Individual Client practice Pillsbury Winthrop Shaw Pittman, NYC & Palo Alto, Calif., 2005—. Trustee Charitable Founds. and Trusts and advisor to numerous high net worth individuals; spkr. in field on estate and tax planning and adminstrn. Co-author: Estate Planning for Authors and Artists, 1998; contbr. chpt. to Estate Tax Techniques. Steering com., Planned Giving Adv. Com., The Mus. of Modern Art; mem. Profl. Advisor's Coun., Lincoln Ctr., Inc.; trustee League for the Hard of Hearing, N.Y.C., 1992-2003, East Side House Settlement, Bronx, N.Y., 1995-2002, Chapin Sch., N.Y.C., 1998-2001; chairperson Ethel Gray Stringfellow Art Case Com., N.Y.C.; bd. trustees San Francisco Ballet. Fellow Am. Coll. Trust and Estate Counsel; mem. ABA (real property, probate and trust law sects.), N.Y. State Bar Assn. (com. on trusts and estates adminstrn.; chairperson subcom. on proposed legislation on executor's commns.), Calif. State Bar Assn. Office: Pillsbury Winthrop Shaw Pittman 2470 Hanover St Palo Alto CA 94304-1114 also: Pillsbury Winthrop Shaw Pittman 1540 Broadway New York NY 10036 Office Phone: 650-233-4020. Office Fax: 650-233-4545. Business E-Mail: jenniferjordan.mccall@pillsburylaw.com.

MCCALL, JUNIETTA BAKER, psychotherapist, minister; d. Cecil Stanford and Katherine Violet Baker; m. John Cornwall Pearson; children: Jonathan Seth, Jeremiah Brierly. BA, Beloit Coll., 1968; MDiv, Andover Newton Theol. Sch., Newton Centre, Mass., 1985, D of Ministry, 1991. Ordained min. United Ch. of Christ, 1983; cert. pastoral psychotherapist N.H., diplomate Am. Assn. Pastoral Counselors. Assoc. pastor South Congl. Ch., Concord, NH, 1980—85; dir. pastoral svcs. N.H. Hosp., Concord, 1985—. Dir. tng. Journeys Pastoral Counseling Ctr., Durham, NH, 1993—96; adj. faculty Andover Newton Theol. Sch., 1993—96. Author: Grief Education for Caregivers of the Elderly, 1999, A Practical Guide to Hospital Ministry, 2002, Bereavement Counseling, 2004. Avocations: qulting, gardening, antiques and collectibles. Office: NH Hosp 36 Clinton St Concord NH 03301 Office Phone: 603-271-5413. Business E-Mail: jmccall@dhhs.state.nh.us.

MCCALL, LOUISE HARRUP, artist; b. Oklahoma City, July 8, 1925; d. Paul Louis and Lucile (Martin) Harrup; m. Robert Theodore McCall, July 20, 1945; children: Linda Louise, Catherine Anne. Student, Okla. State U., 1943-44, U. N.Mex., 1944-45, Art Inst., 1946; pvt. study, N.Y., 1955-65. Freelance artist, Chgo., 1946—48, Tarrytown, NY, 1949—53, Chappaqua, NY, 1953-67, 68-71, London, 1967, Paradise Valley, Ariz., 1971—; owner McCall Studios, Inc., Paradise Valley, 1986—. Exhibitions include Ariz. State U., 1999, Grace Mus., Abilene, Tex., 1999, Sky Harbor Millenium Traveling Show, 1999—2000, Ariz. State U. Club, 1999, Women Artists of Ariz., Wickenburg, 2001; artist with husband (murals) Air and Space Mus., Washington, 1975—76, Johnson Space Ctr., Houston, 1978, Disney Epcot Ctr., L.A., 1983, Phoenix Indsl. Commn., 1987, designed with husband windows of Valley Presbyn. Chapel, Scottsdale, Ariz., 1984, 2002, stained glass window Valley Presbyn. Ch. Libr., 2002, window of Sky Harbor Airport, Phoenix, 1998, Phippen Art Mus., Prescott, Ariz., 2003, artist (paintings in pvt. collections) H.R.H. Prince Fahd Bin Salman and H.R. Prince Sultan Bin Salman of Saudi Arabia, Mayo Clinic Collection, Scottsdale, 1997, designer meditation chapel for new cancer ctr., 2001; exhibitions include West Valley Art Mus., Phoenix, 2002, 2006; designed (stained glass window) Valley Presbyn. Ch. Libr., 2003, Libr. Valley Presbyn. Ch., 2002, designer Chapel for Va. G-Piper Cancer Ctr., Scottsdale, logo for Phoenix Art Mus. fund raiser, 2006. Fundraiser Crisis Nursery, Phoenix, 1984, Ariz. Hist. Soc., Phoenix, 1986, Scottsdale Cultural Ctr. 1990-92, Phoenix Art Mus., 1993-94, Scottsdale Art. Sch., 1996, 1994 Art Show O'Brien's Gallery, 1995 Art Show Peoria Sch. Dist.; ann. fund raiser Hospice Phoenix, 1983-92, Bot. Gardens Phoenix. Winner 1st Prize, State of Tex., 1943, 1st Prize, Jr. League Artists No. Westchester and N.Y., 1961. Mem. NASA Permanent Art Collection, Nat. Mus. Women in the Arts, Jr. League of Phoenix, Paradise Valley Country Club. Republican. Presbyterian. Avocation: speaking. Home and Office: 4816 E Moonlight Way Paradise Valley AZ 85253 Fax: 480-991-2099. Office Phone: 480-991-0385. E-mail: robtmccall@cox.net.

MCCALL, MAXINE COOPER, publisher, minister, educator, writer; d. Lloyd Edison and Minnie Belle (Rector) Cooper; m. Donald Jackson McCall, Oct. 15, 1960. BS in English magna cum laude, Appalachian State U., 1960, MA in English, 1965. English tchr. Appalachian State U., Boone, NC, 1959—60; tchr., adminstr. Burke County Pub. Schs., Morganton, NC, 1960—90; English tchr. gifted programs Valdese and Drexel HS, 1960—71; coord. grades K-12 Burke Schs. Coord. for Lang. Arts, Fgn. Lang., Gifted Programs, 1972—90; area adminstr. Ch. of God, NC, 1982—2001; adj. faculty English dept. Western Piedmont CC, Morganton, NC, 1990—; owner C&M Resources, Drexel, NC, 1997—. Ednl. cons. grades K-12 Burke County Pub. Schs., Morganton, NC, 1960—90; coord. state ministries NC Gen. Assembly of Ch. of God (Anderson, Ind.), 1981—2001; Christian edn. cons., conf. leader Ch. of God Ministries, Anderson, Ind., 1982—; cons. ch. growth and planting Bd. of Ch. Extension, Anderson, Ind., 1990—2001. Author: (book) They Won't Hang a Woman, 1972, What Mean These Stones?, 1993 (History Book award from N.C. Soc. of Historians, 1993); editor: A Handful of Stars, 1996; author: Guidebook to the Trail of Faith, 1998; author, graphic designer (book) Etched in Granite, 1999 (Willie Parker Peace History Book award, 2005, Pres. award NC Soc. Historians, 2005); co-author (graphic designer, publ.): (book) Posthumorously Berk, 2000; editor (graphic designer, pub.): Silver Wings and a Gold Star, 2003. Guest spkr. various ch. and civic orgns. in Burke County, NC, 1971—; co-founder, facilitator Christian Broadcasting Hope Nat. Bible Conf. in Western N.C., 1981—; sec. Arca Adminstr. Assn. Ch. of God (Anderson, Ind.), 1983—88, chairperson, state rep., cons. long-range planning, 1984, governance and policy task force and implementation team, 1988—93, task force implementation team, 1997—98; bd. trustees Anderson U., Ind., 1988—2003; bd. dirs. The History Mus. of Burke County, Morganton, NC, 2003—. Mem.: Delta Kappa Gamma. Mem. Ch. Of God (Anderson, Ind.). Avocations: travel, theater, films, antiques, history. Office: C & M Resources PO Box 487 Drexel NC 28619

MCCALL, RUBY ELANE, music educator; b. New Albany, Ind., Apr. 24, 1950; d. William Charles and Mary Ellen Brown; m. Stephen Kim McCall, May 27, 1993; children: Kim Christine Lenard, Kevin Keith Lenard. BA in Music, Mesa State Coll., Grand Junction, Colo., 1992; MA in Creative Arts, Leslie U., Mass., 2003. Lic. tchr. Colo., 1992. Music specialist Sch. Dist. #51, Grand Junction, Colo., 1992—. Singer Grand Valley Choral, Grand Junction, Colo., 2000—06; ch. music dir. VA Hosp., Grand Junction, Colo., 1992—. Composer (gospel): (cd) Ruby and Lovita. Named Outstanding Tchr., Rocky Mountain Elem., 2005. Office: 3260 D1/2 Rd Clifton CO 81520 Office Phone: 970-434-2800. Office Fax: 970-434-2804.

MCCALL, SUSAN ELIZABETH, small business owner; b. Ogden, Utah, Nov. 21, 1945; d. Edward George and Virginia Alene (Davis) Mester; children: Melissa M., Ian E. Spencer. BFA, Utah State U., 1975. Office mgr. Sewing Dist., Phoenix, 1969-70; art tchr. North Ogden City Schs., 1970-71; graphic arts Permaloy Corp., Ogden, 1972-74; regional purchasing agt. USDA Forest Service, Ogden, 1976; owner, mgr. The Flower Co., Albuquerque, 1976-89; dir. dist. 8-J Florists Transworld Delivery Assn., 1988-89; mgr. Spring Flowers, Sydney, 1990-91; owner, mgr. Floral Arts Design Sch. N. Mex., 1994-96; prin. broker Compass Realty, Portland, Oreg. Recipient First Place award Utah Soc. Art, 1964. Mem. West Tex. Florist Assn., N.Mex. Floral Assn., Albuquerque Vis.' Conv. (mktg. com. 1986-90), Fla. Transworld Delivery Assn. (dir. Dist. 8-J, 1988), Profl. Women in Bus. Avocation: master gardener.

MCCALLA, SANDRA ANN, principal; b. Shreveport, La., Nov. 6, 1939; d. Earl Gray and Dorothy Edna (Adams) McC. BS, Northwestern La. State U., 1960; MA, U. No. Colo., 1968; EdD, Tex. A&M U., 1987. With Caddo Parish

Sch. Bd., Shreveport, 1960-88; asst. prin. Capt. Shreve H.S., 1977-79, prin., 1979-88, 94—; dir., dean divsn. edn. Northwestern State U., Natchitoches, La., 1988-94; instr. math. La. State U., 1979-81. Mem. adv. bd. Sta. KDAQ Pub. Radio, 1985-89, Shreveport Women's Commn., 1983-89. Named Educator of Yr. Shreveport Tmes-Caddo Tchrs. Assn., 1966, La H.S. Prin. of Yr., 1985, 87; recipient Excellence in Edn. award Capt. Shreve H.S., 1982-83; Danforth fellow, 1982-83. Mem. nat. Assn. Secondary Sch. prins., La. Assn. Prins. (Prin. of Yr. 1985), La. Assn. Sch. Execs. (Disting. Svc. award 1983), Times-Caddo Educators Assn. (Educator of Yr. 1984), Phi Delta Kappa, Kappa Delta Pi. Republican.

MCCALLEY, BARBARA VAGLIA DOUGHERTY, secondary school educator; b. Sharon, Pa., Nov. 11, 1939; d. Lawrence and Clara Marie (Santell) Vaglia; m. Bruce W. McCalley, Aug. 9, 1991. BS in Edn., Slippery Rock U., 1961; postgrad., U. Pitts., 1987-90. Tchr. Hickory Twp. Schs., Hermitage, Pa., 1961-63, Shaler (Pa.) Area Schs., 1963—96; culinary instr., 1997—. Bd. dirs. North Dists. Cmty. Credit Union, Pitts., 1990—. Mem. Model T Ford Club Am. (pres. 1987-89, bd. dirs. 1984—). Republican. Avocations: catering, cook book writing and pub., antique car restoring.

MCCALLION, ANNE DEWEY, finance executive, accountant; b. Erie, Pa., July 19, 1954; d. Paul Marvin and Eleanor (Waldinger) Dewey; m. Timothy Joseph McCallion, Dec. 29, 1973; children: Brian, Keith. BS in Acctg. summa cum laude, Gannon U., 1974; MBA, Ashland (Ohio) Coll., 1983. CPA, Pa., Ohio, Ind., Hawaii, Calif. Sr. acct., mgr. Fargo Dowling Pashke & Twargowski, CPAs, Erie, 1974-82; acct. supr. Mayflower Corp., Carmel, Ind., 1982-84; asst. project mgr. Fin. Acctg. Standards Bd., Stamford, Conn., 1984-86; sr. audit mgr. Deloitte & Touche, Woodland Hills, Calif., 1986-90; v.p. fin. Califone Internat. Inc., Chatsworth, Calif., 1990-91; dir. fin. acctg. Countrywide Credit Industries, Pasadena, Calif., 1991—. Part-time mem. faculty Gannon U., Erie, 1978-80, Mercyhurst Coll., Erie, 1978-80. Contbr. articles to profl. jours. Mem. AICPAs. Avocations: reading, travel.

MCCALL-RODRIGUEZ, LEONOR, healthcare services company executive, entrepreneur; b. Chgo., Feb. 21, 1958; d. Sixto Rodriguez Hernandez and Dolores Leonor Jimenez de Rodriguez; m. Dean W. McCall, July 14, 2002; stepchildren: Samantha Lynn McCall, Christopher Dean McCall. Licenciatura in Econs., Universidad Nacional Autónoma de México, Mexico City, 1982; MBA, Universidad de Las Americas, Mexico City, 1998. Lic. economist Secretaria de Educación Publica, Mexico. Mktg. mgr. Casa Pedro Domecq, Mexico City, 1984—90, Braun divsn. Gillette, Mexico City, 1990—91, PepsiCo-Frito Lay, Mexico City, 1991—97, La Opinion, L.A., 1999—2000; pres. Bus. and Mktg. Solutions, Mexico City, 1997—99; v.p. Face to Face Mktg., Inc., Pasadena, Calif., 2000—03; gen. mgr. Walker Advt., Inc., San Pedro, Calif., 2000; pres., founder Mira Promo, Inc., Redondo Beach, Calif., 2003—04, Latino Speakers Bur., Redondo Beach, 2003—; v.p., emerging mkts. WellPoint Inc., Indianapolis, Ind., 2004—. Adj. prof. econs. Universidad Nacional Autónoma de México, Mexico City, 1982—84. Author: (short stories) Cuentos de Juanita La Ranita, 2004; editor, translator: novel La Quileña, 2004. Vol. art tchr. 1736 Family Crisis Ctr., L.A., 2000—03; nat. bus. adv. coun. Rainbow Push Coalition. Named Corp. Leader of the Yr., Nat. Latina Bus. Women Assn., 2006. Mem.: Mexican Am. Nat. Assn. (assoc.), Women's Bus. Entrepreneurs Nat. Coun. (assoc.), Nat. Assn. Women Bus. Owners (assoc.), Latin Bus. Assn. (assoc.). Democrat. Roman Catholic. Avocations: writing, reef aquaria, travel. Office: WellPoint Inc 120 Monument Cir Indianapolis IN 46204

MCCALLUM, JANET ANN ANDERSON, retired hardware store owner; b. Minot, N.D., Sept. 19, 1944; d. Alton C. and Jennie C. (Rygg) Anderson; m. Robert W. McCallum, June 12, 1965; children: Laura Ann, Lisa Kay. BSBA, U. N.D., 1966. Co-owner, v.p. Anderson Ace Hardware, Inc., Bismarck, ND, 1977—96. Mem. exec. bd. US West Communications, 1989-1993. Bd. dirs. United Way, Bismarck, 1987-1990, Bismarck Downtowner's Assn., 1988-1992; active adv. bd. Salvation Army, Bismarck, 1978-2002, chmn., 1985-88; elder, deacon 1st Presbyn. Ch., Bismarck, 1979-85. Mem. AAUW, Job Svc. Adv. Coun. (employer rep. 1985-89), P.E.O. Sisterhood (pres. chpt. AX 1982-84), Zonta Club Bismarck. Republican. Home: 103 Osage Ave Bismarck ND 58501-2672

MCCALLUM, LAURIE RIACH, state government lawyer; b. Virginia, Minn., Aug. 19, 1950; d. Keith Kelvin and Maybelle Louella (Hanson) Riach; m. J. Scott McCallum, June 19, 1979; children: Zachary, Rory, Cara. BA, U. Ariz., 1972; JD, So. Meth. U., 1977. Bar: Wis. 1977. Consumer atty. Office of Commr. of Ins., Madison, Wis., 1977-79; asst. legal counsel Gov. of Wis., Madison, Wis., 1979-82; mng. ptnr. Petri and McCallum Law Firm, Fond du Lac, Wis., 1979-80; exec. dir. Wis. Coun. on Criminal Justice, Madison, 1981-82; commr. Wis. Pers. Commn., Madison, 1982—2002, chairperson, 1988—2002; commr. Wis. Labor and Industry Rev. Commn., 2002—03, sr. rev. atty., 2003—. Mem. gov.'s jud. selection com. Supreme Ct., 1993; dir. State Bar Labor Law Sect., Madison, 1988-91; faculty U. Wis. Law Sch., Madison, 1992, 93. Dir. Prevent Blindness Wis., Madison Symphony Orch., Wis. Women in Govt. Republican. Office: LIRC PO Box 8126 Madison WI 53708-8126 Office Phone: 608-266-9850. Business E-mail: mccalla@dwd.state.wi.us.

MCCAMLEY, SHERRY SMITH, entertainer, actor, vocalist, voice educator; d. Barry Wayne Smith and Patricia Louise Krieger; m. Stephen Alan McCamley, Oct. 14, 1977; children: Patrick Stephen, Erin Louise. BS, Pa. State U., University Park, 1977. Entertainer self-employed, Cin., 1973—; vocal music tchr. Cin. Country Day Sch., 2004—06; dir. of theatre Anderson H.S., 1997—2004. Singer: (cabaret act) Performances; actor: (plays, musicals); musician: (piano/keyboards/vocalist) rock/pop bands; dir.: (plays, musicals). Fundraiser/vol. Aids Vols. of Cin., 1998—2006. Mem.: Ednl. Theatre Assn., Music Educators Nat. Conf., Theatre Comm. Group, Pa. State Alumni Assn. (life), Alpha Sigma Alpha. Avocations: music, swimming, travel, reading, theater. Home: 1501 Huntcrest Dr Cincinnati OH 45255 Personal E-mail: mcsmitty23@aol.com.

MCCAMY, SHARON GROVE, English educator; b. Fredericksburg, Va., May 31, 1961; d. Howard E. and Vivian R. Grove; m. Michael D. McCamy, Jan. 10, 1986; 1 child, Katherine Howard. BA in English, U. Va., 1983; MA in English, George Mason U., 1994. Devel. asst. Corcoran Gallery of Art, Washington, 1983-84; coord. individual giving Nat. Parks Conservation Assn., Washington, 1984-87; dir. devel. Piedmont Environ. Coun., Warrenton, Va., 1991-94; lectr. in English Mary Washington Coll., Fredericksburg, Va., 1996-99; head Divsn Arts and Scis. No. Va. Campus ECPI Coll. Tech., 2005—, dir. edn. No. Va. Campus, 2006—. Mem. Fauquier County Bd. Suprs., 2000—03; mem. bd. Fauquier County Water and Sewer Authority, 2000—03; mem. com. Fauquier Rep. Com., 1997—; bd. dirs. Fauquier County Pub. Libr., Warrenton, 1996—2000, Libr. Va., 1998—2003, Libr. Va. Found., 1999—2003, Va. Ctr. Book, 2000—03. Mem.: Piedmont Rep. Women's Club (sec. 1998—2000, v.p. 2004—06). Home: PO Box 10 Sumerduck VA 22742 Personal E-mail: sharonmccamy@direcway.com.

MC CANDLESS, BARBARA J., tax consultant; b. Cottonwood Falls, Kans., Oct. 25, 1931; d. Arch G. and Grace (Kittle) McCandless; m. Allyn O. Lockner, 1969. BS, Kans. State U., 1953; MS, Cornell U., 1959; postgrad. U. Minn., 1962-66, U. Calif., Berkeley, 1971-72. Enrolled agt. IRS. Home demonstration agt. Kans. State U., 1953-57; teaching asst. Cornell U., 1957-58, asst. extension home economist in marketing, 1958-59; consumer mktg. specialist, asst. prof. Oreg. State U., 1959-62; instr. home econs. U. Minn., 1962-63, research asst. agrl. econs., 1963-66; asst. prof. U. R.I., 1966-67; assoc. prof. family econs., mgmt., housing, equipment dept. head S.D. State U., 1967-73; asst. to sec. Dept. Commerce and Consumer Affairs, S.D., 1973-79, tax cons., 1980-91; revenue auditor Kans. Dept. Revenue, Topeka, 1991-2000; tax cons., 2001—. Mem. Am. Agrl. Econs. Assn., Am. Assn. Family and Consumer Scis., Am. Coun. Consumer Interests, Nat. Coun. on Family Rels., LWV, Kans. State U. Alumni Assn., Pi Gamma Mu, Sierra Club. Address: 2135 SW Potomac Dr Topeka KS 66611-1450 E-mail: bmccandless@cox.net.

MCCANDLESS, CAROLYN KELLER, retired human resources specialist; b. Patuxent River, Md., June 6, 1945; d. Stevens Henry and Betty Jane (Bethune) Keller; m. Stephen Porter McCandless, Apr. 22, 1972; children: Peter Keller, Deborah Marion. BA, Stanford U., Calif., 1967; MBA, Harvard U., Cambridge, Mass., 1969. Fin. analyst Time Inc., N.Y.C., 1969-72, mgr. budgets and fin. analysis, 1972-78, asst. sec., dir. internat. adminstrn., 1978-85, v.p., dir. employee benefits, 1985-90; v.p human resources and adminstrn. Time Warner, Inc., N.Y.C., 1990—2001; ret., 2001. Bd. dirs., treas. Friends and Relatives Institutionalized Aged; bd. dirs., mem. exec. com. Svc. Program Older People, Inc., Annie Eaton Soc.; adv. bd. Booker T. Washington Learning Ctr. and Pres. Coun. Nat. Pub. Radio; bd. dirs. Time-Life Alumni Soc. Democrat. Unitarian.

MC CANN, CECILE NELKEN, writer, artist; b. New Orleans; d. Abraham and Leona Nelken; children: Dorothy Collins, Cecile Isaacs, Annette Arnold, Denise Bachman, Albert Hews III. Student, Vassar Coll., Tulane U.; BA, San Jose State Coll., 1963, MA, 1964; postgrad., U. Calif.-Berkeley, 1966-67; doctorate (hon.), San Francisco Art Inst., 1989. Tool designer Convair Corp., New Orleans, 1942-45; archtl. draftsman, various companies New Orleans and Clinton, Iowa, 1945-47, 51-53; owner, operator ceramics studio Clinton, 1953-58; instr. San Jose State Coll., 1964-65, Calif. State U., Hayward, 1964-65, Chabot Coll., Hayward, 1966-69, Laney Coll., 1967-70, San Francisco State U., 1977-78; founder, editor, pub. Artweek mag., Oakland, Calif., 1970-89; freelance writer, art advisor Kensington, Calif., 1989—. Cons. Nat. Endowment Arts, 1974—78, fellow in art criticism, 1976; panelist numerous confs. and workshops. One-woman shows include Davenport Mus. Art, Robert North Galleries, Chgo., Crocker Art Mus., Sacramento, Calif. Coll. Arts and Crafts, Oakland, exhibited in group shows at DeYoung Mus., San Francisco, Everson Mus. Art, Syracuse, N.Y., Oakland Mus., Pasadena Mus., Los Angeles County Mus. Art, Represented in permanent collections San Jose State Coll., Mills Coll., Coll. Holy Names, City of San Francisco, State of Calif. Trustee emerita Rene and Veronica di Rosa Found.; mem. Pub. Art Adv. Com., Oakland. Recipient Vesta award, Woman's Bldg., 1988, Media award, Bay Area Visual Arts Coalition, 1989. Mem.: Internat. Assn. Art Critics, Art Table (Honor award 1988, Achievement award 1992). E-mail: cilem@citycom.com.

MCCANN, DIANA RAE, secondary school educator; b. Huron, S.D., Nov. 16, 1948; d. Ralph Henry and Rosina Agnes (Rowen) Yager; m. Gregory Charles McCann, 1974; children: Grant Christopher, Holly Ann. BS, S.D. State U., 1972. Tchr. Bon Homme 4-2, Tyndall, SD, 1972—74, 1976—, Avon (S.D.) Sch., 1975—76. Math. curriculum adv. bd., SD, 1992—; coord. Presdl. awards in math., SD, 1998—. Leader 4-H Club, 1986—; sec.-treas. 4-H Leaders Assn., 1992—2000; tournament coord. Bon Homme Youth Wrestling Club, 1986—93. Recipient Elem. Math. Presdl. award for Excellence in Math. Tchgs., NSF, 1993, Disting. Svc. award for Math. in S.D., 2003, Bon Homme Outstanding Tchr. award, 2005. Mem.: S.D. Coun. Tchrs. Math. (pres.-elect 1990—92, pres. 1992—94, treas. 1999—), Nat. Coun. Tchrs. Math. Avocation: gardening. Personal E-mail: dm57062@valyou.net.

MCCANN, ELIZABETH IRELAND, theater producer, television producer, motion picture producer; b. NYC, Mar. 29, 1931; d. Patrick and Rebecca (Henry) McC. BA, Manhattanville Coll., 1952, PhD hon., 1983; MA, Columbia U., 1954; LLD, Fordham U., 1966; ArtsD (hon.), Manhattanville Coll., 1987; LitD (hon.), Marymount Coll., 1993. Bar: N.Y. 1966. Assoc. firm Paul, Weiss, Rifkind, Wharton & Garrison, N.Y.C., 1965-66; assoc. numerous theater mgmts. Robert Joffrey, Hal Prince, Saint Suber, Maurice Evans, 1956-68; mng. dir. Nederlander Orgn., N.Y.C., 1968-76; pres. McCann & Nugent Prodns., Inc., N.Y.C., 1976-86; mng. prodr. Tony Awards, N.Y.C., 2001—. Bd. dirs. City Ctr. Music and Dance, Marymount Coll. Prodr.: (play) My Fat Friend, 1975, Dracula (Tony award for most innovative prodn. revival, 1978), The Elephant Man, 1978 (Tony award for best play, 1979, Drama Critics award, 1978, Drama Desk award, 1978, Outer Critics Circle award 1978, Obie award 1978), Night and Day, 1979, Home, 1980 (Adelco award, 1980), Morning's at Seven, 1980 (Tony award for reproduction play/musical, 1980), Amadeus, 1980 (Tony award for best play, 1981, Drama Desk award, 1980), The Philadelphia Story, 1980, Piaf, 1981, Rose, 1981, The Dresser, 1981, Mass Appeal, 1981, Macbeth, 1981, The Floating Light Bulb, 1981, The Life and Adventures of Nicholas Nickleby, 1981 (Tony award for best play, 1982, Drama Critics Circle award, 1981), Good, 1982, All's Well That Ends Well, 1983, The Glass Menagerie, 1983, Total Abandon, 1983, Painting Churches, 1983, The Lady and the Clarinet, 1983, Cyrano de Bergerac/Much Ado About Nothing, 1984, Pacific Overtures, 1984, Leader of the Pack, 1985, Les Liaisons Dangereuses, 1987 (Drama Critics Circle award, 1987), Stepping Out, 1987, Orpheus Descending, 1989, Nick & Nora, 1991, Three Tall Women, 1995, A Midsummer Night's Dream, 1995, In the West End with Robert Fox, Ltd., 1996, Who's Afraid of Virginia Woolf?, 1996, A Delicate Balance, 1997, A View from the Bridge, 1998 (Tony award for best revival play, 1998), The Unexpected Man, 1998, A View from the Bridge (Tony award), 1999, Copenhagen, 2000 (Tony award for best play, 2000), Cobb, 2000, The Play About the Baby, 2001, Tuesdays with Morrie, 2002, The Goat, or Who is Sylvia?, 2002 (Tony award for best play, 2002), The Smell of the Kill, 2002, Beckee/Albee, 2003, Well-, 2005, Who's Afraid of Virginia Woolf?, 2005; TV show Piaf, 1981, Morning's at Seven, 1982, Pilobolus Dance Theatre, 1982; assoc. prodr. Orpheus Descending, 1990. Recipient Entrepreneurial Woman award Women Bus. Owners of N.Y., 1981, 82, James J. and Jame Hoey award for Interracial Justice, 1981, Spl Drama League award for co-producing the Life and Adventures of Nicholas Nickleby on Broadway, 1982, Dr Louis M. Spadero award Fordham Grad. Sch. Bus., 1982 E-mail: liz@weproduce.biz.

MCCANN, EVELYN LOUISE JOHNSON, retired minister, retired counselor; b. Hawkins, Tex., Aug. 17, 1941; d. Saron and Alberta Johnson; m. Lovorn McCann, Aug. 1, 1960; children: Everett Stephon, Marcus Darwin. Cert. in Stenography, Tyler Comml. Coll., Tex., 1972; cert. in leadership and devel., Dallas Theol. Sem., 1984; cert. completion, Phillip Sch. Theology, Atlanta, 1998. Ordained to ministry Tex., 1976, ordained to chaplain/counselor Tex., 1999. Utility operator/tng. new employees Sewing Rm., Mineola, Tex., 1966—75; seamestry Fashion Clothing, Mineola, Tex., 1975—76; pastor Gladewater, Tex., 1980—84, Lindale, Tex., 1984—87, Wills Point, Tex., 1987—2000; ret., 2000. Instr., Hawkins, Tex., 1976—84. Dir. workshops, Mineola, 2000. Methodist. Avocations: travel, ministering/counseling, cooking, shopping. Home: PO Box 232 309 McDaniel St Mineola TX 75773 Personal E-mail: evemccann@phonecol.net.

MC CANN, FRANCES VERONICA, physiologist, educator; b. Manchester, Conn., Jan. 15, 1927; d. John Joseph and Grace E. (Tuttle) Mc C.; m. Elden J. Murray, Sept. 20, 1962 (dec. Nov. 1975). AB with distinction and honors, U. Conn., 1952, PhD, 1959; MS, U. Ill., 1954; MA (hon.), Dartmouth Coll., 1973. Investigator Marine Biol. Lab., Woods Hole, Mass., 1952-62; instr. physiology Dartmouth Med. Sch., Hanover, N.H., 1959-61, asst. prof., 1961-67, assoc. prof., 1967-73, prof., 1973—98; adj. prof. biol. scis. Dartmouth Coll., 1974—80, prof. emerita. Mem., cons. physiology study sect. NIH, 1973-77, mem. biomed. rsch. devel. com., 1978-82, chmn, 1979; cons. Hayer Inst., 1979—; cons. staff Hitchcock Hosp., Hanover, 1980—, sr. staff rsch. Norris Cotton Cancer Ctr., 1980—; mem. NRC, 1982-86; chmn. Symposium on Comparative Physiology of the Heart, 1968; course leader, mem. curriculum com. Inst. Lifelong Edn., Dartmouth Coll., 2000--. Editor: Comparative Physiology of the Heart: Current Trends, 1965; contbr. numerous articles to profl. jours. Trustee Lebanon Coll., 1970-73, Montshire Mus. Sic., Hanover, 1975-80, Hanover Health Coun., 1976, Lebanon Coll., 1978-80; incorporator Howe Libr., 1975—; active LWV, 1980—, Conservation Coun., 1983—, Hist. Soc., 1975—, N.H. Lakes Assn., 1992—; pres. Armington Lake Assn., 1991-93. Nat. Heart Inst. fellow, 1959; NIH rsch. grantee, 1959-98, Nat. Heart Inst., 1960, N.H. Heart Assn., 1964-65, Vt. Heart Assn., 1966-68. Mem. AAAS, Am. Assn. Advancement of Lab. Animal Care, Am. Physiol. Soc., Soc. Gen. Physiologists, Biophys. Soc., Am. Heart Assn. (coun. basic sci., exec. coun. Dallas chpt. 1982-86), Soc. Neurosci. Marine Biol. Lab., LWV, Sigma Xi, Phi Kappa Phi. Avocations: sailing, hiking, reading, keyaking, skiing. Office: Dartmouth Med Sch Lebanon NH 03756

MCCANN, GAIL ELIZABETH, lawyer; b. Boston, Aug. 25, 1953; d. Joseph and Ruth E. (Lagerquist) McC.; m. Stanley J. Lukasiewicz. AB, Brown U., 1975; JD, U. Pa., Phila., 1978. Bar: RI 1978, Mass. 1984, US Dist. Ct. RI 1978, US Dist. Ct. Mass. 1990. Ptnr. Edwards Angell Palmer & Dodge LLP, Providence, 1978—. Bd. dirs. Caritas House, Inc.; mem. R.I. adv. coun. New Eng. Legal Found. Mem.: Am. Coll. Mortgage Attys. (RI state chair), RI Bar Assn., Brown U. Alumni Assn. (past pres.). Avocations: hiking, travel, yoga. Office: Edwards Angell Palmer & Dodge LLP 2800 Financial Plz Providence RI 02903 Office Phone: 401-274-9200.

MCCANN, HEATHER, orthopedic surgeon, physician; b. Wilmington, Del. d. Neal and Suzanne McCann. BS, U. NC, Chapel Hill, 1993, BA, 1997, MD, 2002. Resident Med. U. SC, Charleston, 2002—, rsch. resident Dept. Orthop. Surgery, 2003—04. Resident rep. alt. Grad. Med. Edn. Internal Residency Rev. Com., Charleston, 2003—04. Author: jour. articles to profl. jours.; editor, author: Med. U. SC Orthop. Jour., Sigling Soc. Newsletter. Recipient Applause award, Med. U. SC, 2002, 2003, 2004, Resident Rsch. award, SC Orthop. Assn., 2004, First Pl. Clin. Rsch. award, Med. U. SC Dept. Orthop. Surgery, 2004; Resident Rsch. grantee, Med. U. SC, 2004. Office: Med U SC 96 Jonathan Lucas St CSB 708 Charleston SC 29425

MCCANN, JEAN FRIEDRICHS, artist, educator; b. NYC, Dec. 6, 1937; d. Herbert Joseph and Catherine Brady (Ward) Friedrichs; m. William Joseph McCann, May 14, 1960; children: Kevin, Brian, Maureen McCann Breslin, William, James, Denis Gerard, Kathleen. Student, Caton-Rose Inst. Fine Arts, 1955—57; AAS, SUNY, Farmingdale, 1959; BS, SUNY-Empire State Coll., Binghamton, 1986; MA summa cum laude, Marywood Coll., 1987, MFA in Art summa cum laude, 1989; completed Kellogg Leadership Program, Sch. Mgmt., SUNY, Binghamton, 1992; PhD, Nova Coll., 1995. Designer Patton Corp., N.Y.C., 1959—66; sub. art tchr. Owego-Apalachin Sch. Dist., 1968—88; tutor, evaluator Empire State Coll. SUNY, 1987—; dir. ArtSpace Gallery, Owego, NY, 1992—94. V.p. bd. dirs. Tioga County Coun. on Arts, 1990—91, pres., 1992—95; demonstrator for various schs., ednl. TV and county museums. One-woman shows include IBM, Owego, 1972, Tioga Hist. Soc. Mus., 1975, Nat. Hist. Ct. House, 1982, Visual Arts Ctr., Scranton, Pa., 1989—90, ArtSpace, Owego, N.Y., 1991, MacDonald Art Gallery, Coll. Misericordia, Dallas, Pa., 1992, Plaza Gallery, Binghamton, 1992, Krembs Gallery, 1993, 2000, 2003, Wilson Gallery, Johnson City, N.Y., 1994, 2001, 2003, Countryside Gallery, Owego, N.Y., 1996, 2002, Meml. Gallery, SUNY, Farmingdale, 1998, juried groups show, Roberson Mus., Binghamton, N.Y., 1972, Arnot Art Mus., Elmira, N.Y., 1974, 1989, 1992, Arena Nat. Exhibits, Binghamton, 1974—76, Pennino's Gallery, Burlington, Vt., 1975—77, Riise Gallery, St. Thomas, 1975—78, Grand Concourse Gallery, Albany, 1987, Schweinfurth Meml. Art Ctr., Auburn, N.Y., 2002, numerous pvt. and pub. collections. Bd. dirs. Birthright of Owego, 1993—2003. Recipient N.Y. State Artisans award, 1982, Nat. Strathmore award, 1989, 1st pl. in Graphic Arts award Jericho Arts Coun., 1994. Mem. Nat. Mus. Women in Arts (charter), Kappa Pi (pres. Zeta Omicron chpt. 1987-89, life), Artists Guild. Avocations: travel, reading. Home (Winter): 1776 Atwater Ct Kissimmee FL 34746 Home: 6403 Roberts Dr Victor NY 14564

MCCANN, JOYCE JEANNINE, retired elementary school educator; b. Council Bluffs, Iowa, Dec. 15, 1926; d. Clyde Oliver and Reva Arleta (Myers) Tisher; m. Daniel Steven McCann, Aug. 14, 1960 (div. 1968); children: Marianne Rose, Daniel Patrick. BA, UCLA, 1955. Elem. tchr. L.A. Unified Sch. Dist., 1968-92. Recipient grant L.A. Bd. Edn., 1986-87. Mem.: Profl. Educators L.A., PEO Sisterhood, Delta Kappa Gamma (pres. Zeta Xi chpt. 2000—01). Republican. Avocation: violinist.

MCCANN, KIM LOU M., theater educator, director; b. Joplin, Mo., Dec. 8, 1954; d. James Cleland McCann and Mary Earline (Campbell) Kelley; m. Mark A. Lawson, Sr., Feb. 15, 2003. AA in Drama, Diablo Valley Coll., 1974; BA in Theater, Calif. State U., 1976; MFA in Drama, U. Calif., Davis, 1981. Artist, instr., asst. program dir. Short Ctr. South, Sacramento, 1982—; theater, film lectr., resident dir. Sacramento City Coll., City Theatre and Sacramento Shakespeare Festival, 1984—. Pres theatre alumni chpt. bd. Calif. State U., Sacramento. Dir. Twelfth Night, Love's Labour's Lost, Hamlet, Cyrano DeBergerac, Measure for Measure, Midsummer Night's Dream, Three Musketeers, Much Ado About Nothing, Twelfth Night, Shrew, Equus, As You LIke It, Blood Wedding, and 60 others; actor in over 100 prodns. including Mother Courage, Top Girls, Dancing at Lughnasa, Our Town, Hay Fever, Midsummer Night's Dream, The Matchmaker, Merry Wives, Winter's Tale, others. Chmn. bd. dirs. City Theater, 1985—. Avocations: pets, music, reading. Office: Sacramento City College ACTH 3 3835 Freeport Blvd Sacramento CA 95822-1386 Business E-Mail: mccannk@scc.losrios.edu.

MCCANN, LOUISE A., mathematics educator; d. Oswald Frank and Bertha Agnes Becherer; m. Gerald Jerome McCann, Aug. 9, 1969; children: Kelly McCann Epperson, Jackie McCann Chase, Shawn McCann Zonavetch. BS, Ill. State U., 1968; MA, Bradley, 1996. Tchr. math. Edwardsville High Sch., Ill., 1968—69, Peoria High Sch., 1969—70, 1984—2002. Mem. Cursillo Steering Com., Peoria, 2003—; tutor Friendship Ho., Peoria, 2003—; active Book Buddy Program, 2003—; participant Just Faith, 2005—06; tchr. St. Jude's Cath. Ch., Dunlap, 1977—84. Mem.: Phi Kappa Phi. Avocations: sewing, hiking, yoga. Home: 1713 Blue Spruce Ct Dunlap IL 61525

MCCANN, MARGARET ANN, sister, educator; b. Port Arthur, Tex., June 3, 1953; d. Donald Joseph and Elizabeth Ann McCann. BA, Coll. of St. Elizabeth, 1996; MA, Montclair State U., 2002; postgrad., Marquette U., 2003—04. Cert. bereavement counselor Archdiocese of Newark, 2001; secondary edn. tchr. N.J., 1996. Tchr. H.S. English, Marylawn Acad. of the Oranges, South Orange, NJ, 1996—97, Acad. of Sacred Heart, Hoboken, NJ, 1997—98; adj. instr. English, Montclair State U., NJ, 1998—2002; instr. English composition, intro. to lit. Coll. of St. Elizabeth, Convent Station, NJ, 2001—02; tchr. H.S. English, Marylawn Acad. of the Oranges, South Orange, NJ, 2002—03. Panelist, presenter Mid-Atlantic Popular/Am. Culture Assn., Syracuse, NY, 1995, 17th Ann. Nat. Conf. of Peer Tutoring in Writing, Merrimack Coll., North Andover, Mass., 2000, 9th Ann. Meeting of the Group for Early Mod. Cultural Studies, Phila., Ctrl. NY Conf. on Lang. and Lit., SUNY, Cortland, 2002; moderator of panel 11th Ann. Conf.: Women's Studies Program: Women and Creativity, 2005; presenter in field. Presenter (paper) Women Addressing Male Hierarchies, Thirteenth ann. 18th and 19th Century British Women Writers Conf., 2005, Money Matters in Jane Austen's Sense and Sensibilty, 2005. Sister of charity, tchr. Sisters of Charity of St. Elizabeth, Convent Station, NJ, 1990—2004; mem. catechetical team Gesu Roman Cath. Ch., Milw., 2003—04. Grad. assistantship, Montclair State U., 1998-2000. Mem.: Womens Writers Assn., Nat. Coun. Tchrs. of English, Kappa Gamma Pi (assoc.). Republican. Roman Catholic. Avocations: teaching, writing, poetry, travel, films. Personal E-mail: sistermccann@hotmail.com.

MCCANN, PEGGY S., physical education educator; b. Galesburg, Ill., June 6, 1964; d. Jerry A. McCann and Janet R. Leaf. PhD, Mich. State U., East Lansing, 2005. Adj. prof. U. Mich., Ann Arbor, 2005—, Wayne State U., Detroit, 2005; asst. prof. sports mgmt. Siena Heights U., Adrian, Mich., 2006—. Cons. Mich. H.S. Athletic Assn., Lansing, 2003—. Author: (book chpt.) Motivation and Outcomes of Youth Participation in Sport; contbr. articles to profl. jours. Mem. Faculty Profl. Women's Assn., East Lansing, Mich., 2003—05. Recipient Coll. of Edn. Kinesiology fellowship, Mich. State U., 2003—04, William Wohlgamuth Meml. Scholarship for Study of Youth Sports, Mich. State U. Inst. for Study of Youth Sports, 2002—03, Student/Mentor Rsch. award, Ill. Alliance of Phys. Edn., Recreation, and Dance, 2000, Dissertation Completion fellowship, 2005. Mem.: AAPHERD,

Nat. Assn. for Girls and Women in Sport, Assn. for Advancement of Applied Sport Psychology, Phi Kappa Phi. Office: U Mich 401 Washtenaw Ann Arbor MI 48109 Office Phone: 517-264-7627. Business E-Mail: pmccann@sienahts.edu.

MCCANN, RENETTA, advertising executive; b. Chgo., Dec. 8, 1956; d. Aditha Lorraine Collymore Walker; married; 2 children. BS in Speech, Northwestern U., 1978. Client svc. trainee Starcom, 1978, v.p., 1988, media dir., 1989, sr. v.p., 1995; CEO Starcom N.Am., Chgo., 1999—2004; CEO Americas Starcom MediaVest Group, 2004—. Bd. mem. Audit Bur. Circulations Northwestern U., mem. adv. bd. Media Mgmt. Ctr.; bd. mem. Chgo. United. Named Media Maven, Advt. Age, 2001, Corp. Exec. of Yr., Black Enterprise, 2002, Advt. Woman of Yr., Women's Advt. Club Chgo., 2002; named one of 50 Women Who Are Changing the World, Essence, 2003, 50 Women to Watch, Wall Street Journal, 2005, Most Influential Black Americans, Ebony mag., 2006; recipient Outstanding Women in Comm. award, Ebony, Vanguard award, Chgo. Mags. Assn., Media Strategies award, Bus. Week, Matrix award for advertising, NY Women in Comm. Inc., 2006. Mem.: Am. Advt. Fedn. (mem. multicultural bus. practices leadership coun.), Am. Assn. Advt. Agys. (chair media policy com.). Office: Starcom NAm 35 W Wacker Dr Chicago IL 60601*

MCCANN, VONYA B., federal agency administrator, telecommunications industry executive; BA, U. Calif., L.A., 1976; MA in Pub. Policy, U. Calif., Berkeley, 1979, JD, 1980. Bar: D.C., 1980. Law clk. Commr. Tyrone Brown, Fed. Comm. Commn.; policy analyst Nat. Telecommunications and Info. Adminstrn. Dept. Commerce; ptnr. Arent, Fox, Kintner, Plotkin and Kahn; amb., dep. asst. sec. internat. comm. & info. policy Dept. State, 1994—99, prin. dep. asst. sec. of state for econ. and bus. affairs, 1997—99; sr. v.p., fed. external affairs Sprint Corp., Overland, Kans., 1999—2005; v.p. govt. affairs Sprint Nextel Corp., Overland, 2005—. Office: Sprint World Hdqrs 6200 Sprint Pkwy Overland Park KS 66251

MCCARDEL, CONNIE SHIRLEY, music educator; b. Toccoa, Ga., Jan. 31, 1963; m. James Russell McCardel, June 27, 1987; children: James Brett, Rachel Elizabeth. MusB, U. of Ga., 1981—85. Certified Teacher Ga., 1985. Dir. of bands Towers H.S., Redan, Ga., 1985—86, J.J. Daniell Mid. Sch., Marietta, Ga., 1986—2000, Am. Heritage Acad., Canton, Ga., 2002—. Concert band clinician/adjudicator Ga. Music Educators Assn.; pvt. clarinet instr. Mid. And H.S. Students, Metro Atlanta, Ga.; free lance clarinetist, Metro Atlanta, Ga. Recipient J.J. Daniell Mid. Sch. Tchr. of the Yr., Cobb County Sch. Sys., 1990—91, Winner of UGA Solo Concerto Competition, U. of Ga., 1984; Presser Fellow, 1985. Mem.: Ga. Music Educators Assn.

MCCAREY, WILMA RUTH, retired lawyer; b. St. Louis, Dec. 7, 1943; d. Ferdinand Martin and Ruth Anna Cora Kirsch; m. Michael Carl McCarey, Aug. 21, 1965; children: Darren Michael, David Brian. BS in Math. with honors, Valparaiso U., Ind., 1965; JD with honors, George Washington U., 1978. Bar: DC, Va., U.S. Dist. Ct. Md., U.S. Dist. Ct. DC, U.S. Ct. Appeals (DC cir.), U.S. Ct. Appeals (4th cir.). Computer sys. analyst Tech. Ops., Inc., Rosslyn, Va., 1965—66, Kroger Co., Cin., 1966—69; rsch. asst. govt. contracts George Washington Nat. Law Ctr., 1976—78; atty. C&P Telephone/Bell Atlantic (now Verizon), 1978—83; sr. atty. AT&T Corp. Mid Atlantic Region, 1983—85, gen. atty., 1985—95, v.p. govt. affairs, pres. comm. Va., Md., W.Va. and DC, 1995—2001; ret., 2001. Bd. dirs. Fairfax Edn. Found., Fairfax C. of C., Fairfax Synphony, Juvenile Diabetes Rsch. Found., No. Va. Luth. Campus Ministries, Va. Econ. Bridge, Vol. Fairfax, Character Counts; mem. adv. bd. Women Execs. in State Govt. Mem.: Va. Telephone Industry Assn. (sec., treas. exec. bd.). Lutheran. Avocations: sailing, golf, travel, exercise, volunteering.

MCCARGAR, ELEANOR BARKER, artist; b. Presque Isle, Maine, Aug. 30, 1913; d. Roy and Lucy Ellen (Hayward) Barker; m. John Albert McCargar, Feb. 18, 1947; children: Margaret, Lucy, Mary. Cert. elem. sch. tchg., Aroostook State Normal Sch., Presque Isle, 1933; student, Acadia U., 1935-36; B of Sociology, Colby Coll., 1937; summer student, Harvard U., 1939; and, Cambridge Sch. Art, 1939; studied portrait painting with Kenneth Washburn, Thomas Leighton, Maria von Ridelstein, Jean Henry, 1957-67. Ltd. svc. credential in fine and applied arts and related tchs. Calif. C.C. Tchr. sci. and geography Limestone (Maine) Jr. H.S., 1937-41; ins. claim adjuster Liberty Mut. Ins. Co., Boston, 1941-42, Portland, Maine, 1943; ARC hosp. worker 20th Gen. Hosp., Ledo, Assam, India, 1944-45; portrait painter Burlingame and Apple Valley, Calif., 1958—. Commns. include more than 800 portraits in 10 states and 4 fgn. countries. Recipient M. Grumbacher Inc. Merit award for outstanding contbn. to arts, 1977; named Univ. of Maine Disting. Alumnus in Arts, 1981. Avocations: canoeing, camping, travel, studying.

MCCARRELL, LYNETTE MARIE, music educator, director; b. Fox River Grove, Ill., Nov. 7, 1979; d. James Clifford and Loretta Marie Wagner; m. Kyle Leman McCarrell, July 3, 2004. B of Music Edn., Cedarville U., Ohio, 2002. Band dir. Lake Ctr. Christian Sch., Hartville, Ohio, 2002—03, Franlin Monroe Schs., Pittsburg, Ohio, 2003—. Mem.: Music Educators Nat. Conf. Republican. Avocations: reading, jogging, flute. Home: 331 Misty Oaks Ct Dayton OH 45415

MCCARROLL, KATHLEEN ANN, radiologist, educator; b. Lincoln, Nebr., July 7, 1948; d. James Richard and Ruth B. (Wagenknecht) McC.; m. Steven Mark Beerbohm, July 10, 1977 (div. 1991); 1 child, Palmer Brooke; m. Lawrence Arthur Weis, Aug. 28, 2004 BS, Wayne State U., 1974; MD, Mich. State U., 1978. Diplomate Am. Bd. Radiology. Intern/resident in diagnostic radiology William Beaumont Hosp., Royal Oak, Mich., 1978-82, fellow in computed tomography and ultrasound, 1983, dir. divsn. emergency radiology, 2001—; radiologist, dir. radiologic edn. Detroit Receiving Hosp., 1984-2001, vice-chief dept. radiology, 1988-96, chief dept. radiology, 1996-2001. Pres.-elect med. staff Detroit Receiving Hosp., 1992-94, pres., 1994-96; mem. admissions com. Wayne State U. Coll. Medicine, Detroit, 1991-2001; trustee Detroit Med. Ctr., 1996-2001, dir. med. staff consolidation, 1996-97, mem. consol. med. exec. com., 1998-2001, chmn. credentials com., 1998-99, joint conf. com., 1998-99; officer bd. dirs. Dr. L. Reynolds Assoc., P.C., Detroit, 1991-94, 96-2001; presenter profl. confs.; assoc. prof. radiology Wayne State U. Sch. Medicine, Detroit, 1995—; health care cons./med. staff affairs, 1998-2006. Editor: Critical Care Clinics, 1992; mem. editl. bd. Emergency Radiology, 1998-2006; contbr. articles to profl. publs. Named to Crain's Bus. Detroit, Detroit's 100 Most Influential Women, 1997. Mem.: AMA, Wayne/Oakland County Med. Soc., Mich. State Med. Soc., Am. Soc. Emergency Radiologists (bd. dirs. 1996—2001, exec. com. 1998—2001, bylaws com. 2001—05), Am. Roentgen Ray Soc., Radio. Soc. N.Am., Am. Coll. Radiology (Mich. chpt. sec. 1995—98, alt. councilor 1999—2002, councilor 2002—, plain film and fluoroscopy accreditation com. 2003—05), Phi Beta Kappa. Avocations: travel, skiing, reading. Office: Wm Beaumont Hosp Dept Diag Radiology 3601 W 13 Mile Rd Royal Oak MI 48073

MCCARTHY, AIMEE LAMAR, science educator; b. Jacksonville, Fla., Jan. 4, 1977; d. Michael David and Debra Thompson Reynolds; m. Patrick Colin McCarthy, Mar. 5, 2001; children: Kieran Reese, Quinn Christian. Bachelors, Calif. State U., Chico, 2000. Tchr. sci., math. Duval County Pub. Schs., Jacksonville, Fla., 2000—02; tchr. sci. Episcopal H.S. Jacksonville, Fla., 2002—. Asst. sci. fair coord. Episcopal H.S., Jacksonville, Fla., 2005—; mem. adv. bd. selection com. Nat. Jr. Honor Soc., Jacksonville, Fla., 2006. Mem.: NSTA. Avocation: spending time with family. Business E-Mail: mccarthya@episcopalhigh.org.

MCCARTHY, ANN PRICE, lawyer; b. LA, Jan. 30, 1947; d. Frank Judson and Marianna (Chase) Price; 1 child, Sundae Jan Cloe; m. Joseph Stephen McCarthy, Dec. 15, 1974; 1 child, Caitlin Price. BA, Old Coll., Reno, 1983; JD, Nev. Sch. Law, 1987. Bar: Nev. 1987, Calif. 1988, U.S. Dist. Ct. (no. dist.) Calif. 1988, U.S. Ct. Appeals (9th cir.) 1989. Legal asst. Aebi, FitzSimmons & Lambrose, Carson City, Nev., 1981-84; ind. legal researcher Reno, 1985; law clk. Martin H. Wiener, Esquire, Reno, 1985-87, Hon. Robin C. Wright, Reno, 1987-88, Hon. John C. Mowbray, Carson City, 1988; ptnr. Eck & McCarthy, Carson City, 1988-90; pvt. practice Ann Price McCarthy, Ltd., Carson City, 1990-91; ptnr. Aebi & McCarthy, Carson City, 1991—. Lectr. Nat. Bus. Inst., Reno, 1992, 93; instr. Juvenile Drug and Alcohol Edn. Program, Carson City, 1992. Bd. dirs., sec. Brewery Arts Ctr., Carson City, 1992, bd. dirs., pres., 1993-95. Mem. Am. Trial Lawyers Assn., Nev. Trial Lawyers Assn., Washoe County Bar Assn., First Jud. Dist. Bar Assn. (pres. 1991-92, 92-93), State Bar of Nev. (pres. 2004). Address: Ann Price McCarthy & Assoc 777 E William St Ste 201 Carson City NV 89701 Office: Aebi and McCarthy Ste 201 777 E William St Carson City NV 89701-4058

MCCARTHY, CAROLE SULLIVAN, retired special education educator, consultant, educational evaluator; b. Norwich, Conn., June 3, 1950; d. John Joseph and Marion Williamson Sullivan; m. Richard Joseph McCarthy, July 10, 1980. BS in Spl. Edn., So. Conn. State Coll., New Haven, 1972; MS in Spl. Edn., So. Conn. State U., New Haven, 1978, degree in reading, 1997. Cert. in spl. edn. State of Conn., in reading State of Conn., 1997. Spl. edn. tchr. Groton Bd. Edn., Conn., 1972—2003. Rep. Town Meeting, Groton, 2005—07; mem. Big Bros./Big Sisters Southeastern Conn., Groton, 1991—2000, com. chair, 1991—2000. Mem.: Internat. Reading Assn. Democrat-Npl. Avocations: bicycling, art, travel, reading.

MCCARTHY, CAROLYN, congresswoman; b. Bklyn., Jan. 5, 1944; m. Dennis McCarthy (dec. Dec. 1993); 1 child. LPN, Glen Cove Nursing Sch., NY, 1964. LPN St. Francis and Winthrop Hosp., 1964—93; gun safety activist, 1994—97; mem. US Congress from 4th NY dist., 1997—. Mem. edn. and the workforce com., US Congress, mem. fin. svcs. com. Recipient numerous awards, including being named one of Newsday's 100 LI Influentials, Congl. Quarterly's 50 Most Effective Legislators in Congress, one of nine Redbook Mag.'s "Mothers and Shakers", Ladies' Home Jour. list of America's 100 Most Important Women, and Advertising Age's list of Most Impact by Women in 1999; also honored by US Women's Soccer Team and Oprah Winfrey. Mem.: New Yorkers Against Gun Violence, NYC Stop the Violence Campaign, Guns for Goods, Ams. Against Gun Violence (hon.). Democrat. Roman Catholic. Office: US Ho Reps 106 Cannon Ho Office Bldg Washington DC 20515-3204 Office Phone: 202-225-5516.*

MCCARTHY, CONNIE KEARNS, university librarian; BA, Rosary Coll., Ill., 1968; MSLS, Catholic U., 1972. Past cataloger Folger U. Shakespeare Libr.; asst. univ. libr. for collections George Washingtn U.; assoc. univ. libr. William R. Perkins Libr. Duke U.; now dean univ. libr. Coll. William and Mary, 1997—. Chair steering com. Virtual Libr. of Va.; chair edtl. bd. CHOICE jour. Mem.: ALA. Office: Earl Gregg Swem Libr Coll William and Mary PO Box 8794 Williamsburg VA 23187-8794 Office Phone: 757-221-3055. Office Fax: 757-221-2635. E-mail: ckmcca@wm.edu.*

MCCARTHY, DENISE EILEEN, clinical psychologist; b. Syracuse, N.Y., Jan. 25, 1941; d. Raymond Dennis McCarthy and Elizabeth Dorne MacBrearty. BS, Cornell U., 1962; MA, Syracuse U., 1969; postgrad., SUNY, Albany, 1977-83; D in Clin. Psychology, Antioch/New Eng. Grad. Sch., Keene, N.H., 1988; postgrad., The Beck Inst., Bala Cynwyd, Pa., 1994-95. Lic. psychologist, N.Y. Home econ. Monroe County Extension Svc., Rochester, N.Y., 1962-65; team leader, sr. counselor N.Y. State Dept. Labor, Albany, Syracuse, 1966-73; rehab. counselor N.Y. State Office Vocat. Rehab., Albany, 1973-80; dir. community support systems Schenectady Shared Svs., 1981-82; masters level psychologist O.D. Heck Devel. Ctr., Schenectady, 1982-83, A.I.M., Saratoga Springs, N.Y., 1983-84; staff counselor Siena Coll., Loudonville, N.Y., 1985; asst. psychologist Capital Dist. Psychiat. Ctr., Cairo, N.Y., 1985-88, assoc. psychologist, 1988-93; pvt. practice Albany, 1990—. Co-founder Ctr. for Cognitive Therapy of the Capital Dist. Bd. dir. Dominion House, Schenectady, 1981-82. Fellow: Acad. Cognitive Therapy (founding fellow); mem.: APA, Nat. Registry Health Svc. Providers, N.Y. State Psychol. Assn. Avocations: reading, piano, skiing, travel. Office: Ctr Cognitive Therapy 1 Pinnacle Pl Ste 207 Albany NY 12203-3496 Office Phone: 518-482-1815. E-mail: drdmccarthy@aol.com.

MCCARTHY, DOROTHY A. (LANDERS), social studies educator; d. Dorthy Landers; m. Philip Francis McCarthy; children: Colleen, Timothy, Kevin, Shawn. BA, Elms Coll., Chicopee, Mass., 1971; MEd, Nat. Louis U., Heidelberg, Germany, 1990. Tchr. Rochester Cath. Sch., NH, 1979—80, Dept. Def. Schs., Wuerzbu1rg, Germany, 1980—83, Vogelweh, 1983—86, Ramstein, 1986—90, Naples, Italy, 1990—2004, Ft. Stewart, Ga., 2004—. Adv., students of Dept. Def. Schs. Nat. Honor Soc., Italy & Germany, 1980—2004; social studies task mem. Dept. Def. Schs.; visitation team mem. NCAA, coord. global svc. and humanitarian project. Mem. Italia chpt. pres. Phi Delta Kappa, 1992. Mem.: Nat. Coun. Social Studies, Fed. Edn. Assn. Roman Catholic. Avocation: travel. Office: Brittin Elem Sch 2772 Hero Rd Fort Stewart GA 31313 Office Phone: 912-368-3324.

MCCARTHY, JANE MCGINNIS, retired government agency administrator; b. Cleve., June 17, 1946; d. William Ashley and Dorothy Haverick McGinnis; m. Albert Gregory McCarthy III, May 23, 1981. AAS, Marymount U. (formerly Marymount Coll. of Va.), 1966. Adminstrv. asst. to the pres. and mgr. Marymount Coll. Va., Arlington, Va., 1966—72; confidential asst. to the exec. dir. Am. Inst. of Planners, Washington, 1972—76; exec. asst. Hunter Corp., 1976—77; office mgr., account exec. Koch Associates, Inc., 1977—81; intergovtl. rels. officer, office of the dep. undersecretary for intergovtl. rels. US HUD, 1981—82; cons. pvt. practice, Arlington, 1981—. Bd. dirs., mem. exec. com. Marymount Coll. Va. (now Marymount U.), Arlington, 1976—86; founding mem., rec. sec., chmn. Friends of Capital Children's Mus., Washington, 1981—88; bd. dirs., chair Support Our Aging Religious, Silver Spring, Md., 1993—99, mem. devel. com., 1999—; campaign adminstr. St. Charles Borromeo Cath. Ch., Arlington, 2000—; tournament coord. Archbishop Borders Ann. Clergy Golf Tournament, Balt., 2000—02; vol. advisor, capital campaign Holy Cross Abbey, Berryville, Va., 2002—05; vice chair Washington met. area adv. bd. All Hallows Coll., Dublin, 2003—. Named Outstanding Young Women in Am., 1976, 1982; recipient Alumni Achievement award, Marymount U., 1994, award of Merit, Marymount U. Alumni Assn., 1985—91. Independent. Roman Catholic. Avocations: golf, travel. Home and Office: 4531 4th Rd N Arlington VA 22203 E-mail: auntiegreat@verizon.net.

MCCARTHY, JENNY, actress; b. Chgo., Nov. 1, 1972; m. John Mallory Asher, Sept. 11, 1999 (div. 2005); 1 child, Evan Joseph Asher. Student Sch. Nursing, So. Ill. U. Spokeswoman Jose Cuervo Tequila. Appeared in films Things to Do in Denver When You're Dead, 1995, The Stupids, 1996, BASEketball, 1998, Diamonds, 1999, Scream 3, 2000, Dirty Love, 2005, John Tucker Must Die, 2006; TV shows The Jenny McCarthy Show, 1997, Jenny, 1997-98, The Bad Girl's Guide, 2005; host game show Singled Out, MTV, 1995-96, Party @ the Palms, 2005; featured photographs in Playboy mag., 1993-96, 98, 05, including as Miss Oct. 1993, then as Playmate of Yr., 1994; author Jen-X, 1997, Belly Laughs: The Naked Truth About Pregnancy and Childbirth, 2004 (NY Times Bestseller list, 2004), Baby Laughs: The Naked Truth About the First Year of Mommyhood, 2005 (NY Times Bestseller list, 2005). Named one of 50 Most Beautiful People in the World, People mag., 1996. Avocation: kickboxing. Address: c/o United Talent Agy 9560 Wilshire Blvd Ste 500 Beverly Hills CA 90212-2427*

MCCARTHY, KAREN P., former congresswoman, former state legislator; b. Mass., Mar. 18, 1947; BS in English, Biology, U. Kans., 1969, MBA, 1985; MEd in English, U. Mo., Kansas City, 1976. Tchr. Shawnee Mission (Kans.) South High Sch., 1969-75, The Sunset Hill (Kans.) Sch., 1975-76; mem. Mo. House of Reps., Jefferson City, 1977-94; cons. govt. affairs Marion Labs., Kansas City, Mo., 1986-93; mem. U.S. Congress from 5th Mo. dist., Washington, 1995—2005; mem. commerce com.; mem. Ho. Select Com. on Homeland Security. Rsch. analyst pub. fin. dept. Stearn Bros. & Co., 1984-85, Kansas City, Mo.; rsch. analyst Midwest Rsch. Inst., econs. and mgmt. scis. dept., Kansas City, 1985-86. Del. Dem. Nat. Conv., 1992, Dem. Nat. Party Conf., 1982, Dem. Nat. Policy Com. Policy Commn., 1985-86; mem. Ho. Commerce Com. Energy and Power, Telecom., Trade and Consumer Protection; co-chair Dem. Caucus Task Health Care Reform. Recipient Outstanding Young Woman Am. award, 1977, Outstanding Woman Mo. award Phi Chi Theta, Woman of Achievement award Mid-Continent Coun. Girl Scouts U.S., 1983, 87, Annie Baxter Leadership award, 1993; named Conservation Legislator of Yr., Conservation Fed. Mo., 1987. Fellow Inst. of Politics; mem. Nat. Inst. of Politics; mem. Nat. Conf. on State Legis. (del. on trade and econ. devel. to Fed. Republic of Germany, Bulgaria, Japan, France and Italy, mem. energy com. 1978-84, fed. taxation, trade and econ. devel. com. 1986, chmn. fed. budget and taxation com. 1987, vice chmn. state fed. assembly 1988, pres.-elect 1993, pres. 1994), Nat. Dem. Inst. for Internat. Affairs (instr. No. Ireland 1988, Baltic Republics 1992, Hungary 1993). Democrat.

MCCARTHY, KATHLEEN MARIE, priest, nurse; b. Redwood Falls, Minn., July 5, 1932; d. Edward Leo Dunlevy and Agnes Florence Trembley; children: Kevin John, Mary Jo McComas. BSN, Cath. U. Am., Washington, D.C., 1959; D in Ministry, U. Creation Spirituality, Oakland, Calif., 2000. Cert. pub. health nurse Calif.; RN Calif. Home care nurse Vis. Nurse Assn. of The Inland Counties, Palm Desert, Calif., 1982—; co-pastor Pathfinder Cmty. of the Risen Christ, Bermuda Dunes, Calif., 2000—. Tchr., retreat team Pathfinder Cmty., Palm Desert, Calif., 1988—; vicar for Pacific region Ecumenical Cath. Communion, Orange, Calif., 2006—. Co-author: The Church for the New Millennium, 1996. Pres. Interfaith Coun., Mid-Valley, 1996—2000. Democrat. Ecumenical Catholic. Avocations: liturgical dancing, swimming, walking. Home: 82061 Hanson Dr Indio CA 92201 Office: Pathfinder Communities of Risen Christ 78125 Ave 42 Bermuda Dunes CA 92203 E-mail: imkathymac@aol.com.

MCCARTHY, KELLI P., music educator; d. Andrew and Diane Perkins; m. Arin E. McCarthy, July 28, 2000; children: Nathan, Sara. BS in Phys. Edn. and Athletic Tng., Brigham Young U., Provo, Utah, 1997, MS in Phys. Edn. and Athletic Tng., 2000. Head athletic trainer Fountain Hills H.S., Spooner and Shaft Phys. Therapy, Ariz., 2000—01; rehab. specialist Integrated Therapeutic Svcs., Houston, 2001—03; mem. faculty U. Phoenix, Houston, 2002—; pvt. piano and voice instr. Houston, 2004—. Singer: Handel's Messiah - Rejoice O Daughters of Zion; pianist: pvt. weddings, parties, receptions. Sunday sch. tchr. LDS Ch., Houston, 2006, music chmn., choir dir., organist Pitts., 2005—06. Scholar Fran Livingston award, Corona Norco Unified Sch. Dist., 1993; Academic scholar, Brigham Young U., 1993—97. Mem.: Nat. Athletic Trainers Assn. Avocations: reading, running, sewing, piano, singing.

MCCARTHY, LISA, communications executive; m. Sean McCarthy; children: Caroline, Tara. BS, Georgetown U., 1988. With USB Securities, Paramount TV, Turner Broadcasting, JMW Consultants; sr. v.p. Viacom Plus, 1998—2002, exec. v.p. N.Y.C., 2002—. Named to, Crain's New York Bus. "40 under 40", 2004; recipient Women to Watch award, N.Y. Advt. Age and Advt. Women N.Y., 2003. Office: Viacom Inc 1515 Broadway New York NY 10036

MCCARTHY, LYNN COWAN, genealogist, researcher; b. Panama City, Panama, Mar. 18, 1940; d. John Linus and Rose (Cowan) McC. BA, Mary Washington Coll., 1961; MSW, Va. Commonwealth U., 1969. Pub. asst. social worker Social Svc. Bur., Norfolk, Va., 1961-62; grad. resident advisor U. Ky., Lexington, 1962-63, head resident, 1963-64; child welfare worker Commonwealth of Ky., Lexington, 1964-67; asst. tng. specialist Commonwealth of Ky. Cabinet for Human Resources, Frankfort, 1969-71, tng. adminstr., 1971-74, child protective svcs. cons., 1974-81, employer svcs. supr., 1981-83; grants and contracts adminstr. Commonwealth of Ky. Dept. Librs. and Archives, Frankfort, 1983-94; profl. genealogist Frankfort, 1994—2002. Sec., exec. bd. Friends of Ky. Pub. Archives, Frankfort, 1994. Rschr. (TV prodn.) The Hatfields and McCoys: An American Feud, 1996; prodr. (video) The Family of Rose and Jack McCarthy, 1998. Vol. Habitat for Humanity, Inc., Ky., 1997-2000. Named Col. Hon. Order of Ky. Cols., 1994, Outstanding Profls. in Human Svcs., Am. Acad. Human Svcs., 1973. Mem. NASW, Nat. Geneal. Soc., Ky. Hist. Soc., Ky. Geneal. Soc., Va. Geneal. Soc., N.C. Geneal. Soc., Friends of Ky. Pub. Archives, Ky. Pub. Retirees, Acad. Cert. Social Workers, Assn. Profl. Geneaologists, Ky. Network Profl. Genealogists (co-founder 1999). Democrat. Methodist. Avocations: travel, bird-watching, photography, landscaping, spectator sports. Home: 929 Brookhaven Dr Frankfort KY 40601-4439

MCCARTHY, MARY ANN, counselor, educator; b. Barstow, Calif., Jan. 16, 1954; d. Thomas Edward and Helen C. (Krutell) McC. BA in Psychology, San Francisco State U., 1975; MS in Counseling, Calif. State U., Fullerton, 1995. Cert. pupil pers. svcs., 1995. Br. mgr., asst. v.p. Great American First Savings, Orange County, Calif., 1981-88, dist. mgr., v.p., 1988-90; dir. re-entry ctr. Saddleback Coll., Mission Viejo, Calif., 1995; intern coord. Orange Coast Coll., Costa Mesa, Calif., 1995—2000, adj. counselor, 1997—; assoc. prof. counseling, counselor Saddleback Coll., Mission Viejo, 1996—, Irvine Valley Coll., Calif., 2004—05. Vol. Beverly Manor Convalescent Hosp., Laguna Hills, Calif., 1989-94, Mission Viejo Animal Shelter, 1996-97, Big sister Big Bros./Big Sisters Am., Mission Viejo, 1980-83; vol. and cmty. rep. Trauma Intervention Program, 2002—; mem scholarship and ednl. coms. Saddleback Valley C. of C., Laguna Hills, 1982-86; spkr. local schs. Saddleback Valley Vol. Network, Mission Viejo, 1982-86; scholarship com Orange Coast Coll., 1997—. Recipient Outstanding Young Woman Am. award, 1983, Outstanding Part-time Faculty Orange Coast Coll., 2005-06; named Saddleback Valley Young Careerist, Bus. & Profl. Women, 1983. Mem. AAUW (past pres., editor, scholarship chair, pub. info. officer, sec. 1996-97), Am. Counseling Assn., Am. Coll. Counseling Assn., Calif. C.C. Counselor Assn., Calif. Assn. Counseling and Devel. Avocations: reading, travel. Home: 5 Martinique St Laguna Niguel CA 92677-5804 Office: Orange Coast Coll 2701 Fairview Rd Costa Mesa CA 92626-5563 also: Saddleback Coll 28000 Marquerite Pkwy Mission Viejo CA 92692

MCCARTHY, MARY ELIZABETH (BETH) CONSTANCE, conductor, music educator; b. Chgo., Apr. 8, 1961; d. Thomas Joseph and Loretta Ann McCarthy. BA, North Ctrl. Coll., 1983; postgrad., Goethe Inst., 1991, Ea. Ill. U., 1993; MusM in Choral and Instrumental Edn. and Cognition and Vocal Performance, Northwestern U., 1999. Profl. cantor Joliet/Rockford Dioceses, Ill., 1979—; assoc. condr. Chorus Orch. Band Ill. Math. and Sci. Acad., Aurora, 1989—2000; site coord. gifted program Ill. Math. and Sci. Acad. at Ea. Ill. U., Charleston, 1990—95; soloist Lincoln Opera Co., Chgo., 1991—94; chmn. Dept. Fine Arts Rosary H.S., Aurora, 1993—; dept. chair music Aurora U., 1995—; condr., artistic dir. Fox Valley Festival Chorus, Aurora, 1999—. Profl. role coach pvt. students, Ill., 1989—; condr., music dir. dinner theatres, summer stock, Ill., 1990—; artistic cons. oratory and recitals, Ill., 1993—; adjudicator orchs., chorus, bands, Ill., 1993—; cons. to critique Nat. Stds. for the Arts, Ill., 1994; master class clinician various choral orgns., Ill., 1995—; guest condr. fine arts festivals, Ill., 2001—; host Cath. Conf. Fine Arts Festival Rosary H.S., Aurora, 2002. Contbr. rsch. articles to profl. publs.; author original scripts; music arranger:. Sec. The Beta Fin. Group, Sycamore, Ill., 1995—2002; conservation mem. Salmon Unlimited-Ill. chpt., 1997; religious edn. tchr. St. Peter and Paul Ch., Naperville, Ill., 1980—, cantor, 1976—, Rite of Christian Initiation for Adults sponsor, 1995. Recipient Internat. Bel-Canto Vocal Competition Opera award, Bel-Canto Found., 1995; fellow Richter fellow for internat. rsch./study, North Ctrl. Coll., 1982. Mem.: ASCD, AAUW, Lyric Opera Chgo., Ill. Music Educators' Assn., Music Educators' Nat. Conf., Fox Valley Music Educators' Assn., North Ctrl. Coll. Alumni Assn., Northwestern U. Music Sch. Alumni Assn. (bd. dirs. 1998—2001), Northwestern Club Chgo., Alpha Psi Omega, Beta Beta Beta, Phi Alpha Theta. Avocations: art, travel, running, boating, reading.

MCCARTHY, MARY LYNN, social work educator; b. Buffalo, Sept. 26, 1950; d. Joseph Timothy and Jean Marie (Weber) McC.; m. David R. Gardam; children: Rachel Lamb, Ethan Gardam. BA, SUNY, Oswego, 1973; MSW, SUNY, Albany, 1982. Cert. social woker. Asst. program dir. Huntington Family Ctr., Syracuse, N.Y., 1973-75; caseworker child protection

Onondaga County Dept. Social Svcs., Syracuse, 1975; coord. Community Svc. Alliance, Syracuse, 1976-79; asst. and assoc. human svcs. Profl. Devel. Program - SUNY, Albany, N.Y., 1979-84; intake coord., dir. parent aides St. Catherines Ctr. for Children, Albany, 1983-84; edn. asst. N.Y. State Edn. Dept., Albany, 1984-87; field edn. asst. coord., instr. SUNY Sch. of Social Welfare, Albany, 1987-93, asst. dean student svcs., 1990—, undergrad. field coord., 1993—. Chmn. Child Welfare Issues Com., Albany, 1983-88; com. mem. N.Y. State Welfare Adv. Coun., Albany, 1983-84. Recipient Disabled Student Svcs. Achievement award U. Albany, 1993. Mem. NASW (sec. 1983-85, v.p. 1985-88, pres. N.E. divsn. 1988-90, nat. trustee Polit. Action for Candidate Election 1989-96, nat. nominations and leadership identification, 1996-99, chair 1994-96, N.Y. state trustee 199 3—, treas. 1990-92, mem. nat. strategic planning com. 1990-91, Social Worker of Yr. N.E. divsn. N.Y. state chpt. 1992), N.Y. State Social Work Edn. Assn. (bd. dirs. 1989), Coun. on Social Work Edn., Interfaith Partnership for the Homeless (bd. dirs. 1995—, chair mission com.). Avocations: canoeing, camping, gardening. Office: Rockefeller Coll Sch Social Welfare 114 Richardson Hl Albany NY 12222-0001

MCCARTHY, NOBU, actress, performing company executive, educator; Adj. prof. Calif. State U. Artistic dir.: East West Players in Los Angeles, As The Crow Flies (Drama-Logue award), Sarcophagus, Come Back Little Sheba; dir. The Chairman's Wife, Webster Street Blues, And the Soul Shall Dance, (TV) China Beach, Island Son, Magnum P.I., Quincy, Farell to Manzanar, Playhouse 90, (feature films) Geisha Boy, Wake Me When It's Over, Karate Kid II, Pacific Heights.

MCCARTHY, PAMELA MAFFEI, magazine editor; b. NYC, May 28, 1952; d. Rudolph Paul Maffei and Mary Frances Maresca; m. Joseph Matthews McCarthy, Sept. 16, 1978; 2 children. Student, Trinity Coll., Dublin, Ireland, 1972-73; BA, Mt. Holyoke Coll., 1974. Copy staff Esquire mag., N.Y.C., 1974-76, copy editor, 1976-79, exec. editor, 1978-84; mng. editor Vanity Fair mag., N.Y.C., 1984-92, The New Yorker, N.Y.C., 1992-95, 1995—, dep. editor. Mem. Am. Soc. Mag. Editors Office: The New Yorker Advance Publications Inc 4 Times Sq New York NY 10036-6561

MCCARTHY, SHERRI NEVADA, psychologist, educator, educational consultant; b. Topeka, June 2, 1958; d. Wallace Gene and Lois Elaine (McDyson) McCarthy; m. Scott Newlin Tucker, Feb. 14, 1983 (div. Feb. 2001); children: Colin Apollo, Chrysallis Altair; m. Brian David Ewing, Feb. 5, 2006. AA in Liberal Arts, Phoenix Coll., 1981; BA in Psychology, Ariz. State U., 1984, BEd in English Lit., 1985, MA in Spl. Edn., 1987, PhD in Ednl. Psychology, 1995. Cert. kindergarten -12 spl. edn., ESL tchr., Ariz. Mng. editor Scottsdale (Ariz.) Free Press, 1977-78; instr. English Skills Ctr. Phoenix C.C., 1978-80; spl. instr. Title I Creighton Sch. Dist., Phoenix, 1980-81; lit. instr. CTY program Johns Hopkins U., 1985; gifted specialist Fountain Hills (Ariz.) Schs., 1985-87; writing instr. Ariz. State U. Ctr. Acad. Precocity, 1986; tchr. ESL Chandler-Gilbert C.C., Chandler, Ariz., 1986-87; tchr. of gifted Chandler (Ariz.) Unified Schs., 1987-90; psychology tchr., cons. Maricopa County C.C., Tempe, Ariz., 1988-96; prof. ednl. psychology No. Ariz. U., Yuma, 1993—. Freelance writer, 1974—; spl. edn. tchr. Hawaii Dept. Edn., 1990-91; faculty assoc. ednl. psychology Ariz. State U., Phoenix, 1992-96; tchr. English Mesa (Ariz.) C.C., 1993-96; advisor, asst. honors coord. Phi Theta Kappa, 1994-96; gifted ednl. specialist Kyrene Pub. Schs., Chandler, Ariz., 1995-96; vis. prof. adolescent psychology Fed. U., Porto Alegre, Brazil, 2002-03; sr. lectr., rschr. Vologola State U., Russia, 2003-2004. Author: Metamorphosis-A Collection of Poems, 1975, Speed Communication, 1979, A Matter of Time, 1980, A Death in the Family, 1988, Coping with Special Needs Classmates, 1993; staff writer Ariz. Hwy. Patrolman mag., Phoenix, 1979-82; newsletter editor Ednl. Opportunity Ctr., Tempe, Ariz., 1982-83; contbr. articles to profl. jours. Bd. dirs. Young Astronauts, Fountain Hills, 1985-87. Fellow APA (CIRP liaison 1992—), Internat. Coun. Psychologists (bd. dirs. 1998—), Internat. Coun. Psychology Educators (conf. organizer 2000-2005); mem. Am. Ednl. Rsch. Orgn. (bd. dirs. 1997—), Ariz. English Tchrs. Assn. (bd. dirs. 1998—), Odyssey of the Mind (mem. bd. govs. 1987-89, Creativity award 1986, 87). Democrat. Roman Catholic. Avocations: writing, guitar, camping, travel, piano. Office: No Ariz Univ at Yuma PO Box 6236 Yuma AZ 85366-6236 E-mail: sherri.mccarthy@nau.edu.

MCCARTNEY, ALISON RIOS MILLETT, political science professor; d. Jeremy John and Margot Rios Millett; m. Paul Thomas McCartney; 1 child, Tyler New. PhD, U. Va., Charlottesville, 2000. Asst editor Miller Ctr. Pub. Affairs, Charlottesville, 1994—99, Koscuiszko fellow Polish studies, 1999—2000; grad. rsch. fellow Ctr. Transatlantic Fgn. and Security Policy, Free U. Berlin, 1998; instr. U. Va., 1999—2000; rsch. fellow Havighurst Ctr. for Russian and Post-Soviet Studies, Oxford, Ohio, 2000—01; vis. asst prof. Miami U., Oxford, Ohio, 2000—01; asst. prof. Towson U., Md., 2001—, dir., internat. studies, 2004—. Contbr. articles, essays to profl. publs. Co-director and co-founder Towson U.-Baltimore County Pub. Schools Model UN, 2002—06. Recipient Towson Elite Faculty award, Student Govt. Assn., Towson U., 2004—05, Coll. of Liberal Arts Outstanding Svc. Recognition award, Towson U., 2005; Dorothy Danforth Compton fellow, Inst. for the Study of World Politics, 1991—94, Dwight D. Eisenhower/Clifford Roberts Grad. fellow, Eisenhower World Affairs Inst., 1996—97, Ted and Walter Wysocki scholar Jagiellonian U., Kosciuszko Found., 1997, Rsch. fellow, German Academic Exch. Svc., 1998, German Lang. Study fellow U. Bayreuth, 1996, H.B. Earhart fellow, Earhart Found., 1995—96. Mem.: European Studies Assn., Am. Assn. Advancement of Slavic Studies, German Studies Assn., Women in Internat. Security, Internat. Studies Assn., Am. Polit. Sci. Assn. Office: Towson U Dept Polit Sci 8000 York Rd Towson MD 21252 Office Phone: 410-704-5284. Office Fax: 410-704-2960. Business E-Mail: amccartney@towson.edu.

MCCARTNEY, KATHLEEN, dean, education educator; m. William Hagen; children: Pres, Sam, Kaitlin, Kimberly. BA summa cum laude, Tufts Univ.; MS psychology, PhD psychology, Yale Univ. Asst. prof. psychology dept. Harvard U., 1982—87, mem. faculty edn., 2000—, Gerald S. Lesser prof. early childhood edn., academic dean, 2004—05, acting dean Grad. Sch. Edn., 2005—06, dean Grad. Sch. Edn., 2006—; dir. Child Study and Development Ctr. U. NH; prin. investigator Nat. Inst. Child Health & Human Devel. Vis. rsch. scholar Ctr. for Rsch. on Women, Wellesley Coll. Editl. bd. Child Devel. Jour., Devel. Psychology; contbr. articles tp profl. jours. Grantee Am. Psychological Soc., Bush Fellow, Yale Univ. Fellow: Am. Psychological Soc.; mem.: Soc. Research Child Devel. (co-chmn.). Office: Harvard U Human Devel & Psychology 7th Fl Larsen Hall Cambridge MA 02138 Office Phone: 617-495-3401. Office Fax: 617-496-1182. E-mail: kathleen_mccartney@gse.harvard.edu.*

MCCARTNEY, RHODA HUXSOL, farm manager; b. Floyd County, Iowa, June 30, 1928; d. Julius Franklin and Ruth Ada (Carney) Huxsol; m. Ralph Farnham McCartney, June 25, 1950; children: Ralph, Julia, David. AA, Frances Shimer, 1948; BA, U. Iowa, 1950. Mng. dir. McCartney-Huxsol Farms, Charles City, Iowa, 1969—; prin. trustee J.F. Huxsol Trusts, Charles City, Iowa, 1984—. Pres. Nat. 19th Amendment Soc., Charles City, 1991-2002, past pres., 2002—; mem. Terace Hill Commn., Des Moines, 1988-94; bd. dirs. Iowa Children and Family Svcs., Des Moines, 1963-68; mem. Iowa Arts Coun., Des Moines, 1974-78. Named Woman of Yr., local C. of C., 2000. Mem. AAUW, Iowa LWV, PEO. Congregationalist. Avocations: church work, gardening, travel. Home: 1828 Cedar View Dr Charles City IA 50616-9129 Office: McCartney-Huxsol Farms 1828 Cedarview Rd Charles City IA 50616

MCCARTY, DIANE MARY, education educator; d. Herman J. Kuennen and Clotiel L. Frana Kuennen; m. John A. McCarty, June 28, 1975; children: Michael, Bryan. BA, William Penn Coll., Oskaloosa, Iowa, 1976; MA in Edn., U. No. Iowa, Cedar Falls, 1988, EdD, 2002. Tchr. Collins-Maxwell Sch., Iowa, 1977—79, Bondurant-Farrar Sch., Bondurant, Iowa, 1979—83, Denver Cmty. Sch., Iowa, 1983—90; master tchr. Price Lab. Sch. U. No. Iowa, Cedar Falls, Iowa, 1990—99; prin. elem. sch. Kittrell Elem., Waterloo, Iowa, 1999—2001; prof. Dept. Edn. Wartburg Coll., Waverly, Iowa, 2001—. Active voices from classroom Iowa Dept. Edn. Commn., Iowa, 1995—99; rep. ednl. partnership Wartburg Coll., 2005; cons. in social studies; presenter in math. and social studies. Author: Math Around the World, 1993, Math Talks, 1993, Math: A Fair, 1993. Reader for blind Iowa Radio Info. Sys. Finalist Tchr. of Yr. award, Iowa Dept. Edn., 1995; named Gold Star Tchr., 1993, Social Studies Tchr. of Yr., 1994; recipient Golden Poet award, 1989, 1992; grantee, Fulbright Meml. Fund, 1999, Dept. Edn., 2000. Mem.: Nat. Coun. Social Studies (chmn. 2005—06, mem. panel notable book award). Avocations: reading, writing, walking, bicycling. Business E-Mail: diane.mccarty@rtburg.edu.

MCCARTY, DIXIE RAYLE, science educator; b. Elberton, Ga., Nov. 16, 1966; m. David McCarty; children: TyRayle, Reed. BA, Piedmont Coll., Demorest, Ga., 1998. Tchr. sci. grade 8 Elbert County Mid. Sch., Elberton, Ga., 1998—. Vol. horse club leader Elbert County 4-H, Elberton, 2003—. Recipient Tchr. of Yr., Elbert County Mid. Sch., 2004—05, Vol. of Yr., Elbert County 4-H, 2004. United Methodist Church. Office: Elbert County Mid Sch 1108 Athens Tech Rd Elberton GA 30635 Office Phone: 706-213-4200. Business E-Mail: dmccarty@elbert.k12.ga.us.

MCCARTY, LOIS LEONE, retired sociologist; b. Oakland, Calif., Feb. 28, 1939; d. Richard Oliver McCarty and Nina Lea Wiley; m. Donald Greene (div. 1976). BA in Psychology, San Jose State U., Calif., 1960, MS in Sociology, 1962; postgrad. in Sociology, Psychology and Human Resource Mgmt., U. Calif., Berkeley, Santa Clara U., Calif. Cert. tchr. Calif. Prof. sociology Foothill Coll., Los Altos Hills, Calif., 1965—2000; juvenile probation officer Santa Cruz County, Calif., 1962—63; adult probation officer San Mateo County, Redwood City, Calif., 1963—67; prof. sociology Santa Rosa Jr. Coll., Calif., 1964—65; adminstrv. evaluator Foothill Coll., Los Altos Hills, Calif., 2000—05; ret., 2005. Recipient SALGO-NOREN Found. award for Tchg. Excellence, 1975, NIDSO Tchg. Excellence award, 1993, 1994, Pres.'s award for acad. excellence, Foothill Coll., 2000, Appreciation plaque, Foothill Coll. Faculty, Students and Staff of Women's Studies, 2000. Mem.: Am. Sociol. Assn., Lodi Women's Club. Avocations: travel, interior decorating, volunteerism, music. Home: 9303 N Hildreth Ln Stockton CA 95212 Office Phone: 209-931-3590. Personal E-mail: lomccr@aol.com.

MCCARTY, SHIRLEY CAROLYN, consumer products company executive; b. Minot, N.D., May 2, 1934; d. Harry and Cecelia Marie (Engene) Wolhowe; m. John Myron McCarty, Apr. 3, 1958. BS in Bus. Adminstrn., U. N.D., Grand Forks, 1958. Mem. tech. staff Douglas Aircraft, El Segundo, Calif., 1960-62, The Aerospace Corp., El Segundo, 1962-72, mgr., 1972-73, dir., 1973-79, prin. dir., 1979-89, gen. mgr., 1989—96; ret., 1996; pres. Shamrock Consulting, 1996—. Mem. adv. coun. Calif. State U., Northridge, 1979—2001, chmn., 1984-86; mem. indsl. adv. bd. Purdue U. Soc. Women Engrs., West Lafayette, Ind., 1979-82, 1985—; apptd. mem. aerospace safety adv. panel NASA, 1998, chair, 2002-03; spkr. in field. Named Woman of Yr. The Aerospace Corp., 1976, Pres.'s award, 1987; named to Hall of Fame Women in Tech. Internat., 2003; recipient Spl. Judges Award for Leadership, Los Angeles YWCA, 1977, Sioux Alumni Award, U. N.D, 1982, Achievement award Los Angeles County Commn. for Women, 1987. Fellow Soc. Women Engrs.; mem. IEEE, Assn. for Computing Machinery, Soc. Women Engrs., Bus. and Profl. Women (Woman of Achievement 1984, Golden Nike award 1985), Women in Bus.(corp. achievement award, 1987), Women in Computing (founding mem., bd. dirs.). Avocations: raising and training siberian huskies, travel, writing, architecture. Home: 357 Valley St El Segundo CA 90245-2932 Office Phone: 310-336-1781. E-mail: mccartys@earthlink.net.

MCCARTY, V. K., publishing executive, chaplain, librarian; b. Boston, June 26, 1948; d. Charles Osner and Dorothy June (McAlister) Long. BM, Mich. State U., 1969; MM, U. Louisville, 1972; cert. in theatre arts, U. London, 1972; intern in clin. pastoral edn., St. Luke's Roosevelt Hosp., 1989, resident in clin. pastoral edn., 1995; student, Congl. Devel. Inst. Tng., Diocese of Newark, 2003. Advt. asst. Lansing (Mich.) State Jour., 1968-69; market rsch. cons. Sta. WKLO, Louisville, 1969-70; libr. Louisville Free Pub. Libr., 1970-72; v.p. assoc. pub. Gen. Media Inc., N.Y.C., 1979-2000; acquisitions libr. Gen. Theol. Sem. St. Mark's Libr., N.Y.C., 2000—; part-time acquisitions libr. Union Theol. Sem. Burke Libr., N.Y.C., 2001—02; dir. Christian Formation, St. Paul's Ch., Chatham, NJ, 2002—03. Bd. dirs. B.F.T., Inc., N.Y.C. Dance editor Saturday Review Mag. Online, 1993-95. Master of ceremonies St. Ignatius of Antioch, N.Y.C., 1984-98; chaplaincy coord. St. Luke's Roosevelt Hosp., N.Y.C. Mem. N.Y. Liturgical Music Found. (steering com. 1982-84), N.Y. Ch. Club. Avocations: Biblical languages, riding, ballet, preservation of Benedictine monasticism, Byzantine art. Office: Gen Theol Sem St Mark's Libr 175 9th Ave New York NY 10011-4977

MCCASKEY, VIRGINIA HALAS, professional sports team executive; b. 1923; d. Georges Hala; m. Edward W. McCaskey (dec. 2003); 11 children. Owner Chgo. Bears Football team, 1983—. Sec. bd. dir. Chgo. Bears Football. Named one of Chicago's 100 Most Influential Women, Crain's Chgo. Bus. mag., 2004. Cath. Office: Halas Hall 1000 Football Dr Lake Forest IL 60045-4829

MCCASLAND, TERESA, secondary school educator, director; b. Dallas, Dec. 14, 1959; d. Edward and Louise Wheat Luttrull; m. Robert C. McCasland, Apr. 28, 1978; children: Bethenna, Cameron, Jillian, Abbie. AA cum laude, Tyler Jr. Coll., Tex.; BS with hons., Tex. A&M U., Commerce, Tex. Cert. tchr. theater Tex., 2000. Dir. theatre Terrell (Tex.) Ind. Sch. Dist., 2000—; airline agt. Am. Airlines, DFW Airport, Tex. Cons. Region 10 Edn. Ctr., Richardson, Tex.; spkr. in field. Dir.: (plays) Edgewood (Tex.) Hist. Soc., 1988—92. Dir. drama ministry First Bapt. Ch., Edgewood, Tex., youth leader. Nominee Tchr. of Yr., Disney, 2001; recipient Dist. UIL OAP Advancing Play award, Tex. U. Interscholastic League, 2006, Tchr. of Yr. award, Walmart Corp., 2006. Mem.: Tchr. Retirement Sys. (assoc.), Tex. Ednl. Theatre Assn. (assoc.). Bapt. Avocations: theater, travel, literature, languages, sign language. Home: 900 Vzcr 3215 Wills Point TX 75169 Office: Terrell ISD 400 Poetry Road Terrell TX 75160 Office Phone: 972-563-7525. Home Fax: 972-563-7525; Office Fax: 972-563-6318. Personal E-mail: mccaslat@terrell.ednet10.net.

MCCASLIN, ELIZABETH ANN, athletic trainer; b. Murfreesboro, Tenn., May 12, 1979; d. James Donald and Edwina Hassell McCaslin. BS in Athletic Tng., East Tenn. State U., Johnson City, 2001; postgrad., U. SC, Columbia, 2006—. Cert. athletic trainer Nat. Athletic Trainers' Assn. Head camp mgr. Universal Cheerleaders Assn., Memphis, 2000—01; athletic tng. fellow Steadman Hawkins Clinic, Vail, Colo., 2002—03, clin. coord., 2003—05; athletic trainer, med. asst. Moore Orthopedic Clinic, Columbia, SC, 2006—. Contbr. articles to profl. jours. Mem.: US Tennis Assn. (vol. 2006), SE Athletic Trainers Assn., SC Athletic Trainers Assn., Nat. Athletic Trainers Assn. (cert.). Avocations: tennis, golf, skiing, travel. Home: 1100 Pulaski St # 524 Columbia SC 29201 Office: Moore Orthopedic Clinic 14 Medical Park Ste 200 Columbia SC 29203 Personal E-mail: lizatc01@msn.com.

MCCASLIN, KATHLEEN DENISE, child abuse educator; m. David Wayne McCaslin, Sept. 27, 1986 (dec. Oct. 1990); 1 child, LeAnn; m. Larry Thomas Ward, July 14, 1998. BA, Adelphi Coll., 1984. Pub. speaker Impact Seminars, Littlestown, Pa., 1987-96; exec. dir. McCaslin Internat., Guffey, Colo., 1994—; pub. speaker The Family Advocate, Guffey, Colo., 1997—. Founder We the People, Colorado Springs, Colo., 1982; vol. counselor/facilitator Beginning Experience, Harrisburg, Pa., 1991-94; spkr. Internat. Child Advocacy Resources Enterprises, 2003—. Author: (books) Trusting in God, 1993, Respecting Yourself, 1993, Loss and Recovery, 1992, (cd audio) One Child's Journey to Freedom, 1998. Troop leader Girl Scouts U.S., Guffey, Colo., 1998-2000. Recipient Outstanding Grad. award Adelphi Coll., Colorado Springs, 1984. Mem. ASCPA, World Wildlife Fedn., Arbor Day Found., S.W. Indian Found. Avocations: reading, hiking, needlecrafts, gourmet cooking, gardening.

MCCASLIN, TERESA EVE, human resources specialist; b. Jersey City, Nov. 22, 1949; d. Felix F. and Ann E. (Golaszewski) Hrynkiewicz; m. Gary A. McCue. BA, Marymount Coll., 1971; MBA, L.I. U., 1981. Adminstrv. officer Civil Service Commn., Fed. Republic Germany, 1972-76; personnel dir. Oceanroutes, Inc., Palo Alto, Calif., 1976-78; mgr., coll. relations Continental Grain Co., N.Y.C., 1978-79, corp. personnel mgr., 1979-81, dir. bus. redesign, internal cons., 1981-84; dir., human resources Grow Group, Inc., N.Y.C., 1984-85, v.p. human resources, 1985-86, v.p. adminstrn., 1986-89; corp. v.p. human resources Avery Dennison Corp., Pasadena, Calif., 1989-94; v.p. human resources Monsanto Co., St. Louis, 1994-97; sr. v.p. human resources, mem. mgmt. com. Conti Group Cos. (formerly Continental Grain Co.), N.Y.C., 1997—, exec. v.p. human resources & info. tech., 1999. Mem. global adv. bd. Am. Grad. Sch. Internat. Mgmt.; bd. dirs. Am. Arbitrator Assn., 2005. Mem. Am. Mgmt. Assn. (chair bd. trustees, fin. and exec. com.), Human Resources Coun. Roman Catholic. Avocations: skiing, travel, golf. Office: Conti Group Cos 277 Park Ave New York NY 10172-0003 Business E-Mail: teri.mccaslin@conti.com.

MCCAUGHAN, DELLA MARIE, retired science educator; b. Pass Christian, Miss., Apr. 10, 1928; d. John Jeff and Nora Bell Sims; m. Finley Brandt McCaughan, Aug. 2, 1952; children: Leona Grace McCaughan Clawson, Diana Kay McCaughan Rodwig. Assocs. Degree, Miss. Gulf Coast C.C., Perkinston, Miss., 1949; BS, U. So. Miss., 1951, MS, 1959, specialist degree in sci. edn., 1979. Cert. elem. and secondary edn. in sci. Miss. Sci. educator Biloxi (Miss.) Pub. Schs., 1951—58, chairperson dept. sci., educator, 1959—95; ret., 1995. Adj. instr. biology for gifted secondary students Johns Hopkins U., Balt., 1988—91; ind. contractor Miss.-Ala. Sea Grant Consortium, Biloxi, 1980—84; edn. advisor U.S. Senate (Office Senator Thad Cochran), Washington, 1991—92; ind. contractor, author Miss. Dept. Marine Resources, Biloxi, 1996—99. Author: Program of Studies on Drug Education, 1973, Accountability and Instructional Management Plan, 1983, Guide to Federal Programs for Mississippi Educators, 1992, Marine Resources and History of the Mississippi Gulf Coast (vols. 1-4), 1998—99; editor: Marine Resources and History of the Mississippi Gulf Coast, vols. I, II, III, IV, 1998; co-author: Book I, The Wetlands: A Student's View, 1982, Book II, Planning A Visit To The Barrier Islands, 1982, Book III, What A Day, 1982, Book IV, Oystering On The Mississippi, 1982, Book V, Seafood Processing: A Factory Visit, 1982, Book VI, The Invertebrates, 1984, Book VII, Kathy's Journal: The Vertebrates, 1984, Book X, Jeremy And The Dolphins, 1989, Book XII, Learning About The Tides, 1991, A Guide to the Marine Resources of Mississippi, 1975; contbr. articles to profl. jours. Finalist Nat. Tchrs. Hall of Fame, 2002; named Congl. Einstein fellow, U.S. Senate, Washington, 1991—92; named to Miss. Hall of Master Tchrs., 1991; recipient Presdl. award for excellence in sci. and math. tchg., Washington, 1984, Tandy Tech. Scholars award, Tandy Corp., L.A., 1991. Mem.: Nat. Sci. Tchrs. Assn. (Nat. Disting. Svc. citation 1976), Assn. Presdl. Awardees in Sci. Tchg., Benevolent Protective Order of Elks. Achievements include discovery of catalepsy in Opsanus beta. Avocations: reading, travel. Home: 134 St Jude St Biloxi MS 39530 Office Phone: 228-326-3095. Personal E-mail: dmccaughan@cableone.net.

MCCAUGHEY ROSS, ELIZABETH P. (BETSY MCCAUGHEY), former lieutenant governor; b. Oct. 20, 1948; d. Albert Peterkin; m. Thomas McCaughey, 1972 (div. 1994); children: Amanda, Caroline, Diana. BA, Vassar Coll., 1970; MA, Columbia Univ., 1972, PhD, 1976. Public policy expert Manhattan Inst., N.Y.C.; lt. gov. State of N.Y., 1995—99. Asst. prof. Vassar Coll., 1979, Columbia U., 1980-84; chmn. Governor's Medicaid Task Force, 1994. Author: From Loyalist to Founding Father, 1980, Government By Choice, 1987; also articles including an article in The New Republic (Nat. Mag. award for Pub. Policy 1995). Recipient Bancroft Dissertation award, Richard B. Morris prize; Woodrow Wilson fellow, Herbert H. Lehman fellow, Honorary Vassar fellow, John Jay fellow, Post Doctoral Rsch. fellow NEH, 1984, John M. Olin fellow Manhattan Inst., 1993, sr. fellow Ctr. Study of the Presidency. Republican.

MCCAUL, ELIZABETH, investment advisor, former state agency administrator; BA in econ., Boston U., 1985; postgrad., Georgetown U. Congl. intern, 1981; investment banker, v.p. Goldman, Sachs & Co., 1985—95; chief of staff N.Y. State Banking Dept., 1995—96, first dep. supt. banks, 1996—97, acting supt. banks, 1997-2000, supt. banks, 2000—03; ptnr. Promontory Fin. Group, 2003—. Dir. Empire State Devel. Corp., State N.Y. Mortgage Agy., N.Y. State Job Devel. Authority, Harlem Cmty. Devel. Corp.; statutory mem. Cmty. Facilities Project Guarantee Fund. Scholar European Econ. Cmty., Inst. European Studies, Freiburg, Germany. Mem. Conf. State Bank Suprs. (bd. dirs., supervisory chmn., 2001-02, internat. bankers adv. bd.), Fed. Fin. Inst. Examination Coun., 2002-03. Office: Promotory Fin Group 1201 Pennsylvania Ave NW Ste 617 Washington DC 20004

MCCAULEY, ANN, lawyer; b. Washington, July 28, 1950; BA, Clark U., 1972; JD, Columbia Univ., 1978. Bar: NY 1979, US Dist. Ct. (so. dist. NY) 1979. Assoc. Cadwalader Wickersham & Taft, N.Y.C., 1978—80; atty. Port Authority of N.Y. & N.J., 1980—83; sr. v.p., chief corp. gen. counsel TJX Companies, Framingham, Mass. Mem.: New Eng. Corp. Counsel Assn., NY State Bar Assn. Office: TJX Companies 770 Cochituate Rd Framingham MA 01701 Office Fax: 508-390-2457. Business E-Mail: ann_mccauley@tjx.com.

MCCAULEY, BETTY BAILEY, school system administrator; b. Hazard, Ky., Mar. 21, 1942; d. Odem Bailey and Emma Whitaker-Bailey; children: Amy, Emily. BS, Western Mich. U., Kalamazoo, 1965; MA, Ctrl. Mich. U., Mt. Pleasant, 2005. Cert. ednl. adminstrn. Elem. art tchr. Detroit Pub. Schs., 1965; art tchr. Leslie (Mich.) Pub. Schs., 1965—67; elem. art tchr. Utica (Mich.) Cmty. Schs., 1967—69; fine arts tchr. Mt. Clemens (Mich.) Cmty. Schs., 1972—74; dir. early childhood programs Lapeer (Mich.) Cmty. Schs., 1991—96; exec. dir. Willows Earth Edn. Ctr., Lapeer, 1996—; dir., founder Chatfield Sch., Lapeer, 1997—. Mem. Mott C.C. Scholarship Bd., Flint, Mich., 1998—. Commr. City Lapeer Planning Com., 1999—; founding mem. City Lapeer Nature Area Steering Com., 1998—; guest Worldwide Webcast Voice of Am., 2005; bd. mem. Lapeer Art Gallery, 2005—. Named Administrator of Yr., Mich. Assn. Public Sch. Administrators, 2006; recipient Great Tchr. award, Lapeer County Great Tchr. Foundation, 1996; Fed. Dissemination grant, Mich. Dept. Edn., 2005—. Mem.: Nat. Assn. Multiage Edn., Nat. Assn. Supervision and Curriculum Devel., Econ. Club of Lapeer. Office: Chatfield Sch 231 Lake Dr Lapeer MI 48446 Office Phone: 810-667-8970. Office Fax: 810-667-8983. Business E-Mail: betmac-1999@yahoo.com.

MCCAULEY, ELIZABETH ANNE, art educator; BA summa cum laude, Wellesley Coll., 1972; MA, Yale U., 1974, PhD, 1980. Lectr. U. N.Mex., Albuquerque, 1978-80, asst. prof. art, 1980-81; asst. dir. U. N.Mex. Art Mus., Albuquerque, 1978-81; asst. prof. art U. Tex., Austin, 1981-86, assoc. prof. art, 1987-88; vis. assoc. prof. U. Mass., Boston, 1988, assoc. prof. art, 1988-95, chair dept. art, 1995-98, prof. art, 1995—2002; McAlpin prof. art Princeton U., 2002—. Pub. lectr. in field; cons. Mathew Brady exhbn., Nat. Portrait Gallery, Washington, 1995, J. Paul Getty Art Info. Thesaurus Project, photography sect., 1989; consulting reader numerous univ. presses; mem. numerous univ. coms. Author: A.A.E. Disderi and the Carte de Visite Portrait Photograph, 1985, Industrial Madness: Commercial Photography in Paris, 1848-71, 1994: co-author Gondola Days: Isabelle Stewart Gardner and the Palazzo Barbero Circle, 2004; author numerous exhbn. catalogues; contbr. chpts. to books, articles and revs. to profl. jours.; contbg. editor History of Photography, 1992—, Etudes photographiques, 1995—, Coll. Art Assn. on-line jour., 1998—; mem. adv. bd. Exposure, 1991. Grantee Mass. Found. Humanities and Pub. Policy, 1989, Healey grantee, 1997-98, Guggenheim fellow, 1998-99, Smithsonian Instn. short-term visitor Nat. Portrait Gallery, 1999; recipient numerous U. Mass. Faculty Devel. grants; recipient George Wittenborn and Ruth Emery awards, 1994. Office: Art and Acrhaeology Dept McCormick Hall Princeton U Princeton NJ 08540

MCCAULLEY, CYNTHIA JANE, elementary art educator; b. Altoona, Pa., Sept. 2, 1948; d. William Thomas and Leta Mae (Yingling) Eisenhower; m. Daniel Robert McCaulley, Aug. 7, 1970; 1 child, Matthew Thomas. BS, Grace

Coll., 1970; MA, Ball State U., 1978; postgrad., Ind. U., 1992—94. Cert. elem., art tchr., Ind. Elem. art tchr. Maconaquah Sch. Corp., Bunker Hill, Ind., 1970—. Conf. presenter; piloted gifted art program Maconaquah Sch. Corp., Bunker Hill, 1992. Contbg.-author (curriculum) A Community of Tchrs., 1993, Making A Difference, 1994. Chmn. Christian edn. bd. 1st Bapt. Ch., Bunker Hill, 1989-93, chmn. youth bd., 1995; mem. Cole Porter Scholarship Com., Peru, 1988, 91, 94. Recipient Miami County Soil and Water Conservation award to Outstanding Tchr., 2000, Art Edn. Assn. of Ind. Outstanding Art Educator of Yr. award, 2000, Pres. award, 2000, Youth Art Month award of merit Coun. for Art Edn., Inc.; Ind. Dept. Edn. scholar, 1992, 93. Mem. Nat. Art Edn. Assn., Art Edn. Assn. Ind. (youth art month state coord. 1997-2001, dist. 2 rep. 1998-2001, Outstanding Art Educator of Yr. 2000, Pres.'s award 2000), Delta Kappa Gamm. Avocations: family, church, painting, travel, gardening. Home: 3183 W 500 S Peru IN 46970 Office: Pipe Creek Elem 3036 W 400 Peru Peru IN 46970 E-mail: mccaulleyj@mail.maconaquah.k12.in.us, danandjane417@cs.com.

MCCAW, SUSAN RASINSKI, ambassador; b. Orange City, Calif. m. Craig McCaw; 3 children. BA, Stanford U.; MBA, Harvard U., 1988. Bus. analyst McKinsey & Co., NY, Hong Kong; assoc. Robertson Stephens' Venture Capital Group; principal Robertson Stephens & Co., San Francisco; pres. COM Investments, Wash.; mng. ptnr. Eagle Creek Capital; US amb. to Austria U.S. Dept. State, Vienna, 2005—. Mem. exec. bd. Stanford Alumni Assn. Office: US Dept State 9900 Vienna Pl Washington DC 20521-9900*

MCCAW, WENDY PETRAK, publishing executive; b. 1952; m. Craig Oliver McCaw, Aug. 18, 1974 (div. 1997). BA, Stanford U., 1973. Co-owner Cellular One Comm., Wash.; founder, CEO Ampersand Holdings LLC, Santa Barbara, Calif., 1998—; owner & CEO Santa Barbara (Calif.) News-Press, 2000—, co-publisher, 2006—. Pres. Wendy P. McCaw Found. (formerly Craig & Wendy McCaw Found.), Santa Barbara, Calif. Named one of America's Richest People, Forbes, 1999, World's Richest People, 2000. Avocations: environmentalism, vegetarianism. Mailing: Santa Barbara News-Press PO Box 1359 Santa Barbara CA 93102 Office: Santa Barbara News-Press 715 Anacapa St Santa Barbara CA 93101 Office Phone: 805-564-5200. Office Fax: 805-966-6258. E-mail: wmccaw@newspress.com.*

MCCHESNEY, S. ELAINE, lawyer; b. Bowling Green, Ky., Sept. 14, 1954; d. Kelsey H. McChesney and Lorraine (Carter) Durey; m. Paul Boylan; children: Michael, Jessica, Andrew. AB summa cum laude, Western Ky. U., 1975; JD, Harvard U., 1978. With Bingham Dana, LLP, Boston, 1978—, ptnr., Litig. Area, 1985—, co-chair, Appellate Practice Group. Chair joint MBA/BBA bar com. on jud. appts., 1988-89, 90-91; trial practice advisor moot ct. exercises Harvard Law Sch.; moot ct. judge Harvard Law Sch., Boston U., Suffolk U. Author: (with Gordon and Rainer) Massachusetts Civil Practice: Discovery, 1996, (with Lauriat, Gordon and Rainer) Massachusetts Practice: Discovery, 2001; bd. editors Mass. Lawyer's Weekly, 1987-88; panelist, speaker in field; contbr. articles to profl. jours. Treas., bd. dirs. St. Paul's Nursery Sch., Dedham, Mass., 1990-95; parent rep., trustee Charles River Sch., Dover, Mass., 1997-2000, vol. numerous coms.; vol. Am. Heart Found., March of Dimes; vol. street canvassing on zoning issues. Mem. ABA (labor law sect. subcom. individual rights in the workplace 1982—, comml. banking or fin. transactions litigation 1982), Mass. Bar Assn., Boston Bar Assn. (coun. 1994—, law sch. liaison com. 1984-85, IOLTA com., co-chair ann. mtg.), Women's Bar Assn. (editor calendar 1988-92, bd. dirs. 1999—). Office: Bingham Dana LLP 150 Federal St Fl 15 Boston MA 02110-1745 Office Phone: 617-951-8501. Office Fax: 617-951-8736. E-mail: semcchesney@bingham.com.

MCCLAIN, BRENDA C., pain management physician; b. Wilson, NC, July 17, 1954; MD, U. NC, Chapel Hill, 1984. Cert. Pain Mgmt., Am. Bd. Anesthesiology, diplomate Am. Bd. Pain Medicine. Intern, anesthesia John Hopkins Hosp., Baltimore, Md., 1984—85, resident, anesthesiology and critical care medicine, 1985—87; fellow pediatric anesthesiology Children's Hosp. Pitts., 1987—88; asst. prof. Med. Coll. Ga., Augusta; dir. pediatric pain Vanderbilt U.; dir., pediatric pain mgmt. services, attending physician pediatric anesthesiology Yale-New Haven Hosp.; assoc. prof., anesthesiology and pediatrics Yale U., 1998—. Chairperson Yale New Haven Hosp. Sedation Analgesia Coun.; mem. examination coun. Am. Bd. Pain Medicine; spkr. in field. Contbr. articles to profl. jours., chapters to books; mem. several editl. boards. Mem.: Am. Pain Soc. (mem. pediatric pain pre-conference prog. com.), Am. Cancer Soc., Am. Acad. Pain Medicine. Office: Yale U 333 Cedar St TMP3 PO Box 208051 New Haven CT 06520-8051 Office Fax: 203-785-2802, 203-785-6664. Business E-Mail: brenda.mcclain@yale.edu.*

MCCLAIN, CINDY DUNSTAN, music educator; d. Kenneth Warren and Janet Lou Dunstan; children: Melinda Wrye Washington, John Michael Kritos. MusB in Vocal and Instrumental Edn. K-12, Lincoln U. of Mo., Jefferson City, 1977; MA in Piano performance, Ctrl. Mo. State U., 1995. Dir., coord. music, adjudicator State Fair Coll., Sedalia, Mo., 1988—2003; dir. music, coord. fine arts Westminster Coll., Fulton, Mo., 2003—. Dir. Jefferson City (Mo.) Cantorum. Recipient Governor's award for excellence in tchg., State of Mo., 2000. Mem.: Mo. Assn. Dept. Schs. of Music, Mo. C.C. Assn., Music Educators Nat. Conf., Am. Choral Dirs. Assn. Office: Westminster Coll 501 Westminster Ave Fulton MO 65251 Office Phone: 573-592-5214. Personal E-mail: cmcclain@socket.net. E-mail: mcclaic@westminster_mo.edu.

MCCLAIN, JENNIFER C., middle school educator; b. Spokane, Wash., Oct. 5, 1973; d. Richard and Patricia Perry; m. W. Richard McClain. BA in English, Ea. Oreg. U., La Grande, 1997. Cert. secondary edn. Idaho. Tchr. Les Bois Jr. HS, Boise, Idaho, 2002—. Co-advisor Nat. Jr. Honor Soc., Boise, 2002—. Century scholar, Boise Rotary Club, 2006. Mem.: NEA, Idaho Edn. Assn., Boise Edn. Assn., Idaho Coun. Tchrs. of English. Democrat. Roman Catholic. Avocations: travel, reading. Office: Les Bois Jr HS 4150 E Grand Forest Dr Boise ID 83716

MCCLAIN, JUANITA, library director; b. Montgomery County, Ala., Oct. 6, 1949; BS, Ala. State U., 1972, MEd, 1979; MLS, Atlanta U., 1984. Dir. pub. libr. Macon-Tuskegee County, Macon, Ala., 1978-88, br. head, 1989-94; dir. Montgomery City-County Pub. Libr., 1994—. Recipient Black Role Model award Montgomery-Tuskegee Times, 1996; Ala. Pub. Libr. Svc. scholar, 1984, Atlanta U. fellow, 1983. Mem. ALA, Ala. Libr. Assn. (sec. 2001-02, pres.-elect 2002—). Office: Montgomery City-County Pub Libr PO Box 1950 Montgomery AL 36102-1950

MCCLAIN, LENA ALEXANDRIA, protective services official; b. Toledo, Ohio, Aug. 15, 1966; d. Lee Earl McClain, Mattie May Roberts-McClain; m. David Angelo Neyland, Aug. 4, 1990 (div. July 1995). AAS in Criminal Justice Adminstrn., Pikes Peak C.C., Colorado Springs, Colo., 1994; postgrad., U. Colo., 1994—95; BS in Criminology, U. So. Colo., 1996; postgrad., Spring Arbor U., Mich., 2001—02; postgrad. in Social Work, Lourdes Coll., Toledo, OH, 2003—. Corrections officer Colo. Dept. Corrections, Colorado Springs, 1994—96, sgt., 1996—97, case mgr./lt., 1997—99; sr. resident specialist coord. N.W. Cmty. Corrections Ctr., Bowling Green, Ohio, 1999—2000; shift supr. Lucas County Dept. Wk. Release, Toledo, 2000—. Employee counsel, bd. dirs. Delta Correctional Ctr., 1998—99. Mem. Colo. Grievance Team, 1998; trio mem. Townsend Learning Ctr.; bd. dirs. Pub. Arts Commn., Delta, Colo., 1999; bd. dirs., liaison Nat. Assn. Blacks in Criminal Justice, Delta, 1998. With U.S. Army, 1987—90. Mem.: Am. Correctional Assn., Correctional Peace Officers Found., Social Work Nat. Honor Soc., Phi Theta Kappa. Democrat. Avocations: golf, basketball, softball, chess, writing. E-mail: brealis37@aol.com, brealis@toast.net.

MCCLAIN, PAULA DENICE, political scientist, educator; b. Louisville, Jan. 3, 1950; d. Robert Landis and Mabel (Molock) McC.; stepdau. of Annette Williams McClain; m. Paul C. Jacobson, Jan. 30, 1988; children: Kristina L., Jessica A. BA, Howard U., Washington, 1972; MA, Howard U., 1974, PhD, 1977; postgrad., U. Pa., 1981—82. Asst. prof. dept. polit. sci. U. Wis., Milw., 1977-82; assoc. prof. and prof. pub. affairs Ariz. State U., Tempe, 1982-91; prof. govt. and fgn. affairs U. Va., Charlottesville, 1991-2000, chair govt. and fgn. affairs, 1994-97; prof. dept. polit. sci. Duke U., Durham, NC, 2000—. Co-author: Can We All Get Along? Racial and Ethnic Minorities in American Politics, 1995, 4th edit. 2005, Race, Place and Risk: Black Homicide in Urban America, 990; editor: Minority Group Influence, 1993; co-editor: Urban Minority Administrators, 1988. Mem. Nat. Conf. Black Polit. Scientists (pres. 1989-90), Am. Polit. Sci. Assn. (exec. coun. 1985-87, v.p. 1993-94), So. Polit. Sci. Assn. (exec. coun. 1992-95, v.p. 2002-03, pres. elect 2004, pres. 2005), Internat. Polit. Sci. Assn. (exec. com. 1997-2003, v.p. 1997-2003), Midwest Polit. Sci. Assn. (v.p. 2002-04). Office: Duke U Dept Polit Sci Perkins Libr PO Box 90204 Durham NC 27708-0204 Office Phone: 919-660-4303. E-mail: pmcclain@duke.edu.

MCCLAIN, SYLVIA NANCY (NANCY JO GRIMM), voice educator, vocalist; b. Worthington, Minn., July 16, 1943; d. Walter Deming and Naomi Leona (Deters) Grimm.; m. Joseph T. McClain (div. Feb. 1994); children: Raimund, Hermine. MusB with honors, Ind. U., 1966, MusM with honors, 1969; D of Musical Arts with commendation, U. Tex., Austin, 1989. Apprentice artist Santa Fe (N.Mex.) Opera, 1968-69; performing singer various concert and opera venues, Germany, 1970-78; asst. prof. dept. music Howard Payne U., Brownwood, Tex., 1980-82; asst. prof. voice dept. fine arts Southwestern U., Georgetown, Tex., 1986-91; assoc prof., chair voice dept. sch. music Hardin-Simmons U., Abilene, Tex., 1992-98; assoc. prof. music, coord. voice and opera U. Conn., Storrs, 1998—. Performer: (recital) Portraits of Women in Songs of Hugo Wolf. Vol. cons. Austin Lyric Opera, 1983—92. Fulbright scholar, Stadtliche Hochschule für Musik, Stuttgart, Germany, 1969-70. Mem. Nat. Assn. Tchrs. Singing, Phi Kappa Lambda. Avocations: exercise, reading, travel.

MCCLAIN, THERESA L., language educator; d. H.D. and Sallie Howard; children: Amy, Derrick. BA, Tex. State U., San Marcos, 1974. Cert. tchr. Tex., Ohio. Writing tchr. U. Tex., San Antonio, 1984—88; English tchr. Converse/Judson H.S., Tex., 1974—79, Greenon H.S., Springfield, Ohio, 1980—83, 1989—, Southwest H.S., San Antonio, 1988—89. Writing adj. Wright State U., Fairborn, Ohio, 1989—97; English unit leader Greenon H.S, 2003—. Author: (book) Never Too Late, 1988, Forever After, 1990; contbr. chapters to books, articles to mags. Recipient Change Course Program grant, NEA, 1995, NEH Summer grant, 2004, Aprise award for contbg. to lives of students, Wittenberg U., 2006. Mem.: Am. Fedn. Tchrs. Baptist.

MCCLANAHAN, CONNIE DEA, pastoral minister; b. Detroit, Mar. 1, 1948; d. Manford Bryce and Dorothy Maxine (Keely) McC. BA, Marygrove Coll., 1969; MRE, Seattle U., 1978; D Ministry, St. Mary Sem. and U., Balt., 1988. Cert. in spiritual direction, youth ministry, advanced catechist. Campus minister Flint (Mich.) Newman Ctr., 1970-80; coord. religious edn. Blessed Sacrament Ch., Burton, Mich., 1981-84; pastoral assoc. Good Shepherd Cath. Ch., Montrose, Mich., 1984-90; pastor Sacred Heart Ch., Flint, 1990—2001; dir. faith formation St. Matthew Ch., 2003—. Music min. New Light Prayer Cmty., Flint, 1979-97; co-chaplain Dukette Cath. Sch., Flint, 1991-97; ind. spiritual dir., 1988—; rep. Diocesan Regional Adult Edn., 1993-96; mem. Nat., State and Lansing Diocese Catholic Campus Ministry Assns., 1970-80; mem. campus ministry task force Interfaith Metro. Agy. for Planning, 1974-76; mem. Lansing Diocesan Liturgical Commn., 1977-80; mem. Flint Cath. Urban Ministry, 1977-80, 90-2001, co-chair, 1992-94; mem. Flint Cath. Healing Prayer Team, 1977-84; coord. nat. study week Cath. Campus Ministry Assn., 1978; mem. steering com. All-Mich. Cath. Charismatic Conf., 1984-86; convener Diocesan Lay Ministry Com. on Cert./Continuing Edn./Spirituality, 1985-86; mem. Diocesan Com. to Update Catechist Formation Handbook, 1989-91; mem. Diocesan All Family Conf. Steering Com., 1990-91; mem. Lansing Diocese svc. com. of Cath. Charismatic Renewal, 1979-85, 95-99, chair, 1996-98. Founding mem. P.O.W.E.R., Inc. (formerly Flint/Genesee Organizing Project), 1996-2001, treas., 1998-2000, sec. 2000-01. Mem. Assn. Cath. Lay Ministers (co-chair Region III 1986-87), Profl. Pastoral Ministers Assn. (founding meme., co-chair 1988-90), Nat. Assn. Lay Ministry. Roman Catholic. Avocations: guitar, singing, leather crafting, reading. Office: St Matthew Ch 706 Beach St Flint MI 48502 Office Phone: 810-232-0880. Personal E-mail: cdcmc2@yahoo.com.

MCCLANAHAN, KAY MARIE, government official, lawyer; b. Arkadelphia, Ark., Feb. 17, 1944; d. Allen William and Dorothy H. (Boon) McC.; m. George Townes Weaver, Jr., Aug. 20, 1966 (div. July 1987); 1 child, Shannon Marie Weaver Flanagan. B in Edn., U. Ark., 1966, JD, 1990; MA in Spanish, U. N.H., 1976. Bar: Ark. 1990. Staff atty. Adminstrv. Office Cts., Little Rock, 1990-92; acting dep. dir. Nat. Women's Bus. Coun., Washington, 1993-94; sr. program officer Devel. Assocs., Arlington, Va., 1995-96; confidential asst. to adminstr. Fgn. Agrl. Svc. USDA, Washington, 1996-97; U.S. rep. Inter-Am. Inst. Coop. Agr., Washington, 1997-99, coord. interregional instnl. rels. San Jose, Costa Rica, 1999—. Spkr. U.S. Info. Agy., Chile and Paraguay, 1994; election observer UN, El Salvador, 1994, OAS, Dominican Republic, 1996, 2000. Bd. dirs. Spanish Ednl. Devel. Ctr., Washington, 1996-99; commr. Sister Cities Commn., Little Rock, 1993; mem. Clinton-Gore Campaign, Ark. and Tex., 1992; dir. Alliance for Am., Nat. Order Women Legislators, Washington, 1994-95. Recipient scholarship Ark. Bar Found., 1988; fellow U. N.H., 1977. Mem. Ark. Womens Lawyers Assn. (exec. bd. dirs. 1992-93), Ark. Bar Assn., Pulaski County Bar Assn. Avocations: singing, dance, nature activities, hiking. E-mail: kaymcclan@hotmail.com.

MCCLANAHAN, RUE (EDDI-RUE MCCLANAHAN), actress; b. Healdton, Okla., Feb. 21, 1934; d. William Edwin and Dreda Rheua-Nell (Medaris) McC.; m. Tom Bish, 1958; 1 child, Mark Thomas Bish; m. Norman Hartweg; m. Peter DeMaio; m. Gus Fisher, 1976; m. Tom Keel, 1984 (div. 1985); m. Morrow Wilson, 1997. BA in German & Theatre Arts cum laude, U. Tulsa, 1956. Appearances include (theatre) Lottice and Lovage, Vienna, 1993, Harvey (London); (Broadway) Jimmy Shine, 1968-69, Sticks and Bones, 1972, California Suite, 1977, After-Play, 1995, The Women, 2002, Wicked, 2005—; (TV series) Maude, 1973-78, Apple Pie, 1978, Mama's Family, 1982-84, Golden Girls, 1985-92, Golden Palace, 1992-93, Safe Harbor, 1999; (TV movies) Having Babies III, 1978, Sgt. Matlowch vs. the U.S. Air Force, 1978, Rainbow, 1978, Topper, 1979, The Great American Traffic Jam, 1980, Word of Honor, 1981, The Day the Bubble Burst, 1982, The Little Match Girl, 1987, Liberace, 1988, Take My Daughters Please, 1988, Let Me Hear You Whisper, 1988, To the Heroes, 1989, After the Shock, 1990, Children of the Bride, 1990, To My Daughter, 1990, The Dreamer of Oz, 1990, Baby of the Bride, 1991, Mother of the Bride, 1993, Danielle Steele's Message from Nam, 1993, Burning Passion: The Margaret Mitchell Story, 1994, Nunsense, 1995, A Holiday to Remember, 1995, Columbo: Ashes to Ashes, 1998; (films) The People Next Door, 1970, They Might Be Giants, 1971, The Pursuit of Happiness, 1971, Modern Love, 1990, This World, Then the Fireworks, 1996, Dear God, 1996, Out to Sea, 1997, Rusty: A Dog's Tale, 1997, Starship Troopers, 1997, Border to Border, 1998, Columbo: Ashes to Ashes, 1998, A Saintly Switch, 1999, The Moving of Sophia Miles, 2000, (off-Broadway prodn.) The Vagina Monologues, 2001, (mini-series) Innocent Victims, 1995. Recipient Obie award for leading off-Broadway role in Who's Happy Now, 1970; Emmy award Best Actress in a comedy, 1987; named Woman of Yr., Pasadena Playhouse, 1986; Spl. scholar Pasadena (Calif.) Playhouse, 1959, Phi Beta Gamma scholar, 1955. Mem. Actors Studio, Actors Equity Assn., AFTRA, Screen Actors Guild. Office Phone: 212-372-1270.

MCCLANAHAN, TINA ANNETTE, elementary school educator, consultant; b. Charleston, W.Va., Jan. 8, 1966; d. Delbert Hershel, Jr. and Dimple Kay (Williams) Miller; m. Jerry Franklin McClanahan II, July 17, 1987; children: Amanda Lynn, Alyssa Katherine. BS in Elem. Edn., Early Childhood Edn., W.Va. State Coll., 1988. Cert. reading recovery, 1992, Nat. Bd. Cert. Early Childhood Generalist, 2001. Kindergarten tchr. Charlotte-Mecklenberg Schs., Charlotte, N.C., 1988-89, 1st grade tchr., 1989, 2nd grade chpt. I tchr., 1989-90, 3rd grade chpt. I tchr., 1990-91, 1st grade chpt. I tchr., 1991-92; local, state, regional and nat. literacy presentor, 1991—; reading recovery tchr. Charlotte-Mecklenberg Schs., NC, 1992—98, literacy tchr., 1992—2002, reading recovery tchr., literacy cons., 1993-94, 94—. Assoc. author, cons. Basic Early Literacy Skills Tchg. Resource, 2003-06; ednl. cons. Skylink Learning Theater, 2003- Grantee, U. NC at Charlotte Behavior and Reading Improvement Ctr., 2002—06, Positive Unified Behavior Support, 2005—06. Mem. Internat. Reading Asn. Avocations: literature, swimming, landscaping. Home: 501 E Matthews St Matthews NC 28105-1304

MCCLEARY, BERYL NOWLIN, volunteer, travel company executive; b. Ft. Worth, Feb. 22, 1929; d. Henry Bryant and Phyllis (Tenney) Nowlin; m. Henry Glenn McCleary, May 29, 1950; children: Laura Gail, Glenn Nowlin, Neil Ray, Paul Tenney. BS in Zoology, Tex. Tech U., 1950. Owner, mgr. Beryl McCleary Travels, Chicago, 1975-81, Denver, 1981-84. Treas. Kappa Alpha Theta Ednl. Found., Tex. Christian U., Ft. Worth, 1958-61; pres. study club Jr. Woman's Club, Ft. Worth, 1959-60; pres. Symphony League, Ft. Worth, 1961-62; v.p., dir. Ft. Worth Symphony Orch. Assn. Inc., 1961; treas. Jr. Pro-Am Tarrant County, 1961-62; corr. sec. Ft. Worth Children's Mus. Guild, 1961; sec. Tarrant County (Tex.) Democratic Exec. Com., 1956-62; pres. guild, bd. dirs. Maadi Community Ch., Cairo, 1964-66; mem. women's bd. Lincoln Park Zool. Soc., Chgo, 1976-81; mem. Episcopal Ch. Women's Diocesan Bd., Chgo., 1976-79; pres., charter mem. Rainbow Investment Club, London, 1970-71, travel dir. Over the Hill Gang Ski Team Internat., Denver, 1982-84. Mem. AAAS, DAR, Geol. Geophys. Aux., Service Club Chgo., Jr. League Denver, Denver Symphony Guild, Central City Opera Guild, Houston Symphony League, Alpha Epsilon Delta, Kappa Alpha Theta (charter mem. Gamma Phi chpt. 1953). Home: Apt F209 2501 Westerland DR Houston TX 77063-2276 E-mail: berylmcc@sbcglobal.net.

MCCLELLAN, BETTY, retired county official; b. Norborne, Mo., Oct. 10, 1940; d. William Edwin and Kathryn Louise England; m. Gerald Louis McClellan, Dec. 6, 1958; childre; Tamela Stanek, Marsha Junge. Grad. high sch., Troy, Mo. Receptionist Nat. Pet Supply, St. Louis, 1958, Lincoln County Meml. Hosp., Troy, Mo., 1958-59; factory worker The Artemis Co., Troy, Mo., 1963-64; hatchery worker Trojan Hatchery, Troy, Mo., 1965-69; bookkeeper Silex (Mo.) Elevator, 1969-74, Agri-Foods, Troy, 1974-79; deputy recorder deeds Lincoln County Recorder, Troy, 1979-83; treas. Lincoln County, Troy, 1983—2002. Treas. Lincoln County Dem. Com., 1989-97, treas. women's club, 1974-80; bd. dirs., treas. Lincoln County Fair, 1996-98; coord. steering com. Congressman Harold Volkmer, Hannibal, Mo., 1977-95. Mem. Mo. County Treas. Assn., Order Ea. Star (sec. Silex chpt. 1986-93). Presbyterian. Avocations: crocheting, crafts, doll collecting, travel. Home: 721 Hwy E Silex MO 63377-2425 Office: Lincoln County Treas 201 Main St Troy MO 63379-1127

MCCLELLAN, CAROLE ANN, retired school nurse; d. Ernest Henry Samuel and Mildred Sophie Lily Alice (Stricker) Battelle; m. Charles Ross McClellan, Dec. 20, 1958; children: Karen Ruth, Carole Lynne McClellan Shaw. Diploma in nursing, Evangelical Deaconess Hosp. Sch. Nursing, 1958. RN Mo. Staff nurse Evang. Deaconess Hosp., St. Louis, 1958—60; nurse St. Joseph (Mo.) Sch. Dist., 1973—99; ret., 1999. Pres. Women's Fellowship Faith Ch., St. Joseph, 1980. Mem.: Nat. Assn. Sch. Nurses, Mo. Assn. Sch. Nurses, Oreg. Calif. Trails Assn. (v.p.), Soc. Memories Doll Mus. (pres., sec.), Questers (sec.). Avocations: water sports, sewing, genealogy.

MC CLELLAN, CATHARINE, anthropologist, educator; b. York, Pa., Mar. 1, 1921; d. William Smith and Josephine (Niles) McClellan; m. John Thayer Hitchcock, June 6, 1974. AB magna cum laude in Classical Archaeology, Bryn Mawr Coll., 1942; PhD (Anthropology fellow), U. Calif., Berkeley, 1950. Vis. asst. prof. U. Mo. at Columbia, 1952; asst. prof. anthropology U. Wash., Seattle, 1952-56; anthrop. cons. USPHS, Arctic Health Research Center, Alaska, 1956; asst. prof. anthropology, chmn. dept. anthropology Barnard Coll., Columbia U., 1956-61; asso. prof. anthropology U. Wis. at Madison, 1961-65, prof., 1965-83, prof. emeritus, 1983—, John Bascom prof., 1973. Vis. lectr. Bryn Mawr (Pa.) Coll., 1954; vis. prof. U. Alaska, 1973, 87. Assoc. editor: Arctic Anthropology, 1961; editor, 1975-82; assoc. editor: The Western Canadian Jour. of Anthropology, 1970-73. Served to lt. WAVES, 1942-46. Margaret Snell fellow AAUW, 1950-51; Am. Acad. Arts and Scis. grantee, 1963-64, Nat. Mus. Can. grantee, 1948-74 Fellow Am. Anthrop. Assn., Royal Anthrop. Inst. Gt. Britain and Ireland, AAAS, Arctic Inst. N.Am.; mem. Am. Ethnol. Soc. (sec.-treas. 1958-59, v.p. 1964, pres. 1965), Kroeber Anthrop. Soc., Am. Folklore Soc., Am. Soc. Ethnohistory (exec. com. 1968-71), Sigma Xi. Achievements include research in archaeological and ethnographic field investigations in Alaska and Yukon Territory in Canada.

MCCLELLAN, DIXIE, secondary school educator; b. Freeburn, Ky., Dec. 4, 1940; d. Albert Eugene and Pauline (Lusk) McC.; m. Edward Lee Jessee, June 13, 1969 (div. Apr. 1975); m. Richard Joel McDuffee, July 2, 1996. BS in Edn., Concord Coll., Athens, W.Va.; MA in Polit. Sci., W.Va. U., 1972. Cert. secondary edn. tchr. Tchr. Roanoke County Schs., Salem, Va., 1959-62, Wyoming County Schs., Pineville, W.Va., 1962-64, Garrett County Schs., Oakland, Md., 1964-69, Preston County Schs., Kingwood, W.Va., 1969-72; Appalachian edn. specialist Appalachian Reigonal Com., Washington, 1972-77; rural devel. dir. Tenco Devel., Shelbyville, Tenn., 1977-81; exec. dir. Tenn. Export Devl. Assn., Nashville, 1982-85; pvt. cons. Nashville, 1985-89; tchr. Williamson County Schs., Nashville, 1989—. Chmn. Bedford County Adult Activity Ctr., Shelbyville, 1977-81; mem. Balance of State CETA Bd., Nashville, 1980-81; bd. dirs. Clan McClellan in Am., 1980-83. Writer monograph, grants, articles. Named to Outstanding Young Women of Am., 1979. Mem. Am. Polit. Sci. Assn., Profl. Educators Tenn. Republican. Episcopalian. Avocations: reading, gourmet cooking. Home: 2936 Spanntown Rd Arrington TN 37014-9123 Office: Centennial HS 5050 Mallory Ln Franklin TN 37067-1398 E-mail: McDuffee@mindspring.com.

MCCLELLAN, JOAN C. OSMUNDSON, art educator; b. Milw., Jan. 5, 1934; d. Henry and Alma (Oyaas) Osmundson; m. Robert J. McClellan, Apr. 2, 1955 (dec.); children: Michael J., Linda A., Katherine M., Mary M. BS, SUNY, Buffalo, 1956; MA, Adelphi U., 1968; postgrad., SUNY, Buffalo, 1961, Hofstra U., 1966. Tchr. Harris Hill (N.Y.) Elem. Sch., 1957; art specialist Huth Rd. Sch., Grand Island, N.Y., 1958-59; art educator Prospect Ave Sch., East Meadow, N.Y., 1959-89, W.T. Clarke High Sch., East Meadow, 1959-89. Exhibited in group shows including Sarasota Art Assn., 1989, Art League of Manatee County, 1989, Federated Woman's Club, 1990, Englewood Artisan Guild, 1990 (Best of the Best award). Vol. English tchr. to Spanish immigrants, L.I., N.Y., 1987-88; vol. soup kitchen, Wyndauch, L.I., 1987-88. Mem.: AAUW, Sarasota Art Assn., Nat. Mus. Women in Arts, Englewood Artisan Guild (rec. sec. 1989—90, chair publicity com. 1997—98, bd. dirs.), Nat. League Pen Women (chair S.C. art com.), Venice Art League, Sea Grape Gallery, Charlotte County Art Guild, Rotonda West Federated Woman's Club (past pres., arts chmn. 1989—). Republican. Roman Catholic. Avocations: travel, cooking, gardening, computers, painting. Home and Studio: 12 Red Leaf Ln Lancaster PA 17602

MCCLELLAN, LEANNE, music educator; b. Brigham, Utah, Apr. 26, 1946; d. Floyd William and Wanda (Jeppsen) Adams; m. Myron (Mike) Lee McClellan, Aug. 2, 1968; children: Eric Lane, Nathan Lee, Dustin Levi, Derek Lincoln, Derek Lincoln, Chad Lawrence, Todd Landon McClean, Christopher Lynn McClean. BS, Utah State Univ., Logan, Utah, 1968; MA, Lesley Univ., Cambridge, Mass., 2005. Dance tchr. Box Elder H.S., Brigham City, Utah, 1968—70; pvt. dance tchr. Lacy, Wash., 1984—85; subsititue tchr. Co-op & Dodd's Oversea, Olympia, Wash., 1987—96; drama tchr. Woodland Elem. Sch., Lacy, Wash., 1992—97; music and fine arts tchr. Southworth Elem. Sch., Yelm, Wash., 1996—2005. Pres. Officers Wives (Air Force), Adana, Turkey; sec. P.T.A., Woodland Elem. Sch.; com. treas. Social Com. Chairperson of Assemblies; pres. Young Women, Colo. Springs, Fla., Lacy, Relief Soc., Adana, Turkey, 1987—89; activities chairperson Lacy's 1st Ward, Lacey, Wash. Recipient Elem. Tchr. Yr., Southworth Elem. Sch., 2005—06. Republican. Lds. Avocations: sports, camping, sewing, dance, cooking.

MCCLELLAN, MARY ANN, pediatric nurse practitioner; b. Mar. 29, 1942; BS, Tex. Woman's U., 1964; MN, U. Wash., 1968-69; cert., U. Tex., Arlington, 1997. Cert. family life educator, CPNP, pediatric nurse practitioner; advanced RN practitioner, Okla. Charge nurse Baylor U. Med. Ctr., Dallas, 1964—65; pub. health staff nurse Dallas County Health Dept., Dallas, 1965—68; supervising nurse Okla. State Dept. Health, Oklahoma City, 1969—70, maternal-child health nurse cons., 1971; asst. prof. U. Okla. Coll. Nursing, Oklahoma City, 1971—72; from instr. to asst. prof. Harris Coll. Nursing Tex. Christian U., Ft. Worth, 1972—75; asst. prof. continuing edn. U. Okla. Coll. Nursing, Oklahoma City, 1976—79, asst. prof. baccalaureate program, 1979—96, mem. grad. faculty, 1991—. Cons. and lectr. in field. Contbr. chpts. to books, articles to profl. jours. Mem. Nat. Coun. on Family Rels., Okla. Family Resources Coalition, Nat. Assn. Pediatric Nurse Assocs. and Practitioners (Okla. chpt.), Assn. Faculty of Pediat. Nurse Practitioner Programs, So. Early Childhood Assn., Okla. Coun. on Family Rels., Okla. Early Childhood Assn., Sigma Theta Tau., Phi Kappa Phi. Office: U Okla Coll Nursing PO Box 26901 Oklahoma City OK 73126-0901

MCCLELLAN, STEPHANIE ANN, speech pathology/audiology services professional; b. Colorado Springs, Colo., Sept. 13, 1962; d. Jay and Ruthann Rash; m. Michael Allen McClellan, Sept. 14, 2001; 1 child, Evan James. AS in Interpreting for the Deaf, Northwestern Conn. C.C., Winsted, 1982; BS in Secondary Edn., Northwest Mo. State U., 1985; MS in Speech Lang. Pathology, Gallaudet U., 1990. Cert. clin. competence Am. Speech Lang. and Hearing Assn., 1991, lic. Del. State Bd. of Profl. Regulation, 2000. Speech lang. pathologist S.C. Sch. for the Deaf and Blind, Spartanburg, SC, 1990—93; chief of speech pathology svcs. in Europe USAF, RAF Lakenheath, England, 1993—99; speech lang. pathologist Smyrna, Del., 1999—. Pvt. practice interpreter, Lawrence, Kans., 1982—2003. Translator interpreter for the deaf. Cons. Smyrna Ch. of Christ Sch., Smyrna, Del., 2000—03. Capt. USAF, 1993—99, RAF Lakenheath, England. Recipient Vol. of Yr. award, S.C. Assn. for the Deaf, 1992. Mem.: Am. Speech Lang. Hearing Assn. (assoc.). Republican. Avocations: quilting, piano, travel, cooking. Home and Office: Speech and Lang Svcs 102 Hunting Way Smyrna DE 19977

MCCLELLAND, AMY KENNARD, elementary school educator; b. Phoenix, Mar. 27, 1963; d. James Robert and Noreen Mary (Neale) Kennard; m. Thomas Melville McClelland, Oct. 23, 1993. BA in Elem. Edn., Purdue U., 1987, MS in Elem. Edn., 1992. 4th grade tchr. Mequon-Thiensville (Wis.) Sch. Dist., 1987-88, 5th grade tchr., 1988-89, gifted and talented specialist, 1989-91; grad. rsch. asst., grad. teaching asst. Purdue U., West Lafayette, Ind., 1991-92; 3d grade tchr. MSD Lawrence Twp., Indpls., 1992—. Bd. dirs. tchr. adv. com. on outreach Purdue U., 1993—; tchr. rep. Indpls. Children's Mus., 1993—; profl. devel. schs. mentor Ind. U./Purdue U. of Indpls., 1993—. Contbr. articles to profl. jours.; patentee Imaginehouses. Youth min. St. Monica Cath. Ch., Indpls., 1994—. Recipient Presdl. award for excellence in sci. and math. teaching NSF, 1994. Mem. Soc. for Elem. Presdl. Awardees, Assn. for Presdl. Awardees in Sci. Teaching, Nat. Sci. Tchrs. Assn., Coun. for Elem. Sci. Internat. (Muriel Green award for outstanding new tchrs. of elem. sci. 1988), Hoosier Assn. for Sci. Tchrs. Inc., Purdue Edn. Alumni Assn. (bd. dirs. 1992—), Kappa Delta Pi. Roman Catholic. Avocations: piano, music, drama, reading, astronomy. Office: Indian Creek Elem Sch 10833 E 56th St Indianapolis IN 46235-9748

MCCLELLAND, DANIELLE, performing company executive; b. Topeka, Kans., Mar. 7, 1968; d. Harold Dean and Saxon McClelland; life ptnr. Susan Maria Ferentinos, Nov. 5, 1992. BA in English and Theater, Lewis & Clark Coll., Portland, Oreg., 1990. Founder Hundredth Monkey Theater Collective, Portland, 1991—94; owner Howling Frog Performance Space, Portland, 1992—94; festival coord. Fronterafest, Austin, Tex., 1995—96; bus. mgr. Windfall Dancers, Bloomington, Ind., 1996—98; program dir. Columbus Area Arts Coun., Ind., 1998—2001; exec. dir. Buskirk-Chumley Theater/BCT Mgmt., Inc., Bloomington, 2001—. Address: Po Box 1323 Bloomington IN 47402-1323

MCCLELLAND, HELEN, music educator; b. Chgo., Dec. 5, 1951; d. Leon Leroy and Willie Jo (Darnell) McC.; (div. Sept. 1981); 1 child, Tasha Renee. Diploma in arts, Kennedy-King Coll., 1971; cert. in voice, Sherwood Music Coll., 1971-73; BS, Chgo. State U., 1975, MA in Adminstrn., 1983; D in Adminstrn. and Supervision, U. Calif., 1993. Tchr. Faulkner Sch., Chgo., 1975-78; tchr. music Harvey (Ill.) Pub. Sch. Dist. 152, 1978—. Dir. music Pleasant Green Missionary Bapt. Ch., Chgo., 1971—; mem. sch. bd. New World Christian Acad., Chgo., 1988—; bd. dirs. South Shore Drill Team, Chgo. Author: operetta So You Want to Be a Star, 1987. Cmty. worker People United to Save Humanity, Chgo., 1973, Harold Washington Orgn., Chgo., 1987; cmty. educator Chgo. Planned Parenthood, 1988; cmty. counselor Lincoln Cmty. Ctr., Chgo., 1975; mem. sch. bd. Dist. 160, 1994, now v.p.; mem. Ill. State Sch. Bd., 1997-98; bd. dirs. Operation P.U.S.H.; vice chmn. Ill. Assn. Sch. Bds., Ill. State Assn. Bd.; bd. dirs. Ill. State Assn. Bd., So. Cook Div., 2003-; v.p. Sch. Dist. #160;; mem. Grace M.B. Ch. Named Tchr. of the Yr., Faulkner Sch., 1976; recipient Nat. Sch. Bd. award for Disting. Svc., Ill. State Assn. Bd., 2003. Mem. Ill. Edn. Assn., NEA, Harvey Edn. Assn., Tennis Club, Traveling Club, Phi Delta Kappa, Pi Lambda Theta. Democrat. Baptist. Avocations: singing, bowling, piano. Home: 18029 Ravisloe Ter Country Club Hills IL 60478-5169

MCCLENDON, MELINDA WHITE, medical/surgical nurse; b. Nashville, Tenn., Nov. 19, 1960; d. Lee Campbell and Lucy (Cooper) White; m. David Edward McClendon, May 26, 1990; one child: Lindsey Carol. BS in Nursing, U. Tenn., Memphis, 1982. Cert. RN Intravenous (CRNI), 1998. Charge nurse Bapt. Hosp., Nashville, head nurse, med./surg. fl.; staff nurse med. short stay unit. Home: 6007 Forrest Ct Greenbrier TN 37073-4594 E-mail: dmcmmc@comcast.net.

MCCLENNEN, MIRIAM J., former state official; b. Seattle, Sept. 16, 1923; d. Phillip and Frieda (Golub) Jacobs; m. Louis McClennen, Apr. 25, 1969; stepchildren: Adams Peter, James C.A., Helen, Persis, Crane, Emery. BA, U. Wash., 1945; MBA, Northwestern U., 1947. Exec. trainee Marshall Field & Co., Chgo., 1945-47; buyer Frederick & Nelson (subs. of Marshall Field), 1949-57, Goldwaters, Phoenix, 1963—67; adminstrv. asst. to pres. Ariz. State Senate, Phoenix, 1973-76; dir. publs. Office of Sec. of State, Phoenix, 1976-87. Chairwoman legis. subcom. adminstrv. procedure Ariz. State Legislature, Phoenix, 1984-85. Original compiler, codifier, editor publ. Ariz. Adminstrv. Code, 1973-87, Ariz. Adminstrv. Register, 1976-87. Bd. dirs., mem. Phoenix Art Mus. League, 1972—90; bd. dirs., mem. exec. bd. Phoenix Symphony Guild, 1969—88; bd. dirs., sec. Combined Met. Phoenix Arts and Scis., 1974—90, mem. adv. bd., 1990—95; bd. dirs. Phoenix Art Coun., 1973—78, Master Apprentice Programs, 1980—83; bd. dirs., mem. exec. bd. Heard Mus., 1982—88, 1990—; mem. adv. bd. Ariz. State Hist. Records, 1987—90, Ariz. Commn. on Arts, 1989—96, Phoenix Art Mus., 1966—; bd. dirs. Arizonans for Cultural Devel., 1996—2002; mem. Cape Mus. Fine Arts, 1996—. Recipient Disting. Svc. award Atty. Gen. Ariz., 1987, Outstanding Svc. to People, Ariz. State Senate, 1987, Nat. Assn. Secs. of State award, 1987. Mem.: Univ. Club, Ariz. Club, Phoenix Country Club, Charter 100 (bd. dirs. 1981—85). Personal E-mail: mjmlm@earthlink.net.

MCCLERKLIN-MOTLEY, SHIRLEY, social sciences educator; b. Columbia, SC, May 15, 1949; d. Willie S. and Juanita D. McClerklin; children: Patryce Lorelle Harvey, George Motley. MSW, U SC, 1990. Program dir. SC Dept. Social Svcs., Columbia, 1995—2000; asst. prof. Coker Coll., Hartsville, SC, 2000—. Dir. West Metro Youth Leadership Inst., West Columbia, SC, 1990—. Pres. Cayce (SC) Cmty. Coalition, 1999—2003. Recipient Cmty. Activism award, Glory Comm., 2002. Mem.: Coun. Social Work Edn. (assoc.). Avocation: travel. Office: Coker Coll 300 East College Ave Hartsville SC 29550 Office Phone: 843-383-8084.

MCCLINTOCK, MARTHA K., biologist, educator; AB, Wellesley College, 1969; MA in Psychology, U. Penn., 1972, PhD in Psychology, 1974. With U. Chgo., 1976—, asst. prof., psychology and human devel., 1976, David Lee Shillinglaw Distinguished Svc. Prof. Psychology, dir., Inst. Mind & Biology; co-dir. Ctr. Interdisciplinary Health Disparities Rsch. Chmn. biopsychology com., 1986—99; mem. neurobiology com., evolutionary biology com., human develop. com. Contbr. articles to profl. jours. Recipient Disting. Sci. Award for Early Career Contbn. to Psychology, APA, 1982, MERIT Award, NIMH, 1992, Edith Krieger Wolf Disting. Vis. Prof., Northwestern Univ., 2000, Henry G. Walter Sense of Smell Award, Sense of Smell Inst., 2001. elected mem., Inst. of Medicine, 1999, Acad. of Arts and Sciences, 1999. Office: U Chgo 5730 S Woodlawn Ave Chicago IL 60637

MCCLINTOCK, SANDRA JANISE, writer, editor, book designer; b. Connersville, Ind., July 28, 1938; d. Owen Dale and Mary Janis (Tierney) M.; m. Harvey Miles Garrison, Jr., Aug. 1, 1959 (div. 1967); children: Heidi, Katherine, H. Miles III; m. Joseph Lloyd Fagen, May 15, 1969; 1 child, Adam Joseph. BA, Drake U., 1960; postgrad., Calif. State U., Fullerton, 1966—67; cert., Am. Grad. U., 1987. Lic. gen. contractor. Coord. copy desk Time Mag., N.Y.C., 1960-62; mem. graphics prodn. staff Times-Mirror Co., L.A., 1962-64; mgr. prodn. Miller Freeman Publs., Long Beach, Calif., 1964-68; supr. Design Svc., Anaheim, Calif., 1968-73; prin. Fagen Graphics, Long Beach, 1973-77, Palomar Publs., Ranchita, Calif., 1977-84; cons. Cons. & Designers, Anaheim, 1984-87; mgr. publs. Tracor Flight Systems, Inc., Santa Ana, Calif., 1987-88; coord. publs. Rockwell Internat. Corp., Anaheim, 1988-92; dir. comms. Terra Christa Comms., Tucson, 1992-93; tech. writer CH2M Hill, Santa Ana, Calif., 1993—97; editor South Coast Mags., San Clemente, Calif., 1993—; assoc. dir. SBC Comm., 1998—2005; COO MB Dolphin & Assocs., LLC, 2005—. Cons. Aerotest, Inc., Mojave, Calif., 1986, Voice Telecom Corp., Laguna Beach, Calif., 1986, Northrup-Grumman, El Segundo, Calif., 2006. Editor: Psychopharmacology, 1984; Joseph of Aramathea, 1982, Who is Who at the Earth Summit, 1992; guest editor Interface Age mag., 1976; contbg. editor Rockwell News in U.S. and Can., 1988. Bd. dirs. Vol. Fire Dept., Ranchita, 1979; fund raiser Dem. candidate Calif. Assembly, Orange county, 1964; mem. Religious Sci. Practitioner Mem. Nat. Mgmt. Assn., So. Calif. Astrological Network, Soc. for Tech. Comm. Avocations: architecture, astronomy, travel, tennis. Home: 29491 Dry Dock Cv Laguna Niguel CA 92677-1643 Personal E-mail: starkid1@pacbell.net.

MCCLINTON, DOROTHY HARDAWAY, retired finance educator; b. Seguin, Tex., Jan. 4, 1925; d. George Washington and Rosetta (Hodge) Hardaway; m. Marion N. Hopkins Sr., Oct. 27, 1951 (div. Dec. 1982); 1 child, Marion N. Jr.; m. Elmer McClinton, Aug. 12, 1986; children: Thomas, Evelyn M., Nathaniel. BS, Huston-Tillotson Coll., 1947; MBEd, Tex. So. U., 1960. Tchr. Ball Elem. Sch., Seguin, 1947-49, Ball Mid. Sch., Seguin, 1949-54; clk., typist Kelly AFB, San Antonio, 1956-57; tchr. Ball High Sch., Seguin, 1957-64; tchr., dept. chair St. Philips Community Coll., San Antonio, 1964-86, prof. emeritus, 1986—. Audio visual tutorial cons. Media Systems Corp. subs. Harcourt Brace Jovanovich, Inc., 1978-86; mem. nat. rsch. rev. panel Ohio State U., 1983-84. Chair telethon United Negro Coll. Fund, San Antonio, 1990-92, 98; trustee Huston-Tillotson Coll., 1990—. Recipient Bus. Tchr. of Yr. award Tex. Bus. Edn. Assn., Austin, 1981-82, Acad. Achievement award Huston-Tillotson Coll., 1990-91; Inst. for Ednl. Ledership fellow St. Philip's Coll., San Antonio, 1984-85, Lifetime Achievement award San Antonio Black Achievement Awards, 1996; named Woman of Yr. St. Paul UMC, 1991; inductee Educators' Hall of Fame, Gamma Tau chpt. Phi Delta Kappa, 1993-94. Mem. Alamo Community Coll. Retirees, Top Ladies of Distinction (sgt.-at-arms 1987-92), Huston-Tillotson Coll. Alumni (pres. 1982-91, nat. pres. 1985-87) Delta Sigma Theta, Inc. (pres. 1972-74).

MCCLOSKEY, DIXIE MAY, retired medical/surgical nurse; b. Buffalo, N.Y., Jan. 4, 1942; d. William David and Jennie Lee (Ross) McC. Diploma, RN, Charity Hosp. Sch. Nursing, New Orleans, 1972; student, La. State U., Baton Rouge. RN, La.; cert. paralegal. Charge nurse emergency room Med. Ctr. Baton Rouge, La., 1985-87; staff nurse Ochsner Family Practice, Baton Rouge, La., 1987-88; supr. hosp. unit Hunt correction ctr. La. State Dept. of Corrections, St. Gabriel, La., 1988-89; charge nurse, med./surg., telemetry Riverview Med. Ctr., Gonzales, La., 1989-95; paralegal, med. rschr. law firm, Baton Rouge, 1997—. 2d lt. Nurse Corps U.S. Army, 1979-81. Mem. Emergency Dept. Nurses Assn. of Baton Rouge (sec. 1972-73). Personal E-mail: kitcat3@msn.com.

MCCLOY, SHIRLEY, physical education educator; b. Riverton, Utah, May 30, 1972; d. Ronald J. and LaFawn Stepan; m. Scott Alexander McCloy, May 14, 1994; children: Makenna, Tamika. AA, Coll. So. Idaho, Twin Falls, 1993; BS, U. Utah, Salt Lake City, 2005, MS, 2006. Cert. tchr. Utah. Coach Globe Unified Sch. Dist., Ariz., 1995—96, Jordan Sch. Dist., Salt Lake City, 1997—98; claims processor Unibase, Salt Lake City, 1999—2000; referee Tooele Jr. Jazz, Utah, 2000; stocker/receiver Maceys Grocery, Tooele, Utah, 2000—02; coach Tooele Sch. Dist., Utah, 2000—03; asst. coord. UFIT U. Utah, Salt Lake City, 2005—. Coord. UFIT-U. Utah, Salt Lake City, 2006. Mem. Lds Ch. Avocations: spending time with family, golf, camping, hiking, basketball. E-mail: macnstep@comcast.net.

MCCLURE, CAROLYN F., psychologist; d. John Alvin and Catherine Dimitrea Wiandt; m. Douglas E. McClure (div.); children: Erin Michelle, Aubrey Catherine, Lea Christine. BA, Coll. Wooster, Ohio, 1986; EdM, Akron U., Ohio, 1989; post M cert. in Sch. Psychology, Ohio State U., Columbus, 2000. Lic. social worker Ohio; cert. sch. psychologist. Case mgr. Counseling Ctr. Wayne Holmes Ctrs., Wooster, Ohio, 1988—93; dir. substance abuse mental illness svcs. Nova Behavioral Health, Massillon, 1993—94; case mgr. Wooster City Schs., 1995—97; sch. psychologist Tri-County Ednl. Svc. Ctr., 2000—. Pvt. therapist The Recovery Ctr., Wooster, Ohio, 1992; cons. psychologist Wooster Cmty. Hosp., 2005—; cmty. edn. Ohio crisis team Ohio Sch. Psychologists Assn., Columbus, 2005—. Mem.: Nat. Assn. Sch. Psychologists. Avocations: travel, walking, music, sports, cultural studies. Office: TriCounty Ednl Ctr 741 Winkler Wooster OH 44691

MCCLURE, CONNIE DIANE, elementary school educator; b. Huntsville, Tex., July 4, 1956; d. Albert Joseph and Alpha Lee (Ash) Davis; m. Ronnie Preston McClure, May 20, 1978; children: Micah Lindsay, Matthew Christopher. BS in Edn., Howard Payne U., 1978; MS in Art Edn., U. North Tex., 1996. Cert. elem. tchr., Tex. Tchr. Brownwood (Tex.) Ind. Sch. Dist., 1980-82; interviewer Tex. Employment Commn., Ft. Worth, 1983-85, investigator, 1985-87, job search tng. seminar facilitator, 1987-89; elem. art tchr. Ft. Worth Ind. Sch. Dist., 1989-97; workshop leader North Tex. Getty Inst. Visual Arts Edn., 1992-94; tchr. elem. art Hurst-Euless-Bedford Ind. Sch. Dist., 1997—. Vol. Brownwood Cmty.Cultural Affairs Commn., 1980-82; coord. Tex. Rangers Baseball Club Summer Acad., 1997—. Marcus fellow Sch. Visual Arts, U. North Tex., 1995-96. Mem.: NAEA, NEA, Am. Fedn. Tchg. Profl., Tex. Art Edn. Assn., Tex. Classroom Tchrs. Assn., Alpha Rho Tau (sec. 1976—77). Republican. Baptist. Avocations: ceramics, drawing, writing, reading, sewing. Home: 6500 Red Bud Rd Fort Worth TX 76135-5372 Office: 1600 Donley Dr Euless TX 76039

MCCLURE, ERIN E., music educator; b. Rancocas, N.J., Sept. 12, 1983; d. Robert G. and Barbara L. McClure. MusB magna cum laude, William Paterson U., 2005. Asst. band dir. Red Bank Regional H.S., 2002—04; marching band staff mem. So. Regional H.S., Manahawkin, 2004; band dir. West Orange (N.J.) H.S., 2006—. Mem. Hawthorne Caballeros Drum and Bugle Corps, Hawthorne, NJ, 2001—03; clarinetist, bass clarinetist High Mountain Symphony, William Paterson U., Wayne, 2003—04. Edward J. Bloustein Disting. scholar, 2001—05, Presdl. scholar, William Paterson U., 2001—05. Mem.: NEA, N.J. Music Educators Assn., Music Educators' Nat. Conf., Sigma Alpha Iota. Avocation: drum corps. Office Phone: 973-669-5301 ext. 239. Business E-Mail: emcclure@woboe.org.

MCCLURE, EVELYN SUSAN, historian, photographer; b. Milw., Mar. 11, 1940; d. Henry F. and Blanche E. Schuster; m. John C. McClure, Oct. 26, 1967; 1 child, Heather. BS, U. Wis., Milw., 1964. Cert. fine art photography, U. Calif. Adminstrv. asst. Northwestern U., Chgo., 1964-66, KGO-TV, San Francisco, 1966-70, Crocker Bank, San Francisco, 1980-86, Wells Fargo Bank, San Francisco, 1986-93; pub. Belle View Press, Sebastopol, Calif., 1993—. Author, photographer: Sebastopol, California - History, Homes & People 1855-1920, 1995 (Historic Scholarship award Sonoma County Hist. Soc. 1997), Sebastopol's Historic Cemetery, 2000; columnist Sonoma West Times and News, Sebastopol, 1998-2005. Exhbn. com. Sebastopol Ctr. Arts, 1995-97; bd. mem., publicity chair, newsletter editor, vol. Western Sonoma County Hist. Soc., Sebastopol, 1996; curator W. Co. Mus., 1999—. Roman Catholic. Avocation: gardening. E-mail: belleview@monitor.net.

MCCLURE, JULIE ANNE, literature educator; b. Naperville, Ill., Mar. 9, 1967; d. Paul Robert and Linda Kay (Schlytter) McClure. BS in English, No. Ariz. U., 1989; AA in Paralegal Studies, Am. Inst., Phoenix, Ariz., 1991. Cert. tchr. Ill., Ariz. Paralegal/payroll profl. Corp. Personnel Svcs., Phoenix, 1992—92; paralegal Robert A. Kelley Jr. & Assocs., Scottsdale, Ariz., 1993—94; English educator Long Wood Acad., Chgo., 1998—99; corp. sec. MacWilliams Corp., Benton Harbor, Mich., 1993—; English educator Maria H.S., Chgo., 1999—. Office: Regina Dominican High Sch 701 Locust Rd Wilmette IL 60091-2298

MCCLURE, TERI PLUMMER, lawyer; b. Kansas City, Kans., Dec. 31, 1963; m. Roderick McClure; 2 children. BS, BA, Washington U., 1985; JD, Emory U., 1988. Bar: Ga. 1988. Employment counsel United Parcel Svc. Inc., 1995—98, coord. labor and practice group, 1998—2003, mgr. ctrl. Fla. dist., 2003—05, gen. counsel, sr. v.p., mgmt. com. mem., 2005—. Bd. dirs. Jr. Achievement Ga., Anne E. Casey Found., UPS Found., Ctr. for Working Families. Mem.: Nat. Employment Law Counsel (mem. coord. com.), State Bar Ga. (mem. labor and employment law sect.), Am. Corp. Counsel Assn., Atlanta Bar Assn. Office: United Parcel Svc Inc 55 Glenlake Pkwy NE Atlanta GA 30328*

MCCLURG, PATRICIA A., minister; b. Bay City, Tex., Mar. 14, 1939; d. T.H. and Margaret (Smith) McC. BA, Austin Coll., 1961; M in Christian Edn., Presbyn. Sch. of Christian Edn., 1963; BD, Austin Presbyn. Theol. Sem., 1967; postgrad., So. Meth. U., 1971-73; DD (hon.), Austin Coll., 1978. Dir. Christian edn. 2d Presbyn. Ch., Newport News, Va., 1963-65; asst. pastor Westminster Presbyn. Ch., Beaumont, Tex., 1967-69; assoc. pastor 1st Presbyn. Ch., Pasadena, Tex., 1969-71; assoc. exec. Synod of Red River, Denton, Tex., 1973-75; dir. gen. assembly mission bd. Presbyn. Ch., Atlanta, 1975-86; assoc. exec. for mission The Presbytery of Elizabeth, Plainfield, N.J., 1986-91; exec. presbyter Presbytery of New Castle, Newark, Del., 1992—2001. Pres. Nat. Coun. Chs. of Christ in the U.S.A., N.Y.C., 1988-89, v.p., 1985-87; del., budget com. chmn. World Coun. Chs. Assembly, Vancouver, Can., 1985; sect. leader World Coun. Chs. Mission and Evang. Confs., Melbourne, Australia, 1980. Contbr. articles to prof. jours. Mem. chs. spl. commn. on South Africa, N.Y.C., 1985—, Anti-Pollution Campaign, Pasadena, 1970. Recipient Disting. Alumni award Austin Coll., 1979. Mem.: Rotary. Democrat. Presbyterian. Avocations: shell collecting, reading, minor house repairs.

MCCLYMONDS, JEAN ELLEN, marketing professional; b. Richmond, Calif. d. Rollin John Lepley and Doris Ellen Baughman; m. Gareth Lynn McClymonds, Sept. 18, 1981. BS in Edn., U. Calif., Berkeley, 1970; M Bus. Communications, San Jose State U., 1987. Adminstr. sales Dohrmann Div. Envirotech, Santa Clara, Calif., 1970-74; supr. order processing Molectron Corp., Sunnyvale, Calif., 1974-79; mgr. mktg. svcs. Gould-Biomation, Santa Clara, 1979-84; dir. corp. communications Madic Corp., Santa Clara, 1984-86; dir. mktg. nat. accounts Skyway Freight Systems, Inc., Watsonville, Calif., 1986-89; pres. Just Mktg., Sonora, Calif., 1989—. Pub. speaker various local orgns., 1984—. Contbr. articles industry jours., 1986—. Mem. Am. Trucking Assn. (outstanding svc. award 1997), Bus. Profl. Advt. Assn., Nat. Assn. Quality Control, Coun. Logistics Mgmt. Republican. Avocations: speaking, dance, travel. Office: 18440 Olov Rd Sonora CA 95370 Office Phone: 209-533-7800. Personal E-mail: justmktng@aol.com.

MCCOLGAN, ELLYN, investment company executive; b. Jersey City; BA in Psychology, Montclair State Coll., NJ; MBA, Harvard Bus. Sch. With Shearson Lehman Bros., NYC, 1983, Bank of New Eng., Fidelity Brokerage Co., 1990—, pres. fin. fidelity intermediary svcs., pres., 2002—. Mem. bd. dir. Securities Industry Assn. Trustee Babson Coll. Named one of 50 Most Powerful Women in Bus., Fortune mag., 2006. Office: Fidelity Investments 82 Devonshire Boston MA 02109 Office Phone: 617-563-7000. Office Fax: 617-476-6152.*

MCCOLL, TERRIE LEE, library director; b. Hackensack, NJ, Sept. 12, 1957; d. Paul and Beverly Ann Harrsch; m. William Michael Ashley, Nov. 26, 1976 (div. Apr. 30, 2002); children: Emily Ashley Haberman, Austin James Ashley; m. William Grady McColl, May 26, 2003. AA in Broadcasting, Bergen C.C., Paramus, NJ, 1989; BA in Philosophy, Columbia U., 1993; MLS, Pratt Inst., 1996. Libr. asst. Am. Mus. Natural History, N.Y.C., 1982—87; media asst. Met. Opera, N.Y.C., 1987—94; supr. access svcs. Barnard Coll., N.Y.C., 1989—97; head, access svcs. Hunter Coll., N.Y.C., 1997—2000; libr. dir. Palisades Pk. (NJ) Pub. Libr., 2000—. Mem. selection com. Works by Women: Film and Video Festival Barnard Coll., N.Y.C., 1989—90; del. for Hunter Coll. Libr. Assn. of City of NY, 1998—99; evening session coun., del. for libr. Hunter Coll., N.Y.C., 1997—98, circulation roundtable CUNY, 1998—2000, faculty del. assembly, del. for libr., 1999—2000; mem. ESL com. Bergen County Coop. Libr. Sys., NJ, 2003—, policy and procedures com., NJ, 2004—, outreach com. mem., NJ, 2005—. Warden, vestry mem. All Saints Episc. Ch., Leonia, NJ, 1999—2005. Mem.: ALA, NJ. Libr. Assn., Pub. Libr. Assn. Episcopalian. Avocation: travel. Office: Palisades Pk Pub Libr 257 2nd St Palisades Park NJ 07650 Office Phone: 201-585-4150. Office Fax: 201-585-2151. E-mail: mccoll@bccls.org.

MCCOLLAM, MARION ANDRUS, consulting firm executive, educator; b. New Orleans, Feb. 8, 1931; d. Gerald Louis and Lucile Gordon (Isacks) Andrus; m. Andrew McCollam, Jr., Jan. 29, 1955 (div. 1978); children: Andrew III, Gerald Andrus, Marion Cage. BA, Tulane U., 1952; M. Urban and Reg. Planning, U. New Orleans, 1978. Human affairs coord. Office of the Mayor, City of New Orleans, 1978, arts coord., 1978-80; dir. planning, prin. cons. Duncan Plaza Design Project, New Orleans, 1978-80; dir. planning Downtown Devel. Dist., New Orleans, 1980-81; pres. Andrus and Roberts Inc., Phoenix, New Orleans, 1980-84; exec. dir. Arts Coun. New Orleans, 1981-90, Cultural Arts Coun. of Houston and Harris County, 1991-98; pres. McCollam Cons., LLC, 1998—. Adj. lectr. in arts adminstrn. Goucher Coll., 1998—2004, mem. nat. adv. com., 2005—; cons. in field. Mem. nat. adv. com. Working Capital Fund, Mpls., 1995-99, Nat. Arts Stabilization, Balt., 1998—; adv. panel design Nat. Endowment for the Arts, Washington, 1995, adv. and chair local arts agencies, 1992-94; bd. dirs., sr. fellow Am. Leadership Forum, Houston, 1994-2000; mem. cmty. assessment com. United Way of Tex. Gulf Coast, 1995-99; bd. dirs. Urban League of New Orleans, 1984-89; pres. Jr. League of New Orleans, 1969-70. Recipient Arts Adminstr. of Yr. award Arts Mgmt. Inst./Nat. News Svc., 1987, Award for Sustained Mgmt. Excellence, Greater New Orleans Found., 1989. Mem. Am. Inst. Cert. Planners, AIA (hon.), U.S. Urban Arts Fedn. (pres. 1988), Nat. Assembly of Local Arts Agencies (vice chmn. bd. dirs. 1988-94, Chairman's award 1992). Avocations: music, art, reading, travel. Office: 1914 Bissonnet St Houston TX 77005-1645

MCCOLLAM, SHARON L., retail executive; BS in Acctg. CPA. Former acctg. Ernst and Young; divisional v.p., CFO Dole Food Co., Inc., 1993—2000; v.p. fin. Williams-Sonoma, Inc., San Francisco, 2000—01, sr. v.p., CFO, 2001—03, exec. v.p., CFO, 2003—. Office: Williams-Sonoma Inc 3250 Van Ness Ave San Francisco CA 94109

MCCOLLIN, MICHELLE J., special education educator; d. Henry and Janet McCollin. BS, Syracuse U., 1986; MEd in Early Childhood and Elem. Edn., LI U., Bklyn., 1988; PhD in Spl. Edn., So. U. and A & M Coll., 2004. Asst. prof. Slippery Rock U., Slippery Rock, Pa., 2004—; ednl. adminstr. sr.

level NYC Bd. Edn., Bklyn., 1989—2004. Cons./motivational spkr. McCollin & Associates, Slippery Rock, Pa. Adv. bd. mem. LRE Adv. Panel for Gaskin's Case, Harrisburgh, Pa., 2005; chair of ednl. comm. NAACP-National Assn. for the Advancement of Colored People, Meadville, PR, 2006; bd. mem. Butler (Pa.) Assn. Retarded Citizens, 2006. Named Collegiate All Am. scholar-at large, US Achievement Acad., 2004; recipient City Coun. Citation, NYC Coun., 2000, Nat. Collegiate Edn. award, US Achievement Acad., 2004; Minority Doctoral fellow, U.S. Dept. Edn., 2002—04. Mem.: NAACP (life; chmn. ednl. com. 2006—), Coun. Exceptional Children (assoc.; chmn. membership com. 2004). Republican. Avocations: singing, travel, reading, dancing. Home: 284 Kelly Blvd Slippery Rock PA 16057 Office: Slippery Rock U 105 Dinger Hall-Special Education Bldg Slippery Rock PA 16057 Office Phone: 724-738-2462. Office Fax: 724-738-4395. Personal E-mail: mjmccollin@aol.com. Business E-Mail: michelle.mccollin@sru.edu.

MCCOLLUM, BETTY, congresswoman; b. Mpls., July 12, 1954; m. Douglas McCollum; 2 children. BS in Edn., Coll. St. Catherine, 1987. Retail store mgr., Minn.; mem. Minn. Ho. Reps., 1992-2000, mem. edn. com., environ. and natural resources com., mem. gen. legis. com., vet. affairs and elections com., mem. transportation and transit com., asst. majority leader, chair legis. commn. on econ. status of women, mem. rules and adminstrv. legis. com.; mem. U.S. Congress from Minn. 4th Dist., Washington, 2001—; mem. edn. and workforce com., resources com.; mem. Com. on Internat. Relations. Mem. St. Croix Valley Coun. Girl Scouts. Mem.: Am. Legion Aux., VFW Aux. Democrat. Office: US Ho Reps 1029 Longworth Ho Office Bldg Washington DC 20515-2304

MCCOLLUM, JEAN HUBBLE, medical technician; b. Peoria, Ill., Oct. 21, 1934; d. Claude Ambrose and Josephine Mildred (Beiter) Hubble; m. Everett Monroe Patton, Sept. 4, 1960 (div. Jan. 1969); 1 child, Linda Joanne; m. James Ward McCollum, Jan. 2, 1971; 1 child, Steven Ward. Student, Bradley U., Ill. Cen. Coll. Stenographer Caterpillar Tractor Co., Peoria, 1952-53, supr. stenographer pool, 1953-55, adminstrv. sec., treas., 1955-60, sec., asst. dept. mgr., 1969-71; med. staff sec. Proctor Cmty. Hosp., Peoria, 1978-82; med. asst. Drs. Taylor, Fox and Morgan, Peoria, 1982-84; freelance med. asst. Meth. Hosp. and numerous physicians, Peoria, 1984-89; office mgr. bus. office Dr. Danehower, McLelland and Stone, Peoria, 1989—2006. Vol. tutor Northmoor Sch., Peoria, 1974-78; bd. dirs., mem. exec. com., chmn. patient rels. com., com. chmn. Planned Parenthood, Peoria, 1990-92; judge Region 2 Ill. State History Fair, Bradley U., 2004, 05; hon. mem. scholarship com. Am. Indian Edn. Found. Recipient Outstanding Performance award Proctor Hosp., 1981, also various awards for svc. to schs., ch. and hosps. for mentally ill. Mem. Nat. Wildlife Fedn., Mensa Internat. (publs. officer, scholarship com., editor 1987-89, scholar com. 1993), Mothers League (treas. 1977), Willow Knolls Country Club (social com. 1989-90), Nature Conservancy (Seasons of the River event com. 2000—), World Wildlife Fund, Forest Park Found., Nat. Trust for Historic Preservation, Natural Resources Def. Coun., Religious Coalition for Reproductive Rights, USO, Am. Indian Educators Found. (hon., scholar com. 2004). Methodist. Avocations: reading, travel, theater, yoga. Home: 6501 N Brookwood Ln Peoria IL 61614-2401

MCCOMB, LEANN MARIE, middle school educator; b. Port Angeles, Wash., Feb. 18, 1956; d. George and Dorothy (Fiddler) McC. BA in Hist., Seattle Pacific U., 1979, postgrad., 1983. Tchr. Stevens Middle Sch., Port Angeles, 1979—, outdoor edn. coord., 1981—, history day coord., 1982—, adv. coord., 1982-86. Regional contest coord. Nat. History Day in Wash. State, 1985—, exec. com. mem., 1986—, vice chmn., 1988-89, sec., 1988-89, contest judge, 1989-90, state chmn., 1990—; dist. instl. material secretion com. mem., Port Angeles, 1985—; mem. social studies dist. curriculum com., 1990—. Participant World Trade Seminar, Wash. State Econ. Coun., 1987. Active Stevens Bldg. Drug and Alcohol Team, Port Angeles, 1988—; dist. rep. PRIDE Drug. Conf., Orlando, Fla., 1990; childrens' ch. tchr. Ind. Bible Ch., Port Angeles, 1988—; vol. leader Young Life on Olympic Peninsula, Port Angeles, 1989-92. Recipient Inst. award NEH, 1991, Wash. State History Tchr. of Merit award, 1992, Inst. World War II, Dept. Def., 1993. Mem. NEA, Nat. Coun. Social Studies, Wash. Edn. Assn., Wash. State Coun. Social Studies, Port Angeles Edn. Assn., Delta Kappa Gamma Upsilon Chpt. Avocations: reading, cooking, crocheting, hiking. Home: 1026 W 11th St Port Angeles WA 98363-7209

MCCOMBS, KELLY FRITZ, dietician; b. Flemington, N.J., Sept. 23, 1968; d. John Frederick Fritz III and Joy Elaine Gallagher; m. Timothy Ronald McCombs, Aug. 31, 1996. BS, Ohio State U., 1997, MS, 1999. Cert. pharmacy technician. Pharmacy technician Riverside Meth. Hosp., Columbus, Ohio, 1989-99, med. rsch. asst., 1996-99; oncology pharmacy technician St. Anthony Regional Oncology Ctr., Columbus, 1990-91; intern Ohio State U., 1998—99; family and consumer sci. agt. N.C. Coop. Ext., Elizabeth City, 1999—2002; diabetes and health promotion dietitian Albemarle Regional Diabetes Care, Elizabeth City, 2003—. Co-author: Jour. Food Quality. Recipient Florence Hall award, 2000, Early Career award, 2002. Mem.: Am. Diabetes Assn., Coastal Diabetes Educators Assn., N.C. Extension Assn. Family and Consumer Scis., Soc. Nutrition Educators, N.C. Dietetic Assn., Am. Dietetic Assn., Elizabeth City Jr. Women's Club. Avocations: gardening, cooking.

MCCONNELL, MARY JOAN, civilian military employee; b. McCormick, S.C., Oct. 3, 1946; d. John Leslie and Annie Ruby (White) McConnell; m. Akhilesh Kumar, Dec. 15, 1979 (div. Dec. 1999). BA in English, Lander Coll., 1976. Civil service employee Randolph Air Force Base, San Antonio, 1983—2004; ret., 2004. Personal E-mail: bittymcc@aol.com, mmcconnell5@satx.rr.com.

MCCONNELL, MARY PATRICIA, lawyer; b. Mpls., Sept. 30, 1952; BS, U. Minn., 1978; JD, William Mitchell Coll. Law, St. Paul, 1984. Bar: Minn. 1988. Sr. biologist C.E., U.S. Army, St. Paul, 1979-84; asst. county atty. Dakota County, Hastings, Minn., 1985—92; ptnr. Lindquist & Vennum, Mpls., 1992—95; from v.p. environ. and regulatory affairs to sr. v.p., gen. counsel, sec. Genmar Holdings, Inc., 1995—2002; gen. counsel control products divsn. Honeywell, 2002—03; v.p., gen. counsel Polaris Industries, Inc., Medinia, Minn., 2003—. Master gardener U. Minn. Ext., St. Paul, 1992—. Contbr. articles to profl. jours. Dir. Wetlands Forum, Mpls., 1990—. Mem. Minn. Bar Assn. (governing coun. environ. and natural resources 1990—, law sect.), Mpls. C. of C. (Leadership Mpls. 1992). Office: Polaris Industries Inc 2100 Highway 55 Medina MN 55340 Office Phone: 763-542-0500. Office Fax: 763-542-0599. E-mail: mary.mcconnell@polarisind.com.

MCCONNELL SERIO, SUZIE THERESA, former professional basketball player, professional basketball coach; b. Pitts., July 29, 1966; married; 4 children. BA, Pa. State U., 1988. Coach Oakland Cath. High Sch., Pitts.; guard Cleve. Rockers, WNBA, 1998—2000; head coach Oakland Cath. H.S., 1990—2003, Minn. Lynx, WNBA, 2003—. Recipient Gold medal Olympic Games, Barcelona, 1988, Bronze medal Olympic Games, Seoul, 1992, Sportsmanship award WNBA, 1998, 1999, Newcomer award, 1998; named to All-WNBA 1st team, 1988. Office: Minn Lynx 600 First Ave North Minneapolis MN 55403

MCCONNEY, MARY E., information technology executive; BA in physics & Environ. Studies, Whitman Coll., 1976; M in Econ., U. Pa., 1979, M in Urban Planning, 1980, PhD in Spatial Econ., 1983. Applied statistician U. Wash., 1977—85, U. Pa., 1977—85; applied statistician & database design NAS, 1985—88; pres. HiroSoft Internat. Corp., 1988—; CFO Sunhawk.com, Seattle, 1992—99, treas., 1999—; with Freehand Systems, Inc. Contbr. articles to profl. jours. Office: Freehand Music Inc 1463 E Republican St Seattle WA 98112-4517

MCCONNON, VIRGINIA FIX, dietician; b. Aberdeen, S.D., July 20, 1932; d. Lavern Clyde and Janette Clare (Schmidt) Fix; m. Thomas James McConnon, Oct. 28, 1955; children: James Renaud, John Thomas, Paul Wilson. BS in Home Econ. (hon.), S.D. State U., Brookings, 1954. Registered dietitian Am. Dietetic Assn., 1955; cert. dietitian/nutritionist, N.Y., 1995. Dietetic intern U. Minn. Hosps., Mpls., 1955; therapeutic dietitian Northwestern Hosp., Mpls., 1955; dietitian Riley County Hosp., Manhattan, Kans., 1956; cons. dietitian Chautauqua County Office for the Aging, Mayville, N.Y., 1975-89. Treas. Aging Svcs. Dietitians of N.Y. State, 1976-90; mem. Chautauqua County Nutrition Coun., 1990-98. Bd. dirs. Hall Meml. Housing Corp., Jamestown, N.Y., 1995-2001, 03—, Harbor House, Jamestown, 1975-80, Chautauqua Region Multiple Sclerosis Soc., Jamestown, 1983-86, Chautauqua Area Adult Day Care Ctrs., Jamestown, Dunkirk and Westfield, N.Y., 1990—; ch. clk., 1990-93, 2004—, diaconate, 1993-96, mem. ch. coun., 1997-2006, ch. choir, 1946—. Named Chautauqua County Sr. Citizen of Yr., 1995. Mem. Am. Dietetic Assn., N.Y. State Dietetic Assn., Western N.Y. Dietetic Assn. Republican. Congregationalist. Avocations: singing, bridge, reading, travel. Home: 4465 Baker Street Ext Lakewood NY 14750-9762 E-mail: mcconnon@stny.rr.com.

MCCOOK, KATHLEEN DE LA PEÑA, librarian, educator; b. Chgo. d. Frank Eugene and Margaret L. (de la Peña) McEntee; m. Philip G. Heim, Mar. 20, 1972 (div.); 1 child, Margaret Marie; m. William Woodrow Lee McCook, Oct. 12, 1991; stepchildren: Cecilia, Billie Jean, Nicole. BA, U. Ill., Chgo.; MA, Marquette U., U. Chgo.; PhD, U. Wis.-Madison. Reference librarian Elmhurst Coll. Libr., Ill.; dir. pub. svcs. Dominican U., River Forest, Ill.; lectr. U. Wis., Madison; asst. prof. library sci. U. Ill., Urbana; dean, prof. La. State U. Sch. Libr. and Info. Sci., Baton Rouge; dean grad. sch. La. State U.; dir. Sch. Libr. and Info. Sci., U. South Fla., 1993-99, prof., 1993—, coord. cmty. outreach, 2000—02, disting. univ. prof., 2002—; McCusker lectr. Dominican U., 2003—. Author: (wth K. Weibel) Role of Women in Librarianship, 1978, (with L. Estabrook) Career Profiles, 1983, (with William E. Moen) Occupational Entry, 1989, Adult Services, 1990, (with Gary O. Rolstad) Developing Readers' Advisory Services, 1993, Toward a Just and Productive Soc., 1994, Opportunities in Library and Information Science, 1997, (with B. Ford) Global Reach: Local Touch, 1998, Women of Color in Librarianship, 1998, (with B. Immroth) Library Services to Youth of Hispanic Heritage, 2000, A Place at the Table, 2000, Introduction To Public Libraries, 2004; mem. editl. bd. Cath. Lib. World Jour., 2005—; contbr. essays to books, articles to profl. jours. Chmn. Equal Rights Amendment Task Force, Ill., 1977-79, South Count Coalition for Cmty. Concerns, 1996-; active Eugene McCarthy campaign, U. Ill., Chgo., 1968, Bill Clinton campaign, 1992, 96, Al Gore campaign, 2000, Bill McBride campaign, Fla., 2002; Betty Castor campaign, 2004; John F. Kerry campaign, 2004; mem. La. Gov.'s Commn.for Women, 1985-88; bd. dirs. La. Endowment for Humanities, 1991-92; mem. exec. bd. Rural Social Svcs. Partnership, Hillsborough County, 1998-2001; mem. dem. exec. com., Hillsborough County, 2001-04; dem. del. Fla. State Convention, 2002-03; Ruskin Neigborhood Adv. Com., Fla., 2003-, Hillsborough County, Citizen's Action Bd., 2004—; mem. collective bargaining com. United Faculty Fla., 2003-; mem. Cmty. Action Bd., 2004—. Recipient Disting. Alumnus award U. Wis., 1991, award of merit Trejo Foster Found., 1999; named Bradshaw scholar Tex. Woman's Univ., 1994; named scholar in residence Chgo. Pub. Libr., 2003. Mem. ALA (com. chmn. 1980—, editor RQ jour. 1982-88, Pub. Librs. Jour. 1989-90, Am. Librs. adv. com. 1994-96, contbg. editor Am. Librs. 1999-2001, column editor RUSQ 2000-06, Notable Books Coun. 2001-06), Progressive Librs. Guild. (coord. com., editl. bd., 2005—), REFORMA (bd. dirs. 1997-98, Latino Libr. of Yr. 2002, Equality award 1987, Monroe Adult Svc. award 1991, Futas Catalyst for Change award 1998, Achievement in Diversity Rsch. award 2004), Assn. for Libr. and Info. Sci. Edn. (com. chmn. 1981—, pres. 1987-88, Pres. award 1997), Fla. Libr. Assn. (bd. dirs. 1995-98, Transformer award 1996), Tampa Bay Libr. Consortium (bd. dirs. 1994-97), Women Libr. Workers, Ruskin Civic Assn. (sec. 1997-99), Ill. Libr. Assn. (treas. 1981-83), Progressive LIbrarians Guild (coord. com. 2004-06), Beta Phi Mu (50th Anniversary Disting. Mem. 1999, Dist. Lectr. award 2002, Disting. Svc. to Edn. for Librarianship 2003), Cath. Libr. Assn. (Brubaker award for Outstanding Article 2003). Democrat. Roman Catholic. Avocation: reading. Office: U South Fla Sch Libr and Info Sci 4202 E Fowler Ave Stop CIS1040 Tampa FL 33620-7800 Personal E-mail: kmccook@tampabay.rr.com.

MCCOOL, COURTNEY, Olympic athlete; b. Kansas City, Apr. 1, 1988; Mem. U.S. Nat. Gymnastics Team, 2002—; gymnast Team USA, Athens Olympic Games, 2004. Achievements include mem. U.S. Championship Team, Pan Am. Games, 2003; invention of Athens Test Event, 1st in all-around, 2004; Silver medal, Olympics. Office: c/o USOC One Olympic Plz Colorado Springs CO 80909

MCCORD, FRANCINE NICHOLE, elementary school educator; b. Sweetwater, Tenn., Dec. 23, 1979; d. Debbie Laurine and Gary Lynn Scruggs (Stepfather); m. Adriel D.J. McCord, June 8, 2002; 1 child, Jaydan Cole. BA, Maryville Coll., Tenn., 2002; MA, Lincoln Meml. U., Harrogate, Tenn., 2004, Edn. Specialist degree, 2005. Tchr. math. and sci. Maryville Mid. Sch., Maryville, 2002—06. Coach cheerleading Maryville Mid. Sch., 2002—06. Children's leader First Bapt. Ch., Maryville, 2002—06. Home: 1602 Manheim Circle Maryville TN 37804

MCCORD, JEAN ELLEN, art educator; b. Ilion, NY, Oct. 20, 1952; d. Harold Shepard and Marian Alice (Bernier) Shepard; m. Colin McCord, May 10, 1977 (div. Sept. 1993). AA, Mohawk Valley C.C., Utica, NY, 1972; BA, SUNY, New Paltz, 1975, postgrad., 1976—77; student, Coll. Santa Reparata Sch. Art, Florence, Italy, 2001. Cert. art educator, NY. Jr. kindergarten tchr. Norfolk (Va.) Naval Base, 1978-79; jr. kindergarten and art tchr. Sunnybrook Day Sch., Virginia Beach, Va., 1979-81; tchr. art Fisher Elem. Sch., Mohawk, NY, 1982-84, Mechanicstown Sch., Middletown, NY, 1984-88, Middletown Start Ctr., 1986-87; tchr. art, synergetic edn. Middletown Tchr. Ctr., 1986-87; pvt. portfolio tutor Middletown, 1989-91; tchr. art Middletown Elem. Summer Sch., 1989—, Middletown H.S., 1987-97; tchr. Maple Hill Elem., 1997—; instr. Creative Studio, Middletown, 2006. Sec. of policy and exec. bds. Middletown Tchr. Ctr., 1988—91, chmn. policy and exec. bds., 1991—92, mem. policy bd., 2004—; com. mem. Bicentennial of Edn.; advisor Nat. Art Honor Soc., 1989—97; coord. After Sch. Program for Youth at Risk, 1995—; tchr., curriculum writer for interdisciplinary art, 1992—94; creator 3-vol. curriculum companion, 2004; internat. com. for comm. Cambridge U., 2001, Cultural Ednl. Exch., Japan, U.S., 2004; coord. 1st child's sculpture garden by children Maple Hill Elem. Sch.; presenter in field; collaborator with Ryoyu Takeda A Whispering Wind from Kasami Village (poetry book), 2004. Actress, vocalist, designer in regional theatre, 1970—; artistic designer sch. plays and Creative Theatre Group; writer, dir. for local cabarets and charities; set designer (off broadway) in NYC including Mother Posture, Seedless Grapes, The Pelican, New Village Prodns. benefit for AIDS, marquee 1st Theatre Mus. Village, Monroe, NY; performer Cancer Soc. Fundraiser, 1997, John Brigham Meml. Scholarship Fundraiser, Ruthie Dino Marshall Fundraiser, others; prodr., dir. Follies/Toys for Tots Campaign, 1997; exhibited in shows Lisbon, Portugal, 2001, Paramount Theatre, Middletown, Cambridge, Eng., 2001, Vancouver, 2002, Middletown Ctr., 2004, Middletown Culture Ctr., 2004; executed mural Middletown H.S., 2001; set designer, Dracula, 2003, Twin Towers Mid. Sch. Mystery Dinner Theatre, 2005; set painter drama workshop Sullivan County, 2005. County svc. coord. Orange County Youth-In-Govt. (adv. 1988-91), Goshen, NY, 1991-93; Odyssey of the Mind Coach, 1984-92; chair edn. and cultural sem., Lisbon, Portugal, 1999; chair edn. and culture comm., Vancouver, Can.; art and music comm., Vancouver; chair, internat. comm. com. Internat. Edn. Culture Com.; mem. Internat. Art and Music Com., Vancouver, 2002, multi-cultural com., 2002-03, edn. and culture chair Dublin, Ireland, 2004, Honolulu, 2005; curriculum writer Middletown City Schs., 2003; mem. Wall of Tolerance, Birmingham, Ala., 2003; policy bd. Middletown Tchr. Ctr., 2004-06; founder 1st Children's Sculpture Garden, Maple Hill Sch., 2006. Named for outstanding set design Times Herald Record, 1994; honored by Bd. Edn. Outstanding Educator, 1992, Apple award, 1999; named in S.W. Arts Mag., 2001; recipient Legion of Honor award United Cultural Conv., 2005 Mem. Marine Corps League (hon.), NJROTC (hon. cadet 1997, Outstanding Contbn. to Arts award, Millenium Medal of Honor 2000), Am. Biog. Inst. (chmn. ednl. culture com. 1999, 2004-05, comm. com., chmn. edn. and culture com. 2002, art and music com., multicultural com. 2002, Educator Yr. 2003), World Peace Diplomacy Forum (founding mem.). Episcopalian. Avocations: theatrical design, singing, calligraphy. Home: PO Box 4429 Middletown NY 10941-8429 Office: Middletown City Schs Wisner Ave Middletown NY 10940 Personal E-mail: jmccord@hvc.rr.com. Business E-Mail: jmccord@ecsdm.org.

MCCORD, RITA RAE, elementary school educator; b. Cedar Rapids, Iowa, Aug. 18, 1979; d. Raymond Henry and Rena Krug; m. Richard Christopher McCord, July 15, 2000. BA in Elem. Edn., U. Iowa, Iowa City, 2003. Tchr. Hiawatha Elem. Sch., Iowa City, Iowa, 2003—. Grantee Sheila E. McFahrland scholarship, U. Iowa, 2003. Mem.: Internat. Reading Assn., Pi Lambda Theta.

MCCORDUCK, PAMELA ANN, writer, educator; b. Liverpool, Eng., Oct. 27, 1940; came to U.S., 1946; d. William John and Hilda May (Bond) McC.; m. Joseph F. Traub, Dec. 6, 1969. Lectr. Columbia U., 1980-90. Author: Familiar Relations, 1971, Working to the End, 1972, Machines Who Think, 1979, rev. 25th anniversary edit., 2004, The Fifth Generation, 1983, The Universal Machine, 1985, The Rise of the Expert Company, 1988, Aaron's Code, 1990, The Futures of Women, 1996. Mem. Am. PEN (bd. dirs. N.Y.C. chpt., 1986-94, v.p. 1994-96). Home: 445 Riverside Dr # 71 New York NY 10027-6801

MCCORKLE, PAMELA LOVERIDGE, elementary school educator; b. Augusta, Ga., Feb. 16, 1959; d. David Roger Loveridge, Sr. and Lucille Lucky Loveridge; m. Michael Wayne McCorkle; 1 stepchild, Jered 1 child, Caleb Stovall. B of Music Edn., Augusta State U., 1998. Cert. tchr. Pk-12 Ga. Music tchr. Columbia County Bd. Edn., Appling, Ga., 1998—2000, Harlem, Ga., 2000—. Recipient 1st pl. award, Nat. Assn. Tchrs. Singing, 1997, Louise Proctor Character Acting award, Augusta Players, 1989, Best Actress award, Augusta Players, 1993. Home: 4546 Glennwood Dr Evans GA 30809 Business E-Mail: pmccorkle@ccboe.net.

MCCORKLE, RUTH, oncological nurse, educator, researcher; BS, U. Md., 1968; MA, U. Iowa, 1972, PhD, 1975. Staff nurse CCU Vanvouver (Wash.) Med. Hosp., 1968-69; oncological clin. nurse specialist U. Iowa Hosps. and Clinics, Iowa City, 1971-73; instr. psychiat. nursing and oncological nursing Sch. Nursing, U. Iowa, Iowa City, 1974-75; from asst. prof. to prof. dept. cmty. health care sys. U. Wash., Seattle, 1975-85; prof. adult health and illness divsn. Sch. Nursing, U. Pa., Phila., 1986—98, chairperson, 1988-89, dir. Ctr. Advancing Care in Serious Illness, 1989—98, dir. cancer control Cancer Comprehensive Ctr., 1990-98; prof. nursing, chmn. doc program, dir. Ctr. Chronic Illness Sch. Yale U., New Haven, 1998—. Mem. nursing sci. rev. com. Nat. Ctr. Nursing Rsch., 1988-92. Contbr. articles to profl. jours. Fellow Am. Acad. Nursing; mem. ANA, NAS, Internat. Soc. Nurses Cancer Care (dir.-at-large 1983-89), Am. Assn. Cancer Edn., Am. Psychosocial Oncology Soc. (charter mem., dir.-at-large 1998-), Oncology Nursing Soc. (charter mem., mem. rsch. com. 1981-82, dir.-at-large 1983-85). Office: Yale U 100 Church St S PO Box 9740 New Haven CT 06536-0740 Business E-Mail: ruth.mccorkle@yale.edu.

MCCORMACK, LOWELL RAY, oil industry executive, corporate financial executive, consultant; b. Ladonia, Tex., Oct. 26, 1925; d. Lowell and Orianna (McDonnold) Coney; m. Paul H. McCormack, June 4, 1948; children: Sharron Ann, Lowell Henry. At, Rutherford Met. Coll., Dallas, 1962, U. Tex., Arlington and Dallas, Eastfield Coll., Dallas, Cooke County Coll., Gainesville, Tex., 1989—; AA, Wm. Alexander Art, 1991. Master graphoanalyst Internat. Graphoanalysis Soc. Bookeeper Jot-Em-Down Gin Corp., Pecan Gap, Tex., 1947, Shedd-Bartush Foods, Dallas, 1948—52; v.p. and sec.-treas. Safari Oil Co., 1954—88, pres., 1989—; acct. and credit mgr. J. P. Ashcraft Co., Inc., 1956—65; v.p., sec.-treas. and CFO Dallas Title Co., 1965—83; treas. First Nat. Bank, Cooper, Tex., 1986—87; pres. Scorpio Oil Co., 1987—. Treas. Butterfield Stage, Gainesville, Tex.; acctg. cons. to atty.; lectr. in field. Author: Stories of Growing Up in the Coney Family, 2005; featured writer Tex. State Hist. Assn. Web Site, 2005. Troop leader Girl Scouts USA, 1955—65; founder Yarn Spinners, Gainesville, Tex., 1988; mem. Newcomers Club, 1986—, pres., 1989—; columnist Cooke County Leader, 1988; founding mem. Gainesville Area Visual Arts; mem. Baptist Choir, Centennial Cir. Mem.: Internat. Platform Assn., North Tex. Oil and Gas Assn., Internat. Graphoanalysis Soc. (life; v.p. Tex. chpt. 1978, pres. 1979, Graphoanalyst of Yr. 1987, keynote spkr. 1987, Okla. seminar leader 1990), Red Hat. Soc., Crosstimbers Geneal. Soc., MENSA, Gainesville C. of C., Cooke County Heritage Soc., Kiwanis (one of 1st women mems. Gainesville chpt. 1988, v.p. 1990—91, pres. 1991—92), Zonta Club (co-chmn. fin. com. 1982, dir. and 2d v.p. 1983—84), Soroptimist Club, Toastmistress (pres. 1981, com. chmn. internat. conv 1984), Phi Theta Kappa (treas. Psi Iota chpt. 1990, acad. all-Am. 3d team for cmty. tech. and jr. colls. 1992). Baptist. Home: 631 S Lindsay St Gainesville TX 76240-5336 Personal E-mail: l.r.mccormack@sbcglobal.net.

MCCORMACK, PATRICIA MARIE, retired thoracic surgeon; b. Canton, Ohio, Mar. 5, 1929; d. Thomas Edward and Anna Agatha (Lhota) Fitzmaurice; m. John H. McCormack. BA, Manhattanville Coll., 1954; MD, Georgetown U., 1958. Resident in surgery St. Elizabeth's Hosp., Boston, 1958-61; chief med. officer Maryknoll Hosp., Hong Kong, 1961-71; surg. oncology officer Sloan-Kettering Meml. Hosp., N.Y.C., 1971-76, cardiothoracic resident, 1974-76; clin. asst. surgeon Sloan-Kettering Meml. Hosp. and N.Y. Hosp., N.Y.C., 1976-80, asst. surgeon, 1980-84, assoc. surgeon, 1984-93, attending surgeon, 1993—. Mem. peer rev. com. N.Y. County Med. Assn., 1985—. Author (book) Surgery for Metsto Lung, 1984; contbr. chpts. to books; contbr. articles to profl. jours. Fellow ACS, Am. Coll. Chest Physicians. Home: 9 Acorn Path P O Box 192 East Quogue NY 11942-4712 Office: Sloan-Kettering Meml Cancer Ctr 1275 York Ave New York NY 10021-6094

MCCORMACK, PATRICIA SEGER, editor, journalist; b. Pitts., June 11, 1927; d. Arthur John and Anne Irene (McCaffrey) Seger; m. Donald P. McCormack, Apr. 28, 1951; 1 son, Christopher Paul. BA, U. Pitts., 1949; certificate, A.P. Inst. Seminar, 1967. News editor weekly newspapers, Mt. Lebanon, Pa., 1950-52; med. editor Pitts. Sun Telegraph, 1952-57; med. sci. editor INS, N.Y.C., 1958-59; columnist, family, health and edn. editor UPI, 1959-84, sr. editor, 1987-90. Mem. Boy of Year selection com. Boys Clubs Am., 1966; mem. Coty Fashion award jury, 1965-72, nat. selection com. Century III Leader Scholarship Competition Nat. Assn. Secondary Sch. Prins., 1986. Recipient Biennial Media award Family Service Assn. Am., 1965, Freedom Found. medal; 1st place Sci. Writing award Am. Dental Assn., 1976; Nat. Media award United Negro Coll. Fund, 1977; John Swett award for disting. educating reporting Calif. Edn. Assn., 1981 Mem. Nat. Assn. Sci. Writers (life), Edn. Writers Assn., Women's Forum Inc. (N.Y.C.), Nat. Fedn. Press Women (Comm. Achievement medal 1993), Conn. Press Club (v.p., Communicator of Achievement 1993), Conn. Women's Forum., N.Y. Acad. Scis. Home and Office: PO Box 3539 Westport CT 06880-8539

MCCORMICK, CAROLYN, actress; b. Midland, Tex., Sept. 19, 1959; BFA with honors, Williams Coll.; MFA, Am. Conservatory Theatre; student, Ctr. d'Etudes Francais, Avignon, France. Actress Am. Conservatory Theatre Co., 1983-85, Denver Ctr. Theatre Co., 1989-90; newscaster Channel 39 News, Houston, 1976—77. Appearances include (films) Enemy Mine, 1985, Rain Without Thunder, 1993, A Simple Twist of Fate, 1994, Loverboy, 2004, Spectropia, 2004, (TV series) Spenser: For Hire, 1986-87, Law and Order, 1991-2006, Cracker, 1997, (TV movies) Victim of Rage, 1994, The Osiris Chronicles, (TV episodes) Star Trek: The Next Generation, 1988, 90, Homocide: Life on The Street, 1996, (stage) In Perpetuality Throughout the Universe, 1988-89, There's One in Every Marriage, 1988, The Importance of Being Earnest, 1988-89, Much Ado About Nothing, 1990-91, Dinner Party, 1999, Dinner with Friends, 1999, Evolution, 2004, Privilege, 2005, Celebration, 2005. Office: Bresler Kelly & Assocs 11500 W Olympic Blvd Ste 510 Los Angeles CA 90064-1578

MCCORMICK, DALE, state official; b. N.Y., Jan. 17, 1947; BA, U. Iowa, 1970. Mem. Maine State Senate from 18th dist, 1991-96; treas. State of Maine, Augusta, 1997—2004; dir. State Housing Aithority, Maine, 2004—. Author: Against the Grain, a Carpentry Manual for Women, 1977. Office: Maine State Housing Authority 353 Water St Augusta ME 04330-4633

MCCORMICK, DONNA LYNN, social worker; b. Austin, Minn., Aug. 13, 1944; d. Raymond Alois and Grace Eleanor (Hayes) Schrom; m. James Michael McCormick, Jan. 15, 1972. BA in Psychology, Coll. St. Catherine, 1966. Cert. substitute tchr. Camden County Coll., 2001. Caseworker Phila. County Bd. Pub. Assistance, 1968-70; sr. social worker San Francisco Dept. Human Svcs., 1986-97; interviewer dept. epidemiology and biostats. U. Pa., Phila., 1998-2000. Mem. Emily's List. Mem.: Nat Trust Hist. Preservation, San Francisco Opera Guild, Nat. Mus. Women Arts. Democrat. Avocations: reading, walking, wine tasting, memoir and letter writing, opera. Office Phone: 541-665-4854. Personal E-mail: jdcormick@charter.net.

MCCORMICK, KAREN LOUISE, savings and loan association executive; b. San Jose, Calif., Nov. 22, 1954; d. Clifford Kaye Jr. and Margaret Elizabeth (Bigler) McC.; children: Crystal DeAnne, Sheralyn Rose McCormick. Grad. high sch., Mountain View, Calif., 1973; cert. Inst. Fin. Edn., Ariz. State U., 1987. Cashier, loan officer Santa Clara County Employees' Credit Union, San Jose, 1973-77; teller, loan officer First Fed. Savs. & Loan Assn. Port Angeles, Wash., 1977-83, v.p., br. mgr., 1983-87, v.p., adminstr. loan prodn., 1987-89, v.p., ass. dir. lending, 1989-90, sr. v.p., dir. lending, 1990—97, pres., CEO, 1997—. Bd. dirs., chair opns. com. Wash. Community Reinvestment Assn., Seattle, 1992-95.; mem. Wash. Savs. League Affordable Housing com., 1991; vice chair Wash. Fin. League, 2003-; chair bd. dirs. WFL Services (subsid. corp. of Wash. Fin. League), 2003-; past bd. mem. & pres. Thrift Inst. Adv. Coun. Contbr. articles to newspapers, 1989-91. Bd. dirs. Clallam County YMCA, 1992-95, Diversified Industries, Inc., Port Angeles, 1985-87, Port Angeles C of C; mem. Queen of Angels sch. bd., 1988-90; co-founder Olympic Peninsula Housing Coalition, 1992—; treas. Peninsula Coll. Found., past pres. Nor'Wester Rotary Club of Port Angeles. Named one of The Top 25 Most Powerful Women in Banking, US Banker mag., 2003. Mem.: America's Cmty. Bankers (pres. 2003). Avocations: creative writing, reading, music, travel. Office: First Fed Savs Port Angeles PO Box 351 Port Angeles WA 98362-0055

MCCORMICK, KATHRYN ELLEN, prosecutor; b. Milw., Dec. 27, 1952; d. James Patrick and Kathryn Goss McCormick; 1 child, Joshua Patrick-Edwin Davis. BS cum laude, Ariz. State U., 1989; JD, U. Ariz., 1994. Bar: Ariz. 1994, U.S. Dist. Ct. Ariz. 1994; cert. peace officer Ariz. Police officer Scottsdale Police Dept., Ariz., 1972—77; investigator Maricopa County Atty.'s Office, Phoenix, 1977—80; spl. agt. Ariz. Atty. Gen.'s Office, Phoenix, 1980—91; def. atty. Maricopa County Pub. Defenders Office, Phoenix, 1994—98; prosecutor Securities divsn. Ariz. Corp. Commn., Phoenix, 1998—2002; dep. county atty. Office of County Counsel Govt. Rels., Phoenix, 2002—. Mem. consumer protection com. Ariz. State Bar, Phoenix, 1999—, mem. UPL adv. com., 2003—. Mem., former pres. Tumbleweed Ctr. for Youth Devel., Phoenix, 1998—; commr. Phoenix Women's Commn., 1999—. Named Police Office of the Yr., Phoenix Exchange Club, 1975. Mem.: Ariz. Alliance for the Mentally Ill, Nat. Alliance for the Mentally Ill, Ariz. Women Lawyers Assn. Avocations: gardening, swimming, hiking, reading. Home: 2034 W Edgemont Phoenix AZ 85009-1944 Office: Office of County Counsel 222 North Central Ste 1100 Phoenix AZ 85004 Office Phone: 602-506-8581. Business E-Mail: mccormk@mcao.maricopa.gov.

MCCORMICK, MARGARET C., science educator; b. Albany, N.Y., Sept. 1, 1978; d. Regina and Alfred McCormick. BS Biology, Bucknell U., Lewisburg, Pa., 2000; MA in tchg. secondary sci., Tchrs. Coll. Columbia U., N.Y.C., 2002. Cert. Tchr. Gen. Sci., Biology, Chemistry N.Y. Tchr. sci. Edgemont H.S., Scarsdale, NY, 2003—. Grantee development project, Greening of Edgemont, Scarsdale Tchrs. Inst., 2005. Mem.: N.Y. State Sci. Tchrs. Home: 346 Richbell Rd Mamaroneck NY 10543 Personal E-mail: maggie_c_mccormick@hotmail.com.

MCCORMICK, MARIE CLARE, pediatrician, educator; b. Winchester, Mass., Jan. 7, 1946; d. Richard John and Clare Bernadine (Keleher) McC.; m. Robert Jay Blendon, Dec. 30, 1977. BA magna cum laude, Emmanuel Coll., 1967, LHD (hon.), 2006; MD, Johns Hopkins U., 1971, ScD, 1978; MA, Harvard U., 1991; D of Humane Letters (hon.), Emmanuel Coll., Boston, 2006. Diplomate Am. Bd. Pediat. Pediatric resident, fellow Johns Hopkins Hosp., Balt., 1971-75, rsch. fellow, 1972-75; asst. prof. U. Ill. Schs. Medicine & Pub. Health, Chgo., 1975-76; pediat. instr. Johns Hopkins Med. Sch., Balt., 1976-78; asst. prof. healthcare orgn. Johns Hopkins Sch. Hygiene & Pub. Health, 1978-81; asst. prof. pediat. U. Pa., Phila., 1981-86, assoc. prof. pediat., 1986-87, Harvard Med. Sch., Boston, 1987-91, prof. pediat., 1992—, 1st Sumner and Esther Feldberg prof. maternal/child health, 1996—; prof. Harvard Sch. Pub. Health, Boston, 1992—2003, chair maternal and child health, 1992—2003, prof. Soc., Human Devel. and Health, 2003—. Adj. assoc. prof. pediat. U. Pa., 1987-92; active attending physician, Johns Hopkins Hosp., 1976-81, asst. physician Children's Hosp. Phila., 1981-84, assoc. physician, 1984-86, sr. physician, 1986-87, assoc. pediatrician Brigham & Women's Hosp., 1987—; sr. assoc. in medicine Children's Hosp., 1987—; sr. assoc. in pediat. Beth Israel Deaconess Med. Ctr., 1987—; vis. prof. Wash. U., St. Louis, 1993; editl. bds. Health Svcs. Rsch., 1985-94, Pediat. in Rev., 1986-91, Pediat., 1993-99; assoc. editor Jour. Ambulatory Pediatric Assn., 1999—; adv. coun. Ctr. Perinatal & Family Health Brigham & Women's Hosp., 1991—; cons. to numerous coms., orgns. and bds. Contbr. articles to profl. jours. Adv. The David and Lucile Packard Found., 1993-95; bd. dirs. Family Planning Coun. S.E. Pa., 1984-87; chair com. child health Mayor's Commn. Phila., 1982-83. Named Henry Strong Denison scholar, Johns Hopkins Sch. Medicine, 1971, Leonard Davis Inst.; recipient Johns Hopkins U. Soc. Scholars award, 1995, award, Nat. Assn. of Nat. Acads., 2001, David Rall award, Inst. Medicine, 2005; Health Econs. fellow, U. Pa., 1984. Fellow Am. Acad. Pediat.; mem. AAAS, Inst. Medicine of NAS, Ambulatory Pediat. Assn. (Rsch. award 1996), Soc. Pediatric Rsch. (sr., Douglas K. Richardson award 2006), Am. Pediatric Soc., Am. Pub. Health Assn., Internat. Epidemiol. Assn., Assn. Health Svcs. Rsch., Ea. Soc. Pediatric Rsch., Soc. Pediatric Epidemiologic Rsch., Assn. Tchrs. Maternal and Child Health, Mass. Med. Soc., Norfolk Dist. Med. Soc., Mass. Pub. Health Assn., Johns Hopkins U. Soc. Scholars. Office: Harvard Sch Pub Health 677 Huntington Ave Boston MA 02115-6096 Business E-Mail: mmccormi@hsph.harvard.edu.

MCCORMICK, MARY F., church administrator; b. Cheraw, S.C., Aug. 4, 1942; d. James Nathaniel and Lillie (Pegues) Floyd; 1 child, Pamala Renee McCormick-Steward. BS, Morris Coll., Sumter, S.C., 1965; Master's degree, Antioch Coll., Yellowsprings, Ohio, 1975. Coord. day camp F.R.E.S.H. summer recreational program St. Paul Cmty. Bapt. Ch., Bklyn., 1986—91, dir. of discipleship, 1987—. Tchr. 1st grade Wash. St. Elem. Sch., Hartsville, SC, 1965—69; group tchr., ednl. specialist Western Queens Nursery Sch., L.I., 1971—83; coord. christians quality edn. tutorial program St. Paul Cmty. Bapt. Ch., Bklyn., 1986—89. Chaplain Brookdale U. Hosp. and Med. Ctr., Bklyn., 2004—06. Recipient Recognition award for drama ministry, St. Paul Cmty. Bapt. Ch., 1987—95, Tchg. Ministry award, Bethlehem Bapt. Ch. Tchg. Ministry, 1992, Mother of Yr. award, St. Paul Cmty. Bapt. Ch., 1982. Mem.: So. Christian Leadership Conf. Democrat. Avocations: shopping, listening to music, reading, good conversation, watching television. Office: St Paul Cmty Bapt Ch 859 Hendrix St Brooklyn NY 11207-7901 Office Phone: 718-257-1300. Home Fax: 718-257-2988; Office Fax: 718-257-2988. Personal E-mail: mmccormick@spcbc.com.

MCCORMICK, MAUREEN OLIVEA, computer systems programmer; b. Toledo, Mar. 24, 1956; d. Richard Ernest and Rita Maureen (Pratt) McCormick. BS in Elem. Edn., Kent State U., 1978, MA Reading Specialization, 1980. Reading instr. Elyria City Schs., Elyria, Ohio, 1975-79; tchr. Wellington Village Schs., Wellington, Ohio, 1979-80; devel. edn. instr. Lorain County C.C., Elyria, 1980-83; computer programmer analyst Navy Fin. Ctr., Cleve., 1981-86, Naval Mil. Pers. Command, Arlington, Va., 1986; computer systems analyst Marine Corps Cen. Design & Programming Activity/MCDEC, Quantico, Va., 1986-87; computer systems programmer Navy Fin. Ctr., Cleve., 1987-91, Def. Fin. and Acctg. Svc.-Cleve./Info. and Tech., 1991-92, 1992-93, supervisory computer specialist, 1993—. Mem. Am. Soc. Mil. Compts., TransAtlantic Brides & Parents Assn. Avocations: swimming, travel, crafts, golf. Home: 153 Burns Rd Elyria OH 44035-1510 Office: DFAS-TSO/CL 1240 E 9th St Cleveland OH 44199-2001 Office Phone: 216-204-4912.

MCCORMICK, MOLLY, elementary school educator; d. Ron Miller and Madge Franklin; m. Joel McCormick, Oct. 30, 1960; children: Blake-Elizabeth, Jacob. BSc, U. Houston, Clear Lake, 2000. Cert. tchr. Bd. Edn. Tex., 2000. Tchr. Pine Dr. Christian Sch., Dickinson, Tex., 1995—2000, Angleton Mid. Sch., Tex., 2000—. Cons. Discovery Channel, Silver Spring, Md., 2006. Tchr., vbs dir. local ch., Angleton, Tex., 1990—. Recipient Educator award, Earthwatch Inst., 2005. Office Phone: 979-849-8594. Business E-Mail: mmccormick@angletonisd.net.

MCCORMICK, QUEEN ESTHER WILLIAMS, clergyman; b. Apr. 5, 1941; BA in Theology, Internat. Sem., 1986; MA in Theology, Logos Bible Coll., 1993, PhD in Ministry, 1996. Adj. prof. Internat. Sem., Plymouth, Fla., 1987,91,98; founder, pastor New Birth House of Prayer for All People, Ft. Lauderdale, Fla., 1980—; pres. CEO Compassionate Hearts-Serving Hands, 2000. Radio/TV min., 1974-97; gospel singer, 1946—. Author: The Elect Lady in Ministry, 3d edit., 1998. Office: PO Box 5712 Fort Lauderdale FL 33310-5712

MCCORMICK, STEPHANIE L. BELL, music educator; b. Battle Creek, Mich., Sept. 11, 1954; children: Jillian Maureen, David John, Rebekah L. BA Music, U. San Diego, 1976. Cert. Elem., Music tchr. Oreg., 1990. Tchr. music Corvallis Sch. Dist., Oreg., 1990—. Dir. choir Heart of the Valley Children's Choir, Corvallis, 1986—; dir. music St. Mary's Cath. Ch., Corvallis, 1981—. Named Who's Who Am. Tchrs.; Who's Who, 2006. Mem.: Oreg. Music Educators Assn., Music Educators Nat. Conf., Am. Choral Dirs. Assn., Flute Soc. Portland. Roman Catholic. Avocations: photography, hiking, camping, travel. Office: Corvallis School District 35th Street Corvallis OR 97330 Personal E-mail: stephanie@corvallis.k12.or.us.

MCCORMICK, SUSAN KONN, retired publishing executive; b. Cleve., Dec. 13, 1953; d. Frank Andrew and Mary Lou (Dunn) Konn; m. Michael F. McCormick, May 25, 1985; children: Amanda, James. BS, Ind. U., 1976; MBA, Stanford U., 1983. CPA, N.Y. Acct. Deloitte Haskins & Sells, Indpls., 1975-77; fin. analyst GM, N.Y.C., 1977-83; exec. Brown Bros. Harriman, N.Y.C., 1983-84; v.p. Bankers Trust Co., N.Y.C., 1984-85; treas. Scholastic, Inc., N.Y.C., 1985-94; now ret., 1994. Mem. AICPA, N.Y. State Soc. CPA's, Risk Ins. Mgmt. Soc., Stanford U. Alumni Assn., N.Y. Treas.'s Club. E-mail: mccormsk@aol.com.

MCCOSHAM, JOYCE L., secondary school educator; b. Norwood, Ohio, Dec. 25, 1927; d. Stanley James and Mary Emily Chambers; m. William Duncan McCosham, June 12, 1948 (dec.); children: Lynn Colleen Hamberg, Kyle Maureen Hellman. BS in Edn., U. Cin., 1948, MEd, 1972. Lic. profl. counselor Ohio, 1986. Instr. water safety, cmty. ctr. leader Cin. Recreation Commn., 1948—74; tchr. phys. edn., health, coach North College Hill Schs., 1948—52; tchr. phys. edn., health, coach, athletic dir., counselor, asst. prin. Mother of Mercy High Sch. and Acad., 1952—92; instr., tchr. edn. Edgecliff Coll., 1959—74; counselor Oak Hills High Sch., 1992—99. Elder Mt. Auburn Presbyb. Ch., Cin., 1974—, recreation program, 1965—70. Named Disting. Alumni, U. Cin. Coll. Edn., 1998, in her honor Joyce McCosham Day, Mayor Roxanne Qualls, Cin., 1999; named to Ath. Hall Fame, Mother of Mercy HS, 1987; recipient cert. of Merit, Ohio Counseling Assn., 1999. Mem.: Mother of Mercy Athletic Hall of Fame, Oak Hills Ret. Tchrs. Assn., Mercy Ret. Tchrs. Assn., Ohio Edn. Assn., Nat. Edn. Assn., Hamilton County Ret. Tchrs. Assn., Greater Cin. Counseling Assn. (pres., v.p., sec.-treas. 1972—, Mary Corre Foster award 1994), Nat. Hole-in-One Assn., U. Cin. Golden Bearcat Club, Kappa Delta Pi Nat. Hon. Avocations: boating, water-skiing, golf, bowling, travel.

MCCOURT, LISA, writer; b. Jacksonville, Fla., Sept. 2, 1964; d. Michael Lee and Bettye Jean McCourt; m. Gregory Vincent Combs; children: Lily-Kate Combs children: Tucker Combs. BS, Drew U., Madison, N.J., 1986. Author: (children's book) I Love You, Stinky Face, 1997 (National Parenting Publication Award (Nappa) Honors Award, 1998), The Rain Forest Counts!, 1997, The Long and Short of It, 1998 (chosen for The Original Art by the Society of Illustrators, 1998), Raptors!, 1997, Deadly Snakes, 1998, I Miss You, Stinky Face, 1999 (a PBS "Between the Lions" selection, 2001), Candy Counting, 1999, Rocket to the Moon, 1999, Construction Buddies; Dozer to the Rescue!, 1999, It's Time for School, Stinky Face, 2000, Construction Buddies; Dozer's Wild Adventure, 2000, Chicken Soup for Little Souls; The Best Night Out with Dad, 1997, Chicken Soup for Little Souls; The Never-Forgotten Doll, 1997 (Storytelling World Award; Honor Title, 1998), Chicken Soup for Little Souls; The Goodness Gorillas, 1997, Chicken Soup for Little Souls; The Braids Girl, 1998, Chicken Soup for Little Souls, A Dog of My Own, 1998 (IRA/CBC Children's Choice Award, 1998), Chicken Soup for Little Souls; The New Kid and the Cookie Thief, 1998, Chicken Soup for Little Souls; Della Splatnuk, Birthday Girl, 1999 (Storytelling World Award, Honor Title, 2000), Chicken Soup for Little Souls Family Collection, 1999, Chicken Soup for the Little Souls; 3 Colorful Stories to Warm the Hearts of Children, 2000, Love You Until., 1999, (parenting book) 101 Ways to Raise a Happy Baby, 1999, (preteen book) Attitude--How to Be the Coolest Girl You Know, 2000, (children's book) Weird in the Wild; Wet 'n' Weird, 2000, Weird in the Wild; Hairy 'n' Weird, 2000, (parenting book) 101 Ways to Raise a Happy Toddler, 2000, (children's book) Good Night, Princess Pruney Toes, 2001, I Love You, Stinky Face board book, 2002, Merry Christmas, Stinky Face, 2002, (children's book) What's Inside My Body?, 2000, (children's book) Mysterious Space, 2000. Personal E-mail: lisa@lisamccourt.com.

MCCOY, AMY L., special education educator; d. Robert and Barbara McCoy. BA in Counseling, Bob Jones U., Greenville, SC, 2001, MA in Tchg. Spl. Edn., 2003. Cert. tchr. SC, 2004. Tchr. emotionally disabled, self-contain tchr. Slater-Marietta Elem., Marietta, SC, 2004; tchr. learning disabledes, resource Cherrydale Elem., Greenville, 2004—. Co-chmn. United Way, Greenville, SC, 2005—. Mentor Hampton Pk. Bapt. Ch., Greenville, SC, 1999—2001. Mem.: Internat. Reading Assn., Coun. Exceptional Children. Home: 2320 Northway Denton TX 76207

MCCOY, ANN, artist; b. Boulder, Colo., July 8, 1946; d. Abram Armstrong McC. and Ruthanna (Eames) Evans. B.F.A., U. Colo., 1969; MA, UCLA, 1972. Instr. dept. art history Barnard Coll., N.Y.C., 1980—. One-woman shows include Fourcade, Droll Inc., N.Y.C., 1974, Inst. Contemporary Art, Boston, 1977, Mus. Ludwig, Cologne, Germany, 1977, Portland (Oreg.) Ctr. for the Visual Arts, 1979, The Arts Club, Chgo., 1979, Margo Leavin Gallery, L.A., 1979, Brooke Alexander, Inc., 1979, 81, 82, 84, 85, Met. Mus. Art, N.Y.C., 1982, Galerie Kornfeld, Bern, Switzerland, 1983, Greenville (S.C.) County Mus. Art, 1984, Eugene Binder Gallery, Dallas, 1986, A.C.A., N.Y.C., 1988, Arnold Herstand Gallery, N.Y.C., 1990, The Contemporary Mus., Honolulu, 1991, Ctrl. Fine Arts, N.Y.C., 1998; exhibited in group shows at Oberlin Coll., 1973, Whitney Mus. Am. Art, 1973, 79, The N.Y. Cultural Ctr., 1974, Indpls. Mus. Art, 1974, The Contemporary Art Ctr., Cin., 1974, Corcoran Gallery of Art, 1976, Crysler Mus., 1982, L.A. County Mus., 1983, P.S. 1, N.Y.C., 1986, San Francisco Mus. Art, 1986, Venice (Italy) Biennale, 1986, Nat. Mus. Am. Art, Washington, 1989, La Jolla (Calif.) Mus. Contemporary Art, 1989, High Mus. Art, Atlanta, 1989, M. Gutierrez Fine Arts, Miami, Fla., 1993, Mus. Contemporary Religious Art, St. Louis, 1993, New Orleans Mus. Art, 1995, Nuberger Mus. Art, Purchase, 1995, The Equitable Gallery, N.Y.C., 1996, A.C.A. Gallery, N.Y.C., 1997, Z Gallery, N.Y.C., 1997; represented in permanent collections at Hirshorn Mus., Met. Mus., Dallas Art Mus., Honolulu Acad. Arts, Indpls. Mus. Art, L.A. County Mus. Art, Mus. Modern Art, Whitney Mus., Newberger Mus., Des Moines Art Ctr., Nat. Gallery Australia, Powis Gallery, Lannan Found., San Francisco Mus. Modern Art, New Orleans Mus. Recipient Contemporary Art Council New Talent award Los Angeles County Mus. Art, 1972, EA award, 1978, award in visual arts Prix de Rome, NEA, E.D. Found., 1989, Alice Baber award, 1990, Pollock Krasner award, 1993, 98; grantee Adolph and Esther Gottlieb Found., 1996. Address: PO Box 1907 Long Island City NY 11101 Office Phone: 646-249-5937. Business E-Mail: annartistmccoy@earthlink.net.

MCCOY, CAROL P., psychologist, training executive; b. Bronxville, NY, June 14, 1948; d. Rawley Deering and Jane (Wiske) McC.; m. Lanny Gordon Foster, Nov. 29, 1975 (div. 1985). BA, Conn. Coll., 1970; MS in Psychology, Rutgers U., 1974, PhD in Psychology, 1980. Adj. instr. psychology Rutgers U., New Brunswick, N.J., 1974-75; faculty chair dept. social sci. Misericordia Hosp. Sch. Nursing, Bronx, N.Y., 1976-79; tng. and devel. cons. Chase Manhattan Bank N.A., N.Y.C., 1980-85, tng. mgr. internat. consumer banking div., 1985-88, tng. mgr. individual banking, 1988-91; dir. corp. tng. UNUM Life Ins. Co. Am., Portland, Maine, 1991-97, mgr. tng. quality assurance, 1997-99; pres. McCoy Trng./Devel. Resources, Falmouth, Maine, 1999—. Pres. Find-Your-Roots.com, 2002—. Author: Managing a Small HRD Department, 1993; editor: Managing the Small Training Staff, 1998. Mem.: APA, ASTD. Avocations: genealogy, music, baseball cards. Home and Office: 28 Lone Pine Ln Yarmouth ME 04096 Office Phone: 207-847-3271. Personal E-mail: cmccoy3333@aol.com.

MCCOY, DEBRA MARLENE BLACK, sales executive; b. Pitts., Nov. 6, 1953; d. Donald T. and Doris A. (Porter) B.; m. Edward B. McCoy, Aug. 8, 1998. BA, Ky. Wesleyan Coll., 1975; MA, Western Ky. U., 1983. Cert. elem. tchr., kindergarten endorsement, Ky. Tchr. kindergarten Owensboro Ind. Schs., Ky., 1975-79, Owensboro-Daviess County Child Care, 1987-88; elem. tchr. Ohio County Bd. Edn., Hartford, Ky., 1979-80; substitute tchr. Owensboro Ind. Schs., 1980-86; tchr. kindergarten Daviess County Bd. Edn., Owensboro, 1988-91; preschool tchr. Mary Mitchell Preschool, Owensboro, 1992—96; sales assoc. Bacons Dept. Stores, 1991—98; area sales mgr. Famous Barr divsn. May Co., Owensboro, Ky., 1998—2006, Macy's, Owensboro, Ky., 2006—. Named Area Sales Mgr. of Yr., 2003. Mem. Beta Sigma Phi (chpt. pres. 1988-91, Woman of Yr. award 1990). Republican. Presbyterian. Avocations: reading, cross stitch, sewing. E-mail: demccoy@bellsouth.net.

MCCOY, DIANN L., information technology acquisition executive; BS in Math. and Computer Sci., Wright State U., Fairborn, Ohio, 1974; MS in Acquisition Logistics, Air Force Inst.Tech., Wright Patterson AFB, 1978; postgrad., MIT, Boston, 1987—88. Cert. profl. logistician Soc. of Logistics Engrs. Various Air Force Logistics Command, Dayton, Ohio, 1971—86, various sr. mgmt. postions, 1989—91; dep. for comm. electronics Sacramento Air Logistics Ctr., Sacramento, 1986—89; dir. Std. Systems Ctr., Montgomery, Ala., 1992—93; dep. mgr. Nat. Comm. Sys., Arlington, Va., 1999—2001; prin. dir. acquisition engring. Def. Info. Sys. Agy., Arlington, Va., 2001—03; component acquistion exec. Def. Info. Systems Agy., Falls Church, Va., 2002—. Recipient varoius presdl. Rank awrds, Fed. Government-OPM, 1993, 2002, 2004, Women in Tech. Award for Govt. Leadership, Disting. Civilian award, Dept. of Def., Meritorious Civilian Svc. award, 1986. Mem.: AFCEA (life), Delta Sigma Theta.

MCCOY, DOROTHY ELOISE, writer, educator; b. Houston, Sept. 4, 1916; d. Robert Major and Evie Letha (Grimes) Morgan; m. Roy McCoy, May 22, 1942; children: Roy Jr., Robert Nicholas (dec.). BA, Rice U., 1938; MA, Tex. A&I U., 1968; postgrad., Ind. U., 1971, U. Calif., Berkeley, 1972, U. Calif., Santa Cruz, 1977. Cert. secondary tchr. BA Corpus Christi (Tex.) Independent Schs., 1958-84, MA, 1985; freelance writer Corpus Christi, 1987—; co-owner United Iron and Machine Works, Corpus Christi, 1946-82. Freelance lectr.; master tchr. Nat. Coun. Tchrs. English, 1971, Nat. Humanities Faculty, Concord Mass., 1977-78; mem. steering com. Edn. Summit, Corpus Christi, 1990-91, mem. summit update, 1991. Author: A Teacher Talks Back, 1990, Let's Restructure the Schools, 1992; contbr. articles and columns to profl. jours. Sr. advisor to U.S. Congress, Washington, 1982-85; trustee Corpus Christi Librs., 1987-90; mem. Corpus Christi Mus.; mem. Friends Corpus Christi Librs., chmn. publicity com., 1988; participant Walk to Emmaus Group, 1990, UPDATE, U. Tex., 1978-92; cons. Libr. Bd. Democracy competition Am. 2000; sec. adminstrv. bd. First United Meth. Ch., 1992-93. Recipient Teacher of Yr. Paul Caplan Humanitarian award, 1981, Advanced Senior Option Program award, 1968. Mem. AAUW, LWV, Phi Beta Kappa. Avocations: gardening, writing. Office Phone: 361-852-0726.

MCCOY, DOROTHY VIRGINIA, psychotherapist, consultant; d. Fred McCoy, Jr. and Dorothy McGrath; BA, U. S.C., Columbia, 1986; MEd, The Citadel, Charleston, S.C., 1990; EdD, U. Sarasota, Fla., 2001. Diplomate Am. Acad. Experts in Traumatic Stress. Psychotherapist, Boone, NC, 1991—; cons. Boone Police Dept., 2003—; instr. S.C. Criminal Justice Acad., Columbia, SC, 2006—. Commr. Western Carolina Higher Edn. Commn., Waterboro-Allendale, SC, 1987—2005; presenter at internat. confs. Author: From Shyness to Social Butterfly, 2001, The Ultimate Personality Test, 2005, The Manipulative Man, 2006. Mem.: Soc. Criminal Psychology. Avocations: travel, gardening, hiking, weightlifting. Home: 119 Timbercrest Trail Fleetwood NC 28626 Office: State Criminal Justice Acad Broad St Columbia SC 29201 Office Phone: 828-334-6373.

MCCOY, JEANIE SHEARER, analytical chemist, consultant; b. Mancelona, Mich., May 27, 1921; d. Theophil R. and Goldie Margaret (Halladay) Schroeder; m. Theodore R. Shearer, June 14, 1958 (div. 1964); 1 child, Blair Barnett; m. George Altha McCoy, July 23, 1966. AA, North Park Coll., 1941; BS, Northwestern U., 1944; MS, No. Ill. U., 1970. Jr. analytical chemist Buick Motor divsn. GM, Melrose Park, Ill., 1944—45; asst. rsch. chemist Hodson Oil Corp., Chgo., 1945—47; asst. analytical chemist Internat. Harvester Co., Melrose Park, 1947—49, analytical chemist, 1949—60, prin. chemist, 1961—74, supr. metal process control, 1974—82; cons. cutting fluid mgmt. divsn. JMT, Inc., Lombard, Ill., 1983—2003; cons. Jeanie McCoy Cutting Fluid Mgmt. Co., Lombard, 2004—. Editor: Lubrication Engring. Mag., 1979—2000; contbr. chapters to books. Fellow: Soc. Tribologists and Lubrication Engrs. (Allan Mantafel award Chgo sect. 1987, P. M. KU award 1991, Internat. award 2000); mem.: AAUW, Soc. Mfg. Engrs., Abrasive Engring. Soc., Am. Chem. Soc., Soc. Automotive Engrs. Avocations: seashell collecting, stamp collecting/philately, fitness activities. Home and Office: 654 N West Rd Lombard IL 60148-1547 Office Phone: 630-627-2721. Personal E-mail: j10mccoy@aol.com.

MCCOY, JENNIE EILEEN, elementary school educator; b. San Diego, Feb. 20, 1964; d. Jerry and Joy Aucoin; m. Russ McCoy, July 10, 1998; children: Madison, Taylor Bray. BA in Liberal Studies, Point Loma Coll., San Diego, 1986; MA in Tchg. and Learning, Point Loma U., San Diego, 1987. Elem. sch. tchr. Hesperia Unified Sch. Dist., 1986—2000; tchr. Big Bear Mid. Sch., Calif., 2000—. Home: PO Box 1583 Big Bear Lake CA 92315 Office: Big Bear Middle School PO Box 1607 Big Bear Lake CA 92315 E-mail: jennie_mccoy@bigbear.k12.ca.us.

MCCOY, JENNIFER, artistic collaborator, educator; b. Sacramento, Calif., 1968; Attended Critical Studies Film Program with CIEE, U. Paris III, Paris, France, 1990; BA in Theater Arts, Cornell U., Ithaca, 1990; MFA in Electronic Arts, Rensselaer Polytechnic Inst., Troy, NY, 1994. Asst. prof. computer graphics Brooklyn Coll. Artistic collaborator with Kevin McCoy (making a wide range of video, installation, new media and performance works dealing with the cultural manifestations of technology in the world), (solo exhibitions) We Like to Watch, Postmasters Gallery, NYC, 2002, Love and Terror, Butler Art Inst., Youngstown, Ohio, 2002, We Like to Watch, Van Laere Contemporary Art Gallery, Antwerp, Belgium, 2002, Stardust, San Jose State U. Art Gallery, Calif., 2003, Soft Rains, FACT (catalog), Liverpool, UK, 2003, Galerie Guy Bartschi, Geneva, Switzerland, 2003, Soft Rains, Postmasters Gallery, NY, 2004, Learning to Watch, Sala Rekalde, Bilbao (catalog), 2004, (video screening) Cluster Images, Werkleitz Geselschaft, Tornitz, Germany, 1996, Video Room Video Festival, Brooklyn, NY, 1998, (web project-solo exhibition) Maintenance/Web, The Thing, NYC, 1997, (web project) Airworld, Walker Art Ctr., Mpls., MN, 1999, (interactive video installation) Tomorrow's Homes Today, Mus. of Sci. and Industry, Manchester, Eng., 1998, (interactive installation) Viper Internat. Media Festival, Lucerne, Switzerland, 1999, Toys and Noise, OK Ctr. for Contemporary Art, Linz, Austria, 1999, (electronic sculpture) Subject to Sound, The Rotunda Gallery, Brooklyn, NY, 2000, (performance) Verbal 3, The Kitchen, NYC, 2000, (screening) Video Viewpoints, Mus. of Modern Art, 2001, Robert Flaherty Film Seminar, Durham, NC, 1999, (group shows) New Acquisitions, Dept. of Photographs, Mus. of Modern Art, 2002, American Dream, Ronald Feldman Gallery, NY, 2002, Tag Team, White Box, 2003, Game Show, James Cohan Gallery, 2004, Open House: Working in Brooklyn, Brooklyn Mus., 2004, Our Grotesque, curated by Rob Storr, 5th Internat. Biennial, SITE Santa Fe, NMex., 2004, and several others. Co-recipient Rave award in Art, WIRED, 2005. Address: c/o Postmaster Gallery 459 W 19th St at 10th Ave New York NY 10001

MCCOY, LILYS D., lawyer; b. San Diego, Calif., Sept. 23, 1967; d. Walter Lee, Jr. and Leoné Doris McCoy; children: Joshua Thomas Moses-McCoy, Jonathan Lee Moses-McCoy. BA with distinction, U. Calif., San Diego, 1987; JD, U. Ariz., Tucson, 1991. Of counsel Law Offices of Frederick Meiser, San Diego, 1992—94; assoc. Law Offices of Gregory Jon Anthony, San Diego, 1994—96; of counsel Barmick, Rutherford and Scott, San Diego, 1996—99; assoc. Rosner Law and Mansfield, San Diego, 1999—2003; shareholder McCoy, Turnage & Robertson APLC, San Diego, 2003—. Pres. Lawyers Club of San Diego, 2002—03, adv. bd., 2002—, judicial endorsements, 2002—, chair, 2005. Named one of Top Attys., San Diego Daily Transcript, 2006. Mem.: Conf. of Delegates (bd. mem. 2004—), Tom Homann Law Assn. (co-pres. 2005—). Democrat. Episcopalian. Office: McCoy Turnage & Robertson APLC 5469 Kearny Village Rd #206 San Diego CA 92123 Office Phone: 585-300-1900. Business E-Mail: ldm@mtrlaw.com.

MCCOY, LOIS CLARK, retired social services administrator, retired county official, editor; b. New Haven, Oct. 1, 1920; m. Herbert Irving McCoy, Oct. 17, 1943; children: Whitney, Kevin, Marianne, Tori, Debra, Sally, Daniel. BS, Skidmore Coll., 1942; student, Nat. Search and Rescue Sch., 1974. Asst. buyer R.H. Macy & Co., N.Y.C., 1942-44, assoc. buyer, 1944-48; instr. Mountain Medicine & Survival, U. Calif., San Diego, 1973-74; cons. editor Search & Rescue Mag., 1975, Rescue Mag., 1988-97, editor, 1992-94, Press On Newsletter, 1992—2000. Coord. San Diego Mountain Rescue Team, La Jolla, Calif., 1973-75; exec. sec. Nat. Assn. for Search and Rescue, Inc., Nashville, La Jolla, 1975-80, comptr., 1980-82; disaster officer San Diego County, 1980-86, Santa Barbara County, 1985-91, ret.; pres. Nat. Inst. Urban Search & Rescue, Inc., 1987—; assoc. dir. Armed Forces Commns. and Electronics Assn., 2003—; mem. project info. techs. to enhance disaster mgmt., NAS, 2005, group using info. tech. to enhance crisis preparedness and response, Nat. Rsch. Coun., 2005; lectr. in field. Author: Search and Rescue Glossary, 1974, The Last Desperado, 2005, Kiss, Shoot, Aim, 2006; contbr. editor Rescue Mag., 1989-97; editor-in-chief Response! mag., 1982-86; editor Press On! Electronic mag., 1994-2001; adv. bd. Hazard Monthly, 1991-99; contbr. articles to profl. jours. Cons. law enforcement divsn. Calif. Office Emergency Svcs., 1976-77; pres. San Diego Com. for L.A. Philharm. Orch., 1957-58; bd. dirs. Search and Rescue of the Californias, 1976-77, Nat. Assn. for Search and Rescue, Inc., 1980-87, pres., 1985-87, trustee, 1987-90, mem. Calif. OES strategic com., 1992-96; CEO Nat. Inst. for Urban Search, 1989—; mem. Gov.'s Task Force on Earthquakes, 1981-82, Earthquake Preparedness Task Force, Seismic Safety Commn., 1982-85, Army Sci. and Tech. Commn., 2003; mem. adv. coun. Nat. Meml. Inst. for the Protection from Terrorism; named to NSF Project "Info. Tech. to Enhance Disaster Mgmt.", 2005. Recipient Hall Foss Outstanding Svc. to Search and Rescue award, 1982, Diamond Safety award, 1996, Superior Performance award AFCEA, 2004, Rep. Senatorial Freedom medal, 2004, Congl. Order merit Rep. Congl. Del., 2005; named to The Fed. 100, 2002. Mem.: IEEE, Armed Forces Comm. and Electronics Assn. (named to Army Sci. and Tech. com. for Homeland Def. 2003—04, bd. dirs. 2003—), San Diego Mountain Rescue (life), Nat. Assn. Search and Rescue (life Svc. award 1985, 2002), Santa Barbara Amateur Radio Club. Episcopalian. Office: PO Box 91648 Santa Barbara CA 93190-1648 Office Phone: 800-767-0093. Personal E-mail: niusr@cox.net.

MCCOY, MARILYN, director; b. Providence, Mar. 18, 1948; d. James Francis and Eleanor (Regan) McC.; m. Charles R. Thomas, Jan. 28, 1983. BA in Econs. cum laude, Smith Coll., 1970; M in Pub. Policy, U. Mich., 1972. Dir. Nat. Ctr. for Higher Edn. Mgmt. Systems, Boulder, Colo., 1972-80; dir. planning and policy devel. U. Colo., Boulder, 1981-85; v.p. adminstrn. and planning Northwestern U., Evanston, Ill., 1985—. Trustee JPMorgan Funds. Co-author: Financing Higher Education in the Fifty States, 1976, 3d edit., 1982. Bd. dir. Evanston Northwestern HealthCare Rsch. Inst., 1988—, Mather Found., 1995—; trustee Carleton Coll., 2003—. Mem. Soc. for Coll. and Univ. Planning (pres., v.p., sec., bd. dir. 1980—), Assn. for Instnl. Rsch. (pres., v.p., exec. com., publ. bd. 1978-87), Chgo. Network (chmn. 1992-93), Chgo. Econ. Club. Home: 1100 N Lake Shore Dr Chicago IL 60611-1070 Office: Northwestern U 633 Clark St Evanston IL 60208-0001

MCCOY, MARY ANN, state official; b. Duluth, Minn., Oct. 13, 1924; d. Homer Burke and Avis (Woodworth) Hursh; m. Charles Ramon McCoy, June 11, 1949; children: Jeffrey, Mary, Jeremy. BA, Grinnell Coll., 1946; postgrad., Laval U., 1946, Mankato State U., 1964-65. Cert.: Minn. Supreme Ct. (neutral mediator) 1996. Exec. trainee Younkers, Inc., Des Moines, 1946; advt. copywriter Des Moines Register & Tribune, 1947; field dir. Duluth Girl Scout Coun., 1947-49; with merchandising dept. Dayton's Inc., Mpls., 1966-75; dir. election and legis. manual divsn. Office Sec. State of Minn., St. Paul, 1975-81; exec. dir. Minn. State Ethical Practices Bd., St. Paul, 1981-95, cons., 1996—. Sec. State Rev. Bd. Nominations to Nat. Register, 1976—89; mem. Minn. Supreme Ct. Bd. Continuing Legal Edn., 1981—87. Editor: Minn. Legis. Manual, 1975—81. Mem.: Am. Assn. State and Local History, Women Historians Midwest, Internat. Assn. Facilitators, Am. Judicature Soc., Minn. Assn. Pub. Adminstrs., Coun. Govt. Ethics Laws (hon.; mem. steering com. 1986—89, treas. 1987—88), Minn. Hist. Soc. (life; hon. coun., mem. exec. coun. 1972—81, 1982—90). Personal E-mail: crmamccoy@att.net.

MCCOY, MARY JANE, retired principal; d. Albert Louis Haley and Della Muriel (Haley-Skinner) Smith; m. Edgar Allen McCoy, Aug. 31, 1957; children: Kim Michelle, Shelley Anne. AA, San Bernardino Valley Jr. Coll., Calif., 1965; BS, Calif. State U., San Bernardino, 1967; MS, Pepperdine U., 1976. Tchg. credential Calif., Wash., adminstrv. credential Calif., Wash. Tchr. San Bernardino Unified, 1968—76, resource reading specialist, 1972—76, elem. vice prin., 1976—78, elem. prin., 1978—92; tchr. Dist. 81, Spokane, Wash., 1992—95. Mem.: NAACP (life), Spokane Women's Coalition, The Links, Inc. (1st v.p. Spokane chpt. 2004—, pres. Spokane chpt. 2000—04, v.p.), Soroptimists, Delta Sigma Theta (sec. 2002—), Phi Delta Kappa (regional dir. far west 1994—95, pres. 1995—, pres. perpetual scholarship found. 1995—). Avocations: reading, crafts, sewing, cross stitch.

MCCOY, MARY NELL, music educator; d. James Albert Swope Jr. and Marjorie Gayle Swope; m. Gary Wayne McCoy, Nov. 28, 1968; children: Amy Annelle, Jason Todd, Joyce Elaine. MusB in Edn., Ctrl. Mo. State U., 1968; M in Ch. Music, S.W. Bapt. Theol. Sem., 1972. Cert. crosscultural, lang. and academic devel. State of Calif., 2000. Elem. music tchr. Knob Noster (Mo.) Elem. Sch., 1968—70; music cons. Internat. Mission Bd., Richmond, 1974—91; elem. music tchr. Bay Elem. Sch. San Lorenzo United Sch. Dist., Calif., 1995—; co-chair San Lorenzo United Sch. Dist., 2006—. Support provider for new tchrs. Beginning Tchr. Support and Assessment, San Lorenzo, 2001—; mentor tchr. Peer Assessment and Rev., San Lorenzo, 2001—; rep. Gifted and Talented Program, San Lorenzo, 2000—; adj. prof. Golden Gate Bapt. Theol. Sem., Mill Valley, Calif. Min. music First Bapt. Ch., Novato, Calif., 1992—96; interim min. music Petaluma (Calif.) Valley Bapt. Ch., 1997—99; children's choir leader Concord Korean Bapt. Ch., Martinez, Calif., 2000—03. Mem.: Calif. Tchrs. Assn. (assoc.), Calif. Music Educator's Conv. (assoc.), Music Educator's Nat. Conv. (assoc.), Calif. Parents, Tchrs. Assn., Phi Kappa Lambda. Democrat. Baptist. Office Phone: 510-317-4328. Personal E-mail: marynell.mccoy@comcast.net.

MCCOY, PATRICIA A., retired clinical special educator, art and culture critic, writer; b. Seattle, Dec. 20, 1951; d. Robert Wilson and Barbara (Foss) McC. BS, U. Nev., 1974; MA, NYU, 1983; postgrad., Ctr. for Psychoanalytic Studies; postgrad. in applied linguistics, NYU. Lectr. in English CUNY, N.Y.C., 1984-88, John Jay Coll. of Criminal Justice, N.Y.C., 1988-91; clin. educator August Aichhorn Resdl. Treatment Ctr., N.Y.C., 1991-93, St. Vincent's Hosp., Puerto Rican Family Inst.; Louise Wise, 1993—2002. Lectr. contemporary art New Arts Program and others, east coast, 1991—; ind. curator, 1987—; instr. NYU. Editor: N.A.P. Texts jour., 1993—; contbr. articles to profl. jours., including Modern Psychoanalysis, Orthopsychiatry's Readings. Grantee N.Y. State Found. for the Arts, 1987, Pa. Coun. for the Arts, 1991, Mid-Atlantic, 1991, Nat. Endowment for the Arts for Text(s), 1992, Pew Charitable Trust for Text(s), 1993; Dean's grantee in grad. rsch. NYU, 2005. Mem. Nat. Soc. Modern Psychoanalysts, Assn. Internat. des Critiques d'Art, Am. Orthopsychiatric Assn., N.Y. State Coun. Humanities Scholars Directory.

MCCOY, SUE, retired surgeon, biochemist, bioethicist; b. Charlottesville, Va., Nov. 14, 1935; d. Hulburt Christopher and Evelyn (Savage) McC. AB, Radcliffe Coll., 1957; PhD, Johns Hopkins U., 1964; MD, U. Va., 1980, postgrad., 2001—. Diplomate Am. Bd. Surgery. Fellow in physiol. chemistry Johns Hopkins U., Balt., 1964-67; asst. prof. chemistry U. South Fla., Tampa, 1967-69; asst. prof. orthopedics U. Va., Charlottesville, 1969-73, asst. prof. surgery, 1973-78; resident in surgery Hosp. U. Pa., Phila., 1980-83; resident in surgery Cooper Hosp. Rutgers U. Med. Sch., Camden, N.J., 1983-85, asst. prof. surgery, 1985-86, East Tenn. State U., Johnson City, 1986-91, assoc. prof., 1991-2000, prof., 2000—01; ret., 2001. Fellow: ACS; mem.: Assn. for Women Surgeons, Southeastern Surg. Congress, Shock Soc., Assn. for Acad. Surgery, Royal Soc. Chemistry, N.Y. Acad. Sci., Am. Chem. Soc., Sigma Xi. Achievements include research in hemorrhagic shock, aging, oxygen transport. Home: 8658 Batesville Rd Afton VA 22920

MCCRACKEN, CARON FRANCIS, information technology consultant; b. Detroit, Jan. 12, 1951; d. WIlliam Joseph and Constance Irene (Kramer) McC. AS, Mott C.C., 1971; BS, Ctrl. Mich. U., 1973; MA, U. Mich., 1978; MBA in Fin. with hons., Wayne State U., 2003. Tchr. Elkton, Pigeon, Bayport (Mich.) High Sch., 1973—74, Davison (Mich.) Jr. High Sch., 1974-75; instr. Mott C.C., Flint, Mich., 1974-78; planning and rsch. specialist Flint Police Dept., 1977-79; campus coord., programmer Systems & Computer Tech. Corp. (now SunGard Data Sys., Inc.), Detroit, 1981-82; acad. specialist computing systems Systems & Computer Tech. Corp., Detroit, 1982-83, mgr. acad. computing systems, 1983-84, mgr. adminstrv. computing systems, 1984-85; communications analyst Fruehauf Corp., Detroit, 1985-86, sr. comms. analyst, 1986-87; account tech. cons. US Sprint Communications Co., Detroit, 1987-89; account mgr. US Sprint Communications Corp., Detroit, 1989-90; sr. mgr. Technology Specialists, Inc., Phila., 1990-91; sr. cons. info. tech. practice. tech. delivery svcs. PriceWaterhouseCoopers LLP, Detroit, 1992—. Adv. bd. CONTEL Bus. Networks, Atlanta, 1987, spkr. in field. Contbr. articles to profl. jours. Vol. charitable and homeless orgns. including Coalition on Temporary Shelter, Core Cities, Paint the Town; undergrad. computer lab. cons., student mgr. computer sci. dept. Wayne State U., 1993-95, vol. computer cons. Bus. Sch., 1997-98; vol. tech. advisor on 1992 elections project City of Detroit; vol. St. Joseph's Mercy Hosp., Pontiac, Mich., 1995; chair of bd., pres., treas. Bloomfield Courts Condominium Assn., 1996-98; vol. Pub. TV WTVS, Detroit, 1996-99, vol., Pub. Radio Sta. WDET, Detroit, 1996-98; elected precinct del. for 4th precinct Bloomfield Twp., 2002—; vol. State Senatorial and U.S. Congressional re-election campaigns, 2002-2004, 2006—; vol. writer, rschr. 2004—. Named to Beta Gamma Sigma MBA Hon. Soc., 2001. Mem.: Detroit Zool. Soc., Detroit Inst. Arts, Assn. Computing Machinery, Data Processing Mgmt. Assn., Alumni Assn. Wayne State U., Smithsonian Instn. (assoc.), Alumni Assn. U. Mich., Adventure Cycling Assn. (Missoula, Mont.), Women's Econ. Club of Met. Detroit (fin. com. 1999), Beta Gamma Sigma. Avocations: athletics, travel. Home: 100 W Hickory Grove H4 Bloomfield Hills MI 48304-2169 Office: PricewaterhouseCoopers LLP 400 Renaissance Ctr Ste 780 Detroit MI 48243-1501

MCCRACKEN, KATHRYN ANGELA, clinical social worker; b. Steubenville, Ohio, Apr. 24, 1943; d. Ned Edward and Anna Lucy (Cortez) White; m. William Floyd Grandinetti, Dec. 14, 1961 (div. 1971); children: Natalie, Jane Elizabeth; m. Dudley Ral McCracken, Aug. 13, 1972; children: Anne Louise, Dori Kate. AS in Fine Arts, Washtenaw Community Coll., Ypsilanti, Mich., 1986; MSW, U. Mich., 1988. Supr. nursing svc. Ypsilanti State Hosp., 1972-88; client svc. mgr. Monroe (Mich.) County Cmty. Mental Health, 1989-98, outpatient therapist, 1998-2000; pvt. practice, 2000—. Mem. NASW, APA. Democrat. Roman Catholic. Avocation: book collector. Office: EJ Wasilewski & Assocs 708 S Monroe St Monroe MI 48161-1420

MCCRACKEN, LINDA, artist, writer; b. Rochester, N.Y., Apr. 13, 1948; d. Frederick Hugh Craig and Shirley Betty (Shacter) Bickford; m. Alan Cheah, June 13, 1972 (div. 1978); m. Bruce E. McCracken, Sept. 23, 1978 (div. 1985); 1 child, Karen Elizabeth. BA in History, SUNY, Geneseo, 1970, MLS, 1970. Libr. reference Northeastern U., Boston, 1971—72; asst. libr. Burlington Pub. Libr., Mass., 1972—74; artist, writer, rschr. McCracken's, Marlow, NH, 1972—; rsch. asst. Data Resources, Inc., Lexington, Mass., 1974—76; asst. libr. N.H. Vocat.-Tech. Coll., Manchester, 1985—87; libr. N.H. Hosp., Concord, 1987—99; med. libr. New London Hosp., NH, 1999—2001; spiritual healer Spiritual Web Comm., Marlow, NH, 2005—. Participant paintings Horseheads Mall Art Show (3d pl. award 1968); graphic artist Rare Coin Rev. mag., 1983; layout artist Market Media Guide, 1979; market rschr. Delahaye Group, Newington, N.H., 1993-94; author Burlington Times-Union, 1973, Pleasant News, 1987-88, Breene Briefings, 1998-99, Occasional Moose, 2005. Treas. Village Players, Wolfeboro, 1982-83; mem. pub. rels. com. Gov.'s Arts Coun., Wolfeboro, 1982. Mem. State Employees Assn. N.H., New Eng. Audio Theatre (sec. 2004-05), Mensa. Avocations: reading, hiking, kayaking, theater. Home and Office: PO Box 235 Marlow NH 03456 Personal E-mail: lmccracken2002@yahoo.com.

MCCRACKEN, TERRI, elementary school educator; b. Lubbock, Tex., Oct. 26, 1969; d. Ray and Theresa Poage; m. Norman McCracken, May 18, 2002. BA in Polit. Sci., U. Tex. Permian Basin, Odessa, Tex., 1994. Tchr. Tex. history Abell Jr. H.S., Midland, Tex., 2003—05; reading tchr. Travis Elem. Sch., 2005—. Sunday sch. tchr., Midland, Tex. Mem.: Midland Reading Coun. Avocations: reading, travel. Home: 5501 Hillcrest Midland TX 79707 E-mail: terrimichele@sbcglobal.net.

MCCRACKEN, URSULA E., museum director; Degree in Art History, Wellesley Coll.; Masters Degree, Johns Hopkins U. With Coll. Notre Dame, Balt., Walters Art Gallery, Balt.; curatorial asst. Albright-Knox Art Gallery, Balt.; dir. Textile Mus., Washington, 1987—.

MCCRADY, BARBARA SACHS, psychologist, educator; b. Evanston, Ill., May 7, 1949; d. James Frederick and Margaret Maxine (Miller) Sachs; m. Dennis D. McCrady, June 13, 1969; 1 child, Eric Paul. BS, Purdue U., 1969; PhD, U. R.I., 1975. Lic. clin. psychologist. Clin. project evaluator Butler Hosp., Providence, 1974-75, chief psychol. assessment program, 1975-76, chief problem drinkers' project, 1976-83; assoc. prof. psychology Rutgers U., Piscataway, NJ, 1983-89, prof. psychology, 1989-2000, prof. II, 2000—. From instr. to assoc. prof. psychiatry Brown U., Providence, 1975—83; acting dir. Rutgers Ctr. Alcohol Studies, Piscataway, 1990—92, dir. clin. tng. dept. psychology, 1993—2005, chair dept. psychology, 2005—; reviewer Nat. Inst. on Alcohol Abuse and Alcoholism, Washington, 1979—82, extramural sci. adv. bd., 1989—93; cons. Inst. Medicine, Washington, 1988—89. Author: The Alcoholic Marriage, 1977; editor: Marriage and Marital Therapy, 1978, Directions in Alcohol Abuse Treatment Research, 1985, Research on Alcoholics Anonymous: Opportunities and Alternatives, 1993, Addictions: A Comprehensive Guidebook, 1999. Grantee Nat. Inst. on Alcohol Abuse and Alcoholism, 1979-83, 1988—. Fellow Am. Psychol. Assn. (past pres. divsn. addictions); mem. Assn. for Advancement Behavior Therapy, Rsch. Soc. on Alcoholism (bd. dirs., 1999-2003). Avocations: horseback riding, skiing, piano. Office: Rutgers U Ctr Alcohol Studies 607 Allison Rd Piscataway NJ 08854-8001 Office Phone: 732-445-0667. E-mail: bmccrady@rci.rutgers.edu.

MCCRAE, JOCELYN DIANE, psychologist; b. Elizabeth, NJ, Dec. 19, 1957; d. John Christopher and Edna Mae McCrae. BA, Temple U., 1980; MSc, Villanova U., 1987; PhD, Wayne State U., 1996. Lic. Psychologist Mich., 2000. Clin. psychologist Children's Hosp. Mich., Detroit, 1993—. Bd. mem., cmty. mental health bd. Phila. Cmty. Coun., 1978—79. Contbr. articles to profl. jours. Tel. crisis counselor Contact Teleministries, Phila., 1986—87. Recipient Legion Honor award, Chapel Four Chaplains, 1983, Recognition cert., Contact Teleministries, 1986; fellow, Wayne State U., 1991—92; Thomas C. Rumble Grad. fellow, 1988—89, Rsch. grant, 1994, Martin Luther King, Jr.-Cesar Chavez-Rosa Parks fellow, 1991—92. Mem.: APA, Soc. Pediatric Psychology. Methodist. Achievements include facilitating the formation of a martial arts support group for children with sickle cell disease. Office: Childrens Hosp Michigan 3901 Beaubien Blvd Detroit MI 48201 Personal E-mail: jocelynmccrae@netscape.net.

MCCRARY, EUGENIA LESTER (MRS. DENNIS DAUGHTRY MCCRARY), civic worker, writer; b. Annapolis, Md., Mar. 23, 1929; d. John Campbell and Eugenia (Potts) Lester; m. John Campbell Howard, July 15, 1955 (dec. Sept. 1965); m. Dennis Daughtry McCrary, June 28, 1969; 1 child, Dennis Campbell. AB cum laude, Radcliffe Coll.-Harvard U., 1950; MA, Johns Hopkins U., 1952; postgrad., Harvard U., 1953, Pa. State U., 1953—54, Drew U., 1957—58, Inst. Study of USSR, Munich, 1964. Grad. asst. dept. Romance langs. Pa. State U., 1953—54; tchr. dept. math. The Brearley Sch., N.Y.C., 1954—57; dir. Sch. Langs., Inc., Summit, NJ, 1958—69, trustee, 1960—69. Co-author: Nom de Plume: Eugenia Campbell Lester, (with Allegra Branson) Frontiers Aflame, 1987; film script adaptation (with John Gallagher) Frontier, 1998. Dist. dir. Ea. Pa. and NJ auditions Met. Opera Nat. Coun., NYC, 1960-66, dist. dir. publicity, 1966-67, nat. vice chmn. publicity, 1967-71, nat. chmn. public rels., 1972-75, hon. nat. chmn. pub. rels., 1976-99; bd. govs., chmn. Van Cortlandt House Mus., 1985-90 Mem. Nat. Soc. Colonial Dames Am. (bd. mgrs. NY 1985-90), Met. Opera Nat. Coun., Soc. Mayflower Descs. (former bd. dirs. NY soc., chmn. house com. 1986-89), Soc. Daus. Holland Dames (bd. dirs. 1982-87, 96—, 3d directress gen. 1987-92, directress gen. 1992-96), L'Eglise du St.-Esprit (vestry 1985-88, sr. warden 1988-90), Huguenot Soc. Am. (governing coun. 1984-90, 2000-03, 2004-05, asst. treas. 1990-91, sec. 1991-95, 2d v.p. 1995-2000), Colonial Dames Am., Daus. of Cin., Colony Club (bd. govs. 1988-96), Causeries du Lundi, The Acorn Found. (bd. mem.), The Hereditary Order Descendants of Colonial Govs. Republican. Episcopalian. Home: 24 Central Park S New York NY 10019-1629 Personal E-mail: elmccrary@aol.com.

MCCRARY, JUDY HALE, education educator; b. Tuscaloosa, Ala., Oct. 16, 1955; d. Rogene Bae and Berta Inez (Smelley) Hale. BA, David Lipscomb U., 1978; MEd, Ala. A&M U., 1989; PhD, Miss. State U., 1994. Art tchr. grades 7-8 Scottsboro (Ala.) Jr. High, 1978-81; headstart tchr. Bridgeport (Ala.) Elem. Sch., 1983-84, tchr. grade 1, 1984-87; migrant tchr. grades K-6 Stevenson (Ala.) Elem. Sch., 1987-89, kindergarten tchr., 1989-91; tchg. asst. Miss. State U., Starkville, 1991-94; asst. prof. Jacksonville (Ala.) State U., 1994—2000, assoc. prof., 2000—06, prof., 2006—. Owner, operator The Art Studio, Scottsboro, 1981-83; presenter in field. Mem. beautification coun. C. of C., Scottsboro, 1983; mem., v.p. Doctoral Student's Assn., Starkville, 1991-94. Faculty Rsch. grantee Jacksonville State U., 1994-96. Mem. AAUW (sec. 1987-89, pres. 1989-91), DAR, Mid South Ednl. Rsch. Assn., Beta Phi, Delta Kappa Gamma, Phi Delta Kappa (historian 1993-94). Avocations: travel, home decorating, gardening, creative arts. Office: Jacksonville State Univ Ramona Wood Bldg 700 Pelham Rd N Jacksonville AL 36265-1623 Office Phone: 256-782-5167. Business E-Mail: jhale@jsu.edu.

MCCRARY, LORI SUE, secondary school educator; b. Columbus, Ohio, Apr. 9, 1961; d. Gerald Lee and Patricia Irene Williams; m. David Edward McCrary, Sept. 30, 1993; children: Nicole Elizabeth Moire, John David, Erin Patricia Moire, Matthew Hunter. BA, U. Ala., Birmingham, 2006. Educator/asst. adminstr. Garywood Christian Sch., Hueytown, Ala., 1996—2004; educator Pleasant Grove H.S., Ala., 2005—. Pres., v.p. Gideons Internat., Bessemer, Ala., 1995—2006. Scholar Holocaust Studies, Birmingham and Nat. Holocaust Found., 2006. Independent. Baptist. Avocations: travel, reading, hiking. Home: 5782 Lake Cyrus Blvd Hoover AL 35244 Office: Pleasant Grove High School 805 7th Ave Pleasant Grove AL 35127 Office Phone: 205-379-5250. Office Fax: 205-379-5295. Personal E-mail: lori_mccrary@yahoo.com. Business E-Mail: lmccrary@jefcoed.com.

MCCRAVEN, EVA STEWART MAPES, health service administrator; b. LA, Sept. 26, 1936; d. Paul Melvin and Wilma Zech (Ziegler) Stewart; m. Carl Clarke McCraven, Mar. 18, 1978; children: David Anthony, Lawrence James, Maria Lynn Mapes. ABS magna cum laude, Calif. State U., Northridge, 1974; MS, Cambridge Grad. Sch. Psycholoy, 1987, PhD, 1991. Dir. spl. projects Pacoima Meml. Hosp., 1969—71, dir. health edn., 1971—74; asst. exec. dir., v.p. Hillview Cmty. Mental Health Ctr., Lakeview Terrace, Calif., 1974—99, exec. dir., 1999—2004, CEO and pres., 2004—. Past dir. dept. consultation and edn. Hillview Ctr., developer, mgr. long-term residential program, 1986-90; former program mgr. crisis residential program, transititional residential program and day treatment program for mentally ill offenders, past dir. mentally ill offenders svcs.; former program dir. Valley Homeless Shelter Mental Health Counseling Program; dir. Integrated Svcs. Agy., Hillview Mental Health Ctr., Inc., 1993-98, dir. clin. programs, 1996-99, exec. dir. 1999— Former pres. San Fernando Valley Coordinating Coun. Area Assn., Sunland-Tujunga Coordinating Coun.; bd. advisors Pacoima Sr. Citizens Multi-Purpose Ctr.; bd. dirs. N.E. Valley Health Corp., 1970-73, Golden Gate Cmty. Mental Health Ctr., 1970-73 Recipient Resolution of Commendation State of Calif., 1988, Commendation award, 1988, Spl. Mayor's plaque, 1988, Cmty. Svcs. Commendation awards City of L.A., 1989, County of Los Angeles, 1989, Calif. Assembly, 1989, Calif. Senate, 1989, award Sunland-Tujunga Police Support Coun., 1989 Mem. Health Svcs. Adminstrn. Alumni Assn. (past v.p.), Sunland-Tujunga Bus. and Profl. Women (Women of Achievement award 1990), LWV, Valley Philharm. Soc Office: Hillview Cmty Mental Health Ctr 11500 Eldridge Ave Lake View Terrace CA 91342-6523

MCCRAW, KATHY, elementary school educator, special education educator; b. Spartanburg, S.C., Dec. 30, 1954; d. Perry Robert and Lillie Belle Stevens; children: Brooke Kathryn, Courtney Nicole. BA with highest honor, Clemson U., 1977; MA, Converse Coll., 1984. Tchr. spl. edn. Lugoff-Elgin Mid. Sch., Camden, S.C., 1977-80; resource tchr. Spartanburg H.S., 1980-97; resource tchr. and tchr. earth and phys. sci. Houston Elem. Sch. and McCracken Jr. H.S., Spartanburg, 1998; tchr. modified lang. arts Whitlock Jr. H.S., Spartanburg, 1999—, tchr. lang. arts, 2002—. Mem. com. writing state stds. for alternative diploma program and developing curriculum and materials. Mem. Coun. for Exceptional Children. Republican. Baptist. Avocation: painting. Home: 588 Chattooga Rd Roebuck SC 29376-3384

MCCRAY, DORIS RAINES, minister; b. Petersburg, Va., July 1, 1940; d. Linwood and Florence Raines; m. John McCray, Aug. 29, 1958; children: Ronald, Deborah Ramsey, Wayne, Donald. Student, Va. State U., 1980; BA, Richmond Va. Sem., 1986, MDiv, 1988. Notary pub. Va. Assoc. min. Met. Ch., Petersburg, Va., 1982—84, 1990—2000; assoc. pastor Good Shepherd Ch., 1985—86, asst. pastor, 1986—87, interim pastor, 1987—90; assoc. pastor Olive Br. Ch., Dinwiddie, 2000—. Counselor Southside Mental Health, Petersburg, 1984—90, Southside Area Family Counseling, 1984—90; chaplain Southside Regional Hosp., 1983—95. Sr. citizen mem. Sr. Adv. Com., Richmond, Va., 2002; ct. apptd. spl. advocate, 2001—; counselor Contact

Tri-City Teleministry, 1978—87; mem. Am. Baptist Churches, 1983—91, Min. Coun., 1989, Petersburg Area Clergy, 1982—2004, pres., 1989; founder, advisor Cmty. Out-Reach Mighty Ministerial Advocacy, 2000—04. Mem.: AARP, Nat. Notary Assn., Nat. Women's History Mus. (charter mem.), U. Va. Alumni Assn. (assoc.). Democrat. Baptist. Avocations: reading, travel. Home: 1712 W Clara Dr Petersburg VA 23803 Office: Olive Br Ch 11119 Boydton Plank Rd Dinwiddie VA 23841 Personal E-mail: preacherdot@hotmail.com.

MCCRAY, GLENDA ELAINE, elementary school educator; d. James Paul and Agerene Lindsey McCray. BS in Edn., Lamar U., Beaumont, Tex., 1991; MEd, Tex. A&M U., 1995. Tchr. 2d grade French Elem., Beaumont; tchr. Beaumont Ind. Sch. Dist., 1991—. Mentor I Have a Dream, Beaumont, 1999—2006. Mem.: Beaumont Tchrs. Assn. (corr.; bd. mem. 2002—04), Sci. Tchrs. Assn. Tex. (assoc.). Home: 890 Norwood Dr Beaumont TX 77706 Office: French Elementary 3525 Cleveland Beaumont TX 77703 Office Phone: 409-832-6631. Personal E-mail: glenda.mccray@sbcglobal.net.

MCCRAY, NIKKI KESANGAME, professional basketball player; b. Collierville, Tenn., Dec. 17, 1971; BA in Sports Mktg. and Edn., U. Tenn., 1995. Basketball player USA Women's Nat. Team, 1996; guard Washington Mystics WNBA, 1998—2001, Ind. Fever WNBA, 2003—03, Phoenix Mercury WNBA, 2004, San Antonio Silver Stars WNBA, 2005—. Recipient Gold Medalist, Atlanta Olympic Games, 1996, Sydney Olympic Games, 2000. Achievements include a park named in her honor in hometown of Colliersville, Tenn. Avocation: singing. Mailing: San Antonion Silver Stars One SBC Center San Antonio TX 78219

MCCREA, MELISSA LAUREN, elementary school educator; b. Balt., Dec. 23, 1976; d. Leigh Ann McCusker and Stephen Bruce Ackerman; m. Bryan Shawn McCrea, June 21, 2003. BS in Phys. Edn., Towson U., Md., 1999. Phys. edn. tchr. Emmorton Elem. Sch., Bel Air, Md., 1999—; track and field coach Bel Air H.S., Md., 2000—. Recipient Simon McNeeley award, Md. Assn. for Health, Phys. Edn., Recreation and Dance, 2005. Mem.: AAHPERD (assoc.), Nat. Assn. for Sport and Phys. Edn. (assoc.), Md. Assn. for Health, Phys. Edn., Recreation and Dance (assoc.). Avocations: running, skiing, recreational sports. Office Phone: 410-638-3920.

MCCREA, SHAUN S., lawyer; b. 1956; d. Robert McCrea. BA, U. Oreg.; JD, 1983. Bar: Oreg. Atty. McCrea P.C., Eugene, Oreg. Vice chmn. Oreg. Pub. Def. Svcs. Commn. Mem.: Nat. Assn. Criminal Def. Lawyers, Oreg. Criminal Def. Lawyers Assn. (past pres.). Avocation: mythology. Office: McCrea PC 1147 High St Eugene OR 97401 Office Phone: 541-485-1182. Office Fax: 541-485-6847. E-mail: smccrea@callatg.com.

MCCREARY, BRENDA KAY, elementary school educator; b. Jerseyville, Ill., Dec. 31, 1960; d. Duey Lee and Peggy Joann Skinner; children: Katelyn Louise, Meghan Nicole, Danah Rae. Masters, Rockford Coll., Ill. Cert. middle sch. tchr. Ill. Health/phys. edn. tchr. Illini Mid. Sch., Jerseyville, 1990—. Home: 908 East Prairie Jerseyville IL 62052 Office: Illini Middle School 1101 S Liberty Jerseyville IL 62052 Personal E-mail: bmccreary@gtec.com.

MCCREARY, JEAN HUTCHINSON, lawyer; b. Harrisburg, Pa., 1955; BA, U. Rochester, 1977; JD, U. Fla., 1982. Bar: Fla. 1982, NY 1985, cert.: Profl. Environ. Auditor 1997. Ptnr., practice group leader Energy & Environ. Practice Nixon Peabody LLP, Rochester, NY. Pres. The Auditing Roundtable, 1995—96; commr. Rochester Health Commn. Mem.: Environ. Auditing Roundtable, Monroe Bar Assn., NY Bar Assn. Office: Nixon Peabody LLP 1300 Clinton Sq Rochester NY 14604-1792 Office Phone: 585-263-1611. Office Fax: 585-263-1600. E-mail: jmccreary@nixonpeabody.com.

MCCRYSTAL, ANN MARIE, community health nurse, administrator; b. Jersey City, Jan. 5, 1937; d. Robert W. and Sybilla M. (Koenig) Bouse; m. Hugh K. McCrystal, Sept. 14, 1963; children: Carolyn, Hugh K., Kelly Ann. BSN, U. Miami, 1959. Office mgr., sec.-treas. Indian River Urology Assocs., P.C., Vero Beach, Fla.; chmn. bd. Vis. Nurse Assn. of the Treasure Coast, Vero Beach. Chmn. Vis. Nurse Assn. Treasure Coast Found., 1991, adv. coun. Vis. Nurse Assn. of Am., 1994; chmn. bd. dirs. Vis. Nurse Assn./Hospice Found. Named Indian River County Woman of Distinction, Girl Scouts Am., 1998, Vol. Fundraiser of Yr., Treasure Coast Nat. Soc. Fundraising Execs., 1999, Book of Golden Deeds award Exch. Club Vero Beach, 2000; recipient C. of C. Cmty. Svc. award, 2000, Nat. award for Cmty. Svc., Nat. Soc. Colonial Dames VXII Cadbury, 2005. Mem. Fla. Nurses Assn. (Dist. 17 Nurse of Yr. 2004), Am. Urol. Assn. Allied, Am. Cancer Soc. (life hon.), Vis. Nurse Assn. Am. (chmn. bd. dirs. 1995—, adv. coun., edn. com., Vol. of Yr. 1991), Sigma Theta Tau. Home: 511 Bay Dr Vero Beach FL 32963-2163 Personal E-mail: ammccrystal@yahoo.com.

MCCUBBIN, SUSAN BRUBECK, lawyer, advertising executive; b. Decatur, Ill., Mar. 16, 1948; d. Rodney Earl Brubeck and Marilyn Jean (McMahon) Hopkins; 1 child, Martin Charles Jr. LLB, Western State U., Fullerton, Calif., 1977. Bar: Calif. 1977; lic. real estate broker, Calif. Ptnr. Blue Chip Constrn. Co., Santa Ana, Calif., 1969-73; pres. Brubeck Co., San Francisco and Newport Beach, Calif., 1973-78; sole practice San Francisco, 1978-79; sr. mktg. cons., broker Grubb & Ellis Co., San Francisco, 1979-87; pres. Greenwich Corp., San Rafael, Calif., 1987—; broker officer Orion Ptnrs. Ltd., 1996—2002; pres. Brubeck Comm., Sausalito, Calif., 1996—, Sausalito Signs, 2002—, Media3, Sausalito, 2005—. Columnist Automotive Age Mag., 1974-75. Chmn. U.S. Senate Primary Campaign, Orange County, Calif., 1976. Mem.: Rotary Club. Republican. Avocations: computers/videography, tennis, historical study, travel, music. Office Phone: 415-332-4560. E-mail: susan@media3.cc.

MCCUE, JUDITH W., lawyer; b. Phila., Apr. 7, 1948; d. Emanuel Leo and Rebecca (Raffel) Weiss; m. Howard M. McCue III, Apr. 3, 1971; children: Howard, Leigh. BA cum laude, U. Pa., 1969; JD, Harvard U., 1972. Bar: Ill. 1972, U.S. Tax Ct. 1984. Ptnr. McDermott Will & Emery LLP, Chgo., 1995—. Dir. Schawk, Inc., Des Plaines, Ill.; past pres. Chgo. Estate Planning Coun. Trustee Chgo. Symphony Orch., 1995—, vice chmn., 1998—2001, 2005—. Mem.: Chgo. Bar Assn. (chmn. probate practice com. 1984—85, chmn. estate and gift tax divsn. of fed. tax com. 1988—89), Am. Coll. Trust and Estate Counsel (com. chmn. 1991—94, regent 1993—2000, com. chmn. 1998—2001, pres. 2005—06, immediate past pres. 2006—). Office: McDermott Will & Emery LLP 227 W Monroe St Ste 3100 Chicago IL 60606-5096 E-mail: jmccue@mwe.com.

MCCUISTION, PEG OREM, retired health facility administrator; b. Houston, July 28, 1930; d. William Darby and Dorothy Mildred (Beckett) Orem; m. Palmer Day McCuistion, Sept. 4, 1949 (div. 1960); 1 child, Leanne E. BBA, Southwest Tex. State, 1963; MBA, George Washington U., 1968; EdD, Wayne State U., 1989. Patient care adminstr. Holy Cross Hosp., Silver Spring, Md., 1968-79; exec. dir. Hospice of S.E. Mich., Southfield, 1979-86, Hospice Austin, Tex., 1987-94; CEO EMBI, Inc., Arlington, Tex., 1994—98; gen. mgr. Hospice Home Care, San Antonio, 2001—04, ret., 2004. Bd. dirs. Cmty. Home for the Elderly, Austin, 1989-92. Fellow Am. Coll. Health Care Execs. (membership com.); mem. Internat. Hospice Inst. (assoc.), Nat. Hospice Orgn. (chair standards and accreditation com.), Tex. Hospice Orgn. (pres. 1993-94), exec. com., standards and ethics com., edn. com., chair legis. com.), Mich. Hospice Orgn. (chair edn. com., bd. dirs.). Personal E-mail: pegomc@wimberley-tx.com.

MCCULLOCH, ANGELA JEAN, theater educator, music educator; b. New Bedford, Mass., Dec. 24, 1976; d. McCulloch Edward Robert and Judith Lee McCulloch. EdB, U. Conn., Storrs, BA in Music, 2000. Cert. provisional educator Conn. Theatre arts and music educator Broadview Mid. Sch., Danbury, Conn., 2002—. Musical dir. Somers HS, Conn., 2001—02. Prodr., musician: (plays) Tales from Da Hood, Snoopy, Godspell, Jr.; musician: (plays) Funny Girl. Mem.: ACDA. Home: 11 Mannions Ln Danbury CT 06810 Office: Broadview Mid Sch 72 Hospital Ave Danbury CT 06810 Office Phone: (203)790-2808. Home Fax: 203-798-7390. Personal E-mail: racerchiquita76m@gmail.com. Business E-Mail: mccula@danbury.k12.ct.us.

MCCULLOCH, LINDA, school system administrator; b. Mont., Dec. 21, 1954; m. Bill McCulloch, 1978. BA in Elem. Edn., U. Mont., 1982, MA in Elem. Edn., 1990. Tchr. Pub. Schs, Mont., Ashland, Missoula, Bonner, 1978—95; rep. Mont. Ho. of Reps., 1995—2001; supt. pub. instrn. Mont., 2002—. Mem. juvenile justice, mental health, judiciary, Indian Affairs coms. Mont. Ho. Reps., 1997; minority caucus leader Ho. Reps., Helena, Mont., 1999; vice chair edn. com. Mont. Ho. Reps., 1999. Mem., officer PTA Assn., Helena, 1985—; bd. dirs. Missoula Developmental Svcs. Corp.; mem. adv. com. Missoula Youth Homes Foster Care. Recipient Mike and Maureen Mansfield Libr. scholaship, 1981, J.C. Penny Vol. Program award, 1998. Mem.: AAUW, LWV, Five Valleys Reading Assn., Mont. State Reading Coun., Mont. Fedn. Tchrs., Mont. Ednl. Assn., Mont. Libr. Assn. (Legislator of Yr. award 1997), Mont. Family Union, Montana Dem. Womens Club. Office: Mont Office Pub Instruction PO box 202501 1227 11th Ave Helena MT 59620-2501 Office Fax: 406-444-5658. Business E-Mail: opisupt@mt.gov.

MCCULLOCH, RACHEL, economist, educator; b. 1942; m. Gary Edward Chamberlain; children: Laura Chamberlain Gehl, Neil Dudley Chamberlain BA, U. Pa., 1962; MA in Teaching, U. Chgo., 1965, MA, 1971, PhD, 1973; student, MIT, 1966-67. Economist Cabinet Task Force on Oil Import Control, Washington, 1969; instr., then asst. prof. Grad. Sch. Bus. U. Chgo., 1971-73; asst. prof., then assoc. prof. econs. Harvard U., Cambridge, Mass., 1973-79; assoc. prof., then prof. econs. U. Wis., Madison, 1979-87; prof. Brandeis U., Waltham, Mass., 1987—, Rosen Family prof., 1989—, dir. Lemberg Program in Internat. Econs. and Fin., 1990-91, dir. PhD program Grad. Sch. Internat. Econs. and Fin., 1994—2001, chair dept. econs., 2006—. Mem. Pres.'s Commn. on Indsl. Competitiveness, 1983-84; mem. adv. coun. Office Tech. Assessment, U.S. Congress, 1979-88; cons. World Bank, Washington, 1984-86, 2004-05; mem. com. on internat. rels. studies with People's Republic of China, 1984-91; rsch. assoc. Nat. Bur. Econ. Rsch., Cambridge, 1985-93; mem. adv. com. Inst. for Internat. Econs., Washington, 1987—; faculty Advanced Mgmt. Network, La Jolla, Calif., 1985-92; mem. com. examiners econs. test Grad. Record Exam. Ednl. Testing Svc., 1990-96, chair, 1992-96; mem. discipline adv. com. for Fulbright scholar awards in econs. Coun. Internat. Exch. Scholars, 1991-93, chair, 1992-93; mem. adv. com. for Fulbright Chairs Program, 1997; cons. Global Economy Project, Edn. Film Ctr., 1993-94; mem. study group on pvt. capital flows to developing and transitional economies Coun. Fgn. Rels., 1995-96, acad. adv. panel, Fed. Reserve Bank of Boston, 1999—; faculty assoc. Harvard Inst. for Internat. Devel., 1997-2000; fellow Internat. Leadership Forum, 2001-; AGIP prof. internat. econs. Sch. Advanced Internat. Studies, Bologna Ctr., Johns Hopkins U., 2004-05. Author: Research and Development as a Determinant of U.S. International Competitiveness, 1978; contbr. articles to profl. jours. and books. Grantee NSF, 1975-79, Hoover Inst., 1984-85, German Marshall Fund of U.S., 1985, Ford Found., 1985-88, U.S. Dept. Edn., 1990-91, Schulhof Found., 2001-02. Mem. Am. Econ. Assn. (dir. summer program for minority students 1983-84, mem. executive com., 1997-2000), Internat. Trade and Fin. Assn. (bd. dirs. 1993-95). Office: Brandeis U Dept Econs MS 021 PO Box 549110 Waltham MA 02454-9110 Business E-Mail: mcculloch@brandeis.edu.

MCCULLOH, JUDITH MARIE, editor; b. Spring Valley, Ill., Aug. 16, 1935; d. Henry A. and Edna Mae (Traub) Binkele; m. Leon Royce McCulloh, Aug. 26, 1961. BA, Ohio Wesleyan U., 1956; MA, Ohio State U., 1957; PhD, Ind. U., 1970. Asst. to dir. Archives of Traditional Music, Bloomington, Ind., 1964-65; asst. editor U. Ill. Press, Champaign, 1972-77, assoc. editor, 1977-82, sr. editor, 1982-85, exec. editor, 1985—, dir. devel., 1992—2003; asst. dir., 1997—. Advisor John Edwards Meml. Forum, LA, 1973—. Mem. Editorial Bd. Am. Music, 1980-89, Jour. Am. Folklore, Washington, 1986-90; co-editor Stars of Country Music, 1975; editor (LP) Green Fields of Ill., 1963, (LP) Hell-Bound Train, 1964, Ethnic Recordings in America, 1982; gen. editor Music in American Life series. Trustee Am. Folklife Ctr., Libr. of Congress, Washington, 1986—2004, chair, 1990—92, 1996—98, trustee emerita, 2004—. Fulbright grantee, 1958-59; NDEA grantee, 1961, 62-63; grantee Nat. Endowment for the Humanities, 1978; recipient Disting. Achievement citation Ohio Wesleyan U. Alumni Assn., Disting. Svc. award Soc. for Am. Music, Lifetime Achievement award Belmont U. Curb Music Industry, Disting. Achievement award Internat. Bluegrass Music Assn. Fellow: Am. Folklore Soc. (exec. bd. 1974—79, pres. 1986—87, exec. bd. 2001—03); mem.: Am. Musicological Soc. (mem. coun. 2005—), Am. Anthropol. Assn., Soc. Ethnomusicology (hon.; treas. 1982—86), Soc. Am. Music (1st v.p. 1989—93, coun. 2005—). Democrat. Office: U Ill Press 1325 S Oak St Champaign IL 61820-6903 Business E-Mail: jmmccull@uillinois.edu.

MCCULLOUGH, ALICIA, English language educator; b. Covington, Ky., May 1, 1948; d. William Prentice and Rosella Custard McCullough. BA in English, Hampton U., Va., 1970; MA in Edn., U. NC, Charlotte, 1976. English tchr. 4th grade and reading Our Lady of Consolation Sch., Charlotte, 1971—73; reading tchr. Kings Mountain Sch. Sys., NC, 1974—76; English instr. NC Cen. U., Durham, 1976—85; instr. African Am. studies U. NC, Charlotte, 1985—90; English instr. Gaston Coll., Dallas, NC, 1993—. Pres. Minority Affairs Com. Gaston Coll., 2006—; bd. dirs. The Women's Shelter, Charlotte, 1990—92. Named Divisional Instr. of Yr., Gaston Coll. Arts & Scis., 2006; recipient rsch. study grant, NEH, 2005. Mem.: Nat. Coun. Tchrs. of English, 2-Yr. Coll. English Assn., Delta Sigma Theta. Democrat. Baptist. Avocations: sewing, cooking, reading, history. Office: Gaston Coll 201 Hwy 321 S Dallas NC 28034 Office Phone: 704-922-6459.

MCCULLOUGH, EILEEN (EILEEN MCCULLOUGH LEPAGE, ELLI MCCULLOUGH), financial consultant, writer, editor, educator; b. Phila., Oct. 16, 1946; d. Charles Norman and Marie Teresa (Inglesby) McCullough; m. Clifford Bennett LePage Jr., Mar. 6, 1970; children: Clifford Bennett III, Alexander Pierce. BA in English and Secondary Edn., George Washington U., Washington, D.C., 1969; MEd in Spl. Edn., Temple U., Phila., 1972. Cert. secondary sch. tchr.; registered securities rep. Record-keeper child growth and devel. program Children's Hosp. of Phila., 1965; with advt. dept. Phila. Inquirer, 1966-67; with ops. control U.S. Civil Svc. Commn., Washington, 1967-69; mgr. N.J. Bell Telephone, Trenton, 1969; rschr. Temple U., Phila., 1969-71; tchr. Wyomissing, Pa., 1972-77; fin. cons. various orgns., 1984-93; cons. EMLC, Reading, 1994—. Adj. instr. Reading (Pa.) Area C.C., 1978-81; lectr. English Albright Coll., Reading, 1981-84; founding mem. Common Cents Investment Club, 1983-93; founding and mng. ptnr. Klein LePage McCullough Partnership, Ocean City, N.J., 1982-96; presenter in field. Author: The Clue in the Snow, 1959; editor: 1st Complete Pocket Guide to Atlantic City Casinos, 1984, The Autobiography of Capt. Michael Kevolic, 1986; photographer Cherry Hill Mtg. Bd. dirs. Nat. Found. March of Dimes, Reading, 1969-75, chmn., 1974-75; bd. sch. dirs. Wyomissing Area Sch. Dist., 1984-92; bd. dirs. Wyomissing Pub. Libr., Reading, 1980-85; asst. chmn Region 8 Pa. Sch. Bds. Assn., 1989-91; dir. Saturday Morning Sch., Assn. for Children with Learning Disabilities, Reading, 1970; acting sec. Berks County Commn. for Women, Reading, 1993; active Reading Community Players, 1980; past bd. mem. Berks Ballet Theatre; past vol. Berks C. of C.; vol. mus. guide Reading Pub. Mus. and Art Gallery, 1999-2002, Berks County Chpt Am. Red Cross, 1997; presenter Green Circle, Reading Berks Human Rels. coun., Reading Pub. Schs., 1998-99. Fellow Pa. writing project; mem. AAUW (life; topic chmn.), Am. Assn. Individual Investors (life), Internat. Platform Soc., Women's Internat. Fedn. for World Peace. Avocations: dance, singing. Home and Office: EMLC 10 Phoebe Dr Reading PA 19610-2857 E-mail: emlco@comcast.net.

MCCULLOUGH, MARY W., social work educator, therapist; b. Phila., Aug. 14, 1945; d. Harry and Mildred (Steel) Werner; children: Phoebe, Abbé. BA, Millersville (Pa.) U., 1968; MSW, U. N.C., 1971; PhD, Temple U., 1991. LCSW Pa. Caseworker Dept. Pub. Welfare, Reading, Pa., 1968-69, social worker Chester, Pa., 1971-73, Mental Health Ctr., Chester, 1973-76, Phila. Family Ctr., 1976-77; asst. prof. West Chester (Pa.) U., 1977-94, assoc. prof., 1994-97, prof., 1997—. Author: Black and White Women as Friends: Building Cross-race Friendships, 1999. With Nat. Guard. Recipient various acad. and svc. awards. Mem.: Nat. Comm. Assn. (chair women's caucus 1995—97). Democrat. Avocations: travel, gardening, snorkeling. Office: West Chester U 509 Main St West Chester PA 19383-0001 Home: 700 N Franklin St #222 West Chester PA 19380-2334

MCCULLY, EMILY ARNOLD, illustrator, writer; b. Galesburg, Ill., 1939; d. Wade E. and Kathryn (Maher) Arnold; m. George E. McCully, 1961 (div. 1975); children: Nathaniel, Tad. BA, Brown U., 1961; MA, Columbia U., 1964; LittD (hon.), Brown U., 2002. Author: How's Your Vacuum Cleaner Working? O'Henry Collection, 1977, A Craving, 1982, (novel) Picnic, 1984 (Christopher award), First Snow, 1985, (novel) Life Drawing, 1986, The Show Must Go On, 1987, School, 1987, You Lucky Duck!, 1988, New Baby, 1988, The Grandma Mix-up, 1988, The Christmas Gift, 1988, Zaza's Big Break, 1989, Grandma's at the Lake, 1990, The Evil Spell, 1990, Speak Up, Blanche!, 1991, Mirette on the Highwire, 1992 (Caldecott medal 1992), Grandma's at Bat, 1993, The Amazing Felix, 1993, My Real Family, 1994, Crossing The New Bridge, 1994, Little Kit, or: The Industrious Flea Circus Girl, 1995, The Pirate Queen, 1995, The Ballot Box Battle, 1996, The Bobbin Girl, 1996, Popcorn at the Palace, 1997, Starring Mirette and Bellini, 1997, an Outlaw Thanksgiving, 1998, Beautiful Warrior, 1998, Mouse Practice, 1999, Monk Camps Out, 2000, The Orphan Singer, 2001, Four Hungry Kittens, 2001, Squirrel and John Muir, 2004; illustrator: Sea Beach Express, 1966, The Seventeenth Street Gang, 1966, Rex, 1967, Luigi of the Streets, 1967, That Mean Man, 1968, Gooney, 1968, Journey From Peppermint Street, 1968 (Nat. Book award 1969), The Mouse and the Elephant, 1969, The Fisherman, 1969, Tales from the Rue Brocca, 1969, Here I Am, 1969, Twin Spell, 1969, Hobo Toad and the Motorcycle Gang, 1970, Slip! Slop! Gobble!, 1970, Friday Night is Papa Night, 1970, Maxie, 1970, Steffie and Me, 1970, The Cat and the Parrot, 1970, Gertrude's Pocket, 1970, Go and Hush the Baby, 1971, Finders Keepers, 1971, Ma n Da La, 1971 (Bklyn. Mus. award 1976, N.Y. Pub. Libr. award 1976), Hurray for Captain Jane!, 1971, Michael Is Brave, 1971, Finding Out With Your Senses, 1971, Henry's Pennies, 1972, Jane's Blanket, 1972, Grandpa's Long Red Underwear, 1972, Girls Can Too!, 1972, The Boyhood of Grace Jones, 1972, Black Is Brown Is Tan, 1973, Isabelle the Itch, 1973, When Violet Died, 1973, That New Boy, 1973, How To Eat Fried Worms, 1973, Jenny's Revenge, 1974, Her Majesty, Grace Jones, 1974, Tree House Town, 1974, I Want Mama, 1974, Amanda, the Panda and the Redhead, 1975, The Bed Book, 1976, My Street's A Morning Cool Street, 1976, Professor Coconut and the Thief, 1977, Martha's Mad Dog, 1977, That's Mine, 1977, Where Wild Willie, 1978, No Help At All, 1978, Partners, 1978, The Twenty-Elephant Restaurant, 1978, What I Did Last Summer, 1978, The Highest Hit, 1978, I and Spraggy, 1978, Edward Troy and the Witch Cat, 1978, My Island Grandma, 1979, Whatever Happened to Beverly Bigler's Birthday?, 1979, Last Look, 1979, Ookie-Spooky, 1979, The Black Dog Who Went Into the Woods, 1980, How I Found Myself at the Fair, 1980, How We Got Our First Cat, 1980, Oliver and Allison's Week, 1980, Pajama Walking, 1981, The April Fool, 1981, I Dance in My Red Pajamas, 1982, The Halloween Candy Mystery, 1982, Go and Mush the Baby, 1982, Mitzi and the Terrible Tyrannosaurus Rex, 1983, Best Friend Insurance, 1983, Mail-Order Wings, 1984, Gertrude's Pocket, 1984, Fifth Grade Magic, 1984, The Ghastly Glasses, 1985, Fourth of July, 1985, The Explorer of Barkham Street, 1985, Wheels, 1986, Lulu and the Witch Baby, 1986, Richard and the Vratch, 1987, Molly, 1987, Molly Goes Hiking, 1987, Jam Day, 1987, The Boston Coffee Party, 1988, The Take-Along Dog, 1989, Selene Goes Home, 1989, The Magic Mean Machine, 1989, It Always Happens to Leona, 1989, The Grandpa Days, 1989, Dinah's Mad, Bad Wishes, 1989, Stepbrother Sabotage, 1990, Lulu Goes to Witch School, 1990, The Day Chubby Became Charles, 1990, The Christmas Present Mystery, 1990, Sky Guys to White Cat, 1991, Meatball, 1991, Leona and Ike, 1991, The Butterfly Birthday, 1991, Yankee Doodle Drumsticks, 1992, One Very Best Valentine's Day, 1992, Meet the Lincoln Lions Band, 1992, Jingle Bells Jam, 1992, In My Tent, 1992, Anne Flies the Birthday Bike, 1993, Amzat and His Brothers, 1993, Leo the Magnificent, 1996, Old Home Day, 1996, The Divide, 1997, Rabbit Pirates, 1999, Sing a Song of Piglets: A Calender in Verse, 2002, One, Two, ILove You, 2004.

MCCUNE, LINDA WILLIAMS, artist, educator; b. Dyersburg, Tenn., Sept. 29, 1950; d. Willard Charles and Margie Harrison Williams; m. William Derryman McCune II, Dec. 30, 1972; children: Nova Lauran, Tayce Caitlin. BFA, U. Tenn., 1974, postgrad., 1974-77; MFA, U. S.C., 1982. Cert. tchr. Tenn., S.C. Artist-illustrator U. Tenn., Knoxville, 1970-72; art history commentator Sta. WSJK-TV, Knoxville, 1971-72; artistic designer Morristown (Tenn.) Theatre Guild, 1971-78; artist in residence Morristown City Sch. Sys., 1972-77; asst. prof. art Walters State C.C., Morristown, 1973-77; display designer Laminite-Laminall Corp., Morristown, Tenn., 1975-76; co-owner Upstairs Gallery, Morristown, 1976-78; art cons. Allendale (S.C.) County Sch. Sys., 1979-80; co-owner Studio III Frame Shop, Allendale, 1979-86; grad. asst. U. S.C., Columbia, 1980-82, teaching assoc. Allendale, Walterboro, 1980-86; dir. Summer Art Series for Youth, Tryon, N.C., 1987-89; artist in residence S.C. Arts Commn. Residency Program, Columbia, 1987-89; mem. art faculty, leader fine arts Greenville (S.C.) Technical Coll., 1989—; grad. student advisor Vt. Coll., Montpelier, 1996—. Mem. fine arts com. Morristown C. of C., 1974—79, bicentennial com., 1975—76; sec. visual and environ. design panel Tenn. Arts Commn., Nashville, 1975—79; mem. fine arts com. Cmty. Devel. Bd., Allendale, 1980, downtown renovations com., 80; chmn. exhbns. com. Allendale County Arts Gallery and Mus., Allendale County Arts Coun., 1984—; mem. bd. Southeastern Art Assn., New Art Examiner Mag., Chgo., 1989—90; lectr. in field. One person shows include Archtl. Bldg. Gallery, U. Tenn., Knoxville, 1970, Morristown-Hamblen Libr., 1971, Walters State C.C., Morristown, 1974, 78, Jonesboro (Tenn.) Gallery, 1975, Appalachia State U., Boone, N.C., 1976, Emory and Henry Coll., Bristol, Va., 1976, Carrol Reese Mus. ETSU, Johnson City, Tenn., 1976, Kingsport (Tenn.) Fed., 1977, Rose Cultural Ctr. Mus., Morristown, 1978, U. S.C., Allendale, 1979, Weekend Gallery, Columbia Mus., 1980, Barnwell (S.C.) County Mus., 1982, Copland Wahl House, Columbia, 1982, Columbia Mus. Arts and Scis., 1983, Spirit Sq. Art Ctr., Charlotte, 1985, Nexus Contemporary Arts Ctr., Atlanta, 1986, Asheville (N.C.) Art Mus. Civic Ctr., 1990, Converse (S.C.) Coll., 1995, 291 Gallery, Greenville, 1996, Taylors (S.C.) First Bapt. Ch., 1997, Coastal Carolina U., Myrtle Beach, S.C., 1997, U. S.C., Spartanburg, 1997, S.C. Archives and History Ctr., Columbia, 1998, Pickens Mus., 2000, North Greenville Coll., 2002, Fine Arts Ctr. Kershaw, Conn., 2001, Union U., Jackson, Tenn.; exhibited in group shows at Dulin Art Mus., Knoxville, 1974, Austin Peay State U., Nashville, 1976, Spoletto Festival at Dock St. Theatre, Charleston, S.C., 1979, Beaufort (S.C.) Art Assn., 1979, 80, 81, Miss. Mus. Art, Jackson, 1981, Tampa (Fla.) Mus., 1983, Alexandria Mus. Art, La., 1983, Roanoke (Va.) Mus. Fine Arts, 1983, McKissick Mus., Columbia, 1982, 83, 93, 95, 96, 98, 2000, Tucson Mus., 1983, Hunter Mus. Art, Chattanooga, 1985, Arrowmont Sch. Arts and Crafts, Gatlinburg, Tenn., 1985, Spartanburg (S.C.) Arts Ctr., 1985, Allendale County Mus., 1986, Columbia Mus. Arts and Scis., 1986, 90, The Upstairs Gallery, Tryon, N.C., 1987, 88, Women's Art Registry Minn., Mpls., 1986, Furman U., Greenville, 1988, 93, 97, 99, S.C. State Mus., Columbia, 1989, 92, 94, 99, 2000, 01, 04, U. Ky., Lexington, 1990, Vista Arts Gallery, Columbia, 1991, Ownesboro (Ky.) Mus. Fine Arts, 1991, 2004, Havens Gallery, Columbia, 1992, Asheville Art Mus., 1993, Greenville County Mus., 1990, 93, 2001, 2002, Lee Hall Gallery, Clemson (S.C.) U., 1985, 95, Greenville Tech. Coll., 1996, 97, 99, 2000, 01, 03, U. S.C., Spartanburg, 1996, Columbia, 1996, Mobile (Ala.) Mus. Art, 1996, NationsBank Plz., Columbia, 1997, 2000, Rocky Mount (N.C.) Art Ctr., 1997, Fayetteville (N.C.) Mus. Art, 1997, Koller Gallery, Washington, 1997, The White House, Washington, 1998, 2001, Greensboro (S.C.) Cultural Art Ctr., 1998, Zone One Contemporary Gallery, Asheville, 1998, Lander U., Greenwood, S.C., 1998, 2004, North Charleston (S.C.) Rhodes Cultural Ctr., 1999, Wachovia Bank Bldg. Gallery, Greenville, 1999, Ashville, N.C., Arboretum, 2000, Burroughs-Chapin Mus., Myrtle Beach, S.C., 1999, Longwood Ctr. in the Visual Arts Farmville, Virginia, 2001, Brevard Coll., Brevard, N.C., 2000, Hartz Witzer Gallery, Charlotte, N.C., 2001, Wingate U., Wingate, N.C., 2001, Accessibility,

Sumpter, S.C., 2001, 02, Moore Coll. Art and Design, Phila., Pa., 2002, W.H. Moring Gallery, Ashboro, N.C., 2002, Fine Arts Ctr., Greenville, S.C., 2003, Anderson Co. Art Ctr., 1999, 2000, 02, 03, Florence Mus. Art, S.C., 2003, Elon Coll., Burlington, N.C., 2003, U. N.C., Asheville, 2003, Meredith Coll., Raleigh, 2003, City Gallery and Redux Gallery, Charleston, 2003, Eastern Carolina U. Sch. Art, 2004, Caldwell Art Ctr., Lenoir City, N.C., 2004, Kinston (N.C.) Art Ctr., 2004, Delta State U., Cleveland, Miss., 2004, Corban Estates Art Ctr., Waitakere City, New Zealand, 2004, many others; contbr. articles to various publs. Tchr. Taylors (S.C.) First Bapt. Ch., 1988—; active PTA Bd., Buena Vista Elem., Greer, S.C., 1991-92. Recipient award, Tenn. Water Color All-State Show, 1974, Beaufort Art Assn. Exhbn., 1979, 1980, 1981, McKissisk Mus. Exhbn., 1982, Sandoz SCRA Regional Exhbn., 1986, Seneca County Art Coun. Exhibit, 1998, 1999, Upstate Visual Arts Millenium Exhbn., 2000, Andenson Arts Coun., 1999, 100 yrs. 100 artist award, S.C. State Mus., 2000; grantee, S.C. Visual Arts, 2001—02, S.C. Visual Arts Commn., 2001. Mem. Nat. Art Edn. Assn., Southeastern Coll. Art Assn., Upstate Visual Artists, Tri State Sculptors (S.C. state rep.), Wash. Sculptors Group, Met. Arts Coun. Avocations: travel, visiting antique shows, collecting vintage broaches. Office: Greenville Tech Coll Visual Arts Dept PO Box 5616 Greenville SC 29606-5616 Office Phone: 864-848-2025. Business E-Mail: linda.mccune@gvltec.edu.

MCCUNE, MARY JOAN HUXLEY, microbiology educator; b. Lewistown, Mont., Jan. 14, 1932; d. Thomas Leonard and Anna Dorothy (Hardie) Huxley; m. Ronald William McCune, June 7, 1965; children: Anna Orpha, Heather Jean. BS, Mont. State Coll., 1953; MS, Wash. State U., 1955; PhD, Purdue U., 1965. Rsch. technician VA Hosp., Oakland, Calif., 1956-59; bacteriologist U.S. Naval Radiol. Def. Lab., San Francisco, 1959-61; tchg. assoc. Purdue U., West Lafayette, Ind., 1961-65, vis. asst. prof., 1965-66; asst. prof. Occidental Coll., L.A., 1966-69; asst. rsch. bacteriologist II UCLA, 1969-70; affiliate asst. prof. Idaho State U., Pocatello, 1970-80, from asst. prof. to prof. microbiology, 1980—2001; prof. emeritus, 2001. Instr. U. Calif., Davis, 1964. Contbr. articles to profl. jours. Pres. AK chpt. PEO, Pocatello, 1988-89; chair faculty senate Idaho State U., 1994-95. David Ross fellow Purdue U., 1964; named Outstanding Alumna, Assn. Women Students, Mont. State U., 1975. Mem. AAAS, N.Y. Acad. Sci., Idaho Acad. Sci. (trustee 1989-95, v.p. 1992-93, pres. 1993-94), Am. Soc. for Microbiology (v.p. Intermountain br. 1988-89, pres. 1989-90, sec.-treas. 2000-01), Idaho Edn. Alliance for Sci. (bd. dirs.), Sigma Xi, Sigma Delta Epsilon. Presbyterian. Home: 30 Colgate St Pocatello ID 83201-3459 Office: Idaho State U Dept Biol Scis Pocatello ID 83209-0001 E-mail: mccujoan@isu.edu.

MCCURDY, PAULETTE QUICK, nurse anesthetist; b. Columbia, S.C., May 12, 1953; d. Ansel Ray and Bertie Lee (Wadford) Quick; 1 child, Charles William McCurdy II. BSN, U. S.C., Columbia, 1974; cert., Richland Meml. Sch. Nurse Anesthesia, 1982. Charge nurse emergency rm. Richland Meml. Hosp., Columbia, S.C., 1974-76, head nurse, 1976-77, supr., 1977-79, asst. DON, 1979-80, nurse anesthetist, 1982-86, Anesthesiologists of Columbia, P.A., Columbia, 1986—88, 1992—2001, Logan Meml. Hosps., Russellville, Ky., 1988-92, Palmetto Health Bapt. Hosp., Columbia, 2001—. Recipient Agatha Hodgins award Richland Meml. Hosp. Sch. Nurse Anesthesia, 1982, Donald H. Harwood award for clin. instr., 1983. Mem. Am. Assn. Nurse Anesthetist. Home: 307 S Chimney Ln Columbia SC 29209-1986 Office: Palmetto Health Bapt Marion at Taylor Columbia SC 29220

MCCURLEY, MARY JOHANNA, lawyer; b. Baton Rouge, La., Oct. 3, 1953; d. William Edward and Leora Elizabeth (Block) Trice; m. Carl Michael McCurley, June 6, 1983; 1 stepchild, Melissa Reneé McCurley. BA, Centenary Coll., 1975; JD, St. Mary's U., 1979. Bar: Tex. 1979; cert. family law. Assoc. Martin, Withers & Box, Dallas, 1979-82, Raggio & Raggio, Inc., Dallas, 1982-83; ptnr. Bruner, McColl, McColloch & McCurley, Dallas, 1983-87; assoc., ptnr. Selligson & Douglass, Dallas, 1987-90; jr. ptnr. Koons, Fuller, McCurley & VanderEykel, Dallas, 1990-92; ptnr. McCurley, Orsinger, McCurley,. Nelson & Downing, Dallas, 1992—. Contbr. articles to profl. jours. Adv. Women's Service League, Dallas, 1993—. Master: Annette Stewart Am. Inn. Ct. (sec.-treas. 2003—04); mem.: Dallas Bar Assn., Tex. Acad. Family Law Specialist, Tex. State Bar Assn. (sec. 2001, vice-chair 2001, treas. 2001, chair 2003—, family law coun.), Dallas Bar Assn. (chair family law sect. 1985), Am. Acad. Matrimonial Lawyers (treas. Tex. chpt. 1993—95, sec. 1995—96, pres. 1997, pres. Tex. chpt. 1997—98, bd. govs. 2000, nat. sec. 2000—02, nat. v.p. 2002—, nat. bd. dirs.). Methodist. Avocations: golf, travel, jogging, horseback riding. Home: 4076 Hanover Ave Dallas TX 75225-7009 Office: McCurley Orsinger McCurley Nelson & Downing LLP 5950 Sherry Ln Ste 800 Dallas TX 75225-6533 Office Phone: 214-273-2400.

MCCURRY, MARGARET IRENE, architect, educator, furniture designer, interior designer; b. Chgo., Sept. 26, 1942; d. Paul D. and Irene B. McC.; m. Stanley Tigerman, Mar. 17, 1979. BA, Vassar Coll., 1964. Registered architect, Ill., Mass., Mich., Tex., Wis., Pa., Ind., Fla.; registered interior designer, Ill. Design coord. Quaker Oats Co., Chgo., 1964-66; sr. interior designer Skidmore, Owings & Merrill, Chgo., 1966-77; pvt. practice architect Margaret I, Chgo., 1977-82; ptnr. Tigerman, McCurry, Chgo., 1982—. Vis. studio critic Art Inst. Chgo., 1985-86, 88, 98, lectr., 1988, 98; vis. studio critic U. Ill., Chgo., Miami U., Oxford, Ohio, 1990; juror Internat. furniture awards Progressive Architecture mag., N.Y.C., 1986, advt. awards, 1988; juror design grants Nat. Endowment for Arts, Washington, 1983; NEA Challenge Design Rev., 1992; peer reviewer design excellence program Gen. Svcs. Administrn., 1992—; juror, Wis., Minn., Calif., Va., Washington, Pitts., Ky., Ga. Conn. Soc. Architects, Detroit, N.Y.C., Memphis, Austin, L.A., Toledo, Jacksonville chpts. AIA, Am. Wood Coun., AIA Students Design Competition, 1993. Author: Margaret McCurry: Constructing 25 Short Stories, 2000; contbr. Chgo. Archtl. Club Jour.; designer, contbr. archtl. exhibit Art Inst. Chgo., 1983-85, 93, 99, 2005, Chgo. Hist. Soc., 1984, Gulbenkian Found., Lisbon Portugal, 1989, Chgo. Athenaeum, 1990, Gwenda Jay Gallery, 1992, Women of Design Traveling Exhbn., 1992-96; archtl. drawings and models in permanent collection Art Inst. Chgo. and Deutsches Architektur Mus., Frankfurt. Chmn. furniture sect. fundraising auction Sta. WTTW-TV, PBS, Chgo., 1975-76; mem. Chgo. Beautiful Com., 1968-70; pres. alumni coun. Grad. Sch. Design, Harvard U., 1997-2000; bd. dirs. Architecture and Design Soc. Art Inst. Chgo., 1988-97, mem. textile adv. bd. textile dept. Loeb fellow Harvard U., 1986-87; recipient Builders Choice Grand award Builders Mag., 1985, Interior Design award Interiors Mag., 1983, Dean of Architecture award Chgo. Design Source and the Merchandise Mart, 1989, Designer of Distinction award ASID, 2002; named a Dean of Design, Archtl. Digest, 2005; inducted into Interior Design Hall of Fame, Interior Design Mag., 1990, ASID Design Excellence Residential Ill Chptr award, 2005, Hist. Preservation award, 2005, Corp. Office award, 2005 Fellow AIA (mem. coll. fellows, v.p. bd. dirs. Chgo. chpt. 1984-89, chair 1993, nat. design com., lectr. Colo. chpt. 1985, nat. conv. 1988, 97-98, Monterey Design Conf. 1989, Washington Design Ctr. 1989, Nat. Honor award 1984, Nat. Interior Architecture award 1992, 98, Disting. Bldg. award Chgo. chpt. 1984, 86, 91, 94, 99-2000, Disting. Interior Architecture award 1981, 83, 88, 91, 97, product display Neocon award 1985, 88, Gold award best of Neocon 1998, Associated Licensed Archs. Silver Medal Design award 2003), Internat. Interior Design Assn., Chgo. Network, Am. Soc. Interior Designers (v.p. bd. dirs. Chgo. chpt., Nat. Design award 1992, 94, Ill. chpt. Design award 1994, 2005, Design Excellence award in hist. preservation, 2005, in corp. interiors, 2005), Chgo. Archtl. Club, Arts Club Chgo., Harvard Alumni Assn. (dir. 2000-06, v.p. Chgo., 2004-06, pres., 2006-). Episcopalian. Avocations: drawing, writing, travel, golf, gardening. Office: Tigerman McCurry Archs 444 N Wells St Chicago IL 60610-4501 Office Phone: 312-644-5880. Business E-Mail: mimccurry@tigerman-mccurry.com.

MCCUTCHAN, PATRICIA LYNN, physician; b. Toledo, Nov. 18, 1957; d. James G. and Frances (Przystup) McC. Cert., St. Vincent Hosp., Toledo, 1978; B in Individualized Studies with honors, Lourdes Coll., 1989; MD, Med. Coll. Ohio, 1994. Spl. procedures technologist Wood County Hosp., Bowling Green, Ohio, 1978-94; resident in diagnostic radiology Providence Hosp., Southfield, Mich., 1994-98. Instr. anatomy and physiology Providence Hosp. Sch. Radiologic Tech., Southfield, 1994-98. Mem. AMA, Am. Coll. Radiology, Radiol. Soc. N.Am., Kappa Gamma Pi. Avocations: piano, golf, bowling, travel, animals. Office: Wood County Hosp 950 W Wooster St Bowling Green OH 43402-2603

MCCUTCHEON, JADE ROSINA, performing arts educator; d. Joana Lutzen McCutcheon. Diploma in Directing, Nat. Inst. Dramatic Art, Sydney, Australia, 1989; M in Creative Arts, U. Wollongong, Australia, 1990; D in Creative Arts, U. Tech. Sydney, Australia, 2000. Dir., lectr. Charles Sturt U., Bathurst, New South Wales, Australia, 1992—2001; asst. prof. U. Calif., Davis, 2003—. Dir.: (drama) Myth, Propoganda and Disaster in Nazi Germany and Contemporary America. Dir. Voices for Youth, Bathurst, 1999—2000. Mem.: Internat. Fedn. Theatre Rsch. (convenor 2003—06). Concerns Of People. Avocations: photography, poetry, walking. Office: Univ Calif Davis One Shields Ave Davis CA 95616 Office Phone: 530 7520891. Personal E-mail: jrmccutcheon@ucdavis.edu.

MCDADE, ROBERTA CLARK, secondary school educator; b. Balt., Dec. 19, 1951; d. Joseph Thomas and Esther Claire Clark; children: Edward Matthew Day, Rebecca Marie Day. BA in English and Elem. Edn., Salisbury State Coll., Md., 1973; MEd in Secondary Math., U. Del., Newark, Del., 1976. Lic. profl. tchr. Colo. Dept. Edn., 2002. Resident asst. Salisbury State Coll., Md., 1971—73; tchr. Kent County Pub. Schs., Chestertown, Md., 1973—76; home daycare provider Chestertown, Md., 1976—82; instr. math. Chesapeake Coll., Wye Mills, Md., 1982—83; tchr. Anne Arundel County Pub. Schs., Annapolis, Md., 1983—87; substitute tchr. Colo. Springs, 1987—88; instr. Basic Skills Edn. Program, Fort Carson, Colo., 1989; tchr. Colo. Springs Dist. 11, Colo., 1990—. Mem. com. Md. State Dept. Edn., Balt., 1980—83; participant step program NASA, Houston, 1996. Coach baseball Severna Pk. (Md.) Little League, 1986; coach wrestling Severna Pk. (Md.) Parks and Recreation, 1985—86; sec. Boy Scouts Am., Cape St Claire, Md., 1986—87, mem. troop com. Pikes Peak Coun. Colo. Springs, 1989—2006; leader Girl Scouts Am., Arnold, Md., 1986—87, leader wagon wheel coun. Colo. Springs, 1992—97; host parent Am. Field Svc., Colo. Springs, 1991—2000; adv. youth Sr. H.S. Chapel at Peterson AFB, Colo. Springs, 1987—89, Asbury United Meth. Fellowship, Salisbury, Md., 1970—73; tchr. christian edn. St Francis Assisi Ch., 1994—97, coord. christian edn., 1998—2001, mem. discernment com., 2005—06. Home: 1811 Summernight Terr Colorado Springs CO 80909-2725 Office: Sprng Creek Youth Svcs Ctr 3190 E Las Vegas St Colorado Springs CO 80906 Office Phone: 719-328-6753. Office Fax: 719-328-6619. Personal E-mail: beccyesmom@hotmail.com. Business E-Mail: ackerrc@d11.org.

MCDADE, TURINA L., principal; b. Bkyln., Sept. 25, 1979; d. Turia M. McDade. BA, SUNY, Albany, 2001; MS, U. Albany, 2002, MS, 2006. Cert. Provisional K-6 Tchg. NY, SAS NY. Grad. intern NY State Edn., Albany, 2001; asst. tchr. St. Catherine's Sch., Albany, 1999—2002, cirrculm coord., 2002—05, prin., 2005—. Mem.: Phi Delta Kappa. Office: St Catherines Ctr for Children 30 N Main Ave Albany NY 12203

MCDANIEL, ANNA S., language educator; b. Van Buren, Ark., Dec. 10, 1940; d. John Dean and Virginia (Linn) Maurer; m. Johnny F. McDaniel, June 30, 1987; children: Johnny Lee, Elisabeth Rice, Kyle Page. BA, Sonoma State U., 1978; MEd, Texas A&M, 1989. Cert. Tex. tchr. Educator- English Spkrs. Other Langs. Dallas Ind. Sch. Dist., Dallas, 1987—2004; coord. Critical World Langs. Bryan Adams H.S., Dallas, 1989—; ret., 2004. Contbr. mags. including Education West Mag., 2001. Named Outstanding Russian Facilitator, Russian Am. Ctr., Dallas, Tex., 2000, Tchr. of Yr., Bryan Adams HS, 2000; recipient Process Innovation award, Kenesis Corp., 2001. Mem.: DAR, Lions (sec. 2006—). Conservative. Episcopalian. Avocation: travel.

MCDANIEL, HELEN MARIE, retired social worker; b. Columbus, Ohio, Nov. 6, 1918; d. Dennis Samuel and Marie (Carter) McDaniel; m. Never Marriet. BSc in Social Work, Ohio State U., Columbus, Ohio, 1941, MA in Social Adminstrn., 1942, PhD in Social Work, 1969; LHD (hon.), Ohio Dominican, Columbus, Ohio, 1985. Dir. girls work Franklin Settlement, Detroit, 1942—44; with Cath. Social Svcs., Inc., Columbus, 1946—71, exec. dir., 1971—85, ret., 1985. Adv. coun. alumni Ohio State U.; mem. Bishop's planning com. Diocese of Columbus; mem. fin. com. St. Mary Magdalene Parish; mem. numerous offices and coms. Conf. Cath. Charities, 1964—83. Lt. jg. USN, 1944—46, ret. USN, 1956. Named Woman of Yr., Pilot Club Columbus, Ohio, 1983; recipient Outstanding Alumnus award, Coll. Social Work, Ohio State U., 1982, Pro-Ecclesiae at Pontifice medal, 1983, Outstanding Work in Cmty. award, City Columbus, 1984, Outstanding Leader award, Christ Child Soc., 1985. Home: 419 Derrer Rd Columbus OH 43204

MCDANIEL, KAY, education educator, writer; d. William Bill and Frances Josephine McDaniel. MS in Sports Sci., U.S. Sports Acad., Daphe, Ala., 1995. Asst. prof. edn. Honor Soc. Edn., Cleve., Tenn., 2002—. Adv. Lee U., Cleve., 2003—06. Contbr. columns in newspapers, articles to jours. and mags. Vol. Spl. Olympics, Cleve., 1985—2006; dir. free clinics Kay McDaniel Tennis Clinics, Cleve., 2003—06. Named to Internat. Libr. Photography, 2005; recipient Profl. Tennis Tournament award, Womens Profl. Tour, 1980—86, Honor an Educator award, Honor Soc. Edn., 2003—06. Mem.: So. Tennis Assn. (life Lifetime Achievement award), U.S. Tennis Assn. (life named Women's Tennis Assn. Fastest Serve in Women's Profl. Tennis 1995), Christian Writers Guild, Christian Golf Assn. (hon.; bd. dirs. 2003—06), Kappa Delta Pi (hon. Honor an Educator award 2003), Delta Zeta Tau (hon.), Theta Delta Kapa (hon.), Kappa Psi Nu (hon.; head sponsor 1996—2006). Republican. Office: Lee University/College of Education 1120 N Ocoee Street Cleveland TN 37320 Office Phone: 423-614-8475. Office Fax: 423-614-8180. Business E-Mail: kmcdaniel@leeuniversity.edu.

MCDANIEL, KRISTEN, secondary school educator; d. Sue Leitzke and Richard Fulmer; m. Mark McDaniel, July 26, 1997. BS in Secondary Edn., U. Wis., Milw., 1989—93, MS in Curriculum & Instrn., 2000—04. Tchr. Sci. Acad. of South Tex., Mercedes, 1994—98; edn. therapist Rogers Meml. Hosp., Oconomowoc, Wis., 2000—02; tchr. Ft. Atkinson HS, Wis., 2002—. Fellow Summer Inst. on Environ. History, NEH, 1996. Mem.: Global Assn. Tchrs of Econs. (assoc.), Wis. Coun. of Social Studies (assoc.; rep. 2005). Office: Fort Atkinson HS 925 Lexington Blvd Fort Atkinson WI 53538 Office Phone: 920-563-7811 2028. Business E-Mail: mcdanielk@mail.fortschools.org.

MCDANIEL, MILDRED GAGE, elementary school educator; b. Marion, N.C., June 6, 1938; d. William James and Nellie Ruth (Davis) Ledbetter; m. Keith S. Gage, June 13, 1959 (dec. May 1976); children: Wendy Carver, Tammy Butler; m. William Royce McDaniel, Apr. 23, 1983 (dec. July 2005). BS, Towson U., 1960; masters equiv., Johns Hopkins U., U. Md., 1972. Tchr., grade 6 Balt. (Md.) County Bd. Edn., 1960-66, reading tchr., 1968-73, reading specialist, 1974—98. Recipient Vol. Svc. award Gov. of Md., 1988, Thanks to Tchrs. Excellence award, 1990. Mem. Internat. Reading Assn., Women Educators Baltimore County, Vol. Network (mem. vol. adv. com. 1994-2003, chmn. vol. partnership adv. com. Baltimore County Bd. Edn. 2001-03) Baptist. Home: 22 Dihedral Dr Baltimore MD 21220-4611

MCDANIEL, MIRIAM LEE MCCAIN, anesthetist; b. Montgomery, Ala., June 24, 1962; d. Thomas and Betty (Rutledge) McCain; m. Ronald Ralph McDaniel, Mar. 5, 1994; children: Tanner Irving, Tucker Lee (twins). BSN, U. Ala., 1984; cert. anesthesia, Bay Med. Sch. Nurse Anesthesia, 1988. Staff anesthetist U. Med. Ctr., Jacksonville, Fla., 1988-92, Charlton Meml. Hosp., Folkston, Ga., 1993-96; obstetric anesthetist Winn Army Cmty. Hosp., Ft. Stewart, Ga., 1993-97; relief anesthetist D.W. McMillan Hosp., Brewton, Ala., 1997-2000; ptnr. Palm Coast Anesthesia Svc.; staff anesthetist Montgomery Anesthesia Assocs., 2000, D.W. McMillan Hosp., Brewton, Ala., 2001—. Office: 1301 Belleville Ave Brewton AL 36426

MCDANIEL, MYRA ATWELL, lawyer, former state official; b. Phila., Dec. 13, 1932; d. Eva Lucinda (Yores) Atwell; m. Reuben Roosevelt McDaniel Jr., Feb. 20, 1955; children: Diane Lorraine, Reuben Roosevelt III. BA, U. Pa., 1954; JD, U. Tex., 1975; LLD, Huston-Tillotson Coll., 1984, Jarvis Christian Coll., 1986. Bar: Tex. 1975, U.S. Dist. Ct. (we. dist.) Tex. 1977, U.S. Dist. Ct. (so. and no. dists.) Tex. 1978, U.S. Ct. Appeals (5th cir.) 1978, U.S. Supreme Ct. 1978, U.S. Dist. Ct. (ea. dist.) Tex. 1979. Asst atty. gen. State of Tex., Austin, 1975-81, chief taxation div., 1979-81, gen. counsel to gov., 1983-84, sec. of state, 1984-87; asst. gen. counsel Tex. R.R. Commn., Austin, 1981-82; gen. counsel Wilson Cos., San Antonio and Midland, Tex., 1982; assoc. Bickerstaff, Heath & Smiley, Austin, 1984, ptnr., 1987-96; mng. ptnr. Bickerstaff, Heath, Smiley, Pollan, Kever & McDaniel, Austin, Tex., 1996—2000, of counsel, 2003. Mem. asset. mgmt. adv. com. State Treasury, Austin, 1984-86; mem. legal affairs com. Criminal Justice Policy Coun., Austin, 1984-8, Inter-State Oil Compact, Oklahoma City, 1984-86; bd. dirs. Austin Cons. Group, 1983-86; mem. Jud. Efficiency Coun., Austin, 1995-96; lectr. in field. Contbr. articles to profl. jours., chpts. to books Del. Tex. Conf. on Librs. and Info. Sci., Austin, 1978, White House Conf. on Librs. and Info. Scis., Washington, 1979; mem. Libr. Svcs. and Constrn. Act Adv. Coun., 1980-84, chmn., 1983-84; mem. long range plan task force Brackenridge Hosp., Austin, 1981; clk. vestry bd. St. James Episcopal Ch., Austin, 1981-83, 89-90; bd. visitors U. Tex. Law Sch., 1983-87, vice chmn., 1983-85; bd. dirs. Friends of Ronald McDonald House Ctrl. Tex., Women's Advocacy, Inc., Capital Area Rehab. Ctr.; trustee Episcopal Found. Tex., 1986-89, St. Edward's U., Austin, 1986—, chmn. acad. com., 1988-2002, vice chair, 2002-04, chmn. 2004—; chmn. divsn. capital area campaign United Way, 1986; active nat. adv. bd. Leadership Am.; trustee Episcopal Sem. S.W., 1990-96, Assn. Governing Bds. Univs. and Colls., Leadership Edn. Arts Program, 1995-2004; adv. bd. mem. Women Basketball Coaches Assn., 1996-99; bd. dirs. U.Tex. Law Sch. Found., 1997-98, Wells Fargo Cmty. Bd., Ctrl. Tex., 2000-03; trustee Episcopal Health Charities, 1997—. Recipient Tribute to 28 Black Women award Concepts Unltd., 1983; Focus on women honoree Serwa Yetu chpt. Mt. Olive grand chpt. Order of Eastern Star, 1979, Woman of Yr. Longview Metro C. of C., 1985, Woman of Yr. Austin chpt. Internat. Tng. in Communication, 1985, Citizen of Yr. Epsilon Iona chpt. Omega Psi Phi, Lone Star Girl Scout Coun. Women of Distinction, 1997, Profiles in Power Austin Bus. Jour., 1999, Silent Samaritan award Samaritan Counseling Ctr., 2000. Master Inns of Ct.; mem. ABA, Am. Bar Found., Tex. Bar Found. (trustee 1986-89), Travis County Bar Assn., Travis County Women Lawyers' Assn., Austin Black Lawyers Assn., State Bar Tex. (chmn. Profl. Efficiency & Econ. Rsch. subcom. 1976-84), Golden Key Nat. Honor Soc., Longhorn Assocs. for Excellence in Women's Athletes (adv. coun. 1988—), Order of Coif (hon. mem.), Omicron Delta Kappa, Delta Phi Alpha. Democrat. Office: Bickerstaff Heath Smiley Pollan Keever & McDaniels 1700 First Bank Plz 816 Congress Ave Austin TX 78701-2443 Office Phone: 512-472-8021. Business E-Mail: mmcdaniel@bickerstaff.com.

MCDANIEL, SARA SHERWOOD (SALLY MCDANIEL), trainer, consultant; b. St. Louis, Apr. 24, 1943; d. Edward Leighton and Dolores Edic (Pitts) Sherwood; m. Allen Polk McDaniel, Dec. 29, 1967; children: James Polk, Fontaine Maury. AA, Mt. Vernon Coll., 1963; BS, Vanderbilt U., 1965. Tchr. Kanawha Valley Schools, Charleston, W.Va., 1965-66, Fulton County Schools, Atlanta, 1966-68, Trinity Sch., 1969-71; tournament dir. Atlanta Classic, 1972-77; dir. alumni affairs Leadership Atlanta, 1988-89; pvt. practice cons., trainer Atlanta, 1988—. Bd. dirs. AID Atlanta, The High Mus. Art, Leadership Coun. Kennedy Ctr. of Vanderbilt U., UNICEF-Atlanta, The Atlanta Women's Found., Leadership Atlanta. Bd. dirs. Girl Scouts U.S., Ga., High Mus. Art, Atlanta Opera, UNICEF Atlanta, Aid Atlanta, Fine Art Collectors; active Com. on Women and Minorities for 1996 Olympics; mem. exec. com. Leadership Atlanta, Jr. League; mem. Friends of Spelman; trustee Mt. Vernon Coll.; bd. chair Atlanta Women's Fund; bd. dirs. Pub. Leadership Edn. Network, Ga. Women of Achievement. Mem. Am. Soc. Trainers and Dirs., Atlanta Women's Network (bd. dirs., pres.), Vanderbilt U. Alumni Assn., Alumni Assn. Peabody Coll., The Atlanta Girls Sch. Presbyterian.

MCDANIEL, SARAH A., lawyer; b. Wolfsboro, N.H., Mar. 13, 1971; d. William Balch Cole and Mary Susana Bamford; m. Jonathan A. McDaniel, Apr. 5, 2003; 1 child, Rosalie Marie. BA in Human Ecology, Coll. of Atlantic, Bar Harbor, Maine, 1993; M Environ. Studies, Yale Sch. Forestry and Environ. Studies, New Haven, 1995; JD, Harvard Law Sch., Cambridge, Mass., 2003. Bar: Maine, U.S. Dist. Ct. Maine, U.S. Circuit Ct. (1st cir.) Appeals. Land protection specialist The Trustees of Reservations, Beverly, Mass., 1997—99; assoc. Murray Plumb & Murray, Portland, Maine, 2003—. Bd. mem. Environ. League Mass., Boston, 1998—2001; trustee Coll. of Atlantic, Bar Harbor, Maine, 2004—. Mem.: ABA, Maine State Bar Assn. Office: Murray Plumb and Murray 75 Pearl St Portland ME 04104

MCDANIEL, SHARON TOLIVER, social welfare administrator, foundation administrator; BA, Penn. State U.; MPA, U. Pitts.; Cert. in Non-Profit Mgmt., Heinz Sch. Public Policy, Carnegie-Mellon U.; D.Ed., NOVA Southeastern U. Former caseworker, supervisor and court liaison Allegheny County Children Youth and Family Svc.; former caseworker and program dir. Black Adoption Svc. Program of Three Rivers Adoption Council; pres., CEO, founder A Second Chance Inc., 1994—. Co-chair Task Force of Kinship Care; co-facilitator Allegheny County Foster Care and Kinship Initiative; bd. mem. Black Administrators in Child Welfare; adv. Children's Defense Fund. Co-investigator, author Subsidized Legal Guardianship: A Permanency Planning Option Study for Children Placed in Kinship Care, Subsidized Legal Guardianship Update. Trustee Casey Family Programs, 2005—. Recipient Nubabian Queen Mother award, Girl Scouts of Southwestern Pa. award. Office: A Second Chance Inc 204 N Highland Ave Pittsburgh PA 15206*

MCDANIEL, SUE POWELL, writer; b. Jefferson City, Mo., Mar. 13, 1946; d. Ernest Gayle and Ruth Angeline (Raithel) Powell; m. Walter Lee Zimmerman, Aug. 14, 1966 (div. 1980); m. Olin Cleve McDaniel, June 23, 1985 (div. 2002). BS in Edn., U. Mo., 1968, MEd in Edn., 1977, EdS, 1980, PhD, 1985. Cert. tchr., Mo. Tchr. Jefferson City Pub. Schs., 1968-80; fiscal assoc. Mo. Coordinating Bd. for Higher Edn., Jefferson City, 1980-90; exec. dir. Mo. Women's Coun., Jefferson City, 1990-99; exec. dir. Skillpath Seminars, 2000—03; pres. Alternatives, Jefferson City, Mo., 1999—; dir. Heisinger Hope Found., 2004. Author: (with C. Dixon) Learning, Changing, Leading: Keep to Success in the 21st Century, 1998, Missouri Women Today, 1993, Status of the Women, 1994, I.M. Heart, 2006. Mem. Zonta Internat. Avocations: reading, music, drawing, flower garden, photography. Home: 1600 Stadium Blvd Jefferson City MO 65109-2418

MCDANIEL, SUSAN HOLMES, psychologist; b. Jersey City, Oct. 31, 1951; d. Grover Cleveland and Anna Lou (Toms) McD.; m. David Morton Siegel, July 22, 1984; children: Hanna, Marisa. BA, Duke U., 1973; PhD, U. N.C., 1979. Fellow in family therapy Tex. Rsch. Inst. Mental Scis., Houston, 1980; Supr., staff psychologist W. Monroe Mental Health Ctr., Rochester, N.Y., 1980-82; pvt. practice psychologist Rochester, 1980-88; prof. psychiatry and family medicine U. Rochester Sch. Medicine, 1987—, co-dir. psychosocial edn. dept. family medicine, dir. family therapy tng. program dept. psychiatry, 1988-94, assoc. dir. div. family programs, 1994-96, dir. divsn. family programs, 1996—, dir. Wyme Ctr. for Family Rsch., 1997—, assoc. chair of family medicine, 2003—. Co-author: Systems Consultation, 1986, Family-oriented Primary Care, 1990, 2d edt. 2005, Medical Family Therapy, 1992, Counseling Families with Chronic Illness, 1995, Integrating Family Therapy, 1995, The Shared Experience of Illness, 1997, Casebook for Integrating Family Therapy, 2001, The Biopsychosocial Approach, 2003, Primary Care Psychology, 2004; co-editor Families, Systems & Health, 1995—; contbr. articles to profl. jours. Recipient Nat. Patient Care award for innovation in family med. edn. Patient Care, Soc. for Tchrs. Family Medicine, 1988; fellow Pub. Health Svc. Primary Care Policy, 1998. Mem. APA (bd. family divsn., Family Psychologist of Yr. 1995), Am. Family Therapy Acad. (bd. dirs., innovative contributions to family therapy award 2000), Commn. on Accreditation for Marriage and Family Therapy Tng. and Edn. (chair

1993-98), Soc. for Tchrs. Family Medicine, Dist. Achieve. in Edn. Assn. Med. Sch. Psychologists Democrat. Avocations: jogging, films. Office: Dept Family Medicine 777 S Clinton Ave Rochester NY 14620 Office Phone: 585-279-4820.

MCDARRAH, GLORIA SCHOFFEL, editor, writer; b. Bronx, N.Y., June 22, 1932; d. Louis and Rose Schoffel; m. Fred W. McDarrah, Nov. 5, 1960; children: Timothy, Patrick. BA in French, Pa. State U., 1953; MA in French, NYU, 1966. Editorial asst. Crowell-Collier, N.Y.C., 1957-59; exec. asst. to pub. Time Inc., N.Y.C., 1959-61; libr., tchr. N.Y.C. Pub. Schs. and St. Luke's Sch., 1972-76; exec. asst. to pres. Capital Cities Communications Inc., N.Y.C., 1972-76; analyst N.Y.C. Landmarks Preservation Commn., 1976-79; project editor Grosset & Dunlap Inc., N.Y.C., 1979-80; sr. editor Prentice Hall trade div. Simon & Schuster Inc., N.Y.C., 1980-88; pres. McDarrah Media Assocs., N.Y.C., 1988—. Editor book rev. The Picture Profl., 1989—; book reviewer Pub.'s Weekly, 1994—. Author: Frommer's Guide to Va., 1992, Frommer's Guide to Va. 2d edit., 1994—95, Frommer's Atlantic City and Cape May, 1984, Frommer's Atlantic City and Cape May 4th edit., 1991, Frommer's Atlantic City and Cape May 5th edit., 1993—95, The Artist's World 2d edit., 1988, Photography Encyclopedia, 1999; co-author: Museums in N.Y. 5th edit., 1990, Photography Marketplace, 1975, The Beat Generation: Glory Days in Greenwich Village, 1996, Anarchy, Protest and Rebellion and the Counter-Culture That Changed Am., 2003; co-editor: Exec. Desk Diary Saturday Rev., 1962—64; contbg. editor (quar.): Dollarwise Traveler, Fodor's Cancun, Cozumel, Yucatan Peninsula, Fodor's Ariz.

MCDAVID, JANET LOUISE, lawyer; b. Mpls., Jan. 24, 1950; d. Robert Matthew and Lois May (Bratt) Kurzeka; m. John Gary McDavid, June 9, 1973; 1 child, Matthew Collins McDavid. BA, Northwestern U., 1971; JD, Georgetown U., 1974. Bar D.C. 1975, U.S. Ct. Appeals (fed. cir.) 1975 (D.C. cir. 1976), U.S. Supreme Ct. 1980, U.S. Ct. Appeals (5th cir.) 1983, (9th cir.) 1986. Assoc. Hogan & Harston, Washington, 1974-83, ptnr., 1984—. Gen. counsel ERAmerica, 1977-83; mem. antitrust task force Dept. Defense, 1993-94, 96-97; mem. antitrust coun. U.S. C. of C., 1994—; advisor Bush adminstrn. transition team, 2001. Contbr. articles to profl. jours. Participant Clinton and Bush adminstrn. transition team FTC. Mem. ABA (antitrust sect., vice chmn. civil practice com. 1986-89, sect. 2 com. 1989-90, chmn. franchising com. 1990-91, coun. mem. 1991-94, program officer 1994-97, vice chair 1997-98, chair-elect 1998-99, chair 1999-2000, immediate past chair, governing com. of forum on franchising 1991-97), ACLU, U.S. C. of C. (antitrust coun. 1995—), Washington Coun. Lawyers, D.C. Bar Assn., Fed. Bar Assn., Womens Legal Def. fund. Democrat. Office: Hogan & Hartson 555 13th St NW Washington DC 20004-1109 Office Phone: 202-637-8780. Business E-Mail: jlmcdavid@hhlaw.com.

MCDAVID, SARA JUNE, librarian; b. Atlanta, Dec. 21, 1945; d. William Harvey and June (Threadgill) McRae; m. Michael Wright McDavid, Mar. 20, 1971. BA, Mercer U., 1967; MLS, Emory U., 1969. Head librarian Fernbank Sci. Ctr., Atlanta, 1969-77; dir. rsch. libr. Fed. Res. Bank of Atlanta, 1977-81; mgr. mem. services SOLINET, Atlanta, 1981-82; media specialist Parkview High Sch., Atlanta, 1982-84; ptnr. Interncontinental Travel, Atlanta, 1984-85; librarian Wesleyan Day Sch., Atlanta, 1985-86; mgr. info. svcs. Internat. Assn. Fin. Planning, Atlanta, 1986-90; dir. rsch. Korn Ferry Internat., Atlanta, 1990-95; Atlanta rsch. coord. Lamalie Amrop Internat., Atlanta, 1995-98; dir. practice splty. teams LAI Ward Howell, 1998; prin. McDavid Rsch. Assocs., Atlanta, 1998-99; lead rschr. The Boston Consulting Group, Atlanta, 1999—. Bd. dirs. Southeastern Library Network, Atlanta, 1977-80, vice chmn. bd., 1979-80. Contbr. articles to profl. jours. Pres., mem. exec. com. Atlanta Humane Soc., 1985-86, bd. dirs. aux., 1978-90. Mem. Ga. Libr. Assn. (v.p. 1981-83), Spl. Librs. Assn. (treas. libr. mgmt. divsn. 1998-2000, editor Libr. Mgmt. Quar. 1996-98, 2002). Home: 1535 Knob Hill Dr NE Atlanta GA 30329-3206 Office: Boston Consulting Group Inc 600 Peachtree St NE Ste 3800 Atlanta GA 30308-2218 Office Phone: 404-877-5200. Business E-Mail: mcdavid.sara@bcg.com.

MCDEMMOND, MARIE VALENTINE, academic administrator, consultant; b. New Orleans, Feb. 4, 1946; d. George Graham and Marie Valentine (Prudeaux) McD.; m. Louis Saulny, June 15, 1966 (div. 1972); children: Alan Peter, Eric W. Reid; m. Roy Russell Mouton, Sept. 18, 1987. BA, Xavier U., 1968; MEd, U. New Orleans, 1971; postgrad, SUNY, Albany; EdD, U. Mass., 1985. Tchr. Kohn Jr. High Sch., New Orleans, 1968-70; dir. Community Leadership Program, New Rochelle, N.Y., 1970-72, Community Leadership Consortium, Westchester County, N.Y., 1972-73; assoc. Higher Edn. Opportunity Program Office, Albany, N.Y., 1973-74; instr. dept. edn. Ithaca (N.Y.) Coll., 1974; with bus. office, dept. acctg. Bronx (N.Y.) Phychiatric Ctr., 1974-77; assoc. higher edn. N.Y. State Bd. Regents, Albany, 1977-78; dir. fin. Mass. Bd. Regional Community Colls., Boston, 1979-80; assoc. vice chancellor U. Mass., Amherst, 1980-84; v.p. budget & fin. Atlanta U., 1984-85; asst. v.p. for fin. Emory U., Atlanta, 1985-86; pres. McDemmond & Assoc., Boca Raton, Fla., 1986-89; asst. prof. edn. U. New Orleans, 1987-88; asst. v.p. adminstrn. & fin. Fla. Atlantic U., Boca Raton, 1988-89, v.p. adminstrn. & fin., 1990-96; pres. Norfolk (Va.) State U., 1996—. Adj. asst. prof. Coll. New Rochelle, N.Y., 1971-73; adj. prof. edn. U. Mass., Amherst, 1984; hostess Sta. WTCC, Springfield, Mass., 1983-84; lectr. in economic redevel., 1989; adv. bd. mem. Historically Black Coll. and U. Author tng. course. Civil svc. examiner State N.Y., Albany, 1976-78; precinct coord. Democrats for Jackson, Amherst, 1984; advisor Palm Beach Judicial Bldg., West Palm Beach, Fla., 1991; bd. dirs. Lumina Found., United Way, Urban League, Hampton Roads. Named Fla. Woman Who Makes a Difference Nat. Assn. Women Bus. Owners, 1990, Adminstr. of Yr. Va. Assn. Ed. Office Profl.; recipient Pioneer award Outstanding Profl. Women of Hampton Roads. Mem. Bus. and Profl. Women's Club Am. (Woman of Achievement award 1991), New England Minority Women (pres. 1982-84), So. Assn. Coll. and Bus. Officers (exec. com. 1991—), Nat. Assn. Coll. and Univ. Bus. Officers, Coun. Minority Edn. (pres. 1982-84). Roman Catholic. Avocations: gardening, reading. Office: Norfolk State U 700 Park Ave Norfolk VA 23504-8090*

MCDERMID, MARGARET E., information technology executive, engineer; B in bus., Mary Baldwin Coll.; MBA, U. Richmond. With Stone and Webster Engrng. Corp.; joined Va. Power, 1982, various positions engrng. & construction dept., 1982—86, dir. adminstrv. svcs., 1986—98; v.p. info. tech., CIO Dominion Resources Inc., 1998—2000, sr. v.p. info. tech., CIO, 2000—. Mem. apptd. by Gov. Gilmore CIO Adv. Bd., 2000. Active with United Way, Big Brothers, Big Sisters; bd. trustees Mary Baldwin Coll.; found. bd. J. Sargeant Reynolds Cmty. Coll.; bd. dirs. Greater Richmond Tech. Coun., Children's Mus. Richmond Bus. Com., CIO Forum; mem. Va. Rsch. and Tech. Adv. Coun. Achievements include first woman to enter the Apprentice Program at Newport News Shipyard where she completed the Patternmaker's program. Office: Dominion Resources Inc 120 Tredegar St Richmond VA 23219 Office Phone: 804-819-2000.

MCDERMOTT, AGNES CHARLENE SENAPE, philosophy educator; b. Hazelton, Pa., Mar. 11, 1937; d. Charles G. and Conjetta (Ranieri) Senape; children: Robert C., Lisa G., Jamie C. BA, U. Pa., 1956, PhD, 1964; postgrad., U. Calif.-Berkeley, 1960—61, U. Amsterdam, Netherlands, 1965, U. Wis., 1967—69. Instr. math. Drexel Inst. Tech., Phila., 1962-63; asst. prof. philosophy SUNY-Buffalo, 1964-65, Hampton Inst., Va., 1966-67; asst. prof. U. Wis.-Milw., 1967-70; assoc. prof. philosophy U. N.Mex., Albuquerque, 1970-80, prof., dean grad. studies, 1981-86; dean in residence Coun. of Grad. Schs., Washington, 1985-86; provost, v.p. acad. affairs CUNY, 1986-89, prof. philosophy, 1986-91; dean for acad. and student affairs, cons. Albuquerque Acad., 1991-93; ind. cons. Corrales, N.Mex., 1993—. Vis. assoc. prof. U. Wash., Seattle, 1974, U. Calif.-Berkeley, 1973-74, U. Hawaii, Honolulu, 1975; vis. prof. U. Calif.-Berkeley, 1980; vis. prof. Semester at Sea, U. Pitts., fall 1994; bd. dir. Juvenile Diabetes Rsch. Found.; lectr., panelist in field. Author: An Eleventh Century Buddhist Logic of 'Exists', 1969, Boethius' Treatise on the Modes of Signifying, 1980; compiler, editor anthology: Comparative Philosophy: Selected Essays, 1983; rev. editor Phil. East West, 1986—; contbr. articles and stories to profl. and literary jours. Active Albuquerque Care Alliance, 1988—2000; state leader Juvenile Diabetes Rsch. Found., N.Mex. AAUW postdoctoral fellow, 1965-66; NEH Younger Humanist fellow, 1971-72; faculty rsch. fellow U. N.Mex., 1978, 79, 80; U. Pa. grad. fellow, 1961-62; S. Fels Found. fellow, 1963-64; U. Pa. tuition scholar; Pa. Hist. Soc. scholar Mem. N.Y. Acad. Scis., Am. Philos. Soc., Am. Philos. Assn. (exec. com. 1977-80), Assn. Asian Studies (exec. com. 1977-80), Am. Oriental Soc., Western Assn. Grad. Schs. (pres. 1986-87), Phi Beta Kappa, Pi Mu Epsilon. Democrat. Avocations: skiing, fly fishing. Personal E-mail: mcdcott@netzero.com.

MCDERMOTT, ALICE, writer; b. Bklyn., June 27, 1953; married; 3 children. BA, SUNY, Oswego, 1975; MA, U. N.H., 1978. Instr. U. Calif., San Diego, Am. U., Washington; lectr. in English U. N.H.; writer-in-residence Lynchburg Coll., Va., Hollins Coll., Va., Johns Hopkins U., Balt. Author: A Bigamist's Daughter, 1982, That Night, 1987 (Pulitzer Prize finalist, Nat. Book Award finalist, L.A. Times Book Prize finalist), At Weddings and Wakes, 1992, Charming Billy, 1998 (Nat. Book Award), After This, 2006; contbr. short stories to numerous profl. publs. Recipient Whiting Writers award. Office: Farrar Straus and Giroux 19 Union Sq W New York NY 10003*

MCDERMOTT, KATHLEEN E., lawyer; b. 1949; BS in fgn. svc., Georgetown U., JD. Bar: 1975. Assoc. Collier, Shannon, Rill & Scott, Washington, 1975—81, ptnr., 1981—93; exec. v.p., chief legal officer Am. Stores Inc (now Albertson's Inc.), Salt Lake City, 1993—99; ptnr. Collier Shannon Scott PLLC, Washington; sr. v.p., gen. counsel Nash Finch Inc., Mpls., 2002—. Mem.: ABA (vice chair corp. counseling com. antitrust sect.). Office: Nash Finch Co 7600 France Ave S Minneapolis MN 55440-0355

MCDERMOTT, LUCINDA MARY, ecumenical minister, educator, psychologist, poet, philosopher; b. Lynwood, Calif., June 3, 1947; d. R. Harry and Cathrine Jaynne (Redmond) Boand. BA, U. So. Calif., L.A., 1969; MS, Calif. State U., Long Beach, 1975; PhD, Saybrook Inst., San Francisco, 1978. Pres. Environ. Health Systems, Newport Beach, Calif., 1976-90; founder, pres. Forerunner Publs., Newport Beach, 1985—, Life-Skills Learning Ctr., Newport Beach, 1985—; founder, dir. Newport Beach Ecumenical Ctr., 1993—. Founder, dir., Tri Delta Mgmt.; pres. bd. dirs., The Boand Family Found. Author: Bridges to Another Place, 1972, Honor Thy Self, Vol. I and II, 1973, Hello-My-Love-Good Bye, 1973, Life-Skills for Adults, 1982, Au Courants, 1983, Life-Skills for Children, 1984, Myrika-An Autobiographical Novel, 1989, White Knights and Shining Halos: Beyond Pair Bonding, 1996, (musical screen play) The Good Life, 1997. Mem. APA, Calif. Psychol. Assn., Truthsayer Minstrels (founder, dir. 1996—), Alpha Kappa Delta, Kappa Kappa Gamma. Office Phone: 949-759-1217. Personal E-mail: Dr.McD@sbcglobal.net.

MCDERMOTT, MARY ANN, nursing educator; b. La Junta, Colo., June 23, 1938; d. George O. and Alice Agnes (Nohelty) Kelley; m. Dennis J. McDermott; children: Dennis, Michael, Sarah, William. BSN, Loyola U., 1960, MSN, 1969; EdD, No. Ill. U., 1980. RN, Ill. Staff nurse Evanston (Ill.) Vis. Nurse Assn., 1960-63, St. Francis Hosp., Sch. Nursing, Evanston, 1963-67; nurse, tchr. Head Start, Chgo. Bd. Edn., 1967-68; faculty mem. Niehoff Sch. Nursing Loyola U., Chgo., 1969—2004, prof. emeritus, 2004—, dir., Ctr. Faith and Mission, 1998—2002, faculty liaison Evoke project, 2004—; pres., nursing and humanities Hecktoen Inst. Medicine, Chgo. Bd. dirs. Park Ridge Ctr. Study Health, Faith and Ethics; adv. coun. Chgo. Dept. Aging, 1995—99; prin. Quality Life Tng., 2002—. Co-editor: Parish Nursing: The Developing Practice, 1990, Parish Nursing: Promoting Whole Person Health Within Faith Communities, 1998, Parish Nursing: Development, Education, Preparation and Administration, 2005. Adv. bd. St. Scholastica Acad., Chgo., 1996-2005; adv. coun. Chgo. Schweizer Urban Fellows, 1996-99; chair Civic Affairs com. U. Club. Chgo., 2001-03. Recipient Ill. Nurse Leader/Power of Nursing award, 2002. Fellow: Am. Acad. Nursing; mem.: ANA, Health Ministries Assn. (adv. bd. 1989—99), Ill. Nurses Assn., Am. Hosp. Assn. (nominating com. 1995—97). Democrat. Roman Catholic. Office: Loyola U Sch Nursing Damen Hall 6525 N Sheridan Rd Chicago IL 60626-5344 Office Phone: 773-508-2904. Personal E-mail: maryannmcdermott@msn.com. Business E-Mail: mmcderm@luc.edu.

MCDERMOTT, MARY ELLEN, insurance agent; b. Hyannis, Mass., July 5, 1946; d. Edward James McDermott and Doris Wilbur Chase. BA, Nasson Coll., 1968; MA, Tufts U., 1970. Cert. justice of the peace Mass. Asst. assessor Town of Orleans, Mass., 1971—88; ins. broker Pike Ins. Agy. Inc., Orleans, 1988—. Author: Tapestry, 1978, Handle With Care, 1988. Mem. bd. assessors Town of Orleans, 2000—03. Mem.: Nickerson Family Assn., Mass. Soc. Mayflower Descendants, Mensa. Episcopalian. Avocations: genealogy, reading, cooking. Home: 97 S Orleans Rd Orleans MA 02653 Office: Pike Ins Agy Inc PO Box 2743 Orleans MA 02653 Office Phone: 508-255-7880. E-mail: insurancepoet@hotmail.com.

MCDERMOTT, MARY KATHERYN, science educator; b. Evanston, Ill., Nov. 17, 1956; d. James Arthur and Shirley Doris Wise; m. Stephen Douglas McDermott; children: Stephanie Adair, Sean James. BS in Biology, Whitworth Coll., Spokane, Wash., 1979. Lic. tchr. Oreg. Teachers and Practices Commn. Sci. tchr. Blackfoot Jr. H.S., 1979—84, Bonneville Jr. H.S., Idaho Falls, 1984—85, Bend Sr. H.S., 1985—. Named Tchr. of Yr., Walmart, 1997, 2006, Oreg. Activity Dir. of Yr., Oreg. Assn. of Student Couns., 1997—98, Jr. High Tchr. of Yr., Blackfoot Sch. Dist., 1981, 1984; recipient Student Achievement award, Coll. of Edn. U. Oreg., 1998. Mem.: NEA (assoc.), Bend Edn. Assn. (assoc.), Oreg. Edn. Assn. (assoc.; rep.), Beta Sigma Phi. Republican. Methodist. Avocations: gardening, reading. Home: 2634 NW Scandia Loop Bend OR 97701 Office: Bend Sr HS 230 NE 6th St Bend OR 97701 Office Phone: 541-383-6324. Business E-Mail: mmcdermo@bend.k12.or.us.

MCDERMOTT, MOLLY, lay minister; b. Cloquet, Minn., Aug. 19, 1932; d. Harry W. McD.; children: Elizabeth Sanders Hellenbrand, Sarah Sanders McKinley, Mary Sanders Day, Margaret Kathleen Sanders Lorfeld. Student, Oreg. State Coll., 1951, U. Minn., Duluth, 1953. Claims specialist Cuna Mut. Ins. Soc., Madison, Wis., 1975-2001. Propr. Molly's Garden. Vol. Holy Redeemer Ch. Mem.: Univ. League, Middleton Garden Club. Roman Catholic. Home: 1724 Parmenter St Middleton WI 53562-3153

MCDERMOTT, PATRICIA ANN, nursing administrator; b. Bklyn., July 10, 1943; d. John J. and Lillian J. (Sweeney) Skelly; m. Joseph Kevin McDermott, Oct. 5, 1963; children: Colleen Mary, John Joseph. Diploma, Kings County Hosp Sch. Nursing, Bklyn., 1963; BS in Health Care Adminstrn., St. Francis Coll., Bklyn., 1979. Staff nurse Kings County Hosp., Bklyn., 1963-66, head nurse outpatient dept., 1966-74; evening supr. Park Nursing Home, Rockaway Park, N.Y., 1974-83; day supr. Hyde Park Nursing Home, Staatsburg, NY, 1984-85, DON, 1985—96, Victory Lake Nursing Ctr., Hyde Park, N.Y., 1996-97. NY State evaluator for nurses aides, 1988—; PRI assessor; MDS coord. Active local Girl Scouts U.S.A., 1971-78, Boy Scouts Am., 1978-82, Stella Maris Parents Club, 1978-82, St. Francis de Sales Altar and Rosary Soc., 1970-83; active St. Francis de Sales Little League, 1978-80, also softball coach, 1974-77; elected tax collector Town of Clinton, N.Y., 1999—; dance com. chair St. Peter's, Hyde Park, N.Y., 1998-2002. Dutchess County Salute to Women honoree, 1997. Mem.: Town of Clinton Ladies Rep. Club, Town of Clinton Hist. Soc. Home: 184 Shadblow Ln Clinton Corners NY 12514-2834

MCDEVITT, SHEILA MARIE, lawyer, energy executive; b. St. Petersburg, Fla., Jan. 15, 1947; d. Frank Davis and Marie (Barfield) McD. AA, St. Petersburg Jr. Coll., 1966; BA in Govt., Fla. State U., 1968, JD, 1978. Bar: Fla. 1978. Research asst. Fla. Legis. Reference Bur., Tallahassee, 1968-69; adminstr., research assoc. Constitution Revision Commn. Ga. Gen. Assembly, Atlanta, 1969-70; adminstrv. asst., analyst Fla. State Sen., Tallahassee, Tampa, 1970-79; assoc. McClain, Walkley & Stuart, P.A., Tampa, Seminole, Fla., 1979-81; govtl. affairs counsel Tampa Electric Co., 1981-82, corp. counsel, 1982-86; sr. corp. counsel TECO Energy, Inc., Tampa, 1986-89, asst. v.p., 1989-92, v.p., asst. gen. counsel, 1992-99, corp. compliance officer, 1993-99, v.p., gen. counsel Tampa, 1999—2001, sr. v.p., gen. counsel, chief legal officer, 2001—. Mem. Worker's Compensation adv. coun. Fla. Dept. Labor, Tallahassee, 1984-86; trustee St. Leo U., 1999—, vice chair, 2001-2005, chair 2005-; mem. bd. visitors Fla. State U. Coll. Law, 1996—, chmn., 2003-2005; mem. bd. advisors The Centre for Women, 1998—, Met. Ministries, 1996-99; mem. ethics adv. bd. U. Tampa Ctr. for Ethics, 1997-99; mem. jud. nominating commn. 13th Jud. Cir., 2001-2003; mem. Fla. bd. govs. State Univ. sys., 2003, vice chair, 2006-. Bd. dirs. Vol. Ctr. Hillsborough County, Tampa, 1984-85, Fla. Aquarium, 1999-2000; bd. dirs. Lowry Park Zoo Soc., 1999-2004, chmn., trustee, 1986-94, also legal advisor; bd. dirs. Hillsborough County Easter Seal Soc., 1994-95; mem. Fla. Rep. Exec. Com., Tallahassee, 1974-75, Hillsborough County Rep. Exec. Com., 1974-75; mem. transition team for Fla. Gov. Bob Martinez, 1986-87; mem. Fed. Jud. Adv. Commn., 1989-93; mem. Fla. Humanities Coun., 2000-2004; mem. WW Women's Leadership, 2004—; bd. trustees Fla. Orch., 2004—. Mem ABA, Fla. Bar (vice chmn., then chmn. energy law com. 1984-87, jud. nominating procedures com. 1986-91, jud. adminstrn. selection and tenure com. 1991-93), Hillsborough Bar Found. (trustee 2002-), Hillsborough County Bar Assn. (chmn. law week com. 1990, corp. counsel com. 1986-87, internat. law com. 1994-95, corporate counsel of the yr. award, 2001-02, Spl. Achievment award), Am. Corp. Counsel Assn. (bd. dirs. Ctrl. Fla. chpt. 1986-87), Hillsborough County Bar Found., Tampa Club, Tiger Bay Club, Tampa Yacht and Country Club. Roman Catholic. Avocations: bicycling, reading. Office: TECO Energy Inc PO Box 111 702 N Franklin St Fl 5 Tampa FL 33602-4440 Business E-Mail: smmcdevitt@tecoenergy.com.

MCDIARMID, LUCY, literature educator, writer; b. Louisville, Mar. 29, 1947; BA, Swarthmore (Pa.) Coll., 1968; MA, Harvard U., 1969, PhD, 1972. Asst. prof. Boston U., 1972-74; from asst. prof. to assoc. prof. Swarthmore Coll., 1974-81; asst. prof. U. Md. Baltimore County, Balt., 1982-84; prof. Villanova (Pa.) U., 1984—. Vis. prof. English Princeton U., 1995; Carole and Gordon Segal vis. chair Irish lit. Northwestern U., 2005; mem. exec. com. Am. Conf. for Irish Studies, 1987-91, v.p., 1995-97, pres., 1997-99, past pres., internat. rep., 1999—2001. Author: Saving Civilization: Yeats, Eliot and Auden Between the Wars, 1984, Auden's Apologies for Poetry, 1990, The Irish Art of Controversy, 2005; co-editor: Selected Writings of Lady Gregory, 1995, High and Low Moderns: Literature and Culture, 1889-1939, 1996; contbr. articles to profl. jours. ACLS grantee, 1976; NEH fellow, 1981-82, Bunting Inst. fellow, 1981-82, Guggenheim fellow, 1993-94, vis. fellow N.Y. Inst. Humanities, 1993-95, fellow Dorothy and Louis B. Cullman Ctr. Scholars and Writers, NY Pub. Libr., 2005-06. Mem. MLA (exec. com. Twentieth Century Lit. divsn.), Internat. Assn. for Study Anglo-Irish Lit. (Am. sec.-treas. 1994-96), Phi Beta Kappa. Home: 1931 Panama St Philadelphia PA 19103-6609

MCDOLE, SYDNEY BOSWORTH, lawyer; b. Chgo., 1947; BA summa cum laude, Vassar Coll., 1970; MA, Middlebury Coll., 1971; JD magna cum laude, Northwestern Univ., 1974. Bar: Ill. 1974, Tex. 1986, admitted to practice: US Fed. Courts 1974, US Supreme Ct. 1983. Ptnr., gen. litigation and energy issues Jones Day, Chgo., now ptnr., gen. litigation and energy issues Dallas. Coord., new associates group Jones Day. Editor-in-chief Law Rev., Harvard Univ., 1974. Mem.: Ill. State Bar Assn., State Bar of Tex., Order of Coif, Phi Beta Kappa. Office: Jones Day 2727 N Harwood St Dallas TX 75201-1515 Office Phone: 214-969-3785. Office Fax: 214-969-5100.

MCDONALD, ARLYS LORRAINE, retired librarian; b. Edison, Neb., Jan. 6, 1932; d. Leo Richard and Christine Mae (Hays) McDonald. BMus, St. Mary Plains Coll., 1963; MMus, U. Ill., 1965. Asst. prof. St. Mary Plains Coll., Dodge City, Kans., 1965-68; head, music libr. Ariz. State U., Tempe, 1968—95; ret. libr. emeritus, 1995. Author: Ned Rorem, 1989; contbg. author: Phoenix in Grove's Dictionary of American Music and Musicians, 1986, Grove's Dictionary of Music and Musicians, 2000. Mem. Music Libr. Assn., Music Libr. Assn. Mt. Plains Chpt., Internat. Assn.Music Librs., Sisters of St. Joseph of Wichita. Democrat.

MCDONALD, AUDRA ANN, actress, vocalist; b. Berlin, July 3, 1970; d. Stanley and Kathryn McDonald; m. Peter Donovan, Sept. 10, 2000; 1 child, Zoe Madeline Donovan. BFA in Voice, Juilliard Sch., 1993; attended, Sch. Arts., Calif. Stage appearances include (regional) Man of La Mancha, Evita, The Wiz, A Chorus Line, Grease, Anything Goes, The Real Inspector Hound, Anyone Can Whistle, 2005;(Broadway) The Secret Garden, Man of La Mancha, 1989, Carousel, 1994 (Tony award best featured actress in a musical, 1994, Outer Critics Circle award outstanding actress in a musical, 1994), Master Class, 1995-97 (Tony award best featured actress in a musical, 1996, LA Ovation award best featured actress in a musical, 1996), Ragtime, 1998-99 (Tony award best featured actress in a musical, 1998), Sweeney Todd, 2000, A Raisin in the Sun, 2004 (Tony award best featured actress in a play, 2004, Drama Desk award best featured actress in a play, 2004), See What I Wanna See (formerly titled R Shomon), 2005; (TV series) Bill Cosby pilot, 1996, Mister Sterling, 2003; (TV Movies) Having Our Say: The Delaney Sisters' First 100 Years, 1999, Annie, 1999, The Last Debate, 2000, Wit, 2001 (Emmy award nom. best supporting actress, 2001); (films) Seven Servants, 1996, The Object of My Affection, 1998, Cradle Will Rock, 1999, It Runs in the Family, 2003, The Best Thief in the World, 2004; concert performances include S'Wonderful, Some Enchanted Evening, Christa Ludwig and James Levine Recital, Revelation in Courthouse Park, Requiem Canticles; singer: (albums) Leonard Bernstien's New York, 1996, Sings Rodgers & Hart, 1996, George & Ira Gershwin: Standards & Gems, 1998, George Gershwin: 100th Birthday Celebration, 1998, Broadway in Love, 2000, Marie Christine: A New Musical, 2000, Broadway Cares: Home for the Holidays, 2001, Dreamgirls in Concert, 2002, (solo albums) Way Back to Paradise, 1998, How Glory Goes, 2000, Happy Songs, 2002, Build a Bridge, 2006. Recipient Theatre World award, 1994, Drama League award distinguished achievement in musical theatre, 2000. Office: Gersh Agency Inc 41 Madison Ave Fl 33 New York NY 10010-2210

MCDONALD, BRENDA DENISE, librarian; b. Waco, Tex., Feb. 15, 1954; d. William Dale and Ella Mae (Parrish) Maness; m. Jeffrey L. McDonald, May 26, 1979; 1 child, Sean Thomas BA History, William Jewell Coll., 1975; MLS, U. Okla., 1978; MA History, U. Tex., El Paso, 1988. Libr. govt. documents and periodicals Hardin Simmons U., Abilene, Tex., 1977—79; head documents and maps libr. U. Tex., El Paso, 1978—84; law libr. Scott Hulse Marshall Feuille Finger and Thurmond, El Paso, 1984—88; libr. govt. documents St. Louis Pub. Libr., 1988—90, coord. info. svcs., 1990—95, dir. ctrl. pub. svcs., 1995—98, dir. ctrl. and regional svcs., 1999—. Jamestown Soc. fellow, 1988 Mem. ALA, Am. Law Libr. Assn., Spl. Libraries Assn., Beta Phi Mu Office: St Louis Pub Library 1301 Olive St Saint Louis MO 63103-2389 Office Phone: 314-539-0348. Business E-Mail: bmcdonald@slpl.org.

MCDONALD, CASSANDRA BURNS, lawyer; b. Aberdeen, Md., Aug. 28, 1963; d. Charles Franklin and Elizabeth (Connor) Burns; children: Christopher, Jordan. AB, Dartmouth Coll., Hanover, N.H., 1985; JD, Cornell U., 1990. Bar: Conn. 1991, U.S. Dist. Ct. Conn. 1992, U.S. Dist. Ct. (ea. and so. dists) N.Y. 1992. Atty. Cummings & Lockwood, Stamford, Conn., 1990—94, 1996—2002; v.p. legal affairs & compliance Luxury Mortgage Corp., Stamford, 2002—. Active Women's Leadership Conf., Conn., 1998—; 1st v.p. The Links, Inc., Fairfield County, 2000—04; v.p. Stamford/Norwalk chpt. Jack and Jill of Am., Inc., 2002—05; bd. dirs. Waveny Care Ctr., New Canaan, Conn., 2000—05, Fairfield County Cmty. Found., 2001—04. Mem.: ABA, Dartmouth Lawyers Assn., Lawyers for Children Am., Inc., Fairfield County Bar Assn., Conn. Bar Assn., Nat. Bar Assn., Black Alumni Dartmouth, Dartmouth Club of Fairfield County, Delta Sigma Theta. Baptist. Avocations: travel, reading, tennis. Office: Luxury Mortgage Corp 1 Landmark Sq Ste 100 Stamford CT 06901 Office Phone: 203-327-6000. Business E-Mail: cbmcdonald@luxurymortgage.com.

MCDONALD, CHRISTIE ANNE, literature and language professor, writer; b. NYC, May 4, 1942; d. John Denis and Dorothy (Eisner) McD.; m. Eugene Augustus Vance, June 11, 1965 (div. June 1986); children: Adam Vance, Jacob Vance; m. Michael David Rosengarten, Dec. 4, 1987. AB, Mt. Holyoke Coll., 1964; PhD, Yale U., 1969; MA (hon.), Harvard Coll., 1994. Acting instr. Yale U., New Haven, 1968-69; asst. prof. French U. Montreal, Que., Canada, 1969-77, assoc. prof. French Que., 1977-83, prof. Que., 1983, 86-93; prof. modern langs. Emory U., Atlanta, 1984-86; prof. romance langs. and. lits. Harvard U., Cambridge, Mass., 1994—, chmn. romance langs. and lits., 2000—. Author: The Dialogue of Writing, 1985, Dispositions, 1986, The Proustian Fabric, 1991; editor: The Ear of the Other, 1988, Transpositions, 1994, Images of Congo, 2005. Decorated chevalier Order Palmes Academiques; recipient Clifford prize Am. Assn. 18th-Century Studies, 1994-95. Mem.: Royal Soc. Can. Office: Harvard U 431 Boylston Hall Cambridge MA 02138 Office Phone: 617-497-0826.

MCDONALD, CHRISTY, newscaster; m. Jamie Samuelsen, 2001. B in Polit. Philosophy, Mich. State U. Prodn. asst. WJBK, Southfield, Mich., 1994—95; prodr. WXYZ, 1996—98; with WJRT-TV, Flint, Mich., 1998—2000; co-anchor Action News at 7pm WXYZ TV, 2000—. Recipient Best Breaking News Reporting award, AP, award, Mich. Assn. Broadcasters, Detroit Press Club. Office: WXYZ-TV 20777 W Ten Mile Rd Southfield MI 48037

MCDONALD, DEBORAH ALYSE, mathematics educator; d. Harold Rollins and Lois Rajab; m. Sam Anthony McDonald, May 1, 1977; children: Sam Anthony Jr., Clifford Leo. MPA, Troy State U., Ala., 2001. Cert. tchr. math. Ga, tchr. music NJ. Music tchr. Newton St. Elem. Sch., Newark, 1972—77; math. and music tchr. Edison Jr. HS, LA, 1978—80; math. tchr. Headland HS, East Point, Ga., 1980—84, MD Collins HS, College Park, Ga., 1984—89, Benjamin Banneker HS, College Park, 1989—. Named Tchr. of Yr., Benjamin Banneker HS, 2002—03. Home: 6645 Kimberly Mill Ln College Park GA 30349 Office: Benjamin Banneker HS 5935 Feldwood Rd College Park GA 30349 Office Phone: 770-969-3410 ext 263. Office Fax: 770-969-3418. Personal E-mail: eskie@bellsouth.net. E-mail: mcdonaldd@fulton.k12.ga.us.

MC DONALD, GAIL FABER, musician, educator; b. Jersey City, Oct. 24, 1917; d. Samuel and Jennie (Weiss) Faber; m. George Walther, Nov. 17, 2000; children from previous marriage: Lora McDonald Ferguson, Charles McDonald, Henry McDonald. Diploma, Mannes Music Sch., N.Y.C., 1938; BA, U. Md., 1962; MusM, Cath. U., 1968; DMus Arts, U. Md., 1977. Legis. asst. Capitol Hill, 1943-46; pvt. tchr. piano and music theory Washington and Md., 1950—. Piano soloist Nat. Gallery Art, 1977; rec. artist Educo Records; lectr., performer Bach Sinfonias and Mendelssohn's Complete Songs Without Words; recorded complete solo piano works of Daniel Gregory Mason. Author: Muzio Clementi and the Gradus Ad Parnassum, 1968. Mem. D.C. Music Tchrs. Assn., Md. Music Tchrs. Assn. (pres. 1977-1981), D.C. Fedn. Music Clubs, Nat. Guild Piano Tchrs. (adjudicator 1972-2005), Friday Morning Music Club (performing mem.). Address: 801 N Monroe St Apt 601 Arlington VA 22201-2372 E-mail: gailmcdonald@comcast.net.

MCDONALD, GERRI VAN PELT, elementary school educator; b. Mobile, Ala., Mar. 15, 1956; d. James Grout and Doris Mae Van Pelt; children: Russell William Stewart, Patrick Ryan Stewart, Melanie Lorraine. M in elem. edn., U. West Fla., 1991; AA, Pensacola Jr. Coll., 1976. Nat. bd. cert. tchr. Tchr. kindergarten Okaloosa County Schs., Eglin Air Force Base, Fla., 1981—83; tchr. physical edn. Monterrey Pennesula Sch. dist., Calif., 1983—84; tchr. 3rd grade and kindergarten Tullahoma city Schools, Tenn., 1986—89; tchr. 1st and 4th grades Escambia County Schs., Century, Fla., 1989—98; tchr. writing Escambia County Sch. Sys., Century, 1998—2001; tchr. project jubilee and humanities K-8th grades Baldwin County Sch. Sys., Perdido, Ala., 2001—, soccer coach, 2004—05. Scholars' bowl coach Perdido Sch., Ala., 2001—05. Vol. Rep. Nat. Com., Pensacola, Fla., 2004—05. Recipient Parent Vol. of Yr., Ernest Ward Sch., 1996. Mem.: Ala. Humanities Found. (assoc. Jenice C. Riley Scholarship 2003), Phi Lambda Theta, Kappa Delta Pi (assoc.), Gamma Beta Pi (assoc.). R-Consevative. Baptist. Avocations: piano, hiking, reading, travel. Home: 8791 Hwy 97 Century FL 32535 Office: Perdido Elementary/Middle School PO Box 28 Perdido AL 36562 Office Phone: 251-937-8456. Personal E-mail: gmcdonald@bcbe.org.

MCDONALD, JANE THERESA, athletic trainer, educator; b. Boston, Apr. 30, 1976; d. John Francis and Shirley Jane McDonald. BS, Boston U., 1999, MEd, 2001. Athletic trainer Sport/Rx, Chesapeake, Va., 2001—02; athletic trainer, lectr. Boston U., 2002—04, Milton Acad., Mass., 2004—. Office: 122C W 7th St Boston MA 02127-2559

MCDONALD, JINX, interior designer; b. Kingston, Jamaica, Aug. 5, 1946; d. Leonard Fraser and Norma Dawn (Phillips) McConnell; m. C. John McDonald, Dec. 20, 1965 (div. Nov. 1993); children: Sarah, Minka. Interior design/journalism, St. Godric's Coll., Hampstead, Eng., 1967; interior design, Tuxedo Ctr., Atlanta, 1986. Owner/pres. Internat. Accents, Inc., Atlanta, 1986—91; interior designer Style, Inc., Naples, 1991—95, Forum Design group, Inc., Naples, Fla., 1995—2000; prin., owner Jinx McDonald Designs, Inc., Naples, Fla., 2000—. Cons. interior design. Recipient Sand Dollar award, Collier Bldg. Industry Assn., 1999, 2002, 2003, Design of Distinction, Naples Illustrated, 2002, Pinacle award, 2003. Mem. Am. Soc. Interior Design (allied mem.), Interior Design Soc., Nat. Abortion and Reproductive Rights Action League, Natural Resources Def. Coun. Democrat. Anglican. Home and Studio: 7536 San Miguel Way Naples FL 34109-7162 Office: Jinx McDonald Designs Inc 5603 Naples Blvd Naples FL 34109-2023 E-mail: jinxmcdonald@yahoo.com.

MCDONALD, KRISTEN, lawyer; b. Newport Beach, Calif., Oct. 3, 1973; BA summa cum laude, UCLA, 1995; JD, George Washington Univ., 1999. Bar: Ga. State Ct., Ga. Superior Ct., U.S. Ct. Appeals Eleventh Dist., U.S. Dist. Ct. Middle, No. Dists. Ga. Assoc. atty., health care law Epstein, Becker & Green, P.C., 1999—. Mem.: ABA, Am. Health Lawyers Assn. Office: Epstein Becker and Green PC Ste 2700 Resurgens Plz 945 East Paces Ferry Rd Atlanta GA 30326 Fax: 404-323-9099.*

MCDONALD, LAURA WITEK, science educator; b. Princeton, N.J., Apr. 9, 1975; d. Joseph Thomas Witek and Constance Ann Hayes; m. Michael Glen McDonald, Mar. 20, 1999; 1 child, Aaron Michael. BA in Biology and Environ. Studies, Kenyon Coll., Gambier, Ohio, 1997; MS in Elem. Edn., SW Mo. State U., Springfield, 2001. Cert. scuba diver, advanced scuba diver, rescue diver, underwater photography. Marine biology tchr. Northfield Mt. Hermon Sch., Mass., 1998; sci. tchr. Thomas Jefferson Ind. Day Sch., Joplin, Mo., 1997—. Contbr. articles to profl. jours. Mem.: Nat. Sci. Tchrs. Assn., Cousteau Soc. Avocations: scuba diving, photography, golf, hiking. Office: Thomas Jefferson Ind Day Sch 3401 Newman Rd Joplin MO 64801 Office Phone: 417-781-5124, 417-781-1949. Business E-Mail: lmcdonald@tjeffschool.org.

MCDONALD, LINDA L., massage therapist; b. Morgantown, W.Va., Dec. 18, 1946; d. Bonita Viola Wittebort; children from previous marriage: Tatiana Denning, Leo Konchesky, Chad. BSc in Psychology, Davis Elkins Coll., 1985; degree in Therapeutic Massage, Cayce/Reilly Sch. of Masseotherapy, 1999. Cert. massage therapist, colon therapist, hypnotherapist 2005. Lab. asst. Monogahela Gen. Hosp., Morgantown, W.Va., 1965—66; doctor's aide Meml. Gen. Hosp., Elkins, W.Va., 1977—81; direct care provider Immediate Crisis Intervention Ctr., Elkins, 1995—96; massage therapist Cayce/Reilly Sch. of Masseotherapy, Va. Beach, Va., 1999—; pvt. practice Va. Beach, 1999—. Hospice vol. Elkins, W.Va., 1995—; vol. Adult Literacy Coun., Fairbanks, Ala., 1996—, Chrysler Ctr., Va. Beach, 1999—, Options Self-Actualizing Ctr., Shefield, Mass., 2001. Author: Song's On The Wind, 1997, Shadow Walker, 1999. Vol. Adult Literacy Coun., Fairbanks, Alaska, 1996, Hospice, Elkins, W.Va., 1995. Mem.: Internat. Massage Therapist Assn. Avocations: painting, writing, travel, nutrition/alternative medicine, reading. Office: Heritage Holistic Ctr 314 Laskin Rd Virginia Beach VA 23457 Home: 315 33rd St Apt 6 Virginia Beach VA 23451-2945 Personal E-mail: dolphynspirit@yahoo.com.

MCDONALD, LOIS ALICE, elementary school educator; b. Grand Rapids, Mich., Feb. 19, 1930; d. Embert and Ruth Alfareta (Priest) Grooters; m. Ronald Gerard McDonald, July 17, 1954; children: Rodney Mark, Wendy Louise. BS, Western Mich. U., 1952, MA, 1974. Cert. elem. permanent tchr., Mich. Kindergarten and elem. tchr. Chalmers Sch., Algoma Twp., Sparta, Mich., 1952-54; elem. tchr. Loucks Sch., Peoria, Ill., 1955-56, Lakeside Sch., East Grand Rapids, Mich., 1957-58, Clyde Park Sch., Wyoming, Mich., 1958-63, 64-76; tchr. kindergarten Gladiola Sch., Wyoming, 1963-64; elem. tchr. Pinery Park Elem. Sch., Wyoming, 1976-85, Rogers Lane Sch., Wyoming, 1985-91; ret., 1991. Dir. John Knox Food Pantry, 1991—96; vol. Red Cross & West Mich. Trails of Girl Scouts, 1998—2002; ch. sch. supt. John Knox Presbyn. Ch., 1968—73; mem. Chancel Choir, 1977—98; bd. of dir. Second Harvest Gleaners of West Mich., 1993—2001. Mem.: DAR, MEA-NEA (life), Beta Sigma Phi (life). Home: 33 13 Mile Rd NE Sparta MI 49345-9342

MCDONALD, MARIANNE, classicist; b. Chgo., Jan. 2, 1937; d. Eugene Francis and Inez (Riddle) McD.; children: Eugene, James, Bryan, Bridget, Kirstie (dec.), Hiroshi. BA magna cum laude, Bryn Mawr Coll., 1958; MA, U. Chgo., 1960; PhD, U. Calif., Irvine, 1975; doctorate (hon.), Am. Coll. Greece, 1988; diploma (hon.), Am. Archaeol. Assn.; DLitt (hon.), U. Athens, 1994, U. Dublin, 1994, Aristotle U., 1997, U. Thessalonika, 1997, Nat. U. Ireland, 2001. Instr. Greek, Latin, English, mythology, cinema U. Calif., Irvine, 1975-79; founder, rsch. fellow Thesaurus Linguae Graecae Project, 1975-97. Tchg. asst. U. Calif., Irvine, 1972-74; vis. prof. U. Ulster, Ireland, 1997, U. Dublin, 1990—, Univ. Coll. Dublin, 1999, 2002, U. Cork, 1999-; adj. prof. theatre U. Calif., San Diego, 1992-94, prof. theatre and classics, 1994—; bd. dirs. Centrum. Author: (novels) Semilemmatized Concordances to Euripides' Alcestis, 1977, Semilemmatized Concordance to Euripides Cyclops, 1978, Terms for Happiness in Euripides, 1978, Cyclops, Andromache, Medea, 1978, Heraclidae, Hippolytus, 1979, Hecuba, 1984, (play) And Then He Met A Woodcutter, 2005 (San Diego Critics Cir. award for best play, 2005), (critical works) Hercules Furens, 1984, Electra, 1984, Ion, 1985, Trojan Women, 1988, Iphigenia in Taurus, 1988, Euripides in Cinema: The Heart Made Visible, 1983, The Living Art of Greek Tragedy, 2003; translator: The Cost of Kindness and Other Fabulous Tales (Shinichi Hoshi), 1986, Views of Clytemnestra, Ancient and Modern, 1990, Classics and Cinema, 1990, Modern Critical Theory and Classical Literature, 1994, A Challenge to Democracy, 1994, Ancient Sun/Modern Light: Greek Drama on the Modern Stage, 1990, Star Myths: Tales of the Constellations, 1996, Sole Antico Luce Moderna, 1999, Mythology of the Zodiac: Tales of the Constellations, 2000, Antigone by Sophocles, 2000, Mythology of the Zodiac, 2000, Sing Sorrow: Classics, History, Heroines in Opera, 2001; translator: (with Michael Walton) Euripides Andromache, 2001; translator: Euripides' Electra, 2004, Euripides' Hecuba, 2005; editor (with M. McDonald and Michael Walton): Six Greek Tragedies, 2002; editor: (with Michael Walton) Amid Our Troubles: Irish Versions of Greek Tragedy, 2002, Canta la tua Pena, 2002; contbr. chapters to books, articles in field to profl. jours., reviews. Bd. dirs. Am. Coll. of Greece, 1981-90, Scripps Hosp., 1981, Am. Sch. Classical Studies, 1986-; mem. bd. overseers U. Calif., San Diego, 1985-; nat. bd. advisors Am. Biog. Inst., 1982—; pres. Soc. for the Preservation of the Greek Heritage, 1990-, Asian Am. Repertory Theatre, 2003; founder Hajime Mori Chair for Japanese Studies, U. Calif., San Diego, 1985, McDonald Ctr. for Alcohol and Substance Abuse, 1984, Thesaurus Linguarum Hiberniae, 1991-, Hiroshi McDonald Mori Performing Arts Ctr. Recipient Ellen Browning Scripps Humanitarian award, 1975, Disting. Svc. award U. Calif., Irvine, 1982, 2001, Irvine medal, 1987; named one of the Cmty. Leaders Am., 1979-80, Philanthropist of Yr., 1985, Headliner San Diego Press Club, 1985, Philanthropist of Yr. Honorary Nat. Conf. Christians and Jews, 1986, Woman of Yr. AHEPA, 1988, San Diego Woman of Distinction, 1990, Woman of Yr. AXIOS, 1991; recipient Bravissimo gold medal San Diego Opera, 1990, Gold Medal Soc. Internationalization of Greek Lang., 1990, Athens medal, 1991, Piraeus medal, 1991, award Desmoi, 1992, award Hellenic Assn. of Univ. Women, 1992, Acad. of Achievement award AHEPA, 1992, Woman of Delphi award European Cultural Ctr. Delphi, 1992, Civis Universitatis award U. Calif., San Diego, 1993, Hypatia award Hellenic U. Women, 1993, Am.-Ireland Fund Heritage award, 1994, Contbn. to Greek Letters award Aristotle U. Thessaloniki, 1994, Mirabella Mag. Readers Choice One of 1000 Women for the Nineties, 1994, citations from U.S. Congress and Calif. Senate, Alexander the Gt. award Hellenic Cultural Soc., 1995, made hon. citizen of Delphi and gold medal of the Amphiktuonon, Del. Bus. award for Fine Arts San Diego Bus. Jour., 1995, Vol. of Decade Women's Internat. Ctr., 1994, 96, Gold Star award San Diego Arts League, 1997, Golden Aeschylus award Inst. Nat. Drama Antkg. Siracusa, 1998, Women Who Mean Bus., Fine Arts award San Diego Bus. Jour., 1998, Fulbright award, 1999, Ellis Island award, 1999, Spirit of Scripps award 1999; Theatre Excellence award KPBS Patte, 2001, Laud and Laurels, U. Calif. Disting. Alumni award Hellenic Cultural Soc. San Diego, 2003, Sledgehammer Theatre award, 2003, New Path award, 2003, Egeria award Women's Internat. Ctr., 2004, Billie award, 2004, Patté award, 2004. Mem. MLA, AAUP, Am. Philol. Assn. (disting. svc. award 1999), Soc. for the Preservation of the Greek Heritage (pres.), Libr. of Am., Am. Classical League, Philol. Assn. Pacific Coast, Am. Comparative Lit. Assn., Modern and Classical Lang. Assn. So. Calif., Hellenic Soc. (coun. award 2000), Calif. Fgn. Lang. Tchrs. Assn., Internat. Platform Assn., Royal Irish Acad., Greece's Order of the Phoenix (comdr. 1994), KPBS Prodrs. Club, Hellenic Univ. Club (bd. dirs.). Avocations: Karate, harp (medieval), skiing, diving. Home: PO Box 929 Rancho Santa Fe CA 92067-0929 Office: U Calif at San Diego Dept Theatre La Jolla CA 92093 Office Phone: 858-481-0107. E-mail: mmcdonald@ucsd.edu.

MCDONALD, MARILYN A., academic assistant; b. Des Moines, Nov. 7, 1932; d. Edmund and Alice Groomes; m. Thomas Edwin McDonald, Feb. 12, 1955 (dec. June 1991); children: Deborah Sue, Thomas Groomes, Sarah Alice, Janet Louise. BS, Iowa State U., 1954. Instr. Sch. Home Econs. Iowa State U., Ames, 1955; tchr. civics and English Evanston Twp. H.S., Evanston, 1956; home economist Pub. Svc. Co., Northbrook, Ill., 1957; substitute tchr. Ft. Worth Ind. Sch. Dist., 1973—76, mid. sch. tchr., 1976—92; exec. asst. dept. neurosurgery U. Tex. Med. Sch., Houston, 1994—. Founding mem., mem. issues com. Save Our ER, Houston, 2001; mem., discussion leader Bible Study Fellowship, Ft. Worth and Houston, 1983—2000; elder First Presbyn. Ch., Houston. Mem.: Mortar Bd., Omicron Nu, Phi Kappa Phi. Avocations: tennis, reading, travel. Office: U Tex Med Sch Dept Neurosurgery 6431 Fannin Ste 7 148 Houston TX 77030

MC DONALD, MEG, public relations executive; b. Santa Monica, Calif., Oct. 11, 1948; Dir. radio & TV svcs. Fran Hynds Pub. Rels., 1969-75; owner, CEO Mc Donald Media Svcs., 1975—. Recipient Buccaneer award PIRATES, 1980, 82, Prisms award Pub. Rels. Soc. Am., 1981, Pro awards Publicity Clubs. of L.A. Mem. Pub. Rels. Soc. Am. (sec. 1985), Radio and TV News Assn. of So. Calif. (mem. bd. dirs. 1973-88), Publicity Club of L.A. (pres. 1979-80), L.A. Advt. Women (v.p. 1984-85), Print Interactive Radio and TV Ednl. Soc. (pres. 1998-00), Radio and TV News Assn. Office: Mc Donald Media Svcs 11076 Fruitland Dr Studio City CA 91604-3541 Business E-Mail: mcdmedia@earthlink.net.

MCDONALD, PAMELA JANE, educational media specialist; d. Edd Reed and Dortha Mae McDonald. BA, Fla. State U., 1974, MS, 1981. Cert. profl. educator's cert. pre-K-12 Dept. Edn., Fla. Ednl. media specialist Max Bruner, Jr. Mid. Sch., Ft. Walton Beach, Fla., 1974—. Recipient extended access grant, Dept. Edn., 2001. Mem.: ALA, Fla. Assn. for Media in Edn. Avocations: travel, genealogy, reading. Office: Max Bruner Jr Mid Sch 322 Holmes Blvd NW Fort Walton Beach FL 32548

MCDONALD, SHARON HOLLIDAY, special education educator; b. Farmington, Mo., Jan. 15, 1948; d. Charles Douglas and Edythe Murriel Holliday; m. Gayle Dean McDonald, Feb. 14, 1969; children: Leslie Douglas, Mry Elizabeth. BS in Edn., U. Mo., 1969; MS in Edn., Kans. State U., 1973. Cert. K-9 tchr., learning disabilities, behavioral disabilities, mental retardation, social studies, composition, Kans. Tchr. spl. edn. Ottumwa (Iowa) Pub. Schs., 1969, Washington (Iowa) Cmty. Schs., 1969-71, Unified Sch. Dist. 336, Holton, Kans., 1971-75, 80-81, 82—. Mem. student improvement team Jackson Heights Elem. Sch., Holton, 1999—. Sunday sch. tchr. 1st United Meth. Ch., Holton, 1991-95, mem. Lady Belles, 1993—, chmn. adminstrv. coun., 1995, del. ann. conf., 1996. Named Outstanding Nutrition Educator, Midland Dairy Coun., 1994. Mem. NEA, Coun. for Exceptional Children (cert. profl. recognized spl. educator), Kans. Edn. Assn., Holton Edn. Assn., Pilot Club (pres. Holton 1980, 2000), Delta Kappa Gamma (membership com. Holton 1998-00). Republican. Avocations: music, needlecrafts, reading. Home: 15587 222nd Rd Holton KS 66436-1406 Office: Jackson Heights Elem Sch 12763 266th Rd Holton KS 66436-8717

MC DONALD, SHIRLEY PETERSON, social worker; b. Indpls., July 7, 1934; d. Harry and Marcella Iona (Kober) Peterson; B.A., Denison U., 1956; teaching credentials Chgo. State U., Nat. Coll. Edn., Prairie State U.; M.S.W., U. Ill., 1976; LCSW; cert. mediator ednl. disputes, Ill. State Bd. Edn.; m. Stanford Laurel McDonald, Apr. 26, 1964; children— Stacia Elizabeth Virginia, Jeffrey Jared Stern, Kathleen Shirley, Patricia Marie. Tchr., Chgo. Public Schs., 1962-64, Flossmoor, Ill., 1972-74; communication devel. program social worker S. Met. Assn., Harvey, Ill., 1976-79; sch. social worker S.W. Cook County Coop. Spl. Edn., Oak Forest, Ill., 1979-87; prof., field liaison Jane Addams Coll. of Social Work, U. Ill. at Chgo., 1987-2000, clin. assoc. prof. emeritus, 2000—, pvt. clin. practice, Park Forest, Ill., 1980—. Cons. sch. social work issues, pratice & litigation; supr. candidates for lic. in clin. social work; presenter in field. Editor: School Social Work: Practaice, Policy and Research Perspectives, 2d and 6th edits.; editor Sch. Social Work Jour. Religious edn. dir. All Souls Unitarian Ch., 1968-71; religious edn. dir. Unitarian Universalist Cmty. Ch., Park Forest, 1975-79, bd. dirs., 1978-81, chmn. bldg. feasibility com., 1981, chmn. bldg. com., 1981-82, also adv. to bd. Mem. Acad. Cert. Social Workers, Nat. Assn. Social Workers, Ill. Assn. Sch. Social Workers (area rep.; mem. com. consultation service, program com. state conf. 1981, adv. 1981-83, pres.-elect 1982-83, pres. 1983-84), Kappa Kappa Gamma, Women's Internat. League Peace and Freedom (past chpt. pres.), Pi Sigma Alpha. E-mail: smcdo12602@ameritech.net.

MCDONALD, SUSAN B., psychologist; b. Ft. Erie, Ont., Can., July 15, 1956; d. Charles A. and Doris F. (Staples) McD. BA hon. upper second class, Queens U., Kingston, Ont., 1978; MS, Fla. State U., 1982. Lic. psychologist, Wis.; bd. cert. forensic examiner; diplomate Am. Coll. Forensic Examiners, lic. profl. counselor; cert. profl. counselor, Wis. Intern Wis. Dept. Corrections, Madison, 1983-84, cons., 1984-85, project specialist, 1985-86; psychologist Waupun Correctional Instn., Wis., 1986-89, Genesis Counseling Svcs., Ltd., Janesville, Wis., 1989—2002, Sand Ridge Secure Treatment Ctr., Wis., 2002—03; founder, ptnr. Cmty. Psych. Svc. LLC, 1996—. Psychol. cons. Wis. Div. Probation and Parole, Janesville, 1991—; psychologist-ptnr. Cmty. Psychol. Svcs., LLC, 1996—; cons. Waupun Correctional Inst., 1996—; exec. dir. Wis. Sex Offender Treatment Network, Inc., 1999-2001. Fellow Wis. Sex Offender Treatment Network (grad.), Am. Coll. Forensic Examiners; mem. APA (assoc.), Assn. Treatment Sexual Abusers (clin. mem.), Phi Kappa Phi, Mu Alpha Theta. Avocations: art, volleyball, reading, painting. Office: Cmty Psychol Svcs LLC PO Box 259096 Madison WI 53725-9096

MCDONALD, THERESA BEATRICE PIERCE (MRS. OLLIE MCDONALD), church official, minister; b. Vicksburg, Miss., Apr. 11, 1929; d. Leonard C. Pierce and Ernestine Morris Templeton Pierce; m. Ollie McDonald, Apr. 23, 1966. Student, Tougaloo Coll., 1946-47, U. Chgo. Indsl. Rels. Ctr., 1963-64; BA in Sociology with deptl. honors, Roosevelt U., 1997; student, Chgo. Theol. Sem., 1997—. Ordained to Gospel Ministry, 1997. Vol. rep. Liberty Bapt. Ch., Am. Legion Aux., VA West Side Hosp., Chgo., 1971-73; nat. instr. ushers dept. Prog. Nat. Bapt. Conv. Inc., Washington, 1973-75, nat. sec. ushers dept., 1975-76, v.p. at large, 1980-82, chmn. pers. com., 1982-84; mem. faculty Congress of Christian Edn., 1978-85; mem. pub. rels. staff Liberty Bapt. Ch., Chgo., 1973-79, trustee, 1987-91; asst. Christian edn. dir. Maryland Ave. Bapt. Ch., Chgo., 1995-99; assoc. min. Md. Ave. Bapt. Ch., Chgo., 1997—; Tchr. Tng. Instr., 1998, 2000; dir. Christian edn. Md. Ave. Bapt. Ch., Chgo., 2000—02. Cons., lectr. in field; Sunday ch. sch. tchr.; bible class instr.; guest speaker TV and radio programs. Participant White House Regional Confs., 1961. Recipient Christian Svc. award Prog. Nat. Bapt. Conv. Inc., 1986, 92, 94, Disting. Svc. award, 1990-94, Dedicated Svc. award, 1998. Mem. VFW (life mem. Hunt aux. 2024), Bethlehem Bapt. Dist. Assn. Chgo. (asst. sec. 1982-84), Ch. Women United in Greater Chgo. (Ecumenical Actions com. 1981-83), Am. Legion (Outstanding Svc. award 1972, 73), Bapt. State Conv. Ill. (life), Order Ea. Star. Address: 9810 S Calumet Ave Chicago IL 60628-1432

MCDONALD, THERESA ELIZABETH, secondary school educator; b. Logan, W.Va., Dec. 24, 1947; d. John Grant and Constance (Babock) Thornbury; m. Daniel K. McDonald, Sept. 26, 1970; 1 child, John Clark. BA in Secondary Social Studies, W.Va. Inst. Tech., 1972; MA in Elem. Edn., Marshall U., 1976. Cert. tchr., W.Va., Fla. Elem. tchr. Logan County Bd. Edn., Logan, 1972-85; secondary social studies tchr. Brevard County Bd. Edn., Viera, Fla., 1985—, peer counseling/dropout prevention instr. Logan, 1992-94; dept. chmn. social studies Astronaut H.S., Titusville, Fla., 1996—. Adult edn. instr. North Area Brevard C.C., Titusville, Fla., 1986-90. Author world history program, world history curriculum standards, others; reviewer Curriculum Rev. for Social Studies in Fla., 1988. Vol., March of Dimes, Titusville, 1988—, Astronaut High Sch. Sports Program, Titusville, 1988—. Grantee in field. Mem. ASCD, Brevard Fedn. Tchrs., Nat. Coun. Social Studies, Fla. Coun. Social Studies, Brevard County Coun. Social Studies (sec. 1989-92). Republican. Baptist. Avocations: genealogy, travel, reading, people watching. Office: Astronaut High Sch 800 War Eagle Blvd Titusville FL 32796-2398 Home: 5 Indian River Ave Apt 1105 Titusville FL 32796

MCDONALD, VIVIAN, minister; b. Gainesville, Fla., June 26, 1949; d. Preston and Pearl Williams; m. Frankie McDonald (dec.); children: Tilwanna Renee Brown, Anita Tyese Mann; adopted children: Cassandra Abbott, Calvin LaMar Abbott, Isaiah K. Phillips. Degree in ministerial enrichment, Bible Inst., 1982. ETA approved tchr. Evangelical Tng. Assn., 1997. Ministerial intern Ch. of God, Tifton, Ga., 1992—93, pastor Dawson, Ga., 1993—. Recipient Women Making Magic, Southwest Ga. Living, 2004. Mem.: Black Ministries. Avocations: sewing, reading, puzzles. Personal E-mail: ladymackie@aol.com.

MCDONALD-POCHIBA, ELIZABETH J., secondary school educator; b. McKeesport, Pa., Aug. 31, 1978; d. Randall C and Joyce A McDonald; m. Brian M Pochiba, Dec. 30, 2005. BA, U. of Pitts., Johnstown, 2000. Cert. tchr. Pa., 2001. Tchr. McKeesport Area H.S., McKeesport, Pa., 2001—; coach dance team, 2005—.

MCDONALD TERLAJE, PATRICIA, counselor; b. Tamuning, Mar. 16, 1962; d. Charles H. and Lucia G. McDonald; m. Paul J. Terlaje, Jan. 11, 2001; children: Pedro C. Lizama, Allen M. McDonald, Trinity E. Terlaje. BA in Secondary Edn. English (hon.), U. Guam, Mangilao, 1985, MA in Counseling, 2001. Tchr. English Guam Pub. Sch. Sys., Hagatna, Guam, 1985—99; counselor Acad. Our Lady Guam, 2000—01, Guam C.C., Mangilao, 2002—. Career resource network counselor U.S. Dept. Edn. Perkins Act, Mangilao, 2002—03. Mem.: Am. Coll. Counseling Assn., Guam Sch. Counselor Assn., Am. Sch. Counselor Assn., Am. Counseling Assn. Home: 557 Chalan Macajna Agana Heights GU 96910 Office: Guam CC PO Box 23069 Barrigada GU 96921 Office Phone: 671-735-5564. Home Fax: 671-734-5238; Office Fax: 671-734-5238. Business E-Mail: pterlaje@guamcc.edu.

MCDONNELL, G. DARLENE, retired business educator; b. South Bend, Ind., Mar. 3, 1939; d. Roy Edward and Gizella Elizabeth Stroup; m. Dennis Eugene McDonnell, June 22, 1968; children: Lori, Jamie. BS, MA, Ball State U., 1962. Lic. real estate broker. Tchr. bus. edn. South Bend Tchr. Sch. Corp., 1962—2002, ret., 2002. Chmn. dept. bus. edn. LaSalle H.S., South Bend Cmty. Sch. Corp., 1972—95, BOA adv. bd., 1973—93. Co-editor (bus. edn. practice set simulation): Aaron's Insurance Agency, 1981. Mem.: Ind. Bus. Edn. Assn. (membership chmn.), Ind. State Tchrs. Assn., Bus. Office Assn. (intracurricular student sponsorship 1972—95), Delta Kappa Gamma, Kappa Delt Pi, Delta Pi Epsilon. Avocations: reading, golf. Home: 20440 Miller Rd South Bend IN 46614

MCDONNELL, KATHLEEN A., supervisor; b. Binghamton, NY, Jan. 24, 1941; d. Banjamin Harrison Bensley and Helen Irene Bensley Mainella; m. Patrick J. McDonnell, Aug. 11, 1962; children: Joseph P., Patrick C., Michael C. BS in Edn., SUNY, NYC, 1962; MS in Reading Edn., Syracyse U., NY, 1976. Tchr. 2d grade Waterville Ctrl. Sch. Dist., NY, 1962—64; tchr. title I Sauquoit Valley Elem. Sch., 1965; tchr. title I, 4th-6th grades Brookfield Ctrl. Sch., 1967—70; owner, operator Barron Apt. Complex, Waterville, 1971—79; tchr. title I Blue Hills Homes Corp., Kansas City, Mo., 1981—89, supr. title I, 1989—2003, Non-Pub. Edn. Svcs., Inc., St. Louis, 2003—05; ret., 2005. Mem.: Internat. Reading Assn. Avocations: reading, walking, bicycling, boating, swimming. Home: 445 Nantucket Dr Saint Charles MO 63301

MCDONNELL, MARY, actress; b. Wilkes-Barre, Pa., Apr. 28, 1952; m. Randle Mell; 2 children. Attended, SUNY, Fredonia, NY. Appearences include (theatre) Buried Child, 1978-79, Letters Home, 1979, Still Life, 1981 (Obie award 1981), The Death of a Miner, 1981-82, A Weekend Near Madison, 1982-83, Red River, 1982-83, Black Angel, 1982-83, All Night Long, 1984, The Three Sisters, 1984-85, Savage in Limbo, 1985, Stitchers and Starlight Talkers, 1985-86, Execution of Justice, 1986, A Doll's House, 1986-87, Three Ways Home, 1988, The Heidi Chronicles, 1990, Summer and Smoke, 1996 (TV series) High Society, 1995, ER, 2001, Battlestar Galactica, 2004-, (TV films) Money on the Side, 1982, Courage, 1986, O, Pioneers!, 1991, The American Clock, 1993, Blue Chips, 1993, Behind the Mask, 1999, A Father's Choice, 2000, For All Time, 2000, Chestnut Hill, 2001, The Locket, 2002, Mrs. Harris, 2005, (films) Garbo Talks, 1984, Matewan, 1987, Tiger Warsaw, 1988, Dances with Wolves, 1990 (Golden Globe award nomination 1990, Acad. Award nomination 1990), Grand Canyon, 1991, Sneakers, 1992, Passion Fish, 1992 (Acad. Award nomination 1993), Blue Chips, 1994, Independence Day, 1996, Mumford, 1999, Donnie Darko, 2001, Crazy Like a Fox, 2004. Office: William Morris Agy 151 S El Camino Dr Beverly Hills CA 90212-2775*

MCDONNELL, MARY THERESA, travel company executive; b. N.Y.C., Nov. 9, 1949; d. John J. and Mary B. (Lunney) McDonnell; m. Robert T. Barber, Oct. 7, 1989 (dec. Nov. 7, 1999). Mgr. Kramer Travel Agy., White Plains, NY, 1967-79; owner, mgr. New Trends Travel, Rye, NY, 1979-90, Honey Travel Inc., Rye, 1990—. Office: Honey Travel Inc 11 Elm Pl Rye NY 10580-2918 Office Phone: 914-921-0455. Personal E-mail: honeytravel@yahoo.com.

MCDONOUGH, ANN PATRICE, ice skater; b. Korea, May 29, 1985; Grad. high sch. Figure skater competing numerous events including State Farm U.S. Championships, 1999—, Jr. Grand Prix, Norway, Mex., 2000, World Jr. Championships, 2001—02, Four Continents Championships, 2002—03, Campbell's Classic, 2002—03, Smart Ones Skate Am., 2002, ABC Sports Internat. Figure Skating Challenge, 2003, Cup of China, 2003, numerous other competitions. Recipient numerous 1st place awards including, Gardena Spring Trophy, Southwestern Sectional, Midwestern Sectional, Jr. Grand Prix Final, Southwestern Regional, World Jr. Championships, numerous 2d place awards including, Jr. GLlrand Prix Norway, World Jr. Championships, Nebelhorn Trophy, Campbell's Class, Smart Ones Skate Am. Office: US Figure Skating Hdqrs 20 First St Colorado Springs CO 80906

MCDONOUGH, BRIDGET ANN, music theatre company director; b. Milw., June 19, 1956; d. James and Lois (Hunzinger) McD.; m. Gregory Paul Opelka, Sept. 20, 1986 (div. Aug. 1993); m. Robert Markey, Feb. 29, 2000. BS, Northwestern U., 1978. Bus. mgr. Organic Theater Co., Chgo., 1979-80; mng. dir., founder Light Opera Works, Evanston, Ill., 1980—. U.S. rep. European Congress Musical Theatre, 1995. Founder, mem. Chgo. Music Alliance, 1984—, pres., 1995-98; mem. Ill. Arts Alliance; bd. dirs., Nat. Alliance for Musical Theatre, 2001-2005, sec., 2001—04; bd. dirs. Evanston Convention Visitors Bur., 1999-2002; mem. alumni adv. bd. Northwestern U. Sch. Speech, 1999-2002; bd. dirs. Around the Coyote Arts Festival, 2002—. Recipient Women on the Move award Evanston YWCA, 1991. Mem. Evanston C. of C. (bd. dirs., 1993-99), North Shore Internat. Network, Rotary (pres. Evanston chpt. 1999-00), Union League Club. Avocation: birdwatching. Office: Light Opera Works 927 Noyes St Evanston IL 60201-6206

MCDONOUGH, CHERYL YORK, principal, educational consultant; b. Melrose, Mass. d. E. Stanley and Marilyn E. York; m. Stephen G. McDonough, Aug. 3, 1982; children: Stephen, Katherine, John. BS in Edn., Keene State Coll., N.H., 1980; cert. in adminstrn., Rivier Coll., Nashua, N.H., 2001; JD, Mass. U., Andover, 1994. Bar: N.H., Mass.; cert. sch. supt. N.H., sch. prin. N.H., educator N.H. Prin. Great Bay Charter, Exeter, NH; cons. Collins Edn., West Newbury, Maine; curriculum dir. SAU 17, Kingston, NH; humanities chair Sanborn H.S., Kingston, NH; English tchr. Timberland H.S., Plaistow, NH. Contbr. articles to profl. jours. Chair Sch. Bd. of Kensington, NH, 1996—2005; mem. Sch. Bd. SAU 16, Exeter, NH, 1996—2005. Grantee, Mass. Sch. Law, 1994. Avocations: writing, newfoundland dogs, reading, travel. Office: Great Bay Learning Charter 56 Linden St Exeter NH 03833 Office Phone: 603-775-8638. Business E-Mail: chmcdonough@sau16.org.

MCDONOUGH, JEAN WHITNEY, personal trainer, sports medicine physician; b. Kealakekua, Hawaii, June 18, 1959; d. Sidney Joseph Weinrich and Marjorie Jane Rundahl; m. Robert E.P. McDonough, June 4; children: Conor W., Robert M. BS in Secondary Edn. and Phys. Edn., U. Hawaii, Honolulu, 1982; MS in Oriental Medicine, Traditional Coll. Cinese Medicine, Hawaii, 2001. Nurse aide Hawaii Prep Acad., Kamuela, athletic trainer, various schs.; phys. therapy assoc. San Diego Kamuela Kona, Jeans Athletic Injury Care, Kamuela, Hawaii. Home: PO Box 1195 Kamuela HI 96743

MCDORMAND, FRANCES, actress; b. Chgo., June 23, 1957; m. Joel Coen, 1984; 2 children. BA, Bethany Coll., 1979; MFA, Yale U. Sch. Drama, 1982. Stage appearances include Awake and Sing!, N.Y.C., 1984, Painting Churches, N.Y.C., 1984, The Three Sisters, Mpls., 1985, N.J., 1991, All My Sons, New Haven, 1986, A Streetcar Named Desire, N.Y.C., 1988, Moon for the Misbegotten, 1992, Sisters Rosensweig, N.Y.C., 1993, The Swan, N.Y.C., 1993, To You, the Birdie!, 2002, Far Away, 2002; TV appearances include The Twilight Zone, The Equalizer, Spencer: For Hire, Hill Street Blues, (series) Hunter, 1984, Legwork, 1986-87, Twilight Zone, 1986, State of Grace, 2001; film appearances include Blood Simple, 1984, Crime Wave, 1986, Raising Arizona, 1987, Mississippi Burning, 1988 (Academy award nominee), Chattahoochee, 1990, Darkman, 1990, Miller's Crossing, 1990, Hidden Agenda, 1990, The Butcher's Wife, 1991, Passed Away, 1992, Short Cuts, 1993, Beyond Rangoon, 1995, Plain Pleasures, 1996, Fargo, 1996 (Academy award for Best Actress in a Leading Role, 1997), Lone Star, 1996, Primal Fear, 1996, Palookaville, 1996, Paradise Road, 1997, Johnny Skidmarks, 1998, Madeline, 1998, Talk of Angels, 1998, Wonder Boys, 1999, Almost Famous (Academy award nominee, Brit. Acad. award nominee, Golden Globe nominee, SAG nominee), Man Who Wasn't There, 2001, City by the Sea, 2002, Something's Gotta Give, 2003, Last Night, 2004, North Country, 2005, Aeon Flux, 2005, Friends With Money, 2006, (TV movies) Scandal Sheet, 1985, Vengeance: The Story of Tony Cimo, 1986, Crazy In Love, 1992, Good Old Boys, 1995, Hidden in America, 1996, (narrator) Precinct Hollywood, 2005.*

MCDOUGALL, GAY, lawyer; b. Atlanta, Aug. 13, 1947; BA, Bennington Coll., 1969; JD, Yale U., 1972; LLM, London Sch. Econs., 1978. Bar: Court Appeals State NY 1974, US Dist. Ct. So. Dist. NY 1977, US Supreme Ct. 1979, DC 1994. Assoc. Debevoise, Plimton, Lyons and Gates, NYC, 1972—74; gen. counsel Nat. Conf. Black Lawyers, NYC, 1975—76; staff atty. minimum standards unit Bd. Corrections, NYC, 1976—77; assoc. counsel Office Dep. Mayor Criminal Justice, NYC, 1979—80; dir. So. Africa project The Lawyer's Com. Civil Rights Under the Law, Washington, 1980—94; exec. dir. Global Rights (formerly Internat. Human Rights Law Group), Washington, 1994—2006; ind. expert on minority issues UN, 2005—. Dir. So. Africa Project, Lawyers' Com. for Civil Rights Under Law, 1980-94; mem. Ind. Electoral Commn. South African Elections, 1994. Founder Commn. Independence for Nambia; mem. com. on elimination of racial discrimination UN, spl. rapporteur on systematic rape and sexual slavery in armed conflict, sub commn. on human rights, 1997-2000; mem. sub-Commission prevention discrimination and protection minorities human rights commn., UN, 1995-2000; ind. expert treaty body that oversees the internat. convention elimination of all forms racial discrimination, UN, 1997-2001; Bd. dirs. Global Fund for Women, 2005-, Africare, 2005-, CARE USA, CARE Internat., Robert F. Kennedy Meml. Found., internat. human rights coun., Jimmy Carter Presidential Ctr. Fellow MacArthur Found., 1999. Mem.: Am. Soc. Internat. Law (president's advisory panel, Judges Panel three major Honors and Medals 2003—), Coun. Fgn. Relations (Africa Program Advisory Panel Ctr. Preventive Action). Office: Palais des Nations CH-1211 Geneva Switzerland*

MCDOUGALL-GIBBS, MARY ELIZABETH (BETSY MCDOUGALL-GIBBS), early childhood special education educator; b. Storm Lake, Iowa, Dec. 30, 1951; d. James Robert and Yvonne Marie (Welch) McDougall; m. Leonard Earl Gibbs, July 9, 1988; children: Martin Daniel, Jeffrey Robert. BA in Speech/Lang. Pathology, U. Minn., Duluth, 1974; MA in Speech/Lang. Pathology, We. Mich. U., 1975; student, U. Wis., Whitewater, 1980. Cert. in early childhood and exceptional edn. needs, Wis. Speech/lang. pathologist Spencer (Wis.) Pub. Schs., 1975-79, Devel. Learning Ctr. Early Intervention Program, Dakota County, Minn., 1980-84, Waisman Ctr., Madison, Wis., 1984-85; instr., supr. tchr. tng. program in early intervention U. Wis., Eau Claire, 1985-88; program support tchr. Early Childhood: Exceptional Edn. Needs Eau Claire Area Sch. Dist., 1988—. Mem. spl. edn. parent adv. bd. Eau Claire Area Sch. Dist., 1988-91; mem. local coordinating coun. for early childhood Chippewa Valley, Eau Claire, 1990—; mem. adv. com. Birth to Three program Eau Claire County, 1992—; mem. devel. and tng. ctr. Integrated Childcare Ctr., Eau Claire, 1991—. Mem. Eau Chaire Early Learning Initiative, coord. access grant com., chair ops. com., site criteria, goverance develop. kindergarten program; bd. dirs. Eau Claire Coalition for Families, 2000—05; mem. Wis. Initiative for Infant Mental Health, 2000—05; spl. edn. adv. com. Head Start, 2002—05, health adv. com., 2003—05; chair tng. and edn. com. Chippewa Valley Children's Mental Health Alliance, 2004—05; mem. tng. and edn. com. Wis. Initiative for Infant Mental Health. Mem. Am. Speech, Lang. and Hearing Assn., Coun. for Exceptional Children, Wis. Div. for Early Childhood (newsletter editor 1988-91). Avocations: bicycling, cross country skiing, travel, puppetry. Home: 2460 Quail Run Rd Eau Claire WI 54701 Office: Eau Claire Area Sch Dist Bd Office 500 Main St Eau Claire WI 54701-3770

MCDOWELL, ANGELA LORENE, counselor; b. Murfreesboro, Tenn., Oct. 30, 1966; d. William Thomas Kendrick Jr. and Jo Carol (Hipp) Leach. AA, Lincoln Land Community Coll., 1987; BS, Ill. State U., 1989; MS, So. Ill. U., 1990. Lic. clin. profl. counselor, 1997—; nat. cert. counselor, 1996—; cert. alcohol and drug counselor, Ill., 1992—, cert. substitute tchr., 2005—; bd. registered counselor II, Mental Ill./Substance Abuse, 2001—. Adult and adolescent counselor, evaluator The Recovery Ctr., Jerseyville, Ill., 1991-95; counselor Tri-County Counseling Ctr., Dept. Alcohol & Substance Abuse, Jerseyville, Ill., 1995-96; utilization mgmr. coord. Chesnut Health Systems, Granite City, Ill., 1996—; counselor Chestnut Health Syt., 1996—2004; substitute tchr., 2005—; office mgr. Jacoby Arts Ctr., 2006—; pvt. practice counseling, 2006—. Grad. asst. Rehab. Inst., So. Ill. U., Carbondale, 1989-90. Mem.: Ill. Counseling Assn., Am. Counseling Assn. Methodist. Avocations: hiking, camping, reading, walking. Home: 4707 Village Dr Godfrey IL 62035-1324 Office Phone: 619-465-9747.

MCDOWELL, BARBARA, lawyer; b. Oakland, Calif., Apr. 5, 1952; d. James Martin and Joyce (Benson) McD.; m. Robert S. Peck, Dec. 19, 1976. BA, George Washington U., 1974; JD, Yale U., 1985. Bar: Pa. 1986, D.C. 1988. Law clk. to judge U.S. Dist. Ct. Conn., New Haven, 1985-86; law clk. to Hon. Ralph Winter U.S. Ct. Appeals (2d cir.), N.Y.C., 1986-87; law clk. to Justice Byron R. White U.S. Supreme Ct., Washington, 1987-88; assoc. Jones, Day, Reavis & Pogue, Washington, 1988—97; asst. to the solicitor gen. US Dept. Justice, Washington, 1997—2004; staff atty., appellate advocacy program Legal Aid Soc., Washington, 2004—. Mem. ABA. Democrat. Congregationalist. Office: 666 11th St NW Ste 800 Washington DC 20001

MCDOWELL, BARBARA, artist; b. Paducah, Ky., Jan. 6, 1921; d. William Bryan Rouse and Mary Marguerite Thomasson; m. William Wells McDowell, Jan. 6, 1944 (dec. 1976). AA, Delmar Coll., Corpus Christi, 1940; BA with hons., Corpus Christi State U., 1986; MA in Studio Art, Tex. A&M U., Corpus Christi, 2003. Artist Davison Paxon, Atlanta, 1944—45; layout artist Tucker Wayne & Co., Atlanta, 1945—46; fashion illustrator Lichtenstein's, Corpus Christi, 1948—49, 1951—52; artist, art dir. Adcraft Advt. Agy., Corpus Christi, 1952—79; owner, artist, writer B. McDowell Graphic Design, Corpus Christi, 1979—2000. One-woman shows include Corpus Christi Mus. Sci. and History, 1973, Bayfront Plz Auditorium, Corpus Christi, 1976, Art Ctr. of Corpus Christi, 1983, 2003, 2006, Tex. A&M U., Kingsville, 1990, Galeria LaVentana, Corpus Christi, 1992—94, Galvan House, 2001, 2002, 2004, exhibited in group shows at S. Tex. Art League, 1972—2006, S.W. Sculpture Soc., 1972—2006, Tex. Watercolor Soc., San Antonio, 1968, 1978, 1982, 1998, Tex. Fine Arts Assn., Austin, 1975, 1979, 1986, Southwestern Watercolor Soc., Dallas, 1985, Hill Country Arts Found., Igram, Tex., 1990, Art Mus. S. Tex., 1990, 2000, 2006, Tex. A&M U. Alumni Show, Corpus Christi, 1992, Upstairs Gallery, 1992, 1996, Third Biennial Gulf of Mex. Symposium, 1995, Gallery Leszarts - Les Cerveux Sous Passavant, France, 1998, Watercolor Art Soc. Houston, 1998, Estelle Stair Art Gallery, Rockport, Tex., 1999, Rockport Ctr. for Arts, 2000, Wilhelmi-Holland Art Gallery, 2000, Watercolor Soc. of S. Texas, Corpus Christi. Donor Art Ctr. Coll. Design, Pasadena, Calif., 1979—, Corpus Christi Botanical Gardens, 1991—, Driscoll Children's Hosp., Corpus Christi, 1995—, Art Mus. S. Tex., 1995, Tex. A & M U., Corpus Christi, 2000—; mem. Rockport Ctr. for Arts; pres. Art Ctr. of Corpus Christi, 2004—05; mem. Art Mus. of S. Tex., Corpus Christi, 1994—, bd. govs., 2005—; mem., com. chair Mcpl. Arts Commn., Corpus Christi, 1986—92. Recipient Nat. Drawing and Sculpture award, Del Mar Coll., 1986, 1993, 1998, Vol. Cert. of Excellence, Caller Times, 1993, prize, NCECA Regional Juried Ceramics Exhibit, Arlington Mus. Art, Ft. Worth, 1995, Purchase award, Tex. A&M U., Corpus Christi, 2002. Mem.: S.W. Sculpture Soc., Watercolor Soc. S. Tex. (pres. 1977—), S. Tex. Art League (chmn. 1976—). Avocations: gardening, ceramics, painting. Home: 302 Glenmore St Corpus Christi TX 78412

MCDOWELL, ELAINE, retired federal government executive, educator; b. Balt., June 28, 1942; d. McKinley and Lena (Blue) McDowell; children: Nathan H. Jr. Murphy, Michael W. Murphy. BA, Morgan State U., Balt., 1965; MSW, U. Md., 1971, PhD, 1988. Drug abuse adminstr., acting regional dir. State Md. Drug Abuse Adminstrn., Balt., 1971-72; social sci. analyst, pub. health advisor Nat. Inst. Drug Abuse, Rockville, MD, 1972-76, dep. dir., dir. div. community assistance, 1976-82, dep. assoc. dir. for policy devel., 1981-82, dir. div. prevention and communications, 1982-85; exec. asst. to adminstr. Alcohol, Drug Abuse & Mental Health Adminstrn., Rockville, Md., 1985; dep. dir. Nat. Inst. on Drug Abuse, Rockville, MD, 1985-88; dir. Ctr. for Substance Abuse Prevention, 1988-96; acting adminstr. Alcohol, Drug Abuse and Mental Health Adminstrn., Rockville, Md., 1992, Substance Abuse and Mental Health Svcs. Adminstrn., Rockville, Md., 1992-94. Expert cons. in substance abuse, treatment, and mental health fields; prof. Morgan State U., Balt. Chmn. non-alcoholic internat. gen. svc. bd. Alcoholics Anonymous, 2001—05, trustee emeritus, 2005—; active Presbyn. Ch. U.S.A., Balt., 1998—; bd. dirs. Rosalynn Carter Inst. for Human Devel. Recipient Outstanding Leadership in Improving Health Care in Black Cmty. award Nat. Med. Assn., 1989, Sec.'s commendation HHS, 1989, Disting. Svc. award, 1990, Nat. Coun. on Alcoholism and Drug Dependence Ind., Pres. award for outstanding fed. leadership, 1991, Presdl. Meritorious Exec. Rank award, 1991, Presdl. Meritorious Disting. Rank award, 1993, Clyde Bailey, Sr. Meml. award Nat. African Am. Drug Policy Coalition, 2006. Mem.: NASW, Sr. Execs. Assn. Personal E-mail: JLuvenia@aol.com.

MCDOWELL, ELIZABETH MARY, retired pathology educator; b. Kew Gardens, Surrey, Eng., Mar. 30, 1940; arrived in U.S., 1971; d. Arthur and Peggy (Bryant) McD. B Vet. Medicine, Royal Vet. Coll., London, 1963; BA, Cambridge U., 1968, PhD, 1971. Gen. practice vet. medicine, 1964-66; Nuffield Found. tng. scholar Cambridge (Eng.) U., 1966-71; instr. dept. pathology U. Md., Balt., 1971-73, asst. prof., 1973-76, assoc. prof., 1976-80, prof., 1980-96, ret., 1996. Co-author: Biopsy Pathology of the Bronchi, 1987; editor: Lung Carcinomas, 1987; contbr. over 120 articles to sci. jours., chpts. to books. Rsch. grantee, NIH, 1979—92. Avocations: conservation education, gardening, swimming.

MCDOWELL, HEATHER L., lawyer; b. Pitts., Apr. 12, 1965; BS with distinction, Pa. State Univ., 1987; JD, George Washington Univ., 1990. Bar: Md. 1990, Va. 1991, DC 1993. Ptnr., adv., mktg., new media communications Venable LLP, Washington, 2000—. Mem. FTC, 1991—94, FCC, 1994—96. Office: Venable LLP 575 Seventh St NW Washington DC 20004 Office Phone: 202-344-4897. Office Fax: 202-344-8300. Business E-Mail: hlmcdowell@venable.com.

MCDOWELL, JENNIFER, sociologist, composer, playwright; b. Albuquerque; d. Willard A. and Margaret Frances (Garrison) McD.; m. Milton Loventhal, July 2, 1973. BA, U. Calif., 1957; MA, San Diego State U., 1958; postgrad., Sorbonne, Paris, 1959; MLS, U. Calif., 1963; PhD, U. Oreg., 1973. Tchr. English Abraham Lincoln H.S., San Jose, Calif., 1960-61; free-lance editor Soviet field, Berkeley, Calif., 1961-63; editor, pub. Merlin Papers, San Jose, 1969-80, Merlin Press, San Jose, 1973—; rsch. cons. sociology San Jose, 1973—; music pub. Lipstick and Toy Balloons Pub. Co., San Jose, 1978—, Abbie & Dolley Records, 2003—; composer Paramount Pictures, 1982-88. Tchr. writing workshops; poetry readings, 1969-73; co-producer radio show lit. and culture Sta. KALX, Berkeley, 1971-72. Author: (with Milton Loventhal) Black Politics: A Study and Annotated Bibliography of the Mississippi Freedom Democratic Party, 1971 (Smithsonian Inst. 1992), Contemporary Women Poets, 1977; co-author: (plays off-off Broadway) Betsy and Phyllis, 1986, Mack the Knife Your Friendly Dentist, 1986, The Estrogen Party To End War, 1986, The Oatmeal Party Comes to Order, 1986, (plays) Betsy Meets the Wacky Iraqi, 1991, Bella and Phyllis, 1994; author numerous poems; contbr. articles and short stories to profl. jours, local newspapers; writer: (songs) Money Makes a Woman Free!, 1976, 2004; 3 songs featured in Parade of Am. Music, 1976-77; co-creator mus. comedy Russia's Secret Plot To Take Back Alaska, 1988; (Cassingle) Intern Girl, 1998, Smithsonian, 2002; (CDs) Our Women Are Strong, 2000, 02, The Wearing of the Green Burkas, 2003; (musical revs., CD) She, A Tapestry of Women's Lives, 2004. Recipient 8 awards Am. Song Festival, 1976-79, Service to Poetry award, 1977, Bill Casey award in Letters (Soviet Studies), 1980, SHE award, Calif. State U.-ERFA Found., 2004, collected by Nobel Inst. for 2003 Nobel Peace Prize laureate Shirin Ebadi; doctoral fellow AAUW, 1971-73; grantee Calif. Arts Coun., 1976-77. Mem. AAUW, Am. Assn. for Advancement of Slavic Studies, Soc. Sci. Study of Religion, Am. Sociol. Assn., Dramatists Guild, Phi Beta Kappa, Sigma Alpha Iota, Beta Phi Mu, Kappa Kappa Gamma. Democrat. Office: care Abbie and Dolley Records PO Box 5602 San Jose CA 95150-5602 Personal E-mail: jeditorphd@earthlink.net.

MCDOWELL, KAREN ANN, lawyer; b. Ruston, La., Oct. 4, 1945; d. Paul and Opal Elizabeth (Davis) Bauer; m. Gary Lee McDowell, Dec. 22, 1979. BA, U. La., Monroe, 1967; JD, U. Mich., 1971; diploma, John Robert Powers Sch., Chgo., 1976, Nat. Inst. Trial Advocacy, 1990. Bar: Ill. 1973, Colo. 1977, U.S. Dist. Ct. (so. dist.) Ill. 1973, U.S. Dist. Ct. Colo. 1977. Reference libr. assoc. Ill. State Library, Springfield, 1972-73; asst. atty. gen. State of Ill., Springfield, 1973-75; pvt. practice Boulder, Colo., 1978-79, Denver, 1979—. Mem. hate violence task force, Colo. Lawyers Com.; foster mom for young kittens Recycled Critter Rescue. Mem.: DAR, ABA, Colo. Women's Bar Assn. (editor newsletter 1982—84), Denver Bar Assn., Colo. Bar Assn., Am. Assn. Retired Persons, Humane Soc. U.S., Survivors United Network (legal coord. 1992—93), Ams. of Royal Descent, Toastmasters Internat. (Able Toastmaster Bronze 1992), Colonial Dames, Survivors United Network Profls. (exec. com. 1992), Mensa (local sect. Ann Arbor, Mich. 1968), Nat. Soc. Magna Carta Dames, Colonial Order of Crown, Sovereign Colonial Soc., Alpha Lambda Delta, Sigma Tau Delta, Phi Alpha Theta. Avocations: stamp collecting/philately, chess, needlecrafts, dinosaurs, horatio alger stories. Office: 1525 Josephine St Denver CO 80206-1406 Office Phone: 303-830-2627. Business E-Mail: kamcdowell@qwest.net.

MCDOWELL-CRAIG, VANESSA DENNISE, supervisor, consultant; b. Washington, Dec. 9, 1954; d. John David and Ossie Ola McDowell; m. John Maurice Craig, May 19, 1984. BS, U. DC, 1995; MEd, Trinity U., Washington, 2000; postgrad., Gallaudet U., 2001—. Cert. mgmt. change leadership Gallaudet U., elem. edn. DC, emergins leaders program DC. ednl. rsch. and dissemination program Am. Fedn. Tchrs. Tng. instr. Blue Cross - Blue Shield, Washington, 1980—87; claims supr. Mut. Omaha, Washington, 1987—88, Health Plus, Riverdale, Md., 1988—89; supr., team mgr. Humana Group Health Plan, Washington, 1989—93; elem. tchr. grades 1-6 DC Pub. Sch. Sys., 1993—2001, instrnl. facilitator, supr., 2002—, spl. edn. coord., supr., cons. Cons. TechAgility LLC, Washington, 2004—. Mem.: ASCD (assoc.), Assn. Childhood Edn. Internat. (assoc.), Internat. Reading Assn. (assoc.; corr. sec. DC reading coun. 1999—2002), Delta Sigma Theta (life). Democrat. African Methodist Episcopal. Avocations: travel, reading, bicycling, singing, dance. Home: 7134 Marbury Court District Heights MD 20747 Office: DC Pub Sch Sys Turner Elem Sch 3264 Staton Rd SE Washington DC 20020 Office Phone: 202-698-1167. Home Fax: 301-736-2365; Office Fax: 202-698-1166. Personal E-mail: vannettie@aol.com. Business E-Mail: vanessa.craig@k12.dc.us.

MCDUNN, ADRIENNE, human behavior consultant; b. Moorhead, Minn., June 16, 1953; d. Adrian James and Virginia Ann McDunn. Student, U. Lancaster, Eng., 1976; BA, U. Minn., 1981; M of Adult Edn., N.C. State U., 1992. Cert. in divorce, family, civil mediation; facilitation; diversity application. Tng. mgr. Cambar Bus. Sys., Charleston, S.C., 1983-85; sr. application cons. Mgmt. Sci. Am., Hamden, Conn., 1985-89; sr. engagement mgr. McKinsey & Co., Atlanta, 1989-91; cons., mediator Dispute Settlement Ct., Durham, N.C., 1991-93; exec. v.p. Personalysis Corp., Houston, 1993—2003; v.p. strategic learning Providence Health Sys., Seattle, 2003—. Mediator in dist. ct. Civil Ct. Sys., Raleigh and Durham, 1991-93; guest lectr. Student Leadership Ctr., N.C. State U., Raleigh, 1992-93. Mem. ASTD (membership dir. 1992), Orgn. Devel. Network, Phi Kappa Phi.

MCEACHERN, JOAN, medical association administrator; b. East Los Angeles, Calif., Feb. 28, 1937; d. Chester Manwell Biffi and Doris May Horrocks; m. Wayne Emery McEachern, Sept. 8, 1961 (dec. Mar. 1992); children: Marc Alan, David Wayne, Eric John. AA, East Los Angeles Coll., 1957. Sec. Flour Corp., City of Commerce, Calif., 1957-61; volunteer art tchr. Yorkville Schs., Yorkville, IL, 1975-1983; office supr. McKeoun-Dunn Ambulance, Oswego, Ill., 1992-97. Author: Illinois Association for Education and Community Education—An Aim for the Homemaker: 75 Years of Education and Outreach, 1999. Mem. Kendall County 4-H, various coms., 1975-2006, mem. Ill. 4-H Found., 1988-97, sec. exec. com. 1990-97; del. Ill. 4-H Salute to Excellence, Washington, 1985; mem. various state coms. in 4-H, 1979-94, developed 4-H project books; ext. adv. coun. U. Ill., 1994-97; pres. Kendall County Homemakers Ext. Assn., 1982-84, Kendall County Assn. Home and

Cmty. Edn., 2003—; adv. coun. Four County Conservation Found., 2003—, Yorkville Schs. Curriculum Com., 1974-76, pres. 1975-76; started Picture Person Art Appreciation program, Yorkville Schs., 1976, chmn., 1975-81; vol. art tchr., 1975-83. Recipient Yorkville Area Humanitarian award City of Yorkville Human Svcs. Com., 1983, Disting. Svc. award Kendall County Homemakers Ext. Assn., 1985, Kendall County Friend of 4-H award, 1989, numerous others. Mem.: Am. Women for Internat. Understanding (bd. dirs. 2002—, membership chair 2003—, v.p. 2003—), Associated County Women of World (pubs. and promotions com. 2001—04), Ill. Assn. Home and Cmty. Edn (pres. 1994—97), Nat. Vol. Outreach Network (pres. 1998—2001), Kendall County Rep. Women, Yorkville Garden Club, Kendall County Hist. Soc. (newsletter editor 1992—), Yorkville Women's Club. Avocations: water color painting, skiing, photography, travel, reading. Home and Office: 137 Riverside Dr Yorkville IL 60560-9471 Personal E-mail: mcskikat@yahoo.com.

MCEACHERN, SUSAN MARY, physician assistant; b. Royal Oak, Mich., May 3, 1960; d. Donald Keith and Lois Jean (Robison) McE.; m. James Paul Corbett, Jan. 8, 1983 (div. 1999). BS, Mich. State U., 1982; MBA, New Mex. State U., 1985. APN-RN, Cmty. Coll. Denver, 2004. From acct. adminstr. trainee to acct. adminstr. IBM, El Paso, Tex., 1985-89, customer support rep. Southfield, Mich., 1989-90, sr. adminstrv. specialist, 1991-92, adv. customer support rep., 1992-93, fin. analyst Boulder, Colo., 1993-95, database adminstr., analyst, 1995, team leader, 1995-2000, project mgr., internet, 2000—02; nurse Spalding Rehab. Hosp., Westminster, Colo., 2004—05; physician asst. St. Anthony Hosp., Westminster, 2005—. Cons. Integrated Sys. Solutions Co., Dallas, 1990-93. Author: Treasury of Poetry, 1992; editor-in-chief Online Newsletter for Polycystic Ovarian Syndrome Assn., 1998-2000; asst. editor Bull. for Nat. Polycystic Ovarian Syndrome Assn., 1998-2000; profl. flutist PSC Players, 1997-2001; prin. flutist Celebration Christian Ctr., 1996-2000. Vol. supr. Easter Seals, Southfield Mich., El Paso, Tex., 1978-88, Crisis Pregnancy, Las Cruces, New Mex., 1982-86, Multiple Sclerosis, Mich., 1983, Longmont (Colo.) Vol. Assn., 1994. Recipient Photography award Mich. State Fair, 1991, 92. Mem. IBM Club (v.p.), Creative Designs (pres. 1994—, Nat. Sci. and Engring. vol. rep. 1994), Polycystic Ovarian Syndrome Assn. (pres. Colo. chpt. 1997-2000, Outstanding Vol. award 1999, Internat. Dir. Med. Rsch.), Women of the Moose (chair health awareness 1998-99, apptd. officer Argus 1999-2000, Acad. Friendship award 2000). Avocations: computers, swimming, white-water rafting, photography, flute. Home: 12711 Colorado Blvd #505 Thornton CO 80241 E-mail: sbrightandsunny@aol.com.

MCELDOWNEY, NANCY, diplomat; b. Fla. m. Tim Hayes; 1 child, Jessica. BA, New Coll.; grad., Columbia U., Nat. Def. U. With Office of Sec. Def. Pentagon; Office of Soviet Affairs US Dept. State, Office of European Security Affairs, Front Office, European Bur., Office of Dep. Sec.; dir. European Affairs, Nat. Security Coun. White House; dep. chief of mission, US Embassy in Baku US Dept. State, Azerbaijan, dep. chief US Mission to Turkey Ankara, 2005—, chargé d'affaires in Turkey. Recipient Disting. Writing award, Nat. War Coll., Sinclair Linguistic award, Superior Honor award, US Dept. State. Mailing: 7000 Ankara Pl Washington DC 20521-7000*

MCELHANNON, NETTIE MARIE, retired orthopaedic nurse; b. Horatio, Ark., July 11, 1946; d. Arlis Victor and Gladys Louise (Daniel) Rowton; m. Kenneth G. McElhannon, July 9, 1972 (dec.); children: Joyce, Lois, Sheila. ADN, Texarkana Coll., 1988; BS in Nursing, U. Tex., 1990. Charge nurse, staff RN St. Michael Hosp., Texarkana, 1987—. Mem. Phi Theta Kappa, Sigma Theta Tau.

MCELHATTEN, BETTY SHREVE, writer, illustrator; b. Union City, Pa., June 4, 1930; d. Earl Milton and Rachel Wilson Shreve; m. Nelson McElhatten, June 4, 1953 (dec. 1994). RN, City Hosp. Sch. Nursing, Meadville, Pa., 1951. Emergency room and surg. scrub nurse Meadville City Hosp., 1951—53; pvt. duty RN U. Pa. Hosp., Phila., 1953—54; gen. duty RN Vets. Hosp., Phila., 1953—54. Scenic designer drama dept. Byram Hills H.S., Armonk, NY, 1970—73; mem. arts forum Village Gallery, San Diego, 1994—. Co-author: The General's Women: MacArthur's' Loves, 2004; co-author, illustrator Stringer and the Blue Bat Mystery, 2003 (finalist San Diego Book award, 2004), illustrator (storyboards) Miss Billy's Story Hour TV show, N.Y.C., 1972, numerous cookbooks, brochures, ads, directories, 1962—74. Neighborhood chair Girl Scouts Am., Mt. Kisco, NY, 1970—71; troop leader Hillside Ch. Pioneer Girls, Armonk, NY, 1971—73; facilitator bereavement support group Rancho Bernardo Presbyn. Ch., San Diego, 1990—93, deacon. Mem.: Am. Pen Women, Press Club North San Diego County. Avocations: art projects, snorkeling, cruising, reading.

MCELHINNEY, SUSAN KAY (KATE ECHEVERRIA) (KATE MCELHINNEY), executive assistant; b. Greeley, Colo., May 20, 1947; d. Glenn Eugene and Maxine (Filkins) McE.; m. Ben Echeverria, 1997. Student, U. N.C., 1965-67, U. Kans., 1969, U. Colo., 1971-72, 80. Adminstrv. sec. Colo. Pub. Defender, Denver, 1970-74; clk. Colo. Dist. Ct., Boulder, 1974-80; legal asst., office mgr. Law Office Ben Echeverria, San Marcos, Calif., 1986-97; exec. asst. Palomar (Calif.) C.C., 1997—. Mem. black tie fund raising com. Palomar C.C., 1991-92. Republican. Avocations: reading, golf, travel, animal advocate, gardening. Home: 8 Santa Ana Dr Placitas NM 87043-9458

MCELLIGOTT, ANN THERESA, accountant; b. Portland, Oreg., Nov. 18, 1942; d. Frank J. and Florence L. (Swanson) McE.; m. Forrest G. Hawkins, Sept. 9, 1961 (div. Sept. 1982); children: Michelle, Brenda, Sandra; m. Bruce N. Braunsten, Dec. 10, 1999. Student, Portland Community Coll., 1971-72; BS, Portland State U., 1974; MS, U. Oreg., 1994. CPA, Oreg. Staff acct. Coopers & Lybrand, Portland, 1974-76, in-charge acct., 1976-78, audit mgr., 1978-83; reporting and gen. ledger mgr. Tektronix, Beaverton, Oreg., 1983-86, group acctg. mgr., 1986-97, dir. facilities gen. svcs., 1997—. Bd. dirs. Campfire Girls, Portland, 1979-81, treas., 1988-91, v.p.; bd. dirs. Neighborhood House, 1998—, treas., 1999—. Recipient Guleck award Campfire Girls, 1986. Mem. AICPA, Oreg. Soc. CPA's. Avocations: bridge, walking, theater.

MCELLIGOTT, CARROLL A.A., writer, horse breeder, rancher; b. Hattiesburg, Miss., Aug. 5, 1946; d. Willie Nash and Elva Graham Ainsworth; m. Ronald John McElligott II, June 28, 1979; 1 child, Deborah Marie. BA, William Carey Coll., 1970. Rsch. asst. Miss. Dept. Archives and History, Jackson, 1970-72; dep. clk. U.S. Ct. Appeals (5th cir.), New Orleans, 1972-74; paralegal Miss. Bar Legal Svcs., Jackson, 1974-75, Law Office of William H. Ferguson, San Antonio, 1976-81; pub. Carroll Ainsworth Enterprises, El Paso, Tex., 1981-83, Harleyville, S.C., 1984-91; horse breeder, rancher Mesilla, N.Mex., 1991-94, Alpine, Tex., 1994-98, Bunkie, La., 1998—. Libr. asst. La. State U. Med. Sch., New Orleans, 1972; substitute tchr., vol. libr. Bowman (SC) Acad., 1987—90. Author: Name Index to the Session Acts of the Mississippi Territory, 1988, Charleston Residents: 1782-1794, 1998, Residents of the Natchez District: 1784, 1988, Residents of the Natchez District: 1787, 1988; co-author: A Guide to the Pre-Civil War Land Records of Colleton County, South Carolina, 2000; editor The Lott Family Newsletter, 1984-88, Geneal. and Hist. Mag. of the South, 1984-88 (1st place quar. divsn. Tex. State Geneal. Soc. 1985); contbr. articles to profl. jours. Leader Ridgerunners 4-H Club, Dona Ana County, N.Mex., 1992-93; vol. tchrs. asst. Zia Mid. Sch., Las Cruces, N.Mex., 1994-95. Mem.: DAR, AAUW, Hist. Soc. N.Mex., Tex. State Hist. Assn., Am. Qtr. Horse Assn.

MCELRATH, AH QUON, academic administrator;

MCELROY, ABBY LUCILLE WOLMAN, financial advisor; b. Washington, Oct. 16, 1957; d. M. Gordon and Elaine (Mielke) Wolman; m. Peter J. McElroy, Mar. 15, 1986; children: Abel Hurst, Leo Frederick. BA, St. Lawrence U., 1979; MS, Ind. U., 1981. 1st v.p. investment Salomon Smith Barney, Westport, Conn., 1986-99, Pridential Securities Inc., Westport, 1999—. London Group Study Exch. grantee Rotary Internat., 1989. Avocations: golf, squash, tennis, lacrosse, swimming, skiing, painting, art history, langs. Office: Wachovia Securities One Morningside Dr N Westport CT 06880

MCELROY, BIRDIE MARIA, artist, graphics designer; d. Carl Maria Rossow and Edith Elizabeth Johnson; m. Jerome Lathrop McElroy, Dec. 31, 1971; children: Jacqueline Elizabeth, Christopher Jerome. BA, Mundelein Coll., Chgo., 1963; MA, U. VI, St. Thomas, 1976; AA, Ivy Tech. State Coll., South Bend, Ind., 1986. Tchr. SAC, Omaha, 1963—66; prodn. asst. Cath. Radio/TV Office, St. Louis, 1966—67; lit. editor Theology Digest, St. Louis U., 1966—67; tchr. Visitation Acad., St. Louis, 1968—69, migrant worker children, Longmont, Colo., 1969—71; coord., tchr. Early Childhood/Antilles Sch., St. Thomas, 1976—80; pres., owner Birdie Designs, South Bend, 1986—. Prin. works include (mural) Ctr. for Homeless, prin. works include (triptych) St. Joseph Regional Med. Ctr. Emergency Dept., Represented in permanent collections South Bend Orthop. Assocs., Cressy & Everett Offices, Dunbar Mortgage & Assocs., commns. include, Ara Parseghian Med. Rsch. Found. benefit, Nat. Fischoff Chamber Music Assn., 2003. Bd. dirs. Mental Health Assn., St. Thomas, 1975—77, Devel. Coun. Sisters of St. Joseph, South Bend, 1985—90, The Montessori Acad., Mishawska, Ind., 1985—87. Named Woman of Yr., YWCA, St. Joseph County, Ind., 2004. Mem.: South Bend Regional Art Ctr., Nat. Mus. Women in Arts, Art Inst. Chgo. Democrat. Avocations: travel, reading, cooking. Home and Office: Birdie Designs 2036 Portage Ave South Bend IN 46616 Office Phone: 574-234-2827. Fax: 574-234-2827. E-mail: birdiedesigns@yahoo.com.

MCELROY, LINDA SUE, retired elementary school educator; b. Stephenville, Tex., Sept. 14, 1945; d. E. J. McElroy Sr. and Margaret Walsworth McElroy. BME, Tarleton State U., 1974, MEd, 1980. Cert. English as Second Lang. 1992, Elem. Edn. 1980. With Evant (Tex.) Ind. Sch. Dist., 1978—80, tchr. k-2, 1979—80; tchr. 1st and 2nd grade Lingleville (Tex.) Ind. Sch. Dist., 1981—85; elem. music tchr. Granbury Ind. Sch. Dist., Granbury, Tex., 1985—86; spl. edn. tchr. Mineral Wells Ind. Sch. Dist., Mineral Wells, Tex., 1987—88; tchr. ESL and music Huckabay Ind. Sch. Dist., Stephenville, 1988—2003; mgr. Stephenville Mus., 2003—. Sec./treas. Tex. State Gospel Singing Conv. Mem.: AAUW (pres. 1988), Assn. Tex. Profl. Educators. Methodist. Avocations: singing, reading. Home: 2643 W Washington Stephenville TX 76401 Office: Stephenville Mus 525 E Washington Stephenville TX 76401

MCELROY, MARY M. (MICKIE MCELROY), educational writer; b. Ft. Worth, June 29, 1944; d. Kennedy King and Maurine (Davenport) McElroy; m. James William Salterio Jr., Aug. 24, 1966 (div. Aug. 1968); m. Michael John Waters, Dec. 13, 1975 (div. Aug. 1983). BA, U. Tex., 1966, MA, 1970; M in Ednl. Adminstrn., Western Wash. U., 1989. Cert. secondary sch. adminstr., classrm. tchr. math., Latin, history. Classrm. tchr. various schs., Wash. and Tex., 1970-78, 80-89; instrnl. cons. in math. Region XIII Ednl. Svc. Ctr., West Tex., 1979-80; asst. prin. Stevens Mid. Sch., Port Angeles, Wash., 1989-90; bus. owner Office on Call, Seattle, 1991-96; dir. edn. Tex. Soc. Profl. Engrs., Austin, 1996-98; curriculum developer Tchg. Tech., Inc., Austin, 1998-99, corp. trainer, 1998-99; devel. editor Thinkwell, Austin, 1999—2001; editor, writer Kamico Instrnl. Media, Austin, 2001—. Dir. Regional Math. Competition, Everett, Wash., 1981-84; chair Com. to Improve Comm., Everett, 1986-87. Author: Powerpoint for Educators, 1998, The Internet and Social Studies in the Classroom, 1999, Designing Web Pages for Libraries, 1998. Dir. Magnolia Summerfest, Magnolia C. of C., Seattle, 1992-94; bd. dirs. Big Bros., Big Sisters, Port Angeles, Wash., 1989-90. Named Networker of Yr., Western Wash. Entrepreneurs Assn., 1992. Mem. Nat. Coun. Tchrs. Math., Wild Bunch, Beta Sigma Phi. Democrat. Avocations: painting, reading, travel, photography. Home: 2712 Deeringhill Dr Austin TX 78745-5112 E-mail: mickiemc@alumni.utexas.net.

MCELVEEN-HUNTER, BONNIE, international relief organization executive; b. SC, Jan. 1945; m. Bynum Merritt Hunter, Sr.; 1 child, Bynum Merritt Hunter Jr. Pres., CEO, owner Pace Comm., Inc.; US amb. to Finland Dept. of State, Helsinki, 2001—03; chair Am. Red Cross, Washington, 2004—. Chmn. Alexis de Tocqueville Soc., United Way Greater Greensboro, NC; bd. mem. United Way Am., chair nat. women's leadership giving campaign; chair Women in Philanthropy Summit, Washington; internat. bd. mem. Habitat for Humanity; bd. mem. Internat. Women Build Habitat for Humanity, Habitat for Humanity First Ladies Build. Named Comdr. Grand Cross Order of Lion, Pres. of Finland; recipient Dr. Carl--Christian Rosenbröijer award. Office: American Red Cross National Headquarters 2025 E St NW Washington DC 20006 Office Phone: 202-737-8300.*

MCELWAINE, THERESA WEEDY, academic administrator, artist; b. Culver City, Calif., Nov. 15, 1950; d. Victor Louis and Doris Yvonne Weedy; m. James William McElwaine, Jan. 1, 1989. BA, Calif. State U., Fullerton, 1972, cert. secondary tchr., 1974; MFA in Photography, San Francisco Art Inst., 1981. Bookstore mgr., 1978-81; asst. dir. San Francisco Camerawork, 1981-83; exec. dir. Collective for Living Cinema, N.Y.C., 1984-85; dir. mktg. Am. Internat. Artists Mgmt., N.Y.C., 1986-87; asst. dean cont. edn. SUNY, Purchase, 1987-97, dir. comm., 1997—. Cons. Parabola Arts Foun., N.Y.C., 1985-86, Clarity Ednl. Prodns., San Francisco, 1983, N.Y. State Coun. on Arts, 1986-91. Exhibited in group and solo shows at San Francisco Camerawork, Inc., Foto Gallery, N.Y.C., U. Calif., Berkeley, San Francisco Mus. Modern Art, Plymouth (England) Arts Ctr., Ariz. State U., Tempe, Vanderbilt U., Nashville, Floating Found. Photography, N.Y.C. Bd. dirs. San Francisco Camerawork, 1977-81; bd. advisors Collective of Living Cinema, 1985-87, Parabola Arts Found., 1986-92. Recipient Excellence awards Am. Inst. Graphic Arts, 1982-83. Home: 64A Valley Rd Cos Cob CT 06807-2533

MCELWEE, DORIS RYAN, psychotherapist; b. Calif., Feb. 15, 1931; d. Dennis M. and Emma A. (Klockau) Ryan; m. Charles B. McElwee, Feb. 6, 1959; children: Brent, Gregg, Cynthia; m. Craig A. Thomson, May 6, 1988. BA, Millikin U., Decatur, Ill.; MA, U. Ariz.; PhD, U. So. Calif., UCLA, Temple U. Sr. therapist Am. Inst. Family Rels., Burbank, Calif., 1969—, grad. faculty, 1972-85; psychotherapist in pvt. practice Burbank and Arcadia, Calif., 1970—; grad. faculty Chapman Coll., 1973-75, Pepperdine U., L.A., 1975-78; psychotherapist Calif. Family Study Ctr., Burbank, 1985-90. Guest expert Phil Donahue Show. Co-author: Techniques of Marriage and Family Counseling, Suicide Prevention for College Students, A Place to Rest Your Heart; contbr. articles to Ladies Home Jour. Bd. dirs. NOW, Pasadena, Calif.; mem. Arcadia Assistance League, Las Alas Orgn. Recipient Merit award, Millikin U., 1983. Mem.: Self Esteem Task Force, So. Calif. Assn. Marriage and Family Therapy, Calif. Assn. Marriage and Family Therapists, Am. Assn. Marriage and Family Therapy, Group Psychotherapy Assn. So. Calif. (v.p., exec. bd. dirs.), Panhellenic Assn., Psi Chi, Pi Beta Phi. Republican. Lutheran. Avocations: travel, gardening.

MCELWREATH, SALLY CHIN, corporate communications executive; b. N.Y.C., Oct. 15, 1940; d. Toon Guey and Jean B. (Wong) Chin; m. Joseph F. Callo, Mar. 17, 1979; 1 child, R.J. McElwreath III. BA, Pace Coll., 1963; MBA, Pace U., 1969. Copywriter O.E. McIntyre, N.Y.C., 1963-65; editl. asst. Sinclair Oil Corp., N.Y.C., 1966-70; account exec. Muller, Jordan & Herrick, N.Y.C., 1970-71; regional mgr. pub. rels. United Airlines, N.Y.C., 1971-79; dir. corp. comm. Trans World Airlines, N.Y.C., 1979-86; v.p. pub. rels. TWA Mktg. Svcs., Inc The Travel Ch. Divsn., N.Y.C., 1986-88; ptnr. The Comm. Group, N.Y.C., 1988-90; gen. mgr. corp. comm. Ofcl. Airline Guides, 1990-91; v.p. corp. comm. Macmillan, Inc., 1991-93; cons. N.Y.C., 1993-94; sr. v.p. corp. comm. Aquila Inc., 1994—2005. Pub. affairs officer USNR, 1973-2000. Ret. Capt. Named Woman of Yr., YWCA, 1980, Alumnus of Yr., Pace U., 1976. Mem. N.Am. Pub. Rels. Assn. (vice chair 2003-05), Wings Club (N.Y.C.). Avocations: sailing, skiing, harpsichord. Personal E-mail: sallymc79@aol.com.

MCENTEE, CHRISTINE W., architecture association administrator, former medical association administrator; married; 2 children. BS in Nursing, Georgetown Univ., 1977; MS in Health Adminstrn., George Washington U., 1982; student adv. exec. program, Kellogg Sch. Mgmt., Northwestern Univ. Dir., office constituency rels. Am. Hosp. Assn., 1986—90, v.p., dep. dir., fed. rels., 1990—94, exec. v.p., 1994—98; CEO Am. Coll. Cardiology, Bethesda, Md., 1998—2005; exec. v.p., CEO Am. Inst. Architects, Washington, 2006—. Named an Under 40 Mover and Shaker, Crain's Chgo. Bus., 1994; recipient Annual Achievement in Health Care Mgmt. award, Women Health Execs. Network, 1997. Mem.: Greater Washington Soc. Assn. Execs., European Soc. Cardiology (nurse fellow). Office: Am Inst Architects 1735 New York Ave NW Washington DC 20006 Office Phone: 301-897-5400.*

MCENTEGART, JUDY R., gifted and talented educator; d. James William Copithorne Jr. and E. Winnetta Copithorne; m. John Thomas McEntegart; children: Jodi Elizabeth, Penny Ruth, Sean James. BS, U. Mass., 1969; postgrad., U. of the South, 1987, Framingham State U., 1993—. Cert. K-12 tchr. Mass. Tchr. Framingham Sch. Dept., 1969—71, ch. I tchr., 1989—93, lang. arts tchr., 1993—. Christian edn. coord. St. Andrew's Ch., Framingham, 1978—93, chapel leader, 1990—; adult leader Boys Scouts Am., Framingham, 1993—. Recipient St. George's medal, Boys Scouts Am., Leaders Merit award. Avocations: sewing, reading, theater. Office: Walsh Mid Sch 301 Brook St Framingham MA 01701

MCENTIRE, BETTY, health facility administrator; Exec. dir. Am. SIDS Inst., Marietta, Ga. Lectr. in field. Contbr. to articles in profl. jours. Office: Am SIDS Inst 509 Augusta Dr SE Marietta GA 30067-8205 Office Phone: 770-426-8746. Office Fax: 770-426-1369.

MCENTIRE, JEAN REYNOLDS, music educator; b. Farmville, Va., Oct. 11, 1943; d. Thomas Pierce and Nancy Noel Reynolds; m. Dennis Pierce McEntire, July 30, 1966; children: Ann-Janette M. Lacatell, David Glenn, Jeremy Reynolds. BS in Music Edn., U. Richmond, 1966; MusM, Va. Commonwealth U., 1996. Tchr. music Itasca (Tex.) Ind. Sch. Dist., 1966-68, Jefferson County Pub. Schs., Ky., 1968-70; fgn. missionary Fgn. Mission Bd., Richmond, Va., 1970-93; pvt. music tchr. Highland Springs, Va., 1992—2003; dir., owner Talent Developing Studio, Hanover Courthouse, Va., 1992—. Workshop instr. Richmond Bapt. Assn., 1996, 98, 99; wellness cons. Nikken, Highland Springs, 1999—2003, Hanover, 2003—; trainer Personality Plus, 2001—; referring travel agt. Your Travel Bus., 2005—. Min. music Hillcrest Bapt. Ch., Mechanicsville, Va., 1994—2000, early childhood music edn. specialist, 2005—. Paul Harris fellow, Rotary, 1997. Mem.: Early Childhood Music and Movement Assn., Music Tchrs. Nat. Assn., Am. Coll. Musicians, Family Friendly Bus. Network, Nat. Fedn. Music Study Clubs. Avocations: music, internet, pets, Rving, bicycling. Office: The Talent Developing Studio PO Box 1598 Mechanicsville VA 23116 Home: 13358 Depot Rd Hanover VA 23069 Office Phone: 804-537-5800. Personal E-mail: jmcen@comcast.net.

MCENTIRE, REBA NELL, musician, actress; b. McAlester, Okla., Mar. 28, 1955; d. Clark Vincent and Jacqueline (Smith) McE.; m. Charlie Battles June 21, 1976 (div. 1987); m. Narvel Blackstock, 1989; 1 child, Shelby Steven McEntire Blackstock; 3 stepchildren. Student elem. edn., music, Southeastern State U., Durant, Okla., 1976. Rec. artist Mercury Records, 1978-83, MCA Records, 1984—. Albums include Whoever's in New England (Gold award), 1986, What Am I Gonna Do About You (Gold award), 1987, Greatest Hits (Gold award, Platinum award (U.S., Can.), 1987, Merry Christmas To You, 1987, The Last One To Know (Gold award), 1988, Reba (Gold award 1988), Sweet 16 (Gold award 1989, U.S.), Rumor Has It (Gold award 1991, Platinum award 1992, Double Platinum 1992), Reba Live (Gold award 1990, Gold award 1991, Platinum award 1991), For My Broken Heart, 1991, Forever in Your Eyes, 1992, It's Your Call, 1992, Read My Mind, 1994, Starting Over, 1995, What If It's You, 1996, If You See Him, 1998, Forever Reba, 1998, Star Profile, 1999, So Good Together, 1999, I'll Be, 2001, Room to Breathe, 2003; Reba compilation video (Gold award, Platinum award 1992), Reba Live (video), 1995, What If It's You, 1996, Celebrating 20 Years (video), 1996; author: (with Tom Carter) Reba: My Story, 1994; actress: (stage) South Pacific, 2005, (films) Tremors, 1990, The Little Rascals, 1994, North, 1994, One Night at McCool's, 2000, (TV films) The Gambler Returns: The Luck of the Draw, 1991, The Man From Left Field, 1993, Is There Life Out There?, 1994, Forever Love, 1998, Secret of Giving, 1999; (TV series) Disney's Hercules, 1998, A Salute to Dustin Hoffman, 1999, Reba (also prodr.), 2001-; other TV appearances include Country Gold, 1982, Bob Hope Winterfest Christmas Show, 1987, (video) Wrestlemania VIII, 1992; appeared on TV series Evening Shade, 1993, Frasier, 1994, The Roseanne Show, 1998, One Life to Live; (host) Acad. County Music awards, 2004. Spokesperson Middle Tenn. United Way, 1988, Nat. and State 4-H Alumni, Bob Hope's Hope for a Drug Free Am.; Nat. spokesperson Am. Lung Assn., 1990-91. Recipient numerous awards in Country music including Disting. Alumni award Southeastern State U., Female vocalist award Country Music Assn., 1984, 85, 86, 87, Grammy award for Best Country Vocal Performance, 1987, 2 Grammy nominations, 1994, Grammy award, Best Country Vocal Collaboration for "Does He Love You" with Linda Davis, 1994, Entertainer of Yr. award Country Radio Awards, 1994, Female Vocalist award, 1994; named Entertainer of Yr., Country Music Assn., 1986, Female Vocalist of Yr. Acad. Country Music, 1984, 85, 86, 87, 92, Top Female Vocalist, 1984, 85, 86, 87, 1991, 94, Am. Music award favorite female country singer, 1988, 90, 91, 92, 93, Am. Music award, 1989, 90, 91, 92, Best Album, 1991, Favorite Female Vocalist, 1994, Favorite Female Vocalist, Peoples Choice Award, 1992, Favorite Female Country Vocalist, 1992, 93, Favorite Female Vocalist, TNN Viewer's Choice Awards, 1993, Favorite Female Country Artist, Billboard, 1994, Favorite Country Album award Am. Music Awards, 1995, Favorite Female Country Vocalist, 1995, Favorite Female Artist-Country, 2004, Favorite Female Vocalist award People's Choice Awards, 1995, Top Female Vocalist of Yr. award Acad. Country Music, 1995, Entertainer of Yr. award Acad. Country Music, 1995, Favorite Female Vocalist award TNN Viewer's Choice Awards, 1995, Star on the Walk of Fame, 1999. Mem. Country Music Assn., Acad. County Music, Nat. Acad. Rec. Arts and Scis., Grand Ol' Opry, AFTRA, Nashville Songwriters Assn. Inc. Avocations: golf, shopping, being with narvel and shelby, horse racing, raising horses.

MCEVERS, ALLISON H., psychologist; b. Evanston, Ill., Jan. 19, 1962; d. Robert Darwin and Joan Allison (Manning) McEvers; m. Jerome M. Newquist; children: Robin McEvers Newquist, Genevieve McEvers Newquist. BA, Trinity U., San Antonio, 1984; PsyD, Ill. Sch. Profl. Psychology, Chgo., 1994. Therapy practicum Ill. State Psychiat. Inst., Chgo., 1989—90; pre-doctoral clin. intern Allendale Assocs., Lake Villa, Ill., 1990—91, therapist II, 1991—94, therapist III, 1994—96, psychologist II, 1996, Bradley Counseling Ctr., Lake Villa, 1996—99; clin. psychologist in pvt. practice Arlington Heights, Ill., 1997—. Mem.: APA. Office: 3250 N Arlington Heights Rd #112 Arlington Heights IL 60004 Office Phone: 847-517-6365. E-mail: drallisonmcevers@yahoo.com.

MCEVOY, FRANCES JANE COMAN, writer, editor; b. Phoenix, May 11, 1929; d. James Lindley Coman and Pearl Catherine Bruns; m. Joseph Francis McEvoy, Nov. 10, 1956 (dec. Oct. 1997); children: David L., Stephen C., Anne G. BA, Ariz. State U., 1951; postgrad., Boston U., 1959—60. Editor Helios Lit. Mag. Ariz. State U., Tempe, 1948—50; editor Am. Acad. Arts and Scis., Boston, 1951—52; reporter Waltham News Tribune Dailey, Mass., 1952—54, State House News Svc., Boston, 1952—55; press sec. Senator Leslie B. Cutler, Boston, 1954—55; asst. dir. publicity Boston U., 1955—56; writer features Boston Herald, 1975—80; writer, contbr. Dell Horoscope Astrologers Newsletter, 1980—98; editor Geocosmic Mag. Nat. Coun. Geocosmic Rsch., 1984—. Author: Power of Yod & Quincuux, 1998, Out of Bounds Moon and Planets, 2002; contbr. articles to jours.; portrait artist, 1970—2002. Mem. pub. rels com. Greater Boston Com., 1954, Rep. State Com., Boston, 1955. Mem.: Women's Edn. and Ind. Union, De Cordova Mus.

(Lincoln, Mass.), Boston Mus. Fine Arts, Bostonian Soc., DAR, Tenn. Hist. Soc., New Eng. Hist. and Geneal. Soc., Daus. Colonial Wars. Avocations: painting, writing, historic research. Home and Office: 209 Common St Belmont MA 02478

MCEVOY, LORRAINE KATHERINE, oncology nurse; b. S.I., N.Y., Mar. 24, 1950; d. Edward Donald and Josephine (Boyle) McMahon; children: Kelly Ann, Kevin Michael. RN, St. Vincent's Sch. Nursing, 1970; BSN, Seton Hall U., 1994; MSN, Kean U. N.J., 1997. RN, N.J. Staff nurse St. Joseph's Hosp. and Med. Ctr., Paterson, N.J., 1981-88, nurse mgr. oncology, bone marrow transplant, 1988—, cons., educator devel. bone marrow, stem cell and cord blood transplant programs, 1995-98. Adj. prof. Kean U., 1997-98. Recipient Disting. Alumni award Kean U., 1999; Susan G. Komen Breast Cancer Found. grantee, 1997, 98, 99. Mem. Oncology Nursing Soc., Transcultural Nursing Soc., Tri-State Bone Marrow Transplant Nurses Assn., Breast Cancer Connection, Sigma Theta Tau.

MCEVOY, SHARLENE ANN, law educator; b. Derby, Conn., July 6, 1950; d. Peter Henry Jr. and Madaline Elizabeth (McCabe) McE. BA magna cum laude, Albertus Magnus Coll., 1972; JD, U. Conn., West Hartford, 1975; MA, Trinity Coll., Hartford, 1980, UCLA, 1982, PhD, 1985. Bar: Conn., 1975. Pvt. practice, Derby, 1984—; asst. prof. bus. law Fairfield (Conn.) U. Sch. Bus., 1986—92; adj. prof. bus. law, polit. sci. Albertus Magnus Coll., New Haven, 1978-80, U. Conn., Stamford, 1984-86; acting chmn. polit. sci. dept. Albertus Magnus Coll., 1980; assoc. prof. law Fairfield U., 1992-98, prof. bus. law, 1998—. Chmn. Women's Resource Ctr., Fairfield U., 1989-91. Staff editor Jour. Legal Studies Edn., 1989-94; reviewer Am. Bus. Law Assn. jour., 1988—, staff editor, 1995—; sr. articles editor N.E. Jour. Legal Studies in Bus., 1995-96; editor-in-chief N.E. Jour. Legal Studies, 2003—. Active Derby Tercentennial Commn., 1973—74; justice of the peace City of Derby, 1975—83; alt. mem. Parks and Recreation Commn., Woodbury, 1995—99; v.p. N.E. Acad. Legal Studies in Bus., 2001—02, 2006—, pres.-elect., program chair, 2003, pres., 2003—04; treas. Woodbury Dem. Town Com., 1995—96, corr. sec., 1996—98; bd. dirs. Valley Transit Dist., Derby, 1975—77. Recipient Best Paper award N.E. Regional Bus. Law Assn., 1990, Best Paper award Tri-State Regional Bus. Law Assn., 1991; Fairfield U. Sch. Bus. rsch. grantee 1989, 91, 92, Fairfield U. rsch. grantee, 1994. Mem. ABA, Conn. Bar Assn., Acad. Legal Studies in Bus., Mensa (coord. SINISTRAL spl. interest group 1977—). Democrat. Roman Catholic. Avocations: sailing, tennis, swimming. Office: 198 Emmett Ave Derby CT 06418-1258 Office Phone: 203-254-4000 ext. 2836. Business E-Mail: samcevoy@mail.fairfield.edu.

MCEWAN, DAWN MARIE, secondary school educator; d. Dennis R. and Lydia J. McEwan. BS in Environ. Sci. Secondary Edn., Trinity Coll. Vt., 2001. Sci. tchr. Mt. Anthony Union HS, Bennington, Vt., 2001—. Advisor Lapidary Club, Bennington, 2005—. Recipient I Dare You Leadership award, Montgomery County, 1996, Environ. Quality award, EPA Region II, 1997. Mem.: NSTA, Trinity Coll. Alumni Assn. (bd. dirs. 2004—), Vt. Sci. Tchrs. Assn., Tri-Beta Biol. Honor Soc. Office: Mt Anthony Union HS Park St Bennington VT 05201

MCEWEN, LAURA, publishing executive; m. James McEwen; 1 child, Sean. BA, Fordham U. Pub. New Woman, Snow Country Mag.; sr. pub. Harpers Bazaar, Family Circle; pub. YM Mag., 2000—03; v.p., pub. dir. Readers Digest Mag., 2003—. Mem., planning com. Mag. Pub. of Am., 2003. Mem.: Fragrance Found., N.Y. Advt. Club, Advt. Women of N.Y., Fashion Group Internat. (bd. dirs.), Cosmetic Exec. Women (bd. dirs.). Office: Readers Digest Mag Box 200 Pleasantville NY 10572-0200 Office Fax: 914-244-7599, 212-850-7275, 914-238-4559. E-mail: laura_mcewen@rd.com.*

MCFADDEN, CYNTHIA ANN BELLVILLE, middle school educator; b. Atlanta, Sept. 25, 1957; d. John Perry and Betty Louisa Bellville; m. Keith Wayne McFadden, June 11, 1977; children: Jessica Louise, Kristina Joy. BS in Mid. Grades Edn., Brenau U., Gainesville, Ga., 1997; MS in Edn., Walden U., 2006. Paraprofl. Gwinnett County Bd. Edn., Lawrenceville, Ga., 1991—97, mid. grades educator, 1997—. Mem.: Alpha Delta Kappa (pres.-elect 2006—, sgt.-at-arms Iota chpt. 2004—06). Baptist. Avocations: travel, reading, gardening. Office Phone: 770-995-0864.

MCFADDEN, CYNTHIA GRAHAM, news correspondent, journalist; b. Lewiston, Maine, May 27, 1956; d. Warren Graham and Arlene McFadden; m. James Hoge (div.); 1 child; m. Michael Davies, 1998 (div.). BA summa cum laude, Bowdoin Coll., 1978; JD, Columbia U., 1984. Exec. prodr. Media and Soc. Columbia U., NYC, 1984-90; sr. prodr., anchor Court TV, NYC, 1990-94; legal corr. ABC News, NYC, 1994—96, sr. legal corr., 1996—, corr. PrimeTime Live, 1996—2004, co-anchor PrimeTime, 2004—, co-anchor Nightline, 2005—. Mem. gov. bd. dirs. Bowdoin Coll., Brunswick, Maine, 1989-95. Recipient Woman of Distinction award Crohns and Colitis Found. Am., 1997, George Foster Peabody award, six CINE Golden Eagle awards, Ohio State award, two Silver Gavel awards ABA, 1987-88, Grand award N.Y. Film Festival, Blue Ribbon Am. Film Festival, Dupont Award, 2001-02, Emmy, Fgn. Press Club award Mem.: Phi Beta Kappa. Office: ABC News 147 Columbus Ave New York NY 10023-5999

MCFADDEN, MARGARET H., education educator, writer; b. Lafayette, Ind., Aug. 1, 1941; d. William Allen and Glenora English McFadden; m. Leslie Eldridge Gerber, Sept. 2, 1967 (div. Feb. 2002); 1 child, Leslie Noel McFadden-Gerber. BA summa cum laude, U. Denver, 1963; MA in English Lang. and Lit., Boston U., 1964; PhD in Humanities, Emory U., 1973. Instr. English No. Mich. U., Marquette, 1964—66, Clark Coll., Atlanta, 1966—67; from instr. to asst. prof. English Spelman Coll., Atlanta, 1969—71; lectr. English U. Md., 1971—73, U. Colo., Colorado Springs, 1974—75; from asst. prof. to prof. interdisciplinary studies and women's studies Appalachian State U., Boone, NC, 1975—. Editor: Nat Womens Studies Assn. Jour., 1997—2003, Women's Issues, 2000; author: Loren Eiseley, 1983, Golden Cables of Sympathy: The Transatlantic Sources of 19th Century Feminism, 1999. Fellow, Sallie Bingham Ctr. for Women's History and Culture, Duke U., 2004; scholar, Fulbright Found., 1991—92, 2004. Mem.: AAUP, NOW. Episcopalian. Office: Appalachian State Univ Dept Interdisciplinary Studies 216 LLA Boone NC 28608 Office Phone: 828-262-2493. Business E-Mail: mcfaddenmh@appstate.edu.

MCFADDEN, MARY JOSEPHINE, fashion industry executive; b. NYC, Oct. 1, 1938; d. Alexander Bloomfield and Mary Josephine (Cutting) McF.; m. Philip Harari; 1 child, Justine. Student, Sorbonne, Paris, Traphagen Sch. Design, 1957, Columbia, 1959-62; DFA, Internat. Fine Arts Coll., 1984. Pub. rels. dir. Christian Dior, N.Y.C., 1962—64; merchandising editor Vogue South Africa, 1964—65, editor, 1965—69; polit. and travel columnist Rand (South Africa) Daily Mail, 1965—68; founder sculptural workshop Vukutu, Zimbabwe, 1968—70; spl. projects editor Vogue U.S.A., 1973; pres. Mary McFadden, Inc., N.Y.C., 1976—; ptnr. MMcF Collection by Mary McFadden, 1991—. Bd. dirs., advisor Sch. Design and Merchandising Kent State U., Eugene O'Neill Meml. Theatre Ctr.; mem. profl. com. Cooper-Hewitt Mus., Smithsonian Inst., Nat. Mus. of Design; designer Collection by Mary McFadden, 2000, Mary McFadden Collection, 2003, Earth-BOUND, N.Y.C., 2003; lectr. U. Phila., 2004, Dept. Ancient Near Eastern Art, Met. Mus. Art, 2004, Sackler Mus., Japan Soc., 2004, U. Archeology and Anthropology, Pa., 2005, Newark Mus., 2005, Freer Gallery, 2006, RMA, N.Y., 2006, Parrish Mus., 2006, CUNY Grad. Sch., 2006, Phipps Westbury Gardens, 2006, Rubin Mus., Queens Coll., NYC, others. Fashion and jewelry designer, 1973—; maj. retrospective of fashion, textiles and jewels at Allentown (Pa.) Art Mus., 2004; author introduction Mary McFadden High Priestess of High Fashion, 2004; artist (exhbn.) Dixon Mus. and Garden, Memphis, 2005. Advisor Nat. Endowment for Arts; active local Police Athletic League, We Care About N.Y., CFDA-Vogue Breast Cancer Initiative, Beth Israel Hosp., The Chemotherapy Found.; curator emeritus Lannan Found., 1973-85; founding trustee Robert Redford's Sundance Inst., 1978-83; trustee Devi Ahilya Bai Holkal Meml. Charitable Trust, Maheshwar, Indore, India. Recipient Am. Fashion Critics award-Coty award, 1976, 78, 79, Audemars Piguet Fashion award, 1976, Rex award, 1977, award More Coll. Art, 1977, Pa. Gov.'s award, 1977, Roscoe award, 1978, Pres.'s Fellows award RISD, 1979, Neiman-Marcus award of excellence, 1979, Design Excellence award Pratt Inst., 1993, award N.Y. Landmarks Conservancy, 1994, NU Breed Fashion award, 1996, Marymount Coll. Fashion award, 1996, Legends award N.Y., 2001, Lifetime Achievement award South Am. Press Assn., Miami, Fla., 2002, Pratt Legions award, 2002, Spirit of Design award Phila. U., 2004; named to Fashion Hall of Fame, 1979; fellow RISD. Mem. Fashion Group (bd. dirs. 1981-82), Council of Fashion Designers Am. (past pres., I Can award). Office: Mary McFadden Inc 525 E 72nd St New York NY 10021 E-mail: mcfcouture@aol.com.

MCFADDEN, ROSEMARY THERESA, retired lawyer, financial services executive; b. Oct. 1, 1948; came to U.S., 1951, naturalized, 1967; d. John and Winifred (Quinn) McFadden; m. Brian Doherty, May 26, 1973. BA, Rutgers U., 1970, MBA, 1974; JD, Seton Hall U., 1978; doctorate (hon.), St. Elizabeth's Coll., Convent Station, NJ, 1985. Bar: N.J. 1978, U.S. Dist. Ct. N.J. 1978. Spl. asst. Office of the Mayor, Jersey City, 1973-76; exec. dir. Hudson Health Sys., Jersey City, 1976-81; assoc. legal counsel N.Y. Merc. Exch., N.Y.C., 1981-82, exec. v.p., 1982-84, pres., 1984-89, spl. policy advisor to bd. dirs., 1989-91; of counsel Shulman, Hanlon and Doherty, Jersey City and N.Y.C., 1989-97; sr. mgr. Price Waterhouse Internat. Practice Group, 1993-97; sr. v.p. Donaldson Lufkin & Jenrette/Pershing, Jersey City, 1997-98; mng. dir. global devel. CSFBdirect, Jersey City, 1999—2005; ret. Mem. deans adv. coun. Rutgers U. Grad Sch. Mgmt., Newark, 1985; bd. dirs., chmn. audit com. Liberty Health Corp., 2003—. Bd. dirs. Jersey City Med. Ctr., 1985-87, UNICEF, 1989-92, Futures Industry Assn., 1989-90, St. Anthony HS 2003—; bd. dirs., chair audit com. Liberty Health Corp. 2003-. Named Alumna of Yr., Rutgers U., 1985, Seton Hall U. Mem. ABA, N.J. Bar Assn., Futures Industry Assn., Securities Industry Assn., Rutgers U. Alumni Assn. Roman Catholic. Avocations: travel, antiques.

MCFADIN, HELEN LOZETTA, retired elementary school educator; b. Tucumcari, N.Mex., Sept. 7, 1923; d. Henry J. and LaRue Altha (Ford) Stockton; m. John Reece McFadin, July 3, 1946; 1 child, Janice Lynn McFadin Koenig. AB in Edn./Psychology, Highlands U., Las Vegas, N.Mex., 1956; MA in Teaching, N.Mex. State U., 1968; postgrad., U. N.D., 1965, St. Leo's Coll., St. Leo, Fla., 1970. Cert. tchr., K-12 reading/psychology specialist, N.Mex. Tchr. 1st and 2d grades Grant County Schs., Bayard, N.Mex., 1943-44; tchr. 4th grade Durango (Colo.) Pub. Schs., 1946-48; tchr. 2d grade Artesia Pub. Schs., Loco Hills, N.Mex., 1955; tchr. 3d grade Alamogordo (N.Mex.) Pub. Schs., 1957-66, h.s. reading specialist, 1966-72, elem. reading specialist, 1972-77, tchr. 4th grade, 1977-82, reading tchr. 7th grade, dept. chair, 1982-87; ret. N.Mex. State U., Alamogordo, 1987, instr. edn., 1987-90. Organizer reading labs. h.s., elem. schs., Alamogordo, 1966-77, designer programs and curriculum, 1957-89; presenter/cons. in field; cons. Mary Kay Cosmetics; rep. Excel Telecomms., Inc. Contbr. articles to profl. jours. Local and dist. judge spelling bees and sci. fairs Alamogordo Pub. Schs., 1987-98. Recipient Literacy award Otero County Reading Coun., 1986; named to Women's Hall of Fame, Alamogordo Women's Clubs, 1989. Mem. Am. Bus. Women's Assn. (pres. 1986-87, v.p. local chpt. 1999-00, named Woman of the Yr. 1988, 2003), NEA (del. 1957-87, Dedicated Svc. award 1987), N.Mex. Edn. Assn., Internat. Reading Assn. (mem. Spl. League of the Honored 1985, pres. 1975-76), N.Mex. Reading Assn. (bd. dirs. 1988-94, del. to 1st Russian reading conf. 1992, Dedicated Svc. award 1994), Tularosa Basin Hist. Soc., Beta Sigma Phi (pres. local chpt. 1998-99, formed new master chpt. 1999, Golden Cir. Anniversary award 2002), Kappa Kappa Iota (local pres. Kappa Conclave 1998-00, state officer, nat. com., co-chair nat. conv. 2000-02, Disting. Educator Emeritus Cert. of Merit 1988, VIP award 2000, 2002). Republican. Baptist. Avocations: reading, fashion modeling. Home: 2364 Union Ave Alamogordo NM 88310-3848

MCFALL, CATHERINE GARDNER, poet, critic, educator; b. Jacksonville, Fla., July 10, 1952; d. Albert Dodge and Joan (Livingston) McF.; m. Peter Forbes Olberg, Oct. 21, 1978; 1 child, Amanda Olberg. Baccalaureat, U. Paris, 1973; AB magna cum laude, Wheaton Coll., Norton, Mass., 1974; MA, Johns Hopkins U., 1975; PhD, NYU, 1990. Editl. asst., short story editor Ladies' Home Jour., N.Y.C., 1975-77; adminstrv. dir. Poetry Soc. Am., N.Y.C., 1981-83; instr. writing NYU, N.Y.C., 1983-87, asst. dir. Poetics Inst., 1984-86; asst. prof. humanities Cooper Union, N.Y.C., 1990-98. Adj. asst. prof. English, Hunter Coll., N.Y.C. Author: Jonathan's Cloud, 1986, Discovery, 1989 (Nation award), Naming the Animals, 1994, The Pilot's Daughter, 1996; editor: Made with Words, 1998; contbr. poetry and revs. to mags. including Paris Rev., Atlantic Monthly, N.Y. Times, others. Bd. dirs. Yaddo, 2003—. MacDowell Colony fellow, 1980, 86, Yaddo fellow, 1981, 84, 91, 93, 97, 99, Nat. Arts Club Poetry scholar Bread Loaf Writers Conf., 1983. Mem. MLA, Poets and Writers, Poetry Soc. Am.

MCFARLAND, JANE ELIZABETH, librarian; b. Athens, Tenn., June 22, 1937; d. John Homer and Martha Virginia (Large) McFarland. AB, Smith Coll., 1959; M in Divinity, Yale U., 1963; MS in LS, U. N.C., 1971. Tchr. hist. and religion Northfield Schs., Mass., 1961-62; head librarian reference and circulation Yale Divinity Library, New Haven, Conn., 1963-71; head librarian Bradford (Mass.) Coll., 1972-77; reference librarian U. Tenn., Chattanooga, Tenn., 1977-80; head librarian reference dept Chattanooga-Hamilton County Bicentennial Library, Tenn., 1980-86, acting dir. Tenn., 1986, dir. Tenn., 1986—. Mem. Chattanooga Library Assn., Tenn. Library Assn., Southeastern Library Assn., Am. Library Assn., Phi Beta Kappa. Democrat. Roman Catholic. Avocations: reading, travel, needlecrafts. Office: Chattanooga-Hamilton County Libr 1001 Broad St Chattanooga TN 37402-2620 Home: 17 Fairway Dr Rehoboth Beach DE 19971-9678

MCFARLAND, KATHLEEN TROIA (KT MCFARLAND), government defense consultant; b. Madison, Wis., July 22, 1951; d. August Joseph and Edith (Fuller) Troia; m. Alan Roberts McFarland, Jr., Jan. 12, 1985; 5 children. BA, George Washington U., 1973; MA, Oxford U., Eng., 1978; postgrad., MIT, 1978-81. Research asst. to Dr. H. A. Kissinger Nat. Security Council, Washington, 1970-73; staff mem. Senate Armed Services Com., Washington, 1981-82; asst. to sec. def. Dept. Def., Washington, 1982-83, dep. asst. sec. def., 1983-84, cons., 1985. Campaign for US Senate NY, 2006—. Student trustee George Washington U., 1971-73 Fellow Ford Found., 1979-81, Arms Control and Disarmament Agy., 1980-81, Inst. for Study World Politics, 1980-81 Mem. Council on Fgn. Relations Republican. Episcopalian. Office: KT McFarland for Senate 954 Lexington Ave Box 135 New York NY 10021*

MCFARLAND, KAY ELEANOR, state supreme court chief justice; b. Coffeyville, Kans., July 20, 1935; d. Kenneth W. and Margaret E. (Thrall) McF BA in English & History, Washburn U., Topeka, 1957, JD, 1964. Bar: Kans. 1964. Sole practice, Topeka, 1964-71; probate and juvenile judge Shawnee County, Topeka, 1971-73; dist. judge Topeka, 1973-77; assoc. justice Kans. Supreme Ct., 1977-95, chief justice, 1995—. Mem. Kans. Bar Assn., Women Attys. Assn. Topeka., Topeka Bar Assn First woman appointed justice of Kans. Supreme Ct. Office: Kans Supreme Ct Kans Jud Ctr 301 SW 10th Ave Topeka KS 66612-1507 Fax: (785) 291-3274.

MCFARLAND, MARCIE ALLRED, lawyer; b. Macon, Ga., Jan. 17, 1970; m. Charles McFarland; 1 child. BBA with highest honors, U. Tex., 1992, MBA with highest honors, 1993, JD with high honors, 2000. CPA 1994; bar: Tex. 2000, US Dist. Ct. (so. and we. dists. Tex.). Tax assoc. to tax sr. Ernst & Young, 1993—97; with fin. grp. Continental Airlines, 1997; atty. Baker Botts, Houston, 2000—03; assoc. Rusty Hardin & Assocs., P.C., Houston, 2003—. Named a Rising Star, Tex. Super Lawyers mag., 2006. Mem.: Houston Young Lawyers Assn., Houston Bar Assn. Avocations: movies, walking, music, reading. Office: Rusty Hardin & Assocs PC 1401 McKinney Ste 2250 Houston TX 77010 Office Phone: 713-652-9000.*

MCFARLANE, BETH LUCETTA TROESTER, retired mayor; b. Osterdock, Iowa, Mar. 9, 1918; d. Francis Charles and Ella Carrie (Moser) Troester; m. George Evert McFarlane, June 20, 1943 (dec. May 1972); children: Douglas, Steven(dec.), Susan, George. EdB, U. No. Iowa, Cedar Falls, 1962, MEd, 1971. Cert. tchr. Tchr. rural and elem. schs., Iowa, 1936-50, 55-56; elem. tchr. Oelwein Cmty. Schs., Iowa, 1956-64, jr. high reading tchr., 1964—71, 1983; city council Oelwein, 1981-82; mayor of Oelwein, 1982-89; ret. Evaluator N. Ctrl. Accreditation Assn. Ednl. Programs; mem. planning team confs. Iowa cities N.E. Iowa, 1985; v.p. N.E. Iowa Regional Coun. Econ. Devel., 1986—89; mem. area econ. devel. com. N.E. Iowa, 1985, mem. legis. interim study com. rural devel., 1987—88; mem. policy com. Iowa League Municipalities, 1987—88. V.p. Fayette County Tourism Coun., 1987—88; mem. Iowa State steering com. road use tax financing, 1988—89; chmn. bd. govs. Oelwein Cmty. Ctr., 1990—94, bd. govs., 2001—; chmn. bldg. and fin. com. Reorganized LDS/Cmty. Christ Ch. Bldg., 1980—, dist. ch. fin. com., 1992—2001, dist. ch. revolving loan com., 1982—2000. Named Iowa Reading Tchr. of Yr., Internat. Reading Assn. Iowa, 1978; recipient Outstanding Contbn. to Reading Coun. Acitivities award, Internat. Reading Assn. N.E. Iowa, 1978, State of Iowa's Gov.'s Leadership award, 1988. Mem.: Oelwein Bus. and Profl. Women (Woman of Yr. 1983), MacDowell Music and Arts Orgn. (pres. 1978—80), N.E. Iowa Reading Coun. (pres. 1975—77), Area Univ. Women (pres. 1999—2000), Oelwein Area Ret. Sch. Pers. (pres. 1994—96), Oelwien Area C. of C. (bd. dirs. 1986—89, Humanitarian award 1987), Delta Kappa Gamma (pres. 1980—82). Republican. Mem. Cmty. Of Christ Ch. Avocations: hiking, refinishing antiques, gardening, walking, creative sewing. Home: 512 7th Ave NE Oelwein IA 50662-1326

MCFARLANE, DANA B., science educator, secondary school educator; b. NYC, Nov. 25, 1965; d. Allen C. and Jann D. Friedman; m. J. Bruce McFarlane, July 14, 1990; children: Carleigh Bryce, Harrison Scott, Reese Meredith. BS, U. Ctrl. Fla., Orlando, 1988. Sci. tchr. JP Taravella H.S., Coral Springs, Fla., 1988—90, Attucks Mid. Sch., Dania Beach, Fla., 1990—93, Westpine Mid. Sch., Sunrise, Fla., 1993—97; magnet sci. tchr. Crystal Lake Mid. Sch., Pompano Beach, Fla., 2000—. Mem.: Nat. Sci. Tchr. Assn. (assoc.). Home: 3761 NW 102 Ave Coral Springs FL 33065 Personal E-mail: dbmcfarlane@yahoo.com.

MCFARLIN, DIANE HOOTEN, publisher; b. Lake Wales, Fla., July 10, 1954; d. Ruffie Denton Hooten and Anna Loraine (Peeples) Huff; m. Henry Briggs McFarlin, Aug. 28, 1976 (div. 1993). BS, U. Fla., 1976. Reporter Sarasota (Fla.) Jour., 1976-77, asst. news editor, 1977-78, city editor, 1978-82; asst. mng. editor Sarasota (Fla.) Herald Tribune, 1983-84, mng. editor, 1985-87; exec. editor Gainesville (Fla.) Sun, 1987-90; from exec. editor to assoc. publ. Sarasota Herald-Tribune, 1990-99, publ., 1999—. Adv. bd. U. Fla. Coll. Journalism and Comm., 1987—; Pulitzer juror Columbia U., 1995-96, 2001-02. Mem. accrediting coun. Edn. in Journalism and Mass Comms., 1994-96. Recipient Alumna of Distinction award U. Fla., 1999. Mem. Am. Soc. Newspaper Editors (com. chair 1992, 94, 96, 2000, bd. dirs. 1994—, treas., sec., v.p. 2001, pres. 2002), Fla. Soc. Newspaper Editors (sec.-treas. 1993, v.p. 1994, pres. 1995). Office: Sarasota Herald-Tribune PO Box 1719 Sarasota FL 34230-1719 also: 801 S Tamiami Trail Sarasota FL 34236-7824

MCFARLIN, SHANNON DIANNE, writer, researcher; b. St. Louis, Mo., May 26, 1954; d. Marion Amos and Dolores Jeannette McFarlin; m. David Lamar Maywhoor, Mar. 17, 1973 (div.). BA cum laude, Murray State U., Murray, Ky., 2002; MA in Pub. History, Murray State U., 2004. Newspaper reporter Daily Std., Celina, Ohio, 1973—96, Wapakoneta Daily News, Wapakoneta, Ohio, 1996—96. Writer Bowling Green State U. Pub. Rels. Office, Bowling Green, Ohio, 1997—99, Paris Post-Intelligencer, Paris, 2003—05; contbg. editor Paris Mag., 2005—; featured spkr. on vanished black communities for Black History Month Ohio State Univ., Lima, Ohio, 1999; panelist The Journal, WBGU-TV, Bowling Green, 1999; featured spkr. Ohio Valley History Conf., Murray, Ky., 2006; writer The Henry Countian Com., 2006—. Sec. Henry County Dem. Women, Paris, Tenn., 2000—03. Nominee Pulitzer Prize, 1991; recipient Winner, Hellman/Hammett Award, Human Rights Watch, 2000, First Pl., Investigative Reporting, Ohio AP, 1991, Hon. Mention, Writer's Digest Writing Competition, 2005; grantee Vanished Black Communities Project, The Ohio Hist. Preservation Soc., 1980. Mem.: Alpha Sigma Lambda, Alpha Chi, Pi Sigma Alpha, Phi Alpha Theta. D-Liberal. Achievements include research in vanished black communities in pre and post Civil War era, funded by Ohio Historical Preservation Society; Frances Wright and her experimental community in Nashoba, Tennessee. Avocation: writing. Home: 713 Park St Paris TN 38242 Personal E-mail: shannonmcfarlin@hotmail.com.

MCFARLING, USHA LEE, newswriter; BA, Brown U., 1988; MA, U. Calif. Berkeley, 1998. With Boston Globe, San Antonio Light; science writer planetary and earth sciences L.A. Times. Mem. sci. and soc. journalism awards com. Nat. Assn. Sci. Writers, Inc.; mem. judging com. Wistar Inst., 2004—; spkr. in field. Recipient award, Wistar Inst., 2004; fellow Knight Sci. Journalism, MIT, 1992—93. Office: LA Times 202 W First St Los Angeles CA 90012 Office Fax: 213-237-4712. Business E-Mail: usha.mcfarling@latimes.com.*

MCFARLIN-KOSIEC, BARBARA ANN, secondary school educator, literature and language professor, small business owner; b. Lamesa, Tex., Oct. 4, 1937; d. Roy W. and Laura Corine (Daniel) McFarlin; m. Leonard E. Kosiec; 1 child, James Daniel. BA in Spanish, Tex. Christian U., Ft. Worth, 1960; attended, Instituto Tecnologico and Estudios Superiores Monterrey, Mex., 1961, Instituto Tecnologico and Estudios Superiores Monterrey, 1962, Pan Am. Coll., Edinburgh, Tex., 1962, Ea. Wash. State U., Cheney, 1963, attended, 1972, attended, 1974, attended, 1977, attended, 1989, Ctrl. Washington State U., Ellensburg, 1971, attended, 1973, attended, 1976, attended, 1977, attended, 1987, attended, 1988, U. of Ams., Mex. City, Mex., 1966, U. San Carlos, Guatemala City, Guatemala, 1967; MA in Spanish, Tex. Christian U., Ft. Worth, 1964; PhD in Leadership in Edn., Gonzaga U., Spokane, Wash., 1985. Tchr. 2d grade Mercedes (Tex.) Pub. Schs., 1962; tchr. English Instituto Tecnologico and Estudios Superiores Monterrey, Mexico, 1962; tchr. Spanish, English and social studies Dayton (Wash.) HS, 1963—65; tchr. Spanish, Mexican and Latin Am. history Peninsula CC, Port Angeles, Wash., 1965-68; tchr. grades 4-12 Spanish, English and social studies Burbank (Wash.) Pub. Schs., 1968-73; tchr. Spanish, ESL and multicultural rels. evening staff mem. Columbia Basin CC, Pasco, 1973—80; tchr. 1st, 2d, 3d, 4th, 5th and 6th grades, bilingual and migrant edn. programs Pasco (Wash.) Pub. Schs., 1973-82, 1993—95; tchr. Tex.-Wash. migrant edn. program Pasco HS, 1975—77; sub. tchr. Fernie Pub. Schs., East Kootenay CC, BC, Canada, 1982—85, Fernie Pub. Schs., 1990—92; tchr. grade 3 bilingual edn. Othello Pub. Schs., Wash., 1985—93; pres. McFarlin-Kosiec Enterprises, Fernie, 1986—; tchr. Spanish grades 1-8 St. Joseph Sch., Kennewick, Wash., 1995—96; tchr. Spanish, history and psychology Mt. Baker Secondary Sch. Southeast Kootenay Sch. dist. 5, Cranbrook, Canada, 1997—2004. Instr. English as second lang. Inst. Tech. y de Estudios Superios de Monterrey, Mex., 1962, Spanish Big Bend CC, Moses Lake, Wash., 1986-87, Seattle Pacific U., 1986, Columbia Bain CC, Pasco, Wash., 1973-80, 87-89; edn. editor El Sol newspaper, Pasco; writer Temos, Buenos Aires; cons. in field; freelance writer Fernie Free Press; adj. prof. second lang. and culture Seattle Pacific U., 1980; mem. Tri-Cities Higher Edn. Orgn., 1987-88, Kennewick Schs. Facilities Com., 1990-96; activist State Com., Wash., 1995-96; del. ann. gen. meeting BC Tchrs.' Fedn., 2002; labour affiliation rep. Cranbrook Dist. Tchrs.' Assn., 2001-02, rep. Cranbrook Tchrs. Assn. to BC Fedn. Labour Capilano Coll. Labour studies program, 2002; mem. Growth Mgmt. Act Com., Kennewick, 1990-96; v.p. Elk Valley and South Country Health Care Coalition, 2004-05, pres., 2005-06; com. mem. Can. Day, Fernie; guest spkr. and cons. in field. Performer: Recess; choreographer, dir. Phantom of the Opera Ballet Lutacoga Modern Dance Troup, 1991, Hook, 1992; choreographer: Desert, Art of Noise, Water, Fire, Rejoice, Autumn Leaves, Sunday in the Parkm Military Celebration, Snow, Meet Me in St. Louis, 1993; artistic dir.: Desert Storm Charity Show, Pasco, 1991; exhbns. include The US Bank,

Othello, 1992, City Hall, Othello, 1993, Mark Twain Elem. Sch., Pasco, 1993, The Fernie Arts Co-op; contbr. articles to profl. jours.; contbr. short stories various programs. Bd. dirs. Mid Columbia Regional Ballet Co., Richland, Wash.; precinct com. mem. Cen. Com., Benton County, 1991—; del. Benton County and Washington State Dem. Convs., 1988, 92, 94, 96, 04; active various Rep. convs.; deaconess Disciples of Christ Ch., Richland; mem. Columbia Chorale, Kennewick, Wash.; mem. negotiations com. Othello Sch. Dist., 1990—; artistic dir. benefit show Persian Gulf War Vets, UNICEF, 1991, Lutacaga Modern Dance Troupe, 1991—, founder; mem. Arts Coun., Fernie, BC, 1991, Writers' Guild Fernie, 1991; facility com. Kennewick Schs., Kennewick, Wash., 1989—; media and urban design planning commr. Kennewick, Wash., 1991—; parks and rec. commn. Kennewick, Wash., 1991—; active mem. Wash. Recreation and Park Assn, 1993—; pianist, organist, vocalist, dancer, performer Not For Profit Theater; organist Christ Ch. (Anglican), Fernie, 2004-06; precinct committeewoman Dem. Party, 1988-06; mem. Electoral Coll., Wash., 1996, Washington Assn. Fgn. Lang. Tchrs., 1962-90; commr. Parks and Recreation, Kennewick, 1990-96; vol. costumes Royal Winnipeg Balley Key City Theater, Cranbrook, 2000; scrutineer East Kootenay Electoral Dist., 2001, 05; sec. East Kootenay constituency exec. com. New Dem. Party, 2002-06, alt. del. provincial coun., 2002-03, del., 2003, chair nomination conv., 2005, master of ceremonies fundraiser, 2005; master of ceremonies fundraiser Elk Valley and South Country Health Care Coalition, 2005; coord. dance divsn. Performing Arts Festival 2001-05, presenter awards, 2001-06, sec., 2002-04, mem. bd., 2005; dir. Fernie Arts Coop.; mem. Royal Can. Legion, Fernie, 2004, 05; vol. The Can. Cancer Soc., 2005, 06; mem. Fernie Arts Coun., Columbia Chorale, Kennewick, 1990-93; mem. Allied Arts Gallery, Richland, Wash. Honored Spanish Embassy rsch. Lope de Vega, 1962; recipient Helen Gibbs award most talented Miss Walla Walla, 1965, award Assn. Quality Participation, 1989, 90, 91, 92, award Rainbow Rockers to Lutacaga Dance Troupe, Othello, 1992, Recognition award Mayor of Othello, Recognition award Othello City Libr., Recognition award Columbia Basin CC. Mem. AAUW (scholarship, legis. conf. 1977), NEA, Wash. Edn. Assn. (exec. bd. 1992—), Pasco Edn. Assn. (grievance rep. 1975-77, bldg. rep. 1980), Columbia Edn. Assn. (legis. com. 1968-73), Peninsula CC Edn. Assn. (profl. rights and negotiations com. 1966-68), Can. Fedn. U. Women, Internat. Platform Assn., Assn. Quality and Participation (chmn. edn. com. 1991, mem. awards com., v.p. 1996-97), Dance Educators Assn. Washington, Tri Cities Higher Edn. Orgn. (bd. dirs. 1987), Prevential Intermediate Tchr.'s Assn., Tchrs.' Fedn. and Coll. of Tchrs. (chmn. unemployed tchrs. Fernie dist. 1984-85, activist sub. tchrs.), BC Ret. Tchrs.'s Assn., Writer's Guild. Achievements include research in advanced statistics and research design. Avocations: arranging solo piano music, teaching modern dance. Home and Office: PO Box 1275 Fernie BC Canada V0B 1M0 E-mail: bkosiec@telus.net.

MCFATE, PATRICIA ANN, foundation executive, science educator; b. Detroit, Mar. 19, 1936; d. John Earle and Mary Louise (Bliss) McF.; m. Sidney Norman Graybeal, Sept. 10, 1988. BA (Alumni scholar), Mich. State U., 1954; MA, Northwestern U., 1956, PhD, 1965; MA (hon.), U. Pa., 1977. Assoc. prof. English, asst. dean liberal arts and scis. U. Ill., Chgo., 1967-74, assoc. prof. English, assoc. vice chancellor acad. affairs, 1974-75; assoc. prof. folklore Faculty Arts and Scis., U. Pa., Phila., 1975-81; prof. tech. and soc. Coll. Engring. and Applied Sci., 1975-81, vice provost, 1975-78; dep. chmn. Nat. Endowment for Humanities, Washington, 1978-81; exec. v.p. Am.-Scandinavian Found., N.Y.C., 1981-82, pres., 1982-88; sr. scientist Sci. Applications Internat. Corp., Mc Lean, Va., 1988—, program dir. Ctr. for Nat. Security Negotiations, 1988—; cons. UN, 1994-95. Vis. assoc. prof. dept. medicine Rush U., Chgo., 1970-85; bd. dirs. First Union Corp.; mem. sr. adv. panel Dept. Def., 1998—. Author: The Writings of James Stephens, 1979, Uncollected Prose of James Stephens, 1983; exec. producer Northern Stars, 1985, Diego Rivera: I Paint What I See, 1989, The Bear in the Skies, 1998; contbr. articles in fields of sci. policy and lit. to various jours. Mem. Arms Control and Non-Proliferation Adv. Bd., Dept. of State, 1995-2001; mem. disting. adv. panel Sandia Nat. Labs.; bd. dirs. Raoul Wallenberg Com. of U.S., Swedish Coun. Am., Santa Fe Cmty. Found., Santa Fe Opera, Lensic Performing Arts Ctr. Decorated officer Order of Leopold II Belgium, comdr. Order Icelandic Falcon, comdr. Royal Order of Polar Star (Sweden), comdr. Order of Lion (Finland), comdr. Royal Norwegian Order Merit, Knight 1st class Royal Order Dannebrog (Denmark); U. Ill. Grad. Coll. faculty fellow, 1968; Swedish Bicentennial Fund grantee, 1981 Fellow N.Y. Acad. Scis.; mem. AAAS (chmn. com. on sci., engring. and pub. policy 1984-87, com. on sci. and internat. security 1976-79, 88-93), Coun. on Fgn. Rels., Acad. Scis. Phila. (founding mem., corr. sec. 1977-79), Theta Alpha Phi, Omega Beta Pi, Delta Delta Delta. E-mail: patricia.a.mcfate@saic.com.

MCFAYDEN, SHANNON W., bank holding company executive; b. Sept. 21, 1960; BA in psychology, Davidson Coll. Head human resources Fla. Bank (merged with Wachovia); with Wachovia Corp., 1982—, dir. human resources client svc., 1998—2001, dir. cmty. affairs, 2001—04, sr. v.p., 2004—, head corp. and cmty. affairs, 2004—. Mem. steering com. Bus. Strengthening Am. Bd. dirs. United Way Capital Campaign Planning, KinderMourn, Cmty. Sch. Arts and Child Care Resources, Charlotte -Mecklenburg Pub. Schs. Found. Mem.: Davidson Coll. Alumni Assn. Office: Wachovia Corp 1 Wachovia Ctr Charlotte NC 28288 E-mail: shannon.mcfayden@wachovia.com.

MCFEATTERS, ANN CAREY, journalist; b. Colorado Springs, Colo., June 27, 1944; d. Norman Cromer and Mildred Harriet Carey; m. Dale B. McFeatters, Sept. 27, 1969; children: Dale C., Matthew C., Kirsten C. BA, Marquette U., 1966. Reporter Evansville (Ind.) Press, 1966-68, Pitts. Press, 1969, Washington Daily News, 1969-70, Scripps Howard News Svc., Washington, 1970-99; Washington bur. chief The Pitts. Post-Gazette and The Toledo Blade, Washington, 1999—. Author: Sandra Day O'Connor: Justice In The Balance, 2006. Named to Hall of Fame Soc. Profl. Journalists, 1998; recipient Disting. Svc. award Scripps Howard News Svc., 1999. Mem. Nat. Press Found. (chmn. 1996-98), Washington Press Club (pres. 1980-81), The Gridiron Club. Office: Block News Alliance 529 14th St NW Ste 955 Washington DC 20045 E-mail: amcfeatters@nationalpress.com.

MCFERRAN, DEBRA BRADY, parochial school educator; d. William Edward and Ida Helen Brady; m. James Calvin McFerran, June 7, 1996; m. Bennie Webb Jackson, Jr., June 21, 1974 (div. Nov. 23, 1995); children: Jordan Lee Jackson, Nicholas Alexander Jackson. AA, U. Louisville, Ky., 1975, BA, 1980, MAT, 1982. Cert. tchr. Ky. Dept. Edn. Substitute Tchr. Jefferson County Pub. Schs., Louisville, 1982—83; tchr. St. Xavier HS, Louisville, 1983—91, Ky. Country Day Sch., Louisville, 1991—98, Christian Acad. of Louisville, 1999—. Founder, tutor Home Enrichment & Learning Practice, Prospect, 1994—. Methodist. Avocations: piano, cooking, gardening, water sports, tennis. Home: 3125 English Way Prospect KY 40059

MCGANN, LISA B. NAPOLI, language educator; b. West Hartford, Conn., Sept. 07; d. James Napoli; m. Edward Harrison McGann, Jr. BA, Vassar Coll., 1980; MA, Columbia U., 1983, postgrad., 1991-95; MA, Middlebury Coll., 1987. Cert. tchr. French, ESL and Italian, Conn. Cmty. English program coord. Tchrs. Coll. Columbia U., N.Y.C., 1982-83; mgr. English tchg. com. Jr. League N.Y., N.Y.C., 1983-84; asst. dir. ESL Fordham U., N.Y.C., 1988-89; ESL instr. Laguardia C.C., CUNY, Long Island City, NY, 1983—, Columbia U., 1983-96. ESL instr. Yale U., 1988, 89; ESL specialist, tchr. UN, N.Y.C., 1990. Big sister Highland Hts., New Haven, 1976-77; ESL tchr. Boys and Girls Club, Astoria, N.Y., 1992. Recipient awards and scholarships. Mem. Nat. TESOL Soc., Am. Assn. Tchrs. Italian, Italian-Am. Hist. Soc., Nat. Italian Am. Found. (coun.), The Statue of Liberty-Ellis Island Found., Inc. Roman Catholic. Avocations: ballet, reading, travel, real estate, tennis.

MCGAREL-WARKOCKI, LYNN M., history educator; b. Evergreen Park, Ill., Jan. 12, 1966; d. Owen F. McGarel and Lillian Levri-McGarel; m. Robert J. Warkocki, June 23, 1990; children: Elizabeth Lynn Warkocki, Ana Jo Warkocki. Bachelor's, U. Ill., Chgo., 1989; Master's, St. Xavier U., Chgo., 2000. Tchr. social studies Jerling Jr. HS, Orland Park, Ill., 1990—91; tchr. history Amos Alonzo Stagg HS, Palos Hills, Ill., 1991—. Dir. Dist. 230 Age Group Gymnastics, Palos Hills, 1991—97. Mem.: NEA, Nat. Coun. for Social Studies, Sports Car Club of Am., Phi Alpha Theta (founder, sponsor Dist. 230 chpt. 2004—). Avocations: reading, exercise. Office: Amas Alonzo Stagg HS 111th & Roberts Rd Palos Hills IL 60465 E-mail: lmcgarel@d230.org.

MCGARRY, CARMEN RACINE, historian, artist; b. Plattsburgh, N.Y., Dec. 15, 1941; d. Allyre Joseph and Annette Cecile (Roy) Racine; sep.; children: Suzanne, John Jr., Annette, Patrick. BA, Coll. St. Rose, 1962. Tchg. cert. Ill.; lic. real estate broker, Ill.; cert. interior designer, Ill. Tchr. Chgo. Bd. Edn., 1962-69; comptr., mgr., broker K&G Bldg. Mgmt., Chgo., 1969-90; rsch. asst. U. Chgo., 1985-89. Bd. dirs. Gread Banc Trust Co. Author: Magnificent Mile: A History of Hillsboro Beach, 1998; designer and creator stained glass windows St. Anne's Shrine, Isle La Motte, Vt., 1995. V.p. Women's History Coalition, Broward County, Ft. Lauderdale, Fla., 1993—2002; com. mem. County Health Fair, Broward County, 1994—; bd. dirs. Hillsboro Lighthouse Com., 1994—, pres., 2005—; bd. dirs. Broward 2000, Broward County League of Cities, 1998-2003; chmn., bd. mem. adv. coun. Area Agy. on Aging, Ft. Lauderdale, 1996—, chmn., 1998—; mem. adv. bd. Fla. Dept. Elder Affairs, 2003-06; chmn. for women's hall of fame Broward County, 1996-98; rep. for srs. on transp. Disadvantaged Coord. Bd. Broward County, 1999—; town commr. Hillsboro Beach, 1999-2003; pres. Hillsboro Lighthouse Assn., 2006—. Recipient Cmty. Svc. award Cystic Fibrosis Found., 1999, First Lady of Broward County award 2000; named to Women's Hall of Fame Broward County, 2001. Golden Choice award from Gov. Bush, 2003, 2004, Sun-Sentinel Vol. award, 2002, 2004; named to Sr. Hall of Fame of Broward, 2004. Mem. ASID, Stained Glass Assn. Am., Women's League Hillsboro (bd. dirs. 1993-2004), Broward County Hist. Commn., Hillsboro Beach Hist. Commn. (founder, pres.), Deerfield Beach Rotary (dir. 1996—, pres. 1999-2000, Cooper-Kirk award for hist. rsch. and preservation 1999), First Ladies of Broward County, 1991. Avocations: travel, writing. Home: 1073 Hillsboro Mile Hillsboro Beach FL 33062-2139 E-mail: ctlm@aol.com.

MCGARRY, FRANCES LORRAINE, education educator; b. Northport, NY, Aug. 5, 1951; d. Louis Joseph Beccaria and Philomena Marie Barile; m. Donald L. McGarry, July 31, 1976; 1 child, Donald P. BS, SUNY, Oneonta, NY, 1973; MA, SUNY, Stony Brook, NY, 1979; PhD, NYU, 2001. Cert. speech and theater edn. NY, Eng. secondary edn. NY, program dir. creative arts team N.Y.C. Wolf Trap Site, 1973, program dir. through the arts N.Y.C. Wolf Trap Site, 2005. English/theater faculty Northport-East Northport Sch. Dist. 4, Northport, NY, 1975—2004; adj. faculty Nassau CC, Garden City, NY, 2001—, NYU, 2003—. Actress various stage, screen, TV roles, NYC, 1997—. Vol. NYU Breakout Com., NYC, 2003; choir St. Anthony of Padua Ch., East Northport, NY, 1999—; vol. Ecumenical Lay Coun., Northport, NY, 2004. Mem.: Drama League, Assn. Theater in Higher Edn. (awards com. 1997—2004), Am. Alliance for Theater and Edn. (adjudicator awards com. 1993—95, John C. Barrer Theater Tchr. of Yr. 1993). Achievements include successfully marketing theatrical program into an on-going event; planning, coordinating and producing an interdisplinary program and a children's theater company for secondary school students. Avocation: boating. Home: 2 Heather Dr Northport NY 11768

MCGARRY, MARCIA, retired community service coordinator; b. Washington, Dec. 9, 1941; d. Emil Sylvester and Bernice B. (Bland) Busey. BS, Morgan State U., 1964. Cert. tchr., law enforcement officer, Fla. Payroll clk., jr. acct. U.S. Dept. Labor, Washington, 1964-65; English tchr. Taiwan, 1968-70; tchr. Monroe County Sch. Bd., Key West, Fla., 1971-81; exec. dir. Monroe Assn. Retarded Citizens, Key West, 1977-79; dep. sheriff Monroe County Sheriff's Dept., Key West, 1979-83, 86-90; probation/parole officer Fla. State Dept. Corrections, Key West, 1983-91; law enforcement instr. Fla. Keys C.C., 1983-91; cmty. svc. coord. City of Bradenton, 1991-2000; domestic violence specialist II Broward County Sheriff Dept., 2001—. Mem. rev. bd. City of Bradenton Police Dept., 1996—2000, mem. cmty. rels. com., 1996—2000. Active local polit. campaigns; co-founder day schs. for underprivileged children; former mem. Big Bros./Big Sisters Am., mem. com., 1985-86, former bd. dirs., Spouse Abuse, former bd. dirs.; bd. dirs. Adv. Coun. Orange-Ridge Elem., 1991-93; bd. dirs. mayor's com., chmn. task force Drug Free Cmtys., 1991-94, bd. dirs., 1996-2001; bd. dirs. Human Rels. Commn., 1991-93, Drug Free Schs. and Cmty. Adv. Coun., 1991-98, T.O.T.S. (These Our Tots), Inc., 1998-2000; former mem. adv. coun. Byrd Edn. Found., Sweet Adelines Internat., 1992-94, commr. 12th Jud. Nominating Commn., 1992-99, cons., facilitator Cultural Diversity Conflict Resolution Workshops, Manatee County High Schs. and Bradenton Police Dept.; attendance adv. com. Bayshore High, 1993, multicultural com., 1994, former rep. Women's Forum; former dir. choir Luth. Ch.; founding mem. Comprehensive Neighborhood Support Network; mem. adv. bd. Manatee County Sheriff's Dept., 1994-2000, mem. hiring rev. bd., 1997-2000. Recipient Appreciation cert., Lions Club, 1978, 1979, Career Week award, Harris Elem. Sch., 1981, Glynn Archer Elem. Sch., 1989, Trainers award, Probation/Parole Acad., 1987, Cert. of Acknowledgement for Cmty. Svc., AAUW, 1995, awadrd, Vol. Army for the War on Drugs, 1989. Mem. NAFE, Fla. Police Benevolent Assn., Fla. Women in Govt. (mem. Manatee County chpt.), Ecumanical Luth. Ch. of Am. (elected consultation comm. Fla. Synod 1989), Key West Profls., Luth. Ch. Women, Delta Sigma Theta (v.p. 1990-91, corr. sec. 1993-95). Office Phone: 954-831-7045. Personal E-mail: marciadnc@aol.com.

MCGARRY, MARTHA E., lawyer; b. Boston, 1951; BA cum laude, Middlebury Coll., 1973; JD, Fordham U., 1977. Bar: N.Y. 1978. Ptnr. Skadden, Arps, Slate, Meagher & Flom, N.Y.C. Office: Skadden Arps Slate Meagher & Flom 4 Times Sq Fl 24 New York NY 10036-6595

MCGARRY, REBECCA A., music educator; d. Dell B. and Ruth Anderson; children: Rachel, Vanessa, Benjamin, Bethany, Jonathan, Daniel, Jacob, Jessica, Jennifer, Jacqueline. AA, Snow Coll., Ephraim, Utah, 1976; MusB, U. Utah, Salt Lake City, 1979, MusM, 1986. Instr. music Snow Coll., Ephraim, Utah, 1999—. Avocations: hiking, dancing, reading, travel, cooking. Office: Snow Coll Humanities Divsn 150 Coll Ave Ephraim UT 84627-1299

MCGARRY-CORL, KELLY JO, counselor, marriage and family therapist, consultant; b. Johnstown, Pa., Feb. 13, 1971; d. Joseph Nicholus Onder and Elizabeth L. Crum. BS, St. Francis Coll., Loretto, Pa., 1993; MA, Liberty U., 2000. Cert. Nat. Cert. Counselor, lic. Profl. Counselor. Counselor So. Allegheny Acad., Portage, Pa., 1993-94; social worker Valley View Nursing Home, Altoona, Pa., 1994-98; geriatric social worker Garvey Manor, Hollidaysburg, Pa., 1998-2001; therapist Family Svcs. Blair, Altoona, 1999-2000; mobile family therapist Children's Paraclete, Johnstown, Pa., 2000—. Mem. Am. Psychotherapy Assn. (diplomat), Am. Counseling Assn., Am. Assn. Christian Counselors, Assn. Spiritual Ethical Religious Values Counseling, Pa. Counselor Assn., Pa. Geriatric Interest Network. Home: 1404 Spruce St Hollidaysburg PA 16648-2340 Office: Children Paraclete Inc 227 Franklin St Ste 300 Johnstown PA 15901-1916

MCGARVEY, VIRGINIA CLAIRE LANCASTER, volunteer; b. Erie, Pa., Feb. 10, 1934; d. Walter Joseph and Clara Marguerite (Johannesen) Lancaster; m. Raymond Leroy McGarvey, Sept. 3, 1955; children: Keith Thomas, Emy Sue, Stephen Bruce. Cert., Thiel Coll., 1954; BS in Bus. Edn., U. Ill., 1957. Sec. P.A. Meyer & Sons, Erie, 1952, Thiel Coll., Greenville, 1953-55; sec. coord. placement office U. Ill., Champaign, 1955-59; tchr. adult edn. Champaign Sch. Dist., 1957-58; dir. Sarah A. Reed Retirement Ctr., Erie, 1972—, chmn., 1980-83, endowment treas., 1984-96, treas., 1996—; dir. Meadow Brook Dairy Co., Erie, 1975-91. Bd. dirs. Country Fair, Inc., Erie. Bd. dirs. Erie County Hist. Soc., 1989-96, treas. 1989-94, 96-99, 2d v.p. 2000—; mem. Harborcreek (Pa.) Zoning Bd., 1990—; grand marshall Harborfest Parade, 1997; chmn., supt. Wesley United Meth. Ch. Christian Edn., 1960-84, chmn. adminstrv. bd., 1986-95; commr. Greater Erie Bicentennial Commn., 1994-95, Millennium Commn., 1999-2000. Recipient Edward C. Doll Cmty. Svc. award, 1994; named to Pa. Honor Roll of Women, 1996; named Disting. Pennsylvanian, Gannon U., 1997. Mem. AAUW (pres. 1970-72, Woman of Yr. 1981), Greater Erie YMCA (bd. dirs. 1981—, pres. elect 1991-93, chmn. 1993-96, trustee 1996—, Woman of Yr. 1987). Republican.

MCGARY, DARIA L., foreign languages educator; b. Antwerp, Belgium, Aug. 1, 1930; came to U.S., 1954; d. William Reynolds and Daria Louise (Bowles) Marshall; m. Frank Joseph McG., Oct. 6, 1951; children: Sharon, Kevin, Marc, Christopher. Interpreter to gen. Mil. Assistance Adv. Group, Brussels, 1950-54; tchr. German, French, Spanish Padua Franciscan Sch., Cleve., 1974-79; tchr. Bishop Ready H.S., Columbus, Ohio, 1979-82; tchr. French, Spanish, dept. chair The Wellington Sch., Columbus, 1982-94. Lectr. French Club, Cleve., 1951-89. Avocations: art history, equestrian, dressage. Home: 3367 Durkin Cir Dublin OH 43017-3645

MCGAVOCK, BRENDA WEISHAAR, clinical psychologist; b. Kansas City, Mo., Jan. 14, 1952; d. Williston Penfield and Alice (Mitchell) Bunting; m. Douglas John Weishaar, june 15, 1978 (div. Apr. 1986); children: Cara, Josephine; m. Robert Kent McGavock, Aug. 10, 1991. BA with honors in Psychology, U. Kans., 1974; MS in Clin. Psychology, U. Wyo., 1978, PhD in Clin. Psychology, 1980. Lic. psychologist, Mo. Staff psychologist Mental Hygiene Clnic, Harry S. Truman Meml. VA Hosp., Columbia, Mo., 1980-83; dir. psychology Charter Hillside Hosp., Columbia, 1984-85; pvt. practice Ctr. for Family & Individual Coun., Columbia, 1982-89; staff mem. Boone Hosp. Ctr., Columbia, 1987—; pvt. practice Fletcher & Weishaar, Columbia, 1990—. Treas., bd. dirs. Mo. Behavioral and Mental Health Specialists, Columbia, 1993-2000; stress mgmt. cons. Boone Hosp. Ctr., Columbia, 1987—; asst. trainer Neuro-Linguistic Programming, Columbus, Ohio, 1988-89; mem. profl. rev. panel Counseling Svcs., U. Mo., Columbia, 1987—. Dir. fed. women's program Harry S. Truman Meml. VA Hosp., Columbia, 1980-83; dist. commr. Hinkson Valley Pony Club, Columbia, 1990-97; vol. Sexually Abused Women, Columbia, 1995; Sunday sch. tchr. Unity Ctr. Columbia, 1987. Mem. APA, ASTD, Am. Soc. Clin. Hypnosis, Mo. Psychol. Assn., Nat. Register Health Svc. Providers in Psychology, Women's Network Columbia C. of C. Avocations: gardening, reading. Office: Fletcher & Weishaar 2716 Forum Blvd Ste 2B Columbia MO 65203-5450 Office Phone: 573-446-4039.

MCGEARY, BARBARA JOYCE, artist, educator; b. Ellwood City, Pa., June 26, 1932; d. Harold Raymond and Helma Joyce Conner; m. Clyde Mills McGeary, Aug. 25, 1954; children: Melinda, Martha, Marilee, Clyde. BS, Ind. U. Pa., 1954; postgrad., U. Pitts., 1962—64, Temple U., 1975—77, Pa. Dept. Edn., 1978. Cert. tchr. art, supr. Pa. Tchr. secondary art North Allegheny Schs., Pitts., 1954—55; supr. art Laurel Joint Schs., New Castle, Pa., 1955—56, New Kensington, Arnold Schs., Pa., 1963; instr. U. Manitoba, Winnipeg, Canada, 1965; thcr. art Harrisburg Schs., Harrisburg, Pa., 1970—72; tchr. art Mechanicsburg Schs., Pa., 1967—69; dir. Arts Magnet Sch., Harrisburg Schs., Pa., 1972—89, supr. arts, 1974—89. Assoc. McGeary Consulting Group, Camp Hill, Pa., 1988—93; spl. advisor/cons. Pa. Dept. Edn., Harrisburg, 1989. Co-author (text series): My World of Art, 1963, Learning Through Art, 1972. Chmn. judges Scholastic Arts, Harrisburg, Pa., 1975—90; mem. edn. com. Susquehanna Art Mus., Harrisburg, Pa., 1995—2005; co-chair fine arts Cumberland County 250th, Carlisle, Pa., 2000; ruling elder Camp Hill Presbyn. Ch., Pa., 1970—76. Named one of Outstanding Women Who Work, Harrisburg Patriot-News, 1980; recipient Disting. Svc. in the Arts award, Harrisburg Theatre Assn., 1995. Mem.: Pa. Art Edn. Assn. (chmn, pres. 1969—75), Nat. Art Edn. Assn., Cosmopolitan Internat. (founding mem., Capital region pres. 1995—96), Tuscarora Forest Property Owners Assn. (1st female pres. 2001—03). Republican. Presbyterian. Avocations: historic preservation, environmental projects, gardening, interior decorating, landscape design. Home: 248 Willow Ave Camp Hill PA 17011 Office: McGeary Assocs 248 Willow Ave Camp Hill PA 17011 Personal E-mail: cbmcgeary@pa.net.

MCGEE, CAROL A., retired elementary school educator; b. Huntsville, Ala., Aug. 4, 1942; BS, U. North Ala., 1964; MEd, Mid. Tenn. State U., 1976; postgrad., Tex. A&M U., 1992. Cert. tchr. Tenn., Ala., S.C., Tex. Tchr. Tuscaloosa County Schs., Ala., 1962-63, Cartagena Colombia/Am. Sch., Colombia, 1963-64, Franklin County Schs., Russellville, Ala., 1964-67, Decatur City Schs., Ala., 1967-71, Rutherford County Schs., Murfreesboro, Tenn., 1971-79, Charleston County Schs., SC, 1979-82, Huntsville Pub. Sch., Tex., 1982—88, Huntsville City Schs., 1982—89, Windham Prison Schs., Huntsville, 1989—91, Conroe Pub. Schs., Tex., 1991—97; libr. Internat. Sch. of Aruba, 1997—99. Bd. dirs. SHARC, Huntsville. Author two books in field; contbr. articles to profl. jours. Campaign chmn. Sch. Bd. Candidate, Walker County, Tex., 1988, 91, 94; mem. Walker County Hy. Commn., Huntsville, 1990—; adult leader Boy Scouts of Am., Walker County, 1982—; state reading adv. com. Tex. Edn. Agy., Austin, 1985-86; vol. Westhill Inst. Mexico City, Mexico, 2000-2005 Mem. Sam Houston Area Reading Coun. (pres. 1987-88, bd. dirs. 1985—), Tex. State Tchrs. Assn. (bldg. rep. 1988-90). Republican. Baptist. Avocations: sewing, travel, reading. Home: 660 Elkins Lk Huntsville TX 77340-7316

MCGEE, JANE MARIE, retired elementary school educator; b. Paducah, Ky., Nov. 3, 1926; d. William Penn and Mary Virginia (Martin) Roberts; m. Hugh Donald McGee, Oct. 11, 1946; children: Catherine Jane McGee Bacon, Nancy Ann McGee McManus. BS in Elem. Edn., Murray State U., 1948; cert. in gifted edn., Nat. Coll. Edn., 1976. Tchr. Hazel (Ky.) Pub. Schs., 1948-49, Pittsford (Mich.) Pub. Schs., 1949-50, Leal Elem. Sch., Urbana, Ill., 1950-53, Cleveland Elem. Sch., Skokie, Ill., 1953-57; pvt. tutor, pre-sch. tchr., 1953-61; tchr. Woodland Park Elem. Sch., Deerfield, Ill., 1968-83; ret., 1983; beauty and skin care cons. Mary Kay Cosmetics, Gunnison, Colo., 1984—; co-owner Eagles Nest B&B, 1996—2002. Soprano Western State Coll. and Cmty. Chorus, Gunnison, 1986-97, European concert tour, 1990. Mem. AAUW, Top o' the World Garden Club (sec. 1984-2002, winner first place at numerous garden club shows). Baptist. Avocations: flower arranging, crafts, knitting, bird watching, rock collecting. Home: 109 San Juan Dr Sequim WA 98382-9326

MCGEE, LINDA MACE, judge, lawyer; b. Marion, NC, Mar. 20, 1949; d. Cecil Adam and Norma Jean (Hogan) Mace; m. B. Gary McGee, Dec. 19, 1970; children: Scott Adam, Jeffrey Sean. BA, U. N.C., 1971, JD, 1973. Bar: N.C. 1973. Exec. dir. N.C. Acad. Trial Lawyers, Raleigh, 1973-78; assoc. Finger, Watson & di Santi, Boone, NC, 1978-80; ptnr. Finger, Watson, di Santi & McGee, Boone, 1980-89, di Santi, Watson & McGee, Boone, 1989-95; judge N.C. Ct. of Appeals, 1995—. Mem. trustee panel U.S. Bankruptcy Ct., Greensboro, N.C., 1980-82; bd. dirs. Legal Services of N.C., Raleigh, 1980-84; mem. N.C. Bd. Law Examiners, 1986-93. Vice-chairperson Watauga County Coun. on Status of Women, Boone, 1979-82; trustee Caldwell C.C. and Tech. Inst., Hudson, N.C., 1980-89; mem. exec. bd. N.C. Assn. C.C. Trustees, 1983-85; trustee Caldwell C.C., 1981-89; mem. Pub. Edn. Commn., 2000—. Mem. ABA, ATLA, AAUW, LWV, ABA Found., Am. Law Inst., N.C. Assn. Women Attys. (charter, treas. 1980-84, chair jud. divsn. 1997, Gwyneth B. Davis award 1997, Outstanding Judge of Yr. award 1999), N.C. Bar Assn. (bd. govs. 1983-86, co-chair lawyers in schs. com., Pro Bono Svc. award, 1992, jud. divsn. Outstanding Judge of Yr. award 1999), N.C. Acad. Trial Lawyers (bd. govs. 1993-95), N.C. State Bar, Boone C. of C. (bd. dirs. 1982-85), N.C. Bus. and Profl. Womens Clubs (chair polit. action com. 1982-83, Young Career Woman 1980), Boone Bus. and Profl. Women's Club (Woman of Yr. 1980), N.C. Women's Forum. Democrat. Presbyterian. Home: PO Box 508 Corolla NC 27927 Office: PO Box 888 Raleigh NC 27602-0888

MCGEE, LYNDA PLANT, college counselor; b. L.A., Nov. 22, 1960; d. Larry Earle and Dolores (Balin) Plant; m. William Granville McGee, Dec. 21, 1996; 1 child, Roman Earle. BA in English Edn. cum laude, Xavier U., 1984; MEd in Counseling Psychology, U. Ill., 1986; cert. in coll. counseling, UCLA, 1997. Pupil pers. svcs. credential in counseling. English tchr., decathalon coach Dorsey H.S., L.A., 1986-94; English tchr. St. Monica Cath. H.S., Santa Monica, Calif., 1994-98, Downtown Magnets H.S., LA, 1998—2000, guidance counselor, 2000—; faculty advisor Teach for Am.,

2003. Instr. Crenshaw-Dorsey Adult Sch., 1988-89; ind. coll. counselor, L.A., 1999—. Author: Active Learning Through Teacher Research, 1997. Mem. sch. decision making coun. Downtown Magnets H.S., L.A., 1998-99; bd. dirs. urban schs. com. UCLA, mem. h.s. initiative com., 2000. Fellow Nat. Endowment, 1994, 2000, UCLA, 1996, 97. Mem. Nat. Assn. Coll. Admission Counselors, Calif. Assn. Sch. Counselors, West of Westwood Homeowners Assn. (bd. mem.),Together for Cultural Diversity, Western Assn. Coll. & Admission Counselors, Order Ea. Star, Zeta Phi Beta. Democrat. Avocations: reading, travel, acting. Office: Downtown Magnets HS 1081 W Temple St Los Angeles CA 90012-1513 Office Phone: 213-481-0371 ext. 5126.

MCGEE, MARY ALICE, health science research administrator; b. Winston-Salem, N.C., Oct. 14, 1950; d. C.L. Jr. and Mary Hilda (Shelton) McG. AB, Meredith Coll., 1972. Tchr. Augusta (Ga.) Schs., 1972-73; specialist grants Med. Sch. Brown U., Providence, R.I., 1974-76; profl. basketball player, 1975-76; dir. research adminstn. Med. Sch. Brown U., Providence, 1976-94; tchr., coach Providence Country Day Sch., East Providence, RI, 1995—2005. Bd. dirs. Sojourner House, Providence, 1983-91, v.p., 1986, 91, treas. 1987-89. Mem. Nat. Coun. Tchrs. Math., Soc. Rsch. Adminstrs., Nat. Coun. U. Rsch. Adminstrs., R.I. Assn. Women in Edn., Womens Basketball Coaches Am. Avocations: sports, travel, dogs. Home: 121 Plain St Rehoboth MA 02769-2540 Office Phone: 508-252-4248. E-mail: Mary_Alice_McGee@verizon.net.

MCGEE, MEGAN E., coach, consultant; BS in Animal Sci., Calif. Poly., San Luis Obispo, 1983. Cert. eventing and dressage steward Fedn. Equestrian Internat., 1995. Head coach equestrian team S.D. State U., Brookings, 2004—. Office: SD State Univ HPER Box 2820 Brookings SD 57007-1497 Office Phone: 605-688-6856. E-mail: megan.mcgee@sdstate.edu.

MCGEE, NANCY PYLE, college administrator, fashion designer, department chairman, artist; d. Milton Melross Pyle. BFA in Fashion Design, U. of the Arts, Phila., 1961; studied weaving, U. Mont., Missoula, 1973; MFA, Temple U., Phila., 1978. Prof., chair fashion design dept. Moore Coll. Art and Design, Phila., 1965—96, dean, 1990—93; dir. Dept. Stylisme Ecole Parsons a Parsons, Paris, 1986—88; mem. faculty then assoc. chair Dept. Fashion Design Parsons Sch. Design, NYC, 1978—2004, acting chair Dept. Fashion Design, 1999—2000, dir. spl. projects, 2000—01; chair Dept. Fashion Design Internat. Acad. Design and Tech., Tampa, Fla., 2004—. Mem.: Fashion Group Internat. (mem. bd. dirs. Phila. chpt. 1968—71, mem. bd. dirs. 2006). Avocations: genealogy, playing the piano and organ, needlepoint. Home: 9923 Bridgeton Dr Tampa FL 33626 Office: Internat Acad Design and Tech 5104 Eisenhower Blvd Tampa FL 33634

MCGEER, EDITH GRAEF, retired neurological science educator; b. N.Y.C., Nov. 18, 1923; d. Charles and Charlotte Annie (Ruhl) Graef; m. Patrick L. McGeer, Apr. 15, 1954; children: Patrick Charles, Brian Theodore, Victoria Lynn. BA, Swarthmore Coll., 1944; PhD, U. Va., 1946; DSc (hon.), U. Victoria, 1987, U. B.C., 2000. Rsch. chemist E.I. DuPont de Nemours & Co., Wilmington, Va., 1946—54; rsch. assoc. divsn. neurol. sci. U. B.C., Vancouver, Canada, 1954-74, assoc. prof., 1974—76, prof., acting head, 1976—83, prof., head, 1983—89, prof. emerita, 1989—. Author: (with others) Molecular Neurobiology of the Mammalian Brain, 1978, 2d edit., 1987; editor: (with others) Kainic Acid as a Tool in Neurobiology, 1978, Glutamine, Glutamate, and GABA, 1983; contbr. articles to profl. jours. Decorated officer Order of B.C., Order of Can.; recipient citation, Am. Chem. Soc., 1958, Rsch. award, Clarke Inst., 1992, Lifetime Achievement award, Sci. Coun. B.C., 1995, Hon. Alumnus award, 1996, cert., Internat. Sci. Inst., 2001, medal of svc., Dr. Cam Coady Found., 2003, Lifetime Achievement award, U. B.C. Med. Faculty, 2006. Fellow Can. Coll. Neuropsychopharmacology, Royal Soc. Can.; mem. Can. Biochem. Soc., Internat. Brain Rsch. Orgn., Internat. Soc. Neurochemistry, Soc. Neurosci., Am. Neurochem. Soc. (councilor 1979-83), North Pacific Soc. Neurology and Psychiatry (hon. fellow), Lychnos Soc., Sigma Xi, Phi Beta Kappa. Office: U BC Divsn Neurol Sci 2255 Wesbrook Mall Vancouver BC Canada V6T 1Z3 Office Phone: 604-822-7380. Business E-Mail: mcgeer@interchange.ubc.ca.

MCGERVEY, TERESA ANN, technical information specialist; b. Pitts., Sept. 27, 1964; d. Walter James and Janet Sarah (Donehue) McG. BS in Geology, Calif. U. Pa., 1986, MS in Earth Sci., 1988; MLS, Cath. U. Am., 1998. Phys. sci. technician U.S. Geol. Survey, Reston, Va., 1989-90; editor, indexer Am. Geol. Inst., Alexandria, Va., 1990-91; cartographer Def. Mapping Agy., Reston, 1991-93; tech. info. specialist Nat. Tech. Info. Svc., Springfield, Va., 1993-2000, Dept. of Def., Arlington, Va., 2000—04, FBI, Washington, 2004—06, Joint Staff, Arlington, 2006—. Intern dept. mineral scis. Smithsonian Instn., 1985—86. Mem.: AAUW, ALA, Geosci. Info. Soc. Office: Joint Staff 935 Pennsylvania Ave NW Washington DC Personal E-mail: tamcgervey@juno.com.

MCGHEE, DIANE BAUMANN, dance instructor, consultant; b. Salem, NJ, 1954; d. Nelson Paul and Alice Elizabeth Baumann; children: Christine, Jonathan, Michael Porcaro. BS, Madison Coll., 1972—76; MS, James Madison U., 1976—78. Phys. edn. and dance instr. Salisbury State Coll., Md., 1978—82; resident choreographer; booking and tour mgr. Mandala Folk Ensemble, Boston, 1984—88; dir. of sch. outreach programs and tchr. MJT Dance Co., Boston, 1988—94; sr. tchr. Boston Renaissance/Edison Project Partnership Sch., 1994—97; dir. SE Ctr. for Dance Edn., Columbia Coll., 1997—2000; assoc. prof. Dept. of Theatre and Dance, Winthrop U., Rock Hill, SC, 2000—02; dir., arts for children interdisciplinary program; assoc. prof. of dance SUNY Coll. at Brockport, Brockport, NY, 2002—. Steering and coordinating committees Arts in Basic Curriculum Project, cons., arts edn. leadership inst.; adv. bd. and cons. Am. Dance Legacy Inst.; edn. cons. NY State Summer Sch. of the Arts Sch. of Dance; dir. Etudes Ednl. Project; exec. bd. Project U.N.I.Q.U.E., arts learning lab; art edn. roundtable Greater Rochester Arts and Cultural Coun. Author: (dance education lesson studies) Roots & Branches: Exploring an Evolving Dance Legacy, (dance unit of study) Civil War to Civil Rights: A Lesson in Humanity, Making Connections: Technology, Education, and Dance, American Indian Dance; A Celebration of Survival and Adaptation, Structuring Time and Space: A Dance Hypothesis. Recipient Presdl. Leadership award in Dance, SC. Dance Assn., 1998, Contbn. to Dance Edn., Fidelity Investments (Am. Ballet Gala, Boston), 1999, Artistic Vision, Comittment to Children, Dedication to Dance Edn., MJT Dance Co., 1994. Mem.: Internat. Assn. for Health, Phys. Edn., Recreation, Sport and Dance, SC Dept. Edn. (co-chair, arts tech. standards com., mem. task force, visual and performing arts curricular standards, arts report card task force, SAT improvement com.), Nat. Dance Edn. Org. (exec. bd. and charter mem.). Office: SUNY Brockport 350 New Campus Dr Brockport NY 14420 Office Phone: 585-395-5304. Business E-Mail: dmcghee@brockport.edu.

MCGHEE, KATHRYN ANN, foundation administrator; m. Truman McGhee, Mar. 20, 1942; children: Heather McGhee Kelley, Timothy S. Tate McGhee. BA, U. Conn., 1966; MPA magna cum laude, NOVA U., 1981. Adminstrn. and mktg. exec. Devel. Ctr., St. Petersburg, Fla., 1984-90; pres. Lincoln Learning Labs., Clearwater, Fla., 1987-90; v.p. Pinellas Assn. Retarded Children, St. Petersburg, 1976-84, 1992—2005, v.p. programs, 2005—. Amb. United Way; mem. adv. bd. Jr. League. Mem. Am. Mgmt. Assn., Nat. Assn. Female Execs., Nat. Assn. Fund-raising Execs. (bd. dirs., editor newsletter). Home: 17854 Lee Ave Apt 202 Redington Shores FL 33708-1169

MCGILL, CARLA ANN, language educator; b. Fontana, Calif., Feb. 13, 1955; d. Robert Coldiron and Ruth Marie Peavy; m. David William McGill, Jul. 26, 1980. BA English, Calif. State U., San Bernardino, 1986; MA English, U. Calif., Riverside, 1988, PhD English, 1993. Tchg. asst. U. Calif., Riverside, 1988-91; sr. lectr. Biola U., La Mirada, Calif., 1993-97; instr. Biola BOLD Prog., La Mirada, Calif., 1995-97; sr. lectr. Azusa Pacific U., Azusa, Calif., 1998—2000; lectr. Calif. State U., San Bernadino, 1999—2001, U. Calif., Riverside, 1999—2001; instr. Corinthian Colls., Santa Ana, 2003—; lectr. U. Redlands, Redlands, Calif., 2006—. Author: Thomas Shepard's "Confessions" dissertation, 1993; contr. book reviews, poems, articles to mags. Mem. Live Poets' Soc. at the Huntington Libr. Michael J. Connell Foun. Fellow, Huntington Libr., 1993. Mem. Am. Lit. Assn., Modern Lang. Assn., Soc. Early Americanists, Colloquium for Study of Amer. Culture. Avocations: poetry, fiction, screenwriting. E-mail: cmcgill215@aol.com.

MCGILL, GRACE ANITA, retired occupational health nurse; b. Lawrence, Mass., Mar. 8, 1943; d. Joseph John and Tina Mary (Sicurella) Tabacco; m. Howard L. McGill, Jr., Feb. 28, 1965 (dec. Mar. 2003); children: Cynthia, Deborah, David. RN, Mass. Gen. Hosp., 1963; BS, Lesley Coll., 1987; MS in Mgmt., Lesley Grad. Sch., 1990. Cert. occupl. health nurse Am. Bd. Occupl. Health Nurses, Inc. Nurse Phillips Acad., Andover, Mass., 1963-65, 97th Gen. Hosp., Frankfurt, Germany, 1966, Highsmith-Rainey Hosp., Fayetteville, N.C., 1968, Lawrence (Mass.) Gen. Hosp., 1969-78, Baldpate Psychiat. Hosp., Georgetown, Mass., 1978-79; nursing staff St. Joseph's Hosp., Lowell, Mass., 1980-81, head nurse, 1981-83; occupl. health nurse Wang Labs., Inc., Lowell, 1983-87, corp. safety specialist, 1987-90; health svcs. adminstr. Loral Infrared and Imaging Sys., Inc., Lexington, Mass., 1990-93; supr. health svcs. Osram Sylvania, Inc., Danvers, Mass., 1993-95; occupl. health nurse Occupl. Health Strategies, Inc., Chelmsford, Mass., 1995—98; ret., 1998. Contract instr. Sch. Pub. Health Harvard U.; occupl. health nurse Sts. Meml. Med. Hosp.; past chair Am. Bd. Occupational Health Nurses, 1997—99. Pres. Cape Cod Hosp. Aux., 2001—03; dir. Cape Cod Healthcare Found. Bd., 2001—03; vestry St. David's Episcopal Ch., South Yarmouth, Mass., 2006—. Recipient MA Medique Leadership grant, 1999. Mem. Am. Assn. Occupl. Health Nurses, Mass. Gen. Hosp. Nurses Alumnae Assn., Lesley Coll. Alumnae. Avocations: music, piano, organ. Home: 30 Marsh Side Dr Yarmouth Port MA 02675 E-mail: mcgilljg@comcast.net.

MCGILL, SYLVIETTE DELPHINE, editor; b. Southern Pines, N.C., Feb. 17, 1964; d. Sylvester Nicholson and Josephine Graham Flowers; m. Michael Anthony McGill, Aug. 7, 1982; children: Vindell, Miranda. BS in Bus., Liberty U., 1992. Tchr. Aldine Sch. Dist., Houston, 1993-94; mng. editor Upscale mag., Atlanta, 1995—. Mem. Mag. Assn. Ga., Atlanta Assn. Black Journalists (Soft Feature award 1998), Nat. Coun. Negro Women. Avocations: singing, travel. Office: Upscale Mag 600 Bronner Bros Way SW Atlanta GA 30310-2040

MCGILLICUDDY, JOAN MARIE, psychotherapist, consultant; b. Chgo., June 23, 1952; d. James Neal and Muriel (Joy) McG. BA, U. Ariz., 1974, MS, 1976; PhD, Walden U., 1996. Cert. nat. counselor. Counselor ACTION, Tucson, 1976; counselor, clin. supr. Behavioral Health Agy. Cen. Ariz., Casa Grande, 1976-81; instr. psychology Cen. Ariz. Coll., Casa Grande, 1978-83; therapist, co-dir. Helping Assocs., Inc., Casa Grande, 1982—, v.p., sec., 1982—; cert. instr. Silva Method Mind Devel., Tucson, 1986—. Active Mayor's Com. for Handicapped, Casa Grande, 1989-90, Human Svcs. Planning, Casa Grande, 1985-95, Pinal Gila Sr. Coun. Found., 2005—. Named Outstanding Am. Lectr. Silva Mind Internat., 1988-99. Mem. ACA. Avocations: jogging, singing. Office: Helping Assocs Inc 1901 N Trekell Rd Casa Grande AZ 85222-1706 Office Phone: 520-836-1029. E-mail: haicg@c212.com.

MCGILLIVRAY, KAREN, retired elementary school educator; b. Richland, Oreg., Aug. 24, 1936; d. Kenneth Melton and Catharina (Sass) McG. BS in Edn. cum laude, Ea. Oreg. State U., LaGrande, 1958; MRE, Pacific Sch. Religion, Berkeley, Calif., 1963. Cert. tchr., Oreg. 4th grade tchr. Salem (Oreg.)-Keizer Pub. Schs.; ret., 1995. Contbr. articles to profl. jours. U.S. Govt. grantee. Mem.: NEA (rep. assembly), Salem Edn. Assn. (officer), Oreg. Ret. Educators Assn. (officer), Oreg. Edn. Assn. (rep. assembly), NEA-Ret. Oreg. (state officer), Wash. State Scottish Terrier Club, Cascade Scottish Terrier Club, Scottish Terrier Club Am., Phi Delta Kappa (officer), Delta Kappa Gamma (officer). United Methodist. Home: 1301 Fulton St Apt 143 Newberg OR 97132-1868 E-mail: karen@mcgillivray.org.

MCGINLEY, MARJORIE, writer; b. Nyack, NY, May 3, 1939; d. Frank Gerard and Ida Mae McGinley; m. Ernest R. Carosella, Sept. 9, 1960; children: Douglas Carosella, Sharon Carosella Clark. BS, We. Conn. State U., 1961. Tchr. William Strong Sch., Southington, Conn., 1967—71. Author: (novels) John Crust and Snuffling Pig, 1998, Rattlesnake Gulch, 1999, Footloose Conroy, 1999, Casey's Journey, 2000, The Gift of the Mestizo, 2001, Close Enough to Kill, 2002. Recipient First prize, Playreaders Theatre, 1995, Second prize, 1997. Mem.: We. Writers Am. Home: 39 Sunnybrook Ln Clinton CT 06413

MCGINN, EILEEN, public health service officer, researcher; b. Phila., Mar. 29, 1947; BA cum laude, CUNY, 1968; MPH, U. Pitts., 1974. Cert. aging Brookdale Ctr. Hunter Coll., CUNY. Tchr. English Peace Corps, Dogondoutchi, Niger, 1968-70; tchr. sci. Diocese of Bklyn., 1971-72; clinic dir. Monsour Med. Ctr., Jeannette, Pa., 1974-76; grants officer Assn. for Voluntary Surg. Contraception, N.Y.C., 1976-79; program officer Planned Parenthood Fedn., N.Y.C., 1979-81; chief of party USAID/Zaire, Kinshasa, 1983-85; dep. chief of party John Snow, Inc., Nepal, Kathmandu, 1986-89; program mgr. Asia Assn. Voluntary Surg. Contraception, N.Y.C., 1989-92; cons., 1992—. Cons. Ctr. Devel. and Pop. Activities, Washington, 1985, Population Svcs. Internat., Washington, 1985, Assn. Voluntary Surg. Contraception, Kenya and Tanzania, 1982, Bangladesh, 1989, USAID, Togo, 1993, John Snow/Svc. Expansion and Tech. Support, Papua New Guinea, 1994; chair neighborhood adv. bd. Manhattan 6, 1996-99; founding bd. dirs., treas. N.Y. Fibromyalgia Connection, 1996-99, bd. mem. cmty. adv. bd. region 7, N.Y.C., 2001—. Author: Field Worker's Manual, 1989, Nurse's Manual, 1989; contbr. articles to profl. jours. Mem. exec. bd. African Art, 2000—; docent Mus. for African Art, 2000-02; mem. exec. bd. Samuel Tilden Dem. Club, 1999—; chair, bd. dirs. Neighborhood Adv. Bd. Manhattan #6, 1994-2000; mem. cmty. action bd. NYC Dept. Youth and Cmty. Devel., 2000-05; English conversation ptnr. Internat. Ctr. and Manhattan Comprehensive Day and Night H.S., 2005—. N.Y.S. State Regents scholar, 1964-68, NYU scholar, 1982; USPHS grantee, 1972-73. Avocations: reading, writing, sewing. Office: 210 E 15th St New York NY 10003-3922 Office Phone: 212-982-4348.

MCGINN, MARY J., lawyer, insurance company executive; b. St. Louis, Apr. 9, 1947; d. Martin J. and Janet McGinn; m. Bernard H. Shapiro, Sept. 6, 1971; children: Sara, Colleen, Molly, Daniel. BA, Dominican U., River Forest, Ill., 1967; JD, St. Louis U., 1970. Bar: Mo. 1970, Ill. 1971. Atty. tax div. U.S. Dept. Justice, Washington, 1970-73; atty. Allstate Ins. Co., Northbrook, Ill., 1973—, v.p., dep. gen. counsel, 1980—. Mem. ABA, Am. Coll. Investment Counsel, Assn. Life Ins. Counsel. Roman Catholic. Home: 155 N Buckley Rd Barrington IL 60010-2607 Office: Allstate Ins Co 3075 Sanders Rd Ste G5A Northbrook IL 60062-7127 E-mail: mmcginn@allstate.com.

MCGINN, MARY LYN, real estate company executive; b. New Orleans, Aug. 12, 1949; d. Dan Creedon and Millicent Virginia (White) Midgett; m. Walter Lee McGinn, Mar. 14, 1985. BA, La. State U., 1970, MA, 1972; PhD, U. So. Miss., 1976; MBA, Loyola Coll., 1990. Cert. comml.-investment mem., cert. property mgr., master appraiser. Dir., prof. Dillard U., New Orleans, 1972-76, Loyola U., New Orleans, 1976-80; sr. v.p. Equity Investment Svcs., Inc., New Orleans, 1980-84; pres. Mgmt. Svcs. Group, Inc., New Orleans, 1984-85, Assoc. Investment Svcs. Inc., New Orleans, 1985-87, Northshore Property Mgmt., Inc., New Orleans, 1985-87; asst. v.p. USF&G Realty, Balt., 1987-89, v.p., 1989-90; exec. mng. dir. Galbreath Co., 1990—98; exec. v.p. CB Richard Ellis, 1998—2001; pres. Lin-Chris Assocs., L.P., 2001—. Cons. colls. and univs., 1976—. Bd. dirs. Pitts. Zoo, Salvation Army, Jr. Achievement. Mem. Nat. Assn. Corporate Real Estate Execs., Bldg. Owners and Mgrs. Assn., Comml.-Investment Council, Nat. Assn. Master Appraisers. Avocations: tennis, golf, skiing. Office Phone: 412-215-4000.

MCGINNIS, MARCY ANN, broadcast executive; b. Long Branch, N.J., Apr. 9, 1950; d. Joseph Arthur and Ruth (Thomas) McG. AAS, Marymount U., 1970, PhD (hon.), Hofstra U. Exec. sec. news Sta. CBS News, N.Y.C., 1970-71; adminstrv. asst. Sta. CBS TV, N.Y.C., 1971-73, asst. producer, 1973-76, assoc. producer, 1976-82, producer, 1982-85, sr. producer, 1985-89, exec. producer, 1989-92; dep. bur. chief London, dir. CBS NEWSNET Europe, 1992-95, TV news exec. prodr., v.p. and London bur. chief, 1995—97; v.p. news coverage CBS News, 1997—2001, sr. v.p. news coverage, 2001—05. Bd. dirs. Internat. Women's Media Found., La. State U. Manship Sch. Mass. Comm. Mem. NATAS, NAFE, TV and Radio Working Press Assn. Roman Catholic.*

MCGINNIS, PATRICIA ANNE, secondary school educator, biologist; b. Monterey, Calif., June 2, 1958; d. Robert Wilhem and Geraldine Sullivan Carius; m. Robert Michael McGinnis, June 14, 1986; children: Kathleen, Matthew, Marybeth. BS in Biology, Wash. State U., Pullman, 1980; MS in Biology, George Mason U., Fairfax, Va., 1985. Cert. tchr. Pa., 1990. Tchr. sci. Manasses Pk. (Va.) Schs., 1981—83, Fairfax (Va.) County Pub. Schs., 1983—87; dir. childcare Phoenixville (Pa.) YMCA, 1990—95; tchr. sci. Methacton Sch. Dist., Norristown, Pa., 1996—. Adv. sci. fair Methacton Sch. Dist., 2004—. Contbr. articles to mags. Finalist Tchr. of Yr. award, Pa., 2003; recipient Unsung Heroes award, 2000, Environ. Excellence award, Elmood Pk. Zoo, 2002, Educator 500 award, 3D Inst., West Chester (Pa.) U., 2005; grantee, Del. Valley McDonald's Assn., 2000, 2001, Pa. Dept. Edn., 2001, Pa. Dept. Environ. Protection, 2002, Toshiba Found., 2002, 2005. Fellow: Paul F. Brandwein Inst.; mem.: Pa. Sci. Tchr. Assn., Nat. Mid. Level Sci. Tchr. Assn. (Paul DeHart Hurd award 2003), Montgomery County Sci. Tchr. Assn. (named Montgomery County Mid. Sch. Sci. Tchr. of Yr. 2004), Nat. Sci. Tchrs. Assn. (tapestry amb. 2002—, mem. judging com. 2004—, mem. com. 1996—. grantee 2002, 2003), Alpha Delta Pi Alumna Assn. (pres. 1990). Roman Cath. Avocations: reading, birdwatching. Office: Arcola Intermed Sch 4000 Eagleville Rd Norristown PA 19403 Business E-Mail: pmcginnis@methacton.org.

MCGINNIS, PATRICIA GWALTNEY, non-profit organization executive; b. Goldsboro, N.C., July 19, 1947; d. Thomas McKim Gwaltney and Patricia Anne (Watkins) Schools; m. James Michael McGinnis, Aug. 4, 1978; children: J. Brian, Katherine B. BA, Mary Washington Coll., 1969; MPA, Harvard U., 1975. Dir. spl. studies U.S. Dept. Commerce, Washington, 1975-76; prof. staff mem. U.S. Senate Budge Com., Washington, 1976-77; dep. assoc. dir. U.S. Office Mgmt. and Budget, Washington, 1977-81; sr. cons. Cresap, McCormick and Paget, Inc., Washington, 1981-82; prin. The FMR Group, Inc., Washington, 1982-94; pres., CEO Coun. for Excellence in Govt., Washington, 1994—. Mem. exec. alumni coun. Kennedy Sch. Govt., Harvard U., Cambridge, Mass., 1992-96; dir. Primark Corp., Waltham, Mass., 1995-2000; mem. assoc. coun. George Washington Sch. Bus. and Pub. Adminstrn., 1996-99; bd. dirs. Brown Shoe Co., St. Louis, Imagitas, Inc., Newton, Mass.; bd. visitors U. Md. Sch. Pub. Affairs; dir. Logistics Mgmt. Inst., McLean, Va. Contbr. articles to profl. jours. Fellow: Nat. Acad. Pub. Adminstrn. Office: Coun for Excellence in Govt 1301 K St NW Ste 450W Washington DC 20005-3397

MCGINNIS, SUSAN PAULIENE, music teacher; b. Kansas City, Kans., Dec. 15, 1956; d. Bobbie Joe and Beulah Allene (Armstrong) McG.; m. Gary Allen Leney, Mar. 29, 1987 (div. Dec. 1993). MusB, U. North Tex., 1981, M in Music Edn., 1986. Cert. all-level provisional tchr. of string music. Tchr. strings Dallas Ind. Sch. Dist., 1983—. Performer (1st violin): Garland (Tex.) Symphony, 1982—85, Mesquite (Tex.) Symphony, 1987—, New Philharm. of Irving, 2000—02; performer: (2d violin) East Tex. Symphony, 1982—84; performer: (CD) Potluck-Roly Poly, 2003, Gospel Bluegrass Will there be any stars, 2004, A Few Favorites, Ashokau Farewell, 2005; dir.: Fiddlers North, 1995—, 2005—. Founding charter mem. Mesquite Symphony Guild, 1988-89; founding mem. Mesquite Symphony, 1987—; soprano II rep. Lovers Lane Sanctuary Choir, 1997—; bd. dirs., tchr. rep. Cabell Elem., 1996-2000. Scholar Meth. Ch., San Angelo, Tex., 1976-77. Mem.: Tex. Music Educators Assn., Music Educators Nat. Conf., Am. String Tchrs. Assn., Sigma Alpha Iota (scholarship com. 1985—97, Marion Flagg scholar 1984—85). Methodist. Avocations: sewing, walking, reading, travel.

MCGINNITY, MAUREEN ANNELL, lawyer; b. Monroe, Wis., Apr. 6, 1956; d. James Arthur and Marie Beatrice (Novak) McG.; m. Richard W. Ziervogel, July 17, 1982; 1 child, Brigitte Kathleen. BS, U. Wis., Milw., 1977; JD, U. Wis., 1982. Bar: Wis. 1982, U.S. Dist. Ct. (ea. and we. dists.) Wis. 1982, U.S. Ct. Appeals (7th cir.) 1989, U.S. Ct. Appeals (1st cir.) 1991, U.S. Tax Ct. 1995, U.S. Supreme Ct. 1991. Assoc. Foley & Lardner LLP, Milw., 1982-91, ptnr., 1991—, chairperson tax valuation & fiduciary litig. practice group. Mem. Wis. Supreme Ct. Planning and Policy Adv. Com., Madison, 1991-94; adv. bd. Domestic Violence Legal Clinic, Milw., 1991—. Treas. Waukesha (Wis.) Food Pantry, 1988-94; trustee Boys & Girls Club Greater Milw., 1991—; bd. dirs. Task Force on Battered Women & Children, Inc., 1994-2006. Recipient Outstanding Svc. award Legal Action Wis., Milw., 1984, 93 Outstanding Fundraising awards Boys & Girls Club Greater Milw., 1987-92, Cert. Recognition, Common Coun. Task Force on Sexual Assault & Domestic Violence, Milw., 1991, Cert. Appreciation, Wis. Equal Justice Task Force, Madison, 1991, Cmty. Svc. award Wis. Law Found., 1995. Mem. ABA, State Bar Wis. (bd. govs. 1992-96, Pro Bono award 1990, chair 1993-94), Assn. for Women Lawyers (various offices, pres. 1992-93), Milw. Young Lawyers Assn. (bd. dirs. 1987-92, pres. 1990-91, Pres.' award 1991), Profl. Dimensions. Office: Foley & Lardner LLP 777 E Wisconsin Ave Ste 3800 Milwaukee WI 53202-5367 Office Phone: 414-297-5510. Office Fax: 414-297-4900. Business E-Mail: mmcginnity@foley.com.

MCGINN MILLER, JANET SCRIVNER, retired elementary school educator, writer; d. Roy Bert Scrivner and Wanda Lou Jeffcoat; m. Glenn Richard Miller, Dec. 29, 2000; m. David George McGinn, Aug. 8, 1987 (dec. Nov. 21, 1993); children: Bryan George Loveless, Kyle Andrew McGinn, Kelly Anita Molly McGinn. BS magna cum laude, Slippery Rock State U., 1980; MEd, U. Ariz., 1995. Cert. tchr. Ariz. Eighth grade tech. tchr. Tucson Unified Sch. Dist., 2001—, math improvement tchr., 2001; eighth grade math tchr. Sunnyside Sch. Dist., Tucson, 1986—94; sixth grade math/sci. tchr. Window Rock Unified Sch. Dist., Ft. Defiance, Ariz., 1984—86. Sponsor Falcon Crest presents (student movie projects) Booth-Fickett Magent Sci. Mid. Sch., Tucson, 2001—. Author: (book) Widowed Without Warning, (screenplay) A Part of We. Mem. PTA, Tucson, 2002—03. Mem.: NYC Writers Assn., Soc. Southwestern Authors, Tucson Edn. Assn., Lambda Epsilon Delta. Liberal. Avocations: web page designer, sewing.

MCGLOWN, BRENDA PRYOR, special education educator; b. Memphis, Tenn., Oct. 31, 1946; d. George and John Ella (Hobbs) Pryor; m. Andrew McGlown III, Dec. 29, 1979; 1 child, Toya Angeliqué. BA, LeMoyne-Owen, 1970; MEd, Memphis State U., 1977. Cert. tchr., Tenn. Tchr. Memphis (Tenn.) City Schs., 1970—. Mem. Inservice Com. Spl. Edn., Memphis, 1990-91, Adminstrv. Adv. Com., Memphis, 1992-93. Author: (test) Adaptive Reading Special Needs, 1986-87, (curriculum) Adaptive Social Studies, 1991-92. Mem. Dist. 33 Adv. Bd., Memphis, 1990-92; officer Shelby County Election Commn., Memphis, 1991-92, election official, 1996-97; mem. People's Rescue Mission, South Memphis, 1989-90; vol. Spl. Olympics, 1990. Recipient Tchr. Excellence award Memphis Rotary Club, 1993; named Tchr. of Yr., Coun. of Exceptional Children, 1988; grantee Memphis Rotary Club, 1988-89, 91-92, 96-97, 97-98. Mem. NEA, Tenn. Edn. Assn., Memphis Edn. Assn., Tenn. Assn. for Children with Learning Disabilities, Zeta Phi Beta Sorority. Avocations: reading, cooking. Home: 5819 W Fox Bend Cv Memphis TN 38115-3804 Office: Grahamwood Elem Sch 3950 Summer Ave Memphis TN 38122-5210

MCGLYNN, ELIZABETH A., health policy analyst; PhD, RAND Grad. Sch., 1988; MPP, U. Mich. Assoc. dir. RAND Health, Santa Monica, Calif.; dir. Ctr. Rsch. on Quality in Health Care, Santa Monica, Calif. Adv. com. Nat. Com. for Quality Assurance (NCQA), Nat. Quality Forum (NQF). Coun. Accountable Physician Practices, Am. Med. Group Assn.; editorial bd. Health Svcs. Rsch., Milbank Meml. Fund Quarterly. Mem.: Inst. Medicine. Achievements include development of QA Tools. Office: RAND Health Communications PO Box 2138 1776 Main St Santa Monica CA 90407-2138*

MCGLYNN, MARGARET G., pharmaceutical executive; BS in Pharmacy, SUNY, Buffalo, 1982, MBA in Mktg., 1983. Profl. rep. Merck & Co., Inc., Whitehouse Sta., NJ, 1983—84, mktg. analyst, 1985—86, promotion mgr., 1986, product mgr., 1987—89, dir. bus. devel., 1987—89, 1989—90, sr. dir. mkt. planning, 1990—91, exec., dir. nat. consumer mktg. U.S. human health, 1991—93, v.p. bus. mgmt. and devel. U.S. human health, 1993, sr. v.p. managed care U.S. human health, 1994—95, sr. v.p. bus. planning proposals and analysis Merck-Medco Managed Care, 1994, sr. v.p. health and utilization mgmt., Merck-Medco Managed Care L.L.C., Whitehouse Sta, 1995—98, sr. v.p. world wide human health mktg., 1998—2001, exec. v.p. customer mktg. and sales U.S. human health, 2001—02, pres. U.S. human health, 2003—05; pres. Merck Vaccines, 2005—. Bd. dir. Air Products and Chemicals. Corp. exec. bd. Phila. Mus. Art; mem. dean's adv. coun. U. Buffalo Sch. Mgmt. Office: Merck & Co Inc One Merck Dr PO Box 100 Whitehouse Station NJ 08889-0100*

MCGLYNN, MAUREEN SCALLEY, history educator; b. Berea, Ohio, July 17, 1951; d. Robert Edward and Norma Ellen (Archibald) Scalley; m. Thomas Mark McGlynn, Apr. 27, 1974; children: Edward Thomas, Charles Geoffrey. BA in History, Cleve. State U., 1973, MA in History, 1983. Cert. history tchr., Ohio. Casework aide adoption dept. Cath. Family and Childrens' Svcs., Cleve., 1973-74; social studies tchr. St. Vincent DePaul Sch., Cleve., 1974-78; customer counselor savs. dept. Cardinal Fed. Savs. & Loan Assn., Lakewood, Ohio, 1978-79; history tchr. and chmn. dept. social studies St. Augustine Acad., 1979—2005; substitute tchr. Padua Franciscan H.S., Parma, 2006—. Coord. Closeup Found. St. Augustine Acad., Lakewood, 1979—82; instr. Townsend Learning Ctr., Westlake, Ohio, 1988., Westlake, 1988; tchr. summer sch. St. Edward H.S., Lakewood, 2001, 02, 04, 05. Mem. Our Lady of the Angels Sch. Parent Tchr. Unit, Cleve., 1991—; vol. fall festival Our Lady of the Angels, Cleve., 1990, 91, 92; mem. Kammco/Neighborhood Devel. Corp., Cleve., 1991-92; vol. Crimewatch, Cleve., 1988, 91. Stratford Hall summer seminar grantee, 1983. Mem. Nat. Coun. Social Studies, Ohio Coun. Social Studies, Greater Cleve. Coun. for Social Studies (treas. 1982-83), Phi Alpha Theta. Roman Catholic. Avocations: sewing, swimming, reading, history, furniture restoration. Home: 3448 Tuttle Ave Cleveland OH 44111-3027 Office: St Augustine Academy 1426 Orchard Grove Ave Lakewood OH 44107-3726 E-mail: mscalleymcglyn@sbcglobal.net.

MCGOLDRICK, JANE R., psychologist, writer, editor; b. Monongahela, Pa., Sept. 3, 1948; d. William H. Robinson and Margaret Taylor; m. Lawrence Frances McGoldrick, 1977; 1 child, Daniel. BA, Agnes Scott Coll., 1970; MA, U. Chgo., 1971, State U. West Ga., 1995; PsyD, Argosy U., 2002. Lic. psychologist, counselor, cert. coreSomatics practitioner Somatic Inst. Pitts. Editor Nat. Geog. Soc., Washington, 1983-95; instr. George Washington U., Washington, 1992-95; contbg. editor Common Boundary Mag., Chevy Chase, Md., 1997-99; founder, owner The Gooseberry Co., Silver Spring, Md., 1995—; assoc. Christine A. Courtois, PhD & Assoc., Washington, 2003—. Psychotherapist Washington Assessment & Therapy Svcs., Germantown, Md., 2003—05; pvt. practice, Burtonsville, Md., 2005—. Author: (book) Animal Clowns, 1989; mng. editor: (books) A Nation's Pride: Art in the White House, 1992, U.S. Senate Catalogue of Fine Art, 2002; contbr. nonfiction articles to mags. Mem. APA, ACA, Internat. Soc. for Study of Subtle Energies and Energy Medicine, D.C. Guild Body Psychotherapists, Md. Psychol. Assn., Am. Soc. Clin. Hypnosis, Internat. Soc. Study of Dissociation, Internat. Soc. Traumatic Stress Studies, Assn. for Comprehensive Energy Psychology. Office: Christine A Courtois PhD and Assoc Ste 513 5225 Wisconsin Ave NW Washington DC 20015 Office Phone: 202-362-2776. E-mail: jane@docmcg.com.

MCGOUGH, MARYLEE, marketing professional; b. Herlong, Calif., Nov. 22, 1944; d. Rufus McGough and Mattie Lee Lett. Degree in liberal arts & speech comm., Fresno City Coll., 1997—2000; BA, Calif. State U., Fresno, 2000—06. Sales exec., buyer Antille Poi, Milan, 1986—88; mktg., pub. rels. and buyer Bamos Pret e Poter, Milan, 1988—2000. Organizer Women's Resource Ctr., Fresno, 2000—05. Dir.: (poetry venue) Poetry Jam (Women's Resource award, 2004). Trustee, senator Student Govt., Fresno, Calif., 1998—2002. Home: 2551 S Bardell Fresno CA 93706 Office: Women's Resource Ctr 5240 N Jackson Ave M/S UC35 Fresno CA 93740-8023 Office Fax: 559-278-7358. Business E-Mail: marylee@csufresno.edu.

MCGOVERN, LORE HARP, communications executive, philanthropist; m. Patrick J. McGovern. Undergrad., Calif. State Univ.; MBA, Pepperdine Univ. Co-founder Vector Graphics Inc., 1976; founder Pacific Tech. Venture Fund, San Francisco, 1981, dir., 1983—85; founder Aplex Corp., 1985—89; CEO Good Morning Teacher! Pub., 1990—99; mem. bd. dir. Internat. Data Group. Chmn. bd. assoc. Whitehead Inst. MIT; mem. bd. advisors Women.com, Blue Pumpkin Software, Skillsvillage.com. Named one of 50 Most Generous Philanthropists, Fortune Mag., 2005; recipient Entrepreneur Yr., 1983. Mem.: Am. Elec. Assn. (former dir.). Office: IDG One Exeter Plz Boston MA 02116 Office Fax: 617-423-0240.*

MC GOVERN, MAUREEN THERESE, entertainer; b. Youngstown, Ohio, July 27, 1949; d. James Terrence and Mary Rita (Welsh) Mc Govern. Student pub. schs., Youngstown. Exec. sec. Youngstown Cartage Co., 1968-69; sec. Assocs. in Anesthesiology, Youngstown, 1970-71. Entertainer, 1972—, (stage appearances plays) The Sound of Music, 1981—, The Pirates of Penzance, 1981, South Pacific, 1982, Nine, 1984, Brownstone, 1984, Guys and Dolls, 1984, Three Penny Opera, 1989, cameo appearance in movie The Towering Inferno, 1975, appeared in film Ky. Fried Theater's Airplane, 1979; singer: (albums) The Morning After, 1973 (Gold Record award), Nice To Be Around, 1974 (Academy Award Performance, 1975), Maureen McGovern, 1979, Another Woman In Love, 1987, Naughty Baby, 1989, Baby I'm Yours, 1992, Music Never Ends, 1997, The Pleasure of His Company, 1998; composer: Midnight Storm, 1973, If I Wrote You a Song, 1973, All I Want, 1974, Memory, 1974, Little Boys and Men, 1974, Love Knots, 1974, You Love Me Too Late, 1979, Thief in the Night, 1979, Don't Stop Now, 1979, Hello Again, 1979, Halfway Home, 1980, others. Recipient Gold Record for single The Morning After, Record Industry Assn. Am., 1973, Can. RPM Gold Leaf award, 1973, Australian gold award, 1975, resolution for bringing fame and recognition to Ohio, Ohio Senate, 1974, Grand prize Tokyo Music Festival, 1975. Mem.: AFTRA, ASCAP, Screen Actors Guild, Am. Fedn. Musicians. Office: c/o Warner Bros Records 3300 Warner Blvd Burbank CA 91505-4632

MCGOVERN, MEGHAN MARIE, athletic trainer; b. Chgo., Mar. 27, 1978; d. Daniel George and Jane Ellen McGovern. BS, Ea. Ill. U., Charleston, 2000; MS, Ea. Ill. U.; MEd, DePaul U., Chgo., 2006. Cert. athletic trainer NATABOC. Asst. mgr. sports medicine Accelerated Rehab. Ctrs., Chgo.; head athletic trainer Accelerated Rehab. Ctrs./Glenbard South HS, Chgo. Mem.: Gt. Lakes Athletic Trainers Assn., Ill. Athletic Trainers Assn., Nat. Athletic Trainers Assn. Office: Accelerated Rehab Ctrs 23W200 Butterfield Rd Glen Ellyn IL 60137 Office Phone: 630-942-6809.

MCGOVERN, REBECCA MAPLES, chamber of commerce executive; b. West Frankfort, Ill., July 3, 1934; d. Joseph Edward and Celia Belle (Gill) McGovern. BA magna cum laude, So. Ill. U., 1956; postgrad., Boston U., 1956—57. Advt. mgr. Beacon Press, Boston, 1962—65; dir. press mktg. MIT, Cambridge, Mass., 1965—74; pres. Mariposa Enterprises, San Juan Bautista, Calif., 1974—82; mktg. dir. San Juan Magazette, San Juan Bautista, 1982—. Bd. dirs. San Benito Econ. Devel. Corp., Chamber Music San Juan Found., Cabrillo Music Festival. Home: 102-104 The Alameda San Juan Bautista CA 95045

MCGOVERN-SCATURO, DIANE JOAN, psychotherapist; d. Francis Michael and Joan Veronica (Quinn) McCarthy; m. Thomas Joseph McGovern (dec.); children: Judith Ann McGovern, Robert Thomas McGovern; m. Christopher John Scaturo, Aug. 1, 1992. BA, Trinity U., Washington, 1953; MEd, U. Pitts., 1956; MS in Edn., St. Bonaventure U., N.Y., 1992. Lic. mental health counselor N.Y. State Edn. Dept., cert. group psychotherapist Nat. Registry Cert. Group Psychotherapists, CA N.Y. State OASAS, AC N.Y. State OASAS, CRMFT Nat. Assn. Cognitive Behavioral Therapists, CRAT Nat. Assn. Cognitive Behavioral Therapists. Family svcs. coord. Cattaraugus County Coun. on Alcoholism and Substance Abuse, Olean, 1987—92; behavioral health therapist Charter Behavioral Health Sys. Winston-Salem, NC, 1994—96; behavioral health therapist, group psychotherapist Olean Gen. Hosp. Behavioral Health Unit, 2000—. Oral panel examiner Credentialled Alcoholism Counselor Exam., Credentialling Application Svcs., Albany, NY, 1992. Mem., bd. dirs. Olean Gen. Hosp. Found., 2000—, sec., bd. dirs., 2005—; mem., adv. bd. Salvation Army, Olean, 1959—86, chmn., adv. bd., 1972—77. Mem.: ACA, Am. Group Psychotherapy Assn. (clin. mem.), Rochester Group Psychotherapy Soc., Am. Psychotherapy Assn. (diplomate). Avocations: golf, downhill skiing. Office: Olean Gen Hosp Behavioral Health Unit 515 Main St Olean NY 14760

MCGOWAN, ANGELA KAY, government agency administrator, researcher; b. Decatur, Ga., Sept. 6, 1970; d. John E. McGowan, Jr. and Linda Kay (Hudson) McGowan. BA, Coll. William & Mary, 1992; JD, Vanderbilt U., 1995; MPH, Emory U., 1998. Bar: Ga. 1995. Atty. Troutman Sanders, LLP, Atlanta, 1996—97; legal svcs. officer Divsn. Pub. Health Ga. Dept. Human Resources, Atlanta, 1999—2002; epidemic intelligence svc. officer Ctrs. for Disease Control & Prevention, Atlanta, 2002—04, pub. health law analyst, 2004—. Pres. Atlanta chpt. William & Mary Alumni Club, 1999—2000; alumni bd. govs. Rollins Sch. Pub. Health, Emory U., Atlanta, 2004—. Mem.: Ga. Bar Assn., Pub. Health Law Assn., Am. Pub. Health Assn. Office: Centers for Disease Control & Prevention 4770 Buford Hwy K-40 Atlanta GA 30341 Office Phone: 770-488-8210. Personal E-mail: angiemcgowan@cs.com. Business E-Mail: amcgowan@cdc.gov.

MCGOWAN, ROSE, actress; b. Florence, Italy, Sept. 5, 1973; Actor: (films) Encino Man, 1992, The Doom Generation, 1995, Bio-Dome, 1996, Kiss & Tell, 1996, Scream, 1996, Going All The Way, 1997, Nowhere, 1997, Lewis & Clark & George, 1997, Seed, 1997, Phantoms, 1998, Southie, 1998, Devil in the Flesh, 1998, Jawbreaker, 1999, Sleeping Beauties, 1999, Ready to Rumble, 2000, The Last Stop, 2000, Monkeybone, 2001, Strange Hearts, 2001, Vacuums, 2002, The Black Dahlia, 2006; (TV films) God Is In the T.V., 1999, The Killing Yard, 2001, Elvis, 2005; (TV series) Charmed, 2001—06, (TV appearances) True Colors, 1990, What About Joan, 2001.*

MCGOWAN, SUSAN, gifted and talented educator; b. Alameda, Calif., May 12, 1959; d. Thomas and Gladys Mae (Prutzman) McG.; m. Warren Howard Jones, Oct. 31, 1980 (div.); children: Kelly Hardcastle, Reilly James; m. Barry William McLaughlin, May 22, 2004 AS in Edn., No. Va. Community Coll., 1988; BA in Russian Area Studies, George Mason U., 1991; MEd, Marymount U., 1994; postgrad., Coll. William & Mary, 2003—. Cert. tchr. Va. Data processor Tracor, Inc., Virginia Beach, Va., 1982-83; computer operator Hughes, Bendix, Holmes and Narver, Virginia Beach, 1983-84; data analyst Tracor, Inc., Virginia Beach, 1984; systems analyst Advanced Tech., Inc., Virginia Beach, 1984-85, computer programmer Reston, Va., 1986-87; tech. writer Swiger Group, Reston, 1987; tchr. 3rd grade Loudoun Country Day Sch., Leesburg, Va., 1991-93; tchr. 4th and 5th grade Loudoun County Pub. Schs., 1994—2000, Va. Beach City Pub. Sch., 2001—. Master tchr. Nat. Tech. Tchr. Inst., WNVT, Fairfax, 1998-99; translation cons. Systems Ctr., Inc., Reston, 1990— Recipient Presdl. award, Va. Gov.'s Sch., 2005. Mem. ASCD, World Affairs Coun., Golden Key, Phi Theta Kappa, Alpha Chi. Personal E-mail: smjones59@aol.com. Business E-Mail: smmcgo@wm.edu.

MCGOWEN, LORRAINE S., lawyer; b. Phila., 1960; m. Gailon McGowen; 4 children. BS, Georgetown U., 1983; JD, Columbia U., 1986. Bar: N.Y. 1987, U.S. Dist. Ct., So. Dist. N.Y. 1988, U.S. Dist. Ct., Ea. Dist. N.Y. 1988, D.C. 1994, U.S. Ct. Appeals, Second Cir. 1994. Ptnr. Orrick, Herrington & Sutcliffe LLP, NYC, 1996—2001, co-chair Bankruptcy and Debt Restructuring Group, 2001—. Mem.: Am. Coll. Investment Counsel, Am. Bankruptcy Inst., DC Bar, Assn. Bar City NY, ABA (bus. law com.). Office: Orrick Herrington & Sutcliffe LLP 666 Fifth Ave New York NY 10103 Office Phone: 212-506-5114. Office Fax: 212-506-5151. Business E-Mail: lmcgowen@orrick.com.

MCGRADY, CORINNE YOUNG, design company executive; b. N.Y.C., May 6, 1938; d. Albert I. and Reda (Bromberg) Young; m. Michael Robinson McGrady; children: Sean, Siobhan, Liam. Student, Bard Coll., Annandale-on-Hudson, N.Y., 1960, Harvard U., 1968—69. Founder, pres. Corinne McGrady Designs; designer Corinneware (joint venture Corinne McGrady Designs and Boston Warehouse Trading Corp.), East Northport, NY, 1970—. Exhibited in group shows at Mus. Contemporary Crafts, N.Y.C., 1969—70, Smithsonian Instn., 1970—71, Pompidou Ctr., Paris, 1971, Mus. Sci. and Industry, 1970, exhibitions include Guild Hall Show, Southampton, N.Y., 1968, Hecksher Mus., 1968; patentee cookbook stand. V.p. Women's Internat. League for Peace and Freedom, Huntington, NY, 1971; mem. bldg. com. Timberland Lib Hoodsport, 1996—97. Recipient Design Rev. award, Indsl. Design, 1969, 1970, Instant Supergraphic Indsl. Design Rev. award, 1971. Home and Office: PO Box 27 Lilliwaup WA 98555-0027

MCGRADY, PHYLLIS, television producer; Exec. prodr. PrimeTime Live, N.Y.C., Turning Point; with ABC, 1977—; v.p. and exec. prodr. spl. programming ABC News, 1998—2000; exec.-in-charge Good Morning Am., 1999—; sr. v.p. primetime, early morning and news program devel. ABC News, 2000—. Office: PrimeTime Live 147 Columbus Ave Fl 3D New York NY 10023-5900

MCGRAIL, JEANE KATHRYN, artist; b. Mpls., May 1, 1947; d. Robert Vern and Mary Virginia (Kees) McGrail. BS, U. Wis.-River Falls, 1970; MFA, Cranbrook Acad. Art, 1972; postgrad., Sch. of Art Inst. of Chgo., 1985, Ill. Inst. Tech., 1993. Tchr. Inst. Contemporary Art. Group exhbn. include Saginaw Art Mus., Mich., 1972, Met. Mus. Art, Miami, Fla., 1974, Lowe Mus. Art, Coral Gables, Fla., 1974, 76, Miller Galleries, Coconut Grove, Fla., 1978, 80, Cicchinelli Gallery, NYC, 1980-82, Harper Coll., 1984, Contemporary Art Ctr. Arlington, Arlington Heights, Ill., 1984, 85, 86, 94, Evanston Art Ctr., 1985, South Shore Cultural Ctr., Chgo., 1990, N.A.M.E. Gallery, 1990, Artemisia Gallery, Chgo., 1991, 92, 93, 94, North Lakeside Art Ctr., Chgo., 1991, 94, 95, Ceres Gallery, NYC, 1992, Harper Coll., Ill., 1993, Environ. Concerns, Chgo., 1993, North Pk. Coll., Chgo., 1993, Franklin Square Gallery, Chgo., 1994, 95, 96, Space 900 Gallery, Chgo., 1994, 95, 96, 97, 98, 99, Chuck Levitan Gallery, NYC, 1995, Riverwest Art Ctr., Milw., 1995, Nat. Mus. Women in the Arts, Wash., 1996, Gallery 1040, 1997-, "Red", Chgo., 1998, Oakton Coll. Gallery, Ill., 1999-, Women's Works, Woodstock, Ill., 1999, "Paint It Siver", ARC Gallery, Chgo., 1999, Past/Present, Chgo., 1999, "Blue", Northeastern Ill. U.,Chgo., 2000, Then and Now, Chgo., 1999, Norris Cultural Ctr., St. Charles, Ill., 1999, others; represented in permanent collections at Chgo. Mus. Sci. and Industry, U. Chgo., Mus. Photography, Chgo., Miami-Dade Pub. Libr., U. Wis.-River Falls, MacGregor Found., Printmakers Workshop, NYC, Norman R. Eppnik Art Gallery Emporia State U., Kans., 2000, Mini Print Internat. Exhbn., Binghamton, NY, 2000, Yale U. Med. Libr., 2000, Columbia U. Med. Ctr., 2000, 06, Mini Print Internat. of Cadaques, Spain, Macy Gallery, Providence, RI, 2000, Brickton Gallery, Pk. Ridge, Fla., 2001, Mini Print Internat. of Cadaques, Spain, 2001—, Last of Primaries, Coll. of Lake Co., 2003-, Ukrainian Mus. Contemporary Art, Chgo., 2003, Chautauqua Nat. Exhbn., N.Y., 2004, others; solo exhbn. include Gallery at the Commons, Chgo., 1982, Truman Coll. Gallery, Chgo., 1991, C.G. Jung Inst., Evanston, Ill., 1992, Carlson Tower Gallery, Chgo., 1994, Olcott Ctr. Gallery, Theosophical Soc. Am., Wheaton, Ill., 2001; pub. "Mosaic", 1992, The Best of Printmaking, 1997; contbr. publ. to profl. jour. Cranbrook Acad. Art scholar, 1971; CAAP grantee Dept. Cultural Affairs City Chgo, 1992; recipient Poster Competition award Vizcaya Mus., 1974; Print award Auction WPBT, 1979, Tchr. Inst. Contemporary Art, Art Inst. Chgo., 2004. Mem. Coll. Art Assn., Chgo. Women's Caucus for Art (bd. dirs. 1992-95, sec.), Chgo. Artists Coalition. Independent. Studio: 1040 W Huron St LL5 Chicago IL 60622-6591 Office Phone: 312-882-8512. E-mail: whoswho@jeanemcgrail.com.

MCGRATH, ANNA FIELDS, retired librarian; b. Westfield, Maine, July 4, 1932; d. Fred Elber and Nancy Phyllis (Tarbell) Fields; m. Bernard McGrath (div.); children: Timothy, Maureen, Patricia, Colleen, Rebecca. BA, U. Maine, Presque Isle, 1976; MEd, U. So. Maine, 1979; MLS, U. R.I., 1982. Libr. U. Maine, Presque Isle, 1976-86, assoc. libr. dir., 1986-89, interim libr. dir., 1989-92, dir., 1992-94, spl. collection libr., 1994-97, ret., 1997. Editor: County: Land of Promise, 1989. Mem. Friends of Aroostook County Hist. Ctr. at Libr., U. Maine-Presque Isle; mem. Plymouth (Mass.) Spiritualist Ch. Mem. Inst. Noetic Scis., Am. Mensa. E-mail: amcgrath@maine.edu.

MCGRATH, BARBARA GATES, city manager; m. Pat McGrath; 1 child, Caitlin. BS summa cum laude, Ohio State U., 1976; JD magna cum laude, Capital U., 1979. Bar: Ohio 1979. Asst. city atty. Columbus (Ohio) City Atty.'s Office, 1979-85; dep. dir. Civil Svc. Commn. City of Columbus, 1985-90, exec. dir. Civil Svc. Commn., 1990—. Past chair bd. dirs. Lifescapes, Inc., A Place to Grow; grad. Columbus Area Leadership Program, 1989. Mem. Columbus Bar Assn. Office: City of Columbus Civil Svc Commn 50 W Gay St Fl 5 Columbus OH 43215-2821

MCGRATH, JUDY (JUDITH ANN MCGRATH), broadcast executive; b. Scranton, Pa., July 2, 1952; BA in English Lit., Cedar Crest Coll. Copy chief Glamour mag.; sr. writer Mademoiselle; copywriter Nat. Advt., Phila.; copywriter, on-air promotion Warner Amex Satellite Entertainment Corp. (predecessor to MTV), 1981; editl. dir. MTV, sr. v.p., creative dir., 1988—92, exec. v.p., creative dir., 1992—93, co-pres., creative dir., 1993—94, pres., 1994—96, MTV, MTV2, 1996—2000, pres. MTV Group, chmn. Interactive Music, 2000—02; pres. MTV Networks Music Group, 2002—04, chmn., CEO, 2004—. Hon. chair Cable Positive. Trustee emeritus Nat. Campaign to Prevent Teen Pregnancy; bd. dirs. Rock the Vote. Named Humanitarian of Yr., T.J. Martell Found. Leukemia, Cancer and AIDS Rsch., 2003; named one of 100 Most Powerful Women in Entertainment, Hollywood Reporter, 2004, 2005, Most Powerful Women in Bus., Fortune mag., 2005, 100 Most Powerful Women, Forbes Mag., 2006, 50 Most Powerful Women in Bus., Fortune mag., 2006; recipient Cable Ace Award, 1993, Founders award, Rock the Vote, 2001, Friend of the Children award, Harlem Children's Zone, 2001. Office: MTV 1515 Broadway Fl 28 New York NY 10036-8901

MCGRATH, KATHRYN BRADLEY, lawyer; b. Norfolk, Va., Sept. 2, 1944; d. James Pierce and Kathryn (Hoyle) Bradley; children: Ian M., James D. AB, Mt. Holyoke Coll., 1966; JD, Georgetown U., 1969. Ptnr. Gardner, Carton & Douglas, Washington, 1979-83; dir. div. investment mgmt. SEC, Washington, 1983-90; ptnr. Morgan Lewis, Washington, 1990—2002, Crowell & Moring, LLP, Washington, 2002—05, Mayer, Brown, Rowe & Maw LLP, Washington, 2005—. Named Disting. Exec., Pres. Reagan, 1987. Mem. Fed. Bar Assn. (exec. council securities law com.). Office: Mayer Brown Rowe & Maw LLP 1909 K St NW Washington DC 20006 Office Phone: 202-263-3374. Business E-Mail: kmcgrath@mayerbrownrowe.com.

MCGRATH, MARY HELENA, plastic surgeon, educator; b. NYC, Apr. 12, 1945; d. Vincent J. and Mary M. (Manning) McG.; children: Margaret E. Simon, Richard M. Simon. BA, Coll. New Rochelle, 1966; MD, St. Louis U., 1970; MPH, George Washington U., 1994. Diplomate Am. Bd. Surgery, Am. Bd. Plastic Surgery, lic. physician Calif. Resident in surg. pathology U. Colo. Med. Ctr., Denver, 1970-71, intern in gen. surgery, 1971-72, resident in gen. surgery, 1971-75, chief resident in gen. surgery, 1975-76; resident in plastic and reconstructive surgery Yale U. Sch. Medicine, New Haven, 1976-77, chief resident plastic and reconstructive surgery, 1977-78; fellow in hand surgery U. Conn.-Yale U., New Haven, 1978; instr. in surgery divsn. plastic and reconstructive surgery Yale U. Sch. Medicine, New Haven, 1977-78, asst. prof. plastic surgery, 1978-80; attending in plastic and reconstructive surgery Yale-New Haven Hosp., 1978-80, Columbia-Presbyn. Hosp., N.Y.C., 1980-84, George Washington U. Med. Ctr., Washington, 1984-2000, Children's Nat. Med. Ctr., Washington, 1985-2000, Loyola U. Med. Ctr., 2000—02, Hines VA Hosp., 2001—02, U. Calif., San Francisco, 2003—, San Francisco VA Ctr., 2003—, San Francisco Gen. Hosp., 2003—; asst. prof. plastic surgery Columbia U., N.Y.C., 1980-84; assoc. prof. plastic surgery Sch. Medicine, George Washington U., Washington, 1984-87, prof. plastic surgery, 1987-2000, Loyola U. Med. Ctr., 2000—02, U. Calif., San Francisco, 2003—. Bd. dirs. Am. Bd. Plastic Surgery, 1989-95, historian, 1991-95; examiner certifying exam., 1986—; mem. Residency Rev. Com. Plastic Surgery, 2006—; senator med. faculty senate George Washington U., bd. govs. Med. Faculty Assocs.; presenter, cons. in field. Co-editor: (with M.L. Turner) Dermatology for Plastic Surgeons, 1993; assoc. editor: The Jour. of Hand Surgery, 1984-89, Annals of Plastic Surgery, 1984-87, Plastic and Reconstructive Surgery, 1989-95, Contemporary Surgery, 1999-2006, Archives of Surgery, 2004—; advt. editor Plastic and Reconstructive Surgery, 2003—; guest reviewer numerous jours.; contbr. chpts. to books and articles to profl. jours Recipient numerous rsch. grants, 1978—. Fellow ACS (D.C. chpt. program ann. meeting chmn., 1992, pres. 1994-95, bd. govs. 1995-98, exec. com. 1996-97, chmn. adv. coun. plastic surgery 1995-98, regent 1997—, vice-chair bd. regents 2005-06)); mem. AAAS, Am. Surg. Assn., Am. Assn. Hand Surgery, Am. Assn. Plastic Surgeons (trustee 1997-00), Am. Burn Assn., Am. Soc. for Aesthetic Plastic Surgery, Am. Soc. Maxillofacial Surgeons, Am. Soc. Plastic and Reconstructive Surgery (chmn. ethics com. 1985-87, chmn. device/tech. evaluation com. 1993-94, chmn. workforce task force 1997-00, bd. dirs. 1994-96, chmn. endowment bd. dirs. 2000-04, trustee 2004—, ednl. found. bd. dirs. 1985-96, treas. 1989-92, v.p. 1992-93, pres.-elect 1993-94, pres. 1994-95), Am. Soc. Reconstructive Microsurgery (edn. com. 1992-94), Am. Soc. Surgery of Hand (chmn. 1987 ann. residents' and fellows conf. 1986-87, rsch. com. 1988-90), Assn. Acad. Chmn. Plastic Surgery (bd. dirs. 1999—), Assn. Acad. Surgery, Chgo. Soc. Plastic Surgeons (treas. 2001-02), Calif. Soc. Plastic Surgeons, San Francisco Surg. Soc., Chgo. Surg. Soc., Internat. Soc. Reconstructive Surgery, Met. D.C. Soc. Surgery Hand (pres. 1995-97), N.Y. Surg. Soc., Northeastern Soc. Plastic Surgeons (treas. 1993-96, pres. 1997-98), Pacific Coast Surg. Assn., Plastic Surgery Rsch. Coun. (chmn. 1990), Surg. Biology Club III, The Wound Healing Soc Office Phone: 415-353-4389. Business E-Mail: mcgrathm@surgery.ucsf.edu.

MCGRATTAN, MARY K., state legislator; b. NYC; married; 6 children. RN, St. Catherine's Hosp. Sch. of Nursing. RN NY, Conn.; cert. notary pub., justice of the peace. Mem. town coun. Town of Ledyard, Conn., 1977-83, mayor, 1983—91; pres. Conn. Conf. of Municipalities, 1990-91; mem. Conn. Ho. of Reps., Hartford, 1993—2002; cons. Ledyard Obesity Prevention Project, 2003; coord. Faith in Action Network, 2003—. Vol. Ledyard Fair, Our Lady of Lourdes Festival; event coord. Crop Walk for Hunger; chair Ledyard HEart Fund Charity Dr.; mem. Ledyard Dem. Town Com. Named Legislator of Yr., Conn. Nurses Assn.; recipient cert. of appreciation, C. of C., Breath of Life award, Am. Lung Assn., award of appreciation, Conn. Assn. Optometrists, Nightingale award for excellence in nursing, 2003; Paul Harris fellow, Rotary. Mem.: Avalonia Land Conservancy, Ledyard Libr. Friends, Ledyard Hist. Soc., Rotary. Avocations: reading, sewing, cooking. Address: 13 Lynn Dr Ledyard CT 06339-1312 Office Phone: 860-442-0733. E-mail: mary@community-partnerships.com.

MCGRAW, LAVINIA MORGAN, retired retail company executive; b. Detroit, Feb. 26, 1924; d. Will Curtis and Margaret Coulter (Oliphant) McG. AB, Radcliffe Coll., 1945. Mem. Phi Beta Kappa.

MCGRAW, PHYLLIS MAE, psychologist, geriatric specialist; b. Longview, Wash., May 14, 1930; d. Frans Aldevin and Ellen Ingeborg (Hermans) Laulainen; m. Arthur Melvin McGraw, Mar. 3, 1950; children: Stephen Whittier, Julie Anne Winslow, John Philip. BS in Clin. Psychology, Portland State U., 1978, MS in Clin. Psychology, 1980, postgrad., 1980; PhD in Clin. Psychology, Columbia Pacific U., 1988. Lic. marriage, family, child counselor, Calif. Pvt. practice, Portland, Oreg., 1980—; geriatric and mental health specialist Orange County Mental Health Agy., Santa Ana, Calif., 1985-86; geriatric specialist Adult Day Care Ctr. Eisenhower Med. Ctr., Rancho Mirage, Calif., 1986-87; dir. psychosocial svcs. chronic mentally ill Garten Found., Salem, Oreg., 1987-88; geriatric cons. long-term care ins. mktg. John

Hancock Mut. Life Ins. Co., Portland, 1988—. Sr. task force Eisenhower Med. Ctr., Rancho Mirage, 1986-87; chairperson 15th Annual Desert Conf. on Aging, Palm Springs, 1987; speaker 34th Annual Conf. Am. Soc. on Aging, San Diego, 1988, 35th Annual Conf., Washington, 1989, St. Vincent's Hosp., Portland, 1990; key note speaker Marion County Mental Health Salem Housing Forum, 1991; profl. vol. VIEWS (Vols. Interested in Emotional Well-Being of Srs.), Multnomah County, Portland; tualatin trainer sr. peer counseling program Meridian Pk. Hosp. Mem. State Calif. Anti-Stigma Campaign, Palm Springs, 1987; adv. coun. Riversied County Office Aging, sec, treas Riverside County Found. Aging; grandchildren task force Riverside County Grandparents; mental health co-chair Riverside County Regional Access Found, co-chair grant com. Educare scholar U. So. Calif. Sch. Edn., 1982. Mem. APA (assoc.), Am. Soc. on Aging, Oreg. Gerontol. Assn., Am. Assn. Ret. Persons, Oreg. Ret. Educators Assn. (pres. Unit 34 1990-91), Portland City Club (pres. 1990-91), Portland Life Underwriters, Hon. Women in Edn., Phi Delta Kappa. Lutheran. Avocations: painting, sewing, reading, family. Home: PO Box 1088 La Quinta CA 92247-1088 Office: Waddell & Reed Fin Svcs 45-150 Club Dr Indian Wells CA 92210

MCGRAW, SUSAN CATHERINE, interior designer; b. Long Beach, Calif., Apr. 16, 1945; d. Thomas Printis and Mary Ruth (Reese) Gregg; m. Don George McGraw, Nov. 21, 1964; children: DeAnna Coulombe, Katrina Daymude. Dental assistant diploma, Career Tng. Inst., 1964. Cert. interior designer, 1993. Ptnr., buyer The Corner, Garden Grove, Calif., 1971-79; interior designer Kris Noel & Assoc., Huntington Beach, Calif., 1980-85; owner, designer A.I. Designs, Huntington Beach, Calif., 1986-94; ptnr., designer Ross-McGraw Studio, Huntington Beach, Calif., 1994—, owner, designer, 1994—. Pres., ptnr. Red Tee Golf, Huntington Beach, 1998-2001. Bd. dirs. Parent Help USA, Huntington Beach, 1992; sec. Seacliff Home Owners Assn., Huntington Beach, 1992-93; v.p. ways and means Friends of Huntington Youth Guild, Huntington Beach, 1994-96, pres., 1996-98; v.p. ways and means com. Friends of Huntington Youth Shelter, 2003-2004. Mem. Am. Soc. Interior Design (profl. mem.). Office Phone: 714-840-1779. Business E-Mail: suemcgraw@socal.rr.com.

MCGREEVEY, LISA S., investment company executive; BA, So. Methodist U. Spl. asst. to Pres. for polit. & intergovernmental affairs The White House, Washington; sr. legis. mgr. US Dept. Treasury, Washington, 1988—92; with Conf. State Bank Supervisors, 1992—99; exec. v.p. for external affairs, pres. Govt. Affairs Coun. The Fin. Services Roundtable, Washington, 1999—2006; exec. v.p., COO Managed Funds Assn., Washington, 2006—. Named one of The Top 40 Lobbyists, The Hill, 2004, The Most Powerful Women in Washington, US Banker, 2005. Office: Managed Funds Assn 2025 M st NW Ste 800 Washington DC 20036*

MCGREEVY, MARY SHARRON, former psychology educator; b. Kansas City, Kans., Nov. 10, 1935; d. Donald and Emmy Lou (Neubert) McG.; m. Phillip Rosenbaum (dec.); children: David, Steve, Mariya, Chay, Allyn, Jacob, Dora. BA in English with honors, Vassar Coll., 1957; postgrad., New Sch. for Social Rsch., NYU, 1958-59, Columbia U., 1959-60, U. P.R., 1963-65, U. Mo., 1965-68, U. Kans.; PhD with distinction, U. Calif., Berkeley, 1969. Exec. Doubleday & Co., N.Y.C., 1957—60; chief libr. San Juan Sch., PR, 1962—63; NIMH drug rschr. Russell Sage Found., Clinico de los Addictos, Rio Piedras, PR, 1963—65; psychiat. rschr. U. PR Med. Sch., PR, 1963—65; psychiat. researcher U. Kans. Med. Ctr., Kansas City, 1966—68; rsch. assoc. Ednl. Rsch., 1965—69; from assoc. prof. to disting. prof. U. Calif., Berkeley, 1968—69, ret., 1969. Yacht owner Encore; lectr. in philosophy; founder Simone de Beauvoir Cir., Inc. Author: (poetry) To a Sailor, 1989, Dreams and Illusions, 1993, Wedding: A Celebration, 1998, The Red Hibiscus, 2000, Irish Poems, 2000, The Swan, 2001, Sea Poems, 2002, Memoir of Annette Van Howe, 2002; contbr. articles to profl. jours. Donor Naval Air Sta. Ft. Lauderdale Hist. Assn., 1994—, Fla. Atlantic U. Found., 1993—; founder, exec. dir. Dora Achenbach McGreevy Poetry and Philosophy Found., Inc., 1989—. Recipient Cert. for Svc. Broward County Hist. Commn., 1994, Nat. Women's History Project award, 1995; honored by Broward County Women's Hist. Coalition, 1996; Sproul fellow, Bancroft Libr. fellow, Russell Sage Found. fellow; postdoctoral grant U. Calif. Mem.: AAUW (corr. sec. 1991—95, bd. dirs. 1991—2001, Jeanne Faiks meml. scholarship fund com. 1992—98, Nat. Ednl. Found. book brunch com. 1994—98, chair cultural events 1995—, chair 1998, rec. sec. 1998—2002, book brunch com. 2000—01, photographer, honoree Ednl. Found. Fund 1993, cert. appreciation 2000), Fla. Philosophy Assn. (spkr. 1991, 1993, chair self in philosophy 1994), Vassar Alumni Assn. Democrat. Roman Catholic. Achievements include first to use methodone treatment and rehabilitation at drug clinic in Puerto Rico. Avocations: poetry, painting, sailing, tennis, the beach. Home: 700 Antioch Ave 14 Fort Lauderdale FL 33304

MCGREGOR, JACQUELINE CARINHAS, psychiatrist; b. San Antonio, Tex., May 25, 1962; d. Joseph Gomes and Mary Jeanne (Haggard) Carinhas; m. Jon Brant McGregor, June 15, 1991; children: Hollis Elizabeth, Lachlan Gray. BBA, U. Tex., Austin, 1984; MD, U. Tex. Med. Br., Galveston, 1993. CPA Tex., 1987; diplomate Am. Bd. of Psychiatry and Neurology, 2002, Am. Bd. of Psychiatry and Neurology, 2003. Adult psychiatry resident Baylor Coll. Medicine, Houston, 1997—2000; child and adolescent psychiatry fellow U. Tex., Houston, 2000—02, chief resident, 2001—02; dir. child and adolescent psychiatry clinic Baylor Coll. Medicine, 2002—05; pvt. practice Houston, 2005—. Clin. faculty Baylor Coll. of Medicine, Houston, 2005—. Legislative aide Tex. State Ho. of Representatives, Austin, 1985. Recipient Laughlin Found. Disting. fellow, Laughlin Found., 2000. Mem.: Tex. Soc. of Psychiat. Physicians, Am. Psychoanalytic Assn. (treas., affiliate coun. 2005—), Am. Assn. of Child and Adolescent Psychiatry, Am. Psychiat. Assn. Office: 3642 University Blvd Ste 200 Houston TX 77005 Office Phone: 713-667-3887.

MCGREGOR, RUTH VAN ROEKEL, state supreme court justice; b. Le Mars, Iowa, Apr. 4, 1943; d. Bernard and Marie Frances (Janssen) Van Roekel; m. Robert James McGregor, Aug. 15, 1965. BA summa cum laude, U. Iowa, 1964, MA, 1965; JD summa cum laude, Ariz. State U., 1974; LLM, U. Va., 1998. Bar: Ariz. 1974, U.S. Dist. Ct. Ariz. 1974, U.S. Ct. Appeals (9th cir.), U.S. Supreme Ct. 1982. Assoc. Fennemore, Craig, von Ammon, Udall & Powers, Phoenix, 1974-79, ptnr., 1980-81, 82-89; law clk. to justice Sandra Day O'Connor U.S. Supreme Ct., Washington, 1981-82; judge Ariz. Ct. Appeals, 1989-98, vice chief judge, 1993-95, chief judge, 1995-98; justice Ariz. Supreme Ct., 1998—, vice chief justice, 2002—05, chief justice, 2005—. Mem. disciplinary commn. Ariz. Supreme Ct., 1984-89, City of Mesa jud. adv. bd., 1997. Mem., newsletter editor Charter 100, Phoenix, 1981—; bd. dirs., mem. Ctr. for Law in Pub. Interest, Phoenix, 1977-80. Named Dwight D. Operman award for Top Judge in the Nation, Am. Judicature Soc., 2005. Mem. ABA (chmn. state memberships 1985-89; named fellow), Ariz. Bar Assn. (disciplinary com. 1984-89), Ariz. Judges Assn. (exec. com. 1990-98, sec. 1991-92, v.p. 1992-93, pres. 1993-94), Nat. Assn. Women Judges (chair first time attendees com. 1990-91, 1994 conv. com.; exec. com. 1995—), Ariz. Woman Lawyers Assn., 1975-. Democrat. Lutheran. Office: Ariz Supreme Ct 1501 W Washington St Phoenix AZ 85007-3231*

MCGREGOR, WENDOLYN SUZANNE, elementary school educator, mathematician; b. The Dalles, Oreg., Aug. 25, 1964; d. Delbert Eugene and Mary Ann Trowbridge; m. Brian Lee McGregor, Sept. 10, 1983 (dec. Apr. 28, 2003); children: Stephanie Nicole, Nathan Jeffrey. AA in Edn., Coll. So. Idaho, 1998, AA in History, 1999; BA in History, Idaho State U., 1999, BS in Elem. Edn., 2001, BS in Secondary Edn., 2006. Cert. elem. and secondary tchr. Idaho, 2000. Computer operator Coll. So. Idaho, Twin Falls, Idaho, 1987—88; payroll clk. Amalgamated Sugar, Twin Falls, 1989—90; 5th grade tchr. Kimberly (Idaho) Sch. Dist., 2000—03; 4th grade tchr. Twin Falls (Idaho) Sch. Dist., 2003—. Bookkeeper Garnard Mktg., Twin Falls, 1987—89; tutor Coll. So. Idaho, 1997—99; mem. math. curriculum com. Kimberly (Idaho) Sch. Dist., 2000—03, mem. tech. com., 2000—03. Asst. leader Girl Scouts Am., Filer, 1992—94; leader Cloverlands 4-H, Filer, 1991—92; bible club dir. Filer (Idaho) First Bapt. Ch., 1991—96; children's leader Bible Study Fellowship, Twin Falls, 1993—96. Scholar Zobell-Albion scholar, Idaho State U., 1999. Mem.: Golden Key Nat. Honor Soc. (Peat Marwick scholar 1999), Nat. Job Corp. Alumni Assn. (Outstanding Student scholar 1999), Phi Theta Kappa. Avocations: reading, time with family, computers, astronomy, college classes. Office: Bickel Elem 607 2nd Ave E Twin Falls ID 83301 Business E-Mail: mcgrwend@isu.edu.

MCGRORY, MARY KATHLEEN, humanities educator, retired academic administrator; b. NYC, Mar. 22, 1933; d. Patrick Joseph and Mary Kate (Gilvary) McG. BA, Pace U., 1957; MA, U. Notre Dame, 1962; PhD, Columbia U., 1969; DHL, Albertus Magnus Coll., 1984; LLD, Briarwood Coll., 1990; DHL, Trinity Coll., 1991. Prof. English Western Conn. State U., Danbury, 1969-78; dean arts and scis. Ea. Conn. State U., Willimantic, 1978-80, v.p. for acad. affairs, 1981-85; pres. Hartford (Conn.) Coll. for Women, 1985-91; sr. fellow U. Va. Commonwealth Ctr., Charlottesville, 1991-92; exec. dir. Soc. Values in Higher Edn./Georgetown U., Washington, 1992-96; chair dept. rhetoric, lang. and culture U. Hartford, dir. profl. and tech. writing, humanies and writing educator, 1999—, adj. faculty dept. rhetoric, lang., culture, 1999—. Pres. MKM Assocs., Holland, Mass., 1983—. Author: Yeats, Joyce & Beckett, 1975. Bd. dirs. Hartford Hosp., 1985-93; chmn. bd. govs. Greater Hartford Consortium Higher Edn., 1989-90. Fels Found. fellow, 1966-67, NEH summer fellow, 1975; Ludwig Vogelstein Found. travel grantee, 1973. Mem. New Eng. Jr. Community and Tech. Coll. Coun. (v.p. 1988-91), Am. Assn. Higher Edn., Med. Acad. of Am., Greater Hartford C. of C. (bd. dirs. 1989-91), Hartford Club (bd. dirs. 1988-91). Avocations: writing, swimming, piano. Address: 44 Forest Dr Holland MA 01521-9702 Office: U Hartford 2000 Bloomfield Ave West Hartford CT 06117 Office Phone: 860-768-4415.

MCGRUDER, TECIA ADRIENNE, assistant principal; b. LaGrange, Ga., Nov. 20, 1967; d. Ruben McGruder and McGruder Avery Janice; m. Arthur Kennard McKay. BS in Edn., Ft. Valley State Coll., 1990; MEd, Ga. State U., 1997, EdD, 2002. Tchr., Alaska, 1993—94, Ga., 1990—2000; instrnl. support specialist Ga. Dept. Edn., Atlanta, 2000—04; asst. prin. Johnson County Schs., Wrightsville, Ga., 2004—. Cons., workshop presenter Nat. Ctr. Edn., The Economy, LA, 2004. Southeastern region undergraduate coord. Zeta Phi Beta Sorority, Inc., Washington, 2005—06, Ga. undergraduate coord., 2003—05; pres. Zeta Phi Beta Sorority, Inc. Kappa Iota Zeta Chpt., Atlanta, 2004—06. Recipient Metro Atlanta Hall Fame, Zeta Phi Beta Sorority, Inc. Kappa Iota Zeta Chpt., 2000. Mem.: Pilot Internat., Zeta Phi Beta Sorority, Inc. Home: 402 Westchester Dr Dublin GA 31021 Personal E-mail: zetat11@aol.com.

MCGUAN, KATHLEEN H., lawyer; b. May 9, 1954; BA, Am. U., 1975; MA in hist. musicology, U. Pa., 1978; JD, Cath. U., 1981. Bar: DC. Joined Reed Smith LLP, Washington, 1991, ptnr., 1994—. Office: Reed Smith LLP 1301 K St NW, Ste 1100 - East Tower Washington DC 20005 Office Phone: 202-414-9230. Office Fax: 202-414-9299. Business E-Mail: kmcguan@reedsmith.com.

MCGUE, ROCHELLE LEE, music educator, rental manager; b. Cleve., Oct. 7, 1965; d. Leo Charles and Gloria Helen Boes; m. Larry E. McGue, Nov. 26, 2004; children: Stacia, Thomas, Emily, Kristin, Jacob. BE, Bowling Green State U., 1988, MEd, 2004; M in curriculum and tchg., Bowling Green U., 2004. Tchr. Norwalk City Schools, Ohio, 1988—89, Western Res. Schools, Collins, Ohio, 1999—. Band dir. Western Res. Schools, Collins, Ohio, 1999—, jr. class adv., 1999—. Spl. events coord. park and recreation City of Norwalk, Ohio, 1980—. Mem.: Ohio Edn. Assn., Ohio Music Educators Assn. Protestant. Avocations: softball, volleyball, music performances. Home: 587 Townline Rd #151 Norwalk OH 44857 Office Phone: 419-668-8470. E-mail: smcgue@mo.rr.com.

MCGUINNESS, NANETTE MICHELE COOPER, singer, voice educator, writer, translator; b. Boston, Mar. 14, 1959; d. Alan Bruce Cooper and Corinne Faith Whitaker; m. David Patrick McGuinness, Apr. 4, 1957; 1 child, Nicholas Matthew Cooper. AB, Cornell U., 1980; MA, U. Calif., Berkeley, 1982; MM, Holy Names Coll., 1987; PhD, U. Calif., Berkeley, 1990; student, Ctr. Internat.de Formation Musicale, France. Opera and classical singer various, including Athena Trio, Berkeley, 1989—; voice tchr. McGuinness Voice Studio, 1986—; writer and freelance translator Athena Translations & Writing, 2001—. Opera in the schs. performer Opera San Jose, 1990—92; artistic adv. bd. mem. Livermore Valley Opera, Calif., 1991—93; student corr. Current Musicology, 1985—86; east bay/north bay critique group coord. Soc. of Children's Book Writers and Illustrators of No. CA, Berkeley, 2003—. Singer: (cd) Music by William Ludtke: Li Bai Songs; singer: (writer and translator for liner notes) Fabulous Femmes (music by 19th and 20th century women composers), with the Athena Trio; contbr. book; translator: (book) Humanizing Development; singer: (performance) Gianni Schicchi (West Bay Opera), (role of Nella), (role of Despina) Cosi fan Tutte (Livermore Valley Opera), (performance) Festival Musica delle Donne, La Boheme: role of Mimi (Silesian State Opera, Czech Republic), La Boheme: role of Musetta (Societa dei Concerti, Santa Margherita Ligure, Italy), Gianni Schicchi/ Le Villi: roles of Lauretta and Anna (Pacific Repertory Opera), Christmas Suite (San Jose Symphony, Joanne Falletta Conducting), Messiah (Solano Choral Society), soprano soloist, Christmas Oratorio (Saint Saens), soprano soloist (Monterey Peninsula Choral Society), Gaia Sophia: role of Gaia (opera by William Ludtke), numerous other performances. Reader, recorder of books for children Cath. Charities of the East Bay, 1998—2002; vol. East Bay 4 Kerry, Oakland, Calif., 2004—04; bd. mem., several functions Translators 4 Kids, 2005—05; translator Eurotexte/ Medecins sans Frontieres, Paris, 2001—05; co-chair, caring comm, vol. Bentley H.S., Lafayette, 2003—05; Alameda County chair, other vol. functions Cornell U. Alumni Assn., Berkeley, 1980—2005; host family Cultural Homestay Internat., 1997—2005; vol. KQED, San Francisco, 2001—03, Prospect Sierra Sch., El Cerrito, Calif., 1994—2003. Recipient First Prize, Martinez Opera Competition, 1990, First prize, Santa Clara Art Song Festival, 1991, Hon. Mention, Haiku Competition, Byline Mag., 2002, 2005; scholar Mary Gibbs Jones scholar, Mary Gibbs Jones Scholarship Fund, 1976-80; Chancellor's Patent Fund grant, U. of Calif. at Berkeley, 1985-6, Hertz fellow, 1982, Cross Meml. fellow, U. of Calif., 1980-1. Mem.: Proz, Chamber Music Am., Opera Am., Soc. of Children's Book Writers and Illustrators, Calif. Writers' Club, Am. Translators Assn. (assoc.), Mensa, Cornell Club of No. Calif., U. of Calif. Alumni Assn. (life). Avocations: hiking, skiing, travel, computers, card games, board games. Personal E-mail: nmc22@cornell.edu. E-mail: nanette22@gmail.com.

MCGUIRE, ANDREA BULLARD, social studies educator; b. High Point, N.C., Sept. 17, 1965; d. Gary Wayne and Georgette Dowd Bullard; children: Christina, Andrew Jernigan. BS summa cum laude, Wingate Coll., N.C., 1986; MA in Tchg., We. Governors U., Salt Lake City, 2005. Cert. early adolescent social studies, history Nat. Bd. Profl. Tchg. Stds., 1999. Tchr. Guilford County Sch., Greensboro, NC, 1987—2002; leadership team chair N.W. Mid. Sch., Greensboro, 2000—02; tchr. Winston-Salem/Forsyth County Sch., Kernersville, NC, 2002—; social studies dept. chair S.E. Mid. Sch., Kernersville, 1998—. Coach N.C. History Bowl, Sedalia, 1996—. H.s. youth coun. Abbotts Creek Missionary Bapt. Ch., High Point, NC, 2005—. Recipient H.K. Helms award, Wingate Coll., 1986; grantee, Kay Chem., 2003; Bright Ideas grant, Energy United, 2005. Mem.: N.C. Coun. for Social Studies. Baptist. Avocations: reading, travel. Office: Southeast Mid Sch 1200 Old Salem Rd Kernersville NC 27284 Office Phone: 336-996-5848. Office Fax: 336-996-0148. Personal E-mail: abmcguire@wsfcs.k12.nc.us.

MCGUIRE, ANNE C., theology studies educator; b. Wisner, Nebr., June 8, 1951; d. Richard Joseph and Margaret Elizabeth McGuire; 1 child, Katherine Elizabeth Shiqi. M Liturgical Studies, St. John's U., Collegeville, Minn., 1981; PhD in Theology, U. Notre Dame, South Bend, Ind., 1994. Liturgist, music dir. St. Olaf Parish, Eau Claire, Wis., 1978—84, Newman Ctr., U. Minn., Mpls., 1984—90, Visitation Parish, Kansas City, Mo., 1996—98; music dir. St. Charles Parish, Chippewa Falls, Wis., 1994—96; asst. prof. theology Loras Coll., Dubuque, Iowa, 1998—2004; assoc. prof. theology St. Gregory's U., Shawnee, Okla., 2004—. Cons., trainer St. Benedict Parish, Shawnee, 2004—06; treas. bd. dirs. Okla. Alliance for Liturgy and the Arts, Oklahoma City, 2005—06. Mem.: Cath. Acad. of Liturgy (assoc.), Societas Liturgica (assoc.), North Am. Acad. Liturgy (assoc.). Roman Catholic. Avocations: singing, piano, travel, reading. Home: 824 N Beard Shawnee OK 74801 Office: St Gregory's U 1900 West MacArthur Shawnee OK 74804 Office Phone: 405-878-5229. Business E-Mail: acmcguire@stgregorys.edu.

MCGUIRE, KATHLEEN ALISON, conductor; b. Melbourne, Australia, May 22, 1965; d. Frank Leonard McGuire and Jeanette Mary Tilson; life ptnr. Stephanie Lynne Smith. MusB, U. Melbourne, 1987; grad. diploma arts in music, Victorian Coll. Arts, U. Melbourne, 1990; grad. diploma in edn., Monash U., Melbourne, 1992; MusM with Distinction, U. Surrey, Guildford, UK, 1995; Dr. in Mus. Arts, U. Colo., 2000. Cert. preparing future faculty U. of Colo. at Boulder, 2000, grad. tchr. cert. U. Colo., Boulder, 2000. Music educator Sacre Coeur Girls' Sch., Melbourne, Victoria, Australia, 1983—86; educator Our Lady of Mercy Coll., 1986; music dir. Mentone Old Time Theatre Soc., Melbourne, Victoria, Australia, 1985—88; educator Killester Coll., Melbourne, Victoria, Australia, 1987; music educator Sacred Heart Regional Girls' Coll., Melbourne, Victoria, Australia, 1988; educator Mentone Girls' Secondary Coll., Melbourne, Victoria, Australia, 1988—89; music tchr. McKinnon Secondary Coll., Melbourne, Victoria, Australia, 1988—90, Mentone Girls' Grammar Sch., Melbourne, Victoria, Australia, 1990—94; dir. of music Sandringham East Primary Sch., Melbourne, Victoria, Australia, 1988—89; condr. Musical Theatre Soc., U. Surrey, Guildford, Sussex, England, 1994—95; asst. condr. Symphony Orch., U. Surrey, Guildford, Sussex, England, 1994—95; condr. Wind Symphony, U. of Surrey, Guildford, Sussex, 1994—95; educator Parkdale Secondary Coll., Melbourne, Victoria, Australia, 1995; music dir. St. Aidan's Episcopal Ch., Boulder, Colo., 1996—2000; asst. condr. U. of Colo. at Boulder Symphony Orch., Boulder, Colo., 1996—2000; assoc. condr. Lakewood Symphony Orch., Denver, 1996—2000; artistic dir./condr. The Rainbow Chorus, Fort Collins, Colo., 1997—2000; asst. condr. Lyric Theatre, U. Colo., Boulder, Colo., 1997—2000; assoc. condr. New Music Ensemble, U. of Colo., Boulder, Colo., 1998—2000; lead grad. tchr. U. of Colo. at Boulder, 1999—2000; assoc. condr. Boulder Youth Symphony, Boulder, Colo., 1999—2000; artistic dir., condr. San Francisco Gay Men's Chorus, 2000—; condr. Opera By the Bay, Marin, Calif., 2001, Cmty. Women's Orch., San Francisco, 2005—; music tchr. Convent of the Sacred Heart H.S., San Francisco, 2004—; music dir. Melbourne U. Choral Soc., Melbourne, Victoria, Australia, Mordialloc Light Opera Co., Melbourne, Victoria, Australia, Nova Theatre, Melbourne, Victoria, Australia, Whitehorse Mus. Theatre, Melbourne, Victoria, Australia; condr., founder Victorian Women's Orch., Melbourne, Victoria, Australia; condr. Kew Philharm. Orch., Melbourne, Victoria, Australia, Steamboat Springs Cmty. Orch.; music dir. Festival Theatre Co., Melbourne, Victoria, Australia, Renaissance Opera Co., Melbourne, Victoria, Australia, Viola Operatic Soc., Melbourne, Victoria, Australia, Melbourne Opera Co., Melbourne, Victoria, Australia, Melbourne Dancers Co., Melbourne, Victoria, Australia, CLOC Musical Theatre, Melbourne, Victoria, Australia, Gilbert and Sullivan Soc., Melbourne, Victoria, Australia, Melbourne U. Gilbert and Sullivan Soc., Melbourne, Victoria, Australia; asst. condr. St. Aidan's Anglican Ch., Melbourne, Victoria, Australia; music dir. Altona City Theatre, Melbourne, Victoria, Australia, Lyric Opera, Melbourne, Victoria, Australia. Instrumentalist Marie Wilson Band, Melbourne, Victoria, Australia, 1992—94; guest condr. for lighting Guildford Philharm., Guildford, Surrey, England, 1995; guest condr. Rocky Mountain Ctr. Mus. Arts, Boulder, Colo., 1996, Boulder Philharm., Boulder, 1996; condr. & founder Colo. Quilt Chorus, Denver, 1997; guest condr. Golden Gate Opera, San Francisco, 2001, Women's Philharm., San Francisco, 2001—02, Sacramento Ballet & Empyrean Ensemble, Sacramento, 2002, Gay Games & Cultural Festival, Sydney, New South Wales, Australia, 2002, Goat Hill Prodns., San Francisco, 2002, Cmty. Women's Orch., San Francisco, 2005, Victorian Music Theatre Guild Awards, Melbourne, Victoria, Australia, Royal Women's Hosp. Fundraiser, Melbourne, Fairfield Hosp. Fundraiser, Melbourne, Ann. AIDS Requiem Svcs., Melbourne; asst. condr. Byrd-Cage Singers, Melbourne; cantor Toorak Uniting Ch. Choir, Melbourne; condr. Malvern City Coun. - ann. fundraiser, Melbourne; instrumentalist Frankston City Band, Melbourne, Mordialloc City Band, Melbourne, Moomba Youth Band, Melbourne, Victoria, Australia; asst. condr. Intervarsity Choral Festival, Melbourne; instrumentalist Yamaha Youth Music Festival, Melbourne. Arranger (choral music concert suite) SFGMC Does Queen, (choral music) We Shall Overcome, Turn the World Around by Harry Belafonte, Every Time I Feel the Spirit, Harriet Tubman, Silent Night, Land of the Free, Peace Like a River; editor: (choral music) (by Gareth Valentine) Requiem in Memory of Those Who Have Died of AIDS; contbr. article to profl. jour., CD insert, ednl. pubs., electronic newsletter; prodr.: (comml. compact disc recording) Home for the Holidays (winner, OutMusic award, Outstanding New Choral Recording, 2006), Oh, Happy Day! (finalist OutMusic awards, Outstanding New Recording, choir or chorus, 2005), Closer Than Ever (winner, OutMusic Awards, Outstanding New Recording, choir or chorus, 2005); prodr.: (comml. compact disc recording) Divas' Revenge; prodr.(and arranger): (comml. compact disc recording) SFGMC Does Queen (finalist, Outstanding new choral rec., OutMusic awards, 2002); contbr. comml. compact disc recording (Wash. Area Music award and finalist, Outstanding New Rec., OutMusic awards, 2001); composer: (choral music) Magnificat, On Love, May God Shield You, Don't Ask, Don't Tell; music dir. (comml. compact disc recordings) Beginnings, Five Years for Freedom, St. Aidan's Prayer for Lindisfarne. Mem. Bay Area Cmty. Women, San Francisco; grand marshal San Francisco Pride, 2006; musician City of Refuge United Ch. Christ, San Francisco, 2004—; bd. mem. Gay and Lesbian Assn. Choruses, Washington, 2002—03; ex-officio bd. mem. Golden Gate Performing Arts, Inc., San Francisco, 2000—. Fellow Enrollment Enhancement fellowship, U. of Colo., Coll. of Music, 1996 - 1997; Ambassadorial fellow, Rotary Internat., 1994 - 1995, Writing fellow, Choral Jour., Florence Bradford scholar, U. Melbourne, 1991, Ivy-May Pendlebury scholar, 1985. Mem.: ASCAP, Coll. Music Soc., Am. Choral Dirs. Assn., Gay and Lesbian Assn. Choruses, Inc., Am. Symphony Orch. League, Conductors Guild, Vancouver Men's Chorus, Lesbian/Gay Chorus of San Francisco, Seattle Men's Chorus, San Diego Men's Chorus, Atlanta Gay Men's Chorus, Buffalo Gay Men's Chorus, Coun. Oaks Men's Chorale, Houston Gay Men's Chorus, Oakland East Bay Gay Men's Chorus, Rochester Gay Men's Chorus, Philadelphia Gay Men's Chorus, Triad Men's Chorus, Twin Cities Gay Men's Chorus, Pi Kappa Lambda. Achievements include first appointed woman conductor and artistic director of the world's oldest and largest openly gay men's chorus (founded 1978); along with life partner, was one of the same-sex couples married at San Francisco City Hall, February 23, 2004; conducted the Australian premiere of the rock opera, Metropolis; conducted the U.S. and Australian premieres of the world's first AIDS Requiem (by Gareth Valentine - composed in 1991); conducted the Australian premiere of The Apple Tree by Jerry Bock; arranged for men's chorus and conducted John Rutter's renowned Gloria in honor of the work's 30th anniversary (December, 2004); founder of Australia's first women's orchestra; conducted performances at Carnegie Hall (NY), Kennedy Center (DC), Davies Symphony Hall (San Francisco), Salle Wilfrid Pelletier (Montreal, Canada), Grace Cathedral (San Francisco); conducted the Sacramento Ballet and the Empyrean Ensemble at the inaugural season of the Mondavi Center, Sacramento, CA; conducted a choir of 560 voices at the Sydney Opera House (Australia) for Gay Games VI (November, 2002); opening ceremonies Chgo. Gay Games VII (July 2006); performed with many celebrities, including: Carol Channing, Sir Ian McKellen, Alan Cumming, Joanna Gleason, Sharon Gless, B.D. Wong, Armistead Maupin, Nichelle Nichols, Julie Newmar, Cris Williamson; arranged music that has been performed by premier artists, including: Turtle Creek Chorale, Pot Pourri, Les Ms, Boston Gay Men's Chorus, Men Alive, Metropolitan Community Church Choir of San Francisco; arranged music performed by artists including: San Diego Men's Chorus, Atlanta Gay Men's Chorus, Buffalo Gay Men's Chorus, Seattle Men's Chorus, Houston Gay Men's Chorus, Twin Cities Gay Men's Chorus; arranged music performed by artists including: Lesbian/Gay Chorus San Francisco, Oakland Eastbay Gay Men's Chorus, Phila. Gay Men's Chorus, Rochester Gay Men's Chorus, Vancouver Men's Chorus; conducted a choir of 80 at Rosie O'Donnell's wedding at San Francisco City Hall, February 2004; completed AIDS Life Cycle V 585 mile bicycle ride from San Francisco to Los Angeles June 2006. Avocations: travel, culinary arts, outdoor sports, crossword puzzles. Office: Golden Gate Performing Arts Inc 1800 Market St PMB 1000 San Francisco CA 94102 Office Phone: 415-865-3650. Office Fax: 415-865-3655.

MCGUIRE, LESIL L., state representative; b. Portland, Oreg., Jan. 22, 1971; Degree in Speech Comm. and Polit. Sci., Willamette U., 1993, JD, 1998. Legis. and press aide U.S. Senator Ted Stevens, 1993—95; legal intern U.S. Atty., 1996; law clk. Oreg. Dept. Justice, 1996—98; mem. Alaska Ho. of Reps., 2000—, judiciary com. Vol. Habitat for Humanity; mentor Bush Elem. Sch. Mentor Program; vol. Salem's Women's Crisis Ctr. Mem.: Young Rep., Anchorage Rep. Women's Club, Am. Diabetes Assn. Republican. Avocations: fishing, skiing, flying, scuba diving, reading. Office: Rm 118 State Capitol Juneau AK 99801-1182 Address: 716 W 4th Ave Ste 430 Anchorage AK 99501-2133 Office Phone: 907-269-0250. E-mail: lesilmcguire@yahoo.com.

MCGUIRE, LILLIAN HILL (LILLIAN ELIZABETH HILL MCGUIRE), historian, researcher, retired education educator, writer; b. Middlesex County, Va., 1928; d. Howard Garfield Hill, Sr. and Malissie O'Neal (Carter) Hill; m. Charles Edward McGuire, Aug. 11, 1957 (dec. July 30, 1997); children: Brenda Colette, Gina Renae, Laura Jane Fortune Battle. Student, Hampton Inst., 1946—48; BS, Morgan State U., 1951. Primary and Secondary Tchg. Cert. Va. Dept. of Edn. Classroom tchr. Richmond County Sch. Sys., Warsaw, Va., 1951—65, Essex County Sch. Sys., Tappahannock, Va., 1965—88; adult edn. tchr. Rappahannock C.C., Warsaw, Va., 1989—94; adult edn. tchr. Essex County Sch. Sys., Tappahannock, 1989—94. Pres. Essex Edn. Assn., Tappahannock, 1982—86, editor-news letter, 1982—88; historian Va. Ret. Tchrs. Assn., Blacksburg, 1995—97. Author: (book) The Vista of a Century: History of the Southside Rappahannock Baptist Association and Allied Bodies, 1977, Our Spiritual Heritage: History of First Baptist Church Tappahannock, VA, 1993, Uprooted & Transplanted: From Africa to America; Focus on African Americans in Essex County, VA, 2000, In Retrospect, 2005; contbr. poetry to Twilight Musings, chapters to books. Charter mem. Mid. Peninsula African-Am. Geneaol. and Hist. Soc. Va., 2005—. Essex County Mus., Tappahannock, 1996—2006, mem. bd. dir., 1996—2006; mem. adv. coun. Essex County Mus. Hist. Soc., Tappahannock, 2006—; mem. NAACP Essex County Br., Tappahannock, 1950. Named Outstanding Elem. Sch. Tchr. of Am., Bd. of Advisors, Washington, 1974; recipient Honor award, Essex Edn. Assn., Tappahannock, 1977, Disting. Svc. award, 1982. Mem.: Internat. Soc. Poets, Mid. Peninsula Geneal. and Hist. Soc. Va. (charter mem.), Rappahannock Indsl. Acad. Alumni Assn. (historian 1975), Morgan State U. Nat. Alumni Assn., Dist. A of Va. Ret. Tchrs. (life; historian 1988). Baptist. Avocations: writing, puzzles, travel, exercise. Home: 445 Marsh St PO Box 143 Tappahannock VA 22560

MCGUIRE, MARY PATRICIA, political science professor; b. Syracuse, NY, Jan. 19, 1958; d. Donald A. and Cecilia F. McGuire; 1 child, Leah. BA, Syracuse U., 1980, MPA, 1993, PhD, 2000. Assoc. Lazard Freres and Co., N.Y.C., 1985—89; asst. v.p. Scudder Stevenson and Clock, N.Y.C., 1989—91; faculty Hobart and William Smith Coll., Geneva, NY, 1999—2001; political sci. educator SUNY, Cortland, 2001—. Cons. Cortland County Legislature, 2005—06, Cayuga County, Auburn, NY, 2005. Co-author (with Jeffery M. Stone): The Emergence of State Government, 2003. Mem.: Midwest Polit. Sci. Assn., Am. Polit. Sci. Assn. Office: SUNY PO Box 2000 Cortland NY 13045 Business E-Mail: mcguirem@cortland.edu.

MCGUIRE, MAUREEN A., artist; b. Flushing, N.Y., July 13, 1941; d. Leo T. and Cecilia A. (Danz) McGuire. BFA, Alfred U., 1963; MA, Pope Pius XII Inst., Florence, Italy, 1964. Apprentice designer, crafts Glassart Studio, Scottsdale, Ariz., 1964—68; ind. designer Phoenix, 1968—. Liturgical designer Papal Mass during Pope John Paul II U.S. Tour, Phoenix, 1987. Recipient Outstanding Alumni citation, Alfred U., 1983. Mem.: Interfaith Forum on Religious Art and Architecture (regional dir. 1983—84, bd. dirs. 1987, Stained Glass award 1979, Outstanding Leadership award 1983, Citation award 1986, Merit awards 1987). Republican. Roman Catholic. Home and Office: 924 E Bethany Home Rd Phoenix AZ 85014-2147

MCGUIRE, PAMELA COTTAM, lawyer; b. Aug. 25, 1947; d. Robert D. and Marion E. (Swift) Cottam; m. Eugene G. McGuire, Sept. 14, 1969; children: Lauren Lambert, Christopher Cottam. BA, Vassar Coll., 1969; MS in urban planning, Columbia U., 1973, JD, 1973. Bar: NY 1974, US Dist. Ct. Ea. Dist. NY 1974, US. Dist. Ct. So. Dist. NY 1974, US Ct. Appeals 2nd Cir. 1974. Law clk to presiding judge US Dist. Ct. Ea. Dist. NY, Bklyn., 1973—74; asst. US atty. US Atty.'s Office, Bklyn., 1974—75; staff counsel Moreland Commn., NYC, 1975—76; assoc. Hughes, Hubbard & Reed, NYC, 1976—77; joined PepsiCo. Inc., Purchase, NY, 1977, v.p., divsn. counsel, 1989—98, v.p., assoc. gen. counsel, 1998; sr. v.p., dep. gen. counsel PepsiCo Inc., 2006—; sr. v.p., gen. counsel, sec. The Pepsi Bottling Group Inc., Somers, 1998—2006. Fellow, Woodrow Wilson Found., 1973. Office: The Pepsi Bottling Group Inc 1 Pepsi Way Somers NY 10589

MCGUIRE, SANDRA LYNN, nursing educator; b. Jan. 28, 1947; d. Donald Armstrong and Mary Lue (Harvey) Johnson; m. Joseph L. McGuire, Mar. 6, 1976; children: Matthew, Kelly, Kerry. BSN, U. Mich., 1969, MPH, 1973, EdD, 1988, MSN, 1997. Staff nurse Univ. Hosp., Ann Arbor, Mich., 1969; pub. health nurse Wayne County Health Dept., Eloise, Mich., 1969—72; instr. Madonna Coll., Livonia, Mich., 1973; pub. health coord. Plymouth Ctr. for Human devel., Northville, Mich., 1974—75; asst. prof. cmty. health nursing U. Mich., Ann Arbor, 1975—83; asst. prof. U. Tenn., Knoxville, 1983—88, assoc. prof., 1990—, coord. gerontol. nurse practitioners program, 1998—, chair MSN program Coll. Nursing. Dir. Kids Are Tomorrow's Srs. Program, 1988—; resource person Gov.'s Com. Unification of Mental Health Svcs. in Mich.; spkr. profl. assns. and workshops. Author (with S. Clemen-Stone and D. Eigsti)): Comprehensive Community Health Nursing, 1981, Comprehensive Community Health Nursing, 5th edit., 1998, Comprehensive Community Health Nursing, 6th edit., 2002. Bd. dirs. Ctr. Understanding Aging, 1987-93, v.p., 1995; bd. dirs. Mich. chpt. ARC, 1980-83, Knoxville chpt., 1984-85; founder Knoxville Intergenerational Network, 1989; coun. mem. AARP Nat. Policy, 2006-. Recipient John W. Runyan, Jr. Cmty. Health Nursing award U. Tenn. Memphis, 2002, Outstanding Svc. award U. Tenn. Knoxville Libr. Friends, 2004; USPHS fellow, 1972-73, Robert Woodruff fellow Emory U., 1996-97, Hewlett Innovative Tech. fellow U. Tenn., Knoxville, 1999-00, Profl. Devel. awardee U. Tenn. Knoxville, 1996-97, 99-2000. Mem. ANA, AARP Nat. Policy Coun., Tenn. Nurses Assn., Soc. Gerontological Soc. Am., Assn. Gerontology, Nat. Conf. Gerontol. Nurse Practitioners, Nat. Gerontol. Nursing Assn., Mich. Pub. Health Assn. (chmn. mental health sect. 1976, dir., co-chmn. residential svcs. com. 1976-79, chmn. health svcs. 1979-82), Nat. Assn. Retarded Citizens, Mich. Assn. Retarded Citizens, Nat. Coun. on Aging, Ctr. for Understanding Aging (v.p. 1994-95), Plymouth (chmn. residential svcs. com. 1975-77), Tenn. Assn. Retarded Citizens, So. Nursing Rsch. Soc., Sigma Theta Tau, Pi Lambda Theta, Phi Kappa Phi. Home: 11008 Crosswind Dr Knoxville TN 37934 Office: 1200 Volunteer Blvd Knoxville TN 37996 Office Phone: 865-974-7589. Business E-Mail: smcguire@utk.edu.

MCGUIRE-RIGGS, SHEILA, Democratic party chairman; Chmn. Iowa Democrat Party, Iowa. Democrat. Mailing: 5661 Fleur Dr Des Moines IA 50321 E-mail: smriggs@iowademocrats.org.

MCGUIRL, MARLENE DANA CALLIS, law librarian, educator; b. Hammond, Ind., Mar. 22, 1938; d. Daniel David and Helen Elizabeth (Baludis) Callis; m. James Franklin McGuirl, Apr. 24, 1965. AB, Ind. U., 1959; JD, DePaul U., 1963; MALS, Rosary Coll., 1965; LLM, George Washington U., 1978; postgrad., Harvard U., 1985. Bar: Ill. 1963, Ind. 1964, D.C. 1972. Asst. DePaul Coll. of Law Libr., 1961-62, asst. law libr., 1962-65; ref. law librarian Boston Coll. Sch. Law, 1965-66; libr. dir. D.C. Bar Libr., 1966-70; asst. chief Am.-Brit. Law Divsn. Libr. of Congress, Washington, 1970, chief, 1970-90, environ. cons., 1990—; counsel Cooter & Gell, 1992-93; adminstr. Washington Met. Transit Authority, 1994—2004. Libr. cons. Nat. Clearinghouse on Proverty Law, OEO, Washington, 1967-69, Northwestern U. Nat. Inst. Edn. in Law and Poverty, 1969, D.C. Office of Corp. Counsel, 1969-70; instr. law librarianship Grad. Sch. of U.S. Dept. of Agr., 1968-72; lectr. legal lit. Cath. U., 1972; adj. asst. prof., 1973-91; assoc. prof. environ. law George Washington U., 1979—; judge Nat. and Internat. Law Moot Ct. Competition, 1976-78, 90—; pres. Hamburger Heaven, Inc., Palm Beach, Fla., 1981-91, L'Image de Marlene Ltd., 1986-92, Clinique de Beauté Inc., 1987-92, Heads & Hands Inc., 1987-92, Horizon Design & Mfg. Co., Inc., 1987—; dir. Stoneridge Farm Inc., Gt. Falls, Va., 1984—. Contbr. articles to profl. jours. Mem. Georgetown Citizens Assn.; trustee D.C. Law Students in Ct.; del. Ind. Democratic Conv., 1964. Recipient Meritorious Svc. award Libr. on Congress, 1974, letter of commendation Dirs. of Pers., 1976, cert. of appreciation, 1981-84. Mem. ABA (facilities law libr. Congress com. 1976-89), Fed. Bar Assn. (chpt. council 1972-76), Ill. Bar Assn., Women's Bar Assn. (pres. 1972-73, exec. bd. 1973-77, Outstanding Contbn. to Human Rights award 1975), D.C. Bar Assn., Am. Bar Found., Nat. Assn. Women Lawyers, Am. Assn. Law Libraries (exec. bd. 1973-77), Law Librarians Soc. of Washington (pres. 1971-73), Exec. Women in Govt. Home: 3416 P St NW Washington DC 20007-2705 Personal E-mail: marlenemcguirl@aol.com.

MCGULPIN, ELIZABETH JANE, nurse; b. Toledo, Ohio, Oct. 18, 1932; d. James Orville and Leah Fayne (Helton) Welden; m. David Nelson Buster, Apr. 9, 1956 (div. Nov. 1960); children: David Hugh, James Ray, Mark Stephen; m. Fredrick Gordon McGulpin, Oct. 7, 1973. AA in Nursing, Pasadena City Coll., 1968. RN, Wash. Lic. nurse Las Encinas Hosp., Pasadena, Calif.; nurse Hopi Indian Reservation HEW, Keams Canyon, Ariz., 1969—70; nurse, enterostomal therapist Pasadena Vis. Nurse Assn., 1972—74; nurse Seattle King County Pub. Health, 1977—81; home care nurse Victorville, Calif., 1983—85; nurse Adult Family Home, Woodinville, Wash., 1986—. Vol. nurse, counselor Child Protective Svcs., Victorville, 1984; realtor Century 21, Lynden, Wash., 1993—. Vol. nurse Am. Cancer Soc., Pasadena, 1973-75, United Ostomy Assn., Los Angeles, Victorville, 1973-84; RN, ARC, 1996—. Am. Cancer Soc. grantee. Mem. Nat. Assn. Realtors, Wash. Assn. Realtors, Whatcom County Assn. Realtors, Vis. Nurse Assn. (Enterostomal Therpay grantee 1973). Avocations: reading, gardening, travel. Home: 18238 Deauville Dr Victorville CA 92392 Personal E-mail: spunky@intlaccess.com.

MCGURK, CATHERINE S., insurance adjuster, paralegal; b. Atlantic County, NJ, Jan. 23, 1967; d. Edward W. and Mary Ann Wilczynski; children: Mark Jr., Elise, Martha. BBA, Atlantic Cape Coll., Mays Landing, NJ, 2002; postgrad., Post U., Walden, Conn., 2006. Casino scheduling coord. Claridge Hotel/Casino, Atlantic City, 1988—90; paralegal Horn, Goldberg, Gorn & Daniels, Atlantic City, 1990—93, Law Office of Philip Perskie, Atlantic City, 1993—95, Law Office of Alfred Bennington, Northfield, NJ, 2000—03, Somers Point, NJ, 2003—06; liability claims adjuster Scibal Assocs., Somers Point, 2006—. Cons. hist. ho. rsch., preservation and restoration. Mem.: Phi Theta Kappa. Avocation: historical preservation and research. Personal E-mail: csm228@verizon.net.

MCHALE, CATHERINE A., lawyer; b. Chgo., Aug. 20, 1964; d. Edward Michael and Nancy Ruth (Martin) McH. BA, Fordham U., 1992; MDiv, Harvard U., 1996; JD, Columbia U., 1999. Press attaché Karl Lagerfeld N.A., N.Y.C., 1988-90; tutor The Learning Ctr., N.Y.C., 1990-92; curatorial asst. Peabody Mus., Cambridge, Mass., 1993-95; asst. to dir. Harvard Native Am. Program, Cambridge, 1995-96; cons. The Drawing Ctr., N.Y.C., 1996-97; with Sonnenschein Nath & Rosenthal, N.Y.C., 1998—2000, Kay & Boose LLP, N.Y.C., 2000—. Author book chpt., poems, articles. Vol. The Repatriation Found., N.Y.C., 1997-99, Vol. Lawyers for the Arts, N.Y.C., 1997-99; mentor Mock Trial Program, N.Y.C., 1999; vol. N.Y. Cares, 2000—, N.Y. Hospice, 2001—. Charlotte Newcombe scholar, 1989, Vera Bellus scholar, 1994, Harland Fiske Stone scholar, 1999. Mem. Am. Acad. Religion, Soc. for Study of Native Am. Religious Traditions. Democrat. Avocations: reading, skiing, cooking. Office: Kay & Boose LLP 1 Dag Hammarskjold Plaza New York NY 10017 Home: 120 Brentwood St Lakewood CO 80226-1350

MCHALE, JUDITH A. (JUDITH OTTALLORAN), broadcast executive, lawyer; b. N.Y.C., 1947; m. Michael McHale; 2 children. B in Politics, U. Nottingham, Eng.; JD, Fordham U.Law Sch., 1979. Atty. Battle, Fowler, N.Y.C.; gen. counsel MTV networks, Discovery Comm., Inc., 1987, sr. v.p., gen. counsel, exec. v.p., gen. counsel, pres., COO, 1995—2004, pres., CEO, 2004—. Mem. Md. State Bd. of Edn., 1997—2001; bd. dirs. Polo Ralph Lauren, John Hancock Co., Potomac Electric Power Co., Host Marriott Corp., Cable in the Classroom, Vital Voices Global Partnership, Africa Soc., Africare, Sister-to-Sister Everyone Has a Heart Found. Office: Discovery Comm 7700 Wisconsin Ave Bethesda MD 20814*

MCHENRY, ANITA PETEI, historian, archaeologist; b. Coffeyville, Kans., Mar. 2, 1949; d. Woodrow Wilson Gordon and Erva Odile (Crevier) Hardy; m. Gray Richard McHenry, Dec. 12, 1981; children: Carrie Ann, Thomas Owen. BS in Anthropology, U. Calif., Riverside, 1992; MA in History, U. San Diego, 1997. Archaeologist, historian Gallegos & Assocs., Carlsbad, Calif., 1990-96; pub., owner GP Mktg., Escondido, Calif., 1996—. Exec. dir. Valley Ctr. (Calif.) History Mus., 2001—; vol. archivist Valley Ctr. Libr., 1996—; v.p. hist. com. Friends of Valley Ctr. Libr., 1996—. Author: History of Valley Center, 1997, San Diego and Honolulu, A PhotoJournal Through a Sailor's Eye 1920-1943, 2002, Ed: From the Ashes of paradise: The San Diego Firestorm, 2003. Active Nat. Trust Historic Preservation. Fellowship grant, U. San Diego, 1995—96. Mem. Soc. Calif. Archaeology, San Diego Hist. Soc., Smithsonian Assn., San Diego County Archaeol. Soc., Nat. League of Am. Pen Women, Register of Profl. Archaeologists, Phi Alpha Theta. Avocations: historical research, genealogy, archaeology, reading. Home and Office: GP Mktg 28338 Mountain Meadow Rd Escondido CA 92026-6907 E-mail: gpmch@att.net.

MCHENRY, ESTHER ANN, artist; b. New Milford, N.J., July 7, 1940; d. Howard Scott McHenry and Elizabeth Ann Sheasby; children: Scott K. Sailor, Graham K. Sailor. BFA, Pratt Inst., Bklyn., N.Y., 1962. Art tchr. N.Y.C. Bd. Edn., N.Y.C., 1962—64; insurance claims Safeco, Royal, Inc., NJ, 1967—97; tchr./painting NJ, 1967—. Mem., trustee Art Ctr. No. N.J., New Milford, 2000—06. Exhibitions include Ridgewood Art Inst., 2002, one-woman shows include Bruised Apple, 2004, Fairleigh Dickinson U., 2005. Vol. grant writer Art Ctr. No. N.J., 2000—06; juror Ft. Lee Artists Assn., 2003, Bergenfield Taste of the Arts, 2004. Mem.: Nat. Mus. Women in Arts. Avocation: target shooting. Home: 324 William St New Milford NJ 07646-1829

MCHOES, ANN MCIVER, academic administrator, computer engineer; b. San Diego, June 17, 1950; d. Donald Anthony and Ann Mae McIver; children: A. Genevieve, Katherine Marie. BS in Math., U. Pitts., 1973, MS in Info. Sci., 1986. Tech. writer Westinghouse Electric Corp., Pitts., 1973—79; pres. McHoes & Assocs., Pitts., 1981—; dir. enrollment svcs. Chatham Coll., Pitts., 2002—. Mem. adj. faculty computer sci., Carlow Coll., Pitts., 1992—, Duquesne U., 1997-99; cons. Westinghouse Electric Corp., 1988-99, PNC Bank, Pitts., 1988—, CBS Corp., 1996-99, Intel, 1998—, McDonalds Corp., 1998-2001, commonwealth of Pa. Healthy Women Project, 1998—; vis. lectr. Pa. State U., State College, 1990-91; judge Pa. Jr. Acad. Sci., Pitts., 1993—; vol. tutor Greater Pitts. Literacy Coun., 1996-98; webmaster NVR Mortgage, 1998-2000; bd. dirs. Pitts. Playback Theatre, 2000-2001. Co-author: Understanding Operating Systems, 1991, 2d edit., 1997, 3d edit., 2000 (used in colleges and univs., North Am., Europe, Africa, Asia and Australia); assoc. editor: (4-vol. ency.) Computer Science for Students, 2002. Recipient 2001 Texty Excellence award Text and Academic Authors Assn., 2001. Mem. IEEE Computer Soc., Assn. Computing Machinery, Info. Sys. Security Assn. (chpt. sec. 1991-94, v.p. 1995-96, membership chair 1994—), Pa. Mid. Sch. Assn. (conf. exhibit chair 1996-97). Avocations: travel, tennis, golf.

MCHOLD, SHARON LAWRENCE, lawyer, mediator; b. Albion, Mich., Mar. 26, 1941; d. Ted E. and Ruth M. McHold; m. Frank H. Lawrence (div. July 1987); children: Christopher, Brian, Kimberly. BS, U. Del., 1963; MS, Tufts U., 1965; JD, U. Maine, 1983. Rschr. U. Ind. Med. Sch., Indpls., 1966-67; instr. Marian Coll., Indpls., 1967-70, Westbrook Coll., Portland, Maine, 1973-79; with Curtis Thaxter, Portland, assoc., 1985-91; law clk. Superior Ct., 1983—84; pvt. practice Yarmouth, Maine, 1991-93; mediator Conflict Solutions, Portland, 1993—. Trustee Maine Audubon Soc., Falmouth, Maine, 1977-80; clk. Island Inst., Rockland, Maine, 1985-92; trustee Maine Island Trail Assn., Portland, 1993-94, Oceanside Conservation Trust, 1993-2002; pres. Yarmouth Land Trust, 2002-, Royal River Conservation Trust, 2002—. Nat. Def. fellow, 1963-65. Mem.: Assn. for Conflict Resolution, Maine Bar Assn. Office: Conflict Solutions 30 Riverbend Dr Yarmouth ME 04096 Office Phone: 207-846-5128. Business E-Mail: sharon@conflictsolutionsinc.com.

MCHUGH, ANNETTE S., artist, educator, playwright, writer; b. Greensburg, Pa., May 31, 1926; d. Daniel Karl Shirey and Marian Grabill Kurtz; m. John Edward McHugh Jr., Nov. 24, 1948. Student, Ind. State Tchrs. Coll., Pa., 1945—47, Pa. State U., 1947—49, State Coll. Pa., 1980, student, 1981, Art Alliance Ctrl. Pa., 1981—85, student, 1985—90. File & locate clk. FBI, Washington, 1944—45; sec. to asst. dean edn. Pa. State U., University Park, 1947—49, sec. to exec. dir., 1962, pers. sec. phys. plant; test adminstr. Pa. State Employment Office, Bellefonte, 1962—65; editl. asst., prodn. sec. Sta. WPSX-TV, 1977—79; tchr. traditional chinese brush painting Art Alliance Ctrl. Pa., Lemont, Pa., 2001—03. Playwright, dir.: Those Were the Days, 1979, We've Come A Long Way Ladies, 1984, Every Night is Opening Night on Broadway, 1989, Madame Pres.Ladies of the Club, 1994, Celebrate State College, 1996. V.p., bd. dirs. Univ. Park Airport, University Park, 1957—62; bd. dirs., flower show chmn. Penn. State Garden Days, University Park, 1957—59; bd. dirs. Art Alliance Ctrl. Pa., 1981—82, pres., 1983, Nittany Coun. Rep. Women, 1961; pres. women's assn. State Coll. Presbyn. Ch., State Coll., Pa., 1971—73, deacon State College, Pa., 1965—71, elder, 1971—74, bd. sec. Recipient State of Pa. award, Pa. Coun. Rep. Women, 1961—62, Pub. Rels. award, Am. Cancer Soc., 1980, 2d pl. art award, Pa. Fedn. Women's Club, 1987. Mem.: Pa. State U. Woman's Club (chair book and play rev., co-editor), State Coll. Woman's Club (pres. 1959—61, past v.p., past pres., art, garden and drama dept. chair). Republican. Presbyterian. Avocations: gardening, photography, reading, golf.

MCHUGH, CARIL EISENSTEIN DREYFUSS, art dealer, art gallery director, consultant; b. New Haven; d. Irving and Gertrude (Lax) Eisenstein; m. Barney Dreyfuss II (div.); children: Caryn, Barney III (Terry), Andrew, Evan; m. James Marshall McHugh Jr., Dec. 31, 1976. BA, Smith Coll. Libr. archivist, mem. staff art rental Washington Gallery of Modern Art, 1963-67; asst. to curator of prints and drawings Nat. Mus. Am. Art, Washington, 1967-69; dir. Studio Gallery, Washington, 1970-75; dir., ptnr. Parsons-Dreyfuss Gallery, N.Y.C., 1976-80; dir. Frank Marino Gallery, N.Y.C., 1981, Humphrey Fine Art, N.Y.C., 1988-90, Gregory Gallery, N.Y.C., 1995-96; freelance curator, adv. bd. Hugo de Pagano Gallery, 1997—2000; rschr. Barnett Newman Found., N.Y.C., 2001—. Art cons., writer, N.Y.C., 1982—; arranger exhbns. Nat. Mus. Am. Art, Washington, 1968-69, USIA, Washington, 1976, Automation House, N.Y.C., 1983; curator Creative Works Exhbn., Smith Coll., 2005. An Homage to Betty Parsons exhbn., 2000, Portraits by Tom Block/Amnesty Internat. Exhbn., 2002, essays to catalogs, articles to profl. mags. Bd. dirs. Women's Nat. Dem. Club, Washington, 1972-76, Friends of the Corcoran, Washington, 1972-76, Smith Club of Washington, 1974-76; Sophia Smith Assoc. Smith Coll., Northampton, Mass., 1985, 90, 95, 2000, 2005, Women in the Arts, 1995—. Avocations: reading, hiking, swimming, poetry. Home: 241 Central Park W Apt 9C New York NY 10024-4545 E-mail: carilmchugh@msn.com.

MCHUGH, MAURA, professional basketball coach; b. Worcester, Mass. m. Greg Olson. Grad. magna cum laude, Old Dominion U., 1975; MS in Phys. Edn., Pa. State U., 1977. Grad. asst. Pa. State U., Univ. Pk., 1977, asst. basketball coach, 1978-80; basketball coach U. Okla., Norman, Ariz. State, Tempe, 1988-93; exec. dir. Bus. Coun. for Alcohol Edn., Phoenix, 1993-97; head basketball coach Long Beach (Calif.) StingRays, 1997—. Named Big Eight Coach of Year, 1977, Converse Nat. Coach of Year, 1977. Achievements include being awarded one of first ever women's basketball scholarships at Old Dominion U.; No. 1 ranking academically at Old Dominion U.; advancing to NCAA Sweet 16 postseason play in 1986.

MCILVAIN, ISABEL, sculptor, art educator; b. 1943; BA, Smith Coll.; MFA, Pratt Inst. Asst. prof. & artist-in-residence Washington & Lee Univ., 1975—82; assoc. prof. Sch. Visual Arts, Boston Univ., 1982—. Vis. assoc. prof. Sweet Briar Coll., 1977. Exhibitions include Robert Schoelkopf Gallery, NYC, 1982-87, Moore Gallery, Phila., 1993, Arnot Art Mus., Elmira N.Y.; Numerous group exhibitions in N.Y., Pa. and Va.; JFK Commission 1989. Grantee Sculpture Fellowship award, Artists Found., Boston, 1984. Mem.: NAD (academician). Office: School of Visual Arts Room 552 855 Commonwealth Ave Boston MA 02215

MCILVAINE, PATRICIA MORROW, physician; b. Pitts., Feb. 4, 1947; d. James Morrow McIlvaine and Virginia Fuller Tucker. BS in Chemistry, Simmons Coll., 1969; MD, U. Utah, 1984. Rsch. technician Mass. Gen. Hosp., Boston, 1969-70, MIT, Cambridge, 1970-75, Utah State U., Logan, 1975-80; resident in internal medicine U. Mass. Hosp., Worcester, 1984-87; pvt. practice, Monson, Mass., 1987-2001; mem. pvt. group practice Walla Walla (Wash.) Clinic, 2002—. Staff physician Wing Meml. Hosp., Palmer, Mass., 1987-2001. Vol., trainer IRBIS Enterprises, Mongolia, 1998-2004. NFS summer scholar, 1968, Helena Rubinstein scholar Simmons Coll., 1968-69. Mem. ACP/Am. Soc. Internal Medicine, Sigma Xi. Avocations: fiber crafts, international travel, hiking, gardening, sailing. Home: 913 Bonnie Brae Walla Walla WA 99362

MCILWAIN, ANNA KEITT, elementary school educator, researcher; b. Newberry, SC, Sept. 14, 1938; d. Joseph Lawrence and Margaret Kinard Keitt; m. James Wade McIlwain, Nov. 28, 1968; children: James Wade McIlwain, Jr., Margaret McIlwain Trammell, Mary McIlwain Hadley. BA, U. S.C., Columbia, 1960; MA, Presbyn. Sch. Christian Edn., Richmond, Va., 1962; MS, Jacksonville State U., Ala., 1993. Cert. libr. media at master's level. Dir. Christian edn. Steele Creek Presbyn. Ch., Charlotte, NC, 1962—63; 7th grade social studies tchr. Brooklyn-Cayce Jr. H.S., Cayce, SC, 1964; English tchr. A.C. Flora H.S., Columbia, 1964—67; field rep. Congaree Girl Scout Coun., Columbia, 1967—68; English tchr. Morton H.S., Miss., 1969—71; job counselor Talladega City Schs., Ala.; English and social studies tchr. Talladega Mid. Sch., Dixon Mid. Sch. and Zora Ellis Jr. H.S., 1983—92; tchr., libr. Salter Elem. Sch., Talladega, 1992—98; ret., 1998. Vol. elem. schs. RSVP in Talladega, 1998—2000; Brownie leader Girl Scouts U.S.; moderator presbytery's Presbyn. Women, 2005—; elder Session of First Presbyn. Ch., Talladega, 2005—; commr. Gen. Assembly Presbyn. Ch. U.S., Richmond, 2004; bd. trustees Heritage Hall, Talladega, 2002—. Fellow Tchg. fellow, Jacksonville State U.; grantee, State of Ala. Dept. Edn., 1992; scholar, Ala. Coun. Tchrs. English, 1990. Mem.: Highland City Club (sec. 2001—02, pres. 2003—04), Kappa Kappa Iota. Democrat. Presbyterian. Avocations: reading, writing, canoeing, gardening, birding. Home: 106 Hickory Ln Talladega AL 35160

MCILWAIN, CLARA EVANS, agricultural economist, consultant; b. Jacksonville, Fla., Apr. 5, 1919; d. Waymon and Jerusha Lee (Dickson) Evans; m. Ivy McIlwain, May 15, 1942 (dec. 1987); children: Ronald E., Carol A. McIlwain Edwards, Marilyn E. McIlwain Moody, Ivy J. McIlwain Lindsay. BS, U. D.C., 1939; MS Agrl. Econs., U. Fla., 1972; DHL, Breakthrough Bible Coll., 2005. Notary pub., Va.; lic. life and health ins. agt., Md., Va., D.C. Statis. asst. Hist. and Statis. Analysis Div., Washington, 1962-67; statistician Econ Devel. Div. USDA, Washington, 1967-70, 72, agrl. economist, 1972-74; program analyst Office Equal Opportunity, USDA, Washington, 1974-79; staff writer Sci. Weekly, Chevy Chase, Md., 1988-89; ins. agt. A.L. Williams, Primerica, Camp Springs, Md., 1990-95; min. New Light Mission Ministries, Clinton, Md., 1995—; prof. English Potomac Coll., Herndon, Va., 2003. Workshop coord. Author: Steps to Eloquence, 1989; co-author (Min. Carol M. Edwards): Blazing the Trail to the Kingdom of God, Old Testament and New Testament, 2001: contbr. to profl. publs. Dist. coord., instr. Youth Leadership and Speechcraft, Toastmasters Internat., Washington area, 1972-78; tchr., bd.

dirs. Sat. Tutorial Enrichment Program, Arlington, Va., 1988-89; mem. network Christian women; min. to sr. citizens New Light Mission Mins., Clinton, Md., 1999-2002; asst. in strategic bus. planning advanced environ. rsch., 1995-2002. Rockefeller Found. scholar, 1970-72. Mem.: Internat. Assn. Home Bus. Entrepreneurs, Nat. Assn. Agrl. Econs., So. Assn. Agrl. Economists, Am. Assn. Notaries, Internat. Platform Assn., Toastmasters Internat. (past pres. Potomac club, Gavel award 1976, Able Toastmaster award 1978). Avocations: teaching public speaking, tutoring, attending conventions. Office: Evans Unlimited 6612 Denny Pl Mc Lean VA 22101-5505 Office Phone: 703-883-0664. Personal E-mail: bunnieduck@aol.com.

MCINNIS, CAROLYN CRAWFORD, real estate broker; b. Fayetteville, Tenn., Oct. 30, 1937; d. Sidney Johnson and Winnie Grace Jean Crawford; m. Bobby Jack Graben, June 30, 1960 (div. Aug. 1975); children: Niles Crawford, Nancy Carol, Norman Curtis. BS, No. Ala. U., 1960; MA in Edn., Tenn. State, 1972. Real estate agt. McKinney Realty World, Dallas, 1979—80; tchr. Comstock Middle Sch., 1976—82; broker Carolyn McInnis, Inc., Realtors, 1982—. Membership chmn. Buckner Ter. Homeowners Assn., Dallas, 1983, publicity chmn., 1980—81; mem. Economic Devel. City of Dallas, 1985—89; crime reduction chair for neighborhood, 2006; elder Eastminster Presbyn., 2005. Mem.: Greater Dallas Bd. Realtors, Kappa Omicron Phi. Republican. Presbyn. Home: 6903 Glacier Dr Dallas TX 75227-1763 Office: Carolyn McInnis Properties 6903 Glacier Ave Dallas TX 75227 Office Phone: 214-381-0469. Personal E-mail: carolyn.m@sbcglobal.net.

MCINTIRE, LINDA CAROLE, mental health and substance abuse counselor; b. Portales, N.Mex., Dec. 29, 1939; d. John Maury and Irva Taylor Sanders; m. Jerald Gene McIntire; children: Christian Tilghman, Ross Andrew, John Patrick. BA in Drama, Speech and English, Ea. N.Mex U., Portales, 1961; student in Theatre, Dallas Theatre Ctr., Baylor U., 1962—63; MA in Psychology and Pers. Svcs., Ea. N.Mex U., Portales, 1976. Lic. alcohol and drug abuse counselor N.Mex., profl. counselor N.Mex. English tchr. Alamogordo Ind. Sch. Dist., N.Mex., 1965—67; reading and English tchr. Grants Ind. Sch. Dist., N.Mex., 1967—68; speech and pub. speaking tchr. Ea. N.Mex U., Portales, 1968—70; spl. edn. tchr. Villa Solano Sch. for Retarded Boys, Hagerman, N.Mex., 1970—71; clothing store mgr. Alamogordo, 1972—74; tchr. Operation SER/ Hispanic Social Svc. Agy., Dallas, 1978—82; pvt. practice therapist Dallas, 1979—91; counseling specialist III U. Tex., Arlington, 1982—89; counselor II Ft. Stanton Women's Facility N.Mex Dept. Corrections, 1996—2001, counselor II Rowell Facility Hagerman, 1996—2001; mgr. facility mental health/addictions RCC, 2001—06, clin. counselor supr., 2006—. Mem. Humane Soc., Va., 2004; vol. Tex. Assn. to Prevent Teenage Pregnancies, Dallas, 1985—87; vol. counselor Shelter for Abused Women and Children, Dallas, 1984—87; mem. adv. bd. Downtown Dallas Family Shelter', 1984—89; vol. counselor City of Dallas Homeless Shelter, 1988—89; speech advisor Rep. candidates, Roswell, 1970; mem. Best Friends, Moab, Utah, 2004. Mem.: Nat. Humane Soc., Northshore Animal League, Sierra Club. Democrat. Episcopalian. Avocations: reading, music, films. Office: NMex Dept Corrections/RCC 578 W Chickasaw Rd Hagerman NM 88232 Office Phone: 505-625-3119.

MCINTIRE, PENNY A. KENDALL, education educator; b. Dixon, Ill., Aug. 27, 1952; d. Carrol William and Ethel Myrtle (Ferrill) M.; m. William F. Kendall, Aug. 18, 1974 (div. 1998); children: Shelley, Abigail AS, Sauk Valley Coll., Dixon, 1973; B Gen. Studies, No. Ill. U., DeKalb, 1977; MS, No. Ill. U., 1982. Owner, mgr. Down To Earth, Dixon, 1975—77; dir. data processing KSB Hosp., Dixon, 1978—79; instr. No. Ill. U., 1982—99, asst. to chair and undergrad. advisor Dept. Computer Sci., 1998—. Cons., Oregon, Ill., 1978—; mem. steering com. Excelerator Acad. User's Group, 1988-90 Author: Introduction to Systems Analysis and Design, 1987, 3d edit., 1996, Student Guide and Casebook for Systems Analysis and Design, 1987, 2d edit., 1992 Asst. leader Brownie Scouts Am., 1987-92. Avocations: restoring old houses, antiques, gardening, skiing, genealogy. Office: No Ill U Dept Computer Sci Dekalb IL 60115 Office Phone: 815-753-6495. E-mail: pmcintire@niu.edu.

MCINTOSH, DEBORAH V., elementary school educator; b. Detroit, Feb. 3, 1950; d. Hubert Harvey and Lillian Ethel Mobley; divorced; Courtney James, Carlyn D'Nita, Corey Harvey. BS, U. Mich., 1974; MEd, U. Detroit, 1994. Cert. elem. edn. tchr. K-8. Employment counselor Businessman's Clearinghouse, Chgo., 1977-79; corp. mgr. trainee Sears, Roebuck & Co., Chgo., 1977-78, retail dept. mgr. Hamilton, Ohio, 1978-81; asst. store mgr. Kayo Oil, Ft. Worth, 1983-84; substitute tchr. St. Brigid & St. Cecilia Schs., Detroit, 1986-92; classroom tchr. Highland Park (Mich.) Pub. Schs., 1994—. Tchr. facilitator Project Link, Highland Park, 1997—; mem. edn. & tech. team Jason Project, Lamphere/Highland Park Sch. Dist., 1998-2000; mem. elem. sci. curriculum devel. team Highland Park Pub. Schs., 1998—; co-chairperson Cortland Acad. Social Comm., Highland Park, 1999-2000; mem. Web-based Sci. Rsch. Grant (Eisenhower Found.), Lawrence Technical Inst., Southfield, Mich., 1999-2000. Vol. Mothers Against Drunk Driving, Livonia, Mich., 1993-96; Earth Day chairperson Cortland Acad. chpt. Earth Day Orgn., Highland Park, Mich., 1999-2000. Named for Excellence in Edn., Wayne County Rsch. Edn. Svc. Agy., 1998, 99. Mem. ASCD, Benjamin Banneker Assn., Detroit Area Coun. Tchrs. Math., Met. Detroit Sci. Tchrs. Assn., Highland Park Fedn. of Tchrs. (strategy team 1994), Alpha Kappa Alpha. Democrat. Avocations: reading, poetry and short story writing, gardening, collecting crystal miniatures. Office: Cortland Acad 138 Cortland St Detroit MI 48203-3511

MCINTOSH, ELAINE VIRGINIA, nutrition educator; b. Webster, SD, Jan. 30, 1924; d. Louis James and Cora Boletta (Bakke) Nelson; m. Thomas Henry McIntosh, Aug. 28, 1955; children: James George, Ronald Thomas, Charles Nelson. BA magna cum laude, Augustana Coll., Sioux Falls, S.D., 1945; MA, U. S.D., 1949; PhD, Iowa State U., 1954. Instr., asst. prof. Sioux Falls Coll., 1945-48; instr. Iowa State U., Ames, 1949-53, rsch. assoc., 1955-62; postdoctoral rsch. assoc. U. Ill., Urbana, 1954-55; asst. prof. human biology U. Wis., Green Bay, 1968-72, assoc. prof., 1972-85, prof., 1985-90, emeritus prof., 1990—, writer, cons., 1990—, chmn. human biology dept., 1975-80, asst. to vice chancellor, asst. to chancellor, 1974-76. Author 3 books including American Food Habits in Historical Perspective, 1995, Lewis and Clark: Food, Nutrition, and Health, 2003; contbr. numerous articles on bacterial metabolism, meat biochemistry and nutrition edn. to profl. jours. Fellow USPHS, 1948-49. Avocation: travel. Office: LS 455 Human Biology U Wis Green Bay 2420 Nicolet Dr Green Bay WI 54311-7001

MCINTOSH, JULIE DEAN, science educator; d. William Dean and Marilyn Smith; m. William McIntosh, Mar. 16, 1991; 1 child, Britney. BA, U. Findlay, 1990; MEd, Bowling Green State U., Ohio, 1994, EdD, 2002. Permanent tchg. lic. Ohio, lic. asst. supt. Ohio. Environ. engr. Ohio EPA, Bowling Green, 1990—92; tchr. Bowling Green H.S., 1992—97, Findlay H. S., 1997—2002; prof. Bowling Green State U., 2002—03; asst. prof. U. Findlay, 2003—, dir. adolescent young adult and multi-age program. Contbr. articles to profl. jours. Youth chair March of Dimes, Findlay, 2001—04. Recipient Old Main Alumni award, U. Findlay, 2001, Disting. Alumni award, Make a Difference award, Findlay HS Acad. Boosters, 2002. Mem.: Ohio Assn. Tchr. Educators, Nat. Assn. for Rsch. in Sci. Edn., Nat. Sci. Tchrs. Assn., U. Findlay Alumni Assn. (pres. 2004—). Office: U Findlay 1000 N Main St Findlay OH 45840 Office Phone: 419-434-4062. Business E-Mail: mcintosh@findlay.edu.

MCINTOSH, KELLI LEE, physics educator; b. Flint, Mich., June 2, 1980; d. Gary Norman Gordon and Vicki Lee Quist, Albert Conway Price (Stepfather) and Linda Louise Gordon (Stepmother); m. Scott Michael McIntosh, June 11, 2005. BS in Edn., U. of Mich., Ann Arbor, 2002. Advanced profl. cert. Md. Tchr. physics Walkersville H.S., Md., 2002—. Sponsor sophomore class Walkersville H.S., 2004—. Office Phone: 240-236-7273.

MCINTOSH, KELLI MARIE, elementary school educator; b. Middletown, Ohio, Nov. 14, 1979; d. Larry Laverne and Beautrice Marie Fox; m. Jesse Schuyler McIntosh, Aug. 4, 2001; 1 child, Kyle Schuyler. BS in Edn., Miami U., Ohio, 1998—2002; MA, Nova Southeastern U., Fla., 2004—05. Tchr. Mason City Schs., Ohio, 2002—.

MCINTOSH, TERRIE TUCKETT, lawyer; b. Ft. Lewis, Wash., July 20, 1944; d. Robert LeRoy and Elda Tuckett; m. Clifton Dennis McIntosh, Oct. 13, 1969; children: Alison, John. BA, U. Utah, 1967; MA, U. Ill., 1970; JD, Harvard U., 1978. Bar: NY 1979, Utah 1980. Assoc. Hughes, Hubbard & Reed, N.Y.C., 1978-79, Fabian & Clendenin, Salt Lake City, 1979-84, shareholder, 1984-86; staff atty. Questar Corp., Salt Lake City, 1986-88, sr. atty., 1988-92, sr. corp. counsel, 1992—. Instr. philosophy Douglass Coll. Rutgers U., New Brunswick, N.J., 1971-72; mem. adv. com. civil procedure Utah Supreme Ct., Salt Lake City, 1987—; mem. jud. nominating com. 5th Cir. Ct., Salt Lake City, 1986-88. Mem. Utah State Bar (ethics and discipline screening panel 1989-96, vice chair ethics and discipline com. 1996-99, 2006—, co-chair law related edn. com. 1985-86, bar examiner rev. com. 2005—), Women Lawyers of Utah (chair exec. com. 1986-87, Woman Lawyer of Yr. award 2005), Salt Lake Legal Aid Soc. (trustee 1999—), Harvard Alumni Assn. Utah (bd. dirs. 1987—), Phi Beta Kappa, Phi Kappa Phi Office Phone: 801-324-5532.

MCINTYRE, ELIZABETH JONES, retired multi-media specialist, educator; b. Teaneck, N.J., July 17, 1939; d. Paul J. Jones and Ann Cecilia O'Leary; m. John Peter McIntyre, Jan. 30, 1960; children: John P. III, Paul M., Patricia M., Maura M. Student, Rosemont Coll., 1957—59; BS in Edn., Seton Hall U., 1961; degree, Caldwell Coll., 1976. Cert. Tchr. N.J., 1976, Libr. N.J., 1976. Tchr. 4th grade Corpus Christi Sch., Hasbrouck Heights, NJ, 1960—61; media specialist Gould & Grandview Sch., North Caldwell, NJ, 1961—63, Parsippany Twp. Sch., Parsippany, NJ, 1974—2000; ret., 2000. Grantee, Parsippany Bd. Edn., 1981, 1989. Mem.: AAUW, Women of Irish Heritage. Republican. Roman Catholic. Avocations: gardening, reading.

MCINTYRE, JERILYN SUE, academic administrator; b. June 24, 1942; d. Frank Otto and Maxine (Ward) McIntyre; m. W. David Smith. Student, Stanford U., Italy, 1962; AB in History with distinction, Stanford U., 1964, MA in Journalism, 1965, cert. Summer Radio-TV Inst., 1965, tchrs. cert., 1968; PhD in Comms., U. Washington, 1973; postgrad. Inst. Ednl. Mgmt., Harvard U., 1993. Corr. World News Bureau McGraw-Hill Pub. Co., L.A., 1965-67; asst. prof. dept. mass comm. Chico (Calif.) State Coll., 1968-70; asst. prof. Sch. Journalism U. Iowa, Iowa City, 1973-77; assoc. prof., prof. dept. comm. U. Utah, Salt Lake City, 1977-2000, assoc. dean Coll. Humanities, 1984-88, assoc. v.p. acad. affairs, 1988-90, interim pres., 1997, v.p. acad. affairs, 1990-98; pres. Ctrl. Wash. U., Ellensburg, 2000—. Dir. Wall St. Jour. Publs. Workshop, Chico State Coll., 1968; mem. edn. adv. bd. NFL, 1996; mem. exec. com. coun. acad. affairs Nat. Assn. State Univs. and Land Grant Coll., 1995—98, chair, 1997; mem. steering com. Utah Edn. Network, 1995—98. Editl. asst. Chemical Week Mag., 1965-66, World News Bureau, 1966-67; mem. editl. bd. Journalism History; co-author: Symbols & Society; contbr. articles to profl. jours., chpts. to books. Mem. Utah Women's Forum. Named a David P. Gardner fellow, 1984; recipient Yesterday's Girl Scout Today's Successful Woman, Utah Girl Scout Coun., 1996, Salt Lake City chpt. Disting. Woman, AAUW, 1994. Mem.: Assn. Edn. in Journalism and Mass Comm. Office: 400 E University Way Ellensburg WA 98926-7501 E-mail: mcintyrej@cwu.edu.

MCINTYRE, JUDY, social worker, state representative; b. Tulsa, Okla., May 31, 1945; d. Garland O. Eason, Del (Stepfather) and Jeanne (Hughes) Phillips; BS in Social Work, U. Okla., 1967, MS in Social Work, 1979. Social worker Dept. Human Svcs. in Child Welfare, Okla.; rep. Ho. Reps., State of Okla., Okla. City, 2002—. Mem. speaker's leadership team Okla. Ho. Reps., Okla. City, 2002—, mem. common edn., higher edn., human svcs., pub. health coms., 2002—. 1921 Race Riot Design Com.; Greenwood Redevel. Authority; mem., pres. Tulsa Sch. Bd. Named Fellow, Ctr. for Am. Women and Politics/Eagleton Inst. Politics, Rutgers U. Leadership Inst., 2002. Mem.: Com. Workers of Am., NAACP. Democrat.

MCINTYRE, LINDA M., healthcare risk analyst; b. Pitts., Nov. 23, 1950; d. John and Genevieve D. Lizon; m. Dennis D. McIntyre, Apr. 26, 1969; children: Lisa M. Morrocco, Shannon M., Ryan D. AS in Nursing, C.C. of Allegheny County, Pitts., 1980; BS in Nursing, California U. of Pa., 2000; MS in Nursing, Carlow U., Pitts., 2004. RN Pa. RN staff nurse Divine Providence Hosp., Pitts., 1980—81, St. Clair Hosp., Pitts., 1981—2000, RN mgr., 2000—02, healthcare risk analyst, 2004—; RN mgr. Mercy Hosp., Pitts., 2002—04. Recipient Nursing Scholarship and Leadership award, Nursing Alumni of California U. of Pa., 2000. Mem.: Assn. Women's Health, Ob. and Neonatal Nurses (Pa. sect. sec.-treas. 1996—2000), Sigma Theta Tau. Avocations: reading, travel. Office Phone: 412-942-1837.

MCINTYRE, LINNEA ANDREN, small business owner; b. Point Pleasant, N.J., July 21, 1950; d. Carl Walter and Eva Helen (ReMillong) Andren; m. Kevin McIntyre, 1987; 1 child, Kasara Megan. BS in Elem. Edn., Trenton State Coll., 1972; cert. master gardener, Pa. State U. Owner Plants by Design, Upper Black Eddy, Pa., 1975—. Mem. Am. Hort. Soc., Pa. Hort. Soc. Avocations: sailing, skiing, gardening. Home and Office: Plants by Design 1306 River Rd Upper Black Eddy PA 18972 Office: Plants by Design 1306 River Rd Upper Black Eddy PA 18972 Office Phone: 610-982-9215. Business E-Mail: linnea@plantsbydesign.com.

MCINTYRE, LOLA MAZZA, music educator; b. Hammond, Ind., Sept. 23, 1955; d. Tony and Isabell Emma Mazza, Wanda Marie Mazza (Stepmother); m. William Russell McIntyre; children: William, Alexander. BMus, Hope Coll., Holland, Michigan, 1978; MMus, U. Tenn., 1989. Cert. nat. cert. piano 1991, Mich. Music Tchg. K-12 1978, Ind. applied music tchg. 2002. Music tchr. Saugatuck (Mich.) Pub. Schs., 1978—79; owner, tchr. The Studio of Holland, Holland, Mich., 1979—81; parish dir. music ministries Lafayette Diocese of Ind., Carmel, Ind., 1991—97; pvt. piano tchr. Carmel, Ind., 1976—; assoc. adj. prof. piano U. Indpls., 2001—. Prodr.: (Audio Recording) Alleluia!, 1996; author: (Multi-media Instructional CD-ROM) Bach's Musette, 2000. Friend Mus. Miniature Enthusiasts, Carmel, 2001—; docent Indpls. Symphony Orch., 1999. Recipient Concerto Competition award, Hope Coll., 1977. Mem.: Ind. Piano Tchrs. Guild (web designer, webmaster 2001—), Gtr. Indpls. Piano Tchrs. Assn. (v.p., theory chmn. 2000—02), Ind. Music Tchrs. Assn. (state advisor, music tech. 2001—02), Music Tchrs. Nat. Assn., Delta Omicron (life; chpt. pres. 1977—78, Star of Delta Omicron 1978). Roman Catholic. Avocations: miniatures, golf, quilting, travel, concerts. Office: U Indpls Music Dept 1400 E Hanna Ave Indianapolis IN Office Phone: 317-788-3255. Personal E-mail: lmcintyre@indy.rr.com. Business E-Mail: lmcintyre@uindy.edu.

MCINTYRE, LOUISE S., income tax consultant; b. Cin., Jan. 29, 1924; d. George Washington and Bertha (McDaniels) Sullivan; m. Harry McIntyre Jr., Jan. 18, 1947; children: Carol L., Patricia A., Harriet L., Harry J., Brenda R. AA, Mira Costa Coll., Oceanside, Calif., 1972; grad. in auditing, Nat. Tax Practice Inst., 1989. Enrolled agt. Hydraulic testor Paterson Field, Fairfield, Ohio, 1942-45; control clk. Hickam Field, Honolulu, 1945-47; clk.-typist Patterson Field, Fairfield, 1947-49, Camp LeJeune, Jacksonville, NC, 1951-56; sec., bookkeeper Mission Bowl, Oceanside, 1973-79; income tax cons. Oceanside, 1974—. Mem. Oceanside Human Rels. Commn., 1970; bd. dirs. Armed Forces YMCA, Oceanside, 1969-71, Oceanside Christian Women's Club, 1988-91, North County Concert Assn. Aux., 1993-96; active PTA, Girl Scout U.S. Mem. Inland Soc. Tax Cons. (bd. dirs. 1988—), Am. Soc. Women Accts. (v.p. 1989-90), Enrolled Agts. Palomar, Nat. Assn. Enrolled Agts., Nat. Soc. Pub. Accts., Calif. Assn. Ind. Accts., Palmquist PTA (hon. life). Avocations: bowling, dance, crafts, interior decorating, cake decorating. Home: 328 Camelot Dr Oceanside CA 92054-4515

MCINTYRE, MEGAN D., lawyer; BS, Pa. State Univ., 1991; JD magna cum laude, Dickinson Sch. Law, 1994. Bar: Del. 1984, US Dist. Ct. (Del. dist. 1995, ea. dist. Mich. 2002), US Ct. Appeals (11th cir.) 2002. Assoc. Skadden Arps Slate Meagher & Flom, Wilmington, Del., 1994—95, Blank Rome Comisky & McCauley, Wilmington, Del., 1995—97; ptnr., corp., securities & comml. litig. practices Grant & Eishnhofer PA, Wilmington, Del., 1997—. Editor (articles): Dickinson Law Rev.; contbr. articles to profl. jours. Mem.: Del. State Bar Assn. Office: Grant E Eisenhofer Pa PO Box 752 Wilmington DE 19899-0752 Office Phone: 302-622-7020. Office Fax: 302-622-7100. Business E-Mail: mmcintyre@gelaw.com.

MCINTYRE, VIRGIE M., elementary school educator; b. Chesnee, SC, Feb. 27, 1923; d. Ed Lawson and Etta Rebecca (Jones) Mahaffey; m. Henry Bryson McIntyre, June 8, 1947; children: Teresa, Dawn. BA in edn., Berea Coll., 1945; M in supr. and adminstrn., Western Carolina U., 1964. Cert. advanced standing (reading) Syracuse U., 1968. Elem. tchr. Polk County Pub. Sch., Columbus, NC, 1945—53, 1957—65, Rutherfordton County, Spindale, NC, 1953—56; suprv. Polk County, 1965—67, reading cons., title 1 dir., 1968—70; reading ctr. prof. Western Carolina U., Cullowhee, NC, 1971—84; ret., 1984. Dir. reading conf. Western Carolina U., Cullowhee, NC, 1971—84, reading cons., 1971—84. Author: Reading Strategies and Enrichment Activities for Grades 4-9, 1979, Split Level Christians, 1993; contbr. articles various profl. jours. Vol. Outreach Min., Columbus, NC, 2000, Green Creek Computer Ctr., Tryon, NC, 2002; vol., dir, pianist Ch. Choir, Columbus, NC, 1984—99. Fellowship grant, Syracuse U., 1969. Mem.: Christian Writer's Group, NC Retired Employee Group. Independent. Avocations: painting, travel, swimming, music, volunteerism. Personal E-mail: tvtmacbd@alltel.com.

MCINTYRE-IVY, JOAN CAROL, data processing executive; b. Port Chester, N.Y., Mar. 1, 1939; d. John Henry and Molly Elizabeth (Gates) Daugherty; m. Stanley Donald McIntyre, Aug. 24, 1957 (div. Jan. 1986); children: Michael Stanley McIntyre, David John McIntyre, Sharon Lynne McIntyre; m. James Morrow Ivy IV, June 1, 1988. Student, Northwestern U., 1956-57, U. Ill., 1957-58. Assoc. editor Writer's Digest, Cin., 1966-68; instr. creative writing U. Ala., Huntsville, 1974-75; editor Strode Pubs., Huntsville, 1974-75; paralegal Smith, Huckaby & Graves (now Bradley, Arant, Rose & White), Huntsville, 1976-82; exec. v.p. Micro Craft, Inc., Huntsville, 1982-85, pres., 1985-89, ceo, chmn. bd., 1989—; also bd. dirs., co-owner. Author: numerous computer operating manuals for law office software, 1978—; co-author: Alabama and Federal Complaint Forms, 1979; editor: Alabama Law for the Layman, 1975; contbr. numerous articles to profl. jours. and short stories to mags. and lit. mags. Hon. scholar Medill Sch. Journalism Northwestern U., 1956. Mem. Huntsville Literary Soc. (bd. dirs. 1976-77). Republican. Methodist. Office: 123 Fairington Rd NW Huntsville AL 35806-2249 Office Phone: 800-225-3147. Personal E-mail: verdictsales@aol.com.

MCIVER, BEVERLY JEAN, art educator, artist; b. Greensboro, N.C., Dec. 14, 1962; d. Ethel Mae (McMaster) McI. BA, N.C. Ctrl. U., 1987; MFA, Pa. State U., 1992. Asst. prof. art Duke U., Durham, N.C., 1995—. Artist-in-residence Vt. Studio Ctr., 1992, Atlantic Ctr. for Arts, 1992, 94, Headlands Ctr. for Arts, Sausalito, Calif., 1995; adj. lectr. N.C. Ctrl. U., Durham, 1992-95; adminstrv. facilitator N.C. Arts Coun., 1994—, panelist, 1995—; juror in field. One woman shows include Durham Art Guild, 1991, Paul Robeson Cultural Ctr., Pa. State U., 1992, Bivins Gallery, Duke U., 1993, 96, Formal Gallery, Pa. State U., 1994, Tyndall Galleries, Durham, N.C., 1994, Glaxo Inc., Research Triangle Park, N.C., 1995, Western Carolina U., Cullowhee, N.C., 1996, Invisible Me, Kent Gallery, 2006; group shows include Appalachian State U., Boone, N.C., 1990, Zoller Gallery, Pa. State U., 1990, The Cotton Exch. Gallery, 1993, The Greensboro Artist League, 1993, Sunshine Cultural Ctr., Raleigh, N.C., 1993, Green Hill Ctr. for N.C. Art, Greensboro, 1994, N.C. State U., 1994, Fayetteville (N.C.) Mus., 1994, 95, Stedman Art Gallery Rutgers U., 1994, Duke U. Mus. Art, 1994, Wilson (N.C.) Art Ctr., 1995, Durham Art Guild, 1995, Tyndall Galleries, 1996, Soho 20 Gallery, N.Y.C., 1996, many others. Fellow Pa. State U., 1989, Visual Artist fellow N.C. Arts Coun., 1994; grantee Durham Arts Coun., 1994; ednl. scholar St. James Bapt. Ch., 1990, Headlands Ctr. for Arts, 1995. Mem. Coll. Arts Assn., Durham Art Guild (bd. dirs. 1993), City Gallery (bd. dirs. 1993). Baptist. Avocations: movies, shopping, art exhbns.*

MCIVER, DEBORAH KAY, tax specialist, entrepreneur, small business owner; b. Des Moines, Iowa, May 6, 1948; d. Floyd Malcolm and Nora Marguerite McIver. BS, N.Mex. Inst. Mining and Tech., 1970; MBA, Pepperdine U., 1981; postgrad., U. N.Mex., 1985—87. Chem. control technician McGaw Labs., Glendale, Calif., 1971—72; statistician Northrop Corp., Hawthorne, 1972—73; math. analyst TRW Sys. Group, Redondo Beach, 1973—76; sci. programmer ISS/Sperry Univac, Cupertino, 1976—77; mem. tech. staff TRW Sys. Group, Sunnyvale, 1977—78, ArgoSys., 1978—79; sr. sci. programmer Finnigan-MAT Corp., San Jose, 1979—82; software engr. Ford Aerospace Co., Sunnyvale, 1982—83; v.p. software ops. controller Askeri, Inc., Santa Clara, 1983; owner McIver Enterprises, 1983—86, Deborah K. McIver, MBA, EA, 1990—. Gen. contractor own home, 1994—95. Active Sea Scouts Am., L.A., 1975—76; friendly visitor United Way, L.A., 1977—79; judge Santa Clara County Sci. and Engring. Sci. Fair, 1980, 1982, 1984; instr., coord. AARP Tax-Aide, 1992—, Colo. state coord., 2004—. Mem.: Soc. Women Engrs. (v.p. San Francisco Bay Area sect. 1980—81, pres. 1981—82, sect. rep. 1982—83), N.Mex. Inst. Mining and Tech. Alumni Assn. (life; pres. No. Calif. chpt. 1980—81). Republican. Disciples Of Christ. Home and Office: PO Box 889 Monument CO 80132-0889 Office Phone: 719-488-3022.

MCJUNKINS, KRISTIN R., academic administrator; b. Lake Forest, Ill., July 16, 1969; d. Phillip R. and Eleanor G. (Soule) McJ. BS, Widener U., 1992, MEd, 1995. Asst. dir. univ. ctr. Widener U., Chester, Pa., 1992-95, dir. univ. ctr., 1995—99; clin. counselor Keystone Ctr., Chester, 1995—2001; asst. dir. freshman svcs. U. Pa., Phila., 1999—2004; pre-profl. advisor Johns Hopkins U., Balt., 2004—. Contbr. article to profl. jour. Mem. Assn. Coll. Unions Internat., Assn. Coll. Conf. & Events Dirs., Kappa Delta Pi. Avocations: exercise, travel, reading, movies. Office: Widener U 1 University Pl Chester PA 19013-5792 E-mail: krmcjunk@msn.com.

MCKAGUE, SHIRLEY, state representative; b. Nampa, Idaho, Dec. 4, 1935; m. Paul McKague; children: Rhonda, Van, Dan, Randy, Rick, Robert. Grad., Nampa H.S. Legal sec. Carey Nixon, 1964—78; columnist Valley Times, 1980—82; co-owner Paul's Meridian Stinker, 1970—; state rep. dist. 20B Idaho Ho. of Reps., Boise, 1996—, mem., vice chmn. commerce and human resources, and transp. and def. coms., revenue and taxation com. Mem. Miss Meridian Pageant com.; mem. Rep. Precinct Com., 1986—. Mem.: Meridian C. of C., Idaho Farm Bur. Republican. Office: State Capitol PO Box 83720 Boise ID 83720-0038

MCKAIN, MAGGIE MARIE, music educator; b. Great Bend, Kans., Nov. 21, 1959; d. Joseph Ray and Darlene Adeline Boley; m. Clifford Jerome McKain, June 8, 1985; children: Michelle, Jerome, Melissa, Megan. B in music edn., Fort Hays State U., 1983. Music tchr. Unified Sch. Dist., Osborne, Kans., 1983—85, Ellis, Kans., 1985—89, Cawker City, Kans., 1989—97, music specialist Overland Park, Kans., 1997—2006; elem. music specialist USD 367, Osawatomie, Kans., 2006—. Adv. bd. Kans. State U. Music Symposium, Manhattan, Kans., 2002—. Contbr. articles various profl. jours. Mentor to 1st yr. music tchrs. Kans. Music Educators Assn., Kans., 2003—. Mem.: Kans. Music Educators Assn. Achievements include state and nat. panel speaker promoting "Tchg. Through the Art of Performing". Home: 1129 3rd St Osawatomie KS 66064 Office: Unified Sch Dist # 229 Sunset Ridge Elem 14901 England Ave Overland Park KS 66221 Office Phone: 913-755-4133. E-mail: mmckain@bluevalleyk12.org, mckain@usd367.k12.ks.us.

MCKANE, BEATRIX, accountant; m. Bob McKane; children: Cynthia, Derek. BA in History, C.W. Post Coll.; MS in Acct., Roth Grad. Bus. Sch., LI Univ. Audit ptnr., not-for-profit and health care svcs. divsn. Holtz Rubenstein & Co. LLP, Melville, NY. Apptd. to Liaison Com. to the IRS Exempt Orgn. NE Region divsn., Com. which develop. the first CFR Audit Guidelines Manual for NY State; spkr. in field. Bd. dir. several charitable orgn. Named one of Top 50 Women In Business on LI, 2001, 2004. Mem.: Am. Inst. CPA, LI Ctr. Bus. & Profl. Women (Achievement award 1996), NY State Soc. CPA (past pres. exec. bd. Suffolk chpt., apptd. to various ad hoc com., bd. dir. statewide, Outstanding Discussion Leader award 1996—97). Office: Holtz Rubenstein & Co LLP 125 Baylis RD Melville NY 11747-3823 also: Holtz Rubenstein & Co LLP 1120 Ave of Americas New York NY 10036-6773 Office Phone: 631-752-7400 ext. 350, 212-398-7600. Office Fax: 631-752-1742. Business E-Mail: bmckane@hrrlip.com.

MCKAUGHAN, MOLLY, writer, consultant; b. Phila., Jan. 20, 1945; d. Jesse Alfred and Elizabeth Hoffman (Honness) McK.; m. William H. Plummer Jr., May 13, 1978 (div. Aug. 1990); children: Nicholas F., Samantha S BA, Smith Coll., 1967. Mng. editor The Paris Rev., N.Y.C., 1974—76, Quest Mag., N.Y.C., 1976—80, Next Mag., N.Y.C., 1980—81; sr. editor N.Y. Mag., N.Y.C., 1982—83; cons. Montclair, NJ, 1983—98; editor, spl. program officer Robert Wood Johnson Found., Princeton, NJ, 1998—. Cons. Commonwealth Fund, N.Y.C., 1981-82, 88-90, program officer, 1990-91; cons. Grantmakers In Health, 1984-96, ICF Inc., Washington, 1991-93, Robert Wood Johnson Found., 1996-98; vis. prof. Syracuse (N.Y.) U., 1982 Author: The Biological Clock, 1987; adv. editor The Paris Rev., 1976—; author numerous poems; contbr. articles to popular mags Home: 6 Carteret St Montclair NJ 07043-1304 Office: Robert Wood Johnson Found Grant Results Reporting Unit PO Box 2316 Princeton NJ 08543

MC KAY, EMILY GANTZ, civil rights and nonprofit professional; b. Columbus, Ohio, Mar. 13, 1945; d. Harry S. and Edwina (Bookwalter) Gantz; m. Jack Alexander McKay, July 3, 1965. BA, Stanford U., 1966, MA, 1967. From pub. info. specialist to rsch. assoc. Cmty. Action Pitts., 1967—70; freelance cons., 1969—70; pub. rels. and materials specialist Met. Cleve. JOBS Coun., 1971—72; rsch. and mgmt. cons. BLK Group, Inc., Washington, 1970—73; dir. tech. products Am. Tech. Assistance Corp., McLean, Va., 1973—74; rsch. and mgmt. cons. CONSAD Rsch. Corp., Pitts., 1974—76, v.p., 1976—78; spl. asst. to pres. for planning and eval. Nat. Coun. La Raza, Washington, 1978—82, v.p. rsch., advocacy & legislation, 1981—88, exec. v.p., 1983—88, cons. to pres., 1988—90, v.p. instl. devel., 1991—93, sr. v.p. instl. devel., 1993—94. Pres. Mosaica: Ctr. for Nonprofit Devel. and Pluralism, 1994—; cons. resource devel. New Israel Fund, 1989-91; cons. City of Cleve., Nat. Assn. Cmty. Devel., Nat. Coun. La Raza, 1975-78, Ford Found., 1989, Nat. AIDS Network, 1988-89, Am. Cultural Ctr., Israel, 1990, Nat. Hispana Leadership Inst., 1993; vol. orgnl. cons. SHATIL, Jerusalem and cmty. based groups in Israel, 1987—; guest faculty Union Inst. Grad. Sch., 1975-78; adj. faculty Sch. Internat. Svc. Am. U., Washington, 1995—; mem. faculty Salzburg (Austria) Seminar on Leadership, 2003. Author orgnl. devel. tng. materials and HIV/AIDS tech. assistance materials. Co-chmn. Citizens Adv. Com. to D.C. Bar, 1986-87; mem. Mayor's Commn. Coop. Econ. Devel., 1981-83; non-lawyer bd. govs. D.C. Bar, 1982-85; exec. com., bd. dirs. Indochina Resource Action Ctr., 1982-92; bd. dirs. exec. com. Southeast Asia Resource Action Ctr., 1993-97; co-chmn. Citizens Commn. Adminstrn. Justice, 1982-84; exec. com. Coalition on Human Needs, 1981-88; Washington area steering com. New Israel Fund, 1989-91; co-chmn. adv. com. to Washington dist. office dir. Immigration and Naturalization Svc., 1984-88; chair Refugee Women in Devel., 1987-90, vice-chair, 1990-94; nat. adv. bd. Project Blueprint United Way of Am., 1992-94, diversity com., 1994-96; vice-chair, treas. Fund for Future of Our Children, 1994—; sec. bd. dirs. New Bosnia Fund, 1995-99, U.S. vice-chair, 1997-99; bd. advisors Internat. Ctr. for Residential Edn., 1994-96; bd. dirs. Mary's Ctr. Maternal and Child Care, 1995-2000, treas., 1996-2000; treas., bd. dirs. AVODAH: The Jewish Svc. Corps., 1996-99; bd. dirs. Acad. of Hope, 2001—; bd. dirs. Nat. Hispana Leadership Inst., 1997-2003, treas., 1998-2003, Hispanic Link Journalism Found., Washington, D.C., 2004—; working group Memorandum of Understanding between HHS and Israeli Ministry of Labour and Social Welfare, 1990-94, chair subcom. Youth at Risk, 1992-94; adv. merit sel. panel Superior Ct. D.C., 1987-90; planning task force U.S.-Israel Women to Women, 2000-01. Recipient I. Pat Rios award Guadalupe Ctr., 1988, Milagros Beanfield award Ayuda, 2004; Ford Found. nat. honors fellow, 1966-67. Mem. NAACP, Nat. Coun. La Raza, Phi Beta Kappa. Democrat. Home: 3200 19th St NW Washington DC 20010-1006 Office: 1522 K St NW Ste 1130 Washington DC 20005-1225 Office Phone: 202-887-0620. Business E-Mail: Emily@mosaica.org.

MCKAY, JOANE WILLIAMS, dean; b. New Underwood, S.D., June 5, 1939; d. Gene Edward and Saxon Molly (Guptill) Williams; m. Donald Jerome McKay, June 5, 1964; children: Marc Donald, Troy Daniel. BA, Augustana Coll., Sioux Falls, S.D., 1961; MS, Iowa State U., 1986, PhD, 1990. Pub. sch. tchr., Wyo., Iowa and S.D., 1980-89; dir. field experience Iowa State U., Ames, 1989-91; grad. coord. U. Nev., Las Vegas, 1991-94; assoc. dean U. No. Iowa, Cedar Falls, 1994-97; dean St. Cloud (Minn.) State U., 1997—. Columnist, Riverton (Wyo.) Ranger, 1966-72, Ames Daily Tribune, 1974-84. Named Tchr. of Yr., Nat. Tchr. of Yr. Awards, 1988. Mem. Assn. Tchr. Educators (chair global task force 1996), Am. Assn. Colls. for Tchr. Edn. (chair spl. interest group 1997). Office: St Cloud State U 720 4th Ave S Saint Cloud MN 56301-4498

MCKAY, LAURA L., bank executive, consultant; b. Watonga, Okla., Mar. 3, 1947; d. Frank Bradford and Elizabeth Jane (Smith) Drew; m. Cecil O. McKay, Sept. 20, 1969; 1 child, Leslie. BSBA, Oreg. State U., 1969. Cert. cash mgr., Treasury Mgmt. Assn. New br. rsch. U.S. Bank, Portland, Oreg., 1969-80, cash mgmt. officer, 1980-82, asst. v.p., 1982-87, v.p., 1987-94; founder, cons. LLM Cons., Milw., 1994-97; co-founder, mng. ptnr. DMC & Assocs. LLC, Portland, 1997—2001; v.p. treasury mgmt., sales mgr. West Coast Bank, 2000—. Cert. trainer Achieve Global and Edge Learning. Chmn. Budget Com., North Clackamas Sch. Dist., 1982-84. Mem. ASTD, Assn. for Fin. Profls., Nat. Assn. Bank Women (chmn. Oreg. group l979-80), Portland Treasury Mgrs. Assn., Portland C. of C. Republican. Office: Ste 100 5000 Meadows Rd Lake Oswego OR 97034 Office Phone: 503-603-8052. E-mail: mckayl@wcb.com.

MCKAY, MARGO MARQUITA, federal agency administrator, lawyer; b. Baltimore, Md., Oct. 9, 1946; d. Gordon and Gary Venetia (Jones) M.; m. James Phillip Allen, Jr., June 10, 1978; children: Marja Allen, Eric Allen, Kaila Allen. BA, Fisk U., Nashville, Tenn., 1968; JD, Georgetown U., Washington, D.C., 1975. Bar: Penn. 1975, Va. 1982. Trial atty. US Dept. Justice, Washington, 1975-78; atty. Am. Legal Cons., 1979; br. chief Dept. Army US Dept. Def., 1980-81; mng. atty. Legal Serv. No. Va., Alexandria, 1982-83; exec. asst. to vice-chmn., sr. advisor, US Merit Systems Protection Bd., Washington, 1983-91; dep. dir. for ethics US Dept. Housing & Urban Devel., Washington, 1990; adminstrv. judge, temp. panel Office Employee Appeals, DC; dir. compliance, assoc. gen. counsel Fannie Mae; asst. sec. for civil rights USDA, Washington, 2006—. Author (high sch. textbook): Street Law, 1975. Recipient numerous employment awards, 1970—. Mem. ABA, Federal Circuit Bar Assoc. Office: USDA Jamie L Whitten Bldg 14th St & Independence Ave SW Rm 240-W Washington DC 20250*

MCKAY, MELINDA, hotel executive; b. Sydney, Australia, 1974; Corp. mktg. devel., rsch. svcs. Jones Lang LaSalle Hotels Asia Pacific; mktg. rsch. Jones Lang LaSalle Hotels, rsch. mgr. Chgo., 1997—99, sr. v.p., 2001—. Named one of 40 Under Forty, Crain's Chgo. Bus., 2005. Office: Jones Lang Lasalle Hotels 190 S LaSalle St Chicago IL 60603*

MCKAY, PATRICIA A., corporate financial executive; CPA. V.p., fin., controller Dole Food Co., 1993—96; sr. v.p. fin. AutoNation Inc.; exec. v.p., CFO Restoration Hardware Inc., 2003—05, Office Depot, Delray Beach, Fla., 2005—. Bd. dir. Office Depot, 2004—05. Office: Office Depot 2200 Old germantown Rd Delray Beach FL 33445*

MCKAY, RENEE, artist; b. Montreal, Que., Can. came to U.S., 1946, naturalized, 1954; d. Frederick Garvin and Mildred Gladys (Higgins) Smith; m. Kenneth Gardiner McKay, July 25, 1942; children: Margaret Craig, Kenneth Gardner. BA, McGill U., 1941. Tchr. art Peck Sch., Morristown, NJ, 1955-56. One woman shows include Pen and Brush Club, N.Y.C., 1957, Cosmopolitan Club, N.Y.C., 1958; group shows include Weyhe Gallery, N.Y.C., 1978, Newark Mus., 1955, 59, Montclair (N.J.) Mus., 1955-58, Nat. Assn. Women Artists, Nat. Acad. Galleries, 1954-78, N.Y. World's Fair, 1964-65, Audubon Artists, N.Y.C., 1955-62, 74-79, N.Y. Soc. Women Artists, 1979-80, Provincetown (Mass.) Art Assn. and Mus., 1975-79; traveling shows in France, Belgium, Italy, Scotland, Can., Japan; represented in permanent collections: Slater Meml. Mus., Norwich, Conn., Norfolk (Va.) Mus., Butler Inst. Am. Art, Youngstown, Ohio, Lydia Drake Libr., Pembroke, Mass., Nat. Arts Club, N.Y.C., Provinceton Mus.- Mass., Provincetown, many pvt. collections. Recipient Jane Peterson prize in oils Nat. Assn. Women Artists, 1954, Famous Artists Sch. prize in watercolor, 1959, Grumbacher Artists Watercolor award 1970, Solo award Pen and Brush, 1957, Sadie-Max Tesser award in watercolor Audubon Artists, 1975, Peterson prize in oils, 1980, Michael Engel prize Nat. Soc. Painters in Casein and Acrylic, 1983. Mem. Nat. Assn. Women Artists (2d v.p. 1969-70, adv. bd. 1974-76), Audubon Artists (pres. 1979, dir. oils 1986-88), Artist Equity (dir. 1977-79, v.p. 1979-81), N.Y. Soc. Women Artists, Pen and Brush, Nat. Soc. Painters in Casein and Acrylic M.J. Kaplan prize 1984, Nat. Arts Club, Provincetown Art Assn. and Mus., Key West Art Assn., Cosmopolitan Club.

MCKAY, SUSAN BOGART, social worker, consultant, artist; b. Miami, Fla., Sept. 25, 1957; d. Frederic Stanley and Jeanette Sophie (Braka) B. AAS, Westchester C.C., 1986; BS in Social Work magna cum laude, Mercy Coll., 1988. Child care counselor Oaklane Day Care, Chapagua, N.Y., Children's Village, Dobbs Ferry, N.Y.; swim instr. for blind and visually impaired teens and adults YMCA, White Plains, N.Y.; group leader spl. svcs. programs, supr. teens vol. programs YM and YWHA of Mid-Westchester, Scarsdale, N.Y.; healthcare and benefit cons. in pvt. practice, Mamaroneck, N.Y. Cons. Midland Credit Corp., N.Y.C. Exhibited art works, Westchester, N.Y., 1997-99. Participant human rights commn. Nat. UN Model Conf., 1987. Mem. NASW, Mercy Coll. Alumni Assn., Alpha Chi.

MCKAY-COX, MARIANNE, secondary school educator; d. Robert Riggs and Frances Ellen Anderson McKay; 1 child, Robert McKay Cox. BS, U. Utah, Salt Lake City, 1969, MS, 1986. Cert. secondary tchr. Ariz., 1986, prin. Ariz., 1995, Maricopa County C.C. instr. Ariz., 1998. Tchr. Scottsdale Unified Sch. Dist. #48, Ariz., 1986—. Adj. prof. Scottsdale C.C., Ariz., 1999—2000; tchr. Scottsdale Ednl. Enrichment Svcs. Summer Sch., Ariz., 1988—96, Scottsdale Unified Sch. Dist. Summer Sch., Ariz., 1988—2006, Mesa Unified Sch. Dist. Night Sch., Ariz., 1996—96, Mesa Unified Sch. Dist. Summer Sch., Ariz., 1996—96; adj. prof. Rio Salado C.C., Tempe, Ariz., 1998—2001; curriculum developer in field. Grad. mem. Mesa Leadership Tng. Orgn., Ariz., 1996—96; elected precinct committeeman Rep. Party, Scottsdale, Ariz., 2004—06. Named an Outstanding Teenage Rep. Advisor U.S.A., 2001, 2006, Outstanding Ariz. Teenage Rep. Club Advisor, 2002, 2003, 2004, 2005, 2006; recipient Achievement and Excellence in Tchg. award, Nat. Soc. HS Scholars, 2004. Mem.: Chi Omega Sorority (life). Avocations: tutor homebound students, travel, gym workouts, yoga, hiking. Home: Unit 1009 10115 E Mountain View Rd Scottsdale AZ 85258 Office: Scottsdale Unified Sch Dist # 48 6250 N 82nd St Scottsdale AZ 85258 Office Phone: 480-484-7100 5113. E-mail: mmckay-cox@susd.org.

MCKAY-WILKINSON, JULIE ANN, minister, marriage and family therapist; b. Washington, D.C., Feb. 26, 1953; d. Charles William and Evelyn Loretta (Starr) McKay; m. Grover Gene Wilkinson, Jan. 13, 1990; 1 child, Angela Starr Gotti. AS, Camden County Coll., 1975; BA, Rowan U., 1978; grad., Unity Sch. Christianity, Lee's Summit, Mo., 1997. Cert. pastoral addictions counselor, and lic. addictions counselor, co-dependency counselor. Probation officer York County Probation, Pa., 1983—86; therapist pvt. practice, York, 1985—90, New Insights, York, 1985—87, Clare Ctr., York, 1987—90; founder, min., therapist Unity Christ Ch., Lubbock, Tex., 1997—2003. Editor: (monthly newsletter) Spiritual Lifelines, 1997—2003. Chairperson Christmas toy dr. Unity Christ Ch., 1997—2003, founder, Christmas bear dr., 2003—. Mem.: Lubbock Ecimenical Orgn. Democrat. Avocations: gardening, music, movies. Office: Christ Unity Church 7300 Mallard Creek Rd Charlotte NC 28262 Home: 2540 Pickway Dr Charlotte NC 28269 Office Phone: 704-599-1180. Personal E-mail: revjulie3@carolina.rr.com.

MCKEAGE, ALICE JANE, computer programmer; b. Saginaw, Mich., Mar. 27, 1948; d. Donald William and Genevieve Francis McK. BS in Edn., Ctrl. Mich. U., Mt. Pleasant, Mich., 1970. Tchr. Madison Dist. Pub. Schs., Madison Heights, Mich., 1970—79; computer programmer Retail Mgmt. Svcs., Birmingham, Mich., 1980—82, 3 PM, Livonia, Mich., 1982—85, Am. Fin. Cons. Co., Troy, Mich., 1985—87, Cats Co., Troy, 1988—90, Ford Motor Co., Dearborn, Mich., 1990—. Interviewee (TV show) Straight Talk About Gays in the Workplace, 2001. Co-founder gay, lesbian, bisexual transgender employee network Ford Motor Co., 1994; co-founder Race Matters, Detroit gay, lesbian, bisexual, transgender discussion group on racism and sexism, 2000; mem. human rights campaign Nat. Gay and Lesbian Task Force, Gay and Lesbian Alliance Against Defamation; mem. steering com. Main St. Pride, Royal Oak, Mich., 1996, outreach co-chair, 1997; bd. dirs. Affirmations Gay Lesbian Bisexual Transgender Cmty. Ctr., Ferndale, 2000—03. Recipient Cmty. Svc. award, Gay Lesbian Bisexual Transgender Pride, 1999, Spirit of Detroit award, Detroit City Coun., 2001, Unity award, Race Matters Gay, Lesbian, Bisexual Transgender Pride awards, 2002, Jan Stevenson award, Affirmations Gay and Lesbian Cmty. Center, 2004. Mem.: NOW, Out and Equal Workplace Advs. Democrat. Avocations: senior softball, gardening, hiking. Office: Ford Motor Co The American Rd Dearborn MI 48121

MCKEE, BETTY DAVIS, English language educator; b. St. Pauls, N.C., June 30, 1946; d. John Chesley and Ernestene King Davis; m. Danny Lee McKee, July 13, 1980; children: Brooke Elizabeth Burgess, Ginger Rae Fears, Amanda Lea. AA, Chowan Coll., Murfreesboro, N.C., 1966; BA, Campbell Coll., Buies Creek, N.C., 1968. Cert. Collegiate Profl. Va., 1970. Tchr. Pinkston Street Sch., Henderson, NC, 1968—70, We. Br. H.S., Chesapeake, Va., 1970—71, Western Branch Jr. High Sch., Chesapeake, 1971—73, Deep Creek Jr. H.S., Chesapeake, 1974—75, We. Br. Jr. H.S., Chesapeake, 1975—91, Western Branch Middle Sch., Chesapeake, 1991—2006. Chair English dept. We. Br. Jr. H.S., 1976—80, 1990—91, We. Br. Mid. Sch., 1991—, team leader, 1991—, co-sponsor Nat. Honor Soc., 2000—05, mem. faculty adv. com.; internal coord. We. Br. Mid. Sch. So. Assn. Colls. and Schs., Chesapeake, 2004—. Mem. AAUW, Portsmouth, Va., 2001—05; bd. dirs. Campbell U. Alumni Assn., Buies Creek, 1978—94; yearbook sponsor, 1971—85; pres. Tidewater chpt. Campbell U. Alumni Assn., Chesapeake, 1978—98. Named Tchr. of Yr., We. Br. Jr. H.S., 1987. Mem.: NEA, PTA (life), Chesapeake Edn. Assn. (treas. 2000—04), Va. Edn. Assn., Delta Kappa Gamma Beta Iota (assoc.; pres. 2002—04, recording sec. 2000—02). Avocations: reading mystery novels, travel, collecting cookbooks.

MCKEE, ELEANOR SWETNAM, retired principal; b. Del Norte, Colo., Oct. 21, 1934; d. William Wayne and Harriet Norris Swetnam; children: Tim, David, Christopher. BA in Secondary Edn., Adams State Coll., 1960; MA in Elem. Edn., U. So. Colo., 1976; postgrad., U. Hawaii, 1976—78. Tchr. Nenana Schs., Alaska, 1964—76; prin. Railroad Sch. Dist., Healy, Alaska, 1976—89; journalist Prism Enterprises, LaJunta, Colo., 1991—95; curriculum writer Internat. Found. for Edn. and Self Help, Malawi, Africa, 1998—99; prin. Am. Grade Schs., Phoenix, 1998—99; tchr. Phoenix Christian Acad., 1999—2001; prin. Beaver Sch./Yukon Flats Sch. Dist., Ft. Yukon, Alaska, 2001—02; ret., 2002. Contbr. articles to profl. jours. Tchr. vol. Migrant Edn., Rocky Rd., Colo., 1991—95. Mem.: N.C. Writers Network, Alaska Edn. Assn. (sec. 1979—80), Orton Soc. Republican. Episcopalian. Avocations: hiking, theater, cooking, piano, mountain biking. Home: PO Box 233 Sugar City CO 81076-0233

MCKEE, JUDITH NELSON, elementary school educator, educational consultant; b. Iowa Falls, Iowa, Nov. 8, 1939; d. Herbert and Emma (Czako) Nelson; m. Bernard B. McKee, Oct. 20, 1962; children: Susan Jennifer Ziegler, Blair David. BA, U. No. Iowa, 1961; MA, Roosevelt U., 1967; postgrad., Ill. State U., Nat. Louis U. Cert. tchr. K-9, learning disabilities K-12. Tchr. 2d grade Dist. 25 Pub. Schs., Arlington Heights, Ill., 1961-67; itinerant tchr. learning disabilities N.W. Suburban Spl. Edn. Dist., Palatine, Ill., 1968-72; tchr. Winnetka (Ill.) Pub. Sch. Nursery, 1974-75; tchr. spl. edn. North Suburban Spl. Edn. Dist., Glenview, Ill., 1975-76; tchr. gifted Worlds of Wisdom and Wonder, Evanston, Ill., 1985-87; instr. astronomy North Cook County Ednl. Svc. Ctr., Glenview, 1987; mem. faculty Nat. Louis U., Evanston, Ill., 1991—2004, DePaul U., Chgo., 2000—01; tchr. primary grades dist. 39 Wilmette, Ill., 1976—99; faculty U. No. Iowa, Cedar Falls, 2002—. Presenter, cons. state, nat. and internat. confs. Co-author: Integrating Instruction: Literacy and Science, 2005; author (with others): Physical Science Activities for Elementary and Middle School, 1987, Fact, Fiction, and Fantasy, 1995; contbr. articles to profl. jours. Named Ill. Honors Sci. Tchr. NSF, Ill. State. U., 1989-91. Mem. Internat. Reading Assn., Nat. Reading Conf., Nat. Sci. Tchrs. Assn. (ret. adv. bd. 2000-03, chair 2002-03), Coun. Elem. Sci. Internat., Ill. Sci. Tchrs. Assn., Phi Delta Kappa. Presbyterian. Home: 315 Fairview Ave Winnetka IL 60093-4210

MCKEE, KATHRYN DIAN GRANT, human resources consultant; b. LA, Sept. 12, 1937; d. Clifford William and Amelia Rosalie (Shacher) G.; m. Paul Eugene McKee, June 17, 1961; children: Scott Alexander, Grant Christopher. BA, U. Calif., Santa Barbara, 1959; grad. Anderson Sch. Mgmt. Exec. Program, UCLA, 1979. Cert. compensation and benefits. Mgr. Mattel, Inc., Hawthorne, Calif., 1963-74; dir. Twentieth Century Fox Film Corp., L.A., 1975-80; sr. v.p. 1st Interstate Bank, Ltd., L.A., 1980-93; sr. v.p. and human resources dir. Am.'s Std. Chartered Bank, 1993-95; pres. Human Resources Consortia, Santa Barbara, Calif., 1995—. V.p. cons. Right Mgmt. Cons., 1997-98; dir. Accordia benefits of Southern Calif., 1991-96, mem. exec. com. H.R. div. of Am. Bankers Assn., 1991-93; bd. dirs. Bank Certification Inst. Am. Bankers Assn., 1992-94; treas. Pers. Accreditation Inst., 1983-86, pres., 1986. Contbr. articles to profl. jours. Pres. GEM Theatre Guild, Garden Grove, Calif., 1984-86; bd. dirs. Vis. Nurses Assn., L.A., 1984-88, SHRM, 1986-92, treas., 1989, vice-chmn., 1990, chmn., 1991, pres. SHRM Found., 1994, 95; bd. dirs. Laguna Playhouse, 1996-2000, pres., 1998-99; dir. Old Spanish Days, 2001-, Ensemble Theatre Co., 2002-; mem. U. Calif. Santa Barbara Found., 2001-, vice chmn. stewardship, 2001-. Recipient Sr. Honor Key award U. Calif., Santa Barbara, 1959, William Winter award Am. Compensation Assn., 1986, Excellence award L.A. Pers. Indsl. Rels. Assn., 1990, Profl. Excellence award SHRM, 1994; named Outstanding Sr. Woman, 1959. Mem. Internat. Assn. Pers. Women (various offices, past nat. pres., Mem. of Yr. 1986), U. Calif. Santa Barbara Alumni Assn. (bd. dirs. 1995-2001, pres.-elect 1999, pres. 1999-2000). Office: Human Resources Consortia 3730 Cedar Vis Santa Barbara CA 93110-1578 E-mail: kmckee3730@cox.net.

MCKEE, LYNN B., human resources specialist; B in Acctg., St. Joseph's U.; MBA, Drexel U. Various positions including dir. employee rels., dir. human resources and exec. devel. Aramark Corp., Phila., 1980—86, mgr. hqtrs. human resources, 1986—89, dir. human resources, 1989, v.p. exec. devel. and compensation, 1998—2001, sr. v.p. human resources, 2001—04, exec. v.p. human resources, 2004—. Mem. human resources roundtable group; mem. conf. bd. advisory coun. human resources mgmt. Office: Aramark Corp Aramark Tower 1101 Market St Philadelphia PA 19107-2988 Office Phone: 215-238-3000. Office Fax: 215-238-3333.

MCKEE, MARGARET JEAN, federal agency administrator; b. New Haven, June 20, 1929; d. Waldo McCutcheon and Elizabeth McKee. AB, Vassar Coll., 1951. Staff asst. United Rep. Fin. Com., N.Y.C., 1952, N.Y. Rep. State Com., N.Y.C., 1953—55, Crusade for Freedom (name later changed to Radio Free Europe Fund), N.Y.C., 1955—57; researcher Stricker & Henning Rsch. Assocs., Inc., N.Y.C., 1957—59; exec. sec. New Yorkers for Nixon (name later changed to N.Y. State Ind. Citizens for Nixon Lodge), N.Y.C., 1959—60; asst. to Raymond Moley, polit. columnist N.Y.C., 1961; asst. campaign com. Louis J. Lefkowitz for Mayor, N.Y.C., 1961; rsch. programmer, treas. Consensus, Inc., N.Y.C., 1962—67; spl. asst. to U. S. Senator Jacob K. Javits NY, 1967—73; adminstr. asst. NY, 1973—75; dep. adminstr. Am. Revolution Bicentennial Adminstrn., 1976, acting adminstr., 1976—77; chief of staff Perry B. Duryea (minority leader) N.Y. State Assembly, 1978; pub. affairs cons., 1979—80; dir. govt. rels. Gen. Mills Restaurant Group, Inc., 1980—83; exec. dir. Fed. Mediation and Conciliation Svc., 1983—86; mem. Fed. Labor Rels. Authority, 1986—89, chmn., 1989—94; mem. Nat. Partnership Coun., 1993—94; chmn. adv. bd. Workplace Solutions, 1996—98. Mem. U.S. Adv.Commn. on Pub. Diplomacy, 1972—82; dir. scheduling and spkrs.' bur. N.Y. Com. to Re-elect the Pres., 1972; mem. bd. govs. Women's Nat. Rep. Club, N.Y.C., 1963—66; mem. N.Y. State Bingo Control Commn., 1965—72; pres. Bklyn. Heights Slope Young Rep. Club, 1955—56; co-chmn. Bklyn. Citizens for Eisenhower-Nixon, 1956; chmn. 2nd Jud. Dist. Assn. N.Y. State Young Rep. Clubs, Inc., 1957—58, vice chmn., mem. bd. govs., 1958—60, v.p., 1960—62, pres., 1962—64; mem. exec. com. Fedn. Women's Rep. Clubs N.Y. State, Inc., 1960—64; asst. campaign mgr. Kenneth B. Keating for Judge Ct. Appeals, NY, 1965; dir. scheduling Gov. Rockefeller campaign, 1966, Sen. Charles E. Goodell campaign, 1970; dir. planning and strategy Conn. Reagan-Bush campaign, Hartford, 1980; mem annual fund adv. com. Vassar Coll., 1992—96, chmn. 50th Reunion, 2001. Mem.: Conn. Olmsted Heritage Alliance (treas. 2005—), Nat. Assn. Olmsted Parks (trustee 2003—), New Eng. Hist. Geneal. Soc. (mem. adv. coun. 2001—03, trustee 2003—06, mem. adv. coun. 2006—, 2006—), Nat. Women's Edn. Fund. (former mem. bd.), Exec. Women on Govt. (chmn. 1986), Nat. Soc. Colonial Dames, Vassar Club (past dir., Bklyn.), Am. Newspaper Women's Club, Jr. League of Bklyn. (past dir.). Republican. Episcopalian. also: 3001 Veazey Ter NW Apt 1225 Washington DC 20008-5407 Address: 532 S Brooksvale Rd Cheshire CT 06410

MCKEE, RHONDA LOUISE, mathematics professor; b. Lamar, Mo., Apr. 23, 1960; d. Ivan Wayne McKee and Ella Mae (Walker) Cooper. BS, BS in Edn., Mo. So. State Coll., 1982; MS in Applied Math., U. Mo., Rolla, 1984, PhD in Topology, 1989. Cert. secondary tchr., Mo. Grad. teaching asst. U. Mo., Rolla, 1982-84, 86-89; instr. math. Cen. Mo. State U., Warrensburg, 1984-86, asst. prof., 1989, prof. math. Referee Mo. Jour. Math. Scis., 1989—. Contbr. articles to profl. jours. Mem. singles coun., editor Corner Notes newsletter Grover Park Bapt. Ch., Warrensburg, 1989—. Chancellor's fellow U. Mo., Rolla, 1982-84, 86-89, faculty rsch. grantee, 1988, 89. Mem. Math. Assn. Am., Am. Math. Soc., Assn. for Women in Math. Office: Cen Mo State U Office WCM 225 Dept Math and Computer Sci Warrensburg MO 64093 Office Phone: 816-543-8929. Office Fax: 660-543-8013. Business E-Mail: mckee@cmsu.edu, mckee@cmsul.csmu.edu.*

MCKEEL, LILLIAN PHILLIPS, retired education educator; b. Rocky Mount, N.C., Aug. 23, 1932; d. Ellis Elma and Lillian Bonner (Archbell) Phillips; m. James Thomas McKeel Jr., July 23, 1955; children: Sarah Lillian McKeel Youngblood, Mary Kathleen McKeel Welch. BA, U. N.C., 1954; MEd, Pa. State U., 1977, DEd, 1993. Tchr. State Coll. (Pa.) Area Schs., 1964-90; instr. Pa. State U., University Park, 1990-93; asst. prof. Shippensburg (Pa.) U., 1993—2001; ret., 2001. Mem. of panel NSTA Book Rev. Panel/Outstanding Sci. Tradebooks for Children, Washington, 1992; faculty sponsor Shippensburg U. Sch. Study Coun., 1993-95. Contbr. articles to profl. jours. Recipient Presdl. award for Excellence in Sci. and Math. Tchng., NSF, Washington, 1990; finalist Tchr. of Yr. program Pa. Dept. Edn., Harrisburg, 1992, cert. Recognition, Hon. Robert Casey/Gov., Harrisburg, Pa., 1991; named Achieving Women of Penn State, Pa. State U., 1993. Mem. Nat. Sci. Tchrs. Assn., Soc. Presdl. Awardees, Assn. Edn. Tchrs. in Sci., Coun. Elem. Sci. Internat., Phi Delta Kappa (Disting. Svc. award 1992), Pi Lambda Theta, Phi Kappa Phi. Avocations: photography, collecting antique toys. Home: 3222 Shellers Bend Unit 230 State College PA 16801-3227 E-mail: lmcke637@aol.com.

MCKEEL, SHERYL WILSON, pharmacist; b. Nashville, Apr. 6, 1957; d. Robert Lewis and Norma Anne (Cox) Wilson; m. Vaughn Allen McKeel, Apr. 22, 2000. BS in Biology, David Lipscomb U., 1979; BS in Pharmacy, Auburn U., 1985. Lic. pharmacist, Tenn. Student extern/intern East Alabama Med. Ctr., Opelika, Ala., 1982-86; staff pharmacist Metro Nashville Gen. Hosp., 1987-95, PharmaThera, Inc., Nashville, 1995-99, Mid. Tenn. Mental Health Inst., Nashville, 1999-2000. Flutist Nashville Cmty. Concert Band, 1973-97; presch. tchr. Donelson Ch. of Christ, 1988—; active Lipscomb U. Cmty. Chorus, 1998—. Mem. Am. Pharm. Assn., Am. Soc. Health Sys. Pharmacists, Am. Soc. Parenteral and Enteral Nutrition, Tenn. Soc. Health Sys. Pharmacists, Nashville Area Pharmacists Assn. Democrat. Avocations: art, music, reading, cooking, sewing. Home: 1439 McGavock Pike Nashville TN 37216-3231 Personal E-mail: mckeelsw@prodigy.net.

MCKEEN, CATHERINE A., humanities educator; b. Queens, NY, Sept. 27, 1965; MA, Washington U., St. Louis, 1991; PhD, Rutgers U., New Brunswick, NJ, 2001. Asst. prof. SUNY Coll. Brockport, 2001—, dir. women's studies, 2005—. Office: SUNY College at Brockport New Campus Dr Brockport NY 14420 Office Phone: 585-395-2026.

MCKEEN, ELISABETH ANNE, oncologist; b. New Castle, Pa., Oct. 13, 1950; d. Richard Douglas and Harriette Elisabeth McK; m. Barry Nixon Walker; children: Anne, Matthew. BS in Biology, Rensselaer Polytech. Inst., 1974; MD, Albany Med. Coll., 1974. Diplomate Nat. Bd. Med. Examiners, Am. Bd. Internal Medicine, Am. Bd. Med. Oncology, Am. Bd. Hospice and Palliative Medicine; cert. in familial cancer assessment and mgmt. Intern Emory U. Affiliated Hosps., Atlanta, 1974-75, resident, 1975-76; fellow cancer epidemiology Nat. Cancer Inst., Bethesda, Md., 1976-78; fellow med. oncology Georgetown U. Hosp., Washington, 1978-79; clin. instr. in medicine Georgetwon U. Hosp., Washington, 1979-82; clin. asst. prof. U. Fla., Gainesville, 1987—; from assoc. to ptnr. Harris & McKeen MDs, P.A., W. Palm Beach, Fla., 1982-90; Palm Beach Oncology/Hematology Good Samaritan Med. Ctr., W. Palm Beach, 1993—, Helen and Harry Gray Cancer Inst., 1997—. Clin. investigator Nat. Cancer Inst., Bethesda, Md. 1979-82; med. dir. Hospice Palm Beach County, 1985-93, faculty, 1990; chmn. med. edn. com. Palm Beach County chpt., 1983—; cons. assoc. dept. medicine Duke U., Durham, N.C., 1994—; med. dir. cancer genetics and counseling, Dr. Mary Tarzian Cancer Genetic Program, 1997—; med. dir. Norma E. and Miles M. Zisson Comprehensive Breast Ctr. Good Samaritan Med. Ctr., W. Palm Beach, 1997—; staff mem. St. Mary's Hosp., West Palm Beach, chair pharmacy and therapeutic com., 1992-93, transfusion com. 1989-90; mem. quality assurance, 1987-88, pharmacy and therapeutic 1991-92, continuing edn. com., 1992-93; cons. Palm Beach Gardens Med. Ctr., Palm Beach Gardens, Fla., 1982—; co-chmn. breast com. Duke Comprehensive Cancer Ctr., 1993—. Contbr. articles to profl. jours. including Am. Jour. Human Genetics, Am. Soc. Human Gentics, Proceedings Am. Soc. Clin. Oncology, Am. Assn. Cancer Rsch., Jour. Nat. Cancer Inst., Lancet, Annals Internal Medicine, Internat. Jour. Cancer; speaker to sci. groups and in ednl. insts. Fla. Chmn. med. edn. com. Am. Cancer Soc., Palm Beach County, 1983—, bd. dirs. 1984-88; mem. speaker's bur. VNA, 1984-88; bd. dir. S. Fla. chpt. Susan G. Komen Breast Cancer Found., Dallas, 1991—; peer reviewer cancer related pain guideline for health care providers Agy. for Health Care Policy and Rsch. and Pain Mgmt. Panel, 1992. Fellow ACP; mem. AMA, Am. Acad. Hospice Physicians (bd. dirs. 1988—, chmn. edn. and tng. com. 1988—), So. Assn. for Oncology, Fla. Soc. Clin. Oncology (bd. dirs. 1991-93, legis., legal and ethics com. 1992-93), Israel Cancer Assn. (regional sci. bd.), Am. Soc. Breast Disease, Am. Soc. Clin. Oncology, Palm Beach County Med. Soc., Am. Soc. Internal Medicine, Fla. Cancer Control and Rsch. Adv. Bd., Gilda's Club of S. Fla. (profl. adv. bd.). Office: Helen & Harry Cancer Inst Palm BEach Cancer Institute 1309 N Flagler Dr West Palm Beach FL 33401-3406 E-mail: elisabeth.mckeen@pbcancer.com.

MCKEEN, SALLY WERST, volunteer; b. Phila., July 28, 1934; d. Harry Kenneth and Doris Callaway Werst; m. Chester M. McKeen, Jr., Nov. 6, 1999 (div.); 1 child, Stephen Harry Werst. BFA, U. Tex., 1956; postgrad., U. Wis., 1975. Intern UN, N.Y.C., 1956; adminstrv. asst. Free Europe Com., Munich, 1958—59; writer, editor U.S. Army Forces Southern Command, Fort Amador, Canal Zone, 1963—75; editor 5th Army Inf. Divsn. Mech., Fort Polk, La., 1975—76; dep. chief of pub. affairs U.S. Army Corps. of Engrs., Dallas, 1976—79, chief pub. affairs Memphis, 1979—83, Fort Worth, Tex., 1983—94. Vol. Harris Meth. Hosp.; bd. dirs. Union Gospel Mission; active U. Christian Ch., deacon, Stephen Minister; bd. dirs. Boy Scouts Am., Women's Policy Forum, YMCA Camp Carter, Ct. Apptd. Spl. Advocates for Children, ARC, Exec. Svc. Corps., Tarrant Area Food Bank; regional dir. Leadership Tex.; chair Leadership Fort Worth, Huguley Meml. Med. Ctr. Hospice, Salvation Army Fort Worth/Tarrant Area; bd. dirs., chair Cancer Care Svcs.; bd. dirs. Cmty. Found. North Tex.; sec. bd. dirs. Meals on Wheels Endowment, Women's Ctr. Tarrant County; bd. dirs. Girl Scouts Am.; mem. capital campaign steering com. Goodwill Industries; active in pub. rels. and devel. coms. Crime Prevention Resource Ctr.; coms. Alzheimer's Assn.; bd. visitors McDonald Observatory U. Tex.; bd. dirs. Learning Ctr. North Tex., Cmty. Hospice of Tex.; commr. Tex. Commn. on Law Enforcement. Decorated Meritorious Civilian Svc. medal U.S. Army; named Outstanding Women of Fort Worth, 1998; recipient Nat. Leadership award, Nat. Assn. for Cmty. Leadership, 1999, Citizen of the Week award, KRLD Dallas, 1998, Sr. Vol. of Yr. award, United Way, 1997, Vol. of Yr. award, Salvation Army, 1977. Mem.: Panamanian/Am. Soc., Pub. Rels. Soc. Am. (Fort Worth co founder, pres., Silver Anvil and Silver Quill awards 1983), Nat. Soc. Fundraising Execs. (bd. dirs., Vol. Fundraiser of Yr. award 1998), Fort Worth Rotary Club (dir., sec. 1993—95, Paul Harris fellow), Kappa Alpha Theta. Republican. Home: 2310 Woodsong Trail Arlington TX 76016 Personal E-mail: swerstmckeen@aol.com.

MCKELVEY, JUDY EILEEN, language educator; b. Britton, S.D., Nov. 19, 1948; d. Kenneth Maurice and Ethel Josephine Hickok; m. Richard Goss McKelvey, Jan. 24, 1981; children: Paul Richard Upjohn, Andrew Kenneth. AA, San Joaquin Delta Coll., Calif., 1969; BA, Calif. State U., Chico, 1971; JD, Humphreys Sch. of Law, Calif., 1981. Cert. State Tchg. Credential Elem. and Secondary Calif., 1971. English tchr. Lodi Unified Schs., Calif., 1971—. Advisor Calif. Jr. Scholarship Fedn., Lodi, 1976—2006. Sunday sch. tchr., jr. choir leader local ch., Lodi, Calif., 1974—79; v.p. Delta Kappa Gamma, Lodi, Calif., 2000—06. Mem.: Calif. Tchrs. Assn. (area rep. 1974—76), BSA (advancement coord., den leader 1990—2006), Delta Kappa Gamma (v.p. 2001—04), P.E.O. Lutheran. Avocations: literature, travel, needlecrafts, calligraphy. Home: 1024 Geneva Ln Lodi CA 95242-9697 Office: Lodi Unified Sch Dist - LMS 945 S Ham Ln Lodi CA 95242 Office Phone: 209-331-7540.

MCKELWAY, JANET BARBARA, music educator, retired; b. Wilkinsburg, Pa., May 11, 1938; d. Dalziel and Jessie Wilson (Gass) McK. BFA in Music Performance, Carnegie Inst. Tech., 1961, BFA in Music Edn., 1961; MFA in Music Edn., Carnegie Mellon U., 1970. Vocal music tchr./piano tchr. El Salaam Sch. for Girls, Assiut, Egypt, 1961-65; music tchr. Carlynton Sch. Dist., Carnegie, Pa., 1965-68; organist Bakerstown (Pa.) Presbyn. Ch., 1965-72; organist, choir dir. Trinity Luth. Ch., Gibsonia, Pa., 1972-92; elem. vocal music tchr. Hampton Twp. Sch. Dist., Allison Park, Pa., 1968-97; organist, assoc. music dir. Community Presbyn. Ch. of Ben Avon, Pitts., 1992—. Contbr. articles to The Am. Organist mag. Recipient Vol. in Arts award, Dominion Found., 2003. Mem. Organ Artists Series of Pitts. (chmn. 1979-84, chmn., 1999-2003), Am. Guild Organists (pres. Pitts. chpt. 1988-90, dir. Pipe Organ Encounter 1990-91, dir. Com. on the New Organist 1993-2001), Pa. State Edn. Assn. (performer), Sigma Alpha Iota (pres. Pitts. alumnae chpt. 1966-68). Republican. Presbyterian. Avocations: attending concerts, theater, swimming, reading, travel. Home: 352 Hawthorn Ct Pittsburgh PA 15237-2618

MCKENNA, ANN K., nutritionist, educator; d. Mary Giannavola and Joseph Peter Kupchak; m. Robert William McKenna, Aug. 10, 1963; children: Rodney William, Scot Robert, Stacy McKenna Brazil, Alison McKenna Rothwell, Cynthia McKenna Holmes. BS in Nutrition and Edn., Marywood Coll., Pa., 1959, MS in Nutrition and Dietetics, 1992. Registered Dietitian Am. Dietetic Assn., 1968, Cert.in Family and Consumer Sci. Am. Assn. of Family and Consumer Sci., 1985, lic. Dietitian, Nutritionist Pa., 2002. Adminstrv. dietitian Flower & Fifth Ave. Hosp., NYC, 1959—62; clin. dietitian Moses Taylor Hosp., Scranton, Pa., 1971—82; cons. dietitian, self employed in long term care facilities and home health orgns. Pa., 1982—; nutrition cons. Scranton Head Start Program, Scranton, 1984—; part-time faculty Marywood U., 1984—; clin. dietitian, educator Moses Taylor Hosp. Diabetes Edn. Program, 1998—2004. Bd. mem. NE Pa. Dietetic Assn., Scranton, Wilkes-Barre, Pa., 1995—; health adv. bd. mem. Scranton Lackawanna Head Start Program, Scranton, 1990—; coordinating cabinet mem. Marywood U. Nutrition and Dietetics Program, 1990—. Recipient Kappa Kappa Nu, Honor Soc. for Nutrition Grads. through Marywood Coll., 1992, Anita Owen award for Dietetic Profls., N.E. Pa. Dietetic Assn., 1998, Outstanding Dietetic Educator, Pa. Dietetic Assn., 1999, Dietetic Educators of Am. Dietetic Assn., 1999, Woman Yr., Head Start Program Scranton Lackawanna Human Devel. Agy., 2000. Mem.: Am. Assn. of Family and Consumer Sci. (assoc.), Am. Dietetic Assn. (assoc.), Pa. Dietetic Assn. (assoc.; bd. mem. 1999—2000), NE Pa. Dietetic Assn. (assoc.; career guidance, job referral chair 1996—2005). Avocations: fitness, gourmet cooking, reading. Home: 1329 Electric St Dunmore PA 18509 Office: Marywood Univ Adams Ave Scranton PA 18509 Office Phone: 570-346-6422. Home Fax: 570-346-6422. Personal E-mail: akmrd@aol.com.

MCKENNA, JEANETTE ANN, archaeologist; b. N.Y.C., Aug. 6, 1953; d. Edward Patrick and Ann Jeanette (O'Brien) McKenna; children: Stephanie Jane, Daniel Glen Edward. AA in Phys. Edn., Mount San Antonio Jr. Coll., 1974; BA in Anthropology, Calif. State U., Fullerton, 1977, MA in Anthropology, 1982; postgrad., Ariz. State U., 1981-84, U. Calif., Riverside, 1991-92. Field archaeologist Archaeol. Rsch., Inc., Costa Mesa, Calif., 1976-79; rsch. asst. Calif. State U., 1979; lab. dir. Environ. Rsch. Archaeologists, L.A., 1978-79; staff archaeologist Ariz. State U., Tempe, 1979-82; rsch. archaeologist Soil Systems, Inc., Phoenix, 1982-84, Sci. Resource Surveys, Huntington Beach, Calif., 1984-87; co-owner, prin. Hatheway & McKenna, Mission Viejo, Calif., 1987-89; owner, prin. McKenna et al., Whittier, Calif., 1989—; dir. Divsn. Cultural Resource Mgmt. Svcs. EIP Assocs., Chino, Calif., 1996-97. Contbr. numerous articles to profl. jours. and reports. Bd. dirs. Whittier Conservancy, 1987-98, interim treas., 1994, pres., 1994-95, bd. dirs. Residents' Voice, 1998—. Recipient Gov.'s award for Hist. Preservation/Calif., The Whittier Conservancy, 1995, Woman of Achievement award for sci. and rsch. YWCA San Gabriel Valley, 2006. Mem. Soc. Profl. Archaeologists (bd. dirs. 1993-97), Archaeol. Inst. Am., Am. Soc. Conservation Archaeology, Am. Mus. Natural History, Soc. Am. Anthropology, Ariz. Archaeol. Coun., Ariz. Hist. Found., Calif. Hist. Soc., Nat. Arbor Day Found., Nat. Parks and Conservation Assn., Nat. Trust for Historic Preservation, Soc. Calif. Archaeology, Soc. Hist. Archaeology, S.W. Mus. Assn., Wilderness Soc., Whittier Conservancy, Southwestern Anthrop. Assn., Gene Autry Western Heritage Mus. Assn., Nature Conservancy, Smithsonian Assocs., Sierra Club, others. Democrat. Roman Catholic. Avocations: travel, reading, hiking, camping, gardening. Office: McKenna et al 6008 Friends Ave Whittier CA 90601-3724 Office Phone: 562-696-3852. Business E-Mail: jmckena@earthlink.net.

MCKENNA, KATHLEEN KWASNIK, artist; b. Detroit, Nov. 6, 1946; d. John J. and Eleanor H. (Ciosek) K.; m. Frank J. McKenna, Jr., Mar. 16, 1968. Cert., Cooper Sch. Art, Cleve., 1973; student, Art Students' League, N.Y.C., 1972, 74. Instr. portrait painting Baycrafters, Bay Village, Ohio, 1976-79; self-employed painter, 1972—; part-time mem. faculty fine arts dept. Lakeland C.C., Kirtland, Ohio, 1996—. One-person shows include Ctrl. Nat. Bank, Cleve., 1975, Women's City Club Gallery, Cleve., 1979, Kennedy Ctr. Art Gallery, Hiram, Ohio, 1980, Chime Art Gallery, Summit, NJ, 1985, Bolton Art Gallery, Cleve., 1986, 91, Lakeland C.C. Gallery, Kirtland, Ohio, 1996, 2002; group shows include Butler Inst. Am. Art, 1981, 89, 91, 93, Mansfield (Ohio) Art Ctr., 1990, 98, Circle Gallery, NYC, 1978, Canton (Ohio) Art Inst., 1990, Art in Embassies Program, 2004—, others Recipient Pres.'s award Am. Artists Profl. League, 1993, other awards. Mem. Catharine Lorillard Wolfe Art Club (Pastel Soc. plaque 1989, Mae Berlind Bach award 1983, Cert. of Merit 1981), Allied Artists Am. (assoc.; Gold medal of Honor 1989). Roman Catholic. Avocations: art-related travel, tennis, skiing. Studio: 15914 Chadbourne Rd Shaker Heights OH 44120

MCKENNA, MARGARET ANNE, academic administrator; b. RI, June 3, 1945; d. Joseph John and Mary (Burns) McK.; children: Michael Aaron McKenna Miller, David Christopher McKenna Miller. BA in Sociology, Emmanuel Coll., 1967; postgrad., Boston Coll. Law Sch., 1968; JD, So. Meth. U., 1971; LLD (hon.), U. Upsala, NJ, 1978, Fitchburg State Coll., Mass., 1979, Regis Coll., 1982; LLD (hon.), Emmanuel Coll., 2000, Episcopal Divinity Sch., 2005. Bar: Tex. 1971, D.C. 1973. Atty. Dept. Justice, Washington, 1971-73; exec. dir. Internat. Assn. Ofcl. Human Rights Agys., Washington, 1973-74; mgmt. cons. Dept. Treasury, Washington, 1975-76; dep. council to Pres. White House, Washington, 1976-79; dep. undersec. Dept. Edn., Washington, 1979-81; dir. Mary Ingraham Bunting Inst., Radcliffe Coll., Cambridge, Mass., 1981-85; v.p. program planning Radcliffe Coll., Cambridge, 1982-85; pres. Lesley U., Cambridge, 1985—. Bd. dirs. Dominion Resources, Inc., Cisco Learning Inst. Bd. dirs. Am. Assn. Coll. for Tchr. Edn., Coun. for Higher Edn. Accreditation, Datatel Scholars Found.; chmn. higher edn. task force Clinton Transition, 1992-93; chmn. edn. task force Mayor Thomas Menino Transition Com., 1994; mem. Princeton Adv. Bd. ACE Policy Adv. Com., Campus Compact Policy Com., MassNetworks. Recipient Outstanding Contribution award Civil Rights Leadership Conf., 1978; named Woman of Yr. Women's Equity Action League, 1979, Outstanding Woman of Yr. Big Sister Assn., 1986, Pinnacle award for Lifetime Achievement, Lelia J. Robinson award Women's Bar Assn. Mass., 1996, Valeria Addams Knapp award, The Coll. Club, 1995; named Margaret A. McKenna Day, Gov. DePrete, R.I. Mem. Boys Scouts Am., Big Sisters Assn. Boston, Y.W.C.A. Cambridge, Women's Equity Action League, Nat. Women's Polit. Conf., Nat. Assn. Official Human Rights Agencies. Democrat. Office: Lesley Univ Office of President 29 Everett St Cambridge MA 02138-2702

MCKENNA, MARGARET MARY, foundation administrator; b. Teaneck, NJ, May 26, 1930; d. Walter F. and Stella M. (Schnell) McKenna. BA, Chestnut Hill Coll., 1955; MA, Notre Dame U., 1960; PhD, U. Pa., 1980. Med. Mission sister 1948. Art editor Med. Missionary Mag., Phila., 1956—65; prof., dean St. Theresa's Inst., Phila., 1961—62; formation dir. Med. Mission Sisters, Phila., 1962—67; asst. prof. La Salle U., Phila., 1970—75; founder Shofar House Cmty., Phila., 1970—76; founder, dir. Peacemaker's Reflection Cmty., Phila., 1983—88; founder, program dir. New Jerusalem Laura, Phila., 1989—. Faculty mem. Women at Grailville, Loveland, Ohio, 1974—75. Author: Women of the Church, 1967, If It Matters, 1965. Mem. Govs. Commn. on Women, Harrisburg, Pa., 1966; bd. mem. Other Side Mag., Phila., 1973—74; sec. Health Ctr. #5, Phila., 1998—2006; pres. Simple Way, Phila., 2000; dir. Alternative to Violence Program, Phila., 1992—2006. Mem.: Soc. Biblical Literature, Catholic Biblical Assn., Atlantic Life Cmty. Green Party. Roman Cath. Avocations: swimming, gardening, art, peace activist, research. Home and Office: New Jerusalem Laura 2011 W Norris St Philadelphia PA 19121 Personal E-mail: njlmargaret@verizon.net.

MCKENZIE, DIANE M., science educator; b. Burlington, Ontario, Canada, Apr. 4, 1964; d. Brian Meredith and Midge F. Cooper; m. Gary J. McKenzie, Aug. 22, 1997. BS, Ind. U., 1987; BEd, U. Windsor, Ont., Canada, 2002; M Multidisciplinary Sci., Wayne State U., 2005. Cert. pers. trainer Am. Coll. Exercise, athletic trainer. Fitness dir. SkyDome Fitness Club, Toronto, Ont., 1992—95; cardiac rehab. mgr. City of Southfield, Mich., 1994—98; membership sales rep. Sports Clubs of Can. - Bloor Pk. Club, Toronto, 1995—98; supr. health club Casino Windsor, 1998—2001; biology tchr. Southeastern HS Tech., Detroit, 2001—. Mem.: MTA, OCT, MSTA, NSTA, MDSTA. Office: Southeastern HS Tech 3030 Fairview St Detroit MI 48211 Office Phone: 313-866-4500. Business E-Mail: diane.mcknezie@detroitk12.org.

MCKENZIE, ELLEN PORTER, elementary school educator, consultant; d. George W. Porter and Mildred L. Watson; m. James W. McKenzie, Aug. 25, 1962; children: Tim, Deborah, Chris. BS, Ind. U., Indpls., 1981, MS, 1984; EdD, Ind. U., Bloomington, 1997; EPPSP, Butler U., Indpls., 1988. Tchr. Brownsburg Pub. Schs., Ind., 1981—. Lectr. Ind. U., Butler, 1990—2000; cons., 1997—, Ind. Dept. Edn., Indpls., 1999—2004. Recipient Tchr. of the Yr., Brownsburg Sch. Corp., 1986. Mem.: Reading Assn., Optimists Club (pres. 2004—05, v.p. 2005—06), Phi Delta Kappa. Home: 7158 Walnut Creek Crossing Avon IN 46123-8266 E-mail: DrELPM@aol.com.

MCKENZIE, KAY BRANCH, public relations executive; b. Atlanta, Feb. 12, 1936; d. William Harllee and Katherine (Hunter) Branch; m. Harold Cantrell McKenzie, Jr., Apr. 11, 1958; children: Ansley, Katherine, Harold Cantrell III. Student, Sweet Briar Coll., 1955, Emory U., 1956-57. Account exec. Hill and Knowlton Inc., Atlanta, 1979-80, account supr./dir. S.E. govt. rels., 1981-83; ptnr. McKenzie, Gordon & Potter, Atlanta, 1983-85; pres. McKenzie & Assocs. Inc., Atlanta, 1986-89; sr. v.p. Manning Selvage & Lee, Atlanta, 1989-93; v.p. comm. and creative svcs. 1996 Atlanta Paralympic Games, 1993-96; v.p. comm. and devel. U.S. Disabled Athletes Fund, 1997—. Mem. Commn. on Future of South, 1974; co-chmn. John Lewis for Congress, Atlanta, 1986; regional bd. dirs. Inst. Internat. Edn., 1987-93. Fellow Soc. Internat. Bus. Fellows (bd. dirs. 1983-85, 92-93, v.p. 1986-88); mem. Pub. Rels. Soc. Am., Ga. C. of C. (bd. dirs. 1983-97), Leadership Atlanta, Ga. Internat. Horse Park Found. (bd. dirs. 1993-98). Democrat. Episcopalian. Office: 280 Interstate N Cir Ste 450 Atlanta GA 30339 Home: 670 Crossfire Ridge Marietta GA 30064 E-mail: kmckenzie@blazesports.com.

MCKENZIE, MARY BETH, artist; b. Cleve. d. William Jennings and Mary Elizabeth (McCray) McK.; m. Tony Mysak, May 8, 1974; children: Zsuzsa McKenzie Mysak, Maria McKenzie Mysak. Student, Mus. Fine Arts, Boston, 1964-65, Cooper Sch. Art, Cleve., 1965-67; diploma, NAD, N.Y.C., 1974. Painting instr. NAD, 1981—, Art Students League, 1995—. Author: A Painterly Approach, 1987; contbr. articles to profl. jours.; one-woman shows include Nat. Arts Club, N.Y.C., 1976, FAR Gallery, 1980, Perin and Sharpe Gallery, New Canaan, Conn., 1981, Frank Caro Gallery, N.Y.C., 1988—89, Joseph Keiffer Gallery, 1991, Union County Coll., 1998, exhibited in group shows at Sindin Gallery, N.Y.C., 1985—86, Ice Collection, 1995—96, Met. Mus. Art, 2001, Represented in permanent collections The Butler Mus. Am. Art, Met. Mus. Art, N.Y.C., Mus. City of N.Y., NAD, Art Students League of N.Y., Nat. Mus. Women in the Arts, Nat. Mus. Am. Art, Smithsonian Instn., Bklyn. Mus. Art, New Britain Mus. Am. Art, N.Y. Hist. Soc., Spanierman Gallery, N.Y.C., exhibitions include Met. Mus. Art, 2001. Recipient Nat. Scholastic award Mus. Fine Arts, Boston, numerous awards including Thomas B. Clark prize and the Isaac N. Maynard prize Nat. Acad. Design, Greenshields Found. grantee, Stacey Found. grantee. Mem. Nat. Acad. Design, Pastel Soc. Am. (Best In Show, Award of Exceptional Merit, Exhbn. Com. award), Allied Artists Am. (Gold medal, The Jane Peterson award, Grumbacher Cash award, Silver medal), Audubon Artists (Pastel Soc. Am. award). Home: 525 W 45th St New York NY 10036-3414 Personal E-mail: mckenzie525@netscape.net.

MCKENZIE-ANDERSON, RITA LYNN, psychologist; b. Boston, Nov. 25, 1952; d. Wallace Andrew and Angelina Rita (Bagnoli) McK; m. Brien Anderson, Oct. 22, 1994; 1 child, Liam Wallace. BA, Framingham State Coll., 1974; MEd, Northeastern U., 1975; PhD, Temple U., 1983. Lic. psychologist, Mass. Pvt. practice, Fairfield, Conn., 1984-86; psychologist Johnson Life Ctr., Springfield, Mass., 1986-87, dir. outpatient therapy, 1987-88; investigator Springfield (Mass.) Juvenile Ct., 1989—2000; pvt. practice Springfield, 1989—. Adj. faculty Holyoke (Mass.) Community Coll., 1989-90, Springfield Tech. Community Coll., 1989-90; dir. day treatment DuBois Day Treatment Ctr., Stamford, Conn., 1982-86; cons. psychologist Community Care Mental Health Ctr., Springfield, 1989-97, Spofford Hall Treatment Ctr., Ludlow, Mass., 1991-92. Trustee Northampton (Mass.) State Hosp., 1989-93; mem. organizing com. Week of Young Child, Springfield, 1988-93; bd. dirs. Stop Abuse Against Kids. Mem. Women Bus. Owners Alliance, Zonta Internat. Office: 380 Union St Ste 14 West Springfield MA 01089-4123 Office Phone: 413-731-1110. Fax: 413-731-1125. E-mail: blrgroup@yahoo.com.

MCKENZIE-SWARTS, MOLLY, human resources specialist, hotel executive; b. Calif. BA, U. So. Calif. Dir. human resources Berkhemer & Kline Pub. Rels., LA; various human resources positions in employment, facilities, adminstrn., compensation, benefits, and human resource info. systems Hilton Hotels Corp., Beverly Hills, Calif., sr. v.p. human resources, 1999—. Mem. Juniors of Social Svc., Nat. Charity League. Office: Hilton Hotels Corp 9336 Civic Center Dr Beverly Hills CA 90210 Office Phone: 310-278-4321. Office Fax: 310-205-7678.

MCKEOUGH, SUSAN ANNE, elementary school educator; d. Richard Blair McKeough and Barbara Jean McKeough. BS, St. Francis Coll., Biddeford, Maine, 1976; MA, Sacred Heart U., Bridgeport, Conn., 1982. Cert. tchr. Conn. Supr. tchr. Child Devel. Ctr., Bellefonte, Pa., 1976—78; tchr. St. Gabriel Sch., Stamford, Conn., 1978—85, Greenwich (Conn.) Cath., 1986—88, Saxe Mid. Sch., New Canaan, Conn., 1988—97, 2001—, Grace Episcopal Sch., Ocala, Fla., 1998—2000. Spl. edn. aide, sub- tchr. Saxe Mid. Sch., New Canaan, 1985—86. Recipient Sci. award, State of Fla., 1998. Home: 3 Valley View Rd #17 Norwalk CT 06851 Office: Saxe Mid Sch 468 South Ave New Canaan CT 06840 Office Phone: 203-594-4500. Personal E-mail: smckeo2621@aol.com.

MCKEOWN, ASHLEY, biological anthropologist, educator; PhD, U. Tenn., Knoxville, 2000. Biological anthropologist, faculty mem. U. Mont., Missoula, Mont. Office: Dept Anthropology U Mont 32 Campus Dr Missoula MT 59812 Office Phone: 406-243-2145. Business E-Mail: ashley.mckeown@umontana.edu.

MCKEOWN, H. MARY, lawyer, law educator; b. West Palm Beach, Fla., Sept. 17, 1952; d. Honore Stephen McKeown and Margaret Berg McKeown Growney; m. Jon Henry Barber, Sept. 18, 1981; children: Sean Patrick, Mary Kathleen. AA, St. Petersburg Jr. Coll., Fla., 1970; BA in Polit. Sci. and Sociology, U. South Fla., 1972; JD cum laude, Samford U., 1976. Bar: Fla. 1976, U.S. Dist. Ct. (mid. dist.) Fla. 1977, U.S. Ct. Appeals (5th and 11th cirs.) 1981, U.S. Supreme Ct. 1992. Asst. state atty. 6th Jud. Ct., Clearwater, Fla., 1976-90; ptnr. Growney, McKeown & Barber, St. Petersburg, 1976—. Adj. prof. Stetson Coll. of Law, St. Petersburg, 1990—. Chairperson Child Welfare Std. and Tng. Coun., 1995—98; mem. nominee qualifications rev. com. Health and Human Svcs. Bd. Dist. 5, 1992—2000; mem. Study Commn. Child Welfare, 1990—91; leader Girl Scouts U.S., 1991—2001. Recipient Victim Advocacy award Pinellas County Victims Rights Coalition, 1984, Law and Order award Elks, Pinellas County, 1991. Mem.: St. Petersburg Bar Assn., Fla. Bar Assn., Acad. Fla. Trial Lawyers, Phi Alpha Delta. Office: 7455 38th Ave N Saint Petersburg FL 33710-1228

MCKEOWN, MARY ELIZABETH, retired educational association administrator; m. James Edward McKeown, Aug. 6, 1955. BS, U. Chgo., 1946; MS, DePaul U., Chgo., 1953. Supr. h.s. dept. Am. Sch., 1948-68, prin., 1968-99, trustee, 1975, v.p., 1979, ednl. dir., 1979—2002, exec. v.p., 1992—2002, cons., 2002—. Author study guides for algebra, geometry, and calculus. Mem.: Distance Edn. and Tng. Coun. (chair person rsch. and edn. com. 1988—93), N. Ctrl. Assn. Colls. and Schs. (exec. bd. 1990—93), NASSP, LWV.

MCKEOWN, MARY MARGARET, federal judge; b. Casper, Wyo., May 11, 1951; d. Robert Mark and Evelyn Margaret (Lipsack) McKeown; m. Peter Francis Cowhey, June 29, 1985; 1 child, Megan Margaret. BA in Internat. Affairs and Spanish, U. Wyo., 1972; JD, Georgetown U., 1975. Bar: Wash. 1975, D.C. 1982. Assoc. Perkins Coie, Seattle, 1975—79, Washington, 1979—80; spl. asst. US Dept. Interior, Washington, 1980—81, The White House, Washington, 1980—81; ptnr., mem. exec. com. Perkins Coie, Seattle,

1981—98, mng. dir. strategic planning and client rels., 1990—95; judge US Ct. Appeals (9th Cir.), San Diego, 1998—. Trustee The Pub. Defender, Seattle, 1982—85; rep. 9th Cir. Judicial Conf., San Francisco, 1985—89; mem. gender bias task force, 1992—93; jud. conf. Com. on Codes of Conduct, 2001—; exec. com. 9th Cir., 2001—; lect. U. Wash. Law Sch., 2000—01; adj. prof. U. San Diego, 2003—; bd. dirs. RAND Inst. for Civil Justice, 2003—. Author: Girl Scout's Guide to New York, 1990; contbr. chpt. to book and articles to profl. jours. Nat. bd. dirs. Girl Scouts U.S., N.Y.C., 1976—87; mem. exec. com. Corp. Coun. for the Arts, Seattle, 1988—98; bd. gen. counsel Downtown Seattle Assn., 1986—89; mem. exec. com. Wash. Coun. Internat. Trade, 1994—; bd. dirs. YMCA Greater Seattle, 1998—, Family Svcs., Seattle, 1982—84. Named one of 100 Young Women of Promise, Good Housekeeping, 1985, Washington's Winningest Trial Lawyers, Washington Jour., 1992, Top 50 Women Lawyers, Nat. Law Jour., 1998; recipient Rising Stars of the 80's award, Legal Times Washington, 1983; fellow Japan leadership, 1992—93. Fellow: ABA (ho. of dels. 1990—, Jud. Adv. Com. to Standing Com. on Ethics 2000—, chair 2002—, Joint Commn. to Evaluate Code of Jud. Conduct 2003—); mem.: Louis M. Welsh Chpt. Am. Inns of Ct., Am. Judicature Soc. (bd. dirs. 2001—), Assn. Bus. Trial Lawyers (bd. dirs. 2003—), Am. Intellectual Property Law Assoc., Am. Law Institute, Nat. Assn. Iolta Programs (bd. dirs. 1989—91), Wash. Women Lawyers (bd. dirs., pres. 1978—79), Legal Found. Wash. (trustee, pres. 1989—90), Seattle-King County Bar Assn. (trustee, sec. 1984—85, Outstanding Lawyer award 1992), Wash. Bar Assn. (chmn. jud. recommendations 1989—90), Fed. Bar Assn. (trustee western dist. Wash. 1980—90), White House Fellows Found. (bd. dirs. 1998—, pres. 2000—01). Avocations: travel, classical piano, hiking, gourmet cooking, tennis. Office: US Ct Appeals 401 West A St Ste 2000 San Diego CA 92101-7908 E-mail: Judge_McKeown@ca9.uscourts.gov.*

MCKEOWN-MOAK, MARY PARK, educational consultant; d. John Paton and Sophie Cichon Park; m. Lynn Martin Moak, Oct. 4, 1997; children: David Lynn Moak, Susan Marie Moak; m. James Charles McKeown, Jan. 2, 1965 (div.); children: Jeffrey Charles McKeown, Pamela Lynn McKeown; m. Kenneth Forbis Jordan, Jan. 2, 1982 (div. Sept. 1993). BA, MA, Mich. State U., East Lansing, 1966; PhD, U. Ill., Urbana-Champaign, 1974. Cert. tchr. Mich., 1966, real estate agent Ill., 1977. Bus. mgr. U. Ill. Found., Champaign, 1974—77; sch. fin. specialist, asst. prof. pub. adminstrn. Ill. Bd. Edn., Sangamon State U., Springfield, 1977—80; assoc. dir. fin. and facilities Md. State Bd. Higher Edn., Annapolis, 1980—87; dir. strategic planning Ariz. State U., Tempe, 1987—94; assoc. exec. dir., sr. fin. officer Ariz. Bd. Regents, Phoenix, 1994—98; ptnr. MGT Am., Inc., Austin, Tex., 1998—. Pres. Fiscal Issues Spl. Interest Group Am. Edn. Rsch. Assn., Washington, 1990—91, pres., chair Futures Planning Spl. Interest Group, 1992—93; pres. Am. Edn. Fin. Assn., Denver, 1996—97. Contbr. articles to profl. jours. Pres. Coll. Bus. Faculty Wives, Champaign, 1971—73; troop leader Girl Scouts, Boy Scouts, Champaign, 1974—78; treas. Champaign-Urbana PTA Coun., 1978—80; pres. Alameda Estates Homeowners Assn., Tempe, Ariz., 1988—95, v.p., 1988—95, sec., 1988—95. Mem.: Travis Audubon Soc., Phi Delta Kappa (sec. Ariz. chpt. 1987—91). Avocations: gardening, travel, birdwatching. Home: 8800 Gallant Fox Road Austin TX 78737 Office: MGT Am Inc 502 E 11th Street Ste 300 Austin TX 78701 Office Phone: 512-476-4697. Business E-Mail: mmoak@mgtamer.com.

MCKERROW, AMANDA, ballet dancer; b. Albuquerque; d. Alan and Constance McKerrow; m. John Gardner. Student, Met. Acad. Ballet, Bethesda, Md., Washington Sch. Ballet. With Washington Ballet Co., 1980-82, Am. Ballet Theatre, N.Y.C., 1982—, soloist, from 1983, prin. dancer, 1987—2005. Toured Europe with Washington Ballet; teacher and instr. ballet dancing; danced in Margot Fonteyn Gala at Metropolitan Opera House; featured in Pavlova Tribute film, also many guest appearances; leading roles in Ballet Imperial, La Bayadere, Manon, Birthday Offering, Dim Lustre, Donizetti Variations, Giselle, Graduation Ball, The Leaves Are Fading, Nine Sinatra Songs, The Nutcracker, Pillar of Fire, Requiem, Romeo and Juliet, The Sleeping Beauty, Les Sylphides, Push Comes to Shove, Symphony Concertante, Symphonic Variations, Theme and Variations, Stravinsky Violin Concerto, Swan Lake, Triad, Duets, Etudes, Coppelia, Voluntaries and Rodeo, Don Quixote; created leading role in Bruch Violin Concerto No. 1, Some Assembly Required and Agnus De Mille's The Other. Recipient Princess Grace Dance Fell., 1986, N.Y. Woman award for dance, 1991; co-winner gold prize for women Moscow Internat. Ballet Competition, 1981. Office: Am Ballet Theatre 890 Broadway New York NY 10003

MCKILLIP, MARY, physical education educator; b. Deadwood, S.D., July 15, 1954; d. John P. Wood and Edith (Wham) Shepherd; m. Terry O. McKillip, Oct. 8, 1977. BS, Chadron State Coll., 1976. Cert. tchr., Wyo. Tchr. Crook County Sch. Dist. 1, Moorcroft, Wyo., 1976—. Coord. Jump Rope for Heart, Moorcroft, 1980—; mem. Wyo. AIDS Com., Gillette, 1990-93. Mem. NEA, Wyo. Edn. Assn., AAHPERD, Wyo. Alliance Health, Phys. Edn., Recreation and Dance (v.p. health 1984-85, treas. 1985-87, Honor award 1990). Avocations: skiing, sewing, horseback riding, gardening, bicycling. Home: 16921 Us Highway 14 Moorcroft WY 82721-8703 Office: Phys Edn Dept 101 S Belle Fourche Ave Moorcroft WY 82721

MCKILLIP, PATRICIA CLAIRE, operatic soloist; b. Milw., Apr. 28; d. Lester J. and Ruth J. (Lohneis) McK.; m. Mark Richard McKillip, June 16, 1990. BA in English-Drama, Creative Writing, Lit., Alverno Coll., 1980, MusB in Applied Music, 1981; postgrad., Wis. Conservatory of Mus., 1981-82; MS in Fine Arts Edn., U. Wis., Milw., 1996; postgrad., The Juilliard Sch., 1982-84, Am. Acad. Dramatic Arts, 1983-84, Adelphi U., 1984; MA in English-Creative Writing and Lit., U. Wis., Milw., 1997; postgrad., Milw. Inst. Art and Design, 2003—. Soloist Amadeus Opera Co.; instr. vocal music seminars various high schs., NY. Co-founder, co-dir. The Masque Consort, N.Y.C., 1990-91, exec. v.p., 1991; v.p., co-founder Creative Learning Assocs.; instr. Cardinal Stritch Coll., Milw., 1994—. Performer Florentine Opera Co., Music Under the Stars Prodns., Milw. Opera Co., Westchester Lyric Opera Co., Profl. Opera Workshop at Lincoln Ctr., Met. Opera Co., N.Y. Grand Opera Co., Monteverdi Opera Guild Prodns., Republic Opera Co., La Puma Opera Co., others; puppeteer, costumer, designer Puppet Art Troupe; author: (poetry and artwork) Springdrift, 2003; author numerous poems. Exec. v.p. Masque Consort, a multi-media theatrical orgn. Music dept. scholar Alverno U.; named Woman of Yr., Am. Biographical Inst. Bd. Internat. Rsch., 2003. Mem. AFTRA, SAG, Nat. Assn. Music Tchrs., Music Educators Nat. Conf. (treas.), Internat. Platform Assn., Wis. Fedn. Music Clubs, Music Clubs Am., Am. Guild Mus. Artists, Q'ahal-Liturgical Music Soc., Acad. Am. Poets, Milw. Artists Resource Network, Walker's Point Ctr. for Arts, Delta Omicron (v.p., chaplain, warden Gamma Gamma chpt., WMA State and Regional Vocal award 1978, Star of Delta Omicron award 1980, 40 music medals from state and dist. WSMA), Alpha Sigma Tau. Democrat. Roman Catholic. Avocations: dance, creative writing, art. Home: 4860 S 69th St Greenfield WI 53220-4452 Personal E-mail: celticdramaticsoprano@yahoo.com.

MCKILLOP, SUSAN REGAN, art educator; d. William M. and Susan C. Regan; m. Allan A. McKillop, June 30, 1954; children: Mary A., Allan M. PhD, Harvard U., Cambridge, Mass., 1966. Prof. art history Sonoma State U., Rohnert Park, Calif., 1978—, chmn. Dept. Art, 1980—83. Senator academic senate Calif. State U., 1996—2004, chmn. senate task force, 2001—03, vice chmn. senate faculty affairs com., 1998—99, vice chmn. senate fiscal and govtl. affairs com., 2002—04. Author: Franciabigio, 1974. Bd. dirs. Crocker Art Mus., Sacramento. Recipient Faculty Rsch. award, Sonoma State U., 1992, Excellence in Tchg. award, 1999, Wang Family Excellence award, Trustees Calif. State U., 2004. Mem.: Italian Art Soc., Renaissance Soc. Am., Coll. Art Assn. Home: 535 Miller Drive Davis CA 95616 Office: Sonoma State University 1801 East Cotati Avenue Rohnert Park CA 94928 Office Phone: 707-664-2251. Business E-Mail: susan.mckillop@sonoma.edu.

MCKIM, RUTH ANN, financial planner; b. Keokuk, Iowa, Nov. 26, 1932; d. Carl Edward and Ruby Irene (Martin) McKim; m. William James Ashbrook, Aug. 15, 1959 (div. 1974); children: Leslie, Diane Hodges. BS, U. Louisville, 1955, MS in Cmty. Devel., 1977. Dir. art therapy Ky. Bapt. Hosp., Louisville, 1955—56; co-dir. art therapy Norton-Children's Hosps. Inc., 1956—57; dir. art therapy NKC Hosps., 1957—59; rschr. Bd. Aldermen, 1976; pub. rels. staff Dept. Consumer Affairs, 1976—78; realtor assoc. Century 21, 1979—86; fin. planner Nat. Life Vt., 1986—. Tutor Ky. Assn. Specific Perceptual-Motor Disability, Louisville, 1970—74. Author: Banking Survey, 1977. Arts festival com., 1975—77; coord. Louisville Food Day, 1978; vol. and art donor PBS, 1985—88; voter registration canvasser, 1976, 1978, 1982; active Rep. Nat. Com., Rep. Presdl. Task Force, Nat. Rep. Senatorial Com., Nat. Rep. Congl. Com. Com.; sec., treas. St. Francis in the Fields Espicopal Ch., Louisville, 1975—76. Recipient Rep. Presdl. Legion of Merit medal, Order of Merit; scholar Allen R. Hite Art Inst., 1952—54; Bd. Realtors scholar, 1979—. Mem.: Inst. Community Devel. Assn., Ky. Artists and Craftsmen, Louisville Craftsmans Guild (life), U. Louisville Alumni Assn. Republican. Episcopalian. Avocation: oil and acrylic painting. Home: No 43 410 Mockingbird Valley Rd Louisville KY 40207-1318

MCKINLEY, ANNE C., lawyer; b. 1974; m. John R. Wickstrom, May 6, 2000. BA, Northwestern U., 1996; grad., U. Ill. Coll. Law. With US SEC, Chgo., 1998—, br. chief enforcement divsn., 2003—. Named one of 40 Under 40, Crain's Chgo. Bus., 2006. Office: US SEC Midwest Regional Office Ste 900 175 W Jackson Blvd Chicago IL 60604 Office Phone: 312-353-7390. E-mail: chicago@sec.gov.*

MCKINLEY, CAMILLE DOMBROWSKI, psychologist; b. Buffalo, May 6, 1922; d. Eugene Anthony and Anne Victoria (Sliwinska) Dombrowski; m. Thomas Leroy Smith, Dec. 30, 1944 (div. 1977); children: Thomas Dan, Cynthia Camille (dec.), Pamela Susan; m. William Frank McKinley, Oct. 7, 1984 (dec. Mar. 1985); m. Stuart Peebles Parker, Dec. 20, 1996. BA, Syracuse U., 1943; MA, Boston U., 1947; edn. specialist, Mich. State U., 1970, PhD, 1978. Acad. advisor Mich. State U., East Lansing, 1966-70, dir. Career Ctr., 1970-81, counseling psychologist Counseling Ctr., 1981-91; pres. Priam Pubs., 1978—. Mem. Career Planning and Placement Coun. Mich. State U., 1970-91. Editor: The Mich. State Univ. Referral Directory, 1970-91, The Gracious Reader, 1970-80; editor, publisher The CAM Report, 1978—. Founding pres. Greater Lansing chpt. Planned Parenthood, Mich., 1967; v.p. Opera Co. of Mid-Mich., 1983-85; mem. inner cir. Wharton Ctr. for Performing Arts, Mich. State U., mem. Platinum Cir. Mem. Mich. State U. Pres.'s Club and Beaumont Tower Soc., Zonta Internat., Zeta Tau Alpha. Home: PO Box 1862 East Lansing MI 48826-1862 Fax: 517-351-9054. E-mail: mckinl18@msu.edu.

MCKINLEY, DEBRA LYNN MCKINNEY, small business owner, dog show judge, real estate agent, artist; b. Albuquerque, July 8, 1954; d. Francis Marion and Bonnie Marie (Byard) McKinney; m. René John Krier II, Sept. 7, 1974 (div. June 1989); children: René John Krier III, Lynn Marie Krier Lyne; m. Eugene Randon McKinley, Sept. 7, 1991 (dec. Aug. 26, 2000). Grad., Taunton (Mass.) H.S., 1972, John Powers, Phila., 1973. Lic. judge Am. Kennel Club, real estate agent S.C. Judge Am. Kennel Club, N.Y.C., 1983—; owner, pres. Charleston (SC) Gas Light LLC. Contbr. articles to jours. in field; artist exhibited Robert Lange Studio, Charleston, S.C. Founder Taunton Young Reps., 1971-72; com. woman Taunton Rep. Party, 1972; treas. Rowan Rep. Women, Salisbury, N.C., 1993-94; treas. Salisbury Symphony Guild, 1991-94, pres., 1994-95; pres. bd. dirs. Salisbury Symphony Soc., 1996-97; pres. concert choir, 1994-95. Named Miss Rehobeth Mass., Miss Am. Pageants, Taunton, 1972, Miss Lansdale, Pa., Miss USA Pageants, 1973. Mem. DAR (sec. Elizabeth Maxwell chpt. 1997-98), Cabarrus Kennel Club (pres. 1984). Presbyterian. Avocations: master gardener, showing championship dogs, entertaining, volunteer work, genealogy. Home: One Ocean Point Isle Of Palms SC 29451 Office Phone: 877-427-5483. Office Fax: 888-958-0023. E-mail: dmckinley@mindspring.com.

MCKINLEY, ELLEN BACON, priest; b. Milw., June 9, 1929; d. Edward Alsted and Lorraine Goodrich (Graham) Bacon; m. Richard Smallbrook McKinley, III, June 16, 1951 (div. Oct. 1977); children: Richard, Ellen Graham, David Todd, Edward Bacon. BA cum laude, Bryn Mawr Coll., 1951; MDiv, Yale U., 1976; STM, Gen. Theol. Sem., N.Y.C., 1979; PhD, Union Theol. Sem., N.Y.C., 1988. Ordained deacon Episcopal Ch., 1980, as priest Episcopal Ch., 1981. Intern St. Francis Ch., Stamford, Conn., 1976-77; pastoral asst. St. Paul's Ch., Riverside, Conn., 1979-80, curate, 1980-81; asst. St. Saviour's Ch., Old Greenwich, Conn., 1982-90; interim asst. Trinity Ch., Princeton, NJ, 1990—91; priest assoc. All Saints Ch., Princeton, NJ, 1992—97, St. Christophers Ch., Chatham, Mass., 1997—. Episc. election com. Diocese of Conn., 1986—87, com. on human sexuality, 1987—90, donations and bequests com., 1987—90; major chpt. mem. Trinity Cathedral, Trenton, NJ, 1992—96; interim rector All Saints Ch., Princeton, NJ, 1993. Sec. Greenwich Com. Drugs, 1970—71; active Episcopal Women's Caucus; bd. dirs. Greenwich YWCA, 1971—72, Chatham Old Village Assn., 1998—2004. Mem.: Colonial Dames Am.

MCKINNEY, CARA LYNN, music educator; b. Lake Forest, Ill., Mar. 19, 1967; d. Gordon LeRoy and Jeanne Crista Nereim; m. Franklin Connor McKinney, July 31, 1988. BA in Music Edn., U. Ctrl. Fla., 1990, Master's in Ednl. Leadership, 1997. Cert. music educator K-12 Fla. Band dir. Deltona H.S., Fla., 1990—94, Deltona Mid. Sch., 1994—2006. Chair Volusia All County Band Volusia County Schs., Fla., 1995—97, Fla., 2002—06. Named Tchr. of Yr., Deltona Middle Sch., 2002. Mem.: Music Educators Nat. Conf., Fla. Music Educators Assn., Fla. Bandmasters Assn. (dist. chair 1998—2000, exec. bd. dirs. 1998—2000). Presbyterian. Avocations: gardening, camping, hiking.

MCKINNEY, CAROLYN, educational association administrator, educator; BS in Early Childhood Edn., U. N.C., Greensboro; M in Elem. Edn., Gardner-Webb U. Elem. sch. tchr. Winston-Salem/Forsyth County Schs.; elem. tchr. Sedge Garden Sch. Math. and Sci.; 2n and 3d gr. tchr. Kernersville Elem. Sch.; tchr. Gen. Greene Sch., Guilford County; pres. N.C. Assn. Educators, Raleigh, 2001—. Mem.: NEA (alt. dir. bd. dirs.), N.C. Assn. Educators (bd. dirs., Terry Sanford award for excellence in edn. 1997), Forsyth Assn. Classroom Tchrs. (pres.). Office: NC Assn Educators PO Box 27347 Raleigh NC 27611

MCKINNEY, CYNTHIA ANN, congresswoman; b. Atlanta, Ga., Mar. 17, 1955; d. Billy and Leola McKinney; 1 child, Coy Grandison. BA in internat. rels., U. So. Calif., 1978; MA, Tufts U. Fletcher Sch. Law & Diplomacy; postgrad., Ga. State U., U. Wis. Former instr. Clark Atlanta U., Atlanta Met. Coll.; mem. Ga. Ho. Reps., 1988-92, US Congress from 4th Ga. dist., 1993—2003, 2005—, mem. com. on armed svc., com. on budget. Mem. HIV Health Services Planning Coun., Atlanta, 1991—92; Frank H.T. Rhodes vis. prof. Cornell U., Ithaca, NY, 2003—04. Named a Diplomatic fellow, Spellman Coll., 1984; named one of Most Influential Black Americans, Ebony mag., 2006; recipient Edgar Wayburn award, Sierra Club, 1998, Outstanding Contribution award, Nat. Orgn. Sierra Leonians in N Am., 2000. Mem.: Progressive Caucus, Congl. Black Caucus, Agrl. Com., Sierra Club, Nat. Coun. Negro Women, Metro Atlanta, NAACP. Democrat. Roman Catholic. Achievements include the first African American woman elected to Congress from Georgia. Office: US Ho Reps 320 Cannon Ho Office Bldg Washington DC 20515-1004 also: N DeKalb Mall Ste D-46 2050 Lawrenceville Hwy Decatur GA 30033 Office Phone: 202-225-1605. Office Fax: 202-226-0691.*

MCKINNEY, MELISSA A., lawyer; 1 child. BS in Criminal Justice, U. North Tex., 1999; JD, So. Meth. U. Dedman Sch. Law, 2003. Bar: Tex. 2003. Assoc. Barrett, Burke, Wilson, Castle, Daffin & Frappier, L.L.P., Addison, Tex. Named a Rising Star, Tex. Super Lawyers mag., 2006. Mem.: Dallas Young Lawyers Assn., Dallas Bar Assn. Office: Barrett Burke Wilson Castle Daffin & Frappier LLP 15000 Surveyor Blvd Ste 100 Addison TX 75001 Office Phone: 972-386-5040.*

MCKINNEY, SALLY VITKUS, state official; b. Muncie, Ind., Aug. 6, 1944; d. Robert Brookins and Mary (Mann) Gooden; m. Alan George Vitkus (div. Jan. 1979); m. James Larry McKinney, Feb. 1, 1986. AA, William Woods U., 1964; BS, U. Ariz., 1966; postgrad., U. Nev., Las Vegas, 1966-68. Tchr. Las Vegas Day Sch., 1972—76; salesperson Globe Realty, Las Vegas, 1976—79; owner, pres. Realty West, Las Vegas, 1979—96; chief investigator State of Nev. Real Estate Divsn., 1996—2000; prin., owner McKinney Realty, Las Vegas, 2000—; corp. broker, dir. bus. and devel. Real Estate Temps, Las Vegas. Rec. sec. Clark County Rep. Cen. Com., Las Vegas, 1982, 1st vice chmn., 1985; vice-chmn. Nev. Rep. com., 1986, chmn., 1987-88; active Assistance League Las Vegas; state chmn. Nev. Rep. Party. Mem. Nat. Assn. Realtors, Nat. Assn. Home Builders, Las Vegas Bd. Realtors, Greater Las Vegas C. of C., Gen. Fedn. Womens Clubs (nominee Outstanding Young Woman Am. 1979, exec. bd. 1980-82), Jr. League Las Vegas (sustaining), Mesquite Club (chmn. pub. affairs com. 1986-87, past pres., secret witness exec. bd. 1994-96, vice chmn.). Presbyterian. Avocations: bridge, fly fishing. Home: 511 Mountain Dell Ave Henderson NV 89012-2509

MCKINNEY, THERESA, secondary school educator; BA in Psychology, Oakland U., Rochester Hills, Mich., 1982; MA in Edn., Wayne State U., Detroit, 1990. Continuing edn. cert. Mich. H.s. tchr. Utica Cmty. Schs., Sterling Heights, Mich., 1985—. Mem.: Nat. Coun. Social Studies (assoc.). Avocations: motorcycling, ballroom dancing. Office: Stevenon HS 39701 Dodge Park Rd Sterling Heights MI 48313 Office Phone: 586-797-2063.

MCKINNEY, VENORA WARE, librarian; b. Meridian, Okla., June 16, 1937; BA, Langston U., 1959; MLS, U. Ill., 1965. Librarian Milw. Pub. Library, 1962-68, br. librarian, 1979-83, dep. city librarian, 1983—; librarian Peoria Pub. Schs., Ill., 1969, Milw. Pub. Schs., 1972-79. Adj. faculty U. Wis., Milw.; mem. Wis. Govs. Coun. on Libr. Devel., 1983-93; bd. dirs. V.E. Carter Child Devel. Group, 1992-96. Bd. dirs. Milw. Repertory Theatre; coun. adv. Sch. Libr. and Info. Sci., U. Wis., Madison, 1992-96. Nat. Forum for Black Pub. Adminstrs. fellow Exec. Leadership Inst., George Mason U. Mem. ALA Black Caucus, Wis. Libr. Assn. (v.p. 1994, pres. 1995—, bd. dirs. 1996), Wis. Black Librs. Network, ALA Pub. Libr. Assn., Links, Delta Sigma Theta. Baptist. Office: Milw Pub Libr 814 W Wisconsin Ave Milwaukee WI 53233-2309

MCKINNEY, VIRGINIA ELAINE ZUCCARO, educational administrator; b. San Francisco, Nov. 18, 1924; d. Salvadore John and Elaine Agnes (Shepard) Zuccaro; B.A., Calif. State U.-Los Angeles, 1968; M.A., Calif. State U., Northridge, 1969; Ph.D., Claremont Grad. Sch., 1983; children—Joe, Walter Clifton Official ct. reporter Los Angeles County Superior Cts., 1948-59; tchr. speech-reading, adult edn. Los Angeles Bd. Edn., 1966-71; lang., reading specialist Marlton Sch. for the Deaf, Los Angeles, 1971-79; founder, pres., dir. communication skills program Center for Communicative Devel., Inc., Los Angeles, 1969-; part-time lectr. spl. edn. Calif. State U., Los Angeles, 1971-1978; cons. for various univs. and programs for the hearing-impaired; mem. State Ind. Living Coun., 1993-2000, adv. com. for deaf Calif. Dept. Rehab., 1979—1984, Atty.'s Gen. Commn. on Disability, 1987-1990. Recipient Leadership award Nat. Leadership Tng. Program in Area of Deaf, Calif. State U., Northridge, 1974; NEA Project Life grantee, 1970, Gallaudet Coll. Center for Continuing Edn. grantee, 1974. Mem. Calif. Educators for Deaf and Hard of Hearing, Calif. Assn. For Postsecondary Edn. and Disability, Beverly-Hollywood (Calif.) Hearing Soc. (pres. 1967-68). Republican. Presbyterian. Author: The Picture Plus Dictionary, 1997, (CD) Picture Plus Vocabulary, 2000, developer, producer audio-visual media, including 22 films and 4 books, to aid in speechreading and auditory tng., 1963-68; participant research project with Project Life on devel. of communication skills for multiply-handicapped deaf adults, 1970; developer, pub. Toe-Hold Literacy Packet, 1973, Linguistics 36, interactive computer lang. devel. program, 1986. Office: 2550 Beverly Blvd Los Angeles CA 90057-1019 Home: 3460 Wilshire Blvd Ste 200 Los Angeles CA 90010 Office Phone: 213-738-8176. Personal E-mail: ccdcom40@yahoo.com.

MCKINSEY, ELIZABETH, humanities educator, consultant; b. Columbia, Mo., Aug. 10, 1947; d. J. Wendell and A. Ruhamah (Peret) McK.; m. Thomas N. Clough, June 18, 1977; children: Emily, Peter. BA, Radcliffe Coll., 1970; PhD, Harvard U., 1976. From instr. to asst. prof. English Bryn Mawr (Pa.) Coll., 1975-77; from asst. to assoc. prof. English Harvard U., Cambridge, Mass., 1977-85; dir. Bunting Inst. Radcliffe Coll., Cambridge, 1985-89; dean Carleton Coll., Northfield, Minn., 1989—2002, prof., 2002—. Author: Niagara Falls: Icon of the American Sublime, 1985; contbr. articles and revs. to profl. jours. and lit. mags. NEH fellow, 1980; Carnegie Found. for the Advancement of Tchg. vis. scholar, 2003. Mem. MLA, Am. Conf. Acad. Deans, Nat. Coun. for Rsch. on Women (assoc.), Am. Studies Assn., Nat. Assn. Women in Edn., Phi Beta Kappa (pres. Iota of Mass. chpt. 1986-89). Home: 801 Mayflower Ct Northfield MN 55057-2308 Office: Carleton Coll 1 N College St Northfield MN 55057-4001 Office Phone: 507-646-5900. E-mail: emckinse@carleton.edu.

MCKNIGHT, PAMELA ANN, art educator; b. Morristown, N.J., Sept. 29, 1959; d. Edward Harold Spreen and Juliet Ann Dorigo; m. William A. McKnight, Mar. 11, 1995; m. Benjamin A. Mall, May 25, 1985 (div. Aug. 15, 1994); children: Victoria A. Mall, Katherine Rose Mall. BA, Oral Roberts U., Tulsa, 1981; MA in Art Edn., U. North Tex., 2004. Cert. tchr. all level art Tex., 1981, elem. tchr. 1-8 Tex. Art tchr. Our Lady of Sorrows Sch., McAllen, Tex., 1983—87, Mary Hoge Jr. High Sch., Weslaco, Tex., 1987—89, Lamar Jr. High Sch., McAllen, Tex., 1989—90, Martha Turner Reilly Elem. Sch., Dallas, 1991—2001, Bradfield Elem. Sch., Highland Park, Tex., 2002—. Art tchr. Dallas Mus. of Art, Dallas, 2002—. Recipient Profl. Achievement Award, Highland Pk. Ind. Sch. Dist., 2003, 2004, 2005, 2006; Marcus fellow, Edward and Betty Marcus Found. and North Tex. Inst. for Educators on the Visual Arts, 2001. Mem.: Nat. Art Edn. Assn. (assoc.), Tex. Art Edn. Assn. (assoc.; regional rep. 2001—03), Tex. Parent Tchr. Assn. (life; cultural arts chair 1996—2001, Life Membership Award 2000), Phi Kappa Phi (assoc.). Avocations: travel, reading, art. Office: Highland Park ISD 4300 Southern Ave Dallas TX 75205 E-mail: mcknigp@hpisd.org.

MCKNIGHT, PATRICIA GAYLE, musician, artist, writer, educator; b. Rochester, Minn., Aug. 9, 1935; d. William Robert and Maxine Matilda (Hutchings) McK.; m. James Russell Grittner, Nov. 24, 1962; children: Leah Kristin, Rachel Anne. BS in Music, U. Wis., Superior, 1982, MA in Art, 1990, MA in Art History, 1993; postgrad. in Musicology, U. Iowa, 1982—83. Asst. MS editor Am. Acad. Ophthalmology and Otolaryngology, Rochester, Minn., 1958-63. Musician U. Iowa Symphony Orch., U. Iowa Opera Orch., U. of Iowa Small Ensembles, U. Wis. Superior Symphony Orch., Rochester Symphony Orch. Exhibited in group shows including Kruk Gallery, Rochester Cmty. Coll., Duluth Art Inst. Biennial, 1988, 90, Port Wing (Wis.) Gallery, Tile Show, 2006; author: Zenith City Arts newspaper. Mem. historic preservation com. City of Superior, 1996—. Avocations: playing cello, viola da gamba. Home: 2325 Hughitt Ave Superior WI 54880-4920

MCKOWEN, DOROTHY KEETON, librarian, educator; b. Bonne Terre, Mo., Oct. 5, 1948; d. John Richard and Dorothy (Spoonhour) Keeton; m. Paul Edwin McKowen, Dec. 19, 1970; children: Richard James, Mark David. BS, Pacific Christian Coll., 1970; MLS, U. So. Calif., 1973; MA in English, Purdue U., 1985, PhD, 2003. Libr.-specialist Doheny Libr., U. So. Calif., L.A., 1973-74; asst. libr. Pacific Christian Coll., 1974-78; serials cataloger Purdue U. Librs., 1978-88; head children's and young adult svcs. Kokomo-Howard County Pub. Libr., Ind., 1988-89, coord. children's and tech. svcs. Ind., 1989-91; cataloger, network libr. Ind. Coop. Libr. Svcs. Authority, 1991-2001. Mem. adj. faculty Ivy Tech. C.C. of Ind., 2001—; lectr. Purdue U., 2003—. Mem. ALA, MLA, Soc. Early Americanists, Assn. for Libr. Collections and Tech. Svcs. (bd. dirs. 1986-90, 95-96, vice chair, chair-elect coun. of regional groups 1986-88, chair 1988-90, conf. program com. 1986-88, internat. rels. com. 1986-88, micropub. com. 1986-87, subject analysis com., membership com. 1988-90, planning and rsch. com. 1988-90, chair program initiatives com. 1991-93, orgn. and bylaws com. 1991-92, 99-2001), Network OCLC Svc. Mgrs. (MARC Task Force 2000-01), Ind.

Coun. Libr. Automation (bibliog. stds. task force), Ind. Libr. Fedn. (chair tech. svcs. divsn. 1984-85), Ohio Valley Group Tech. Svcs. Libr. (chmn. 1985-86). Republican. Home: 7625 Summit Ln Lafayette IN 47905-9729 E-mail: mckowens2@yahoo.com.

MCKOWN, MARTHA, minister, writer; b. Dixie, Ky., May 29, 1933; d. John William and Dora Ellen (Melton) Powell; m. Leslie Henry McKown, June 22, 1957; children: Karen Marie McKown, Liana Jane McKown Edenfield. AB in English, Evansville Coll., 1955; M of Religious Edn., Boston U., 1957; MDiv, Christian Theol. Sem., 1978. Ordained elder Meth. Ch., 1979. Dir. ch. edn. Maple St. Congl. Ch., Danvers, Mass., 1957-58, Temple United Meth. Ch., Terre Haute, Ind., 1973-75; pastor East Park United Meth. Ch., Indpls., 1979-80; assoc. pastor Trinity United Meth. Ch., Evansville, Ind., 1980-82; pastor Faith United Meth. Ch., Princeton, Ind., 1982-85, St. Paul United Meth. Ch., Poseyville, Ind., 1985-89. Author: Palm Sunday Parade, 1995; contbr. articles to various pubs. Pastoral counselor Pike County (Ind.) Hospice, 1993-96; mem. So. Ind. Conf. United Meth. Ch.; rep. Red Bird Missionary Conf., 1995—2002; pres. joint archives North and South Ind. confs., 1998-99, South Ind. Conf. United Meth. Hist. Soc., 2000-03; mem. Southern Ind. Conf. Archives pres. South Ind. Conf. United Meth. Hist. Soc., 2000-03, Southern Ins. Conf. Archives History Commn., 1996-2004; bd. dirs. Evansville United Meth. Youth Home, 1994-2002. Mem. Ohio Valley Writers Guild, Princeton Ministerial Assn. (pres. 1984), Tri-State Geneal. Soc., Woman's Club, Browning Club (pres. 1996-97). Democrat. Avocations: gardening, swimming, walking, reading, genealogy. Home and Office: 7944 Meadow Ln Newburgh IN 47630-2842

MCLACHLAN, SARAH, musician, composer; b. Halifax, Nova Scotia, Jan. 28, 1968; m. Ashwin Sood, Feb. 7, 1997; 1 child, India. Founder, performer Lilith Fair. Albums include Touch, 1989, Solace, 1991, Live EP, 1992, Fumbling Towards Ecstasy, 1994, Freedom Sessions, 1995, Rarities, B-Sides, and Other Stuff, 1996, Surfacing, 1997, Mirrorball, 1999, Sarah McLachlan Remixed, 2001, Afterglow, 2003, Wintersong, 2006, Mirrorball: The Complete Concert, 2006; appearances include Gravity, 1991, Island of Circles: A Nettwork C, 1991, No Alternative, 1993, Christmas at Mountain Stage, 1994, Testimonial Dinner: the Songs of Xt, 1995, Memories of the Soul Shack Survivor, 1996, Heroine, 1996, Bloom, 2005; worked with Delerium, Donovan. Recipient Order of Canada, Best Female Pop Vocal Performance award Grammy, 1997, 1999, Best Pop Instrumental Performance award, 1997; nominated for Grammy for Best Female Pop Vocal Performance for "Fallen," 2003. Achievements include founding Lilith Fair, all-female peformance concert tour, 1997-1999. Office: Nettwerk Mgmt 1650 W 2nd Ave Vancouver BC V6J 4R3 Canada

MCLACHLIN, BEVERLEY, Canadian supreme court chief justice; b. Pincher Creek, Alta., Can., Sept. 7, 1943; m. Roderick McLachlin (dec. 1988); 1 child, Angus; m. Frank E. McArdle, 1992. BA, U. Alta., MA in Philosophy, LLB, LLD (hon.), 1991, U. B.C., 1990, U. Toronto, 1995, York U., 1999, Law Soc. Upper Can., 2000, U. Ottawa, 2000, U. Calgary, 2000, Brock U., 2000, Simon Fraser U., 2000, U. Victoria, 2000, U. Alberta, 2000, U. Lethbridge, 2001, Bridgewater State Coll., 2001, Mt. St. Vincent U., 2002, U. PEI, 2002, U. Montreal, 2003, U. Man., 2004, Queen's U., Belfast, 2004, Dalhousie U., 2004, Carleton U., 2004, U. Ft. Kent, Maine, 2005. Bar: Alta. 1969, B.C. 1971. Assoc. Wood, Moir, Hyde and Ross, Edmonton, Alta., Canada, 1969—71, Thomas, Herdy, Mitchell & Co., Fort St. John, B.C., Canada, 1971—72, Bull, Housser and Tupper, Vancouver, 1972—75; from lectr. to prof. U. B.C., 1974—81; appointed to County Ct., Vancouver, 1981; justice Supreme Ct. of B.C., 1981—85, B.C. Ct. of Appeal, Canada, 1985—88; chief justice Supreme Ct. of B.C., Canada, 1988; justice Supreme Ct. Can., Ottawa, Ont., Canada, 1989—2000, chief justice Can., 2000—. Co-author: B.C. Supreme Court Practice, B.C. Court Forms, Canadian Law of Arch. and Engring.; contbr. articles to profl. jours. Office: Supreme Ct Bldg 301 Wellington St Ottawa ON Canada K1A 0J1 Office Phone: 613-992-6940.*

MCLAINE, BARBARA BISHOP, counselor assistant; b. Walterboro, S.C., Jan. 2, 1954; d. Murry Eugene and Rosine (Johns) Bishop; m. Joseph Lee McLaine, Mar. 10, 1974; 1 child, Matthew Jason. Grad., Walterboro (S.C.) High Sch., 1972. Tchr.'s aide Cen. Elem. Sch., Cottageville, S.C., 1972-73; counselor asst. Vocat. Rehab. Dept., Walterboro, S.C., 1973—; ret., 2001. Democrat. Methodist. Avocations: reading, birdwatching.

MCLANE-ILES, BETTY LOUISE, academic administrator, language educator, writer; b. Chgo., Mar. 15, 1951; d. Clifford I. (Mac) and Genevieve (Cohn) McLane; m. Lawrence (Larry) Irvine Iles, Dec. 28, 1983. BA, French U., Ariz., 1973, MA, 1975; PhD, French U., Ill., 1982. French instr. U. Ariz., Tucson, 1973—76, U. Ill., Champaign-Urbana, 1976—77; adminstr. asst., rschr. small bus. com. Ho. of Reps., Washington, 1977—78; French instr. U. Ill., Champaign-Urbana, 1978—79; lectr. Lycée Henri IV, Paris, 1979—80; French instr. U. Ill., Champaign-Urbana, 1980—81; prof. French, Truman State U., Kirksville, Mo., 1982—. Rsch. asst. econ. and bus. rsch. divsn. U. Ariz., Tucson, 1970—73; co-chairperson fgn. lang. dept. Truman State U., 1996—98, chairperson French dept., 1982—88, 1990—92, 1999—2000. Author: Uprooting and Integration in the Writings of Simone Weil, 1987, (plays) The Last Duchess, 1996; contbr. articles to profl. jours. Faculty advisor Amnesty Internat., Kirkville, Mo., 1997—; faculty advisor Coll. Greens, Truman State U., 1998—2003. Mem.: MLA, Chgo. Playwrights Network, Assn. internationale des Études Québécoises, Nat. Fraternity of Student Musicians, Internat. Women Playwrights Assn., Mo. Writers Guild, Pi Delta Phi (founder, faculty co-advisor Iota Tau chpt. 1984—), Phi Kappa Phi, Phi Beta Kappa. Jewish. Avocations: writing, swimming, travel, drawing. Office: Truman State Univ Dept French Kirksville MO 63501 Business E-Mail: bmclanei@truman.edu.

MCLAREN, RUTH, bank executive; Grad., Dominican U. Sr. v.p. retail banking Cmty. Bank of Oak Park River Forest, Ill. Mem.: GALA Fireworks Orgn., Rotary Club of OPRF. Office: Cmty Bank Oak Park River Forest 1001 Lake St Oak Park IL 60301 E-mail: ruthm@cboprf.com.

MCLAUCHLEN, JENNIFER, art dealer; b. Montclair, N.J., May 19, 1966; d. James Robert III and Kathleen Ann Carew McLauchlen; m. Joseph Robert de Sane, June 21, 1998. BA, Marymount Coll., 1986, Stony Brook U., 1993. Studio asst. Elaine de Kooning, Easthampton, N.Y., 1987-88, Willem de Kooning, Easthampton, 1988-93; archives dept. rschr. Leo Castelle Gallery, N.Y.C., 1993; lic. appraiser Hamptons Appraisal Corp., Southampton, N.Y., 1994-98; sales assoc. McLauchlen Real Estate, Southampton, 1994-98; owner McLauchlen Gallery, Ltd., Southampton, 1998—. Staff reporter The Easthampton Star, 1994-96. Benefit chairperson Water Mill (N.Y.) Cmty. Club, 1993-94; benefits com. mem. Parrish Art Mus., Southampton, 1995-97, Southampton Cultural Ctr., 1998-99, bd. dirs., 1999—, Guild Hall Easthampton. Mem. Water Mill Cmty. Club Home: 18 Old Fort Ln Southampton NY 11968-4409

MCLAUGHLIN, CAROLYN LUCILE, elementary school educator; b. Pensacola, Fla., June 16, 1947; d. John Franklin and Mamie Lou (Rayburn) Wells; m. Richard Allen McLaughlin, Sept. 5, 1969; children: Allen Wayne, Kristen Lynn. BA, U. West Fla., 1970. Cert. early childhood, elem. edn. tchr., ESOL. Elem. tchr. Santa Rosa Sch. Bd., Milton, Fla., 1970—2003, reading specialist tchr., 2002—03. Lobbyist for edn. State Fla. Legis. Com., 2001—03. Mem. County Tchr. Edn. Coun., Santa Rosa, v.p., 1995—97, pres., 1998—2000, 2001—03; youth ch. tng. tchr., music and youth dir., Sunday sch. youth tchr. Billory Bapt. Ch., East Bay Bapt. Ch., Midway Bapt. Ch., 1970—95, Navarre Bapt. Ch.; dir. Bible Sch. Holley Assembly God, 2001. Grantee Jr. League 1986, 91-99, Chpt. II Fed. grantee Elem. and Secondary Edn. Act, 1992. Mem.: Santa Rosa Reading Assn. (treas. 2001—03), Santa Rosa Profl. Educators (dist VII rep., negotiations team com., county calendar com., sec. county restructuring steering com., county curriculum com., tchr. of yr. com.), Fla. Reading Assn., Internat. Reading Assn. (v.p. Santa Rosa chpt. 1998—99, pres.-elect 1999—2000, pres. 2001—03), Navarre C. of C. (edn. com. 1998—2001, 2001—03), Kiwanis (children priority one com. 1998—2001). Home: 3586 Ginger Ln Navarre FL 32566-9616 E-mail: richcarol@cs.com, mclaughlincl@mail.santarosa.klz-fl.us.

MCLAUGHLIN, CATHERINE G., healthcare educator; AB, Randolph-Macon Woman's Coll., 1971; MS in Econs., U. Wis., 1978, PhD in Econs., 1980. Prof. health mgmt. and policy U. Mich., 1983—, dir. Econ. Rsch. Initiative on the Uninsured, prof. dept. health mgmt. and policy, dir. Robert Wood Johnson Found. Scholars in Health Policy Rsch. Program. Dir. U. Mich. component Agy. for Healthcare Rsch. and Quality's Ctr. of Excellence on Managed Care Markets and Quality. Contbr. articles to profl. jours.; sr. assoc. editor Health Svcs. Rsch. Office: U Mich Dept Health Mgmt and Policy 109 S Observatory M3166 SPH II Ann Arbor MI 48109-2029 Business E-Mail: cmcl@umich.edu.

MCLAUGHLIN, ELAINE M., elementary school educator; b. Toms River, NJ, Apr. 21, 1947; d. James Charles McLaughlin and Marie Eleanor Mullaney. BS, So. Conn. State U., New Haven, 1970, MS, 1972; postgrad., Sacred Heart U., Bridgeport, Conn., 2000. Cert. tchr. Conn. Tchr. Naugatuck Sch. Sys., Conn. Home: 344 King St Naugatuck CT 06770-1554

MCLAUGHLIN, ELLEN MCGEHEE, playwright, educator, actor; b. Boston, Nov. 9, 1957; d. Charles Capen and Ann Landis McLaughlin; m. Rinde Williams Eckert, Aug. 14, 1994. BA summa cum laude, Yale U., New Haven, 1980. Prof. playwrighting dept. English Barnard Coll., NYC, 1995—. Adj. prof. Yale U. Sch. Drama, 1999—2000, Middlebury Sch. English Breadloaf, Vt., 1999, Princeton U., NJ, 2006; playwright resident Juilliard Sch., 1986—87. Author: (plays) A Narrow Bed, 1987 (co-winner Susan Smith Blackburn prize, 1987), Tongue of a Bird, 1999, The Greek Plays, 2006; actor: (Broadway plays) Angels in America, (off-Broadway plays) String of Pearls, Blue Window, A Bright Room Called Day, The Bacchae, (numerous regional theatrical prodns.); (films) Everything Relative, The Bed You Sleep In, Boys On the Side, Junior; (TV series) Law and Order. Recipient Writer's award, Lila Wallace-Reader's Digest Fund, 1995, Berilla Kerr Playwrighting award, 2000; grantee, Nat. Endowment for Arts, 1987; winner, Great Am. Play Contest, 1985.

MCLAUGHLIN, GOLDIE CARTER, music educator; b. Martinsville, Mo., Aug. 15, 1906; d. Silas Franklin and Fannie Elizabeth (Creekmore) Carter; m. William Coleman McLaughlin, Jan. 5, 1935 (dec. 1970). AA, Palmer Coll., Albany, Mo., 1925; student, U. N.Mex., 1929-31, State Coll., Maryville, Mo., 1930, U. Calif., San Diego. Cert. tchr. Mo., N.Mex., Calif. Grade sch. tchr. Pawnee (Mo.) Sch. Dist., 1927-28; tchr. Hollister (Mo.) City Schs., 1925-29, Russelville (Mo.) Pub. Schs., 1929-30, Dona Ana County Pub. Schs., Las Cruces, N.Mex., 1930-35; engineering draftman Tool Design Dept. North Island Naval Air Station, 1942-46; pvt. music tchr. Napa, Calif. and El Paso, Tex., 1972—.

MCLAUGHLIN, JEAN WALLACE, art director, artist; b. Charlotte, N.C., Dec. 19, 1950; d. John Mason and Caroline (Garner) McL.; m. Thomas Hudson Spleth, Jan. 1991. BA, U. N.C., 1972; postgrad., Calif. Coll. Arts & Crafts, 1983-85; MA, N.C. State U., 1994. Spl. projects coord. Divsn. of the Arts, Dept. Cultural Resources, Raleigh, N.C., 1975-77; arts program coord. Gov.'s Adv. Coun. for Persons with Disabilities, Raleigh, 1978-79; visual and literary arts coord. N.C. Arts Coun., Raleigh, 1979-82; pvt. practice arts cons. San Francisco, 1982-85; visual arts sect. dir. N.C. Arts Coun., Raleigh, 1985-98; dir. Penland (N.C.) Sch. Crafts, 1998—. Art educator Charlotte (N.C.) Latin Sch., 1973-75; panelist and spkr. in field. Author: The Arts in the Churches and Synagogues of North Carolina, 1976; prodr. (book) Public Art Dialogue: SE, 1988. Bd. mem. New Langton Arts, San Francisco, 1983-85, N.C. World Ctr., Raleigh, 1988-91; program com. mem. Fiberworks, Berkeley, 1984-85. Mem. Nat. Assn. Artists Orgns., N.C. Ats Advs., Am. Assn. Mus., Am. Crafts Coun., New Langton Arts, Internat Sculpture Ctr., Art Table, Inc., N.C. Mus. Art, Southeastern Ctr. for Contemporary Art, Mint Mus. Craft and Design, Smithsonian. Avocations: gardening, travel, reading, writing, making art.

MCLAUGHLIN, MARGARET BROWN, adult education educator, writer; b. Miami Beach, Fla., Aug. 24, 1926; d. J. Clifford and Grace Lindsey (DuPre) Brown; m. Francis Edward McLaughlin, Oct. 30, 1982 (dec.). BA cum laude, U. Miami, 1946; MA, Duke U., Durham, N.C., 1949; PhD, Tulane U., New Orleans, 1976. Instr., lectr. in English U. Miami, Coral Gables, Fla., 1946-47, 56-61, 73-91, 2000; English tchr. Narimasu Am. Sch., Tokyo, 1963-65; asst. prof. Manchester Coll., North Manchester, Ind., 1965-67; instr. Miami-Dade C.C., 1977, 81; dir. writing workshop for fgn. students U. Miami Sch. Medicine, 1991-92; adj. prof. English, Asian and Liberal Studies and Acad. Lifelong Learning, Fla. Internat. U., Miami, Fla., 1997—; instr. humanities Barry U., Miami, 2004. Prodr. Dade County Cable TV series Caribbean Writers and Their Art, 1991; prodr., host cable tv series Haiti Cherie, 1993-94. Contbr. articles to popular Japanese and U.S. mags. and newspapers; contbr. play reviews to Internet pub. Trustee Mus. Sci., Miami, 1977-78. Mem. Am. Lit. Assn. (Henry Adams Soc.), Egyptology and Asian Civilizations Soc. Miami (bd. dirs., pres. 1976-78, 83-85), South Fla. Internat. Press Club (scholarship chmn. 2002—), South Fla. Writers' Assn. Avocations: writing, travel, editing. Home and Office: 1621 S Bayshore Dr Miami FL 33133-4201 Office Phone: 305-858-7224. Personal E-mail: mjmbjb711@aol.com.

MCLAUGHLIN, PATRICIA A., social services administrator; b. Balt., Mar. 29, 1943; BA, Coll. Notre Dame of Md., 1966; MA, Manhattanville Coll., 1973. Mem. Inst. Notre Dame, 1990—92, chair, 1992—96; mem. Coll. Notre Dame, 1996—; v.p. St. William of York Sch. Bd., 1997—2000; sec. Sch. Sisters Notre Dame Charitable Trust Bd., 1995—; mem. employment adv. com. Hist. East Balt. Cmty. Action Coalition, 1998—; Bd. dirs. Sch. Sisters of Notre Dame, 1987—96, Marian House, 1987—96. Named one of Md.'s Top 100 Women, Daily Record, 1999. Office: 900 Sommerset St Baltimore MD 21202

MCLAUGHLIN, PHOEBE, mathematics professor; BA, Nat. Taiwan U.; MS, PhD, U. Iowa. Prof. meth. Ctrl. Mo. State U., Warrensburg. Sponsor The Actuarial Orgn. Assoc. editor in algebra and number theory Missouri Journal of Mathematical Sciences, referee. Mem.: TeX Users Group, Assn. for Women in Math., Math. Assn. Am., An. Math. Soc. Office: Ctrl Mo State U Office WCM 227 Dept Math and Computer Science Warrensburg MO 64093 Office Phone: 660-543-8931. Office Fax: 660-543-8013. Business E-Mail: pmclaughlin@csmu.edu.*

MCLAUGHLIN, SYLVIA CRANMER, volunteer, environmentalist; b. Denver, Dec. 24, 1916; d. George Ernest and Jean Louise (Chappell) Cranmer; m. Donald Hamilton McLaughlin, Dec. 29, 1948; children: Jean Katherine McLaughlin Shaterian, George Cranmer McLaughlin. AB, Vassar Coll., 1939. Co-founder Save San Francisco Bay Assn., Berkeley-Oakland, Calif., 1961-99, pres., 1993-95. Mem. waterfront adv. com. City of Berkeley, Calif., 1964—68; sec., bd. dirs. Resource Renewal Inst., 1989—, Citizens for East Shore State Pks., 1984—2005, 2005—; founder, bd. dirs. Pub. Trust Group, Oakland, Calif., 1997—; mem. awards com. Berkeley Cmty. Fund, 1998—; mem. adv. bd. Greenbelt Alliance, San Francisco, 1982—; mem. nat. adv. coun. Trust for Pub. Land, San Francisco, 1986—, Ecocity Builders, Berkeley, 1990—; bd. dirs. Ptnrs. for Liveable Cmtys., Washington, 1975—78. Mem. Nat. Audubon Soc. (bd. dirs. 1970-76), Nat. Recreation and Parks Assn. (bd. dirs. 1974-78), East Bay Conservation Corps (bd. dirs. 1985-97), Student Conservation Assn. (bd. dirs. 1979-84). Avocations: reading, travel, grandchildren, environmental causes. Home: 1450 Hawthorne Ter Berkeley CA 94708-1804

MCLAURIN, TONI MARIE, orthopedist, surgeon, educator; b. Ann Arbor, Mich., Jan. 27, 1963; d. Jasper E. and Doris M. McLaurin. AB, Harvard and Radcliffe Colls., Cambridge, 1985; MD, U. Mich., Ann Arbor, 1991. Diplomate Am. Bd. Orthop. Surgery, 2000. Intern then resident Grand Rapids Orthop. Surgery Residency Program, Grand Rapids, Mich., 1991—96; fellowship in orthop. trauma Emory U. Sch. Medicine, Atlanta, 1996—97, chief orthop. trauma, 1997—2002; asst. prof. Sch. Medicine N.Y. U., N.Y.C., 2003—. Fellow: Am. Acad. Orthopaedic Surgeons. Office: NYU Hospital for Joint Diseases 550 First Avenue NBV 21W37 New York NY 10016 Office Phone: 212-598-6047. Office Fax: 212-263-8217. Business E-Mail: toni.mclaurin@med.nyu.edu.

MCLEAN, CHERYL L., physics educator; d. Howard D. Johnston and Dorothy H. Gray-Johnston; m. Hugh B. McLean, Oct. 18, 1986; children: Pamela A., Daniel M., Katherine M. BS in Materials Sci. Engring., Purdue U., West Lafayette, Ind., 1984. Lic. tchr. Profl. Stds. Bd. Ind., 2003. Metall. engr. GM, LaGrange, Ill., 1984—87; tchr. Tippecanoe Sch. Corp., Lafayette, Ind., 2004—. Coord. QuarkNet - Purdue, West Lafayette, 2004—06. Mem., vol. Evang. Covenant Ch., Lafayette, 1992—2006. Grantee, Bright Ideas - Payton Manning Found., 2005. Mem.: Am. Assn. Physics Tchrs. Office: McCutcheon HS 4951 Old US Hwy 231 Lafayette IN 47909 Office Phone: 765-474-1488.

MCLEAN, JODIE W., investment company executive; b. Chgo. BS in Fin. and Mgmt. with honors, U. S.C. With Edens & Avants, Columbia, SC, 1990—, chief investment officer, 1997—, pres., 2002—. Office: Edens & Avant 900 Bank of America Plaza 1901 Main St Columbia SC 29201

MCLEAN, JULIANNE DREW, concert pianist, educator; b. Stoneham, Mass., Sept. 12, 1928; d. Benjamin Drew and Elizabeth Anna McLean; m. Carmelo Addario, Oct. 18, 1958 (dec.); 1 child, Angela Elizabeth Addario. BMusic, Conservatory of Music, Kansas City, Mo., 1949, MMusic, 1950. Concert pianist NAC, U.S., Europe, Near and Far East, 1956—; tchr. pvt. classes, Kans., Hawaii, Va., 1956—; rec. artist Wichita State U., 1987—; lectr. in field. Musician: appearances on TV; musician: (invited pianist) Survivors of Andrea Doria Reunion; musician: live on Vatican Radio. Bd. dirs. Maud Powell Found., Falls Church, Va., 1995—. Recipient scholarships. Mem. Mu Phi Epsilon. Roman Catholic. Avocation: cooking.

MCLEAN, KATHERINE, artist, photographer; b. Washington, Feb. 6, 1950; d. Melvin Anselm and Louise Victoria-Ruth (Kiefer) J.; m. Gordon Kennedy McLean, Dec. 30, 1970; children: Jason Richard, Jesse J. Student, Phila. Coll. Art, 1970; BA summa cum laude, U. Pa., 1986. Freelance designer, med. illustrator, Phila., 1975-86; freelance photographer, artist Phila., Pitts., 1985—. Asst. film editor, prodn. asst. Visionaries Film & Video, Phila., 1984-87; coord. membership and edn. Silver Eye Ctr. for Photography, Pitts., 1993-94. Painter: Art of the State, 1997 (1st pl. award 1997), Wonder Boy, 1999; photographer: Photo Opportunity, 1991 (Juror's award 1991). Vol. Associated Artists Pitts., 1990-99. Mem. Group A, Pitts. Soc. Artists (Juror's award 1992). Avocations: reading, gardening, travel, movies.

MCLEAN, SUSAN O'BRIEN, artist; b. Bronxville, N.Y., Dec. 13, 1944; d. Francis Joseph O'Brien and Mildred Maud Brooks; m. John Allan McLean, Oct. 2, 1965; children: John Allan Cameron, Jennifer Brooks, Christopher O'Brien. Student, Chestnut Hill Coll., Pa., 1962-63, Church Stile Studio Schs., Cobham, Surrey, Eng., 1981-86, St. Martins Sch. Art, London, 1982-83. One-woman show include Boathouse Gallery, Walton-on-Thames, 1989; exhibited in group shows at Royal Inst. Painters in Watercolor, London, Royal Soc. Portrait Painters, London, 1987, Pastel Soc., London, 1985, 86, Cape Cod Art Assn., Falmouth Artist's Guild, Creative Arts Ctr., Chatham, Copley Soc., Duxbury Art Complex; represented in permanent collection Cape Mus. of Fine Arts, Dennis. Mem. Copley Soc. (Copley Artist), Cape Cod Art Assn. (artist mem., Grumbacher Gold Medal award for painting All New Eng. Show 1997). Home: 36 Donna Ave Osterville MA 02655-1714 E-mail: jacsusie@mindspring.com.

MCLEER, LAUREEN DOROTHY, drug development and pharmaceutical professional; b. N.Y.C., Feb. 5, 1955; d. William Myers and Una Lee (Massey) McLeer. BS, Columbia U., 1977; MBA, U. London, 1981. RN N.Y., D.C., state reg. nurse, Eng., registered state nurse, Wales. Staff nurse NYU Med. Ctr., N.Y.C., 1977-78; charge nurse Scripps Clinic and Rsch. Found., La Jolla, Calif., 1979-80; clin. rschr. Ayerst Labs., N.Y.C., 1982; sales rep. Pfizer, Inc., N.Y.C., 1983-87, Cahners Pub. Co., N.Y.C., 1988-89; dir. bus. devel. Pro Clinica, N.Y.C., 1990-91; account supr. Salthouse Torre Norton, Inc., Rutherford, N.J., 1992-93; dir. bus. devel. Med. & Tech. Rsch. Assocs., Inc., Wellesley, Mass., 1993-94; sr. project dir. Quiltiles Inc., Arlington, Va., 1994-99; project mgr. product devel. and commercialization Aventis Pharms., Inc., Berwyn, Pa., 1999—2002; clin. trial mgmt. leader AstraZeneca, LP, Wilmington, Del., 2002—, assoc. dir., 2005—. Mem. com. for healthcare issues and legis. United Hosp. Fund, N.Y.C., 1992—94. Chmn. Help Our Neighbors Eat Yr. 'Round, N.Y.C., 1987—89; trustee Murray Hill Comn., N.Y.C., 1988—90; bd. dirs. East Midtown Svcs. for Older People, 1987—94; vol. nurse Whitman Walker Clinic, 1995—99; bd. dirs. Cecil Land Trust, 2002—06, Eastern Shore Land Conservancy, 2003—, treas., exec. bd. dirs., 2005—. Named Md. Wildlife Farmer of Yr., Md. Dept. Natural Resources, 2004. Mem.: Drug Info. Assn., Regulatory Affairs Profl. Soc. Home: PO Box 681 Chesapeake City MD 21915 Office: AstraZeneca LP 1800 Concorde Pike Wilmington DE 19802-4034 Office Phone: 302-885-5213. Business E-Mail: laureen.mcleer@astrazeneca.com.

MCLELLAN, A. ANNE, Canadian government official; b. Hants County, N.S., Can., Aug. 31, 1950; d. Howard Gilmore and Joan Mary (Pullan) McL. BA, Dalhousie U., LLB, 1974; LLM, King's Coll., U. London, 1975. Bar: N.S., 1976. Asst. prof. law U. N.B., Can., 1976-80; assoc. prof. law U. Alta., Edmonton, Can., 1980-89, assoc. dean faculty of law, 1985-87, prof. law, 1989-93, acting dean, 1991-92; M.P. for Edmonton West Ho. of Commons, Can., 1993—; min. of nat. resources Govt. of Canada, Ottawa, 1993—97, min. of energy, mines and resources, 1993—95, min. of forestry, 1993—95, fed. interlocutor for metis and non-status Indians, 1993—97, min. justice and atty. gen. of Canada Ottawa, Canada, 1997—2002, min. of health, 2002—03, dep. prime min., 2003—06, min. of public safety and emergency preparedness, 2003—06; disting. scholar in residence U. Alberta, 2006—; counsel Bennett Jones LLP, Edmonton, Canada, 2006—. Commentator on Can. Charter of Rights and Freedoms and on human rights issues. Contbr. articles to profl. publs. Past bd. dirs. Can. Civil Liberties Assn., Alta. Legal Aid; past v.p. U. Alta. Faculty Assn.; bd. dir. Nexen Inc., 2006-, Agrium Inc., 2006-. E-mail: McLellan.A@parloge.ca.*

MCLEMORE, ELLEN H., music educator; b. Munich, May 30, 1964; d. Thomas R. and Lena Elizabeth Hogle; m. James R. McLemore, June 13, 1987; children: Martha Easton, Anne Elizabeth, James Richard, William Thomas. B in Music Edn., Wesleyan Coll., Macon, Ga., 1985. Piano instr. Ga. Music, Macon, 1985—86; pvt. piano tchr. Macon, 1985—95; music specialist Bibb County Schs., Macon, 1986—91; interim min. music 1st Presbyn. Ch., Macon, 1994—95; dir. children's choirs Ingleside Bapt. Ch., Macon, 2004—05; choral dir. 1st Presbyn. Day Sch., Macon, 2003—. Mem. Jr. League, Macon, Ga., 1988—94; pres. Macon Concert Assn., Macon, Ga., 1994—95. Mem.: Music Educators Nat. Assn. Avocations: singing, travel, choral directing. Home: 4951 Wellington Dr Macon GA 31210 Office: 1st Presbyn Day Sch 5671 Calvin Dr Macon GA 31210 Office Phone: 478-477-6505. E-mail: emclemore@fpdmacon.org.

MCLEMORE, JOAN MEADOWS, librarian, consultant; b. Bivens, Tex., Aug. 24, 1929; d. James Leon Jr. and Dell (Crawford) Meadows; m. Kenneth Lyons McLemore, May 6, 1950 (dec.); 1 child, Ken Malcolm. Student, Miss. State Coll. for Women, 1947-49; BS, U. So. Miss., 1976, MLS, 1983. Libr. Franklin County Pub. Libr., Meadville, Miss., 1976-90; libr. dir. Copiah-Lincoln C.C., Natchez, Miss., 1990—2003. Story teller, presenter conf. The Delta Kappa Gamma Soc. Internat., Louisville, 1991, Nashville, 1994; internat. spkr. Delta Kappa Soc., Red Deer, Can., 1994; mem. faculty Elderhostel, Natchez, Miss., 1990—; presenter Southeastern Regional Conf., Delta Kappa Gamma Soc. Internat., Charleston, S.C, 1997; pres. Franklinc. Mus., 1999-2004, Franklin County Mus., Meadville, Miss., 2002—, Inst. Lng. in Retirement, 2003—. Contbr. articles to profl. jours. Libr. trustee

Franklin County, Meadville, 1962-76, Lincoln-Lawrence-Franklin Regional Libr., Brookhaven, Miss., 1971-76; trustee Franklin County Meml. Hosp., 1997-2001, jury com., 1998-2001; deacon Presbyn.Ch., 2003—; Miss. com. Humanities Spkrs. Roster, 2004— Mem. Miss. Libr. Assn. (com. chair, exec. dir. libr. week activities 1989), Colonial Dames (gov. George Harlan chpt., 2nd v.p. 2002-05, parliamentarian 2005—), DAR (Homochitlo River chpt. 1979-1999, Natchez chpt. 2000—), Dames of the Ct. of Honor (treas. 2001—, chaplain 1999-2003), Mis. Soc. DAMES of the South, Daughters of Soc. of War of 1812, Natchez Garden Club, Natchez Hist. Soc. (trustee 2005—), Miss. Hist. Soc., Order of the First Families of Miss.: 1619-1817 (chaplain 2002-05, historian 2005—), First Families Twin Territories, Delta Kappa Gamma (pres. 1979-80, 1979-97 Rho chpt.), Delta Kappa Gamma Soc. Internat. (Alpha Omicron chpt.), Progressive Study Club (sec. 2006-), Natchez Women's Book Soc., Friends of Armstrong Libr., Rose Craft Club, Scottish Heritage Soc., Natchez Retriee Partnership. Avocations: genealogy, reading, baking, historial research, story telling. Home: Apt A 310 S Dr Ml King Jr St Natchez MS 39120-3533 E-mail: joanmcl1@bellsouth.net.

MCLENDON, KATHLEEN MARY, elementary school educator; b. Louisville, Ky., Dec. 11, 1949; d. William Arthur McCue and Carolyn Lillian Goetz; m. Stephen Douglas McLendon, July 8, 1983; children: Tammy McLendon Giusti, Stephen Douglas II. BSc in Elem. Edn., Grand Canyon U., 1992; MEd in Elem. Curriculum and Instruction, Chapman U., 1995. Cert. tchr. State Bd. Edn., Ariz. Adminstrv. asst. U.S. West, Phoenix, 1983—90; tchr. Palm Lane Elem. Sch. Cartwright Sch. Dist., Phoenix, 1992—. Mentor Rodel Found., Scottsdale, Ariz., 2005—. Named Employee of Month, Cartwright Sch. Dist., 1996, Rodel Exemplary Tchr., Rodel Found., 2005. Mem.: Cartwright Edn. Assn. Avocations: reading, scrapbooks. Home: 20297 N 108th Lane Sun City AZ 85373 Office: Palm Lane School 2043 N 64th Dr Phoenix AZ 85035

MCLENDON, MARY KATHRYN, athletic trainer; b. Montgomery, Ala., Oct. 15, 1973; d. Wayne and Shari Lee McLendon. BS, U. Colo., Boulder, 1994; M Exercise and Sport Sci., U. Fla., Gainesville, 1996. Cert. athletic trainer Bd. Certification, Inc., 1994, lic. Miss., 1996, cert. Nat. Certification Bd. Therapeutic Massage and Bodywork, 1995. Asst. athletic trainer Miss. State U., Starkville, 1996—. Recipient Grad. Achievement award, Rocky Mountain Athletic Trainers' Assn., 1994. Mem.: Miss. Athletic Trainers' Assn., Southeastern Athletic Trainers' Assn., Nat. Athletic Trainers' Assn. (dist. chmn. women in athletic com. 2005—). Avocations: reading, movies, travel. Office: PO Box 5327 Mississippi State MS 39762 Office Phone: 662-325-0657. Business E-Mail: mkm13@msstate.edu.

MCLENDON, SUSAN MICHELLE, lawyer; b. NYC, Mar. 5, 1964; d. James McLendon, Sr. BSN, SUNY, 1986; JD, Temple U., 1990. Bar: NJ (adm.) 1991, Wash., DC 1998, NY 2000; RN NY, 1986. Asst. regional counsel Social Security Adminstrn., Office Gen. Counsel, NYC, 1990-98; pvt. practice, 2000—. Cons. in field. Editor-in-chief: Environ. Law Digest, 1989—90. Named Landmark Affirmative Action Baby, 1967, World's Smartest Genius, 1967; scholar, NY State Regents, 1982—86, 1982—86, 1989—90. Avocations: singing, writing, running, tennis, skiing.

MCLENNAN, BARBARA NANCY, tax specialist; b. NYC, Mar. 25, 1940; d. Sol and Gertrude (Rochkind) Miller; m. Kenneth McLennan, Aug. 14, 1962; children: Gordon, Laura. BA magna cum laude, CCNY, 1961; MS, U. Wis., 1962, PhD, 1965; JD, Georgetown U., 1983. Bar: DC 1983, U.S. Ct. Internat. Trade 1988, U.S. Ct. Appeals (DC cir.) 1988, U.S. Supreme Ct. 1988, Va. 1991; cert. accredited valuation analyst Nat. Assn. Cert. Valuation Analysts, 2004. From asst. prof. to assoc. prof. Temple U., Phila., 1965—78; budget analyst Com. Budget, U.S. Ho. of Reps., Washington, 1978—81; legis. asst. fin. and budget Senator Dan Quayle, Washington, 1981—84; internat. tax specialist IRS U.S. Dept. Treasury, Washington, 1984—89; dep. asst. sec. trade, info. and analysis U.S. Dept. Commerce, Washington, 1989—91; prin., atty.-at-law Bitonti and Wilhelm, PC., McLean, Va., 1991—93; staff v.p. govt.-legal affairs consumer electronics group Electronic Industries Assn., Washington, 1993—94, staff v.p. tech. policy, consumer electronics group, 1994—95; v.p. Van Scoyoc Assocs., Washington, 1995—96; cons. on tax related issues in U.S., former Soviet Union, and West Bank and Gaza McLean, Va., 1996—. Adj. prof. Coll. William and Mary, 2005—; sr. polit. scientist SRI-Internat., Arlington, Va., 1971—74; vis. prof. Am. Coll., Paris, 1975—76; cons. UNESCO, Paris, 1977—78. Author: (book) Comparative Political Systems, 1975; contbr. articles to profl. jours. Mem. parents adv. coun. Randolph-Macon Coll., Ashland, Va., 1989—92. Fellow NDEA, 1962—65. Mem.: ABA, Va. Bar Assn., Fed. Bar Assn., DC Bar Assn., Am. Soc. Assn. Execs., Phi Beta Kappa. Home: 1620 Harbor Rd Williamsburg VA 23185 E-mail: barb.mcl@cox.net.

MCLEOD, CAROLYN LOUISE, artist; b. Palo Alto, Calif., Sept. 26, 1946; d. James and Virginia McLeod; m. William Bailey, Nov. 19, 1965 (div. 1969); 1 child, William; m. Peter Johnson, Dec. 31, 1987 AA in Art with honors, Foothill Coll., 1972; postgrad., Sonoma State U., 1973-74; BA in Art with honors, San Jose State U., 1976, postgrad., 1976-77, Truckee Meadows C.C., 1995—. Sec. Stanford (Calif.) U., 1982-87, U.S. Geol. Survey, Menlo Park, Calif., 1988-92. One-woman shows include Hollister (Calif.) City Hall, 1983, King St. Gallery, Carson City, Nev., 1995, Nev. State Libr. & Archives, Carson City, 1997, Clay Nichols Gallery, Reno, 2006, McKinley Arts and Culture Ctr., 2006, exhibited in group shows at Sacramento Fine Arts Ctr., Carmichael, Calif., 1994 (Excellence award), Carl Cherry Ctr. for Arts, Carmel, Calif., 1994, Las Vegas (N.Mex.) Arts Coun., 1995, 1997, Poudre Valley Art League, Lincoln Ctr., Ft. Collins, Colo., 1995, River Gallery, Reno, 1995 (Best of Show), Nat. Assn. Women Artists, NYC, 1995—2005, Nat. Mus. Women Arts, Washington, 1996, China World Trade Ctr., Beijing, 1995, Sierra Arts, Reno, 1996, Artists' Atelier of Atlanta, 1999, Sierra Arts Ctr., Reno, 1999, Roswell Mus. and Art Ctr., N.Mex., 2000, Mus. of Fine Arts, St. Petersburg, Fla., 2000, Atelier 14, NYC, 2000, Paris Gibson Sq. Mus. Art, Gt. Falls, Mont., 2001, Binney Smith Gallery, Bethlehem, Pa., 2002, UN, NYC, 2002, Gulf Coast Mus. Art, Largo, Fla., 2003, Strathmore Hall Arts Ctr., North Bethesda, Md., 2004, Leepa-Rattner Mus. Art, Fla., 2004, Smithsonian Instn., Washington, 2004, Dunedin (Fla.) Fine Art Ctr., 2005, King St. Gallery, Carson City, Nev., 2006 (2 1st pl. awards), Clay Nichols Group, Reno, Nev., 2006. Dean's scholar San Jose State U., 1976. Mem.: Cider Painters Am., Miniature Art Soc. Fla., Nev. Mus. Art, Sierra Arts Found., Nat. Mus. Women in Arts, Nev. Artists Assn. (newsletter editor 1996—99, Recognition award 1997—98), Nat. Assn. Women Artists (Mary K. Karasick Meml. award 2001, Myra Bigger Staff award 2002). Home: 2512 Plumas St Reno NV 89509-4255

MCLEOD, CHERYL O'HALLORAN, artist, art educator; b. Greensburg, Pa., Nov. 12, 1944; d. Benton Homer and Dorothy Lavern (McClain) Sams; children: Jeffrey, Brian. BA in Art Edn., Ind. U., Pa., 1966; postgrad., Mass. Coll. Art, 1983-84, Boston U., 1967. Represented by Swain Galleries, Plainfield, NJ, Olde Clinton Falls Gallery, Clinton, NJ, Craft Masters Gallery, Montclair, NJ; workshop tchr. N.Mex. Art League, Albuquerque; elem. art instr. Westford, Mass., 1966—69; tchr. Catskill Art Soc., Hurleyville, NY, Adult Continuing Edn. Programs, Edison, NJ, Mother Seton Reg. Girls Catholic HS, Clark, NJ, 1989—96; workshop tchr. Ghost Ranch Conf. Ctr., Abiquiu, N.Mex., 1989—89; HS art instr. Reading, Mass., 1981—84. Art instr. Mother Seton Regional Girls Cath. High Sch., Clark, NJ, 1990-96; pvt. instr. The Art Alcove; workship instr. Ghost Ranch Conf. Ctr., Abiquiu, N.Mex., 1988-89, Mid-West Pastel Soc., Palatine, Ill., 1989, Wilmette Hist. Soc., Ill., 1988, N.Mex. Art League, Albuquerque, 1987; high sch. art instr., Reading, Mass., 1981-84; elem. sch. art instr., Westford, Mass., 1966-68. One-woman shows include Tohono Chul Park, Tucson, 1987, U. Ariz, 1988, Kemper Group, Long Grove, Ill., 1989, Valley Cottage Libr. Gallery, NY, 1992, Valley Coll., NY, 1992, Poricy Park, Middletown, NJ, 1993, Burgdorff Realtors Corp. Gallery, Murray Hill, NJ, 1994, Georgian Court Coll., Lakewood, NJ, 1994, Swain Gallery, Plainfield, NJ, 1995, Union County Arts Ctr., Rahway, NJ, 1997, Lucca's Backroom Gallery, Metuchen, NJ, 1998, Palmer Mus., Springfield, NJ, 1998, Aberjona River Gallery, Winchester, Mass, 2005; group shows include Ariz. Aqueous '88, Tubac, 1988, Pastel Soc. Am., NYC, 1988, 89, 91, 93, Am. Artist Profl. League Grand Nat. Show, NY, 1988, 90, Midwest Pastel Soc. Mems. Show, Libertyville, Ill., 1989, Studio-in-the-Woods, Wauconda, Ill., 1989, Talman Home Savs. Instn., Chgo., 1989, Art Ctr., Elk Grove, Ill., 1989, Levy Ctr., Evanston, Ill., 1989, Rockland County Arts Coun., Spring Valley, NY, 1990, Visual Arts '90, Union County, NJ, 1990, Am. Artists Profl. League, 1990, 93, Ringwood Exhbn., NJ, 1991, Roman Cath. Diocese of Albany, NY, 1991, Kean Coll., Union, NJ, 1992, Johnson & Johnson World Hdqs., New Brunswick, NJ, 1992, Barron Arts Ctr., Woodbridge, NJ, 1993, Jersey City State Coll., 1993, Arts Ctr. No. NJ, New Milford, 1993, Newark Mus., 1994, Chubb Corp., Warren, NJ, 1994, Lever House Gallery, NYC, 1995, others; prin. works represented at Delta Corp. Svcs., Cogen Techs., Libr. Coop. Group, Abbott Labs., First Nat. Bank Shawnee, Oklahoma City Allergy Clinic, Nat. Cowgirl Hall of Fame, T.R. Roof & Assocs., Butler & Stein Attys., Petroleum Abstract & Title Co. Recipient First place, Nat. Small Painting Exhbn., Albuquerque, 1986, MW Pastel Soc. Show, Libertyville, Ill., 1989, Ctrl. NJ C. of C. Festival of Art award 1992, 94, 95, Catherine Lorillard Wolfe Art Club. Corp. award, 1997; grantee, Plainfield Cultural and Heritage Commn., NJ, 1998. Fellow Am. Artist Profl. League (Paul Bransom award 1993, Nat. award 1994, Merit award 1992, 93); mem. Pastel Soc. Am. (full juried signature mem., H.M. Hurlimann-Armstrong award 1993, Klimberger Meml. award 1995), Allied Artists Am. Home: 162 Middlesex Ave Wilmington MA 01887-2737 Personal E-mail: cmcleod44@aol.com.

MCLEOD, DEBRA ANN, librarian, mail order book company executive; b. St. Louis, Apr. 21, 1952; d. Frank Joseph and Virginia Veronica (Jasso) Osterloh; m. Bradley J. McLeod, June 24, 1977; children: Catherine Rose, Elizabeth Lauren. BA in History, U. Mo., St. Louis, 1974; MSLS, U. Ill., 1975. Research asst. Grad. Sch. Library Sci., U. Ill., Urbana, 1974; children's librarian St. Louis Pub. Library, 1976-77, Kent County Library System, Grand Rapids, Mich., 1977-81; children's specialist Johnson County Library, Shawnee Mission, Kans., 1981-83, coordinator children's collections, 1983-90, youth collections specialist, 1991-, libr. Holy Trinity Cath. Sch., Lenexa, Kans, 1990-94; mng. ptnr. The Book Tree, Lenexa, Kans., 1982—; library cons. Family Services of Kent County (Mich.), 1977-79. Contbg. editor Kansas City Parent, 1986-90, Parent's Guide to Media, 1995-2001; AV reviewer Booklist, 1995- Mem. ALA, Assn. for Library Service to Children (intellectual freedom com. 1984-88, co-chair video pre-conf. 1989, film and video evaluation com. 1989-92, chair 1992, Newbery award com. 1983, Caldecott award com. 1993, Carnegie medal com., chair 1995, edn. com., chair 1996-97, connectivity pre-conf. 1998, liaison with organ. serving the child com. 1998-2002, bd. dirs. 2002-05, new awards task force, chair 2005-, Scribner award 1980), Freedom to Read Found., U.S. Pony Club (nat. games com. 2002-, chair 2006), Roman Catholic. Office: Johnson Coutny Libr Sys 9875 W 87th St Pkwy Shawnee Mission KS 66212 Office Phone: 913-495-2437. Business E-Mail: mcleodd@jocolibrary.org.

MCLIN, RHINE LANA, mayor, former state legislator; b. Dayton, Ohio, Oct. 3, 1948; d. C. Josef, Jr. and Bernice (Cottman) McL. BA in Sociology, Parsons Coll., 1969; MEd, Xavier U., 1972; postgrad. in law, U. Dayton, 1974-76; AA in Mortuary Sci., Cin. Coll., 1988. Lic. funeral dir. Tchr. Dayton Bd. Edn., 1970-72; divorce counselor Domestic Rels. Ct., Dayton, 1972-73; law clk. Montgomery Common Pleas Ct., Dayton, 1973-74; v.p., dir., embalmer McLin Funeral Homes, Dayton, 1972—; mem. Ohio Ho. of Reps. from 36th & 38th dists., Columbus, 1988-94, Ohio Senate from 5th dist., Columbus, 1994—2002; mem. Ways & Means Com.; controlling bd., ins. commerce comn. ranking mem.; state and local govt. com. Columbus; minority whip Ohio Senate, Columbus, 1994—2001; mayor City of Dayton, 2002—. Instr. Central State U., Wilberforce, Ohio, 1982-97; mem. Ohio Tuition Trust Authority. Mem. Dem. Nat. Com., Children's Def. Fund. Toll fellow; Paul Harris fellow; Flemming fellow; BLLD fellow; named Ohio Legislator of Yr., Ohio Social Workers Assn., 1999. Mem. Nat. Funeral Dirs. Assn., Ohio Funeral Dirs. Assn., Montgomery County Hist. Soc., NAACP (life), Nat. Coun. Negro Women (life), Delta Sigma Theta. Achievements include being first female mayor of Dayton. Office: City Hall 2nd Fl 101 W Third St Dayton OH 45402 Office Phone: 937-333-3653. Business E-Mail: Rhine.McLin@cityofDayton.org.

MCLIN-MITCHELL, VELMA ELAINE, language educator, literature educator; b. Florence, Miss., June 1, 1932; d. McCullough McLin and Marie Cannon-McLin; m. Claude Mitchell, June 29, 1968; children: Gary Delano Mitchell, Joyce Marie Mitchell. BS in Lang. Arts, Jackson State U., Miss., 1953; MA in English and Am. Lit., Howard U., Washington, 1964, PhD in Linguistics, 1970; cert. in reading, U. Chgo., 1965; cert. in comparative edn. (hon.), Cambridge U., Eng., 1998. Tchr. Steep Bank Sch., Florence, Miss., 1950; tchr. English Walnut Grove Hickory H.S., Miss., 1953—54; tchr. math. Carter H.S., Brandon, Miss., 1954—56; tchr. English Tougaloo Coll., Miss.; tchr. English, libr. Hickory HS, Miss., 1956—61; grad. asst. Howard U., 1956—61; tchr. comp. and lit. Mpls. Jr. Coll.; prof. linguistics and adult edn. Cheyney U., Pa., 1977—2000. Dir. freshman English Howard U.; chairperson English dept. Cheyney U.; cons., instr. Acad. Academic Excellence, Cheyney U.; spkr. Jackson State U. Centennial celebration, NCNW Nat. Conv., 1975. Contbr. articles to profl. publs. Pres. Studevan Plus, Inc., Darby Township, Pa., 1978—, Jackson State U. Alumni Chpt., 1970—79, NCNW, St. Paul, 1971—76. Named to Wall of Tolerance, Ala.; recipient plaque, AME Ch., Darby Township, Pa., NAACP, Golden dipl., Jackson State U., 2003. Mem.: Nat. Coun. Negro Women (pres. Del. sect. 1979—99, Mary McLeod Bethune award 1981), NAACP. Democrat. Protestant-Baptist. Avocations: reading, travel, community service. Home: 114 Marie McLin Lane Florence MS 39073 Personal E-mail: vimi805@aol.com.

MCMAHON, CATHERINE DRISCOLL, lawyer; b. Mineola, N.Y., Apr. 28, 1950; d. Matthew Joseph and Elizabeth (Driscoll) McM.; m. Gregory Arthur McGrath, Sept. 10, 1977 (div. 1991); children: Elizabeth Driscoll, Kerry Margaret, Michael Riley. BA, Simmons Coll., 1972; JD, Boston Coll., 1975; postgrad., Suffolk U., 1972-73; LLM, NYU, 1980. Bar: N.Y. 1976, D.C. 1979, U.S. Supreme Ct. 1980, U.S. Tax Ct. 1991. Tax atty. asst. Exxon Corp., N.Y.C., 1975-76, asst. tax atty., 1976-77, sr. tax atty., 1979-81; tax atty. Exxon Internat. Co., N.Y.C., 1977-79; sr. tax counsel Florham Park, NJ, 1990-92, Exxon Co. U.S.A., Houston, 1992—98, Exxon Coal and Minerals Co., Houston, 1998—2002, Exxon Mobil Corp., 2003—. Tax mgr. Exxon Rsch. & Engrng. Co., Florham Park, 1981-90. Bd. dirs. S.E. Morris chpt. ARC, Madison, N.J., 1983. Recipient TWIN award YMCA, Plainfield/Westfield, N.J., 1983. Mem. ABA, N.Y. State Bar Assn., D.C. Bar Assn. Roman Catholic. Office: Exxon Mobil Corp 800 Bell St Houston TX 77002-7497 Business E-Mail: catherine.d.mcmahon@exxonmobil.com.

MCMAHON, COLLEEN, federal judge; b. Columbus, Ohio, July 18, 1951; d. John Patrick and Patricia Paterson (McDanel) McM.; m. Frank V. Sica, May 16, 1981; children: Moira Catherine, Patrick McMahon, Brian Vincent. BA summa cum laude, Ohio State U., 1973; JD cum laude, Harvard U., 1976. Bar: N.Y. 1977, U.S. Dist. Ct. (so. and ea. dists.) N.Y. 1977, U.S. Ct. Appeals (2d cir.) 1978, U.S. Supreme Ct. 1980, U.S. Ct. Appeals (5th cir.) 1985, D.C. 1985. Spl. asst. U.S. mission to the UN, N.Y.C., 1979-80; assoc. Paul, Weiss, Rifkind, Wharton & Garrison, N.Y.C., 1976-79, 80-84, ptnr., 1984-95; judge N.Y. Ct. Claims, N.Y.C., 1995-98; acting justice N.Y. Supreme Ct., 1995-98; judge U.S. Dist. Ct. (So. Dist.), White Plains, NY, 1998—. Chair The Jury Project, N.Y. Office Ct. Adminstrn., 1993-94; mem. 1st jud. dist. com. Litigation Delay Reduction, 1997. Bd. dirs. Vol. Lawyers for the Arts, N.Y.C., 1979-83, Dance Theater Workshop, 1978-83; vice chancellor Episcopal Diocese of N.Y., 1992-95. Mem. ABA, Assn. of Bar of City of N.Y. (mem. coun. on jud. adminstrn. 1983-87, chmn. com. on state cts. of superior jurisdiction 1984-87, com. on women profession 1989-95, chmn. 1992-95, chmn. nominating com. 1996, mem. ad hoc com. jud. conduct 1996—), Am. Law Inst., Am. Judicature Soc., Westchester County Bar Assn., N.Y. State Bar Assn. (mem. ho. of dels. 1986-89), Fed. Bar Coun., N.Y. County Lawyers Assn. (chmn. com. changing trends in the profession 1998). Republican. Episcopalian. Office: United States Courthouse 300 Quarropas St White Plains NY 10601-4140

MCMAHON, ELIZABETH MILDRED, educator; b. Bridgeport, Conn., June 16, 1918; d. Frederick Francis and Elizabeth Mildred (Collins) McM. AB, Coll. New Rochelle, 1940; MA, Fairfield U., 1952, cert. advanced study, 1963. Tchr. English Roger Ludlow Jr. High Sch., East Norwalk, Conn., 1942-43, Ctr. Jr. High Sch., Norwalk, Conn., 1943, counselor, tchr., 1945-53; head guidance counselor Nathan Hale Mid. Sch., Norwalk, 1953-92; ret. Instr. Danbury State Tchrs. Coll., Danbury, Conn., 1953-54. Mem. Tchr. Certification Adv. Bd., 1967-72, chmn. 1969; vol. Norwalk Hosp, Lockwood Mathews Mansion Mus., Regina A. Quick Ctr. for the Arts, Fairfield U.; mem. adv. bd. St. Thomas the Apostle Ch. Parish, 1994-97 GE fellow, 1959, U.S. State Dept. fellow, 1965, Ford Found. fellow, 1966; recipient Tchr. Honor Roll award, Norwalk H.S. Alumni Assn., 2004. Mem. AACD, NEA (life), AAUW (life), Am. Sch. Counselor Assn., Conn. Edn. Assn. (life, bd. dirs. 1964-88), Conn. Assn. Counseling and Devel., Norwalk Tchrs. Assn. (pres. 1957-60) Coll. New Rochelle Alumni Assn. (pres. 1985—, bd. dirs. 1994-97) Democrat. Roman Catholic. Home: 128 Gregory Blvd Norwalk CT 06855-2515

MCMAHON, JANET MANKIEWICH, critical care nurse; b. Rockville Centre, N.Y., Apr. 23, 1957; d. Matthew J. and Lois May (Johns) Mankiewich; m. Michael T. McMahon, July 12, 1985; children: Shannon and Sandy (twins), Patrick. BSN, Adelphi U., 1980. RN, N.Y., Va.; cert. BLS instr., ACLS. Nurse St. Francis Hosp., Roslyn, NY; charge nurse L.I. Jewish Hillside Med. Ctr., New Hyde Park, NY, Alexandria (Va.) Hosp., Mary Washington Hosp., Fredricksberg, Va., Mt. Vernon (Va.) Hosp., George Washington U. Hosp., Washington; nurse Potomac Hosp., Woodbridge, Va. Mem. AACCN. Home: 4803 Kempair Ct Woodbridge VA 22193-4631

MCMAHON, LINDA E., sports association executive; b. New Bern, N.C., Oct. 4, 1948; d. Henry and Evelyn Edwards; m. Vincent K. McMahon, Aug. 6, 1966; children: Shane, Stephanie. BA French, East Carolina U., 1969. Co-founder, bd. dirs. World Wrestling Entertainment, Inc., Stamford, Conn., 1980—, pres., 1993—2000, CEO, 1997—. Prodr.: (TV series) WWE: Raw is War, 1997—, WWE: Sunday Night Heat, 1998—, WWE: Smackdown!, 1999—; exec. prodr.: WWE Experience, 2004. Office: World Wrestling Entertainment Inc Titan Towers 1241 E Main St Stamford CT 06902

MCMAHON, MARGOT ANN, sculptor, art educator; b. Lake Forest, Ill., Apr. 15, 1957; d. William Franklin and Irene Mary (Leahy) McM.; m. Daniel Joseph Burke, June 25, 1988; children: Brendan McMahon Burke, Mary Irene McMahon Burke, Aubrey McMahon Burke. BA, Hamline U., 1979; MFA, Yale U., 1984. Sculpture asst. Hamline U., St. Paul, 1978; editl. artist World Book Ency., Chgo., 1979-82; tchg. asst. Yale U., New Haven, 1982-84; tchr. Yale Summer Sch., Norfolk, Conn., 1983; mem. sculpture faculty Sch. of Art Inst., Chgo., 1986-89; lectr. Art Inst. Assocs., Chgo., 1989—, DePaul U., Chgo., 1998. Vis. artist Sch. of Art Inst., 1992, 96, St. Xavier Coll., Chgo, 1995; presenter in field. Prin. works include sculptures and mural at St. Patrick Ch., Lake Forest, Ill., John D. MacArthur State Park, North Palm Beach., Fla., DePaul U., One Northfield Plz., Northfield, Ill., Lake Bluff, Ill., St. Mary's Sch., Lake Forest, Robert Irwin Park, Homewood, Ill., Highwood (Ill.) Pub. Libr., St. Francis Retreat Ctr., Oak Brook, Ill., Chgo. Botanic Garden, Northfield Pub. Libr., Beye Sch., Oak Park, Ill.; represented in permanent collections Chgo. Hist. Soc., Chgo. Horticultural Mus., DePaul U., John D. and Catherine T. MacArthur Found., Lake Forest H.S., Mobil Oil Internat., Fairfax, Va., Mus. Contemporary Art, Chgo., Nat. Portrait Gallery, Smithsonian Instn., Washington, Sch. of St. Mary, Lake Forest, Silberline Co., Inc., Tamaqua, Pa., Tuthill Corp., Hinsdale, Ill., Yale U., and numerous pvt. collections; represented in DeBilzan Gallery, Santa Fe, N.Mex. Bd. dirs. Palette and Chisel, Chgo., 1989, Oak Park Area Arts Coun., 1999, Nat. Mus. of Women in the Arts, 1999—; mem., exhibitor Deerpath Art League, Lake Forest, 1990-00, Hyde Park Art Ctr., Chgo., 1992—, Oak Park Area Arts Coun., 1992—, Chgo. Arts Club. Recipient Fellowship award Barat Coll., 2000, Rose Phillipine Duchasne award, 2000; grantee Retirement Rsch. Found., Chgo., 1989, Ragdale Found., 1993, Steans Family Found., 1991. Mem. Internat. Sculpture Soc., Nat. Sculpture Soc. (Alex B. Hexter award 1991), Renaissance Soc., Ragdale Found., Mus. Contemporary Art, Arts Club of Chgo. Roman Catholic. Avocations: book clubs, sailing, music, softball. Home: 310 S Humphrey Ave Oak Park IL 60302-3528 E-mail: mmcmahom@mediaone.net.

MCMAHON, SUSANNA ROSEMARY, clinical psychologist, author; b. Lisbon, Portugal, Apr. 19, 1947; came to U.S., 1955; d. G. Harvey Summ and Joan Helena Quarm; m. Terry Phillip Gardner, Sept. 3, 1966 (div. Aug. 1980); children: Jennifer Joan, Catherine Mary Gardner Watson; m. John Timothy McMahon, June 9, 1985; 1 stepchild, K. Kelly McMahon. BA in Psychology, U. Houston, 1978, MA in Psychology, 1982, PhD in Psychology, 1983. Lic. clin. psychologist, Tex. Clin. cons. Adult-Adolescent Rehab. Ctr., Houston, 1984-85; staff psychologist VA Med. Ctr., Houston, 1984-85; child clin. psychologist U.S. Dept. Def., Heidelberg, Germany, 1985-89; dir. Cmty. Mental Health Program, Madrid, 1990-92; pvt. practice Houston, 1992—. Author: The Portable Therapist, 1994, Having Healthy Relationships, 1996, Coping with Life's Stressors, 1996, The Portable Pilgrim, 1998. Mem. Am. Psychol. Assn., Pen-West, U.S.A., Charter 100 (founder, Madrid, Houston). Avocations: world traveling, reading, writing. Home and Office: 2001 Holcombe Blvd Unit 2604 Houston TX 77030-4218 Office Phone: 713-796-0530. Business E-Mail: ibu.one@sbcglobal.net.

MCMAHON MASTRODDI, MARCIA A., secondary school educator, artist, writer; b. Akron, Ohio, Dec. 26, 1953; d. James R. and Marla June McMahon; m. Dennis W. Mastroddi, Aug. 22, 1987. BA in Art, Ursuline Coll., 1978; MA in Art, Case Western Res. U., 1980; student, Cleve. Inst. Art. Cert. K-12 art tchr., Ill. Instr. art Cuyahoga C.C., Warrensville Heights, Ohio, 1978-87; lectr. art Spoon River Coll., Canton, Ill., 1989, Ill. Ctrl. Coll., Peoria, 1990; tchr. art CBS Alternative H.S., Beardstown, Ill., 1993-95, Ursuline Acad., Springfield, Ill., 1996-97, Dist. 186, Springfield, 1997-98; tchr. art, chmn. dept. Tower Hill (Ill) Consol. Unified Sch. Dist. 66, 1999—. Lectr. art for gifted Lincoln Land C.C., Springfield, part-time 1995-98, Art Inst. Online, divsn. Pitts. Art Inst.; featured guest spkr. Case Western Res. U., Cleve., 1980, Shard Hill Art Gallery, Farmington, Ill., 1989, Bot. Garden, 1998, Ursuline Coll., Cleve., 1979, Peoria Art Guild, 1990—. Ill. State Mus., Springfield, 1995—, Unity Gallery, 1999—, Rushville (Ill.) Arts Coun., 1999, Taste of Champaign (Ill.) Art Ctr. Sq. Show, 1999, Lincoln Prairie Trail Art Show, 2001; author: Diana Speaks to the World, 2002, Princess Diana's Message of Peace: An Extraordinary Message of Peace for Our Current World, 2004; prin. works include, U.S., Europe, and Can.; pub. in (with Princess Diana's messages) Channeling Anthoogy for September 11th (www.spiritwritings.com). Houseparent Am. Youth Hostels, 1988-89. Recipient svc. award for tchr. Cuyahoga C.C., 1989, Rosie Richmond award Springfield Area Arts Coun., 1998. Mem. Prairie State Orchid Soc., Ill. state Mus. Soc., Washington Park Bot. Gardens, Tower Hill Art Club. Mem. Unity Ch. Avocations: designing jewelry, hiking, sketching, portraiture, collecting antiques. E-mail: marcia@ctitech.com, dianaspeaks@hotmail.com.

MCMANIGAL, PENNY, artist; b. Orange, Calif., 1936; d. Howard R. and Helen L. Hineman; m. Paul G. McManigal, Aug. 22, 1959; children: Lisa Anne, Scott Paul. BA, Pomona Coll., 1958. Tchr. Fern Dr. Elem. Sch., Fullerton, Calif., 1958—59, Springhill Elem., Lafayette, Calif., 1959—63; master tchr. San Jose State U., Lafayette, 1962—63; tchr.-writer art curriculum Eastbluff Elem., Newport Beach, Calif., 1974—79. Mem. faculty Social Artistry Summer Leadership Conf., So. Oreg. U.; presenter in field. One-woman shows include Newport Beach (Calif.) Civic Ctr. Gallery, 1966, Sherman Gardens Gallery, Corona del Mar, Calif., 1967, Pomona Coll., Claremont, Calif., 1979, Galerie France, Bordeaux, 1982, Civic Ctr. Gallery, Buena Park, Calif., 1984, Pennswood Gallery, Newtown, Pa., 1990, Internat. Mus. 20th Century Art & Culture, Laguna Beach, Calif., 1991, U. Calif., Irvine, 1992, The Beckman Ctr., 1993, Peace Tent, UN 4th NGO World Conf. on Women, China, 1995, Claremont Forum Gallery, Claremont, Calif., 1999, Calif. State U., Long Beach, 2000, UN Ch. Ctr., NYC, 2002, St. Paul's Chapel, 2002, numerous internat. locations, world co-creative interactive project Weaving the Dream!, 1997—2003, Founder's Hall Gallery, Soka U., Aliso Viejo, Calif., 2005—06, The Costa Mesa Country Club, Conn., exhibited in group shows at Mont. Gallery, Pomona Coll., Claremont, 1989, City of San Diego-USSR Cultural Exch., 1990, Irvine Fine Arts Ctr., Irvine, Calif., 1994, Anaheim Mus., Anaheim, Calif., 1999, L.A. County Fair, Edn. Bldg., 2000, dA Gallery, Pomona, Calif., 2001, 2002, numerous others, Peace for Our Children painting presented to Mikhail Gorbachev, Pres. George H.W. Bush, Desmond Tutu, others, one-woman shows include N.Y.C. Phoenix Bird Dream Catcher (interactive sculpture) UN Ch. Ctr., N.Y.C., 2002; featured artist painting featured on Axis Mundi mag., Greece, 2006, painting also in internat. mag. in Eng.; contbr. poems pub. to profl. jour. Artistic amb. People to People Internat., 2000; spkr. Calif. State Long Beach, Art Affiliates, 1991, Rembrandt Club, Pomona Coll., 1996, SCA, Irvine Fine Arts Ctr., Irvine, Calif., 1999, Claremont Forum, Claremont, Calif., 1999, The People's Network Television, Dallas, 1996, Presbyn. Western Synod, San Diego, 1996, Social Artistry Summer Leadership Conf., Southern Oreg. U., 2003; planning com. The Millionth Cir., 2001—, Gather the Women Internat. Congress, San Francisco, 2003, Dallas, 2004, Using Art as a Daily Meditation, Dallas, 2004; co-founder Orange County Circle Gatherings, 2004—; mem. Newport Beach City Arts Com., 1965—71; co-chair Newport Beach City Arts Festival, 1970; mem. Pomona Coll. Alumni Coun., 1978—82; del. and group co-creative leader UN 4th NGO World Conf. on Women, China, 1995; rep. NGO Pathways to Peace UN Dept. Pub. Info./NGO Conf., 2002; del. and group co-creative leader UN Commn. on the Status of Women, NY, 2002, del. co-leader Millionth Cir. NY, 2002; founder and pres. Parents Who Care, Newport Beach, 1982—86; city arts commr. City of Newport Beach, 1966—71. Named Outstanding Young Women of Am., 1967; named to Hall of Fame, Fullerton Union H.S., 1985; recipient Outstanding Vol. Svc. to the Arts award, City Coun., 1982, Silver Anchor award for outstanding cmty. svc., C. of C. Newport Beach, 1985, Outstanding Contbn. to Edn. award, Orange County Dept. Edn., 1988, Clara Barton Spectrum awards, Orange County chpt. ARC, 1995, Artistic Contbn. award, 1995. Mem.: Orange County Circle Gatherings, Southern Calif. Artist Assn., The Millionth Circle, Conveners, Nat. Mus. of Women in the Arts, Internat. Soc. Poets. Achievements include creator world's first interactive Internet cyberquilt; creator of many new forms of interactive LiveArt. Avocations: genealogy, writing, travel, poetry. Home: 16 Inverness Ln Newport Beach CA 92660 Office: PO Box 9426 Newport Beach CA 92658-9426 Office Phone: 949-721-8059. Personal E-mail: paxweave@aol.com.

MCMANIGAL, SHIRLEY ANN, retired dean; b. Deering, Mo., May 4, 1938; d. Jadie C. and Willie B. (Groves) Naile. BS, Ark. State U., 1971; MS, U. Okla., 1976, PhD, 1979. Med. technologist, 1958—75; chair dept. med. tech. U. So. Miss., Hattiesburg, 1979—83, Tex. Tech U. Health Scis. Ctr., Lubbock, 1983—87, dean Sch. Allied Health, 1987—97. Gov.'s appointee to statewide health coord. coun., 1994-97. Leadership Tex., 1992; Lt. Alumnae Regl. dir., 1994-97. Recipient Citation, State of Tex., 1988; named Woman of Yr., AAUW, Tex. divsn., 1990, Woman of Excellence in Edn. YWCA, Lubbock, 1990. Mem.: AAUW (Tex. bd. dirs. 1990—94, mem. ednl. found. internat. fellows panel 1994—98, chair 1998—2001), Tex. Soc. Med. Tech. (Educator of Yr. 1990), Tex. Soc. Allied Health Professions (pres. 1990—91), So. Assn. Allied Health Deans at Acad. Health Ctrs., Nat. Assn. Women in Edn., Am. Soc. Med. Tech., Clin. Lab. Mgmt. Assn. (chair edn. com. 1989, 1991), Phi Beta Delta, Alpha Eta. Home: 612 S 72d St Broken Arrow OK 74014 Personal E-mail: smcmanigal1@cox.net.

MCMANNESS, LINDA MARIE, language educator; b. St. Louis, Mo., June 11, 1955; d. Donald R. and Gloria Jean McManness. BA, S.W. Baptist U., 1977; MA, U. Wash., 1987, PhD, 1990. Tchr. Spanish & Eng. Lamar H.S., Lamar, Mo., 1977—81; mgr. Lerner NY, Joplin, Mo., 1980—81, Springfield, Mo., 1981—83, Tulsa, 1981—85; acct. U. Wash., Seattle, 1985—86, grad. tchg. asst., 1986—90; assoc. prof. Spanish & Portuguese Baylor U., Waco, Tex., 1990—. Dir. Spanish grad. studies Baylor U., 1996—99. Author: Lexical Categories in Spanish: The Determiner, 1996, book reviews to profl. jours. Co-pres. Cen-Tex Foreign Lang. Collaborative, Waco, 1994—96; cook Meals on Wheels, Waco, 1997—; dir. global Christian ventures Baylor U., 1999—. Mem.: AAUP, Southwest Conf. Latin Am. Studies, South Ctrl. Modern Lang. Assn. Office: Baylor U PO Box 97393 Waco TX 76798 Office Phone: 254-710-4426.

MCMANUS, DEBRA LYNNE, secondary school educator; b. Pauls Valley, Okla., June 7, 1954; m. Larry R. McManus, June 15, 1973; children: Courtney, Jared. BA, East Ctrl. U., Ada, Okla., 1977, M in Secondary Edn., 1992. English tchr. Maysville (Okla.) Pub. Schs., 1980—82, Pauls Valley Pub. Schs., 1984—. Mem.: NEA, Nat. Coun. Tchrs. English, Pauls Valley Edn. Assn., Okla. Edn. Assn. Office: Pauls Valley High School North St Pauls Valley OK 73075 Office Phone: 405-238-6497. Business E-Mail: dmcmanus@paulsvalley.k12.ok.us.

MCMANUS, DELANA ANN, elementary school educator; b. Tulsa, Okla., Mar. 9, 1970; d. Richard Lee and Mary Alice Campbell; m. Sean Michael McManus, June 17, 1995; children: Alexandra, Pete. BA in early childhood Edn., Northeastern State U., Tahlequah, Okla., 1993; MS, Okla. State U., Stillwater, 1996; EdD, Okla. State U., 1999. Cert. early Childhood Edn., Reading specialist, Elem. Edn. First grade tchr. Tulsa Pub. Schs., Tulsa, Okla., 1993—97; reading specialist titleI coord. Bixby Pub. Sch., Bixby, Okla., 1997—. Contbr. scientific papers. Mem.: NEA, Bixby Edn. Assn. Republican. Avocations: reading, travel, scrapbooks. Office: Bixby Pub Schs 501 S Riverview Bixby OK 74008 Business E-Mail: dmcmanus@bixbyps.org.

MCMASTER, BELLE MILLER, religious organization administrator; b. Atlanta, May 24, 1932; d. Patrick Dwight and Lila (Bonner) Miller; m. George R. McMaster, June 19, 1953; children: Lisa McMaster Stork, George Neel, Patrick Miller. BA, Agnes Scott Coll., 1953; MA, U. Louisville, 1970, PhD, 1974. Assoc. corp. witness Presbyn. Ch. USA, Atlanta, 1974-77, dir. corp. witness, 1977-81, dir. div. corp. and social mission, 1981-87, dir. social justice and peacemaking unit Louisville, 1987-93; acting dir. program women in theology and ministry Candler Sch. Theology Emory U., 1993-96, dir. advanced studies Candler Sch. Theology, 1995—2003. Vice-moderator chs. commn. internat. affairs World Coun. Chs., 1984-91, mem. justice, peace and creation commn., 1991-99; chair commn. internat. affairs Nat. Coun. Chs., NYC, 1986-89, v.p., 1990-95, exec. bd., 1986-2003, chair ch. world svc. and witness unit com., 1990-2003; chair fin. com. Ch. World Svc. and Witness Unit Com., NC, 1997-99, bd. dirs., 1995-2003. Author: Witnessing to the Kingdom, 1982, book columnist "What I Have Been Reading" in Church and Society Magazine, 1993-2001; contbr. articles to profl. jours. Pres. League of Women Voters, Greenville, S.C., 1963-64; bd. dirs. Interfaith Housing, Atlanta, 1975-81. Danforth fellow, 1969-74. Mem.: MLA, Soc. for Values in Higher Edn., Acad. Am. Religion, Phi Beta Kappa. Presbyterian. Business E-Mail: bmcmast@emory.edu.

MCMASTER, JANET LYNN, psychologist; b. Pittsburgh, Pa., Sept. 3, 1951; d. Louis McClurg and Erma Esther (Leech) McM.; 1 child, Lindsey Jordan McMaster. AB in Psychology with honors, Grove City Coll., 1973; MS, Duquesne U., 1974; PhD, U. Pitts., 1988. Cert. tchr., sch. psychologist, Pa.; nat. cert. sch. psychologist, 1988. Self-employed psychologist, Pa., 1979—. Vol. rschr. Inst. for the Black Family, Pitts., 1988-91, U. Pitts. Cancer Inst., 1999-2003 Co-author: (with others) Measurements of Marital Quality, 1989. Mem. Nat. Assn. Sch. Psychologists, Assn. Sch. Psychologists Pa., Assn. Doctoral Educators, Spinone Club Am., Am. Spinone Club. Home and Office: 16 Linn Farm Rd Canonsburg PA 15317-5114 Office: 16 Linn Farm Rd Canonsburg PA 15317-5114

MCMASTER, JULIET SYLVIA, English language educator; b. Kisumu, Kenya, Aug. 2, 1937; emigrated to Can., 1961, naturalized, 1976; d. Sydney Herbert and Sylvia (Hook) Fazan; m. Rowland McMaster, May 10, 1968; children: Rawdon, Lindsey. BA with honors, Oxford U., Eng., 1959; MA, U. Alta., Can., 1963, PhD, 1965. Asst. prof. English U. Alta., Edmonton, Canada, 1965—70, assoc. prof., 1970—76, prof. English, 1976—86, univ. prof., 1986—2000, prof. emeritus, 2000—. Author: Thackeray: The Major Novels, 1971, Jane Austen on Love, 1978, Trollope's Palliser Novels, 1978; author: (with R.D. McMaster) The Novel from Sterne to James, 1981; author: Dickens the Designer, 1987, Jane Austen the Novelist, 1995, Reading the Body in the Eighteenth Century Novel, 2004, Woman Behind the Painter: The Diaries of Rosalie, Mrs. James Clarke-Hook, 2006; co-editor: Jane Austen's Business, 1996, Cambridge Companion to Jane Austen, 1997, The Child Writer From Austen to Woolf, 2005; gen. editor: Juvenilia Press, 1993—2002, illustrator/editor: children's picture book (by Jane Austen) The Beautifull Cassandra, 1993; contbr. articles to profl. jours. Fellow Can. Coun., 1969-70, Guggenheim Found., 1976-77, Killam Found., 1987-89; recipient Molson prize in Humanities for Outstanding Contbn. to Canadian Culture, 1994, Alberta Centennial medal, 2005. Fellow Royal Soc. Can.; mem. Victorian Studies Assn. Western Can. (founding pres. 1972), Assn. Can. Univ. Tchrs. English (pres. 1976-78), MLA, Jane Austen Soc. N.Am. (dir. 1980-91). Office Phone: 708-436-5284. Business E-Mail: juliet.mcmaster@ualberta.ca.

MCMASTERS, GLENETTA G., science educator; d. Glen C. and Anna M. Klein; children: Jesse K., Jonathan D., Joshua G., Joseph L. BS Natural Scis., Cameron U., Lawton, Okla., 1997. Cert. Tchr. Okla. State Bd. Edn., 1997. Tchr. jr. h.s. sci. Lawton Pub. Schs., 1997—2000; tchr. h.s. sci. Elgin Pub. Schs., Okla., 2000—. Conservative-R. Baptist. Avocations: reading, sewing, camping, gardening. Office: Elgin Public Schools PO Box 369 Elgin OK 73538-0369

MCMATH, ELIZABETH MOORE, graphic artist; b. Iredell, Tex., Feb. 20, 1930; d. Fred William and Elizabeth Carol (Smith) Moore; m. Charles Wallis McMath, Jan. 16, 1978 (dec. Dec. 1990); children: Charles Wallis, John Seals. BA, BS in Advt. Design, Tex. Woman's U., Denton, 1951; grad. gemologist, Gemol. Inst. Am., L.A., 1977. Layout artist Leonard's Dept. Store, Ft. Worth, Tex., 1951-52; artist/bookkeeper Bud Biggs Studio, Dallas, 1953; sec./artist Squire Haskins Studio, Dallas, 1953-54; artist/art dir. Dowdell-Merrill, Inc., Dallas, 1954-58; owner/artist Moore Co., Dallas, 1958-90. Mem. Stemmons Corridor Bus. Assn., Dallas, 1988-89. Mem. Dallas/Ft. Worth Soc. Visual Comm. (founder), Tex. Woman's U. Nat. Alumnae Assn., Greater North Tex. Orchid Soc. (treas. 1987), Daylily Growers of Dallas (sec. 1989-90, 1st v.p. and program chmn. 1992), Internat. Bulb Soc., Native Plant Soc. Tex. (publicity chmn. Trinity Forks chpt. 1991-02, pres. 1998, sec. 1999-2003, Elm Fork chpt., master naturalist 2001—), Fort Worth Orchid Soc. Presbyterian. Avocations: ranching, horticulture, plant propagation, lost wax casting, gemstone cutting. Home: PO Box 1068 Denton TX 76202-1068 E-mail: elizabeth.mcmath@sbcglobal.net.

MCMATH, LULA WRAY, retired elementary school educator, realtor; b. Grenada, Miss., Apr. 27, 1933; d. Alva and Augusta McMath; m. Jesse C. Terry; 1 child, Damita. BS in Edn., Chgo. State U., 1971, MS in Urban Edn., 1972, MS in Corrections, 1974. Lic. realtor Chgo. (Ill.) Bd. Realtors, 1986. Seamstress Hart Schaffner and Marx, Chgo., 1952—65; tchr. Chgo. (Ill.) Bd. Edn., 1965—93; realtor Ronald Waters, Chgo., 1986—. Author: How 8th Grade Students View Discipline, 1973, Places I Have Visited, 1994, My Lovely Garden, 1994. Vol. gardener City of Chgo., 1989; vol. literacy educator Roosevelt U., Chgo., 1993; ballot giver Dem. Party, Chgo., 1988, poll watcher, 1984, judge, 1990, registrar, 1988. Recipient Valuable Svc. award, Faith Temple Ch., 1975, Meritorious award, United Negro Colls., 1991. Mem.: Am. Fedn., Ret. Tchrs. Avocations: gardening, singing, dance, interior decorating. Home: 10621 S Wood St Chicago IL 60643-2717

MCMEANS, SARAH DORNIN WILKINSON, communications regulatory specialist; b. Berkeley, Calif., Apr. 20, 1939; d. Winsor Dornin and Mabel Florence (Sutton) Wilkinson; m. David McMeans, Dec. 12, 1969. BA, U. Calif. Davis, 1961. Vol. US Peace Corps, Moalboal, Philippines, 1962—64; jr. officer US Dept of State, Caracas, Venezuela, 1965—66, vice consul Guatamala City, Guatemala, 1966—68; paralegal, comm. regulatory specialist Covington & Burling LLP, Wash., 1968—. Bd. mem. Peace Corps Alumni, Found. for Philippine Devel., Wash., DC, 1997—. Mem.: Nat. Peace Corps Assn. Home: 3025 Ontario Rd NW 404 Washington DC 20009-6034 Office: Covington & Burling LLP 1201 Pa Ave NW Washington DC 20004-2401 Office Phone: 202-662-5015. Business E-Mail: smcmeans@cov.com.

MCMEEKIN, DOROTHY, botanist, plant pathologist, educator; b. Boston, Feb. 24, 1932; d. Thomas LeRoy and Vera (Crockatt) McM. BA, Wilson Coll., 1953; MA, Wellesley Coll., 1955; PhD, Cornell U., 1959. Asst. prof. Upsala Coll., East Orange, NJ, 1959-64, Bowling Green State U., Ohio, 1964-66; prof. natural sci. Mich. State U., East Lansing, 1966-89, prof. botany, plant pathology, 1989—. Author: Diego Rivera: Science and Creativity, 1985; contbr. articles to profl. jours. Mem. Am. Phytopath. Soc., Mycol. Soc. Am., Soc. Econ. Bot., Mich. Bot. Soc. (former bd. dirs.), Mich. Women's Studies Assn., Sigma Xi, Phi Kappa Phi. Avocations: gardening, sewing, travel, drawing. Home: 1055 Marigold Ave East Lansing MI 48823-5128 Office: Mich State U Dept Botany-Plant Pathology 100 N Kedzie Hall East Lansing MI 48824-1031 E-mail: mcmeekin@msu.edu.

MCMEEN, SHEILA TAENZLER, retired lawyer; b. Morristown, N.J., Aug. 26, 1946; d. William Paul and Mary Cunningham Taenzler; m. E. Ellsworth McMeen, III, July 31, 1971; children: Jonathan, Daniel, James, Mary. AB summa cum laude, Muhlenberg Coll., Allentown, Pa., 1968; JD cum laude, U. Pa., 1971. Bar: N.Y. 1972, U.S. Supreme Ct. 1979. Assoc. Davis Polk & Wardwell, N.Y.C., 1971—80; ret. Editor: U. Pa. Law Rev. Pastoral care vol. staff Andover (N.J.) Rehab Ctr., 2004—; mem. Bd. of Edn., Mountain Lakes, NJ, 1993—2001, Sussex County Child Placement Rev. Bd., Newton, NJ, 2003—. Mem.: Phi Beta Kappa. Avocations: needlework, cryptic puzzles, reading. Home: 34 Angelo Dr Sparta NJ 07871 E-mail: elmcmeen@ptd.net.

MCMICHAEL, MARIA MADELYN, publishing executive; b. Camden, NJ, May 2, 1968; d. William Richard McMichael and Angela Nita Bovo. BA, Chestnut Hill Coll., Phila., 1990. Editl. asst. Current Sci., Phila., 1990—91, prodn. editor, 1991—92, sr. editor, 1992—95; sr. tng. editor Rapid Sci. Pubs., Phila., 1995—97; mng. editor Internat. Thompson Pub., Phila., 1997—98; pub. Lippincott Williams & Wilkins, Phila., 1998—2003; sr. pub. Walters Lluvver, Phila., 2003—. Home: 19 N Logan Ave Audubon NJ 08106-1036

MCMILLAN, ADELL, retired academic administrator; b. Portland, Oreg., June 22, 1933; d. John and Eunice A. (Hoyt) McM. AB in Social Sci., Whitman Coll., 1955; MS in Recreation Mgmt., U. Oreg., 1963. Program dir. Erb Meml. Union, U. Oreg., Eugen, 1955-68; program cons. Willard Straight Hall, Cornell U., Ithaca, N.Y., 1966-67; assoc. dir. Erb Meml. Union, U. Oreg., Eugene, 1968-75, dir., 1975-91, dir. emeritus, 1992—. Editor, co-author: College Unions: Seventy-Five Years, 1989; interviewer, editor oral history interviews, 1978, 92-94, 96; author: A Common Ground--Erb Memorial Union 1950-2000, 2004—. Bd. dirs. United Way, Lane County, Oreg., 1976-83, 87-97, 98—, pres., 1982-83, 88-90; commr. Eugene City Planning Commn., 1992-2004; mem. Hist. Rev. Bd., 1992-2004; mem. Tree Commn., 1992-93; bd. dirs., treas., 1994-95, Eugene Opera Co., 1992-2000; bd. dirs. Eugene Pub. Libr. Found., 2002—; pres.-elect City Club of Eugene, 2003-04, pres., 2004-2005. Named Woman of Yr. Lane County Coun. Orgns., Eugene, Oreg., 1985; re-named Erb Meml. Union Art Gallery, U. Oreg. as Adell McMillan Art Gallery, 1998. Mem. Assn. Coll. Unions-Internat. (v.p. 1977-80, pres. 1981-82, Butts-Whiting award 1987, hon. 1992, editor Vets. newsletter, 1993-2000, internat. ednl. rsch. found. bd. dirs. 2004—), Zonta Club of Eugene, Zonta Internat. (pres. 1984-86, dist. treas. 1990-92, 92-94), Emerald Valley Women's Golf Club (pres. 1995). Democrat. Episcopalian. Avocations: golf, reading. Office: 55 W 39th Ave Eugene OR 97405-3344 Office Phone: 541-344-6305. Business E-Mail: adellmcm@uoregon.edu.

MCMILLAN, BETTIE BARNEY, language educator; b. Fayetteville, N.C., Mar. 14, 1941; d. Booker T. and Sarah Estelle (Barney) McM.; children: Gregory L., Kenneth A., Ronald D., Pamela M., Deirdre Y., Michael A. BA in Psychology/Sociology, Meth. Coll., 1978. Program supr. Adminstrv. Office of the Cts.-Guardian Ad Litem Program, Raleigh, N.C.; English instr. Cmty. Coll., Fayetteville, N.C.; info. specialist, case mgr. Big Bros./Big Sisters, Fayetteville. Author: A Plea For Love, 1995, The Language of Love (award of merit 2002), Fires of Passion (Pres. award for literary excellence, Nat. Authors Registry, 2003), (song) Love Is Waiting, 2003, (poems) I Am Love, Language of Love, 2002, (featured on Sound of Poetry album) Did You See?, My Brother-You Are Not Alone, 2004; contbr. Celebrations of Honor: a collection of poems and essays from around the world, 2003, (poems) Eternal Portraits, 2005, Invoking the Muse, 2005. Leader, nat. officer United Order of Tents, Norfolk, Va., 1982-92; vol. N.C. Guardian Ad Litem, Raleigh, 1992—; mem. Atlanta Com. for Olympic Games, 1996. Recipient Copyright award plaque Copywright award, 1996, Poet Merit award Nat. Libr. Congress, 1995, Shakespeare Trophy of Excellence, 2002, 04, Poet of Yr. Medallion, 2002, Pres. award for Lit. Excellence, 2003. Mem. Internat. Soc. of Poets (Disting. mem., 1995-96, Poets Choice award 1995, Outstanding Achievement in Poetry award 2005), Sigma Omega Chi. Baptist. Avocations: reading, writing, literary works, community volunteer, gardening, travel. Home: 5509 Ramshorn Dr Fayetteville NC 28303-2736

MCMILLAN, EILEEN MARGARET, daycare administrator, educator; b. Denville, N.J., Oct. 10, 1954; d. Thomas Henry and Barbara Ann (Mead) Ahlers; children: Shane, Kelly, Sadie, Troy. BS in Health and Phys. Edn., Slippery Rock U., 1977; postgrad., East Shroudsburg U., 1982—83, U. Mont., 1987—88, Salish Kootenai Coll., 1987, Antioch U., 1998—99; AAS in Early Childhood, U. Mont., 2004. Tchr. health & phys. edn. North Warren Regional High Sch., Blairstown, NJ, 1977—83; sec., asst. phys. therapy St. Joseph Hosp., Polson, Mont., 1983—86; phys. edn. aide Dist. #28, St. Ignatius, 1986—88; owner, operator Custom Fitness, Ronan, 1988—92; substitute tchr. Dist. #30, 1992—2000; dir. daycare, tchr. presch. Dixon Sch., 2000—. Com. mem. 21st Century After Sch. Program, Dixon, 2000—05; com. mem. early learning guidelines Dept. Pub. Health & Human Svcs., Helena, 2003—04. Pres., v.p., sec. Dist. 30 PTA, Ronan, 1999—2000; mem. reading incentive program com. Dist. 30, 1991—99, coord. mileage club, 1996—2004; tchr. Sunday sch. Sacred Heart Cath. Ch., 1990—94; leader Boy Scouts Am., 1993—95. Recipient Merit Tng. award, Dept. Pub. Health & Human Svcs., Helena, 2002—03, 2003—04; scholar, Early Childhood Project, Bozeman, Mont., 2002. Mem.: Nat. Assn. Edn. Young Children. Republican. Avocations: horseback riding, bicycling, travel, reading, swimming. Home: 238 Back Rd Ronan MT 59864 Office: Dixon Sch PO Box 10 B St Dixon MT 59831 Office Phone: 406-246-3370. E-mail: dixondaycam@blackfoot.net.

MCMILLAN, HELEN BERNEICE, sales executive; b. Huntington, Ark., Jan. 27, 1932; d. James Louis and Edna Lorene (Repass) Harrison; m. James Edward McMillan, May 10, 1950; children: Dianna Kaye Carter, Connie Sue Sadler. BBA, Dallas Bapt. U., 1993. Sewing machine operator Bobbinoak Corp., Fort Smith, Ark., 1949-50; greeting card decorator Hallmark Corp., Leavenworth, Kans., 1950-54; office clk. Sears Roebuck & Co., Lawton, Okla., 1955-57; grocery checker Safeway Grocery, Moberly, Mo., 1957-58; asst. retail mgr. Army & Air Force Exch., Leesville, La., 1962-74, buyer ladieswear Dallas, 1974-90, merchandise mgr. Munich, 1990-93; sales assoc. Hallmark Cards, Grand Prairie, Tex., 1994—. Recipient Achievement award Nat. Assn. Purchasing Mgmt., Dallas, 1988. Mem. NAFE, Fashion Group Internat. Republican. Avocations: doll collecting, ceramics, aerobics, gardening, fashion. Home: 609 Redwood Dr Grand Prairie TX 75052-6734

MCMILLAN, MARY BIGELOW, retired minister, volunteer; b. St. Paul, July 30, 1919; d. Charles Henry and Allison (McKibbin) Bigelow; m. Richard McMillan, June 26, 1943; children: Richard Jr., Charles B., Douglas D., M. Allison, Anne E. BA, Vassar Coll., 1941; MDiv, United Theol. Sem. Twin Cities, 1978, DDiv (hon.), 1989. Ordained to ministry Presbyn. Ch., 1978. Asst. min. House of Hope Presbyn. Ch., St. Paul, 1978-82; interim pres. United Theol. Sem. Twin Cities, New Brighton, Minn., 1982-83, ret., 1987. Contbg. author The Good Steward, 1983. Regional dir. Assn. Jr. Leagues, N.Y.C., 1959—61, pres. St. Paul chpt., 1957—59; vice chair Ramsey County Welfare Bd., St. Paul, 1962—66, St. Paul Health and Welfare Planning Coun., 1964—70, F.R. Bigelow Found., St. Paul, 1988—95, also 1st vice chair; 1st vice chair, trustee Wilder Found., 1973—89; active Presbyn. Homes Found., 1996—; trustee Minn. Ch. Found., Mpls., 1984—99, United Theol. Sem. Twin Cities, 1977—89, also chmn. bd. trustees; bd. dirs. Inst. for Ecumenical and Cultural Rsch., Collegeville, Minn., 1982—2003. Recipient award for cmty. planning United Way, 1965, also for yr. round leadership, 1973, Leadership in Cmty. Svc. award YWCA, 1980, Sisterhood award NCCJ, Mpls., 1989, Outstanding Vol. Fundraiser award Minn., 2005; named Disting Alumna, St. Paul Acad. and Summit Sch., 1988 Mem.: Univ. Club, New Century Club. Avocations: knitting, reading. Home: 2925 Lincoln Dr #713 Roseville MN 55113 Personal E-mail: mbmcmo@comcast.net.

MCMILLAN, TERRY L., writer, educator; b. Port Huron, Mich., Oct. 18, 1951; d. Edward McMillan and Madeline Washington Tillman; 1 child, Solomon Welch; m. Jonathan Plummer, 1998 (div. 2005). BA in Journalism, U. Calif., Berkeley, 1979; postgrad., Columbia Univ., N.Y.C., 1979. Instr. U. Wyoming, Laramie, 1987-88; prof. U. Ariz., Tucson, 1988-91. Author: Mama, 1987 (Nat. Book award Before Columbus Found.), Disappearing Acts, 1989, Waiting to Exhale, 1992, How Stella Got Her Groove Back, 1996, A Day Late & A Dollar Short, 2001, The Interruption of Everything, 2005 (NY Times and Publishers Weekly hardcover bestseller list); editor: Breaking Ice: An Anthropology of Contemporary African-American Fiction, 1990; screenwriter (with Ron Bass) (movies) Waiting to Exhale, 1995, How Stella Got Her Groove Back, 1998. Recipient NY Found.for the Arts Fellowship, 1986, Nat.Endowment for the Arts fellowship, 1988, Doubleday/Columbia Univ. Lit. Fellowship, MacDowell Colony fellow, Yaddo Artist Colony fellow (three times).

MCMILLAN, TOBI A., career planning administrator; b. Lubbock, Tex., July 11, 1973; d. Dennis R. McMillan and Barbara K. Hintergardt. BS, Tex. Tech U., Lubbock, 1995, MS, 2003. Sci. tchr. Roosevelt Ind. Sch. Dist., Lubbock, Tex., 1996—2000, Lubbock-Cooper Ind. Sch. Dist., 2000—04; coord. precoll. outreach Tex. Tech U.-Howard Hughes Med. Inst., 2004—. Vol. Backyard Mission, 1997—2006; vol. leader Young Life, Lubbock, 2002—05. Named Tchr. You Can Count On, News Channel 11, 2000; recipient Gentry Lynn Excellence award, Tex. Tech U.- Howard Hughes Med. Inst., 2003—04; fellow, 2000—01; grantee, Tex. Higher Edn. Coordinating Bd., 2002—03. Mem.: Sci. Tchrs. Assn. Tex. (assoc.; region 17 pres., sec. 2000—04), Sigma Phi Lambda (mem. alumni coun. 1996—2006). Independent. Avocations: travel, reading, writing, mission work. Office: Texas Tech University-HHMI Box 43131 Lubbock TX 79409 Office Phone: 806-742-2784. Personal E-mail: tobimac711@yahoo.com.

MCMILLEN, ELIZABETH CASHIN, artist; b. Chgo. d. James Blaine and Hortense (Fears) Cashin; m. John Stephen Jerabek; 1 child, Michael N. Student, Western Coll. for Women, 1961-63; BA, Bard Coll., 1965. Coord. com. and juror Spectra I, sponsor state exhbn. women artists Westbrook Coll., Portland, Maine, 1979; dir. Hancock County Auditorium Art Gallery, Ellsworth, Maine, 1984, 85. Exhibited at Frick Gallery, Belfast, Maine, 1993, 94, Maine Coast Artists Juried Show, Rockport, 1994, Portland Children's Mus., 1995, Lakes Gallery, Sebago, Maine, 1995—, Maine Coast Artists, Rockport, 1998, Portland Mus. Art, 1998, 2001, American Embassy Santiago Chili, 1998—, Maine Art Gallery, Wiscasset, 2001, Payson Gallery, Portland, 2002, June Fitzpatrick at MECA, Portland, 2004, U. Maine Mus. Art., Bangor, 2005, Ctr. for Maine Contemporary ARt, Rockport, 2005; one-person shows include Area Gallery, Portland, 1994, Frick Gallery, Belfast, Maine, 1995, Lakes Gallery, Sebago, Maine, 1997, June Fitzpatrick Alternative, Portland, 1999, June Fitzpatrick Gallery, Portland, 2001, 04; two persons show Maine Coast Artists, Rockport, 1996. Dem. chair Town of Lamoine, Maine, 1984-85, 86-87, 88-89; legislation coord. Amnesty Internat., Ellsworth, 1991-97. Democrat. Episcopalian. Avocations: writing, politics, teaching, African-American history.

MCMILLER, ANITA WILLIAMS, leasing company executive; b. Chgo., Dec. 23, 1946; d. Chester Leon and Marion Claudette (Martin) Williams; m. Robert Melvin McMiller, July 29, 1967 (div. 1980). BS in Edn., No. Ill. U., 1968; MBA, Fla. Inst. Tech., 1979; M of Mil. Arts and Sci., U.S. Army

Command & Gen. Staff Coll., 1990; postgrad., U.S. Army War Coll., Carlisle, Pa., 1993-94. Social worker Cook County, Chgo., 1968-69; recruiter analyst, dir. pers. State of Ill., Chgo., 1969-75; commd. 1st lt. U.S. Army, 1975, advanced through grades to col., 1996; dep. comdr., ops. officer Bremerhaven (Germany) Terminal, Ft. Eustis, Va. and Okinawa; comdr. 1320th Port Batt, 1991-93; comdr. 1320th Port Battalion U.K. Terminal, Felixstowe, Great Britain, 1991-93; dep. legis. asst. to Chmn. Joint Chiefs of Staff The Pentagon, Washington, 1994-98; pres., CEO Trove Internat., 1999—2002; v.p. ATC Leasing, Kenosha, Wis., 1999—; cons. Trove Internat., Washington, 2002—. Instr. Ctrl. Tex. Coll., Hanau, Germany, 1981-83, Phillips Bus. Coll., Alexandria, Va., 1983-84, City Colls. Chgo., 1987-89. Editor: Rocks, Inc. Pictoral Album, 1996, Alpha Kappa Alpha 75th Commemorative Album, 1997; contbr. articles to profl. jours. Child adv., foster mother Army Cmty. Svc., Hanau, 1980-83; tutor Parent-Tchr. Club Hanau Schs., 1981-83; vol. Vis. Nurses Assn. No. Va., 1983-85; coord., English tutor Adopt-a-Sch. Project, Washington, 1983-85; treas. Bremerhaven Girl Scouts Coun., 1987-89; bd. dirs. Project 2000, Boys and Girls Club of Kenosha. Mem.: NAACP, Internat. Coach Fedn., Links, Inc., Nat. Coun. Negro Women, Army Women's Profl. Assn., Internat. Platform Assn., Am. Hist. Assn., Rocks, Inc., Fedn. Bus. Profl. Women, Am. Mgmt. Assn., Am. Soc. for Quality, Assn. U.S. Army, World Affairs Coun., Nat. Def. Transp. Assn. (bd. dirs., v.p.), Army-Navy Club (Washington), Jr. League Washington, Am. Legion, Alpha Kappa Alpha. Avocations: golf, historical research. Home: 404 129th Infantry Dr Joliet IL 60435-5174

MCMILLIN, LISA SULLIVAN, education educator; b. Louisville, Miss., Feb. 4, 1961; d. Paul Burnard and Barbara Luke Sullivan; m. James Richard McMillin, Jr., Mar. 6, 1982; children: Jay, Paul, Barbara. BS, Miss. State U., Starkville, 1981; MEd, Miss. State U., 1983, EdD, 1992. Tchr. Winston/Louisville Vo-Tech, Louisville, 1986—90; grad. asst. Miss. State U., Starkville, 1990—91; tchr. Winston Acad., Louisville, 1991—93; asst. prof. U. West Ala., Livington, 1993—94; salesperson Temtco Steel, Louisville, 1994—97; faculty East Ctrl. C.C., Louisville. Baptist. Avocations: walking, tennis, singing. Home: 107 McMillin Dr Louisville MS 39339 Office: East Central Community College 107 McMillin Dr Louisville MS 39339

MCMILLION, MARGARET KIM, foreign service officer; b. New Brighton, Pa., Nov. 4, 1951; d. Theodore M. and Margaret Jane (Houlette) McM. BA, Eisenhower Coll., 1973; MPIA, U. Pitts., 1975; cert., Nat. War Coll., 1990. Analyst, intern Gulf Oil Corp., Pitts., 1974; polit. and consular officer U.S. Embassy, Kigali, Rwanda, 1975-77, consular officer Taipei, Taiwan, 1977-79; travel svcs. officer Am. Inst. in Taiwan, Taipei, 1979; desk officer Office of West African Affairs U.S. Dept. of State, Washington, 1979-81; with tng. dept. Fgn. Svc. Inst., Washington, 1981—82; polit. officer. U.S. Embassy, Pretoria, South Africa, 1982—85; with Thai lang. tng. dept., Washington, 1985-86; prin. officer U.S. Consulate, Udorn, Thailand, 1986—89; asst. dir. Office of Korean Affairs, Washington, 1990—91; spl. asst. under sec. for polit. affairs U.S. Dept. State, Washington, 1991—92; polit. counselor U.S. Embassy, Bangkok, 1992—95; dep. chief Mission in Vientiane, Laos, 1996—99; dir. Office for Analysis of Africa, Bur. Intelligence and Rsch., 1999—2001; U.S. amb. to Rwanda, 2001—04; dep. comdr. internat. affairs U.S. Army War Coll., 2004—06; ret. State Dept., 2006. Presbyterian. Achievements include speaks French, Afrikaans, Thai and Lao. Avocations: swimming, hiking, music, reading. Office: 191 Surawangse Rd Bangkok 10500 Thailand Office Phone: 66-8-061073260. Personal E-mail: mkmcmillion@aol.com.

MCMINN, VIRGINIA ANN, human resources consulting company executive; b. Champaign, Ill., Apr. 7, 1948; d. Richard Henry and Esther Lucille (Ellis) Taylor; m. Michael Lee McMinn, Dec. 29, 1973. BA in Teaching of English, U. Ill., 1969; MS in Indsl. Rels., Loyola U., Chgo., 1985. Pers. sec. Solo Cup Co., Urbana, Ill., 1972-74; pers. asst. Rust-Oleum Corp., Evanston, Ill., 1974-75, asst. pers. mgr., 1974-80, mgr. employee rels. Vernon Hills, Ill., 1980-81, mgr. human resources, 1981-84; dir. human resources Field Container Corp., Elk Grove Village, Ill., 1984-87; regional mgr. human resources Hartford Ins. Corp., Chgo., 1987-90; owner, pres. McMinn HR, Gilbert, Ariz., 1988—; state cert. dir. Ariz. SHRM, 2006; mem. Inst. Mgmt. Cons., 2006; cons. Hispanic 50/50 Bus. Coalition, 2006, Shared Vision Network, 2006. Instr. bus. and mgmt. divsn. Trinity Coll., Deerfield, Ill., 1984-85; instr. bus. and social scis. Harper Coll., Palatine, Ill., 1990-93; bd. dirs. Nierman's Hard-To-Find Sizes Shoes, Chgo., Ariz. SmallBus. Assn.; practitioner faculty U. Phoenix Online, 2000—; spkr. in field. Bd. dirs. Ill. Crossroads coun. Girls Scouts USA, Elk Grove, 1988-92, Ariz. Small Bus. Assn., 2004—; mem. Ill. Com. to Implement Clean Indoor Air Act, Chgo., 1990-91; past mem. adv. bd. Coll. of Lake County, 1982-84. Mem. Nat. Assn. Women Bus. Owners (Phoenix bd. dirs. 2005-06), Soc. for Human Resource Mgmt., Nat. Network Sales Profls. (program chmn. 1990-93), Women in Mgmt. (chpt. Leadership award corp. category, past pres.), Ariz. Small Bus. Assn. (bd. dirs.), Nat. Assn. Women Bus. Owners (prgram chair). Avocations: reading, golf, crafts. Office Phone: 480-726-0343. Business E-Mail: ginny@mcminnhr.com.

MCMORRIS, CATHY, congresswoman; b. Salem, Oreg., May 22, 1969; BA in Pre-Law, Pensacola Christian Coll., Fla., 1990; MBA, U. Wash., 2002. Mem. Wash. State Ho. Reps. from 7th Dist., 1994—2004; minority leader Wash. State Ho. Reps., 7th Dist., 2002—03; mem. US Congress 5th Wash. dist., 2005—, mem. armed svcs. com., mem. resources com., mem. edn. and the workforce com. Recipient Cornerstone award, Assn. Wash. Bus., 1995—96, Sentinal award, Wash. State Law Enforcement Assn., 1996, Guardian of Small Bus. award, Nat. Fedn. Ind. Bus., 1996, Gold Medal, Ind. Bus. Assn., 1996. Mem.: Wash. Women for Survival of Agr., Wash. Rural Health Assn., Wash. State Farm Bur. (Legislator of the Year 1997), Wash. State Cattlemen's Assn., N.E. Wash. Women in Timber. Republican. Office: US Ho Reps 1708 Longworth Ho Office Bldg Washington DC 20515-4705 Office Phone: 202-225-2006.*

MCMORRIS, CYCELIA A., elementary school educator; m. Don McMorris; children: Dondres, Diondre. BA in English, U. Anchorage, Alaska, 2000; MA in Curriculum and Instrn., U. Anchorage, 2006; MA in Tchr. K-8 (hon.), Alaska Pacific U., Anchorage, 2002. English tchr. Anchorage Sch. Dist., 2002—. Pvt. tutor. Mem.: Nat. Coun. Tchrs. Math. Office: Wendler Mid Sch 2905 Lake Otis Pkwy Anchorage AK 99503 Office Phone: 907-742-7300.

MCMORROW, MARY ANN GROHWIN, retired state supreme court justice; b. Chgo., Jan. 16, 1930; m. Emmett J. McMorrow, May 5, 1962; 1 dau., Mary Ann. Attended, Rosary Coll., 1948—50; JD, Loyola U., 1953. Bar: Ill. 1953, U.S. Dist. Ct. (7th dist.) Ill. 1960, U.S. Supreme Ct. 1976. Atty. Riordan & Linklater Law Offices, Chgo., 1954—56; asst. state's atty. Cook County, Chgo., 1956-63; sole practice Chgo., 1963-76; judge Cir. Ct. Cook County, 1976-85, Ill. Appellate Ct., 1985-92; justice Ill. Supreme Ct., 1992—2006, chief justice, 2002—05. Faculty adv. Nat. Jud. Coll., U. Nev., 1984. Contbr. articles to profl. jours. Mem. Chgo. Bar Assn., Ill. State Bar Assn., Women's Bar Assn. of Ill. (pres. 1975-76, bd. dirs. 1970-78), Am. Judicature Soc., Northwestern U. Assocs., Ill. Judges Assn., Nat. Assn. Women Judges, Advocates Soc., Northwest Suburban Bar Assn., West Suburban Bar Assn., Loyola Law Alumni Assn. (bd. govs. 1985—), Ill. Judges Assn. (bd. dirs.), Cath. Lawyers Guild (v.p.), The Law Club of the City of Chgo., Inns of Ct.

MCMULLEN, JENNIFER ANNE, secondary school educator; b. Abilene, Tex., May 16, 1970; d. Robert Milton McMullen, Sr. and Ouida Anne (Mitchell) McMullen. BA cum laude, Harding U., 1992, MEd, 1994. Tchr. Ctrl. Ark. Christian Sch., North Little Rock, 1994—95; instr. First Class Driving Sch., Bossier City, La., 1995—; tchr. for homebound, hospitalized teenagers Caddo Parish Sch. Bd., Shreveport, La., 2001—; tchr. BASE Ctr., Bossier Parish Sch. Bd., La., 2002—. Mem.: ASCAP, Southern Songwriters Guild (sec.). Avocations: singer, songwriter, musician, youth group support team mem. Personal E-mail: dixiegarden@aol.com.

MCMULLEN, MELINDA KAE, public relations executive; b. Japan, July 20, 1957; d. Paul K. and Valerie C. McMullen. BA in Communications, U. Pacific, 1979. Account exec. Ketchum Communications, San Francisco, 1979-80, Burson-Marsteller, N.Y.C., 1980-81; mgr. pub. relations Am. Express, N.Y.C., 1981-86; dir. pub. relations Firemans Fund Ins., Novato, Calif., 1986-87; formerly sr. v.p. Edelman Pub. Relations, San Francisco, Los Angeles. Recipient Silver Anvil Pub. Relations Soc. Am., 1979. Mem. Nat. Investor Relations Inst. Office: Bob Thomas and Assocs 228 Manhattan Beach Blvd Manhattan Beach CA 90266-5347 also: 5670 Wilshire Blvd Los Angeles CA 90036-5679

MCMULLEN, SHARON JOY ABEL, retired marriage and family therapist; b. Peoria, Ill., June 21, 1933; d. Richard Glen Abel and Harriet Bernice Copland; m. David Winston McMullen, Dec. 27, 1956; children: David Paul, Jeniffer Joy. BA, UCLA, 1955; MA in Marriage and Family Therapy, St. Joseph Coll., 1996. Lic. marriage and family therapist, Conn.; life cert. tchr. Calif. Marriage and family therapist First Ch. of Christ, Wethersfield, Conn., 1996—2003, Stafford Family Svcs., Stafford Springs, Conn., 1996—2003. Vol. staff asst. Master Therapists Workshop Series, U. Conn. Health Ctr., 1996—2003. Chair counseling task force 1st Ch. of Christ, Wethersfield, 1997-98, co-founder, team tchr. couples ministry, co-facilitator, 1997-2002. Mem.: Internat. Coaching Fedn. Democrat. Avocations: reading, genealogy, walking, blogging. Home: 1755 Vallecito Dr San Pedro CA 90732 Office Phone: 310-833-2014. Personal E-mail: sharon@designyourmarriagetolast.com.

MCMULLIN, RUTH RONEY, retired publishing executive; b. NYC, Feb. 9, 1942; d. Richard Thomas and Virginia (Goodwin) Roney; m. Thomas Ryan McMullin, Apr. 27, 1968; 1 child, David Patrick. BA, Conn. Coll., 1963; M Pub. and Pvt. Mgmt., Yale U., 1979. Market rschr. Aviation Week Mag., McGraw-Hill Co., N.Y.C., 1962-64; assoc. editor, bus. mgr. Doubleday & Co., N.Y.C., 1964-66; mgr. Natural History Press, 1967-70; v.p., treas. Weston (Conn.) Woods, Inc., 1970-71; staff assoc. GE, Fairfield, Conn., 1979-82; mng. fin. analyst GECC Transp., Stamford, Conn., 1982—84; credit analyst corp. fin. dept. GECC, Stamford, Conn., 1984-85; sr. v.p. GECC Capital Markets Group, Inc., N.Y.C., 1985-87; exec. v.p., COO, CEO, John Wiley & Sons, N.Y.C., 1987—90, pres., CEO; CEO Harvard Bus. Sch. Pub. Corp., Boston, 1991-94; mem. chmn.'s com., acting CEO UNR Industries Inc., Chgo., 1991-92, also bd. dirs.; mgmt. fellow, vis. prof. Sch. Mgmt. Yale U., New Haven, 1994-95; chairperson trustees Eagle-Picher Personal Injury Settlement Trust, 1996—; chairperson Claims Procesing Facility, Inc., 1998—. Bd. dirs. Bausch & Lomb, Rochester, N.Y.; vis. prof. Sch. Mgmt., Yale U., New Haven, 1994-95. Mem. dean's adv. bd. Sch. Mgmt. Yale U., 1985—92; bd. dirs. Yale U. Alumni fund, 1986—92, Yale U. Press, 1988—99, Math. Scis. Edn. Bd., 1990—93; bd. dirs., treas. Mighty Eighth Air Force Heritage Mus., 2000—03; chmn. Mighty Eighth Found., 2003—; bd. dirs. Savannah Symphony, 1999—2003, The Landings Club, 2002—04. Mem. N.Y. Yacht Club, Stamford Yacht Club, Yale Club. Avocations: sailing, skiing, golf, tennis. Home: 8 Breckinridge Ln Savannah GA 31411-1701 Office: Eagle Picher Trust P O box 206 652 Main St Cincinnati OH 45202-2542 Personal E-mail: rrmcmullin@aya.yale.edu. Business E-Mail: ruthmcmullin@direcway.com.

MCMUNN, NANCY LEE, parochial school educator; b. Kittanning, Pa., July 16, 1942; d. Russell Earl and Dorothy May McMunn. BA, Grace Coll., Winona Lake, Ind., 1964; MALS, Valparaiso U., Ind.; diploma, Centre Missionnaire, Albertville, France, 1982. Tchr. Rensselaer Jr. H.S., Ind., 1964—66, Hobart Jr. H.S., Ind., 1966—68, Pine Jr. H.S., Anaheim, Calif., 1968—70, Fegely Middle Sch., Portage, Ind., 1970—74, Milner Meml. Sch., Central African Republic, 1975—76, Culver H.S., Ind., 1976—77, Highland Jr. H.S., Ind., 1977—81, Lakeland Christian Acad., Winona Lake, Ind. Mem.: Nat. Coun. Tchrs. English. Office: Lakeland Christian Acad 1093 S 250 E Winona Lake IN 46590

MCMURRAY, CLAUDIA ANNE, federal agency administrator, lawyer; d. Raymond D. and Sally Kathryn (Martin) McM.; m. Donald V. Moorehead, June 6, 1987. AB with honors, Smith Coll., 1980; JD, Georgetown U., 1984. Bar: D.C. 1985. Legis. asst. to Rep. Bill Emerson US Ho. Reps, Washington, 1980-81; law clk. Office of Counsel to the Pres. The White House, Washington, 1983-84; atty. Patton, Boggs & Blow LLP, 1984-87, Kirkland & Ellis LLP, 1987-89; legis. counsel to Senator John W. Warner US Senate, 1989-90, minority counsel Com. on Environment and Pub. Works, 1991—95, gen. counsel to Senator Fred Thompson, 1996—98; v.p. Van Scoyoc Associates, Inc., 1998—2000; assoc. dep. adminstr. & chief of staff to dep. adminstr. EPA, 2000—03; dep. asst. sec for environ., Bur. Oceans & Internat. Environ. & Sci. Affairs US Dept. State, Washington, 2003—06, asst. sec. for oceans, internat. environ., & scientific affairs, 2006—. Editor The Tax Lawyer. Office: US Dept State Harry S Truman Bldg 2201 C St NW Rm 7831 Washington DC 20520*

MCMURRAY, JUSTINE, elementary school educator; b. Pontiac, Mich., Mar. 22, 1965; d. Tom Jackson and Evonne Casser; m. David McMurray, June 24, 1989. BS in Elem. Edn. magna cum laude, Wash. State U., Pullman. Tchr. mid. sch. sci. & math. Lockland Mid. Sch., Nashville, 1993—2001; tchr. 6th grade sci. and history Meigs Magnet Sch., 2001—. Coach volleyball & track Metro Davidson County Schs., Nashville, 2001—; presenter in field. Mem.: Nat. Tchrs. Math., Tenn. Tchrs. Sci., Phi Kappa Phi. Avocations: travel, reading, volleyball, running. Home: 133 Lake Terrace Hendersonville TN 37075 Office: Meigs Magnet School 713 Ramsey Street Nashville TN Office Phone: (615) 271-3222. Personal E-mail: justine.mcmurray@mnps.org.

MCMURRY, IDANELLE SAM, educational consultant; b. Morganfield, Ky., Dec. 6, 1924; d. Sam Anderson and Aurelia Marie (Robertson) McM. BA, Vanderbilt U., 1945, MA, 1946. Tchr. English Abbot Acad., Andover, Mass., 1946-50, Hockaday Sch., Dallas, 1951-54, San Jacinto High Sch., Houston, 1954-55; dean of girls Kinkaid Sch., Houston, 1955-63; headmistress Harpeth Hall Sch., Nashville, 1963-79, Hockaday Sch., Dallas, 1979-89; ret.; now pvt. sch. cons. The Edn. Group, Dallas. Bd. dirs. Ednl. Records Bur., 1979-85, trustee, 1980-85. Bd. dirs. Tex. council Girl Scouts U.S., 1980-82, Town North YMCA; trustee Winston Sch., 1979-85, Spl. Care Sch., 1979-81, Asheville Sch., Manzano Day Sch. Mem. Nat. Study Sch. Evaluation (bd. dirs. 1979-83), Headmasters Assn., Nat. Assn. Ind. Schs. (bd. dirs. 1974-84, acad. com. 1974-79, sec. 1978-80, chmn. 1980-84), So. Assn. Ind. Schs. (pres. 1974-75), Tenn. Assn. Ind. Schs. (pres. 1967-68), Mid-South Assn. Ind. Schs. (pres. 1972-73), Ind. Schs. Assn. S.W. (v.p. 1967—), Nat. Assn. Prins. Schs. for Girls (sec. 1970-72, pres. 1975-77, coun. 1970-79), Nat. Assn. Secondary Sch. Prins., Country Day Sch. Headmasters Assn. (exe. com. 1984-87, v.p. 1988-89), So. Assn. Colls. and Schs. (adminstrv. coun. 1974-77, ctrl. reviewing com. 1972-77, vice chmn. secondary commn. 1975-76, chmn. 1976-77, bd. dirs. 1976-81), Ladies Hermitage Assn., Vanderilt Aid Soc. (sec. 1971-73, pres. 1994-96), Ind. Edn. Svcs. (trustee 1980-88, chmn. 1986-88), Susan Komen Found. (adv. bd.), Belle Meade Club, Centennial Club, Phi Beta Kappa, Pi Beta Phi. Democrat. Presbyterian. Office: 5 Strawberry Hill Nashville TN 37215-4118

MCNABB, CORRINE RADTKE, librarian; b. Detroit, Dec. 18, 1956; d. Eugene R. and Dorothy A. (Dorosz) Radtke; children: Brynne Catherine, Kalen Daniel. BA, Aquinas Coll., 1978; MS, Drexel U., 1982, cert. advanced study, 1997. Cert. tchr. Pa., SC. Assoc. Nat. Libr. Medicine, Bethesda, Md., 1982-83; dir. libr. svcs. Carbondale (Pa.) Gen. Hosp., 1983-85; libr. dir. Interboro Libr., Peckville, Pa., 1985-86; reference libr. U. Scranton, Pa., 1986-87; libr. Cmty. Med. Ctr., Scranton, 1987-95; elem. libr. Carbondale Area Sch. Dist., 1995-96, Mountain View Sch. Dist., Kingsley, Pa., 1996—; adj. faculty Univ. Scranton, 2002—. Bd. dirs. Carbondale Pub. Libr., 1993—. Mem. ASCD, ALA, Pa. Sch. Librs. Assn. Roman Catholic. Avocations: reading, travel, walking. Home: 214 Stoney Creek Rd Clarks Summit PA 18411 Office: Mountain View Elem Libr RR 1 Box 339A Kingsley PA 18826-9778 Office Phone: 570-434-2181. Personal E-mail: santafe13@hotmail.com.

MCNAIR, EMMA LOUISE, minister; b. Ellisville, Miss., Mar. 11, 1935; d. Will and Chanie Prince Bell; m. Willie Charles McNair Jr., Mar. 16, 1956 (dec. Dec. 1967); children: Ruth, Channie, Willie C. Jr., Victor D., Karen L., Yul L. AA in Edn., Prentiss Inst., Miss., 1974; BA in Social Work, Rust Coll., 1979; MDiv, Memphis Theol. Sem., 1983; cert., East Miss. State Hosp., 1991. Ordained deacon 1981, ordained elder 1993. Pastor Victor/Taylor Charge, Senatobia, Miss., 1981—83, Marion/Walhall Parish, Columbia, Miss., 1983—84, Enterprise (Miss.) Cir., Brookhaven (Miss.) Charge, 1988—89; staff chaplain East Miss. Hosp., Meridian, Meth. Med. Ctr., Jackson, Miss., 1991—2000. Address: 153 Dacetown Rd Ellisville MS 39437

MCNAIR, MARCIA L., language educator, writer, editor; BA in English, Dartmouth Coll., Hanover, 1980; MA in Writing, NYU, NYC, 1989. Asst. editor Essence Mag., NYC, 1980—83; program coord. NYU, NYC, 1984—87; program coord., adj. lectr. CUNY, NYC, 1987—94; asst. prof. English Nassau CC, Garden City, NY, 1995—. Adj. prof. Molloy Coll., Rockville Center, NY, 2002—; ednl. cons. African Am. Mus., Hempstead, NY, 2005—; workshop facilitator Nassau CC, 2005, lectr., 06. Contbr. essays; creative dir.: Diary of a Mad Black Feminist; author: E-males; editor (arts and entertainment): Lakeview Cmty. News, 2006—. Coord. Nassau Cmty. Co. Nat. African Am. Read In, Garden City, NY, 2002—. Recipient Hon. Mention, New Millenium Writers Creative Non-Fiction Contest, 2002; grantee, LI Coun. Arts, 2006. Mem.: Schomburg Ctr. Rsch. Black Culture, Assn. Black Women Higher Edn., LI Writers Guild, Sigma Delta Chi. Office: Nassau CC English Dept One Education Dr Garden City NY 11530

MCNAIR, SUZETTE JORDAN, elementary school educator; d. Jimmie Carlton and Beretta Hooks Jordan; m. Suzette Jordan McNair, June 9, 2002. BS, East Carolina U., Greenville, N.C., 1987. Math tchr. Warren Co. Sch., Warrenton, NC, 1988—93, Wake Co. Pub. Sch., Raleigh, NC, 1993—. Choir mem., youth advisor, christian women's fellowship St. James Christian Ch., Wilson, 1975—2006. Scholar, Delta Sigma Theta, 1982. Mem.: NCAE. Office: Zebulon GT Magnet Mid 1000 Sheperd School Rd Zebulon NC 27597 Office Phone: 919-404-3630.

MCNAIRN, PEGGI JEAN, speech pathologist, educator; b. Dallas, Sept. 22, 1954; d. Glenn Alton Harmon and Anna Eugenia (McVay) Hicks; m. Kerry Glen McNairn, Jan. 27, 1979; children: Micah Jay, Nathan Corey. BS in Speech Pathology, Tex. Christian U., 1977, MS in Communications Pathology, 1978; PhD in Edn., Kennedy Western U., 1991. Cert. speech pathologist, mid mgmt., asst. tech. practitioner. Staff speech pathologist, asst. dir. infant program Easter Seal Soc. for Crippled Children and Adults Tarrant County, Ft. Worth, 1978-80; staff speech pathologist, spl. edn. lead tchr. Sherrod Elem. Sch. Arlington (Tex.) Ind. Sch. Dist., 1981-84, secondary speech/lang. specialist, early childhood assessment staff, 1984-89, mem. state forms com., 1985-86, chairperson assessment com., 1986-87; owner, dir. Speech Assocs., 1989—92; cons. augmentative communication Prentke Romich Co., 1992-97; distance learning coord. Edn. Svc. Ctr., Tex. Womens U., 1998—2001; asst. tech. specialist, ednl. cons. Edn. Svc. Ctr., Ft. Worth, 2001—. Adj. prof., clin. supr. Tex. Christian U., Ft. Worth, 1978-79; clin. speech pathologist North Tex. Home Health Assn., Ft. Worth, 1980-92; adj. prof. Tex. Women's Univ., 1997-2001. Author: Quick Tech Activities for Literacy, 1993, Readable, Repeatable Stories and Activities, 1994, Quick Tech Magic: Music-Based Literacy Activities, 1996, AAC Feature Match Software, 1996, A First Course in Dysphagia, 2001, Quick Tech Readable, Repeatable Stories & Software, 2004. Chair United Cerebral Palsy Toy Lending Libr., 1989-90; dir. comms. & tech. Easter Seal Soc. for Children & Adults; sunday sch. tchr. 1st United Meth. Ch., Arlington, 1982-87; active South Arlington Homeowners Assn., Arlington, 1985-87; 3rd v.p. Bebensee Elem. PTA. Recipient Outstanding Svc. to Handicapped Am. Biog. Inst., 1989; Cert. of Achievement John Hopkins U. for computing to assist persons with disabilities, 1991. Mem. Internat. U.S. Tex. Socs. for Augmentative and Alternate Comm. (sec. Tex. branch, exec. bd. mem. 1996-98), Neurodevelopmental Assn., Assn. for Curriculum and Supervision, Am. Speech and Hearing Assn., Tex. Speech-Lang.-Hearing Assn., Tex. Speech and Hearing Assn. (task force mem for augmentative comm.) Teaching Tex. Tots Consortium, Tex. Christian U. Speech and Hearing Alumni Assn., Kappa Delta Pi, Alpha Lambda Delta. Democrat. Avocations: doll making, sewing. Home: 4924 Brazoswood Cir Arlington TX 76017-1094 Office: Mansfield ISD 1016 Magnolia Mansfield TX 76063

MCNAIR-STYLES, KIMBERLY RENÉ, secondary school educator; b. Las Vegas, Nev., Oct. 8, 1964; d. William Ray and Sharon Jane McNair; m. Daren James Styles, Apr. 2, 2006; children: Ryan Dennis Conaty, Kyle William Conaty. BS in Bus., Edn. and Math., U. Nev., Las Vegas, 1992; M in Adminstrn. with high honors, U. Phoenix, Las Vegas, 2000. Cert. educator Nev., 1992. Bus. owner KC's Bookkeeping, Las Vegas, 1984—; tchr. C.C. So. Nev., Las Vegas, 1990—91, Clark County Sch. Dist., Las Vegas, 1992—; office asst., acct. McNair & Assocs., Las Vegas, 2000—04. Mem.: NBEA (assoc.). Democrat. Avocations: shopping, collecting, travel. Home: 4800 E Cheyenne #238 Las Vegas NV 89115 Office: A-TECH High School (CCSD) 2500 Vegas Dr Las Vegas NV 89106 Office Phone: 702-799-7870. Personal E-mail: ltlbunz2@cox.net.

MCNALLY, CONNIE BENSON, magazine editor, publisher, antiques dealer; b. Chgo., d. Peter D. and Joanna Agriostathes; m. Dick Benson, Nov. 19, 1955 (div. mar. 1961); 1 child, Douglas; m. William C. McNally, July 27, 1975. Student, Univ. Wis., 1954-55; BA, Baylor, 1962. Midwest supr. Slenderella Internat., Chgo., 1955-59; dir. John Roberts Powers Sch., Dallas, 1960-62; backgammon tchr., profl. Racquet Club, Palm Springs, Calif., 1969-75, La Costa (Calif.) Resort, 1973-75; antique dealer Palm Springs, 1975—; ptnr. Carriage Trade Antiques, 1975-78; owner, mgr. McNally Co. Antiques, 1978—; editor, pub. Silver Mag., Inc., Rancho Santa Fe, Calif, 1993—. Mem. Am. Assn. Antique Dealers, Antique Dealers Assn. Calif., Country Firends (vol. chair 1985-87, area dir. 1988-89, publicity chair 1990-91, program chair 1992-93, corr. sec. 1994-95, bd. dirs.), Social Svc. League La Jolla, Soc. Am. Silversmiths, Rancho Santa Fe Rep. Women's Club. Avocations: equestrian, gourmet cooking.

MCNALLY, MICHELE, editor, photographer; Sales rep. Sygma Photo News, 1977; picture editor Time Life's Mag. Develop. Group, Fortune Mag., 1986—2004; dir. photography The New York Times, 2004—05, asst. mng. editor, 2005—. Judge Pictures of the Year Contest, White House News Photographers Contest, World Press Photography Contest, Overseas Pres Club Photography Contest, Am. Photography Contest; nominating com. mem. W. Eugene Smith Grant in Humanistic Photography; chair, US divsn. World Press; featured spkr., vis. prof. Duke U., U. N.C., Chapel Hill, Syracuse U., Parsons Sch. Design, NYU, Internat. Ctr. Photography. Editor: Day in the Life series. Office: The New York Times 229 West 43rd St New York NY 10003 Office Phone: 212-556-1234.*

MCNAMARA, ANN DOWD, medical technician; b. Detroit, Oct. 17, 1924; d. Frank Raymond and Frances Mae (Ayling) Sullivan; m. Thomas Stephen Dowd, Apr. 23, 1949 (dec. 1980); children: Cynthia Dowd Restuccia, Kevin Thomas Dowd; m. Robert A. McNamara, June 15, 1985. BS, Wayne State U., 1947. Med. technologist Woman's Hosp. (now Hutzel Hosp.), Detroit, 1946-52, St. James Clin. Lab., Detroit, 1960-62; supr. histo-pathology lab. Hutzel Hosp., Detroit, 1962-72, Mt. Carmel Mercy Hosp., 1972-87, ret., 1987. Docent Domino's Ctr. Architecture & Design, Ann Arbor, Mich. 1988. Mem. Am. Soc. Clin. Pathologists, Am. Soc. Med. Technology, Mich. Soc. Med. Technology, Nat. Soc. Histotechnology, Mich. Soc. Histotechnologists, Wayne State U. Alumni Assn., Smithsonian Assos., Detroit Inst. Arts Founders Soc. Home: 2488 Signature Dr Pinckney MI 48169

MCNAMARA, JULIA MARY, academic administrator, foreign language educator; b. N.Y.C., Dec. 13, 1941; d. John P. and Julia (Dowd) McNamara. BA in History and French, Ohio Dominican Coll., 1965; MA in French, Middlebury Coll., 1972; MPhil, Yale U., PhD in French Lang. and Lit., 1980; DHL (hon.), Sacred Heart U., Hamden, Conn., 1984. Mem. faculty St.

William Sch., Pitts., 1963-64, Holy Spirit Sch., Columbus, Ohio, 1964-65, Newark (Ohio) Cath. High Sch., 1965-66, Northwest Cath. High Sch., West Hartford, Conn., 1966-69, St. Vincent Ferrer High Sch., N.Y.C., 1969-70, St. Mary's High Sch., New Haven, 1971-74; lectr. french Albertus Magnus Coll., New Haven, 1976-80, dean of students, 1980-82, acting pres., 1982-83, pres., 1983—. Prof. French Albertus Magnus Coll., 1981—; mem. Conn. Health and Edn. Facilities Authority, Hartford, 1983—; chair Conn. Conf. Ind. Colls., Hartford, 1990-92, sec.-treas. 1986—, chmn., 1990-92; lectr. in field; assoc. fellow Yale U., Morse Coll.; bd. dirs. New Haven Savs. Bank. Chairperson United Way Greater New Haven, 1987; bd. dirs. St. Mary's High Sch., New Haven, 1982-91, ARC, New Haven Savs. Bank, 1990—; trustee Yale-New Haven Hosp., 1984— (chair med. com., 1989-91 vice chair bd., 1991-), chair, Yale-New Haven Health Sys.; adv. bd. Bank of Boston-Conn., 1983-87; adv. com. Jr. League Greater New Haven, 1985; trustee Hartford Sem., 1985-91. Fulbright fellow, Paris, 1977-78; Yale U. fellow, 1974-78, Am. Council on Edn. fellow, 1981; recipient Disting. Woman in Leadership award New Haven YWCA, 1984, Veritas award Providence Coll., 1987, Greater New Haven Jr. Achievement Ann. award, 1990. Mem. Fulbright Alumni Assn., New Haven C. of C. (bd. dirs. 1984-90), New England Assn. Schs. and Colls. (appeals bd. 1986-88). Roman Catholic. Office: Albertus Magnus Coll Office of the President 700 Prospect St New Haven CT 06511-1224

MCNAMARA, KIMBERLY DIANE, science educator, department chairman; b. Chgo., June 1, 1975; d. John and Ramona Krzystof; m. Robert McNamara, June 5, 1998; children: Brenna, Kyle, Isabella. BS, Ea. Ill. U., Charleston, 1998; M in Edn. and Leadership, St. Xavier U., Chgo., 2005. Biology tchr. Thornridge H.S., Dolton, Ill., 1999—2006, sci. dept. chair, 2005—. Home: 9616 S Knox Ave Oak Lawn IL 60453 Office: Thornridge High School 15000 Cottage Grove Dolton IL 60419 Office Phone: 708-271-4539. Personal E-mail: mcnamara.kimberly@district 205.net.

MCNAMARA, MARY ELLEN, not-for-profit executive; b. Mpls., Dec. 18, 1943; d. Edward Emmanuel and Gladys Theresa (Mattson) Bjorklund; m. Peter Alexander McNamara II (div.); children: Peter Alexander III, Nathaniel Paul. BA, Carleton Coll., 1965; MDiv, Harvard U., 1968. Cert. fin. planner. Program dir. St. Peter's Ch., NYC, 1968-72, program dir., dep. exec., 1977-80; program dir. Ctr. Ch. on-the-Green, 1972-74; program developer Westminster Presbyn. Ch., Springfield, Ill., 1974-77; assoc. Gen. Assembly Coun. Presbyn. Ch. (USA), NYC, 1980—86; dir. not-for-profit sector City of NY, 1986—90; pres., exec. dir. Interchurch Ctr., NYC, 1990-99; interim pres. Union Theol. Sem., NYC, 1998—99, exec. v.p., 1999—; mem. exec. com. Assn. Theol. Sch., 2003—. V.p. Pathways for Youth, Bronx, NY, 1987—96; pres. Morningside Area Alliance, N.Y.C., 1991—98; parish assoc. Fifth Ave. Presbyn. Ch., 1998—2002. Moderator Presbyn. NYC, 1995—96, chair com. on ministry, 1992—95, chair implementation task force, 1996—98, chair nominating com., 2005—; chmn. bd. dirs. exec. com. Presbyn. Conf. Ctr., Stony Point, NY, 1996—2002, chmn. nominating com., 2005—; bd. dirs. Blanton/Peale Inst. on Religion and Health, 1994—2001, Wartburg Adult Care Cmty., 1999—, chair elect, 2001—03, chair, 2003—, chmn. pers. com., exec. com., 2001—03. Mem.: Assn. Theol. Seminaries (exec. com. 2004—, bd. dirs. 2005—). Home: 99 Claremont Ave Apt 621 New York NY 10027-5711 Office: Union Theol Sem 3041 Broadway New York NY 10027-5710

MCNAMARA-RINGEWALD, MARY ANN THÉRÈSE, artist, educator; b. Hempstead, N.Y., Apr. 11, 1935; d. William George Schlichtig and Alice Agnes Rakeman; m. Raymond Anthony McNamara, Apr. 22, 1957 (div. Sept. 1975); children: Thomas William, Raymond Gerard, William Daniel, Peter Joseph, James Francis Jude; m. John Drew Ringewald, Feb. 17, 1984. BS, Fordham U., 1957, Barbizon Sch., NYC, 1953; M in Studio Arts, Adelphi U., 1972; postgrad., Parsons Sch. Design, 1973-75; student, Art Students League, N.Y.C., 1973-74; postgrad., Goddard Coll., Calif., 1986-87; student, Progoff Intensive Jour. Program, N.Y.C., 1999—, Cape Cod Sch., 1993. Cert. elem. edn. and art N.Y. Elem. sch. art tchr. Dept. Edn., Freeport, NY, 1957-58, Farmingdale, NY, 1967; jr. and h.s. art tchr. Massapequa (N.Y.) Sch. Dist., 1970-90; owner, pres. South Shore Creative Arts Ctr., Massapequa, 1975; pvt. art tchr. various locations, 1970-90. Illustrator Doubleday, Inc., N.Y.C.; art advisory bd. Chesapeake Coll, Wye Mills, Md., 1995— (lectr., 1998, 99, 2000), Snow Princess, Fordham U., 1954; symposium coord. Hofstra U., N.Y.; lectr. Naples Philharm., 1992; judge, lectr. in field; architectural designer, M.E, 1977, M.D., 1988-, F.L., 1990. One-woman shows include Fordham U., 1954, Andonia Gallery, Massepequa, N.Y., 1974, Isis Gallery, Islip, N.Y., 1974, For the Birds, Salisbury, Conn., 1978, Harguen Gallery, Pt. Jefferson, N.Y., 1979, Adelphi U., Garden City, N.Y., 1992, Wohlfarth Gallery, Washington, 1994-95, SpanBauer Gallery Naples, Fla., 1996, Naples Philharmonic, Naples, Fla., 1992, Gallery 44, Millbrook, N.Y., 1997-98; groups shows: Acad. of Arts, Easton, Md., 1993. works exhibited at Kennedy Gallery, Key West, Fla., 1997-99, Chesapeake Coll., Md., 1998-99; represented in pvt. collections General Motors, The Benedictines, Prudential Life, St. Michael's Maritime Mus., Yupo Corp., Japan; illustrator: From a Lighthouse Window, Chesapeake Bay Maritime Mus., 1992 (Best of Balt. Book award 1993, Book award Tabasco N.Y.C. 1994); original poetry published. Pres. AAUW, L.I., 1969-71; bd. dirs. L.I. (N.Y.) Art Tchrs. Assn., 1973-76; docent U.S. Fish and Wildlife Svc., Washington, 1994-95; mem. Am. Farmland Trust; vol. Delmarva Chpt., ARC, 2001-. Recipient Nat. Middle Sch. Art Tchrs. award, Nassau County Middle Sch. Art Tchrs. Assn., 1988, Very Spl. Arts Festival for Handicapped, 1977, Festival of Creation, Diocese of RVC, 1975, Catalyst, 1975; named to Outstanding Young Women of Am., 1969; works featured in Nat. Anthology of Poetry, 1953. Mem. Internat. Welcome Fla. Assn. Series (lectr. 1994—), Nat. League Am. Pen Women (founder, pres. Naples, Fla. br. 1995—), Nat. Gallery Art (copyist 1993—), Order of the Benedictines (oblate 1990—), Working Artists Forum (Easton, Md.), NY State Art Tchrs. Assn. (bd. mem. 1972-80). Roman Catholic. Avocations: horticulture, travel, illuminations, music, poetry. Address: Marafour 5493 Anderby Dr Royal Oak MD 21662 Office: Marafour Studio 27098 Del Ln Bonita Springs FL 34135-4409

MCNAMEE, SISTER CATHERINE, theology studies educator; b. Troy, N.Y., Nov. 13, 1931; d. Thomas Ignatius McNamee and Kathryn McNamee Marois. BA, Coll. of St. Rose, 1953, DHL (hon.), 1975; MEd, Boston Coll., 1955, MA, 1958; PhD, U. Madrid, 1967. Grad. asst. Boston Coll., 1954-55, asst. registrar Grad. Sch., 1955-57; mem. faculty Coll. St. Rose, Albany, NY, 1960-65, acad. v.p., 1968-75; dir. liberal arts Thomas Edison Coll., Trenton, 1975-76; pres. Trinity Coll., Burlington, Vt., 1976-79, Coll. St. Catherine, St. Paul, 1979-84; dean Dexter Hanley Coll., U. Scranton, Pa., 1984-86; pres. Nat. Cath. Ednl. Assn., Washington, 1986-96; sr. scholar Ctr. for Cath. Studies, U. St. Thomas, St. Paul, 1996-2000; prof. U. Catolica, Talca, Chile, 2000—. Bd. dirs. Am. Forum for Global Edn. Trustee assoc. Boston Coll. Spanish Govt. grantee, 1965-67; OAS grantee, 1967-68; Fulbright grantee, 1972-73 Mem. Inter-Am. Confedn. Cath. Edn., Internat. Orgn. Cath. Edn., Nat. Cath. Ednl. Assn., Internat. Fedn. Cath. Univs., Delta Epsilon Sigma. Roman Catholic. Home: 1880 Randolph Ave Saint Paul MN 55101 Personal E-mail: cmncsj@hotmail.com.

MCNAMEE, LINDA ROSE, broadcast executive; b. Holyoke, Mass., Oct. 1, 1969; d. Robert Dean and Jacqueline Marguerite Mashia. BA, Smith Coll., 1991; CSS, Harvard U., 2002. Cert. elem. tchr. level 1-6 Mass., FCC restricted radiotelephone operator permit. Instr. Learning Skills, Inc., Northampton, Mass., 1991-92; traffic asst. Sta. WGBY-TV, Springfield, Mass., 1992-93, air/traffic contr., 1993-94, asst. dir. broadcast ops., 1994-95; learning resources coord. Sta. WXEL-TV, West Palm Beach, Fla., 1995-96, ops. mgr., 1996-97, dir. ops., 1997; broadcasting coord. Sta. WGBH-TV, Boston, 1997-2000, traffic supr., 2000—03, devel. coord., 2003—. Mem. PBS Traffic Adv. Com., Alexandria, 1998—2001, vice chmn., 2000—01, mem., 2003. Dist. com. mem. Squanto dist. Boy Scouts Am., Brockton, Mass., 1997—99, Knox Trail Coun., 2000—; assoc. advisor Stoughton (Mass.) Police Explorer Post # 57, 1998—2000, Newton (Mass.) Police Explorer Post # 300, 1999—2001, Emergency Svcs. Post # 525, Waltham, Mass., 2001—; dir. Children's Handbell Choir, 1998—2003. Home: 5 Manning St Burlington MA 01803- Office: Sta WGBH 125 Western Ave Boston MA 02134-1008 Fax: 617-300-1022. E-mail: linda_mcnamee@wgbh.org.

MCNAUGHT, JUDITH, author; b. San Luis Obispo, Calif., May 10, 1944; d. Clifford Harris and Rosetta (Prince) Spath; m. J. Michael McNaught, June 1, 1974 (dec. 1983); children: Whitney, Clayton. BS, Northwestern U., 1966. Pres. Pro-Temps, Inc., St. Louis, 1983-84, Eagle Syndication, Inc., Dallas, 1987. Author Tender Triumph, 1983 (Critics Choice award 1983); Double Standards, 1984; Whitney, My Love (Best Hist. Novelist 1985), Once and Always, 1987 (Best Hist. Novel 1987), Something Wonderful 1988 (NY Times Best seller, Critics Choice award Best Hist. Novel 1988), A Kingdom of Dreams, 1989 (NY Times Bestseller, Award for Best Hist. Novel 1989), Almost Heaven, 1990 (NY Times #1 Bestseller, Persie award, Romantic Times award), Paradise, 1991 (NY Times Bestseller award for best hardcover contemporary romance, Romantic Times award), Perfect, 1993 (NY Times Bestseller), Until You, 1994, Holiday of Love, 1996, (NY Times Bestseller), Remember When, 1996 (NY Times Bestseller), Night Whispers, 1998, Every Breath You Take, 2005. Mem. Novelists, Inc. Roman Catholic. Avocations: racquetball, skiing. Home: Dallas TX Mailing: Ballentine Books Author Mail 18th Floor 1745 Broadway New York NY 10019*

MCNEAL, JANE ERSKINE, music educator, musician; b. Somers Point, NJ, Oct. 29, 1958; d. James Kelley and Jane Emma McNeal. BA Psychology, Stockton State Coll., 1983; music studies, Wheaton Coll., Ill., 1976—78; Kindermusik Cert., Westminster Choir Coll., Princeton, NJ, 1997; Crescendo Music Cert., Acad. Cmty. Music, Ft. Washington, Pa., 2005. Choir dir., NJ, 1991—95; piano instr. NJ, 1975—; vocal instr. Vineland, NJ, 1999—; profl. accompanist NJ, 1976—; ch. and synagogue organist NJ, 1983—; organ and piano recitalist NJ, 1989—. Advocate for mentally ill. Scholar Nat. Merit Corp. Scholarship, Sun Shipbuilding, Chester, Pa., 1976—78; music scholar, Wheaton Coll., 1976. Mem.: Local Musicians Union, Am. Guild Organists, Nat. Guild Piano Tchrs., Psi Chi. Avocations: walking, classical music, jazz, reading. Home: 529 Sassafras St Millville NJ 08332 Office: St Bernadette Cath Ch 1421 New Rd Northfield NJ 08225 Office Phone: 609-646-5611.

MCNEAL, MARY KAY, secondary school educator; b. Denver, June 28, 1957; d. Elizabeth Ann and Charles Edwin Willis (Stepfather); m. Johnny Ray McNeal, Feb. 17, 1978; children: Joshua Allen, Sarah Nicole. BA in History and Edn., Augusta State U., Ga., 1986; MA in Tchg. and Learning, Nova Southeastern U., Orlando, Fla., 2002. Nat. bd. cert. tchr. 1999. Tchr. Greenwood Lakes Mid. Sch., Lake Mary, Fla., 1986—90, Rock Lake Mid. Sch., Longwood, Fla., 1991—92, Indian Trails Mid. Sch., Winter Springs, Fla., 1992—. Fundraiser Southeastern Guide Dogs, Inc., Palmetto, Fla., 1990—2006; women's leader Dorcus, Sanford, Fla., 1996—97. With U.S. Army, 1976—79. Named Indian Trails Mid. Sch. Tchr. of Year, 1996, Indian Trails Mid. Sch. Social Studies Tchr. of Year, 2000, Orlando Sentinel Tchr. of Week, 2001. Mem.: NEA (assoc.), Fla. Geog. Alliance (assoc.), Nat. Coun. for the Social Studies (assoc.). Republican. Lutheran. Avocations: reading, gardening. Home: 105 Garden Ct Sanford FL 32771 Office: Indian Trails Middle School 415 Tuskawilla Rd Winter Springs FL 32708 Office Phone: 407-320-4348. Personal E-mail: mmcneal728@aol.com. Business E-Mail: mary_mcneal@scps.k12.fl.us.

MCNEAL, PHYLLIS PAULETTE, parole agent; d. Earline Brown. BA in Psychology, Calif. State U., Long Beach, 1982; MSW, Calif. State U., San Bernardino, 2003. Mental health intern Jenesse Domestic Violence Ctr., LA, 2001—01, Los Padrinos Juvenile Hall, Downey, Calif., 2002—03; group supr. Calif. Youth Authority, Norwalk, 1981—84, youth counselor Ontario, 1984—89; parole agt. I parole and cmty. svcs. divsn. Calif. Dept. Corrections, Inglewood, 1989—99, asst. unit supr. LA, 1999—. Sponsor Calif. Youth Authoity, Ontario, 1986—89; small group tng. instr. Calif. Youth Authority, Onartio, 1986—89; founder, CEO Straight Talk Program, Inc., Corona, Calif., 1990—; coll. internship coord. parole and cmty. svcs. divsn. Calif. Dept. Corrections, Ingelwood, 1990—98, defensive tactics instr., LA, 1991—99. Author: Corrections in America an Introduction, 9th edit. (Correctional Champions, 2001); editor: Corrections Today Mag. (Best in the Bus., 1998). Prison min. Abundant Living Family Ch., Rancho Cucamonga, Calif., 2003—05; prison com. mem. Nat. Assn. Equal Justice in Am., Compton, Calif., 2002—05; bd. dirs. Cornerstone Accelerated Learning Acad., LA, 2001—05. Named Parole Agt. of the Yr., Calif. Probation, Parole, and Correctional Assn., 1998, Citizen of the Week, KNX Newsradio CBS, 1998, Hero Of the Week, UPN Channel 13, 1998; recipient Cmty. Stars award, Staples, 1999, award, Freedom Jour., 2000, Trailblazer Award, First AME Ch., 2004, amb. of Progress, Blackwall St., 2005. Local Heroes Neighborhood Excellence award, Bank of Am., 2005. Mem.: Save Our Sons (assoc.; publicity com. mem. 2000—05), Black Women 's Network (assoc.), Delta Sigma Theta (life; dean pledge 1980). Office: Straight Talk Program Inc PO Box 5693 Norco CA 92860 Business E-Mail: straighttalkprogram@charter.net.

MCNEELY, BONNIE L. (K.W. ROWE JR.), retired internist; b. Cin., Nov. 26, 1930; d. William Vernuel and Lydia LaBelle McNeely; m. Kenneth Wyer Rowe, Jr., Sept. 18, 1969; children: Christopher, Amy, Gregory, Laurel. BS, U. Cin., 1952, MD, 1956. Intern Cin. Gen. Hosp., 1956-57, resident in surgery, 1957-58, resident in internal medicine, 1958-60, fellow in cardiology, 1960-61; mem. faculty, dir. med. ctr. health svc. U. Cin. Coll. Medicine, 1961-88; dir. pers. health and employee health svcs. Conemaugh Meml. Med. Ctr., Johnstown, Pa., 1989-97; ret., 1997. Elder, Seventh Presbyn. Ch., Cin. Republican. Avocations: carpentry, outdoor activities, reading, gardening.

MCNEELY, DELORES, banker; b. Ft. Bragg, N.C., Dec. 28, 1949; d. Rayfield O. and Ann Gloria Ozier; m. James Leon Bell, Sept. 21, 1968 (div. June 1986); 1 child, Jeffrey Demarco; m. Robert Arthur McNeely, June 25, 1988. Human resources cert., San Diego State U., 1984; cert. in banking, Pacific Coast Banking Sch., 1997. From mgmt. trainee to sr. v.p. Union Bank of Calif., San Diego, 1972—. Chief of staff San Diego Urban Bankers, 1989-99, pres. 1993-94; mem. Econ. Devel. task force, 1993. Home: 922 Cordova St San Diego CA 92107-4224 Office: Union Bank of Calif 530 B St Ste 1610 San Diego CA 92101-4410

MCNEELY, JUANITA, artist; b. St. Louis; d. Robert Hunt and Alta B. (Green) McN.; m. Jeremy Lebensohn, Mar., 1982. BFA, Washington U. St. Louis, 1959; MFA, So. Ill. U., 1964. Prof. figure drawing So. Ill. U., Carbondale, 1962-64; prof. drawing Chgo. Art Inst., 1964-65; prof. drawing and painting Western Ill. U., Macomb, 1965-67; prof. painting Suffolk (N.Y.) Coll., 1969-82; artist, 1959—; art tchr., 1962—. Adj. prof. painting Parsons Sch. Art, N.Y.C., NYU; artist-judge art exhbn. White House, Washington, 1994; art judge, spkr. Very Spl. Arts, Washington, 1990-96. One-woman shows include Prince St. Gallery, N.Y.C., 1970—80, Evelyn Amis Gallery, Can., 1980—84, Soho 20 Gallery, N.Y.C., 1980—82, Elaine Benson Gallery, Bridgehampton, L.I., N.Y., 1994, Mitchell Algus Gallery, N.Y.C., 2006, Represented in permanent collections Nat. Mus. Art, Taipei, Taiwan, Palacio de Las Bellas Artes, Mex. City, Oakleigh Collection, Boston, Bryn Mawr Coll., and others, Mitchell Algus Gallery, N.Y.C., Nat. Acad. Mus., included in books, including Self Portrait by Women Painters, Feminist Art Criticism, An Anthology: At Last a Mainstream Female Art Movement, 1989. Recipient Ellen P. Speyer prize for painting, 179th Invitational Contemporary Am. Painting Exhbn.; honored for major contribution to the Second Wave Feminist Revolution 1966-1980 (exhibit and placed on honor roll), Veteran Feminists of Am., NY Coun. for Arts award, 1976-77, Jackson Pollack-Lee Krasner Found. for Painting, 1986-87, Aldolph and Ester Gottieb Found. for Painting, 1984-87. Studio: 463 West St New York NY 10014-2010

MCNEELY, PATRICIA GANTT, communications educator; b. Winnsboro, S.C., Dec. 2, 1939; d. William Adolphus and Alice (Woodson) Gantt; m. Alfred Raymond McNeely, Apr. 8, 1960; children: Allison Patricia, Alan David. BA, Furman U., 1960; MA, U. S.C., 1975. Reporter Greenville (S.C.) News, 1958-60, Columbia (S.C.) Record, 1960-66, 66-72, news editor, 1979-80; reporter The State, Columbia, 1965-66; prof. journalism U. S.C., Columbia, 1972—, Eleanor M. and R. Frank Mundy prof. of journalism, 2000—, dir. print and electronic sequence, 2000—. State mgr. Voter News Svc., N.Y., 1972—; workshop dir. Reader's Digest, Pleasantville, N.Y., 1985—. Author: Fighting Words: A History of the Media of South Carolina, The Palmetto Press: The History of South Carolina's Newspapers and the Press Association. Mem. Assn. for Edn. in Journalism and Mass Comm. (sec. mag. divsn. 1995-96, head newspaper divsn. 1988-89, standing profl. freedom and responsibility com. 1995-98). Office: Univ SC Coll Journalism Mass Comm Blossom At Assembly Sts Columbia SC 29208-0001

MCNEES, PAT (PATRICIA ANN MCNEES), writer, editor; b. Riverside, Calif., Jan. 30, 1940; d. Glenn Harold and Eleanor Maxine (McCoskrie) McN.; m. Anthony V. Mancini, Apr. 22, 1967 (div. 1978), 1 child, Romana Mancini BA, UCLA, 1961; postgrad., Stanford U., 1961—63. Instr. English Stanford U., Palo Alto, Calif., 1962—63; assoc. editor Harper & Row, N.Y.C., 1963—66; editor Fawcett Pubs., N.Y.C., 1966—70; ind. writer and editor N.Y.C., Washington, 1970—. Cons. clients World Bank, 1987—, UN, Rockefeller Found., Nat. Sci. Found., Libr. Congress, U.S. Inst. Peace, NIH. Author: Dancing: A Guide to the Capital Area, 1987, An American Biography: An Industrialist Remembers the 20th Century, 1995, By Design, 1997, YPO: The First 50 Years, 2000, New Formulas for America's Workforce: Girls in Science and Engineering, 2003, Building Ten at Fifty: 50 Years of Clinical Research at the NIH Clinical Center, 2003; editor: (anthologies) Contemporary Latin American Short Stories, 1974, Dying: A Book of Comfort, 1996; contbr. articles to mags. including New York Mag., Washington Post Mem. Am. Soc. Journalists and Authors, Authors Guild, PEN, Nat. Assn. Sci. Writers Avocations: cooking, dancing. Business E-Mail: pmcnees@nasw.org.

MCNEESE, BEVERLY DIANE, language educator; b. Turlock, Calif., Apr. 4, 1952; d. Jesse Audry and Willie Jean Doty; m. Timothy Dean McNeese; children: Noah Michael, Summer Elizabeth. AA, York Coll., Nebr., 1973, BA in English, 1995; MA in Edn., Drury U., Springfield, Mo., 2003. With White County Libr., Searey, Ark., 1974—75; presch. tchr. East Grand Ch. of Christ, Springfield, Mo., 1976—91; learning disabilities para-profl. Strafford Pub. Schs., Mo., 1991—92; libr. aide Levitt Libr., York Coll., Nebr., 1992—94; adj. faculty dept. English, York Coll., 1995—2002, asst. prof. English, 2003—. Mem.: Kappa Omicron Nu, Sigma Tau Delta (York Coll. chpt. pres. 1995—96, York Coll. chpt. faculty sponsor 1998—2006). Republican. Mem. Ch. Of Christ. Avocations: refinishing antiques, reading, travel. Home: 5 Arbor Ct York NE 68467 Office: York Coll Dept English 1125 E Eighth St York NE 68467 Office Phone: 402-363-5690. Office Fax: 402-363-5699. E-mail: bdmcneese@york.edu.

MCNEIL, AMY, language educator, web site designer; b. Glen Ridge, Nj, June 1, 1979; d. Thomas and Freda Bowman; m. Michael McNeil, Apr. 23, 2004. Master's, NYU, 2003. Webmaster ALK Technologies, Princeton, NJ, 2003—04; instr. English Surry C.C., Dobson, NC, 2004—. Office: Surry CC 630 S Main St Dobson NC 27017 Office Phone: 336-386-3375. Business E-Mail: mcneila@surry.edu.

MCNEIL, JENNIFER JAYNE, music educator; b. Seaford, NY, Feb. 21, 1979; d. Valerie Jayne and Robert Stephan Sikora. M of Liberal Studies, Stony Brook U., 2004. Music tchr. Smithtown Ctrl. Sch. Dist., NY, 2001—. Pvt. clarinet studio self-employed, Smithtown, 2001—. Treas. Smithtown Alumni Assn., 2003—05. Mem.: ASCD (assoc.), N.Y. State Band Dirs. Assn. (assoc.), N.Y. State Schs. Music Assn. (assoc.), Suffolk County Music Educators Assn. (assoc.). Avocations: reading, exercise. Office: Accompset Mid Sch 660 Meadow Rd Smithtown NY 11787-1656 Office Phone: 631-382-2700, 631-382-2300. E-mail: jsikora@smithtown.k12.ny.us.

MCNEIL, SUE, transportation system educator; b. Newcastle, Australia, June 17, 1955; d. George Peers and Norma (Avard) McGeachie; m. John Franklin McNeil, Dec. 4, 1976; children: Sarah, Emily. BS, U. Newcastle, Newcastle, Australia, 1976; B.E., U. Newcastle, 1978; MS, Carnegie Mellon U., 1981, PhD, 1983. Registered profl. engr., N.J. Asst. works engr. N.S.W. Dept. Main Rds., Singleton, Australia, 1977-79; transp. engr. Garmen Assocs., Montville, N.J., 1983-84; vis. lectr. Princeton U., Princeton, N.J., 1984-85; asst. prof. MIT, Cambridge, Mass., 1985-87, Carnegie Mellon U., Pitts., 1988-90, assoc. prof. to prof., 1990—2000; dir. The Brownfields Ctr., Mellon U. Carnegie, 1998—2000; dir. Urban Transp. Ctr. U. Ill., Chgo.; prof. Coll. Urban Planning and Pub. Affairs, 2000—05, Univ. Del., 2005—. Assoc. editor Jour. Infrastructure Sys.; contbr. articles to profl. jours. Doctoral dissertation fellow AAUW, 1982-83; named Presdl. Young Investigator, NSF, 1987-92. Mem.: ASCE (chmn. facilities mgmt. com. 1988—94), Transp. Rsch. Bd. (exec. com. 2004—), INFORMS (assoc.), Inst. Transp. Engrs. (assoc.). Office: Univ Del Dept Civil & Environ Engring 301 W Dupont Hall Newark DE 19716 Office Phone: 302-831-6578. Business E-Mail: smcneil@udel.edu.

MCNEIL, VICKI LAUGHTER, student affairs administrator; b. Pawnee, Okla., Sept. 24, 1955; d. Fred Raymond and Ilena (Brant) Laughter; m. Wayne K. McNeil, Nov. 16, 1954. BME, Okla. State U., 1977, MS, 1978, EdD, 1981. Career counselor Univ. Okla., Norman, 1981-82; dir. Student Assistance Ctr. Temple U., Phila., 1982-87, acting asst. dean of students, 1986-87, assoc. dean of students, 1987-88; assoc. v.p. for student affairs Loyola U., New Orleans, 1988—. Cons. Community Coll. of Phila., 1984-86. Contbr. articles to profl. jours. Named to Outstanding Young Women of Am., 1982. Mem. Am. Coll. Pers. Assn. (bd. dirs. commn. IV 1983-85), Nat. Assn. Coll. Student Pers., Nat. Assn. Student Pers. Adminstrs. (com. mem. 1990—, finalist Dissertation of Yr. award 1982), Omicron Delta Kappa, Kappa Delta Pi, Delta Zeta. Avocation: photography. Office: Loyola U Danna Ctr Rm 205 6363 Saint Charles Ave New Orleans LA 70118-6195 Office Phone: 504-865-3030. Business E-Mail: mcneil@loyno.edu.

MCNEIL, WENDY LAWSON-JOHNSTON, foundation administrator; d. Peter and Dorothy Stevenson Hammond Lawson-Johnston; m. Thomas K. McNeil; 1 child, Lawson Johnston McNeil Wijesooriya. V.p. Solomon R. Guggenheim Found. Bd. trustees Solomon R. Guggenheim Mus. Office: Solomon R Guggenheim Found 1071 Fifth Ave New York NY 10128

MCNEILL, SUSAN, marketing professional, real estate professional, sales professional; b. Prescott, Ariz., Feb. 26, 1936; d. Glenn S. and Alma Johnson Hunter; m. Richard G. Bryant, Dec. 19,1 956 (div. Apr. 1971); children: Robert (dec.), Kathleen; m. Kenneth I. McNeill, Nov. 23, 1972; 1 child, John. BA, U. Ariz., Tucson, 1957. Real estate owner Seaview Properties, Palos Verdes, Calif., 1978-82; real estate mktg. staff Coldwell Banker, Palos Verdes, 1982-99, Summit Group, Palos Verdes, 1999-2000, ReMax, Palos Verdes, 2001—. Art tchr., dir. Arts Unlimited Chadwick Sch., Palos Verdes, 1982-90; owner Bright Ideas, Palos Verdes, 1982—; founder Art At Your Fingertips, Palos Verdes. Bd. dirs. Norris Theater, Palos Verdes C. of C. Recipient Cmty. Svc. award City of L.A., 1993; named Palos Verdes Citizen of Yr., 2000. Mem. Palos Verdes Arts Ctr. (bd. dirs., exhbn. curator). Home: 32735 Seagate Dr Palos Verdes Peninsula CA 90275-5886 also: PO Box 2370 Palos Verdes Peninsula CA 90274-8370 Office: 63 Malaga Cove Plz Palos Verdes Estates CA 90274 Office Phone: 310-378-1922. Business E-Mail: smcneill@remaxpv.com.

MCNEILL-MURRAY, JOAN REAGIN, volunteer, consultant; b. Atlanta, July 8, 1936; d. Arthur Edward and Annie May (Busby) Reagin; children: Thomas Pinckney, Clyde Reagin. Student, U. Louisville, 1955-57; BA, U. Tenn., Chattanooga, 1976; D of Music Mgmt. (hon.), Kharkov Philharm. Inst. Music, 2002. Founding pres. Family and Children's Svcs. Assocs., Chattanooga, 1987-88, bd. dirs., 1996—; bd. dirs. Chattanooga Symphony and Opera Assn., 1984-88, 99—, pres., 1984-87, 05-; pres. Chattanooga Ballet Assn., 1986-88; bd. dirs. U. Chattanooga Found., 1986-89, A.I.M. Ctr. of Chattanooga, 1997-04, Eos Orch., N.Y.C., 1998-04, Chattanooga Little Theater, 2003—; v.p. devel. Chattanooga Cares, 1997-04; chair Spl. Needs and Svcs. for the Elderly of Chattanooga, 1997-04; mem. bd. dirs. Hosanna House, 2001-2004; mem. vol. coun. bd. dirs. Am. Symphony Orch. League, N.Y.C., 1986-96; pres.-elect, 1992-93, pres., 1993-95; bd. dirs. Hosanna House of Chattanooga, pres., 2002-; pres. Internat. Conducting Competition Philharm., 2002—, Vakhtang Jordania Music Found., 2003—, U.S., 2006—; judge Internat. Music Competition, Ibla, Sicily, 2004-06, Ibla Grand Prize. Recipient Outstanding Svc. award U. Tenn., Chattanooga, 1988; named Chattanooga's Disting. Woman, 1999. Mem. U. Tenn. Chattanooga Alumni Assn. (pres. 1985-86), Golden Key, Order of Omega, Sigma Kappa Found. (trustee 1992-98, sec. 1993-94, pres. 1994-98, Colby award for volunteerism 1990). Republican. Episcopalian. Office: 7457 Preston Cir Chattanooga TN 37421-1839 Personal E-mail: clownjoni@aol.com.

MCNEMAR, ROBIN M., chemistry educator; d. Robert W. and Helen M. McNemar; m. Michael S. Liebman, Apr. 3, 1998; 1 child, Jeffrey Liebman. BS, Elizabethtown Coll., Pa., 1989; EdM, East Stroudsburg U., Pa., 1996; M in Chemistry, U. Pa., Phila., 2004. Cert. chemistry and math. edn. Pa., 1989. Chemistry tchr. Lower Moreland H.S., Huntingdon Valley, Pa., 1996—; webpage design tchr. U. Pa., Phila., 2005—. Vestry St Jude and the Nativity Episcopal Ch., Lafayette Hill, Pa., 2001—06. Mem.: Am. Chem. Soc. Office: Lower Moreland High School 555 Red Lion Rd Huntingdon Valley PA 19006 Personal E-mail: mcnemar@aol.com. Business E-Mail: rmcnemar@mciu.org.

MCNEW, JILL HASTY, performing company executive, educator; d. Billy Keith and Carolyn Erlene Hasty; m. Brian Ray McNew; children: Sara, Laine, Lakin. BS in Elem. Edn., Miss. Coll., Clinton, 1990. Cert. tchr. dance Dance Masters of Am. Tchr. grade 1 Timberlawn Elem. Sch., Jackson, Miss., 1990—91; tchr. grade 6 Huntsville Mid. Sch., Ala., 1991—95; owner/dir. Jill's Studio of Dance, Huntsville, 1995—. Mem. Arts Coun., Huntsville, 1998—; bd. dirs. Dance Masters of Am., Ala., Tenn., Ga., 2002—. Mem. Jr. League, Huntsville, 1996—. Named Top Fifty Studios on the Move, Dance Spirit and Dance Tchr. mag.; recipient Dance Educator award, 2006, numerous choreography awards, Dance Masters of Am., Dance Educators Am., Danoply Arts Festival. Mem.: Gothic Guild Huntsville. Achievements include students winning two National Championships in 2002 and 2005. Office: Jill's Studio of Dance 7900 G Bailey Cove Rd Huntsville AL 35802 Office Phone: 256-883-1633. Office Fax: 256-883-2037. Business E-Mail: jill.mcnew@jills.com.

MCNICHOLS, MARY ALICE, humanities educator; d. Frank William McNichols and Alice Anne Parker; m. William W. Webb, Aug. 7, 1983; 1 child, Alexander McNichols Webb. BA, MA, U. Mich., Ann Arbor, 1970, Wayne State U., Detroit, 1988; PhD, Union Inst., Cin., 1988. Prof. Coll. Creative Studies, Detroit, 1973—, assoc. academic dean, 1987—93, interim chmn. liberal arts dept., 2005—06. Contbr. articles to profl. publs. Parliamentarian Ahs Cmty. Services, Detroit, 2005—06. Mem.: Midwest Art History Soc., Coll. Art Assn. Roman Catholic. Avocation: horseback riding. Office: Coll Creative Studies 201 E Kirby Detroit MI 48202 Office Phone: 313-664-7640. Business E-Mail: mmcnic@ccscad.edu.

MCNISH, SUSAN KIRK, retired lawyer; b. San Jose, Calif., Nov. 4, 1940; d. Wallace Garland and Dorothy (Kirk) Shaw; m. Thomas A. McNish, May 12, 1989; children: Jenifer, Michael. BA, U. Calif., 1962; JD, U. Santa Clara, Calif., 1981; postgrad., Stanford U., 1979, U. Mich., 1981. Bar: Mich. 1981, U.S. Dist. Ct. (ea. dist.) Mich. 1981. Various positions Stanford (Calif.) U., 1968-79; law clk. U.S. Dist. Ct. (no. dist.) Calif., San Francisco, 1979; atty. Consumers Power Co., Jackson, Mich., 1981-88; v.p., gen. counsel, corp. sec. Mich. Consol. Gas Co., Detroit, 1988-98; ret. Mem. clin. svcs. adv. bd. Detroit Med. Ctr., Wayne State U.; dir. Vista Maria Corp., Dearborn Heights, Mich. Mem. Am. Arbitration Assn. (arbitrator, Mich. adv. panel). Home: 1809 Bay Meadow Ct Raleigh NC 27615-5482 E-mail: susankmcnish@yahoo.com.

MCNULTY, KATHLEEN ANNE, social worker, consultant, psychotherapist; b. Hackensack, N.J., Oct. 6, 1958; d. Alfred Edward and Gertrude Natalie (Currie) McN.; m. Henry Stanislaw Kowal, Sept. 16, 1988. BA, Rutgers U., 1980; MSW, Smith Coll., 1984; postgrad., Fielding Grad. Inst., 2001—. Lic. marriage and family therapist; lic. clin. social worker; lic. psychologist. Mental health aide Belleville (N.J.) Mental Health Clinic, 1980-82; clin. social worker Albert Einstein Coll. Medicine, Bronx, N.Y., 1984-86, Family Guidance Bergen, Hackensack, 1986-87, Cliffwood Mental Health Ctr., Englewood, N.J., 1986-87; pvt. practice Rutherford, N.J., 1987-99, Ridgewood, N.J., 1999—. Cons. Meadowlands Weight Control, Rutherford, 1988—, St. Lukes-Roosevelt Hosp. Ctr., N.Y.C., 1988. Contbr. articles to profl. jours. Mem. Am. Orthopsychiat. Assn., Acad. Cert. Social Workers (cert.), Nat. Assn. Social Workers. Avocations: painting, singing, sports, poetry. Office Phone: 201-444-4010. E-mail: kam1058@aol.com, relationsconnect@aol.com.

MCNUTT, DEBORAH MATOY, history educator; b. Talaquah, Okla., Jan. 16, 1954; d. Jay Wallace Matoy and Peggy Sue Pointer; m. Tom McNutt, July 16, 1997; children: Kristian Blair Stiles, Ashlye Nannett Stiles. BA in History, Sam Houston State U., Huntsville Tex., 2002. Cert. tchr. Tex., 2003. Nat. sales mgr. Continental Airlines, Houston, 1990—2001; tchr. U.S. history Conroe Ind. Sch. Dist., 2003—. Mem.: Nat. Orgn. Historians (assoc.). Democrat. Avocations: politics, travel. Home: 1591 Pine Oak Conroe TX 77304 Office: Conroe High School 3200 West Davis Conroe TX 77304

MCNUTT, EDITH RICHARDS, psychiatrist; b. Pasadena, Calif., June 17, 1942; d. Clark Leslie and Margaret Gilkey Richards; m. Neil Scott McNutt, June 10, 1967. BA, Wellesley U., Mass., 1964; MD, Harvard U., Boston, 1968. Clin. asst. prof. psychiatry Weill Cornell Med. Ctr., NYC, 1983—; tng. & supv. analyst NY Psychoanalytic Soc. & Inst., 1993—. Mem.: NY Psychoanalytic Soc. & Inst. (treas. 1993—95, Charles Brenner Tchg. award 2005), Am. Psychiatric Assn. Office: 210 E 47th St #1G New York NY 10017 Office Phone: 212-688-5595.

MCNUTT, MARCIA KEMPER, geophysicist; b. Mpls., Minn., Feb. 19, 1952; widowed, 1988; 3 children. BA in Physics, Colo. Coll., 1973; PhD in Earth Sciences, Scripps Inst. Oceanography, 1978; DSc (hon.), Colo. Coll., 1988. Geophysicist US Geol. Survey, 1979-82; asst. prof. geophysics MIT, 1982-86, assoc. prof., 1986-89, prof. geophysics, 1989—95, Griswold prof., 1991, assoc. dir. Sea Grant Coll. Program, 1993—95; pres. & CEO Monterey Bay Aquarium Rsch. Inst., 1997—; prof. geophysics Stanford U., 1998—. Bd. dirs. Monterey Bay Aquarium, 1998—; chmn. Pres. Com. on Ocean Exploration, 2000—; mem. exploration of the seas com. Nat. Rsch. Coun., 2001—. Sr. editl. bd. Science mag., 2000—. Mem. Am. Geophys. Union (pres. tectonophysics sect., 1994, pres., 2000-02, chmn., Macelwane award com., 1996-98, Macelevane award 1988), NAS. Office: MBARI 7700 Sandholt Rd Moss Landing CA 95039-9644*

MCNUTT, MARGARET H. HONAKER, secondary school educator; b. W.Va., July 7, 1935; d. Vanus Jerome and M. Montague (Humphrey) Honaker; m. Alfred Dudley McNutt; children: Mary Margaret McNutt Sirchia, Marilyn Diane McNutt Furubotten. BS, Concord Coll., 1957; MS, Va. Poly. Inst. and State U., 1965. Tchr. Mercer County Schs., Bluefield, W.Va., 1957-63; tchr., chair dept. L.A. Unified Sch. Dist., 1964-99; ret., 1999. Supr. student tchg. secondary edn. Calif. State U., Northridge. Advisor Future Bus. Leaders Am., 1981-91. Grantee State of Calif., 1975; named Faculty Role Model, Calif. Assn. CPAs, 1988, L.A. chpg., 1988. Mem. NEA, DAR, United Tchrs. L.A., Calif. Tchrs. Assn., United Daus. of Confederacy, Order Ea. Star, Sigma Sigma Sigma. Presbyterian. Avocations: writing, reading, tennis, dance, painting. Personal E-mail: MHMcNutt@aol.com.

MCNUTT, SUZANNE MICHAELENE, music educator; b. Detroit, Mich., Feb. 20, 1952; d. Orville James Corf and Annie Angeline Mikolayek; m. Robert Wayne McNutt, Nov. 21, 1987; 1 child, Christopher Robert Cort. BA, Wayne State U., Detroit, 1979. Piano and organ tchr., Detroit, 1970—2006; pianist and organist Various churches, Detroit, 1970—2006; sub. tchr. Southwestern City Schools, 2004—06. Accompanist Kinderchor, Columbus, Ohio, 2003—05; piano judge OMEA, Ohio, 2001—06; judge piano competition Roscoe Village, Ohio, 1998—2005. Mem. Leadership in Coshocton, 1998. Recipient Nat. Honor Roll, Am. Coll. Musicians, 2003—06. Mem.: Ohio Music Tchr. Assn., Am. Guild Organists, Ohio Music Educators Assn., Music Tchr. Nat. Assn. Avocations: travel, walking, music. Home: 5946 Groff Ct Hilliard OH 43026

MCPARTLAND, PATRICIA ANN, educational association administrator, health educator; b. Passaic, N.J. d. Daniel and Josephine McP. BA, U. Mo., 1971; MCRP, Ohio State U., 1975, MS in Preventive Medicine, 1975; EdD in Higher and Adult Edn., Columbia U., 1988; cert. distance edn., Tex. A&M U., 2000, cert. distance edn. web pub. cert., 2001. Cert. health edn. specialist, distance edn. web pub., grants specialist; workforce devel. profl. Sr. health planner Merrimack Valley HSA, Lawrence, Mass., 1977—79; planning cons., adminstr. Children's Hosp., Boston, 1979—80; exec. dir. Assn. Workforce Alternatives, Rsch. & Devel., Inc., Marion, Mass., 1980—; evening sch. dir. Upper Cape Cod Regional Tech. Sch., Bourne, Mass., 2005—. V.p., cons. New Bedford (Mass.) Cmty. Health Ctr, 1993—94; chmn. edn. and tng. com. Health and Human Svc. Coalition, 1988—89; mem. project expert panel Office of Minority Health, 1997—2003; mem. New Eng. Regional Minority Health Conf. Com., 1997—99; vis. lectr. Bridgewater State Coll.; lectr. in field; project expert panel Office Minority Health's Culturally and Linguistically Appropriate Svcs.; mem. New Eng. Regional Minority Health Conf. Com., 2001—03; rev. editor Jour. Workforce Devel., Internat. Electronic Jour. Health Edn. Mem. editl. bd. Jour. Healthcare Edn. and Tng., 1989-93, Jour. of Workforce Devel.; author: Promoting Health in the Workplace, 1991; reviewer Qualitative Health Rsch. Jour.; contbr. articles to profl. jours. Vol. spkr. March of Dimes Found., Wareham, Mass., 1992-93; coll.-wide vocat. Cape Cod C.C., Hyannis, Mass., 1989—; planning adv. 2nd Internat. Symposium, Pasco, Wash., 1992; v.p. New Bedford chpt. Am. Cancer Soc., 1985-90. Recipient award Excellence in Continuing Edn. Nat. AHEC Ctr. Dirs. Assn., 1994, 95, 96, 97, Sec.'s awards for Outstanding Progam in Community Health, Nat. Cancer Inst., Washington, 1990. Mem.: APHA, Nat. Assn. Workforce Devel. Profls. (bd. dirs.), Nat. Planning Conf. (mem. com. 1984—87), Southeastern Mass. Health Planning (bd. dirs., sec. 1982—87), Inst. for Disease Prevention (steering com. 1982—). Avocations: writing, acting, dance, theater, travel. Home: PO Box 1116 Marion MA 02738-0020 Office: Assn for Workforce Alternatives R&D Inc PO Box 69 2 Spring St Marion MA 02738-1519 Office Phone: 508-759-7711 ext. 258. Personal E-mail: pmcpartland@comcast.net. Business E-Mail: smahec@tiac.net, pmcpartland@uppercapetech.org.

MCPETERS, SHARON JENISE, artist, writer; b. San Bernardino, Calif., Oct. 17, 1951; d. Cecil L. and Mary I. (Tanner) McP.; 1 child, Angela M. Benders. BA in Journalism and English, U. So. Calif., 1981. Proofreader Ventura (Calif.) Coll., 1979. Prin. works include My Professors, 1993, Interpretations, 1994, The Thoughts of Socrates, 1995, Self Portrait, 1995, Happiness, 1996, My True Self, 1998, Czechoslovakia 1923, 1999, Liszt, 1999, Portrait of Ten Artists, 2000; author: (autobiography) A Human Mind, 1997, (novels) Domestic Symphonies, 1986, The Broken Heart of the World, 1999, An Illuminated Manuscript, 1994, (short stories) The Library of Heaven, 2000, A Girl Without A Name, 2001, A Sanctified Heart, Selected Poems, 1974-2002, 2003, An Intellect's Goodness, 2004, Professor Scapegoat Speaks, 2006. Avocations: classical music, philosophy.

MCPHAIL, JOANN WINSTEAD, writer, art dealer; b. Trenton, Fla., Feb. 17, 1941; d. William Emerson and Donna Mae (Crawford) Winstead; m. James Michael McPhail, June 15, 1963; children: Angela C. McPhail Morris, Dana Denise McPhail Gaizutis, Whitney Gold Student, Fla. So. Coll., 1959—60, St. John's River Jr. Coll., Palatka, Fla., 1960—61, Houston C.C. With Jim Walter Corp., Houston, 1961—62; receptionist, land lease sec. Oil and Gas Property Mgmt. Inc., Houston, 1962—63; sec. to mng. atty. State Farm Ins. Co., Houston, 1963—64; saleswoman, decorator Oneil-Anderson, Houston, 1973; sec. Law Offices of Ed Christensen, Houston, 1980—82; advt. mgr. Egalitarian Houston C.C. Sys., 1981; fashion display artist, 1985—86; entrepreneur, writer, art agt. Golden Galleries and Antiques, Houston, 1990—95; owner, property mgr. APT Investments, 1994—98; lyricist, pub. Anna Gold Classics, 1995—, writer song lyrics, 1996—. Freelance writer, photographer: Elegance of Needlepoint, 1970, S.W. Art Mag., A Touch of Greatness, 1973, Sweet 70's Anthology, The Budding of Tomorrow, 1974 (award); columnist, photographer: Egalitarian: Names Can be Symbols, Design Your Wall Covering, Student Profile, 1981, National Library of Poetry, Fireworks (award), 1995; contbr. poetry various publs.; playwright, 1993—; screenwriter, 1996—; writer, pub. The Missing Crown, religious drama World Wide Christian Radio, Sta. KCBI-FM, KYND-AM, and other radio stas., 1996—, baby publ. Hello.World.Hello, 1997; author: (poetry) The Budding of Tomorrow, 1997; music pub., 1999—. Vol. PTO bd. Sharptown Middle Sch. Mem. ASCAP, Manuscriptors Guild, Mus. Fine Arts Houston Methodist. Avocations: antiques, art. Home: 361 N Post Oak Ln Apt 333 Houston TX 77024-5950 E-mail: joannmcphail@yahoo.com.

MCPHAIL-GEIST, KARIN RUTH, secondary school educator, real estate agent, musician; b. Urbana, Ill., Nov. 23, 1938; d. Wilber Harold and Bertha Amanda Sofia (Helander) Tammeus; m. David Pendleton McPhail, Sept. 7, 1958 (div. 1972); children: Julia Elizabeth, Mark Andrew; m. John Charles Geist, June 4, 1989 (div. 1995). BS, Juilliard Sch. Music, 1962; postgrad., Stanford U., 1983-84, L'Academia, Florence and Pistoia, Italy, 1984-85, Calif. State U., 1986-87, U. Calif., Berkeley, 1991, 92. Cert. tchr., Calif.; lic. real estate agt., Calif. Tchr. Woodstock Sch., Musoorie, India, 1957, Canadian, Tex., 1962-66, Head Royce Sch., Oakland, Calif., 1975-79, 87—, Sleepy Hollow Sch., Orinda, Calif., 1985-2001; realtor Freeholders, Berkeley, Calif., 1971-85, Northbrae, Berkeley, Calif., 1985-92, Templeton Co., Berkeley, 1992—99. Organist Kellogg Meml., Musoorie, 1956-57, Mills Coll. Chapel, Oakland, 1972—; cashier Trinity U., San Antonio, 1957-58; cen. records sec. Riverside Ch., N.Y.C., 1958-60; sec. Dr. Rollo May, N.Y.C., 1959-62, United Presbyn. Nat. Missions, N.Y.C., 1960, United Presbyn. Ecumenical Mission, N.Y.C., 1961, Nat. Coun. Chs., N.Y.C., 1962; choral dir. First Presbyn. Ch., Canadian, Tex., 1962-66; assoc. in music Montclair Presbyn. Ch., Oakland, 1972-88; site coord., artist, collaborator Calif. Arts Coun. Artist; cons. music edn. videos and CD Roms Clearvue EAV, Chgo., 1993—. Artist: produced and performed major choral and orchestral works, 1972-88; prodr. Paradiso, Kronos Quartet, 1985, Magdalena, 1991, 92, Children's Quest, 1993—. Grantee Orinda Union Sch. Dist., 1988. Mem. Berkeley Bd. Realtors, East Bay Regional Multiple Listing Svc., Calif. Tchrs. Assn., Commonwealth Club (San Francisco). Democrat. Home: 7360 Claremont Ave Berkeley CA 94705-1429

MCPHEARSON, GERALDINE JUNE, retired medical/surgical nurse; b. Red Bud, Ill., June 3, 1938; d. Arthur and Viola (Liefer) Althoff; children: Deborah, Michael, Belinda, Sabrina. Diploma, Evang. Deaconess Hosp. Sch. Nursing, St. Louis, 1959. RN. Sch. nurse San Antonio Ind. Sch. Dist.; head nurse Bethesda Gen. Hosp., St. Louis; supr. Am. Blood Components, Inc., St. Louis; nurse mgr. Meml. Hosp., Belleville, Ill.; ret., 2005. Coord. arthritis svc. staff Meml. Hosp. Mem. Nat. Assn. Orthopaedic Nurses (1st pres., sec., v.p., organizer Ill. chpt.).

MCPHEE, JOAN, lawyer; b. May 29, 1958; BA, Princeton Univ., 1980; JD magna cum laude, Harvard Univ., 1984. Bar: Mass. 1986, N.Y. 1986, R.I. 1991. Law clk. Judge Abraham D. Sofaer, US Dist. Ct. So. N.Y.; asst. U.S. atty. & dep. chief appeals unit U.S. Dept. Justice, So. Dist. N.Y.; ptnr. litigation dept. Ropes & Gray, Boston, 1990—, chair diversity com. Co-chair Govt. Enforcement Practice Group. Editor (articles): Harvard Law Rev. Mem.: ABA, R.I. Bar Assn., Boston Bar Assn., Phi Beta Kappa. Office: Ropes & Gray 1 International Pl Boston MA 02110-2624 Office Phone: 617-951-7535. Office Fax: 617-951-7050. Business E-Mail: jmcphee@ropesgray.com.

MCPHEE, KATHARINE HOPE, singer; b. Sherman Oaks, Calif., Mar. 25, 1984; d. Peisha Burch and Daniel McPhee. Contestant & second-place winner American Idol, 2006; signed to 19 Recordings Ltd./RCA Records, 2006—. Singer: (singles) Somewhere Over the Rainbow/My Destiny, 2006; actor: (plays) Annie Get Your Gun, The Ghost & Mrs. Muir, 2005; (films) Crazy, 2006. Office: 19 Entertainment Ltd 33 Ransomes Dock 35-37 Parkgate Rd London SW11 4NP England Office Phone: 818-788-3056.

MCPHEE, PENELOPE L. ORTNER, foundation administrator, television producer, writer; b. Louisville, Nov. 24, 1947; d. Alvin B. and Loyce L. Ortner; m. Raymond Hunter McPhee, Aug. 25, 1973; 1 child, Cameron McPhee Baker. BA with honors, Wellesley Coll., 1969; MS in Journalism, Columbia U., 1970. Dir. pub. rels. Am. Sch. in Switzerland, Lugano, 1970-71; writer, rschr. Sta. WTVJ-TV, Miami, Fla., 1972-73; prof. journalism and film Fleming Coll., Florence, Italy, 1972-73; freelance writer, prodr. Miami, 1973-80; exec. prodr. for cultural programming Sta. WPBT-TV, Miami, 1980-88; instr. documentary filmmaking Fla. Internat. U., 1987-88; ind. TV prodr., cons., 1988-90; program officer arts and culture Knight Found., Miami, 1990-96, v.p., chief program officer, 1996—. Author: Martin Luther King, Jr.: A Documentary, Montgomery to Memphis, 1976 (Best of Books award ALA 1983), Beauty Ency., 1978, King Remembered, 1986, Your Future in Space, 1986; contbg. author: Underwater Photography for Everyone, 1978. Trustee Dade County Art in Pub. Places Trust, 1985, vice chmn., 1988-89, chmn., 1989-90; trustee Grantmakers in the Arts, 1992-98, chmn. 1995-96, Southeastern Coun. on Foundations, 1999—, Coun. on Founds., 1998-2002; adviser Indep. Sector Comm. com., 1999—. Recipient Iris award Nat. Assn. TV Program Execs., 1983, Children's Programming award Corp. for Pub. Broadcasting, 1982, local program award Corp. Pub. Broadcasting, 1984, 90, Emmy award, 1984, 88, N.Y. State Martin Luther King, Jr. Medal of Freedom, 1986; Sackett scholar Columbia U., 1970. Mem. Miami Wellesley (v.p. 1976-80, admissions rep. 1980-85, 1989-90). Office: John S & James L Knight Foundation 200 S Biscayne Blvd Ste 3300 Miami FL 33131-2349 E-mail: Mcphee@knightfdn.org.

MCPHERSON, ALICE RUTH, ophthalmologist, educator; b. Regina, Sask., Can., June 30, 1926; came to U.S., 1938, naturalized, 1958; d. Gordon and Viola (Hoover) McP. BS, U. Wis., 1948, MD, 1951, DSc (hon.), 1997. Diplomate Am. Bd. Ophthalmology. Intern Santa Barbara (Calif.) Cottage Hosp., 1951-52; resident anesthesiology Hartford (Conn.) Hosp., 1952; resident ophthalmology Chgo. Eye, Ear, Nose and Throat Hosp., 1953, U. Wis. Hosps., 1953-55; ophthalmologist Davis and Duehr Eye Clinic, Madison, Wis., 1956-57; clin. instr. U. Wis., 1956-57; fellow retina svc. Mass. Eye and Ear Infirmary, 1957-58; ophthalmologist Scott and White Clinic, Temple, Tex., 1958-60; practice medicine specializing in ophthalmology and retinal diseases Houston, 1960—. Staff Meth., St. Luke's, Tex. Children's Hosps., Harris County Hosp. Dist., Houston; clin. asst. prof. Baylor Coll. Medicine, Houston, 1959-61, asst. prof. ophthalmology, 1961-69, clin. assoc. prof., 1969-75, clin. prof., 1975-98, prof., 1998—; cons. retinal diseases VA Hosp., Houston, 1960—, Ben Taub Hosp., Houston, 1960—; mem. adv. com. for active staff appt. sect. ophthalmology Meth. Hosp., 1986-91, mem equipment com., 1993-95, mem. grievance panel, 1997; vol. clin. faculty appts. and promotions com., 1993; bd. dirs. Highlights of Ophthalmology; v.p. N.Am. Highlights of Ophthalmology Internat. Editor: New and Controversial Aspects of Retinal Detachment, 1968, New and Controversial Aspects of Vitreoretinal Surgery, 1977, Retinopathy of Prematurity: Current Concepts and Controversies, 1986. Amb. Houston Ballet, mem. Houston Ballet Found.; mem. pres.'s coun. Houston Grand Opera; condrs. cir. Houston Symphony, mem. Houston Symphony Soc.; mem. campaign for 80s Baylor Coll. Medicine; mem. Assn. for Cmty. TV, BBB, Physicians' Benevolent Fund, South Tex. Diabetes Assn. Inc., Jr. League Houston; bd. dirs. U. Wis. Found., Madison. Recipient Award of appreciation KT Eye Found., 1978, Woodlands Medal for Outstanding Contbn. to the Econ. Devel. of Cmty., 1988, spl. recognition award Assn. for Rsch. in Vision in Ophthalmology, Crystal award Recognizing Generous Support-Ptnrs. with an Eye for Vision Found. Am. Acad. Ophthalmology, 2000, Benjamin Boyd Humanitarian award Pan Am. Assn. Ophthalmology, 2001, Philip Corboy Meml. award Disting. Svc. Ophthalmology, 2002, Women of Vision Houston Delta Gamma Found., 2002; Alice R. Mc Pherson Lab. for Retina Rsch. dedicated Baylor Ctr. for Biotech., 1988; Alice R. Mc Pherson Day proclaimed in her honor Mayor of City of Houston, Mar. 12, 1988. Fellow: ACS (credentials and Tex. credentials com., com. on applications), Am. Acad. Ophthalmology (2nd v.p. 1979, vice chmn. program devel. found. bd. trustees 1993—, nominating com. subspecialty/specialized sect. of coun. 2001, com. for pub. and profl. rels., bd. dirs. opthalmology ednl. trust fund found., laureate award selection com., mem. coun. representing PAAO, honor award 1956, sr. honor award 1986, guest of honor 1998 meeting, Visionary Soc. Gold Mem.); mem.: AMA, Highlights Ophthal. Internat., Schepens Internat. Soc. (sec. 1986—93, v.p. 1993—95, pres. 1995—97), U. Wis. Ophthal. Alumni Assn. (founding pres. 1990—93, founded Alice R. McPherson lectureship 1994), Assn. Rsch. Surgeons, Pan Am. Assn. Ophthalmology Found., Tex. Ophthal. Assn., So. Med. Soc., Rsch. to Prevent Blindness, Pan Am. Assn. Opthalmology (v.p. 1991—92, pres. elect 1992—95, AJO lectr. 1993, pres. 1995—97, pres. found. 1997, bd. dirs., membership com., Benjamin Boyd Humanitarian award 2001), Macula Soc. (credentialing com. 1992), Internat. Soc. Eye Rsch. (credentials com. 1992), Houston Ophthal. Soc. (pres. 1990—91, credentials com.), Harris County Med. Soc., Am. Bd. Laser Surgery, Am. Soc. Contemporary Ophthalmology (Charles Schepens Hon. award), Internat. Coll. Ocular Surgeons (vice regent 1991), Retina Soc. (v.p. 1976—77, pres. 1978—79, credentials com.), Am. Med. Women's Assn., Internat. Coll. Surgeons (vice regent 1991—), Tex. Med. Assn., Vitreous Soc., Jules Gonin Club. Achievements include research in vision and ophthalmology. Office: Tex Med Ctr 6560 Fannin St Ste 2200 Houston TX 77030-2715 E-mail: alicem@bcm.tmc.edu.

MCPHERSON, GAIL, publishing executive, real estate executive; b. Ft. Worth; d. Garland and Daphne McP. Student, U. Tex.-Austin; BA, MS, CUNY. Advt. sales exec. Harper's Bazaar mag., NYC, 1974—76; sr. v.p., fashion mktg. dir. L'Officiel/ USA mag., NYC, 1976—80; fashion mgr. Town & Country Mag., NYC, 1980—82; v.p. advt. and mktg. Ultra mag., NYC, 1982—84; fragrance, jewelry and imported automotive mgr. M. Mag., NYC, Tex., 1984—85; sr. real estate sales exec. Fredric M. Reed & Co., Inc., NYC, Tex., 1985—88; AT&T security system rep. Home-Watch Inc., Amarillo, Tex., 1989—92; sales rep. Universal Comm., Dallas, 1992—94; acct. exec. Corp. Mktg., Inc., Dallas, 1994—98; sales rep. Pub. Concepts, Dallas, 1998—. NY sponsor Southampton Hosp. Benefit Com.; jr. com. Mannes Sch. Music, NYC, Henry St. Settlement; mem. Dallas Mus. Art League. Mem. Fashion Group NY, Advt. Women NY, Real Estate Bd. NY, U. Tex. Alumni Assn. of NY (v.p.), Corviglia Club (St. Moritz, Switzerland), Doubles, El Morocco Club (jr. com.), Le Club. Republican. Presbyterian. Home: 17850 Sunmeadow Dr #2009 Dallas TX 75252-5382

MCPHERSON, JOANNE FRANCES, art educator, artist, special education educator; b. St. Paul, Apr. 26, 1946; d. Tony J. and Frances L. Kushlan; m. Robert Waite McPherson Sr.; children: Robert Waite McPherson, Jr., Melanie Anne McPherson. BS, St. Cloud State U., 1969; MEd, U. Minn., 1986. Licensed art tchr. grades K-12, Minn.; licensed spl. edn. tchr. Art educator Rocori H.S., Cold Spring, Minn., 1969-70; fed. title 1 tchr. Juvenile Correctional Facility, Lino Lakes, Minn., 1970-72; art educator Ind. Sch. Dist. 622, Maplewood, Minn., 1972-89, chairperson curriculum coordination coun., 1986-89, 95—; spl. edn. educator Tartan H.S., Oakdale, Minn., 1989-95; art, spl. edn. educator North St. Paul (Minn.) Sr. H.S., 1995—. Instr. Creative Learning Ctr., Roseville, Minn., 1986-89; vol. artist Ind. Sch. Dist. #622, North St. Paul and Maplewood, Minn., 1989-2005, ret., 2006. Mem. Coon Rapids Fine Arts Commn., 1979-83. Prof. opportunity program grantee Minn. Coun. Arts Edn. State of Minn., 1994, found. grantee Dist. 622, 1997, 99; recipient certification of appreciation Coon Rapids Fine Arts Commn., 1990. Mem. Minn. Edn. Assn., Mpls. Woman's Club, St. Andrew's Soc. Minn. (pres. 1997-99), Phi Delta Kappa, Alpha Delta Kappa. Avocations: painting, gourmet cooking, bicycling, photography, travel, creative writing.

MCPHERSON, KATHARYN ROSS, elementary school educator; b. Aug. 3, 1949; BBA, Tex Tech. U., 1971, MEd, 1981. Bus. tchr. U.S. Army, 1971-76; tchr. fourth grade Beaumont (Tex.) Ind. Sch. Dist., 1978-79; math. tchr. fifth grade Killeen (Tex.) Ind. Sch. Dist., 1979—. Presenter of workshops, Tex. and Miss., 1992—; speaker at math. tchrs. convs. and confs.; mem. curriculum coms., Killeen, Tex., 1978—, Project ABCD Curriculum Fellows (first computerized math. curriculum for state of Tex.), 1991. Author: 3 problem solving strategies books, numerous games and posters, 1992-98. Mem. Nat. Coun. Tchrs. of Math. (spkr. 1998), Rio Grande Valley Conf. Tchrs. of Math. Home: 3100 June St Killeen TX 76543-4913 Office Phone: 254-690-4487. E-mail: makemathfun@yahoo.com.

MCPHERSON, LINDA, music educator; b. Lawrence, Kans., Jan. 3, 1960; d. Lois and Thomas F. Rogers; m. Richard McPherson, Jan. 18, 1958; children: Jared, Nolan. B of Music Edn., Okla. Bapt. U., Shawnee, 1982; MAS, Baker U., Baldwin, Kans., 2003. Cert. Orff level I tchr. AOSA, Tex., 1984, Orff level II tchr. AOSA, Tex., 2003, k-12 vocal music tchr. Kans., 1990, adminstr. Kans., 2003. Tchr. music Duncanville Sch. Dist., Hastings Elem., Tex., 1982—90, De Soto USD 232, Woodsonia Elem., Shawnee, Kans., 1990—95; tchr. vocal music Monticello Trails Mid. Sch., Shawnee, Kans., 1995—98; tchr. music Woodsonia Elem., Shawnee, Kans., 1998—2000, Mize Elem., Shawnee, Kans., 2000—. Dir. handbell choir 1st Bapt. Ch. of Olathe, Kans., 1994—2004, dir. children's choir, 2000—04; bldg. rep. De Soto Tchr. Assn., Kans., 2000—03; coord. Kans. tchr. of yr. De Soto USD 232, Shawnee, Kans., 2002—, coord. Horizon award, Kans., 2005—, coord. profl. devel., 2006—; chair North Ctrl. Accrediation, Mize Elem., Shawnee, Kans., 2002—. Composer: (music publication, activity) Instrument Hold Up Music K-8 Vol. 5 #5, You've Gotta Talk Music K-8 Vo. 3 #1; dir.: (beat keepers perform at kmea) Live with Bobby McFerrin, Kansas Music Educators Conference. Mem. Kans. Exemplary Edns. Network, Topeka, 2002—06. Finalist Elem. Tchr. of Yr., Kans., 2002; recipient Outstanding Tchr. of Yr. award, Okla. Bapt. U., 1982, Outstanding Tchr. award, De Soto USD 232, 1991, Risk Taker award, 1999, 2002, 2004; Rhythm and Drumming grant, Greenbush, 2001, Reading and Music grant, De Soto USD 232, 2003, 2005, Music Comes Alive grant, Sprint Grant, 2005. Mem.: NEA, Kans. Orff Chpt. (bd. dirs. 2004—06), Kans. Music Educators Assn. Avocations: travel, reading, music. Home: 14526 S Roth Cir Olathe KS 66062 Office: Mize Elem 7301 Mize Rd Shawnee KS 66227 Office Phone: 913-441-0880. Office Fax: 913-441-9452. Personal E-mail: rlmcpherso@comcast.net. E-mail: lmcpherson@usd232.org.

MCPHERSON, MARY E., social studies educator; d. Joseph Edward and Barbara Ellen McPherson. BS in History, U. W.Ga., Carrollton, 1976, MEd, 1986. Lic. secondary tchr. Ga. Dept. Edn., 1976. Social studies chairperson Haralson County H.S., Tallapoosa, Ga., 1976—. Bd. trustees Bremen First United Meth. Ch., 2006—; bd. dirs. Our Ho. for Kids, Inc., Bremen, Ga. Named Haralson County Tchr. of Yr., Ga. Dept. Edn., 2003. Mem.: Ga. Assn. Econ. Educators, Ga. Educators Assn. Office Phone: 770-574-7647.

MCPHERSON, MONA SUE, science educator, department chairman; d. Merle Adrian and Montez Genell Trimm; children: Sean, Kelly. BS, Lipscomb U., Nashville, Tenn., 1966—68; MEd, Tenn. State U., Nashville, 1976—78. Tchr. Litton Jr. High, Nashville, 1969—70, Valley Sta. High, Louisville, Ky., 1970—71, Hawkins Jr. High, Hendersonville, Tenn., 1971—90; tchr., sci. dept. chairperson Hendersonville HS, 1990—2006. Coord. Tenn. space week Tenn. Edn. Assn., Sumner Co-Ed Assn., Nashville, 1990—2002; curriculum writer Vanderbilt Dyer Observatory, Nashville, 2004—06, Rsch. One, Nashville, 2006. Contbr. articles to profl. pubs. Coord., aerospace days Sumner County Regional Airport Authority, Gallatin, 1998, coord., first flight, 2003, sec., bd. mem., 1998—2006. Recipient Sumner County Tchr. of Yr., Sumner County Bd. Edn., Gallatin, 1988, Aerospace Educator of Yr., Nat. Space Found., Colorado Springs, Colo., 2003; grantee Tenn. Space Week grant, Tenn. Edn. Assn., 1999, 2001, 2005, Christa McAuliffe fellowship, Nat. Sci. Tchrs.-State Schs., Washington, DC, 1998—99; Smart Kids grant, 2005. Mem.: Sumner County Edn. Assn. (bd. mem., pres. 1988—89), Tenn. Assn. Sci., Tenn. Sci. Tchrs. Assn. (bd. mem. 1994—). Mem. Christian Ch. Avocations: flying, scuba diving, travel, cooking, gardening. Office: Hendersonville HS 123 Cherokee Rd Hendersonville TN 37075

MCPHERSON, RENEE, meteorologist; b. Madison, Wis. BS in Math. and Meteorology, U. Wis., Madison; MS in Meteorology, U. Okla., Norman; PhD in Meteorology, U. okla., Norman. Asst. dir. Okla. Climatol. Survey, Norman, 1995—2001, co-dir. Project Earthstorm, 1996—99, assoc. dir., 2001—04, acting dir., 2004—; asst. dir. Coop. Inst. for Mesoscale Meteorol. Studies, Norman, 2003—04. Mem. pastor's coun. Grace Fellowship Ch., Norman. Recipient Amelia Earhart Fellowship award, Zonta Internat., 1988, June Bacon-Bercey scholarship in Atmospheric Scis. for Women, Am. Geophys. Union, 1988, Macelwane award in Meteorology, Am. Meteorol. Soc., 1988, Innovations in Am. Govt. award, Harvard U., 2001, Douglas Lilly award for Best PhD Publ., Sch. Meteorology, U. Okla., 2004, Spl. award to the Okla. Climatol. Survey, Am. Meteorol. Soc., 2000, Spl. award to the Okla. Mesonet, 2005. Mem.: Am. Meteorol. Soc.

MCPHERSON, SANDRA JEAN, poet, educator; b. San Jose, Calif., Aug. 2, 1943; d. John Emmet and Joyce (Turney) Todd, adopted d. Walter James and Frances K. (Gibson) McPherson; m. Henry D. Carlile, 1966 (div. 1985); 1 child, Phoebe; m. Walter D. Pavlich, 1995 (dec. 2002). BA in English, San Jose (Calif.) State U., 1965; postgrad., U. Wash., 1965-66. Vis. lectr. U. Iowa Writers Workshop, 1974-76, 78-80; Holloway lectr. U. Calif., Berkeley, 1981; tchr. poetry workshop Oreg. Writers Workshop, Portland, 1981-85; prof. English U. Calif., Davis, 1985—. Editor and pub. Swan Scythe Press. Author: (poetry) Elegies for the Hot Season, 1970, Radiation, 1973, The Year of Our Birth, 1978, Patron Happiness, 1983, Streamers, 1988, The God of Indeterminacy, 1993, The Spaces Between Birds: Mother/Daughter Poems, 1996, Edge Effect: Trails and portrayals, 1996, A Visit to Civilization, 2002. Recipient Nat. Endowment for the Arts awards; award in lit. Am. Acad. and Inst. Arts and Letters, 1987; Ingram Merrill Found. fellow; grantee Guggenheim Found., 1976, Oreg. Arts Commn., 1984-85. Democrat. Avocation: collector and exhibitor of African-Am. quilts. Office: Univ Calif Dept English 1 Shields Ave Dept English Davis CA 95616-5271

MCPHERSON, SHERRY LYNN, social worker; b. Bklyn., Mar. 8, 1969; d. George Cephano and Mary Sue McPherson. BA, Hofstra U., 1992; MSW, Adelphi U., 1996. Cert. sch. social worker. Program coord. Colonial Youth and Family Svcs., Mastic, NY, 1993; sch. social worker Cmty. Counseling Ctr., Franklin Square, NY, 1996—97; cons. Elmont Pre-Kindergarten, NY, 1997, Glen Cove Child Day Care, NY, 1997—98; sch. social worker Patchogue-Medford Schs., NY, 1997—. Bd. dirs. Pronto L.I. Mem. sub com. on youth criminal justice Criminal Justice Coordinating Counsel Suffolk County; mem. site based mgmt. Patchogue-Medford High. Mem.: NASW, NAACP, Sch. Social Work Assn. Am., Nat. Assn. Black Social Workers (treas. 2002—04), Black/Hispanic Alumni Assn. Hofstra U., Lupus Alliance. Roman Catholic. Avocations: travel, baseball. Office: Patchogue Medford Sch Sys 241 S Ocean Ave Patchogue NY 11772 Personal E-mail: senigma8@aol.com.

MCPHERSON, VANZETTA PENN, magistrate judge; b. Montgomery, Ala., May 26, 1947; d. Luther Lincoln and Sadie Lee (Gardner) P.; m. Winston D. Durant, Aug. 17, 1968 (div. Apr. 1979); 1 child, Raegan Winston; m. Thomas McPherson Jr., Nov. 16, 1985. BS in Speech Pathology, Howard U., Washington, 1969; MA in Speech Pathology, Columbia U., 1971, JD, 1974. Bar: N.Y. 1975, Ala. 1976, U.S. Dist. Ct. (so. dist.) N.Y. 1975, U.S. Dist. Ct. (mid. dist.) Ala. 1980, U.S. Ct. Appeals (2d cir.) 1975, U.S. Ct. Appeals (11th cir.) 1981, U.S. Supreme Ct. Assoc. Hughes, Hubbard & Reed, N.Y.C., 1974-75; asst. atty. gen. Ala. Atty. Gen. Office, Montgomery, 1975-78; pvt. practice Montgomery, 1978-92; magistrate judge U.S. Dist. Ct. (mid. dist.) Ala., Montgomery, 1992—. Former co-owner Roots & Wings, A Cultural Bookplace, Montgomery, 1989—2000. Dir. Ala. Shakespeare Festival, Montgomery, 1987—, Montgomery Symphony Orch., 1995-98; chmn. trustees Dexter Ave. King Meml. Bapt. Ch., Montgomery, 1988; chmn. Leadership Montgomery; bd. mem. Lighthouse Counseling Ctr., Montgomery, 1981-84, Montgomery County Pub. Libr., 1989-90; v.p. Lanier H.S. Parent Tchr. Student Assn., Montgomery, 1990-91, Metro-Montgomery YMCA, 2000—, Ala. Arts Coun., 2001-. Recipient cert. Ala. Jud. Coll.; named Woman of Achievement Montgomery Advertiser, 1989, Boss of Yr. Montgomery Assn. Legal Secs., 1992. Mem. ABA (law office design award 1985), FBA (pres. Montgomery chpt.), Nat. Bar Assn., Ala. State Bar Assn. (chmn. family law sect. 1989-90), N.Y. State Bar Assn., Montgomery Inn of Cts. (master bencher 1992—), Ala. Black Lawyers Assn. (pres. 1979-80). Office: US Dist Ct Mid Dist Ala PO Box 1629 One Church St Montgomery AL 36104

MCQUAID, PATRICIA A., information systems educator; b. Cleve., May 19, 1954; d. Thomas F. and Sophia (Mihailoff) McQ. BS in Acctg., Case-Western Res. U., 1978; MBA, Eastern Mich. U., 1982; MS in Computer Sci. and Engring., Auburn U., 1988, PhD in Computer Sci. and Engring., 1996. Cert. info. sys. auditor. Sr. EDP audit analyst COMERICA Bank, Detroit, 1978-81; sr. EDP auditor The Bendix Corp., Southfield, Mich., 1981-83; lectr. in acctg. Ea. Mich. U., Ypsilanti, 1983-84; instr. info. sys. U. Cin., 1984-85; instr. computer sci. and engring. Auburn (Ala.) U., 1985-92; instr. info. sys. Auburn U., Montgomery, 1992-96; assoc. prof. Calif. Poly. State U., San Luis Obispo, 1996—. Chair program com. North, Ctrl., South Am. 2nd World Congress for Software Quality; spkr. in field. Contbr. articles to profl. jours. Recipient Best Rsch. Paper in Field of Software Metrics Fifth European Conf. Software Quality European Orgn. Quality, 1996. Mem. Am. Soc. Quality (software divsn., program com. N.Am., C.Am., S.Am. 1998—). Avocations: raising lizards, pool, golf. Office: Calif Poly State U Coll Bus - MIS San Luis Obispo CA 93407

MCQUARRIE, MEGAN, science educator; d. Allen and Carole McQuarrie. BA, U. RI, 1993; MS, Duke U., 1998. Cons. USGS, Menlo Park, Calif., 1998—; instr. Cerritos Coll., Norwalk, Calif., 2001—; exec. dir. Elixir Fund, Inc., Long Beach, Calif., 2003—. Chair bd., exec. dir., founder Elixir Fund, Inc., 2003—06. Office Phone: 562-860-2451 5037.

MCQUEEN, PAMELA, principal; BA in English, No. Ky. U., MA in Secondary Edn. and English. Cert. rank I in secondary adminstrn. Xavier U. Tchr., prin.; prin. Villa Madonna Acad. H.S., Villa Hills, Ky., 1996—. Office: Villa Madonna Acad HS 2500 Amsterdam Rd Fort Mitchell KY 41017-5316

MCQUEEN, REGENIA, writer; b. Summerville, SC, Oct. 29, 1945; d. William and Mary (Stoutamire) McQueen; m. John Ray Sanders Teasley, Oct. 11, 1961; children: John Ray Sanders Teasley, Tonya Teasley, Ieishia Teasley, Nairobi Teasley, Rhodesia Teasley, Donnish Lindsey Teasley, DeJong Lindsey Teasley. A, Cin. Tech. Coll., 1985; cert., Blackstone Sch. of Law, Dallas, 2000; BA, No. Ky. U., 2005. Clk. Western-So. Life Ins., Cin., 1967—72, IRS, Covington, Ky., 1985-87. Author: Regenia McQueen: Born to Search, 2000, Nairobi Teasley: 1-1/2 Hour Defenseless Lamb, 2001, Witnesses to the Impossible Dreams, 2002, Regenia McQueen: Life Stolen, Name, Land, City Government and History Theft in South Carolina, 2003, Reginia McQueen's Documents, Name, Land, Oil, Government and History Theft of William McQueen in South Carolina vol. 1-4, 2004, John Teasley and Nairobi Teasley: Unlawfully Made Guilty until Lawfully Proven Innocent vol. 1 and 2, 2004, Regenia McQueen, One of the Richest Women in the World yet, I Have Not a Dime to Spend, 2006, Regenia McQueen A Queen that Lives in the Ghetto, 2006. V.p. 13th St. Tenant Assn., 1979—85; Rosa Parks co-chmn.; trustee Owning the Realty, 1983—85. Recipient Achievement award, Ho. of Reps., Ohio, 2000, Wall of Tolerance award, Nat. Campaign Tolerance, 2002. Avocation: researching. Mailing: PO Box 15311 Covington KY 41015 E-mail: rteasley-3204@fuse.net.

MCQUEEN, SHARON, library and information scientist, educator; b. Port Washington, Wis., Jan. 6, 1961; d. Robert Joseph and Alice Ann Sauer; m. Richard Douglas Wambold, Sept. 18, 2005; m. David Alan Cecsarini, June 12, 1988 (div. June 13, 1995); m. Robert Douglas McQueen, Nov. 12, 1982 (div. Sept. 8, 1987). BA, U. Wis., Milw., 1997, MLS, 1999; PhD, U. Wis., Madison, 2006. Freelance actress, N.Y.C., 1980—82; founder, prodr. and artistic dir. Clavis Theatre, Milw., 1983, Theatre Tesseract, 1984—91; libr. Milw. Pub. Libr., 1993—95; lectr. Sch. Libr. and Info. Studies U. Wis., Madison, 2001; asst. prof. Sch. Libr. and Info. Sci. U. Ky., Lexington, 2005—. Adj. instr. Sch. Libr. and Info. Sci. U. Wis., Milw., 1998—2000; dir. McConnell ctr. study youth lit. Sch. Libr. and Info. Sci. U. Ky., Lexington, 2005—; vis. lectr. Sch. Libr. and Info. Sci. U. Iowa, Iowa City, 2005. Author: (monograph (manual/book) In-House Bookbinding & Repair, (literary spoof published in a monograph) The Annotated Pyrocodex. Founder Wis. chpt. Adopt a Grandparent, Grafton, 1974—76. Recipient Leadership and Svc. award, Am. Legion, 1979, citation Achievement and Outstanding Leadership, Grafton Jaycettes, 1979, Mayor's Landscape award, City of Milw., 2000, 2003; fellow, U. Wis., Madison, 2005; grantee, Performing Arts Ctr. & Milw. Sentinel, 1984; Vida Cummins Stanton scholar, Wis. Libr. Assn., 1998, Beth Mason scholar, AAUW, 1998, Dean's scholar, U. Wis., Milw., 1998, Judy Pitts scholar, Conf. Co-Chairs Treasure Mountain, 2002. Mem.: ALA (mem. nat. planning spl. collections com. 2003—05, advisor Michael Gorman's presdl. libr. edn. initiative 2005—, mem. Carnegie award sel. com. 2005—06), Soc. History Children and Youth, Children's Lit. Assn., Ky. Libr. Assn., Soc. History Authorship, Reading & Pub., Assn. Libr. and Info. Sci. Edn. (chair doctoral students spl. interest group 2001—02, membership com. 2001—03, chair youth svcs. spl. interest group 2003—04, chair new faculty special interest group 2006, chair nominating com.), Phi Kappa Phi, Beta Phi Mu. Independent. Avocations: gardening, krumhorn, flute, piccolo, recorder, bassoon, washboard. Office: UK School of Library & Info Sci 520 King Library Lexington KY 40506-0039 Office Phone: 859-257-3771. Office Fax: 859-257-4205.

MCQUIGG, MICHELE BERGER, state legislator; b. Bay Shore, N.Y., Sept. 2, 1947; children: Heather Lukes, Katie Schneider. BS, Mary Washington Coll., 1968; MS, Va. Polytech. Inst. & State U., 1978. Mem. Va. State Legis., 1998—, mem. cts. of justice com., mem. counties cities & towns com., vice chair gen. laws com., mem. sci. and tech. com. Republican. Episcopalian. Office: Gen Assembly Bldg PO Box 406 Richmond VA 23218-0406 E-mail: del_mcquigg@house.state.va.us, michele@mcquigg.com.

MCQUOWN, ELOISE, librarian; b. Santa Monica, Calif. d. Franklyn King and Paula (Rogers) McQ. BA, U. Utah, Salt Lake City, 1965; MLS, Rutgers U., New Brunswick, N.J., 1968; MS, U. Utah, Salt Lake City, 1976. Libr. U. Utah Librs., Salt Lake City, 1969-80, head access svcs., 1980-84; asst. dir.adminstrv. svcs. San Francisco State U., 1984-89, libr. instrnl. and rsch. svcs., 1989—. Conf. workshop leader Calif. Libr. Assn., Oakland, 1993; conf. spkr. Utah Libr. Assn., St. George, 1989, Am. Libr. Assn., Chgo., 1984, libr. cons. Children's Ctr., Salt lake City, 1970-73. Author: Business Information, 1974; contbg. editor: Network, 1978-84; contbr. articles to profl. jours. Del. Dem. Nat. Conv., N.Y.C., 1976, 80; candidate Utah State Legis., Salt Lake City, 1980. Recipient Susa Young Gates award Utah Women's Polit. Caucus, 1975; named Disting. Woman of Yr. in Utah., Salt Lake City, 1979. Mem. Calif. Faculty Assn. (chair polit. action, legis. com. 1995—, dir. voter registration project. 1996, chair statewide legis. polit. action com. 1999—2003, statewide bd. dirs. 1999—), Am. Assn. of U. Prof. (govt. rels. com. 2002—). Democrat. Avocations: travel, tennis, human rights. Office: San Francisco State U Library 1630 Holloway Ave San Francisco CA 94132-1722 Office Phone: 415-338-2131. Business E-Mail: emcquown@sfsu.edu.

MCQUOWN, JUDITH HERSHKOWITZ, writer, consultant, financial planner; b. NYC, Apr. 8, 1941; d. Frederick Ephraim and Pearl (Rosenberg) H.; m. Michael L. McQuown, Jan. 13, 1969 (div. 1980); m. Harrison Roth, Dec. 8, 1985 (dec. 1997); m. Harold Allen Lightman, Jan. 2, 2005. AB, Hunter Coll., 1963; postgrad., N.Y. Inst. Fin., N.Y.C., 1965-67. Chief underwriting div. mcpl. securities City of N.Y., 1972-73; CEO Judith H. McQuown & Co., Inc., N.Y.C., 1973—. Author: Tax Shelters That Work for Everyone, 1979, The Fashion Survival Manual, 1981, Playing the Takeover Market, 1982, How to Profit After You Inc. Yourself, 1985, Keep One Suitcase Empty: The Bargain Shopper's Guide to the Finest Factory Outlets in the British Isles, 1987, Keep One Suitcase Empty: The Bargain Shopper's Guide to the Finest Factory Outlets in Europe, 1988, Use Your Own Corporation to Get Rich, 1991, Inc. Yourself: How to Profit by Setting Up Your Own Corporation, 10th edit., 2002, 1,001 Tips for Living Well with Diabetes: Firsthand Advice That Really Works, 2004; contbg. editor: Boardroom Reports, Physician's Fin. News, Physician's Guide to Money Mgmt.; contbr. seminars The Learning Annex, seminars The Discovery Ctr., seminars Boston Ctr. for Adult Edn., seminars First Class, seminars Learning Connection, seminars Knowledge Network. Mem. Am. Soc. Journalists and Authors. Home and Office: One Gracie Ter Apt 9C New York NY 10028

MCQUOWN, KIMBERLY ALYSE, elementary school educator; b. Banning, Calif., Aug. 26, 1981; d. John Charles and Susan Elaine McQuown. BA in Elem. Edn., U. Ariz., Tucson, 2003. Cert. elem. edn. Ariz. Dept. Edn., 2003. Student tchr. Amphi Unified Sch. Dist., Tucson, 2003—03; tchr. 4th grade Altar Valley Sch. Dist., 2003—04; tchr. 5th grade Scottsdale Unified Sch. Dist., 2004—, tchr. 6th grade, 2006—. Named Tchr. of Yr., Altar Valley Sch. Dist., 2003—04. Mem.: Scottsdale Educators Assn. (assoc.), Am. Edn. Assn. (assoc.). Home: 9750 N 94th Place #208 Scottsdale AZ 85258 Office: Scottsdale Unified School District 3811 N 44th Street Phoenix AZ 85018 Office Phone: 480-484-6100. Personal E-mail: kmcquown@susd.org.

MCRAE, MARION ELEANOR, critical care nurse; b. Kingston, Ont., Can., Sept. 19, 1960; d. James Malcolm and Madeline Eleanor (MacNamara) McR. BSN, Queen's U., Kingston, 1982; MSN, U. Toronto, 1989, ACNP diploma, 2001. RN, Calif., CCRN; cert. BCLS, ACLS, CMC, CSC, ANA cardiac/vascular; advanced practice RN; bd. cert. acute care nurse practitioner. Staff nurse thoracic surgery Toronto (Can.) Gen. Hosp., 1982-83, staff nurse cardiovascular ICU, 1983-85; nurse clinician critical care Michael's Hosp., Toronto, 1985-87; external critical care clin. tchr. Ryerson Poly. Inst., Toronto, 1986-87; staff nurse cardiovascular ICU The Toronto Hosp.-Toronto Gen. Divsn., 1987-89; clin. nurse specialist cardiac surgery The Toronto Hosp., 1989-90; clin. nurse II cardiothoracic ICU UCLA Med. Ctr., 1990-92, clin. nurse III cardiothoracic ICU, 1992-2000; nurse practitioner cardiovasc. surgery Toronto Gen. Hosp., 2000—; clin. assoc. faculty nursing U. Toronto, Ont., 2004—. Mem. critical care nursing adv. bd. George Brown Coll., Toronto, 1987-88. Contbr. articles to profl. nursing jours. Recipient Open Master's fellowship U. Toronto, 1987-88, M. Keyes bursary Toronto Gen. Hosp., 1988-89, Nursing fellowship Heart and Stroke Found. Ont., 1988-89, Outstanding Svc. award UCLA Med. Ctr., 1994, Cardiothoracic ICU Nurse of Yr. award UCLA, 1995. Mem. AACN, Am. Heart Assn. Coun. on Cardiovascular Nursing. Office: Toronto Gen Hosp 4C 452 585 University Ave Toronto ON Canada M5G 2N2 E-mail: marion.mcrae@uhn.on.ca.

MCRANEY, JOAN KATHERINE, artist; b. Magee, Miss., Mar. 21, 1936; d. Harold Bryce and Ruth Katherine (Graves) McRaney; m. William Cummings Hollis, Mar. 14, 1966 (div. June 1970); m. Richard Felder, 1997. BFA, Inst. Allende, San Miguel de Allende, Mex., 1975; postgrad., U. So. Miss., Hattiesburg, 1990—; studied with sculptor Dan Askew, 1999—2000. Profl. portrait artist and contemporary sculptor, McComb, Hattiesburg, Miss., 1979—. Lectr. Lauren Rogers Mus. Art, Laurel, Miss., 1996. Exhibitions include Inst. Allende Gallery, 1973, Bellas Artes Gallery, San Miguel de Allende, 1974, Gulf South Gallery, McComb, 1982—84, New Orleans World Fair, 1984, Cottonlandia Mus., Greenwood, Miss., 1985—86, Woods Gallery U. So. Miss., 1990, Saenger Gallery, Hattiesburg, 1990, Woods and Locke Gallery U. So. Miss., 1992—96, Lucille Parker Gallery, William Carey Coll., 1993, Lauren Rogers Mus. Art, Laurel, Miss., 1996, 1999, Meridian (Miss.) Mus. Arts, 1997, USM Mus. Art, 1998, Meridian Mus. Art, 1999, Exit Gallery, Hattiesburg Downtown Gallery Walk, 1999—2000, Impressions Gallery, 2000—01, McComb Pub. Libr., 2000, Southwest C.C., 2002, one-woman shows include Gulf South Gallery, McComb, 2003, Meridian Mus. Art, 2004, Impressions Gallery, 2004, Edgewood Gallery, McComb, 2005—06, Good Karma Gallery, 2005—06, New Yokel Mkt., Represented in permanent collections Ole Miss Law Sch. Named winner juried competition, Laurel Arts League, 1999; recipient Louie B. Holmes Meml. award, McComb, 1980, 1981, Hon. Mention, Nat. Portrait Seminar, 1981, 1st pl. Pastel award, S. Miss. Art Assn. Cloverleaf Show, 1992, 1st pl. Drawing award, 1992, Dean's Outstanding Creativity award, 1993, 1994, 1st pl. Painting award, Umpteenth Ann. Student Show, Woods Gallery, 1995, Fred A. Walts Endowment, 1995, 1st Pl. Drawing award, 1995, Best of Show award Mixed Media Sculpture, Miss. Collegiate Art Competition, 1997, Best Sculpture award, Dept. Art Annual Student Exhbn., 1998, Honor, Hattiesburg Arts Coun., 1998, winner juried competition, Meridian Mus. Art, 1999. Mem.: Golden Key Soc., Kappa Delta. Avocations: gardening, photography, yoga, meditation, cooking. Home and Studio: 308 2nd Ave Hattiesburg MS 39401-3879 Office Phone: 601-818-4131. Personal E-mail: mcraneyart@comcast.net.

MCSORLEY, RITA ELIZABETH, adult education educator; b. Baraboo, Wis., Feb. 13, 1947; d. Charles Gervase and Bertie Ellen (Baker) Collins; m. William David McSorley III, June 6, 1967; children: William David IV, Kathryn Rita, Stephen Charles, Matthew Thomas. B Liberal Studies, Mary Washington Coll., Fredericksburg, Va., 1988; MEd, U. Va., Charlottesville, 1994. Adult edn. instr. Waipahu (Hawaii) Cmty. Sch. for Adults, 1989-91, literacy coord., 1990-91; dir. religious edn. Marine Meml. Chapel, Quantico, Va., 1992-94; adult edn. instr. Prince William County Schs., Quantico, 1992-93; coord. computer assisted lang. learning project Literacy Coun. No. Va., Falls Church, 1995-96; ednl. cons. Fairfield Lang. Techs., Harrisonburg, Va., 1996-97; adult edn. coord. N.E. Ind. Sch. Sys., San Antonio, 2000—; part-time tng. staff Tex. Ednl. Svc. Ctr. Region XX, 2004—. Presenter Ednl. Svc. Ctr., San Antonio, 2004—; lectr. in field. Mem. sch. bd. Quantico Dependent Schs., 1980-82; vol. Boy Scouts Am., Quantico and Pearl City, Hawaii, 1985-97. Mem. TESOL, U. Va. Alumni Assn. Roman Catholic. Avocations: quilting, genealogy, travel. Office: NEISD 10333 Broadway San Antonio TX 78217 E-mail: rmcsor@neisd.net.

MCSPADDEN, JODY SODD, lawyer; b. Corsicana, Tex., Feb. 21, 1975; BS, Tex. A&M U., 1998; JD, Baylor U. Law Sch., 2002. Bar: Tex. 2002. Assoc. Dawson & Sodd, P.C., Corsicana, Tex. Named a Rising Star, Tex. Super Lawyers mag., 2006. Office: Dawson & Sodd PC 121 N Main St PO Box 837 Corsicana TX 75151 Office Phone: 903-872-8181. E-mail: jody@dawsonsodd.com.*

MCSWAIN, GEORGIA HAYGOOD, educational program specialist, consultant; b. Huntsville, Ala., Oct. 2, 1948; d. Richard Erskin and Ira Stone Haygood; m. John Ivery McSwain, Jr., June 19, 1975 (div. June 21, 1994); 1 child, John Ivery III. BA, U. Ala., Huntsville, 1971; MEd, Ga. State U., Atlanta, 1985, Edn. Specialist Degree, 1987. Cert. English educator Ga., 2002, gifted edn. endorsement Ga. Profl. Standards Commn., 1999, cert. ednl. leadership P-12 Ga. Profl. Standards Commn., 1999. Lang. arts tchr. Huntsville City Schs., Ala., 1971—75; bookkeeper Exxon Co., USA, Atlanta, 1975—76; lang. arts tchr. Fulton County Schs., Atlanta, 1976—99, adminstrv. asst., 1999—2000, asst. prin., 2000—04; program specialist Ga. Dept. Edn., Atlanta, 2004—. Curriculum developer Fulton County Schs., 1976—2000, student tchr. supr., 1990—97, adminstrv. leadership program intern, 1998; cons. writing aross the curriculum Atlanta Pub. Schs., Atlanta, 1988; graduation sponsor M.D.Collins & Banneker High Schs., College Park, Ga., 1989—93; coord. African Am. Read-In Young Matrons Mt. Moriah, Atlanta, 1990—93; yearbook sponsor Banneker HS, College Park, Ga., 1991—97, SACS steering com. chairperson, 1994—98; lang. arts instr. Atlanta Met. Coll.'s Upward Bound Program, 1994—2000; program specialist Ga. Dept. Edn.-Innovative Academic Programs, Atlanta, 2004—; sch. of excellence chairperson Tri-Cities HS, East Point, Ga., 2002—03, coord. Coll. Bd.'s Inspiration award, 2002—03. Mem. NAACP, Balt., 1994—, Mt. Moriah Bapt. Ch., Atlanta, 1976—. Recipient Student Tchr. Achievement Recognition, Bus. Coun. Ga., 1988, 1991, HOPE scholarship for Tchrs., Ga. Fin.

Commn., 1997—98; fellow, Nat. Endowment for the Humanities, 1994; grantee, Fulton County Schs., 1990, 2003. Mem.: Nat. Coun. Tchrs. English, ASCD, Ga. State Alumni Assn., Pi Lambda Theta. Achievements include first 4-year African American graduate from University of Alabama, Huntsville, 1971. Home: 1862 Silver Creek Dr Lithia Springs GA 30122-2800 Office: Ga Dept Edn 1770 Twin Towers E 205 Jesse Hill Dr Atlanta GA 30334-5040 Business E-Mail: gmcswain@doe.k12.ga.us.

MCSWEENEY, FRANCES KAYE, psychology professor; b. Rochester, NY, Feb. 6, 1948; d. Edward William and Elsie Winifred (Kingston) McSweeney. BA, Smith Coll., 1969; MA, Harvard U., 1972, PhD, 1974. Lectr. McMaster U., Hamilton, Ont., Canada, 1973—74; asst. prof. Wash. State U., Pullman, 1974—79, assoc. prof., 1979—83, prof. psychology, 1983—2004, Regents prof. psychology, 2004—, chmn. dept. psychology, 1986—94, vice provost for faculty affairs, 2003—. Cons. in field. Contbr. articles to profl. jours. Woodrow Wilson fellow, Sloan fellow, 1968—69, NIMH fellow, 1973. Fellow: APA, Assn. Behavior Analysis (pres. 2005—06), Assn. for Psychol. Sci.; mem.: Psychonomic Soc., Phi Kappa Phi, Sigma Xi, Phi Beta Kappa. Home: 860 SW Alcora Dr Pullman WA 99163-2053 Office: Wash State U Dept Psychology Pullman WA 99164-4820 Office Phone: 509-335-2738. Business E-Mail: fkmcs@mail.wsu.edu.

MCSWEENY, DOROTHY PIERCE, art association administrator; b. Montgomery, Ala., Apr. 17, 1940; d. George Everill and Mary Dorothy Goodrich Pierce; m. William Francis McSweeny, Jan. 20, 1969; children: Ethan Madden Maverick, Terrell Pierce. BA, Brown U., Providence, 1962. Exec. tng. program U.S. Treasury Dept., Washington, 1962—64; officer Agy. Internat. Devel. U.S. Overseas Mission, Saigon, Vietnam, 1964—65; edn. writer The Boston Globe, 1965—67; presdl. oral historian The White Ho., Washington, 1967—69; Lyndon Johnson oral history project U. Tex., Austin, 1969—70; spl. counsel to spkr. U.S. Ho. Reps., Washington, 1970—72; cons. oral historian, 1972—90; chair D.C. Commn. on the Arts & Humanities, Washington, 1995—. Presdl. trustee John F Kennedy Ctr. Performing Arts, Washington, 1976—81; trustee and v.p. Nat. Symphony Orch., 1981—; founder, trustee and chair Washington Episcopal Sch., Bethesda, Md., 1985—; dir. and vice chair The Washington Ballet, 1986—; founder and vice chair Discovery Creek Children's Mus., 1993—; vice chair Mid Atlantic Arts Found., Balt., 1999—; dir. Nat. Assembly State Art Agencies, Washington, 2002—05; dir. and D.C. chair Nat. Mus. Am. Indian, 2002—06; D.C. cultural del. Senegal, Washington, 2006—, Ghana, 2006—, South Africa, 2006—. Founding dir. Nat. Race for the Cure, 1989—2006; founding mem. and mem. women's com. Nat. Mus. Women in the Arts, Washington, 1986—2006; co-chair Lombardi Cancer Rsch. Ctr. Georgetown U. Hosp., Washington, 1994—96; inaugural hdqs. com. Nat. Coun. Negro Women, Washington, 1996—2000; adv. coun. Katzen Arts Ctr. Am. U., 2003—06; eucharistic lay minister Episcopal Ch.; bd. dir. Boston U. Sch. Medicine, 1988—2000; founding mem. Lady Bird Johnson Wildflower Rsch. Ctr., Austin, Tex., 1988—2006; founder, chair, then vice chair EnvironMentors Nat. Environ. Edn. and Tng. Found., Washington, 1993—2006. Named Washingtonian of the Yr., Washingtonian Mag., 1995, Outstanding Fundraising Vol., Nat. Capital Philanthropy, 2002; recipient Founders award, Washington Episcopal Sch., 1999, Lifetime Achievement award, DC Youth Orch., 1999, Patron of the Arts award, Cultural Alliance of Greater Washington, 2000, Laura Phillips Angel of the Arts award, Cathedral Choral Arts Soc., 2004. Mem.: Fed. City Coun. (trustee 2000—06), D.C. C. of C. (trustee 2000—05), Women's Nat. Dem. Club (life), Order St. John of Jerusalem (comdr. 1987), Internat. Neighbors Club III (pres. then v.p. 1993—2006). Episcopalian-Eucharistic Lay Minister. Avocations: scuba diving, skiing, hiking, reading, tennis. Home: 5021 Millwood Lane NW Washington DC 20016 Office: DC Commn Arts & Humanities 410 Eighth St NW Washington DC 20004 Office Phone: 202-724-5613. Office Fax: 202-724-4135.

MCTAGUE-DOUGHERTY, AMY ELIZABETH, speech pathology/audiology services professional; d. Edward Patrick and Eileen Frances McTague; m. Patrick C. Dougherty, July 12, 1997; 1 child, Emma Louise Dougherty. BS, Loyola Coll., Balt., 1993, MS, 1995. Cert. clin. competence Am. Speech Lang. Hearing Assn., speech lang. pathologist N.J. Augmentative comm. specialist Cerebral Palsy of Monmouth and Ocean Counties, Inc., Wanamassa, NJ, 1995—; augmentative comm. cons. Prentke Romich Co., Wooster, Ohio, 1997—99; comm. instr. Temple U., Phila., 1999. Adj. prof. Richard Stockton Coll. N.J., Pomona, 1999—2001. Named Employee of the Quarter, Cerebral Palsy of Monmouth and Ocean Counties, 1996. Mem.: Am. Speech Lang. Hearing Assn., Internat. Soc. of Augmentative and Alternative Comm., U.S. Soc. of Augmentative and Alternative Comm., N.J. Speech Lang. Hearing Assn. (co-chair augmentative and alternative comm. com. 1998—99). Roman Catholic. Achievements include development of Vocabulary program for communication devices. Avocations: bicycling, gardening, walking. Office: Ladacin Network 1701 Kneeley Blvd Wanamassa NJ 07712 Office Phone: 732-493-5900. Personal E-mail: pat.doug@verizon.net.

MCTAGUE-STOCK, NANCY A., painter, printmaker; b. Brooklyn, Dec. 26, 1957; d. Walter James McTague and Mary Louise Tazewell; m. Robert Stock, Oct. 2, 1982; children: Benjamin Stock, Rebecca Stock. BFA, Va. Commonwealth U., 1979. V.p. of design R.S. Designs, Inc., New York, NY, 1985—92; art hist. lectr. Weston Public Schs., Conn.; originator and facilitator Landscapes into Tuscany Painting Tours, Italy, 1997—99; self-employed painter and printmaker Wilton, Conn., 1996—; faculty mem. Silvermine Sch. of Art, New Canaan, Conn., 2000—. Vis. artist lectr. Wilton Arts Festival, Wilton, Conn., 2000—01; lectr. Silvermine Sch. Art, New Canaan, Conn., 2001; monotype instructor Creative Arts Festival, Westport, Conn., 2001; lectr. Art Lecture Series, Conn., 2000; mem. faculty Green Farms Acad., Conn., 2002—. Exhibitions include Hamsphire Coll. Main Gallery, Mass., 2001, The Swedish Am. Mus., Chgo., 2001, Silvermine Galleries, Conn., 2001, Milford Ctr. Arts, Milford, Conn., 2001, Catherine J. Smith Gallery, Appalachian State Univ., N.C., 2001, Solon H. Borghlum Galley, Conn., 2001, Laura Barton Gallery, Westport, Conn., 2001, Left of the Bank Gallery, Old Greenwich, Conn., 2001, John Slade Ely Gallery, New Haven, Conn., 2001, Conn. Graphic Arts Ctr., Norwalk, Conn., 2001, Attleboro (Mass.) Mus., 2002, Am. Print Alliance Traveling Exhbn., 2002, U. Conn., Stamford, 2002, Jeffrey Weiss Gallery, Conn., 2002 (Drawing award Nat. Arts Program), Ctr. Contemporary Printmaking, Norwalk, Conn., 2002, Westport (Conn.) Arts Ctr., 2002, Higgins Art Gallery, Cape Cod, Mass., 2002, Capital C.C., Hartford, Conn., 2003, Silvermine Hays Gallery, Conn., 2003, Carriage Barn Gallery, New Cannan, Conn., 2003, Hays Gallery, New Canaan, 2003, Attleboro Mus., 2003, numerous others; contbr. articles The Weston Forum, 1998, to jours., 2001; exhibitions include Ctr. for Contemporary Printmaking, Norwalk, Conn., 2002, Westport Arts Ctr., Conn., 2002, Hays Gallery, New Canaan, Conn., 2003, Carriage Barn Gallery, Conn., 2003, Capital Cmty. Coll., Hartford, Conn., 2003. Named landscape painter, Darien Land Trust, Conn.; recipient Juror's award, 21 Ann. Conn. Artists Exhbn., 2001, Honorable Mention award, Stamford Mus., 2000, Rembrandt Award for Excellence in Graphic Art, Silvermine Galleries, 1999, Printmaking award, Landscape, Stamford Art Assn., 1997, Drawing award, Nat. Arts Educators' Exhbn., 2003. Mem.: Conn. Women Artists, Women's Caucus of Art, Monotype Guild of New England, Am. Print Alliance. Avocations: art history, cooking, gardening. Business E-Mail: nmsstudio1@aol.com.

MCTEE, CINDY, classical musician, educator; b. 1953; BM, Pacific Luth. U., 1976, studied with David Robbins; MM, Yale U., 1978, studied with Krzysztof Pendereckl, Jacob Druckman, and Bruce MacCombie; PhD, U. Iowa, 1981, studied with Richard Hervig; studied with Penderecki, Marek Stachowski, and Krystyna Moszumanska-Nazar, Higher Sch. Music, Cracow, Poland. Tchr. Pacific Luth. U., Tacoma, 1981-84; asst. to full prof. music composition U. North Tex., Denton, 1984—. Fulbright-Hayes Sr. Lectr. fellow in computer music Acad. Music, Cracow, 1990. Recipient comms. from Dallas Symphony Orch., Nat. Symphony Orch., Big Eight Band Dirs. Assn., Voices of Change, Barlow Endowment for Music Composition, Am. Guild Organists, Coll. Band Dirs. Nat. Assn., Phi Kappa Lambda Bd. Regents; works performed by Dallas Symphony Orch., Am. Symphony Orch., Detroit Symphony Orch., Chgo. Symphony Orch., Indpls. Symphony Orch., Nat. Repertory Orch., St. Louis Symphony, Memphis Symphony, Honolulu Symphony, Pitts. New Music Ensemble, Nat. Symphony Orch., Nippon Housou Kyoukai (NHK) Symphony Orch., Philharm. Orch., London. Recipient BMI award, Guggenheim Fellowship, 2001; grantee Wash. State Arts Commn.; Composers fellow NEA, Goddard Lieberson fellow AAAL; Acad. award in Music, AAAL, 2002; winner Louisville Orch. Composition Competition, 2001. Home: 1217 Piping Rock St Denton TX 76205-8126

MCTYER-CLARKE, WANDA KATHLEEN, interior designer; b. St. Louis, Apr. 06; d. Wiley and Lorain Howard. BSBA, St. Louis U., 1982; MS in Econs., So. Ill. U., Edwardsville, 1989; postgrad., Sheffield Sch. Interior Design, N.Y.C.; MBA in Organizational Behavior, Heriot-Watt U. Sch. Bus. Edinburgh Sch., Scotland, 1997; cert., N.Y. Sch. of Interior Design, 1995. Cert. nutritionist, aerobic dance instr., folk art paint technique instr.; decorative painters cert. Plaid Co. OSCI. Sec. clk. St. Louis U.; substitute tchr., aerobic dance instr. St. Louis Bd. Edn.; caseworker Mo. Div. Family Social Svcs., St. Louis; interior designer St. Louis; with McTyer-Clarke Designs, 1992-96. Block capt. Operation Brightside (cert. of appreciation); Ms. Mahogany Social Clubs 2d Runner Up, 1981-82, Miss Galaxy 1st Runner-Up, 1984. Alpha Kappa Alpha scholar, Sigma Ghamma Rho scholar, Washington Tabernacle Ch. scholar, Cotillion de Leon's Alternate scholar.

MCVEIGH, GLENNA FAYE, minister; b. Holts Summit, Mo., Oct. 3, 1936; d. Frank Edward and Ila Francis Morris; children: Randall, Richard, Kenneth. Student, Southwest Bapt. Coll., 1995, Saint Paul Sch. Theology, 1993—97. Reporter Memphis (Mo.) Dem. Newspaper, 1981—85, editor, 1985—89; receptionist, sec. Fulton (Mo.) Police Dept., 1990—92; minister Bethel United Meth. Ch., Montgomery City, Mo., 1992, Mountain View (Mo.) United Meth. Ch., 1992—2004, Pleasant Grove (Mo.) United Meth. Ch., 1992—2002, Keytesville/Dalton (Mo.) United Meth. Ch., 2004—. V.p. Ministerial Alliance, Mountain View, 2000—04; chaplain Mountain View (Mo.) Healthcare Ctr., 1997—2004. Editor: United Meth. Ch. Jefferson City/Rolla Dist. Newsletter, 1996—99. Bd. dirs. Agape House, Mountain View, 2002—04, FEED Program, Mountain View, 2000—04. Named day in honor, City Mountain View, 2002; recipient Denman Evangelism, Dist. United Meth. Ch., 1995. Mem.: Keytesville (Mo.) C. of C. Avocations: sewing, singing, reading. Home and Office: Keytesville Dalton Immanuel United Methodist 408 West Finnell Dr Keytesville MO 65261

MCVEIGH-PETTIGREW, SHARON CHRISTINE, communications consultant; b. San Francisco, Feb. 6, 1949; d. Martin Allen and Frances (Roddy) McVeigh; m. John Wallace Pettigrew, Mar. 27, 1971; children: Benjamin Thomas Pettigrew, Margaret Mary Pettigrew. BA with honors, U. Calif.-Berkeley, 1971; diploma of edn., Monash U., Australia, 1975; MBA, Golden Gate U., 1985. Tchr., adminstr. Victorian Edn. Dept., Victoria, Australia, 1972—79; supr. Network Control Ctr. GTE Sprint Comms., Burlingame, Calif., 1979—81, mgr. customer assistance, 1981—84, mgr. state legis. ops., 1984—85, dir. revenue programs, 1986—87; comm. cons. Flores, Pettigrew & Co., San Mateo, Calif., 1987—89; telemktg. Apple Computer Inc., Cupertino, Calif., 1989—94; prin. The Call Ctr. Group, San Mateo, Calif., 1995—. Telecomm. cons. PPG Svcs., 1994—; telecomm. spkr. Dept. Consumer Affairs, Sacramento, 1984. Panelist Wash. Gov.'s Citizens Coun., 1984; founding mem. Maroondah Women's Shelter, Victoria, 1978; organizer nat. conf. Bus. Women and the Polit. Process, New Orleans, 1986; mem. sch. bd. Boronia Tech. Sch., Victoria, 1979. Recipient Tchr. Spl. Responsibilities award, Victoria Edn. Dept., 1979. Mem.: Women's Econ. Action League, Am. Telemktg. Assn. (bd. dirs. 1992), Peninsula Profl. Women's Network, Am. Mgmt. Assn., Women in Telecom. (panel moderator San Francisco 1984). Democrat. Roman Catholic. Office Phone: 650-579-1298.

MCVETY, LINDA DOW, music educator; b. Melrose, Mass., Dec. 23, 1954; d. Robert Arthur and Eleanor May Dow; m. David James McVety, June 18, 1983; children: Robert, Christopher, Matthew. BS in Music Edn., U. Maine, Orono, 1976; M in Creative Arts, Lesley U., Cambridge, Mass, 2004. Cellist Bangor Symphony, Bangor, Maine, 1974—79; tchr. k-12 music MSAD #3 Mt. View, Unity, 1978—80; specialist k-12 gen. and string music MSAD #17 Oxford Hills, 1980—85; elem. music specialist MSAD #61 Songo Locks Elem., Naples, 1989—. Mem.: Nat. Tchrs. Assn. Avocations: cello, reading, crafts. Office: MSAD #61 Songo Locks Elementary Box 25 Songo School Road Naples ME 04055 Office Phone: 207-693-6828. Personal E-mail: lmcvety@sad61.k12.me.us.

MCVEY, ALICE LLOYD, social worker; b. N.Y.C., Mar. 21, 1935; d. George John and Alice Wood (Lloyd) Mc Vey. MS, Syracuse U., 1970; M of Profl. Svc., N.Y. Theol. Sem., 1977; cert. pastoral counseling, Postgrad. Ctr. Mental Health, 1977; cert. in gerontology, Adelphi U., 1983; MSW, Fordham U., 1991. Tchr. elem. Schs. in Diocese of Bklyn., 1955-66; tchr. biology Holy Family High Sch., Huntington, N.Y., 1966-75; regional superior Sisters of St. Joseph, Brentwood, N.Y., 1975-82; pastoral minister to older adults Our Lady of Grace Ch., West Babylon, N.Y., 1982-96, dir. parish social min. office, 1996—. Mem. Acad. Cert. Social Workers. Avocations: gardening, birding, hiking.

MCVEY, DIANE ELAINE, accountant; b. Wilmington, Del., Apr. 20, 1953; d. C. Granville and Margaret M. (Lindell) McV. AA in Acctg., Goldey Beacom Coll. (Del.), 1973, BS in Acctg., 1980; MBA in Mgmt., Fairleigh Dickinson U., 1985. Acct. Audio Visual Arts, Wilmington, Del., 1973; cost acct. FMC Corp., Kennett Square, Pa., 1973-75; asst. acct. NVF Corp., Kennett Square, 1978—80; staff analyst GPU Nuclear, Parsippany, NJ, 1980—93, staff acct., 1993—95, GPU Svc., Morristown, 1995—2000, Reading, Pa., 2000—, FirstEnergy, 2001—04, sr. accountant, 2004—. Owner, Demac Cons., Dover, N.J., 1988-2000, Reading, 2000—. Elder First Presbyn. Ch., Rockaway, N.J., 1986—, session mem., 1986-91; commr. to bd. adjustment, Dover, N.J., 1994-2000. With U.S. Army, 1975-78. Mem. Assn. MBA Execs. Republican. Presbyterian. Avocations: reading mystery books, writing and performing music, needlecrafts. Office: 2800 Pottsville Pike Reading PA 19601 Office Phone: 610-921-6560. E-mail: dmcvey@firstenergy.com.

MCVICKER, MARY ELLEN HARSHBARGER, museum director, art educator; b. Mexico, Mo., May 5, 1951; d. Don Milton and Harriet Pauline (Mossholder) Harshbarger; m. Wiley Ray McVicker, June 2, 1973; children: Laura Elizabeth, Todd Michael. BA with honors, U. Mo., 1973, MA, 1975, PhD, 1989. Instr. Ctrl. Meth. Coll., Fayette, Mo., 1978-85, mus. dir., 1980-85; project dir. Mo. Com. Humanities, Fayette, 1981-85, Mo. Dept. Natural Resources Office Hist. Preservation, 1978-85; owner Memories of Mo. and Tour Tyme, Inc., 1986-96; prof. history Kemper Mil. Coll., 1993-2000; dir. devel. The Salvation Army, Columbia, Mo., 2000-01; exec. dir. Friends of Historic Boonville, 2001—06; prof. history Columbia campus Moberly Area C.C., Mo., 2006—. Author: History Book, 1984. V.p. Friends Hist. Boonville, Mo., 1982-87, pres., 1989-90; bd. dors. Mus. Assocs. Mo. U., Columbia, 1981-83, Mo. Meth. Soc., Fayette, 1981-84; chmn. Bicentennial Celebration Methodism, Boonville, Mo., 1984; pres. Arts and Sci. Alumni, U. Mo., 1992-94; bd. dirs. Mo. Humanities Coun., 1993-97. Recipient Gov.'s award Excellence in Coll. Teaching, 1998. Mem. Mo. Alliance Hist. Preservation (charter), AAUW (treas. 1977-79), Am. Assn. Mus., Centralia Hist. Soc. (project dir. 1978), Mus. Assocs. United Meth. Ch. (charter, bd. dir. 1981-83), Mortar Bd., Women's Club (treas. 1977-79), United Meth. Women's Group (charter), Phi Beta Kappa. Democrat. Avocations: collecting antiques, gardening, family farming, singing, travel. Home: 22151 Highway 98 Boonville MO 65233-3022 Office: Moberly Area CC 805 E Walnut Columbia MO 65201 Business E-Mail: phd89@iland.net.

MCVICKER, MELISSA QUICK, counseling administrator, educator; b. Monroe, NC, Aug. 9, 1969; d. Richard Smith Quick and Terry Elaine Richardson; m. Michael Patrick McVicker, May 24, 1997; children: Shelby Madison, Sydney Paige. BA, Wingate Coll., 1994; M Theol. Studies cum laude, Gordon-Conwell Theol. Sem., 1999; D Ministry, Christian Life Sch. Theology, 2004. Counseling intern First Step Recovery Ctr., Monroe; counselor Piedmont Behavioral Healthcare, Monroe; clin. supr. BHC First Step, Monroe; clin. dir. SAIL, Inc., Charlotte, NC. Bd. dirs. Rivendell Counseling, Charlotte; cons. Summit Counseling Svcs., Waynesville, NC; presenter in field; musician various conventions and confs. Risden P. Reece scholar, Wingate Coll., 1994. Avocations: drums, motorcycling, hiking, jet skiing. Office: SAIL 5601 Executive Center Dr Ste 101 Charlotte NC 28212

MC VIE, CHRISTINE PERFECT, musician; b. Eng., July 12, 1943; m. John McVie (div.); m. Eddy Quintela. Student art sch., pvt. student sculpture. Singer, keyboardist, Fleetwood Mac, from 1970; albums with Fleetwood Mac include: Fleetwood Mac, 1968, Fleetwood Mac in Chicago, 1969, Then Play On, 1969, English Rose, 1969, Kiln House, 1970, Future Games, 1971, Bare Trees, 1972, Penguin, Mystery To Me, 1973, Heroes Are Hard to Find, 1974, Fleetwood Mac, 1975, Rumours, 1977, Tusk, 1979, Fleetwood Mac Live, 1980, Mirage, 1982, Jumping at Shadows, 1985, Tango in the Night, 1987, Greatest Hits, 1988, Behind the Mask, 1990, The Dance, 1997; solo albums include Christine Perfect, 1969, Christine McVie, 1984; composer: songs including Spare Me a Little of Your Love, Don't Stop, You Make Loving Fun, Over and Over, Hold Me, Songbird, Got a Hold on Me, Heroes Are Hard to Find, Little Lies, As Long as You Follow, Save Me, Skies the Limit. Office: care Warner Bros Records 3300 Warner Blvd Burbank CA 91505-4632

MCWEENY, JEN, philosopher, educator; b. Boston, Oct. 8, 1976; d. William McWeeny and Cameron DeMarche, Thomas DeMarche (Stepfather) and Caren Plank (Stepmother). BA in Philosophy, Colo. Coll., Colorado Springs, BA in Biology, 1998; MA in Philosophy, U. Hawaii, Manoa, 2000; cert. in women's and gender studies, U. Oreg., Eugene, MA in French Lit., 2003, PhD, 2005. Asst. prof. John Carroll U., University Heights, Ohio, 2004—. Co-author: Simone de Beauvoir's The Mandarins. Gary E. Smith Summer grantee, U. Oreg., 2003. Mem.: Am. Philos. Assn., Merleau-Ponty Cir. (assoc.), Soc. Asian and Comparative Philosophy (assoc.), Feminist Ethics and Social Theory (assoc.), Simone de Beauvoir Soc. (assoc.), Soc. Phenomenology and Existentialist Philosophy (assoc.), Soc. Women Philosophy (assoc.; sec. eastern divsn. 2006—). Avocations: running, hiking, soccer, travel.

MCWETHY, PATRICIA JOAN, educational association administrator; b. Chgo., Feb. 27, 1946; d. Frank E. and Emma (Kuehne) McW.; m. H. Frank Eden; children: Kristin Beth, Justin Nicholas. BA, Northwestern U., 1968; MA, U. Minn., 1970; MBA, George Washington U., 1981. Geog. analyst CIA, McLean, Va., 1970-71; rsch. asst. NSF, Washington, 1972-74, spl. asst. to dir., 1975, assoc. program dir. human geography and regional sci. program, 1976-79; exec. dir, Assn. Am. Geographers, Washington., 1979-84, Nat. Assn. Biology Tchrs., Reston, Va., 1984-95, Nat. Sci. Edn. Leadership Assn., Arlington, Va., 1995-97; edn. dir. Nat. Alliance for Mentally Ill, Arlington, 1998-99. Prin. investigator grant on biotech. equipment ednl. resource partnership NSF, 1989-93, NSF funded internat. symposium on Basic Biol. Concepts: What Should the World's Children Know?, 1992-94; co-prin. investigator NSF grant, 1995-97; mem. chmn.'s adv. com. Nat. Com. Sci. Stds. and Assessment, 1992-95; mem. Commn. for Biology Edn., Internat. Union Biol. Sci., 1988-97; mem. exec. com. Alliance for Environ. Edn., 1987-90, chmn. program com., 1990; condr. seminars in field; lectr. in field. Author monograph and papers in field; editor handbook. NSF grantee, 1989-93, 95-97; NSF fellow, 1968-69; recipient Outstanding Performance award, NSF, 1973. Mem. Phi Beta Kappa.

MCWHINNEY, DEBORAH, finance company executive; BA, U. Mont.; grad., Pacific Coast Banking Sch. With consumer electronic banking divsn. Bank Am. Corp. 17 yrs.; exec. v.p. bus. planning and strategy Visa Internat., 1995—99; group pres. Engage Media Svc., 1999—2001; pres., exec. com. mem. Schwab Instl., Schwab & Co., Inc., 2001—. Exec. advisor to bd. and exec. team Hitachi Data Sys. and Hitachi Ltd., 2003; chair bd. trustees U. Mont. Found.; former bd. chair Electronic Funds Tranfer Assn.; bd. dirs. Novadigm, Inc., PLUS Sys., Touch Am. Holdings, Inc.; past fin. chair Women's Mus.; founding investor, former dir. First Bank Idaho. Named one of 100 Most Influential Women in Bay Area Bus., San Francisco Bus. Times, 2002, 2003, 2004, 25 Most Influential People in Planning Profession, Investment Advisor List, 2004; recipient Movers & Shakers award Fin. Planning, 2004. Achievements include apptd. by Pres. Bush to Securities Investor Protection Corp. (SIPC), 2002.

MCWHINNEY, MADELINE H. (MRS. JOHN DENNY DALE), economist, director; b. Denver, Mar. 11, 1922; d. Leroy and Alice (Houston) McW.; m. John D. Dale, June 23, 1961; 1 child, Thomas Denny. BA, Smith Coll., 1943; MBA, NYU, 1947. Economist Fed. Res. Bank, NYC, 1943-73, chief fin. trade statis. divsn., 1955-59, mgr. market stats. dept., 1960-65, asst. v.p., 1965-73; pres. First Women's Bank, NYC, 1974-76, Dale, Elliott & Co., Inc., Red Bank, NJ, 1977-97. Trustee Retirement System Fed. Res. Bank, 1955-58; vis. lectr. NYU Grad. Sch. Bus., 1976-77; mem. NJ Casino Control Commn., 1980-82, Women's Econ. Round Table, 1978-89, chmn. 1987-88; bd. govs. Am. Stock Exch., 1977-81; trustee Monmouth Mus., 1995—, Vis. Nurse Assn. Ctrl. Jersey, 1995-2004, Planned Parenthood Ctrl. Jersey, 1995-2003, Carnegie Corp. NY, 1974-82, Central Savs. Bank NY, 1980-82, Monmouth Conservatory Music, 2002-; trustee Charles F. Kettering Found., 1975-93, chmn. 1987-91; trustee Inst. Internat. Edn., 1975-, Investor Responsibility Rsch. Ctr., Inc., 1974-81; asst. dir. Whitney Mus. Am. Art, 1983-86; dir. Atlantic Energy Co., 1983-93; trustee Mgrs. Funds, 1983-2004; mem. adv. com. profl. ethics NJ Supreme Ct., 1983-98. Recipient Smith Coll. medal, 1971, Alumni Achievement award NYU Grad. Sch. Bus. Adminstrn. Alumni Assn., 1971, NYU Crystal award, 1982. Mem. Am. Fin. Assn. (past dir.), Money Marketeers (v.p. 1960, pres. 1961-62), Alumni Assn. Grad. Sch. Bus. Adminstrn. NYU (dir. 1951-63, pres. 1957-59), Soc. Meml. Ctr., NJ Com. Humanities, Phi Beta Kappa Fellows (v.p. 1979-87). Office: PO Box 458 Red Bank NJ 07701-0458 Home: 192 Heritage Court Little Silver NJ 07739 Personal E-mail: mdale38569@comcast.net.

MCWHIRTER, GLENNA SUZANNE (NICKIE MCWHIRTER), retired columnist; b. Peoria, Ill., June 28, 1929; d. Alfred Leon and Garnet Lorene (Short) Sotier; m. Edward Ford McWhirter (div.); children: Suzanne McWhirter Orlicki, Charles Edward, James Richard. BS in English Lang. and Lit., U. Mich., postgrad., 1960-63. Editl. asst. McGraw-Hill Pub. Co., Detroit, 1951-54; staff writer Detroit Free Press, Inc., Detroit, 1963-70, asst. city editor, 1971-77, columnist, 1977-88, Detroit News Inc., Detroit, 1988-97; advt. copy writer Campbell-Ewald Co., Detroit, 1967-68; ret., 1997. Author: Pea Soup, 1984 Winner 1st Place Commentary award UPI, Mich., 1979; 1st Place Columns AP, Mich., 1978, 81; 1st Place Columns Detroit Press Club Found., Mich., 1978; Disting. Service award State of Mich., 1985 Mem. Women in Comm. (Headliner award 1978), Alpha Gamma Delta. Avocations: flower gardening, interior design. Home: 495 Lake Shore Ln Grosse Pointe Woods MI 48236

MCWHORTER, DIANE, writer; b. Tupelo, Miss., Nov. 1, 1952; BA in Comparative Lit., Wellesley Coll. Writer, NYC. Contbr. The NY Times, USA Today (Op-Ed page), The Nation, Slate; contbg. author: Carry Me Home: Birmingham, Alabama,The Climactic Battle of the Civil Rights Revolution, 2001 (Pulitzer prize for gen. nonfiction, 2002, named NY Times Notable Book, winner, Southern Book Critics Circle award, 2001, J. Anthony Lukas Book prize, 2002, English Speaking Union Ambassador award, 2002, Sidney Hillman Found. award, 2002), A Dream of Freedom: The Civil Rights Movement from 1954 to 1968, 2004 (NY Times Notable Children's Book, 2004, USA Today Best Children's History, 2004, on ALA Best New Book for Young Adults list, 2004), These United States, 2003, Stories from the Blue Moon Cafe, 2005. Recipient Clarence Cason award, 2003. Personal E-mail: dmcwhorter@earthlink.net.

MCWHORTER, ELSIE JEAN, retired art educator, artist; b. Laurel, Miss., Apr. 5, 1932; d. Benjamin Collen and Elsie McWhorter. BFA, U. Ga., Athens, Ga., 1954, MA, 1956; student, Bklyn. Mus. Art Sch., N.Y. Asst. prof. Morningside Coll., Sioux City, Iowa, 1958—61; tchr. art Mus. Art Sch., Columbia, SC, 1961—84; asst. prof. Benedict Coll., Columbia, SC, 1984—94, ret., 1994. Home: 5419 Sylvan Dr Columbia SC 29206-1405

MCWHORTER, RUTH ALICE, counselor, marriage and family therapist; b. Norfolk, Va., May 14, 1946; d. Lester Arthur and Mabel (Hopwood) Gorman; m. Brent Wilson McWhorter, Aug. 16, 1986; stepchildren: Daniel Chastin, Kenley Reid, Scott Jason; BA in Edn., Ariz. State U., 1970, M of Counseling Psychology, 1979. Lic. profl. counselor Ariz., marriage and family therapist Ariz., nat. cert. counselor, eye movement desensitization reprocessing therapist. Tchr. lang. arts Globe Mid. Sch., Ariz., 1969-72; tchr. English Isaac Jr. HS, Phoenix, 1973-74; real estate salesperson Phoenix, 1975-76; overnight counselor The New Found., Phoenix, 1978-80; family therapist Youth Svc. Bur., Phoenix, 1980-81; owner, corp. officer, profl. counselor/marriage & family therapist Family Devel. Resources, Phoenix, 1981—. Cons., vol. counselor Deseret Industries, Phoenix, 1992-96. Bd. dirs. Westside Mental Health Svcs., Phoenix, 1982-87; vol. facilitator Ariz. Multiple Sclerosis Soc., Phoenix, 1988; vol. disaster mental health team ARC-Ctrl. Divsn., Phoenix, 1996—. Mem.: ACA, Ariz. Assn. Marriage and Family Therapists, Assn. Mormon Counselors and Psychotherapists (sec.-treas. Ariz. 1990—2000), Ariz. Mental Health Counselors Assn. (sec.-treas. ctrl. chpt. 1982, sec. ctrl. chpt. 1995), Ariz. Counselors Assn., Am. Mental Health Counselors Assn., Am. Assn. Marriage and Family Therapists. Avocations: antiques and collectibles, movies, reading, golf, genealogy. Office: Family Devel Resources PC 6140 E Voltaire Ave Phoenix AZ 85254-3807 Office Phone: 480-483-7884.

MCWILLIAM, JOANNE ELIZABETH, retired theology studies educator; b. Toronto, Ont., Can., Dec. 10, 1928; d. Cecil Edward and Edna Viola (Archer) McW.; children, Leslie Mary Giroday, Elizabeth Dewart, Sean Dewart, Colin Dewart; m. C. Peter Slater, June 6, 1987. BA, U. Toronto, 1951, MA, 1953, U. St. Michael's, Toronto, 1966, PhD, 1968; DD honoris causa, Queen's U., Kingston, Ont., 2003. Asst. prof. religious studies U. Toronto, 1968-74, assoc. prof., 1974-87, prof., 1987, chairperson dept. religious studies, 1990-92, 93-94; Mary Crooke Hoffman prof. of Dogmatic Theology The Gen. Theol. Sem., N.Y.C, 1994-99; ret., 1999. Author: The Theology of Grace of Theodore of Mopsuestia, 1971, Death and Resurrection in the Fathers, 1986; editor: Augustine: Rhetor to Theologian, 1991, Toronto Jour. Theology. Mem. Can. Soc. for Patristic Studies (pres. 1987-90), Conf. Anglican Theologians (pres. 1990-91), Can. Soc. for the Study of Religion, Can. Theol. Soc., Am. Theol. Soc., Am. Acad. Religion. Anglican. Home: 59 Duggan Ave Toronto ON Canada M4V 1Y1 E-mail: joanne.mcwilliam@utoronto.ca.

MCWILLIAMS, BETTY JANE, science administrator, speech pathology/audiology services professional, educator; b. Martins Ferry, Ohio; d. Harry J. and Martha (McClure) McW. BS, Ohio State U., 1949; MS, U. Pitts., 1950, PhD, 1953. Prof. emerita U. Pitts., 1991—, dir. Cleft Palate-Craniofacial Ctr., 1969—91, dir. emerita, 1993—. Recipient Herbert Cooper Meml. award Cooper Clinic, 1979, award of recognition Pa. Acad. Dentistry for Children, 1989, award of recognition Pa. Dental Soc., 1991, Disting. Alumni award U. Pitts., 2004. Fellow Am. Speech, Lang. and Hearing Assn. (cert. clin. competence, Frank R. Kleffner Career award 1995); mem. Am. Coll. Dentists; mem. APA, Am. Cleft Palate-Craniofacial Assn. (pres. 1965, asst. sec. gen. 1st internat. congress 1969, editor 1975-81, pres. Cleft Palate Found. 1982-83, svc. award 1975, Honors of Assn. 1987), Pa. Fedn. Cleft Palate Clinics (pres. 1980-82, 89-90). Home and Office: 328 Overlook Dr Verona PA 15147-3852 Office Phone: 412-826-4997. E-mail: bj@relymail.com.

MCWILLIAMS, CHERYL A., music educator; d. Albert and Mary Goyette; m. Timothy McWilliams; children: Kevin, Kurt, Krystle. BA in Music, RI Coll., Providence, 1981, EdM, 1997. Cert. elem. tchg. RI, life profl. tchg. RI, prin. secondary, mid. and elem. sch. RI, edn. adminstrn. Providence Coll., 2006. Tchr. Pawtucket Sch. Dept., RI; music tchr. William E. Tolman HS. Mem.: ASCD, Am. Choral Dirs. Assn., Music Educators Nat. Conf. Mailing: Tolman HS 678 Benefit St Pawtucket RI 02861-1553

MCWILLIAMS, ELIZABETH ANN, elementary school educator; b. Sheffield, Ala., Sept. 12, 1950; d. Johnny Clarence and Flora (Despigno) Brumley; m. Andy Christopher McWilliams, July 4, 1974; 1 child, Amanda Elizabeth. BS in Edn., U. North Ala., 1973, MA in Edn., 1976, AA cert. in edn., 1986. Residence hall asst. U. North Ala., Florence, 1973-74; tchr. Colbert County Bd. Edn., Tuscumbia, Ala., 1974—2005; ret. Tchr. Growing Health Program, Tuscumbia, 1989—; presenter to tchrs. U.S. Space Camp, Huntsville, Ala., 1990—. Chpt. II grantee Ala. Dept. Edn., 1987. Fellow NEA; mem. Ala Edn. Assn. (faculty rep. 1990—2000, del. assembly 1993-2004, treas. dist. 4 uniserv), Colbert County Edn. Assn. (sch. rep. to exec. bd., sec. 1997-2003), Colbert County Ret. Tchrs. Assn. (v.p. 2006—), Ala. Edn. Assn. Ret. Tchrs., Phi Delta Kappa, Alpha Delta Kappa (rec. sec. 1992-94, corr. sec. 1994—). Mem. Ch. Of Christ. Avocations: reading, swimming, jogging. Home: 2120 Red Rock Rd Tuscumbia AL 35674-7021

MCWILLIAMS, MARGARET ANN, home economist, educator, writer; b. Osage, Iowa, May 26, 1929; d. Alvin Randall and Mildred Irene Edgar; children: Roger, Kathleen. BS, Iowa State U., 1951, MS, 1953; PhD, Oreg. State U., 1968. Registered dietitian. Asst. prof. home econs. Calif. State U., L.A., 1961-66, assoc. prof., 1966-68, prof., 1968-92, prof. emeritus, 1992—, chmn. dept., 1968-76; pres. Plycon Press, 1978—. Author: Food Fundamentals, 1966, 8th edit., 2006, Nutrition for the Growing Years, 1967, Experimental Foods Laboratory Manual, 1977, 5th edit., 2000, 6th edit., 2005, Lifelong Nutrition, 2001, (with L. Kotschevar) Understanding Food, 1969, Illustrated Guide to Food Preparation, 1970, 8th edit., 1998, 9th edit., 2005, (with L. Davis) Food for You, 1971, 2d edit., 1976, The Meatless Cookbook, 1973, (with F. Stare) Living Nutrition, 1973, 4th edit., 1984, Nutrition for Good Health, 1974, 2d edit., 1982, (with H. Paine) Modern Food Preservation, 1977, Fundamentals of Meal Management, 1978, 4th edit., 2005, (with H. Heller) The World of Nutrition, 1984, Foods: Experimental Perspectives, 1989, 4th edit. 2000, 5th edit., 2005, Food Around the World: A Cultural Perspective, 2003. Chmn. bd. Beach Cities Symphony, 1991-94. Recipient Alumni Centennial award Iowa State U., 1971, Profl. Achievement award, 1977; Phi Upsilon Omicron Nat. Founders fellow, 1964; Home Economist in Bus. Nat. Found. fellow, 1967; Outstanding Prof. award Calif. State U., 1976. Mem. Am. Dietetic Assn., Inst. Food Technologists, Phi Kappa Phi, Phi Upsilon Omicron, Omicron Nu, Iota Sigma Pi, Sigma Delta Epsilon, Sigma Alpha Iota. Home: PO Box 220 Redondo Beach CA 90277-0220 Personal E-mail: mmcwredondo@aol.com.

MEACHAM, DOLORES ANN (SISSY MEACHAM), elementary librarian; b. Monticello, Ark., Sept. 16, 1950; d. Macel Dean and Mildred Eloise (Alldread) Baker; m. William Kirby Meacham, Jr., July 24, 1948; children: Amber, Joseph. BS in Edn., U. Ark., 1981. Sec. Monroe County Extension Office, Clarendon, Ark., 1971-78; tchr. 4th grade Clarendon (Ark.) Pub. Sch., 1980-84, elem. libr., 1984—. Mem. women's com. Monroe County Farm Bur., 1989-90. Mem. ASCD, Delta Kappa Gamma (2d v.p. 1990—). Democrat. Mem. Ch. of Christ. Avocations: reading, travel. Office: Clarendon Pub Sch 316 N 6th St Clarendon AR 72029-2412

MEAD, SUSANAH M., dean; BA, Smith Coll., 1969; JD, Indiana U. Sch. Law, Indianapolis, 1976. Law for Honorable Paul H. Buchanan Jr, chief judge Indiana Court of Appeals, 1976—78; lecturer, legal writing program Indiana U. Sch. Law, Indianapolis, 1978, dir. legal writing, 1980—81, assoc. dean academic affairs, 1997—2004, interim dean, 2005—. Office: Indian U Sch Law Lawrence W Inlow Hall Rm 307 530 W New York St Indianapolis IN 46202-3225 Office Phone: 317-274-2581. Office Fax: 317-374-3955. E-mail: smead@iupui.edu.

MEADE, DOROTHY WINIFRED, retired educational administrator; b. N.Y.C., Jan. 26, 1935; d. Percival and Fraulien Franklin; m. Gerald H. Meade (dec. 2004); 1 child, Myrla E. BA in Am. History, Queens Coll., Flushing, N.Y., 1970; MA in Corrective Reading, Bklyn. Coll., 1975; BA in Religious Edn., United Christian Coll., Bklyn., 1980; postgrad., Bklyn. Coll., 1984; MDiv, N.Y. Theol. Sem., 2004. Tchr. social studies cluster Pub. Sch. 137, Bklyn., 1979-83, curriculum coord. Follow Through Program, 1984-88, adminstrv. intern, 1983-84; staff developer social studies Cen. Sch. Dist. 23, Bklyn., 1988-89, dist. coord. Project Child, 1989-91. Mem. faculty Coll. of New Rochelle, Bklyn., 1994-97. Participant Crossroads Africa, 1958; active Agape Tabernack Internat. Fellowship, 2000; former mem. Ch. of the Master; theol. intern Mt. Lebanon Bapt. Ch., 2001. Mem. African Christian Tchrs., N.Y. Pub. Sch. Early Childhood Edn., N.Y. Geography Inst., Women Organizing, Mobilizing, Bldg. Pentecostal. Avocations: bicycling, swimming, roller skating, singing, travel. Home: 538 E 86th St Brooklyn NY 11236

MEADE, PATRICIA SUE, marketing professional; b. Columbus, Ohio, Mar. 14, 1960; d. Harold Eugene and Glenna Rhae (Croaff) M. BS in Communications, Ohio U., 1982, M in Sports Adminstrn., 1984, MS in Communications, 1986. Dir. advt. The Pensacola (Fla.) Civic Ctr., 1984-85; asst. dir. mktg. Ohio Ctr. Co., Columbus, 1985-86; asst. v.p. mktg. Doctors Hosp., Columbus, 1986-88; regional mgr. mktg. Jacobs, Visconsi & Jacobs Co., Cleve., 1988-89; dir. bus. devel. and pub. affairs Deaconess Hosp., Cleve., 1989-91; div. head mktg. and pub. affairs Lake Metroparks, Concord Township, Ohio, 1991-93; sr. health care cons. Cohen & Co., Cleve., 1993-95; pres. Creative Works, Inc., Cleve., 1995—. Author: Healthcare Advertising & Marketing: A Practical Approach to Effective Communications, 1999. Mem. Cleve. Mus. Art, Cleve. Bot. Garden. Mem.: Graphic Artists Guild, Cleve. Mus. Art., Collinwood Art, Lake Erie Artists. Office Phone: 216-268-1900. Business E-Mail: pat@cre8veworks.com.

MEADERS, NOBUKO YOSHIZAWA, psychotherapist; b. Kobe, Hyogo-ken, Japan, Mar. 2, 1942; d. Shigenobu and Ayako (Takahashi) Tsuchiya; m. Wilson E. Meaders, Apr. 2, 1976 (div. Apr. 1985); m. Takeshi Yoshizawa, June 15, 1989. AA, Seiwa Coll., Nishinomiya, Japan, 1965, Warren Wilson Coll., Swannanoa, N.C., 1967; BA, So. Meth. U., Dallas, 1969; MS in Social Work, U. Tex., Arlington, 1971; cert. psychotherapy-psychoanalysis, Postgrad. Ctr. Mental Health, N.Y.C., 1977, cert. in supervision psychotherapeutic processes, 1979. Cert. social worker N.Y., diplomate Am. Bd. Examiners Clin. Social Work. Psychiat. social worker Killgore Children's Psychiat. Hosp., Amarillo, Tex., 1971-73, Jewish Child Care Assn., Childville div., N.Y.C., 1973-74; supr. social work, social work dept. Bellevue Hosp., N.Y.C., 1974-76; asst. dir. tng. Postgrad. Ctr. Mental Health, N.Y.C., 1979-82, assoc. supr., 1979-82, supr., 1982-85, sr. supr., 1985—, tng. analyst, 1989—; pvt. practice psychotherapy and psychoanalysis N.Y.C., 1976—. Clin. cons. Pace U. Personal Devel. Ctr., N.Y.C., 1987—. Fellow: N.Y. Soc. Clin. Social Work Psychotherapists; mem.: NASW, Acad. Cert. Social Workers. Avocations: sculpting, drawing, gardening, writing. Personal E-mail: nobukomeaders@aol.com.

MEADOW, LYNNE (CAROLYN MEADOW), theater producer; b. New Haven, Nov. 12, 1946; d. Frank and Virginia R. Meadow. BA cum laude, Bryn Mawr Coll., 1968; postgrad., Yale U., 1968-70. Dir. Theatre Communications Group, 1978-80. Adj. prof. SUNY, Stony Brook, 1975-76, Yale U., Circle in the Sq., 1977-78, 89-91, NYU, 1977-80; theatre and music/theatre panelist Nat. Endowment for Arts, 1977-88; artistic advisor Fund for New Am. Plays, 1988-90. Artistic dir. Manhattan Theatre Club, N.Y.C., 1972—; guest dir. Nat. Playwrights Conf., Eugene O'Neill Theatre Ctr., 1975-77, Phoenix Theatre, 1976; dir. Ashes for Manhattan Theatre Club and N.Y. Shakespeare Festival, 1977; prodr. off-Broadway shows Ain't Misbehavin', 1978, Crimes of the Heart, 1981, Miss Firecracker Contest, 1984, Frankie and Johnny, 1987, Eastern Standard, 1988, Lisbon Traviata, 1989, Lips Together, Teeth Apart, 1991, Four Dogs and a Bone, 1993, Love! Valour! Compassion!, 1994; dir. Principia Scritoriae, 1986, Woman in Mind, 1988 (Drama Desk award), Eleemosynary, 1989, Absent Friends, 1991; dir. Broadway prodn. A Small Family Business, 1992, The Loman Family Picnic, 1993, Nine Armenians, 1996 (Drama Desk nominee), Captains Courageous: The Musical, 1999, The Tale of the Allergist's Wife, 2000; (dir. Broadway prodn. and nat. tour), Last Dance, 2003, Rose's Dilemma, 2003, Moonlight and Magnolias, 2005; co-prodr. Off-Broadway and Broadway show Mass Appeal, 1981. Recipient Citation of Merit Nat. Coun. Women, 1976, Outer Circle Critics award 1977, Drama Desk award, 1977, Obie award for Ashes, 1977, Margo Jones award for Continued Encouragement New Playwrights, 1981, Critics Circle award Outstanding Revival on or off Broadway for Loot, 1986, Lucille Lortel award for Outstanding Achievement, 1987, Spl. Drama Desk award, 1989, N.Y. Drama Critics Circle award Best Fgn. Play for Aristocrats, 1989, Torch of Hope award, 1989, Manhattan Mag. award, 1994, Lee Reynolds award League Profl. Theatre Women, 1994; named Northwood Inst. Disting. Woman of Yr., 1990, Person of Yr., Nat. Theatre Conf., 1992, SDCF "Mr. Abbott" award, 2003. Office: Manhattan Theatre Club 311 W 43rd St Fl 8 New York NY 10036-6413 Office Phone: 212-399-3000 x 114.

MEADOWS, GWENDOLYN JOANN, retired behavioral disorders educator; b. Nov. 20, 1944; d. Guss Lee and Bennie Jolene Treadaway; children: Terence Lee Bradley, Melissa Ann Bradley Davis. AA, Norman Coll.; BA, Berry Coll.; M in Behavior Disorders, West Ga. Coll.; ednl. splty. degree in mild learning handicaps, Jacksonville State U., 1988; postgrad. in Adminstrn., U. Ala.; EdD in Human Svcs. and Counseling, U. Sarasota. Cert. tchr. Tchr. Pres. Hillhouse Garden Club, United Daus. of The Confederacy; life mem., bd. dirs. Calhoun Hist. Soc.; life mem. The Deep South Garden Clubs of Ga.; organizer Homebound program for Local Sheriff's Office; mem. Calhoun Red Hats Soc., Calhoun First Bapt. Ch.; bd. dirs. Calhoun Beautification Bd., Garden Club Ga., 2003—04. Named one of Ga. Women of Achievement, 1999. Mem.: Calhoun-Gordon County Ret. Educators Assn., VFW (life), Am. Legion Aux. (pres., 1st v.p., 2d v.p., historian, parliamentarian, chaplain, pres. dept. Ga. 2005—06), Kappa Kappa Iota (1st v.p.). Baptist. Avocations: reading, gardening.

MEADOWS, JOYCE KATHERINE, nurse; b. Detroit, Mich., Aug. 12, 1944; d. Jesse O. and Katherine Rita Meadows; 1 child from previous marriage, Katherine Cherine. Diploma LAC USC Sch. Nursing, 1977, Enterostomal Therapy Cert., 1979. RN. RN, cons., educator, Calif., 1968—97; nurse Jerry Pettis Meml. Vets. Hosp., Loma Linda, Calif., 1978—81; educator, specialist, Vis. Nurse Assn., Inland County, Riverside, Calif., 1981—84; educator, specialist Vis. Nurse Assn., Sacramento, 1984—86, Vis. Nurse Assn., Orange County, Tustin, Calif., 1986—90; wound, ostomy specialist, educator Vis. Nurse Assn., Inland County, Riverside, Calif., 1997—. Chair nursing subcom. Dept. of Aging, Sacrament0, Calif., 1991; cons. to FHP model for govt. HMO system, Fountain Valley, Calif., 1990—96; spkr. in field. Contbr. articles to profl. publs. Educator, cons. Ostomy Assn., Riverside, Calif., 1981—84. Recipient Hands and Heart award with commendation, Max Cleland VA Adminstrn., Washington, D.C., 1980. Avocation: candlemaking, writing poetry and stories. Office: Vis Nurse of Inland County PO Box 1649 Riverside CA 92502

MEADOWS, JUDITH ADAMS, law librarian, educator; b. Spartanburg, SC, June 5, 1945; d. Thomas Taylor and Virginia (Dayton) Adams; m. Bruce R. Meadows; children: Beth Ann Blackwood, Ted Adams Meadows. BA, Am. U., 1967; MLS, U. Md., 1979. Law libr. Aspen Sys. Corp., Gaithersburg, Md., 1979-81; dir. Fairfax (Va.) Law Libr., 1981-84, State Law Libr., Helena, Mont., 1984—. Vis. prof. U. Wash., Seattle, 1994; adj. prof. U. Great Falls, Mont., 1989-96; presiding ofcl. Gov.'s Conf. on Libr. Info. Svc., Helena, Mont., 1991; cons. Nat. Ctr. for State Cts., 2000—; mem. Mont. Commn. Continuing Legal Edn., 2006—. Author: (book chpts.) From Yellow Pads to Computers, 1991, Law Librarianship, 1994; contbr. articles to profl. jours. Bd. dirs. Helena Presents, 1986-92, Holter Mus. Art, 1995-2002, Mont. Supreme Ct. Commn. on Tech., Mont. Equal Justice Task Force, 2001-; bd. dirs. Helena Edn. Found., v.p., 2003, pres. 2005-06; chair Mont. Supreme Ct. Commn. on Self-Represented Litigants, 2004—; mem. Mont. Commn. Continuing Legal Edn., 2006—. Recipient Disting. Svc. award State Bar of Mont., 1991, Pro Bono Pub. award, 2002. Mem. Am. Assn. Law Librs. (treas. 1992-95, v.p. 1996—, pres. 1997-98, past pres. 1998—), N.W. Consortium of Law Librs. (pres.), Mont. Libr. Assn. (sec. 1986-88). Office: State Law Libr Mont PO Box 203004 Helena MT 59620-3004

MEADOWS, PATRICIA BLACHLY, curator, civic worker; b. Amarillo, Tex., Nov. 12, 1938; d. William Douglas and Irene Bond Blachly; m. Curtis Washington Meadows, Jr., June 10, 1961; children: Michael Lee, John Morgan. BA in English and History, U. Tex., 1960. Program dir. Ex-Students Assn., Austin, Tex., 1960-61; co-founder, dir. Dallas Visual Art Ctr., 1981-86, curator, 1987-98, bd. dirs., 1981-99, pres. bd. dirs., 1982-85, founder The Collectors, 1988; founder, prin. cons. Art Connections, Dallas, 1996—; sr. v.p. Hall Fin. Group Ltd., 1999—. Exhbn. dir. Tex. bd. Nat. Mus. Women in Arts, Washington, 1986-91; mem. acquisition com. Dallas Mus. Art, 1988-92; chmn. adv. bd. Oaks Bank and Trust, 1993-96; juror numerous exhibits, Dallas and Tex.; spkr. on arts subjects; cons. city, state and nat. project concerning arts; chmn. bd. dirs. State-Thomas TIF Zone #1, 1994-99, bd. dirs. 1989-99. Author: (art catalogues) Critic's Choice, 1983-97, Texas Women, 1989-90, Texas: reflections, rituals, 1991; organizer many exhbns. including Presenting Nine, D-Art Visual Art Ctr., 1984, Mosaics, 1991-97, Senses Beyond Sight, 1992-93. Bd. dirs. Mid-Am. Arts Alliance, Kansas City, Mo., 1989-93, Tex. Bd. Commerce, Austin, 1991-93, Women's Issues Network, Dallas, 1994-96; bd. dirs. Dallas Summit, 1989-95, pres., 1993-94, mem. 1988—; mem. Charter 100, 1993—, Dallas Assembly, 1993—, Leadership Tex., 1987; co-founder, mem. steering com. Emergency Artists Support League, Dallas, 1992-99; mem. originating task force Dallas Coalition for Arts, 1984; also others. Recipient Dedication to Arts award Tex. Fine Arts Assn., 1984, Assn. Artists and Craftsmen, 1984, Southwestern Watercolor Soc., 1985, Flora award Dallas Civic Garden Ctr., 1987, James K. Wilson award TACA, 1988, Maura award Women's Ctr. Dallas, 1991, Disting. Woman award Northwood U., 1993, Excellence in the Arts award Dallas Hist. Soc., 1993, Legend award Dallas Visual Art Ctr., 1996. Mem. Tex. Assn. Mus., Arts Dist. Mgmt. Assn. (bd. dirs., exec. com. 1984-92, Artists and Craftsmen Assn. (pres. bd. dirs. 1982-83), Dallas Art Dealer's Assn. (pres. 1997-99). Presbyterian. Office: Hall Financial Group 6801 Gaylord Pkwy Ste 100 Frisco TX 75034-8545 Business E-Mail: pmeadows@hallfinancial.com.

MEADOWS, VICKERS B., federal agency administrator; Grad., Green Mountain Coll. Procuremen, dir. presdl. gifts The White House, Washington, 1985—87, spl. asst. to the v.p. for adminstrn., 1987—89; dep. dir., dir. exec. svc. US Dept. Transp., Washington, 1989—93; dir. adminstrn. to Gov. Bush State of Tex., 1995—2000; spl. asst. to Pres., dir. White House Mgmt. The White House, Washington, 2001, dir. adminstrn. Bush-Cheney Transition; asst. sec. for adminstrn. office, CIO, chief human capital officer US Dept. Housing & Urban Devel., Washington, 2002—04; chief adminstrv. officer, US Patent & Trademark Office US Dept. Commerce, Washington, 2005—. Republican. Office: US Patent & Trademark Office 2121 Crystal Dr Arlington VA 22202

MEADS, MINDY, merchandising and design executive; BS, U. Ill. With Denver Dry Goods, 1974—78; sr. v.p., v.p., merchandising administr., v.p., store mgr., jeans collection buyer R.H. Macy and Company Inc., 1978—89; operating exec. The Limited, 1989—90; v.p., gen. merchandising mgr. Lands End, 1991—94, sr. v.p. merchandising and design, 1994—96; sr. v.p., gen. merchandising mgr., merchandising design planning and allocation Gymboree Corp., 1996—98; exec. v.p. merchandising and design Lands End, 1998—2003; gen. mgr. apparel Sears Roebuck and Co., 2003—04, exec. v.p., 2003—; pres. Lands End, 2003—, CEO, 2004—. Office: Sears Roebuck and Co 3333 Beverly Rd Hoffman Estates IL 60179

MEAGHER, DEIRDRA M., lawyer; b. N.Y.C., Aug. 15, 1949; d. Pearse P. and Katherine M. Meagher. BA, Mercy Coll., Dobbs Ferry, N.Y., 1970; MS, Mich. State U., East Lansing, 1972; JD, Seton Hall U. Sch. of Law, Newark, 1992. Bar: N.J. 1994, D.C. 1994, U.S. Patent and Trademark Office 2000. Systems engr. EDS Corp., Plano, Tex., 1973—77; tech. assoc. Merck & Co., Inc., Rahway, NJ, 1977—81; info. tech. cons. Fords, NJ, 1981—85; project leader Hartz Mountain Corp., Secaucus, NJ, 1985—88; summer law assoc. Friedman Siegelbaum, Roseland, NJ, 1991—91; assoc., law clk. Selitto, Behr & Kim, Metuchen, NJ, 1991—95; assoc. Glynn & Assocs., P.C., Flemington, NJ, 1995—2004, GlynnTech, Inc., Flemington, NJ, 2005—. Author: Vendor's Guide to Computer Contracting. Chair cmty. affairs commn. Metuchen Diocesan Coun. of Cath. Women, Metuchen, NJ, 1983—89; greeter Interfaith Hospitality Network, Somerset County, NJ, 1998—2000; recorder Rec. for the Blind and Dyslexic, Princeton, NJ, 1999—2000; com. mem. Condominium Assn. Bldg. and Grounds Com., Flemington, NJ, 2001—04; mem. Ladies Ancient Order of Hibernians, Somerville, NJ, 2001—04; del. No. N.J. Square Dance Assn., 2003—; Confraternity of Christian Doctrine tchr. St. James Ch., Woodbridge, NJ, 1986—87; parish pastoral coun. rep., sec. St. Joseph Ch., East Millstone, NJ, 1995—98; lector, visitor to homebound, and rosary altar soc. mem. St. Magdalen de Pazzi Ch., Flemington, NJ, 2000—04. Roman Catholic. Achievements include developed system specifications and workflows on numerous computer systems including manufacturing, telephony, pharmaceutical and medical systems; software, electrical, mechanical, and biochemical arts; drafted and prosecuted trademark applications; developed software, licensing, employment and confidentiality agreements. Avocations: swimming, folk dancing, tennis. Home and Office: 4 Colts Ln Flemington NJ 08822 Personal E-mail: drdmeag@netzero.com.

MEAL, LARIE, chemistry professor, researcher, consultant; b. Cin., June 15, 1939; d. George Lawrence Meal and Dorothy Louise (Heileman) Fitzpatrick. BS in Chemistry, U. Cin., 1961, PhD, 1966. Rsch. chemist U.S. Indsl. Chems., Cin., 1966-67; instr. chemistry U. Cin., 1968-69, asst. prof., 1969-75, assoc. prof., 1975-90, prof., 1990—, rschr., 1980—. Cons. in field. Contbr. articles to profl. jours. Mem. AAAS, N.Y. Acad. Scis., Am. Chem. Soc., NOW, Planned Parenthood, Iota Sigma Pi. Democrat. Avocation: gardening. Home: 2231 Slane Ave Norwood OH 45212-3615 Office: U Cin 2220 Victory Pky Cincinnati OH 45206-2822 Office Phone: 513-556-4364. Business E-Mail: meall@uc.edu.

MEANY, ANGELINA MARIE, dancer, educator; b. Santa Monica, Calif., Nov. 23, 1966; d. John Oliver and Rose Marie Meany. BA, Loyola Marymount U., L.A., 1990. Instr. ballet Young Stars Gym and Arts, L.A., 1992—95; modern dancer and tchr. Donna Sternberg and Dancers, Santa Monica, 1997—2002; freelance instr./coach ballet L.A., 1998—; instr. ballet Zeal Studios, L.A., 2001—04; faculty tchr. ballet Pasadena City Coll., Calif., 2004—05, faculty tchr. contemporary dance; pvt. instr. Collenette Sch. Ballet, San Marino, Calif., 2004—; faculty tchr. ballet Santa Monica Coll., 1998—, faculty tchr. modern dance, 2004. Guest lectr. Calif. Educators' Dance and Movement Workshop, Irvine; adjudicator Santa Monica Coll., 2000—; guest instr. Westside Acad. Ballet, Santa Monica, 2001. Dancer (ensemble ballet piece) Shubertiad, Les Coquettes, (ensemble contemporary dance piece) The 4 Adagios. Mem.: Faculty Assn. Calif. Cmty. Colls. Avocations: travel, oenology, writing. Office: Santa Monica College 1900 Pico Blvd Santa Monica CA 90405 Business E-Mail: meany_angelina@smc.edu.

MEARA, ANNE, actress, playwright, writer; b. Bklyn., Sept. 20; d. Edward Joseph and Mary (Dempsey) M.; m. Gerald Stiller, Sept. 14, 1954; children: Amy, Benjamin. Student, Herbert Berghoff Studio, 1953-54. Apprentice in summer stock, Southold, L.I. and Woodstock, N.Y., 1950-53; off-Broadway appearances include A Month in the Country, 1954, Maedchen in Uniform, 1955 (Show Bus. off-Broadway award), Ulysses in Nightown, 1958, The House of Blue Leaves, 1970, Bosoms and Neglect, 1986, After-Play, 1996; Shakespeare Co., Two Gentlemen of Verona, Ctrl. Park, N.Y.C., 1957, Romeo and Juliet, 1988; Broadway plays: Spookhouse, 1982, Eastern Standard, 1989, Anna Christie, 1993 (Tony nomination Best Supporting Actress); film appearances include The Out-of-Towners, 1968, Lovers and Other Strangers, 1969, The Boys From Brazil, 1978, Fame, 1979, Nasty Habits (with husband Jerry Stiller), 1976, An Open Window, 1990, Mia, 1990, Awakenings, 1991, Reality Bites, 1994, Daytrippers, 1997, The Fish in the Bathtub, 1998, Southie, 1999, The Independent, 2001, Like Mike, 2002, comedy act, 1963—;

appearances Happy Medium and Medium Rare, Chgo., 1960-61, Village Gate, Phase Two and Blue Angel, N.Y.C., 1963, The Establishment, London, 1963, QE II, 1990; syndicated TV series Take Five with Stiller and Meara, 1977-78; numerous appearances on TV game and talk shows, also spls. and variety shows; rec. numerous commls. for TV and radio (co-recipient Voice of Imagery award Advt. Bur. N.Y.); star TV series Kate McShane, 1975, Archie Bunker's Place, 1979, Alf, 1986-88; other TV appearances The Sunset Gang, 1990, Avenue Z Afternoon, 1991, Murphy Brown, 1994, Homicide, 1996 (Emmy nomination), Will and Grace, 2002, Sex in the City, 2002-04, The King of Queens, 2003-05, Good Morning Miami, 2003; (TV movie) Jitters, 1997, All My Children, 1994-99, (TV movie) What Makes a Family, 2001; writer, actress TV movie The Other Woman, 1983 (co-recipient Writer's Guild Outstanding Achievement award 1983), Alf, To Make Up to Break Up, The Stiller and Meara pilot; author, actor (play) After-Play, 1996; author (play) Down the Garden Paths, 2000; video host (with Jerry Stiller) So You Want to Be an Actor? Recipient Outer Critic's Cir. Playwriting award for After-Play, 1995, 4th ann. Alan King award in Jewish Humor, 2003, Productive Aging award Jewish Coun. Aging, 2004, Thalia award (w/ Jerry Stiller) Humbert Coll. Toronto.

MEARES, TRACEY LOUISE, law educator; b. 1967; BS in Gen. Engring., U. Ill., Urbana-Champaign, 1988; JD cum laude, U. Chgo., 1991. Bar: Ill. 1991. Law clk. to Judge Harlington Wood, Jr. US Ct. Appeals 7th Cir., 1991—92; trial atty. antitrust divsn. US Dept. Justice, 1992—93; asst. prof. law U. Chgo. Law Sch., 1994—99, prof., 1999—, dir. Ctr. for Studies in Criminal Justice, 2000—. Vis. asst. prof. law U. Chgo. Law Sch., 1993—94; vis. prof. law U. Mich. Law Sch., 1998; rsch. fellow Am. Bar Found. & U. Chgo., 1999—. Co-author (with D. Kahan): Urgent Times: Policing and Rights in Inner City Communities, 1999. Mem.: ABA, Law and Soc. Assn., Chgo. Coun. Lawyers, Ill. Bar Assn. Office: U Chgo Law Sch 1111 E 60th St Chicago IL 60637 Office Phone: 773-702-9582. E-mail: tlmeares@midway.uchicago.edu.*

MEARS, JOYCE LUND, educational counselor; b. Davenport, Iowa, Aug. 20, 1937; d. Hilding Eugene and Thelma (Peitscher) Lund; m. Walter R. Mears, Aug. 4, 1963 (div. Dec. 1983); children: Stephanie Joy, Susan Marie. BFA, Drake U., 1960; postgrad., U. Va., 1984; MS in Edn., Va. Poly. Inst. and State U., 1992. Cert. tchr., Iowa. Travel coord. Kennedy Summer White House, Hyannis, Mass., 1961; sec. Bank Am., Los Angeles, 1962; quality control Census Bur., Dept. Commerce, L.A., No. Va., 1980; owner, mgr. cons. firm J.L. Mears, Inc., McLean, Va., 1981-86; ednl. counselor Fairfax County Adult and Cmty. Edn., Fairfax, Va., 1992—. Patentee tech cart. Bd. dirs. Deborah's Pl., Washington, 1982, Fairfax County (Va.) PTA, 1978, 84; coun. mem. Zion Luth. Ch., Princeton, Iowa. Grantee Ctr. for Innovative Tech., 1988. Mem. MIT Enterprise Forum Washington/Balt., Met. Area Career/Life Planning Network (steering com.), Iowa Bar Found., La Claire Iowa C. of C., Mortar Bd., Kappa Kappa Gamma. Lutheran. Home: 23580 Great River Rd Le Claire IA 52753-9142

MEBANE, BARBARA MARGOT, artistic director, choreographer; b. Sylacauga, Ala., July 21, 1947; d. Audrey Dixon and Mary Ellen (Yaikow) Baxley; m. James Lewis Mebane, Dec. 31, 1971; 1 child, Cieson Brooke. Grad., Brookhaven Coll., Dallas. Line performer J. Taylor Dance Co., Miami, Fla., 1964-65; sales mgr. Dixie Readers Svc., Jackson, Miss., 1965-67; regional sales mgr. Robertson Products Co., Texarkana, Tex., 1967-75; owner, pres. Telco Sales, Svc. and Supply, Dallas, 1976-90; dir. The Dance Factory performing co., Lewisville, Tex.; owner, artistic dir. Dancers Workshop Studios, Inc., Lewisville; founder DWSI, a 501c3 corp. working with youth at risk and financially challenged families. Mgr., choreographer music videos for pay/cable TV, 1985—; prodr. theatrical/musical shows to profl. theatre, coll. dists. and high schs; pub. spkr. in field of positive thinking for women; dir. dancers workshop studies, 1993—. Author: Paper on Positive Thinking, 1983. Sponsor Cancer Rsch. Ctr., Dallas, Flower Mound Bus. Womens Group; hon. chmn. Rep. State Com., Tex.; founder arts devel. and outreach Dancers Workshop Studies Inc. for underpriveledged children. Named Bus. Woman of the Yr., Gov. Anne Richards, Tex., 1994. Mem. Internat. Register of Profiles Cambridge, Eng., Female and Minority Owned Bus. League, PDTA (Dallas Dance Coun.), Old Town Bus. Assn. (Pres.'s adv. com. 2003-04). Avocations: working with children, teaching dance, writing. Office: Dancers Workshop 705 S Mill Lewisville TX 75057

MEBANE, JULIE S., lawyer; b. San Antonio, Mar. 13, 1957; d. John Cummins and Mildred (Hill) Mebane; m. Kenneth Jerome Stipanov, Jan. 21, 1984; children: Thomas Kenneth Stipanov, Kristen Hill Stipanov. BA in Polit. Sci., UCLA, 1978, JD, 1981. Bar: Calif. 1981, U.S. Dist. Ct. (so. dist.) Calif. 1981. Assoc. Gray, Cary, Ames & Frye, San Diego, 1981-85, Sheppard, Mullin, Richter & Hampton, San Diego, 1986-90; ptnr. Scalone, Stipanov, Yaffa & Mebane, San Diego, 1990-94, Stipanov & Mebane, San Diego, 1994—2004, Duane Morris LLP, San Diego, 2005—. Panelist Calif. Continuing Edn. Bar, 2000—01. Bd. dirs. Episcopal Diocese San Diego, 1992—95, Francis Parker Sch., 2003—. Mem.: San Diego Lawyers Club, San Diego County Bar Assn., ABA, Nat. Assn. Women Bus. Owners (bd. dirs. San Diego chpt. 1996—97), UCLA Alumni Assn. (gen. counsel, bd. dirs. 1992—96), Phi Beta Kappa, Kappa Alpha Theta. Avocations: sports, travel. Office: Duane Morris LLP 101 W Broadway Ste 900 San Diego CA 92101-3544 Office Phone: 619-744-2211. E-mail: jmebane@duanemorris.com.

MECHANECK, RUTH SARA, clinical psychologist; b. N.Y.C., Feb. 4, 1941; d. Isidore and Anna (Nadler) M.; 1 child, Christopher. BA, Brandeis U., 1961; MA, U. Minn., 1963; PhD, CUNY, 1976. Cert. psychologist, N.Y. Jr. rsch. assoc. Inst. Devel. Studies, N.Y.C., 1963—65; rsch. assoc. William Alanson White Inst., 1965—68; instr. Briarcliff Coll., Briarcliff Manor, 1975—76; staff psychologist Met. Ctr. Mental Health, N.Y.C., 1979—81; pvt. practice, 1981—; sch. psychologist Solomon Schechter Sch. Manhattan, 2005—. Project dir. rsch. Single Mothers by Choice, N.Y., 1983-87; cons. Childrens Def. Fund, N.Y., 1975-77, child abuse task force N.Y. State Assembly, 1975-77; adj. asst. prof. psychology Hunter Coll., N.Y.C., 1991. Author: (with others) Single Mothers, 1987. NICHD fellow CUNY, 1969-71. Mem. APA, N.Y. State Psychol. Assn., Nat. Register of Health Svc. Providers in Psychology, Assn. Advancement Psychology. Avocations: piano, skiing, tennis, creative writing. Home and Office: 340 E 93rd St Apt 22M New York NY 10128-5555

MECHLING, BRENDA L., voice educator, director; d. N. Dale and Averial Williams; m. George J. Mechling, Sept. 5, 1978; children: Paige, Preston, Parish, Darrin, Jason. Student, U. Okla., 1975, Northwestern Okla. State U., 1976; AA, Rose State Coll., 1994; MusB in Edn., U. Ctrl. Okla., 1996. Sec. health sci. divsn. Rose State Coll., Midwest City, Okla., 1981—85; owner, dir. Voice Plus Pvt. Studio, Midwest City, 1986—97; youth choir dir., nursery coord. First Presbyn. Ch., Midwest City, 1990—95; vocal music dir. Carl Albert Jr. HS, Midwest City, 1996—2004, Carl Albert HS, 2004—. Mem. curriculum com. Mid-Del Schs., Midwest City, 2004—; mem. adv. bd. Okla. Ctr. Fine Arts Edn., Edmond, 2004—05; mem. student bd. Chopin Soc., Edmond, 1994—96. Promoter/advocate Nat. Anthem Project, Okla., 2005. Named to Mixed Chorus Honor Choir, Okla. Music Educator Assn., 2000, Women's Honor Choir, 2003, Honor Show Choir, Okla. Choir Dir. Assn., 2002. Mem.: Okla. Choral Dir. Assn., Okla. Music Educator Assn., Am. Choral Dir. Assn., Nat. Assn. Music Edn. Democrat. Presbyterian. Achievements include choir selected for state honors; voice students named to state, regional and national honor choirs. Avocations: singing, dance, theater, piano, music. Office: Carl Albert HS 2009 S Post Rd Midwest City OK 73130 Personal E-mail: bmechling@cox.net.

MECK, J. KAREN, retired elementary school educator; b. Elmira, N.Y., Jan. 26, 1945; d. Edward John Meck and Mary Aurelia Ryan. BS English, Nazareth Coll., Rochester, N.Y., 1970; MS Edn., Nazareth Coll., 1976. Tchr. grade 1 St. Thomas the Apostle Sch., Irondequoit, NY, 1967—68, St. Mary's Sch., Corning, NY, 1968—70; tchr. spl. edn. Holy Childhood Sch., Rochester, 1971—73; tchr. reading grade 6 Rogers Mid. Sch., Irondequoit, 1974; tchr. reading grade 2 and 4, jr. high, h.s. Honeoye Ctrl. Sch., NY, 1975—99; ret., 1999. Set up reading program grade 1 St. Mary's Sch., Corning, 1968—69; set up reading program jr. high Honeoye Ctrl. Sch., 1977—78. Insp. voting Dem. Nat. Com., Mendon, NY, 1999, 2001. Elem. Libr. grant, N.Y. State Edn. Dept., Honeoye, 1976—77. Mem.: Honeoye United Ret. Tchrs., N.Y. State United Tchrs. Roman Catholic. Avocations: travel, gardening, reading, bicycling, swimming. Home: 77 Huxley Way Fairport NY 14450

MECKES, KIMBERLY JO, music educator; b. Stroudsburg, Pa., Apr. 12, 1970; BS in Music Edn., Ind. U. Pa., 1992. Band dir. New Hope Solebury Sch. Dist., Pocono Mountain Sch. Dist., Swiftwater, Pa.; dir. 5th grade band East Windsor Sch. Dist., 2005—06; tchr. Bradley Beach Sch. Dist., NJ, 2006—. Recipient Gift Of Time award. Mem.: Music Educators Nat. Conf. (pres. 1991—92), Nat. Flute Assn. (life), Delta Omicron (life; pres. 1992—92). Home: 43 Long Rd Freehold NJ 07728 Personal E-mail: kmeckes@optonline.net.

MEDAGLIA, ELIZABETH ELLEN, small business owner; b. Boston, Jan. 22, 1970; d. Anthony Joseph Medaglia, Jr. and Catherine Louise (Nardelli) Medaglia. BA in Sociology, Coll. of the Holy Cross, 1991; postgrad., Cornell U., 1995—97; cert. in therapeutic massage and hydrotherapy, Finger Lakes Sch. Massage, 1999; M in Acupuncture, Acad. for Five Element Acupuncture, 2003. Lic. massage therapist N.Y., acupuncturist Mass., diplomate acupuncture (NCCAOM), cert. MT educator Finger Lakes Sch. Massage, 2nd degree Reiki, clean needle technique Council Coll. Acupuncture and Oriental, Pan Gu Shengong instr. Litig. legal asst. Ropes & Gray, Boston, 1991—95; founder, pres. DancingPhoenix LLC, Hingham, Mass., 2003—. Fundraiser, cmty. vol. City Year, Mass., 1992—95; intake test vol. Literacy Vol. Am., Mass., 1994—95; rape crisis counselor, adv. Boston Area Rape Crisis Ctr., 1995. Mem.: Am. Acupuncture Coun., Ctr. for Balance, Theosophical Soc. Boston, Acupuncture and Oriental Medicine Alliance, South Shore C. of C., Better Bus. Bur. Office Phone: 617-869-6371.

MEDAGLIA, MARY-ELIZABETH, lawyer; b. Suffern, N.Y., Oct. 13, 1947; d. Joseph Mario and Edith Elizabeth (Price) Medaglia. BA, Sweet Briar Coll., 1969; JD, U. Va., 1972. Bar: Va. 1972, D.C. 1974, U.S. Ct. Appeals (D.C. cir.) 1974, U.S. Supreme Ct. 1980, U.S. Ct. Appeals (4th, 5th, 9th and 11th cirs.) 1981, U.S. Ct. Appeals (10th cir.) 1982, Md. 1990, U.S. Ct. Appeals (2d cir.) 1998. Law clk. to judge D.C. Ct. Appeals, Washington, 1972-74; asst. atty. U.S. Atty.'s Office, Washington, 1974-79; deputy solicitor Fed. Labor Relations Authority, Washington, 1979-82, acting solicitor, 1982; assoc. Jackson & Campbell P.C., Washington, 1982-84, ptnr., 1984—. Sec. D.C. Bar, 1983—84, bd. govs., 1984—87. Fellow Am. Bar Found.; mem. ABA (chmn. TIPS com. on ins. coverage litigation 1989-91, ho. of dels. 1981-83), D.C. Bar Assn. (bd. dirs. 1980-83, chmn. young lawyers sect. 1980-81), Women's Bar Assn. D.C. (pres. 1982-83), Charles Fahy Am. Inn of Ct. (pres. 1990-92), Fedn. Def. and Corp. Counsel, The Barristrs (pres. 2004-05), Lawyers' Club Washington, Phi Beta Kappa. Office: Jackson & Campbell PC South Tower 1120 20th St NW Ste 300S Washington DC 20036-3437 Office Phone: 202-457-1612. Business E-Mail: LMedaglia@jackscamp.com.

MEDEIROS, DONNA, assistant principal; BS, Bridgewater State Coll., 1986, MS, 2001, CAGS summa cum laude, 2005. Tchr. Sandwich Pub. Sch., Forestdale, Mass., 1986—; asst. prin. Harwich Mid. Sch., Mass. Pres. Hyannis Bridgewater (Mass.) P.E. Alumni, 1998—. Recipient Paul Wright Leadership award, Bridgewater State Coll., 2005. Office: 204 Sisson Rd Harwich MA 02645-2617 Office Phone: 508-430-7212. Business E-Mail: dmedeiros@sandwich.k12.ma.us.

MEDEIROS, JENNIFER LYNN, school psychologist, consultant; b. New Bedford, Mass., Feb. 5, 1974; d. Antone and Joan Elaine Medeiros. BA in Psychology, Bridgewater State Coll., 1995; MEd, U. Mass., Boston, 2004. Tchr. I.H. Schwartz Children's Rehab. Ctr., New Bedford, Mass., 1995—97; children's intensive support services mgr. TILL, Inc., Dedham, Mass., 1997—2001; therapeutic mentor Family Intervention Network, Wakefield, Mass., 1999—2002; cons. Charles River Assn. for Retarded Citizens, Needham, Mass., 2001—; rsch. asst. Ctr. for Social Devel. and Edn., Boston, 2001—04; sch. psychologist Boston Pub. Schools, 2004—. Student rep. Ctr. for Exceptional Children Divsn. of Rsch., Arlington, Va., 2003—04. Mem.: Coun. for Exceptional Children (student rep.divsn. of rsch. 2003—04), Mass. Assn. of Sch. Psychologists, Nat. Assn. Sch. Psychologists. Home: 90A Dexter Ave Watertown MA 02472 Office: Boston Pub Sch 443 Warren St Dorchester MA 02121 Office Phone: 617-635-9676. Personal E-mail: jen_medeiros@yahoo.com.

MEDEL, REBECCA ROSALIE, artist; b. Denver, Mar. 26, 1947; d. Natividad and Josefa (Apodaca) Medel. BFA, Ariz. State U., 1970; MFA, UCLA, 1982. Asst. prof. fibers dept. head Tenn. Technol. U., Smithville, 1983-88; lectr. Dept. of Design, UCLA, 1989-91; studio artist, 1991—; prof. Tyler Sch. Art Temple U., 1995—. Lectr. N.C. State U., Raleigh, San Diego State U., SUNY, Purchase, 1992, Penland Sch. Asheville, N.C., Textile Study Group, N.Y.C., Calif. Coll. of Arts & Crafts, Oakland, Calif., San Jose State U., Am. Ctr., Kyoto, Japan, City Ctr., Sapporo, Japan, 1986; vis. artist U. N.D., 1985. One-woman shows include Thirteen Moons Gallery, Santa Fe, 2003, 05, Brown Grotta Gallery, Wilton, Conn., 1996, Neuberger Mus. of Art, Purchase, N.Y., 1992-93, Bellas Artes Gallery, N.Y.C., 1991, N.D. Mus. Art, Grand Forks, 1985, Maya Behn Galerie, Zurich, 1984, UCLA, 1982, Thirteen Moons Gallery, Santa Fe, 2003, 05; group shows include Bellas Artes Gallery, Santa Fe, N.Mex., 1992, N.C. State U. Gallery, 1992, Portland Art Mus., 1995, Madison (Wis.) Art Ctr., 1995, Santa Monica (Calif.) Art Gallery, 1995, Maya Behn Gallerie, 1991, Mus. Van Bommel-Van Dam, Venlo, Netherlands, 1990, Palo Alto Cultural Ctr., 1990, Barbican Ctr. Concourse Gallery, London, 1998, Montclair (N.J.) State U. Gallery, 1998, Art Inst. Chgo., 1999, Yokohama (Japan) Mus. Art, 1999, Biennial 2000, Del. Art Mus., Wilmington, L.A. Mus. Art, 2000, Soc. Contemporary Crafts, Pitts., 2001, Westport Arts Ctr., Conn., 2003, many others. Recipient bronze medal Triennial of Tapestry, 1985; visual artist fellow Nat. Endowment for Arts, 1986, 88, fellow for emerging visual artists So. Arts Fedn. NEA, 1985; Pew fellow in the arts, 1999, 2003, fellow Pa. Coun. on Arts, 2001, 03; scholar to Arcosanti, Nat. Endowment for Arts, 1986, 88. Home: 2920 Meyer Ave Glenside PA 19038-1920 Office Phone: 215-782-2728. Business E-Mail: rmedel@temple.edu.

MEDERICH, AMY MARIE, social studies educator; b. Des Plaines, Ill., Mar. 14, 1975; d. Paul Mederich and Sharon Collord. BS in History, DePaul U., Chgo., 1997; MS, Roosevelt U., Lake Forest Coll. Social studies tchr. Conant H.S., Hoffman Estates, Ill., 1998—. Cross-country and soccer coach Conant H.S., Hoffman Estates, Afghanistan, 1998—. Active Habitat For Humanity, Santo Domingo, Dominican Republic, 2003.

MEDEROS, CAROLINA LUISA, public policy consultant; b. Rochester, Minn., July 1, 1947; d. Luis O. and Carolina (del Valle) Mederos. BA, Vanderbilt U., 1969; MA, U. Chgo., 1971. Adminstrv. asst. Lt. Gov. of Ill., Chgo., 1972; sr. research assoc. U. Chgo., 1972; project mgr., cons. Urban Dynamics, Inner City Fund and Community Programs Inc., Chgo., 1972-73; legis. asst. to Senate pres. Ill. State Senate, Chgo. and Springfield, 1973-76; program analyst Dept. Transp., Washington, 1976-79, chief, trans. assistance programs div., 1979-81, dir. programs and evaluation, 1981-88, chairwoman, sec.'s safety rev. task force, 1985-88, deputy asst. sec. for safety, 1988-89; cons. Patton Boggs LLP, Washington, 1990—. Recipient award for Meritorious Achievement, Sec. Transp. 1980, Superior Achievement award U.S. Dept. Transp., 1981, Sec.'s Gold Medal award for Outstanding Achievement, 1986, Presdl. Rank award, 1987. Home: 2723 O St NW Washington DC 20007-3128 Office: Patton Boggs LLP 2550 M St NW Washington DC 20037-1350 Office Phone: 202-457-5653. E-mail: cmederos@pattonboggs.com.

MEDICI, ROCHELLE, psychologist, brain researcher; b. Morris, Minn., Dec. 31, 1933; d. Albert and Johanna (Ulvestad) Johnson; m. Michael A. Medici, July 4, 1970 (div. 1995); 1 child, Bianca Cristina. BA magna cum laude, U. Minn., 1954, PhD, 1962. Lic. psychologist, Calif. USPHS postdoctoral fellow U. Minn., Mpls., 1965-67; asst. biologist Calif. Inst. Tech., Pasadena, 1967-68; assoc. prof. anatomy Brain Rsch. Inst., UCLA, 1968-79; pvt. practice neuropsychology, San Marino, Calif., 1980—. Cons. AEC, Washington, 1976, WHO, Washington, 1976, Neurosci. Rsch. Program, Boston, 1977. Rschr. numerous publs.; contbr. articles to profl. jours (Nature, Brain Research, et al) Mem. APA, AAAS, Explorers Club, Phi Beta Kappa. Democrat. Avocations: music, art, travel, politics, literature. Home: 2220 El Molino Pl San Marino CA 91108-2317

MEDIN, JULIA ADELE, mathematics professor, researcher; b. Dayton, Ohio, Jan. 16, 1929; d. Caroline (Feinberg) Levitt; m. A. Louis Medin, Dec. 24, 1950; children: Douglas, David, Thomas, Linda. BS in Maths. Edn., Ohio State U., 1951; MA in Higher Edn., George Washington U., 1977; PhD in Counseling and Math. Edn., Am. U., 1985. Cert. tchr., Fla., Md. Rsch. engr. Sun Oil Co., Marcus Hook, Pa., 1951-53; tchr. maths. Montgomery County Pub. Schs., Rockville, Md., 1973-88; asst. prof. maths. U. Ctrl. Fla., Orlando, 1988-90, sr. ednl. technologist Inst. for Simulation and Tng., 1990-99; sr. assoc. Mgmt. and Ednl. Tech. Assocs., 1999—. Adv. steering com. U.S. Dept. Edn. Title II, Washington, 1985-89; sr. math. educator, rschr. Inst. for Simulation and Tng., Orlando, 1988-90; judge, co-chair GII Nar. Awards; co-acad. advisor I/ITSEC Conf.; condr. nationwide rsch. project on effective use of technology in the classroom; spkr. in field Author: Loc. of Cont. and Test Anxiety of Mar. Math. Studies, 1985, Single Sex Public Schools, Who Needs Them and Why, 2005; co-author: Single Sex Public Schools, 2005; contbg. author: Math for 14 & 17 Yr. Olds, 1987; editor: Simulation and Computer-Based Technology for Education; contbr. articles to profl. jours. Dem. committeewoman Town of Monroeville, Pa., 1962; religious sch. dir. Beth Tikva Religious Sch., Rockville, 1971; cons. Monroeville Mental Health, 1960 Mem. Nat. Coun. Tchrs. Math., Math. Assn. Am. (task force on minorities in math.), Women in Math. in Edn., Nat. Coalition for Tech. in Edn. and Tng., Phi Delta Kappa, Kappa Delta Pi. Home and Office: 11401 Ridge Mist Ter Potomac MD 20854-7002 Personal E-mail: jmedin@comcast.net.

MEDINA, JANIE, not-for-profit fundraiser; b. Bronx, June 24, 1956; d. Luis A. and Aida Diaz Medina. Paralegal Cert., CUNY, 1997, BA, 1988. Adminstrv. asst. Planned Parenthood of N.Y.C., 1979—83; events coord. Mt. Sinai Children's Ctr. Found., N.Y.C., 1984—98; spl. events assoc. Mt. Sinai NYU Health, N.Y.C., 1998—. Cons. Latino Heritage Mo. Mt. Sinai Med. Ctr., 2000—01. Lobbyist, 1981—83; recording sec. Mt. Sinai Children's Ctr. Found., N.Y.C., 1991—98; vol. Mike Bloomberg for Mayor, N.Y.C., 2001, Latino Expo, 2001, Kids of NYU, 2000—01; pres. 615 Pelham Pkwy. North Tenants Assn., 1981—82; vol. Fundraising Day N.Y., 2002, N.Y. Internat. Latino Film Festival, 2002. Mem.: N.Y. Women's Agenda, Coun. of Protocol Execs., Women in Devel., Alpha Sigma Lambda.

MEDINA, KATHRYN BACH, book editor; b. Plainfield, NJ; d. F. Earl and Elizabeth E. Bach; 1 child. BA, Smith Coll.; MA, NYU. With Doubleday Pub. Co., Inc., NYC, 1965-85; exec. editl. dir., sr. v.p. Random House, NYC, 1985—. Assoc. fellow Jonathan Edwards Coll., Yale U., New Haven, 1982—; fellow Bunting Inst., 1994—95; cons., 1995—96, Coun. Fgn. Rels. Editor: books by James Atlas, Peter Benchley, Elizabeth Berg, Amy Bloom, Bill Bradley, Tom Brokaw, Anita Brookner, Ethan Canin, Michael Chabon, Robert Coles, Agnes deMille, E.L. Doctorow, Jane Fonda, Max Frankel, Charles Frazier, Henry Louis Gates, Jr., Carol Gilligan, Mary Gordon, David Halberstam, Kathryn Harrison, John Irving, Tracy Kidder, Wynton Marsalis, Bobbie Ann Mason, Jon Meacham, James A. Michener, Sandra Day O'Connor, Jane Pauley, Anna Quindlen, Nancy Reagan, James Reston, William Safire, Maggie Scarf, Gloria Steinem, Christopher Tilghman, Alice Walker, Daniel Yergin.

MEDINA, SANDRA, social worker, educator; b. Tulsa, Oct. 4, 1947; d. James and Erleen (Austin) Meeks; m. Michael Sellman, 1966 (div. 1979); children: Rhainnie, Morgan; m. Ernest Medina, Aug. 21, 1985; 1 child, Brendyn. Cert., Community Coll. of Denver, 1975; BS summa cum laude, Met. State Coll., Denver, 1981; MSW, U. Denver, 1983, postgrad. Lic. clin. social worker, Colo. Dir. Lafayette (Colo.) Presch./Playtime, 1973-75, Bennett (Colo.) Non-Denominational Presch., 1975-76; intern. in clin. social work Brighton (Colo.) Schs., 1981-82; adminstrv. social work intern Jefferson County (Colo.) Schs., 1982-83; med. social worker Las Animas County Health Dept., Trinidad, Colo., 1985-85; psychiat. social worker Colo. State Hosp., Pueblo, 1985-89; clin. social worker PsychCare, Greeley, 1990-92; counselor high sch. U. Northern Colo. Lab. Sch. Instr. Trinidad State Jr. Coll., 1984-85; field instr. N.Mex. Highlands U., Las Vegas, 1986-87, U. So. Colo., Pueblo, 1988-89; adj. prof. social work U. Denver, 1996-97; asst. prof. social work, practicum coord. Chadron State Coll., 1997-99. Mem. exec. com. Gov.'s Task Force on Child Abuse, Denver, 1985; bd. dirs. Adams County Rep. Advs. for Children Today, Denver, 1978-79; chairperson membership com. Met. Child Protection Coun., Denver, 1982-83. Mem. NASW. Democrat. Presbyterian. E-mail: bestmedfam@netscape.net.

MEDINA-HAMILTON, GINNY EVELYN, music educator; b. Miami, Fla., Oct. 25, 1973; d. Rina Olazabal and Julio Cesar Medina; m. Harvie Douglas Hamilton, III, May 12, 2001; children: Michael Hamilton, Laura Hamilton. BA, U. New Orleans, 1996. Cert. K-12 La., music La. Dir. choirs Vandebilt Cath. H.S., Houma, La., 1996—2005; tchr. talented in music Terrebonne Parish Sch. Dist., Houma, La., 2005—. Adminstrv. dir. South La. Ctr. for Arts, Houma, 2003—04. Musician (guest choral conductor): St. Charles Parish Mid. Sch. Honor Choir; actor: (musical theatre) Le Petit Theatre of Terrebonne Summer Musicals. Sec. St. Matthew's Episcopal Ch. Vestry, Houma, 2002—06. Recipient Teenager of Yr., Elk Lodge, Houma, 1990, Music Dept. Outstanding Sr. Classical Divsn. award, U. New Orleans, 1996, Patriotic award, KC, 1991; scholar Sch., Area, State, Region Good Citizen award, DAR, 1991; Vocal Music scholar, U. New Orleans, 1991—95. Mem.: Music Educators Nat. Conf., Am. Choral Dirs. Assn. (pres., sec. dist. VII 1998—2006). Episcopalian.

MEDLER, MARY ANN L., federal judge; JD, St. Louis U., 1983. Atty. Thompson Coburn, St. Louis, 1983-85; asst. cir. atty. Office of Cir. Atty. of City of St. Louis, 1985-92; atty. Union Pacific R.R., St. Louis, 1992-93; magistrate judge U.S. Dist. Ct. (ea. dist.) Mo., St. Louis. Office: 111 S 10th St Rm 13S Saint Louis MO 63102 Office Phone: 314-244-7490. Business E-Mail: Mary_Ann_Medler@moed.uscourts.gov.

MEDLOCK, ANN, not-for-profit developer, writer; b. Portsmouth, Va., May 6, 1933; d. Frank Wesley and Olive Edna (Litz) Medlock; m. Thomas Proctor Crawford, Mar. 5, 1955 (div.); 1 child, Philip Courtney; m. John Peasley Miraglia, June 22, 1966 (div.); children: Cynthia Medlock, David Medlock; m. John A. Graham, June 13, 1982. BA magna cum laude, U. Md., 1964. Free-lance writer, N.Y.C., Princeton (N.J.) and Saigon, Republic of Vietnam, 1959-65; editor Vietnam Presse, Saigon, 1959-61, Macmillan Pub. Inc., N.Y.C., 1966-69; founder Medlock & Co. Pub. Rels., 1972-82; speechwriter the Aga Khan, N.Y.C., 1979-80; editor-in-chief Children's Express, N.Y.C., 1978-79; founder, pres. The Giraffe Project, N.Y.C. and Whidbey Island, Wash., 1983—. Judge Creative Altruism Awards, Sausalito, Calif., 1988-92, Eddie Bauer Heroes for the Earth Award, 1990-93. Author: Arias, Riffs and Whispers, 2003; editor: The Giraffe Gazette, 1983-92. Mem. planning bd. City of Langley, Wash., 1986-88; co-founder Citizens for Sensible Devel., Whidbey Island, 1988; mem. bd. advisors Cmty. Action Network, 1986-94, Windstar Found., Snowmass, Colo., 1984-92, U.S.-Soviet Ptnrs. Project, Seattle, 1989-92; bd. dirs. Hedgebrook Writers' Colony, 1994-1997, Context Inst., 1996-1998. Recipient Pub. Svc. award Am. Values, 1989, 1st Pl. award Wash. Press Assn., 1991, Temple award for Creative Altruism, Noetics Inst., 1996, Nat. Caring award, Caring Inst., 1998. Avocations: painting, designing. Office: The Giraffe Project 197 Second St PO Box 759 Langley WA 98260-0759

MEDOWS, RHONDA M., state agency administrator, public health service officer; married; 3 children. BS, Cornell Univ.; MD, Morehouse Sch. Med., Atlanta. Cert. family medicine. Residency Univ. Hosp., Stony Brook, NY; physician Kaiser Permanente, Atlanta, 1989—93; private practice Mayo Clinic, Jacksonville, Fla., 1993—2000; med. dir. Blue Cross Blue Shield Fla., Jacksonville, 2000—01; sec. Fla. Agy. Health Care Adminstrn., 2001—04; chief med. officer Centers for Medicare & Medicaid Svc. Region IV, Atlanta, 2004—05; commr. Ga. Dept. Cmty. Health, Atlanta, 2005—. Instr. Univ. Fla., Fla. State Univ. Mem.: Am. Acad. Family Physicians, Nat. Med. Assn., Am. Coll. Physician Executives, Fla. Med. Assn., Fla. Acad. Family physicians, Nat. Assn. Managed Care Physicians. Office: Dept Cmty Health 40th Fl 2 Peachtree St NW Atlanta GA 30303

MEDVECKY, PATRICIA, retired elementary school educator; b. N.Y.C., Feb. 2, 1936; d. Patrick and Katherine Conneally; m. Thomas E. Medvecky, Aug. 25, 1967; 1 child, Thomas E. II. BA, Hunter Coll., 1961, MS in Edn., 1965. Cert. notary pub. Conn. Tchr. elem. sch. Bd. Edn., N.Y.C., 1961—67, Ridgefield, Conn., 1967—73, ret., 1973; real property abstractor Law Office of T.E. Medvecky, Bethel, Conn., 1973—96. Mem.: Hunter Coll. Alumni Assn., Sheffield Art League. Republican. Roman Catholic. Avocations: history, watercolor painting and etching. Home: PO Box 23 99 Washinee Heights Rd Taconic CT 06079 Personal E-mail: oldpatsy@yahoo.com.

MEDVEDOW, JILL, museum director; BA, Colgate U., 1976; M of Art History, Inst. Fine Arts N.Y., 1978. With Met. Mus. Art, N.Y.C., Franklin Furnace; founder Contemporary Art Ctr., Seattle; program mgr. New Eng. Found. Arts, Boston; dep. dir. contemporary art Isabella Stewart Gardner Mus., Boston, 1991-97; dir. Inst. Contemporary Art, Boston, 1998—. Founder Vita Brevis. Office: Inst Contemporary Art 955 Boylston St Boston MA 02115-3194 E-mail: info@icaboston.org.

MEDVIDOVICH, SUZANNE F., human resources specialist; Letter carrier U.S. Postal Svc., New Cumberland, Pa., 1974—99, v.p. area ops. Midwest area, 1999—2001, sr. v.p. human resources Washington, 2001—. Office: US Postal Svc 475 Lenfant Plz SW Washington DC 20260-0010 Office Phone: 202-268-2500. Office Fax: 202-268-4860.

MEDWICK, DEBRA LOU, special education services professional; b. Louisville, Ky., June 23, 1953; d. Charles Basil and Virginia Isabelle Graff; m. Lee Noel Medwick, May 12, 1973; children: Stephanie, Kristen. BS in Soc. Work, U. Ala., 1975; M of Spl. Edn., Ga. State U., 1981. Cert. ednl. specialist Ga. State U., 1997, T-6 Profl. Stds. Commn. Ga., Nat. Bd. Cert. Tchrs. 2004. Spl. edn. tchr. Parkview High Sch., Liburn, Ga., 1978—, spl. edn. dept. chair., 2000—. Student coun. advisor Parkview High Sch., Liburn, 1979—; first responder Gwinnett H. County Fire and Emergency Svcs., Ga., 1998—; tchr., mentor Parkview High Sch., Liburn, 1996—2002. Pres. Gwinnett Ballet Guild, Snellville, Ga., 1999—2002, sec., 1997—99; bd. dirs. Gwinnett Ballet, 1999—2002. Recipient Torchlighter award, Camp Fire Girls, 1993. Mem.: Gwinnett Ballet Guild, Coun. for Exception Children, Pi Lambda Theta. Avocations: swimming, reading, art.

MEE, MAUREEN ADELE See DOZE, MAUREEN

MEED, RITA GOLDWASSER, clinical psychologist; b. Lodz, Poland, Jan. 27, 1951; d. Israel and Tauba (Zylberman) Goldwasser; m. Steven David Meed, Aug. 19, 1973; children: Jessica Tsesha, Chava Leah, Jonathan Lev. BA, U. Chgo., 1973; MA, L.I. U., 1977, PhD, 1988; cert., Tng. Inst. Psychotherapies, N.Y.C., 1992. Lic. psychologist, N.Y. Researcher U. Chgo., 1969-73; microbiologist N.Y.C. Pub. Health Lab., 1973-75; psychology intern Wash. U. and Malcolm Bliss Mental Health Ctr., St. Louis, 1977-78; psychologist West End Psychneuro. Svcs., N.Y.C., 1987—; pvt. practice N.Y.C. Columnist: Can This Marriage Be Saved?, 1990, Ladies Home Jour., 1993. Chair, liaison Heschel Sch., N.Y.C., 1989-91; bd. dirs. Roosevelt Jewish Corp., 1988-91; chair bd. dirs. Roosevelt Island Day Nursery, 1995—; exec. com. Am. Friends of Lolomei Hagetaot. Mem. APA, Internat. Network of Children of Holocaust Survivors (chair kinship group St. Louis and N.Y.C. 1975-89). Democrat. Jewish. Avocations: reading, politics, gardening, skiing. Home: 531 Main St New York NY 10044-0105 also: 110 E 59th St New York NY 10022-1304 Office: 150 E 58th St 18th Flr New York NY 10155

MEEHAN, JEAN MARIE ROSS, human resources, occupational health and safety management consultant; b. Chgo., Mar. 16, 1954; d. A. Ronald Gonzalez and Barbara Marx Shipley; m. John J. Meehan, 1993; 1 child, Jenna A.; 1 child from previous marriage, Justin L. Ross. Diploma in Nursing, St. Mary of Nazareth Hosp., Chgo., 1974; BS in Health Arts with high honors, U. St. Francis, 1988; MPA with honors, Roosevelt U., 2000. Cert. occupl. health nurse specialist, cert. pharmacy technician (CPhT); ordained minister Universal Life Ch., 2003; cert. senior professional in human resources. Staff nurse St. Mary of Nazareth Hosp., Chgo., 1973—75; head nurse ambulatory care Edgebrook Med. Diagnostic Ctr., Chgo., 1975—76; occupl. health nurse Williams Electronics, Inc., Chgo., 1976—84; adminstr. safety and benefits Reliable Power Products, Franklin Park, Ill., 1984—90; dir. corp. human resources MacLean-Fogg Co., Mundelein, Ill., 1990—2005, Navitus Health Solutions LLC, Madison, Wis., 2005—. Pres. Auriel Mgmt. Group, LLC, Island Lake, Ill., 1992—, Claim Masters, LLC, 1998—99; adv. bd. dir. Gt. Lakes Health Care Alliance, 1996—97; spkr. in workshops. Poetry included in Visions of Beauty, 1999 (Editor's Choice award 1999), Tides of Memory, 2000, America at the Millennium—The Best Poems and Poets of the 20th Century, 2000. Guest spkr. local schs. and environ. groups, also I.E.P.A. and U.S. E.P.A. workshops; mem. Ill. Pollution Prevention Adv. Coun., Springfield, Ill., 1993-98; mem. Lake County Employer Coun. Bus./Govt. Partnership, 1996-99; faculty Am. Occupl. Health Conf., 2003-04. Recipient Leadership Civic citation United Way Charities of Lake County, 1993, 94. Mem. Am. Assn. Occupl. Health Nurses, Soc. for Human Resources Mgmt., Lake County Violence Intervention and Prevention, Lake County Employer Coun. Avocations: parenting, interior design, reading, art. Office: Auriel Mgmt Group LLC PO Box 86 Wauconda IL 60084 Office Phone: 608-827-7567. Personal E-mail: hrpro@email.com.

MEEHAN, LIL EUPHRASIA THERESE, poet; b. Boston, Nov. 14, 1942; d. George Leo Meehan and Elizabeth Catherine Dalton Meehan; m. Daniel Charles McGrath, Dec. 19, 1964 (div. Aug. 1968); 1 child, Christopher. Prodn. staff U.S. Mint, San Francisco, 1980—85; freelance author, 1985—. Author (song poems): The True American, 1986, The Robe, 2000, Eyes, 2000, Emblem of Your Character, 2000, Peace Be With You, 2000, That's Our Baby Tim, 2000, Ten Years Ago That Day, 2000, So Beautiful and Rare, 2000, Even Though, 2001, Don't Let Go, 2001, Bubbles, 2001, The Best Present, 2001, You Have Arisen, 2001, Heartfelt Love in USA, 2001, Winds of Winter, 2001, Mother of Mercy, 2002, Reflections, 2004, The Root, 2005. With Nat. Guard U.S. Army, 1976. Democrat. Roman Catholic. Avocations: reading, writing, swimming, basketball.

MEEHAN, SANDRA GOTHAM, corporate financial executive, consultant, writer; b. Tokyo, June 9, 1948; d. Fred C. and Evelyn (Dirr) Gotham; m. James P. Jenkins, June 15, 1970 (div.); m. Dayton T. Carr, Dec. 27, 1986 (div. 1989), m. Michael J. Meehan, II, Jan. 16, 1992. Student, Stanford-in-France, Tours, 1968-69; BA, Stanford U., 1970, MA, 1971. Acct. exec. Young & Rubicam Inc., N.Y.C., 1972-78, acct. supr., 1978-80; pres. Gotham Prodns., N.Y.C., 1980-82; v.p., mgmt. supr. Ogilvy & Mather, N.Y.C., 1982-85; v.p. Steuben Glass, N.Y.C., 1985-88; sr. v.p. Siegel & Gale, N.Y.C., 1988-92; prin., mng. ptnr. Gotham Meehan Ptnrs., N.Y.C., 1992—. Sr. v.p., dir. corp. comm. Bionutrics, Inc., 1997-98; cons. Congl. coms., FDA, FTC for exec. program Am. Assn. Advt. Agys., Washington, 1978-80; cons. Ctr. Arctic Studies Sorbonne, Paris, in U.S. and Can., 1980-82; seminar dir. N.Y. chpt. Women in Bus., N.Y.C., 1983-84. Author, editor: TV documentary Inuit! The Universal Cry of the Eskimo People, 1981. Trustee, bd. dirs. Rensselaerville (N.Y.) Inst.; exec. com., bd. dirs. Checkerboard Film Found.; NYC Mayor's rep. to bd. dirs. Bot. Gardens; bd. dirs. Paris Rev. Mag., The Accompanied Literary Soc., NYC, Agora Found. Home: 220 E 73rd St New York NY 10021-4319 Office: Gotham Meehan Ptnrs 220 E 73rd St Ste 5G New York NY 10021-4319 Office Phone: 212-628-6810. Office Fax: 212-628-6747. Personal E-mail: gmp7777@aol.com.

MEEK, AMY GERTRUDE, retired elementary school educator; b. Frostburg, Md., Jan. 3, 1928; d. Arthur Stewart and Amy Laura (Brain) M. BS, Frostburg State U., 1950; MEd, U. Md., 1956; postgrad., Columbia U., 1964, Am. U., 1968-70. Cert. tchr., Md. Tchr. elem. sch. Prince Georges County Schs., Bradbury Heights, Md., 1950-51, Allegany County Schs., Cumberland, Md., 1951-60, Frostburg, 1960-84; now ret. Author (with others): Stir Into Flame, 1991; contbr. articles to profl. jours. Mem. Frostburg Hosp. Aux., 1987-91; bd. dirs. Frostburg Hist. Mus., 1989—; bd. dirs. Coun. of Alleghenies, 1991, sec., 1991-2003; sec. Braddock Estates Civic Assn., Frostburg, 1988; mem. com. Frostburg Libr., 1989; tchr. Ch. Conf. Schs. Missions, 1970; vol. tutor, 1986-92; pres. Ch. Women United, Frostburg, 1989-95; trustee Frostburg United Meth. Ch., 1992-2005; pres. Cumberland-Hagerstown dist. United Meth. Women, 1985-89, coord. spiritual life, 2006—, chmn. fin. interpretation Balt. Conf., 1990-94; lay spkr. United Meth. Ch., 1975—, endowment fund com. Balt. conf., 1992-2003, bd. ordained ministry Cumberland-Hagerstown dist., 2000—; pres. bd. dirs. Frostburg Mus., 2000—; bd. dirs. Found. for Frostburg, 2000. Mem. AAUW (pres. 1993-95, treas. Md. divsn. 1974-76, Woman of Yr. award Frostburg br. 1980, New Frostburg Libr. Bldg. Com. 1994-98, chair pub. policy com. Frostburg br. 2001-03,, pres. Frostburg br. 2006, treas. libr. fund 2002—). Republican. Avocations: travel, reading, gardening, genealogy, historical research.

MEEK, CARRIE P., former congresswoman; b. Tallahassee, Fla., Apr. 29, 1926; 3 children. BS, Fla. A&M U., 1946; MS, U. Mich., 1948. Mem. Fla. Ho. of Reps., Tallahassee, 1979-82, Fla. Senate, Tallahassee, 1982—93, U.S. Congress from 17th Fla. dist., 1993—2002; mem. appropriations com.; mem. subcommittee on Treasury, Postal Svc. and Gen. Gov., subcommittee on VA, HUD, and Ind. Agencies. Named to Florida Women's Hall of Fame, 1992; recipient Benjamin Franklin award for outstanding pub. svc., Suncoast Tiger Bay Club, 2004. Democrat.

MEEK, CARROLL LEE LARSON, psychologist, graphic designer; b. Whitehall, Mont., Oct. 6, 1942; d. Leland Carroll and Doris Grace (Husband) Larson; m. Saul Matthew Spiro, July 31, 1982. BA, Whitman Coll., 1964; MS, Ind. U., 1966; PhD, U. Idaho, 1972. Lic. psychologist, Wash. Counselor U. Wis., OshKosh, 1966-68, U. Idaho Counseling Ctr., Moscow, 1968-69; psychologist Wash. State U., Pullman, 1969-82; counselor Ctr. for Personal & Family Counseling, Moscow, 1972-74; owner Graphed Charts and Kits for Miniature Needlepoint Tapestries, 1987—; pvt. practice psychologist Pullman, 1982—92, Anacortes, Wash., 1992—. Mem. people/pet partnership Wash. State U., Pullman, 1979—; coord. crisis and rape intervention task force, 1980-84. Editor: Post-Traumatic Stress Disorder, 1990; contbr. articles to profl. jous. Sponsor & coord. Hedgehogs N.W. Ann. Internat. Hedgehog Show, Anacortes, 2003—. Mem. Am. Psychol. Assn., Am. Assn. Sex Educators, Counselors and Therapists, Nat. Register Health Svc., Nat. Assn. Miniature Enthusits. Avocations: needlecrafts, miniatures, Japanese koi, gardening. Office Phone: 360-293-8176.

MEEK, VIOLET IMHOF, retired dean; b. Geneva, Ill., June 12, 1939; d. John and Violet (Krepel) Imhof; m. Devon W. Meek, Aug. 21, 1965 (dec. 1988); children: Brian, Karen; m. Don M. Dell, Jan. 4, 1992. BA summa cum laude, St. Olaf Coll., 1960; MS, U. Ill., 1962, PhD in Chemistry, 1964. Instr. chemistry Mount Holyoke Coll., South Hadley, Mass., 1964-65; asst. prof. to prof. Ohio Wesleyan U., Delaware, Ohio, 1965-84, dean for ednl. svcs., 1980-84; dir. annual programs Coun. Ind. Colls., Washington, 1984-86; assoc. dir. sponsored programs devel. Rsch. Found. Ohio State U., Columbus, 1986-91, dean, dir. Lima, 1992—2003; ret., 2003. Vis. dean U. Calif., Berkeley, 1982, Stanford U., Palo Alto, Calif., 1982, reviewer GTE Sci. and Tech. Program, Princeton, N.J., 1986-92, Goldwater Nat. Fellowships, Princeton, 1990-98. Co-author: Experimental General Chemistry, 1984; contbr. articles to profl. jours. Bd. dirs. Luth. Campus Ministries, Columbus, 1988-91, Luth. Social Svcs., 1988-91, Americom Bank, Lima, 1992-98, Art Space, Lima, 1993—, Allen Lima Leadership, 1993—, Am. House, 1992—, Lima Vets. Meml. Civic Ctr. Found., 1992—; chmn. synodical coms. Evang. Luth. Ch. Am., Columbus, 1982; bd. trustees Trinity Luth. Sem., Columbus, 1996—; chmn. Allen County C. of C., 1995—, chair bd. dirs., 1999; bd. dirs. Lima Syphomy Orch., 1993—, pres. bd. dirs., 1997— Recipient Woodrow Wilson Fellowship, 1960. Mem.: Am. Assn. Higher Edn., Nat. Coun. Rsch. Adminstrs. (named Outstanding New Profl. midwest region 1990), Phi Beta Kappa. Avocations: music, skiing, woodworking, civil war history, travel. Home: 209 W Beechwold Blvd Columbus OH 43214-2012 Office: Ohio State Lima 8521 Libra Rd Dublin OH 43016-9022

MEEKER, CAROL LOUISE, special education educator, consultant; d. Alva David O'Connell and Rosemary Carol Strohbehn; m. Arlo Harry Meeker, Aug. 26, 1967; children: Kevin, Kyle, Kimberly. BA, Empire State Coll., 1990; MS in Edn., Binghamton U., 1991. Spl. edn. Bd. of Coop. Ednl. Svcs., Binghamton, NY, 1991—92, Windsor (N.Y.) Ctrl. Sch., 1992—. Cons. tchr. Com. Presch. Spl. Edn., Windsor, 2003—. Dir. Awana, Windsor, 1993—; dir. drama West Windsor Bapt. Ch., 2000—. Mem.: Binghamton Area Reading Coun. Avocation: travel. Office: CR Weeks Elem Sch 440 Foley Rd Windsor NY 13865 E-mail: cmeeker@windsor-csd.org.

MEEKER, MARY G., brokerage house executive; b. Portland, Ind., Sept. 1959; BA in Psychology, DePauw U., 1981; MBA in Fin., Cornell U., 1986. Stockbroker Merrill Lynch, Chgo., 1982; tech. rsch. analyst Salomon Bros., 1989, Cowen & Co., 1990—91; mng. dir. Internet, new media and PC software equity rsch. Morgan Stanley, Dean Witter, Discover & Co. (now Morgan Stanley), N.Y.C., 1991—. Named Queen of the Net, Barron's. Avocations: golf, fishing, skiing. Office: Morgan Stanley 1585 Broadway New York NY 10036-8200 Fax: 212-761-0472. E-mail: mmeeker@ms.com.

MEEKISON, MARYFRAN, writer; b. Napoleon, Ohio, Apr. 9, 1919; d. Frank J. and Elizabeth (Keyes) Shaff; m. David Meekison, June 17, 1939; children: Maureen Meekison Houppert, David Francis, Beth Ann. Student, St. Mary's Coll., Notre Dame, Ind., 1936-39. Hist. writer, photographer, Napoleon, 1963—, St. Augustine Ch., 1983—; mem. citizen com. Napoleon Area H.S. Award, 2005—. Author: (photographer) Canal Days to Modern Ways Revisited, 1984, History of St. Augustine's 1882-1982, History of St. Augustine Ch., 1983, centennial edit.; (brochure) Canal Days to Modern Ways, 1963; mem. editorial adv. bd. Courier mag., 1989-91; contbr. articles to numerous mags. Steering com. Napoleon Susquicentennial, 1984; trustee Napoleon Pub. Lib., 1976-01. Recipient Spl. citation Courier Alumnae mag., also numerous photography and writing awards, Pres.'s medal, St. Mary's Coll., Notre Dame, Ind., 1991; named Citizen of Yr., Napoleain Area C. of C., 1990; named to St. Mary's Coll. Athletic Hall of Fame Notre Dame, 2001. Mem. Alumnae Assn. St. Mary's Coll. (bd. dirs. 1985-91), Literary Club. Democrat. Roman Catholic. Avocations: tennis, sailing. Home: PO Box 253 Napoleon OH 43545-0253

MEEKS, DONNA MARIE, art educator; b. Louisville, Jan. 14, 1960; d. Ernest and Marilyn Elizabeth (Breckel) M.; 1 child, Christopher Michael Passmore BA Drawing honors, U. Louisville, 1982, MA Tchg., 1984; MFA Painting, Sculpture, U. Wis., Milw., 1986. Cert. tchr. art kindergarten to 12th grade, English 7th to 12th grade, Ky., art 7th to 12th grade, English 7th to 12th grade, Wis. Grad. asst. Sch. Edn., U. Louisville, 1982—84; tchg. asst. art dept. U. Wis., 1984—85, project asst. Art Mus., 1985—86; substitute tchr. Milw. Pub. Schs., 1986—87; curator edn. Tarble Arts Ctr., instr. art dept. Coll. Fine Arts, Ea. Ill. U., Charleston, 1987—93; dir. edn. Am. Acad. Art, Chgo., 1993—95; prof., chair art dept. Lamar U., Beaumont, Tex., 1995—. Guest artist Am. Acad. Art, Chgo., 1992; artist in residence art dept. Alverno Coll., Milw., 1991, Fundacion Torre Pujales, Corme, Galicia, Spain, 2005; vis. artist Wabash Coll., Crawfordsville, Ind., 1996, Knight Found. fellowship Brandywine Workshop, Phila., 2001; mem. adv. panel Arts in Edn. Arts Roster Ill. Arts Coun., 1993, 94. One-person shows at Dorothea Theil Gallery, South Suburban Coll., South Holland, Ill., 1989, Ill. Ctrl. Coll., East Peoria, 1989, Wright St. Gallery, Milw., 1989, Perkinson Gallery, Kirkland Fine Arts Ctr., Millikin U., Decatur, Ill., 1994, Robinson Galleries, Houston, 1999, Dishman Art Mus., Beaumont, 2000; two-person show Montgomery Coll. Art Gallery, Conroe, Tex., 2006; exhibited in group shows at Space Gallery, Chgo., 1992, Rockville (Md.) Arts Pl., 1993, South Bend (Ind.) Regional Mus. Art., 1993, Ga. So. U., Ink People Gallery, Eureka, Calif., 1994, Woman Made Gallery, Chgo., Summitt, Denise Bibro Fine Art, N.Y.C., 1997, Visual Arts Ctr. Boise State U.1998, Alternative Mus., N.Y.C., 1999, Orange County Ctr. Contemporary Art, Santa Ana, Calif., 2001, Montgomery Armory Art Ctr., West Palm Beach, Fla., 2001, 2002, Butler Inst. Am. Art, Youngstown, Ohio, 2003, Brad Cooper Gallery, Tampa, Fla., Lankersham Art Gallery, North Hollywood, Calif., 2004, Touchstone Gallery, Washington, 2005, N.J. Ctr. for the Visual arts, Summit, 2005; represented in permanent collections at Hoyt Inst. Fine Arts, New Castle, Pa., Millikin U., Decatur, Fundacion Torre Pujales, Corme, Spain, Art Mus. Southeast Tex., Beaumont, Brandywine Workshop, Phila. Mem. Nat. Coun. Arts Adminstrs., Coll. Art Assn Democrat. Office: Lamar U Dept Art PO Box 10027 Beaumont TX 77710-0027 Business E-Mail: donna.meeks@lamar.edu.

MEEKS, JACQUELYNN, city health department administrator; MPH, Tulane U.; DPH, Harvard U. Corp. dir. quality assurance Mutual of Omaha; dir. quality improvement Group Health Plan, Inc.; rsch. assoc. Washington U. Sch. Medicine; dir. dept. health St. Louis County, 2001—04; health dir. Maricopa County, Ariz., 2005—. Office: Maricopa County Dept Health 4041 N Central Ste 1400 Phoenix AZ 85012 Office Phone: 602-506-6902. Office Fax: 602-506-0272. Business E-Mail: jacquelynnmeeks@mail.maricopa.gov.*

MEEROPOL, RACHEL, lawyer; BA, Wesleyan U., 1997; JD, NYU, 2002. Staff atty., fellow Ctr. Constitutional Rights, 2002—. Author, co-editor: Jailhouse Lawyers Handbook; editor: America's Disappeared: Secret Imprisonment, Detainees, and the "War on Terror". Named one of Top 40 Lawyers Under 40, Nat. Law Jour., 2005. Mem.: Nat. Lawyers Guild NYC Chpt. (v.p.). Office: Nat Lawyers Guild 143 Madison Ave 4th Fl New York NY 10016 also: Ctr Constitutional Rights 666 Broadway New York NY 10012 Office Phone: 212-679-6018, 212-614-6420. Office Fax: 212-679-6178.

MEERS, ELIZABETH BLOSSOM, lawyer; b. Cleve., Jan. 12, 1952; BA summa cum laude, Radcliffe Coll., 1975; JD magna cum laude, Georgetown U. Law Ctr., 1980; cert. theological studies, Georgetown U. Sch. Summer & Continuing Edn., 1994. Bar: Fla. 1983, D.C. 1980, U.S. Ct. Appeals, D.C. Cir. Law clk. Hon. John M. Ferren, D.C. Ct. Appeals, Washington, 1980—81; ptnr. Hogan & Hartson LLP, Washington, 1982—, edn. practice group dir. Mem.: Nat. Assn. Coll. & U. Atty. (interim exec. dir. 2000—01), Fed. Bar Assn. (chmn. & vice chmn., fed. grants com. pub. contract sect. 1985—97), ABA, Georgetown U. (bd. regents, Alumni Achievement Award 1999), Radcliffe Coll. (trustee 1979—87), William Bingham Found., Catholic Cmty. Svc. Archdiocese-Washington (adv. coun., Archdiocesan legal network), John Carroll Soc. (bd. dirs.). Office: Hogan & Hartson LLP Columbia Sq 555 Thirteenth St NW Washington DC 20004-1109 Office Phone: 202-637-8676. Office Fax: 202-637-5910. Business E-Mail: ebmeers@hhlaw.com.

MEERS, THERESA MARY, nursing educator, science educator; b. 7/6/57, Ny; d. Edward J. and Patricia N. O'Connor; m. Robert F. Meers, May 8, 1993; children: Casey E. O'Connor, Michaela J., Kaelan Robert. BS in Nursing, Salem State Coll., Mass., 1984; MAT, Union Coll., Schenectady, N.Y., 1997. Registered nurse, N.Y., Mass., 1979; cert. biology and earth sci. tchr. N.Y., 1997. Earth sci./biology tchr. Mohonsen H.S., Schenectady, NY, 2002; nursing instr. Maria Coll., Albany, 2006—. Eucharistic min. Immaculate Conception Ch., Schenectady, 1998. Recipient New Tchr. of Yr., STANYS, 1999. Mem.: St. Elizabeth's Auxillary (assoc.). Independent-Republican. Catholic. Achievements include research in effects of estrogen on learning and behavior. Office Phone: 518-355-0350.

MEESE, FRANCES MILDRED, library administrator; b. Ottawa, Ohio, Feb. 5, 1915; d. Berl Butler Blauvelt and Clara Bell Atkinson-Blauvelt; m. Ward Richard Meese; children: John Butler, Paul Richard, Jane Claire Meese-Jones. BS Edn., U. Colo., Colorado Springs, CO, 1974. Certified Teacher Colo. State, 1974, Tutor Certificate Laubach Literacy Action, Colo. Springs, 1986, Choral & Music Direction U. Denver, Library Science So. Colo. State, Organ Music Technique Colo. Coll., 1974. Dental asst. Dr. John R. White, DDS, Ft. Wayne, Ind., 1934—42; bigade chapel organist Ft. Carson Army Post, Fort Carson, Colo., 1961—73; med. libr. (original organizer) Meml. Hosp., Colorado Springs, Colo., 1958—85; tchr., english as a second lang. Sch. Dist. #3, Security, Colo., 1985—98. Leader Cub Scouts, Girl Scouts; charter mem. Soli Deo Gloria Choir, Colorado Springs, Colo., 1973; mem. Colo. Springs Chorus, Colorado Springs, Colo., 1957—58, Colo. Springs Chorale, Colorado Springs, Colo., 1958—74. Avocation: church organist. Home: 808 Dahlia Dr Colorado Springs CO 80911

MEESTER, HOLLY, elementary school educator, music educator, sales executive; b. Grafton, N.D., Sept. 1, 1966; d. Gordon and (Alice) Jane Thompson; m. Brent Meester, Sept. 27, 1991; children: Emily, Daniel. BS in Music Edn., N.D. State U., 1989; MA in Music Edn., U. St. Thomas, 2003. Lic. profl. educator N.D., 1989. Asst. dir. Red River Boy Choir, Fargo, ND, 1988—90; tchr. elem. music Fargo Pub. Schs., 1989—; founder, music dir. Lake Agassiz Girls Choir, Fargo, 1990—97. Ind. cons. Mary Kay Cosmetics, Fargo, 1993—; mentor Fargo Pub. Schs., 1999—2002, dir. elem. hand chimes performing group, 1991—, dir. elem. choir, 1989—; adj. prof. Minn. State U., Moorhead, 2004—. Bldg. liaison Fargo Edn. Assn.; bd. mem. Lake Agassiz Girls Choir, Fargo, 1990—98; steering com. mem. North Ctrl. Accreditation - Lewis & Clark Elem., 1992—2005. Mem.: N.D. Music Educators Assn. (state pres. collegiate chpt. 1988—89, Outstanding Collegiate Music Educator 1989), Music Educators Nat. Conf., Orgn. Am. Kodaly Educators, No. Plains Kodaly Chpt. (pres., v.p., past pres., member-at-large 1997—2005), Kappa Delta (life; corr. sec. 1986—87), Sigma Alpha Iota (life). Achievements include Performance at National Organization of American Kodaly Educators while Director of Lake Agassiz Girls Choir. Avocations: reading, piano, scrapbooks, choir. Office: Fargo Pub Schs 1040 29th St N Fargo ND 58102 Office Phone: 701-446-4854.

MEFFORD, NAOMI RUTH DOLBEARE, secondary school educator, elementary school educator; b. Pittsfield, Ill., Feb. 10, 1944; d. Donald Pryor and Ruth Allyne (Utter) Dolbeare; m. Clark L. Mefford, Feb. 8, 1964; children: Joseph Clark, Christopher Lee. BA, William Penn Coll., 1977; MA, N.E. Mo. State U., 1986, EdS, 1991. Cert. profl. tchr., adminstr., Iowa. Undergrad. instr. Buena Vista, Ottumwa, Iowa, 1984-87; grad. instr. So. Prairie AEA and Marycrest Coll., Ottumwa, 1988-92; tchr. Ottumwa Schs., 1985—; adj. inst. in edn. Indian Hills C.C., 1998, 2000. Dir. summer sch. Ottumwa, 1991-93, Organizer Outdoor Edn. Camp. 2002. Chmn. Hosp. Major Fund Raiser, Ottumwa, 1995. Mem. AAUW (pres. Iowa chpt. 1996—1998), Delta Kappa Gamma. Home: 8 Country Club Pl Ottumwa IA 52501-1417 Office: Eisenhower Sch 2624 Marilyn Rd Ottumwa IA 52501-1400

MEGA, LESLY TAMARIN, psychiatrist, educator; b. 1944; married; 2 children. AB, MD, Boston U., 1962—68. Cert. Gen. Psychiatry, 1974, Child Psychiatry, 1976, lic. NY, Va., NJ, NC. Resident gen. psychiatry NY Med. Coll., Met. Hosp. Ctr., 1969—70; fellowship child and adolescent psychiatry Med. Coll. of Va., Va. Treatment Ctr. for Children, Richmond, 1970—72; prof. child and adolescent psychiatric medicine Brody Sch. Med., East Carolina U., 1982—, dir. Med. Student Edn. in Psychiatric Medicine. Contbr. articles to profl. jours. Fellow: Am. Psychiatric Assn.; mem.: NC Psychiatric Assn. (pres. 1993—94), Am. Med. Women's Assn. (Bertha VanHoosen Award 2005). Office: Brody Sch Medicine at E Carolina U Dept Psychiatric Medicine 600 Moye Blvd, Brody 4E-98 Greenville NC 27834 Office Phone: 252-744-3772. Office Fax: 252-744-3815. E-mail: megal@mail.ecu.edu.*

MEGAHY, DIANE ALAIRE, physician; b. Des Moines, Iowa, Oct. 12, 1943; d. Edwin and Georgiana Lee Raygor; m. Mohamed H. Saleh Megahy, Sept. 20, 1969; children: Hassan, Hamed, Hala, Heba. MD, U. Alexandria, Egypt, 1981. Diplomate Am. Bd. Family Practice. Intern Univ. Hosp., Alexandria, Egypt, 1982-83; resident Siu Family Practice, Belleville, Ill., 1987—90; physician St. Joseph's Hosp., Highland, Ill., 1988—2001; med. coord. Tri-County Radiation Oncology, 2001—. Mem. steering com. on domestic violence 3d Jud. Cir. Ct., co-chmn. health care subcom. Mem. emergency med. svcs. coun. Madison and St. Clair Counties, Ill.; active Am. Cancer Soc. Mem.: AAUW, AMA (Excellence in Medicine I.M.G. Leadership award 2004), St. Clair County Med. Soc. (pres. elect 2006—), Ill. Rural Health Assn., Ill. State Med. Soc. (del. internat. med. grad. com.), So. Ill. Med. Assn. (past pres.), Ill. Coalition for Injury Prevention, Safe Kid Ill. Home: 2 Bay Meadow Pl Belleville IL 62223 Office: 7300 Twin Pyramid Pky Belleville IL 62223 Office Fax: 618-234-1793. Personal E-mail: dialmeg@msn.com.

MEGERIAN, TALENE, lawyer; BA, Loyola Coll., 1998; JD, Villanova U., 2002. Bar: Pa., NY, NJ, Ct. Appeals of NY, Supreme Ct. of Pa., Supreme Ct. of NJ. Assoc. Rawle & Henderson LLP, Phila. Office: Rawle & Henderson LLP The Widener Bldg One S Penn Sq Philadelphia PA 19107 Office Phone: 215-575-4388. Office Fax: 215-563-2583. E-mail: tmegerian@rawle.com.*

MEGGERS, BETTY JANE, anthropologist, researcher; b. Washington, Dec. 5, 1921; d. William Frederick and Edith (Raddant) M.; m. Clifford Evans, Sept. 13, 1946. AB, U. Pa., 1943; MA, U. Mich., 1944; PhD, Columbia U., 1952; D (hon.), U. de Guayaquil, Ecuador, 1987, U. Fed. Rio de Janeiro, Brazil, 1994, U. Nat. La Plata, Argentina, 1997, U. Católica de Goiás, Brazil, 1999. Instr. anthropology Am. U., Washington, 1950-51; rsch. assoc. Smithsonian Instn., 1954—, expert, 1981—; founder, pres. Taraxacum Inc., 1977—. Hon. prof. U. de Azuay, Ecuador, 1991. Author: Environmental Limitation on the Development of Culture, 1954, Ecuador, 1966, Amazonia, 1971, 2d edit., 1996, Prehistoric America, 1972, Evolucion y Difusion Cultural, 1998, Ecologia y Biogeografia de la Amazonia, 1999, (with Clifford Evans) Archeological Investigations at the Mouth of the Amazon, 1957, Archeological Investigations in British Guiana, 1960, (with Clifford Evans and Emilio Estrada) Early Formative Period of Coastal Ecuador, 1965, (with Clifford Evans) Archeological Investigations on the Rio Napo, Eastern Ecuador, 1968; editor: Prehistoria Sudamericana, 1992. Recipient award for sci. achievement Washington Acad. Sci., 1956; gold medal 37th Internat. Congress of Americanists, 1966; Order Al Merito Govt. Ecuador, 1966; Order Bernardo O'Higgins Govt. Chile, 1985; Sec.'s Gold medal for exceptional service Smithsonian Instn., 1986; Order Andres Bello Govt. Venezuela, 1988; Order Al Mérito por Servicios Distinguidos Govt. Peru, 1989, Order Al Mérito Científico, Casa de la Cultura Ecuatoriana, 2006. Fellow: AAAS, Assn. Tropical Biology (hon.; councilor 1976—78, pres.-elect 1982, pres. 1983); mem.: Ecol. Soc. Am., New Eng. Antiquities Rsch. Assn., Academia Nacional Historia Ecuador (corr.), Am. Anthrop. Assn. (exec. sec. 1959—61), Museo Antropológico de la Cultura Andina (hon.), Soc. Am. Archaeology (exec. bd. 1962—64), Am. Ethnol. Soc., Anthrop. Soc. Wash. (treas. 1955—60, v.p. 1965—66, pres. 1966—68), Phi Beta Kappa, Sigma Xi. Home: 1227 30th St NW Washington DC 20007-3410 Office: Smithsonian Instn Washington DC 20560-0001

MEGGINSON, ELIZABETH R., legislative staff member, director, lawyer; b. Clarksdale, Miss., Oct. 27, 1947; d. Mitford Ray and Cleo Ruth (Faggard) M.; m. Mark W. Menezes; children: Paige Jennings, Marisa Menezes. BM, La. State U., 1969, MM, 1970, JD, 1977. Pvt. practice, 1977-78; counsel natural resources com. La. Ho. Reps., 1978-81, legis. svc. coord. comml. regulation divsn., 1981-84; asst. atty. gen. environ. enforcement divsn. La. Dept. Justice, 1984-88; asst. sec. for office legal affairs and enforcement La. Dept. Environ. Quality, 1988-89; adminstrv. asst. to Rep. W.J. Billy Tauzin, Washington, 1989-90; staff dir. counsel Subcommittee on Coast Guard and Navigation Com. on Merchant Marine and Fisheries, U.S. Ho. Rep., Washington, 1990—95; counsel to chair Com. on Resources, U.S. Ho. Rep., Washington, 1995—96, chief counsel, 1997—2000, Com. on Transp. & Infrastructure, U.S. Ho. Rep., Washington, 2001—. Mem. Phi Kappa Phi. Office: Committee on Transportation & Infrastructure Room 2165 Rayburn House Office Building Washington DC 20515-6256

MEGHERIAN, YEFKIN, sculptor; b. Troy, NY, Mar. 23, 1924; d. Haroutiun DerBedrosian and Nevart DerVartanian; m. Vartan Megherian, Nov. 30, 1947 (dec. Jan. 1984); children: Gay Zarman, Lori Christine, Narrek Khachig, Talin Yefkin. BA, SUNY, Albany, 1945, MA, 1946; AS in Fine Arts, Queensborough C.C., N.Y.C., 1994. Cert. tchr. secondary schs. N.Y., tchr. primary grades N.Y., ancillary cert. tchr. art Bd. Edn., N.Y.C. H.S. sci. tchr. Warwick (N.Y.) Valley Ctrl. Sch., 1946—47; tchr. N.Y.C. Bd. Edn., 1967—85; sculptor, 1986—. Ch. sch. supr. St. James Armenian Ch., Evanston, Ill., 1947—55, Armenian Ch. of the Holy Martyrs, Bayside, NY, 1955—72; sec. coun. for religious edn. Diocese Armenian Ch., N.Y.C., 1956—61, mem. adv. bd. for bronze doors of cathedral, 2002—. Prin. works include Statue of Pope John Paul II, Vatican Mus., Rome, Bust of Vazken I, Catholicos of All Armenians, St. Gregory Illuminator Ch., Westchester, N.Y., Bust of Archbishop Tiran Nersoyan, Libr. Armenian Seminary, Westchester, Bas-relief, St. Vartan Armenian Cathedral, N.Y.C., St. Peter Armenian Ch., Watervliet, N.Y., medallion, Med. Mus., Wroclaw, Poland, Alex Manoogian Mus., St. John Armenian Ch., Southfield, Mich., exhibitions include Pen and Brush Gallery, NYC, 1995—2003, Canon House Office Bldg. Rotunda, Washington, 1996, Newark Mus., 1996, Nordic Heritage Mus., Seattle, 2004, Nat. Assn. Women Artists, Reading, Pa., 2004—05, Forest Lawn Mus., Calif., 2005, Padded Cell Gallery, Royal Oak, Mich., 2005, Queensborough CC, NYC, 2000, pvt. collections. Mem.: Nat. Assn. Women Artists, Pen and Brush, Inc. (Tallix Foundry award 1996, Merit award 2000, Compleat Sculptor 2003), Fedn. Internat. de la Medaille, Nat. Mus. Women in the Arts, Am. Medallic Sculpture Assn. (bd. dirs. 1997—2000, co-chair medallic sculpture exhbn. 2000), Nat. Sculpture Soc. Avocations: painting, travel, opera, ceramics, reading. Home: 218-37 Grand Central Pkwy Queens Village NY 11427 Office Phone: 718-217-6285. Personal E-mail: yefkin323@aol.com.

MEGLI, LISA L., assistant principal; d. Max and Linda Megli. B, Southwestern Okla. State U., Weatherford, 1985, M, 1995. Ops. rsch. analyst US Dept. Def., Ft. Sill, Okla., 1985—88; math. tchr. Wichita Falls Ind. Sch. Dist., Tex., 1989—92, Yukon Pub. Schs., Okla., 1992—2001, asst. prin., 2001—. Ch. pianist, Sunday sch. tchr. Alfalfa Bapt. Ch., Carnegie, Okla., 1977—. Mem.: Okla. Assn. Secondary Sch. Prins., Coop. Coun. for Okla. Sch. Adminstrn. (fellow Prin.'s Leadership Acad. 2006), Nat. Assn. Secondary Sch. Prins. Office: Yukon HS 9-10 1029 Garth Brooks Blvd Yukon OK 73099 Office Phone: 405-354-6692.

MEHLTRETTER, KATHLEEN M., former prosecutor; b. 1954; BS, Univ. of Dayton; JD, State Univ. of NY at Buffalo. Bar: New York 1979. U.S. atty. (we. dist.) NY U.S. Dept. Justice, Buffalo, 2005—06.*

MEHR, VICKI JOYCE, music educator; b. Bklyn., Nov. 18, 1953; d. Riva Mehr. MusB, SUNY, Fredonia, 1975, MusM, 1979. Cert. tchr. music edn. K-12 NY. String instrumental music tchr. Lewiston-Porter Ctrl. Schs., Youngstown, NY, 1975—. Chairperson and condr. of Niagara County elem. string orch.; performances with sch. orch. at Kleinhans Music Hall in buffalo. Musician free-lance musician, Sara Brightman Show, Smokey Robinson Show; musician: (musicals, opera at artpark-lewiston, ny). Mem.: ASTA, N.Y. State United Tchrs., Music Educators Nat. Conf., Phi Delta Kappa, Kappa Delta Pi. Avocation: health and fitness. Office: Lewiston-Porter Central Schools 4061 Creek Rd Youngstown NY 14174 Office Phone: 716-754-4743 3109. E-mail: mehrv@lew-port.com.

MEHRETU, JULIE, artist; b. Addis Ababa, Ethiopia, 1970; Attended, U. Cheik Anta Diop, Dakar, Senegal, 1990—91; BA, Kalamazoo Coll., 1992; MFA with honors, RI Sch. Design, 1997. Greater New York, P.S.1 Contemporary Arts Ctr., NY, 2000, exhibited in group shows, Ctr. Curatorial Studies, Bard College, Annandale-on-Hudson, 2000, Free Style, Studio Mus. Harlem, 2001, The Americans, Barbican Gallery, London, 2001, Busan Biennale, Korea, 2002, 8th Baltic Triennial Vilnius, Lithuania, 2002, Drawing Now: Eight Propositions, Mus. Modern Art, 2002, Painting at the Edge of the World, Walker Art Ctr., 2003, one-woman shows include, Sol Kofler Gallery, Providence, RI, 1995, Ancestral Reflections, Archive Gallery, NY, 1995, Bombastic Righteous Passively Become Apparent Absurdities, Sol Kofler Gallery, Providence, RI, 1996, Recent Work, Barbara Davis Gallery, Houston, 1998, Module, Project Row Houses, Houston, 1999, The Project, NYC, 2001, Art Pace, San Antonio, Tex., 2001, White Cube, London, 2002, Julie Mehretu: Drawing into Painting, Walker Art Ctr. (travelling), 2003, REDCAT, LA, Calif., 2004, Albright-Knox Art Gallery, Buffalo, NY, 2004, Matrix, U. Calif. Berkeley Art Mus., 2004, earlier 1 gebauer, Berlin, Germany, 2004, Drawing, The Project, NYC, 2005, Current, St. Louis Art Mus., 2005, exhibited in group shows at Carnegie Internat., Carnegie Mus. Art, Pitts., Pa., 2004, Sao Paulo Biennial, San Paulo, Brazil, 2004, Whitney Biennal, The Whitney Mus. Am. Art, NYC, 2004, Back to Paint, C&M Arts, NYC, 2004, Firewall, Ausstellungshalle Zeitgenössische Kunst, Munster, Germany, 2004. Recipient Cry of My Birth, Visiting Artist Residency Project, Sch. Art Inst. Chgo., 1999, Excellence Award, RI Sch. Design, 1996, Penny McCall Award, 2001; Core Fellowship, Artist in Residence, Glassell Sch. Art, Mus. Fine Arts, Houston, 1997—99, MacArthur Fellow, John D. and Catherine T. MacArthur Found., 2005. Address: 37 W 57th St 3rd Fl New York NY 10019

MEHRING, NANCY, medical/surgical nurse, administrator; b. Lorain, Ohio, June 13, 1943; d. d. Stacy C. and Mary B. (Sascik) Jezewski; m. Frank Mehring, July 16, 1966; children: Gregory M., Stacey M. Diploma, M.B. Johnson Sch. Nursing, Elyria, Ohio, 1964; BSN, U. Akron, 1984. Staff nurse, asst. head nurse, head nurse Elyria Meml. Hosp., 1964-84, admission coord., mgr., 1984-2000; nurse mgr. P.A.T. and Ambulatory Care Ctr.; onsite mgr. Amherst (Ohio) Hosp., 2000—. Mem. adv. com. U. Akron Outreach Program. Mem. ANA, Ohio Nurses Assn., M.B. Johnson Sch. Nursing Alumni Assn., Lorain County Dist. Nurses Assn., Sigma Theta Tau.

MEHTA, EILEEN ROSE, lawyer; b. Colver, Pa., Apr. 1, 1953; d. Richard Glenn and Helen (Wahna) Ball; m. Abdul Rashid Mehta, Aug. 31, 1973. Student, Miami U., 1971-73; BA with distinction, Fla. Internat. U., 1974; JD cum laude, U. Miami, 1977. Bar: Fla. 1977, U.S. Dist. Ct. (so. dist.) Fla. 1977, U.S. Ct. Appeals (11th cir.) 1981. Law clk. to presiding judge U.S. Dist. Ct. (so. dist.) Fla., Miami, 1977-79; asst. atty. County of Dade, Miami, 1979-89; shareholder Fine Jacobson Schwartz Nash Block & England, Miami, Fla., 1989-94; ptnr. Eckert Seamans Cherin & Mellott, Miami, 1994-98, Bilzin Sumberg Baena Price & Axelrod, Miami, 1998—. Lectr. in field; v.p., bd. dirs. Shalimar Homes Inc., Anderson, S.C. Miami U. scholar, 1971-73. Mem. Fla. Bar Assn., Dade County Bar Assn. Office: Bilzin Sumberg Baena Price & Axelrod 2500 Wachovia Fin Ctr Miami FL 33131 Office Phone: 305-350-2380. Business E-Mail: emehta@bilzin.com.

MEHTA, LINN CARY, literature educator; b. Chgo., Aug. 8, 1955; d. William Lucius and Katherine L.F. (Cooper) Cary; m. Ved Mehta, Dec. 17, 1983; children: Alexandra Sage, Natasha Cary. BA in English and French, Yale U., 1977; MA in English, Oxford U., 1979; MPhil in Comparative Lit., Columbia U., 1989, PhD in Comparative Lit., 2004. Asst. to pres. Ford Found., N.Y.C., 1980—82, asst. program officer, 1982—85; preceptor Columbia U., N.Y.C., 1990—91; instr. Yale U., New Haven, 1993; instr., adj. asst. prof. English dept. Vassar Coll., Poughkeepsie, NY, 1994—97; lectr. English dept. Barnard Coll., N.Y.C., 2000—. Chair bd. Am. Friends St. Hilda's Coll., Boston, 1995-02; sec. bd. alumnae Wrexham Found., New Haven, 1988-94; lit. advisor English adaptation Theater New City, 2006—. Actor: (English adaptation of play) Allende, Theater for a New City, 2006. Bd. pres. Ctr. for Traditional Music and Dance, NYC, 1989-94, v.p., 2000—, Lexington 79th Corp., NYC, 1993-97; bd. dirs. Norman Rockwell Mus., Stockbridge, Mass., 1991-96, NY Soc. Libr., 2002—; adv. bd. Appalshop, Whitesburg, Ky., 1990-92. Mem. MLA, Am. Comparative Lit. Assn., Thursday Evening Club (pres. 1998-2001) Avocations: music, running, languages. Home: 139 E 79th St New York NY 10021-0324 Office: English Dept Barnard Coll Columbia U 3009 Broadway New York NY 10027 Business E-Mail: lmehta@barnard.edu.

MEIDES, HOLLY SUE, music educator; b. Buffalo, Dec. 15, 1968; d. Richard Henry and Margaret Ann Meides. MusB, Potsdam Coll., N.Y., 1991; MusM, Potsdam Coll., 1992. Cert. tchr. music K-12 NY, 1991. Gen. music tchr. Amherst Ctrl. Schs., NY, 1993; orch./band dir., tchr. Lancaster Ctrl. Schs., Lancaster, NY, 1993—. Sec./clarinetist Akron Cmty. Band, Akron, NY, 1984—; solo adjudicator Erie County Music Educator's Assn., East Aurora, NY, 1995—. Recipient Departmental scholar, Crane Sch. of Music, 1991, Presdl. scholar, Potsdam Coll., 1987—91, Presdl. fellow, 1991—92, Gold award, Girl Scouts of Am., 1986. Mem.: NY State Sch. Music Assn., Am. String Tchrs. Assn., Erie County Music Educators Assn., Music Educators Nat. Conf., Maroon Key Soc. (hon.), Pi Kappa Lambda (hon.), Kappa Delta Pi (hon.), Gamma Sigma Sigma (life), Sigma Alpha Iota (life). Roman Catholic. Home: 7061 Maple Rd Akron NY 14001 Office: William Street Sch 5201 William St Lancaster NY 14086 Office Phone: 716-686-3800. Personal E-mail: strings15@aol.com.

MEIER, BEVERLY JOYCE LOEFFLER, science educator, educational consultant; b. Balt., Md., June 28, 1941; d. John Thomas and Frances Lillian Loeffler; m. Thomas Meier, June 8, 1963; children: Thomas Jr., John H. BS, U. Colo., Boulder, Colo., 1963; MA, U. Colo., 1969. Sci. tchr. Cherry Creek Sch. Dist., Denever, Colo., 1963—65; potter Boulder Potter's Guild, Boulder, Colo., 1970—77; part owner Sturtz Copeland Florist, Boulder, Colo., 1970—75; sci. tchr. Boulder Valley Sch. Dist., Boulder, Colo., 1977—. Cons. sci. edn. Nat. Oceanic Atmosphere Adminstrn., Boulder, Colo., 1993—, Nat. Renewal Energy Lab, Golden, Colo., 1989—90; cons. Am. Indian Sci. Engr. Soc., Boulder, Colo., 1994. Contbr. articles to profl. jour. Adv. bd. Colo. Sci. and Engring. Fair, Ft. Collin., 1990—; dir. sci. fair Boulder Valley Sch. Dist., 1982—. Grantee Boulder Valley Impact grant, 2000, Toyota Tapestry-NSTA, 1998, Boulder Valley Impact on Edn. grant, 2006. Mem.: NSTA, Phi Delta Kappa. Avocations: anthropology, archaeology. Office: Broomfield Heights Mid Sch 1555 Daphne St Boulder CO 80305

MEIER, ENGE, pre-school educator; b. N.Y.C., Jan. 17; d. Rudolf and Kate (Furstenow) Pietschyck; children: Kenneth Randolph, Philip Alan. BBA, Western States U., 1987, MBA, 1989. Tchr. nursery sch., Neu Ulm, Fed. Republic Germany, 1963-64; sec. Brewster (N.Y.) Mid. Sch., 1969-72; teaching asst. Brewster Elem. Sch., 1972-73; office asst. Bd. Coop. Edn., Yorktown Heights, N.Y., 1973-76; sec. Am. Can. Co., Greenwich, Conn., 1976-77, adminstrv. sec., 1977-79, exec. sec., 1979-84; adminstrv. asst. U. Tex., Austin, 1984-85, 88-90, adminstrv. assoc., 1985-86, sr. adminstrv. assoc., 1986-88; exec. asst. DTM Corp., Austin, 1990; funds asst. mgr. Tex. Assn. Sch. Bds., Austin, 1991-92; nursery sch. tchr. Westlake Presbyn. Sch., Austin, 1992-95; tchr. Grace Covenant Christian Sch., 1995-96; office mgr. Dr. G. Roebuck, Austin, 1996—. Docent LBJ Libr. and Mus., Austin, 1984—; mem. Women's Polit. Caucus, 1988—; bd. dirs. Leadership, Edn. and Devel., 1991. Mem. Women in Mgmt., Bus. and Profl. Women (pres. 1989, bd. dirs. Austin chpt. 1987—), Women's C. of C. Presbyterian. Avocations: golf, swimming. E-mail: enge@austin.rr.com.

MEIER, KATHRYN ELAINE, pharmacologist, educator; b. San Mateo, Calif., Apr. 28, 1953; d. Robert E. and I. Dorothy Hunt; m. G. Patrick Meier, June 16, 1975; children: Adam M., Andrea D. BA in Biology, U. Calif., San Diego, 1975; PhD in Pharmacology, U. Wis., Madison, 1981. Lab. asst., tchg. asst., rsch. fellow U. Calif. San Diego, La Jolla, 1971-75; rsch. asst., fellow U. Wis., Madison, 1975-81; NIH postdoctoral fellow U. Calif. San Diego, La Jolla, 1981-84; assoc., sr. assoc. Howard Hughes Med. Inst., Seattle, 1984-89; rsch. asst. prof. U. Wash., Seattle, 1988-91; asst. prof. Med. U. S.C., Charleston, 1991-96, assoc. prof. pharmacology, 1996—2003; prof. dept. pharm. sci. Wash. State U., Pullman, 2003—, chair dept. pharm. sci., 2003—05. Scientist reviewer Dept. Def., Ft. Detrick, Md., 1996-2005, VA Merit Review, 1999— Mem. editl. bd. Jour. Biol. Chemistry, 1993-98, Am. Jour. Physiology, 1996—, Jour. Pharmacology and Exptl. Therapeutics, 1998-2000, Molecular Pharmacology, 2004—; contbr. articles to profl. jours. Recipient Tchg. Excellence award Med. U. SC, 2001; NIH fellow, 1981-84; Rsch. grantee NIH, 1993-96, 2004—, Dept. Def., 1998—. Mem. Am. Soc. Biochemistry and Molecular Biology, Am. Soc. Pharmacology and Exptl. Therapeutics, Am. Soc. Physiology, Am. Assn. Coll. Pharmacy. Office: Washington State Univ Dept Pharm Scis Wegner Hall PO Box 646534 Pullman WA 99164-6534 Business E-Mail: kmeier@wsu.edu.

MEIER, LISA M., lawyer; b. Springfield, Vt., Aug. 22, 1977; BA in Hist. and Russian Lang. and Lit., Smith Coll., 1999; JD, William Mitchell Coll. Law, 2002. Bar: Minn. 2002. Children's prog. intern Minn. Advocates for Human Rights, Mpls., 2000; devel. asst. Office of Instl. Advancement William Mitchell Coll. Law, St. Paul, 2000; law clk. Honsa & Michales, P.A., Mpls., 2001—02, atty., 2002—. Named a Rising Star, Minn. Super Lawyers mag., 2006. Mem.: Dakota County Bar Assn., ABA, Minn. State Bar Assn. (mem. family law sect.), Ramsey County Bar Assn. (mem. family law sect.), Hennepin County Bar Assn. (mem. family law sect., sec. family law exec. com.). Avocations: reading, hiking, walking. Office: Anne M Honsa 5500 Wayzata Blvd Ste 1075 Minneapolis MN 55416 Office Phone: 763-797-9855.*

MEIERHENRY, JUDITH KNITTEL, state supreme court justice; b. Burke, SD, Jan. 20, 1944; m. Mark Vernon Meierhenry, May 14, 1961; children: Todd, Mary. BA in English, U. S.D., 1966, MA, 1968, JD, 1977. Bar: S.D. 1977. H.S. tchr. English Plattsmouth (Nebr.) Pub. Schs., 1966-67; instr. U. SD, 1968-70, Hiram Scott Coll., Scottbluff, Nebr., 1970; tchr. Todd County Pub. Schs., Mission, SD, 1971-74; ptnr. Meierhenry, DeVaney, Krueger & Meierhenry, Vermillion, SD, 1977-79; cabinet sec. SD Dept. Labor, Pierre, 1980-84; sr. mgr., asst. gen. counsel Citibank SD, 1985-88; cabinet sec. edn. and cultural affairs State SD, 1983-84, cir. ct. judge, 1988—2002; justice SD Supreme Ct., 2002—. Mem.: Nat. Assn. Women Judges, SD Bar Assn. Office: SD Supreme Ct 500 E Capital Ave Pierre SD 57501*

MEIKLE, DORA QUINN ARNEY, retired physical education educator; b. Springfield, Mo., Jan. 15, 1929; d. George and Lida Louise (Whitlock) Quinn; m. Nelson D. Arney (dec. 1970); children: David Rex, Rex Allen; m. James Lane Meikle, Aug. 20, 1977. BS, S.W. Mo. State U., 1950; MEd, U. Ark., 1970; postgrad., U. Mo., U. Pa. Tchr. St. Charles (Mo.) Pub. Schs., 1950-51, Greenwood Tng. Sch., Springfield, 1954-55, Camdenton (Mo.) High Sch., 1955-56, Barstow Pub. Schs., Kansas City, Mo., 1956-60, Mountain Grove (Mo.) Pub. Schs., 1960-62, Park Hill Pub. Schs., Parkville, Mo., 1962-63; instr. Lindenwood Coll., St. Charles, 1951-53, U. Mo., Kansas City, 1956-60; assoc. prof. Coll. of the Ozarks, Point Lookout, Mo., 1965-94, prof. emeritus. With Kiwanis Twin Lakes Art & Crafts Camp, Plymouth, Ind., Camp Thunderbird, Bemidji, Minn., First Women's Sports Del. to Russia, 1993. Water safety trainer Taney County unit ARC, 1971—, lifeguard trainer, 1983—, health svc. trainer, 1986—. Recipient 30 and 40-yr. pin ARC; named to Coll. of the Ozarks Sports Hall of Fame, 1992, Nat. Red Cross Hall of Fame, 1993. Mem. AAHPERD, Nat. Instn. Recreational Sports Assn., Nat. Aquatic Com., Delta Kappa Gamma. Democrat. Presbyterian. Avocations: outdoor activities, water sports. Home: HC 9 Box 1414 Branson MO 65616-8509

MEIKLEJOHN, MINDY JUNE (LORRAINE MEIKLEJOHN), political organizer, realtor; b. Staunton, Ill., June 9, 1929; d. Edward H. and Erna E. (Schwabe) Mindrup; m. Alvin J. Meiklejohn, Apr. 25, 1953; children: Pamela, Shelley, Bruce, Scott. Student, Ill. Bus. Coll., 1948, Red Rocks C.C., 1980-81. Pvt. sec. Ill. Liquor Commn., 1948-51, David M. Wilson, Ill. Sec. of State's Office, 1951-52; flight attendant Continental Airlines, 1952-53, pvt. sec. to mgr. flight svcs. office, 1953-54; orgnl. dir. Colo. Rep. Party, Denver, 1981-85, mem. Ctrl. Com., 1987—. Campaign coord. Hank Brown's Exploratory Campaign for Gov., 1985, mgr. Hank Brown for Congress, 1985-86; dep. campaign dir. Steve Schuck for Gov., 1985-86; vice chmn. 2d Congl. Ctrl. Com. Colo.; active campaigns; del., alt. to various county, state, dist. and nat. assemblies and convs.; Colo. chmn. Citizens for Am., 1987-96; realtor, sales assoc. Metro Brokers, Inc.; mem. polit. action com. Jefferson County Bd. Realtors; bd. dirs. Humphrey Meml. Park and Mus., 1996—, Sci. and Cultural Facilities Dist., 1989-94, Jefferson County chpt. Am. Cancer Soc., 1987-91, Jefferson Found., 1991-97; apptd. trustee Harry S. Truman scholarship Found., 1991; mem. Jefferson County Hist. Commn., Colo., 1974-82, pres., 1979; vol. Jefferson County Legal Aid Soc., 1970-74; vice chmn. Jefferson County Rep. Party, 1977-81, exec. com., 1987; vice chmn. Colo. State Rep. Party, 1981-85; chmn. Rep. Nat. Pilot Project on Volunteerism, 1981; mem. adv. coun. Peace Corps, 1982-84; sect. chmn. Jefferson County United Way Fund Drive; mem. exec. bd. Colo. Fedn. Rep. Women; pres. Operation Shelter, Inc., 1983-99; chair bd. dirs. Rocky Mountain Butterfly Consortium, 1996-2004, bd. dirs., 2005—; state chair Citizens for Am., 1987-96. Mem. Jefferson County Women's Rep. (edn. chmn. 1987-91). Home: 7540 Kline Dr Arvada CO 80005-3732 Personal E-mail: mindymeiklejohn@aol.com.

MEILAN, CELIA, food products executive; b. Bklyn., Jan. 21, 1920; d. Ventura Lorenzo and Susana (Prego) Meilan. Student, CCNY, 1943—46. Codes and ciphers translator security divsn. U.S. Censorship Office, N.Y.C., 1942—46; sec., treas. Albumina Supply Co., N.Y.C., 1946—55; co-founder, co-owner, sec., treas., fin. officer Internat. Proteins Corp. (now AnimalFeeds Internat. Corp.), Clark, NJ, 1955—86, exec. v.p., 1986—92, pres., 1992—94, chair emeritus, bd. dirs., 1994—, v.p., co-owner, 1998—. Bd. dirs. Pesquera Taboquilla, Panama City, Panama, Inversiones Pesqueras S.A., British Virgin Islands; v.p., bd. dirs. Atlantic Shipers of Tex. Inc., Port Arthur, 1989; bd. dirs. Atlantic Shippers Inc., Morehead City, NC, Empacadora Nacional S.A., Panama City; v.p., dir. AnimalFeeds, Internat., Santiago, Chile. Named One of Top 50 Women Bus. Owners, Working Woman Mag./Nat. Found. Women Bus. Owners, 1994, 1995. Mem.: Nat. Found. Women Bus. Owners, Spanish Benevolent Soc. (bd. dirs. 1955—62). Avocation: Avocations: travel, hand crafts, backgammon, puzzles. Office Fax: 732-827-0188.

MEILI, BARBARA, lawyer; b. Rhinebeck, NY; BA, Bennington Coll., 1980; JD magna cum laude, NY Law Sch., 1983. Bar: NY 1984. Shareholder, corp. and securities tech., media and telecom. Greenberg Traurig LLP, NYC. Mem.: ABA, Assn. Bar of NYC, Women in Cable and Telecom. Office: Greenberg Traurig MetLife Bldg 200 Park Ave New York NY 10166-1400 Office Phone: 212-801-9200. Office Fax: 212-801-6400. Business E-Mail: meilib@gtlaw.com.

MEILINK, JACQUELINE RAE, music educator; b. St. Louis, Mo., Mar. 4, 1956; d. Raymond John and Dorothy Virginia Meiners; m. Michael Steven Meilink, May 19, 1979; children: Steven M., Kristin R. BMusEd, U. Mo., Kansas City, 1978, MMusEd, 1999. Pvt. piano tchr., 1971—94; tchr. music North Kansas City Sch. Dist., Kansas City, Mo., 1978—85; choir dir. Northminster Presbyn. Ch., 1983—85; dir. children's choir Northgate Bapt. Ch., 1987—94, ch. pianister, 1988—2002; music tchr. North Kansas City Sch. Dist., 1994—. Sponsor Jr. Achievement, Kansas City, 2005—06; cultural art chmn. Oakwood Manor Parent Tchr. Student Assn., Kansas City, Mo.; reflections chmn. Antioch Mid. Sch. Parent Tchr. Student Assn., Gladstone, 1997, Maple Park Mid. Sch. Parent Tchr. Student Assn., Kansas City, 1998. Mem.: Am. Choral Dirs., Music Educators Nat. Conf., Mu Phi Epsilon (pres. Alpha Kappa chpt. 1977, Outstanding Jr. 1977). Republican. Baptist. Avocations: bicycling, exercise, reading, piano. Office: Northgate Mid Sch NE 48th St Kansas City MO 64118

MEILTON, SANDRA L., lawyer; b. 1946; BA, Bethany Coll., 1968; attended, U. Pitts.; JD, Dickinson Sch. Law, 1980. Bar: Pa. 1980. Assoc. Hepford, Swartz and Morgan, 1980—87, ptnr., 1987—98; shareholder Tucker Arensberg, P.C., 1998—. Bd. dirs. Mechanicsburg Children's Home. Named one of Best Lawyers in Am., 2005. Mem.: ABA, Dauphin County Bar Assn., Am. Acad. Matrimonial Lawyers. Office: Tucker Arensberg PO Box 889 111 N Front St Harrisburg PA 17108-0889 Office Phone: 717-234-4121. Business E-Mail: smeilton@tuckerlaw.com.

MEINER, SUE ELLEN THOMPSON, adult nurse practitioner, consultant, gerontologist; b. Ironton, Mo., Oct. 24, 1943; d. Louis Raymond and Verna Mae Thompson; m. Robert Edward Meiner, Mar. 5, 1971; children: Diane Romeril, Suzanne. AAS, Meramec C.C., 1970; BSN, St. Louis U., 1978, MSN, 1983; EdD, So. Ill. U., Edwardsville, 1991. RN, Nev.; cert. gerontol. nurse practitioner; cert. clin. specialist in gerontol. nursing. Staff RN St. Joseph's Hosp., St. Charles, Mo., 1976-78; nursing supr. Bethesda Gen. Hosp., St. Louis, 1975-76, 71-74; adult med. dir. Family Care Ctr.-Carondelet, St. Louis, 1978-79; program dir., lectr. Webster Coll./Bethesda Hosp., Webster Groves, Mo., 1979-82; diabetes clin. specialist Washington U. Sch. Medicine, St. Louis, 1982; asst. prof. St. Louis C.C., 1983-88; vis. nurse assoc. St. Louis, 1970—71; chmn. dept. nursing, asst. prof. Barnes Hosp. Sch. Nursing, 1988-89; instr. U. Mo., St. Louis, 1989; assoc. prof. St. Charles County C.C., St. Peters, Mo., 1990-92, Deaconess Coll. of Nursing, 1991-93; patient care mgr. Deaconess Hosp., St. Louis, 1993-94; assoc. prof. Jewish Hosp. Coll. of Nursing and Allied Health, 1994-99; gerontol. nurse, rschr. Wash. U. Sch. Med., St. Louis, 1996-2000; asst. prof. nursing U. Nev. Coll. Health Scis., Las Vegas, 2000—05; pvt. practice Nev., 2005—. Nat. dir. edn. Nat. Assn. Practical Nurse Edn. and Svc., Inc., St. Louis, 1984-86; mem. task force St. Louis Met. Hosp. Assn., 1987-88; mem. adv. com. Bd. Edn. Sch. Nursing, St. Louis, 1986-90; grant coord. Kellogg Found. Gerontology and Nursing, 1991-92; project dir. NIH, NIA Grant Washington U. Sch. Medicine, St. Louis, 1996-00; mem. editorial bd. Geriatric Nursing Journ., 1999-02; legal nurse cons. Author and editor profl. books; contbr. articles to profl. jours. Chmn. bd. dirs. Creve Coeur Fire Protection Dist. Mo., 1984-89; vice chmn. Bd. Cen. St. Louis County Emergency Dispatch Svc., 1985-87; asst. leader Girl Scouts U.S., St. Louis, 1975; treas. Older Women's League, St. Louis, 1992-93. Recipient Woman of Worth award Gateway chpt. Older Women's League, 1993. Mem.: ANA, Am. Soc. of Aging, Nat. League for Nursing, Am. Nurses Found., Am. Coll. Nurse Practitioners, Am. Acad. Nurse Practitioners, Job's Daus. (guardian 1979—80), Order Ea. Star (chaplain 1970), Creve Coeur C. of C., Sigma Theta Tau (fin. chmn. 1984, archivist 1985—87, Zeta Kappa chpt. v.p. 2001—03), Kappa Delta Pi, Sigma Phi Omega (Iota chpt. pres. 1990—91). Avocations: travel, reading. Home and Office: 3722 Violet Rose Ct Las Vegas NV 89147-7400 Personal E-mail: agingwell@earthlink.net.

MEINHARDT, CAROL JEAN, education educator; b. Grand Rapids, Mich., July 2, 1943; d. Donald Lee Price and Dorothy Lucille Shawgo; m. Joseph Randall Meinhardt, July 1, 1971; children: Tracie Lynn Meinhardt-Todd, David Randall. BA, Ctrl. Mich. U., Mt. Pleasant; MA, Ctrl. Mich. U., 1972. Cert. tchr. Mich., 1962. Tchr. Jefferson Intermediate Sch., Midland, Mich., 1967—73; adj. prof. Delta Coll., University Center, Mich., 1991—96; prof. edn. Northwood U., Midland. Profl. standards com. Northwood U.; acad. advisor Delta Zeta Sorority, Midland, 2000—, S.A.F.E., Midland, 2003—. Co-chair Midland Art Fair; tchg. leader Bible Study Fellowship, Midland, 1996—2002. Mem.: Delta Mu Delta (life), P.E.O. Protestant. Home: 5009 Plainfield Midland MI 48642 Office: Northwood University 4000 Whiting Dr Midland MI 48642 Office Phone: 1-989-837-4830. E-mail: meinhardt@northwood.edu.

MEIROWITZ, CLAIRE CECILE, publishing executive; b. Frankfurt, Germany, Jan. 14, 1934; came to U.S., 1939; d. Karl and Margot Bier; m. Richard Meirowitz, Sept. 12, 1954 (div., July, 1969); children: Diane, Laura, Linda; m. Joseph, Apr. 20, 1975. AA, Nassau C.C., 1971; BA magna cum laude, Hofstra U., 1976; postgrad., N.Y. Inst. Tech., 1987-90. Pres., owner, editor, writer, pub. rels. and mktg. cons. Profl. Editing Svcs., Babylon, NY, 1972-76, 92—; editl. asst. United Tech. Publs., Garden City, NY, 1976-77; publs. assoc. N.Y. Inst. Tech., Old Westbury, NY, 1977-79; asst. dir. coll. rels., dir. publs. SUNY, Old Westbury, 1979-87, dir. cmty. rels. and publs., 1987-92. Pres. SUNY Coun. for Univ. Affairs and Devel., 1987-89; cons. Guarino Graphics, Greenville, N.Y., 1985-92, editor, copywriter, 1986-92. Manuscript editor Jour. of Collective Negotiations in Pub. Sector, 1972-91, editr., 1991—, Jour. of Individual Employment Rights, 1992—; editor art catalog South Africa/South Bronx, 1981 (art excellence award 1982); author: New Student Prospectus, The College at Old Westbury, 1979, Labor-Management Relations Among Government Workers, 1983; co-editor: Strategies for Impasse Resolution, 1992; editor Alzheimer's Assn. L.I. chpt. newsletter; contbr. articles to profl. jours. V.p., treas., sec., Taxpayers Edn. Assn., Hicksville, N.Y., 1962-68; mem. The Nature Conservancy, Cold Spring Harbor, N.Y., 1980-91; tutor Lit. Vols. Am. Suffolk County Chpt., 1996-99; newsletter editor Babylon Breast Cancer Coalition, 1997—, The Active Retiree, United Univ. Professions, 1999-2002. Recipient Excellence in Profl. Svc. award SUNY, Albany, 1987, Disting. Svc. award SUNY Coun. Univ. Affairs, 1989, award for excellence in communications SUNY Westbury Alumni Assn., 1992, award for disting. leadership L.I. Women's Coun. for Equal Edn., Employment and Tng., 1992, award for newsletter excellence N.Y. State United Tchrs., 2001. Mem. L.I. Communicators Assn., Internat. Assn. of Bus. Communicators (steering com., sec., v.p. L.I. Women's Coun. 1990-99), Babylon Village Womens Club, Babylon Bus. and Profl. Women's Assn. Democrat. Jewish. Avocation: computers. Home: 167 Cadman Ave Babylon NY 11702-1607 Office Phone: 631-422-6804. E-mail: cmeirowitz@yahoo.com.

MEIS, JEANETTE KAY, elementary educator; b. Greeley, Colo., July 16, 1959; d. Gerald Martin and Kathryn Ella Jean (Chessmore) M. BA, U. No. Colo., 1980, MA, 1986. Cert. elem. tchr., Colo. Tchr. kindergarten Hugo (Colo.) Pub. Sch., 1981, tchr. 4th grade, 1981-82; tchr. Greeley Pub. Schs., 1982-83, tchr. 2d grade, 1983-88, tchr. kindergarten, 1988—. Activity coord. Colo. Camp Cherith, Woodland Park, 1978-88, dir., 1988-2000. Mem. Alpha Delta Kappa, Colo. Orgn. Kindergarten Tchrs. (founding mem.). Baptist. Home: 1622 14th Ave Greeley CO 80631-5302 Personal E-mail: jeanettemeis@aol.com.

MEIS, NANCY RUTH, marketing executive; b. Iowa City, Aug. 6, 1952; d. Donald J. and Theresa (Dee) M.; m. Paul L. Wenske, Oct. 14, 1978; children: Alexis Wenske Burdick, Christopher Meis Wenske. BA, Clarke Coll., 1974; MBA, U. Okla., 1981. Cultural program supr. City of Dubuque, Iowa, 1974—76; from cmty. svc. dir. to program dir. State Arts Coun. of Okla. City, 1976—79; mgr. Cimarron Circuit Opera Co., Norman, Okla., 1979—82; accout exec. Bell System, Kansas City, Mo., 1980; mgr. spl. svc. Children Internat., Kansas City, Mo., 1983—86, dir. mktg. and fund raising, 1986—87, dir. devel., 1987—88, v.p. devel., 1988—90; dir. mktg., consulting svc. uni-media divsn. Universal Press Syndicate, Kansas City, Mo., 1990—95; dir. mktg. universal new media divsn. Andrews McMeel Universal, 1996—2000; v.p. content and licensing Active Buddy, Inc., N.Y.C., 2000—01; pres., co-founder Electric Prairie, LLC, 2001—. Pres. Electric Idea Cons.; cons., spkr. in field; exec. dir. Arts in Prison, Inc., 2004—.

MEISELAS, SUSAN CLAY, photographer; b. Balt., June 21, 1948; d. Leonard and Murrayl (Groh) M. BA, Sarah Lawrence Coll., 1970; EdM, Harvard U., 1971; DFA (hon.), Parsons Sch./New Sch., N.Y.C., 1988, Art Inst. of Boston, 1996, Trinity Coll., Hartford, 1999. Photographic cons. Cmty. Resources Inst., N.Y.C., 1972-74; artist-in-residence S.C. Arts Commn., 1974-75; photography tchr. New Sch., N.Y.C., 1975; free-lance photographer Magnum Photos, N.Y.C., 1976—, v.p., 1986-91. Author: Carnival Strippers, 1976, revised 2d edit., 2003, Nicaragua, 1981, Kurdistan: In the Shadow of History, 1997, Pandora's Box, 2001, Encounters with The Dani, 2003; co-editor: El Salvador, 1983; editor: Chile from Within, 1991; editor Learn to See, 1974, Voyages, 1984; co-dir.: (film) Living at Risk, 1985, Pictures from a Revolution, 1991. Recipient Robert Capa gold medal Overseas Press Club, 1979, Leica award of excellence New Sch., 1981, Photojournalist of Yr. award Am. Soc. Mag. Photographers, 1981, award Nat Endowment for Arts, 1987, Hasselblad Found., 1994, Maria Moors Cabot prize Columbia U., 1994, Cornell Capa Infinity award, 2005; MacArthur fellow, 1992. Office: Magnum Photos Inc 151 W 25th St New York NY 10001-7204 Office Phone: 212-929-6000. E-mail: susan@magnumphotos.com.

MEISINGER, SUSAN, human resources specialist; BA, Mary Washington Coll.; JD, George Washington U. Cert. sr. profl. Human Resources Certification Inst. Spl. legal counsel Associated Builders and Contractors, Washington; dep. under sec. employment standards adminstrn. U.S. Dept. Labor, Washington; v.p. govt. and pub. affairs Soc. Human Resource Mgmt., Alexandria, Va., 1987—97, sr. v.p., 1997—99, exec. v.p., COO, 1999—2002, pres., CEO, 2002—. Mem.: DC Bar Assn. Office: Soc Human Resource Mgmt 1800 Duke St Alexandria VA 22314

MEISNER, MARY JO, foundation administrator, former newspaper editor; b. Chgo., Dec. 24, 1951; d. Robert Joseph and Mary Elizabeth (Casey) M.; 1 child, Thomas Joseph Gradel. BS in Journalism, U. Ill., 1974, MS in Journalism, 1976. Copy editor Wilmington (Del.) News Jour., 1975-76, labor and bus. reporter, 1976-79; labor and gen. assignment reporter Phila. Daily News, 1979, city editor, 1979-83, met. editor, 1983-85; PM city editor San Jose (Calif.) Mercury News, 1985-86, met. editor, 1986-87; city editor The Washington Post, 1987-90; mng. editor The Ft. Worth Star-Telegram, 1991-93; editor and v.p. The Milw. Jour., 1993-95; editor, sr. v.p The Milw. Jour. Sentinel, 1995-97; editor, vice chmn. Cmty. Newspaper Co., Needham, Mass., 1997—2001; v.p., comm., external affairs Boston Found., 2001—. Mem. AP Mng. Editors (bd. dirs. 1992-95), Am. Soc. Newspaper Editors, Internat. Press Inst. (bd. dirs. 1994-2000, Pulitzer prize juror 1994, 96). Mass. Newspaper Pubs. Assn. (bd. dirs.); bd. dir., WorldBoston. Office: Boston Foundation 10th Fl 75 Arlington St Boston MA 02116 Business E-Mail: mjm@tbf.org.

MEISNER, PATRICIA ANN, assistant principal; d. Edward Charles and Eileen Cull Meisner. BS in elem. edn., Ohio U., 1969; M in ednl. adminstrn., U. Hawaii, 1982. Cert. elem. prin. Ohio, elem. tchr. Ohio. Tchr. Northwest Local Sch., Cin., 1969—72, Star of Sea, Honolulu, 1972—83, St. Bartholomew Sch., Cin., 1987—2002; prin. St. Catharine of Siena, Cin., 1983—86; asst. prin. St. Ursula Villa, Cin., 2002—. Trustee N.Am. Ursuline Ednl. Svcs., 2004—. Mem.: Nat. Cath. Edn. Assn., Assn. Supervision and Curriculum Devel. Avocation: travel. Office: St Ursula Villa 3660 Vineyard Pl Cincinnati OH 45226 Office Phone: 513-871-7218 ext. 127. Business E-Mail: p.meisner@stursulavilla.org.

MEISSINGER, ELLEN MURRAY, artist, educator; b. Raleigh, N.C., June 19, 1947; d. William Don and Sarah (Elliott) Murray; m. Lonnie Dean Meissinger, Jan. 10, 1975; children: Logan Don, Jordan Daniel. BFA, U. N.C., Greensboro, 1969, MFA, 1971. Prof. Okla. State U., Stillwater, 1971-86, Ariz. State U. Sch. of Art, Tempe, 1986—. Juror Rocky Mountain Nat. Water Media Exhibit Foothills Art Ctr., Golden, Colo., 1997; mem. painting and print commn. and drawing area Ariz. State U., Tempe; juror Ariz. Aqueous Internat. Exhbn., Tubac Ctr. for the Arts, 2006. Invitational exhbns. include Am. Still Life Painting, 1998, Watercolor Now V/Springfield Art Mus., 1997, Shemer Art Ctr. and Mus., Phoenix, 2005, M.A. Doran Gallery, Tulsa, 2005, Park Central Gallery, Springfield, Mo., 2005, Mo. State U. Art and Design Gallery, Springfield, 2006; featured in books: Best of Watercolor Painting Composition, 1997, Best of Watercolor Painting Texture, 1997. Mem.: Watercolor Honor Soc. (bd. dirs.), Nat. Soc. Arts and Letters (greater Ariz. regional art chmn.), Coll. Art Assn., Watercolor USA Honor Soc. (pres. 1993—95, bd. dirs. 1995—2004), Nat. Watercolor Soc. Avocation: gardening. Office: Ariz State U Sch of Art PO Box 871505 Tempe AZ 85287-1505 Business E-Mail: e.murray@asu.edu.

MEISSNER, ANN LORING, psychologist, educator; b. Richland Center, Wis., Nov. 26, 1924; d. Frank Gilson Woodworth and Leona Bergman; m. Hans Meissner, July 4, 1946 (div. 1953); children: Edie, John Arthur; m. Corbin Sherwood Kidder, Oct. 28,1979. BS, U. Mich., 1953; MS, U. Wis., 1960, PhD, 1965; MPH, U. Calif., Berkeley, 1969; diploma, Gestalt Inst., Cleve., 1974, U. Minn., 1993; D for Life Long Learning (hon.), St. Mary's U., Winona, Minn., 2001. Lic. psychologist, Minn. Assoc. dir. Coop. Sch. Rehab. Ctr., Mpls., 1965-72; assoc. prof. W.Va. U., 1972-74; psychologist Alternative Behavior Assn., Mpls., 1974-79, Judson Family Ctr., Mpls., 1979-84; pvt. practice St. Paul, 1984—. Dir. nursing Augsburg U., Mpls., 1974-76; adj. prof. St. Mary's U., Mpls., 1979-2004; mem. staff Gestalt Inst. Twin Cities, Mpls., 1978-88; dir. Today Per., Mpls., 1980-91; mem. State Bd. Psychology, Mpls., 1982-86. Recipient Disting. Human Svc. Profl. award N. Hennepin C.C., Mpls., 1981. Mem. APA, Elder Zest (pres. 2002). Episcopalian. Office: 332 Minn St 1255 Saint Paul MN 55101-1314 Home: 1840 U Ave W Apt 301 Saint Paul MN 55104 Personal E-mail: croneann@mac.com.

MEISSNER, KATHERINE GONG, municipal official; b. Stockton, Calif., 1955; BA, U. Phoenix, Stockton, Calif., 1999. Mem. comty. planning dept. staff City of Stockton, Calif., 1982-85, exec. asst. city clk., 1985-96, city clk., 1996—. Office: City Stockton Office City Clk 425 N El Dorado St Stockton CA 95202-1997 Office Phone: 209-937-8458. Business E-Mail: city.clerk@ci.stockton.ca.us.

MEISTER, KAREN OLIVIA, secondary school educator; b. Newark, May 19, 1944; d. Bernice Hendricks Huebner; children: Christin, Brian, Erin. BA, Kean Coll., 1966, MA, 1987. Tchr. Union (N.J.) Bd. Edn., 1970-74; instr. Roselle (N.J.) Bd. Edn., 1982—; adj. prof. Union County Coll., 1987—92, Raritan Valley Cmty. Coll., Somerset, 1992—; Ind. Cons. Mary Kay Inc. Trainer Lit. Vol. Am., 1989-91. Mem. NEA, N.J. Edn. Assn., Internat. Reading Assn., N.J. Reading Assn., Suburban Reading Coun. Avocation: antiques. Office: Harrison Sch 310 Harrison Ave Roselle NJ 07203-1495

MEIT, HEATHER TONIA, psychologist; d. James and Patricia Anderson; 1 child, Maxwell Harold. BA, Ea. Ill. U., 1981—85; MA, Bradley U., 1985—87; PhD, W.Va. U., 1996—2001. Lic. psychologist W.Va.; profl. counselor W.Va., cert. employee assistance profl. Program dir. Salvation Army Domestic Violence Program, Cocoa, Fla., 1987—88; children's clinician La Frontera Mental Health Ctr., Tucson, Ariz., 1988—89; therapist Alternatives for Children & Families, Flint, Mich., 1989—90; cons. Nat. Employee Assistance Services, Waukesha, Wis., 1991—92; sr. account mgr. United HealthCare Corp. (IHR Divsn.), Brookfield, Wis., 1992—94; readjustment counseling therapist Louis A. Johnson VA Med. Ctr., Clarksburg, W.Va., 2001—. Mem. Women's Ctr., Waukesha, Wis., 1993—94; co-chair Combined Fed. Campaign Louis A. Johnson VA Med. Ctr., Clarksburg, W.Va., 2004—05. Mem.: APA (assoc.), Employee Assistance Profls. Assn. (assoc.; pres. 2005—, West Va. chpt.), W.Va. Psychol. Assn. (assoc.), Psi Chi (assoc.; sec., treas., pres. 1982—85, East Ill. U. chpt.). Avocations: running, reading.

MEITNER, PAMELA, lawyer, educator; b. Phila., Aug. 23, 1950; d. Alfred Victor Meitner and Claire Jane (Carroll) Harmer; m. William Bruce Larson, Sept. 13, 1980; 1 child, William Bruce, Jr. BS in chem. engring., Drexel U., 1973; JD, Del. Law Sch., 1977. Bar: Del. 1977, U.S. Dist. Ct. Del. 1977, U.S. Patent and Trademark Office 1977. Engr. DuPont Co., Deepwater, N.J., 1973-77, lawyer Wilmington, Del., 1977. Prof. Del. Law Sch., Wilmington, 1985-89. Commr. State Emergency Response Com., Dover, Del., 1986-90, 97—. Mem. Del. Bar Assn. Clubs: DuPont Country (Wilmington) (bd. govs. 1984-85). Home: 211 Welwyn Rd Wilmington DE 19803-2951 Office: DuPont Co Legal Dept 1007 S Market St Wilmington DE 19801-5227 Office Phone: 302-774-8720. Business E-Mail: pamela.meitner@usa.dupont.com.

MEJIA, BARBARA OVIEDO, retired chemistry professor; b. San Francisco, Apr. 14, 1946; d. Louis Jerome and Alice May (Beall) O. AA, Sierra Coll., 1967; BS, U. Calif., Davis, 1969, PhD, 1973. Cert. community coll. tchr., Calif. Lectr. U. Calif., Davis, summer 1977, Calif. State U., Chico, 1973-76, asst. prof., 1976-80, assoc. prof., 1980-85, prof., 1985—2001, emeritus, 2001—. Contbr. articles to profl. jours. Judge Calif. Cen. Valley Sci.-Engring. Fair, Chico, 1977, 89, 81, 81, 88, bd. dirs., 1978-79; judge Butte County Sci. Fair, Chico, 1985-90. Mem. AAAS, Am. Chem. Soc., Congress of Faculty Assns., Cal Aggie Alumni Assn., Assn. Calif. State Univ. Profs., Sigma Xi. Home: 6 Laguna Ct Chico CA 95928-7431 Office: Calif State U Dept Chemistry Chico CA 95929-0001 Business E-Mail: Bmejia@csuchico.edu.

MEJIA, MIGDALIA TERESA, psychologist, performing arts educator; b. San Juan, PR, Nov. 18, 1968; d. Diego Mejia and Migdalia Costa. BA in Psychology, U. PR, 1990, BA in Pedagogy, 1996; M in Clin. Psychology, Carlos Albiza U., 2003. Tchr. asst. spl. edn. La Esperanza Sch., Rio Piedras, 1991—93; tchr. drama Car-Le Pre-sch., Rio Piedras, 1995—96, Juanita Peraza Sch., Rio Piedras, 1996—2004; evaluator U. PR, 2004—05; intern psychology Mental Health Clinic, San Juan, 2005—. Actor: (plays) Theatre Workshop Rondon & O'Neill, 1992—94; dir.: (theatre play) Prohibido Suicidarse en Primavera, 1994. Chorus singer Santa Luis's Ch., Rio Piedras, 1995—2005. All-Am. scholar, Carlos Albiza U., 2000—02. Mem.: Am. Counseling Assn. Avocations: dance, reading, writing, movies, theater. Home: B23 D St Ext Alameda San Juan PR 00926 Personal E-mail: mejiamigdalia@yahoo.com.

MELAMED, CAROL DRESCHER, lawyer; b. NYC, July 12, 1946; d. Raymond A. and Ruth W. (Schwartz) Drescher; m. Arthur Douglas Melamed, May 26, 1983; children: Kathryn, Elizabeth;children from previous marriage: Stephanie Weisman, D. Wynne Brown. AB, Brown U., 1967; MAT, Harvard U., 1969; JD, Cath. U. Am., 1974. Bar: Md. 1974, D.C. 1975, U.S. Ct. Appeals (D.C. cir.) 1975, U.S. Dist. Ct. D.C. 1981, U.S. Supreme Ct. 1982. Tchr. English Wellesley (Mass.) H.S., 1968-69; law clk. U.S. Ct. Appeals (D.C. cir.), Washington, 1974-75; assoc. Wilmer, Cutler & Pickering, Washington, 1975-79; assoc. counsel The Washington Post, 1979-95, v.p. govt. affairs, 1995—2006. Mem. Phi Beta Kappa.

MELANÇON, RENÉE M., lawyer; b. Lakenheath, Eng., May 23, 1971; BS cum laude, U. Fla., 1992; MS, U. Ariz., 1997, JD magna cum laude, 1997. Bar: Tex. 2002. Jud. law clk. to Hon. Robert E. Jones US Dist. Ct. (dist. Oreg.), 1998—99; jud. law clk. to Hon. Martha Craug Daughtrey US Ct. Appeals (6th cir.), 2000—01; assoc. appellate sect. Baron & Budd, P.C., Dallas. Contbr. articles to profl. publs. Named a Rising Star, Tex. Super Lawyers mag., 2006. Mem.: Dallas Bar Assn., Dallas Trial Lawyers Assn., Tex. Trial Lawyers Assn., Trial Lawyers for Pub. Justice, Am. Trial Lawyers Assn., ABA, Phi Beta Kappa. Office: Baron & Budd PC 3102 Oak Lawn Ave Ste 1100 Dallas TX 75219 Office Phone: 214-521-3605.*

MELANCON, WANDA LORIE, secondary educator; b. Hahnville, La., Oct. 15, 1941; d. Ted and Ada (Millet) Lorie; divorced; children: Kim, Michelle, Charles, Brent, Susan, Mark, Michael, Jessica, Amanda. BA, Nicholls Coll., Thidadaux, La., 1975. Cert. English and speech tchr., talented drama tchr., La. Tchr. English and talented drama Hahnville High Sch., Boutte, La., 1976—. Presenter in field, 1984—. Vol. Girl Scouts U.S.A., Luling, La., 1989-92; tchr. Holy Family Ch., Luling, 1992—. Named Tchr. of Yr., Hahnville High Sch., 1988, Tchr. of Month, 1992. Avocations: cooking, theater, jazz, travel, gardening. Office: Hahnville High Sch 200 Tiger Dr Boutte LA 70039-3520

MELANSON, KATHLEEN JEAN, nutritionist, educator; b. Boston, Mass., Sept. 23, 1963; d. Henry Louis and Alice Elizabeth Melanson; m. Bjorn Olof Carlsson, Aug. 17, 2002; 1 child, Sebastian Axel Carlsson. BS in animal sci., U. New Hampshire, 1983, BS in nutrition sci., 1987; MS in nutrition sci., Pa. State U., 1990; PhD in nutrition sci., Tufts U. Sch. of Nutrition, 1996. Registered dietitian, lic. Diet tech. Spaulding Rehab. Hosp., Boston, 1987—88; grad. rsch. asst. Pa. State U., State Coll., Pa., 1987—90, Tufts U. Sch. Nutrition, Boston, 1990—96; post doctorate rsch. fellow Maastricht U., Maastricht, Netherlands, 1996—99; sr. scientist Rippe Lifestyle Inst., Shrewsbury, Mass., 1999—2001; asst. prof. nutrition U. RI, Kingston, RI, 2001—. Sr. nutrition sci. cons. Rippe Lifestyle Inst., Shrewsbury, Mass., 2001—. Contbr. articles to profl. jours., chapters to books. Conf. speaker com. chair Am. Overseas Dietetic Assn., 1999; invited lectr. various schs. cmty. ctrs., 1999—; aerobics instr. various gyms, Boston, 1992—; ski instr. Tenney Mt., Plymouth, NH, 1985—2003. Recipient Outstanding Young Am. Woman, 1988; 4 Grad. scholarships, Am. Dietetic Assn., 1993—94, 2 grad. scholarships, Mass. Dietetic Assn., 1992—93. Mem.: Soc. for the Study of Ingestive Behavior, No. Am. Assn. for the Study of Obesity, Am. Dietetic Assn. (New Investigator award 1992). Office: U RI Nutrition Food Sci Dept 106 Ranger Hall Kingston RI 02881-1966 Business E-Mail: kmelanson@uri.edu.

MELANSON, SUSAN CHAPMAN, small business owner; b. Boston, May 6, 1946; d. Arthur Wood and Marion (Saunders) Chapman; m. Arthur S. Melanson. AA, Colby-Sawyer Coll., 1966; BA, Hiram Coll., 1970. Founder, pres. Gem Island Software, Reading, Mass., 1985-90, dir. Carlisle, Mass., 1990-93; property mgr. Finard & Co., Burlington, Mass., 1993-98; founder, herbalist Oak Hill Farm, South Hiram, Maine, 1995—; co-owner High Acres Maple Syrup. Co-owner Washington Kennel, Oak Hill Farm Bed and Breakfast Cottages; breeder, trainer, racer Siberian and Alaskan Huskies. Author: Wentworth-By-The-Sea, 1969, Nepal: A Three Week Cultural and Shamanic Immersion, 2006. Class historian Wellesley High Class, 1964. Mem.: Omicron Beta. Avocations: genealogy, collecting Inuit art, Native American Studies.

MELBERG, SHARON ELAINE, nurse; b. Brainerd, Minn., Mar. 12, 1947; d. Clinton Elsworth and Betty Lou (Smiddy) Melberg; m. Daniel D. Degner, April 7, 1966; children: Daniel Michael, Emberly Michele, Erik Christopher. B of English, Calif. State U., 1970; ADN, Golden West Coll., 1975; MPA, U. San Francisco, 1987. Tchr. English and drama St. Anthony's High Sch., Long Beach, Calif, 1970-72; Staff nurse St. Mary's Med. Ctr., Long Beach, 1975-76; mobile intensive care nurse, charge nurse emergency dept. Huntington Intercommunity Hosp., Huntington Beach, Calif., 1976-77, asst. dir. nursing, 1977-78; supr. nursing svcs. Hoag Meml. Hosp., Newport Beach, Calif., 1978, adminstrv. coord., 1978-80; nurse mgr. U. Calif. Davis Med. Ctr., Sacramento, 1980-84, asst. dir. hosps. and clinics, 1984—; asst. clin. prof., rural outreach coord. Dept. Int. Med., West Coast Ctr. for Palliative Edn. Founder jr. nurse vols., opener AIDS unit U. Calif. Davis Med. Ctr.; bd. dirs., pres. Spinal Cord and Head Injury Prevention Program, 1989—92; lectr. health care and mgmt. topics. Contbr. articles to profl. jours.; editor: U. Calif. Davis Nurse. Democrat. Roman Catholic. Avocations: decoy carving, horsemanship, hiking, painting, writing. Office: U Calif Davis Med Ctr 2315 Stockton Blvd Sacramento CA 95817-2201

MELBY, BARBARA MURPHY, lawyer; b. Nov. 22, 1965; BA, Vassar Coll., 1987; JD, Boston U., 1991. Bar: NY 1992, DC 1998, Pa. 2001. Ptnr. Global Outsourcing Group Morgan, Lewis & Bockius LLP, Phila. Co-author: Business Process Outsourcing: Process, Strategies, and Contracts, 2000, Information Technology Outsourcing: Process, Strategies, and Contracts, 2001; contbr. articles to profl. jours. Office: Morgan, Lewis & Bockius LLP 1701 Market St Philadelphia PA 19103 Office Phone: 215-963-5053. Office Fax: 215-963-5001. E-mail: bmelby@morganlewis.com.

MELBY, DONNA D., lawyer; b. 1950; BA, U. Calif., Santa Barbara, 1972; attended, Loyola U. Sch. Law, 1977—78, Calif. Western Sch. Law, 1975—77, JD, 1978. Bar: Calif. 1979. Ptnr. Sonnenschein Nath & Rosenthal LLP, LA, 2002—05. Mem. Calif. Judicial Selection Adv. Coun., 2004. Named one of The Most Influential & Talented Women Trial Lawyers in Calif., LA Daily Jour. & San Francisco Recorder, 2002, 2003, 2004, 16 leading litigators in the US, Minority Corp. Counsel Assn., 2004, The 100 Most Influential Attorneys in State of Calif., LA Daily Jour. & San Francisco Recorder, 2004; named to Top 5% So. Calif. Super Lawyers, LA Mag., 2003—05; recipient Rothchild Pro Bono Award, Sonnenschein Nath & Rosenthall LLP, 2004. Fellow: Internat. Soc. Barristers, Am. Coll. Trial Lawyers; mem.: Fed. Bar Assn., Women Lawyers of LA, Calif. Women Lawyers, Assn. Bus. Trial Lawyers, Assn. So. Calif. Def. Counsel, Def. Rsch. Inst. (labor & employment com.), Fedn. Def. and Corp. Counsel, Internat.

Assn. Def. Counsel (faculty mem. trial sch.), Am. Bd. Trial Advocates (faculty mem. trial sch. 1993—, mem. bd. dirs. 1994—, mem. found. bd. trustees 2001—, v.p. 2003, pres.-elect 2004, pres. 2005, pres. LA chpt. 2004), Chancery Club. Office: Sonnenschein Nath & Rosenthal LLP 601 S Figueroa St, Ste 1500 Los Angeles CA 90017 Office Fax: 213-892-5027. Business E-Mail: dmelby@sonnenschein.com.

MELCHER, ELIZABETH, musician; b. Phoenixville, Pa., Oct. 1, 1965; d. William Diehl Lober and Caroline Merroth Melcher; 1 child, Amy Elizabeth Winger. MusB, The Curtis Inst. Music, 1987; MusM, The Juilliard Sch., 1990; DMA, Eastman Sch. Music, 1994. Fellow in ch. music Christ and St. Stephen's Episc. Ch., NYC, 1988—89; asst. organist Brick Presbyn. Ch., NYC, 1989—90; organist/choirmaster Ch. of Ascension, Rochester, NY, 1991—94; min. music Ascension Luth. Ch., Balt., 1994—97; dir. music The Luth. Ch. St. Andrew, Silver Spring, 1997—2001; min. music The Ch. Good Shepherd, Burke, Va., 2001—03; organist/choirmaster Grace and Holy Trinity Episc. Ch., Richmond, Va., 2003—. Asst. organist John Wanamaker Grand Ct. Organ, Phila., 1985—87; pvt. tchr. organ and piano, 1999—. Organist: CD recording Pageant, 2001. Recipient 2d prize, Naples (Fla.) Internat. Organ Festival Competition, 1993, Arthur Poister Nat. Organ Competition, 1995, 1988. Mem.: Am. Guild Organists (recitalist, adjudicator various competitions, 1st prize Nat. Young Artists competition, Region III 1991, Finalist Nat. Young Artists competition 1996). Avocations: tennis, swimming, reading, concerts, travel. Office: Grace and Holy Trinity Episc Church 8 North Laurel St Richmond VA 23220-4797 Office Phone: 804-359-5628 ext. 20. Office Fax: 804-353-2348. Business E-Mail: emelcher@ghtc.org.

MELCHER, KIRSTEN JEGSEN, physical therapist, consultant, small business owner; b. Aarhus, Denmark, Aug. 8, 1934; came to U.S., 1959; d. Henry Feifer and Karen Marie (Petersen) Jegsen; m. Richard Allen Melcher, Mar. 10, 1962; children: Michael Jegsen, Peter Jegsen. Grad. in phys. therapy, Theilman, Copenhagen, 1959. Phys. therapist Copenhagen Community Hosp., 1959, George Washington U. Hosp., Washington, 1959-61, Riksforsikringsverkets Hosp., Sweden, 1961-62, Shaughnessy Hosp., Vancouver, B.C., Can., 1962-63; chief phys. therapy L. B. Johnson Hosp., Pago Pago, Samoa, 1964-70; phys. therapist Rehab. Hosp. Pacific, Honolulu, 1970-72; owner Phys. Therapy Svcs., Honolulu, 1972—. Mem. Am. Phys. Therapy Assn., Danske Fysioterapeut, Honolulu Acad. Art, Planned Parenthood, Outdoor Circle, Rebild Nat. Park Soc., Waikiki Yacht Club. Avocations: paddle tennis, bridge, sailing. Office: Physical Therapy Svcs 850 W Hind Dr # 106-108 Honolulu HI 96821-1855 Home: 6009 Kalanianaole Hwy Honolulu HI 96821-2311

MELCHER, TRINI URTUZUASTEGUI, retired finance educator; b. Somerton, Ariz., Dec. 1, 1931; d. Francisco Juan and Dolores (Barraza) Urtuzuastegui; m. Arlyn Melcher, Aug. 3, 1957 (div. Feb. 1972); children: Teresa Dolores, Michael Francis, Jocelyn Marie. BS, Ariz. State U., 1954, PhD, 1977; MBA, Kent State U., 1964. Acct. CPA firm, LA, 1954—56; instr. LA Sch. Dist., 1956—58, Dolton (Ill.) Sch. Dist., 1958—61; asst. prof. Kent (Ohio) State U., 1962—72; prof. Calif. State U., Fullerton, 1976—89, founding faculty mem. San Marcos, 1990—, prof. emeritus, 2003—. Author: Intermediate Accounting Study Guide, 1984; co-author: International Accounting: A Global Perspective, 1997. Treas. Cmty. Devel. Coun., Santa Ana, Calif., 1985-88, chmn. bd., 1989; mem. com. U.S. Dept. Labor, 1989—. Named Outstanding Educator, League of United Latin Am. Citizens, Stanton, Calif., 1987, Mex. Am. Women's Nat. Assn., Irvine, Calif., 1987, One of Ten Women of Merit, N. County Times, 1999, One of 80 Elite Hispanic Women, Hispanic Bus., 2002; recipient Outstanding Faculty award Calif. State U. Sch. Bus., 1983, Pub. Svc. award Am. Soc. Women CPAs, San Antonio, 1996; Affirmative Action grantee, 1990. Mem. AICPA (editl. bd. The Woman CPA), Am. Acctg. Assn., Calif. Soc. CPAs (Merit award 1991), Hispanic CPAs. Avocations: music, travel. Home: 2024 Sequoia St San Marcos CA 92078-5454 Office: Calif State U San Marcos CA 92096-0001 Office Phone: 760-750-4213. Business E-Mail: tmelcher@csusm.edu.

MELCONIAN, LINDA JEAN, state senator, lawyer, educator; b. Springfield, Mass. d. George and Virginia Elaine (Noble) Melconian. BA, Mt. Holyoke Coll.; MA, George Washington U.; JD, George Mason U. Asst. counsel to Spkr. Thomas P. O'Neill, Jr. U.S. Ho. of Reps., Washington; pros. atty. Hampden County Dist. Atty., Springfield, Mass.; state senator Mass. Gen. Ct., Boston, 1983—2004, majority leader emeritus Mass. State Senate. Instr. Mt. Holyoke Coll., Am. Internat. Coll.; vis. asst. prof. Suffolk U., Boston. Ex Officio trustee Ella T. Grasso Found., Conn.; active Dem. State Com., Mass. Home: 465 Dwight Rd Springfield MA 01108 Office Phone: 413-374-3671. Business E-Mail: lindamelconian@comcast.net, lindamelconi@suffolk.edu. E-mail: lmelconi@suffolk.edu.

MELE, JOANNE THERESA, dentist; b. Chgo., Dec. 5, 1943; d. Andrew and Josephine Jeanette (Calabrese). Diploma, St. Elizabeth's Sch. Nursing, Chgo., 1964; diploma in dental hygiene, Northwestern U., 1977; AS, Triton Coll., 1979; DDS, Loyola U., 1983. RN; registered dental hygienist. Staff nurse medicine/surgery St. Elizabeth's Hosp., Chgo., 1964-66, oper. room nurse, 1966-67; head nurse oper. room Cook County Hosp., Chgo., 1967-76, head nurse ICU, 1976-77; dental hygienist Mele Dental Assocs., Ltd., Oakbrook, Ill., 1977-79, practice dentistry, 1983—. Clin. asst. prof. Loyola U., Chgo., 1988-93. Recipient Northwestern U. Dental Hygiene Clinic award, 1977; Dr. Duxler Humanitarian scholar Loyola U., 1982. Mem. Chgo. Dental Soc., Ill. State Dental Soc., Acad. Gen. Dentistry, Acad. Operative Dentistry, Am. Prosthodontic Soc., Internat. Congress Oral Implantologists, Psi Omega (Kappa chpt.). Roman Catholic. Avocations: reading, music, gardening. Office Phone: 630-573-0420.

MELENDEZ, SONIA IVETTE, counselor; b. Rio Piedras, P.R., Dec. 12, 1952; d. Ramon Melendez and Bienvenida Miray. Faith educator, ISTEPA, Rio Piedros, 1983; Psychology Social Work, Career Stratford Inst., Washington, 2001; child psychology, Career Stratford Inst., 2002, Sex and Drug Counselor, 2003. Tchr. Colegio San Antonio, Rio Piedros, 1983—85, Colegio Catolice Notre Dame, Cigues, PR, 1985—89; spiritual counselor Casa Cristo Redentor, Aguas Buenas, PR, 1990—2001; cons., trainer Family Devel. Dept. Families P.R., San Juan, 1995—2006; pres. San Agustin Coqui Inc., Aguas Buenas, 1991—. Chaplain CAP, Bayamon, PR, 2000—06. Mem.: ACA, Assn. Puertarriqueni de Psicologia Individual, Am. Type Assn. Roman Catholic. Avocations: music, sports, gardening, tai chi. Office: San Agustin Coqui Inc Aguas Buenas PR 00703 E-mail: agustins13@prtc.net.

MELICIA, KITTY, human resources administrator, foundation administrator; b. San Jose, Calif., June 25, 1955; d. Philip Louis and Jeanne Cattano; m. Salvatore James Melicia, Dec. 31, 1983 (div. Oct. 1999); children: Jessica, Krystyne. AAS in Computer Bus., Heald Bus. Coll., 1997-98. Office mgr. Southland Corp., San Jose, 1978-83; human resources admin. Sierracin EOI, San Jose, 1983-85; founder, exec. dir., pres. Candlelighters Childhood Cancer Found., Seaside, Calif., 1994—; human resources adminstr. SPCA Monterey County, Monterey, Calif., 1999—. Bd. dirs. Monterey County (Calif.) Bd. Health. Contbr. essay to profl. pub. Pres. PTA Ord Terrace Sch., Monterey, 1993-96. Mem. Ctrl. Coast Human Resource Assn., Soc. Human Resources Mgmt. E-mail: buzymom@hotmail.com, kmelicia@spcamc.org.

MELKVIK, JENNIFER KENT, retired mathematics educator; b. Detroit, Mich., Jan. 3, 1953; d. Edgar James and Mary Norton Kent; m. Leslie R Melkvik, July 12, 1980; children: Jennifer M. Thibeault, Sarah J., Jason E., Chelsie V. BA in edn., Western Mich. U., 1970—74; MS, Ea. Mich. U., 1975—79. Professional Teaching Certification Dept. of Edn./Mich., 1974. Mid. sch. math tchr. East Mid. Sch., Plymouth, Mich., 1974—2006; ret., 2006. Math dept. chmn. East Mid. Sch., Plymouth, Mich., 1987—; Wayne county rep. Mich. Math Leaders Acad., 2002—; coach, mathcounts team East Mid. Sch., Plymouth, Mich., 1995—; cooperating tchr. Ea. Mich. U., 1997—; founding mem. Girls Excel in Math. and Sci. Com. Plymouth-Canton Schools, Mich., 1992—. Youth leader Chilson Hills, Am. Bapt. Ch., Brighton, Mich., 1996—2005. Recipient Edythe May Sliffe award, 2004, Math Leadership award for Wayne County Teachers, 2004, Plymouth-Canton Cmty. Schools Extra Miler award, 2003, Detroit Metro Coaching award, Mathcounts, 2003, 2004, 2005. Mem.: Nat. Coun. of Teachers of Math., Mich. Coun. of Teachers of Math., Detroit Area Coun. of Teachers of Math., Math. Assn. of Am. (hon.), Delta Kappa Gamma. Christian. Avocations: exercise, boating, swimming. Home: 10820 Gamewood Dr South Lyon MI 48178 Office: East Middle School 1042 S Mill St Plymouth MI 48170 Office Fax: 734-416-4949. Personal E-mail: jmelkvik@hotmail.com. E-mail: melkvij@pccs.k12.mi.us.

MELL, PATRICIA, dean; b. Cleve., Dec. 15, 1953; d. Julian Cooper and Thelma (Webb) M.; m. Michael Steven Ragland. AB with honors, Wellesley Coll., 1975; JD, Case Western Res. U., 1978. Bar: Ohio 1979, Pa. 1988, U.S. Dist. Ct. (so. and no. dists.) Ohio 1979. Asst. atty. gen. State of Ohio, Columbus, 1978-82, sec. of state corps. counsel, 1982-84; vis. asst. prof. Capital U. Law Sch., Columbus, 1984-85, U. Toledo Law Sch., 1985-86; asst. prof. law Widener U. (formerly Delaware Law Sch.), Wilmington, 1986—88; assoc. prof. law Mich. State U. Detroit Coll. of Law, East Lansing, Mich., 1992—2003, prof. law, 1996—2003, assoc. dean for academic affairs, 2000—02; dean John Marshall Law Sch., Chicago, Ill., 2003—. Mediator night prosecutor's program, Columbus, 1984-85. Mem. scholarship screening com. Black Am. Law Student Assn. U. Toledo Law Sch., 1985-86, governing bd. Case Western Res. U. Law Sch., Cleve., 1985-88, Alliance of Black Women, Columbus, 1983-85, Capers for Judge com., Cleve., 1980-86, century club Ohio Dems., 1985-86; chmn. law student com. Young Black Dems., Columbus, 1982-84; coordinator minority affiliations subcom. Citizens for Brown for Gov., Columbus, 1981-82; mem. Nat. Beach MBA, 1986—. Named Chgo. Midwest Honoree, Nat. Coun. Negro Women, 2003, one of Chgo.s 100 Most Influentianl Women, Crain's Chgo. Bus., 2004; recipient award, 2d Bapt. Ch., Evanston, 2003, Internat. Assn. Corps. Adminstrs., 1983, C.F. Stradford award, 2005. Mem. ABA, Nat. Bar Assn., Nat. Conf. Black Lawyers, Am. Arbitration Assn. (comml. arbitrator 1986—), Nat. Black MBA's, 1986-91. Lutheran. Avocations: modern languages, stained glass work, fencing, tennis, piano. Office: John Marshall Law Sch 315 S Plymouth Court Chicago IL 60604

MELLAN, OLIVIA JULIE (OLIVIA JULIE SHAPIRO), psychotherapist; b. Bklyn., Oct. 14, 1946; d. Eli N. and Sara Blossom (Tepper) M.; m. Anand Mundra (div. 1984); children: Aniel; m. Michael Shapiro, May 17, 1987. BA in French cum laude, Mt. Holyoke Coll., 1968; MS in French, Georgetown U., 1973, postgrad. Pvt. practice psychotherapy Washington Therapy Guild, Washington, 1975—; cons., spkr., trainer psychotherapy Olivia Mellan & Assocs., Inc., Washington, 1982—. Keynote speaker nat. and regional confs. for fin. planners, 1986-91; trainer therapists; vol. Psychologists for Social Responsibility, Washington, 1986—. Author: Money Harmony: Resolving Money Conflicts in Your Life and Relationships, 1994, Overcoming Overspending: A Winning Plan for Spenders and Their Partners, 1996, Money Shy To Money Sure: A Woman's Road Map To Financial Well-Being, 2001, The Advisors Guide To Money Psychology, 2d edit, 2005; (audiocassette) Finding Balance in Your Moneylife: Money Harmony for Individuals and Couples, 1988, Money Psychology Tips for Financial Planners; ((audio CD) Money Harmoney For You And Your Family, 2006video) In the Prime: Couples & Money with Olivia Mellan, 1996. Mem. Washington Ethical Soc. Democrat. Jewish. Avocations: spoof songwriting, choreography, jewelry making. Office: Olivia Mellan & Assocs Inc 2607 Connecticut Ave NW Washington DC 20008-1543

MELLEN, JOAN, author; b. N.Y.C. BA, Hunter Coll., 1962; MA, CUNY, 1964, PhD, 1968. Prof. Temple U., Phila., 1967—. Author: The Battle of Algiers, 1972, Marilyn Monroe, 1973, Women and their Sexuality in the New Film, 1974, Voices from the Japanese Cinema, 1975, The Waves at Genji's Door, 1976, Big Bad Wolves: Masculinity in the American Film, 1978; editor: The World of Luis Buñuel, 1978, Privilege: The Enigma of Sasha Bruce, 1980, Natural Tendencies: A Novel, 1981, Bob Knight: His Own Man, 1988, Kay Boyle: Author of Herself, 1994, Hellman and Hammett: The Legendary Passion of Lillian Hellman and Dashiell Hammett, 1996, The Seven Samurai, 2002, In the Realm of the Senses, 2004, A Farewell to Justice: Jim Garrison, JFK's Assasination and the Case That Should Have Changed History, 2005, Modern Times, 2006. Home: PO Box 359 Pennington NJ 08534-0359 Office: Temple U Anderson Hall Dept English Philadelphia PA 19122 Office Phone: 215-204-1802. E-mail: joanmellen@aol.com.

MELLERT, LUCIE ANNE, writer, photographer; b. Charleston, W.Va., June 6, 1932; d. Wilbur Conant and Grace Martin (Taylor) Frame; m. William Jennings Mellert, March 15, 1957; 1 child, James Floyd Kelly III. Student, Mason Coll. of Music Fine Arts, Charleston, 1937-49, W.Va. U., Morgantown, 1950-51. Pub. rels. exec., asst. treas., office mgr. J. H. Milam, Inc., Dunbar, W.Va., 1959-71; pub. rels. exec., office mgr. Hallcraft, Inc., Dunbar, 1972-74; office mgr. Kanawha Stone Co. Inc., Nitro, W.Va., 1975-78; freelance writer Dunbar, 1978—; freelance writer, photographer Charleston, W.Va., 1978—. Vol. photographer Charleston Gazette, 1997—. Beautification commr. City of Dunbar, 1969-72; activity coordinator, program dir. Dunbar Bicentennial Com., 1971; founder, coordinator Dunbar City wide Beautification and Improvement Com., 1969-72; coord. Kanawha County Elem. Students Anti-Litter Program, Planting the Seed, 1996-2003; pres. United Meth. Women of St. Marks; active U. Charleston Builders, Friends of Avampato Discovery Mus., W.Va. Humanities Coun., Friends of W. Va. Culture and History; judge various cmty. events, 1995-2004; commr. Kanawha County Pks. and Recreation Commn., 2000—; vol. photographer Charleston Gazette On the Town, 1997-. Named Disting. Mountaineer, W.Va. Gov. Joe Manchin III, 2005; recipient West Virginian award, Gov. Cecil Underwood, 2000, Gov. Bob Wise, 2001, West Va. Vol. Spirit award, W. Va. Women's Commn., 2003, commendation for vol. svc., W.Va. Gov. Bob Wise, 2004. Mem. Nat. Mus. Women in the Arts, Nat. Fedn. Press Women, Pioneer Women's (past pres.), Libr. of Congress Assn., Kanawha Valley and Nat. Trust Hist. and Preservation Soc., East End Assn., Women of Moose, Woman's Club Charleston, W.Va. Soc.Assn. Execs., Mental Health Assn., Mid Atlantic Arts Found. Methodist. Avocations: church activities, piano, music, travel, art. Home: 1604 Virginia St E Charleston WV 25311-2114

MELLI, MARYGOLD SHIRE, law educator; b. Rhinelander, Wis., Feb. 8, 1926; d. Osborne and May (Bonnie) Shire; m. Joseph Alexander Melli, Apr. 8, 1950; children: Joseph, Sarah Bonnie, Sylvia Anne, James Alexander. BA, U. Wis., 1947, LLB, 1950. Bar: Wis. 1950. Dir. children's code revision Wis. Legis. Coun., Madison, 1950-53; exec. dir. Wis. Jud. Coun., Madison, 1955-59; asst. prof. law U. Wis., Madison, 1959-66, assoc. prof., 1966-67, prof., 1967-84, Voss-Bascom prof., 1985-93, emerita, 1993—. Assoc. dean U. Wis., 1970-72, rsch. affiliate Inst. for Rsch. on Poverty, 1980—; mem. spl. rev. bd. Dept. Health and Social Svcs., State of Wis., Madison, 1973—2002. Author: (pamphlet) The Legal Status of Women in Wisconsin, 1977, (book) Wisconsin Juvenile Court Practice, 1978, rev. edit., 1983, (with others) Child Support & Alimony, 1988, The Case for Transracial Adoption, 1994; co-editor: Child Support: The Next Frontier, 1999; contbr. articles to profl. jours. Bd. dirs. Am. Humane Assn., 1985-95, Frank Lloyd Wright - Wis., 2004; chair A Fund for Women, Madison, Wis., 2002, 2003. Named one of five Outstanding Young Women in Wis., Jaycees, 1961; rsch. grantee NSF, 1983; recipient Belle Case LaFollette award for outstanding svc. to the profession, 1994, award for Outstanding Contbn. to Advancement of Women in Higher Edn., 1991, award for Lifelong Contbn. to Advancement of Women in the Legal Prof., 1994, Rotary Sr. Svc. award, Madison, Wis., 2002. Fellow Am. Acad. Matrimonial Lawyers (exec. editor jour. 1985-90); mem. Am. Law Inst. (cons. project on law of family dissolution), Internat. Soc. Family Law (v.p. 1994-2000, 2002-05), Wis. State Bar Assn. (reporter family law sect., 1976—), Nat. Conf. Bar Examiners (chmn. bd. mgrs. 1989, editl. adv. com.). Democrat. Roman Catholic. Avocations: walking, swimming, collecting art. Home: 2904 Waunona Way Madison WI 53713-2238 Office: U Wis Law Sch Madison WI 53706 Office Phone: 608-262-1610. Business E-Mail: msmelli@wisc.edu.

MELLISH, JO-ANNE ELIZABETH, marine biologist, researcher; b. Halifax, Nova Scotia, Can. arrived in U.S., 1999; d. Merrill Reginald and Margaret Helen Mellish; m. Stephen Ahgeak MacLean; 1 child, Gwendolyn Sirrouna MacLean. BSc in Biology with honors, Dalhousie U., Halifax, Nova Scotia, Can., 1994, PhD in Biology, 1999. Post doctoral fellow Tex. Inst. Oceanography, Galveston, 1999—2001; scientist Alaska Sea Life Ctr., Seward, 2001—; asst. rsch. prof. U. Alaska, Fairbanks, 2001—. Mem.: Soc. Marine Mammalogy, Comparative Nutrition Soc., Am. Physiological Soc. Office: Sch Fisheries and Ocean Sci Univ Alaska PO Box 757220 Fairbanks AK 99775-7220

MELLO, DAWN, retail executive; b. Lynn, Mass. Student, Modern Sch. Fashion and Design, Boston. Model; asst. to fashion dir. B. Altman & Co., N.Y.C., fashion dir., 1971—75; from corp. buying officer to v.p. and gen. merchandise mgr. May Dept. Stores Co.; v.p., fashion dir. to exec. v.p., dir. fashion merchandising Bergdorf Goodman, N.Y.C., 1975—84, pres., 1984—89, 1994—99; creative dir. Gucci, 1989—94; cons. Dawn Mello and Assocs., N.Y.C., 1999—. Recipient Eleanor Lambert award, Coun. Fashion Designer's Am., 2001. Office: Dawn Mello and Assocs Inc 12 W 57th St # 802 New York NY 10019*

MELLOR, KATHY, English as a second language educator; b. Providence; BS in Elem. Edn., RI Coll., 1970, MEd, 1977; MA in Teaching, with ESL and Cross Cultural studies, Brown U., 1989. Substitute tchr. Cranston, RI Sch. Dept., 1970—74; ESL tchr. Internat. Inst. RI, 1980—85; continuing edn. tchr., english dept. RI Coll., 1985—86; cons. for ESL North Kingstown Sch. Dept., RI, 1985; ESL tchr. Hamilton Elem. Sch., North Kingstown, RI, Davisville Mid. Sch., North Kingstown, RI, 1985—. Nat. and internat. spokesperson for education, 2004—. Named Nat. Tchr. of Yr., Coun. Chief State Sch. Officers, 2004. Achievements include redesigning her school's ESL program, which provides each student with one to three periods per day in classes for English learners. The amount of instruction given depends on their skill level; providing help to students and their families by forming a local parents group called the "Ladybugs" for speakers of other languages. This improved their ability to help their children; has instructed students from virtually every part of the globe (Laos, Korea, Bolivia, Brazil, Puerto Rico, the Philippines and the Dominican Republic); hosts an International Picnic where her students and their families gather to celebrate their achievements during the school year. Office: Davisville Mid Sch 200 School St North Kingstown RI 02852 Office Phone: 401-541-6300.

MELNICK, ALICE JEAN (AJ MELNICK), counselor; b. St. Louis, Dec. 25, 1931; d. Nathan and Henrietta (Hausfater) Fisher; m. Harold Melnick, May 24, 1953; children: Susan, Vikki, Patrice. BJ, U. Tex., Austin, 1952; MEd, U. North Tex., Denton, 1974. Reporter San Antonio Light, 1952-53; instr. journalism project Upward Bound So. Meth. U., Dallas, 1967-71. Instr. writing El Centro Dallas County C.C., Dallas, part time 1972-74; instr. human devel. Richland C.C., Dallas, part-time 1974-79; tchr. English, journalism and psychology Dallas Ind. Sch. Dist., 1969-81; counselor Ursuline Acad., 1981-94; part-time instr. human devel. Sante Fe C.C.; freelance documentary photographer. Author: They Changed the World: People of the Manhattan Project, 2006. Mem. Dallas Sports Car Club, N.Mex. Jewish Hist. Soc., Temple Beth Shalom. Jewish. Home: 101 Monte Alto Rd Santa Fe NM 87508-8865 Personal E-mail: aj@melnick.net.

MELNICK, JANE FISHER, writer, educator, photographer; b. Boston, Sept. 26, 1939; d. Richard T. and Mary (Holcombe) Fisher; m. Burton A. Melnick, Dec. 1962 (div. 1969); 1 child, Benjamin A.; life ptnr. Eileen Willenborg, 1978—. BA cum laude, Radcliffe Coll., 1962; MA, NYU, 1985, PhD in Am. Studies, 1991. News writer, photographer, freelance editor, 1962—75; editor, writer, photographer In These Times, Chgo., 1976-78; grapnics editor, writer Seven Days, N.Y.C., 1978-81; instr. writing, journalism, Am. lit. and history NYU, 1981-86; instr. writing, Am. lit. Loyola U., Chgo., 1988-91; asst. prof. Elmhurst (Ill.) Coll., 1991-96; writer, coll. prep. tutor Chgo., 1997—2004. Recipient Phi Beta Kappa award for best creative work by an undergrad. Radcliffe Coll., 1959; Mademoiselle mag. fiction contest award, 1962, NEA grantee, 1973, dean's dissertation fellow NYU, 1987. Mem. MLA, Mid-Am. Am. Studies Assn. (exec. bd.) Avocations: home renovation, travel. Home: 5000 N Marine Dr Apt 15A Chicago IL 60640-3226

MELOY, JUDITH MARIE, humanities educator; b. Pitts., Oct. 22, 1951; d. John C. and Miriam Meloy. BA, Denison U., 1973; MST, U. Dayton, 1982; PhD, Ind. U., 1986. Admissions counselor Denison U., Granville, Ohio, 1973—74; tchr. Centerville (Ohio) City Schs., 1978—83; program evaluation Conn. State Dept. Edn., Hartford, 1987—89; prof. Vt. State Colls., Castleton, 1989—. Dept. chair, 1994—95; chair tchg. and scholarship com., 2001—03; faculty fellow, 1996—97. Author: (book) Writing the Qualitative Dissertation: Understanding by Doing, 1994, Writing the Qualitative Dissertation: Understanding by Doing, 2d edit., 2002. Comty. Svc., Castleton, 1998—; mem. Hayes Found. Bd., 1992—. Recipient Outstanding Faculty award, Castleton State Coll. Alumni Assn., 2005. Mem.: Am. Ednl. Rsch. Assn. (chmn. qualitative rsch. spl. interest group 2004—06). Office: Castleton State Coll Castleton VT 05735 Business E-Mail: judy.meloy@castleton.edu.

MELOY, PATRICIA, vocational school educator, art educator; b. St. Louis, Sept. 5, 1951; d. Clyde and Mildred Schoue; m. Loyd R. Meloy, July 28, 1978; children: Jason Patrick, Kenda Renee. BS in Indsl. Arts and Fine Arts, S.E. Mo. State U.; MA in Tchg. Arts, Webster U. Shop tchr. Parkway Sch. Dist., St. Louis, 1974—75; shop and art tchr. Seckman Middle Sch., Imperial, Mo., 1975—. Safety tabulator Mo. Cheerleader Coaches Assn., 1999—2006; coach grades 7-9 and 10-12 poms, cheerleaders, and freshman volleyball. Safety judge Mo. Dance Team Assn. Named Tchr. of Month, Seckman Middle Sch., 2001, Outstanding Educator, Fox C-6 Sch. Bd., Arnold, Mo., 2002. Mem.: Mo.Dance Team Assn., Mo. State Tchrs. Assn. (bldg. rep. 2000—05), NEA (bldg. rep. 2005—). Avocations: harp, painting. Office: Seckman Middle Sch 2840 Seckman Rd Imperial MO 63052 Business E-Mail: schoue@fox.k12.mo.us.

MELOY, SYBIL PISKUR, retired lawyer; b. Chgo., Dec. 1, 1939; d. Michael M. and Laura (Stevenson) Piskur; children: William S., Bradley M. BS with honors, U. Ill., 1961; JD, Chgo. Kent Coll. Law, 1965. Bar: Ill. 1965, Fla. 1985, D.C. 1995, U.S. Dist. Ct. (no. dist.) Ill. 1965, U.S. Supreme Ct. 1972, U.S. Ct. Appeals (fed. cir.) 1983, U.S. Dist. Ct. (so. dist.) Fla. 1985, D.C. 1995. Patent chemist, patent atty., sr. atty., internat. counsel G.D. Searle & Co., Skokie, Ill., 1961-72; regional counsel Abbott Labs., North Chicago, Ill., 1972-78; pvt. practice Arlington Heights, Ill., 1978-79; asst. gen. counsel Alberto Culver Co., Melrose Park, Ill., 1979-83; corp. counsel Key Pharms., Inc., Miami, Fla., 1983-86; assoc. Ruden, Barnett, McCloskey, Smith, Schuster and Russell, Pa., 1987-89, ptnr. Pa., 1990-91, Foley & Lardner, Miami, Washington, 1991—2001. Adj. prof. Univ. of Miami Sch. of Law, 1986-92. Contbr. article on fertility control and abortion laws, book rev. on arbitration to law revs. Recipient Abbott Presdl. award, 1977; Bur. Nat. Affairs prize, 1965; Law Rev. prize for best article. Mem. ABA, Chgo. Bar Assn. (chmn.-elect and vice chmn. internat. and fgn. law com.), Am. Patent Law Assn., Am. Chem. Soc., Licencing Execs. Soc., Phi Beta Kappa, Phi Kappa Phi. Patentee oral contraceptive, 1965. Office: 1676 32d St NW Washington DC 20007-2960

MELROY, PAMELA ANN, astronaut; b. Palo Alto, Calif., Sept. 17, 1961; d. David and Helen M.; married BS in Physics and Astronomy, Wellesley Coll., 1983; MSc in Earth and Planetary Scis., MIT, 1984. Commd. 2nd lt. USAF, 1983, advanced through grades to lt. col.; co-pilot KC-10, aircraft comdr., instr. pilot Barksdale AFB, Bossier City, La.; test pilot C-17 Combined Test Force; shuttle pilot NASA, Houston, pilot STS-92 (Discovery), 2000, pilot STS-112 (Atlantis), 2002, shuttle comdr. STS-120 to Internat. Space Station, 2006, selected as astronaut, 1994, astronaut, 1995—. Bd. trustee Wellesley Coll. Decorated Air Force Meritorious Svc. medal with oak leaf cluster, Air medal with oak leaf cluster, Aerial Achievement medal with oak leaf cluster, Expeditionary medal with oak leaf cluster. Mem. Soc. Exptl. Test Pilots, Order of Daedalians, 99s. Achievements include being the second female astronaut to command a US orbiter. Avocations: theater, tap and jazz dancing, reading, cooking, flying. Office: Astronaut Office/CB NASA Lyndon B Johnson Space Ctr Houston TX 77058*

MELTEBEKE, RENETTE, career counselor; b. Portland, Oreg., Apr. 20, 1948; d. Rene and Gretchen (Hartwig) M. BS in Sociology, Portland State U., 1970; MA in Counseling Psychology, Lewis and Clark Coll., 1985. Lic. profl. counselor, Oreg.; nat. cert. counselor; Veriditas trained labyrinth facilitator. Secondary tchr. Portland Pub. Schs., 1970-80; project coord. Multi-Wash CETA, Hillsboro, Oreg., 1980-81; coop. edn. specialist Portland C.C., 1981-91; pvt. practice career counseling, owner Career Guidance Specialists, Lake Oswego, Oreg., 1988—. Mem. adj. faculty Marylhurst (Oreg.) U., 2003—, Portland State U., 1994-98, Lewis and Clark Coll., 2001—; assoc. Drake Beam Morin Inc., Portland, 1993-96; career cons. Managed Health Network, 1994-98, Career Devel. Svcs., 1990-95, Life Dimensions, Inc., 1994; presenter Internat. Conf., St. Petersburg, Russia, 1995. Rotating columnist Lake Oswego Rev., 1995-99; creator video presentation on work in Am. in 5 langs., 1981; pub. in "Chicken Soup to Inspire a Woman's Soul, 2004. Pres. Citizens for Quality Living, Sherwood, Oreg., 1989; mem. Leadership Roundtable on Sustainability for Sherwood, 1994-95; bd. dirs. Bus. for Social Responsibility for Oreg. and Southwestern Wash., 1999, 2000. Recipient Esther Matthews award for outstanding contbn. to field of career devel., 1998. Mem.: Assn. for Humanistic Psychology (presenter nat. conf. Tacoma 1996), Oreg. Career Devel. Assn. (pres. 1990), Nat. Career Devel. Assn., Willamette Writers. Avocations: walking, swimming, bicycling, cross country skiing, photography. Office: Career Guidance Specialists 15800 Boones Ferry Rd Ste C104 Lake Oswego OR 97035-3492 Home: 15117 SW Merryman St Sherwood OR 97140 Office Phone: 503-625-7513. E-mail: Renette@responsiblestewardship.com.

MELTON, AMANDA LOUISE, science educator; b. St. Louis, Mo., July 30, 1979; d. Russell Robert and Patricia Ann Roehr; m. Matthew Carl Melton, July 29, 2006. BS in Biology, Truman State U., Kirksville, Mo., 2001, MA in Secondary Edn./Unified Sci.-Biology, 2003. Sci. tchr. McCluer HS, Florissant, Mo., 2002—. Recipient Inspirational Tchr. of Yr. award, 2005. Mem.: NEA, NSTA, Nat. Assn. Biology Tchrs. Avocations: reading, dance.

MELTON, BENGI BIBER, psychiatrist, educator; d. Ahmet Biber; m. Arvin Basil Melton, 1998; 1 child, Brent Berkin. MD, Ankara U., Turkey, 1991. Asst. prof. U. Tex. Med. Br., Galveston, Tex., 2004—. Mem.: Am. Psychiat. Assn. Office: Utmb 301 University Blvd Galveston TX 77555 Office Phone: 409-747-9667. Personal E-mail: bb_melton@yahoo.com. Business E-Mail: bbmelton@utmb.edu.

MELTON, CAROL A., communications executive; b. St. Augustine, Fla., 1954; m. Joseph M. Hassett; children: Matthew, Meredith Hassett. BA with honors, Wake Forest U., 1976; MA in Journalism and Comm., U. Fla., 1977; JD with honors, Am. U., 1981. Assoc. in comm. grp. Hogan and Hartson, Washington, 1981-82; asst. gen. counsel Nat. Cable TV Assn., 1983-86; legal adv. to Chmn. Mark Fowler FCC, Washington, 1986-87; Washington counsel Warner Comm., 1987-91; v.p. law and pub. policy Time Warner Inc., Washington, 1992-97, exec. v.p. global pub. policy, exec. officer, 2005—; exec. v.p. govt. rels., exec. officer Viacom, Inc., Washington, 1997—2005. Trustee The Media Inst., Washington, 1997—2005, Washington Performing Arts Soc., 1997—99, The Potomac Sch., McLean, Va., 1999—2000, Meridian Internat. Ctr., 2001—03; mem. Fed. City Coun., 1997—, Coun. on Fgn. Rels., 2006—. Office: Time Warner Inc 800 Connecticut Ave NW Washington DC 20006

MELTON, EMMA ALEXANDER, educational consultant, retired elementary school educator; b. Louisville, Ky., Aug. 26, 1933; d. Jesse Wilson and Reella Odessa Alexander; m. Brady Melton Jr., Apr. 17, 1960; children: Brady Aldred, Tia Meychelle. BA in English and Speech, Ctrl. State Coll., 1954; MA in Elem. Edn., Ohio State U., 1962; cert. in reading, John Carroll U. English tchr. Xenia (Ohio) City Sch., 1955—57; elem. tchr. Cleve. Pub. Sch., 1957—63, reading cons., 1969—90; social skills cons. Soc. Prevention of Violence, Cleve., 1990—92; diversity trainer of educators Anti-Defamation League, Cleve., 1992—97; worksh. Workshop facilitator Inst. Cultural Affairs Internat., various locations, 1970—2000; spkr. at nat. and internat. conf. and workshops, 1984—. Contbg. author: Sister to Sister, 1999. Adv. bd. Nuc. Age Resource Ctr., Cleve., 1994—2004; deacon First Bapt. Ch., Cleve., 1980—; advocacy bd. Interreligious Ptnrs. in Action, Cleve., 2000—; mem. adv. bd. Cleve. Ecumenical Inst. for Religious Studies, 2006—. Recipient Ecumenical award, Interchurch Coun., Cleve., 1998; grantee, Cleve. Edn. Fund, 1987; Martha Holden Jennings scholar, Jennings Found., 1981. Mem.: Delta Sigma Theta. Democrat. Baptist. Avocations: reading, travel, singing.

MELTON, JUNE MARIE, nursing educator; b. St. Louis, Oct. 16, 1927; d. Thomas Jasper and Alice Marie (Sloas) Hayes; m. Malcolm Adrian Essen, July 12, 1947 (dec. July 1978); children: Alison, William, Terrence, Mark, Cathleen, Melodie; m. Denver A. Melton, Sept. 6, 1989 (dec.). Grad., Jewish Hosp. Sch. Nursing, 1948; student, U. Mo., Lincoln U., U. Colo., Stephens Coll., U. S.W. RN, Mo.; nurse ARC. Instr. home nursing U. Mo., Columbia, 1948-49; acting dir. nurses, 1957-68; supr. instr., obstet. supr. Charles E. Still Hosp., Jefferson City, Mo.; supr. nurse ICU, primary nurse St. Mary's Health Ctr., Jefferson City; health dir. Algoa Correctional Instn., Jefferson City, 1979-83; home health vis. nurse A&M Home Health, Jefferson City, 1983-96, parish nurse, 1998—. Mem. adv. bd. A&M Home Nursing, Jefferson City; instr. GED Lincoln U., Jefferson City; participant study of premature baby nursing U. Colo., 1964. Vol. ARC, Belle-Rolla, Mo., instr. home nursing; missionary to Togo, West Africa Mo. Synod. Luth. Ch., 1996—97, parish nurse, 1998—, harvester for Christ, 1999—; parish nurse Ysleta Luth. Mission, 2002. Mem.: U.S. Nurse Corps. Democrat. Lutheran. Avocations: fishing, sewing, reading, travel. Home: 704 Golden Village Apt 1-D New Bloomfield MO 65063

MELTON, NANCY KERLEY, medical, surgical, and oncological nurse; b. Lamesa, Tex., Nov. 13, 1949; d. Ralph Burton Sr. and Edna Dale (Bearden) K.; 1 child, Stacey Dale Kent. LVN, Paris (Tex.) Jr. Coll., 1987, ADN, 1990. RN; ACLS. Team leader St. Joseph's Hosp., Paris, 1996—, Regional Med. Ctr. Hosp., 1990—.

MELTON, STEPHANIE ANN, music educator; d. Francis Hobart and Amanda Ruth Means; m. Raymond Lee Melton, Dec. 28, 1991; children: Kyle, Kimberly, Ryan. AA, Eastern Okla. State Jr. Coll., 1979; MusB in edn., Ctrl. State U., Okla., 1981, MusM in edn., 1985. Cert. music edn. tchr. Oka. Music aid Hefner Jr. High, Oklahoma City, 1981—82; music tchr. Highland Park Elem., Del City, Okla., 1982—97, Country Estates Elem., Midwest City, Okla., 1997—2006. Pres. Mid-Del Elem. Music Tchrs., Midwest City, Okla., 1987, 1999; accompanist Midwest Choral Soc., Midwest City, Okla., 2004—05. Grantee Classroom Grant, Mid-Del Schs. Found., 2000—01. Republican. Southern Baptist.

MELTZER, E. ALYNE, elementary school educator, social worker, volunteer; b. Jersey City, May 16, 1934; d. Abraham Samuel and Fannie Ruth (Nydick) Meltzer. BA, Mich. State U., 1956. Acctg. clk. Louis Marx Co. Inc., N.Y.C., 1957-60; tchr. social studies Haverstraw HS, NY, 1960-61; tchr. Sachem Ctrl. Sch. Dist., Farmingville, NY, 1961-63, East Paterson Sch. Dist., NJ, 1964-65; case worker dept. social svc. Human Resource Adminstrn., N.Y.C., 1966-89. Mem. Yorkville Civic Coun., 1988—93; policy advisor Senator Roy Goodman Adv. Com., Albany, 1987—90; mem. Temple Shaaray Tefila. Recipient Sabra Soc. Plaque award, State of Israel New Leadership Divsn., N.Y.C., 1979, Prime Min. Club Plaque award, State of Israel Bonds, 1986—87, 1996, Pin award, 1986—87, 1990, 1994—96, others. Mem.: AAUW, Jewish Genealogy Soc., Assn. Ref. Zionists Am., Am. Jewish Com., Internat. Coun. Jewish Women (participant Jerusalem seminar 1991, N.Am. region anti semitism seminar 2005), Nat. Coun. Jewish Women (life; rep. evening br. inter br. bd. 1972—74, chmn. program N.Y. sectr. evening br. 1973—74, participant nat. conv. 1987, Albany Inst. 1987, Washington Inst. 1987, N.E. dist. conv. 1988, Albany Inst. 1988, Israel Summit V 1988, Washington Inst. 1989, sec. pub. affairs com. 1990—93, mem. state pub. affairs com. 1990—98, sec. pub. affairs com. 1990—, Albany Inst. 1991, Washington Mission 1991, co-chair Hunger Program Sunday Family Soup Kitchen 1991—93, nat. Israel affairs com. 1991—96, bd. dirs. N.Y. sect. 1991—, Jewish/Israel affairs com. sect. 1991—, Washington Inst. 1992, participant nat. conv. 1993, Albany Inst. 1993, chair Roosevelt Island Svcs. 1993—2003, participant nat. conv. 1996, Israel Roundtable 1996—99, co-chair fundraising jour. 1998—2000, co-chair sec. Yad B'Yad (Hand in Hand with Israel) cmty. svc. project 1999—2005, film festival com. Eleanor Leff Jewish Women's Resource Ctr. 2001—02, co-chair sec. Jewish/Israel Affairs com. 2001—04, advisor sec. Jewish Israeli Affairs com. 2004—, participant nat. conv. 2005, life mem. N.Y. and Rockland County sects., Outstanding Vol. award 1973—74, 1990—91, Donor award 1987—93, 1996), People for the Am. Way, Mich. State U. Alumni Orgn. (life; sec. N.Y. chpt. 1959—60), Women's League for Israel (life), Jewish Hist. Soc. N.Y., Mothers and Others, Hadassah (life), Rockland County Jewish Home for the Aged (life), Sierra Club.

MELVIN, MARY BELLE, religious studies educator, director; b. Old Hickory, Tenn., May 11, 1952; d. Mary Tabitha and Murray Trice Melvin. MEd, Tenn. State U., Nashville, 1987. Cert. tchr. Tenn. Spiritual life dir. Donelson Christian Acad., Nashville, 1975; edn. and adminstr. coord. New Hope Bapt. Ch., Hermitage, Tenn., 2005—. Youth coun. Nashville Bapt. Assn., 1995—96. Named Coach of Yr., Tenn. Secondary Schools Athletic Assn., 1987, 1990. Office: Donelson Christian Acad 300 Danyacrest Dr Nashville TN 37214 Office Phone: 615-577-1226. Business E-Mail: mmelvin@dcanet.org.

MEMBIELA, ROYMI VICTORIA, marketing professional, consultant; b. Havana, Cuba, June 25, 1957; arrived in U.S., 1970; d. Rolando Angel Membiela and Migdalia Amand; m. Terry D McCandlish, July 22, 2003. BS in Mktg., Barry U., 1986. Lic. real estate assoc. Fla. Dir. new bus. and Hispanic market devel. specialist Miami (Fla.) Herald Pub. Co., 1977—94; pres. Mktg. Americas Group, Coral Gables, Fla., 1994—98; cons. Internat. Consulting Partners, Inc, Miami, 1998—99; sr. v.p. Kelley Swofford Roy, Coral Gables, 1999—2002; pres. Roymi Membiela & Associates, Inc, Miami Beach, Fla., 2002—. Community activist (mentorship of women) Miami Dade County Parks & Recreation (In the Co. of Women, 2003). Bd. mem. UNIDAD Hispana, Miami Beach, Fla., 2001—03, Spanish-Am. League Against Discrimination, Miami, 1999—2003; bd. dirs. Vizcaya Trust Fund, Miami, 2000—02; cmty. activist, women's mentor Miami Dade County Parks & Recreation; chmn. Cmty. Rels. Bd. City of Miami Beach, 2002—03; mem. State of Fla. Bd. of Architecture and Interior Design, Tallahassee, 2002—03; bd. dirs. Miami Dade County Housing Fin. Authority, Miami, 2002—03; chmn. Miami Dade County Hispanic Affairs Adv. Bd., Miami, 1998—2002; mem. Miami Dade County Cmty. Rels. Bd., Miami, 2001—02; bd. dirs. Miami-Dade Expy. Auth., 2004—, Miami Beach Cultural Arts Coun., 2004—. Recipient Achievement award for Hispanic Women, VISTA Mag., 1997, Corp. Hispanic Bus. Adv. award, U.S. Hispanic Chamber of Commerce, 1993. Mem.: Greater Miami C. of C. (assoc.), Pub. Rels. Soc. of Am. (assoc.), Camara Comercio Latina (assoc.), Assn. Women in Comm. (assoc.). Avocations: travel, reading, public speaking, mentoring. Office: Roymi Membiela & Associates 6538 Collins Avenue #125 Miami Beach FL 33141 Office Phone: 305-868-1655. E-mail: roymi@membiela.com.

MENA, MICHELE M., counselor, educator; b. Paterson, NJ, Nov. 24, 1953; d. Rev. Miguel Mena and Catalina Alvarez. MA in Counseling, Montclair State U., 1978; MA in Health Edn., NYU, 1985; PhD in Clin. Christian Counseling, Fla. Christian U., 2004. Vocat. rehab. counselor Addiction Rsch. Treatment Corp., NYC, 1984—88; instr. Boricua Coll., NYC, 1988—90; dir. counseling and human svcs. Iron Bd. Edn. Cultural Ctr., Newark, 1992—94; N.G.O. (philanthrope) UN Earth Summit, 1994—; counselor, educator Bridges of Am., Fla., 2003—. Author: (poetry) Internat. Libr. of Poetry. Guest Presdl. Inaugural-Reagan/Bush, 1984, Nat. Repub. Convention, New Orleans, 1988; mem. Repub. Com. Task Force, Montclair Repub. Com., 1981—91. Recipient grad. assistantship, Dept. Adult Edn., Montclair State U., 1977—78. Mem.: Nat. Assn. Forensic Counselors, Ctrl. Fla. Mental Health Assn., Am. Assn. Christian Counselors, Montclair Historical Soc., Eagle Forum, White House Historical Soc., Montclair State U. Alumni Assn., Nat. Trust for Historic Preservation, Nat. Geographic Soc., The Audubon Soc., Nat. Wildlife Fund., World Wildlife Fund, Williamsburg Colonial Found., The Nature Conservancy, Am. Nat. World War II Mus., Women's Club Upper Montclair, Nat. Garden Club. Republican. Protestant. Avocations: gardening, antiques, poetry, archaeology. Home: 2009 S Magnolia Ave Sanford FL 32771 Office: 500 Smith Holly Ave Sanford FL 32771

MENAGE, CAROLYN LEE, elementary school educator; b. Sioux Falls, SD, June 26, 1948; d. Ralph Wayne and Betty Jean Warner; m. Michael Lee Menage, Sept. 21, 1968; children: Scott Dean, Brad Allan. BS in Edn., Black Hills State Coll., Spearfish, SD, 1970. Fourth and fifth grade Hemet Unified Sch. Dist., Calif., 1970—72; first grade Wall Lake Cmty. Sch., Wall Lake, Iowa, 1972—73; Title I Odebolt Arthur, Odebolt, Iowa, 1974—, curriculum coord., 1974—96. Tech. com. Prairie Lakes AEA, Ft. Dodge, Iowa, 2002—03, prof. devel. com., 2005—06. Mem.: NEA, Assn. Supervision and Curriculum Devel., Internat. Reading Assn., Delta Kappa Gamma, Alpha Delta Kappa. Avocation: reading. Office: Odebolt Arthur CSD 600 S Maple St Odebolt IA 51458

MENCER, JETTA, lawyer; b. Coshocton, Ohio, Apr. 7, 1959; d. William J. and Virginia M. (Fry) M. BS, Ohio State U., 1980, JD, 1983. Bar: Ohio, U.S. Dist. Ct. (so. dist.) Ohio. Assoc. Berry, Owens & Manning, Coshocton, 1983-86; asst. pros. atty. Coshocton County, 1983-86, Licking County, Newark, Ohio, 1986-88, asst. atty. gen., 1988-95; pvt. practice Coshocton, 1995-96; prosecuting atty. Coshocton County (Ohio) Prosecutor's Office, 1997-2001; atty. Lee Smith & Assocs., Columbus, Ohio, 2001—03; pvt. practice Columbus, 2003—. Treas. Coshocton County Dem. Cen. & Exec. Coms., 1984-86; chmn., 1986-88; sec., bd. dirs. Heart Ohio Girl Scout Council, Inc., Zanesville, Ohio, 1985-87; fin. chmn., bd. dirs. YMCA, Coshocton, 1985-87. Mem. Ohio State Bar Assn., Coshocton County Bar Assn., Lions Club. Democrat. Methodist. Office: One S Park Pl Newark OH 43055 Office Phone: 740-345-5171. Personal E-mail: jmencer@columbus.rr.com.

MENCER, SUE (CONSTANCE SUZANNE MENCER), former federal agency administrator; b. Nov. 15, 1947; m. John Mencer; children: Jessie, Alex. BA in Spanish, Ohio St. U., 1968; Grad., JFK Sch. Govt., Harvard U., 2003. Tchr. Spanish, 1968—78; spl. agt. FBI, 1978—85, supervisory spl. agt., 1985—90, supr., 1990—98; pvt. cons. Anti-Terrorism Tng., Denver; exec. dir. dept. pub. safety State of Colo., Denver, 2000—03; exec. dir. Office of State & Local Govt. Coordination & Preparedness US Dept. Homeland Security, Washington, 2003—05; sr. policy advisor govt. rels. group Brownstein Hyatt & Farber, PC, Denver, 2005—. Mem.: Commn. on Jud. Discipline, Soc. Former Spl. Agents. Office: Brownstein Hyatt & Farber PC 410 17th St 22nd Fl Denver CO 80202 E-mail: smencer@bhf-law.com.*

MENCK, J CLAIRE, chef, consultant; b. Elgin, Ill., June 12, 1970; d. Werner Hans Menck and Willa Marie Widerborg-Menck. BA in German Lit. and Sociology, U. Wis., Madison, 1993; AOS in Culinary Arts, New Eng. Culinary Inst., Montpelier, Vt., 1998; M in Bus. Adminstrn., U. Phoenix, 2004. Kitchen mgr. in charge of tng. Legal Sea Foods, Boston, 1998—99; food, beverage mgr. Riverbarge Excursion Lines, New Orleans, 1999—2000, Radisson Hotels, Milw., 1999—99; dist. area mgr. Wash. Inventory Svc., Wash., Kans. City, Milw., 2000—03; chef owner Girlchef, Inc., Independence, Kans., 2000—06; chef instr. New Eng. Culinary Inst., Essex, Vt., 2006—. Recipient Young Restaurateur of the World, Internat. Hotel and Restaurant Assn., 1999; James Beard Student scholar, James Beard Found., 1997, Student scholar, Internat. Food Editl. Coun., 1996, Fellowship, U. Wis.-Madison, German Dept., 1991. Mem.: Assn. of Transpersonal Psychology, Chef's Collaborative, Soc. for Psychol. Study of Social Issues, Women Chefs and Restauranteurs, Alpha Kappa Delta. Office Phone: 888-4RL-CHEF. Personal E-mail: claire@girlchef.com.

MENCONI, MARGUERITE L., customer service logistics; b. Battle Creek, Mich., Jan. 14, 1950; d. Donald Mayo and Helen (Moog) Putnam; m. Carl W. Menconi, Oct. 10, 1998. BSBA, Babson Coll., 1976, MBA, 1977. Dir. customer svc. logistics Prime Computer, Natick, Mass.; materials mgr. Digital Computer, Maynard, Mass.; quality mgr. Polaroid Corp., Waltham, Mass.; dir. customer svc. edn. Prime Computer, Natick; rsch. dir. AMR Research, Boston; transportation dir. Teradyne, Boston. With USN, 1968-71. Mem. Logistics Mgmt. Coun., Beta Gamma.

MENDE, MAGGIE SARAH, elementary school educator; b. Aniston, Ala., May 8, 1961; d. Henry Thomas and Mary Margaret Uhrig; m. Kevin Madison Mende, May 19, 1984; children: Jesse G., Sarah M., Jared H. BS in Elem. Edn., UTEP, El Paso, Tex., 1990. Tchr. 4th grade El Paso Sch. Dist., 1990—95; kindergarten tchr. Mt. Franklin Christian Sch., El Paso, 1998—.

MENDELSOHN, CAROL S., television producer; Student, Smith Coll., Cornell U. Writer CSI and CSI: Miami CBS, LA; with Securities and Exchange Commn.; atty. Washington; writer Fame NBC, LA; with Stephen J. Cannell; exec. prodr. Melrose Pl. NBC, 1990—99; exec. prodr. CSI CBS, LA, 2000—. Author: (TV series) Clifford the Big Red Dog, CSI (nominated Emmy Outstanding Drama Series award, 2002, 2003, nominated TV Prodr. of Yr. award, 2003, 2004), CSI: Miami, Gabriel's Fire, Hardcastle & McCormick, J.J. Starbuck, Melrose Place, Providence, Stingray, Teenage Mutant Ninja Turtles, Wiseguy, (films) To Brave Alaska.

MENDELSON, BARBARA R., lawyer; BS, Rensselaer Polytech. Inst., 1976; JD, U. Mich., 1981. Bar: N.Y. 1982, U.S. Dist. Ct., So. Dist. N.Y. 1983. Atty. Fed. Reserve Bank N.Y., 1981; ptnr. Morrison & Foerster LLP, N.Y.C., 1995—, leader fin. svc. practice group. Mem.: Assn. Bar City N.Y. Office: Morrison & Foerster LLP 1290 Avenue of the Americas New York NY 10104-0185 Office Phone: 212-468-8118. Office Fax: 212-468-7900. Business E-Mail: bmendelson@mofo.com.

MENDELSON, ELLEN B., radiologist, educator; MD, Northwestern U. Feinberg Sch. Medicine, 1980. Cert. diagnostic radiology 1984. Intern to resident, diagnostic radiology NW U. Meml. Hosp., Chgo., 1981—84, fellowship, 1984—85; radiologist Western Penn Hosp., Pitts.; bd. mem. Monongahela Valley Hosp., Pa.; assoc. prof., radiology U. Pitts. Sch. Medicine; prof. radiology NW U., Feinberg Sch. Medicine, Chgo.; dir. breast imaging NW Meml. Hosp. Office: NW U Feinberg Sch Medicine 675 N St Clair Galter 13th Fl Chicago IL 60611 Address: NW Meml Hosp 251 E Huron St Chicago IL 60611

MENDELSON, JOAN RINTEL, lawyer; b. N.Y.C., July 19, 1941; d. Leon and Myra Rintel; m. Neil H. Mendelson, July 30, 1959; children: Debora C., Marie Mendelson Piccarreta. BA with high distinction, with honors in Zoology, Ind. U., 1962, MA, 1963; JD, U. Ariz., 1974. Bar: Ariz. 1975. Co-founder and co-dir. Catonsville Coop. Nursery Sch., Md., 1967—69; assoc. Law Offices of Ann Bowen, Tucson, 1975—76; pvt. practice Tucson, 1977—80; asst. atty. gen. Office of Atty. Gen., Tucson, 1980—2000. Instr. biology U. Md. Balt. County, Catonsville, 1968; spl. magistrate Tucson City Ct., 1984—91; mem. Pima County Child Fatality Rev. Bd., Tucson, 1982—; mem. legal counsel Gov.'s Task Force on Sch. Age Child Care, Phoenix, 1984—86; mem. Pima County Citizen Rev. Bd., Tucson, 2000—; mem. child abuse team Ariz. Health Scis. Ctr., Tucson, 1983—2000; mem. ad hoc com. on child protective svcs. and related child welfare issues Ariz. Legislature, Phoenix, 1994—2000, mem. legal and statutory reform subcom. ad hoc com. on child protective svcs. and related child welfare issues, 1994—2000, chair sys. and policy changes subcom. ad hoc com. on child protective svcs. and related child welfare issues, 1996—2000; mem. model ct. steering com. Pima County Juvenile Ct., Tucson, 1996—2000, mem. model ct. workgroup, 1998—2000; mem. emergency juvenile rules com. Ariz. Supreme Ct., Phoenix, 1998—99, mem. juvenile rules com., 1999—2000, mem. ct. improvement project adv. workgroup, 1998—2003; mem. Pima County Interagency Task Forces on Custodial Interference, Tucson, 1997—2000, Pima County Child Adv. Ctr. Adv. Bd., Tucson, 1997—99; mem. child adv. clinic adv. bd. Coll. Law U. Ariz., Tucson, 1998. Fellow, Ford Found., 1961, NSF, 1962; N.Y. State Regents scholar, 1958. Mem.: Sigma Xi, Phi Beta Kappa. Personal E-mail: njmend@earthlink.net.

MENDELSON, LOTTIE M., retired pediatric nurse practitioner, writer; b. Portland, Oreg., June 4, 1937; d. Esther Layton-Murphy, James A. Murphy; m. Robert Mendelson, June 22, 1958; children: David, Tamara Mendelson-Hefetz, Mark, Michelle Rosenbloom. BS, U. Portland, 1958; MS, Oreg. Health Scis. U., 1972, Pediat. Nurse Practitioner, 1978. RN 1958, cert. pediat. nurse practitioner, 1978. Pediat. nurse practitioner Pediat. Assocs., Portland, Oreg., 1980—98; ret., 1998. Co-author: Raising Your Baby and Young Child, The New Parent's Question and Answer Book, 1992, editor (founder) Pediat. newsletter, 1984-97. Bd. dirs. Jewish Family and Child Svc., Portland, 1993—98. Mem.: Woman's Divsn. Oreg. Israel Bonds (chairperson 1981—85). Avocations: tennis, travel. Home: 5455 SW 87th Ave Portland OR 97225-1713 Personal E-mail: bbxmnr@aol.com.

MENDELSON, NINA, law educator; AB summa cum laude, Harvard U.; JD, Yale U. Law clk. for Judge Pierre Leval So. Dist. NY; for Judge John Walker Jr., Second Cir.; atty. Heller, Ehrman, White & McAuliffe, Seattle, US Dept. Justice, Environment and Natural Resources Div.; prof. law U. Mich Law Sch., Ann Arbor. Fellow Senate Com. on Environment and Pub. Works. Contbr. articles to law jours. Recipient Thomas Neville Award, Wash. State Bar Assn. Mem.: Phi Beta Kappa. Office: U Mich Law Sch 339 Hutchins Hall 625 S State St Ann Arbor MI 48109-1215 Office Phone: 734-936-5071. Office Fax: 734-763-9375. E-mail: nmendel@umich.edu.

MENDENHALL, NANCY PRICE, radiologist, educator; b. Eldorado, Ark., Apr. 18, 1951; d. Delton E. and Betty Jean Price; m. William M. Mendenhall; children: Marisa, Elena. BA in English Lit., U. Fla., 1973, MD, 1980. Diplomate Am. Bd. Radiology. Intern, radiation therapy U. Fla., Gainesville, 1980—81, resident, radiation therapy, 1981—84; asst. prof. dept. radiation oncology U. Fla. Coll. Medicine, Gainesville, 1984-89, assoc. prof., 1989-94, prof., 1994—, chmn. dept. radiation oncology, 1992—; med. dir. Fla. Proton Therapy Inst., also bd. dir.; assoc. chair, radiation oncology U. Fla. Coll. Medicine, Jacksonville. Editor: The Breast; prodr., author video for Am. Coll. Surgeons; contbr. articles to profl. jours. Active Trinity United Meth. Ch.; mem. dean's com., Dept. Veteran Affairs; bd. dir. Am. Cancer Soc., Alachua County; mem. Children's Oncology Group (mem. Hodgkin's com.) Mem. Am. Soc. for Therapeutic Radiology and Oncology (human resources com. 1995, by-laws com. 1995-96), Soc. Chmn. of Academic Radiation Oncology Programs, Am. Radium Soc., Gilbert H. Fletcher Soc., Alachua County Med. Soc., Fla. Soc. Clin. Oncology, Am. Coll. Radiology, Phi Beta Kappa; fellow Am. Coll. Radiology. Methodist. Avocations: horseback riding, sewing, cooking, piano. Office: U Fla Dept Radiation Oncology 2000 SW Archer Rd Dept Gainesville FL 32608-1136 also: UF Coll Medicine Jacksonville 653-1 W Eighth St Jacksonville FL 32209 also: U Fla Proton Therapy Inst 2015 N Jefferson St Jacksonville FL 32206*

MENDES, EVA, actress; b. Houston, Mar. 5, 1974; Spokesperson Revlon Cosmetics. Actor: (films) A Night at the Roxbury, 1998, My Brother the Pig, 1999, Urban Legends: Final Cut, 2000, Exit Wounds, 2001, Training Day, 2001, All About the Benjamins, 2002, 2 Fast 2 Furious, 2003, Once Upon a Time in Mexico, 2003, Out of Time, 2003, Stuck on You, 2003, Hitch, 2005; (TV films) The Disciples, 2000; TV appearances include: ER, 1998; Mortal Kombat: Conquest, 1998; VIP, 1999. Office: Creative Artist Agency 9830 Wilshire Blvd Beverly Hills CA 90212-1825

MENDEZ, DEBORAH, parochial school educator; b. Delran, N.J., Mar. 7, 1973; d. Robert Barry and Mary Lou Sause; m. John Mendez, Mar. 7, 1997. BS, St. John's U., 1995; postgrad., Nova Southeastern U., Ft. Lauderdale, Fla. Cert. tchr., Fla. Tchr. Our Lady of Refuge Sch., Bklyn., 1996-97, Annunciation Sch., Hollywood, Fla., 1997—. Active Annunciation Parish, 1997—. Mem. St. John's U. Alumni Assn. Roman Catholic. Home: 7161 SW 10th St Pembroke Pines FL 33023-1644 Office: Annunciation Sch 3751 SW 39th St Hollywood FL 33023-6252 E-mail: jmendez6@bellsouth.net.

MENDEZ, MIRIAM ROMAN, elementary school educator; b. Ponce, P.R., May 29, 1950; d. Pedro Juan Roman and Antonia Garcia-Roman; m. Carlos Mario Mendez, Dec. 19, 1980; children: Richard Isidoro, Cassie D. BA with hons., Caldwell Colllge, NJ, 1974; MA in Counseling Svcs., Rider U., Lawerenville, N.J., 1997; MEd in Curriculum and Instrn., Houston Bapt. U., Tex., 2001; MA in Edn. Adminstrn., Cranyon U., Ariz., 2005. Cert. tchr. handicapped Dept Edn., N.J., 1990. Placement counselor Youth Chance Mt. Carmel Guild, Newark, 1972—81; tchr. handicapped spl. edn. Grace A. Dunn Mid. Sch., Trenton, 1986—, guidance counselor, 2000—04. Chmn. career fair Grace A. Dunn Mid. Sch., 1990—92. Named Tchr. of Yr., Trenton (N.J.) Bd. Edn., 1998; recipient Tchr. Recognition award, Mayor City of Trenton, 1994. Mem.: Trenton (N.J.) Edn. Assn. (assoc.; bd. trustees 1990—2006, mid. sch. rep. 1990—2006). Avocations: interior decorating, crafts. Home: 2 Atrium Drive Yardville NJ 08620 Office: Grace A Dunn Middle School 401 Dayton Street Trenton NJ 08620 Office Phone: 1 609 656 4700. Personal E-mail: rim14@comcast.net. Business E-Mail: mmendez@trenton.k12.nj.us.

MENDIBLE, MYRA, literature educator, researcher; d. Gonzalo Bobadilla and Silvia Garcia; m. Ernesto Mendible, Dec. 15, 1979. PhD, U. Miami, Fla., 1993. Lectr. U. Miami, 1993—94; assoc prof. Fla. Gulf Coast U., Ft. Myers, 1994—. Editor: (anthology) From Bananas to Buttocks: The Latina Body in Popular Culture; contbr. articles to profl. jours. Participant Am. Democracy Project, Ft.Myers. Nat. Hispanic scholar, Postdoctoral fellow, AAUW. Mem.: Humiliation and Human Dignity Orgn. (affiliate global scholars network 2005—06). Avocations: stained glass art, gardening. Office: Florida Gulf Coast University 10501 FGCU Blvd South Fort Myers FL 33965 Office Phone: 239-590-7182.

MENDIOLA, ANNA MARIA G., mathematics educator; b. Laredo, Tex., Dec. 21, 1948; d. Alberto and Aurora (Benavides) Gonzalez; m. Alfonso Mendiola Jr., Aug. 11, 1973; children: Alfonso, Alberto. AA, Laredo C.C., Tex., 1967; BA, Tex. Woman's U., 1969, MS, 1974. Tchr. math. Laredo Ind. Sch. Dist., 1969-81; instr. math. Laredo C.C., 1981—, organizer Jaime Escalante program, 1991-92; tech. prep. com. mem., 1991-92; ednl. coun., sec. Christen Mid. Campus, 1992-94; mem. site based campus com. Martin H.S., 1994-2000. Vis. instr. St. Augustine Sch., Laredo. 1987-88; evaluator So. Assn., Corpus Christi, 1981, So. Assn. Colls. and Schs., United H.S., 1991; mem. quality improvement coun. Laredo C.C., 1993-94; mem. instrn. coun. Laredo C.C., 1995-96; participant SC3 Calculus Reform Inst., NSF, 1996; mem. adv. com. on core curriculum Tex. Higher Edn. Coord. Bd., 1997-99, mem. adv. com. on transfer issues and field of study, 2000-05; mem. Laredo C.C. self-study steering com. So. Assn. Colls. and Schs. Reaffirmation, 1997-99, coord. honors program, 1999-2004; math. dept. chair 2002-; faculty assoc. NSF-LCC Rio Grande River Project, 1998-2000. V.p., bd. dirs. Our Lady of Guadalupe Sch., Laredo, 1988-91; sec. Laredo C.C. Faculty Senate, 1986-87, v.p., 1995-96, pres., 1996-97, mem. fin. com., 2006—, mem. curriculum com., 2003—; rep. Laredo Ind. Sch. Dist. Parent Adv. Coun., 1997-98; mem. math focus team Laredo Ind. Sch. Dist., 2005— Recipient Teaching Excellence award NISOD, 1993; named LCC Innovator of the Month, 1998. Mem. AAUW (pres. 1979-81, v.p. 1987-89, scholarship chair 1993-94, membership chair 1994-95, bylaws chair 1996-97, pub. policy chair 1997-99), Am. Math. Assn. Two-Yr. Colls., Tex. State Tchrs. Assn., Tex. C.C. Tchrs. Assn. (campus rep., sec. math. sect. 1997-98, vice chair math. sect. 1998-99, chair math. sect. 1999-2000, chair audit com. 1999-2000, co-chair membership com. 2001-02, mem. profl. devel. com., 2003-05, nominating com. 2005-2006, chair convention com., 2006—), Tex. Woman's U. Alumnae Assn., Blessed Sacrament Altar Soc., Delta Kappa Gamma (membership chair 1993-96, v.p. 2000-02, corr. sec. 2004—2006), Math Assn. Am. Democrat. Roman Catholic. Office: Laredo CC West End Washington St Laredo TX 78040 Business E-Mail: amendiola@laredo.edu.

MENDIUS, PATRICIA DODD WINTER, editor, educator, writer; b. Davenport, Iowa, July 9, 1924; d. Otho Edward and Helen Rose (Dodd) Winter; m. John Richard Mendius, June 19, 1947; children: Richard, Catherine M. Graber, Louise, Karen M. Chooljian. BA cum laude, UCLA, 1946; MA cum laude, U. N.Mex., 1966. Cert. secondary edn. tchr., Calif., N.Mex. English tchg. asst. UCLA, 1946—47; English tchr. Marlborough Sch. for Girls, LA, 1947—50, Aztec (N.Mex.) HS, 1953—55, Farmington (N.Mex.) HS, 1955—63; chair English dept. Los Alamos (N.Mex.) HS, 1963—86; sr. technical writer, editor Los Alamos Nat. Lab., 1987—2005. Adj. prof. English, U. N.Mex., Los Alamos, 1970-72, Albuquerque, 1982-85; English cons. S.W. Regional Coll. Bd., Austin, Tex., 1975—; writer, editor, cons. advanced placement English test devel. com. Nat. Coll. Bd., 1982-86, reader, 1982-86, project equality cons., 1985-88; book selection cons. Scholastic mag., 1980-82. Author: Preparing for the Advanced Placement English Exams, 1975; editor Los Alamos Arts Coun. bull., 1986-91. Chair Los Alamos Art Pub. Places Bd., 1987-92; chair adv. bd. trustees U. N.Mex., Los Alamos, 1987-93; pres. Los Alamos Concert Assn., 1972-73, 95-98, 2000-04, pres., 2003-04; chair Los Alamos Mesa Pub. Libr. Bd., 1990-94, chair endowment com., 1995-99. Named Living Treasure of Los Alamos, 2005. Mem. Soc. Tech. Communicators, AAUW (pres. 1961-63, state bd. dirs. 1959-63, Los Alamos coordinating coun. 1992-93, pres. 1993-94, 2002-04, sec. 2001-04), DAR, Order Ea. Star, Mortar Bd., Phi Beta Kappa (pres. Los Alamos chpt. 1969-72, 99, v.p. 1996-99, pres. 2000-01, dir. 2002—), Phi Kappa Phi, Delta Kappa Gamma, Gamma Phi Beta. Avocations: swimming, reading, hiking, astronomy, singing. Home: 124 Rover Blvd Los Alamos NM 87544-3634 Office: Los Alamos Nat Lab Diamond Dr Los Alamos NM 87544 E-mail: pmendius@cybermesa.com.

MENDON, KAREN JEANETTE, elementary school educator; b. Oct. 22, 1949; AA, Mt. San Antonio Jr. Coll., 1969; BA, Calif. State U., Long Beach, 1972; std. elem. credential, U. Calif., Irvine, 1976; MA in Curriculum and Devel., Coll. St. Thomas, 1984; Lang Devel. Specialist cert., UCLA, 1993. Phys. edn. tchr. Montebello Intermediate Montebello Unified Sch. Dist., 1972—. Phys. edn. mentor tchr. Montebello Unified Sch. Dist., 1990-93, site adminstrv. internship, 1989-90, demonstration sch. coord., 1991—; mem. Healthy Kids Healthy Calif. ad hoc com., health cirruculum ad hoc com., mentor tchr., earthquake com., planning com., faculty club, recreation adv. com., coord. personal best program, leadership team, disaster search and rescue team; chair discipline com.; presenter in field. Author: Ideas, Activities and Games to Expend, Enrich and Enhance Your Physical Education Program (grades 3-8). Recipient L.A. County Healthy Fitness Leader award, 1994, Am. Tchr. Honoree award Walt Disney, 1995. Mem. ASCD, NEA, AAHPERD, PTA (Sch. Svc. award 1977), Calif. Assn. Health, Phys. Edn., Recreation & Dance (Unit 413 Outstanding Mid. Sch. Phys. Educator award 1993, Southern Dist. Outstanding Mid. Sch. Phys. Educator award 1993, Calif. Outstanding Mid. Sch. Phys. Educator award 1994).

MENDOZA, JULIE C., lawyer; BA summa cum laude, Tufts U., 1977; JD, U. Chgo., 1981. Bar: DC 1981, US Ct. Internat. Trade, US Ct. Appeals, Fed. Cir. Ptnr., co-chair Internat. Trade Group Kaye Scholer LLP, Washington, DC. Office: Kaye Scholer LLP McPherson Bldg 901 Fifteenth St, NW, Ste 1100 Washington DC 20005 Office Phone: 202-682-3640. E-mail: jmendoza@kayescholer.com.

MENDOZA, KAREN LYNN, special education educator; b. Artesia, New Mex., Feb. 5, 1970; d. Fred Torrez and Esperanza-Mariscal Alvarez; m. Ramon Mendoza; children: Eris, Jadyn. BSc, Eastern New Mex. U., 1993. Cert. tchr. Tex. Tchr., San Antonio, 1993—97; tchr. Arnett Elem. Sch. Lubbock (Tex.) Ind. Sch. Dist., 1997—. Avocations: scrapbooks, photography, reading. Personal E-mail: kamendoza@cox.net.

MENDOZA, MARTHA, reporter; b. LA, 1969; BA, U. Calif. Santa Cruz, 1988. Reporter Madera Tribune, Bay City News Svc., Santa Cruz County Sentinel; nat. investigative reporter Associated Press, San Jose, Calif., 1995—. Co-author: The Bridge at No Gun Ril: A Hidden Nightmare from the Korean War, 2001. Recipient Pulitzer prize, 2000, Alumni Achievment award, U. Calif. Santa Cruz, 2002; John S. Knight fellow, Stanford U., 2001. Office: Associated Press 675 N 1st St San Jose CA 95112

MENEES, KATHERINE DETERMAN, parochial school educator; b. Keyser, W.Va., Mar. 22, 1941; d. Alphonsus William and Bernadette Cosgrove Determan; m. Timothy Ryan Menees, Aug. 24, 1968; children: Timothy Marion, Rebecca Menees Ciccio. BS, Frostburg State U., Md., 1963. Tchr. Surrattsville Jr. HS, Clinton, Md., 1963—69; substitute tchr. Incirlik Am. Sch., Turkey, 1970—71, Bainbridge Island HS, Wash., 1973—74; tchr. St. Valentine Sch., Bethel Park, Pa., 1985—. Forensics team moderator, coach Southwestern Pa. Forensics League, Pitts., 1995—; advisor St. Valentine Sch. Newspaper, 1996—. Tchr., student advisor St. Mary of Mercy at Meny Red Door Program, Pitts., 1987, 1988, 1999, 2005, Food Bank, McKeesport, Pa., 1990; bd. dirs. Children's Ctr. for Theater Arts, Mt. Lebanon, Pa., 1981—90. MAC grantee, McDonalds, Bethel Park, 2004. Mem.: Nat. Cath. Ednl. Assn., Western Pa. Coun. Tchrs. of English, Nat. Coun. Tchrs. of English. Roman Catholic. Avocations: piano, sewing, gardening, reading. Home: 5001 Highland Ave Bethel Park PA 15102 Office: St Valentine Sch 2709 Mesta St Bethel Park PA 15102 Office Phone: 412-835-3780. E-mail: detcat322@aol.com.

MENEFEE, LINNEA-NORMA, antique dealer; b. Mpls., Mar. 5, 1924; d. Arthur Wesley and Elsie Ida Buck. Student, U. Minn., Mpls., U. Minn., Duluth, McPhail Sch. Music, Mpls. Chmn. State Vet. Home, Buffalo. Founder Albert Lea (Minn.) Art Ctr., 1959; county chairwoman Goldwater for Pres., Albert Lea. Recipient Conscientious award, 2001. Mem. AAUW, Am. Med. Assn. Alliance, Nat. Fedn. Rep. Women, Nat. Women of the Arts, Nat. Am. Legion Aux., Nat. VFW Aux., Nat. Assn. Family and Cmty. Edn., Order of Ea. Star, Gillette Blue Blades, Kiwanis Internat., Zeta Phi Eta, Omega Upsilon, Zeta Beta Chi. Episcopalian. Avocations: writing, reading, painting, sculpting, travel.

MENENDEZ, BELINDA, broadcast executive; Student, St. Andrews U., Scotland. With internat. TV sales Televisa, 1986—95; mgr. TV sales Cisneros; internat. tv distbn. ops. mgr. Michael Solomon's S.I.E.; exec. v.p. sales Studio Canal (formerly Canal Plus DA); co-pres. Universal TV Distbn., Universal City, Calif., 2001—. Office: Universal TV Distbn USA Bldg 1440/3030 100 Universal City Plaza Universal City CA 91608-1002

MENENDEZ, SHIRLEY CORBIN, writer; b. Richmond, Va., Feb. 5, 1937; d. Daniel and Madeline Euting Corbin; m. Albert John Menendez, June 15, 1974. BA, Mary Baldwin Coll., Staunton, Va., 1961; M in Libr. Sci., Drexel U., 1965. Cataloger, reference libr. Fed. Res. Bank, Phila., 1963—65; libr. Prince George's County Meml. Libr. Sys., Hyattsville, Md., 1965—78; asst. dir. Westchester Libr. Sys., Hartsdale, NY, 1979—81; coord. of adminstrv. svcs. Kennedy Inst. of Ethics, Washington, 1981—82; adminstrv. asst. to U. pres. Georgetown U., 1982—86, dir. of housing svcs., 1987—2004. Author: Allie, the Christmas Spider, B is for Blue Crab: A Maryland Alphabet; co-author (with Albert Menendez): Maryland Trivia, New Jersey Trivia, South Carolina Trivia, Christmas Songs Made in America: Favorite Holiday Melodies and the Stories of Their Origins, Joy to the World: Sacred Christmas Songs Through the Ages. Mem.: Soc. Children's Book Writers and Illustrators. Achievements include Vicennial Medal, Georgetown University, 2003. Home: 12625 Timonium Terr North Potomac MD 20878-3428

MENENDEZ CAMBO, PATRICIA, lawyer; b. N.Y.C., June 7, 1966; BBA, U. Miami, 1986; JD, U. Pa., 1989. Bar: Fla. 1991, DC 1993. With Greenberg Traurig, PA, Miami, 1994—2000; chief U.S. legal counsel Telefónica S.A., 2000—02; shareholder, chair internat. practice group Greenberg Traurig, PA, Miami, 2002—. Bd. dirs. Coun. of Americas. Contbr. articles to profl. jours. Trustee Nat. Alliance for Autism Rsch. Named one of Top Up and Comers in So. Fla., So. Fla. Legal Guide, 2004, Top 40 Lawyers Under 40, Nat. Law Jour., 2005. Office: Greenberg Traurig 1221 Brickell Ave Miami FL 33131 Office Phone: 305-579-0766. Office Fax: 305-579-0717. Business E-Mail: pmc@gtlaw.com.

MENG, M. KATHRYN, lawyer; JD, Fordham U. Former dist. ct. bur. chief criminal divsn. Legal Aid Soc. Nassau County; ptnr. Cianciulli Meng & Panos P.C., Garden City, NY, 1992—. Dean Nassau Acad. Law; adj. prof. Nassau C.C., 1992—. Columnist Nassau Lawyer. Bd. dirs. Sara's Ctr.; mem. outreach adv. com. St. Brigid's Ch., Westbury, eucharistic ministr. Mem.: ABA (del.), 2d Jud. Dept. Com. on Character and Fitness Adminstrn. Attys. to the Bar, Nassau Legal Aid Soc. (former pres., former bd. dirs.), Attys. to the Bar, Criminal Cts. Bar Assn. (former pres., bd. dirs.), N.Y. State Bar Assn. (del.), Nassau County Bar Assn. (pres., chair civil rights com., former chair lawyers assistance com., former mem. judiciary com.). Office: Cianciulli Meng & Panos PC 99 Quentin Roosevelt Blvd Ste 201 Garden City NY 11530 Office Fax: 516-683-0907. Business E-Mail: kmeng@cmlawgroup.net.

MENGES, SUSAN DEBRA FAVREAU, management consultant, retired protective services official; b. Cleve., Dec. 15, 1955; d. Donald Francis and Helen Patricia (Rafferty) F.; m. William J. Menges, Nov. 17, 2001. Cert., N.Y. State Police Acad., 1974; student, Cornell U., 1984, SUNY, 1986. Comm. specialist N.Y. State Police, Loudonville, 1974—87, comm. specialist divsn. hdqrs., 1987—98; mgmt. cons., sec.-treas., dir. Don Favreau Assocs., Inc., Clifton Park, NY, 1983—86, v.p., 1986—; comm. specialist divsn. hdqrs. N.Y. State Police, Albany, 1987—98, sys. support specialist divsn. hdqrs., 1998—2005, ret., 2005. Adj. faculty Internat. Assn. Chiefs Police; NYSPIN coord. FBI/Nat. Crime Info. Ctr. cert. program, 1986—; ind. sr. beauty cons. Mary Kay Cosmetics, 2003 Author: Teamwork in the Telecommunication Center, 1986, One More Time: How to be a Mature and Successful Telecommunications Manager, 1987, Law Enforcement Terminal Security, 1991; also NYSPIN cert. manuals. Vol. Suncoast Seabird Sanctuary, Indian Shores, Fla., 2005—06. Recipient Dirs. Commendation N.Y. State Police Acad., 1977, Commendation N.Y. State Police, 1978, Supt.'s Commendation, 1986, Y2K Commendation Gov. George Pataki, 2000 Mem. NAFE, N.Y. State Civil Svc. Assn., Emergency Communicators Profl. Assn. (adv. bd.), Colonie Police Benevolent Assn. (hon.), Am. Soc. Law Enforcement Trainers, Assoc. Pub. Safety Comm. Officers (planning commn. Atlantic chpt. 1991, registration chair ann. N.E. conf. 1991), N.Y. State Troopers Police Benevolent Assn. (hon.), Nat. Bus. Women Am., Internat. Assn. Chiefs Police, Am. Horse Shows Assn., Am. Soc. Law Enforcement Trainers, Capital Dist. Hunter/Jumper Coun Republican. Roman Catholic. Avocations: horseback riding, target shooting, reading, sewing. Office: Hdqrs NY State Police State Office Bldg Campus Bldg # 22 Albany NY 12226 Home: 19701 Gulf Blvd Apt 307 Indian Shores FL 33785-2385 E-mail: susan9g6@aol.com.

MENINGALL, EVELYN L., retired educational media specialist; b. Dothan, Ala., July 22, 1935; d. Earl and Luella Koonce; m. A. Richard Meningall, Jan. 17, 1958; children: Dawn, Tracy, Richard. BS in Edn., Wayne State U., 1975; MLS, Rutgers U., 1979. Cert. ednl. media specialist Dept. Edn. State N.J., elem. sch. dept. Dept. Edn. State N.J., profl. librs. cert. Dept. Edn. State N.J. Tchr. Detroit Bd. Edn., 1975—76; libr. East Brunswick (N.J.) Pub. Libr., 1978—80; ednl. media specialist Piscataway (N.J.) Bd. Edn., 1980—98; ret., 1998. Author: A Way of Life: An Anthology of Poems, 2004, Reflections: A Collection of Poems, 2005. Active New Detroit, Inc., Delta Sigma Theta Sorority Ctrl. Jersey; vol. tutor/reader pub. schs.; vol. to holisitic score English tests Plainfield (N.J.) H.S.; recording sec. Scholarship Fund of St. Paul AME Ch. Mem.: ALA (life), Ednl. Media Assn., Nat. Edn. Assn. (life), NJ Edn. Assn. (life), Nat. Sorority Phi Delta Kappa, Inc. (life; basileus 1987—89, exec. advisor 1989—91), Delta Sigma Theta (life). St. Paul Ame Church. Avocations: poetry, reading, fishing. Home: 23 Vauxhall Rd East Brunswick NJ 08816-1719

MENIUS, JOY VICTORIA, musician, music educator; b. Asheboro, N.C., Sept. 1, 1954; d. Victor Hal and Elizabeth (Purvis) Hussey; m. John White Menius, III, June 16, 1979; children: Alexander White, Meredith Megan Victoria. MusB Organ Performance and Music Edn., Meredith Coll., Raleigh, N.C., 1976; MusM in Organ Performance, U. N.C., Greenville, 1985. Organist 1st Bapt. Ch., Robbins, NC, 1970—72, Dogwood Acres Presbyn. Ch., Asheboro, NC, 1978—79, 1st Bapt. Ch., Asheboro, 1979—83, Episcopal Ch. Good Shepherd, Asheboro, 1983—89, Ctrl. U. Meth. Ch., Asheboro, 1989—; tchr. music Randolph County Schs., Asheboro, 1977—79, 2000—. Pvt. piano tchr., Asheboro, 1970—. Mem.: Music Educators Nat. Conf., Am. Guild Organists (sub-dean, dean 1988—90), Am. Fedn. Music Clubs (sec., v.p., pres. 1979—94), Rotary Club (Paul Harris fellow 2004). Democrat. Methodist. Avocations: reading, needlework, music. Home: 1036 Oakmont Dr Asheboro NC 27205

MENJIVAR, CECILIA, social sciences educator; arrived in U.S., 1978; d. Jose and Mercedes Menjivar; m. Victor Agadjanian, Mar. 27, 1992. BA in Psychology and Sociology, U. of So. Calif., L.A., 1981, MS in Internat. Ednl. Devel., 1983; MA in Sociology, U. of Calif., Davis, 1986, PhD in Sociology, 1992. Postdoctoral fellow U. of Calif., Berkeley, 1992—94; postdoctoral rschr., cons. RAND Corp., Santa Monica, Calif., 1994—95; assoc. prof. Ariz. State U., Tempe, 1996—. Mem., com. on the status of women Ariz. State U., Tempe, Ariz., 2001—02; co-chair Cen. Am. sect. Latin Am. Studies Assn., 2002—. Author: Fragmented Ties: Salvadoran Immigrant Networks in America, 2000 (William J. Goode Book award Am. Sociol. Assn. Family Sect., 2001, Hon. Mention Internat. Migration Sect., Outstanding Acad. Title in Social and Behavioral Scis. award, CHOICE award, 02); editor: Through the Eyes of Women: Gender, Social Networks, Family and Structural Change in Latin America and the Caribbean, 2003; mem. editl. bd.: Gender and Identity; co-editor: When States Kill: Latin America, The US, and Technologies of Terror, 2005; contbr. articles to profl. jours. Mem.: Pacific Sociol. Assn. (mem. com. on coms. 2004—), Latin Am. Studies Assn. (mem. coun. sect. on gender 2004—), Soc. Study of Social Problems (chmn. minority fellowship selection com. 2001—02), Am. Sociol. Assn. (mem. coun. internat. migration sect. 2003—, mem. editl. bd. Am. Sociol. Rev., chair Latinola section 2005—). Office: Ariz State U Dept Sociology Tempe AZ 85287-4802 Business E-Mail: menjivar@asu.edu.

MENKEL-MEADOW, CARRIE JOAN, law educator; b. N.Y.C., Dec. 24, 1949; d. Gary G. and Margot (Sinn) Menkel; m. Robert Gary Meadow, Aug. 22, 1971. AB magna cum laude, Columbia U., 1971; JD cum laude, U. Pa., 1974; LLD (hon.), Quinnipiac Coll. Law, 1995. Bar: Pa. 1974, U.S. Ct. Appeals (3d cir.) 1975, Calif. 1979, D.C., 1997. Dir. legal writing U. Pa. Law Sch., Phila., 1974-75, clin. supt., lectr., 1976-79; staff atty. Cmty. Legal Svcs., Phila., 1975-77; prof. UCLA, 1979—, prof. law, 1979-99, Georgetown Law Ctr., Washington, 1996—, A.B. Chettle Jr. chair prof. dispute resolution civil procedure, 2005—; holder Phyllis Beck chair Temple U. Law Sch., Phila., 1999. Cons. ABA, Chgo., 1979—84; panel mem. NAS, Washington, 1986—87, NSF, Washington, 1987—90; vis. prof. law Stanford Law Sch., 1990, Harvard Law Sch., 2001, U. Fribourg, Switzerland, 2003; dir. UCLA Ctr. for Conflict Resolution, 1994—99, Georgetown-Hewlett Program on Conflict Resolution and Problem Solving, 2001—. Author: Mediation: Theory, Practice and Policy, 2000, Dispute Processing: Theory, Practice and Policy, 2003, What's Fair: Ethics for Negotiators, 2004, Dispute Resolution: Beyond the Adversarial Model, 2004, Negotiation: Processes for Problem Solving, 2005, Mediation: Practice, Policy and Ethics, 2005; editor-in-chief Jour. Legal Edn., 2003—; editor-in-chief: Internat. Jour. Law in Context, 2004—; contbr. articles to profl. jours. Chairperson Ctr. for Study of Women, UCLA; chair CPR Commn. on Ethics and ADR; bd. dirs. Western Ctr. on Law and Poverty, LA, 1980—86. Recipient William Rutter Found. for Tchg. award UCLA, 1992, 1st prize for Acad. Scholarship on Alternative Dispute Resolution Ctr. for Pub. Resources, 1983, 91, 98, Frank Flegal award for tchg., Georgetown U., 2006. Mem.: Acad. Civil Trial Mediators, Am. Law Inst., Am. Bar Found. (bd. dir., sec., exec. com. 1994—), Law and Soc. Assn. (trustee), Ctr. for Law and Human Values (bd. dir.), Assn. Am. Law Schs. (alt. dispute resolution sect., law and social sci. sect., women in law sect., accreditation com. 1987—90, editor-in-chief Jour. of Legal Edn. 2004—), Soc. Am. Law Tchrs. (trustee), Phi Beta Kappa. Democrat. Office: Georgetown Law Ctr 600 New Jersey Ave NW Washington DC 20001-2075 Office Phone: 202-662-9379. E-mail: meadow@law.georgetown.edu.

MENKEN, JANE AVA, demographer, educator; b. Phila., Nov. 29, 1939; d. Isaac Nathan and Rose Ida (Sarvetnick) Golubitsky; m. Matthew Menken, 1960 (div. 1985); children: Kenneth Lloyd, Kathryn Lee; m. Richard Jessor, Nov. 13, 1992. AB, U. Pa., 1960; MS, Harvard U., 1962; PhD, Princeton U., NJ, 1975. Asst. in biostats. Harvard U. Sch. Pub. Health, Boston, 1962-64; math. statistician NIMH, Bethesda, Md., 1964-66; rsch. assoc. dept. biostats. Columbia U., N.Y.C., 1966-69; mem. rsch. staff Office of Population Rsch. Princeton U., 1969-71, 75-87, asst. dir., 1978-86, assoc. dir., 1986-87, prof. sociology, 1980-82, prof. sociology and pub. affairs, 1982-87; prof. sociology and demography U. Pa., Phila., 1987-97, UPS Found. prof. social scis., 1987-97, dir. Population Studies Ctr., 1989-95; prof. sociology U. Colo., Boulder, 1997—, faculty assoc. Population Program, Inst. Behavioral Sci., 1997—; dir. Population Aging Ctr., 2000—, Inst. Behavioral Sci., 2001—, disting. prof., 2002—. Mem. social scis. and population study sect., NIH, Bethesda, 1978-82, chmn., 1980-82, dirs. adv. com., 1995-2000, Nat. Adv. Child Health and Human Devel. Coun., 1988-91, adv. com. Fogarty Internat. Ctr., 2000-02, population adv. com. Rockefeller Found., NYC, 1981-93, com. on population and demography, NAS, Washington, 1978-83, com. on population, 1983-85, 1996-2002, chair 1998-2002, com. nat. stats., 1983-89, com. on AIDS rsch., 1987-93, chair 1990-93; co-chair panel data and rsch. priorities for arresting AIDS in sub-Saharan Africa, 1994-96, Com. on Behavioral and Social Scis. and Edn., 1991-97, chair, steering com., workshop on aging in Africa, 2003-06, chair, sci. adv. com., INDEPTH newtwork, 2002-; cons. Internat. Centre for Diarrhoeal Disease Rsch., Bangladesh, Dhaka, 1984—. Author: (with Mindel C. Sheps) Mathematical Models of Conception and Birth, 1973, (with Ann Blanc and Cynthia Lloyd) Training and Support of Developing Country Population Scientists, 2002; editor: (with Henri Leridon) Natural Fertility, 1979, (with Frank Furstenberg, Jr. and Richard Lincoln) Teenage Sexuality, Pregnancy and Childbearing, 1981, World Population and U.S. Policy: The Choices Ahead, 1986, (with Barney Cohen) Aging in Sub-Saharan Africa: Recommendations for Furthering Research, 2006; contbr. articles to profl. jours. Bd. dirs. Alan Guttmacher Inst., NYC, 1981-90, 93-2000, African Population and Health Rsch. Ctr., Nairobi, Kenya, 2000—. Nat. Merit scholar, 1957; John Simon Guggenheim Found. fellow, 1992-93, Ctr. for Advanced Study in Behavioral Scis. fellow, 1995-96. Fellow AAAS, Am. Statis. Assn.; mem. NAS, Inst. of Medicine, Am. Acad. Arts and Scis., Population Assn. Am. (pres. 1985, Mindel Sheps award 1982), Am. Pub. Health Assn. (Mortimer Spiegelman award 1975), Am. Sociol. Assn., Soc. for Study of Social Biology, Internat. Union for Sci. Study of Population (coun. 1989-97), Sociol. Rsch. Assn. (exec. com. 1991-96, pres. 1996). Office: U Colo IBS#1 483 UCB Boulder CO 80309-0483 Office Phone: 303-492-8148. Business E-Mail: menken@colorado.edu.

MENKES, SHERYL R., lawyer; b. Mt. Vernon, NY, Sept. 21, 1950; d. Maximillian Oscar and Dita Menkes. BA, Case Western Res. U., Cleve., 1972; MBA, Columbia U., NYC, 1984; JD, Bklyn. Law Sch., 1989; LLM, NYU, 1992. With media, mktg. Doubleday, Ted Bates Interpublic, NYC, 1973—86; assoc. atty. Zurchuk and Zelermyer, White Plains, NY, 1989—90, Kroll and Tract, NYC, 1990—91. Spkr. in field. Mem.: Am. Trial Lawyers Assn. (nursing home group), NY State Trial Lawyers (bd. dirs. 2005—). Avocations: gardening, painting. Office: Menkes Law Firm 150 Broadway 14th Fl New York NY 10038

MENKIN, EVA L., marriage and family therapist; b. Berlin, June 26, 1923; came to the U.S., 1934; d. Henry O. and Tamara G. Fuchs; m. Fred Landecker, Sept. 10, 1942 (div. 1972); children: Judy Hoffman, David, Anita, Peter; m. David B. Menkin, Feb. 17, 1974. BA in Psychology, Goddard Coll., 1971, MA in Marriage and Family Counseling, 1973. Lic. marriage and family therapist. Intern Beverly Manor Convalescent House, L.A., 1972,

Winsor Manor Retirement Home, Glendale, Calif., 1972; intern, counselor So. Calif. Counseling Ctr., L.A., 1973-76; pvt. practice Westchester Ctr. for Counseling and Psychotherapy, L.A., 1975-76; pvt. practice psychotherapy Santa Barbara, Calif., 1976—. Coord. daytime programs for older adults Rutgers U., 1968-70; instr. UCLA Ext., 1974, Felicia Mahood Ctr., L.A., 1975, U. Calif., Santa Barbara, 1977-78; field faculty Goddard and Antioch Colls., 1976-81; cons., therapist Arthritis Found., Santa Barbara, 1976-80; cons. Sanctuary House, 1976-80, Santa Barbara City Coll., 1981, Casa Dorinda Residential Retirement Home, Santa Barbara, 1983-84. Co-authro: (with B. Weininger) Aging is a Lifelong Affair, 1978; contbr. articles to profl. jours. Mem. Am. Assn. Marriage and Family Therapy, Calif. Assn. Marriage and Family Therapists, Gerontol. Soc. Am. Home: 1011 Mission Ridge Rd Santa Barbara CA 93103-1618 E-mail: dmenkin@aol.com.

MENLOVE, FRANCES LEE, psychologist; b. Salt Lake City, June 4, 1936; d. Edwin Fred and Pernecy Greaves Anderson; children: Stephen, Lynelle, Spencer, Lauren. BA, Stanford U., Calif.; PhD, U. Mich., 1963; cert. in Profl. Ethics, Pacific Sch. Religion, 1990, MDiv, 1998. Lic. psychologist N.Mex., 1976, Oreg., 1990, cert. in profl. quality psychology Calif., 2001. Founder, dir. Coun. Alcholism, Los Alamos, N.Mex., 1973—74; chief psychologist U. Calif., Los Alamos, 1974—86, dir. human resources, 1986—96; ethicist Bioethics Consultation Group, Berkeley, Calif., 1997—2000; asst. min. United Ch. Christ Congl., Lincoln City, Oreg., 2002—. Tchr. ethics U. N.Mex., Los Alamos, 1991—92; trustee Dialogue Jour., Palo Alto, Calif., 1965—72; cons. N.Mex. Dept. Corrections, Albuquerque, 1972—72; dir. Called to Care, Lincoln City, Oreg., 2002—05; psychologist Am. Red Cross, Lincoln City, 2001—; adv. bd. U. N.Mex., Los Alamos, N.Mex., 1993—96. Author: A Challenge of Honesty, 1987, A Challenge of Honesty-Watershed Articles 35 Years of Dialogue, 2001, Sunstone, 2004; manuscript editor Quar. Jour. Dialogue, 1963—65; editor: Jour. Morman Thought, 1963—65; contbr. articles to profl. jours. Recipient Danforth award, Danforth Found., 1954; fellow, Woodrow Wilson Found., 1959. Mem.: APA (life), Phi Beta Kappa. Avocations: reading, whale watching, travel.

MENNA, SÁRI, artist, educator; b. San Fracisco, Sept. 29, 1932; m. Ferdinand Carl Menna, Mar. 10, 1949; children: Mark, Diane Menna Clarke. BFA cum laude, Hunter Coll. of CUNY, N.Y.C., 1968, MFA, 1974; post grad., N.Y. U., N.Y.C., 1987—93. Lic. tchr. N.Y. Bd. Edn., 1971. Substitute tchr. Massapequa Pub. Schs., L.I., NY, 1968—69; tchr. art N.Y.C. Bd. Edn., 1971—95; ret., 1995. Vol. art tchr. Pres.' Econ. Opportunity Ctr., L.I., 1967—68; organizer juried art shows Amity Art League, 1964—67; tchr. cultural workshop Amityville Workshop, L.I., 1968. Mini-park, N.Y.C., 1974, calendar and cover art, Women Artists, 1983, exhibitions include Salute to Women, Washington and Nairobi, 1991, Women's Art, N.Y.C., 1992, Paintings and Paperworks, CUNY, 1992, Small Works, Kirkland, Wash., 1993, Garden of Delights, Bklyn., 1994, Family Values, N.Y.C., 1994, Hallelujah 94, 1994, Visions of Reality, Madison, N.J., 1995, A Woman's Pl., N.Y.C., 1995, Points of View, 1995, ADA: Women and Info. Tech., Chgo., 1995—96, The World's Women On Line, Beijing, Tempe, Ariz. and online, 1995—96, Fine Arts Mus., L.I., 1996, Openings 96, N.Y.C., 1996, Diversity, 1997, Small Statement Show, Bklyn., 1997, Painterly Forms, N.Y.C., 1997, BWAC 4th Ann. Pier Show, NJ, 1998, Flat Iron Gallery, Peekskill, N.Y., 1999, Broome St. Gallery, Soho, N.Y.C., 2000, WIA PART II, Canojohri, N.Y., 2000, Broome St. Gallery, NYC, 2004, Williamsburg Art and Hist. Ctr., Bklyn., 2004, Taller Boriqua Galleries, Julia de Burgos Cultural Ctr., NYC, 2005, Medeung Gallery, Korea, 2005, exhibited in group shows at Pier Show, N.Y.C., N.Y., 2006, Represented in permanent collections Nat. Mus. of Women in the Arts, Washington, Women's Interart Collections, N.Y.C., in pvt. collections, online exhibitions. Pres. Creative Women's Collective, N.Y.C., 1982—85; mem. Women's Caucus Art (N.Y.C. chpt.), 1982—91; mem. Queens Coun. on Art, 2001—06. Mem.: Creative Women's Collective, Women in the Arts Found, Inc., Women's Studio Ctr., Artists Equity.

MENSH, SUZANNE COOPER, state official; b. Atlantic City, Aug. 29, 1929; d. Paul Joel and Jennie Jean Cooper; m. H. David Mensh, Dec. 18, 1949; children: Paul Jay, Spencer Lee; m. Saul Brown, Feb. 17, 1985. Grad. high sch., Balt. Assoc. judge Orphans' Ct., Balt., 1962-66, chief judge, 1966-85; clk. of ct. Circuit Ct. for Baltimore County, Balt., 1986—. Mem. jud. ethics com. Judiciary of Md., Balt., 1992-99. Active Balt. Dem. Com., 1962—; mem. Nat. Coun. Jewish Women; pres. Balt. Zionist Fedn., 1989-93; former mem. found. bd. Towson State U.; former mem. bd. dirs. Jewish Nat. Fund; former condr. estate planning seminars N.W. Hosp. Ctr., also formr mem. found. bd. Named Woman of Yr. Aux. Baltimore County Gen. Hosp. (now N.W. Hosp. Ctr.), 1989. Mem. Md. Circuit Ct. Clks. Assn. (past pres.), Hadassah (life), Na'Amat (life). Jewish. Avocations: walking, decorating, entertaining, violin. Home: 303 Glatisant Pl Baltimore MD 21208-1400 Office: Circuit Ct Clk's Office County Cts Bldg 401 Bosley Ave Baltimore MD 21204-4420

MENTON, TANYA LIA, lawyer, educator; b. Chgo., Sept. 13, 1964; d. Joseph Bernard and Rosalind Marie (Macey) M. BA magna cum laude, Northwestern U., 1986, JD, 1989. Bar: Calif. 1989, N.Y. 1993. Counsel Townley and Updike, N.Y.C., 1991—96; v.p. litigation and employment practices ABC, Inc., L.A., 1995—. Adj. prof. Mercy Coll., Dobbs Ferry, N.Y., 1993-2000; lectr. on sexual harassment, discrimination and mgmt. tng. various orgns. Editor: (legal publ.) California Employment Law Letter, 1989-91. Nat. Harry S. Truman scholar, 1982-86. Mem. ABA, Calif. Bar Assn. (labor and employment sect.), N.Y. State Bar Assn. (labor and employment sect.). Democrat. Avocation: horseback riding. Home: # 17P 301 E 79th St Apt 17P New York NY 10021-0940 Office: ABC Inc 77 W 66th St New York NY 10023-6201 Office Phone: 212-456-6178.

MENTZER, ROSLYN, academic administrator; b. N.Y.C., Oct. 26, 1935; d. Morris and Etta B. (Greenberg) Moskowitz; m. Alan D. Mentzer, June 21, 1953; children: Michelle, Stuart. BA, Queens Coll., 1965; MA, UCLA, 1968. Instr. L.A. Community Coll. Dist., 1968-69; v.p. United Coll. of Bus., L.A., 1969—. Pres. CAPPS, Calif., 1984-87. Mem. LWV (v.p. Beverly Hills, Calif. chpt. 1969), Phi Beta Kappa. Avocations: tennis, bridge, writing. Home: 61 Cascade Ky Bellevue WA 98006-1023 Office: United Coll of Bus 445 S Figueroa St Bldg 2400 Los Angeles CA 90071-1602

MENUTIS, RUTH ANN, small business owner; b. Lafayette, La., Aug. 7, 1939; d. Minus and Annie (Duhon) Pellerin; ed. S.W. La. Inst., Patricia Stevens Sch. Modeling; m. Jimmie Menutis, Feb. 15, 1960; children: Jamie, Marika, Dimitri. Comml. announcer, traffic mgr. KLFY-TV, 1957-58; hostess Trans Tex./Tex. Internat. Airlines, also model Dallas Apparel Mart, 1958-68; owner, mgr. Playgril Shop of Am. and Ruth Ann Fashion, New Orleans, 1960—; owner Natural Energy Unltd., Inc. (doing bus. as Grove), 1980-2004; owner Menutis Investments, Lafayette, La.; pres. Branded Works Inc.; acting pres. French Market Corp.; real estate investor; real estate salesman French Quarter Realty; clothing designer Miss Jane of Miami. Bd. dirs. Better Bus. Bur., Contemporary Arts Ctr.; chmn. La. del. to White House Small Bus. Conf., 1980; vice chmn. midwest U.S.A. Small Bus. Nat. Unity Council; chmn. New Orleans Mayor's, French Quar. Task Force. Mem. Vieux Carre Action Assn. (v.p.), Bourbon Mchts. Assn. (pres.), New Orleans C. of C. (dir.). Greek Orthodox. Office: 110 Travis St # 121 Lafayette LA 70503-2453 Office Phone: 504-525-6887. E-mail: rmenutis@brandedworksinc.com.

MENZEL, BARBARA EDWINA, systems analyst; b. Indpls., Jan. 3, 1951; d. Harold William and Winifred Anne Bradford Menzel. BS in Accountancy, No. Ariz. U., Flagstaff, 1985; MEd, Ariz. State U., Tempe, 1992. Computer programmer analyst Rocky Mountain Forest and Range Expt. Sta., Flagstaff, Ariz., 1980—86, USGS, Tucson, 1986—88; auditor Def. Contract Audit Agy., Scottsdale, Ariz., 1988—89; computer programmer analyst Self-employed, Tucson, 1989—90; grad. asst. Ariz. State U., Tempe, 1991—92; tchr. Red Rocks C.C., Lakewood, Colo., 1992—94; computer programmer analyst USDA Forest Svc., Fort Collins, Colo., 1995—. Mem.: No. Colo. Artist's Assn., Am. Bus. Women's Assn., Inst. of Noetic Scis., The Planetary Soc. Independent. Unitarian. Avocations: quilting, hiking, photography. Home: 3298 Williamsburg St Loveland CO 80538 Office: USDA Forest Service 2150 Centre Ave Suite 341-A Fort Collins CO 80526 Office Phone: 970-295-5775. Personal E-mail: b.e.menzel@att.net.

MENZEL, IDINA, actress, singer; b. Syosset, May 30, 1971; d. Stuart and Helene Mentzel; m. Taye Diggs, Jan. 11, 2003. BFA in Drama, NYU. Actor: (Broadway plays) RENT, 1995—97 (Tony award nominee), Aida, 2001, Funny Girl, 2002, Wicked, 2003—05 (Tony award best actress in a musical, 2004); (plays) The Wild Party, 1999, Summer of '42, 2000, Hair, 2001, The Vagina Monologues, 2002, See What I Wanna See, 2005; singer: (albums) Still I Can't Be Still, 1998, Here, 2004; actor: (films) Kissing Jessica Stein, 2001, Just a Kiss, 2002, The Tollbooth, 2004, Rent, 2005; composer: (songs) Follow If You Lead for film "The Other Sister", 1999.*

MENZEL, MARYBELLE PROCTOR, volunteer; b. Milledgeville, Ga., Feb. 5, 1940; d. Ennis Hall Proctor and Sara (Evans) McCarthy; m. Robert John Menzel, Sept. 1, 1961; children: Blake, John, Craig. BA cum laude, Wesleyan Coll., Macon, Ga., 1962; MA with highest distinction, U. Ctrl. Fla., 1986. Cert. highest level tchr. Fla. Tchr. Spaulding Jr. HS, Griffin, Ga., 1962, East Syracuse (NY) Minoa HS, 1964—65, Coral Gables (Fla.) HS, 1965—66; dir. Gerber Child Care Ctr., Indialantic, Fla., 1981, Brevard CC Coop Presch., Melbourne, Fla., 1982—85; adj. instr. English and Humanities Brevard CC, Cocoa, Fla., 1985. Host, guide, amb. Denver Art Mus., 2006—. Named Million Dollar Woman, Wesleyan Coll., 2005. Mem.: AAUW (Nat. award Fundraising AAUW Ednl. Found. 2001, Garden of Victories award 1993), Colo. AAUW (dir. ednl. found. 2000—01, pres. elect 2001—02, pres. 2002—04, past pres. 2004—05, pub. policy com. 2004—, women's legis. breakfast com. 2005—, state exec. bd., mem. women's lobby), Wesleyan Coll. Million Dollar Women, Nat. Mus. Women in the Arts (friend), Nat. Mus. Women's History (charter), Nat. Trust for Historic Preservation, Phi Kappa Phi. Democrat. Methodist.

MÉRAS, PHYLLIS LESLIE, journalist; b. Bklyn., May 10, 1931; d. Edmond Albert and Leslie Trousdale (Ross) M.; BA, Wellesley Coll., 1955; MS in Journalism, Columbia U., 1954; Swiss Govt. Exchange fellow, Inst. Higher Internat. Studies, Geneva, 1957; m. Thomas H. Cocroft, Nov. 3, 1968. Reporter, copy editor Providence Jour., 1954-57, 59-61; feature writer Ladies Home Jour. mag., 1957-58; editor Weekly Tribune, Geneva, Switzerland, 1961-62; copyeditor, travel sect. N.Y. Times, 1962-68; mng. editor Vineyard Gazette, Edgartown, Mass., 1970-74, contbg. editor, 1974—; assoc. editor Rhode Islander, Providence, 1970-76; travel editor Providence Jour., 1976-95; editor Wellesley Alumnae mag., 1979-96; assoc. in journalism U. R.I., 1974-75; adj. instr. Columbia U. Sch. Journalism, 1975-76. Author: First Spring: A Martha's Vineyard Journal, 1972, A Yankee Way With Wood, 1975, Miniatures: How to Make Them, Use Them, Sell Them, 1976, Vacation Crafts, 1978, The Mermaids of Chenonceaux and 828 Other Tales: An Anecdotal Guide to Europe, 1982, Exploring Rhode Island, 1984, Castles, Keeps and Leprechauns: Tales, Myths and Legends of Historic Sites in Great Britain and Ireland, 1988, Eastern Europe: A Traveler's Companion, 1991; co-author: Christmas Angels, 1979, Carry-out Cuisine, 1982, New Carry Out Cuisine, 1986, Rhode Island Explorer's Guide, 2004, Country Editor: Henry Beetle Hough and the Vineyard Gazette, 2006. Pulitzer fellow in critical writing, 1967. Mem. Soc. Am. Travel Writers. Home: Music St PO Box 215 West Tisbury MA 02575-0215 Office Phone: 508-693-1439. E-mail: pmcocroft@aol.com.

MERCADO, MARY GONZALES, cardiologist; b. Houston, July 9, 1959; d. Frank Reyes and Joyce (Byrd) Gonzales; m. Antonio Gonzalez Mercado, May 25, 1985. BS magna cum laude, U. Tex., San Antonio, 1987; MD with honors, Baylor Coll. of Medicine, 1992. Diplomate Am. Bd. Internal Medicine, Am. Bd. Cardiovasc. Diseases, Am. Bd. Nuclear Cardiology. Intern U. Tex. Affiliated Hosps., San Antonio, 1992-93, resident, 1993-95, chief resident, 1995-96, fellow in cardiology, 1996-99; pvt. practice, Ozark, Ala. Presenter confs. and symposiums. Contbr. articles to med. publs. Mem. AMA, Am. Soc. Echocardiography, Am. Coll. Cardiology, Am. Soc. Nuc. Cardiology, Tex. Med. Assn., Ala. Med. Assn., Bexar County Med. Soc., Dale County Med. Soc. E-mail: mgmercado@charter.net.

MERCEDE, NEVIN, art educator, artist; b. Phila., Oct. 31, 1953; d. Philip Bausman and Patricia Clark Schaeffer. BFA, Calif. Coll. Arts and Crafts, 1976; MFA, U. Mont., 1984. Adj. prof. Mt. Wachusett CC, Gardner, Mass., 1986—87, Md. Inst. Coll. Art, Balt., 1988—90; asst. prof. Ind. U. Pa., 1990—93; vis. asst. prof. Wash. U. St. Louis, 1993—94, U. South Fla., Tampa, 1994—96; vis. faculty Ringling Sch. Art and Design, Sarasota, 1997—98; assoc. prof. Antioch Coll., Yellow Springs, Ohio, 1998—. V.p. bus. procs. Founds. Art: Theory and Edn., Charleston, Ill., 1993—2003, editl. bd., 1997—2000; dir. Herndon Gallery, Antioch Coll., Yellow Springs, Ohio, 1999—2003; outside reviewer Art Acad. Cin., 2000; adj. prof. Springfield (Mass.) Coll., 1984—86; cons. in field. Curator Katherine Kadish Recent Works, Recent MFAs Series, Materially Reconsidered, Monsters and Metaphors, Identity Memories, Of Two Worlds; author, artist: essay and photographs Positive Women an excerpt; exhibitions include Giving Art (Con)Text, 2005, one-woman shows include The Siva Series, 1984, The Vishnumena Series, 1986, Nimesa Color Studies, 1988, The Nimes Project Installation, 1992, Positive Women, 1994, Drawings from the Nimesa Project, 1999, The Relection Series, 2000, From the Nimesa Series, 2001. Com. mem. Coll. Art Assn. Women in Arts, NYC, 1991—94; bd. dirs. Cmty. Svc. Inc., Yellow Springs, 2000—04, trustee, 2000—04. Grantee Faculty Fund grant, Antioch Coll., 2006; Artist Residency scholarship, M M Karolyi Found., Vence, France, 1988, CityArts grant, Balt. City, 1990, Travel grant, Ind. U. Pa., 1991, Rsch. grant, 1991, 1993, Profl. Devel. grant, Antioch Coll., 1998-2005, Artist in Residence grant, Bethesda Chevy Chase HS, Travel and Edn. fellowship, Global Ptnrs., Russia, 2004, Faculty Fund grant, Antioch Coll., 2004. Mem.: Coll. Art Assn. Independent. Avocations: travel, reading, walking, films, theater. Home: PO Box 264 Yellow Springs OH 45387 Office: Antioch Coll 795 Livermore St Yellow Springs OH 45387 Business E-Mail: nmercede@antioch-college.edu.

MERCER, DOROTHY L., psychology educator, consultant; b. Charlevoix, Mich. d. Hoy M. Dewey. BA, Adrian (Mich.) Coll., 1963; MA, U. Mich., 1964; PhD, Mich. State U., 1986. Lic. psychologist, Ky. Tchr. spl. edn. Prince Georges County Schs., College Park, Md., 1965—68; mental health therapist Tri-County Community Mental Health, Lansing, Mich., 1980; psychologist Jackson-Hillsdale (Mich.) Cmty. Mental Health, 1980-84; counselor Mich. State U., East Lansing, 1985-87; prof. psychology Ea. Ky. U., Richmond, 1987—. Psychol. cons. Mothers Against Drunk Driving, Hurst, Tex., 1989—. Mem. Am. Psychol. Assn., Am. Death Educators and Counselors (cert.), Ky. Psychol. Assn Office: Ea Ky U 127 Cammack Bldg Richmond KY 40475 Business E-Mail: dorothy.mercer@eku.edu.

MERCER, DOROTHY MAY, real estate company executive; b. Spring Arbor, Mich., June 12, 0192; d. Leon Luther and Esther Elizabeth (Dodes) Douglas; m. David Neal Mercer, Mar. 17, 1951; children: Shelley Lynn, Ann Elizabeth. AA, Grand Rapids Jr. Coll., Mich., 1975; MusB summa cum laude, Western Mich. U., Kalamazoo, 1981; postgrad., Perkins Sch. Theology, Highland Park, Tex., 1987. Cert. dir. mus. and healing and wholeness ministries United Meth. Ch. Dir. music Grandville United Meth. Ch., Grandville, Mich., 1979—80, Burton Hts. United Meth. Ch., Grand Rapids, Mich., 1980—81, Faith United Meth. Ch., Grand Rapids, 1981—88, Northland United Meth. Ch., Stanwood, 1994—2004; pvt. tchr. piano, voice and guitar Grand Rapids and Stanwood, 1970—2005; pres. Mercer Pubs., Inc., Stanwood, 1986—, Swains Lake Farms, Inc., Concord, Mich., 1992—. Deacon United Meth. Ch., 1997—; cons. in healing and wholeness ministries; condr. seminars and workshops in field; dir. MerriMen Chorus, Canadian Lakes, Mich., 1995—. Composer: numerous piano, guitar and choral works; author: numerous books on healing and wholeness. Fundraiser Habitat for Humanity, Mecosta County, Mich., 1993—; leader Girls Scouts U.S., Grand Rapids, 1962—70; fundraiser WWII Meml., Washington, 2000—05; pres. Swains Lake Farms Property Owners Assn., Concord, 2003—05; chmn. bd. diaconal ministry West Mich. Conf., United Meth. Ch., 1994. Republican. Methodist.

MERCER, EVELYN LOIS, retired counseling administrator; b. Ellensboro, N.C., Apr. 25, 1934; d. Milton Bernadine Robinson Sr. and Lois Lenora Robinson; m. Theodore Roosevelt Mercer Sr. (div. June 1978); children: Theodore Roosevelt Jr., Brian Vincent, David Lemuel. BS in Math., Livingstone Coll., 1957; MEd in Guidance and Counseling, U. Cin., 1972; student, U. Akron, 1973, Miami U., Ohio, 1973—75, U. Akron, 1974. Cert. math tchr. Ohio, 1963, guidance counselor Ohio, 1972, lic. profl. counselor Ohio Counselor & Social Worker Bd., 1984. Math tchr. Jackson County Pub. Schs., Gumberry, NC, 1957—60, Cin. Pub. Schs., Cin., 1963—72, guidance counselor, 1972—73, Winton Woods City Sch. Dist., Cin., 1973—94, ret., 1994. Mem. adv. com. conselor edn. U. Cin., Cin., 1975—76; admissions adv. bd. Cin. Tech. Coll., Cin., 1975—81, The Ohio State U., Columbus, Ohio, 1982—85; nursing sch. adv. bd. Deaconess Hosp. Sch. Nursing, Cin., 1983—88; dir. Sch. Counseling Cons. Svc., Cin., 1994—, Charlotte, NC, 1994—. Mem. housing commn. City of Forest Park, Cin., 1974—76; Dem. precinct exec. Hamilton County Bd. Elections, Cin., 1974—96. Named Outstanding Counselor of Yr., Inroads of Cin., 1984. Mem.: NEA, AAUW (pres. Charlotte br. 2001—03), Am. Assn. U. Women of NC (v.p. membership 2004—), Am. Assn Coll. Admissions Counselors, Ohio Assn. Coll. Admissions Counselors, Ohio Sch. Counselors Assn., Ohio Edn. Assn., Livingstone Coll. Alumni Assn., U. Cin. Alumni Assn., Nat. Assn. Advancement for Colored People, Les Birdies Golf Club Charlotte (founder 1999, pres. 1999—2001), Order of Eastern Star, Zeta Phi Beta. Democrat. Methodist. Avocations: golf, travel, bridge, volunteering, gardening. Home and Office: 4101 Rye Mill Ct Charlotte NC 28277

MERCER, FRANCES DECOURCY, artist, educator; b. Centreville, Miss., June 14, 1944; d. John Homer Jr. and Patricia Powers (Given) Mercer. BA in English Lit., U. Miami, 1969, MA in History of Art, 1971; MFA in Painting, San Francisco Art Inst., 1974. Cert. tchr. Fla. Instr. South Fla. Art Inst., Hollywood, Fla., 1979—81; tchg. asst. San Francisco Art Inst., 1974; instr. Broward C.C., Ft. Lauderdale, Fla., 1979—83; owner 17th St. Galleries, Ft. Lauderdale, 1984—91; tchr. Broward County Sch. Bd., 1980—82; adj. prof. Fla. Atlantic U., 1979—80. Exhibited in group shows at Grove Art Gallery, Coconut Grove, Fla., 1973, Emanuel Walter Gallery, San Francisco, 1975, The Lucian LaBaudt Gallery, 1976, The Both Up Gallery, Berkeley, Calif., 1976, Discover Ctr., Ft. Lauderdale, 1980, Nova U. Artoberfest, Art and Culture Ctr. Hollywood, 1981, Indian Hammock Hunt and Riding Club, Okeechobee, Fla., 1998, A.E. Backus Gallery and Mus., Ft. Pierce, Fla., 2000, pvt. collections. Scholar Tuition scholar, San Francisco Art Inst., 1972, 1973, 1974. Avocations: photography, trail hiking, kayaking, golf, sailing. E-mail: fmercer@floridawatercolors.com.

MERCHANT, NATALIE ANNE, musician, singer; b. Jamestown, N.Y., Oct. 26, 1963; d. Tony and Ann Merchant; 1 child. Lead singer band 10,000 Maniacs, 1981-1993; solo artist, 1993—; founder Myth Amer. Records LLC, 2003—. Albums with 10,000 Maniacs include Human Conflict Number Five, 1982, Secrets of the I Ching, 1983, The Wishing Chair, 1986, In My Tribe, 1987, Blind Man's Zoo, 1989, Hope Chest, 1990, Our Time in Eden, 1992, 10,000 Maniacs MTV Unplugged, 1993; solo album Tigerlily, 1995, Ophelia, 1998, Live In Concert, 1999, Motherland, 2001, Natalie Merchant, 2001, Motherland, 2001, The House Carpenter's Daughter, 2003; composer soundtracks: Felicity, 1998, Earthlings, 2003. Office: Myth Amer Records 660 Madison Ave 10th Fl New York NY 10021

MERCIER, EILEEN ANN, corporate financial executive; b. Toronto, Ont., Can., July 7, 1947; d. Thomas Sidley and Frances Katherine (Boone) Falconer; m. Ernest Cochrane Mercier, Feb. 8, 1980; children: Jenny, Sheelagh, Peter, Michael, Stuart. BA with honors, Waterloo Luth. U., 1968; MA, U. Alta., Can., 1969; fellow, Instn. Can. Bankers, 1975; MBA, York U., 1977. Mgr. corp. fin. Toronto-Dominion Bank, 1972-78, portfolio mgr. TD capital; dir., U.S. comm. ops. Canwest Capital Corp., Toronto, 1978-81; mgr. fin. strategy & planning Gulf Can. Ltd., Toronto, 1981-86, mgr. corp. fin.; v.p. The Pagurian Corp., Toronto, 1986-87; v.p., treas. Abitibi-Price, Inc., Toronto, 1987-88, v.p. corp. devel., 1989-90, sr. v.p., CFO, 1990-95. Bd. dirs. Hydro One, Inc., TeeKay Shipping Corp., The CGI Group Inc., ING Bank Can., ING Can., Inc., Shermag Ltd., Ont. Tchrs. Pension Plan. Past chmn., mem. bd. govs. Wilfrid Laurier U., Waterloo, Ont., York U., U. Health Network. Recipient Outstanding Bus. Leader award Wilfrid Laurier U., 1991, Award for Outstanding Contbn. Schulich Sch. of Bus. York U., 1997. Office: 199 Cranbrooke Ave Toronto ON Canada M5M 1M6

MERCIER, LINDA ANN, secondary school educator; b. Salem, Mass., Nov. 6, 1947; d. Joseph Emile and Maroin Ann (Freeman) Mercier. BS in Secondary Edn., Salem State Coll., 1972; MS in Edn., Lesley Coll., 1997. Advanced cert. tchg. social studies 1998. Tchr. St. John's, Peabody, Mass., 1972—76, St. Pius, Lynn, Mass., 1986—91, Palo Verde H.S., Las Vegas, 1991—. V.p. Social Studies Coun. Nev., 1998—. Scholar Fulbright Meml. Fund, Japan, 2001. Avocations: photography, writing. Home: 3208 Beaconshores Cir Las Vegas NV 89117 Office: 333 S Pavilion Center Dr Las Vegas NV 89144-4001

MERCK, GERRY ELIZABETH, counselor; b. Rutherfordton, N.C., July 10, 1951; d. Charles Hedrick Stanley and Elizabeth Ann (Lovelace) Cash; adopted children: Joshua Jordan Matheson, Miles Alexander. BS in Psychology, BS in Art, Western Carolina U., 1974; MHDL, U. N.C., Charlotte, 1990—. Dir. activities Rutherford County Convalescent Ctr., Rutherfordton, 1974-82, Meadowbrook Manor, Cherryville, N.C., 1982-85; coord. adult svcs. Child Abuse Prevention Svcs. Cleveland County, Shelby, N.C., 1985-89; therapeutic foster parent Lifegains, Inc., Morganton, N.C., 1982—. Program cons. Cleveland Vocat. Industries, Lawndale, N.C., 1988-95; therapist Employee Assistance Program of Cleve. County, 1996—. Writer songs. Recipient gov.'s vol. award State of N.C., 1982. Mem. ACA, Assn. for Multicultural Counseling Devel., N.C. Counseling Assn., Am. Mensa, Psi Chi, Phi Kappa Phi, Chi Sigma Iota. Democrat. Episcopalian. Avocations: amateur astronomy, pottery, celtic harp, songwriting, native american flute. Home: 301 Iowa St Utica NE 68456-6047

MERCKER, MARY ALICE, aviation school administrator; b. Kansas City, Mo., June 29, 1932; d. Kenneth Foster Rhees and Catherine Mary Henel; m. Reid Martin, Nov. 23, 1950 (div. Nov. 1969); children: Reid J., Kenneth C., Mark T., Mary M., Theodore H., Sylvia R., Ben X., Teresa I. Student, Phoenix Coll., 1949-50; AA, Pima Coll., 1990-93; student, U. Ariz., 1994. Fed. aviation adminstr.; comml. pilot; cert. flight instr. Instr. Ariz. Sch. Aviation, Tucson, 1979, Tucson Cmdr., 1980, AVRA Flt. Ctr., Marana, Ariz., 1976-78; pres., founder Alpha Air, Inc., Tucson, 1980—; sec., treas. Manasco Inc., Tucson, 1987—. Aviation cons., Tucson, 1987—; adj. profl aviation Pima C.C., Tucson, 1988-94, curriculum cons., 1988-93. Author: Northumberland Dreaming, 1998, numerous poems. Recipient 2nd Place Sparrowgrass Poetry Forum, 1996, 1st Place Sparrowgrass Chapbook award, 2001. Mem. Ariz. Pilots Assn., Aircraft Owners and Pilots Assn., 99's (life). Home: 6220 W Belmont Rd Tucson AZ 85743-9212 Office: Alpha Air Inc HC 2 Box 282 Tucson AZ 85735-9709 Personal E-mail: alphair@msn.com.

MERCURI, JOAN B., museum administrator; b. NYC; BA, Va. Commonwealth U., 1984. Mgmt. positions various corps., Ill., 1986-96; exec. dir. Frank Lloyd Wright Home and Studio Found., Oak Park, Ill., 1996—; pres., CEO Frank Lloyd Wright Preservation Trust, Oak Park, 2000—. Dir. Oak Park Area Conv. and Vis. Bur. Mem. Am. Assn. Museums, Nat. Trust for Hist. Preservation, Employment Mgmt. Assn., Soc. Human Resource Mgmt., Frank Lloyd Wright Bldg. Conservancy, Assn. Fundraising Profls., Board Source. Office Phone: 708-848-1976. Business E-Mail: mercuri@wrightplus.org.

MERCURI, THERESA B., mathematician, educator; d. Antoni and Wladyslawa Zawadzki; m. Jeffrey Mercuri, Aug. 20, 1988; children: Jeffrey Allen, Samantha Anne, Rebecca Anne. BS in Acctg., D'Youville Coll., Buffalo, N.Y., 1988, MEd, 2001; M in Edn. Adminstrn., Canisius Coll., Buffalo, N.Y., 2005. Cert. 7-12 math. tchr. N.Y., 2001, 7-12 bus. tchr. N.Y., 2001, sch. adminstr., supr. N.Y., sch. dist. adminstr. N.Y. Operational/acctg. analyst Del. North Cos., Buffalo, 1990—2001; tchr. math. Hamburg Mid. Sch., NY, 2001—02, Depew Mid. Sch., NY, 2002—. Bd. mem. Lancaster Youth Bur., NY. Mem.: Nat. Coun. of Tchrs. of Math., Nat. Assn. of Secondary Sch. Prins. Office: Depew Mid Sch 5201 S Transit Rd Depew NY 14043 Office Phone: 716-686-2442.

MEREDITH, JOANNE CUSICK, special education educator, director; b. Pitts., Pa., Dec. 2, 1952; d. Joseph Francis and Anne Amelia (Fiorillo) Cusick; m. Richard Burdette Meredith, Nov. 25, 2001. BS in speech and hearing, Ind. U. of Pa., 1974, MS in Speech Pathology, 1979. Cert. spl. edn. supr. Slippery Rock U. Pa., 1987, sch. psychologist Duquesne U., Pa., 1992, speech correction profl. level II Ind. U. Pa., supr. spl. edn. profl. level II Slippery Rock U. of Pa., 1987, sch. psychologist level I. Speech/lang. therapist Seneca Valley Sch. Dist., Harmony, Pa., 1974—96; part-time speech pathologist Rehab. Specialists, Pitts., 1980—81; sch. psychologist intern Seneca Valley Sch. Dist., Harmony, Pa., 1991—92, dir. spl. edn., 1996—. Pres. Seneca Valley Edn. Assn., Harmony, Pa., 1986—90, chief negotiator, 1989—95, v.p., 1990—92. Recipient Gift of Time award, Am. Family Inst., ACE award, Am. Speech/Lang./Hearing Assn., Appreciation award, Pa. State Assn. for Health, PE, Recreation and Dance, 1995. Mem.: ASCD, Mid. Sch. Assn., Pa. State Assn. for Health, Coun. for Exceptional Children, Pa. Speech/Lang. Assn., Am. Speech, Lang. and Hearing Assn., Phi Delta Kappa. Democrat. Avocations: beach, shopping, motorcycling, cruises. Home: 345 Beacon Rd Renfrew PA 16053 Office: Seneca Valley Sch Dist 124 Seneca Sch Rd Harmony PA 16037 Office Phone: 724-452-6040 x 221.

MEREDITH, LISA ANN MARIE, social studies educator, consultant; b. Reading, Pa., May 2, 1969; d. Robert Lee and Carol Ann Meredith; life ptnr. Thomas J. Unrath. BA, Alvernia Coll., Reading, Pa., 1990—91. Cert. elem. sch. tchr. Commonwealth of Pa., 1991, mid. sch. tchr. Commonwealth of Pa., 2005. Tchr. Reading Sch. Dist., Pa., 1991—2003, Sch. Dist. Phila., 2001—; edn. coord. Nat. Constn. Ctr., Phila., 2003—04. Asst. coord. Ctr. for Civic Edn., Phila., 2003—04; cons. Pa. Gov.'s Inst. for Social Studies Educators, Harrisburg, 2004—. Mem. Champions for Caring, Phila., 2003—04; activist, rep. Reading Edn. Assn., Pa., 1998—2000; activist Phila. (Pa.) Citizens Children and Youth, 2002—03, Phila. Fedn. Tchrs., 2004—05. Grantee, Eisenhower Grants, 1995—96, Tchg. Am. History, 2002—03. Mem.: Nat. Coun. Social Studies Tchrs. (assoc.), Phila. Fedn. Tchrs. (assoc.). Liberal. Lutheran. Avocations: history, travel, golf, reading. Office: Sch Dist Phila 238 E Wyoming Ave Philadelphia PA 19120 Office Phone: 215-456-3012. Personal E-mail: lamm34@comcast.net. Business E-Mail: lameredith@phila.k12.pa.us.

MEREDITH, MERI HILL, reference librarian, educator; b. Riverside, Calif., May 30, 1943; d. William Beans and Marie Louise (Zantzinger) Hill; m. William Rinehardt Meredith, Mar. 17, 1970 (div.); children William Rinehardt III, Sarah Daingerfield Meredith. AB in French, George Washington U., Washington, 1967; MLS, Ind. U., 1980. Cataloger Ind. U., Bloomington, 1980-81; bus. libr. Cummins Engine Co., Columbus, Ind., 1981-88; pres. Info. and Comm. Rsch., Inc., Columbus, 1989-92; reference libr. Ohio State U. Bus. Libr., 1992—. Bd. dirs. Sch. of Libr. and Info. Sci., Ind. U., Bloomington; pres., co-founder Ind. On-Line Users Group, Indpls. Mem. AAUP, Spl. Librs. Assn., Acad. Libr. Assn. of Ohio. Republican. Roman Catholic. Home: 1800 Lafayette Pl Apt A1 Columbus OH 43212-1609 Office: Ohio State U Bus Libr Raymond E Mason Hall 250 W Woodruff Ave Columbus OH 43210-1133 Office Phone: 614-292-2136. Business E-Mail: meredith.18@osu.edu.

MERGLER, NANCY L., academic administrator; BA in Psychology, Syracuse U., 1972, MA in Developmental Psychology, 1975, PhD in Developmental Psychology, 1977. Tchg. asst. dept. psychology Syracuse U., 1973—75; asst. prof. dept. psychology Washington Coll., 1976—83, assoc. prof., 1984—94; prof. dept. psychology U. Okla., 1995—, sr. v.p., provost, 1995—. Contbr. articles to profl. jours. Mem.: APA, Okla. Psychol. Assn., Southwestern Psychol. Assn., Ea. Psychol. Assn., Gerontol. Soc. Office: Provosts Office 104 Evans Hall Univ Okla Norman OK 73019-0390

MERIDETH, SUSAN CAROL, business administration educator; b. St. Louis, May 25, 1956; d. George Getzel Brody and Jacquie Jean Lammers; m. John Wolf Merideth, July 28, 1979; children: Laura, Michelle. AAS, St. Louis C.C., 1977; BS, Fontbonne U., 1979; Master of Bus. Adminstrn., Maryville U., 1994. Presch. tchr. various instns., San Diego, 1979—82, Greater San Diego Health Plan, San Diego, 1985—87; supr. Cmty. Care Network, San Diego, 1987—90; mgr. St. John's Mercy Med. Ctr., St. Louis, 1990—95; contracts mgr. Nashua Eye Assocs., Nashua, 1996—98; practice mgr. Found. Med. Ptnrs., Nashua, 1998—99; assoc. prof. bus. adminstrn. Hesser Coll., Manchester, NH, 2000—. Mem.: AAUP, Nat. Bus. Edn. Assn., New England Regional Adv. Bd., Phi Theta Kappa (faculty advisor Alpha Nu Upsilon chpt. 2002—, mem. Pi Kappa chpt.). Office: Hesser Coll 3 Sundial Ave Manchester NH 03103 Office Phone: 603-668-6660. Business E-Mail: susan.merideth@ptk.org.

MERINI, RAFIKA, humanities educator, writer, language educator; b. Morocco; arrived in U.S., 1972; d. Mohamed M. and Fatima Merini. BA in English cum laude, U. Utah, 1978, MA in Romance Langs. and Lits., 1981; postgrad., U. Wash., 1980-82; cert. in translation, SUNY, Binghamton, 1988, PhD in Comparative Lit., 1992. Tchg. asst. U. Utah, Salt Lake City, 1978-80, U. Wash., Seattle, 1980-82; adminstrv. asst., tchr. French, interpreter The Lang. Sch., Seattle, 1982-83; lectr. Pacific Luth. U., Tacoma, 1983; instr. French and Spanish Ft. Steilacoom C.C. (now Pierce C.C.), 1983—85; tchg. asst. dept. romance langs. SUNY, Binghamton, 1985-87, tchg. asst. women's studies dept., 1988, tchg. asst. comparative lit. dept., 1986-88; vis. instr. humanities and French Union Coll., Schenectady, NY, 1988—89; vis. instr. dept. fgn. langs. and lits. Skidmore Coll., Saratoga Springs, NY, 1989-90; asst. prof. dept. modern and classical langs. State U. Coll., Buffalo, 1990—96, assoc. prof. dept. modern and classical langs., 1996—. Coord. Buffalo State Coll. women's studies interdiscipinary unit State U. Coll., Buffalo, 1993-99, adviser French Club, 1990-93; founder, dir. Trois-Pistoles French Immersion Program, U. Western Ont.-Buffalo State Coll., London, 1994, 95; presenter, spkr., conf. organizer in field. Author: Two Major Francophone Women Writers, Assia Djébar and Leïla Sebbar: A Thematic Study of Their Works, 1999, 2d printing, paperback edit., 2001; mem. editl. bd. Jour. Middle Eastern and North African Intellectual and Cultural Studies; contbr. articles to profl. jours Grantee Nat. Defense Student award U. Utah, 1974; also numerous other grants and awards. Mem. MLA, Pi Delta Phi. Office: State Univ Coll-Buffalo Modern & Classical Langs 1300 Elmwood Ave Buffalo NY 14222-1095 E-mail: merinir@buffalostate.edu.

MERK, ELIZABETH THOLE, investment company executive; b. Salt Lake City, July 29, 1950; d. John Bernard and Emily Josephine (Knotek) Thole; m. J. Eliot Merk, July 26, 1996 (div.); 1 child from previous marriage, William Lance Ulich. BA, U. Hawaii, Hilo, 1984, paralegal cert. cum laude, 1989; postgrad., U. Hawaii, Manoa, 1985-86. Lic. gen. agt. Hawaii; registered investment advisor, stock broker Hawaii, Calif., Ariz., lic. mortgage broker Hawaii, prin. Regional archtl. rep. Lightolier, Inc., Salt Lake City, 1978-80; group sales rep. FHP/Utah, Salt Lake City, 1980-81; health net rep. Blue Cross Corp., L.A., 1981-82; v.p. fin. Bus. Support Systems, Hilo, 1983-89; rep. Prudential Ins. and Fin. Svcs., Honolulu, 1989-97; registered rep. Pruco Securities Corp. subs. Prudential Ins. & Fin. Svcs., 1989—97; acct. exec. Dean Witter Reynolds, 1997—98; adv. assoc., registered prin. Mutual Svc. Corp., 1998—2001; adv. assoc., prin., rep. Hawaii, Centaurus Fin. Inc., 2001—; realtor assoc. Clark Realty Corp., 1998—. Docent Lyman House, 1984-85, L.A. County Mus. of Art, 1980-81, S.L.C. Art Mus., 1970-80; bd. dirs. YWCA, Hawaii Island, 1980-91, 1st v.p., 1988. Named YWCA Vol. of Yr., 1991, Top 25 Women owned Firms in Hawaii, Pacific Bus. News, 2001, 02, 03, 04, 05, 06, Women Who Mean Bus. in Hawaii, Pacific Bus. News, 2001, 02, 03, 04, 05, 06; recipient Nat. Quality award 1991, 92, 93, 94, Nat. Sales Achievement award NAIFA, 1992, 93; Paul Harris fellow Rotary Internat., 1997. Fellow: Life Underwriters Tng. Coun.; mem.: AAUW (bd. dirs. Hilo chpt. 1987—89, fundraiser chmn. Kona chpt. 1992, Steven Bufton grantee 1985), Securities Industry Assn., Million Dollar Round Table (mem. Ct. of the Table 2000, mem. Top of the Table 2001—06), Nat. Assn. Ins. and Fin. Advisors (charter mem.), Nat. Assn. Life Underwriters (legis. rep. West Hawaii chpt. 1995—97), Am. Bus. Women's Assn. (pres. Nani O Hilo chpt. 1995—96, membership chmn. 1996—97, inner circle 1997—), Outdoor Circle, Soroptimists. Roman Catholic. Office: 65-1231 Opelo Rd Ste 3 Waimea HI 96743

MERK, P. EVELYN, librarian; b. Macon, Ga., Dec. 8, 1943; d. Charlie B. and Gladys (Perry) M. BA, Mercer U., 1966; MEd, U. Ga., 1973; MLS, Emory U., 1987. Tchr. East Laurens High Sch., Dublin, Ga., 1966-68, Westside Sch., McDonough, Ga., 1968-70, Brantley County High Sch., Nahunta, Ga., 1970-72; sch. media specialist Mary Persons Sch., Forsyth, Ga., 1973-75; tech. services librarian Houston County Pub. Library, Warner Robins, Ga., 1975-76, reference librarian, 1976-77, libr., 1977—96, asst. dir., 1996—2002, libr. cons./trainer, 2002—. Bd. dirs. Warner Robins Day Care Ctr. Inc., chmn. 1984-85, 91. Mem. ALA, AAUW, Southeastern Library Assn., Ga. Library Assn., Warner Robins Pioneers. Avocations: reading, candle making. Home: 293 Peachtree Cir Warner Robins GA 31088-4448 Office: Houston County Pub Libr 721 Watson Blvd Warner Robins GA 31093-3413 E-mail: evelynmerk@aol.com.

MERKEL, ANNE D., science educator; b. Wilmington, Del., Nov. 4, 1942; d. George and Eileen Davis; m. James A. Merkel, June 3, 1970. BS, U. Del., Newark, 1964; MEd in Chemistry, U. Del., 1971. Registered Med. Technologist ASCP, Chgo., 2006. Dir. med. assisting program Beal Coll., Bangor, Maine, 1979—81; instr. Ea. Maine C.C., Bangor, 1981—. Grader for coll. bd. essays in ap biology Ednl. Testing Svcs., Newark, 2002—04; program dir. med. lab. tech. Ea. Maine C.C., Bangor, 1996—2001; supr. microbiology dept. Maine Coast Meml. Hosp., Ellsworth, 1977—79; rsch. assoc. virology DuPont Co., Newark, 1965—69. Mem.: NEA, Maine Tchrs. Assn. Independent. Roman Catholic. Achievements include curriculum development for programs at Jackson Laboratory, Beal College and East Maine Community College; Served on accrediting teams for New England Association of Schools and Colleges. Avocations: jogging, swimming, travel and cruising. Home: 298 Ohio St Bangor ME 04401 Office: Eastern Maine Cmty Coll 354 Hogan Rd Bangor ME 04401 Office Phone: 207-974-4645. Business E-Mail: amerkel@emcc.edu.

MERKEL, PATRICIA MAE, retired school system administrator; b. Spokane, Wash., June 18, 1935; d. Hugo Oscar and Mary Jane (Blackwelder) Koenig; m. Gordon Henry, Nov. 10, 1956 (div. 1973); children: Katherine Marie Merkel Fisk, Karol Ann Merkel Korte, John Henry. BA cum laude, Ea. Washington U., 1989. Cert. ednl. office employee. Acctg. clk. Pacific N.W. Bell, Spokane, 1954-56; book-keeper Edwall (Wash.) Sch. Dist., 1969-75, Reardan (Wash.)-Edwall Sch. Dist., 1975-78, bus. mgr., 1978-82; asst. to supr. fin. Dayton (Wash.) Sch. Dist., 1982-99. Mem. Town of Reardan Planning Commn., 1977-82, sec., 1978-82; treas. Citizens for Edn. Com., Dayton, 1983-91, Columbia County Courthouse Restoration Project, Dayton, 1988-99; fin. adv. com. Dayton Gen. Hosp., 1986-90, Dayton City Coun., 1986-87; vocat. bus. adv. com. Dayton HS, 1990-96. Recipient Mary Shields Wilson Medallion award; George F. Hixson fellow, 2005. Mem. AAUW, Wash. Assn. Sch. Ednl. Office Profls. (treas. 1984-86, pres.-elect 1986-87, pres. 1987-88, Ednl. Office Profl. of Yr. award 1990), Nat. Assn. Ednl. Office Profls. (Ednl. Office Profl. of Yr. award 1990), Assn. Sch. Bus. Ofcls. (chmn. com. 1978-81), S.C. Assn. Ednl. Office Profls. (pres. 1991-92), Blue Mountain Assn. Ednl. Office Profls., Assn. Sch. Bus. Ofcls. Internat. (com. 1984-86, scholar 1987), Order of Eagles, Kiwanis (sec. 1991-99, pres.-elect Tri Cities 2002-03, pres. 2003-04, Kiwaniain of Yr. 1993, 99). Democrat. Methodist. Avocations: reading, quilting, needle work, doll and bear making. Home: 3324 W 19th Ave Trlr 102 Kennewick WA 99338-2292 Personal E-mail: patmmerkel@aol.com.

MERKERSON, S. EPATHA, actress; b. Saginaw, Mich., Nov. 28, 1952; BFA, Wayne State U. Broadway and Off-Broadway productions include The Piano Lesson, I'm Not Stupid (Obie award 1992), The Old Settler, Birdie Blue, 2005 (OBIE award Village Voice 2006); appeared in films including Terminator II, Jacob's Ladder, Navy Seals, Loose Cannons, Random Hearts, 1999, The Rising Place, 2001, Radio, 2003, Jersey Girl, 2004; television guest appearances include The Cosby Show, Equal Justice, Elysian Fields, Moe's World; television series roles include Pee Wee's Playhouse, Mann & Machine, Here & Now, Law & Order (Outstanding Supporting Actress in a Drama Series, NAACP Image award, 2006), A Place for Annie, 1994, A Mother's Prayer, 1995, Breaking Through, 1996, An Unexpected Life, 1998, Exiled, 1998, Lackawanna Blues, 2005 (Emmy award for outstanding lead actress in a miniseries or a movie, 2005, best performance by an actress in a mini-series or motion picture made for television, Hollywood Fgn. Press Assn. (Golden Globe award), 2006, outstanding performance by an female actor in a TV movie or miniseries, Screen Actors Guild award, 2006, Outstanding Actress in a TV Movie, Mini-Series, or Dramatic Spl., NAACP Image awards, 2006). Nominated for Tony award, 1990, Drama Desk award, 1990, Helen Hayes award, 1990, L.A. Theater Critics award, 1990. Office: Law & Order c/o Universal Television 100 Universal City Plz Universal City CA 91608-1002*

MERKL, ELISSA FRANCES, visual artist, editor, publishing executive; b. Colo. Springs, July 2, 1949; d. Ellis Francis and Marie Ermelinda (Varrone) Merkl. BA, Marymount Coll., 1971. Visual artist self-employed, Gillette, 1971—; silk screen demonstrator various N.J. art orgns., 1973—; co-owner, v.p. Travel Designers, Inc., Springfield, N.J., 1986—94; visual arts critiquer Union County Teen Arts, Summit, N.J., 1996—2002; instr. Newark, 2001—02; pub./editor Cultural Events N.J., Gillette, 2001—. Bd. trustees Art Gallery of South Orange, 1975—85, Millburn-Short Hills Arts Ctr., 1985—2003, pres., 1998—2001. Exhibited in group shows at Color!, Nova Gallery, N.J., 3rd Annual Nat. Small Works Exhibit, Creede Arts Coun., Colo., 4th Annual Nat. Small Works Exhibit, 5th Annual Nat. Small Works Exhibit, 6th Annual Nat. Small Works Exhibit, Expression Through Contours, Agora Gallery, N.Y., Nat. Juried Printmaking Exhbns., Hunterdon Mus. Art, N.J., Invitational Two-Person Show, Schoharie Arts Coun., N.Y., Springfield Art Mus., Mo., Monmouth Mus., NJ, Stonemetal Press, Tex., Salmagundi Club, NYC, 2006, one-woman shows include Back to the Future-A Retrospective, Les Malamut Gallery, N.J., Recent Serigraphs by Elissa F. Merkl, Johnson & Johnson, N.J., Current Printmaking/Printmaking Currents, Ol d Ch. Cultural Ctr., N.J. Founder art fair C. of C., Millburn, 1978—2000, initiator scholarship fund-art fair, 1986—2005. Recipient Mem. of Yr., Millburn-Short Hills C. of C., 1992, Purchase award, Print Club of Albany, 1998, award of Excellence, Graphics, Tone Gallery, Bangladesh, 1998, 1st Pl., Chambersburg Arts Coun., Pa., 1999, award of Excellence, Sussex County Cultural & Heritage, N.J., 2002, 1st prize, Archtl. Miniature Art Soc. Fla., 2006. Mem.: Millburn-Short Hills Arts Ctr. (arts exhbn. chmn. 1991—93, Vol. of Yr. 1992, Award of Excellence 2005), Westfield Art Assn., N.J. Ctr. Visual Arts (publicity chmn. 1974—76), Printmaking Coun. N.J. Home and Office: Cultural Events of NJ 325 Morristown Rd Gillette NJ 07933 Office Phone: 908-647-0318. Office Fax: 908-647-0389. Personal E-mail: merklarts@aol.com. Business E-Mail: culturaleventsnj@aol.com.

MERMELSTEIN, ISABEL MAE ROSENBERG, financial consultant; b. Houston, Aug. 20, 1934; d. Joe Hyman and Sylvia (Lincove) Rosenberg; m. Robert Jay Mermelstein, Sept. 6, 1953 (div. July 1975); children: William, Linda, Jody. Student, U. Ariz., 1952, Mich. State U., 1974, Lansing CC, Mich., 1975. Exec. dir. Shiawassee County YWCA, Owosso, Mich., 1975—78; real estate developer F&S Devel. Corp., Lansing, Mich., 1978—79, Corum Devel. Corp., Houston, 1979—81; adminstrv. fin. planner, sr. citizen cons. Investec Asset Mgmt. Group, Inc.; owner Ins. Filling Svcs. Sr. Citizens, 1985—98; guardian VA, 1990—. Author: For You! I Killed the Chicken, 1972. Mem. Older Women's League, Houston, 1st Ecumenical Coun. Lansing, Nat. Mus. Women in Arts, Judaica Mus., Houston, Mus. Fine Arts, Houston, Mus. Natural Sci., Houston; bd. mem. Holocaust Mus., Houston; mem. African-Jewish Dialogue Group, Houston; trustee Congregation Beth Yeshurn Cemetery Assn., 2002-. Recipient State of Mich. Flag, 1972, Key to City, City of Lansing, 1972-73. Mem. Nat. Assn. Claims Assistance Profls., Afro-Am. Jewish Dialogue Group, Internat. Women's Pilot Orgn. (the 99's), Jewish Geneal. Soc., Tex. Jewish Hist. Assn., Internat. Directorate Disting. Leadership, Zonta, Licoma, B'nai B'rith, Hadassah, Nat. Fedn. Temple Sisterhoods, Wellington Soc., Flew All Women's Transcontinental Air Race (Powder Puff Derby 1972, 73). Republican. Jewish. Avocations: flying, gourmet cooking, needlepoint, knitting, skiing. Home: 1400 Hermann Dr Unit 16B Houston TX 77004-7138

MERMELSTEIN, PAULA, broadcasting executive; b. N.Y.C., Nov. 8, 1947; d. Robert and Dorothy Blanche (Asch) M.; m. Francis W. James, Fr., Nov. 23, 1975; 1 son, Robert Austin. BA cum laude, Bklyn. Coll., 1968. Promotion writer, producer NBC, N.Y.C., 1970-78, supervising writer, producer, 1978-79, dir. on-air promotion, 1979, v.p. on-air promotion, 1979-80, v.p. on-air promotion and print copy, 1980-82, creative dir. East Coast, 1982-87, exec. dir. copy, 1985-87; free-lance advt. writer and producer N.Y.C., 1987; creative group head broadcast advt. Spring, O'Brien, House, N.Y.C., 1988—; assoc. creative dir. Hal Riney & Ptnrs., N.Y.C., 1988-89; freelance writer and producer N.Y.C., 1989—; sr. writer, prodr., creative dir. Showtime Networks, 1991—. Mem. editorial staff Joe Garagiola's Memory Game quiz show; prodn. asst. Macy's Thanksgiving Day Parade, 1969. Author: (Reader column) Glamour mag., 1970. 1st Place in News Promo U.S. TV Comms. Festival, 1977; recipient Silver award Broadcasters Promotion Assn., 1983, Gold award Chgo. Internat. Film Festival, 1986, 2 Gold awards Broadcast Promotion and Mktg. Execs., 1987, Gold award N.Y. Festivals, 1991, Silver award Chgo. Film Festival, 1995, Grand trophy NY Festivals, 1999, Gold and Silver awards, N.Y. Festival, 2002. Mem. Writers Guild Am. Jewish.

MERRIER, HELEN, actress, writer; b. Chgo., Mar. 10, 1932; d. Miner Thompson and Helen (Hembree) Coburn; m. Tim Meier, Dec. 23, 1954; 1 child, William Frank (dec.). BA, Mills Coll., 1954; BS, Northwestern U., 1955. Radio roles include Ma Perkins, One Man's Family, Standard School House of the Air, 1934-52; stage roles include Finian's Rainbow, 1952, The Happy Time, 1952, The Night of January 16th, 1952, No Exit, 1953, Tiger at the Gates, 1953, Caeser and Cleopatra, 1953, The Cocktail Party, 1953, Streetcar Named Desire, 1953, Misalliance, 1956, Cry the Beloved Country, 1956, Cat in a Tin Roof, 1963, Take Me Along, 1966, Caucasian Chalk Circle, 1967, The Devils, 1968, Electra, 1969, Jean Harlow and Billy the Kid, 1969, Three-Penny Opera, 1969, A Shot in the Dark, 1970, Private Lives, 1970, The Importance of Being Earnest, 1971, Forty Carats, 1972, Paris is Out!, 1972, A Christmas Carol, 1973, The Sea Gull, 1975, Something more than Ordinary, 1976, Three Dollar Bill, 1976, Maid to Marry, 1977, Scrooge, the musical, 1984, Prisoner of Second Avenue, 1985, Tom Sawyer, 1986, Comedy of Errors, 1987, Juno and the Paycock, 1987, Woman of the Year, 1989, Time and the Conways, 1991, Cinderella, 1991, Sweeney Todd, 1991, The Birds, 1993, Dreams of Defiance (rev.), 1994, Lady Lucinda's Scrapbook (solo play), 1996-98, As You Like It hike, 1998-99, A Midsummer Night's Dream hike, 1999, 2001, Vieux Carre, 1999, Woman Talk (cabaret), 1999—, Healthy- Minded Little Old Lady Songs (solo cabaret), 2000—, William Inge Festival, 2000, Robin Hood hike, 2000-01, Rip van Winkle hike, 2001, Stephen Foster in Song and Story (solo cabaret), 2001—, Eleemosynary, 2002, Some Americans Abroad, 2004, Romeo and Juliet, 2004, Ancestral Voices, 2004-2005, All I Really Need to Know I Learned in Kindergarten, 2004. Recipient The Spirit of Theater award, 2000, Disting. Svc. award The Salvation Army, 2000. Mem. Victory Svcs. Club (London), Arts Club Chgo. Home: 915 Linden Ave Wilmette IL 60091-2712 Personal E-mail: hmerrier@worldnet.att.net.

MERRILL, CONNIE LANGE, chemical company executive; b. Baytown, Tex., Oct. 18, 1950; d. Monroe Edison and Doris Marie Lange; m. James Tyler Merrill, Jan. 1, 1977; m. William Edward Terry, Sept. 19, 1969 (div. 1975); 1 child, Adam Maxwell. BS in Chemistry, N.C. State U., 1977; PhD in Chemistry, Rice U., 1981. Rsch. chemist detergents Shell Chem. Co., Houston, 1981-88, venture devel. mgr. olefins and detergents, 1988-90, quality performance mgr., 1990-93, coatings mktg. mgr. resins, 1993-96, global bus. coord. thermoset performance products, 1996-98; practice leader global diversity consultancy Shell Group of Cos., London, 1998-99; mgr. mergers and acquisitions Shell Chems. Ltd., Houston, 1999—. Spkr. in field. Inventor R&D detergent; contbr. articles to profl. jours. Mem. Am. Chem. Soc. (bd. dirs. local chpt. 1983-88), Chem. Specialty Mfrs. Assn. (chmn. 1986-90), Houston Bus. Forum (bd. dirs. 1991-93), Nat. Paint and Coatings Assn. Avocations: scuba diving, underwater photography, travel. Office: Shell Chems 910 Louisiana St Houston TX 77002-4916

MERRILL, HEATHER ANNE, geography and anthropology educator; d. Jack Kenneth Merrill and Aurelia Mary Worton; m. Donald Martin Carter; children: Nicolas Janos Carter, Eliana Julia Aurelia Merril Carter. BA, NYU, NYC, 1981; MA, Columbia U., NYC, 1985, U. Chgo., 1992, U. Calif., Berkeley, 1996, Ph.D, 1999. Assoc. prof. geography and anthropology Dickinson Coll., Carlisle, Pa., 2006—, exec. dir. Clarke Ctr. for Interdisciplinary Study of Contemporary Issues, 2006—. Author: An Alliance of Women: Immigration and the Politics of Race, 2006. Vol. US Peace Corps, Washington, 1982—84. Mem.: Assn. Am. Geographers (co-director qualitative rsch. splty. group 2003—05). Democrat. Office: Dickinson Coll Clarke Center 255 Louther St Carlisle PA 17013 Office Phone: 717-245-1846.

MERRILL, JEAN FAIRBANKS, writer; b. Rochester, NY, Jan. 27, 1923; d. Earl Dwight and Elsie (Fairbanks) M. BA, Allegheny Coll., 1944; MA, Wellesley Coll., 1945. Feature editor Scholastic Mags., 1947-50; editor Lit. Cavalcade, 1956-57; publs. div. Bank St. Coll. Edn., 1964-65. Children's books include Henry, the Hand-Painted Mouse, 1951, The Woover, 1952, Boxes, 1953, The Tree House of Jimmy Domino, 1955, The Travels of Marco, 1956, A Song for Gar, 1957, The Very Nice Things, 1959, Blue's Broken Heart, 1960, Shan's Lucky Knife (Jr. Lit. Guild selection), Emily Emerson's Moon, 1960 (Jr. Lit. Guild selection), The Superlative Horse (Jr. Lit. Guild selection), 1961 (Lewis Carroll Shelf award 1963), Tell About the Cowbarn, Daddy, 1963, The Pushcart War (Lewis Carroll Shelf award), 1964 (Boys Club Am. Jr. Book award), High, Wide & Handsome, 1964 (Jr. Lit. Guild selection), The Elephant Who Liked to Smash Small Cars, 1967, Red Riding, 1968, The Black Sheep, 1969, Here I Come-Ready or Not!, 1970, Mary, Come Running, 1970, How Many Kids are Hiding on My Block?, 1970, Please, Don't Eat My Cabin, 1971, The Toothpaste Millionaire (Dorothy Canfield Fisher Meml. award 1975-76), 1972 (Sequoyah award 1977), The Second Greatest Clown in the World, 1972, The Jackpot, 1972, The Bumper Sticker Book, 1973, Maria's House, 1974, The Girl Who Loved Caterpillars, 1992; poetry books edited include A Few Flies and I, 1969; libretto for chamber opera Mary Come Running, 1983. Fulbright fellow, India, 1952—53. Mem. Authors League, Vt. Arts. Coun., Vt. Inst. Natural Sci., Vt. Nat. Resources Coun., Fulbright Assn., Acad. Am. Poets, Women's Internat. League Peace and Justice, Sierra Club, Audobon Soc., Women's Internat. League Peace and Justice, Phi Beta Kappa. Office Phone: 802-728-9549.

MERRILL, JUDITH ALLYN, small business owner; b. Miami, Fla., Oct. 16, 1944; d. George H. and Barbara (Cosgrove) Keyser; m. H. Taylor Merrill, Mar. 25, 1967; children: Todd Arthur, Kathryn Merver. AB, Mich. State U., 1966; MBA, La Grange (Ga.) Coll., 1989. Computer programmer analyst AT&T Long Lines, Kansas City, Mo., 1966-69; talk show host Sta. Cable 9, Wooster, Ohio, 1971-74; owner, operator Ockfuskee Plastics, La Grange, 1974-84; ptnr. Dairy Queen of Troup County, La Grange, 1982—; computer sci. instr. La Grange Coll., 1989—; corp. sec. Ultra Ventures, La Grange, Ga., 1990—. Pres. New Ventures; grad. advisor Students in Free Enterprise;

advisor Jr. Achievement; pres. PTA; pres. GOP County Women; pres. Camp Viola, LaGrange; pres. LaGraye Symphony Orch., 1996-99; pres. Leadership Troup, 1999-2001. Home: 717 Camellia Dr Lagrange GA 30240-1646

MERRILL, LYNDA MAE, real estate broker; b. Bklyn., Jan. 30, 1948; d. Bernard and Edith Zucker; m. Dennis Alan Merrill, Feb. 14, 2000; m. Joe John Romero, Apr. 28, 1979 (dec. Apr. 18, 1996); children: Jason Matthew Romero, Derek Austin Romero. AA, L.A. City Coll., 1967. Cert. accreditation Relocation Resources, Inc., 1994. Legal sec. Heaton & Wright, Las Vegas, Nev., 1978—82, Lionel, Sawyer & Collins, Las Vegas, 1982—85; broker, saleswoman Western Properties, ERA, Las Vegas, 1985—90; broker, co-owner Properties Plus, Inc., Las Vegas, 1990—93; broker, saleswoman Coldwell Banker Premier, Las Vegas, 1993—2000, Merit Realty, Las Vegas, 2000—; broker, owner Merrill Realty Group, Inc., Las Vegas, 2002—. Author: (poetry) Reflections of The Inward Silence, The Fisherman, Night Stalker. Chairwoman residential com. North Las Vegas (Nev.) C. of C., 1990—91; mem. sponsorship com. Silverado Little League, Las Vegas, 1995—97; programs Comml. Real Estate Women, Las Vegas, 2003—03. Recipient Most Sales award, Greater Las Vegas Assn. Realtors, 1988, 1990. Mem.: Nat. Assn. Realtors, Nev. Assn. Realtors, Comml. Real Estate Women. Avocations: golf, writing, drawing. Office: Merrill Realty Group Inc 2700 E Sonnet Rd #11 Las Vegas NV 89120 Office Phone: 702-895-7427. E-mail: lynda@merrillrealty.lvcoxmail.com.

MERRILL, MARTHA, library and information scientist; b. Anniston, Ala., Apr. 21, 1946; d. Walter James and Polly (McCarty) M. BA, Birmingham-So. Coll., 1968; MS, Jacksonville (Ala.) State U., 1974; PhD, U. Pitts., 1979. Social worker Tuscaloosa (Ala.) County Dept. Human Resources, 1968-71, Calhoun County Dept. Human Resources, Anniston, 1971-73; social scis./bus. libr. Jacksonville State U., 1974-86, prof. instrnl. media, 1987—. Editor: Reference Services and Media, 1999; co-author: Dictionary for School Library Media Specialists, 2001. Mem. Friends of Libr. bd. Anniston-Calhoun County Pub. Libr., 1984—. Recipient Ala./SIRS Intellectual Freedom award, Intellectual Freedom Com., Ala. Libr. Assn., 1992, Ala. Beta Phi Mu chpt. Libr. of Yr. award, 1997. Mem. ALA (exec. bd., Intellectual Freedom Round Table 1987-93), Ala. Libr. Assn. (pres. 1990-91, Disting. Svc. award 1995 Outstanding Publ. award, 2004), Ala. Assn. Coll. and Spcl. Librs. (pres. 1989-90), Southeastern Libr. Assn. (chair intellectual freedom com. 1986-88, chair resolutions com. 1990-92). Office: Jacksonville State U Coll Edn Dept Ednl Resources Jacksonville AL 36265 Office Phone: 256-782-5011. E-mail: mmerrill@jsucc.jsu.edu.

MERRILL, MARY H. See BOYD, MARY

MERRILL, NORMA, video poducer, copy writer; b. Whittier, Calif., Apr. 7, 1925; d. Parmer Leroy and Roosevelt Miller; m. Zadoc Ensign Merrill, Nov. 13, 1944; children: Cindy, Sally, Libby, Dadoc Ensign, Tawny. Grad., Albany (Oreg.) H.S., 1942. Asst. society editor Dem.-Herald, Albany, 1944-45; video prodn. coord. Upstairs Prodns., Portland, Oreg., 1980-91; video assoc. prodr. ZM Assocs., Portland, 1991—. Bd. dirs. Upstairs Prodns. Lyricist; copy writer for TV and vidio prodns. The Winter Winds of Hell, 1998. Republican. Mem. Four-Square Christian Ch. Avocation: travel. Home: 4062 SW Pendleton St Portland OR 97221-3449

MERRILL, SUSAN L., lawyer; b. 1957; Grad. cum laude, U. Md., 1979; JD summa cum laude, Bklyn. Law Sch., 1986. Law clk. to Hon. Francis L. Van Dusen US Ct. Appeals (3rd cir.), 1986—87; assoc. Davis Polk & Wardwell, 1987—2004, ptnr., 1994—2004; exec. v.p. enforcement NYSE Group, Inc. (formerly NY Stock Exch.), 2004—. Office: NYSE Group Inc 11 Wall St New York NY 10005 Office Phone: 212-656-3000.*

MERRILL, TRISTA MARIE, literature and language professor, writer; b. Rochester, N.Y., June 9, 1973; d. Gary Dennis and Sharon Lois (Arnold) Merrill. BA in English, SUNY, Potsdam, NY, 1995; MA in English, SUNY, Binghamton, 1998; PhD in English, SUNY, 2003. Instr. of record SUNY, Binghamton, 1998—2005; adj. faculty Genesee CC, Arcade, 2003—04, Keuka Coll., Keuka Pk., NY, 2003—04; asst. prof. English Finger Lakes CC, Canandaigua, 2004—. Com. mem. mentor Finger Lakes CC, 2005—. Author: Popular Contemporary Writers, 2005. Team capt. Nat. MS Soc., Canandaigua, 2005. Mem.: Popluar Culture Assn., Popluar Culture Assn. Australia. Independent. Avocations: reading, writing, computers, films. Office: Finger Lakes CC 4355 Lakeshore Dr Canandaigua NY 14424

MERRILL, WENDY JANE, financial services company executive; b. Waterbury, Conn., Dec. 4, 1961; d. David Kenneth and Jane Joy (Nevius) Merrill; m. Aidan T. Harrison (div. Nov. 1998); children: Christopher Harrison, Charlotte Harrison, Ryan Harrison; m. Michael G. Kelly, Oct. 2, 1999 (dissolved Nov. 2004). BA in Journalism, George Washington U., 1981; MBA in mgmt., Cornell U., 1992. Intern edn. HEW, Washington, 1978, writer, 1979; rsch. asst. dept. health svcs. adminstrn. George Washington U., Washington, 1979—81; sec. Nat. Assn. Beverage Importers, Washington, 1981; account exec. Staff Design, Washington, 1982; adminstrv. aide Internat. Food Policy Rsch. Inst., Washington, 1983—86; program assoc. Acad. for Ednl. Devel., Washington, 1986—87; pvt. practice cons. Washington, 1987—88; adminstrv. mgr. food and nutrition policy program Cornell U., Ithaca, NY, 1988—92; cons. mgmt. of med. practices Med. Bus. Mgmt., Ithaca, 1994—95; realtor Century 21 Alpha, 1995—97; compensation mgr. Santa Clara U., Calif., 1996—98; sr. compensation analyst Stanford U., Calif., 1998—99; human resources cons. Siemens Info. and Comm. Networks, 2000; compensation and benefits mgr. Kana Comms., 2000—01; U.S. compensation mgr. KLA-Tencor, 2001—02; pres. Total Solutions Ins. Agy., Inc., Calif., 2003—, Total Solutions Comml. Ventures, Inc., 2003—, Total Solutions Settlement Ptnrs., Inc., 2003—. Cons., editor George Washington U., 1986; cons., rapporteur Internat. Food Policy Restaurant Inst., Washington and Copenhagen, Denmark, 1987; cons., adminstr. Hansell & Post, Washington, 1987-88, Cornell U., Washington and Ithaca, 1988; pvt. practice cons., 2001—. Sponsor Worldvision, Tanzania, 1988-91. George Washington U. scholar, 1979-81. Mem. AMA, Soc. for Human Resources Mgmt., Zonta Club (charter pres. Silicon Valley chpt. 2006—), Sigma Delta Xi (scholar 1980). Democrat. Episcopalian. Avocations: piano, hiking, swimming. Home: 745 S Mary Ave Sunnyvale CA 94087 Office Phone: 408-830-9300. Business E-Mail: wendy@totalsolutionscv.com.

MERRILL WARNER, VERONIQUE, psychologist; b. Dansville, NY, Mar. 14, 1965; d. Raymond Greiner Merrill and Monique Marcelle Francette Monnot; m. Michael V. Warner, May 17, 1991; children: Jeremy Raymond Warner, Miranda Caline Warner, Valerie Cosette Warner. B cum laude, Occidental Coll., 1987; MA, Calif. Sch. Profl. Psychology, L.A., 1997, D in Psychology, 1999. Lic. psychologist Calif. Bd. of Psychology, 2001. Bookkeeper Carol L. Strop, CPA, Glendale, Calif., 1987—91, Very-unique Bus. Svcs., Sierra Madre, Calif., 1991—99; lic. psychologist-contractor Bienvenidos Children's Ctr., Altadena, Calif., 2001; outpatient unit coord. Enki Health and Rsch. Systems, Inc., Covina, Calif., 1999—2001, supervising psychologist, 2001, clinic mgr. Pico Rivera, El Monte, Calif., 2001—06, program developer, 2006—. Testing supr. Enki Health & Rsch. Systems, Inc., Pico Rivera, 2001—; field tng. supr. U. of La Verne, Calif., 2001—; ambs. of change task force mem. Enki Health & Rsch. Systems, Inc., Covina, 2000—01; tchr. asst. Assessment Lab. Calif. Sch. of Profl. Psychology, L.A., 1997—99, field tng. supr., 2003—; mem. dissertationcom. U. La Verne. Author (singer/songwriter): (compact disc/songbook) I'm a Kid, Too. Vol. Pasadena (Calif.) Mental Health Ctr., 1994—95; team mom Am. Youth Soccer Org.; vol. Grace Miller Elem. Sch., La Verne, Calif., 2002—03, Sierra Madre Sch., Sierra Madre, Calif., 2000—02. Mem.: APA (licentiate), Psi Chi (pres. 1987). Democrat. Avocations: singing, theater, writing, reading, gardening. Office: Enki Youth & Family Svcs 3208 Rosemead Blvd Ste 200 El Monte CA 91731 Office Phone: 626-227-7014 x 205. Personal E-mail: doc.vmw@verizon.net.

MERRILL-WASHINGTON, VICTORIA, elementary school educator, consultant; children: Victor Washington, Steven Washington. BA, Calumet Coll., Whiting, Ind., 1981; MA, Purdue Calumet, Hammond, Ind., 1991; student, U. Phoenix, Ariz., 2005. Cert. counselor Nat. Bd. Cert. Instr. Purdue Calumet, Hammond, Ind., 2001; tchr. Gary (Ind.) Cmty. Sch. Corp., 2001—, counselor, 2001—. Judge Amateur Confederation Roller Skating, 2003; bd. dirs. Ind. Ballet N.W., Crown Point, Ind., 2002—04. Recipient Achievement cert., Ind., 2002, Meritorious Svc. award, USA Roller Sports, 2003. Mem.: Ind. Sch. Counselor Assn. (conf. chmn. 2002), Ind. Counseling Assn. (region rep. 2004—06), Am. Fedn. Tchrs., Crown Point C. of C. Avocations: dance, artistic roller skating. Home and Office: VMW Cons Svcs PO Box 11393 Merrillville IN 46410

MERRIM, LOUISE MEYEROWITZ, artist, actress; b. N.Y.C. d. Leo and Jeanette (Harris) Meyerowitz; m. Lewis Jay Merrim, June 27, 1948; children: Stephanie, Andrea Merrim Goff (dec.). BFA, Pratt Inst., 1947; MFA, Columbia U., 1951; postgrad., Post Coll., 1971-72, New Sch., 1977-78. Art tchr. pub. schs., N.Y.C., 1947-51, Port Washington, NY, 1970-83. One-woman shows include Plandome Gallery, L.I., Isis Gallery, N.Y., San Diego art Inst., Pan Pacific Hotel, San Diego; exhibited in group shows at Nassau County Fine Arts Mus. (Bronze award), Heckscher Mus. (Nora Mirmont award), Nat. Acad., Nat. Assn. Women Artists (Medal of Honor, Charlotte Whinston award), Audubon Artists (Stephen Hirsch Meml. award), Cork Gallery, Warner Comm. Gallery, L.I. Art Tchrs. (two awards of excellence), L.I. Art Tchrs. Award Winners Show, Pt. Washington Libr. Invitational, Glen Cove (2nd prize), Manhasset Art Assn. (best in show, five 1st prizes), San Diego Art Inst., San Diego Mus. Art (Gold award), Oceanside Mus. Art, Hank Baum Gallery, San Francisco, Tarbox Gallery, Clark Gallery, Knowles Gallery, San Diego, Golden Pacific Arts Gallery, San Diego, Henry Chastain Gallery, Scottsdale, Boehm Gallery/Palomar Coll., Hyde Gallery/Grossmont Coll., Timmons Gallery, Rancho Santa Fe, Calif.; included in permanent collection of San Diego Mus. Art; appeared in numerous theatrical prodns. including Fiddler on the Roof, Barefoot in the Park, N.Y., Anything Goes, The Musical Comedy Murders of 1940, Anastasia (Drama award), Fiddler on the Roof, The Music Man, What's Wrong With this Picture?, Marvin's Room, San Diego, The Foreigner; dir. Under Milkwood; dir., appeared in Spoon River Anthology. Mem.: Nat. Assn. Women Artists, NY Soc. of Women Artists, Contemporary Artists Guild of NY, Audubon Artist (NY), San Diego Art Inst., Artists Guild of San Diego Art Mus. (pres. 1993), Artists Equity, Actors Alliance. Avocations: tennis, poetry, travel. Home: 3330 Caminito Vasto La Jolla CA 92037-2929 E-mail: louisemer@hotmail.com.

MERRITT, CAROLYN, government agency administrator; Diploma, Radford U. Mngr. of solid and hazardous waste and environmental health and safety Champion Intl. Corp., 1988—94; sr. project mngr. RMT/Jones and Neuse, Inc., Houston, 1994; sr. v.p. for Environment, Health and Safety IMC Global Inc., Northbrook, Ill.; chmn, CEO U.S. Chemical Safety and Hazard Investigation Board, 2002—. Office: 2175 K Street NW Ste 400 Washington DC 20037 Office Phone: 202-261-7600.

MERRITT, EDITH BRADFORD, elementary school educator; b. Athens, Ga., June 14, 1945; d. Duane Elton and Frances Edith (McCart) Bradford; m. Thomas Wayne Merritt Jr., Jan. 24, 1970; children: Theresa, Jennifer, David, Penny. BS, Auburn U., 1976; MS, Troy State U., 1989. Cert. elem. tchr., Nat. Bd. Edn., 2000. 2d, 4th and 5th grade tchr. Lee-Scott Acad., Auburn, Ala.; tchr. accelerated sci. and social studies 4th gr. Auburn City Schs., tchr. elem. schs. Tuscaloosa, Ala. Workshop presenter ASTA State Conf., U. Ala. In-Svc. Ctr. Finalist Ala. State Tchr. of Yr., 1988-89; recipient commendation for profl. in teaching Ala. Ho. of Reps., 1989, Profl. Best Leadership award Learning Mag.; named Ala. Outstanding Elem. Tchr., 1995. Home: 140 Barnes Lane Eutaw AL 35462-1227

MERRITT, HELEN HENRY, retired art educator, sculptor, ceramist, art historian; b. Norfolk, Va., June 15, 1920; d. John Crockett and Mabel Deborah (Richards) Henry; m. James Willis Merritt, Jan. 22, 1946; 1 child, Deborah Branan Merritt Aldrich. BA, Colby Coll., Waterville, Maine, 1942; MA, Rockford Coll., Ill., 1956; MFA, No. Ill. U., DeKalb, 1964; postgrad., Tokyo U. Fine Arts, Cambridge (Eng.) U. Sec. U.S. Naval Hosp., Norfolk, 1942-46; art tchr. DeKalb (Ill.) Schs., 1956-57; instr. art history No. Ill. U., DeKalb, 1964, asst. prof., 1965-71, assoc. prof., 1972-79, prof., 1980-90. Ceramic sculptor, DeKalb, 1952—. Author: Guiding Free Expression in Children's Art, 1964, Modern Japanese Woodblock Prints, 1990, Guide to Modern Japanese Woodblock Prints, 1992, Woodblock Kuchi-E Prints—Reflections of Meiji Culture, 2000; contbr. articles to profl. jours. Founding mem. Gurler Heritage Assn., DeKalb, 1978—; cmty. activist DeKalb Pond, Fisk Block Group, 1989—. Recipient Excellence in Tchg. award, No. Ill. U., 1990, Humanitarian award for cmty. svc., 1997, James Foster Cmty. Svc. award, 2003. Mem.: Rotary. Home: 419 Garden Rd Dekalb IL 60115-6206 Business E-Mail: hmerritt@niu.edu.

MERRITT, MARY JANE, community volunteer; b. Milford, Mass., Feb. 6, 1942; d. Theodore and Rosemary Edith (Box) Bothfeld; m. Thomas Butler Merritt, July 23, 1966; children: Thomas Butler Jr., Haidee Soule, Theodore Bothfeld. AB, Boston U., 1964. Tchr. Perceptual Edn. Rsch. Ctr., Inc., Sherborn, Mass., 1964-66, Tenacre Country Day Sch., Wellesley, Mass., 1966-67, Head Start, Nashua, N.H., 1995-96; with ARC Bloodmobile, 1997-2001. Pres. Colonial Garden Club, Hollis, N. H., 1987-90; chmn. Governing Com. of Charles J. Nichols Fund, Hollis, N.H., 1989-95; mem. Master Plan Study com., Hollis, N.H., 1989-91; pres. Amherst Villagers Chpt. of The Questers, Inc., Amherst, N.H., 1995-97; pres. Hollis Woman's Club, 1999-2001. Recipient Community Svc. award Town of Hollis, N.H., 1993. Mem. Alpha Phi. Home: PO Box 516 Littleton NH 03561-0516

MERRITT, NANCY-JO, lawyer; b. Phoenix, Sept. 24, 1942; d. Robert Nelson Meeker and Violet Adele Gibson; children: Sidney Kathryn, Kurt, Douglas. BA, Ariz. State U., 1964, MA, 1974, JD, 1978. Bar: Ariz. 1978, U.S. Dist. Ct. Ariz. 1978, U.S. Ct. Appeals (9th cir.) 1984. Shareholder Fennemore Craig, P.C., Phoenix. Author: Understanding Immigration Law, 1993; sr. editor: Immigration and National Law Handbook, 1993—; contbr. articles to profl. jours. Chair bd. dirs. TERROS, 1995-97. Fellow Ariz. Bar Found.; mem. ABA, Am. Immigration Lawyers Assn. (chairperson Ariz. chpt. 1985-87, several coms., Pro Bono award), Ariz. Bar Assn. (immigration sect.), Nucleus Club. Democrat. Avocations: modern literature, south american literature, hiking, gardening. Office Phone: 602-916-5411, 702-692-8003. Business E-Mail: njmerritt@fclaw.com.

MERRITT, SANDRA LEE, educational consultant; b. Manchester, Iowa, Sept. 16, 1949; d. Roy Thomas Atkinson and Lavon Blanche Williams; m. William Joseph Merritt, June 18, 1988; children: Michelle Ann McClure, Staci Lynn Shaffer. MA in Edn., U. No. Iowa, 1999. Endorsement in elem. admin. 2004. First grade tchr. Center Point (Iowa)-Urbana Schools, 1971—2002, reading recovery tchr., 2000—02; inclusion resource specialist Grant Wood Area Edn. Agy., Cedar Rapids, Iowa, 2002—. Contbr. articles to profl. jours. Recipient Spl. Tchr. award, Greater Cedar Rapids Cmty. Found., 2002. Mem.: NEA, ASCD, Coun. for Exceptional Children, Iowa State Edn. Assn., Iowa Assn. for the Edn. of Young Children (sec. 1999—2002). Home: 900 Maplewood Dr Center Point IA 52213 Office: Grant Wood Area Education Agency 4401 6th St SW Cedar Rapids IA 52404 Office Phone: 319-399-6783. Personal E-mail: slmerritt@msn.com. E-mail: smerritt@aea10.k12.ia.us.

MERRITT, SUSAN MARY, computer science educator, dean; b. New London, Conn., July 28, 1946; d. Nelson Alfred and Mary (Cory) M. BA summa cum laude, Cath. U. Am., 1968; MS, NYU, 1969, PhD, 1982; Cert., Inst. for Edn. Mgmt., Harvard U., 1985. Joined Sisters of Divine Compassion, 1975; permanent cert. tchr., N.Y. Systems programmer Digital Equipment Corp., Maynard, Mass., 1969-70; tchr. Good Counsel Acad. High Sch., White Plains, N.Y., 1970-75; adj. instr. computer sci. Pace U., 1972-78, asst. prof. White Plains, 1978-82, assoc. prof., 1982-85, prof., 1985—, chmn. dept., 1981-83, dean Sch. Computer Sci., 1983—. Spkr. in field, mem. gen. coun. Sisters Divine Compassion, 1988-92. Contbr. articles to profl. jours. Recipient Carol S. Russett Award for Disting. Svcs., ACE Nat. Women's Leadership Network, Recipient Cert. of Appreciation, IEEE, 1990. Mem. Assn. for Computing Machinery (edn. bd. 1988—), Phi Beta Kappa, Sigma Xi. Roman Catholic.

MERRIWEATHER, FREDA E., education educator; d. Oscar and Eura Merriweather; m. William M. Norvell, III, Apr. 30, 1961 (div.); children: Stacy LePrix Norvell, Tracy Norvell Dukes. BS, So. Ill. U., 1964; MS, U. Wis., Milwaukee, 1971; EdD, U. Louisville, 1992. Cert. tchr. So. Ill. U., 1964, Principal U. Wis., 1972, Superintendent State of Ky., 1991. Tchr. Siefert Elem. Sch., Milw., 1964—73; prin. Md. Ave. Sch., Milw., 1974—76, James Whit Comb Riley, Milw., 1977—80, Price Elem. Sch. - JCPS, Louisville, 1984—87; vice-principal William McKinley Internat. Sch., Milw., 1976—80; edn. cons. Ingham Internat. Sch. Dist., Holt, Mich., 1982—84; dir. Jefferson County Pub. Sch., Louisville, 1987—91, exec. dir., 1991—93, asst. supt., 1993—2002, 1993—2002; practitioner in residence U. Louisville, Louisville, 2002—. Mem. Gov.'s Literacy Task Force, Frankfort, Ky.; alumni bd. U. Louisville, 1993—95; alumni Supt. Prepared-McKenzie Group, Washington, 1995. Mem. Jr. Achieve., Louisville, Urban League, Louisville. Recipient Adminstrv. Leadership award, Collaborative for Tchg. and Learning, 2001, award, Sarah Scott Leadership, 1978, Valedictorian, H.S. Class, Alumni Fellow, Coll. of Edn., U. Louisville, 1999, Bingham Fellows, 1993, Grad. Sch. Dean's Citation, 1991, Ky. Edn. Leadership Inst., 1990, Outstanding Prin., Nat. Schools of Excellence, 1987; grantee, Leadership Louisville, 1992, Bd. of Alderman, 1992; Doctoral Program scholarship, Scottish Rites Found. Mem.: NAACP, Greater Louisville Alliance of Black Sch. Educators, Nat. Alliance of Black Sch. Educators, Urban League (dir.), Louisville Chpt. of Moles (parliamentation), Delta Sigma Theta Sorority. Avocations: dancing, card games, reading. Office Phone: 502-852-0635. Personal E-mail: femerr01@aol.com.

MERRYMAN-MARR, MELISSA JO, social studies educator; b. Hopkinsville, Ky., Oct. 3, 1970; d. Edward (Ted) Hughes and JoAnn Merryman; m. Bryan Christopher Marr, Dec. 18, 1999; 1 child, Gabriel Scott Marr. EdM, Western Ky. U., Bowling Green, 1999. Social studies tchr. Warren East High, Bowling Green, 1994—. Avocations: tennis, reading. Home: 263 Payne Rd Park City KY 42160 Office: Warren East High School 6867 Louisville Rd Bowling Green KY 42101 Office Phone: 270-781-1277. Personal E-mail: bmarr@scrtc.com. Business E-Mail: melissa.marr@warren.kyschools.us.

MERSEL, MARJORIE KATHRYN PEDERSEN, lawyer; b. Manila, Utah, June 17, 1923; d. Leo Henry and Kathryn Anna (Reed) Pedersen; m. Jules Mersel, Apr. 12, 1950; 1 child, Jonathan. AB, U. Calif., 1948; LLB, U. San Francisco, 1948. Bar: D.C. 1952, Calif. 1955. Pvt. practice, Beverly Hills, Calif., 1961—71, L.A., 1997—; staff counsel Dept. Real Estate State of Calif., L.A., 1971—97. Pub. counsel, 2000—02. Active L.A.-Guangzhou Sister City. Mem.: ABA, Current Affairs Forum, World Affairs Coun., So. Calif. Women Lawyers Assn. (treas. 1962—63), Trial Lawyers Assn., L.A. County Bar Assn., Beverly Hills Bar Assn., Beverly Hills C. of C., L.A.-Guanghou Sister City Assn., Sierra Club, L.A. Athletic Club. Home: 13007 Hartsook St Sherman Oaks CA 91423-1616 Office: Dept Real Estate 107 S Broadway Ste 8107 Los Angeles CA 90012-4402

MERSEREAU, SUSAN, information systems company executive, data processing executive; b. Portland, Oreg., Sept. 5, 1946; d. Roland William Mersereau and Barbara Munro; m. Robert Stier, June 19, 1968; 1 child, Arran Elizabeth; m. Philip White, Nov. 17, 1989; children: Richard, Brandon. BA in History, Scripps, 1968; MAT in Edn. History, U. Chgo., 1971; MA in Whole Systems Design, Antioch, 1990. Tchr. South Shore High Sch., Chgo., 1969-70; adminstrv. asst. U. Ill., Chgo., 1970; rsch. analyst U. Wash., Seattle, 1971-72; dir. planning rsch. and evaluation Seattle Sch. Dist., 1972-80; program mgr. Weyerhauser Co., Tacoma, 1980-81, mgr. advanced tech., 1981-83, dir. telecom., 1983-88; gen. mgr., v.p. Weyerhauser Info. Systems, Tacoma, 1988-92, v.p. total quality region adminstrv. svcs. and aviation, 1992—98; v.p. organizational effectiveness Weyerhauser Co., Federal Way, Wash., 1998—2003, sr. v.p. info. tech, chief info. officer, 2003—. Bd. dirs. King County Jr. Achievemen, King County United Way. Avocations: skiing, art, hiking, tennis, fishing. Office: Weyerhaeuser Co 33663 Weyerhaeuser Way S PO Box 9777 Federal Way WA 98063-9777 Office Phone: 253-924-2345.*

MERSEREAU, SUSAN S., clinical psychologist; b. Atlanta, Apr. 9, 1947; d. John Andy Jr. and Dorothy Grace (Smith) Smith; m. Peter Roland Mersereau, May 30, 1970; children: Barrett, Travis, Courtney. AB, Vassar Coll., 1969; MSEd, Elmira Coll., 1973; D in Psychology, Pacific U., 1989. Lic. psychologist, Oreg.; diplomate Am. Coll. Forensic Medicine, Nat. Registry of Cert. Group Psychotherapists. Psychology intern Pacific Gateway Hosp., Portland, Oreg., 1987-88, Psychol. Svcs. Ctr., Hillsboro, Oreg., 1988-89; psychology resident Lee Doppelt, Beaverton, Oreg., 1990-91; staff Pac. Gateway Hosp., 1990—99; pvt. practice psychologist Beaverton, 1991-93; dir. Pacific Ctr. for Attention and Learning, Beaverton, 1993—. Mem. Neuropsychology Delegation to South Africa, 1996. Tchr. Incentive grantee Guam Dept. Edn., 1979. Mem. APA, Oreg. Psychol. Assn., Nat. Register Health Svc. Providers, Am. Coll. Forensic Examiners (diplomate), Nat. Registry Group Psychotherapist (cert. group psychotherapist), Vassar Club Oreg. (admissions com. 1984—, pres. 1984-88). Avocations: gardening, orchid growing. Office: Pacific Ctr Attention & Learning Lincoln Ctr 10300 SW Greenburg Rd Ste 430 Portland OR 97223-5453 Office Phone: 503-244-2599.

MERSETH, KATHERINE K., mathematician, education educator; BA in Math., Cornell U.; MS in Math., Boston Coll.; EdD, Harvard U. Sr. lectr. edn. Harvard U., dir. Tchr. Edn. Program, 1983—88, 2001—. Author: Case Studies in Educational Administration, 1997; contbr. articles to profl. jours. Advisor Roxbury (Mass.) Cmty. Prep Charter Sch., 2001—; bd. dirs. Media and Arts Tech. Charter H.S., Allston, Mass., Shackleton Schs., Boston, Consortium on Math Applications Project, Lexington, Mass. Recipient Morningstar Award for Excellence in Tchg., 2001; grantee Math. Case Devel. Project, NSF, Tchr. Edn. Addressing Math. and Sci. in Boston and Cambridge Project. Mem.: Nat. Coun. Tchrs. Math., Am. Assn. Ednl. Rsch. Avocation: Avocation: rowing. Office: Harvard Grad Sch Edn Tchr Edn Longfellow 310 Cambridge MA 02138

MERSKEY-ZEGER, MARIE GERTRUDE FINE, retired librarian; b. Kimberley, South Africa, Oct. 10, 1914; came to U.S., 1960, naturalized, 1965; d. Herman and Annie Myra (Wigoder) Fine; m. Clarence Merskey, Oct. 8, 1939 (dec. 1982); children: Hilary Pamela Merskey Nathe, Susan Heather Merskey Sinistore, Joan Margaret Merskey Schneiderman; m. Jack I. Zeger, July 15, 1984 (dec. Jan. 1997). Grad., Underwood Bus. Sch., Cape Town, South Africa, 1934; BA, U. Cape Town, 1958, Diploma in Librarianship, 1960. Sec. to Chief Rabbi Israel Abrahams, South Africa, 1945-49; sec. Jewish Sheltered Employment Coun., 1954-56; reference libr. New Rochelle (N.Y.) Pub. Libr., 1960-63; rsch. libr. Consumers Union, Mt. Vernon, NY, 1963-66; asst. readers svcs., head union catalog Westchester Libr. Sys., 1966-69, trustee, 1989-93, v.p., 1991; dir. Harrison (N.Y.) Pub. Libr. and West Harrison Br., 1969-84; acting dir. Mamaroneck (N.Y.) Free Libr., 1987-88, also trustee, 1988-93. Author: History of the Harrison Libraries, 1980; contbg. author: Celebration, Village of Mamaroneck Centennial, 1895-1995, History of Town/Village of Harrison Tricennial, 1696-1996; editor: Harrison Highlights and Anecdotes, 1989, (cookbook) On Harrison's Table, 1976; author articles. Pub. edn. officer USCG Aux Flotilla 63; bd. dirs Shore Acres Point Corp., Mamaroneck, 1985-89; program dir. Friends of the Mamaroneck Libr., 1993—. Recipient Brotherhood award B'nai B'rith, 1974; named Woman of Yr., Harrison, 1984. Mem. ALA, N.Y. Libr. Assn. (adult edn. com. for continuing edn. 1971-75, adult svcs. com. 1973-75, vice chmn. 1975, exec. bd. 1981-82), Westchester Libr. Assn., Pub. Libr. Dirs. Assn. (tech. svcs. com. chmn. Westchester County 1971, exec. bd. 1974-75, vice chmn. 1975), Charles Dawson History Ctr. (co-founder 1980, bd. dirs.), Harrison Hist. Soc. Home: 316 S Barry Ave Mamaroneck NY 10543-4201

MERSZEI, AIMÉE MÖRNER, not-for-profit fundraiser; b. N.Y.C., July 20, 1944; d. Gustav Hampus and Florence Lacombe Mörner; m. Zoltan Merszei, May 15, 1982; 1 child, Kevin Zoltan. AB, Mt. Holyoke Coll., 1966. With Union Trust Co., Greenwich, Conn., 1963—66; jr. underwriter Chubb & Son Inc., N.Y.C., 1966—67; asst. to sr. rsch. analysts Smith Barney & Co. Inc., N.Y.C., 1968—70; writer, editor Fortune Mag., N.Y.C., 1971—83; co-chair, bd. trustee, chair various coms. Nat. Childhood Cancer Found., Arcadia, Calif., 1991—2001; bd. trustees, mem. strategic planning com., chmn. investment com. The Marrow Found., Washington, 2001—. Bd. trustees, chair parents com., devel. com. Eaglebrook Sch., Deerfield, Mass., 1997—99. Named Helen and Richard DeVos Disting. Lectr. in Pediat. Oncology, DeVos Children's Hosp., 1999; recipient Disting. Women's award, Northwood U., 2000. Mem.: Fin. Women's Assn. Republican. Avocations: fitness, tennis, skiing, skeet shooting, travel.

MERTENS, JOAN R., museum curator, art historian; b. NYC, Oct. 10, 1946; d. Otto R. and Helen H. M. BA, Radcliffe Coll., 1967; PhD, Harvard U., 1972. Curatorial asst. Met. Mus. Art, N.Y.C., 1972-73, asst. curator, 1973-76, assoc. curator, 1976-81, curator Greek and Roman dept., 1981—, curator, adminstr., 1983-90, mem. editorial bd. Mus. Jour., 1976—. Lectr. NYU, Inst. Fine Arts, 1992—. Author: Attic White-Ground*Its Development, 1977, Greek Bronzes in the Metropolitan Museum of Art, 1985, (with others) Ancient Art from Cyprus: The Cesnola Collection in the Metropolitan Museum of Art, 2000, (with others) The Cesnola Collection: Terracottas, 2004. Mem. Archaeol. Inst. Am., German Archael. Inst. (corr. mem.) Home: 124 E 84th St New York NY 10028-0915 Office: Met Mus Art Fifth Ave at 82nd St New York NY 10028

MERVIS, BONNIE AARON, social worker; b. Chgo., Apr. 2, 1945; d. Herman Leonard Aaron and Rosalie (Zakroff) Ovson; m. Charles L. Mervis, May 25, 1975; children: Aaron, Jessica BS, Cornell U., 1967; MA, U. Chgo., 1974; PhD, Inst. Clin. Social Work, Chgo., 1997. LCSW; cert. sch. social worker, Ill., bd. cert. diplomate. Tchr. Head Start, Elmira, NY, 1967—68; tchr. elem. sch. various cities, 1968—70; team leader Forest Hosp., Des Plaines, Ill., 1970—72; instr. dept. med. social work U. Ill. Hosp., Chgo., 1974—76; social worker Spl. Edn. Dist. North Lake County, Gurnee, Ill., 1979—82, Sch. Dist. 107 (now Sch. Dist. 112), Highland Park, Ill., 1982—2006; adj. faculty Sch. Social Work Loyola U., Chgo., 2006—. Pvt. practice, Highland Park, 1982—; assoc. faculty Chgo. Ctr. for Family Health, 1998-2006; field instr. U. Chgo. Sch. Social Svc. Adminstrn., 1990-2006; presenter at profl. confs Contbr. articles to profl. jours Mem. Ill. Assn. Sch. Social Workers, NASW, NEA. Avocation: fiction book reviewing. Home: 70 Hastings Ave Highland Park IL 60035 Business E-Mail: bmervis@nssd112.org. E-mail: merviss@comcast.net.

MERY, NAOMI MARIE, music educator; b. El Paso, Tex., Jan. 13, 1959; d. Arturo and Maria Refugio de la Torre; m. Robert Charles Mery, July 16, 1983; 1 child, Robert Joseph. MusB in piano, U. Tex., El Paso, 1983. Tchg. k-12 Tex., 1983, tchg. music Ed K-12 Colo., 2001. Instr. cert. yamaha piano Phoenix Yamaha Sch., 1985—85, Rocky Mt. Yamaha Sch., Denver, 1985—88; tchr. pvt. piano Schroeder Baldwin Studios, El Paso, Tex., 1980—83, Home Studio, Co. Springs, Colo., 1989—93, 2001—02; tchr. music Divine Redeemer Cath. Sch., Co. Springs, 1990—2002; choir, music, theatre Gorman Pub. Mid. Sch., Co. Springs, 2002—04; vocal music dir., choral tchr., piano lab. instr. Fox Meadow Mid. Sch., Colorado Springs, 2002—. Studio supr. Schroeder Baldwin Studios, El Paso, Tex., 1980—83; arts assembly coord. Divine Redeemer Cath. Sch., Colorado Springs, Colo., 1996—2002. Dir.: (plays) Elem Mid. Sch. Theatre. Music tchr. Divine Redeemer Cath. Sch., Co. Springs, Colo., 1990—2002. Recipient Mortar Bd. Honor Roll Assn. award, Mortar Bd. honor Roll Assoc., 1981, 1982; scholar Piano Competition, 1st Place, Sigma Alpha Iota Music Frat., 1982; Piano Dept. scholarship, U. Tex. El Paso, 1978—80. Mem.: Colo. Music Educators Assn. (licentiate), Music Educators Nat. Conf. (licentiate), Music Teachers Nat. Assoc. (corr.). Avocations: sewing, movies, concerts. Home: 1935 Chapel Hills Dr Colorado Springs CO 80920 Personal E-mail: naomimery@pcisys.net.

MESCH, DEBRA J., finance educator; m. James M. Ayers, Sept. 6, 1998. BS, U. Cin., 1974; MS, Vanderbilt U., Nashville, 1976; MBA, Ind. U., Bloomington, 1989, PhD, 1990. Asst. prof. edn. Simmons Coll., Boston, 1977—83, clin. assoc. prof., 1984—85; asst. prof. bus. adminstrn. Northeastern U., Boston, 1990—92; assoc. prof. pub. and nonprofit mgmt. IUPUI-Sch. Pub. and Environ. Affairs, Indpls., 1992—. Dir. secondary sch. tchr. tng. program Simmons Coll. and Boston Pub. Schs., 1981—85; dir. grad. programs SPEA-IUPUI, Indpls., 2003—05, dir. pub. affairs, 2005—; chair philanthropic studies faculty Ind. U., Indpls., 1999—2003, chair policy and adminstrn. faculty SPEA, 1999—2000, bd. Ctr. on Philanthropy, 1999—2003. Contbr. chapters to books, articles to profl. jours. Exec. com., bd. mem. Ctrl. Ind. Big Bros. Big Sisters, Indpls., 1998—; active Ctr. on Philanthropy, Indpls., 1999—2003. Office: Indiana University Purdue University Ind 801 W Michigan St Indianapolis IN 46202 Office Phone: 317-274-8635.

MESCHKE, DEBRA JOANN, polymer chemist; b. Elyria, Ohio, Oct. 22, 1952; d. Loren Willis and JoAnne Elizabeth (Meyer) M. BS, U. Cin., 1974; MS, Case Western Res. U., 1976, PhD, 1979. Sr. chemist Union Carbide Corp., South Charleston, W.Va., 1979—82, project scientist, 1982—85, chair R&D Exempt Women's Group, 1980—81, chair R&D Ctr. Safety Team, 1981—82, coord. Polymer Methods Course, 1982—83, project scientist Tarrytown, NY, 1985—86; sr. prin. rsch. chemist Air Products and Chems. Inc., Allentown, Pa., 1986—88, chmn. waste disposal com., 1986—88; rsch. scientist Union Carbide Corp., South Charleston, W.Va., 1988—95, sr. rsch. scientist, 1995—2001; process leader Dow Chem. Co., 2001—06; ret., 2006. Author chpts. in textbooks; patentee in field. Bd. dirs. Overbrook Home Owners Assn., Macungie, Pa., 1987. Case Western Res. U. grad. fellow, 1974-79. Mem. AAAS, Am. Chem. Soc. (Polymer div.), Iota Sigma Pi. Avocations: gardening, reading, automobiles, water sports, skiing. Home: 2022 Parkwood Rd Charleston WV 25314-2244 Office Phone: 304-747-3934. Personal E-mail: dmeschke@msn.com.

MESENGRING, TAMMIE LYNN, elementary school educator; b. Kankakee, Ill., Nov. 27, 1965; d. Charles James and Sandra Lynn (Pawlowski) Drazy; m. Kurt Hilton Mesenbring, Nov. 28, 1992; 1 child, Kathleen Elizabeth. B in Zoology, Eastern Ill. U., 1987. Tchr. St. Joseph Sch., Bradley, 1987—. Safety chmn. Joliet Diocesan Sci. Tchr. Assn. Mem. ch. coun. St. Paul's Luth. Ch., Kankaee, Ill., mem. youth bd.; mem. Girl Scouts Am. Mem.: Beta Beta Beta. Republican. Luth. Home: 421 Deer Pass Ridge Bourbonnais IL 60914 Office: St Joseph Sch 247 N Center Ave Bradley IL 60915

MESERVE, MARILYN MOSES, retired pediatrician; b. Ticonderoga, NY, Oct. 2, 1926; d. Luther Horace and Marion (Card) Moses; m. Edwin Copp Meserve, Dec. 18, 1948; children: John, William, Donald, Thomas, Mary Beth, Charles. AA, Green Mt. Coll., Poultney, Vt.; BS in Biology, Boston U., 1946, MD, 1950. Pvt. practice, Southboro, Mass., 1953—88; ret., 1989. Bd. dirs. Teen Canteen, Southboro, 1970—75. Named Citizen of Yr., Rotary, Southboro, 1974. Mem.: Mass. Med. Soc. Democrat.

MESHI, ALEXIS, psychiatrist; b. Santa Monica, Calif., June 9, 1973; d. Joseph and Estera Hinda Meshi. BA, Wellesley Coll., 1995; MD, AUC Sch. Medicine, 2000. Lic. Med. Calif. Postdoctoral fellow U. Calif., Irvine, Calif., 2000—01; med. internship UCLA, Northridge (Calif.) Family Medicine Residency Program, 2002—03; med. resident Morehouse Sch. Medicine, Atlanta, 2004—. Nominee Assn. Women Psychiatrists Wyeth Pharm. fellowship, Morehouse Sch. Medicine, Dept. Psychiatry, 2005, Am. Psychiat. Inst. Rsch., Education's fellowship Program, 2006; recipient Emory, Pfizer Resident Rsch. award, Emory U. Dept. Psychiatry, 2004, Bipolar Minifellowship award, 2006, Travel award, Morehouse Sch. Medicine, Dept. Psychiatry, 2004. Mem.: Am. Psychiat. Assn., Ga. Psychiat. Physicians Assn., Assn. Women Psychiat. Office: Morehouse Sch Medicine 720 Westview Dr SW Atlanta GA 30310

MESHULAM, DEBORAH R., lawyer; b. Lancaster, Pa., Nov. 25, 1956; BA magna cum laude, Univ. Va., 1978; JD, Columbia Univ., 1981. Bar: NY 1982, DC 1988, US Dist. Ct. (so. & ea. NY, Md., DC dist.), US Ct. Appeals (2d, 11th, DC cir.), US Supreme Ct. Asst. chief litigation counsel SEC, Washington, 1990—97; ptnr, head of Litigation group DLA Piper Rudnick Gray Cary, Washington. Co-author: Plain English Guidebook to SEC Recordkeeping & Retention, 2003; contbr. articles to profl. jours. Harlan Fiske Stone scholar. Office: DLA Piper Rudnick Gray Cary 1200 19th St NW Washington DC 20036-2412 Office Phone: 202-861-6470. Office Fax: 202-223-2085. Business E-Mail: deborah.meshulam@dlapiper.com.

MESKE, SANDY, government agency administrator; BSBA. From clk. to tech. asst. Dryden Flight Rsch. Ctr. NASA, Edwards AFB, Calif., 1985—2000, adminstrv. ops. specialist Dryden Flight Rsch. Ctr., 2000—. Office: NASA Dryden Flight Rsch Ctr PO Box 273 MS 2004 Edwards AFB CA 93523-0273

MESMER, KAREN LUANN, elementary school educator; b. Columbus, Ohio, July 13, 1958; d. Andrew and Bonnie Lisko; m. David O. Pfaff, Jan. 5, 2002; children: Alex, Jaclyn. BA, Capital U., 1980; Masters, U. Wis., 1992, PhD in Curriculum and Instrn., Sci. Edn., 2003. Sci. tchr. NW Arctic Borough Sch. Dist., Kotzebue, Alaska, 1980—88, Jack Young Mid. Sch., Baraboo, Wis., 1988—. Educator Tchr. Enhancement Program, Madison, Wis., 2003—06. Contbr. chapters to books, articles to profl. jours. Named Outstanding Tchr., Tchr. Enhancement Program U. Wis.-Madison, 1998, Disting. Alumni, U. Wis.-Madison Edn. Dept., 1999; recipient Severn Rinkob Tchr. of Yr. award, Baraboo Sch. Dist., 1994, Presdl. award for Excellence in Sci. Tchg., The White Ho. and the NSF, 1997, Ohaus award for Mid. Sch. Sci., Ohaus and the Nat. Sci. Tchr. Assn., 2002; fellow, Kohl Found., 1997. Mem.: Nat. Assn. Biology Tchrs., Wis. Soc. Sci. Tchrs. (com. mem., Regional Sci. Tchr. award 1999), Nat. Mid. Level Sci. Tchrs. Assn. (pres. 2000—01), Nat. Sci. Tchrs. Assn. (bd. dirs. 2000—01). Progressive. Avocations: kayaking, hiking, gardening. Office: Jack Young Middle School 1531 Draper St Baraboo WI 53913 Office Phone: 608-355-3930. Business E-Mail: kmesmer@baraboo.k12.wi.us.

MESQUITA, ROSALYN, artist, educator; b. Belen, N.Mex., Aug. 21, 1945; d. Trinidad José and Margaret Anaya; m. Theodore Mesquita (dec. Aug. 1997); children: John, Richard, Larry, Thresa. AA, Pierce Coll., Woodland Hills, Calif., 1969; BA, Calif. State U., Northridge, 1973; MFA, U. Calif., Irvine, 1976. Instr. Santa Monica (Calif.) Coll., 1987-91; prof. art El Camino Coll., Torrance, Calif., 1991—. Exhibits include N.Mex. Mus. Art, Santa Fe, Capitol Round House Mus., Santa Fe, Barnsdall Mus. Art, L.A., Boston Libr., Boston, Calif. Poly. U. Gallery Mus., Pomona, Franklin Gallery, N.Y.C. Mem. Santa Monica Arts Commn., 1991-95; bd. dirs., advisor, curator Nongovernmental orgn. UN Women's World Conf., Nairobi, Kenya, 1985, bd. dirs., art advisor, Beijing, 1995. Named col. adc State of N.Mex., 1986-72; recipient Chancellor Arts award U. Calif., 1978, Latin tchr. award L.A. City Coun., 1998, L.A. County Tchr. of the Yr. award, Cal State U., 1999. Avocation: travel. Home: 6845 Ranchito Ave Van Nuys CA 91405-4160 Office: El Camino Coll 16007 Crenshaw Blvd Torrance CA 90506-0001

MESROBIAN, ARPENA SACHAKLIAN, publishing executive, consultant, editor; b. Boston; d. Aaron H. and Eliza Sachaklian; m. William J. Mesrobian, June 22, 1940 (dec.); children: William S.(dec.), Marian Elizabeth (Mrs. Bruce MacCurdy). Student, Armenian Coll. of Beirut, Lebanon, 1937-38; AA, Univ. Coll., Syracuse U., NY, 1959, BA magna cum laude, 1971; MSsc, Syracuse U., 1993. Editor Syracuse U. Press, 1955-58, exec. editor, 1958-61, asst. dir., 1961-65, acting dir., 1965-66, editor, 1968-85, assoc. dir., 1968-75, dir., 1975-85, 87-88, dir. emeritus, 1985. Dir. workshop on univ. press. pub. U. Malaysia, Kuala Lumpur, 1985; cons. Empire State Coll. Book rev. editor: Armenian Rev., 1967-75; author: Like One Family: The Armenians of Syracuse, 2000; mem. publs. bd. Courier, 1970-94; mem. adv. bd. Armenian Rev., 1981-83; contbr. to Ency. of NY State, 2005; contbr. numerous articles, revs. to profl. jours. Pres. Syracuse chpt. Armenian Relief Soc., 1972-74; sponsor Armenian Assembly, Washington, 1975; mem. mktg. task force Office of Spl. Edn., Dept. Edn., 1979-84, Adminstrn. of Developmental Disabilities, HHS; mem. publs. panel Nat. Endowment for Humanities, Washington; bd. dirs. Syracuse Girls Club, 1982-87; pres. trustees St. John the Bapt. Armenian Apostolic Ch. and Cmty. Ctr., 1991-95. Named Post-Standard Woman of Achievement, 1980; recipient Chancellor's award for disting. service Syracuse U., 1985; Nat. award U.S. sect. World Edn. Fellowship, 1986; N.Y. State Humanities scholar. Mem. Women in Communications, Soc. Armenian Studies (adminstrv. council 1976-78, 85-87, sec. 1978, 85-87), Syracuse U. Library Assocs. (v.p. 1983-88), Am. Univ. Press Services (dir. 1976-77), Armenian Lit. Soc., Armenian Community Center, Assn. Am. Univ. Presses (v.p. 1976-77), UN Assn. (bd. dirs. 1983-88, v.p. 1985), Phi Kappa Phi, Alpha Sigma Lambda. Mem. Armenian Apostolic Ch. (past trustee). Club: Zonta of Syracuse (pres. 1979-80, 1st v.p. 1985-86, dist. historian Dist. 2 Zonta Internat. 1993-96).

MESROP, ALIDA YOLANDE, academic administrator; b. N.Y.C., Dec. 23, 1931; d. Umberto and Jessica (Subrizi) R.; m. Alden Mesrop, Nov. 25, 1954; children: Andrea Francesca, Alison Bianca, Claudia Anne. BA cum laude, Hunter Coll., 1952. Freelance writer-cons., 1960-66; prodn. asst. Today Show, Nat. Broadcasting System, N.Y.C., 1952-54; pub. rels. coord. Tonight Show, Nat. Broadcasting System, N.Y.C., 1954-59; pub. rels. dir. Sta. WPIX-TV, N.Y.C., 1959-60; spl. asst. to pres. Coll. for Human Svcs., N.Y.C., 1966-79, dean, 1979-96, pres., 1996—; pres. emerita Audrey Cohen Coll. (now Met. Coll. N.Y.). PTA com. chair, Pelham, N.Y., 1969-79; rep. Dem. Party, Pelham, 1977-80; pub. rels. dir. Coalition on Environment, Pelham, 1978-82. Mem. Exec. Women in Human Svcs., Phi Beta Kappa. Avocations: travel, tennis, literature, photography.

MESSALINE, WENDY JEAN, retail chain official; b. New Bedford, Mass., Feb. 10, 1966; d. Robert Milton and Judith Louise (Rayno) M. Student, Butera Sch. Art, Boston, 1984-85; BS in Mgmt., U. Mass., 2005. Cashier Sears, Roebuck & Co., North Dartmouth, Mass., 1984-88, sales mgr. trainee Dedham, Mass., 1988-90, mgr. automotive svc., 1990-91, mgr. automotive ctr. Concord, N.H., 1991-93, Sears, Roebuck and Co., Nashua, N.H., 1993-96; human resource mgr. Sears Roebuck & Co., Taunton, Mass., 1996—2005; acct. Bridgewater State Coll., NH, 2005—. Mem. NAFE, Am. Bus. Women's Assn., Mchts. Assn. N.H. (bd. dirs.). Home: 21 Lakeside Ave Lakeville MA 02347-2416 Office: Sears Roebuck & Co 8 Galleria Mall Dr Taunton MA 02780-6988 E-mail: wendy.messaline@bridgew.edu.

MESSÉ, MADELYN RENÉE, clinical psychologist, consultant; b. N.Y.C., Sept. 13, 1957; d. Abba Messé and Carolyn Fielding. BA in Psychology, Biology, Vassar Coll., 1978; MA in Clin. Psychology, SUNY Stony Brook, 1981; PhD in Clin. Psychology, SUNY, Stony Brook, 1983. Diplomate Am. Bd. Med. Psychotherapy. Instr. Mt. Sinai Sch. Medicine, N.Y.C., 1984-86; clin. rsch. psychologist Nat. Cancer Inst., N.Y.C., 1984-86; pvt. practice N.Y.C., 1986—. Cons. to industry, 1986—. Author: (chpt.) Behavioral Medicine and Clinical Psychology: Overlapping Disciplines, 1982; contbr. articles to profl. jours. including Oncology Digest, Cancer, Psychosomatic Medicine, Proceedings of APA, and others. Fellow Internat. Soc. Philos. Enquiry; mem. APA, Sigma Xi (Sci. Rsch. award 1982). Avocations: photography, travel, art, music, reading.

MESSENGER, BARBARA BEALL, artist; d. John Murray and Anne Bryant (Dorsey) Beall; m. Donald White Messenger, Aug. 16, 1960; children: Colleen Beall Messenger-Baldwin, Melanie Dorsey Messenger Davis. BS, Western Md. Coll., 1960; postgrad., Md. Inst. Art, 1978, Howard C.C., Columbia, Md., 1979—80. Art educator, dept. chair Md. Pub. Sch. Sys., New Carrollton, 1960—66; art dir. Bellassai Gallery, Ellicott City, Md., 1980—84; proprietor Art and Frame Shop Ellicott Mills Gallery, Ellicott City, 1984—2000. Set, costume and program designer Calverton Players, Beltsville, Md., 1970—73; art critic, writer Laurel (Md.) Newsleader, 1974—80; substitute tchr. Howard County Sch. Sys., Ellicott City, 1984, Ellicott City, 85; publicity chmn. Laurel Art Guild. Exhibited in group shows at Laurel Art Guild, 1979, Bellassai Gallery, 1980—84, Villa Julia, Stevenson, Md., 1983, exhibited in group shows, Camden, Maine, 1988, exhibitions include Ellicott Mills Gallery, Md., Represented in permanent collections, Honduras, Turkey, Italy, German, U.S.A., and many islands. Active PTA, Howard County; membership chmn., v.p. Howard County Rep. Women; events coord. Howard County Rep. Party. Recipient Best of Balt. Art Gallery, Balt. Mag., 1980. Mem.: Am. Craft Coun., Howard County Arts Coun., Md. State Arts Coun. (bd. mem. 2003—), Nat. Mus. Women in the Arts (charter). Avocations: painting, crafts, reading, writing, photography. Home and Office: 616 Traveller Ct Lothian MD 20711 Office Phone: 410-741-0959. E-mail: bobbiemessenger@aol.com.

MESSER, BONNIE JEANNE, psychologist; b. Brookings, S.D., Apr. 29, 1943; d. Wanita J. Halstead Nagel; m. Donald E. Messer, Aug. 30, 1964; children: Christine, Kent. BS, Morningside Coll., Sioux City, Iowa, 1964; MS in Social Sci., Boston U., 1966; PhD, U. Denver, 1986. Lic. psychologist Colo. Social worker United Day Care Ctrs., Boston, 1966-69; instr. to asst. prof. Dakota Wesleyan U., Mitchell, S.D., 1972-81; instr. and adj. prof. U. Denver, 1986—91; counselor, assoc. dir Counseling Ctr., U. Denver, 1984-90; pvt. practice Denver, 1985—91. Author: Dealing with Change, 1996; co-author: Manual for the Adult Self-Perception Profile, 1986; contbr. chpt. to book. Recipient Bonnie Nagel Messer Social Wk. medal Dakota Wesleyan U., 1977. Mem. APA, Colo. Psychol. Assn. Democrat. Methodist. Office: 9000 E Nichols Ste 240 Centennial CO 80112

MESSERLE, JUDITH ROSE, retired medical librarian, retired public relations executive; b. Litchfield, Ill., Jan. 16, 1943; d. Richard Douglas and Nelrose B. Wilcox; m. Darrell Wayne Messerle, Apr. 26, 1968; children: Kurt Norman, Katherine Lynn. BA in Zoology, So. Ill. U., 1966; MLS, U. Ill., 1967. Cert. med. libr. Libr. St. Joseph's Sch. Nursing, Alton, Ill., 1967-71, dir. med. info. ctr., 1971-76, dir. info. svcs., 1976-79; dir. ednl. resources and cmty. rels. St. Joseph's Hosp., 1979-84; dir. Med. Ctr. Libr. St. Louis U., 1985-88; libr. Francis A. Countway Libr. Harvard Med. Sch. and Boston Med. Libr., 1989—2004; ret. Cons., 1973—; instr. Lewis and Clark Coll., 1975, Med. Libr. Assn. Bd. dirs. Family Svcs. and Vis. Nurses Assn., Alton, 1976-79. Fellow AAAS, Med. Libr. Assn. (search com. for exec. dir. 1979, dir. 1981-84, pres. 1986-87, legis. task force 1986-90, task force for knowledge and skills 1988-92, nominating com. 1996); mem. OCLC (spl. libr. adv. com. 1994-98), AMA (com. on allied health edn. and accreditation 1991-94), Assn. Acad. Health Sci. Libr. Dirs. (editl. bd. for ann. stats. 1989-94, Region 8 adv. bd. 1992-93, joint legis. task force 1992-96, pres. 1993, charting the future task force 2001-03, scholarly communication task force 2003-05), Am. Med. Informatics Assn. (planning com. 1990, publs. com. 1994-96, ann. mtg. com. 1996-98), Ill. State Libr. Adv. Com., Midwest Health Sci. Libr. Network (divsn. health sci. coun.), St. Louis Med. Librs., Hosp. Pub. Rels. Soc. St. Louis, Nat. Libr. Medicine (biomed. libr. rev. com. 1988-92).

MESSERLY, JENNIFER, science educator; MS in Edn., Ohio State U., Columbus. Sci. tchr. Bexley City Schs., Ohio, 1998—. Office Phone: 614-231-4591.

MESSERSMITH, STEPHANIE HUNT, nursing administrator; b. Key West, Fla. BSN, U. Hawaii, 1978; MSN, George Mason U., 1996. RN, Md., Va., DC; cert. case mgr.; diplomate Am. Bd. Quality Assurance & Utilization Rev. Physicians. Staff nurse Paul H. Weisshaar, MD, Burke, Va., 1986-89; nurse case mgr. Resource Opportunities, Inc., Vienna, Va., 1989-92; analyst State and Fed. Assocs., Vienna, Va., 1992-95; cons. Springfield, Va., 1995-97; ambulatory case mgr. Kaiser Permanent, Springfield, Va., 1997-98, quality improvement coord. Rockville, Md., 1998-99, project mgr., 1999-2000, sr. mgr. Springfield, Va., 2000—. Mem. People to People, Managed Helath Care Del., South Africa, 2000. Co-author: (coloring book for children with cancer) Do You Know What This Is All About?, 1978 (Best Regional Project Am. Cancer Soc. 1978). Mem. Am. Bd. Quality Assurance and Utilization Review Physicians, 1998—, Case Mgmt. Soc. Am., Case Mgmt. Soc. Nat. Capital Area (bd. dirs. 1994). Office: Kaiser Permanente Mid-Atlantic States 2101 E Jefferson St Rockville MD 20852-4908

MESSIN, MARLENE ANN, plastics company executive; b. St. Paul, Oct. 6, 1935; d. Edgar Leander and Luella Johanna (Rahn) Johnson; m. Eugene Carlson (div. 1972); children: Rick, Debora, Ronald, Lori; m. Willard Smith (dec. 1975); m. Frank Messin, Sept. 24, 1982; 5 stepchildren. Bookkeeper Jeans Implement Co., Forest Lake, Minn., 1952-53, 1953—57, Great Plains Supply, St. Paul, 1960-62, Plastic Products Co., Inc., Lindstrom, Minn., 1962-75, pres., 1975—; co-owner, treas. Gustaf's Fine Gifts, Lindstrom, 1985—. Bookkeeper Trinity Luth. Ch., Lindstrom, 1976-81. Recipient award, Diversity 2000/Woman-Owned Bus. in Minn. Mem. Soc. Plastic Engrs., Swedish Inst., Soc. Plastic Industry, Minn. State Hist. Soc., Chgo. County Hist. Soc. Home: 28968 Olinda Trl Lindstrom MN 55045-9429 Office: 30355 Akerson St Lindstrom MN 55045-9456

MESSINA, NANCE ANN, primary school educator; b. Somerville, Mass., Oct. 26, 1956; d. Ralph Cosmo and Anna Marie (Capadonno) Tucci; m. Lucian Vito Messina, May 28, 1977; children: Jason, Peter. BS in Edn., Boston State Coll., 1978; MEd, Leslie U., Cambridge, Mass., 1997. Cert. advanced grad. studies Fitchburg State Coll., Mass., 2006. Tchr. St. Mary Sch., Clinton, Mass., 1992—97, Green Meadow Sch., Maynard, Mass., 1997—. Grantee, Maynard Edn. Found., 2002. Home: 4 Marychris Dr Hudson MA 01749 Office: Green Meadow Sch 5 Tiger Dr Maynard MA 01754

MESSING, CAROL SUE, communications educator; b. Bronx, N.Y. d. Isidore and Esther Florence (Burtoff) Weinberg; m. Sheldon H. Messing; children: Lauren, Robyn. BA, Bklyn. Coll., N.Y., 1967, MS, 1970. Tchr. N.Y.C. Bd. Edn., 1967-72; prof. lang. arts Northwood U., Midland, Mich., 1973—2004, prof., 1993—. Owner Job Match, Midland, 1983-85; cons. Mich. Credit Union League, Saginaw, 1984-87, Nat. Hotel & Restaurant, Midland, 1985-89, Univ. Coll. program, Continuing Edn. program, Northwood U., 1986—, Dow Chem. Employee's Credit Union, 1988—. Author: (anthology) Symbiosis, 1985, rev. edit., 1987, Controlling Communication, 1987, rev. edit., 1993, Creating Effective Team Presentations, 1995; co-author: PRIMIS, 1993. Mem.: LWV, Nat Coun. Tchrs. English, Kappa Delta Pi, Delta Mu Delta (advisor). Avocations: reading, sewing. Office: Northwood U 4000 Whiting Dr Midland MI 48640-2311 Office Phone: 989-837-4829. Business E-Mail: messing@northwood.edu.

MESSING, DEBRA, actress; b. Bklyn., Aug. 15, 1968; m. Daniel Zelman, Sept. 3, 2000; 1 child. Grad., Brandeis U.; M in Drama, NYU. Actor: (films) Walk in the Clouds, 1995, McHale's Navy, 1997, Prey, 1997, Celebrity, 1998, Mothman Prophecies, 2002, Hollywood Ending, 2002, Along Came Polly, 2004, (voice) Garfield, 2004, The Wedding Date, 2005; (TV series) Ned and Stacey, 1995, Prey, 1998, Will & Grace, 1998—2006 (Emmy award best actress in a comedy, 2003); TV appearances include: NYPD Blue, 1994, 1995; Partners, 1995; Seinfeld, 1996, 1997; (voice) King of the Hill, 2002. Office: c/o Gersh Agy 232 N Canon Dr Beverly Hills CA 90210*

MESSING, ELLEN JEAN, lawyer; b. Springfield, Mass. AB cum laude, Harvard U., 1973; JD cum laude, Boston U., 1977. Bar: Mass. 1977, U.S. Dist. Ct. (Mass.) 1980, U.S. Ct. Appeals (1st cir.) 1994. Staff atty. Mass. Dept. Pub. Utilities, Boston, 1977-78, Southeastern Mass. Legal Assistance Corp., New Bedford, 1978-79; sole practice Boston, 1979-80; staff atty., clin. instr. U. Mich., Ann Arbor, 1980-82; clin. instr. Boston U. Sch. Law, 1982-83; assoc., of counsel Schreiber & Assocs., Boston, 1983-85; of counsel Westwater & Hernandez, Boston, 1985-86, Stern & Shapiro, Boston, 1986-88; ptnr. Messing & Rudavsky, P.C., Boston, 1988—, Messing, Rudavsky & Weliky PC, Boston. Author: Executive Compensation Packages: An Overview from the Employee's Point of View, The Practical Lawyer, 2002, The Ethical Constraints on Talking to Potential Witnesses, 2003, Representing Plaintiffs in Title VII Actions; contbr. numerous articles to profl. jours. Co-founder, co-chair Alliance for Future of Brookline Schs., Boston, 1991—. Recipient Faculty Award for Exceptional Dedication to Ideals of Community Svc. Boston U. Sch. Law, 1977; named one of Boston's top lawyers Boston Mag. 2004. Mem.: ABA (adv. coun. commn. evaluation rules or profl. conduct ethics commn. 2000), Mass. Bar Assn. (co-chair ethics com. labor & employment law sect. 1988—91, vice chair 1990—91, chair labor and employment law sect. 1991—92), Boston Bar Assn. (co-chair CLE com. labor law sect. 1988—91), Coll. Labor and Employment Lawyers, Boston Inn of Ct. (program dir. 1992—94, co-pres.-elect 1994—95, co-pres. 1995—96), Nat. Employment Lawyers Assn. (chair ethics and sanctions com. 1991—, pres. Mass. chpt. 1992—99, exec. bd. 1992—, co-chair affiliate rels. com. 1993—95, nat. sec. 2002—). Office: Messing Rudavsky & Weliky PC 44 School St Boston MA 02108-4201 Office Phone: 617-742-0004. Business E-Mail: mail@mrwemploymentlaw.com, emessing@mrwemployment.com.

MESSING, KAREN, occupational health researcher; b. Springfield, Mass., Feb. 2, 1943; BA, Harvard U., 1963; MSc, McGill U., 1970, PhD in Biology, 1975. Rsch. asst. biochemistry Jewish Gen. Hosp., Montreal, Can., 1970-71; NIH fellow genetics Boyce Thompson Inst. Plant Rsch., 1975-76; prof. ergonomics U. Quebec, Montreal, 1976—, dir. Ctr. Stu Biol. Interactions & Environ. Health, 1990—95, 2000—03, dir. grad. ergonomics program, 1999-2000. Disting. fellow Que. Coun. for Social Rsch., 1995-97, Can. Inst. Health Rsch., 2001—; invited rschr. Inst. Cancer Montreal, 1983-95, Sweden Nat. Inst. Working Life, 1997-98; mem. bd. dirs. Quebec Sci. & Tech. Mus., 1984-86, Quebec Coun. Social Affairs, 1984-90. Author: One-Eyed Science: Occupational Health and Working Women, 1998, Integrating Gender in Ergonomic Analysis, 1999; editor: Women and Health, Policy and Practice in Health and Safety, Internat. Jour. Health Svcs., Recherches Feministes Salud y Trabajo, Policy and Practice in Health and Safety; co-editor: Women's Health at Work, 1998. Mem. Am. Pub. Health Assn., Assn. Can. Ergonomists. Office: Univ Que at Montreal CP 8888 succursale Centre-ville Montreal PQ Canada H3C 3P8 Office Phone: 514-987-3000 x 3334. Business E-Mail: messing.karen@uqam.ca.

MESSINGER, HOLLY LYNN, secondary school educator; b. Ft. Benning, Ga., July 2, 1954; d. Frank Dana and Helen Ruth (White) Proctor; m. Lucien B. Messinger, June 15, 1974; children: Kara Elizabeth Grace, Ryan Casselden. BS in Secondary Edn., Old Dominion U., 1976; MEd in Ednl. Lea..ip, George Mason U., 1998. Tchr. bus. Lake Braddock Secondary Sch., Burke, Va., 1977-84, Madison H.S., Vienna, Va., 1984-85; chmn. bus. dept., coord. coop. office edn. Falls Church H.S., Va., 1985—95; curriculum resource tchr. Fairfax County Pub. Schs., 1995—99; asst. prin. Centreville H.S., Clifton, Va., 1999—2003, Woodson H.S., Fairfax, Va., 2003—04, Westfield H.S., Chantilly, Va., 2004—. Curriculum chmn. Fairfax County Pub. Schs., 1992—; presenter South Western Pub. Co., Cin., 1991—. Pres. Fairfax County Jr. Woman's Club, Fairfax, Va., 1987. Mem. Nat. Bus. Edn. Assn., Va. Bus. Edn. Assn. (editor 1993-94, No. Va. rep. 1994—), Fairfax County Bus. Tchrs. Assn. (pres. 1990-91, treas. 1993-94), No. Va. Assn. Secondary Sch. Adminstrs. Republican. Methodist. Avocation: reading. Office: Westfield HS 4700 Stonecroft Blvd Chantilly VA 20151-1716

MESSMER, MELINDA ELLEN, elementary school educator; b. Kansas City, Mo., Dec. 7, 1970; d. William E. and Juanita E. Messmer. Bachelor's in Edn., Pittsburg State U., Kans., 1993; Master's in Liberal Arts, Baker U., Baldwin, Kans. Cert. elem. tchr. Kans., 1993. Tchr. grade 2 Brookwood Elem., Leawood, Kans., 1993—96; tchr. grade 7 Westridge Mid. Sch., Overland Park, Kans., 1996—. Mem. Jr. League of Wyandotte and Johnson Counties, Kansas City, Kans., 2003—06. Named Outstanding Faculty Mem., Westridge Mid. Sch., 1999—2000, Friend of Spl. Edn., Shawnee Mission Sch. Dist., 2005, Shawnee Mission Tchr. of Yr., Shawnee Mission Pub. Schs., 2003—04, Tchr. of Yr., Lenexa Rotary Club, 2004; recipient Lifetime Mem. award, PTA, 1999—2000, Tchr. of Month, Star 102, 2005. Mem.: NEA (assoc.), Kans. Exemplary Edn. Assn., Jr. League (assoc. Extra Mile award 2006), Am. Legion Aux. (assoc.). Home: 6604 Hallet Shawnee KS 66216 Office: Westridge Middle School 9300 Nieman Overland Park KS 66214 Office Phone: 913-993-1200.

MESSNER, YVONNE F., physical education educator; widowed; 3 children. BA cum laude in Elem. Edn. and Phys. Edn., Wheaton Coll.; MS cum laude in Phys. Edn., Ind. U., D in Phys. Edn. in Recreation and Health with honors. Tchr. West Ward Elem. Sch., Warsaw, Ind., 1955—56; phys. edn. tchr., coach Warsaw Jr. and Sr. H.S., 1956—57; instr. health and phys. edn. Grace Coll., Winona Lake, Ind., 1957—63, dir. women's intramural and extramural sports, 1957—63, asst. prof. phys. edn., 1963—76, dir. intramural sports program, 1963—76, women's athletic dir., 1963—76, assoc. prof. phys. edn., chair health and phys. edn. dept., women's athletic dir., 1977—85; assoc. prof. phys. edn., dir. fitness Ball State U., Muncie, Ind., 1986—87; asst. prof. phys. edn. Winthrop U., Rock Hill, SC, 1988—96, Azusa (Calif.) Pacific U., 1996—2003. Author: Campfire Cooking, 1973, Camp Devotions, 1974, Swimming Everyone, 1989, Swimming Everyone, 2d edit., 1992; contbr. articles to profl. jours. Mem.: S.C. Pk. and Recreation Assn., S.C. Alliance Health, Phys. Edn., Recreation and Dance, Am. Alliance Health, Phys. Edn., Recreation and Dance. Home: 4303 Shady Ln Oceanside CA 92056-4803

MESTA, PAMELA ANNE, supervisor, consultant; b. Titusville, Pa., Dec. 24, 1973; d. James Ernest and Michaelene Ann Mesta; m. Stephen William Curry, Aug. 11. BA in Comm., Pa. State U., Erie, 1995; MS in Edn. with honors, U. Pa., Edinboro, 1998. Tchr. Prince George's County Pub. Schs., Riverdale, Md., 1998—2000, Carroll County Pub. Schs., Westminster, Md., 2000—02, ESOL program coord., 2002—. Presenter in field. Mem.: TESOL, ASCD, Nat. Coun. Tchrs. Math., Nat. Assn. for Bilingual Edn., Internat. Reading Assn., Coun. Ednl. Adminstrv. Supervisory Orgns. Md., Md. ASCD (conf. planning com.), Kappa Delta Pi, Pi Lambda Theta. Home: 2203 E Mayberry Rd Westminster MD 21158 Office: Carroll County Pub Schs 125 N Court St Westminster MD 21157

MESTEL, SHERRY Y., social worker, school psychologist, art therapist; b. Bklyn., Dec. 7, 1952; d. Robert and Miriam Mestel; children: Jessica, Iris. MSc in Bilingual Edn., CCNY, 1976; MSW, SUNY, Stonybrook, 1979; MSC in Sch. Psychology, LI U., 1992; PhD, Nat. Inst. Expressive Therapy, 1995; cert. in traumatic brain injury and children, Mt. Sinai Hosp. and Hunter Coll., 1999. Lic. social worker; cert. bilingual Spanish/English elem. tchr. NY, sch. psychologist NY. Puppeteer NYC Dept. Pks., 1972—74; elem. sch. tchr. NYC Bd. Edn., 1974—75, sch. social worker, 1987—92; psychiat. social worker Rockland Children's Psychiat. Ctr., Orangeburg, NY, 1979—81; psychotherapist NY Psychotherapy & Counseling Ctr., Bklyn., 1981—87; sch. psychologist NYC Dept. Edn., Bklyn., 1992—; social worker For the Children, Para los Ninos, PLLC, Bklyn., 2000—. Spkr. NY State Early Childhood Conf., Bklyn., 1999—, YAI, NYC, 1999—; owner Early Intervention, Bklyn., 2000—. Editor: Herbal Remedies, 1978, Women's Rituals, 1979; exhibitions include A.I.R. Gallery, NYC, B.W.A.I.C., Bklyn. Recipient Elem. Sch. Book award, Queens Coll., Flushing, NY, 1974. Mem.: NASP, NASW, Am. Art Therapy Assn. (cert.), Nat. Expressive Therapy Assn., Assn. Humanistic Psychology, Nuyagi Keetowah Soc., Bklyn. Women's Chorus, Bklyn. Working Artist Coalition, Backyard Garden.

MESTRES, JEAN L. See SULC, JEAN LUENA

MESUK, ELAINE M., music educator; b. Pompton Plains, NJ, Jan. 14, 1969; d. John M. and Gloria V. Milko; m. Paul A. Mesuk, Aug. 7, 1999; 1 child, Julia Mae. Assoc., Coll. Misericordia, Dallas, Pa., 1988; MusB, William Paterson U., Wayne, NJ, 1992. Cert. K-12 music edn. NJ, 1992. Music tchr. Bloomfield (NJ) Pub. Schs., 1992—, interim fine arts coord., 2006—; music tchr. Ridgewood (NJ) Pub. Schs., 2000—02. Vocalist Berkshire Choral Festival, Sheffield, Mass., 1991—2000, Oratorio Soc. NJ, Montclair, 1994—98, Starlite Chorale, Clark, NJ, 2005—06; cellist NJ Intergenerational Orch., Cranford, NJ, 1994—96. Composer, arranger: string orchestra (levels 1-2) Contemporary Progressions. Vocalist St. Thomas the Apostle Ch., Bloomfield, 2002—06. Mem.: Music Educators Nat. Conf. (pres. collegiate chpts. 1989—91). Roman Catholic. Avocations: saltwater fishing, gardening, bargain shopping, downhill skiing. Office: Music Department 150 Garrabrant Ave Bloomfield NJ 07003 Office Phone: 973-680-8590. Business E-Mail: emesuk@bloomfield.k12.nj.us.

METALLO, FRANCES ROSEBELL, mathematics professor; b. Jersey City; d. Vincenzo James and Lucille (Frank) M. BA in Math., Jersey City State Coll., 1985, MA in Math. Edn., 1987. Math. tchr. Emerson HS, Union City, NJ, 1990-92; math tchr. gifted/talented program Jefferson Annex Woodrow Wilson Sch. Dist. Union City, 1992-95; math tchr. Woodrow Wilson Sch., Dist. Union City, 1995—. Adj. tchr. math. Hudson County CC, 1987—, Jersey City State Coll., 1986—, tutor, 1983-86; reviewer for Nat. Coun. Tchrs. Math mag., A Plus for Kids Tchr. Network, 1994, grantee 1993, 96 Contbr. articles to profl. publs.; author, History of the Abacus and Study of Soroban, 1987, The Abacus: It's History and Application Module 17, 1990, A Concise Dictionary of Math and Symbols, 1992, Smile, Basic Algebra is Fun, 1999. Nominee Pres. award for sci. and math tchg., 1996, EWT Com. of NJ, 1996; named Most Admired Woman of Decade; recipient St. Jude's Children's Rsch. Hosp. award, 1995, 1996. Mem. Nat. Coun. Tchrs. Math., Assn. Math. Tchrs. of NJ, Alumni Assn. Jersey City State Coll., Math. Assn. Am., Am. Soc. Prevention of Cruelty to Animals, Assn. of Women in Math., Am. Math. Soc., Dozenal Soc., Kappa Delta Pi (mem. Wall of Tolerance, 2005, 06), Phi Delta Kappa. Avocations: crochet, embroidery, piano. Home: 201 Hancock Ave Jersey City NJ 07307-1916

METCALF, AMY BOLLING, secondary school educator; b. Huntington, W.Va., Nov. 10, 1952; d. Richard Norman Bolling and Ella Juanita Baisden; m. Walter Hahn Metcalf. BA, N.C. State U., Raleigh, 1974; MEd, Ariz. State U., Tempe, 1999. Cert. tchr. Ariz. Flight attendant TWA, N.Y.C., 1975—90; English dept. chair Cactus Shadows H.S., Cave Creek, Ariz., 1997—. Mem.: Kappa Delta Pi (life). Office: Cactus Shadows HS PO Box 426 Cave Creek AZ 85327-0426 Office Phone: 480-575-2491. E-mail: ametcalf@ccusd93.org.

METCALF, GINGER (VIRGINIA) ARVAN, psychotherapist, consultant; b. Decorah, Iowa, Aug. 19, 1953; d. Theodore Gerald Arvan and Norma Jean Ellickson; m. Michael James Metcalf, Feb. 22, 1985; children: Jason Alan, Rachel Teresa Metcalf-Lange; children: Matthew Lee Canterbury, Aimee Elizabeth Canterbury. BS cum laude in Nursing, Wash. State U., 1975; MS magna cum laude in Clin. Psychology, Ea. Wash. U., 1990. Lic. mental health counselor Nat. Bd. Counselor Certification, Wash., 1993. Therapist, case mgr. Spokane (Wash.) Mental Health, 1990—94; pvt. practice psychotherapist Spokane, 1994—. Cons. Mentor Program, Spokane, 1996; clin. cons. Luth. Cmty. Svc., Spokane, 2001—. Ct. apptd. spl. adv. Spokane (Wash.) Juvenile Ct., 1984—90. Mem.: Am. Profl. Soc. Abuse of Children. Democrat. Lutheran. Avocations: sprint triathalons, quilting. Office: 807 W 7th Ave Spokane WA 99204 Office Phone: 509-455-7654. Fax: 509-455-4112. Personal E-mail: gingamet@comcast.net.

METCALF, KAREN, retired foundation executive; b. Reading, Mass., Dec. 12, 1936; d. Albion Edmund and Natalie Viola (Ives) M. AB, Vassar Coll., 1958; MBA, Harvard U., 1968. CFA. Sec. Radio Liberty Com., N.Y.C., 1958-60; rsch. asst. Air Inc., Cambridge, Mass., 1960-64; sys. analyst Keydata Corp., Watertown, Mass., 1964-66; customer edn. cons. Interactive Data Corp., N.Y.C., 1968; portfolio mgr. Scudder, Stevens & Clark, N.Y.C., 1969-81; v.p. fin. and adminstrn. N.Y. Cmty. Trust, N.Y.C., 1981—2002. Episcopalian. Avocations: travel, opera.

METCALF, PAULINE CABOT, architectural historian; b. Providence, Mar. 31, 1939; d. George Pierce Metcalf and Pauline Pumpelly (Cabot) Metcalf Wykeham-Fiennes. BA, Sarah Lawrence Coll., 1960; MS in Hist. Preservation, Columbia U., 1978. Interior decorator Thedlow, Inc., N.Y.C., 1962-65; assoc. ptnr. Richard A. Nelson, Inc., N.Y.C., 1966-75; pvt. practice PCM Interiors, N.Y.C., 1975—. Cons. for interior restorations and renovations for hist. bldgs.; lectr. in field. Author, editor: Ogden Codman and the Decoration of Houses, 1988. Trustee RISD, Providence, 1989—, Preservation Soc. Newport Co., 1998—; bd. dirs. Victorian Soc. Am., 1984-94, adv. bd., 1995—; bd. dirs. Edith Wharton Restoration, Lenox, Mass., 1984—. Winterthur fellow, 1995-96. Mem. Canterbury Choral Soc., Nat. Soc. Colonial Dames, Decorator's Club, Art Club Providence, Cosmopolitan Club. Avocations: choral singing, gardening, skiing, tennis.

METCALF, SUSAN STIMMEL, community volunteer; b. San Francisco, May 6, 1926; d. George Stimmel and Elsie (Bishop) Higgins; m. Lawrence Vincent Metcalf, Jan. 27, 1950; children: John Brockway, Elsie (dec.). BS, U. Calif., Berkeley, 1947. Pres. bd. Jr. League San Francisco, 1953-54, Edgewood Children's Home, San Francisco, 1959-61, The Heritage, San Francisco, 1967-76; sec. health adv. bd. City and County San Francisco, 1966-77; chmn. bd. Four Winds Found., Seattle, 1976-82, San Francisco Found., 1986-88; bd. dirs. San Francisco Opera, 1985-91, Ft. Mason Ctr., San Francisco, 1989-91; bd. govs. San Francisco Symphony, 1991—, Fioli Ctr., 1991— . Recipient Rosalie M. Stern award for Women U. Calif., Berkeley, 1957. Mem. Town and Country Club, San Francisco Golf Club.

METCALFE, ELIZABETH BROKAW, art educator; b. St. Louis, Feb. 14, 1941; d. Augustus Van Liew and Elizabeth Cabell Gray Brokaw; m. James Walter Metcalfe, June 7, 1969; children: James Kenneth Brokaw, Elizabeth Cabell. BA, Washington U., St. Louis, 1962, MA, 1965. Instr. Pierce Coll., Athens, Greece, 1966; instr. art history Maryville U., St. Louis, 1968—72, 1981—. Lectr. and book reviewer. Mem. St. Louis Art Mus., 1970—, Chgo. Art Inst., 1970—. Mem.: Archeol. Inst. Am., Nat. Soc. Colonial Dames Am. Republican. Episcopalian. Avocations: reading, walking, running, travel, hiking. Home: 65 Berry Rd Pk Saint Louis MO 63122 Office: Maryville Univ 13550 Conway Rd Saint Louis MO 63141 Personal E-mail: stlouis65@juno.com.

METLTZOFF, NANCY JEAN, education educator; b. N.Y.C., Mar. 26, 1952; d. Julian and Judith (Novikoff) M.; children: Kimberly, Adam, Jesse Buckingham. PhD, U. Oreg. Coord. Super Summer Program, Eugene, Oreg., 1989; dir. Starts Program, 1990-91; asst. prof. of edn. Willamette U., Salem, 1991-93; coord. grad. program, asst. prof. edn. Pacific U., Eugene, 1994—2002, assoc. prof. edn., 2002—. Author: (novel) A Sense of Balance, 1978. Mem.: Nat. Assn. Multicultural Edn. Avocation: dance. Office: Pacific U 40 E Broadway Eugene OR 97401-3135

METOYER, PAMELA PARADIS, scientific editor, writer; b. Hutchinson, Minn., Sept. 1, 1955; d. Paul Edward, Sr. and Mary LaVerne (Hebert) Paradis; m. Jeffrey Johns Powell, June 17, 1977 (div. July 1982); m. Christopher Allen Tice, Aug. 25, 1997 (div. Sept. 2004),; m. Grady Wilson Metoyer, June 3, 2006. BA, Coll. of St. Scholastica, 1977. Statis./sec. U. Tex. M.D. Anderson Cancer Ctr., Houston, 1978-87; data coord. Baylor Coll. Medicine, Houston, 1987-88, editl. asst., 1988-90, sr. editor, 1992-2000, rsch. assoc., 2000—; dept. editor U. Tex. Med. Sch., Houston, 1990-91; editor, Houston medicine HCA Ctr. for Health Excell., Houston, 1991-92; exec. asst. U. Tex. Sch. Nursing, Houston, 1991-92. Mem. scope and mandate task force, Coun. of Sci. Editors, Chgo., 1996. Editor-in-chief: Am. Med. Writers Assn. Jour., 1992-95 (Apex awards 1995, 96, 97, Matrix award 1996, 2000, 2001, others). Recipient Presdl. Alumni award, Coll. of St. Scholastica, 2003. Mem. Am. Med. Writers Assn. (chpt. sec. 1989-90, chpt. treas. 1990-92, chpt. pres.-elect 1992-93, chpt. pres. 1993-94, chpt. past pres. 1994-95, chpt. dir.-at-large 2001-2003, chair McGovern Award com. 2003—, Chpt. Svc. award 1994, Assn. Pres. award 1993, Assn. Leadership award 1995), Coun. of Sci. Editors, Bd. of Editors in the Life Scis. (diplomate 2002). Office Phone: 713-798-1087. Business E-Mail: pptice@bcm.tmc.edu.

METTEE-MCCUTCHON, ILA, municipal official, retired military officer; b. Mobile, Ala., May 1, 1945; d. John Martin and Anna Ruth (Cleveland) Mettee; m. John Robert McCutchon, Oct. 13, 1974; 1 child, Erin Tempest. BS, Auburn U., Ala., 1967, MS, 1969; grad., various army schs. Rsch. psychologist VA Hosp., Tuskegee, Ala., 1967-69; clin. psychologist U. Ala. Med. Ctr., Birmingham, 1969-71; commd. 1st lt. U.S. Army, 1971, advanced through grades to col., 1992. Officer in charge Alcohol and Drug Abuse Rehab. Ctr., Presidio, San Francisco, 1971-73; strategic intelligence officer 8th Psychol. Bn., 1973-75; tactical intelligence officer, ops. officer, co. comdr. 525th MI Brigade (Airborne), Ft. Bragg, N.C., 1976-79; project officer Command, Control, Comms. and Intelligence Directorate, Combined Arms Combat Devel. Activity, Ft. Leavenworth, Kans., 1979-82; student Command and Gen. Staff Coll., 1982-83; ops. officer Army Spl. Security Group, Washington, 1983-86; Def. Lang. Inst. Presidio of Monterey, 1986-87; chief U.S. So. command Joint Intelligence Ctr., Republic of Panama, 1987-89; comdr. 741st M.I. Bn., Ft. Meade, Md., 1989-91; U.S. Army War Coll., 1991-92; strategic intelligence officer Internat. Mil. Staff NATO, Brussels, 1992-94; comdr. Presidio of Monterey and Ft. Ord, Calif., 1994-96, chief base realignment and closure/environ. mgmt., 1996-97, ret. with honors, 1997. Elected to Marina City Coun., 1998, Rep. ctrl. com. Monterey County, 2000, Mayor City of Marina, 2002—, reelected, 2004; apptd. housing cmty. and econ. devel. policy com. League Calif. Cities', 1999—; chair bd. dirs. Ftord Reuse Auth., 2004 Decorated Army Commendation medal (3), Meritorious Svc. medal (4), Def. Meritorious Svc. medal, Army Achievement award (2), Legion of Merit (2), Def. Superior Svc. medal; named Woman of Yr. Marina, 2001, Philanthropist of Yr., 2001. Mem. NAFE, Nat. Assn. Univ. Women, Nat. Women's Polit. Caucus, VFW, Assn. U.S. Army, Alumni Assn. U.S. Army War Coll., WAC Found., Women in NATO, Am. Legion (post 694), Ft. Ord Alumni Assn. (adv. bd.), Girl Scouts of Monterey Bay (bd. dirs.), Cmty. Human Svcs. (bd. dirs.), Rotary Internat. (local chpt.), Monterey Rep. Women, Marina C. of C., Marina Bus. Assn., Marina Larger Libr. Com. Home: 3181 DeForest Rd Marina CA 93933 Office: City Hall City of Marina 211 Hillcrest Ave Marina CA 93933-3534 Office Phone: 831-884-1278.

METZ, MARY SEAWELL, retired foundation administrator, retired academic administrator; b. Rockhill, SC, May 7, 1937; d. Columbus Jackson and Mary (Dunlap) Seawell; m. F. Eugene Metz, Dec. 21, 1957; 1 dau., Mary Eugena. BA summa cum laude in French and English, Furman U., 1958; postgrad., Institut Phonetique, Paris, 1962-63, Sorbonne, 1962-63; PhD magna cum laude in French, La. State U., 1966; HHD (hon.), Furman U., 1984; LLD (hon.), Chapman Coll., 1985; DLT (hon.), Converse Coll., 1988. Instr. French La. State U., 1965-66, asst. prof., 1966-67, 1968-72, assoc. prof., 1972-76, dir. elem. and intermediate French programs, 1966-74, spl. asst. to chancellor, 1974-75, asst. to chancellor, 1975-76; prof. French Hood Coll., Frederick, Md., 1976-81, provost, dean acad. affairs, 1976-81; pres. Mills Coll., Oakland, Calif., 1981-90; dean of extension U. Calif., Berkeley, 1991-98; pres. S.H. Cowell Found., San Francisco, 1999—. Vis. asst. prof. U. Calif.-Berkeley, 1967-68; mem. commn. on leadership devel. Am. Coun. on Edn., 1981-90, adv. coun. Stanford Rsch. Inst., 1985-90, adv. coun. Grad. Sch. Bus., Stanford U.; bd. dirs. PG&E, AT&T, Inc., Union Bank, Longs Drug Stores. Author: Reflets du monde francais, 1971, 78, Cahier d'exercices: Reflets du monde francais, 1972, 78, (with Helstrom) Le Francais a decouvrir, 1972, 78, Le Francais a vivre, 1972, 78, Cahier d'exercices: Le Francais a vivre, 1972, 78; standardized tests; mem. editorial bd. Liberal Edn., 1982—. Trustee Am. Conservatory Theater. NDEA fellow, 1960-62, 1963-64; Fulbright fellow, 1962-63; Am. Council Edn. fellow, 1974-75 Mem. Western Coll. Assn. (v.p. 1982-84, pres. 1984-86), Assn. Ind. Calif. Colls. and Univs. (exec. com. 1982-90), Nat. Assn. Ind. Colls. and Univs. (govt. rels. adv. coun. 1982-85), So. Conf. Lang. Teaching (chmn. 1976-77), World Affairs Coun. No. Calif. (bd. dirs. 1984-93), Bus.-Higher Edn. Forum, Women's Forum West, Women's Coll. Coalition (exec. com. 1984-88), Phi Kappa Phi, Phi Beta Kappa. Address: PO Box 686 Stinson Beach CA 94970-0686 also: 9 Regulus Ct Alameda CA 94501-1015

METZ, PATRICIA A., retired bank executive; b. Portland, Oreg., Apr. 22, 1938; d. Frank K. Seely and Margaret L. Hosmer; m. Leroy Heinrichs, Dec. 10, 1957 (div. Dec. 1, 1959); 1 child, Kenneth N. Heinrichs; m. Dan Metz, Mar. 17, 1972 (dec. Jan. 2, 1976); 1 child, Daniel W. A, Dominican Coll., San Rafael, Calif., 1958. V.p. Wells Fargo Bank, NA, Medford, Oreg., 1968—2000. Dir. Rogue Valley Manor, Medford, 1988—2006, Access, Medford, 1994—2006; ct. apptd. spl. advocate for children CASA, Medford, 2006.

METZCAR, VIRGINIA JOYCE, social worker; b. Richmond, Ind., Feb. 5, 1947; d. John Edward and Norma Irene Hoch; m. Edward H. Metzcar, Oct. 2, 1965; children: Vincent, Alan, William, Anne, Aaron, Jeremiah, Jessica. BSW, St. Mary of Woods Coll., Terre Haute, Ind., 1992. Lic. social worker, cert. case mgr. Income maintenance worker Darke County Human Svcs., Greenville, Ohio, 1980—88; case mgr. Cath. Social Svcs., Sidney, Ohio, 1988—91; dir. social svcs. Brookhaven Retirement Cmty., Brookville, Ohio, 1991—92; med. social worker Maria Joseph Home Care, Dayton, Ohio, 1990—92; home care/hospice social worker Reid Hosp., Richmond, Ind., 1992—98, oncology social worker, 1998—2002; administrator Oakley House Assisted Living, Greenville, Ohio, 2002—03; dir. social svcs. Heartland of Greenville, 2003—. Facilitator Tools to Live with Cancer Support Group, Richmond, Ind., 2000—; bd. mem. Cancer Health Ministry, Richmond. Corr.: news column Greenville Daily Adv. Pres. Friends of Libr., New Madison, Ohio, 2000—02; v.p. Money Mgmt. Adv. Bd., Richmond, Ind., 2001—02; sec. Cancer Assn. Darke County, 2005; chairperson Nurses Seminar; bd. mem. Cancer Assn. Darke County, 2003—. Mem.: NASW, Ind. Oncology Social Workers, Assn. Oncology Social Workers. Roman Catholic. Avocations: cooking, needlecrafts, reading. Office: Heartland Greenville 243 Marion Dr Greenville OH 45331

METZER, PATRICIA ANN, lawyer; b. Phila., Mar. 10, 1941; d. Freeman Weeks and Evelyn (Heap) M.; m. Karl Hormann, June 30, 1980. BA with distinction, U. Pa., 1963, LLB cum laude, 1966. Bar: Mass. 1966, D.C. 1972, U.S. Tax Ct. 1988. Assoc., then ptnr. Mintz, Levin, Cohn, Glovsky and Popeo, Boston, 1966—75; assoc. tax legis. counsel U.S. Treasury Dept., Washington, 1975-78; shareholder, dir. Goulston & Storrs, P.C., Boston, 1978-98; stockholder Hutchins, Wheeler & Dittmar, P.C., Boston, 1998—2002; of counsel Vacovec, Mayotte & Singer LLP, Newton, Mass., 2003—. Lectr. program continuing legal edn. Boston Coll. Law Sch., Chestnut Hill, Mass., spring, 1974; lectr. grad. tax program Boston U. Law Sch., 2001—03; adv. com. NYU Inst. Fed. Taxation, NYC, 1981—87; practitioner liaison com. Mass. Dept. Revenue, 1985—90; spkr. in field. Author: Federal Income Taxation of Individuals, 1984; authors' panel Jour. Passthrough Entities, 2003—; mem. editl. bd. Am. Jour. Tax Policy, 1995-98; mem. adv. bd. Corp. Tax and Bus. Planning Rev., 1996—; contbr. articles to profl. jours., chpts. to books. Bd. mgrs. Barrington Ct. Condominium, Cambridge, Mass., 1985-86; bd. dirs. Univ. Rd. Parking Assn., Cambridge, 1988—; trustee Social Law Libr., Boston, 1989-93. Mem. ABA (tax sect., vice-chair publs. 2000-02, mem. coun. 1996-99, chair subcom. allocations and distbns. partnership com. 1978-82, vice-chair legis. 1991-93, chair 1993-95, com. govt. submissions, vice liaison 1993-94, liaison 1994-95, North Atlantic region, co-liaison 1995-96, N.E. region, regional liaison meetings com.), FBA (coun. on taxation, chmn. corp. taxation com. 1977-81, chair com. partnership taxation 1981-87), Mass. Bar Assn. (coun. taxation law sect. 2001-06, chair coun. taxation law sect. 2006—), Boston Bar Assn. (coun. 1987-89, chair tax sect. 1989-91, steering com. solo and small firm sect. 2005—), Am. Coll. Tax Counsel (bd. regents 1999-2004), Boston Estate Planning Coun. (exec. com. 1975, 79-82). Avocation: vocal performances (as soloist and with choral groups). Office: Vacovec Mayotte & Singer LLP Two Newton Pl Ste 340 255 Washington St Newton MA 02458-1634 Office Phone: 617-964-0500. Business E-Mail: pmetzer@vacovec.com.

METZGER, DELORES VIRGINIA, social services professional; b. Balt., Feb. 25, 1952; d. Arthur Willard and Delores Fredricka Maxwell; m. Albert Timothy Metzger, Apr. 15, 1972; children: Brian Timothy, Damien Phillip. AA degrees, Dundalk C.C., 1975, 89; BA, U. Balt., 1992; MSW, U. Md., 1994. Lic. social worker. Child support enforcement agt. Dept. Human Resources, Balt., 1983-85, adminstrv. reviewer Family Investment Adminstrn., 1985-87, asst. field supr., 1987-90, field supr., 1990-95, program mgr., 1995-96, mgmt. analyst, 1997-99, program analyst Social Svcs. Adminstrn., 1999—. Chair hospitality com. PTA High Point Elem. Sch., 1980-90; ch. vol. Our Daily Bread, Balt. Mem. Loyal Order of the Moose. Avocations: reading, bowling, contestant on wheel of fortune. Office: Dept Human Resources 311 W Saratoga St Baltimore MD 21201-3500

METZGER, EVELYN BORCHARD, artist; b. N.Y.C., June 8, 1911; d. Samuel and Eva (Rose) Borchard; m. H. A. Metzger, June 28, 1934 (dec. 1974); children: James Borchard, Edward Arthur, Eva Metzger Lanier. AB, Vassar Coll., 1932. One-woman shows include Galeria Muller, Buenos Aires, 1950, S.A.G. Gallery, N.Y.C., 1962, Gallerie Bellechasse, Paris, 1963, Vassar Coll. Art Gallery, Poughkeepsie, N.Y., 1963, Everhart Mus., Scranton, Pa., 1963, Frank Partridge Gallery, N.Y.C., 1964, Norfolk (Va.) Mus. Art, 1965, Van Diemen-Lilienfeld Gallery, N.Y., 1966, Columbus Mus., Ga., 1966, Ga. Mus. Fine Arts, Athens, Ga., 1966, Mex.-Am. Cultural Inst., Mexico City, 1967, Telfair Acad. Arts, Savannah, Ga., 1966, U. Maine, Orono, 1967, Slater Meml. Mus., Norwich, Conn., 1967, Albion (Mich.) Coll., 1969, Graham-Eches Sch., Palm Beach, Fla., 1970, Bartholet Gallery, N.Y.C., 1973, Arsenal Gallery, N.Y.C., 1983, Quogue Libr., N.Y., 1988, Nat. Mus. Women in the Arts, Washington 1997, 2002, Joan Whalen Gallery, N.Y.C., 1997, Cornell U., 1998, Washington County Mus. Fine Art, Hagerstown, Md., 1999, Curzen Gallery, Boca Raton, Fla., 2001, AnnNorton Sculpture Garden, Fla., 2001, Am. Norton Sculptur Gardens, West Palm Beach, Fla., 2001, Nat. Mus. Women in Arts, Washington, 2002; represented in permanent collections including Art in Embassies program, U.S. Dept. State. Mem. Artists Equity, Cosmopolitan Club. Avocation: travel. Home: 815 Park Ave New York NY 10021-3276

METZGER, JAMIE B., science educator; b. Troy, Ohio, Apr. 23, 1975; d. Keith E. and Carma Jo Kauffman; m. J. Scott Metzger, Aug. 21, 1999; 1 child, Dalton S. BS, Ohio State U., Columbus, 1998, Ohio U., 2005. Cert. tchr. integrated sci. Ohio, 2001. Precision agrl. specialist Premium Agrl. Commodities Inc., Washington Court Ho., Ohio, 1998—2001; sci. tchr. Chillicothe City Schs., 2001—. Mem.: Ohio Edn. Assn., Chillicothe Edn. Assn. Home: 7966 Williamsport Pk Williamsport OH 43164 Office: Chillicothe City Schs 421 Yoctangee Pkwy Chillicothe OH 45601 Office Phone: 740-702-2287. Personal E-mail: smetzger@bright.net.

METZGER, KATHLEEN ANN, computer systems specialist; b. Orchard Park, N.Y., Aug. 4, 1949; d. Charles Milton and Anna Irene (Matwijow) Wetherby; m. Robert George Metzger, Aug. 29, 1970 (div. June 1988). BS in Edn. cum laude, SUNY Coll., Buffalo, 1970; postgrad., SUNY, Fredonia, 1975. Cert. secondary tchr. Math. tchr. Crestwood High Sch., Mantua, Ohio, 1970-71; sec., bookkeeper Maple Bay Marina, Lakewood, NY, 1972; math., bus. tchr. Falconer (N.Y.) High Sch., 1972-76; bookkeeper Darling Jewelers, Lakewood, 1977-78; computer operator Ethan Allen Inc., Jamestown, NY, 1978-79, So. Tier Bldg. Trades, Jamestown, 1979; program analyst TRW Bearings Divsn., Inc., Jamestown, 1980-82; cons. Fla. Power Corp., St. Petersburg, 1982-2000; lead IT analyst Progress Energy, St. Petersburg, 2000—05; poll worker, instr. Pinellas County Elections Office, 2006—. Vol. Christmas Toy Shop. Mem. Assn. Info. Tech. Profls., St. Petersburg Second Time Arounders Marching Band Color Guard, Kappa Delta Pi. Republican. Roman Catholic. Avocations: travel, photography, boating, watching football and hockey, driving corvette. Home: 8701 Blind Pass Rd Apt 110 Saint Petersburg FL 33706-1463

METZKE, LINDA KUZAN, education educator; b. Dekalb, Ill., May 6, 1944; d. Frank R. and Mary Florence (McCabe) Kuzan; m. Frank M. Metzke, Aug. 16, 1967; children: Michell, Frank David, Mark. BS, U. Wis., Madison, 1966; MS, U. Wis., Whitewater, 1984; PhD, Marquette U., 1988. Cert. spl. edn. English tchr., Wis. Tchr. English Delavan-Darien High Sch. (Wis.), 1966-71; rsch. asst. U. Wis., Whitewater, 1982-84, rsch. assoc., 1987-88; learning disabilities tchr. North High Sch., Waukesha, Wis., 1984-87; asst. prof. Lyndon State Coll., Lyndonville, Vt., 1988—; co-dir. Northeast Kingdom Sch. Devel. Ctr., 2000—. Contbr. articles to profl. jours. Bd. mem. Area Agy. on Aging, St. Johnsbury, Vt., 1988-2000, Northeast Kingdom Mental Health, Newport, Vt., 1989—; trainer Girl Scouts USA, East Troy, Wis., 1972-82; leader La Leche League, Mukwonago, Wis., 1973-80; bd. mem. St. Peter's Sch. Com., East Troy, 1982-84. Mem. ASCD, Coun. for Exceptional Children, Internat. Soc. for Exploring Teaching Alternatives, Caledonia Essex Local Tchr. Standards Bd., Internat. Assn. for study of Cooperation in Edn., Phi Kappa Phi, Phi Delta Kappa, Pi Lambda Theta, Delta Kappa Gamma. Democrat. Roman Catholic. Avocation: gardening. Home: PO Box 58 Concord VT 05824 E-mail: linda.metzke@lyndonstate.edu.

METZKER, JULIA, chemistry professor; d. Gerald John Moberg and Mary Ann Bennett; m. Joseph Metzker, Oct. 11, 1998. PhD in Chemistry, U. Ariz., Tucson, 2001. Asst. prof. chemistry Ga. Coll. & State U., Milledgeville, 2004—. Mem. Haddock Cmty. Action Program, Ga., 2004—06; chair Ariz. State Green Party, Pheonix, 2000—01. Fellow, U. York, England, 2001—03. Mem.: Am. Chem. Soc. Avocation: crafts. Office: Georgia College & State University 231 W Hancock Street Milledgeville GA 31061 Office Phone: 478-445-5208.

METZLER, RUTH HORTON, genealogical educator; b. Eden, New York, Aug. 4, 1927; d. John Morris and Bernice Louise (Horton); m. Henry George Metzler, Sept. 4, 1948; children: Kathleen, Ronald, Janice, Margaret. Attended, Wheaton Coll., 1945-48; BA (hon.), Wilmington Coll., 1956; MLS, State Univ. of N.Y., Geneseo, 1962. Cert. tchr., libr. media specialist, N.Y. Cataloging typist Peoria Pub. Libr., Ill., 1949-52; cataloging asst. Wilmington Coll. Libr., Ohio, 1953-56; sch. libr. K-12 Nunda Ctrl. Sch., NY, 1956-65; head libr. media ctr. Irondequoit H.S., Rochester, NY, 1965-84; pres. Rochester Geneal. Soc., NY, 1989-93; instr., lectr. Rochester Mus. and Sci. Ctr., NY, 1990—. Author of several family histories. Organizing instr. Genealogy workshops, Rochester Mus. and Sci. Ctr; contbg. lectr. Nat. Geneal. Conf., Rochester, 1990; others. Mem. N.Y. Libr. Assn.,;N.Y. State Tchr. Retirement Sys.; New Eng. Hist. and Geneal. Soc.; Kodak Geneal. Soc., N.Y.; State Coun. of Geneal.; Genealogy Round Table of Monroe County (del. 1996—); Rochester Geneal. Soc.; Geneal. Educators (organizing mem. 1996). Republican. Baptist. Avocations: genealogy, writing.

MEYER, ALICE VIRGINIA, state official; b. NYC, Mar. 15, 1921; d. Martin G. and Marguerite Helene (Houzé) Kliemand; m. Theodore Harry Meyer, June 28, 1947; children: Robert Charles, John Edward. BA, Barnard Coll., 1941; MA, Columbia U., 1942; D of Humanitarian Svcs. (hon.), Briarwood Coll., 2006. Tchr. pub. schs., Elmont, N.Y., 1942-43; tchr. Fairlawn (N.J.) High Sch., 1943-47; office mgr., sales rep. N.Y.C., 1948-55; substitute tchr. Pub. Schs., Easton, Conn., 1965-72; state rep., asst. minority leader Conn. State Legislature, Hartford, 1976-93. Mem. Ct. Bd. of Govs. Higher Edn., 1993-05, vice-chair, chair. bd. govs. higher edn.; bd. dirs. 3030 Fairfield Health Ctr., 1994-06. Mem. Edn. Commn. of the States, 1985—87; life trustee Discovery Mus., 1980—; trustee United Way Regional Youth Substance Abuse Project, Bridgeport, 1983—93; mem. strategic planning com. Town of Easton, 1993—96; vice chmn. ct. adv. coun. on intergovtl. rels., 1988—; mem. Conn. Commn. on Quality Edn., 1992—93; supporter Conn. Small Towns, 1988; mem. Conn. Humanities Coun., 1974—76, Conn. Film Commn., 1985—88; co-chair Com. on State Plan of Conservation and Devel., 1985—87; mem. Lt. Gov.'s Commn. on Mandate Reduction, 1995; sec. Easton Free Sch. Scholarship Fund, 1980—; pres. Barnard Class of 1941, 1996—; justice of the peace, 2001—; ct. adv. coun. career and vocat. edn., 1980—88; mem. Easton Rep. Town Com., 1965—, vice chmn., 1970—78; bd. dirs. 3030 Park, 1993—2006; Fairfield County Lit. Coalition Bridgeport, 1988—94. Named Legislator of Yr. Conn. Libr. Assn., 1985; Guardian Small Bus. grantee Nat. Fedn. Ind. Bus., 1987; honoree Fairfield YWCA Salute to Women, 1988, Conn. Assn. Small Towns, 1990; named grant to AAUW Fellowship Fund, Bridgeport Br., 1970, Conn. State AAUW, 1974; recipient Conn. Friends of Libr. Hon. award, 1984, Disting. Svc. award Conn. State Coun. on Voc/Tech. Edn., 1986, Sacred Heart U. Ctr. for Policy Issues award, 1988, citation Conn. Bd. for Acad. Affairs, 1992, citation Charter Oak Coll., 1993, Spl. Day Recognition, Town of Weston, 1993, Cert. of Recognition, Town of Westport, 1993, Citation for Fostering Open Access to Higher Edn., AAUW, 1994, Disting. Rep. award Easton Rep. Town Com., 2000, Pub. Svc. award Conn. Sec. of State, 2003, others; named in her honor Alice U. Meyer Day, Conn., 2005; scholarship named in her honor, 2006. Mem.: LWV, AAUW (local pres. 1976, bd. dirs. 1982), Nat. Order Women Legislators (regional dir. 1987—91, past pres. Conn. chpt.), Conn. Assn. Sch. Adminstrs. (hon.), Bus. and Profl. Women. Congregationalist. Avocations: swimming, sailing, bridge. Home: 18 Lantern Hill Rd Easton CT 06612-2218

MEYER, ALICIA, special education educator; b. Massapequa, NY, 1961; d. Edmund and Kate (McHugh) Bembenek; m. Ronald Meyer, July 8, 1989. AA in Liberal Arts, Nassau C.C., Garden City, N.Y., 1981; BS in Elem. Edn., SUNY, Old Westbury, 1985; MA in Spl. Edn. magna cum laude, Hofstra U., 1987. Counselor Assn. for Children with Learning Disabilities, Westbury, N.Y., 1987-88; tchr. spl. edn. Bd. Coop. Ednl. Svcs. Nassau County, Massapequa, N.Y., 1987-89; tchr. early childhood learning disabled N.Y.C. Bd. Edn., S.I., 1989-92; fourth grade tchr. Prairie Sch., Racine, Wis., 2000—05. Mem. Coun. for Exceptional Children. Home: 4843 Hampton Ct Racine WI 53403-9429

MEYER, ANN JANE, human development educator; b. NYC, Mar. 11, 1942; d. Louis John and Theresa Meyer. BA, U. Mich., 1964; MA, U. Calif., Berkeley, 1967, PhD, 1971. Asst. prof. dept. human devel. Calif. State U., Hayward, 1972-77, assoc. prof., 1977-84, prof., 1984—. Mem. APA. Office: Calif State U Dept Human Devel Hayward CA 94542 Office Phone: 500-885-3076. Business E-Mail: ameyer@csuhayward.edu.

MEYER, BARBARA, psychologist; arrived in U.S., 1994; d. Ulrich Meyer and Gertrud Meyer-Waelli. AA in Bibl. Studies, Life Bible Coll., San Dimas, Calif., 1996; BA in Psychology magna cum laude, Azusa Pacific U., Calif., 1998; MA in Clin. Psychology, Calif. Sch. Profl. Psychology Alliant Internat. U., Alhambra, 2001, PhD in Clin. Psychology, 2003. Lic. psychologist Calif. Bd. Psychology, 2005. Relief counselor River Cmty., Azusa, Calif., 1999—2000; practicum trainee St. Francis Med. Ctr., Lynwood, 2000—01; internship trainee Las Encinas Hosp., Pasadena, 2001—02; predoctoral psychology intern Augustus F. Hawkins Cmty. Mental Health Ctr., L.A., 2002—03; psychologist and mental health therapist The Children's Collective Inc., 2002—04; Spanish speaking clin. psychologist LA County Dept. Mental Health, 2004—05; psychologist Calif. Hosp. Med. Ctr., 2005; clinician Casa Pacifica, 2005—. Adj. faculty Azusa Pacific U., 2002; grad. tchg. asst. Calif. Sch. Profl. Psychology Alliant Internat. U., Alhambra, 2000—01. Vol. paraprofl. counselor Pasadena Mental Health Ctr., Calif., 1998—99; vol. support group facilitator Internat. Child Abuse Network, Canoga Park, 1999—2000; vol. social skills group facilitator Hogar de Transito, Quito, Ecuador, 2001. Mem.: APA (assoc.), Ventura County Psychol. Assn., Sierra Club. Avocations: rock climbing, skiing, sailing, tennis, travel. Office: Casa Pacifica 1722 S Lewis Rd Camarillo CA 93012 Personal E-mail: barmeyer@hotmail.com. Business E-Mail: bmeyer@casapacifica.org.

MEYER, CAROL FRANCES, retired pediatrician, allergist; b. Berea, Ky., June 2, 1936; d. Harvey Kessler and Jessie Irene (Hamm) Meyer; m. Daniel Baker Cox, June 5, 1955 (div. Apr. 1962). AA, U. Fla., 1955; BA, Duke U., 1957; MD, Med. Coll. Ga., 1967. Diplomate Am. Bd. Pediatrics, Am. Bd. Allergy and Immunology. Intern in pediat. Med. Coll. Ga., Augusta, 1967-68; resident in pediat. Gorgas Hosp., Canal Zone, 1968-69; fellow in pediat. respiratory disease Med. Coll. Ga., 1969-71, instr. pediat., 1971-72; med. officer pediat. Canal Zone Govt., 1972-79, Dept. of Army, Panama, 1979-82, med. officer allergy, 1982-89, physician in charge allergy clinic, 1984-89; asst. prof. pediat. and medicine Med. Coll. Ga., Augusta, 1990-2000, med. dir. Telemedicine Ctr., 2000-01; ret. Mem. Bd. of Canal Zone Merit Sys. Examiners, 1976-79. Contbr. articles to profl. jours. Mem. First Bapt. Ch. Orch., 1992-2000; founding mem., violoncello Curundu Chamber Ensemble, 1979-89. Recipient U.S. Army Exceptional Performance awards, 1985, 86, 89, Merck award Med. Coll. Ga., 1967; U. Fla. J. Hillis Miller scholar, 1954. Mem.: Am. Lung Assn. (Ga. East Ctrl. br. exec. bd. 1990—98), Ga. Ornithol. Soc., Panama Canal Soc. Fla., Am. Acad. Pediat., Am. Acad. Allergy, Asthma and Immunology, Am. Coll. Allergy, Asthma and Immunology, Ga. Pediat. Soc., Hispanic-Am. Allergy and Immunology Assn., Allergy and Immunology Soc. Ga., Am. Coll. Rheumatology, Willow Run Homeowner's Assn. (pres. 1994—99), Augusta Audbubon Soc., Nat. Assn. Ret. Fed. Employees, Nature Conservancy, Am. Assn. Ret. Persons, Royal Soc. for Preservation Birds, Nat. Audubon Soc., Hawks Nest Village Assn. (1st v.p. 2000—01), Alpha Omega Alpha.

MEYER, CATHERINE DIEFFENBACH, lawyer; b. Seattle, Mar. 27, 1951; d. Patrick Andrew and Hope Dieffenbach; m. Michael E. Meyer, Nov. 21, 1982; children: AB, Bryn Mawr Coll., 1973; JD, Northwestern U., 1979. Bar: Calif. 1979, U.S. Dist. Ct. (cen. dist.) Calif., 1979, U.S. Ct. Appeals (9th cir.) 1982, U.S. Dist. Ct. (ea., no. and so. dists.) Calif. 1987. Assoc. Lillick, McHose & Charles, L.A., 1979-85, ptnr., 1985-88, Lillick & McHose, L.A., 1988-90, Pillsbury Madison & Sutro, L.A., 1990—2001, Pillsbury Winthrop LLP, L.A., 2001—05; past co-chmn. Privacy & Data Protection practice, co-chmn. LA Bus. dept. Pillsbury Winthrop Shaw Pittman LLP, L.A., 2005—, counsel, 2005—. Bd. dirs. House Ear Inst. Mem.: ABA (past co-chmn. Extraterritorial Application of Law subcommittee), LA County Bar Assn. Office: Pillsbury Winthrop Shaw Pittman Suite 2800 725 S Figueroa St Los Angeles CA 90017 Office Phone: 213-488-7362. Office Fax: 213-629-1033. Business E-Mail: catherine.meyer@pillsburylaw.com.

MEYER, CHERYL LORRAINE, music educator; b. Camp Breckenridge, Ky., Feb. 10, 1953; d. Stanley O. and Arliss L. Boyum; m. Jon C. Meyer, Aug. 1973; children: Sarah, Erik. MusB, U. Wis., Madison, 1975. Elem. music specialist Sch. Dist. 102 of La Grange, La Grange Park, Ill., 1975—76, Sch. Dist. 92 1/2, Westchester, Ill., 1976—77, Appleton (Wis.) Area Sch. Dist., 1985—. Conductor Lawrence Arts Acad. Girl Choir, Appleton, 1992—. Named Appleton Elem. Educator of Yr., Mielke Found., 2001. Mem.: Wis Choral Dirs. Assn., Am. Choral Dirs. Assn., Music Educators Nat. Conf. Office: Jefferson Elem Sch 1000 S Mason St Appleton WI 54914 Office Phone: 920-832-6260.

MEYER, DARLA ANNE, accountant; b. Dallas, Tex., Sept. 24, 1964; d. Charles Robert and Carol Jean Smith; m. Tim Martin Meyer, May 26, 1984; children: Robert Terry, Paul Michael. BBA in Acctg., Computer Sci., Math summa cum laude, U. Tex.-Tyler, 1994. CPA Tex. Bd. Accountancy, 2003. Teller Plains Nat. Bank, Lubbock, Tex., 1984—86; computer operator Moody Nat. Bank, Galveston, Tex., 1990—92; Citizens Nat. Bank, Crockett, Tex., 2000—01; acct. Bonner, Bolton, Sullivan, & Taylor, LLP, Palestine, Tex., 2002—. Mem. Houston County Career Women, Crockett, 1998—2002, Houston County Rep. Women, Crockett, 1995—2005; treas. Christian Women Assn., Crockett, 1996—2000, Grace Bible Ch., Grapeland, Tex., 1997—2002, East Tex. Tres Dias, Grapeland, 2004—. Recipient Rookie of Yr., Houston County Career Women, 1999. Mem.: Tex. Soc. CPAs, AICPA. Conservative. Protestant. Avocations: reading, travel, church activities, puzzles. Home: RR 5 Box 611 Crockett TX 75835 Office: Bonner Bolton Sullivan & Taylor LLP 1023 N Mallard Palestine TX 75802 Office Phone: 903-729-2229. Business E-Mail: dmeyer@bbstcpa.com.

MEYER, DEBORA LYNN, music educator; d. Ronald James and Lorraine Gott; m. Marcus Joseph Meyer, Dec. 20, 1986. BA in K-12 vocal music edn. and vocal performance, Carthage Coll., Kenosha, Wis., 1976; MME in Music Edn., Holy Names Coll., Oakland, Calif., 1990. Cert. Kodaly Orgn. of Am. Kodaly Educators. Pvt. music instr. voice, piano, organ, and guitar, Kenosha and Milwaukee Counties, Wis., 1969—87; profl. vocalist Kenosha, Racine, Milw., Waukesha and Winnebago counties, Wis., 1970—; vocal music specialist K-8, dir. of music St. George Sch. and Ch., Kenosha, Wis., 1976—82; vocal music specialist K-8 St. Stephen Sch., Milw., 1982—87; vocal music specialist K-6, choral dir. Banting Sch. Sch. Dist. Waukesha, Wis., 1987—; clinician music listening, singing sci., children's choral pedagogy Orgn. of Am. Kodaly Educators, Wis. Choral Dirs., Wis. Sci. Tchrs., 1990—. Music mentor acad. decathlon - music mentor Waukesha West H.S., 2001—. Bldg. chairperson campaign United Way of Waukesha County, 2001—05. Recipient Kohl Tchr. Fellowship award, Sen. Herb Kohl, 1998. Mem.: NEA (assoc.), Am. Orff-Schulwerk Assn. (assoc.), Midwest Kodaly Music Educators Assn. (assoc.), Orgn. Am. Kodaly Educators (assoc.; regional rep. mid-west 1 1993—95), Wis. Choral Dirs. Assn. (assoc.; state chair Singing in Wis. and Children's Conv. Choir 1991—94, state chair Conv. Children's Honor Choir 1991—94, rep. Southeastern dist. 1992—94), Am. Choral Dirs. Assn. (assoc.), Nat. Assn. Tchrs. of Singing (assoc.), Wis. Music Educators Assn. (assoc.), Edn. Assn. of Waukesha (assoc.; bldg. union rep. 2000—, NEA del. to nat. assembly in New Orleans 2003), Music Educators Nat. Conf. (assoc.), Sigma Alpha Iota (assoc.). Office: Banting Elem Sch 2019 Butler Dr Waukesha WI 53186-2634 Office Phone: 262-970-1250. Personal E-mail: musicmeyer@wi.rr.com. E-mail: dmeyer@waukesha.k12.wi.us.

MEYER, DONNA W., medical educator, director; b. Louisville, Ky., Feb. 8, 1953; d. Alexander J. and Teresita Russ Walker; children: Michelle, Shari. BS, U. Ky., Lexington, 1975; MS, Tex. A&M U., Corpus Christi, 1997. Cert. MT ASCP, tchr., supr. Tex. With St. Joseph's Hosp., Lexington, Ky.; rsch. asst. U. Ky., Lexington; med. technologist Ctrl. Bapt. Hosp., Lexington; tchr. Silva Health Magnet H.S., El Paso, Tex.; health sci. program specialist Tex. Edn. Agy., Austin; tchr. McNeil H.S., Austin; edn. coord. MD Anderson Cancer Ctr., U. Tex., Smithville. Mem. adv. bd. ACC-Biotechnology, Austin, Tex.; nat. bd. HOSA; legislative and policy com. ACTE-HOE, Washington. Author: (state sci. course) Scientific Research and Design, 1996. Recipient Tchr. of Yr. award, EPISD, 1998—99. Mem.: ASCD, ILS, NASSP, ASCP. Roman Catholic. Avocations: gardening, photography, travel. Home: 8301 Pilgrims Pl Austin TX 78759 Office: Univ Tex MD Anderson Cancer Ctr 1808 Park Rd 1C Smithville TX 78957 Office Phone: 512-237-9377. E-mail: donnawmeyer@earthlink.net.

MEYER, DOROTHY VIRGINIA, retired education educator; b. Boston, Apr. 15, 1930; d. Arnold S. and Hilda M. (Cann) M. BA, Houghton (N.Y.) Coll., 1952; MEd, Boston U., 1959, EdD, 1976. Tchr. Wellesley Pub. Schs., Mass., 1954-69; dir. edn. Cambridge Model Cities, Mass., 1969-71, dir. program ops., 1971-73; asst. prof. Newton Coll., Mass., 1973-75, Grad. Sch. Edn. U. Mass.-Lowell, Mass., 1975-79, assoc. prof. and coord. Ctr. Adminstrn., Planning and Policy Mass., 1979—99, chmn. faculty Edn., 1983, 84-88, prof. emerita, 2000. Bd. dirs. Mass. Coun. Pub. Schs., 1963-66, Mass. Coun. Tchr. Edn., 1964-66; mem. adv. com. U.S. Office Edn. Nat. Tchr. Corps, 1970-72, panel cons.'s Ednl. Personnel Devel. Div., 1967-69, Mass. Bi-Lingual Adv. Bd., 1971-75. Contbr. articles to ednl. jours. Bd. dirs. Bishop Guetrin High Sch., Nashua, N.H., 1987-93, Commn. on Ministry to Higher Edn. Mass. Episc. Diocese, 1983-90. Mem. NEA (commr. nat. commn. tchr. edn. and profl. standards 1966-70, chmn. 1968-69, bd. dirs. Ctr. for Study Instrn. 1967-71, co-editor publ., 1980), Mass. Soc. Profs., Mass. Tchrs. Assn. (bd. dirs. 1957-67, exec. com. 1963-67, v.p. 1962-65, pres. 1965-66), Nat. Assn. State Edn. Assns. (exec. com. 1965-67, v.p. 1967-68), Internat. Soc. Ednl. Planning, Nat. Coun. Accreditation Tchr. Edn. (mem. coordinating bd. 1968-70, mem. evaluation bd. 1971-74) Home: 43 Linnaean St Cambridge MA 02138-1544 Business E-Mail: dorothy_Meyer@uml.edu.

MEYER, ELLEN L., academic administrator; BA and MS Geo Wash U. Vp for mktg and exten, dean of cont studies and dir of exten prog and summer sch Minneapolis College of Art and Design; dir of cont ed and spec prog RI Sch of Design; pres. Atlanta Coll. Art, 1992—. Mem.: National Black Arts Festival Bd of Dir, Metro Atlanta Arts Fund Adv Bd, vice chair, bd of dir, Atl Reg Consortium for Higher Ed. Achievements include 1992-93 graduate, Midtown Leadership Program, Atlanta; 1994 graduate, Leadership-Atlanta. Office: Atlanta Coll Art 1280 Peachtree St NE Atlanta GA 30309-3502

MEYER, FRANCES MARGARET ANTHONY, educational consultant; b. Stella, Va., Nov. 15, 1947; d. Arthur Abner Jr. and Emmie Adeline (Murray) Anthony; m. Stephen Leroy Meyer, Aug. 2, 1975. BS, Longwood Coll., 1970; MS, Va. Commonwealth U., 1982, PhD, 1996. Cert. tchr. Va. Tchr, health, phys. edn., and dance Fredericksburg City Pub. Schs., Va., 1970—89; coord. AIDS edn. Va. Dept. Edn., Richmond, 1989—90, specialist health edn., 1990—94, specialist comprehensive sch. health program, 1994—2003; ednl. cons. Fredericksburg, Va., 2003—. Mem. rev. bd. Nat. Commn. for Health Edn. and Credentialing, Inc., conf. and profl. devel. rev., 1996-2000. Author, editor: Dance Education, What is it? Why is it important?, 2002; author (with others): Elementary Physical Education: Growing through Movement-A Curriculum Guide, 1982; contbr. articles to profl. jours. Dir. Va. Children's Dance Festival, 1981—96, 1997—99; vol. ARC, Fredericksburg, 1976—84, 1997—2001, Va. affiliate AHA, 1982—93, 1999—2001; mem. ctrl. steering com. Health, Mental Health and Safety in Schs. Nat. Guidelines Project, Am. Acad. Pediat., 2000—02; Va. Affiliate Am. Cancer Soc. Richmond, Va.; mem. Public Health Edn.Coun., Comprehensive Sch. Health Edn. Team, Va. Alliance Adolescents and Sch. Health, 1990—2004; health com. Va. Healthy Pathways Coalition, 2004—; mem. Am. Heart Assn., 2004—; bd. dirs. Va. HIV/AIDS Network ARC, 1997—2001. Recipient gov.'s medal for substance abuse and prevention edn. State of Va., 1997, Alumni Cmty. Svc. award Va. Commonwealth U., 1998, Youth Edn. award for Leadership in the healthy devel. of children Am. Cancer Soc., 2002, Disting. Leadership in Phys. Edn. award Nat. Assn. Sport and Phys. Edn., 2004, Profls. Who Make A Difference award Coll. Edn. & Human Svcs., Longwood U., 2006; Nat. Pub. Health Leadership Inst. fellow, 2000; Va. Coordinated Sch. Health Leadership fellow, 2006. Fellow: N.Am. Soc. Health, Phys. Edn., Recreation, Sport and Dance (hon.); mem.: AAPHERD (chmn. divsn. 1970—, chmn. so. dist. applied strategic planning com. 2002—04, pres. so. dist. 2005—, past v.p., strategic planning com., social justice com., nominating com., pres.'s recognition award 1997, svc. award 1997, nat. honor award 1999), ASCD, AAUW (com. 1989—90, 1995—), NEA, Dance Edn. Orgn. (charter), Va. Assn. for Health, Phys. Edn., Recreation and Dance (various coms. 1970—, health edn. editor Va. Jour. 1994—2003, past pres., Tchr. of Yr. 1983, Va. Honor award 1988, Va. Pioneer award 2003), Va. Alliance for Arts Edn. (adv. bd. 1980—83, 1989—90, 1994—96), Am. Coll. Health Assn. (curriculum and tng. rev. panel 1992—94), Soc. State Dirs. Health, Phys. Edn. and Recreation (legis. affairs com. 1994—98, applied strategic planning com. 1994—2001, pres.-elect 1997, pres. 1998, past pres. 1999, think tank chair 2000—02, Healthis acad. rev. com. 2001—03, applied policy & legis. com. 2002—, Presdl. award 1996, Presdl. Recognition award 1997, 2000, Simon A. McNeely Honor award 2000, Julian B. Smith award 2004), Va. Health Promotion and Edn. Coun. (bd. dirs. 1990—96), Internat. Coun. for Health, Phys. Edn., Recreation, Sport and Dance (internat. commns. for health edn. and commn. for dance and dance edn., jour. articles rev. com.), Va. Mid. Sch. Assn., Va. Edn. Assn., Nat. Mid. Sch. Assn., Nat. Dance Assn. (bd. dirs., pres. 2001—03, Presdl. citation 1998, svc. award 1998, 2000, Pres.'s Merit award 2001), Nat. Network for Youth Svcs. (adv. bd. 1994—98, rev. panel), Longwood Coll. Alumni Coun. (bd. dirs. 1987—90), Delta Kappa Gamma (pres. Beta Eta chpt. 1988—90). Baptist. Avocations: travel, dance, swimming, reading, theatrical performances.

MEYER, FREMONTA LEE, psychiatrist; b. Toledo, Aug. 10, 1979; d. Richard John and Mary Bell Meyer. BA in Chemistry and German Studies, Dartmouth Coll., Hanover, N.H., 2000; MD, Dartmouth Coll., Lebanon, NH, 2004. Resident Cambridge (Mass.) Health Alliance, 2004—. Mem. instl. rev. bd. Cambridge Health Alliance, 2005—. Recipient Excellence in Neurology award, Am. Acad. Neurology, 2004, Glasgow-Rubin Achievement citation, Am. Med. Women's Assn., 2004; Rolf F. Syvertson scholar, Dartmouth Med. Sch., 2004. Mem.: Phi Beta Kappa, Alpha Omega Alpha. Avocations: violin, hiking, exercise. Home: 11 Park Dr #31 Boston MA 02215 Personal E-mail: fertinator@hotmail.com.

MEYER, GAIL BARRY, retired real estate broker; b. Athens, Ga., Oct. 13, 1940; d. John Carlton and Addie Lorene (Harris) Barry; m. Leo Marcus Meyer Jr., July 2, 1960; Rand Marcus, Brian Kevin, Kelli Paige Cert., Grad. Realtors Inst., 1979. Cert. residential specialist, rape counselor. Assoc. broker, owner So. Realty, Statesboro, Ga., 1977—80; assoc. broker Zetterower-Olliff Realty, Statesboro, 1980—84, Century 21, Johnny Cobb Realty, Statesboro, 1984—99. Pres., v.p., treas. Citizens Against Crime, Statesboro, 1990—; pres. Victim Witness Assistance Program, Statesboro, 1990—; mem. Georgians for Victims Justice, Parents and Childrens Counsel, 1998-2004 Recipient Deen Day Smith award C. of C. and Statesboro Herald News, 1989 Mem.: AAUW, MADD, NOW (pres. 1980—, v.p., treas.). Roman Catholic. Avocation: reading. Home: 274 Parkway Dr Athens GA 30606-4950 E-mail: gail586@charter.net.

MEYER, HELEN M., state supreme court justice; BSW, U. Minn.; JD, William Mitchell Coll. Law. Ptnr. Pritzker & Meyer, 1987—96, Meyer and Assocs., 1996—2002; assoc. justice Minn. Supreme Ct., St. Paul, 2002—. Office: Minn Jud Ctr 25 Rev Dr Martin Luther King Jr Blv Saint Paul MN 55155

MEYER, JANIS M., lawyer; b. NYC, Apr. 29, 1947; BA, SUNY, Stony Brook, 1969; MA, Ohio State Univ., 1971; JD with distinction, Hofstra Univ., 1981. Bar: N.Y. 1982, US Dist. Ct. (ea. & so. dist. N.Y., no. dist. Ill.), US Ct. Appeals (2d, 7th, 9th cir.). Law clerk, Judge George C. Pratt, US Dist. Ct. ea. N.Y. & US Ct. Appeals, 2d cir.; ptnr. litigation & diversity affairs Dewey Ballantine LLP, N.Y.C., 1995—. Contbr. chapters to books. Bd. trustees Hofstra Univ., 1993—, vice chmn., 1996—99, 2002—. Mem.: ABA (vice chmn. Internat. Litigation com. 1993—94), Assn. Bar City of N.Y. Office: Dewey Ballantine LLP 1301 Ave of the Americas New York NY 10019-6092 Office Phone: 212-259-6030. Office Fax: 212-259-6333. Business E-Mail: jmeyer@dbllp.com.

MEYER, JUDY L., science educator, director; BS in Zoology, U. Mich.; MS in Zoology, U. Hawaii; PhD in Ecology, Cornell U. Co-dir. River Basin Sci. and Policy Ctr., Athens, Ga.; Disting. Rsch. prof. Inst. Ecology U. Ga. Mem. com. Nat. Acad. Scis./NRC; mem. Improving Nat. Water Quality Assessment Program USGS; elected U.S. nat. rep. Internat. Assn. Theoretical and Applied Limnology; chair sci. and tech. adv. com., bd. dirs. Am. Rivers; chair edn. and sci. adv. com., bd. dirs. Upper Chattahoochee Riverkeeper; bd. dirs. Ga. Land Trust Svc. Ctr. Recipient Creative Rsch. medal, U. Ga. Rsch. Foun.; grantee, NSF, EPA, U.S. Dept. Agr., U.S. Dept. Energy, U.S. Forest Svc., U.S. Geol. Survey, U.S. Fish and Wildlife Svc., Ga. Dept. Natural Resources, Turner Found. Fellow: AAAS; mem.: Nat. Coun. Sci. Soc. Pres. (exec. com.), Ecol. Soc. Am. (v.p., pres.). Office: River Basin Sci and Policy Ctr 201 N Milledge Ave Athens GA 30602-5482

MEYER, KATHERINE ANNE, lawyer; BA, Manhattanville Coll., 1973; JD, Columbus Sch. Law, Cath. U. Am., 1976. Bar: DC, Md. With Swankin & Turner, 1976—77, Ctr. for Auto Safety, 1977—79, Pub. Citizen Litigation Group, 1979—89, Harmon, Curran, Gallagher & Spielberg, 1989—93; ptnr. Meyer Glitzenstein & Crystal, Washington, 1993—. Chmn. litigation com. Defenders of Wildlife; adj. prof. law Georgetown U. Law Ctr. (Civil Litigation and Pub. Interest Advocacy), 1986—92; bd. dir. Defenders of Wildlife, Ctr. for Auto Safety, Wildlife Advocacy Project; with DC Cir. Advisory Com. Procedures, 1995—2001; bd. dirs. Ctr. Biol. Diversity. Named one of Best 75 Lawyers in Washington, Washingtonian Mag., 2002. Office: Mayer Glitzenstein & Crystal 1601 Connecticut Ave NW Ste 700 Washington DC 20009-1056 Office Phone: 202-588-5206. Office Fax: 202-588-5049.

MEYER, LINDSAY BEARDSWORTH, lawyer; b. Bridgeport, Conn., Apr. 11, 1961; Student, Universite de Rouen, France, 1982; BS cum laude, Univ. Conn., 1983; JD, George Washington Univ., 1987. Bar: Va. 1987, DC 1988; lic. US Customs Svc. Broker. Assoc. Venable, Baetjer, Howard & Civiletti LLP (now Venable LLP), Washington; ptnr., adv., mktg., new media, homeland security practice areas Venable LLP, Washington, and head, internat. trade practice group. Mem. Md.-Washington Dist. Export Coun. Mem.: ABA (chair, internat. trade and customs com.), DC Bar Assn., Va. Bar Assn., Am. Assn. Exporters and Importers, Beta Gamma Sigma. Office: Venable LLP 575 Seventh St NW Washington DC 20004 Office Phone: 202-344-4829. Office Fax: 202-344-8300. Business E-Mail: lbmeyer@venable.com.

MEYER, LISA MARIE, elementary school educator; b. Livonia, Mich., Nov. 15, 1961; d. James Theo and Dolores Lola Bishop; m. John Melville Meyer, May 22, 1982; children: Jessica Ellen, Brittany Allyssa. AA, Henry Ford C.C., Dearborn, Mich., 1981; B in Music Edn., Ea. Mich. U., 1987; M in Elem. Edn., Wayne State U., 1991. Cert. tchr. music edn., elem. edn. Mich. Elem. music tchr. Detroit Pub. Schs., 1987—89; music tchr. Dearborn Pub. Schs., 1989—95, music resource tchr., 1995—. Adj. instr. William Tyndale Coll., Farmington Hills, Mich., 1986—; cons. Ideas, LLC, West Norwalk, Conn., 2000—; mem. adv. bd. Ward Pre-Sch., Northville, Mich., 1987—90. Named one of Best 100 for Music Edn. in Am., Music Tchr. Nat. Assn., 2001; recipient Named one of Best of 100 for Music Edn. in Am., 2002. Mem.: Mich. Music Educator Assn. (Outstanding Adminstr. award 2001, 2002), Am. Orff Schulwerk Assn., Nat. Assn. Music Edn. Avocations: singing, camping, hiking. Home: 43069 Devon Ln Canton MI 48187 Office: Dearborn Pub Schs 18700 Audette Dearborn MI 48124 E-mail: meyerl@dearborn.k12.mi.us.

MEYER, LYNN NIX, lawyer; b. Vinita, Okla., Aug. 10, 1948; d. William Armour and Joan Ross Nix; children: Veronica, Victoria, David. BA, Baldwin Wallace Coll., 1978; JD, Case Western Res. U., 1981. Bar: Ky. 1982, Colo. 1984. Paralegal Texaco Devel., Austin, Tex., 1976-77; legal asst. Alcan Aluminum, Cleve., 1977-79; assoc. Wyatt, Tarrant & Combs, Lexington, Ky., 1982-83; ptnr. Meyer, Meyer & Assocs., P.C., Denver, 1984-85; gen. counsel Carbon Fuels Corp., 1985-95; in pvt. practice Denver, 1996-97; asst. gen. counsel products Gambro, Inc. (now Gambro BCT), Lakewood, Colo., 1997—. Mem. ABA, Colo. Bar Assn., Ky. Bar Assn., Arapahoe County Bar Assn. Home: 10487 E Ida Ave Englewood CO 80111-3746 Office: Gambro BCT 10810 W Collins Ave Lakewood CO 80215-4439 E-mail: lynn.meyer@gambrobct.com.

MEYER, MADELINE ANNA, librarian; b. Great Bend, Kans., Mar. 26, 1948; d. George Albert and Anna Millicent (Noel) M. Student, Cambridge U., Eng., 1967-68; BA, Valparaiso U., 1970; MA, U. Denver, 1981. Libr. Denver Pub. Library, 1971-76; lease records mgr. Vantage Cos., Dallas, 1976-77; libr. Lytham-St. Annes Coll., St. Annes-on-Sea, Lancashire, Eng., 1977-78; lease records asst. J. Grynberg & Assocs., Denver, 1978-79; travel cons. Free Spirit Travel, Aurora, Colo., 1979-82; libr. Aurora Pub. Library, 1982-83; customer svc. rep. Western Air Lines, Denver, 1983-85; libr. Mesa (Ariz.) Pub. Library, 1985-87, Scottsdale (Ariz.) Pub. Library, 1987—. Dep. registrar Election Com., Phoenix, 1985—. Mem. Ariz. State Library Assn., Nat. Mgmt. Assn., Cen. Ariz. Tall Soc. Democrat. Lutheran. Avocation: travel. Office: Scottsdale Pub Libr 3839 N Civic Center Blvd Scottsdale AZ 85251-4405

MEYER, MARA ELLICE, special education educator, consultant, academic administrator; b. Chgo., Oct. 28, 1952; d. David and Harriett (Lazar) Einhorn; m. Leonard X. Meyer, July 20, 1986; children: Hayley Rebecca, David Joseph. BS in Speech and Hearing Sci., U. Ill., 1974, MS in Speech and Lang. Pathology, 1975, postgrad. in pub. policy PhD program, 1990—. Cert. speech and lang. pathologist, spl. edn. tchr., reading tchr. Speech and lang. pathologist Macon-Piatt Spl. Edn. Dist., Decatur, Ill., 1975-76; speech and lang. pathologist, reading specialist, learning disabilities coord. Community Consolidated Sch. Dist. # 59, Arlington Heights, Ill., 1976-87; test cons. Psychol. Corp., San Antonio, 1987-89; adj. prof. Nat.-Louis U., Evanston, Ill., 1985-87, 2003—; ednl. cons. The Psychol. Corp., 1987-89, Am. Guidance Svc., Circle Pines, Minn., 1989-94; pvt. practice ednl. cons. Deerfield, Ill., 1994—; prin. edn. cons. Ill. Bd. Edn., 2004—06. Project dir. Riverside Pub. Co., Chgo., 1993-94; mem. adv. coun. to Headstart, Dept. Human Svsc., City of Chgo., 1990-99; cons. Spl. Edn. Dist. of Lake County, 1995—, Waukegan (Ill.) Pub. Schs., 1997; cons. Lake Zurich Pub. Schs., 1996-98; asst. prin., inclusion coord. Mundelein (Ill.) Sch. Dist., 1999-2001; spl. edn. adminstr. Wilmette Schs., 2001-2003; spl. cons. Avoca Sch. Dist. 37, Wilmette, Ill., 2003—; prin. cons. Ill. State Bd. Edn., 2004—06. Area coord. Dem. Party, Lake County, Ill., 1978—; pres. Park West Condo Assn., Lake County, 1983-88. Mem. NEA, ASCD, Nat. Assn. Elem. Prins., Nat. Family Partnership Network, Am. Speech-Lang. and Hearing Assn., Ill. Speech-Lang. and Hearing Assn., Ill. Prins. Assn., Internat. Reading Assn., Coun. on Exceptional Children. Avocations: swimming official, leisure reading, technical reading. Home: 1540 Central Ave Deerfield IL 60015-3963 Office Phone: 847-431-0767. Personal E-mail: maraemeyer@comcast.net. Business E-Mail: mara.meyer@nl.edu.

MEYER, MARGARET ELEANOR, retired microbiologist; b. Westwood, Calif., Feb. 8, 1923; d. Herman Henry and Eleanor (Dobson) M. BS, U. Calif., Berkeley, 1945; PhD, U. Calif., Davis, 1961. Pub. health analyst USPHS, Bethesda, Md., 1945-46; swine Brucellosis control agt. Dept. Agr., Davis, 1946-47; bacteriologist U. Calif., Davis, 1947-61; research microbiologist U. Calif. (Sch. Vet. Medicine), 1961-77, prof. vet. pub. health and microbiologist exptl. sta., 1977—; rsch. microbiologist U. Calif. Med. Sch., L.A., 1961-77; supr. Brucella identifications lab. WHO, U. Calif., Davis, 1964—87, prof. vet. pub. health, 1973—87, dir. program in preventive vet. medicine, 1987; ret., 1987. Cons. subcom. on Brucella Internat. Com. Bacterial Taxonomy, 1962—, mem., 1966—; mem. 5th Pan Am. Congress Veterinary Medicine, Venezuela, 1966; mem. Internat. Congress Microbiology, Moscow, 1966, Mexico City, 1970, Munich, Ger., 1978, mem., officer, Eng., 1986; mem. Internat. Conf. Culture Collections, Tokyo, 1968; mem. adv. com. to Bergey's Manual Determative Bacteriology, 1967; cons. in resident Pan Am. Health Orgn., Zoonoses Lab., Buenos Aires, 1968; mem. brucellosis tech. adv. com. U.S. Animal Health Assn., 1977; FAO cons. on brucellosis control in dairy animals, Tripoli, Libya, 1981, mem. 3d internat. brucellosis symposium, Algiers, 1983; cons. Alaska Dept. Fish and Game, 1976, FAO, Libya, 1981, Bering Straits Reindeer Herders Assn., Nome, Alaska, 1981; invited speaker Internat. Symposium on Advances in Brucellosis Rsch., Tex. A&M U., 1989, Internat. Bison Conf.; resident cons. on brucellosis control in sheep and goats Am. Near East Refugee Aid, East Jerusalem, 1989; cons. on brucellosis in Yellowstone Nat. Pk., Nat. Pk. Svc., 1991—; invited mem. nat. symposium on brucellosis in the Greater Yellowstone Area, Jackson Hole, Wyo., 1994; cons. on brucellosis control in livestock for Armenia, 1994—. Contbr. articles to profl. jours. Bd. dirs. Carmichael Park and Recreation Dist., Calif., 1975; mem. Sacramento County Grand Jury, 1999-2000. Recipient Research Career Devel. award USPHS-NIH, 1963 Fellow Am. Pub. Health Assn., Am. Acad. Microbiology; mem. Soc. Am. Microbiologists, N.Am. Conf. Animal Disease Research Workers, Am. Coll. Vet. Microbiologists (hon. affiliate), U.S. Animal Health Assn. (chmn. brucellosis tech. advisory com. 1978-79), Internat. Assn. Microbiol. Socs. (mem. 1st intersect. congress 1974), AAUW, No. Calif. Women's Golf Assn., U. Calif. Alumni Assn., Sigma Xi. Clubs: U. Calif. Faculty (Davis); El Dorado Royal Country (Shingle Springs, Calif.); Reno Women's Golf. Home: 5611 Fair Oaks Blvd Carmichael CA 95608-5503 Office: U Calif Sch Vet Medicine Dept Epidemiology & Preventive Medicine Davis CA 95616

MEYER, MARGARET VAUGHAN, librarian, educator; b. Phila., Mar. 13, 1919; d. Clifford and Fannie (Lehman) Vaughan; m. Donald Robert Meyer, Sept. 3, 1949 (dec. Mar. 2002); children: Karen, Frederick E., Julie Meyer; m. Arnoldo Ramos, 1985; 3 children; m. Shelly Brogden, 2000. BEd, UCLA, 1942; MLS, U. So. Calif., 1967. Elem. tchr. Indio Sch. Dist., Indio, Calif., 1942-43, Lawndale Sch. Dist., Lawndale, Calif., 1943-44, L.A. Unified Schs., 1946-53; program libr. City of Pasadena Libr., Pasadena, Calif., 1965-85. Co-author (Spanish-English): Centeno Collection-Annotated, 1977; author (biog. and notes, 2 CDs): Clifford Vaughan classical music. Organizer, chmn. libr. com. PTA, L.A., 1961—64, hon. life mem., 1964; vol. Com. Solidarity People of El Salvadore, L.A., 1985—97; mem. Citizens Com. Save Elysian Park, L.A., 1987—, L.A. County Mus. Art, 1986—2003, Friends of Pasadena Pub. Libr., 1986—, Food Bank, Washington, 2004—. Mem.: ALA (del. 1967—80), L.A. Pub. Libr., Libr. Found. (charter mem.), Calif. Libr. Assn., Am. Fedn. Tchrs. (exec. bd. L.A. chpt.), Denishawn Repertory Dancers (hon. bd. dirs.), Sierra Club. Avocations: music, reading, swimming, gardening, games. Home: 1525 Upshur-NW Washington DC 20011

MEYER, NORMA, secondary school educator; b. Cambria, Wis., Sept. 16, 1944; d. Willard Vander Galien and Jessie Stiemsma; m. Thomas Jay Vander Galien, June 4, 1966; children: Christopher Jon, Matthew Galien, Melissa Beth Adams. Masters, U. Denver, Colo., 1998. Cert. tchr. Colo., 1986. Tchr. Edmonson Jr. H.S., Willow Run, Colo., 1966—69, Emily Griffith H.S., Denver, 1986—. Sunday sch. tchr., worship com., social justice com. Third Christian Ref. Ch., Denver, 1974—2005. Mem.: Nat. Coun. for Social Studies. Independent. Reformed. Avocations: travel, reading, photography, exercise, hiking. Office: Emily Griffith HS 1250 Welton St Denver CO 80204 Office Phone: 720-423-4757.

MEYER, PATRICIA HANES, social worker; b. Champaign, Ill., Feb. 10, 1947; d. Walter Ernest and Mary Kathryn (Kemp) Hanes; m. Scott Kimbrough Meyer, June 15, 1969; children: Jennifer Suzanne, Claire Catherine, John Andrew. BA, Carroll Coll., Waukesha, Wis., 1969; MSW, Cath. U. Am., 1976. Dir. family therapy program Fairfax County Juvenile Ct., Fairfax, Va., 1970-77; clin. instr. Georgetown U. Med. Sch., Washington, 1976-84; pvt. practice family therapy Reston, Va., 1976—. Adv. editor The Family, 1977-84, The Journey to Solid Self Series, 2000-. Office: 11800 Sunrise Valley Dr Ste 312 Reston VA 20191-5302 Office Phone: 703-715-2202. Business E-Mail: phm@phmlcsw.com.

MEYER, PAULA JEAN, music educator; b. Lawton, Okla., Aug. 19, 1954; d. Donald Ellsworth and Truda Faye Hines; m. Jefferson Allen Meyer, May 8, 1976; children: Matthew Allen, Melissa Ann. MusB in Edn., U. Ctrl. Okla., Edmond, 1976. Cert. K-12 music tchr. Okla., 1976. Tchr. voice, piano, Edmond and Norman, Okla., 1974—90; tchr. gifted and talented Norman Pub. Schs., Irving Mid. Sch., Okla., 1978—81; tchr. music Moore Pub. Schs., Houchin Elem. Sch., Okla., 1990—; ch. pianist/organist Emmaus Bapt. Ch., Oklahoma City, 1996—. Musician for weddings, funerals, soloists, Edmond, Norman, Moore, and Oklahoma City, Okla., 1972—; dir. children's choirs 1st Bapt. Ch., Moore, Okla., dir. women's ensemble. Author children's mus. Christmas play; writer - arranger (voice parts for women's trio). Mem. Moore H.S. Touchdown Club, Okla., 1997—2000; rehearsal condr. Moore All-City Elem. Honor Choir, Okla., 2000—06. Mem.: Moore Elem. Music Orgn., Houchin PTA. Southern Baptist. Avocations: dog lover, cross-stitch, embroidery. Personal E-mail: jmeyer52@cox.net.

MEYER, PEARL, compensation executive consultant; b. NYC; d. Allen Charles and Rose Weissman; m. Ira A. Meyer. BA cum laude, NYU, postgrad. Statis. specialist, exec. comp. div. Gen. Foods Corp., White Plains, NY; exec. v.p. and cons. Handy Assocs., Inc., N.Y.C., NY; founder, chair Pearl Meyer & Ptnrs., N.Y.C., NY, 1989—. Lectr. exec. compensation confs. and seminars. Contbr. articles to profl. jours. Recipient Woman of Achievement award, Women Bus. Owners NY, Legal Momentum Aiming High award, 2003. Mem.: Pers. Accreditation Inst., Women's Econ. Roundtable, Soc. Human Resources Mgmt. (cert. accredited pers. diplomate), WorldatWork, Am. Mgmt. Assn., Women's Forum, Sky Club, Sedgewood Club, Phi Beta Kappa, Beta Gamma Sigma, Pi Mu Epsilon. Office: Pearl Meyer & Ptnrs 445 Park Ave New York NY 10022-2606

MEYER, PRISCILLA ANN, literature and language professor; b. Aug. 26, 1942; d. Herbert Edward and Marjorie Rose (Wolff) M.; m. William L. Trousdale, Sept. 15, 1974; 1 dau., Rachel V. BA, U. Calif., Berkeley, 1964; MA, Princeton U., 1966; PhD, 1971. Lectr. in Russian lang. and lit. Wesleyan U., Middletown, Conn., 1968-71, asst. prof., 1971-75, assoc. prof., 1975-88, prof., 1988—. Vis. asst. prof. Yale U., 1973, adv. coun. dept. Slavic lang. and lit. Princeton U., 1998-2002. Co-editor: Dostoevsky and Gogol, 1979; editor: Life in Windy Weather (by Andrei Bitov), 1986, author: Find What the Sailor Has Hidden: Vladimir Nabokov's Pale Fire, 1988; co-editor: Essays on Gogol: Logos and the Russian Word, 1992, Nabokov's World, 2001, Yuz! Essays on the Occasion of the 75th Birthday of Yuz Aleshkovsky, 2005; translator stories; mem. editl. bd. Slavic and East European Jour., 1999—; contbr. articles to profl. jours. Scholar Internat. Rsch. and Exch. Bd., 1973; grantee Ford Found., 1964-68, 70; hon. vis. fellow Sch. Slavonic and East European Studies London U., 1997, 2001. Mem. Am. Coun. Tchrs. Russian (dir. 1983-86), Am. Assn. Tchrs. Slavic and East European Studies, Internat. Vladimir Nabokov Soc. (v.p. 1983-85, 2002-04, pres. 1985-87, 2004-06), Tolstoi Soc., Dostoevsky Soc., Conn. Acad. Arts and Scis. Office: Russian Dept Wesleyan U Middletown CT 06459-0001 Office Phone: 860-685-3127. E-mail: pmeyer@wesleyan.edu.

MEYER, PUCCI, editor; b. NYC, Sept. 1, 1944; d. Charles Albert and Lollo (Offer) M.; m. Michael V. McGill, Oct. 28, 2001. BA, U. Wis., 1966. Asst. editor Look mag., N.Y.C., 1970-71, editorial asst. Paris, 1967-69; reporter Newsday, Garden City, L.I., NY, 1971-73; style editor N.Y. Daily News Sunday Mag., N.Y.C., 1974-76, assoc. editor, 1977-82, editor, 1983-86; sr. editor Prodigy, White Plains, NY, 1987; spl. projects editor N.Y. Post, N.Y.C., 1988-89, style editor, 1990-92, food editor, 1992-93, assoc. features editor, 1993—94, travel editor, 1994—2004. Contbr. articles to various nat. mags. Recipient Pulitzer prize as mem. Newsday investigative team that wrote articles and book The Heroin Trail, 1973.

MEYER, RACHEL ABIJAH, foundation administrator, artist, poet; b. Job's Corners, Pa., Aug. 18, 1963; d. Jacob Owen and Velma Ruth (Foreman) M.; children: Andrew Carson, Peter Franklin. Student, Lebanon Valley Coll. Restaurant owner Purcy's Place, Ono, Pa.; restaurant mgr. King's Table Buffet, Citrus Heights, Calif.; product finalizer TransWorld Enterprises, Blaine, Wash.; dir., support svcs. adminstr. Tacticar Found., Sacramento, 1991—; tchr. Tacticar Inst., 1995; chair Coniremis, Sacramento, 1996—. Author: Year of the Unicorn, 1994. Avocations: researching, writing, painting. Personal E-mail: ihopinsac@yahoo.com.

MEYER, ROBERTA, mediator, communication consultant; b. San Francisco, July 27, 1936; d. Theodore Robert and Virginia (Organ) Meyer; m. G. William Sheldon; children: Megan McDougall Radeski, Deborah Ann Guerra. Student, U. Utah, 1974. Cert. mediator. Founder, pres., exec. dir. Roberta Meyer Communication Cons., Inc., San Francisco, 1977—. Presenter numerous workshops in alcoholism and communication; nat. spkr. Nat. Found. Alcoholism Comm.; keynote spkr. Calif. Women's Comm. Alcoholism, 1981; mem. adv. bd. Soviet Am. Alliance Alcoholism and Other Addictions; founder Youth Dance Experience, 1999. Author: (book) Facts About Booze and Other Drugs, 1980, The Parent Connection: How to Communicate with Your Child about Alcohol and Other Drugs, 1984, Listen to the Heart, 1989, (screenplays) Understanding Addition, 1988, Better Relationships Through Effective Communication, 1991; numerous radio and TV appearances; dir.: Meyer Method Dance Program for ballroom dancers, One Meyer Method Dance Training Video, 1998. Mem. adv. bd. Marin Svcs. Women, 1980; vol. Calif. Pacific Med. Ctr., San Francisco Ballet Aux.; mem. N.Y.C. and San Francisco Ballet Cos., 1950—56, San Francisco Ballet Sch., 1956—65; founder, dir. Ballet Arts San Francisco, 1965—78, San Francisco Ballroom Dance Theatre and the accelerated dance programs, 1994—. Named 56th Point of Light, Pres. Bush, 1990; recipient award, Optimists Club. Mem.: Childrens Theatre Assn., Nat. Coun. Alcoholism and Drug Dependence Calif. (pres. 1988—91), San Francisco Womens Rehab. Assn. (pres. 1975—76, dir., founder Youth Dance Project 1999), Nat. Coun. Alcoholism (co-chmn. pub. info. com. 1985—, v.p. Bay area 1988—, bd. dirs. Teen Kick Off 1987—, Alcoholism and Drug Rsch. Comm. Ctr. 1990—, pres. 1988—, creator, cons. youth aware program 1974—), Nat. Collaborative Planning and Cmty. Svc. (cert.), San Francisco C. of C. Address: 2625 Alcatraz Ave #283 Berkeley CA 94705-2702

MEYER, RUTH KRUEGER, museum director, educator, art historian; b. Chicago Heights, Ill., Aug. 20, 1940; d. Harold Rohe and Ruth Halbert (Bateman) Krueger; m. Kenneth R. Meyer, June 15, 1963 (div. 1978); 1 child, Karl Augustus. BFA, U. Cin., 1963; MA, Brown U., Providence, 1968; PhD, U. Minn., 1980. Lectr. Walker Art Ctr., Mpls., 1970—72; instr. U. Cin., 1973—75; curator Contemporary Arts Ctr., Cin., 1976—80; dir. Ohio Found. Arts, Columbus, 1980—83, Taft Mus., Cin., 1983—93; prof. Miyazaki (Japan) Internat. Coll., 1994—2001; sr. curator Solway Gallery, Cin., 2003—05; prof. Art Acad. Cin., 2002—. Adj. prof. The Union Inst., Cin., 1994. Pub. Dialogue Mag., Columbus, 1980-83; author: (exhbn. catalogues) Sandy Rosen Vestal Vases, 1986, Oblique Illusion: An Installation by Rick Paul, 1986, David Black an American Sculptor, 1985, Brad Davis: The Pines, 1984, The American Weigh, 1983, New Epiphanies, 1982, (with others) The Tafts Collection: The First Ten Years of Its Development, 1988, The Tafts of Pike St., 1988, (exhbn. catalogue) The History of Travel: Paintings by William Wegman, 1985-90, 1990, The Artist Face to Face: Two Centuries of Self-Portraits from the Paris Collection of Gerald Shurr, 1989, Tributes to the Tafts, 1991, The Taft Museum: Its Collection and Its History, 1995; (with Madeleine Fidell-Beaufort) Collecting in the Gilded Age: Art Patronage in Pittsburgh, 1997, Water de Gruyter BErlin, 2000, others; contbr. articles to profl. jours. Recipient Rsch. award Kress Found., 1967, 76; named Chevalier in the Order of Arts and Letters, Govt. of France, 1989. Mem. Internat. Assn. Art Critics, Coll. Art Assn. Democrat. Office Phone: 513-621-0069. Business E-Mail: ruth@solwaygallery.com. E-mail: ruthkmeyer@yahoo.com.

MEYER, SUSAN MOON, speech pathologist, educator; b. Hazleton, Pa., Mar. 8, 1949; d. Robert A. and Jane W. (Walters) Moon; m. John C. Meyer Jr., Feb. 16, 1989; children: Chris, Scott. BS, Pa. State U., 1971, MS, 1972; PhD, Temple U., 1983. Cert. tchr., Pa. Speech-lang. pathologist, instr. Elmira (N.Y.) Coll., 1973-74; speech-lang. pathologist Arnot-Ogden Hosp., Elmira, 1973-74; supr. Sacred Heart Hosp. Speech and Hearing Ctr., Allentown, Pa., 1974-75; speech-lang. pathology instr. Kutztown (Pa.) U., 1975-78, asst. prof., 1978-82, assoc. prof., 1982-85, prof., 1985—. Owner Speech and Lang. Svcs., Allentown, 1975-87; cons. Vis. Nurses Assn., Allentown, 1975-85, Home Care, Allentown, 1975-85. Author: Survival Guide for the Speech-Language Clinician, 1998, 2004. Mem. Am. Speech-Lang.-Hearing Assn. (cert., councilor 1986-89, numerous Continuing Edn. awards), Pa. Speech-Lang.-Hearing Assn. (cert., v.p. profl. preparation 1985-89, Appreciation award 1987-89, 2001), Northea. Speech and Hearing Assn. Pa. (pres. 1984-86, Outstanding Dedication award 1985, Honors of the Assn. award 1999), Coun. Suprs. Speech-Lang. Pathology and Audiology. Avocations: cross country skiing, reading, water gardening. Office: Kutztown U Dept Speech-Lang Kutztown PA 19530 Office Phone: 610-683-4297. Business E-Mail: smeyer@kutztown.edu.

MEYER, URSULA, retired library director; b. Nov. 6, 1927; came to U.S., 1941; d. Herman S. and Gertrud (Rosenfeld) M. BA, UCLA, 1949; MLS, U. So. Calif., 1953; postgrad., U. Wis., 1969. Librarian Butte County (Calif.) Libr., 1961-68; asst. pub. librs. divsn. libr. devel. N.Y. State Libr., Albany, 1969-72; coord. Mountain Valley Coop. Sys., Sacramento, Calif., 1972-73; chmn. 49-99 Coop. Libr. Sys., Stockton, Calif., 1974-85; dir. libr. svcs. Stockton-San Joaquin County Pub. Libr., 1974-94. Active Freedom to Read Found. Higher Edn. Title II fellow, 1968-69. Mem. ALA (council 1979-83, chmn. nominating com. 1982-83, legis. com. 1985-87), AAUW, LWV, Calif. Libr. Assn. (pres. 1978, council 1974-82), Am. Assn. Pub. Adminstrs., Sierra Club, Common Cause, Rotary, Soroptimists.

MEYER, VIRGINIA MAURINE, music educator; b. Longview, Tex., Nov. 15, 1954; d. Eugene Victor and Genevieve (Mayberry) Ericson; m. Philip F. Brodersen (div.); children: Christian Brodersen, Robert Brodersen, Paul Brodersen, Bethany Brodersen; m. James Dale Meyer, June 28, 1997; 1 child, Andy. B Music Edn. cum laude, No. Ariz. U.; MA, Tulsa U. Cert. tchr. Ariz., Calif., Vt., Okla. Vocal music dir. Skiatook (Okla.) Pub. Schs., 2002—05, Chelsea Pub. Schs., 1994—2002; vocal performance tchr., adj. faculty mem. Colo. Christian U., Denver, 1983—90; pvt. voice tchr. Ariz., Colo. and Okla., 1983—2005; music tchr. Terra Bella, Calif., 1981—82, Concord, Waterford and Gilman, Vt., 1980; choral and gen. music tchr. Flagstaff (Ariz.) Pub.

Schs., 1977—79. Actor: Tulsa Gilbert & Sullivan Soc., 1994—95. Solo and choral performer First Bapt. Ch., Claremore, 1995—2005. Scholar, No. Ariz. U., Tulsa U. Mem.: NEA, Am. Choral Dirs. Assn., Okla. Music Edn. Assn., Okla. Edn. Assn., Music Educators Nat. Conf., NE Choral Dirs. Assn. (pres. 2005). Republican. Avocations: handwork, horseback riding, motorcycling. Home: 15650 Red Rock Ranch Rd Claremore OK 74017 Office: Siatook Pub Schs 355 S Osage Skiatook OK 74070 E-mail: gingermeyer@earthlink.net.

MEYERINK, VICTORIA PAIGE, film producer, actress; b. Santa Barbara, Calif., Dec. 27, 1960; d. William Joseph Meyerink and Jeanne Baird; m. Lawrence David Foldes, Apr. 24, 1983. Student, U. So. Calif., 1978-80. Actress, 1962—; v.p. Star Cinema Prodn. Group, Inc., 1981-85; pres. Star Entertainment Group, Inc., L.A., 1985—. Mem. faculty Internat. Film & TV Workshops, 1991—; lectr. colls. & film festivals. Prodr. (motion pictures) The Great Skycopter Rescue, 1982, Young Warriors, 1984, Night Force, 1987, Prima Donnas, 1996, Finding Home, 2004; actress (TV series) The Danny Kaye Show, Green Acres, My Three Sons, Family Affair, The FBI, Adam 12, (motion pictures) Speedway, Night of The Grizzly, Seconds, Brainstorm, The Littlest Hobo, (TV spl.) It Isn't Easy Being a Teenage Millionairess, numerous commls. Recipient Mayoral Proclamation for Outstanding Achievement, City of L.A., Cert. of Recognition for 25 Yrs. Outstanding Contbns. to the Entertainment Industry, City of L.A., Outstanding Achievement award Acad. Family Films & TV. Mem. Acad. Motion Picture Arts & Scis. (exec. com. Student Acad. Awards 1996—), L.A. Film Tchrs. Assn. Avocations: languages, travel, music, scuba diving, gourmet cooking.

MEYERS, ABBEY S., foundation administrator; b. Bklyn., Apr. 11, 1944; m. Jerrold B. Meyers, Oct. 23, 1966; children: David, Adam, Laura. AAS, N.Y.C. Community Coll., 1962; LHD (hon.), Alfred U., 1994. Comml. artist various advt. agys., N.Y.C., 1962-65; dir. patient svcs. Tourette Syndrome Assn., Bayside, NY, 1980-85; exec. dir., founder Nat. Org. for Rare Disorders, Danbury, Conn., 1985—, pres. U.S. commr. Nat. Commn. on Orphan Diseases, Washington, 1986-89; subcom. human gene therapy NIH, Bethesda, Md., 1989-92, recombinant DNA adv. com., 1992-96; mem. Health Care Payor Adv. Commn. on Conn. Commn. on Hosps. and Health Care, 1992-94; mem. FDA Biol. Response Modifiers Com., 1995-99; DHHS Nat. Human Rsch. Protection Adv. Com., 2000-2002; Partnership for Human Rsch. Protection Pub. Adv. Coun., 2005—. Author: (with others) Orphan Drugs and Orphan Diseases: Clinical Reality and Public Policy, 1983, (with others) Cooperative Approaches to Research and Development of Orphan Drugs, 1985, (with others) Tourette Syndrome: Clinical Understanding and Treatment, 1988, (with others) Physicians Guide to Rare Diseases, 1992. Bd. dirs. Nat. Orphan Drug and Device Found., N.Y.C., 1982-85; leader Coalition to Pass Orphan Drug Act of 1983, 1979-82. Recipient Pub. Health Svc. award HHS, 1985, Commr.'s Spl. citation FDA, 1988. Mem. Nat. Health Coun. (bd. dirs. 1989-94), Alliance of Genetic Support Groups (bd. dirs. 1987-89), European Orgn. for Rare Disorders (hon. pres. 1997—). Avocations: reading, horseback riding. Office: Nat Orgn for Rare Disorders PO Box 1968 Danbury CT 06813-1968 E-mail: orphan@rarediseases.org.

MEYERS, AMY, museum director; m. Jack Meyers; 1 child, Rachel. BA, U. Chgo.; PhD in Am. Studies, Yale U. Rschr. Dumbarton Oaks; rschr. Ctr. for Advanced Study in Visual Arts, Nat. Gallery; curator Am. Art, Henry E. Huntington Libr., Art Collections and Bot. Gardens, San Marino, Calif.; dir. Yale Ctr. for Brit. Art; prof. art Yale U. Adj. faculty Calif. Inst. Tech.; vice chair, Huntington rep. Assn. Rsch. Insts. in History of Art, 1995—2000. Editor (with Margaret Pritchard): Empire's Nature: Mark Catesby's New World Vision; editor: (with Alan Trachtenberg) Classic Essays on Photography. Office: Yale Ctr for Brit Art PO Box 208280 1080 Chapel St New Haven CT 06520-8280

MEYERS, CAROLYN WINSTEAD, academic administrator, mechanical engineer, educator; b. Hampton, Va., May 11, 1946; d. John Selner and Eva Carroll (Tonsler) Winstead; divorced; m. James E. Cofield, Jr.; children: Timothy C. III, Leslie C., Lisa A.; m. James E. Cofield, Jr. BSME, Howard U., 1968; MSME, Ga. Inst. Tech., 1979, PhD in Metallurgy, 1984. Steam generator analyst Machinery Apparatus Operation div. Machinery Apparatus Ops. div. GE, Schenectady, 1968; systems analyst Info. Svcs. div. Info. Svcs. div. GE, Bethesda, Md., 1969; instr. Atlanta U. Ctr. Corp., 1972-77; instr. mech. engring. Ga. Inst. Tech., Atlanta, 1979-84, asst. prof., 1984-90, assoc. prof., 1990-96; dir. SUCCEED Coalition Ctr. for Profl. Success, 1992-93; assoc. dean rsch. Coll. Engring. Ga. Inst. Tech., Atlanta, 1993-96; dean Coll. Engring. NC A&T State U., Greensboro, 1996, prof. mech. engring., 1996—2006, vice chancellor acad. affairs, 2000—06, provost, 2001—06; pres. Norfolk State U., Va., 2006—. Summer faculty fellow USAF Materials Lab., Wright-Patterson AFB, Ohio, 1988; program officer NSF, 1996-99. Contbr. articles to profl. jours. Chmn. waste volume reduction subcom. Atlanta Mayor's Commn. on Solid Waste Disposal, 1989-92; trustee Westminster Schs., Atlanta, 1989-93; program dir. divsn. undergrad edn. NSF, 1997-99, divsn. human resources devel., Arlington, V., 1999—; bd. dirs. Piedmont Triad Coun. Internat. Visitors, N.C. Sch. Sci. and Math, 2000-, Moses Cone Health Sys., 2003-, United Way Greater Greensboro, 2002-03, Rsch. Triangle Inst., MentorNet; chair, bd. dirs. Nat. Inst. Aerospace, 2003—. Recipient Faculty award for women NSF, 1991, Disting. Alumni award Atlanta-Howard U. Alumni Assn., 1992; named Black Engr. of Yr. in Higher Edn. U.S. Black Engr. Mag. and Coun. Engring Deans, 1990; Pres. Young Investigator grantee NSF, 1988; inducted to Acad. of Disting. Engring. Alumni Ga. Tech. U., 1996; honored alumna in edn. on Charter Day Howard U., 1997. Fellow ASME (Engr. of Yr. 1990); mem. AIME, SAE (Ralph Teetor Ednl. award 1986), Am. Soc. Engr. Edn. (v.p. pub. affairs 2001-2003), Foundry Ednl. Found. (key prof. 1985-95), Soc. Women Engrs. (state pres. Atlanta sect. 1987-90), Am. Foundrymen's Soc. (sponsor student sect. 1987-95, aluminum divsn. sci. merit award 1994), Soc. Black Engrs. (Golden Torch award 2002, Emerald honors Women in Sci and Tech. 2003), Links (pres. Atlanta chpt. 1987-89), Jack and Jill Am., The Girl Friends, Golden Key, Sigma Xi, Tau Beta Pi, Phi Kappa Phi, Alpha Kappa Alpha, Beta Gamma Sigma. Roman Catholic. Office: Office of Pres Norfolk State U 700 Park Ave Norfolk VA 23504 E-mail: president@nsu.edu.

MEYERS, CHRISTINE LAINE, marketing and media executive, consultant; b. Detroit, Mar. 7, 1946; d. Ernest Robert and Eva Elizabeth (Laine) M.; 1 child, Kathryn Laine; m. Oliver S. Moore III, May 12, 1990. BA, U. Mich., 1968. Editor indsl. rels. diesel divsn. Gen. Motors Corp., Detroit, 1968; nat. advt. mgr. J.L. Hudson Co., Detroit, 1969-76, mgr. internal sales promotion, 1972-73, dir. pub., 1973-76; nat. advt. mgr. Pontiac Motor divsn., Mich., 1976-78; pres., owner Laine Meyers Mktg. Cos., Inc., Troy, Mich., 1978—; founder, owner CORP! Mag., 1998—. Dir. Internat. Inst. Met. Detroit, Inc. Contbr. articles to profl. publs. Bus. adv. coun. Ctrl. Mich. U., 1977-79; pub. adv. com. on jud. candidates Oakland County Bar Assn.; adv. bd. Birmingham Cmty. Hosp., Bank of Am., 1999-2001; bd. dirs. YMCA, Mich., 1992-98, Haven, 1997—, Automation Alley, Oakland County, 1999—. Named Mich. Ad Woman of Yr., 1976, one of Top 10 Working Women, Glamour mag., 1978, one of 100 Best and Brightest Advt. Age, 1987, one of Mich.'s top 25 female bus. owners Nat. Assn. Women Bus. Owners, One of Top 10 Women Owned Bus., Mich., 1994; recipient Vanguard award Women in Comm., 1986, Lifetime Achievement award Northwood U., 2002. Mem. Internat. Assn. Bus. Communicators, Adcraft Club, Women's Advt. Club (1st v.p. 1975), Women's Econ. Club (pres. 1976-77), Internat. Women's Forum Mich. (founding pres. 1986-97), Internat. Inst. Detroit (bd. dirs. 1986-89), Detroit C. of C., Troy C. of C., Mortar Bd., Quill and Scroll, Pub. Rels. Com. Women for United Found., Founders Soc. Detroit Inst. Arts, Fashion Group, Pub. Rels. Soc. Am., First Soc. Detroit (exec. com. 1970-71), Kappa Tau Alpha. Home: 5165 Longmeadow Rd Bloomfield Hills MI 48304-3657 Office: Laine Meyers Mktg Cos Inc 3645 Crooks Rd Troy MI 48084-1642 Office Phone: 248-458-2677 ext.301. Business E-Mail: cmyers@corpmagazine.com.

MEYERS, DALE (MRS. MARIO COOPER), artist; b. Chgo. d. Walter Herman and Gertude (Pettee) Wetterer; m. Mario Cooper, Oct. 11, 1964; children: Dale, Steven R. Student, Glendale Coll., Corcoran Gallery Sch. Art, Washington, 1962-63, Art Student's League, N.Y.C., 1964-78. Instr. Art Students League, 1979—; ofcl. artist NASA, USCG.; lectr. Parson's Sch. Design, Nat. Acad. Sch. Author The Sketchbook, 1983; contbr.: Watercolor Bold and Free, Am. Artist mag, Diversion mag.; solo exhbns. include, West Wing Gallery, Ringwood (N.J.) State Park, 1970, Manor Club, Pelham Manor, N.Y., 1970, Apollo Art Gallery, Oklahoma City, 1972, Quadrangle Gallery, Dallas, 1972, Galveston Ctr. for Arts, 1974, Fla. Gulf Coast Art Ctr., 1977, 86, Okura Hotel, Tokyo, Japan, 1977, Owensboro Mus. Art, 1983, Salmagundi Club, 1986, 88, Stehle-Reed Gallery, Midland, Tex., 1987, others; artist-in-residence, Galveston Arts Ctr., 1974, Owensboro Mus. Art, 1983, Asilomar, Calif., 1983, 84; group exhbns. include Two Hundred Years of Watercolor Painting in Am. Met. Mus. Art, 1966, Eyewitness to Space, Nat. Gallery Art, Washington, 1969, Smithsonian Instn., 1961-63, Corcoran Gallery, 1963, Museo de la Acuarela, Mexico City, 1968, 89, London (Ont., Can.) Mus. Art, 1971-72, Art Gallery Hamilton, Ont., Can., 1971-72, Ont. Inst. Edn., 1971-72, Butler Inst. Art, 1962—, Frye Mus., 1962—; represented in permanent collections, Calif. Palace of Legion of Honor, San Francisco, Nat. Acad. N.Y.C., Avon Fine Arts Collection, NASA, EPA, Museo de la Acuarela, Schumacher Gallery, Columbus, Ohio, Slater Mus., Conn., Portland (Maine) Mus., U. Utah Fine Arts Collection, Frye Mus., Seattle, Owensboro Mus. Art, Coll. Misericordia, Dallas, Pa, Canton Art Inst., Ohio, Arnot Mus., Elmira, N.Y.; internat. watercolor exhbn. Can., U.S., Gt. Britain, 1991-94, Chung Cheng Gallery, Taipei, 1994. Recipient Henry W. Ranger award Nat. Acad. Design, 1968, Samuel F.B. Morse medal, 1973, Anna Hyatt Huntington Bronze medal, 1971, Knickerbocker Artists Gold medal, 1981, 88, Allied Artists Am. award, 1969, Gold medal honor Nat. Arts Club, 1972, Anna Hyatt Huntington Gold medal, 1974, Adolf and Cara Obrig award Nat. Acad., 1974, 81, Walter Biggs award, 1976, Allied Arts Gold medal, 1978, Audubon ARtists Silver medal, 1984. Fellow Royal Soc. Arts (Grumbocher Gold medals 1988, 90); mem. Am. Watercolor Soc. (pres. 1993-03, pres. emeritus 2003-, editor jours. 1962-79, Bronze medal honor award 1968, awards 1970, 72, 78, 79, 81, 82, 83, 85, 87, 89, 93, 98, High Winds medal 2001, 05, Dolphin medal 2000), Nat. Acad. (academician), Allied Artists Am. (pres. 1975-78), Art Students League N.Y., La. Watercolor Soc. (hon.), Ky. Watercolor Soc., Ohio Watercolor Soc. (hon.), Watercolor Soc. Mex., Fla. Watercolor Soc. (hon.), Audubon Artists, Salimagundi Club (medal of honor 1994). Office: Art Students League 215 W 57th St New York NY 10019

MEYERS, ELSIE FLINT, anesthesiologist; b. Wolcottville, Ind., Oct. 9, 1922; d. Truman Sutton and Birdena (Healey) Flint; m. Robert Weigel Meyers, Mar. 1, 1951; children: Linda Ann Ginzer, Deborah Ellen, Cynthia Ruth. AB, Ind. U., Bloomington, 1947; MD, Ind. U. Sch. Medicine, 1950. Rotating intern U. Pa. Hosp., Phila., 1950—51, resident anesthesiology, 1951—52, Jewish Hosp. St. Louis, 1970—71; fellow Anesthesiology Children's Hosp. Phila., 1971; ret., 1971. From instr. to prof. Anesthesiology Washington U., St. Louis. Recipient award, Alpha Omega Alpha, 1950. Mem.: Am. Soc. Anesthesiologists (life). Avocations: travel, music, quilting.

MEYERS, JAN, retired congresswoman; b. Lincoln, Nebr., July 20, 1928; m. Louis Meyers; children: Valerie, Philip AA in Fine Arts cum laude, William Woods Coll., 1948; BA in Communications (hon.), U. Nebr.-Lincoln, 1951; LittD, William Woods Coll., 1986; LLD (hon.), Baker U., 1993. Mem. Overland Park (Kans.) City Coun., 1967-72; pres. Overland (Kans.) Park City Council; mem. Kans. Senate, 1972-84, chmn. pub. health and welfare com., local govt. com.; mem. 99th-103rd Congresses from 3rd Kans. Dist., 1985-97, mem. com. internat. rels., chmn. sml. bus. com., mem. com. on econ. and ednl. opportunities. Chmn. pub. health and welfare com., chmn. local govt. com., vice chmn. transp. com., vice chmn. utilities com. Kans. Senate. 3rd Dist. co-chmn. Bob Dole for U.S. Senate, 1968; chmn. Johnson County Bob Bennett For Gov., 1974; mem. Johnson County Cmty. Coll. Found.; bd. dirs. Johnson County Mental Health Assn.; mem. fundraising com. Johnson County Am. Cancer Soc.; mem. com. for Ctr. for Aging, Kans. U. Med. Ctr.; bd. dirs. Johnson County Libr. Assn. Recipient Outstanding Elected Ofcl. of Yr. award Assn. Cmty. Mental Health Ctrs. Kans., Woman of Achievement Matrix award Women in Communications, Disting. Service award Bus. and Profl. Women Kansas City, William Woods Alumna award of distinction, Cmty. Svc. award Jr. League Kansas City, 1st Disting. Legislator award Kans. Assn. C.C.s, Outstanding Svc. award Kans. Library Assn., United Community Services, Kans. Pub. Health Assn., award Gov.'s Conf. Child Abuse and Neglect, Outstanding Legislator award Kans. Action for Children, Friend award Nat. Assn. County Park and Recreation Ofcls., 1987, Disting. Alumna award, 1991, Spirit of Enterprise award U.S. C. of C., Guardian of Small Bus. award Nat. Fedn. Ind. Bus. Mem. LWV (past pres. Shawnee Mission) Methodist.

MEYERS, KAREN DIANE, lawyer, educator; b. Cin., July 8, 1950; d. Willard Paul and Camille Jeannette (Schutte) M.; m. William J. Jones, Mar. 27, 1978. BA summa cum laude, Thomas More Coll., 1971; MBA, MEd, Xavier U., 1978; JD, U. Ky., Covington, 1978. Bar: Ohio 1978, Ky. 1978; CLU; CPCU; cert. structured settlement cons. Clk. to mgr. Baldwin Co., Cin., 1970-78; adj. prof. bus. Thomas More Coll., Crestview Hill, Ky., 1978—, CSSC-U. Notre Dame, 1994, CSSC, 1994; asst. sec., asst. v.p., sr. counsel The Ohio Life Ins. Co., Hamilton, 1978-91; prin. KD Meyers & Assocs., 1991; v.p. Benefit Designs, Inc., 1991-96, Little, Meyers & Assocs., Ltd., Cin., 1996—; adj. prof. Miami U., 1998—. Adj. lectr. U. Notre Dame, South Bend, Ind., 2005—. Bd. dirs. ARC, Hamilton, 1978-83, vol., 1978—; bd. dirs. YWCA, Hamilton, 1985-91. Gardner Found. fellow, 1968-71; recipient Ind. Progress award Bus. & Profl. Women, 1990. Fellow Life Mgmt. Inst. Atlanta; mem. ABA, Soc. Chartered Property Casualty Underwriters (instr. 1987—), Cin. Bar Assn., Butler County Bar Assn., Ohio Bar Assn., Ky. Bar Assn. Roman Catholic. Avocations: aerobics, jogging, crafts. Home: 7903 Hickory Hill Ln Cincinnati OH 45241-1363

MEYERS, KAREN EVANS, gifted and talented educator; children: Andrew, Leland. BS, Edinboro Coll., 1974; MA, Pa. State U., 1976. Tchr. gifted students West Allegheny Sch. Dist., Imperial, Pa., 1974—. Part-time tchr. Carnegie Mellon U., 2005—06. Mem.: Pa. State Edn. Assn., West Allegheny Edn. Assn. (sec. 1994—), Montour Band Parents Assn. (treas. 1998—99, recording sec. 2000—02, v.p. 2004—05). Avocations: reading, travel, walking. Office: West Allegheny Sch Dist West Allegheny Edn Assn Imperial PA 15126

MEYERS, LAUREN ANCEL, biologist; BA, Harvard U., 1996; PhD in biol. scis., Stanford U., 2000. Asst. prof. section integrative biology U. Tex., Austin. Contbr. articles to profl. jour. Named one of Top 100 Young Innovators, MIT Tech. Review, 2004. Office: U Tex Section Integrative Biology PAT 638 1 University Station C0930 Austin TX 78712 Business E-Mail: laurenmeyers@mail.utexas.edu.

MEYERS, LINDA DEE, non-profit administrator, researcher; b. Chgo., Dec. 31, 1945; m. L. Richard Meyers; 2 children. BA in Phys. Edn. & Health with honors, Goshen Coll., 1968; MS in Nutrition, Colo. State U., 1974; PhD in Human Nutrition, Cornell U., 1978. Tchr. Swaneng Hill Secondary Sch., 1968-71; staff Bioteko Rural Coop., Serowe, Botswana, 1972; rsch. asst. dept. food sci. and nutrition Colo. State U., 1973-74; scientist Nat. Ctr. Health Statistics HHS, Washington, 1976-78, sr. nutrition advisor, 1986—, dep. dir. and team leader nutrn., environ. hlth. & sci. coord., 1996—2001; dep. dir. food and nutrition Inst. of Med. of Nat. Acads., Washington, 2001—03, exec. dir., food and nutrition bd., 2003—. Contbr. articles to profl. jours. Mem. APHA, IFT, Am. Soc. Nutrition, Omicron Nu, Phi Kappa Phi. Office: Inst of Med 500 Fifth St NW Washington DC 20001

MEYERS, MARLENE O., retired hospital administrator; m. Eugene Meyers; children: Lori, Lisa, Dean. BSN, U. Sask., 1962; postgrad., U. Oslo, Norway, 1973; MSc, U. Calgary, Alta., Can., 1976; continuing edn., Harvard U., 1980, Banff Sch. Mgmt., 1985, U. Western Ont., Can., 1993; EMT-B, Scottsdale C.C., 2000. RN, Ariz. Various nursing positions, Alta. and B.C., Can., 1962-69; instr., chair Mount Royal Coll. Allied Health, Calgary, 1969-82; asst. exec. dir. Rockyview Hosp., Calgary, 1982-85; v.p. patient svcs. Calgary Gen. Hosp., 1985-91, pres., CEO, 1991-95, Meyers and Assocs. Health Care Mgmt. Cons., Calgary, 1995—98; clin. nurse Scottsdale Behavioral Health Ctr., 1999—. Surveyor Can. Coun. on Health Facilities Accreditation, 1986-97; mem. adv. com. for South Caucasus Health info. project, Can. Adv. Com. Named Calgary Woman of Yr. in field of Health, 1982; recipient Heritage of Svc. award, 1992. Mem. Alta. Assn. RNs (hon.), Can. Coll. Health Svcs. Orgn., Can. Exec. Svcs. Orgn., Can. Soc. for Internat. Health (bd. dirs. 1997-2001, South Caucasus adv. com. 2001—), Rotary Internat. also: 10464 E Cannon Dr Scottsdale AZ 85258-4929

MEYERS, MARSHA LYNN, retired social worker; b. Springfield, Ohio, Dec. 3, 1948; d. Dennis Wathan and Juanita E. (Ratliff) Easterling; m. Wade Trent Meyers, Oct. 5, 1974; children: Lindsay Dionne, Whitney Jane. BA in Sociology, Olivet Nazarene U., 1972. Lic. social worker, Ohio. Formerly social work coord. Mercy Meml. Hosp. and Home Health Care, Urbana, Ohio. Former bd. dirs. Champaign County chpt. Am. Cancer Soc.; mem. adv. bd. Mercy Meml. Hosp. Home Health Care Hospice. Named Social Worker of the Yr. for excellence in small depts. Ohio Soc. Hops. Social Workers, 1995, Social Worker of Yr., Cedarville U. chpt. Phi Alpha Theta, 2000. Mem. Soc. of Hosp. Social Work Dirs., Nat. Assn. Christian Social Workers (past v.p.). Home: 223 College St Urbana OH 43078-2405

MEYERS, MARY ANN, foundation administrator, consultant, writer; b. Sodus, NY, Sept. 30, 1937; d. Harold Galpin and Clarice Mildred (Daniel) Dye; m. John Matthew Meyers, Aug. 22, 1959; children: Andrew Christopher, Anne Kathryn. BA magna cum laude, Syracuse U., 1959; MA, U. Pa., 1965, PhD, 1976. Editorial asst. Ladies' Home Jour., Phila., 1959-62; editor, asst. dir. news bur. U. Pa., Phila., 1962-65, asst. to pres., 1973-75, univ. sec., lectr. Am. civilization, 1980-90; contbg. writer The Pennsylvania Gazette, Phila., 1965—97; dir. coll. rels., editor Haverford Horizons, lectr. in religion Haverford (Pa.) Coll., 1977-80; pres. The Annenberg Found., St. Davids, Pa., 1990-92; v.p. for external affairs Moore Coll. Art and Design, Phila., 1995-97; sr. fellow The John Templeton Found., Radnor, Pa., 1997—. Vis. com. dept. biology U. Pa., 1996—2002; mem. bd. advisors The Peter Gruber Found., St. Thomas, U.S. V.I., 2001—. Author: A New World Jerusalem, 1983, Art, Education and African American Culture: Albert Barnes and the Science of Philanthropy, 2004, 06; contbg. author: Death in America, 1975, Gladly Learn, Gladly Teach, 1978, Coping with Serious Illness, 1980, Religion in American Life, 1987; contbr. articles to profl. jours. Judge recognition program Coun. for Advancement and Support Edn., Washington, 1977—78, chair creative editing and writing workshop, 1978; mem. Picker Found. Program on Human Qualities in Medicine, N.Y.C., Phila., 1980—83; del. Phila.-Leningrad Sister Cities Project, 1986; trustee U. Pa. Press., 1985—2003; vice chmn. U. Pa. 250th Anniversary Commn., 1987—90; mem. steering com. of bd. trustees U. Pa., Annenberg Sch. for Comm., 1990—92; mem. adv. bd. U. Pa., Annenberg Ctr. for the Performing Arts, 1990—98; mem. bd. overseers U. Pa., Sch. Arts and Scis., 1990—97; mem. steering com. of bd. trustees Annenberg Ctr. for Comm., U. So. Calif., L.A., 1990—92, The Annenberg Washington Program in Comm. Policy Studies of Northwestern U., Washington, 1990—92; dir., sec. Am. Acad. Polit. and Social Sci., 1992—, World Affairs Coun. Phila., 1990—95; dir. Diagnostic and Rehab. Ctr., Phila., 1993—2002. Recipient Excellence award Women in Communications, Inc., 1973-74, award for pub. affairs reporting Newsweek/Coun. for Advancement and Support Edn., 1977, Silver medal Coun. for Advancement and Support Edn., 1986. Mem. Am. Acad. Polit. and Social Sci. (sec. and dir. 1992-), Cosmopolitan Club, Sunday Breakfast Club, Phi Beta Kappa (mem. steering com. Delaware Valley chpt. 1995-97). Roman Catholic. Home: 217 Gypsy Ln Wynnewood PA 19096-1112

MEYERS, MAY LOU, retired psychologist, educational consultant; b. Austin, Tex., May 21, 1930; d. Ira William and Gertrude (Tebbs) Wilke; m. Carol Hansford Meyers, Mar. 22, 1951; children: Donna Michelle Spillers, Duane Randall. BA, U. Tex., 1951, MS, 1978. Lic. assoc. psychologist, Tex., 1978; lic. specialist in sch. psychology, Tex., 1996; lic. psychol. examiner, Ark. Psychol. assoc. Charles T. Fries, Tyler, Tex., 1979-88; assoc. sch. psychologist Whitehouse (Tex.) Ind. Sch. Dist., 1980-95; ret. Mem. Phi Beta Kappa, Pi Lambda Theta. Methodist. Avocations: music, music composition, gardening, sewing.

MEYERS, MIRIAM WATKINS, retired language educator; b. Atlanta, Jan. 22, 1941; d. William Craton Watkins and Carolyn Grey (Franklin) Burtz; m. Chester Albert Meyers, July 29, 1967. AB with honors, Peabody Coll., 1962; MS, Georgetown U., 1968; postgrad., Yale U., U. Minn., Hamline U., Met. State U. Tchr. English, French Fairfax (Va.) County Pub. Schs., 1962-66; jr. editor, writer NASA Hdqrs., Washington, 1966-67; supr. practice teaching, instr. Yale U., New Haven, 1967-68; asst. to dir. and research coordinator Inst. for Interdisciplinary Studies, Mpls., 1969-71; exec. asst. to pres. Met. State U., St. Paul, 1971-72, asst. prof., 1971-76, assoc. prof., 1976-83, prof., 1983—2001, prof. emerita, 2001—. Author: A Bite off Mama's Place, 2001; mem. editl. bd. Women and Lang.; contbr. articles to profl. jours., chpts. to books. Vol. Minn. Civil Liberties Union, 1970-80. Recipient Algernon Sidney Sullivan award Peabody Coll., 1962, Teaching Excellence citation Met. State U., 1980, 86; named Outstanding Faculty Advisor Met. State U., 1983. Mem. Am. Dialect Soc., Minn. Assn. for Continuing Adult Edn. (sec. 1983-84, bd. dirs. 1983-84, 86-87), Orgn. for Study of Comm., Lang. and Gender (bd. dirs. 1990-91). Democrat. Home: 2000 W 21st St Minneapolis MN 55405-2414

MEYERS, NANCY JANE, screenwriter, producer, director; b. Phila., Dec. 8, 1949; d. Irving H. and Patricia (Lemisch) M. BA, Am. U., Washington, 1971. Dir.: (films) The Parent Trap, 1998, What Women Want, 2000, Somethings Gotta Give, 2003; prodr.: (films) Private Benjamin (Acad. award nominee, Writers Guild award 1980), Baby Boom, 1987, Father of the Bride, 1991, A Place to be Loved (assoc. prodr.), 1991, I Love Trouble, 1994, Father of the Bride Part II, 1995, Ted Hawkins: Amazing Grace (co-prodr.), 1996, What Women Want, 2000, The Affair of the Necklace, 2001, Something's Gotta Give, 2003; wrote.: (films) Private Benjamin, 1980, Irreconcilable Differences, 1984, Protocol, 1985, Baby Boom, 1987, Father of the Bride, 1991, Once Upon A Crime., 1992, I Love Trouble, 1994, Father of the Bride Part II, 1995, The Parent Trap, 1998, Something's Gotta Give, 2003. Mem. ASCAP, Acad. Motion Picture Arts and Scis., Writers Guild Am. West. Office: Creative Artists Agy 9830 Wilshire Blvd Beverly Hills CA 90212-1825

MEYERS, PAMELA SUE, lawyer; b. Lakewood, N.J., June 13, 1951; d. Morris Leon and Isabel (Leibowitz) M.; m. Gerald Stephen Greenberg, Aug. 24, 1975; children: David Stuart Greenberg, Allison Brooke Greenberg. AB with distinction, Cornell U., 1973; JD cum laude, Harvard U., 1976. Bar: N.Y. 1977, Ohio 1990. Assoc. Stroock & Stroock & Lavan, N.Y.C., 1976-80; staff v.p., asst. gen. counsel Am. Premier Underwriters, Inc., Cin., 1980-96; legal counsel Citizens Fed. Bank, Dayton, Ohio, 1997-98; gen. counsel, sec. Mosler Inc., Hamilton, Ohio, 1998—2001. Bd. dirs. Hamilton County Alcohol and Drug Addiction Svc. Bd., 1996-2000, Adath Israel Congregation, 1999-2005; dir. Gorman Heritage Farm Found., 2006—; trustee Carpenters Creek Civic Assn., 2004-06; mem. Village Evendale Recreation Commn., 2006—. Mem. Cin. Bar Assn., Harvard Club of Cin. (pres. 1998-99, bd. dirs. 1993-2000), Phi Beta Kappa. Jewish. Avocations: piano, reading, tennis. Home: 3633 Carpenters Creek Dr Cincinnati OH 45241-3824 Personal E-mail: psmeyers@fuse.net.

MEYERS, PAMELA SUE, elementary school educator; b. Tiffin, Ohio, Dec. 30, 1980; d. Carl Albert and Donna Jean Meyers. BS in Edn., Ashland U., 2003. Cert. intervention specialist moderate to intensive K-12 Ohio, 2004. Mulitiple disabilities tchr. grades K-3 Shiloh Elem. Sch., Ohio, 2003—. Mulitiple disabilities thcr. summer camp Fairway Sch., Bucyrus, Ohio, 2003—04. Grantee Multiple Disablities, North Ctrl. Electric Cooperation, 2004. Mem.: Coun. for Exceptional Children, Coll. Edn., Alpha Delta Pi (music chair 2001—02), Alpha Lambda (hon.), Rho Lambda (hon.), Kappa Kappa Psi (hon.; fundraiser chair 2002—03). Avocations: singing, exercise, playing flute, sports, coaching. Office: Shiloh Elem Sch 26 Mechanic St Shiloh OH 44878 Home: 447 Lake Shore Dr Willard OH 44890 Office Phone: 419-896-2691. Personal E-mail: missmeyers1980@yahoo.com.

MEYERS, REBECKA LOUISE, pediatric general surgeon; b. Salt Lake City, May 11, 1958; MD, Oreg. Health Sciences U. Sch. Medicine, 1985. Cert. Gen. Surgery, Pediatric Gen. Surgery. Intern, gen. surgery U. Calif. Med. Ctr., San Francisco, 1985—88, fellow, cardiovascular diseases, 1988—90, resident, gen. surgery, 1990—92; fellow St. Christopher's Hosp. for Children in Pediatric Surgery, Phila., 1992—94; pediatric surgeon Primary Children's Med. Ctr., Salt Lake City, 1994—; chief, divsn. pediatric surgery Univ. Utah Hosp. (now called U. Utah Health Sciences Ctr.), Salt Lake City, 2001—; asst. prof. U. Utah, Salt Lake City, 1994—99, assoc. prof., 1999. Mem.: Utah Med. Assn., Pacific Assn. of Pediatric Surgeons, Internat. Pediatric Endosurgery Group, Assn. Women Surgeons, Am. Pediatric Surgical Assn., Am. Coll. Surgeons, Am. Acad. Pediatrics. Office: Primary Childrens Med Ctr 100 N Medical Dr Ste 2600 Salt Lake City UT 84113 also: U Utah Health Services Ctr 50 N Medical Dr Salt Lake City UT 84132 Office Phone: 801-588-3350.*

MEYERS, SHARON MAY, sales executive; b. Whittier, Calif., Feb. 8, 1946; d. Hubert Miller and Garnet May (Prater) Jones; m. Gary Lee Klink, June 18, 1966 (div.); children: Robert Douglas, Jeffrey Loren; m. Carl Eugene Meyers, Dec. 16, 1989. Student, Pasadena Coll., 1963—65; AA, Rio Hondo Coll., 1978; student, Calif. State U. Fullerton, 1978; BSBA, U. Redlands, 1982. Sec. Armorlite Lens Co., Pasadena, 1963—64, James, Pond & Clark, Pasadena, 1964—65; sales sec. Fiberboard Paper, Commerce, Calif., 1965—67; instr. aide East Whittier Sch. Dist., Calif., 1974—78; sales rep. Gen. Can Co., Montebello, Calif., 1978—86, Brouse-Whited Creative Packaging, Marina del Rey, Calif., 1986; br. mgr. Gen. Can Inc., Hayward, Calif., 1986—88; bus. banking mgr. Wells Fargo Bank NA, San Jose, Calif., 1988—89; sales rep. Moore Bus. Products, Colorado Springs, Colo., 1990—93, Assoc. Bus. Products, Santa Rosa, Calif., 1993—94, Advantage Bus. Forms, Oreg., 1994—96, Tekprinting Svcs., Inc., Medford, Oreg., 1996—2006; personal banker US Bank, Medford. Sec. ch. bd. Ch. of the Nazarene, 1973-76, childrens dir., 1965-69; youth dir. Womens Christian Temperance Union, 1965-69; treas. PTA, 1977-79; bd. dirs. Bay Area Crisis Nursery, Concord, Calif.; vol. Valley Meml. Hosp. Emergency Rm., Livermore, Calif., vol. lunch buddy program Washington Elem. Sch., Oak Grove Elem. Sch. 1999-. Named Sales Rep of Yr. Moore Bus. Products, 1991. Republican. Avocations: writing, cooking. Home: 227 St Ives Dr Talent OR 97540 Office Phone: 541-779-6764.

MEYERSON, AMY LIN, lawyer; b. New Orleans, May 26, 1967; m. Brandon Aaron Meyerson, Mar. 25, 1995. AB with Distinction, Duke U., 1989; JD, U. Conn. Sch. Law, 1994. Bar: Ga. 1994, D.C. 1997, U.S. Dist. Ct. (No. Dist.) Ga. 1995, Conn., 2000. Cert. legal intern Disability Law Legal Clinic; repr. Student Bar Assn.; corp. legal asst. White & Case, NYC; summer law clerk for Judge Thomas P. Smith US Magistrate, Hartford, Conn.; law clerk Aetna Life & Casualty, Hartford, Conn.; atty. Appelbaum & LaRoss, Atlanta, 1994-95; assoc. Gerry, Friend & Sapronov LLP, Atlanta, 1995, Martin, Lucas & Chioffi, Stamford, Conn.; sole practitioner Weston, Conn. Spkr. in field. Adminstrv. editor Conn. Jour. Internat. Law, 1992—94; contbr. articles to profl. law jours. Bd. dir. U. Conn. Sch. Law Alumni Assn., 2001—02. Named one of Best Lawyers Under 40 award, Nat. Asian Pacific Am. Bar Assn., 2003; recipient George and Lorraine Schatzki award, 1994, New Leaders in the Law award, Conn. Law Tribune, 2002, Edwin Archer Randolph Diversity award, 2006. Mem. ABA (coun., dir. gen. practice, small firm and solo divsn.), Nat. Asian Pacific Am. Bar Assn. (Ga. chpt. dir. 1996-97, pres. 2005-06), State Bar of Ga. (elections com. 1997-2000), Conn. Asian Pacific Am. Bar Assn. (founder, past pres., 2000-03, bd. dir., 2000-), Conn. Bar Assn. (nominating com., 2002-06; long range planning com., 2002-06, young lawyers sect. exec. com., 2002-03), DC Bar Assn., Adv. Com., TEAM Westport, Conn., Phi Delta Phi. Office: 20 Old Stagecoach Rd Weston CT 06883-1908 Address: Nat Asian Pacific Am Bar Assn 910 17th St NW Ste 315 Washington DC 20006 Office Phone: 203-232-4322, 202-775-9555. Office Fax: 203-548-9213, 202-775-9333. E-mail: amy@almesq.com.

MEYERSON, BARBARA TOBIAS, elementary school educator; b. Rockville Centre, NY, May 17, 1928; d. Sol and Hermine (Sternberg) Tobias; m. Daniel Meyerson, Sept. 4, 1962 (dec. Apr. 1989); children: George D., Barbara Meyerson Ayers. BEd, SUNY, New Paltz, 1948; postgrad., NYU, Hofstra U. Tchr. kindergarten Dix Hills (N.Y.) pub. schs., Hicksville (N.Y.) pub. schs., Valley Stream (N.Y.) pub. schs.; tchr. 6th grade Flushing (N.Y.) Bd. Edn. Dist. commr. Boy Scouts Am., tng. staff, organizer new units; founder, sec. Repertory Theatre, Rio Rancho, N.Mex.; bd. dirs. Italian Am. Assn., Rio Rancho; vol. Rio Rancho City Hall Pub. Offices; vol. reading and spl. edn. classes Rio Rancho Pub. Schs; vice-chair Rio Rancho Park and Recreation Bd. Commrs.; dep. publicity chair State of N.Mex. VFW Aux., Mayor's Com. Study Health, 2004-2005. Recipient Lt. Gov. Civic Vol. award, State of N.Mex., 2005. Mem. ACE, VFW Aux. (pres. dist. II), United Fedn. Tchrs. Home: 6127 Cottontail Rd NE Rio Rancho NM 87144-1545 Personal E-mail: barbtobias1@aol.com.

MEYROWITZ, CAROL, retail executive; Joined The TJX Cos., Inc., Framingham, Mass., 1983—; exec. v.p. merchandising Chadwick's of Boston (divsn. previously held by TJX), 1996—99; sr. v.p. merchandising, Marmaxx group The TJX Cos., Inc., 1999—2000, exec. v.p. merchandising, Marmaxx group Framingham, Mass., 2000—01, exec. v.p., pres. Marmaxx group, 2001—04, sr. exec. v.p., 2004—05, adv. cons., 2005, pres., 2005—. Bd. dirs. Yankee Candle, 2004—. Named one of 50 Most Powerful Women in Business, Fortune mag., 2006, 50 Most Powerful Women in Bus., 2006. Office: TJX Companies 770 Cochituate Rd Framingham MA 01701*

MEZACAPA, EDNA S., music educator, elementary school educator; b. Flint, Mich., Jan. 23, 1948; d. Jack E. and Vlasta A. Tremayne; m. Nicklas A. Mezacapa, July 25, 1970; children: Amy Anne, Sara Marie. MusB, Heidelberg Coll., Tiffin, Ohio, 1970. Gen. music tchr. Bellevue (Ohio) City Schs., 1969—73; youth choir dir. Findlay Episc. Ch., Findlay, Ohio, 1975—78; subs. tchr. Rochester (N.Y.) Schs., 1979—81; youth choir dir. Ch. of the Epiphany, Rochester, 1979—81; music tchr., K-8 St. Mary's Cath. Sch., Kalamazoo, 1981—82, St. Ludmila Cath. Sch., Cedar Rapids, Iowa, 1984—86; tchr. Christian edn. Calvary Episc. Ch., Rochester, Minn., 1986—87; subs. music tchr., 1-6 Rochester City Schs., Rochester, Minn., 1988—90, music tchr., 1-6, 1990—. Dir. Calvary Episc. Youth Choir, 1995—96, Suzuki Orch., 2001—03. Dir. youth choir Calvary Episcopal Ch., 1996—97; dir. Suzuki Orch., 2001—03.

MEZOUGHEM, CLAIRE VIRGINIA, economist; b. Portsmouth, NH, July 13, 1970; d. Louis Herman and Virginia Herman Klotz; m. Lyes Mezoughem, Aug. 5, 2005. BA, Mt. Holyoke Coll., South Hadley, Mass., 1992; MS, Purdue U., West Lafayette, Ind., 1996. Economist US Dept. Agr./Agrl. Mktg. Svc., Washington, 1998—2001; agrl. mktg. specialist US Dept. of Agr./Fgn. Agrl. Svc., Washington, 2001—04, economist, 2004—. Editor: Livestock and Poultry: World Markets and Trade; author: How to Direct Market Farm Products on the Internet; editor: Farmer Direct Marketing Newsletter; author: Improving and Facilitating a Farmers Market in a Low-Income Urban Neighborhood: A Washington, DC Case Study. Nat. Security Edn. Program fellow, 1994—95. Mem.: Mensa. Office: USDA-Fgn Agrl Svc 1400 Independence Ave SW Stop 1052 Washington DC 20250 Office Phone: 202-720-7715.

MIAH, JAMILA SIKANDER, social worker, researcher; d. Sikander and Hamida Begum Miah; children: Sikander Rahman, Jehan Rahman. MSW (hon.), Fordham U., 2005. LCSW NY. Safety coord. Lifespire, NYC, 2000—01; treatment coord. Westchester ARC, Peekskill, NY, 2001—04; access svc. rep. NY Presbyn. Hosp., White Plains, 2004—05, social worker, 2005—06, VA Hudson Valley Healthcare Sys., Montrose, NY, 2006—. Rschr. NY Presbyn. Hosp., 2005—. Mem.: NASW (assoc.), NY Soc. Clin. Social Work (editor newsletter, grantee 2005), Am. Group Psychotherapy Assn. (assoc.). Avocation: travel. Office: Hudson Valley Healthcare SYs 100 Albany Post Rd Montrose NY 10548 Office Phone: 914-737-4400.

MICEK, ISABELLE, music educator; b. Shelby, Nebr., July 28, 1922; d. Thomas Adolph and Julia Lucy (Triba) M. MusB in Piano Performance, St. Louis Inst. Music, 1943; postgrad., Peabody Conservatory, 1971; MusM in Piano Pedagogy, St. Louis Inst. Music, 1972. Instrumental/vocal tchr. various elem. and secondary schs., Hull, Ill., 1943-45, Oakland, Iowa, 1945-46; pvt. piano/vocal/theory instr. Columbus, Nebr., 1946—. Participated internat. workshops, Honolulu, 1980, Calgary, 1990, Graz, Austria, 2000. Pres. N.E. Dist. Nebr. Music Tchrs. Assn., 1949-56, Cmty. Concert Assn., Columbus, 1965-67; advisor Birthright Columbus, 1992—. Recipient Medallion of Merit award Art Publ. Soc., St. Louis, 1957; scholar U. Mexico, Mexico City, 1950, Royal Conservatory, London, 1952, Staatlichen Hochschule, Munich, 1963, St. Cecilia Conservatory, Rome, 1966, Manuel de Falla Conservatore, Buenos Aires, 1974. Mem. Music Tchrs. Nat. Assn., Nebr. Music Tchrs. Assn., Nat. Guild (adjudicator 1993-98). Democrat. Roman Catholic. Avocations: gardening, reading, concerts, speaker for modern problems high school classes. Home: 2115 18th St Columbus NE 68601-4531

MICHAEL, CLAIRE PATRICIA, director; b. Atlanta, May 22, 1970; d. Herman Perry and Patricia Cagle Michael. BEd in Spanish Edn., U. Ga., Athens, 1994, MEd in Ednl. Leadership, 2001; postgrad., Ga. State U., Atlanta. Spanish tchr. Barrow County Sch., Winder, Ga., 1994—2001, asst. prin., 2000—01, secondary curriculum coord., 2001—05, exec. curriculum dir., 2005—06. Contbr. articles to profl. jours. Mem. Teen Pregnancy Prevention Bd., Barrow County, Ga., 2004—06. Mem.: Profl. Assn. Ga. Educators, Ga. Assn. Ednl. Tchrs., Am. Ednl. Rsch. Assn. Republican. Baptist. Avocations: running, cooking, reading, hiking. Home: 5548 Trace Views Dr Norcross GA 30071 Office: Barrow County Sch 179 W Athens St Winder GA 30680 Office Phone: 770-864-4527. Office Fax: 770-867-4519. Business E-Mail: cmichael@barrow.k12.ga.us.

MICHAEL, DOROTHY ANN, nursing administrator, military officer; b. Lancaster, Pa., Sept. 20, 1950; d. Richard Linus and Mary Ruth (Hahn) M.; m. Juan Roberto Morales, July 15, 1995. Diploma, RN, Montgomery Hosp. Sch. Nursing, Norristown, Pa., 1971; BSN, George Mason U., 1980; MSN, U. Tex. Health Sci. Ctr., 1985. Commd. ensign USN, 1970, advanced through grades to capt. Nurse Corps, 1994, staff nurse Nat. Naval Med. Ctr. Bethesda, Md., 1971-73, charge nurse Naval Hosp. Guantanamo Bay, Cuba, 1973-74, charge nurse Naval Regional Med. Ctr. Phila., 1974-76, charge nurse Naval Hosp. Keflavik, Iceland, 1977, Bethesda, Md., 1980-84; sr. nurse, asst. officer-in-charge Br. Med. Clinic Naval Weapons Ctr., China Lake, Calif., 1986-89; coord. quality assurance Naval Hosp., Oakland, Calif., 1989-92, assoc. dir. inpatient nursing, 1992-93; divsn. officer USNS Mercy, Persian Gulf, 1990-91; assoc. dir. surg. nursing Naval Hosp., Oakland, 1993-95, dir. nursing svc. Great Lakes, Ill., 1995-98; dep. comdr. Naval Ambulatory Care Ctr., Newport, R.I., 1998-2001; ret. Splty. advisor to dir. Navy Nurse Corp., Navy Med. Command, Washington, 1983-84. V.p. Deepwood Homeowners Assn., Reston, Va., 1978-82; advisor, com. mem. Reston Found., 1979. Decorated Navy Commendation medal, Meritorious Svc. medal, Legion of Merit; recipient R.W. Bjorklund Mgmt. Innovator award, Kern County, Calif., 1988, Comdr.'s award for outstanding professionalism in pub. health support, 1988. Mem. VFW, Vietnam Vets. Am., Am. Legion, Sigma Theta Tau. Roman Catholic. Home: 3324 Susquehanna Rd Dresher PA 19025 E-mail: dotjuan1@msn.com.

MICHAEL, JEAN, mathematics educator; d. Marvin Burgraff; m. James Michael, May 9, 1998; 1 child, Samantha. MS, St. Cloud State U., Minn., 1995—99. Math tchr. Apollo HS, St. Cloud, 1994—.

MICHAEL, MARILYN CORLISS, music educator, mezzo soprano; d. Charles Bernard and Peggy Clarice Michael. MusB in Voice, U. Kans., 1976, MusM in Vocal Performance, 1977; EdD in Curriculum and Instrn., U. Sarasota, Argosy U., 2002. Instr. voice U. Kans., Lawrence, 1976—77, dir. vocal program Midwest Music and Art Camp, 1976—77; prof. voice Eckerd Coll., St. Petersburg, Fla., 1980—88; prof. voice, opera and hon., humanities St. Petersburg Coll., 1994—; artistic dir. New Century Opera, Tarpon Springs, Fla.; founder dir. Summer Vocal Inst. St. Petersburg Coll., 2003—. Dir. music, organist Chapel By-the-Sea, Clearwater Beach, Fla., 1980—. Singer (mezzo-soprano soloist): Carnegie Hall debut, New Eng. Chamber Orch. and Bethany Choir; singer: (CD) Von ewiger Liebe, and other songs by Johannes Brahms, (Operas) Suncoast Opera Guild (1st Pl. winner, 1980); singer: (soloist) Mahler Symphony no. 2, London Bach Choir, Stuttgart Sommerfest, Toynbee Hall. Mem.: Am. Guild Organists, Opera Am., Pinellas Opera League, Pi Kappa Lambda, Phi Kappa Phi. Conservative. Roman Catholic. Achievements include development of Summer Vocal Institute in collaboration with leading Metropolitan Opera tenor, Enrico di Giuseppe and leadingMet. Opera baritone Sherrill Milnes. Avocations: swimming, dogs, antiques. Home: 2935 Robinwood Ln Palm Harbor FL 34684 Office: St Petersburg Coll 6605 5th Ave N Saint Petersburg FL 33710 Office Phone: 727-341-4679. Business E-Mail: michaelm@spcollege.edu.

MICHAEL, NOREEN, school system administrator; PhD in Ednl. Psychology, U. Ill. Commr. of edn. Virgin Islands Dept. Edn., Charlotte, Amalie, Virgin Islands, 2002—. Office: Commr of Education 44-46 Kongena Gade St Thomas VI 00802

MICHAEL, SANDRA DALE, biomedical educator, researcher; b. Sacramento, Jan. 23, 1945; d. Gordon G. and Ruby F. (Johnson) M.; m. Dennis P. Murr, Aug. 12, 1967 (div. 1974). BA, Calif. State Coll., Sonoma, 1967; PhD, U. Calif., Davis, 1970. NIH predoctoral fellow U. Calif., Davis, 1967—70, NIH postdoctoral fellow, 1970—73, asst. rsch. geneticist, 1973—74; asst. prof. Binghamton U., SUNY, 1974—81, assoc. prof., 1981—88, prof. reproductive endocrinology, 1988—2005, disting. svc. prof., 2005—, dept. chair, 1992—2000, dir. grad. studies, 2004—. Adj. prof. dept. ob-gyn. SUNY Upstate Med. U., Syracuse; mem. NIH Reproductive Endocrinology Study Sect., 1991-95; cons., presenter in field; grant reviewer NIH, NSF, USDA and others. Mem. editl. bd. Reproductive Biology and Endocrinology, Am. Jour. Reproductive Immunology; contbr. articles to profl. jours. Bd. dirs. Tri Cities Opera, Binghamton Summer Music Festival/So. Tier Celebrates; convener Episc. Ch. Network for Sci., Tech. and Faith, 2004—; vice chair Tri Cities Opera Guild, Binghamton, 1987—90, chair, 1990—92; mem. SUNY Found., Binghamton, 1990—96, Harpur Forum, Binghamton, 1987—. Fulbright Sr. scholar Czech Republic, 1994; grantee NIMH, 1976-79, Nat. Cancer Inst., 1977-80, 83-87, Nat. Inst. Environ. Health Scis., 1979-80, NSF, 1981-83, NIH, 1987—. Fellow: AAAS; mem.: N.Y. Acad. Sci., Soc. for Exptl. Biology and Medicine, Women in Endocrinology, Am. Soc. for Immunology of Reprodn. (editl. bd., treas. 2005—), Soc. for Study of Fertility, Soc. for Study of Reprodn., Endocrine Soc., Sigma Xi. Avocations: golf, bridge, opera, literature, travel. Office: Binghamton U Dept Biol Scis Binghamton NY 13902 Office Phone: 607-777-6517. Business E-Mail: smichael@binghamton.edu.

MICHAELIS, BETTY JANE, sculptor, retired small business owner; b. Champaign County, Ohio, Feb. 6, 1928; d. Charles Edward and Mable Augusta (Stevens) Hendricks; m. Philip Alvin Russell, July 25, 1947 (div. Feb. 1965); children: Barbara Ann Russell Clifford, Karen Sue Russell Geist, Philip Edward; m. Larry Edward Michaelis, Nov. 29, 1986. Student, Sinclair C.C., 1987-88. 2d v.p. Credit Life Ins., Springfield, Ohio, 1984-86; sculptor of public art Miamisburg, Ohio, 1987—. Avocation: reading. Home: 9616 Yorkridge Ct Miamisburg OH 45342-5208

MICHAELIS, GABRIELLE DEMONCEAU, mathematics professor; b. NYC, Jan. 14, 1960; d. Lansing Michaelis and Arlette Lydie deMonceau-Michaelis; m. Daniel Cifoni, July 4, 2004; children: Dj Scheid, Josephine Arlette Scheid. AA (hon.), Manatee C.C., Bradenton. Fla., 1992; BA (hon.), U. South Fla., Tampa, 1995, M of Art & Scis., 2001. Tchr. h.s. math. Manatee County Sch. Bd., Bradenton, Fla., 1995—98; math. prof. Cumberland County Coll., Vineland, NJ, 2001—. Adj. Manatee C.C., Bradenton, Fla., 1998—2001. Author: Mathematics Workbook. Office Phone: 856-691-8600 419. Personal E-mail: gmichaelis@cccnj.edu.

MICHAELS, JENNIFER, choreographer, dancer, educator; b. Hinsdale, Ill., June 4, 1978; d. Cynthia and Richard Sproul; m. Joshua Michaels, June 18, 2005. BFA in dance performance, No. Ill. U., 2000. Profl. dancer, instr. Chattanooga Ballet, 2001—06; resident choreographer, modern and jazz dance instr. Chattanooga HS Ctr. for Creative Arts, 2001—06. Dancer (profl. union performance) The Chicago Tribune Charities The Nutcracker, (musical) State Fair. Scholar Talent, Academic Scholarship, No. Ill. U., 1997—2000. Home: 1451 Belmont St NW 211 Washington DC 20009 Personal E-mail: jen@michaelsinc.net.

MICHAELS, JENNIFER TONKS, foreign language educator; b. Sedgley, England, May 19, 1945; d. Frank Gordon and Dorothy (Compston) Tonks; m. Eric Michaels, 1973; children: Joseph, David, Ellen. MA, U. Edinburgh, 1967, McGill U., 1971, PhD, 1974. Teaching asst. German dept. Wesleyan U., 1967-68; instr. German dept. Bucknell (Pa.) U., 1968-69; teaching asst. German dept. McGill U., Canada, 1969-72; prodn. asst. Pub. TV News and Polit. program, Schenectady, NY, 1974-75; from asst. prof. to assoc. prof. Grinnell (Iowa) Coll., 1975-87, prof., 1987—. Vis. cons. German dept. Hamilton Coll., 1981; cons. Modern Lang. dept. Colby Coll.; panelist NEH, 1985; spkr. in field. Author: D.H. Lawrence, The Polarity of North and South, 1976, Anarchy and Eros: Otto Gross' Impact on German Expressionist Writers, 1983, Franz Jung: Expressionist, Dadaist, Revolutionary and Outsider, 1989, Franz Werfel and the Critics, 1994; contbr. numerous articles, revs. to profl. jours. Mem. MLA, Rocky Mt. MLA (v.p. 2005), Am. Assn. Tchrs. of German, Soc. Exile Studies, German Studies Assn. (sec. treas. 1991-92, v.p. 1992-94, pres. 1995-96, numerous coms.). Democrat. Avocations: music, travel, reading. Office: Grinnell Coll German Dept PO Box 805 Grinnell IA 50112-0805 Business E-Mail: michaels@grinnell.edu.

MICHAELS, MARION CECELIA, newswriter, editor, news syndicate executive; b. Black River Falls, Wis. d. Leonard N. and Estelle O. (Payne) Doud; m. Charles Webb (div.); children: Charles, David, Robert; m. Mark J. Michaels (div.); 1 child, Merry A. BS in Bus. Edn., U. Wis., 1978, MS in Spl. Edn., 1981. Mgr., instr. bus. program Blackwell Job Corps Ctr., 1987-89; mgr. Michaels Secretarial Svc., Black River Falls, Wis., 1979-83; columnist, editor Michaels News, Black River Falls, 1983—, pres., 1989—. Hon. appt. rsch. bd. advisors Am. Biog. Inst., 1996-2001. Author: The Little Cowboy: Pursuing Dana's Dream, 1998, September's Song, 2003—, Dana's Dream, 2004, Loving Lisa, 2005; columnist Single Parenting, 1983—94, Parenting Plus, 1990—2004, editor, contbr. (column) Surviving Single, 1990—95, To Read or Not (Fiction), 1985—, To Read or Not (Non-Fiction), 1985—2004, Report From Planet Earth, 1985—, Travel Tidbits, 1991—95, Surviving Sane, 1995—98. Chmn. Brockway Cmty. Orgn., 1969-71; chair, counselor Brockway Youth Group, 1970-72; chmn. labor com. Dem. Platform Com., Wis., 1975-76; candidate State Assembly, 1978, 82; co-founder Franklin Delano Roosevelt Meml., 1997; mem. LWV. Named to Internat. Poetry Hall of Fame, 1997. Mem.: Assn. Rsch. and Enlightenment, Physicians for Social Responsibility, Union Concerned Scientists, Internat. Soc. Poets (founding laureate mem. 2006, Internat. Poet of Merit award 1999, Outstanding achievement in poetry award 2005, 2006), Humane Soc. of U.S., Nat. Com. to Protect Soc. Security and Medicare, Peale Ctr. for Positive Living, Friends of the Earth, Nat. Trust for Pub. Edn., Smithsonian (assoc.), Pub. Citizen, Am. United, Nat. Parks, Clean Wis., So. Poverty Law Ctr., Natural Resources Def. Coun., Co-op Am., Amnesty Internat., Inst. for Noetic Sci., League of Conservation Voters, Wilson Ctr., Common Cause, Internat. Fund for Animals, Women's History Mus. (charter mem.), Phi Delta Kappa, Pi Omega Pi. Avocations: singing, dance, walking, swimming.

MICHALAK, JO-ANN, library director; Grad., Syracuse U., U. Ill., Columbia U. Libr. U. Ill., Ind. U., Columbia U., U. Pitts.; now dir. Tisch Libr. Tufts. U., Medford, Mass. Pres. Boston Libr. Consortium, 2006—; mem. adv. bd. for univ. librs. Carnegie Mellon U., 2006—; bd. dirs. NELINET. Mem.: Soc. For Scholarly Pub. Office: Tisch Libr Tufts U 35 Professors Row Medford MA 02155 Office Phone: 617-627-3345. Office Fax: 617-627-3002. E-mail: jo-ann.michalak@tufts.edu.*

MICHALAK, SARAH C., university librarian; BA in English, Univ. Calif. Riverside, 1969; MLS, UCLA, 1970. Previous head Bio-Agrl. Dept. Univ. Calif. Riverside; previous libr. Univ. Wash., Seattle; dir. J. Willard Marriot Libr. Univ. UT, Salt Lake City, 1995—2004; univ. libr. and assoc. provost for univ. libraries U. NC, Chapel Hill, 2004—. Mem.: Scholarly Pub. and Academic Resources Coalition (steering com.), Libr. Adminstrn. and Mgmt. Assn., Assn. Rsch. Libr. Office: CB 3900 Davis Libr Univ NC Chapel Hill NC 27514 Office Phone: 919-962-1301. E-mail: smichala@email.unc.edu.*

MICHALEK, TINA A., social studies educator; b. Evergreen Park, Ill., Aug. 12, 1978; d. James Peter and Pamela Ann Michalek. BA in Psychology, St. Xavier U., Chgo., 2002; MA in Edn., Lewis U., Romeoville, Ill., 2006. Spl. edn. tchrs. asst. Oak Lawn Cmty. H.S., Ill., 2002—04; social studies tchr. Waubonsie Valley H.S., Aurora, Ill., 2004—. Student coun. co-sponsor Waubonsie Valley H.S., Aurora, 2004—. Recipient Indian Prairie Scholars award, Waubonsie Valley H.S., 2005; scholar, St. Xavier U., 1999—2002, Moraine Valley C.C., 1996—99. Office Phone: 630-375-3551.

MICHAUD, PHYLLIS CAROL, school counselor; b. Dallas, Mar. 26, 1955; d. Donald Cecil and Sarah Jane Horton; m. Timothy Cyr Michaud, June 24, 1978; children: Andrew Jason, Eric Thomas, Sarah Margaret. BA, Mt. Union Coll., 1977; EdM in Guidance and Counseling, U. Ctrl. Okla., 2002. Cert. sch. counselor Okla. State Dept. Edn. Caseworker Trumbull County Children Svcs. Bd., Warren, Ohio, 1977—78; intake caseworker Summit City Children Svcs. Bd., Akron, Ohio, 1979; substitute tchr. Norman (Okla.) Pub. Schs., 1996—97, 2002—03, tchrs. asst., 1997—2002, sch. counselor, 2003—. Student assistance program/drug prevention counselor Norman North H.S., 2003—, Baby Steps Coalition, Norman, 2003—. Outreach chair area mgmt. team Okla. Spl. Olympics, Norman, 2004—; mem. mission team United Meth. Vols. in Mission, Rio Bravo, Mexico, 2001, 2002; mem. various coms. Goodrich United Meth. Ch., Norman, 2002—, group facilitator Moms of Teens, 2004—, chmn. ch. coun., 2006. Mem.: Okla. Counseling Assn., Profl. Educators Norman, Chi Sigma Iota. Avocations: reading, sewing, crafts, hiking, camping. Home: 1427 Cherry Stone St Norman OK 73072 Office: Norman North High Sch 1309 Stubbeman Ave Norman OK 73069

MICHEL, DONNA TONTY, education educator; b. Washington, D.C., Sept. 21, 1952; d. Carl Joseph and Kathryn May Tonty; m. William III Michel, Aug. 17, 1974; children: Kathleen, Victoria. BS in Edn., Towson State Coll., Balt., 1974; MS in comm. disorders/reading, Johns Hopkins U., Balt., 1982. Tchr. Wicomico County Pub. Schs., Salisbury, Md., 1974—75; instructional asst. Howard County Pub. Sch., Columbia, Md., 1975—76, tchr., 1976—82, reading specialist Ellicott City, Md., 1982—, adj. prof. Columbia, Md., 2003—. Project coord. implementation reading and learning styles instruction Howard County Pub. Schs., Ellicott City, Md., 1986—87, project coord. devel. cohesive spelling program, 1997—99, profject coord. effect of 6 trait writing on reading comprehension, 2004—05. Conf. presenter Md. Reading Inst./State of Md. Internat. Reading Assn., 1988, 1993; cons. U. Md. Tchg. Effectiveness Network, 1990; pres. Howard County Reading Assn., Ellicott, Md., 1997—99; cons. prescription for reading program Howard County Gen. Hosp., Columbia, Md., 1997—98; developer Books for Babies Howard County Gen. Hosp./Howard County Reading Assn., Columbia, Md., 1997; v.p. Centennial HS Band Parents, Ellicott, Md., 2004—05; chairperson, bd. dirs. State of Md. Internat. Reading Assn. Recipient Reading By 9 Tchr. award, Balt. Sun Newspaper, 1999; Artist in Residence grant, Wal-Mart Corp., 2005, Title V Rsch. grant, U.S. Dept. Edn., 2004—05. Mem.: Internat. Reading Assn., State of Md. Reading Assn., Delta Kappa Gamma. Avocations: reading, baseball, concerts, theater, sports. Home: 10249 Little Brick House Ct Ellicott City MD 21042 Office: Howard County Pub Schs Northfield Elem Sch 9125 Northfield Rd Ellicott City MD 21042 Personal E-mail: michel@connext.net, donna_michel@hcps.org.

MICHEL, ELIZABETH CHENEY, social reform consultant; b. Pitts., Feb. 11, 1951; d. George Philip and Charlotte Elizabeth (Cowser) Cheney; m. Raymond Joseph Michel, Oct. 21, 1973 (div. June 1997); children: Keith Raymond, Grant Petersen. BA, Rollins Coll., 1973; M in Comm., U. Ctrl. Fla., 1988, PhD, 1992. Vis. prof. Univ. Ctrl. Fla., Orlando, Fla., 1989-92; assoc. prof., chair comm. program Mars Hill (N.C.) Coll., 1993-99; comms. cons., v.p. Comms. Strategies-Healthcare.com, Corp., 1999-2000; dir. change mgmt. Ga. Tech. Authority, 2001—. Pres. Kairos Commn. Strategies, Atlanta, 1998—; bd. dirs. Biltmore Inst., 1997—, cons., 1996—; bd. dirs. Commn. on Industries of the Mind, Atlanta; vice-chair 21st Century Comm., 1996—; project coord. for joint comm. with Chinese Acad. Social Scis., China; del. to Consortium for Global Edn., China, 1998; vis. prof. comm. Kennesaw State U.; mem. internat. del. to Conf. on Environ. Sustainability, Shanghai, 2000, Implementation Strategies for SMEs, Networking 2000, Paris, 2000; v.p. Systems and Strategies; mem. bd. advisor Atlantic U. Chinese Medicine, 2000—, chair bd. dirs., 2001—. Author: 4 Simple Steps to Communications that Connect! and Kairos Community Strategies Interactive CD-ROM, 2000; chief editor: An Orchestra of Voices: Making the Argument for Press and Speech Freedom in the People's Republic of China, 2000; contbr. articles to mag. Bd. dirs. Atlanta Women's Network, 2000—01. Internat. Rsch. grant Appalachian Coll. Assn., 1994, 96, 97, Mellon Found., 1994, 95, 96, 97; Vis. Rsch. fellow Chinese Acad. Social Scis., 1996, 97. Mem.: Women's Network, Brit. Am. Bus. Group, Am. Educators Journalism and Mass Comm., Nat. Comm. Assn., Atlanta Coun. on Internat. Rels., Dem. Women's forum, Metro Atlanta C. of C., Women's Commerce Club, Ga. Exec. Women's Network, Atlanta Women's Network-Strategic Planning, Kappa Delta Phi, Phi Kappa Phi. Presbyterian. Avocations: acting, music, drawing.

MICHEL, JACQUELINE, geochemist; BS, U. SC, Columbia, 1974, MS, 1976, PhD in Geochemistry, 1980. Registered geologist SC. Prin. investigator NOAA Hazardous Materials Response and Assessment Divsn., Seattle, 1978—; project mgr. Office of Pipeline Safety, 1996—; pres. Rsch. Planning Inc., 2000—. Mem. com. spills on nonfloating oil NRC, 1998—99, mem. com. oil in the sea, 1999—2002, chmn. com. spills of emulsified fuels: risks and responses, 2001; mem. Oceans Study Bd. NAS; mem. sci. adv. panel US Commn. Ocean Policy; adj. prof. U. SC School of Environment. Contbr. articles to profl. jours., chapters to books. Mem.: Carolina Geol. Soc., Sigma Xi. Office: RPI Louisiana Inc Twin Heights Office Pk Ste E 27999 Old S Walker Rd Walker LA 70785*

MICHEL, MARY ANN KEDZUF, nursing educator; b. Evergreen Park, Ill., June 1, 1939; d. John Roman and Mary Kedzuf; m. Jean Paul Michel, 1974. Diploma in nursing, Little Company of Mary Hosp., Evergreen Park, 1960; BSN, Loyola U., Chgo., 1964; MS, No. Ill. U., 1968, EdD, 1971. Staff nurse Little Co. of Mary Hosp., 1960-64; instr. Little Co. of Mary Hosp. Sch. Nursing, 1964-67, No. Ill. U., DeKalb, 1968-69, asst. prof., 1969-71; chmn. dept. nursing U. Nev., Las Vegas, 1971-73, prof. nursing, 1975—, dean Coll. Health Scis., 1973-90; pres. PERC, Inc.; mgmt. cons., 1993—95. Mgmt. cons. Nev. Donor Network, 1993; mem. So. Nev. Health Manpower Task Force, 1975; mem. manpower com. Plan Devel. Commn., Clark County Health Sys. Agy., 1977-79, mem. governing body, 1981-86; mem. Nev. Health Coordinating Coun., Western Inst. Nursing, 1971-85; mem. coordinating com. assembly instnl. adminstrs. dept. allied health edn. and accreditation AMA, 1985-88; mem. bd. advisors So. Nev. Vocat. Tech. Ctr., 1976-80; sec.-treas. Nev. Donor Network, 1988-89, chmn. bd., 1988-90. Contbr. articles to profl. jours. Trustee Desert Spring Hosp., Las Vegas, 1976-85; bd. dirs. Nathan Adelson Hospice, 1982-88, Bridge Counseling Assocs., 1982, Everywoman's Ctr., 1984-86; chair Nev. Commn. on Nursing Edn., 1972-73, Nursing Articulation Com., 1972-73, Yr. of Nurse Com., 1978; moderator Invitational Conf. Continuing Edn., Am. Soc. Allied Health Professions, 1978; mgmt. cons. Nev. Donor Network, 1994-95, Donor Organ Recovery Svc., Transplant Recipient Internat. Orgn., S.W. Eye Bank, S.W. Tissue Bank. Named Outstanding Alumnus, Loyola U., 1983; NIMH fellow, 1967-68. Fellow Am. Soc. Allied Health Professions, 1991, (chair nat. resolutions com. 1981-84, treas. 1988-90, sec's. award com. 1982-83, 92-93, nat. by-laws com. 1985, conv. chair 1987); mem. AAUP, Am. Nurses Assn., Nev. Nurses Assn. (dir. 1975-77, treas. 1977-79, conv. chair 1978), So. Nev. Area Health Edn. Coun., Western Health Deans (co-organizer 1985, chair, 1988-90), Nat. League Nursing, Nev. Heart Assn., So. Nev. Mem. Hosps. (nursing recruitment com. 1981-83, mem. nursing practice com. 1983-85), Las Vegas C. of C. (named Woman of Yr. Edn.) 1988, Slovak Catholic Sokols, Phi Kappa Phi (chpt. sec. 1981-83, pres.-elect 1983, pres. 1984, v.p. Western region 1989-95, editl. bd. jour. Nat. Forum 1989-93), Alpha Beta Gamma (hon.), Sigma Theta Tau, Zeta Kappa. Office: U Nev Las Vegas 4505 S Maryland Pky Las Vegas NV 89154-9900 Office Phone: 702-895-3719. Personal E-mail: m.a.michel@worldnet.att.com.

MICHELINI, SYLVIA HAMILTON, auditor; b. Decatur, Ala., May 16, 1946; d. George Borum and Dorothy Rose (Swatzell) Hamilton; m. H. Stewart Michelini, June 4, 1964; children: Stewart Anthony, Cynthia Leigh. BSBA summa cum laude, U. Ala., Huntsville, 1987. CPA, Ala.; cert. govt. fin. mgr., fraud examiner. Acct. Ray McCay, CPA, Huntsville, 1987-88; auditor Def. Contract Audit Agy., Huntsville, 1989-92; auditor-office of inspector general George C. Marshall Space Flight, Center, Ala., 1992-97; contr. Hamilton Hotels, Inc., 1997-2001; ret. Exec. bd. Decatur City PTA, 1976-78; pres., v.p. Elem. Sch. PTA, Decatur, 1977-79; leader Girl Scouts U.S. and Cub Scouts, Decatur, 1972-77; active local ARC, 1973-77. Mem.: AAUW (chpt. treas. 1988—90), AICPA, Inst. Mgmt. Accts. (v.p. comm., dir. program book 1991—94, Dixie coun. dir. newsletters 1992—93, dir. ednl. programs 1992—93, 1993—94, nat. com. ethics 1990—97, nat. fin. com. 1997—98, nat. bd. dirs. 1994—97), Inst. Internal Auditors (dir. awards and recognition 1996—97, sec. 1999—2001, 2003—04), Ala. Soc. CPAs (profl. ethics com. 1993—94, govtl. acctg. and auditing com. 1994—95), Assn. Govt. Accts. (sec. 1992—93, chmn. pub. rels. 1993—94), Am. Soc. Women Accts. (chpt. treas. 1989—90, dir. chpt. devel. 1989—90), Nat. Notary Assn., Nat. Assn. Accts. (dir. cmty. svc. 1987—88, v.p. adminstrn. and fin. 1988—89, pres. 1989—90, nat. com. on ethics 1990—91), Phi Kappa Phi. Baptist. Avocations: reading, walking, sewing, research, music. Home and Office: 2801 Sylvia Dr SE Decatur AL 35603-5643 E-mail: nimi@hiway.net.

MICHELS, EILEEN MANNING, retired art educator, curator, writer; b. Fargo, ND, Mar. 27, 1926; d. Walter James and Agnes Maybelle Manning; m. Joseph Emmanuel Michels, Mar. 9, 1955; 1 child, James. BA magna cum laude, U. Minn., Mpls., 1947, MA in Art History, 1953, MA in Lib. Sci., 1959, PhD in Art History, 1971. Art librarian U. Minn., Mpls., 1948—53, curator univ. gallery, 1954—55; asst. prof. U. Wis., River Falls, 1966—70; curator architecture Minn. Mus. Art, St. Paul, 1971—72; vis. asst. prof. Stanford U., Calif., 1972—73; assoc. dir. Minn. Mus. Art, St. Paul, 1973; assoc. prof., dept. chair U. St. Thomas, St. Paul, 1978—88, prof., 1989—92, prof. emerita, 1992—. Freelance rsch., writer, cons. Corning Mus. Glass, Corning, NY, Carleton Coll., Northfield, Minn., Gustavus Adolphus Coll., St. Peter, Minn., Mpls. Inst. Arts. Contbr. chapters to books; author: Edwin Hugh Lundie FAIA, 1972, An Architectural View: The Minneapolis Society of Fine Arts, 1883-1974, 1974, A Landmark Reclaimed: The Old Federal Courts Building, 1977, Reconfiguring Harvey Ellis, 2004. Mem. State Review Bd., 1976—90, St. Paul Heritage Preservation Commn., 1982—86. Recipient U.S. Govt. Fulbright award, Paris, 1956—57, Vincent Scully Jr. Rsch. award, Archtl. History Found., 1994. Mem.: Coll. Art Assn., Soc. Architectural Historians (dir. 1976—79, sec. 1982—86), Ramsey County Hist. Soc. (cons. 1977), Delta Phi Delta, Phi Beta Kappa. Achievements include establishment of the department of art history at the University of St. Thomas in St. Paul, Minnesota in 1978. Avocation: decorative arts collecting. Home: 2183 Hendon Ave Saint Paul MN 55108 Personal E-mail: epmichels@visi.com.

MICHELS, MARY PAT, music educator; d. Joseph Stephen and Sharon Rose Subjak; m. Drew Peter Michels, July 13, 2002. BA, U. Wis., 1995. Cert. music edn. U. Wis., 1996. Admin. asst. tchr. Milw. Youth Symphony Orch., 1991—2000; program coord. bands, orch. U. Wis., Milw., 1993—97; viola section player, libr. Waukesha Symphony Orch., 1995—; music educator West Allis Sch. Dist., West Allis, 1997—; principal viola Racine Symphony Orch., Wis., 2000—; organist St. Pius V Roman Cath. Ch., Mukwongo, Wis., 2000—. Mgr., violinist Lakeside Strings, New Berlin, Wis., 0995—. Mem.: Wis. Music Educators, Music Educators Nat. Conf., Am. String Tchrs. Assn. Roman Catholic.

MICHELS, RUTH YVONNE, retired cytologist; b. Denver, Aug. 23, 1942; d. James John Crumb and Ruth Marie Hoglund; m. Robert Allen Michels, June 5, 1960; children: Danna Lynn Michels Hardy, Anita Kay Michels Bornschein. AS, Mesa State Coll., Grand Junction, Colo., 1973. Registered cytotechnologist Am. Soc. of Clin. Pathologist, 1974. Rsch. cytotechnologist St. Mary's Hosp. & Med. Ctr., Grand Junction, Colo., 1973—83, clin. cytotechnologist, 1983—85, cytology/histology supr., 1985—93; edn. coord. -cytology program Grand Junction campus U. Utah, Salt Lake City, 1987—88, clin. instr., 1988—93; cons. Shandon, Inc., Pitts., 1988—99; dir. of ops. Saccomanno Rsch. Inst., Grand Junction, Colo., 1993—99; cons. Bayer Diagnostic, Emeryville, Calif., 1999—2001; cytotechnologist - call in position Cmty. Hosp., Grand Junction, Colo., 2000—; cons. Inspire Pharms., Inc., Durham, NC, 2000—01; rsch. cons. Opacity, Inc. (Bio-Imaging Tech.), Grand Junction, Colo., 2001—03; contract employee Mesa County Dept. Pub. Health, 2005—. Mem. nat. adv. com. Am. Soc. of Cytology, Phila., 1990—92; chmn. quality assurance com. on pap smears Colo. State Dept. of Health Women's Health Initiative, Denver, 1991—94; mem. adv. com. on papanicolaou technique: approved guidelines Nat. Com. for Clin. Lab. Stds., Wayne, Pa., 1993—94; human subjects adv. com. mem. U.S. Dept. of Energy, Washington, 1993—99; exec. com. ASSIST - Colo. Dept. of Pub. Health, Denver, 1994—99; developer mass fatalities plan Mesa County Coroner's Office, 2005. Author: (sci. paper) Cancer in Children, Pulmonary Cytologic Specimens using the Shandon Megafunnel (Nat. Soc. of Histology Sci. Paper of the yr., 1998), Geno Saccomanno, MD, Ph.D. Pioneer Pathologist 1915 -1999, Examination of p53 Alterations and Cytokeratin Expression in Sputa Collected from Patients Prior to Histologic Diagnosis of Squamous Cell Carcinoma., Concurrent Flourescence In Situ Hybridization and Immunocytochemistry for the Detection of Chromosome Abberations in Exfoliated Bronchial Epithelial Cells., Cytologic Evaluations of Pulmonary Infiltrates: Tumor vs. Inflammation, (tech. video) The Saccomanno Brush Wash Collection Tube; contbr. documentary film - universal studios Early Warning Lung Cancer; author (presenter): (presentation) Early Detection of Lung Cancer, (human subjects meeting) Educating the Nations IRBS, (lung cancer seminar) Where Do We Go From Here?; author: (sci. paper) The Cytologic Diagnosis of Small Cell Carcinoma of the Lung., A comparison of Saccomanno Smear Slides and the New Large Format Cytospin, Megafunnel Slides of sputum Specimens. Co-chmn. Drug Free Mesa County, Grand Junction, Colo., 1999—2003; mem. Rocky Mountain Divsn., Am. Cancer Soc., Denver, 1995—2003, Colo. Divsn. Am. Cancer Soc., Denver, 1974—95; chmn. bd. dirs. Colo. Divsn., Am. Cancer Soc., Denver, 1991—92; stakeholder on peer rev. grant application com. - cell cycle and growth Nat. Home Office - Am. Cancer Soc., Atlanta, 2000—04. Named Vol. of Yr., Colo. divsn. Am. Cancer Soc., 1982; recipient St. Geroge medal, Nat. Home Office, Am. Cancer Soc., 1995, Bonnie Forquer award for substance abuse prevention, Drug Free Mesa County and the Mesa County Dept. of Pub. Health, 2002, Disting. Alumni award, Mesa State Coll., 2003. Mem.: Internat. Acad. of Cytology (assoc.), Am. Soc. of Cytology (assoc.), Sigma Xi Sci. Rsch. Soc. (assoc.). Independent-Republican. Lutheran. Achievements include patents for Cell Block Collection Method and Apparatus for Cytology Specimens; Cytological Sampling Method and Device using a liquid Based Fixative for Pap smears; Cytological Sampling Method and Device for non gynecological cytology specimens. Avocations: creative writing, reading, bike riding, outdoors activities. Home: 2151 Hawthorne Ave Grand Junction CO 81506-4164 Personal E-mail: rmichels@acsol.net.

MICHELSEN, CLEO, retired education educator, writer; b. Jan. 22, 1909; d. Hamilton Michelsen and Elizabeth Havens; m. Auriel Bessemer (div.). BA in English, George Washington U., Washington, 1943, MA in Theater Arts, 1952. Tchr. D.C. Pub. Schs., Washington, 1931—45; Eng. instr. U. Calif., Berkeley, 1945—47; asst. prof., supr. of student tchg. D.C. Tchr.'s Coll., 1958—65. Instr., creative dramatics George Washington U., 1953—54; dir., children's playhouse Radio Sta. WCFM, Washington, 1948—49. Co-author: (textbook series) Enjoying English, 1961—. Membership chair World Assn. for World Fedn., Amsterdam, Netherlands, 1982—84; pres., so. Calif. region World Federalist Assn., L.A., 1980—86, pres., Va. chpt., 1987—2000. Mem.: World Federalist Assn. (adv. bd. 2000—, pres. 1995), Earth Action (internat. bd. mem. 2003—), Dem. World Federalists (brain trust 2003—). Democrat. Unitarian. Avocations: writing, reading, walking, theater. Home: 3440 S Jefferson St Falls Church VA 22041 E-mail: 1world@cox.net.

MICHELSON, GERTRUDE GERALDINE, retired retail executive; b. Jamestown, NY, June 3, 1925; d. Thomas and Celia Rosen; m. Horace Michelson, Mar. 28, 1947 (dec. Apr. 2002); children: Martha Ann (dec.), Barbara Jane. BA, Pa. State U., 1945; LLB, Columbia U., 1947; LLD with honors, Adelphi U., 1981; DHL with honors, New Rochelle Coll., 1983; LLD with honors, Marymount Manhattan Coll., 1988; PhD in Policy Analysis, Rand Grad. Sch., 2002. Mgmt. trainee Macy's NY, 1947-48, various mgmt. positions, v.p. employee personnel, 1963-70, sr. v.p. labor consumer rels., 1970—72; sr. v.p. pers. labor consumer rels. Macy & Co., Inc., 1972-79, sr. v.p. external affairs, 1979-80, R.H. Macy & Co., Inc., 1980-92, sr. advisor, 1992-94; ret., 1995. Chmn. Helena Rubinstein Found.; bd. dirs. Markle Found.; chmn. emeritus bd. trustees Columbia U.; life trustee Spelman Coll.; past pres. bd. overseers Tchrs. Ins. Annuity Assn. Am. Coll. Retirement Equities Fund. Recipient Disting. Svc. medal Pa. State U., 1969. Mem. NYC Ptnrship. (vice chmn.), Women's Forum, Econ. Club NY Home: 70 E 10th St New York NY 10003-5102 Office: Federated Dept Stores Inc 151 W 34th St New York NY 10001-2101

MICHELSON, LILLIAN, librarian, researcher; b. NYC, June 21, 1928; d. Louis and Dora (Keller) Farber; m. Harold Michelson, Dec. 14, 1947; children: Alan Bruce, Eric Neil, Dennis Paul. Vol. Goldwyn Libr., Hollywood, Calif., 1961-69; owner Former Goldwyn Rsch. Libr., Hollywood, 1969—; ind. location scout, 1973—. Mem. Motion Picture Libr. Found., 2002—, Friends L.A. Pub. Libr. Mem.: Acad. Motion Picture Arts and Scis. Office: c/o Dreamworks SKG Rsch Libr 1000 Flower St Glendale CA 91201-3007 Office Phone: 818-695-6445. E-mail: hmichelson@dreamworks.com.

MICHNICH, MARIE E., health policy analyst, consultant, educator; M Health Svs. Adminstrn., UCLA, DrPH Health Svs. Rsch. Asst. prof. health svs. U. Washington; sr. exec. v.p. Health Policy, Am. Coll. Cardiology Clin. Practice and Sci. Svs. Divsn.; dir. Health Policy Programs and Fellowships Nat. Acad. Scis. Inst. Medicine, 2002—. Cons, spkr. in field; legis. asst. health policy Medicare, Medicaid, maternal and child health; legis. asst. U.S. Senate Majority Leader Robert Dole; mem. several nat. health policy groups. Robert Wood Johnson Health Policy fellow. Mem.: Am. Pharm. Assn. Found. (1st pub. mem. bd. dirs. 2002—), Robert Wood Johnson Health Policy Fellows Program (mem. adv. bd., dir.), Health Care Quality Alliance (former chmn.). Office: Office Health Policy Programs Fellowship 500 5th St NW Washington DC 20001

MICHON, KATHERINE J., lawyer; b. 1964; BA, U. Mass.; JD, New Eng. Sch. Law. Bar: Mass. 1992. Atty. Shilepsky, Messing & Rudavsky, P.C., Dwyer & Collora, LLP; co-founder & ptnr. Kimball, Brousseau & Michon, Boston. Named one of best employment lawyers, Boston Mag., 2002, top Boston lawyers, 2004. Mem.: Mass. Bar Assn.-Labor & Employment Sect. (chairperson Brown Bag Lunch program, employee rights & responsibilities com.). Office: Kimball Brousseau & Michon One Washington Mall 14th Fl Boston MA 02108 Office Phone: 617-367-9449. Office Fax: 617-367-9468.

MICKATAVAGE, JANE CLINE, director; b. Yonkers, N.Y., July 12, 1932; d. George Edward and Lillian Katherine Cline; m. Robert Charles Mickatavage, Mar. 31, 1956; children: Robert, George, Jill, Phebe. BA, Susquehanna U., Selinsgrove, Pa., 1954; MS, Coll. New Rochelle, N.Y., 1986. Cert. family therapy Ctr. for Family Learning. Tchr. elem. edn. various N.J. schs., New Market and Palmyra, 1954—58; reporter Rye Record, NY, 1985—91; coord. comty. svc. Rye County Day Sch., 1985—91; sch. psychologist Rye H.S., 1986—88; family therapist Samaritan Coun., Rye, 1986—96; coord. comty. svc. Rye H.S., 1988—. Leader parenting group Rye H.S. Ch. elder, deacon Rye Presbyn. Ch.; bd. dirs. FIRST, White Plains, NY, 1980—84; co-pres. ICARE, Rye, 1985—; pres. Twig Orgn., United Hosp., 2002—04; mem. human rights com. City Coun., Rye, 2000—. Recipient Samaritan award, Samaritan Counseling Ctr., Rye Youth Coun. award. Mem.: ACA. Avocations: reading, needlecrafts. Home: 81 Hillside Rd Rye NY 10580

MICKELSON, RHODA ANN, speech pathology/audiology services professional; b. Rugby, ND, Oct. 22, 1952; d. Oliver Roger and Doris Marie Stutrud; m. Edward Carl Mickelson, June 27, 1981; children: Alison Marie, Brittany Ann, Elizabeth Ann Marie. BS, Minot State Univ., N.D., 1974; MEd, Univ. N.D., Grand Forks, N.D., 1996. Speech lang. pathologist Lake Region Spl. Edn. Unit, Cavalier County, ND, 1974—76; elem. edn. tchr. Mt. Pleasant Schs., Rolla, ND, 1976—80; elem. tchr. Larimore Pub. Sch., ND, 1980—81; speech lang. pathologist Turtle Mountain Cmty. Sch., Belcourt, ND, 1981—82; disabilities coord., speech pathologist Turtle Mountain Head Start, Belcourt, ND, 1982—91; speech lang. pathologist Turtle Mountain Cmty. Sch., Belcourt, ND, 1991—2006, preschool spl. need tchr., 2006—. Bd. dirs. Internat. Ragtop Festival, Rolla, ND, 1997; com. mem. Boys & Girls Club of Am., Rolla, ND, 2001. Mem.: CEC, WELCA, Elks. Luth. Avocations: travel, reading. Office Phone: 701-477-5546 x 12. E-mail: Rhoda.A.Mickelson@sendit.nodak.edu.

MICKI, BACKSTEIN LYNN, social worker; b. Decatur, Ill., Apr. 15, 1979; d. Richard Eugene and Laura Cay Backstein. BA in Sociology/Psychology, DePaul U., 2004. Mgmt. methods analyst U. Ill., Chgo., 2002—04; sass crisis team Grand Prairie Behavioral Health Svcs., Flossimer, Ill., 2004—. Mental health profl. Grand Prairie Svcs., Flossimer, 2004—. Luth. Avocations: tennis, travel, interior decorating, jewelry making. Home: 1822 S Bishop St #207 Chicago IL 60608 Office: Grand Prairie Behavioral Health Svcs 19530 S Kedzie Ave Flossmoor IL 60422

MICKLE, DELORIS B., retired credit manager, artist; b. Erwin, N.C., Mar. 3, 1951; d. Lewis Hart and Essie Lee Blue; m. Joseph Mickle, Feb. 22, 1970 (div. Jan. 7, 1976); children: Joseph Mickle Jr., Miranda Lanette. Grad. in Graphic Comml. Art, Nova U., 1990; cert. in Electronic Comm., Innovative Tng. Inc., 1998; cert. in Intranet Ware 4.11 Adminstrn., Ctrl. Piedmont C.C., 1998. Sec., key punch op. IBM, White Plains, NY, 1969—73; pheripheral and computer op. S.C. Dept. Mental Health, Columbia, 1973—77; record clk. AT&T, White Plains, 1980—84, reports clk. White Plains and Herndon, Va., 1984—94, billing clk. Charlotte, NC, 1994—2001; ret., 2001. Artist, designer (book cover) 10 Minutes Past Too Late, 2001, photographer (pub.) The Awakening At Hains Point, 2000, patentee in field. Mem. Pioneers, Charlotte, 1990—. Recipient award, Internat. Libr. Photography, 2001. Mem.: Nat. Mus. Women in Arts. Home: 6220 Tiara Ln Apt 102 Charlotte NC 28212-8416 Personal E-mail: delorisdee3@peoplepc.com.

MICKLOS, JANET M., state agency administrator, human services director; b. Jacksonville, Fla., July 24, 1947; d. Thomas Anthony and Yolanda Mae (Murphy) Micklos; married; children: Shawn E. Satterthwaite, Ryan W. Satterthwaite; m. Terry Mercer Maisey, May 28, 1988. BA, U. No. Colo., 1969; MA disting. grad., Webster U., 1985; grad., N.H. Part-Time Police Acad., 1995. Phys. edn. tchr. Terrell Wells Mid. Sch., San Antonio, 1969-70; fitness instr./gymnastic coach Victor Valley C.C., Apple Valley, Calif., 1977-79; dir. phys. dept. Victor Valley YMCA, Victorville, Calif., 1978-79; secretarial support joint U.S. mil. mission aid to Turkey Ankara, Turkey, 1981-82; secretarial support U.S. Logistics Group, Ankara, 1982-83; pub. edn. dir. Alamo Area Rape Crisis Ctr., San Antonio, 1986-88; admissions coord. Horizon Hosp., San Antonio, 1988; psychiat. counselor Portsmouth (N.H.) Pavilion, 1988-89; dir. human svcs. Rockingham County (N.H.) Dept. of Corrections, Brentwood, 1989—. Mem. adv. task force N.H. Coun. Chs., 1992; mem. gov.'s coun. on volunteerism, Seacoast, 1990-93; chmn. outreach commn. 1st United Meth. Ch., Portsmouth, 1990-93; mem. task force on victim restitution Rockingham County, 1992-2000; spl. dep. Rockingham County Sheriff's Dept., 1995-2000; police officer Newfields Police Dept., 1995-2000; trustee Newfields Cmty. Ch. 1994-2000; mem. N.H. Sex Offender Mgmt. Adv. Com., 2004—. Mem. Am. Correctional Assn., Am. Jail Assn. Avocations: archery, gardening, reading, skiing. Office: Rockingham County Dept Corrections 99 North Rd Brentwood NH 03833-6613

MIDCAP, LINDA LUREE, social studies educator; b. Sidney, Nebr., Mar. 6, 1952; d. Ivan Harold and Ardith Luree Gillham; m. Michael Ray Midcap, June 15, 1974; children: Elizabeth(dec.), Sarah, Luke(dec.). AA, Northeastern Jr. Coll., Sterling, Colo., 1972; BA, U. No. Colo., Greeley, 1974. Elem. endorsement U. No. Colo., 1989. Tchr. art Weld Ctrl. H.S., Keenesburg, Colo., 1974—76; tchr. Title I Wiggins Elem. Sch., 1989—91; tchr. history and govt. Wiggins H.S., 1991—. Bd. dirs. Blue Horizons. Office: Wiggins Jr HS 320 Chapman St Wiggins CO 80654-1374

MIDDLEBROOK, DIANE WOOD, English language educator, writer; b. Pocatello, Idaho, Apr. 16, 1939; d. Thomas Isaac and Helen Loretta (Downey) Wood; m. Jonathan Middlebrook, June 15, 1963 (annulled 1976); 1 child, Leah Wood; m. Carl Djerassi, June 21, 1985. BA, U. Wash., 1961; MA, Yale U., 1962, PhD, 1968; LittD (hon.), Kenyon Coll., 1999, U. Mass., Dartmouth, 2005. Asst. prof. Stanford (Calif.) U., 1966—73, assoc. prof., 1978—83, prof., 1983—2001, prof. emerita, 2002—, dir. Ctr. for Rsch. on Women, 1977—79. Author: Walt Whitman and Wallace Stevens, 1974, Worlds into Words: Understanding Modern Poems, 1980, Anne Sexton, A Biography, 1991, Suits Me: The Double Life of Billy Tipton, 1998, Her Husband: Hughes and Plath, a Marriage, 2003; editor: Coming to Light: American Women Poets in the Twentieth Century, 1985; author: (poetry) Gin Considered as a Demon, 1983. Founding trustee Djerassi Resident Artists Program, Woodside, Calif., 1980—83, chair, 1994; trustee San Francisco Art Inst, 1993. Finalist Nat. Book award, 1991; recipient Yale Prize for Poetry; fellow Ind. Study, NEH, 1982—83, Bunting Inst., Radcliffe Coll., 1982—83, Guggenheim Found., 1988—89, Rockefeller Study Ctr., 1990. Fellow: Royal Soc. Lit.; mem.: MLA, Authors Guild, Christs Coll. Cambridge (hon.), The Athenaeum Club, Biographers Club. Avocations: collecting art, theater. Home: 1101 Green St Apt 1501 San Francisco CA 94109-2012 Office: Agent Georges Borchardt 136 E 57th St New York NY 10022 Office Phone: 415-474-1866. E-mail: dwm@stanford.edu.

MIDDLEBROOKS, DELORIS JEANETTE, retired nursing educator; b. Cedar Rapids, Iowa, Apr. 9, 1931; d. Harland R. and Rosa V. (Anderson) Hickey; m. Johnnie L. Middlebrooks, Apr. 25, 1962 (dec.); children: James, Kathleen. Diploma, Evang. Hosp. Sch. Nursing, 1956; BSN, State U. Iowa, 1958; MS in Nursing, U. Calif., San Francisco, 1960; EdD, U. Nev., Las Vegas, 1985. Instr., coord. Nev. State Hosp. Sch. Practical Nursing, Sparks, 1963-66; staff nurse St. Mary's Hosp., Reno, 1968; instr., coord. Reno VA Sch. Practical Nursing, 1968-72; instr., coord. health occupations Wooster High Sch., 1972-73; nursing faculty Truckee Meadows C.C., 1973-94, ret., 1994; intermittent staff nurse VA Hosp., 1984-86; instr., review course Stanley Kaplan Ednl. Ctr., 1987-89; clin. nursing faculty Western Nev. C.C., Carson City, 1987, Northern Nev. C.C., Elko, 1979-93; guest assoc. prof. nursing Lewis-Clark State Coll., Lewiston, Idaho, 1989. Cons. Irish Bd. Nursing, Dublin, Ireland, 1985. Nominated Nev. Voc. Tchr. of Yr., 1975, 79, 88, 89; Recipient March of Dimes Community Leadership award, 1990. Mem.: ANA, Am. Assn. for the History of Nursing, Nev. Nurses Assn., Phi Kappa Phi, Sigma Theta Tau. Home: 1385 Ebbetts Dr Reno NV 89503-1918

MIDDLETON, DAWN E., education educator; b. Pottstown, Pa. d. William H. and Sara G. Bowman; m. Stephen R. Mourar, June 1983; children: William Middleton, Shelly Mourar. AA in Early Childhood Edn., Montgomery Community Coll., 1972; BS in Elem. Edn., West Chester State Coll., 1974; MA in Edn. Curriculum and Instrn. Edn., Pa. State U., 1982, DEd, 1984. Instr. Continuing Edn. Pa. State U., University Park; dir. specialized early childhood programs and svcs. Wiley House, Bethlehem, Pa.; dir. Children's Sch.

of Cabrini Coll., Radnor, Pa.; dept. chmn., prof. edn. Cabrini Coll., Radnor. Home: 208 Bethel Rd Spring City PA 19475-3200 Office Phone: 610-902-8350. E-mail: dawn.middleton@cabrini.edu.

MIDDLETON, DENISE, restaurant owner, real estate agent, educator; b. Camden, N.J., Apr. 28, 1954; d. Anthony Elton and Geraldine Lucille (Meritt) Vail; m. Robert Warner Middleton Jr., Jan. 11, 1975; children: Robert III, Ryan, Ashley. BA in Elem. Edn., Glassboro State Coll., 1976; nursery cert., Glassboro State U., 1982, reading cert., 1984. Owner Larry's Restaurant, Vineland, N.J., 1975-88, Larry's II Restaurant, Vineland, 1987—; tchr. Edgarton Meml. Sch., Newfield, N.J., 1976-77; substitute tchr. Vineland (N.J.) Pub. Schs., 1991-97; real estate agt. Coldwell Banker McClain Heller, Vineland, 1994—. Mem. Vineland (N.J.) Dist. steering com., 1991, U.N. Day Com., Vineland, 1991, Quality Edn. Act., Com., Vineland, 1991. Mem. Vineland Jaycettes, 1975-78; den leader South Jersey coun. Boy Scouts Am., Vineland; coach, pub. rels. Vineland Soccer Assn., 1984-89; referee U.S. Soccer Fedn., 1986-91; v.p. Vineland Mcpl. Alliance, 1990-91, edn. chair, 1987-92; mem. governing bd. Christian and Missionary Alliance Ch., 2001-2005, trustee, 2002-. Mem. Vineland (N.J.) C. of C. (edn. chairperson 1987-92, Pres.' award 1987, Outstanding Chairperson award 1991, Small Bus. of Yr. award 1992). Mem. Christian and Missionary Alliance Ch. Avocations: golf, music, theater, reading. Office: Larrys II Restaurant 907 N Main Rd Bldg A Vineland NJ 08360-8200

MIDDLETON-DOWNING, LAURA, psychiatric social worker, artist, small business owner; b. Edinburg, Ind., Apr. 20, 1935; d. John Thomas Jr. and Rowene Elizabeth (Baker) Middleton; m. George Charles Downing, 1974 (div. 1986). BA in English Lit., U. Colo., 1966, MFA, 1969, BA in Psychology, 1988; MSW, U. Denver, 1992; Doctor of Clin. Hypnotherapy, Am. Inst. Hypnotherapy, 1995. Cert. clin. hypnotherapist, Calif., Colo.; cert. past life therapist, Colo., In ternat. Bd. for Regression Therapy-Level II cert. Profl. artist, Silver Plume and Boulder, Colo., 1965—; profl. photographer Silver Plume, Boulder, 1975—; art tchr. U. Colo., Boulder and Longmont, 1971-73; mem. survey crew Bur. of Land Mgmt., Empire, Colo., 1984-85; cons. social work and psychotherapy Boulder, 1992—; psychiat. and med. social worker Good Samaritan Health Agy., Boulder, 1993-97; pvt. practice clin. hypnotherapy Boulder, 1995—; pvt. practice past-life therapist, 1995—. Pres. Phoenix LG, Inc., 1998-2004 Author, photographer Frontiers, Vol. IV, No. 1, 1979; works exhibited in 15 one-woman shows, 1969—; numerous group exhbns. including group exhbn., Colo. History Mus., Denver, 1997-98. Trustee Town of Silver Plume, Colo., 1975-84; co-founder, pres. Alma Holm Rogers Nat. Orgn. Women, Clear Creek County, 1975-82; mem. Ctrl. Mountain Coun., Clear Creek County, 1980; chairperson Mary Ellen Barnes Cmty. Ctr. Project, Silver Plume, Colo., 1983; vol. Rape Crisis Team, Boulder, 1989-90, Child & Family Advocacy Program, Boulder, 1992-97; adv. bd. mem. Good Samaritan Agy., Boulder, 1993-97; caring minister vol. First Congl. Ch., Boulder, 1995-98; founding mem. Front Range Women in the Visual Arts, Boulder, Colo., 1974. Recipient Juried Exhbn. Merit award Colo. Women in the Arts, 1979; Women's Incentive scholar U. Colo., Boulder, 1989; Grad. Sch. Social Work scholar U. Denver, 1991; Colo. Grad. grantee U. Denver, 1992. Mem. AAUW, NASW, DAR, Colo. Advs. for Responsible Mental Health Svcs., Eye Movement Desensitization Reprocessing Network, Internat. Assn. for Regression Rsch. and Therapies, Inc. (Ecocycle, Colo. block leader), Natural Resources Def. Coun., The Nature Conservancy, World Wildlife Fedn., Bus. Women's Leadership Group, Sierra Club, Defender of Wildlife, Psi Chi. Avocations: skipping, photography, travel, volunteerism, bicycling. Office: PO Box 2312 Boulder CO 80306-2312

MIDKIFF, DINAH LEE, retired elementary and middle school educator; b. Ashland, Ky., Dec. 23, 1954; d. Marie Ramey Midkiff. AA, Ashland Cmty. Coll, 1974; BA, Morehead State U., 1976, MA, 1978, cert. in adminstrn. and supervision, 1980. Tchr. Boyd County Bd. Edn., Ashland, 1976—85, Boone County Bd. Edn., Hebron, Ky., 1989—90, Franklin County Bd. Edn., Frankfort, Ky., 1990—2003, Jessamine County Bd. Edn., Nicholasville, Ky., 2003—04; ret., 2004—. Cons. Ky. Dept. Edn., Frankfort, Ky., 1986—89. Co-author: Jazz Up Reading: A Conference Overview, Informal Selection Process for Grade One Placement. Named Ky. Col., 2001, Maker's Mark Amb., 2005; recipient Drug Abuse Resistance Edn. award, 2002. Mem.: NOW, AAUW, Am. Assn. Ret. Persons, Ky. Ret. Tchr. Assn., Sierra Club (mem. mission trips to Ky., SD, Tex., Mexico, Jamaica). Democrat. Avocations: travel, reading. Home: 1338 Shun Pike Nicholasville KY 40356

MIDLER, BETTE, singer, entertainer, actress; b. Honolulu, Dec. 1, 1945; m. Martin von Haselberg, 1984; 1 child, Sophie. Student, U. Hawaii. Debut as actress (films), Hawaii, 1965, mem. cast Fiddler on the Roof, N.Y.C, 1966—69, Salvation, 1970, Tommy, Seattle Opera Co., 1971, nightclub concert performer on tour U.S., from 1972; appearance Palace Theatre, N.Y.C., 1973, Radio City Music Hall, 1993, TV appearances include The Tonight Show, Bette Midler: Old Red Hair is Back, 1978, Gypsy, 1993 (Golden Globe award best actress in a mini-series or movie made for television, 1994, Emmy nomination, Lead Actress - Special, 1994), Seinfeld, 1996, Diva Las Vegas, 1997, Murphy Brown, 1998, appeared Clams on The Half-Shell Revue, N.Y.C., 1975, recs. include The Divine Miss M, 1972, Bette Midler, 1973, Broken Blossom, 1977, Live at Last, 1977, The Rose, Thighs and Whispers, 1979, Songs for the New Depression, 1979, Divine Madness, 1980, No Frills, 1984, Mud Will Be Flung Tonight, 1985, Beaches (soundtrack), 1989, Some People's Lives, 1990, Bette of Roses, 1995, Bathhouse Betty, 1998, Bette, 2000, Bette Midler Sings The Rosemary Clooney Songbook, 2003; actor: (films) Hawaii, 1966, The Rose, 1979 (Academy award nomination best actress, 1979), Divine Madness, 1980, Jinxed, 1982, Down and Out in Beverly Hills, 1986, Ruthless People, 1986, Outrageous Fortune, 1987, Oliver and Company (voice), 1988, Big Business, 1988, Beaches, 1988, Stella, 1990, Scenes From a Mall, 1991, For the Boys, 1991 (Academy award nomination best actress, 1991), Hocus Pocus, 1993, Get Shorty, 1995, The First Wives Club, 1996, That Old Feeling, 1997, Get Bruce, 1999, Isn't She Great, 1999, Drowning Mona, 2000, Isn't She Great, 2000, The Stepford Wives, 2004; appeared in cable TV (HBO) prodn. Bette Midler's Mondo Beyondo, 1988; author: A View From A Broad, 1980, The Saga of Baby Divine, 1983; exec. prodr., composer (TV show) Bette, 2000, exec. prodr. Some of My Best Friends, 2001, (films) Divine Secret of the Ya-Ya Sisterhood, 2002. Recipient After Dark Ruby award, 1973, Grammy awards, 1973, 1990, spl. Tony award, 1973, Emmy award for NBC Spl., Ol' Red Hair is Back, 1978, 2 Golden Globe awards for The Rose, 1979, Golden Globe award for The Boys, 1991, Emmy award The Tonight Show appearance, 1992.

MIEARS-CUTSINGER, MARY ELLEN, artist, art gallery owner; b. Ratliff, Okla., Jan. 23, 1931; d. Elmer Cecil and Ruth Collins Miears; m. Leroy Gene Meyers (dec.); children: Kathryn, Melissa, Mary Teresa, Marsha, Donna; m. Charles Wesley Cutsinger, Oct. 10, 1979. Student, Mt. San Antonio Coll., Walnut, Calif., 1975—76. Freelance comml. and portrait artist, 1949—76; staff artist Pomona (Calif.) Progress Bull., 1976—77; studio artist Miears Fine Art, Ridgecrest, Calif., 1979—; art tchr. Studio Eight, Ridgecrest, 1989—96; studio artist Miears Fine Art and Studio Eight Gallery, Ridgecrest, 1979—. Mem. gallery com. Maturango Mus., Ridgecrest, 1990. Recipient Top 100 Paintings award, Premier Arts for the Parks Nat., 1987, Wingspread Guide to N.Mex. award, Ann. Art Exhbn., 2000, 2d pl. award, Sierra Pastel Soc. Internat., 2004. Mem.: Allied Artists, Pastel Soc. West Coast (signature mem.), Catharine Lorillard Wolfe Art club (signature mem.). Home: 1125 W Benson Ridgecrest CA 93555 Office: 995 N Norma St Ste # Ridgecrest CA 93555 Office Phone: 760-446-7977. E-mail: mary@kuanyin-images.com.

MIEKKA, JEANETTE ANN, retired science educator; b. Kenmore, NY, Aug. 25, 1931; d. Harry Whittier and Beulah Laura Lambe; m. Richard George Miekka, June 22, 1958; children: James Richard, Frederick Noah, Cynthia Marie Bordas-Miekka. BSc, Boston U., 1949—53, MEd, 1954—57. Teacher of All Sciences Mass., 1954. Tchr. of chemistry, physics, biology, gen. sci. Meridith H.S., Meridity, NH, 1953—54; sci. tchr. and dept. chmn. Hicksville Jr. H.S., 1954—56; biology and physiology tchr. Newton H.S., Mass., 1956—60; instr. of comparative physiology Allied Health Jr. Coll., Holliston, Mass., 1978—79; ret., 1979. Sophomore class advisor Meridith H.S., NH, 1953—54; supr. of student teachers Newton H.S., Mass., 1957—60, advisor, future teachers of am., 1956—60. Contbr. articles to profl. jours. Pres. Am. Field Svc., Natick, Mass., 1964—65; dir. F.I.S.H., Natick, Mass., 1964—65; chmn., publicity Sudbury Women's Club, Mass., 1971—74; mem. Sun Coast Opera Guild; cons. St. Francis Sch., Loiseau, Haiti, 2002—05; assoc. St. Margaret's Convent, Boston; lay eucharistic min. St. Matthews Ch., St. Petersburg, Fla., 2004—05. Mem.: Internat. Women's Writing Guild (assoc.). Episcopal. Avocations: travel, bridge, book club, cooking, writing.

MIELKE, NANCY E., music educator; b. Savanna, Ill., Apr. 13, 1944; d. Edward H. and Isabelle M. Mielke. BS in Elem. Edn. and Music with honors, Western Mont. Coll., 1965; M with hons. in Music Edn., U. Mont., 1974; postgrad., U. Nev. Cert. tchr. Nev. 2d grade tchr. Missoula (Mont.) Sch. Dist., 1965—69, Washoe County Sch. Dist., Reno, 1969—70; elem. gen. music tchr. grades K-6 and spl. edn., mid. sch. choral and handbell dir. grades 6-8 Carson City (Nev.) Sch. Dist., 1970—. Presenter in field. Music dir., childrens, adult and handbell choirs, organist, pianist First United Meth. Ch., Carson City, 1973—. Named Tchr. of Yr., Carson City Schs., 1984, 2004; recipient Outstanding Handbells in Edn. Nat. award, 2000. Mem.: Voice Care Network, Am. Guild English Handbell Ringers (Nat. Exemplary award 2000), Am. Guild Organists, Am. Choral Dirs. Assn., Internat. Soc. for Music Edn., Music Educators Nat. Conf., Delta Kappa Gamma (chpt. pres. 1995—99, state music chair 1995—97, Rose of Recognition 1998). Republican. United Methodist. Avocations: gardening, hiking, reading, antiques. Home: 4098 Northgate Ln Carson City NV 89706

MIERA, LUCILLE CATHERINE MIERA, artist, retired art educator; b. Socorro, N.Mex., Nov. 25, 1931; d. Stephen Maurice and Carmen Rosela (Baca) Miera; m. Vito Modesto Miera Jr., Aug. 22, 1953; children: Stephanie Lucille Miera Mansfield, Jennifer Ann Miera Eberhart. BA, U. N.Mex., 1973, MA, 1976, Ednl. Specialist Sch. Adminstrn., 1984. Cert. tchr., adminstr., N.Mex. Apprentice land surveying and draftsmen Stephen M. Miera, Regional Land Surveyor, Albuquerque, 1946-49; typist Albuquerque Abstract & Title, 1950; typist, engrng. draftsman U.S. Army Corps Engrs., Albuquerque, 1950-57; engrng. draftsman U.S. Dept. Interior, Albuquerque, 1957-59; art tchr., art dept. chair Albuquerque Pub. Sch. Sys., 1973-93, reviewer curriculum devel. plan jr. high schs.; reviewer mid. schs.; ret. Prof. asst. U. N.Mex., Albuquerque, 1974; mid. sch. articulation rep. Taylor Middle Sch., Albuquerque, 1974-83; art rep. North Ctrl. Evaluation Middle Sch., Albuquerque, 1978; pres., art tchr. N.Mex Art League, Albuquerque, 1996, 97, 99; founder art program Emeritus Acad., Tech. Vocat. Inst., 1997, art. tchr., bd. dirs. 1997—. Exhibitions include Mus. Art, Toledo, Ohio, 1964, Kirtland AFB Officers Club, Albuquerque, 1967—68, U. N.Mex., 1969—76, 1999—2000, Albuquerque Pub. Schs. Adminstrn. Bldg., 1973—93, United Bank N.Mex., 1982, Albuquerque C. of C., 1999, exhibited in group shows at N.Mex. State Fair Fine Arts Gallery, N.Mex. State Fair Hispanic Art Gallery, Scottsdale Village Cir. Art Gallery, Old Town Albuquerque De Colores Soaring Eagle and La Hacienda Galleries, Coronado Airport Gallery. Mem., flyer distbr. Rep. Party, Albuquerque, 1954; poll clk. Bernalillo County, Albuquerque, 1960; leader Campfire USA, Albuquerque, 1966, 80; treas. Manzano Band, Albuquerque, 1977; pres. Glenwood Neighborhood Assn., Albuquerque, 1984-87; pres., nat. area dir. Res. Officers Assn. Ladies, Washington, 1989-91. Mem. Nat. Mus. Women's Art (charter), Nat. Hist. Soc., N.Mex. Assn. Educators Ret., N.Mex. Watercolor Soc., N.Mex. Res. Officer Ladies (pres.), N.Mex. Archdiocesan Coun. Cath. Women (pres. 1974), Epsilon Sigma Alpha. Avocations: travel, instructing and displaying art to promote art in the community. Home: 4405 Glenwood Hills Dr NE Albuquerque NM 87111-4260 E-mail: lmierart@aol.com.

MIERAS, ELVIA F., dietician, educator; d. Humberto Saldivar and Rose Martha Flores; m. James Edward Mieras, Jr., Jan. 4, 1992; 1 child, James Edward II. BS in Dietetics and Food Adminstrn., Calif. State U., 1982, MS, 1984. Registered Commn. Dietetic Registration, 1984. Dietetic technician Long Beach (Calif.) Meml. Hosp., 1979—84; dietary supr. Woodruff Convalescent Hosp., Bellflower, Calif., 1984—86; dietician Daibetes Treatment Ctr., Lakewood, Calif., 1986—89, Diabetes Mgmt. and Rsch. Ctr., Center City, Calif., 1989—91; instr. Long Beach City Coll., 1992—. Grantee, Long Beach City Coll., 1999—2000; Carl Perkins-Vatea grant, 1994—96, 1999. Mem.: Am. Dietetic Assn. Roman Catholic. Avocations: golf, tennis, exercise, reading, cooking. Office: Long Beach City Coll 4901 E Carson St Long Beach CA 90808 Office Phone: 562-938-4193. Business E-Mail: emieras@lbcc.edu.

MIERS, HARRIET ELLAN, federal official, lawyer; b. Dallas, Aug. 10, 1945; BS in Mathematics, So. Meth. U., 1967, JD, 1970. Bar: Tex. 1970. Law clk. to Hon. Joe E. Estes US Dist. Ct. (no. dist.) Tex., 1970—72; assoc. Locke Purnell Rain Harrell (formerly Locke, Purnell, Boren, Laney & Neely PC), Dallas, 1972—78, ptnr, 1978—99, pres., 1996—99; mng. ptnr. Locke Liddell & Sapp L.L.P., 1999—2001; asst. to Pres. & staff sec The White House, Washington, 2001—03, asst. to Pres. & dep. chief of staff for policy, 2003—05, gen. counsel to Pres., 2005—; nominee for assoc. justice US Supreme Ct., 2005, withdrew nomination, 2005. Chairwoman, Tex. Lottery Commn., 1995-2000; mem. bd. dirs. Capstead Mortgage Corp., Coamerica Bank, Tex. Comments editor Southwestern Law Jour., 1969-70. Mem.-at-large Dallas City Coun., 1989-91; trustee Southwestern Legal Found. Named 1 of Top 50 Most Influential Lawyers Nat. Law Jour., 1998; named Outstanding Young Lawyer of Dallas, Dallas Assn. of Young Lawyers, 1978, Woman of the Year, Today's Dallas Woman, 1997; Woman of Excellence award, Woman's Enterprise Mag., Louise B. Raggio award, Dallas Women Lawyers Assn., Jurisprudence award, Anti-Defamation League, 1996, Hon. Merrill Hartman award, Legal Svcs. of No. Tex., Sarah T. Hughes award, Women in Law Section State Bat of Tex., Am. Jewish Comm. Human Relations award, DBA's Justinian award for Community Svc. Fellow Am. Bar Found., Tex. Bar Found. (life); mem. ABA (jour. bd. editors, ho. dels., chair credentials and admissions com., election law com., bus. and cmty. activities), Dallas Bar Found., Dallas Bar Assn. (chmn. bd. dirs. 1981, pres., 1985-90), State Bar Tex. (pres. 1992-93, dir. 1986-89), Attys. Liability Assurance Soc. (bd. dirs.). Office: The White House 1600 Pennsylvania Ave NW 2nd Fl Washington DC 20502

MIESLE, ANGELA DENISE, elementary school educator; b. Ft. Wayne, Ind., Oct. 17, 1974; d. Dennis James and Ruth Mary Miesle; 1 child, Madeline Adele. BA in History and Phys. Edn., St. Francis Coll., Ft. Wayne, 1998; MEd in Tchg., Chapman Coll., Pitts., 2001. Program dir. YMCA, Dayton, Ohio, 1998—2000, Ft. Wayne, 1998—2000; tchr. St. James Cathedral Sch., Orlando, Fla., 2002—03, New Haven Mid. Sch., Ind., 2003—. Vol. United Way Allen County, Ft. Wayne, 2004—, UMCA Camp Potawatomi, 2003—05. Avocations: art, travel.

MIGALA, LUCYNA J., journalist, broadcast executive, artistic director; b. Krakow, Poland, May 22, 1944; came to U.S., 1947, naturalized, 1955; d. Joseph and Estelle (Suwala) M.; m. Frank A. Cizon, Oct. 9, 1998. Student, Loyola U., Chgo., 1962-63, Chgo. Conservatory of Music, 1963-70; BS in Journalism, Northwestern U., 1966. Radio announcer, prodr. Sta. WOPA, Oak Park, Ill., 1963—66; writer, reporter, prodr. NBC News, Chgo., 1966—69, 1969—71; prodr. NBC local news, Washington, 1969; prodr., coord. NBC network news, Cleve., 1971—78, field prodr. Chgo., 1978—79; v.p. Migala Comm. Corp., 1979—. Program and news dir., on-air personality Sta. WCEV, Cicero, Ill, 1979—; lectr. City Colls., Chgo., 1981, Morton Coll., 1988. Columnist Free Press, Chgo., 1984-87. Founder, artistic dir., gen. mgr. Lira Ensemble (formerly The Lira Singers), Chgo., 1965—. Artist-in-residence, Loyola U., Chgo.; mem., chmn. various cultural coms. Polish Am. Congress, 1970-80; bd. dir. Nationalities Svcs. Ctr., Cleve., 1973-78; bd. dir., v.p. Cicero-Berwyn Fine Arts Coun., Cicero, Ill., 1980-87; mem. City Arts I and II panels Chgo. Office Fine Arts, 1986-89, 94; v.p. Chgo. chpt. Kosciuszko Found., 1983-86; bd. dir. Polish Women's Alliance Am., 1983-87, Ill. Humanities Coun., 1983-89, mem. exec. com., 1986-87; bd. dir. Ill. Arts Alliance, 1989-92; founder, gen. chmn. Midwest Chopin Piano Competition (later Chgo. Chopin Competition), 1984-86; founding mem. ethnic and folk arts panel Ill. Arts Coun., 1984-87, 92-94; mem. Polonia Census 2000 Com.; bd. dir.Polish-Am. Leadership Initiative, Chgo., 2001—; trustee Lincoln Acad. Ill., 2005—. Fellow Washington Journalism Ctr., 1969; decorated Cavalier's Cross of Merit Govt. Poland; recipient AP Broadcasters award, 1973, Emmy award NATAS, 1974, Cultural Achievement award Am. Coun. Polish Culture, 1990, award of merit Advocates Soc. Polish Am. Attys., 1991, Human Rels. Media award City of Chgo., 1992, Outstanding Achievement award Minister Fgn. Affairs Rep. of Poland, 1994, Civic Achievement award Polish Am. Hist. Assn., 2000, Nat. Creative Arts award Polish Am. Hist. Soc., 2003, Beautiful Spirit award Keep Chgo. Beautiful, Inc., 2005. Mem. Soc. Profl. Journalists. Office: Sta WCEV 5356 W Belmont Ave Chicago IL 60641-4103 also: The Lira Ensemble 6525 N Sheridan Rd # Sky905 Chicago IL 60626-5344 Business E-Mail: lmigala@liraensemble.com.

MIGAS, ROSALIE ANN, social worker; b. Stevens Point, Wis., Apr. 18, 1951; m. Raymond Fonck, Aug. 22, 1977. BA in Social Work and Polit. Sci., U. Wis., 1973, MSSW, 1975. Lic. clin. ind. social worker. House fellow U. Wis., Madison, 1974-75; social worker Kenosha (Wis.) Sch. Dist., 1975-76, Bethesda Luth. Home, Watertown, Wis., 1976-78; supr. coding dept. Gallup Orgn., Princeton, N.J., 1979; supr. casework svcs. Big Bros./Big Sisters Mercer County, Trenton, N.J., 1985-86; social worker Bordentown (N.J.) Sch. Dist., 1979-85, 86-89; AODA/SAP coord. Wis. Heights Sch. Dist., Mazomanie, 1989-91; program mgr. Wis. Assn. on Alcohol and Other Drug Abuse, Madison, 1993-96; program dir. Children's Svc. Soc. Wis., 1997—2005. Adj. instr. Edgewood Coll.; pres. NASW Wis. Chpt., 2002—04; bd. mem. CASA Wis., 2005—. NIMH fellow, 1974. Mem.: NASW (nat. leadership identification com. 1995, chair south ctrl. br. 1998—2001, pres. 2001—04, bd. mem. 2006). Avocations: ice skating, hiking, cross country skiing. Home: 5913 S Hill Dr Madison WI 53705-4447 Business E-Mail: rmigas@edgewood.edu.

MIGEON, BARBARA RUBEN, pediatrician, geneticist, educator; b. Rochester, NY, July 31, 1931; d. William Saul and Sara (Gitin) Ruben; m. Claude Jean Migeon, Apr. 2, 1960; children: Jacques Claude, Jean-Paul, Nicole. BA, Smith Coll., Northampton, Mass., 1952; MD, SUNY, Buffalo, 1956. Diplomate Am. Bd. Pediatrics; cert. in med. genetics. Pediatric residency The Johns Hopkins U., Balt., 1956-59; fellow in endocrinology Harvard U. Med. Sch., Boston, 1959-60; fellow in genetics The Johns Hopkins Sch. Medicine, Balt., 1960-62, assoc. prof. pediatrics, 1970-79, joint appointment in biology, 1978—, prof., 1979—, founding dir. PhD program in human genetics and molecular biology, 1979-89; Exch. prof. Guys Hosp., 1986. Mem. Genetics Study Sect., NIH, Bethesda, Md., 1975-77, Mammalian Genetics Study Sect., NIH, Bethesda, 1977-79, Human Genome Study Sect., NIH, Bethesda, 1991-93; vis. investigator Carnegie Instn. Washington, 1975. Contbr. more than 100 rsch. papers to profl. publs. Recipient Outstanding Woman Physician award Med. Coll. Pa. Mem. Am. Soc. Human Genetics. Office: Inst Genetic Medicine BRB 459 The Johns Hopkins U Baltimore MD 21205 Office Phone: 410-955-3049. Business E-Mail: bmigeon@jhmi.edu.

MIGIELICZ, GERALYN, photojournalist; b. St. Louis, Feb. 15, 1958; d. Edward J. and Mary Ann (McCarthy) M. BJ, U. Mo., 1979. Photographer Emporia (Kans.) Gazette, 1979-80; chief photographer St. Joseph (Mo.) News-Press & Gazette, 1980-83; photo editor, photographer Seattle Times, 1984; picture editor Rocky Mountain News, Denver, 1985-86; graphics editor San Jose (Calif.) Mercury News, 1986-92, dir. photography, 1992—. Mem. faculty Poynter Inst., U. Mo. Workshop, Latin Am. Photojournalism Conf., Stan Kalish Picture Editing Workshop. Knight fellow Stanford U., 2005; recipient Individual Editing awards Soc. Newspaper Designers, 1988-04, Editing awards, 91-01; named for Overall Excellence in Editing, Picture of Yr. Contest, U. Mo., 1993. Office: San Jose Mercury News 750 Ridder Park Dr San Jose CA 95131-2432

MIGIMOTO, FUMIYO KODANI, retired secondary school educator; b. Oxnard, Calif, Jan. 2, 1918; d. Katsutaro and Yoshio Kodani; m. Tadao Migimoto, June 1956. BA, UCLA, 1939, cert. teaching, 1940; MA, Oberlin Coll., 1953; cert. in teaching, U. Hawaii, 1956. Cert. secondary tchr., Calif., Hawaii. Asst. to dean of coll. Oberlin Coll., Ohio; English tchr. Jackson Coll., Honolulu, Hawaii State Dept. Edn., Honolulu; retired. Mem. textbook evaluation com., Hawaii. Author many poems, editor, military newsletters 1993-1999. Grantee, Hawaii State Dept. Edn. Mem ASCD, Internat. Soc. Poets, Pan-Pacific S.E. Asia Women's Assn. Hawaii (past exec. v.p.), Hawaii Edn. Assn., Hawaii State Retired Tchr. Assn., Oahu Retired Tchr. Assn., Alliance for Drama Edn., UCLA Alumni Assn., Oberlin Alumni Assn., Poetry Acad., Alpha Delta Kappa (past chpt. exec. pres., chmn. frat. edn.). Home: 999 Wilder Ave Apt 303 Honolulu HI 96822-2628

MIGLIORINO, CAROLINE MILANO, nursing consultant; b. Shaker Heights, Ohio; d. Albino and Albina (Tognaccini) Milano; m. Mauro A. Miglorino; children: Paul P., Monica M., Marc J., Laura E. ADN, Prairie State Jr. Coll., Chicago Heights, Ill., 1974; BSN, Gov.'s State U., University Park, Ill., 1977, MSN, 1984; PhD med. candidate anthropology, U. Minn., 1999; PhD (hon.), Cambridge U., 2005. Cert. in addictions. Dir. health svcs. Art Inst. Chgo., 1978-84; managed care specialist dept. psychiatry Christ Hosp., Oak Lawn, Ill., 1990-93; counselor chem. dependence and addictions Oak Lawn; prof. med. psychiatry & addictions; adj. prof. clin. psychiatry South Suburban Jr. Coll., South Holland, Ill., 1994—, Joliet (Ill.) Jr. Coll., 1994—. Managed care specialist Christ Hosp., Oak Lawn; adj. prof. South Suburban Jr. Coll., Joliet Jr. Coll. Recipient Acad. award Gov.'s State U. Alumni Assn., 1984. Mem. ANA, Ill. Nurses Assn., Nat. Nurses Soc. on Addictions. Home: 37 S Stough St Hinsdale IL 60521-3014

MIHALIK, PHYLLIS ANN, management consultant, systems analyst, educator; b. Cleve., Mar. 11, 1952; d. Henry Arvon and Dorothy (Markovich) Trepal; m. John P. Mihalik, Aug. 5, 1972. AA, Lakeland Coll., 1982; BS in Computer Sci., Lake Erie Coll., 1986; Exec. Masters in Bus. Adminstrn., Case Western Res. U., 1992. Acct. Picker Internat., Highland Heights, Ohio, 1977-80, programmer, analyst, 1980-82, fin. systems analyst, 1982-83; sr. systems analyst Harris, Solon, Ohio, 1983-84, mgr. systems and programming, 1984-86, dir. internal audit, 1986-88; pres., owner Productivity & Mgmt. Cons., Chardon, Ohio, 1988—; owner PM Cons. and Remodeling, Chardon, 2000—. Faculty mem. Lakeland Coll., Mentor, Ohio, 1987—. Author: Introduction to PC's, 1989, Managing the PC Work Environment, 1989. Adv. bd. chmn. Master Garden OSO Deaga Co., 2004—. Mem. Data Processing Mgmt. Assn., Assn. for Systems Mgmt., Women Bus. Owners. Avocations: horticulture, travel, stained glass, interior design. Office: Productivity and Mgmt Cons 11457 Fowlers Mill Rd Chardon OH 44024-8720 Office Phone: 440-285-9487.

MIHELIC, TRACEY L., lawyer; b. Lake Forest, Ill., Sept. 12, 1965; BA, Ill., 1990. With Gardner, Carton & Douglas, Chgo., 1990—2000, ptnr., 1998—2000, Baker & McKenzie, Chgo., 2000—. Mem.: ABA, Internat. Emissions Trading Assn., Emissions Mktg. Assn., Ill. State Bar Assn. Office: Baker and McKenzie One Prudential Plz 130 E Randolph Dr Chicago IL 60601

MIHURA, JONI LYNN, psychologist, educator; BS in Psychology, Okla. State U., Stillwater, 1987, PhD, 1995. Lic. clin. psychologist Ohio. Assoc. prof. psychology U. Toledo, 1996—. Rschr. in field; pvt. practice psychotherapy. Predoctoral fellow, Ford Found., 1990—93. Mem.: APA (fellow 1999—2000), Soc. Psychotherapy Rsch., Soc. Personality Assessment (Samuel J. and Anne G. Beck award for outstanding early career sch. in personality assessment 2002). Office: U Toledo 2801 W Bancroft St Toledo OH 43606

MIILLER, SUSAN DIANE, artist; b. NYC; d. Charles and Alyce Mary (Gebhardt) Knapp. BFA, SUNY, 1988; MFA, U. North Tex., Denton, 1992. Scenic designer Forestburgh Playhouse, NY, 1989; adj. prof. Tex. Christian U., Ft. Worth, 1992-94; lectr. U. Tex., Dallas, 1995-99, SUNY, New Paltz, 1999—. Treas. mem. 500X Gallery, Dallas, 1991-92. One-woman shows include Western Tex. Coll., 1993, Brazos Gallery, Richland Coll., 1993, Women & Their Work Gallery, 1995 (Gallery Artists Series award, 1995), A.I.R. Gallery, 1996, Milagros Contemporary Art, 1996, Pentimenti Gallery, Pa., 1997, Plano Art Ctr., 1999, Orange County C.C., 2000, Continental Gallery, 2001, Marie Park Studios, 2001, Weir Farm Trust, Plano Art Ctr., 2003, SUNY New Paltz, 2004, Catskill Art Gallery, 2005, Honor's Ctr., SUNY, New Paltz, Karpeles Mus., Newburgh, N.Y., 2006; resident artist Weir Farm Nat. Hist. Trust, Catskill Ctr. for Conservation, 2006. Recipient 4th Nat. Biennial Exhbns. Grand Purchase award, 1991, Mus. Abilene award, 1992, Lubbock Art Festival Merit award, 1992, 2d pl. award, Matrix Gallery, 1995, Hon. Mention award 3d Biennial Gulf of Mex. Exhbn., 1995, 1st place award, Soho Gallery, 1996, Juror's Choice award, Bucking the Texan Myth Exhbn., 1998, hon. mention, Susquehanna Art Mus., 1998, 1999, Faculty Devel. award, 2001, 2004, 2006, NYSCA award, 2003, 2d pl. award, Orange County Exhibit, 2005, Individual Devel. award, SUNY, 2006. Mem. Coll. Art Assn., Greene County Coun. on Arts, NY Acad. Arts, Del. Valley Arts Alliance. Business E-Mail: miillers@newpaltz.edu.

MIKEL, SARAH ANN, librarian; b. Bklyn., Aug. 29, 1947; d. Robert H. and Sarah A. (Saver) Whalen; m. John R. Mikel, Oct. 21, 1977; 1 dau., Katherine Ann. B.A., U. Miami, 1969; M.A., U. Fla., 1971; M.A.L.S., Rosary Coll., River Forest, Ill., 1973. Editorial researcher Field Ednl. Enterprises, Chgo., 1971-72; librarian Purdue U., West Lafayette, Ind., 1973-75, U.S. Army Corps of Engrs., Rock Island, Ill., 1975-76, chief librarian, Washington, 1976-87, major command librarian, 1987-91; libr. dir. Nat. Def. Libr., Washington, 1991—; chmn. FEDLINK Users Group, 1980-83; mem. exec. adv. coun. FEDLINK, 1988-90; program chmn. Fed. Interagy. Field Librs. Workshop, 1983-84; mem. com. Fed. Libr. and Info. Ctr., 1992-95; mem. mil. edn. coordinating com. Libr. Group. Mem. Spl. Libr. Assn. (chmn. mil. librs. 1978-79), Army Libr. Inst. (chmn. 1988, 94, Army dep. functional chiefs rep. 1992-94, vice chair, federal libr. and info. ctr. commn., 2003). Home: 3343 Reservoir Rd NW Washington DC 20007-2312 Office: Nat Def Univ Ft Leslie J McNair 4th & P St SW Washington DC 20319-0001 Office Phone: 202-685-3948. E-mail: mikels@ndu.edu.

MIKELL, MARTHA SIMMS, secondary school educator; b. Fredericksburg, Va., Oct. 6, 1975; d. Albert E. Simms, Jr. and Jane C. Sthreshley, James B. Sthreshley (Stepfather) and Lois A. Simms (Stepmother); m. Stephen Abraham Mikell, June 21, 2003. BS Kinesiology, Coll. William & Mary, Williamsburg, Va., 1993—97; MEd, Old Dominion U., Norfolk, Va., 2000—02. Cert. athletic trainer Bd. Cert. Athletic Trainers, 1997, strength & conditioning specialist Nat. Strength & Conditioning Assn., 2005, BLS healthcare provider and heartsaver first aid instr. Am. Heart Assn., 2004. Sci. tchr., athletic trainer, adv. coord. Hampton Roads Acad., Newport News, Va., 1997—2006; athletic trainer Augusta County Pub. Schs., Stuarts Draft, Va., 2006—. Bd. certification home study reviewer Bd. Cert. Athletic Trainers, 2005—. Vol. Animal Aid Soc., Hampton, Va., 2004—06. Recipient, Phi Kappa Phi Honor Soc., 2002. Mem.: Nat. Strength & Conditioning Assn., Va. Athletic Trainers Assn., Nat. Athletic Trainers Assn. Home: 45 Flory Ave Stuarts Draft VA 24477 Personal E-mail: themikells@yahoo.com.

MIKELS, JO, science educator; b. Findlay, Ohio, Oct. 24, 1952; d. A. Robert and Mary Welsh Kostyo; m. John Kenneth Mikels, Aug. 28, 1952; children: Shana, Erin. BA, U. Tex. at Pan Am., Edinburg, 1974. Cert. tchr. Tex., 1974, early adolescence, sci. tchr. Nat. Bd. for Profl. Tchg. Stds., 2003. Tchr. Austin Ind. Sch. Dist., Tex., 1982—. Tchr., cons. Tex. Mining and Reclaimation Assn., Austin, 2001—. Recipient Tchr. of Yr. award, Mendez Mid. Sch., 1998, Mid. Sch. Tchr. of Yr. award, Tex. Mining and Reclaimation Assn., 2002. Mem.: Edn. Austin, Phi Delta Kappa, Delta Kappa Gamma (Alpha State Lambda Iota chpt. pres. 2006—). Avocation: reading. Home: 7205 Towering Oaks Dr Austin TX 78745 Office: Clint Small Jr Mid Sch 4801 Monterey Oaks Blvd Austin TX 78749 Office Phone: 512-841-6739. Office Fax: 512-841-6703. Personal E-mail: koszmik@gmail.com. E-mail: jmikels@austinisd.org.

MIKESELL, MARY (JANE MIKESELL), psychotherapist; b. Oct. 29, 1943; d. John and Mary C. (Leighty) Wagner. BA, Calif. State U., Northridge, 1967; MA, Pacific Oaks Coll., 1980; PhD, Calif. Grad. Inst. Psychology, 1989. Tchr. L.A. pub. schs., 1966-69; photog. lab. dir. Oceanograficos de Honduras, Roatan, 1969-70; supr. L.A. Life Ins. Co., 1970-72; customer svc. rep. Beverly Hills Fed. Savs. & Loans, Calif., 1972-73; mem. staff counseling ctr. Calif. State U., Northridge, 1974-78; head office svcs. Pacific Oaks Coll., Pasadena, Calif., 1978-79; prodn. supr. Frito-Lay, Inc., L.A., 1979-81; circulation supr. Daily News, Van Nuys, Calif., 1981-82; ednl. therapist, marriage, family and child counselor intern Barr Counseling Ctr., 1982-86, Victory-Tampa Psychol. Ctr. (now Ctr. for Human Devel.), San Fernando Valley, Calif., 1982-89; project coord. Carlson Rockey & Assocs., Brentwood, Calif., 1983-84; staff mem. Southland Olympic News Bur., Sub-Ctr. Steward Press Ops., Olympic Water Polo Venue, LAOOC, 1983-84; project coord., comms. and sys. specialist Student Ins. divsn. William F. Hooper, Inc., Brentwood, 1985-87; child counselor The Poinsetta Found., Ventura, Calif., 1990-91, The Calabasas Acad., Calif., 1991, prin., 1992-95, Hillside Acad., 1995-96; child counselor Brighton Acad., 1992-93; prin., CEO S.F. Space and Mil. Sci. Acad., Inc., 1996-98; marriage, family and child therapist Project Genesis, com-cart, project hope and part time programs mgr. Interface, Inc., Camarillo, Calif., 1999—2006; dir. diagnostics Children's Mental Health Diagnostics and Treatment Svcs. of Ventura County, Inc., Simi Valley, Calif., 2006—. Cons. Designer Collection by Pingy, 1985, others; dir. vocat. program Brighton Acad., 1992-93. Photographer. Mem. APA, Am. Assn. for Counseling and Devel., Calif. Scholarship Fedn., Calif. Grad. Inst. Psychology Student Assn. (v.p. 1985-88), Nat. Space Soc., CSUN Anthropology Club. Republican. Avocations: photography, writing, theoretical physics, astronomy, sports. Office: Childrens Mental Health Diagnostics and Treatment Svcs PO Box 2181 Simi Valley CA 93062

MIKIEWICZ, ANNA DANIELLA, marketing and international business export manager; b. Chgo., Dec. 22, 1960; d. Zdislaw and Lucy (Magnusweska) M. BS in Mktg., Elmhurst Coll., 1982; postgrad., Triton Coll. Asst. to midwestern regional mgr. Melster Pub. Co., Chgo., 1983; sales rep. First Impressions, Elk Grove, Ill., 1984; asst. to Midwestern dist. mgr. Airco Ind. Gases, Broadview, Carol Stream, Ill., 1985; customer svc. & ops. mgr. Yamazen USA, Inc., Schaumburg, Ill., 1985-88; nat. sales & mktg. coord. Kitamura Machinery U.S.A. Inc., 1988-95; mktg. mgr. Beth Lee Boutique, 1995-97; internat. bus. export control sales coord. MHI Machine Tool USA, Inc. subs. Mistubishi Heavy Industries, 1997-99; internat. bus. asst. to exec. v.p. sales America Excel, Inc., Elk Grove Village, Ill., 1999—; internat. bus. Brazil Market JST Sales Am., Inc., Waukegan, Ill., 2000—04; internat. export bus. mgr. global worldwide market Anixter, Inc., 2005—. Named Chgo. Polish Queen Polish Am. Culture Club, 1983-84. Mem.: NAFE. Republican. Roman Catholic.

MIKKELSEN, BARBARA BERRY, retired retail executive, rancher; b. Wichita Falls, Tex., June 16, 1942; d. Marshall Keith Berry and Louie Arlene Williams; m. John Hardie Mikkelsen, Nov. 24, 1967. BA, Tulane U., New Orleans, La., 1965. Pres. White Rabbit, Inc, Vernon, Tex., 1980—96, Plum Creek Farms, Inc, Vernon, Tex., 1985—. Adv. bd. Vernon Humane Soc., Tex., 1983—2003; mem. Adv. Bd. for Vernon State Hosp., Vernon, Tex., 1974; mem. of bd. Vernon Boys and Girls Club, Vernon, Tex., 1969—2003; chmn. spl. events Santa Fe Opera, 2003—05, mem. of bd., 2003—, Anson County Hist. Soc., Wadesboro, NC, 1988—89, Red River Valley Mus., Vernon, Tex., 1983—2000, Wilbarger Country Hist. Soc., Vernon, Tex., 1988—99; pres. Vernon Jr. League, Vernon, Tex., 1969—71, mem. of bd., 1971—76, Broadway Theatre League, Wichita Falls, Tex., 1970—72. Recipient 25 Yr. Award, Vernon Boys and Girls Club, 1994, Donor, Vernon Humane Soc., 1984. Avocations: raising and training horses, art, travel, opera, theater. Office: 2429 Texas St Vernon TX 76384 Home: 8 Altazano Dr Santa Fe NM 87505 Personal E-mail: eagle505@earthlink.net.

MIKKELSEN, NINA ELIZABETH MARKOWITZ, writer, researcher; b. Mullens, W.Va., Dec. 3, 1942; d. Paul and Martha (Sullivan) Markowitz; m. Vincent Peter Mikkelsen, Aug. 16, 1965; children: Vincent Peter, Mark Evin. BS, Concord Coll., 1964; MA, Fla. State U., 1966, PhD, 1971. English educator Fla. State U., Tallahassee, 1964-70, East Carolina U., Greenville, N.C., 1978-80, 82-83, Ind. (Pa.) U., 1986-91, 98-99. Cons. lit. and literacy Ea. N.C. Sch. Dists., 1980-85. Author: Virginia Hamilton, 1994, Susan Cooper, 1998, Words and Pictures, 1999, Powerful Magic: Learning From Children's Responses to Fantasy Literature, 2005; contbr. articles to profl. jours. and books. Mem. MLA, Nat. Coun. Tchrs. English. Home: 104 Williams St Emerald Isle NC 28594-3649

MIKLES, CHRIS, secondary school educator; b. Annapolis, Md., Apr. 23, 1950; d. Robert Edward and Ruth Baier (McBride) Melhorn; m. Scott Allen Mikles, Jan. 5, 1974; children: Andrew Christopher, Allen Scott. AA, Ventura Coll., 1970; BS, Calif. Poly. State Univ., 1972. Cert. tchr., Calif., Idaho, Wash. Tchr. St. Thomas Aquinas Sch., Ojai, Calif., 1972-76, Rio Sch. Dist., El Rio, Calif., 1976-79, Ventura (Calif.) H.S., 1985-95, Univ. Idaho, Coeur d'Alene, 1996—; dir. tchrs. edn. CPM Ednl. Program, Sacramento, 1995—. Cons. math. State Calif., Ventura. Bd. dirs. PTA, Am. Youth Soccer Assn., Ventura, 1987-90, soccer coach, 1990-94; chairperson Non-Traditional Career Day, Ventura, 1990-95; coach Ventura Youth Basketball, 1994. Finalist Pres. award for excellence in tchg. and math., 1994. Mem. AAUW (v.p., pres., pres Corerd'Alena br. 1997-99, Eleanor Roosevelt Tchr. fellow 1994), Nat. Coun. Tchrs. Math., Wash. Math. Coun., Calif. Math. Coun., Idaho Math. Coun., Ventura County Math. Coun. (bd. dirs., Tchr. of Yr. 1993), Nat. Coun. Sup. Math, Nat. Mid. Sch. Assn. Republican. Avocations: sports, crafts, camping. Home: 8102 N Spokane St Post Falls ID 83854-4519 Office Phone: 888-808-4276.

MIKSIS, CHRISTINA BARBARA, psychologist; b. Elmhurst, Ill., Jan. 17, 1971; d. Albert Charles Miksis and Regina Vyga Suhr. BS, U. Iowa, 1993; MA, Ill. Sch. Profl. Psychology, 1997, D in Psychology, 2001. Lic. clin. psychologist Ill. Bd. Regulations, 2002. Asst. clin. dir. The MENTA Group, Inc./Fox Tech, North Aurora, Ill., 2002—03; clin. dir. The MENTA Group, Inc/Fox Tech, 2003—04; outpatient coord., clin. tng. coord. Alexian Ctr. Mental Health, Arlington Heights, 2004—. Mem.: APA. E-mail: christina.miksis@abnwmhc.net.

MIKULAK, MARCIA LEE, anthropologist, educator; m. Robert R. West, Aug. 19, 2002. MusB, San Francisco Conservatory Music, 1970; MFA, Mills Coll., Oakland, Calif., 1974; PhD, U. N.Mex, Albuquerque, 2002. Rsch. asst. U. N.Mex, Albuquerque, 1998—2001; asst. prof. U. ND, Grand Forks, 2002—. Dir. Santa Fe Rsch., 1984—2000. Musician: (concert pianist solo rec.) American Contemporary Music of Dane Rudhyar. Faculty mem., multi-cultural activities com. U. ND, Grand Forks, 2004—06; mem. Amnesty Internat., 1999—2006; active Cmty. Violence Intervention Ctr., Grand Forks, 2004—06. Mem.: Am. Anthropological Assn. (assoc.; mem.). Achievements include research in the social construction of disposable children, street and working children in Minas Gerais, Brazil. Office: U ND Babcock Hall 236 Centennial Dr Stop 8374 Grand Forks ND 58202 Office Phone: 701-777-4718. Office Fax: 701-777-4006. E-mail: marcia.mikulak@und.nodak.edu.

MIKULSKI, BARBARA ANN, senator; b. Balt., July 20, 1936; d. William and Christine (Kutz) M. BA in Sociology, Mt. St. Agnes Coll., 1958; MSW, U. Md., 1965; LLD (hon.), Goucher Coll., 1973, Hood Coll., 1978, Bowie State U., 1989, Morgan State U., 1990, U. Mass., 1991; DHL (hon.), Pratt Inst., 1974. Tchr. Vista Tng. Ctr. Mount St. Mary's Sem., Balt.; social worker Balt. Dept. Social Services, 1961-63, 66-70; mem. Balt. City Council, 1971-76, 95th-99th Congresses from 3d Md. Dist., 1977-87; US Senator from Md., 1987—; sec. Dem. Conf. 104th-106th Congress. Adj. prof. Loyola Coll., 1972-76; mem. U.S. Senate labor and human resources com., 1987—, ranking mem. subcom. on aging, 1993—; mem. appropriations com., 1987, ranking mem. subcom. on vets., housing, and ind. agys., 1987—. Bd. visitors U.S. Naval Acad.; bd. adv. Space Awareness Alliance. Recipient Nat. Citizen of Yr. award Buffalo Am.-Polit. Eagle, 1973, Woman of Yr. Bus. & Profl. Women's Club Assn., 1973, Outstanding Alumnus U. Md. Sch. Social Work, 1973, Govt. Social Responsibility award, 1991, Disting. Svc. award Ctrl. and East European Coalition, 1996, Louis D. Brandeis award Baltimore, Md. Zionist Dist., 1996, Public Svc. award Am. Inst. Aeronautics and Astronautics, 1998, Order of Merit Commanders Cross with Star Govt. Poland, 2001, Good Housekeeping/Wyeth award women's health, 2002, Connie Mack Lifetime Avhievement award Susan G. Komen Breast Cancer Found., 2003, Elmer P. Martin Public Svc. award Great Blacks in Wax Mus., 2003, Public Svc. award Emergency Nurses Assn., 2004, Nat. Leadership award Big Brothers and Big Sisters of Ctrl. Md., 2005. Mem. LWV. Democrat. Roman Catholic. Office: US Senate 503 Hart Sen Office Bldg Washington DC 20510-0001 also: Brown's Wharf Ste 400 1629 Thames St Baltimore MD 21231 Office Phone: 202-224-4654, 410-962-4510. Office Fax: 202-224-8858, 410-962-4760.*

MIKUMO, AKIKO, lawyer; b. Kyoto, June 18, 1953; BA, U. Calif., Berkeley, 1978; JD, NYU, 1982. Assoc. Weil, Gotshal & Manges LLP, N.Y.C., 1982—90, ptnr., 1990—, head U.S. practice London, 1998—2000. Mem.: ABA (mem. com. on corp. law 1993—), Assn. of the Bar of the City of N.Y. Office: Weil Gotshal & Manges LLP 767 Fifth Ave New York NY 10153 Office Phone: 212-310-8000.

MIKUS, ELEANORE ANN, artist; b. Detroit, July 25, 1927; d. Joseph and Bertha (Englot) M.; m. Richard Burns, July 6, 1949 (div. 1963); children: Richard, Hillary, Gabrielle. Student, Mich. State U., 1946-49, U. Mex., summer 1948; B.F.A., U. Denver, 1957, MA, 1967; postgrad., Art Students League, 1958, NYU, 1959-60. Asst. prof. Cornell U., Ithaca, NY, 1979-80, assoc. prof., 1980-92, prof. art, 1992-94, prof. emerita, 1994—. Asst. prof. art Monmouth Coll., West Long Branch, N.J., 1966-70, prof. Cornell, Rome, 1989; vis. lectr. painting Cooper Union, N.Y.C., 1970-72, Central Sch. Art and Design, London, 1973-77, Kensington Inst., London, 1974-77, Harrow (Eng.) Coll. Tech. and Art, 1975-76. One-woman shows at Pace Gallery, NYC (1963, 64, 65) and O.K. Harris Gallery (1971, 72, 73, 74), NYC, Baskett Gallery, Cin., 1982, 84-85, Claudia Carr Gallery, 1998—, Mitchell Algus Gallery, NYC, 1998, 2003, 04, Drawing Ctr., NYC, 2006; represented in permanent collections including Met. Mus. Art, NYC, Mus. Modern Art, NYC, Whitney Mus., NYC, Los Angeles County Mus., Cin. Mus., Birmingham Mus. Art, Ala., Norton Simon Mus., Pasadena, Bklyn. Mus., Honolulu Acad. Arts, Indpls. Mus. Art, Nat. Gallery Art, Washington, Victoria and Albert Mus., London, Libr. of Congress, Washington, Tucson Mus. of Art, Blanton Mus. U. Tex., U. Ariz. Mus. Art, Tucson, Univ. Ariz., Tucson, De Cordova Mus., Lincoln, Mass.; subject of book Eleanore Mikus, Shadows of the Real (by Robert Hobbs and Judith Bernstock), 1991. Fellow, Guggenheim, 1966—67, Tamarind, 1968, McDowell, 1969, Yaddo drawing and painting, 2004. Home: PO Box 4775 Ithaca NY 14852-4775 Office: Cornell U Dept Art Tjaden Hall Ithaca NY 14853 also: 270 Luce Rd Groton NY 13073-9747 Office Phone: 607-533-7766. Personal E-mail: mikusart44@hotmail.com.

MILAM, MELISSA GAIL, elementary school educator; b. Cin., Oct. 16, 1982; d. James C. and Deborah A. Funk; m. Daniel Joel Milam, June 25, 2005. BS, Lipscomb U., Nashville, 2001—05. Cert. Tchr. K-8 Tenn. Dept. Edn., 2005. Extended tchr./camp counselor Franklin Rd. Acad., Nashville, 2001—; third grade tchr. Met. Nashville Pub. Schs., 2005—. Office Phone: 615-333-5043. Business E-Mail: melissa.milam@mnps.org.

MILAN, ELLEN JUDITH, artist; b. Bronx, N.Y., Mar. 23, 1937; d. Joseph B. and Kay (Rosenblum); m. Donald Barnard Milan, April 27, 1957; children: Janice Moore, Sharon. BS in Art Edn., U. Wis., 1958. Cert. tchr., Mass., Wis. Art tchr. Madison (Wis.) Sch. System, 1957-58, Madison Tech. Coll., 1968-70, Newton (Mass.) Pub. Schs., 1985—2003, Cultural Edn. Collaborative, Boston, 1987—. Leader workshop Brookline (Mass.) High Sch., 1988; lectr. in field. One woman shows include U. Wis., Madison, Beloit (Wis.) Coll., Hebrew Coll., Brookline, Mass., Aquinas Jr. Coll., Newton, Mass., Waltham (Mass.) Pub. Libr., Harvard Neighbors, Cambridge, Mass., Lexington (Mass.) Pub. Libr.; exhibited in group shows at IVV Grand Prix Internat., D'Art, Monaco, 1971, Florence Biennali, 1972, Zurich Exhbn. Jerusalem Artists, 1973, Mus. Modern Art, Haifa, Mass. Bay Community Coll., Wellesley, 1987, Schlesinger Libr., Radcliffe Coll., 1991. Recipient 1st prize Municipality of Jerusalem, 1971, prize Nat. Print Exhbn., Big Bend Nat. Art Exhbn. Mem.: Concord Art Assn. Home and Office: 152 Chestnut Cir Lincoln MA 01773-4918

MILANA PANOPOULOS, MARIA, artist; b. Oceanside, NY, Nov. 13, 1965; d. Thomas F. and Angelina M. Milana; m. Michael S. Panopoulos, May 1988; children, Thomas, Nicholas Student, Kingsborough C.C., Manhattan Beach, N.Y., 1983-84, Nassau C.C., Garden City, N.Y., 1984-85. Freelance model, N.Y., Fla., 1981—; model Home Shopping Network, N.Y., Fla., 1992-93; owner Artistic Creations, Custom Faux You, Maria Panopoulos,owner, 2006—. Poet. Mem. adv. bd. Trinity Oaks Homeowners Assn., New Port Richey, Fla., 1992-93. Mem. Tarpon Springs Art Assn. (bd. dirs. 1998—), Herbal Healer Acad. Republican. Roman Catholic. Achievements include patent for knee brace. Business E-Mail: cre8tive@tampabay.rr.com.

MILANO, ALYSSA, actress; b. N.Y.C., Dec. 19, 1972; d. Thomas M. and Lin Milano.; m. Cinjun August Tate, Jan. 1, 1999 (div. Nov. 20, 1999). Student, Bel Air Prep. Sch., L.A. Appeared on TV series Who's the Boss?, 1984-92, Melrose Place, 1997-98, Charmed, 1998-2006 (also prodr.); appeared in TV movies The Canterville Ghost, 1986, Dance'Til Dawn, 1988, Conflict of Interest, 1992, Candles in the Dark, 1993, Casualties of Love: The Long Island Lolita Story, 1993, Confessions of a Sorority Girl, 1994; appeared in various TV spls.; on TV shows Body by Jake, 1988, The Arsenio Hall Show, 1989, various shows for American Treasury, 1989, To Brave Alaska, 1996; film actress Old Enough, 1982, Commando, 1985, Speed Zone, 1989, Where the Day Takes You, 1992, Little Sister, 1992, Double Dragon, 1993, Embrace of the Vampire, 1995, At Home with the Webbers, 1993, The Surrogate, 1995, Public Enemy # 1, 1995, No Fear, 1996, Glory Daze, 1996, Jimmy Zip, 1996, Below Utopia, 1997, Hugo Pool, 1997, Buying the Cow, 2002, Kiss the Bride, 2002, Dickie Roberts: Former Child Star, 2003, (voice) Dinotopia: Quest for the Ruby Sunstone, 2005; stage debut in Annie, various cities, 1980-81; stage appearances include All Night Long, Second Stage Theatre Co., N.Y.C., 1984, Jane Eyre, Theatre Opera Music Inst., N.Y.C., others; TV guest appearances include The Outer Limits, 1995, Spin City, 1996, Fantasy Island, 1998; prodr. Below Utopia, 1997. Recipient Best Supporting Actress award Youth Films Awards; Silver prize Tokyo Music Festival, 1989. Mem. SAG, AFTRA, Actors' Equity Assn.*

MILANOVICH, LYNN ESTHER, counselor; b. Sewickley, Pa., May 8, 1949; d. Steve and Alice (Thomas) Michael; m. Rodney J. Milanovich, Sept. 3, 1971; children: Dave, Kimberly, Dianne. BS in Elem. and Spl. Edn., Duquesne U., 1971, MSED in Counseling, 1976, cert. in sch. counseling, 1986; postgrad., Western Psychiat. Inst., 1986, 87-88, C.C. Beaver County, 1986, 88. Tchr. Ctr. Area Sch. Dist., Monaca, Pa., 1971-72; subs. tchr. South Side Sch. Dist., Hookstown, Pa., 1985-87, Hopewell Area Sch. Dist., Aliquippa, Pa., 1980-87, counselor 5th-8th grade, 1987—, chmn. Dept. Counseling, 2006—. Cons. stress mgmt. C.C. Beaver County Prevention Project, Monaca, 1986. Active PTSA, Hopewell Jr. HS; mem. PTA Raccoon & Ind. Elem. Schs. Mem. ACA, Am. Sch. Counselors Assn., Pa. State Edn. Assn., Pa. Sch. Counselors Assn., Allegheny County Counselors Assn., Beaver County Counselors Assn., Hopewell Edn. Assn. Home: 442 Independence Rd Aliquippa PA 15001-5758 Office: Hopewell Area Schs 2354 Brodhead Rd Aliquippa PA 15001-4669 Office Phone: 724-375-3201.

MILANOVICH, NORMA JOANNE, training services executive; b. Littlefork, Minn., June 4, 1945; d. Lyle Albert and Loretta (Leona) Drake; m. Rudolph William Milanovich, Mar. 18, 1943 (dec.); 1 child, Rudolph William Jr. BS in Home Econs., U. Wis., Stout, 1968; MA in Curriculum and Instrn., U. Houston, 1973, EdD in Curriculum and Program Devel., 1982. Instr. human svcs. dept. U. Houston, 1971-75; dir. videos project U. N.Mex., Albuquerque, 1976-78, dir. vocat. edn. equity ctr., 1978-88, asst. prof. occupational edn., 1982-88, coord. occupational vocat. edn. programs, 1983-88, dir. consortium rsch. and devel. in occupational edn., 1984-88; pres. Alpha Connection Tng. Corp., Albuquerque, 1988—; exec. dir. Trinity Found., 1991—; pres. Athena Leadership Ctr., 1994—. Adj. instr. Cen. Tng. Acad., Dept. Energy, Wackenhut; faculty U. Phoenix; adj. faculty So. Ill. U., Lesley Coll., Boston; lectr. in field Author: Model Equitable Behavior in the Classroom, 1983, Handbook for Vocational-Technical Certification in New Mexico, 1985, A Vision for Kansas: Systems of Measures and Standards of Performance, 1992, Workplace Skills: The Employability Factor, 1993; editor: Choosing What's Best for You, 1982, A Handbook for Handling Conflict in the Classroom, 1983, Starting Out.A Job Finding Handbook for Teen Parents, Going to Work.Job Rights for Teens; author: JTPA Strategic Marketing Plan, 1990, We, The Arcturians, 1990, Sacred Journey to Atlantis, 1991, The Light Shall Set You Free, 1996; editor: Majestic Raise newsletter, 1996—, Celestial Voices newsletter, 1991—; conf. presenter in field. Del. Youth for Understanding Internat. Program, 1985—90; adv. bd. Southwestern Indian Poly. Inst., 1984—88; com. mem. Region VI Consumer Exch. Com., 1982—84; coord. various countries Worldwide Conf. for Peace on Earth, 1999—2006; coord. Customized Leadership Programs, 2003—06; bd. dirs. Albuquerque Single Parent Occupational Scholarship Program, 1984—86. Grantee N.Mex. Dept. Edn., 1976-86, HEW, 1979-81, 83-87 Mem. ASTD, Am. Vocat. Assn., Vocat. Edn. Equity Coun., Nat. Coalition for Sex Equity Edn., Am. Home Econs. Assn., Inst. Noetic Scis., N.Mex. Home Econs. Assn., N.Mex. Vocat. Edn. Assn., N.Mex. Adv. Coun. on Vocat. Edn., Greater Albuquerque C. of C., NAFE, Phi Delta Kappa, Phi Upsilon Omicron, Phi Theta Kappa. Democrat. Roman Catholic. Office: Athena Leadership Ctr Scottsdale AZ 85259 Office Phone: 480-767-5346. Business E-Mail: info@athenalctr.com.

MILBOURNE, MELINDA D., elementary school educator, researcher; b. Pasadena, Tex., Jan. 17, 1957; d. R. L. and R. M. Dedman; 1 child, Rachel. BS in Biology Edn., Miami U., Oxford, Ohio, 1988. Labtech Lonza Chem., Bayport, Tex., 1979—81, Miami U., Oxford, 1982—88; rsch. asst. Fla. Tech., Melbourne, 1989—90; sci. tchr. St. Marys Sch., Rockledge, Fla., 1990—2000, 2004—, Holy Name of Jesus, Fla., 2000—04. Instr. Rover workship Keystone Inst., Denver, 2005; rschr., tchr. Brevard Internat. Sci. and Engring. Fair, Brevard County, Fla., 1990—. Active Heifer Project Inter Schs., 2004—; liturgical music dir. St. Patricks Pageant. Recipient Sci. Tchr. award, Fla. Sci. Tchrs. Assn., 1995—96, 1998; grantee, Orlando Sci. Ctr., 2002. Democrat. Methodist. Avocations: music, art, reading.

MILBRATH, MARY MERRILL LEMKE, quality assurance professional; b. Evanston, Ill., Aug. 13, 1940; d. William Frederick and Martha Merrill (Slagel) Lemke; m. Gene McCoy Milbrath, Aug. 22, 1964; children: Elizabeth Ann, Sarah Toril Jeanne. BA in Biology, Albion Coll., 1962; MS in Plant Pathology, U. Ariz., 1966. Microbiologist Abbott Labs., North Chicago, Ill., 1962; toxicologist U. Ariz., Tucson, 1965-67, U. Ill., Urbana, 1976-77, entomologist, 1978; plant pathologist State of Oreg., Salem, 1979, chemist, 1980-82; quality auditor Siltec Corp., Salem, 1983-84, quality control supr., 1985-91, quality auditing mgr., 1992-97, implementor ISO 9002, 1995, implementor ISO 9001 Quality Std., 1996, quality assurance dir., 1997—2002; implementor ISO 14001 Siltec Corp., Salem, 1998; pres. MLM Enterprises, Salem, 2002—. Active Ill. Emergency Svcs.toxic sub task force U. Ill., Urbana, 1978; mem. Responsible Corp. Citizens Com., Salem, 1989-96. Mem. citizens adv. com. Sch. Bd., Urbana, 1976-78; campaigner Oreg. 5th Dist. Race, Salem, 1984, Oreg. Nat. Abortion Rights Assn. League, Salem, 1986; bd. dirs. Tribute to Outstanding Women, YWCA, 1992, 93, 94, 95; vol. Tree Giving, 1991, 92. NDEA fellow U.S. Dept. Def., 1962; elected Woman of Achievement, YWCA, 1997. Mem. AAUW (chmn. interest group), Am. Soc. for Quality (cert. quality auditor exam writing com. 1993, 95, exam rev. 1996, 98, 2002, spkr. nat. conf. 1999), Willamette U. House Corp. (treas. 1982-85, v.p. 1991-96, 2001—, mem.-at-large 2000—, treas. 2001--), Delta Gamma (treas. Salem Alumnae chpt. 1981-85, pres. Salem Alumnae chpt. 1987-89, scholarship advisor Willamette U. chpt. 1986-90). Avocation: travel. Office: 3225 Holiday Dr Salem OR 97302-4105

MILBRETT, TIFFENY CARLEEN, professional soccer player; b. Portland, Oreg., Oct. 23, 1972; Degree in comms. mgmt., U. Portland. Mem. U.S. Women's Nat. Soccer Team; profl. soccer player N.Y. Power, 2001—03. Mem. championship team, Montricoux, France, 1993. Named World Cup Champion, 1999; recipient Gold medal, Centennial Olympic Games, 1996, 3d place medal, 1995, Silver medal, World Univ. Games, 1993, Sydney Olympic Games, 2000. Office: c/o US Soccer Fedn 1801 S Prairie Ave # 1811 Chicago IL 60616-1319

MILDVAN, DONNA, infectious diseases physician; b. Phila., June 20, 1942; d. Carl David and Gertrude M.; m. Rolf Dirk Hamann; 1 child, Gabriella Kay. AB magna cum laude, Bryn Mawr Coll., 1963; MD, Johns Hopkins U., 1967. Diplomate Am. Bd. Internal Medicine and Infectious Diseases. Intern, resident Mt. Sinai Hosp., N.Y.C., 1967-70, fellow, infectious diseases, 1970-72; asst., assoc. prof. clin. medicine Mt. Sinai Sch. Medicine, N.Y.C., 1972-87; prof. clinical medicine Dept. Medicine, Mt. Sinai Sch. Medicine, N.Y.C., 1987-88, prof. medicine, 1988-94; physician-in-charge infectious diseases Beth Israel Med. Ctr., N.Y.C., 1972-79, chief, div. infectious diseases, 1980—; prof. medicine Albert Einstein Coll. of Medicine, N.Y.C., 1994—. Mem. AIDS charter rev. com., NIH/Nat. Inst. Allergy and Infectious Diseases, Bethesda, 1987—; cons. FDA, Rockville, 1987—, Ctrs. for Disease Control, Atlanta, 1985-86; among first to describe AIDS, "Pre-AIDS", AIDS Dementia, 1982, among first to study AZT, 1986; Keynote speaker, II Internat. Conf. on AIDS, Paris, 1986 and other achievements in field; Sophie Jones Meml. lectr. in infectious diseases U. Mich. Hosps., 1984. Contbr. numerous articles to profl. jours; co-editor two books, many book chpts. and abstracts on infectious diseases and AIDS; editor: Atlas of AIDS, edits. 1-3. Grantee N.Y. State AIDS Inst., 1986-87; Henry Strong Denison scholar Johns Hopkins U. Sch. Medicine, 1967; recipient Woman of Achievement award AAUW, 1987, Hero in Medicine award Internat. Assn. Physicians in AIDS Care, 2000; contract for antiviral therapy in AIDS, Nat. Cancer Inst./Nat. Inst. Allergy and Infectious Diseases, 1985-86, subcontract Nat. Inst. Allergy and Infectious Diseases, ACTU, 1987-99, prin. investigator, 2000—. Fellow Infectious Diseases Soc. Am.; mem. Am. Soc. Microbiology, AAAS, Harvey Soc., Internat. AIDS Soc. Democrat. Jewish. Avocation: old movies. Office: Beth Israel Med Ctr 1st Ave New York NY 10003-7903

MILES, AMY E., recreational facility executive; With PricewaterhouseCoopers, LLC, 1989—98; sr. mgr. Deloitte & Touche, 1998—99; from sr. v.p. fin. to exec. v.p., CFO, treas. Regal Entertainment Group, Englewood, Colo., 1999—2000, exec. v.p., 2000—, CFO, 2000—, treas., 2000—. Office: Regal Entertainment Group 9110 East Nichols Ave Ste 200 Englewood CO 80112

MILES, CAROLE HARRISON, artist; b. Richmond, Va., Mar. 13, 1946; d. Edward Eaton Jr. and Gayla Delsia (Smith) Harrison; m. Avrel Franklin Seabolt, Jr., Jan. 26, 1967 (dec. Jan 1975); 1 child, Elizabeth Louise; m. Steven Dale Martinie, Nov. 26, 1978 (div. Oct. 1993); children: Melissa Leigh Harrison and Michelle Lorraine Harrison (twins), Rebecca Gayle Harrison; m. Louis Paul Miles, June 2006 BS cum laude, Longwood Coll., Farmville, Va., 1967; M Art Edn., Va. Commonwealth U., Richmond, 1971; MArch, Va. Tech., Blacksburg, 1982; DEd, U. Va., 1983; degree in Acoustical Engring., Old Dominion U., 1975. Lic. tchr. art, history, instrnl. tech., Wis. Tchr. history and art Prince George (Va.) Jr. H.S., 1967-70; illustrator U.S. Army Troop Support Agy., Ft. Lee, Va., 1972-78; edn. specialist, visual info. U.S. Army Quartermaster Sch., Ft. Lee, 1972-78; grad. asst. U. Va., Charlottesville, 1978-80, art edn. curriculum cons., grad. tchg. asst., 1979-80; grad. asst. Learning Resource Ctr. Va. Poly. Inst. and State U., Blacksburg, 1980-82; freelance artist, cons. designer Va. and Wis., 1967—; designer Pace Architects, Milw. and Chgo., 1990-91, 92; Idea Ctr. designer, cons. Builders Square, Milw., 1994—; art tchr. Learning Enterprize H.S. Vol. designer Esperanza Unida; vol. mem. AIA Search for Shelter Com.; former substitute tchr., Milw., Shorewood and Whitefish Bay pub. schs.; instr. Richard Bland Coll., Coll. William and Mary, Petersburg; part-time art tchr. Milw. Art Mus. Exhibited in group shows at Va. Mus. Fine Arts, Richmond, Poplar Lawn Art Show, Petersburg, others, 1967—; composer, writer contemporary folk songs for Sing in Celebration, 1976. Home and Office: Gaines Mill 6430 Cold Harbor Rd Mechanicsvlle VA 23111-3242

MILES, CHRISTINE MARIE, museum director; b. Madison, Ind., Mar. 2, 1951; d. Leland Weber and Mary Virginia (Geyer) M. BA, Boston U., 1973; MA, George Washington U., 1982; postgrad., Mus. Mgmt. Inst., 1985. Curatorial asst. Mus. City of N.Y., 1973-75; art gallery dir. South Street Seaport Mus., N.Y.C., 1975-77; rschr. The Octagon, AIA Found., Washington, 1978-80; dir. Fraunces Tavern Mus., Washington, 1980-86, Albany (N.Y.) Inst. History and Art, 1986—. Bd. dirs. SUNY-Albany Found. Author, writer/coordinator, compiler of catalogs in field. Mem. Arts Commn. City of Albany; pres. Gallery Assn. N.Y. State, 1991-93, Mus. Assn. N.Y. State. Mem. Am. Assn. Mus. Office: Albany Inst History and Art 125 Washington Ave Albany NY 12210-2296

MILES, ELIZABETH JANE, social worker; b. Upper Fairmount, Md., Mar. 13, 1927; d. Harry Budd Miles and Elizabeth Thomas. AA, St. Mary's Coll., St. Mary's City, Md., 1947; BA, Scarritt Coll., 1949; MSW, Vanderbilt U., 1951. Dir. Christian edn. Meth. Ch., Gaithersberg, Md., 1952—53; mgr., owner Edn. Assn., Pitts., 1954—60, Frontier Press, Balt., 1960—70; social worker, bd. dirs. Home-Coming Mental Health, Bel Air, Md., 1970—90; resident supr. VA Home Programs, Perry Point, Md., 1990; pvt. cons. in field. Mem. bd. Commn. on Aging, Somerset County, Md., 1990—; deaconess Meth. Ch., Balt., 1951—52; bd. dirs. Country Retreat-Christian Retreat, Bradenton, Fla., 1991—. Scholar, Md. State Senator, 1945, Meth. Missionary Bd. Mem.: Nat. Hist. Trust Assn., Bus. and Profl. Club. Republican. Methodist. Avocations: horses, antiques, restoring family home. Home (Summer): PO Box 144 Manokin MD 21836

MILES, HELEN, oncological nurse; b. Pitts., Dec. 17, 1936; d. John Michael and Mary (Kurtz) Sharak; m. James Robert Miles, June 3, 1956 (div. 1974); children: Ron, Dave, Kevin, Susan, Tina. Grad., Allegheny C.C., 1976; LPN, Connelly Skill Learning Ctr., 1981. Sec. Bd. Edn., Pitts., 1970-80; staff nurse oncology Mercy Hosp., Pitts., 1981-85; pvt. duty nurse Quality Care, Pitts., 1985; staff nurse oncology Naples (Fla.) Cmty. Hosp., 1986-96; pvt. practice oncol. nurse Naples, 1996—. Notary pub., Pa., 1975-83; counseling asst. Tom Connelly Med, CAP, Pitts., Naples, 1984-86; assoc. producer, co-host TC Prodns., Pitts., 1984-85; preceptor oncology unit, Naples Hosp., 1990-96, mem. adv. bds., 1986-96. Author: (poetry) Walk Through Paradise, 1995; (with others) The Voice Within, Where Dawn Lingers, 1996. Vol. Naples Hotline, 1987-88; environ. def. mem. Nat. Trust for Historic Preservation. Recipient Clin. Excellence award, 1995, cert. appreciation Project Hotline, 1993, Nat. Humane Edn. Soc., 1995, Cmmdrs. Club Bronze Leader award DAV, 1996, Hon. Guardian of Nature award World Wildlife Found., 1996, cert. of appreciation Nat. Park Trust, 1997; named to Internat. Poetry Hall of Fame. Mem. Nat. Parks Conservation Assn., Ctr. for Marine Conservation, Smithsonian Assn., Internat. Soc. Poets (Internat. Poet of Merit award 1995, 96, Editor's Choice award 1995, 96), The Conservancy, Nat. Geographic Soc., Swarovski Crystal Soc. Republican. Avocations: travel, writing, theater, music. Home: Royal Pk Villas 6 Hackney Ln Naples FL 34112-0625

MILES, JOAN, state agency administrator, former state legislator, lawyer; BS, SUNY, Albany, 1971; MS, Univ. Mont., 1979; JD, McGeorge Sch. Law Univ. Pacific, 1992. Bar: Calif., Mont. Law clk. Mont. Supreme Ct.; rep. Mont. Legislature, 1984—88; dir. Lewis & Clark City-County Health Dept., Mont., 1994—2005, Mont. Dept. Health & Human Svc., Helena, 2005—. Mailing: Dept Health & Human Svcs PO Box 4210 Helena MT 59604*

MILES, JOANNA, actress, playwright, director; b. Nice, France, Mar. 6, 1940; came to U.S., 1941, naturalized, 1941; d. Johannes Schiefer and Jeanne Miles; m. William Burns, May 23, 1970 (div. 1977); m. Michael Brandman, Apr. 29, 1978; 1 child, Miles. Grad. H.S., Putney, Vt., 1958. Mem. Actors Studio, Playwrites and Dirs. Workshop, NYC, 1966; co-founder, mem. LA Classic Theatre, 1986; playwright, dir. Unit Actor's Studio, LA, 2002—05. Founder, mem. Playwrights Group/LAWW, 1991-98, L.A. Writer's Workshop, 1996-98. Starred in: (motion pictures) The Way We Live Now, 1969, Bug, 1975, The Ultimate Warrior, 1975, Golden Girl, 1978, Cross Creek, 1983, As Is, 1986, Blackout, 1988, Rosencrants and Guildenstern are Dead, 1991, The Rhinghart Theory, 1994, Judge Dredd, 1994, Alone, 1996, Sex & Breakfast, 2006; numerous television films including In What America, 1965, My Mothers House, 1963, Glass Managerie, 1974, Born Innocent, 1974, Aloha Means Goodbye, 1974, The Trial of Chaplain Jensen, 1975, Harvest Home, 1977, Fire in the Sky, 1978, Sophisticated Gents, 1979, Promise of Love, 1982, Sound of Murder, 1983, All My Sons, 1987, The Right to Die, 1987, The Habitation of Dragons, 1991, Heart of Justice, 1991, Water Engine, 1991, Cooperstown, 1992, Legionnaires, 1992, Life Lessons, 1992, Willing to Kill, 1992, The American Clock, 1993, Dark Reflections, 1993, Outcry, 1994, Everything to Gain, 1995, Small Vices, 1998, Crossfire Trail, 1999, Thin Aire, 1999, Monty Walsh, 2002, Jane Doe: Shaken & Stirred, 2006; episodes in numerous TV series including: Barney Miller, Dallas, St. Elsewhere, The Hulk, Trapper John, Kaz, Cagney and Lacey, Studio 5B, 1989, Star Trek: The Next Generation, 1990, 91, Life Stories, 1991, HBO Life Stories, 1993, Total Security, 1997, Nothing Sacred, 1998, Chicago Hope, 1998-99, ER, 2000, 01, Family Law, 2000, Judging Amy, 2003; stage plays include Once in a Life Time, 1963, Cave Dwellers, 1964, Drums in the Night, 1968, Dracula, 1968, Home Free, 1964, One Night Stands of a Noisy Passenger, 1972, Dylan, 1973, Dancing for the Kaiser, 1976, Debutante Ball, 1985, Kramer, 1977, One Flew Over the Cuckoo's Nest, 1989, Growing Gracefully, 1990, Cut Flowers, 1994; performed in radio shows Sta. KCRW Once in a Lifetime, 1987, Babbit, 1987, Sta. KPFK, Grapes of Wrath, 1989, The White Plague, Sta. KCRW, 1991, Chekhov Short Stories, Sta. KCRW, 1992; playwright, v.p. Brandman Productions; author: (plays) Ethanasia, A Woman in Reconstruction, Hostages, Feathers, On the Shelf, (films) An Offereing of Oranges, Breaking the Rules. Pres. Children Giving to Children. Recipient 2 Emmy awards, 1974, Women in Radio and TV award, 1974, Actors Studio Achievement award, 1980, Dramalogue award, 1996, Vision award 2003; nominated Golden Globe, 1974. Mem. Acad. Motion Picture Arts and Scis. Office: Brandman Prodns 2062 Vine St Apt 5 Hollywood CA 90068-3928 Office Phone: 323-463-3224. Personal E-mail: jmilesb@aol.com.

MILES, LAVEDA ANN, advertising executive; b. Greenville, S.C., Nov. 21, 1945; d. Grady Lewis and Edna Sylvia (Mahaffey) Bruce; m. Charles Thomas Miles, Nov. 10, 1974; 1 child, Joshua Bruce. A in Bus. Adminstrn., North Greenville Jr. Coll. Traffic mgr. WFBV-TV, Greenville, 1968-74; pub. svc. dir., traffic mgr. WTCG-TV, Atlanta, 1974-75; traffic mgr. Henderson Advt. Co., Greenville, 1975-77, broadcast coord., 1977-79, dir. broadcast bus., 1979-82, v.p., dir. broadcast bus., 1982-89, bus. mgr. creative dept., 1989-91, dir. creative svcs., 1991-93, sr. v.p., 1994-96, v.p., dir. creative svcs., 2000—; owner Altamont Mktg., 1996-99. Mem. Leadership S.C., 1994-95; bd. dirs. Boys Home of the South, 2003—. Named one of 100 Best and Brightest Women, Ad Age and Advt. Women of N.Y., 1988. Mem. Advt. Fedn. Greenville (sec. 1979-81), Greenville Ad Club (sec. 1999-2000, pres. 2000—, Silver medal awrd 2003). Republican. Baptist.

MILES, MARY ELLEN, retired human resources specialist; d. Monroe and Leona (Simmons) Jackson; m. Monte Sanford, Sept. 21, 1956 (div.); children: Dean Sanford, Marisa Sanford(dec.), Mark Sanford. Degree in secretarial sci., Orlando (Fla.) Jr. Coll., 1962. Cert. OSHA inspector, EEO investigator. Exec. sec. Dept of Def./AAFES, Montgomery, Ala., 1974, employee devel. specialist Wright Patterson AFB, Ohio, 1974—77, tech. publs. writer/editor Munich, 1977—79, pers. asst Ft. Rucker, Ala., 1979—82, pers. asst, employee devel. specialist Langley AFB, Va., 1982—85, human resources mgr. Ft. Eustis, Va., 1985—87, Ft. Knox, Ky., 1987—91, Ft. Carson, Colo., 1990—93, Ft. Hood, Tex., 1993—95, Hickam AFB, Hawaii, 1995—98, sr. human resources policy specialist/policy devel. Dallas, 1998—2002. HR subject matter expert, cons., Decatur, Ala., 2002. Author: (cookbook) From the Heart. Newsletter writer, editor Newport News Literacy Coun., Va., 1985—86, Clean Cmty. Commn., Newport News, 1985—86; mem. Mayor's Coun. Handicapped Employment, Newport News, 1985—87; vol. Duncanville Pub. Libr., Tex., 2002, Carnegie Visual Arts Ctr., Decatur, 2003; mem. Ala. Citizens for Constn. Reform, Huntsville, 2003—06, Acad. for Lifetime Learning, U. Ala., Huntsville, 2003—05, Leadership Coun., So. Poverty Law Ctr., Montgomery, Ala., 2003, Morgan County Diversity Coun., 2004, Princess Theater, Decatur, 2006; vol. Decatur City Schs., 2004—06, Cmty. Free Clinic, Decatur, 2005, Habitat for Humanity, Decatur, 2006, Morgan County Pub. Libr., Decatur, 2006; docent Carnegie Visual Arts Ctr., 2003. Recipient Commander's Coin, Cold War Recognition Cert. for Fed. Govt. Svc. Mem.: Am. Bus. Women's Assn. Republican. Avocations: reading, writing, art, antiques, collectibles, cooking.

MILES, MICHELE LESLIE, physician assistant; b. Orange, Calif., Dec. 11, 1962; d. David Moffat Miles and Molly Patricia Gallagher. BS, Alderson Broaddus Coll., 1987, MS, 1996. Cert. physician asst. Physician asst. Samuel K. Roberto MD, Elkins, W.Va., 1987-92, La Clinica del Cariño, Hood River, Oreg., 1992-95; physician asst., adminstr. Grant County Meml. Hosp., Petersburg, W.Va., 1995-96, Hardy County Med. Svcs., Moorefield, W.Va., 1995-96; physician asst. Cornerstone Family Physician, Tacoma, Wash., 1997-98; med. officer U.S. Peace Corps, Santo Domingo, Dominican Republic, 1999—. Adminstrv. grant writer Grant Meml. Hosp., Petersburg, 1995-96; dir. Mission Med. Internat., Maple Valley, Wash., 1998-99. Fellow Wash. State Med. Assn. Avocations: internatl medical missions, poetry, swimming. Home: 10962 W Wild Iris St Star ID 83669-5387

MILES-LA GRANGE, VICKI, judge; b. Oklahoma City, Okla., Sept. 30, 1953; d. Charles and Mary (Greenard) Miles. BA, Vassar Coll., 1974; LLB, Howard U., 1977; cert., U. Ghana, West Africa; DHL (hon.), Oklahoma City U., 1995. Legis. aide Spkr. House Rep. Carl Albert, 1974-76; law clerk Judge Woodrow Seals U.S. Dist. Ct. (so. dist.), Tex., 1977-79; fellow, atty. criminal divsn. U.S. Dept. Justice, Washington, 1979-83; asst. dist. atty. Dist. Atty.'s Office, Oklahoma County, 1983-86; pvt. practice Oklahoma City, 1986-93; mem. Okla. Senate (Dist. 48), 1987-93; U.S. atty. U.S. Dept. Justice, Oklahoma City, Okla., 1993-94; judge U.S. Dist. Ct. (we. dist.), Oklahoma City, 1994—. Bd. trustees Vassar Coll. Mem. ABA, Nat. Bar Assn., Okla. Bar Assn., Am. Inns Ct. Democrat. Baptist. Office: US Dist Judge US Courthouse 200 NW 4th St Ste 5011 Oklahoma City OK 73102-3031

MILEWSKI, BARBARA ANNE, pediatrics nurse, neonatal/perinatal nurse practitioner, critical care nurse; b. Chgo., Sept. 11, 1934; d. Anthony and LaVerne (Sepp) Witt; m. Leonard A. Milewski, Feb. 23, 1952; children: Pamela, Robert, Diane, Timothy. ADN, Harper Coll., Palatine, Ill., 1982; BS, Northern Ill. U., 1992; postgrad., North Park Coll. RN Ill., cert. CPR instr. Staff nurse N.W. Cmty. Hosp., Arlington Heights, Ill., Resurrection Hosp., Chgo.; nurse neonatal ICU Children's Meml. Hosp., Chgo.; day care cons. Cook County Dept. Pub. Health; owner, CEO Child Care Health Cons. CPR instr. Stewart Oxygen Svcs., Chgo., Harper Coll., Children's Meml. Hosp.; instr., organizer parenting and well baby classes and clinics; health coord. CEDA Head Start; mem. adv. bd. Cook County Child Care Resource and Referral; dir. Albany Park Head Start. Vol. Children's Meml. Hosp., Boy Scouts Am. Mem.: Am. Mortar Bd., Sigma Theta Tau. Personal E-mail: barbmilewski@aol.com.

MILFORD, NANCY WINSTON, writer, literature educator; b. Dearborn, Mich. d. Joseph Leo and Vivienne Winston; m. Kenneth Hans Milford, Mar. 24, 1962 (div. 1985); children: Matthew, Kate, Nell. BA, U. Mich.; MA, Columbia U., N.Y.C., 1964, PhD, 1972. Prof. English and writing Bard Coll., Annandale-on-Hudson, N.Y., 1983-90; vis. prof. English Vassar Coll., Poughkeepsie, N.Y., 1984; adj. prof. English grad. program in creative writing NYU, N.Y.C., 1991-94; vis. prof. English U. Mich., Ann Arbor, 1993, 94; Annenberg fellow Brown U., Providence, 1995—; Am. studies program Princeton U., 2002; vis. prof. Hunter Coll., CUNY, 2002—03, distinguished lectr. English, 2003—. Founder, mem. Writers Room, Inc., 1978—, bd. dirs., past pres. Author: Zelda, A Biography, 1970, Savage Beauty, The Life of Edna St. Vincent Millay, 2001; contbr. revs., essays and articles to various publs. Lit. panelist N.Y. State Coun. on Arts, N.Y.C., 1976-79. Guggenheim fellow, 1978, Lila Wallace-Reader's Digest writing fellow, 1992-95, Woodrow Wilson vis. fellow U.S. Govt./USIA, S.C., 1995, Fulbright fellow, 1996-97, 1999—; recipient Lit. Lion award N.Y. Pub. Libr., 1984. Mem. PEN, Author's Guild (mem. exec. coun. 1971-89), Soc. Am. Historians (exec. bd. dirs. 1971-88). Avocations: fencing, sailing. Office: ICM 40 W 57th St New York NY 10020

MILHOAN, SUSANA, mathematics educator; d. Angel Castillo and Guillermina Chavez; m. Susana G. Castillo, Aug. 28, 1982; children: Charlie children: Neysa Otts. BS in Math., U. Utah, Salt Lake City, 1994. Tchr. math. Indian Hills, Sandi Utah, Utah, 1994—97, Wylie H.S., 1999—. Mem. Lds Ch. Office: Wylie High School 2550 W Fm 544 Wylie TX 75098 Office Phone: 972-429-3000. E-mail: wylieisd.net.

MILIANI, LORENNA, secondary school educator, social studies educator, writer; 1 child, Luna Elena Turchi Miliani. BA, Tufts U., 1995. Lic. mortgage broker Fla., 2005, cert. social studies educator Fla., 2003. Tchr. social studies Dade County Pub. Schs., Miami, Fla., 2000—. Country dir., sec. Amazonian Project, Miami, Fla. Author: marialionza website. Office: HD McMillan Middle 13100 Sw 59 St Miami FL 33183 Office Phone: 305-385-6877. Personal E-mail: mlore@bellsouth.net.

MILITO, CONNIE MARIE, education administrator, government relations administrator; b. Tampa, Fla., Nov. 12, 1958; d. Frederick Anthony and Costantina Milito. BA, U. South Fla., 1981; MA, Nova U., 1990. Cert. adminstrn. and supervision early childhood edn. Elem. tchr. Sch. Dist. Hillsborough County, Tampa, Fla., 1982—90, acting supr. early childhood edn., 1990—92, dir. govt. rels., 1993—. Mem. exec. com. Cmty. Advocates for Resources for Edn. and Social Svcs., Tampa, 1993—2002; mem. Horace Mann League, 1994—, Tiger Bay Club Tampa; mem. exec. bd. Bipartisan Polit. Club, 2000—02. Mem.: Fla. Edn. Legis. Liaisons (pres. 1998—99, exec. bd. 1996—2002), Phi Delta Kappa, Kappa Delta Phi. Office: Sch Dist Hillsborough County 901 E Kennedy Blvd Tampa FL 33602 Office Phone: 813-272-4519. Business E-Mail: milito_c@firn.edu.

MILKE, LINDA JEAN, elementary school educator; b. Muskegon, Mich., Sept. 30; d. John Carl and Helen Maxine Milke. BA, Western Mich. U., Kalamazoo, 1973; MEd in Curriculum and Instrn., Ariz. State U., Tempe, 2002. Tchr. in sch. intervention Gililland Mid. Sch., Tempe, Ariz., 1998—2003, tchr. 6th grade social studies, 2003—. Co-chair pride com. Gililland Mid. Sch., 2000—, co-chair leadership team, 2003—04. Mem.: NEA (assoc.), Nat. Assn. Bilingual Educators (assoc.), Phi Kappa Phi. Avocations: antiques, trivia, home decorating, reading. Home: 7026 E Kiva Avenue Mesa AZ 85209 Office: Gililland Middle School 1025 S Beck Avenue Tempe AZ 85281 Office Phone: 480-966-7114 5895. Personal E-mail: lindamilke@msn.com. E-mail: lindamilke@tempeschools.org.

MILKEY, VIRGINIA A., state legislator; b. Brattleboro, Vt., Jan. 27, 1950; BA, Middlebury Coll., 1972. Mem. Vt. Ho. of Reps., Montpelier, 1991—. Co-founder, bd. dirs. Bonnyvale Environ. Edn. Ctr.; bd. dirs. Alliance for Bldg. Cmty.; mem. Brattleboro Agrl. Adv. Com.; mem., exec., health, life, property and casualty and state/fed. rels. coms. of Nat. Conf. Ins. Legislators. Rep. Brattleboro Town Meeting; corporator Brattleboro Meml. Hosp. Home: 266 Meadowbrook Rd Brattleboro VT 05301-2581

MILKMAN, MARIANNE FRIEDENTHAL, retired city planner; b. Berlin, May 13, 1931; arrived in US, 1957; d. Ernst Leopold and Margarethe (Goldschmidt) Friedenthal; m. Roger Dawson Milkman, Oct. 18, 1958; children: Ruth, Louise, Janet, Paul. BA, Cambridge (Eng.) U., 1952, MA, 1956; teaching diploma, London U., 1953. Tchr. biology Milham Ford High Sch., Oxford, Eng., 1953-57; teaching fellow, rsch. asst. U. Mich., Ann Arbor, 1957-59; sci. dir. Children's Sch. Sci., Woods Hole, Mass., 1971-72; planning technician dept. planning and program devel. City of Iowa City, 1975-76, planner I, 1976-79, assoc. planner, 1979-85, coord. comty. devel., 1986-96; ret., 1996. Bikeways chmn Project Green, Iowa City, 1968—75; chmn. comprehensive plan com. Town of Falmouth, 2002—. Fellow, English Speaking Union, 1957—58; scholar State, Cambridge Univ and London Univ, 1949—53, Fulbright Traveling, Univ Mich, 1957. Mem.: Nat Community Develop Asn, Nat Asn Housing and Redevelopment Offs, Am Planning Asn (secy-treas Iowa chpt 1982—84, vpres 1984—86, pres 1986—88, chmn univ relations comt 1987—91, Pres's Award 1988). Jewish. Avocations: mountain hiking, wild flowers, music. Home: 12 Fells Rd Falmouth MA 02540-1626

MILLANE, LYNN, retired municipal official; b. Buffalo, Oct. 14, 1928; d. Robert P. and Justine A. Schermerhorn; m. J. Vaughan Millane Jr., Aug. 16, 1952; children: Maureen, Michele, John, Mark, Kathleen. EdB, U. Buffalo, 1949, EdM in Health Edn., 1951. Coun. mem. Amherst Town Bd., NY, 1982—96, dep. town supr., 1990-96, supr., 1996. Founder, liaison 1st adult day svcs. adv. bd. Town of Amherst, 1988, liaison to ad hoc cable TV com., 1992—96, liaison to Amherst C. of C., 1993—96, 1st records mgmt. adv. bd., liaison ethics bd., 1994—96; legis. liaison SUNY Family Violence Clin. Sch. Law, Buffalo, 1997—98; pres. E.J. Meyer Hosp. Jr. Bd., 1962—64; commr. (apptd. by Gov. George Pataki) NY State Ethics Commn., 1999—2004, 2004—; adv. bd. NY State Office Aging, 1996—2005, chair adv. bd., 1997—2005; spkr. in field. Pres. Aux. to Erie County Bar Assn., 1966-68, Womens Com. Buffalo Philharm. Orch., 1976-78, v.p. adminstrn., 1975-76, v.p. pub. affairs, 1974-75, chair. adv. bd., 1979-82; v.p. Buffalo Philharm. Orch. Soc., Inc., 1976-78, coun. mem., trustee, 1979-87, bd. overseers, 1987-92; dir. 8th jud. dist. NY State Assn. Large Towns, 1989-91; bd. dirs. oper. bd. Millard Fillmore Suburban Hosp., 1992-98; 1st v.p. Fams for 17, 1980-82, Friends of Baird Hall SUNY, Buffalo, 1980-82; exec. bd. Womens Exec. Coun. Erie County Rep. Com., 1969-71, Longview Protestant Home for Children, 1979-85, 2d v.p., 1982-85; bd. dirs. Amherst br. ARC, 1982-91, by-laws com., 1981, 84, chair sr. concerns com., 1982-91, liaison code of ethics com., 1987-89; nat. music com. Womens Assn. for Symphony Orchs. in Am. and Can., 1977-79; coun. mem. Am. Symphony Orch. League; sec. Amherst Sr. Citizens Adv. Bd., 1980-81, liaison from Amherst Town Bd., 1982-96; liaison to the Alternate Fuel and Clean Cities Com., 1994-96; dir.-at-large cmty. adv. coun. SUNY, Buffalo, 1981-91; co-assoc. chair maj. gift divsn. capital campaign Daemen Coll., 1983-84, trustee, 1998-; chair mem. com. Daemen Coll Trustees, 2003—; co-chair Women United Against Drugs Campaign, 1970-72; founding mem. Lunch and Issues, Amherst, 1981—; edn. com., bd. dirs. Network in Aging of Western N.Y., Inc., 1982-89, housing com., 1987-89; bd. dirs. Amherst Elderly Transp. Corp., 1982-99; committeeman dist. Town of Amherst Rep. Com.; treas. Town and Country Rep. Club, 1980-81; nominating com. Fedn. Rep. Womens Clubs Erie County, 1980; del. N.Y. State Govs. Conf. on Aging, 1995, White House Conf. on Aging, 1995, named mem. aging svcs.; mem. Erie County Indsl. Devel. Agy. Erie County Regional Devel. Corp., 1996-97; mem. adv. bd. Amherst Symphony Orch., 2003-; vol. life project Greater Buffalo chpt. ARC, 2002-05, mem. svc. to older adults com., 2002-05. Named Homemaker of Yr., Family Circle mag., 1969, Woman of Substance, 20th Century Rep. Women, 1983, Woman of Yr., Buffalo Philharm. Orch. Soc., Inc., 1982, Outstanding Woman in Cmty. Svc., SUNY, Buffalo, 1985; recipient Good Neighbor award, Courier Express, 1978, Merit award, Buffalo Philharm. Orch., 1978, Edn. Rep. Womens Clubs Erie County award, 1982, Disting. Svc. award, Town of Amherst Sr. Ctr., 1985, Amherst Adult Day Care and Vis. Nurses Assn., 1994, Susan B. Anthony award, Interclub Coun. Western NY, 1991, Cmty. Svc. award, Amherst Rep. Com., 1991, D.A.R.E. award, Town of Amherst Police Dept., 1994, Amherst South Rotary Club, 1997, Outstanding Cmty. Svc. award, Amherst Sr. Citizen Found., 1997, Lynn Millane Cmty. Svc. award named in her honor, Rep. honoree, award for svc., Town of Amherst Youth Bd., 1996, award for care and assistance to sr. citizens of N.Y. State, Batavia Nursing Home, 2000, Woman of Distinction award, NY State Senate, 2003; hon. Paul Harris fellow. Mem. Amherst C. of C. (VIP dinner com. 1984), LWV, SUNY Buffalo Alumni Assn. (life, presdl. advisor 1977-79), Amherst Symphony Orch. Assn. (bd. dirs. 1981-87, roster chair. 1982-84, nominating chair 1985-86, vice-chair 50th ann. com. 1994-96, adv. com. 2003-), Niagara Connect, Amherst Rep. Womens Club (bd. dirs. 1963-65, 99), Zonta (pres. Amherst chpt. 1986-88, Zontian of Yr. 1992), Pi Lambda Theta (hon.).

MILLARD, JERI KILLOUGH, educational consultant; d. Robert Earl and Linda Ruthven Killough; m. Marshall Nathan Millard; children from previous marriage: J. Tanner Word, J. Robert Word. BS in Elem. Edn. and Speech Therapy, Tex. A&M, Kingsville, 1978; MS in Curriculum and Instrn., Tex. A&M, Corpus Christi, 1985. Cert. ednl. diagnostician, lang and learning disabilities. Speech pathologist Corpus Christi Ind. Sch. Dist., 1979—85, ednl. diagnostician, 1985—88; child find specialist Duval County Pub. Schs., Jacksonville, 1988—93; child find preschool specialist Fairfax (Va.) County Pub. Schs., 1993—97; bus. owner, ednl. diagnostician Rainbow Dianostic Svcs., Ponte Vedra, Fla., 1997—. Dir. resource devel. US U. N. Fla., Jacksonville, 2004—. Mem.: Learning Disabilities Assn., Internat. Dyslexia Assn., Coun. Exceptional Children. Methodist. Avocations: reading, water sports, interior decorating. Office: Rainbow Diagnostic Svcs 175 Roscoe Blvd N Ponte Vedra Beach FL 32082 Personal E-mail: jeri.ruld@comcast.net.

MILLENDER-MCDONALD, JUANITA, congresswoman; b. Birmingham, Ala., Sept. 7, 1938; d. Shelly and Everlina (Dortch) M.; m. James McDonald III, July 26, 1955; children: Valeria, Angela, Sherryll, Michael, Roderick. BS, U. Redlands, Calif., 1980; MS in Edn., Calif. State U., L.A., 1986; postgrad., U. So. Calif. Manuscript editor Calif. State Dept. Edn., Sacramento; dir. gender equity programs L.A. Unified Sch. Dist.; mem. U.S. Congress from 37th Calif dist., Washington, 1996—; mem. small bus. com., transp. and infrastructure com.; mem. Ho. Com. on Ho. Adminstrn.; tchr., sch. adminstr., 1981—90; Carson mayor pro-tempore; mem. Calif. Assembly, 1992—96, Jt. Com. Libr., Dem. Homeland Security Task Force, New Democrat Coalition, Regional Whip. City councilwoman, Carson; bd. dirs. S.C.L.C. Pvt. Industry Coun. Policy Bd., West Basin Mcpl. Water Dist., Cities Legis. League (vice chmn.; mem. Nat. Women's Polit. Caucus; mem. adv. bd. Comparative Ethnic Tng. U. So. Calif.; founder, exec. dir. Young Advocates So. Calif. Recipient Most Influential Black Americans, Ebony mag., 2006. Mem. NAACP, NEA, Nat. Assn. Minority Polit. Women, NAFE, Nat. Fedn. Bus. and Profl. Women, Assn. Calif. Sch. Adminstrs., Am. Mgmt. Assn., League African Women, L.A. World Affairs Coun., Nat. Female Execs., Nat. Coun. Jewish Women, Carson C. of C., Phi Delta Kappa. Democrat. Office: 2445 Rayburn HOB Washington DC 20515-0537 also: 970 W 190 St Ste 900 Torrance CA 90502 Office Phone: 202-225-7924. Office Fax: 202-225-7926.*

MILLER, ALISA DOROTHY NORTON, artist; b. Wellsville, N.Y., Nov. 18, 1920; d. Oak Duke and Gladys Virginia (Dexter) Norton; Rochester Inst. Tech., 1968-69, San Jose State U., 1981; A.A. in Fine Arts, West Valley Coll., Saratoga, Calif., 1983; m. Robert E. Miller, Oct. 12, 1974; children by previous marriage— Richard, Linda, Michael. Airline stewardess Colonial Airlines, N.Y.C., 1944-45; art supr. Eastman Kodak Co., Rochester, 1962-70; exec. sec. 3M Corp., Rochester, 1970-72; med. sec., asst., Los Gatos, Calif., 1972-76; portrait artist Art Studio, Los Gatos, 1976—1990; one-man show: Norton Gallery, Rochester, 1972; group shows include: Glossinger Cultural Mus., Xenia, Ohio, 1964, Rosicrucian Mus., San Jose, Calif., 1981, Triton Mus., Santa Clara, Calif., 1982; represented in permanent collections: Glossinger Cultural Mus., also numerous pvt. collections. Home and Office: 2561 Sadies Drive Hollister CA 95023-8320

(MARBACH) MILLER, AMANDA JOY, educator; b. San Antonio, Tex., July 28, 1975; d. Jerome Claude and Elizabeth (Betty) Ann Marbach; m. John Boswell Miller, Apr. 30, 2005. BA in Interdisciplinary Studies, U. Tex., 1999. Tchr. Our Lady Perpetual Help Sch., Selma, Tex., 1999—. Home: 112 Avenue B Converse TX 78109 Office: Our Lady Perpetual Help School 16075 N Evans Rd Selma TX 78154 Office Phone: 210-651-6811. Personal E-mail: amanda.marbach@sbcglobal.net. E-mail: millera@olphselma.org.

MILLER, ANDREA LYNN, library science educator; b. Warren, Pa., Sept. 25, 1957; d. Harlan Kermit and Hazel Adeline Samuelson; m. Michael Edward Miller, oct. 16, 1953; 1 child, Lena. BS in Edn., Clarion U., 1978, MA in English, 1982, MSLS, 1991; PhD in Info. Scis., U. Pitts., 1997. English tchr. Redbank Valley Sch. Dist., New Bethlehem, Pa., 1979-86, sch. libr. media specialist, 1986-92; prof. libr. sci. Clarion (Pa.) U., 1992—, dir. Inst. for Study and Devel. of Sci. Libr. Info. Ctrs., 2000—, chmn., dir. program dir. Dept. Libr. Sci., 2002—05. Contbg. author: Powerful Public Relations with Full-time Results, 2d edit., 2001; author profl. devel. workshop in field. Trustee Clarion Free Pub. Libr., 1993-99. Recipient Laura Braun scholarship, 1993; grantee Pa. State Sys. Higher Edn., 1999. Mem. ALA, ASCD, Assn. Libr. and Info. Sci. Edn., Pa. Assn. Ednl. Comms. and Tech., Assn. Pa. State Coll. and Univ. Facilities (chmn. nominating com. 1995-97), Assn. Libr. Svc. to Childen, Young Sch. Librarians (chmn. Highsmith rsch. grant award 1999-2001), Pa. Sch. Librarians Assn. (co-chmn. state curriculum com. 1998-2002), Internat. Assn. Sch. Librarians, Assn. Ednl. Comms. and Tech., Delta Kappa Gamma. Democrat. Baptist. Avocations: travel, golf, biking. Home: 35 Ross St Clarion PA 16214 Office: Clarion U Pa 840 Wood St Clarion PA 16214 Office Phone: 814-393-2271. Office Fax: (814) 393-2150. Business E-Mail: amiller@clarion.edu.

MILLER, ANGELA, art educator; b. La. d. Dean and Ann Marie Miller. BFA, Boston U., 1998, MFA in Studio Art Tchg., 1999. Cert. tchr. art K-12 Mass., 1999. Art educator Quincy Pub. Schs., Mass., 2001—, Fitchburg Pulic Schs. Adviser art club and art gallery club. Painter, various paintings. Grantee Excellence In Tchg. grant, Great Idea grant, Quincy Pub. Schs., 2002—06. Mem.: Mass. Tchrs. Assn., Nat. Art Education Assn.

MILLER, ANGELA D., secondary school educator; b. Springfield, Mo., Oct. 11, 1972; d. Gary G. and Sandra K. Wingo; m. Jeffrey D. Miller, June 15, 2001; 1 child, Seth Thomas. BS in Edn., Mo. State U., Springfield, 1996, MA in Theater, 2000, MA in History, 2004. Cert. tchr. Mo. Tchr. Springfield Pub. Schs., 1996—.

MILLER, ANGELA MARIE, elementary school educator; b. Tiffin, Ohio, Aug. 22, 1969; d. Molly Forry and Ralph Troiano; m. Steven Miller, Oct. 17, 1992; children: Kristi, Candace, Stephanie, Simone, Hannah, Heath. MEd, Bowling Green State U., Ohio. Tchr. Upper Sandusky Schs., Ohio, 1995. Summer sch. dir. Upper Sandusky Schs. Singer: (performer) Messiah. Pres. Wynford PTO, Bucyrus, Ohio, 2005—06. Recipient N.W. Ohio Tchr. of Yr., Time Warner Cable, 2002, Nominee Tchr. of Yr., Ohio Dept. Edn., 2003. Mem.: Phi Kappa Phi, East Ctrl. Ohio Mensa. Office: Upper Sandusky Schs 390 W Walker St Upper Sandusky OH 43351 Office Phone: 419-294-5721. Personal E-mail: amiller@udata.com.

MILLER, ANITA DIANE, psychologist; b. Lewistown, Pa., Oct. 31, 1968; d. Fred A. and Sarah A. Miller; life ptnr. James McMartin Long; 1 child, Hannah Nicole Keener. BA, Bucknell U.; PhD, Vanderbilt U., 1998. Lic. clin. psychologist NY, 2002. Rsch. cons. James Long Co., Caroga Lake, NY, 2002—05; asst. prof. Skidmore Coll., Saratoga Springs, 2005—. Contbr. articles to profl. jours. Mem. Resident's Com. Protect Adirondacks, Blue Mountain Lake, NY, 2004—05, Adirondack Nature Conservancy, Keene Valley, 2004—05. Recipient Still prize, Bucknell U., 1989, Nat. Rsch. Svc. award, NIMH, 1994—97, 1999—2002, Rsch. award, 1999, Young Investigator award, Nat. Alliance for Rsch. on Schizophrenia and Depression, 2000—03; fellow, Pew Sci. Found., 1989, U. Pitts., 1998—2002; scholar, U. Wis., 1999. Mem.: APA (assoc.), Am. Psychol. Soc., NY Psychol. Assn. (assoc.), Soc. Rsch. Child Devel. (assoc.), Soc. Neurosci. (assoc.), Soc. Rsch. Psychopathology (assoc.), Internat. Neuropsychological Soc. (assoc.), Soc. Psychophysiological Rsch. (assoc.), Sigma Xi, Phi Beta Kappa, Psi Chi, Alpha Lambda Delta, Phi Eta Sigma. Achievements include research in Psychophysiology Device Development, with James Long. Home: PO Box 685 Caroga Lake NY 12032-0685 Office: Skidmore Coll 815 North Broadway Saratoga Springs NY 12866-1632 Personal E-mail: anita_miller_phd@yahoo.com.

MILLER, ANN CLINTON, communications educator; d. Everett Dean Gerwig and Mary Jane Boyles; m. James William Miller, June 27, 1970; children: James Hunter, Courtney Ellen. BA, U. Charleston; MA, U. Del., 1984. Dir. WD Comm., Red Bank, NJ; writing instr. U. Del., Newark, 1984—85. Author: Training Resource Manual. Mem.: ASTD. Achievements include development of Corporate Training Programs. Avocations: music, travel, reading. Office Phone: 732-530-2076. Personal E-mail: amiller@wdcommunications.com.

MILLER, ANN G., lawyer; b. San Francisco, Nov. 1, 1944; BA, U. San Diego, 1966; JD, U. San Francisco, 1970. Bar: Calif. 1971. Law clk. U.S. Dist. Ct. (no. dist.) Calif., 1970-71; ptnr. Lillick & Charles, San Francisco, Nixon Peabody LLP, San Francisco, 2001—. Mem. Ninth Cir. Judicial Nominating Com. Mem.: ABA, Computer Law Assn., Bar Assn. San Francisco, Maritime Law Assn. (chair Passenger Vessel and Cruise Com.). Office: Nixon Peabody LLP Two Embarcadero Ctr San Francisco CA 94111-3996 Office Phone: 415-984-8236. Office Fax: 415-984-8300. E-mail: amiller@nixonpeabody.com.

MILLER, ANNIE CHRISTMAS, secondary school educator; b. Greenville, N.C., Dec. 22, 1947; d. Oliver Miller and Maggie Gaylord; children: Kwan, Kia. BS, Elizabeth City State U., 1970; MA, U. D.C., 1977. Expungent aide FBI, Washington, 1982—86; tchr. D.C. Pub. Schs., Washington, 1987—. Adv. mem. World Wildlife Fund, Washington, 1985—, Teen Life Choices, Washington, 1997—; gleaners Washington Area Gleaning Network, Arlington, Va., 1990—; mem. Nat. Campaign for Tolerance, Washington, 2000—. Named Internat. Tchr. of Yr., World Affairs Coun., 2001, D.C. state History Tchr. of Yr., 2004; recipient Kelly Miller Pen Pal Club award, Samuel Pardoe Found., 1996, Program Excellence award, Ptnrs. Am., 1997; fellow Ptnrs. Am. Internat. fellow, W.K. Kellogg Found., 1998; scholar Fulbright scholar, World Affairs Coun., 2001. Democrat. Avocations: reading, travel. Home: 531 42nd St NE Washington DC 20019

MILLER, APRIL D., special education educator; b. McKeesport, Pa., Apr. 11, 1961; d. Albert L. and Mary M. Roney. BS, Ohio State U., 1983, MA, 1988, PhD, 1992. Cert. tchr. K-12 reading, K-12 spl. edn., supervision, Ohio. Mem. adj. faculty Ashland U., Columbus, Ohio, 1989-92, Wright State U., Dayton, Ohio, 1991-92, Ohio Dominican Coll., Columbus, 1991-92; asst. prof. U. So. Miss., Hattiesburg, 1992-96, assoc. prof., chair dept. spl. edn., 1996—2000, prof., spl. edn., 2000—03, assoc. dean Coll. Edn. and Psychology, 2000—03; prof., dean Tex. Woman's U. Coll. Prof. Edn., 2003—06; prof., asst. dean Coll. Edn., Morehead State U., Ky., 2006—. Presenter convs. various nat. profl. orgns.; ednl. cons. local edn. agys., 1992—. Contbr. articles to profl. jours. Faculty senator U. So. Miss., 1995-96; mem. coun. U. So. Miss. Tchr. Edn. Coun., 1994-2003; vol. Assn. for Retarded Citizens, Very Spl. Arts Festival, Spl. Olympics, 1992-2003, bd. dirs. Denton County chpt., 2004— Mem. Coun. for Exceptional Children (nominee Susan Phillips Gorin award 1996, faculty advisor 1992-98), Assn. for Behavioral Analysis (Outstanding Svcs. award 1994, com. chair profl. devel. 1995-97, coord. internat. sci. and engring. fair initiative 1993-97), Phi Delta Kappa (conf. planner U. So. Miss. 1996, v.p. programs chpt. 75 1994-95, pres. 1995-96). Office: 100 Ginger Hall Morehead KY 40351

MILLER, ARLENE, psychotherapist, mental health facility director; b. Phila., Oct. 10; d. Nathan Sydel and Bella (Schuman) M. BA in Polit. Sci., U. Miami (Fla.), 1964-65; M in Social Work, U. Md., Balt., 1969-71. Diplomate Am. Bd. Clin. Social Work, Am. Bd. Cert. Managed Care Providers; diplomate clin. social work NASW; lic. clin. social worker. Dir. sr. adults program Jewish Community Ctrs. of South Fla., 1972-76; adminstrv. coord. Early Childhood Day Sch., Miami, Fla., 1974-76; project dir. Sr. AIDES Program Dade County, Miami, Fla., 1976-83; exec. dir. Pentland Hall Discovery Program, Miami, Fla., 1983-85; real estate closing processor Mark Buchbinder, Atty., Miami, Fla., 1985-86; dir. Anxiety and Stress Mgmt. Ctr., Miami, Fla., 1986—; co-owner, v.p., bd. dirs. Ctr. for Cognitive Behavioral Therapy, Inc., Plantation, Fla., 1994—. Cons. Child Anxiety and Phobia Ctr., Fla. Internat. U., Miami, 1991. Fellow NIMH, U. Md.; recipient Honor award City of Miami Fire Dept., Outstanding Svc. award Metro/Dade County, City of Miami, Pub. Svc. award NCSC, Citizen of the Day award WINZ radio. Mem. ACA, NASW, Anxiety Disorders Assn. Am., Fla. Soc. Clin. Social Workers, Clin. Social Work Assn. So. Fla., Fla. Anxiety Disorders Assn. (bd. dirs.), Fla. Assn. Family Mediators, Dade County Alliance Against Domestic Violence, Phi Sigma Alpha (hon.). Avocations: golf, reading, painting. Office: 8525 SW 92nd St Ste A3 Miami FL 33156-7374 Office Phone: 305-279-1715.

MILLER, ARLYN HOCHBERG, psychologist; b. N.Y.C., Dec. 2, 1925; d. Nathaniel and Marie (Weinstein) Hochberg; m. Arthur M. Miller, May 29, 1947 (div. June 1971); children: David, Eve. BS in Edn., CCNY, 1946, MS in Psychology, 1949; EdD in Psychology, Temple U., 1965. Lic. sch. psychologist, N.J., N.Y., Pa., lic. pvt. practice psychologist, N.J., Pa. Faculty Littaur Hosp., Gloversville, N.Y., 1954-58; sch. psychologist Cherry Hill, N.J., 1958-63, Collingswood, Glassboro, Delran, N.J., 1958-65; staff psychologist Children's Hosp., Pa., 1963-64; sr. psychologist Camden County Child Guidance Clinic, 1964-69; psychologist N.J. Divsn. Youth and Family Svcs., 1965-85; pvt. practice N.J., Pa., 1965—; supr. clin. tng. Sch. Psychology Rutgers U., 1968-70; psychologist N.J. Divsn. Vocat. Rehab., 1970-85; prof. Hahnemann Hosp., 1975—. Bd. dirs. N.J. Assn. Children with Learning Disabilities, psychologist, 1968-74; bd. dirs. Camden County Mental Health Assn., mem. profl. adv. bd.; N.Y. state bd. dirs. Assn. for Help of Retarded Children; bd. dirs. Sch. for Retarded Children, Fulton County, N.Y.; adj. prof. Drexel U., 1969-70, Glassboro Coll., 1972-74, Our Lady of Lourdes Hosp., 1974-75, Temple U., 1975-81; cons. to tech. adv. svc. to attys., 1991—; presenter numerous seminars. Author: (booklets) Guidelines for Divorcing Parents, 1986, Guidelines for Step-Parents, 1986; contbr. articles and tapes to profl. jours. Founder, coord. Hemlock Soc. Delaware Valley, 1991-92; bd. dirs. Camden County divsn. Parents without Partners, 1987; mem. profl. adv. bd. Single Parents Soc. Fellow in sex counseling and therapy Internat. Coun. Sex Edn. and Parenthood. Mem. APA, Am. Soc. Sex Educators, Counselors and Therapists (cert. sex therapist), N.J. Psychol. Assn., Phila. Soc. Clin. Psychologists, Camden County Psychol. Assn. (charter, founder), Victorian Soc. Am., Internat. Profl. Exch., Am. Bd. forensic Examiners. Home and Office: 1420 Locust St 31D Philadelphia PA 19102-4223

MILLER, BARBARA JEAN, health facility administrator; b. Viroqua, Wis., June 27, 1961; d. Alan Wayne and Sharon Joan (Phillips) Bennett; m. Leonard Ralf Miller, May 5, 1984; children: Kari Elizabeth, Ronald Alan. BSN, Viterbo Coll., La Crosse, Wis., 1983. RN, Mich.; cert. nephrology nurse, peritoneal dialysis nurse, clin. advancement sys. Level IV nurse. Nursing asst. Bethany St. Joseph Health Care Ctr, La Crosse, 1978—81; staff and charge nurse Butterworth Hosp., Grand Rapids, Mich., 1983—84; hemodialysis charge nurse St. Mary's Health Svcs., Grand Rapids, 1984—90, peritoneal dialysis nurse, 1990—98; clin. mgr. peritoneal dialysis home tng. Gambro Healthcare Patient Svcs., Wyoming, Mich., 1998—2000; ctr. dir. Gamgro Healthcare Grand Rapids Clinic, Mich., 2000—01, Physicians Dialysis, Inc., Grand Rapids, 2001—. Speaker, educator in field. Bd. dirs., health chmn. Sparta (Mich.) Presch., 1992-94; bd. dirs. Sparta Schs. Parent Tchr. Commn., 1997-99. Mem.: Nat. Kidney Found. (coun. nephrology nurses 1991—), Am. Nephrology Nurses Assn. (edn. com. Mich. chpt. 1986—). Republican. Roman Catholic. Home: 3825 13 Mile Rd NW Sparta MI 49345-9792

MILLER, BARBARA KENTON, retired librarian; b. N.Y.C., Sept. 21, 1934; d. Robert Alfred and Kathleen Hope (Levy) Kenton; m. John Arnold Miller, June 15, 1955; children: Valerie Ann Miller, Jennifer Karen Kraft. BA distinction, Finch Coll., 1960; MLS, C.W. Post, 1976. Cert. libr., N.Y. Libr., cons. archivist Coun. Fgn. Rels., N.Y.C., 1977—2000; ret., 2000. Cons. archivist Coun. on Fgn. Rels. Mem. Spl. Librs. Assn., Beta Phi Mu. Avocations: dogs, golf. Office: Coun Fgn Rels 58 E 68 St New York NY 10021-5953 Personal E-mail: bkmiller55@aol.com.

MILLER, BERTHA HAMPTON, history professor; d. James Robert Hampton and Millie Lucinda Lynch; m. Bobby Hugh Miller, June 12, 1971. BS in sociology, Hampton U., 1960; MA in am. hist., Case Western Res. U., 1970; PhD in am. hist., Duke U., 1981. Tchr. history Portsmouth (Va.) Pub. Sch., Portsmouth, Va., 1960—65, Roanoke Pub. Sch., 1967—71; instr. of hist. and dept. chair A&T State U., Greensboro, NC, 1971—84; dep. dir. bur. history Mich. Dept. State, Lansing, 1985—88; dean sch. edn. Fayetteville State U., NC, 1988—94, act. vice chancellor acad. affairs, 1994—96, dean, coll. arts and scis., 1996—2004, prof. hist., 2004—. Mem. bicentennial of the constn. com. Mich. Dept. State, Lansing, 1985—86; mem. Mich. Coun. Humanities, Lansing, Mich., 1986—88; mem. state program approval team N.C. Dept. Pub. Instrn., Raleigh, 1989—; mem. bd. examiners NCATE, Washington, 1994—2003. Editor: (hist. publication) Pathways to Michigan's Black Hist.; author: A History of Fayetteville State University 1867-2003. Spkr. Civic Clubs, Ch., Sch., Cumberland County, NC, 1988—2005. Named to Chancellor's Million Dollar Club Grantsmanship, N.C.; grantee, Sloan Found., 1982—83, Ford Found., 1994—2000, N.C. Dept. Pub. Instrn., 1994—2000, NSF, 1996—2004. Mem.: Assn. for the Study of African-Am. Life and Hist., AACTE, NAACP, Sigma Delta Phi, Delta Mu Delta, Kappa Delta Phi, Phi Alpha Theta. Methodist. Home: 6135 Lochview Dr Fayetteville NC 28311 Office: Fayetteville State U 1200 Murchison Rd Fayetteville NC 28301-4242 Office Phone: 910-672-1837. Home Fax: 910-672-1470. E-mail: bmiller@uncfsu.edu.

MILLER, BETH MCCARTHY, television director; Dir.: (TV series) Saturday Night Live, 1975, 1995—, The Jon Stewart Show, 1993—, The Colin Quinn Show, 2002, (TV spl.) Eagles: Hell Freezes Over, 1994—, Nirvana Unplugged, 1994—, James Taylor Live, 1998—, Saturday Night Live: The Best of Adam Sandler, 1999—, Saturday Night Live Christmas, 1999—, Saturday Night Live: 25th Anniversary, 1999, America: A Tribute to Heroes, 2001, NBC 75th Anniversary Spl., 2002, Saturday Night Live: The Best of Will Ferrell, 2002, GQ Men of the Yr. Awards, 2003; dir., prodr.: MTV Video Music Awards, 2003. Nominee Outstanding Directorial Achievement in Musical/Variety award, DGA, 2000, 2004, Emmy award, 1999, 2000, 2003; recipient Outstanding Directorial Achievement in Musical/Variety award, DGA, 2001, 2002. Office: Saturday Night Live 30 Rockefeller Plaza 50th St and 6th Ave New York NY 10112

MILLER, BETTY, elementary school educator; d. Winsol and Jewel Mitchell; m. James Miller, June 2, 1972; children: Michael Dale, April Amanda Verdoni, Amy Annette Sanders. MS, Miss. Coll., Clinton, 1990. 6th grade tchr. Coleman Elem. Sch., Columbus, Miss., 1987—88; 3rd grade tchr. Bradley Elem. Sch., Jackson, Miss., 1988—97; 6th and 7th grade tchr. Forrest Sch., Chapel Hill, Tenn., 1998—. Workshop presenter in field. Mem.: Delta Kappa Gamma. Home: 1771 Wade Brown Rd Lewisburg TN 37091 Office: Forrest School 310 North Horton Pkwy Chapel Hill TN 37034 Personal E-mail: millerb44@k12tn.net.

MILLER, BETTY BROWN, freelance writer; b. Altus, Ark., Dec. 21, 1926; d. Carlos William and Arlie Gertrude (Sublett) Brown; m. Robert Wiley Miller, Nov. 15, 1953; children: Janet Ruth, Stephen Wiley. BS, Okla. State U., 1949; MS, U. Tulsa, 1953; postgrad., Am. U., 1966—68. Tchr. LeFlore (Okla.) H.S., 1947-48, Osage Indian Reservation H.S., Hominy, Okla., 1948-50, Jenks (Okla.) HS, 1950—51; instr. Sch. Bus. U. Tulsa, 1950-51; tchr. Tulsa pub. schs., 1951-54; faculty mem. Burdette Coll., Boston, 1954-55; reporter Bethesda-Chevy Chase Tribune, Montgomery County, Md., 1970-73; freelance writer, contbr. newspapers and mags., 1973—. V.p. Kenwood Park (Md.) Citizens Assn., 1960; mem. Ft. Sumner Citizens Assn., editor newsletter, 1969; mem. Md. State PTA, editl. coord. leadership conf., 1973-74; founder, chair Montgomery County Forum Edn., 1970-75; trustee Friends Valley Forge Nat. Hist. Park; bd. dirs. Friends Curtis Inst. Music; active Nat. Mus. Women in the Arts, Musical Fund Soc. Phila.; trustee adv. Help the Aged Internat. Mem.: DAR, PEO, Union League Phila. (past mem. ladies com., mem. ladies adv. com.), The Nat. Gravel Soc., Internat. Platform Assn., Montgomery County Press Assn., Nat. Soc. Arts & Letters (past editor mag., bd. dirs. pub rels., past nat. corr. sec.), Huguenot Soc. Pa. (v.p. 1989—92, pres. 1993—95, past bd. dirs., hon. pres. 1997—), Nat. League Am. Pen Women (former nat. budget chmn., past nat. treas.), Soc. Descendants of Washington's Army at Valley Forge (past. nat. comdr. in chief, past inspector gen. Nat. Huguenot Soc., past. mem. gen. coun.), Acorn Club Phila., Sedgeley Club (pres. Phila. 1985—88), Washington Club, U.D.C., Adventures Unltd. (chmn. Washington chpt.), Capital Spkrs. Club Washington (past pres.), Melba T. Croft Music Club, Order Ea. Star (life). Republican. Address: PO Box 573 Valley Forge PA 19481-0573

MILLER, BEVERLY WHITE, former college president, educational consultant; b. Willoughby, Ohio, 1923; d. Joseph Martin and Marguerite Sarah (Storer) White; m. Lynn Martin Miller, Oct. 11, 1945 (dec. 1986); children: Michaela Ann, Craig Martin, Todd Daniel, Cass Timothy, Simone Agnes. AB, Western Res. U., 1945; MA, Mich. State U., 1957; PhD, U. Toledo, 1967; LHD (hon.), Coll. St. Benedict, St. Joseph, Minn., 1979; LLD (hon.), U. Toledo, 1988. Chem. and biol. researcher, 1945-57; tchr. schs. in Mich., also Mercy Sch. Nursing, St. Lawrence Hosp., Lansing, Mich., 1957-58; mem. chemistry and biology faculty Mary Manse Coll., Toledo, 1958-71, dean grad. div., 1968-71, exec. v.p., 1968-71; acad. dean Salve Regina Coll., Newport, RI, 1971-74; pres. Coll. St. Benedict, St. Joseph, Minn., 1974-79, Western New Eng. Coll., Springfield, Mass., 1980-96, pres. emerita, 1996—. Higher edn. cons., 1996—; cons. U.S. Office Edn., 1980; mem. Springfield Pvt. Industry Coun./Regional Employment Bd., exec. com., 1982-94; mem. Minn. Pvt. Coll. Coun., 1974-79, sec., 1974-75, vice chmn., 1975-76, chmn., 1976-77; cons. in field. Author papers and books in field. Corporator Mercy Hosp., Springfield, Mass. Recipient President's citation St. John's U., Minn., 1979; also various service awards; named disting. alumna of yr. U. Toledo, 1998. Mem. AAAS, Am. Assn. Higher Edn., Assn. Cath. Colls. and Univs. (exec. bd.), Internat. Assn. Sci. Edn., Nat. Assn. Ind. Colls. and Univs. (govt. rels. adv. com., bd. dirs. 1990-93, exec. com. 1991-93, treas. 1992-93), Nat. Assn. Biology Tchrs., Assn. Ind. Colls. and Univs. of Mass. (exec. com. 1981-96, vice chmn. 1985-86, chmn. 1986-87), Nat. Assn. Rsch. Sci. Tchg., Springfield C. of C. (bd. dirs.), Am. Assn. Univ. Adminstrs. (bd. dirs. 1989-92), Delta Kappa Gamma, Sigma Delta Epsilon. Office: 6713 County Road M Delta OH 43515-9778

MILLER, BLONDELL STEPHENSON, social worker, minister; b. Hartsville, S.C. d. Johnnie and Marie Belvin Stephenson; m. James Lee Miller, Apr. 6, 1974; children: Taris Lydell, James Richard, Brandon Jerel. BA in History, Morris Coll., 1973; degree in Social Work, Winthrop U., 1980; student in Religious Edn., Duke U., 2004—05. Lic. pastor S.C. Conf. United Meth. Ch., 2003; LCSW S.C. Bd. Social Work, 1989. Tchr. Lee County Bd. Edn., Bishipville, SC, 1973—74; social worker Lee County Dept. Social Svc., Bishipville, 1974—2005; pastor Hartsville (S.C.) Dist. United Meth., 2000—. Chmn. bd. FEMA, Bishopville; bd. dir. Lee First Step, Bishopville, Waterse Head Start Program Health, Sumter, SC. Mem.: NAACP, Morris Coll. Alumni (sec.), Ea. Star (treas.), Delta Sigma Theta (chaplin 1986—). Meth. Avocations: cooking, reading, singing, travel, basketball. Home: 503 Pleasantview Dr Hartsville SC 29550 Office: Lee County Dept Social Svc 820 Brown St Bishopville SC 29010 Office Phone: 803-484-5376. Personal E-mail: blon1949@aol.com.

MILLER, BONNIE RUTH, retired elementary school educator; b. Sherman, Tex., Jan. 14, 1939; d. Bonnie Charles and Virginia Ruth (Brannum) May; m. Bruce A. Miller, June 25, 1960; children: Kevin Bruce, Daniel Jesse, Rainee Lynette. BA, Austin Coll., 1961. Cert. elem. tchr., Tex. Kindergarten tchr. So. Kern Unified Sch. Dist., Rosamond, Calif.; 4th grade tchr. Schertz (Tex.)-Cibolo-Universal City Ind. Sch. Dist.; ret., 1999. Mem. NEA, Tex. State Tchrs. Assn. CVEA, Internat. Reading Assn., State Coun. Internat. Reading Assn. (pres.). Home: 260 Fm 477 Seguin TX 78155-1026

MILLER, BONNIE SEWELL, marketing professional, writer; b. Junction City, Ky., July 24, 1932; d. William Andrew and Lillian Irene (McCowan) Sewell; m. William Gustave Tournade Jr., Nov. 5, 1950 (div. 1974); children:

Bonnie Sue Tournade Zaner, William Gustave III, Sharon Irene Tournade Leach; m. Bruce George Miller, Nov. 15, 1981. BA, U. South Fla., 1968, MA, 1973. Cert. tchr., Fla. Chair dept. English Tampa Cath. H.S., Fla., 1972—78; tchr. Clearwater H.S., Fla., 1978—80; mgr. prodn. svcs. Paradyne Corp., Largo, Fla., 1980—83; freelance writer, cons. Tampa, 1983—84; mgr. product documentation PPS, Inc., Largo, 1984—86, mgr. mktg. comm., 1986—87; writer Nixdorf Computer Corp., Tampa, 1988—89; mktg. dir. Suncoast Schs. Fed. Credit Union, Tampa, 1989—98; co-owner, v.p., writer, cons. Need-A-Writer, Inc., Tampa, 1998—; instr. profl. and tech. writing U. South Fla., 2004—. Instr. English, Hillsborough C.C., Tampa, Fla., 1975—87; cons. bus. writing Coronet Instrnl. Media Writing Project, 1976, Nat. Mgmt. Assn., 1981—87; adj. instr. profl. writing U. South Fla., 1993; adj. instr. tech. writing U. Tampa, 2002—, English instr., 2002—; adj. instr. profl. and tech. writing U. South Fla., 2004—. Author: Youth Financial Literacy, 1999, Effective Business Writing for Credit Unions, 2000, Meeting for a Lifetime, 2006; contbr. articles to profl. jours. Bd. dir. SERVE, Tampa, Credit Union Mktg. Assn. Coun., Sing Parent Displaced Homemakers Group; legis. chair Tampa PTA, 1965; judge speech contest Am. Legion, Tampa, 1976; vol. North Tampa Vol. Libr., 1988. NEH fellow, 1975. Mem. NAFE, Soc. Tech. Communicators, Am. Assn. Bus. Women, Kappa Delta Pi. Democrat. Methodist. Avocations: writing, sewing, gardening, travel, decorating. Home and Office: 516 2d Ave SE Lutz FL 33549 Business E-Mail: bsmiller@sunstarcom.net.

MILLER, BRENDA, real estate investment analyst; b. Gary, Ind., Dec. 31, 1957; d. Earl Miller and Essie Birdsong Hill; m. Petion Michael Nemorin, Feb. 14, 1987 (div. Mar. 1989); 1 child, Chris. BA, Howard U., 1979; JD, U. West L.A., 1995. Domestic violence cert. adv. Haven Hills Shelter, 1999. 60 Minutes archives asst. CBS Broadcast Ctr., N.Y.C., 1978; mdse. supr. Universal Studio Tour, Universal City, Calif., 1981—83; employment liaison specialist Mayor's Office for the Disabled, L.A., 1984—86; ind. sales contractor various orgns., L.A., 1988—98; nutrition team mem. Whole Foods Market, Woodland Hills, Calif., 1999—2001; in-house security L.A. Family Housing Shelter, North Hollywood, 2002—04; Home Mag. staff writer Womens Care Cottage Shelter, North Hollywood, Calif., 2002—04; sr. investment analyst 1031 Commercial Exchange, Beverly Hills, Calif., 2003—. Resident adv. com. mem. Haven Hills Shelter, Canoga Park, Calif.; mentor for youth prison Calif. Youth Authority, Camarillo; adv. for women's prison Calif. Instn. for Women, Corona. Author poetry. Pro-bono legal work San Fernando Valley Legal Aide, Pacoima, Calif., 1994; pub. rels. co-chair Lawyers for Human Rights, L.A., 1995; domestic abuse response team Haven Hills Shelter/L.A. Police Dept., Van Nuys, Calif., 1999; Infinite Way meditation tape group leader, 1998—; mem. Living Praise Christian Ctr., Chatsworth, Calif. Recipient Wiley M. Manuel for Pro Bono Legal Svc., State Bar Calif., 1994—95, Battered Women's Svc. award, Convicted Women Against Abuse, Calif. State Prison, 2000, Courageous Achievers award, Billy Blanks Found., 2001. Mem.: Living Praise Chrisitian Ctr., Alpha Kappa Alpha (Sigma Lamda Omega chpt. San Fernando Valley). Democrat. Home: 7727 Lankershim Blvd #142 North Hollywood CA 91605

MILLER, BRIDGET A., lawyer; BA, Ursuline Coll.; JD, Cleveland State U. Bar: Ohio 1983. Assoc. Mansour, Gavin, Gerlack & Manos, LPA, Cleveland; corp. insurance risk mgr. Invacare Inc., Elyria, Ohio, 1993, asst. gen. counsel, dir. risk mgmt., v.p., gen. counsel, 2002—. Mem.: ABA, Soc. Chartered Property Casualty Underwriters, Cleveland Bar Assn., Ohio State Bar Assn., Lorain County Bar Assn. Office: Invacare Corp One Invacare Way Elyria OH 44036

MILLER, CAMILLE M., lawyer; b. Paoli, Pa., Apr. 29, 1965; BA, Franklin & Marshall Coll., 1987; JD with honors, Chgo.-Kent Coll. Law, 1991. Bar: Ill. 1991, Pa. 1997, U.S. Dist. Ct. No. Ill. 1991, U.S. Dist. Ct. Ea. Pa. 1997, U.S. Ct. Appeals 7th cir. 1994, U.S. Ct. Appeals 3rd cir. 1997, U.S. Ct. Appeals Fed. cir. 1998, U.S. Ct. Appeals 4th cir. 2000. Ptnr. Woodcock Washburn, Phila.; mem. Cozen O'Connor, Phila., 2002—. Named one of Lawyers on the Fast Track, Am. Lawyer Media, 2004; recipient Am. Legion award. Mem.: ABA, Pa. Bar Assn., Phila. Intellectual Property Law Assn., Intellectual Property Org., Copyright Soc. U.S.A., Internat. Trademark Assn., Phila. Bar Assn. Office: Cozen O'Connor 1900 Market St Philadelphia PA 19103 Business E-Mail: cmiller@cozen.com.

MILLER, CANDICE S., congresswoman; b. Clair Shores, Mich., May 7, 1954; m. Donald G. Miller; 1 child, Wendy Nicole. Student, Macomb County C.C., 1973—74, Northwood U., 1974. Sec., treas. D.B. Snider, Inc., 1972-79; trustee Harrison Twp., 1979-80, supr., 1980-92; treas. Macomb County, 1992-95; sec. of state State of Mich., Lansing, 1995—2003; mem. US Congress from 10th Mich. dist., 2003—. Mem. Lake St. Clair Blue Ribbon Commn. Chair John Engler for Gov. campaign, Macomb County; del. Rep. Nat. Conv., 1996; co-chair Rep. Platform Com., 1996, Dole/Kemp Presdl. Campaign, Mich., 1996, Bush/Cheney Presdl. Campaign, Mich., 2000; mem. Carehouse-Macomb County Child Adv. Ctr., Selfridge Air Nat. Guard Base Cmty. Coun., Detroit Econ. Club; mem. adminstrv. bd. Mich. State, mem. safety commn. Recipient Macomb Citizen of Yr. award, March of Dimes, 1997, Woman of Distinction award, Macomb County Girl Scouts, Adjutant General's Patriot award, Mich. Nat. Guard, 2002, GH award women in govt., Good Housekeeping mag., 2003, Econ. Excellence award, Macomb C. of C.; Paul Harris Internat. fellow. Mem.: Nat. Assn. Secretaries of State, Boat Town Assn. Republican. Presbyterian. Avocations: boating, yacht racing. Office: US Congress 228 Cannon HOB Washington DC 20515 also: District Office 48653 Van Dyke Ave Shelby Township MI 48317-2560 Office Phone: 202-225-2106, 586-997-5010. Office Fax: 202-226-1169, 586-997-5013.*

MILLER, CAROL, elementary school educator, counselor; b. Bklyn., N.Y., Jan. 10, 1939; d. Maurice and Bess (Strauss) Shapiro; m. Stephen Herschel Miller (div.); children: Mark Alan, David Charles. MS in Elem. Edn., Ohio State U., Columbus, 1959; grad. work-edn., Queens Coll., Flushing, N.Y., 1959—61; MA in Counseling Psychology, Lewis & Clark Coll., Portland, Oreg., 1988. Cert. tchr. k-3 N.Y. Bd. Edn., 1959, tchr. k-6 Calif. Bd. Edn., 1966, basic counselor Personnel Svcs., Oreg., 1988. Kindergarten tchr. Hampton St. Sch., Mineola, NY, 1959—61; tchr, (k-3) Roosevelt Elem. Sch., Santa Monica, Calif., 1961—66; elem. sch. tchr. Horace Mann Sch., Beverly Hills, 1966—67; substitute elem. sch. tchr. San Diego Sch. Dist., 1967—68, 1990—91; cancer support group facilitator Am. Cancer Soc., San Diego, 1992—99; breast cancer support group facilitator Scripps Meml. Hosp., LaJolla, 2000—02; adv. bd. mem. Am. Cancer Soc., San Diego, 1994—96; adv. bd. mem., breast cancer ctr. Scripps Meml. Hosp., LaJolla, 1999—2001; adv. bd. mem. St. Germaine Aux. for Child Abuse Prevention, San Diego, 1998—. Contbr. papers to profl. jours. and pubs. Leader Boy Scouts Am., Hershey, Pa./Lake Oswego, Oreg., 1977—83; vol. Reach to Recovery, Pa., 1982—, Oreg., 1982—, Calif., 1982—; coord. Reach to Recovery Program, San Diego, Calif., 1991—93; vol. Polinsky Children's Ctr., San Diego, 1991—2005, U. Calif. San Diego, Moores Cancer Ctr., LaJolla, 2005—; com. mem. Citizen Involvement, Lake Oswego, Oreg., 1982. Recipient Terese Lasser award, Am. Cancer Soc., San Diego, 1993, Vol. of Yr., Health & Human Svcs., San Diego, 2002. Mem.: LWV, Psi Chi. Democrat. Jewish. Avocations: tennis, dance, reading, travel. Home: 6555 Caminito Northland La Jolla CA 92037

MILLER, CAROL LYNN, librarian; b. Kingsville, Tex., Mar. 31, 1961; d. Walter Edward, Jr. and Emma Lee (Nelson) Miller. BS in Early Childhood Edn., So. Nazerene U., 1985; M in Early Childhood Edn., Ala. A & M U., 1987; MLS, U. Ala., 1993. Office worker Salvation Army, Huntsville, Ala., 1979—83; libr. Madison (Ala.) Br. Libr., 1985, br. head, 1987—92; sub. tchr. Huntsville City and Madison County Sch. Sys., 1986—87; br. head Madison Sq. Mall Br. Libr., Huntsville, 1992—2000; head adult svcs./reference, asst. br. mgr. Madison Pub. Libr., 2000—02; libr. supr. Bold and Cool Satellite Librs. Ft. Worth Pub. Libr., 2002—. Methodist. Office: Ft Worth Pub Libr 1801 North/South Fwy Fort Worth TX 76102 Personal E-mail: carlyntx@sbcglobal.net.

MILLER, CAROLINE, editor-in-chief; Exec. editor Variety mag., NYC, 1989—92; editor-in-chief Lear's mag., NYC, 1992—94, Seventeen mag., NYC, 1994—96, New York mag., NYC, 1996—2004; editl. dir. Absolute Publ. USA, NYC, 2004—. Office: Absolute Publ 10 East 34th St New York NY 10016

MILLER, CAROLYN, secondary education educator, composer; b. Cin. m. Gary G. Miller; children: Jeffrey, Daniel, Randall. BS in Music Edn., U. Cin., 1963; MEd, Xavier U., Cin., 1991. Cert. in piano, 1963. Tchr. grades 4-6 Cin. Pub. Schs., 1963-67; tchr. K-6 Finneytown Schs., Cin., 1980-81, tchr. grade 5, 1981-82; tchr. grade 1-8 St. John the Evangelist, Cin., 1984-89; tchr. grades 9-12 Sycamore Schs., Cin., 1989—. Min. of music North College Hill United Meth. Ch., Cin., 1964—; accompanist Sycamore H.S. Show Choir, 1987—. Composer (piano solos, performed by Regis Philbin on nat. TV) Rolling River, 1992, Fireflies, 1993; composer over 80 piano solos and duets, many were selected for Nat. Fedn. Music Clubs Contest, 1995-97; composer: (piano solo books) Just Play It Boogie, 1997, Just Play It with Feeling, 1997, Just Play It Attitudes, 1997, Just Play It For Fun, 1997, Arpeggios Rule, 1997, Student Favorites, 1997, Student Favorites Book 2, 1999, Scales Rule, 1997, 5 Finger Patterns Rule, 1997, Syncopation Rules, 1997, Sportacular Warm-ups Book 1-4, 1998, Just Play It Together, 1998, Chords Rule, 1998, Just Play it Together Book 2, 1999, Teaching Little Fingers to Play Christmas, 2000, Teaching Little Fingers to Play Boogie and Blues, 2001, Teaching Little Fingers to Play Recital Pieces, 2006; composer 6 piano duets chosen for performance at All Ohio Piano Ensemble, 1998. Sec. Kindervelt #37, Finneytown, 1996—. Mem. NEA, Music Tchrs. Nat. Assn. (workshop presenter conv. Dallas 1997), Sycamore Edn. Assn., Ohio Music Educators Assn., Music Educators Nat. Conf. Avocations: travel, planting flowers, playing piano, walking, singing.

MILLER, CAROLYN LYONS, microbiologist, military officer; b. Birmingham, Ala., June 28, 1955; d. John Henry and Annie Lois Lyons; m. Brian Lenny Miller, July 28, 1984; 1 child, Brian Lenny Miller, Jr. BS, U. Ala., 1977; MS, Ala. A&M U., 1979; PhD, Rutgers U., 1984; degree, Air U., 2000. Lic. medical technologist Am. Soc. Clin. Pathologists, 1984, cert. clin. lab. scientist Nat. Certification Agy, Lenexa, KS, 1984. Student asst. Dept. Biology and Microbiology U. Ala., Birmingham, Ala., 1973—77; rsch. asst. Dept of Biology and Food Sci. and Tech. Ala. A&M U., Normal, Ala., 1977—79; rsch. asst. Dept Pedodontics Sch. of Dentistry U. Ala., 1980; tchg. asst. biology and microbiology Cook Coll. Rutgers U., New Brunswick, NJ, 1980—83, asst. area coord. student life Douglass Coll., 1983—84; med. tech. intern Wilford Hall Med. Ctr., Lackland Air Force Base, Tex., 1985—86; chief quality control/epidemiology divsn. Air Force Sch. Aerospace Medicine, Brooks Air Force Base, Tex., 1986—89; comdr. 421st med. svc. squadron Wilford Hall Med. Ctr., Lackland Air Force Base, 1997—98; assoc. prof. Dept. Biology USAF Acad., Colorado Springs, Colo., 1989—93, exec. officer to the dean of the faculty, 1993—95; exec. officer to the comdr. Human Sys. Ctr., Brooks Air Force Base, Tex., 1995—97; ops. staff officer/dir., quality assurance & regulatory affairs 59th Med. Diagnostics and Therapeutics Group, Lackland Air Force Base, Tex., 1998—99; v.p. recruitment & diversity affairs Uniformed Svcs. U. Health Scis., Bethesda, Md., 1999—2002; pathology flight comdr. 375th Med. Group, Scott AFB, Ill., 2002—05; dep. med. support squadron comdr. 375th Med. Support Squadron, Scott Air Force Base, Ill., 2002—05; biomed. sci. corps exec. 375th Airlift Wing, Scott AFB, Ill., 2002—05; dir. chem., biol., nuc. and clin. surveilance Air Force Inst. for Operational Health, Brooks City AFB, Tex., 2005—. Faculty advisor for vol. cmty. med. clinic Med. Sch. Uniformed Svcs. U., Bethesda, 1999—2002; coach odyssey of the mind White Oaks Elem. Sch., Burke, Va., 2000—02; vol. instr. Incarnate Word Coll., San Antonio, 1995—97; chmn. parent adv. com. Child Devel. Ctr., Colorado Springs, Colo., 1991—95; mem., leadership coun. for cmty. svc. Alamo Fed. Exec. Bd., San Antonio, 1995—99; cons. in field. Contbr. articles to profl. jours. Cmty. mem. Alamo Fed. Exec. Bd., San Antonio, Tex., 1995—99; ch. med. vol. Emmanuel Ch., San Antonio, Tex., 1985—89; advisor to the bd. Uniformed Svcs Med. Sch., Bethesda, Md., 1999—2002; mil. deployment Mil., Overseas, Non-U.S., Classified, 2003—03. Col. USAF, 1985, Scott and various other Air Force Bases, over 20 years of service. Decorated Expeditionary Svc. Ribbon with Gold Border USAF, Air Force Outstanding Unit Award with Valor US; fellow, 81Rutgers U., 1984; Pell grant, U. of Ala., 1974—77. Master: Biomedical Scis. Corps (licentiate; licensure 1985, Chief Mastery badge 1995); mem.: Soc. Armed Forces Mil. Lab. Scientists (sr. mem. 1986, Best Rsch. Poster Presentation 1999), Am. Soc. Microbiologists (corr.; mem. 1978, Grad. Student award 1983), Assn.Mil. Surgeons of U.S. (corr.; mem. 1996), Am. Soc. Clin. Pathologists (assoc. mem. 1990), Officers Club (assoc.; mem. 1986), Beta Beta Beta (hon.; honor mem. 1979), Phi Beta (corr.; pres. 1975—77, Cmty. Charity Supporter 1976). Achievements include research in converting urine to potable water to prevent discharge in space; development of medical laboratory in deployed location; first to tri-service military and federal medical school recruitment to help meet nation's need for physicians, women and minorities. Avocations: reading, horseback riding, running, walking, interior decorating. Home: 23003 Whisper Canyon San Antonio TX 78258-3211 Office: 2350 Gillingham Dr Brooks City-Base TX 78235 Office Phone: 210-536-8305. Personal E-mail: bbcmiller@earthlink.net. Business E-Mail: carolyn.miller@brooks.af.mil.

MILLER, CARRIE SIMS, music educator; b. Pensacola, Fla., Jan. 19, 1978; d. J. Larry and Maria Sims; m. Robert Ward Miller, Jr., July 7, 2001. MusB in Edn., Auburn U., Ala., 2001; MEd, Ariz. State U., Tempe, 2003. Cert. tchr. Ala. State Dept. Edn., 2001. Music tchr., band dir. Frank Sch., Guadalupe, Ariz., 2001—03; band dir. Andalusia Mid. Sch., Ala., 2003—04; music tchr. Concord Elem. Sch., Bessemer, Ala., 2005, North Highland Elem. Sch., Hueytown, Ala., 2005—. Mem.: Birmingham Cmty. Concert Band Assn., Am. Fedn. Tchrs., Collegiate Music Educators Nat. Conf. (sec., treas. 2000—01, Outstanding Achievement award 2000), Music Educators Nat. Conf., Nat. Orff-Schulwerk Assn., Auburn Alumni Assn. (life). Avocation: ballroom dancing. Office: North Highland Elem Sch 2021 29th Ave N Bessemer AL 35023 Personal E-mail: csmiller@jefcoed.com.

MILLER, CATHERINE H., nursing administrator, property manager; d. Lawrence James Gleason, Jr. and Arlene Joan Woolsey; m. Thomas Dewayne Keyser (div.); children: Kenneth James Keyser, Kerry Lee Keyser, Gary Wayne Keyser; m. James H. Miller, Dec. 14, 1996. Certificate acctg., Brown's Bus. Sch., Hempstead, N.Y., 1966; certificate cmty. health agt., certificate nursing asst., Dabney S. Lancaster C.C., Clifton Forge, Va., 1977, AAS, 1981. RN Va., 1981. Sec., bookkeeper Aluminum Specialties Home Improvement, Levittown, NY, 1960—76; cert. nursing asst. Liberty House Nursing Home, Clifton Forge, 1977—79, RN charge nurse, 1981—83, 1985—97, RN supr., 1997—2005; staff devel. dir. Alleghany Rehab./Health Care, Clifton Forge, 2006; RN supr. Beverly Health Care, Alleghany Rehab./Health Care, Clifton Forge, 2006—. Nurse, adult CPR instr. Am. Red Cross, Covington, Va., 1997—. Worthy matron Order of Ea. Star Martha chpt. 21, Covington, 1985. Named to Wall of Tolerance, Nat. Campaign for Tolerance, founding chair Rosa Parks, 2005. Avocation: painting. Office: Alleghany Highlands Cmty Svcs Adult Day Ctr 550 Pine St Clifton Forge VA 24422

MILLER, CHARLOTTE FAYE, speech pathology/audiology services professional; b. Weir, Miss., Feb. 19, 1959; d. John Samuel and Gertha Lee (Warren) Miller; m. Phillip William Miller, July 14, 1978. BS, Jackson State U., 1981; MS, Miss. State U., 1996. Cert. sch. clinician, sch. adminstr. Miss. Speech lang. pathologist Choctaw County Schs., Ackerman, Miss., 1981-90, Attala County Schs., Kosciusko, Miss., 1990—. Ins. salesperson Pre Paid Legal Svcs., Inc., Jackson, Miss., 1996—. Chairperson spl. edn. svcs. Greenlee Elem. Sch., McCool, Miss., 1996—98, Image Award Martin Luther King Celebration, Kosciusko, 1997—98; lay spkr. United Meth. Ch.; dir. Miss Black Choctaw County Pageant, Weir, 1983—93; coord. Buttons and Beaus Pageant, Ehtel, Miss., 1996—98; property mgr. Millers - Colemans - Satterfields Found., Inc. Named Woman of the Yr., Star Herald Newspaper, 1992; recipient Gratitude award, Attala County Assn. Educators, 1995. Mem.: Miss. Assn. Educators (local pres. 1993—95, Outstanding Achievement award 1993), Miss. Speech Hearing Assn., Nat. Coun. Negro Women (membership chair 1996—, pres. 1998—, award 1996), Heroines of Jericho (jr. matron 1988—, dist. sec. 1994—95), Zeta Phi Beta (local, state, regional officer 1990—98, Appreciation award 1990, 1993, 1997, 1998). Democrat. Methodist. Avocations: travel, quilting, houseplants. Home: 2472 Allala Rd 2126 Mc Cool MS 39108 Office: Greenlee Elem Sch RR 3 Box 66 Mc Cool MS 39108-9110

MILLER, CHERYL DEANN, former professional basketball coach, broadcaster; b. Riverside, Calif., Jan. 3, 1964; BA in Broadcast Journalism, U. So. Calif., 1985. Basketball player Jr. Nat. Team, 1981, U.S. Nat. Team, 1982, U.S. Olympics, 1984; commentator ABC Sports; head coach women's basketball U. So. Calif., 1993-94; commentator TNT Sports, Atlanta, 1996; gen. mgr., head coach Phoenix Mercury, 1997—2000. Player JC Penney All-Am. Team Five, U. So. Calif. Women's Basketball Team, World Championship Team, 1983. Recipient Sports Illustrated Player of Yr., 1986, Naismith Player of Yr. award, Kodak All-Am. award, more than 1,140 trophies and 125 plaques including Nat. Sports Festival, 1981, Pan Am. Games, 1983, FIBA World Championship, Goodwill Games, gold medal 1984 Olympic Games; elected to Naismith Basketball Hall of Fame, 1995.

MILLER, CHERYL MARIE, special education educator, small business owner; b. Syracuse, N.Y., Sept. 3, 1969; d. Lawrence J. and Georgia Ann (Smith) Gola; m. Wendell L. Miller, June 8, 1991; 1 child, Ian William. BS in Edn., SUNY, Geneseo, 1991; MS in Edn., SUNY, Oswego, 1995. Cert. spl. edn. tchr., reading tchr., N.Y. Spl. edn. tchr. South Jefferson Ctrl. Sch., Adams Center, N.Y., 1991-93; mental health case mgr. Oswego County Health Dept., Oswego, N.Y., 1994-98; spl. edn. aide Sandy Creek (N.Y.) Ctrl. Sch., 1998-99; spl. edn. tchr Rehab Resources, Oswego, 1999—. Mem. Coun. for Exceptional Children, Internat. Reading Assn. Avocations: reading, archery. Home: 391 Kehoe Rd Sandy Creek NY 13145-2172

MILLER, CHRISTINE LEE, psychotherapist; b. New Orleans, Oct. 13, 1948; d. Leo Miller and Janice (Mathews) Pizzolato; m. Harold Butler, Nov. 22, 1969 (div. 1980); m. Michael Kevin Brown, Mar. 26, 1983 (div. 2006); 1 child, Elizabeth Miller Brown. Student, Hollins Coll., 1966-69; BA, La. State U., 1970; MEd, Boston U., 1972. Cert. mental health counselor., lic. clin. mental health counselor. Administrv. asst. psychiat. pavilion St. Elizabeth's Hosp., Brighton, Mass., 1970-72; juvenile group supr. Hillcrest Juvenile Hall, Belmont, Calif., 1973; counselor, tchr. cons. Manchester (N.H.) Sch. Dept., 1973-74; dir. social svcs. Manchester Family Planning, 1974-77; dir. Child & Family Svcs. Group Home, Concord, N.H., 1980-87; pvt. practice Manchester, 1989—. Adj. faculty N.H. Tech. Inst., Concord, New England Coll., Henniker, N.H., 1977-84; cons. Resolve, Inc., N.H., 1990-92; grant reviewer U.S. Dept. HHS, Washington, 1981-84; workshop presenter U. N.H., 2000—. Elected del. Dem. Nat. Conv., N.Y.C., 1992; city chair Clinton for Pres., Concord, 1992; vol. N.H. Nat. Abortion Rights Action League, Concord, 1985-2001. Mem. Nat. Acad. Cert. Clin. Mental Health Counselors, AACD. Episcopalian. Avocation: politics. Office: 201 Riverway Pl Bedford NH 03110-6741

MILLER, CHRISTINE MARIE, marketing executive, public relations executive; b. Williamsport, Pa., Dec. 7, 1950; d. Frederick James and Mary (Wurster) M.; m. Robert M. Ancell, Mar. 30, 1985. BA, U. Kans., Lawrence, 1972; MA, Northwestern U., Evanston, Ill., 1978, PhD, 1982. Pub. rels. asst. Bedford County Commr., Pa., 1972—73; tchg. asst. Northwestern U., Evanston, Ill., 1977—80; asst. prof. U. Ala., Tuscaloosa, 1980—82, Loyola U., New Orleans, 1982—85; vis. prof. Ind. U. Sch. Journalism, Bloomington, 1985—86; dir. mktg. Nat. Inst. Fitness & Sport, Indpls., 1986—88; mgmt. assoc. cmty. and media rels. Subaru-Isuzu Automotive, Inc., Lafayette, Ind., 1988—91; dir. pub. rels. Giddings & Lewis, Fond Du Lac, Wis., 1991—93; v.p. comm. and enrollment mgmt. Milton Hershey Sch., Pa., 1993—94, dir. adminstrn., 1994—95; account mgr. WorldCom Govt. Markets, Vienna, Va., 1995—. Program dir. Nat. Entrepreneurship Acad., Bloomington, 1986—88. Co-author: The Biographical Dictionary of World War II General and Flag Officers, 1996; contbr. articles to profl. jours. Bd. dirs. Indpls. Entrepreneurship Acad., 1988-91, Area IV Agy., Greater Lafayette Mus. Art, 1989-91. With USN, 1973-77, capt. USNR, 1977—. Mem. Armed Forces Comm. Electronics Assn., Pub. Rels. Soc. Am., Naval Order of the U.S. (nat. pub. affairs com.), U.S. Naval Pub. Affairs Alumnae Assn. (bd. dirs.), Naval Res. Assn., Res. Officers Assn. Presbyterian. Avocations: cooking, swimming, reading, travel, bicycling. Home: 11419 S Lakes Dr Reston VA 20191 Office: MCI Govt Mkts Ste 7055 1945 Old Gallows Rd Vienna VA 22182-3931 Office Phone: 703-343-6051. Business E-Mail: christine.m.miller@verizonbusiness.com.

MILLER, CHRISTINE ODELL COOK, federal judge; b. Oakland, Calif., Aug. 26, 1944; m. Dennis F. Miller; 2 children. BA in Polit. Sci., Stanford U., 1966; JD, U. Utah, 1969. Bar: D.C., Calif. Law clk. to Hon. David T. Lewis U.S. Ct. Appeals (10th cir.), Salt Lake City; trial atty. U.S. Dept. Justice, U.S. Ct. Claims; team leader atty. FTC; atty. Hogan & Hartson, Washington; spl. counsel Pension Benefit Guaranty Corp.; dep. gen. counsel U.S. Ry. Assn.; ptnr. Shack & Kimball, Washington; judge U.S. Ct. Fed. Claims, Washington, 1982—. Comment editor Utah law Rev. Scholar U. Utah Coll. Law. Mem. D.C. Bar Assn., Calif. State Bar, Order of Coif, Univ. Club, Cosmos Club. Avocation: genealogy. Office: US Ct Fed Claims 717 Madison Pl NW Ste 716 Washington DC 20005-1011

MILLER, CLAIRE ELLEN, editor, educator, writer; b. Milw., July 17, 1936; d. Emil George Benjamin and Phyllis Dorothy (Rahn) Holtzen; m. Gerald Ray Miller, June 21, 1958; children: Karin, Russell. BS in Edn., Concordia U., 1961. Tchr. Grace Episcopal Day Sch., Silver Spring, Md., 1971-77, The Norwood Sch., Bethesda, Md., 1977-79; writer Media Materials, Balt., 1980; project editor Ednl. Challenges, Alexandria, Va., 1981; asst. mng. editor Ranger Rick Mag., Nat. Wildlife Fedn., Vienna, Va., 1981-87, mng. editor, 1988-2001, contbg. editor, 2002—; propr. Claire Ellen Miller, Writer and Editor, Rockville, Md., 2001—. Author numerous activity books for presch. thru mid. sch., 1979-80; project editor 6 vocabulary books, 1981; author numerous children's mag. and newspaper stories and books, 1981—. Mem. Assn. Ednl. Pubs., Md. Ornithol. Soc. Democrat. Lutheran. Avocation: birding. Home and Office: 17501 Kirk Ln Rockville MD 20853-1033 Personal E-mail: clairemiller@erols.com.

MILLER, CONNIE JOY, assistant real estate officer, real estate broker; b. Martinez, Calif., May 7, 1949; d. Lee Issac James and Lela Martha (Carter) James Poe; m. Avery Jared Miller Oct. 22, 1967 (div. Mar. 1988); children: Elaine Paula Miller Bond, Alfred Saul Jacob Miller. AA, Contra Costa Coll., San Pablo; BA, St. Mary's Coll. Lic. real estate broker. Acct. AT&T, San Francisco, 1967; real estate broker, mgr. Berkeley and El Cerrito, Calif., 1979-93; CFO A.J. Miller & Assocs., Berkeley, Calif., 1978-87; auditor UCOP, Oakland, 1987-88, benefits acct., 1988, exec. asst. to assoc. v.p., 1988—94, sr. real estate analyst, 1994—2001, asst. real estate officer, 2001—. Past chair Cmty. Resources for Children; past pres. El Cerrito Soccer, Tilden chpt. ORT; past v.p. Berkeley Hadassah. Mem. NAR, AAUW, Calif. Assn. Realtors, Berkeley Assn. Realtors. Avocations: gardening, travel, art, cooking. Home: 7300 Pomona Ct El Cerrito CA 94530 Office: UC Office of Pres 1111 Franklin St 6th Fl Oakland CA 94607-5200

MILLER, CONSTANCE JOHNSON, elementary school educator; b. Jacksonville, Fla., Mar. 16, 1948; d. Shepheard and Victoria (Fisher) Johnson; children: Rodney Johnson, Larry Miller. BS, Fla. Meml. Coll., 1972. Tchr., family planning educator Urban League of Greater Miami, Fla., 1972-73; recreation leader YMCA of Greater Miami, 1973-74; recreation therapist Dade County Corrections and Rehab., 1974-76; tchr. Broward County Sch. Bd., Ft. Lauderdale, Fla., 1976—, Hollywood Hills H.S., Hollywood, Fla., 1986—. Coach McNicol and Hallandale Middle Sch., Hollywood, Fla., 176-87, Hollywood Hills Sr. H.S., 1992-97; asst. athletic dir. Hollywood Hills H.S., 1998—. Assoc. min. New Birth Bapt. Ch., Miami; mem. NAACP. Democrat. Avocations: cooking, collecting oldies, decorating, golf, travel. Home: 20680 NE 4th Ct Apt 202 Miami FL 33179-1880

MILLER, DARCY M., publishing executive; b. Glen Ridge, N.J., June 17, 1953; d. Paul Richardson and Susan (Alling) Miller; m. James R. Donaldson III, Feb. 6, 1988 (div.); 1 child, Zoe Alling Donaldson; m. Richard G. Powers, Aug. 23, 2003. Co-founder, assoc. pub. Mus. Mag., N.Y.C., 1979-83; pub. Crop Protection Chems. Ref., N.Y.C., 1983-85; assoc. pub. Chief Exec. Mag., N.Y.C., 1986-87, pub., 1987-89, exec. v.p., 1989-96; pub. Stagebill, N.Y.C., 1996-97; group pub. Am. Baby Group, 1997-2000, pres., 2000—01; pres. corp. sales Primedia Inc., N.Y.C., 2001—03; sabbatical, 2003—. Mem.: ASCAP, Advt. Women of N.Y. Democrat. Episcopalian.

MILLER, DAWN MARIE, retired meteorologist; b. Hartford, Conn., Sept. 17, 1963; d. Eugene E. Miller and Audrey E. (Flagg) Laurel; m. Dennis James Miller, Sept. 9, 1989; children: Zackarey, Amanda. BS in Meteorology, SUNY, Oneonta, 1985. Customer support specialist WSI Corp., Bedford, Mass., 1985-87, from media TV mktg. to product mktg. specialist-data svcs. Billerica, Mass., 1987-97, sr. meteorologist, product mktg. specialist, 1997-99, sr. meteorologist, assoc. product mgr., 1999—2001, sr. meteorologist, media mktg. and promotion, 2001—03, ret., 2004; salon coord. Shear Class, LLC, Hudson, NH, 2005—. Mem.: Nat. Weather Assn., Am. Meteorol. Soc., Am. Hort. Soc., Nature Conservancy, Nat. Audubon Soc., Nat. Arbor Day Found., Oneonta Alumni Assn. Republican. Episcopalian. Avocations: meteorology, astronomy, photography, gardening, bird watching. Home: 37 Wren Dr Litchfield NH 03052-2540 E-mail: dawn.miller@gmail.com.

MILLER, DEANE GUYNES, salon and cosmetic studio owner; b. El Paso, Tex., Jan. 12, 1927; d. James Tillman and Margaret (Brady) Guynes; m. Richard George Miller, Apr. 12, 1947; children: J. Michael, Marcia Deane. Degree in bus. adminstrn., U. Tex., El Paso, 1949. Owner four Merle Norman Cosmetic Studios, El Paso, 1967-96; pres. The Velvet Door, Inc., El Paso, 1967-96. Pres., bd. dirs. YWCA, 1967; v.p. Sun Bowl Assn., 1970; bd. dirs. El Paso Symphony Assn.; bd. dirs., treas. El Paso Mus. Art, trustee, 1990, pres., 1990—93; chmn. bd. El Paso Internat. Airport; bd. dirs., sec. Armed Svc. YMCA, 1987, 1st v.p., 1990; trustee Internat. Mus. Art, 1999, pres., 2003, 2004—05. Named Outstanding Woman field of civic endeavor El Paso Herald Post. Mem. Women's C. of C. (pres. 1969), Pan Am. Round Table (dir., pres. 1987), Internat. Assn. for Visual Arts (v.p. 1998, 2000), Internat. Mus. Art (pres. 2004-05) Home: 1 Silent Crest Dr El Paso TX 79902-2160 Office: 1211 Montana Ave El Paso TX 79902

MILLER, DEBBIE SUE, special education educator; b. Uniontown, Pa., Mar. 9, 1955; m. David W. Miller, Sept. 18, 1979; children: Jason, Jennifer. BS, Pa. State U., 1977; MEd, California (Pa.) State U., 1990. Tchr. spl. edn. McKeesport (Pa.) Area Sch. Dist., 1990—. Mem. Coun. Exceptional Children, Phi Kappa Phi, Sigma Pi Epsilon Delta. Home: RR 1 Box 108A Lemont Furnace PA 15456-9717

MILLER, DEBORAH, medical surgical nurse; b. Townsend, Vt., Nov. 6, 1961; d. Duane and Evelyn (Bean) Gorham; m. Arthur Miller, Oct. 29, 1988; children: Lindsay, Anthony AS, Vt. Coll., 1981. RN, Fla.; cert. med.-surg. nurse, 2005. Nurse home health care and pediat. All Children's Hosp., St. Petersburg, Fla.; charge nurse Tex. Children's Hosp., Houston; travelling nurse Flying Nurses, Brownsville, Tex.; staff nurse med.-surg. unit Largo Med. Ctr., Fla.; staff nurse pediat. Mease Dunedin; DON All Caring Nurses, MedLink Inc., Clearwater, Fla. Mem. staff Physician's Health HMO, Tampa, Fla Home: 372 Tavernier Cir Oldsmar FL 34677-4627

MILLER, DEBRA LYNN, political scientist; b. Chgo., Dec. 8, 1952; d. Arnold and Beverly S. Miller; children: Abigail Suzanne Davidow, Molly Hannah Davidow stepchildren: Elizabeth Brooks Davidow, Judith Loraine Davidow. AB, U. Calif., Berkeley, 1974; PhD, Harvard U., Cambridge, Mass., 1979. Intern Office of Senator Birch Bayh, Washington, 1973, Office of Congressman John M. Murphy, 1973, U.S. Dept. State, 1974; asst. prof. Barnard Coll. and Columbia U., N.Y.C., 1979—87; internat. economist Office of Indsl. Trade U.S. Dept. Commerce, Washington, 1988—90; sr. fellow and project dir. Ctr. Strategic and Internat. Studies, 1990—93, program dir., 1993—94, polit. scientist, 2003—. Cons. Ednl. Testing Svc., Princeton, NJ, 1984, 85; v.p. Tech. Strategy Group, 1987—88; dir. Strengthening of Am. Commn., Washington, 1990—94; adj. faculty George Mason U., Fairfax, Va., 1990—97; faculty Salzburg Seminar on a changing Europe, 1990; spkr. internat. politics Intellectual Property Rights Internat. Trade. Author: Principles for Health Care Reform: The Second Report of the CSIS Strengthening of America Commission, 1994; editor: A Commerce Department Analysis of European Community Directives vols. 1-3, 1989—90; contbr. chapters to books, articles to profl. jours. John Compton Predoctoral fellow, Princeton U., 1977—78, Dorothy Danforth Compton fellow, Inst. Study of World Politics, 1977—78, Mellon grant non-tenured faculty, Barnard Coll., 1980. Mem.: Coun. Fgn. Rels. Home: 340 Tappan St Apt 4 Brookline MA 02445

MILLER, DEMETRA FAY PELAT, elementary school educator, city official; b. Painesville, Ohio, June 15, 1933; d. William Anthony and Helen (Mimo) Pelat. Grad., Monticello Jr. Coll., Alton, Ill., 1953; BS in Edn., Kent State U., 1955, postgrad., 1957-63, John Carroll U., 1957-63. Tchr. Grant Elem. Sch., Cuyahoga Falls, Ohio, 1955-57, Benjamin Franklin Elem. Sch., Euclid, Ohio, 1957-58, Meml. Park Elem. Sch., Euclid, 1958-87, Lincoln Elem. Sch., Euclid, 1987—. Mem. Euclid City Coun., 1983—; sec. Citizens' Pet Responsibility Com., 1978—; trustee Shore Civic Cultural Ctr., 1988—; treas. Euclid Women's Caucus, 1978-79, v.p., 1981-83, pres., 1983; bd. dirs. YwCA-YMCA, Euclid, 1985—; mem. women's jr. bd., vol. Euclid Gen. Hosp., 1967—; mem. Euclid Devel. Corp., Euclid Recreation Commn., 1985—; former mem. citizens adv. bd. Regional Transit Authority; past mem. Euclid Charter Rev. Commn.; chmn. Euclid City Growth, Devel. and Zoning Commn., 1989—. Named Woman of Yr., Euclid Women's Caucus, 1985, Euclid Citizen of Yr., Am. Legion Post 343, 1986, cert. of appreciation YWCA-YMCA, 1989, One of Most Interesting People award Cleve. Mag., 1990. Mem. NEA (nat. del. 1978-89), Ohio Edn. Assn. (del. 1977—), Euclid Tchrs. Assn. (pres. 1978-79, 83-84, Outstanding Educator award 1979), Ednl. Coun. Cuyahoga County (pres. 1981-82), Coalition Major Ednl. Orgns., Delta Kappa Gamma. Greek Orthodox. Home: 25601 Zeman Ave Cleveland OH 44132-1816 Office: Euclid Bd Edn 651 E 222nd St Euclid OH 44123-2000

MILLER, DIANE FAYE, art education educator, business owner; b. Wauseon, Ohio, Dec. 10, 1966; d. Richard Lee and Twila Fern (Bontrager) Beck; m. Wendell Eugene Miller, June 29, 1991. BS in Art Edn. (cum laude) hons., Grace Coll., Winona Lake, Ind., 1989. Gen. edn., art edn. tchr. New Horizons Ministries, Marion, Ind., 1989-90; art edn., ceramics tchr. Warsaw Cmty. HS, Ind., 1990-94; instr. studio painting I art dept. Grace Coll., spring 1997. Sponsor Art Club, Warsaw Cmty. HS, 1992-94, chairperson Student Asst. Program, 1992-94; coord. Tri Kappa HS Art Show, Warsaw, 1992-94; speaker Fellowship of Christian Athletes, Warsaw, 1992, 93. Vol. freelance artist, decorator bulletin bds., artwork local elem. sch. Recipient 1st Pl. People's Choice award in Interior Decorating, Parade of Homes Exhbn., 2000, 2005, 2nd Pl. People's Choice award, Dec. Parade of Homes Exhbn., 2006. Mem. Nat. Art Edn. Assn., Warsaw Cmty. Edn. Assn., Warsaw Christian Women's Club (exec. bd. dirs. 1995-97). Republican. Mennonite. Avocations: ceramics, basket weaving, skiing, antiques, cooking. E-mail: wdmiller@comcast.net.

MILLER, DIANE WILMARTH, retired human resources director; b. Clarinda, Iowa, Mar. 12, 1940; d. Donald and Floy Pauline (Madden) W.; m. Robert Nolen Miller, Aug. 21, 1965; children: Robert Wilmarth, Anne Elizabeth. AA, Colo. Women's Coll., 1960; BBA, U. Iowa, 1962; MA, U. No. Colo., 1994. Cert. tchr., Colo.; vocat. credential, Colo.; cert. sr. profl. in human resources; lic. real estate broker. Prodr. Sec.-counselor U. S.C. Rep., Myrtle Beach AFB, 1968-69; instr. Coastal Carolina Campus U. S.C., Conway, 1967-69; tchr. bus. Poudre Sch. Dist. R-1, Ft. Collins, Colo., 1970-71; travel cons. United Bank Travel Svc., Greeley, Colo., 1972-74; dir. human resources Aims C.C., Greeley, 1984—2001, ret., 2001. Instr. Aims CC, 1972—89; bd. dirs. U. No. Colo. Found., Greeley, 2003—. Bd. trustees 1st Congl. Ch., Greeley, 2005—. Mem.: Philanthropic Ednl. Orgn. (pres. 1988—89), Women's Panhellenic Assn. (pres. 1983—84), Questers (pres. 2002—04), WTK Club (pres. 2006—), Scroll and Fan Club (pres. 1985—86). Home: 3542 Wagon Trail Rd Greeley CO 80634-3405

MILLER, DIXIE DAVIS, elementary school educator; b. Lubbock, Tex., June 3, 1940; d. Leroy and Sara Edna (Lightfoot) Davis; m. Greg Miller, Aug. 10, 1968; 1 child, Jason Davis. BS in Edn., Tex. Christian U., 1961, MEd, 1967; postgrad., Tex. Wesleyan U. Cert. elem., early childhood, secondary English tchr., Tex. Elem. tchr. Denver Pub. Schs., Ft. Worth Pub. Schs., Albuquerque Pub. Schs., Birmingham (Mich.) Pub. Schs., Aledo (Tex.) Ind. Sch. Dist., Gwinnett County Pub. Schs., Lawrenceville, Ga. Group leader Young Author's Conf.; insvc. leader creative writing; presenter in field. Active PTA, PTO. Named Tchr. of Yr., Dyer Elem. Sch., Lawrenceville, 1979, 82, Grayson Elem. Sch., 1986, Educator of Yr. award Lawrenceville Jaycees, 1981, Les Evans Chpt. award Tex. Assn. for Supervision and Curriculum Devel., 1989, Excellence in Tchg. award Tex. State Reading Assn., 1998. Mem. NEA, Internat. Reading Assn., Assn. Childhood Edn. Internat., Ga. Assn. Educators, Mich. Edn. Assn., Tex. Tchrs. Assn. Home: 113 Squaw Creek Rd Weatherford TX 76087-8240

MILLER, DONNA KAYE, mental health services professional, real estate investor; b. Livingston County, Ky., Feb. 21, 1943; d. Jessie Otis "Pat" and Mary Emma (Thompson) Champion; m. Jimmy Don Miller, July 18, 1965; children: Cheryl Lynne Lassiter, Kenneth Mance, Karl Edwin. BA in Humanities, Purdue U., West Lafayette, Ind., 1965; MS in Mental Health Counseling, Nova Southea. U., Ft. Lauderdale, Fla., 1998. Lic. mental health counselor. Social worker Dept. Pensions and Security, State Ala., Dadeville, 1966—68; vol, tutor Pahokee, Fla., 1969—96; vol. 45th St. Mental Health Clinic, Rivera Beach, Fla., 1997—98; case mgr. Pahokee Youth Devel. Ctr., 1996—98, mental health profl., 1998—2000; psychol. specialist South Bay Correctional Facility, Fla., 2001—03; juvenile ct. liaison East Ala. Family Children Svcs., Opelika, 2005—. Shelter mgr. Katrina relief Am. Red Cross, Opelika, 2005; mem. Nat. Resources Defense Coun., N.Y.C., 2005—. Named to Wall of Tolerance, So. Poverty Law Ctr., Montgomery, Ala., 2005. Mem.: Internat. Schizophrena Found., Ala. Counseling Assn., Am. Mental Health Counselors Assn. Independent. Office: East Ala Mental Health Family Children Svcs 2300 Center Hill Dr Bldg 2 Opelika AL 36801

MILLER, DONNA REED, city official; married; children: Tari McSween (dec.), Shakira. Mem. Dem. exec. com. 59th Ward, Phila., 1970—2005, leader, 1999—; city councilwoman dist. 8 Phila., 1996—. Chair Parks and Recreation com., cultural com. Phila. City Coun., vice chair edn. com. Office: Room 312 City Hall Philadelphia PA 19107-3201 E-mail: donna.miller@phila.gov.

MILLER, DOROTHEA HELEN, librarian, educator; b. Macedonia, Iowa, Mar. 10, 1925; d. Carl Hamilton and Dorothy Marie (Wilson) Stempel; m. Ruben Roy Miller, Sept. 30, 1945 (dec. May 1987); children: Cecilia Rogge, Catherine Miller-King, Constance Miller. Student, U. Denver, 1942-45, State U. Iowa, 1960; BA with honors, Kearney (Nebr.) State Coll., 1966; ME, U. Nebr., 1970. Cert. media specialist Nebr. Libr. Oakland (Iowa) Pub. Libr., 1956-61; elem. libr. Grand Island (Nebr.) Pub. Schs., 1962-65, elem. libr. supr., 1965-78, media specialist, 1978-86; ret., 1986. Cons. Nat. Def. Edn. Act Inst. for Advanced Study in Ednl. Media Concordia Coll., 1967. Vol. Denver Mus. of Natural History, 1994-96, Nat. Def. Edn. Act Inst. Libr. Materials for Minority Students, Queens Coll., N.Y. Named Outstanding Educator in Am. Acad. Am. Educators, 1973-74; Rsch. grantee Howard Sch., 1966. Mem. AAUW, Nebr. Congress Parents and Tchrs. (hon. life), Order Ea. Star (assoc. matron), Cherry Creek Womans Club. Democrat. Avocations: genealogy, watercolors, calligraphy, poetry. Home: 13991 E Marina Dr Apt 303 Aurora CO 80014-3788 Personal E-mail: TheaMil03@aol.com.

MILLER, DOROTHY ANNE SMITH, retired cytogenetics educator; b. N.Y.C., Oct. 20, 1931; d. John Philip and Anna Elizabeth (Hellberg) Smith; m. Orlando Jack Miller, July 10, 1954; children: Richard L., Cynthia K., Karen A. BA in Chemistry magna cum laude, Wilson Coll., Chambersburg, Pa., 1952; PhD in Biochemistry, Yale U., 1957. Rsch. assoc. dept. ob-gyn Columbia U., N.Y.C., 1964-72, from rsch. assoc. to asst. prof. dept. human genetics-devel., 1973-85; prof. dept. molecular biology and genetics Wayne State U., Detroit, 1985-94, prof. dept. pathology, 1985-96, prof. Ctr. for Molecular Medicine and Genetics, 1994-96. Vis. scientist clin. and population cytogenetics unit Med. Rsch. Coun., Edinburgh, Scotland, 1983-84; vis. prof. dept. genetics and molecular biology U. la Sapienza, Rome, 1988; vis. disting. fellow La Trobe U., Melbourne, Australia, 1992. Contbr. numerous articles to sci. jours. Grantee March of Dimes Birth Defects Found., 1974-93, NSF, 1983-84. Mem. Am. Soc. Human Genetics, Genetics Soc. Am., Genetics Soc. Australia, Phi Beta Kappa. Presbyterian. Home: 19365 Cypress Ridge Terr #817 Lansdowne VA 20176 Personal E-mail: damiller@smartneighborhood.net.

MILLER, DOROTHY ELOISE, education educator; b. Ft. Pierce, Fla., Apr. 13, 1944; d. Robert Foy and Aline (Mahon) Wilkes. BS in Edn., Bloomsburg U., 1966, MEd, 1969; MLA, Johns Hopkins U., 1978; EdD, Columbia U., 1991. Tchr. Cen. Dauphin East H.S., Harrisburg, Pa., 1966-68, Aberdeen (Md.) H.S., 1968-69; asst. dean of coll., prof. Harford C.C., Bel Air, Md., 1969—. Owner Ideas by Design, 1995—; mem. accreditation team Mid. States Commn., 1995—; statewide writing skills assessment com., statewide English stds. com. Md. Higher Edn. Commn. 1997-2001, English composition com., 1997—, English alignment com., 2002—; adj. prof. U. Balt., 2001. Editor: Renewing the American Community Colleges, 1984; contbr. articles to profl. jours. Pres. Harlan Sq. Condominium Assn., Bel Air, 1982, 90-96, Md. internat. divsn. St. Petersburg Sister State Com., 1993-2001; edn. liaison AAUW, Harford County, Md., 1982-92; cen. com. mem. Rep. Party, Harford County, 1974-78; crusade co-chair Am. Cancer Soc., Harford County, 1976-78; mem. faculty adv. com. Md. Higher Edn. Commn., 1993-96; people's adv. coun. Harford County Coun., 1994-2003. Recipient Nat. Tchg. Excellence award Nat. Inst. for Staff and Orgn. Devel., U. Tex.-Austin, 1992. Mem. Nat. Mus. Women in the Arts (charter). Republican. Methodist. Avocations: skiing, swimming, golf, reading, image consulting. Office: Harford Community Coll 401 Thomas Run Rd Bel Air MD 21015-1627 Business E-Mail: demiller@harford.edu.

MILLER, EDITH FISHER, special education educator; b. Pottsville, Pa., Aug. 9, 1946; d. Lewis Walter and Elsie Lu (Haas) Fisher; m. Charles Edward Miller, July 6, 1968; 1 child, Charmagne Elsie Miller Webb. BA, Gettysburg (Pa.) Coll., 1968; MEd, East Stroudsburg (Pa.) U., 1985; EdD, Temple U., Phila., 1994. Cert. English, spl. edn., reading, program specialist. Tchr. English Mifflin County Sch. Dist., Lewistown, Pa., 1968-69; substitute tchr. various dists., Monroe County, Pa., 1975-82; tchr. spl. edn. Intermediate Unit # 20, Nazareth, Pa., 1982-84, itinerant learning disabilities tchr., 1984-85, ednl. cons. Easton, Pa., 1985-90; Am. with Disabilities Act coord. East Stroudsburg U., 1992-98, disability svcs. coord., 1990—. Mem. adv. bd. LDA of Monroe County, Stroudsburg, Pa., 1994-97; cons. C & E Miller Assocs., Bethlehem, 1997—. Author: Effective Strategies for Tutoring Students and LD and ADHD, 1998. Presenter Vols. for Literacy, Jim Thrope, Pa., 1993, Parent Assn., Pine Grove, Pa., 1995, Higher Edn. & Disability, Innsbruck, Austria, 1995. Mem. Internat. Reading Assn., Assn. Higher Edn. and Disability, Nat. Tutoring Assn. (program chair 1993-94, Pres. award 1998), Phi Delta Kappa (pres. elect 1999-2000, Educator of Yr. Pocono chpt. 1995, C. of C. (ADA workshop organizer 1992). Democrat. Lutheran. Avocations: travel, snorkeling, reading medieval mysteries, cats. Home: 5540 Montauk Ln Bethlehem PA 18017-8909 Office: East Stroudsburg U 200 Prospect St East Stroudsburg PA 18301-2999 E-mail: emiller@po-box.esu.edu.

MILLER, EDNA RAE ATKINS, secondary school educator; b. Clarksville, Ark., Dec. 28, 1915; d. Sammie Lawrence and Dora May (Turner) Atkins; m. Oscar E. Miller, Feb. 27, 1936; children: Myrna Sue Miller Hanses, William Samuel. BE, Sacramento State Coll., 1966. Tchr. one rm. sch., Johnson County, Ark., 1933-35; tchr. elem. Placerville, Calif., 1953-61; tchr. spl. edn. and mentally retarded County of El Dorado, Placerville, Calif., 1961-74; ret. El Dorado (Calif.) County, 1974. Author: Mother Lode of Learning: One Room Schools of El Dorado County, 1990. Mem. Friends of the Libr. of El Dorado County, Placerville, 1974—; historian People-to-People Internat., 1975-90, Sister City Program, 1975-90. Recipient Cert. of Appreciation, Lung Assn. Sacramento and Emmagrant Trails, 1978, Cert. of Appreciation, Ret. Tchrs. of El Dorado County, 1984, 86, 88. Mem. El Dorado County Hist. Soc., Children's Home Soc. (assoc.), Epsilon Chi chpt. Delta Kappa Gamma (pres. Placerville chpt. 1966-68). Democrat. Baptist. Avocations: research, gardening, painting, cake decorating, quilting. Home: 4301 Golden Center Dr Placerville CA 95667-6260

MILLER, ELAINE WOLFORD, writer; b. Rochester, Pa., Oct. 1, 1948; d. Glen Leon and Mary Isabelle Wolford; m. Daniel Dwight Miller, Oct. 12, 1970; children: Joanna, Elizabeth, Samuel. Assoc., Robert Moore Jr. Coll., Coraopolis, Pa., 1968, Tompkins Cortland C.C., Dryden, NY, 1976. Sec. U.S. Treasury Dept., Washington, 1968—70; adminstrv. asst. Cornell U., Ithaca, NY, 1970—75; spkr., 1986—; writer, 2003—. Founder South View Writers' Group, Horseheads, NY, 2004. Author: Splashes of Serenity, 2005; writer (mag.) At the Center, 0205. Missions chmn. Maranatha Bible Chapel, Horseheads, NY, 1998—; tchr. vacation Bible sch. Gabon, 2001. Republican. Home: 204 Robins Rd Horseheads NY 14845 Personal E-mail: miller970@stny.rr.com.

MILLER, ELEANORA GENEVIEVE, freelance/self-employed poet; b. Gowrie, Iowa, Nov. 17, 1916; d. Alfred Theodore and Jennie Wilhelmina (Carlon) Liljegren; m. Chester Forest Miller, June 1, 1941; children: Carolin Miller Gibson, Loring. BA, Augustana Coll., Rock Island, Ill., 1938; MA, Drake U., 1983. Tchr. English and speech Keota (Iowa) High Sch., 1938-39, Moulton (Iowa) High Sch., 1940-41; reporter Des Moines Register, 1956—; bookkeeper Miller Ins. Ltd., Leon, Iowa, 1980—98; writer pvt. practice, Leon, 1938—. Author: (books of poetry) Poems in Iowa Annual of Lyrical Poetry, 1955, Interviewing the Ghosts, 2001, numerous poems published; winner of over 18 awards for poetry, (book) Interviewing the Ghosts, 2001; editor (newsletter) For Front, 1971-75. Vol. ARC, 1962-73; sec. South Ctrl. Iowa Theatre, Leon, 1978—; mem. Iowa Gov.'s Civil Rights Commn., 1961-65; state chmn. Iowa Citizens for Human Rights, 1965; mem. bd. ch. and society Iowa Conf., United Meth. Ch., 1985-90; lay speaker United Meth. Ch., Creston Dist., 1980—. Mem. VFW Aux. (Iowa state pres 1955-56), Nat. League of Am. Penwomen (br. pres. 1964-66, state pres. 1966-68, 1st pl. lyric poetry 1972), Iowa Poetry Assn. (state pres. 1972-74). Republican. Avocations: vocal music, book collecting. Home: 1405 NW Church St Leon IA 50144-1267

MILLER, ELIZABETH J., mathematician, educator; b. Vienna; arrived in U.S., 1941; MA in Math. Edn., CUNY, N.Y.C., 1965; MEd in Guidance, Columbia U., N.Y.C., 1977, postgrad., 1978—81. Cert. tchr., sch. counselor N.Y. Tchr. math. George Washington H.S., 1960—73, H.S. Truman H.S., 1973—78; guidance counselor Office of H.S. Admissions, 1978—82, Evander Childs H.S., Bronx, NY, 1982—. Home: 5143 Post Rd Bronx NY 10471 Office: Evander Childs HS 800 E Gun Hill Rd Bronx NY 10467 Office Phone: 212-547-7700.

MILLER, ELIZABETH JOAN, artist, guidance counselor; b. Vienna, Austria, Nov. 2, 1925; arrived in U.S., 1941; d. Joseph Ronald Ehrlich and Martha Eleanor Lamm-Ehrlich; m. Alfred Abraham Miller; children: Mark M., Steven H. B in Chem. Engring., City Coll., N.Y.C., 1947, MA in Math. Edn., 1965; MEd in Human Devel., Tchrs. Coll., Columbia U., N.Y.C., 1977. Asst. to chief physicist Air Reduction Co., NYC, 1947—53; tchr., HS math. NYC Bd. Edn., 1960—77, guidance counselor, 1977—90. Mem. Westlake Village Art Guild, 1992—; pres. (sisterhood) Riverdale Temple, Bronx, NY, 1988—90; sec., then pres. Soc. Women Engrs., NE Region, 1950—56. Mem.: Buena Ventura Art Assn., Calif. Gold Coast Watercolor Soc., Peripheral Neuropathy Support (recording sec. 2000—06). Achievements include patents for visually learning mathematics operations with signed numbers. Home: 2478 Chaucer Pl Thousand Oaks CA 91362

MILLER, ELIZABETH RODRIGUEZ, city official; b. Tucson, Feb. 22, 1954; d. Tony S. Martinez and Maria (Corral) Rodriguez; m. Marc Alan Miller, Nov. 5, 1972; children: Andrea Eve, Matthew Luke, Meredith C. BA in Spanish, U. Ariz., 1976, MLS, 1978. Unit mgr. S. Tucson Libr., 1978-80; activities coord. community cable com. City of Tucson, 1980; info./reference mgr. Tucson Pub. Libr., 1981-84, agy. mgr., 1984-85, regional mgr., 1985-87, asst. dir. pub. svcs., 1987-89; dep. exec. dir. divsn. ALA Libr. Adminstrn. & Mgmt. Assn., Chgo., 1990; dep. dir. Tucson Pima Libr., 1990-91, libr. dir., 1991-96; asst. city mgr. City of Tucson, 1996—. Co-editor: Great Library Promotion Ideas V, 1990; contbr. articles to profl. jours. Mem. adv. bd. libr. power grant Tucson Unified Sch. Dist., 1992-95; bd. dirs. Tucson area Literacy Coalition, 1992-95, YWCA, 1998—2001; active Hispanic Profl. Action Com., 1992—. Mem. ALA (mem. pres. program com. 1987, mem. nominating com. 1991-93), REFORMA (chair elections com. 1983-84, 85, chair conf. program 1987, pres. 1987-88), Libr. Adminstrn. and Mgmt. Assn. (mem. cultural diversity com. 1991-92, chair 1992-93, mem. nominating com. 1992-93), Pub. Libr. Assn. (mem. Pub. Libr. Assn.-Libr. Adminstrn. and Mgmt. Assn. cert. com. 1991-92, chair 1992-93, chair Allie Beth Martin Award com. 1987-88, mem. 1989), Ariz. Libr. Assn. (Libr. of Yr. 1995), Ariz. State Libr. Assn. (chair svcs. to Spanish-speaking Roundtable 1980-82, pres. pub. libr. divsn. 1984-85, chair ann. conf. 1986), Internat. City/County Mgmt. Assn. (assoc., participant Comparative Performance Measurement Consortium 1994-96, U. Ariz. Hispanic Alumni Assn., Women at the Top (mem. Carondelet health network fin. com). Office: City Hall 255 W Alameda St Tucson AZ 85701 Office Phone: 520-791-4204. Office Fax: 520-791-5198.

MILLER, ELLEN KATHERINE, music educator; b. St. Louis, June 18, 1955; d. Samuel and Lydia Ann Boda; m. John Walter Miller, June 25, 1978; children: Katherina Ruth, Matthew John. BA in Edn., Concordia U., River Forest, Ill., 1977; level I cert. Orff music tchr., Webster U.; postgrad., N.W. Mo. U. and U. Miami. Dir. mid. sch. band Walther Luth. H.S., Melrose Park, Ill., 1977—81; tchr. 3d grade St. John Luth. Sch., Lombard, Ill., 1978—79; sec. Luth. Child and Family Svcs., Forest Park, Ill., 1980—81; med. sec. West Suburban Family Practice, Elmwood Park, Ill., 1988—98; instr. mid. sch. band Luth. H.S. South, St. Louis, 1998—. Pvt. flute instr., St. Louis, 1974—; freelance flutist, Chgo. and St. Louis, 1974—. Mem.: Mo. Music Educators Assn. Lutheran. Avocations: playing flute, swimming, gardening. Office: Luth H S South 9515 Tesson Ferry Rd Saint Louis MO 63123

MILLER, ELLEN S., marketing executive; b. Indpls., June 28, 1954; d. Harold Edward and Lilian (Gantner) M. BA, DePauw U., 1976; postgrad., Sch. Visual Arts, N.Y.C., 1981-82. Editorial asst. Daisy mag., N.Y.C., 1976-77; asst. dept. mgr., Christmas hiring mgr. Bloomingdale's, N.Y.C., 1978; sales rep. Rosenthal USA Ltd., N.Y.C., 1979, mktg. asst., 1980-81, dir. mktg. comms., 1982-90; mgr. consumer mktg. Creamer Dickson Basford, Providence, 1990, v.p., 1991-94; prin. E.S. Miller Comm., Providence, 1994—. Instr. Learning Connection. Editor Community Prep. Sch. newsletter, 1993. Trustee Cmty. Prep Sch., Providence, 1993—, mem. exec. com., 1997—. Recipient Bell Ringer award New Eng. Pub. Club, 1992, 93, Iris award N.J. chpt. Internat. Assn. Bus. Communicators, 1993, Silver Quill award Dist. I, 1993, Holland award Ctrl. Mass. Advt. Club, 1997. Mem. Pub. Rels. Soc. Am., Nat. Tabletop Assn. (com. chair 1989), Internat. Tabletop Awards (bd. dirs. 1989), Rotary Club. Republican. Presbyterian. Office Phone: 401-724-3773. E-mail: ellensmiller@att.net.

MILLER, EMILIE F., former state senator, consultant; b. Chgo., Aug. 11, 1936; d. Bruno C. and Etta M. (Senese) Feiza; m. Dean E. Miller; children: Desireé M., Edward C. BSBA, Drake U., 1958. Asst. buyer Jordan Marsh Co., Boston, 1958-60, Carson, Pirie, Scott & Co., Chgo., 1960-62; dept. mgr., asst. buyer Woodward & Lothrop, Washington, 1962-64; state labor coord. Robb Davis Daliles Joint Campaign; legis. aide Senator Adelard Brandt, Va., 1980-83; fin. dir. Saslaw for Congress, 1984; legis. cons. Va. Fedn. Bus. Profl.

Women, 1986-87, 98-00; senator Va. Gen. Assembly, Richmond, 1988-92; cons. apptd. by Gov. Wilder to bd. dirs. Innovative Tech. Authority, 1992-94, Ctr. for Innovative Tech., 1992-94; cons., 1992—; sr. mgr. Thompson, Cobb, Bazilio & Assocs., 1999—. Bus. tng. seminars, Moscow, Nizhny Novgorod, Russia, 1993, Novgorod, St. Petersburg, 95; cons. in field. Guest editl. writer No. Va. Sun, 1981; host, prodr. weekly TV program, Channel 61. Active State Ctrl. Com. Dem. Party Va., Richmond, 1974—2005, steering com., 2000—, chair 11th congrl. dist., 2001—; mem. Fairfax County Dem. Com., 1968—, chair, 1976-80, 98-2000, Presdl. Inaugural Com., 1977, 1992 Dem. Nat. Platform Com., Va., Dem. Adv. Com. Robb-Spong Commn., 1978-79; chair 11th Congrl. Dist. Dem. Com., 2001—; founder, chair Va. Assoc. Dem. County and City Chmn., 1976-80; chmn. Fairfax County Dem. Com., 1976-80, 1998-00; security supr. 1980 Dem. Nat. Conv.; v.p. Va. Fedn. Dem. Women, 1992-94; bd. dirs. Stop Child Abuse Now, 1988, Ctr. Innovative Tech., 1992-94, Ct. Apptd. Spl. Advs., 1993-96; nat. alumni bd. J.A. Achievement, BRAVO adv. com. for the first Gov.'s Awards for Arts in Va., 1979-80; lay tchr. St. Ambrose Cath. Ch., 1963-80; del. to White House Conf. on Children, 1970; chair Va. Coalition for Mentally Disabled, 1992-94; com. of 100, Va. Opera Bd., 1994-99; bd. dirs. Social Action Linking Together. Recipient Disting. Grad. award Jr. Achievement, 1973, Woman of Achievement award Fairfax (Va.) Bd. Suprs. and Fairfax County Commn. for Women, 1982, Cmty. Svc. award Friends of Victims Assistance Network, 1988, Founders award Fairfax County Coun. of Arts, 1989, Mental Health Assn. of Northern Va. Warren Stambaugh award, 1991, Ann. Svc. award Va. Assn. for Marriage and Family Therapy, 1991, Psychology Soc. of Washington Cmty. Svc. award, 1993, pacesetter award So. Women in Pub. Leadership Conf., 1996. Mem. NOW, Nat. Mus. Women in the Arts, Va. Assn. Female Execs. (mem. adv. bd., bd. dirs., v.p. 1992-99), Va. Assn. Cmty. Svc. Bds. (chmn. 1980-82), North Va. Assn. Cmty. Bds. (chmn. 1978-79, 95-98), Fairfax County Coun. Arts (v.p. 1980—, mem. exec. com. internat. children's festival, Founders award 1989), Fairfax County C. of C. (mem. legis. com.), Greater Merrifield Bus. and Profl. Assn., Mental Health Assn. No.Va. (bd. dirs.), Ctrl. Fairfax C. of C., Falls Church C. of C., Bus. and Profl. Women's Fedn. Va., Mantua Citizens Assn. (exec. bd.), Bus. and Profl. Women's Club (pres. Falls Church chpt. 1994-96, Woman of Yr. award 1990), Women's Nat. Dem. Club (past v.p., mem. bd. govs.), Downtown Club (Richmond), Va. Assn. Female Execs. (bd. dirs. 1992-99), Phi Gamma Nu. Democrat. Roman Catholic. Avocations: tennis, art, baseball. Home: 8701 Duvall St Fairfax VA 22031-2711 Office Phone: 703-560-0291. Personal E-mail: emiliemiller@cs.com.

MILLER, EMILY JOSEPHINE, retired secondary school educator; b. San Francisco, Nov. 29, 1937; d. Emil Albert Tarradas and Louis Marie Loshuertos; m. David Charles Miller, Jr. (dec.); 1 child, Colin Albert. BA, Dominican U., San Rafael, Calif., 1968. Cert. Spanish tchr. Calif. Tchr. math., sci., Spanish, English, phys. edn. Martin County Office Edn., San Rafael, 1979—99; ret., 1999. Mem.: Young Ladies Inst., Los Robles Mobile Home Park (pres. 1996—2003). Democrat. Roman Cath. Home: 20 Oceano Pl Novato CA 94949

MILLER, ERIKA VITTUR, secondary school educator, language educator; b. Bressanane, Italy, Sept. 7, 1952; arrived in U.S., 1974; d. Heinrich Vittur and Theodora Unterfrauner; m. Andrew K. Miller, Feb. 16, 1974; children: Christina T., Alexander E. BA in German and French, Millersville U., Pa., 1990, MA in German, 1992. Tchr. Lancaster (Pa.) Waldorf Sch., 1984—86; tchr. German, French Pequea Valley H.S., Kinzers, Pa., 1990—93, John Piersol McCaskey H.S., Lancaster, 1993—. Coord. exchange program JPMC Caskey H.S., 1997—, dept. facilitator, 2002—05. Named Tchr. of Yr., Pequea Valley H.S., 1993; recipient Duden award, 2001. Mem.: Lancaster (Pa.) Edn. Assn. (bldg. rep. 1990—), Am. Assn. Tchrs. French (pres. Pa. chpt. 2002—04, v.p. 2002), Am. Assn. Tchrs. German. Avocations: gardening, travel, reading, crafts, hiking. Office: JPMC Caskey HS 445 N Reservoir St Lancaster PA 17551

MILLER, EUNICE A., marriage and family therapist, sex therapist, foundation administrator; b. Phila., Mar. 29, 1940; d. Henry and Elizabeth Eisenberg; m. Melvin Norman Miller, May 12, 1963; children: Emily, Rachel, Deborah. BA, Adelphi U., 1961; MSW, U. Pa., 1965. Dir. Crossroads Counseling Ctr., Malvern, Pa., 1979—. Book reviewer Dan's Papers, 2005—, talk show host Plain Wrapper, Voiceamerica Health and Wellness Channel, 2005—. Mem. Lower Merion Twp. (Pa.) Cable Adv. Com., 1985—97; pres. Melvin and Eunice A. Miller Found., Malvern, 1996—. Mem.: Counselors and Therapists (book reviewer, cert. sex therapist), Am. Assn. Sex Educators. Personal E-mail: eunicemiller@hotmail.com.

MILLER, GENEVIEVE, retired medical historian; b. Butler, Pa., Oct. 15, 1914; d. Charles Russell and Genevieve (Wolford) Miller. AB, Goucher Coll., Balt., 1935; MA, Johns Hopkins U., Balt., 1939; PhD, Cornell U., Ithaca, N.Y., 1955. Asst. in history medicine Johns Hopkins Inst. History of Medicine, Balt., 1943—44, instr., 1945—48, rsch. assoc., 1979—94; asst. prof. history of sci. Case Western Res. U. Sch. Medicine, Cleve., 1953-67, assoc. prof., 1967-79, assoc. prof. emeritus, 1979—; rsch. assoc. med. history Clevel. Med. Libr. Assn., 1953-62; curator Howard Dittrick Mus. Hist. Medicine, 1962-67, dir., 1967-79. Author: William Beaumont's Formative Years: Two Early Notebooks 1811-1821, 1946; The Adoption of Inoculation for Smallpox in England and France, 1957 (William H. Welch medal Am. Assn. History Medicine 1962), Bibliography of the History of Medicine of the U.S. and Canada, 1939-1960, 1964, Bibliography of the Writings of Henry E. Sigerist, 1966, Letters of Edward Jenner and Other Documents Concerning the Early History of Vaccination, 1983; assoc. editor Bull. of History of Medicine, 1944-48, acting editor, 1948, mem. adv. editl. bd., 1960-92; mem. bd. editors Jour. History of Medicine & Allied Scis., 1948-65; editor Newsletter Am. Assn. History of Medicine, 1986-96; contbr. articles to profl. jours. Alumna trustee Goucher Coll., Balt., 1966-69; trustee Judson Retirement Cmty., Clevel., 1993-99, Am. Coun. Learned Socs. fellow, 1948-50, Dean Van Meter fellow, Goucher Coll., 1953-54. Fellow Cleve. Med. Libr. Assn. (hon.); mem. Am. Assn. History Medicine (pres. 1978-80, mem. coun. 1960-63, Lifetime Achievement award 1999), Am. Hist. Assn., Internat. Soc. History of Medicine, Soc. Archtl. Historians, Phi Beta Kappa. Democrat. Home and Office: Judson Manor Apt 616 1890 E 107th St Cleveland OH 44106-2251

MILLER, GERALDINE, clinical psychologist; b. Jersey City, Nov. 30, 1946; d. Gerard and Nora Miller; m. Walter Greenberg, Apr. 1984. BA magna cum laude, CCNY, 1971; MPh, CUNY, 1979, PhD, 1980. Lic. psychologist NY. Clin. intern Columbia Presbyn. Med. Ctr., N.Y. State Psychiat. Inst., N.Y.C., 1974-75; staff psychologist substance abuse svc. Albert Einstein Med. Coll., Bronx, N.Y., 1978-79; assoc. psychologist Pilgrim Psychiat. Ctr., West Brentwood, 1980—2001, leader treatment team, 1984—91, psychologist, 2001—. Sec., patient rels. com. Presbyn. Hosp. Cmty. Health Coun., 1979-82. Recipient numerous awards CCNY, Employee Recognition award Pilgrim Psychiat. Ctr., 1981, 84, 87, 89. Mem. APA (membership chmn. clin. psychology sect. 1982-86), Ea. Psychol. Assn., N.Y. State Psychol. Assn., Suffolk County Psychol. Assn., Phi Beta Kappa.

MILLER, GERALDINE ALICE, psychologist, educator; d. Gordon Wyman Miller and Adeline Ella Splitgerber; m. Ronald Roy Hood. BA, Moorhead State U., 1977; MSE, U. Wis. at River Falls, 1986; PhD in Counseling Psychology, Ball State U., 1990. Chem. dependency counselor Met. Clinic of Counseling, Mpls., 1983—86; psychologist Appalachian State U., Boone, NC, 1993—96, 2000—04; vol. psychologist Watauga County Health Dept., 1993—; asst. prof. ND State U., 1990—92, Appalachian State U., 1992—96, assoc. prof., 1996—2002, prof., 2002—. Mem. NC Substance Abuse Profl. Practice Bd., 2000—. Author: Learning the Language of Addiction Counseling, 2005, 1999, Incorporating Spirituality in Counseling and Psychotherapy, 2004. Bd. dirs., lead disaster mental health ARC, 2004—. Recipient Cert. of Appreciation, ARC, 2004, Spl. Citation for Exceptional Vol. Svc., 2002, Mentor of the Yr. award, Appalachian State U. Grad. Student Assn., 2000—01, Outstanding Scholarship award, Reich Coll. Edn., 2002. Mem.: ACA, APA. Avocations: needlecrafts, piano, jogging, reading. Home: P O Box 8 Fleetwood NC 28626 Office: Appalachian State U Edwin Duncan Hall Boone NC 28608

MILLER, GERALDINE B., music educator; b. Johnstown, Pa., Sept. 30, 1917; d. Samuel George Felton and Jennie Aurora Ling; m. Walter Randolph Miller, Mar. 19, 1916; children: W. Bruce, Diane Miller Jackson. BA, Ursinus Coll., Collegeville, Pa., 1939; MusB, Phila. Conservatory of Music, 1964. Piano tchr. Lancaster Conservatory of Music, Lancaster, Pa., 1959—62; pvt. piano tchr. Bala Cynwyd, Pa., 1959—2001. Recipient 1st prize winner Tri-Concerts Assn., 1968, 2d prize Pa. Music Tchrs. Assn., 1977. Mem. Phila. Music Tchrs. Assn. (v.p. 1986-90, pres. 1990-92, publicity chmn.), Musical Coterie of Wayne (jr. coterie chmn. 1969-87), Music Study Club. Avocations: sewing, needlecrafts, gardening. Home: 3300 Darby Rd #2210 Haverford PA 19041-1068

MILLER, GWENDOLYN DORIS, retired special education educator; b. NYC, Oct. 22, 1933; d. Raymond Addison and Hattie Bryant; m. Leo Miller Jr., Oct. 22, 1955 (dec. Oct. 1999); children: Steven, Debra, Scott, Derek. BA, Hunter Coll., 1961; MS in Edn., L.I. U., 1978, profl. diploma, 1979. Cert. sch. adminstr., supr., NY. Tchr. trainer NYC Dept. Edn., Divsn. Spl. Edn., 1978-80; supr. spl. edn. Sch. Dist. #22, Bklyn., 1980-92; owner, prin. Travel Network, Jamaica, NY, 1989-97; v.p., curator Ebony Treasures and Art Gallery Inc., Jamaica, 1997—2006; ret., 2006. Mem. bd. examiners Bd. Edn., Bklyn., 1986-92, cons., 1992-93; adj. profl St. John's U., Queens, NY, 1995-2001; edn. dir. UPK, 2001-03. Bd. dirs. York Coll., Queens, 1993-95, Hillside Eastern Queens Mental Health Coun., 1983-89; treas., bd. dirs. Jamaica Day Nursery Inc., 1993—; sec. bd. dirs. Reach Into Cultural Heights Inc., Queens, 1994—; mem. task force on South Africa, Presbytery of NY, 1993—; mem. NY State jud. com., Queens Dem. Orgn., 1976, county com., 1975; active Boy Scouts Am., 1972, Girl Scouts of U.S., 1973; elder, Christian edn., Sunday Sch., Presbyn. Ch. Mem. Africa Travel Assn., Phi Delta Kappa, Protestant Tchrs. Assn. NYC, Rotary of South Eastern Queens (founding mem.). Avocations: collecting art from Africa, internat. travel, different cultures.

MILLER, HEIDI G., diversified financial company executive; b. 1951; married; 2 children. BA in History, Princeton U., 1974; PhD in History, Yale U., 1979. Various positions to mng. dir. emerging markets structured finance group Chemical Bank, 1979—92; joined as v.p. and asst. to the pres. Travelers Group, 1992, CFO, 1995—98, Citigroup (merger of Citibank and Travelers Group), NYC, 1998—2000; CFO, sr. exec. v.p. strategic planning and adminstrn. Priceline.com, Norwalk, Conn., 2000; vice chmn. Marsh & McLennan Co., Inc., NYC, 2001—02; exec. v.p. strategy and devel., CFO Bank One Corp., 2002—04; exec. v.p., CEO, treasury & securities div. J.P. Morgan Chase & Co. (merger of Bank One Corp. and J.P. Morgan Chase & Co.), NYC, 2004—. Bd. dirs. General Mills Inc., 1999—, Merck & Co., Inc., 2000—04, Bank One Corp., 2000—02, Local Initiatives Support Corp., 2004—. Trustee Princeton U., NYU Med. Sch. Named one of 50 Most Powerful Women in Bus., Fortune mag., 2006. Office: JP Morgan Chase & Co 270 Park Ave New York NY 10017*

MILLER, HELEN, state representative, lawyer; b. Newark, Nov. 1945; BA, Howard U.; MS, Our Lady of the Lake U.; JD, Georgetown U. Bar: (D.C.), (Iowa). Atty.; state rep. dist. 49 Iowa Ho. of Reps., 2003—, mem. internat. rels.com., mem. econ. growth com., mem. agr. com., mem. appropriations com., mem. adminstrn. and rules com., asst. minority leader. Vol. Cmty. Sch. Improvement Adv. Bd., Webster County Crime Stoppers; bd. govs. Leadership Iowa; cmty. task force adv. bd. Ft. Dodge Correctional Facility; exec. dir., bd. dirs. Young At Art. Democrat. Office: State Capitol East 12th and Grand Des Moines IA 50319 Address: PO Box 675 Fort Dodge IA 50501 Office Phone: 515-281-3221.

MILLER, HELEN ELIZABETH, art educator, adult education educator, artist; b. Granit City, Ill., Feb. 18, 1969; d. David Allen Busch and Christine Delores Mistarz; m. Todd Charles Miller, Apr. 25, 1967; 1 child, Samantha Alexandria. BA magna cum laude, Calumet Coll., 1995; MA, Ind. U., 1999. Tchr. art Waukegan (Ill.) Sch. Sys., 2002—03, 2004—, Round Lake (Ill.) H.S., 2003—04. Organizer clothing drive Carman Buckner Sch., Waukegan, Ill., 2004. Prin. works include mural, Waukegan (Ill.) Sch. Sys. Grantee, Walmart, 2004. Avocations: painting, drawing, scuba diving, bicycling, ceramics. Home: 330 Greenview Ln Lake Villa IL 60046 Office: Waukegan School Dist Sheridan Rd Waukegan IL 60046 Office Phone: 847-336-3100. Personal E-mail: helenemiller@yahoo.com.

MILLER, HELEN F., music educator, musician; b. Lewistown, Mont., May 29, 1918; d. Otis Willard Freeman and Laura Olive Cowell; m. Paul Gilbert Miller, June 10, 1938; children: Don Paul, Barbara Helen. MusB, U. Wis., 1938; MusM in Edn., Immaculate Heart Coll., 1968. Mem. So. Symphony, Columbia, S.C., 1940, Music Under Stars Symphony, Milw., 1944-46; concert master Waukesha (Wis.) Symphony, 1948-51; mem. N.J. Symphony, Orange, 1952-54, Colonial Symphony, Madison, N.J., 1952-54; soloist U. Ariz. Symphony, Tucson, 1959; mem. Santa Monica (Calif.) Symphony, 1960-61. Pvt. violin tchr., 1938—; tchr. music Immaculate Heart Coll. Prep. Sch., L.A., 1960-67, Mt. Gleason Jr. High, Tujunga, Calif., 1961-62, Immaculate Heart Coll., L.A., 1963-66, Sch. Dist. #91, Idaho Falls, 1967-70, Rick's Coll. Music Camp, Rexburg, Idaho, summers 1968-69, Taipei (Taiwan) Am. Sch., 1970-71, Dept. Def., Secondary Schs., Seoul, 1972-73, U. Catolica, Valparaiso, Chile, 1973-80, Coll of the Desert, Palm Desert, Calif., 1982-88. Solo violin performances, Cheney, Wash., 1934-37, Clemson, S.C., 1939, Milw. Mus., 1947, Orange, N.J., 1955, U. Ariz. Symphony, Tucson, 1959, Immaculate Heart Coll., L.A., 1961-66, Idaho Falls Symphony, 1968, Taipei, 1971, Tsing Hwa U., Hsinchu, Taiwan, 1971, U. Law, Taipei, 1971, U. Catolica and U. Chile sede Valparaiso, 1973-80; violinist Westbrook Trio, N.J., N.Y., Conn., 1954-58, Angeles String Trio, L.A. Mus. Concert, 1961, Seoul Nat. U. Sch. Music, 1973; organizer, performer Twilight Festival of Music, Idaho Falls, summers 1967, 68, 69 Choir dir. Meth. Ch., Oconomowoc, Wis., 1958-61, Cmty. Meth. Ch., Tujunga, 1963-64, St. Philips Luth. Ch., Pacoima, Calif., 1964-67; organizer, founder Youth String Competition, Riverside, Calif., 1998, 99. Scholar U. Wis., U. Ariz.; tchg. fellow Immaculate Heart Coll. Home: 39517 Cedarwood Dr Murrieta CA 92563-5305

MILLER, INABETH, educational administrator, librarian, technology consultant; b. Providence; m. William Howard; children— Cathy, Scott, Jeffrey, Marcy AB, Brown U., 1956; MS, Simmons Coll., 1969; Ed.D., Boston U., 1982. Cert. librarian, tchr., edn. adminstr. Tchr. Lab. Sch., U. Chgo., 1955-56; librarian Boston U., 1956-58, Holliston Pub. Schs., Mass., 1969-71; media dir. Watertown Pub. Schs., Mass., 1971-78; library dir. Harvard U., Cambridge, Mass., 1978-85, educator, Boston Coll., 1972-80, Simmons Coll., Boston, 1969-71, Boston U., 1971-75, 1986—; head ednl. tech. and outreach program Boston Mus. Sci., 1985—. Adminstr. Nat. Database in Interactive Tech. Author: Microcomputers in School Media Centers, 1984, 20th Century Theories in American Education, 1987; editor: Video Games and Human Development, 1984; contbr. articles and chpts. to profl. publs. Bd. dirs. Ctr. for Coastal Study Nat. Geog. Kids Network. Mem. ALA, Am. Ednl. Research Assn., AAM. Home: 10 Bushnell Dr Lexington MA 02421-4930

MILLER, IRENE M., physician assistant; b. Berlin; arrived in U.S., 1955; d. Siegfried and Anneliese Mueller; m. Harold E. Miller (div.); children: Deborah, Duane, Kirstie. Student, Phila. Coll. Performing Arts, 1956—58, Musikakademie, Berlin, 1958, West Chester U., 1977—79; BS Physician Asst., Hahnemann U., 1981. Lic. physician asst. Mass., Maine, NH, NC, NY, cert. ACLS, ATLS. Resident in surgery Norwalk Hosp./Yale U. Sch. Medicine, New Haven, 1981—82; physician asst. dept. neurosurgery U. Pitts., 1982—83; physician asst. Family Medicine and Bariatrics, Fairfield, Conn., 1984—86; physician asst. dept. medicine Hall-Brooke Hosp., Westport, Conn., 1987—89; physician asst. occupl. medicine Bankers Trust Co., N.Y.C., 1989—90; physician asst. Okemo Mountain Ski Clinic, Emergency Svcs. of New England, Springfield, Vt., 1990—91; physician asst. Jaffrey (NH) Family Medicine, 1991—95, CompHealth, Salt Lake City, 1995—98; fgn. svc. med. officer Am. Embassy U.S. State Dept., Kampala, Uganda, 1998—2000; pvt. practice internal medicine/holistic medicine Keene, NH, 2000—. Lectr., spkr., presenter in field; cellist symphony orchs. U.S. and Europe. Author: Love Letters from Uganda, 2003. Mem. med. mission, China, 1994. Grantee, London Grove Quaker Meeting, 1979; scholar, Phila. Music Acad., 1956—58. Fellow: Am. Acad. Physician Assts.; mem.: NH Soc. Physician Assts. (pres. 1993—94). Avocations: hiking, dance, painting. Home: 105 Lampman Rd Harrisville NH 03450

MILLER, JACQUELINE WINSLOW, library director; b. N.Y.C., Apr. 15, 1935; d. Lynward Roosevelt and Sarah Ellen (Grevious) W.; 1 child, Percy Scott. BA, Morgan State Coll., 1957; MLS, Pratt Inst., 1960; grad. profl. seminar, U. Md., 1973. Cert. profl. libr. With Bklyn. Pub. Libr., 1957-68; head ext. svcs. New Rochelle (N.Y.) Pub. Libr., 1969-70; br. adminstr. Grinton Will Yonkers (N.Y.) Pub. Libr., 1970-75; dir. Yonkers Pub. Libr., 1975-96. Mem. adj. faculty grad. libr. studies Queens Coll., CUNY, 1989, 90. Mem. commr.'s com. Statewide Libr. Devel., Albany, N.Y., 1980; mem. N.Y. Gov.'s Commn. on Librs., 1990, 91; bd. dirs. Cmty. Planning Coun., Yonkers, N.Y., 1987; mem. Yonkers Black Women's Polit. Caucus, 1987; pres. bd. Literacy Vols. of Westchester County, 1991-92; mem. fair campaign practices com. LWV, 1996—. Recipient Yonkers Citizen award Ch. of Our Saviour, 1980, 2d Ann. Mae Morgan Robinson award Yonkers chpt. Westchester Black Women's Polit. Caucus, 1992, 3d Ann. Equality Day award City of Yonkers, 1992, African-Am. Heritage 1st award YWCA, 1994; named Outstanding Profl. Woman Nat. Assn. Negro Bus. and Profl. Women's Clubs Inc., 1981. Mem. ALA (councilor 1987-91), N.Y. State Libr. Assn., Pub. Libr. Dirs. Assn. (exec. bd.), N.Y. State Pub. Libr. Dirs. Assn., Westchester Libr. Assn., Yonkers C. of C. (bd. dirs. 1992-95), Educate the Girls, Inc. (bd. dirs., 2003—) Rotary (Yonkers chpt.). Personal E-mail: jacki@sprynet.com.

MILLER, JACQUIE HAYNES, musician, educator; d. Vonnie Lee and Henrietta Brown Haynes; m. Seth Thomas Miller, May 28, 1999. BA in Music, Western Ky. U., Bowling Green, 1999; postgrad., Campbellsville (Ky.) U., 2003—. Min. of music Irvington Bapt. Ch., Ky., 1999—2005; freelance musician, 1999—; prodn. mgr. Weekly Shopper Publs. and TMS Mktg., Elizabethtown, Ky., 2000—02; music tchr. St. Romuald Sch., Hardinsburg, Ky., 2005—06; min. of music Rock Haven Bapt. Ch., Brandenburg, Ky., 2006—. Performer Ky. Bapt. Assn. Women's Chorale and Orch., 2001—; music dir. Salem Assn. of Bapts., Ky., 2003; participant mission to Europe Ky. Bapt. Conv. Women's Chorale, 2002; pvt. flute tchr. Composer, arranger Vision, 2006. Leader, co-leader Girl Scouts of USA, 1998—; trainer for leaders Girl Scouts of Kentuckiana, Elizabethtown, 2002—; organizer, dir. Praise Pipers Flute Choir, 2002—. Recipient Girl Scout Gold award, Girl Scouts of Kentuckiana, 1994, Daisy award, 2001, Pillar of Support award, 2005. Mem.: Delta Omicron. Avocations: flute, pet birds, music arranging. Home: 104 E Walnut St Irvington KY 40146 Office Phone: 270-547-8541. E-mail: jlhmiller@bbtcl.com.

MILLER, JANEL HOWELL, psychologist; b. Boone, N.C., May 18, 1947; d. John Estle and Grace Louise (Hemberger) Howell; m. C. Rick Miller, Nov. 24, 1968; children: Kimberly, Brian, Audrey, Rachel. BA, DePauw U., 1969; postgrad., Rice U., 1969; MA, U. Houston, 1972; PhD, Tex. A&M U., 1979. Lic. clin. psychologist, sch. psychologist Tex. Assoc. sch. psychologist Houston Ind. Sch. Dist., 1971-74; rsch. psychologist VA Hosp., Houston, 1972; assoc. sch. psychologist Clear Creek (Tex.) Ind. Sch. Dist., 1974-76; instr. psychology, counseling psychology intern Tex. A&M U., 1976-77; clin. psychology intern VA Hosp., Houston, 1977-78; coord. psychol. svcs. Clear Creek Ind. Sch. Dist., 1978-81, assoc. dir. psychol. svcs., 1981-82; pvt. practice Houston, 1982—. Faculty U. Houston-Clear Lake, 1984—; adolescent suicide cons., 1984—. DePauw U. Alumni scholar, 1965-69; NIMH fellow U. Houston, 1970-71. Mem. APA, Am. Assn. Marriage and Family Therapists, Soc. for Personality Assessment, Am. Coll. Forensic Examiners, Internat. Rorschach Soc., Tex. Psychol. Assn., Tex. Assn. Marriage and Family Therapists, Houston Psychol. Assn. (media rep. 1984-85), Houston Assn. Marriage and Family Therapists. Home: 806 Walbrook Dr Houston TX 77062-4030 Office: 16854 Royal Crest Dr Houston TX 77058-2529 Office Phone: 281-461-4098. Business E-Mail: shrinkskate@sbcglobal.net.

MILLER, JANET LUTZ, mathematics professor, department chairman; d. Faye Hogge Lutz; m. Benjamin Ely Miller, Jr.; 1 child, Thomas Burks Kessinge III. BS in Math., Western Ky. U., 1987; EdD, U. Ky., Lexington, 1999. Prof. math. Campbellsville U., Ky., 1987—. Chmn. math. and computer sci. dept. Campbellsville U., 2005—. PEW fellowship, Appalachian Coll. Assn. Mem.: Nat. Coun. Tchrs. of Math. Office: Cambellsville Univ 1 University Dr Campbellsville KY 42718

MILLER, JANETH MAUK, retired secondary education educator; b. Kansas City, Mo., Mar. 31, 1941; d. Harold E. and Frances Rose (McCarter) Mauk; m. Edbert Wayne Miller, Sept. 2, 1962; children: Susan Rae Miller Dyer, Richard Wayne Miller. BS, U. Kans., 1963; MLS, Emporia State U., 1972. Media specialist Shawnee Heights H.S., Tecumseh, Kans., 1967-97, ret., 1997. Co-author: Standards for School Libraries, 1975. Vol. camera operator KTWU-TV, Topeka, 1982—. Avocations: lacemaking, reading, gardening, woodworking. Home: 6838 SE Berryton Rd Berryton KS 66409-9572

MILLER, JANICE BRICE, art educator; d. Clyde Allie Booker and Hazel Louise Moffitt; m. Robert B. Brice (dec.); children: Jan Alesa Brice Thorp, Robert Benjamin Brice, Chera Nell Brice Cox; m. James Clyde Miller (dec.). BS, East Tenn. State U., 1973, MA, 1974, EdD, 1981; postgrad., Duke U., 1995—96. Cert. tchr. Tenn. Instr. Lees-McRae Coll., Banner Elk, NC, 1982—86, dir. external res., 1996—97; JTPA svc. delivery area adminstr. Region D Coun. Govts., Boone, NC, 1986—87; dean Grad. Sch. Bristol (Tenn.) U., 1988; dir. orgnl. mgmt. program Milligan Coll., Johnson City, 1989—90; dir. Milligan Coll., Knoxville Campus, 1989—90; coord. spl. rsch. programs East Tenn. State U. Coll. Medicine, Johnson City, 1991—92; advancement officer Va. Highlands C.C., Abingdon, 1994—95, prof., 2000—. Mem. pres. cabinet Lees-McRae Coll., Banner Elk, 1996—97, head Office of Advancement, 1996—97. Author: The Strange Gift of Grief, 2004; pub., editor: newspaper The Pinnacle, 1995—97. V.p. Jaycee Wives Club, 1966—67; fundraiser Lees-McRae Coll., Banner Elk, 1996—97, Christian Med. and Dental Assns., Bristol, Tenn., 2005, 2006; arts adhoc com. C of C., Elizabethton, 1998—99. Doctoral fellow, East Tenn. State U., 1975—78. Mem.: Appalachian Ctr. for Poets and Writers, Elizabethton Book Club (sec. 2003—04), Phi Kappa Phi. Avocations: reading, walking, travel. Home: 603 Holston Ave Elizabethton TN 37643 Office: Va Highlands CC PO Box 828 Abingdon VA 24212

MILLER, JEAN RUTH, retired librarian; b. St. Helena, Calif., Aug. 4, 1927; d. William Leonard and Jean (Stanton) M. BA, Occidental Coll., 1950; MLS, U. So. Calif., Los Angeles, 1952. Base librarian USAF, Wethersfield, Eng., 1952-55; post librarian USMC Air Sta., El Toro, Calif., 1955-63; data systems librarian Autonetics (Rockwell), Anaheim, Calif., 1963-65; mgr. library services Beckman Instruments, Inc., Fullerton, Calif., 1966-92. Mem. adv. com. Library Technician Program, Fullerton Coll., 1969-1995. Author: (bibliography) Field Air Traffic Control, 1965, Electrical Shock Hazards, 1974. Chair Fullerton Are U. So. Calif. Scholarship Alumni Interview Program, Fullerton, 1974-1993; vol. Beckman Heritage Ctr. Mem. Orange County Libr. Assn., Spl. Libraries Assn. (pres. So. Calif. chpt. 1975-76, chair Sci./Tech. Div. 1985-86), Santa Ana Elks Lodge (scholarship chair 2003—). Republican. Avocations: travel, reading, swimming. Home: 4701 E Fairfield St Anaheim CA 92807-3651

MILLER, JEANNE-MARIE ANDERSON (MRS. NATHAN J. MILLER), language educator, academic administrator; b. Washington, Feb. 18, 1937; d. William and Agnes Catherine (Johns) Anderson; m. Nathan John Miller, Oct. 2, 1960. BA, Howard U., 1959, MA, 1963, PhD, 1976. Instr. dept.

English Howard U., Washington, 1963-76, asst. prof., 1976-79, assoc. prof., 1979-92, prof., 1992-97, prof. emeritus, 1997—, asst. dir. Inst. Arts and Humanities, 1973-75, asst. acad. planning, office v.p. for acad. affairs, 1976-90. Cons. Am. Studies Assn., 1972—75, Silver Burdett Pub. Co., NEH, 1978—; mem. adv. bd. D.C. Libr. for Arts, 1973—. Editor, Black Theatre Bull., 1977-86; Realism to Ritual: Form and Style in Black Theatre, 1983; assoc. editor Theatre Jour., 1980-81; contbr. articles to profl. jours., chpts. to books. Mem. Washington Performing Arts Soc., 1971—, Friends of Sta. WETA-TV, 1971—, Mus. African Art, 1971—, Arena Stage Assocs., 1972—, Washington Opera Guild, 1982—, Wolf Trap Assocs., 1982—, Drama League N.Y., 1995, Shakespeare Theatre, 2001—, Met. Opera Guild, 2002—. Ford Found. fellow, 1970-72, So. Fellowships Fund fellow, 1973-74; Howard U. rsch. grant, 1975-76, 94-97, ACLS grant, 1978-79, NEH grant, 1981-84. Mem.: LWV, MLA, ACLU, AAUP, Nat. Archives Found., Folger Shakespeare Libr., Acad. Am. Poets, Am. Theatre and Drama Soc., Studio Mus. Harlem, Nat. Mus. Women in Arts, Nat. Bldg. Mus., Winterthur Guild, Hist. Soc. Washington, D.C. Preservation League, Nat. Trust Historic Preservation, Zora Neale Hurston Soc., Langston Hughes Soc., Ibsen Soc., Friends of Kennedy Ctr. for Performing Arts, Am. Assn. Higher Edn., Coll. Lang. Assn., Common Cause, Am. Assn. Higher Edn., Am. Studies Assn., Coll. English Assn., Nat. Coun. Tchrs. English, Sierra Club, Pi Lambda Theta. Democrat. Episcopalian. Home: 504 24th St NE Washington DC 20002-4818 E-mail: jmamiller@verizon.net.

MILLER, JENEFER ARDELL, elementary school educator, choreographer; b. Royal Oak, Mich., Feb. 22, 1975; d. Raymond George and Judith Ardell Stickradt; m. Christopher John Miller, June 21, 2002. BA in Performing Arts, Oakland U., Rochester, Mich., 1933; MA in Elem. Edn., U. Phoenix, Ariz., 2003. Dance tchr./choreographer Deborah's Stage Door Dance Ctr., Rochester Hills, Mich., 1993—97, Copeland Dance Acad., St. Charles, Ill., 1997—2001, Plumb Performing Arts Ctr., Scottsdale, Ariz., 2001—05, Betty Johnson Sch. of Dance, Phoenix, 2001—06; tchr. 4th grade Hearn Acad. - A Ball Charter Sch., Phoenix, 2003—05; tchr. 7th grade lang. arts Akimel A-al Mid. Sch., Phoenix, 2005—. Mem. Kyrene Edn. Assn., Phoenix, 2005—; dir. Ratller Players Drama Club for Youth, Phoenix, 2005—. Choreographer/tchr. Down on Wall Street (Showstopper Am. Dance Champions - 1st Pl., 1997). Mem. Young Dems. of Ariz., Phoenix, 2005—06. Dance scholarship, Oakland U., 1993-1996. Democrat-Npl. Avocations: dancing, hiking, volunteering with stray animals, reading, running. Office Phone: 480-783-1600. Personal E-mail: jenk360@msn.com.

MILLER, JENNIFER L., elementary school educator, small business owner; d. Frank L. and Patricia M. Warfel; m. Ryan G. Miller, July 2, 1994; children: Calleigh L., Garrett R., Trevor R. BA in Elem. Edn. (hon.), U. Portland, 1992. Cert. tchr. A-regular classroom Alaska, spl. edn. endorsement. Dir. summer recreation City of Wrangell, 1990—91; summer acad. tchr. geology; pvt. tutor Wrangell, 1991—92; 1st grade tchr. Wrangell City Schs., 1992—95, asst. coach h.s. girls basketball, 1993—94, multiage tchr. 1-2, 1995—96, multiage tchr. 2-3, 1996—2002; substitute tchr., 1998—92; multiage tchr. 1-2-3 Wrangell City Schs., 2002—03, multiage tchr. 2-3, 2003—04; tchr. 3rd grade Wrangell (Alaska) City Schs., 2004—; co-owner Clearwater Packing. Benchmark cut score com. dept. edn. State of Alaska, benchmark test bias com. edn. and early devel., stds. based assessment validation com., 2004—, content rev. com., 2005—, mem. dept. edn. data review com., 2006; adv. bd. Evergreen Elem., 2002—. Co-founder Evergreen Agtrl. Testing Site; leader Girl Scouts, Wrangell, 2002; active Friends of the Libr., Wrangell, Master Gardener's, Alaska; cmty. fair vendor Alaska, 1997; vol. Wrangell Little League, 2002, Alaskans for Drug Free Youth, Alaska, 1991, Hershey Track and Field, Alaska, 1990—91, Stikine River Rats Swim Team, Alaska, 1992; judge Wrangell H.S. Cheerleaders, Alaska, 1990—92. Recipient Youth Garden grant, Nat. Gardening Assn., 1999, Clay Muralist grant, Alaska Arts in Edn. Mem.: ASCD, NEA, NSTA, Alaska State Literacy Assn., Alaska Coun. Tchrs. Math., Internat. Reading Assn., Wrangell Tchr.'s Assn. (sec. 2000—, negotiations com., bldg. rep., Tchr. of Yr. 1997, 2001, 2006), Nat. Coun. Tchrs. English, Assn. for Childhood Edn. Internat., Juneau-Haines Reading Coun., Nat. Coun. Tchrs. Math., Elk. Home: PO Box 1899 25 Mile Zimovia Hwy Wrangell AK 99929 Home Fax: 907-874-3182. Personal E-mail: rjcgmill@aptalaska.net.

MILLER, JO CAROLYN DENDY, family and marriage counselor, educator; b. Gorman, Tex., Sept. 16, 1942; d. Leonard Lee and Vera Vertie (Robison) Dendy; m. Douglas Terry Barnes, June 1, 1963 (div. June 1975); children: Douglas Alan, Bradley Jason; m. Walton Sansom Miller, Sept. 19, 1982. BA, Tarleton State U., Stephenville, Tex., 1964; MEd, U. North State, 1977; PhD, Tex. Woman's U., 1993. Tchr. Mineral Wells (Tex.) H.S., 1964-65, Weatherford (Tex.) Mid. Sch., 1969-74; counselor, instr. psychology Tarrant County Jr. Coll., Hurst, Tex., 1977-82; pvt. practice Dallas, 1982—. Author: (with Velma Baker, Jeannene Ward) Becoming: A Human Relations Workbook, 1981. Mem. ACA, Tex. State Bd. Examiners Profl. Counselors, Tex. State Bd. Marriage and Family Therapists, Tex. Counseling Assn., North Ctrl. Tex. Counseling Assn., Dallas Symphony Orch. League, Nat. Coun. Family Rels., Tex. Mental Health Counselors Assn., Internat. Assn. for Marriage and Family Counselors. Methodist. Office: 8222 Douglas Ave Ste 777 Dallas TX 75225-5938 Office Phone: 214-691-0400. Personal E-mail: jcdmphd@sbcglobal.net.

MILLER, JUDITH A. (JUDY MILLER), retired journalist; b. NYC, 1948; m. Jason Epstein, 1993. BA in Economics, Barnard Coll., 1969; MA, Princeton U., 1971. Corr. The Progressive, Nat. Pub. Radio; reporter, Washington Bur. NY Times, Washington, 1977, chief Cairo Bur. Egypt, 1983, Paris correspondent France, 1986—87, news editor and dep. bur. chief, Washington Bur., 1987—88, spl. correspondent to Persian Gulf crisis, 1990, spl. correspondent, Sunday Mag., 1990, sr. writer; ret., 2005. Lectr. in field. Author: One, By One, By One, 1990, God Has Ninety-Nine Names, 1996; co-author (with Laurie Mylroie): Saddam Hussein and the Crisis in the Gulf, 1990; co-author: (with William Broad and Stephen Engelberg) Biological Weapons & America's Secret War, 2002. Co-recipient Pulitzer Prize, explanatory journalism, 2002; recipient Emmy award, 2002, DuPont award, 2002. Achievements include first woman to be named chief of NY Times Cairo Bur. E-mail: miller@nytimes.com.*

MILLER, JUDITH BRAFFMAN, writer; b. St. Louis, Feb. 21, 1947; d. William and Lorraine Shirley Braffman; m. Mark Ellis Miller, June 9, 1968. BA, U. Calif., Berkeley, 1969. Freelance writer, 1978—. Active Amnesty Internat., NYC, 2002—, Am. Friends Svc. Com., 2005. Fellow: Royal Astron. Soc. Gt. Britain; mem.: AIAA, ACLU, AAAS, Internat. Dark Sky Assn., Astron. Soc. of the Pacific, Nat. Space Soc., Planetary Soc., Am. Inst. Physics, Brit. Astron. Assn., Am. Astron. Soc., Am. Chem. Soc., NY Acad. Scis., Am. Soc. Journalists and Authors, Union Concerned Scientists. Avocations: naturalist, poetry, politics. Home and Office: 1149 Partridge Ave Saint Louis MO 63130 Office Phone: 314-725-7096.

MILLER, KAREN, clinical psychologist, neuropsychologist; b. Tucson, Dec. 9, 1969; d. Keith Lee and Marlene Jean Miller. BS in Psychology, U. Ariz., 1992; MA in Theology, MA in Psychology, Fuller Sem., Pasadena, Calif., 1996, PhD in Clin. Psychology, 1998. Psychologist UCLA, 1994—, dir. neuropsychology externship tng. MPAC, 2003—; therapist VA West Los Angeles, Calif., 1996—2000; clin. faculty mem., supr. Fuller Psychol. and Family Svcs., Pasadena, Calif., 2000—. Dir. externship tng. for neuropsychology. Contbr. articles to profl. jours. John P. Schaeffer and Regents scholar, 1988-92. Mem.: APA, Calif. Psychol. Assn., Internat. Neuropsychol. Soc., Mortar Bd., Phi Beta Kappa. Home: 760 La Vina Ln Altadena CA 91001

MILLER, KARLA PATRICIA, elementary school educator; b. Takoma Park, Md., Apr. 6, 1968; d. James Roland and Patricia Melvin Miller. BS, U. Md., 1990, MEd, 1994, postgrad., 1997—2005. Advanced profl. cert. elem. grades and reading Md. State Dept. Edn., 2001. Tchr. 1st and 2d grade Montgomery County Pub. Schs., Olney, Md., 1991—95, reading specialist Silver Spring, 1995—98, tchr. 1st grade, 1998—2005. Mem. travel group observe best practices schs. Australia and New Zealand Montgomery County Pub. Schs., Rockville, 1993, first grade team leader, 1999—2000; mem. travel group observe schs. Australia and New Zealand, IRA's world congress Jr. Class Learning, Auckland, 2000; lect. Am. U., Washington, 2003; clin. supr. reading U. Md., College Park, 1997; cons. Md. State Dept. Edn., Balt., 1996—97. Participant Out of the Darkness Pallotta Teamworks, Washington, 2002. Mem.: IRA's Publ. Com., Internat. Reading Assn. (young author's chair Montgomery County coun. 1994—95, v.p. Montgomery County coun. 1995—96, pres.-elect Montgomery County coun. 1996—97, pres. Montgomery County coun. 1997—98, mem. internat. reading assn. pub. com. 1998—2000), Am. Edn. Rsch. Assn., Golden Key Nat. Honor Soc., Kappa Delta Pi, Phi Delta Kappa. Avocations: French, reading, writing. Office: Montgomery County Pub Schs 2111 Porter Rd Silver Spring MD 20910 Personal E-mail: kmiller4@umd.edu.

MILLER, KATHLEEN ELIZABETH, college administrator; b. Missoula, Mont., Oct. 12, 1942; d. Lyman Wellington and Kathryn Henrietta (Freyler) M. BS, Syracuse U., 1964; MS, U. Iowa, 1966, PhD, 1971. Instr. Western State U., Gunnison, Colo., 1964-65; from instr. to asst. prof. U. Iowa, Iowa City, 1966-70, 71-77; from asst. to prof. U. Mont., Missoula, 1977—, acting dean sch. edn., 1985-87, assoc. dean sch. edn., 1987—. Cons. Police Officer Standards and Tng. div. Dept. Justice, Helena, Mont., 1980—. Contbr. articles to profl. jours. Grantee Mont. Dept. Highways, 1985, N.W. Regional Ednl. Lab., 1989, 92. Mem. Am. Alliance for Health, Phys. Edn., Recreation and Dance, Internat. Soc. Biomechanics for Sports, Mont. Assn. for Health, Phys. Edn., Recreation and Dance. Avocations: fishing, hunting, hiking, gardening. Office: U Mont Mcgill # 205 Missoula MT 59812-0001

MILLER, KATHLEEN MAE, educational association administrator; b. Flint, Mich., Sept. 1, 1966; d. Joseph Casper and Karen Sue Shovels; m. James Stuart Miller, Mar. 30, 1991; children: Susan Marie, Rebecca Mae. BS in Edn. with honors, U. Mich., 1988; M in Ednl. Leadership, Ea. Mich. U., Michigan, 2002; grad., Leadership Shiawassee, 2002—03. Cert. tchg. K-8 Mich., 1988, tchg. 7-12 Mich., 1996. Assessment & tech. specialist Shiawassee Regional Svc. Dist., Corunna, Mich., 1999—2000; coord. of curriculum & assessment Shiawassee Regional Ednl. Svc. Dist., Corunna, Mich., 2000—03, dir. instrnl. svs., 2003—. Instr., office mgr., supr., program developer Learning Ctr. SW Flint, Mich., 1988—91; tchr. adult edn., program coord. Beecher Cmty. Schs., 1991—92, tchr. 3-4, 1992—95; tchr. 7-8 Swartz Creek Cmty. Schs., Swartz Creek, 1995—97; core curriculum support position Swartz Creek Cmty. Sch. Dist., 1997—99. Mem. Genesee County Queen Genesee County, Mich., 1987; co-dir. children's programs Chapin United Meth. Ch., Henderson, 2002; mem. Leadership Shiawassee, Ann Arbor, 1999. Recipient James B. Angell scholar, U. Mich., Branstorm Prize, Branstorm Assn.; grantee Regent's Alumni scholar, U. of Mich.; scholar Genesee Adminstrv. Tng. Acad. Mem.: Mich. Inst. for Ednl. Mgmt., Capital Quality Initiative, Assn. Supervision Curriculum Devel., Mich. Staff Devel. Coun. (assoc.), Mich. Ednl. Rsch. Assn. (assoc.), Am. Ednl. Rsch. Assn. (assoc.), Kappa Delta Phi, Phi Kappa Phi. Avocations: horseback riding, swimming, gardening, travel, fishing. Office: Shiawassee RESD 1025 N Shiawassee St Henderson MI 48817 E-mail: millerk@sresd.k12.mi.us.

MILLER, KATHLEEN S., project engineer; b. Pitts., Nov. 6, 1958; d. Herbert Ellsworth and Elizabeth Lorraine (McKean) Shaffer; m. Richard Joseph Miller, Sept. 27, 1986; 1 child, Melissa Ann. AAS, Cmty. Coll. Beaver County, 1996; BA, Robert Morris Coll., 1998. Asst. project engr. Power Piping Co., Pitts., 1977-94; project engr. McCarl's Inc., 1997—. Home: 146 Irwin Rd Georgetown PA 15043-9521 Office: 1413 9th Ave Beaver Falls PA 15010-4106

MILLER, KENDRA DANETTE, art services business owner, consultant; b. Jackson, Miss., Jan. 24, 1970; d. William Jerome Miller and Linda B. Walker. BA, Northwestern U., 1992; MA in Arts Adminstrn., Sch. of Art Inst. Chgo., 1997. Cert. fine and decorative art appraisal studies George Wash. U. Ctr for Profl. Devel., D.C., 2004. External affairs dir. Pinchot Inst. for Conservation, Wash., 2000—04; prin. Strata Fine Art Svcs., Silver Spring, Md., 2004—. Docent Nat. Mus. Women in the Arts, Wash., 2000—; vol. Nativity Youth Ctr., Wash., 2004—05; adv. bd. McClinton Musical Theatre Arts Found., Bucharest, Romania, 2003—05; bd. mem. Woman Made Gallery, Chgo., 1997—99, treas., 1999; bd. mem. Imani Found. & Art Gallery, Kent, Ohio, Better Existence with HIV, Evanston, Ill., 1992—94. Scholar, Assn. Fundraising Profls., Greater N.Y. chpt., 2000, Nat. Capital Gift Planning Coun., 2002. Mem.: Am. Soc. Appraisers (assoc.). Conservative. Avocations: scuba diving, tennis, reading, art, travel. Office: Strata Fine Art Svcs LLC 8201 Schrider St Ste 4 Silver Spring MD 20910-4637 Office Phone: 240-271-5036. Business E-Mail: info@stratafineartservices.com.

MILLER, KIMBERLY M., social studies educator; b. Hammond, Ind., June 15, 1973; d. Dennis Philip and Alice Louise Faverty; m. Daniel Eugene Miller, Apr. 2, 2005. BA in History, Purdue U., West Lafayette, Ind., 1995. Cert. tchr. Ind. Americorps mem. 21st Century Scholars, Knox, Ind., 1997—99; h.s. tchr. North Judson (Ind.) San Pierre Schs., 2000—. Mem.: PEO (rec. sec. 2004—06), Delta Kappa Gamma. Baptist. Office: North Judson San Pierre Cmty Sch 1 Bluejay Dr North Judson IN 46366 Personal E-mail: outtatime_73@hotmail.com. E-mail: kmiller@njsp.k12.in.us.

MILLER, LARA T., dance educator; b. Abilene, Tex., Aug. 6, 1976; d. Susan and Steve Turner; m. Jeff Miller, July 28, 2001; 1 child, Morgan Leigh. A, Kilgore Jr. Coll., 1996; B, U. Tex., Austin, 1999. Cert. tchr. Tex., 1999. Tchr., dance team dir. James Bowie HS, Austin, 1999—2003; with Regional Ednl. Lab. Network, 2003—. Named Secondary Student Tchr. of Yr., U. Tex., 1999; named to Nat. Honor Roll of Tchrs., 2006. Mem.: Tex. Dance Tchrs. Assn. (assoc.), Rangerettes Forever (life). Methodist. Office: Robert E Lee High Sch 411 ESE Loop 323 Tyler TX 75762 Home Fax: 903-262-2630. Personal E-mail: lara.miller@tylerisd.org.

MILLER, LAURA, mayor, journalist; b. Balt., Nov. 18, 1958; m. Steven Wolens; children: Alex, Lily, Maxwell. Grad., U. Wis., Madison. Mem. Dallas City Coun., 1998—2002; mayor City of Dallas, 2002—. Columnist, investigative reporter Dallas Observer, metro columnist Dallas Times Herald, New York Daily News, The Dallas Morning News, The Miami Herald; freelance writer: The Miami Herald. Recipient H.L. Mencken Writing award, Balt. Sun, 1995, 6 Katie awards, Dallas Press Club, 2 Tex. Headliner awards, 2 Philbin awards, Dallas Bar Assn., cert. of merit, ABA. Office: Dallas City Hall 1500 Marilla St Rm 5EN Dallas TX 75201-6390

MILLER, LAURA JEAN, federal agency administrator; b. Louisville, Nov. 11, 1946; d. Arthur and Marion (Adams) M.; m. Garrett Van Koughnett; children: Michael J. Uhlik, Caroline E. Uhlik. BA, U. Mo., Columbia, 1970; MPA, U. Mo., Kansas City, 1978. Presdl. mgmt. intern U.S. Dept. Vets. Affairs, Topeka, 1978-79, Kansas City, Mo., 1979-80, asst. to chief of staff, 1980-86, regional quality assurance mgr. Grand Prairie, Tex., 1986-89, assoc. dir. trainee Dallas, 1989-90, asst. med. ctr. dir., 1990-91, assoc. med. ctr. dir. Salem, Va., 1991-94, med. ctr. dir. Pitts., 1994, dir. Veterans Integrated Svc. Network 10 Cin., asst. dep. under sec. of heath Washington, DC, 2001—02, dep. under sec. for heath for ops. and mgmt., 2002—. Mem. exec. planning coun. U. Pitts., Western Psychiat. Inst. and Clinic, 1995—; mem.adv. bd. Vietnam Vets. Leadership Program Western Pa., Pitts., 1995—. Mem. Am. Coll. Healthcare Execs., Health Exec. Forum of Southwestern Pa., Interagy. Healthcare Inst. Alumnni. Office: US Dept Vet Affairs 810 Vermont Ave Washington DC 20420

MILLER, LESLIE ANNE, lawyer; b. Franklin, Ind., Nov. 4, 1951; d. G. Thomas and Anne (Gaines) Miller; m. Richard B. Worley, Feb. 14, 1987. AB cum laude, Mt. Holyoke Coll., 1973; MA in Polit. Sci., Rutgers U., 1974; JD, Dickinson Sch. Law, 1977; LLM with honors, Temple U., 1994; LLD (hon.), Thomas Jefferson U. Coll. Health Profls., 2002; HHD (hon.), Wilson Coll., 2001. Bar: Pa. 1977, U.S. Dist. Ct. (ea. dist.) Pa. 1977, U.S. Ct. Appeals (3d cir.) 1980, U.S. Dist. Ct. (ea. dist.) Pa. 1987. Assoc. LaBrum & Doak, Phila., 1977—81, ptnr., 1982—86, Goldfein & Joseph, Phila., 1986—95, McKissock & Hoffman, P.C., Phila., 1995—2003; gen. counsel Gov. Pa., 2002—. Bd. dirs. WHYY-TV, 1996—; del. Third Circuit Jud. Conf., 1981, 82, 85; mem. Jud. Inquiry and Rev. Bd., 1990-94, chair, 1993-94; mem. faculty trial advocacy program Dickinson Sch. Law, 1992, 94; mem. hearing com., disciplinary bd. Supreme Ct. Pa., 1996—; mem. faculty Acad. Advocacy Temple U., 1994—; judge pro tem Ct. of Common Pleas; interm pres. Kimmel Ctr. for the Performing Arts, 2001-02 Mem. acad. ball com. Phila. Orch., 1986-87, 89-91, 95-96, mem. acad. music com. 1998—; mem. Open Space Task Force Com., Lower Merion Twp., Pa., 1990, bd. dirs., 1990-94, mem. counsel, 1990, Lower Merion Conservancy, 1995-97, 2000—, others; bd. dirs. Med. Coll. Pa., 1985-96, sec., 1987-92, chair presdl. search com., 1993, chair presdl. inauguration, 1987, chair com. on acad. affairs, 1989-95, chair dean's search com., 1994-95, chair nomenclature com., 1996; bd. dirs. Med. Coll. Hosps., 1991-96, Allegheny Health Edn. and Rsch. Found., 1993-96, Hahnemann U. Med. Sch., 1994-96, Pa. Ballet, 1994—, St. Christopher's Hosp. for Children, 1991-94, vice chair, 1990-94; bd. dirs. Phila. Free Libr., 1997—, bd. dirs. Kimmel Ctr. for the Performing Arts, 1999—, interim pres., 2001-02, vice chair bd. dirs., 2002—; hon. chair Pa. Breast Cancer Coalition, 2003, exec. v.p. Pa. chpt., 2005; bd. trustees Mt. Holyoke Coll., 2000—, chair, 2005—; bd. govs. Dickinson Sch. Law, Pa. State U., 2001—. Recipient Mary Lyon award Mt. Holyoke Alumni Assn., 1985, Alumnae Medal of Honor, 1988, Hon. Alumnae award, 1989, Pres.'s award Med. Coll. Pa., 1993, Sylvia Rambo award Dickinson Sch. of Law, 1997, Star award Forum of Exec. Women, 1998, Ann Alpern award PBA Women in the Profession, 1999, Sandra Day O'Connor award Phila. Bar Assn., 1999, Outstanding Leadership in Support of Legal Svcs. award Pa. Legal Svcs., 1999, Women Making History Nat. Assn. of Women Bus. Owners, 2002, Women of Distinction award, Phila. Bus. Jour., 2001, Internat. Women's Forum "Women Who Make a Difference" award, 2003, Pink Ribbon award Pa. Breast Cancer Coalition, 2003, Woman One award Drexel U. Inst. for Women's Health and Leadership, 2004, Pa. Meritorious Svc. medal, 2005; named to Pa. Honor Roll of Women, 1996; named Disting. Dau. of Pa., Gov. of Pa., 1999. Fellow Am. Bar Found., Pa. Bar Found.; mem. ABA, Phila. Bar Assn. (exec. com. divsn. young lawyers 1982-85, bicentennial com. 1986-87, bd. govs. 1990-93, gender bias task force 1993-97, chair com. on jud. selection and retention 1987-89, vice chair 1985-87, investigative divsn. 1982-85, chair Andrew Hamilton Ball 1989, trustee Phila. Bar Found. 1990-97, co-chair century three commn. 1995-97, others), Pa. Bar Assn. (found. ho. dels. life fellow, bd. govs. 1980-83, 84-87, 91-93, chair young lawyers divsn. 1982-83, long range planning com. 1985-87, com. on professionalism, 1987-91, vice chmn. jud. inquiry and rev. bd. study com. 1989-91, sec. 1984-87, chair ho. dels. 1991-93, chair commn. on women in the profession 1993-95, v.p. 1996-97, pres. 1998-99, immediate past pres. 1999—, apptd. mem. ct. jud. discipline 1999), Pa. Bar Inst. (faculty, course planner), Phila. Assn. Def. Counsel (exec. coun. 1987-90, 94, joint trial demonstration with Phila. Trial Lawyers Assn. 1993), Def. Rsch. Inst. (spkr. toxic torts seminar 1983), Phila. Bar Edn. Advocacy Women Litigators (course planner, faculty 1995), Women's Assn. Women's Alternatives (bd. dirs. 1983-94, vice chair 1985-94), Phila. Forum Exec. Women, Pa. Women's Forum (pres. 2002-04), Com. of Seventy, Mt. Holyoke Alumnae Assn. (bd. dirs. 1986-89, 1999—). Democrat. Lutheran. Avocations: collecting American antiques, gardening, running. Office: Governors Office of Gen Counsel 225 Main Capitol Bldg Harrisburg PA 17120 Office Phone: 610-940-5325. Personal E-mail: millesq@aol.com.

MILLER, LESLIE R., obstetrician, gynecologist, educator; MD, U. Washington, 1990. Lic. Washington, 1992, cert. Obstetrics and Gynecology, 1996. Resident, obstetrics and gynecology U. Washington, Seattle, 1994, joined, 1994, assoc. prof., women's health. Contbr. articles to profl. jours. Recipient Med. Student Tchg. award, Assn. Prof. Gynecology and Obstetrics, 1996, Cert. Achievement, Reproductive Epidemiology and Clinical Trial Design Program, Berlex Found., 1997. Mem.: Assn. Reproductive Health Professionals, Alpha Omega Alpha Soc., King County Med. Soc., Washington State Med. Assn., Am. Coll. Obstetrics and Gynecologists (ACOG-Elsevier Sci., Inc., Dept. Recognition award 2001, Roy M. Pitkin award, ACOG: One of the four outstanding papers published in Obstetrics and Gynecology 2002, Parke-Davis Rsch. award to Advance the Mgmt. of Women's Health Care 1997). Office: Harborview Women's Clinic Harborview Med Ctr Box 359854 Seattle WA 98104-2499 Office Phone: 206-731-3319, 206-731-3367.*

MILLER, LILLIAN MAY, psychologist; b. Milw., Mar. 22, 1946; d. Erviin Frank and Elizabeth Kurnat Miller; 1 child, Zoe. BA cum laude, Harvard U., Cambridge, Mass., 1967; PhD, U. Mass., Amherst, 1976. Lic. clin. psychologist Mass., registered sch. psychologist N.H. Dir. Austin Riggs Nursery Sch., Stockbridge, Mass., 1969—71; clin. fellow dept. psychiatry Harvard Med. Sch., Boston, 1973—74; clin. psychologist North Shore Guidance Ctr., Salem, Mass., 1974—77, VA Outpatient Clin., Boston, 1977—85, BU Counseling Ctr., Boston, 1988—89; sch. psychologist Exeter Hampton NH, Exeter, NH, 1989—90, 1993—94; clin. psychologist pvt. practice, Mass., 1979—93, EDIS US Army, Heidelberg, Germany, 1994—2002, FFSC US Navy, Naples, Italy, 2002—. Asst. clin. prof. Tufts Med. Sch., Boston, 1979—85; adj. asst. prof. Univ. Md., overseas, 1999—. Overseas interviewer Harvard Coll., Germany, Italy; EEO counselor US Army, Heildelberg, Germany, 1997—2002. Recipient achievement and monetary awards, US Army and Navy, 1997—2002, 2005. Mem.: Harvard Alumni, Am. Psychol. Assn. Avocations: reading, gardening, travel.

MILLER, LINDA B., political scientist; b. Manchester, NH, Aug. 7, 1937; d. Louis and Helene (Chase) M. AB cum laude, Radcliffe Coll., 1959; MA, Columbia U., 1961, PhD, 1965. Asst. prof. Barnard Coll., 1964-67; rsch. assoc. Princeton U., 1966-67, Harvard U., 1967-71, 76-81, lectr. polit. sci., 1968-69; assoc. prof. Wellesley (Mass.) Coll., 1969-75, prof. polit. sci., 1975—2004, chmn. dept., 1985-89. Vis. prof. rsch. Watson Inst., Brown U., 1997, adj. prof. internat. rels., 1998—2000, 2003—, sr. fellow, 2000—03; vis. prof. polit. sci. Brown U., 1997. Author: World Order and Local Disorder: The United Nations and Internal Conflicts, 1967, Dynamics of World Politics: Studies in the Resolution of Conflicts, 1968, Cyprus: The Law and Politics of Civil Strife, 1968; co-author, co-editor: Ideas and Ideals: Essays on Politics in Honor of Stanley Hoffmann, 1993; editor Internat. Studies Rev., 1999-2002; contbr. articles to profl. jours. Internat. Affairs fellow Coun. Fng. Rels., 1973-74, Rockefeller Found. fellow, 1976-77, Oceanographic Instn. sr. fellow, 1979-80, 82-83, NATO social sci. rsch. fellow, 1982-83. Mem. Inst. Strategic Studies, Internat. Studies Assn., Coun. Fgn. Rels., Phi Beta Kappa. Home: PO Box 415 South Wellfleet MA 02663-0415 Office: Wellesley Coll Dept Polit Sci Wellesley MA 02482 also: Watson Inst Brown U PO Box 1970 Providence RI 02912-1970 Office Phone: 401-863-1598. Business E-Mail: Linda_Miller@brown.edu.

MILLER, LINDA B., administrator; Pres. Vol. Trustees Found., Washington. Mem.: Inst. Medicine ((in conjunction w/NRC) mem. adv. com. Human Embryonic Stem Cell Rsch. 2006—). Office: Vol Trustees Fond 818 18th St NW Ste 410 Washington DC 20006 Office Phone: 202-659-0338, 202-659-0116.*

MILLER, LINDA H., accountant; b. Bklyn., July 21, 1945; d. Irwin and Ruth Miller. BBA, CCNY, NYC, 1968. Prodn. acct. various networks and studios, 1978—; assoc. prodr. Dreamworks, 2005—. Assoc. prodr.: Spitfire Grill; Law and Order: Special Victims Unit, 2005—. Mem.: NY Women in Film and Television. Democrat. Jewish. Avocations: theater, dance, embroidery.

MILLER, LINDA KAREN, retired secondary school educator, social studies educator, law educator; b. Kansas City, Jan. 22, 1948; d. Bennie Chris and Thelma Jane (Richey) M. B of Secondary Edn., U. Kans., 1970; M of Secondary Edn., U. Va., 1978, EdD, 1991. Tchr. social studies Pierson Jr. H.S., Kansas City, 1970—72; substitute tchr. Fairfax Pub. Schs., Va., 1972—73; reading aide Lake Braddock Secondary Sch., Burke, Va., 1973—74; tchr. social studies Mark Twain Intermediate Sch., Alexandria, Va., 1974—75, Herndon Intermediate Sch., Va., 1975—78, Fairfax H.S., 1978—86, 1987—2002; ret., 2002. Cons. in field; instr. Sch. Law Cmty. Coll.

So. Nev., Las Vegas, 2003; del. People to People, China, 2005. Ambassador to China People to People, 2003; Nev. coord. Nat. Coun. for History Edn., 2005. Named Pre-Collegiate Tchr. of Yr., Orgn. Am. Historians, 1996, Secondary Tchr. of Yr., Nat. Coun. for Social Studies, 1996, U. Va., 1997, Outstanding Secondary Tchr., Va. Hist. Soc., 1998, Va. Geography Tchr. of Yr., 1999, Global Technet Tchr. of Yr., Nat. Peace Corps Assn., 1999, Nat. Peace Educator, 2002; recipient George Washington medal, Valley Forge Freedom Found., 1988, Excellence in Tchg. award, U. Kans. Sch. Edn., 1999, Celebrating Tchg. Excellence award, Am. Coun. Tchrs. Russian, 1998, World History Tchg. prize, World History Assn., 2002, Humanities Leadership award, NEH, 2003; fellow, Korean Soc., 2000, 2004, Am. Revolution fellow, NY Hist. Soc., 2001. Mem. Nat. Coun. Social Studies (curriculum com. 1991-94), Am. Legal History Soc., Orgn. Am. Historians, Nat. Coun. for History Edn., Nev. Coun. Social Studies, U. Va. Alumni Assn. Republican. Episcopalian. Avocation: doll collecting.

MILLER, LINDA LOU, education administrator, communications specialist; b. Pottsville, Pa., Feb. 5, 1955; d. Cletus Isaac and Erma Ruth (Brown) M.; m. William Joseph Murray Jr., July 23, 1989; 1 stepchild, Nathan Andrew BA, Shippensburg U., Pa., 1977; MEd, Pa. State U., 1998. Copywriter, media buyer Williams & Assocs., Harrisburg, Pa., 1977—78; dir. comm. Pa. Newspaper Pub.'s Assn., Harrisburg, 1978—82; dir. alumni affairs Shippensburg U., Pa., 1982—85, adj. instr., dir. major gifts, 2002—, mem. performing arts adv. coun., adv. coun., 1990; exec. v.p. Pa. Soc. Assn. Execs., Harrisburg, 1985—90; dir. comm. The Milton Hershey Sch., Pa., 1990—2001; adj. instr. Lebanon Valley Coll., Pa.; sales coord. Messiah Village/Grantham Heights, 2001—02. Pers. chair Chapel Hill United Ch. of Christ, 1992-94, ops. commn., 1992-94; mem. Milton Hershey Postage Stamp Celebration Com., 1995; editor 100th Ann. Memories Book, St. Peter's UCC, Pine Grove, Pa., 2000-01; mem. alumni bd. Shippensburg U., 2000-04, mem. disting. alumni award selection ctr. Recipient Disting. Alumnus award, Pine Grove Area Alumni Assn., 2002, Outstanding Achievement award, U. Shippensburg Pa., 1998. Mem. PRSA, NAFE, Pa. Soc. Assn. Execs., Coun. for Advancement and Support of Edn., Am. Soc. Assn. Execs. (bd. dirs. 1989, cert.), Conf. Assn. Soc. Execs. (pres. 1988-89), Allied Socs. Coun. (chmn. 1988-89), Exec. Club Ctrl. Pa. (bd. dirs. 1988-90), Rotary Club, Order Ea. Star (Trio Chpt.) Avocations: reading, walking, travel, genealogy. Home: 27 Conway Dr Mechanicsburg PA 17055-6136 Office: Shippensburg Univ Found 1871 Old Main Dr Shippensburg PA 17257

MILLER, LISA ANN, lawyer; b. Bayshore, NY, Dec. 23, 1959; d. Harold Douglas and Joan Marie Miller; m. Michael E. Millhoan (div.); children: Shane E. Millhoan, Clayton W. Perry. BA in Polit. Sci., Ohio No. Coll., Ada, 1998; JD, U. Toledo, Toledo, Ohio, 2002. Bar: Ohio, Ohio (Supreme Ct.) 2002. Asst. to advertising dir. Good Housekeeping Mag., NY, 1985—88; asst. mktg. dir. Family Circle Mag., NY Times, NY, 1988—90; assoc. atty. Wise & Dorner LLC, Toledo, 2000—03; staff atty. Seneca County Dept. Family Svcs., Tiffin, Ohio, 2003—04; pvt. practice Findlay, Ohio, 2004—. Pres. Seneca County Bar Assoc., Tiffin, Ohio, 2006, v.p., 2004—05; law libr. trustee Seneca County Law Libr. Assoc., Tiffin, Ohio, 2004—06. Atty. advisor St. Wendelin HS Mock Trial Team, Fostonia, Ohio, 2006; voting rights staff Voter Protection Program, Fostonia, Ohio, 2004. Mem.: Southern Poverty Law Ctr., Ohio Assn. Criminal Defense Atty., Ohio State Bar Assn. Office Phone: 419-424-5553.

MILLER, LISA FRIEDMAN, psychology educator; b. Iowa City, Iowa, July 25, 1966; m. Philip Roger Miller. BA, Yale U., 1988; PhD, U. Pa., 1994. Assoc. prof. Tchrs. Coll. Columbia U., N.Y.C., 1998—. Contbr. articles to profl. jours., chapters to books. Grantee, William T. Grant Found., N.Y.C., 1999—, NIMH, N.Y.C., 1999—. Mem.: APA (exec. com. divsn. 36 2001—02, WT Grant Faculty Scholars Award 1999-2003). Avocations: running, theater, museums. Office: Tchrs Coll Columbia U 525 W 120th St New York NY 10027 Business E-Mail: drlfm@yahoo.com.

MILLER, LYNN FIELDMAN, lawyer; b. Newark, Oct. 9, 1938; d. George Martin and Helene G. (Friedman) Fieldman; m. Arthur Harold Miller, Aug. 24, 1958; children: Jennifer Lyn, Jonathan Daniel. BA in English, Barnard Coll., 1959; MLS, Rutgers U., 1971, MA in Theater Arts, 1977, JD, 1990. Bar: N.J. 1990, U.S. Dist. Ct. N.J. 1990, U.S. Ct. Appeals (3d cir.) 1992. Head libr. Alma White Coll., Zarapheth, N.J., 1971; reference libr. Douglas Coll., New Brunswick, N.J., 1971-79; media libr. Rutgers U., New Brunswick, 1979-87; intern Hon. Anne E. Thompson Fed. Dist. Ct., Trenton, NJ, 1988; assoc. Wilentz, Goldman & Spitzer, Woodbridge, NJ, 1989, Greenbaum, Rowe, Smith, Woodbridge, 1990-91, Miller & Littman, New Brunswick, 1991-93; ptnr. Miller & Miller, New Brunswick, 1993-2001, Miller, Miller & Tucker, P.A., 2001—. Editor in chief: (jour.) Women's Rights Law Reporter, 1989-90. Active Highland Park (NJ) Environ. Commn., 1991-97, Supreme Ct. Com. on Women in the Cts.; trustee Middlesex County Bar Found., 2002—. Mem. NJ State Bar Assn. (trustee 2000-06, individual rights com. 1989-95, chair individual rights com. 1995-97, dir. entertainment and arts law sect. 1992-96, bd. trustees Women in the Profession sect. 1997-98, sec. 1998-99, chmn. 2000-01, chair spl. com. consumer protection law 2002-2004), Middlesex County Bar Assn. (chair women lawyers sect. 1995-96, bd. trustees 1996-2002, treas. 2003-04, 2d v.p. 2004-05, 1st v.p. 2005-06, pres.-elect 2006—). Avocations: walking, bicycling. Office: 96 Paterson St New Brunswick NJ 08901-2109 Office Phone: 732-828-2234. Business E-Mail: lmiller@millerandmiller.com.

MILLER, LYNN RUTH, writer, artist, comedian; b. Toledo, Ohio, Oct. 11, 1933; d. Irwin Rudolph and Ida Ruth Miller. BA in Edn., U. Mich., Ann Arbor, 1955; MEd, U. Toledo, Ohio, 1960; MA in Comm., Stanford U., Calif., 1964. Cert. tchr. Ohio, 1955. Elem. sch. tchr. Bd. of Edn., Cleveland Heights, Ohio, 1955—56, Brookline, Mass., 1957—59, Toledo, Ohio, 1959—60, Ottawa Hills, Ohio, 1959—62; prof. U. of Toledo Cmty. and Tech. Coll., 1965—70; free lance writer, 1970—. Author: (novels) Starving Hearts, 1999, Thoughts While Walking the Dog, 2000, More Thoughts While Walking the Dog, 2003, The Late Bloomer, 2005; stand-up comic, storyteller (Bay Area show) Farewell to the Tooth Fairy. Art tchrs., reader Pacifica Pub. Schools, Pacifica, Calif. Home: 441 Brighton Rd Pacifica CA 94044 Personal E-mail: lynnruth@pacbell.net.

MILLER, LYNNE MARIE, environmental services administrator; b. NYC, Aug. 4, 1951; d. David Jr. and Evelyn (Gulbransen) M. AB, Wellesley Coll., 1973; MS, Rutgers U., 1976. Analyst Franklin Inst., Phila., 1976-78; dir. hazardous waste div. Clement Assocs., Washington, 1978-81; pres. Risk Sci. Internat., Washington, 1981-86; CEO, Environ. Strategies Consulting, LLC, Reston, Va., 1986—. Bd. dirs. Scana Corp., Adams Nat. Bank. Editor: Insurance Claims for Environmental Damages, 1989, editor-in-chief Environ. Claims Jour.; contbr. chpts. to books. Named Ins. Woman of Yr. Assn. Profl. Ins. Women, 1983. Mem.: Wellesley Bus. Leadership Coun. Office: Environ Strategies Consulting LLC 11911 Freedom Dr Ste 900 Reston VA 20190-5631 E-mail: lmiller@escva.com.

MILLER, MARGARET ALISON, education educator; b. L.A., Dec. 17, 1944; d. Richard Crump and Virginia Margaret (Dudley) M.; m. Spencer Hall, Aug. 21, 1967 (div. 1977); 1 child, Justin Robinson; m. Alan Blair Howard, Oct. 7, 1990. BA in English summa cum laude, UCLA, 1966; postgrad., Stanford U., 1966-67; PhD in English, U. Va., 1971. Instr. English U. Va., Charlottesville, 1971-72; from asst. prof. to assoc. prof. U. Mass., Dartmouth, 1972-83; prof. English, 1983-86, co-dir. women's studies program, 1981-83, asst. to dean arts and scis., 1983-85, asst. to pres., 1985-86; acad. affairs coord. State Coun. Higher Edn. for Va., Richmond, 1986-87, assoc. dir. for acad. affairs, 1987-97; pres. Am. Assn. for Higher Edn., Washington, 1997-2000; pres. emerita Am. Assn. Higher Edn., Washington, 2000—; prof. higher edn. policy U. Va., Charlottesville, 2001—, dir. Ctr. for Study of Higher Edn., 2005—. Head English sect. transitional summer program Brown U., 1976; instr. honors program Va. Commonwealth U., 1991-93; cons. Coun. Rectors, Budapest, 1993, Minn. State U. System, Mpls., 1992, U.S. Dept. Edn., Washington, 1990—, S.C. Higher Edn. Commn., 1989-90, Edn. Commn. States, Denver, 1994-2000; presenter in field; participant UNESCO World Conf. on Higher Edn., 1998; adv. commr. Edn. Commn. of the States, 1998-2000; chair steering com. Washington Higher Edn. Secretariat, 1997-2000; mem. Nat. Postsecondary Edn. Cooperative, 1997-2000; cons. Nat. Ctr. for Pub. Policy and Higher Edn., 1998—; bd. dirs. Nat. Ctr. for Edn. Mgmt. Sys., 2001—; participant Aspen Inst., 1998; exec. editor Change mag., 2000—; judge Tchrs. Ins. Annuity Assn./Coll. Retirement Equity Fund Hesburgh awards, 1999—; dir. Nat. Forum on Coll. Level. Learning, 2002-04. Contbr. articles to profl. jours. Mem. Am. Assn. Higher Edn. (leadership coun.), Am. Coun. on Edn. (exec. com. identification program in Va. 1988-97, participant nat. identification program's 41st nat. forum for women leaders in higher edn. 1989, adv. bd. Policy Inst.), Phi Beta Kappa. Avocations: reading, gardening, travel. Home: 2176 Lindsay Rd Gordonsville VA 22942-1620 Office: Curry Sch Edn U Va 405 Emmett St S Charlottesville VA 22903 Office Phone: 434-243-8882. E-mail: pmiller@virginia.edu.

MILLER, MARGERY, psychologist, educator, speech pathology/audiology services professional, mental health services professional; m. Donald F. Moores; children: Kip Lee, Tige Justice. BA, Elmira Coll., 1971; MA, NYU, 1972; EdS, MS, SUNY, Albany, 1975; MA, Towson State U., 1987; PhD, Georgetown U., 1991. Lic. speech pathologist Md., psychologist Md.; cert. tchr. nursery-6th grades, spl. edn. N.Y., nationally cert. sch. psychologist. Speech and lang. pathologist Mental Retardation Inst. Flower and Fifth Ave. Hosp., NYC, 1971—72; cmty. speech/lang. pathologist, dir. speech and hearing svc. NY State Dept. Mental Hygiene, Troy, 1972—74; instr. comm. disorders dept. Coll. St. Rose, Albany, NY, 1975—77; clin. supr. U. Md., College Park, 1978; speech/lang. pathologist Md. Sch. for Deaf, Frederick, 1978—84; auditory devel. specialist Montgomery County Pub. Schs., Rockville, Md., 1984—87; coord. Family Life program Nat. Acad. Gallaudet U., Washington, 1987—88, interim dir., 1988—89; dir. Counseling and Devel. Ctr. N.W. Campus, Washington, 1989—93; prof. psychology, coord. psychology internship program, dir. undergrad. psychology program Gallaudet U., Washington, 1993—; lic. practicing psychologist Bethesda, Md., 1998—. Instr. sign-lang. program Frederick CC; dance instr. for deaf adolescents; diagnostic cons. psychology and speech pathology; presenter at confs.; profl. coaching, Md., Fla., 2002—. Author: It's O.K. to be Angry, 1976; co-author: Cognition, Education and Deafness: Directions for Research and Instruction, 1985; mem. editl. rev. com. Gov.'s Devel. Disabilities Coun., Md.; contbr. articles to profl. jours. Vol., choreographer Miss Deaf Am. Pageant, 1984. Office Edn. Children's Bur. fellow, 1971. Mem.: APA, Montgomery County Md. Mental Health Assn., Am. Assn. Higher Edn., Nat. Assn. Sch. Psychologists, Nat. Assn. Deaf, Am. Speech, Lang. and Hearing Assn. (cert. clin. competence in speech/lang. pathology). Office: Gallaudet U 800 Florida Ave NE Washington DC 20002-3660 Office Phone: 202-651-5540. Business E-Mail: margery.miller@gallaudet.edu.

MILLER, MARIA B., retired educator; b. Chgo., Nov. 19, 1931; d. Maurice and Violet (Finley) Brasseur; m. William V. Miller, Apr. 25, 1952; children: Deborah Miller King, Suellen F. BA, San Jose (Calif.) State U., 1967, MA, 1969. Prof., coord. speech program Jefferson C.C., Louisville, 1971-76, coord. spl. svcs. program, 1977-82, coord. adv. program, 1982-86, coord. speech program, 1987-93; prof. emeritus, 1994—. Cons., Louisville, 1974—. Co-author: (books) You're Speaking, Who's Listening, 1980, BASIC-LY Speaking, 1990, Student Workbook for Interpersonal Communication, 1992; contbr. articles to profl. jours. Bd. dirs. Louisville YWCA, 1984-87. Mem. Speech Comm. Assn. (Outstanding C.C. Educator, C.C. sect. 1991). Home: 2556 Claremont St Port Townsend WA 98368-1041

MILLER, MARIAN, professional society administrator; Grad., Ind. U. 3rd v.p., sec. Nat. Fedn. Rep. Women, Alexandria, Va., 1st v.p., mem. exec. com., also bd. dirs., pres., 2000—01. Chair program by-laws, sr. Am. and leadership coms., regent Nat. Fedn. Rep. Women. Advisor to Suellen Reed State Supt. Com., to Steve Goldsmith for Gov. Campaign; statewide vol. coord. for v.p. Dan Quayle's 1st U.S. Senate campaign, U.S. Senator Dan Coats, Gov. Otis Bowen, John Murtz for Gov. Campaigns; del. Rep. Nat. Convs., 1988, 92, 96; precinct committeewoman Tippecanoe County; pres. Tippecanoe County RWC; active Ind. Com. Humanities, Gov.'s Adv. Com. on Pub. Welfare, Pension Mgmt. Legis. Study Commn.; active gov. rels. com. Ind. Hosp. Assn.; bd. dirs. United Way Ind.; del. to White House Conf. on Aging; chmn. Ind. Commn. on Aging; del. to Nat. Forum on Excellence in Edn.; founder Hoosier Assocs., 1975—. Recipient Pres.'s award Ind. U. Alumni Assn., Sagamore of the Wabash award Gov. Ind.

MILLER, MARILYN JANE, music educator; b. Lancaster, Pa., Dec. 20, 1946; d. Kenneth Billett and Vern June Strominger; m. Gerald Lester Miller, Apr. 3, 1976. BA in Sacred Music, Messiah Coll., Grantham, Pa, 1970, BS in Music Edn., 1970. Pvt. voice and piano instr., Pa.; secondary music tchr. Boiling Springs H.S., Pa., 1970—72; choral dir. and soloist Trinity Presbyn. Ch., Cherry Hill, NJ, 1988—89. Choir dir. Luth., Meth. and Presbyn. Churches, Pa., 1966—88; recitalist and presenter. Performer: Music of Women Composers. Mem. chancel choir Pine St. Presbyn. Ch., 1991—2004; benefit recitalist Downtown Daily Bread Pine St. Presbyn. Ch.; bd. mem. Harrisburg Singers, Pa., 1994—96. Mem.: Wednesday Club Master Recital Program, Pa. Music Teachers Assn. (Capital area chpt), Music Tchrs. Nat. Assn., Am. Choral Directors Assn., Grantham Oratorio Soc., Nat. Assn. Tchrs. of Singing, Lancaster Chamber Singers, Ephrata Cloister Chorus and Vorspiel Prodn., Lebanon Valley Coll. Alumni Chorale. Home: 1816 Hearthstone Lane Middletown PA 17057 E-mail: orglvoce@comcast.net.

MILLER, MARILYN LEA, library and information scientist, educator; AA, Graceland Coll., 1950; BS in English, U. Kans., 1952; AMLS, U. Mich., 1959, PhD of Librarianship and Higher Edn., 1976. Bldg.-level sch. libr. Wellsville HS, Kans., 1952-54; tchr.-libr. Arthur Capper Jr. HS, Topeka, 1954-56; head libr. Topeka HS, Topeka, 1956-62; sch. libr. cons. State of Kans. Dept. of Pub. Instrn., 1962-67; from asst. to assoc. prof. Sch. Librarianship Western Mich. U., Kalamazoo, 1967-77; assoc. prof. libr. sci. U. NC, Chapel Hill, 1977-87, prof., chair dept. libr. and info. studies Greensboro, 1987-95, prof. emeritus, 1996—. Vis. faculty Kans. State Tchrs., Emporia, 1960, 63, 64, 66, U. Minn., Mpls., 1971, U. Manitoba, Winnipeg, Can., 1971; vis. prof. Appalachian State U., Boone, NC, 1987; adv. bd. sch. libr. media program Nat. Ctr. for Edtl. Stats., 1989, user rev. panel, 1990; chair assoc. dean search com. Sch. Edn., 1988, coord. Piedmont young writers conf., 1989-94, 97-99, chair race and gender com., 1990-93, SACS planning and evaluation com., 1990-91, learning resources ctr. adv. com., 1991-93; hearing panel for honor code U. NC Greensboro, 1988-91, assn. women faculty and administrv. staff, 1987-95, faculty coun., 1987-95, chair, 1994-95, univ. libr. com., 1987-88, com. faculty devel. in race and gender scholarship, 1990-92; lectr. and cons. in field. Editor: Pioneers and Leaders in Library Service to Youth, 2003; mem. editl. bd. The Emergency Librarian, 1981-97, Collection Building: Studies in the Development and Effective Use of Library Resources, 1978-96; contbr. chpt. to books, articles to profl. jour. Children's libr. specialists to visit Russian sch. and pub. libr., book publs., Moscow, Leningrad, Tashkent, 1979; hon. del. White House Conf. on Libr. and Info. Svcs., Washington, 1991; head del. Romanian Summer Inst. on Librarianship in U.S., 1991; citizen amb. People to People Internat. Program, People's Republic of China, 1992, Russian and Poland, 1992, Russia, 1994, Barcelona, 1995; exec. bd. dirs. Friends of Greensboro Pub. Libr., 1996-99, chair gift shop and coffee shop adv. com., 1996-2002, v.p., 2003-05, pres. 2005—; chair Citizens Materials Adv. com., 1999-; chair Citizens Strategic Long Range Planning com., 1994-95, 2001-03, chair, 2003, 06, Sch. Pub. Libr. com., 2002—, chair, 2003—; pub. libr. trustee, 2005-, NC State Libr. Commn., 2006-. Recipient Freedom Found. medal, 1962, Disting. Svc. to Sch. Librs. award Kans. Assn. Sch. Librs., 1982, Disting. Svc. award Graceland Coll., 1992, Disting. Alumnus award Sch. Libr. and Info. Studies, U. Mich., 1988, Contribution to Libr. Info. Sci. award Assn. Libr. Info. Sci., 1999; Delta Kappa Gamma scholar, 1972. Mem.: ALA (awards com. 1971—72, chair Chgo. conf. resolutions 1972, chair 1973—75, resolutions com. 1976—78, adv. com. Nat. Ctr. Ednl. Stats. 1984, standing com. libr. edn. 1987—91, yearbook adv. com. 1988—90, chair 1989—90, pres. 1992—93, exec. dir. 1994, chair rsch. com., chair search com., Disting. Svc. award Am. Assn. Sch. Librs. 1993), Friends of N.C. Pub. Librs. (bd. dirs. 2000—), So. Assn. Colls. and Schs. (accreditation team 1988), Southeastern Libr. Assn. (chair libr. educators sect. 1990—92), N.C. Assn. Sch. Librs. (Disting. Svc. award 2004), Assn. Libr Svc. to Children (bd. dirs. 1976—81, pres. 1979—80, rsch. com. 1982—85, chair 1984—85, Disting. Svc. award 2005), Assn. Ednl. Comms. and Tech., Am. Assn. Sch. Librs. (nominating com. 1980, pub. com. 1981—82, chair search com. exec. dir. 1985, v.p., pres.-elect 1985—86, pres. 1986—87, coord. coms. nat. stds. vision and implementation 1995—98), N.C. Libr. Assn. (life; edn. libr. com. 1978—80, 1982—86, bd. dirs. 1987—99, exec. bd. status women roundtable 1989—2003, chmn.-elect 1995—97, chmn. 1997—99, commn. on status of sch. librs. 1999—2000). Personal E-mail: marilynl@bellsouth.net.

MILLER, MARJORIE LYMAN, editor; b. Aug. 7, 1929; married; 4 children. BA, George Washington U., 1950; postgrad., U. Calif., L.A, 1952. Field dir. Long Beach Coun. Camp Fire Girls, Inc., Calif., 1951—53, Potomac Area Coun. Camp Fire Girls, Inc., Arlington, Va., 1953—56; recruitment rep. blood svc. ARC, Phila., 1978, adminstr. east Del. county br., 1978—81, adminstr. east Chester county. br., 1981—84, adminstr. greater Del. county br., 1984—88; ptnr. Bylines, 1988—. Co-author: 7 books; contbr. articles to jours. and mags. Bd. dirs., publicity dir., adminstr World Affairs Coun. Greater Valley Forge, 1992—; apptd. Chester County Open Space and Environ. Task Force, 1989—90, Chester County Pk. and Recreation Bd., 1977—94, pres., 1990—94; bd. dirs. Maysie's Farm Conf. Ctr., 2000—, Main Line Symphpny Orch., 1996—. Mem.: LWV (membership chair 1966—70, chair state conv. 1970—73, co-chair 50th ann. nat. conv. 1972, bd. trustees 1973—74, 1st vice chair 1974), Assn. Retirees ARC (pres. ea. Pa. unit 1991—93, nat. bd. dirs. 1993—, v.p. 1999, pres. 1999—2003, 2001—03, chmn. Ea. Pa. unit 1991—93, 2004—), Soroptimist Internat., Pi Beta Phi. Home: 12 Grant Ln Wayne PA 19087

MILLER, MARTHA GLENN, academic administrator, consultant; b. Roswell, N.Mex., Aug. 20, 1951; d. Frank Chester and Mary Elizabeth (Russell) W.; m. Robert John Cox (div. 1980); m. William Robert Claybaugh II, May 12, 1984; children: William Robert III, David Miller. BA, Ind. U., 1974; PhD, Harvard U., 1979. Asst. prof. Yale Sch. of Orgn. and Mgmt., New Haven, Conn., 1980-84, asst. dean, 1984-85, assoc. dean, 1985-86; asst. dean Anderson Grad. Sch. Mgmt. UCLA, Los Angeles, 1987-91; assoc. dean, 1991—. Lectr. Harvard U., Cambridge, Mass., 1979-80; sr. assoc. Good Measure, Inc., Cambridge, 1976—. Fellow Danforth Found., 1974-78; Disting. scholar Ind. U. and Gen. Motors Corp., Bloomington, 1970-74; recipient Disting. Alumna Award, Ind. U., 1974. Mem. Am. Sociol. Assn., Internat. Jour. of Small Group Research, Phi Beta Kappa. Avocation: cross country skiing. Home: 2426 Inglewood Ct Falls Church VA 22043-3223

MILLER, MARY HELEN, retired state government administrator; b. Smiths Grove, Ky., June 30, 1936; d. Walter Frank and Lottie Belle (Russell) Huddleston; m. George Ward Wilson, Sept. 12, 1958 (div. Sept. 1973); children: Ward Glenn, Amy Elizabeth Huddleston; m. Francis Guion Miller Jr., June 6, 1981. BA, Western Ky. U., 1958. Tchr. Fayette County Schs., Lexington, Ky., 1958-60, Seneca High Sch., Louisville, 1960-63, Shelby County High Sch., Shelbyville, Ky., 1963-69; rsch. analyst Legis. Rsch. Com., Frankfort, Ky., 1973-79, asst. dir., 1979-83, 90-91; chief exec. asst. Office Gov., Frankfort, 1983-87, 93-95, legis. liaison, 1991-93; cabinet sec. Natural Resources and Environ. Protection Cabinet, Frankfort, 1987-88; sales assoc. W. Wagner, Jr. Comml. Real Estate, Louisville, 1989-91; ret., 1996. Author: (constl. revision) Citizens Guide To/Perspective, 1978, (booklet) A Look at Kentucky General Assembly, 1979, A Guide to Education Reform, 1990, (handbook) Gubernatorial Transition in Kentucky, 1991. Mem. Leadershi Ky. Alumni, Frankfort, 1986, Waterfront Devel. Corp. Bd., Louisville, 1986—87, Greater Louis Partnership Econ. Devel., 1988—92, Shelbyville 2000 Found. Bd., 1991—92; mem., sec. Regional Airport Authority Bd., Louisville, 1986—89; mem. Shelby County Cmty. Theatre Bd., Shelbyville, 1978—83, 1988—91, treas., 1979—83, pres., 1989—91; chair Shelby County Cmty. Found., 1995—2000; mem. Ky. Long Term Policy Bd., 1992—99, chair, 1995; mem. Ky. Hist. Properties Commn., 1995—99; exec. com. Ky. Hist. Soc., 2002—, v.p., 2004—; mem. Shelby Devel. Found., 2003—05. Recipient Vic Hellard Jr. Pub. Svc. in Ky. award, 1999; named Shelbyville Citizen of Yr., 1998. Mem. Caryatid Book Club (pres. 1999), Women's Initiative Networking Groups (pres. 1998), Western Ky. U. Alumni Assn. (bd. dirs. 1992-95). Democrat. Episcopalian. Avocations: reading, theater, gardening, antiques. Home: 1116 Main St Shelbyville KY 40065-1420 E-mail: mhm1116@aol.com.

MILLER, MARY RITA, retired adult education educator; b. Williamsburg, Iowa, Mar. 4, 1920; d. James Carl and Bernadette (O'Meara) Rush; m. Clarence Glenn Miller, June 2, 1947 (dec. Aug. 1987); 1 child, Ronald Rush; m. William J. Gibbons, July 14, 1992 (dec. June 2001). BA, U. Iowa, 1941; MA, Denver U., 1959; PhD, Georgetown U., 1969. From instr. to asst. prof. Regis Coll., Denver, 1962-65; from asst. prof. to prof. U. Md., College Park, 1968-91, prof. emeritus, 1991—. Author: Children of the Salt River, 1977, Place—Names of the Northern Neck of Virginia, 1983; contbr. numerous articles and revs. Avocations: research, travel, reading, farming. Home: 2825 29th Pl NW Washington DC 20008-3501

MILLER, MARY-EMILY, history educator; b. Wilmington, Del., Mar. 7, 1934; B.A. in History with distinction, U. Del., 1955; cert. Harvard-Radcliffe Program Bus. Adminstrn., 1956; M.A., Boston U., 1959, Ph.D., 1962. Sec. research com. Lemuel Shattuck Hosp., Harvard U., 1956-58; mem. staff registrar's office Radcliffe Coll., 1958-59; resident asst. Boston U., 1959-61; asst. prof. history, dean women Methodist Coll., Fayetteville, N.C., 1962-64, chmn. history dept. and social sci. area, 1963-64; asst. prof., dean women Park Coll., Parkville, Mo., 1964-66, acting chmn. dept., 1965; prof. history Salem (Mass.) State Coll., 1966-92, chmn. dept., liaison to Salem Partnership re Russia, 1989-92; part-time prof. history U. Del., 1992—. Recipient Family Bus. Longevity award DESmall Bus. Bur., 2003. Contbr. numerous articles to profl. jours. Mem. Tercentennery Commn., Cumberland County, N.C., 1963, Kent County (Del.) Tricentennial Commn. and Exec. Bd., 1983; active Bicentennial and Bicentennial of Constn. activities in Mass. and Del.; mem. Fayetteville Symphony Orch., 1962-64, St. Joseph Symphony Orch., 1964-66, Hollis (N.H.) Town Band, 1970-83, Middlesex Wind Ensemble, 1978-81, U. Del. Alumni Band, Boston U. Alumni Band, 1978—; Mem. AAUP (chpt. pres. 1979-92), Am. Hist. Assn., Orgn. Am. Historians, Assn. Counseling and Devel., Am. Coll. Pers. Assn., New Eng. Hist. Assn., Soc. History Discoveries, N.Am. Oceanic History Assn., Peabody-Essex Mus., Blue Hen Power Squad. (treas. 1996—), Renaissance Assn., English-Speaking Union, Harvard Bus. Sch. Alumni Assn., Lewes Yacht Club, Phi Alpha Theta, Delta Tau Kappa, others. Home and Office: Box 287 113 S Market St Frederica DE 19946-0287 Office Phone: 302-335-5229.

MILLER, MAUREEN CHERTOW, science educator; b. Chgo., Sept. 18, 1968; d. Bruce Sherwin and Janice Elaine Chertow; m. Jeffrey Miller, June 11, 2005. BA in Biology, Ind. U., Bloomington, 1991; MEd in Tech. in Edn., Nat. Louis U., Evanston, Ill., 2001; cert. in ednl. leadership, Loyola U., Chgo., 2004. Biology tchr. Rustburg H.S., Va., 1992—93, Waukegan H.S., Ill., 1994—98; sci. tchr. Edgewood Mid. Sch., Highland Park, Ill., 1998—. Adj. faculty Nat. Louis U., Chgo., 2004. Mem.: Northshore Edn. Assn. (sec. 2003—). D-Liberal. Jewish. Avocations: volleyball, travel, photography. Office: Edgewood Mid Sch 929 Edgewood Rd Highland Park IL 60035 Office Phone: 847-432-3858.

MILLER, MAXINE LYNCH, retired home economist, retired interior designer, educator; b. Ellensburg, Wash., Feb. 15, 1921; d. Ralph A. Lynch and Bertha Sorenson; m. Harlan LeRoy Miller, Aug. 29, 1950 (div. June 1965). BA in Home Econs., Wash. State U., Pullman, 1942; MA in Home Econs., U. Wash., Seattle, 1959. Asst. prof. to prof. Calif. State U., LA, 1955—80; prof. emeritus, 1980. Chair program accreditation team, nat. treas. Interior Design Educators Coun., Inc. Recipient Interior Design Educators

Coun. Emeritus Letter of Commendation award, Found. Interior Design Edn. Rsch., 1959; scholar, Am. Soc. Internat. Design, 1968. Mem.: Nat. Soc. DAR. Avocations: genealogy, photography, art, crafts. Home: 913 Chamith Ln Ellensburg WA 98926

MILLER, MICHELLE D., lawyer; b. 1952; BA cum laude, Boston Univ., 1974; JD magna cum laude, Boston Coll., 1979. Bar: Mass. 1979. Law clk. Judge Paul J. Liacos, Supreme Judicial Ct. Mass., 1979—80; assoc. to ptnr. Wilmer Cutler Pickering Hale & Dorr, Boston, 1980—, vice chmn. Litigation dept., vice chmn. Antitrust & Competition dept., mem. exec. com. Contbr. articles to profl. jours. Named one of Top 50 Female Mass. Lawyers, Boston Mag., 2004. Mem.: ABA, Boston Bar Assn. (former co-chmn. Antitrust com.), Order of the Coif. Office: Wilmer Cutler Pickering Hale & Dorr 60 State St Boston MA 02109 Office Phone: 617-526-6116. Office Fax: 617-526-5000. Business E-Mail: michelle.miller@wilmerhale.com.

MILLER, MONICA LISA, social studies educator; b. Orlando, Fla., Feb. 22, 1972; d. Maurena L. Fluellyn; m. Hoyt Horace Harper, Jr., May 19, 2005; 1 child, Jalen Juwan Harper. BS, Fla. A&M U., Tallahassee, 1995. Cert. Profl. Educator Fla., 2003. Tchr. social studies grades 6-8 Westridge Mid. Sch., Orlando, 1999—. Personal E-mail: millerml72@yahoo.com.

MILLER, NANCY ELLEN, computer scientist, consultant; b. Detroit, Aug. 30, 1956; d. George Jacob and Charlotte M. Miller. BS in Computer and Comm. Scis., U. Mich., 1978; MS in Computer Scis., U. Wis., 1981. Product engr. Ford Motor Co., Dearborn, Mich., 1977; computer programmer Unique Bus. Sys., Inc., Southfield, Mich., 1978; tchg. asst. U. Wis., Computer Scis. Dept., Madison, 1978—82; computer scientist Lister Hill Nat. Ctr. Biomed. Commns., Nat. Libr. Medicine, NIH, Bethesda, Md., 1984—88; pvt. practice West Bloomfield, Mich., 1993—. Recipient Jour. of Am. Soc. for Info. Sci. Best Paper award, 1988. Mem. Assn. for Computing Machinery (sec. S.E. Mich. spl. interest group on artificial intelligence 1993-94), Am. Assn. for Artificial Intelligence, Assn. for Logic Programming, U. Wis. Alumni Assn. (life), U. Mich. Alumni Assn. (life), Am. Contract Bridge League, Nat. Women's Polit. Caucus, NARAL Pro-Choice Am., Jewish Fedn. Met. Detroit, Planned Parenthood Fed. Am., Hadassah: The Women's Zionist Orgn. Am. (life). Democrat. Jewish. Address: PO Box 4224 Southfield MI 48037-4224

MILLER, NANCY JO., science educator; b. Callaway, Nebr., May 1, 1953; d. Stanley Earl and Donna Marie Helberg; m. Larry Mike Miller, Nov. 11, 1978; children: Travis, Lisa, Amanda. BS, Chadion State Coll., Nebr., 1975. Tchr. Pine Ridge (SD) Mid. Sch., 1975—77, Little World Sch., Kyle, SD, 1977—78, Dix (Nebr.) Pub. Sch., Nebr., 1979—86, Potter-Dix Pub. Sch., 1986—. Co-founder Potter-Dix Cmty. Svc. Award, 2001; presenter Nebr. Assn. Tchrs. Sci. Named Tchr. of Yr., Farm Bureau, 2006; Therapy Balls grant, U. Nebr. Med. Ctr., 2004. Mem.: NEA, Potter-Dix Edn. Assn. (pres. 2004—06), Nat. Sci. Tchrs. Assn. Democrat. Luth. Avocation: swimming. Home: 2645 Rd 63E Dix NE 69133 Office: Potter Dix Schs 303 Walnut Potter NE 69156 Office Phone: 308-879-4434. Office Fax: 308-682-5227. Business E-Mail: nmiller@panesu.org.

MILLER, NANCY LOIS, senior pastor; b. Lancaster, Pa., July 20, 1954; d. William Martin and Dorothy DeBoer Miller. BA, Lebanon Valley Coll., 1976; MDiv, Garrett-Evangelical Theol. Sem., 1980. Cert. deacon Ea. Pa. Ann. Conf. United Meth. Ch., 1977, elder Ea. Pa. Ann. Conf. United Meth. Ch., 1981, basic quarter clin. pastoral edn. Rush Presbyn. St. Luke's Med. Ctr., Ill., 1979. Student asst. pastor Cmty. Ch. Wilmette, Ill., 1977—78; vesper intern Vesper Soc., San Leandro, Calif., 1978—79; sr. pastor Milton Grove United Meth. Ch., Mount Joy, Pa., 1980—82, Bellegrove United Meth. Ch., Annville, Pa., 1992—94, Water Works United Meth. Ch., Cleona, Pa., 1992—94, Radnor United Meth. Ch., Rosemont, Pa., 1994—98, Coventryville United Meth. Ch., Pottstown, Pa., 1998—2003, Messiah United Meth. Ch., Lafayette Hill, Pa., 2003—; assoc. in resident svs., assoc. chaplain Cornwall Manor Retirement Cmty., Pa., 1983—84; founding pastor Faith United Meth. Ch., Lititz, Pa., 1984—92. Mem. dist. com. min. Lancaster Dist. United Meth. Ch., Pa., 1981—83; chairperson Evaluation Com. Conf. Coun. on Mins. of The Ethnic Minority Local Ch. Task Force, Valley Forge, Pa., 1982—82; chairperson, mem. commn. Comission on Status & Role Women Ea. Pa. Ann. Conf. The United Meth. Ch., Valley Forge, Pa., 2000—; mem. United Meth. Ch. Camp Pocono Plateau Site Com., Cresco, Pa., 1981—85; co-chair Harry Hosier Dist. Ministerium of The United Meth. Ch., Phila., 1994—96; chair worship com. & retreat com., mem. of steering com. Women of Faith (sub-com. The Met. Christian Coun. of Phila.), 1994—98. Actor: (plays) Musical Carnival. Founding pastor Faith United Methodist Ch. Mem.: Conshohocken Bus. and Profl. Women, Whitemarsh Twp. Bus. Assn. Democrat. Avocations: travel, camping, needlework, singing, piano. Office: Messiah United Meth Ch 527 Ridge Pike Lafayette Hill PA 19444 Office Phone: 610-828-0118. Office Fax: 610-828-2463. Personal E-mail: nancymiller@verizon.net.

MILLER, NANCY SUZANNE, technology consultant, artist; b. Springfield, Mass., Nov. 8, 1946; d. Harry J. and Helen G. (Golden) Corwin; m. Daniel B. Morgan, May 26, 1983; children: Jillian Morgan, Bradley Morgan. BA, Columbia U., 1969; postgrad., NYU, 1972-74; MFA, CCNY, 1998. Tech. cons. J.P. Morgan, N.Y.C., 1986—; tchr. N.Y.C. Bd. Edn., 1996—. One-woman shows include Ingrid Cusson Gallery, N.Y.C., 1989, Pines Gallery, 1990, Z Gallery, N.Y.C., 1991, New World Gallery, Boston, 1992, R.M. Bradley & Co., Boston, 1994, Mulberry Gallery, N.Y.C., 1995, Aquasource Gallery, N.Y.C., 1995; exhibited in group shows at Daniel Gallery, Ft. Lauderdale, Fla., 1988, Soha Open Studio Show, N.Y.C., 1988, Whitehall Gallery, Palm Springs, Calif., 1989, Peabody Gallery, Boston, 1989, AIR Gallery, N.Y.C., 1989, Tallahassee Gallery, 1990, Valerie Miller Gallery, Palm Springs, 1990, 91, Gallery Gaudi, Watermill, N.Y., 1991, Z Gallery, N.Y.C., 1992, C.W. Post Coll., 1993, Soha Art Gallery, 1993, New England Fine Arts Inst., Boston, 1993, Benton Gallery, Southampton, N.Y., 1993, Zimerlee Mus., Rutgers U., N.J., 1993, Viva Galeria, N.Y.C., 1994, Ann Harper Gallery, East Hampton, 1995, Bob Blackburn and CCNY Prinmakers, NYC, 1996, Arthur Danzinger Gallery, Soho, 1996, AIR Gallery, NYC, 1997, 2005, 27 West Gallery, 1998, Venezuelan Ctr., N.Y.C., 2003, Cork Gallery, N.Y.C., 2003, Queen's Coun. on Arts, 2003, Broome St. Gallery, 2004, Bertoni Gallery, 2004, LI City Open Studios, 2004, CCNY Alumni and Student Biennial, 2005, Godwin-Ternbach Mus. Queens Cill. N.Y., 2005; represented in permanent collections Bankers Trust Co., N.Y., Morgan Stanley, Bryan Cave McPheeters & McRoberts, N.Y., Cellular One, Boston, Citibank, N.Y., Daiwa Am. Securities, N.Y., Equitable, N.Y., Gen. Instruments, N.Y., John Hancock, Boston, IBM, N.Y., Irving Trust, N.Y., others. Vol. fund raiser Pub. Sch. 87, 1990-92, vol. art tchr., 1995-96; dir. spring soccer Am. Youth Soccer Orgn., 1995; PTA treas., 2001-03. Mem.: Barnard Bus. and Profl. Women. Jewish. Avocations: scuba diving, skiing, soccer team parent, computer graphics. Home: 527 W 110th St New York NY 10025-2081 E-mail: nmiller@yahoo.com.

MILLER, NICOLE, art columnist; "Arts Beat" columnist Washington Post, visual arts columnist for Sunday Source. Office: Washington Post 1150 15th St NW Washington DC 20071 Business E-Mail: millern@washpost.com.

MILLER, NICOLE JACQUELINE, fashion designer; b. Ft. Worth, Mar. 20, 1951; d. Grier Bovey and Jacqueline (Mahieu) M. BFA, RISD, 1973; cert. de coursspeciale, École de la Chambre Syndicale de la Couture Parisienne, Paris, 1971. Opened boutique Gamine, Stockbridge, Mass., 1973—74; asst. designer Clovis Ruffin, NYC, 1974; designer Raincheetahs, NYC, 1974—75, P.J. Walsh, NYC, 1975-82, Nicole Miller, NYC, 1982—, millergirl sportswear line, 2003—, Nicole by Nicole Miller, J.C. Penney, 2005—. Mem. Sports Commn. of N.Y., Commn. of Status of Women; bd. trustees R.I. Sch. of Design. Bd. dirs. Smith's Food and Drug. Recipient Dallas Fashion award, 1991, Earnie award for children's wear, Michael award for fashion. Mem. Fashion Group, Fashion Roundtable, Coun. of Fashion Designers of Am., N.Y. Athletic Club. Avocations: skiing, ice skating, waterskiing, wind surfing. Office: 525 7th Ave Fl 20 New York NY 10018-4901*

MILLER, NIDI R., artist, sculptor, educator; b. Camaguey, Cuba, Feb. 6, 1958; d. Robert A. and Nydian R. Ynda; m. William R. Miller, July 4, 1991; children: Alexis C., Albert R., Patrick R. BA in Fgn. Langs., BA in Art and Sculpture, George Mason U., 2004. Artist, sculptor, educator Fairfax County, Centreville, Va., 2000—. Exhibitions include Group House/Earl House Exhibit, mural, September 11 Commemoration. Vol. Fairfax Area Christian Emergency and Transitional Svcs., 2000—01, Centreville United Meth. Ch., 1999—2002. Recipient Vision awards for acad. excellence, Office of Diversity Programs and Svcs., 2004. Mem.: Alpha Chi (hon.), Golden Key (hon.).

MILLER, PAMELA GUNDERSEN, retired mayor; b. Cambridge, Mass., Sept. 7, 1938; d. Sven M. and Harriet Adams Gundersen; m. Ralph E. Miller, July 7, 1962; children: Alexander, Erik, Karen. AB magna cum laude, Smith Coll., 1960. Feature writer Congl. Quar., Washington, 1962-65; dir. cable TV franchising Storer Broadcasting Co., Louisville, Lexington, Ky., 1978—80; mem. 4th dist. Lexington Fayette County Urban Coun., 1973-77; councilwoman-at-large, 1982-93; vice mayor, 1984-86, 89-93; mayor, 1993—2003. Dep. commr. Ky. Dept. Local Govt., Frankfort, 1980-81; pres. Pam Miller, Inc., 1984-94, Cmty. Ventures Corp., 1985-95. Mem. Fayette County Bd. Health, 1975—77, Downtown Devel. Commn., 1975—77; bd. dirs. YMCA, Lexington, 1975—77, 1985—90, Fund for the Arts, 1984—93, Coun. of Arts, 1978—80, Sister Cities, 1978—80; chmn. Prichard Com. for Acad. Excellence, 2004—; treas. Planned Parenthood, 2003—, Fayette Edn. Found., 2005—; alt. del. Dem. Nat. Com., 1976; bd. dirs. Lexington Opera Soc., 2003—; chair Fund for Arts Campaign, 2003—04. Named woman of achievement YWCA, 1984, outstanding Woman of Blue Grass AAUW, 1984. Mem. LWV (dir. 1970-73), Profl. Women's Forum. Home: 140 Cherokee Park Lexington KY 40503-1304

MILLER, PATRICIA A., music educator, opera and concert artist; b. Washington, June 16; d. Robert Lee and Bernice (Echols) Miller. MusB, Boston U.; MusM, New Eng. Conservatory; artist's diploma, Accademia di Santa Cecilia, Rome; postdoctoral diploma, Mozarteum, Salzburg. Artist Thea Dispeker Artist's Mgmt., Inc., N.Y.C., 1981—95; assoc. prof. music, artist-in-residence U. Mo., Columbia, 1983—85; prof. music, dir. vocal studies, artist-in-residence George Mason U., Fairfax, Va., 1991—; prof. voice Oberlin Coll. Conservatory, Oberlin, Ohio, 2000—01. Dir. vocal studies George Mason U., 1995—, prodr. opera theater, 2000—, dir. Inst. Vocal Arts, 2004—; lectr. Smithsonian, Wash., DC, 2000—02. Performer: (Operas) ERCOLE Amante, 1986, Carmen, 1985, Porgy & Bess, 1996,; concert/recital artist Kennedy Ctr., Washington, 2000, Kiev, 2002, Austrian Embassy, 2003, Salzburg, Austria, 2004, Kaynon Concert Hall, Seoul, Korea, 2005; performer (soloist): Schloss Leopolskron Great Hall, 2004, Kiev Philharmonic Orch., 2004, New Strathmore Music Ctr., 2005, Nat. Philharmonic Orch. and Chorus, 2005. Mem. opera panel Nat. Endowment for the Arts, 2003—04; mem. panel Va. Commn. for the Arts, 2004—05. Recipient Shining Star Cmty Svc. award, Nat. Urban League, Sojourner Truth Leadership award, George Mason U., 2004; grantee, Am. Embassy, 2002; Fulbright scholar, Rome. Mem.: Fulbright Assn. (bd. dirs. Nat. Capitol area), Nat. Assn. Tchrs. Singing (state bd. dirs.), Sigma Alpha Iota (Alumni Artistry Leadership award 2004, Outstanding Artist award 2004). Methodist. Avocations: travel, walking, swimming, cooking. Office: George Mason Univ Dept Music MSN-3E3 4400 University Dr Fairfax VA 22030-4444 Office Phone: 703-993-1382. Personal E-mail: labellavoce1@aol.com. Business E-Mail: pmiller@gmu.edu.

MILLER, PATRICIA ANN, secondary school educator; b. Charleston, W.Va., Oct. 26, 1938; d. William Jennings and Frankie Marguerite (Bragg) Nutter; m. Maurice E. Miller, July 20, 1963; children: Elizabeth, Jeffrey, Joel. BS Mus Edn., Charleston U., 1961; postgrad., Cin. Conservatory Music, 1962, 63, Miami U., Oxford, Ohio, 1965. Tchr. Ross (Ohio) High Sch., 1961-65, Hamilton (Ohio) Pub. Schs., 1973-95; retired, 1995. Choir dir, Immanuel Bapt. Ch., Hamilton, 1968-84, 1986-94, Grace United Meth. Ch., Hamilton, 1994-1998; featured soloist Hamilton Symphony Chorale. Mem. Music Educators Nat. Conf., Ohio Music Edn. Assn., Great Miami Choral Soc. (featured soloist), Am. Choral Dir's. Assn. Home (Winter): 1590 E Firestone Dr Chandler AZ 85249-4382

MILLER, PATRICIA ANNE, speech and language pathologist; b. Lamesa, Tex., Aug. 19, 1957; d. Warren Layton and Evelyn Joyce (Pearson) Oliver; m. John Ernest Roberts, May 25, 1979 (div.); 1 child, Jason Aaron; m. Michael David Miller, Nov. 30, 1984; children: Jennifer Anne, Catherine Denise. BS, Howard Payne Coll., 1979; postgrad., Baylor U., 1983. Cert. tchr., Tex.; lic. speech-lang. pathologist, Tex. Speech therapist Crosbyton (Tex.) Ctrl. Ind. Sch. Dist., 1980-81, Hillsboro (Tex.) Spl. Edn. Coop., 1981, speech therapy cons., 1982-83; speech therapist Cleburne (Tex.) Ind. Sch. Dist., 1987-89, Levelland (Tex.) Ind. Sch. Dist. Coop., 1989; speech therapist Speech, Lang. and Hearing Ctr. Lamesa Ind. Sch. Dist., Lubbock, Tex., 1990-95; speech-lang. pathologist Sundance Rehab. Corp., Lamesa, Tex., 1995-96, Lamesa Ind. Sch. Dist. and Seminole Ind. Sch. Dist., 1997—2002, The Weston Group, Inc., Lubbock, 2002—. Baptist. Avocations: flute, tennis. Office: Weston-Rehab Inc 9812 Vinton Ave Lubbock TX 79414

MILLER, PATRICIA ANNE, physician assistant; b. Aug. 24, 1957; d. George Albert and Lillian Mamie M.; children: Christian Arthur Turner. BS, George Washington U., Washinton, 1989; BS physician asst. studies, George Washington U., 1991; MS in Rural Primary Care, Alderson-Broaddus Coll., 2000. Cert. Nat. Cert. Com. Physician Assn. Med. officer/adminstrv. officer USS Monongahela AO-178, Norfolk, Va., 1991-93; divsn. officer acute care dept. Branch Clin. NAS Oceana, Va. Beach, 1993-95; instr. Intersvc. Physician Asst. Program, San Antonio, 1996-98; physician asst. Broaddus Hosp., Philippi, W.V., 1998-99, West Taylor Primary Care Ctr., Flemington, W.Va., 1999—. Assoc. prof. George Washington U., Washington, 1996-98, U. Nebr., 1996-98, Lt. USN, 1975—. Recipient Army Commendation Medal, San Antonio, 1998, Navay Commendation Medal, 1988, 93, 96. Fellow Naval Assn. Physician Assts. (pres. 1997—), Bexar County Soc. Physician Assts. (sec. 1996-97), Am. Acad. Physician Assts. (del. 1996—). Avocations: camping, music, reading. Office: West Taylor Primary Care Ctr Flemington WV 26347 Address: C/O W Taylor Primary Care Service PO Box 247 Flemington WV 26347-0247 E-mail: hugapa@aol.com.

MILLER, PATRICIA HACKNEY, psychology educator; b. Wellington, Kans., Aug. 24, 1945; d. Robert Holmes and Mary (Welsch) Hackney; m. Scott Anthony Miller, Dec. 17, 1967; children: Erica, Kevin. BA, U. Kans., 1966; PhD, U. Minn., 1970. Lectr. U. Mich., Ann Arbor, 1970—73, asst. prof., 1973—77; assoc. prof. U. Fla., Gainesville, 1979—86, dir. devel. psychology, 1982—92, 1994—95, prof., 1986—2001, U. Ga., 2001—, dept. head, 2005—. Author: Theories of Developmental Psychology, 1983, rev. edit., 1989, 3rd edit., 1993; co-author: Cognitive Development, 3rd eidt., 1993; contbr. chpts. to book and articles to profl. jours. Rsch. grantee NIMH, 1979-82, NSF, 1987-90, NIH rsch. tng. grantee, 1982-93, 93—. Fellow APA (exec. com. divsn. 7 1990-1992); mem. Am. Psychol. Soc., Soc. for Rsch. in Child Devel., Jean Piaget Soc. (bd. dirs. 1990-97). Democrat. Home: 17 Plantation Dr Ne Atlanta GA 30324-2935

MILLER, PATRICIA HOFFMAN, human services administrator, finance educator; b. Lancaster, Pa., June 6, 1947; d. Ralph J. and Anne M. Reeves; m. David E. Hoffman; m. Gary N. Miller Sr., Dec. 24, 1984; children: Dawn, Gary, Maia, David Ellson, Sean Kevin. BS in Bus., Chgo. State U., 1974; MPA in Pub. Adminstrn., Roosevelt U., Chgo., 1976; ABD, U. Iowa, Iowa City, 1980; PhD in Ednl. Policy, The Union Inst., 2001. Human resources coord. The Pillsbury Corp., Mpls., 1973-76; asst. prof. mgmt. Chgo. State U., 1976-79; human resource mgr. Rockwell Internat., Cedar Rapids, Iowa, 1979-81; pres. Matrix Solutions, Harrisburg, Pa., 1981—; secondary educator Harrisburg (Pa.) Sch. Dist., 1998—2001; primary prof. Ea. Coll., St. Davids, Pa., 1997—2001; exec. dir. human resources Gay (Ind.) Cmty. Sch. Corp., 2002. Cons. Mallay St. Apts., SBA, Phila., U. Wis., Madison, U. No. Iowa, Waterloo. Mem. Acad. Polit. Sci., Phi Delta Sigma. Democrat. Baptist.

MILLER, PATRICIA LOUISE, state legislator, nurse; b. Bellefontaine, Ohio, July 4, 1936; d. Richard William and Rachel Orpha (Williams) M.; m. Kenneth Orlan Miller, July 3, 1960; children: Tamara Sue, Matthew Ivan. RN, Meth. Hosp. Sch. Nursing, Indpls., 1957; BS, Ind. U., 1960. Staff nurse Cmty. Hosp., Indpls., 1958, Meth. Hosp., Indpls., 1959; office nurse A.D. Dennison, MD, 1960-61; rep. State of Ind. Dist. 50, Indpls., 1982-83; senator State of Ind. Dist. 32, Indpls., 1983—, chair senate health and provider svcs. com., 1999—; mem. labor and pension com., 1985—94; mem. edn. com., 1989—92; legis. appt. and elections com., chmn. interim study com. pub. health and mental health Ind. Gen. Assembly, 1986; chair Senate Environl. Affairs, 1990—91; health and environ affairs, 1992—; mem. election com., 1992—; mem. budget subcom. Senate Fin. Com., 1995—. Mem. Bd. Edn. Met. Sch. Dist., Warren Twop., 1974-82, pres., 1979-80, 80-81; mem. Warren Twp. Citizens Screening Com. for Sch. Bd. Candidates, 1972-84, Met. Zoning Bd. Appeals, Divsn. I, apptd. mem. City-County Coun. on Aging, Indpls. 1977-80; mem. State Bd. Vocat. and Tech. Edn., 1978-82, sec., 1980-82; mem. gov.'s Select Adv. Commn. for Primary and Secondary Edn., 1983; precinct committeeman Rep. Party, 1967-74, ward vice-chmn., 1974-78, ward chmn., 1978-85, twp. chmn., 1985-87; vice chmn. Marion County Rep., 1986-2000; sgt. at arms, 1982, mem. platform com., 1984, 88, 90, 92, co-chmn. Ind. Rep. Platform Com., 1992; rep. Presdl. Elector Alternate, 1992; active various polit. campaigns; bd. dirs. PTA, 1967-81; pres. Grassy Creek PTA, 1971-72; state del. Ind. PTA, 1978; mem. child car adv. com. Walker Career Ctr., 1976-80, others; bd. dirs. Ch. Fedn. Greater Indpls., 1979-82, Christian Justice Ctr., Inc., 1983-85, Gideon Internat. Aux., 1977, Ctrl. Ind. Coun. Aging; mem. United Meth. Bd. Missions Aux. Indpls., 1974-80, v.p., 1974-76, mem. nominating com., 1977; bd. dirs. Lucille Raines Residence, Inc., 1977-80; exec. com. S. Ind. Conf. United Meth. Women, 1977-80, lay del. s. Ind. Conf. United Meth. Ch., 1977—, fin. and adminstrn. com., 1979-88, planning and rsch. com., 1980-88, co-chmn. law adv. com., chmn. health and welfare, conf. coun. ministries, also mem. task force, bd. ordained ministry, also panel, chmn. com. on dist. superintendency, dist. coun. on ministries; sec. Indpls. S.E. Dist. Council on Minstries, 1977-78, pres. 1982; chmn. council on ministries Cumberland United Meth. Ch., 1969-76; chmn. stewardship com. Old Bethal United Meth. Ch., 1982-85, fin. com., 1982-85, adminstrv. bd., mem. council on ministries, 1981-85; co-chair Evangelism Com., 1994—; jurisdictional del. United Meth. Ch., 1988, 92, 96-2000; alternate del. United Methodist Ch. Gen. Conf., 1988, del. 1992; mem. adv. com. Warren Fine Arts Found., 1991—; mem. adv. bd. St. Francis Hosp., 1992-2005; mem. health and human svcs. com. Midwest Legis. Conf., 1995; del rep. various confs. and convs. Recipient Lambda Theta Honor for Outstanding contbr. in fiedl of end., 1976; named Woman of Yr. Cumberland Bus. and Profl. Women, 1979; Ind. Vocat. Assn. citation award, 1984, others. Mem. Indpls. dist. Dental Soc. Women's Aux., Ind. Dental Assn. Women's Aux., Am. Dental Assn. Women's Aux., Coun. State Govt. (intergovtl. affairs com.), Nat. Conf. State Legis. (vice chmn. health com. 1994—), Warren Twp. Rep., Franklin Rep., Lawrence Rep., Center Twp. Rep., Fall Creek Valley Rep, Marion County Coun. Rep. Women (3rd v.p. 1986-89), Ind. Women's Rep. (legis. chair 1988-89), Nat. Fedn. rep. Women, Beech Grove Rep., Perry Twp. Rep., Indpls. Women's Rep. Club (3rd v.p. 1989—), Indpls. Press Club. Office Phone: 317-232-9400. Business E-Mail: s32@in.gov.

MILLER, PEGGY GORDON ELLIOTT, academic administrator; b. Matewan, W.Va., May 27, 1937; d. Herbert Hunt and Mary Ann (Renfro) Gordon; m. Robert Lawrence Miller, Nov. 23, 2001; stepchildren: Rohn J., Robert K.;children from previous marriage: Scott Vandling Elliott III, Anne Gordon Elliott. BA, Transylvania Coll., 1959; MA, Northwestern U., 1964; EdD, Ind. U., 1975; degree (hon.), Transylvania U., 1993, Chungnam Nat. U., Korea, 2000. Tchr. Horace Mann H.S., Gary, Ind., 1959-64; instr. English Am. Inst. Banking, Gary, 1969-70, Ind. U. N.W., Gary, 1965-69, lectr. Edn., 1973-74, asst. prof. edn., 1975-78, assoc. prof., 1978-80, supr. secondary student tchg., 1973-74, dir. student tchg., 1975-77, dir. Office Field Experiences, 1977-78, dir. profl. devel., 1978-80, spl. asst. to chancellor, 1981-83, asst. to chancellor, 1983-84, acting chancellor, 1983-84, chancellor, 1984-92; pres. U. Akron, Ohio, 1992-96, SD State U., 1998—. Sr. fellow Nat. Ctr. for Higher Edn., 1996-97; vis. prof. U. Ark., 1979-80, U. Alaska, 1982; bd. dirs. Lubrizol Corp., A. Schulman Corp., Commn. on Women in Higher Edn., SD Mus. Art, Akron Tomorrow, Ohio Aerospace Consortium, Ohio Super Computer Com., Brookings C. of C.; holder VA Harrington disting. chair in edn., 1994-96, Charles G. Herbrich chair in leadership mgmt., 1996—; chmn. Growth partnership Rsch. Pk. Author: (with C. Smith) Reading Activities for Middle and Secondary Schools: A Handbook for Teachers, 1979, Reading Instruction for Secondary Schools, 1986, How to Improve Your Scores on Reading Competency Tests, 1981, (with C. Smith and G. Ingersoll) Trends in Educational Materials: Traditionals and the New Technologies, 1983, The Urban Campus: Educating a New Majority for a New Century, 1994, also numerous articles. Bd. dirs. Am. Humanics Meth. Hosp., N.W. Ind. Forum, N.W. Ind. Symphony, S.D. Art Mus., Boys Club N.W. Ind., Akron Symphony, NBD Bank, John S. Knight Conv. Ctr., Inventure Pl., Akron Roundtable, Cleve. Com. Higher Edn., 4-H Found., S.D. Art Mus., S.D. Value. Recipient Disting. Alumni award Northwestern U., UA Disting. Alumni award, 1994, Dist. Alumni award, Ind. U., 2004, Disting. Hon. Alumni, S.D. State U.; numerous grants; Am. Council on Edn. fellow in acad. adminstrn. Ind. U., Bloomington, 1980-81. Mem. Assn. Tchr. Educators (nat. pres. 1984-85, Disting. Mem. 1990), Ind. Assn. Tchr. Educators (past pres.), North Ctrl. Assn. (mem. commn. at large), Am. Assn. State Colls. and Univs. (acting v.p. divsn. acad. and internat. programs 1997, bd. dirs., treas., chmn. global priorities commn.), Am. Coun. Edn. (bd. dirs., exec. com.), Leadership Devel. Coun. ACE, Office Women Higher Edn. (mem. emerita of exec. bd), Am. Humanics (bd. dirs.), Ohio Inter Univ. Coun. (chairperson), Internat. Reading Assn., Akron Urban League (bd. dirs.), P.E.O., Cosmos Club, Phi Delta Kappa (Outstanding Young Educator award), Delta Kappa Gamma (Leadership/Mgmt. fellow 1980), Pi Lambda Theta, Pi Kappa Phi, Chi Omega. Episcopalian. Avocation: music. Home: 929 Harvey Dunn St Brookings SD 57006-1347 Office: Office of the Pres South Dakota State Univ Adminstrn Bldg 201 Brookings SD 57007-0001 Office Phone: 605-688-4111, 605-688-4112. Business E-Mail: Peggy_Miller@sdstate.edu.

MILLER, PEGGY MCLAREN, retired management educator; b. Tomahawk, Wis., Jan. 12, 1931; d. Cecil Glenn and Gladys Lucille (Bame) McLaren; m. Richard Irwin Miller, June 25, 1955; children: Joan Marie, Diane Lee, Janine Louise. BS, Iowa State U., 1953; MA, Am. U., 1959; MBA, Rochester Inst. Tech., 1979; PhD, Ohio U., 1987. Instr. Beirut Coll. for Women, 1953-55, U. Ky., Lexington, 1964-66, S.W. Tex. State U., San Marcos, 1981-84; home economist Borden Co., N.Y.C., 1955-58; cons. Consumer Cons., Chgo., Springfield, Ill., 1972-77; sr. mktg. rep. N.Y. State Dept. Agr., Rochester, 1978-79; asst. prof., coord. bus. and mgmt. Keuka Coll., Keuka Park, N.Y., 1979-81; lectr. mgmt. Ohio U., Athens, 1984-2000; ret., 2000. Home: 17 Briarwood Dr Athens OH 45701-1302 E-mail: pmmiller@aol.com.

MILLER, RITA, personnel consultant, diecasting company executive; b. Bklyn., Jan. 15, 1925; d. Joseph and Etta M.; BA, Bklyn. Coll., 1947; MA, Boston U., 1949; children: Erika Greenwald, Roy Barnet Glickman. Personnel officer, sec. to pres. Marine Elec. Corp., Bklyn., 1943-47; script writer Song Debut, Boston, 1949-50; dir. Writers' Workshops, interviewer pub. opinion surveys, New Rochelle, N.Y., 1962-64; dir. pers. and indsl. rels. Dynacast divsn. Coats & Clark, Inc., Yorktown Heights, 1966-89. Mem. Am. Soc. Personnel Adminstrn., Westchester Personnel Mgmt. Assn. (dir.), Personnel Council New Rochelle, Bus. and Profl. Women U.S.A., Nat. Sociology Hon. Soc. Editor: The Management Consultant (George Kenning), 1965; contbr. articles to profl. jours. Home: 29-I Windsor Ct Keene NH 03431

MILLER, ROBERTA ANN, gastroenterology nurse; b. Saginaw, Mich., Mar. 5, 1955; d. Frank William and Elizabeth Martha (Zimmerman) Carelli; m. Mark Clifford Miller, July, 1977; children: Matthew Gerald, Sarah Rose. BSN, No. Mich. U., 1977. RN, Mich.; cert. gastroenterology clinician. Staff nurse med./surg. unit St. Anthony Med. Ctr., Columbus, Ohio, 1977-78, staff nurse surg. ICU, 1978-85, staff nurse vascular lab., 1985-86, gastroenterology clinician, 1986-92; supr. digestive disease ctr. Grant Med. Ctr., 1994—.

Contbr. articles to profl. jours. Mem. Hosp. Mgmt. Assn., Soc. Gastroenterology Nurses ans Assocs. (mem. rsch. com., dir. edn. 1998—), Ohio Soc. Gastrointestinal Nurses and Assocs. (pres. 1993-98). E-mail: b.miller@ohiohealth.com.

MILLER, ROSALIND ELAINE, librarian, educator; b. Neosho, Mo., June 15, 1929; d. Charles Roland and Ruby (Bushner) Baugher; m. Edgar Miller, Jan. 1953 (div. 1967); children: Mary, David. BA in English, Drury Coll., 1951; MA in English Edn., Washington U., 1967; MLS, U. Ill., 1967; PhD, St. Louis U., 1972. Libr. Fairview High Sch., 1959-66, Florissant (Mo.) Valley C.C., 1966-67; instr. evening sch. dist. Washington U., St. Louis, 1969-71; summer lectr. U. Ill. Grad. Sch. Libr. Sci., Urbana, 1968-70; instr. Sch. Edn. St. Louis U., summer 1971; dir. libr. Clayton (Mo.) High Sch., 1967-72; prof. Libr. Media Edn., Coll. Edn. Ga. State U., Atlanta, 1972—. Cons. Dekalb (Ga.) Sch. Dist., 1987-88, Gwinnett (Ga.) Sch. Dist., 1989-92, Rockdale County Sch. Dist., Rockdale, Ga., 1992, U. No. Iowa, Watertown, 1992. Author: (with Terwillegar) Commonsense Cataloging, 4th edit., 1990; contbr. articles to profl. jours., chpts. to books. Recipient Outstanding Profl. Writing prize Sch. Libr. Media Ann., Librs. Unltd., 1989; grantee Ga. State U., 1985, 87; Fulbright prof., Cyrus, 1983, India, 1989, 93. Mem. ALA, Am. Assn. Sch. Librs. (bd. dirs. 1985-86, 89-91, exec. bd. 1991-92), Ga. Libr. Media Assn. (editor jour. 1989—, William M. Patterson award 1989). Avocations: reading, exercise, duplicate bridge. Home: 222 Forkner Dr Apt 15 Decatur GA 30030-1656 Office: Ga State U Univ Plaza Atlanta GA 30303

MILLER, RUBY SILLS, retired gerontologist; b. Montpelier, Ind., July 7, 1919; d. Elijah Bert and Alma (Beeks) Sills; m. Glenn Kenneth Miller, Mar. 26, 1966. BS in Edn., Ball State Tchrs. Coll., 1957; MBA, U. Wis., 1958; MPS, New Sch. Social Rsch., 1983; post-masters cert., Hunter Brookdale Ctr. on Aging, 1988. Reporter Montpelier Herald, 1937-41; soc. editor, reporter Hartford City News-Times, Ind., 1941-44, bus. office supr., 1945-57; asst. to dean, instr. U. Wis. Sch. Bus., 1958-60; exec. dir. Nat. Fedn. Bus. and Profl. Women's Clubs, 1960-64; asst. to nat. exec. dir. Girl Scouts U.S.A., NYC, 1964-66, spl. asst. to nat. exec. dir., 1972-74; dir. exptl. project for adminstrv. trainees Camp Fire Girls, Inc. and Girl Scouts U.S.A., 1966-68; dir. regional confs. Nat. Assembly for Social Policy and Devel., Inc., 1968-71; project dir. Nat. Ctr. for Vol. Action, 1971-72; cons. Nat. Coun. for Homemaker-Home Health Aide Svc., Inc., 1972, 76; asst. dir. Gustavus Adolphus Cmty. Lounge Sr. Ctr., 1977-78; cmty. program officer Queens County NYC Dept. Aging, 1978-89; gerontologist cons., 1989—. Sec. Hartford City Retailers Assn., 1951-54 Mem. bd. life mem. Bellevue Day Care Ctr., 1979—, pres., 1980—82; bd. mem. Bellevue Hosp. Adv. Coun., 1978—82, 1991—97; region 1 field rep. NY State Wide Sr. Action Coun., 1989—91, bd. trustees, 1992—2002, region 1 pres., 1996—98, state pres., 1996—98; coord. vol. nat. study guardianship system NY Older Women's League and Ctr. Social Gerontology, Ann Arbor, Mich., 1990—91; pres. Ind. Bapt. Youth Fellowship, 1944—46; supt. Sunday sch. 1st Bapt. Ch. in Montpelier Bapt. Ch., 1949—51; bd. trustees Cmty Ch., Unitarian-Universalist, 1987—92, 1998—2003, vice chair, 1999—2002. Mem.: State Soc. Aging NY. Home: 165 E 32nd St Apt 5G New York NY 10016-6009 Personal E-mail: RMille7030@aol.com.

MILLER, RUTH ANN, artist; b. Columbia, Mo., Dec. 7, 1930; d. Carl Elmer and Marjorie May (Harris) Miller; m. Rowland Procter Elzea, June 1958 (div.); children: Jessica Mary, Cathlin Suzanne, Lucas James; m. Andrew Murray Forge, Dec. 24, 1974. BA, U. Mo., 1954; student, Art Students League, N.Y.C., 1954-56. Tchr., adj. prof. Queens Coll., N.Y.C., 1974-75, U. Hartford, Conn., 1975-78, N.Y. Studio Sch., N.Y.C., 1973—, Parsons Sch. Design, N.Y.C., 1991-93. One-person exhbns. include Lincoln Gallery, Westchester, Pa., 1964, Del. Art Mus., Wilmington, 1967, Washington Art Assn., N.Y. Studio Gallery, 1979, 88, Washington Depot, Conn., 1982, 92, Bowery Gallery, N.Y.C., 1993, others; group shows include Am. Acad. and Ist. Arts and Letters, N.Y.C., 1990, N.Y. Studio Sch. Gallery, N.Y.C., 1990, Waterbury (Conn.) Arts, 1991, NAD, N.Y.C., 1992, 93, 94, 95, Bryn Mawr Coll., 1993, N.D. Mus. Art, 1993; works in collections at Del. Art Mus., U. Del., Corcoran Gallery, pvt. collections. Ingram Merril Found. grantee, 1981, 95. Mem. NAD (academician), Washington Art Assn.

MILLER, SABRINA WARES, librarian; d. Margaret Ann Bonds and Edson Brigham Wares; children: Adrian Matthew, Brandon Thomas. BA, Sul Ross State U., Alpine, Tex., 1992; MLS, NC Ctrl. U., Durham, 2000. Cert. health info. profl. Med. Libr. Assn., 2005. Med. libr. intern Laupus Libr., East Carolina U. Sch. of Medicine, Greenville, NC, 2000—00; edn. ctr. libr. Mid-Am. Cancer Ctr., Springfield, Mo., 2000—01; pub. svcs. med. libr. John B. Coleman, M.D., Health Scis. Libr., Houston CC, 2001—06; tech. libr. Champion Techs., Fresno, Tex., 2006—. Accreditation cons. Acad. of HealthCare Professions, Houston, 2004—. Vol. Poe Elem. Sch., Houston, 2003; vol. charity work Salvation Army. Bedichek Faculty Devel. grant, Houston C.C. Sys., 2001, 2003. Mem.: Spl. Libr. Assn., Mensa Internat., Acad. Health Info. Profls., Tex. Med. Ctr. Health Scis. Libr. Consortium, Med. Libr. Assn. Democrat. Office: PO Box 450499 Houston TX 77245 Office Phone: 281-431-2561.

MILLER, SANDRA PERRY, middle school educator, department chair; b. Nashville, Aug. 3, 1951; d. James Ralph and Pauline (Williams) Perry; m. William Kerley Miller, June 22, 1974. BS, David Lipscomb U., 1973; MEd, Tenn. State U., 1983, cert. in spl. edn., reading splty., 1986. Cert. tchr., Tenn. Tchr. Clyde Riggs Elem. Sch., Portland, Tenn., 1973—86; tchr. social studies Portland Mid. Sch., 1986—, chmn. dept. history/social studies, 2004—05. Adv. bd. tech. and comm. in edn. Sumner County Sch. Bd., Gallatin, Tenn., 1990—; co-dir., cons. Tenn. Students-at-Risk, Nashville, 1991—; assoc. edn. cons. Edn. Fgn. Inst. Cultural Exch., 1991-92; fellow World History Inst., Princeton (N.J.) U., 1992—; awards com. Tenn. Dept. Edn., Nashville, 1992; U.S. edn. amb. E.F. Ednl. Tours, Eng., France, Germany, Belgium, Holland, 1991; ednl. cons. HoughtonMifflin Co., Boston; apptd. Tenn. Mini-Grants award com., Tenn. 21st Century Tech. Com.; mem. Tenn. Textbook Com., 1995, Think-Tank on 21st Century Edn., Tenn. and Milliken Nat. Educator Found.; apptd. to Gov.'s Task Force Commn. on 21st Schs., Gov.'s Task Force for Anti-Drug and Alcohol Abuse Among Teens; mem. nat. com. for instnl. tech. devel. Milken Family Found. Nat. Edn. Conf., 1996; apptd. to Instrnl. Tech. Devel.-Project Strand, 1996 Milken Family Found., Nat. Edn. Conf.; appointed curriculum com. Bicentennial WW II Meml., 1996-97; developed State Model Drop-Out Prevent Program, 1996-97; U.S. tchr. amb. to Ukraine, Am. Coun. for Internat. Edn.; Sumner County music dir. Sumner Enrichment Program, 2001-02; mem. awards com. for U.S., Am. Couns. for Internat. Edn., Washington, 2002; chmn. history dept. Portland Mid. Sch.; adj. faculty Vol. State C.C., Gallatin, Tenn., 2005—06; adv. bd. McDougal Littel/Houghton Mifflin, 2006—. Author curriculum materials; presenter creative crafts segment local TV sta., 1990-93; producer, dir. documentary on edn. PBS, Corona, Calif., 1990. Mem. nat. com. instnl. tech. devel. project Strand of the 1996 Milken Family Found. Nat. Edn. Conf., L.A., 1996; performer Nashville Symphony Orch., 1970—73; leader Sumner County 4-H Club, 1976—86; mem. Woodrow Wilson Nat. Fellowship Found. on Am. History, Princeton U., 1994; co-chair Inter Media Cable Commn.; apptd. tchr. mentoring program Midd Tenn. State U. and Tenn. State U. Dept. Edn.; chmn. Comcast Cable Commn., Portland area, 2001—05. Recipient Excellence in Tchg. award U. Tenn., 1992, 93, award for Outstanding Teaching in Humanities Tenn. Humanities Coun., 1994; named Tchr. of Yr. Upper Cumberland dist. Tenn. Dept. Edn., 1991-92, 92-93, Mid. Tenn. Educator of Yr. Tenn. Assn. Mid. Schs., 1991, Tenn. Tchr. of Yr. Tenn. Dept. Edn., 1992, Nat. Educator of Yr. Milken Family Found., 1992, U.S. Tchr. Ambassador to Ukraine, Am. Coun. Internat. Edn., Washington; named one of Top 100 Geography Tchrs. in Tenn. Nat. Geog. Soc., 2005; grantee Tenn. Dept. Edn. for Devel. of Model Drop Out Prevention Program, 1996. Mem. NEA, ASCD, Sumner County Edn. Assn. (sch. rep. 1973—, Disting. Tchr. of Yr. 1992), Tenn. Edn. Assn. (rep. 1973—), Nat. Geographic Tenn. Alliance (rep. 1990—, grantee 1990), Tenn. Humanities Coun. (rep. 1990—), Nat. Coun. Social Studies, Internat. Platform Assn. Baptist. Avocations: crafts, doll collecting, reading, music, fashion modeling. Office: Portland Mid Sch 604 S Broadway Portland TN 37148-1624 Office Phone: 615-325-4146. Business E-Mail: sandy@sandyabc.com.

MILLER, SANDRA RITCHIE, artist, art therapist; b. Downers Grove, Ill., Aug. 15, 1940; d. Joseph Edgar and Ruby Irene (McAllister) Ritchie; m. David Martin Miller, Dec. 13, 1968; 1 child, Ritchie Wayne. Student, Cambridge U., Eng., 1975-76, U. Minn., 1971; AA in Art, Glendale Coll., 1979; BS in Psychology, Ariz. State U., 1982. Adminstrv. asst. Rand Corp., Santa Monica, Calif., 1959, System Devel. Corp., Santa Monica, Calif., 1965-69; art tchr. Wheelersburg, Ohio, 1983-85; artist, 1970—; art person, therapist Oak Meadow Nursing Home, Alexandria, Va., 1987—94, Woodbine Healthcare and Rehab., Alexandria, 1992—. Bd. dirs., v.p. Gallery West, Alexandria. One-woman shows include Gallery West, Alexandria, Va., 1992, 1993, 1995, 1996, Hamilton Gallery, Alexandria, 1991, Yarrow Gallery, Oundie, Eng., 1998, Parish Gallery, Washington, 1999, 2002, 2004, Willow Gallery, Annapolis, Md., 2003, 2005, Md. Fedn. Art, Annapolis, 2005, AAAS, 2006, exhibitions include Women's Internat. League for Peace and Freedom Calendar, 1983, Nat. Mus. Women in Arts archives, 1994—, Mus. Contemporary Art, Washington, 1996, Internat. Artists' Support Group, 1996—, Amsterdam Whitney Gallery, NYC, Google Artworks, Pa., Farmington Art Mus., 2006, AAAS, 2006. Vol. USAF Family Svcs., Duluth, Minn., 1970-72, RAF Alconbury, Eng., 1972-75, Friends of the Earth, San Francisco, 1980-81, Child Assault Prevention Program, Portsmouth, Ohio, 1983-85; bd. dirs. Art League/Torpedo Factory, Alexandria, 1989-91, Belle Haven on the Green, Alexandria, 1988-92, pres. 1991-92. Mem. Ward Nasse Gallery, Knickerbocker Artists, Washington Project for the Arts, Mus. Contemporary Art, Nat. Assn. Women Artists. Democrat. Avocations: travel, reading, study. Home: 5747 Blaine Rd Churchton MD 20733-9656 Office: 5747 Blaine Rd Churchton MD 20733-9656 Office Phone: 301-261-5045. E-mail: sdra1@hotmail.com.

MILLER, SARABETH, secondary school educator; b. Apr. 6, 1927; d. Clayton Everett and Margaret (Noland) Reif; m. Lloyd Melvin Miller, Dec. 2, 1944; children: Virginia, Shirley, Judith, John, Nola, Steven. BA, Valparaiso U., 1972, MA in L.S, 1977; postgrad., Purdue U., 1983, Ind. U., 1986, postgrad., 1991, Art Inst. Ft. Lauderdale, Fla., 1992, Ind. State U., 1996, postgrad., 1997, St. Joseph U., 1998. Lic. tchr. Ind., cert. data processing. Office employee Porter County Herald, Hebron, Ind., 1954—55, Little Co. of Mary Hosp. and Home, San Pierre, Ind., 1960—65, Jasper County Co-op, Tefft, Ind., 1965—69, Hannon's, Valparaiso, 1969—72; tchr. art DeMotte (Ind.) elem. sch., 1972—76, Kankakee Valley High Sch., Wheatfield, Ind., 1976—. Participant Lilly Creative Tchr.'s Workshop. Participant (art and lit. mag.) Mirage, No. Region Artists Invitational; contbr. articles and photographs to local newspapers. Leader 4-H Club, Kouts; participant North Ctrl. Regional Forum, 1991, 1992, 1993; participant archeol. dig K.V. Hist. Soc. and Notre Dame; mem., elder Kouts Presbyn. Ch.; mem. adv. com. secondary sch. showcase Valparaiso U. Recipient various prizes, Lake Ctrl. (Ind.) Fair, 1975, 1980, photography award, Ind. Dept. Tourism, 1976, Porter County Fair, 1989, 1996, 1998, 2000, 2001, 2004, Gainer Bank Calendar award, 4-H Alumni award, 2002, 4-H 45 yr. leader tenure award, 1994; grantee, Nat. Gallery of Art, 1993; Lilly Endowment fellow, Lilly Extending Tchr. Creativity Inst., 1987, 1994, 1995, 1996, 2002, 2003, 2004, 2005. Mem.: AIA, NEA, North Ctrl. Assn. Secondary Schs. (mem. evaln. team), Kankakee Valley Tchrs. Assn., Ind. Art Edn. Assn., Ind. Tchrs. Assn., Nat. Art Edn. Assn., Nat. Mus. American Indians, Smithsonian Instn., Hist. Landmarks, Kankakee Valley Hist. Soc. Presbyterian. Home: 1056 S Baums Bridge Rd Kouts IN 46347-9712

MILLER, SARAH PEARL, librarian; b. Wilkensburg, Pa., Aug. 31, 1938; d. Samuel Henry and Anna Deborah (Shirley) Lyons; m. Paul Victor Miller, Apr. 15, 1989; children: Cheryl, Michael, Daniel, Lorel. BS, Indiana U. of Pa., 1960; MREM, Denver Conservative Bapt. Sem., 1965; MA, U. Denver, 1966. Libr. Denver Conservative Bapt. Sem., 1966—. Mem. Am. Theol. Libr. Assn. (bd. dirs. 1978-81, 90-91, index bd. 1983-90). Home: 15707 E Grand Ave Aurora CO 80015-1708

MILLER, SHARI ANN, art educator; b. Friend, Nebr., Aug. 3, 1959; d. Roger Dean and Jane Suzanne Johnson; m. William Joseph Miller, July 11, 1980; children: Derek Ryan, Shannon Suzanne. B in Art Edn., Doane Coll., 1981. Art tchr. Bruning (Nebr.) Pub. Sch., 1982—83, Harvard (Nebr.) Pub. Sch., 1985—, Aurora (Nebr.) Pub. Sch., 2002—. V.p., sec. Honey Do's Ext. Club, Clay Center, Nebr.; v.p. Altar Soc. Ch., Harvard. Mem.: NSEA, NEA, Harvard Edn. Assn. (sec.), Clay Ctr. Cmty. Club. Republican. Roman Catholic. Avocations: camping, boating, bicycling, horseback riding, fishing. Office: Harvard Pub Sch Aurora Pub Sch 300 L St Aurora NE 68818

MILLER, SHARON LEA, art educator; b. Topeka, Kans., Sept. 6, 1956; d. Forrest Edwin and Eula Mae Cowell. BA in Theatre, Washburn U., Topeka, 1978; MS in Ednl. Tech., Kans. State U., Manhattan, 1989. Cert. tchr. Kans., 1985, Mary Kay color Mary Kay Nat. Sales Dir., 2006. Tech. theatre dir.; Helen Hocker Theatre Topeka Parks nad Recreation Dept., Topeka, 1978—83; 5th grade tchr. Pauline South Mid. Sch., Pauline, Kans., 1985—86; 6th and 7th math tchr Auburn Mid. Sch., Kans., 1986—87; 5th grade tchr. Auburn Elem. Sch., Kans., 1987—97; 7th and 8th grade art tchr. Washburn Rural Mid. Sch., Topeka, 1997—. Drama sponsor/theatre dir. Washburn Rural Mid. Sch., Topeka, 1997—2004; beauty cons. Mary Kay, Inc., Dallas, 2004—. Recipient Excellence in First Yr. Tchg., Sallie Mae, 1986, Award of Excellence for Outstanding Mid. Level Math Educator of the Yr., N.E. Kans. Assn. of Tchrs. Math, 1996, Mary Kay Queen of Personal Sales; Kunis Unit, Mary Kay Cosmetics, 2006. Mem.: Auburn-Washburn Nat. Ednl. Assn. (co-pres. 2003—04), Kans. Prairie Packers (bd. of dirs. 2003—06), Phi Kappa Phi. Methodist. Avocations: travel, camping, raising horses, singing, gardening. Office: Auburn-Washburn USD #437; Middle School 5620 SW 61st St Topeka KS 66619 Office Phone: 785-339-4351. Office Fax: 785-339-4325. E-mail: millesha@usd437.net.

MILLER, SHEILA, state legislator; d. Vernon and Mildred M.; m. Michael Miller; 1 child, Emilie C. BS cum laude, Pa. State U., 1974. Rep. dist. 129 State of Pa., 1993—. Bd. dirs. Berks County Farmland Preservation. Mem. Nat. Cattlemens Assn., Berks Farm Bur., Berks Cattlemens Assn., Pa. Cattlemens Assn., Heidelberg Heritage Soc., Berks County Rep. Women, Phi Kappa Phi, Gamma Sigma Delta Agrl. Alumni Soc. Republican. Office: Pa Ho of Reps PO Box 202020 Harrisburg PA 17120-2020

MILLER, SHEILA DIANE, language educator; b. Missoula, Mont., Nov. 24, 1957; d. Ray and Barbara Miller; m. Walter James Orzepowski, July 2, 1994. BA Polit. Sci. and Spanish, U. Idaho, Moscow, 1980; M, Boise State U., Idaho, 2002. Cert. Tchr. Secondary Edn. Idaho, 2002. Tchr. Bishop Kelly H.S., Boise, 1984—87, Kwassui Gakuin, Nagasaki, Kyushu, Japan, 1987—89; tchr. Japanese, Spanish, sheltered U.S. history Boise Pub. Schs., 1990—. Bd. mem. Cmty. Ho. Homeless Shelter, Boise, 1995—98; mem. choir St John's Ch., Boise, 1991—2006; v.p., bd. mem. Jr. League Boise, 1992—2003; bd. mem. Japanese Assn. Lang. Tchrs., Nagasaki, 1986—88. Recipient Golden Nugget, Jr. League Boise, 1995; grantee, Boise Schs. Found., 1995. Mem.: Idaho Assn. Tchrs. Lang. Culture (assoc.; pres., v.p., sect. leader 1995—2006, bd. dirs.), Alpha Chi Omega (life). D-Liberal. Roman Catholic. Avocations: travel, camping, gardening, politics. Home: 4170 N Azalea Lane Boise ID 83703 Office: Borah High School 6001 Cassia Boise ID 83709 Office Fax: 208-322-7371. E-mail: sheila.miller@boiseschools.org.

MILLER, SHERRY DUNCAN, elementary school educator; b. Lexington, Va., Nov. 28, 1962; d. John Houston Duncan and Ann Mackey Ewing; m. Ronald Lee Miller, Dec. 21, 1985; children: Reba Diane, Payton Lee. BS, Mary Baldwin Coll., Staunton, Va., 1984; M of Reading, U. Va., Charlottesville, 1991. Reading specialist, tchr. H. Waddell Elem. Sch., Lexington, Va., 1985—. Mem.: Internat. Reading Assn. Home: 733 S Main St Lexington VA 24450 Office: H Waddell Elem Sch 100 Pendleton Pl Lexington VA 24450

MILLER, SONJA GLAASER, counselor; b. Coos Bay, Oreg., Oct. 16, 1953; d. Eduard Glaaser and Gwendolyn (Elrod) Michael; m. David Weston Miller, Oct. 8, 1988; children: Benjamin Frank, Nicolas Johann, Alexandra Jane. BS in Bus. Fin., U. Oreg., 1978; MA in Counseling/Psychology, Lewis & Clark Coll., 1994. nat. cert. counselor; lic. profl. counselor, Oreg., 2001. Personal property appraiser Lane County Assessors, Eugene, Oreg., 1979; residential appraiser Jackson County Assessor, Medford, Oreg., 1979-82; camp dir., asst. dir. Silver Sage Girl Scout Coun., Boise, Idaho, summer 1983, 84; young program dir. Ch. of the Good Samaritan, Corvallis, Oreg., 1983-84; youth program cons. Corvallis, Oreg., 1983-86; alcohol and drug abuse counselor DePaul Adolescent Treatment Program, Portland, Oreg., 1987-88; social worker White Shield Ctr., Salvation Army, Portland, Oreg., 1994-99; counselor Chem. Dependency Svcs. Providence Portland Med. Ctr., 1999—2002; acute care coord. Multnomah County, 2002—05, sr. program devel. specialist, 2005—. Author: The Director's Handbook for Youth Conferences, 1983. Mem. youth commn. Diocese of Oreg., Portland, 1980-84, chair, 1984-86, program and budget com., 1993-96, Metro-east convocation, pres., 1996-98, ministry of all baptised task force, 1995-99; youth dir. vol. St. Mark's Ch., Medford, 1979-83; counselor vol. William Temple House, Portland, 1994; co-pres. MOMS Club Portland, 1993-94; sr. warden St. Michael All Angels Ch., Portland, 1993, mem. vestry, 1990-93, convener women's group, 1994-95, lay eucharistic min., 1996-99; mem. vestry All Saints Episc. Ch., 2002-05, lay eucharistic min., 2000—03, sr. warden 2002-03 Mem. ACA Democrat. Episcopalian. Avocations: sewing, gardening, reading, walking, cooking. E-mail: xalapa@teleport.com.

MILLER, SUE, information technology executive; Owner Sue Miller & Assoc., Atlanta. Leadership roles Tech. Assn. Ga., Digital Ball Exec. Com. Mem.: Women in Tech. Found. (pres.), Women in Tech. (pres. 2000, interim pres. 2006—, v.p., dir. fin.). Office: Women in Tech Ste A Box 473 4780 Ashford Dunwoody Rd Atlanta GA 30338-5504 Office Phone: 678-234-7329.*

MILLER, SUSAN ANN, retired school system administrator; b. Cleve., Nov. 24, 1947; d. Earl Wilbur and Marie Coletta (Hendershot) M. BS in Edn., Kent State U., 1969; MEd, Cleve. State U., 1975; PhD, Kent State U., 1993. Cert. supt.; cert. elem. prin., cert. elem. supervisor; cert. Learning Disabled/Behavior Disabled tchr.; cert. tchr. grades 1-8; cert. sch. counselor; lic. counselor. Tchr., guidance counselor, interim prin. North Royalton City Schs., Ohio, 1969-84; dir. elem. and spl. edn., acting supt., asst. supt. Ednl. Svc. Ctr. of Cuyahoga County, Valley View, Ohio, 1984—. Contbr. articles to profl. jours. Grantee Latchkey Program, State Dept. Edn., North Coast Leadership Forum, Peer Assistance and Rev., Entry Yr. Program, Alt. H.S. Mem. ASCD, Coun. Exceptional Children, Phi Delta Kappa. Office: ESC Cuyahoga County 5700 W Canal Rd Valley View OH 44125-3326 Home: 7236 Morning Star Trail Sagamore Hills OH 44067 Personal E-mail: sumrtoi47@yahoo.com.

MILLER, SUSAN LAURA, real estate company executive, retired special education educator; d. Martin and Bertha (Bottenstein) Fried; m. Carl William Miller, Apr. 5, 1970; children: Ryan Scott, Brent Todd. BA, Western Ky. U., 1970, MA in Spl. Edn., 1973. Cert. Tchr. in English, Spl. Edn., Psychology NY, Fla., Ga. Spl. edn. tchr. Morgantown Schs., Ky., 1970—73, Clayton County Schs., Jonesboro, Ga., 1973—80, Mid. Island Longwood HS, LI, NY, 1980—2001; v.p. Carl Miller Am. Yearbook Inc., 1992—2005; mktg. dir. Classic Experience; pres., owner Island Coastal Properties Mgmt. LLC, 2002—. Asst. developer spl. edn. curriculum. Mem. planning com. Ga. Spl. Olympics. Mem.: N.Y. State Retired tchrs. Assn., Flagler Point Condo Assn., Silver Sands Condominium Assn. (v.p. 2004—05), Ga. Jaycettes (Woman of Yr. 1976), Eau Gallie Yacht Club, Women's Club of Brevard, Sigma Kappa. Avocations: world travel, yachting, home designing. Home: 795 Loggerhead Island Way Satellite Beach FL 32937

MILLER, SUSAN M., telecommunications industry executive; BA in English Lit. and Art History, Dickinson Coll., 1981; JD, Cath. U. Columbus Sch. Law, 1984. Counsel telecomm. Weil, Gotshal, & Manges, N.Y.C.; counsel GTE; v.p., gen. counsel ATIS, Washington, 1988—99, pres., CEO, 1999—. Rep. ATIS FCC, Am. Nat. Stds. Inst., N.Am. Numbering Coun., Network Reliability and Interoperability Coun., Internat. Engring. Consortium Adv. Coun. Office: ATIS 1200 G St NW Ste 500 Washington DC 20005

MILLER, SUZANNE EVAGASH, education educator; b. Norfolk, Va., Dec. 15, 1943; d. Julius Joseph and Agnes Catherine (Klobuchar) Evagash; m. H. Curtis Miller Jr., July 31, 1965; children: Kimberly Suzanne Miller McLoughlin, Curtis Geoffrey. BS, Ind. U. Pa., 1965; MEd, Pa. State U., 1988; D, Duquesne U., 1997. Cert. elem. and secondary tchr., Pa. Tchr. Jefferson Union High Sch., Richmond, Ohio, 1965-66, Rocky Grove High Sch., Franklin, Pa., 1966-67; tchr. elem. Connellsville (Pa.) Area Sch. Dist., 1967-68; instr. C.C. Allegheny County, Pitts., 1973-83; head dept. Boyd Sch., Pitts., 1984-85; tchr. jr. high Shaler Area Sch.Dit., Glenshaw, Pa., 1985-87; tchr. North Catholic High Sch., Pitts., 1987-89; prof. Point Park U., Pitts., 1989—. Cons. Pa. Dept. Edn., Harrisburg; speaker workshop C.C. Allegheny County. Mem. utilization com. North Hills Sch. Dist., Pitts. Mem. ASCD, Pa. Assn. Coll. Tchr. Educators, Faculty Devel. Resource Assn., Phi Delta Kappa. Avocations: reading, walking, flea marketing. Office: Point Park U 201 Wood St Pittsburgh PA 15222-1984

MILLER, SUZANNE MARIE, library director, educator; b. Feb. 25, 1954; d. John Gordon and Dorothy Margaret (Sabatka) M.; 1 child, Altinay Marie. BA in English, U. S.D., 1975; MA in Library Sci., U. Denver, 1976, postgrad. in law, 1984. Librarian II U. S.D. Sch. of Law, Vermillion, 1977-78; law libr. U. LaVerne, Calif., 1978-85, instr. in law Calif., 1980-85; asst. libr. tech. svcs. McGeorge Sch. Law, Calif., 1985-99, prof. advanced legal rsch. Calif., 1994-99; state librarian S.D. State Library, Pierre, 1999—2004; state libr. Minn. State Libr. Svcs. and Sch. Tech., Roseville, 2004—. Co-author (with Elizabeth J. Pokorny) U.S. Government Documents: A Practical Guide for Library Assistants in Academic and Public Libraries, 1988; contbr. chpt. to book, articles to profl. jours. Pres. Short Grass Arts Coun., 2001—03; bd. dirs. Black Hills Playhouse Bd., 1999—2004, S.D. Ctr. for the Book Bd., 2002—04. Recipient A. Jurisprudence award Bancroft Whitney Pub. Co., 1983. Mem.: ALA, Minn. Ednl. Media Orgn., Minn. Libr. Assn., Western Coun. State Librs. (sec. 2001—02), Chief Officers of State Libr. Agys. (sec. 2002—04), Western Pacific Assn. Law Librs. (sec. 1990—94, pres. elect 1994—95, pres. 1995—96, local arrangements chair 1997), No. Calif. Assn. Law Librs. (mem. program com., inst. 1988), Mt. Plains Libr. Assn. (S.D. rep. to exec. bd. 2001—04), So. Calif. Assn. Law Librs. (arrangements com. 1981—82), Am. Assn. Law Librs., S.D. Libr. Assn. Roman Catholic. Home: 448 McCarrons Blvd So Roseville MN 55113 Office: Minn Dept Edn 1500 Hwy 36 West Roseville MN 55113-4266 Office Phone: 651-582-8251. Business E-Mail: suzanne.miller@state.mn.us.

MILLER, TANYA JOY, art educator; d. Jon Edwin and Helen Emma Stafsholt; m. Richard Eugene Miller, Aug. 3, 1996; children: Anna Lynn, Emma Lee. BA, Concordia Coll., Moorhead, Minn., 1993; MA, Bemidji State U., Minn., 2004; MFA, Minn. State U. Moorhead, 2005. Tchr. Clearbrook-Gonvick H.S., Minn., 1993—94, Park Rapids Area Schs., Minn., 1994—. Speech coach Park Rapids Area Schs., 1993—. Mem. Calvary Luth. Ch., Park Rapids, 1994—2006. Dfl. Office: Park Rapids Area School 401 Huntsinger Ave Park Rapids MN 56470

MILLER, THERESA L., library director; b. Port Huron, Mich., Apr. 2, 1959; d. David R. Miller and Mary Louise Preininger. AA, AS, St. Clair County C.C., Port Huron, Mich., 1990; BS, Wayne State U., 1992, MLIS, 1994. Support tutor St. Clair County C.C., 1988-89, master tutor, 1989-91; circulation supr. Baker Coll. of Port Huron, 1992-95, faculty math., 1998, faculty blackboard, ethics, libr., computers, 2005—, co-chair pres. adv. coun., 2005—; pub. spkr. Mich., 1988—; investigative asst. Huffmaster Cos., Port Huron, 1998-2000; libr. dir. Baker Coll. of Pt. Huron, 1995—; judge Bus. Profs. of Am., St. Clair County, 1994—2000, 2003—04. Baker coll. rep. County Tech. Adv. Com., St. Clair County, 1997—2003; mem. adv. bd. Baker Coll. of Port Huron Career Svcs., 1997—2003; judge Port Huron HS Writing Competition, 1997—2001. Editor: (newsletter) Baker Beacon, 1997; author: (newsletter) LUC News, 1993-96; author: (book) A Reference Librarians User Guide to the Internet, 1993. Recorder for the blind Libr. of Mich., Lansing, 1996-2004; mem. gov. bd. Seaway Cmty. Freenet, St. Clair County, 1995-96; pres., founding bd. dirs. First Night of Port Huron, 2001-04; bd. dirs. Girl Scouts Mich. Waterways Council, 2006—; mem. St. Clair County Pub. Libr. Friends, 2004-. Mem.: AAUW, ALA, Internat. Libr. Support Group (founder 1999—2005, chmn.), Librs. Using Computers/Mich. (chair 1994—96), Mich. Libr. Assn., Optimists (Port Huron bd. dir. 1997—99, pres. Pt. Huron chpt. 2000—01, lt. gov. Mich. 2001—04, Port Huron bd. dir. 2004—05), St. Clair County Pub. Libr. Friends, Phi Theta Kappa (treas. 1989—90, founding alumni pres. St. Clair C.C. chpt. 1991). Avocations: singing professionally, collecting jewelry, auctions, theater, investing. Office: Baker Coll Port Huron Libr 3403 Lapeer Rd Port Huron MI 48060 Office Phone: 810-989-2122. Business E-Mail: theresa.miller@baker.edu.

MILLER, VALERIE CAROL, journalist; b. Chgo. d. V. Heinz and Arlene Elizabeth Miller. A in Gen. Studies, C.C. So. Nev.; BA Comms., U. Nev., 1998. Travel coord. Great Escape Travel, Las Vegas, 1996—97; staff writer, reporter U. Nev. Las Vegas Rebel Yell Students Newspaper, 1997—98; travel coord. World Travel and Accessories, Las Vegas, 1998—2000; reporter, freelance writer, intern Las Vegas Sun Newspaper, 1998—2000; broadcaster, disk jockey Sta. KLAV AM 1230, Las Vegas, 1997—; reporter, staff writer Las Vegas Bus. Press Newspaper, 2000—; staff writer Las Vegas Sr. Press. Host radio show Valerie's Music Magic. Vol. Shade Tree Shelter, Las Vegas, 2002; vol. writer Nev. Times Newspaper, Las Vegas, 1995, 1997. Nominee Journalist of Merit award, Nev. Press Assn., 2002, 2003, Small Bus. Journalist of Yr., Nev. Small Bus. Adminstrn., 2003; recipient Best Feature Story award third prize, Nev. Press Assn., 2001, Small Bus. Journalist of Yr. award for Nev., U.S. Small Bus. Assn., 2002, Merit award for news writing, Internat. Assn. Bus. Comm., 2003, Merit award for series writing, 2003, 2005, Best Bus. Story award, Nev. Press. Assn., 2002, 2004. Fellow: Soc. for the Advanced Placement of Materials, Working in Comms., Soc. Profl. Journalists, 3rd Wave Nev., Tortois Group; mem.: Phi Lambda Eta. Avocations: travel, writing poems and song lyrics, movies. Office: Las Vegas Bus Press 1385 Pama Ln Ste 111 Las Vegas NV 89119 Office Phone: 702-871-6780 ext. 331. Personal E-mail: millerv52@hotmail.com. Business E-Mail: vmiller@lvpress.com.

MILLER, VIRGINIA IRENE, fine art galleries executive; b. Tampa, Fla., May 29, 1943; d. Chester Howard and Marie M.; A.A., Miami-Dade Community Coll., 1969; B.A. in Psychology, U. Miami, 1973; m. William Robert DuPriest, June 16, 1974. Art cons., organizer, dir. numerous art exhbns. for leading charities, fin. instns., Dade County, Fla., 1969-73; owner, dir. Virginia Miller Galleries, Inc., Coconut Grove, Fla., 1974-84; owner, dir. ArtSpace/Virginia Miller Galleries, Coral Gables, Fla., 1981—; guest lectr. Miami-Dade Community Coll. Ctr. Continuing Edn. of Women, 1984, U. Miami, 1985, Fla. Internat. U., 1985; pres. MACH I, Met. Mus. and Art Ctrs., Coral Gables, 1979-80, also mem. community relations com.; panelist, New Sch., N.Y.C., 1978; juror Artist's Day Competition, Coconut Grove 110th Birthday Celebration, 1984, Mus. of Sci. Left Bank Art; curator Miami ARTSfest, 1985; guest panelist Spl. Assignment: The Outlook for the Arts, WLRN-TV, 1985, art writer Women's Almanac newspaper, 1978-79; del. Gov.'s Conf. on Small Bus., 1983; community relations com., dir. Met. Mus. and Art Centers, 1979-80; mem. loan com. Fla. Feminist Credit Union, Miami, 1978-79; mem. adv. bd. The Coral Gables City Beautiful mag., 1983-85; bd. dirs. Miami Forum, 1984—; mem. exec. com. South Fla. Wilderness Camp, 1983, Jack and Ruth Eckerd Found.; press delegate White House Conf. on small bus., Washington. Mem. Coral Gables C. of C. (mem. beautification com., 1977, chmn. cultural affairs com. 1979-81), Coconut Grove C. of C. (dir., chmn. cultural affairs com. 1978-79, chmn. tourism com. 1979-80), Greater Miami C. of C. (mem. econ. devel. com., 1985-86), Nat. Found. for the Advancement of the Arts (mem. Com. of 1000, panelist Fla. Cultural Conf., 1984), Art Dealers Assn. South Fla. (treas. 1978-79), Phi Kappa Phi, Psi Chi. Address: Artspace 169 Madeira Ave Coral Gables FL 33134 Office Phone: 305-444-4493. Office Fax: 305-444-9844.

MILLER, VIRGINIA MEREDITH, secondary school educator; b. Tulsa, Dec. 15, 1944; d. Russell Porter Hester and June Constance Calhoun; m. Walter Arthur Miller, Aug. 2, 1969; 1 child, Hester. BS in Bus. Adminstrn. and Econs., McPherson Coll., Kans., 1967; MS in Edn., Pittsburg State U., Kans., 1985. Sec. Farmland Industries, McPherson, Kans., 1968—69; tchr. Chelsea Pub. Schs., Okla., 1970—74; owner, mgr. Chelsea Const., Okla., 1974—96; tchr., career and tech. edn. Coffeyville Pub. Schs., Kans., 1987—. Mem., ASSET bd. Dept. Commerce, Independence, Kans., 1998—; mem. adv. bd. Coffeyville CC, Kans., 1999—; grantwriter, coord. Indian edn. and career and tech. edn., Coffeyville; owner, mgr. Chelsea Constrn., Leasing and Equipment Co., Coffeyville. Life mem., coun. mem. Girl Scouts Am., Kans., 1951—. Mem.: NEA, Cherokee Nation. Avocations: travel, Southwest Indian art and jewelery, house restoration. Address: 1110 W 8th St Coffeyville KS 67337 Business E-Mail: millerv@cvilleschools.com.

MILLER, WILMA HILDRUTH, education educator; b. Dixon, Ill., Mar. 8, 1936; d. William Alexander and Ruth Karin (Hanson) M. BS in Edn., No. Ill. U., DeKalb, 1958, MS in Edn., 1961; DEd, U. Ariz., 1967. Cert. reading specialist. Elem. tchr. Dist. 170, Dixon, Ill., 1958-63, Dist. 1, Tucson, Ariz., 1963-64; asst. prof. edn. Wis. State U., Whitewater, 1965-68; assoc. prof. edn. Ill. State U., Normal, 1968-72, prof., 1972-98, prof. emeritus, 1998—. Author: Diagnosing and Correcting Reading Difficulties in Children, 1988, Reading Comprehension, 1990, Complete Reading Disabilities Handbook, 1993, Alternative Assessment Techniques in Reading and Writing, 1995, Reading and Writing Remediation Kit, 1997, The Reading Teacher's Survival Kit, 2001, Reading Skills Problem Solver, 2002, Survival Reading Skills for Secondary School Students, 2003, 101 Ways for Developing Emergent Literacy, 2004, others; contbr. over 225 articles to profl. jours. Altar Guild, usher, greeter, communion asst. Our Saviour Luth. Ch., Normal, 1990—. Recipient Outstanding Contbn. to Edn. award No. Ill. U., 1998. Mem. Internat. Reading Assn. (parent and reading com. 1972-74, editl. adv. bd. 1995-98, Outstanding Dissertation award 1968), Mid-State Reading Coun. (editl. adv. bd. 1991-98), Alpha Upsilon Alpha (advisor Reading chpt. 1993-98), Pi Lambda Theta, Kappa Delta Pi, Phi Delta Kappa. Avocations: travel, writing, reading, antiques. Home: 302 N Coolidge St Normal IL 61761-2435 Personal E-mail: whmille@ilstu.edu.

MILLER, YVONNE BOND, state legislator, educator; b. Edenton, NC; d. John and Pency Bond. BS, Va. State Coll., Petersburg, 1956; postgrad., Va. State Coll., Norfolk, 1966; MA, Columbia U., 1962; PhD, U. Pitts., 1973; postgrad., CCNY, 1976. Tchr. Norfolk Pub. Schs., 1956-68; asst. prof. Norfolk State U., 1968-71, assoc. prof., 1971-74, prof., 1974-88, head dept. early childhood/elem. edn., 1984-87; mem. Va. Ho. Dels., Richmond, 1984-87, mem. edn. com., health, welfare and instns. com., militia and police com., 1983-87; mem. Va. Senate, Richmond, 1988—. Commerce and labor com., gen. laws com., transp. com., rehab. and social svcs. com. Va. Senate, HIV subcom., remediation subcom., unemployment compensation act subcom., infants and toddlers with disabilities subcom.; mem. intergovtl. coop. commn., youth commn., disability commn., Va. Coun. Coord. Prevention commn.; cons. in field. Commr. Ea. Va. Med. Authority; adv. bd. Va. Divsn. Children; active Faith Temple Ch. of God in Christ. 1st black woman to be elected to Ho. of Dels. Legislature, 1983, 1st black woman to be elected to Va. Senate, 1987. Mem. Nat. Alliance Black Sch. Educators (life; bd. dirs.), Va. Assn. for Early Childhood Edn., Nat. Assn. Dem. Chairs, Zeta Phi Beta (past officer). Office: 2539 Corprew Ave Norfolk VA 23504-3909 also: 555 Fenchurch St # 403 Norfolk VA 23510 also: Va Senate Gen Assembly Bldg Rm 315 Richmond VA 23219 Office Phone: 757-627-4212. Fax: 757-627-7203. Personal E-mail: senatorybmiller@verizon.net. E-mail: ybmiller1@aol.com.

MILLER, ZOYA DICKINS, civic worker, consultant; b. Washington, July 15, 1923; d. Randolph and Zoya Pavlovna (Klementinovska) Dickins; m. Hilliard Eve Miller, Jr., Dec. 6, 1943; children: Jeffrey Arnot, Hilliard Eve III. Grad., Stuart Sch. Costume Design, Washington, 1942; student, Cochran Galleries of Fine Arts, 1942, Sophie Newcomb Coll., 1944, New Eng. Conservatory Music, 1946, Colo. Coll., 1965; grad., Internat. Sch. Reading, 1969; student, Cochran Galleries of Fine Arts, 1942. Lic. pvt. pilot. Instr. Stuart Summer Sch. Costume Design, Washington, 1942; fashion coord. Julius Garfinckel, Washington, 1942-43; fashion coord., cons. Mademoiselle mag., 1942-44; star TV show Cowbelle Kitchen, 1957-58, Flair for Living, 1958-59; model mags. and comml. films, also nat. comml. recs., 1956-80; dir. rsch. devel. Webb-Waring Inst. Cancer, Aging and Antioxidant Rsch., Denver, 1973—2006, devel. cons., 2006—. Contbr. articles, lectrs. on health care sys. and fund raising. Mem. exec. com., bd. dirs. El Paso County chpt. Am. Lung Assn. Colo., 1965—84, bd. dirs., 1965—87, chmn. radio and TV coun., 1963—70, mem. med. affairs com., 1965—70, pres., 1965—66, procurer found. funds, 1965—70; developer nat. radio ednl. prodns. for internat. use Am. Lung Assn., 1963—70, coord. statewide pulmonary screening programs Colo., other states, 1965—72; chmn. benefit fund raising El Paso County Cancer Soc., 1963; co-founder, coord. Colorado Springs Debutante Ball, 1967—; coord. Nat. Gov.'s Comprehensive Health Planning Coun., 1967—74, chmn., 1971—72, Colo. Chronic Care Com., 1969—73, chmn. fund raising, 1970—72, chmn. spl. com. conl. studies on nat. health bills, 1971—73; mem. Colo.-Wyo. Regional Med. Program Adv. Coun., 1969—73, Colo. Med. Found. Consumers Adv. Coun., 1972—78; mem. decorative arts com. Colorado Springs Fine Arts Ctr., 1972—75; founder, state coord. Nov. Noel Pediat. Benefit Am. Lung Assn., 1973—87; founder, chmn. bd. dirs. Newborn Hope, Inc., 1987—; mem. adv. bd. Wagon Wheel Girl Scouts, 1991—94; mem. cmty. adv. coun. Beth-El Nursing Sch., 1998—; chmn. Colo. Festival World Theatre Gala, 2005; gala chmn. Colorado Festival World Theatre, 2005; maj. donor devel. dir. Meml. Health Sys., Colorado Springs, 2006—; bd. dirs. Episcopal Columbarium Assn., 2001, The Family Attachment Ctr., Inc., Meml. Hosp. Found., Colo. Springs, Colo., 2004; hon. bd. mem. KCME 88.7 FM, Colorado Springs, Colo., 2004; gala chmn. Colo. Festival of World Theatre, 2005; maj. donor devel. dir. Meml. Health Sys., Colo. Springs, 2006—. Zoya Dickins Miller Vol. of Yr. award established Am. Lung Assn. of Colo., 1979; recipient James J. Waring award Colo. Conf. on Respiratory Disease Workers, 1963, Nat. Pub. Rels. award Am. Lung Assn., 1979, Gold Double Bar Cross award, 1980, 83, Jefferson award Am. Inst. Pub. Svc., 1991, Thousand Points of Light award The White House, 1992, Recognition award So. Colo. Women's C. of C., 1994, Silver Spur Cmty. award Pikes Peak Range Riders, 1994, Silver Bell award Assistance League Colorado Springs, 1996, Svc. to Mankind award Centennial Sertoma Club, 1997, Help Can't Wait award Pikes Peak chpt. ARC, 1997, Cmty. Weaver award The Independent News, 1997, Apgar award Colo. March of Dimes, 1998; named Humanitarian of Yr., Am. Lung Assn. of Colo., 1987, El Pomar Found. award for Excellence, Russell Tutt Leadership award, 2004. Mem.: Nat. Soc. Fund Raising Execs., Denver Round Table for Planned Giving, Colo. Assn. Fund Raisers, Nat. Soc. Colonial Dames, The Family Attachment Ctr., Nat. Cowbell Assn. (El Paso county pres. 1954, TV chmn., chmn. nat. Father of Yr. contest Colo. 1956—57), Broadmoor Garden Club, Garden of the Gods Club, Cheyenne Mountain Country Club. Home: 74 W Cheyenne Mountain Blvd Colorado Springs CO 80906-4336 E-mail: hope4455@adelphia.net.

MILLER-DREUSICKE, CONNIE ANNE, special education educator; b. Danville, Ill., Oct. 14, 1960; d. Arthur John Rudolph and Jane Ellen (Patterson) Dreusicke; children: Drew Arthur Miller, Blake Aaron Miller, Hannah Marie Miller. BS in Spl. Edn., Ill. State U., Normal, 1982; MS in Human Resource Devel., Clemson U., SC, 1995. Spl. edn. tchr. McKinley Sch., Danville, 1982—85; spl. edn. tchr., dept. head West Ashley High, Charleston, SC, 1985—. Summer camp dir. ARC, Summerville, SC, 1985—88. Basketball coach Upwards-Charleston Bapt. Ch., Charleston, 2005—06; coach Spl. Olympics, Ill., 1985—, SC, 1985—; sec., bd. dirs. PTA, Danville, 1982—85. Mem.: Coun. for Exceptional Children (sec. 1987—89).

MILLER-DUFFY, MERRITT, insurance agent, camp director; b. Summit, N.J., July 16, 1966; d. Bertram B. and Lynne Clutsam Miller; m. James F. Duffy, Aug. 8, 1987; 1 child, Heather Ogden Duffy. BA, Cedar Crest Coll., 1988. Sr. underwriter St. Paul Fire & Marine Ins. Co., Iselin, N.J., 1988-93; v.p. B.B. Miller & Co., Elizabeth, N.J., 1993—. Asst. dir. Adirondack Camp, Putnam Sta., N.Y., 1999—, mem. adv. bd., 1996—. Vol. Jr. League of Summit, 1988-91; trustee CMI Cmty. Ctr., Inc., Elizabeth, 1999—; bd. dirs., vol. Jr. Achievement of Union County, N.J., Elizabeth, 1996—. Dir. of Distinction award, 1999. Recipient Vol. of Yr. award Jr. Achievement of Union County, 1996-97, Silver Life Card award Union County Conf. of PBA Dels., 1999. Mem. Ind. Ins. Agts., Nat. Assn. Ins. Women (cert. profl. ins. woman, sec. N.J. chpt. 1995-96, cert. ins. counselor), Young Agts. Coun. (county rep. 1996-97), 200 Club of Union County, Inc. (officer, trustee 1993—), N.J. State PBA (hon., life). Avocations: painting, gardening, community volunteer work. Office: B B Miller Co PO Box 260 Elizabeth NJ 07207-0260

MILLER-ENGEL, MARJORIE, foundation administrator, commissioner, small business owner; d. David Harry Siegel and Ruth Joan Gord; m. Robert Alan Engel, May 4, 1984; 1 child, Liana Laura Engel. BA, Syracuse U.; cert. in interior design, N.Y. Sch. Interior Design. Assoc. dir. devel. Planned Parenthood Fedn., N.Y.C.; account exec. Harold Oram Consulting, N.Y.C.; pres., owner Marjorie Miller Pub. Rels., N.Y.C.; founder, chmn. Life Ctr. Youth, Inc., Santa Fe, 1982—; pres., owner M. M. Designs, Inc., Santa Fe, 1989—. Co-owner Greenkey Property Investments, Santa Fe, 1989—. Commr. N.Mex Commn. Status Women, 2003—. Mem.: Intl. Women's Forum. Office: Life Ctr Youth Inc PO Box 8718 2725 Agua Fria St Santa Fe NM 87504

MILLER-LACHMANN, LYN, editor; b. Lubbock, Tex., July 31, 1956; d. Arnold Myron Miller and Suzanne Selber Miler; m. Richard William Lachmann, July 30, 1993; children: Derrick Karl, Madeleine Margaret. BA, Princeton U., N.J., 1978; MA, Yale U., New Haven, Conn., 1981; MLS, U. Wis., 1990. Tchr. N.Y.C. Pub. Schs., 1981—83; ref. libr. Siena Coll., Loudonville, NY, 1990—94; editor-in-chief Multicultural Rev., Tampa, Fla., 1994—. Author: Hiding Places, 1988, Dirt Cheap, 2006; co-author: Schools for All: Educating Children in a Diverse Society, 1995, Downsized But Not Defeated: The Family Guide to Living on Less, 1997; editor: Our Family, Our Friends, Our World: An Annotated Guide to Significant Multicultural Books for Children and Teenagers, 1993, Global Voices, Global Visions: A Core Collection of Multicultural Books, 1995, Once Upon a Cuento: Short Stories for Children by Latino Writers, 2004; author: (plays) Murder on the Campaign Trail, 2003. Supr. team, referral specialist CAPTAIN Shenendohowa, Clifton Pk., NY, 1990—2005; tchr. religous sch. Cong. Gates Heaven, Schenectady, NY, 1999—; bd. liaison Freedom To Read Found., Chgo., 2003—. Grantee, Puffin Found., 2004. Mem.: ALA (bd. dirs. roundtable 1998—2002, Dinali Press award 1993), Soc. Children's Book Writers and Illustrators (Work in Progress award 1989), Internat. Women Writers Guild. Democrat. Jewish. Avocations: bicycling, hiking. Office: Goldman Group 4125 Gunn Hwy Ste B1 Tampa FL 33618 Office Phone: 518-729-3976. Personal E-mail: mcreview@aol.com.

MILLER-LANE, BARBARA See LANE, BARBARA

MILLER-LERMAN, LINDSEY, state supreme court justice; b. L.A., July 30, 1947; BA, Wellesley Coll., 1968; JD, Columbia U., 1973; LHD (hon.), Coll. of St. Mary, Omaha, 1993. Bar: N.Y. 1974, U.S. Dist. Ct. (so. dist.) N.Y. 1974, U.S. Ct. Appeals (2d cir.) 1974, Nebr. 1976, U.S. Dist. Ct. (ea. dist.) N.Y. 1975, U.S. Dist. Ct. Nebr. 1976, U.S. Ct. Appeals (8th cir.) 1979, U.S. Supreme Ct. 1982, U.S. Ct. Appeals (6th cir.) 1984, U.S. Ct. Appeals (10th cir.) 1987. Law clk. U.S. Dist. Ct., N.Y.C., 1973-75; from assoc. to ptnr. Kutak Rock, Omaha, 1975-92; judge Nebr. Ct. Appeals, Lincoln, 1992-98, chief judge, 1996-98; justice Nebr. Supreme Ct., 1998—. Contbr. articles to profl. jours. Bd. dirs. Tuesday Musical, Omaha, 1985—. Office: Nebr Supreme Ct State Capitol Rm 2222 Lincoln NE 68509 Office Phone: 402-471-3734.

MILLER-PERRIN, CINDY LOU, psychology professor; b. McKeesport, Pa., Feb. 26, 1962; d. Emerson and Helen Francis (Beck) M.; m. Robin D. Perrin, Aug. 3, 1985; children: Jacob, Madison. BA, Pepperdine U., Malibu, Calif., 1983; MS, Washington State Univ., 1987; PhD, Washington State U., 1991. Psychology intern Univ. Wash., Seattle, 1990-91, postdoctoral fellow, 1991-92; asst. prof. Pepperdine Univ., Malibu, Calif., 1992-96, assoc. prof., 1996—2002, prof. psychology, 2002—. Author: Preventing Child Sexual Abuse: Sharing., 1992, Family Violence Across the Lifespan, 1997, 2d edit. 2005, Child Maltreatment, 1999, 2d edit. 2006; contbr. articles to profl. jours. Mem. APA, Am. Psychol. Soc., Western Psychol. Assn., Internat. Soc. Prevention of Child Abuse Neglect, Am. Profl. Soc. on the Abuse of Children, Sigma Xi. Avocations: hiking, backpacking, golf, travel. Office: Pepperdine Univ Social Sci Div Malibu CA 90263 Office Phone: 310-506-4027. Business E-Mail: cindy.perrin@pepperdine.edu.

MILLER SCHEAR, ANNICE MARA, music educator; d. Trina C. and Herbert K Miller; 1 child, Ilana T. Schear. MusM, Cleve. State U., Cleve. Ohio, 1998—2002; MusB Edn., Kent State U., Kent, Ohio, 1990—93; BA in Comm. Arts, U. of Cin., Cin., Ohio, 1981—85. Orff Music Certification 1999, Kodaly Music Certification 2001, cert. nat. bd. cert. tchr. early adolescent/young adult Nat. Bd. for Profl. Tchg. Stds., 2004. Music educator St. Ann Ch., Cleve. Heights, 1993—94, St. Joan of Arc Ch., Chagrin Falls, Ohio, 1993—94, Hebrew Acad. of Cleve., 1994—95; vocal music dir. Nathan Hale Mid. Sch., Cleve., 1995—. Dept. chairperson of fine arts Nathan Hale Mid. Sch., Cleveland, Ohio, 2000—, profl. devel. presenter, 2001—, acad. AAP facilitator, 2002—, mem. acad. AAP team, 1996—2002; music dir. Beachwood Cmty. Theater, 2003—; asst. dir. jr. choir Anshe Chesed Fairmount Temple, 2003—. Author: (jour. article) OMEA - TRIAD Jour. Mem. Anshe Chesed - Fairmount Temple, Beachwood, Ohio, 1986—. Recipient Tchr. Recognition of the Yr., Nathan Hale Mid. Sch., 2002, PTA Reflections Chairperson Recognition, Southlyn Elem. Sch., 2003, Lifetime Achievement award, Ohio PTA, 2005; grantee Monetary award for multicultural music materials, The Huntington Nat. Bank, 2002, Computer Lab, Cleve. Mcpl. Sch. Dist., 1999—2001, Monetary grant for Character Edn., City of Cleve. - Neighborhood Block Grant, 1996—98. Mem.: South Euclid Lyndhurst PTA (1st v.p. coun. 2004—), Ohio Music Educators Assn. (multicultural rep. 1999—), Ohio Music Educators Assn. (sec. 2002—04), The Nat. Assn. of Music Educators, Anshe Chesed - Fairmount Temple Chorale (music com.), Meml. Jr. H.S. PTA (pres. 2005—), Greenview Upper Elementary PTA (pres. 2003—05), Southlyn Elem. PTA (v.p. 2000—02), Sigma Delta Tau Soc. Avocations: musical theater, board games, travel, inline skating, exercise. Home: 4102 Ellison Road South Euclid OH 44121 Personal E-mail: amschear@aol.com.

MILLER-SEDA, RHONDA GRACE, elementary school educator; b. Everett, Pa., June 29, 1953; d. Ronald W. Miller and N. Grace Miller, (nee Hartle); m. E. Elliott Seda, Sept. 1, 1979. BS in Music Edn., Elizabethtown Coll., Elizabethtown, Pa., 1975; MEd, Penn State U., State College, Pa., 1980. Tchr. elem. vocal music Dover Area Sch. Dist., Pa., 1980—. Home: 12 Rumford Court Lancaster PA 17602 Office: Dover Area School District School Lane Dover PA 17315 Office Phone: 717-292-3671.

MILLER-SYDNEY, AUDREY YVONNE, music educator; d. Joseph Horace Miller and Edith Mae Gibson-Miller. BA, Va. State U., Petersburg, 1960; MusM, Manhattan Sch. Music, NYC, 1966. Cert. tchr. NY. Choral and music instr. Irving N. Taylor Jr. HS, Danville, Va., 1960—62, NYC Pub. Schs., NYC, 1963—65; vocal and instrumental tchr. Union Settlement Music Sch., NYC, 1963—67; music tchr. Joan of Arc Jr. HS, NYC, 1967—68; project coord. Salem Crescent Learning Ctr., NYC, 1979—80; chmn. music, magnet coord. Dr. Alfred M. Franko Magnet Sch., Mt. Vernon, NY, 1978—97; adj. prof. music appreciation Coll. New Rochelle, NY, 2002—. Home: Apt 4B 730 Riverside Dr New York NY 10031-2444 E-mail: amsydney02@verizon.net.

MILLER UDELL, BRONWYN, judge; b. Danbury, Conn., Aug. 7, 1972; BA, Barnard Coll., Columbia U., 1994; JD, U. Miami, 1997. Bar: (Fla.) 1997. Asst. state atty. State of Fla., Miami, 1997—2005; judge Dade County, 2005—. Adj. faculty Fla. Internat. U., 2001—02; mem. Witness Justice Adv. Bd. Mem. Cmtys. in Schs. Miami Mentoring Program, Coral Gables Sr. H.S. Parent Tchr. Assn.; co-chair Expert Corps. Vol. Mem.: League of Prosecutors (bd. dir.), Fla. Assn. Women Lawyers, Fla. Pros. Attys. Assn., Federalist Soc. Lawyer's Divsn., Elephant Forum, Phi Delta Phi. Office: South Dade Justice Ctr 10710 SW 211th St Miami FL 33189 Office Phone: 305-252-5840.

MILLETT, KATE (KATHERINE MURRAY MILLETT), political activist, sculptor, artist, writer; b. St. Paul, Sept. 14, 1934; m. Fumio Yoshimura, 1965. BA magna cum laude, U. Minn., 1956; postgrad. with 1st class honors, St. Hilda's Coll. Oxford, Eng., 1956-58; PhD with distinction, Columbia U., 1970. Instr. English U. N.C. at Greensboro, 1958; file clk. N.Y.C.; kindergarten tchr., 1960-61; sculptor, Tokyo, 1961-63; tchr. Barnard Coll., 1964-70; tchr. English Bryn Mawr (Pa.) Coll., 1970. Disting. vis. prof. Sacramento State Coll., 1972—73; adj. prof. NYU, N.Y.C.; founder Women's Art Colony Farm, Poughkeepsie, NY; rep. as non-govtl. orgn. on behalf of human rights UN. Author: Sexual Politics, 1970, The Prostitution Papers, 1973, Flying, 1974, Sita, 1977, The Basement, 1979, Going to Iran, 1982, The Loony Bin Trip, 1990, The Politics of Cruelty, 1994, A.D., 1995, Mother Millett, 2001; co-prodr., co-dir. film Three Lives, 1970; one-woman shows Minami Gallery, Tokyo, Judson Gallery, N.Y.C., 1967, Noho Gallery, N.Y.C., 1976, 79, 80, 82, 84, 86, 93, 99, 2001, Women's Bldg., L.A., 1977; drawings Andre Wanters Gallery, Berlin, 1980, Courtland Jessup Gallery, Provincetown, Mass., 1991, 92, 93, 94, 95, 98, 99, Retrospective Exhbn., U. Md., 1997, Hunter Coll., 1998, Northampton Ctr. for the Arts, 1998, John Jay Coll., N.Y.C., 1998, Nohs Gallery, 2002. Mem. Congress of Racial Equality; chmn. edn. com. NOW, 1966; active supporter gay and women's liberation groups, also mental patients liberation and political prisoners; UN rep. for polit. prisoners. Mem. Phi Beta Kappa.

MILLICAN, FRANCES KENNEDY, psychiatrist; b. Steubenville, Ohio, Nov. 17, 1918; d. John Luther and Maude (Silliman) Kennedy; m. Roscoe Carl Millican, Dec. 27, 1945 (dec. 1964); children: Mary Carol, Jean Madeleine, Adrienne Frances. BS, Peabody Coll., Nashville, 1938; MS, U. Tenn., Memphis, 1946; MD, U. Tenn., 1948. Intern St. Elizabeth Hosp., Washington, 1948—49, resident, 1949—50, VA Op, 1950—51, Children's Hosp., Washington, 1954—56; psychiatrist VA Outpatient Clinic, Washington, 1952-53; research/faculty assoc. Children's Hosp. of D.C., 1956-75; clin. assoc. prof. psychiatry Georgetown U., Washington, 1965—2004; pvt. practice psychiatry Bethesda, Md., 1956—2004; supr. adult and child Seattle Psychoanalytic Inst., 2005—. Supervising and tng. analyst Washington Psychoanalytic Inst., 1970-2004; cons. NIMH, Bethesda, 1975-1996. Contbr. articles to profl. jours. Fellow Am. Psychiatric Assn.; mem. Am. Psychoanalytic Assn., Assn. for Child Psychoanalysis, Am. Acad. Child and Adolescent Psychiatry, Washington Psychoanalytic Soc. (pres. 1981-83), Washington Psychoanalytic Inst. (chmn. edn. com. 1986-89), Alpha Omega Alpha. Unitarian Universalist. Office Phone: 206-325-2237.

MILLIGAN, KRISTA, drafting educator; B off Tech., No. Mont. Coll., Havre, 1990. Drafting instr. ITT Edn. Svcs., San Bernardino, Calif., 1990—2000, Mont. State U.-No., Havre, 2002—. Mem.: Am. Design Drafting Assn.

MILLIGAN, MARGARET ERIN, science educator; b. Grand Rapids, Mich., Aug. 31, 1979; d. Nell Milligan. BS in Biology, Mich. State U., E. Lansing, 2001. Sci. tchr./robotics mentor Oak Pk. Sch. Dist., Mich., 2002—. Office Phone: 248-691-8412.

MILLIGAN, SISTER MARY, theology studies educator, consultant; b. LA, Jan. 23, 1935; d. Bernard Joseph and Carolyn (Krebs) M. BA, Marymount Coll., 1956; Dr. de l'Univ., U. Paris, 1959; MA in Theology, St. Mary's Coll., Notre Dame, Ind., 1966; STD, Gregorian U., 1975; D. honoris causa, Marymount U., 1988. Tchr. Cours Marymount, Neuilly, France, 1956-59; asst. prof. Marymount Coll., Los Angeles, 1959-67; gen. councillor Religious of Sacred Heart of Mary, Rome, 1969-75, gen. superior, 1980-85; asst. prof. Loyola Marymount U., Los Angeles, 1977-78, provost, 1986-90, prof., 1990—96, dean liberal arts, 1992-97, provincial superior, 1997—2003; prof. St. John's Sem., 2003—. Pres. bd. dirs. St. John's Sem., Camarillo, Calif., 1986-89; mem. exec. com. Internat. Union Superiors Gen., Rome, 1983-85; mem. planning bd. spiritual renewal program Loyola Marymount U., Los Angeles, 1976-78. Author: That They May Have Life, 1975; compiler analytical index Ways of Peace, 1986; contbr. articles to profl. jours. Vis. scholar Grad. Theol. Union, Berkeley, 1986. Mem. Coll. Theology Soc., Cath. Biblical Assn. Democrat. Roman Catholic. Business E-Mail: mmilligan@stjohnsem.edu.

MILLIKEN, MARY SUE, chef, television personality, writer; Former mem. staff Le Perroquet, Chgo., Restaurant d'Olympe, Paris; formerly chef, co-owner City Cafe, L.A.; chef, co-owner CITY, L.A., 1985—94, Border Grill, L.A., 1985—91, Santa Monica, 1990—. Co-host (TV series) Too Hot Tamales, 1995—, Tamales' World Tour, (radio show) Good Food; co-author: City Cuisine, 1989, Mesa Mexicana, 1994, Cantina, 1996, Cooking with Too Hot Tamales, 1997; guest appearances (TV series) Oprah Winfrey Show, Maury Povich, Today Show, Sabrina the Teenage Witch, featured in USA Today, People Mag., Entertainment Weekly. Active Scleroderma Rsch. Found. Named Chef of Yr., Calif. Restaurant Writers, 1993. Mem.: Chef's Collaborative 2000, Women Chefs and Restaurateurs. Office: Border Grill 1445 4th St Santa Monica CA 90401*

MILLION, CHARLENE R., music educator, church administrator; b. Warsaw, Mo. d. Charles Raymond and Betty Sue O'Laughlin; m. Kevin Million; 1 child, Ashley; 1 child, Amanda Ballard. BEd, Hannibal Lagrange Coll., 1989; MEd, Central Mo. State U., 1996. Elem. music tchr. Warsaw K-9 Sch., 1989—2005, h.s. vocal music tchr., 2005—; music dir. Warsaw Baptist Ch., 1999—2005. Mem.: MNEA, Music Educators Nat. Conf. Avocations: singing, reading, boating, bicycling. Office: Warsaw R-9 Sch PO Box 248 Warsaw MO 65355 Office Phone: 660-438-7351. Business E-Mail: million@warsaw.k12.mo.us.

MILLMAN, AMY J., government official; b. Bklyn., June 12, 1954; m. Aug. 3, 1984; 2 children. BA in History, Carnegie Mellon U., 1976; MPA, George Washington U., 1978. Rschr. Congl. Quar., Inc., Washington, 1976-79; analyst OSHA, Dept. Labor, Washington, 1979-81; Washington rep. The Philip Morris Cos., Inc., 1981-91; dir. legis. affairs The Am. Trucking Assn., Inc., Washington, 1991-93; exec. dir. Nat. Women's Bus. Coun., Washington, 1993—2001; pres. Springboard Enterprises, 2001—. Adj. prof. George Washington U., Sch. Bus. and Public Mgmt., 2001—; bd. advisors Enterprising Woman Magazine, 2001—. Mem. Phi Kappa Phi.

MILLMAN, LAURA DIANE, federal official; b. NYC, Apr. 23, 1946; BA cum laude, City Coll., 1966; MA, Lehman Coll., 1969; JD cum laude, Fordham U., 1976. Bar: N.Y. 1977, D.C. 1978, Md. 1987. Honors program trial atty. US Dept. Justice, NYC, Washington, 1976-88; ptnr. West & Galebach, Gaithersburg, Md., 1988-91; spl. master US Ct. Fed. Claims, Washington, 1991—. Avocations: synchronized swimming, walking. Office: Office Spl Master US Ct Fed Claims 717 Madison Pl NW Washington DC 20005

MILLMAN, MARILYN ESTELLE, elementary school educator; b. Lynn, MA, Nov. 28, 1936; d. Benjamin and Dora (Goldman) Millman. BS, Boston U., 1958. Elem. tchr. Beverly (Mass.) Sch. Dist., 1958—64, Lagunitas (Calif.) Sch. Dist., 1964—65, San Rafael (Calif.) City Schs., 1965—97; founder, pres. Marilyn Millman Scholarship Found., 1997—. Vol. chair and bd. dirs. Susan G. Komen Breast Cancer Found.

MILLNER, F. ANN, academic administrator; BS, Univ. Tenn.; MS, Southwest Tex. State Univ.; EdD, Brigham Young Univ. Assoc. dean, asst. v.p., dir. outreach edn. Weber State Univ., Ogden, Utah, 1982—93, v.p. univ. rels., 1993—2002, pres., 2002—. Trustee Intermountain Health Care; past pres. Ogden/Weber C. of C. Recipient Athena award, Ogden/Weber C. of C. Mem.: Phi Kappa Phi. Office: Weber State Univ President's Office 3850 University Circle Ogden UT 84408

MILLNER, RACHEL ERIN, psychology educator, occupational therapist; b. Phila., Oct. 12, 1977; d. Martin S. and Jane Cohen Millner. D of Psychology magna cum alude, Alliant Internat. U., San Diego, Calif., 2004. Practicum student Calif. State U., San Marcos, Calif., 2000—01; intern Interfaith Cmty. Svcs., Escondido, 2001—03; intern- apa approved U. Buffalo Counseling and Psychol. Svcs., Buffalo, 2003—04; psychology fellow U. Pa. Counseling and Psychol. Svcs., Philadelphia. Supervision group leader U. of Pa., Philadelphia, Pa., 2004—; lectr. U. of Pa.- Sch. of Edn., Philadelphia, Pa., 2005—; vol. Healing Connections, San Diego, 1999; admissions interviewer Calif. Sch. of Profl. Psychology, San Diego; presenter in field. Vol. Sunshine Lady Found., 1998—2005. Recipient Outstanding Vol. Award, Healing Connections, 1999. Mem.: APA (assoc.), Psi Chi. Democrat. Jewish. Achievements include research in Poster Presentation at the Am. Psychol. Assn. Nat. Conf., 2004. Home: 943 Randolph Dr Yardley PA 19067 Office Phone: 215-932-9885. Personal E-mail: drmillner@rachelmillner.com.

MILLS, BETHANY S., psychologist, educator; b. Circleville, Ohio, May 6, 1975; d. Donald E. and Brenda S. Reams; m. Dwayne P. Mlls, Aug. 5, 1995; children: Ethan, Evan. BA in Psychology, Mt. Vernon Nazarene Coll., Ohio, 1996; MS in Counseling, Ind. U., Bloomington, 2000; D in Psychology, Spalding U., Louisville, 2005. Assessment assoc. Christopher & Assocs., Seymour, Ind., 2003—05; dir. counsel svcs Olivet Nazarene U., Bourbonnais, Ill., 2005—06, asst. prof. psychology, 2005—. Worship leader Coll Ch. Nazarene, Bourbonnais, 2006. Mem.: Am. Assn. Christian Counselors. Office: Olivet Nazarene U 1 Univ Ave Bourbonnais IL 60914

MILLS, CAROL MARGARET, public relations executive, consultant; b. Salt Lake City, Aug. 31, 1943; d. Samuel Lawrence and Beth (Neilson) M. BS magna cum laude, U. Utah, 1965. With W.S. Hatch Co., Woods Cross, Utah, 1965-87, corp. sec., 1970-87, traffic mgr., 1969-87, dir. publicity, 1974-87, cons. various orgns., 1988—. Bd. dirs. Intermountain Tariff Bur. Inc., 1978-88, chmn., 1981-82, 1986-87; bd. dirs. Mountainwest Venture Group. Fund raiser March of Dimes, Am. Cancer Soc., Am. Heart Assn.; active senatorial campaign, 1976, gubernatorial campaign, 1984, 88, congl. campaign, 1990, 92, 94, vice chair voting dist., 1988-90, congl. campaign, 1994, chmn. 1990-92, chmn. party caucus legis. dist.; witness transp. com. Utah State Legislature, 1984, 85; apptd. by gov. to bd. trustees Utah Tech. Fin. Corp., 1986—, corp. sec., mem. exec. com., 1988—; mem. expdn. to Antaractica, 1996, Titanic '96 expdn.; mem. Iceland and Greenland expdn., 2001; mem. Pioneer Theatre Guld, 1985--. Recipient Svc. awards W.S. Hatch Co., 1971, 80; VIP chpt. Easter Seal Telethon, 1989, 90, Outstanding Vol. Svc. award Easter Seal Soc. Utah, 1989, 90. Mem. Nat. Tank Truck Carriers, Transp. Club Salt Lake City, Am. Trucking Assn. (mem. pub. rels. coun.), Utah Motor Transport Assn. (bd. dirs. 1982-88), Internat. Platform Assn., Traveler's Century Club, Titanic Internat., Beta Gamma Sigma, Phi Kappa Phi, Phi Chi Theta. Home: HC 11 Box 329 Kamiah ID 83536-9410

MILLS, CELESTE LOUISE, occupational therapist; b. LA, May 16, 1952; d. Emery John and Helen Louise (Bradbury) W.; m. Robert Richardson Feigel, Apr. 11, 1971 (div. 1973); m. Peter Alexander Mills, June 12, 1991 (div. 1992). BBA, Western State U., Doniphan, Mo., 1987; PhD in Religion, Universal Life Ch. Univ., 1987; grad., Hypnotism Tng. Inst., Glendale, Calif., 1990. Cert. hypnotherapist. Credit mgr. accounts receivable Gensler-Lee Diamonds, Santa Barbara, Calif., 1973-74, Terry Hinge and Hardware, Van Nuys, Calif., 1975-78; credit mgr., fin. analyst Peanut Butter Fashions, Chatsworth, Calif., 1978-82; personal mgr. Charter Mgmt. Co., Beverly Hills, Calif., 1982-83; co-owner, v.p. Noreen Jenney Communicates, Beverly Hills, 1983-85; corp. credit mgr., fin. analyst Ctrl. Diagnostic Lab., Tarzana, Calif., 1985-89; credit mgr., fin. analyst Metwest Clin. Lab., Inc., Tarzana, Calif., 1989-90; pvt. practice, clin. hypnotherapist Sherman Oaks, Calif., 1990—. Cons. Results Now, Inc., Tarzana, 1986-87; profl. magician Magic Castle, Hollywood, 1989—, Prodr., host (TV) Brainstorm, 1993—, Dances with Woofs, 2003. Media spokesperson Am. Cancer Soc., 1990—. Mem. NAFE, NOW, Nat. Humane Ednl. Found., Credit Mgrs. Assn. Trade Groups (bd. govs. 1988-89), Nat. Clin. Lab. Trade Group (chmn. 1988-89), Med. and Surg. Suppliers Trade Group (vice chmn. 1988-89, chmn. 1989-90), Soc. Am. Magicians, Acad. Magical Arts, Internat. Brotherhood of Magicians, Assn. Advanced Ethical Hypnosis, Am. Coun. Hypnotist Examiners, Golden Retriever Club of Am. (bd. dirs. LA chpt. 2002—, v.p. 2005-06), Ventura Dog Fancy, Valley Hills Dog Obedience Club. Avocations: scuba diving, sailing. Office Phone: 818-989-7999. E-mail: qnwoof@aol.com.

MILLS, CHERYL E., education educator; b. New Orleans; d. Russell Mills, Sr and Gloria Muse-Mills; 1 child, Jason D. Amos. BA cum laude, Dillard U., New Orleans, 1969; M of Social Work, NYU, NYC, 1971; PhD in Sociology, Tulane U., New Orleans, 1997. Cert. Bd. Cert. Social Worker La State Bd. of Examiners, 1982. Caseworker Children's Aid Soc., NY; adminstrv. social worker Bloomfield ctr. for emotionally disturbed children, Bloomfield, NJ; asst. prof./dir. of student internships Rutgers Univ. sch. of social work; adj. prof. Fairleigh Dickinson U., Teaneck, NJ, Bergen C.C., Paramas; project dir. for la statewide child abuse and neglect tng. program for social svc. profls. So. U. Sch. of Social Work, New Orleans; sch. social worker Newark Bd. of Edn., Dept. of Child Guidance, Newark; asst. dean/ dir. of student affairs So. U. Sch. of Social Work, New Orleans, asst. prof. Site visitor for accreditation of sch. of social work Coun. on Social Work Edn., Alexanderia, Va.; adv. bd. mem. La State Dept. of Edn. Spl. Populations, Baton Rouge, Jefferson Parish Dept. of Juvenile Svcs., Metarie, La., Youth Study Ctr., New Orleans; project dir., welfare to work program La Office of Family Svcs. and Support, New Orleans; adv. bd. mem. One Ch. - One Child for the Adoption of Minority Children, New Orleans; cons./trainer for mentors of children of incarcerated parents Cmty. Orgn. Svc., New Orleans. Mem. NAACP, New Orleans; 2nd v.p. YWCA, New Orleans; state pres., la black caucas of sch. bd. mem. La Sch. Boards Assn., Baton Rouge; pres., v.p. orleans parish sch. bd. New Orleans Pub. Schs., New Orleans, 1998—2004. Recipient YWCA Role Model, YWCA, 1997, Bethune, Tubman, Truth Woman of the Yr. Award, La Chpt. Nat. Assn. of Black Social Workers, 1999, Social Worker of the Yr., La. State Legis., 1999, Educator of the Yr., Nat. Coun. of Negro Women La Chpt., 2001; fellow Dr, Martin Luther King Jr Fellowship, N.Y. U., Tulane U. Mem.: Am. Profl. Soc. on the Abuse of Children, Nat. Assn. of U. Women, Nat. assn. of Forensic Social Workers, Nat. Assn. of Black Social Workers La Chpt., Southwestern Sociol. Assn., Coun. on Social Work Edn., Nat. Associaton of Social Workers, Nat. Coalition of 100 Black Women, Nat. Coun. of Negro Women (life). Democrat. Lutheran. Avocations: music, art, literature, dance. Office: Southern Univ New Orleans 6400 Press Dr New Orleans LA 70126 Office Phone: 504-286-5376. Office Fax: 504-286-5387. Personal E-mail: phdcm@msn.com. Business E-Mail: cemills@suno.edu.

MILLS, CORINNE C., music educator; d. William P. and Cynthia L. Channon; children: Kristen Danielle, Pamela Dawn. MusB, Hartt Sch., West Hartford, Conn., 1977. Cert. Conn. Dept. Edn. Traffic coord. Fafair Bearing Co., New Britain, Conn., 1980—82; cello tchr. U. Conn. Cmty. Sch. Arts, Storrs, 1990—93; music tchr. Hartford (Conn.) Pub. Sch., 1995—2001, dist. music coach, 2001—; cello tchr., ensemble coach Hartford Conservatory, 1992—2006. Tchr., coach, dir. summer program Hartford Conservatory, Conn., 1992—2000. Musician (asst. prin. cellist): Ea. Conn. Symphony Orch., 1982—; musician: (cellist) Oakdale Music Theater, 1991—, Andrea Bocelli Am. Tour, 2001—; co-author: Teaching Music in the Urban Classroom: A Guide to Survival, Success and Reform, 2006. Mem.: Am. Orff Schulwerk Assn., Am. Fedn. Tchrs., Am. Fedn. Musicians, Alpha Chi. Democrat. Avocation: gardening. Office: Hartford Pub Sch 960 Main St Hartford CT 06103 Office Phone: 860-695-8724. Business E-Mail: millcoo1@hartfordschools.org.

MILLS, DALE DOUGLAS, journalist; b. Seattle, Oct. 4, 1930; d. Donald Emery and Antoinette (Kinleyside) Douglas; m. William Russell Mills, Aug. 13, 1955; children: Lida Susan, William Tad Jr., Peter Donald, Jane Douglas. BA, U. Wash., Seattle, 1952. Reporter Seattle Times, 1954-55, 74-83; asst. libr. Harvard U., 1955-56; editor Puget Soundings mag., 1968-71. Author: Deliver Us From Squid Roe, 1995. Mem. com. sign control Seattle City Coun., 1970-72; rsch. dir. City Coun. campaign; bd. mgrs. King County Juvenile Ct.; trustee Allied Arts Seattle; bd. dirs. King County Coun. for Prevention of Child Abuse and Neglect. Recipient awards for excellence in journalism Wash. Press Assn., Nat. Fedn. Press Women, Allied Daily Newspapers, C.B. Blethen Meml. award for disting. investigative reporting, Excellence award Soc. Profl. Journalists/Sigma Delta Chi; named Disting. Alumnus Lakeside-St. Nicholas Sch., 1984. Mem.: Jr. League Seattle, Helen T. Bush Children's Hosp Guild, Earthjustice, Sunset Club, Seattle Yacht Club, Kappa Kappa Gamma. E-mail: ddmills@comcast.net.

MILLS, DORA ANNE, public health service officer; BA, Bowdoin Coll.; MD, Univ. Vt. Coll. Med. Residency Children's Hosp., LA; dir. & chief medical officer Maine Bureau of Health, Augusta, 1996—. Recipient Lightship award, Maine Public Rels. Council. Office: Health & Human Svc Dept 11 State House Sta Augusta ME 04333*

MILLS, DOROTHY ALLEN, investor; b. New Brunswick, N.J., Dec. 14, 1920; d. James R. and Bertha Lovilla (Porter) Allen; m. George M. Mills, Apr. 21, 1945; children: Dianne Adele McKay, Dorothy Louise Sphatt. BA, Douglass Coll., New Brunswick, N.J., 1943. Investment reviewer Ctrl. Hanover Bank, N.Y.C., 1943-44; asst. to dir. of admissions and sec. undergrad. yrs. Douglass Coll., New Brunswick, 1944-45; sec., regional dir. O.P.A., Ventura, Calif., 1945-46; corp. sec. George M. Mills Inc., Highland Park, NJ, 1946-75; pvt. investor N. Brunswick, 1975—. Sr. v.p. Children Am. Revolution, N.J., 1965; active alumni com. Douglass Coll., 1990—. Recipient Douglass Alumni award, 1992. Mem. AAUW, New Brunswick Hist. Soc., DAR, English Speaking Union, Rutgers Alumni Faculty Club, Woman's League of Rutgers U., Princeton-Douglass Alumni Club, N. Brunswick Women's Club, Auxiliary Robert Wood Johnson Hosp. and Med. Sch. Republican. Mem. Dutch Reformed Ch. Avocations: travel, gardening, bridge. Home: 1054 Hoover Dr New Brunswick NJ 08902-3244

MILLS, ELIZABETH JENNINGS, art educator; b. Baton Rouge, La., Feb. 19, 1947; d. Robert Bernard Jennings and Virginia Adelia (Lobdell) Jennings; m. Wilmer Riddle Millsm Dec. 28, 1967; children: Wilmer Hastings, Evelyn Kate, Virginia Young, John Jennings. BA in Art and English, La. State Univ., 1969. Agrl. missionary to Brazil S.Am. Presbyn. Ch. in U.S., La., 1972-80. Weaving demonstrator ch. and civic groups, St. Francisville, La., 1983—; guest lectr. James Madison U., Harrisonburg, Va., 1995. Dramatic monologue Fanny Mendlesolhm, 2004; exhbns. include Zeigler Mus., Jennings, La., 1993, La. State U., 1995, Cabaret Theater, 1995, La. Arts and Science Ctr. Mus., 1996; weaving exhibit Magnolia Mound Plantation, 2000; portrait show Eight First Ladies and Lecture, 2000; juried art show Grand Isle, La., 2003, 2004. Mem., officer, tchr. The Plains Presbyn. Ch., Zachary, La., 1980—; mem., officer Study Clubs/Book Clubs, Baton Rouge and Zachary, 1982—; vol. Baton Rouge Symphony, 1987-90; tour guide Plantation Homes St. Francisville Pilgrimage, West Feliciana, La., 1985-90, c. 1790 house on McHugh House tour, 2004, film location of Dukes of Hazard movie, 2004-05; mem. award grants panel, E.B.R. Parish, 2003, art com. Zachary Sch. Sys., 2004. Mem. Assoc. Women in the Arts (sec. 1991-93), Artist Guild of West Feliciana (bd. dirs. 1992—), The Weaving Group. Avocations: writing, poetry, weaving, book making, travelling to museums. Home: 22552 Old Scenic Hwy # 964 Zachary LA 70791-6222

MILLS, ELIZABETH SHOWN, historical writer, genealogist; b. Cleve., Miss., Dec. 29, 1944; d. Floyd Finley Shown and Elizabeth Thulmar (Jeffcoat) Carver; m. Gary B. Mills, 1963; children: Clayton Bernard, Donna Rachal, Daniel Garland. BA, U. Ala., 1980. Cert. genealogist, geneal. lectr. Hist. writer, educator, 1972—; editor Nat. Geneal. Soc. Quar., Arlington, Va., 1987—2002. Faculty Samford U. Inst. of Genealogy and Hist. Rsch., Birmingham, Ala., 1980—; trustee Assn. for Promotion of Scholarship in Genealogy, N.Y., 1984-90; contract dir., cons. U. Ala., 1985-92; faculty Nat. Inst. of Geneal. Rsch., 1985-97. Author, editor, translator Cane River Creole Series, 6 vols.; author: Evidence: Citation and Analysis for the Family Historian, 1997, Professional Genealogy: A Manual for Researchers, Writers, Editors, Lecturers, and Librarians, 2001, Isle of Canes: A Historical Novel, 2004; contbr. articles to profl. jours. Trustee Nat. Bd. Certification Genealogists, 1984—, v.p., 1989-94, pres., 1994-96; trustee Assn. Profl. Genealogists, 1984-90, 92-94, regional v.p., 1988-89. Named Outstanding Young Women of Am. Jaycees, Gadsden, 1976, Outstanding Alumna award U. Ala. New Coll., Tuscaloosa, 1990. Fellow Am. Soc. Geneal. (sec. 1992-95, v.p. 1995-98, pres. 1998-2001), Nat. Geneal. Soc. (councilor 1987-92), Utah Geneal. Assn., Grady McWhiney Rsch. Found. (sr.); mem. Assn. Profl. Genealogists (Smallwood Svc. award, 1989). Republican. Roman Catholic.

MILLS, GLORIA ADAMS, energy executive, consultant; b. Chgo., Mar. 1, 1940; d. Edward Charles and Olive Margaret (McCarty) Adams; m. Peter Mills, Dec. 29, 1962 (div. July 1986). BA, Rosary Coll., River Forest, Ill., 1962, MALS, 1970; MBA, U. Chgo., 1976. Lit. chemist UOP, Inc., Des Plaines, Ill., 1962-70, suprr. patent libr., 1970-77, mktg. engr., 1977-81, mgr. project devel., 1981-83; v.p. mktg. Covanta Waste to Energy, Inc., Fairfield, N.J., 1983-87, sr. v.p. mktg., 1987-89, exec. v.p. mktg., 1989-94, exec. v.p. bus. devel., 1994-01, ret., 2001. Chmn. of bd. Ambiente 2000 S.r.l., 1998-01, mem. indsl. adv. bd. So. Ill. U. Coll. Engring. and Tech., Carbondale, 1985-90, 2000—; chmn. cmty. sta. bd. WHTJ Charlottesville PBS, 2005—. Contbr. articles to profl. jours. Mem. ASME (solid waste processing div., medal of achievement 2001), Am. Chem. Soc. Avocations: travel, reading. E-mail: littlemeadow1@aol.com.

MILLS, HELENE AUDREY, retired education educator; b. Oct. 6, 1933; d. Paul Albert and Mabel Meister; m. Ray Mills, Apr. 17, 1954; children: Keith, Katherine(dec.), Kevin. BS in Family Life Edn., Wayne State U., Detroit, 1954; MEd in Human Resources, Wayne State U., 1965, EdD in Gen. Adminstrn., 1980. Supr., instr. Wayne State Coll. Edn., 1958-67; tchr. life studies, health edn. Seaholm HS, Birmingham, Mich., 1967-72, 74-77, asst. to prin., 1974-77, asst. prin., 1978-79, prin., 1990-97, Derby Mid. Sch., Birmingham, 1980-90; asst. prof. Oakland U., Rochester Hills, Mich., 1997—2002; ret., 2002. Adj. prof. Oakland U., Rochester, 1985—89, Wayne State U., Detroit, 1989—91; consulting editor Clearing Ho., 1985—97. Contbr. articles to profl. jours. Mem. steering com. Meadowbrook Leadership Acad., 1984—87; mem. Detroit Strategic Planning Task Force, 1986—88; mem. exec. bd. Oakland County Youth Assistance, 1987—90; v.p. Cmty. Ho. Sr. Women's Club, Birmingham, Mich., 2004—; program chairperson women's group Northbrooke Ch., 1997—99, mem. adult ministries purpose com., 1998—99. Recipient PTSA Coun. Pres. award, 1982, Celebration of Women award, Greater Detroit Coun. NA'AMAT U.S., 1986, Exemplary Secondary Sch. award, State of Mich., 1991. Mem.: NASCD, Oakland County Secondary Prins. Assn. (pres. 1983—85, Prin. of the Yr. 1991), Mich. Secondary Prins. Assn., Mich. Coun. Family Rels., Mich. Assn. Supervision and Curriculum Devel., Nat. Secondary Prins. Assn., Nat. Staff Devel. Assn., Birmingham Area Sr. Citizens Assn. (bd. mem., program chair 2003—), Phi Delta Kappa (chmn. mem. Oakland br. 1998—2002).

MILLS, IANTHER MARIE, minister; b. Washington, Nov. 27, 1956; d. Jimmie Lee Williamson and Sarah Edna House; m. Hilton Earl Mills, Oct. 8, 1992. BS in math., Georgetown U., 1978; MS in computer sci., U. of NC, 1983; MBA, U. of Okla., 1987; MDiv summa cum laude, Wesley Theol. Sem., 1997, DMin, 2003. Ordained Elder United Meth. Ch., 2000, Ordained Deacon United Meth. Ch., 1997. Sr. software engr. TRW Inc, Hanover, Md., 1980—85; sr. cons. Booz, Allen, & Hamilton, Vienna, Va., 1986—87; sect. head/program mgr. TRW, Inc., Columbia, Md., 1987—90; dept./program mgr. GTE Govt. Systems, Rockville, Md., 1990—95; assoc. pastor Catonsville U.M. Ch., Md., 1997—2000; sr. pastor Good Hope Union U.M. Ch., Silver Spring, Md., 2000—05; dist. supt. Balt.-Washington Conf. United Meth. Ch., 2005—. Mem. Black Clergywomen of the U.M.C., 1997—; mem., bd. of dirs. Suburban Pastoral Counseling Ctr., Catonsville, Md., 1997—2000. Mem. NAACP. Recipient Dalghren medal, Georgetown U., 1978; scholar Yokey award, U. of Okla., 1985—86; Pogue fellowship, U. of NC at Chapel Hill, 1978—79. Democrat-Npl. United Methodist. Avocations: golf, quilting. Office: Balt-Washington Conf 7178 Columbia Gateway Dr Columbia MD 21046-2132 Office Phone: 410-309-3400.

MILLS, INGA-BRITTA, artist; b. Eskilstuna, Sweden, Sept. 14, 1925; came to U.S., 1954; d. Gerhard Valdemar and Märta Kristina (Söderberg) Stenhäll; m. Mogens Schiött, June, 1950 (div. 1952); m. Victor Moore Mills, June 6, 1956; children: Karl-Olof, Victoria Inga Kristina Attended, U. Gothenburg, Sweden, 0946—1948; BA, MA, Montclair State Coll., 1979; postgrad., Temple U., 1980—82. Sec. to dir. Port Authority, Gothenburg, 1952—54; adminstrv. asst. UN, N.Y.C., 1954—55. One-person shows include Montclair (N.J.) Pub. Libr., 1977, UN Food and Agr. Orgn., Rome, 1979, Libr. Arts Ctr., Newport, N.H., 1984, Ariel Gallery, Soho, N.Y.C., 1986, Stamford Mus. and Nature Ctr., 1989, Burnham Libr., Bridgewater, Conn., 1991, Westover Sch., Middlebury, Conn., 1993, Roxbury Libr., 1995, Gallery AE, Gothenburg, 1995, Conn. Housing Fin. Authority, Rockyhill; exhibited in group shows including Am. Women's Assn. Rome, 1982, Marian Graves Mugar Gallery, Colby-Sawyer Coll., New London, N.H., 1984, Artworks Gallery, Hartford, Conn., 1986, Greene Gallery, Guilford, Conn., 1989, The Discovery Mus., Bridgeport, Conn., 1990, Silvermine Galleries, New Canaan, Conn., 1990, Ward-Nasse Gallery, Soho, 1991, 92, Internat. Juried Print Exhibit, Somers, N.Y., 1992, Grand Prix Fine Art de Paris, 1993, Stamford Hist. Soc., 1993, Montserrat Gallery, Soho, 1994, Internat. Print Biennial, Cracow, Poland, 1994, Trenton (N.J.) State Coll., 1995, New Haven Paint and Clay Club, 1995, Conn. Women Artists, New Britain Mus. Am. Art, 1995, Internat Print Triennial, Cracow, 1997, 4th Ann. Internat. Graphics Addition, Stockholm, 1997; represented in collections Corning & Co., N.Y.C., New Haven Paint and Clay Club, Somerstown Gallery, Somers; represented in pvt. collections, U.S., Europe, Japan, and Australia Recipient Marjorie Frances Meml. award Stamford Mus. and Nature Ctr., 1990, Faber-Birren Color award Stamford Art Assn., 1990 Mem. Wash. Art Assn Democrat. Avocations: gardening, reading, music, theater.

MILLS, JEAN D., education educator; b. Crown City, Ohio, Nov. 9, 1929; d. Stanley B. and Effie B. (Day) Dillon; m. Robert W. MIlls, Nov. 29, 1949; children: Brenda Harman, Vanessa, Matthew D. BA, Marshall U., 1958; postgrad., Ohio State U., 1979-83, Ohio Dominican, 1978-79. Cert. profl. tchr., Ohio. Tchr. math. and English Deercreek Bd. Edn., Williamsport, Ohio, 1948-50, 51-54; tchr. sci. and math. Logan Elem. Bd. Edn., Circleville, Ohio, 1956-87; adj. prof. sci./math. Circleville Bible Coll., 1988-95. Mem. Pickaway County Ret. Tchr. Assn. (pres. 1990-92), Ohio Ret. Tchr. Assn. (pres. 1999), Delta Kappa Gamma (hon.). Republican. Meth. Avocations: reading, travel.

MILLS, MARSHA LEE, retired secondary school educator; b. Independence, Kans., Dec. 28, 1948; d. Arthur Robert and Thelma Louise (Esch) M. BS in Edn., Truman U., 1970, MA, 1974; real estate cert., Ind. Career Inst., Westport, Mo., 1991. Part time tchr. NMSU Mo. U., Kirksville, 1970-72; jr. high art educator Lincoln County R-3 Schs., Troy, Mo., 1972—2006; ret., 2006; realtor assoc. Century 21 Coose, Troy, 1991—. Exhibitor: (ceramics)

Mo. Coll. Art Students, 1969, Mo. Artists and Coll. Educators, 1970 (hon. mention), (multi media) N.E. Mo. U., 1974. Mus. friend St. Louis Art Mus., 1978—; badge cons. Boy Scouts Am., St. Louis Coun., 1978—; trustee Moscow Mills (Mo.) Meth. Ch., 1992—. Recipient I Dare You award Purina, 1966, Regents scholarship NMSU, Kirksville, 1966, Art Guild scholarship NMSU Art Guild, Kirksville, 1969. Mem. Mo. State Tchrs. Assn. (v.p., pres., dist. officer 1987-93), Greater St. Louis Tchrs. Assn. (2nd v.p. 1994, 95, pres. 1996-1998), Nat. Art Edn. Assn. (coun. 1978—), St. Charles Bd. Realtors, Alpha Delta Kappa (Beta Chi chpt. treas., sec., v.p. 1987-93, pres. 1994-2000), Delta Kappa Gamma. Democrat. Avocations: investments, computers, fine arts, baseball, walking. Home: 444 Highway Mm Moscow Mills MO 63362-1502 Office: 43 Ellis Ave Troy MO 63379 Office Phone: 314-528-8941 228. Personal E-mail: me-mar@att.net.

MILLS, MELANIE MARIE, elementary school educator; b. Houma, La., Feb. 18, 1973; d. Richard Fred and Helen Pellegrin Mills; 1 child, Besse Meryl. MEd, Nicholls State U., Thibodaux, La., 2006. Tchr. Terrebonne Parish Schs., Houma, La., 1996—. Mem.: La. Sci. Tchrs. Assn.

MILLS, NINA ROSALIE, social worker; b. Huntington, W.Va., July 17, 1953; d. Lloyd William and Violet Macil (Elkins) Fowler; m. Homer Chester Bartoe, Jan. 30, 1972 (div. Dec. 1979); m. Gary Michael Lovejoy, Aug. 9, 1982 (div. Mar. 1989); m. Raymond Wesley Perkins, Apr. 14, 1989 (div. Nov. 1989); m. Kermit Mills Jr., June 24, 2004; 1 child, Homer David. BSW, Marshall U., 1982; postgrad., W.Va. U., 1989-95. Lic. social worker, W.Va.; cert. personal care provider. Child care worker Charles W. Cammack Children's Ctr., Huntington, 1983-84; ins. underwriter Mut. of Omaha, Shreveport, La., 1984-86; banquet mgr. Ramada Inn, Shreveport, 1986-87; ctr. coord. Cabell County Cmty. Svcs. Orgn., Inc., Huntington, 1987-90, case mgr. sr. svcs., 1990-92; minority AIDS program coord. W.Va. Dept. Health, Charleston, 1988-90, cons. instr., 1990-92; social worker, dir. social svcs., Frank E. Hanshaw Geriatric Ctr. Marshall U. Sch. Medicine, Huntington, 1990—, rsch. study coord., 1998—2000; owner, adminstr. Sr. Care Mgmt. Svcs., Huntington, W.Va., 1991-92; dir. social svcs. Wayne Continuous Care Ctr., 1992—97. Charter mem. Cabell County Com. for Drug Info., Huntington, 1990—; mem. Huntington Area AIDS Task Force, 1988—; social work cons. for Region 2, Area Agy. on Aging Adv. Com.; cons. and guest lectr., 1991-96; mem. ethics com. W.Va. Dept. HHS Office Social Svcs., 1995-97; mem. partial hospitilization adv. com. Prestera Ctr. Mental Health. Bd. dirs. Cabell County Cmty. Svcs.; mem. Dem. Women's Club; sr. forum Cabell County. Recipient Cert. for Concerned Citizenship, State of W.Va., 1982. Mem. NAFE, Internat. Plaform Assn., Inst. Noetic Scis. Democrat. Baptist. Avocations: gardening, writing, swimming, reading. Office: Frank Hanshaw Geriatric Ctr 1600 Med Ctr Dr Ste 6150 Huntington WV 25701 Business E-Mail: perkinsn@marshall.edu.

MILLS, PATRICIA JAGENTOWICZ, philosophy scholar, educator, writer; b. Newark, Mar. 18, 1944; d. Alexander A. and Louise A. (Breunig) Jagentowicz; 1 child, Holland. BA, Rutgers U., 1973; MA, SUNY, Stony Brook, 1975; PhD, York U., Toronto, Ont., Can., 1984. Lectr. U. Toronto, 1984—85, vis. scholar, 1985—86, asst. prof. philosophy, 1986—88; asst. prof. polit. theory U. Mass., Amherst, 1988—91, assoc. prof. polit. theory, 1991—. Vis. scholar Pembroke Ctr. for Tchg. and Rsch. on Women, Brown U., 1999-2000; lectr. philosophy dept. Smith Coll., spring 1992; manuscript referee Social Scis. and Humanities Rsch. Coun. Can., 1985-86, 87-88, 91-92, Polity: Jour. of Northeastern Polit. Sci. Assn., 1990, 91; invited spkr. New Sch. for Social Rsch., 1990, Coll. Holy Cross, 1991, NEH seminar, Mt. Holyoke Coll., 1992, U. Pitts., 1993, Antigone Conf., SUNY Buffalo, 1997; presenter paper 20th World Congress Philosophy, 1998. Author: Woman, Nature, and Psyche, 1987; editor: Feminist Interpretations of G.W.F. Hegel, 1996; author, contbr.: (book chpts.) The Sexism of Social and Political Theory: Women and Reproduction from Plato to Nietzsche, 1979, Ethnicity in a Technological Age, 1988, Taking Our Time: Feminist Perspectives on Temporality, 1989, Renewing the Earth: The Promise of Social Ecology, 1990, The Future of Continental Philosophy and the Politics of Difference, 1991, Ecological Feminist Philosophies, 1996, The Phenomenology of Spirit Reader, 1998, Hegel and Law, 2002; contbr. articles to profl. jours. Dir. Drop-In Ctr., Newark, 1972-73; mem. N.J. Abortion Project, 1971-73; mem. Fortune Soc., N.J., 1972; grassroots organizer against the war in Vietnam, N.J., 1970-71; grassroots organizer women's movement, N.J. and N.Y., 1971-73. Recipient Disting. Tchg. award Delta Lambda chpt. Pi Sigma Alpha Honor Soc., U. Mass., 1997; postdoctoral fellow Social Scis. and Humanities Rsch. Coun. Can., 1983-85; scholar York U., 1975; faculty grantee for tchg. U. Mass., 1991-92. Mem. Am. Philos. Assn. (conf. presenter 1995 meeting), Soc. for Phenomenology and Existential Philosophy (presenter conf. papers 1988, 91, 92), Hegel Soc., Ancient Philosophy Soc., Soc. for the Study of Women Philosophers. Office: U Mass Thompson Hall Dept Polit Sci Amherst MA 01003 E-mail: pjmills@polsci.umass.edu.

MILLS, PATRICIA LYNN, theater director, educator; d. Ed and Zee Mills. BFA, U. of Tex., Austin, 1986. Cert. tchr. Tex. Edn. Assn. Tech. theater dir. Newman Smith H.S., Carrollton, Tex., 1986—; cons. theater and libr. design Lovejoy Ind. Sch. Dist., Tex., 2003. Chair fine arts dept. Newman Smith H.S., Carrollton, 1997—99, instrnl. facilitator, 1999—2003, chair fine arts dept., 2001—02; leaderfine arts cluster Carrollton-Farmers Br. Ind. Sch. Dist., 1999—2003. Techn. dir.: (one-act play) Murder in the Cathedral (One of Top 8 Plays in State, 1992); dir.: Song at the Scaffold (State Meet Qualifier, 1998); designer, stage mgr., dir.: Carrollton-Farmers Br. Ind. Sch. Dist. Convocation. Tech. coord. NSHS and RLT Carrollton Police-Shattered Dreams, 1999—2002; performer coord. Carrollton Fire Dept., 1999. Named VIP Tchr., Carrollton-Farmers Br. Ind. Sch. Dist., 1996, Educator of Distinction, Nat. Soc. of H.S. Scholars, 2004, 2005. Mem.: NEA, Tex. State Tchrs. Assn., Internat. Thespian Soc. (life; chpt. sponsor 1986—2006). Avocations: quilting, reading, gardening, travel. Home: 2213 Spring Leaf Dr Carrollton TX 75006 Office: Newman Smith HS 2335 N Josey Ln Carrollton TX 75006 Office Phone: 972-968-5200. Home Fax: 972-968-5210; Office Fax: 972-968-5210. Business E-Mail: millsp@cfbisd.edu.

MILLS, STEPHANIE ELLEN, writer; b. Berkeley, Calif., Sept. 11, 1948; d. Robert C. and Edith (Garrison) M.; m. Philip Thiel (div. 1990). BA, Mills Coll., 1969. Campus organizer Planned Parenthood, Alameda, San Francisco, Calif., 1969-70; editor in chief Earth Times, San Francisco, 1970; story editor Earth, San Francisco, 1971; conference facilitator Mills Coll., Oakland, 1973-74; writer family planning program Emory Univ., Atlanta, 1974; dir. outings program Friends of the Earth, San Francisco, 1975-76, dir. membership devel., 1976-78; fellow Found. for Nat. Progress, San Francisco, 1978-80; from asst. editor to editor CoEvolution Quar., Sausalito, Calif., 1980-82; editor in chief, rsch. dir. Calif. Tomorrow, San Francisco, 1982-83; dir. devel. World Coll. West, San Rafael, Calif., 1983-84; freelance writer, lectr., 1984—; adj. prof. Grand Valley State Univ., Traverse City, Mich., 2002. V.p. Earth First! Found., 1986-89; pres. No. Mich. Environ. Action Coun., 1987-88; mem. planning com. Great Lakes Bioregional Congress, 1991; pres. bd. dirs. Oryana Natural Foods Coop., 1992-93; mem. adv. coun. Earth Island Inst., mem. adv. bd. Orion Soc., mem. Am. for Maine Woods, Nat. Park Adv. com., Northwoods Wilderness Recovery. Author: In Service of the Wild: Restoring and Reinhabiting Damaged Land, 1995, Whatever Happened to Ecology?, 1989, Epicurean Simplicity, 2002; editor: Turning Away from Technology: A New Vision for the Twenty-first Century, 1997 (Utne Visionary award 1996); editor, contbr. In Praise of Nature, 1990; corr. Wild Earth; editor-in-chief Not Man Apart newsletter from Friends of the Earth, 1978; editl. adv. E; contbr. to Ency. Brit. Book of Yr., 1998; contbr. articles to popular mags. Bd. dirs. Planned Parenthood Fedn. Am., 1970-76. Recipient award Mademoiselle, 1969, Friends of UN Environ. Program, 1987; grantee Point Found., 1972, IRA-HITI Found., 1992; resident Blue Mountain Ctr., 1983, 86. Avocations: swimming, cooking. Office: care Katinka Matson Brockman Inc 5 E 59th St New York NY 10022-1027

MILLS, SYLVIA JANET, secondary education educator; b. Chgo., Oct. 5, 1954; d. Clarence Thomas and Janet Lucille (Curry) Mills; children: Ean O'Harrel Mills, Raymond Echols II. BA in Journalism, Columbia Coll., Chgo., 1979; MA in Instructional Design, U. Iowa, 1993, secondary tchg. cert. in journalism, 1996. Edn. Beat reporter Chgo. Daily Defender Newspapers, 1979-80; tech. writer/editor, data mgmt. supr., ops./planning analyst Sonicraft, Inc., Chgo., 1983-88; sec. and pub. rels. officer Female Entrepreneurs of Chgo., 1988-89; adminstrv. asst./editor Student Devel. Office, City Colls. of Chgo., 1989-91; rsch. intern Am. Coll. Testing, Inc., Iowa City, 1991-93; grad. asst. U. Iowa Grad. Coll., Iowa City, 1993-95; lang. arts reading instr. Keokuk Cmty. Sch., 1996—. Rsch. asst. Ctr. for Evaluation and Assessment, U. Iowa, 1995-96. Bd. dirs. All in a Kid's Day Summer Immersion Program, Iowa City, 1994; mem. PTA Beasley Acad. Ctr., Chgo., 1988-90, PTO, Iowa City, 1992-93. Mem. ASCD, Alpha Kappa Alpha (treas., dean of pledges 1973-74). Avocations: reading, writing. Home: PO Box 742 Keokuk IA 52632-0742

MILLS-NOVOA, BEVERLY A., psychologist, consultant; b. Indpls., Apr. 23, 1954; d. Paul Gerald and Arzella Mills; m. Avelino Mills-Novoa, Aug. 27, 1977; children: Nicole, Megan. BA, Earlham Coll., 1976; MA, U. Minn., 1979, PhD, 1980. Lic. psychologist. Cons. Control Data Corp., Mpls., 1980-83; sr. cons. Control Data Bus. Advisors, Mpls., 1983-87; cons. McLagan Internat., Mpls., 1987-88; asst. prof. U. St. Thomas, St. Paul, 1988—94; prin. cons. Mills-Novoa & Assocs., Mpls., 1989—. Bd. dirs. Minn. Career Develop. Assn., Mpls., 1983-86. Author: (play) The Last Laugh, 1972, (manual/booklet) Striving for Success, 1992. Mem.: APA. Avocations: writing, walking, reading. Office: PO Box 16373 Saint Louis Park MN 55416-0373 Office Phone: 952-292-8550. Business E-Mail: bmillsnovoa@mn.rr.com.

MILLS-SCHREIBER, ROBIN KATE, law librarian; b. Chgo., Jan. 10, 1947; d. Dumont Cromwell and Virginia Anne (Nordeng) M.; A.B., Ind. U., 1969, M.L.S., 1970; J.D., U. S.C., 1976. Circulation/reference librarian Ind. U. Sch. Law, Bloomington, 1970-73; asst. law librarian U. S.C. Sch. Law, Columbia, 1973-76, asst. prof. law and law librarian, 1976-81, asso. prof. law and law librarian, 1981-84; assoc. prof. law, law librarian, 1984-87; prof. law, law libr. Emory U. Sch. Law, Atlanta, 1987—, assoc. dean library services. Mem. Am. Assn. Law Libraries (chpt. pres. 1980-82), Am. Bar Assn., S.C. Bar Assn. Office: Emory U Law Libr Gambrell Hl Atlanta GA 30322-0001

MILLSTEIN, ROBERTA L., humanities educator; AB, Dartmouth Coll., Hanover, N.H., 1988; PhD, U. of Minn., Mpls., 1997. Assoc. prof. dept. philosophy Calif. State U.-East Bay, Hayward, 1997—2006, U. Calif., Davis, 2006—. Contbr. articles to profl. jours. Faculty Support grantee, Calif. State U., Hayward, 1999, 2001, 2001. Mem.: Internat. Soc. for Environ. Ethics, Am. Philos. Assn., History of Sci. Soc., Internat. Soc. for the History, Philosophy, and Social Studies of Biology (listserv moderator 2001—, webmaster 2002—05), Philosophy of Sci. Assn. (program com. 2004, nominating com. 2006—).

MILMAN, DORIS HOPE, retired pediatrician, psychiatrist, educator; b. NYC, Nov. 17, 1917; d. Barnet S. and Rose (Smoleroff) Milman; m. Nathan Kreeger, June 15, 1941; 1 child, Elizabeth Kreeger Goldman. BA, Barnard Coll., 1938; MD, NYU, 1942. Diplomate Am. Bd. Pediat.; lic. physician, N.Y. Intern Jewish Hosp., Bklyn., 1942-43, resident, 1944-46, fellow in pediat., 1946-47; postgrad. extern in psychiatry Bellevue Hosp., N.Y.C., 1947-49; attending pediat. psychiatrist Jewish Hosp., Bklyn., 1950-56; asst. prof. pediat. Health Sci. Ctr. at Bklyn. SUNY, 1956-67, assoc. prof., 1967-73, prof., 1973-93, prof. emeritus, 1993—, acting chmn. dept. pediat., 1973-75, 82. Pvt. practice child and adolescent psychiatry, Bklyn., 1950-90; vis. prof. Ben Gurion U. of the Negev, Beersheva, Israel, 1977. Co-editor: AAP Adolescent Newsletter, 1993—; copyeditor: Bellevue Lit. Rev., 2001—. Mem. adv. bd. N.Y. Assn. for the Learning Disabled, N.Y.C., 1975-80. Recipient Disting. Alumna award Barnard Coll., 1986, Solomon R. Berson Achievement award NYU Sch. Medicine, 1991; Grace Potter Rice fellow Barnard Coll., 1938-39. Fellow Am. Acad. Pediat. (emeritus), Am. Psychiat. Assn. (disting. life fellow); mem. AAAS, Am. Orthopsychiat. Assn. (life), Am. Pediat. Soc. (emeritus), N.Y. Pediat. Soc. (emeritus), Phi Beta Kappa, Alpha Omega Alpha. Home: 2373 Broadway Apt 2028 New York NY 10024-2842

MILNE, JENNIFER ANNE, literature and language educator; b. Jefferson City, Mo., Oct. 31, 1950; d. Charles and Josephine Anne Czarlinsky; m. Erwin Lance Milne, Apr. 2, 1983; children: Elizabeth Hockaday Dudenhoeffer, Edmund Calvert Fine, Jordan Claire, Brendan Ainsley. BS in English Edn., U. Mo., Columbia, 1972; MEd, Lincoln U., Jefferson City, Mo., 1984. Cert. Mo. Dept. Elem. and Secondary Edn., 1972. Instr. William Woods U., Fulton, Mo.; instr. English Lincoln U., Jefferson City, 1986—90, Jefferson City Pub. Schs., 1998—. Bd. mem. Children's Hosp. Bd., U. Mo. Med. Ctr., Columbia, Spl. Learning Ctr., Jefferson City, 1993—96. Recipient Tchr. Yr., Jefferson City Pub. Schs., 2000. Home: 1210 Moreau Drive Jefferson City MO 65101 Office: Jefferson City High School 609 Union Street Jefferson City MO 65101 Office Phone: 573-659-3050. Personal E-mail: emilne@mchsi.com.

MILNE, KAREN LOUISE, science educator; b. Phoenix, Apr. 26, 1947; d. Jean Raisch Stewart; children: Jamie Barbara Roberson, Benjamin Morrison. BA in Edn., Ariz. State U., Tempe, 1972. Sci./math tchr. 5th grade Manzanita Sch., Phoenix, 1969—74; sci./math tchr. 8th grade Cactus Wren Sch., Phoenix, 1980—84; sci. tchr. 7th grade Cholla Mid. Sch., Phoenix, 1984—96; sci. tchr. 7th and 8th grade Sweetwater Sch., Glendale, Ariz., 1996—. Mid. sch. biology instr. Woodrow Wilson Nat. Fellowship Found., Princeton, NJ, 1995—98. Student coun. advisor Sweetwater Sch., 1996—2006; treas. Cholla Sch. PTO, Phoenix, 1984—85; sec. Sweetwater PTO, Glendale, 1997—98, Sweetwater Site Coun., Glendale, 2000—02, mem., 2002—04; yearbook advisor Sweetwater Sch., 1996—2006. Recipient Sci. Tchr. of Yr., Ariz. Sci. Tchrs. Assn., 1994; grantee, Woodrow Wilson Nat. Fellowship Found., 1994, Ariz. Game and Fish Dept., 1994. Mem.: Ariz. Profl. Educators, NEA, Nat. Biology Tchrs. Assn., Nat. Sci. Tchrs. Assn. Office: Sweetwater Sch 4602 W Sweetwater Ave Glendale AZ 85304 Office Phone: 602-896-6500. Business E-Mail: kmilne@sw.wesd.k12.az.us.

MILNE, LORNA, Canadian legislator; b. Toronto, Ont., Can., Dec. 13, 1934; BS in Agr., U. Guelph. Adminstr., lectr. Physics Dept. U. Guelph; senator The Senate of Can., Ottawa, 1995—. Trustee, vice-chair Peel County Bd. Edn. Bd. dirs. Peel County Mus., Brampton and Dist. YM-YWCA and Rapport House; former chair Brampton and Dist. Assn. for Mentally Retarded; former pres. Brampton and Dist. Univ. Women's Club. Mem.: Heart and Stroke Found. Ont. (residential coord.), Ont. Automobile Ins. Bd. Liberal. Office: 247 East Block The Senate of Canada Ottawa ON Canada K1A 0A4 Office Phone: 613-947-7695. Business E-Mail: milnel@sen.parl.gc.ca.

MILNER, BEVERLY JANE, retired medical/surgical nurse; b. Webster, S.D., Oct. 30, 1939; d. Anton and Josephine (Wika) Boik; m. Roger W. Milner, Nov. 26, 1960; children: Robert A., Michael. Diploma, Presentation Sch. Nursing, Aberdeen, S.D., 1960; BS, Laverne U., 1986. Oper. rm. staff nurse St. Francis Hosp., Lynwood, Calif., 1961-62; oper. rm. supr. Corona Cmty. Hosp., Calif., 1969-92; relief supr. oper. rm. Fallbrook Dist. Hosp., 1993—96; ret., 1996. Mem. Assn. Operating Rm. Nurses (bd. dirs., sec., treas., v.p., pres. Inland Valley chpt.).

MILNER, JOAN W., retired elementary school educator; b. Marion, Ohio, Mar. 23, 1930; d. Fred R. and Genevieve Agnes White; m. J. Stanley Zucker (dec.); m. Raymond Milner, Mar. 28, 1978 (dec.). Student, Ohio State U., Columbus, 1948—51; BS, Ohio No. U., Ada, 1969. Cert. tchr. Ohio. Tchr. Marion City Sch., 1959—85; ret., 1985. Sec., v.p., pres. Marion Edn. Assn., 1962—68; pres. bd. dirs. Friends of Pres. Harding, Marion, 1996—98; mem. Twig 3 & 6, Marion Gen. Hosp., 1982—84. Recipient Vol. award Harding Home, Dept. of Army, Marion, 1997; Jennings scholar, Martha Holden Jennings Found., Columbus, 1980—81. Mem.: DAR, PEO, All Children's Hosp. Guild (life), Alpha Chi Omega (pres. 1982—85). Methodist. Avocations: photography, rubber stamping, reading, knitting.

MILNOR, HAZEL, nurse; b. Marble, Ark., Apr. 2, 1921; d. Andrew Jackson and Laura Jane (Davis) Spencer; m. John Champion Milnor, June 21, 1951 (dec. Aug. 1989); children: Mary Christine, Jean Ann Laura. RN, Calif., Hawaii. Nurse pvt. duty, Calif., 1942—; surg. nurse Queen's Hosp., Hawaii, 1944-46; flight attendant United Airlines, San Francisco, 1946-51. Author: Entertaining in Hawaii, 1977, (poetry) As Angels Watch, 1997. Founding pres. Spl. Angels Ministry, Hawaii; chair develop. com. Spl. Angels; vol. various orgns., 1951—. Recipient Disting. Svc. award Assn. for Retarded Citizens in Hawaii, 2005; inducted Internat. Poetry Hall of Fame. Mem. Assn. Retarded Citizens, Clipped Wings (mem.-at-large, mem. coms.), Internat. Soc. Poets (disting.), Oahu Country Club. Republican. Episcopalian. Avocations: collecting angels, travel.

MILOY, LEATHA FAYE, university program director; b. Marlin, Tex., Mar. 12, 1936; d. J. D. and Leola Hazel (Rhudy) Hill; m. John Miloy, June 20, 1960; children: Tyler Hill, David Reed, Nancy Lee. BA, Sam Houston State U., 1957; MS, Tex. A&M U., 1967, PhD, 1978. Dir. pub. affairs Gulf Univs. Rsch. Corp., College Station, Tex., 1966-69; asst. dir. Ctr. for Marine Resources Tex. A&M U., College Station, 1974-76, dir. edn. svcs., 1974-78; dir. info. and spl. svcs. Tex. Woman's U., Denton, 1978-79; asst. v.p. univ. advancement S.W. Tex. State U., San Marcos, 1979-83, asst. to pres., 1983-84, v.p. student and instl. rels., 1984-90, v.p. univ. advancement, 1990-93, dir. capital campaign, 1993-98. Vis. lectr. humanities and sea U. Va., 1972-73; cons. Office Tech. Assessment, Washington, 1976-86, Tex. A&M U., Galveston, 1979-82, Bemidji State U., Glassboro State Coll., 1984; mem. Task Force on Edn. and Pub. Interest, 1987-88. Editor: The Ocean From Space, 1969; author, editor Sea Grant 70's, 1970-79 (Sea Grant award 1973-74); contbr. articles to profl. jours. Ad hoc mem. Marine Resources Coun. Tex., Austin, 1971-72, Tex. Energy Adv. Coun., 1974-75; chmn. United Way, Bryan, Tex., 1976; com. mem. various local elections, 1974-78. NSF grantee, 1970-78; recipient Marine Resources Info. award NSF, 1969-71, Tex. Energy Info. award Gov.'s Office, 1974-75, Tex. Water Info. award Dept. Interior, 1977-79. Mem. Nat. Soc. Fundraising Execs., Coun. for the Advancement and Support Edn. (bd. dirs. 1979-81, Disting. Achievement award 1998), Coun. Student Svcs. (v.p. Tex. 1988-90, Case IV Hall Fame 2004), Tex. Fedn. Porcelain Artists (bd. dirs. 2005—), Highland Lakes Porcelain Guild (pres. 2005—). Avocations: reading, painting, fishing. Home: PO Box 752 Buchanan Dam TX 78609-0752 E-mail: lmiloy@tstar.net.

MILTON, BARBARA ELLA, II, psychotherapist; b. Camden, NJ, May 13, 1959; d. Barbara Ella Milton Sr.; m. S.Kay Osborn, Jan. 8, 2002; children: Tania Kirkman, Ian Kirkman. BA, Seton Hill Coll., 1982; MSW, Rutgers U., 2001; postgrad., CUNY/Hunter Coll. Lic. social workder NJ. Lic. social worker State Bd. of Social Work Examiners, Trenton, NJ, 2001, cert. social worker, 1994—2001; school social worker Dept. Edn., Trenton, 2001. Pres. Imani Comms., Jersey City, 1995—. Mem. NAACP; workforce investment bd. YWCA of Central NJ, Hackensack, 1996—98; mem. Human Svcs. Adv. Coun., Hackensack, 1996—98; bd. dirs. YWCA of Central NJ, New Brunswick, 1992—95. Recipient Mark Foreman award, Rutgers U., 2001; fellow, CUNY Hunter Coll., 2001. Mem.: NASW, Juvenile Detention Assn., Avanta-Satir Network. Avocations: travel, sports. Office: Jersey City Med Ctr Liberty Health Sys 50 Baldwin St II-Ctr Bldg Jersey City NJ 07304

MILTON, CAROL LYNNE, artist; b. NYC, June 23, 1947; d. August William Thiel and Ruth Elizabeth Gilbert; m. Thomas Macon Milton, Mar. 31, 1973; 1 child, Nicholas John. Sec. Herndon (Va.) Oldtown Gallery, 1989-90, treas., 1990-91; pres. Reston (Va.) Arts Gallery, 1991-92, treas., 1992-93; v.p. Vienna (Va.) Arts Soc. Inc., 1994-95, pres., 1995-98, bd. dirs., 1998-2001. Art program provider Gt. Falls. (Va.) Womens Club, Mobil Wife's Club; chair VAS Gallery, 2000-01, dir., 2001—. Watercolor painter, 1993—; exhbns. include Herndon (Va.) Old Town Gallery, 1988, Reston (Va.) Art Gallery, 1991, 92, Reston Health Club, 1992, Patrick Henry Libr., Vienna, Va., 1991, 97, 99, Reston Cmty. Art Ctr., 1992, Cameron Glenn Ctr., Reston, 1992, Vienna Town Hall, 1995, Hannabils Coffee House, Vienna, 1996, Thomas Jefferson Libr., Falls Church, Va., 1996. Art show provider Arts in Pub. Places, metro D.C. area, 1989—; mural painter Our Lady of Good Coun., Vienna, 1996; calendar artist Town of Vienna, 1998, mem. mural project com. Town of Vienna, 1999. Mem.: Vienna Art Soc. (chmn. bd. dirs. 2001, dir. gallery 2001—04, workshop coord. Vienna Art Ctr. 2004—). Avocations: gardening, gourmet cooking, antiques, travel. Studio: 10311 Yellow Pine Dr Vienna VA 22182-1344 Personal E-mail: miltons22182@yahoo.com.

MILTON, CATHERINE HIGGS, entrepreneur; b. NYC, Jan. 6, 1943; d. Edgar Homer and Josephine (Doughty) Higgs; m. A. Fenner Milton (div.); m. Thomas F. McBride, Aug. 25, 1974 (dec. Oct. 31, 2003); children: Raphael McBride, Luke McBride. BA, Mt. Holyoke Coll., 1964, PhD (hon.), 1992. Reporter, travel writer Boston Globe, 1964-68; with Internat. Assn. Chiefs Police, Washington, 1968-70; asst. dir. Police Found., Washington, 1970-75; spl. asst. US Treasury Dept., Washington, 1977-80; project staff Spl. Com. Aging/Senate, Washington, 1980-81; spl. asst. to pres., founder/exec. dir. Stanford U. Haas Ctr. for Public, Calif., 1981-91; exec. dir. Commn. for Nat. and Cmty. Svc., Washington, 1991-93; v.p. Corp. for Nat. Svc., Washington, 1993-95; exec. dir. Presidio Leadership Ctr., 1995-96; exec. dir. US Programs Save the Children, Westport, Conn., 1996—2002; pres. Friends of the Children, Portland, Oreg., 2002—05. Mem. US Atty. General's Task Force on Family Violence, 1981-82; chair nat. forum Kellogg Found., 1990; bd. dirs. Inst. Higher Edn. Policy, Generation United. Author: Women in Policing, 1972, Police Use of Deadly Force, 1976; co-author: History of Black Americans, 1965, Team Policing, Little Sisters and the Law, 1970. Bd. dirs. Youth Svc. Calif., L.A., 1986-91, Trauma Found., San Francisco, 1982-90, Generation United, 1985-, Inst. Higher Edn. Policy, 1985-; spl. advisor Campus Compact, 1986-91. Nat. Kellogg Found. fellow, Battle Creek, Mich., 1985-88; recipient Dedication and Outstanding Efforts award Bd. Suprs., Santa Clara, Calif., 1989, Outstanding Vol. Contbn. award Strive for Five, San Francisco, 1991, Dinkelspiel award Stanford U., 1991; named Outstanding Campus Adminstr. COOL, 1987. Avocations: backpacking, skiing, hiking, travel. Home: 3652 SE Oak St Portland OR 97214

MILTON-JONES, DELISHA, professional basketball player; b. Riceboro, Ga., Sept. 11, 1974; d. Beverly Milton; m. Roland Jones, June 30, 2003. BA in Sports Mgmt., U. Fla. Forward Portland Power, 1997—99, L.A. Sparks, 1999—. Forward Ekaterinburg team/EuroLeague, Russia, 2002—; mem. USA Basketball Women's Sr. Nat. Team, 2004. Recipient gold medal, Olympic Games, 2000, World Championships, 1998, 2002, U.S. Olympic Cub, 1999, World Univ. Games, 1997, U.S. Olympic Festival, 1994. Office: Los Angeles Sparks 555 N Nash St El Segundo CA 90245

MIMI, HAAS, volunteer; BA in Polit. Sci., George Washington U., 1968. Pres. Miriam and Peter Haas Fund, 1981—; trustee, chair, mem. accessions com. San Francisco Mus. Modern Art, 1986—; mem. nat. adv. bd. Stanford (Calif.) U. Haas Ctr. for Pub. Svc., 1986—; bd. visitors Terry Sanford Inst. for Pub. Policy Duke U., 1995—; bd. advisors Paul H. Nitze Sch. Internat. Studies, Johns Hopkins U., Balt., 1998—; trustee N.Y. Mus. Modern Art, 1999—. Coord. Citizens Waterfront Com., 1970-71; docent San Francisco Mus. Modern Art, 1974-82; chair enabling funds com. Jr. League, 1981-83; mem. corps. emergency fund com. No. Calif. Grantmakers Found., 1981-86; mem. San Francisco coun. Archives of Am. Art, 1984-89; bd. govs. San Francisco Symphony, 1985-89; trustee San Francisco U. H.S., 1986-96, Summerbridge Nat., 1992-95, Children Now, 1993-97, Dia Ctr. for Arts, N.Y., 1994-97. Address: 2800 Broadway St San Francisco CA 94115-1061

MIMS, CLARICE ROBERTA, financial advisor; b. New York, Dec. 26, 1947; d. Clarence Robert Mims and Victoria Antoinette Tynes; 1 child, Dawn Imani Dawson. BS in Art Edn., Hampton Inst., 1969; MS in Urban Edn., Syracuse U., 1972; postgrad. in bus., NYU, 1972-74; Cert. Computer Techs., MIT, 1985; MEd in Supervision and Adminstrn., Bank St. Coll. Edn., 1995. Lic. securities, life and health ins.; cert. tchr. Acct. exec. 3M Corp., Caldwell, N.J., 1976-78; acct. exec., tech. cons. AT&T, New York, 1978-85; pres., cons. Mims Cons., New York, 1985-87; educator N.Y.C. Bd. Edn., Bklyn., 1987-95, cons. Chancellor's Dist., 1996-98; personal fin. adv. Am. Express Fin. Advs., Langhorne, Pa., 1999—. Pres., owner Loral Devel. Corp., N.Y.C., 1983-84, DSL Mortgage Co., N.Y.C., 1990-92. V.p. mktg. Black Edn. Network, N.Y.C., 1996-99; mem. adv. bd. African Am. Leadership Summit, Bklyn., 1995-97. Mem. Am. Bridge Assn., Alpha Kappa Alpha. Avocations: art, writing, bridge, guitar, piano.

MIMS, JOYCE ELAINE, lawyer; b. Chgo., Mar. 6, 1942; d. Thomas Samuel Mims and Hortense Bernice Miller; m. John Young. BA, U. Wis., 1964; MA, Northwestern U., 1965; JD, NYU, 1975. Bar: Ill. 1976. Tchr. Lane Tech. High Sch., Chgo. Bd. Edn., 1965—67; edn. specialist IBM World Trade Corp., NYC, 1968—69; adminstr. lectr. CUNY-Brooklyn, 1969—75; assoc. firm Bell, Boyd & Lloyd, Chgo., 1975—78; atty. Am. Hosp. Supply Corp., Evanston, Ill., 1978—82, div. counsel, 1982—83, asst. gen. counsel, 1983—89; gen. counsel Ancilla Systems Inc., 1989—95, sr. v.p., gen. counsel, 1995—98; v.p., gen. counsel, sec. Ryerson Tull, Inc., Chgo., 1999—2001, v.p., gen. counsel, 2001—. Mem. Evanston Zoning Bd. Appeals, 1977—82; mem. bd. dirs. Evanston Community Devel. Corp., Evanston Hosp. Corp. Mem.: ABA, Chgo. Bar Assn. Office: Ryerson Tull Inc 2621 W 15th Pl Chicago IL 60608

MIN, JANICE BYUNG, editor-in-chief; b. Atlanta, 1969; m. Peter Sheehy, 1997; 1 child. BA in Journalism, Columbia U., NYC, 1990. Reporter, Westchester County, NY, 1990—92; writer to sr. editor People mag., NYC, 1992—97; with Life mag., NYC, 1997—98; asst. mng. editor In Style mag., NYC, 1998—2001; exec. editor Us Weekly mag., NYC, 2002—03, editor-in-chief, 2003—. Named one of 40 Under 40, Crain's NY Bus., 2006; recipient Editor of Yr., AdWeek mag., 2005. Office: Us Weekly 1290 Ave of Americas New York NY 10104-0298 Office Phone: 800-283-3956. Office Fax: 212-651-7890.*

MINAHAN, JANICE TERRY, science educator; d. Donald LaRue and Maerine Tompkins McCarty; m. Michael Lester Terry (div.); m. Patrick McCormick Minahan, Sr., June 15, 2002; 1 child, Patrick McCormick Jr. BS in Biology, Columbus Coll., Ga., 1981, MEd in Secondary Sci., 1985; PhD in Secondary Sci. Edn., Auburn U., Ala., 1994. Cert. secondary sci. composite grades 6-12 Tex., 2003, secondary biology grades 6-12 Tex., 2003, gifted and talented Tex., 2003, sci. and biology NT 4, 5, PBT 4, 5, 6, 7 Ga. Tchr. sci. Shaw H.S., Muscogee County Sch. Dist., Columbus, 1985—2002, Aledo H.S., Aledo Ind. Sch. Dist., Tex., 2002—. Instr. Applied Biology and Chemistry I Workshop for Tchrs., Doughville, Ga., 1994, Applied Biology and Chemistry II Workshop for Tchrs., Doughville, Ga., 1995; asst. test adminstr. Nat. Found. System Tchr. Cert. Exam., Columbus, 1994—96; part-time sci. instr. Ga. Mil. Coll., Ft. Benning, 1997—2000; part-time biology instr. Chattahochee Valley C.C., Phenix City, Ala., 2000—01; H.S. sci. tchr. rep. Sci. Book Adoption Com., Aledo, 2002—03; mem./tchr. rep. Sch. Health Adv. Com., Aledo, 2002—. Author (presenter): Phys. Sci. Labs. for H.S., 1990; author: (article) What Factors Affect Attitudes Toward Women in Science Held by High School Biology Students, 1997. Treas. Columbus Track Club, 1992—93, 1995—97; vol. Coca-Cola Sci. Space Ctr., Columbus, 1995—2002; site leader Help the Hooch River Clean Up, Columbus, 1998—2002; vol. Team Diabetes Kua Hawaii Marathon, 1999—2000. Named Miss Columbus Coll., 1980—81; recipient Makes A Difference award, Shaw High PTA, 1991—92, Top Tchrs. award, Sara Spano Assn., 1994—95. Mem.: Valley Area Sci. Tchrs. (pres. 2000—01), Nat. Sci. Tchrs. Assn., Auburn U. Alumni Assn., Columbus Coll. Alumni Assn., Phi Delta Kappa. Democrat. Baptist. Avocations: antiques, walking. Business E-Mail: jminahan@aledo.k12.tx.us.

MINARDI, ANN SEGURA, lawyer, musician; d. William A. and Mary Louise Segura; m. John Christopher Minardi, June 10, 1983; children: Christine Ann, Angela Rose. BA, U. Mich., 1980; JD, Boston U., 1984. Bar: Md. 1988, U.S. Ct. Internat. Trade 1988, U.S. Ct. Appeals (fed. cir.) 1988, U.S. Supreme Ct. 1989. Atty. Office of Regulations and Rulings, Washington, 1988—. Musician: (professional flutist) Friday Morning Music Club, 1998—. Recipient Academic award, U. Mich., 1980. Mem.: Customs Lawyers Assn. (chair, program com. 2004—05). Avocation: equestrian sports. Office: Customs and Border Protection 1300 Pennsylvania Ave NW Washington DC 20229

MINARIK, ELSE HOLMELUND (BIGART MINARIK), author; b. Aarhus, Denmark, Sept. 13, 1920; d. Kaj Marius and Helga Holmelund; m. Walter Minarik, July 14, 1940 (dec.); 1 child, Brooke Ellen; m. Homer Bigart, Oct. 3, 1970 (dec.). BA, Queens Coll., 1942. Tchr. 1st grade, art Commack (N.Y.) Pub. Schs., 1950-54. Author children's books: Little Bear, 1957, Father Bear Comes Home, 1959, Little Bear's Friend, 1960, Little Bear's Visit, 1961, No Fighting, No Biting, 1958, Cat and Dog, 1960, The Winds That Come From Far Away, 1960, The Little Giant Girl and the Elf Boy, 1963, A Kiss for Little Bear, 1968, What If, 1987, Percy and the Five Houses, 1988, It's Spring, 1989, The Little Girl and the Dragon, 1991, Am I Beautiful, 1992. Mem. PEN Club. Home: 30 Gebig Rd Nottingham NH 03290 Office: care Greenwillow Books 1350 Ave Americas New York NY 10019

MINASIAN, MAUREEN, physical education educator; d. Bernard and Jane Barrows; m. Warren Minasian, Aug. 0, 2000; children: Rick Collins, Meghan Chiasson. BS in Phys. Edn., Bridgewater State Coll., Mass., 1988, MS in Phys. Edn., 2001. Tchr. phys. edn. Bridgewater-Raynham Sch. Dist., Mass., 1991—; instr. Cambridge Coll., 2003—. Land steward Conservation Commn., Bridgewater, 2002—06; fundraiser NRTB, 2001—06; past pres., v.p. Bridgewater State PE Alumni, 1997—2005; mem. BSC Alumni Assn., 1996—2002. Mem.: NEA, BCEA, PCEA, MAHPERD, AAHPERD, MTA, BREA (licentiate; v.p. polit. action 2002—06). Office: Geo Mitchell Elem School 500 South St Bridgewater MA 02324

MINCE, CAROL KIRKHAM, history educator; b. Clarksville, Tenn., Aug. 1, 1961; d. Lawrence Ray and Mary Virginia Cox; m. John William Mince Jr., Apr. 23, 1992. BS, Austin Peay State U., 1982, MA in Edn., 1984. Cert. tchr. Tenn. Asst. mgr. Kelley's Food City, Clarksville, 1980—93; social studies tchr. New Providence Mid. Sch., Clarksville, 1993—2005; world history tchr. Montgomery Ctrl. HS, Cunningham, Tenn., 2005—. Named Tchr. of Yr. at Bldg. Level, Tenn. Dept. Edn., 2000, 2004. Mem.: NEA, ASPCA, Tenn. Geog. Alliance, Nat. Coun. Social Studies., Clarksville-Montgomery County Edn. Assn. (Disting. Classroom Tchr. award 2000, 2004), Tenn. Edn. Assn., Nat. Humane Edn. Soc., Am. Humane Assn., Humane Soc. US, Phi Kappa Phi. Avocations: reading, hiking, antiques, photography. Office: Montgomery Ctrl HS 3955 Hwy 48 Cunningham TN 37052

MINCH, DONNA RUTH BLACK, director; d. Ian Robert Birse and Ruth Ann Black; m. Steven Henry Minch, Apr. 16, 1977; children: Jessica Dawn, Rebecca Leigh Minch Green. Profl. diploma, Ritner's Sch. of Floral Design, Boston, 1973; BS in Plant Sci., Utah State U., Logan, 1977. Instr. floral design Utah State U., 1973—77, coord. off-campus horticulture degree program, student advisor, 1995—; owner landscape design firm Aurora, Colo., 1977—79; hort. cons. Miotello Farms, Caldogno, Italy, 1980—83; dir. purchasing Apple Tree Florist, Plano, Tex., 1984—87; adult edn. instr. Plano, 1984—87; instr. Norman (Okla.) Pub. Schs., 1988—91; horticulturist Utah State U. Bot. Garden, Farmington, 1992—95; adult edn. instr. Pks. and Recreation, Layton, Utah, 1995. Internat. lectr. floral design Caserma Ederle, Vicenza, Italy, 1980—83; cons. horticulture Farmington City, Utah, 1992—; mem. curriculum com. horticulture Davis County Schs., Farmington, 2000—; mem. edn. com. Utah State U. Bot. Ctr., Kaysville, 1998—; mem. adv. com. FFA/4-H, Logan, 2002—06; mem. horticulture curriculum com. PSB dept. Utah State U., 2002—, mem. advising assessment com., 2005—; mem. adv. bd. Univ. Ctr., Salt Lake CC, Salt Lake City, 2004—; endorser Utah Nursery and Landscape Assn. Cert. Nursery Profl., Salt Lake City, 1995—. Pres. Utah State Coll. Agr. Alumni Assn., Logan, 2003—05; mem. adv. com. Utah State Future Farmers of Am., Logan, 1995—2006; mem. PTA, Norman, 1988—91, Plano, 1984—87; vol. Girl Scouts Am., Plano, 1984—87; editor yearbook elem. schs., Norman, 1988—91; pres. Young Women's LDS Ch., Norman, 1988—91; primary tchr. LDS Ch., Farmington, 1992—2006; mem. Medway (Mass.) HS Alumni Assn., 1972—2006; host family Angels Minor League Baseball, Farmington, 2002—06; vol. Children's Aid Soc., Ogden, Utah, 2000—06. Finalist Robbins award, Utah State U., 2003—04; named Pillsbury Outstanding Student, 1975, Advisor of Yr., Utah State U. Continuing Edn., 2004; recipient award for svc. to faculty and students, Coll. of Agr. Utah State U., 2001. Mem.: Nat. Academic Advising Assn. (assoc.), Life Flight: Grounded Ones, Utah State Alumni Assn. (life), Davis County Master Gardener Assn. Avocations: gardening, travel, skiing, hiking, baseball. Office: Utah State U PSB Dept 4820 Old Main Hill Logan UT 84322-4820 Office Phone: 801-451-4604. E-mail: donnam@ext.usu.edu.

MINCO, DEBRA THOMPSON, chemistry educator; m. Leonard Minco; children: John Thompson, Lauren Marie. BS in Nutritional Sci., U. Calif., Berkeley, 1978. Therapeutic dietitian El Camino Hosp., Mountainview, Calif., 1978—79, Santa Teresa Hosp., San Jose, Calif., 1979—80; rsch. dietitian VA Hosp., Lexington, Ky., 1980—81. Office Phone: 817-305-4700.

MINDES, GAYLE DEAN, education educator; b. Kansas City, Mo., Feb. 11, 1942; d. Elton Burnett and Juanita Maxine (Mangold) Taylor; m. Marvin William Mindes, June 20, 1969 (dec.); 1 child, Jonathan Seth; m. Matilde Delich-Funes Mindes Jun. 27, 2002. BS, U. Kans., Lawrence, 1964; MS, U. Wis., Madison, 1965; EdD, Loyola U., Chgo., 1979. Tchr. pub. schs., Newburgh, N.Y., 1965-67; spl. educator Ill. Dept. Mental Health, Chgo., 1967-69; spl. edn. supr. Evanston (Ill.) Dist. 65 Schs., 1969-74; lectr. Loyola U., Chgo., 1974-76, Coll. St. Francis, Joliet, Ill., 1976-79; asst. prof. edn. Oklahoma City U., 1979-80; prof. sch. edn. DePaul U., 1993-99, acting dean, 1998-99, prof. edn., 1999—, dir. EdD program, 2000—02, chair tchr. edn., 2003. Lectr. Northeastern Ill., U. Chgo, 1974, North Park Coll., Chgo., 1978; vis. asst. prof., rsch. assoc. Roosevelt U. Coll. Edn., Chgo, 1983-87, Albert A. Robin campus prof., dir. R&D dir. tchr. edn., dir. early childhood, dir. grad. edn. ctr., 1993; senate chair Roosevelt U., 1986-89, trustee Roosevelt U., 1987-93; search com. multicultural affairs v.p. advancement, DePaul U., co-chair tchg., learning, tech. com, 2000—, strategic planning univ. com., 2004, search com., 2004, sr. v.p. advancement, 2004, faculty coun. budget com., 2004—, univ. tenure and promotion bd., 2005—, pres. com. tech., 2005—, sch. edn. NCA com., 2005-06; co-chair ILAEYC Bldg. Bridges; faculty adv. com. to univ. plan. and info. tech. DePaul U. Sch. Edn., panel on grievances, 1995-99, comprehensive pers. devel. com., 1995-99; tng. sub-com. adv. Ill. Dept. Children & Family Svcs., 1993-95; panel of advisers comprehensive pers. devel. sys. Ill. State Bd. Edn., 1995-99; mentor, cons. to partnerships project tng. early intervention svcs. U. Ill., Champaign; panelist Ill. Initiative for Articulation between Ill. Bd. Higher Edn. and Ill. CC Bd., Early Childhood Assessment Sys.; co-chair, panelist Bansenville Pub. Schs.; cons. in field; project evaluator Chgo. Tchr. Collaborative, Dept. Edn., 1999-2004; chair U. Tchg. Learning Tech. com., 2001—; mem. partnership com. Ill. State Bd. Ednl., 2002, content expert panel, 2003; faculty coun. De Paul Budget Com., 2004—; active Sch. Edn. North Ctrl. Assn. Commn., 2005—; cons. Heinemann Libraries. Author: Assessing Young Children, 1996, 2d edit., 2003, Teaching Young Children Social Studies, 2006; co-author: (with Marie Donovan) Building Character: Five Enduring Themes for a Stronger Early Childhood Curriculum PK-3, 2000; (with Allan C. Ornstein and Thomas Lesley II) Secondary and Middle School Methods, 2005; editor: DePaul U. Sch. Edn. Newsletter; co-author: Planning a Theme Based Curriculum for 4's or 5's, 1993, Assessing Young Children: 1996, Encyclopedia of Children's Play, 1997, 2d edit., 2006; mem. editl. bd. Ill. Sch. R&D, Ill. Divsn. Early Childhood Edn. Adv. Com. to Ill. Bd. Edn.; cons. editor: NAEYC, 2003; contbr. articles to profl. jours. Bd. dir. North Side Family Day Care, 1981; northside affiliate Mus. Contemporary Art, 1991-96; active Gov's Task Force on Alternative Rts. to Cert., 1999; edn. adv. com. Okla. Dept. Edn., 1979-80; adv. bd. bilingual early childhood program Oakton C.C.; adv. bd. early childood tech. assistance project Chgo. Pub. Schs., Lake View Mental Health, 1986-90; planning com. Lake View Citizens Coun. Day Care Ctr., 1978-79; local planning coun. Ill. Dept. Child and Family Svcs.; childcare block grant tng. sub. com.; chair teen com. Florence G. Heller JCC, membership com.; adv. bd. Harold Washington Coll. Child Devel., regional tech. assistance grant LICA; parents. com. Francis W. Parker Sch.; assessment task force Dept. Human Svcs., City of Chgo., 2001-02; trustee Congregation Kol Ami., 2000-03; vol. gardener Lincoln Park Zoo, 2002—; resale shop vol. Mt. Sinai Hosp., 2004—. U. Kans. scholar, 1960, Cerebral Palsy Assn. scholar, 1965; U. Wis. fellow, 1964-65. Fellow: Am. Orthopsychiat. Assn.; mem.: ASCD, North Ctrl. Assn. (mem. sch. bd. com. 2005—), Found. for Excellence in Tchg. (selection com. Golden Apple 1989—94), Ill. Assn. for Edn. Young Children (co-chair bldg. bridges project), Ill. Coun. for Exceptional Children, Coun. for Exceptional Children, Am. Ednl. Rsch. Assn., Nat. Assn. for Edn. Young Children (tchr. edn. bd. 1990—94, editl. panel 2003—, editl. rev. bd.), Pi Lambda Theta, Phi Delta Kappa, Alpha Sigma Nu. Office: DePaul Univ Sch Of Edn Chicago IL 60614 Office Phone: 773-325-7769. Business E-Mail: gmindes@depaul.edu.

MINDLIN, SUSAN W., small business owner, educator; b. Milw., Nov. 27, 1931; d. Julius Weinberg and Marjorie D. Alshuler; m. Richard Barnett Mindlin, Feb. 6, 1954; children: Steven, Edward, Andrew. BA, Conn. Coll., New London, Conn., 1953. Mem. exec. tng. program Bloomingdale's, NY, 1953; co-owner Coach House Stores Inc., Kans. City, 1955; owner VIP Customized Tours and Imaging, 1993—. Docent, Nelson=Atkins Mus. of Art, Kans. City, 1980—; bd. advs. Children's Mercy Hosp., Kans. City, 2002—. Bd. chmn. Univ. Assoc. U. Mo., Kans. City, 1975—77, Children's Rehab. U. Kans. City Med. Ctr., 1970—72; pres. Aux. Menorah Med. Ctr., Kans. City, 1980—82; bd. Am. Red Cross, Kans. City, 1996—2002. Mem.: Am. Mus. Women in the Arts, YouthFriends Kans. City, Nelson Atkins Mus. of Art. Avocation: golf. Office: VIP Customized Tours and Imaging 4101 W 90 St Shawnee Mission KS 66207

MINDNICH, ELLEN, sales executive; b. Red Bank, N.J., Apr. 2, 1962; d. James Robert and Ann Marie M. BS in Bus. Mgmt., W. Chester U. Sales mgr. U.S. Healthcare, N.Y., 1991-96; sales recruiter Paragon Computer, N.Y., 1996-97; ins. agt., 1998—. Home: 205 W End Ave Apt 24 Long Branch NJ 07740-5243

MINDT, MICHELE L.M., music educator; d. Myron and Kathleen Mindt. BS in Music Edn., U. Mary, 1994; MiusM in Clarinet Performance, U. Iowa, 1996. Cert. music tchr. ND, 1996, in gifted and talented tchg. U. ND, 1996. Instr. U. ND, Grand Forks; tchr. music Standing Rock Sch., Fort Yates, ND, Wilton Pub. Sch., ND, Sykeston Pub. Sch., ND, Midway Pub. Sch., Inkster, ND; gifted and talented tchr. Standing Rock Elem. Sch., Fort Yates, ND. Tchr. After Sch. Program Sykeston (N.D.) Pub. Sch. Musician: Bismarck-Mandan (N.D.) Symphony Orch., Grand Forks (N.D.) Symphony Orch., U. Iowa Orch., Mo. River Cmty. Band. Avocations: gardening, walking, birdwatching, rodeos, church.

MINEHAN, CATHY ELIZABETH, bank executive; b. Jersey City, Feb. 15, 1947; d. Harry Manford Jones and Rita Jane (Decora) Jones Leary; m. Gerald Paul Minehan, July 18, 1970; children: Melissa Jane, Brian Patrick. BA, U. Rochester, 1968; MBA, NYU, 1977. Various positions to sr. v.p. Fed. Reserve Bank N.Y., N.Y.C., 1968—75, ops. analysis officer, 1975, mgr. mgmt. info. dept., 1976—78, asst. v.p., 1979—82, v.p., 1982—87, sr. v.p., 1987—91; chief operating officer Fed. Reserve Bank Boston, 1991-94, pres., 1994—. Cons. IMF, Washington, 1990-91; bd. dirs. Boston Mcpl. Rsch. Bur., Park St. Corp., The New Eng. Coun.; mem. Gov.'s Coun. Econ. Growth and Tech. Bd. dirs. Boston Pvt. Industry Council, Boston Mcpl. Rsch. Bur., Jobs for Mass., New Eng. Council, Boston Pub. Libr. Found.; mem. Mass. Women's Forum, Boston, 1991—; bd. advisors Caroll Sch. Mgmt. Boston Coll.; trustee Bentley Coll., 1992—; trustee coun. U. Rochester, 1993—. Mem. Pub. Securities Assn. (ex officio, govt. ops. com. 1986-91), Beta Gamma Sigma. Democrat. Roman Catholic. Avocations: golf, skiing, jogging. Office: Fed Res Bank Boston PO Box 2076 600 Atlantic Ave Ste 100 Boston MA 02210-2204*

MINEHART, JEAN BESSE, tax accountant; b. Cleve., Nov. 8, 1937; d. Ralph and Augusta Besse; m. Ralph Conrad Minehart, Aug. 28, 1959; children: Patricia Minehart Miron, Deborah Minehart Rust, Elizabeth Minehart Biedermann, Stephen. BA, Mass. Wellesley Coll., Wellesley, 1959; MEd, U. Va., Charlottesville, 1971. Rsch. assoc. Age Ctr. of New Eng., Boston, 1959-61; substitute tchr. Charlottesville Sch. Sys., Va., 1976-81; tax acct. H&R Block, Charlottesville, 1982-94, Huey & Bjorn, Charlottesville, 1994—2006; ret., 2006. Past pres. Ephphatha Village Housing for the Deaf, Charlottesville, 1984-87; bd. dirs. Tues. Evening Concert Series, Charlottesville, 1990-94; sec., bd. dirs. Family Svc., Inc., Charlottesville, 1987-91; bd. dirs. Westminster Organ Concert Series; elder Westminster Presbyn. Ch., 1979-81, 94-96, trustee, 2005— Scholar, Wellesley Coll. scholar. Mem. LWV (v.p., treas. 1991-95) Blue Ridge Wellesley Club (pres. Charlottesvillechpt. 1989-91, dorm rep. 1996-2004). Avocations: reading, music. Home: 1714 Yorktown Dr Charlottesville VA 22901 Office Phone: 434-971-7642.

MINEKA, SUSAN, psychology professor; b. Ithaca, N.Y., June 2, 1948; d. Francis Edward and Muriel Leota (McGregor) M. BA in Psychology magna cum laude, Cornell U., 1970; PhD, U. Pa., 1974. Lic. psychologist Ill. Prof. psychology U. Wis., Madison, 1974-85, U. Tex., Austin, 1986-87; prof. Northwestern U., Evanston, Ill., 1987—. Co-dir. Panic Treatment Ctr., Evanston Hosp., 1988—99; co-dir. Anxiety and Panic Treatment Clinic Northwestern U., 2001—; mem. NIH Panic Consensus Panel, 1991. Editor: Jour. Abnormal Psychology, 1990—94; assoc. editor Emotion, 2003—; contbr. articles to profl. jours. Fellow, Ctr. for Advanced Study in the Behavioral Scis., Stanford, Calif., 1997—98; grantee, NSF and NIMH, 1978—. Fellow APA (bd. sci. affairs 1992-94, chair 1994, pres. divsn. 12, sect. 3 1995), Am. Psychol. Soc. (bd. dirs. 2001-04); mem. Assn. for Advancement Behavior Therapy, Midwestern Psychol. Assn. (pres. 1996-97), Soc. for Rsch. in Psychopathology (mem. exec. bd. 1992-94, 2000-03), Phi Beta Kappa, Sigma Xi. Democrat. Office: Northwestern U Psychology Dept Evanston IL 60208-0001

MINELLI, HELENE MARIE, artist; b. Sonoma, Calif., Sept. 26, 1918; d. Adolph Herman Trappe and Maria Barbara Hilzinger; m. Louie Minelli, Mar. 4, 1939 (dec. Aug. 1993); children: Ernest, Carol, Michael. Student, Santa Rosa Jr. Coll. Bd. trustees Calif. Exposition Adv. Coun., Sacramento, 1984—89; artistic treas. Cultural Fine Arts Commn., Sonoma Valley, 1989. Named one of 60 Pastel Artists of World, Internat. Pastel Mag. Mem.: Soc. We. Artists (bd. trustees 1988—), Nat. League Am. Pen Women (pres. 1995—96), Gen. Fedn. Women's Club (past state art chmn.), Sonoma Valley Art (past pres.). Home: 200 Malaga St Sonoma CA 95476

MINER, ALICE E., medial/surgical, geriatric and charge nurse; b. Gregory, S.D., Feb. 13, 1956; d. Richard Lyle and Eleanor Virginia (Beavers) Vakiner; m. Gordon Dennis Miner, Dec. 17, 1988; children: Kris, Scott, Holly, Allen. BA, Dakota Wesleyan U., 1978, AA, 1985. Cert. provider ACLS, Am. Heart Assn., cert. provider CPR, ARC. Staff, charge nurse Lundberg Meml. Hosp., Creighton, Nebr.; evening supr. Firesteel Health Care Ctr., Mitchell, SD; RN, charge nurse Cmty. Meml. Hosp., Burke, SD; staff nurse Winner Nursing Home, SD; nurse Schramm Med. Clinic, Winner. Established Diabetes Outreach Clinic for Cmty. Vol. cancer awareness edn. for cmty.; ednl. coord. county level, state bd. dirs. Am. Cancer Soc., pres. county. Home: 33550 302nd St Gregory SD 57533 Office: Rock County Hosp PO BOX 300 Bassett NE 68714

MINER, ALLISON PATRICE, physical therapist; b. Van Nuys, Calif., July 14, 1971; d. Gordon Brainard, Jr. Miner and Anne Elizabeth Eschrich. BS in Kinesiology, San Diego State U., Calif., 2000; D in Physical Therapy, U. Puget Sound, Wash., 2004. Cert. physical therapist and athletic trainer Calif. Stage crew, carpenter Moonlight Ampitheatre, Vista, Calif., 1987—90; waitress, mgr. Feliccia's Italian Deli/Restaurant, Vista, Calif., 1989—2001; athletic trainer Valley Ctrl. HS, Calif., 2000—01, U. Puget Sound, Tacoma, 2001—03; physical therapist Scripps Meml. Hosp., Encinidas, Calif., 2004—; physical therapist, athletic trainer San Diego State U., 2006—. Adj. faculty San Diego State U., 2005—, accredited clinical instr., 2005—. Author: (rsch. article) Neurology Report, 2003. Leader of usher/greeters The Rock Ch., San Diego, 1999—2000. Grantee Roth Meml. Scholarship, U. Puget Sound, 2003. Republican. Avocations: outrigger canoeing, hiking, surfing, musical theatre, script writing. Office: San Diego State U Dept Athletics 5500 Campanile Dr San Diego CA 92182

MINER, JACQUELINE, political consultant; b. Dec. 10, 1936; d. Ralph E. and Agnes (McGee) Mariani; m. Roger J. Miner, Aug. 11, 1975; children: Laurence, Ronald Carmichael, Ralph Carmichael, Mark. Ind. polit. cons., Hudson, NY; instr. history and polit. sci. SUNY, Hudson, 1974—79. Mem. nat. steering com. Fund for Am.'s Future, 2d cir. Hist. Com.; mem. White House Outreach Working Group on Central Am.; candidate for Rep. nomination U.S. Senate, 1982; co-chair N.Y. state steering com. George Bush for Pres. campaign, 1986—88; del. Rep. Conv., 1992, GOP Conv., 1992; Rep. county committeewoman, 1958—76; vice chmn. N.Y. State Ronald Reagan campaign, 1980, N.Y. State Rep. Com., 1991—93; co-chmn. N.Y. State Reagan Roundup Campaign, 1984—86; chmn. Coll. Consortium for Internat. Studies. Mem.: PEO, U.S. Supreme Ct. Hist. Soc. Address: 1 Merlins Way Hudson NY 12534-4157

MING, JENNY J., former retail executive; b. Canton, China, 1955; arrived in US, 1964; married; 3 children. BA in Clothing Merchandising, San Jose State U. Mdse. mgr. brand activewear Gap Inc., 1986—89, v.p., divsn. mdse. mgr., 1989—94, sr. v.p. merchandising, Old Navy, 1994—96, exec. v.p. merchandising, Old Navy, 1996—99, pres., Old Navy, 1999—2006, mem., sr. oper. com., 1999—2006. Bd. dirs. Epiphany, Inc., 2001—. Bd. dirs. Big Brothers Big Sisters, San Francisco; mem. Com. of 100. Named one of 50 Most Powerful Women in Am. Bus., Fortune mag., 2003; recipient Award for Leadership in Bus. & Community Svc., Merage Found. for the American Dream, 2006.*

MING-NA, actress; b. Coloane Island, Macau, Nov. 20, 1963; m. Eric Michael Zee, June 16, 1995; 1 child, Michaela. BA, Carnegie Mellon U. Actor: (TV series) As the World Turns, 1988—91, The Single Guy, 1995, (voice) Spawn, 1997, Outreach, 1999, ER, 1995, 2000—04, (voice) The Batman, 2004, Inconceivable, 2005—; (films) Rain Without Thunder, 1992, The Joy Luck Club, 1993, Terminal Voyage, 1994, Hong Kong 97, 1994, Street Fighter, 1994, Street Fighter: The Movie, 1994, One Night Stand, 1997, Mulan Story Studio, 1998, 12 Bucks, 1998, (voice) Mulan, 1998, Spawn 3: Ultimate Battle, 1999, (Aki's Dream) Aki's Dream, 2001, (voice) Final Fantasy: The Spirits Within, 2001, A Ribbon of Dreams, 2002, Teddy Bears' Picnic, 2002, Perfection, 2004, (voice) Mulan II, 2004,; (TV films) Blind Spot, 1993, Vanishing Son II, 1994, Vanishing Son IV, 1994, Tempting Fate, 1998.

MINGUS, CHERIE LYNN, home economics educator; b. La Rochelle, France, June 24, 1954; came to U.S., 1956; d. Shafter and Margie (Vannatter) Watts; m. Gordon Mitchell Mingus, July 9, 1977; children: Michael Gordon, Cherise Michelle. BS, U. Ky., 1976; MS, Western Ky. U., 1985. Cert. home economist, Ky. Home econs. tchr. Radcliff (Ky.) Mid. Sch., 1976-77, J. T. Alton Mid. Sch., Vine Grove, Ky., 1983-84, West Hardin High Sch., Stephensburg, Ky., 1984-90, Cen. Hardin High Sch., Cecilia, Ky., 1990—. Mem. Project Future Adv. Bd., Elizabethtown, Ky., 1989—94, Ky. Family Career and Cmty. Leaders of Am., Frankfort, 1991—92. Mem. Assn. Career and Tech. Edn., Nat. Tchrs. Family and Consumer Scis., Am. Home Econs. Assn., Ky. Vocat. Assn. (regional pres. 1991-92), Ky. Assn. Vocat. Home Econs. Tchrs. (state pres. 1991-92), Am. Assn. Family and Consumer Scis.(com. mem.). Democrat. Baptist. Avocations: cross stitch, reading, walking, bowling, being with family.

MINGUS, LOIS KAGAN, actor, dancer, singer, choreographer, playwright; b. Boston; d. Bert S. and Edith B. (Greene) Kagan. Co. mem., actor, dancer, singer The Living Theatre, N.Y.C., 1988—; acting co. mem. Dadanewyork,

N.Y.C., 1993—; acting co. mem., singer The Wycherly Sisters, N.Y.C., 1993—; acting co. mem. The Theatre of Dreams, N.Y.C., 1996—. Co-prodr. The Living Theatre at the Jewish Mus., N.Y.C., 1996; choreographer, Dadanewyork and The Living Theatre, 1993—; spkr. in field Actor (plays) The Tablets, 1990, We Should.(A Lie), 1991, Humanity, 1991, Utopia, 1996, Mysteries and Smaller Pieces, 1996, (cabarets) Dadanewyork, 1997, The Theatre of Dreams, 1996-97. Actor/activities The Living Theatre, N.Y.C. and Europe, 1988—; co-founder workshop Action Racket Theatre Recipient hon. mention Lamia Ink Internat. One Page Play Festival, 2001.

MINICH, JACQUELINE HUTTON, science educator; b. Buffalo, Aug. 9, 1954; d. Alice Francis and John Russell Hutton; m. Mark Owen Minich, Mar. 22, 1975; children: Christine Renee, Joseph Elmer, Cheryl Alice, Angela Joy. B, Tri-State U., Ind., 1986. BS Physical Edn., Biology, Sci. and Health Dept. of Edn., Fla., 1986. Sci. instr. North Ft. Myers HS, Fla., 1985—87; sci. instr., sci. dept. head Mariner HS, Cape Coral, Fla., 1987—. Com. mem. Christ Luth. Ch., Cape Coral, Fla., 1985—2006. Recipient Tchr. of Yr. award, Lee County Sci. Bd., 1991, 1994, Invention award, Thomas Alva Edison Regional Sci. Invention Bd., 1999, 2006, Tchr. of Yr. award, C. of C. Edn. Com., 2004. Mem.: Nat. Sci. Tchr. Assn. Conservative. Lutheran. Avocations: travel, boating, reading. Home: 5210 SW 12th Pl Cape Coral FL 33914 Office: Mariner HS 701 N Chiquita Blvd Cape Coral FL 33993 Office Phone: 239-772-3324. Business E-Mail: jackiem2@lee.k12.fl.us.

MINKLEIN, SHARON ELIZABETH, elementary school educator; b. Buffalo, Apr. 6, 1939; d. Theodore William and Marian Elizabeth Minklein. BS, D'Youville Coll., Buffalo, 1962; MEd, SUNY, Buffalo, 1967; cert. in creative studies, State Tchrs. Coll., Buffalo, 1994. Permanent tchg. cert. K-6 NY. Mem. clin. faculty U. Buffalo, 1990—96; elem. tchr. Williamsville Ctrl., Amherst, NY, 1962—2000, gifted program specialist, 1994—2000. Edn. chair Buffalo Lille Orgn., 1999—. Mem. Erie County Commn. on Status of Women, Buffalo, 1998—; vol. spl. exhibits Albright Knox Art Gallery, Buffalo, 2000—; pres. Williamsville (NY) Edn. Found., 2001—05; vice chair St. Benedict's Sch. Bd., Amherst, NY, 2002—. Named to, Internat. Amateur Photography, 2001, 2003; recipient Outstanding Achievement award, 2004. Mem.: AAUW, Twentieth Century Club, Phi Delta Kappa (10 yr. award 1989). Avocations: tennis, travel, photography, literature. Home: 32 Bernhardt Dr Amherst NY 14226 Personal E-mail: sminklein@adelphia.net.

MINKOFF, JILL S., small business owner, educator, entrepreneur; b. July 12, 1953; d. Julius Burt and Eloise Joy (Shlensky) Minkoff; m. Barry Charles Goldman, Jan. 30, 1982 (div. Nov. 1995); children: Joshua Scott Goldman, Elise Lynn Goldman. Certificat d'Assiduite, U. Grenoble, France, 1968; BA, Pomona Coll., 1974; MA, Siegal Coll., 2006. Cert. spiritual counselor Am. Bd. Hypnotherapy. Mktg. rep. IBM, Riverside, Calif., 1974-77, San Francisco, 1978-79; dir. store sys. Neiman Marcus, Dallas, 1979-81; dir. end-user computing svcs. Marion Labs., Kansas City, Mo., 1982-89, dir. info. sys. data and techs., 1989. Dir. corp. info. systems Marion Merrell Dow Inc., 1989-91; dir. Bus. Process Improvement, 1992-93; pres. Visions Connections, Inc., Kans., 1993-2000, Aleph Sys., 2000—. Sch. pres. ARC, Kansas City, Mo., 1966-67; v.p. chpt. B'nai B'rith Girls, Kansas City, 1968-69; mem. Nat. Coun. Jewish Women, 2001, bd. dirs. Kansas City chpt., 2002-03. Mem. Silicon Prairie Tech. Assn. (bd. dirs. 1992-99, adv. bd. creative courseware 1995-2002). Home and Office: 600 E 8 Street 5S Kansas City MO 64106 Personal E-mail: mjsminkoff@aol.com.

MINNA, MARIA, member of Canadian Parliament; b. Pofi, Frosinone, Italy, Mar. 14, 1948; arrived in Can., 1957. Grad. in Sociology with honors, U. Toronto. Policy advisor to former Ont. Premier David Peterson; pres. COSTI-IIAS Immigrant Svcs.; v.p. pub. affairs cons. co., Toronto; M.P. from Beaches-Woodbine dist. Ho. of Commons, Toronto, 1993-97, MP from Beaches-East York dist. Ottawa, Ont., Can., 1997—; parliamentary sec. Min. Citizenship and Immigration, 1996—98; chmn. to social policy com. Nat. Liberal Caucus, 1998—99, min. for internat. cooperation, 1999—2002. Life-long liberal, mem. Nat. Platform Com., 1988; apptd. vice chair standing com. Human Resources Devel., 1994. Contbr. reports on cmty. devel. and provision of svcs. to immigrants and minority groups. Former mem. campaign cabinet United Way Gtr. Toronto; former dir. Nat. Coun. Welfare Recipient Premio Italia nel Mondo award, 2001, President's Award, Indo-Canada Chamber of Commerce, 2001, Outstanding Leadership Award, RESULTS Canada, 2002. Mem. Nat. Congress Italian-Canadians (former exec. dir. Toronto dist., former pres.). Liberal. Office: House of Commons 406 West Block Ottawa ON Canada K1A 0A6 also: 1912 Danforth Ave M4C1J4 Toronto ON Canada E-mail: Minna.M@parl.gc.ca.

MINNELLI, LIZA, singer, actress; b. Los Angeles, Mar. 12, 1946; d. Vincente and Judy (Garland) M.; m. Peter Allen, Mar. 3, 1967 (div. June 24, 1972); m. Jack Haley Jr., Sept. 15, 1974 (div. 1979); m. Mark Gero, Dec. 4, 1979 (div. 1992); m. David Gest, Mar. 16, 2002 (div. 2003). Appeared in Off-Broadway revival of Best Foot Forward, 1963; appeared with mother at London Palladium, 1964; nightclub debut at Shoreham Hotel, Washington, 1965; appeared in Flora, the Red Menace, 1965 (Tony award), The Act, 1977 (Tony award), The Rink, 1984, Victor Victoria; films include Charlie Bubbles, 1967, The Sterile Cuckoo, 1969, Tell Me That You Love Me, Junie Moon, 1970, Cabaret, 1972 (Oscar award), That's Entertainment, 1974, Lucky Lady, 1975, A Matter of Time, 1976, Silent Movie, 1976, New York, New York, 1977, Arthur, 1981, Rent A Cop, Arthur on the Rocks, 1988, Stepping Out, 1991, The OH in Ohio, 2006; recorded You Are For Loving, 1963, Tropical Nights, 1977, Liza Minnelli at Carnegie Hall, 1987, Results, 1989, Maybe This Time, 1996, Gently, 1996, Minnelli on Minnelli, 2000, (with Herbie Hancock, Johnny Mathis, Donna Summer), Liza's Back!, 2003; (TV films) Parallel Lives, 1994, The West Side Waltz, 1995, Jackie's Back!, 1999; appeared on TV in own spl. Liza With a Z, 1972 (Recipient Emmy award); other TV appearances include Goldie and Liza Together, 1980, Baryshnikov on Broadway, 1980, The Princess and the Pea, Showtime, 1983, A Time to Live, 1985, Sam Found Out, 1988, Liza Minnelli Live from Radio City Music Hall, PBS (Emmy nomination, Music Program Performance, 1993), The Wonderful World of Oz: 50 Years of Magic, 1990, A Century of Cinema, 1994, My Favorite Broadway: The Leading Ladies, 1999, (TV series) Arrested Development, 2003-05; guest appearance Law & Order: Criminal Intent, 2006; internat. tour with Frank Sinatra, Sammy Davis Jr., 1988. Awarded the Brit. equivalent of the Oscar for Best Actress, 1972, Italy's David di Donatello award (twice), the Valentino award. Address: Capitol Records Inc 1750 Vine St Hollywood CA 90028-5209 also: Angel EMI Guardian Records 304 Park Ave S New York NY 10010-5339*

MINNER, RUTH ANN, governor; b. Melford, Del., Jan. 17, 1935; m. Frank Ingram (dec. 1967); 3 children; m. Roger Minner (dec. 1991). Student, Del. Tech. and Community Coll. Office receptionist to Gov, State of Del., Dover, 1972—74; mem. Del. Ho. of Reps., Dover, 1974—82, Del. State Senate, Dover, 1982—92; lt. gov. State of Del., Dover, 1993—2001, gov., 2001—. Mem.: Dem. Nat. Com. Democrat. Office: Office Gov William Penn St Tatnall Bldg 3d Fl Dover DE 19901 Office Phone: 302-744-4101. Office Fax: 302-739-2775.*

MINNEY, GLORIA JOAN, massage therapist, holistic health practitioner; b. Eugene, Oreg., Dec. 31, 1936; d. Arthur Benjamin Minney and Anna Lucille Hart Minney; m. Jack Junior Curtis, Dec. 20, 1958 (div. Jan. 1962); m. Michael Jacob Meils, June 19, 1965 (div. Nov. 4, 1980); children: Joanna Dianna Meils, Minney Sosa. BS, U. Oreg., 1959, MS, 1962; postgrad., Ariz. State U., 1964—67, John Ben Shepperd Pub. Leadership Inst., 1999—2000, U. Tex.-Permian Basin, El Paso C.C., 1973—. Cert. tchg., health, P.E., art, social studies Oreg., Ariz., New Mex., Tex., lic. massage therapist, instr. Tex., New Mex. Tchr. Lowell H.S., Oreg., 1959—62; instr. Colo. State Coll., Greeley, Colo., 1962—64; tchr. Camelback H.S., Phoenix, 1964—67, White Mid. Sch., El Paso, Tex., 1968—70; instr. Jacksonville State Univ., Ala., 1970—73, El Paso C.C., 1973—; tchr. De Valle H.S., El Paso, Tex., 1989—. Instr. Univ. Tex., El Paso, Tex., 1979; curriculum devel. El Paso C.C., 1973—95; massage therapist, holistic health practitioner, Tex., 1984—, N.Mex., 1984—. Painting, printmaking, jewerly, (best show);, performer dance, drama; choreographer, tchr. (modern, folk, square social). Sec., treas., pres., v.p. 4-H Clubs, 1945—55. Mem.: Nat. Edn. Assn., Am. Assn. for Health, Physical Edn. and Dance, Am. Massage Therapy Assn. Independent. Roman Catholic. Avocations: painting, printmaking, travel, sewing, gardening. Home: Box 31143 El Paso TX 79931 Office: Del Valle H S 950 Bordeaux Dr El Paso TX 79907

MINNICH, DIANE KAY, legal association administrator; b. Iowa City, Feb. 17, 1956; d. Ralph Maynard Minnich and Kathryn Jane (Obye) Tompkins. BA in Behavioral Sci., San Jose State U., 1978. Tutorial program coord./instr. Operation SHARE/La Valley Coll., Van Nuys, Calif., 1979-81; field exec. Silver Sage Girl Scout Coun., Boise, Idaho, 1981-85; continuing legal edn. dir. Idaho State Bar/Idaho Law Found. Inc., Boise, 1985-88, dep. dir., 1988-90, exec. dir., 1990—. Sec.-treas. Western States Bar Conf., 2001-2005; bd. dirs. Atty. Liability Protection Soc.--A Fmily of Profl. Svc. Cos.; mem. adv. bd. legal asst. program Boise State U. Mem. Assn. CLE Adminstrs., Chgo., 1985-90; bd. dirs. Silver Sage coun. Girl Scouts, Boise, 1990-93, 99-2001, mem. nominating com., 1990-94, 97-2001, chair nominating com., 1991-92; mem. legal asst. program adv. bd. Boise State U.; bd. dirs. Boise Schs. Found., 2004—. Named one of Outstanding Young Women in Am., 1991. Mem. ABA (standing com. on pub. edn. adv. commn. 2004—), Nat. Orgn. Bar Execs. (membership com. 1992-97, chair 1996-97), Zonta Club Boise (pres. 1991-92, bd. dirs. 1989-93), Rotary Club Boise (chair mem. com. 1994-97, bd. dirs. 1996-97, 99—, pres. 2003-04). Avocations: jogging, golf. Office: Idaho State Bar Idaho Law Found PO Box 895 525 W Jefferson St Boise ID 83702-5931 Home: 1118 Harrison Blvd Boise ID 83702-3448 Office Phone: 208-334-4500. E-mail: dminnich@isb.idaho.gov.

MINNICK, MARY E., beverage company executive; b. Evanston, Ill., Nov. 27, 1959; BS in Bus., Bowling Green St. U., 1981; MBA, Duke U., 1983. With fountain sales, bottle/can divsn. Coca-Cola USA; asst. v.p., dir non-carbonated beverages The Coca-Cola Co., 1993—95, v.p., Middle & Far East mktg., 1996—97, pres. South Pacific divsn., 1997—2000, pres., Coca-Cola Japan, 2000—01, pres., COO, Asia Group, 2001—05, exec. v.p., 2002—, pres. mktg., strategy & innovation, 2005—. Mem. Dean's Coun. John F. Kennedy Sch. Bus., Harvard U.; bd. visitors Fuqua Sch. Bus. Named one of 50 Most Powerful Women in Bus., Fortune mag., 2005, 2006, 100 Most Powerful Women in World, Forbes mag., 2005, 25 Masters of Innovation, BusinessWeek, 2006. Office: The Coca-Cola Co PO Box 1734 Atlanta GA 30301*

MINNICK, SALLY SCHAEFER, director; b. St. Louis, Dec. 31, 1943; d. Kenneth M. and Miriam (Glaze) Schaefer; m. Randall Wayne Minnick, Sept. 5, 1964; children: Randall Kenneth (dec.), Mark Wayne. BS in Edn., U. Mo., 1965. Life cert. grades K-8 contained class and grades 1-8 French. Tchr. grade 6 Parkade Sch., Columbia, Mo., 1965; tchr. grade 7 Polo (Mo.) Sch., 1965-68; tchr. grade 1 Tina (Mo.)-Avalon Sch., 1968-69; tchr. grade 5 Tri-County R-7, Jamesport, Mo., 1981—2000; regional assessment program facilitator Mo. Dept. Elem. and Secondary Edn., Jefferson City, 2000—. State grant reader Mo. Dept. Elem. and Secondary Edn., Jefferson City, 1991-94, state writing assessment scorer, 1992-94, state ad hoc stds. com., 1993-95; presenter in field; reviewer in field. Columnist (book revs.) Middle Sch. Reading Spl. Interest Group Newsletter, 1993—. Mem., Sunday sch. tchr. Jamesport (Mo.) Meth. Ch., 1974-94; project leader Jamesport (Mo.) 4-H Club, 1974-94, cmty. leader, 1979-89. State Incentive grantee Mo. Dept. Elem. and Secondary Edn., Jefferson City, 1992, 93, 94, 85, 96, 97, 98. Mem. Internat. Reading Assn. (coun. pres. 1992-94, chairperson Mark Twain com. 1992-93, chairperson state literacy com. 1993-95, coun. sec. 1994-95, zone coord. 1996-2000), Mo. State Tchrs. Assn. (local pres. 1991-93, regional rep. Mo. staff devel. coun. 2000-03). Avocations: crafts, sewing, reading, swimming, exercising. Office: Tri-County R-7 Sch 701 South St Jamesport MO 64648-9219

MINNIS, KAREN, state representative; b. Portland, Oreg., July 20, 1954; m. John Minnis, 1972; 3 children. Legis. aide State Rep. John Minnis, 1987—98; mem. Oreg. Ho. of Reps., 1998—; majority leader, 2001—03. Spkr. of the Ho., 2003—. Republican. Office: 900 Court St NE Rm 269 Salem OR 97301 Office Phone: 503-986-1200.

MINOR, ADDINE E., civic leader; b. Tupelo, Miss., June 22, 1919; d. George Bradley and Myrtle (Guyton) Jones; m. William Minor, Oct. 11, 1941; children: Ramona June Warhurst, Deborah Merle Ruff, William Bradley Minor, Bonnie Sue Shannon. Grad., Bandy's Secretarial Sch., Osceola, 1937; AA, So. Bapt. U., 1974; student, Parke Coll. Sec., bookkeeper Sinclair Refining Co., Osceola, Ark., 1948-53, Judge A.F. Barham, Osceola, 1953-59; sec., then welfare counselor State of Ark., Blytheville and Osceola, 1959-63, substitute tchr. Luxora and Osceola, 1983-86; sec., counselor U.S. Govt., Blytheville AFB, 1963-83; exec. sec. Calvary Bapt. Ch., Osceola, 1986—; substitute tchr. Rivercrest Jr. H.S., Wilson, 1994; tchr.'s asst. North Elem. Sch., Osceola, 1995; adminstrv. sec. Workforce Alliance, Blytheville, 1998—, asst. Class sec. bible study First Bapt. Ch., Osceola, 1985-86; mem. Calvary Bapt. Ch. 1971—, libr. tng. union, 1986—, tng. union dir., 1988—, served baptismal com., 1986-88; ch. clk., 1988—. Mem. First Bapt. Ch., Miss. County Literacy Coun.; vol. AmeriCorps. Recipient English award State Miss., 1936, PMIT Golden Fingers award Hdqrs. SAC Offutt AFB NE, 1978, 79, 80, Presdl. Cert. U.S. Govt., Washington, 1983. Mem. Explorer Bible First Bapt. Ch., Home Bible Study, Women's Missionary Union, Farm Bur., Nat. Assn. Female Execs., Homemaker's Extension Club (sec., treas. to 1987), Gen. Fedn. Women's Clubs, Profl. Women's Orgn. (sec.), Worldwide Communications. Republican. Avocations: reading, creative writing, needlepoint, croquet, golf.

MINOR, MARIAN THOMAS, educational consultant, retired elementary school educator, retired secondary school educator; b. Richmond, Va., Apr. 16, 1933; d. James Madison and Florence Elwood (Edwards) M. BS, U. Va., 1955; MEd, William and Mary Coll., 1968; postgrad., Va. Commonwealth U., 1987-88. Cert. guidance, health and phys. edn. Educator Richmond (Va.) Pub. Schs., 1955-90, ednl. cons., 1990—. Educator Sch. Nursing Med. Coll. Va., Richmond, 1958-68; camp dir. Manakin, Va., 1956-68; nat. basketball ofcl. Richmond (Va.) Bd. Ofcls., 1952-77; mem. faculty adv. com. Albert Hill Middle Sch., Richmond, 1965-90, dept. chmn., 1960-90, Tchr. of Yr., 1980; textbook adoption Richmond (Va.) Pub. Sch., 1975, 85, curriculum planner, 1978-79, 82-83, 84-85; PTA coord. Albert Hill Middle Sch., Richmond, 1985-89, chmn. self-study and accreditation team, 1987-88. Chmn. basketball ofcl. examiners Richmond Bd. Women Ofcls., 1966-76; bd. dirs., homeowner adv., constrn. crewman, family svcs. com. Habitat for Humanity, 1994-2002, Blitz Build 2000 adv. chmn.; mem. exec. com. Northminster Bapt. Ch., 1991-94, 99-2002, deacon, clk., 97-99, worship team, 1999—, premises chair, 1991-94, mem. by-laws revision com., 1986, 98, 99, srs. task force chmn., pres. sr. fellowship, 2006—, regional adv. coun. Befriender Ministry. Recipient J.C. Penney Golden Rule award, 1996, Outstanding Vol. award Habitat for Humanity, 1998, Outstanding Svc. award Albert Hill PTA, 1988. Mem. AAUW, AAHPERD, Va. Health Phys. Edn. Assn., Va. Ret. Tchrs. Assn., Train Collectors Assn., Sherwood Park Civic Assn., King and Queen Hist. Soc., Mortar Bd., Alpha Phi Sigma, Kappa Delta Pi. Republican. Avocations: genealogy, history. Home and Office: 1507 Brookland Pky Richmond VA 23227-4707

MINOR, V. CHRISTINE MAHAFFEY, science educator; b. Greenville, SC, Mar. 27, 1969; d. Janet Bock and William Larry Mahaffey; m. John Charles Minor, Nov. 6, 1992; 1 child, Savannah Nicole. BS in Biology, U. SC, Spartanburg, 1991; MS in Biol. Sci., Iowa State U., 1997. Lab. coord. Iowa State U., Ames, 1993—98; sr. lectr. Clemson U., SC, 1998—. Various roles Carolina Basset Hound Rescue, Charleston, SC, 1998—2006; coach Tiger Town Troublemakers Lego League, Clemson, SC, 2004—06. Mem.: NSTA (assoc.), Nat. Assn. of Biology Tchrs. (assoc.). Avocations: woodturning, crafting, gardening. Home: 116 Wigington St Clemson SC 29631 Office: Clemson Univ 330C Long Hall Clemson SC 29634 Office Phone: 864-656-3837. Personal E-mail: mminor@clemson.edu.

MINOW, JOSEPHINE BASKIN, civic volunteer; b. Chgo., Nov. 3, 1926; d. Salem N. and Bessie (Sampson) Baskin; m. Newton N. Minow, May 29, 1949; children: Nell, Martha, Mary. BS, Northwestern U., Evanston, Ill., 1948. Asst. to advt. dir. Mandel Brothers Dept. Store, Chgo., 1948-49; tchr. Francis W. Parker Sch., Chgo., 1949-50; vol. in civil and charitable activities, 1950—; bd. dirs. Juvenile Protective Assn., Chgo., 1958—, pres., 1973-75. Bd. dirs. Parnham Trust, Beaminster, Dorset, England. Author: Marty the Broken Hearted Artichoke, 1997. Founder, coord. Children's divsn. Hospitality and Info. Svc., Washington, 1961-63; mem. Caucus Com., Glencoe, Ill., 1965-69; co-chmn. spl. study on juvenile justice Chgo. Cmty. Trust, 1978-80; chmn. Know Your Chgo., 1980-83; bd. dirs. Chgo. Coun. Fgn. Rels., 1977-2003, hon. life mem., 2003; trustee Chgo. Hist. Soc., Ravinia Festival Assn.; mem. women's bd. Field Mus., U. Chgo.; founding mem., v.p. women's bd. Northwestern U., 1978; bd. govs. Chgo. Symphony, 1966-73, 76-; mem. Citizens Com. Juvenile Ct. of Cook County, 1985-96; exec. com. Northwestern U. Libr. Coun., 1974-96; co-chair grandparents' adv. com. Chgo. Children's Mus., 1999; bd. dirs. Jane Addams Juvenile Ct. Found.; dir. Abraham Lincoln Presdl. Libr. and Mus., 2005—. Recipient spl. award Chgo. Sch. and Workshop for Retarded, 1975, Children's Guardian award Juvenile Protective Assn., 1993. Mem. Hebrew Immigrant Aid Soc. (bd. dirs. 1977-98, award 1988), Friday Club, The Arts Club. Democrat. Jewish. Office: Chgo Hist Museum Clark St at North Ave Chicago IL 60614

MINOW, MARTHA LOUISE, law educator; b. Highland Pk., Ill., Dec. 6, 1954; AB in History, U. Mich., 1975; EdM, Harvard U., 1976; JD, Yale U., 1979; EdD (hon.), Wheelock Coll., 1998. Bar: Mass. 1981. Law clk. to Judge David L. Bazelon US Ct. Appeals DC Cir., 1979-80; law clk. to Assoc. Justice Thurgood Marshall US Supreme Ct., 1980-81; asst. prof. law Harvard Law Sch., Cambridge, Mass., 1981-86, prof., 1986—, William Henry Bloomberg prof. law, 2003—; acting dir. program on ethics and the professions Harvard U., Cambridge, Mass., 1993—94, acting dir. ctr. on ethics and the professions, 2000—01; co-dir. Children's Studies at Harvard, 1996—99. Sr. fellow, Harvard Soc. Fellows, 1997-. Author: Making All the Difference: Inclusion, Exclusion, and American Law, 1990, Not Only For Myself: Identity, Politics, and Law, 1997, Between Vengeance and Forgiveness: Facing History After Genocide and Mass Violence, 1998, Partners, Not Rivals: Privatization and the Public Good, 2002; co-author: Teacher's Manual, Civil Procedure: Doctrine, Practice, and Context, 2004; editor: Family Matters: Readings on Family Lives and the Law, 1993; co-editor: Narrative, Violence, and the Law, 1992, Law Stories, 1996, The Free Exercise of Culture, 2001, Engaging in Cultural Differences, 2002, Imagine Coexistence: Restoring Humanity After Violent Ethnic Conflict, 2003, Mary Joe Frug's Women and the Law, 2004. Trustee emeritus Judge Baker Children's Ctr.; trustee William T. Grant Found.; bd. dirs. Judge David L. Bazelon Ctr. for Mental Health Law, The Covenant Found, Am. Bar Found, 1985-94. Mem. Law and Soc. Assn. Office: Harvard Law Sch 1563 Massachusetts Ave Cambridge MA 02138 Office Phone: 617-495-4276. Office Fax: 617-496-5156. Business E-Mail: minow@law.harvard.edu.

MINSHALL, DOROTHY KATHLEEN, music educator; b. Bakersfield, Calif., Feb. 6, 1967; d. Donna Kathleen Bigler, Robert Lynn Bigler; m. Todd Allen Minshall; children: Eric, Rhett. BMus-flute and voice performance, Dallas Bapt. U., 1989; Associates in Theatre, Eastern Okla. State Coll., 2005. Owner, tchr. Dottie's Studio for Fine Arts, Snow, Okla., 1989—; guest artist, guest instr. drama, music and choreography Eastern Okla. State U., 2003—. Cons. Music and Arts Okla. Task Force on Edn., 1991—92. Dir.(musical prodns.): For God and Country, 1992 (Outstanding Children's Prodn., 1992); musician: flute sub for two symphony orchestras; actor(musical theatre): My Fair Lady, 1989 (Best Actress, 1989); dir.(children's theatre): A Season of Giving, 2000 (Best Dir.--Best Overall Prodn.). Tchr. Sun. sch. Nashoba Valley Bapt. Ch., Nashoba, Okla., 1989—. Nominee Irene Ryan, ACTF, 2004. Mem.: Okla. Music Tchrs. Assn. (cert. 1990), Music Tchrs. Nat. Assn. (cert. 1990). Baptist. Avocation: jewelry designer. Home: PO Box 1132 Wilburton OK 74578-1132 Office: Dottie's Studio for Fine Arts 3279 Roger Davis Rd Wilburton OK 74578-1132 Personal E-mail: dminshall@pisp.net, dminshall67@yahoo.com.

MINTICH, MARY R., art educator, sculptor; b. Detroit; d. Clayton Harris and Mary Inez (Barber) Ringelberg; m. George Mintich, Mar. 9, 1954; children: Barbara, Mark. MFA, U. N.C., Greensboro, 1971. Tchr. Charlotte(N.C.)-Mecklenburg Schs., 1961-66, Sacred Heart Coll., Belmont, N.C., 1967-72; prof. Winthrop U., Rock Hill, SC, 1973—. One and two artist shows include Greenville County Mus. Art, Mint Mus. Art, Southeastern Ctr. Contemporary Art, Asheville Mus. Art, St. John's Mus., Clemson U. Recipient Ferro Purchase award Everson Mus., Purchase awards Mint Mus., S.C. State Art Collection, Nations Bank, St. Johns Mus., Capitol Ctr., Raleigh, N.C. Mem. Coll. Art Assn., Piedmont Craftsmen Inc., Tri-State Sculptors, Soc. N. Am. Goldsmiths. Home: 515 Dogwood Ln Belmont NC 28012-3710 Office: Winthrop U Oakland Ave Rock Hill SC 29733-0001

MINTON, JANE ISABELLE, education educator; b. Pinckneyville, Ill., Aug. 1, 1946; d. James Scott and Isabella Boeheim Templeton; m. Walter J. Minton (div.); 1 child, James Isaac. BA in Psychology, McKendree Coll., Lebanon, Ill.; BA in Bus. Adminstrn., U. Md., Far East Divsn., Okinawa, Japan; MA in Gerontology, U. South Fla., Tampa, 1975. Acad. advisor, counselor, term faculty mem. John A. Logan Coll., Carterville, Ill., 1989—. Contbr. articles to profl. jours. and pubs. Bd. mem. 5 Star Industries, Du Quoin, Ill., 1978—80; pres., bd. mem. Unit Dist. 300 Sch. Bd., Du Quoin, 1995—2004; sec., treas. Ill. Sch. Dist. Agy. Bd. Regents, Chgo., 1998—2004. Home: Du Quoin IL 62832 Office: John A Logan Coll 700 Logan College Rd Carterville IL 62918 Office Phone: 618-985-3741. Business E-Mail: janeminton@jalc.edu.

MINTON, JENNIFER, information technology executive; Various positions audit divsn. Arthur Andersen LLP, 1983; various fin. positions including asst. corp. controller Oracle Corp., Redwood City, Calif., 1989—98, corp. controller, 1998—, v.p., 1995, sr. v.p., 2000—. Office: acle Corp 500 Oracle Pkwy Redwood City CA 94085

MINTZ, GWENDOLYN JOYCE, writer, actress, comedian; b. White Sands, N.Mex, July 23, 1961; BA with distinction, N.Mex State U., 1984. Lic. ednl. asst. N.Mex. Teddy bear artist, owner Teddy Hugs & Things, Las Cruces, N.Mex., 1983—; field rschr. Smithsonian Folklife Program, 1991—92; instr. Dona Ana Br. CC, Las Cruces, 1992—95, 2002; supr., activity asst. U. Ter. Good Samaritan Village, Las Cruces, 1997—99; news writer Las Cruces Bull., 1997—2000. Asst. fiction editor: Small Spiral Notebook, 2002—04; editor: Scrivener's Pen Libr. Jour., 2003—; contbr. poetry, short stories, articles to publs.; actor: Ofay Watcher, 2004, Vagina Monologues, 2004. Vol. Univ. Hills Elem., Las Cruces, 1999—2002, Ctrl. Elem., Las Cruces, 2002—03. Named Outstanding Young Women in Am., 1985, Flash Fiction Extraordinaire, Fiction Warehouse, 2004; recipient Hon. Mention, Writer's Digest Mag. Short Story Competition, 1981, 2001, 4th Ann. Mandy Poetry Contest, 2003, Black Scholar award, Office Black Programs N.Mex State U., 1986, 1990, 2001, 2d pl., The Ink/Border Book Festival Poetry Competition, 2001, Comedy Lab/Pontiac Coll. Comedy Bake-off winner, 2001, Winner, Comedy Lab/Pontiac Coll. Comedy Bake-off NMSU, 2001; scholar, Inst. Gerontol. Rsch. and Edn., 1986, Sarah Lawrence Coll., 2001; Crimson scholar, N.Mex State U., 1980—81. Personal E-mail: gwendolynjoycemintz@yahoo.com.

MINTZ, LENORE CHAICE (LEA MINTZ), consultant; b. N.Y.C., Aug. 6, 1925; d. Abraham and Dr. Eva (Kornblith) Chaice; m. Lewis R. Mintz, July 4, 1944 (dec. Aug. 1996); children: Richard Lewis, Alan Lee, Douglas Chaice. Student, U. Mich., 1942-44; BA magna cum laude, U. Bridgeport, 1976. Cert. personnel cons. Office mgr., personnel cons. Golden Door, Inc., Norwalk, Conn., 1970-78; v.p. permanent div. Aubrey Thomas, Inc., Stamford and Norwalk, 1978-84; sr. v.p. Aubrey Thomas Temps., N.Y., N.J., Conn., Pa., 1984-88; area v.p. Mid-Atlantic div. Talent Tree Personnel Svcs., 1988-89; v.p. bus. devel. Human Resources, Inc., Norwalk, Stamford, Statford and North Haven, 1989-90; prin. Lea Mintz & Assocs., Norwalk, 1990—. Spkr., panel mem., condr. workshop and seminars in field; justice of peace, Fairfield County, Conn., 1954—94; mem. adv. bd. Norwalk Savs. Soc., 1987—98, U.S. Surg. Corp. (now Tyco Corp.), 1991—; instl. animal care and use com. Bayer Corp., 2002—. Loaned exec. United Way of Norwalk & Wilton, Conn., 1991-92; mem. Norwalk Bd. Edn., 1966-72, chmn., 1969, Norwalk Planning and Zoning Commn., 1971-73, Conn. Edn. Coun., 1979-83, Conn. Small Bus. Adv. Coun., 1984-86; mem. regional adv. coun. Norwalk C.C., 1988-90; past pres. Norwalk Cmty. Tech. Coll. Found., 1988-90, bd. dirs. 1964-94, life hon. bd. dirs., 1995—; del. numerous Dem. state and county convs.; Clinton del. Dem. Nat. Conv., 1992; mem. adv. coun. displaced homemakers Bridgeport YWCA, 1988-90; v.p. Greater Norwalk Cmty. Coun., 1973-75; life mem. Women's Aux. Jewish Home for Aged in Conn.; cmty. rels. cons. Family & Children's Aid Mid-Fairfield County, Conn., 1992—; chair Mayor's Com. Hist. Preservation, Norwalk, 2003; dir. vols. fin. divsn. Dem. Nat. Conv., Boston, 2004; mem. social events com. Dedication Clinton Libr., Little Rock, 2004; active numerous other orgns. Recipient numerous awards including Woman of Yr. award Norwalk Bus. and Profl. Womens Club, 1984, Outstanding Woman of Decade award UN Assn. Conn., 1987, Outstanding Svc. award Conn. Cmty. and Tech. Coll. Bd. Trustees, 1991 (1st honoree), Successful Aging award Conn. Cmty. Care Inc., 1999, Woman of Substance award Conn. Post Newspaper, 2000. Mem. Women in Mgmt. (pres. 1990, Ann. Recognition award Conn. and Met. N.Y. area 1988), Internat. Assn. Personnel Women, Greater Norwalk C. of C. (bd. dirs. 1980-84, 1st Athena award 1986), Nat. Coun. Jewish Women (life), LWV, Midday Club Stamford, B'nai B'rith (life), Alpha Sigma Lambda. Avocations: reading, knitting, travel, golf. Home and Office: 1205 Foxboro Dr Norwalk CT 06851 E-mail: leamintz@optonline.net.

MINTZ, MARILYN D., artist, writer; b. Phila., Mar. 18; d. Milton A. and Mildred L. Mintz. Attended, U. Calif., Santa Barbara, 1968—70, BFA in Theater, 1972; MA in Film and TV, U. Calif., L.A., 1975. Prin., owner M.D.M. Co., Studio City, Calif., 1981, The Sweetheart Arts Co., Inc., Los Gatos, Calif., 1990—. Author: The Martial Arts Films, 1978, 2nd edit., 1983; author: (creator) Cartoon Pictures, 1979, The Cartoonist, 1980; contbr. columns in newspapers. Achievements include patents for doll and associated products. Office: The Sweathearts Arts Co Inc PO Box 1411 Los Gatos CA 95031

MINTZ, SUSAN ASHINOFF, apparel manufacturing company executive; b. NYC, Dec. 7, 1949; d. Lawrence and Thelma Ashinoff; m. Robert Mintz; children: Geoffrey, Tyler. BA, Finch Coll., 1971; MPA, NYU, 1977. Menswear advt. asst. New Yorker Mag., N.Y.C., 1971-72; assoc. Staub Warmbold & Assocs., Inc., exec. search co., N.Y.C., 1972-80; exec. v.p. Muhammad Ali Sportswear, Ltd., N.Y.C., 1980-81; pres. Forum Sportswear, Ltd., N.Y.C. and Portsmouth, Va., 1981—; group v.p., bd. dirs. Coronet Group, Portsmouth, 1985—. Trustee Dean Coll. Named to Outstanding Young Women in Am., U.S. Jaycees, 1980. Mem.: Essex Country Club.

MINTZ, SUZANNE, association executive; b. Feb. 1946; m. Steven Mintz. BA, Queens Coll., City U. NY; MS, U. Md. Architect; pres., co-founder Nat. Family Caregivers Assn., Wash., DC, 1993—. Bd. dirs. Nat. Patient Safety Found.; adv. bd. Easter Seals, Nat. Assn. Hosp. Hospitality Houses. Author: Love, Honor and Value: A Family Caregiver Speaks Out About the Choices and Challenges of Caregiving, 2002; writer about caregiver issues. Recipient Lilly Welcome Back award for lifetime achievement, 2004. Achievements include has testified before Congress about caregiver issues. Office: Nat Family Caregivers Assn 10400 Conn Ave #500 Kensington MD 20895-3944 Office Phone: 800-896-3650. Office Fax: 301-942-2302.

MINTZ-HITTNER, HELEN ANN, physician, researcher; b. Houston, Aug. 12, 1944; d. Bert and Jeanette (Haydis) Mintz; m. David Hittner, Sept. 8, 1968 (div. May 11, 1989); children: Miriam Annette Hittner Tondera, Susan Michelle Hittner, George Jacob Hittner. BA, Rice U., 1965; MD, Baylor Coll. Medicine, 1969. Lic. Tex. Bd. of Med. Examiners, 1969. Intern pediat. Baylor Affiliated Hosps., Houston, 1969—70, resident ophthalmology, 1970—73; fellow pediat. ophthalmology Tex. Children's Hosp., Houston, 1973—74; pediat. ophthalmologist Houston, 1974—95; Alfred W. Lasher III prof. pediat. ophthalmology U. Tex. Houston Med. Sch., 1995—. Author: several rsch. reports and jour. articles. Fellow: Am. Acad. Ophthalmology (Honor award 1986, Sr. Honor award 2005); mem.: N.Y. Acad. Medicine, N.Y. Acad. Sci., Ciba Found., Soc. Heed Fellows (life), Assn. Rsch. in Vision and Ophthalmology, Am. Assn. Pediat. Ophthalmology and Strabismus, Phi Beta Kappa (life), Alpha Omega Alpha (life). Liberal. Jewish. Achievements include discovery of Primary etiology of retinopathy of prematurity; research in Genetic linkage of aniridia to chromosome 11p13 (PAX6); Genetic identification of anterior segment dysgenesis on chromosome 10q25 (PITX3); Genetic identification of anterior segment dysgenesis on chromosome 1p32 (FOXE3); Genetic identification of anterior segment dysgenesis on chromosome 20p11.2 (VSX1). Home: 2400 N Braeswood Blvd #125 Houston TX 77030-4357 Office: U of Tex-Houston Med Sch 6410 Fannin St #920 Houston TX 77030-5204 Personal E-mail: mintzhittner@aol.com. Business E-Mail: Helen.A.Mintz-Hittner@uth.tmc.edu.

MINUDRI, REGINA URSULA, librarian, consultant; b. San Francisco, May 9, 1937; d. John C. and Molly (Halter) M. BA, San Francisco Coll. for Women, 1958; MLS, U. Calif., Berkeley, 1959. Reference libr. Menlo Park (Calif.) Pub. Libr., 1959-62; regional libr. Santa Clara County (Calif.) Libr., 1962-68; project coord. Fed. Young Adult Libr. Svcs. Project, Mountain View, Calif., 1968-71; dir. profl. svcs. Alameda County (Calif.) Libr., 1971, asst. county libr., 1972-77; libr. dir. Berkeley Pub. Libr., 1977-94; city libr. San Francisco Pub. Libr., 1997-2000. Lectr. U. San Francisco, 1970-72, U. Calif., Berkeley, 1977-81, 91-93, San Jose State U., 1994-97; cons., 1975-90; mem. adv. bd. Miles Cutter Ednl., 1992-98. Author: Getting It Together, A Young Adult Bibliography, 1970; contbr. articles to publs. including Sch. Libr. Jour., Wilson Libr. Bull. Bd. dirs. No. Calif. ACLU, 1994-96, Cmty. Memory, 1989-91, Berkeley Pub. Libr. Found., 1996-99; bd. dirs. Berkeley Cmty. Fund, 1995-99, chair youth com., 1994-96; mem. bd. mgrs. ctrl. br. Berkeley YMCA, 1988-93. Recipient proclamation Mayor of Berkeley, 1985, 86, 94, Citation of Merit, Calif. State Assembly, 1994; named Woman of Yr., Alameda County North chpt. Nat. Women's Polit. Caucus, 1985, Outstanding Alumna, U. Calif. Sch. Libr. and Info. Scis., Berkeley, 1987, Lifetime Achievement award Berkeley Cmty. Fund, 2001. Mem. ALA (pres. 1986-87, exec. bd. 1980-89, coun. 1979-88, 90-94, Grolier award 1974), Calif. Libr. Assn. (pres. 1981, coun. 1965-69, 79-82), LWV (dir. Berkeley chpt. 1980-81, v.p. comm. svcs. 1995-97). Office: Reality Mgmt 836 The Alameda Berkeley CA 94707-1916

MINYARD, LIZ, food products executive; BBA, Tex. Christian U., 1975. CEO Minyard Food Stores, Coppell, Tex., 1976—; dir. consumer affairs Minyard Food Stores Inc., Coppell, Tex., v.p. consumer affairs, 1980, v.p. corp. rels., 1983, also vice-chmn. bd. dirs., also co-chmn. bd. dirs. Trustee Boys and Girls Clubs of Am., 1995; chmn. United Way Dallas and Tarrant Counties, 1978, 1983—95; sect. chmn. United Way Tarrant County, 1983—84; chmn. mcht. divsn. United Way Dallas County, 1987, bd. dirs., 1995; bd. mem. Goodwill Industries of Dallas, Inc., 1981—94, mem. exec. com., 1987—88, 1993—95, vice chmn., 1992—94, chmn., 1995; mem. spring campaign drive YWCA, Dallas, 1982, chmn. campaign, 1983—85, co-chmn. capital campaign, 1995, co-chmn. mayor's summer youth employment commn., 1994, chmn. mayor's summer youth employment commn., 1995, bd. dirs., 1995; v.p. Dallas Urban League, 1989—91, bd. dirs., 1985—95, chmn. bd. dirs., 1992—93, chmn. bldg. com., 1995; mem. Dallas Citizens Coun., 1988—94, bd. dirs. exec. com., 1992—95; bd. dirs. Leukemia Assn. of North Ctrl. Tex., 1988—95; mem. Dallas Assembly, 1989—95; bd. dirs. Baylor Hosp. Found., 1989—95; mem. Dallas Summit, 1992—95, Dallas Together Forum, 1993—95, Dallas Women's Forum, 1994—95; bd. dirs. Zale Lipshy Hosp., 1993—95, Am. Heart Assn., 1991—94; chmn. City of Dallas Bond Program, 1995. Recipient Dallas/Ft. Worth Dist. Women in Bus. Adv. of Yr. award, U.S. Small Bus. Adminstrn., 1995, Tex. Family Bus. of Yr.-Cmty. Involvement award, Tex. Inst. Family Bus., 1995, Bus. award for Cmty. Involvement, Martin Luther King Jr. Cmty Ctr., 1995, Contbrs. award, Black State Employees Assn. of Tex., 1995, Art of Achievement award, Nat. Fedn. ow Women Bus. Owners, 1995. Mem.: North Tex. Commn. (bd. dirs. 1992—95), CIES The Food Bus. Forum (ann. congress com. mem. 1996), Tex. Food Mktg. Assn. (v.p. 1981—82, pres. 1982—84), Food Mktg. Inst. (consumer coun. 1977—88, steering com. 1982, pub. affairs com. 1989—90, bd. dirs. 1991—95), Greater Dallas C. of C. (leadership program 1982—83, bd. dirs. 1987—90, women's bus. issues exec. com. 1994—95, Women's Convenant Diamond Cutters award 1995), Second Harvest (Chgo. bd. dirs. 1992—95), North Tex. Food Bank (founding bd. mem., sec. 1981—83, bd. mem. 1982—95, pres. 1984, v.p. devel. 1987, chmn. hunger link program 1989—90). Office: Minyard Food Stores Inc PO Box 518 Coppell TX 75019-0518

MINZNER, PAMELA BURGY, state supreme court justice; b. Meridian, Miss., Nov. 19, 1943; BA cum laude, Miami U., 1965; LLB, Harvard U., 1968. Bar: Mass. 1968, N.Mex. 1972. Pvt. practice, Mass., 1968—71, Albuquerque, 1971—73; adj. prof. law U. N.Mex., Albuquerque, 1972—73, asst. prof., 1973—77, assoc. prof., 1977—80, prof. law, 1980—84; judge N.Mex. Ct. Appeals, Albuquerque, 1984—94, chief judge, 1993—94; justice N.Mex. Supreme Ct., Santa Fe, 1994—, chief justice, 1999—2001. Mem. faculty Inst. Preparativo Legal U., N.Mex. Sch. Law, 1975, 79; participant NEH Summer Seminars for Law Tchrs. Stanford Law Sch., 1982, U. Chgo. Law Sch., 1978. Author (with Robert T. Laurence): A Student's Guide to Estates in Land and Future Interests: Text, Examples, Problems & Answers, 1981, 2d edit., 1993. Mem.: ABA, State Bar N.Mex. (co-editor newsletter 1979—83, bd. dirs. 1978—79, 1983—84, sect. on women's legal rights and obligations), Gamma Phi Beta. Democrat. Avocations: reading, bridge, movies. Office: Supreme Ct NMex PO Box 848 Santa Fe NM 87501-0848*

MIORI, VIRGINIA MARIE, finance educator; d. Eugene and Mary Ann Miori. BA in Math., Hiram Coll., Ohio, 1983; MS in Ops. Rsch., Case Western Res. U., Cleve., 1986; MS in Transp., U. Pa., Phila., 1991; PhD in Ops. Rsch., Drexel U., Phila., 2006. Logistics cons. in field, Phila., 1989—99; math. tchr. Merion Mercy Acad., Merion Station, Pa., 1999—2002; adj. faculty Villanova U., Pa., 2002—06; asst. prof. St. Joseph U., Phila., 2006—. Recipient Drexel Rsch. Day Competition 1st Pl. award, 2004, Drexel Rsch. Day Competition Dean's award, 2005, Outstanding Dissertation award. Mem.: Coun. Supply Chain Mgmt. Profls., Soc. for Indsl. and Applied Math., Inst. for Ops. Rsch. and Mgmt. Scis. Office: St Joseph U Haub Sch Bus 5600 City Ave Philadelphia PA 19131 Personal E-mail: vmiori@comcast.net.

MIORI-MEROLA, DOREEN M., literature and language educator; d. Nilo M. Miori and Rose Sassi Miori; m. Albert Joseph Merola, July 20, 1985; 1 child, Nila Michelle Merola. BS, SUNY, Oswego, 1975; MS, Syracuse U., NY, 1997. Tchr. English Solvay H.S., NY, 1976—. Content specialist Solvay Union Free Sch. Dist., 2004—; agy. trainer ctr. cognitive coaching SUFSD, 2004—. Co-author: 100 Years of Tradition, History of the Village of Solvay. Bd. mem. Dollars for Scholars, Solvay, 2003—06. Grantee, Ctrl. NY Tchg. Ctr., 2004. Mem.: ASCD (assoc.), NY State United Tchrs. (assoc.), Nat. Coun. Tchrs. English (assoc.). Avocations: horseback riding, reading, travel. Office: Solvay High Sch 600 Gertrude Ave Solvay NY 13209 Office Phone: 315-468-2551. Office Fax: 315-468-2551. Personal E-mail: dmerola@solvay.cnyric.org.

MIOTTO, MARY ELIZABETH G., pediatrician; b. NYC, Apr. 9, 1964; MD, George Wash. U. Sch. Medicine, 1992. Intern Children's Nat. Med. Ctr., Washington, 1992—93, resident, 1993—95; attending physician INOVA Fairfax Children's Hosp., Falls Church, Va.; staff Marlborough Hosp., Mass. Mem. working group Pediat. Leadership Alliance. Recipient Excellence in Medicine Leadership award, AMA Found., 2004. Mem.: AMA, Am. Acad. Pediat. Office: Marlborough Hosp 157 Union St Marlborough MA 01752

MIRABAL, NANCY RAQUEL, social sciences educator, researcher; b. L.A., July 5, 1966; d. Servelio and Delia Mirabal. PhD, U. Mich., Ann Arbor, Mich., 1996. Assoc. prof. San Francisco State U., San Francisco, 1996—. Dir. Mission Oral History Gentrification Project, San Francisco; postdoctoral fellow U. Calif., Berkeley, Calif., 2001—03. Author: Ser de Aqui: Beyond the Cuban Exile Model, Technofuturos: Critical Interventions in Latina/o Studies. Bd. dirs. The Edge Project, San Francisco, 2005—06. Fellow, Social Sci. Rsch. Coun., 2003—04; grantee, Orgn. Am. Historian, 2005—; Cesar Chavez Dissertation fellow, Dartmouth Coll., 1995—96. Mem.: Latin Am. Studies Assn. (assoc.). Office: San Francisco State University 1600 Holloway Ave San Francisco CA 94132 Office Phone: 415-338-6804. Business E-Mail: nmirabal@sfsu.edu.

MIRACLE, DORIS JEAN, retired medical/surgical nurse; b. Louisville, July 23, 1931; d. Bernard Louis and Catherine Federle; m. Earl Miracle, Aug. 31, 1951; 1 child, David. Surg. nurse Norton Hosp., Louisville, 1951, Norton-Children's Hosp., Louisville, 1969—86; ret., 1986. Poetry (albums) Sounds of Poetry, 2003; author: numerous poems; contbr. articles to profl. jours. Recipient Editors Choice award, 2003, 2006. Mem.: Wilderness Rd. Writers, Gaslight Writers, Ky. Writer's Coalition, Internat. Soc. of Poets, Soc. Children's Book Writers and Illustrators, Louisville Astronomical Soc. Avocations: reading, poetry, astronomy, art, music. Personal E-mail: doriskitm@aol.com.

MIRACLE, SHEILA GIBBS, science educator; d. John Leslie Gibbs, Sr. and Joanne Cowan Gibbs; m. Eddy Philip Miracle, Dec. 11, 1997; children: Jeremy, Lauren. BA in Microbiology, U. Tenn., Knoxville, 1979, BA in Med. Tech., 1980; MEd in Biology, Lincoln Meml. U., Harrogate, Tenn., 1985. Hematologist Am. Soc. Clin. Pathologists, clin. lab. scientist, clin. lab. supr. NCA, med. technologist, supr. Tenn. Med. technologist, supr. blood bank and hematology Pineville Comty. Hosp., Ky., 1980—93; prof. S.E. Ky. Comty. and Tech. Coll., Cumberland, 1993—. Author: (book) Environmental Effects on Wood Lice, 1985. Recipient Tchg. Excellence award, Nat. Inst. for Staff and Orgnl. Devel. Mem.: Ky. Assn. Blood Banks, Tenn. Assn. Blood Banks, Am. Soc. Clin. Pathologists. Avocations: cooking, reading. Office: S E Ky Comty and Tech Coll 1300 Chichester Ave Middlesboro KY 40965

MIRAN, PATRICIA MARIE, art educator; b. Seattle, Apr. 6, 1951; d. Robert Glenroy Hancock and Bernice Iris Brisky; m. Maynard Alvin Miran, May 1, 1983; children: Maxwell, Jacob, Emma. Diploma in fine arts illustration, Art Students League, N.Y.C., 1974; BS cum laude, Excelsior Coll., 2001. Childrens story hr. dir. Sayre Libr., 1989—95; exec. dir. Lincoln Acad., Waverly, NY, 1998—2004; tchr. Jewish Cmty. Sch., Elmira, NY, 1999—. Libr. dir. Cady Libr., Nichols, NY, 1996; tutor, remedial reading M-G Edn., Elmira, 2001—; instr. Elmira Bus. Inst., 2005—06, pvt. painting lessons, 2006—. Rep. 4-H Cornell Coop. Ext., Owego, NY, 1989—2001. Grantee, N.Y. State Coun. on Arts, 1994—96; scholar, Calif. Coll. Arts and Crafts, 1969—70, Art Student League, 1971. Mem.: Arnot Art Mus. Avocations: gardening, birdwatching, hiking, canoeing, painting. Home and Studio: 21 Lincoln St Waverly NY 14892 Office: Jewish Cmty Sch PO Box 3087 1008 W Water St Elmira NY 14905 Personal E-mail: mmiran@stny.rr.com.

MIRANDA, M. JEANNE, psychiatrist; BS, Idaho State U., 1976; MA, U. Kansas, 1983, PhD, 1986. Asst. clin. prof. psychology U. Calif. San Francisco (UCSF), 1988—95, asst. prof. in residence in psychology, 1992—95; assoc. prof. psychology Georgetown U., Washington, 1995—2001; assoc. prof. biobehavioral sciences & psychiatry UCLA Neuropsychiatric Inst., 2001—, assoc. dir. Health Svcs. Rsch. Ctr. Sr. scientific editor Mental Health: Culture, Race, & Ethnicity, 2001. Recipient Interdisciplinary Achievement award, LPPI-UCSF Alumni-Faculty Assn., 1986, R.E. Harris award, UCSF, 1986; fellow, Rehabilitation Svc. Adminstrn., 1980—84; NIMH Clin. Svcs. Rsch. Fellowship, 1986—88. Mem.: Inst. Medicine. Office: Health Svcs Rsch Ctr UCLA Wilshire Ctr Ste 300 10920 Wilshire Blvd Los Angeles CA 90024-6505 Office Phone: 310-794-3710. E-mail: mirandaj@ucla.edu.*

MIRANDA, MINDA, chemist, pharmacy technologist; b. Alabat, Quezon, The Philippines, Apr. 7, 1955; came to U.S., 1990; d. Macario and Engracia (Malapajo) Felisco; m. Danilo E. Miranda, June 10, 1979; children: Mary Eisser, Dann Keoffer. BSChemE, Nat.U., Manila, The Philippines, 1977. Instr. Nat. U., Manila, 1977-90; pharm. technician Automated Pharm. Svcs., Moorestown, N.J., 1990-95; quality control lab. technician Marsam Pharms., Cherry Hill, N.J., 1995-96, assoc. stability chemist, 1996-97, stability chemist I, 1997—. Scholar Nat. U., 1972-75. Mem. Am. Chem. Soc. Home: 142 Cooper Ave Oaklyn NJ 08107-2246

MIRANDA-DIAZ, ALEJANDRA GUILLERMINA, surgeon, medical educator, researcher; b. Guadalajara Jalisco, Mexico, Mar. 23, 1952; d. Francisco Miranda Camacho and María Antonia Diáz Diaz. MBBS, Sch. Medicine U. Guadelajara, Jalisco, Mex., 1977; MBCh, U. Guadelajara, Mex., 1983, MS, 1993, MD, 2003. Gen. surgeon Mexican Inst. Social Security, Ocotlan, 1983—84, Guadalajara, Mexico, Mexican Inst. Social Security Ctrl. Med. Hosp., 1985—93; chief dept. surgery Mexican Inst. Social Security, 1993—96, sub dir., 1996—98; coord. masters degree in sci. U. Guadalajara, 2001—. Pvt. practice gen. surgery Agrupacion de Medicos Especialistas AC, 1983—; rsch. prof. U. Guadalajara, 2005—. Contbr. scientific papers, articles to profl. jours. Grantee PIFI 2.0, U. Guadalajara, 2002, NIVEL 1, Nat. Investigator Sys., 2005, Nat. Bd. Sci. and Tech., 2006. Fellow: Am. Coll. Surgeons; mem.: Mex. Assn. Surgery. Roman Cath. Avocation: painting. Office: Agruupacion de Medicos Especialistas AC Av La Paz No 2758 44500 Guadalajara Jalisco Mexico

MIRANDA-EVANS, VALETTA LEE, social worker, human services manager; d. Leland James and Mary Miranda; m. Bruce Claude Evans, Aug. 23, 1986; children: Darcel Lynette Murray, Adam Bruce Evans, Kristina L. Evans. BA, Boston U., 1977; MSW, Boston Coll., 1979. LCSW 1986, CEAP 1983, PHR 2000. Program specialist Nat. Clearinghouse for Alcohol/Drug Info., Rockville, Md., 1979—82; employee assistance counselor Prince George's County Health Dept., Beltsville, Md., 1982—84; substance abuse program coord. Social Security Adminstrn., Balt., 1984—88; dir. employee assistance program ARC, Washington, 1988—92; employee assistance cons. DuPont, Richmond, Va., 1992—96, human resource mgr., 1996—2002, employee assistance cons. Wilmington, Del., 2002—. Office: DuPont Rte 141 CRP 700/32 Wilmington DE 19808

MIRANDA-MORGART, LYNDA CHRISTINE, elementary school educator; b. Leominister, Mass., Jan. 2, 1977; d. Jose Armando Miranda and Carmencita Llado' Miranda; 1 child, Isabella Maria Morgart. BS in Interdisciplinary Studies, Tex. A&M U., College Station, 2000. Cert. self-contained classroom tchr. Tex. Bd. Edn., 2000, English instrn. 1-8 Tex. Bd. Edn., 2000, reading instrn. 1-8 Tex. Bd. Edn., 2000, ESL Tex. Bd. Edn., 2001. Tchr. grade 1 Sheridan Elem., Katy, Tex., 2000—04, Huggins Elem., Fulshear, Tex., 2004—. Mem.: Tex. Classroom Tchrs. Assn. Liberal.

MIRENDA, ROSALIE M., academic administrator, nursing educator; b. Phila., Sept. 22, 1937; d. Achille and Anna Pierotti; m. Anthony D. Mirenda, Sept. 9, 1961; children: Anthony D. Jr., John A., Rosalie A. BSN, Villanova U., 1959; MS in Nursing, U. Pa., 1978; DNSc, Widener U., 1992. Staff nurse, tchr. St. Agnes Med. Ctr., Phila., Mercy Cath. Med. Ctr., Darby, Pa.; instr. Nursing Div. Our Lady of Angels Coll. (now Neumann Coll.), Aston, Pa., 1973—86, prof., chair Nursing Div., 1986, prof., v.p. for acad. affairs, 1990, pres., 1996—. Pres. Neuman Systems Model Trustee Group Inc. Contbr. articles to profl. jours. Chmn. bd. trustees Sch. Holy Child, Drexel. Recipient Bronze medal; named Prof. of Yr. Coun. Adv. Support Edn., 1987, Outstanding Educator of Am., 1975, Outstanding Nurse award, 1990. Mem. ANA, NLN, AAUW, Sigma Theta Tau, Delta Tau. Office: Neumann Coll 1 Neumann Dr Aston PA 19014-1277 E-mail: RMIRENDA@neumann.edu.

MIRIPOL, JERILYN ELISE, poet, writer, writing therapist; b. Chgo., Jan. 22; d. Albert and Janice (Tuchin) M.; m. Richard Palmer Van Duyne, Dec. 30, 1986. BA in English Lit., Northeastern Ill. U., 1974. Writing therapist Northshore Retirement Hotel, Evanston, Ill., 1983; creative writing tchr. Oakton Community Coll., Evanston, 1985—; writing therapist St. Francis Hosp., Evanston, 1989—. Artist-writer-in-residence Dawes Sch., Evanston, 1985; artist-in-residence Evanston Twp. High Sch., 1988; writing facilitator for individual students, Chgo., 1987—; tchr. writing therapy to mental health profls. and caregivers U. Wis., Milw., 1989; presenter writing therapy workshop, 1990, Nat. Assn. Poetry-Therapy, Chgo., 1991. Author: Discovering Self-Awareness Through Poetry, 1987, (poetry) The Sounds Were Distilled, 1977; author numerous poems; contbr. articles to profl. jours. Vol. Ridgeview Nursing Home, Evanston, 1982-83; advocate of children of abuse, human and civil rights. Talent scholar in creative writing Northeastern Ill. U., Squaw Valley Community Writers scholar, 1980, Radgale Found. scholar, 1985, Aspen Writer's Workshop Breadloaf Writer's Conf. scholar; Danforth fellow nominee; Dawes Sch. grantee, 1987. Mem. NOW, PEN, UNICEF, ACLU, Nat. Assn. Poetry Therapy, Women's Internat. League for Peace, Humanitas Internat. (human rights com.), Amnesty Internat., Am. Acad. Poets, Ill. Alliance of Arts, Pan Pacific Southeast Asia Women's Assn. (v.p.), 11th Ann. Poetry Therapy Conf. (keynote speaker), Greenpeace, Death Penalty Foes. Avocations: music, dance, art, reading, drama, films. Home: 1520 Washington Ave Wilmette IL 60091-2417 Office Phone: 847-251-6721. Personal E-mail: jmiripol@webtv.net.

MIRISOLA, LISA HEINEMANN, air quality engineer; b. Glendale, Calif., Mar. 25, 1963; d. J. Herbert and Betty Jane (Howson) Heinemann; m. Daniel Carl Mirisola, June 27, 1987; 1 child, Ian Cataldo. BSME, UCLA, 1986. Cert. engr.-in-tng., Calif. Air quality engr. South Coast Air Quality Mgmt. Dist., Diamond Bar, Calif., 1988—. Chancellor's scholar UCLA, 1981. Mem. ASME, SAE, Soc. Women Engrs. Office: South Coast Air Quality Mgmt Dist 21865 Copley Dr Diamond Bar CA 91765-4178 Office Phone: 909-396-2638. E-mail: lmirisola@aqmd.gov.

MIRK, JUDY ANN, retired elementary school educator; b. Victorville, Calif., June 10, 1944; d. Richard Nesbit and Corrine (Berghoefer). BA in Social Sci., San Jose (Calif.) State U., 1966, cert. in teaching, 1967; MA in Edn., Calif. State U., Chico, 1980. Cert. elem. edn. tchr. Calif. Profl. psychology trainee John F. Kennedy U., Orinda, Calif., 1997—99; tchr. Cupertino (Calif.) Union Sch. Dist., 1967-95; lead tchr. lang. arts Dilworth Sch., San Jose, 1988-90, mem. supt.'s adv. team, 1986-90, mem. student study team, 1987-95; ret. Mem. student study team, 1987-95; mem. Dilworth Sch. Site Coun., 1981-95. Mem.: The Commonwealth Club of Calif., Phi Mu. Independent. Avocations: photography, natural history, watercolors.

MIROSEVICH, TONI, writer, educator; life ptnr. Shotsy Faust. BA in Liberal Studies, Antioch U., San Francisco, 1988; MA in English, MFA, San Francisco State U., 1992. Assoc. dir. poetry ctr. San Francisco State U., 1996—98, assoc. prof., 1998—. Author: (books of poetry) My Oblique Strategies (Frank O'Hara Chapbook Competition award, 2005), Queer Street, (book of poetry and prose) The Rooms We Make Our Own. Judge of writer applications Djerassi Found., San Francisco, 2006—; author Bay Area Poets For Peace, San Francisco, 2002—. Finalist Peninsula Found. grantee; named Emerging Lesbian Writer in Fiction, Astraea Found., 1999; recipient Acad. Am. Poets award, San Francisco State U., 1994, Poetry prize, Ams. Rev., 1994; fellow MacDowell Colony, 2004, Willard R. Espy Lit. Found., 2004, Djerassi Found., 2005. Office: San Francisco State U 1600 Holloway Ave San Francisco CA 94132 Office Phone: 415-338-7439. E-mail: tonimiro@sfsu.edu.

MIRRA, SUZANNE SAMUELS, pathologist; BA, Hunter Coll., 1962; MD, SUNY, Bklyn., 1967. Instr. pathology Yale U. Sch. Medicine, New Haven, 1971-73; staff pathologist Atlanta VA Med. Ctr., Decatur, Ga., 1973-97; asst. prof. pathology Emory U. Sch. Medicine, Atlanta, 1973-80, assoc. prof. pathology, 1981-93, prof. pathology, 1993-97; prof., chair dept. pathology SUNY Health Sci. Ctr., Bklyn., 1997—. Dir., prin. investor Emory Alzheimer's Disease Ctr., Atlanta, 1991—97. Mem. editl. bd. Arch Pathol. Lab.

Med., 1988-2000, Jour. Neuropathology Exptl. Neurology, 1991-95, Brain Pathology, 1995-99, Alzheimer's Disease Reviews, 1995-2000. Recipient Albert E. Levy Sci. Faculty Rsch. award Emory U., 1987, Disting. Alumnus Achievement award SUNY, 1992; named to Hunter Coll. Hall of Fame, 1996. Fellow Coll. Am. Pathologists (Presdl. award 1987,89, Herbert Lansky award 1990, chair neuropathology commn. 1992-95); mem. Am. Assn. Neuropathologists (v.p. profl. affairs 1992-97, pres. 1999-2000, Meritorious Contributions to Neuropathology award, 2005), Alzheimer's Assn. (bd. dir. Atlanta chpt. 1987-97, nat. bd. dir. 1997-05), Alpha Omega Alpha. Office: SUNY Health Sci Ctr 450 Clarkson Ave Brooklyn NY 11203-2056 Business E-Mail: suzanne.mirra@downstate.edu.

MIRRER, LOUISE, language educator, consultant; b. NYC, Apr. 27, 1953; d. Gerald Paul and Mildred (Friedelbaum) M.; m. Philip Singer, Sept. 1, 1974 (div. Nov., 1984); 1 child, Philip Mirrer-Singer; m. David Halle, Mar. 6, 1947; children: Carla, Malcolm. BA, U. Pa., 1973; Diploma in Linguistics, Cambridge U., Eng., 1975; MA, Stanford U., 1977, PhD, 1980. Asst. prof. Spanish and Portuguese Fordham U., NYC, 1979-86, assoc. prof., 1986-91, prof. and dept. chair, 1991-94; prof. and chair Spanish & Portuguese dept. U. Minn., Mpls., 1994—95, prof. Spanish & Portuguese, 1994—99, vice provost arts, sci. & engring., 1995—97; vice chancellor for academic affairs CUNY, NY, 1997—2000, prof. Hispanic & Luso-Brazilian studies & medieval studies NY, 1997—. Bd. advisors Medieval Feminist Newsletter, 1991—; project dir. Japan Found. Grant, 1992-94; editorial bd. mem. Hispanic Issues U. Minnesota Press, 1995-; pres. NY Historical Soc., 2004- Author The Language of Evaluation: A Sociolinguistic Approach to the Story of Pedro el Cruel in Ballad and Chronicle, 1986, Women, Jews, and Muslims in the Texts of Reconquest Castile, 1996; co-author (with David Halle) Prints of Power, 1991; editor Upon My Husband's Death: Widows in the Literature and Histories of Medieval Europe, 1992; contributor Medieval Crime and Social Control, 1999, Women in Medieval Western European Culture, 1999, Charting Memory: Recalling Medieval Spain, 1999. Recipient McKnight fellowship, U. Minn., 1995, YWCA Women Achievers award, 2000, Leadership award Asian-Am. Rsch. Institution, 2003; grantee Littauer Found., 1993, NY Coun. for Humanities, 1994, fellow council on Institutional Cooperation, 1995-96; named one of 50 Most Influential Women in NY, NY Post, 2003. Mem. Governor's Interagency Council on Women, NY State Commissioner's Policy Advisory Com. Governing Bd. (vice chair), Alliance for Minority Participation, NY Acad. of Sci. Working Group for NY Tech. Council, Exec. Com. Modern Language Assn. Div. on Medieval Spanish Literature (chair 1999-2000, mem. delegate assembly 1988-91), Nominating Com. Internat. Assocn. of Hispanists, 1999-, bd. dirs. NY Structural Biology Ctr., bd. advisors Gateway Inst. for Pre-Coll. Edn., Asian-Am. Rsch. Inst., Soc. Medieval Feminist Scholarship, 1991-. Achievements include application of sociolinguistic methodology to orally composed texts; feminist approaches to medieval Spanish literature. Office: CUNY 535 E 80th St New York NY 10021

MIRSKY, PHYLLIS SIMON, librarian; b. Petach Tikva, Israel, Dec. 18, 1940; d. Allan and Lea (Prizant) Simon; m. Edward Mirsky, Oct. 21, 1967; 1 child, Seth (dec.). BS in Social Welfare, Ohio State U., 1962; postgrad., Columbia U., 1962-63; AMLS, U. Mich., 1965. Caseworker field placement Children's Aid Soc., N.Y.C., 1962-63; hosp. libr. hosp. and instns. divsn. Cleve. Pub. Libr., 1963-64; reference libr. UCLA Biomed. Libr., 1965-68, reference/acquisitions libr., 1968-69, head cons./continuing edn. Pacific S.W. Regl. Med. Libr. Sv., 1969-71, asst. dir. Pacific S.W. Regl. Med. Libr. Sv., 1971-73, faculty coord. Biomed. Libr. program Cen. San Joaquin Valley Area Health Edn. Ctr., 1973-77, assoc. dir. Pacific S.W. Regl. Med. Libr. Sv., 1973-79; head reference sect., coord. libr. assoc. program Nat. Libr. of Medicine, Bethesda, Md., 1979-81; asst. univ. libr., scis. U. Calif.-San Diego, La Jolla, 1981-86, acting univ. libr., 1985, 92-93, 98-99, asst. univ. libr. adminstrv. and pub. svcs., 1986-87, assoc. univ. libr. adminstrv. and pub. svcs., 1987-92, assoc. univ. libr., 1993-95; dep. univ. libr., 1995—. Guest lectr. Libr. Schs. UCLA and U. So. Calif., 1967-78, Grad. Sch. Libr. Sci. Cath. U., Washington, 1980, Grad. Sch. Libr. and Info. Sci. UCLA, 1984; mem. task force on role of spl. libr. nationwide network and coop. programs Nat. Commn. on Libr. and Info. Svcs./Spl. Libr. Assn., 1981-83; facilitator AASLD/MLA Guidelines Scenario Writing Session, L.A., 1984; mem. users coun. OCLC Online Computer Libr. Ctr., Inc., 1991-94; U. Calif.-San Diego rep. Coalition for Networked Info., 1992—; instr. Assn. Rsch. Librs., Office Mgmt. Studies, Mgmt. Inst., 1987; peer reviewer Coll. Libr. Tech. and Cooperation Grant Program U.S. Dept. Edn., 1988-94; cons. Nat. Libr. Medicine, Bethesda, Md., 1988, San Diego Mus. Contemporary Art Libr., La Jolla, Calif., 1993, Salk Inst., 1995; mem. Libr. of Congress Network Adv. Com., 1994-96, chair steering com., 1995-96. Contbr. articles to profl. jours. and bulls. Mem. fin. com. City of Del Mar, 1995-98, chair, 1997-98, facility adv. com., 2000—. NIH fellow Columbia U., 1962-63; sr. fellow UCLA/Coun. on Libr. Resources, 1987. Fellow Med. Libr. Assn. (bd. dirs. 1977-80); mem. ALA (site visitors panel com. on accreditation 1990-92, libr. adminstrn. and mgmt. assn. 1990-92), Med. Libr. Group Soc. Calif. and Ariz. (sec. 1970-71, v.p. 1971-72, pres. 1972-73), Documentation Abstracts, Inc. (bd. dirs. 1985-90, vice chair bd. dirs. 1988-90), Med. Libr. Assn. (pres. 1984-85), U. Mich. Sch. Libr. Sci. Alumni Assn. Office: U Calif San Diego U Libr 0175G 9500 Gilman Dr La Jolla CA 92093-0175

MIRVAHABI, FARIN, lawyer; b. Tehran, Iran; d. Ali and Azar Mirvahabi; m. Richard C. Powell; children: Bobby Naemi, Jimmy Naemi. Degree in Law, Tehran U., Iran, 1968; M of Comparative Law, Georgetown U., 1972; LLM, George Washington U., 1976; JSD, NYU, 1978; diploma, The Hague Acad. Internat. Law, 1983. Bar: Va. 1989, U.S. Dist. Ct. (ea. and we. dists.) Va. 1990, D.C. 1990, U.S. Dist. Ct. D.C. 1990, U.S. Supreme Ct. 1997. With Gold & Cutner, N.Y.C., 1979-80; in-house counsel IRA Engring. and Constrn., Tehran, London, 1981-82; legal advisor Bank Markazi, Tehran, 1981-82; practiced law The Hague, The Netherlands, 1982-87; arbitrator Iran Air-Pan Am Arbitration Tribunal, Paris, 1984-87; legal cons. Rooney, Barry & Fogerty, Washington, 1987-88; atty. sole practice, Washington, 1989—. Law prof. No. Va. Law Sch., Alexandria, 1989-90; instr. Paralegal Inst., Arlington, Va., 1988-89; prof. Tehran U., 1982; panelist Am. Arbitration Assn.; guest speaker in field; life dep. gov. Am. Biog. Inst. Rsch. Assn., 19995—. Contbr. numerous articles to profl. jours. Named Maxplank fellow Maxplank Inst. of Internat. Law, 1986; recipient Clyde Eagleton award NYU, 1977, Woman of Yr. medallion honoring Cmty. Svc. and Profl. Achievement, 1995, Spl. Merit award DC Bar, 2005. Mem. ABA, Internat. Bar Assn., Arbitration Forum Inc., D.C. Bar Assn. (panelist client-atty. arbitration bd. 1990—), D.C. Bar & Lawyers Assn., Trial Lawyers Assn., Va. Bar Found., Am. Soc. Internat. Law, Am. Film Inst. The Kennedy Ctr. Avocations: reading, writing, Broadway shows, picnic, swimming. Office: Ste 613-6 1000 Connecticut Ave NW Washington DC 20036 Office Phone: 703-534-6677.

MISCELLA, MARIA DIANA, humanities educator; b. NYC, July 11, 1929; d. Nicola and Giovanna (Tangorra) Torelli; m. Emilio Miscella, Feb. 27, 1954 (dec. Sept. 30, 1996); children: Delia, Marisa, Giuliana. Tchr. Degree, Istituto Magistrale, Lecce, Italy, 1946; postgrad., U. Naples, 1946-48; BA, Hunter Coll., 1954, MA, 1972. Cert. secondary educator NY. English corr. GE Co., Rome, 1950-51; corr. Spanish & French Pettinos Import & Export Co., N.Y.C., 1952-53; tchr. Italian Harrison (N.Y.) H.S., 1967-87, St. John's U., Queens, NY, 1987-89; lectr. Italian various orgsn., N.Y. State, 1987—; lectr. Italian lit. and history various colls. and univs., NY, 1987—. Moderator of club Harrison (N.Y.) H.S., 1967-87. Mem. Little Neck (N.Y.) Civic Assn., 1970-95, Am. Assn. Ret. People, Douglaston, N.Y., 1994—; founder, treas. Italian Am. Women's Ctr., 1997—. Recipient scholarship Columbia U., 1954, Letter of Commendation, Bd. Regents, Albany, N.Y., 1980, Cert. Recognition and Gratitude for Contbn. to the Arts and Dedication to Cmty., N.Y.C. Coun., 2004, Spl. Lit. Contest prize The Salt Queen Found., 2005; named Woman of Yr., Consortium of L.I. Italian Am. Orgns., 1992. Mem. AAUW (hostess, v.p. 1990-93, cert. of commendation 1996), Am. Assn. Tchrs. of Italian (sec. Societa Onoraria Italica 1979-91), Ams. Italian Heritage (bd. mem. 1982—, Women of the Yr. 2004), Sons of Italy (John Marino Lodge cultural com. mem 1994—, Merit award 1995), Assn. Italian Am. Educators (dir./historian by-laws com. 2000), N.Y. State United Tchrs., Am. Fedn. Tchrs., Nat. Italian Am. Found., Douglaston Women Club, Retirees Club. Roman Catholic. Avocations: reading, writing, travel, going to theatre, playing bridge.

MISCHIA, MARIETTA COCHRAN, retired principal; d. George W. Bradford and Mae Jetter (Bradford) Rogan; m. Francesco Mischia, Aug. 12, 1972; 1 child, Steve Wayne Cochran. AA, Miami Dade Coll., 1964; BS, Fla. Atlantic U., Boca Raton, 1965; MS, Fla. Internat. U., 1975; EdD, Nova Southeastern U., Ft. Lauderdale, Fla., 1992. Cert. elem. sch. tchr. Fla., elem. sch. prin. Fla. Tchr. elem. sch. Miami Dade Schs., 1965—75, asst. prin. elem. sch., 1975—81, prin. elem. sch., 1982—93; ednl. cons. Zeta Tau Royal Comty. Ctr., 2000—; bd. dirs. Fla. Health and Human Svcs., Lutz. Vice-chair Comty. Based Care Alliance, Dept. Children and Families, Miami, 2001—; mem. adv. com. Alliance for Human Svcs., Miami, 1999—. Recipient Cert. Recognition, Honor, Appreciation and Dedicated Svc., Fla. Dept. Children and Families, United Way of Miami-Dade, Fla. Dept. Health, Alliance for Human Svcs., others, Outstanding/Dedicated Svc. award, Comty. Based Care Alliance, 2005, Dedicated Svc. award, Miami-Dade Black Affairs Adv. Bd., 2003. Mem.: Phi Delta Kappa, Beta Tau Zeta. Avocations: reading, gardening, fishing, sewing. Home: 10355 NW 32d Pl Miami FL 33147

MISER, ANN, retired government researcher; b. Balt., Jan. 29, 1935; d. Robert and Lucile Miser; 1 adopted child, Janna. BS in Fine Arts and Edn., U. N.C., Chapel Hill, 1956; student, Earlham Coll., Richmond, 1952—54, Johns Hopkins U., Balt., 1960. Art tchr. Md. State Dept. Edn., Balt., 1958—60, N.Y. State Dept. Edn., N.Y.C., 1961—62; owner Lady Baltimore Temporary Agy. and Miss Liberty Inc., London, 1963—75; U.S. govt. rschr. Commerce Dept., Phila., 1975—2005; ret., 2005. Mem.: U. N.C. Alumni Assn., Lymphoma Soc. Democrat. Quaker. Avocations: travel, reading, sports. Home: 6101 Allwood Ct Baltimore MD 21210 Office Phone: 410-377-4151.

MISERANDINO, MARIANNE, psychology educator; b. Rockville Centre, N.Y., July 1, 1960; d. Dominick Alfred and Catherine Margaret (Healy) M. BA, U. Rochester, 1982; PhD, Cornell U., 1987. Teaching asst., statis. cons. Cornell U., Ithaca, N.Y., 1983-87; asst. prof. psychology Hobart and William Smith Colls., Geneva, N.Y., 1987-90; rsch. assoc. U. Rochester, N.Y., 1990-92; asst. prof. Beaver Coll., Glenside, Pa., 1992—2001; assoc. prof. Arcadia U., Glenside, Pa., 2001—. Adj. faculty Tompkins-Cortland Community Coll., Dryden, N.Y., 1986-87. Contbr. articles to profl. jours. Mem. Am. Psychol. Assn. (div. teaching of psychology, div. social and personality), Am. Psychol. Soc. Office: Arcadia U Dept Psychology Glenside PA 19038

MISHER STENZLER, SHARI, youth activities organization administrator; d. Sheldon and Joan Misher; m. Andy Mark Stenzler, 2000. BA, Syracuse Univ.; MFA in Film, New York Univ. Co-founder, pres. Kidville NY, 2003—. Named one of 40 Under 40, Crain's NY Bus. Mag., 2006. Office: Kidville NY 163 E 84th St New York NY 10028*

MISHINA, MIZUHO, artist; b. Osaka, Japan, Nov. 21, 1942; came to U.S., 1979; d. Kakusen Mah and Fumiko Hayashi; m. Masanori Mishina, Mar. 14, 1968; children: Yuri, Mayu. Degree in home econs., Kawamura Women's Coll., Tokyo, 1963; BA in art, No. Ill. U., 1986. Sec. Inst. for Nuclear Study, U. Tokyo, 1965-69; gallery asst. Charles Bennett Gallery, Geneva, Ill., 1984-85; artist Geneva, 1986—. Exhbn. com. mem. Fermi Nat. Lab., Batavia, Ill., 1981-94, landscape com. mem., 1984-88, Nalwo bd. mem., 1981, 89, auditorium com. mem., 1982-84. One-person shows include Chgo. Atty. Gen. Office, 1991, Beverly Art Ctr., Chgo., 1991, Geneva (Ill.) Pub. Libr., 1991, 94, Independence Arts Coun. Gallery, Kans., 1991, Rolling Meadows (Ill.) Pub. Libr., 1992, Batavia (Ill.) Pub. Libr., 1992, Borders Books, Naperville, Ill., 1995, Glen Ellyn, 97, Geneva, 99, Fermilab, Batavia, Ill., 2001; exhibited in group shows Fermi Nat. Lab., Batavia, Ill., 1987, Galeria Mesa, Ariz., 1988, Miami EXPO 89, Fla., 1989, Kiwshwaukee (Ill.) Coll. Art Gallery, 1993, Roberta Campbell Cultural Arts Ctr., Geneva, 1993, Art in Embossier, Majuro, Marshal Island, 1996, Borders Books, Wheaton, Ill., 1997, Coll. DuPage, Glen Ellyn, 1998, Norris Gallery, St. Charles, Ill., 1999, Internat. Libr. of Photography, Owings, Md., 1999, Geneva C. of C., 2000, Coll. of Dupage, Glen Ellyn, 2001, Coll. Dupage Juried Show, 2003. Recipient jewelry award Coll. of DuPage, 1996, 97. 98, First Place award, United Art Glass Competition, Naperville, Ill., 2005. Mem.: Soc. N.Am. Goldsmiths, Chgo. Metal Arts Guild, Glass Art Soc. Avocations: travel, snorkeling. Home: 322 Grant Ave Geneva IL 60134-1115

MISKILL, DEE SHELTON, graphics designer; b. N.Y.C., Dec. 30, 1948; d. Nicholas T. and Estelle Shelton; m. Donald Keepers Miskill Jr., May 23, 1980; children: Nathan, Rachael, Justin, Colin. Student, Marymount Jr. Coll., 1966-67; BA in Sociology, Adelphi U., 1970. Naval reservist multiple units, Mass., Maine and Va., 1976-92; sr. advisor ARC, Sigonella, Sicily, Italy, 1992-94; subs. tchr. Stephen Decatur Sch., Sigonella, Sicily, Italy, 1993-94; pub. info. specialist Mid Coast Health Svcs., Brunswick, Maine, 1995-98; dir. devel. Mid Coast chpt. ARC, Brunswick, 1998-99; pres. Deesign Graphics, Orrs Island, Maine, 2000—. Co-chmn. ARC Annual Ball, Brunswick, 1995-97, chair adv. com. to Brunswick Naval Air Sta., 1987-92. Lt. USN, 1975-76. Mem. Naval Res. Assn. (life). Roman Catholic. Avocations: snowshoeing, cooking, hiking.

MISKIMEN, THERESA MARIE, psychiatrist, educator; b. Mayaguez, P.R., Sept. 5, 1964; d. George William and Carmen M. (Rivera) M.; m. Juan Carlos Ortiz. BS in Biology magna cum laude, U. P.R., 1986, MD, 1990. Diplomate Am. Bd. Psychiatry and Neurology. Instr. psychiatry U. Medicine and Dentistry N.J., Newark, 1994-97, asst. prof. psychiatry, 1997—2000; assoc. prof. psychiatry RWJ Med. Sch., Piscataway, 2000—. Mem. pharmacy and therapeutic com. U. Medicine and Dentistry U. Hosp., Newark, 1995-99; lectr. Acad. Medicine N.J., Princeton, 1999-; med. dir., acute inpatient unit, UBHC, 2004-, v.p., med. svcs., 2006-. Resident column editor N.J. Psychiat. News, 1993. Active Nat. Hispanic Mentor Recruitment Network, Interamerican Coll. Physicians and Surgeons, Newark, 1996-99. Am. Assn. Med. Colls. fellow, 1997. Fellow Am. Psychiat. Assn. (disting., chairperson early career psychiatry com. 1997-98); mem. N.J. Psychiat. Assn. (treas. 2004-06, v.p. 2006-), Beta Beta Beta. Business E-Mail: miskimtm@umdnj.edu.

MISNER, CHARLOTTE BLANCHE RUCKMAN, retired community organization administrator; b. Gifford, Idaho, Aug. 30, 1937; d. Richard Steele and Arizona (Hill) Ruckman; m. G. Arthur Misner, Jr., Aug. 29, 1959; children: Michelle, Mary, Jennifer. BS in Psychology, U. Idaho, 1959. Vol. numerous orgns., India, Mexico, The Philippines, 1962-70; sec., v.p., pres., trustee St. Luke's Hosp., Manila, 1970-84; founding mem., 3d v.p., pres. Am. Women's Club of Philippines, 1980-84; exec. dir. Friends of Oakland (Calif.) Parks and Recreation, 1986-2000, ret., 2000. Active Lincoln Child Ctr., Oakland, 1984—. Recipient Vol. Svc. award Women's Bd. St. Luke's Hosp., 1977, Mid. Sch. Vol. award Internat. Sch.-Manila, 1980. Me. Alpha Gamma Delta (alumnae treas., pres. East Bay 1985-89, province dir. alumnae 1989-98, bd. dirs. alumni devel. 1998-2005, mem. steering com. centennial capital campaign 1999—), Cum Laude Soc. (hon.).

MISRA, MADHUSMITA, pediatric neuroendocrinologist, educator; d. Sachidananda and Seema Misra; m. Sidhartha Pani, Nov. 27, 1990; 1 child, Sarthak Pani. MBBS with Hons., Utkal U., Orissa, India, 1987; MD, Inst. Med. Sci., Varanasi, India, 1991; MPH, Harvard Sch. Pub. Health, Boston, 2005. Cert. in pediat. Am. Bd. Pediat., 1999, in pediatric endocrinology Am. Bd. Pediat., 2003. Lectr., ob-gyn. Kasturba Med. Coll., Manipal, 1992; med. officer, ob-gyn. JLN Hosp. & Rsch. Ctr., Bhilai, 1992—96; clin. rsch. fellow Mass. Gen. Hosp., Boston, 1998—2002, asst., pediatrics, 2002—, asst., biology, 2002—; instr., pediatrics Harvard Med. Sch., Boston, 2002—05, asst. prof., pediatrics, 2005—. Com. mem. Mass. Med. Soc., 2005; presenter in field. Contbr. chapters to books, numerous articles and papers to profl. jours. and pubs. Recipient award, NIH, 2004; grantee Post-Grad. Travel grant, Pharmacia, 2001, Rita M. Kelly fellowship, Mass. Gen. Hosp., 2003, Claflin Disting. scholarship, 2006. Mem.: Lawson Wilkins Pediatric Endocrine Soc. (com. mem. drugs and therapeutics 2005—, Travel grant 2001), Endocrine Soc. (Travel grant 2004), Women in Endocrinology (Janet McArthur award 2003). Avocations: music, reading, stamp collecting/philately. Office: Mass Gen Hosp 55 Fruit St Boston MA 02114

MISRACK, TANA MARIE, counselor, minister, writer; b. Toledo, July 25, 1954; d. Anthony James and Isabelle (Drinkhou[illegible]ards; m. Robert Aaron Misrack, June 30, 1996. AS in Interior Desig[illegible]est Valley Coll., 1979. Ordained to ministry Universal Ch. of Master, 1986. Owner, designer Interiors by Tana Marie, Saratoga, Calif., 1979-88; min., profl. intuitive counselor Monterey, Calif., 1988—; CEO, cons. Strategies for Success, Monterey, Calif., 1994—; CEO, Tana Marie's Passion Island, 2002—. Lectr., seminar leader, Monterey, 1988—; radio personality Sta. KNRY-1240 Cannery Row, Monterey, 2000—; profl. intuitive counselor. Author: Isle of Fantasies, 1995, Mating Games:Stop Playing and Start Loving, 1999, Guy Code: Understand Your Man, 2000; contbr. articles to profl. jours. Amb. San Jose (Calif.) C. of C., 1993-2000; mem. Mountain View (Calif.) Chamber, 1994-98. Mem. Women's Fund (1st v.p. 1994-98, pres. 1998-2000), Monterey C. of C. Avocations: bicycling, photography, writing. Office Phone: 831-646-1137. Personal E-mail: TM@Tanamarie.com.

MISSAKIAN, ILONA VIRGINIA, secondary school educator; b. Huntington Park, Calif., July 16, 1968; d. Garo Garabed and Brigitte Renate Anne Marie (Kunkel) M. AA with honors, Mt. San Antonio Coll., 1991; BA with honors, Calif. State U., 1993; MA, Calif. State U., Fullerton, 1997. Tchg. credential. Instr. Alexandra Ballet Acad., Hacienda Heights, Calif., 1985—92, Dellos Dance and Performing Arts Ctr., Walnut, Calif., 1989—91; apprentice Les Ballets Classiques, Montreal, Canada, 1987—88; bookkeeper Garo's German Auto Repair, Walnut, 1986—; tchr. Brea Olinda H.S., Calif., 1994—. Instr. Dance En l'Air, Glendora, Calif., 1998—; tchr. Mt. San Antonio (Calif.) Coll., 1999-2003, Rio Hondo (Calif.) Coll., 2003—; assoc. dir. Calif. Classical Youth Ballet, 2001-; writing project fellow U. Calif., 2003. Mem. MLA, Calif. Lit. Project, Calif. State Fullerton Alumni, Alpha Gamma Sigma (sec., news editor 1988-91). Avocations: ballet, visual arts. Office: Brea Olinda HS 789 Wildcat Way Brea CA 92821-7402

MISSELE, BRENDA MARIE, secondary school educator; b. Elgin, Ill., Oct. 23, 1978; d. Carl and Chris Missele. BA in History, Carthage Coll., Kenosha, Wis., 2001. Cert. secondary tchr. Ill. Tchr. asst. Elgin Sch. Dist., 2001—04, tchr., 2005—; tutor Huntington Learning Ctr., Elgin, 2006—. Intern Geneva History Ctr., 2000. History fellow, Carthage Coll., 1999, Wingspread fellow, 1999. Mem.: Nat. Coun. Social Studies, Nat. Coun. History Edn.

MISTACCO, VICKI E., foreign language educator; b. Bklyn., Nov. 18, 1942; d. Anthony Sebastian and Lucia (Lalli) M. BA, NYU, 1963; MA, Middlebury Coll., 1964; M of Philosophy, Yale U., 1968, PhD, 1972. Instr. French Wellesley Coll., Mass., 1968-72, asst. prof. French, 1972-78, assoc. prof. French, 1978-84, prof. French, 1984—, chmn., 1978-81. Nat. adv. bd. Sweet Briar Jr. Yr. in France, Va., 1978—. Author: Women and Literary Tradition: Anthology from the Middle Ages to the Present, 2006—; contbr. articles to profl. jours. Fulbright fellow, 1963-64, Woodrow Wilson fellow, 1964-67; NEH fellow, 1983-84, 94-95. Mem.: N.E. MLA, MLA, Soc. Internat. pour l'Etude des Femmes de l'Ancien Regime, Women in French, Am. Assn. Tchrs. French, Phi Beta Kappa. Democrat. Roman Catholic. Avocations: photography, travel. Office: Wellesley Coll Dept French 106 Central St Wellesley MA 02481-8268 Office Phone: 781-283-2406. Business E-Mail: vmistacco@wellesley.edu.

MITCHAM, CARLA J., utilities executive; BS in Indsl. Distbn., Tex. A&M U., MS in Indsl. Tech.; JD, U. Houston. Pres. Reliant Energy ERCOT Supply Reliant Resources, Inc., Houston. Office: Reliant Energy Exec Office PO Box 2286 Houston TX 77252-2286

MITCHARD, JACQUELYN, writer; b. 1953; H.S. English tchr., 1974—76; mng. editor, reporter Pioneer Press, Chgo., 1976—79; reporter The Capital Times, Madison, Wis., 1979—84; metro reporter, columnist Milw. Jour., 1984—88; speechwriter for Donna Shalala, 1989—93. Author: Mother Less Child, 1985, Jane Addams: Pioneer in Social Reform and Activist for World Peace, 1991, Jane Addams: Peace Activist, 1992, The Deep End of the Ocean, 1996, The Rest of Us: Dispatches from the Mothership, 1997, The Most Wanted, 1998, A Theory of Relativity, 2001, Twelve Times Blessed, 2003, Christmas Present, 2003, Starring Prima!, 2004, Baby Bat's Lullaby, 2004, The Breakdown Lane, 2005, Cage of Stars, 2006.

MITCHELL, ADA MAE BOYD, legal assistant; b. Nov. 23, 1927; d. Allen T. Boyd and Marjorie (Bigger) Mills Boyd; 1 child, Joseph W. Student, NYU, 1972-73. Supr. Faberge, Inc., Mahwah, NJ; mgr. Demonstration Svcs. and Promotional Monies; mgr. accts. receivables, credit mgr. Faberge, Inc., Mahwah, NJ, 1946-89; legal asst. Wright Patterson Med. Ctr., Dayton, Ohio, 1990—. Pres. Urban League Guild, Bergen County, NJ, 1982—83, bd. dirs., 1982—83; founder N.J. Coalition of 100 Black Women, 1982; dtr. Isis Akbar Ct. # 33, 1995—; vol. WPAFB, Ohio-Legal Office/Med. Group, 1990—, Nat. Notary Assn., 1990—, Heroines of Jericho P.H.A. Burning Bush Ct., 1997, Truth Guild #2 Heroines of Temple Crusades, 1997; active Dayton Urban League Guild, 1991; treas. Bethany Presbyn. Ch., Englewood, NJ, 1975, fin. sect., 1966—67, chair bldg. and renovation com., 1978—81, choir mem., elder, 1979—, clk. of session, 1980—85; 1st Black woman moderator Presbytery of Palisades-Presbyn. Ch., 1986; mem. self devel. of people com. Presbyn. Ch. Miami Presbytery, Dayton; active Jarvis Soc. Nat. Presbyn. Ch. Mem. NAFE, NAACP, Order Eastern Star (Queen of Sheba chpt. 4, Worthy Matron 1972-73), Daughters of Isis (illustrious commandress Akbar Ct. #33 2002-).

MITCHELL, ALICE JOYCE, secondary school educator, dietician; b. W.Va., Jan. 27, 1936; d. Edgar Dunbar and Mildred Edna Jones; m. Ernest Lopez Mitchell. BS in Home Econs., W.Va. State Coll., Institute, 1957; degree in Higher Edn. Adminstrn., N.Y.U., Hofstra U. Dietician Kings County Hosp., Bklyn., 1957—58, Montefiore Hosp., Bronx, 1958—66; substitute tchr. home econs. Bd. Edn. Bronx, 1966—68; tchr. home econs. N.Y.C. Bd. Edn., 1968—91; ret., 1991. Chairperson home econs. dept. Jr. H.S. 117, Bklyn., 1971—75, Bklyn., 1979—85, dean of girls, 1976—79; tchr. mentor 117 Intermediate Sch., Bklyn., 1989—91. Served Coast Guard Aux., 1977—78, Bayside, N.Y. Named Master Tchr., Prin. 117 Bklyn., 1971, 1972, 1973, 1974, 1975, 1979, 1980, 1981, 1982, 1985. Mem.: Sr. Coalition, TREA Sr. Citizens League, W.Va. State U. Alumni Club, Acorn, 55+ Club. Republican. Catholic. Avocations: sewing, gardening, travel. Home: 572 S Main St Freeport NY 11520

MITCHELL, ANDREA, journalist; b. NYC, Oct. 30, 1946; d. Sydney and Cecile Mitchell; m. Alan Greenspan, Apr. 6, 1997. BA in English Literature, U. Pa., 1967. Polit. reporter KYW Newsradio, Phila., 1967-76; polit. corr. Sta. KYW-TV, Phila., 1972-76; corr. Sta. WTOP-TV, Washington, 1977-78; gen. assignment and energy corr. NBC News, Washington, 1978-81, White House corr., 1981-88, chief congl. corr., 1989-92, chief White House corr., 1993-94, chief fgn. affairs corr. Washington, 1995—. Substitute host Meet the Press, 1988-; host MSNBC The Mitchell Report, Decision 2000. Author: (book) Talking Back:.to Presidents, Dictators, and Assorted Scoundrels, 2005. Trustee U. Pa., 1995—. Recipient award for pub. affairs reporting Am. Polit. Sci. Assn., 1969, Pub. Affairs Reporting award AP, 1976, AP Broadcast award, 1977; named Communicator of the Yr., Phila. chpt. Women in Comms., 1976, Woman of the Yr., Phila. chpt. Am. Women in Radio and TV, 1989, Lucretia Mott award Woman's Way, 1991, Welles Hangen award superior achievement journalism, Brown U., 2003, Lifetime Achievement award RTNDA, 2004, Harvard U. Goldsmith Career Achievement prize, 2005. Office: NBC News 4001 Nebraska Ave NW Washington DC 20016-2733

MITCHELL, ANGELA D., education educator; b. Hillsboro, Ohio, May 24, 1975; d. Thomas R. Kessinger and Doris J. Kesinger; 1 child, Thomas E. MBA, Thomas More Coll., Ky., 2001. Sr. rschr. Procter & Gamble, Cin., 1997—2002; prof. Wilmington Coll., Ohio, 2002—. Pres. Big Bros. and Sisters, Lebanon, Ohio, 1997—2004. Office: Wilmington Coll 251 Ludovic St # 1312 Wilmington OH 45177 Office Phone: 937-382-6661. Business E-Mail: angela_mitchell@wilmington.edu.

MITCHELL, ANNA-MARIE RAJALA, quality/outcomes analyst; b. Detroit; d. Ruben Victor and Janie Elizabeth Rajala; m. Robert David Mitchell, Jan. 22, 1994; children: Kimberly, Andrew. BS in Med. Tech., U. Mich., 1986, M Health Svcs. Adminstrn., 1992. Cert. med. technologist Am. Soc. Clin. Pathologists. Med. technologist U. Mich. Med. Ctr., Ann Arbor, 1986-94; med. data analyst Blue Care Network, Southfield, Mich., 1994-98; quality/outcomes analyst M-CARE, Ann Arbor, 1998—. Mem. Jr. League of Ann Arbor, 1993-95. Mem. APHA, ACHE, S.E. Suburban Mothers of Twins Club (state rep., resale chairwoman 1997—). Office: M-CARE 2301 Commonwealth Blvd Fl 2 Ann Arbor MI 48105-2955 Fax: 734-747-7153. E-mail: armitch@umich.edu.

MITCHELL, ANNE S., music educator; d. James. W. and Ruby K. Smithey; m. Steven D. Mitchell, Nov. 20, 1987. MusB Edn., Shorter Coll., 1971; grad. work, U. Ga., 1973, Ga. State U., 1973—75; Continuing Edn., Utah State U., 1992—93. Cert. music tchr. grades K-12 Wyo. Dept. Edn., 1990. Music tchr. Whitfield County Bd. Edn., Dalton, Ga., 1971—78, Sublette Sch. Dist. # 9, Big Piney, Wyo., 1991—. Dir. Big Piney Jazz Band, 1996—, Big Piney Jazz Choir, 2002—04. Recipient Presdl. Disting. Tchr., White Ho. Commn. on Presdl. Scholars, 1995. Mem.: Wyo. Music Educators Assn. (assoc.), Music Educator's Nat. Conf. (assoc.), Phi Beta Mu (assoc.). Avocation: breeding, raising, showing American paint horses. Home: P O Box 1177 Big Piney WY 83113-1177 Office: Sublette Sch Dist # 9 P O Box 769 Big Piney WY 83113-0769 Office Phone: 307-276-3322. Business E-Mail: amitchell@bp.k12.wy.us.

MITCHELL, BARBARA ANNE, librarian; b. Wilkes-Barre, Pa., June 10, 1948; d. Frederic Edward and Elizabeth Anne (Postupack) M. BA in Journalism, Am. U., 1970; M.L.S., U. Mich., 1974, MA in Am. History, 1986. Asst. manuscript curator William L. Clements Library, U. Mich., Ann Arbor, 1977-82, curator maps, prints and newspapers, 1982-83; librarian Ctr. for Internat. Affairs, Harvard Inst. Internat. Devel., Ctr. Middle Eastern Studies, Harvard U., Cambridge, Mass., 1983—. Author: (with others) Guide to the Manuscript Collections of the William L. Clements Library, 1978 Home: 362 Commonwealth Ave Boston MA 02115-2157 Office: Ctr Internat Affairs Harvard Univ 1737 Cambridge St Cambridge MA 02138-3016

MITCHELL, BETTIE PHAENON, religious organization administrator; b. Colorado Springs, Colo., June 6, 1934; d. Roy William and Laura Lee (Costin) Roberts; m. Gerald Mitchell, May 3, 1952; children: Michelle Carter Smith, Laura Sweitz, Jennie Grenzer, Mohammad Bader. BS in Edn., Lewis & Clark Coll., 1954; postgrad., Portland State U., 1962-72; MA in Religion summa cum laude, Warner Pacific Coll., 1979. Cert. counselor, Oreg. Elem. tchr. Quincy Sch. Dist., Clatskanie, Oreg., 1955-56; substitute tchr. Beaverton (Oreg.) and Washington County Schs., 1956-77; tchr. of the Bible Portland (Oreg.) C.C., 1974-92; counseling and healing ministry, 1977-79; founder, exec. dir. Good Samaritan Ministries, Beaverton, 1979—2005, founder, internat. exec. dir., 1988—2005. Tchr. Christian Renewal Ctr. Workshops, 1977-2002; spkr., presenter in field; leader tours in the Mid. East; developing counselor edn. programs Spain, Ghana, Pakistan, Ukraine, Jordan, Egypt, Kenya, numerous other countries. Author: Who Is My Neighbor? A Parable, 1988, The Power of Conflict and Sacrifice, A Therapy Manual for Christian Marriage, 1988, Good Samaritan Training Handbook, 1989, Be Still and Listen to His Voice, The Story of Prayer and Faith, 1990, A Need for Understanding - International Counselor Training Manual, 1993, The Heros of Vietnam, The Children They Touched. Mem. Israel Task Force, Portland, 1974-80; Leader Camp Fire Internat., 1962-73, elem. sch. coord., 1962-68; asst. dir. Washington County Civil Def., 1961-63; precinct committeewoman Rep. Party, 1960; bd. dirs. Beaverton Fish, 1966-74; v.p. NCCJ, Portland, 1983-85; chmn., speaker's bur. Near East Task Force for Israel; chmn. fire bond issue campaign City of Beaverton, mgr. mayoral campaign, 1960; sunday sch. tchr., speaker, organizer Sharing and Caring program Bethel Ch., 1974-79. Mem. Am. Christian Counseling Assn., Christian Assn. for Psychol. Studies, Oreg. Counseling Assn. Republican. Avocations: historical research, writing, photography. Home: 6550 SW Imperial Dr Beaverton OR 97008-5311 Office: Good Samaritan Ministries 7929 SW Cirrus Dr Ste 23 Beaverton OR 97008-5973 Office Phone: 503-644-2339. Business E-Mail: bettie@gsmusa.org.

MITCHELL, BEVERLY SHRIVER, hematologist, oncologist, educator; b. Balt., May 14, 1944; m. John Robert Pringle; children: Robert Mitchell, Elizabeth Greene. AB summa cum laude in Biochemistry, Smith Coll., 1965; MD, Harvard U., 1969. Hematology fellow U. Mich., Ann Arbor, 1975-77, from instr. to asst. prof. internal medicine, 1977-81, assoc. prof., 1981-87, prof. internal medicine and pharmacology, 1987-91, U. N.C., Chapel Hill, 1991—, divsn. chief hematology/oncology, 1994—2003; assoc. dir. Lineberger Cancer Ctr., Chapel Hill, 1994—2005; deputy dir. Stanford Cancer Ctr., Stanford U., 2005—. Mem. bd. sci. counselors Cancer Treatment divsn. Nat. Cancer Inst. Vice chair med. and sci. affairs Leukemia and Lymphoma Soc., 2003—05. Recipient Stohlman award Leukemia Soc., 1988. Mem. Am. Soc. Hematology (treas. 1991-96, v.p. 1998, pres. 2000), Phi Beta, Inst. Medicine. Achievements include research in nucleotide metabolism and the development of novel therapies for hematologic malignancies. Office: Stanford Cancer Ctr 800 Welch Rd Stanford CA 94305-5796 Office Phone: 650-725-9621. Business E-Mail: bmitchell@stanford.edu.

MITCHELL, BIKI-RAY, physical education educator; b. Stephenville, Newfoundland, Can., Sept. 18, 1954; arrived in U.S., 1976; d. Claxton and Ola-Gay Ray; m. Larry F.C. Mitchell, Mar. 22, 1975; children: Clint, Garret. BS Edn., U. Ala. Tuscaloosa, 1978; MS Sports Medicine, U.S. Sports Acad., Mobile, Ala., 1979. Cert. CPR, instr. Am. Mgmt. Assn., instr. Bike Smart Va. Dept. Edn., instr. Am. Heart Assn., instr. fishing, instr. in-line skating Va. Dept. Edn., ATC Va. Bd. Medicine. Head women's ATC Athletic dept. U. Fla., Gainesville, 1979—80; asst. women's ATC Athletic dept. La. State U., Baton Rouge, 1982—83; tchr., coach H.F. Byrd Mid. Sch., Richmond, Va., 1986—90, H.J. MacDonald Mid. Sch., New Bern, NC, 1993—94; tchr., coach, dept. chair Brookland Mid. Sch., Richmond, 1994—2005; tchr. Robious Mid. Sch., Midlothian, Va., 2005—. Mem. Rhythmic Gymnastics com. U.S. Olympic Com., 1984. Mem. adult ministry team Young Life, Hanover, Va., 1994—. Named Tchr. of Yr., Wal-Mart, 2005, Secondary Tchr. of Yr., Henrico County Pub. Schs., 2003, Master Tchr., 2001. Mem.: AAHPERD, Va. AHPERD, Nat. Athletic Trainers Assn. Avocation: quilting. Office: Robious Mid Sch 2701 Robious Crossing Dr Midlothian VA 23113

MITCHELL, BRENDA KING, training services executive; b. NYC, Jan. 9, 1943; d. William Franklin and Ola Mae (Ross) K.; divorced; 1 child, Corrie Nelson. BA, Fordham U., 1973; MA, Hunter Coll., 1977; PhD in Pub. Adminstrn., Nova U., 1981. Dir. manpower planning Addictive Disease Agy., N.Y.C., 1973-77; project and contract mgr. Pub./Pvt. Ventures Corp., Phila., 1978-80; exec. dir. Econ. Devel. Corp., Phila., 1980-84; bus. mgr. Control Data Corp., Mpls., 1984-87; dep. sec. Pa. Dept. Comm., 1987—91; spl. asst. to Gov. of Pa. in community econ. devel. initiatives, 1989—91; sec. Commonwealth of Pa., Harrisburg, 1991-94; pres., CEO African Am. Delaware Valley Port Corp., Phila., 1993—94, Mgmt. & Environ. Tech. Inc., Phila., 1995—; co-founder, mng. ptnr. Cmty Leadership Devel. Inst., Allegheny County, Pa., 1999—. Sole propr. bus. in real estate devel. & property mgmt., Phila., Harrisburg, adv. coun. US Dept. Commerce Industry sector, 1994-, bd. dir. Penns Landing Corp, 2001-, adv. bd. Benjamin Franklin Tech. Ptnrs., 2002-. Author: They Crossed Together, 1975. Recipient citation for Outstanding Leadership in Econ. Devel., City of Phila. Mayor's Office, 1987; named for Outstanding Leadership, People United to Serve Humanity, Inc., 1991, Disting. Alumni, Nova U., 1992, Policy Advocate of Yr., Nat. Assn. Bus. Women Owners, 1992. Mem. NAACP (life), Nat. Congress of Black Women, Nat. Forum Black Pub. Adminstrs. (pres. 1987), Forum Exec. Women, Black Women's Leadership Conf. Home: 5204 Overbrook Ave Philadelphia PA 19131-2409 Office: Mgmt & Environ Tech Inc Ste 1108 1315 Walnut St Philadelphia PA 19107 Office Phone: 215-546-7991. Office Fax: 215-546-7995.

MITCHELL, BRENDA MARIE, humanities educator; PhD, U. Ill., Urbana-Champaign. Assoc. prof. Indiana U. of Pa., 1994—. Tchg. and Rsch. fellow, Nagoya U., Japan, 2002, 2005—06. Mem.: NAACP, AAUW, Nat. Women's Studies Assn., Coll. Art Assn.

MITCHELL, BRYCE MAHONEY, psychotherapist, counselor; b. Fitzgerald, Ga., Aug. 31, 1946; d. James Wilson Mahoney and Bennie Elizabeth (Gatliff) Mann; m. Robert David Mitchell, Oct. 15, 1966 (div. June 1977); children: Syne Vallor, Ryel Paldin; m. Stanley Joseph Wnukowski, July 22, 1989, (div. Nov. 2001). BA, Fla. State U., 1966, MA, 1967, PhD, 1971; MS Counseling, U. Wisc.-Madison, 1999. Cert. tchr., profl. counselor, clin. mental health counselor, group psychotherapist. Assoc. prof. Jackson (Miss.) State U., 1972-78; tchr. Monroe County Schs., Key West, Fla., 1979-87, spl. areas dept. head, 1984-87; prof. St. Leo Coll., Key West, Fla., 1980-87; tchr. Holmdel (N.J.) Schs., 1987-89; editor, pub. Recovery and Discovery, Madison, Wis., 1990-92; counselor Ctr. for Exptl. Learning, Madison, 1990-93; owner Wellspring Psychotherapy & Counseling Ctr., Madison, 1993—. Mem. speakers bur. Rape Crisis Ctr., Madison, 1989-92. Contbr. articles to profl. jours. Mem. edn. com. Wis. Coalition Against Sexual Assault, Madison, 1989-90. N.J. Gov.'s Office grantee, 1988; Dane County Youth Commn. grantee, 1990. Mem. ACA, Am. Profl. Soc. on Abuse of Children, Internat. Soc. for Philos. Enquiry, MENSA, Triple Nine Soc. Eckankar religion. Eckankar religion. Office: Wellspring 458 S Owen Dr Madison WI 53711-1550 Office Phone: 608-274-5888.

MITCHELL, CARMENCITA C., literature and language professor; b. NYC, Dec. 27, 1969; BA in Humanities, NYU, 1998; MA in English, St. John's U., 2001; student, Fla. Atlantic U., 2003—. Admissions clerk, receptionist NYU, NYC, 1996—99; grad. tchg., rsch. asst. St. John's U., Jamaica, NY, 1999—2001; adj. asst. prof. English Hofstra U., Hempstead, NY, 2001—03, writing ctr. tutor, 2001—03; instr. English Fla. Atlantic U., Boca Raton, Fla., 2003—. Freelance ESL tutor, 2000—; adj. instr. English, speech St. John's U., Jamaica, NY, 2002—03; presenter in field. Poet (collections in field). Vol. career mentor Girl Scouts Am., Bklyn., 2000—. Mem.: Nat. Women's Studies Assn. (25th ann. conf. presenter 2004, Travel award 2004). Roman Catholic. Avocations: Middle Eastern dance, fashion design, writing, opera. Home: PO Box 8129 New York NY 10150 Office: Fla Atlantic Univ 777 Glades Rd Boca Raton FL 33431

MITCHELL, CAROL ANN, nursing educator; b. Portsmouth, Va., Aug. 31, 1942; d. William Howell and Eleanor Bertha (Wesarg) M.; m. David Alan Friedman, June 17, 1971 (div. 1988). Diploma, NYU, 1963; BS, Columbia U., 1968, MA, 1971, EdM, 1974, EdD, 1980; MS, SUNY, Stony Brook, 1990. Charge nurse Nassau County Med. Ctr., East Meadow, N.Y., 1963-65; staff nurse Meml. Hosp., N.Y.C., 1965-68; head nurse, supr. Cmty. at Glen Cove (N.Y.), 1969-71; assoc. prof. dept. nursing Queensborough C.C. CUNY, Bayside, 1971-80; assoc. prof. Marion A. Buckley Sch. Nursing Adelphi U., Garden City, N.Y., 1981-88; ednl. cons. Nat. League for Nursing, N.Y.C., 1980-81; prof. sch. nursing SUNY, Stony Brook, 1988-92, chmn. adult nursing, 1988-92; prof. chair Coll. Nursing East Tenn. State U., 1992-95, mem faculty, 1995-96; geriat. nurse practitioner, dir. geriat. evaluation unit Vet. Affairs Med. Ctr., Mountain Home, Tenn., 1997—. Mem. faculty Regents Coll. degrees in nursing program USNY, Albany, 1978-91, cons., 1978—; faculty cons. geriats. Montefiore Med. Ctr., 1991-93. Editor emeritus: Scholarly Inquiry in Nursing Practice, 1983—; contbr. articles to profl. jours. Robert Wood Johnson clin. nurse scholar postdoctoral fellow U. Rochester (N.Y.), 1983-85. Mem.: Am. Geriatrics Soc., Am. Nurses Assn. Avocations: reading, gardening, bicycling, travel, cooking.

MITCHELL, CAROL L., lawyer; b. 1955; BA, Boston Coll., 1978; JD, U. Maine, 1987. Bar: Maine 1988. Sr. v.p. legal affairs Peoples Heritage Fin. Group, 1991—99; exec. v.p., chief adminstrn. officer, gen. counsel, corp. clerk Banknorth Group, Inc., Portland, Maine, 2000—. Dir. New Eng. Legal Found.; mem. Gov.'s Bus. Adv. Coun.; mem. bd. visitors U. Maine Sch. Law; spkr. in field. Mem.: Am. Soc. Corp. Secs., Internat. Women's Forum (treas.). Office: Banknorth Group Inc Two Portland Sq Portland ME 04101 Office Phone: 207-761-8500. E-mail: cmitchell@banknorth.com.

MITCHELL, CAROLYN COCHRAN, administrative assistant; b. Atlanta, Dec. 27, 1943; d. Clemern Covell and Agnes Emily (Veal) Cochran; m. W. Alan Mitchell, Aug. 30, 1964; 1 child, Teri Marie. AB magna cum laude, Mercer U., 1965, M in Svc. Mgmt., 1989. Caseworker Ga. Dept. Family & Children Svc., Macon, 1965-67, Covington, 1967-69; presch. dir. Southwestern Theol. Sem., Ft. Worth, 1969-70; presch. tchr., dir. Noah's Ark Day Care, Bowden, Ga., 1970-72, First Bapt. Ch., Bremen, Ga., 1972-75; preschool tchr., dir. Roebuck Pk. Bapt. Ch., Birmingham, Ala., 1975-79; freelance office mgr. and bookkeeper Macon, 1979-84; asst. to pres. Ga. Wesleyan Coll., Macon, 1984-98; asst. to pres., CEO Medcen Cmty. Health Found., Macon, 1998—. Exec. dir. Ga. Women of Achievement, 1991-95; dir. Macon Arts Alliance, 1987-91; mem. Cultural Plan Oversight Com., 1989-90. Active Get Out the Vote Task Force, Macon, 1981-95, Macon Symphony Guild, 1986-91; dep. registrar Bibb County Bd. Elections, Macon, 1981-95; asst. sec. Ronald McDonald House Ctrl. Ga., 1999-2000; charter mem. Nat. Mus. Am. Indian. Mem. AAUW (bd. dirs. Ga. chpt., v.p. 1991-93, chair coll.-univ. rels. com. 1993-94, bylaws com. 1991-92, v.p., sec., treas., historian, newsletter editor, Macon chpt., Named Gift Honoree 1988, 2000), NAFE, NOW, Women's Network for Change, Am. Mgmt. Assn., Presdl. Assts. in Higher Edn., Religious Coalition for Reproductive Choice, The Interfaith Alliance, Women's Polit. Orgn. Macon, Sigma Mu. Democrat. Baptist. Office Phone: 478-633-7395. Business E-Mail: mitchell.carolyn@mccg.org.

MITCHELL, CATHY (C.C.) CHRISTINE, art educator; b. Phoenixville, Pa., 1954; d. William Douglas and Christine (Donshietz) Mitchell. AA, Cuyahoga C.C., Parma Heights, Ohio, 1975; BFA, Sch. of the Art Inst. Chgo., 1987, MA in Art Edn., 1994. Cert. art tchr. grades K-12 Ill., 1987, Ohio, 1998. Dir./arts coord. Howland Sch. Arts, Chgo. Pub. Schs., 1987—98; interim coord. dept. edn. Wexner Ctr. for the Arts, Columbus, Ohio, 1998—2000; arts educator - visual art Columbus (Ohio) Pub. Schs., 2000—. Mem. adv. bd. Art Inst. Chgo., 1991—98; mem. edn. bd. Mus. Contemporary Art, Chgo., 1997—99; adj. faculty dept. art edn. Elmhurst (Ill.) Coll., 1997. Co-prodr., writer (video) School Improvement Planning, Chicago Public Schools. Mem. Cliff Dwellers, Chgo., 1997; com. chair Columbus Arts Festival, 1998—; trustee Parkview NE Condominium Assn., Lewis Center, Ohio, 2001—; active Joel Hall Dance Co., Chgo., 1997—2001. Recipient Nat. Grand prize, Tchr.-Student Photography, Canon Photography with USA Today, 1997, Outstanding Svc. in Arts Edn. for the State of Ill. award, Ill. Alliance for the Arts, 1997, Art Tchr. of Yr., Ill. Alliance for Arts, 1997. Mem.: NEA (assoc.), Ohio Edn. Assn. (assoc.), Nat. Art Edn. Assn. (assoc.). Office: CC Mitchell PO Box 1674 Powell OH 43065-1674 Personal E-mail: box1674@ameritech.net.

MITCHELL, ELLEN CLABAUGH, investment executive; b. Omaha, Mar. 2, 1942; d. Joseph Franklin and Dorothy (Newton) Carpenter; m. Dixon L. Mitchell, Aug. 25, 1962; 1 child, Lara Ellen. BS in Fin. & Econs., U. Nebr., Omaha, 1965; MBA, Va. Poly. Inst., 1983. Chartered Fin. Analyst. Asst. v.p. Firstier Fin., Omaha, 1965-69, 1971-75, Bridges Investments, Omaha, 1970-71; analyst U.S. Securities and Exchange Commn., Washington, 1983-85; v.p. Nat. Bank of Washington, 1985-87, Foxhall Investment Mgmt., Washington, 1987-93; pres. Mitchell Advisors Inc., Reston, Va., 1993—. Mem. Washington Soc. Investment Analysts, Inst. Chartered Fin. Analysts, Garden Club (v.p., treas. 1980). Episcopalian. Home: 2017 Turtle Pond Dr Reston VA 20191-4045 Office: Mitchell Advisors Inc 2017 Turtle Pond Dr Reston VA 20191-4045

MITCHELL, GWENDOLYN ANN, mathematics educator; b. Fort Payne, Ala., July 13, 1973; d. Stephen Randall and Patricia Brisendine Mitchell. BA, U. Ala.-Huntsville, 1995; MA, U. Ala., 2002, EdS, 2004. Cert. math. tchr. Math. tchr. Fort Payne HS, 1995—. Adj. math prof. N.E. Ala. CC, Rainsville, Ala., 2004—. Mem. missions team New Oreg. United Meth. Ch., Fort Payne, 1989—. Mem.: Math. Assn. Am., Nat. Coun. Tchrs. Math., Fort Payne Edn. Assn. (sec. 2004—05), Delta Kappa Gamma. Democrat. United Methodist. Avocation: travel. Home: 408 15th St NW Fort Payne AL 35967 Office Phone: 256-845-0535. Personal E-mail: moonpi@bellsouth.net.

MITCHELL, HELEN DERAMUS, public health administrator; b. Montgomery, Ala., Aug. 12; d. James Alexander and Elizabeth Harriet (Brown) deR.; m. William Andrew Mitchell, June 9, 1943; 1 child, Michael J. BS, U. Chgo., 1941, MS, 1943; MA, Columbia U., 1947, MPH, 1958; EdD, NYU, 1953. Prof. biology and hygiene U. Md., Princess Anne, 1942-45; sr. public health educator N.Y.C. Dept. of Health, 1947-66; exec. dir. Hunts Point divsn. N.Y.C. Human Resources Adminstrn., 1966-68, asst. commr., 1968-71; sr. comprehensive health coord. N.Y.C. Dept. of Health, 1974-76; spl. asst. to pres. Health and Hosp. Corp., N.Y.C., 1977-78; sr. cons. dept. mental health N.Y.C. Dept. of Mental Health, 1979-81; spl. asst. to dep. asst. commr. City of N.Y. Human Resources Adminstrn., 1981-86, assoc. staff analyst for medicaid program, 1989-95; instr. preventive medicine N.Y. Med. Coll., N.Y.C., 1948-58; instr. health counseling NYU, 1953-54. Participant bus boycott, Montgomery, Ala., 1956; bd. dirs. Bronx Cath. Interracial Coun., Inc., 1961-75; pres. cmty. com. Forest Neighborhood House, Bronx, 1962-63; chair edn. and narcotics coms. Cmty. Planning Bd. #2, N.Y.C., 1964-66; mem. local sch. bd., 1961-66; com. Urban League of Greater N.Y., Bronx, 1961-66; mem. Women's City Club, N.Y.C., 1963-90; bd. dirs. Coll. of Human Svcs., N.Y.C. (Audrey Cohen Coll.), 1970; program com. Cmty. Coun. of Greater N.Y., 1963-65; organizer, coord. Cath. Archdiocese of N.Y. March on Washington, 1963; mem. WMAC Radio and Nat. Coun. of Negro Women, N.Y.C., 1963-64; vol. Spl. Voter Registration, N.Y.C.; mem. Coalition of 100 Black Women; chair program and issues com. Fred Samuel Dem. Club, Harlem, N.Y., 1983-87. Recipient Public Health Educator award Public Health Assn. Fellow Am. Public Health Assn. (chair com. on rsch. proposals); mem. Fred Samuel Dem. Club (life), U. Chgo. Alumni Assn., Nat. Med. Assn., NYU Alumni Assn., Ladies of Charity Archdiocese of N.Y., Alpha Kappa Alpha (Tau Omega chpt.). Democrat. Roman Catholic. Avocations: current activities, cyberspace activities. Home: 8 Peter Cooper Rd New York NY 10010-6711

MITCHELL, IRA JOAN, nutritionist; b. Oklahoma City, Jan. 8, 1945; d. John Ira and Eunice (Henderson) M.; 1 child, Mark Anthony. AA, Oscar Rose Jr. Coll., Oklahoma City, 1975. Therapeutic supr. Okla. U. Med. Ctr., Oklahoma City, 1970-74; clinical diet technician U. Hosp., Oklahoma City, 1974-79; adminstrv. technician Okla. Meml. Hosp., Oklahoma City, 1979-95; clin. technician U. Hosp., Oklahoma City, 1995—. Program planner Office of the Gov., Oklahoma City, 1977; practitioner Commn. on Dietetic Registration, Chgo., 1988. Com. mem. Am. Heart Assn., Oklahoma City, 1996; vol. March of Dimes, Oklahoma City, 1994—, Heart Assn. Am., Oklahoma City, 1994—; treas. women's missionary union Tabernacle Bapt. Ch., Oklahoma City, 1997—, pres. adult ushers, 1996—. Mem. Am. Dietetic Assn., Commn. on Dietetic Registration, Okla. Dietetic Assn. (bd. dirs. 1988-90, Technician of Yr. 1988). Democrat. Baptist. Avocations: cooking, golf, travel, exercise. Home: 108 NW 81st St Oklahoma City OK 73114-3202 Office: U Hosp 800 NE 13th St Oklahoma City OK 73104-5006

MITCHELL, JO KATHRYN, retired hospital technical supervisor; b. Clarksville, Ark., Dec. 1, 1934; d. Vintris Franklin and Melissa Lucile (Edwards) Clark; m. James M. Mitchell, June 4, 1955 (dec. Feb. 1973); children: James, Karen Ann, Leslie Kay, Vicki Lynn. Student, U. Ark., Fayetteville, 1952-53; student, Coll. Ozarks, 1953-54, U. Ark., 1954-55, Little Rock U., 1958. Technologist clin. chemistry U. Hosp., Little Rock, 1956-57, asst. supr., 1957-59, rsch. technologist, 1960-62, asst. supr. clin. chemistry, 1979-82, supr. clin. chemistry, 1982—2003; technologist Conway County Hosp., Morrilton, Ark., 1959; office mgr., co-owner Medic Pharmacy, Little Rock, 1962-71; owner The Cheese Shop, Little Rock, 1977-80. Adult advisor Order Rainbow Girls local, Little Rock, 1970-84, state, Ark., 1977-84. Mem. Pharmacy Aux. (pres. 1967-69), Order Eastern Star. Methodist. Avocations: reading, needlecrafts, genealogy, travel. Home: 6908 Lucerne Dr Little Rock AR 72205-5029 Personal E-mail: jkmitch@sbcglobal.net.

MITCHELL, JOYCE FAYE, writer, editor; b. Town Creek, Ala., Sept. 13, 1944; d. Charles Hatton Dawson and Elizabeth Cole; m. William Jackson Mitchell, Sept. 2, 1965; children: Suzanna Michelle, Charlotte Lynn, William Michael, Lora Elizabeth. Student, U. North Ala., 1965. Author, editor: (books) Olden Times of Colbert and Franklin County, Alabama, vols. 1 and 2, 1991, vol. 3, 1993, Olden Times of Lawrence County, Alabama, vols. 1 and 2, 1989; asst. editor Carpenter Jours., 1980-88. Treas. Natchez Trace Soc., Florence, Ala., 1986-87; dir. Family History Ctr., Florence, Ala., 1996-2000; pres. Relief Soc., 1968-70, Primary Orgn., 1985-87; leader Cub Scouts, 1985-87; counselor, youth leader Young Women's Orgn., 1988-94; rsch. fundraiser, 2003-06.; achievement leader for youth, 2003-06. Named Ky. Col., Gov. John Y. Brown Jr., 1983. Mem. DAR. Home: 6150 Woodmont Dr Tuscumbia AL 35674-4631

MITCHELL, JUDITH ANN, education educator; b. Pasadena, Calif., Aug. 11, 1941; d. Theodore Woodrow and Alice Sylvia (Nees) M. AB, UCLA, 1963; MS, U. Wis., Madison, 1971, PhD, 1977. Cert. elem. tchr., Calif. Tchr. Santa Monica (Calif.) Pub. Schs., 1963-67, Madison Pub. Schs., 1967-68, Fountain Valley Pub. Schs., Huntington Beach, Calif., 1968-70; program developer Southwest Regional Labs, Los Alamitos, Calif., 1972-73; asst. prof. Austin Coll., Sherman, Tex., 1976-78, Kennesaw State Coll., Marietta, Ga., 1978-83, assoc. prof., 1983-88, coordinator edn. field experiences, 1978-85, chair dept. curriculum and instrn., 1983-88, prof. edn., 1988—, dir. Regional Inst. Sch. Enhancement, 1994—. Chairperson faculty caucus Kennesaw State Coll., 1992-95. Contbr. articles to profl. jours. Mem. exec. bd. Cobb County Youth Mus., Marietta, 1980—. Mem. ASCD, Am. Ednl. Rsch. Assn., Assn. Tchr. Educators (chmn. resolutions com. 1988-94, chair-elect ATE Coun. of Unit Pres.), Ga. Assn. Tchr. Educators (exec. bd. 1984—, pres.), Phi Delta Kappa, Golden Key. Democrat. Lutheran. Avocations: gardening, reading. Office: Kennesaw State Coll 1000 Chastain Rd NW Kennesaw GA 30144-5588

MITCHELL, KAREN LEE, special education educator, consultant; b. Hudson, Mass., Nov. 23, 1949; d. Leon E. and Barbara V. (Jusseaume) LaFlamme; m. Ernest L. Mitchell, July 24, 1971; 1 child, Jeremy R. BS in Edn., Fitchburg (Mass.) State Coll., 1971; MA in Psychology, Anna Maria Coll., 1982. Cert. spl. edn. tchr., elem. tchr., sch. guidance counselor. Tchr. spl. needs Quaboag Regional Jr./Sr. High Sch., Warren, Mass., 1971-73; specialize care foster parent Mass. Dept. Social Svcs., 1973-81; tchr. gifted and talented Oxford Acad., Northborough, Mass., 1981-89, test adminstr., cons., 1985-89; tchr. Here We Grow Pre-Sch., Auburn, Mass., 1990—94; tchr. spl. edn. Bartlett Jr./Sr. H.S., Webster, Mass., 1994—. Pvt. practice ednl. cons., Auburn, 1989—90. Sunday Sch. tchr. First Congl. Ch., Auburn, 1974-78, trustee, 1980; den leader Boy Scouts Am., Auburn, 1982-85. Avocations: photography, cross country skiing, biking, swimming, camping. Home: 71 Hill St Auburn MA 01501-3335 Personal E-mail: teachem_1@msn.com. E-mail: teachem_1@charter.net.

MITCHELL, KATHLEEN, medical/surgical and geriatrics nurse; b. Memphis, Aug. 4, 1943; d. David D. and Louise R. (McKinny) M.; children: Mary A. King Kinler, Margaret A. King Wetzel. BSN, La. State U., 1976,

MNursing, 1983, D of Nursing Sci., 1989; MEd, William Carey Coll., 1996. Cert. nurse practitioner. Staff nurse SNU & REHAB units Meml. Med. Ctr. (Baptist Campus), New Orleans; gerontol. clin. nurse specialist So. Bapt. Hosp., New Orleans, clin. nurse; prof. nursing William Carey Coll. Sch. Nursing. Fellow in discipline of nursing La. Geriatric Ctr. Contbr. articles to profl. jours. Mem. ANA (coun. gerontol. nurses), La. State Nurses Assn., Nat. Gerontol. Nursing Assn., New Orleans Dist. Nurses Assn., New Orleans Coun. on Aging, So. Gerontol. Soc., S.W. Soc. on Aging, Nat. Coun. on Aging, Sigma Theta Tau. E-mail: kathleen.mitchel@wmcarey.edu.

MITCHELL, LILLIAN ADASSA, principal; b. Oct. 20, 1951; BS in Elem. Edn., W.I. Coll., 1982; MA, Andrew's U., 1987. Asst. prin. Bklyn. Sch., 1991-97; prin. Whispering Pines Sch., Old Westbury, NY, 1997—2002, Greater NY Acad., 2002—. Recipient Zappara Excellence in Tchg. award, 1992. Home: 3206 Bayswater Ct Far Rockaway NY 11691-1606

MITCHELL, LINDA MARLENE, education educator; b. Atchison, Kans., June 18, 1952; d. Frank Fayne and Marlene Marie Riley; m. John Lee Mitchell Jr., Oct. 16, 1971; children: John Michael, Joseph Lee, Jessica Nicole. BA, Wichita State U., 1986, MA, 1990; PhD, U. Kans., 1997. Cert. neonatal assessment scale; lic. speech lang. pathologist, cert. legal asst. Legal asst. Woodard, Baylock & HErnandez, Wichita, 1979-87; legal asst. to corp. counsel Pizza Hut, Inc., Wichita, 1987-89; infant-toddler svcs. coord., speech/lang. pathologist Rainbows United, Inc., Wichita, 1990-93; rsch. asst. U. Kans., Lawrence, 1993-96; v.p. Futures Unltd., Inc., Wellington, Kans., 1996-97; assoc. prof. dept. curriculum & instrn. Wichita State U., 1997—. Presenter and rschr. in field early childhood special edn.; spl. edn. due process hearing officer State of Kans. Mem. editl. bd.: Young Exceptional Children. Grantee multiple grant recipient. Mem. ASCD, Am. Speech-Lang.-Hearing Assn., Nat. Assn. Edn. Young Children, Am. Asn. People with Disabilities, Coun. Exceptional Children, Assn. Persons With Severe Handicaps. Democrat. Avocations: walking, weightlifting, flower gardening, bird watching, hiking, crochet. Office: Wichita State U 1845 Fairmount St Wichita KS 67260-0028 Business E-Mail: linda.mitchell@wichita.edu.

MITCHELL, LOUISE TYNDALL, special education educator; b. St. Louis, Oct. 25; d. Walter Eugene and Nellie May (Otey) Tyndall; m. Felix Mitchell Sr., Sept. 30, 1958; children: Felix Jr., Jeane Mitchell-Carr. AA, Stowe Tchrs. Coll., St. Louis, 1947; BA, Harris Tchrs. Coll., St. Louis, 1958; MA, St. Louis U., 1965. Cert. elem. tchr., secondary English and math., reading clinician. Tchr. math. Hadley High Sch., St. Louis, 1958-59; tchr. Emerson Elem. Sch., St. Louis, 1969-67; head dept. spl. edn. Laclede Elem. Sch., St. Louis, 1967-68, coord. curriculum, 1968-70; adminstrv. asst. Delmar High Sch., St. Louis, 1970-72; assoc. prof., reading clinician, mgr. apprentice tchrs. Harris Tchrs. Coll., 1972-78; chair dept. spl. edn. Cleveland High Sch., St. Louis, 1978-84, chmn. faculty, 1982-84; head dept. spl. edn. S.W. High Sch., St. Louis, 1984-87, tchr., mentor, 1987—. Mentor St. Louis Pub. Schs., 1988-89. Author: (handbook) Teachers Aide, 1987, curriculum guides, 1974, 78; co-author (curriculum guide) Fundamental Curriculum, 1990. Chair Rsch. and Status Black Women, St. Louis, 1974; charter mem. Triagle Club YWCA, 1970. Recipient Community Svc. award Top Ladies Distinction, St. Louis, 1981, 50 Yrs. Outstanding Svc. award A.M.E. Ch., St. Louis, 1987, Salute to Excellence in Edn. recognition St. Louis Am. Newspaper, 1991. Mem. NAACP, Am. Fedn. Tchrs., Nat. Coun. Negro Women, Colored Womens' Fed. Clubs, Women Achievement (coord. youth 1989), St. Louis U. Alumni Assn., (Svc. award 1986), Ch. Women United, Order Ea. Star (past Worthy Matron 1978), Sigma Gamma Rho (chaplain 1988-90), Phi Delta Kappa. Avocations: reading, writing, drama, singing, public speaking. Home: 4537 Fair Ave # A Saint Louis MO 63115-3054

MITCHELL, LUCILLE ANNE, retired elementary school educator; b. Dayton Corners, Ill., Oct. 19, 1928; d. Roy Rollin and Edna May (Whitehouse) Sheppard; m. Donald L. Mitchell; children: David, Diane, Barbara Rock, Patricia Reaves. BS in Edn., Augustana Coll., 1966; MS in Edn., Western Ill. U., 1972, Edn. Specialist, 1974. Tchr. Carbon Cliff (Ill.) Elem. Sch., 1962-65, Moline (Ill.) Bd. Edn., 1967-92. Mem. textbook selection com. Moline Bd. Edn., 1967-84, rep. Moline Bd. Edn., Ill. Network Sch. Devel., 1973. Author: numerous poems. Counselor to pastor Cmty. of Christ, 2001—02, elder in priesthood. Named Ill. Master Tchr., State of Ill., 1984; recipient Internat. Peace prize United Cultural Convention, 2005 Mem. Ill. Edn. Assn. (com. mem.), Moline Edn. Assn. (com. mem.), Delta Kappa Gamma (program chmn. 1978-79, recording sec. 1980-81) Avocations: organ, piano, oil and water color painting, poetry, teaching Bible study classes. Home: 3214 55th Street Ct Moline IL 61265-5740 Personal E-mail: donnlucy@mchsi.com.

MITCHELL, M. YVONNE, paraprofessional; b. San Francisco, July 4, 1957; d. Richard Henry Mitchell and Mary Rose Mitchell Young; children: Janelle A. Fenall, C. Monique Jessie. BS, Univ. Santa Clara, 1978; PhD, O.I.T., Klameth Falls, Oreg., 1995. Lic. CNA, 1995, 1997. CNA MWMC, Klamath Falls, Oreg., 1995—97; caregiver Est. of JA Phillips, Klamath Falls, Oreg., 1998—2003; tchrs. asst. Riverside Elem. Sch., Klamath Falls, Oreg., 1999—2000, KYDC, Klamath Falls, Oreg., 2000—03; paraprofessional Mills Elem. sch., Klamath Falls, Oreg., 2003—05. Exec. bd. KFACE, Klamath Falls, Oreg., 2003—05, bldg. rep., 2001—05; RA rep. OEA, Klamath Falls, Oreg., 2003—05. Mem. Ch.; vol. Salvation Army. Recipient Vol. of the Yr., United Way, 2003. Mem.: NEA, Oreg. Coun. of Edn. Support Profl., Family Empowerment. Democrat. Bapt.

MITCHELL, MADELEINE ENID, retired nutritionist; b. Jamaica, West Indies, Dec. 14, 1941; came to U.S., 1963, naturalized, 1974. d. William Keith and Doris Christine (Levey) M. B.Sc. in Home Econs., McGill U., Montreal, Que., Can., 1963; MS, Cornell U., 1965, PhD, 1968. Asst. prof. Wash. State U., Pullman, 1969-77, assoc. prof., 1978—2004, acting. chmn. home econs. rsch. ctr., 1981-83; ret., 2004. Nutrition scientist U.S. Dept. Agr., Washington, 1980-81. Author: Jamaican Ancestry: How to Find Out More, 1998. Mem.: Am. Dietetics Assn. Episcopalian. Avocations: genealogy, music. Personal E-mail: mitchelm@pullman.com.

MITCHELL, MARGARET YVONNE, forester; b. Niagara Falls, NY, June 4, 1963; d. Reece Graham and Judith Ann Mitchell. BS in Landscape Architecture, Colo. State U., 1986; MS in Forestry, U. Idaho, 1989. Landscape architect Wenatchee Nat. Forest, Wenatchee, Wash., 1982—87; tchg./rsch. asst. U. Idaho, Moscow, 1988—89; landscape architect Wenatchee Nat. Forest, Cle Elum, Wash., 1989—91, Tongass Nat. Forest, Wrangell, Ala., 1991—92, dist. planning staff officer, 1992—97, dist. ranger, 1997—2000, Wallowa-Whitman Nat. Forest/USDA Forest Svc., Enterprise, Oreg., 2000—.

MITCHELL, MARY ANN CARRICO, poet; b. Louisville, Aug. 1, 1937; d. Bernard and Catherine (Steinlockner) Carrico; m. William Ray Mitchell, Aug. 25, 1962; children: Michael, Anne Marie, Katherine. RN, St. Joseph Sch. Nursing, Louisville, 1958; BSN, U. Colo., 1962. Head nurse Our Lady of Peace Hosp., Louisville, 1960; mgr. collections Point Loma Credit Union, San Diego, 1974-77; charge nurse Mercy Hosp., San Diego, 1977-78; managerial sec. Gulf Oil, Denver, 1977-81; exec. sec. Phillips Petrol, Denver, 1981-82; adminstrv. asst. Reliance Petroleum, Denver, 1982-84. Author: (poems) Meeshak, 1997, My First Vertical, 1997, White Tail-a-Flyin', 1997, Friends, 1997. Mem. DAR, AAUW, Nat. League Am. Penwomen (founder, pres. Bluegrass of Ky. br.). Roman Catholic. Avocations: painting, sewing, quilting, gardening, poetry. Home: 494 Lea View Ave Campbellsburg KY 40011-7545 E-mail: macmky@aol.com.

MITCHELL, MARY JENKINS, public health service officer; b. Rochester, NY; d. Hudson and Clara May Jenkins; m. Floyd Mitchell, Aug. 24, 1991; 1 child, Derek Scot. B Cmty. Health, St. Joseph's Coll., Bklyn., 1984; MPA, LI U., Bklyn., 1999. Cert. non-profit mgmt. Columbia U., 1986. Asst. to pres. Bklyn. Borough Pres.' Office, 1987—95; dir., health careers inst. LI U., 1995—2000; regional v.p. Am. Cancer Soc., Bklyn., 2000—03; exec. dir. MSI Area Health Edn. Ctr., NYC, 2004—. Adj. prof. LI U., Brooklyn, NY, 1998—2000; student cons. Pub. Svc. Commn., Pretoria, South Africa, 1998. V.p. Justice Works Cmty., Inc., Bklyn., 1995—2000; deaconess Flatbush Tompkins Congl. Ch., Bklyn., 1997—2004; bd. dirs. NY Women's Found., NYC, 1993—95. Recipient Ability, Accomplishment and Cmty. Svc. award, Outstanding Young Women Am., 1986, Cmty. Leadership award, Bklyn Exec. Bus. Women's Assoc., 2004. Mem.: Pi Alpha Alpha (life). Office: Manhattan-State Area Health Educ Ctr 43 Central Park North New York NY 10026 Office Phone: 212-534-2432. Personal E-mail: mljm1@excite.com. Business E-Mail: mary@msiahec.org.

MITCHELL, MOZELLA GORDON, language educator, minister; b. Starkville, Miss., Aug. 14, 1936; d. John Thomas and Odena Mae (Graham) Gordon; m. Edrick R. Woodson, Mar. 20, 1951 (div. 1974); children: Cynthia LaVern, Marcia Delores Woodson Miller. AB, LeMoyne Coll., 1959; MA in English, U. Mich., 1963; MA in Religious Studies, Colgate-Rochester Divinity Sch., 1973; PhD, Emory U., 1980. Instr. in English and Speech Alcorn A&M Coll., Lorman, Miss., 1960-61; instr. English, chmn. dept. Owen Jr. Coll., Memphis, 1961-65; asst. prof. English and religion Norfolk State Coll. U. Norfolk, Va., 1965—81; assoc. prof. U. South Fla., Tampa, 1981—93, prof., 1993—, chmn.-elect religious studies dept., 2005—, chair religious studies dept., 2006—; pastor Mount Sinai AME Zion Ch., 1882—89; presiding elder Tampa dist. AME Zion Ch., 1988—; pastor, founder Love of Christ AME Zion Tabernacle, Branden, 1993—; candidate for bishop AME Zion Ch., 2003—04, presiding Elder, 1998—2004. Vis. assoc. prof. Hood Theol. Sem., Salisbury, N.C., 1979-80, St. Louis U., 1992-93; vis. asst. lectr. U. Rochester, N.Y., 1972-73; co-dir. Ghent VISTA Project, Norfolk, 1969-71; cons. Black Women and Ministry Interdenominational Theol. Ctr; lectr. Fla. Humanities Coun., 1994-95; Meml. lectr. Mordecai Johnson Inst., Colgate Rochester Div. Sch., 1997. Author: Spiritual Dynamics of Howard Thurman's Theology, 1985, Howard Thurman and the Quest for Freedom, Proc. 2d Ann. Howard Thurman Convocation (Peter Lang), 1992, African American Religious History in Tampa Bay, 1992;, New Africa in America: The Blending of African and American Religious and Social Traditions Among Black People in Meridian, Mississippi and Surrounding Counties (Peter Lang), 1994, Crucial Issues in Caribbean Religions (Peter Lang), 2006, Crucial Issues in Caribbean Religion, 2006; editor: Martin Luther King Meml. Series in Religion, Culture and Social Devel.; editorial bd. Cornucopia Reprint Series; contr. articles and essays in field. Mem. Tampa-Hillsborough County Human Rels. Coun., 1987—; founder Women at the Well, Inc.; del. 7th assembly World Coun. Chs., Canberra, Australia, 1991, 17th World Meth. Coun., Rio de Janiero, 1996; del. 18th World Meth. Coun., Brighton, England, 2001; mem. connectional coun. A.M.E. Zion Ch., Charlotte, 1984—, staff writer Sunday sch. lit., 1981—, mem. jud. coun., candidate for bishop, 2002—04; pres. Fla. Coun. Chs., Orlando, Fla., 1988—90, pres.-elect, 1998—, pres. exec. bd., 2000. Recipient ecumenical leadership citation Fla. Coun. Chs., 1990, Inaugural lectr. award Geddes Hanson Black Cultural Ctr. Princeton Theol. Sem., 1993; fellow Nat. Doctoral Fund, 1978-80; grantee NEH, 1981, Fla. Endowment for Humanities, 1990—, U. South Fla. Rsch. Coun., 1990—. Mem. Coll. Theology Soc., Am. Acad. Religion, Soc. for the Study of Black Religion (pres. 1992-96), Joint Ctr. for Polit. Studies, Black Women in Ch. and Soc., Alpha Kappa Alpha. Phi Kappa Phi. Democrat. Methodist. Avocations: piano, poetry, tennis, bicycling, Scrabble. Office: Univ South Florida Religious Studies Dept CPR 107 Tampa FL 33620 Office Phone: 813-974-1852. Business E-Mail: mozellam@aol.com.

MITCHELL, PAMELA ANN, airline pilot; b. Otis AFB, Mass., May 6, 1955; d. Gene Thomas and Rose Margaret (Jones) Mitchell. BFA, Colo. State U., 1975; postgrad., Webster Coll., 1981. Lic. pilot Ill., comml. instr., airline transport pilot, jet rating, Boeing 747 and 727, Boeing 747-400, McDonnell Douglas DC-10. Flight attendant United Airlines, Chgo., 1976-80; owner, operator Deliverance, Unltd. Ferry Co., Aurora, Ill., 1978-81; flight test pilot Cessna Aircraft Co., Wichita, Kans., 1981-82, nat. spokeswoman, 1982-83; airline pilot Rep. Airlines, Mpls., 1983-84; airline pilot, captain Northwest Airlines, Mpls., 1985—; owner, pres. The Global Nomad LLC, 1997—. Mem. Safety Coun. Airline Pilots Assn., 99's Internat. Women Pilots Assn., Internat. Soc. Women Airline Pilots (bd. dirs. 1994-96), Nat. Aviation Club, N.W. Airline Ski Team (capt. 1989-94), Kappa Kappa Gamma. Republican. Presbyterian. Avocations: piano, skiing, tennis, travel, golf.

MITCHELL, PATRICIA ANN, education educator; b. Washington, Sept. 17, 1946; d. James Garnell and Ruth Estella (Harper) Turner; m. Larry Wayne Mitchell, June 29, 1977; children— Candyce, Jason, Jeremy. B.S. in Edn., Morgan State Coll., 1968; M.S. in Edn. (fellow), So. Ill. U., 1970; Ph.D. (fellow), Cath. U. Am., 1978. Cert. pub. sch., jr. coll. tchr., Calif., Md. Tchr. 1st grade Prince George's County (Md.) Pub. Schs., 1968, reading specialist, 1970-77; instr. U. San Francisco, 1977-78, asst. prof. edn., 1978—94, assoc. prof., 1994—, chair, orgn. and leadership dept., 1999—; coordinator Elem. edn. program, 1987—. Bd. dirs. Sem Yeta chpt. Camp Fire Inc.; mem. edn. com. Am. Cancer Soc. Solano County. Mem. NAACP, Nat. Urban League. Mem. Am. Ednl. Research Assn., Nat. Assn. Female Execs., Internat. Reading Assn., Calif. Women in Higher Edn. Assn., Coll. Reading Assn., Alpha Kappa Alpha. Democrat. Baptist. Office: Sch Edn U San Francisco 2130 Fulton St San Francisco CA 94117-1080 Office Phone: 415-422-2079.

MITCHELL, PATRICIA EDENFIELD, broadcast museum administrator; b. Swainsboro, Ga., Jan. 20, 1943; d. James Otis and Bernice Tucker Edenfield; m. Jay Addison Mitchell, Aug. 20, 1964 (div. June 1970); 1 child, Mark Addison. BA magna cum laude, U. Ga., 1964, MA, 1965. English instr. U. Ga., Athens, 1965—69; English, drama instr. Va. Commonwealth U., Richmond, 1969—70; researcher, writer LOOK Mag., NYC, 1970; cons., speech writer Garth Assocs., NYC, 1970—71; TV prodr., reporter WB2-TV, Boston, 1971—77; anchor, talk show host WTTG-TV, Washington, 1977—79; corr. NBC-TV Today, NYC, 1984—89, CBS-TV Sunday Morning, NYC, 1989—90; exec. prodr., writer documentaries VU Prodns., LA, 1990; pres. CNN Prodns. and Time Inc. TV TBS, 1992—2000; pres., CEO PBS, 2000—06; pres. Mus. TV & Radio, 2006—. Creator, prodr., host, owner Woman to Woman (nationally syndicated program), L.A., 1983—; spkr., conf. leader on women's issues, 1973—; bd. trustees Sundance Inst.; former mem. exec. com. TBS, Inc., CNN Exec. Com.; bd. mem. Internews, 2002—. Mem. adv. com. Nat. Coun. on Rsch. on Women, N.Y.C., 1990—92; mem. adv. bd. Schlesinger Libr. on History of Women, Radcliffe Coll., Cambridge, Mass., 1985—92; media com. Hollywood Women's Polit. Com., L.A., 1989—92; former trustee Metro Atlanta YMCA, High Mus. Art, Atlanta; mem. adv. bd. Santa Barbara Sch. Comm. U. Calif.; pres. Global Green USA (Am. affiliate Mikhail Gorbachev's worldwide conservation orgn.); nat. bd. mem. Girls Inc. Named One of the 100 Most Powerful Women in Television, The Hollywood Reporter; recipient Emmy for Best Daytime Program, TV Acad., 1984, Emmy for Best Host-Daytime, 1971, numerous film festival awards, 1989—92, Women in Cable & Broadcasting Woman of the Year, CINE Golden Eagle for Lifetime Achievement, Sandra Day O'Connor award for Leadership. Avocations: hiking, bicycling, horseback riding, reading. Office: Mus TV & Radio 25 W 52nd St New York NY 10019 Office Phone: 212-621-6800.*

MITCHELL, PATSY MALIER, religious school founder, administrator; b. Greenwood, Miss., Aug. 28, 1948; d. William Lonal and Lillian (Walker) Malier; m. Charles E. Mitchell, Apr. 20, 1970; children: Christopher, Kara, Angela. BS in Edn., Delta State U., 1970, MEd, 1974, Edn. Specialist, 1979; MA in Ch. Ministries, Ch. of God Sch. Theology, 1990; PhD in Psychology and Counseling, La. Bapt. U., 1994; D in Edn. Christian Sch. Adminstrn., Baptist Christian U., 1992. Cert. sch. adminstr. Youth, Christian edn. dir. Ch. of God, Minter City, Miss., 1975—, teen talent dir., 1983—, missions rep., 1975—, dist. Christian edn. dir. Cleveland, Miss., 1983-85, sch. adminstr., 1985—. Del. Ch. of God Edn. Leadership, Cleveland, Tenn., 1990; del., spkr. Christian Sch. Internat., Chattanooga, 1991. Contbr. Dir. St. Jude Children's Hosp., Memphis, 1991; vol. 4-H Club, Greenwood, Miss., 1985—91. Named Outstanding Young Women of Am., 1983, Top 10 of 50 Leading Bus. Women in Miss., 2001; recipient Cmty. Pride award, Chevron, 1988, Internat. Woman of Yr. award, 1993, One of One Thousand Greatest Ams., 2004, Top 100 Educators in the World, 2005—06, Internat. Educator of the Yr., 2004. Mem.: NAFE, Ch. of God Edn. Assn., Christian Schs. Internat., Christian Sch. Adminstrs., Gospel Music Assn., Ch. of God Sch. of Theology Alumni assn., Delta State Alumni Assn. Republican. Home: 5642 County Rd 544 Minter City MS 38944 Office Phone: 662-299-4592.

MITCHELL, RUTHIE YVETTE, human services administrator, director; b. Harrisburg, Pa., Nov. 14, 1960; d. Jerry Mitchell and Nina Walters; children: Edmond Vincent, Sharrow, Tyrone, DeAndre Diggs. B in Human Svcs., M in Human Svcs., Lincoln U., 2004; student, Capella U., Mpls., Minn., 2004—. Armed correctional officer supr. DC Dept. Corrections, Lorton, Va., 1985—90; campus police officer Howard U., Washington, 1998—2002; preventive case mgmt. counselor Us Helping Us, Washington, case mgr., 2000—, transitional discharge planner, project mgr., 2002—; exec. dir. Jewel In the Night, Washington. Facilitator Dept. Corrections Tng. Acad., 1985, Fed. Protective Svc. Divsn. Acad., 1998, Ct. Svcs. Offender Supervision Agy., Washington, 2004. Editor: (book) So This Is Nina, 2004. Vol. substance abuse counselor Pilgrim Rest Bapt. Therapeutic Svcs., Washington, 1998—. Recipient Outstanding Performance Duty, HUH Security Divsn., 2000. Mem.: Pi Gamma Mu. Avocations: writing, ballet. Home: 5802 Southern Ave Washington DC 20019 Office: Jewel in Night 5802 Southern Ave Washington DC 20019 Office Phone: 202-446-1105. Office Fax: 202-204-0808. Personal E-mail: ruthiemitchell2002@yahoo.com.

MITCHELL, SHARON, artist; b. Elmira, N.Y., Dec. 5, 1944; d. Earl Arlington Mitchell and Mary Elizabeth Whitney; m. Chet F. Lunner, Aug. 2, 1966 (div. Feb. 1984); children: Kristina, Kimberly; m. John K. Craford, Dec. 3, 1994. Student, U. Maine, Augusta, 1989-91; BFA, RISD, 1994. Exec. dir., chmn. Maine State Housing Authority, Augusta, 1980-83; CEO Fin. Authority Maine, Augusta, 1983-84; v.p. pub. fin. Mossley, Boston, 1984-85; treas. Ctrl. Maine Power, Augusta, 1985-86; pres. Ariel Corp., Augusta, 1986-89; artist, cons. Saybrook, Conn., 1989—; pres., founder Emerald Tara Co., Saybrook, 1999—. Chair child abuse task force, Dept. Housing Svcs., 1983-84; chair Gov.'s Rural Devel. Commn., 1984-85; treas. Coun. State Fin. Agy., 1983-84. Exhibited at group shows a. Jain Maranouchi Gallery, N.Y.C., 1995—, Impact Woman's Gallery, Buffalo, 1996, N.Mex. Art League, Albuquerque, 1996, Assoc. Artists, Southport, N.C., 1999. Mem. Gov.'s Cost Mgmt. Task Force, 1983-84, Gov.'s Telecomms. Task Force, 1983-84, Future Maine Forests, 1984-85. Mem. Alliance for Art, Women Caucus for Art. Home: 463 W Gray St Elmira NY 14905-2527

MITCHELL, SHAWNE MAUREEN, author; b. Tacoma, Wash., Jan. 09; d. F. King and Nona Margaret Burnside (Hayes) M.; m. J.D. Cook, Spt. 4, 1982; children: Travis, Austin. BA, U. Wash.; postgrad., U. Santa Monica, 1997—. CEO Adventures of the Spirit, Santa Barbara, Calif., 1994—; author, spkr. Soul Style, 1995—; columnist Feng Shui-Soul Style, Calif., 1996—. Cons. real estate, Wash., Calif., 1980—; dir. Small Luxury Hotels, L.A., 1986-87; internat. spkr., author on subject of higher consciousness; internat. spkr. on Feng Shui. Author: Soul Style, 1997, Exploring Feng Shui, Ancient Secrets and Modern Insights, 2001, Creating Home Sanctuaries with Feng Shui, 2002, Simple Feng Shui, 2004; editor: Home Sanctuaries mag.; contbr. articles to profl. jours. Bd. dirs. Montecito (Calif.) Ednl. Found., 1997-99, Los Positas Park Found., Santa Barbara, 1995. Mem.: Womens Exec. Network, Santa Barbara Polo Club. Avocations: boating, hiking, travel, music, art. Office: Adventures of the Spirit Inc PO Box 5765 Santa Barbara CA 93150-5765 Office Phone: 805-565-8885. E-mail: shawne@shawnemitchell.com.

MITCHELL, TAWNIA JUANITA, elementary school educator, music educator; b. St. Croix Falls, Wis., July 29, 1969; d. DeWayne Gerhard and Wanda Juanita Gunderson; m. Jeffery Paul Mitchell, Mar. 22, 1997; 1 child, Madelyn Maudene. MusB in Edn., Lawrence U., 1991. Music, vocal tchr. K-12th grade Cambria (Wis.)-Friesland Sch., 1991—93; music, choral tchr. 4th-12th grade Montello (Wis.) Sch. Dist., 1994—96; music, choral tchr. 3rd-12th grade Green Lake (Wis.) Sch. Dist., 1997—, drama dir., 1997—2004. Musician (cellist): Beaver Dam Area Orch., 1992—2003. Mem.: Wis. Choral Dirs. Assn., Music Educators Nat. Conf. Avocations: cello, organ, singing, dance, scrapbooks. Office: Green Lake Sch Dist 612 Mill St PO Box 369 Green Lake WI 54941 Business E-Mail: tmitche2@glsd.k12.wi.us.

MITCHELL, VIRGINIA ANN, investment company executive; b. El Dorado, Ark., June 1, 1951; d. Joseph Grover Mitchell and Wanda Frazier; m. Greg R. Hoban, Dec. 6, 1986 (div. July 5, 1995); children: Aimee Judy, Hunter Hoban. AA, Maui C.C., Hawaii, 1984; BS, Excelsior Coll., Albany, 2001. Owner, mgr. Vamm Enterprises, Miami, 1979—. Editor: Ho'oulu, 1998. Mem. Unity by the Sea; parent vol. Highland Oaks Middle Sch., 2001; parent vol. reading program Kamali'i Elem. Sch., 1998—99. Mem.: Forest Landowners Assn., Fed. Forest Farm Assn., Sigma Tau Delta. Avocations: hiking, scuba diving, boating. Home: # 139 16850-112 Collins Ave Miami FL 33160 Office: Vamm Enterprises 3741 Ne 163rd St # 139 Miami FL 33160 E-mail: vmitc1@aol.com.

MITCHELLL, PAULA RAE, nursing educator, dean; b. Independence, Mo., Jan. 10, 1951; d. Millard Henry and E. Lorene (Denton) Gates; m. Ralph William Mitchell, May 24, 1975. BS in Nursing, Graceland U., 1973; MS in Nursing, U. Tex., 1976; EdD in Ednl. Adminstrn., N.Mex. State U., 1996. RN, Tex., Mo.; cert. childbirth educator. Instr. nursing El Paso (Tex.) C.C., 1979-85, dir. nursing, 1985—2003, acting divsn. chmn. health occupations, 1985-86, divsn. dean, 1998-99, dean health occupations, 1999-2000, curriculum facilitator, 1984—85, dean health occupations, math and sci., campus dean Rio Grande, 2000—. Ob-gyn. nurse practitioner Planned Parenthood, El Paso, 1981-86, med. com., 1986-98; cons. in field, army med. dept. officer Acad. Health Scis.Ft. Author: (with Grippando) Nursing Perspectives and Issues, 1989, 93; contbr. articles to profl. jours. Founder, bd. dirs. Health-CREST, El Paso, 1981—85; mem. pub. edn. com. Am. Cancer Soc., El Paso, 1983—84, mem. profl. activities com., 1992—93; mem. El-Paso City-County Bd. Health, 1989—91; mem. Govt. Applications Rev. Com. Rio Grande Coun. Govts., 1989—91; mem. collaborative coun. El Paso Magnet H.S. for Health Care Professions, 1992—94; co-chair health and human svcs. task force Unite El Paso Health, 1996—98, mem. steering com., 1999—2000; co-chair health taskforce El Paso Cmty. Legis. Agenda, 1997—99; mem. adv. com. Ctr. for Border Health Rsch., Paso del Norte Health Found., 1998—2004; mem. Leadership El Paso, 1999; mem. health profl. shortage task force Greater El Paso C. of C., 2001—, mem. health care coun., 2002—; mem. star adv. com. Canutillo Tex. Ind. Sch. Dist., Canutillo, Tex., 2003—; mem. El Paso County Civil Svc. Commn., 2006—; bd. dirs. Border Health Inst., El Paso, 2001—, sec.-treas., 2003—. Capt. U.S. Army, 1972—78. Decorated Army Commendation medal, Meritorious Svc. medal. Named to Women's Hall of Fame, El Paso Commn., 1999, named Outstanding Alumni, N.Mex. State U. Dept. Edn. Mgmt. and Devel., 2002-03. Mem. Nat. League Nursing (resolutions com. Assocs. Degree coun. 1987-89, accreditation site visitor, AD coun. 1990—, Tex. edn. com. 1991-92, Tex. 3d v.p. 1992-93, Tex. 1st v.p. 1997-99, nominating com. 1999-2000), Am. Soc. Psychoprophylaxis Obstetrics, Nurses Assn. Am. Coll. Ob-Gyn. (cert. in ambulatory women's healthcare, chpt. coord. 1979-83, nat. program rev. com. 1984-86, corr. 1987-89), Advanced Nurse Practitioner Group El Paso (coord. 1980-83, legis. com. 1984), Am. Phys. Therapist Assn. (commn. on accreditation, site visitor for phys. therapist asst. programs 1991-), Orgn. Assoc. Degree Nursing (Tex. membership chmn. 1985-89, chmn. goals com. 1989-2004, nat. bylaws com. 1990-95), Am. Vocat. Assn., Am. Assn. Women Cmty. and Jr. Colls., Tex. Orgn. Nurse Execs., Nat. Coun. Workforce Edn. (articulation task force 1986-89, program standards task force 1991-93), Nat. Coun. Instrnl. Adminstrs., Tex. Soc. Allied Health Profls. (sec., 2004-2005), Tex. Nurses Assn. (pres.-elect dist. one 2002-03, pres. 2003-05), Nat. Soc. Allied Health Profls. (edn. com. 1993-96), El Paso C. of C. (healthcare coun. 2001-05), Sigma Theta Tau, Phi Kappa Phi. Mem. Christian Ch. (Disciples Of Christ). Home: 4616 Cupid Dr El Paso TX 79924-1726 Office: El Paso C C PO Box 20500 El Paso TX 79998-0500 Office Phone: 915-831-4030. Business E-Mail: paulam@epcc.edu.

MITCHEM, CHERYL E., accounting educator; b. South Bend, Ind., June 24, 1947; d. Roy Francis and Marcella Evelyn (Chryst) Drake; m. Allen Pershing Mitchem, Jr., Nov. 28, 1969; children: Michael, Marlo, Megan, Melissa. BA, Tex. Christian U., 1969; MBA, San Diego State U., 1980; PhD, Va. Commonwealth U., 1990. CPA, Va.; cert. mgmt. acct. Vis. prof. acctg. Coll. William and Mary, Williamsburg, Va., 1986-88; adj. prof. acctg. Va. Commonwealth U., Richmond, 1988-89; asst. prof. acctg. Christopher Newport U., Newport News, 1989-91; asst. prof. Va. State U., Petersburg, 1991—98, chair acctg., 1993—2003, assoc. prof., 1998—, acting asst. dean Sch. Bus., 2004—. Contbr. articles to profl. jours. Mem. AICPA, Am. Acctg. Assn., Inst. Mgmt. Accts. Mem. Christian Ch. (Disciples Of Christ). Avocations: travel, reading.

MITRA, ADITI, mathematician, educator; d. Asoke and Ratna Sen; m. Aniruddha Mitra, Apr. 18, 1989; children: Trisha, Ria. BSc, Calcutta U., India, 1988; BS, U. Nev., Reno, 1995, MS, 1999. Rsch. and tchg. asst. U. Nev., Reno, 1995—98; asst. documentation analyst Hytek Microsystems, Carson City, Nev., 2001—02; part time instr. Ogeechee Tech. Coll., Statesboro, Ga., 2003—04, East Ga. Coll., Statesboro, 2004—06, math. instr., 2006—. Home: 504 Springer Ct Statesboro GA 30461 Office: East Ga Coll 1709 Chandler Rd Statesboro GA 30460 Business E-Mail: amitra@ega.edu.

MITTELSTAEDT, JANET RUGEN, music educator, composer; b. Port Washington, NY, Mar. 30, 1941; d. Chester Davis and Harriet Helen (Goodman) Rugen; m. Ronald Edward Mittelstaedt, Aug. 24, 1963; children: Edward D., Amy C. Leimbach, Thomas A. BS in Edn., Bucknell U., 1963; BA in Music, Marylhurst U., 1984; MM in Composition, U. Portland, 1993. Nat. cert. in piano and composition Music Tchrs. Nat. Assn. Tchr. 6th grade Spring Branch Sch. Dist., Houston, 1964-66; piano tchr. Houston, 1964-66, Pitts., 1967-74, Portland, Oreg., 1978—; composition tchr., 1988—. Composer: Solo Snips, 1991, Splashes of Color, 1992, Sonatina for Youth, 1993, Fabric and Frills, 1994, Beehive, 2002, Animal Antics, 2004; contbr. articles to profl. jours. Pianist, music coord. Evergreen Presbyn. Ch., Portland, 1994—2000, dir. children's mus., 1996, 1997; youth choir accompanist First Presbyn. Ch., Portland, 2003—05. Recipient award, Ernest Bloch Composers Symposium, 1993, spl. awards, ASCAP, 1994—95, 1997—2004. Mem.: Oreg. Music Tchrs. Assn. (music composition clinician 1990—, composition adjudicator 1990—, chmn. Portland ensemble 1992—94, state composition 1992—95, Portland composition 1998—99, chair Portland program 1999—2001, syllabus adjudicator 2002—, co-chmn. sylllabus far west area 2004—, chmn. Pt. syllabus 1980, music theory clinician 1980, Composer of Yr. 1994), Oreg. Fedn. Music Clubs (chair composition 1980). Republican. Presbyterian. Avocations: reading, travel, poetry. Home: 4485 NW 187th Ave Portland OR 97229-2911 Personal E-mail: janrm@att.net.

MITTENDORF, KIMBERLY ANN, secondary school educator, real estate consultant; d. K. A. and Jo Mittendorf. BS in Edn., Murray State U., 1980, MA in Edn., 1987. Cert. career and tech. edn. Nat. Bd. Tchr. Certification, 2004, lic. real estate Paducah C.C., 1990. Tchr. Paducah Pub. Schs., Ky., 1982—; real estate specialist Prudential Real Estate, Paducah, 1990—99. Mem. Paducah Bd. Realtors, 1990—2001; mem. edn. com. Challenger Learning Space Ctr., Paducah, 2001—03; mem. fed. res. economics edn. com. Fed. Res., Louisville, 2005—. Affiliate Hon. Order of Ky. Cols., Louisville, 1996—; inductee Paducah C. of C. Leadership Class, 1995—96; mem. Paducah C. of C., 1995—98; mem. funds distbn. com. United Way, Paducah, 1996—97. Recipient Invitation to China, People to People Amb. -Edn. Del. to China, 2005. Mem.: NEA (assoc.), Ky. Edn. Assn. (assoc.), Ky. Assn. Career and Tech. Edn. (assoc.), Pi Lambda Theta. Avocations: literature, architecture and design, fitness, cuisine. Office: McCracken County Pub Schs 435 Berger Rd Paducah KY 42001 Business E-Mail: kim.mittendorf@mccracken.kyschools.us.

MITTLEIDER, REBECCA ANN, elementary school educator; d. Leslie Earl and Bonnie Kay Johnson; m. Randy Wayne Mittleider, Aug. 20, 1988; 1 child, Megan Kate. B Sociology, Western Wash. U., 1988; M Tchg., Wash. State U., 1995. Cert. tchr. Wash. Cmty. corrections officer Dept. Corrections, Kennewick, Wash., 1988—95; mid. sch. tchr. Kennewick (Wash.) Sch. Dist., 1995—96; elem. sch. tchr. Richland Sch. Dist., West Richland, Wash., 1996—. Sci. curriculum coord. Tapteal Elem. Sch., Richland, 2004—05; presenter in field. Vol. pet therapist with miniature horses at local nursing homes, Wash., 2004—05; vol. horse therapist Handicapped Equestrian Riding Team, Kennewick, 1995—95. Recipient Excellence in Tchg. award, KEPR News, 2001; Tchr. Leadership Project grantee, Bill and Melinda Gates Found., 2000. Mem.: NAST, Wash. Orgn. Reading Devel., Am. Miniature Horse Registry (Nat. Top-Ten All Star in Roadster and Obstacle 2004), Columbia Basin Bass Club (bd. dirs., newsletter editor 1998—99), Ctrl. Wash. Miniature Horse Club (Yr. End High Point awards 2004—05), Franklin County Saddle Club. Office Phone: 509-967-6300.

MITTLER, DIANA (DIANA MITTLER-BATTIPAGLIA), music educator, pianist; b. NYC, Oct. 19, 1941; d. Franz and Regina (Schilling) Mittler; m. Victor Battipaglia, Sept. 5, 1965 (div. 1982). BS, Juilliard Sch., 1962, MS, 1963; DMA, Eastman Sch. Music, 1974. Choral dir. William Cowper Jr. H.S. and Springfield Gardens Jr. H.S., Queens, NY, 1963-68; coord. music Flushing H.S., Queens, 1968-79; asst. prin. music Bayside H.S., Queens, 1979-86; assoc. prof. music Lehman Coll., CUNY, 1986-87, prof., 1987—, choral dir., 1986—. Cons. ednl. projects New World Records, 1987—; ednl. cons. Flushing Coun. on Culture and the Arts; cons. Sta. WNET; assoc. condr. Queens Borough-Wide Chorus, 1964-70; pianist, founder Con Brio Chamber Ensemble, 1978; faculty So. Vt. Music Festival, 1979-83; soloist with N.Y. Philharm., 1956; examiner NYC Bd. Edn. Bd. Exams., 1985—. Author: 57 Lessons for the H.S. Music Class, 1983, Franz Mittler: Austro-American Composer, Musician and Humorous Poet, 1993; contbr. articles to profl. jours.; performance Internat. Summer acad. Mozarteum, Salzburg, Austria, 1995, Weill Recital Hall, 1996, Merkin Hall, 1997, Herbert von Karajan Centrum, Vienna, Austria, 1998; rec. Franz Mittler, Preiser Records, Trio and Piano Pieces, 2003; featured on Study with the Best Series, CUNY TV, 2005. Choral dir., accompanist various charitable, religious, mil., civic holiday functions. N.Y. State Regents scholar, 1958-62; scholarships Juilliard Sch. and Eastman Sch. Music; recipient Excellence in Tchg. award, 1993, Prism award, 1996. Mem. Am. Choral Dirs. Assn., Music Edn. Nat. Conf., Golden Key Soc. Democrat. Home: 10857 66th Ave Forest Hills NY 11375-2247 Office: Lehman Coll Music Dept Bedford Pk Blvd W Bronx NY 10468 Office Phone: 718-960-7795. Personal E-mail: dianamittler@aol.com.

MITTY, LIZBETH, artist; b. NYC, Oct. 28, 1952; d. Sol and Anne (Ross) M.; m. Robert Gumenick, Oct. 29, 1995; children: Maris, Dana, Ruby Sue. Student, SUNY, Stony Brook, 1969-71; BS, U. Wis., 1973, MFA, 1975. One-woman shows include Image Gallery, Athens, 1978, Heath Gallery, Atlanta, 1978, Rosa Esman Gallery, N.Y.C., 1982-83, 85, Cheryl Pelavin Gallery, 1998, 2002, 05; exhibited in group shows at Bronx Mus., 1989, Assoc. Am. Artists Gallery, N.Y.C., 1989, Mus. Nat. Arts Found., N.Y.C., 1989, Berkshire Mus., Pittsfield, Mass., 1989, Mus. at Stony Brook, 1990, Tom Cugliani Gallery, N.Y.C., 1990, Trierenberg Art, Traun, Austria, 2005, others; represented in permanent collections Met. Mus. Art, Mint Mus., Newark Mus., Chem. Bank, Zimmerli Archive, Orlando Mus., Prudential, U.S. State Dept., N.Y. Heart Assn., Fidelity Investments, Oak Brook Bank, Ill., Blue Cross, Blue Shield. Office Phone: 212-925-9424. Personal E-mail: lizbethmitty@hotmail.com.

MITZEL, BRENDA RENEE, mathematics educator; b. Cavalier, ND, Oct. 20, 1969; d. Lyle Dennis and JoAnn Lilja Hardy; m. Robert Joseph Mitzel, June 21, 1997. BS in Edn., Valley City State U., N.D., 1992. Tchr. 7-12 math. Wolford Pub. Sch., ND, 1992—, tech. coord., 1995—. Treas. Wolford PTO, ND, 1996—, St. Mary's Ladies Soc., Knox, ND, 1999—. Recipient Small Sch. Tech. Leader of Yr. award, 2005, Cert. of Merit award, Valley City State U., 2005. Roman Catholic. Avocations: bicycling, walking, helping with farm. Office Phone: 701-583-2387. Business E-Mail: brenda.hardy@sendit.nodak.edu.

MITZELFELT, CONNIE J., secondary school educator, principal; d. Donald and Janet Mitzelfelt. BS, So. Utah U., Cedar City, 1991. Tchr. LeRoys Boys Home, Pomona, Calif., 1991—92; tchr., prin. Barstow (Calif.) Seventh-Day Adventist Sch., 1992—95; asst. ednl. dir. Sylvan Learning Ctr., Peoria, Ill., 1995; edn. dir. Project PATCH, Garden Valley, Idaho, 1995—98; tchr., prin. Peoria Adventist Sch., 1998—2003, Lake County Seventh Day Adventist Sch., Gurnee, Ill., 2003—04, Peoria Adventist Sch., 2004—. EMT Tremont Rescue Squad, 1999—2003. Mem.: Assn. Supervision and Curriculum Devel. Seventh-Day Adventist. Office: Peoria Adventist Sch 4019 N Knoxville Ave Peoria IL 61614 Office Phone: 309-303-0280. Personal E-mail: cmitzelfelt@illinoisadventist.org.

MIURA, MASAKO KUSAYANAGI, retired dermatologist; b. Pasadena, Calif., June 29, 1914; d. Takejiro Kusayanagi and Matsu Hoshizaki; m. Kiyoshi Miura, June 29, 1955; m. James Mitsuo Goto (div.); children: Denise Goto Kodani, Hans Masaji Goto. AB, U. So. Calif., L.A., 1936, MD, 1941. Resident dermatology L.A. County Hosp., 1941—42, 1945—49; physician War Relocation Authority, Manzanar, 1942—43, Topaz, 1943—45; sch. physician L.A. Bd. Edn, 1951—54; physician U.S. Army, Oakland, 1954—55, Monterey, 1955—81; ret., 1981; supervising physician Project Scout, Santa Cruz County, 1983—88. Fellow: Pacific Dermatology Assn. (nominating com. 1987); mem.: Internat. Soc. Dermatology, San Francisco Dermatol. Soc., Nat. Assn. Ret. Fed. Employees (program chair 2000), Half-Century Club, Japanese Am. Citizens League, 4-H, Phi Kappa Phi, Phi Beta Kappa. Methodist. Home: 2917 Crocker Ct Aptos CA 95003

MIX, JILL KAYE, secondary school educator, artist; b. Oshkosh, Wis., Apr. 12, 1947; d. Emil Frank and Faye Ione (Wegner) Mix; m. Daniel Charles Knoop (div.); children: Victoria Mae Gonzalez, Valorie Faye Knoop. AA, Riverside CC, 1981; BA, Calif. State U., 1997. Cert. tchr. Calif. Advt. staff Moreno Valley (Calif.) News; pub. rels. staff, photographer Moreno Valley C. of C.; art and art history tchr. Ramona HS, Riverside, Big Bear HS, Big Bear Lake, Calif. Represented in permanent collections Sugar Loaf Park, Grant Elem. Sch., Ramona HS. Sec. Moreno Valley C. of C., 1987. Grantee, Steven G. Mihaylo Edn. Found., 2004. Mem.: NEA, Calif. Tchrs. Assn., Phi Kappa Phi. Avocations: interior decorating, photography, painting. Home: PO Box 3214 432 Booth Way Big Bear City CA 92314 Office: Big Bear High Sch PO Box 1708 Big Bear Lake CA 92315

MIYAGAWA, CHIORI, theater educator, playwright; life ptnr. Hap Tivey. MFA, CUNY, 1989. Asst. lit. mgr. Actors Theatre of Louisville, 1990—91; lit. mgr. Arena Stage, Washington, 1991—92; assoc. artist Pub. Theater, N.Y.C., 1992—93; artistic assoc. N.Y. Theatre Workshop, N.Y.C., 1993—2000; assoc. prof. theater Bard Coll., Annandale-on-Hudson, NY, 2001—. Playwritht-in-residence Yale Sch. Drama, New Haven, 1996—2000; bd. dir. Alliance of Resident Theatre, N.Y.C., 2003—. Author: (plays) America Dreaming, 1995 (Rockefeller Mulit-Artist Prodn. award, 1994), Nothing Forever (Rockefeller Mulit-Artist Prodn. award, 1995), Yesterday's Window, FireDance, 1997, Jamaica Avenue, 1998, Broken Morning, 1998 (TCG Extended Collaboration grant, 1998), Awakening, 1999 (Japan Found. award, 2000), Woman Killer, 2001, Antigone's Red, 2002, Antigone Project/Red Again, 2004; author: (plays) Leaving Eden, 2005. Recipient, Ensemble Studio Theatre/Alfred P. Sloan Found., 2002; fellow, N.Y. Found. for Arts, 1994, Van Lier Playwriting fellow, N.Y. Theatre Workshop, 1997, Asian Cultural Coun., 1999, MacDowell Colony, 2002—03; McKnight Playwriting fellow, Playwrights Ctr., 1998. Democrat. Buddhist. Office: Bard Coll Theater Dept Annandale On Hudson NY 12504 Office Phone: 845-758-7938. E-mail: miyagawa@bard.edu.

MIYAKE, STEPHANIE ANN, psychology professor, director, marriage and family therapist; b. Tulsa, Okla., Feb. 8, 1953; d. Thomas Wayne and Thelma Ann Shank; m. Thomas Masami Miyake, Mar. 19, 1988; children: Jan, Amber, Diann, Chris, Lance. BA, U. Ark., 1988; MA, Phillips Grad. Inst., 1994. Lic. marriage and family therapist Calif., Tex. Bus. mgr., therapist Angeles Cmty. Counseling Ctr., Monrovia, Calif., 1994—2002; marriage and family therapist self employed, 1994—; PsyD program admin. Azusa Pacific U., Azusa, Calif., 1999—2003, dir. MA clin. psych. program, 2001—05, dir. clin. training, 2005—. Trea., bd. mem. Angeles Cmty. Counseling Ctr., Monrovia, Calif., 1998—2002; adv. So. Calif. Consortium of Marriage and Family Therapist Educators, Encino, Calif., 2002—. Editor: Skilled Empathy, 2004; author: Clinical Placement Manual, 2000. Chairperson Claremont HS Grad. Night 2000, Claremont, Calif., 1999—2000; bd. pres. San Gabriel Valley Choral Co., Monrovia, Calif., 1997—99, bd. sec., 2000—03; 1st. v.p. Parent Faculty Assn., Claremont, Calif., 1998—99. Recipient Pres. award, Phillips Grad. Inst., 1994. Mem.: Calif. Assn. of Marriage and Family Therapists, Am. Assn. of Marriage and Family Therapists, Phi Kappa Phi. Achievements include built MA program to be nationally recognized in a 3 year period. Avocations: gardening, singing. Office: Azusa Pacific U Dept of Grad Psych 701 E Foothill Blvd Azusa CA 91702 Office Fax: 628-815-5015. Business E-Mail: smiyake@apu.edu.

MIYAMORI, KEIKO, artist; b. Yokohama, Kanagawa, Japan, Jan. 14, 1964; arrived in U.S., 1998; d. Yukio and Yuriko Miyamori. BFA, U. Tsukuba, Japan, 1993, MFA, 1995. Adj. faculty Pa. Acad. Fine Arts, Phila., 2000—. Artist-in-residence U. Pa., Phila., 1998—99, Soc. Contemporary Craft, Pitts., 2003. Recipient Sculputre Competition award, Frederik Meijer Gardens and Sculpture Park, 2004; grantee, Leeway Found., 2003. Office: PO Box 11771 Philadelphia PA 19101 Office Phone: 215-888-3245. Business E-Mail: info@princewoods.com.

MIZES, MARIA GABRIELA, cultural organization administrator, art historian; b. Buenos Aires, July 11, 1961; d. Jimmy M. and Beatriz Adot BA in art history magna cum laude, Columbia U., 1992. Asst. registrar Mus. Nacional de Bellas Artes, Buenos Aires, 1982-83, asst. curator, 1983-85, asst. dir., 1985-87, registrar, 1987-90; exhbn. asst. Lat. Am. Artists of the Twentieth Century Mus. Modern Art, N.Y.C., 1991-93; assoc. registrar Am. Fedn. Arts, N.Y.C., 1993-94, registrar, 1994-96, Trust for Mus. Exhbns., Washington, 1996—97; ind. registrar, 1998—; mgr. Racine Berkow Assoc., Alexandria, Va., 2003—. Mem. Am. Assn. Mus. (registrars com. 1990), Internat. Coun. Muss., Internat. Documentation Com., Phi Beta Kappa. Roman Catholic. Avocations: collecting magnets, collecting museum buildings' postcards, sunbathing, bird hunting with dogs. Home: 5500 Muncaster Mill Rd Derwood MD 20855-1825

MIZZI, CHARLOTTE H., city director; b. Malta, May 14, 1940; came to the U.S., 1950; d. Ely and Lily Mizzi; m. Robert Haley, May 27, 1961 (div. Feb. 1982); children: Mark, Alan, Audrey. Student, Montclair State Coll., 1958-60, Jersey City State Coll., 1974-79. Price analyst Kueffel & Esser Co., Hoboken, N.J., 1961-64; dir. divsn. tenant/landlord City of Jersey City, N.J., 1973-92, 94—, chief of staff, 1992-93, acting dir. pub. works, 1993-94. Debator League of Municipalities, 1974, 75, 76, 80, panelist, 1991; lectr. N.J. Property Owners Assnb., 1991. Co-editor Ch. Newsletter, 1997—. Elected mem. N.J. State Dem. Com., Trenton, 1974-78; mem. Electoral Coll., 1976; ethnic support coord. Com. to Elect Chris Whitman Gov., Hudson County, 1992-93; co-chairperson Election Com. for Mayor Schundler, Jersey City, 1993; Mayor's alt. to Hackensack Meadowlands Mcpl. Com., 1993—. Mem. N.Y. Tchg. Ctr. (pres., treas. 1997—), Rent Leveling Assn. N.J. (legis. com. 1996—, Presdl. award 1986-92), Rotary Club Jersey City. Avocations: bible studies, reading, horseback riding, hiking, world religions. Office: City of Jersey City 30 Montgomery St Jersey City NJ 07302-3821 E-mail: pwpo.charlotte@mail.cityofjerseycity.com.

MJAGKIJ, NINA, history professor; MA, U. Cin., 1986, PhD, 1990. Prof. history, dir. African Am. studies program Ball State U., Muncie, Ind., 1990—. Co-editor African Am. History series Rowman & Littlefield Pub., Lanham, Md. Author: Light in the Darkness: African-Americans and the YMCA, 1852-1946, 1994; editor: (encyclopedia) Organizing Black America: An Encyclopedia of African American Associations, 2001, Portraits of African American Life since 1865, 2003; co-editor: Men and Women Adrift: The YMCA and the YWCA in the City, 1997. Mem.: Soc. Historians of the Gilded Age and Prog. Era (editl. bd. jour.). Office: Ball State U History Dept Muncie IN 47306 Office Phone: 765-285-8700. Business E-Mail: 00n0mjagkij@bsu.edu.

MKRYAN, SONYA, geophysicist, educator, research scientist; b. Beyrouth, Lebanon, Mar. 1, 1935; arrived in U.S., 1979; d. Vahram and Marie (Topalian) Faradjian; m. Karapet Mkryan, Apr. 11, 1970; children: Marine, Anahit, Lusine. MS in Physics, Pedagogical Inst., 1956; PhD in Tech. Scis., Tbilicy State U., 1970. Physics, math. tchr. HS, Ghaltakchi, 1956-57; libr. Ores Dept., Leninakan, Armenia, 1957-60; geophysicist, rschr. Inst. Geophysics Engring. Seismology, Leninakan, 1960-70; assoc. prof. physics Polytech. Inst., Kirovakan, Armenia, 1970-79; mech. insp. Robertshaw Co., Anaheim, Calif., 1980-82; tchr. Pasadena (Calif.) Sch. Dist., 1983-86; eligibility worker, acting supr. Dept. of Pub. Svcs., Glendale, Calif., 1986-97; social worker home supportive svcs. Glendale, 1997—. Author: (poetry) Ups and Downs of Life, 1987, Incessant Melodies, 1992, Light and Darkness, 1997, (novels) Eternities Travelers, 1998, Man and Its Time, 2006, Paradoxical Reality and My Heartbeats, 2006; one-woman shows include Tekeyan Gallere, Pasadena, Calif., 1989, Pasadena Union of Marash Armenians Hall, 1982—95; exhibited in group shows at Altadena, Pasadena, Downey, Glendale, Ambassador Hotel, L.A. (2d prize, 1987), Wilshir Ebel, 1988. Bd. dirs. Sahag-Mesrob Armenian Christian Sch. Mem.: Armenian Radio and TV Com., Armenian Allied Arts Assn. (1st prize 1982, 1984, 1985, 1987, 1991), Nat. Libr. Poets, Internat. Soc. Poets, Armenian Writers Union Calif. Avocations: writing, walking, reading, cooking, dance. Home: 2723 N Lake Ave Altadena CA 91001-1903

MLAWSKY, KAREN, hospital administrator; Various positions Ohio State Univ. Hosp., 1991—99, Ohio State Univ. Hosp. East, 1999—2000, CFO, 2000—04, assoc. exec. dir., 2004, exec. dir., 2004—. Office: Ohio State Univ Hosps East 1492 E Broad St Columbus OH 43205-1546 Office Phone: 614-257-3000.*

MLAY, MARIAN, retired government official; b. Pitts., Sept. 11, 1935; AB, U. Pitts., 1957; postgrad., Princeton U., 1969-70; JD, Am. U., 1977. Mgmt. intern HEW, Washington, 1961-70, dep. dir. Chgo. region, 1971-72, dir. divsn. consol. funding, 1972-73; dep. dir. office policy devel. and planning USPHS, Washington, 1973-77; dir. program evaluation EPA, Washington, 1978-9, dep. dir. office of drinking water, 1979-84, dir. office of ground water protection, 1984-91, dir. oceans and coastal protection, 1991-95; sr. rsch. assoc. Nat. Acad. Pub. Adminstrn., 1995-97; ret., 1997. Contbr. articles to profl. jours., chpts. to books. Bd. dirs. D.C. United Fund, 1979-80, New Dominion Chorale, 2001--, Davis Meml. Goodwill Book Com., 1999-2002. Princeton U. fellow, 1969-70; recipient Career Edn. award Nat. Inst. Public Affairs, 1960. Mem. ABA, D.C. Bar Assn. (co-chair steering com. energy, environ. and natural resources sect.). Achievements include development of a ground-water protection strategy for EPA establishing a national program to support related state and local efforts and to define a common ground-water protection policy for EPA.

MOBLEY, BROOKE MICHELLE, science educator; d. Jerry Stephens and Cynthia Rebecca Walker; m. Dale Vincent Mobley, May 27, 2005. BS Edn in Secondary Sci. Edn., U. Ga., 2003; postgrad., U. Tenn., Chattanooga, 2005—. Cert. tchr. Ga. Mid. grades spl. edn. math tchr. LaFayette (Ga.) Mid. Sch., 2004, 6th grade math. tchr., 2004—05; secondary sci. tchr. Lakeview-Fort Oglethorpe (Ga.) HS, 2005—, majorette coach. Mem.: NEA, Ga. Assn. Educators, Ga. Sci. Tchrs. Assn., Am. Sch. Counselor Assn., Nat. Sci. Tchrs. Assn., Nat. Exch. Club (hon.), Kappa Delta Epsilon, Delta Epsilon Iota. Baptist. Office: Lakeview-Fort Oglethorpe HS 1850 Battlefield Parkway Fort Oglethorpe GA 30742 Office Phone: 706-866-0342. Personal E-mail: bmwuga@hotmail.com. Business E-Mail: bmobley.lfo@catoosa.k12.ga.us.

MOBLEY, EMILY RUTH, library director, educator, dean; b. Valdosta, Ga., Oct. 1, 1942; d. Emmett and Ruth (Johnson) M. AB in Edn., U. Mich., 1964, AM in Libr. Sci., 1967, postgrad., 1973-76. Tchr. Ecorse (Mich.) Pub. Schs., 1964-65; adminstrv. trainee Chrysler Corp., Highland Park, Mich., 1965-66, engring. libr., 1966-69; libr. II Wayne State U., Detroit, 1969-72, libr. III, 172-75; staff asst. GM Rsch. Labs. Libr., Warren, Mich., 1976-78, supr. reader svcs., 1978-81; libr. dir. GMI Engring. & Mgmt. Inst., Flint, Mich., 1982-86; assoc. dir. for pub. svcs. & collection devel., assoc. prof. libr. sci. Purdue U. Librs., West Lafayette, Ind., 1986-89, acting dir. librs., assoc. prof. libr. sci., 1989, dean librs., prof. libr. sci., 1989—2004; Esther Ellis Norton Disting. Prof. Libr. Sci. Purdue U., West Lafayette, Ind., 1997—. Adj. lectr. U. Mich. Sch. Libr. Sci., Ann Arbor, 1974-75, 83-86; grants reader Libr. of Mich., 1980-81; project dir. Mideastern Mich. Region Libr. Cooperation, 1984-86; cons. Libr. Coop. of Macomb, 1985-86, Clark-Atlanta U., 1990-91; search com. for new dir. of libr. Smithsonian Instn., 1988; mem. GM Pub. Affairs Subcom. on Introducing Minorities to Engring.; presenter in field. Author: Special Libraries at Work, 1984; mem. editl. bd. Reference Svcs. Rev., 1989-2004, Infomanage, 1993-97. Corp. vis. com. for librs. MIT, 1990-2004, Carnegie-Mellon U., 1998—; mem. Ind. Statewide Libr. Automation Task Force, 1989-90; state tech. strategy subcom. on info. tech. and telecomms. Ind. Corp. for Sci. & Tech., 1989; nat. adv. com. Libr. of Congress, 1988; trustee Libr. of Mich., 1983-86, v.p., 1986, long range plan com., 1979-82, task force on document access and delivery, 1977-79; info. project mem. Rep. Nat. Conv., 1980; bd. dirs. Small Farms Assn., Southfield, Mich., Lafayette Symphony Orch., YWCA. Recipient Bausch & Lomb award, 1960, Cert. for Outstanding Performance in Acad. Achievement State of Mich. Ho. of Reps., 1976, Spl. Tribute for Outstanding Contbns. Libr. of Mich. Bd. Trustees, 1986, Disting. Alumnus award U. Mich. Sch. Info. & Libr. Studies, 1989; U. Mich. Regents Alumni scholar, 1960-64; CIC doctoral fellow in libr. sci., 1973-76. Mem. ALA (com. on accreditation, subcom. to rev. 1972, standards for accreditation 1988-89, OLOS minority internship com. 1988-89, nominating com. 1992-93, mem. coun. resolutions com. 1993-97), Assn. Coll. & Rsch. Librs. (task force on libr. sch. curriculum 1988-89, com. on profl. edn. 1990-92), Libr. Adminstrn. & Mgmt. Assn., Assn. Rsch. Librs. (bd. dirs. 1990-93), Spl. Librs. Assn. (pres. 1987-88, fellow 1991, com. mem.), Alpha Kappa Alpha, Phi Kappa Phi, Sigma Xi, Iron Key. Office: Purdue U Librs Stewart Ctr Lafayette IN 47907 Business E-Mail: emobley@purdue.edu.

MOBLEY, KAREN RUTH, art director; b. Cheyenne, Wyo., Aug. 26, 1961; d. David G. and Marlene G. (Franz) M. BFA, U. Wyo., 1983; MFA, U. Oka., 1987. Sales assoc. Morgan Gallery, Kansas City, Mo., 1984-85; grad. asst. U. Okla. Mus. Art, Norman, 1985-87; dir. Univ. Art Gallery N.Mex. State U., Las Cruces, 1988-93; exec. dir. Nicolaysen Art Mus., Casper, Wyo., 1993-96; dir. Spokane Arts Com., 1997—. Guest artist Oklahoma City C.C., 1986. Exhbns. include Phoenix Triennial, 1990, New Am. Talent, Laguna Gloria Art Mus., Austin, Tex., 1992, Adair Margo Gallery, El Paso, 1992-94, Wyo. Arts Coun. Gallery and Casper Coll., 1995, Mont. State U., 1996, Whitworth Coll., 2004, Good Works Gallery, 2005 Trustee Westminster Congl. Ch.; bd. dirs. Spokane Pub. Radio. Wyo. Arts Coun. Individual Artist grantee 1994, Lit. fellow, 1995-96; named Outstanding Young Women Am. Mem. Am. Assn. Mus., Coll. Art Assn., Wash. State Arts Alliance, Rotary 21, Phi Beta Kappa, Phi Kappa Phi. Office: Spokane Arts Com 808 W Spokane Falls Blvd Spokane WA 99203 Office Phone: 509-625-6050. Business E-Mail: kmobley@spokanecity.org.

MOBLEY, ROBIN N., nursing administrator; b. Memphis, May 6, 1963; d. William D. and Virginia Ruth (Sanders) Newsom; m. James N. Mobley, June 22, 1985; children: Virginia Marie, James William. BSN, U. Tenn., Memphis, 1985, MSN, 1988. RN Tenn., cert. ACLS, nursing adminstrn. ANCC, St. Judes Children's Hosp. Staff Meth. Hosp., Memphis, pulmonary patient educator, instr. Sch. of Nursing, pulmonary clin. nurse. Mem. Am. Lung Assn. (bd. dirs.), Sigma Theta Tau. Home: 6952 Surrey Ln Germantown TN 38138-2528

MOCH, PEGGY L., mathematics professor; d. Edward J. and Elma M. Moch; 1 child, Julie A. Weinbloom. AA, Valencia C.C., 1994; BS in Math Edn., U. Ctrl. Fla., 1996, MEd in Math Edn., 1999, PhD in Curriculum and Instrn., 1979—2002. Cert. lab. tech. Colo., 1978, med. tech. Fla., 1979. Mgr. Orlando (Fla.) Plasma Ctr., 1979—81; med. technologist Orlando Gen. Hosp., 1981—90, Princeton Hosp., Orlando, 1990—96; math. tchr. Maynard Evans HS, Orlando, 1996—99; grad. tchg. asst. U. Ctrl. Fla., Orlando, 1999—2002; asst. prof. math. Valdosta (Ga.) State U., 2002—. Math. cons. Lee County Pub. Sch., Ft. Myers, Fla., 2000; math. writer Math. and Sci. Profl. Devel. Project, Orlando, 2001, math. cons., Brevard and Orange County, Fla., 02; logo designer U. Ctrl. Fla. Holmes Partnership, Orlando, 2002; math. & sci. cons. Math. & Sci. Partnership Ctrl. Plains RESA, Ga., 2005—06, Pace HS, Cin., 2006. Author: Mathematics Content for Elementary Teachers, 2005. Recipient Scholars Outstanding Tchr. award, Radio Shack and Tandy, 1998—99. Mem.: Am. Soc. Clin. Pathologists, Sch. Sci. and Math. Assn., Am. Assn. for Tchg. and Curriculum, Math. Assn. Am., Kappa Delta Pi (co-chair convocation com. 2001, mem. convocation com. 2004—05, Alpha Beta Kappa counselor 2004—, Outstanding Svc. to Chpt. award Omicron Lambda chpt. 1997, 1999). Republican. Avocations: guitar, writing poems, songs, and stories. Office: Valdosta State U 1500 N Patterson St Valdosta GA 31698-0040 Office Phone: 229-333-5785. Office Fax: 229-219-1257. E-mail: plmoch@valdosta.edu.

MOCK, BEVERLY A., geneticist, researcher; m. Richard P. Nordan (dec. June 7, 1998); children: Alex, Chris. MS, U. Md., 1980, PhD in zoology, 1983. Studies on the genetics of susceptibility to parasitic diseases Dept. Immunology Walter Reed Army Inst. Rsch.; assoc. dir. sci. planning Ctr. Cancer Rsch., Nat. Cancer Inst., 1999—2004, chief Lab. Genetics, 2004—, head Cancer Genetics Sect., Lab. Genetics. Office: Lab Genetics Ctr Cancer Rsch 37 Convent Dr Bldg 37 Rm 3146 Bethesda MD 20892-4258 Office Phone: 301-496-2360. Office Fax: 301-402-1031. E-mail: bev@helix.nih.gov.

MOCK, CHERRY L., marriage and family therapist; b. Baytown, Tex., June 14, 1951; d. Jack Glenn and Joan Fay (Barry) Sawberger; m. Robert D. Mock, July 3, 1972; 1 child, Rhett Vaughn. BA in Edn., Southwestern Union Coll., Keene, Tex., 1973; MS in Marriage, Family and Child Therapy, Loma Linda U., 1976. Cert. in elem. edn.; lic. profl. counselor. Tchr. 5th grade Redlands (Calif.) Jr. Acad., 1973-75; dir. Meth. Home Svcs., Houston, 1976-79; pvt. practice marriage and family therapy The Mock Clinic, The Woodlands, Tex., 1979-88; Arabian horse breeder Almaz Aseel Arabians, The Woodlands, 1990—. Named Dir. of Yr., Meth. Home Svcs., 1979. Mem. Am. Assn. Marriage and Family Therapy. Republican. Seventh-day Adventist. Home: 10406 Treeridge Pl The Woodlands TX 77380-1338 Office: The Mock Clinic 1120 Medical Plaza Dr Ste 380 The Woodlands TX 77380-3243

MOCK, JOAN BODET, music educator; b. Houston, Dec. 3, 1937; d. Edward Bodet and Dorothy Crawford; m. Donald P. Garrett, 1966 (dec. 1985); children: William Clifford Garrett, Christopher Paul Garrett; m. Raymond Cecil Mock, July 7, 2002; 1 child from previous marriage, Charles H. Edwards II. B Music Edn., Ind. U., 1960; postgrad., U. N.Mex. Cert. tchr. N.Mex. Tchr. Espanola (N.Mex.) H.S., 1963—66, Hope H.S., Albuquerque, 1978—79; tchr. group piano lessons Piano Store Orgn., Colorado Springs, 1969—70; pvt. tchr. Garrett's Sch. Piano and Voice, Albuquerque; substitute tchr. Albuquerque Pub. Schs. Soloist for Ed Sullivan, Houston, 1956. Performer: Houston Little Theater, 1954—56, Acola Theater, 1970—79, The Ballad Hunter TV Program, 1954—56; dir.: O.P.E.R.A., 1978; contbr. poems to lit. pubs. Soloist Christ Unity Ch., Albuquerque, 1988—92. Inst. Work scholar, Ind. U., 1957—60. Mem.: Albuquerque Music Tchrs. Assn., Nat. Music Tchrs. Assn., Nat. Fedn. Music Clubs. Home and Office: 10401 Crosscut Dr NW Albuquerque NM 87114 Office Phone: 505-350-7612.

MOCK, MELANIE LYNN, elementary school educator, music educator; b. Endicott, NY, June 7, 1967; d. Kenneth G. Orchard and Marjorie Lillian Hardin; m. William Glenn Mock, Jan. 8, 1964. MusB, Mid. Tenn. State U., 1989; MA in Edn., Cumberland U., 2001. Lic. lic. Tenn., 1989. Tchr. elem. music Murfreesboro City Schs., Tenn., 1991—. Pvt. instr. flute, Smyrna, Tenn., 1985—; mem. steering com. Northfield Elem., Murfreesboro, 1995—; youth leader First Presbyn. Ch., Smyrna, 1998—. Tchr. Sunday sch. First Presbyn. Ch., Smyrna, dir. music, 1991—2005, worship leader, 1990—2005. Mem.: NEA (corr.), Music Educator's Nat. Conf. (corr.). Conservative. Presbyterian. Avocations: singing, reading, cross stitch, decorating, spending time with family. Home: 635 Greenleaf Ave Smyrna TN 37167 Office: Northfield Elem Sch 550 W Northfield Blvd Murfreesboro TN 37129 Office Phone: 615-895-7324. Personal E-mail: wmmock@aol.com.

MOCK, MELINDA SMITH, orthopedic nurse specialist, consultant; b. Austell, Ga., Nov. 15, 1947; d. Robert Jehu and Emily Dorris (Smith) Smith; m. David Thomas Mock, Oct. 20, 1969. ASN, DeKalb Coll., 1972. RN Ga., orthop. nurse specialist, cert. orthop. nurse; life care planner. Nursing technician Ga. Bapt. Hosp., Atlanta, 1967, staff nurse, 1979; asst. corr. Harcourt, Brace & World Pub. Co., Atlanta, 1968-69; receptionist, sec. Goodbody & Co., Atlanta, 1969-70; nursing asst. DeKalb Gen. Hosp., Decatur, Ga., 1970-71; staff nurse Drs.' Meml. Hosp., Atlanta, 1972-73; staff nurse, relief charge nurse Shallowford Cmty. Hosp., Atlanta, 1973, charge nurse, 1973-76, head nurse, 1976-79, orthop. nurse specialist emergency rm., 1979; rehab. specialist, sr. rehab. specialist Internat. Rehab. Assocs., Inc., Norcross, Ga., 1981, rehab. supr., 1981-82; cons., founder, propr. Healthcare Cost Cons., Inc., Alpharetta, Ga., 1982-83, cons., founder, pres., 1983—. Legis. com. adv. coun. Ga. Bd. Nursing, Atlanta, 1984—85; adv. coun. Milton HS Coop. Bus. Edn., 1986—89; task force profl. liability ins. Nat. Fedn. Splty. Nursing Orgns., 1987—89; mem. Congressman Patrick Swindall Sr. Citizen Adv. Coun., 1988, Congressman Ben Jones Vets. Affairs Adv. Coun., 1989—92, White Ho. Conf. Small Bus., 1995, Congressman Newt Gingrich Small Bus. Adv. Com., 1997—99; apptd. Congl. Small Bus. Summit, 1998; apptd. Congressman Tom Price Health Delivery & Care Advisory Coun., 2005—. Parliamentarian Cherokee County Rep. Women, 2004; atl. del.-at-large Nat. Rep. Conv., 1996; dep. voter registrar Fulton County, Ga., 1983—87; Rep. treas. 23d House Dist.; active various coms. and positions Fulton County Rep. Party, 1989—2001; Rep. treas. 41st House Dist., 1993—97; mem. state exec. com. Ga. Rep. Party, 1997—99; 1st vice chairwoman Rep. 6th Congl. Dist., 1993—97, chmn., 1997—99; vice chair 7th Congl. Dist. Ga. Rep. Party, 2003—05, 7th Dist. GOP com., 2005; del. various convs., 1993—; mem. Chattahoochee Rep. Women, 1989—2001, chmn. campaign com., 1992—94, rec. sec., 1995—2001; chmn. nominating com. House Dist. 23, 1990; mem. steering com. Re-Elect State Rep. Tom Campbell, 1990; mem. campaign staff Re-Elect State Senator Sallie Newbill, 1990, 1992, 1994; mem. health adv. campaign Elect Matt Towery for Lt. Gov., 1990, Elect Bob Barr U.S. Senate, 1991—92; mem. election com. Mark Burkhalter for State Rep.; vol. campaign staff Re-Elect Congressman Newt Gingrich, 1992, 1994, 1996, 1998; mem. Cherokee County Rep. Party, 2001—; asst. poll mgr. Cherokee County Elections, 2004; rules com. mem. Ga. Fedn. Rep. Women; county co-chmn. Price for Congress, 2006; vol. campaign staff Elect Tom Price to State Senate, 1996, Re-Elect Tom Price to U.S. Congress. Recipient Nat. Disting. Svc. Registry award, 1987, Outstanding Alumni award Ga. Perimeter Coll., 2006; named Outstanding Young Women Am., 1984. Mem. Nat. Assn. Orthop. Nurses (nat. policies com. 1981-82, chmn. govt. rels. com. 1987-90, nat. treas. 1991-95, nat. pres. elect 1998-99, pres. 1999-2000, Nurse in Washington intern 1987, 99, legis. contbr. editor news 1989, chmn. legis workshop 1989, co-chmn. legis. workshop 1990, guest editl. Orthop. Nursing Jour. 1988, Ann. Congress del. 1982, 91-94, 96, 98-2001, 2003, 2005, Pres.'s award 1992, Outstanding Contbn. to NAON award 1996, chmn. budget and fin. com. 1991-95, nat. bylaws and policies com. 1995-98, bylaws and policies com. Atlanta chpt. 1994-96, pres-elect Atlanta chpt. 1996-97, 2004-05, pres. 1997-98, 2005-06, program dir. 2002-04), Orthop. Nurses Assn. (nat. bd. dirs. 1977-79, nat. treas. 1979-80), Coun. Splty. Nursing Orgns. Ga. (nominating com. 1976-77), Assn. Rehab. Nurses (bd. dirs. Ga. chpt. 1980-81, del. people-to-people program to China 1981, 2006, 2006), Nat. Fedn. Bus. (guardian 1988—, leadership coun. 1990—, healthcare task force chmn. 1992-2005, vice-chmn./fed. liaison Ga. adv. coun. 1995-2005), Am. Bd. Nursing Specialities (chmn. nominating com. 1993-95, chmn. com. on splty. bd. rev. 1993-95), Ga. Jaycees (dist. 4C rep. Ga. Jaycee Legis. 1984-85), Ga. Seatbelt Coalition, Orthop. Nurses Cert. Bd. (bd. dirs. 1991-96, pres. 1992-93, task force on advanced practice cert. 1991-92), North Fulton C. of C. (vice chmn. health svc. effectiveness alliance 1984-85, chmn. 1985-86, co-chmn./editor periodical 1985, 3rd Quarter Workhorse award 1985), Alpharetta Jaycees (adminstrv. v.p. 1984-85, internal v.p. 1985-86), Alpharetta Jaycee Women (bd. dirs. 1983), Ga. Perimeter Coll. Nursing Alumni Assn. (dir. 2000-05, pres. 2005—), Ga. Perimeter Coll. Alumni Assn. (bd. dirs. 2005—, Outstanding Alumni award 2006), Nat. Assn. Orthopadic Nurses Found. (trustee, treas. 2005—06, pres. 2006—). Baptist. Avocations: reading, community service activities, scrapbooking. Office: Healthcare Cost Cons Inc PO Box 466 Alpharetta GA 30009-0466 Office Phone: 770-475-9454.

MOCKLER, ANNA, writer, ecologist; b. Mahopac, N.Y., Sept. 26, 1955; d. Nils Edward and Adele Rosen Mockler; m. Reuben D. Radding, Dec. 17, 2002. BA in Psychology, Antioch Coll., 1977; MA in Environ. Conservation, NYU, 1991. Cert. profl. wetland scientist. Wetland writer and scientist N.Y.C. Pks., 1990—92; proprietor Mockler Environ., Eugene, Oreg., 1992—96; mitigation specialist King County DDES, Renton, Wash., 1997—98; sr. wetland ecologist Cooke Sci. Svcs., Seattle, 1999—2000; proprietor Upstream Enterprises, Seattle, 2000—02; writer Bklyn., 2002—. Author: (booklet) Freshwater Wetlands of N.Y.C., 1990, Handbook of Sensitive Area Mitigation, 1998, (short stories) Burning Salt, 2003. Recipient Heintzelman Trophy award, Point No Point, 1999. Mem.: Bklyn. Bot. Gardens, Poets and Writers.

MOCKLER, ESTHER JAYNE, state senator; b. Jackson, Wyo., Sept. 21, 1957; d. Franklin and Nancy (Fisher) Mockler. BA in Polit. Sci., Wellesley Coll., 1980. Legal asst., 1981-84; legal adminstr., 1984-87; rschr., cons., 1987—; exec. dir. Wyo. Dem. Party, 1993-95; mem. from Dist. 44 Wyo. Ho. of Reps., Cheyenne, 1992—96; mem. from Dist. 8 Wyo. Senate, Cheyenne, 1996—. Mem. Audubon Wyo. Bd. Office: PO Box 1857 Cheyenne WY 82003-1857 Office Phone: 307-632-5883.

MOCKLER, JENNIFER LYNN, psychologist, education educator; d. Henry Joseph and Linda Diane Grudnik; m. Richard James Mockler, July 20, 2002. BA, U. South Fla., Tampa, Fla., 1998; MAE, U. Fla., Gainesville, Fla., 2001, PhD, EdS, U. Fla., Gainesville, Fla., 2003. Cert. Profl. Sch. Psychologist PK-12 Fla., 2003. Rsch. asst. U. Fla., Gainesville, Fla., 1999—2002; sch. psychologist Broward County Sch. Dist., Ft. Lauderdale, Fla., 2002—; adj. prof. Nova Southeastern U., Ft. Lauderdale, Fla., 2004—. Presentation (poster) Society for Neuroscience Convention; contbr. articles pub. to profl. jour. Recipient Travel Award, Ctr. for Neurobiological Studies, 2001, Grad. Student Coun. Travel Award, U. Fla., 2001; scholar Fla. Academic Scholarship Recipient, Fla., 1994-1998. Mem.: NASP, APA, Broward Assn. of Sch. Psychologists, Fla. Assn. of Sch. Psychologists. Avocations: photography, cooking, hiking, travel.

MOCKLER, JOLEE MARIE, art educator; b. Kenosha, Wis., June 21, 1957; d. Frank A. and Josephine (Pavelich) Bobusch; m. John R. Mockler, Feb. 20, 1982. BA in art edn., Carthage Coll., 1979; MS secondary edn., U. Wis., 2000. Lic. Art Edn. K-12 Wis. Elem. art tchr. Kenosha Unified Sch., Kenosha, Wis., 1979—80; adj. prof. Edgewood Coll., Art Edn. Dept., Madison, Wis., 2003—; art instr., chairperson Reedsburg Area HS, Wis., 1988—; bus. owner Homeworks Furniture and Accents, Reedsburg, Wis., 1991—98. Supr. student tchrs. Edgewood Coll., Madison, Wis., 1996—, Luther Coll., Decorah, Iowa, 2000; art dept. chairperson Reedsburg Sch. Dist., Reedsburg, Wis., 1998—; judge art shows Sauk County Art Assn., Baraboo, 2006. Co-author: Reedsburg Sch. Dist., K-12 Art Curriculum, 1988—89. Judge for rep. Tammy Baldwin's Congressional Art Competition 2nd Congressional, Madison, Wis., 2003; active Sauk County Basset Hound Rescue. Recipient Top Notch Tchr. award, Wis. TV Channel 3, 2003, Excellence in Edn. award, Reedsburg BOE, 1999, Tchr. of Month award, Reedsburg Area HS, 1998, 2003, Outstanding Am. Tchrs. award, Nat. Honor Roll, 2005—06. Mem.: NEA, Sauk County Art Assn., Reedsburg Edn. Assn., Wis. Edn. Assn. Home: PO Box 243 La Valle WI 53941 Office: Reedsburg Area HS 1100 S Albert Ave Reedsburg WI 53959 Office Phone: 608-524-4327 1134. Business E-Mail: jmockler@rsd.k12.wi.us.

MOCK-MORGAN, MAVERA ELIZABETH, artist, art educator; b. McClellan, Fla., May 14, 1926; d. Arthur Charles and Mary Esther (Jones) M.; m. Joseph Mulford Morgan, Nov. 2, 1950; children: Arthur Chester, David Mulford. Student, Stetson U.; BA in Fine Arts, Am. U., 1965; MA in Art Edn., U. Md., 1976. Asst. to gen. counsel Nat. Capitol Planning Commn., Washington, 1955-58; mem. faculty U. Hawaii, 1959-60; adj. faculty Chulalongkorn U., Bangkok, 1958-61; instr. art D.C. Tchrs. Coll., Washington, 1969-70, U. Md., College Park, 1970-71; asst. assoc. prof. art, chmn. D.C. Tchrs. Coll., Washington, 1971-77, prof., 1978; chmn. div. fine arts U. D.C., Harvard-Ga. Campus, Washington, 1974-78, prof., 1978—. Guest prof. Queen's U., Kingston, Ont., Can., 1979-80; cons. lectr. art U. Md.; mem. Washington Com. on Fine Arts, 1976-78 Painter, sculptor, Bangkok, 1960, Washington Art Club, 1974, Artists USA, 1974, 75, 76, 78, 1977-78, author, UDC Graphics Manual, 1977, (with others) Self-Study Manual UDC, 1977, The Historical Study of Theories of Art Education of Arthur Wesley Dow, 1976. Fellow Nat. Arts and Humanities Inst., 1968; fellow Fla. State U., 1968, HEW, 1968 Mem. Nat. Art Edn. Assn., Internat. Soc. Edn. Through Art, U.S. Soc. Edn. Through Art, Miniature Artists Am., Am. Art League, Md. Art Edn. Assn., Asia Soc., Thai Com. (dir.), Am. Nepal Soc., Emerald Schillelagh Marching and Chowder Soc., Phi Delta Gamma (past chpt. pres.) Clubs: Washington-Bangkok Women's (pres. 1965, dir. 1969-74). Home: 3 Carvel Cir Bethesda MD 20816-1808 Office: U DC Van News Campus 4200 Connecticut Ave NW Washington DC 20008

MODEN, JOLEEN, communications executive; B in Bus. Adminstr. and Acctg., Kans. State U. CPA. Ptnr. Coopers & Lybrand; v.p., CFO, treas. Signature Home Care Grp.; dir. corp. audit PepsiCo Inc.; asst. contr. internal audit GTE, 1998—2000; sr. v.p. internal auditing Verizon Comm. Inc., NYC, 2000—. Office: Verizon Comms Inc Verizon Ctr VC44E227 One Verizon Way Basking Ridge NJ 07920-1997 E-mail: joleenmoden@verizon.com.

MODIE, CHRISTINE M., insurance company executive; BS, U. Vt., 1974. V.p. mutual fund info. svcs. State St. Bank and Trust Co., Quincy; chief info. officer Batterymarch Fin. Mgmt., Inc., Boston; verious sr. level positions Aetna Life Ins. Co., Hartford, Conn.; sr. v.p., chief info. officer Travelers Life & Annuity, 1997—99; exec. v.p., chief info. officer Mass. Life Ins. Co., Springfield, 1999—. Office: Mass Life Ins Co 1295 State St Springfield MA 01111-6001

MODISETTE, BARBARA JANE, education educator, psychologist; b. Jacksonville, Tex., Oct. 14, 1938; d. RG and Kathaleen Williams Hensley; m. James Harold Modisette; children: John Philip, James Bret, Jay Hensley. A, Kilgore Coll., 1959; BS in Elem. Edn., Stephen F. Austin State U., 1962, MEd in Guidance and Counseling, 1970; EdD, Tex. A&M, 1983. Adj. prof. LeTourneau U., Longview, Tex., 2004—. Mem.: Tex. Assn. Sch. Psychologists, Am. Bd. Sch. Neuropsychologists, Am. Coun. Assn., Am. Assn. Sports Psychology, Nat. Assn. Sch. Psychologists, Rangerette Forever, Phi Delta Kappa, Alph Delta Kappa. Presbyterian. Avocations: piano, singing. Home: 102 Crystal St Longview TX 75604 Office Phone: 903-759-6147. Personal E-mail: docmod@cablelynx.com.

MODJTABAI, AVID, bank executive; BS in Indsl. Engring., Stanford U.; MBA in Fin., Columbia U. With McKinsey & Co.; exec. vice-pres., dir. internet svcs. Wells Fargo, San Francisco, head online personal fin. svcs., exec. vice-pres., dir. HR. Named one of 25 Most Powerful Women in Banking, US Banker, 2004, 100 Most Influential Women in Bay Area Bus., San Francisco Bus. Times, 2004—05. Office: Wells Fargo 420 Montgomery St San Francisco CA 94104*

MODNY, CYNTHIA JEAN, dermatologist; b. Jan. 23, 1945; d. Michael Theodore and Mary (Tabaka) M. BA, Mt. Holyoke Coll., 1967; MD, U. Va., Charlottesville, 1971. Diplomate Am. Bd. Dermatology. Intern Lenox Hill Hosp., N.Y.C., 1971-72; resident N.Y. Hosp./Cornell Med. Ctr., N.Y.C., 1972-75, instr. dermatology, 1976—81; practice medicine specializing in dermatology Montclair, N.J., 1976-92, Phoenix, 1994—. Pvt. practice cons. undersea medicine, Montclair, 1982-92; clin. instr. dermatology Skin and Cancer Unit, NYU Med. Ctr., N.Y.C., 1981-92; participant Physicians' Undersea Medicine Tng., NOAA, Miami, Fla., 1982; dir. Skin Cancer Inst., Montclair, 1984. Med. editor Dive Travel Report (monthly), 1983-92; contbr. article to Skin Diver mag. Bd. dirs. Montclair Sr. Citizens, 1984. Fellow Am. Acad. Dermatology; mem. Undersea Med. Soc., Am. Soc. Dermatologic Surgery, Princeton Club, Mt. Holyoke Club (N.Y.C.). Office: 1277 E Missouri Ave Ste 114 Phoenix AZ 85014-2916 Home: 2402 E San Miguel Ave Phoenix AZ 85016 Office Phone: 602-266-0266. Personal E-mail: moddoc@cox.net.

MOE, JANET ANNE, elementary school educator, church organist; b. Sacramento, May 24, 1946; d. Joseph Robert and Virginia Lou (Jones) Mangan; m. Edward Earl Moe, Aug. 23, 1969 (dec. Aug. 2002); children: Erik John, Erin Jean Moe Mitchell. BA, Calif. Luth. U., 1968; std. secondary tchg. credential, Calif. State U., Sacramento, 1969, crosscultural, lang. and acad. devel. cert. (CLAD), 1996; cert. in Orff Schulwerk Levels I, II and III, U. Calif. Santa Cruz, 1987; MS, Nat. U., Sacramento, 2001, preliminary adminstrv. credential, 2001. Elem. tchr. Gloria Dei Luth. Sch., Sacramento, 1969—73; elem. music specialist Sacramento City Unified Sch. Dist., 1982—. All-city elem. choir coord. Sacramento City Unified Sch. Dist., 1999—2001; chorus dir. Sierra Mt. Music Camp, 2001; facilitator Calif. dept. edn. model arts project Sacramento City Unified Sch. Dist. Singer: Sacramento City Coll. Choir, 1998—2006;: Sacramento City Coll. Choir, 2002;: Sacramento City Coll. Choir, 2004, 2006. Touring choir So. Calif. and Hawaii Calif. Luth. U., 1967—68; task force to restore music and the fine arts Sacramento City Unified Sch. Dist., 1999—2000; organist Gloria Dei Luth. Ch., 1970—2002, Luth. Ch. of Good Shepherd, 2003—. Recipient Hon. Svc. award, PTA Bear Flag Sch., Sacramento, 1992, VH1 Save the Music grant, 2002, 2005. Mem.: NEA, Sacramento Cmty. Concerts Assn. (bd. dirs. 2006), Calif. Music Educators Assn. (bd. dirs. 2006, elem. rep., mem. bd. Capitol Sect., Outstanding Music Educator award 1996, 2003), Nat. Audubon Soc. Republican. Lutheran. Avocations: birdwatching, travel, yoga, reading, hiking. Home: PO Box 109 Elk Grove CA 95759-0109 Personal E-mail: janetmoe46@yahoo.com.

MOE, JANET KIRSTEN, music educator; b. Viroqua, Wis., Feb. 13, 1962; d. Maurice Neland and Rose Marie Moe. BA, Minn. Bible Coll., Rochester, Minn., 1984; BS in Tchg., Winona State U., Minn., 1986. Classroom/vocal music tchr. Grand Meadow Pub. Sch., Minn., 1986—. Choir dir./pianist Marion Ch. of Christ, Rochester, Minn., 1986—2005; pianist Grace Christian Ch., LeRoy, Minn., 2006. R-Conservative. Christian. Avocations: writing, hiking, reading, farming. Office: Grand Meadow Public School 710 4th Ave NE Grand Meadow MN 55936 Office Phone: 507-754-5318 180. Office Fax: 507-754-5608. E-mail: jmoe@gm.k12.mn.us.

MOE, VIDA DELORES, civic worker; b. Ryder, ND, Feb. 29, 1928; d. John Nelson and Inga Marie (Lewis) Ahlgran; m. Placido Ferdinand, July 28, 1950 (dec. 1997); children: Terrence Paul, Star Marie; m. Edgar Louis Moe, May 24, 1970 (dec. 1983). Student, Minot State U., ND, 1964-66; diploma in interior decorating, LaSalle Ext. U., 1976. Sec. Raleigh Ins., Tacoma, 1949-50; clk. stenographer Army Transp. Office, San Francisco, 1951-52; clk.-typist Base Supply, Minot AFB, N.D., 1960-61; clk.-stenographer Base Housing, Minot AFB, 1961-62, 74; sec MIADS Direction Ctr., Minot AFB, 1962-63; sec. QC Br., Minot AFB, 1963-64, dept. acctg. and fin., Minot AFB, 1964-65; med. sec. USAF Regional Hosp., 1965-66; sec. Minuteman AFSC, 1966-67, 74-75, 5th Bomb Wing, 1967-70, 1st Missile Wing, 1973-74, dept. mil. pers., 1975-76, disaster preparedness (NORAD), 1987-93; ret., 1993; sec., salesperson Allen Realty, Minot, 1980-85. Pres. City Art League, 1977-79, 86-87; chmn. Carnegie Restoration and Art Ctr. Project, 1980-87; bd. dirs. Patrons of Libr., Minot, 1978-87, sec., 1979-80, v.p., 1981, pres., 1982-83; v.p. 40/50 Rep. Women Minot, 1982, chair decorations com., 1983; historian Minot Rep. Women, 1984-86; vol. ARC, 2002-03; quilters com. 1st Lutheran Ch., 2003—; vol. Trinity Hosp. Arts and Crafts Ctr., 2005—. Recipient Superior Performance award 5th Bomb Wing, Minot AFB, 1968, Devotion to Vol. Duty award USAF Regional Hosp., Minot, 1983, 86, Superior Performance Cash award Dept. of Air Force 857 Combat Support Group, 1988-91. Mem. AARP (bd. dir. 1996-97, treas. Ward County chpt. 1996-2000, v.p. 2001-2002, pres. 2002-04), AMVETS, Nat. Assn. Ret. Fed. Employees (chaplain, 2002-04), ND Bus. and Profl. Women's Club (rec. sec. 1978-79, 81-82), Minot Bus. and Profl. Women's Club (pres. 1981-82), Am. Legion Aux. (judge jr. art posters contest 1980-82, pres. 1982-84, chaplain 2006—), Minot Shrine Hosp. Aux. (v.p. 1984-85, pres. 1986-87, 97), Beta Sigma Phi (v.p. Laureate Epsilon chpt. 1981-82, pres. 1983-85, Valentine Queen 1985, Girl of Yr. 1985, preceptor Eta chpt., Girl of Yr. 1980, life), MidState Porcelain Artists Guild (v.p. 1983, 89, pres. 1984, treas. 1997), Order Ea. Star (ND Grand chpt., grand rep. 1979-81, dist. rep. 1982-83, chair credentials com. 1983-84, Grand Martha 1984-85, Grand Electa 1985-86, chmn. registration com. 1986-87, assoc. Grand Conductress 1987-88, Grand Conductress 1989-90, assoc. Grand Matron 1990-91, Worthy Grand Matron 1991-92, Past Worthy Grand Matron, 1992-, Worthy Matron Minot Venus chpt. 1976, 87-89, sec. 1993-94, chaplain 1994-95, assoc. conductress 1995-96, conductress 1996-97, assoc. matron, 1997-98, Worthy Matron 1998-99), Elketts (2d v.p. 1988-89, sec. 1993-94), Sons Norway (social dir. 1993-94, chmn. social dirs. 1994), Eagles Aux. (conductor 1993-94, chaplain 1994-95, v.p. 1995-96, pres. 1996-97, jr. past pres. 1997, past pres. 1997-, chaplain 2006—), Swedish Heritage Soc. (pres. 2001-02). Lutheran. Avocations: porcelain painting, oil painting, sewing, candlemaking, embroidery. Home: 705 25th St NW Minot ND 58703-1733

MOE-FISHBACK, BARBARA ANN, counseling administrator; b. Grand Forks, ND, June 24, 1955; d. Robert Alan and Ruth Ann (Wang) Moe; m. William Martin Fishback; children: Kristen Ann Fishback, William Robert Fishback. BS in Psychology, U. ND, 1977, MA in Counseling and Guidance, 1979, BS in Elem. Edn., 1984. Cert. K-12 counselor Ill. Tchr. United Day Nursery, Grand Forks, 1977-78; social worker Cavalier County Social Svcs., Langdon, N.D., 1979-83; elem. sch. counselor Douglas Sch. Sys., Ellsworth AFB, S.D., 1984-87, Jacksonville (Ill.) Sch. Sys., 1987—2004; h.s. counselor/early years counselor Jacksonville Sch. Dist., 2004—; counselor Jacksonville H.S., 2005—. Vol. Big Sister program, Grand Forks, 1978—84; leader pine to prairie coun. Girls Scouts U.S., 1980—82; tchr. Head Start Program, Grand Forks, 1979; mem. parent com., sec. Abraham Lincoln coun. Boy Scouts Am., 2001—; Sunday sch. tchr., 2001—; leader confirmation team, 2003—. Mem.: ACA, AAUW (local br. newsletter editor 1980—81, br. sec. 1981—83), NEA, Am. Sch. Counselor Assn., Ill. Edn. Assn., Ill. Sch. Counselor Assn., Ill. Counseling Assn., Jaycettes (bd. dirs. 1982—83), Kappa Alpha Theta (newsletter, mag. article editor 1976—77). Avocations: cooking, creative writing, crafts. Home: 291 Sandusky St Jacksonville IL 62650-1844 Office: Jacksonville High Sch 1211 N Diamond Jacksonville IL 62650 Office Phone: 217-243-4384 ext. 2239. Business E-Mail: bfishback@jax117.morgan.k12.il.us.

MOELHMAN, AMY JO, social worker; b. Lafayette, Ind., Mar. 18, 1954; d. Charles and Marian (Young) Moelhman. BS, Ball State U., 1976; MSW, U. Denver, 1979. Lic. clin. social worker, Ind. Social worker Adolescent Crisis Team, Adams County Social Svc., Denver; counselor adolescent boys prog. Pleasant Run Children's Home, Indpls.; group therapist Mothers of Victims of Sexual Abuse, Mid-Town Mental Health, Indpls.; supr. foster care and counseling prog. Children's Bur., Indpls.; mgr. Family Connection Ctr., 1989-90; dir. family programs Vis. Nurse Svc., Indpls., 1990-96; dir. Holy Family Svcs., Cath. Social Svcs., Indpls., 1996—2001; cons. Brown County Family Access Ctr., 1999—; supr. cmty. programs Indpls. Transition Ctr. Casey Family Programs, 2001—03; exec. dir. Ind. Alliance Human Svcs., Indpls., 2004—. Chair Ind. Coalition of Family-based Svcs., 1992-94; co-chair family preservation com. Marion County Stepahead; part-time faculty masters in social work program Ind. U.-Purdue U., Indpls. Contbr. articles to profl. jours. Mem. NASW, Acad. Cert. Social Workers. Home: 818 E 53rd St Indianapolis IN 46220-3104 Office Phone: 317-603-6866. Personal E-mail: amoelhman@aol.com.

MOELLER, AUDREY CAROLYN, retired energy company executive, retired corporate secretary; b. Pitts., May 10, 1935; d. Nicholas William and Edith Tecla (Russman) M. Grad. high sch., Pitts. Legal sec. Equitable Resources Inc., Pitts., 1955-72, asst. corp. sec., 1972-80, corp. sec., 1980-86, v.p., corp. sec., 1986-99; also corp. sec. Equitable Resources Inc. subs.; ret., 1999. Com. mem. United Way Allegheny County, Pa., 1978, United Way Southwestern Pa., 1984. Mem.: Pa. Assn. Notaries, Am. Soc. Corp. Secs. (chmn. membership and asst. sec. Pitts. chpt. 1995, treas. 1996, v.p. and program chmn. 1997, pres. 1998), Loyal Christian Benefit Assn. (nat. coun. 1993, pres. br. 331 2000, nat. auditor 2001—04). Democrat. Roman Catholic. Avocations: singing, golf, travel. Home: 1003 Cherry Hill Dr Presto PA 15142

MOELLER, JUDITH STONE, reading educator, consultant; d. Francis Richard and Helen Mae Bradshaw; m. Roger W. Moeller, Apr. 17, 2004; children: Kristin, Allyson; m. Robert Mark Stone (div.); 1 child, Kelly Stone. BA in Elem. and Spl. Edn., Kean U., 1977, MA in Reading Recovery, 1982; student, So. Conn. State U.; degree in Reading Recovery (hon.), U. Conn., 1995. Spl. edn. tchr. Hopewell Elem., NJ, 1977—79, Pennington Grammar Sch., NJ, 1979—80; reading recovery cons. North Branford Dist., Conn., 1992—95; reading recovery tchr., cons. Sandy Hook Elem., NJ, 1995—99; reading recovery cons., staff developer Bethel Dist., Conn., 1999—2003, Watertown Dist., Conn., 2002—, reading and language arts coord., 2002—. Cons. in field; mem. Reading Recovery Coun. N. Am., 1995—, Nat. Coun. Tchrs. of English, 1999—. Leader, coord. Brownie/Girl Scouts, Newtown, 1989—90. Mem.: Conn. Assn. Reading, Conn. Reading Rsch. Assn., Assn. Supervision & Curriculum Devel., Internat. Reading Assn. Avocations: travel, arts, theater. Home: PO Box 386 Bethlehem CT 06751 Office: John Trumbull Primary Sch 779 Buckingham St Oakville CT 06779

MOELLER, MARY ELLA, retired home economist, retired educator, radio personality; b. Southampton, NY, Mar. 11, 1938; d. Harry Eugene and Edith Leone (Reester) Parsons; m. James Myron Moeller, Aug. 5, 1961; 1 child, Mary Beth. BS in Home Econs., U. Nebr., 1960; MLS, SUNY, Stony Brook, 1977. Tchr. home econs. Port Jefferson Schs., N.Y., 1960-70; home econs. program asst. Suffolk County Coop. Extension of Cornell U., Riverhead, N.Y., 1972-82; tchr. home econs. Eastport (N.Y.) H.S., 1982-85, South County Schs., Bellport Middle Sch., N.Y., 1985-93; sch. coord. N.Y. state mentoring program Bellport Middle Sch., 1992-95. Host Ask Your Neighbor, Sta. WRIV, Riverhead, 1982-87; trainer Home Econs. Entrepreneurship N.Y. State Edn. Dept., 1986-95; mem. home and career skills regional team N.Y. State Edn. Dept., 1984-86; mem. consumer homemaking adv. bd. Bd. Coop. Edn.; friendly svc. chmn. N.Y. State Ret. Tchrs. L.I. Zone, 1995-2003. Contbr. articles to profl. jours. Chairperson policy bd. South Country Tchrs. Ctr.; mem. East Hampton Town Citizens Adv. com., East Hampton Citizens Adv. Commn., East Hampton Sr. Citizen Adv. Com.; v.p. Friendly Svc., 2000-03. Mem.: DAR (historian 1985, parliamentarian East Hampton chpt.), East End Ret. Tchrs. Assn. (chmn. by laws com. 2003—), N.Y. State Ret. Tchrs. Assn. (v.p. Friendly Svc., L.I. Zone 2000—03, chmn. nominations Long Island zone 2003—, health care coord. 2003—), Suffolk County Home Econs. Assn., Am. Home Econs. Assn. (cert. home economist), N.Y. State Home Econs. Assn., East Hampton Ladies Village Improvement Soc. (bd. dirs.), Daus. of the Founders and Patriots of Am., Eastern Gate Garden Club, Eastern Star (matron 1970). Home: 161 Newtown Ln East Hampton NY 11937-2429 Office: Bellport Mid Sch Kreamer St Bellport NY 11713 Office Phone: 631-329-6710. Personal E-mail: jasmoel@aol.com.

MOELLER, MARYANN, music educator; d. John George Moeller, Sr. and Anna Blasick Moeller. B in Music Edn., Northwestern U., 1955; M in Music Edn., Duquesne U., 1960; postgrad., Temple U., 1970, Hofstra U., 1971, Ariz. State U., 1971, SUNY, Stony Brook, 1974, Dowling Coll., 1978. Cert. tchr. N.Y., Pa. Music and chorus tchr. Mellon Jr. H.S., Mt. Lebanon, Pa., 1955—57, Sayville (N.Y.) Jr. H.S. and Cherry Ave. Elem., 1957—59, McMillan, Hillcrest and Meml. Elem. Schs., Bethel Park, Pa., 1959—62, Herricks Jr. H.S., New Hyde Park, NY, 1962—66, Garden City (N.Y.) Jr. H.S., 1966—72, Mt. Pleasant Elem., Smithtown (N.Y.) Elem. and Great Hollow Mid. Sch., 1974—88. Mem. curriculum com. Music Instrnl. Coun., Garden City, 1967, Garden City, 68; mem. chorus festival com. Nassau County Jr. H.S. Chorus Com., 1969; com. mem. Dist. Supt. Com., Garden City, 1971, Garden City, 72. Elsie Eckstein Music scholar, Northwestern U., 1951—55. Mem.: Pa. Music Educators Assn. (life), N.Y. State Sch. Music Assn. (life), Music Educators Nat. Conf. (life), Order Ea. Star, Sigma Alpha Iota. Republican. Avocations: sewing, gardening, singing, piano, walking. Home: 960 Buckingham Dr Allentown PA 18103

MOELLERING, CHARLOTTE LARESON, music educator; d. Charles Gene and LaGreta Stevens Reed; children: Laura Elizabeth, Jane Ann. BMus, Southwestern U., 1980; MEd, U. North Tex., 1996. Orchestra dir. Grand Prairie (Tex.) Ind. Sch. Dist., 1980—84, Irving (Tex.) Ind. Sch. Dist., 1985—86, Carrollton (Tex.) Farmers Br. Ind. Sch. Dist., 1986—. Dir. Nor'kirk Presbyn. Orch., Carrollton, Tex., 2001—. Recipient Cmty. Svc. award, DAR, 2003. Mem.: Am. String Tchrs. Assn. (state sec. 1992—94), Tex. Music Educators Assn., Music Educators Nat. Conf., Tex. Music Adjudicators Assn. (orchestra v.p. 2002—04), Tex. Orchestra Dirs. Assn. (pres. 1996—2001), Phi Delta Kappa, Mu Omicron. Presbyterian. Avocations: church activities, performing on violin, singing, reading. Office: Blalack Middle Sch 1706 Peters Colony Carrollton TX 75007 Office Phone: 972-394-3155.

MOELY, BARBARA E., psychologist, educator; b. Prairie du Sac, Wis., July 17, 1940; d. John Arthur and Loretta Ruth (Giese) M.; children: John Jacob Moely Wiener, David Andrew Moely Wiener. Student, Carroll Coll., 1958-60; BA, U. Wis., 1962, MA, 1964; PhD, U. Minn., 1968. Asst. prof. U. Hawaii, Honolulu, 1967-71; rsch. psychologist UCLA, 1971-72; asst. prof. Tulane U., New Orleans, 1972-75, assoc. prof. psychology, 1975-85, prof., 1985—2004, prof. emerita, 2004—, dept. chmn., 1992-96, dir. Office of Svc. Learning, 1999—2004. Contbr. articles to profl. jours. Grantee U.S. Office Edn., Handicapped Pers. Preparation, 1977-80, Tulane U., 1973, 75, 77-78, 83-84, Inst. for Mental Hygiene, City of New Orleans, 1983-84, 2000, Nat. Inst. Edn., 1983-84, La. Edn. Quality Support Fund, 1988-89, 91-92, 96, HUD, 1997-2003, Annenberg, 1997, HHS, 1997-2002, US Dept. Edn., 1999-2002, Fund for Improvement Post-Secondary Edn., 2000-03, Corp. Nat. and Cmty. Svc., 2003-. Mem. AAUP (v.p. La. conf. 1992-93, sec. 1993-97, v.p. 1998-2000, pres. Tulane 1992-94), Am. Ednl. Rsch. Assn., Southwestern Soc. for Rsch. in Human Devel. (pres. 1986-88), Phi Beta Kappa (pres. Alpha chpt. La. 1981-82, sec. 1995-99) Office: Tulane Univ Ctr for Pub Svc New Orleans LA 70118 Business E-Mail: moely@tulane.edu.

MOEN, CHERYL A., literature and language educator; b. Mason City, Iowa, Jan. 13, 1950; d. Burdett W. and Elaine Wakeman; m. Richard E. Moen, Feb. 12, 1983. BS in English and Speech, U. Wis., La Crosse, 1972. Cert. lang. arts tchr. Minn. Lang. arts tchr. La Crescent HS, Minn., 1972—. Mem. adv. coun. Coll. Edn., U. Wis., La Crosse, 1984—86; apptd. by gov. to state lang. arts 9-12 Graduation Stds. Com. State of Minn., 2003—04; workshop presenter Gt. River Writing Project, La Crosse, 1978—82. Author: (children's book) Johnnie Ollie Carrie Three and His Friend, 1984. Creator Zero-Tolerance for Violence Program, Houston County, Minn., 1996—97. Named La Crescent Tchr. of Yr., 1984, 1997, Minn. Honor Roll Tchr., 1997, Featured Alumna for Spotlight on Excellence, Coll. of Liberal Studies, U. Wis., LaCrosse, 2002; named one of Outstanding Young Women of Am., 1977. Mem.: NEA, La Crescent Edn. Minn., Edn. Minn., Nat. Coun. Tchrs. of English. Home: 165 McIntosh E La Crescent MN 55947 Office: La Crescent HS 1301 Lancer Blvd La Crescent MN 55947 Office Phone: 507-895-5017. Office Fax: 507-895-4490. E-mail: moenc@isd300.k12.mn.us.

MOEN, MARGARET, editor; b. Tokyo, Apr. 2, 1951; arrived in U.S., 1951; d. Raymond Otis and Evelyn (Carr) M. BA in History summa cum laude, Seattle U., 1972; MA in English, U. Minn., Mpls., 1980. Cert. English tchr. St. Paul Cmty. Edn. Assoc. editor Wanderer Printing Co., St. Paul, Minn., 1973—. English tchr. St. Paul Cmty. Edn. Contbr. articles to profl. jours. Mem.: Smithsonian Instn., Minn. Hist. Soc., U. Minn. Alumni Assn. Republican. Roman Catholic. Avocations: Italian language, swing and ballroom dancing, photography, genealogy. E-mail: moeneditor@cs.com.

MOEN, MONICA BALK, lawyer, real estate developer; b. Carroll, Iowa, Dec. 7, 1952; d. Frank Xavier and M. Franziska Balk; m. Marc Bradley Moen (div.). BS in Urban & Regional Planning, Iowa State U., Ames, 1976; JD, U. Iowa Coll. of Law, Iowa City, 1997. Cmty. liaison Linn County Regional Planning Commn., Cedar Rapids, 1976—79; sr. land use planner City of Iowa City, 1982—94; atty. Evans Keane LLP, Boise, Idaho, 1997—2001, Idaho Power Co., Boise, 2001—. Mem. Moen Group, Iowa City. Avocations: travel, reading. Office: Idaho Power Co PO Box 70 Boise ID 83707

MOERTEL, CHERYL ANN, science educator; b. St. Cloud, Minn., Mar. 30, 1959; d. Paul and Mabel Holthaus; m. David Matthew Moertel, May 1, 1882; children: Jessica, Ryan. BA, St. Olaf Coll., Northfield, Minn., 1981; MS in Molecular Biology, Mayo Grad. Sch., Rochester, Minn., 1993; MEd, Winona State U., Minn., 1997. Cert. tchr. life and phys. sci. Minn. Dept. of Edn., 2006, Divemaster Profl. Assn. Dive Instrs., 2002. Rsch. technologist in cytogenetics Mayo Clinic, Rochester, Minn., 1981—93; sci. tchr. Rochester Sch. Dist., 1993—; edn. grad. program faciliator Winona State U., 2003—06; padi divemaster MDC Sports, Rochester, Minn., 2002—; gifted and talented tchr. - coll. for kids Rochester Cmty. and Tech. Coll., 2000—. Venture crew leader - high adventure crew Boy Scouts of Am., Rochester, Minn., 1997—. Bd. dirs. Eagle Bluff Environ. Edn. Ctr., Lanesboro, Minn., 2003—06. Mem.: Minn. Sci. Tchrs. Assn. (Minn. Sci. Tchr. of the Yr. 2003). Office: Century High School 2525 Viola Rd NE Rochester MN 55906 E-mail: chmoertel@rochester.k12.mn.us.

MOEVS, MARIA TERESA MARABINI, archaeologist; b. Rome, Jan. 31, 1926; came to U.S., 1955, naturalized, 1959; d. Giuseppe and Tosca (Toschi) Marabini; Laurea Lettere, U. Bologna, 1947; Ph.D. summa cum laude, U. Rome, 1951; postgrad. Italian Archaeol. Sch., Athens, 1950-51; m. Robert W. Moevs, Oct. 1, 1953; children— Marina F., Christian R. Insp. antiquities Ministry Edn., Italy, Syracuse, Padua, 1952-53; insp. Central Restoration Inst., Rome, 1953-55; instr. Italian, Harvard U., 1956-57, Douglass Coll., 1965-68, asst. prof. Italian, 1968-72, asso. prof., 1972-77, prof., 1977-81, prof. classics and archaeology, 1981—; mem. Inst. Advanced Study, Princeton, N.J., 1977-78; mem. nat. screening com. Fulbright Am. Grad. Study Program, study in Italy, 1978-79, study in Italy-Greece, 1982-83. Recipient Goffredo Bellonci Spl. Prize, Rome Biennium, 1975-77; Italian Govt. fellow Italian Archaeol. Sch., Rome, 1947-50, Italian Archaeol. Sch. fellow, Athens, 1950-51, Fulbright fellow Am. Acad. Rome, 1952-53; Radcliffe Inst. Ind. Study asso. scholar, 1962-64, Am. Acad. Rome. fellow, 1963-64; NEH fellow, 1986-87. Mem. Archaeol. Inst. Am., Princeton Soc. of Archaeol. Inst. Am. (pres. 1986—), Rei Cretariae Romanae Favtores, Soc. Fellows, Am. Acad. Rome. Author: The Roman Thin Walled Pottery from Cosa, 1973; Gabriele D'Annunzio e le estetiche della fine del secolo, 1976; The Italo-Megarian ware from Cosa, 1980; Aco in Northern Etruria, 1980; Le Muse di Ambracia, 1981; Il Kalathos alessandrino di Bologna, 1983; Penteteris e le tre Horainella Pompe di Tolomeo Filadelfo, 1987. Contbr. articles on Roman pottery from excavations at Cosa, Italy to profl. jours, publs.

MOFFAT, MARYBETH, consulting company executive; b. Pitts., July 25, 1951; d. Herbert Franklin and Florence Grafe (Knerem) M.; m. Brian Francis Soulier, Nov. 30, 1974 (div.). BA, Carroll Coll., 1973. Indsl. engring. technician Wis. Centrifugal Co., Waukesha, Wisc., 1976-77; indsl. engr. Utility Products, Inc., Milw., 1977-79; mgr. indsl. engring. Bear Automotive (divsn. SPX Corp.), Bangor, Pa., 1980-90; program mgr. Toyota Johnson Controls, Inc. Automotive Systems Group, 1990-2001; pres., CEO Moffat Enterprises, Inc., 2001—. Group home house parent Headwaters Regional Achievement Ctr., Lake Tomahawk, Wis., 1974. Mem. Am. Inst. Indsl. Engrs., MTM Assn. for Standards Rsch., Indsl. Mgmt. Soc., Alpha Gamma Delta (standards chmn. 1971-72). Republican. Methodist. Avocations: skiing, horseback riding, swimming, reading. Office Phone: 859-272-0056. Personal E-mail: m.moffat@insightbb.com.

MOFFATT, JOYCE ANNE, performing company executive; b. Grand Rapids, Mich., Jan. 3, 1936; d. John Barnard and Ruth Lillian (Pellow) M. BA in Lit., U. Mich., 1957, MA in Theatre, 1960; HHD (hon.), Profl. Sch. Psychology, San Francisco, 1991. Stage mgr., lighting designer Off-Broadway plays; costume, lighting and set designer, stage mgr. stock cos., 1954-62; nat. subscription mgr. Theatre Guild/Am. Theatre Soc., N.Y.C., 1965-67; subscription mgr. Theatre, Inc.-Phoenix Theatre, N.Y.C., 1963-67; cons. N.Y.C. Ballet and N.Y.C. Opera, 1967-70; asst. house mgr. N.Y. State Theater, 1970-72; dir. ticket sales City Ctr. of Music and Drama, Inc., N.Y.C., 1970-72; prodn. mgr. San Antonio's Symphony/Opera, 1973-75; gen. mgr. San Antonio Symphony/Opera, 1975-76, 55th St. Dance Theater Found., Inc., N.Y.C., 1976-77, Ballet Theatre Found., Inc./Am. Ballet Theatre, N.Y.C., 1977-81; v.p. prodn. Radio City Music Hall Prodns., Inc., N.Y.C., 1981-83; artist-in-residence CCNY, 1981—; propr. mgmt. cons. firm for performing arts N.Y.C., 1983—; exec. dir. San Francisco Ballet Assn., 1987-93; mng. dir. Houston Ballet Assoc., 1993-95; gen. mgr. Chgo. Music and Dance Theater, Inc., 1995—2004. Cons. Ford Found., NY State Coun. on Arts, Kennedy Ctr. Performing Arts., Lensic Performing Arts Ctr., Santa Fe, Bloomington Cultural Dist., Ill., Sheboygan (Wis.) Theater Found., The Arts Partnership Spartanburg, SC; mem. dance panels NY State Coun. on Arts, 1979-81; mem. panels for Support to Prominent Orgns. and Dance, Calif. Arts Coun., 1988-92. Appointee San Francisco Cultural Affairs Task Force, 1991; chmn. bd. dir. Tex. Inst. Arts in Edn., 1994—; trustee Internat. Alliance of Theatrical Stage Employees Local 16 Pension and Welfare Fund, 1991-94; bd. dir. Rudolf Nureyev Dance Found., Chgo., 1998—. Mem. Assn. Theatrical Press Agts. and Mgrs., Actors Equity Assn., United Scenic Artists Local 829, San Francisco Visitors and Conv. Bur. (bd. dirs.), Argyle Club (San Antonio). Office Phone: 864-457-4575.

MOFFATT, KATY (KATHERINE LOUELLA MOFFATT), musician, lyricist, vocalist; b. Ft. Worth, Nov. 19, 1950; d. Lester Huger and Sue-Jo (Jarrott) M. Student, Sophie Newcomb Coll., 1968, St. John's Coll., 1969-70. Rec. artist Columbia Records, 1975-79, Permian/MCA Records, 1982-84, Enigma Records, L.A., 1985, Wrestler Records, L.A., 1987-88, Red Moon Records, Switzerland, 1988-93, Philo/Rounder Records, 1989-96, Round Tower Music, U.K., Ireland, Europe, 1993-96, Watermelon Records, U.S., 1994-96, Panther City Records, New Zealand, 1998, Hightone/HMG Records, 1998-2001, Western Jubilee/Dualtone Records, 2001—, Demon/Westside Records, 2002, Fuel Records/Universal Records, 2005. Folksinger, Ft. Worth, 1967-68; musician, vocalist, songwriter, rec. artist: (films) Billy Jack, 1970, Hard Country, 1981, The Thing Called Love, 1993; prodn. asst. film, Sta. KIII-TV, Corpus Christi, 1970, audio engr., Sta. KRIS-TV, Corpus Christi, 1970; musician, vocalist in blues band, Corpus Christi, 1970; receptionist, bookkeeping asst., copywriter, announcer, Sta. KFWT, Ft. Worth, 1971, musician, vocalist, songwriter, Denver, 1971-72, on tour, 1973, 75—, Denver, 1974, on tour, 1976-79, European tour, 1977, Can. tour, 1984-85, on tour in Europe, U.S., Can., Asia and Australia, 1985—; albums include Katy, 1976, Kissin' In The California Sun, Am. release, 1977, internat. release, 1978, A Town South of Bakersfield, 1985, Walkin' on the Moon, European release, 1988, U.S. release, 1989, Child Bride, 1990, (duet album with brother Hugh) Dance Me Outside, 1992, (Switzerland only) Indoor Fireworks, 1992, The Greatest Show On Earth A.K.A. The Evangeline Hotel, 1994, Hearts Gone Wild, 1994, Tulare Dust, 1995, (duet album with Kate Brislin) Sleepless Nights, 1996, Midnight Radio, 1996, Angel Town, 1998, Loose Diamond, 1999, Cowboy Girl, 2001, (reissue on CD) Katy/Kissin' in the California Sun, 2002, Up Close & Personal, 2005; songs include The Magic Ring, 1971; Gerry's Song, 1973, Kansas City Morning, 1974, Take Me Back To Texas, 1975, (Waitin' For) The Real Thing, 1975, Didn't We Have Love, 1976, Kissin' in the California Sun, 1977, Walkin' on the Moon, 1989. Recipient Record World Album award, 1976; named one of 4 Top New Female Vocalists, Cashbox Singles Awards, 1976; nominee for Top New Female Vocalist, Acad. Country Music, 1985; winner best singer-songwriter category Ft. Worth Weekly Mag. Music awards, 1997. Mem. AFTRA, SAG, NARAS, Am. Fedn. Musicians.

MOGABGAB, ROSE-WARREN BERRYMAN, academic administrator, writer; b. Richmond, Va., Mar. 13, 1940; d. Maynard Warren Berryman and Bessie Virginia Edwards; m. William Joseph Mogabgab, July 15, 1988 (dec.); children: Robert Mogabgab Berryman, William Joseph Mogabgab Berryman. AB, Randolph-Macon Woman's Coll., 1962. From mgr. lab. Sch. Medicine to rsch. assoc. Tulane U., New Orleans, 1965—81, rsch. assoc. Sch. Medicine, 1981—92; freelance med. writer and cons. New Orleans, 1993—. Presenter in field. Contbr. articles to profl. jours. Recipient 25 Yr. Svc. award, Tulane U. Sch. Medicine, 1980, Civc award, Mayor New Orleans, 1982. Mem.: Women for a Better La., Randolph Macon Woman's Coll. Alumnae (pres. New Orleans chpt. 1990—2001), Kingsmill Yacht Club, Kappa Alpha Theta. Avocations: antiques, gardening, travel. Home: 1220 Brookhaven Park Pl NE Atlanta GA 30319

MOGAN, CONNIE K., secondary school educator, elementary school educator; b. Malta, Mont., Dec. 6, 1958; d. Floyd L. and Mary H. Eklund; m. Marlin R. Mogan, Nov. 25, 1983; children: Andy, Christina, Lacey. BS in Edn., Mont. State U., Havre, 1981. Sci. tchr. Savage H.S., Mont., 1981—85, Harlem Pub. Sch., Mont., 1986—87; 6th grade and jr. H.S. sci. tchr. Box Elder Pub., Mont., 1989—96; 5th/6th combine and later sci. tchr. Hinsdale Pub. Schs., Mont., 1997—. Leader 4-H, Hinsdale; rep. coun. mem. Hinsdale Luth. Ch. Home: PO Box 93 Hinsdale MT 59241

MOGERMAN, FLORA MAY, music educator, director; b. Buffalo, May 12, 1939; d. Irring Raphael and Ida Snyder; children: Michael, Ida. MusB, Ithaca Coll., NY, 1961; MusM, Manhattan Sch. Music, NY, 1963. Piano tchr., accompanist Scottsdale CC, Ariz., 2003—. Pianist touring shows Erita and Will Rogers Follies Nat. Touring Co., Phoenix, 1997, Phoenix, 98. Pres. B'nai B'rith, Phoenix, 1976—77. Recipient Best Musical Dir., Arizoni Awards Com., 2002, 2004, 2005. Mem.: Am. Fedn. Musicians (life). Avocations: theater, crossword puzzles, reading, travel. Home: 334 W Tonnley Ave Phoenix AZ 85021

MOGGE, HARRIET MORGAN, educational association executive; b. Cleve. d. Russell VanDyke and Grace (Wells) Morgan; m. Robert Arthur Mogge (div.); 1 child, Linda Jean. BME, Northwestern U.; postgrad., Ill. State U. Instr. piano, Evanston, Ill., 1954-58; instr. elem. music pub. schs., Evanston, 1959; editl. asst. archivist Summy-Birchard Co., Evanston, 1964-66, asst. to editor-in-chief, 1966-67, cons., 1968-69, ednl. dir., 1969-74, also historian, 1973-74; supr. vocal music jr. high sch., Watseka, Ill., 1967-68; asst. dir. profl. programs Music Educators Nat. Conf., Reston, Va., 1974-84, dir. meetings and convs., 1984-94, mgr. direct mktg. svc., 1981-89; sr. cons. Conv. Cons. Svc., 1993—2003, ret., 2003—. Mng. editor Am. Suzuki Jour., 1972-74, Gen. Music Today, 1987-91; mgr. display advt. Model T Times, 1971—2006; vice chair editl. bd. Exposition Mgmt., 1991-93. Active various cmty. drives; parish bd. clerk, United Christian Parish, 2001-. Mem. Music Educators Nat. Conf., Am. Choral Dirs. Assn., In and About Chgo., Music Educators Assn. (bd. dirs.1973-74), Suzuki Assn. Ams. (exec. sec. 1972-74, Disting. Svc. award 1996), Internat. Assn. Exposition Mgmt. (cert., mem. edn. com. 1979-88, chmn. edn. com. 1985-87, bd. liaison edn. com. 1987-88, bd. dirs. Washington chpt. 1983-85, nat. bd. dirs. 1986-91, nat. v.p. 1989, nat. pres. 1990, Disting. Svc. award 1996), Bus. and Profl. Women's Club Watseka (bd. dirs. 1968-70), Antique Automobile Club (registrar ann. meeting 1961-86), Model T Ford Club Internat. (v.p. 1971-72, 76-77, pres. 1981, treas. 1983-87, bd. dirs. 1971-87), Mu Phi Epsilon, Kappa Delta (province pres. 1960-66, 72-76, regional chpts. dir. 1976-78, nat. dir. scholarship 1981-84). Republican. Presbyterian. Home and Office: 1919A Villaridge Dr Reston VA 20191-4824 Office Phone: 703-201-1281.

MOGGIO, BARBARA JEAN, health education specialist; b. Bronx, N.Y., July 7, 1953; d. Thomas Francis and Barbara Margaret (Lang) O'Meara; m. Richard Albert Moggio, July 28, 1984; stepchildren: Samuel A., Jonathan F. ADN, Pace U., 1976; BS, Mercy Coll., Dobbs Ferry, N.Y., 1985; MPH, Yale U., 1987. RN, N.Y.; cert. health edn. specialist. Critical care nurse, nursing care coord. Westchester Med. Ctr., Valhalla, N.Y., 1974-85; adj. asst. prof. Iona Coll., New Rochelle, N.Y., 1988-94; proprietor, CEO Health Wave, Inc., Stamford, Conn., 1990—. Author health curriculum Health Promotion Wave, 1987, 88, 95, 96. Mem. APHA, AAUW, Am. Sch. Health Assn., Assn. Advancement of Health Edn. Avocations: opera, golf. Office: Health Wave Inc 39 Davenport St Stamford CT 06902-6702

MOGULL, KIM, real estate company executive; Undergraduate, Northwestern Univ. With Coldwell Banker; founder, pres., CEO Mogull Realty Inc., 1993—. Named one of Forty Under 40, Crain's NY Bus., 2004. Office: Mogull Realty Trump Tower 725 Fifth Ave New York NY 10022 Office Phone: 212-286-5500. Office Fax: 212-308-4228.

MOGY, CATHERINE WADDELL, critical care nurse; b. Florence, SC, Mar. 13, 1964; d. Harold Dean and Sarah Margaret (Windham) Waddell; m. Richard A. Mogy, Sept. 13, 1986; children: Austin Waddell, Sarah Catherine. ADN, Florence-Darlington Tech. Coll., 1985; BSN, Med. U. S.C., Florence, 1989; cert., Richland Meml. Sch. Anesthesia, 1991. Cert. advanced cardiac life support; RN S.C., cert. registered nurse anesthetist. Staff nurse surg. ICU McLeod Regional Med. Ctr., Florence, 1985—86; staff nurse ICU Bruce Hosp., Florence, 1986—89; cert. RN anesthetist Carolina's Hosp. Sys., Florence, 1991—98; staff nurse anesthetist McLeod Regional Med. Ctr., Florence, 1998—. Scholar Alumni scholar, Francis Marion. Mem. Am. Assn. Nurse Anesthetists, ANA, Sigma Theta Tau.

MOHAMMADI, MINA, physician, researcher; b. Tehran, Iran, Nov. 5, 1965; came to the U.S., 1994; d. Jafar and Pouran Mohammadi; m. Bijan Poursharifi, Mar. 31, 1986; children: Pegah, Meelad. BS, Mahmoodzadeh Sch., Tehran, 1982; MBBS, Ambedkar Med. Sch., Bangalore, India, 1989. Diplomate Am. Bd. Internal Medicine, Am. Bd. Pulmonary Diseases. Resident in internal medicine N.Y. Meth. Hosp., Bklyn., 1994-97; fellow in pulmonary medicine Coney Island Hosp., Bklyn., 1997-99; pulmonologist, med. staff mem. North Ctrl. Bronx Hosp., Bronx, NY, 1999—. Faculty apptd. asst. prof. Albert Einstein Coll. Medicine. Fellow Coll. Chest Physician; mem. AMA, Am. Coll. Chest Physicians, Am. Thoracic Soc. Avocations: aerobics, horseback riding, dance, playing chess. Home: 7 Manor Dr Andover NJ 07821 Office Phone: 973-579-8090. E-mail: mina_mohammadi2001@yahoo.com.

MOHANTY, CHRISTINE ANN, retired language educator, actress; b. Coaldale, Pa., Jan. 4, 1945; d. Warren Russell and Helen Hargraves; 1 child, Kasmira. BA, Queens Coll., Flushing, N.Y.; MS Edn., Queens Coll., 1972; PhD English Lit., SUNY, Stony Brook, 1986. Tchr. fgn. langs. Three Village Ctrl. Sch. Dist., Setauket, NY, 1969—2000; assoc. prof. Suffolk County C.C., Selden, NY, 1994—2004, SUNY, Stony Brook, 2004—. Dir.: (plays) Deathtrap, 1992, Snow Queen, 1995; actor: Stepping Out, 1992, Prelude to a Kiss, 1998, Three Blind Mice, 1999, Social Security, 1999, Arsenic and Old Lace, 2000, Phantom of the Opera, 2000, Wuthering Heights, 2001, The Corn is Green, 2002, The Uninvited, 2002, Little Women, 2002, I Hate Hamlet, 2003, Noel Coward One Acts, 2003, Jekyll & Hyde, 2003, Dancing at Lughnasa, 2004, Shadow of a Doubt, 2004, Doll's House, 2005; contbr. articles to profl. jours.; Exhibited in group shows at Bayport Pub. Libr., N.Y., 2001—02. Recipient Educator of Week award, NY55 WLNY-TV, 2000; U. Salamanca scholarship, N.Y. State Edn. Dept., 1990. Mem.: AAUW, Am. Assn. Tchrs. French (pres. Suffolk County 1990—93, scholarship to France 1982), L.I. Lang. Tchrs., Phi Beta Kappa. Avocations: travel, tennis, creative writing, painting. Home: 790 Bretton Woods Dr Coram NY 11727 Personal E-mail: christinemohanty@excite.com.

MOHIN, ANN MARIE, writer; b. Balt., Jan. 31, 1946; d. Edward Joseph and Josephine (Gross) Purcell; m. William Bryan Mohin, July 7, 1978. BA, U. Md., 1976. Freelance writer, novelist, 1980—. Author: (book) The Farm She Was, 1998. Recipient N.Y. Times Notable Book Yr., 1998. Democrat. Avocation: gardening. Home: 1708 Tremont Ct Sun City Center FL 33573-4840

MOHLER, MARY GAIL, magazine editor; b. Milaca, Minn., Dec. 15, 1948; d. Albert and Deane (Vedders) M.; m. Paul Rodes Trautman, June 5, 1976 (div. 1994); children: Elizabeth Deane, David Albert Rodes, Theodore DeForest Lloyd. BA, U. Calif.-Davis, 1974; MA in Lit., SUNY-Stony Brook, 1976. Asst., then editor-reporter Family Circle Mag., N.Y.C., 1979-81; editorial coordinator Ladies' Home Jour., N.Y.C., 1981, assoc. articles editor, 1982, mng. editor, 1982-93, sr. editor, 1994-98; editor in chief Ladies' Home Jour. Parent's Digest; mng. editor Parents Mag., 1999—2001, editor at large, freelance writer, 2001—. Co-author: Those Who Can.Teach, 1999. Medieval philosophy fellow SUNY-Binghamton, 1978 Mem. MLA, Am. Soc. Mag. Editors, Phi Beta Kappa Clubs: Medieval; Overseas Press. Office: Parents Mag 375 Lexington Ave New York NY 10017-5514

MOHN, AMY ELIZABETH BRENNAN, special education educator, retail executive, consultant; b. Manchester, Conn., June 7, 1969; d. William Francis and Judith Elizabeth Benz Brennan; m. Bryan Keith Mohn, Aug. 5, 1995. BA in Psychology, Coll. of William and Mary, 1991, MEd in Spl. Edn., 1992. Cert. tchr. learning disabled and emotionally disturbed K-12. Grade 6 disturbed children Chesterfield County Schs., Va., 1992-93; ednl. prescriptionist Dept. of Def., Republic of Panama, 1993-96; kindergarten tchr. Ft. McClellan (Ala.) Elem. Sch., 1996-97; tchr. exceptional children Devers Elem. Sch., Ft. Bragg, N.C., 1997-98; retail cons. The Gift Shop, Fayetteville, N.C., 1999—. Kindergarten summer camp advisor Jr. League of Fayetteville, 1999; tutor, homeless family advocate Highland Presbyn. Ch., Fayetteville, 1998—; vol. City Coun. Campaign, 1998—. Grantee State of Va., 1991. Mem. Coun. for Exceptional Children. Republican. Avocations: running, travel, cooking, mountain biking, languages. Office: The Gift Shop 1110 Hay St Fayetteville NC 28305-5318 Home: 181 Woodland Rd Southborough MA 01772-2039

MOHNEY, NELL WEBB, religion educator, speaker, author; b. Shelby, N.C., Oct. 31, 1921; d. John Wonnie and Maude (Ferree) Webb; m. Ralph Wilson Mohney, Dec. 31, 1948; children: Richard Bentley, Ralph Wilson Jr. BA, Greensboro Coll., 1943; LHD (hon.), Tenn. Wesleyan Coll., 1982. Dir. youth work Western N.C. Conf., Salisbury, 1945-48; dir. Christian edn. 1st United Meth. Ch., Lenoir, N.C., 1943-45, Washington Pike United Meth. Ch., Knoxville, Tenn., 1952-56; dir. adult ministries 1st Centenary United Meth. Ch., Chattanooga, 1967-73, dir. membership devel., 1973-81, 1st Broad St. United Meth. Ch., Kingsport, Tenn., 1981-87; speaker, seminar leader for bus., profl., religious orgns. S.E. U.S., 1960—. Spkr. Internat. Women's Conf., Crystal Cathedral, 1991, 2001; adj. staff Bd. Discipleship Sect. on Evangelism, Nashville, 1987-96. Author: Inside Story, 1979, Single Out Singles for Ministry, 1989, Don't Put a Period Where God Put a Comma, 1993, How to be Up on Down Days, 1995, Keep on Kicking as Long as You Are Ticking, 1999, Get A Faith Lift, 2000, Develop Your Bounce Back Ability, 2000, From Eve to Esther: What Old Testament Women Say to Women Today, 2001, From Mary to Lydia, 2002, You Can Soar Like An Eagle, 2004, Running the Marathon of Life, 2005; co-author: Parable Churches, 1989, Churches of Vision, 1990, 365 Meditations for Grandmothers, 1996, 365 Meditations for Women, 1997, 2004; contbr. weekly article Chattanooga Free Press, 1977- Recipient Freedom Founds. award for writing, Valley Forge, Pa., 1973, for speaking, 1974, Key to City of Chattanooga, 1979; named Disting. Alumnae Greensboro Coll., 1988, Woman of Distinction in Chattanooga, 1992, Woman of Distinction Hall of Fame, 1993, Tenn. Woman of Yr., 1999. Republican. Home: 1004 Northbridge Ln Chattanooga TN 37405-4214 Office Phone: 423-645-8852. Personal E-mail: rwmsr18@comcast.net.

MOHON, EARLENE MANN, counselor; b. Jackson, Tenn., Sept. 22, 1939; d. German Earl and Lillie Frances (Graves) Mann; m. Robert Troy Mohon, Apr. 21, l961; children: David, Chad. BS, Miss. U. for Women, 1960; MEd in Counseling and Guidance, Miss. Coll., 1968. Tchr. Natchez Pub. Schs., Miss., 1960-61, Leesville Pub. Schs., La., 1961-62, Chapel Hill Pub. Schs., Tex., 1962-63, Judson Pub. Schs., Longview, Tex., 1963-65, Jackson Pub. Schs., Miss., 1965-69; substitute tchr. Mountain Brook Pub. Schs., Ala., 1981-83; counselor Birmingham City Schs., Ala., 1987—2003; ret. Recipient citation for drug free program Mayor of Birmingham, citation for drug free progam in elem. sch. Birmingham Sch. Bd. Mem. NEA, Am. Assn. for Counseling and Devel., Ala. Assn. for Counseling and Devel., Ala. Edn. Assn., Birmingham Edn. Assn., Chi Sigma Iota (sponsor Just Say No Club Ala., 1989). Republican. Baptist. Avocations: painting, needlecrafts. Home: 3516 Crest Brook Rd Birmingham AL 35223-1510 Office: 3136 Norwood Blvd Birmingham AL 35234-2123

MOHR, BARBARA JEANNE, elementary school educator; b. Santa Monica, Calif., Jan. 26, 1953; d. Edgar Kirchner and Beatrice Jeanne (Anderson) M. BA, Calif. State U., Fullerton, 1976, MS, 1982. Multiple Subject Teaching Credential, 1977, Single Subject Tchr. Credential, 1977. Substitute tchr. Fullerton (Calif.) Sch. Dist., 1977-78, tchr., 1978—, mentor, 1984-96. Tchr. calligraphy Laguna Rd. Sch., 1985-92, student coun. advisor, 1988-92, advisor Just Say No Club, 1986-94. Recipient Hon. Svc. award Laguna Rd. Sch. PTA, 1989; named Tchr. of Yr. Fullerton Sch. Dist., 1989, Golden Hill Sch. Tchr. of Yr., 2005; Weingart fellow Nat. Gallery of Art Tchr. Inst., 1996. Mem. NEA, Calif. Tchrs. Assn., Fullerton Elem. Tchrs. Assn., Calif. State U. Alumni Assn., Phi Kappa Phi. Avocations: calligraphy, gardening, travel. Office Phone: 714-447-7715. Personal E-mail: barbmohr26@sbcglobal.net.

MOHR, CHRISTINA, retired economist; b. San Diego, Calif., June 1, 1949; d. Lloyd Crowell and Joan Watkins, Oliver Watkins (Stepfather); m. Peter Joseph Mohr, July 13, 1989; stepchildren: Robert, Tracie 1 child, Oliver Wise. BS in Polit. Sci, U. Pa., Phila., 1971; MA in Internat. Affairs, George Washington U., Washington, DC, 1979; PhD in Econs., U. Md., College Park, 1993. Cons. World Bank, Washington, 1982; analyst sci. resource Nat. Sci. Found., Washington, 1983—86, speech writer for dir., 1987—93; sci. diplomacy fellow US Agy. Internat. Devel., Washington, 1994—95; sr. analyst Nat. Sci. Found., Washington, 1996—2001; ret., 2001. Commr. People with Disabilities Commn., Montgomery County, Md., 1994—96. Home: 2932 Woodstock Ave Silver Spring MD 20910 Personal E-mail: mohr@nist.gov.

MOHR, DORIS JEAN, mathematics professor; d. Emil and Marcella Schipp; m. Ronald Anthony Mohr, Sept. 20, 1975; children: Nicholas Adam, Lucas Anthony. BS, U. So. Ind., Evansville, 1987; MA, Ind. U., Bloomington, 1992; PhD, Ind. U., 2005. Instr. U. So. Ind., 1992—2004, asst. prof. math., 2004—. Treas. Dubois County Mental Health Assn., Ind., 1980—, U. So. Ind. Alumni Assn. of Dubois County, 2000—; Neighbor-to-Neighbor program facilitator St. Vincent de Paul Soc. of St. Ferdinand Parish. Summer rsch. fellow, U. So. Ind.-Pott Coll. Sci. and Engring., 2006. Mem.: Am. Ednl. Rsch. Assn., Internat. Soc. for Tech. in Edn., Assn. Math. Tchr. Educators, Nat. Coun. Tchrs. of Math. Achievements include research in how 4th-graders from Indiana perform on the mathematics portion of the National Assessment of Educational Progress compared to the rest of the nation. Avocations: embroidery, gardening, reading. Office: U So Ind 8600 University Blvd Evansville IN 47712 Office Phone: 812-464-1769. E-mail: djmohr@usi.edu.

MOHR, IRIS, finance educator; b. Tel Aviv, Aug. 1962; d. Joseph and Aviva Mohr; m. Charles Mohr, Feb. 13, 1988 (div.); m. Charles Jackson, Feb. 13, 1988 (div. Sept. 0, 1999); m. Charles Jackson, Feb. 13, 1988 (div. Sept. 0, 1999); children: Erica Ashley Jackson, Erica Ashley Jackson, Erica Ashley Jackson, Erica Ashley Jackson, Joshua Leslie Jackson, Erica Ashley Jackson, Joshua Leslie Jackson, Joshua Leslie Jackson. PhD, CUNY, 1991. Assoc. prof. mktg. St. John's U., Jamaica, NY, 1990—. Entertainment mktg. textbook writer. Author: (textbook) Entertainment and Event Marketing. Office: St John'S Univ 8000 Utopia Parkways Jamaica NY 11439 Office Phone: 718-990-7307. Home Fax: 516-431-4632. Personal E-mail: iris@entmarketingpro.com. Business E-Mail: mohri@stjohns.edu.

MOHR, VICTORIA H., obstetrician; b. Ft. Lauderdale, Fla., May 2, 1969; d. Merle Fredrick and Joan Anna Mohr. BS, Fla. State. U., Tallahassee, 1993; MD, Am. U. Caribbean, St. Maarten, 2000. Diplomate Am. Bd. Ob-Gyn. Resident George Washington U., Washington, 2001—04; staff physician North Fla. Ob-Gyn., Jacksonville, 2004—06, Global Med. Staffing, Ltd., Masterton, New Zealand, 2006—. Recipient Gold Medal, U.S. Figure Skating Assn. Fellow: Am. Coll. Ob-Gyn.; mem.: Am. Assn. Laproscopic Gynecol. Surgeons. Avocations: travel, skiing, rock climbing, diving, skating. Home: 651 Mangrove Point Rd Sarasota FL 34242

MOHRAZ, JUDY JOLLEY, foundation administrator; b. Houston, Oct. 1, 1943; d. John Chesler and Mae (Jackson) Jolley; m. Bijan Mohraz; children: Andrew, Jonathan. BA, Baylor U., 1966, MA, 1968; PhD, U. Ill., 1974. Lectr. history Ill. Wesleyan U., 1972-74; asst. prof. history So. Meth. U., Dallas, 1974-80, coord. women's studies, 1977-81, assoc. prof. history, 1980-94, asst. provost, 1983-88, assoc. provost for student academics, 1988-94; pres. Goucher Coll., Towson, Md., 1994-2000, Virginia G. Piper Charitable Trust, Scottsdale, Ariz., 2000—. Cons. Ednl. Testing Svc., Princeton, NJ, 1984-93, Nat. Park Svcs., Seneca Falls, NY, 1992-93; bd. dirs. Balt. Equitable Soc., 1996-00, The Assocs. First Capital, 1999-00, Coun. Foundations, 2005-; bd. visitors US Naval Acad., 1996-01. Trustee St. Mark's Sch. Tex., 1993-94; adv. bd. U. Tex. Southwestern Med. Sch., 1992-94; active Leadership Dallas, 1994; bd. dirs. Nat. Assn. Ind., The Balt. Cmty. Found., Coun. of Founds., 2005—; pres. Ariz. Grantmakers Forum, 2003-05; mem. Ariz. State Sch. Readiness Bd., 2003—; bd. dirs. Greater Phoenix Leadership, 2005—. Recipient Disting. Alumni award Baylor U., 1993; named Woman of Merit, Omicron Delta Kappa, 1993. Office: Virgina G Piper Charitable Trust 6720 N Scottsdale Rd Ste 350 Scottsdale AZ 85253 Office Phone: 480-948-5853. Business E-Mail: jmohraz@pipertrust.org.

MOHRMAN, KATHRYN J., academic administrator; BA, Grinnell Coll., 1967; MA, U. Wis., 1969; PhD, George Washington U., 1982. Dean undergrad. studies U. Md., College Park, 1988—93; pres. The Colo. Coll., Colorado Springs, 1993—2002; exec. dir. Hopkins-Nanjing Ctr. for Chinese and Am. Studies, Johns Hopkins U., 2003—. Office: 1619 Massachusetts Ave NW Washington DC 20036 Office Phone: 202-663-5801.

MOISTNER, MONA SUE, adult education educator; b. New Castle, Ind., Jan. 11, 1955; d. Kenneth Orlando Jr. and Mary Belle (Williams) M. AA in Liberal Studies/English, Ind. U. East, Richmond, 1997, BA in English, 1999; MLS, Ind. U., 2004. Cert. substitute tchr., Ind. Intern Huddleston Farmhouse Inn Mus., Cambridge City, Ind., 1998; disability accomodations asst. Ind. U. East, Richmond, 1999—2001; mgr. Foster Cmty. Learning and ResourceCtr. Ind. U., Bloomington, Ind., 2001—. Part-time faculty humanities dept. Ivy Tech. State Coll., Richmond, 2000—; staff photographer Huddleston Farmhouse Inn Mus., Hist. Landmarks Found. Ind., Cambridge City, 1998-99; instr. English Ivy Tech. State Coll., Richmond, Ind., 2000, Connersville, Ind., 2000; tutor Ind. U. East, Richmond, Ind., 1998. Dick and Joanne Reynolds scholar Ind. U. East, 1997-2000, Ruth Brown scholar, 1996, Judith Roman scholar, 1994. Mem. Ind. U. Alumni Assn., Hist. Landmarks Found. Ind., Am. Legion Aux. Methodist. Avocations: poetry, literature, travel, writing, promoting literacy.

MOJICA, AGNES, academic administrator; Chancellor Inter Am. U. of PR, San German, P.R. Past chair governing bd. Hispanic Assn. Colls. and Univs., 1995-96, co-chair leadership group; chair governing bd. Intercollegiate Athletic League, 2001-02. Pres., Consortium of Presidents and Chancellors for the Prevention of the Use and Abuse of Drugs and Alcohol, 1998-02; co-chair Am. Cancer Assn. Relay for Life Event, PR, Rsch. Area-Polit. Violence PR. Mem., Assn. Industrialists of P.R., Western C. of C., Am. Assn. Higher Edn., Assn. Profl. Women, Altrusa, Rotary (hon.), Alpha Delta Kappa, Phi Delta Kappa. Office: Inter Am U PO Box 5100 San German PR 00683-9801 Office Phone: 787-264-1912 ext. 73. Business E-Mail: amojica@sg.inter.edu.

MOJTABAI, ANN GRACE, author, educator; b. N.Y.C., June 8, 1937; d. Robert and Naomi (Friedman) Alpher; m. Fathollah Mojtabai, Apr. 27, 1960 (div. 1966); children: Chitra, Ramin. BA in Philosophy, Antioch Coll., 1958; MA in Philosophy, Columbia U., 1968, MS in Libr. Sci., 1970. Lectr. philosophy Hunter Coll., CUNY, 1966-68; libr. CCNY, 1970-76; fellow Radcliffe Inst. Ind. Study, Cambridge, Mass., 1976-78; Briggs-Copeland lectr. on English Harvard U., 1978-83; writer-in-residence U. Tulsa, 1983—2005, Yaddo Found., Saratoga, NY, 1975, 76. Author: Mundome, 1974, The 400 Eels of Sigmund Freud, 1976, A Stopping Place, 1979, Autumn, 1982, Blessed Assurance, 1986, Ordinary Time, 1989, Called Out, 1994, Soon: Tales From Hospice, 1998. Recipient Richard and Hinda Rosenthal award Am. Acad. and Inst. Arts and Letters, 1983, Lillian Smith award So. Regional Coun., 1986, Lit. Acad. award AAAL, 1993; Guggenheim fellow, 1981-82 Mem.: PEN, Mark Twain Soc., Tex. Inst. Letters, Phi Beta Kappa. Home: 2329 Woodside Drive Amarillo TX 79124-1036 Personal E-mail: agmojtabai@aol.com.

MOK, CAROLYN LEE, physician; b. San Antonio, Tex., Jan. 22, 1953; d. Edward and May Lee Mok. AB, Vassar Coll., Poughkeepsie, NY, 1974; MD, U. Tex. Med. Sch., Houston, 1976. Diplomate Am. Bd. Family Physicians. Staff physician Westside Health Svcs., Rochester, NY, 1983—. Vol. St. Thomas' Episcopal Ch., Diocese of Rochester, NY, 1978—. Fellow: Am. Acad. Family Practice. Office: Brown Sq Health Ctr 322 Lake Ave Rochester NY 14608

MOL, GRETCHEN, actress; b. Deep River, Conn., Nov. 8, 1972; d. Janet Mol; m. Tod Williams, June 1, 2004. Grad., Am. Musical & Dramatic Acad. Actor: (films) Girl 6, 1996, The Funeral, 1996, Donnie Brasco, 1997, The Last Time I Committed Suicide, 1997, The Deli, 1997, Bleach, 1998, Too Tired to Die, 1998, Rounders, 1998, New Rose Hotel, 1998, Celebrity, 1998, Finding Graceland, 1998, Music from Another Room, 1998, The Thirteenth Floor, 1999, Cradle Will Rock, 1999, Sweet & Lowdown, 1999, Forever Mine, 1999, Just Looking, 1999, Attraction, 2000, Get Carter, 2000, The Shape of Things, 2003, Heavy Put-Away, 2004, The Notorious Bettie Page, 2005, Puccini for Beginners, 2006; (TV films) Calm at Sunset, 1996, Subway Stories: Tales from the Underground, 1997, Picnic, 2000, Freshening Up, 2002, The Magnificent Ambersons, 2002; (TV miniseries) Dead Man's Walk, 1996; (TV series) Girls Club, 2002. Office: c/o William Morris Agy 1 William Morris Pl Beverly Hills CA 90212 Office Phone: 310-859-4000.*

MOLAD, CLARISSE BEHAR, writer, consultant; b. Jerusalem, June 11, 1951; arrived in U.S., 1973; d. Israel and Draga Behar; m. Ofer Molad, Sept. 9, 1972 (div. May 1987); children: Leital, Danny, Shelley, Mickey. B, Ben Gurion U., Beer Sheva, Israel, 1973; M, U. North Tex., 1975; PhD, Union Inst. & U., Cin., 1996. Pres. Softex, Houston, 1983—85; gen. mgr. SAGA Mgmt. Info. Sys., Houston, 1986—88; bus. analyst MW Kellogg, Houston, 1988—90; R&D specialist Bechtel Corp., Houston, 1990—93; v.p. Plant STEP, Inc., Houston, 1993—95, Data Xchange Technologies, Houston, 1995—97; pres. CBM Cons., Houston, 1997—; dir. The Adizes Inst., Santa Barbara, Calif. Chair Houston Women in Tech. Forum, Houston, 1999—; bd. dirs. Women in Tech. Internat., Houston; adj. prof. U. Phoenix, 2001—04. Contbr. articles. Founder Technitude Competition for Girls; pres. Assn. Women in Computing, Houston, 1999—2000. With Israeli Navy, 1969—71. Named one of Top 20 Women in Tech., Assn. Women in Computing, 1999; Fulbright scholar, U.S. State Dept. Balkan Region, 2005—. Democrat. Jewish. Avocations: travel, reading, scuba diving, dancing. Office: The Adizes Inst 2815 East Valley Rd Santa Barbara CA 93108 Office Phone: 805-565-2901. Business E-Mail: clarisse@adizes.com.

MOLASKY-ARMAN, ALICE ANNE, state commissioner; Commr. ins. State of Nev., 1995—. Office: Divsn Ins 788 Fairview Dr Ste 300 Carson City NV 89701-5491

MOLAY, HILARY S., lawyer; b. 1954; BA, Brandeis U.; JD, U. Miami. Bar: 1980. Law clerk to Judge Rita C. Davidson Md. Ct. of Appeals; trial atty. civil div. US Dept. Justice, Washington; assoc. Shank, Irwin & Conant, Finley, Kumble, Wagner, Heine, Underberg, Manley, Myerson & Casey; counsel J.C. Penney Co., Inc.; v.p., gen. counsel, sec. Zale Corp., Irving, Tex., 2000—05, sr. v.p., gen. counsel, corp. sec., 2005—. Mem. adv. bd. corp. counsel symposium Southern Methodist U., 2004; mem. gen. counsel forum Nat. Retail Federation. Mem.: ABA, Am. Soc. of Corp. Secretaries (mem. corp. practices comm.). Office: Zale Corp 901 W Walnut Hill Ln Irving TX 75038

MOLDEN, A(NNA) JANE, counselor; b. Weeping Water, Nebr. BS, Schauffler Coll.; MA, Princeton (N.J.) Theol. Sem. Cert. adminstr., Iowa. Dir. outreach Chgo. City Union; dir. campus ministry Iowa State U., Ames; dir. Christian edn. 1st Congl. Ch., Ames; dir. community outreach Congl. Chs., Kansas City, Mo.; ctrl. regional dir. Am. Friends Svc., Des Moines; dir. acad. support counseling Grand View Coll., Des Moines; dir. Consortium of Higher Edn., Des Moines. Mem. Health Planing Coun. Ctrl. Iowa; mem. Gov.'s Vocat. Rehab. Adv. Coun., 1993—; mem. Protection and Adv. Pair Adv. Coun., 1993—; bd. dirs. Iowa Protection and Adv. Bd. Dir. Grand View Coll. Dems., 1971-93; active devel. com. for handicapped HUD, Des Moines; bd. dirs. Plymouth Pl.; mem. Dr. Martin Luther King Com., Des Moines, Internat. Black Children's Conf., Iowa Vocat. Rehab. Coun., Iowa Protection and Adv. Coun.; chair Des Moines Human Rights Commn.; mem. study com. LWV; past pres. Citizens Disability Coun.; mem. community adv. bd. McKinley Sch.; mem. George Washington Carver com. Simpson Coll.; bd. dirs. Bernie Lorenz House, Community Focus, Greater Des Moines YWCA, Christian Ednl. Plymouth Congl. Ch.; bd. dirs. Youth Incentives. Named Outstanding Educator Jack and Jill, Inc., Des Moines, Supporting Friend, Learning Disability Coun. Ctrl. Iowa. Mem.: AACD, Edmonds Acad. Fine Arts (mentor), Torch Club Internat. (pres.), Delta Kappa Gamma. Democrat. Mem. United Ch. of Christ.

MOLDENHAUER, JUDITH A., graphic design educator; b. Oak Park, Ill., Feb. 28, 1951; d. Raymond L. and Jean Marie (Carqueville) M. BFA, U. Ill., 1973; MA, Stanford U., 1974; MFA, U. Wis., 1977. Design supr. N.E. Mo. State U., Kirksville, Mo., 1977-79; asst. prof. design Kansas City Art Inst., Mo., 1979-83; asst. prof. art, graphic design Sch. Art U. Mich., Ann Arbor, 1983-92; vis. lectr. Wayne State U., 1990-92, asst. prof. graphic design, 1992-98, assoc. prof. graphic design, 1998—, area coord. graphic design, 1992—. Free-lance designer The Detroit Inst. Arts, Toledo (Ohio) Mus. Art, Burroughs Corp. (Unisys) Detroit, Detroit Focus Gallery; vis. designer N.S. Coll. Art and Design, 1986; juror Ohio Mus. Assn., 1986, Collaborator Presdl. Initiative "Healthy Start": prenatal and pre-conceptional booklets and ednl. modules designs, 1992-1995; mem. organizing group health info. design Design Forum; presenter Congress Women's Health Issues, 1997, 98, Internat. Inst. Info. Design, Schwarzenberg, Austria, 1998, Vienna, 2005, Read Me exhbn., Bern, Switzerland, 1999, Expert Forum Manual Design, Malardalen U., Eskilstuna, Sweden, 2000, Vision Plus II, Internat. Inst. for Info. Design, 2005, others; co-chair info. design edn. Internat. Inst. Info. Design, 2004, faculty/vis. expert Summer Acad., Bolzano, Italy, 2005, co-dir. Summer Acad., Chgo., 2006, Health Comm. Forum, Boston, 2006 Contbr. articles to profl. jours. Recipient award of distinction, merit award Am. Assn. Museums, 1985, 86, Excellence Design award Beckett Paper Co., 1991, gold award for softcover books Printing & Pub. Competition, 1994, Am. Graphic Design award, 1996, 98; Rackham grantee U. Mich., 1987, grantee Nat. Endowment for Arts, 1988; US-EU FIPSE grantee U.S. Dept. Edn. student and faculty exch. info. design, 2003. 19th Internat. Bi-Ann. Graphic Design, Czech Republic, 2001; Fulbright fellow, Sweden, 2006—. Mem. Wood Engraving Network, Univ. and Coll. Designers Assn. (merit award 1979, gold award 1979), Coll. Art Assn. (chmn. panel 1991), Women's Caucus for Art (panel chmn. 1987), Amnesty Internat., Women in Design (excellence award Chgo. 1985, Sierra Club, Audubon Soc., Nat. Inst. Design. Lutheran. Office: Wayne State U Dept Art and Art History 150 Art Bldg Detroit MI 48202 Office Phone: 313-993-8165, 313-577-2980. Personal E-mail: FrogBoggd@aol.com.

MOLDENHAUER, SUSAN, museum director, curator; BFA, No. Ill. U., 1974; MFA, Pa. State U., 1982. Gallery mgr. Sch. Visual Arts, Pa. State U.; exec. dir. Second Street Gallery, Charlottesville, Va.; curator mus. progs. U. Wyo. Art Mus., Laramie, 1991—96, asst. dir., 1996—2000, interim dir., 2000—02, dir., chief curator, 2002—. Office: U Wyo Art Mus 2111 Willett Dr Laramie WY 82071-3807 Office Phone: 307-766-6620. E-mail: uwartmus@uwyo.edu.

MOLER, ELIZABETH ANNE, lawyer; b. Salt Lake City, Jan. 24, 1949; d. Murray McClure and Eleanor Lorraine (Barry) M.; m. Thomas Blake Williams, Oct. 19, 1979; children: Blake Martin Williams, Eleanor Bliss Williams. BA, Am. U., 1971; postgrad., Johns Hopkins U., 1972; JD, George Wash. U., 1977. Bar: D.C. 1978. Chief legis. asst. Senator Floyd Haskell, Washington, 1973-75; law clk. Sharon, Pierson, Semmes, Crolius & Finley, Washington, 1975-76; profl. staff mem. com. on energy and natural resources U.S. Senate, Washington, 1976-77, counsel, 1977-86, sr. counsel, 1987-88; commr. FERC, Washington, 1988-93, chair, 1993-97; dep. sec. Dept. of Energy, Washington, 1997-98, acting sec., 1998; ptnr. Vinson & Elkins, Washington, 1998-99; sr. v.p. Exelon Corp., 2000—02, exec. v.p., 2002—. Mem. ABA, D.C. Bar Assn. Democrat. Office: Exelon Corp Suite 400 East 101 Constitution Ave NW Washington DC 20001 Home: 1537 Forest Ln Mc Lean VA 22101-3317

MOLHOLT, PAT, academic administrator, associate dean; b. Fond du Lac, Wis., Oct. 19, 1943; d. Elmore Harrison and Leona Ann (Reschke) Leu; m. Louis D. Levine; children: Rebecca Marie, Stephanie Anne. BS, U. Wis., 1966, MLS, 1970; PhD, Rensselaer Poly. Inst., 1996. Library intern Milw. Pub. Library, 1966-67; astronomy librarian, dept. astronomy U. Wis., Madison, 1970-73; physics librarian U. Wis. Libraries, Madison, 1973-77; asst. prof., dir. U. Wyo. Sci. and Tech. Library, Laramie, 1977-78; assoc. dir. Rensselaer Poly. Inst. Libraries, Troy, N.Y., 1978-92, affirmative action advisor to pres., 1988-92; asst. v.p., assoc. dean scholarly resources Columbia U., N.Y.C., 1992—; dir., office of edn. Columbia U. Med. Ctr., 2004—. Co-dir. art and architecture thesaurus program J. Paul Getty Trust, Williamstown, Mass., 1983-86; rsch. analyst U.S. Dept. Edn., Washington, 1987-88; pres. Universal Serials and Book Exch., 1988-89; trustee Capital Dist. Libr. Coun., 1986-89; bd. visitors U. Pitts. Sch. Libr. and Info. Studies, 1993-95; mem. adv. bd. libr. sci. program Wayne State U., Detroit, 1992-95; mem. IBM Higher Edn. Customer Adv. Coun., 1995-99; mem. Biomed. Libr. rev. com. Nat. Libr. of Medicine, 1995-99; adv. com. mem. tchg. and learning, EDUCAUSE, 2003-06. Contbr. articles to profl. jours. Mem. adv. bd. Sch. Info. and Pub. Policy, SUNY-Albany, 1989; mem. steering com. N.Y. Gov.'s Conf. on Libr. and Info. Svcs., 1989-90; active N.Y. State Regent's Vis. Com. on State Archives, 1991—. Fellow Spl. Librs. Assn. (pres. 1983-84, John Cotton Dana award 1989); mem. ALA, NSF (mem. adv. bd., divsn. networking comm. rsch. and infrastructure 1991-92), Am. Soc. Info. Sci. (chair tech. program com. mid-yr. meeting, 1994, bd. dirs. 1997-2000, mem. fin. com. 1998-2000), Am. Med. Informatics Assn. (mem. exec. com. edn. working group 2001-), Assn. Am. Med. Coll. (mem. steering com. group info. resources 1999-, GIR survey com. mem. 2003-06). Office: Columbia U Health Scis 701 W 168th St Rm 201 New York NY 10032-2704 Office Phone: 212-305-3688. Business E-Mail: molholt@columbia.edu.

MOLIA, DENISE F., judge; b. N.Y.C. d. Frank and Lena Busi Molia; m. Robert J. Michta. JD, Hofstra U., Hempstead, N.Y., 1984. Bar: N.Y., N.J. Justice N.Y. State Supreme Ct., Riverhead, NY. Office: New York State Supreme Ct 235 Griffing Ave Riverhead NY 11901

MOLINA, GLORIA, municipal official; b. Montebello, Calif., May 31, 1948; d. Leonardo and Concepcion Molina; m. Ron Martinez, 1 child, Valentina Student, East L.A. Coll., 1968, Calif. State U., L.A., 1968-70. Staffing specialist Office Presdl. Pers., Washington, 1977-79; dir. intergovtl and congl. affairs region IX US Dept. Health & Human Services, San Francisco, 1979-81; So. Calif chief dep. Calif. State Rep. Willie L. Brown Jr., 1981; mem. Calif. State Assembly, 1982—86, L.A. City Coun., 1987—91, L.A. County Bd. Supervisors, 1991—, chair, 2005—. Mem. Revenue & Taxation, Labor & Employment, Utilities & Comm. Coms., Select Com. on Small Bus., 1982—, Consumer Protection, 1984—; chairwoman Subcom. Mental Health & Devel. Disabilities, 1984—. Named Hispanic of the Yr. Caminos mag., 1982, Dem. of the Yr. L.A. County Dem. Ctrl. Com., 1983, Woman of the Year Mexican-Am. Opportunity Found., 1983, MS mag, 1984, Woman of the Yr. Hispanic Bus. mag., 2006 Mem. Comision Femenil Mexicana Nacional. Office: LA County 500 W Temple St Ste 856 Los Angeles CA 90012-2723*

MOLINA, TANYA E., school librarian; b. Hamilton, New Zealand, June 2, 1971; arrived in U.S., 1973; d. Cyril Alfred and Karen Dawn Call; 1 child, Christian Michael. BS, No. Ariz. U., 1997, MEd, 1998; MA, U. Ariz., 2000. Tchr. Safford (Ariz.) Unified Sch. Dist., 1997—2001; libr. King City (Calif.) Elem. Sch. Dist., 2001—02; libr. media specialist Avondale (Ariz.) Elem. Sch. Dist., 2002—. Cons. in field. Mem.: ALA, Internat. Reading Assn., Ariz. Libr. Assn. Republican. Lds Ch. Avocations: writing, reading, scrapbooks. Office: Centerra Mirage Sch Goodyear AZ 85338

MOLINARI, ANA MARIA, salon owner; b. Lima, Peru, June 18, 1948; came to U.S., 1970; d. Jorge and Lucy Gonzales; children: Fabiola Guiliana Beckmann, Sergio Antonio Molinari. BA in Edn., Jorge Polar U., Lima, 1966; Cosmetology Degree, Helena Rubenstein, Lima, 1970. Hairstylist John Paul-Garfinkels, Washington, 1973-76; owner, designer Hide and Seek, Sarasota, Fla., 1976-80; co-owner, hairstylist Ambiance, Sarasota, 1980-85; owner, hairstylist Ana Molinari Inc., Sarasota, 1985—; owner LaMariee Bridal Salon, 2002—. Named Best of Best, Sarasota Mag., 1995—2000, Readers Choice, Sarasota Herald Tribune, 1995—2000, Small Bus. of Yr., Longboat Key C. of C., 2001; recipient award of excellence, Bus. Mag., 1993. Mem. Sarasota C. of C., Longboat Key C. of C., Siesta Key C. of C. Avocations: exercise, beach, antique collecting. Office Phone: 877-262-7722. E-mail: ana.molinari@verizon.net.

MOLINARI, CAROL V., writer, investment company executive, educator; b. Bklyn., Oct. 14, 1931; d. Sabino and Anna (Mancusi) M. BS, Douglass Coll., 1953; MEd, Rutgers U., 1962; postgrad., U. Alaska, Anchorage, 1963—. Tchr. Bridgewater Twp. Schs., Bridgewater, N.J., 1953-56, Somerville (N.J.) H.S., 1956-59; tchr. phys. edn., guidance counselor Bridgewater H.S., Raritan, N.J., 1959-62; guidance counselor Anchorage Borough Sch. Dist., 1962-63, Air Force Dependent Sch., Tokyo, 1963-64, Arcturus Jr. H.S., Ft. Richardson, Alaska., 1965-67; asst. dir. student coll. ctr. Douglass Coll., Rutgers U., New Brunswick, N.J., 1967-69; cons., counselor Native Head Start program Alaska Meth. U., Anchorage, 1967-69; adminstr. asst., counselor U. Alaska, Anchorage, 1969-70; office sales mgr. Alcan Realty, Anchorage, 1971-74; dir. Ctr. for Alcohol and Addiction Studies U. Alaska, Anchorage, 1975-79; sales assoc. Century 21 Royal Realty, Anchorage, 1970-83; cons. in the devel. of Now Dimensions Holistic Health Ctr.; pres., dir. Molinari Investments Inc., Anchorage, 1982—. Developer fin. projects, 1978-82; seminar presenter on investing techniques. Author: The Magic of Financing and Investing, 1987, (cookbook) Mom's Italian Recipes, American's Wake Up We Can Heal Our Country, 1996; co-author: Out of Nowhere; contbr. articles to Alaska Tchr., This Alaska, Alcohol Health and Research World, others. Bd. dirs. Alaska region Nat. Coun. on Alcohol, Morning Song; mem. adv. bd. Salvation Army; mem. ch. coun. Holy Family Cathedral. Rutgers U. schoalr, 1975. Mem. NAFE, NEA, Alaska Edn. Assn., Bd. Realtors, Women of Vision and Action, Soroptimist. Avocations: hiking, reading, skiing, fishing, travel. Personal E-mail: cmolin@webtv.net.

MOLINARI, SUSAN, former congresswoman; b. Staten Island, NY, Mar. 27, 1958; d. Guy V. and Marguerite (Wing) Molinari; m. Bill Paxon; 2 children. BA, SUNY, Albany, 1980, MA, 1982. Former intern for State Senator Christopher Mega; former rsch. analyst N.Y. State Senate Fin. Com.; former fin. asst. Nat. Rep. Gov.'s Assn.; ethnic community liaison Rep. Nat. Com., 1983-84; minority leader N.Y.C. Council, 1986-90; mem. 101st-104th Congresses from 14th (now 13th) N.Y. dist., 1990-97, vice-chair House Rep. Conf.; anchor CBS News Sat. Morning, N.Y.C., 1997-98; Chairman, CEO The Washington Group, 2001—. Author: (book) Representative Mom: Balancing Budgets, Bill and Baby in the U.S. Congress, 1998. Roman Catholic. Office: c/o The Washington Group 1401 K Street NW Ste 1000 Washington DC 20005

MOLITOR, KELLEY MARIE, mathematics professor; b. Colusa, Calif., Apr. 24, 1963; d. Thomas Earl Tucker, Jr. and Lila Ann (Mayberry) Tucker; m. Todd David Molitor, Mar. 30, 1996; children: Jeremy Todd, Hannah Suzanne. BA in math., Calif. State U., 1986; MST in math., U. New Hampshire, 1995. Math. tchr. Nevada Union HS, Grass Valley, Calif., 1988—, Sierra Coll., Grass Valley, 1997—, Nat. U., 2006—. Author: Alegebra I Curriculum, 2003. Recipient Tchr. Rsch. Assoc. award, U.S. Dep. Energy, 1992, APLE award, Calif. Student Aid Comm., 1987; Ptnrs in Edn. fellowship, Nevada County Office of Edn., 1991, Congressional Tchr. scholarship, Calif. Student Aid Comm., 1987. Mem.: Math. Assn. Am., Nat. Coun. of Tchrs. of Math. (Dale Seymore Scholarship 1995, Mary Dolciani Scholarship 1994). Office: Nevada Union HS 11761 Ridge Rd Grass Valley CA 95945 Office Phone: 530-273-4431 503. Business E-Mail: kmolitor@nuhsd.k12.ca.us.

MOLL, DEBORAH ADELAIDE, lawyer; b. Wilmington, Del., Jan. 19, 1946; BA, St. John's Coll., Annapolis, Md., 1969; MA, U. Tex., 1972, JD, 1975. Bar: N.Mex. 1977. Law clk. Tex. Ct. Criminal Appeals, Austin, 1975-76, U.S. Ct. Appeals (10th cir.), Santa Fe, 1977-78; asst. atty. gen. N.Mex Atty. Gen., Santa Fe, 1978-84; asst. appellate defender N.Mex Pub. Defender Dept., Santa Fe, 1984-87; staff atty. N.Mex Taxation and Revenue Dept., Santa Fe, 1987-92; shareholder Kemrer-Hayes & Moll, P.A., Albuquerque, 1992; gen. counsel N.Mex Gen. Svcs. Dept., Santa Fe, 1993—. Mem.: N.Mex. State Bar (bd. dirs. bankruptcy sect. 1992, adv. opinion com. 1993—96, bd. dirs. pub. law sect. 1996—, chair pub. law sect. 1997—98, bd. dirs. employment law sect. 1999—2003, chair ad hoc com. 2001, com. establish legal specialization constrn. and pub. contracts 2002—). Avocation: photography. Office: NMex Gen Svcs Dept 715 Alta Vista St Santa Fe NM 87505-4108 Office Phone: 505-827-2000. E-mail: Deborah.Moll@state.nm.us.

MOLL, LAURETTA JANE, guidance counselor; b. Willard, Ohio, Apr. 13, 1954; d. Herman Edward and Sylvia Ann (Topping) M. BA in Psychology, Bus., Covenant Coll., Lookout Mountain, Ga., 1976; MA in Theology, MA in Counseling, Covenant Theol. Sem., St. Louis, 1979; cert. in Bibl. counseling, Columbia (S.C.) Grad. Sch., 1980; cert. in edn., Fla. Atlantic U., 1984. Adminstrv. asst. in devel. Covenant Theol. Sem., 1976-78; portfolio reviewer A.G. Edwards & Sons, Inc., St. Louis, 1978-79; dir. guidance and counseling Ft. Lauderdale (Fla.) Christian Sch., 1979-85; adminstrv. asst. Community Electric of Collier, Inc., Naples, Fla., 1985-87; secondary sch. prin. Naples Christian Acad., 1987-89; psychotherapist Willough at Naples, 1989-90; dir. guidance and counseling Lake Worth (Fla.) Christian Schs., 1990—. Mem. Nat. Right to Life, Morality in Media. Republican. Presbyterian. Avocations: travel, reading, music, sports. Home: 1202 S Lake Dr Apt 205 Lantana FL 33462-5424 Office: Lake Worth Christian Schs 7592 High Ridge Rd Boynton Beach FL 33426-9320

MOLL, SARA H., psychologist, volunteer; b. Oklahoma City, July 4, 1943; d. Virgil Blount and Kathryn (Holland) Hooks; m. Curtis Eric Moll, Nov. 29, 1963; children: Curtis David, Robert Theodore, Charles Merideth, Sara Frances. BA, Case Western Res. U., 1965, MA, 1990, PhD, 1992; MA, Cleve. State U., 1988. Postdoctoral fellow Univ. Hosp., Cleve., 1992-93; instr. Ursuline Coll., Pepper Pike, Ohio, 1994-95; clin. psychologist Ohio Dept. Mental Health, Medina, 1994—; mem. clin. faculty psychiatry Sch. Medicine Case Western Res. U., Cleve., 1994—. Contbr. articles to profl. jours. Mem. Coalition Against Domestic Violence, Cleve., 1993-94; psychotherapist, adult survivor group The City Mission, Cleve., 1994; mem. Clin. Oversight Coun., Medina, Ohio, 1999; chair expansion ministries for women and children The City Mission, Cleve., 1998—, trustee, bd. dirs., 1994—. Estab. Sara H. Moll Christian Youth Ctr., The City Mission, 1994. Mem. APA. Methodist. Avocations: bible study, book club, travel, choir, needlepoint. Office: Ohio Dept Mental Health 3076A Remsen Rd Medina OH 44256-9225

MOLLAND, MARIA U., Internet company executive; b. 1974; BA, Northwestern U.; MBA, Harvard U. With Disney Internet Group, Volpe Brown Whelan; bus. devel. mgr. Yahoo Finance, 2002—05; gen. mgr. MarketWatch, Inc. Dow Jones & Co., San Francisco, 2005—. Office: MarketWatch Inc 825 Battery St San Francisco CA 94111 Office Phone: 415-733-0500. Office Fax: 415-680-1635.*

MOLLEDO, MAGDALENA FERREIRA, elementary school educator; b. Austin, Minn., Mar. 13, 1966; d. Guillermo and Ana Luque Ferreira; m. Francisco Antonio Molledo, Dec. 30, 1989; children: Sara-Maria, Ramon Antonio, Ana Mercedes, Francisco Jose. BS, U. Minn., Mpls., 1988; MA, U. Phoenix, 2005. Cert. tchr. Fla. Tchr. Rosarian Acad., West Palm Beach, Fla., 1989—91, Little Flower Sch., Hollywood, Fla., 1991—92, Bethune Elem. Sch. of the Arts, Dania, Fla., 1993—94, Avon Pk. (Fla.) Mid. Sch., 1994—99, Space Coast Mid. Sch., Cocoa, Fla., 1999—2001, DeLaura Mid. Sch., Satellite Beach, Fla., 2001—. Cons. Holt Reinhart Winston, 2004—05. Named Dist. Tchr. of the Yr., Highlands County Sch. Bd., 1999, Exemplary Sci. Tchr., Brevard Schools Found., 2003; grantee Break the Mold, Fla. Dept. Edn., 1997; Environ. grant, SW Fla. Water Mgmt. Dist., 1995—99. Mem.: NSTA. Roman Catholic. Home: 420 Park Ave Satellite Beach FL 32937 Office: DeLaura Mid Sch 300 Jackson Ave Satellite Beach FL 32937 Office Phone: 321-773-7581. Home Fax: 321-773-0702; Office Fax: 321-773-0702. Personal E-mail: nenmolledo@cfl.rr.com. Business E-Mail: molledom@brevard.k12.fl.us.

MOLLOY, SYLVIA, language educator; b. Buenos Aires, Aug. 29, 1938; came to U.S. 1967; d. Herbert Edward and Margarita Berta (Chasseing) M. Licence es Lettres, U. Paris, 1960, Diplome D'Etudes Superieures, 1961, Doctorat de U. Paris, 1967. Asst. prof. Spanish SUNY, Buffalo, 1967-69; asst. prof. Spanish Vassar Coll., Poughkeepsie, NY, 1969-70, Princeton U., Princeton, NJ, 1970-73, assoc. prof., 1973-81, Emory L. Ford prof., 1981-86; prof. Spanish Yale U., New Haven, 1986-90; Albert Schweitzer prof. of Humanities NYU, 1990—. Author: La Diffusion de la Litterature Hispanoamericaine en France, 1972, Las Letras de Borges, 1979, En Breve Carcel, 1981, At Face Value: Autobiographical Writing in Spanish America, 1991; co-author Women's Writing in Latin America, 1991, Hispanisms and Homosexualities, 1998, El Común Olvido, 2002, Varia Imaginación, 2003; author short stories and contbr. articles to profl. jours.; cons., editorial bd. Revista Iberoamericana, 1979-81, 1985-89, Latin Am. Literary Rev., 1985—, Revista de Filología, Buenos Aires, 1985— Fellow Am. Philos. Soc., 1970, NEH, 1976; Social Sci. Research Council grantee, 1983; Guggenheim Found. fellow, 1986-87 Mem. MLA (pres.), Asociacion Internacional de Hispanistas, Instituto Internacional de Literatura Iberoamericana

MOLNAR, KATHLEEN KAY, management information systems educator; b. El Paso, Sept. 25, 1958; d. Herbert Charles and Maureen MaryAnn (Wood) Finger; m. Jeffrey Allan Molnar, Sept. 22, 1984; children: Steven Charles, Alixandra MaryAnn. BS in Natural Sci. magna cum laude, Xavier U., 1979; MBA, U. Wis., Oshkosh, 1992; PhD in Bus. Adminstrn., Okla. State U., Stillwater, 1997. Air traffic control specialist FAA-Rockford (Ill.) Control Tower, 1979-81; programmer supr. St. Anthony Hosp., Rockford, 1983-84; programmer analyst, cons. Arthur Young, Milw., 1984-85; sys. analyst Columbia Hosp., Milw., 1985, St. Norbert Coll., DePere, Wis., 1986-92, dir. computer svcs., 1989-92, asst. prof., 1997—, U. Ctrl. Okla., Edmond, 1996-97. Contbr. chpts. to books, articles to profl. jours. Mem. AAUW, Decision Scis. Inst., N.E. Wis. Talented and Gifted Orgn. (v.p. 1998—), Phi Kappa Phi, Beta Gamma Sigma. Office: St Norbert Coll 100 Grant St De Pere WI 54115-2002

MOLNAR, MARY ANNE, retired secondary school educator, consultant; m. William; children: Jennifer, Allyson. BA, SUNY, 1966, MA, 1969. Math tchr. Guilderland (N.Y.) Ctrl. High Sch., 1966-69, No. Valley Req High Sch., Demarest, 1969—2003; ret., 2003. Math. cons. Peoples/Wiley Pubs. Vol. local Ch. NSF grantee San Diego State, 1968; recipient Tandy recognition, 1991, Gov.'s award for Excellence in Teaching, 1993, Mid. States AP Tchr. award, 1999. Mem. Math. Assn. Am., Nat. Coun. Tchrs. Math. Avocations: fossil hunting, crafts, hiking, camping, skiing. Personal E-mail: molnar@cybernex.net.

MOLNAR, VIOLET, mental health nurse; b. Budapest, Hungary; arrived in U.S., 1960; d. Janos Molnar and Erzsebeth Krekacs. ADN, Atlantic Union Coll., 1967; BSN, Walla Walla Coll., 1973. RN Mass., Calif. Staff nurse New Eng. Meml. Hosp., Stoneham, Mass., 1968—70; IV therapist Loma Linda U. Med. Hosp., Calif., 1970—72; psychiat. nurse St. Bernardines Med. Ctr., San Bernardino, Calif., 1974—89, Corona Regional Med. Ctr., San Bernardino, 1990—. Pub. spkr. Pres. Lady's Club Friendly Cir., Loma Linda, 1997—99, pres., 2006—; elder, deaconess, greeter Seventh Day Adventist Ch. Loma Linda U., 1975—. Mem.: Rotary Club San Bernardino/Highland (Paul Harris fellow 2001). Avocations: travel, reading, church activities. Home: 11422 Benton St Loma Linda CA 92354 Personal E-mail: imolnar@juno.com.

MOLNAU, CAROL, lieutenant governor; b. Minn., Sept. 17, 1949; m. Steven F. Molnau; 3 children. Attended, U. Minn. Mem. Minn. Ho. of Reps., 1992—2003; commr. Minn. Dept. Transportation; lt. gov. State of Minn., St. Paul, 2003—. Active Corn Growers, Farm Bur., Soybean Growers, Norseland Ch. Mem. Agrl. Com., Econ. Devel., Infrastructure & Regulation Fin.-Transportation Fin. Divsn., Fin. Inst. & Ins.: Internat. Trade & Economic Devel. Republican. Office: Office Lt Governor 130 State Capitol 75 Rev Dr Martin Luther King Jr Blvd Saint Paul MN 55155 Office Phone: 651-296-3391. Office Fax: 651-296-2089.

MOLTER, KAREN S, literature and language educator; d. Edwin Lindlow and Dorothy Mae Rich; m. Michael D. Molter, Sept. 4, 1976; children: Megan Elizabeth, Joshua Michael. BS, Ind. State U., 1973; M, Purdue U., West Lafayette, Ind., 1983. Lang. arts tchr. South Newton Schools, Kentland, Ind., 1982—. Tchr. adv. coun. Learning Points Assoc. North Ctrl. Regional Edn. Labs, Naperville, Ill., 2002—; sec. Ind. State Teachers of Yr., Indianapolis, Ind., 2000—. Coun. pres. Kappa Kappa Kappa, Inc., Indpls.; publicity dir. Newton County Fair Assn., Kentland, Ind., 1995—2006; dir. George Ade Meml. Assn., Kentland, Ind., 2001—06. Recipient Citizen of Yr., Kentland C. of C., 1998. Mem.: Kappa Delta Pi, Delta Kappa Gamma, Nat. Coun. of Teachers of English. Office: South Newton Schools 13100 S 50 E Kentland IN 47951 Office Phone: 219-474-5167.

MOLTZ, BEVERLY ANN, elementary school educator; b. Houston, May 12, 1946; d. Harold Hudson and Mary Dorothy Wood; m. Simon M. Moltz, Apr. 3, 1966; children: Monica, Michelle, April. BS in Homemaking Edn., Southwest Tex. State U., 1968, MEd in Spl. Edn., 1996. Cert. kindergarten tchr. 1987. Homemaking tchr. Schertz Cibalo Unified Sch. Dist., Schertz, Tex., 1968; dir. day care ctr. Travis Pk. United Meth. Ch., San Antonio, 1976—77; kindergarten tchr. East Ctrl. Sch. Dist., San Antonio, 1985—96, spl. edn. facilitator, 1996—. Recipient Sinclair Tchr. of Yr. award, 2004. Mem.: Assn. Tex. Profl. Educators, Embroiderers Guild of Am. Methodist. Achievements include assessor for Nat. Bd. of Tchg. Standards 1997, 1998, 2005. Avocation: embroidery. Office: Sinclair Elem Sch 6126 Sinclair Rd San Antonio TX 78222 Office Phone: 210-648-4620.

MOLYNEAUX, DOROTHY MUNZ, retired education educator, retired speech pathology/audiology services professional; d. Charles George and Dorothy Prekel Munz; m. M. Glenn Molyneaux, Sept. 14, 1945; children: Liane, Andrea, Gregg, Mark, Kent. BA, Univ. Ill., Urbana, Ill., 1944; MS Speech Commn., Northwestern Univ., Evanston, Ill., 1945; PhD, Stanford Univ., Palo Alto, Calif., 1949. Cert. speech, lang. pathology, audiology Am. Speech, Lang., Hearing Assn. Dir. San Francisco Hearing Ctr., San Francisco, 1948—50; speech pathologist pvt. practice, San Francisco, 1950—55; prof., clin. supr., dir. special parent counseling program San Francisco State, San Francisco, 1964—87, prof. emeritus, 1987—. Lang. cons. Preschool Tng. Ctr., San Francisco, 1971—75; profl. adv. mem. Easter Seals Society, Burlingame, Calif., 1976—80. Author: (Univ. textbook) Effective Interviewing, 1982, Successful Interactive Skills for Speech Language, 1990, The Dynamics of Communicative Development, 1992. Vol. Santa Rosa Symphony League; chair and bd. mem. parish edn. Calif.-Nev.-Hawaii dist. Luth. Ch. Mo. Synod, 1979—85, mem. pres. commn. on women, 1986—93; bd. dir. Luth. Care Aging, 1985—. Fellow: Calif. Speech-Lang.-Hearing Assn. (Outstanding Achievement award 1986); mem.: Am. Speech-Lang.-Hearing Assn., Coun. for Exceptional Children, Pi Lambda Theta, Phi Beta Kappa, Zeta Phi Eta, Delta Sigma Rho. Avocation: travel.

MOLZ, CAROL JEAN, elementary school educator; d. Wayne J. and Neva M. Madill; 1 child from previous marriage, Ellie Catherine DeHaven. BE, Pitts. State U., Kans., 1974, EdM, 1991. Phys. edn. tchr. Haysville Jr. HS, Kans.; sec. Madill Carbide, Inc., Wichita; tchr. Unified Sch. Dist. 265, Goddard. Mem. profl. adv. com. Unified Sch. Dist. 265, Goddard, Kans., 1999—2003; grade level dept. head Clark Davidson Elem. Sch.; presenter Character Edn. State Conf., Wichita, 2002; bd. dir. Madill Carbide, Inc. Contbr. articles to profl. jours. Mem. Unified Sch. Dist. 265 PTO, 1998—; chmn. defribrillator fund raising com. Unified Sch. Dist. 265, Kans., chmn. humane society fund raisers; bldg. rep. Susan G. Koman Found.; chmn. Clark Davidson sch. Ronald McDonald Pop-Top Dr. Recipient Tookie Cmty. Svc. award, KDFI FM, Golden Apple award, KAKE TV, Cmty. Svc. award, Goddard Police Dept. Home: 1 Tonjo Ct Goddard KS 67052-9101

MOLZ, REDMOND KATHLEEN, public affairs educator; b. Balt., Mar. 5, 1928; d. Joseph T. and Regina (Barry) M. BS, Johns Hopkins U., Balt., 1949, MA, 1950; MALS, U. Mich., Ann Arbor, 1953; DLS, Columbia U., N.Y.C., 1976. Librarian I and II Enoch Pratt Free Library, Balt., 1953-56; pub. relations officer Free Library of Phila., 1958-62; editor Wilson Library Bull. H.W. Wilson Co., Bronx, NY, 1962-68; chief planning staff Bur. Libraries and Learning Resources U.S. Office Edn., Washington, 1968-73; prof. library sci. Sch. Library Service Columbia U., N.Y.C., 1976-80, Melvil Dewey prof., 1980-93; prof. pub. affairs Sch. Internat. and Pub. Affairs, Columbia U., N.Y.C., 1993-99, prof. emeritus, 2000—. Cons. U.S. Nat. Commn. Librs. and Info. Sci., Washington, 1974-75, U.S. Adv. Commn. Intergovtl. Relations, Washington, 1979-80; mem. nat. adv. coun. The Sheridan Librs., Johns Hopkins U., 1997—. Author: Federal Policy and Library Support, 1976 (Ralph R. Shaw award 1977), National Planning for Library Service, 1935-75, 1984, Library Planning and Policy Making: The Legacy of the Public and Private Sector, 1990, The Federal Roles in Support of Public Library Services, 1990, The Federal Roles in Support of Academic and Research Libraries, 1991; co-author (with Phyllis Dain) Civic Space/Cyberspace: The American Public Library in the Information Age, 1999; co-editor: The Metropolitan Library (anthology), 1972; author TV script Portraits in Print, 1959. Recipient Leadership Tng. award Fund for Adult Edn., 1956-57; recipient Disting. Alumnus award Sch. Library Sci. U. Mich., 1969, George Virgil Fuller award Columbia U., 1975, Johns Hopkins U. scholar, 1949-50, Horace H. Rackham fellow U. Mich., 1952-53, Columbia U. scholar, 1974-76, Tangley Oaks fellow, 1975-76; Council Library Resources Inc. Officers' grantee, 1974 Mem. ALA (councilor 1972-74, 76-80, exec. bd. 1976-80, chmn. legis. com. 1985-86), Freedom to Read Found. (dir. 1972-79, pres. 1977-79) Business E-Mail: rkm2@columbia.edu.

MOMMSEN, KATHARINA, retired literature and language professor, foundation administrator; b. Berlin, Sept. 18, 1925; came to U.S., 1974, naturalized, 1980; d. Hermann and Anna (Johannsen) Zimmer; m. Momme Mommsen, Dec. 23, 1948. DPhil, U. Tübingen, 1956; Dr. habil., Berlin Free U., 1962. Collaborator Acad. Scis., Berlin, 1949—61; assoc. prof. Free U., Berlin, 1962—70; prof. German Carleton U., Ottawa, Canada, 1970—74; Albert Guerard prof. lit. Stanford U., 1974—94, ret., 1995. Vis. prof. U. Giessen, Tech. U. Berlin, 1965, State U. N.Y., Buffalo, 1966, U. Calif., San Diego, 1973; pres. Mommsen Found. Author over 200 publs. on 18th-20th century German and comparative lit.; editor: Germanic Studies in America. Mem. Goethe Soc., Schiller Soc. Home: 980 Palo Alto Ave Palo Alto CA 94301-2223 Office Phone: 650-326-6637. E-mail: k.mommsen@comcast.net, katmom@stanford.edu.

MONACO, KELLY MARIE, actress; b. Phila., May 23, 1976; Actor: (TV series) Baywatch, 1997—98, Port Charles, 1999—2003, General Hospital, 2003—; (films) Idle Hands, 1999, Late Last Night, 1999, Mumford, 1999; dancer (TV series) Dancing with the Stars, 2005 (winner dance compitition, 2005); guest appearance Spin City, 2001, The Tonight Show, 2005, Larry King Live, 2005, Live with Regis and Kelly, 2005, The View, 2005, Jimmy Kimmel Live, 2005. Office: William Morris Agency One William Morris Pl Beverly Hills CA 90212

MONAGHAN, KATHLEEN M., art museum director; b. Waterville, Maine, Sept. 6, 1936; d. Russell Vernon and Gloria Beatrice (LeClair) M. BA in Art History, U. Calif.-Santa Barbara, 1979, MA in Art History, 1981. Curatorial fellow Whitney Mus., N.Y.C., 1979, dir. Equitable Br., 1985-93; asst. curator Santa Barbara Mus., Calif., 1980-81, curator of art Calif., 1983-84; curator, dir. Akron Art Mus., Ohio, 1984-85; dir. The Hyde Collection, Glens Falls, NY, 1994—99; exec. dir. Fresno Metropolitan Museum, Fresno, Calif., 1999—. Mem. Internat. Com. on Mus., Coll. Art Assn. Office: Fresno Met Mus 1515 Van Ness Ave Fresno CA 93721-1200

MONAGHAN, M. PATRICIA, education educator, writer; b. Bklyn., Feb. 15, 1946; d. Edward Joseph and Mary Margaret (Gordon) M. BA in English, U. Minn., 1967, MA in English, 1971; MFA, U. Alaska, 1981; PhD, The Union Inst., 1995. News editor U. Alaska, Fairbanks, 1970-71; pub. rels. dir. Walker Art Ctr., Mpls., 1972; editor Minn. Monthly Minn. Pub. Radio, St. Paul, 1973-74; women's editor Daily News miner, Fairbanks, 1975; lectr., head English dept. Tanana Valley C.C., Fairbanks, 1976-87; instr. writing The Neighborhood Inst., Chgo., 1987-89; dir. cont. edn. St. Xavier U., Chgo., 1990—; assoc. prof. DePaul U. Sch. for New Learning, Chgo. Booklist reviewer ALA, Chgo., 1987—. Author: Book of Goddesses and Heroines, 1981, 2d edit., 90, Working Wisdom, 1994, O Mother Sun New View of Feminine, 1994; (poems) Seasons of the Witch, 1992 (Friends of Lit. award), Meditation: The Complete Guide, 1999, Dancing with Chaos, 2002, The Red Haired Girl from the Bog, 2003 (Pushcart prize 2004). Recipient Rsch. award NUCEA, 1993. Mem. Am. Conf. on Irish Studies, Soc. Midland Authors, Authors Guild. Democrat. Mem. Soc. Of Friends. Office: DePaul Univ Sch for New Learning 16333 S Kilbourn Oak Forest IL 60452 Office Phone: 312-476-3076. E-mail: pmonagha@depaul.edu.

MONAHAN, DANIELLE JOAN, renal nutritionist; b. Tacoma, Feb. 22, 1952; d. Daniel Gustav and Bernice Elizabeth (Nordlund) Anderson; m. Jay Mitchell Littlefield, Nov. 13, 1976 (dec. 1997); children: David, Rachel, Paul; m. Aldrich B. Monahan, Jr., Oct. 30, 1999. BS, Va. Poly. Inst., 1974; MS, U. Md., 1975. Registered dietitian, Va. Therapeutic dietitian Samaritan Hosp., Troy, N.Y., 1976; renal dietitian BMA/Fresenius Med. Care (formerly Nat. Med. Care), Washington, 1977-85, Fairfax Dialysis (formerly BMA of Arlington), 1985—. Cons. Fairfax, 1985—; rep. network coordinating coun. Nat. Kidney Found., Chevy Chase, Md., 1980-84; chmn. BMA Dietitians Group, Washington, 1980-93. Contbr. articles to profl. jours., mags. Del. Va. Rep. Party, Vienna, 1982. Mem. Am. Dietetic Assn., No. Va. Dietetic Assn. Republican. Avocation: cooking. Office: Fairfax Dialysis 8316 Arlington Blvd #108 Fairfax VA 22031-5216 Office Phone: 703-698-8070. Personal E-mail: amonahan445@msn.com.

MONAHAN, SHERRY ANN, writer; d. John Philip and Marilyn Ann Teeter; m. Lawrence A. Monahan, Aug. 24, 1985. Comm. specialist Genworth Mort. Ins., Raleigh, NC, 1990—; writer Willow Spring, NC, 1995—. Author: Wicked West, 2005, Tombstone's Treas., 2007, Pikes Peak, 2002; contbg. editor: True West Mag., History Channel Personality; contbr. articles publ. to profl. jour. Mem. Women Writing the West, Western Writers Am., Author's Guild, N.C. Writers Network. Avocations: cooking, travel, photography. Home: 7049 Landingham Dr Willow Spring NC 27592-8621 Office Phone: 919-577-6399. Business E-Mail: sherry@wildwestinfo.com.

MONASTERO, TINA MARIE, elementary school educator; b. Cleve., Sept. 3, 1965; d. Anthony Ross and Roselyn Louise (Cugini) M. BS, Cleve. State U., 1990; Masters, Marygrove Coll., 2004. Lic. tchr., Ohio. Phys. edn. tchr. kindergarten to 8th grade Incarnate Word Acad., Parma Heights, Ohio, 1990—; 8th grade health, 9th-12th grade physical edn. tchr. Mayfield (Ohio) HS, 1999—. Basketball coach West Geauga Recreation Coun., Chesterland, Ohio, 1988—; softball coach Notre Dame Cathedral Latin, Chardon, Ohio, 1990—; coord. Jump Rope for Your Heart, Parma Heights, 1990—; volleyball coach Incarnate Word Acad., Parma Heights, 1992, girls volleyball coach, 1994; girls soccer coach West Geauga H.S., Chesterland, 1993. Mem ASCD, Ohio Assn. Health, Phys. Edn., Recreation and Dance. Republican. Roman Catholic. Avocations: softball, golf. Home: 5939 Ridgebury Blvd Cleveland OH 44124-1638 Office: Incarnate Word Acad 6618 Pearl Rd Parma Heights OH 44130-3898 Office Phone: 440-995-6837.

MONCRIEF, JACQUELINE C., retired state agency administrator; b. Cin., Ohio, Apr. 27, 1940; d. John L. Craddock and Novella D. Noble; children: David, Vanessa, Orlando. Student, Cen. State U., Wilberforce, Ohio, 1958—61; BA, Capital U., Columbus, Ohio, 1991. Cert. Gospel Lighthouse Sch. Ministry, lic. missionary Bishop Ross, Triedstone Ch. Monetary supr. Ohio Bur. Employment Svcs., Columbus, 1974—2001, initial claims supr., 1974—2001; compliance auditor Ohio Dept. Job and Family Svcs., Columbus, 1974—2001; ret. Mem. various planning teams ODJFS, Columbus. Vol. United Way; tutor, mentor Adopt-a-Sch. program Starling Sch., 1996—99; tutor, mentor Ohio Reads program Sedalia Sch., 1999—2000. Recipient Outstanding Svc. award and trophy, GMWA, 1988, plaque, Luth. Social Svcs., 1985. Mem.: Gospel Music Workshop of Am. Baptist. Avocations: singing in choir, dance, travel, games. Home: 1858 Riverdale Rd Columbus OH 43232

MONCURE, JANE BELK, educator, author, consultant; b. Orlando, Fla., Dec. 16, 1926; d. John Blanton and Jennie Bruce (Wannamaker) Belk; m. James Ashby Moncure; 1 child, James Ashby II. BS in Elem. Edn., Va. Commonwealth U., 1952; MA in Early Childhood Edn., Columbia U., 1954. Tchr., and various directorships schs. and chs., N.Y., Va., 1952-66; instr. early childhood edn. Va. Commonwealth U., Richmond, 1966-72; instr. children's lit. U. Richmond, 1973-74; tchr. early childhood edn. Burlington, N.C., 1974-78. Author, cons. early childhood edn., 1979-93; lectr. seminars and workshops, Va., N.C., Ill., Ind. Author: Word Bird Series for Young Readers, Wise Owl Series for Young Readers, Sound Box Books, Alphabet Books, various lang. arts books including It Happened at Macky's Point, What's So Special About Lauren?, Now I Am Five, Magic Monsters series, Child Development, Creative Dramatics series, Creative Expression series, Special Day Arts and Crafts, Science and Social Science series, Values series, Religious Education series, First Steps to Reading series, First Steps to Math series, Magic Castle Readers Series, Discovery World Series: First Steps to Science. Recipient C.S. Lewis Gold medal Assn. of Christian Schs. Internat., 1984, Outstanding Svc. to Young Children in Va. award, 1979. Mem. Va. Assn. for Early Childhood Edn. (Outstanding Svc. to Young Children in Va.), So. Assn. for Children Under Six, Nat. Assn. for Edn. Young Children. Home and Office: 1613 Aquinas Ct Burlington NC 27215-9308

MONCZEWSKI, MAUREEN R., art educator, visual artist; b. Scranton, Pa., Jan. 14, 1957; d. Walter Albert and Ann Hedwig (Sawicki) M. BA in Profl. Art, Marywood U., 1978, MFA in Painting, 1987. Cert. art educator K-12. Art instr. Internat. Corr. Sch., Scranton, Pa., 1983-98; grad. asst. Marywood U., Scranton, 1985-86; art tchr. Moravian Acad., Bethlehem, Pa., 1989-90; adj. art instr. Penn State U., Lehman, Pa., 1990-91; art tchr. Notre Dame Jr./Sr. High Sch., East Stroudsburg, Pa., 1997—2001; secondary art tchr. Stroudsburg (Pa.) H.S., 2001—. Designer, painter of site specific murals Scranton Redevel. Authority, 1979, Scranton Sr. Activities Ctr., 1986, Carbondale (Pa.) Housing Authority, 1987, Teamsters Local 229, Scranton, 1990, Housing Authority of the County of Lackawanna-Dunmore (Pa.) Sr. Hi-Rise, 1994, The Artist's Studio, Scranton, 1995, Baird's County Kennel, Mehoopany, Pa., 1995, West Side Sr. Activities Ctr., Scranton, 1996, Wyo. Paint and Art Supply, Scranton, 1996, Suz's Marineland, Tunkhannock, Pa., 1996; represented in pvt. collections. Gen. Program grantee Boys & Girls Club, 1992, Housing Authority Mural grantee Lackawanna County, Dunmore, Pa., 1994, Arts to the People grantee Lackawanna County Commrs., Scranton, 1992, 95; recipient Cert. of Excellence award Dept. Labor, 1980. Mem. St. Luke's Art Soc., Kappa Pi. Democrat. Roman Catholic. Avocations: sculpture, writing, design, travel, drawing. Personal E-mail: marsbar@pametrocast.net.

MONDA, MARILYN, statistician, quality assurance professional; b. Paterson, N.J., Aug. 11, 1956; d. Thomas John and Lydia Mary (Dal Santo) M.; m. Lawrence G. Gifford, Jr., Aug. 25, 1984. BA, San Diego State U., 1980; MA, Baylor U., 1984. Math. statistician Navy Pers. R&D Ctr., San Diego, 1984-86; quality engr. Info. Magnetics, Inc., San Diego, 1986-87; mgmt. cons. Process Mgmt. Inst., Inc., Mpls., 1987-89; staff assoc. Luftig & Assocs., Inc., Detroit, 1989-92; founder Quality Disciplines, San Diego, 1992—99, GE Real Estate, Stanford, Conn., 1999—. Lectr. in field. Contbr. articles to profl. jours. Mem. San Diego Deming Users Group, Am. Soc. Quality Consultants, Am. Statistical Assn., Phi Beta Kappa. Avocations: literature, computers. Home and Office: 95 Meadowlawn Rd Stratford CT 06614-1523 Office Phone: 203-961-2332. Personal E-mail: marmonda@optonline.net.

MONDA-AMAYA, LISA ELLEN, education educator; d. Gerald P. and Catherine Monda; m. George I. Amaya, June 16, 1990 BS, MS, Fla. State U., 1982, PhD, 1989. Tchr. spl. edn. St. Johns County Sch. Bd., St. Augustine, Fla., 1982-85; dir. reading clinic Fla. State U., Tallahassee, 1985-86, supr., reading specialist Regional Multidisciplinary Ctr., 1986-87; asst. prof., program coord. CRT program U. Ill., Champaign, 1990—97, assoc. prof., program coord., 1997—. Contbr. articles to scholastic jours. Office: U Ill Dept Spl Edn 288 Education 1310 S 6th St Champaign IL 61820-6925

MONDALE, JOAN ADAMS, wife of former Vice President of United States; b. Eugene, Oreg., Aug. 8, 1930; d. John Maxwell and Eleanor Jane (Hall) Adams; m. Walter F. Mondale, Dec. 27, 1955; children— Theodore, Eleanor Jane, William Hall. BA, Macalester Coll., 1952. Asst. slide librarian Boston Mus. Fine Arts, 1952-53; asst. in edn. Mpls. Inst. of Arts, 1953-57; weekly tour guide Nat. Gallery of Art, Washington, 1965-74; hostess Washington Whirl-A-Round, 1975-76; ambassador to Japan, 1993-96. Author: Politics in Art, 1972, Letters from Japan, 1998. Bd. govs. Women's Nat. Dem. Club; hon. chmn. Fed. Coun. on Arts and Humanities, 1978-80; bd. dirs. Associated Coun. of Arts, 1973-75, Reading Is Fundamental, Am. Craft Coun., NYC, 1981-88, J.F.K. Ctr. Performing Arts, 1981-90, Walker Art Ctr., Mpls., 1987-93, Minn. Orch., Mpls., 1988-93, 97-2003, St. Paul Chamber Orch., 1988-90, Northern Clay Ctr., 1988-93, St. Paul, 1988-93, Nancy Hauser Dance Co., Mpls., 1989-93, Minn. Landmarks, 1991-93, Walker Art Ctr., Mpls., 1997-2003; trustee Macalester Coll., 1986—; mem. commn. Nat. Portrait Gallery, 1997—; chair Hiawatha Light Rail Transit Pub. Art and Design com., 2000-04; active Walker Art Ctr., 2003—, Minn. Orch., 1997—; citizen's stamp adv. com. US Postal Svc., 2005— Mem.: Phi Beta Kappa Epsilon. Democrat. Presbyterian. Home: 2116 Irving Ave S Minneapolis MN 55405-2541 E-mail: joan.mondale@mac.com.

MONDELLO, LISETTE MCSOUD, federal agency administrator; BA, Trinity Coll. Dir. comm. office of Sen. Alfonse D'Amato U.S. Senate, Washington, dir. comm. office of Sen. Kay Bailey Hutchison; sr. advisor office comm. and outreach US Dept. Edn.; asst. sec. pub. & intergovernmental affairs US Dept. Veterans Affairs, 2005—. Office: US Dept Veterans Affairs 810 Vermont Ave NW Rm 900 Washington DC 20420 Office Phone: 202-273-5750. Office Fax: 202-273-5717.

MONES, JOAN MICHELE, pathologist; b. Downey, Calif., Nov. 26, 1952; d. Joseph Morgan and Mary Kathryn (Crisp) Battersby; m. Harris Hal Mones, May 11, 1979 (div. Dec. 1987). BA, UCLA, 1975; DO, U. Osteo. Medicine, 1979. Diplomate Am. Bd. Pathology, Anatomic and Clin. Intern Drs. Gen. Hosp., Plantation, Fla., 1979-80; pvt. practice Coral Gables, Fla., 1980-81; resident in pathology Jackson Meml. Hosp., Miami, 1981-85, fellow in surg. pathology, 1985-86; instr. in pathology U. Miami, 1986-87; asst. lab. dir. North Miami Med. Ctr., 1987-90; attending pathologist Parkway Regional Med. Ctr., North Miami, 1990-97; fellow in dermatopathology Thomas Jefferson U., Phila., 1998-99; med. dir. Ackerman Acad. Dermatopathology, N.Y.C., 1999—. Clin. asst. prof. U. Miami, 1988—, Southeastern U. Osteo. Medicine, Miami, 1989—. Contbr. articles to profl. jours. Fellowship Nat. Cancer Soc., 1985. Fellow Coll. Am. Pathologists, Am. Soc. Clin. Pathologists; mem. U.S. and Canadian Acad. Pathology, Am. Osteo. Coll. Pathology, Am. Osteo. Assn. Office: Ackerman Acad Dermatopathology 145 E 32d St New York NY 10016

MONEY, RUTH ROWNTREE, retired infant development and care specialist, parent/infant programs consultant; b. Brownwood, Tex. m. Lloyd Jean Money; children: Jeffrey, Meredith, Jeannette. BA in Biology, Rice U., 1944; MA in Devel. Psychology, Calif. State U., Long Beach, 1971; BA in Early Childhood Edn., U. D.C., 1979. Rsch. psychologist Early Edn. Project, Capitol Heights, Md., 1971-73; lectr. No. Va. C.C., Anandale, 1973-74; tchr. preschs. Calif. and Va., 1979-81; dir. various preschs., Washington and Va., 1981-85; instr. guided studies Pacific Oaks Coll., Pasadena, Calif., 1986-88; cons. parent/infant programs Resources for Infant Educarers, L.A., 1986—2005; founder, dir. South Bay Infant Ctr., Redondo Beach, Calif., 1988-92; instr. child devel. Harbor Coll., L.A., 1992-93; ret. Bd. dirs. Resources for Infant Educarers, 1986-2005; pres. bd. dirs. South Bay Infant Ctr., Redondo Beach, 1988-94, treas., 1994-98. Producer (ednl. videos) Caring for Infants, 1988—. Mem. League of Women Voters, 1956—, v.p., 1972-76. Mem. Nat. Assn. for Edn. of Young Children, Assn. for Childhood Edn. Internat., Infant Devel. Assn. Calif. Avocations: travel, hiking. Home: 3939 Walnut Ave Carmichael CA 95608 E-mail: ruthmoney@comcast.net.

MONFERRATO, ANGELA MARIA, investor, writer; b. Wissembourg, Alsace-Loraine, France, July 19, 1948; arrived in U.S., 1950; d. Albert Carmen and Anna Maria (Vieri) M. Diplomate, Pensionnat Florissant, Lausanne, Switzerland, 1966—67; BS in Consumer Related Studies, Mktg., Pa. State U., 1971, postgrad. in speech and comm., 1971—72. Simultaneous translator fgn. langs. Inst. for Achievement of Human Potential, Phila., 1976-78; art dir. The Artworks, Sumneytown, Pa., 1976; real property mgr. Plz. 15 Condominium, Ft. Lauderdale, Fla., 1979-80; legal asst. Ft. Lauderdale, 1981-85; owner Rising Sun the Real Estate Corp. South Fla., Ft. Lauderdale, 1986—. Pres. Kideos Video Prodns., 1985—; owner, designer Monferrato Designs, 1988-99. Avocations: writing, designing, yoga, faux painting, restoration of antiques. Office: Monferrato Designs Telluride 200 Front St PO Box 2 Placerville CO 81430

MONGEON, LOUISE BERNADETTE, school nurse; b. Burlington, Vt., June 22, 1957; d. Paul and Rita (Thibault) Dufresne; m. Richard P. Mongeon, June 5, 1982; children: Brian, Adam, Sarah. BS, U. Vt., 1979. RN 1983. Charge nurse Med. Ctr. Hosp. Vt., Burlington, 1984; camp nurse Camp Marycrest, Grand Isle, Vt., 1980-82; staff nurse per diem Fletcher Allen Health Care, Fanny Allen Hosp. Campus, Colchester, Vt., 1988-94; daycare dir. St. Francis Xavier Ext., 1994-99; part time sch. nurse St. Francis Xavier Sch., Winooski, Vt., 1994-99; sch. nurse Winooski Ednl. Ctr., 1999—2005; sch. nurse supr. Burlington Sch. Dist., 2001—05; sch. nurse H.O. Wheeler Elem. Sch., 2005—. 1st lt. U.S. Army, 1980-83. Mem.: ANA, Vt. Sch. Nurses Assn., Nat. Assn. Sch. Nurses (cert.), Vt. State Nurses Assn. Office Phone: 802-865-4172. E-mail: lbmongeon@yahoo.com, lmongeon@bsdvt.org.

MONGES, MIRIAM M., social studies educator; b. Phila., Feb. 1, 1950; d. Walter Holland and Ruth (Harris) Johnson; m. Pedro Chango Monges, Feb. 11, 1974 (div. June 1992); children: Taína Afaph, Caliph Caribe. BA cum laude, Bklyn. Coll., 1973; MSW, Temple U., 1979, PhD in African-Am. Studies, 1995. Project coord. Ctr. Social Policy and Cmty. Devel. Temple U., Phila., 1986-92, adj. prof., 1993-94; exec. dir. Spruce Adolescent Ctr., Phila., 1992-94; assoc. prof. Calif. State U., Chico, 1995—. Mem. adv. coun. Ctr. Multicultural & Gender Studies, Chico, 1995—; cultural resource specialist African Am. Culture XXVI Olympiad, Atlanta, 1996; multicultural cons. social work Bodo (Norway) Coll., 1997. Author: Kush: The Jewel of Nubia, 1997; mem. editl. bd. Jour. Black Studies, 1996—. Named for Disting. Scholarship and Mentoring, Internat. Assn. Women of Color Day, Sacramento, 1999. Mem. Nat. Assn. Black Social Workers, Nat. Assn. African Am. Studies, Nat. Coun. Black Studies. Avocations: spinning, making jewelry. Office: Calif State U Ctr Multicultural & Gender Studies Dept Sociology Social Work Chico CA 95929-0001 Home: 902 Valley Rd Apt 10c Elkins Park PA 19027-3236

MONGIELLO, CHRISTINE, music educator; b. Secaucus, N.J. d. Richard Robert and Catherine Madeline Mongiello. MusB, West Chester U., 2000—04. Cert. tchr. Pa. Bd. Edn. Music tchr. Gen. Music Programs, Wilmington, Del., 2004—05. Mem.: Nat. Assn. Music Edn. Avocations: yoga, swimming.

MONHEISER, CHERYL ANN, retired elementary school educator; b. Trinidad, Colo., Sept. 16, 1945; m. Kenneth Monheiser, June 8, 1969; children: Matthew, David, Mary. BA, U. No. Colo., Greeley, 1967. Cert. tchr. Colo. English tchr. North Junior High, Colorado Springs, 1967—74; title I math tchr. Sterling (Colo.) Mid. Sch., 1989—2006; ret., 2006. Pres. South Platte Edn. Assn., Sterling, 2000—04. Recipient Outstanding Educator award, Dist. Com., 2003. Mem.: Colo. Edn. Assn.

MONIA, JOAN, retired management consultant; d. James Anthony and Anne Linden McCaffrey; m. Charles Anthony Monia, Dec. 30, 1961; 1 child, Clare Ann Woodman. BA, Ohio Dominican U., 1960. Info. specialist Battelle Meml. Inst., Columbus, Ohio, 1960-62; project leader Douglas Aircraft Corp., Huntington Beach, Calif., 1962-64; programmer analyst McDonnell Aircraft Corp., St. Louis, 1965-66; project mgr. Sanders Assocs., Nashua, N.H., 1968-70; database adminstrn. project leader Mass. Blue Cross, Boston, 1970-74; data strategist Factory Mut. Engring. Corp., Norwood, Mass., 1974-78; mgr. data resource planning Digital Equipment Corp., Maynard, Mass., 1978-84; sr. mem. tech. staff GTE Govt. Systems Corp., Needham, Mass., 1984-91; prin. DMR Group, Inc., Waltham, Mass., 1991-96; owner, mgr. Info-Driven Enterprise Structures, Marlborough, Mass., 1997, San Jose, Calif., 1998—2002; ret., 2002. Recipient Sci. medal, Bausch & Lomb, 1956. Avocation: painting. Home: 7553 Morevern Cir San Jose CA 95135-2106

MONICH, MARYLOU, music educator; b. Pitts., Sept. 20, 1981; d. Andrew Thomas and Barbara Hale Monich; m. Todd Alan Bushyager, July 1, 2006. BS in Music Edn., Slippery Rock U., Pa., 2003; postgrad., Carlow U., Pitts., 2005—. Asst. band dir. Sto-Rox HS, McKees Rocks, Pa., 2002—03; chorus tchr., asst. band dir. Perry Tradicional Acad., Pitts., 2004—. Saxophone tchr. Mays Music Shoppe, Butler, Pa., 2001—; dir. All City Elem. Band, Pitts. Pub. Schs., 2005—. Keyboard grantee, Pitts. Pub. Schs. and Carnegie Mellon U., 2006. Mem.: Pa. Music Educators Assn. Democrat. Roman Catholic. Home: 61 N Duane Ave Pittsburgh PA 15205

MONIHAN, MARY ELIZABETH, lawyer; b. Cleve., Mar. 22, 1957; d. Michael Reilley and Donna (Warner) Monihan. BS in Econs., John Carroll U., 1979; JD, Cleve. State U., 1984. Bar: Ohio 1984, U.S. Dist. Ct. (no. dist.) Ohio 1985, U.S. Supreme Ct. 1989. Atty. in office of counsel Ameritrust Co. Nat. Assn., Cleve., 1984-85; assoc. Jones, Day, Reavis & Pogue, Cleve., 1985-89, Squire, Sanders & Dempsey, Cleve., 1989-95; ptnr. Spieth, Bell, McCurdy & Newell, Co., L.P.A., Cleve., 1995—. Pres. Estate Planning Coun. Cleve., 1994-95. Pres., vol. Coun. Cleve. Orch., 1998-2001; trustee Assn. Major Symphony Orch. Vols., 1997-99; trustee Women's Com. of the Cleveland Orch., 2000-2003, Cath. Charities, 2003—. Mem.: ABA, Cleve. Cath. Lawyers Guild (exec. bd. 2001—04), Cleve. Bar Assn., Ohio Bar Assn., Am. Coll. Trust and Estate Counsel, Jr. Com. Cleve. Orch. (pres. 1997—99). Office: Spieth Bell McCurdy & Newell Co LPA 925 Euclid Ave Ste 2000 Cleveland OH 44115-1407 Office Phone: 216-696-4700. E-mail: memonihan@spiethbell.com.

MONK, DEBRA, actress; b. Middletown, Ohio, Feb. 27, 1949; Grad., Frostburg State U. Stage appearances include (Broadway) Ah, Wilderness!, Steel Pier Company, Nick & Nora, Prelude to a Kiss, Pump Boys and Dinettes (also co-author), Redwood Curtain (Tony award featured actress in play 1993), Picnic (Tony nomination featured actress 1994), (theatre) Death Defying Acts, 3 Hotels (Helen Hayes award leading actress 1994), Assassins, Oil City Symphony (co-author, Drama Desk award Best Ensemble 1988), Laughing Wild, 2005, Chicago, 2005, Curtains, 2006; TV appearances include Women & Wallace, 1990, Loving, 1994, Redwood Curtain, 1995, Ellen Foster, 1997, NYPD Blue, 1998-2001 (Emmy award for Outstanding Guest Acress in a Drama Series 1999), The Music Man, 2003, Eloise at the Plaza, 2003, Eloise at Christmastime, 2003, Show People, 2006; films include: Prelude to a Kiss, 1992, For Love or Money, 1993, Fearless, 1993, Quiz Show, 1993, Reckless, 1995, Bridges of Madison County, 1995, Jeffrey, 1995, First Wives Club, 1996, Bed of Roses, 1996, Mrs. Winterbourne, 1996, Substance of Fire, 1996, Devil's Advocate, 1997, Extreme Measures, 1996, In and Out, 1997, Bulworth, 1998, Center Stage, 2000, Briar Patch, 2003, Milwaukee, Minnesota, 2003, Palindromes, 2004, Dark Water, 2005. Office: Gage Group care Steve Unger 315 W 57th St Ste 4H New York NY 10019-3158*

MONK, DIANA CHARLA, small business owner; b. Visalia, Calif., Feb. 25, 1927; d. Charles Edward and Viola Genevieve (Shea) Williams; m. James Alfred Monk, Aug. 11, 1951; children: Kiloran, Sydney, Geoffrey, Anne, Eric. Student, U. Pacific, 1946-47, Sacramento Coll., 1947-48, Calif. Coll. Fine Arts, San Francisco, 1948-51, Calif. Coll. Arts & Crafts, Oakland, 1972. Art tchr. Mt. Diablo Sch. Dist., Concord, Calif., 1958-63; pvt. art tchr. Lafayette, Calif., 1963-70; gallery dir. Jason Aver Gallery, San Francisco, 1970-72; owner, mgr. Monk & Lee Assocs., Lafayette, 1973-80; stable owner, mgr. Longacre Tng. Stables, Santa Rosa, Calif., 1989—. One-person shows include John F. Kennedy U., Orinda, Calif., Civic Arts Gallery, Walnut Creek, Calif., Vallery Art Gallery, Walnut Creek, Sea Ranch Gallery, Gualala, Calif., Jason Aver Gallery, San Francisco; exhibited in group shows at Oakland (Calif.) Art Mus., Crocker Nat. Art Gallery, Sacramento, Le Salon des Nations, Paris. Chair bd. dirs. Walnut Creek (Calif.) Civic Arts, 1972-74, advisor to dir., 1968-72; exhibit chmn. Valley Art Gallery, Walnut Creek, 1977-78; juror Women's Art Show, Walnut Creek, 1970, Oakland Calif. Art. Home and Office: Longacre Tng Stables 1702 Willowside Rd Santa Rosa CA 95401-3922 Office Phone: 707-544-7030. Personal E-mail: longacrestables@msn.com.

MONK, MEREDITH JANE, artistic director, composer, choreographer, filmmaker; b. NYC, Nov. 20, 1942; d. Theodore G. and Audrey Lois (Zellman) Monk. BA, Sarah Lawrence Coll., 1964; ArtsD (hon.), Bard Coll., 1988, U. of the Arts, 1989, Juilliard Sch. Music, 1997, San Francisco Art Inst., 1998, Boston Conservatory, 2001, Bennington Coll., 2002, Cornish Coll. Arts, 2002. Artistic dir., founder Ho. Found. Arts, N.Y.C., 1968—. Bd. dirs. Am. Music Ctr., The Kitchen. Prin. works include 16 Millimeter Earrings, 1966, Vessel, 1971, Quarry, 1976, Recent Ruins, 1979, Turtle Dreams, 1983, The Games, 1983, Book of Days, 1988, Facing North, 1990, Atlas, 1991, Three Heavens and Hells, 1992, Volcano Songs, 1994, American Archeology, 1994, The Politics of Quiet, 1996, Magic Frequencies, 1998, Mercy, 2001, Possible Sky, 2003, Impermanence, 2004, Stringsongs, 2005, exhibitions include Libr. of Performing Arts, Lincoln Ctr., 1996, Walker Art Ctr., Mpls., 1998, Whitney Mus. Art, 2002, Exit Art, 2002. Recipient Obie award, Village Voice, 1972, 1976, 1985, Creative Arts award, Brandeis U., 1974, Villager award, 1980, 1983, Deutches Kritiker preis, 1981, 1986, Bessie award, 1985, Nat. Music Theatre award, 1986, Dance Mag. award, 1993, John D. and Catherine T. MacArthur award, 1995, Sarah Lawrence Disting. Alumna award, 1996, Samuel Scripps award, 1996, Sigma Phi Omega award, 1987; fellow Guggenheim, 1972, 1982, Norton Stevens, 1993—94, MacDowell Colony. Fellow: Am. Acad. Arts and Scis.; mem.: ASCAP (award 1980—2000, Concert Music award 2005, Bessie award 2005). Office: House Found for Arts 306 W 38th St Ste 401 New York NY 10018

MONK, MICHELLE L., secondary school educator; b. Peoria, Ill., Jan. 25, 1975; m. Troy Monk, Nov. 11, 2000; 1 child, Brady. BS in Biology Edn., Ill. State U., Normal, 1998; MA in Edn., St. Xavier U., 2004. Cert. secondary sci. tchr. Ill. Sci. tchr. Hall HS, Spring Valley, Ill., 1998—2000; biology tchr. Tremont Cmty. Sch. Dist., Ill., 2000—, coach dance team, 2002—06, coach boys track team, 2000—02. Mem.: Ill. Sci. Tchrs. Assn. Office: Tremont Cmty Sch Dist 400 W Pearl Tremont IL 61568 Office Phone: 309-925-3823. Personal E-mail: mmonk12@hotmail.com. Business E-Mail: mmonk@roe53.k12.il.us.

MONK, SHARON ANNE, special education educator; b. Boulder City, Nev., Dec. 9, 1948; d. Earl Robert Oxtoby and Katherine Francis Brazil; m. Michael Arthur Monk, July 20, 1968; children: Robert Lee, John Patrick, James Michael. BA with spl. distinction, U. So. Colo., 1979; MA in Spl. Edn. summa cum laude, Azusa Pacific U., Calif., 2004. Cert. elem. sch. tchr. Colo., elem. sch. tchr. regular edn. Calif., regular edn. K-12, early childhood tchr. Calif., No Child Left Behind Act highly qualified tchr. cert. Calif., cert. cross-cultural and academic devel. Calif. Instrnl. asst. Harrison Sch. Dist., Colorado Springs, Colo., 1977—78; preschool tchr. YMCA/La Petite Acad., Sacramento, 1987—89; children's after-sch. tchr. San Juan Unified Sch. Dist., Carmichael, Calif., 1989—94; early intervention tchr. V.I.P.-Tots Presch., Hemet, Calif., 2002—03; primary spl. edn. tchr. Perris (Calif.) Elem. Sch. Dist., 2003—. Profl., parent advocate Parent Helping Parents, Sacramento, 1992—94, Parents of Children with Disabilities, Sacramento, 1992—94. Apple grantee, Calif. Commn. on Tchr. Credentialing, 2002, 2004, 2005, 2006. Mem.: NEA, Calif. Edn. Assn., Coun. on Exceptional Children, Pi Lambda Theta. Avocations: travel, writing, music, research, reading. Office: 250 'D' S Lyon Ave PMB 212 Hemet CA 92543

MONK, SUSAN MARIE, pediatrician, educator; b. York, Pa., May 7, 1945; d. John Spotz and Mary Elizabeth (Shelly) M.; m. Jaime Pacheco, June 5, 1971; children: Benjamin Joaquin, Maria Cristina. AB, Colby Coll., 1967; MD, Jefferson Med. Coll., 1971. Diplomate Am. Bd. Pediatrics. Pediatrician Children's Med. Ctr., Dayton, Ohio, 1975—; asst. clin. prof. pediat. Wright State U., Dayton, 1976—83, assoc. clin. prof. pediat., 1983—2000, asst. prof. pediatrics, 2000—. Mem. bd. dirs. Children's Med. Ctr., Dayton, 1991-96, chief-of-staff, 1992-94. Mem. Am. Acad. Pediatrics, We. Ohio Pediatric Soc., Pediatric Ambulatory Care Soc. Avocations: reading, gardening, travel, movies, theater. Office: Childrens Health Clinic 730 C Valley St Dayton OH 45404-1845 Office Phone: 937-641-5355.

MONK KIDD, SUE, writer; b. 1949; m. Sandy Monk Kidd; 2 children. BS in Nursing, Tex. Christian U., Fort Worth, 1970; studied writing, Emory Univ., Atlanta. Nurse St. Joseph's Hosp., Fort Worth, Tex., Med.Coll. Ga. Contbg. editor: Guideposts; author: God's Joyful Surprise, 1988, When the Heart Waits: Spiritual Direction for Life's Sacred Questions, 1990, The Dance of the Dissident Daughter: A Woman's Journey from Christian Tradition to the Sacred Feminine, 1996, The Secret Life of Bees, 2002 (SEBA Book of Yr. award, 2003, Publishers Weekly Bestseller list, 2003, 2004), The Mermaid

Chair, 2005 (Publishers Weekly Bestseller list, 2005, Quills award for gen. fiction, 2005); contbr. essays to mags. Recipient Katherine Anne Porter Second prize in fiction, Nimrod/Hardman Awards, 1993, S.C. Fiction Projectaward, S.C. Arts Commn., 1993, 1995, 1997, Isak Dineson Creative Non-Fiction award, 1994, Literal Latte Creative Non-Fiction Third prize, 1999, Bread Loaf scholar, Bread Loaf Writers Conf., 1995; fellow, S.C. Arts Commn., 1993—94, S.C. Acad. Authors, 1994, 1996. Office: c/o Carolyn Coleburn Viking Penguin 375 Hudson St New York NY 10014

MONROE, ERIN, psychiatric nurse practitioner; b. Topeka, Kans., Oct. 10, 1958; d. James Arthur and Virginia Marie Monroe. BA Psychology/Sociology magna cum laude, Bethany Coll., 1981; BSN magna cum laude, Washburn U., 1988; MSN summa cum laude, U. Kans., 1997. RN, Kans., Ohio; cert. addictions nurse, psychiatry/mental health nurse; cert. advanced nurse practitioner; cert. group psychotherapist; cert. child psychotherapist. Lic. mental health technician Topeka State Hosp., 1982-87; staff psychiat. nurse Menninger's, Topeka, 1988-98, advanced RN practitioner case mgr., 1998-99, primary clinician, 1999-2001, mem. quality assurance investigative com., 1999, Stormont-Vail Regional Health Ctr., Topeka, 2001—02; advanced practice nurse Cin. Children's Hosp. Med. Ctr., 2002—. Contbr. articles to profl. jours. Town rep. McPherson (Kans.) County Family Life Edn. Com., 1979. Mem. ANA, Am. Psychiat. Nurses Assn., Ohio Assn. Advanced Practice Nurses, Kans. State Nurses Assn., Psi Chi (pres., sec. 1979-81), Phi Kappa Phi, Sigma Theta Tau (Eta and Delta chpts.), Beta Tau Sigma. Democrat. Avocations: reading, films, psychoanalysis, art, walking. Office: Cincinnati Children's Hosp Med Ctr 3333 Burnet Cincinnati OH 45229 Home: 3779 Vineyard Woods Dr Cincinnati OH 45255-4699 Office Phone: 513-636-1007. Personal E-mail: emonroe02@yahoo.com.

MONROE, EVELYN JONES, retired librarian; d. Freeman B. Jones Sr. and Emma Bush Jones; m. Ralph B. Benbow (div.); 1 child, Cheryl Denise; m. Robert Aaron Monroe, June 6, 1966. BS, Ala. State Coll., Montgomery, 1955; MS in Libr. and Info. Scis., U. Wis., Madison, 1964. Cert. life and health ins. agt. Va., 1995. Tchr., libr. Mobile County Sch. Bd., Mobile, Ala., 1955—66; sch. libr. Norfolk Pub. Sch. Sys., Va., 1966—67; adminstrv. libr. FCDSSA, Virginia Beach, Va., 1967—84; tech. libr. Virginia Beach, 1984—94; benefit coord. Benefit Assn., Virginia Beach, 1995—96; asst. instr. Donovan Agy., Virginia Beach, 1996—97; asst. registrar Portsmouth, Va., 1999—2000. Chmn., tng. coord. Coun. Navy Sci. and Tech. Libraries, Dept. Navy, 1987—92; counselor, coord. FCDSSA, Virginia Beach, 1976—86; supr. tech. writers, editors Computer Program Documentation for Delivery to Ship to Shore Activities, 1984—94. Chmn. bd. trustees Hist. Third Bapt. Ch., Portsmouth, Va., 2003—. Recipient award for excellence, NAVSEA EEO, 1984. Mem.: Am. Contract Bridge League, Am. Bridge Assn. (club point coord. 1987—2006), Delta Sigma Theta. Democrat. Avocation: bridge. Home: 37 Lantern Way Portsmouth VA 23703 E-mail: monroeejn@aol.com.

MONROE, JANE D., federal agency administrator; Probation officer; police officer; spl. agt. FBI, Abuquerque, 1985, Tampa, Fla., Washington; spl. agt. criminal divsn. FBI Hdqs., Washington; spl. agt. behavioral sci. unit FBI Acad., Quantico, Va.; supr. white collar crime and pub. corruption squad FBI, San Diego, 1995, coord. hostage negotiation and evidence response teams, 1995—99, asst. spl. agt. in charge Denver, 1999, spl. agt. in charge L.A., 2002, asst. dir. cyber divsn. Washington, 2002—. Office: Fed Bur Investigation J Edgar Hoover Bldg 935 Penn Ave NW Washington DC 20535-0001

MONROE, JUDITH A., state agency administrator, public health service officer; married; 3 children. B, Ea. Ky. Univ., 1975; MD, Univ. Md., 1983. Residency Univ. Cincinnati, 1983—86; physician Nat. Health Svc. Corps, Morgan County, Tenn., 1986—90; fellowship Ea. Tenn. State Univ., 1990; dir. clinics Dept. Family Med., Ind. Univ., 1990—92; dir. primary care ctr. & family med. residency prog. St. Vincent Hosp. & Health Svc., Indpls., 1992—2005; fellowship Univ. Wis., 1993; commr. Ind. Dept. Health, Indpls., 2005—. Office: Dept Health 2 N Meridian St Indianapolis IN 46204*

MONROE, KATHERINE DIANE OSBORNE, secondary school educator; b. Williamson, W.Va., July 2, 1947; d. Bill and Carrie Lorraine (Adkins) Osborne; m. B. Ed Monroe Jr. BS in Edn., Concord Coll., 1969; MEd in Guidance/Counseling, U. Del., 1976; MEd in Adminstrn., Old Dominion U., 1992. Cert. social sci. tchr., guidance counselor and adminstr. Tchr. Ctrl. Mid. Sch., Dover, Del., 1969-78, Princess Ann H.S., Virginia Beach, Va., 1978-81, First Colonial H.S., Virginia Beach, Va., 1981-82, Green Run H.S., Virginia Beach, Va., 1982-89, Salem H.S., Virginia Beach, Va., 1989—2003; ret., 2003. Recipient Excellence in Tchg. Constition, John Marshall Found., Richmond, Va., 1991. Mem. NEA, Va. Edn. Assn., Virginia Beach Edn. Assn., Nat. Coun. Social Studies, Va. Coun. Social Studies (Tidwater region coord. 1979-80). Avocations: reading, cooking, crafts. Home: 1400 Franklin Dr Virginia Beach VA 23454-1532 Personal E-mail: dmonroe@cox.net.

MONROE, MELROSE, retired bank executive; b. Flowery Branch, Ga., Apr. 13, 1919; d. Willis Jeptha and Leila Adell Cash; m. Lynn Austin, June 14, 1942. AB in Edn., Ga. State U., 1968. Negotiator Trust Co. Bank, Atlanta, 1962-89, ret., 1989. Mem. Nat. Women's C. of C. (pres. 1987-88), Atlanta Women's C. of C. (dir. 1965-66, pres. Fidelis SS class 1962-63), Nat. Am. Legion Aux. (so. divsn. chmn. aux. Americanism 1995-96, so. divsn. chmn. aux. emergency fund 1996-97, cmty. svc. com.), Am. Legion Aux. (pres. 5th dist. 1986-87, Ga. state chaplain 1989-90, state historian 1991-92, state 2d v.p. 1992-93, 1st v.p. 1993-94, pres. 1994-95, Americanism chmn. so. divsn. 1995-95, chmn. emergency fund 1996-97, mem. cmty. svc. com. 1997-98, nat. historian 1999-00, v. chmn. nat. poppy com. 2000-01), Order Ea. Star (worthy matron 1951-52). Democrat. Home and Office: 6250 Spout Springs Rd Flowery Branch GA 30542-5031

MONROE, NANCY L., secondary school educator; b. Charleston, W.Va., July 25, 1944; d. James Roy, Sr. and Lee (White) Monroe. BA, Bethany Coll., W.Va., 1966; MA, Northwestern State U., Natchitoches, La., 1974; postgrad., Tex. Christian U., Ft. Worth, 1974. Cert. tchr. Tchr. Allagheny County HS, Covington, Va., Nolan HS, Ft. Worth, Jones St. Jr. High, Alexandria, La., Bolton HS, Alexandria. Named State English Tchr. of Yr., La. Coun. Tchrs. English, 2000. Mem.: La. Assn. Acad. Competition (v.p. 2000—). Democrat. Home: 71 Carolina Dr Boyce LA 71409

MONROE, SANDRA ELAINE, retired secondary art educator, minister; b. Three Rivers, Mich., Apr. 28, 1941; d. Tommee and Margaret (Hoopingarner) Hughes; m. Eugene F. Monroe, Sept. 1, 1962; children: Lisa Monroe Hamilton, Dawn Monroe Walters. BS, Ctrl. Mich. U., 1963; MA, We. Mich. U., 1974; EdS, U. Ga., 1991; MDiv, Columbia Theol. Sem., 2001. Cert. art tchr., Ga. Art tchr. Farwell (Mich.) Area Schs., 1963-66; tchr. art and chemistry Bronson (Mich.) Pub. Schs., 1966-67; art tchr. Muscogee County Sch. Dist., Columbus, Ga., 1967-68, tchr. sci., 1969-70; counselor, art tchr. Deckerville (Mich.) Community Schs., 1974-82; counselor Monroe County Bd. Edn., Forsyth, Ga., 1982-85; fin. planner Jefferson Pilot Fin. Svcs., Greensboro, N.C., 1985-87; art tchr. Twiggs County Bd. Edn., Jeffersonville, Ga., 1987-89, Thomaston/Upson Bd. Edn., Thomaston, Ga., 1989-98; mem. fine arts com., yearbook advisor Upson-Lee Middle Sch., Thomaston, 1990-98, mem. olympic com., 1991-98, mem. tech. com., 1994-98; pastor Cuthbert Presbyn Ch., 2001—04, Cuba Presbyn. Ch., 2001—04, Ft. Valley Presbyn. Ch., 2004—. Sch. Dist. Title IX coord. Deckerville Community Schs., 1978-82, career edn. coord., 1977-82. Contbg. editor Yearbook, 1996. Elder on session First Presbyn. Ch., Deckerville, 1980-82, Forsyth Presbyn. Ch., 1987-90, 94-98; Sunday sch. tchr., youth group advisor Presbyn. chs. in Allegan, Mich., Deckerville and Forsyth, 1973-93; co-pres. women's issues Ministry Group Columbia Theol. Sem., 1999-2000; moderator worship com. Flint River Presbyn., 2002-04, christian edn. com., 2002-05; mem. 5 County Leadership Bd., 2003-04; bd. dirs. Habitat for Humanity, 2003—. Mem. Randolph County Arts Coun. (sec. 2003-04), Randolph County Ministerial Assn. (sec. 2003-04), Early County Ministerial Assn. (sec. 2003-04). Democrat. Avocations: reading, photography, painting, travel, computers. Home: 1501 Knoxville St Fort Valley GA 31030-3590

MONROE, STEPHANIE JOHNSON, federal agency administrator; BA, U. Md., 1980; JD, U. of Baltimore, 1985. Legis. asst. to senator of NH US Senate; chief counsel, staff dir. Com. on Labor & Human Resources, Children, Families, Drugs & Alcoholism Subcommittee, US Senate, 1989—2001; chief counsel Com. on Health, Education, Labor & Pensions, US Senate, 2001—05; profl. staff mem. US Senate Budget Com.; asst. sec. Office for Civil Rights US Dept. Edn., Washington, 2005—. Head Start Quality & Expansion adv. com. US Dept. Health & Human Svcs., 1993—. Office: Office for Civil Rights US Dept Education Potomac Ctr 6th Fl 550 12th St SW Washington DC 20202-1100 Office Phone: 202-245-6700. Office Fax: 202-205-9862.*

MONROE, VIRGINIA MARIE, library media specialist, educator; b. Auburn, Kans., Mar. 18, 1933; d. Kenneth Merle and Hazel Marie (Widau) McConnell; m. James Arthur Monroe, Aug. 29, 1954; children: Erin Pegeen, Elissa Gay. AB in Art and History, Washburn U., 1955; MA in Edn., U. Kans., 1967; MLS, Emporia State U., 1976. Cert. libr. media specialist. Tchr. Highland Park HS, Topeka, 1955-58, Shawnee Heights HS, Tecumseh, Kans., 1964-71; libr. media specialist Jay Shideler Jr. High, Topeka, 1976-80, Shawnee Heights Jr. High, Tecumseh, 1980—97; ret. Com. worker Highland Park Meth. Ch., Topeka, 1986-91; charter mem. Our Saviors Luth. Ch., 1959-80, 1997-, bd. dirs., 2005—; mem. Topeka Jazz Workshop, 1961—; mem., supporter Topeka Civil Theater, 1960—. Mem. NEA, Kans. NEA, Shawnee Hts. Edn. Assn., Kans. Assn. Sch. Librs., Assn. Ednl. Communications and Tech., Non Nobis Solum, Beta Phi Mu, Pi Gamma Mu, Delta Phi Delta, Tau Delta. Avocations: reading, theater, concerts, sewing, gardening. Home: 2221 SW De Sousa Ct Topeka KS 66611-1621 Business E-Mail: vjmonroe@cox.net.

MONROY, GLADYS H., lawyer; b. NYC, Aug. 29, 1937; d. Henry B. and Leonora E. (Low) Chu; m. Jaime L. G. Monroy (div.); m. C. Lawrence Marks, Nov. 29, 1980. BA, Hunter Coll., N.Y., 1957; MS, NYU, 1968, PhD, 1973; JD, U. San Francisco, 1986. Bar: Calif.; registered U.S. Patent and Trademark office. Lab. technician Sloan-Kettering Inst., N.Y., 1957-60, Pub. Health Rsch. Inst., N.Y., 1960-63, rsch. asst., 1963-68; post doctoral fellow Albert Einstein Coll. Medicine, Bronx, NY, 1973-77; asst. prof. N.Y. Med. Coll., Valhalla, 1977-79; acquisitions editor Acad. Press, Inc., 1979-81; reseach assoc. U. Calif., San Francisco, 1981-83; atty. Irell & Manella, Menlo Park, Calif., 1986-90, ptnr., 1990-91, Morrison & Foerster, Palo Alto, Calif., 1991—, co-leader patent practice group. Co-chair I.P. Group, 1997—2002, Life Scis. Group, 1997—. Contbr. articles to profl. jours. Mem. bd. dirs. Project Hogar De Los Ninos, Menlo Park, Calif., 1987, 89, mem. Profl. Women's Network, San Francisco, 1988—90; mem. bd. dirs. Child Advocates of Santa Clara and San Mateo Counties, 1995—99. Mem. ABA, Am. Intellectual Property Law Assn., Am. Soc. Human Genetics, Am. Chem. Soc., Calif. Bar Assn., San Francisco Intellectual Property Law Assn. (chair patent com. 1992-94), Peninsula Patent Law Assn. (program chair 1993-94, treas. 1994-95, sec. 1995-96, v.p. 1996-97, pres. 1997—98), Am. Soc. Microbiology, Phi Alpha Delta. Avocations: swimming, bicycling, skiing, reading, opera. Office: Morrison & Foerster LLP 755 Page Mill Rd Palo Alto CA 94304-1018 Office Phone: 650-813-5600. Office Fax: 650-494-0792. Business E-Mail: gmonroy@mofo.com.

MONSEN, ELAINE RANKER, nutritionist, educator, editor; b. Oakland, Calif., June 6, 1935; d. Emery R. and Irene Stewart (Thorley) Ranker; m. Raymond Joseph Monsen, Jr., Jan. 21, 1959; 1 dau., Maren Ranker Grainger-Monsen. BA, U. Utah, 1956; MS (Mead Johnson grad. scholar), U. Calif., Berkeley, 1959, PhD (NSF fellow), 1961; postgrad. NSF sci. faculty fellow, Harvard U., 1968-69. Dietetic intern Mass. Gen. Hosp., Boston, 1956-57; asst. prof. nutrition, lectr. biochemistry Brigham Young U., Provo, Utah, 1960-63; mem. faculty U. Wash., 1963—, prof. nutrition, adj. prof. medicine, 1976-84, prof. nutrition and medicine, 1984—2004, prof. emeritus, 2004—, chmn. div. human nutrition, dietetics and foods, 1977-82, dir. grad. nutritional scis. program, 1994-99, mem. Council of Coll. Arts and Scis., 1974-78; chmn. Nutrition Studies Commn., 1969-83. Vis. scholar Stanford U., 1971-72; mem. sci. adv. com. food fortification Pan-Am. Health Orgn., São Paulo, Brazil, 1972; tng. grant coordinator NIH, 1976-97. Editor-in-chief Jour. Am. Dietetic Assn., 1983-2003; Editor Emeritus, Jour. Am. Dietetic Assn., 2003—; mem. editorial bd. Coun. Biology Editors, 1992-96; author rsch. papers on lipid metabolism, iron absorption. Bd. dirs. A Contemporary Theatre, Seattle, 1969-72; trustee, bd. dirs. Seattle Found., 1978-95, vice chmn., 1987-91, chmn., 1991-93; pres. Seattle bd. Santa Fe Chamber Music Festival, 1984-85; mem. Puget Sound Blood Ctr. Bd., 1996-99. Grantee Nutrition Found., 1965-68, Agrl. Rsch. Svc., 1969-84; recipient Disting. Alumnus award U. Utah, F. Fischer Meml. Nutrition Lectr. award, 1988, L.F. Cooper Meml. Lectr. award, 1991, L. Hatch Meml. Lectr. award, 1992, Goble Lectr. award Purdue U., 1997. Fellow: Am. Soc. Clin. Nutrition (sec. 1987—90), Am. Inst. Nutrition; mem.: Wash. Heart Assn. (nutrition coun. 1973—76), Am. Soc. Parenteral and Enteral Nutrition, Soc. Nutriton Edn., Am. Dietetic Assn. Office: U Wash PO Box 353410 Seattle WA 98195-3410

MONSON, DIANNE LYNN, literacy educator; b. Minot, ND, Nov. 24, 1934; d. Albert Rachie and Iona Cordelia (Kirk) M. BS, U. Minn., 1956, MA, 1962, PhD, 1966. Tchr. Rochester (Minn.) Pub. Schs., 1956-59, U.S. Dept. Def., Schweinfurt, West Germany, 1959-61, St. Louis Park (Minn.) Schs., 1961-62; instr. U. Minn., Mpls., 1962-66; prof. U. Wash., Seattle, 1966-82; prof. literacy edn. U. Minn., Mpls., 1982-97, prof. emeritus, 1997—. Chmn. curriculum and instrn. U. Minn., 1986—89. Co-author: Scott Foresman Reading, 2000, New Horizons in the Language Arts, 1972, Children and Books, 6th edit., 1981, Experiencing Children's Literature, 1984, Language Arts: Teaching and Learning Effective Use of Language, 1988, Reading Together: Helping Children Get A Good Start With Reading, 1991; assoc. editor: Dictionary of Literacy, 1995; mem. editl. bd. Five Owls Mag., 1997-2005. Bd. adv. Kerlan Collection, 2001—04, Minn. Humanities Commn., 2004—05; bd. dirs. Friends of Kerlan Collection, 2000—04. Recipient Outstanding Educator award U. Minn. Alumni Assn., 1983, Alumni Faculty award U. Minn. Alumni Assn., 1991. Fellow Nat. Conf. Rsch. in English (pres. 1990-91); mem. ALA, Nat. Coun. Tchrs. English (exec. com. 1979-81), Internat. Reading Assn. (dir. 1980-83, Arbuthnot award 1993, Reading Hall of Fame 1997), U.S. Bd. Books for Young People (pres. 1988-90). Lutheran. Home: 515 S Lexington Pkwy # 604 Saint Paul MN 55116 Business E-Mail: monso001@tc.umn.edu.

MONTAGUE, DEBORAH MARIE, elementary school educator, music educator, consultant; b. Cin., July 2, 1953; d. Charles Jay and June Marie Henry; m. Steven A. Montague, Aug. 17, 1979; children: Sarah, Benjamin. BA in Music Edn., Ctrl. Wash. U., 1974; MA in Music Edn., U. Wash. Music educator grades 3-6 Northshore Sch. Dist., Bothell, Wash., 1974—79; music educator grades 5-9 Sumner (Wash.) Sch. Dist., 1979—88; freelance music educator/cons. Alta Loma, Calif., 1988—90; music educator grades 5-9 Northshore Sch. Dist., Kenmore, Wash., 1990—. Dist. honor band chair Northshore Sch. Dist., Bothell, 1990—; member-at-large Cascade Youth Orch. Symphony, Bothell, 1999—; performer N.W. Music Educator's Conf., 1993, 2001, 03, Nat. Music Educator's Conf., 2002. Mem.: NEA, West Ctrl. Music Educators Nat. Conf. (band rep. 1984—85), Music Educators Nat. Conf. Lutheran. Office: Kenmore Jr High 20323 66 Ave NE Kenmore WA 98028

MONTALVO, EILEEN, communications executive; b. 1973; Exec. v.p., Sales and Mktg. GolTV, 2005—06; dir., Mktg. and Comm. Discovery Networks US Hispanic Grp., 2006—. Named one of 40 Executives Under 40, Multichannel News, 2006. Office: Discovery Communications Inc 1 Discovery Pl Silver Spring MD 20910*

MONTAÑEZ, CARMEN LYDIA, Spanish language educator, literature researcher, lawyer; b. Santurce, P.R., Dec. 17, 1944; d. Pablo and Amalia (Falcón) Cotto; m. Carlos Montañez, Nov. 14, 1965; children: Carmen Aracelis, Carlos, Juan-Carlos. BA magna cum laude, U. Turabo, P.R., 1979; JD, Interam. U., P.R., 1983; MA in Spanish Lit., U. Louisville, 1987; PhD, U. Ky., 1995. Assoc. instr. Ind. U., Bloomington, 1987; lectr. U. Louisville, 1985-89; assoc. instr. Ind. U. S.E., New Albany, 1987-89; mem. adj. faculty Troy U., Montgomery, Ala., 1990-91; grad. teaching asst. U. Ky., Lexington, 1991-93; vis. asst. prof. U. Louisville, 1993-94; asst. prof. Ind. State U., Terre Haute, 1994—. Author: El personaje femenino en la cuentística de varias escritoras puertorriquenas: Subversion y creatividad, 1998, De El Fanguito a la loza, 2001, Pelo Bueno, Pelo Malo, 2006; co-editor: Annal del Teatro Puertorriqueño del Ateneo, 1997—99; contbr. short story to Letras femeninas, essays to profl. jours. Mem. MLA (exec. com. discussion group on Puerto Rican lit. and culture 1994—), Am. Assn. Tchrs. Spanish and Portuguese, SIGSA, Asociació de Literature Femenina Hispánica, Instituto Hispanoamericano, Sigma Delta Pi, Phi Kappa Phi. Mem. MLA (exec. com. discussion group on Puerto Rican lit. and culture 1994—), Am. Assn. Tchrs. Spanish and Portuguese, SIGSA, Sigma Delta Pi, Phi Kappa Phi. Office: Ind State Univ Dept Foreign Langs And Lit Terre Haute IN 47809-0001

MONTANEZ-JOHNER, NANCY, federal agency administrator; With profl. ptnrs. program region III behavioral health svcs. Health and Human Svcs. Sys. State of Nebr., 1995—99, adminstr. S.W. svc. area, 1999—2001, CEO We. svc. area, 2001—04, dir., 2004—05; under sec. agr. food, nutrition & consumer services USDA, Washington, 2006—. Bd. dirs. Commodity Credit Corp. USDA, 2006—. Office: USDA Adminstrn Bldg 1400 Independence Ave SW Rm 240-E Washington DC 20250 Office Phone: 202-720-7711. Office Fax: 202-690-3100.*

MONTAÑO, TIFFANY DUNHILL, aerospace production control specialist; d. Richard Shirley and Bonnie Beatrice Finch; m. Popa Dave Christopher Montaño, Dec. 6, 1997. Cert. programmer Computer Learning Ctr., 1991. Prodn. control supr. Northrop Corp., Pico Rivera, Calif., 1975—89; sr. adminstrv. coord. Space Systems Loral, Palo Alto, Calif., 1991—99. Activist, founder Native Am. Sovereignty Recognition and Cultural Pride Movement, Berry Creek, Calif., 2004—05. Mem.: Chico Art Soc. (assoc.). Avocations: art, poetry. Home: 11997 Oro Quincy Hwy Berry Creek CA 95916-9780 Office Phone: 530-859-4667. Personal E-mail: tiffany@tiffanysart.com.

MONTAVON, VICTORIA A., university librarian, dean; b. Cin. m. James M. Myers; 3 children. Libr. Rider U., Temple U., Lindenwood Coll., Carlow Coll., Notre Dame Coll., Ohio; univ. libr. St. Joseph 's U. Libr., Phila., 1990—96, Wright State U., 1996—2001; dean, univ. libr. U. Cin., 2001—. Recipient Pres. Quality Svc. Award, 2003. Office: U Cin U Librs PO Box 210033 Cincinnati OH 45221-0033 E-mail: Victoria.Montavon@uc.edu.*

MONTE, BONNIE J., performing arts company executive, director, educator; b. Stamford, Conn., Nov. 27, 1954; d. Eugene N. and Ruth M. (Thompson) M. BA, Bethany Coll., 1976; diploma, Hartman Conservatory, Stamford, 1978; LHD (hon.), Drew U., 2005. Assoc. artistic dir. Williamstown (Mass.) Theatre Festival, 1981-89; casting dir. Manhattan Theatre Club, N.Y.C., 1989-90; artistic dir. The Shakespeare Theatre of NJ, Madison, 1990—. Mem. faculty Drew U., 1991-96; guest artist-in-residence U. Notre Dame, The New Sch.-Eugene Lang. Coll., U. S.C. Recipient Nat. Soc. of Arts and Letters award, N.J., 1997, Alumni Achievement award for arts mgmt. Bethany Coll., 1999; grantee Lotte Crabtree Found., Boston, 1977. Democrat. Avocations: bicycling, archery, writing, travel. Office: Shakespeare Theatre NJ 36 Madison Ave Madison NJ 07940-1434

MONTEALEGRE, EVA DENISE, artist, writer; b. St. Louis, Mo., May 19, 1957; d. Ronald John Schroder and Patricia Ann Wilson; m. David Anthony Carmichael, July 7, 1992; m. Forest Steven Whitaker (div.). Cert. graphic design West Valley Occupl. Ctr. Prodr., writer and researcher Meta-4 Prodns., Santa Monica, Calif., 1986—87; v.p. Long Beach Arts Gallery, Calif., 2005—. Founding mem. Waterfront Stage, Santa Monica, Calif.; freelance artist. Prodr.: (documentaries) The Shaping of America series, (pub. svc. announcements) American History 1492- (U.S. troops voted best series); prin. works include Lady Starskull Ponders the Cosmos, 2004 (3d prize, 2004), exhibitions include MJ Higgins Gallery, Topanga Studio Tour, Love Bldg. Ventura County Artwalk, World Trade Ctr., Long Beach, Calif., 2005, Canoga Park Youth Exhibit, 2005, Santa Barbara Art Pavilion, 2006; actor: Jump at the Sun, 2004 (Bay Area Critics award); editor: Techno-Noir, 2005. Steering com. and publicity chmn. Left Coast Crime Benefit, 2003. Mem.: Phi Theta Kappa. E-mail: evamontealegre@yahoo.com.

MONTEFERRANTE, JUDITH CATHERINE, cardiologist; b. N.Y., Jan. 27, 1949; d. Stanley and Monica (Vinckus) Sosaris; m. Ronald J. Monteferrante (div.); 1 child, Jason Paul (dec.); m. Roger E. Salisbury, Mar. 3, 1990. BS, Adelphi U., Garden City, 1970; MS, SUNY, Buffalo, 1973; MD, Mt. Sinai, N.Y.C., 1978. Diplomate Cert. Coun. Nuc. Cardiology. Attending N.Y. Med. Coll., Valhalla, NY, 1983—; pvt. practice Primary Care and Cardiovasc. Assocs., divsn. Cardiology Cons. Westchester, White Plains, NY, 1994—. Mem. bd. White Plains Med. Ctr., 1997—2000; spkr. on women and heart disease. Contbr. articles to profl. jours. Past trustee Coll. Mt. St. Vincent, N.Y.C. Fellow: ACP, Am. Heart Assn. (past. pres. 1996—98), Am. Coll. Cardiology (councilor N.Y. state chpt. 2003—); mem.: Am. Soc. Nuc. Cardiology, Salmagundi Club (N.Y.C.), Greenwich Art Soc., Newburyport Art Assn., Rockport Art Assn. Office: 15 N Broadway White Plains NY 10601-2225 Office Phone: 914-428-6000. Business E-Mail: monteferrante@ccwpc.com.

MONTEILA, SHARON CHRISTINE, dancer, educator, choreographer; BA in Dance, Butler U., Indpls., 1987; MFA in Dance, The Boston Conservatory, Mass., 1994. Dance instr. Bradford Coll., Mass., 1994—97; asst. adj. prof. dance Pine Manor, Chestnut Hill, Mass., 1998—. Instr. dance The Brook Sch., North Andover, Mass., 2004—06; instr. the hip hop workshop The Boston Conservatory, 2005; dance workshop leader Boston Children's Mus., 2004—, Milton Acad., Boston, 2004—; coord. choreography award Project Concern Youth Dance Co., Boston, 1997—98. Dancer Boston Dance Collective Young Audiences, 2000—, Boston Dance Co., 2002—; dir.: Pine Manor Coll. Dance Ensemble, 1997—2006; dancer (films) Dance By Design, Pub. Enemy Videos, choreographer jazz dance (Moses Project) Maly Baker Eddy Libr., 2000. Mem.: presentation Mary Acad. Alumni Assn., Boston Conservatory Alumni Assn. Office: Pine Manor Coll 400 Heath St Chestnut Hill MA 02467 Personal E-mail: hiphopballerina@yahoo.com.

MONTEILH, YVETTE MARIE, education educator; b. Ingelwood, Calif., Oct. 2, 1962; d. Stephen Lester and Mary (Metoyer) Bellow; m. Keith Andrew Monteilh, July 9, 1988; children: Desiree Stephanie, Aaron Andrew, Austin Joseph. BA, Calif. Stae U., Long Beach, 1986, MA, 1992. Cert. tchr. Tchr. L.A. Unified Sch. Dist., 1990—. Roman Catholic. E-mail: ymmo118@lausd.k12.ca.us.

MONTEIRO, LOIS ANN, nursing educator; b. Central Falls, R.I., Mar. 22, 1934; d. William Henry and Martha Mae (Leach) Hodgins; m. George Monteiro, Aug. 14, 1958 (div. Feb. 1992); children: Katherine, Stephen, Emily. RN, Roger Williams Hosp., Providence, 1954; BA, Brown U., k1958, PhD, 1970; MS, Boston U., 1960. Asst. prof. Boston U., 1960-65, Brown U., Providence, 1971-77, assoc. prof., 1978-82, prof., 1983—, chmn. dept., 1985—, assoc. dean medicine, 1991—. Vis. prof. U. Va., 1990, U. Miss., 2002; bd. dirs. Harvard Cmty. Health Plan, 1990-95, Harvard Pilgrim Health Care Plan, New Eng., 1995—. Author: Montoring Health Status, 1976, Cardiac Rehabilitation, 1980; contbr. articles to profl. jours. Mem. Commn. State of R.I., Providence, 1989—. NSF grantee, 1969, Robert W. Johnson Found. grantee, Princeton, N.J., 1983, NIH grantee, 1987; Bunting Inst. fellow, Cambridge, Mass., 1981, Congrl. fellow House Vets. Affairs Commn., 1998; recipient Am. Sociol. Assn. Spivack award, 1998. Mem. Am. Sociol. Assn., R.I. State Nurses Assn. (pres. 1974-76), Women in Medicine/Assn. Am. Med. Colls. Democrat. Presbyterian. Avocation: collecting books on nursing history. Office: Brown U Dept Med Sci PO Box G-a413 Providence RI 02912-0001 E-mail: lois_monteiro@brown.edu.

MONTEIRO, PATRICIA M., clinical social worker; BSW, Western New Eng. Coll., Springfield, Mass., 1982; MSW, R.I. Coll., 1988. Cert. HIV counselor. Sr. social worker Dept. Social Svcs., New Bedford, 1982-89, clin. supr. social workers Cape Cod and Islands, 1989-90, clin. supr. social workders Fall River, 1990-94; med. social worker Staff Builders, New Bedford, 1997-98; clin. social worker Greater New Bedford Cmty. Health Ctr., 1998—2003; self-employed ct. investigator, guardian ad litem juvenile and probate cts., Bristol County, Mass., 1994—2003; pvt. practice social worker, 2002—. Mem. Mass. Coun. on Aging, 1996—99, ad hoc com. responsible for sr. ctr., 1995, New Bedford Adolescent Task Force, 1988—89; apptd. legal guardian for elderly in need Bristol County Probate Ct., 2002—. Daisy leader Girl Scouts U.S., 2000—01, Brownie leader, 2001—02; co-pres. PTA com. Mass., 2003—; founder, co-leader Drama Club Ctr. Sch., Mattapoisett, 2002—. Recipient Pride in Performance Recognition award Commr. Mass. Dept. Social Svc., 1992. Mem. NASW, Portuguese-Am. Leadership Coun. U.S.A. Avocations: reading, dinner parties, gardening, aerobics, travel. Office: PO Box 5322 New Bedford MA 02742-5322

MONTEITH, TRACY R., music educator, lay worker; b. Colorado Springs, Colo., Oct. 26, 1966; d. Ron and Sherry Mills; m. Thomas I. Monteith, June 1, 1985; children: Micheil B., Jonathan J., Christopher T., Kaitlyn A. BA in Christian Counseling, Patriot U., Alamosa, Colo. Pvt. piano tchr., Colorado Springs, Colo., 1990—2005; tchr. music history James Irwin Charter Mid. Sch., 2005—06; music tchr. Banning Lewis Ranch Charter Acad., 2006—. Pianist Pleasant Valley Bapt. Ch., Colorado Springs, Colo., 2003—, founder and dir. women's ministries, 2003—. Avocations: photography, pets. Office Phone: 719-635-5811. Personal E-mail: kangarae66@aol.com.

MONTELEONE, PATRICIA L., dean; MD, St. Louis U., 1961; MBA, MHA. V.p. med. affairs Cardinal Glennon Children's Hosp., 1986—93; prof. pediatrics St. Louis U. Sch. Medicine, 1967—, dean, 1994—. Office: St Louis U Sch Medicine 1402 S Grand Blvd Saint Louis MO 63104-1004

MONTERO, LETICIA, social studies educator; b. Nogales, Mexico, June 10, 1979; d. Rosa Lopez and Enrique Montero. BA Edn., U. Ariz., Tucson, 2004. Tchr. social studies Sierra Mid. Sch., Tucson, 2004—. Youth dir. Santa Cruz Ch., Tucson, 1996—. Cmty. involvement (exhibitions) Enciende Una Luz (Recognition, 1999). Dir. Santa Cruz Ch., Tucson, 1999—2006. Home: 5890 S Springbrook Tucson AZ 85746 Office: Sierra Middle School 5801 S Del Moral Tucson AZ 85706

MONTERO, SYLVIA, pharmaceutical executive; b. PR; BA, Columbia U. Barnard Coll., 1972; MA, CUNY Queens Coll., 1976. HS tchr. Spanish and bilingual studies, NYC; prof. lit. Interamerican U., PR; with Pfizer Puerto Rico, 1978—82, Pfizer, Inc., NYC, 1982—, v.p. human resources Animal Health Grp., 1994, sr. v.p. human resources Global Rsch. and Devel., 2003, sr. v.p. human resources, 2005, head worldwide talent devel. and human resources, head human resources leadership team. Bd. mem. Grand St. Settlement. Named one of Top 50 Hispanic Bus. Women, Hispanic Bus. Mag., 2001, 80 Elite Women, 2002, 20 Corp. Elite in US, 2006; recipient Orgullo Latino award, 100 Hispanic Women orgn., 2005. Mem.: Hispanic Fedn. Office: Pfizer Inc 235 E 42nd St New York NY 10017*

MONTGOMERY, ANN D., federal judge, educator; b. Litchfield, Minn., May 9, 1949; m. Theodore Smetak; 2 children; 1 stepchild. BS, U. Kans., 1971; JD, U. Minn., 1974. Bar: Minn. 1974, US Dist. Ct. Minn., US Ct. Appeals (8th cir.), US Supreme Ct. Law clk. DC Ct. Appeals, Washington, 1974-75; asst. US atty. Dist. Minn., Mpls., 1976-83; mcpl. judge Hennepin County, 1983-85; judge Hennepin County Dist. Ct., 1985-94, US Magistrate Ct., 1994-96; federal judge US Dist. Ct., Mpls., 1996—. Adj. prof. U. Minn. Law Sch., Mpls., 1988—; steering com. mem., dir. criminal divsn. Minn. Jud. Coll., 1990-94. Recipient Trial Judge of Yr. award Am. Bd. Trial Advocates, 1996. Mem. FBA, Minn. Dist. Judges Assn., Minn. Bar Assn., Minn. Women Lawyers (Myra Bradwell award 2000), Hennepin County Bar Assn. (Professionalism award 1993), Eighth Cir. Dist. Judges Assn. (pres. 2003-04). Office: US Dist Ct 300 S 4th St Minneapolis MN 55415-1320 Fax: 612-664-5097. E-mail: admontgomery@mnd.uscourts.gov.

MONTGOMERY, BETTY ADAMS, elementary school educator; b. Lexington, Ky., Oct. 27, 1951; d. Ernest and Beulah Mae (Murphy) Adams; m. Joe Gordon Montgomery, May 23, 1970; children: Adam Joseph, Emily Ann. BS, Ea. Ky. U., 1972, MA, 1975. 1st grade tchr. Camp Dick Robinson, Lancaster, Ky., 1972-77; primary tchr. Lancaster Elem., 1977—. Tchr. rep. Site Based Decision Making Coun., Lancaster, 1993—; state math. adv. bd. rep. State Dept. Edn., Frankfort, Ky., 1992-95. Recipient Excellence in Tchg. award Campbellsville Coll., 1991, Presdl. award for excellence in tchg. math. and sci. NSF, 1994, Golden Apple Achiever award Ashland Oil, 1995, Ky. Col. award State of Ky., 1995. Mem. Delta Kappa Gamma (v.p., sec.). Republican. Methodist. Home: 159 Eastland Acres Lancaster KY 40444-9707 Office: Lancaster Elem 205 Lexington St Lancaster KY 40444-1130

MONTGOMERY, BETTY DEE, state auditor, former state attorney general, former state legislator; b. Apr. 3, 1948; BA, Bowling Green State U.; JD, Coll. Law U. Toledo, 1976. Former criminal clk. Lucas County Common Pleas Ct.; former asst. pros. atty. Wood County, Ohio, 1977—78, former pros. atty. Ohio, 1980—88, City of Perrysburg, Ohio, 1978—81; former mem. Ohio Senate, 1988—95; former atty. gen. State of Ohio, Columbus, 1994—2002, auditor, 2002—. Former mem. Econ. Devel. Tech. & Aerospace, Agr. & Ways & Means Com.; former vice-chmn. Judiciary Com. Mem. bd. dirs. Ohio Sch. Bd. Atty. Assn. Recipient Women of Achievement award, Toledo Women in Comms., 1984, Govt. Leaders Against Drunk Drivers, MADD, 1990, Senator of the Year, Ohio Hospice Assn., 1991, Disting. Svc. award, Ohio State Bar Assn., 1992, Ohio Women Hall of Fame award, 1996, Public Svc. award, Ohio Assn. of Big Brothers/Big Sisters, 1999, Advocacy award, Ohio Soc. Healthcare Consumer Advocacy, 1999, Child Adv. of the Year, Ohio Ct. Appointed Spl. Advs./Guardian Ad Litem Assn., 1999, Toledo YWCA Milestones award, Women in Govt., 2001, Presdl. award for Pro Bono Svc., The Ohio Legal Assistance Found., 2002, ABA Pro Bono award, to the Office of the Atty. Gen., 2002, Disting. Alumnus award, Bowling Green State Univ., 2003. Mem.: Ohio Prosecuting Atty. Assn. (mem. 1984), Legis. Com., Internat. Prosecutors Assn., Wood County Bar Assn., Alternative Edn. Adv. Com. (former chmn.), Wood County Child Abuse & Neglect Adv. Bd. (former vice-chmn., chmn.), Sexual Abuse Prevention Project, Wood County Sch. (mem. 1981—), Bowling Green C. of C. Republican. Office: Auditor of State 88 E Broad St 5th Fl Columbus OH 43215

MONTGOMERY, CAROLYN WILLIAMS, retired secondary school educator; b. Houston, Nov. 12, 1940; d. Paul Girard and Nina Jewell (Anderson) Williams; m. James M. Montgomery, Aug. 17, 1963 (div. 1970). BA, Baylor U., 1962. Tchr. China Spring (Tex.) Ind. Sch. Dist., 1964-65, Houston (Tex.) Ind. Sch. Dist., 1962—2005, ret., 2005. Actress, officer Theatre Suburbia, 1974—; actress Country Playhouse, 1976—, various dinner theaters, 1974-85. Baptist.

MONTGOMERY, CONSTANCE O., mathematics educator; d. William Allen and Myra Comer Oates; m. Wallace Montgomery, Aug. 2, 1969; children: Lane children: Alyson Rowland, Anna. M in Math. (hon.), U. Ala., Gadsden, 1982. Tchr. Jersey City (NJ) Bd. Edn., 1970—72, Charlotte-Mechlinburg Bd Edn., 1973—78; tchr. secondary math. Gadsden City Bd. Edn., 1990—. Home: 11431 Duck Springs Rd Attalla AL 35954 Office: Gadsden Mid Sch 612 Tracy St Gadsden AL 35901 E-mail: cmontgom@gcs.k12.al.us.

MONTGOMERY, DENISE KAREN, nurse; b. N.Y.C., Dec. 23, 1951; d. Thomas Cornell and Dorothy Marie (Castine) Simons; m. Timothy Bruce Montgomery, July 19, 1974 (div. Feb. 1981); m. Joseph Samuel Montgomery, Aug. 20, 1983. A in Nursing, San Jacinto Coll., 1971. RN, Tex. Charge nurse Aarons Womens Clinic, Houston, 1977; rsch. asst. dept. ob-gyn. Baylor Coll. Medicine, Houston, 1977-81, nursing supr., 1979-81, program coord. population control program, 1979-81; nurse Dr. Eric J. Haufrect, Houston, 1982-83; office mgr., supr. Dr. Samuel Law, Houston, 1983-84, Dr. J.S. Montgomery III, 1987—. Contbr. articles to profl. jours. Recipient Disting. Pub. Svc. award Am. Heart Assn., 1976; numerous rsch. grants. Mem. Nat. Assn. Coll. Ob-Gyn. Republican. Christian. Home: 8202 N Tahoe Dr Houston TX 77040-1256 Office Phone: 281-955-5330. E-mail: denmnt@houston.rr.com, denmnt@hotmail.com.

MONTGOMERY, DENISE LYNNE, librarian, researcher; b. Greenfield, Ind., Aug. 1, 1953; d. Herbert Walter and Virginia Lou Montgomery. AB, Sweet Briar Coll., 1975; MSLS, Fla. State U., 1981. Readers' svcs. libr. St. Leo Coll., St. Leo, Fla., 1983; assoc. prof., head of interlibr. loan Valdosta State U., Valdosta, Ga., 1984—. Sr. rsch. editor: The Yale Dictionary of Quotations, 2006, contbr.: Royal Visits and War Brides to Britain and the Americas: Culture, Politics and History, 2005; contbr. articles to profl. jours. including Library Trends. Mem.: ALA (fee-based svcs. com. 2001—03, svcs. to adults com. 2003—05, STARS edn. com. 2005—), Ga. Libr. Assn. (chmn. interlibrary loan round table 1992—93). Liberal. Unitarian Universalist. Office: Odum Libr Valdosta State U 1500 N Patterson St Valdosta GA 31698 Office Phone: 229-245-3747. Business E-Mail: dmontgom@valdosta.edu.

MONTGOMERY, JUNE C., musician, composer; b. Columbia, S.C., Dec. 12, 1931; d. Joseph Watts Conyers and Justina Wylding; m. Edwin Fleming Montgomery, Dec. 28, 1954; children: Edwin Fleming III, Joseph Watts, James Leighton. BA in Piano with honors, Fla. State U., 1954; BS, U. Fla., 1968. Pvt. piano tchr., Jasper, Fla., 1954—63, Lake City, Fla., 1975—93; music tchr. Orange Park (Fla.) Elem., 1968—74; composer, author Music Encounters, Lake City, 1984—89, David C. Glover Method CPP/Belwin, Miami, Fla., 1988—90, Alfred Pub. Co., Van Nuys, Calif., 1990—. Carillonneur Stephen Foster Meml., White Springs, Fla., 1954—. Author, composer: FUNdamental Musicianship Skills, 1994, Theory Through the Year, 1995, author, composer with M. Mier: Musical Concepts, 1997, author, composer with M. Hinson: Meet the Great Composers, 1995, author, composer: Meet the Great Composers Repertoire Books, 1997, Stories of the Great Composers, 2000, Piano Camp, 1999, Musical Fantasies, 2001, Stories of the Great Hymns, 2002. Named Outstanding Elem. Tchr. Am., Orange Park, 1973. Mem.: Music Tchrs. Nat. Assn., Am. Coll. Musicians, Delta Kappa Gamma. Democrat. Presbyterian. Avocations: crafts, gardening.

MONTGOMERY, KATHLEEN RAE, counselor; b. Bloomington, Ind., Aug. 15, 1950; d. Raymond Hershel and Helen Kathleen (Trent) Montgomery; m. Steven Myers, Oct. 2, 1970; children: Jason Paul, Lisa Dawn, Stephanie Kathleen. AS in Psychology, Vincennes U., 1970; BS in Social Svcs., Milligan Coll., 1974; MS in Counseling, Ind. U., 1992. Lic. school counselor, mental health counselor. Police dispatcher Ind. State Police, Bloomington, Ind., 1974-76; counselor Cookson Hills Christian Ministries, Kansas, Okla., 1976-78; social worker Health Svcs. Bur., Bloomington, 1982-88; tng. asst. The Associated Group, Indpls., 1990-91; ops. mgr. drug abuse prevention workshops Ind. U., Bloomington, 1991-92; outreach coord., counselor, testing coord. gender equity Ivy Tech. State Coll., Bloomington, 1992-99; counselor N. Putnam H.S., Roachdale, IN, 1999—. Counselor Upward Bound program, Vincennes, Ind., 1970; crisis counselor Matrix Lifeline, 1978-79; field instr. Ind. U. BSW program, Bloomington, 1983-88; support group leader Sherwood Oaks Christian Ch., 1991-92. Mem. adv. bd. Expectant Mother's Program, Bloomington, 1984-86, Parent's Group, Ellettsville, Ind., 1986-88, adv. bd. IMPACT, 1992-93; mem. retention com. Ivy Tech. Coll., 1993-98. Mem. AAUW, Ind. Coll. Counseling Assn., Ind. Counseling Assn., Ind. School Counselors Assn., Ind. Academic Advisors Network, Ind. Higher Edn. Assoc. for Disabiliities. Republican. Avocations: biking, hiking, crafts. Home: 627 Bayberry Ct W Bloomington IN 47401-4673

MONTGOMERY, LANI LYNN, art educator; b. Oceanside, NY, Sept. 24, 1950; d. Warren Andrew and Lucy Marie; m. Bruce Montgomery, Dec. 18, 1976; children: Colin, Kirstin, Kerrin. AA, Suffolk County C.C., NY, 1972; BA, Dowling Coll., Oakdale, NY, 1976; MA, Montclaire State U., NJ, 1997. Tchr. art Bridgewater-Raritan Schs., NJ, Abington Sch. Dist., Pa. Recipient Disting. Tchr. award, Bridgewater-Raritan Schs., 2003, Golden Apple award, 1990, 1993. Fellow: Nat. Art Edn. Assn., NJ Art Edn. Assn.; mem.: NEA, Am. Canoe Assn. (instr. 1999—). Episcopalian. Avocations: kayaking, white-water rafting, cross country skiing, bicycling, hiking.

MONTGOMERY, LINDA BOUDREAUX, artist; b. Crowley, La., July 27, 1947; d. Edward John Boudreaux and Ellender Earle Murrell; children: Scott Allen, Brian Michael. BFA, U. La., 1985. Interpreter Montpelier Found., Montpelier Station, Va., 2003; artist Orange, Va., 2003—; owner, artist Corner House Gallery, Orange, Va., 2006—. Exec. dir. Literacy Coun. of Madison County, Va., 2004. Original painting, Decorations in the Front Hall, Tex. State Capitol, Austin, Tex., 2002 (Ofcl. Tex. Christmas Card for Gov. and Mrs. George Bush), Cities, Suburbs, Countryside, Nat. Bldg., Wash., D.C., 2003 (Hon. Mention for Nat. Trust for Hist. Preservation, 2003); author (illustrator): (children's book) A Colorful Guide to the World Famous Tabasco Pepper Sauce Factory, 1995, A Coloring Guide to the World Famous Jungle Gardens - Wildlife, 1995, A Coloring Guide to the Historic Conrad Rice Mill, 1995, A Colorful Tour of Louisiana's Cajun Country, 1995, A Visit to the Dr. Pepper Museum, 1996, A Visit to the University of Texas at Austin McDonald Observatory, 1996, A Visit to Louisiana's Jean Lafitte National Historic Park & Preserve, 1996, Abbeville - Some Place Special On The Bayou, 1996, A Visit to the Texas Capitol, Austin, Texas, 1997, Una Visita Al Capitolio De Tejas, Austin, Texas, 1997, How Texas Laws Are Made - A Children's Guide, 1997, A Visit to the Alabama Capitol, Montgomery, Alabama, 1997, A Visit to the International UFO Museum & Research Center, Roswell, NM, 1997, A Visit to the Arizona Capitol, Phoenix, Arizona, 1997, A Visit to the California Capitol, Sacramento, California, 1999, A Visit to the Oklahoma Capitol, Oklahoma City, Oklahoma, 2000; commd., James Madison Montpelier South Yard, Slave Cemetery. Office: Corner House Gallery LLC 173 West Main St Orange VA 22960 Personal E-mail: paintings@customart.com.

MONTGOMERY, M. DARLENE, language educator; b. Muskogee, Okla., May 25, 1949; d. William Perry and Nemie Anne (Emery) Dunn; m. Rex Jay Montgomery, June 5, 1971; children: Emory Anne Lobb, April Marie. BA, Northeastern State U., 1971; M in Liberal Studies, U. Okla., 1994. Tchg. cert., Ark., Va., Okla. Journalism, speech, drama and English tchr. Virginia Beach (Va.) Pub. Schs., 1971-74; co-owner Taylor Rental Ctr., Ft. Smith, Ark., 1975-86; English tchr. Ft. Smith Pub. Sch., 1987—. Adj. English prof. Westark C.C., Ft. Smith, 1994-98. Editor (assn. newspaper) The Sounding Board, 1993-99. Choir/video technician Harvest Time Tabernacle, Ft. Smith, 1983-86. Recipient Lifetime PTA award Kimmons Jr. High, Ft. Smith, 1994, 1st place in state for assn. reporting Ark. Edn. Assn., Little Rock, 1996, 97. Mem. Ft. Smith Classroom Tchrs. Assn. (pres., 2000-02, faculty rep. 1992-93, bd. mem. 1993-99, publs. sec./editor 1993-99), Northside PTA, Phi Delta Kappa, Alpha Delta Kappa, Alpha Chi, Rho Theta. Avocations: reading, writing essays and short stories. Home: 3205 S 98th St Fort Smith AR 72903-5714 Office: Ft Smith Pub Schs 2301 N B St Fort Smith AR 72901-3433

MONTGOMERY, SUSAN BARBIERI, lawyer; b. New Haven, Nov. 11, 1949; BFA, RISD, 1971, MAE, 1978; JD, Northeastern U., 1986. Bar: Mass. 1986, U.S. Dist. Ct. Mass. 1987, U.S. Ct. Appeals (D.C. cir.) 1988. Tchr., dept. chmn. Westport (Mass.) Pub. Schs., 1976-83; freelance artist Westport, 1971—; law clk. to Justice J. Harold Flannery Mass. Superior Ct., Boston, 1986; assoc. Foley Hoag LLP, Boston, 1986-94, ptnr., 1995—. Adj. prof. Suffolk U. Law Sch., 1999—; advisor in field. Co-editor: Worldwide Trademark Transfer, 1992—2006. Trustee Vol. Lawyers for Arts, Boston, 1992—; chmn. bldg. com. Westport Arts Group, Inc.; advisor Am. Law Inst. Mem. ABA (chair elect IPL sect., mem. UCITA working group, past chair bus. baw & IPL sect. joint task force), Mass. Bar Assn. (coms. 1987—), Boston Bar Assn. (coms. 1987—), Internat. Trademark Assn. (chmn. publs. com., dir. 1995-97), Copyright Soc. (com. mem. 1991—), Lex Mundi (chair intellectual property practice group). Office: Foley Hoag LLP Seaport World Trade Center West 155 Seaport Blvd Boston MA 02210-2600 Office Phone: 617-832-1222. Business E-Mail: smontgomery@foleyhoag.com.

MONTI, LAURA ANNE, psychology researcher, educator; b. Evanston, Ill., Feb. 28, 1959; d. LeRoy John and Mary Alice (Foley) M. BA in Psychology, U. Ariz., 1981; MA in Cognitive Sci., Loyola U., Chgo., 1986, PhD, 1987; postgrad., Menninger Found., 1988. Mem. bd. dirs., co-owner Monti & Assocs. Inc., Arlington Heights, Ill., 1976—; co-owner MAM Imports and Creative Gifts, Kildeer, Ill., 1986-89; lectr. psychology Loyola U., Chgo., 1986-89; asst. prof. North Park Coll., Chgo., 1989-91; instr. psychology Rush-Presbyn.-St. Luke's Med. Ctr., Chgo., 1992-94, asst. prof., 1995-98. Vis. rsch. specialist U. Ill., Ill. Inst. Devel. Disabilities, 1989-90; cons. Walter H. Sobel FAIA & Assocs., Chgo., 1987—, Yate and Auberle, Oakbrook, Ill., 1987-88; postdoctoral fellow Northwestern U., Evanston, Ill., 1990-92. Contbr. articles to profl. jours.; co-author tech. reports to various orgns. Tuition scholar Loyola U., Chgo., 1983-84; NIH fellow, 1992-94; Loyola U. grad. asst., 1986. Mem. APA (divsn. psychology of women 1989-92, gen. psychology, 1989—), Psi Chi (faculty rep. for North Park Coll. 1989-91), Sigma Alpha Iota. Roman Catholic. Avocations: tennis, piano. Home: 720 Cimarron Dr Cary IL 60013 E-mail: drlmonti@aol.com.

MONTICONE, DIANE THERESE, French educator; b. Teaneck, N.J., Apr. 7, 1941; d. John W. and Ann Claire (Veslany) K.; m. Ronald Charles Monticone, June 10, 1967; children: Ronald Charles Jr., Joanne Mary. BA, Marymount Coll., 1962; MS, Georgetown U., 1965; PhD, Rutgers U., 1980. Cert. tchr. fgn. lang., N.J. Lang. lab. asst. Marymount Coll., Arlington, Va., 1962-63; instr. French Coll. St. Elizabeth, Convent Station, NJ, 1963-66, asst. prof., 1966-80, assoc. prof., 1980—2000. Fellow N.J. Global Edn. Project, 1994. Author: Montesquieu and His Reader, 1989. Fellow Inst. Internat. Edn. and N.J. Dept. Higher Edn., 1989, 90-92; grantee Govt. Que., 1991, Dept. Higher Edn. N.J., 1984-86; French-Am. Found. fellow, 1995. Mem. AAUP, Am. Assn. Tchrs. French, Alliance Française (bd. dirs. Bergen County chpt. 1983—, sec. 1983-85, treas. 1989-91, publicity dir. 1993—). Avocations: travel, gardening. Home: 946 Midland Rd Oradell NJ 07649-1947

MONTIEL, CAROL E., health services administrator; b. Bklyn., Dec. 14, 1944; d. Jack Seymour and Jeanette (Moshen) Rothstein; m. Francisco Jose Montiel, Dec. 24, 1965; children: Deborah, David, Antonio, Daniela. BS, Syracuse U., 1966, MS, 1971. RN. Staff nurse Crouse Irving/Meml. Hosp., Syracuse, N.Y., 1966-71; founder, pres. Rincon De Los Niños, Maracaibo, Venezuela, 1972-76; dir. Healthex, Ft. Lauderdale, Fla., 1981-90; dir. pediatrics Glassrock, Ft. Lauderdale, 1990-92; adminstrv. dir. Kids Med. Club, Ft. Lauderdale, 1992-95, Pediat. Svcs. of Am., Ft. Lauderdale, 1995-97, quality coord. Norcross, Ga., 1997—. Cons., vis. lectr. U. Miami Sch. Medicine, 1985—; adv. bd. mem. Kids Med. Club, West Palm Beach, 1994-97. Contbr. articles to profl. jours. Founding mem. Ventilator Camp, Miami, 1985, Oncology Camp, United Order True Sisters, Miami, 1990; founding bd. dirs. South Fla. SIDS Assn., Miami, 1990. Jewish. Avocations: working with children, tennis, travel, reading. Home: 6360 NE 20th Ter Fort Lauderdale FL 33308-1319 Office: Pediatric Svcs of Am 3159 Campus Dr Norcross GA 30071-1402

MONTOOTH, SHEILA CHRISTINE, state agency administrator; d. Gerald Frank and Janet Laura Montooth. BS, Calif. State U., L.A., 1974; MPA, Calif. State U., 1985. CPA, Calif. From auditor 1 to tax auditor IV State Bd. Equalization Calif. Bd. Equalization, Pasadena, 1974—81, supr. tax auditor I State Bd. of Equalization West L.A., 1981—83, bus. taxes adminstr. III State Bd. of Equalization Lakewood, 1984—87, bus. taxes adminstr. IV State Bd. of Equalization Downey, 1987—92; bus. taxes adminstr. V State Bd. of Equalization, Hollywood, 1992—93, Arcadia, 1994, City of Industry, 1994—2000, V State Bd. Equalization, West Covina, Calif., 2000—. Active Futures for Children, 1994-05. Recipient Bronze award United Way, Los Angeles, 1984, Gold award, 1985. Mem. Nat. Mus. Am. Indian Smithsonian Instn. (charter). Democrat. Roman Catholic. Avocations: reading American history, classic and adventure movies, travel. Office: State Bd Equalization 1521 W Cameron Ave Ste 300 West Covina CA 91790 Office Phone: 626-480-7310. Business E-Mail: sheila.montooth@boe.ca.gov.

MONTOYA, LEIALA, assistant principal; d. Michael J. and Virginia B. Chong; m. Michael S. Montoya, Aug. 31, 1974 (dec. Dec. 24, 1992); 1 child, Aaron. AA, Modesto Jr. Coll., Calif., 1963; BA, Calif. State U., Fresno, 1994; MEdn., Calif. State U., San Bernardino, 1996; postgrad. in EdD program, U. So. Calif., LA, 1996—. Spl. edn. tchr. Cardozo Sch., Riverbank, Calif., 1971—74, Palm View Sch., Coachella, Calif., 1997—2001; asst. prin. John Kelley Sch., Thermal, Calif., 2001—. Mem.: AAUW (assoc.), Nat. Coun. Teachers of English, Internat. Reading Assn. (assoc.), Coun. for Exceptional Children (assoc.), Assn. for Supervison and Curriculum (assoc.), Phi Mu. Democrat. Roman Catholic. Avocations: mentoring teachers, exercise, travel, cooking. Office: John Kelley Elem Sch 87-163 Center St Thermal CA 92274

MONTOYA, REGINA T., association executive, lawyer; b. Tucumcari, N.Mex., Dec. 25, 1953; d Fred and Rosa (Meraz) M.; m. Paul E. Coggins, June 12, 1976; 1 child, Jessica. BA, Wellesley Coll., 1975; JD, Harvard U., 1979. Bar: Tex. 1979. Law clk. to U.S. Dist. Judge Sarah T. Hughes, Dallas, 1979-80; ptnr. Akin, Gump, Strauss, Hauer & Feld, Dallas, 1980-90; shareholder Godwin, Carlton & Maxwell, Dallas, 1990-93; asst. to pres., dir. Office of Intergovernmental Affairs, Washington D.C., 1993; v.p. Westcott Comm., 1994—95; panelist Between the Lines KERA-TV, 1994; public delegate UN Gen. Assembly, 1998; pres. WORKRules, 1995—2005; CEO New Am. Alliance, 2005—. Bd. dirs. Wash. Mut., 2006-. Trustee Wellesley Coll., 1990—; bd. dirs. Dallas Theater Ctr., 2004—, Parkland Found., 2005—. Mem. Student Loan Mktg. Assn. (bd. dirs. 1994-2001). Democrat. Roman Catholic. Office: New America Alliance 1050 Connecticut Ave NW 10th Fl Washington DC 20036 Office Phone: 202-772-1872. Business E-Mail: rmontoya@naaonline.org.

MONTOYA, RUBY, alcohol and drug abuse counselor; b. Medanales, N.Mex., Feb. 8, 1938; d. Eusebio and Agueda Salazar Martinez; m. Fermin L. Herrera (div.); children: Lewis R., Ralph A., Phyllis. Student, WNMU. Lic. alcohol and drug abuse counselor; cert. alcohol and other drug abuse counselor. OD abuse counselor, counselor supr. Residential Tex. Alcoholism-Recovery of Alcoholics Program, Santa Fe, 1986-96; prevention specialist Hoy Alcoholism Program, Espanale, N.Mex., 1992-94. Mem. Alcoholics Anonymous, N.Mex. Alcoholism and Drug Abuse Counselors Assn. (bd. dirs. 1986—, pres.-elect, tng. com.), Rio Arvila Family Care Network. Democrat. Roman Catholic. Avocations: weaving, fishing. Office: Esperanza Home for Battered Families 243 Old Los Alamos Hwy Espanola NM 87532

MONTOYA, VELMA, economist, consultant; b. LA, Apr. 9, 1938; d. Jose Gutierrez and Consuelo (Cavazos) Montoya; m. Earl A. Thompson; 1 child, Bret L. Thompson. BA in Diplomacy and World Affairs, Occidental Coll., 1959, MA in Internat. Rels., 1960; MS in Econs., Stanford U., 1965; PhD in Econs., UCLA, 1977. Asst. prof. econs. Calif. State U., L.A., 1965-68; vis. assoc. prof. U. So. Calif., 1979; instr. UCLA, 1981-82; staff economist The Rand Corp., Santa Monica, Calif., 1973-82; asst. dir. for strategy, White House Office of Policy Devel. Exec. Office of the Pres., 1982-83; expert economist Office Regulatory Analysis, OSHA, U.S. Dept. of Labor, 1983-85; dir. of Studies in Pub. Policy and Assoc. Prof. of Political Economy, Sch. of Bus. Mgmt. Chapman U., 1985-87; adj. prof. Sch. Bus. Mgmt. Pepperdine U., 1987-88; pres. Hispanic-Am. Pub. Policy Inst., 1984-90; assoc. prof. fin. Sch. Bus. Adminstrn., Calif. State Poly. U., Pomona, 1988-90; mem. Occupl. Safety and Health Rev. Commn., 1990-97; cons. on regulatory and econ. policy, 1997—. Cons. Urban Inst., 1974, Mexican-Am. Study Project UCLA, 1966, Grad. and Profl. Fellowships to the Office of Post Secondary Edn., U.S. Dept. Edn.; editl. referee Contemporary Policy Issues, Economic Inquiry, Policy Analysis, Jour. Econ. Lit.; discussion leader Am. Assembly on Rels. Between the U.S. and Mex.; pres. del. White House Conf. on Aging, 1981; reader of 1988 proposals for the U.S. Dept Edn. for the Improvement and

Reform of Schs. and Tchg.; rsch. participant U.S. Dept. Edn. Delphi Assessment of Drug Policies for Use in Minority Neighborhoods, 1989; mem. Hispanic adv. panel Nat. Commn. for Employment Policy, 1981-82; lectr. Brookings Inst. Seminars for U.S. Bus. Leaders; bd. adv. Close-Up Found., 1982-83; discussant Western Econ. Assn. Meetings, 1985, 93; bd. adv. Nat. Rehab. Hosp., 1991-94; nat. exec. adv. bd. Harvard Jour. Hispanic Policy, 1993-95; reader proposals for Hispanic Serving Instns., U.S. Dept. Edn., 2001-2004; regional panel to select White House Fellows, 2002— Mem. census adv. com. on hispanic population for 1990 census, 1988—93; mem. adv. com. Senate Rep. Conf. Task Force on Hispanic Affairs, Washington, 1991—; bd. regents U. Calif., 1994—2005; program rev. com. Los Alamos (N.Mex.) Nat. Lab.; mem. steering com. GetSmarter.org, 1998—99; mem. outreach adv. bd. U. Calif., 1998—2005, mem. coun. friends Bancroft Libr. Berkeley, 2005—; commr. Calif. Postsecondary Edn. Commn., 2000—01, 2004—05; coun. trustees, alumni Inst. Effective Governance Adv. Bd., 2003—. Named One of the 100 U.S. Hispanic Influentials Hispanic Bus. Mag., 1982, 90, 97, Woman of the Yr. Mex.-Am. Oportunity Found., 1983, The East L.A. Com. Union, 1979, one of 80 Elite Hispanic Women, Hispanic Bus. Mag., 2002, 03; recipient Freedom Found. at Valley Forge Honor Econ. Edn. Excellence Cert., 1986, Profl. Achievement award S.E. L.A. Lincoln Club, 2002, Hispanic Leadership award Minorities in Bus. Mag., 2001; Univ. fellow Stanford U., Internat. Rels. fellow Calif. PTA, John Hay Whitney Opportunity fellow; Calif. State Univ. Found. Faculty Rsch. grantee; Marshall scholar, Fulbright scholar. Mem. ASTM (com. on rsch. and tech. planning 1985-87), Am. Econ. Assn. (session chair ann. meetings 1995), Nat. Coun. Hispanic Women (pres. 1997—), Am. Soc. Hispanic Econimists, State Bar of Calif., Calif. State Bar Ct. (exec. com. 1987-89, disciplinary bd. 1986-89), Western Econ. Assn., Indsl. Rsch. Inst. for Pacific Nations (adv. bd. 1988-89), Salesian Boys and Girls Club (bd. dirs. 1989—), Vets. in Com. Svc. (adv. com. 1989-94), Phi Beta Kappa, Omicron Delta Epsilon, Phi Alpha Theta Home: 6970 Los Tilos Rd Los Angeles CA 90068-3107 Office Phone: 213-427-8048. Personal E-mail: velmamontoya@earthlink.net.

MONTPELIER, PAMELA J., bank executive; BS in Bus. Admin., Univ. So. Maine. Retail banker Strata Bank, 1982, CEO, chmn. Franklin, Mass., 2000—. Bd. mem. Nat. Ctr. Family Homelessness; bd. adv. Franklin Performing Arts Co.; mem. leadership coun. United Chamber Commerce; capital campaign mgr. YMCA. Office: Strata Bank 81 Main St Medway MA 02053 Office Phone: 508-533-4343. Office Fax: 508-533-1245.*

MONTUORI, DONA F., retired elementary school educator; d. George Francis and Sarah Lorena (Donovan) McSheehy; children: Kevin Wayne, Kyle Sarena. BS, Fitchburg State Coll., 1964, MS in Edn., 1967, cert. advanced grad. study, 1993; mentorship (hon.), Lowell U., 1995; grad. (hon.), John Robert Powers Sch. Modeling, 1997; grad. Boston Bartender's Sch. Mixology (hon.). Cert. elem. edn., guidance dir., secondary social studies, secondary English principalship Mass. Elem. tchr. City of Fitchburg, Mass., 1964—67, City of Waynesboro, Va., 1967—68, Town of Dracut, Mass., 1968—2001; subsitute elem. tchr. English and reading City of Lowell, Mass., 2004—06; with US Treasury Dept., Andover, Mass., 2004—06. Curriculum com. Dracut Sch. Sys.; exec. bd. Dracut Tchrs. Assn., chmn. health & safety com.; mem. sch. com, drama com. Presentation of Mary H.S., Methuen, Mass.; workshop presenter Dracut Sch. Sys.; dir. playground instrs., Fitchburg. Author: (poems) Windows, 2005, The Howling Wind, 2005, Despotic Love, Shining Stars, 2005, Stalking, 2005, Reminiscences, 2005, Construction, 2005, An Open Window in Spring, 2005; appeared (TV commercial) Sunsetters Awning. Judge Nat. Teen Pageant, Boston, 2002; Eucharist min. St. Joseph Shrine, Lowell, 2005, ch. lector, 2005, mem. ch. choir, 2005; mem. League of Cath. Women. Recipient Internat. Classic Runway Model of Yr., Internat. Modeling & Talent Assn., N.Y., 1997, Editor's Choice award, poetry.com, 2005, Outstanding Achievement in Poetry award, 2005, 2006. Mem.: Nat. Treas. Employees Union, Retired State, County and Mcpl. Employees Assn., Fitchburg State Coll. Alumnae Assn., AARP. Republican. Roman Catholic. Avocations: travel, writing, runway modeling. Personal E-mail: dmontuori@netzero.net.

MONZINGO, AGNES YVONNE, veterinary technician; b. Mangum, Okla., July 16, 1942; d. Ira Lee and Opal Alice (McAlexander) Mayfield; m. Monty Brent Monzingo, Dec. 19, 1959; children: Tara, Dawn, Michael, Kermit. AS, San Antonio Coll., 1969. Registered vet. technician. Mgr. Tupperware Corp., Wichita Falls, Tex., 1966—69; with La Louisiane, San Antonio, 1974—79; counselor Diet Ctr., Duncanville, Tex., 1984—87; vet. technician VCA DeSoto Animal Hosp., Tex., 1985—98, hosp. mgr., 1998—. Author: (weekly column) Happy Tracks, 1981. Commr. Boy Scouts Am., 1988—93, tng. chmn. Wisdom Trail Dist., 1991—98, dist. commr. Wisdom Trail commn., 1998—99; pres. Dallas Stake Primary, 1983—88. Recipient Wood badge Boy Scouts Am., 1987, Wisdom Trail Dist. award of merit, 1990, Silver Beaver award Boy Scouts Am., 1993. Mem. Tex. Assn. Registered Vet. Technicians (v.p. 1991), Tex. Assn. Animal Technicians (pres. 1988, com. chair 1990-92), Tex. Assn. Registered Technicians (pres. 1992), Am. Boxer Club, Dallas Boxers Club (sec. 1982-92), Metroplex Vet. Hosp. Mgr. Assn., mem. Tex. Vet. Medical Assn., 1980-present. Mem. Lds Ch. Avocations: dog show exhibitor, dog breeder. Business E-Mail: agnes.monzingo@vcamail.com.

MOOD, ROSALYN THOMAS, assistant principal; b. Lancaster, SC; d. Fred D. and Anabell Asgill Thomas; children: Adrian Thomas, Kevin Asgill. Bachelor's degree, U. S.C., Columbia, 1980; MA in Tchg., U. of SC., Columbia, 1982; M in Ednl. Leadership, Winthrop U., Rock Hill, S.C., 2004. Sci. tchr. Warren Hills Jr. H.S., NJ, 1982—83; sci. tchr., dept. chairperson E. C. Glass H.S., Lynchburg, Va., 1984—99, Lancaster H.S., 1999—2005, instrnl. mentor, 2003—05, asst. prin., 2005—. Mem. Lancaster County Red Cross, 2006, Lancaster Cmty. Found. Bd., 2006. Named Tchr. of Yr., Lancaster County Sch. Dist., 2002. Mem.: ASCD, NEA, S.C. Assn. of Sch. Adminstrs., Nat. Sci. Tchrs. Assn., SC. Edn. Assn. Methodist. Avocations: reading, travel. Office Phone: 809-283-2001.

MOODIE, JANICE, professional golfer; b. Glasgow, Scotland, May 31, 1973; Degree in psychology, San Jose State U., 1997. Winner Scottish Ladies title, 1992; mem. team Great Britain, 1994, Ireland Curtis Cup, 1996; turned profl., 1996. Avocations: exercise, movies. Office: PGA 100 International Golf Dr Daytona Beach FL 32124-1092

MOODY, FRANCES MARIE, former performing arts educator, musician; b. McComas, W.Va., May 15, 1922; d. Arthur and Della Virginia Moody. BA, Concord Coll., Athens, WV, 1944; MA, Columbia U., New York, NY, 1948. Choral dir. Princeton H.S., Princeton, W.Va., 1944—61; choir dir. Fairmont State Coll., Fairmont, W.Va., 1961—84, music edn. specialist, 1961—84, organ & piano specialist, 1961—84. Pres. W.Va. Am. Choral Directors, W.Va., 1967—68; guest dir. Choral Pl. Festivals, W.Va., 1968—75, accompanist, W.Va., 1968—75; emeritus prof. Fairmont State Coll., W.Va. Recipient Woman of the Yr., Gamma Chpt., Delta Kappa Gamma, 1970, Chosen for Choral Seminar, Phila. Coll. of Performing Arts, 1975. Mem.: Music Educators Nat. Conf., Am. Choral Directors Assn. D-Liberal. Methodist. Avocations: travel, reading, piano and organ performance, dining. Home: 221 College Avenue Princeton WV 24740

MOODY, JACQUELINE ELAINE, music educator; d. Roberta Anita Foster; m. Christopher Moody, Dec. 29, 1981; children: Dominique Elaine, Crystal Simone. BS, Fisk U., Nashville, 1978; MusM, Boston Conservatory of Music, 1980; EdS, U. of Miami, Coral Gables, Fla., 1992. Tchr. Fla. Dept. of Edn. Music instr. Elaine Sch. of Music, Miami, 1988—; music tchr. Perrine Elem., Miami, 1997—; music prof. Miami Dade Coll., Miami, 2006—. Singer Conn. Opera Co., Hartford, 1982—88, Fla. Grand Opera, Miami, 1989—90. Vol. Sweet Home Missionary Bapt., Perrine, Fla., 2003—06. Named Educator of Note, Young Patronessess of the Opera, 2000, Outstanding Educator, Delta Sigma Theta, 2000; recipient Presdl. scholarship, Fisk U., 1974—75, Minority scholarship, U. of Miami, 1988—89, Champion of the Arts award, Nat. Bus. and Profl. Women, 2005. Mem.: Jack and Jill of Am., Inc (corr.; chaplain, chairperson for children's cluster 2002—), Sigma Alpha Iota (corr.; corr. sec. 1999—2000), Delta Sigma Theta (corr. Outstanding Educator 2000). Democrat. Baptist. Avocations: playing the piano, singing, cooking, travel, sewing. Office: Perrine Elem Sc 8891 SW 168 St Miami FL 33157 Office Phone: 305-235-2442.

MOODY, LIZABETH ANN, lawyer, educator; b. Johnson City, Tenn., July 11, 1934; d. Robert Alexander and Clara Pauline (Fine) M.; m. Alan Paul Buchmann, Sept. 5, 1959. AB, Columbia U., 1956; LLB, Yale U., 1959. Bar: Conn. 1959, Ohio 1960, U.S. Dist. Ct. Conn. 1960, U.S. Supreme Ct. 1977, U.S. Dist. Ct. (no. dist.) Ohio 1961. Assoc. Goldstein & Peck, Bridgeport, Conn., 1959-60, Slough & Slough, Cleve., 1960-61, 63-66, Ginsberg, Guren & Meritt, Cleve., 1962; ptnr. Metzenbaum, Gaines, Finley & Stern, Cleve., 1967-71; assoc. prof. Cleve. State U., 1970-73, prof., 1973-94, interim dean and prof., 1987-88; vis. prof. U. Toledo, 1976-77; v.p., dean Coll. Law, prof. Stetson U., 1994-99, Disting. univ. prof., 1998—. Rev. authority on civil rights HEW, Washington, 1973—79; vis. prof. Nat. Law Ctr. George Washington U., 1981—82, U. Hawaii, Honolulu, 1988, Wallace S. Fugiama Disting. prof., 2002; vis. prof. So. Meth. U., 2004; CEO Law Sch. Admission Svcs., Newtown, Pa., 1991—93; v.p. Stetson U., 1994—99; dir., sec., mem. exec. com. Fla. Health Scis. Ctr., Tampa Gen. Hosp., Fla., 1998—2002; chair drafting com. to reverse model Non-Profit Corp. Act, 2000—. Author: Smith's Review of Corps, 1987, Smith's Review of Estates, 1987; contbr. articles to profl. jours. Pres. Cuyahoga County Econ. and Cmty. Devel., Cleve., 1984-88, Task Force on Violent Crime, Cleve., 1987-88; chmn. audit com. Law Sch. Admission Coun., New Town, Pa., 1988-89, bd. trustees Law Sch. Admission Coun., 1989-94, exec. dir., 1991-93, pres., CEO, dir. Law Sch. Admission Svc., 1991-93; commr. Ohio Ethics Commn., Columbus, Ohio, 1988-91, Ohio Pub. Defender Commn.; v.p., trustee Gt. Lakes Theatre Festival, Cleve., 1972-90; dir., sec. exec. com. Fla. Health Scis. Ctr., 1997—; dir. Cleve. Growth Assn., 1987-88; trustee Acad. Prep., St. Petersburg, Fla., 1999—; lay reader Cathedral Ch. of St. Peter's, St. Petersburg, Fla., 2000—. Recipient New Frontier award Ams. for Dem. Action, 1977, YWCA Women of Distinction award, 1988, Josephine Irwin award, 1990, award for Excellence in Governance Fl. Health Sci. Ctr., 2002; Day named in her honor, May 8, 1990, Cleve. Mem.: AAUP, ABA (chair non-profit corp. com. 1987—91, bus. law sect. coun. mem. 1993—94, house of dels. 1994—99, mem. accreditation com. 1994—2000, chair internat. programs com. 1995—99, sr. lawyers divsn. coun. 1997—2001, chair accreditation com. 1999—2000, sect. legal edn. coun. 2000—, chair sr. lawyers divsn. coun. 2003—04, chair 2003—04, specialization standing com. 2001—04, Glass Cutter award 1997), English Speaking Union (trustee 1986—89), Cleve. Bar Assn. (pres. 1987—88, meritorious svc. award 1987), Ohio State Bar Assn. (coun. of dels. 1981—91, Ohio Bar medal 1992), Am. Law Inst. (ALI-ABA com. 1998—2001, adv. com. 2001—, elected mem.), Assn. Am. Law Schs. (exec. com. 1977—81), St. Petersburg Yacht Club. Office: 1401 61st St S Saint Petersburg FL 33707-3246 Office Phone: 727-562-7848. Business E-Mail: moody@law.stetson.edu.

MOODY, LORETTA JEANNE, literature and language educator; b. Washington Court House, Ohio, July 26, 1969; d. Barbara Lee and Russell Allen White; m. Russell H. Moody, July 24, 1966; children: Jonathon Edward, David Jerald, Elizabeth Nicole. BA in English, Ohio U., Athens, 1992. Tchr. English Crooksville (Ohio) H.S., 1994—99, Ohio Hi-Point Vocat. Sch., Bellefontaine, Ohio, 1999—2000, Ridgemont H.S., Ridgeway, Ohio, 2000—. Mem.: Nat. Coun. Tchrs. English. Methodist. Avocations: reading, gardening, poetry, writing. Office: Ridgemont High Sch 162 E Hale St Ridgeway OH 43345 Office Phone: 937-363-2701.

MOODY, MARILYN DALLAS, retired librarian; b. Little Rock, Aug. 28; d. Corbin Luther and Marian Dallas; m. W.I. Moody Jr., June 1, 1970 (div. 1987); m. Jeffry Baumann, 1988 Student, Hendrix Coll, Conway, Ark., 1959, U. Ark., 1960, Drexel U., 1964. Libr. Free Libr. Phila., 1964—70, cons. libr., 1971—76, coord. dist. libr. ctr. svcs., 1976—82, chief ext. svcs. divsn., 1982—91; exec. dir. Bucks County Free Libr., Doylestown, Pa., 1991—2003; ret., 2003. Recipient Cert. of Merit, 1981 Mem. ALA (councilor 1983-86), Pub. Libr. Assn. (legis. com. 1989-93), Pa. Libr. Assn. (legis. com. 1988-90, chair legis. com. 1980-82, coord. Legis. Day 1980-82, 87, 92, pres. pub. libr. divsn. 1995-96, chair scholarship com., treas. 2000-02), Assn. Pa. Pub. Libr. Sys. (chair 2002), Pa. Citizens for Better Librs. (bd. dirs., chair membership com. 2006) Avocations: reading, travel.

MOODY, MARILYN LEAVITT, special education educator; b. Lowell, Mass., Dec. 18, 1937; d. Thomas Augustin and Mary Leavitt; m. Paul Elliot Moody, Mar. 14, 1959; children: Kristann Lee, Paul Elliot Jr., Kathleen Ann. BS in Elem. Edn., U. Mass., Lowell, 1959; postgrad., Brown U., Providence, 1971, postgrad., 1977, U. RI, 1977—78. Cert. tchr. RI, Mass. Tchr. Lexington Pub. Schs., Mass., 1959, Lowell Pub. Schs., Mass., 1959, Barrington Pub. Schs., RI, 1974—78, RI Coll., Providence, 1984—91; head tchr. Children's Perceptual Achievement Ctr., Rumford, RI, 1978—. Author: (booklets) Consumers - Are You Award of Your Rights?, 1978, Chisanbop - Math Finger Calculation, 1990. Mem. Golden Retriever Rescue Inc., Hudson, Mass., 2001—. Recipient Cert. of Appreciation, Barrington Pub. Schs., 1978, cash award, RI Consumer's Coun., Providence, 1978. Mem.: Stevenson Reading Program, Sci. Rsch. Assn., Nat. Wildlife Fedn., Smithsonian Instn., Nat. Trust for Hist. Preservation, Orton Billingham Soc. Roman Catholic. Avocations: reading, cooking, antiques, dogs, birdwatching. Home: 6 Lafayette Rd Barrington RI 02806 Office: Children's Perceptual Achievement Ctr 145 Newport Ave Pawtucket RI 02861

MOODY, MARY DOYLE, elementary school educator; b. Burlington, Wis., Sept. 11, 1954; d. James Joseph Doyle and Barbara Ann Bauer; m. Gregory Charles Moody, June 28, 1980; children: Robert Christopher, Daniel Joseph. BS, U. North Tex., 1977. Cert. Edn. Tex. Kindergarten tchr. St. Maria Goretti Cath. Sch., Arlington, Tex., 1977—82; elem. tchr. St. John the Apostle Cath. Sch., N. Richland Hills, Tex., 1990—2003, 2003—. Dir. religious edn. St. John the Apostle Cath. Ch., 1985—90. Vol. St. John the Apostle Cath. Ch., 1980—2006. Recipient Golden Apple award, NE Tarrant County C. of C., 2000. Mem.: NSTA (assoc.), Nat. Cath. Edn. Assn., Nat. Coun. Tchrs. Math. (assoc.). Home: 7117 Timberlane Dr North Richland Hills TX 76180 Office: St John the Apostle Cath Sch 7421 Glenview Dr North Richland Hills TX 76180 Office Phone: 817-284-2228. Business E-Mail: mmoody@stjs.org.

MOODY, PATRICIA ANN, psychiatric nurse, small business owner, artist; b. Oceana County, Mich., Dec. 16, 1939; d. Herbert Ernest and Dorothy Marie (Allen) Baesch; m. Robert Edward Murray, Sept. 3, 1960 (div. Jan. 1992); children: Deanna Lee Cañas, Adam James Murray, Tara Michelle Murray, Danielle Marie Murray; m. Frank Alan Moody, Sept. 26, 1992. BSN, U. Mich., 1961; MSN, Washington U., St. Louis, 1966; student, Acad. of Art, San Francisco, 1975-78. RN; lic. coast guard, ocean operator. Psychiat. staff nurse U. Mich., Ann Arbor, 1961-62, Langley-Porter Neuro-Psychiat. Inst., San Francisco, 1962-63; instr. nursing Barnes Hosp. Sch. Nursing, St. Louis, 1963; psychiat. nursing instr. Washington U., St. Louis, 1966-68; psychiat. nurse instr. St. Francis Sch. Nursing, San Francisco, 1970-71; psychiat. staff nurse Calif. Pacific Med. Ctr., San Francisco, 1991-97. Psychiat. staff nurse Charter Heights Behavioral Health Sys., Albuquerque, 1996-97, Nurse Finders, 2002-04; owner, cruise cons. Cruise Holidays Albuquerque, 1995—. Oil and watercolors included in various group exhbns., 1982-93. V.p. Belles-Fundraising Orgn., St. Mary's Hosp., San Francisco, 1974; pres. PTO, Commodore Sloat Sch., 1982; docent Albuquerque Mus. Art and History, 1998—. Recipient Honor award Danforth Found., 1954, Freshman award Oreon Scott Found., 1958; merit scholar U. Mich., 1957. Mem. Nat. Alliance for Mental Illness (sec. bd. dirs. 2000), San Francisco Women Artists (Merit award for oil painting 1989), Artist's Equity (bd. dirs. No. Calif. chpt. 1987-89, pres. No. Calif. chpt. 1990), Met. Club. Republican. Lutheran. Avocations: hiking, photography, piano, travel. Home: 219 Spring Creek Ln NE Albuquerque NM 87122-2013 Office: Good Mood Cruises Inc 12231 Acad Rd NE 301-305 Albuquerque NM 87111-3962 Office Phone: 800-803-5288, 505-296-6255. Business E-Mail: patmoody@goodmoodcruises.com, cruises@goodmoodcruises.com.

MOOK, SARAH, retired chemist; b. Bklyn., Oct. 29, 1929; d. Wong and Lie Won (Woo) M. BA, Hunter Coll., N.Y.C., 1952; postgrad., Columbia U., N.Y.C., 1954—57, postgrad., 1962—65, U. Hartford, Conn., 1958—59; grad., N.Y.C. Citizens Police Acad., 2001. Cartographic aide U.S. Geol. Survey Dept. of Interior, Washington, 1952-54; rsch. asst. Mineral Beneficiation Lab. Columbia U., NYC, 1954-57; analytical chemist nuc. divsn. Combustion Engring., Inc., Windsor, Conn., 1957-59; rsch. scientist Radiations Applications Inc., Long Island City, NY, 1959-62; chemist Marks Polarized Corp., Whitestone, NY, 1962-64; sr. chemist NRA Inc. subs. Nuc. Rsch. Assoc., Inc., New Hyde Park, NY, 1964-75; clin. chemist Coney Island Hosp., Bklyn., 1974-84, cmty. bd., 1978-80; assoc. chemist Bellevue Hosp. Ctr., 1984-89, prin. chemist, 1989-95; ret., 1995; instr. ESL, 1999—2005. Contbr. articles to profl. jours. Mem. adv. com. to state assemblyman State of NY, 1970-72; trustee Park Ave. Christian Ch., 1973-82, sec., 1973-80, vice-chair, 1980-81, chair bd. trustees, 1981-82, pres. Christian Women's Fellowship, 1962-65, elder, 1982—; mem. Neighborhood Adv. Bd. for Cmty. Devel., 1996—, sec., 1996-99, chair 2000-02; mem. Cmty. Bd., 2002-04; mem. cmty. adv. bd. Coney Island Hosp., 2004—. Named Woman of Yr., N.Y.C. Coun., 2004; recipient Margaret M. McCord Woman of Yr. Meml. award, Sheepshead Bay Hist. Soc., 2004, Woman of Yr. Humanitarian award, NY State Senate, 2004, Disting. Leadership in Cmty. award, NYC Office of Comptr. Mem. Am. Assn. Clin. Chemistry (sec. NY Met. sect. 1999—), AAAS, Am. Chem. Soc., NY Acad. Sci., Van Slyke Soc., Citizens Police Acad. Alumni Assn. (publicity com. 2004—). Republican. Home: 2042 E 14th St Brooklyn NY 11229-3314

MOOMJY, MAUREEN O'BRIEN, surgeon, educator; d. John Kenneth O'Brien and Marion Helen Castagna; m. Alexander Moomjy, July 13, 1985; children: Nicole, Gregory, Nadine. BS, Elizabethtown Coll., Pa., 1981; M in Devel. Disabilities, NYU, 1982; MD, SUNY, Bklyn., 1989. Cert. ob.-gyn. 1998, reproductive medicine and infertility 1998. Internship, residency Columbia Presbyn. Med. Ctr., 1989—94; asst. prof. Weill-Cornell Med. Ctr., NYC, 1994—; physician and surgeon Madison Women's Health and Fertility, NYC, 2000—; clin. asst. prof. Jamaica Hosp., Queens, NY, 2000—; attending physician NYU-IVF, NYC, 2000—. Contbr. articles to profl. jours. Mem. Disabilities Com., Tenafly, 2000—. Mem.: AMA, Am. Soc. Reproductive Medicine (paper prize 1999). Avocations: travel, Broadway shows, opera, tennis. Office: Madison Women's Health and Fertility 50 E 77th St New York NY 10021 Office Phone: 212-639-9122. Office Fax: 212-639-9413. E-mail: mmoomjy@aol.com.

MOON, GABRIELLE MARIE, biology educator; d. Kenny and Roxy Sovell Moon. BA, U. St. Thomas, St. Paul, 2000—04. Cert. biology tchr. Va., 2004. Biology tchr. Mt. Vernon HS, Alexandria, Va., 2004—. Sci. fair dir. Mt. Vernon HS, 2005—06.

MOON, JANE ANDERSON, systems engineer, consultant; b. Bryn Mawr, Pa., Feb. 6, 1938; d. Karl Leopold and Louise Laylander (Fowler) Anderson; m. Marion Francis Moon, June 28, 1965; children: Douglas Charles Moon, Cary Allen Gordon, Diana Moon Robinson BSc cum laude, U. Calif., Irvine, 1972, MSc, 1976. Programmer Collins Radio Co., Newport Beach, Calif., 1960-63; engring. programmer Hughes Aircraft Co., Fullerton, Calif., 1963-66; software engr. Calif. Computer Products, Anaheim, Calif., 1966-69; prin., owner Moon Mgmt. Consulting, Orange, Calif., 1972-76; lectr. U. Calif., Irvine, 1973-75; software engring. mgr. Burroughs Corp., Santa Ana, Calif., 1976-81; sr. prin. scientist Hughes Aircraft Co., Fullerton, 1981-98; sr. prin. scientist, engr., cons. Raytheon Co., Fullerton, 1998—. Prin. Moon Mgmt. Consulting, Orange, Calif., 1985—; adv. bd. Software Engring. Inst., Pitts., 1993-96, lead assessor, 1996-2004, lead appraiser, 2000—; mem. Capability Maturity Model Integration Product Devel. team, 1998; presenter in field Author: Hughes Aircraft's Widespread Deployment of a Continuously Improving Software Process; contbr. articles to profl. jours Vol. Loma Linda (Calif.) U. Med. Ctr. Children's Hosp., 1996—. Recipient Outstanding Achievement award, Hughes Aircraft Co., 1986, 1990, 1992, 1994, Summit award, 1996, Outstanding Achievement award, Raytheon Co., 1998, One Co. award, 2003. Mem. Internat. Council Systems Engring., Orange County Philharmonic Soc. Avocations: gardening, art quilting, restoring old houses.

MOON, KAREN ROBIN, science educator; d. Harlan Oliver and Martha Ann Smith; m. Karen Robin Smith, Feb. 1, 1986; children: Weston Gary, Landon Dewayne. AA, Wallace State Coll., 1986; BS in Ed., Athens State Coll., 1989; M in Adminstrn., U. Ala., 2004. Chpt. 1 tchr. aide Vinemont Sch., Cullman, Ala., 1990—93; sci., social studies tchr. Parkside Sch., Baileyton, Ala., 1993—. Sponsor Parkside Sch. Jr. Honor Soc., 1993—; chmn. Local, County Sci. Fair, Cullman, 1995—; s.t.a.r. team mem. Parkside Sch., 1997—2003; mem. Parkside Sch. Accelerated Reading, 1999—2004; sponsor Parkside Sch. Scholar's Bowl Team, 2001—; mem. Parkside Sch. Budget Com., 2002—04; sponsor Parkside Sch. Band, 2005—. Mem. Mt. Olive Primitive Bapt. Ch., Cullman, 1974—2005, Mt. Vernon Primitive Bapt. Ch., Cullman, 2005. Mem.: NEA, Cullman County Edn. Assn., Ala. Edn. Assn., Alpha Delta Kappa. Bapt. Avocations: swimming, gardening. Office Phone: 256-796-5568. Business E-Mail: kmoon@ccboe.org.

MOON, KATHLEEN K., language arts educator; m. Gary F. Moon. BA in Elem. Edn. with honors, Georgian Ct. Coll., Lakewood, N.J., 1971. Cert. reading recovery Rutgers U., New Brunswick, 2002. Tchr. grade 3 John Adams Elem. Sch., North Brunswick, 1973—74; tchr. grade 1 Parsons Elem. Sch., North Brunswick, 1971—73, 1974—2001, tchr. reading recovery, 2001—02, tchr. lang. arts academic support, 2002—. Chair TV-Turn-Off Week, NBTEA scholarship com. Parsons Elem. Sch. Mem. Literacy Vols. Am., 1991—; vol. Elijah's Promise Soup Kitchen, New Brunswick; usher Ch. of the Assumption, New Egypt, NJ, 2005—. Mem.: NEA, NJEA, NBTEA, North Brunswick Twp. Ednl. Assn., Middlesex County Ednl. Assn., N.J. Reading Assn., Middlesex Reading Assn., NTEA, NEA, Georgian Ct. U. Alumni Assn., Delta Tau Kappa, Phi Delta Phi. Avocations: reading, walking, boating, cross stitch, kayaking. Office: Parsons Elem Sch 899 Hollywood St North Brunswick NJ 08902

MOON, LORETTA MARIE, recreational therapist; b. Spokane, Wash., Jan. 22, 1952; d. George Edmond and Eva Louise Moon; m. William Roy Rose, 1976 (div. 1989); children: Charlie Ann Rose, Julie Lynn Rose, Jennifer Rene Rose, Nicolle Louise Rose. AS, AA, Big Bend C.C., Moses Lake, Wash., 1974; BA in Recreation Adminstrn., Ea. Wash. U., Cheney, 1976. Cert. recreation therapist Nat. Coun. Therapeutic Recreation, 1989. Lifeguard Spokane County Parks Dept., Wash., 1971—76; recreation leader 2 Interlake Sch. Severe and Profound, Medical Lake, 1989—92; instr. adult swimming class YWCA, Spokane, 1990—92, coord. adaptive aquatic, 1992—94; recreation therapist geriatric unit Ea. State Hosp., Medical Lake, 1992—94; recreation therapist, aquatic therapy specialist Ea. State Hosp./ Wash. State Therapy Pool, 1994—; lifeguard, instr. water safety YWCA, 2002—05; nurse asst. Carol's Adult Family Home, Nine Mile Falls, 2004—06. Mem., pres. Med. Lake Mid. Sch., 2001—02; leader, outdoor chmn. Inland North West Campfire, Spokane, 1983—91; tchr. LDS Ch., 1980—2006. Mem.: US Water Fitness Assn. (Top 100 Aquatic Dirs. US 1997—2005, Top Aquatic Therapy Ctr. US 2003—05), Am. Assn. Phys. Activity (master tchr. 2000—06), Am. Therapeutic Recreation Assn. Mem. Lds Ch. Avocations: swimming, embroidery, crocheting, gardening. Office Phone: 509-299-4283. Personal E-mail: recreationrose@aol.com.

MOON, MARILYN LEE, economist; b. El Dorado, Kans., July 7, 1947; d. Jesse Morris and Shirley Lois M.; m. Douglas Gomery, Jan. 13, 1973. BA in Econs., Colo. Coll., 1969; MS in Econs., U. Wis., 1972, PhD in Econs., 1974. Rsch. assoc. Inst. for Rsch. on Poverty U. Wis., Madison, 1973-74; asst. prof. econs. U. Wis., Milw., 1974-80, assoc. prof. econs., 1980-81; sr. analyst human resources and cmty. devel. divsn. The Congl. Budget Office, Washington, 1981-83; sr. rsch. assoc. Health Policy Ctr. The Urban Inst., Washington, 1983-86; dir. pub. policy inst. AARP, 1986-89; sr. rsch. assoc. The Urban Inst., 1989-94, sr. fellow, 1994—2003; v.p. Am. Insts. for Rsch., 2003—, dir. health program. Cons. The Pepper Commn., 1989. Author: The Measurement of Economic Welfare: Its Application to the Aged, 1977,

Medicare Now and in the Future, 1993, 2d edit., 1996, Medicare: A Policy Primer, 2006; co-author: Balancing Access, Cost and Politics: The American Context for Health System Reform, 1991, Entitlements and the Elderly: Protecting Promises, Recognizing Realities, 1995; editor: Economic Transfers in the United States, vol. 49, 1984; co-editor: Improving Measures of Economic Well-Being, 1977; columnist The Washington Post, 1993-00; contbr. articles to profl. jours. Pub. trustee social security and Medicare trust funds, 1995-00. Ford Found. fellow, 1971-73. Mem. Nat. Acad. Social Ins. (bd. dirs. 1993-00, pres. 2005-), Medicare Rights Ctr. (bd. dirs. 1998, pres. 2005-), Inst. Medicine, Phi Beta Kappa. Avocations: photography, hiking, reading. Office: Am Insts for Rsch 10720 Columbia Pike Silver Spring MD 20901 Office Phone: 301-592-2101. E-mail: mmoon@air.org.

MOON, MONA MCTAGGART, activities educator, consultant; b. Buffalo, N.Y., Oct. 4, 1934; d. William Daniel and Helen Violet (Dubin) McTaggart; m. James McCallum Moon, July 14, 1957; children: Douglas, Melisa, Bruce. BA, UCLA, 1955; MA, San Diego State U., 1985. Lic. tchr., Calif., cert. adminstrn., supervision, Calif. Tchr. high sch. Acalanes High Sch., Lafayette, Calif., 1956-61, San Diego Unified Sch. Dist., 1967-82; pres. Motivation Dynamics, San Diego, 1982—. Contbr. articles to profl. jours. Dir. LWV San Diego, 1967-72. Recipient Outstanding Contbn. award Calif. Assn. Dirs. of Activities; named San Diego County Tchr. of Yr., 1980. Mem. ASTD, Nat. Speakers Assn., Phi Beta Kappa. Democrat. Presbyterian. Office: 7910 Ivanhoe Ave # 29 La Jolla CA 92037-4511 Office Phone: 858-454-5117. E-mail: mona@monamoon.com.

MOON, ROSE ANN, elementary school educator; b. Teague, Republic of Korea, Oct. 25, 1979; d. Michael Reed and Pok Hui Moon. BS, Friends U., Wichita, Kans., 2001; ESOL, Wichita State U., 2004. 2nd grade tchr. Wichita Pub. Schs. Unified Sch. Dist. #259, 2001—04, 6th grade tchr., 2004—.

MOONEY, BETH, bank executive; BA, U. Tex.; MBA, So. Meth. U. Sec. First Republic Bank, Dallas, bank mgr., 1980, Citicorp; head banking group AmSouth Bank, Tenn., No. La., 2000—04, sr. exec. v.p., CFO Birmingham, 2004—06; vice chairwoman KeyCorp, 2006—. Bd. dir. United Way Met. Nashville, 2001—, Vanderbilt Univ. Med. Ctr. Named one of 25 Most Powerful Women in Banking, USBanker Mag., 2005, Top 10 CFOs in Banking, 2006. Office: KeyCorp 127 Public Sq Cleveland OH 44114 Office Phone: 615-748-2214. Office Fax: 205-326-4072.*

MOONEY, JENNIFER, literature educator; b. Rochester, Pa., Dec. 13, 1978; d. Sherryl A. Mooney; 1 child, Rhianna S. BA in English, Robert Morris U., Moon Township, Pa., 2002; MA in English, Slippery Rock U., Pa., 2003. Asst. prof. Robert Morris U., Moon Township, Pa., 2004—, Jefferson C.C., Steubenville, Ohio, 2004—, Point Pk. U., Pitts., 2006—. R-Liberal. Christian. Avocations: horseback riding, reading, writing poetry, music, dance. Office: Robert Morris University 6001 University Blvd Moon Township PA 15108 E-mail: mooney@rmu.edu.

MOONEY, MARILYN, lawyer; b. Pitts., July 29, 1952; d. James Russell and Mary Elizabeth (Cartwright) M. BA summa cum laude, U. Pa., 1973, JD, 1976. Bar: Mass. 1977, D.C. 1985, Pa. 1990, U.S. Dist. Ct. D.C. 1985, U.S. Ct. Appeals (D.C. cir.) 1985, U.S. Supreme Ct. 1986. Atty. E. I. du Pont de Nemours & Co., Wilmington, Del., 1976-84, Washington, 1985; assoc. Fulbright & Jaworski L.L.P., Washington, 1985—89, ptnr., 1990—, ptnr. in charge corp. and securities practice Washington Office, 2005—. Contbr. articles to profl. jours. Mem.: ABA (fed. regulation securities com.), D.C. Bar (corp. fin. and securties law and internat. sections), Internat. Bar Assn. (issues and trading in securities com.), Am. Soc. Corp. Secs. (securities law com.). Office: Fulbright & Jaworski LLP 801 Pennsylvania Ave NW Washington DC 20004-2615 Office Phone: 202-662-4678. E-mail: mmooney@fulbright.com.

MOONEY, PATRICIA ANNE, secondary school educator; b. Bronx, N.Y., June 6, 1948; d. Peter Joseph and Helen (Houlihan) Mooney; m. Anthony John Grasso, Nov. 21, 1970 (div. 1977); 1 child, A. Benjamin Grasso. BA, Coll. New Rochelle, N.Y., 1970, MS, 1975. Tchr. Archdiocese of N.Y., Harrison, 1970-78; salesperson N.Y. Tel., N.Y.C., 1978-82; sales instr. AT&T, Aurora, Colo., 1983, sales mgr. N.Y.C., 1984, mgr. sales support dept., 1985, mgr. pricing and contract support dept. Morristown, NJ, 1986, mgr. new bus. support dept. Bridgewater, NJ, 1987, sales br. mgr. Englewood, Colo., 1988-92, sales change mgmt. orgn. Bridgewater, NJ, 1993, data networking customer svc. process mgmt. Bedminster, NJ, 1994, large bus. customer svc. strategy, 1995-97; bus. process improvement Nextel, McLean, Va., 1997-98; operational process improvement, retention, after-market sales and ordering exec. Aerial (now T Mobile), Tampa, Fla., 1998-2000; operational process improvement Intermedia (now Worldcom), Tampa, 2000—01; tchr. Belleville (N.J.) Sch. Dist., 2002—. Roman Catholic. Avocations: performing arts, travel, hiking. Home: 3 Tulip Ln Morristown NJ 07960-6768 E-mail: pamooney6648@aol.com.

MOONWALKER, TU, minister, counselor, artist; b. Feb. 9, 1948; BA, Calif. State U., Sacramento, 1972; BS, U. Calif., Davis, 1973; MA, Tex. Tech. U., 1978, MS, 1979; postgrad., So. Meth. U., 1979. Chef Fairmont Hotel, San Francisco, 1971—72; rsch. and biopsy technician Tex. Tech. U. and Med. Ctr., Lubbock, 1974—78; Native Am. artist Santa Fe, 1979—87; cons. Am. Indian art Wheelwright Mus., Santa Fe, 1984—87; spiritual counselor, tchr. Ctr. for Universal Beingness, Moriarty, N.Mex., 1988—; min., canon Brigade of Light Ch., Cedar Mountain, NC, 1991—. Tech. advisor Am. Playhouse PBS Spl., Crestone, Colo., 1987; chmn. bd. dirs. Crystal Found., Denver, 1988—92, Profit from the Sun, Moriarity, 1999—2001; co-founder Ctr. for Universal Beingness; cons., spkr. in field. Dir.(writer): Karen Lee Dance Theater, 2000—02. Chairperson bd. dirs. Ednl. Opportunity Program Calif. State U., Sacramento, 1971; mem. art com. chair, bd. dirs. YWCA, Lubbock, 1976—77; coun. mem. Sacramento Indian Ctr., 1971; vol. Talking Talons Youth Group, Tijeras, N.Mex., 2000. Named Outstanding Young Woman Am., 1982; recipient Humanitarian award, Friends for Life, Albuquerque, 1996; Wetlands Devel. Fed. grant, U.S. Wildlife, N.Mex., 1999. Mem.: Inst. Noetic Scis., Astron. Soc. Pacific, N.Y. Acad. Scis., Defenders of Wildlife (Wildlife Guardian), Acad. Am. Poets. Avocations: crafts, woodworking, stained glass, poetry, writing. Office: 30-A Steeldust Ave Moriarty NM 87035

MOORE, ALECIA B. See PINK

MOORE, ALMA C., publishing executive, consultant; b. Cin. d. Henry Paul and Helena Anne (Link) Clausing; m. Roy Moore. Student, Stephens Coll., Parsons Sch. Design, New Sch. Social Rsch., N.Y.C. Women's editor TV Guide mag., N.Y.C., 1962-70; dir. advt., promotion and pub. rels. Yves Saint Laurent Parfums, 1971-72; v.p., promotion and editl. dir. Viva/Omni mags., 1974-80; dir. mktg. comm. Redbook mag., 1980-83; editor, pub. Women Entrepreneur mag., 1983-85; pres. Alma C. Moore & Assocs. Mag. Cons., N.Y.C., 1983—. Co-author: (with Roy Moore) Thomas Jefferson's Journey to the South of France, 1999. Mem. ind. jud. screening panel N.Y.C. Civil Ct. Judges Dem. Com., 1985, Emily's List, Eleanor Roosevelt Legacy Com.; advocate Children's Aid Soc. Mem. ACLU, NOW, LWV, Nat. Trust Hist. Preservation, Advt. Women N.Y., Women's City Club of N.Y. Home and Office: 1040 Park Ave New York NY 10028-1032

MOORE, ALMA DONST, writer, lyricist; Clk. domestic and juvenile ct., spl. dep. county clk. Warren County Bd. Freeholders Ct. Ho., Belvidere, NJ, 1948—58. Lectr. Sen. Garrett W. Hagedorn NJ State Hosp. Contbg. writer: Soul Food, 1999—; founder The Spotlight, 1948; editor: The Spotlight, 1948, Warren Jour., 1948; author: (lyrics) Lifetime; contbr. articles to profl. jour. Cultural arts dir. Hunterdon County, 2005—06; coun. mem. Rambai Mukti Mission, Clinton, NJ, 1998—. Recipient Sliver Poet, World Poetry, 1989, Gold Poet, 1999, Homer Diamond, Famous Poets Soc., 1999, Outstanding Achievement in Poetry, Silver Cup, Internat. Soc. Poets, 2003. Mem.: Inter. Soc. of Poets.

MOORE, ALMA MERLE, association executive; b. Webster Springs, W.Va., Aug. 8, 1937; d. Thomas Wayne and Edna Jane (Bullion) M. AB, Glenville (W.Va.) State Coll., 1960; MLS, U. Pitts., 1969; MPA, W.Va. U., 1977. Sch. libr. Webster County Bd. Edn., Webster Springs, 1959-65, Columbian County Bd. Edn., Lisbon, Ohio, 1965-66; libr. asst. W.Va. Libr. Commn., Charleston, 1966-68; libr. dir. Clarksburg (W.Va.)-Harrison Pub. Libr., 1969-89; dir. Lewis County C. of C., Weston, W.Va., 1990—. Pres. Back Fork Books, Inc., Webster Springs, 1979-90; library dir., chmn. Nat. Mine Health Safety Acad., Beaver, W.V., 1996-2002. ret. 2002. Mem. W.Va. Italian Heritage Festival, Clarksburg, 1979—; mem. W.Va. Humanities Coun., Charleston, 1980-86, v.p., 1985-86; mem. W.Va. Libr. Commn., Charleston, 1990—, chmn., 1995—; mem. vis. com. W.Va. U. Libr., 1987—; Bd. mem. W.V. Mus. Am. Glass, Weston, W.V., 1993-. Named Disting. West Virginian Gov. Gaston Caperton, Charleston, 1988, Hon. Italian, W.Va. Italian Heritage Festival, Clarksburg, 1989. Mem. ALA, W.Va. Libr. Assn. (Dora Ruth Parks award 1987), Sierra Club (treas. W.Va. chpt. 1974-75), W.Va. Highlands Conservancy. Democrat. Avocations: gardening, cooking, reading, hiking. Home: 566 Bell St Webster Springs WV 26288-1197

MOORE, AMANDA LEIGH See MOORE, MANDY

MOORE, AMY NORWOOD, lawyer; b. Durham, NC, Sept. 24, 1953; AB summa cum laude, Mt. Holyoke Coll., 1976; MA in English, U. Va., 1978, JD, 1983. Bar: DC 1984, registered: US Ct. Appeals, DC 1985, US Ct. Appeals (6th cir.) 1985, US Tax Ct. 1998. Law clk. to Frank M. Coffin, U.S. Ct. Appeals (1st cir.), 1983-84; ptnr., Employee Benefits Practice Group Covington & Burling, Washington. Articles editor Va. Law Rev., 1982—83. Mem.: Phi Beta Kappa. Office: Covington & Burling 1201 Pennsylvania Ave NW Washington DC 20004-2401 Office Phone: 202-662-5390. Office Fax: 202-662-6291. Business E-Mail: anmoore@cov.com.

MOORE, ANN ROY, school system administrator; b. Florence, Ala. BA, Hampton U., Va.; MA, EdS, U. No. Ala.; EdD in Curriculum Leadership Pers. and Early Childhood Edn., Vanderbilt U., 1986; cert. in ednl. adminstrn., 1986, cert. in ednl. adminstrn., 1987; cert. supt., Ala. A&M, 1992. Former tchr. pre-sch. and elem. sch. Huntsville (Ala.) City Schs., curriculum specialist, 1978—80, former prin., mgr. elem. edn., dep. supt., 1999—2001, supt., 2001—; former asst. supt. Florence Sch. Sys. Office: Huntsville City Schs 200 White St Huntsville AL 35801

MOORE, ANN S., publishing executive; b. McLean, Va., 1950; d. Monty and Bea Sommovigo; m. Donovan Moore; 1 son, Brendan. BA in Polit. Sci., Vanderbilt U., 1971; MBA, Harvard U., 1978. With Time, Inc., NYC, 1978—; gen. mgr. Sports Illustrated, 1983—89; founding publisher Sports Illustrated for Kids, 1989-91; publisher People mag., 1991—93, pres., 1993—98, People Mag. Group (renamed People/In Style Mag. Group, 2001), 1998—2001; exec. v.p. Time, Inc., 2001—02, chmn., CEO, 2002—. Bd. dirs. Avon Products Inc., 1993; public spkr. bus. and women's issues. Hon. bd. mem. Gilda's Club, N.Y.C.; founder Time to Give Back; bd. dirs. Wallace Found. Named Pub. Exec. of Yr., Adweek, 1998, 2004 Bus. Statesman, Harvard Bus. Sch.; named one of The 50 Most Powerful Women in Am. Bus., Fortune mag., 100 Most Powerful Women, Forbes mag., 2005—06, 50 Women to Watch, Wall Street Journal, 2005, 50 Most Powerful Women in Bus., Fortune mag., 2006; recipient AOL Time Warner Civic Leadership award, 2003. Achievements include guiding People magazine to spin off several popular titles including In Style (domestic and international), Teen People, People en Español, and Real Simple. Office: Time Warner Cable 1 Time Warner Ctr New York NY 10019-6038*

MOORE, ANNE, physician; b. N.Y.C., Apr. 28, 1944; d. John D.J. and Mary Foote Moore; m. Arnold L. Lisio, Sept. 6, 1969; children: Philip Moore, Mary Foote. BA, Smith Coll., 1965; MD, Columbia U., 1969. Diplomate Am. Bd. Internal Medicine, Am. Bd. Hematology (chmn. 1996), Am. Bd. Oncology. Intern dept. medicine N.Y. Hosp., N.Y.C., 1969-73, assoc. attending physician, 1981-95, attending physician, 1996—; postdoctoral fellow Rockefeller U., 1972-73, hematology-oncology fellow, 1973-75; asst. prof. medicine Cornell U. Med. Coll., N.Y.C., 1975-91, assoc. prof. clin. medicine, 1981-95, prof. clin. medicine, 1996—. Cons. Strang Cancer Prevention Ctr.; lectr., cons., in field. Author: Patient's Guide to Breast Cancer Treatment, 1992, rev. edit., 1997; ad hoc reviewer Am. Jour. Clin. Oncology, 1994, New Eng. Jour. Medicine, 1994, 96, 97; contbr. articles to profl. jours., chpts. to books. Trustee St. David's Sch., 1983-89, HealthCare Chaplaincy, Inc., 1991—; bd. dirs. Camilli Found., 1990—, Cure Myeloma Fund, 1988-98, N.Y. Community Trust. Recipient award SHARE, 1992, Wholeness of Life award Hosp. Chaplaincy, 1992, Alumnae award Oak Knoll Sch., 1994, Eileen Dreyer Meml. Lectureship award Sass Found. for Med. Rsch., 1996, Commendation award Office of Exec. Nassau County, 1996, award Artists for Breast Cancer Survival, Inc., 2000. Mem. Am. Bd. Internal Medicine (bd. dirs. 1996—), Am. Soc. Hematology, Am. Soc. Clin. Oncology, N.Y. Acad. Scis., Soc. for Study of Blood (membership chmn. 1979-80), N.Y. Met. Breast Cancer Group (membership chmn. 1992-93, sec.-treas. 1993-95, v.p. 1995-96, pres. 1997—), Soc. for Study of Breast Disease, N.Y. Cancer Soc., N.Y. Acad. Medicine (trustee 1998—). Office: Weill-Cornell Med Ctr 428 E 72nd St New York NY 10021-4635

MOORE, ANNE FRANCES, art administrator, consultant, educator, art appraiser, dealer; b. Jackson, Tennesse, Jan. 6, 1946; d. William Clifton and Frances (Woods) Moore; m. Michael Mezzatesta, Mar. 14, 1970 (div. 1987); children: Philip Moore, Alexander Woods, Marya Frances; m. Ernest Watson Hutton, Jr., Apr. 20, 1996. BA, Columbia Univ., 1969, MFA, 1971; MA in History of Art, Hunter Coll., 1982; Cert. in Mus. Mgmt., Am. Fedn. of the Arts, Berkeley, Calif., 1993. Cert. appraiser fine and decorative arts N.Y., 2003. Lectr., rsch. assoc. Kimbell Art Mus., Ft. Worth, 1980—83; dir. outreach Dallas Mus. Art, 1986—88; curator edn. Allen Art Mus., Oberlin Coll., Ohio, 1988—91, dir. Ohio, 1991—96; lectr. N.Y. Univ., 1999—; project mgr. Peabody Essex Mus., Salem, Mass., 2000—02; owner Anne Frances Moore Fine Art Svc., Bklyn., 2002—, Ancestor Image, Bklyn., 2004—. V.p. bd. trustees Intermus. Conservation Assn., Oberlin, 1994-96, trustee, 1991-94. Editor: Bull. of the Allen Meml. Art Mus., 1991-93. Mem.: Appraisers Assn. Am. Home and Office: Fine Arts Svc 172 Pacific St Brooklyn NY 11201-6214 Office Phone: 718-834-8881. Business E-Mail: annefmoore@mindspring.com.

MOORE, ANNETTE B., legislative staff member; b. Salt Lake City, Nov. 8, 1946; Sec., chief adminstrv. officer Utah State Senate, Salt Lake City, 1994—. Mem.: Am. Soc. Legislative Clks. and Secs. (chair mem. and comm. com. 2000—01, chair profl. com. 2001—02, editor Jour. of Profl. Com. 2002—03, mem. exec. com. 2003, chair site selection 2003—04, vice chair Internat. Com. & Devel. 2004—05). Office: Utah State Senate State Capitol Complex Ste W-115 Salt Lake City UT 84114 Office Phone: 801-538-1458. E-mail: amoore@utahsenate.org.

MOORE, ANTOINETTE MERCEDES, counselor; b. Chgo., June 18, 1942; d. Antonio Macio Moore and Uldyn Mercedes Salter; 1 child, Jacqueline Mercedes Buress. BA in Psychology, U. Mo., St. Louis, 2000, MA in Edn., 2003. Therapeutic asst. New Beginnings C-Star, St. Louis, 1992—93, level I, II and II counselor, 1993—95, clin. supr., 1996—97, sr. counselor, 1998—2005, program dir., 2005—. Mem.: ACA. Office: New Beginnings C-Star 3901 Union Blvd Ste 101 Saint Louis MO 63115-1130

MOORE, BARBARA C., ambassador; b. Buffalo; m. Spencer B. Moore; 1 child. BA, Coll. of New Rochelle, 1973. Tours as info. officer U.S. Info. Agy., Caracas, Venezuela, 1989—93; coun. pub. affairs Santiago, Chile, 1993—97; dep. dir. U.S. Info. Agy. Office of Western Hemisphere Affairs, 1997—98; dep. chief of mission U.S. Embassy, Bogota, Colombia, 1998—2002; amb. to Rep. of Nicaragua, 2002—. Office: DOS Amb 3240 Managua Pl Washington DC 20521-3240 Fax: 011-(505)-2669074.

MOORE, BARBARA C., fraternal organization administrator; V.p. institutional advancement Benedict Coll., Columbia, SC. Bd. mem. Midlands YWCA, Richland County Nat. March of Dimes Found. Named one of Most Influential Black Americans, Ebony mag., 2006. Mem.: Nat. Polit. Congress of Black Women, Inc., Coun. for the Advancement and Support of Edn., Nat. Assn. of Female Execs., Nat. Coun. of Negro Women (Living the Legacy Award 1983), Top Ladies of Distinction, Inc., Zeta Phi Beta Sorority (life; nat. first v.p., chair nat. exec. bd., chmn. Nat. Capital Campaign, Grand Basileus, nat. pres. 2002—). Office: Zeta Phi Beta Sorority, Inc 1734 New Hampshire Ave, NW Washington DC 20009 also: 2nd Fl 145 Kennedy St, NW Washington DC 20011*

MOORE, BEALER GWEN, transcription company executive; b. Roxboro, N.C., Sept. 16, 1944; d. Bealer William and Clara (Wilkins) M.; divorced; 1 child, Steven Todd. Cert., U. N.C., Greensboro, 1963; BSBA, U. S.C., Spartanburg, 1987; MS in Orgnl. Mgmt., Pfeiffer U., 2000. Exec. sec. Container Corp. Am., Greensboro, 1964-67; asst. dir. dept. med. record Spartanburg Regional Med. Ctr., 1986-88, mgr. dept. med. transcription, 1988—; owner Spartanburg Transcription Svc., 1986—. Instr. med. terminology Ctrl. Piedmont C.C., 2001—. Mem. adv. bd. Spartanburg Tech. Coll., 1984-95; mem. Matthews United Meth. Ch. Mem. Am. Med. Record Assn., Am. Med. Transcriptionist Assn. Avocations: tennis, painting. Office: Carolinas Healthcare Sys Dir Transcription Dept 1000 Blythe Blvd Charlotte NC 28203-5812 Home: 6807 Copernicus Cir Charlotte NC 28226-3923

MOORE, BEATRICE, religious organization administrator; b. Somerville, Mass., Oct. 6, 1928; d. George and Christina Turner; m. Wendell Moore, May 9, 1953; children: Karl C., Linda Moore Flewelling, Diane Pearl, Larry. BA in Theology and English, Berkshire Christian Coll., Lenox, Mass., 1950. Pres. The Woman's Home and Foreign Mission Soc., Loudon, NH, past nat. pres. Charlotte, NC, 1987—96, nat. spiritual life chmn., 1997—2005. Sunday sch. tchr., deaconess Loudon Ridge Family Bible Ch.; chair Concord Christian Women's Club, 2002-03, 05-06; prayer coord. Ladies Bible Study leader, 1998-05, Concord Christian Women's Club, 2003-04; active Women's Home and Fgn. Mission Soc., Loudon, past pres. NH Soc., past pres. ea. region; hostess, contact chmn., prayer adv., Bible club guide Stonecroft Ministries, Friendship Bible Study Guide; past leader 4-H Club. Mem.: Concord Christian Womens Club (chair 2005—). Office: Woman's Home & Foreign Mission 845 Loudon Ridge Rd Loudon NH 03307-1712

MOORE, BETH A., education educator; d. Floyd Thomas and Marjorie Catherine Collett; m. James Dale Moore, June 30, 1973; children: Todd, Scott. BS in Acctg., Ind. U., Bloomington, 1973, MS in Elem. Edn., 1979; Gifted & Talented Endorsement, Purdue U., W. Lafayette, Ind., 1989. Tchr. Clark-Pleasant Sch. Corp., Whiteland, Ind., 1979—2004; cons. Sch. Renaissance, Madison, Wis., 1997—2003; instr. of edn. Franklin Coll., Franklin, Ind., 2003—. Dir., math. study ctr. Franklin Coll., 2004—, student adv., 2005—. Fundraiser Habitat for Humanity, Franklin, 2006; musician Fair Haven Christian Ch., Franklin, 2003—. Recipient Reading Master Classroom award, Renaissance Learning, 1999—2004; grantee, Ind. Dept. Econs., 1991—93. Mem.: Phi Lambda Theta. Avocations: music, gardening. Home: 152 S 700 W Morgantown IN 46160 Office: Franklin Coll 101 Branigan Blvd Franklin IN 46131 Business E-Mail: bmoore@franklincollege.edu.

MOORE, BETTY JO, legal assistant; b. Medicine Lodge, Kans., July 10, 1921; d. Joseph Christy and Helen Blanche (Hubbell) Sims; m. Harold Frank Moore, June 19, 1941 (dec.); children: Terrance C., Harold Anthony, Trisha Jo. Cert., U. West L.A., 1978; student, Wichita (Kans.) U., 1940-41. Cert. legal asst./escrow officer. Sec. UCLA, 1949-59; escrow officer Security Pacific Nat. Bank, L.A., 1959-62, Empire Savs. & Loan Assn., Van Nuys, Calif., 1962-64; escrow supr. San Fernando Valley Bank, Van Nuys, 1964; escrow officer Heritage Bank, Westwood, Calif., 1964-66; escrow coord. Land Sys. Corp., Woodland Hills, Calif., 1966-67; escrow officer/asst. mgr., real estate lending officer Security Pacific Nat. Bank, L.A., 1967-80; real estate paralegal Pub. Storage, Pasadena, 1980-81; asst. mgr. escrow dept. First Beverly Bank, Century City, Calif., 1982-84; escrow trainer/officer Moore's Tng. Temps Inc., Canoga Park, Calif., 1984—92, legal asst., 1992—. Participant People to People Amb. Program/Women in Mgmt. to USSR, 1989; observer Internat. Fedn. Bus. and Profl. Women's Congress, Washington, 1965, 81, Nassau, Bahamas, 1989, Narobi, Kenya, 1991, Havana, Cuba, 2004. Adv. bd. escrow edn. Pierce Coll., Woodland Hills, Calif., 1968-80. Recipient Cert. of Appreciation, Pierce Coll., 1979, Calif. Fedn. Bus. and Profl. Women, 1989, Nat. Women's History Project, 1995. Mem. Nat. Fedn. Bus. and Profl. Women's Clubs, Calif. Fedn. Bus. and Profl. Women (pres. dist. 1987-88, Calif. Found. chmn. 1988-89, internat. concerns chmn. 1996-97, 2003), Woodland Hills Bus. and Profl. Women ((pres. 1991-92, 94-95), Valley/Sunset Dist. BPW (v.p. legislation/pub. policy 1997-98, 2001-02, 03, Cert. of Appreciation 2002), Tri Valley Dist. Bus. and Profl. Women (legis. chair 1992-93, exec./corr. sec. 1993-94, 94-95), Internat. Fedn. Bus. and Profl. Women, Nat. Women's Polit. Caucus (coord., sec. San Fernando Valley caucus 1986-87, sec. 1990-2003, legis. co-chair 1991-93), Women's Orgn. Coalition San Fernando Valley (exec. com. L.A. Women's Equality Day 1995, pres. 2002—), San Fernando Valley Escrow Assn. (bd. dirs. 1962-64), L.A. Women's Family Equity Coalition, U. West L.A. Alumni Assn., Rotary, U.N. Assn. (v.p. San Fernando Valley), League of Women Voters. Democrat. Methodist. Avocations: reading, musical theater.

MOORE, BEVERLY ANN, retired librarian; b. Evanston, Wyo., Mar. 17, 1934; d. James H. and Louise M. (Miller) Barrett; m. James O. Moore, Oct. 6, 1957 (div. 1966); children: Louis Barrett, Ann Louise Cushman. AA, Hutchinson (Kans.) Jr. Coll., 1954; BA, U. No. Colo., 1957; MA in Libr. Sci., Denver U., 1970. Br. libr. Pueblo (Colo.) Libr. Dist., 1966-70; documents libr. U. So. Colo., Pueblo, 1970-74, head cataloger, 1974-76, libr. dir., 1976-96, dean libr. svcs., 1996—2001. Mem. ALA, Colo. Assn. Librs., Colo. Libr. Assn. (pres. 1985), Beta Phi Mu. Democrat. Congregationalist.

MOORE, BILLIE JO, minister; b. Centerpoint, Ark., Aug. 15, 1929; d. Willie Corn Henry and Irene Ruby Bevill; m. Warner Conrad Moore, Aug. 14, 1948 (div. Sept. 1967); children: Mark Glenn, Janice Marie Baudat. Student, Maranatha Inst., Inc., Calif., 1995. Ordained minister Rhema Bible Tng. Ctr., Okla., 1984. Clk. City of Long Beach, Calif., 1968—79; missionary to Philippines Billie Moore Ministries, Cypress, Calif., 1984—85; self-employed Calif., 1982—2006; minister Rhema, Broken Arrow, Okla., 1984—2006; prayer coord. Ch. of Claremore, Okla., 1986—87. Area coord. Nat. Day of Prayer, Oakley, Antioch, Calif., 1990—99, Auburn, Calif., 2000—02; dir. jail ministry Billie Moore Ministries, Contra Costa County, Calif., 1995—; tchr./facilitator various chs., Calif., 1979—; chaplain Placer County Chaplaincy, Calif., 2000—05, Auburn Ravine Terrace, Calif., 2003—06. Area facilitator Traditional Values Coalition, Placer County, Calif., 2000—02; ch. svc., nursing Auburn Ravine Terr., Calif., 2003—06; vol. Bread of Life Ministry, Antioch, 1990—94, Friendship Manor Ch. Svc., Antioch, 1993—99. Mem.: Foothills Christian Writers, Rhema Ministerial Assn. Internat., Christian Ministerial Assn. of the Foothills, Women's Aglow Internat. (spkr.), Christian Coalition Am. Republican. Avocations: writing, charity work. Office: Billie Moore Ministries Inc PO Box 71 Auburn CA 95604 Mailing: PO Box 71 Auburn CA 95604

MOORE, CAROL A., academic administrator; b. Newark, N.J., Dec. 8, 1945; d. James Clifford and Helen Mohan Brierley; m. Thomas Eric Moore, Nov. 25, 1967; 1 child, Kimberly Ann. BS in Biology, Montclair St. Coll., N.J., 1967; MA in Biology, Monclair State Coll., N.J., 1972; PhD in Biology, Northeastern Univ., Boston, Mass., 1981. Sci. tchr. H.S. and Jr. H.S., 1967—71; asst. prof. biology Massasoit C.C., Brockton, Mass., 1972—83, divsn. chairperson sci. and tech., asst prof. biology, 1979—83, asst. dean academic affairs, asst. prof. biology, 1983—84; dean academic affairs, chief academic officer, prof. biology Lasell Coll., Newton, Mass., 1984—88; dean undergraduate sch., chief acadmic officer, prof. biology Lesley Coll., Cambridge, Mass., 1988—91; provost & v.p. academic affairs, chief academic officer, prof. biology Mercy Coll., Dobbs Ferry, NY, 1992—98; pres. Lyndon State Coll., Lyndonville, Vt., 1998—. Vis. scientist Marine Sci. Inst.,

Northeastern Univ., Nahant, Mass., 1991—. Contbr. scientific papers to numerous conf., chapters to books, articles to profl. jour. Mem., Vt. higher edn. coun. rep. New Eng. Higher Edn. Bd., 1991—; mem., adv. bd. Vt. Telecom Advancement Ctr. USDA Grant, 2002—, Office of Nursing Workforce Rsch., Planning and Develp., Univ. Vt., 2001—; mem., Vt. bd. dirs. Girl Scout Coun., 2001—; mem. Am. Coun. Edn. Commn. on Women in Higher Edn., 2002—03; mem. Vt. Higher Edn. Coun., 1998—; rep. New Eng. Bd. of Higher Edn., 2002—, pres., 2001—02, v.p., 2000—01, exec. com., 1999—, sec.-treas., 1999—2000, com. on cert. & accreditation, 1998—; bd. dirs. Northeastern Vt. Devel. Assn., 2000—, Northeast Kingdom Learning Svc., 2000—. Grantee Title III Retention Grant, 1995, AAC Cirriculm Devel. Grant, 1990, NSF, 1983. Mem.: Soc. of Devel. and Comparative Immunology, Soc. for Invertebrate Pathology, Nat. Shellfisheries Soc., Am. Soc. of Zoologists (travel award), New Eng. Estuarine Rsch. Soc., Nat/ Assn. for Women Deans, Adminstr., and Counselors, Assn. of Tchr. Educators, Am. Coun. of Edn./ Nat. Identification Program, Nat. Assn. of Academic Affairs Adminstr., Sigma Xi, Phi Sigma. Office: Lyndon State Coll 1001 Coll Rd Lyndonville VT 05851

MOORE, CAROLE IRENE, librarian; b. Berkeley, Calif., Aug. 15, 1944; AB, Stanford U., 1966; MLS, Columbia U., 1967. Reference libr. Columbia U., N.Y.C., 1967-68, U. Toronto, Can., 1968-80, head cataloging, 1980-85, assoc. libr., 1985-86, chief libr., 1986—. Mem. nat. adv. bd. Nat. Libr. Can., Ottawa, 1991-94; bd. dirs. Rsch. Librs. Group. 1994-2000, U. Toronto Press, 1994—. Recipient Disting. Alumni award Columbia U., 1989. Mem. ALA, Can. Libr. Assn., Can. Assn. Rsch. Librs. (pres. 1989-91, bd. dirs. 1996-98). Avocation: gardening. Office: U Toronto Libr 130 Saint George St Toronto ON Canada M5S 1A5

MOORE, CASSANDRA CHRONES, real estate broker; b. Oneonta, N.Y., June 14, 1935; d. Constantine John and Antonia (Laskaris) Chrones; m. Thomas Gale Moore, Dec. 28, 1958; children: Charles Godwin, Antonia Laskaris. BA summa cum laude, Radcliffe Coll., Cambridge, Mass., 1956; MA, Harvard U., 1958; PhD, U. Mich., 1975. Lic. real estate broker Calif. Lectr. Duquesne U., Pitts., 1962-65, Mich. State U., East Lansing, 1966-68; broker, owner Moore Assocs., Palo Alto, Calif., 1983-85; dir. state and mcpl. legislation Nat. Assn. Realtors, Washington, 1985-87; exec. dir. Fed. Interagy. Coun. on Homeless, Washington, 1987-89; adj. scholar Competitive Enterprise Inst., Washington, 1989—, mem. adv. bd., 1995—; adj. scholar Cato Inst., Washington, 1996—. Author: Haunted Housing, 1997. Co-chmn. Radcliffe Alumnae Lectureship Com., Palo Alto and San Francisco, 1984-2000; mem. nat. com. Radcliffe Alumnae Professorship Fund, 2001-02. Recipient Fulbright fellowship U.S. Govt., Washington, 1956-57. Mem.: Calif. Assn. Scholars (mem. adv. bd. 2005—), Palo Alto Bd. Realtors (dir. 1984, 1985), Tsintzinian Soc. (bd. mem. 1999—, alt. bd. mem. 2001—02), Am. Assn. Small Property Owners (bd. mem. 1997—), Radcliffe Club Peninsula (pres. 1980—82), Phi Beta Kappa. Avocations: hiking, swimming, skiing. Office: 415 Cambridge Ave Palo Alto CA 94306 Office Phone: 650-853-0798. Personal E-mail: ccmassoc@comcast.net.

MOORE, CATHLEEN TURNER, retired psychology professor; b. Pretoria, Transvaal, Republic South Africa, Oct. 18, 1944; came to U.S., 1970; d. James William and Kathleen Elizabeth (Diamond) Turner; m. Dan Houston Moore, Feb. 25, 1975. Transvaal diploma, Coll. Edn., Republic South Africa, 1964; BA, Rutgers U., 1974; MEd, Temple U., 1975, EdD, 1979. Assoc. prof. psychology Phila. Coll. Pharmacy and Sci., 1981—2000; prof. U. Scis. Phila., 2000—01, prof. emerita, 2001—; owner, operator 10 room bed and breakfast. Pvt. practice, cons. in human rels. and resources, 1980—; vis. prof. U. Durban-Westville, South Africa. Contbr. articles to profl. jours. Cons., trainer Polish Found. Bus. Sch., Vilnius U., Lithuania. Mem. APA, Am. Phys. Soc., Ea. Psychol. Assn.,Psychologists for Social Responsibility. Home: 286 Pump House Rd Weatherly PA 18255-4848 Personal E-mail: cturnermoore@hazleton.net.

MOORE, CHERYL JEROME (CHERYL MILKES JEROME), lawyer; b. Dallas, Jan. 10, 1951; d. Dean and Marjorie (Wolens) Milkes; m. Edward Jerome, Aug. 21, 1976 (div. 1986); 1 child, Elizabeth Milkes; m. David Moore, Feb. 25, 1995. Student, Tulane U., 1969-70; BA and BSW, Syracuse U., 1972, JD, 1976. Bar: N.Y. 1977, Tex. 1978, U.S. Dist. Ct. (no. dist.) N.Y., U.S. Dist. Ct. (all dists.) Tex., U.S. Ct. Appeals (5th cir.). Law clk. Bogart & Andrews, Syracuse, NY, 1975-76; assoc. Law Office Louis Tarantelli, Horseheads, NY, 1976-78, Glast, Miller & Allen, Dallas, 1985-86; sr. planner, adminstrn. asst. County of Dallas, 1977—78, chief commr. fraud, Dist. Atty.'s Office, 1979-85; ptnr. Hewitt, Jerome & Armstrong, Dallas; ptnr., Securities, Oil & Gas Law, Comml. & Transactional Litigation Patton Boggs LLP, Dallas, dep. chmn. litigation dept., mem. mgmt. com. Adj. prof. So. Meth. U. Coll. Law, Dallas, 1986-2000; tchg. staff Nat. Inst. Trial Advocacy. Contbr. articles to profl. jours. Bd. dirs., legal counsel Cmty. Homes Adults, Inc., Dallas, 1987-2004; bd. dirs. Jewish Fedn. Dallas; chair Legacy Sr. Communities Inc., 2004—. Mem. N.Y. Bar Assn., Dallas Bar Assn. Democrat. Jewish. Office: Patton Boggs LLP Suite 3000 2001 Ross Ave Dallas TX 75201-8001 Office Phone: 214-758-3504. Office Fax: 214-758-1550. Business E-Mail: cmoore@pattonboggs.com.

MOORE, COLLEEN, piano and voice instructor; b. Austin, Tex., Oct. 2, 1928; d. Herbert D. and Alice (Heinen) Bohn; m. Doyle H. Moore, Feb. 2, 1949; children: Sherry, Frosty, Robin. Student, U. Tex., 1946-49. Piano and voice teacher pvt. studio; singer Austin Lyric Opera Chorus, Tex., Liz Carpenter's "Getting Better All the Time" Singers. Mem. exec. com. Austin Symphony, Art Guild (past pres.), Austin Lyric Opera Guild; choir mem., past dir. Westlake Hills Presbyterian Church. Named Tchr. of Yr., Austin Dist. Music Tchrs. Assn.; recipient Plaques of Recognition, Women's Symphony League, Austin Symphony Orch., Austin Lyric Opera Chorus. Mem. Womens Symphony League (past pres.), Wednesday Morning Music Club (past pres.), Austin Woman's Club (pres.), Nat. Piano Guild, Tex. Music Teachers Assn., Nat. Music Teachers Assn., Alpha Delta Pi Sorority, Austin District Music Teachers (past pres.). Republican. Presbyterian. Avocations: grandchildren, lake, ranch, family, friends. Home: 803 Westlake Dr Austin TX 78746-4507

MOORE, DEANA DAIELLO, art educator; b. Easton, Pa., Dec. 19, 1969; d. David Anthony Daiello and Susan Marie Korpics; m. Hayden Nicholas Moore, July 12, 2002; 1 child, Mia Susan. AA in Advt. Design, Northampton CC, Pa., 1993; BS in Art Edn., Kutztown U., Pa., 1993; MA in Adminstrn., N.J. City U., Jersey City, 2004. Art tchr. Pub. Sch., West New York, NJ, 1994—. Cheerleading coach, 1995—96; yearbook adv., 1995, 1999—2003. Recipient cert. of Appreciation, Hudson County Sch. of Tech. Mem.: N.J. Art Assn., N.J. Educator's Assn. Avocations: art, reading, gardening, cooking.

MOORE, DEBORAH CHANTAY, protective services official, psychotherapist; b. Queens, NY, May 9, 1969; d. Charles Edward and Evelyn Elizabeth Moore. AA, LaGuardia C.C., 1989; BA, York Coll., 1994; MEd, Fordham U., 1997; PhD, Capella U., 2004. Police sgt., counselor N.Y.C. Police Dept., 1991—; founder, owner Personal Enrichment Svcs.; psychotherapist D.C. Moore & Assocs., Queens, 1998—; founder, owner Personal Enrichment Counseling, Inc. Cons. mcpl. law enforcement agys., NY, 2000—. Contbr. articles to profl. jours. Recipient Law Enforcement Appreciation award, Kings Dist. Atty. Office, 2001, Congl. Hearing Achievement award, 6th Dist. NY, U.S. Congress Ho. of Reps., 2003, Dem. Achievement award, 2003;, N.Y.C. Police Dept. scholar, 2000. Mem.: Am. Acad. Experts in Traumatic Stress (diplomat), Internat. Assn. Marriage and Family Counselors, Am. Mental Health Counselors Assn., Am. Counseling Assn., Acad. Profl. Law Enforcement, Order Ea. Star. Democrat. Avocations: jogging, travel, reading, soap-making, tennis. Office: Personal Enrichment Counseling Inc DC Moore & Assn Counseling Svcs PO Box 130372 Springfield Gardens NY 11413 Office Phone: 718-288-8548. Personal E-mail: chantay@mindspring.com.

MOORE, DONNA TIPTON, special education educator; b. Cheyenne, Wyo., Feb. 16, 1959; d. Donald Lee and Jovita June Tipton; m. Mikeal Lyn Moore. MA, U. Tex., 2003. Cert. Educator Tex. Spl. edn. tchr. Midland (Tex.) Ind. Sch. Dist., 1998—2004, Winters (Tex.) Ind. Sch. Dist., 2004—. Mentor Big Bros., Big Sisters, Midland, 1991—99. Title VII grant, State Tex., 2000-2003. Mem.: Nat. Reading Assn. (assoc.). Home: 207 S Ch St Winters TX 79567 Personal E-mail: djtmoore@pgrb.com.

MOORE, EARLENE J., school librarian; b. Flint, Mich., Dec. 18, 1943; d. Clifford Thomas and Iola Mildred Moore; children: Weldon Wynne Phillips, David Scott Phillips. AA, Grand Rapids Jr. Coll., Mich., 1973; BA, Grand Valley State U., Allendale, Mich., 1976; M in Info. and Libr. Studies, U. Mich., Ann Arbor, 1993. Page, clerical asst. Kent County Libr. Sys., Grand Rapids, 1960—75; libr. clerical asst. Ctrl. H.S., Grand Rapids, 1977—78; adminstrv. specialist Housing Commn., Equal Opportunity Dept., Grand Rapids, 1978—82; libr. asst. Grand Rapids Pub. Libr., 1983—85; adminstrv. specialist City of Grand Rapids, Equal Opportunity Dept., 1985—86; libr. asst. Grand Rapids C.C., 1987—93, U. Mich., Bus. Sch. Libr., Ann Arbor, 1993—94; libr. U. Tenn., Martin, 1994—. Prodr.: (museum exhibit) West Tennessee Treasures: Women Writers; contbr. articles to profl. jours. Civil rights planning com. U. Tenn., Martin, 2001, mem. women's studies adb. bd., 1996—; adv. bd. mem. Office of Minority Affairs, U. Tenn., Martin, 2005. Recipient Cert. of Merit, Nat. Mus. of Am. Indian, 2004. Mem.: AAUW (diversity chair Tenn. chpt. 2006), W.Tenn. Acad. Libr. Consortium. Home: 775 Howell Martin TN 38237 Office: Univ Tenn Martin 1 Wayne Fisher Dr Martin TN 38238 Office Phone: 731-881-7067. Office Fax: 731-881-7074.

MOORE, EILEEN C., judge, prosecutor; BA, U. Calif., Irvine, 1975; JD, Pepperdine U., 1978; LLM, U. Va., 2004. Assoc. justice Calif. Ct. of Appeal, 2000—; judge Orange County Superior Ct., 1989—2000; atty., civil litigation, 1978—89; rn, 1965—. Lectr. U. Calif., 1990. Contbr. articles to profl. jours. Chmn. Orange County Family Violence Coun., 1995—2000; stay in sch. program vol., 1990—95; op. jumpstart vol., 1995—96; mem. bd. visitors Pepperdine U. 2d lt. U.S. Army Nurse Corps, 1966—. Recipient Vietnam Svc. medal, U.S. Army Nurse Corps, Nat. Def. Svc. medal, Cross of Gallantry with Palm, Am. Jurisprudence award, 1978, Disting. Alumnae award, U. Calif., 1992, Judge of Yr., Orange County Women Lawyers, 1993, Trial Judge Civility award, Am. Bd. of Trial Adv., 1999, Appellate Justice of Yr., Consumer Atty. Assn. of Calif., 2002, Outstanding Svc. award, Vietnam Vet. of Am., 2005, Orange County Citizen of Yr., League of United Latin Am. Citizens, 2005, Leadership and Commn. award, Toastmasters Internat., 2005, Appellate Justice of Yr. award, Consumer Atty. Assn. of Los Angeles, 2006. Mem.: Orange County Family Violence Coun. (chmn. 1995—2000), Celtic Bar Assn., Task Force on Violence to Women, Assn. of Bus. Trial Lawyers (mem. bd. dirs. 2002—05), Jud. Coun. of Calif., Calif. Jud. Coun. (corr.; mem. adv. com. on court interpreters 2001—05, mem. adv. com. on civil and small claims 1997—2000). Office: Fourth Dist Ct of Appeal Divsn 3 925 N Spurgeon St Santa Ana CA 92701

MOORE, ELEANOR S., retired elementary school educator; b. Saginaw, Mich., Sept. 14, 1930; d. Calvin Solon and Eunice Shepherd Sifferd; m. Thomas Edwin Moore; children: Deborah Susan, Melinda Sifferd Kerr. BA with high honors, U. Ill., Urbana, 1952; MA, U. Mich., Ann Arbor, 1962. Tchr. Champaign (Ill.) Pub. Schs., 1952—55; head tchr. Beth Israel Nursery Sch., Ann Arbor, Mich., 1958—61; tchr. Ann Arbor Pub. Schs., 1970—91; ret., 1991. Editor: Living in Ann Arbor, 1968. Pres. Internat. Neighbors, Ann Arbor, Mich., 1968—69, bd. dir., 1965—68, Kempf Ho. Mus., Ann Arbor, 1997—, ops. dir., 1997—2000, dir. vols., 2000—04, pres., 2004—06. Mem.: NEA, Ann Arbor Edn. Assn. (mem. exec. com. King, Newport and Lawton schs. 1970—91), Mich. Edn. Assn., Mortar Bd., Kappa Alpha Theta (bd. dir. 1958—65). Avocations: travel, family horse farm. Home: 4243 N Delhi Rd Ann Arbor MI 48103

MOORE, ELISE LUCILLE, Christian Science practitioner, educator; b. Pitts. d. Ernest Lowell Price and Elizabeth Nell (Goodman) Burton; m. Frank David Moore, Jan. 28, 1983; stepchildren: Doug, Brian. BA in Econs., Mich. State U., 1974. Mktg. mgr. Indsl. Tube Divsn. Westinghouse, Horseheads, N.Y., 1974-76, mktg. 7-Up of Ind. Indpls., 1976-77; sales rep. Microfilm Equipment Divsn. Bell & Howell, Indpls., 1977-79, mktg. mgr. Microfilm Equipment Divsn. Lincolnwood, Ill., 1979-81; nat. sales mgr. Phoenix, 1981; owner Pitts., 1982; practitioner First Ch. of Christ, Scientist, Nashville, 1985—, tchr. Christian Sci., 1997—. Regional rep. Christian Sci. Ch. to coll. orgns. in Tenn., N.C., S.C., 1992; nat. pub. lectr. Christian Sci., 2005, 2006—. Religious columnist Gallatin News Examiner, 1993-1998, Metro. Times, Nashville, 1993-1998; contbr. articles to Christian Sci. publs. Sec. Civitan-Gallatin (Tenn.), 1985-86; pres. Sumner County Literacy Coun., Gallatin, 1988, 89, 90; organizer AIM, Inc., Gallatin, 1989; chaplain Storefront Ministries, Nashville. Mem. Nashville Assn. Rabbis, Priests and Mins., Religious Comm. Coun., Omicron Delta Epsilon. Avocations: speaking Spanish, birdwatching. Office: 1719 W End Ave Ste 718W Nashville TN 37203-5106

MOORE, EMMA SIMS, business educator; b. Branford, Fla., Oct. 27, 1937; d. Lawton Edward and Annie Ruth (Hewitt) Sims; m. H. Dean Moore, Sr., Sept. 30, 1961; 1 child, H. Dean Jr. Secretarial sci., Jones Coll., 1955; B, Butler U., 1984; MS, Ind. Wesleyan U., 1989; MA, Fielding Inst., 1995, EdD, 1996. Cert. profl. sec.; cert. adminstrv. mgr. Sec. to svc. mgr. Buick Motor div. GM, Jacksonville, Fla., 1956-72, Charlotte, N.C., 1972-74; sec. to br. mgr. Motors Holding div. GM, Washington, 1974-78, Phila., 1978-82; exec. sec. to dir. product support Allison Gas Turbine div. GM, Indpls., 1982-92; ret., 1992. Bus. educator Ind. Wesleyan U., 1993-94, 2003—, So. Wesleyan U. Central, S.C., 1995-98, St. Leo U., Lake City, Fla., 1998—. Mem. exec. com. Boy Scouts Am., West Chester, Pa., 1981-82. Profl. Secs. Internat. (v.p. 1986-87, pres. 1987-89, 500 chpt., Sec. of Yr. 1986 500 chpt., 1989 Ind. divs.), CPS Acad., Inst. Certification. Baptist. Home: 1327 NW Scenic Lake Dr Lake City FL 32055

MOORE, ERICA, band director; b. Washington, Dec. 15, 1971; d. Harold Reginald and Shirley Armeda Moore. BA, Bowie State U., 1995, MEd, 2000. Cert. advanced profl. tchr., adminstrn. I. Band dir., gen. music instr. Thomas Johnson Mid. Sch., Lanham, Md., 1995—2001; asst. program coord. Prince George's County Workforce Svcs. Corp., Landover, Md., 1995—99. Musician: (Music MSPAP Curriculum Guide) Maryland State Performance Assessment Curriculum Guide Supplement, 2001. Recipient Cert. Appreciation, Mine, Safety, & Health Adminstrn., 2001, Oasis Program, P.G. County Pub. Schs., 1997, Cert. Recognition, Md. Music Educator's Assn., 2001; scholar Charlotte Bronte Robinson Meml. scholar, Nat. Alumni Assn. for Music Edn. Leadership, Bowie State U., 1984. Mem.: Prince George's County Assn., Md. Music Educators Assn. (Cert. Recognition 2001), Nat. Assn. for Music Educators, Phi Delta Kappa, Sigma Gamma Rho Sorority Inc. (Rhoer Club advisor 2000—02, Outstanding Svc. award (Phi Sigma Chapter) 2001, Youth Symposium Cert. of Appreciation (Eta Iota Sigma chpt. and Zeta Tau Sigma chpt.) 2001, Northeast Region Adv. of Yr. 2002, Nat. Adv. of Yr. 2002, named Rhoer Adv. of Yr. 2003, First Pl. Scrapbook and Exhibit award 2003, Advisor of Yr. N.E. Region 2002—03). African Methodist Episcopal. Avocations: teaching, learning, travel. Office: Thomas Johnson Mid Sch 5401 Barker Pl Lanham Seabrook MD 20706

MOORE, ERIN M., social studies educator; b. Evergreen Park, Ill., Jan. 31, 1976; m. Adam D. Moore, June 15, 2001; 1 child, Declan. BA in Social Sci., Domincan U., River Forest, Ill., 1998; M in Polit. Justice Studies, Gov. State U., University Park, Ill., 2006. Tchr. Mother McAuley H.S., Chgo., 1998—2002, Downers Grove North H.S., Ill., 2002—.

MOORE, FAY, artist; b. Cambridge, Mass., July 26, 1920; d. Lawrence Eldred and Irene (Ketchum) Mowery; m. Roger Eugene Donoghue, Nov. 20, 1960; m. Charles Werner Moore (div.). BA, Bennington Coll., Vt.; postgrad., Yale Grad. Sch. Drama, New Haven. Window designer Bonwit Teller, N.Y.C.; fashion designer B.H. Wragge, N.Y.C.; instr. U. Kansas City, Kans.; instr. drama Carnegie Mellon, Pitts.; fashion designer Samuel Roberts, N.Y.C.; artist pastel workshop Pickett Gallery, Lexington, Ky. One-woman shows include Nat. Art Mus. Sport, N.Y., Ky. Derby Mus., Louisville Connoisseur Gallery, exhibited in group shows at Frost and Reed, London Heike Pickett Gallery, Sporting Gallery, Mickleburg, Va., prin. works include Ky. Basketball Mus., Mus. Solar Energy, Washington, Three Rivers Stadium, Pitts., N.J. Bell Telephone, Represented in permanent collections Nat. Art Mus. Sport, Ky. Derby Mus., Belmont Terrace Rm., Detroit Racecourse, Hialeah Race Track, Sportsman Park, Pocono Downs, U. Va. Field House. Mem.: Scenic Artists Union, Pastel Soc. Am., Nat. Soc. Mural Painters, Artist Alliance East Hampton, Am. Acad. Equine Art, Allied Artists Am. Home: Nat Arts Club 15 Gramercy Pk New York NY 10003

MOORE, FAY LINDA, systems engineer; b. Houston, Apr. 7, 1942; d. Charlie Louis and Esther Mable (Banks) Moore; m. Noel Patrick Walker, Jan. 5, 1963 (div. 1967); 1 child, Trina Nicole Moore. Student, Prairie View Agrl. and Mech. Coll., 1960-61, Tex. So. U., 1961, Our Lady Lake U., 1993, U. Phoenix, 2003. Cert. ISO 9001 Internal Auditor, 1994-97. Instr. Internat. Bus. Coll., Houston, 1965; keypunch operator IBM Corp., Houston, 1965-67, sr. keypunch operator, 1967-70, programmer technician, 1970-72, asst. programmer, 1972-73, assoc. programmer, 1973-74, sr. assoc. programmer, 1984-87, staff programmer, 1987-92, staff sys. analyst, 1992-96; sr. software quality engr. Loral Space Info. Sys., Houston, 1994—96; owner, pres. AFT Co., Houston, 1993—; sr. software quality engr. Lockheed Martin Corp., Houston, 1996-97; software quality engr. Motorola, Inc., Austin, 1998-2001, quality sys. rev. assessor, 1998-2001, info. tech. quality engr., 2000-2001; prin. sys. engr. Titan Corp., Houston, 2001—, ISO 9001 lead internal auditor, 2005—; software quality engr. Software Engring. Inst. Space shuttle flight support team IBM, 1985—92, mem. space sta. team, 1992—93. Recipient Apollo Achievement award, NASA, 1969, Quality and Productivity award, 1986, 1992, Cert. of Recognition, NASA Office of Space Flight, 2004. Democrat. Roman Catholic. Avocation: personal computing.

MOORE, FAYE HALFACRE, jewelry manufacturer; b. Granville, Tenn., Oct. 16, 1941; d. Benton Mack and Dora Mai (Carter) Halfacre; m. Travis Edward Halford, Jan. 2, 1965; children: Kristi Faye, Trent Edward; m. Charles Harold Moore, Jan. 23, 1989. BSBA, Tenn. Technol. U., 1963. Exec. sec. E.I. du Pont de Nemours, Old Hickory, Tenn., 1963-65, Amoco, New Orleans, 1965-66; adminstrv. asst. Thompson & Moss, Atlanta, 1967-72; founder, owner Strictly Natural, Ltd., Atlanta, 1975—, Elegant Accessories, Internat., Atlanta, 1980—. Pres. Sandy Springs Arts and Heritage Soc., Atlanta, 1986; founding dir. Leadership Sandy Springs, 1987; bd. dirs. Lindsey-Wilson Coll., Columbia, Ky., 1989, Cardinal Hill Hosp., Lexington, 1989, Ky. Ednl. TV Authority (vice chmn. 1992), Ky. Literacy Commn., Ky. Literacy Found., chmn. 1991; bd. dirs. Lexington Philharm. Found., 1989, chmn. 1991—' trustee Tenn. Technol. U., 2005—. Named Citizen of Yr. Sandy Springs Jr. Women's Club, 1976. Mem. Women Bus. Owners, Assn. Women Entrepreneurs (founder), Women's Commerce Club, Macro Island Woman's Club (pres., 2003), Remax, 100% Club, Rotary. Democrat. Avocations: harp, piano, reading, painting, gardening. Home: 5900 Russell Cave Rd Lexington KY 40511-8441 Office: 847 N Collier Blvd Marco Island FL 34145 Home: 840 S Collier Marco Island FL 34145 Personal E-mail: marcofaye@aol.com.

MOORE, GWENDOLYNNE S. (GWEN MOORE), congresswoman; b. Racine, Wis., Apr. 18, 1951; 3 children. BA in Polit. Sci., Marquette U., Milw., 1978. Mem. Wis. State Assembly, 1989—92, Wis. State Senate from 4th dist., Madison, 1992—2004, US Congress from 4th Wis. dist., 2005—, mem. small bus. com., mem. fin. svcs. com. Named one of Most Influential Black Americans, Ebony mag., 2006. Democrat. Office: US Ho Reps 1408 Longworth Ho Office Bldg Washington DC 20515-4904 Office Phone: 202-225-4572.*

MOORE, HELEN ELIZABETH, reporter; b. Rush County, Ind., Dec. 19, 1920; d. John Brackenridge and Mary Amelia (Custer) Johnson; m. Harry Evan Moore, May 15, 1954. BS, Ind. U., 1972, MS, 1973. Ofcl. ct. reporter 37th Jud. Cir., Brookville, Ind., 1950-60; freelance reporter Rushvile, Ind., 1960—. Conv. reporter various assns. With USMC, 1943. Recipient Sagamore of the Wabash award Gov. Ind., 1984, 99. Mem. Women Marines Assn. (charter, nat. pres. 1966-68), Am. Legion Aux. (various offices 1950—including Eight Forty nat. sec.-treas., pres. Ind. dept. 1966-67, conv. reporter), Nat. Shorthand Reporters Assn., Ind. Shorthand Reporters Assn., Ind. German Heritage Soc. (state dir. 1984-92, pres. 1990-92), Ind. U. Alumni Assn. Democrat. Methodist. Avocations: reading, genealogy, knitting, crocheting, gardening. Home and Office: PO Box 206 Rushville IN 46173-0206 Office Phone: 765-932-2297. Personal E-mail: hem@lightbound.com.

MOORE, HELEN LUCILLE, adult education educator, consultant; b. Watseka, Ill., July 24, 1930; d. John Kenneth and Thelma Mae (Wollschlaeger) Weidert; m. Harold Junior Gossett, June 24, 1948 (div. May 1971); children: Steven, Joyce, Gary, Ricky, Kenny, Jane; m. Herff Leo Moore, Jr., Nov. 24, 1991. AS in Mgmt., Kankakee (Ill.) Jr. Coll., 1969. Sr. sec. Nimz Transp., Watseka, 1948-57; tchg. aide Glenn Raymond H.S., Watseka, 1964-71; asst. pers. and safety mgr. Gt. Plains Bag Co., Jacksonville, Ark., 1971-81; sr. human resources rep. Maybelline Products Co., Inc. divsn. L'Oreal, North Little Rock, Ark., 1981-2000; recruiting dir. StaffMark, Little Rock, 2000—01; adult edn. cons. Dept. Workforce Edn., Little Rock, 2001—. Chmn. Ark. Human Resource Conf., Hot Springs, 1991-92. Contbr. articles to profl. publs. Bd. dirs. Ark. Urban League, Little Rock, 1985-93; co-founder, exec. bd. dirs. Workforce Alliance for Growth in Economy, 1993—; mem. Ark. Gov.'s Workforce Investment Bd. and Exec. Com., 1999—. Recipient Outstanding Ark. Human Resources Profl. award Ark. Human Resources Coun., 1994; named Sr. Inspirational Employee of Yr., ABLE (Ability Based on Long Experience), 1997. Mem.: Ctrl. Ark. Mfg. Pers. Assn. (chmn. 1990—99, co-founder), Ctrl. Ark. Human Resources Assn. (bd. dirs. 1988—90, profl.), Soc. for Human Resource Mgmt. (profl., Outstanding Profl. Mem. award 1989), Nat. Employer Coun. (Ark. chmn. local employer adv. couns. 1989—2000, sch.-to-work com., focus group 1998, Star Performer award 1999), Am. Legion Aux. (life). Office: Dept Workforce Edn Luther S Hardin Bldg Three Capitol Mall Rm 303 Little Rock AR 72034-3315

MOORE, IRMA D., alcohol and drug counselor, prevention specialist; b. Stringer, Miss., Sept. 21, 1939; d. Joe Lee and Mary Louise (Anderson) McWilliams; m. Jerry B. Moore, Oct. 9, 1959; children: Jerry Randall (dec.), Angela Darlene. Secretaria Degree AA, Draughon's Coll., Jackson, Miss., 1959; AA, Copiah Lincoln Jr. Coll., Natchez, Miss., 1999. Cert. alcohol and drug counselor. Sec. Bapt. Children's Village, Clinton, Miss., 1970-82; med. records sec., officer mgr., prevention specialist Mental Health Ctr., Natchez, 1982—. Organizer support groups for parents of children with ADHD, United Way. Mem. Miss-Lou Mental Health Assn. (pres. 1994-99), Moose Lodge, Natchez C. of C. Democrat. Baptist. Avocations: working with children, teaching sunday school and choir, aerobics, reading, swimming. Home: 111 Overton Rd Natchez MS 39120-5246 E-mail: imoore@smmhe.com.

MOORE, JACQUELYN, art educator; b. Helena, Mont., July 31, 1949; d. John Winfield and Grace Genearl Oswalt Moore. BA in Art, Mont. State U., 1972, tchr. cert., 1980; MA in Art, U. Mont., 1979. Asst. claims adjuster Dept. Fish, Game and Wildlife, Helena, 1968; clk., auditor Dept. Revenue, Helena, 1972-79; instr. Carroll Coll., Helena, 1981-87, asst. dir. Guadalupe Hall, 1984-87; dispatcher Fire Tower Lookout Dept. State Lands, Helena, 1986; designer stained glass Shed Brand Studios, Charlotte, N.C., 1987; art tchr. Cedar Hill (Tex.) Ind. Sch. Dist., 1988—. Artist, co-planner Women's Commemorative Mural, Helena, 1979; artist, designer Carroll Coll., Helena, 1981-87; tchr. cmty. edn. Cedar Hill Ind. Sch. Dist., 1990-95, advisor/planner bldg. com., 1992-2001; asst. to Daniel Hillen, Carroll Coll. with various art exhbns./projects, 1981-2002. Numerous exhibits, including U. Mont., Missoula, 1989, Clay Gallery, Missoula, Mont., 1980, Mont. Hist. Soc., Helena, 1982, Carroll Coll., Helena, 1984, State Fair of Tex., 1992, Zula Bryant Wylie Libr., 1994, St. Catherine's Coll., Oxford U., Eng., 2006, others. Pres. libr. bd. Cedar Hill Zula Bryant Wylie Libr., Tex., 1999, v.p. libr. bd. Tex., 2002—03. Recipient 1st place watercolor award Zula Bryant Wylie Libr., 1994, hon. mention State Fair of Tex., "Hostage", a warvigil watercolor 1992, Vigil quilt, 2d pl., State Fair, Tex., 2003. Mem. CHACA Arts Coun., Dallas Mus. Art,

Kimball Mus./Ft. Worth. Avocations: painting, drawing, travel, gardening, writing letters, accordion. Home: 707 Penn Pl Cedar Hill TX 75104-1747 Office: Beltline Intermediate Sch 504 Beltline Rd Cedar Hill TX 75104 Personal E-mail: jacquelynmoore@sbcglobal.net. E-mail: jacquelyn.moore@chisd.net.

MOORE, JACQUELYN CORNELIA, retired labor union administrator, editor; b. Dec. 25, 1929; d. James C. and Harriette I. Thomas; m. Clarence Carbin Moore, Jan. 19, 1947 (dec. Feb. 1970); children: Clarence Joseph, Janet Elizabeth Moore Marshall. Mail clk. U.S. P.O., Phila., 1966—93; editor Local 509 Newsletter Nat. Alliance of Postal and Fed. Employees, Washington, 1969—74, editl. newsletter chmn., 1969—74, sec. dist. 5, 1972—74, nat. editor Nat. Alliance, 1974—2004, mem. exec. bd., 1974—, union photographer, 1974—2005, ret., 2005. Dir. 202 Housing for Elderly Corp. bds., Chattanooga, New Orleans, 1981—2004, Atlanta, 1988—2004; sec. supervisory com. Nat. Fed. Credit Union, 1977—82, 1984—94, chair, 1994—. Vol. D.C. Voting Rights Corp., Washington, 1979—2004; sustaining mem. Dem. Nat. Com., 1977—2004. Mem.: Nat. Alliance Postel and Fed. Employees. Roman Catholic. Home: 1640 11th St NW 202 Washington DC 20001 E-mail: jacmar5362@aol.com.

MOORE, JANE ROSS, librarian, educator; b. Phila., Apr. 24, 1929; d. John William and Mary M. Ross; m. Cyril Howard Moore, Jr., June 1, 1956 (div. Mar. 1967). AB, Smith Coll., 1951; MLS, Drexel U., 1952; postgrad., Columbia U.; MBA with distinction, NYU, 1965; PhD, Case Western Res. U., 1974. Cataloguer Yale U. Librs., 1952-54; chief tech. processes libr. Lederle Labs., Am. Cyanamid Co., Pearl River, NY, 1954-58; chief serials catalog libr. Bklyn. Coll. Libr., 1958-65, asst. prof., chief catalog divsn., 1965-70, assoc. prof., chief catalog divsn., 1971-73, assoc. prof., assoc. libr. adminstrv. svcs., 1973-76; prof., chief libr. Mina Rees Libr., Grad. Ctr., CUNY, 1976-91, prof., chief libr. emerita, 1991—. Lectr. Syracuse U. Grad. Sch. Libr. Sci., 1967, 69, Queens Coll. Grad. Sch. Libr. and Info. Studies, 1967—69, adj. assoc. prof., 1974—76, adj. prof., 1977—86; HEW Title IIB fellow Case Western Res. U. Sch. Libr. Sci., 1970—72; mem. chancellor's task force librs. CUNY, 1979—81; trustee N.Y. Met. Reference and Rsch. Libr. Agy., 1984—93, 2d v.p., 1985—88, v.p., 1988—90, treas., 1991—93. Elder Presbyn. Ch., clk. session, pres. corp.; bd. dirs. Vis. Nurse Assn. Bklyn., 1984—2006, mem. exec. com., 1987—2006, vice chmn., 2001—06; bd. dirs., mem. exec. com., sec. Vis. Nurse Regional Health Care Sys., Inc., 2001—06. Mem.: AAUW, AAUP, ALA (life; membership com. 1967—71, chmn. coun. regional groups, resources and tech. svcs. divsn. 1968—69, dir. divsn. 1968—70, 1975—76, chmn. divsn. cataloging and classification sect. 1975—76), The Typophiles (sec.-treas. 1996—2006), N.Y. Tech. Svcs. Librs. (pres. 1963—64), Spl. Librs. Assn., Am. Printing History Assn., OCLC Users Coun. (SUNY del. 1981—85), Assn. Coll. and Rsch. Librs. (chmn. univ. librs. sect. 1983—84), N.Y. Libr. Assn. (pres. resources and tech. svcs. sect., councilor 1966—67, sec.-treas. acad. and spl. librs. sect. 1973—75, councilor 1975—76, 1978—81, pres. 1979—80), Chartered Inst. Libr. and Info. Profl. Gt. Britain (life), NYU Grad. Sch. Bus. Adminstrn. Alumni Assn. (rec. sec. 1967—69, dir. 1969—70, 1975—79), Princeton Club N.Y., Smith Coll. Club Bklyn. (pres. 1966—68, class treas. 1976—81), N.Y. Libr. Club (sec. 1964—66, coun. 1966—70, 1973—77, 1979—82, pres. 1980—81), Smith Coll. Club N.Y., Archons of Colophon, Phi Kappa Phi. Home: 103 Kendal Dr Oberlin OH 44074-1905

MOORE, JANET LAMBERT, artist, educator; b. Lowell, Mass., Apr. 25, 1939; d. Chauncey Howard and Virginia Foster Lambert; m. Richard A.J. Moore (dec.); children: Joseph Patrick, Chauncey Richard. BFA, Mass. Coll. Art, Boston, 1960; MEd, State Coll. Salem, Mass., 1962. Artsit, cons., Lowell, Mass., 1960—; art supr., tchr. Dracut H.S., Mass., 1960—69; art supr. Neighborhood Youth Corp., Cmty. Teamwork, Lowell, Mass., 1978—79; artist Brush with History Gllery, Lowell, Mass., 1981—89. Mem. adv. bd. Lowell Art Assn., 1982—88, Lowell Cultural Coun., 1990—96; bd. overseers Merrimack Repertory Theatre, Lowell, 1990—2006. Author, artist: coloring book Lowell, Illustrated, 1979; cookbook, What's Cooking at Girls Inc.?, 1990, The Mill City in Good Taste, 1995, hist. mural, Nesmith House for Middlesex C.C., Lowell, painting, Vet.'s Office, Lowell Meml. Auditorium, over 15 one-woman exhbns. Artist, vol. Lowell Boys and Girls Club, 1980—2006, Lowell Assn. for the Blind, 1990—2006, Whistler House Mus., 1956—2006; artist, vol., muralist Dracut Hist. Soc., Mass. Recipient award, Commonwealth of Mass., U.S. Congl. Office, City of Lowell. Mem.: Lowell Pks. and Conservation Commn., Lowell Hist. Soc. (life), Whistler House Mus. Art (life; bd. dirs. 1985—2006). Avocations: travel, theater, sightseeing, collecting antique postcards, gardening. Home: 14 Lawn Ave Lowell MA 01852 Office: Janet Lambert Moore 14 Lawn Ave Lowell MA 01852 Office Phone: 978-459-4003.

MOORE, JANET L.S., music educator, dean; d. Wallace Milton and Roberta Lee Schulze; m. Marvin Lynn Moore; children: Gregory Scott, Kellia Lynne. MusB, Ea. Ky. U., 1974; MusM, U. N.C., Greensboro, 1977, EdD, 1984. Choral and keyboard instr. Rockingham County Sr. H.S., Wentworth, NC, 1977—80; fine arts supr., cultural arts coord. Rockingham County Schs., Wentworth, 1978—80; elem. music specialist Price Traditional Sch., Greensboro, 1984; asst. prof. music edn. Rutgers U., New Brunswick, NJ, 1985—88, Northwestern U., Evanston, Ill., 1988—89; asst. prof. music Sch. Music U. South Fla., Tampa, 1989—95, coord. music edn., 1995—98, assoc. prof. music, 1995—, assoc. dean Coll. Visual and Performing Arts, 1998—2003, assoc. dean undergrad. studies, 2003—. External evaluator Hillsborough County Sch. Sys., Tampa, 2002—; pres. faculty senate U. South Fla., 1997—99. Author: (music textbook) Understanding Music Through Sound Exploration and Experiments; contbr. music textbook On the Nature of Musical Experience; editor: (state curriculum guide) Introduction to Music Performance. Recipient Tchg. Incentive Program award, Fla. State Legislature and State U. Sys., 1994; grantee, U. South Fla. Rsch. Coun., 1990—97, U. South Fla. Ctr. Tchg. Enhancement, 1998; internat. travel grantee, Inst. on Black Life, U. South Fla., 1993, 1997, summer fellow, Rutgers U. Rsch. Coun., 1987. Mem.: Coun. Colls. Arts and Scis., Fla. Music Educators Assn. (Leadership award 1998), Am. Orff Schulwerk Assn., Internat. Soc. Music Edn. (nat. adv. bd. 1991—94, world conf. adv. bd. 1991—94), Soc. Gen. Music, Soc. Rsch. in Music Edn., Music Educators Nat. Conf. (nat. mem.-at-large Soc. Gen. Music 1997—99, editor Gen. Music Today jour. 2000—03, editl. bd. Soc. Gen. Music), Phi Kappa Phi (life), Pi Kappa Lambda (life; founding pres., Eta Lambda chpt. 1992—94). Office: U South Fla 4202 E Fowler Ave UGS SVC 2002 Tampa FL 33620-6920 Office Phone: 813-974-4051.

MOORE, JEAN E., social worker, academic administrator, educator, radio personality; d. Hugh Huriel and Theodora H. Buchanan Campbell; m. Robert M. Moore, Jr.; children: Robert M. III, Doreen R. Moore Closson. BA, Hunter Coll., 1947; M of Social Svc., Bryn Mawr Coll., 1949; EdD, Temple U., 1978. Cert. social worker Acad. Cert. Social Workers, LCSW Pa., 1989. Social worker Children's Svc., Inc., Phila., 1949—52; asst. chief clin. social work svcs. Region 10 U.S. VA, Phila., 1952—60; social work specialist Ctrl. Relocation Bur., Phila. Redevel. Authority, 1962—67; social work/human svcs. adviser for Model Cities Region III U.S. Dept. Housing and Urban devel. for 6 states and D.C., 1967—69; assoc. prof., grad. faculty, dir. new career ladders Temple U., Phila., dir. program devel. Office of Rsch. and Program Devel., 1969—89, assoc. prof. emerita, 1989—; exec. asst. to pres. Cheyney U. of Pa., 1985—91; v.p. instnl. advancement U. Md. Ea. Shore, Princess Anne, Md., 1991—97; host, exec. prodr. Univ. Forum Temple U. Pub. Radio, Phila., 1997—. Mem. internat. bd. advisors Radio for Peace Internat.; bd. dirs., club dir. Gundaker Found., Inc.; cons., spkr., presenter, lectr. Contbr. articles to profl. publs. Past bd. trustees Lackawanna Jr. Coll., C.C. of Phila.; past pres. Fair Housing Coun. Suburban Phila.; chair vis. accreditation teams Mid. States Assn. Colls. and Schs. Commn. on Higher Edn.; past bd. pres. Spectrum Health Svcs., Inc.; chair State Bd. Pvt. Corresp. Schs.; elder Lansdowne First Presbyn. Ch.; bd. dirs. Children's Svc., Inc. Named Paul Harris fellow, Rotary Found., 2005, Guy Gundaker fellow, Gundaker Found. Rotary Internat. Dist. 7450, 2006; named to Hall of Fame, Hunter Coll., 1999; recipient Documentary Gold award, Internat. Assn. Audio Visual Commns., 1999, Crystal award of Excellence, The Communicator Awards, 1999, 2000, 2002, 2003, 2004, 2005, 1st pl. radio/edn1., Broadcast Edn. Assn., 2000, Documentary award, 2000, Achievement in Radio award, March of Dimes, 2000—04, Gold Cindy award, Internat. Assn. Audio Visual Communicators, 2000, 2002, 2003, Media award, Kelly Anne Dolan Meml. Fund, 2003, Martin Luther King Jr. Humanitarian award, Upper Merion, 2004, Mayor's Fire Prevention medal, City of N.Y., Outstanding Contbn. in Edn. award, Theta Nu Sigma, Image award, Black Women in Sport Found., Radio Program awards, Best Coverage Maternal Health Issues/Problems Risk Pregnancies, numerous academic awards. Mem.: NASW (Golden Membership Disting. Svc. award 2005), Broadcast Pioneers of Phila., Inc., Pa. Abolition Soc. (bd. mgrs.), Rotary Club Upper Darby-Lansdown (bd. dirs. 2001—05), Phi Delta Kappa, Alpha Chi Alpha, Phi Beta Kappa, Delta Sigma Theta. Avocations: international travel, writing, poetry. Office Phone: 215-204-4376.

MOORE, JOYCE WEST, social worker, psychotherapist; b. Anadarko, Okla., Nov. 18, 1936; d. Carl Edwin and Alma (Hunter) West; children: Richard Britain, Cynthia Jane. BS, Okla. U., 1958; MSW, U. Tex., Arlington, 1973. Diplomate in Clin. Social Work; cert. social worker; lic. clin. social worker, Calif. Clin. social worker Baylor U. Med. Ctr., Dallas, 1973-76; psychiat. social worker Tex. Tech. U. Health Scis. Ctr., Lubbock, 1976-78; clinician, supr. Mental Health Svcs. So. Okla., Ada, 1978-83; exec. dir. Area Youth Shelter, Ada, 1983-84; program evaluator, dir. satellite svcs. Taliaferro Ctr., Lawton, Okla., 1984-88; forensic social worker State of Calif. Patton State Hosp., 1988-93; psychotherapist Family Svcs. Agy., San Bernardino, Calif., 1989-91; supervising social worker R.J. Donovan Correction Facility, San Diego, 1993—99; psychotherapist Thomas Curtis, MD, Lancaster, Calif., 2000—05; ret., 2005. Mem. adv. bd. East Cen. Univ., Ada, 1980-83; coord. The Chem. People Project, Ada, 1983; adj. asst. prof. U. Okla., Norman, 1982-83; social work cons. Harmon County Hosp., Hollis, Okla., 1984-88; treas. Okla. State Bd. Lic. Social Workers, 1982-84. V.p. Ada Community Svcs. Coun., 1984; mem. Child Abuse Prevention Task Force, Altus, Okla., 1985, Inland Empire Symphony Assn., San Bernardino, 1990; mem. chancel choir First Congl. Ch., San Bernardino, 1989-90. Mem. Nat. Assn. Social Workers (bd. dirs. 1981-84, Social Worker of Yr. 1986, pres. Okla. chpt. 1981-84, bd. trustees legal def. fund 1985-87, mem. polit. action com. 1981-88), Forensic Mental Health Assn. Calif., Antelope Valley Allied Arts Assn., Lakes and Valleys Art Guild, Antelope Valley Coll. Friends of the Gallery Office: Dept Corrections State of Calif RJ Donovan Correctional Facility 480 Alta Rd San Diego CA 92179-0001

MOORE, JUDY W., music educator, musician; b. Lock Haven, Pa., Apr. 26, 1941; d. Victor Linville and Harriet Inez Williams; m. John Hays Moore, Aug. 10, 1963; children: John Hays IV, Victoria Inez. B in Music Edn., Peabody Conservatory, 1965, M in Music Edn., 1966; PhD, U. Md., College Park, 2004. Music tchr. Eleanor Roosevelt HS, Greenbelt, Md., 1981—2003, dept. chair, 1990—2003; flutist Baroque Artists, Hyattsville, Md., 1981—. Ednl. cons. State of Pa., 1999—2000. Guest condr.: Nat. HS. Flute Choir, 1994. Chair Music at Riverdale, Md., 2004—05; ednl. outreach mem. Prince George's County, Riverdale, 2004—05. Recipient Gov.'s Citation, State of Md., 1991. Mem.: Sigma Alpha Iota. Home: 2383 Oak Leaf Dr State College PA 16803

MOORE, JUEL ANN, retired elementary school educator; d. Lucy Mae Giddens; m. Gene Paul Moore, Mar. 31, 1962; children: Dr. Gina LuChrista Moore-Sanders, Richard Vernon. BA, Fisk U.; PhD, San Diego State U. and Claremont U., 1998. Cert. reading specialist Calif. Tchr. Met. Nashville, 1962—67, Travis Unified Schs., Fairfield, Calif., 1967, San Diego City Schs., 1969—81, prin. coach, 1981—2002, literacy cons. Charter Sch., 2002—. Author: (book chpt.) Black English. Recipient Svc./Cmty. award, Women's Inc., 2003. Master: Assn. African Am. Educators (pres. 2002—03). Presbyterian. Achievements include research in Language Registers of African Americans. Avocations: travel, reading, writing, research, discussion groups. Personal E-mail: gpjamoore@yahoo.com.

MOORE, JULIA GIBERT, retired educational administrator, priest; b. Cleveland, Miss., Jan. 13, 1938; d. Jere T. and Zora C. (Coghlan) Gibert; m. Dana C. Moore Jr., Apr. 19, 1958; 1 child, Kilby. BA in English, History, French cum laude, U. Miss., Oxford, 1958; MEd in Spl. Edn., Delta State U., 1982, EdD, 1984. Cert. supr., adminstr.; lic. lay minister Episcopal Diocese, 1986. Tchr. English Margaret Green Jr. High Sch. Cleveland Sch. Dist., 1958-61; decorator The Fireside Shop, Cleveland, 1963-76; owner needlework shop Cleveland, 1976-79; grad. asst. divsn. curriculum and instrn. Sch. Edn. Delta State U., Cleveland, 1981-83; ednl. cons. curriculum for the gifted Bay County Schs., Panama City, Fla., 1984; edn1. cons. Fla. Diagnostic Learning Resources System, 1984; adj. prof. spl. edn. Ark. State U., Jonesboro, 1985; dir. instrn. Sunflower County Schs., Indianola, Miss., 1985—. Evaluator Gov.'s Sch., Miss. U. Women, 1982; supr. tchrs. Delta State's Summer Scholars Program, 1982; coord. Miss. State Dept. Edn., 1982-84; mem. selection com. Miss. Sch. for Math. and Sci., 1988; cons. Fla. State Dept. Edn., 1983, numerous programs for Miss. State Dept. Edn., West Boliver County Sch. Dist., 1989; instrl. mgmt. evaluator Greenville, 1988, Ranklin County, 1991; presenter numerous workshops on instrl. mgmt., teaching strategies, evaluating curriculum. Contbr. numerous articles and papers on teaching and testing methods, spl. edn. to ednl. jours.; writer several teaching manuals for adult Christian edn. Vestry mem. Calvary Episcopal Ch., Cleve., 1977-80, 89-92, del. to Diocesan Coun., 1986, 91, pres. Episcopal Ch. Women, editor the Cook's Book, tchr. Sunday adult Christian edn., leader, tchr. Disciples of Christ in Community, mentor Edn. for Ministry; life mem. Nat. Assn. Jr. Auxiliaries, nat. pres., regional dir.; pres., sec., arts festival sec. Crosstie Arts Coun.; sec. Friends of Boliver County Libr. Mem. ASCD, Miss. Assn. for Children under Six, Mid-South Ednl. Rsch. Assn., Phi Delta Kappa (officer 1988-89), Delta Coun. for Curriculum and Instrn. (exec. sec. 1989-91). Personal E-mail: jgmoore@cableone.net.

MOORE, JULIANNE (JULIE ANNE SMITH), actress; b. Fayetteville, N.C., Dec. 3, 1960; m. Sundar Chakravarthy, Nov. 21, 1983 (div. Oct. 12, 1985); m. John Gould Rubin, May 3, 1986 (div. Aug. 25, 1995); m. Bart Freundlich, Aug. 23, 2003; 2 children. BFA, Boston Univ. With The Guthrie Theater, 1988-89. Actress: (theatre) Serious Money, 1987, Bone-the-Fish, 1988, Ice Cream with Hot Fudge, 1990, Uncle Vanya, (TV soap operas) As the World Turns (Emmy award outstanding ingenue in daytime drama series 1988), The Edge of Night, (TV movies) Money, Power, Murder, 1989, Lovecraft, 1991, (feature films) The Hand That Rocks the Cradle, 1992, The Gun in Betty Lou's Handbag, 1992, Body of Evidence, 1993, Benny & Joon, 1993, The Fugitive, 1993, Short Cuts, 1993, Vanya on 42nd Street, 1994, Roommates, 1995, Nine Months, 1995, Safe, 1995, Assassins, 1995, Surviving Picasso, 1996, The Myth of Fingerprints, 1997, The Lost World: Jurassic Park, 1997, Hellcab, 1997, Boogie Nights, 1997, Chicago Cab, 1998, The Big Lebowski, 1998, Psycho, 1998, Map of the World, 1999, Magnolia, 1999, Cookie's Fortune, 1999, An Ideal Husband, 1999, The End of the Affair, 1999, Hannibal, 2001, Evolution, 2001, The Shipping News, 2001, Far From Heaven, 2002, The Hours, 2002, Marie and Bruce, 2004, Laws of Attraction, 2004, The Forgotten, 2004, The Prize Winner of Defiance, Ohio, 2005, Freedomland, 2006. Office: Creative Artists Agy care Kevin Huvane 9830 Wilshire Blvd Beverly Hills CA 90212-1825*

MOORE, JULIE L., bibliographer, librarian; b. Sioux City, Iowa, Sept. 11, 1941; d. Mabel (DeRaad) Rude. BA, U. Denver, 1962, MS, 1963. Indexer Conservation Libr., Denver, 1965-67; head libr. Gerontology Libr., U. So. Calif., LA, 1968-85; owner, mgr. Wildlife Info. Svc., Las Cruces, N.Mex., 1971—. Compiler: Thesaurus of Sport-Fish and Wildlife, 1968, Bibliography of Wildlife Theses, 1900-1968, 1970, Bibliography of Reported Biological Phenomena.Attributed to Microwave and Radio-Frequency Radiation, 1984; indexer: Updata Index to U.S. Dept. Agriculture Handbooks, 1980; editor: Abstracts in Social Gerontology, 1989-95; co-producer CD-ROM Wildlife Worldwide, 1990-95, Bibliography of Evapotranspiration with special emphasis on riparian vegetation, 2004. Office Phone: 505-527-2547. E-mail: julmoore@nmsu.edu.

MOORE, KAREN NELSON, judge; AB magna cum laude, Radcliffe Coll., 1970; JD magna cum laude, Harvard U., 1973. Bar: DC 1973, Ohio 1976, U.S. Ct. Appeals (DC cir.) 1974, U.S. Supreme Ct. 1980, U.S. Ct. Appeals (6th cir.) 1984. Law clk. to Hon. Malcolm R. Wilkey U.S. Ct. Appeals (DC Cir.), Washington, 1973—74; law clk. to Hon. Harry A. Blackmun U.S. Supreme Ct., Washington, 1974—75; assoc. Jones, Day, Reavis & Pogue, Cleve., 1975—77; asst. prof. Case Western Res. Law Sch., Cleve., 1977—80, assoc. prof., 1980—82, prof., 1982—95; judge U.S. Ct. Appeals (6th cir.), Cleve., 1995—. Vis. prof. Harvard Law Sch., 1990—91. Mem. Harvard Law Rev., 1971—73; contbr. articles to profl. jours. Trustee Lakewood Hosp., Ohio, 1978—85, Radcliffe Coll., Cambridge, 1980—84. Fellow: Am. Bar Found.; mem.: Harvard U. Alumni Assn. (bd. dirs. 1984—87), Am. Law Inst., Phi Beta Kappa. Office: US Ct Appeals 6th Cir Carl B Stokes US Courthouse 801 W Superior Ave Cleveland OH 44113-1831*

MOORE, KATHY LYNN, elementary school educator; b. London, Ky. d. Billy and Katherine Hacker; 1 child, Austin. BS, Ea. Ky. U., 1988. First grade tchr. South Irvine Elem., Ky., 1988—98, fifth grade tchr., 1998—2002; sixth grade tchr. Estill County Mid. Sch., Irvine, Ky., 2002—. Republican. Home: 140 Eades Dr Irvine KY 40336

MOORE, KELLY ANN, secondary school educator; b. Holyoke, Mass., Mar. 31, 1966; d. Timothy and Dianne Moore. BS, Am. Internat. Coll., Springfield, Mass.; M in Spl. Edn., Westfield State Coll., Mass. Lic. tchr. Mass. Tchr. spl. needs Westfield Mid. Sch., Westfield, Mass., 1993—94; tchr. history West Springfield H.S., 1994—. Advisor and head Ceili Crew, West Springfield, Mass., 2003—; bd. dir. Irish Cultural Ctr., Chicope, Mass., sec., 1998—. Recipient Tchg. Excellence award, Westfield State Coll., 2006. Mem.: Irish Cultural Ctr., John Boyle O'Reilly, Alpha Delta Kappa. Office: W Springfield HS 425 Piper Rd West Springfield MA 01089 Business E-Mail: moore@wsps.org.

MOORE, KIMBERLY ANN, federal judge, law educator; b. Baltimore, Md., 1968; BS in Electrical Engring., MIT, 1990, MS, 1991; JD, Georgetown U., 1994. Bar: Md. 1995, DC. Assoc. Kirkland & Ellis LLP, DC & L.A., 1994—95; law clk. to Hon. Glenn L. Archer Jr. US Ct. Appeals (Fed. Cir.), 1995—97; asst. prof. law Chgo.-Kent Coll. Law, 1997—99, assoc. dir., Intellectual Property Law Program, 1998—99; asst. prof. law U. Md. Sch. Law, 1999—2000; counsel Morgan, Lewis & Bockius LLP, 2000—03; assoc. prof. law George Mason U. Sch. Law, 2000—04, prof. law, 2004—. Assoc. editor Fed. Cir. Bar Journ., 1997—98, editor-in-chief, 1998—2006. Office: US Ct Appeals Fed Cir 717 Madison Pl NW Washington DC 20439

MOORE, LINDA SULLIVAN, social work educator, dean; b. New Castle, Pa., Aug. 29, 1947; d. Joseph Daniel and Alberta Mae (Henderson) Sullivan; m. Willie C. Moore, June 1, 1984; 1 child, Eric J. BA, Eastern Coll., 1969; MSW, Va. Commonwealth, 1975; PhD, Tex. Woman's U., 1994. Lic. social worker Acad. Cert. Social Workers. Caseworker The Glen Mills (Pa.) Schs., 1969-72; social worker Sleighton Farm Sch., Delaware County, Pa., 1972-73, cottage life supr., 1974; instr. social work, field coord. Longwood Coll., Farmville, Va., 1975-77; asst. prof. social work, coord. field edn. Tex. Christian U., Ft. Worth, 1977-81, coord. acad. svcs. for student athletics, 1982-84, assoc. prof. social work, 1981-99, dir. social work program, 1991-98, chair dept. of social work, 1998—, prof., 1999—, assoc. dean. Coll. Health and Human Svcs., 2001—04. Author: (with others) The Family in Texas, 1979; contbr. articles to profl. jours. Program chair campfire for children 1st Tex. Coun., Campfire Inc., Ft. Worth, 1990—; child care com. mem. Tarrant County Youth Collaboration, Ft. Worth, 1990—; pres. Ft. Worth Civil Liberties Union, 1979—81; conf. steering com. Family Svcs., Ft. Worth, 1988; mem. ACLU, pres., 1979—81; mem. NAACP, NOW, Neglect Hurts Task Force, Ft. Worth, 1999—2005; mem. citizens rev. team Tarrant County Child Protective Svcs., 2003—; pres. Tex. Assn. Undergrad. Social Work Educators, 1983—84, Undergrad. Social Work Faculty Assn., N.Y.C., 1983—84; mem. clin. rsch. com. John Peter Smith Hosp., Ft. Worth, 2000—05. Recipient Deans' Tchg. award, Tex. Christian U., 1994, 1995, 2004, Disting. award for rsch., Coll. Health and Human Scis., 2001. Mem.: NASW (pres. Tex. chpt. 1983—85, program com. 1993—95, Social Worker of Yr. Tarrant County chpt. 1983), Assn. Baccalaureate Social Work Program Dirs. (chair nomination com. 1999—2001, pres. 2005—, membership com., editor Journal of Baccelaureate Social Work 2000—05), Tex. Assn. of Social Work Deans and Dirs. (pres.), Coun. on Social Work Edn. (ho. of dels. 1980—83, corr. com. 1990—, nominating com. 2002, commn. on confs. and faculty devel., co-chair 2001 ann. program mtg., chair 2003), Golden Key, Phi Alpha, Alpha Kappa Delta, Phi Kappa Phi, Alpha Delta Mu. Democrat. Avocations: reading, home remodelling. Home: 3533 Plymouth Ave Fort Worth TX 76109-4562 Office: Tex Christian U TCU Box 298750 Fort Worth TX 76129-0001

MOORE, LOIS JEAN, health science facility administrator; married; 1 child. Grad., Prairie View Sch. Nursing, Tex., 1957; BS in Nursing, Tex. Woman's U., 1970; MS in Edn., Tex. So. U., 1974. Nurse Harris County (Tex.) Hosp. Dist., 1957—; pres., chief exec. officer Harris County Hosp.; adminstr. Jefferson Davis Hosp., Houston, 1977-88, exec. v.p., chief ops. officer, 1988—2001; chief adminstr. U. Tex. Harris County Psychiat. Hosp., Houston, 2001—. Mem. adv. bd. Tex. Pub. Hosp. Assn. Contbr. articles to profl. jours. Mem. Mental Health Needs Council Houston and Harris County, Congressman Mickey Leland's Infant Mortality Task Force, Houston Crackdown Com., Gov.'s task force on health care policy, 1991; chairperson Tex. Assn. Pub. and Nonprofit Hosps., 1991, subcom. of Gov.'s task force to identify essential health care svc., 1992; bd. dirs. ARC, 1991—, Greater Houston Hosp. Coun., March of Dimes, United Way. Recipient Pacesetter award North-East C. of C., 1991; named Nurse of Yr. Houston Area League Nursing, 1976-77, Outstanding Black Achiever YMCA Century Club, 1974, Outstanding Women in Medicine YWCA, 1989. Mem. Am. Coll. Hosp. Adminstrs., Tex. Hosp. Assn. (chmn. pub. hosp. com.), Young Hosp. Adminstrs., Nat. Assn. Pub. Hosps. (bd. dirs., mem. exec. com. Tex. assn.), License Vocat. Nurses Assn., sigma Theta Tau. Home: 3730 S Macgregor Way Houston TX 77021-1506 Office: Univ Texas Harris County Psychiatric Ctr 2800 S Macbryor Way Houston TX 77021 Office Phone: 713-741-7803.

MOORE, LORRIE, writer, English professor; b. Glens Falls, NY, Jan. 13, 1957; BA summa cum laude, St. Lawrence U., 1978; MFA, Cornell U., 1982. Now prof. English, U. Wis., Madison. Author: Self-Help, 1985, Anagrams, 1986, The Forgotten Helper, 1987, Like Life, 1990, Who Will Run the Frog Hospital?, 1994, Birds of America, 1998 (Nat. Book Critics Cir. award finalist, Irish Times Internat. Prize for Lit.); editor: I Know Some Things: Stories About Childhood by Contemporary Writers, 1992, The Best American Short Stories 2004; contbr. fiction reviews and essays to NY Times, Harper's, Paris Rev., New Yorker, others. Recipient Nat. Endowment Arts award, 1989, Rea award achievement in short story, 2004, PEN/Malamud award short fiction, 2005; Rockefeller fellow, 1989, Guggenheim fellow, 1991, Lannan Found. fellow, 2001. Mem.: Am. Acad. Arts and Letters. Office: 7187 Helen C White Hall Univ Wis Dept English 600 N Park St Madison WI 53706

MOORE, LOUISE HILL, surgical technologist; b. Knoxville, Tenn., July 9, 1950; d. Mary Elizabeth Hill; m. David Oscar Moore; children: Kimberly Hill, Daveisha. Cert. surg. technologist; cosmetologist, aesthetician. Cosmetologist Millers Dept. Store, Knoxville, 1968—70, Austinian Beauty Shop, Knoxville, 1970—74, Hair Fashions E., Knoxville, 1974—78; gen. laborer Alcoa, Alcoa, Tenn., 1978—94; cert. surg. technologist St. Mary's Med. Ctr., Knoxville, 1995, Ft. Sanders Hosp., Knoxville, U. Tenn. Med. Ctr., Knoxville, 1997, safety coord., slip/pack/utility, 1997—. Mem.: Knoxville Writers Guild, Assn. Surg. Technologists. Home: 225 Grata Rd Knoxville TN 37914 Personal E-mail: elvenia@aol.com.

MOORE, MANDY (AMANDA LEIGH MOORE), actress, singer; b. Nashua, NH, Apr. 10, 1984; d. Don and Stacy Moore. Host MTV show, Mandy, 2000. Actor: (films) Street Rats, 1996, (voice only) Dr. Doolittle 2, 2001, The Princess Diaries, 2001, A Walk to Remember, 2002 (MTV Movie award breakthrough performance-female, 2002, Teen Choice awards choice breakout performance-actress, with Shane West Teen Choice awards choice chemistry, 2002), Try Seventeen, 2002, How to Deal, 2003, Saved!, 2003, (voice only) Racing Stripes, 2005, Chasing Liberty, 2004, First Daughter, 2004, Romance & Cigarettes, 2005, American Dreamz, 2006; (TV films) Summer Music Mania 2001, 2001, (TV appearances) Entourage, 2005; singer: (albums) So Real, 1999, I Wanna Be With You, 2000, Mandy Moore, 2001, Coverage, 2003, The Best of Mandy Moore, 2004, Candy, 2005. Office: William Morris Agy One William Morris Pl Beverly Hills CA 90212*

MOORE, MARGARET D., human resources specialist; b. New Haven, 1948; BA, Smith Coll., 1970; MBA, Columbia U., N.Y.C., 1974. Treasury analyst PepsiCo, 1973—77, asst. treas., 1977—87, v.p. investor rels., 1987—99, sr. v.p. human resources, 1999—; sr. v.p., treas. Pepsi Bottling Group, 1998—99, bd. dirs. Bd. dirs. Michael Foods; mem. corp. adv. coun. Fin. Acctg. Stds. Bd.; spkr. in field. Office: Pepsico Inc 700 Anderson Hill Rd Purchase NY 10577

MOORE, MARILYN ULFERS, social worker; b. Waterloo, Iowa, Aug. 15, 1952; d. Herman Lawrence Hartema and Lucille Jeanette Ohrt; m. Dennis Dale Ulfers (dec. Aug. 1985); children: Dale W. Ulfers II, Kelly C. Burger; m. Donald Vernon Moore, 1996. BSW, U. No. Iowa, 1991. LCSW. Membership asst. Girl Scouts U.S., Waterloo, 1995—96; sec. Allen Hosp., Waterloo, 1996—98; exec. dir. ASPIRE TRP, Inc., Waterloo, 1998—. Mem.: Rotary, Quota Club (sec.). Avocations: reading, walking, ceramics, massage. Office: ASPIRE TRP Inc 8100 Kimball Ave Waterloo IA 50701 E-mail: aspireofc@aol.com.

MOORE, MARSHA LYNN, retired elementary school educator, counseling administrator; b. Washington, May 19, 1946; d. Marshall Alexander and Doris Virginia (Diggs) Moore. BA, Howard U., 1967; MEd, U. Md., 1973. Sch. counseling K-12, cert. tchr. grades 1-6, sci. resource tchr. grades 1-6. 1st grade demonstration tchr. Anne M. Goding Sch. D.C. Pub. Schs., 1967—72; counselor Balt. County Schs., Towson, Md., 1972—77; fashion coord., mgr. Wallach's Ladies' Store, Nanuet, NY and Livingston, NJ, 1977—80; adult edn. cons., counselor East Orange (N.J.) Adult High Sch., 1980—83; coord. lang. arts Faith Hope Christian Sch., 1983—84; minority counselor Essex County C.C., Newark, 1984—85; equal opportunity fund counselor, instr. Kean Coll., Union, NJ, 1985—87; tchr. 5th grade Randle Highlands Elem. Sch., 1987—90; tchr. 5th and 6th grade Brookland Sch., Washington, 1990—98; 5th grade tchr., math. and sci. resource tchr. Shepherd Elem. Sch., Washington, 1998—2002; tchr. 6th grade math. and sci. Bertie Backus Mid. Sch., Washington, 2002—03; tchr./coord. 6th grade math. Friendship-Edison Pub. Charter Sch., Wash., 2004—05; ednl. cons., 2005—. Coord. counselor Summer Youth Program, East Orange, 1982; career fair coord. East Orange Adult H.S., 1981, Essex County C.C., 1985; mem. discipline com. PTA Shepherd Sch., Washington, 1998—2002; liaison, exec. bd., hospitality com., multicultural com. PTA, 2000—02; math.-a-thon coord. St. Jude's, 2000, coord. parent math. workshop, 2000—02; coord. Sci. Careers Expo and 1st Sci. Bee, 2001; co-sponsor Student Coun., 2001—02; facilitator DCACTS, 2001—02; math. tutor, 2000—01; sgt.-at-arms WT Union Sch. Orgn., 2002—03. Editor: Sci. newsletter. Chmn. Teen Lift, NJ, Delteens, Washington; 2d v.p. Washington Pan-Hellenic Coun., 1994—96, fin. sec., 1996—98, co-chair Greek Forum, 1996—98; mentor Best Friends, Inc. Mem.: NAACP, AFT, Internat. Soc. Poets, Washington Tchrs. Union, Nat. Coun. Negro Women, Howard U. Alumni Assn. (reunion planning com. 1967, N.J. coord. 1980—87, v.p. Washington 1989—91, pres. 1991—93, parliamentarian Washington chpt. 1999—2001, chair membership com. Wash. chpt. 2003—04, nat. rec. sec. 2004—, chair fundraising com. 2005—, co-chair pub. rels. com. 2005—, co-chair spl. events com. 2005—, life mem. Washington chpt.), Friends of Andrew Rankin Chapel (adj. sec. 1994—97, newsletter co-chair, fundraising and archives coms.), U.S. Tennis Assn., Kennedy Ctr. for Performing Arts, Delta Sigma Theta (Diamond Life mem.). Episcopalian. Avocations: tennis, gardening, landscape designing, swimming, travel. Office Phone: 202-526-5537. E-mail: marsh6793@msn.com.

MOORE, MARY FRENCH (MUFFY MOORE), potter, advocate; d. John and Rhoda French; m. Alan Baird Minier, 1982; children: Jonathan Corbet, Jennifer Corbet, Michael Corbet. BA cum laude, Colo. U., 1964. Ceramics mfg., Wilson, Wyo., 1969-82, Cheyenne, Wyo., 1982—. Commr. County Teton (Wyo.), 1976-83, chmn. bd. commrs., 1981, 83, mem. dept. pub. assistance and social svc., 1976-82, mem. recreation bd., 1978-81, water quality adv. bd., 1976-82. Bd. dirs. Teton Sci. Sch., 1968-83, vice chmn., 1979-81, chmn., 1982; bd. dirs. Grand Teton Music Festival, 1963-68, Teton Energy Coun., 1978-83, Whitney Gallery of Western Art, Cody, Wyo., 1995—, Opera Colo., 1998—, Opera Colo. Found., 2005-06; mem. water quality adv. bd. Wyo. Dept. Environ. Quality, 1979-83; Dem. precinct committeewoman, 1978-81; mem. Wyo. Dem. Ctrl. Com., 1981-83; vice chmn. Laramie County Dem. Ctrl. Com., 1983-84, Wyo. Dem. nat. committeewoman, 1984-87; chmn. Wyo. Dem. Party, 1987-89; del. Dem. Nat. Conv., 1984, 88, mem. fairness commn. Dem. Nat. Com., 1985, vice-chair western caucus, 1986-89; chmn. platform com. Wyo. Dem. Conv., 1982; mem. Wyo. Dept. Environ. Quality Land Quality Adv. Bd., 1983-86; mem. Gov.'s Steering Com. on Troubled Youth, 1982, dem. nat. com. Compliance Assistance Commn., 1986-87; exec. com. Assn. of State Dem. Chairs, 1989; mem. Wyo. Coun. on the Arts, 1989-95, chmn., 1994-95, Dem. Nat. Com. Jud. Coun., 1989—; legis. aide for Gov. Wyo., 1985, 86; project coord. Gov.'s Com. on Childrens' Svcs., 1985-86; bd. dirs. Wyo. Outdoor Coun., 1984-85; polit. dir., dep. mgr. Schuster for Congress, 1994-95; adminstrv. dir. Freudenthal for Gov., 2002, pers. coord., 2002; mem. pres.' adv. com. on the performing arts John F. Kennedy Ctr. for the Performing Arts, 1999-2001. Recipient Woman of Yr. award Jackson Hole Bus. and Profl. Women, 1981, Dem. of Yr. Nellie Tayloe Ross award Wyo. Dems., 1990. Mem. Alden Kindred of Am., Jackson Hole Art Assn. (bd. dirs., vice chmn. 1981, chmn. 1982), Assn. State Dem. Chairs, Soc. Mayflower Descendents, Pi Sigma Alpha. Home: 8907 Cowpoke Rd Cheyenne WY 82009-1234

MOORE, MARY JOHNSON, nurse; b. West Point, NY, Feb. 8, 1940; d. Robert Phillip and Edith Virginia (Carr) Johnson; m. Prentis Monroe Moore, Dec. 28, 1960 (dec. Jan. 1990); children: Carol Edith, Tracey Marie. Diploma, Boston City Hosp. Sch. Nursing, 1960. RN. Clinic nurse in pediat. and obstetrics Harris County Health Dept./Lyons Clinic, Houston, 1982—85; clinic nurse Tex. Sch. for Deaf, Austin, 1986—87; staff nurse pediat. Ben Taub Hosp., Houston, 1989—92; telephone triage nurse, ob-gyn. McGregor Clinic, Houston, 1992—93; staff nurse pediat. Grant Hosp., Chgo., 1994—96; clinic nurse Columbus-Maryville Hosp., Chgo., 1996—2002; travel nurse Star-Med Profl. Staffing, 2002—03; case mgr. Brockton Neighborhood Health Ctr., Mass., 2003—04. Mem. vol. choir St. Chrysostoms Episcopal Ch., 1997—2002. George Monks Meml. scholar, 1960. Democrat. Avocations: art, music, history, collecting unicorns, angels and lighthouses. Home: 72 Pine St Brockton MA 02302 Personal E-mail: mryjrn@yahoo.com.

MOORE, MARY TYLER, actress; b. Bklyn., Dec. 29, 1936; d. George and Marjorie Moore; m. Richard Meeker, 1955 (div. 1961); 1 child, Richard (dec.); m. Grant Tinker, 1963 (div. 1981); m. Robert Levine, 1983. Chmn. bd. MTM Enterprises, Inc., Studio City, Calif. Stage appearances include (Broadway debut) Breakfast at Tiffany's, 1966, Whose Life Is It, Anyway?, 1980, Sweet Sue, 1988, The Players Club Centennial Salute, 1989, Rose's Dilemma, 2003; appeared in TV series Richard Diamond, Private Eye, 1957-59, Dick Van Dyke Show, 1961-66, Mary Tyler Moore Show, 1970-77, Mary, 1978, Mary Tyler Moore Hour, 1979, Mary, 1985, Annie McGuire, 1988, New York News, 1995, Mary and Rhoda, 1998; miniseries Gore Vidal's Lincoln, 1988, New York News, 1995; in TV movies Love American Style, 1969, Run a Crooked Mile, 1969, First You Cry, 1978, Heartsounds, 1984, Finnegan Begin Again, 1984, The Last Best Year, 1990, Thanksgiving Day, 1990, Stolen Babies, 1993 (Emmy award, Outstanding Supporting Actress in a Miniseries or Special, 1993), Payback, 1997, Mary and Rhoda, 2000, Like Mother, Like Son: The Strange Story of Sante and Kenny Kimes, 2001, Miss Lettie & Me, 2002, The Gin Game, 2003, Blessings, 2003; films: X-15, 1961, Thoroughly Modern Millie, 1967, Don't Just Stand There, 1968, What's So Bad About Feeling Good?, 1968, Change of Habit, 1969, Ordinary People, 1980 (Acad. Award nominee for best actress 1981), Six Weeks, 1982, Just Between Friends, 1986, Keys to Tulsa, 1996, Flirting with Disaster, 1996, Reno Finds Her Mom, 1997, Labor Pains, 1999; appeared on Broadway in Whose Life Is It Anyway?, 1980, Sweet Sue, 1987, Labor Pains, 2000, Cheats, 2002; in TV spl. How to Survive the Seventies, 1978, How To Raise a Drug Free Child; author: After All, 1995. Chair Juvenile Diabetes Found., 1985—. Recipient Emmy award Nat. Acad. TV Arts and Scis. 1964-65, 73-74, 76, Golden Globe award 1965, 81, Star on the Hollywood Walk of Fame, 1992; named to TV Hall of Fame, 1985. Office: William Morris Agy care Betsy Berg 151 S El Camino Dr Beverly Hills CA 90212-2775

MOORE, MARYLOU, researcher; b. El Reno, Okla., July 29, 1937; d. Marion D. and Maria M. Griffith; 1 child, Erin. B, U. Calif., Berkeley, 1989; M, San Francisco State U., 1992; PhD, U. Idaho, 2000. Tutor Price Waterhouse Corp., Tokyo, 1982—86; editing tutor Nippon Telegraph and Telephone Pub. Corp., Yokosuka, 1981—86; editor Office of Naval Rsch., Tokyo, 1980—86; tchg. asst. U. Idaho, 1994; assoc. editor Martin Peace Inst., 1999—2000; statistical asst. U. Idaho, 2000. Contbr. articles to profl. jours. Democrat. Avocations: art, music, literature. Home: 5200 Akron Way #161 Carmichael CA 95608

MOORE, MATTIE H., clergy, folk artist, retired educator; b. Empire, Ga., Apr. 27, 1910; d. Joe and Pearlie (Oneal) Hodge; m. William A. Moore, 1934 (dec. Sept. 1948); chldren: Patricia M. Jones, Iris M., Pinkney, Robert D. Moore. BA in Psychology/Edn., Rutgers U., 1974; MA in Psychology/Edn., Columbia, 1980. Cert. elem. tchr., N.J. Tchr. Newark Pub. Schs., 1965-70; minister African Am. Mth. Episcopal Ch., Newark, 1960—. Adv. bd. Mount Carmel Guild Mental Health Ctr., 1979. Artist producing folk art. Candidate for mayor City of Newark, 1978. Recipient New Cmty. Corp. award, Newark, 1983, People Helping People award Essex County, 1976, Essex Plz. Choir Svc. award, 1976, Anheuser Busch Svc. award for Cmty. Svc., 1995, Outstanding Svc. for Religion award Tau Gamma Delta Sorority, 1995, Outstanding Cmty. Svc. award Urban League of Essex County, 1995, Svc. award Bur. Children Svcs. Day Care Program, Women of Influence award YWCA of Essex and West Hudson, 1999, others. Avocations: reading, painting, internet, writing, playing piano. Home: 78 Richmond St Newark NJ 07103-3424

MOORE, MELANIE RUTH, medical technician; b. San Jose, Calif., Nov. 21, 1955; d. Alan Claude and M. Laverne (Galeener) M. BS in Biol. Sci., U. Calif., Davis, 1977. Registered vet. technician; registered x-ray technician; registered vet. dermatologist. Head registered vet. technician Berryessa Animal Hosp., San Jose, Calif., 1977—. Cons. CARE, Animal Res. Orgn., San Jose, 1994-2000; behavioral study participant Primate Ctr., U. Calif., Davis, 1976-77. Editor, cons. (humor book) Collecting Dead Relatives, 1987, Further Undertakings, 1989. Mem. Human Soc.; petition circulator Three Strikes and You're Out Campaign, San Jose. Mem. ASPCA, Archaeol. Inst. Am., Soc. Expdns. Democrat. Avocations: archaeology, evolutionary biology, world travel, horticulture, reading. Office: Berryessa Animal Hosp 940 Berryessa Rd San Jose CA 95133-1001

MOORE, MILDRED THORPE, dietician; b. St. Louis, July 11, 1924; d. Walter Proctor and Rose Frances (Fiala) Thorpe; m. John Austin Moore, June 7, 1947; children: John A. Jr., Frances Ann, Thomas Thorpe, Lynn Brownell. BS in Dietetics, U. Ala., 1945; postgrad., St. Louis U. Hosps., 1945-46. Registered dietitian. Clin. dietitian Jefferson-Hillman Hosp., Birmingham, Ala., 1946-47, VA Hosp., Tuscaloosa, Ala., 1947-48; teaching dietitian Riverside Hosp. Sch. Nursing, Newport News, Va., 1963-82; cons. registered dietitian Va. Bapt. Retirement Cmty., Newport News, 1975-90, Sarah Bonwell Hudgins Assn. Retarded Citizens, Hampton, Va., 1980—. Sec.-treas. Nutritionists in Nursing Edn., 1979—81; mem. Peninsula Nutrition Coun., 1983—, Gerontol. Nutrition Practice, 1982—. Spkr. in field. Den mother Boy Scouts Am., Newport News, 1963—64; vol. Am. Heart Assn., Am. Cancer Soc., Leukemia Assn., 1959—; pres. PTA, Newport News., 1965, 1968; vol. reading tutor 2d-4th grades, 1994—; elder Presbyn. Ch., 1986—89, 1999—2002, pres., hon. life mem. Presbyn. Women, 1999—2002. Mem.: AAUW, Cons. dietitians Health Care (pres. Hampton br. 1961—63), Tidewater Dietetic Assn. (pres. 1956, 1968), Va. Dietetic Assn. (pres. 1972—74, del. 1976—79, Dietitian of the Yr. 1978), Am. Dietetic Assn. (mem. by-laws com. 1977—79), Va. Peninsula Alumni Zeta Tau Alpha (sec. 1994), Zeta Tau Alpha (alumni pres. 1983, Cert. Merit award 1985, Order of the Shield 1992). Republican. Avocations: travel, walking, antiques, bridge. E-mail: mtmjam@aol.com.

MOORE, NEVALYN, music educator; b. Laurel, Miss., Mar. 12, 1948; d. Shelby Milburn Price Sr. and Neva Trapp; m. James W. Moore, Aug. 29, 1970; children: Christopher, Brian, Bonnie, Jenny K., Matthew. BA in Music, Judson Coll., 1969; MusM in Organ Performance, U. Miss., 1971. Music therapist Dyer County (Tenn.) Sch. System, 1979-80; instr. music Dyersburg (Tenn.) State C.C., 1975-80; asst. prof. music Campbellsville (Ky.) U., 1980—; staff organist Lexington Ave. Bapt., Danville, 1989-96; staff accompanist Danville (Ky.) Children's Choir, 1993-98; asst. music dir. Louisville Youth Choir, 1998-2000; staff organist St. Matthews Bapt. Ch., Louisville, 1998-2000. Keyboard specialist Ky. Bapt. Conv., Louisville, 1989-93; organ cons. Pleasant Hill Bapt. Ch., Campbellsville, 1984-85. Co-compiler: Organ Registration, 1991, Organ Techniques, 1992, Let's Get Back to Basics, 1992; co-compiler, author: The Expressive Organist, 1993. Mem. h.s. restructuring com. Campbellsville H.S., 1993-94, sch. improvement com., 1994-95. Nevalyn Moore scholarship Danville Children's Choir, 1998— Mem. Music Educators Nat. Conf., Ky. Music Educators Assn. (4th dist. Coll./U. Tchr. of Yr., 2000, 02, Coll./U. Tchr. of Yr. 2002), Music Tchrs. Nat. Assn. (cert.), Ky. Music Tchrs. Assn. (master tchr. 1988—), Am. Guild of Organists, Am. Guild of English Handbell Ringers. Baptist. Avocations: sewing and design, bicycle riding, hiking, folk music, pilates. Office: Campbellsville U 1 University Dr Campbellsville KY 42718-2799 Home: 407 Lebanon Ave Campbellsville KY 42718-1803 Office Phone: 270-789-5342.

MOORE, PAMELA RAE, elementary school educator; b. Paulding, Ohio, Feb. 22, 1959; d. Loren J. and Louella I. Thomas; m. Chet Moore, Dec. 10, 1977; children: Amy Renae, Cheryl Kae. BS, Defiance Coll., 1990; MS, St. Francis U., 1995. H.s. learning disabilities tchr., Paulding, 1991—99; mid. sch. reading tchr., 1999—. Home: 819 E Wayne St Paulding OH 45879

MOORE, PATRICIA ANN, alcohol/drug abuse services professional; b. Lake Forest, Ill., Oct. 6, 1953; d. C. Therese Stenson; m. Duane B. Moore, Oct. 9, 1982; children: Kelly Roe Duggan, Katie Marie. AA, Coll. of Lake County, Grayslake, Ill., 1986; Addictions Cert., Coll. of DuPage, Glen Ellyn, Ill., 2000; BA in Human Svc. and Psychology, Nat. Louis U., Wheaton, Ill., 2000; MS in Cmty. Counseling, Nat. Louis U., Lisle, Ill., 2006. Cert. IAODOPCA, CADC. Addictions counselor Cmty. Counseling Ctr., Aurora, Ill., 2000—01; probation officer DuPage County Ct. Svcs., Wheaton, Ill., 2001—03; addictions counselor, probation officer Kane County Drug Rehab. Ct., St. Charles, Ill., 2003—05; case mgr. Breaking Free, Aurora, Ill., 2006—. Trainer Girl Scouts U.S., Naperville, Ill., 1994, troop leader, 1990—95; chairperson blood dr. Lifesource, Deerfield, Ill., 1986; child advocate Ct. Appointed Spl. Advocate, Wheaton, 2000. Recipient Nat. Collegiate award, U.S. Achievement Acad., 2000. Mem.: Nat. Assn. Drug Ct. Profls., Am. Counseling Assn. Avocations: sailing, gardening. Home: 433 Tupelo Dr Naperville IL 60540 Office: Breaking Free 120 Gale St Aurora IL 60506

MOORE, PATRICIA LYNN GRAVES, school system administrator; b. Knoxville, Tenn., Sept. 22, 1956; d. Boyd J. Graves and Lois A. Shipley Graves; m. Steven Clarence Moore, Apr. 19, 1974; 1 child, James Randell. BA in Human Learning and Behavior, U. Tenn., Knoxville, 1993, MA in Curriculum and Instrn., 1994; degree in Ednl. Adminstrn. and Supr., Lincoln Meml. U., 2005. Substitute tchr., aide Knox County Schs., Knoxville, 1985—91, tchr. elem. sch., 1994—2004, facilitator curriculum and instrn., 2004—. Bd. dirs. celebrate literacy Smoky Mt. Coun., Tenn., 2005—06. Named Innovative Elem. Sci. Tchr., Tenn. Student Tchrs. Assn., 1995; grantee, Jr. League, 1999, 2000. Mem.: ASCD, Internat. Reading Assn., Tenn. Reading Assn. Avocations: camping, crafts. Home: 1103 Deaderick Rd Knoxville TN 37920 Office: Mooreland Heights Elem Sch 5315 Magazine Rd Knoxville TN 37920

MOORE, PEARL B., nursing educator; b. Pitts., Aug. 25, 1936; d. Hyman and Ethel (Antis) Friedman; 1 child, Cheryl. BS in Nursing, U. Pitts., 1968, M in Nursing, 1974. Staff nurse Allegheny Gen. Hosp., Pitts., 1957-60; instr. Liliane S. Kaufman Sch. Nursing, Pitts., 1960-70, asst. dir., 1970, dir., 1970-72; cancer nurse specialist Montefiore Hosp., Pitts., 1974-75; coord. Brain Tumor Study Group, Pitts., 1975-83; adj. asst. prof. U. Pitts., 1983—. Contbr. articles in field to profl. publs. Fellow Am. Acad. Nursing; mem. ANA, Oncology Nursing Soc. (exec. dir. 1983—, CEO 1999, Disting. Svc. award 1995), Am. Soc. Clin. Oncology, Am. Soc. Assn. Execs., Nurses Alumnae U. Pitts., Sigma Theta Tau. Home: 5701 Centre Ave Pittsburgh PA 15206 Office: 125 Enterprise Dr Pittsburgh PA 15275

MOORE, PEGGY SUE, small business owner; b. Wichita, Kans., June 16, 1942; d. George Alvin and Marie Aileene (Hoskinson) M. Student, Wichita State U., 1961-63, Wichita Bus. Coll., 1963-64. Contr. Mears Electric Co., Wichita, 1965-69; pres., CEO CPI Corp., Wichita, 1969—2001, also bd. dirs., pres., CEO, 1999—; dir. food svc. Bethel Coll., 2001—; dietary dir. food svcs. PMMA of Midwest U.S., 2002—; ptnr., owner FavMo Inst. Hollistic Health, 2003—. Trustee Fringe Benefits Co., Kansas City, Mo., 1984-85. Active Rep. Nat. Com., Washington, 1985-86, task force, 1986—; treas., bd. dirs. Good Shepherd Luth. Ch., Wichita, 1980-85, mem., 1977—; active Wichita Commn. on Status of Women, 1988. CPI Corp. recipient of Blue Chip Enterprise prize U.S. C. of C., 1996. Mem. NAFE, DAR, Nat. Assn. of Women Bus. Owners, Wichita C. of C., Women's Nat. Bowling Assn. (bd. dirs., pub. com. 1969-76), Internat. Platform Assn., Kans. Purveyors Assn. (bd. dirs. 1988-89), Women's Speakers Bur. Avocations: bowling, golf, fishing. Office: CPI Corp 816 E Funston St Wichita KS 67211-4398

MOORE, PRISCILLA W., gerontological nurse; b. Anderson, S.C., Jan. 7, 1956; d. Stewart Jr. and Laura (Adams) Wilson; m. Broadus Moore Jr., June 28, 1975; children; Laura Jessina, Bridget Reneé, Samantha Christina. BSN, Clemson U., 1987. Cert. dementia specialist ARnold Sch. Pub. Health, SC, 2006. Staff nurse, med. surg. Anderson Meml. Hosp.; staff nurse, emergency rm. Oconee Meml. Hosp., Seneca, S.C.; pub. health nurse Anderson County Health Dept., 1990-91; head nurse Richard M. Campbell Vets. Nursing Home, 1991—. Instr. Tri-County Tech. Coll. Health Care Dept. Continuing Edn., 1991—96. Leader, Brownie Troop 137; min., St. Paul's First Bapt. Ch., 2006—, assoc. pastor, 2006—. Mem. S.C. Pub. Health Assn., AKA. Home: 2015 Donaldson Rd Anderson SC 29621-4318 Office: St Pauls First Bapt Ch 322 West Reed St Anderson SC 29624

MOORE, RACHEL SUZANNE, performing company executive, dancer; b. Davis, Calif., Feb. 19, 1965; d. Charles Vincent and Patricia (Dudley) M. BA, Brown U., 1992; MA, Columbia U., 1994. Dancer Am. Ballet Theatre II, N.Y.C., 1982-84, 1984—88; devel. officer Nat. Cultural Alliance, Wash., 1994—95; dir., coord. Center for Cmty. Devel. & Arts Americans for the Arts, Wash., 1995—97; mng. dir. Ballet Theater of Boston, Boston, 1998; exec. dir. Project STEP, Boston, 1998—2001; dir. Boston Ballet Center for Dance Ed., Boston, 2001—04; exec. dir. Amer. Ballet Theatre, NYC, 2004—. Adjunct dance prof. Emerson Coll., Boston U. Presidential scholar U.S. Dept. of Edn., Washington, 1982. Mem. Am. Guild of Mus. Artists. Democrat. Unitarian Universalist. Office: Am Ballet Theatre 890 Broadway Fl 3D New York NY 10003-1211

MOORE, ROBERTA YORK, secondary school educator, small business owner; d. Robert and Eva M. York; m. James Moore, June 3, 1961; children: Byron, Paula, Landon York Moore-Gran. BA, Campbellsville U., 1967; MA, Western Ky. U., 1971, U. Ky., 1972. Music tchr. Marion County, Lebanon, Ky., 1960—61; tchr. Campbellsville Ind. Sch., 1968—69; English tchr. Taylor County Sch., Campbellsville, 1971—; owner The Elegant Touch, Campbellsville, 1985—. Writing advisor for state Ky. Dept. Edn., Frankfort; reading mentor Taylor County Schs., Campbellsville. Active First United Ch., Campbellsville. Mem.: KCTE, NEA, Campbellsville C. of C., Downtown Bus. Assn., Ky. Edn. Assn. (officer), Campbellsville Women's Club, Campbellsville Country Club. Avocations: horseback riding, gardening, poetry. Home: 434 Friendship Pike Campbellsville KY 42718

MOORE, ROSEMARY KUULEI, art gallery owner; b. San Diego, Apr. 16, 1955; d. Edward James and Rina Larn (Young) M.; m. Richard M. Sword; children: Ian Everest Yannell, Sean Maru Yannell, Michael McKinley Yannell, Sarah Lehua Holter, Aki Sword, Ella Sword. Student, U. So. Calif., L.A., 1975, U. Hawaii, Kahului, 1980. Project coord. Hawaiian Sea Village, Amfac Property Corp., Kaanapali, 1979-80; shopping ctr. mgr. Whalers Village, Amfac Property Corp., Kaanapali, 1980-83; comm. mgr., adminstrv. dir. Amfac Property Corp., Kaanapali, 1983, property mgr., 1983-85; v.p. Kahikinui (Hawaii) Homes Project, 1990-93; chair, com. rels. dir. Haleakala Waldorf Sch., Kula, Hawaii, 1991-92, headmaster, 1992-95; dir. Viewpoints Galleries, Makawao, Hawaii, 1999—2003; owner 'Ano'ano Galleries, Maui, Hawaii, 2003—; pres. Merchants Assocs., 2000—. Author: Lightworker, 1990, Mikey & Cocoa are Friends, 1992; narrator: Cellular Universe (CD), 2006; contbr. articles to profl. jours. Coord. hwy. beautification Dept. Transp., Maui, 1992—; mem. steering com. Valley Isle Voters Assn., Maui, 1994. Mem. Nat. Wildlife Soc., Cousteau Soc. Avocations: writing, surfing, skin diving, hiking, camping.

MOORE, RUTH JOHNSTON, retired medical center official; b. Washington, Pa., Mar. 25, 1939; d. Warren and Wilma Bell (McDaid) Johnston; 1 child, Dean Jason. BS in Nursing, Fla. Internat. U., 1978; MEd, Fla. Atlantic U., 1980, EdS, 1986, EdD, 1987. Adj. faculty health svcs. Broward Community Coll., Ft. Lauderdale, Fla., 1978-80, div. chmn. continuing edn. and health-related professions, 1980-89; v.p. Boca Raton Community Hosp, Boca Raton, FL, 1989-92; prin. Moore Cons., 1992; corp. dir. profl. practice and devel. Charleston (W.Va.) Area Med. Ctr., 1992—98, ret., 1998. Cons. in field. Mem. ANA (edn. com., mem. instr. nursing practice 1993—), Am. Orgn. Nurse Execs., Am. Assn. Deans & Dirs. Nursing Edn., Nat. League Nursing, W.Va. Nurses Assn. (bd. dirs. 1994—), W.Va. Health & Human Resources (task force subcom.), W.Va. Congress on Nursing Practice (chair 1994), Phi Kappa Phi, Sigma Theta Tau. Methodist. Avocations: exercise physiology, biking, skiing, swimming.

MOORE, SALLY FALK, anthropology educator; b. NYC, Jan. 18, 1924; d. Henry Charles and Mildred (Hymanson) Falk; m. Cresap Moore, July 14, 1951; children: Penelope, Nicola. BA, Barnard Coll., 1943; LL.B., Columbia U., 1945, PhD, 1957. Asst. prof. U. So. Calif., Los Angeles, 1963-65, assoc. prof., 1965-70, prof., 1970-77, UCLA, 1977-81; prof. anthropology Harvard U., Cambridge, Mass., 1981—, Victor Thomas prof. anthropology, 1991—, dean Grad. Sch. Arts and Scis., 1985-89. Author: Power and Property in Inca Peru, (Ansley Prize 1957), 1958, Law as Process, 1978, Social Facts and Fabrications, 1986, Moralizing States, 1993, Anthropology and Africa, 1994, Law and Anthropology, 2005. Trustee Barnard Coll., Columbia U., 1991—92; master Dunster House, 1984—89. Grantee Social Sci. Rsch. Coun., 1968-69, NSF, 1972-75, 79-80, Wenner Gren Found., 1983; Guggenheim fellow, 1995-96. Fellow Am. Acad. Arts & Scis., Am. Anthrop. Assn., Royal Anthrop. Inst. (Huxley medallist, lectr. for 1999); mem. Am. Philos. Soc., Assn. Polit. and Legal Anthropology (pres. 1983), Am. Ethnological Soc. (pres. 1987-88), Assn. Africanist Anthropologists (pres.-elect 1995, pres. 1996-98), Law and Soc. Assn. (Kalven prize 2005) Democrat. Office: Harvard U 350 William James Hall Cambridge MA 02138

MOORE, SHANNA LA'VON, chemical company executive; b. Cleveland, Tenn., Oct. 25, 1963; d. Joel Thomas and Minnie Jean (Hall) M. AAS, Cleve. State Community Coll., 1984; BS, U. Tenn., 1988. Tech. svc. rep. Mobil Chem. Co., Pittsford, N.Y., 1990-93, nat. account tech. specialist, 1993-96;

application devel. mgr. Latin Am. Mobile Chem. Co., Sao Paulo, Brazil, 1996—; comml. application devel. leader ExxonMobil Chem. Co., Macedon, N.Y., 2000—. Supr. product and application devel. with South Am. customers. Author: HFF & S Machine Conversions, 1991. Republican. Avocations: exercise, playing piano, sports.

MOORE, SHARON HELEN SCOTT, gerontological nurse; b. L.I., N.Y., Nov. 7, 1947; d. James G. and Bernice Virginia (Conklin) Scott; m. Richard A. Moore Sr., July 5, 1966; children: Brian Keith, Richard A. Jr., Kevin Scott, Shannon Nicole. AAS, Fayetteville (N.C.) Tech. Inst., 1979; BSN, Med. U. S.S., 1993. RN, N.C., S.C., N.Y., Conn.; lic. long term care adminstr.; cert. gerontol. nursing, legal nurse cons. DON Elizabethtown (N.C.) Nursing Home; head nurse VA Med. Ctr., Fayetteville; coord. patient care Hospice Charleston, S.C.; DON, dir. human resources Sea Island Health Care Corp., Johns Island, SC; v.p. Sea Island Comprehensive Health Care Corp.; salsa nurse Marriott Sr. Living Svcs., Stamford, Conn.; owner Moore's Legal Nurse Cons. Svcs. Spkr. in field; bd. dirs. Phoebe Taylor Family Clinic. Active St. Paul AME Ch., Rockville Ctr., N.Y.; pres. family support group S.C. Army NG; vol. ARC, Fayetteville; bd. dirs. CYDC Big Brothers/Big Sisters. Indian Nurse scholar Nat. Soc. Colonial Dames Am., 1992. Mem. Nat. League Nursing, N.C. Nurses Assn., S.C. Nurse Assn. Home: 428 Jefferson Ave Rockville Centre NY 11570 Office: Brighton Gardens Stamford by Marriott 69 Roxbury Rd Stamford CT 06902-1214

MOORE, SHERRY MILLS, lawyer; b. 1951; m. Tim Moore; 2 children. BA, Beloit Coll.; JD, Univ. ND, 1979. Pvt. practice, Bismarck, ND. Bd. mem. Mental Health Assn. of ND, Prevent Child Abuse ND; pres. Bismarck Library Bd.; chair Mayor's Task Force on Methamphetamine. Named Vol. Lawyer of Yr., Big Muddy Bar Assn., 2000. Mem.: State Bar Assn. of ND (pres. 2004). Avocations: photography, reading, jetskiing. Office: 300 N 4th St PO Box 4144 Bismarck ND 58502-4144

MOORE, SHIRLEY THROCKMORTON (MRS. ELMER LEE MOORE), accountant; b. Des Moines, July 4, 1918; d. John Carder and Jessie (Wright) Throckmorton; m. Elmer Lee Moore, Dec. 19, 1946; children: Fay, Lynn Dallas. Student, Iowa State Tchrs. Coll., 1937-38, Madison Coll., 1939-41; MCS, Banjamin Franklin U., 1944. CPA. Asst. bookkeeper Sibley Hosp., Washington, 1941-42, Alvord & Alvord, 1942-46, bookkeeper, 1946-49, chief acct., 1950-64, fin. advisor to sr. ptnr., 1957-64; dir. Allen Oil Co., 1958-74; pvt. practice acctg., 1964—. Contbr. articles to profl. jours. Mem. sch. bd. Takoma Acad., Takoma Park, Md., 1970—; mem. hosp. bd. Washington Adventist Hosp., 1974-85; chmn. worthy student fund Takoma Park Seven Day Adventist Ch., 1987-88; trustee Benson Found., 1963-99; vol. Am. Women's Vol. Svc., 1942-45. Recipient Disting. Grad. award Banjamin Franklin U., 1961. Mem. AICPA, D.C. Inst. CPAs (pub. rels. com. 1976—), Am. Women's Soc. CPAs, Am. Soc. Women Accts. (legis. chmn. 1960-62, nat. dir. 1952-53, nat. treas. 1953-54), Bus. and Profl. Women's Club (treas. D.C. 1967-68), Banjamin Franklin U. Alumni Assn. (Disting. Alumni award 1964, charter, past dir.), DAR, Md. Assn. CPAs (charter chmn. membership com. Montgomery Prince George County 1963-64, chmn. student rels. com. 1964-67, pres. 1968-69, mem. fed. tax com. 1971-73). Mem. Seventh Day Adventist Ch. Home and Office: 2401 Pine Lake Dr West Columbia SC 29169-3737

MOORE, STEPHANIE LAFAYE, advocate, director; d. Victor and Gwendolyn Hillman; m. Galloway Moore, III, June 7, 2003; children: Si'Eirria Di'Voushia Singleton-Moore, A'Mira Masaun-Celeste, Galloway III. Student, Kalamazoo Valley C.C., 1990—92. Program coord. Northside Assn. for Cmty. Devel., Kalamazoo, 1993—95; legis. asst. U.S. Ho. Rep., Rep. Upton 6th Dist., Kalamazoo, 1995—96; exec. dir. Fannie Lou Hamer Project, Kalamazoo, 1999—; field organizing dir. Mich. Citizen Action, Kalamazoo, 1996—2001. Recipient Black Achiever award, Kalamazoo YMCA, 2002. Mem.: LWV (assoc.), NAACP (assoc.; polit. action chair 2003—04), Battle Creek Chpt. A. Phillip Randolph Inst. (assoc.). Avocation: reading. Home: 414 W Paterson St Kalamazoo MI 49007-2513 Office Phone: 269-349-9760. E-mail: smoore@flhp.org.

MOORE, TANNA LYNN, marketing professional; b. Columbus, Ohio, Oct. 19, 1954; d. Richard Owen and Marianne Ruth (Daries) M.; m. Craig Thomas Swaggert, Aug. 3l, 1986; stepchildren: Mitchell, Nickolas. BA in Econs., Kenyon Coll., 1976; MBA, Dartmouth Coll., 1978. Product mgr. Gen. Mills Inc., 1978-82; account exec., sr. v.p. U.S. Comm. Corp., Mpls., 1982-90; sr. v.p. Keewaydin Group, Inc., Mpls., 1990-91; v.p. planning and bus. devel. Ceridian Corp., Mpls., 1991-93, v.p., gen. mgr. human resource svcs. and mktg., 1993-96; v.p. sales and mktg. Ontrack Data Internat., 1997-98; chief mktg. officer RTW Inc., Bloomington, Minn., 1998-2000; v.p. Rooster.com, 2001; COO Digital Mktg., 2002—04; mgmt. cons., 2005—; CEO Meritas, 2006—. Prof. St. Thomas Coll., St. Paul. Bd. dirs. Illusion Theatre, Mpls., 1979—86, Downtown YMCA, Mpls., 1988—92, KTCA TV, 1988—94; commr. Minn. Amateur Sports Commn., 1992—2001; trustee Kenyon Coll., 1997—2001; pres. bd. dirs. Washburn Child Guidance Ctr., Mpls., 2002—. Avocations: skiing, tennis, piano, gardening. Home: 1126 Kenwood Pky Minneapolis MN 55403 E-mail: tannamoore@msn.com.

MOORE, TERESA L., mathematics educator; b. Lousiville, Miss., Aug. 13, 1962; d. Billy Ray and Louise D. Dempsey; m. Larry P. Moore, Dec. 17, 1988; 1 child, Daniel P. BS in Secondary Edn., Miss. State U., 1984. Tchr. Yazoo City Pub. Schs., Miss., 1984—85, 1986—90, Louisville Alt. Program, Miss., 1985—86, Benton Acad., Miss., 1990—. Vol. Miss. Rehab. Ctr., Jackson, 2004—, Martha Laker Convalescent, Yazoo City, 2004—. Named Star Tchr., Miss. Econ. Coun. Methodist. Avocations: gardening, house renovations. Office: Benton Acad 216 Academy Dr Benton MS 39039

MOORE, VERNA, county official; b. Belleville, Ill., June 26, 1926; d. Walter William and Stella Blomenkamp; m. Jay H. Moore, Apr. 5, 1952 (wid.); 1 child, Gail Moore Elmore. Classified advt. mgr., sales rep. The Item, Sumter, S.C., 1966-91; dep. coroner Sumter County, 1975-92, coroner, 1993—. Bd. mem. Elected Ofcls., Columbia. Active S.C. Dem. Party, Sumter, 1966—. Avocations: bowling, golf. Home: 1814 W Oakland Ave Sumter SC 29150-5539 Office: Courthouse 141 N Main St Sumter SC 29150-4965 Office Phone: 803-436-2111.

MOORE, VICTORIA EBERHARD, elementary school educator; b. Atlanta, Mar. 5, 1956; d. Victor John and Elizabeth Jones Eberhard; m. Paul Melvin Moore, Feb. 8, 1951; children: Victor Paul, Andrew William, Blair Elizabeth. BS in Edn., U. Ga., Athens, 1979. Cert. mid. grades edn. Ga. Profl. Stds. Commn., 1995, tchr. support specialist Ga. Profl. Stds. Commn., 2003. Adult edn. coord. Apt. Owners and Mgrs. Assn., Atlanta, 1979—80; dir. pub. rels. ARC, Cleve., 1980—84; dir., founder christian recreation Mt. Pisgah United Meth. Ch., Alpharetta, Ga., 1985—92; tchr. Fulton County Bd. Edn., Atlanta, 1995—. Vol. Hands on Atlanta, 2000—06, Alpharetta United Meth. Ch., 2005—06. Named Tchr. of Yr., Holcomb Bridge Mid. Sch., 1998; grantee, Holcomb Bridge Mid. Sch. PTA, 1997, Haynes Bridge Mid. Sch. PTA, 2004. Mem.: Environ. Educators Ga. (corr.), NASTA (corr.), Order of Ky. Cols., Atlanta Track Club (corr.; vol. 1984—2006), Alpha Omicron Pi (corr.; social chmn. 1974—75). Methodist. Avocations: tennis, reading. Office: Haynes Bridge Mid Sch 10665 Haynes Bridge Rd Alpharetta GA 30022 Office Phone: 770-740-7030.

MOORE, VIRGINIA BRADLEY, librarian; b. Laurens, S.C., May 13, 1932; d. Robert Otis Brown and Queen Esther (Smith) Bradley; m. David Lee Moore, Dec. 27, 1957 (div. 1973). BS, Winston-Salem State U., 1954; MLS, U. Md., 1970. Cert. in libr. sci. edn. Tchr. John R. Hawkins H.S., Warrenton, NC, 1954-55, Happy Plains H.S., Taylorsville, NC, 1955-58, Young and Carver elem. schs., Washington, 1958-65; libr. Davis and Minor elem. schs., Washington, 1965-72, Ballou Sr. H.S., Kramer Jr. H.S., Washington, 1972-75, 78-80, Anacostia Sr. H.S., Washington, 1975-77, 80-95; libr. I, adult svcs. Greenbelt (Md.) Br. Libr., 1997—. Dir. ch. libr. workshops Asbury United Meth. Ch., Washington, 1972—74, 1976; spkr., presenter Ch. and Synagogue Libr. Assn., 1975, 80, 83, spkr. spring workshop, 99, presenter, 2000; mem. serials com. Prince George's County Meml. Libr. Sys., 2000—05; chair-competency based curriculum D.C. pub. schs., 1978—93; chair local arrangements launching Nat. Sch. Libr. Media Month U.S. Capitol, 1985; mem. 1st libr. and info. sci. del. to People's Republic China, 1985; mem. faculty 1st established pub. svc. acad. in nation Anacostia Sr. H.S., 1990—95; coord. Nat. Libr. Week workshop Greenbelt Libr. Prince George's County Meml. Libr. Sys., 2002; presenter in field; host ch. chair Asbury United Meth. Ch., 2004. Author: (bibliography) The Negro in American History, 1619-1968, 1968; (with Helen E. Williams) Books By African-American Authors and Illustrators for Children and Young Adults, 1991; TV script for vacation reading program, 1971, sound/slide presentation D.C. Church Librs.' Bicentennial Celebration, 1976; video script and tchr.'s guide for Nat. Libr. Week Balloon Launch Day, 1983; bibliography Black Literature/Materials, 1987; contbr. articles to profl. jours. [illegible]mn. nat. libr. involvement com. Martin Luther King, Jr. Fed. Holiday C[illegible]n., 1990—99, chmn., 1996—99; trustee LeRoy C. Merritt Humanitarian Fund, 2002—06; libr. Mt. Carmel Bapt. Ch., Washington, 1984, chair ch. libr. com., 2000—05, ad hoc com. for church-wide programs, 2001—05, libr. Sunday Sch. Mother's Day coord., 1990—94, jr. ch. pianist, 1994—97, Sunday Sch. adult dept. pianist, 1984—, co-chmn. African-Am. History Mo. commn., 1996—, chmn. publicity com., 1996—99, com. renovation of Rev. Arthur H. Pace Libr. Multipurpose Rm., vice-chair publicity liaison com., 1999—2005, soprano sanctuary choir, 1995—, soprano soloist women's day and tribute commemoration, 1998, music com., 1998—2005; chmn. social responsibilities roundtable Martin Luther King Jr. holiday task force Am. Libr. Assn., 1999—; rec. sec. Washington Pan-Hellenic Coun., 1975. Named outstanding educator, Mt. Carmel Bapt. Ch., 1984; recipient Outstanding Congl. Libr., Ch. and Synagogue Libr. Assn., 2001, certs. of award, D.C. Pub. Libr., 1980, D.C. Pub. Schs., 1983; fellow Grad. fellow, U. Md., 1969; scholar NDEA scholar, Central State Coll., Edmond, Okla., 1969, U. Ky., 1969, Ball State U., 1969. Mem. ALA (councilor-at-large 1983-91, 96—, com. on coms. 2005, Freedom to Read Honor Roll, 1999, chmn.), LWV (sec. Prince George's County, Md. 1997-99, v.p. 1999-2000, pres. 2000-05, mem. lobby corps. 2004-, nominations chair Nat. Capital area 2005—2006), AARP, Internat. Assn. Sch. Librs., NEA (life), Am. Assn. Sch. Librs. (coms. 1973-83, 1987—), D.C. Assn. Sch. Librs. (pres. 1971-73, citation 1973, newsletter editor 1971-75, 83), Intellectual Freedom Com. (chmn. 1983-99), Freedom to Read Found., Soc. Sch. Librs. Internat. (charter), Intellectual Freedom Roundtable (bd. dirs. exec. com. 1989-91), D.C. Libr. Assn., Md. Libr. Assn., Md. Ednl. Media Orgn., Internat. Platform Assn., S.E. Neighbors Club, Am. First Day Cover Soc., Nat. Coun. Negro Women, Zeta Phi Beta (v.p. chpt. 1972-74), Delta Kappa Gamma (v.p. Alpha chpt. 1990-92, pres. 1992-95, Nu State D.C. membership chmn. 1991-92, 2002-, rec. sec. 1994-95, v.p. 1995-97, liaison U.S. Forum 1995-97, 99—, spkr., state pres. 1997-99, steering com. spkr. Soc. Internat. Legis. seminar 1998, D.C. state del. Nat. Legis. Seminar 2006). Democrat. Achievements include being First Lady Laura Bush's guest at White House to launch Nat. Libr. Week, 2003. Home: 2100 Brooks Dr Apt 721 Forestville MD 20747-1016 Office: Prince Georges County Meml Libr Sys Greenbelt Br Libr 11 Crescent Rd Greenbelt MD 20770-1891 E-mail: vbmoore_99@yahoo.com.

MOORE, VIRGINIA LEE SMITH, elementary school educator; b. Middletown, NY, May 13, 1943; d. James William and Anna Van Alst (Suydam) Smith; m. Thomas J. Moore, Oct. 16, 1965 (div. Apr. 1980); 1 child, Christian Thomas. AA in Liberal Arts, Orange County C.C., 1963; BA in Sociology magna cum laude, SUNY, Buffalo, 1965; MS in Edn., SUNY, New Paltz, 1980; MS in Edn. of Gifted, Coll. New Rochelle, 1990, cert. elem. edn., staff devel., 1994; cert. sch. adminstrn., 1994. Cert. elem. tchr., N.Y. Spl. edn. tchr. The Devereux Found., Glen Loch, Pa., 1965-66; elem. tchr. Harris Sch., Coatesville, Pa., 1967, Pine Bush (N.Y.) Cen. Schs., 1967-70, 78-00, substitute tchr., 1970-71; nursery sch. tchr. Olivet Meth. Nursery Sch., Coatesville, Pa., 1976-78; profl. devel. coord. Pine Bush Sch. Dist., 1998. Participant math., sci. and tech. on elem. level program NSF, 1997—2000; presenter ednl. workshops in various sch. dists. and for orgns. and instns. Contbr. articles to profl. jours. Pres. Redtown Residents' Assn., Middletown, 1988—. Recipient Dean's Acad. Excellence award Coll. of New Rochelle, 1991, Orange County Conservation Tchr. of Yr., 1993, NY State Conservation Tchr. of Yr., 1993, Presdl. award for excellence in math. and sci. tchg. NY State, 1997; Partnership in Edn. grantee Area Fund Orange County, NY, 1991, Energy grantee Orange and Rockland Utilities, 1995, Tech. grantee Mid-Hudson Tchr. Ctr., 1997-98, Energy grantee NY State Electric and Gas, 1998. Mem. NSTA, DAR, Internat. Tech. Edn. Assn. (N.Y. State Elem. Sch. Tchr. Excellence award 1998-99), N.Y. State United Tchrs., Sci. Tchrs. Assn. N.Y. State (Outstanding Sci. Tchr. award 1992, Excellence in Sci. Tchg. award 1995), N.Y. State Tech. Edn. Assn. (Tech. grantee 1999), Orange County Geneal. Soc., Phi Beta Kappa. Baptist. Achievements include development of interactive science museum exhibits. Avocations: piano, reading, genealogy, history. Home: 177 Benedict Rd Montgomery NY 12549

MOORE, WANDA SUE, surgical nurse; b. Glasgow, Ky., Aug. 7, 1949; d. William and Lois Marie (Carver) Mercer; m. Charles E. Moore, Sept. 5, 1970; children: Todd, Missy, Terri. AB, Ms. Kellys Bus. Sch., 1968; cert. oper. rm. technician, Ky. Bapt. Hosp., 1973; ADN, Jefferson Community Coll., 1983; postgrad., Spaulding Coll. RN, Ky., CNOR, CORT. Unit mgr. oper. rm. Ky. Bapt. Hosp., Louisville; charge nurse Bapt. Hosp. Highlands, Louisville; orthopedic coord. Bapt. Hosp. East, Louisville; mgr. surg. svcs. Jewish Hosp., Shelbyville, Ky. Mem. Assn. Oper. Rm. Nurses.

MOORE, ZANA YVONNE, secondary school educator, researcher; b. Carlsbad, N.Mex., June 14, 1955; d. Melvin Eugene and Gayla Jane Switzer; m. David Rogers Moore, Dec. 31, 1976; children: Brandi Dawn Arnold, Braydon Kent, Dagan Terrell. BA in English with honors, Sul Ross State U., Alpine, Tex., 1995, MEd, 2005. Cert. tchr. Tex., prin. Tex. Tel. svc. supr. Sul Ross State U., Alpine, Tex., 1975—80; tel. co. facilitator Big Bend Tel. Co., Inc., Alpine, Tex., 1980—95; English tchr. Alpine HS, 1996—, theatre tchr., 2003—. Dir.: (plays) White Room of My Remembering, The Runner Stumbles, The Insanity of Mary Girard; editor: Sul Ross State U. MELL Grant, 2005—. Pres. Parent/Tchr. Assn., Alpine, 1985—91; campus, dist. site-based com. Alpine Ind. Sch. Dist., 1997—2000, sch. bd. pres., 1992—95; adv. bd., Sunday sch. tchr. First United Meth. Ch., Alpine, 1979—86. Named Tchr. of Yr., Alpine HS, 2004; recipient Southwestern Bell UIL Sponsor Excellence Award Nominee, Southwestern Bell, 2002. Mem.: ATPE, Tex. Ednl. Theatre Assn. Avocation: reading. Home: 2705 N Hwy 118 Alpine TX 79830 Office: Alpine High Sch 300 E Hendryx Ave Alpine TX 79830 Office Phone: 432-837-7710. Office Fax: 432-837-7741. Personal E-mail: superzmom@yahoo.com. Business E-Mail: zmoore@alpine.esc18.net.

MOORE-BERRY, NORMA JEAN, secondary school educator; b. Hampton, Ark., Jan. 7, 1949; d. James E. and Alma Lee (McRae) Moore, Sr.; children: Rhemona Moore, Nerissa Moore. BA in English Edn., U. Ark., Pine Bluff, 1971; MA in Reading Edn., So. Ark. U., 1985; postgrad., Henderson State U., 1986, U. Ark., 1989-90. Cert. mid. and secondary English tchr., adult edn., all levels reading. Tchr. English Chidester (Ark.) Sch. Dist., 1971-73; tchr. English, adult edn. instr. Lewisville (Ark.) Sch. Dist., 1973-92, secondary tchr., 1973-93, reading tutor, 1991—; instr. adult edn. Texarkana (Ark.) Pub. Sch. Dist., 1984-91; tchr. English Ctrl. High Sch., 1984-93, Hall Sr. High Sch., Little Rock, 1987-90. Chmn. English dept. Lewisville Sch. Dist.; instr. English Ctrl. High Sch., summer 1992; tchr. Ctrl. High Sch. Summer Sch., Little Rock Sch. Dist., summer 1994; English and reading secondary instr., 1994-95; reading tchr. Southeast Tech. Coll., Pine Bluff, Ark., 1996. Sponsor sr. class; active sch. charity fund-raising; organizer, sponsor Lewisville Reading Club, Lewisville English Club; bible study group Bethel CME Ch., Stamps, Ark., adult class Sunday sch. tchr.; sponsor, sec. ceo com. Ethnic Club Lewisville High Sch.; v.p. Women's Missionary Soc. Bethel AME Ch., Stamp, Ark., stewardess, sec., 2001-03. Named Tchr. Yr., 1984, Lewisville Mid. Sch. Reading/English Tchr., Woman of Yr. ABI, 1993-94. Mem. ASCD, Nat. Coun. Tchrs. English, Ark. Edn. Assn., Ark. Tchr. Retirement Assn., Ark. Reading Coun. Assn. (lit. coun.), Lewisville Edn. Assn. (treas. 1993-94), Phi Delta Kappa. Home: 1221 Hope Rd Stamps AR 71860-4807 Office: 424 Magnolia Street Stamps AR 71860

MOOREFIELD, JENNIFER MARY, legislative staff member; b. Danville, Va., Nov. 10, 1950; d. Folger Lester and Mildred (Cox) M. BA in Psychology, Averett Coll., 1972; A in Applied Sci., Danville C.C., 1986; MS in Edn., Cmty. and Coll. Counseling, Longwood Coll., 1997. Social worker Henry County Social Svcs., Collinsville, Va., 1972-75, sr. social worker, 1975-80; clk. inventory control Dan River, Inc., Danville, Va., 1981-83; staff asst. U.S. Congressman Dan Daniel, Danville, 1984-88, U.S. Congressman L.F. Payne, Danville, 1988-91, office mgr., casework supr., 1991-96; casework supr., office mgr. U.S. Congressman Virgil H. Goode, Jr., Danville, 1997—. Office mgr. U.S. Congressman L.F. Payne, Danville, 1991-96; webmaster Congressman Virgil Goode and Danville Area Coun. Cmty. Svcs. Bd. rec. sec. Danville Speech and Hearing Ctr., 1988; Sunday sch. tchr. Emmanuel Wesleyan Ch., Danville, 1975-97; dir. Wesleyan Kids for Missions, Danville, 1993-98, Ch. Vacation Bible Sch., Danville, 1993; sec. Danville Area Coun. on Cmty. Svcs., 1997-98; program chmn, Danville Area Coun. on Cmty. Svcs. 1999—; mem. merger plan Emmanuel Weleyan Ch. and Gethseman Wesleyan Ch. to Trinity Wesleyan Ch., 2004, bd. trustees, organist. Recipient recognized and honored by Congressman Goode for 20 yrs. congl. svc., 2004. Mem. Va. Dist.- Pilot Internat. (area fundraising leader 1990-91, dist. chaplain 1993-94), Va. Counselors Assn., Nat. Career Devel. Assn., Pinnacle. Avocations: reading, computers, music, photography, calligraphy. Home: 136 Brookview Rd Danville VA 24540-3408 Office: Office of Congressman Virgil H Goode Jr 437 Main St Danville VA 24541-1109 Office Phone: 434-792-1280. Business E-Mail: jennifer.moorefield@mail.house.gov.

MOORER, ANNETTE JOHNSON See WYNDEWICKE, KIONNE

MOORE-VICULIN, CHARLOTTE ANNE, artist, musician; d. Harry and Virginia Longworth (Dyer) Moore; m. Richard Jerry Viculin, Oct. 15, 1977. Grad., Detroit Conservatory of Music; BFA, postgrad., Wayne State U. Self-employed portrait artist, mural painter; tchr., performer piano, vocalist Detroit, Livonia and Plymouth, Mich.; music arranger, profl. music judge. Fundraiser Plymouth Symphony League, 1980—95; bd. dirs., former sec. Plymouth Symphony, 1991—96. Named Nat. Career Woman of Yr., Nat. Assn. Career Women, 1991. Mem. Am. Soc. Portrait Artists, Portrait Soc. Am., Nat. Guild Piano Tchrs., Nat. Music Tchrs. Assn., Mich. Music Tchrs. Assn., Nat. Fedn. Music Clubs, Mich. Fedn. Music Clubs (officer), Ann Arbor Area Piano Tchrs. Guild (officer), Livonia Area Piano Tchrs. Forum (officer) Home: 27265 Canfield Dr W Dearborn Heights MI 48127-1044 Office: Charlotte Moore-Viculin Studios of Music and Art 352 N Main St Ste 4 Plymouth MI 48170-1270 Office Phone: 734-459-1112.

MOORE-WLEKLINSKI, PATRICIA MARIE, secondary school educator; b. Syracuse, NY, Oct. 10, 1956; d. John William and Mary Jane Moore; m. John Joseph Wleklinski, Aug. 18, 1984; 1 child, Alyssa Jane Wleklinski. BS in Elem. Edn., SUNY, Cortland, 1978, MEd, 1990. Cert. elem. tchr. NY. Elem. tchr. St. Ann's Sch., Syracuse, 1982—85; English tchr. Christian Bros. Acad., Syracuse, 1985—2005. Varsity cheerleading coach West Genesee Sr. HS, Camillus, NY, 1978—85; majorette instr. Liverpool HS, NY, 1975—78, Cicero-North Syracuse HS, Cicero, NY, 1978—81, Syracuse U., 1981—83, Genesee Alumni Bd., 2001, 06. Basketball support chmn. Empire State Games, Syracuse, 1982—2006; religious edn. tchr. St. Joseph's Ch., Camillus, 2001—06, eucharistic min. and lector, 2001—04. Recipient Outstanding Educator for a Merrill Presdl. scholar, Cornell U., 2005, Coach's Achievement award, Onondaga HS League, 1994. Mem.: Nat. Cath. Educators Assn., NY State English Coun., Nat. Coun. Tchrs. English. Roman Catholic. Avocations: reading, music, puzzles, twirling.

MOORHEAD, JENNIFER THERESA, art educator; b. Detroit, June 16, 1956; d. Arthur A. Jr. and Veronica W. (Popiela) DeBlock; m. Jack David Moorhead, Aug. 4, 2000; children: Alison Mary Presley, Jacob Arthur Presley Student, Banff Sch. Fine Arts, Alta., Can., 1974, U. No. Colo., 1974—75, U. Mich., 1977; BFA, We. Mich. U., 1978; MFA, U. Md., 1981. Mgr. Brush Gallery, Houston, 1981—82; adj. instr. North Harris Coll., Houston, 1982—84; program coord. art Kingwood Coll., Tex., 1984—94, divsn. chair, 1988—89, program coord. graphic design, 1992—93; assoc. prof. art U. Evansville, Ind., 1994—; program dir. graphic design and multimedia Westwood Coll. Tech., Denver, 1997—, exec. dir., 2000; adj. Arvada Ctr. Arts and Humanities, Colo., 2001—. Tchg. asst. U. Md., College Park, 1979-81; adminstr. art after sch. program Kingwood Coll., 1984-86; owner DeBlock Design, Evansville, 1986-96, exec. dir. Integrated Svcs., 2000-03; counselor European trips Cultural Heritage Alliance, Phila., 1992—; exec. dir. Alliance Tng. Sys., 2000-03; prin., owner Furtography; dir., instr. Moorhead Studios and Art Sch., 2004—; founder, participant Arvada Art Studio Tour, 2002—; adj. prof. Regis U., Denver, 2003—; presenter in field One-woman shows at Fine Arts Houston, 1982, 83, Ten Brooks Gallery, N.Y.C., 1986, Learning Resource Ctr. Gallery, Kingwood Coll., 1992, Houstonian, 1993, Artswatch, 1997, Denver West Gallery, 2003; exhibited in group shows at Steers Gallery, Kalamazoo, Mich., 1978, We. Mich. U., Kalamazoo, 1978, Glen Oaks Country Club Auction, Birmingham, Mich., 1978, Francis Scott Key Bldg., College Park, Md., 1980, U. Md. Gallery, 1981, Glassel Sch. Art, Houston, 1982, Ctr. for Art and Performance, Houston, 1982, Fine Arts Houston Gallery, 1983, Chocolate Bayou Theater, Houston, 1983, McKowey Gallery, Houston, 1983, Cmty. Art Ctr., West Bend, Wis., 1985, Washington Ave. Gallery, N.Y.C., 1985, Diverse Works, Houston, 1988, Lawndale Annex, U. Houston, 1987-89, Rosenburg Gallery, Galveston, Tex., 1989, Archway Gallery, Houston, 1989, 90, North Harris Coll. Gallery, Houston, 1984-86, 89-93, Two Houston Ctr., 1987, 90-92, Sam Houston State U. Gallery, 1990, Baytown (Tex.) Civic Ctr., 1990, Transco Towers, Houston, 1991, Toni Jones Gallery, Houston, 1991, Brazosport (Tex.) Coll. Gallery, 1992, Art League Gallery, Houston, 1992, Shepherd Plz., Houston, 1993, Firehouse Gallery, Houston, 1993, West End Gallery, Houston, 1994, Dishman Gallery, Lamar U., Beaumont, Tex., 1994, 96, Krannert Gallery Art, U. Evansville, 1994-95, San Francisco Women Artists Gallery, 1994, 96, Evansville Mus. Arts and Scis., 1994-96, Thorns Gallery Art, Ft. Hays State U., Hays, Kans., 1995, L.A. Conv. Ctr., 1995, Indpls. Marriott, 1995, Sawtooth Bldg. Galleries, 1995, S.W. Ind. Artists Collaborative, 1995, Indpls. Art Ctr., 1996, Art Pavilion San Jose (Calif.) Conv. Ctr., 1997, Art Gallery, Marist Coll., Poughkeepsie, N.Y., 1997, A Boy & His Dog, Key West, Fla., 2003, Harrison Gallery, Key West, 2003, Faculty exhibit Regis U., 2005, Dog and Pony Show Arvada Ctr. Arts and Humanities, 2006 U. Md. scholar, 1979-81; recipient Hon. Mention award Tri-State Exhbn., Beaumont, 1986, Galveston Art League, 1988, 89, Top Artist award 4th Ann. East End Show, Lawndale Annex, 1988, 2d Pl. award YMCA Corp. Challenge, 1995, Southwestern Ind. Artists Collaborative, 1995 Mem. Univ. and Coll. Designers Assn., Coll. Art Assn., Founds. Art and Theory in Edn., Amazing Space, Diverse Works, Houston Apple Users' Group, Houston Area Women's Ctr., Southwestern Ind. Artists Collaborative, Women's Caucus for Arts, Visual Arts Alliance, Am. Inst. Graphic Arts Avocations: airplane gliding, snow skiing, horseback riding, sailing, triathlete. Home: 8337 Vivian St Arvada CO 80005-5277 Personal E-mail: jdmoorhead@earthlink.net.

MOORHEAD, LUCY GALPIN, writer; b. N.Y.C., Jan. 24, 1926; d. Perrin Comstock and Stephanie (English) Galpin; children: William S., Lucy Perrin M. Grayson, Stephen G., James B. BA, VAssar Coll., 1946. Author: Entertaining in Washington, 1978, Dolly Appleton, (a novel) In the Town and In the Country (a memoir), 2004. Mem. Chevy Chase Club, Cosmopolitan Club. Episcopalian. Avocations: fox-hunting, painting.

MOORHOUSE, ROBBI PRESSWOOD, elementary school educator; b. Morristown, Tenn., Jan. 26, 1961; d. James Robert and Marian Bailey Presswood; m. Joel Dean Moorhouse, Sr., May 14, 1956; 1 child, Joel Dean II. BS, U. Tenn., Chattanooga, 1983. Cert. tchr. Tenn. Quality assurance mgr. Johnston Coca-Cola Bottling Co., Cleveland, Tenn., 1983—88; tchr. Hamilton County Bd. of Edn., Chattanooga, 1989—2006. Mem. Order of the Ea. Star, Chattanooga, 1990—2006, Freedom's Found., Chattanooga, 1992—2006, DAR, Cleveland, Tenn., 2000—06, UDC, Benton, Tenn., 2000—06. Mem.: Delta Kappa Gamma (treas. 1999—2003). Avocations: antiques, books. Office Phone: 423-238-5221.

MOORMAN, ROSE DRUNELL, county administrator, systems analyst; b. Miami, Fla., May 13, 1945; d. Willie and Claudia (Fluker) M. BA in Mathematics, Fisk U., 1967; MSE in Computer and Info. Scis., U. Pa., 1976. Computer programmer GE, Valley Forge, Pa., 1967-70; programmer/analyst Price Waterhouse Co., Phila., 1970-72; sr. programmer/analyst Inst. Environ. Medicine U. Pa., Phila., 1972-77; systems analyst Honeywell, Ft. Washington, Pa., 1977-78; dir. tech. svcs. Gill Assocs., Inc., Washington, 1978-83; owner, CEO Computer and Info. Mgmt., Inc., Miami, 1983-88; mgr. tech. support City of Miami, 1988-94, coord. diversity, 1994-95; exec. adminstr. to county commr. Metro-Dade County, 1996-97; sr. systems analyst Miami-Dade County, 1997—. Facilitator Women in Info. Processing, Washington, 1979-83; computer edn. adv. panel Dade County Pub. Schs., 1984-88. Editor: (newsletter) Bits and Bytes, 1979-82; co-editor: (newsletter) Ebenezer Speaks, 1992—. Active Ebenezer United Meth. Ch., Miami, 1954—, treas., chair fin. com., 1992—, Family Christian Assn., 1989-94; troop leader Girl Scouts Am., 1990—; pres. Loran Park Sch. PTA, Miami, 1991-93; treas., bd. dirs. Overtown Cmty. Health Clinic, Miami, 1992—, New Miami Group, Inc., 1994—; mem. Dade Heritage Trust, Miami, 1994—; mem. Dade County Hist. Preservation Bd., 1996-98. Recipient Leadership award ARC, 1957, 63, Bronze medallion for Community Svc. NCCJ, 1963, Svc. Excellence award Delta Sigma Theta, 1986. Meritorious Svc. award Fisk U., 1992. Mem. NAACP, Nat. Forum Black Pub. Adminstrs. (bd. dirs., 2d v.p. 1993—), Nat. Coun. Negro Women, Black Data Processing Assocs. South Fla. (pres., bd. dirs. 2001—). Democrat. Avocations: bridge, collecting cookbooks and kaleidoscopes, hunting, gardening, hist. preservation of structures and cultures. Office: Miami-Dade County Enterprise Tech Svcs Dept 5680 SW 87th Ave Miami FL 33173-1618

MOOS, VERNA VIVIAN, special education educator; b. Jamestown, N.D., July 1, 1951; d. Philip and Violena (Schweitzer) M. BS in Edn., Valley City State U., 1973; MEd, U. So. Miss., 1983, EdS, 1988; AA, Minot State U., 1987; postgrad., East Tex. State U., U. Tex., N.D. State U., U. N.D., Kans. State U., McGill U. Supr. recreation Valley City (N.D.) Recreation Dept., 1969-73; tchr. Harvey (N.D.) Pub. Schs., 1973-75; tchr. spl. edn. Belfield (N.D.) Pub. Schs., 1975-77; edn. therapist N.D. Elks Assn., Dawson, 1976-77; tchr. spl. edn. Dickinson (N.D.) pub. Schs., 1977-87; ednl. technician ABLE, Inc., Dickinson, 1984-87; tchr. spl. edn. Pewitt Ind. Sch. Dist., Omaha and Naples, Tex., 1987—; tchr. adult edn. N.E. Tex. C.C., Mt. Pleasant, 1989—. Local and area dir. Tex. Spl. Olympics, Austin, 1988—; local, regional and state dir. N.D. Spl. Olympics, 1972-87; local coord. Very Spl. Arts Festival; mem. Am. Heart Assn., 1979-87, N.D. Heart Assn., 1979-87; mem. adminstrv. bd. First United Meth. Ch., Naples, Tex., 1994—; active Communities-In-Sch. program for at-risk students, 1995—. Named Dickinson Jaycees Outstanding Young Educator, 1979, Dickinson C. of C. Tchr. of Yr., 1985, Dallas area Coach of Yr., Tex. Spl. Olympics, 1993, Dir. of Yr., N.D. Spl. Olympics, 1985. Mem. NEA, Coun. Exceptional Children, Naples C. of C., Delta Kappa Gamma (scholar), Phi Delta Kappa, Kappa Delta Pi. Avocations: travel, reading, working, sports. Home: PO Box 788 Omaha TX 75571-0788 Office: Pewitt CISD PO Box 1106 Omaha TX 75571-1106

MOQUIN, BARBARA E., psychotherapist; b. York, Pa., Nov. 17, 1956; d. Ray Charles and Antoinette Teresa (Mai) Barnes; children: Christiana, David. BSN, Georgetown U., 1978; MSN, Cath. U. Am., 1982. Cert. Reiki master, bio-energy I, therapeutic touch, clin. hypnosis, behavioral medicine. Staff nurse hematology unit U. Chgo.; asst. head nurse oncology unit Arlington (Va.) Hosp.; clinic coord. NCI-Navy Oncology Br., Bethesda, Md.; nurse specialist Naval Hosp., Bethesda, asst. divsn. head behavioral medicine, dept. psychology; pvt. practice. Mem. NAFE, Soc. Behaviorial Meidine, Sigma Theta Tau, Alpha Sigma Nu. Home: 44 Napa Valley Rd Gaithersburg MD 20878-4111

MORA, DAWN ANN, theater educator; b. Ft. Worth, Tex., July 28, 1941; d. William S. Arms and Frances M. Tucker; 1 child, Abraham. BA, MA, San Diego State U.; postgrad., UCLA, U.S. Internat. U., San Diego. Tchr. Goodman Sch. Drama, Chgo.; prof. Northwestern U., Evanston, Ill. Presenter in field. Writer, prodr.: (video) Movement for the Actor; co-dir., co-creator (mus.) The Boy Who Could Not Fly. Recipient Ford Found. grant, McCormick Tchg. Excellence award, Northwestern U., Cira grants. Mem.: Assn. Theater Educators in Higher Edn., Movement Educators of Am. Avocation: dance. Office: Northwestern U Evanston IL 60201

MORA, MARIA, elementary school educator; d. Flor A. and Eduardo Munoz; m. Gabriel Mora, Jan. 7, 2000; children: Amber Nicole, Gabriel. BA in Math., U. Tex. - Pan Am., Edinburg, 1995—2000. Tchr. B.L. Garza Mid. Sch., Edinburg, 2002—. Office Phone: 956-316-3100.

MORA, PAT, writer, speech professional; b. El Paso, Tex., Jan. 19, 1942; d. Raul Antonio and Estella (Delgado) M.; m. William H. Burnside, July 27, 1963 (div. Aug. 1981); children: William Burnside, Elizabeth Burnside, Cecilia Burnside; m. Vernon L. Scarborough, May 25, 1984. BA, Tex. Western Coll., 1963; MA, U. Tex., El Paso, 1967. Lectr. English U. Tex., El Paso, 1979-81, asst. to v.p. for acad. affairs, 1981-89, mus. dir., asst. to pres., 1987-89; cons. W.K. Kellogg Found., Battle Creek, Mich., 1989-91. Advisor Kellogg Nat. Fellowship Program, 1991-93. Author: (poetry) Chants, 1984 (SW Book award 1985), Borders, 1986 (SW Book award 1987), Communion, 1991, Agua Santa: Holy Water, Aunt Carmen's Book of Practical Saints, 1997; (nonfiction) Nepantla: Essays from the Land in the Middle, 1993, House of Houses, 1997; (children's books) Confetti: Poems for Children, Uno, Dos, Tres: One, Two, Three, Listen to the Desert: Oye al Desierto, The Race of Toad and Deer, The Gift of the Poinsettia: El regalo de la flor de nochebuena, The Desert Is My Mother: El desierto es mi madra, Agua, Agua, Agua, Pablo's Tree, A Birthday Basket for Tía, 1992 (SW Book award 1993), Tomás and the Library Lady, 1997, A library for Juana: The World of Sor Juana Inés, 2002 (Tomás Rivera Mexican American Children's Book award, 2002), Dona Flor: A Tall Tale About a Giant Woman with a Great Big Heart, 2005 (Am. Libr. Assn. Pura Belpre Author Honor Book, 2006). Kellogg nat. fellow W.K. Kellogg Found., 1986; Nat. Endowment Arts Creative Writing fellow, 1994; recipient poetry award Conf. Cin. Women, 1990; named to El Paso Herald Post Writers Hall of Fame, 1988. Mem Tex. Inst. Letters, Acad. Am. Poets, Nat. Coun. Tchrs. English, Soc. Children's Book Writers, Poetry Soc. Am. Democrat. Avocations: reading, walking, travel.*

MORACA-SAWICKI, ANNE MARIE, oncology nurse; b. Niagara Falls, N.Y., Sept. 28, 1952; d. Joseph R. and Joan (Forgione) Moraca; m. Richard L. Sawicki, Sept. 15, 1979. BSN, D'Youville Coll., 1974; MS in Nursing, SUNY at Buffalo, 1977. Asst. prof. nursing D'Youville Coll., Buffalo, 1977-81; clin. editor Springhouse (Pa.) Corp., 1981-82; charge nurse Mt. St. Mary's Hosp., Lewiston, N.Y., 1982-84; surg. coord., adminstrv. asst. Dr. Richard L. Sawicki, Niagara Falls, N.Y., 1983—. Clin. cons., externship site supr. Niagara County C.C., Sanborn, N.Y.; bd. dirs. Health Assn. Niagara County, Inc., adult day care program Health Assn. Niagara County Inc. Contbr.: Nurses Legal Handbook, 1985, Pharmacotherapeutics: A Nursing Process Approach, 1986, 2d edit., 1990, 3rd edit., 1994, 4th edit., 1998; clin. editor, contbr. Nurses Ref. Libr. Series Vols. on Drugs, Definitions, Procedures and Practices; clin. reviewer Manual of Med./Sug. Nursing, 1995, contbr., 1996; clin. reviewer Critical Care Handbook and IV Drug Handbook, 1995; clin. cons. Critical Care Plans, 1987, Taber's Cyclopedic Med. Dictionary, 16th edit., 1989; grant writer LaSalle Bus. and Profl. Assn. Mem. Niagara Falls Cmty. Devel. Bd.; bd. dirs. Barbara Zimmer Holiday Wish Show, Barbara Zimmer Holiday Wish Breast Cancer Fund Raiser; co-chairperson LaSalle Bus. and Profl. Cmty. Devel. Fund Raising Com. Recipient Cert. of Appreciation Niagara County C.C., 1988, 91, 92, Cmty. Svc. award Am. Cancer Soc., 1978, Miss Hope award, 1977, Am. Cancer Soc. Nursing Fellowship Grant, 1977, Good Neighbor award Niagara Falls Meml. Med. Ctr., 2003, LaSalle Bus. and Profl. Assn. Cmty. Svc. award, 2003, Pres.'s award, HANEI, 2004; Grad. fellow SUNY, Buffalo, 1976-77; grantee mulitple grants for cmty. devel., beautification and health and safety, LaSalle. Mem. AAUP, N.Y. State Nurse's Assn., Health Assn. Niagara County (chairperson 1995—, bd. dirs. adult day care program), LaSalle Bus. and Prof. Assn. (publicity chairperson), Am. Bus. Women's Assn., Sigma Theta Tau. Home: 4658 Vrooman Dr Lewiston NY 14092-1049 E-mail: ams928@webtv.net.

MORAHAN-MARTIN, JANET MAY, psychologist, educator; b. N.Y.C., Jan. 13, 1944; d. William Timothy and May Rosalind (Tarangelo) Morahan; m. Curtis Harmon Martin, June 2, 1979; 1 child, Gwendolyn May. AB, Rosemont (Pa.) Coll., 1965; MEd, Tufts U., 1968; PhD, Boston Coll., 1978. Asst. mkt. rsch. analyst Compton Advt. Co., N.Y.C., 1965-67; mkt. rsch. analyst Ogilvy & Mather Advt., N.Y.C., 1967; ednl. rsch. asst. Tufts U., Medford, Mass., 1968-69; counselor Psychol. Inst. Bentley Coll., Waltham, Mass., 1971-72; dir. counseling svcs. Bryant U., Smithfield, RI, 1972-75, psychology instr., 1972-76, asst. prof. psychology, 1976-81, assoc. prof. psychology, 1981-91, prof. psychology, 1991—. Bd. dirs. Multi-Svc. Ctr., Newton, Mass., 1980-82. Contbr. articles to profl. jours., chpts. to books; reviewer APA Conv., 1985—, Teaching of Psychology Jour., 1988—, Collegiate Micro-Computer Jour., 1991, 93, Nat. Soc. Sci. Jour., 1991; mem. editl. bd., spl. edit. editor Cyber Psychology and Behavior. Bd. dirs. Wellesley (Mass.) Community Children's Ctr., 1986-90, Coun. for Children, Newton, Mass., 1984-86. NIMH fellow, 1967-68; NSF grantee, 1974-76, U.S. Office Edn. grantee, 1980. Mem. APA, Mass. Audubon Soc., Internat. Soc. for Online Mental Health (founding mem.), Soc. for Tchg. of Psychology, Soc. Computers in Psychology. Avocations: photography, antiques, gardening, literature. Home: 17 Fuller Brook Rd Wellesley MA 02482-7108 Office: Bryant U 1150 Douglas Pike Smithfield RI 02917-1291 Business E-Mail: jmorahan@bryant.edu.

MORALES, DIANE K., former federal agency administrator; b. Houston, July 11, 1946; d. Arthur Clement and Helen Mary (Araiza) Morales, Louie Welch (Stepfather); m. James Neal Glerum. BA, U. Tex.-Austin, 1968. Account exec. Goodwin, Dannenbaum, Littman & Wingfield, Houston, 1968—70; pub. rels. rep. Gittings, Inc., Dallas, 1970—71; asst. buyer, mgr. Neiman-Marcus, Dallas, 1971—80; sr. assoc., mktg. mgr. 3/D Internat., Houston, 1980—81; dep. asst. sec. policy U.S. Dept. Interior, Washington, 1981—83; bd. dirs. CAB, Washington, 1983—86; v.p. govt. rels. Earth Tech. Corp., Washington, 1986—88; pres. Morales Consulting Svc. Co., Washington, 1988—90; dep. asst. sec. def. for logistics U.S. Dept. Def., Washington, 1990—93, dep. under sec. logistics and material readiness, 2001—04; pres. DMS, Inc., Washington, 1993—2001, DMG Enterprises, LLC, Washington, 2004—. Mem. logistics mgmt. com. Nat. Def. Industry Assn., 1995—2001. Pres. Downtown Rep. Women's Club, Dallas, 1975-80; bd. dirs. Dallas County Men's Rep. Club, 1978-80, Dallas Coun. Women's Rep. Club, 1978-80, Houston Interam. C. of C., 1980-81, Christian Embassy, 1990-93, Am. Cancer Soc./NOVA, 2000-04, Wolf Trap Found., 2005—. Nat. Job Corps Assn., 2005—; Project Nehemiah, 1996—, Tex. State Soc., 1996-2001; mem. Rep. Women's Fed. Forum, Rep. Nat. Hispanic Assembly, Conservative Rep. Network, 1985-89. Mem.: Women in Def. Industry. Republican. Presbyterian.

MORALES, MARCIA PAULETTE MERRY, language educator, archaeologist; b. Denver, Dec. 10, 1946; d. Paul Robert Merry and Berneice Roberta Lyddon; m. Jorge Bernardo Morales, Dec. 28, 1977; children: Marcia Paloma, Elisa Berenice, Andrea Paul-Etta. BA, U. Denver, 1969; MA cum laude, U. Am., 1975. Rsch. asst. dept. anthropology U. Ill., Puebla, Mexico, 1972—75; tchr. Eng., art history Escuela Preparatoria, Cuautla, Morclos, Mexico, 1975—76; tchr., coord. Eng. Colegio Oquetza, Cuautla, 1982—91; tchr. anthropology, Eng. Centro Cultural Iberoamericano, Cuernavaca, Mexico, 1992—95; tchr. Spanish Aztec (N.Mex.) HS, 1996—. Instr. Spanish Fort Lewis Coll., Durango, Colo., 1997—. Contbr. chapters to books Ancient Chalcatzingo, 1987. Fellow: Durango Heartbeat (pres. 1997—), San Juan Audubon Soc. (treas. 1996—). Methodist. Avocations: hiking, birdwatching, travel.

MORALES, MARIA CRISTINA, social sciences educator; d. Oscar and Maria Morales; m. Brian Roebuck. BA in Sociology, BA in Psychology, U. Tex., El Paso, 1996; MSc, Tex. A&M U., College Station, 1999, PhD, 2004. Lectr. Tex. A&M U., College Station, 2003, rsch. asst., 1997—2004; asst. prof. sociology U. Nev., Las Vegas, 2004—06, U. Tex., El Paso, 2006—. Grassroots cmty. adv., Las Vegas, 2004—06. Advocate & educator against violence towards women, labor rights, and immigrant rights, Las Vegas, 2004—. Recipient Dissertation Enhancement award, NSF, 2002—04, Dissertation award, Tex. A&M U., 2004; grantee, U. Nev. Las Vegas, 2005—06, 2006—, Stimulation Implementation Transition Enhancement grant, 2005—06, Am. Sociol. Assn., 2006; Conf. fellowships, Am. Assn. of Higher Edn.—Hispanic Caucus, 2000—03, Population Sci. & GIS fellowship, Ctr. for Spatially Integrated Social Sci., 2003. Mem.: Southwestern Sociol. Assn. (exec. coun. 2006—), Am. Sociol. Assn. (Travel award, Session Organizer, Preparing Future Faculty award 2001, 2005, 2006), Students Stand Up, Sociologists Without Borders. Office: Univ Tex Old Main 312 El Paso TX 79968-8900 Office Phone: 915-747-6838. Office Fax: 915-747-5505. Business E-Mail: mcmorales@utep.edu.

MORALES, MARY E., social worker; b. Va., Jan. 14, 1972; d. Juan and Wanda I. Morales. BA in Psychology and BA in Environ. Studies, Yale U., 1994. Social worker Evergreen Children's Svcs., Det., 1994—96; child devel. specialist Klingberg Family Ctr., New Britain, 1998—99; resdl. supr. St. Agnes Family Ctr., West Hartford, Conn., 1997—99; high risk newborn social worker Dept. Children & Families, New Britain, 1999—. Mem. child protection team Bristol (Conn.) Hosp., 1999—. Vol. P.E.P. (Youth at Risk), Plainville, Conn., 1999—; mentor St. Agnes Family Ctr., West Hartford, 1999—. Recipient Conn. Cmty. Svc. award, Yale U., 1991—94, award for outstanding cmty. edn., U. Conn. Med. Sch. Home: 123 Stearns St Bristol CT 06010-5134

MORALES-MARTIN, GISELA, interior designer; b. Miami, Fla., Mar. 14, 1959; d. Oscar and Silvia Morales; m. Richard Martin, Nov. 4, 1987 (div. Jan. 1997); children: Brittany Martin, Anthony Martin. B in Interior Design, Fla. Internat. U. Asst. designer Robison & Assocs., Coral Gables, Fla., 1980—81; sr. designer Dennis Jenkins Assocs., Coral Gables, 1981—85; head designer Blitstein Design Assocs., Coral Gables, 1985—89; owner, pres. Gisela Martin & Assocs., Coral Gables, 1989—. Critic student presentations Fla. Internat. U., Miami, 1993—96. Recipient 1st pl. Comml. Project, Interior Design Guild, 1998. Mem.: Nat. Trust of Historic Preservation, Am. Soc. Interior Design, Mercy Hosp. Aux.Program. Democrat. Roman Catholic. Avocation: Avocations: exercise, gardening, bird watching. Office: 285 Sevilla Ave Coral Gables FL 33134

MORALEZ, JOSELYN HOPE, special education educator; b. Lordsburg, N.Mex., July 7, 1966; d. Mary Lou Chavez. BS, N.Mex. State U., 1988. Instr. elem. spl. edn. Animas Pub. Schs., N.Mex., 1988—90, Lordsburg Pub. Schs., 1990—. Mem. Coun. Exceptional Children, Delta Kappa Gamma. Office: Southside Elem Sch 200E 9th St Lordsburg NM 88045 Office Phone: 505-542-9473. E-mail: jmoralez@lmsed.org.

MORAN, ANNE E., lawyer; b. Rockville Centre, NY, July 9, 1953; BA, Wellesley Coll., 1975; JD, Harvard U., 1978. Bar: DC 1978, NY 1979. Law clk. to Hon. Philip Nichols US Ct. Appeals (Fed. cir.); ptnr. Miller & Chevalier Chartered, Washington, Steptoe & Johnson LLP, Washington. Mem. ERISA adv. coun. US Dept. Labor, 1992-94; tax counsel fin. com. US Senate, 1983-86; adj. prof. LLM prog. Georgetown U. Contbr. articles to profl. jours. Mem. ABA (chmn. joint com. on employee benefits 1989-90), DC Bar (chmn. com. on employee benefits), Phi Beta Kappa. Office: Steptoe & Johnson 1330 Connecticut Ave NW Washington DC 20036-1704 E-mail: amoran@steptoe.com.

MORAN, BARBARA BURNS, librarian, educator; b. Columbus, Miss., July 8, 1944; d. Robert Theron and Joan (Brown) Burns; m. Joseph J. Moran, Sept. 4, 1965; children: Joseph Michael, Brian Matthew. AB, Mount Holyoke Coll., S. Hadley, Mass., 1966; MLS, Emory U., Atlanta, 1973; PhD, SUNY, Buffalo, 1982. Head libr. The Park Sch. of Buffalo, Snyder, NY, 1974-78; prof. Sch. Info. and Libr. Sci. U. N.C., Chapel Hill, 1981—, asst. dean, 1987-90, dean, 1990-98, prof. and dir. internat. programs, 1999—. Bd. govs. U. N.C. Press, 1998—; Fulbright sr. specialist Charles U., Prague, 2006; participant various seminars; evaluator various edn. progs.; cons. in field. Author: (book) Academic Libraries, 1984; author: (with Robert D. Stueart) Library Information Center Management, 6th edit., 2002; contbr. articles to profl. jours., chapters to books; mem. editl. bd.: Jour. Acad. Librarianship, 1992—94, Coll. and Rsch. Librs., 1996—2002, Jour. Edn. Info. and Libr. Sci., 2001—. Grantee Univ. Rsch. Coun., 1983, 1989, Coun. Libr. Resources, 1985, IMLS, 2004; others, Fulbright sr. specialist, Charles U., Prague, 2006. Mem.: ALA, N.C. Libr. Assn., Assn. Libr. And Info. Sci. Edn., Popular Culture Assn., Beta Phi Mu. Home: 1307 Leclair St Chapel Hill NC 27517-3034 Office: Univ NC Sch Info & Libr Sci Chapel Hill NC 27599-0001 Office Phone: 919-962-8062. Business E-Mail: moran@ils.unc.edu.

MORAN, DARA ELAIN, science educator; b. Huntington, W.Va., Apr. 18, 1970; d. Herbert Daniel Cyrus and Dara Sue Harmon; m. Todd Phillip Moran, Feb. 8, 2003; 1 child, Tucker Colin. BE, Marshall U., Huntington, W.Va., 1997. Intermediate sci. tchr. Lawrence County Schs., Louisa, Ky., 1999—. Pride educator/vol. PRIDE The Ctr. Rural Devel., Louisa, Ky., 2003—; sci. leadership support network mem. U. Ky. Partnership Inst. Math., Lexington, 2005—. Vol. Big Sandy Area Bikers, Louisa, Ky., 1999—2006. Recipient Outstanding Tchr. award, Local Bd. of Edn., 2006. Mem.: Hon. Order of Ky. Cols. Nazarene. Avocations: travel, horseback riding. Home: 300 Harley Dr Louisa KY 41230 Office: Fallsburg Elem Sch 6869 N Hwy 3 Louisa KY 41230 Office Phone: 606-686-2351. Personal E-mail: dara.moran@lawrence.kyschools.us.

MORAN, DONNA MARIE, school psychologist, counselor, educator; b. South Bend, Ind., Dec. 11, 1945; d. Raymond P. and Elsie (DeWitte) DeLee; m. Stephen E. Moran, Apr. 10, 1976; 1 child, Kent S. BA in Secondary Edn., St. Francis Coll., 1973, MS in Secondary Edn., 1976, MS in Guidance and Counseling, 1980, MS in Pre-Clin. Psychology, 1984. Jr. high tchr. Immaculate Conception Sch., Union, Mo., 1970-73; tchr. Huntington (Ind.) Cath. H.S., 1973-76; counselor So. Wells Jr. and Sr. H.S., Poneto, Ind., 1976-77; mid. sch. counselor East Allen County Sch., New Haven, Ind., 1977-93, sch. psychologist, 1993—. Bd. dirs. Family and Children's Svc., Ft. Wayne, Ind., 1987-93, A.J. Blaising Social Svc., Ft. Wayne, 1991-95. Mem. ACA, Am. Sch. Counselors Assn., Nat. Assn. Sch. Psychologists, Ind. Counseling Assn. (N.E. region sec., treas., pres.-elect, pres.), Ind. Sch. Counselors Assn. (Counselor of Yr. 1994), Ind. Assn. Sch. Psychologists (Indian Sch. Psychologist of the Yr. 2004). Roman Catholic. Avocations: water-skiing, jogging, reading. Home: 4665 S 050 E Wolcottville IN 46795-9260 Office: East Allen County Schs 1000 Prospect Ave New Haven IN 46774-1625

MORAN, JOAN JENSEN, physical education educator, healthcare educator; b. Chgo., Sept. 25, 1952; d. Axel Fred and Mary J. (Maes) J.; m. Gregory Keith Moran. BS in Edn., Western Ill. U., Macomb, 1974; MS in Edn., No. Ill. U., DeKalb, 1978. Cert. tchr. Ill. Tchr., coach East Coloma Sch., Rock Falls, Ill., 1974—. Recreation specialist Woodhaven Lakes, Sublette, Ill., 1975-79; cons. Ill. State Bd. Edn., Springfield, 1984—; instr. NDEITA, Ill., 1988—; facilitator Project Wild, Ill., 1990—. Instr. ARC, Rock Falls, 1978—, Am. Heart Assn., Rock Falls, 1978—; exec. bd. East Coloma Cmty. Club; fitness del. to Russia and Hungary, 1992; cons. Alcohol Awareness & Occupant Restraint Ill. State Bd. Edn., Substance Abuse Guidance Edn. Com., Rock Falls Drug Free Cmty. Grant com., Whiteside County CPR Coord. com. Recipient Western Ill. U. Alumni Achievement award, 1993, Western Ill. Master Tchr. award, 1993, Svc. award Ill. Assn. Health, Phys. Edn., Recreation and Dance, 1991, 92, Outstanding Young Woman award, 1986, Phys. Educator of Yr. award, 1988; named Mid. Sch. Phys. Edn. Tchr. of Yr. Midwest AAHPERD, 1993, Ill. Assn. Health, Phys. Edn., Recreation and Dance, 1992, Gov.'s Coun. Health and Phys. Edn. award, 1991, Am. Tchr. of Yr. award Walt Disney Co., 1993, Excel award Ill. State Bd. Edn., 1995, finalist Ill. Tchr. of Yr., 1996, Milkin Nat. Educator award, 1997, Health Edn. award and Quarter Century award Ill. Assn. Health, Phys. Edn., Recreation and Dance, 1999, Presidential citation, 1998; named to USA Today Tchr. Team, 2000. Mem.: AAHPERD (Health Tchr. of Yr. midwest chpt. 2001), Environ. Edn. Assn. Ill., East Coloma Edn. Assn. (pres., pub. rels., v.p. 1993—94), Ill. Edn. Assn., No. Dist. Ill. Assn. Health, Phys. Edn., Recreation and Dance (newsletter editor 1984—85, exec. bd. 1985—90, treas. 1985—90), Ill. Assn. Health, Phys. Edn., Recreation and Dance (v.p. teenage youth 1988—90, pres. 1994, past pres., conv. coord. 1995, Honor Fellow award 1996). Democrat. Lutheran. Avocations: skiing, hiking, biking, reading, travel. Home: 1903 E 41st St Sterling IL 61081-9449 Personal E-mail: moran@essex1.com.

MORAN, JULIETTE M., retired chemicals executive; b. NYC, June 12, 1917; d. James Joseph and Louise M. BS, Columbia U., 1938; MS, NYU, 1948. Research asst. Columbia U., 1941; jr. engr. Signal Corps Lab., U.S. Army, 1942-43; with GAF Corp. (formerly Gen. Aniline & Film Corp.), 1943-82; from jr. chemist process devel. dept. to exec. v.p. and dir. GAF Corp., 1953—80, vice chmn., 1982—2002, cons., 1982—95; ret., 1982. Bd. dirs. N.Y. State Sci. and Tech. Found. Recipient Greater N.Y. Advt. award for excellence in communications N.Y. chpt. Assn. Indsl. Advertisers, 1972, Alumni Achievement award N.Y. U. Grad. Sch. Arts and Scis., 1977 Fellow AAAS, Am. Inst. Chemists; mem. Am. Chem. Soc., Comml. Devel. Assn. Home: 10 W 66th St New York NY 10023-6206

MORAN, LINDA, management consultant, researcher; b. Scranton, Pa., Feb. 15, 1957; d. Michael Thomas and Janice Walsh Moran; m. Joseph George Buda, Feb. 13, 1988; children: Joseph Michael Buda, Margaret Anne Buda. BS, Pa. State U., University Park, 1979; MA, U. Md., College Park, 1981; EdD, Columbia U., N.Y.C., 2002. Tng. specialist G.P.U. Nuc., Forked River, NJ, 1981—83; sales tng. specialist Chubb Ins. Co., Warren, NJ, 1983—85; tng. performance cons. Zenger Miller, N.Y.C., 1984—86, client svcs. cons., 1986—90, v.p., client svcs. San Jose, Calif., 1990—94; team practice leader Achieve Internat., Toronto, Canada, 1993—96; exec. cons. Achieve Global, Tampa, Fla., 1996—. Tchr. St. Catherine of Siena, Simsbury, Conn., 2000—05. Co-author: Self-Directed Teams, 1990, Keeping Teams of Track, 2000, Beyond Teams Building, 2003. Office: Achieve Global 6 Apple Ln Simsbury CT 06070 Home: 6 Apple Ln Simsbury CT 06070

MORAN, MARISSA J., law educator; b. Bklyn. m. James Moran; children: James, JonPaul, Justin. JD, Bklyn. Law Sch. Law clk. Hon. Burton R. Lifland, Chief Judge US Bankruptcy Ct. So. Dist. NY, NYC, 1989—91; assoc. Kaye, Scholer, Fierman, Hays & Handler, Emmet, Marvin & Martin; prof. dept. law & paralegal studies NYC Coll. Tech., Bklyn.; adj. prof. Leonard N. Stern Sch. Bus. NYU. Mem.: ABA, Columbian Lawyers Assn., NY State Bar Assn., Am. Assn. Paralegal Educators. Office: NYC Coll Tech Dept Law & Paralegal Studies 300 Jay St Brooklyn NY 11201 Business E-Mail: mmoran@citytech.cuny.edu.

MORAN, NANCY A., ecologist, educator; b. Dallas, Dec. 21, 1954; BA in biology, U. Tex., 1976; MS in zoology, U. Mich., 1978, PhD in zoology, 1982. Asst. prof. entomology U. Ariz., 1986—91, assoc. prof. ecology and evolutionary biology, 1991—96, prof. ecology and evolutionary biology, 1996—2001, regent's prof. ecology and evolutionary biology, 2001—. NSF postdoctoral fellow, No. Ariz. U., 1984-1986, NAS postdoctoral fellow, Inst. Entomology, Czech, 1984, MacArthur Fellow, John D. and Catherine T. MacArthur Found., 1997. Mem. NAS, Soc. Study Evolution (pres. 2002), Am. Naturalists Soc. (v.p. 2001, Pres. award, 1988); fellow Am. Acad. Arts & Sciences Office: U Ariz Dept Ecology & Evolutionary Biology PO Box 210088 Biosciences W 310 1041 E Lowell St Tucson AZ 85721 Office Phone: 520-621-3581. Office Fax: 520-621-9190. E-mail: nmoran@email.arizona.edu.*

MORAN, PATRICIA, lawyer; b. Wilmington, Del., 1959; BS, U. Scranton, 1981; JD, Villanova U., 1984. Bar: Del. 1984. Atty. Skadden, Arps, Slate, Meagher & Flom LLP, N.Y., ptnr., 1994—. Office: Skadden Arps Slate Meagher & Flom LLP Four Times Square New York NY 10036

MORAN, PATRICIA GENEVIEVE, corporate financial executive; b. Evanston, Ill., July 26, 1945; d. James Moran; children: Christine Coyle, Thomas Beddia, Donald Beddia. Student, Marquette U. Dir. corp. transp. JM Family Enterprises, Inc., 1984, corp. assoc. rels. dir., 1985, v.p., 1985-88; group v.p. sales Southeast Toyota, Deerfield Beach, Fla., 1988-89; pres., CEO JM Family Enterprises, Inc., Deerfield Beach, Fla., 1989—2000, chmn., 2000—. Bd. dirs. Am. Heritage Life Ins. Co. Bd. dirs. Take Stock in Children, Boca Raton Resort and Club. Named One of Top 50 Working Women by Working Woman's Mag. Mem. Nat. Assn. Automobile Dealers, Am. Internat. Automobile Dealers Assn., Fla. Council of 100, Com. of 200. Office: JM Family Enterprises 100 NW 12th Ave Deerfield Beach FL 33442

MORAN, RACHEL, law educator; b. Kansas City, Mo., June 27, 1956; d. Thomas Albert and Josephine (Portillo) Moran. AB, Stanford U., 1978; JD, Yale U., 1981. Bar: Calif. 1984. Assoc Heller, Ehrman, White & McAuliffe, San Francisco, 1982-83; prof. law U. Calif., Berkeley, 1984—, Robert D. and Leslie-Kay Raven prof. law, 1998—. Vis. prof. UCLA Sch. Law, 1988, 2002, Stanford (Calif.) U. Law Sch., 1989, NYU Sch. Law, 1996, U. Miami Sch. Law, 1997, U. Tex. Law Sch., 2000, Fordham Law Sch., 2005; chair Chicano/Latino Policy Project, 1993—96; dir. Inst. for Study Social Change, 2003—. Contbr. articles to profl. jours. Recipient Disting. Tchg. award, U. Calif. Mem.: ABA, Calif. Bar Assn., Am. Law Inst., Phi Beta Kappa. Democrat. Unitarian Universalist. Avocations: jogging, aerobics, reading, listening to music. Office: U Calif Sch Law Boalt Hall Berkeley CA 94720 Office Phone: 510-643-6351. Business E-Mail: moran@law.berkeley.edu.

MORAN, SHEILA KATHLEEN, journalist; b. Norwalk, Conn. d. Edmond Joseph and Alice Marie (Laux) M.; m. John Joseph Reynolds, Apr. 2, 1987 (dec. Apr. 1993). BA in European History, Manhattanville Coll., Purchase, N.Y. Sportswriter, reporter AP, N.Y.C., N.Y. Post, N.Y.C., L.A. Times; actress, freelance writer L.A.; prodr. Evensong Assocs., N.Y.C. Freelance reporter USA Today. Vol. VA Hosp., L.A., Meml. Sloan Kettering Cancer Ctr., N.Y.C.; mem. St. Bartholomew's Ch. Mem.: AFTRA, Inner Circle, Prodrs. Group, N.Y.C., Actors' Equity Assn., Screen Actors Guild. Democrat.

MORAN, WENDY JACQUELINE, music educator, musician; b. Chappaqua, N.Y., Jan. 16, 1952; d. Edward Albert and Gladys (Dildarian) Hamilton; m. Brian Vincent Moran, Aug. 5, 1979; children: Melissa Kathleen, Kevin William. Attended, U. N.C., Greensboro, 1970—72; MusB Edn., Westminster Choir Coll., Princeton, N.J., 1975; grad. student in Musicology, NYU, 1978—80. Cert. music specialist Pre-K-12 Dept. Edn. Mass., 2000, N.J., 1975. Music specialist Westminster Choir Coll. (Conservatory divsn.), Princeton, 1975; pvt. instrn. (voice/flute/recorder/eurhythmics) Holliston, Mass., 1975—; music specialist Montessori Children's Rm., Armonk, N.Y., 1975—83, various Montessori schs., music schs., pub. schs., pvt. schs., Md., Mass., N.Y., 1983—89, Christian Family Montessori Sch., Holliston, 1989—, Hopkinton Pub. Schs., Mass., 1996—. Flute soloist in field, 1975—; soprano soloist in field, 1975—; student Kodaly Music Tchrs. Workshops, Princeton, 1975; participant/student Music Educator Workshops/Chamber Music Workshops:Dalcroze Sch. of Music/Mannes Coll. of Music, N.Y., 1978—89; participant master class with Jean-Pierre Rampal, N.Y., 1979, Montessori Music Teacher's Workshop Whitby Sch., Greenwich, Conn., 1980; flutist Southeastern Mass. Concert Band, Medway, Mass., 1990—; singer Berkshire Choral Inst., Sheffield, Mass., 1996—; profl. devel. mgr., exec. bd. New Eng. chpt. Am. Orff-Schulwerk Assn., Lexington, Mass., 1999—2003; singer Heritage Chorale, Framingham, 1999—, chorus rep. bd. dirs., 2003—; singer/flutist Composer's Conf.: Chamber Music Ctr. and Singer's Workshop, Wellesley, Mass., 2003—. Author (co-author): (guidebook) Curriculum Guide for Hopkinton, Mass. Dept. Music; singer: (concerts) choral concerts under the direction of Leonard Bernstein, Pierre Boulez, Antal Dorati, (concert) under Robert Shaw in Mostly Mozart Festival, Lincoln Ctr. Music specialist, volunteered classes in music to support funding for town playground Town of Annapolis, Md., 1988; membership chmn. Medway Newcomer's Club, Mass., 1988—89. Recipient numerous monetary awards given to Hopkinton Edn. Found. in name of Ms. Moran for fostering excellence in edn., Hopkinton, Mass., 1999 - 2005. Mem.: Gone with the Winds woodwind quintet, Cmty. Orch., Arundel Vocal Arts Soc. (Md.), Westchester Choral Soc., Somer's Chorale, Bach Choral Soc., Pleasantville Cantata Singers (N.Y.), Broadmoor Chamber Singers. Achievements include developing a system for music education based upon Kodaly/Orff/Dalcroze methods; researching and developing methods for ear-training and pitch understanding for young children; thirty years of studying and implementing creative approaches of music education based upon the Dalcroze, Kodaly, Orff methods of music learning. Avocations: yoga, swimming, cross-country skiing, hiking, dance. Home: 267 Norfolk St Holliston MA 01746 Office: Hopkinton Public Schools Haydn Rowe St Hopkinton MA 01748 Personal E-mail: wenmora@aol.com. Business E-Mail: wmoran@hopkinton.k12.ma.us.

MORANG, DIANE JUDY, writer, television producer, entrepreneur; b. Chgo., Apr. 28, 1942; d. Anthony Thomas Morang and Laura Ann Andrzejczak. Student, Stevens Finishing Sch., Chgo., 1956, Fox Bus. Coll., 1959-60, UCLA, 1967-69. Mem. staff Chgo. Sun Times, Daily News, 1957, Drury Ln. Theatre, Chgo., 1961-62, AM Show ABC-TV, Hollywood, Calif., 1970-71. Judge 2 categories regional Emmy Awards, 1985, chair, mem. judging panel, 89; prin., owner website company, 2004—06. Author: How to Get into the Movies, 1978; author, creator: The Rainbow Keyboard, 1991, The Translation of the Code of Music Into Numerics; creator: The Best Kids' Show in the World, The Best Dog Treats in the World; contbr. numerous articles to newspapers, mags. Bd. dirs., mem. scholarship com. Ariz. Bruins, UCLA Alumni Assn.; mem. Nat. Mus. Women in the Arts, Washington, D.C.; mem. Nat. Women's Hall of Fame, Seneca Falls, N.Y. Mem. NATAS (mem. Hollywood Emmy Award-winning team Hollywood, Calif. 1971), Ariz. Authors Assn. (bd. dirs.), Amon Carter Mus. Roman Catholic.

MORANT, BRENDA WHITE, publishing executive, small business owner, investor; b. Balt., May 5, 1944; BS, U. Md., 1973; MPA, Cen. Mich. U., 1974. Founder, chief exec. officer Women's Econ. Enterprises, 1988—; publisher Networking Mag., 1990—; bus. devel. The BES Co., 1988—; owner Market Rsch. Cons., Atlanta, 1994—. Cons. U.S. Air Force, Oscoda, Mich., 1977, Greater Mt. Calvery Bapt. Ch., Jackson Miss., 1991—, Options & Opportunities Career Ctr., Greenville, N.C., 1991—. Inventor electro thermo engineered insulated refrigeration container system for heat sensitive products. Organizer Battered Women's Ctr., 1979, Juneteen Celebration in Miss., 1980, Commn. on Women, 1986, Industrial Energy Soc., 1984. With USMC, 1962-64. Named 1st Businesswoman on the front Cover of Miss. Official State Mag., 1987; recipient Innovation award U.S. Dept of Energy, 1985, Governor Miss., 1985. Mem.: NAFE, Alumni Assn. Ctrl. Mich. U. (pres. Atlanta chpt.), Assn. Female Vets. (bd.). Avocations: dance exercising, boating, travel, painting, reading. Office: BES Techs PO Box 162125 Atlanta GA 30321-2125

MORARIU, CORINA, professional tennis player; b. Detroit, Michigan, Jan. 26, 1978; d. Albin and Rodica Morariu; m. Andrew Turcinovich. Grad., St. Andrews H.S., 1996. Mem. U.S. Nat. Tennis team, 1996. Won Jr. Championship Australian, French and U.S. Opens, 1995, Australia, 1994, Wimbledon, doubles, 1999 (with Lindsay Davenport), Australian Open Mixed Doubles (with E. Ferreira), 2001; winner 1 Career Singles Title, 10 Career Doubles Titles, WTA Tour. Office: USTA 70 W Red Oak Ln White Plains NY 10604-3602 also: ATP Tour 201 Atp Tour Blvd Ponte Vedra Beach FL 32082-3211

MORAS, BARBARA J., music educator; b. Schenectady, NY, Dec. 29, 1955; d. Victor and Gloria Capogna. B Music Edn., SUNY, Potsdam, 1977; M Music Edn., La. State U., Baton Rouge, 1984. Choral dir. Destrehan HS, La., 1993—2000; music tchr. High Point Elem. Sch., Atlanta, 2000—02; choral dir. Northview HS, Duluth, Ga., 2002—. Mem.: Internat. Assn. Jazz Educators, Am. Choral Dirs. Assn., Ga. Music Educators Assn. (dist. V choral chmn.). Republican. Roman Catholic. Avocations: writing, piano, singing. Home: 1427 Statnion Center Blvd Suwanee GA 30024 E-mail: moras@fulton.k12.ga.us.

MORAWETZ, CATHLEEN SYNGE, mathematician; b. Toronto, Ont., Can., May 5, 1923; arrived in U.S., 1945, naturalized, 1950; d. John Lighton and Elizabeth Eleanor Mabel (Allen) Synge; m. Herbert Morawetz, Oct. 28, 1945; children: Pegeen Morawetz Rubinstein, John Synge, Lida Morawetz Jeck, Nancy. BA, U. Toronto, 1945; SM, MIT, 1946; PhD, NYU, 1951; degree (hon.), Ea. Mich. U., 1980, Smith Coll., 1982, Brown U., 1982, Princeton U., 1986, Duke U., 1988, N.J. Inst. Tech., 1988, U. Waterloo, 1993, U. Dublin, 1996, U. Toronto, 1996. Research assoc. Courant Inst., NYU, 1952—57, asst. prof. math., 1957—60, assoc. prof., 1960—65, prof., 1965—, assoc. dir., 1978—84, dir., 1984—88. Chmn. bd. Sch. Theoretical Physics Dublin Inst. for Advanced Studies, 1995—2000. Contbr. articles to profl. jours. Trustee Princeton U., 1973—78, Sloan Found., 1980—94. Recipient Nat. medal of Sci., NSF, 1998; fellow Guggenheim, 1967, 1979; grantee Office of Naval Rsch., 1975—90. Fellow: AAAS, Royal Soc. Can.; mem.: NAS, London Math. Soc., Royal Irish Acad., Soc. Indsl. and Applied Math., Am. Philos. Soc., Am. Acad. Arts and Scis., Am. Math. Soc. (term trustee 1975—85, pres. 1995—97, George David Birkhoff prize in Applied Math. (awarded jointly by Am. Math. Soc. and Soc. for Indsl. and Applied Math.) 2006, Steele prize 2004). Achievements include research in applications of partial differential equations, especially transonic flow and scattering theory. Office: CIMS 251 Mercer St New York NY 10012-1110 Office Phone: 212-998-3297. Business E-Mail: morawetz@cims.nyu.edu.

MORBY, JACQUELINE, venture capitalist; b. Sacramento, June 19, 1937; d. Junior Jennings and Bertha (Backer) Collins; m. Jeffrey L. Morby, June 21, 1959; children: Andrew Jennings, Michelle Lorraine. BA in Psychology, Stanford U., 1959; M in Mgmt., Simmons Grad. Mgmt. Sch., Boston, 1978. Assoc. TA Assocs., Boston, 1978-81, gen. ptnr., 1982-89, mng. dir., 1989—2002, prin., 2003—. Bd. dirs. HVL, Inc., Pitts., Softmed Sys. Inc., Bethesda, Md., Ansys, Inc., Canonsburg, Pa., Pacific Life Corp., Newport Beach, Calif., J&B Software, Inc., Bluebell, Pa. Trustee Simmons Coll., Warholl Mus. Mem. Nat. Venture Capital Orgn. Avocations: theater, reading, art, skiing, travel. Office: TA Assocs 125 High St Boston MA 02110-2704 E-mail: jmorby@ta.com.

MORE, KANE JEAN, science educator; b. Norwalk, Ohio, Nov. 19, 1953; d. Charles Norman and Kazue (Miura) M.; m. Steven W. Gong, Nov. 24, 1979; children: Benjamin, Kaylyn. BS, Wright State U., 1976; MS in Zoology, U. Fla., 1982. Cert. tchr., Fla. Rsch. assoc. Dept. Zoology, U. Fla., Gainesville, 1979-86; sci. tchr. Spanish River High Sch., Boca Raton, Fla., 1987-91; sci. dept. chair Olympic Heights High Sch., Boca Raton, 1991—2004; sci. dept. chmn. West Boca Raton (Fla.) HS, 2004—. Sponsor, faculty Nat. Honor Soc., Boca Raton, 1991—. Contbr. articles to Jour. of Exptl. Biology. Recipient Outstanding Tchr. award, 1992-93; Tandy Tech. scholar. Mem. Mount Desert Island Biol. Lab., Fla. Assn. Sci. Tchrs., Sigma Xi. Democrat. Home: 11426 Sundance Ln Boca Raton FL 33428-5518 Office: West Boca Raton HS 12811 Glades Rd Boca Raton FL 33498 E-mail: morek@palmbeach.k12.fl.us.

MOREA, MICHELLE, performing arts educator; b. Smithtown, N.Y., Jan. 29, 1976; d. Robert and Kathy Morea, Larry Kincer (Stepfather). BA, U. Ga., Athens, 1998; MA, Ctrl. Wash. U., Ellensburg, 2005. Cert. tchr. drama K-12 Ga., 2000. Theatre tchr. Pope H.S., Marietta, Ga., 1998—2000, Grayson H.S., Loganville, Ga., 2001—. Dir.: (one act competition) Catfish Moon (State One Act Championship, 2001). Sponsor Red Cross Blood Drive, Loganville, 2002—06; state bd. mem. and local sponsor Ga. Thespian Soc., 2002—06. Office: Grayson HS 50 Hope Hollow Rd Loganville GA 30052 Office Phone: 770-554-7819. Business E-Mail: michelle_morea@gwinnett.k12.ga.us.

MOREAU, PATRICIA D., science educator; b. Ft. Wayne, Ind., Mar. 30, 1955; m. David A. Moreau, Feb. 20, 1976; children: Miranda D. Petrey, Michael D. BS (hon.), Mich. State U., E. Lansing, 1977. Cert. Dept. Edn., Fla., 1998, purchasing mgr. Fla., 1992. Tchr. Tavares H.S., Fla., Mount Dora H.S., Fla., 2006—. Finalist Presdl. Excellence award, Fla., 2005; named Tchr. of Yr., Tavares H.S., 2005—06. Mem.: Alpha Delta Kappa (membership chmn. 2004—06, pres. Beta Gamma chpt. 2006—). Office: Mount Dora High Sch 700 N Highland St Mount Dora FL 32757 Office Phone: 352-383-2177.

MOREDOCK, REBECCA JUANETTE, psychiatrist; d. Paul Lawrence and Loretta Fay Jackson. BS, Oral Roberts U., Tulsa, 1989; MD, U. Louisville, 1994. Diplomate Am. Bd. Psychiatry and Neurology. Intern U. Louisville, 1995—96; resident in psychiatry U. Cin., 1996—98; psychiatrist St. John's Hosp., Anderson, Ind., 1998—2001, Gallahue, Shelbyville, Ind., 2001—05, Cmty. Hosp., Greenfield, Ind., 2001—05; pvt. practice psychiatry Lotus Group, Fishers, Ind., 2003—. Bd. examiner Am. Bd. Psychiatry and Neurology, 2004—. Named one of Top Psychiatrists in the country, Consumer Rsch. Coun. of Am. Mem.: AMA, Am. Psychiat. Assn. Christian Ch. Avocations: weightlifting, running. Office: Lotus Group 11950 Fishers Crossing Dr Fishers IN 46038 Office Phone: 317-595-5555.

MOREHEAD, ANDREA, newscaster; BA in Comm./Journalism, Howard U., 1991; JD, Ind. U., 1996. Prodn. intern Koppel Comm., Washington; reporter, anchor Sta. WGMC-TV, Worchester, Mass., 1992—93; mgnt. coun. law clk. Nat. Football League, NY, 1995; reporter, asst. prodr. assignment editor WXIN-TV, Indpls.; anchor Sta. WOOD-TV, Grand Rapids, Mich., Sta. WTHR-TV, Indpls., 1999—. Recipient Up and Coming award, Ann. Minority Bus. and Profl. Achievers, Recognition award, Ctr. Leadership Devel., Indpls., 2002. Office: WTHR-TV 1000 N Meridian St Indianapolis IN 46204

MOREHOUSE, SARAH MCCALLY, retired political science professor; b. Boston, Jan. 15, 1927; d. Ralph Dewey and Eugenia Whitehead (Norris) Powell; m. W. Bradley Morehouse, Nov. 8, 1969 (div. Nov. 1986); children: Richard, John, Catherine, David; m. Malcolm Edwin Jewell, Dec. 28, 1991. BA in Polit. Sci., Wellesley Coll., 1948; PhD in Polit. Sci., Yale U., 1964. Instr. Conn. Coll., New London, 1964-66; lectr. Hunter Coll., Bronx, N.Y., 1966-69; assoc. prof. Manhattanville Coll., Purchase, N.Y., 1969-75; prof. U. Conn., Stamford, 1976-92, prof. emerita, 1992—. Univ. senator U. Conn., 1982-85, assoc. dir., 1990-91. Author: State Politics, Parties and Policy, 1981, The Governor as Party Leader, 1998; contbr. various articles to profl. jours. Sec. Charter Revision Commn. Fairfield, Conn., 1960; chmn. Ethics Commn., Fairfield, 1984-88; pres. LWV, 1996-98; state LWV sec. bd. dirs. 1998-2001; political parties/elections, 2001. Vis. professorship for women NSF, 1991; fellow Danforth Found., 1960; rsch. grantee Russell Sage Found., 1983; vis. scholar U. Calif, Berkeley, 1991-92. Mem. Wellesley Club. Home: 242 Somerset Ave Fairfield CT 06824-4935 Personal E-mail: macsarahj@worldnet.att.net.

MORELAN, PAULA KAY, choreographer; b. Lafayette, Ind., Nov. 24, 1949; d. Dickie Booth and Marian Maxine (Fetterhoff) M.; m. Kerim Sayan, Aug. 10, 1974. Student, U. Utah, 1968-69; BFA, Tex. Christian U., 1972; postgrad., El Centro Coll., 1969-70. Tchr. Rosello Sch. Ballet, Dallas, 1972-74; mgr., tchr. Ballet Arts Ctr., Dallas, 1974-76; owner, tchr. Ballet Classique, Garland, Tex., 1976-87, Garland Ballet Acad., 1977-87; resident choreographer Garland Civic Theatre, 1988—, lifetime mem., 1998. Asst. to Mythra Rosello Tex. Civic Ballet, Dallas, 1972—74; assoc. artistic dir. Dance Repertory Theatre Dallas, 1974—75, artistic dir., 1975—76, Garland (Tex.) Ballet Assn., 1977—90, Classical Ballet Acad., Performing Arts Sch., 1987—90; artistic dir. musical theatre dept. KD Actors Conservatory, 2005—; founder, chairperson Act IV Guild, 2002—05. Bd. dirs. Garland Civic Theatre, 2000—05. Recipient Leon Rabin award for Best Choreography, Dallas Theatre League, 1996, 1998, 2000, 2001, 2004, Column award, 2004, Best Choreographer award, 2003, Choreographer of Yr. award, 2001, 2002, 2003, 2004. Personal E-mail: pkm@worldnet.att.net.

MORELLA, CONSTANCE ALBANESE, ambassador, former congresswoman; b. Somerville, Mass., Feb. 12, 1931; d. Salvatore and Mary Christine (Fallette) Albanese; m. Anthony C. Morella, Aug. 21, 1954; children: Paul, Mark, Laura; guardians of: Christine, Catherine, Louise, Rachel, Paul, Ursula. AA, Boston U., 1950, AB, 1954; MA, Am. U., 1967, D of Pub. Svc. (hon.), 1988, Norwich U. and Dickinson Coll., 1989, Mt. Vernon Coll., 1995, U. Md. U. Coll., 1996, USUHS, 1997, U. Md., 1997, Elizabethtown Coll., 1999. Tchr. Montgomery County (Md.) Pub. Schs., 1956-60; instr. Am. U., 1968-70; prof. Montgomery Coll., Rockville, Md., 1970-86; mem. Md. Ho. Dels., Annapolis, 1979-86, U.S. Congress from 8th Md. dist., 1987—2003; mem. sci. com., tech. subcom., basic rsch. subcom., govt. reform com., chair D.C. subcom., mem. civil svc. subcom.; visiting fellow Kennedy School, Harvard, 2003; U.S. permanent rep. to Orgn. for Econ. Co-operation & Devel. U.S. Dept. State, Paris, 2003—. Mem. civil svc., adv. bd. Am. Univ., Washington Mem. adv. coun. Montgomery County Hospice Soc.; hon. bd. mem. Nat. Kidney Found; active Human Rights Caucus; Congressional Women's Caucus, Older Ams. Caucus, Population and Devel. Caucus; mem. Bd. Cafritz Found. Named Glamour Woman of Yr. Glamour mag. 1995, Washingtonian of Yr. 1991; named to Md. Women's Hall of Fame, Md. Women's Hall of Fame, 1994. Republican. Avocations: theater, tennis, reading. Home: USOECD PSC 116 APO AE 09777

MORELOCK, JASMINE CRAWFORD, artist; b. Boise, June 30, 1925; d. Graydon Clemson and Doris Cecile (Dinwiddie) Crawford; m. Max Maurice Morelock, Apr. 8, 1950; 1 child, Maurice Max. AA, Stephens Coll., 1945; BA, La. State U., 1948; MA, La. Sch. Tech., 1979; MFA cum laude, Inst. Allende, San Miguel Allende, Guanajuato, Mexico, 1978. Cert. tchr. speech and art, La. Advtsg. writer programming dept. KRMD Radio Sta., Shreveport, La., 1946—47; with Bozell and Jacobs Nat. Advt. Agy., 1949—50; with comml. design Glen Mason Advt. Agy.; asst. prof. fine arts La. State U., Baton Rouge, 1948-49; head art dept. Southfield Sch., Shreveport, La., 1972-74; tchr. portrait classes Bossier C. C., Bossier City, La., 1989-91; tchr. art Caddo Parish Sch. Bd., Shreveport, La., 1975-80; represented by Gallery on the Green, Lexington, Mass., Juleaux Gallery of Fine Arts, Kansas City, WLR Design Co., Shreveport, La., Lytle's, Shreveport, La., Riverwalk Gallery, New Orleans. Presenter workshops Barnwell Art Ctr., Shreveport, La., J&M Studio Groups, Shreveport, Women's Dept. Club, Shreveport, Springhill (La.) Art Assn., 1993. One woman exhbns. include La. State U. Shreveport Gallery, 1992, Cambridge Club, Shreveport, 1993, The Glen Gallery, Shreveport, 1995, Shreve Meml. Libr., Shreveport, 1995, numerous others; group exhbns. include Valerie Originals, KJ's Antiques and Silks, Hot Springs, Ark., 1986, Women Artists of La., Baton Rouge, 1987, Boots Pharmaceutical Co., Cambridge Club, Shreveport, La., 1988, 90, 92, Stoner Arts Ctr., Shreveport, 1989, 90, Gallery on the Green, Lexington, Mass., 1989, Simmers Gallery, Shreveport, 1989, La. Artist Group Show, 1990, Barksdale Air Base, 1990, Turner Art Ctr., 1990, Artport, Shreveport, 1990, 92, 93, 94, Riverside Galleries, Shreveport, Southwestern Watercolor Soc., 1992, 94, Nat. Mus. Art, Washington, 1993, Still River Artists, Danbury, Conn., 1993, Okla. 12th Annual Juried Show, 1995, Shreveport Art Port, 2004-06, Northwest La. Triennial Competition, Meadows Mus., 2006, numerous others; represented in pvt. and pub. collections La. State U. Ctr., St. Luke's Hosp., St. Vincent's Acad., U. Club, Seagull Cos., McGoldrick Oil Co., numerous others; featured in (cover) (Goodloe Stuck) The Shreveport Madam, 1986, Boots Pharm. Art Catalogue, 1990, Behold, I Make All Things New, 1991, Artists of La. Catalogue, 1991, (t.v. show) Focus on the Arts, The Shreveport Times, 1995. Recipient Special Selection award Ark. Arts Ctr., Little Rock, 1984, First Purchase Prize Izora and Thilo Steinschulte Meml. award First Meth. Ch. Alexandria (La.), 1984, First Place Ark-La-Tex-Okla Competition First Meth. Ch., Shreveport, 1984. Mem. Nat. Watercolor Soc., Nat. Assn. Women Artists, Southwestern Watercolor Soc. (Elizabeth Shanon Meml. award 1991), La. Watercolor Soc. Soc. Exptl. Artists, Hoover Watercolor Soc. (v.p., First Place 1984, H.M. award 1993), Registry of La. Artists, La. Artists, Inc., Southeastern Ctr. for Contemporary Art, Coalition of Women's Art (nat., Dallas). Home: 427 Monrovia St Shreveport LA 71106-1607 Office Phone: 318-861-3773. Personal E-mail: jcmore@bellsouth.net.

MORENCY, PAULA J., lawyer; b. Oak Park, Ill., Mar. 13, 1955; AB magna cum laude, Princeton U., 1977; JD, U. Va., 1980. Bar: Ill. 1980, U.S. Dist. Ct. (no. dist.) Ill. 1980, U.S. Ct. Appeals (7th cir.) 1981, U.S. Ct. Appeals (5th cir.) 1990, U.S. Dist. Ct. (ctrl. dist.) Ill. 1999, U.S. Dist. Ct. (ea. dist.) Wis. 2000. Assoc. Mayer, Brown & Platt, Chgo., 1980-86, ptnr., 1987-94, Schiff Hardin & Waite, Chgo., 1994—. Adj. prof. trial advocacy Northwestern U. Sch. Law, Chgo., 1997--; faculty Midwest Regional, Nat. Inst. for Trial Advocacy, 1988—; mem. pres.'s coun. Dominican U., 1998-2002. Author: Cross-Examination of a Franchise Executive, 1995, Insurance Coverage Issues in Franchise and Intellectual Property Litigation, 1996, Re-Emergence of Franchise Class Actions, 1997, Judicial and Legislative Update: ABA Forum on Franchising, 1999, How to Find, Use and Defend Against the Expert Witness, 2000, Dealing With System Change in a High-Tech World, 2001, A Decade After Daubert, 2004. Mem. ABA (forum franchising, governing com. 2001-04, litig. sect., antitrust sect., intellectual property sect., bd. dir.), Chgo. Coun. of Lawyers (bd. govs. 1989-93), Constnl. Rights Found. Chgo. (chair 2001). Office: Schiff Hardin LLP 6600 Sears Tower Chicago IL 60606 Office Phone: 312-258-5549.

MORENO, JEANNE SIMONNE, cardiac nurse; b. Fall River, Mass., July 5, 1968; d. Theodore J. and Simonne Bernier; m. Gabriel Moreno; children: Christopher Michael, Elora Jeanne, Alyssa Paige, Gabriel Matthew. BSN, Southeastern Mass. U., North Dartmouth, 1990. RN, Mass. Nurse Vis. Nurses Assn. Southeastern Mass., Inc., Fall River, 1999—. Clin. nursing instr. Diman Regional Sch. Practical Nursing, 1999—.

MORENO, PATRICIA FRAZIER, lawyer; b. Lebanon, Pa. d. Joseph James and Cariella Agnes (Rothermel) Frazier; m. Camille Quijada Moreno, Dec. 4, 1982; children: William David, Helen Grace, Camille Fitzcarraldo. Student, Millersville U., 1969-71, Cochise Coll., 1992-93; BA in Polit. Sci., U. Ariz., Sierra Vista, 1997; JD, U. Ariz., 2001. Cert.: Nat. Assn. Legal Secs. (profl. legal sec.), Nat. Assn. Legal Assts. (legal asst.), bar: Ariz. 2002. Law clerk John F. Kelliher, Jr. PC, Sierra Vista, Ariz., 1999-2001, assoc., 2002—04; spl. asst. atty. gen. State of Ariz., 2005. Assoc. faculty Cochise Coll., Sierra Vista, 1996—97, U. Ariz. S., 2003—; with Policy-Studies, Inc., 2005. Mem. human rels. commn. City of Sierra Vista, 1982—83; mem. adv. bd. Salvation Army, Sierra Vista, 1988—92. Named Sec. of the Yr., S.E. Ariz. Legal Secs. Assn., 1993, Lawyer of the Yr., Ariz. Vol. Lawyers Program, Alumnus of the Yr., U. Ariz. S., 2006; named one of Top 50 Pro Bono Lawyers, Ariz. Legal Svcs. Found., 2005. Mem.: ACLU, Borderline Mensa (officer 1987—93, scholar 1992). Democrat. Avocations: cyberculture, film history. Office: Child Support Svcs Ariz 7 Bisbee Rd Bisbee AZ 85603 Office Phone: 520-432-3161. Business E-Mail: pmoreno@policy-studies.com. E-mail: patricia.moreno@azbar.org.

MORENO, RENEE TERESA, education educator; b. Washington, July 29, 1955; d. Kenneth Lee and Alice Elizabeth Harriston; m. Jose Enrico Moreno, Mar. 12, 1998; m. Nolley, Aug. 18, 1984 (div. Feb. 0, 1996); children: Michelle Nicole Nolley, Brandon Rene Nolley. BA, Cath. U., DC, 1998. Tchr. St. Mary's Sch., Landover Hills, Md., 1998—2004, St. Ambrose Sch., Cheverly, Md., 2004—05, St. Mary's Sch., 2005—. Home: 3010 Pkwy Cheverly MD 20785 Office: St Mary Cath Sch 7207 Annapolis Rd Landover Hills MD 20784 Office Phone: 301-577-0031.

MORENO, RITA (ROSITA DOLORES ALVERIO), actress; b. Humacao, P.R., Dec. 11, 1931; m. Leonard I. Gordon, June 18, 1965; 1 child, Fernanda Luisa. Spanish dancer since childhood, night club entertainer; appeared on Broadway in The Sign in Sidney Brustein's Window, 1964-65, Gantry, 1969-70, The Last of the Red Hot Lovers, 1970-71, The National Health,

1974, The Ritz, 1975, Wally's Cafe, 1981, The Odd Couple, 1985; (off Broadway) After Play, 1995, (London prodn.) Sunset Blvd., 1996; motion picture debut, 1950, and appeared in numerous films including West Side Story, Carnal Knowledge, The King and I, Singing in the Rain, The Four Seasons, I Like It Like That, 1994, Angus, 1995, Wharf Rat, 1995, Slums of Beverly Hills, 1998, Carlo's Wake, 1999, Blue Moon, 2000, Pinero, 2001, King of the Corner, 2004, Lolo's Cafe, 2006, Play It By Ear, 2006, (TV) The Rockford Files: If It Bleeds.It Leads, 1999, Strong Medicine, 2003, The Guardian, 2003, Copshop, 2004, Law and Order, 2005, (series) American Family, 2002. Recipient Acad. Award for best supporting actress, 1962; Grammy award for best rec., 1973; Antoinette Perry award for best supporting actress Broadway play, 1975; Emmy award, 1977, 78, award Nat. Osteoporosis Found., 2000. Achievements include being in the Guinness Book of World Records as the only female performer to win Acad., Grammy, Tony and Emmy awards. Address: care Agency for Performing Arts 9200 W Sunset Blvd Los Angeles CA 90069-3502*

MORENO, VERONICA, food products executive; m. Eduardo Moreno. Co-founder Olè Mexican Foods, Norcross, Ga., 1987—. Named Nat. Hispanic Businesswoman of Yr., U.S. Hispanic C. of C., 2001, Latina Entrepreneur of Yr., Hispanic Bus. Mag., 2004. Office: Ole Mexican Foods Inc 6585 Crescent Dr Norcross GA 30071

MORENO, ZERKA TOEMAN, psychodrama educator; b. Amsterdam, The Netherlands, June 13, 1917; d. Joseph and Rosalia (Gutwirth) Toeman; m. Jacob L. Moreno, Dec.1949; 1 child, Jonathan D.; 1 stepchild, Regina. Student, Willesden Tech. Coll., 1937-38, NYU, 1948-49. Cert. trainer, educator, practitioner of psychodrama and group psychotherapy Am. Bd. Examiners. Rsch. asst. Psychodramatic and Sociometric Insts., N.Y.C., 1942-51; pres. Moreno Inst., N.Y.C. and Beacon, N.Y., 1951-82; trainer in psychodrama Studiefrämjandet, Stockholm, 1976-83, Finnish Psychodrama Assn., Lahti, Finland, 1976-83. Lectr., trainer, Gt. Britain, Australia, China, New Zealand, Norway, Sweden, Italy, Germany, Japan, 1976-96, Argentina, Brazil, Greece, The Netherlands, Denmark, Belgium, Spain, Israel, Korea and Taiwan, 1977—; hon. pres. Internat. Zerka Moreno Inst., Nanjing, China; acad. advisor mental health Nanjing Brain Hosp., China, 1997. Co-author: Psychodrama, Surplus Reality, and the Art of Healing, 2000, Psychodrama, Vol. II, 1967, Vol. III, 1969, The First Psychodramatic Family, 1964; author: (poetry) Love Songs to Life, 1971, 2d edit., 1993, The Quintessential Zerka, 2006. Named hon. citizen Comune di Roma, Assessorato Alla Cultura, 1983, Municipalidad de la Ciudad de Buenos Aires, 1984, Hon. Mem. Federacao Brasiliero de Psicodrama, Sao Paulo, 1996; first recipient of prize from Astrid Badina Stiftung (Baden-Baden, Germany), 1999 Fellow Am. Soc. Group Psychotherapy and Psychodrama (pres. 1967-69, hon. pres. 1988—, sec.-treas. 1955-66); hon. mem. Internat. Assn. Group Psychotherapy (treas. 1974-76, bd. dirs. 1976-80), Soc. Psicodrama Sao Paulo (hon.), Sociedad Argentina Psicodrama (hon.). Home: The Colonnades C24 2600 Barracks Rd Charlottesville VA 22901-2198

MORENO-DUCHENY, DENISE, state senator; m. Al Ducheny. Student, Univ. Lund, Sweden; BA in History, Pomona Coll.; JD, Southwestern U., 1979. Bar: Calif. Lawyer; trustee San Diego CC Dist. Governing Bd; mem. Calif. State Assembly, 1994—2000, Calif. State Senate, Sacramento, 2002—. Chair Senate Budget Subcom. Health and Human Svcs.; mem. Environ. Cooperation Commn.; commr. San Diego County Regional Governance Efficiency Commn., State Commn. on the Califs.; mem. Latino Legis. Caucus, Women's Caucus; lectr. in field. Trustee Anza-Borrego State Park Found.; bd. dirs. San Diego Natural Hisotry Mus. Mem.: Calif. C.C. Trustees Assn. (bd. dirs.), Assn. Latino C.C. Trustees Calif. (chair, co-founder). Democrat. Office: 637 3rd Ave Ste C Chula Vista CA 91910

MOREY, CHARLOTTE ANN, elementary school educator, music educator; b. Dickinson, N.D., Dec. 1, 1949; d. Clarence William Hartman and Catherine Sills; m. Michael Scott Morey, June 19, 1971; children: Christopher Michael, Melissa Kay. BS, Dickinson State Coll., 1971. Elem. music specialist Slope County Schs., Amidon, ND, 1971—72, New England Pub. Schs., 1972—75, 1980—80; jr. high sch. music specialist McKenzie County Pub. Schs., Watford City, 1976—78; elem. music specialist Hettinger Pub. Sch., 1985—2000, Lincoln Elem. Sch., Fargo, 2000—. Contbr. articles to profl. jours. Flutist cmty. bands, Hettinger, Bismark, Fargo, 1981—; organist Luth. Ch., Regent, New England, Watford City, Hettinger, 1965—2000. Named N.D. Music Educator of Yr., 2001; recipient Disting. Svc. award, Internat. Misic Camp, 1999, Alumni Fellows award, Dickinson State U., 2004. Mem.: Music Educators Assn. N.D. (clinician & adjudicator 1971—), Orgn. Am. Kodaly Educators (clinician 1995—, pres. North Plains chpt.), N.D. Music Educators Assn. (state chair, bd. dirs., exec. bd., Music Educator of Yr. 2001), N.D. Am. Choral Dirs. Assn. (state pres. 2001—, past repertoire & stds. chair). Avocations: cross stitch, gardening, cooking, reading. Office: Lincoln Elem Sch 2120 9th St S Fargo ND 58103

MOREY, SHARON LYNN, psychotherapist, mediator; b. Cherokee, Iowa, Apr. 8, 1948; d. Joseph Glenn and Annie (Bush) M.; m. Edward Devere Beck, July 23, 1988; stepchildren: Mark Edward, Bruce David. Cert. in bus., Mpls. Bus. Coll., 1968; BA in Psychology, Adminstrn., Met. State U., 1988; PhD in Clin. Psychology, The Union Inst., 1992. Exec. dir. Iowa Lakes Regional Orgn., Spirit Lake, 1982-86; peer acad. advisor Met. State U., St. Paul, 1986-88; appointed to mktg. task force Minn. State U. System, St. Paul, 1987-88; crisis phone counselor Lovelines Counseling Ctr., Mpls., 1987-88; mediator North Hennepin Mediation Project, Brooklyn Center, Minn., 1988-93; pvt. practice St. Anthony Mental Health Ctr., Mendota Heights, Minn., 1988-93; intern in clin. psychology Richfield (Minn.) High Sch., 1990-91; psychotherapist, mediator St. Anthony Mental Health Clinic, St. Paul, 1990-93. Cons. Iowa Lakes Regional Orgn., Spirit Lake, 1986-90; group facilitator Toughlove Orgn., Eagan, Minn., 1987-90. Mem. Okoboji Area After 5 Christian Bus. Women, Spirit Lake, 1978-82, Okoboji Lakes Bible and Missionary Conf., Spirit Lake, 1978—, Grad. Sch. of Union Inst. Exec. Learner Coun., Cin., 1990-92; bd. dirs. N.W. Iowa Singles Weekend Conf., Spirit Lake, 1978. Met. State U. scholar, 1987, Highland Park Bus. and Profl. Women scholar, 1987; grantee Dept. Vocat. Rehab., 1986-87, Alliss Edn. Foun., 1986, Pell, 1986-87. Mem. APA, N.Am. Soc. Adlerian Psychologists, Minn. Coun. Mediators (interim v.p. 1990-91), Minn. Psychol. Assn., Grad. Sch. of Union Inst. Alumni Assn., Met. State U. Alumni Assn., Minority and Women Doctoral Directory, Soc. Profls. in Dispute Resolution, Assn. Family and Conciliation Cts. Mem. Christian Ch. Avocations: tennis, golf, walking, singing.

MORFORD, JOANN (JOANN MORFORD-BURG), state senator, investment company executive; b. Miller, S.D., Nov. 26, 1956; d. Darrell Keith Morford and Eleanor May Morford-Steptoe. BS in Agrl.-Bus., Comml. Econs., S.D. State U., 1979; cert. in personal fin. planning, Am. Coll., 1992. CLU; chartered fin. cons. Agrl. loan officer 1st Bank System, Presho, SD, 1980-82, Wessington Springs, SD, 1982-86, Am. State Bank, Wessington Springs, 1986; investment rep. ARM Fin. Svcs. Inc., Wessington Springs, 1986-96, Capital Financial Svcs., Inc., Miller, 1997—; mem. S.D. State Senate, Wessington Springs, 1990-96, majority whip, 1993-94, minority whip, 1995-96, mem., 1990-97, Miller, 1997-98; ins. agt. Western Fraternal Life Assn., 2001—03. Mem. transp. com., commerce com., taxation com. S.D. State Senate, Pierre, 1990—92, mem. appropriations com., 1993—98, chair ops. and audit com., 1993—94, mem. ops. and audit com., 1995—98; mem. fed. issues environ. com. Nat. Conf. State Legislators' Assembly, 1994—98, vice chair, 1996—97. Mem. midwestern-Can. task force Midwest Conf., 1990—94; treas. twp. bd. Wessington Springs, 1990—92; active Wessington Springs Sch. Improvement Coun., 1992—95; bd. dirs. Nyoda Coun. Girls Scouts U.S.; mem. fin. com. United Meth. Ch., Miller, 2001—04. Fleming fellow, Ctr. Policy Alternatives, 1996. Mem.: S.D. Farmers Union, Bus. and Profl. Women (2nd v.p. 2002), Alumni Coun. Young Polit. Leaders (China delegation 1996, host El Salvador delegation 1999), Future Farmers Am. (adv. bd. Wessington Springs chpt. 1984—96), S.D. State U. 4-H Alumni Assn., Order Ea. Star (various offices 1980—). Democrat. Home and Office: 1510 N Parkview Pl Miller SD 57362-0021

MORFORD, LYNN ELLEN, state official; b. Peoria, Ill., June 17, 1953; d. Raymond Scott Jr. and Georgiana (Woodhall) M. BA, Millikin U., 1975; MA, U. Ill. was Sangamon State U., Springfield, Ill., 1984. News reporter Stas. WJBC-WBNQ, Bloomington, Ill., 1975-76, Sta. WSOY-AM-FM, Decatur, Ill., 1976-78, Stas. WXCL-WZRO-FM, Peoria, 1978, Sta. KACY-AM-FM, Ventura, Calif., 1978, Sta. WKAN, Kankakee, Ill., 1979-82; freelance news reporter Sta. WMAQ, Chgo., 1982; news dir. Stas. WXCL-WKQA-FM, Peoria, 1983; press sec. Ill. Ho. of Reps. Rep. Press Office, Springfield, 1984-85; chief Press Office, Ill. Dept. Commerce and Community Affairs, Springfield, 1986-95, comms. coord., 1995—. Mem. adv. bd. Ill. AP, 1983; radio news contest judge Okla. AP, 1983; bd. dirs. Ill. News Broadcasters Assn., 1980-84; mem. Gov.'s Conf. on Mgmt. of Illinois River, 1997—. Mem. adv. bd. Leadership Ill., 1992—, spring conf. chair, 1994; Springfield St. Patrick's Day Parade Com., 1991-99; chmn. pub. rels. film fund raiser Vachel Linds ay Assn., Springfield, 1989; mem. Springfield Jr. League, 1990-91; mem. Samaritans St. John's Hosp., Springfield, 1995—. Ill. River Econ. Devel. Action Team, 1996-97, Orlene Moore Scholarship Com., 1996—, Student of Yr. Selection Com., 1996; pres., bd. trustees Sherman Pub. Libr. Dist., 1995—; elder Buffalo Hart Presbyn. ch., 1998—; pres. Buffalo Hart Women's Assn., 1997—; mem. Town and Country Women's Assn., 1998—. Recipient Best Contbr. award Ill. AP, 1983; Robert Howard scholar Sangamon State U., 1983; named to Hon. Order of Ky. Cols., 1992. Mem. Order of Ea. Star. Presbyterian. Avocations: golf, competitive sewing and baking (state fair champion), vocal music, gardening, decorating. Office: Ill Dept Commerce and Community Affairs 620 E Adams St Springfield IL 62701-1615 Home: 10 Country Club Pl Bloomington IL 61701-3486 E-mail: lmorford@commerce.state.il.us.

MORFORD, MARIE ARLENE, insurance company executive; b. Wichita, Oct. 21, 1929; d. George and Bertha (Wear) Bachman; divorced; children: Stephen, Cheryl, Phillip. Clk. McKesson Robbin Drug, Wichita, 1948-49, Safeway Offices, Wichita, 1952-55; ins. sec. Benfer Ins., Newton, Kans., 1955-70, Ctrl. Agy., Newton, 1970-87; patient admitting operator Halstead (Kans.) Hosp., 1988-90; ins. rep., office mgr., lic. rep. State Farm, Newton, Kans., 1990—. Dir. religious edn. St. Mary's Ch., Newton, 1988, advisor adult religious edn., 1996, eucharistic minister, 1982; rep. Mother to Mother Ministry, Newton, 1988, Harvey County Citizens for Life, Newton, 1989; regent Daus. of Isabella St. Joseph's Cir., Kans., 1993-97, 2005-, treas., 1995—, state vice regent, 1999—; pres. Wichita Diocesan Coun. of Cath. Women, 1993-95; adv. bd. Wichita Diocesan Religious Edn. Mem. Daus. of Isabella (state vice regent 1999-2001, state auditor 2001, regent 2005—, state trustee, 2000—). Home: 1206 Harrison PO Box 135 Newton KS 67114-0135

MORGAN, ANN M., artist, educator; b. Atlanta, July 27, 1918; d. Henry Marchman and Sallie Claude Holden; m. Robert Fleming Carter, July 6, 1952 (dec. Mar. 1955); 1 child, Robert Fleming Jr.; m. Cyril James Morgan, Mar. 13, 1989. BS, Ga. State Coll. Women, 1940, BA, 1941; postgrad., NYU, 1948-49. Cert. bus. edn., fine arts, English lit. and grammar tchr. Instr. Fulton County Pub. Schs., Atlanta; tchr. H.S. and jr. coll. Ramey AFB, P.R., 1939-40; tchr. girls H.S., Fulton County, Ga., 1940-41, S.W. H.S., Dade County Pub. Schs., Miami, Fla., 1957-58; instr. Dade Bus. Coll., Dade County; founder, instr. De Nova Art Sch., Miami. Exhibited in group shows at Lowe Mus., Horte Mus., others. Head blocks program Rockdale (Fla.) Civic Assn.; chmn. Wives of West Point Officers' Aux., 1945-59. Mem. Coral Gables Art Orgn. (membership chmn., various offices), Miami Watercolor Soc. (membership chmn., various offices), soc. Four Arts.

MORGAN, ANN MARIE, psychologist; b. Fresno, Calif., Mar. 8, 1949; d. Charles and Cassie Alvena (Armey) McMurray; m. Stephen Charles Morgan, Sept. 6, 1969; 1 child, Kesley Suzanne. BA, U. LaVerne, 1971, MEd, 1973; MS in Marriage and Family Counseling, U. Laverne, 1999; MA in Psychology, Calif. Sch. Profl. Psychology, 1999, PsyD in Clin. Psychology, 2001. Tchr. Ontario (Calif.)-Montclair Sch. Dist., 1971-78, Cabrillo Unf. Sch. Dist., Half Moon Bay, Calif., 1978-85; project coord. U. La Verne, Calif., 1986—94; dir. program Ctr. Aging Resources, 2004; pvt. practice, 2004. Exec. com. Camp Fire Boys and Girls, Inc., Mount Baldy Region, Claremont, Calif., 1989—, bd. dirs., 1987—; mem. Children's Home Soc., Claremont, 1987-2004; bd. dirs. Ctr. Aging Resources, 2004. Mem.: Pi Gamma Mu. Mem. Ch. of the Brethren. Avocations: reading, gardening, exercise, skiing. Office: 428 W Harrison Ave Ste 101A Claremont CA 91711 Office Phone: 909-399-3402.

MORGAN, ANNE MARIE G., broadcast journalist, educator; b. Paducah, Ky., Apr. 23, 1955; d. Ralph Edward and Vera Christine Gill; m. Michael William Morgan, Nov. 19, 1977; children: Deborah, Jon, James. BA in Govt. and Psychology, Coll. William and Mary, 1976; MA in Polit. Sci., U. Richmond, 1997; postgrad. in Pub. Policy, Va. Commonwealth U., 1998. HS tchr. James-City County Sch., Williamsburg, Va., 1977, Colonial Hts. Sch., Va., 1977-79; TV and radio journalist Capitol News, Richmond, Va., 1984—, Va. Pub. Broadcasting, Richmond, Va., 1987—, WRIC-TV, Richmond, 1994—96, WTVR-TV, Richmond, 1996—2000; broadcast news anchor Va. News Network, Richmond, Va., 2000—02; journalist WVTF Radio, Roanoke, 2002—, Va. Pub. Radio, 2002—. Assoc. prof. polit. sci. U. Richmond, Va., 1998—. Author: (with others) Controversies in American Public Polity, 1999, Opposing Viewpoints Series, 1991. Sec. Parents' Guidance/Pupil Pers. Guidance Com., Powhatan, Va., 1996—98; state bd. dirs. Va. Pub. Broadcasting, Richmond, 2000—02; bd. dirs. Va. Adv. Coun. Adult Edn. and Literacy, Richmond, 1999—2002, Coun. Child Care and Early Childhood Devel., Richmond, 1995—96; chair bd. dirs. State Bd. for Cmty. Colls., Richmond, 1997—2002; chair Va. Coun. Status of Women, Richmond, 1994—2002. Recipient Meritorious award, Va. Assoc. Press Broadcasters, 2002, Disting. Faculty award, U. Richmond Sch. Contg. Studies, 2005, 1st Pl. award, Nat. Fedn. Press Women, 2005; Gov. proclamation Anne Marie Morgan Day in Commonwealth Va., Gov. Va., 1997. Mem.: Soc. Profl. Journalists, Soc. Profl. Journalists (Va. profl. chpt.), Nat. Fedn. Press Women (1st Pl. Prepared Radio Report award 2005), Va. Press Women (1st Pl. award 2005, 1st Pl. award spl. programming radio 2006, 1st Pl. award on the scene report radio 2006, 1st Pl. award prepared report radio 2006), Capitol Corrs. Assn., Am. Polit. Sci. Assn., Pi Sigma Alpha. Avocations: music, singing, mentoring.

MORGAN, ARDYS NORD, school improvement consultant; b. South Bend, Ind., Nov. 1, 1946; d. Arthur August and Janet Ardis (Eide) Nord; children: Elizabeth Elayne, Matthew Richard. BS in Elem. Edn., Ind. U., Bloomington, 1968; MS in Elem. Edn., Ind. U., Indpls., 1972; reading cert., Ind. U., South Bend, 1982; EDS, Ind. U., Bloomington, 1992; adminstr. lic., Ind. U.-Purdue U., Indpls., 1989; EdD in Curriculum and Sch. Adminstrn., Ind. U., 1994. Tchr., South Bend, 1968-69, 73-87; adminstr. dept. instrn. and curriculum, 1987-90; tchr. Indpls., 1969-70; resident lectr. Ind. U./Purdue U., Indpls., 1970-73, adminstr., 1989; mem. adj. faculty Ind. U., South Bend, 1985-90, acting program dir. elem. and secondary edn., 1990-92; asst. supt. schs. Michigan City (Ind.) Area Schs., 1992-94; supt. Union North United Schs. Corp., 1994-96; ednl. cons., tech. and staff devel. in curriculum Lightspan Partnership, San Diego, 1997-99; pres. Sch. Improvement Partnership, Inc., Granger, Ind., 1999—. Cons. in field. Recipient Disting. Alumni award div. edn. Ind. U., South Bend, 1990. Lilly Endowment fellow, 1987. Home: 51550 Stratton Ct Granger IN 46530-8342 Office: Sch Improvement Partnership 51550 Stratton Ct Ste 300 Granger IN 46530-8342

MORGAN, BARBARA R., astronaut; b. Fresno, Calif., Nov. 28, 1951; m. Clay Morgan; 2 children. BA in Human Biology with distinction, Stanford U., 1973; tchg. credential, Coll. Notre Dame, 1974. Tchr. remedial reading and math Flathead Indian Reservation Arlee (Mont.) Elem. Sch., 1974; tchr. reading, math McCall-Donnelly Elem. Sch., Idaho, 1975—78, tchr., 1979—98; tchr. elem. English and sci. Colegio Americano de Quito, Ecuador, 1978—79; astronaut, educator mission specialist candidate NASA, Johnson Space Ctr., Houston, 1998—. Backup candidate for Tchr. in Space Program NASA, 1985; mem. fed. task force for women and minorities in sci. and engring. NSF. Recipient Citizen of Yr. award, USA Today, 1986, Edn. award, Women in Aerospace, 1991, Wright Bros. "Kitty Hawk" Sands of Time Edn. award, L.A. C. of C., 1991, Space Pioneer award for edn., Nat. Space Soc., 1992, Pres.'s Medallion award, U. Idaho, 1998, Idaho Fellowship award, 1998. Mem.: Challenger Ctr. for Space Sci. Edn. (Challenger 7 award 1995), Internat. Tech. Edn. Assn. (Lawrence Prakken Profl. Cooperation award 1996), Internat. Reading Assn., Nat. Sci. Tchrs. Assn., Nat. Coun. Tchrs. Math., Idaho Edn. Assn., Nat. PTA (hon.; life), Phi Beta Kappa. Office: Astronaut Office/CB NASA Johnson Space Ctr Houston TX 77058

MORGAN, BETSY STELLE, lawyer; b. Terre Haute, Ind., Mar. 15, 1963; BA, DePauw U., 1985; JD, John Marshall Law Sch., 1988. Bar: Ill. 1989. With Baker & McKenzie, Chgo., 1988—, counsel, 1997—2002, ptnr., 2002—. Co-chair N.Am. Pro Bono Initiative Baker & McKenzie, Chgo. Author: United States Business Immigration Manual, 2003. Office: Baker and McKenzie One Prudential Plz 130 E Randolph Dr Chicago IL 60601

MORGAN, BEVERLY CARVER, pediatrician, educator; b. NYC, May 29, 1927; d. Jay and Florence (Newkamp) Carver; children: Nancy, Thomas E. III, John E. MD cum laude, Duke U., 1955. Diplomate Am. Bd. Pediat. (oral examiner 1984-90, mem. written examination com. 1990—), Nat. Bd. Med. Examiners. Intern, asst. resident Stanford U. Hosp., San Francisco, 1955-56; clin. fellow pediat., trainee pediatric cardiology Babies Hosp.-Columbia Presbyn. Med. Ctr., NYC, 1956-59; rsch. fellow cardiovasc. diagnostic lab. Columbia-Presbyn. Med. Ctr., NYC, 1959-60; instr. pediat. Coll. Physicians and Surgeons, Columbia U., NYC, 1960; dir. heart sta. Robert B. Green Meml. Hosp., San Antonio, 1960-62; lectr. pediat. U. Tex., 1960-62; spl. rsch. fellow in pediatric cardiology Sch. Medicine, U. Wash., Seattle, 1962-64, from instr. to prof. pediat., 1962-73, chmn. dept. pediat., 1973-80; mem. staff U. Wash. Hosp., chief of staff, 1975-77; mem. staff Harborview Med. Ctr., Children's Orthop. Hosp. and Med. Ctr., dir. dept. medicine, 1974-80; prof., chmn. dept. pediat. U. Calif., Irvine, 1980-88, prof. pediat. and pediatric cardiology, 1980—; pediatrician in chief Children's Hosp. Orange County, 1988. Mem. pulmonary acad. awards panel Nat. Heart and Lung Inst., 1972-75; mem. grad. med. edn. nat. adv. com. to sec. HEW, 1977-80; mem. Coun. on Pediatric Practice; chmn. Task Force on Opportunities for Women in Pediat., 1982; mem. nursing rev. com. NIH, 1987-88. Contbr. articles to profl. jours.; mem. editl. bd. Clin. Pediat., Am. Jour. Diseases of Children, Jour. of Orange County Pediatric Soc., Jour. Am. Acad. Pediat., LA Pediatric Soc. Recipient Women of Achievement award Matrix Table, Seattle, 1974; Disting. Alumnus award Duke U. Med. Sch., 1974; Ann. award Nat. Bd. Med. Coll. Pa., 1977; Career Devel. award USPHS, 1966-71; Moseby scholar, 1955. Mem. Am. Acad. Pediat. (chmn. com. on pediat. manpower 1984-86), Am. Coll. Cardiology, Soc. for Pediat. Rsch., Am. Fedn. Clin. Rsch., Am. Pediat. Soc., Assn. Med. Sch. Pediat. Dept. Chmn. (sec.-treas. 1981-87), Western Soc. for Pediat. Rsch., Alpha Omega Alpha. Office: U Calif Irvine Med Ctr Dept Pediatrics 101 The City Dr S Orange CA 92868-3201 Office Phone: 714-456-6483. Business E-Mail: bcmorgan@uci.edu.

MORGAN, BEVERLY HAMMERSLEY, elementary school educator, artist; b. Wichita Falls, Tex. d. Vernon C. and Melba Marie (Whited) Hammersley; m. Robert Lewis Morgan, Sept. 21, 1957 (div. 1972); children: Janet Claire, Robert David. BA, So. Meth. U.; MA, U. Ala., 1980, AA certification, 1982; postgrad., U. Tex., 1991—. Cert. art tchr., Tex., Ala.; cert. elem. tchr., Ala. Tchr. art Ft. Worth Pub. Schs., 1955-60; tchr. English, Lincoln County Schs., Fayetteville, Tenn., 1961-62; elem. tchr. Huntsville (Ala.) Pub. Schs., 1960-61, 62-68, tchr. art, 1972-92, 93-94. One-woman shows include U. Ala., 1980, Huntsville Art League, 1981, and various other art gallerys, art shows and exhbns. Mem. HAL Gallery, Huntsville, Madison County Sr. Art Gallery. Mem. Huntsville Mus. Art, Am. Contract Bridge League. Republican. Avocations: bridge, travel, collecting Hammersley English bone china. Home: 12027 Chicamauga Trl SE Huntsville AL 35803-1544

MORGAN, DAHLIA, museum director, art educator; BA, McGill U., Montreal, 1958; postgrad., Sir George Williams U., Montreal, 1968-69, U. Miami, Fla., 1974. Lectr. Mus. of Fine Arts, Montreal, 1965-70; lectr./rsch. Sir George Williams U., Montreal, 1968-70; grad. asst. dept. art and art history U. Miami, Fla., 1971-74; adj. prof. visual arts dept. Fla. Internat. U., Miami, 1975-77, vis. rof. visual arts dept., 1978-79, faculty visual arts dept., 1979—, dir. Art in State Bldgs. Program, 1984—, dir. Art Mus., 1980—. Lectr. in field; curator numerous exhbns.; panelist NEA Mus. Grants, 1993, Cultural Advancement Grants, 1990, 92; cons. Fed. Gen. Svcs. Adminstrn., 1992, Metro-Dade Art in Pub. Places Program, 1992. Prodr. numerous catalogues to exhbns. Juror South Miami Art Fair Photo Group; bd. dirs. Nat. Found. for Advancement in the Arts, 1984—; founder Friends of the Frost Art Mus. Support Group at Fla. Internat. U., 1984—; chmn. State of Fla. Art in Bldgs., 1984—; chmn. Art in Pub. Places, Dade County, Fla., 1980-84. Recipient 3d Ann. MAXIE award Miami Arts Exchange, 1990; grantee Fla. Endowment for Humanities, 1986, Metro Dade County Cultural Affairs Coun., 1986, Fla. Internat. U., 1990, 91; U. Miami-Coral Gables merit scholar, fed. scholar. Mem. Assn. Coll. and Univ. Mus. and Galleries, Am. Assn. Mus., Coll. Art Assn. Am., Fla. Mus. Dirs. Assn., Fla. Higher Edn. Arts Network, Internat. Coun. Mus. (fine arts com.), Miami Cultural execs. Coun., Southeastern Mus. Assn., Fla. Cultural Action Alliance, Phi Kappa Phi. Office: Frost Art Mus Fla Internat U University Park PC # 110 11200 SW 8th St Miami FL 33199-0001

MORGAN, DONNA EVENSEN, lawyer; b. Bklyn., Feb. 28, 1957; d. Edward Ivar and Judith (Larsen) Evensen; m. Charles S. Morgan, Sept. 3, 1988. BA, Colgate U., 1979; JD, U. Mich., 1984. Bar: Ill. 1985. Assoc. Chapman and Cutler, Chgo., 1985-86, Kirkland and Ellis, Chgo., 1987-89, Mayer Brown Rowe & Maw LLP, Chgo., 1989—. Office: Mayer Brown Rowe & Maw LLP 71 S Wacker Dr Chicago IL 60606-4637 Office Phone: 312-701-7138. Business E-Mail: dmorgan@mayerbrownrowe.com.

MORGAN, DONNA JEAN, psychotherapist; b. Edgerton, Wis., Nov. 16, 1955; d. Donald Edward and Pearl Elizabeth (Robinson) Garey. BA, U. Wis., Whitewater, 1983, MS, 1985. Lic. psychotherapist, Wis.; lic. mental health and alcohol and drug counselor, Wis.; nat. cert. alcohol and drug abuse counselor; lic. marriage and family therapist, Wis.; lic. ind. social worker; lic. clin. ind. social worker; nat. cert. counselor; lic. profl. counselor; lic. advanced practice social worker. Clin. supr. Stoughton (Wis.) Hosp., 1985-88; pvt. practice Janesville, Wis., 1988-91; prin. Morgan and Assocs., Janesville, Wis., 1991-96; pvt. practice New Focus, Waukesha and Mukwonago, Wis., 1996-97, William N. Watson & Assocs., MD, S.C., Oconomowoc, Waukesha, Wis., 1997—, Morgan Counseling, LLC, Janesville, Wis., 1998—. Mem. underaged drinking violation alternative program Rock County, 1986—96; co-chmn. task force on child sexual abuse, 1989—91; mem. Rock County Multi-disciplinary Team on Child Abuse, 1990—96; mem. spkrs. bur. Rock County C.A.R.E. House, 1990—; adv. bd. Parents Place, Waukesha County, Wis., 1997—99; active ARC, 2001—; vol. Red Cross, 2001—. Mem. APA, ACA, Am. Profl. Soc. on Abuse of Children, Wis. Profl. Soc. on Abuse of Children (bd. dirs. 1994-98, v.p. 1997-98), Am. Assn. Mental Health Counselors, Wis. Assn. Mental Health Counselors, Am. Assn. Marriage and Family Therapy (clin. mem.), Am. Assn. Christian Counselors, Wis. Counseling Assn., Am. Psycotherapy Assn., So. Wis. Ducks Unlimited. (mem. com. 1980—), Wis. Assn. of Mediators, Vest-A-Dog Program, Future Farmers Am. (PALS trainer). Office Phone: 608-757-1994.

MORGAN, ELAINE LUDLUM, minister; b. L.A., May 21, 1927; d. William Francis and Helen Katharine Ludlum; m. Robert Norman Morgan, Apr. 8, 1949; children: Robert Norman Jr., Lorene Elaine. AA, Pasadena C.C., 1947; BA, Pomona Coll., 1949; MA, U. So. Calif. L.A., 1953; postgrad., Diocesan Sch. Theology, Seattle, 1984. Ordained min. Episc. Ch.; cert. secondary tchr. Calif. Instr. English/Journalism Pasadena C.C., 1949—59; deacon All Saints Episc. Ch., Vancouver, Wash., 1984—89, St. Peters Episc. Ch., Carson City, Nev., 1989—95, Coventry Cross Episc. Ch., Minden, Nev., 1995—. Co-owner Crow's Nest Antiques, Greenford Farm, 1980—; chaplain Vancouver Meml. Hosp., 1984—89, Cason-Tahoe Hosp., Carson City, 1993—; chairperson Carson-Tahoe Rehab. Ctr., Carson City, 2001—. Editor: Pipes of Pan, 1947; editor: (cookbook) In the Kitchen With Women of Saint Marks, 1962, Not By Bread Alone, 1987, Coventry Cross Cuisine, 1998.

Recipient scholarship, Pasadena Rotary Club, 1947. Mem.: Carson City Ministerial Assn., P.E.O. (chairperson ways and means com. 2003, pres. 1994—95), Phi Beta Kappa, Phi Lambda Theta. Republican. Avocations: reading, collecting communion tokens and conders. Home and Office: 402 W Robinson St Carson City NV 89703

MORGAN, ELISE FENG-I, science educator; BS, Stanford U., Calif., 1996; MS, U. Calif., Berkeley, 2000, PhD, 2002. Tchr. The Pingry Sch., Martinsville, NJ, 1996—97; postdoctoral rschr. Stanford U., 2002—03; asst. prof. Boston U., 2003—. Recipient Young Investigator award, Internat. Osteoporosis Found. - Servier Rsch. Group, 2005; Grad. fellow, NSF, 1997—2000. Mem.: ASME, ASBMR, ORS, ASEE, Phi Beta Kappa, Tau Beta Pi. Office: Boston University 110 Cummington St Boston MA 02215 Office Phone: 617-353-2791.

MORGAN, ELIZABETH, plastic surgeon; b. Washington, July 9, 1947; d. William James and Antonia (Bell) Morgan; 1 child, Elena. BA magna cum laude, Harvard U., 1967; postgrad. (fellow), Oxford U., 1967, 70; MD, Yale U., 1971; PhD in Psychology, U. Canterbury, Christchurch, New Zealand, 1995. Diplomate Am. Bd. Surgery, Am. Bd. Plastic Surgery. Intern Yale-New Haven Hosp., 1971-72, resident, 1972-73, 76-77, Tufts-New Eng. Med. Center, Boston, 1973-76, Harvard-Cambridge Hosp., Mass., 1977-78; columnist Cosmopolitan mag., 1973-80; pvt. practice specializing in cosmetic plastic surgery Washington, 1978-87, McLean, Va., 1998—2006, Chevy Chase, Md., 1998—2006; chief plastic surgery Beverly Hills Physicians, Calif., 2006—. Faculty dept. psychology U. Md., 1995; assoc. faculty Am. U. Dept. Law, Justice and Soc., 1998. Author: The Making of A Woman Surgeon, 1980, Solo Practice, 1982, Custody, A True Story, 1986, The Complete Book of Cosmetic Surgery for Men, Women and Teens, 1988. Fellow: ACS, Am. Soc. Aesthetic Plastic Surgeons, Am. Soc. Plastic Surgeons; mem.: APA. Episcopalian. Office: 333 S Doheny Dr 202 Los Angeles CA 90048-3527 Business E-Mail: mail@drelizabethmorgan.com. E-mail: morgan52650@gmail.com.

MORGAN, ELIZABETH SEYDEL, writer, educator, retired writer; b. Atlanta, Ga, Feb. 19, 1939; d. John Rutherford and Jane Reynolds Seydel; children: Matthew, John, Elizabeth Borkey. BA, Hollins College, Roanoke, Va, 1956—60; MFA, Virginia Commonwealth University, Richmond, Va, 1983—86. Teacher, english and creative writing St. Catherine's School, Richmond, Va., 1960—93. Author: (,poet,book,) Parties, 1988, (book) The Governor of Desire, 1993, On Long Mountain, 1998 (finalist, Lib. Va. prize, 1999); translator: (part of penn greek drama series) "Electra" by Euripides, 1998; author: (short fiction) "Economics", 1991 (Emily Clark Balch Prize, 1992); contbr. essay Wild In The City: the James River in Richmond, 1999; author: (screenplay) Queen Esther, 1993 (Govs. award, Fa. Film Fest., 1993), (short fiction anthologies) New Stories From The South, 1993. Bd. dir. Richmond Pub. Libr. Found., Richmond, 1999—. Mem.: Fellows Council, Virginia Center for the Creative Arts. Home: 504 Honaker Avenue Richmond VA 23226

MORGAN, ELLEN LOUISE, elementary school educator; b. Sheboygan, Wis., Apr. 10, 1951; d. Robert George and Arlyn Ruth (Zehm) Guehna; m. John Derek Morgan, Oct. 23, 1976; children: Christina, Steven. AA, Concordia Coll., 1969—71; BS, Concordia Tchrs. Coll., 1971—73. Cert. tchr., Ohio. Tchr. 1st and 2d grades Luth. Sch. of Our Redeemer, Cin., 1973—93, interim prin., 1990—91; tchr. 4th and 5th grades Concordia Luth. Sch., Cin., 1993—94, tchr. 2d grade, 1994—, interim prin., 2004—05. Corr. sec. Ohio Dist. Luth. Tchrs., 1991. Bd. missions Ohio Dist. Luth. Ch.-Mo. Synod, 1982-84, mem. Licensure Profl. Devel. Com., 2003—. Mem. Luth. Edn. Assn., Luth. Elem. Tchrs., Choristers Guild. Avocations: needlecrafts, camping, bicycling, baking, reading.

MORGAN, EVELYN BUCK, retired nursing educator; b. Phila., Nov. 3, 1931; d. Kenneth Edward and Evelyn Louise (Rhineberg) Buck; m. John Allen McGeary, Aug. 15, 1958 (div. 1964); children: John Andrew, Jacquelyn Ann McGeary Keplinger; m. Kenneth Dean Morgan, June 26, 1965 (dec. 1975). Grad., Muhlenberg Hosp. Sch. Nursing, Plainfield, N.J., 1955; BSN summa cum laude, Ohio State U., 1972, MS, 1973; EdD, Nova U., 1978. RN, N.J., Ohio, Fla., Calif.; cert. clin. specialist ANCC; cert. advanced RN practitioner, Fla. Staff nurse Muhlenberg Hosp., 1955-57; indsl. nurse Western Electric Co., Columbus, Ohio, 195-59; supr. Mt. Carmel Hosp., Columbus, 1960-65; instr. Grant Hosp. Sch. Nursing, Columbus, 1965-72; cons. Ohio Dept. Health, Columbus, 1972-74; prof. nursing Miami (Fla.)-Dade C.C., 1974-96, prof. emerita, 1996—; pvt. practice family therapy, Ft. Lauderdale, Fla., 1982—. Family therapist Hollywood Pavilion Hosp., 1977-82; founder Elder Reach, Inc., care mgmt. co., 1998. Sustaining mem. Dem. Nat. Com., 1975—. Mem. ANA, Nat. Guild Hypnotists, Am. Nurses Found., Am. Holistic Nurses Assn., Fla. Coun. Psychiat. and Mental Health Clin. Specialists, Sigma Theta Tau. Roman Catholic.

MORGAN, FLORENCE MURDINA, nurse; b. Northern Manchester, Jamaica, Mar. 1, 1936; came to U.S., 1967; d. James William and Juanita Agatha (Lorraine) M. RN, Wanstead Hosp., Hermon Hill London, 1962; State Cert. Midwife, Rochford Hosp., Essex, Eng., 1963; Queens Nurse, Queens Inst. Dist. Nursing, Eng., 1965; BSN cum laude, CUNY, 1989, MSN, 1992. Cert. Childbirth Educator. Staff nurse Toronto Gen. Hosp., 1964-65; jr. supr., queens nurse/midwife Surrey County Coun., Kingston-on-Thames, Eng., 1965-66; staff midwife St. Luke's Hosp., Guildford, Surrey, 1966-67; staff nurse No. Westchester Hosp., Mt. Kisco, N.Y., 1967-70, Vis. Nurse Svc., N.Y.C., 1970-71; pvt. duty med. surg. nurse N.Y.C., 1971-76; staff nurse divsn. substance abuse Beth Israel Med. Ctr., N.Y.C., 1976—. Tb coord., tchr. health, tb. prevention, AIDS prevention Beth Israel Med. Ctr., N.Y.C., 1993—; vol. nursing Spalding Hosp., Jamaica, 1955-57. Vol. Luth. Ch., N.Y.C., 1967-76; vol. 1199 Polit. Action, N.Y.C., 1989-95. Mem. N.Y. Acad. Scis., Hunter-Bellevue Alumni Assn., Sigma Theta Tau. Democrat. Avocations: swimming, tennis, arts and crafts, dance, unpublished poems. Home: 445 E 14th St Apt 3D New York NY 10009-2805

MORGAN, JACQUI, illustrator, painter, art educator, writer; b. NYC, Feb. 22, 1939; d. Henry and Emily (Cook) Morganstern; m. Onnig Kalfayan, Apr. 23, 1967 (div. 1972); m. Tomás Gonda, Jan. 1983 (dec. 1988). BFA with honors, Pratt Inst., Bklyn., 1960; MA, CCNY, 1978. Textile designer M. Lowenstein & Sons, N.Y.C., 1961-62, Fruit of the Loom, N.Y.C., 1962; stylist-design dir. Au Courant, Inc., N.Y.C., 1966—; assoc. prof. Pratt Inst., Bklyn., 1977—. Guest lectr. U. Que., Syracuse U., Warsaw TV & Radio, Poland, NYU, Parsons Sch. Design, N.Y.C., Sch. Visual Arts, N.Y.C., Va. Commonwealth U., Fashion Inst. of Tech., others; mem. profl. juries; curator Tomás Gonda retrospective exhbn.; adj. prof. Fashion Inst. Tech., N.Y.C.; condr. workshops. One-person shows include Soc. Illustrators, N.Y.C., 1977, Art Dirs. Club, N.Y.C., 1978, Gallerie Nowe Miasto, Warsaw, 1978, Gallerie Baumeister, Munich, W.Ger., 1978, Hansen-Feuerman Gallery, N.Y.C., 1980, Krannert Mus./U. Ill., 1998, Art Gallery at Marywood U., Scranton, Pa., 1998, Soc. Illustrators N.Y., 2005; group shows include Mus. Contemporary Crafts, N.Y.C., 1975, Smithsonian Instn., Washington, 1976, Mus. Warsaw, 1976, 78, Mus. Tokyo, 1979, Nat. Watercolor Soc., 1989, Salmagundi Club, 1990, New Eng. Watercolor Soc. Open, 1990, Miss. Watercolor Grand Nat., 1990, Illustration West 29, 1990, Adirondack Nat., 1990, Die Verlassenen Schuhe, 1993, N.Y. restaurant Sch., 1994, Lizan-Tops Gallery, 1996, The Art Club, 2000, Museum at Fashion Inst. Am., 2003, Soc. Illustrators, 2005, Spring Studio, 2006; represented in permanent collections: Smithsonian Instn., Mus. Warsaw; author, illustrator: Watercolor for Illustration; produced 3 instrnl. watercolor videos; series of prints pub., 1995; series of plates publ., 1995; co-curator Tomas Gonda Retrospective, Va. Commonwealth U., Rutgers U., Carnegie Mellon U., others in U.S., Museo Del Arte Moderno, Buenos Aires, Ulmer Mus., Ulm, Germany; illustrator Lights Along the Path, 1999, The Healing Garden, 1999; contbr. articles to profl. jours. Recipient more than 200 awards from various orgns. including Soc. Illustrators, Fed. Design Coun., Comm. Arts Mag., Am. Inst. Graphic Arts, N.Y. Art Dirs. Club, Print Design Ann. Mem.: Graphic Artists Guild (dir. 1975—79), Soc. Illustrators, Women Artists of the West, Pa. Watercolor Soc. Studio: 6940 Yellowstone Blvd 515 Forest Hills NY 11375-3400

MORGAN, JANE HALE, retired library director; b. Dines, Wyo., May 11, 1926; d. Arthur Hale and Billie (Wood) Hale; m. Joseph Charles Morgan, Aug. 12, 1955; children: Joseph Hale, Jane Frances, Ann Michele. BA, Howard U., 1947; MA, U. Denver, 1954. Staff Detroit Pub. Libr., 1954-87, exec. asst. dir., 1973-75, dep. dir., 1975-78, dir., 1978-87; ret., 1987. Mem. Mich. Libr. Consortium Bd.; exec. bd. Southeastern Mich. Regional Film Libr.; vis. prof. Wayne State U., 1989—. Trustee New Detroit, Inc., Delta Dental Plan of Mich., v.p. Delta Dental Fund, Delta Dental Plan of Ohio; v.p. United Southwestern Mich.; pres. Univ.-Cultural Ctr. Assn.; bd. dirs. Rehab. Inst., YWCA, Met. Affairs Corp., Literacy Vols. Am., Detroit, Mich. Ctr. for the Book, Interfaith Coun.; bd. dirs., v.p. United Comty. Svcs. Met. Detroit; chmn. Detroiters for Adult Reading Excellence; chmn. adv. coun. libr. sci. U. Mich.; mem. adv. coun. libr. sci. U. Mich., mem. adv. coun. libr. sci. Wayne State U.; dir. Met. Detroit Youth Found.; chmn. Mich. LSCA adv. coun.; mem. UWA Literacy Com., Attys. Grievance Com., Women's Commn., Mich. Civil Svc. Rev. Com.; vice-chair Mich. Coun. for Humanities; v.p. Commn. for the Greening of Detroit; adv. com. Headstart; mem. Detroit Women's Com., Detroit Women's Forum, Detroit Exec. Svc. Corps.; sec., treas. Delta Dental Fund, pres., 1999. Recipient Anthony Wayne award Wayne State U., 1981, Summit award Greater Detroit C. of C.; named Detroit Howardite of Year, 1983 Mem. ALA, AAUW, Mich. Libr. Assn., Women's Nat. Book Assn., Assn. Mcpl. Profl. Women, NAACP, LWV, Women's Econ. Club (bd. dirs.), Sorosis Club (v.p.), Alpha Kappa Alpha (pres.). Democrat. Episcopalian.

MORGAN, JANET F., elementary school educator; b. Salesville, Ohio, May 19, 1938; d. Cleland Ellsworth and Helen Marie (Lashley) Frame; m. Terry F. MOrgan, Feb. 15, 1958; children: Brenda, Christy, Diana. BS in Edn., Muskingum Coll., postgrad.; MA, Ohio State U., 1991. Tchr. Shady Ln. Sch., Columbus, Ohio, 1958-59, Pleasant City (Ohio) Sch., 1959-60, Quaker City (Ohio) Sch., 1960-61, 68-93, Lore City (Ohio) Sch., 1962-65; retired, 1993. Recipient Martha Holden Jennings award, Oustanding Educator award, Phi Delta Kappa. Avocations: piano, organ. Home: PO Box 175 Quaker City OH 43773-0175

MORGAN, JENNIFER, counselor; d. Larry Ray Kilburn and Nancy Lee Kuhn; m. Mark William Mountford, Jan. 22, 2005. BA, U. Mo., Columbia, 1994—98; MA, Saint Louis U., 1998—2000. Lic. profl. counselor State of Mo., 2002. Lic. profl. counselor Meier Clinic, St. Louis, 2000—04, Morgan Counseling Svcs., St. Louis, 2004—. Mem.: Am. Assn. Christian Counselors, Am. Counseling Assn. Office: Morgan Counseling Svcs 11116 S Towne Sq Ste 105 Saint Louis MO 63123 Office Phone: 314-221-3773.

MORGAN, JOYCE KAYE, social worker; b. Acme, Pa., July 17, 1941; d. Jesse Gray and Lillian (Kubick) Hoyman; m. James Edward Morgan, Oct. 13, 1967. BS in Secondary Edn., Calif. State Coll., 1963; MSW, W.Va. U., 1967. Cert. social worker; lic. social worker, Pa.; bd. cert. diplomate social work. Tchr. Scottdale (Pa.) Jr.-Sr. High Sch., 1963-64, Hempfield Jr. High, Greensburg, Pa., 1966; social worker, supr. Rosewood State Hosp., Owings Mills, Md., 1967-72, Latrobe (Pa.) Area Hosp., 1974-79; pvt. practice Mt. Pleasant, Pa., 1987-2000. Mem. Multi Disciplinary Team Child Abuse, Greensburg, Pa., 1978-79; sec. adv. bd. Westmoreland County Children's Bur., Greensburg, 1979-83. Avocations: gardening, crafts, painting. Home: Happy Hill Farm 113 Sunset View Ln Mount Pleasant PA 15666-8927

MORGAN, KATHRYN DIANE, criminology educator; b. Cameron, Tex., Aug. 14, 1953; children: Moya Elyse, Bria Kathryn. PhD, Fla. State U., Tallahassee, 1991. Assoc. prof. U. Ala., Birmingham, 1991—. Mem. bd., site-based coun. Tuscaloosa City Schs. PTSA, 2000. Patricia Harris fellow, 1986—91. Mem.: Acad. Criminal Justice Scis., Am. Soc. Criminology, Phi Kappa Phi. Baptist. Avocations: cooking, reading. Home: 4714 7th Ct E Tuscaloosa AL 35405 Office: U Ala 210 University Blvd Office Bldg Birmingham AL 35294-4562 Office Phone: 205-934-2069. Home Fax: 205-934-2067. Office Fax: 205-934-2067. Personal E-mail: kmorgan0853@comcast.net. Business E-Mail: kmorgan@uab.edu.

MORGAN, KATHRYN LAWSON, retired historian, educator; 1 child, Susan Morgan Crooks MA, Howard U., 1952, U. Pa., 1967, PhD, 1970. Asst. prof. U. Del., Newark, 1970-71; lectr. Swarthmore Coll., Pa., spring 1970, prof. history and folklore Pa., 1972—95, Sara Lawrence Lightfoot Prof. History emerita Pa., 1995. Vis. assoc. prof. Bryn Mawr Coll., 1972-75, Haverford Coll., 1972-74, U. Calif.-Berkeley, winter 1975; cons. Research for Better Schs., Phila., 1968-69, Black History Mus., Phila., 1966-76, Smithsonian Instn., 1974-76, Ednl. Film Service, 1977 Author: Children of Strangers; Stories of a Black Family, 1980, transl. Brazilian-Portuguese, 2002, Books Across the Seas, Selected for Youth, 1981; contbr. articles to profl. jours., mags. Grantee Smithsonian Instn.-Am. Philos. Soc., 1983; Danforth Found. fellow, 1968—70, sr. rsch. scholar, Swarthmore Coll., 2003. Avocations: travel, storytelling, theater, music. Office: Swarthmore Coll Dept Hist Swarthmore PA 19081

MORGAN, LINDA GAIL, theater producer; b. Tallahassee, May 14, 1952; d. Thomas Mitchell Morgan Sr. and Helen Frances (Rives) Stokes. BS, Fla. State U., 1974. Prodn. mgr. Valley Forge Ballet-5th World Peace Youth Culture Festival, Honolulu, 1985, Salute to Lady Liberty, Madison Square Gardens, 1986, U.S. Constn. 200 Yr. Anniversary Parade, Phila., 1986-89, Columbus Day Parade, N.Y.C., 1988, Gift of the White Bird Parade-Landmark Entertainment, Oita, Japan, 1990-91, 1996 Olympic Opening and Closing Ceremonies-Centenniel Events, Inc., Olympic Stadium, Atlanta, 1996, Super Bowl XXXI Half Time Show, New Orleans, 1997, N.Y. Jets Halftime Show, Meadowlands Stadium, N.J., 1997; prodn. state mgr. Walt Disney Bus. Prodns., 1998; coordinating prodr. (musical) This Is America, The New World, Freedom Music, Santa Monica, Calif., 1989, California Traditional Music Festival, Human Rights Lectr. Series, Soka U. Am., L.A., 1992-95, The Genius and the Great, L.A., 1993, Every Child Deserves a Chance, L.A., 1994, A Tribute to Burt Reynolds, L.A., 1994, Celebrate the Garnet and Gold IV Honoring Charles Nelson Reilly, L.A., 1995, Leisure Quest Internat./Entertainment Devel. Group, Burbank, Calif., 1997; artist agt., co. gen. mgr. Zoli Mgmt., Inc., N.Y.C., 1986-89; orch. prodn. mgr. All Am. Gen. Meeting, Spectrum, Phila., 1987; asst. prodn. mgr. 8th World Peace Culture Festival, Fukuoka, Japan, 1987, This Is America, Madison Square Gardens, 1988, 1991 Olympic Festival Opening Ceremonies Radio City Spl. Events, Dodger Stadium, L.A., 1991; prodn. staff Inauguration Mayor of Atlanta, Civic Ctr., Atlanta, 1998; event mgr. Coke on Ice World of Coca Cola, Atlanta, 1997-98, Disney Events Productions, 1998-2003, Tribeca Film Fest., 2004; prodr. Anheuser-Bush Creative Svcs., 2001-. Mem. Soka Gakkai Internat. (arts divsn. culture dept. 1995-99), Fla. State U. So. Calif. Alumni Assn. (bd. dirs. 1991-95, Garnet/Gold award 1995), Internat. Spl. Event Soc., Alpha Chi Omega. Democrat. Buddhist. Avocations: arts, needlepoint, antiques, piano, gardening. Personal E-mail: lgailmorgan@cs.com.

MORGAN, LUCY WARE, news correspondent, journalist; b. Memphis, Oct. 11, 1940; d. Thomas Allin and Lucile (Sanders) Keen; m. Alton F. Ware, June 26, 1958 (div. Sept. 1967); children: Mary Kathleen, Andrew Allin; m. Richard Alan Morgan, Aug. 9, 1968; children: Lynn Elwell, Kent Morgan AA, Pasco Hernando C.C., New Port Richey, Fla., 1975; student, U. South Fla., 1976-80. Reporter Ocala Star Banner, Fla., 1965-68, St. Petersburg Times, Fla., 1967-86, capitol bur. chief, 1986—2006, sr. corr., 2006—. Assoc. editor and bd. dirs. Times Pub. Co., 1991—2006. Recipient Paul Hansel award Fla. Soc. Newspaper Editors, 1982, First in Pub. Service award Fla. Soc. Newspaper Editors, 1982, First Place award in pub. service Fla. Press Club, 1982, Pulitzer award for investigative reporting Columbia U., 1985, First Place award in investigative reporting Sigma Delta Chi, 1985; named to Kappa Tau Alpha Hall of Fame, 1992, Fla. Women's Hall of Fame, 2006; named Fla. Senate Press Gallery in Morgan's honor, 2005. Home: 7030 Spencer Dr Tallahassee FL 32312-3548 Office: St Petersburg Times 336 E College Ave Tallahassee FL 32301-1551 Office Phone: 850-224-7263. Personal E-mail: lucytimes@aol.com.

MORGAN, LYNN, sports association executive; BS in Mktg., U. Ga. Dir. sales devel., Olympic mktg. mgr. Cox Enterprises, Inc., Atlanta, 1991—2001; pres., CEO Women's United Soccer Assn., N.Y.C., 2001—03. Bd. dirs. Atlanta Sports Coun., Atlanta Thunder; gen. mgr. Atlanta Beat Women's United Soccer Assn. Bd. dirs. Salvation Army, Atlanta Ad Club, Atlanta Arts and Bus. Coun.

MORGAN, M. JANE, computer systems consultant; b. Washington, July 21, 1945; d. Edmond John and Roberta (Livingstone) Dolphin (dec.); 1 child, Sheena Anne. Student, U. Md., 1963-66, Montgomery Coll., 1966-70; BA in Applied Behavioral Sci with honors, Nat.-Louis Univ., 1987, MS in Mgmt., 1991; postgrad. diploma in info. resource mgmt, Am. U., 1995; cert., USDA Grad. Sch., 2000; postgrad. diploma, State U. Calif., Northridge, 2002. With HUD, Washington, 1965-84, computer specialist, 1978-84; pres., CEO Systems and Mgmt. Assocs., 1983-91; dir. systems engrng. Advanced Tech. Systems, Inc., Vienna, Va., 1984-86, sr. cons., 1989; chief tech. staff Tech. and Mgmt. Svcs., Inc., 1986-89; sr. computer scientist Integrated Systems divsn. Computer Scis. Corp., 1989-90; computer systems specialist gen. svcs. adminstrn. U.S. Govt., 1991—2001; divsn. dir. U.S. Gen. Svcs. Adminstrn., 2001—06. Mgmt. cons. Author: Rapid Identification of Critical Staff, 1991. Bd. dirs. PL Active. Mem. Federally Employed Women (life, webmaster, 1996-, nat. exec. v.p. 1998-2000), Order Eastern Star. Episcopalian. Personal E-mail: webwoman@jmorgan.net.

MORGAN, MARABEL, writer; b. Crestline, Ohio, June 25, 1937; d. Howard and Delsa (Smith) Hawk; m. Charles O. Morgan, Jr., June 25, 1964; children— Laura Lynn, Michelle Rene. Student, Ohio State U. Pres. Total Woman, Inc., Miami, Fla., 1970—. Pub. speaker. Author: The Total Woman, 1973, Total Joy, 1976, The Total Woman Cookbook, 1980, The Electric Woman, 1985, The Home on the Range Cookbook, 1995. Office: c/o Total Woman Inc 1300 NW 167th St Ste 3 Miami FL 33169-5738

MORGAN, MARLENE, education educator, consultant; b. Aug. 01; AAS, Lower Columbia Coll., 1992; BA in Human Devel., Wash. State U., 1996; M in Early Childhood, U. Houston, 2004. Cert. master trainer Tex. Head Start State Collaboration Office, 2005. Tchr., spl. ed. coord. Lower Columbia Coll. Head Start, Longview, Wash., 1991—99; trainer, tech. asst. Tex. Tech U. Head Start Quality Info. Ctr., Lubbock, 2000—03; literacy mentor tchr. Galveston Head Start and Cir. Program; early childhood cons. pvt. practice, Houston, 2001—; nat. literacy head start trainer Ctr. Improving Readiness Children Learning and Edn., U. Tex. Med. Br., 2002—02; early head start, head start fed. program reviewer Danya Internat., Washington, 2002—; instr. edn. Lee Coll., Baytown, 2005—. Summer program dir. Kids Coll., Galveston Coll., 2000—00; ednl. sci. intern Space Ctr. Houston, 2004—04; profl. devel. lab instr. Environ. Inst. Houston, Houston, 2003—05. Leader, organizer Apple Ln. Task Force, Kelso, Wash., 1998—99. Named Internat. Student Leader Yr., Assn. Childhood Edn. Internat., 2004, Orientation Leader Yr., U. Houston Clear Lake, 2005; recipient Significant Svc. award Head Start, Lower Columbia Coll., 2000, Presdl. award, U. Houston Clear Lake, 2002—04; grantee, Lakeshore Learning Materials, 2000, Software Edn. Future Tchrs., 2006. Mem.: ASCD (assoc.), Assn. Childhood Edn. Internat. (assoc.; pres., advisor 2003—06), Nat. Assn. Edn. Young Children (assoc.; sec. 1993—2006), Tex. Head Start Assn. (assoc.), Nat. Head Start (assoc.), Kappa Delta Pi (sec., pres. 2004—06), Omicron Delta Kappa (pres. 2004—06, Cir. Leader Yr. 2005), Phi Theta Kappa (life; v.p. 2003—05). Achievements include first to collaborative program with three diverse Education Organizations at the UHCL to reach out to low income familes at an Even Start Program called Reading Parties: Sharing theJoy of Literacy; Connected students and organizations at the University of Houston Clear Lake with children orphaned by AIDS in Kenya to help with their educational needs called Starfish Kenya; first to warehouse clearance book fair twice a year to raise funds to help at risk children in the local community. This collaborative is between Scholastic and an educational organization @ UHCL; development of an Educational Professional Development organization at Lee College for students majoring in Edcuation. Avocation: gardening. Office Phone: 281-425-6486.

MORGAN, MARY DAN, librarian; b. Tallulah, La., Nov. 30, 1943; d. Daniel Boone and Mary Louise (McLeod) M.; m. William Jefferson Day (div. Dec. 1995); 1 child, Forrest Jefferson Day. BA, La. Coll., 1965; MLS, La. State U., 1968; MA Edn., Murray State U., 1976; MSW, U. Louisville, 1992. Cert. social worker, Ky., Ind. Libr. Ascension Parish Schs., Donaldsonville, La., 1966—68, Jefferson County Schs., Louisville, 1968—75; tchr. Webster County Schs., Dixon, Ky., 1975—79, Hardin County Schs., Elizabethtown, Ky., 1979—82, dir. media ctr., 1982—87, tchr. day and residential juvenile facilities, 1987—91, tchr. mid. and sr. high alt. schs., 1991—93; social worker Hospice of Ctrl. Ky., Elizabethtown, 1993—2000, Gentiva Health Svcs., Louisville, 1995, Lincoln Trail Dist. Home Health, Elizabethtown, 1997—98; libr. Luther Luckett Correctional Complex, La Grange, Ky., 2000—. Pres. Webster County Tchrs. Assn., Dixon, Ky., 1977-78; sec. Ky. Libr. Network Bd., Frankfort, 1986-87. Mem.: ALA, AAUW, NASW, NEA (life), Filson Hist. Soc. Office: Luther Luckett Correctional Complex PO Box 6 La Grange KY 40031 Office Phone: 502-222-0363.

MORGAN, MARY E., publishing executive; married; 1 child. B, SUNY Binghamton. Adv. dir. Fitness Mag., 1992—94; assoc. group pub. Parents and Child Mag., 1994—95; assoc. pub. Ladies Home Journal, 1995—97; v.p., pub. Health Mag., 1997—2003, Redbook, 2003—. Mem. editl. bd. Pharmaceutical Executive Magazine. Mem.: Nat. Assn. of Chain Drug Stores, Cosmetic Exec. Women (philanthropy com.), Advt. Women of N.Y. (mem. bd. dirs.), Advt. Club of N.Y. Office: Redbook 224 West 57th St New York NY 10019 Home: Chatham MA Office Phone: 212-649-3450.*

MORGAN, MARY JANE, retired mathematics educator; b. Tulsa, June 12, 1945; d. Cecil E. and Walene May Folks; life ptnr. Raymond Victor Morgan, Aug. 13, 1967; children: Jason Wesley, Jeremy Victor. BS, Southwestern State U., Weatherford, Okla., 1966; M Liberal Arts, So. Meth. U., Dallas, 1972. Cert. Tchr. Tex., 1969. Math. tchr. Columbia Ind. Sch. Dist., Mo., 1967—69, Highland Pk. Ind. Sch. Dist., Dallas, 1969—75, Alpine Ind. Sch. Dist., Tex., 1976—2001, chmn. math. dept., 1992—2001; ret., 2001. Trustee Pilot Internat., Macon, Ga., 2006, bd. dirs., 2004—05; pres. Pilot Club of Alpine, 1989—90; bd. dirs. Alpine Pub. Libr., 2005; program coord. Leadership Big Bend, Alpine, 2001; amb. Alpine C. of C., 2006; sec., trustee Alpine Ind. Sch. Dist., 2003; treas. Ch. of Christ, Alpine, 2001; exec. bd. Tex. State Teachers Assoc., Austin, Tex., 1985—89. Named Tchr. of Yr., Alpine H.S., 1991, Citizen of Yr., Alpine C. of C., 2005. Democrat. Mem. Church Of Christ. Avocations: reading, walking, cooking, volunteer work, travel. Home: PO Box 1341 Alpine TX 79831 Home Fax: 432-837-8367. Personal E-mail: mjmorgan@sulross.edu.

MORGAN, MARY LOU, retired education educator, volunteer; b. Chgo., Mar. 5, 1938; d. William Nicholas and Esther Lucille (Galbraith) Wanmer; m. James Edward Morgan, May 30, 1963. BA in Bus. Edn. and Econs., Wichita State U., 1971, MEd in Student Pers. and Guidance, 1974; postgrad., Kans. State U., 1986. Cert. bus. tchr., Kans. Reservationist Braniff, Wichita, Kans., 1961—62; stenographer, fin. analyst, clk.-typist Boeing Co., Wichita, 1962—68, tng., pers. and records positions, 1979—93; pers. cons. Rita Pers. Svc., Wichita, 1974—75; adminstrv. aide, manpower specialist, job developer City of Wichita, 1975—76; account exec., employment counselor Mgmt. Recruiters, 1976—77; pers. mgr., patient cons. Women's Clinic, 1977; vocat. rehab. counselor State of Kans., Parsons, 1977—79; pvt. detective Investigation Svcs., Wichita, 1981—84; instr. career devel. Wichita State U., 1988—90. Paralegal asst. Turner & Hensley, Wichita, 1975. Coord. funding Women's Crisis Ctr., Wichita, 1975; docent Carver Mus., Hoover Mus.; vice chmn. Hist. Preservation Commn.; founder, coord. Ann. Women's Chautauqua; Precinct committeewoman Wichita Dem. Com., 1992—94; pres. Jasper County-Newton County Dems., 1998; sub., co-chair then chmn. precinct walkers voter registration Grover Beach Dems., 2004—, assembly dist. mem., 2005—, chmn. equal rights com., del. to state; mem. 22,000 Club Calif. State Dem. Coun., 2006—; vol. Dem. Party, San Luis Obispo; bd. dir. City of Wichita Commn. on Status of Women, 1988—91. Mem.: AARP, NOW (founder, 1st pres. and v.p. program chmn. Wichita chpt. 1969—93, asst. state coord. polit. action com. Wichita chpt. 1993—95, at-large state bd. Joplin chpt. 1994—95, 1997—98, 1999—2000, at-large state mem. 2001—04, del. nat. convention 2006), AAUW (bd. dir. edn., equity, women's issues Joplin br. 1999—2000, pres. Grover Beach br. 2002—04, mem. state pub. policy com. 2003—04, br. pub. policy chair 2004—05, v.p. membership 2004—), LWV (v.p. issues study Joplin area league 1998—2000, Grover Beach league 2001—06, off board dir. 2002—03, bd. dir. 2003—04), Alliance Ret. Persons, Dem. Women United, Dem. Women United, Century Club. Avocations: water-skiing, boating, travel.

MORGAN, MARY LOUISE FITZSIMMONS, fund raising executive, lobbyist; b. NYC, July 22, 1946; d. Robert John and Mary Louise (Gordon) Fitzsimmons; m. David William Morgan, Aug. 7, 1971; children: Mallory Siobhan, David William. BA, Marquette U., 1964; MA, Cath. U., 1966; postgrad., Columbia U., 2005. Asst. prof. Monmouth U., West Long Branch, NJ, 1966-69; campaign dir. United Way, NYC, 1969-80; pres. Morgan Communications, NYC, 1980-82; capital campaign dir. YMCA of Greater NY, 1982-85; dir. devel. NY Med. Coll., Valhalla, 1985-88; counsel Challenger Ctr., Va., 1988-89; v.p. Ctr. Molecular Medicine & Immunology, Newark, 1989-92, Garden State Cancer Ctr., Newark, 1989-92; chief devel. and pub. affairs officer Mental Health Assn., White Plains, NY, 1993-95; dir. external affairs St. Vincents Svcs., 1996—, mng. dir., 2006—. Adj. prof. Iona Coll., New Rochelle, NY, 1994-95; dir. Meth Ch. Home for Aged, Riverdale, NY, Casita Maria Inc., NYC, 1975-95; pres., founding dir. Achievement Rewards for Coll. Scientists Inc., 1978-80. Sec. Darien (Conn.) Dem. Town Com., 1984—, vice chmn. Darien nominating com. 1986—. Recipient 50th Anniversary award Casita Maria Inc., N.Y.C., 1984, Iris award Bus. Communicators of Am., 1991, Nat. Depression Awareness Campaign award NMHA, 1994, Am. Graphic Design award, 2002. Mem. Nat. Soc. Fund Raising Execs., Nat. Soc. Hosp. Adminstrn., Spring Lake (NJ) Bath and Tennis Club. Democrat. Roman Catholic. Avocations: golf, gardening, tennis. Office: 66 Boerum Pl Brooklyn NY 11201-5705 Office Phone: 718-422-2255. E-mail: MaryL.Morgan@svs.org.

MORGAN, NICOLE RAE, theater director, educator; b. Pasadena, Tex., Feb. 28, 1970; d. Sandra Ann Cowan; m. Daniel Joseph Cowan, Jan. 4, 1992; children: Colleen Rae, Nathaniel Joseph. BFA, Southwestern U., Georgetown, Tex., 1991. Theater and speech dir. St. Pius X HS, Houston, 1992—99; dir. of theatre arts Meml. HS, Houston, 1999—. Mem. 4th of July steering com. City of Friendswood, Tex., 1990—; cub scout den leader Pack 711, Houston, 2004—; lectr. Mary Queen Cath. Ch., Friendswood, 1985—. Mem.: EDTA (assoc.), Tex. Ednl. Theater Assn. (assoc.), Delta Zeta (assoc.). Avocations: reading, travel. Office Phone: 713-365-5110.

MORGAN, PATRICIA, financial consultant, former Republican party chairman; Chairwoman Rep. Party, East Providence, RI Rep. State Ctrl. Com., West Warwick, 2001—03; fin. cons. Smith Barney, Providence, 2003.

MORGAN, ROBIN EVONNE, poet, writer, journalist, editor; b. Lake Worth, Fla., Jan. 29, 1941; 1 child, Blake Ariel. Grad. with honors, The Wetter Sch., 1956; student, pvt. tutors, 1956-59, Columbia U.; DHL (hon.), U. Conn., 1992. Free-lance book editor, 1961-69; editor Grove Press, 1967-70; editor, columnist World column Ms. Mag., NYC, 1974-87, editor in chief, 1989-93, cons. editor, 1993—, columnist, 2003—04, global editor, 2004—. Vis. chair and guest prof. women's studies New Coll., Sarasota, Fla., 1973; disting. vis. scholar, lectr. Ctr. Critical Analysis of Contemporary Culture, Rutgers U., 1987, U. Canterbury, Christchurch, New Zealand, 1989, U. Denver Grad. Sch. Internat. Affairs, 1996-97; invited spl. cons. UN com. UN Conv. to End All Forms Discrimination Against Women, Sao Paulo and Brasilia, Brazil, 1987; adv. bd. ISIS (internat. network women's internat. cross-cultural exch.); spl. advisor gen. assembly conf. on Gender UN Internat. Sch., 1985-86; free-lance journalist, lectr. cons., editor, 1969—; presenter, spkr. in field Author, compiler, editor: Sisterhood Is Powerful: An Anthology of Writings from the Women's Liberation Movement, 1970, Swedish edit., 1972, Sisterhood Is Global: The International Women's Movement Anthology, 1984, U.K. edit., 1985, Spanish edit., 1994, Feminist Press edit., 1996, Sisterhood Is Forever:The Women's Anthology for A New Millennium, 2003; author: (nonfiction) Going Too Far: The Personal Chronicle of a Feminist, 1978, German edit., 1978, The Anatomy of Freedom: Feminism, Physics and Global Politics, 1982, 2d edit., 1994, fgn. edits. UK, 1984, Germany, 1985, Argentina, 1986, Brazil, 1992, The Demon Lover: On the Sexuality of Terrorism, 1989, UK edit., 1989, Japanese edit., 1992, Italian edit., 1998, rev. US edit., 2002, The Word of a Woman: Feminist Dispatches 1968-91, 1992, 2d edit., 1994, UK edit., 1992, Chinese edit., 1996, A Woman's Creed, English, Arabic, French, Italian, Sanskrit, Hindi, Russian, Spanish, Portuguese, Chinese and Persian edits., 1995, Saturday's Child: A Memoir, 2000, Fighting Words, 2006, (fiction) Dry Your Smile: A Novel, 1987, UK edit., 1988, The Mer-Child: A New Legend, 1991, German edit., 1995, Korean edit., 2000, The Burning Time, 2006, (poetry) Monster: Poems, 1972, Lady of the Beasts: Poems, 1976, Death Benefits: Poems, 1981, Depth Perception: New Poems and a Masque, 1982, Upstairs in the Garden: Selected and New Poems, 1968-88, 1990, A Hot January: Poems 1996-1999, 1999, (plays) In Another Country, 1960, The Duel, 1979; editor: The New Woman: Anthology, 1969; author numerous poems; contbr. articles to profl. jours Mem. 1st women's liberation caucus CORE, 1965, Student Nonviolent Coordinating Com., 1966; organizer 1st feminist demonstration against Miss Am. Pageant, 1968; founder, pres. Sisterhood is Powerful Fund, 1970, NY Women's Law Ctr., 1970; founder NY Women's Ctr., 1969; co-founder, bd. dirs. Feminist Women's Health Network, Nat. Battered Women's Refuge Network, Nat. Network Rape Crisis Ctr.; bd. dirs. Women's Fgn. Policy Coun.; adv. trustee Nat. Women's Inst. for Freedom of Press; founding mem. Nat. Mus. Women in Arts; founder Sisterhood is Global Inst., 1984, officer, 1989-97, chair adv. bd., 1997-2004, pres., 2004—; co-founder Nat. Women's Media Ctr., 2005, Womens Radio Network, 2006; co-organizer, U.S. mem. ofcl. visit Coalition of Philippines Women's Movement, 1988; chair NY state com. Hands Across Am. Com. for Justice and Empowerment, 1988; adv. bd. Global Fund for Women, Equality Now Recipient Front Page award for disting. journalism, Wonder Woman award for internat. peace and understanding, 1982, Feminist of Yr. award Fund for Feminist Majority, 1990; Human Rights Activism Award from Equality NOW, 2002, Feminist Press award, 2003; writer-in-residence grantee Yaddo, 1980; grantee Nat. Endowment for Arts, 1979-80, Ford Found., 1982-84 Mem. Nat. Mus. Women in Arts, Feminist Writers' Guild, Media Women, N.Am. Feminist Coalition, Pan Arab Feminist Solidarity Assn. (hon.), Israeli Feminists Against Occupation (hon.).

MORGAN, RUTH PROUSE, academic administrator, educator; b. Berkeley, Calif., Mar. 30, 1934; d. Ervin Joseph and Thelma Ruth (Prcesang) Prouse; m. Vernon Edward Morgan, June 3, 1956; children: Glenn Edward, Renée Ruth. BA summa cum laude, U. Tex., 1956; MA, La. State U., 1961, PhD, 1966. Asst. prof. Am. govt., politics and theory So. Meth. U., Dallas, 1966-70, assoc. prof., 1970-74, prof., 1974-95; prof. emeritus, 1995—; asst. provost So. Meth. U., Dallas, 1978-82, assoc. provost, 1982—86, provost ad interim, 1986-87, provost, 1987-93, provost emerita, 1993—; v.p. Chem. Abatement Tech., Inc., 1995—. Tex. state polit. analyst ABC, N.Y.C., 1972-84. Author: The President and Civil Rights, 1970, Governance By Decree: The Impact of the Voting Rights Act in Dallas, 2004; mem. editl. bd. Jour. of Politics, 1975-82, Presdl. Studies Quar., 1980-2006; contbr. articles to profl. jours. Mem. Internat. Women's Forum, 1987—, City of Dallas Redistricting Commn., 2001, Greater Dallas Planning Coun, 1997—; mem. adv. bd. Maguire Ctr. for Ethics and Pub. Responsibility; trustee Hockaday Sch., 1988-94, The Kilby Awards Found., 1993-95; bd. dirs. United Way, Met. Dallas, 1993-99; adv. com. U.S. Army Command and Gen. Staff. Coll., 1994-97; founder Archives of Women of the Southwest, 1992, chmn. adv. com. 1995-99; mem. Dallas Women's Found.; adv. bd. Cary M. Maguire Ctr. for Ethics and Pub. Responsibilty, 1998—, The Women's Mus., Dallas, 1999— Mem. Am. Polit. Sci. Assn., So. Polit. Sci. Assn. (mem. exec. coun. 1979-84), Southwestern Polit. Sci. Assn. (pres. 1982-83, mem. exec. coun. 1981-84), The Dallas Assembly, The Dallas Forum of Internat. Women's Forum (pres. 1996-97), Charter 100 Club (pres. 1991-92), Ctr. for the Study of the Presidency, The Women's Mus (charter), Dallas Summit Club (pres. 1992-93), Phi Beta Kappa, Pi Sigma Alpha, Phi Kappa Phi, Theta Sigma Phi. Avocations: photography, travel. Office Phone: 214-691-5944. Personal E-mail: morgan_ruth@yahoo.com.

MORGAN, SHARON LYNN, principal; b. Cumberland, Md., Oct. 9, 1958; d. John Stafford Smith, Jr and Shirley Nightengale Smith; m. Harry Alvin Morgan, Apr. 12, 1980; children: Matthew Allen, Adam James. BS in Elem. Edn., Frostburg State Coll., Md., 1976—80, MEd in Elem. Adminstrn./Supervision, 1981—85. Elem. Edn., grades 1-6 W.Va. Bd. Edn., 1980, Elem. Adminstrng./Supervision W.Va. Bd. Edn., 1985, Elem. Edn., gr. 1-8 Md. Bd. Edn., 1992, Elem. Adminstrn./Supervision Md. Bd. Edn., 1992. Scholarship chair Alpha Delta Kappa, LaVale, Md., 1997—2006. Pianist First United Meth. Ch., Lonaconing, Md., 1996—2006. Mem.: NAESP, Internat. Reading Assn., Phi Delta Kappa. Methodist. Avocations: needlepoint, scouting, music, soccer (son's high school team). Office: Westernport Elem Sch 172 Church St Westernport MD 21562 Office Phone: 301-359-0511.

MORGAN, TIMI SUE, lawyer; b. Parsons, Kans., June 16, 1953; d. James Daniel and Iris Mae (Wilson) Baumgardner; m. Rex Michael Morgan, Oct. 28, 1983; children: Tessa Anne, Camma Elizabeth. BS, U. Kans., 1974; JD, So. Meth. U., 1977. Bar: Tex. 1977, U.S. Dist. Ct. (no. dist.) Tex. 1978, U.S. Ct. Appeals (5th cir.) 1979, U.S. Tax Ct. 1980; cert. tax law specialist. Assoc. Gardere & Wynne, Dallas, 1977-79, Akin, Gump, Strauss, Hauer & Feld, Dallas, 1979-83, ptnr., 1984-86; of counsel Stinson, Mag & Fizzell, Dallas, 1986-88; sole practice Dallas, 1988—. Adj. lectr. law So. Meth. U., 1989-90, 92-98. Bd. dirs. Dallas Urban League Inc., 1987-91. Mem. State Bar Tex. (mem. taxation sect.), Dallas Bar Assn., So. Meth. U. Law Alumni Coun. (sec. 1985-86), Order of Coif, Beta Gamma Sigma. Republican. Episcopalian. Personal E-mail: tsmorganpc@aol.com.

MORGAN, VICTORIA, performing company executive, choreographer; BFA, U. Utah, 1973, MFA magna cum laude, 1976. Prin. dancer Ballet West, 1969-78, San Francisco Ballet, 1978-87; resident choreographer San Francisco Opera, 1987—97; artistic dir. Cin. Ballet, 1997—. Dancer with lead roles in numerous classical, neoclassical and modern ballets including works by George Balanchine, Forsythe, and Kudelka, lead roles for TV and films, choreographer creating over 40 works for 20 ballet and opera cos. across U.S. including Utah Ballet, Pacific Northwest Ballet, Glimmerglass Opera, N.Y.C. Opera and Cin. Opera; creator, prodr. Ballet CD-ROM, choreography featured in documentary The Creation of O.M.O. Office: Cincinnati Ballet 1555 Central Pkwy Cincinnati OH 45214-2863*

MORGAN, VIRGINIA MATTISON, judge; b. 1946; BS, Univ. of Mich., 1968; JD, Univ. of Toledo, 1975. Bar: Mich. 1975, Federal 1975, U.S. Ct. Appeals (6th cir.) 1979. Tchr. Dept. of Interior, Bur. of Indian Affairs, 1968-70, San Diego Unified Schs., 1970-72, Oregon, Ohio, 1972-74; asst. prosecutor Washtenaw County Prosecutor's Office, 1976-79; asst. U.S. atty. Detroit, 1979-85; magistrate judge U.S. Dist. Ct. (Mich. ea. dist.), 6th circuit, Detroit, 1985—. Mem. bd. Fed. Jud. Ctr., 1997-2001; mem. jud. conf. U.S. Com. on Long Range Planning, 1993-96. Recipient Spl. Achievement award Dept. of Justice, Disting. Alumni award U. Toledo, 1993. Fellow Mich. State Bar Found.; mem. FBA (chpt. pres. 1996-97), Fed. Magistrate Judges Assn. (pres. 1995-96). Office: US Courthouse 231 W Lafayette Blvd Detroit MI 48226-2700

MORGAN-GRALA, TERRY LEE, elementary school educator; b. Naiuticoke, Pa., Oct. 28, 1952; d. Edward W. and Ann (Vernitus) Morgan; m. Edward M. Grala, Aug. 1, 1985; children: Morgan Edward, Mariana Leigh. BS in Elem. Edn., Mansfield U., 1974, MEd in English, 1978. Cert. prof., Pa. Tchr. 6th grade lang. arts, social studies Liberty Elem Sch., Pa., 0977—; head tchr. Liberty (Pa.) Elem Sch., 1983—. Mem. lang. arts. curriculum com. So. Tioga Sch. Dist, Blossburg, Pa., 1980—; cooperating. tchr. for student tchrs. Mansfield (Pa.) U., 1987—. Recipient Southern Tioga Sch. Dist. Tchr. Yr., 2004. Fellow Endless Mountains Writing Project (inservice coord. 2006-); mem. Pa. State Edn. Assn., Pa. State Tchrs. Assn., Nat. Wildlife Assn., Nat. Assn. Nat. Parks, Adoptive Families Am. Roman Catholic. Avocations: camping, hiking, gardening, cooking, travel. Office: Liberty Elem Sch 8622 Rte 414 Liberty PA 16930

MORGENSON, GRETCHEN C., reporter; b. State College, Pa., Jan. 2, 1956; married; 1 child. BA in English and History, Saint Olaf Coll., Northfield, Minn., 1976. Asst. editor to writer, fin. columnist Vogue Mag., 1976—81; stock broker Dean Witter Reynolds, NYC, 1981—84; staff writer Money Mag., 1984—86; editor, investigative bus. writer Forbes Mag., 1986—93, press sec. for Forbes for President campaign, 1995—96, asst. mng. editor, 1996—98; exec. editor Worth Mag., 1993—95; asst. bus. and fin. editor NY Times, NYC, 1998, now Market Watch columnist, Sunday Money and Bus. section. Author: Forbes Great Minds of Business, 1997; co-author: The Woman's Guide to the Stock Market, 1981; author: (with Campbell R. Harvey) The New York Times Dictionary of Money and Investing: The Essential A-to-Z Guide to the Language of the New Market, 2002; co-author: (with Allen R. Myerson (editor), Floyd Norris) The New Rules of Personal Investing: How to Prosper in a Changing Economy, 2001. Recipient Gerald Loeb award, 1998, 2002, Pulitzer Prize for beat reporting, 2002, TJFR Group/MasterCard Internat. Bus. News Luminaries award, 2003, Fin. Journalism prize for lifetime achievement, Women's Econ. Round Table, 2003. Office: NY Times 229 W 43d St New York NY 10036

MORI, MARIKO, artist; b. Tokyo, 1967; Student, Bunka Fashion Coll., Tokyo, 1986-88, Byam Shaw Sch. Art, London, 1988-89, Chelsea Coll. Art, 1989-92, Whitney Mus. Am. Art, 1992-93. One-woman shows include Geneva Project Room, N.Y.C., 1993, Shiseido Gallery, Tokyo, 1995, Am. Fine Arts Co., N.Y., 1995, Galerie Emmanuel Perrotin, Paris, 1996, Ctr. Nat. D'Art Contemporain Grenoble, Italy-Nordic Pavilion Venice Biennale, 1997, L.A. County Mus. Art, 1998, Mus. Contemporary Art, Cgo., 1998, Serpentine Gallery, London, 1998, Andy Warhol Mus., Paris, 1998, Bklyn. Mus. Art, Kunstmus. Wolfsburg, 1999, Fondazione Prada, Milan, 1999, Ctr. Pompidou, Paris, Ctr. Nat. Photography, 2000, Mus. Contemporary Art, 2002, Tokyo, 2004.

MORIARTY, KAREN, state agency administrator; b. Mesa, Ariz., June 15, 1957; d. Glenn Federick and Rosalee Mae (Russell) Bowers; m. Brian Logan Moriarty, Aug. 15, 1981; children: Lisa Louise, Kimberly Ann. Cert. pub. mgr. Clk. typist State of Ariz. Indsl. Commn., Phoenix, 1978, acctg. clk., 1978-85, fiscal specialist svcs. I, 1985-96, fiscal speicalist svcs. II, 1996—2002, self-ins. adminstr., 2003—, mgr. self-ins. adminstr., 2005—. Leader, trainer Ariz. Cactus Pine coun. Girl Scouts U.S., 1994—; active United Way, Phoenix, 1996, Big Bros./Big Sisters, Phoenix, 1987-91. Named Vol. of Yr., City of Chandler, 1995. Mem. NAFE, Nat. Assn. of the Deaf, Girl Scouts U.S. (life). Avocations: cross-stitch, swimming. Office: State of Ariz Indsl Commn 800 W Washington St Phoenix AZ 85007-2934 Personal E-mail: karenmori@cox.net.

MORIARTY, LAUREN, ambassador; b. 1955; 2 children. BA, U. Hawaii, 1976; MALD, Fletcher Sch. Law and Diplomacy, 1978. Dep. dir. Office of Develop. Fin., Bur. of Econ., Agr. and Bus. Affairs; trade policy officer Bur. East Asian and Pacific Affairs; head Econ. Sections Am. Inst. in Taiwan, 1994—97, dep. dir., 1997—98; diplomat-in-residence East-West Ctr., Honolulu, 1993—94; head Econ. Sections U.S. Embassy Fgn. Svc., US Dept. State, Beijing, 1999—2001; dir. Office of East African Affairs US Dept. State, 2001—03, sr. official to Asia Pacific Econ. Cooperation (APEC), 2003—04, amb. to APEC, 2004—. Office: APEC US Dept State 2201 C St NW Washington DC 20520

MORIN, KAREN M., geographer, educator; BA, U. Nebr., Lincoln, 1978; PhD in Geography, U. Nebr., 1996; MA in English, Bowling Green State U., Bowling, Ohio, 1982. Editl. asst. U. Nebr., 1990—92, tchg. asst., 1992—95; asst. prof. Bucknell U., 1995—2000, assoc. prof., 2001—. Vis. lectr. U. Waikato, New Zealand, 1995, 1998—99; lectr. in field. Editl. bd. Gender Place and Culture, 2000—, Journal of Historical Geography, 2001—, Historical Geography, 2003—, ACME: An International E-Journal for Critical Geographies, 2002—; contbr. articles numerous to profl. jour., chapters to books, scientific papers. Fellow: Am. Geog. Soc.; mem.: Fulbright Assn., Am. Studies Assn., Internat. Hist. Geographers, Soc. Women Geographers, Assn. Am. Geographers (Glenda Law awards com. 2005—). Office: Dept Geography Bucknell U Lewisburg PA 17837 Business E-Mail: morin@bucknell.edu.

MORIN, KAREN MARIE, education educator, researcher; b. Omaha, Nebr., May 17, 1956; d. Thomas Robert Morin and Margaret Ann Kalin; m. Daniel James Olivetti, Nov. 29, 1986; children: Nina, Nicholas. BA, U. Nebr., Lincoln, 1978; MA, Bowling Green State U., 1982; PhD, U. Nebr., Lincoln, 1996. Asst. prof. Bucknell U., Lewisburg, Pa., 1995—2000, assoc. prof. geography, 2001—. Mem. editl.bd. Gender, Place and Culture, Jour. of Hist. Geography, book review editor Gender, Place and Culture, 2001—05; editor: Historical Geography; contbr. articles to profl. jours. Sec. of bd. Lewisburg Prison Project, 2006—. Fellow, Gilder-Lehrman inst., 2005; grantee, NSF, 2003—06; scholar, Fulbright Assn., 2002, 2006. Fellow: Am. Geographical Soc.; mem.: Fulbright Assn., Assn. Am. Geographers, Soc. Women Geographers. Home: 237 Keila Ave Lewisburg PA 17837 Office: Bucknell U Dept Geography Lewisburg PA 17837

MORIN-MILLER, CARMEN ALINE, writer; b. Montreal, Que., Can., Dec. 20, 1929; came to U.S., 1983, naturalized, 2000; d. J. Gabriel Morin and Marie-Jeanne (Guay Morin) Vincent; m. Benoît H. Massicotte, July 28, 1951 (div. 1975); children: Andrée, Chantal, Joane, Claude, Anne; m. Jack Conway Miller, Sept. 9, 1983. Diploma, U. Laval, Québec City, Can., 1950, C.I.M., 1974; diploma in art, Charles-Huot Sch., Québec City, 1978. Freelance writer, 1954—; info. officer Ministère des Communications of Quebec, Quebec City, 1974-83; gallery owner Morin-Miller Galleries, NYC, 1985-90, Equity Art Svcs., Collegeville, Pa., 1983—. Dir. Amitiés Culturelles, Beauport, Quebec City, 1968-75. Author: Lumière, 1989, Conspiration, 1977; contbr. articles to Perspectives mag., other mags., newspapers. Pres. Assn. des Parents, Beauport, 1964-74. Mem. Nat. Geographic Soc., Am. Rhododendron Soc., Union Ecrivaines et Ecrivains Quebecois, Club Journalistes (pres. com. 1967-69), Assn. Morin d'Amerique (regional dir.). Avocations: reading, music, bridge, travel.

MORISATO, SUSAN CAY, actuary; b. Chgo., Feb. 11, 1955; d. George and Jessie (Fujita) M.; m. Thomas Michael Remec, Mar. 6, 1981. BS, U. Ill., 1975, MS, 1977. Actuarial student Aetna Life & Casualty, Hartford, Conn., 1977-79; actuarial asst. Bankers Life & Casualty Co., Chgo., 1979-80, asst. actuary, 1980-83, assoc. actuary, 1983-85, health product actuary, 1985-86, v.p., 1986-95, sr. v.p., 1996—2004, also bd. dirs., 2000—04; chief operating officer, sr. and retiree svcs. Ovations (a UnitedHealth Group co.), 2005—. Participant individual forum Am.'s Health Ins. Plans, 1983; spkr. in field. Adv. panel on long term care financing Brookings' Inst.; trustee Minn. Zoo Found., 2005—. Fellow Soc. Actuaries (workshop leader 1990, 93, news editor health sect. news 1988-90, conf. spkr. 2001, 02); mem. Am. Acad. Actuaries, Am.'s Health Ins. Plans (long term care task force 1988-2004, chair 1993-95, tech. adv. com. 1991-93, legis. policy com. 1996-99, nominating com. 1996-98, other coms., policy coord. coun. 1999-2003, sr. mktg. task force chair 2000-01, chmn. task force on Medicare modernization 2002-04, exec. com. 2004, bd. dirs. 2004, policy com. 2004, medicare com. 2005—, Founders award 1996), Health Ins. Assn. Am. (conf. spkr. 2000), LIMRA Internat. (strategic mktg. ins. com. 2001—, bd. dirs. 2003—, chmn. compensation and benefits com. 2004-05, vice-chair bd. dirs. 2005-06, chair bd. 2006—), Nat. Assn. Ins. Commrs. (ad hoc actuarial working group for long term care nonforfeiture benefits 1992), Am. Coun. Life Ins. (accelerated benefits/long term care com. 1997-2001), Chgo. Actuarial Assn. (sec. 1983-85, program com. 1987-89), Phi Beta Kappa, Kappa Delta Pi, Phi Kappa Phi. Office: Ovations UnitedHealth Group MN008-T440 9900 Bren Rd E Minnetonka MN 55343 Office Phone: 952-945-7555. Business E-Mail: susan_c_morisato@uhc.com.

MORISON, KATHRYN DIANE, actor, consultant; b. Merced, Calif., Oct. 3, 1962; d. Allan Grant Morison and Diane Griffin; 1 child, Alexander Brannan Pannullo. BA in Bus. Mgmt., Calif. State U., 1987. Actor Sacramento Theatre Co., Calif., 1986—92; mktg. and ops. Q&S Mgmt., Sacramento, 1992—95; actor Portland Repertory Theatre, Oreg., 1995—98; instr. YMCA, Portland, 1996—98; office mgr. Gail Kaufman Cons., Sacramento, 1998—99; owner, CEO Kathryn Morison Cons., Sacramento, 1999—. Cons. Calif. Lectures, Sacramento, 2004—, Cooper Prodns., Boston, 1999—2003, Fairytale Town, Sacramento, 1996—97. Author: (plays) Season Songs, 1994, Holidaze, 1993; prodr.: Stage and Theatre Co., 1988. Mem. East Sacramento Neighborhood Com., 2006; judge Sacramento City Sch. Dist., 2006; vol. Sacramento Food Bank, 1999—. Mem.: AEA, AFTRA. Democrat. Avocations: rollerblading, running, gardening. Home: 1257 Rodeo Way Sacramento CA 95819 Office: Kathryn Morison Cons 1257 Rodeo Way Sacramento CA 95819

MORISSETTE, ALANIS NADINE, singer; b. Ottawa, ON, Canada, June 1, 1974; d. Alan and Georgia Morissette. Singer: (albums) Alanis, 1991, Now is the Time, 1992, Jagged Little Pill, 1995 (Grammy award for Album of Yr., Best Female Rock Vocal Performance, Best Rock Song, Best Rock Album, 1996), Supposed Former Infatuation Junkie, 1998, Space Cakes, 1998, Alanis Unplugged, 1999, Under Rug Swept, 2002, Feast On Scraps, 2002, So-Called Chaos, 2004, Jagged Little Pill Acoustic, 2005, Alanis Morissette: The Collection, 2005; actor: (films) Anything for Love, 1993, Dogma, 1999, Jay and Silent Bob Strike Back, 2001; (TV films) The Great Warming, 2003; (TV series) You Can't Do That on Television, 1986; actor, prodr., writer (TV series) We're with the Band, 2006; actor: (TV appearances) Sex and the City, 2000, American Dreams, 2004, Degrassi: The Next Generation, 2005, Nip/Tuck, 2006; (plays) The Exonerated, 2003. Recipient BRIT award for Best Internat. Newcomer, 1996, MTV European Music award for Best Female Artist, 1996, Juno award for Prodr. of the Yr., 2003. Achievements include inducted into Canadian Walk of Fame, 2005.*

MORIYAMA, KAREN ITO, educational association administrator; d. Sadamu and Sumiko Honma Ito; children: Ryan M., Kristel S. BEd with high honors, U. Hawaii, Manoa, 1970, MEd, 1975. Lic. sch. adminstr. Dept. Edn., Hawaii, sch. counselor Dept. Edn., Hawaii, psychol. examiner Dept. Edn., Hawaii, cert. elem. tchr. Dept. Edn., Hawaii. Tchr. Red Hill Elem., Honolulu, 1971—73, Kipapa Elem. Sch., Mililani, Hawaii, 1973—82; counselor Solomon Elem. Sch., Wahiawa, Hawaii, 1982—85; counseling resource tchr. Dept. Edn., Central District, Hawaii, 1985—87; vice prin. Wheeler Intermediate Sch., Wahiawa, 1987—89; prin. Leihoku Elem. Sch., Waianae, Hawaii, 1989—94, Kanoelani Elem. Sch., Waipahu, Hawaii, 1995—2000; dist. dep. supt. Leeward Dist., Waipahu, 2000—02; complex area supt. Nanakuli-Pearl City, Waipahu, 2002—. Adv. mem. U. Hawaii Counseling and Guidance Adv. Com., Honolulu, 1986. Mem., sec. Waianae Mil./Civilian Adv. Coun., 1991—94; bd. dirs. Joint Venture Edn. Forum, Honolulu, 2002—05, YMCA, Mililani, Hawaii, 1997—2001. Mem.: NAESP (assoc. Leeward Dist. Disting. Prin. award 1994, 1999), Hawaii Assn. Supervision and Curriculum Devel. (assoc.), Delta Kappa Gamma (Beta chpt.) (assoc.; pres., v.p. 1996—2000). Office: Leeward District Dept Edn Rm 418 601 Kamokila Blvd Kapolei HI 96707 Office Phone: 808-692-8000. Office Fax: 808-692-7899. E-mail: karen_moriyama@notes.k12.hi.us.

MORLAN, JOANN G., communications educator; b. Boon, Iowa; d. Jacob and Shirley Faye Boon; m. Joseph C. Morlan, Aug. 19, 1978; children: Jaret Michael, Jessica SueAnn. AA, Des Moines Area C.C., Boone, Iowa, 1975; BA, Iowa State U., Ames, 1977; MA, U. No. Iowa, Cedar Falls, 2005. Tchr. English and Speech Rosalie Pub. Sch., Nebr., 1977—78; dir. vocational-tech. edn. New Hope Village, Iowa, 1980—83, qualified mental retardation profl., 1983—87; speech and drama coach Kuemper Cath. H.S., Carroll, 1981—2002; adj. prof. and ednl. advisor DesMoines Area C.C., 1987—. Advisor Phi Theta Kappa, Carroll, Iowa, 2000—. Contbr. to anthologies; lyricist: Houson the Hill, 1974. Pres. Carroll Cmty. Theatre, Iowa, 1995—2002, v.p., 2003—04, pres., 2004—05. Mem.: Am. Assn. Cmty. Theater, Internat. Listening Assn., Iowa C.C. Student Svc. Assn. (Outstanding Svc. award 1995, Dedicated Svc. award 1995). Independent. Roman Cath. Avocations: quilting, reading, writing, knitting, needlecrafts. Mailing: Des Moines Area CC 906 N Grant Rd Carroll IA 51401-2525

MORLAN, JUDITH JEANNETTE, science eductor; b. Detroit, Mich., Apr. 20, 1939; d. Stanley Arthur and Marion Jeannette (Walker) Green; m. Gordon Elliott Morlan, June 18, 1960; children: Christopher Elliott, Andrew Benjamin Morlan. BA, We. Mich. U., 1961; MA, Wayne State U., 1969, Education Specialist, 1992. Cert. permanent tchr. K-8, Mich. Elem. sch. tchr. Royal Oak, Mich., 1961-64, Portage(Mich.) Sch., 1964-65, Grosse Pointe (Mich.) Sch., Mich., 1975-90, middle sch. tchr., 1991-95, elem. sci. cons., 1991. Contbr. article to profl. jour. Recipient Tchrs. award Optical Soc., 1993; Wayne County grantee, 1993, Field Trip grantee Geo. Hydrology Wayne County, 1994. Mem. Mich. Sci. Tchrs. Assn. (elem. sci. dir., 1985-88, pres. 1989-90, adv. bd. Sci. and Children, 1992-95, sponsored tours 1994—), League of Women Voters (legal chpt., edn. chpt.), Metro Detroit Sci. Tchrs. Assn., Mich. Sci. Edn. Specialists, Mich. Earth Sic. Tchrs. Assoc., Nat. Sci. Tchrs. Assn., Golbar Rivers Environ. Edn. Network, Grosse Pointe Citizens for Recycling, Delta kappa Gamma. Presbyterian. Avocations: english riding, dressage and jumping, sailing, travel. Home: 723 Barrington Rd Grosse Pointe MI 48230-1724 Office: Brownell Middle Sch 260 Chalfonte Ave Detroit MI 48236-3350

MORONEY, LINDA L.S. (MUFFIE), lawyer, educator; b. Washington, May 27, 1943; d. Robert Emmet and Jessie (Robinson) M.; m. Clarence Renshaw II, Mar. 28, 1967 (div. 1977); children: Robert Milnor, Justin W.R. BA, Randolph-Macon Woman's Coll., 1965; JD cum laude, U. Houston, 1982. Bar: Tex. 1982, U.S. Ct. Appeals (5th cir.) 1982, U.S. Dist. Ct. (so. dist.) Tex. 1982, U.S. Supreme Ct. 1988. Law clk. to assoc. justice 14th Ct. Appeals, Houston, 1982-83; assoc. Pannill and Reynolds, Houston, 1983-85, Gilpin, Pohl & Bennett, Houston, 1985-89, Vinson & Elkins, Houston, 1989-92. Adj. prof. law U. Houston, 1986—91, dir. legal rsch. and writing, 1992—96, civil trial and appellate litigation and mediation, 1996—. Bd. dirs. Episcopal Ch. Pub. Co., Planned Parenthood of Houston and S.E. Tex., River Oaks Area Dem. Women (Roadwomen). Mem. ABA, State Bar Tex., Houston Bar Assn., Assn. of Women Attys., Tex. Women Lawyers, Alumnae Assn. Randolph-Macon Women's Coll. (bd. dirs.), Order of the Barons, Phi Delta Phi. Episcopalian. Home and Office: 4010 Whitman St Houston TX 77027-6334 Office Phone: 713-542-5073. Business E-Mail: mmoroney@hal-pc.org.

MORPHEW, DOROTHY RICHARDS-BASSETT, artist, real estate broker; b. Cambridge, Mass., Aug. 4, 1918; d. George and Evangeline Booth Richards; children: Jon Eric Bassett, Marc Alan Bassett, Dana Kimball Bassett. Grad., Boston Art Inst., 1949. Draftsman United Shoe Machinery Co., 1937—42; blueprinter, advt. artist A.C. Lawrence Leather Co., Peabody, Mass., 1949—51; propr. Studio Shop and Studio Potters, Beverly, Mass., 1951—53; tchr. ceramics and art Kingston, NH, 1953—; real estate broker, 1965—81; two-man exhbn. Topsfield (Mass.) Libr., 1960; owner, operator Ceramic Shop, West Stewartstown, NH. With USNR, 1942—44. Recipient Profl. award, New Eng. Ceramic Show, 1975, also numerous certs. in ceramics. Mem.: Englewood (Fla.) Art Guild.

MORREIM, E. HAAVI, medical ethics educator; b. July 21, 1950; d. Paul and Florence Morreim. BA in Philosophy, St. Olaf Coll., 1972; MA in Philosophy, U. Va., 1976, PhD, 1980. Med. philosopher program in human biology and soc. U. Va. Sch. Medicine, Charlottesville, 1980-82, asst. prof. philosophy in medicine, 1982-84; from asst. to assoc. prof. dept. human values and ethics U. Tenn. Coll. Medicine, Memphis, 1988—93, prof. dept. human values and ethics, 1993—. Adj. prof. philosophy Va. Commonwealth U., Richmond, 1980; vis. prof. philosophy St. Olaf Coll., Northfield, Minn., 1982; Andrew Mellon vis. asst. prof. humanities and medicine Georgetown U. Sch. Medicine, Washington, 1983; sr. vis. rsch. scholar Kennedy Inst. Ethics, Georgetown U., 1983; manuscript reviewer; presenter and lectr. in field. Author: Balancing Act: The New Medical Ethics of Medicine's New Economics, 1991, Holding Health Care Accountable: Law and the New Medical Marketplace, 2001; mem. editl. adv. bd. Jour. Medicine and Philosophy; bd. editors: Jour. Law, Medicine and Ethics, IRB: Ethics and Human Research; contbr. articles to profl. jours. Active Hastings Ctr. Mem. Am. Health Lawyers Assn., Am. Soc. Law, Medicine, and Ethics, Am. Soc. for Bioethics and Humanities, Phi Beta Kappa. Avocations: running, high-performance automobile driving, photography, skiing. Office: Univ Tenn Coll Medicine 956 Court Ave Ste B328 Memphis TN 38163-2814 Office Phone: 901-448-5725. Business E-Mail: hmorreim@utmem.edu.

MORRILL, PENNY CHITTIM, art historian; b. San Antonio, Feb. 4, 1947; d. Jack Robert and Dorothy Born (Sutherland) Chittim; m. James Agrippa Morrill, July 12, 1969; children: Jackson Forrest, Julia Chiltipin BA with honors, Tulane U., 1969; MA, U. Pa., 1971; PhD, U. Md., 2001. Program coord. Cancer Rsch. Found. Am., Alexandria, Va., 1990—95; adj. prof. Md. Inst. Coll. Art, Balt., 2000, Corcoran Coll. Art, Washington, 2003, Georgetown U., 2004—05, Hood Coll., Md., 2006—. Author: Silver Masters of Mexico, 1996, Mexican Silver, 1994; curator Carlyle Ho. Mus., Alexandria, 1980; curator, catalogue author traveling exhbn. Maestros de Plata: William Spratling and the Mex. Silver Renaissance, San Antonio Mus. Art., 1998-2004; contbr. articles to profl. jours. Vol. teen pregnancy prevention Nat. ARC, Washington, 1986-98; participant Coro Women in Leadership, Washington, 1988; mem. adv. com. Betty Ford Breast Health Ctr., Washington, 1997-98, adv. bd.; bd. dirs. Nat. Rehab. Hosp., Washington, 1991-2006, pres., 1991-2006; mem. alumnae bd. Newcomb Coll./Tulane U., 1990-94, v.p., 1992-97; v.p. Lyceum Mus., Alexandria, 1992-97, bd. mem., pres.; bd. mem., editor, pres. Hist. Alexandria Found., 1980-89; curator exhbn. Carlyle House Mus., Alexandria, 1980; mem. alumnae bd., v.p. Newcomb Coll. Tulane U., 1991-2006; bd. dirs., pres. Lyceum Mus., Alexandria, 1992-97, Hist. Alexandria Found., 1980-89, editor, 1980-89. Recipient Achievement award Jr. League Phila., 1985, RAP and AMAZE award, Nat. ARC, 1988, Spirit Volunteerism award Jr. League Washington, 1992, Recognition award Nat. Rehab. Hosp., 1997, Bd. Dir. award, 2005 Mem. Coll. Art Assn., Am. Soc. Jewelry Historians Episcopalian. Avocations: knitting, gardening.

MORRILL-CUMMINS, CAROLYN, social worker, consultant; b. Alexandria, Va., June 29, 1957; d. William Ashley and Lois (Birrell) Morrill; m. Joseph Paul Cummins, June 4, 1983; children: Katharine Jean, Cody William. BS in Psychology cum laude, Union Coll., Schenectady, N.Y., 1979; MSW, U. Albany, 1983. LCSW. Ptnr. Marion River Restaurant, Blue Mountain Lake, N.Y., 1979-82; home visitor Warren-Hamilton Counties Head Start, Indian Lake, N.Y., 1983-84; social worker, case mgr. Sunmount Devel. Disabilities Svc. Office, Tupper Lake, N.Y., 1984-86; social worker Wilton Devel. Disabilities Svc. Office, Indian Lake, 1986-93; tchr. asst. Indian Lake Ctrl. Sch., 1993-94; social worker Cmty. Workshop, Inc., Glens Falls, N.Y., 1994-95; clin. social worker Hamilton County Cmty. Svcs. Office, Indian Lake, 1995—. Social work cons. Mercy Healthcare Ctr., Tupper Lake, 1985-86, Warren-Washington ARC, Glens Falls, 1993, Eddy Home Care, Troy, N.Y., 1993-97. Bd. dirs. Hamilton County Cmty. Svcs. Bd., Indian Lake, 1983-84, Warren-Hamilton Counties Head Start, 1984-85, Hudson Headwaters Health Network, Warrensburg, NY, 1993-99, Indian Lake Ctrl. Sch. Bd. Edn., 1999-2004, pres. 2002-04; co-pres. Indian Lake Ctrl. Sch. PTA, 1994-99, pastor parish rels. com. Blue Mountain Lake United Meth. Ch., 1993—. Home: PO Box 993 Sabael NY 12864-0993 Office Phone: 518-648-5355.

MORRIS, CAROL E., biologist, educator; b. N.Y., Oct. 2, 1950; d. Erich Arnold Marx and Erna Lowenberg; m. John A.X. Morris, Aug. 12, 1973; 1 child, Stephan Erich. BA, Binghamton U., NY, 1972; MS, Cornell U., Ithaca, N.Y., 1974. Rsch. specialist Cornell U., 1974—76; prof. Tomokins Cortland C.C., Dryden, NY, 1976—. Land steward Finger Lakes Land Trust, Ithaca, 1995—. Mem.: Empire State Assn. Two Yr. Coll. Biologists. Home: 2449 Gee Hill Rd Dryden NY 13053 Office: TC3 170 North Dryden NY 13053

MORRIS, CAROLYN S., elementary school educator; d. Richard Lee and Henrietta C. Horst; m. Dallas D. Morris, Aug. 2, 1970; children: David L., Allison K. BS, Kans. State Teachers Coll., Emporia, 1970. Cert. tchr. Tex. Tchr. Manhattan Unified Sch. Dist., Kans., 1970—73, Spring Br. Ind. Sch. Dist., Houston, 1973—76, 1980—. Author: (educational book) Research Texas Style. Pres. Spring Br. YWCA, Houston, 1977—78. Recipient Rachel Carson Women in Math and Sci. award, Sky Ranch, Tex. Higher Edn. Coordinating Bd. and Tex. Edn. Agy., 2006. Mem.: AAUW, NEA, Spring Branch Edn. Assn., Tex. State Teachers Assn., Tex. Coun. Social Studies, Spring Branch Coun. Social Studies (pres. 2002—04). Presbyterian. Office: Bendwood Elem Sch 12750 Kimberley Houston TX 77024 Office Phone: 713-365-4990.

MORRIS, CATHLEEN ANN, academic administrator; d. John Lewis and Eloise Williams Morris; m. Ronald Lee Peters, Oct. 15, 2005. BS, U. Wis., La Crosse, 1979; MusB in Edn., U. Wis., River Falls, 1983; MS in Edn., U. Wis., La Crosse, 1984; PhD, Kent State U., Ohio, 1994. Cert. tchr. phys. edn. Dept. Pub. Instrn., Wis., 1979, tchr. music Dept. Pub. Instrn., Wis., 1983. Resident dir. and program advisor Buena Vista U., Storm Lake, Iowa, 1986—87; asst. dir. student activities and coord. student leadership programs Ashland U., Ohio, 1987—89; grad. asst. Kent State U., 1989—90; assoc. dean of students Marquette U., Milw., 1995—99; asst. to v.p. for student devel. Carroll Coll., Waukesha, Wis., 1991—92, acting dean of students, 1992—93, assoc. dean of students, 1993—95, dir. cmty. arts, 1999—2001, dir. outreach programs, 2001—02, dir. outreach programs, internat. student programming, 2002—. Chair Am. Coll. Pers. Assn., Washington, 1994—96. Mem. edn. com. Waukesha Symphony Orch./League, 1996—; vol. East Troy Electric RR, Wis., 2000—; session mem. First Presbyn. Ch., Waukesha, 1992—94; bd. mem. Waukesha Symphony Orch., 1996—2001, Arts Alliance of Waukesha County, 1999—, Waukesha County Art Mus., 2000—; adv. bd. mem. Salvation Army, Waukesha, Wis., 2004—06. Recipient Dedicacion a la Cultura award, Latin Am. Student Orgn., Carroll Coll., 1995. Mem.: Am. AAHPERD (life). Presbyterian. Avocations: singing, golf. Office: Carroll Coll 100 N East Ave Waukesha WI 53186 Office Phone: 262-524-7634. Business E-Mail: morris@cc.edu.

MORRIS, DEBBIE KAY, director, educator; b. Riverside, Calif., Mar. 4, 1957; d. Laurence M. and Alma A. Morris. Bachelors degree, Calif. State U.-Dominguez Hills, Carson, 1979. Tchg. credential State of Calif. Tchr. life scis. South Gate H.S., South Gate, 1985—2004; magnet coord. Orthopaedic Hosp. Med. Magnet H.S., L.A., 2004—. Recipient Earthwatch Tchr. fellowship, 1990, intern fellowship, Cheetah Conservation Fund, 2003. Mem.: Nat. Sci. Tchrs. Assn. Office: Orthopaedic Hosp Med Magnet HS 300 W 23rd St Los Angeles CA 90007 Office Phone: 213-765-2088. Office Fax: 213-742-9694. Personal E-mail: jambodebbie@earthlink.net.

MORRIS, GRETA N., former ambassador; b. 1947; BA, U. Redlands; MA in English, UCLA. Joined Fgn. Svc., US Dept. State, 1980; cultural and exchanges coord. Africa, Ascension; info. ctr. dir. Nairobi, Kenya; dir. Office Pub. Affairs Bur. African Affairs; press attaché Thailand; pub. affairs officer Uganda; counselor for pub. affairs Philippines; dep. dir. Office of Pub. Diplomacy Bureau for East Asian and Pacific Affairs; counselor for pub. affairs Jakarta; US amb. to Republic of Marshall Islands US Dept. State, 2003—06. Avocations: singing, swimming, cello.

MORRIS, HARRIET R., elementary school educator; b. Springfield, Mass., July 4, 1923; d. Walter Dewitt and Ida Ann (Rome) Bearg; m. Samuel Morris, Oct. 14, 1945 (dec. 1993); children: Robert, Julia, Jonathan, Daniel. BS, Am. Internat. Coll., 1944; MS, Butler U., 1973, EdS, 1985. Cert. tchr. K-12 Ind., mentally retarded, emotionally disturbed, LD/neurol. impaired, reading tchr. Ind., lic. sch. psychologist Ind. Tchr. lang. arts, grades 1-6 Children's Ho., Indpls., 1971—72; tchr. Indpls. Pub. Schs., 1972—89; sch. psychologist Avon Sch. Sys., Ind., 1990. Leader cub scouts Boy Scouts Am., Schenectady, NY, 1955—56; leader brownies Girl Scouts U.S., Schenectady, 1957—58; Sunday sch. tchr. Indpls. Hebrew Congregation, 1964—66; bd. dirs. Indpls. chpt. Hadassah, 1990—; guardian ad litem Ind. Advs. for Children, 1994—95; docent Indpls. Children's Mus., 1996—97; vol. Older Adult Svc. and Info. Sys., 1996—98. Mem.: Mensa.

MORRIS, HOLLY, elementary school educator; d. Michael and Carol Sparks; m. Eric Morris, Sept. 19, 1992; children: Alyx, Riley. BA in Secondary Edn., Idaho State U., Pocatello, 2002. Gifted and talented tchr. Am. Falls Sch. Dist., Idaho, 2002—03, 8th grade social studies tchr., 2002—. Leadership/cmty. svc. tchr. Am. Falls Sch. Dist., 2004—. Office Phone: (208)226-5203.

MORRIS, JILL CAROLE, psychotherapist; b. Phila., Sept. 15, 1965; d. Stephen M. and Deborah Sue (Moskovitz) Morris; m. Abraham Glickman, Feb. 14, 1987 (div. Sept. 1993); children: Deanna Justine, Jaisyn Rebecca. BFA in Fine Arts, Fla. Atlantic U., 1989, MEd in Mental Health Counseling, 1994; MS in Edn., Nova Southeastern U., 1992, PhD in Family Therapy, 1998. Lic. mental health counselor, Fla., marriage and family therapist, Fla.; nat. bd. cert. clin. hypnotherapist; diplomate Am. Bd. Child Mental Health Svc. Providers. Arts and crafts specialist Jewish Cmty. Ctr., Boca Raton, Fla., 1989—90, Congregation B'nai Israel, Boca Raton, 1991; head dept. art Ft. Lauderdale Prep. Sch., 1989—91; dir. edn., pub. affairs Planned Parenthood, Boca Raton, 1996—97; family therapist Dania, Fla., 1994—98; tchr. art, guidance counselor Grandview Prep. Sch., Boca Raton, 1997—98; pres., family therapist Every Woman's Place, Boca Raton, 1997—99; pres., family therapist in pvt. practice, 1999—; clin. supr., regional tng. ctr. Children's Aid Soc., Boca Raton, 2002—04. Exec. dir., founder Sage Inst. for Women and Families; family cons. Ann Stork Ctr., Ft. Lauderdale, 1996; pres., dir., founder Sage Inst. Women & Families, 1999-2003; adj. faculty Dept. Family Therapy Nova Southeastern U. Contbr. articles to profl. jours. Vol. counselor Compass, West Palm Beach, Fla., 1994; vol. Palm Beach County Mental Health Assn., 1994-95; sec. South Palm Beach County NOW, Boca Raton, 1997-99, v.p., 1999—. Mem. AAUW, ACLU, ACA, NOW (v.p. South Palm Beach County chpt. 1999—), Am. Mental Health Counselors Assn., Am. Assn. Marriage and Family Therapy, Internat. Assn. Marriage and Family Counselors, Phi Kappa Phi. Democrat. Jewish. Office: PO Box 970162 Boca Raton FL 33497 Office Phone: 561-558-2875. Personal E-mail: jmorrisphd@yahoo.com.

MORRIS, JUDY, artist; b. Calif., 1944; m. Tom Morris; 1 child, Sarah. BS, So. Oreg. State Coll., 1967, MS, 1976. Exhibited in group shows Am. Watercolor Soc., Water Color Soc. of Oreg., N.W. Watercolor Soc., Midwest Watercolor Soc., La. Watercolor Soc., Tex. Watercolor Soc., Nat. Watercolor Soc., Art-USA, Watercolor Art Soc. Houston, Salmagundi Club, N.Y.C., Ariz. Aqueous; works featured in publs. including Artist's Mag., Best of Watercolor, In Watercolor: People, Artist's Guide, Splash 4, Splash 5, Splash 7, The Artistic Touch, Best of Floral Painting 2, Watercolor Highlights 2, others; author: Watercolor Basics, LIGHT. Finalist in portrait, still life and landscape categories The Artist's Mag., 1991, all media competition, 1994, 96. Mem. Am. Watercolor Soc. (signature), Nat. Watercolor Soc. (signature, regional rep.), Watercolor Soc. Oreg., N.W. Watercolor Soc. (signature), West Coast Watercolor Soc., Transparent Watercolor Soc. Am. (signature), Rogue Valley Art Assn. Address: 2404 E Main St Medford OR 97504-6919 Office Phone: 541-779-5306. E-mail: judy@judymorris-art.com.

MORRIS, LAURA, elementary school educator; b. Santa Monica, Calif., Feb. 26, 1948; d. Maurice and Freida (Shiner) Rosenberg; m. Michael William Morris, Dec. 29, 1968; children: Samantha, Leah M. BA in Elem. Edn., U. Mont., 1970. Cert. elem. tchr., Mont. Elem. tchr. various schs., 1971-75; tchr. 1st grade Our Lady of Sorrows Cath. Sch., Rock Springs, Wyo., 1975-76; piano tchr. Laromor Piano Studio, Rock Springs, 1976-86; instr. Western Wyo. Coll., Rock Springs, 1982-84; tchr. 1st grade Westridge Sch., Rock Springs, 1985-86; tchr., accompanist Baker (Mont.) Pub. Schs., 1986—. Mem. gifted and talented adv. com. Baker Elem. Schs., 1994-95. Mem. Music Tchrs. Nat. Assn., Mont. State Music Tchrs. Assn. (v.p. S.E. divsn. 1986—), S.W. Wyo. Music Tchrs. Assn. (pres. 1981-83), Am. Orff Schulwerk Assn., Am. Legion Aux Avocations: reading, writing, drawing, cross country skiing, playing piano.

MORRIS, LISSA CAMILLE, music educator; d. Thomas Melvin Melot and Audrey Camille LaCroix; m. Randall Wyatt Morris, Mar. 15, 1986; children: Thomas Zachary, Linday Alissa, Jesse Randall, Aaron Wyatt. BA, Excelsior Coll., 1995. Music tchr. Village Pkwy. Sch., San Antonio, 1996—97; dir. music St. Michael's Ch., San Antonio, 1997—98, St. George Ch., San Antonio, 1998—2004, ret., 2004; co-owner WOW Sci. Lab., San Antonio, 2003—. Founder Little Mozarts Music Camp, Nishnabec Organic Farm, 2005—06. Contbr. articles to profl. jours.; composer: On the Ledge, 2002. Mem.: Music Educators Nat. Conf., Nat. Piano Guild, San Antonio Music Tchr.'s Assn. (bd. dirs. 1997—98). Republican. Roman Catholic. Avocations: reading, dance. Personal E-mail: lissacamille@yahoo.com.

MORRIS, LOIS LAWSON, retired education educator; b. Antoine, Ark., Nov. 27, 1914; d. Oscar Moran and Dona Alice (Ward) Lawson; m. William D. Morris, July 2, 1932 (dec.); 1 child, Lavonne Morris Howell (dec.). BA, Henderson U., 1948; specialist degree, U. Ark., 1956, MS, 1951, MA, 1966; postgrad., U. Colo., 1954, Am. U., 1958, U. N.C., 1968. History tchr. Delight H.S., Ark., 1942-47; counselor Huntsville Vocat. Sch., 1947-48; guidance dir. Russellville Pub. Sch. Sys., Ark., 1948-55; asst. prof. edn. U. Ark., Fayetteville, 1955-82, prof. emeritus, 1982—. Ednl. cons. Ark. Pub. Schs., 1965—78. Author: Biographical Essays, 2000; contbr. book reviews and articles to mags. and profl. jours. including Ga. Hist. Quar., 1998, Ark. Biography, 2000. Mem. Hist. Preservation Alliance Ark.; pres. Washington County Hist. Soc., 1983-85, Pope County Hist. Assn.; mem. Ark. Symphony Guild; charter mem. Nat. Mus. in Arts; bd. dirs. Potts Inn Mus. Found. Named Ark. Coll. Tchr. of Yr., 1972; recipient Plaque for Outstanding Svcs. to Washington County Hist. Soc., 1984. Mem. LWV, AAUW, NEA, Washington County Hist., Soc. (exec. bd. 1977-80), Ark. Edn. Assn., Ark. Hist. Assn., Pope County Hist. Assn. (pres. 1991-92), The Ga. Hist. Soc., U. Ark. Alumni Assn., Sierra Club, Nature Conservancy, Ark. River Valley Arts Assn., Phi Delta Kappa, Kappa Delta Pi, Phi Alpha Theta. Democrat. Episcopalian. Address: 1601 W 3d St Russellville AR 72801-4725

MORRIS, MARGARET ELIZABETH, marketing professional, small business owner; b. NYC, Nov. 1, 1962; d. John Daniel and Jean Bingham (MacCollom) M. BA in English, Georgetown U., 1984. Cert. Rubenfeld Synergy Method, 1997; cert. scuba diver: openwater, rescue diver, divemaster, emergency first responder instr., PADI open water scuba instr. Mem. staff mktg. programs AT&T Nat. Fed. Mktg., Arlington, Va., 1985; mktg. tech. cons. AT&T Nat. Fed. Systems, Washington, 1985-87; tech. cons. computer mktg. Cin. Bell Tel. Co., 1987-89, mktg. tech. cons., 1989-95; sr. acct. exec.-strategic accts., 1995—. Tutor (vol.) Ptnrs. in Edn. Editor: (newsletter) District Action Project RAP, 1981-82; contbr. chpt. to book. Intern Citizens' Complaint Ctr., Washington, 1981—82; asst. coach River City Volleyball Club; coach CYO Girls Volleyball; vol. tech. amb. Corryville Cath. Sch.; vol. coord. SPCA Cin.; participant Leukemia and Lymphoma Soc. Am. Team in Tng., Suzuki Rock n Roll Marathon, San Diego, 2000, Walt Disney World Marathon, Orlando, Fla., 2001, Flying Pig Marathon, Cin., 2001, Mayor's Midnight Sun Marathon, Anchorage, 2002, Las Vegas Internat. Marathon, 2003, Marine Corps Marathon, 2003, NYC Marathon, 2004, Rock N Roll Arix. Half Marathon, 2004, Flying Pig Half Marathon, 2006. Named Salesperson of Yr., 1997, Corp. Vol. of Yr., SPCA Cin., 2001. Mem.: Telephone Pioneers Am. (Pioneer Vol. of Yr. 2000). Office: Cin Bell Tech Solutions Rm 346-500 4600 Montgomery Rd Cincinnati OH 45212

MORRIS, MARGRETTA ELIZABETH, conservationist; b. Oakland, Calif., Sept. 14, 1950; d. Joseph Francis and Mildred Ruth Madeo; m. Dennis W. Morris, July 22, 1972; children: Matthew B., Roseanna A. BA in Geography, Radford U., 1972. Paralegal Law Office of Henry F. Zwack, Stephentown, N.Y., 1980-91; exec. dir. Ea. Rensselaer County Waste Mgmt. Authority, Stephentown, 1991-97; v.p., founder ERC Cmty. Warehouse, 1996—; mgr. govt. programs EnergyAnswers, Albany, NY, 1997—2005, v.p. govt. programs, 2006—. Co-founder MDM Prodns., Stephentown, 1986—. Councilperson Town of Stephentown, 1987-92; treas. Stephentown Meml. Libr., 2002-03. Mem.: America Recycles (bd. dirs. 2002—, chmn.), Fedn. N.Y. Solid Waste Assns. (chmn. 1997—), N.Y. State Assn. for Reduction, Reuse and Recycling (treas. 1992—), N.Y. State Assn. for Solid Waste Mgmt. (rec. sec. 1992—94), Nat. Recycling Coalition (bd. dirs. 1999—2005, pres.), Antilles H.S. Alumni Assn. (treas. 2002—), Gamma Theta Upsilon. Republican. Roman Catholic. Avocations: cross country skiing, hiking, biking. Office: EnergyAnswers 79 N Pearl St Albany NY 12207-2294

MORRIS, MARILYN LAVONNE, retired elementary school educator, minister; b. Sharon, W.Va., Apr. 24, 1936; d. James Edward and Nina Temperance Adkins; m. Stanley John Morris, June 6, 1964; children: Sara Griffith, Nina Knuckles, James Stanley. BA, MB, Charleston U., 1958. Pub. sch. tchr. Fayette County, Fayetteville, W.Va., 1958—64, Tazewell (Va.) County, 1980—98; sect. rep. Appalachian Dist. A/G., Ghent, W.Va., 1999—2005. Organist, choir dir. Bethel A/G, Richlands, Va., 1968—98, G.S. tchr., 1968—98; pastor Whittaker Ridge A/G, Bandy, Va., 2002—05; dist. tng. coord. Women's Ministry Appalachian Dist. A/G, 2002—05. Named Tchr. of Yr., Tazewell County DARE, 1993, Va. DARE Orgn., 1994. Avocations: piano, cooking, travel, sewing. Home: 504 Barrett St Richlands VA 24641

MORRIS, MARTHA JOSEPHINE, information services administrator; b. LaPorte, Ind., Jan. 16, 1951; d. John J. and Pearl L. Gorski; m. Richard Dale Morris, Sept. 5, 1970; children: Valerie A., Marlene N. ASN, Purdue U., Westville, Ind., 1977; BSN, Nazareth (Mich.) Coll., 1989. Charge nurse alcoholism/med. surg. unit Borgess Med. Ctr., Kalamazoo, 1977-81, asst. clin. mgr. substance abuse, 1981-88, asst. clin. nurse mgr. nephrology, 1988-90, contingency and patient intensity coord., 1990-93, mgr. patient info. tech., 1993-98, clin. analyst, project leader info. svcs., 1998—2002, info. svc. dir. clin. sys., 2002—. Test devel. com. for informatics nursing Am. Nurses Credentialing Ctr., Washington, 1994-2004. Mem.: ANA, Mich. Nurses Assn. Roman Catholic. Avocations: reading, flower gardening. Office: Borgess Med Ctr 1521 Gull Rd Kalamazoo MI 49048-1666 E-mail: marthamorris@borgess.com.

MORRIS, MARTHA MARNEL, music educator; b. Trenton, NJ, Aug. 25, 1948; M Music, American Conservatory, 1977; B Music Edn., St Mary of the Woods Coll., 1972. Co-founder/dir. Flutes Unlimited, Chgo., 1997—; music exec. Saint Xavier U., Chgo., 1984—96; conductor St. Xavier U. Orch., Chgo., 1983—; assoc. prof. music St. Xavier U., 1977—. Presenter in field. Musician: (CD) An Art Song Excursion, 2004, Wind and Song, 2000; arranger (flute, choir, and voices). Recipient various grants, St. Xavier U.; scholar, 2005—06. Achievements include research in application of vocal tract resonance in achieving optimum tone quality in woodwind and brass players. Office Phone: 773-298-3420. Personal E-mail: morris@sxu.edu.

MORRIS, MARY ANN, bookkeeper; b. Great Falls, Mont., Feb. 16, 1946; d. Francis Leonard and Dorothy Irene (Howe) De Lacey; m. Donald Edward Wermuth, June 29, 1968 (div. Jan. 1974); 1 child, Deborah Ann; m. Larry Dallas Morris, Apr. 23, 1977; stepchildren: Serena Jo, Bradley Dwayne, Brian Dale, Bruce Dean. Student, North Idaho Coll., 1985. Sales clk. Dundas Office Supply, Great Falls, 1964-68, Stationer's Office Supply, Tacoma, 1969-70; bookkeeper Miller's Office Supply, Puyallup, Wash., 1971-72, Judge Moving & Storage (Allied), Great Falls, 1973-74; bookkeeper, credit mgr. Meadow Gold Dairy, Great Falls, 1974; pro-rate clk. Builders Transport, Great Falls, 1975-77; bookkeeper C&S Glass, Coeur d'Alene, Idaho, 1978-81, Morris Trucking, Coeur d'Alene, 1977-82, LDM Transport, Hayden Lake, Idaho, 1982—2000, profl. truck driver (class A vehicle), 1988—, sec. and treas., 2000—; operator cons. svc. to small trucking bus. Mem. Women's Retail Credit Mgrs. Assn. Republican. Home and Office: PO Box 2350 Hayden ID 83835-2350

MORRIS, MARY ELIZABETH, pastor; b. Schenectady, N.Y. d. William and Kathryn Dilkes (Wilkins) Simpson; m. David John Stevens, Sept. 10, 1966 (dec. Dec. 1975); children: Jeffrey David, Wendy Elizabeth; m. Gerald Douglas Morris, Apr. 15, 1977; stepchildren: Laura Louise, Douglas Owen. BS with cert. in phys. therapy, Simmons Coll., 1966; MDiv, Boston U. Theology, 1988. Ordained min. 1993. Pvt. phys. therapist Muscular Dystrophy Assn., Dedham, Mass., 1971—93; vicar Holy Trinity Luth. Ch., North Easton, Mass., 1988—89; interim pastoral asst. Zion Luth. Ch., Plymouth, Mass., 1989—91; interim chaplain Symmes Hosp., Arlington, Mass., 1990—91; phys. therapist South Shore Vis. Nurse Assn, Braintree, Mass., 1991—93; pastor Bethany Luth. Ch., Orange, Mass., 1993—98, St. Mark Evangelical Luth. Ch., Woonsocket, RI, 1999—. Dean R.I. Conf. of New Eng. Synod of Evangelical Luth. Ch. in Am., 2002—05; ecumenical rep. R.I. State Coun. Chs., 2001—. Mem. Evangelical Luth. Ch. In Am. Office: St Mark Evangel Luth Ch 871 Harris Ave Woonsocket RI 02895 Office Phone: 401-769-8320.

MORRIS, MAUREEN SAUTER, banker; d. Harold J. and Mary Sauter; m. Jon P. Morris; 1 child, Jeffrey. BEd, U. Miami, 1969; MA, U. W. Fla., 2001. Tchr. Fairfax County Schs., Va., Okaloosa County Schs., Shalimar, Fla.; loan processor Eglin Fed. Credit Union, Ft. Walton Beach, Fla. Bd. dirs. Cmty. Band. Capt. USAF, 1969—74, maj. USAF Res., 1975—82. Mem.: Am. Soc. Mil. Comptrollers, Coun. Exceptional Children, Phi Lambda Theta. Avocations: reading, counted cross stitch, working out, bunko.

MORRIS, NANCY LOIS, elementary school educator; b. Oceanside, N.Y., Jan. 15, 1950; d. Maurice Morris and Sylvia Goodfriend. AAS, Sullivan County C.C., Lock Sheldrake, N.Y., 1970; BS in Elem. Edn., SUNY, Geneseo, 1971; MS in Spl. Edn., Hofstra U., 1975; postgrad., U. Ariz., 1979, Scranton (Pa.) U., 1978, 79, Bowie (Md.) State U., 1983, Nova U., Ft. Lauderdale, Fla., 1987. Lic. in elem. edn., spl. edn., N.Y., Md., D.C., Fla. Tchr. 2d and 3d grades Hempstead (N.Y.) Sch. Dist. 1, 1972-73; tchr., counselor Rhinebeck (N.Y.) Country Sch., 1976-77; tchr. 2d and 4th grades and ESL Bur. Indian Affairs, Phoenix, 1977-79; tchr. emotionally handicapped D.C. Children's Ctr., Laurel, Md., 1979-87, Sch. Bd. of Broward County, Ft. Lauderdale, 1987-88, Sch. Bd. of Palm Beach County, West Palm Beach, Fla., 1988-92; with HRS Divsn. Elder Abuse, Lake Worth, Fla., 1992-93, Am. Cancer Soc., West Palm Beach, 1993-94; substitute tchr. Sch. Bd. Palm Beach County, 1994, tchr. emotionally handicapped, 1994-96; with Ctr. for Info. and Crisis Svcs., Inc., Lantana, Fla., 1997-98; tchr. 6th grade Edison-Russell Sch., Palm Beach Gardens, 1998-2000; investigator The Fla. Dept. of Children and Family, West Palm Beach, Fla., 2001—. Mem. Phi Delta Kappa. Home: 10445 Boynton Place Cir Boynton Beach FL 33437-2627

MORRIS, NAOMI CAROLYN MINNER, clinical pediatrician, medical researcher, educator, health facility administrator; b. Chgo., June 8, 1931; d. Morris George and Carrie Ruth (Auslender) Minner; m. Charles Elliot Morris, June 28, 1951; children: Jonathan Edward, David Carlton. BA magna cum laude, U. Colo., 1952, MD, 1955; MPH magna cum laude, Harvard U., 1959. Diplomate Am. Bd. Preventive Medicine. Rotating intern LA County Gen. Hosp., 1955-56; clin. fellow in pediat. Mass. Gen. Hosp., Boston, 1957; pub. health physician Mass. Dept. Health, Boston, 1957-58; clin. pediatrician Norfolk King's Daus. Hosp., Va., 1959-61; from rsch. assoc. to prof. dept. maternal/child health Sch. Pub. Health, U. NC, Chapel Hill, NC, 1962-70, 71-74, chair dept., 1975-77; prof., dir. cmty. pediat. U. Health Sci., Chgo. Med. Sch., Ill., 1977-80; prof. Sch. Pub. Health, U. Ill., Chgo., 1980—, dir. cmty. health sci. divsn., 1980-95. Advisor to chief pub.health officer, Guam, 1970-71; mem. liaison com. with Lake County Med. Soc. 1978-80; nursing divsn. adv. com. Lake County Health Dept., 1978-98; resource person Ill. 1980 White Ho. Conf. on Children, 1979-80; participant Enrich-A-Life series Chgo. Dept. Health, 1984-85, Ill. Health and Hazardous Substance Registry Pregnancy Outcome Task Force, 1984-86; mem. profl. adv. bd. Beethoven Project Ctr. Child Devel., 1986-96; mem. planning com. for action to reduce infant mortality Chgo. Inst. Medicine, 1986-89; founding mem. Westside Futures Infant Mortality Network, 1986; mem. Ill. vital stats. supplement Ill. Dept. Pub. Health, 1987; investigator and team leader Rev. Mo. Families Maternal and Child Health State Svcs., 1989; mem. children and youth 2000 task force MacArthur Found., 1992—; active Ill. Caucus on Teenage Pregnancies, 1978—, Chgo. Dept. Health Child Health Task Force, 1982-83, HSC Interprofessional Edn. Com., 1983-84, Med. Task Force Project Life, 1988-88, Women's Studies Curriculum Com., 1985-90, Com. Rsch. on Women, 1985-90, Mayor's Adv. Com. on Infant Mortality, 1986-2002, Coun. for Integrated Svc. Sys., 2001-02, Cmty. Access Program, 2002—, Gov. Adv. Coun. on Infant Mortality, 1988-96, Ctr. for Rsch. on Women Fellowship Com., 1993-98; cons. pediat. nursing resources group Ill. Dept. Pub. Health, 1983-84; cons. Cook County Hosp. Study of Preventive Childhood Obesity, 1983-84, Chgo. Dept. Pub. Health Coun. for an Integrated Svc. Sys., 2001-02. founder and dir. MCH training program, 1983-03 Contbr. chapters to books, articles to profl. jours. Mem. Ill. MCH Coalition, 1994—, Voices for Ill. Children, 1993—, Children and Youth 2000, 1992—. Recipient Jonas Salk Lifetime Achievement award, March of Dimes, 2003. Fellow APHA (task force on adolescence maternal and child health sect. 1977-85, sec. 1979-80, cons. manpower project 1982-83, publ. bd. 1985-87, coun. pediat. rsch. to Am. Acad. Pediats. 1985-92, APHA, Martha May Eliot award outstanding contbns. to field of maternal and child health 1999-, Am. Coll. Preventive Medicine, Am. Acad. Pediats. (Ill. chpt. com. on sch. health, 1992-94, and com. adolescent health 1993—); mem. Ambulatory Pediat. Assn., Assn. Tchrs. Maternal and Child Health (exec. com. 1981-87, com. on tng. and continuing edn. needs of MCH/CCS dirs. 1982-83, liaison com. to fed. DCMH office 1983-87, pres. 1983-85), Chgo. Pediat. Soc. (Disting. Svc. award 2002), Phi Beta Kappa, Alpha Omega Alpha, Delta Omega, Sigma Xi. Avocations: photography, swimming, reading, classical music, travel. Office: U Ill Chgo 651 SPHPI M/C 923 1603 W Taylor St Chicago IL 60612-4246

MORRIS, PEGGY ANN, elementary school educator, mathematics educator; m. Dale Wayne Morris, Aug. 20, 1985 (div. Sept. 13, 2001); children: Jennifer Jean Layten, Tasha Ann, Layla Marie. BA in Elem. Edn., Coll. Ozarks, Point Lookout, Mo., 1985; MS in Edn., SW Bapt. U., Bolivar, Mo., 2002. Kindergarten tchr. Laquey Elem. Sch., Mo., 1985—89, parents as tchr., parent educator, 1985—89, elem. libr., 1989—93, fifth grade social studies tchr., 1991—92, title i math tchr., 1993—; h.s. libr. Laquey H.S., Mo., 1992—93. Hyer scholar, 1983—85, Scottish Rite scholar, Masons, 1984, Edn. scholar, First Bapt. Ch., 2001. Mem.: Mo. State Teachers Assn. (assoc.), Alpha Beta Alpha (pres. beta gamma chpt. 1983—84). Democrat. Baptist.

MORRIS, PHYLLIS, legislative staff member; b. Prague, Okla., June 27, 1951; d. Winford J. and Rosalie Magdalen Willoughby; m. Philip Joe Isaacs, June 19, 1976 (div. Oct. 1993); 1 child, Eric Joe; m. Danny Jay Morris, June 14, 1995. Student, S.W. Okla. Coll., 1971. Office mgr. Okla. Health Scis. Ctr., Oklahoma City, 1988-90; legis. asst. Okla. Ho. of Reps., Oklahoma City, 1991—. Fundraiser for numerous politicians Okla. Ho. of Reps., Okla. State Senate, 1991—. Democrat. Roman Catholic. Home: 8311 Blue Jay Rd Norman OK 73026-3762 Office: Okla Ho of Reps 328 State Capitol Oklahoma City OK 73026

MORRIS, RUSTY LEE, architectural consulting firm executive; b. Glenwood Springs, Colo., Nov. 28, 1940; d. Raymond M. and Raylene Pearl Marie (Hendrick) Morris; m. Robert W. Sosa, Nov. 20, 1995; children: Thomas John, Michael Joseph (dec.), Michelle Renee Bentley. Student, York Christian Coll., 1974-75, U. Nebr., 1975-76, Mesa State Coll., 1992-95; BS in Orgnl. Mgmt. summa cum laude, Colo. Christian U., 1996; postgrad., Union Inst., 1996—; MS in Mgmt., Colo. Christian U., Cin., 1997; postgrad. in forensic criminology, Union Inst., Cin. Specialist comm. security Martin-Marietta Corp., Larson AFB, 1962-63; communications security specialist classified def. project Boeing Aerospace Div., Larson AFB, Wash., 1963-64; with F.W. Sickles div. Gen. Instrument Corp., Chicopee, Mass., 1965-68; adminstr. judicial affairs J. Arthur Hickerson, Judge, Springfield, Mass., 1969-71; researcher Mont. United Indian Assn., Helena, 1970-72; adminstrv. asst. Vanderbilt U. Hosp., Nashville, 1980-82; paid bus. supr. Sears Svc. Ctr., Grand Junction, Colo., 1987-89; founder, chief exec. officer Vast Spl. Svcs., Grand Junction, 1988—; courier U.S. Census Bur., Grand Junction, 1990; spl. program coord. Colo. Dept. Parks and Recreation, Ridgway, 1990-91. Acad. athletic program founder, coord. Mesa State Coll., 1992-93, math. and sci. rep., student govt., 1992—, athletic coun., 1993—, student health ctr. com., 1993—, faculty search com., 1993; founder, CEO Rolling Spokes Assn.; world cons. on archtl. contracts for structural and/or outdoor recreational facilities. Author: Abuse of Women with Disabilities, 1996. Vol. Easter Seals Soc., 1964-67, vol. instr. Adult Literacy Program, 1984-87; vol. T.V. host Muscular Dystrophy Assn. Am., 1975-94; bd. dirs. Independent Living Ctr., 1985-87, Handicap Awareness Week, 1989; trails com. Colo. State Parks and Outdoor Recreation, 1988—; condr. seminars Ams. With Disabilites Act, 1989—; cons. Bur. Reclamation, 1988—, Bur. Land Mgmt., 1989—; staff trainer Breckenridge Outdoor Recreation Ctr., 1989-90; emergency svcs. officer Colo. Civil Air Patrol, Thunder Mountain Squadron, 1989—; bd. dirs. Handicap Awareness, 1989; dir. com. Colo. State Trails Commn., 1989-90; mem. Dem. Nat. Com., 1991—; dist. com. Grand Junction Sch. Dist., 1992—; mem. Restore the Com., Avalon, 1993—; bd. dirs., presenter No. Colo. chpt. Colo. Orgn. of Victim Assistance; with victim assistance Mesa County Sheriff's Dept., 1993—. Recipient Hometown Hero award, 1993. Mem. AAUW, Internat. Platform Assn., Handicap Scholarship Assn. (bd. dirs. 1994, award 1993), Nat. Orgn. Victim Assistance (presenter 1988—), Nat. Coun. Alcoholism and Drug Abuse (vol. 1987—), Mother's Against Drunk Driver's (bd. dirs. Mesa County chpt., v.p. 1985—), Concerns of Policy Survivors, Club 20 of Western Colo. (mem. com. status), Great Outdoor Colo., Grand Junction C. of C., Grand Junction Symphony, Mus. Western Colo., Mesa State Coll. Geology Club, Toastmasters (Able Toastmaster, winner speech contests 1985-87). Home and Office: 1617 S Jean St Kennewick WA 99337-4173

MORRIS, SANDRA JOAN, lawyer; b. Chgo., Oct. 13, 1944; d. Bernard and Helene (Davies) Aronson; m. Richard William Morris, May 30, 1965 (div. Jan. 1974); children: Tracy Michelle, Bretton Todd; m. William Mark Bandt, July 12, 1981 (div. Oct. 2004); 1 child, Victoria Elizabeth. BA, U. Ariz., 1965; JD, Calif. Western U., 1969. Bar: Calif. 1970, U.S. Dist. Ct. (so. dist.) Calif. 1970, diplomate: Am. Coll. Family Trial Lawyers. Ptnr. Morris & Morris, APC, San Diego, 1970-74; sole practice San Diego, 1974—. Mem. Adv. Commn. on Family Law, Calif. Senate, 1978—79. Contbr. articles to profl. jours. Pres. San Diego Cmty. Child Abuse Coordinating Coun., 1977; mem. human rsch. rev. bd. Children's Hosp., San Diego, 1977-92. Fellow: Internat. Acad. Matrimonial Lawyers, Am. Acad. Matrimonial Lawyers (chpt. pres. 1987—88, nat. bd. govs. 1987—89, parliamentarian 1989—91, nat. bd. govs. 1993—94, treas. 1994—97, v.p. 1997—2000, 1st v.p. 2000—01, pres. 2002—03); mem.: San Diego Cert. Family Law Specialists (chair 1995—96), State Bar Calif. (cert. family law specialist 1980—), ABA (family law sect. exec. com. marital property 1982—83, 1987—94, faculty mem. Trial Advocacy Inst. 2001—), Lawyers Club San Diego (bd. dirs. 1973). Republican. Jewish. Avocations: art, travel, skiing. Office: 3200 4th Ave Ste 101 San Diego CA 92103-5716 Office Phone: 619-296-6060.

MORRIS, SHARON LOUISE STEWART, emergency medical technician, paramedic; b. Washington, Feb. 9, 1956; d. George Arthur Jr. and Shirley Ann (Dickinson) S. (dec.); m. Brian Stanley Morris, Feb. 9, 1979 (div.); children: Jessica Kristin, Krystle Maria. BS, Atlantic Christian Coll., Wilson, N.C., 1978; student, Wilson County Tech. Coll., 1998; paramedic stud., Nash Community Coll. Cert. tchr. elem. edn. and math., N.C., EMT paramedic, ACLS, Pediatric Advanced Life Support, pediat. edn. prehosp. profls., AHA CPR/BLS instr.; cert. pre-hosp. trauma life support Prehosp. Edn. for Prehosp. Profls.; automatic external defibrilator (AED) instr.; basic trauma life support (BTLS); farm medic. Cashier Safeway Fin., Wilson, 1980-81, Provident Fin., Wilson, 1981-85; mktg. svc. mgr. Beneficial of N.C. Inc., Wilson, 1985-91; ind. carrier Wilson Daily Times, 1991-94; child care provider Crestview Day Sch., Wilson, 1994-95; EMT vol. Elm City, N.C., 1996—; EMT paramedic Wilson County Emergency Med. Svcs., 1998—2004, training office, 2003—04, shift asst. supr., 2004—. Agt. Cen. Nat. Life Ins., Wilson, 1988-91, Olde Republic, 1990; EMT Elm City Emergency Svcs., 1996, attendant, driver Am. Med. Response, 1997; paramedic Sch. Nash Tech. CC, Wayne County EMS, 2006-. Notary pub. State of NC, 1986—2006; bd. dirs. Elm City, 1997, 99; full time paramedic for Johnston Ambulance Svc., 2002-, first responder instr. EMT, 2003; paramedic Wayne County EMS, 2006-. Democrat. Methodist. Avocations: crocheting, cross-stitch, needlepoint, plants, baking. Home: PO Box 9053 Wilson NC 27895 Personal E-mail: emsbabygirl120@peoplepc.com.

MORRIS, SHEILA J., elementary school educator; d. Tommy Jean Hayes and Shirley Jean; m. Gregory Wayne Morris, Dec. 18, 1982; children: Sarah Michelle, Nicholas Warren. AA, Del Mar Jr. Coll., Corpus Christi, Tex., 1981; B in Music Edn., Evangelical U., Springfield, Mo., 1983. Cert. music tchr. Mo., Tex. Music tchr. Brevard Elem., NC, 1991—94; tchr. Carpenter's Kids Presch., Springfield, 1999—2002, kindergarten music tchr., 2001—02; substitute tchr. L-R Upper Elem., Rogersville, Mo., 2002—04, tchr. 3rd grade, 2004—06; music tchr. Logan Rogersville Upper Elem., 2006—. Mem.: Mo. Music Edn. Assn., Nat. Assn. for Music Edn., Am. Choral Dirs. Assn., Mo. State Tchrs. Assn. Avocations: sewing, gardening.

MORRIS, SYLVIA JUNE BURBANK, retired physician; b. Le Roy, Iowa, June 18, 1921; d. Dean Stanley and Myra G. (Douglas) Burbank; m. John Thomas Morris, Jan. 1, 1948 (div.); children: Thomas Dean, Richard Lee, John Douglas. BA in Chemistry, Grinnell Coll., 1942; MD, U. Iowa, 1945; MPH, U. Ala., 1981. Intern Balt. City Hosp., 1945—46; pediat. intern. Johns Hopkins Hosp., 1946—47; pvt. practice Pleasantville, Iowa, 1947—48, Hanceville, Ala., 1949—53; asst. med. dir. Tri-County Health Dept., Decatur, 1972—88, epidemiologist, 1981—88; ret., 1988. Asst. prof. health policy U. Ala. Sch. Pub. Health, Birmingham, 1983—88; mem. children's policy coun. Juvenile Ct., Cullman, Ala., 1994—. Editor: Jerome-Civil War Letters, 1994; author: Doctoring, 1996, Jennifer, 1999, Jennifer Again, 2003, Piggy Flu & Lil' Sam Too: Medical Adventures in Appalacia, 2003, Beth's Song, 2005; editor: Doctoring in Cullman County Before 1900, 1996, Jennifer-A Cat Tale, 2003; contbr. articles to profl. publs. Mem. Cullman County Hist. Soc., Ala. Hist. Assn. Mem.: AMA, Med. Assn. State of Ala. (dist. counselor 1999—), Ala. Writer's Conclave, Ala. Hist. Assn., Cullman County Hist. Soc., Symphony Club. Home: PO Box 305 Cullman AL 35056-0305

MORRIS, TAMMY KAY, bank executive; d. George Allan and Harriet Nadine Zumwalt; m. Vincent Carl Morris, Sept. 14, 1985; children: Vincent Keath, Kerry Lashell. Mortgage banker Wells Fargo Home Mortgage, Show Low, Ariz., 1999—2004; banking ctr. mgr. Bank Am., 2004—. Pres., charter mem. Kiwanis Internat., Show Low, 2005—. Recipient Sales & Svc. Excellence award, Bank Am. Pacific SW Divsn., 2005—. Conservative. Evangelical. Avocation: reading.

MORRIS, TRISHA ANN, librarian; b. Canton, Ohio, Dec. 15, 1941; d. James Warren and Anna Marie (Packa) Lamoreaux; m. Kenneth F. Whitmer, June 5, 1962 (dec. 1971); children: Erica M., Tess A., Clifford K.; m. Nick D. Morris, Oct. 4, 1973; children: Aaron D., Shawn K., Tasha T. BA, Kent State U., 1973, MLS, 1977. Dir. libr. So. Ohio Coll. N.E., Akron, 1985-87; asst. libr. Prestonsburg (Ky.) Community Coll., 1987-90; dir. libr. Pa. State U., Du Bois, 1990-92, Ohio Dominican Coll., Columbus, 1992—. Author: (index) Appalachian Heritage, 1991; contbr. entries Ency. Ky., 1990; columnist Floyd County Times, 1987-90. Mem. ALA, AAUW (editor newsletter 1991), Ohio Libr. Assn., Appalachian Writers Assn., Du Bois Area Librs. (editor union list 1991). Avocations: reading, walking, needlecrafts. Office: Pa State U Du Bois Campus Coll Pl Du Bois PA 15801 also: Spangler Libr Ohio Dominican Coll 1216 Sunbury Rd Columbus OH 43219-2086

MORRIS, VALERIE, news correspondent; b. Phila. BA in journalism, San Jose State U.; M in broadcast journalism, Columbia U. Grad. Sch. Journalism. Morning drive anchor KCBS Radio, LA; anchor KCBS-TV, LA; researcher, gen. assignment reporter, anchor KRON-TV and KGO-TV, San Francisco; gen. assignment reporter, weekend anchor WPIX-TV, NY; with CNN, 1996—. Recipient Three Calif. Emmy awards for breaking news events and special reports, Black Woman Yr. award, Outstanding Contbn. to Broadcasting award, Am. Women in Radio and TV, Award Courage, Nat. Orgn. Women. Mem.: Delta Sigma Theta. Office: One Time Warner Ctr New York NY 10019

MORRIS, VALERIE BONITA, dean; b. Beverly, Mass., May 22, 1947; d. Glen Franklin and Helen (Benjamin) M.; m. Boris Bohun-Chudyniv, Jan. 7, 1975; children: Alexander, Anya. BA, Am. U., 1968, MA, U. Mich., 1972. Promotions dir. McCarter Theatre, Princeton, N.J., 1972-73; assoc. mgr. Jorgensen Auditorium, Storrs, Conn., 1973-74; dir. art mgmt., chair performing arts Am. U., Washington, 1974-98, chair faculty senate, 1989-91; dean Sch. Arts Coll. of Charleston, S.C., 1998—. Exec. editor Jour. Arts Mgmt., Law and Soc., 1982-88, 90—; co-editor: Future of the Arts, 1990, The Arts in an New Millennium, 2003. Bd. dirs. Everyday Theatre, Washington, 1990-93, The Support Ctr., 1980-98, The Theatre Lab, 1994—, Charleston Symphony, 1998—, ABC Project, 1999—, Scaae, 2000-, ICFAD, 2003-05, Charleston Ballet Theatre, 2005—. Named one of Outstanding Women of Am., 1983. Mem. Assn. Arts Adminstrv. Edn. (sec. treas. 1989-91, pres. 1997-98), Am. Coun. for Arts (rsch. adv. coun.), Assn. Performing Arts Presenters, Internat. Coun. Fine Arts Deans, Omicron Delta Kappa. Home: 710 Willow Lake Rd Charleston SC 29412-9164 Office: Coll of Charleston 66 George St Charleston SC 29424-1407 Office Phone: 843-953-8222. Business E-Mail: morrisv@cofc.edu.

MORRIS, VALERIE L., music educator; b. Durham, N.C., May 6, 1965; d. Fred Cotton and Ruth Morris; life ptnr. Carla Gentry. BA in Music, Meth. Coll., Fayetteville, N.C., 1989; BA in Elem. Edn., Meth. Coll., 1989; M.Mus.Edn., Meredith Coll., Raleigh, N.C., 1999. Music tchr. Forest View Elem. Sch., Durham, NC, 1993—2005, kindergarten tchr., 2005—. Interim music dir. Meredith Coll. Girls' Chorus and Chorale, Raleigh, 1995. Mem.: Music Educators Assn. D-Liberal. Methodist. Avocations: music, swimming, computers. Home: 3701 Highgate Dr Apt F Durham NC 27713 Office: Forest View Elementary 3007 Mt Sinai Rd Durham NC 27705 Personal E-mail: musicv@msn.com.

MORRIS, VALERIE LYN, secondary school educator; d. D. E. and Darlene Ann Morris; children: Joshua David, Tamara Taylor. BA, U. Mich., Flint, 1996. Cert. tchr. Mich. Tchr. LakeVille HS, Otisville, Mich., 1998—. Democrat. Lutheran. Avocations: outdoor work, animals, fundraising for kids in need, playing rahjong. Office: Lakeville HS Washburn Rd Otisville MI 48463 Office Phone: 810-591-4022. Personal E-mail: taysmom@alldial.net. E-mail: vmorris@lakevilleschools.com.

MORRIS, VIRGINIA MARY, retired minister; b. Freemont, Mo., Aug. 2, 1920; d. William Homer White and Lizzie B. McBay; m. Charles Morris, 1937; 2 children. H.S., Ellington, Mo., 1935. Pastor Calvary Assembly Ch., Fenton, Mo., 1964—2002. Superior judge Jefferson County, Murphy, Mo. Mem.: Fenton Minstral Alliance (sec. 1980—). Republican. Home: 220 Lee St Fredericktown MO 65045

MORRISEY, MARENA GRANT, art museum administrator; b. Newport News, Va., May 28, 1945; BFA in Interior Design, Va. Commonwealth U., 1967, MA in Art History, 1970. With Orlando (Fla.) Mus. Art, 1970—, exec. dir., 1976—. Former v.p., chmn. mus. svcs. com., mem. ad hoc com. on collections sharing and long range planning com., past chmn. exhbns. and edn. com. Am. Fedn. Arts; former mem. nat. adv. coun. George Washington U. Clearinghouse on Mus. Edn.; former mem. accreditation com. Nat. Found. for Interior Design Edn. Rsch. Former mem. strategic planning adv. coun. Orange County Sch. Dist.; former mem. advt. rev. bd. BBB; former mem. Orlando Pub. Art Adv. Bd., Orlando Leadership Coun., Orlando Hist. Bldg. Commn.; mem. art selection com. Orlando Internat. Airport, former chmn.; former mem. bd. dirs. Sta. WMFE-TV; bd. dirs. New World Sch. of Arts; vol. Sister Cities of Orlando; mem. internat. arts and culture com. Metro Orlando Internat. Affairs Commn.; pub. art review com. Orange County; exec. com. Uptown Dist. Named Orlando's Outstanding Woman of Yr. in Field of Art; recipient Fla. State of Arts award. Mem. Am. Assn. Mus. (former mem. governing bd., accreditation commn., profl. stds. and practices com., internat. coun. of mus.), Assn. Art Mus. Dirs. (comm. and publs. com.), Southeastern Mus. Conf. (past pres.), Fla. Art Mus. Dirs. Assn. (past pres.), Fla. Assn. Mus. (former bd. dirs.), Greater Orlando C. of C. (past mem. steering com. Leadership Orlando), Jr. League Orlando-Winter Park, Rotary Club Orlando (Paul Harris fellow). Office: Orlando Museum of Art 2416 N Mills Ave Orlando FL 32803-1483 Office Phone: 407-896-4231. Business E-Mail: mgmorrisey@omart.org.

MORRISON, AMANDA MARY, music educator; b. Burlington, Vt., Mar. 30, 1971; d. William Steven Cleveland and Marilyn Thompson Dick; m. Christopher Allen Morrison, Dec. 30, 2000; 1 child, Benjamin Christopher. BA, Western Conn. State U., Danbury, 1993; MA, Sacred Heart U., Fairfield, Conn., 2003. Tchr. Broadview and Rogers Park Schs., Danbury, 1993—97, Chalk Hill Sch., Monroe, Conn., 1997—. Mem.: NEA, Am. Choral Dirs. Assn., Conn. Edn. Assn. Roman Catholic. Avocation: cooking. Office: Chalk Hill Sch 375 Fan Hill Rd Monroe CT 06468

MORRISON, AMY MICHELE, secondary school educator; b. Silver Spring, Md., Apr. 24, 1975; d. Arlene Beverly and Elliott Fred Factor (Stepfather). BA in History, Salisbury State U., Md., 1993—97; MEd, Bowie State U., 1999. Tchr. High Point HS, Beltsville, Md., 1998—. Mem.: Prince Georges' County Educators Assn. D-Liberal. Jewish.

MORRISON, ANN HESS, systems administrator; b. Grants Pass, Oreg., Mar. 29, 1944; d. Wilbur Lill and Esther Elaine Groner; m. Robert Thornton Morrison, Apr. 14, 1996; children: David William Hess, William Albert Hess. BSEE, BS in Math., Oreg. State U., 1968; MBA in Info. Tech., Maryville U., St. Louis, 2001. Engr. Lawrence Livermore Lab., Livermore, Calif., 1968-69; owner RBR Scales, Inc., Anaheim, Calif., 1969-84; lead engr. Rockwell Internat., Seal Beach, Calif., 1984-86, '87-88; software engr. GM Hughes, Fullerton, Calif., 1986-87; sr. engr. Logican Eagle Tech., Inc., Eatontown, N.J., 1988-91; owner Holistic Eclectic Software Svc., Orange, Calif., 1991—92; sys. specialist Jacobs-Sverdrup Engring., 1993—2001; owner Homeland Def. 4U Inc., St. Louis, 2002—. Active Calif. Master Chorale, Santa Ana, 1990-92. Mem.: Sigma Beta Delta, Tau Beta Pi, Eta Kappa Nu, Phi Kappa Phi. Presbyn. Avocations: singing, art, gardening. Office: Homeland Def 4U Inc PO Box 581 Chesterfield MO 63006-0581 Office Phone: 314-727-5252. E-mail: ann@homeland-defense4u.com.

MORRISON, BARBARA SHEFFIELD, Japanese translator and interpreter, consultant, educator; b. Morristown, N.J., Dec. 22, 1958; d. Barclay Morrison and Pauline Morison O'Gorman; m. Michael Missiras, Nov. 2, 1991. BA, Wesleyan U., 1980; postgrad., Middlebury Coll., 1983; MA in

Japanese Lit., Columbia U., 1998; PhD in English Lit., U. N.D., 2006. English tchr. Bus. English Ctr., Tokyo, 1980—83; bilingual adminstrv. asst. Chiba Bank, Ltd., NYC, 1985—86; bilingual real estate salesperson Huberth & Peters, Inc., NYC, 1986—88, Joseph Hilton & Assocs., Inc., NYC, 1988—89; bilingual acct. mgr. Sys. Rsch. and Consulting, NYC, 1989—92; owner, operator Redgate, Inc., NYC, 1990—2000, Japan Rsch. and Consulting, Moorhead, Minn., 2000—. Adj. instr. langs. dept. Minn. State U., 1999; instr. English Composition U. N.D., 2001-06; instr. Japanese lang. and culture; lectr. Japanese lang. One woman show, Soho, N.Y., 1992, The Pyramid Gallery, Rochester, N.Y., 1993, Spirit Rm. Gallery, Fargo, N.D., 1999; translator: Coltrane: A Player's Guide to His Harmony, 1994, American House Styles: A Concise Guide, 1997. Mem. Fargo Moorhead Heritage Soc. (sec. 2001-03, v.p., 2003-05), Shingon Vajrayana Sangha (v.p. and sec. 2005-06). Avocation: dog breeding. Home and Office: 702 4th St S Moorhead MN 56560-3403 Business E-Mail: jrconsult6@gmail.com.

MORRISON, GAIL, internist, nephrologist, educator; BA in Biology, Chemistry magna cum laude, Boston U., 1967; MD, U. Pa., 1971. Diplomate Am. Bd. Med. Examiners, Am. Bd. Internal Medicine, Am. Bd. Nephrology. Instr. dept. continuing edn. Boston U., 1966-67; clin. fellow Harvard U., Boston, 1971-72; intern Beth Israel Hosp., Boston, 1971-72; jr. asst. resident Georgetown U. Hosp., Washington, 1972-73; staff physician clin. ctr. NIH, Bethesda, Md., 1973-74, staff assoc. Nat. Heart & Lung Inst., 1973-74; fellow in nephrology renal electrolyte sect. U. Pa. Hosp., Phila., 1974-76, rsch. fellow in nephrology renal electrolyte sect. NIH, 1975-76, asst. prof. medicine, 1982-83; from asst. prof. to assoc. prof. medicine U. Pa. Sch. Medicine, Phila., 1976-94, prof. medicine, 1994—, vice dean edn., 1995—, dir. acad. programs, 1995—; attending Phila. Vets. Adminstrn. Med. Ctr., 1976-77, U. Pa. Health Sys., 1996—. Asst. dir. dialysis unit U. Pa. Hosp., Phila., 1976-77, assoc. dir., 1977-82, dir. renal outpatient prog., 1976-82, dir. outpatient dialysis unit, 1979-84, acting dir. dialysis prog. for inpatient and outpatient dialysis units, 1981-82, dir., 1982-86; acad. coord. dept. medicine U. Pa. Hosp., Phila., 1985-96; assoc. chmn. dept. medicine for student edn. U. Pa. Sch. Medicine, Phila., 1986-96, acting assoc. dean for clin. curriculum, 1991, assoc. dean for clin. curriculum, 1991-95, vice dean for edn., dir. acad. progs., 1995—, mem. numerous acad., search, planning, steering, alumni, budget, nutrition coms., others; cons., advisor in field; presenter, co-dir., tchr., leader workshops, symposiums, confs. Author: (with A. Goroll) Core Medicine Clerkship: A Curriculum Guide, Manual for Curriculum 2000, 1996; editor: (with others) Introduction to Clinical Medicine, 2d rev. edit., 1995, Concepts in Basic Science, 1995, Essentials of Nutrition: A Case-Based Approach, 1995; mem. editorial bd. Am. Jour. Medicine, 1996-99; author papers, reviews, abstracts, chpts. to books; contbr. articles to profl. jours. Recipient Daniel C. Tosteson award for leadership in med. edn., Disting. Aumni Svc. award U. Pa.; grantee Pa. Sch. Nursing, 1989-90, Heinz Endowment Fund, 1990-95, U. Pa. Sch. Medicine, 1993-95, 93-96, 97-98. Fellow ACP, Coll. Physicians of Pa. (mem. sect. on pub. health and preventive medicine 1995—); mem. AAAS, Internat. Soc. Nephrology, Am. Soc. Nephrology, Am. Fedn. for Clin. Rsch., Am. Assn. Med. Colls. Women's Liaison Officer, Pa. Soc. Nephrology (coun. mem. network #24 federally funded end-stage renal disease orgn. 1978-83, mem. facility planning bd. 1979-80, chmn. 1980-82, mem. exec. com. 1980-82, ad-hoc mem. med. review bd. 1980-82, mem. nomination and credential com. 1982-83), Southeastern Nat. Kidney Found. (bd. dirs. 1984-88), Phi Beta Kappa, Sigma Xi, Alpha Omega Alpha. Home: 1040 Stony Ln Gladwyne PA 19035-1136 Fax: 215-573-4289. Office Phone: 215-898-8034. Business E-Mail: morrisog@mailmed.upenn.edu.

MORRISON, JACQUELINE ANN, social worker, psychologist; b. Chattanooga, June 1, 1943; d. Curtis Matthew and Jacqueline Ann (Hurley) Hinsley; m. Randal Charles Morrison, Sept. 16, 1967; 1 child, Laura Jo. BS, Ohio State U., 1965, MSW, 1968, PhD, 1995. Cert. clin. social worker, lic., Ohio; lic. psychologist. Recreation dir., case worker United Meth. Children's Home, Worthington, Ohio, 1968-70; casefinding coord. The Nisonger Ctr./Ohio State, Columbus, 1972-74, social work faculty, 1978-79; project coord. cancer rehab. project Ohio State U. Cancer Ctr., 1974-77; social worker Cen. Ohio Dialysis Ctr., Columbus, 1978; asst. prof. Coll. of Social Work Ohio State U., 1979-81, grad. rsch. assoc., 1987-88; clinician, cons. Netcare, Inc., Columbus, 1986-87; social worker, pvt. practice Cancer and Chronic Illness Counseling, Columbus, 1980—. Adj. faculty Ohio State U., 1976-77, 84-85; cons. Harding Hosp., Columbus, 1994—, psychologist, 1998—; cons. Kids n' Kamp, Columbus, 1988—, Hospice of Columbus, 1983-85, Multiple Sclerosis Arthritis Prog., Columbus, 1982-85, Family Counseling/Crittenden Svcs., Columbus, 1982, Cystic Fibrosis Cen. Ohio, 1983. Author: To Find the Invisible Child; author/editor: Franklin County Community Cancer Resource Guide, 1975; designer/editor: (pamphlet) Make Today Count, 1979; developer breast cancer therapy support group prog., Woman to Woman, 1982-86. Chmn. unit mem. LWV, Columbus, 1972, 73; adv. com. Franklin County Unit Am. Cancer Soc., 1976-84; steering com. Make Today Count (cancer patient group), Columbus, 1977-83, others. Nominated for Jefferson award J.C. Penney, 1982; recipient Outstanding Human Svc. award Ohio State U., 1987. Diplomate Am. Bd. Examiners in Social Work; mem. NASW, Cen. Ohio Psychol. Assn. (membership chairperson), Ohio Psychological Assn., Golden Key. Democrat. Methodist. Avocations: tennis, swimming, cooking, reading, travel, poetry. Home and Office: 1260 Clubview Blvd S Columbus OH 43235-1632

MORRISON, K. JAYDENE, education counseling firm executive; b. Cherokee, Okla., Aug. 22, 1933; d. Jay Frank and Kathryn D. (Johnson) Walker; m. Michael H. Morrison, July 11, 1955 (dec. 1991); children: Jay, Mac. BS, Okla. State U., 1955, MS, 1957; postgrad., U. Colo., 1965, Ctrl. State U., Okla., 1967—70, postgrad., 1984, U. Denver, 1981—82. Lic. coun. Okla., marriage and family therapist, cert. sch. psychologist, counselor. Psychologist Cushing Pub. Schs., Okla., 1955—57, Indpls. Pub. Schs., 1958—59; counselor, tchr. spl. edn. Helena-Goltry Pub. Schs., Okla., 1965—73; psychometrist Okla. State Title III Program, Alva; sch. psychologist Okla. State Dept. Edn., Enid, 1977—85; pres., dir. Ventures in Learning, Inc., Helena, 1984—. Career counselor, Oklahoma City, 1985—86; rural specialist Okla. Conf. Chs. AG LINK, 1986—88; v.p., sec./treas. Okla. Made, Inc., Oklahoma City, 1988—89; sch. psychologist Okla. City Pub. Schs., 1988—93; therapist and pub. sch. liason Chisholm Trail Counseling Svc., 1993—95; coord. Statewide Farm Stress Program, 1994—95; therapist Greenleaf Drug/Alcohol Rehab., 1988—89; sec., treas. Okla. Pure; part-time counselor Clayton Clinic, 1987—89; cons. Okla. Family Inst., 1990—93; with Dept. Edn. Behavior Mgmt. Ctrl. Dist., Hawaii, 1995—. Author: Coping with ADD/ADHD, 1995; co-author: Coping With a Learning Disability, 1992; author: I'm Not Sick, Society Is--A 5 Step Drug-Free Parent/Teacher Guide, 2006. Chmn. Alfalfa County Excise and Equalization Bd., Cherokee, 1979—83; asst. state coord. Okla. Am. Agr. Movement, Oklahoma City, 1982—83; co-chmn. Alfalfa County Dem. Party, Cherokee, 1976—83; sec.-treas. 6th Dist. Okla. Dem. State Exec. Bd., 1983—87; counselor United Meth. Counseling Ctr., 1987—88; mem. Elder Christian Ch. Named Citizen of Yr., Okla. chpt. Nat. Assn. Social Workers, 1988; recipient Tchr. of Yr. award, Helena Masonic Lodge, 1967, Spl. award, Okla. Women for Agr., 1979. Mem.: Okla. Assn. Learning Disabilities, Garfield County Interagy. Task Force, Okla. Sch. Psychologists Assn., Nat. Assn. Sch. Psychologists, Okla. Soc. Advancement Biofeedback, Biofeedback Soc. Am., Chi Omega Alumni, Delta Kappa Gamma. Office: PO Box 917 Nederland CO 80466-0917 Office Phone: 303-258-3976. Business E-Mail: JaydeneMor@aol.com.

MORRISON, KAREN A., music educator; d. Raymond W. and L. Geraldine Watland; m. Patrick L. Morrison, June 4, 1977; children: Rachel D. Ivashchuk, Sara A. BS, ND State U., Fargo, 1979. Cert. tchr. ND. Band tchr. Moorhead Pub. Sch. Dist., Minn., 1979—81; music tchr. West Fargo Pub. Sch. Dist., ND, 1981—. Ch. musician Edgewood United Meth. Ch., Fargo, 2000—; pit orch. dir. West Fargo HS, ND, 1994—. Home: 2026 5th Ave E West Fargo ND 58078 Office: Cheney Middle Sch 825 17th Ave E West Fargo ND 58078 Office Phone: 701-356-2090.

MORRISON, LEE See GLAZER, LEE

MORRISON, LIZ, educational consultant; b. Bradford, Pa., Aug. 1, 1962; d. Don and Shirley Costanzo; m. Rick Morrison, Apr. 9, 1987; 1 child, Carley Holly Lindsey. BS, U. Iowa, 1984; M in Curriculum, Instrnl., U. Mo., 2001. Tchr. Pky. Sch. Dist., Manchester, Mo., 1996—2005, curriculum coord. social studies St. Louis, 2005—. Pres. Mo. Coun. Social Studies, 2004—05. Coord. Kids Voting Pky., St. Louis, 2006. Recipient Tchr. of Yr., Mo. Coun. Social Studies, 1999—2000, Nat. Coun. Social Studies, 2001—02, Christa McAuliff award, 2004—05, award, Save Our History!, 2003—05; grantee Tchg. Am. History, Dept. of Edn., 2005 - 2008. Mem.: Mo. Coun. Social Studies (assoc.; pres. 2003—04). Avocations: travel, reading. Office: Pkwy Sch Dist 12657 Fee Fee Rd Saint Louis MO 63141 Office Phone: 314-415-7032. Business E-Mail: emorrison@pkwy.k12.mo.us.

MORRISON, MARGARET L., artist, educator, consultant; b. Atlanta, Oct. 06; d. Watson Russell Sr and Eva D. Morrison. BS in Edn., U. Ga., Athens, 1970. Cert. tchr., Ga. Supr. KPMG, Atlanta, 1971-97; art tchr. Decatur City Schs., Ga., 1997-99; pvt. instr. in art and edn., 2000—. Pvt. practice cons. interior design, 1998—. Exhbns. include Coastal Ctr. for the Arts, St. Simons Island, Ga., Gallery One, St. Simons Island, Decatur Arts Alliance, Acad. Midi, Paris, The Glynn County Art Assn., Jekyll Island, Ga., L'Orangerie Mus., Paris. Royal patron Hutt River Province, Queensland, Australia, 1995; active High Mus. Art, Atlanta, 1989—; bd. govs. Internat. Biog. Ctr.; adv. bd. Am. Biog. Inst.; mem. consumer panel AC Nielsen. Fellow Acad. Midi (hon.); mem. DAR, NAFE, AAUW, Internat. Platform Assn., Nat. Mus. Women in Arts, Allied Artists of Ga., Pen and Ink, U. Ga. Alumni Soc., AC Nielsen Comsumer Bd. mem., Internat. Biographical Ctr., Bd. of Adv. Office Phone: 404-378-2061.

MORRISON, MARLENA, mathematics educator; b. St. Petersburg, Fla., July 27, 1975; d. J. Ronald and Lynn Moore; m. Chris Morrison, Mar. 1, 2003; 1 child, Christian. BS Math., U. Fla., Gainesville, 1999, MA Edn., 2000. Tchr. Boca Ciega H.S., Gulfport, Fla., 2000—. Mem. New Life Fellowship, St. Petersburg, 2004—06. Office: Boca Ciega High School 924 58th St S Gulfport FL 33707

MORRISON, MARY F., psychiatrist, researcher; d. Herbert and Helen Morrison; m. Michael E. Selzer. BS, Brown U., 1980; MD, Case Western Res. U., 1985; MS in Clin. Epidemiology, U. Pa., ', 2001. Diplomate Am. Bd. Internal Medicine, Am. Bd. Psychiatry and Neurology, added qualifications in geriatric psychiatry Am. Bd. of Psychiatry and Neurology, 1996. Intern U. Pa., Phila, 1985—86, resident in internal medicine, 1985—88, resident in psychiatry, 1990—93, asst. prof. of psychiatry, 1993—2001, cons. in psychiatry and clin. rsch., adj. assoc. prof., 2003—; attending physician in internal medicine Pa. Hosp., Phila., 1988—89, Grad. Hosp., Phila., 1989—90; dir., assoc. dir. clin. neuroscience Merck Rsch. Labs., Blue Bell, Pa., 2001—04; sr. dir., global clin. rsch. Shire Pharm., Wayne, Pa., 2005—06. Editor: Hormones, Gender and the Aging Brain. The Endocrine Basis of Geriatric Psychiatry, 2000. Recipient Career Devel. award, NIMH, 1995—2000; Charles A. Dana fellow in clin. rsch., U. Pa. Sch. Medicine, 1984—85, Laughlin fellow, Am. Coll. Psychiatrists, 1993. Fellow: ACP, Am. Psychiat. Assn. (Disting. Fellow 2003, Burroughs-Wellcome fellow 1991—93); mem.: Am. Assn. Geriatric Psychiatry. Achievements include research in hormones (estrogen and androgens) and mood in aging. Personal E-mail: morrimar@comcast.net.

MORRISON, NANCY JANE, art educator; b. Hannibal, Mo., Oct. 29, 1953; d. Wiley Russell Morrison and Marguerite Grace Taylor; m. Stephen Mark Graboski. BFA, U. Kans., Lawrence, 1976; MFA, Md. Inst. Coll. Art, Balt., 1990. Art instr. Dundalk C.C., Md., 1990—91, Anne Arundel County Continuing Edn., Md., 1991; vis. artist St. Paul Sch. for Girls, Balt., 1991; art instr. Essex C.C., Md., 1991—94, Longview C.C., Lee's Summit, Mo., 1995—, Notre Dame de Sion, Kansas City, Mo., 1995—. Mem. Lee's Summit Arts Coun., 2002, 03; grad. student rep., Gallery Com. Md. Inst. Coll. Art, 1989—90; fine arts chair Student Union Activities Bd., Lawrence, 1974—75; grad. studies asst. to Dir. Mt. Royal Sch. Painting Maryland Inst. Coll. Art, 1989—90. Ltd. edit. book, Sitting In, 1973, exhibitions include Kans. Art Commn., Fox Gallery, MICA, Dundalk Gallery, New Eng. Fine Art Inst., Mulvane Art Mus., Spivia Art Ctr., Nelson-Atkins Mus. Art, Chatauqua Gallery Art, Bauhouse Gallery, Mus. Contemporary Arts, Balt., State of Kansas Collection, Topeka, Md. Fedn. Art. Mem.: Mo. Art Edn. Assn., Nat. Art Edn. Assn., Lee's Summit Garden Club (treas. 2002—04, hospitality chmn. 2006—). Avocations: drawing, painting, gardening, genealogy.

MORRISON, PATRICE BURGERT, lawyer; b. St. Louis, July 8, 1948; d. Frank J. and Loretta (S.) Burgert; m. William Brian Morrison, Aug. 12, 1969; 1 child, W. Brett. AB, U. Miami, 1971, MA, 1972; JD, Am. U., 1975; LLM in Taxation, Georgetown U., 1978. Bar: Fla. 1975, DC 1977, NY 1983. Atty. US Dept. Treas., Washington, 1975-79; atty., ptnr. Nixon Hargrave Devans & Doyle, LLP, Palm Beach County, Fla., 1980-89, Nixon Peabody LLP (formerly Nixon, Hargrave, Devans & Doyle), Rochester, NY, 1989—. Bd. dirs. Rochester Friendly Sr. Svcs., Inc., 1996—. Bd. dirs. Alzheimer's Assn., Rochester, 1990-95, Nat. Women's Hall of Fame, 1990-92; mem. Rochester Women's Network; mem. exec. com. Estate Planning Coun. Rochester, 1992-95; dir. Cloverwood Sr. Living, Inc., 2000—. Mem. Am. Immigration Lawyers Assn. Republican. Office: Nixon Peabody LLP PO Box 31051 Rochester NY 14603-1051

MORRISON, PATRICIA B., information technology executive; BA in Math. & Stats. summa cum laude, Miami Univ., BS in Secondary Edn. Sys. mgmt., IT positions Procter & Gamble; CIO GE Indsl. Sys. Gen. Electric, 1997—2000; CIO Quaker Oats Co., Chgo., 2000—02, Office Depot, Inc., Delray Beach, Fla., 2002—05; sr. v.p., chief info. officer Motorola Inc., 2005—. Bd. dir. Jo-Ann Stores, Inc. Office: Motorola Inc 1303 E Algonquin Rd Schaumburg IL 60196*

MORRISON, PORTIA OWEN, lawyer; b. Charlotte, NC, Apr. 1, 1944; d. Robert Hall Jr. and Josephine Currier (Hutchison) M.; m. Alan Peter Richmond, June 19, 1976; 1 child, Anne Morrison. BA in English, Agnes Scott Coll., 1966; MA, U. Wis., 1967; JD, U. Chgo., 1978. Bar: Ill. 1978. Sr. counsel DLA Piper U.S. LLP, Chgo., 1978—. Lectr. in field. Past pres. Girl Scouts of Chgo. Mem.: ABA, CREW Chgo., Chgo. Fin. Exch., Pension Real Estate Assn., Chgo. Bar Assn. (real property com., subcom. real property fin., alliance for women), Am. Coll. Real Estate Lawyers (past pres. bd. govs., bd. govs.). Office: DLA Piper US LLP 203 N La Salle St Chicago IL 60601-1210 Office Phone: 312-368-4013. Business E-Mail: portia.morrison@dlapiper.com.

MORRISON, SARAH LYDDON, author; b. Rochester, N.Y., May 19, 1939; d. Paul William and Winifred (Cowles) Lyddon. BA, U. Vt., 1961. Sec. asst. Glamour mag., N.Y.C., 1961-63, Vogue mag., N.Y.C., 1963-65; asst. editor Venture mag., N.Y.C., 1966-71; dir. pub. rels. for tourism Commonwealth of P.R., N.Y.C., 1971-75; asst. Am. Legion, Washington, 1988-98; owner Sarah Lyddon Morrison Pub. Rels., Washington, 1999—. Author: The Modern Witch's Spellbook, 1971, Book II, 1983, The Modern Witch's Dream Book, 1985, The Modern Witch's Book of Home Remedies, 1988, The Modern Witch's Book of Symbols, 1997, Modern Witch's Guide to Magic and Spells, 1998 Advisor to nat. security coord. John Kerry Presdl. Campaign, 2003—04. Mem. Women's Nat. Dem. Club, DAR (Emily Nelson chpt.), Colonial Dames XVII Century (refreshment chmn., nat. def. chmn.). Avocations: travel, reading, swimming, rock music, cooking. Office Phone: 202-966-2981. Personal E-mail: sarahlyd@verizon.net.

MORRISON, SHELLEY, actress; b. NYC, Oct. 26, 1936; d. Maurice Nissim and Hortense Mitrani; m. Walter R. Dominguez, Aug. 11, 1973. Student, L.A. City Coll., 1954—56. Presenter Alma awards, 2001—02, Imagan Awards, 2001, Nosotros Golden Eagle awards, 2002. Actress: (films) Interns, 1962, The Greatest Story Ever Told, 1964, Castle of Evil, 1965, Divorce, American Style, 1965, How to Save a Marriage, 1966, Funny Girl, 1967, Three Guns for Texas, 1969, Man and Boy, 1971, Blume in Love, 1972, McKenna's Gold, 1967, Breezy, 1973, People Toys, 1973, Rabbit Test, 1975, Max Dugan Returns, 1982, Troop Beverly Hills, 1988, Fools Rush In, 1996, Shark Tale, 2004, others, (TV movies) The Girl Who Came Giftwrapped, Three's a Crowd, 1969, Once an Eagle, 1974, The Night That Panicked America, 1975, Kids Don't Tell, 1984, Cries From the Heart, 1994, Columbo: It's All In the Game, Lassie: A New Beginning, others, (TV series) Laredo, 1965-67, The Flying Nun, 1966-70, First and Ten, 1987, I'm Home, 1990, The Fanelli Boys, 1990, Love, Lies and Murder, 1990, Playhouse 90, Dr. Kildare, The Fugitive, Gunsmoke, Marcus Welby, General Hospital, and many others, 1960-70, Man of the People, Sisters, 1991, 92, Murder She Wrote, 1992, Johnny Bago, 1993, Columbo, 1993, L.A. Law, 1994, Live Shot, 1995, Courthouse, Home Improvement, 1997, Nothing Sacred, 1997, Prey, 1997, Nearly Yours, 1998; recurring role in Will & Grace, 1998-, series regular 1999-06 (Diversity award 2004, People's Choice award 2005, nominee Golden Globe award 2005, nominee SAG award 2005); TV guest appearances include Prey, Nothing Sacred, L.A. Law, Busting Loose, Marcus Welby, M.D., Occasional Wife, Between the Lines, Home Improvement, Murder, She Wrote, The Bold Ones, Divorce Court, Soap, The Streets of San Francisco, Dr. Kildare, Man of the People, The Partridge Family, My Favorite Martian, The Outer Limits, The Robert Taylor Show, numerous others; (voice over animated cartoon comml.) Handy Manny, 2006 (voice animated cartoon series), (A&E) Letters, 2003, numerous others, (stage prodns.) Pal Joey, 1956, Bus Stop, 1956, Only in America, 1960, Orpheus Descending, 1960, Spring's Awakening, 1962, over 65 other prodns., 1956-1970, also appeared in The Mikado, Pal Joey, Anastasia, Orpheus Descending, A Streetcar Named Desire, Sweet Bird of Youth, The Crucible, Zoo Story, Rashomon, Desk Set, Pygmalian, The Would-Be Gentleman, Comedy of Errors, Tiger at the Gates, The Rose Tattoo, Orpheus Descending, Come Back Little Sheba, The Odd Couple, Only in America, El Camino Real, Hamlet, Country Girl, Romeo and Juliet, Cotton Candy, Point of View, Coney Island of the Mind, Last of the Aztecs, numerous others; prodr., writer, 1975—; prodr. (with husband Walter Dominguez) documentary Mexican culture, 2003. Condr. seminars (with husband Walter Dominquez) about Native Americans to keep traditions and ceremonies flourishing. Honored (with husband Walter Dominguez) for work with homeless City of LA, 1985, for work during LA riots, 1992, Bronx Walk of Fame, 2004, Eternity award Women's Theater Group, 2004; nominated for Alma awards SAG, 2000, 01, 02, 06; recipient Emmy award Best Comedy for Will and Grace, 2000, SAG award for Will and Grace, 2002, Halo award, 2003, People's Choice award for Will and Grace ensemble, 2004, Gladd award for Will and Grace ensemble, 2004, Diversity award for Will and Grace ensemble, 2004. Mem. SAG, AFTRA, Actors Equity Assn. Democrat.

MORRISON, STACEY, information scientist; married; 1 child. BS in Computer Sci. cum laude, Mich. Tech. U.; MS in Computer Sci., U. Houston, 1993. With Mission Ops. Directorate, customer svc. agt.; sys. adminstr. Info. Sys. Directorate; with Office of the CIO Johnson Space Ctr.; deputy chief info. officer NASA Space and Life Sci. Directorate Johnson Space Ctr. Adult choir House of Prayer Luth. Ch., Houston, Sunday sch. tchr. 7th grade; youth group sponsor Celebration Kids; music tchr. Vacation Bible Sch.; coun. mem. House of Prayer Luth. Ch., Houston. Avocations: reading, dance, walking, gardening. Office: NASA Johnson Space Ctr Mailcode JA Houston TX 77058

MORRISON, STACY LYNNE, magazine editor; b. Jenkintown, Pa., Jan. 17, 1969; d. Robert Isaac and Sharon Lee (Wiley) Morrison; m. Christopher Cole Shannon, Oct. 1, 1994. BA, Washington & Lee U., 1990. Editl. asst. Mirabella mag., NYC, 1991-92, asst. editor, 1992-93, assoc. features editor, 1993-95; mng. editor J. Crew Group Inc., NYC, 1995, Time Out New York, NYC, Conde Nast Sports for Women; editor-in-chief Modern Bride, 1998—2000, ONE, 2000—01; exec. editor Marie Claire, NYC, 2001—04; editor-in-chief Redbook, NYC, 2004—. Office: Redbook 224 W 57th St New York NY 10019*

MORRISON, TONI (CHLOE ANTHONY WOFFORD), writer, educator, editor; b. Lorain, Ohio, Feb. 18, 1931; d. George and Ella Ramah (Willis) Wofford; m. Harold Morrison, 1958 (div. 1964); children: Harold Ford, Slade Kevin. BA in English, Howard U., 1953; MA in Am. Lit., Cornell U., 1955; degree (hon.), Harvard U., U. Pa., Sarah Lawrence, Oberlin, Dartmouth, Yale, Georgetown, Columbia U., Brown U., U. Mich., Universite Paris 7-Denis Diderot. Instr. English Tex. So. U., 1955-57, Howard U., 1957-64; assoc. editor Random House, Syracuse, NY, 1965—67, sr. editor NYC, 1967—83; assoc. prof. English SUNY, Purchase, 1971-72, Albert Schweitzer Prof. in the Humanities Albany, NY, 1984-89; Robert F. Goheen Prof. in the Humanities Princeton U., Princeton, NJ, 1989—, dir. Princeton Atelier, 1994—. Vis. lectr. Yale Univ., 1976-77, Bard Coll., 1986-88, Obert C. Tanner Lectr. U. Mich., Ann Arbor, 1988, Jeannette K. Watson Disting. Prof., Syracuse U., 1988; delivered the Clark lectures, Trinity Coll., Cambridge, 1990, Massey Lectures, Harvard U., 1990; Internat. Cordorcet Chair, Ecole Normale Superieure and College de France, 1994. Author: (novels) The Bluest Eye, 1969, Sula, 1973 (National Book Award nomination 1975, Ohioana Book Award 1975), Song of Solomon, 1977 (National Book Critics Circle Award 1977, American Acad. and Inst. of Arts and Letters Award 1977), Tar Baby, 1981, Beloved, 1987 (Pulitzer Prize for fiction 1988, Robert F. Kennedy Meml. Book Award 1988, Melcher Book Award Unitarian Universalist Assn. 1988, National Book Award nomination 1987, National Book Critics Circle Award nomination 1987, Best American Fiction of Past 25 Years, NY Times, 2006), Jazz, 1992, Paradise, 1998, Love, 2003, (children's book) Remember: The Journey to School Integration, 2004 (Coretta Scott King Award ALA, 2005), (play) Dreaming Emmett, 1986, (non-fiction) Playing in the Dark: Whiteness and the Literary Imagination, 1992, (speech) The Dancing Mind, 1996; co-author (with son Slade Kevin) (children's books) The Big Box, 1999, The Book of Mean People, 2002, The Lion or the Mouse?, 2003, The Ant or the Grashopper?, 2003, The Poppy or the Snake?, 2003; editor: The Black Book, 1974, Race-ing Justice, En-Gendering Power: Essays on Anita Hill, Clarence Thomas, and the Construction of Social Reality, 1992, To Die for the People: The Writings of Huey P. Newton, 1995; co-editor Birth of a Nation'Hood: Gaze, Script, Spectacle in the O.J. Simpson Case, 1997; lyricist: Honey and Rue, 1992. Recipient NY State Governor's Art Award, 1986, Elizabeth Cady Stanton Award National Orgn. Women, Nobel Prize in Literature, 1993, Nat. Book Found. Medal for Disting. Contbn. to Am. Letters, 1996, Nat. Humanities Medal, 2000. Mem. Am. Acad. Arts and Letters, Author's Guild (coun.), Nat. Coun. Arts. Achievements include being first African American woman to win the Nobel Prize in Literature.*

MORRISON, WYNONA MARVEL, psychotherapist; BA in Edn., U. Wash., 1969, MSW, 1974. Bd. cert. in clin. social work. Mental health profl. Community Psychiatric Clinic, Seattle, 1974-84; prin. Wynona Morrison, MSW, Edmonds, Wash., 1984—. Mem. NASW, Wash. State Soc. Clin. Social Work (treas. 1987-93), N.W. Alliance Psychoanalytic Study (pres. 1993-95). Office: Wynona Morrison MSW BCD 115 3rd Ave N Edmonds WA 98020-3108

MORRISON-SASSO, PATRICIA BLANCHE, nursing educator and practitioner; b. S.I., N.Y., Aug. 28, 1953; d. Francis X. and Marie (Hayes) Morrison; m. Louis A. Sasso, May 16, 1981; 1 child, Sean. BSN, Hunter Coll., 1975; MA, NYU, 1983; postgrad., Adelphi U., 1994. RN, N.Y., N.J.; cert. adult nurse practitioner, med.-surg. clin. nurse specialist. LPN Midwood Hosp., Bklyn., 1973-75; staff RN med. surg. S.I. Hosp., 1975-76; staff RN med.-surg. ICU, maternal child health N.Y. Infirmary Hosp., 1976-77; nurse II adolescent psychiatry South Beach Psychiat. Ctr., S.I., 1977-78; asst. nurse adminstr. psychiat. med. svcs. South Beach Psychiatric Ctr., S.I., 1978-79, nurse administrator, BCLS/ACLS coord., 1979-81; adminstrv. asst. dir. nursing S.I. Hosp., 1982-84, 85-86, divsn. asst. dir. nursing maternal-child health, 1984-85; assoc. dir. nursing maternal child health/psychiatry Meth. Hosp., Bklyn., 1986-88, nurse facilitator, retention coord., 1987-88; nursing lectr., clin. instr. advanced med.-surg. nursing St. Vincents Med. Ctr. of Richmond, S.I., 1988-90; nurse intake coord. The Richmond Hospice, S.I., 1990-91; adj. nursing instr. med.-surg. nursing Coll. S.I., 1991-92; asst. prof. dept. nursing Kingsborough C.C., Bklyn., 1992—. Mem. adv. bd. S.I. Univ. Hosp. Hospice, 1994—. Sec., exec. bd. Trinity Luth. Sch. PTA, 1988-91, sch. bd. rep., 1991-92; mem. People for Ethical Treatment of Animals, World

Wildlife Fund, Nature Conservancy, Christian Childrens Fund. Mem. ANA, Nat. League for Nursing, N.Y. State Nurses Assn., N.Y. Counties Nurses Assn., N.Y. State Coalition of Nurse Practitioners, Sigma Theta Tau (v.p. 199-93), Choice in Dying, Am. Coll. Nurse Practitioners. Democrat. Home: PO Box 127 Staten Island NY 10305-0127

MORRIS-ROBINSON, DOROTHY KAY, writer; b. Charleston, S.C., Dec. 25, 1935; d. Robert Oliver and Desma Lee (Rudd) M.; m. Andre Maréchal, Aug. 20, 1955 (div. July 1965); children: Désireé Katherine Maréchal, Suzette Maréchal; m. Robert Brig Robinson, Feb. 16, 2006. Pvt. coach competitive horseback riding, 1972-92; credit professional Internat. Credit Unocal Corp., Brea, Calif., 1985—99; ret., 1999. Author: Secret Sins of the Mothers, 1999, Coyotes of Creek Crossing, 2004, The Eighth Evil, 2006; contbr. articles to horsemanship mags. Vol. English tchr., tutor Thai Cmty., L.A., 1986-91; vol. book writing Allexperts.com. Mem.: Nat. Soc. DAR. Libertarian. Office Phone: 661-268-1533. E-mail: dkm122535@sbcglobal.net.

MORRISROE, JULIA MARIE, art gallery director, artist; b. Chgo., Sept. 26, 1961; d. William Rouen and Viola Mae Morrisroe; m. Lance Douglas Warren; children: Katherine, Spencer. BFA, No. Ill. U., 1988; MFA, U. Wash., 1990. Dir. Lill St. Gallery, Chgo., 1991-92; gallery dir. David Adler Cultural Ctr., Livertyville, Ill., 1993-94; instr. Moraine Valley C.C., Palos Park, Ill., 1995-97; dir. Univ. Art Gallery, Ctrl. Mich. U., Mt. Pleasant, 1998—. Adj. faculty W.R. Harper Coll., Palatine, Ill., 1990-98, Ill. State U., Normal. Exhibited works at Appalachian State U., 1999, Saginaw Art Mus., 1999, South Bend Mus. Art, 2001, Pitts. Ctr. Arts, 2001, Acme Art Co., Columbus, 2002, Carnegie Mellon U., 2003, SPACES, Cleve., 2003. Recipient awards for art work; artist grantee City of Chgo., 1994, 95, 96; Faculty Rsch. grantee Ctrl. Mich. U., 1999, 2000. Mem. Coll. Art Assn., Assn. Coll. and Univ. Art Galleries and Mus., Am. Assn. Mus. Office: Ctrl Mich U Art Dept Wi132 Mount Pleasant MI 48859-0001 Fax: 989-774-2278. E-mail: julia.morrisroe@cmich.edu.

MORRISSETTE, DANIELLE, biology educator; b. Joliet, Ill., Nov. 9, 1969; d. James and Kathleen Briscoe; m. Matthew Morrissette, July 22, 1995; 1 child, Emily. BS, U. St. Francis, Joliet, 1991; MS, Govs. State U., 2000. Tchr. Rich South H.S., Richton Park, Ill., 1992—. Home: 119 Julianne Dr Manhattan IL 60442 Office: Rich South High School 5000 Sauk Trail Richton Park IL 60471 Office Phone: 708-679-3161.

MORRISSEY, PATRICIA A., federal agency administrator; AA in Liberal Arts, Hartford CC, 1964; BA in Psychology, Stetson U., 1966; M.Ed. in Spl. Edn., Pa. State U., 1971, PhD in Spl. Edn., 1974. Positions with US Ho. of Reps. Com. on Edn. and Labor, Senate Com. on Health, Edn., Labor, and Pensions; sr. assoc. Booz Allen Hamilton, McLean, Va.; commr. Adminstrn. Devel. Disabilities Adminstrn. Children and Families, HHS, 2001—. Republican. Office: Adminstrn Children and Families Adminstrn Devel Disabilities 370 L'Enfant Promenade SW Washington DC 20447 Office Phone: 202-690-6590. Business E-Mail: pmorrissey@acf.hhs.gov.*

MORRIS-TYNDALL, LUCY, construction executive; married; 2 children. From sec. to cost engr. Swinerton & Walberg, San Francisco, 1977—92, asst. project mgr., 1992—94, with mgmt. and consulting br., 1994—97, v.p., ops. mgr., 1997—99; chief info. officer Swinerton Inc. (formerly Swinerton & Walberg), San Francisco, 1999—. Recipient Julia Morgan award, YWCA of Oakland, 1996, Medal of Excellence, Women at Work, 2002. Mem.: AGC of Calif. (info. tech. task force), Constrn. Info. Execs. Office: Swinerton Inc 260 Townsend St San Francisco CA 94107

MORRIS-WONG, BETH, school librarian, educator; d. Leonard Archie and Sandra Morris; m. Thomas Wong, Jan. 30, 2003. MAT, BS, Fairleigh Dickinson U., Teaneck, NJ, 1994; M in Libr. and Info. Sci., San Jose State U., 1999. Tchr. Edendale Mid. Sch., San Lorenzo, Calif., 1998—2000; libr. media tchr. Hillview Crest Elem. Sch., Hayward, Calif., 2000—. Health and safety instr. ARC, San Francisco, 2005. Mem.: Am. Indian Sci. and Engring. Soc. (life), Girl Scouts USA (life Gold award 1985, Silver award 1984). Office Phone: 510-471-5720. Personal E-mail: skyokwa2000@yahoo.com. E-mail: beth_morris-wong@nhusd.k12.ca.us.

MORROW, ARDYTHE LUXION, adult education educator, researcher; b. Elgin, Ill., Aug. 30, 1955; m. Kenneth R. Haag; children: Winona, Justin, Anna, Emily. PhD, U. Tex., Houston, 1991. Prof. Eastern Va. Med. Sch., Norfolk, 1992—2001; assoc. dir. Ctr. for Pediatric Rsch., Norfolk, 1998—2001; prof. U. Cin. Coll. Medicine, 2001—; dir. Ctr. for Epidemiology and Biostats., Cin. Children's Hosp. Med. Ctr., 2001—. Tech. advisor WHO, 2001—. Co-editor: Protecting Infants through Human Milk: Advancing the Scientific Evidence, 2004; mem. editl. bd.: Jour. Human Lactation, 2004, Jour. of Acad. for Breastfeeding Medicine, 2005—; contbr. articles to profl. jours. Dir. Bang Bao Rsch. Scholarship Program. Recipient Young Investigator award Internat. Soc. for Rsch. in Human Milk and Lactation, 1997, Faculty Rsch. award Eastern Va. Med. Sch., 1999, Human Milk Program Project grant NIH, 2003—; fellow Exec. Leadership in Acad. Medicine program MCP Hahnemann U., 2000-01; Jackie Schnell Meml. scholar Rice U., Brown Coll., 1974. Mem.: Internat. Soc. for Rsch. in Human Milk and Lactation (pres.-elect 2006—, exec. coun.), Milk Club/Pediat. Acad. Soc. (chair 2002—05), Am. Pediat. Soc., Am. Coll. Epidemiology. Bahai Faith. Avocations: travel, music. Office: Ctr Epidemiology and Biostats Cin Children's Hosp 3333 Burnet Ave Cincinnati OH 45229 Home: 4929 Bouton St Cincinnati OH 45208 Office Phone: 513-636-7626. Business E-Mail: ardythe.morrow@cchmc.org.

MORROW, CAROLINE DONOVAN, retired social worker; b. Houston, Tex., Dec. 11, 1937; d. Ira and Verda Ree Donovan; m. Leonard Emery Morrow, June 17, 1967; children: Emery Donovan, April Antionette. BS, Wiley Coll., 1960; MSW, Atlanta U., 1962. LCSW Colo. Counselor Ansel Rd. Golden Age Ctr., Cleve., 1962—67; vol. counselor Rhein Main AFB, Frankfurt, Germany, 1967—69; adminstr. Job Corp. YWCA, Denver, 1970—75; med. social worker Rose Med. Ctr., Denver, 1976—2003, ret., 2003. Cons. in field. Vol. Village East Elem. Sch., Aurora, Colo., 2002—04; vol. presdl. election Dem Com., Denver, 2004; vol. food bank Mt. Gilead Bapt. Ch., Denver, sec., 1999. Recipient Appreciation cert., USAF, 1978, Wall Tolerance, 2004, Recognition cert., NAACP, 2004. Mem.: Order Ea. Star, Alpha Kappa Alpha. Democrat. Avocations: reading, writing, puzzles, collecting recipes, decorating. Home: 1358 So Oswego Ct Aurora CO 80012

MORROW, JENNIFER LEIGH See LEIGH, JENNIFER

MORROW, KATHY ANN, psychologist, social worker; b. Detroit, Aug. 11, 1960; d. Frank Fisher; m. Carl Herman Morrow; children: Kamel Eugene Sherrod-Morrow, Cesalee Olean. BA in Social Work and Psychology, U. Detroit Mercy, 1989; MSW, Wayne State U., Detroit, 1992; PhD in Clin. Psychology, The Union Inst., Cin., Ohio, 2001. LCSW Mich., 1992. Pvt. practice clin. psychologist Reprieve Well-Being Ctr., Inc., Southfield, Mich., 2000—. Clin. psychologist Detroit Pub. Schs., 1992—; adj. prof. Wayne County C.C., Detroit, 2003—. Leader local chpt. Girl Scouts of Am., Southfield, Mich., 1997—2000. Mem.: Detlt Sigma Theta (life). Democrat. Achievements include research in healthy adult adaptation in women who were teen parents; development of relax, reflect, resurrect retreats for women and girls. Avocations: writing, drawing, travel, dance. Home: 20700 Civic Center Dr Ste 170 Southfield MI 48075 Office: Detroit Public Schools/WCCCD 1 West Grand Blvd Detroit MI 48213 Office Phone: 313-886-4306. Home Fax: 248-557-4233. Personal E-mail: drkathymorrow@yahoo.com.

MORROW, SANDRA KAY, librarian; b. Levelland, Tex., Jan. 6, 1944; d. Oran Eiland and Martha Jane Johnson; m. Troy Leon Morrow; children: Paul, Kile. AA, Lubbock Christian U., 1964; BS in Edn., Abilene Christian U., 1966. Cert. libr. sci. U. Tex., 1973. Tchr. Andrews Sch. Dist., Andrews, Tex., 1966—68, New Deal Sch. Dist., New Deal, Tex., 1970—71, Ector County Sch., Odessa, Tex., 1971—72; libr. Austin Sch. Dist., Austin, Tex., 1974—77; tchr. Brentwood Christian Sch., Austin, 1984—. Originator Christian Librarians' Conf., Searcy, Ark., 1996—2003; presenter in field; dir. Yearly Booklist for primary, intermediate and Jr. H.S., 1992—. Creator Children's Crown award, 1992, Lamplighter award, 1996, Children's Crown Gallery award, 2000; ministry leader Westover Hills Ch. of Christ, Austin, 1977—2002, nursery dir., 1975—85. Recipient Disting. Alumni award, Lubbock Christian U., 2002, Abilene Christian U., 2005—. Mem.: Nat. Christian Sch. Assn. (awards dir. 1996—, Christian Educator of Yr. award 2001), Tex. Christian Schools Assn. (Tchr. of Yr. award 2001), Tex. Libr. Assn. Republican. Mem.Church Of Christ. Avocations: reading, gardening, jogging, music. Home: 8308 Grayledge Drive Austin TX 78753 Office: National Christian School Association 11908 North Lamar Boulevard Austin TX 78753 Business E-Mail: smorrow@brentwoodchristian.org.

MORROW, SUSAN BRIND, writer; b. Geneva, N.Y., Apr. 30, 1958; d. David Hutchison and Shirley Jean (Hodgins) Brind; m. Lance Morrow, Oct. 19, 1988. BA, Barnard Coll., 1978; MA, Columbia U., 1983. Fellw Inst. Current World Affairs, Hanover, N.H., 1988-90. Author: The Names of Things: a passage in the Egyptian Desert, 1997, Wolves and Honey: A Hidden History of the Natural World; (play) Mt. Analogue, 2006. Fellow Explorers Club; mem. Soc. Women Geographers, Inst. Human Origins.

MORSE, ANNE BERNADETTE, retired educational consultant; b. Bklyn., May 7, 1925; d. Salvatore and Lucia (Romano) Somma; m. George Morse, Oct. 14, 1951; children: Jonathan, David. BBA in Acctg., CCNY, 1950. Office mgr. Chesterfield Hat Corp., N.Y.C., 1947-54; spl. asst. edn. Office Borough Pres. Queens, N.Y.C., 1975-90; cons. Queensborough C.C. Fund, N.Y.C., 1991-95. Pres. PTA P.S. 188Q, Bayside, NY, 1967-69; founding mem., 1st chair Sch. Dist. 26 Pres. Coun., Queens, 1968-69; v.p. Cmty. Sch. Bd. 26, 1969-75; apptd. mem. N.Y. State Task Force Edn., Albany, 1974-75; founding mem. Alley Pond Environ. Ctr., 1975—; mem. Queens Com. Childrens Svcs., 1976—; bd. dirs. Queens Child Guidance Ctr., 1982—; charter mem. Ams. Italian Heritage, 1982—; adv. bd. Queensborough C.C. Holocaust Rsch. Ctr., 1983—, chair, 1999-2004. Recipient Cert. of Appreciation Girl Scouts Am., 1975, Sonia Strumpf Humanitarian award, 2000. Mem. Coun. Suprs. and Adminstrs. (spl. edn. awards com.). Avocations: travel, opera, reading, walking, theater.

MORSE, GAYLE SKAWENNIO, psychologist, consultant; d. Arthur T. Lamendola and Karonhiosta Thomas; children: Mark T., Catherine Ann, Alexander Granville(dec.). BA, Kennesaw U., Ga., 1992; PhD, SUNY, Albany, 2000. Lic. psychologist N.Y. State Bd. of Edn. Program dir. Crossroads/CDPC/NYS-OMH, Castleton, NY, 2004—; psychologist, cons. mobil team, office of child and family svcs. Capital Dist. Psychiat. Ctr., Albany, NY, 2000—04; asst. prof. The Sage Colls., Albany, NY, 2005—. Cons. N.Y. State Police, Albany, 2000—; adj. faculty SUNY, Albany, 2000—. Contbr. articles to rsch. jours. Mem.: ACA (jour. reviewer Jour. Counseling and Devel. 2003—, interim v.p. Assn. for Multicultural Counseling and Devel., mem. Native Am. concerns com. 1997—98), APA (mem. partnership com. 1999—2002, mem. working group Assn. Grad. Students and Bd. Ednl. Affairs 1999—2002). Achievements include research in Relationships among Culture, Mental Health and Quality of Life. Office Phone: 518-479-3520.

MORSE, JANICE LEA, secondary school educator; BA in Tchg., Sam Houston U., 1971; Masters in Art, U. Houston, Clear Lake, 1999. Cert. secondary bus. and art edn. Art tchr. Houston HS Pasadena Ind. Sch. Dist., 1972-83; art tchr. Pearland (Tex.) Ind. Schs. Dist., 1988—94, Deer Park Ind. Sch. Dist., 1998—2003. Mem. Bay Area Art Educators Assn. (treas. 1991-93, pres. 1993-94). Methodist. Avocations: skiing, fishing, freelance art work. Home: 2214 Erin Glen Ct Deer Park TX 77536-3924

MORSE, JUDITH, music educator, conductor; MusB in Music Performance, Manhattan Sch. Music, 1982; MA in Music Edn., Columbia U., 1983, EdM in Music Edn., 1986. Tchg. asst. to Dr. Samuel Applebaum, 1977—80; music tchr., dir. mid. sch. and HS orchs. Hopewell Valley Regional Schs., Pennington, NJ, 1985—; condr., music dir. Edison (NJ) Symphony Orch., 2000—. Tour condr. Ann Jillian; condr. guitarist Celino Romero, von Trapp Children, Jack Jones, Ft. Worth Symphony Orch., Trenton Sister City Orch.; guest condr. NJ Region Orch., 1996. Recipient Proclamation, NJ State Senate, 1987, Mayor of Edison, 2000, Nat. Gold Orch. award, Boston, 2004, Nat. Music Tchr. award, 2006. Mem.: NJ Music Educators, Music Educators Nat. Conf. Achievements include research in Asian culture and influence on development of arts; relation of study of music and academic progress. Address: 41 Bernard Ave Edison NJ 08837 Office Phone: 732-548-4691. Personal E-mail: jmorse777@hotmail.com.

MORSE, KAREN WILLIAMS, academic administrator; b. Monroe, Mich., May 8, 1940; m. Joseph G. Morse; children: Robert G., Geoffrey E. BS, Denison U., 1962; MS, U. Mich., 1964, PhD, 1967; DSc (hon.), Denison U., 1990. Rsch. chemist Ballistic Rsch. Lab., Aberdeen Proving Ground, Md., 1966-68; lectr. chemistry dept. Utah State U., Logan, 1968-69, from asst. to assoc. prof. chemistry, 1969-83, prof. chemistry dept., 1983-93, dept. head Coll. Sci., 1981-88, dean Coll. Sci., 1988-89, univ. provost, 1989-93; pres. Western Wash. U., Bellingham, 1993—. Mem., chair Grad. Record Exam in chemistry com., Princeton, N.J., 1980-89, Gov.'s Sci. Coun., Salt Lake City, 1986-93, Gov.'s Coun. on Fusion, 1989-91, ACS Com. on Profl. Tng., 1984-92; cons. 1993; nat. ChemLinks adv. com. NSF, 1995; bd. advisor's orgn. com. 2008 summer Olympic Games, Seattle, 1995; faculty Am. Assn. State Colls. and Univs. Pres.'s Acad., 1995, 96; chair Wash. Coun. of Pres., 1995-96; bd. dirs. Whatcom State Bank; NCAA Divsn. II Pres.'s Coun., 1999—, CHEA bd., 2000—; Nat. Rsch. Coun. Chem. Svcs. Roundtable, 1999—. Contbr. articles to profl. jours. Mem. Cache County Sch. Dist. Found., Cache Valley, Logan, 1988-93; swim coach, soccer coach; trustee First United Presbyn. Ch., Logan, 1979-81, 82-85; adv. bd. Sci. Discovery Ctr., Logan, 1993, KCTS-TV, Bellingham, 1996—, Seattle Opera Bd., 1999—; mem. bd. dirs. United Way, Whatcom County, 1993—; exec. com. Bellingham-Whatcom Econ. Devel. Com., 1993—. Recipient Disting. Alumni in Residence award U. Mich., 1989, Francis P. Garvan and John M. Olin medal, 1997. Fellow AAAS; mem. Am. Chem. Soc. (Utah award Salt Lake City and Cen. dists. 1988, Garvan-Olin medal 1997), Am. Assn. State Colls. and Univs. (mem. policy and purposes com. 1995, chair 1996), Bus. and Profl. Women Club (pres. 1984-85), Philanthropic Edn. Orgn., Phi Beta Kappa, Sigma Xi, Phi Beta Kappa Assocs., Phi Kappa Phi, Beta Gamma Sigma. Avocations: skiing, bicycling, photography. Office: Office of the Pres Western Washington U 516 High St Old Main 450 MS 9000 Bellingham WA 98225-5946

MORSE, KERRY W., elementary school educator; b. Danbury, Conn., Aug. 14, 1955; d. John H. and Constance M. Will; m. Bob A. Morse, Apr. 10, 1992; m. Thomas H. Green, Sept. 7, 1985 (div. July 9, 1991); children: Megan A. Green, Amy L. Green. BS, Nichols Coll., Dudley, Mass., 1977. Cert. tchr. Ariz., 1998. Customer svc. Jard Co., Bennington, Vt., 1983—89; exec. asst. ECIII, Yuma, Ariz., 1989—97; contract adminstr. Pyramid Svcs., Yuma, Ariz., 1997—98; tchr. lang. arts Yuma Sch. Dist. 1, Ariz., 1999—. Cheer coach Gila Vista Jr. High, Yuma, Ariz., 2000—. Mem. Strategic Planning Com., Yuma, Ariz., 1992—92; bd. mem. Yuma County Juvenile Probation, Ariz., 2003—06. Recipient 1st Yr. Tchr. of Yr. award, Gila Vista Jr. High, 1999-2000, Tchr. of Yr. award, 2005-2006. Mem.: Nat. Mid. Sch. Assn. (assoc.), Alpha Delta Kappa (assoc.). Office: Gila Vista Jr High 2245 S Arizona Ave Yuma AZ 85364 Office Phone: 928-782-5174. Personal E-mail: kmorse@yumaed.org.

MORSE, KIMBERLY DEANE, artist; b. Fall River, Mass., Mar. 27, 1960; d. Alan Whitney and Elizabeth Mary Morse; 1 child, Alan Fredrick Koechlein. BFA cum laude, Va. Commonwealth Univ., 1978—82, student, 1983. Sub. tchr. Chesterfield County Schs., 1980—83; practicum tchg. Va. Mus. of Fine Arts Richmond City Sch. and Chesterfield County Schs., 1981—82; elem. art tchr. C.E. Curtis Elem., Chesterfield County Schs., 1983—90; art tchr. Dept. Def. Dependent Schs. Elem. and Middle Sch. Tchr., Panama, 1990—95, Woolridge Elem., Chesterfield County Schs., 1995—99; art instr. pvt. practice, Midlothian, Va., 2000—01; pvt. instr. Brandermill Retirement Cmty., 2000—01; art tchr. Mataco Middle Sch., Chesterfield County Schs., 2001—04. Mem. Supt. Comm. Task Force, Chesterfield County Schs., 1988—90; mentor Teachers Need Teachers, Chesterfield County Schs. Contbr. presenter and chairperson in field; one-woman shows include Jewlery Artisan, Vender Shockoe Slip and Cary Town, 1986—90, Jwelery Artisan, Painter and Theatre Prop and Set Designer, Panama, 1990—95, Water Colorist, Outdoor Canvas Painter and Muralist, 1995—2003. Recipient First Place in Panama Art Show for Jewelry, 1990, Nominee Walt Disney Tchr. of The Yr. award, 1994, Nominee, REB award, 1996. Master: The Nat. Art Edn. Assn.; mem.: Brandermill Artist and Writers Assn., Panama Artist and Theater Troupe, Overseas Art Edn. Assn., Parent Tchr. Assn., Va. Art Edn. Assn. Home: 3500 Seven Oaks Rd Midlothian VA 23112-4946

MORSE, TERRI FRASER, mechanical engineer; d. James Howard and Bonnie Lou Fraser; m. Mark Harry Morse, Oct. 19, 1990. BA in Edn./Math. and Music, Ctrl. Wash. U., Ellensburg, 1978. Youth/Christian edn. dir. Kelso (Wash.) Presbyn. Ch., 1978-80; stability and flight controls engr. The Boeing Co., Seattle, 1980-82, avionics computer engr., 1982-85, flight sys. lab. engr. lead, 1985-86, engr. supr., 1986-89, rsch. engring. supr., 1989-90, mech./elec. supr., 1990-95, elec. processes/computing mgr., 1995—. Vol. mission team mem. Africa U., Zimbabwe, 1996; bd. dirs. Multifaith Works, Seattle, 1998—; mem. bishops coun. on children and poverty United Meth. Ch., Seattle, 1998—; loaned exec. Corp. Coun. for the Arts, Seattle, 1993-95, Leadership Tomorrow--Seattle Commerce/United Way, 1997-98. Mem. AIAA (sr.), Soc. Women Engrs. (life; bylaws chair, program chair). Avocations: hiking, camping, skiing, kite-flying, home improvement.

MORSE-MCNEELY, PATRICIA, poet, writer, retired secondary school educator; b. Galveston, Tex., Apr. 2, 1923; d. Bleecker Lansing Sr. and Annie Maud (Pillow) Morse; m. Chalmers Rankin McNeely, Mar. 22, 1949 (div. Aug. 1959); children: David Lansing McNeely, Timothy Ann McNeely Caldwell, Patricia Grace McNeely Dragon, Abigail Rankin McNeely. BS in Edn., U. Tex., 1972; MA in Ednl. Psychology/Spl. Edn., U. Tex. at San Antonio, 1976, MA in Ednl. Psychology/Counseling, 1981. Cert. tchr. Tex., profl. counselor. Sec./adminstrv. sec. various cos., Galveston & Austin, Tex., 1945-49, 60-70; dep. clk. Ct. of Civil Appeals, Galveston, 1947-48; police stenographer Austin Police Dept., 1970-74; history and spl. edn. tchr. N.E. Ind. Sch. Dist., San Antonio, 1974-76; spl. edn. tchr. S.W. Ind. Sch. Dist., San Antonio, 1978-81; vocat. adjustment coord. East Ctrl. Ind. Sch. Dist., San Antonio, 1981-82; counselor, tchr. Stockdale (Tex.) Ind. Sch. Dist., 1982-84; clinic sec. Humana Hosp., Dallas, 1985-87; tchr. history, spl. edn. and lang. arts Dallas Ind. Sch. Dist., 1987-2000; ret., 2000. TSTA/NEA assn. rep. Hill Mid. Sch., Dallas, 1990—91, E.B. Comstock Mid. Sch., Dallas, 1991—2000. Author: (poetry) Texas City, 1947, A Gift of Love, 1978, The Key, 1991, The House Part I, 1995, The Gull's Quill, 2001, 2d edit., 2005, Pat's Portfolio, 2002, The House Parts I and II, 2002, From Mother's Writings, 2005, numerous poems in lit. publs. and anthologies; contbr. articles to newsletters and profl. jours. V.p. zone, corr. sec., libr., various coms. Parents Without Ptnrs., Inc., Austin, 1965—74, 1976—78, chmn. internat. ad hoc com. for writing leadership tng. program, 1968, newsletter editor, 1967—72. Recipient awards for poetry. Mem.: AARP, NEA (life), San Gabriel Writers League, Soc. Children's Book Writers and Illustrators, Nat. Trust for Edn. (trustee), U. Tex. Austin Alumni Assn. (First Bernice Milburn Moore scholarship award 1972), Internat. Libr. Poetry (Hall of Fame 1997), Assn. Am. Poets, Nat. Edn. Assn. (life), Tex. Ret. Tchrs. (life), Tex. State Tchrs. Assn. (life; del. to Tex. State Tchrs. Assn. Conf. 1978—81, 1991—97), Internat. Soc. Poets (life). Episcopalian. Avocations: reading, music, sewing/handcrafts, book collecting. Personal E-mail: pmmcneely@netzero.net.

MORTEN, ANN KEANE, nurse midwife; b. Portland, Oreg. d. Gordon Hunter and Georgia Miller Keane; m. John Adams Bright (div. 1972); children: Amy Elisabeth Bright-Thompson, Kathleen Ann Bright-Freer, Diana Sue Bright-Basye; m. Douglas Lynn Morten, 1981; stepchildren: Lise-Marie, Eric. Student, U. Colo.; BA in Social Scis., Maryhurst U., 1980; ADN, Portland (Oreg.) C.C., 1983; BSN, Oreg. Health Scis. U., 1985, MSN, 1989, cert. nurse midwife, 1991. RN, Wash.; ARNP, Wash., Oreg. Performance musician, 1970-86; counselor Juvenile Dept. Washington County, Hillsboro, Oreg., 1979-80, Boys & Girls Aide Soc., Portland, 1980-83; staff RN labor and delivery Emanuel Hosp., Portland, 1983-91; fullscope cert. nurse midwife Vancouver (Wash.) Clinic, 1991-98; pvt. pratice full scope cert. nurse midwife Portland, 1998—. Active Portland Art Mus., 1980—, Sierra Club and Nat. Pks. Orgn., 1980—, Zero Population, 1980—, Planned Parenthood, 1980—, Nature Conservancy, 1980—, Oreg. Pub. Broadcasting, 1980—. Mem. Am. Coll. Nurse Midwives, Ob-gyn. Jour. Club, Lake Oswego C. of C. Democrat. Episcopalian. Avocations: music (playing guitar and singing), golf, skiing, sailing, tennis. Home: 484 Grey Cliffs Dr Saint Helens OR 97051-1031

MORTENSEN-SAY, MARLYS, retired school system administrator; b. Yankton, S.D., Mar. 11, 1924; d. Melvin A. and Edith L. (Fargo) Mortensen; m. John Theodore Say, June 21, 1951; children: Mary Louise, James Kenneth, John Melvin, Margaret Ann. BA, U. Colo., 1949, MEd, 1953; Adminstrv. Specialist, U. Nebr., 1973. Tchr. Huron (S.D.) Jr. H.S., 1944-48, Lamar (Colo.) Jr. H.S., 1950-52, Norfolk Pub. Sch., 1962-63; sch. supr. Madison County, Madison, Nebr., 1963-79; ret., 1979. Mem. ASCD, NEA (life) AAUW, Am. Assn. Sch. Adminstrs., Dept. Rural Edn., Nebr. Assn. County Supts., N.E. Nebr. County Supts. Assn. Assn. Sch. Bus. Ofcls., Nat. Orgn. Legal Problems in Edn., Nebr. Edn. Assn., Nebr. Sch. Adminstrs. Assn. Republican. Methodist.

MORTENSON, JANICE GAYLE MILLS, business owner, accountant; b. Chgo., Apr. 25, 1949; d. Richard Thomas and Elizabeth Ruth (Sanders) Mills; m. LeRoy A. Mortenson, Apr. 16, 1983 (dec. May 1987); m. James Richard White, Dec. 18, 1993. BA, U. Minn., 1974, BS, 1976; MBA, Seattle U., 1987. CPA Wash. Co-owner Mortenson Co., Kirkland, Wash., 1984—87; contr. NW Composites, Marysville, Wash., 1987—93; owner Postal Boxes Plus, Bothell, Wash., 1993—2001, Woodsilk (JMW Enterprises, Inc.), Seattle, 1993—2001; acct. Cottle & Swanson, CPA, 2002—04; pvt. practice Bothell, 2004—05; with Paul A. Hense, CPA, PC, Grand Rapids, Mich., 2005—. Mem. Wash. State CPA Soc. (bus. and industry com. 1993-94), Mich. Assn. CPA Presbyterian. Office Phone: 616-949-5555. Personal E-mail: janicemortenson@hotmail.com.

MORTENSON, KRISTIN OPPENHEIM, musician; b. San Antonio, Tex., July 14, 1964; d. Russell E. and Martha Kunkel Oppenheim; m. Gary Curtiss Mortenson; children: Leah Marie, Sarah Grace. Attended, U. Tex., 1984; MusB, La. State U., 1987, MusM, 1988. Violinist Austin Symphony Orch., Austin, Tex., 1981—84, Baton Rouge Symphony, Baton Rouge, 1985—89, Wichita Symphony Orch., Wichita, Kans., 1991—93, Des Moines Symphony, Des Moines, 1993—2001; assoc. concertmaster Topeka Symphony Orch., Topeka, 2001—; instr. music Kans. State U., 2004—. Assistant editor The International Trumpet Guild Jour., 2001—, violinist (live performances with) Ray Charles, Dionne Warwick, Bob Hope, Shirley Jones, Marvin Hamlisch, Rich Little. Mem. Lee Sch. Site Coun., Manhattan, Kans., 2000—02; pres. Lee Sch. PTO, Manhattan, Kans., 2000—01, 2005—06, treas., 2004—05. Mem.: Am. String Tchrs. Assn. (state pres. La. 1988—89), Sigma Alpha Iota (life; pres. U. Tex. 1983—84, Coll. Honor award, Sword of Honor 1984). Home: 522 Westview Dr Manhattan KS 66502

MORTHAM, SANDRA BARRINGER, former state official; b. Erie, Pa., Jan. 4, 1951; d. Norman Lyell and Ruth (Harer) Barringer; m. Allen Mortham, Aug. 21, 1950; children: Allen Jr., Jeffrey. AS, St. Petersburg Jr. Coll., 1971; BA, Eckerd Coll. Cons. Capital Formation Counselors, Inc., Bellair Bluffs, Fla., 1972-74; commr. City of Largo, Fla., 1982-86, vice mayor Fla., 1985-86; mem. Fla. Ho. of Reps., 1986-94, Rep. leader pro tempore, 1990-92, Rep. leader, 1992-94; Sec. of State State of Fla., 1995-98; pub. affairs dir., CEO, exec. v.p. Fla. Med. Assn., 1999—. Bd. dirs. Performing Arts Ctr. & Theatre,

Clearwater, Fla.; exec. com. Pinellas County Rep. Com., Rep. Nat. Com. Named Citizen of Yr., 1990; recipient Tax Watch Competitive Govt. award, 1994, Bus. and Profl. Women "Break the Glass Ceiling" award, 1995, Fla. League of Cities Quality Floridian award, 1995, also numerous outstanding legislator awards, achievement among women awards from civic and profl. orgns. Mem. Am. Legis. Exch. Coun., Nat. Rep. Legislators Assn., Largo C. of C. (bd. dirs. 1987—, pres.), Largo Jr. Woman's Club (pres., Woman of Yr. award 1979), Suncoast Community Woman's Club (pres., Outstanding Svc. award 1981, Woman of Yr. award 1986), Suncoast Tiger Bay, Greater Largo Rep., Belleair Rep. Woman's, Clearwater Rep. Woman's, Tallahassee Rep. Woman's Club (pres. 1999-2000), Fla. Fedn. Rep. Women (2d v.p.). Republican. Presbyterian. Home: 6675 Weeping Willow Way Tallahassee FL 32311-8795 Office Phone: 850-224-6496. E-mail: smortham@aol.com.

MORTIMER, ANITA LOUISE, minister; b. Jefferson City, Mo., July 2, 1950; m. Ross Maitland Snell and Viola Alice (Leigh) M.; children: Caleb Ross, Hannah Erin (dec.). BA, Graceland Coll., 1973; JD, Washburn U., 1976; MA in Religion with honors, Park Coll., 1992. Bar: Kans. 1976, U.S. Dist. Ct. Kans. 1976, Mo. 1980, U.S. Dist. Ct. (we. dist.) Mo. 1980, U.S. Ct. Appeals (8th cir.) 1980, U.S. Supreme Ct. 1980; ordained to ministry Cmty. of Christ, 1993. Tng. cons. Orgn. to Counter Sexual Assault, Mo., Iowa, Kans., Ill., 1979-80; asst. dist. atty. Wyandotte County, Kansas City, Kans., 1976-80; asst. U.S. atty. U.S. Dept. Justice, Kansas City, Mo., 1980-97; min. Cmty. of Christ, 1998—. Appointee Organized Crime and Drug Enforcement Task Force, 1988; cons. Govs. Task Force on Rape Prevention, Mo., 1979-80; instr. Nat. Coll. Dist. Attys., 1980, various camps and retreats, family-related topics, various seminars for fed. agts.; bd. dirs. SHARE, Inc. Contbr. articles to profl. jours. Bd. dirs. Met. Orgn. to Counter Sexual Assault, Kansas City, 1976-80, Outreach Internat., 1995-99, Graceland Ctr. for Profl. Devel., 1994—; apptd. to Presdl. Com. on Status of Women, 1979-80; trustee Independence (Mo.) Regional Health Ctr., 1990-94; mem. Ctr. Stake Strategic Planning Commn. RLDS, 1989-90; apptd. chair World Ch. Task Force on Singles' Ministry RLDS, 1990—; chair del. caucus RLDS World Conf., 1992, 94, 96, 98, 00; trustee Graceland Coll., 1994-2000, chair, 1998-2000; mem. Friends of the Zoo. Named to Honorable Order of Ky. Cols., Gov., 1980. Mem. ABA, Mo. Bar Assn., Assn. Women Lawyers, Kansas City Met. Bar Assn.; Alumni Assn. Graceland Coll. (bd. dirs. 1987, pres. 1988), John Whitmer Hist. Soc. Clubs: MOCSA (Kansas City), Friends of Art. Office: Peace and Justice Ministries Community of Christ 1001 W Walnut Independence MO 64050 Home: 3044 NE 60th Ave Portland OR 97213 Business E-Mail: amortimer@cofchrist.org.

MORTIMER, ANN O., executive secretary; b. Mt. Kisco, NY, Oct. 15, 1943; d. Owen A and Agnes (Brennan) O'Hare; m. Donald A. Mortimer, June 17, 1967. Degree in secretarial sci., Berkeley Sch.Westchester, White Plains, N.Y., 1962. Exec. sec. to CEO Gen. Foods Corp., White Plains, NY, 1967—81; adminstrv. asst. to CEO Avco Corp., Greenwich, Conn., 1981—86; exec. asst. to chmn./CEO Reader's Digest Assn., Inc., Pleasantville, NY, 1986—97; asst. to chmn./CEO IBM Corp., Armonk, NY, 1997—2002; adminstrv. asst. to David Rockefeller, N.Y.C., 2003—. Vice-chair Leonard Park Com., Mt. Kisco, NY, 1987—97. Mem.: Seraphic Soc. (pres. 1992—94). Office: 30 Rockefeller Pl Rm 5600 New York NY 10112

MORTON, LINDA JUNE, academic administrator; b. Nashville, Jan. 21, 1943; d. William Taylor Morton and Ruby Grayson (Maiden name-Page) Morton. BA, George Peabody Coll., 1964, MS, 1976; PhD, Vanderbilt U., 1981. Cert. ednl. adminstr. Tenn., 1981, tchr. English 7-12 Tenn., 1964, tchr. music K-12 Tenn., 1964, career ladder III tchr. Tenn., 1985. Tchr. high sch. English, music Metro Nashville Pub. Schs., 1964—67, tchr. mid. sch. tchr. music, 1967—89, asst. prin., 1989—2000. Chair, McGavock cluster prins. Metro Nashville Pub. Schools, 1990—91, spl. edn. prins. adv. com. mem., 1992—94; chair curriculum com. 10 yr. sacs evaluation McGavock H.S., 1992—92. Wrote and compiled (7th grade music curriculum outline) 7th Grade Music Curriculum Outline. Dir. Jr. Dept. Woman's Club Nashville, 1972—74; vice-moderator, bd. trustees Memphis Theol. Sem., 1998—2003; mem. bd. dirs. Kidney Found. Mid. Tenn., 1981—83. Mem.: Fla. Oceanographic Soc., Aerospace Edn., Internat. Soc. Music Edn., U. Club Nashville, Woman's Club Nashville (life), Phi Delta Kappa, Alpha Delta Kappa. Avocations: photography, swimming, travel, music, scuba diving. Home: 6740 Currywood Dr Nashville TN 37205 Office Phone: 772-225-1599. Personal E-mail: laquarius@aol.com.

MORTON, MARILYN MILLER, retired genealogy educator, researcher, retired history professor, travel company executive; b. Water Valley, Miss, Dec. 2, 1929; d. Julius Brunner and Irma Faye (Magee) Miller; m. Perry Wilkes Morton Jr., July 2, 1958; children: Dent Miller Morton, Nancy Marilyn Morton Driggers, E. Perian Morton Dyar. BA in English, Miss. U. for Women, 1952; MS in History, Miss. State U., 1955. Cert. secondary tchr. Tchr. English, speech and history Starkville (Miss.) H.S., 1952-58; part-time instr. Miss. State U., 1953-55; spl. collection staff Samford U. Libr., Birmingham, Ala., 1984-92; lectr. genealogy and history, instr. Inst. Genealogy & Hist. Rsch., Samford U., Birmingham, 1985-93, assoc. dir., 1985-88, exec. dir., 1988-93; founding dir. SU Brit. and Irish Inst. Genealogy & Hist. Rsch. Samford U., Birmingham, 1986-93; owner, dir. Marilyn Miller Morton Brit-Ire-U.S. Genealogy, Birmingham, 1994—95, British Virgin Islands, 1994—95. Instr. genealogy classes Samford U. Metro Coll., 1986-94; former lectr. nat. conf. Fedn. of Geneal. Soc. Contbr. articles to profl. jours. Miss. state pres. Future Homemakers Am., 1947-48; active Birmingham chpt. Salvation Army Aux., 1982-87. Named to Miss. U. for Women Hall of Fame, 1952. Fellow Irish Geneal. Rsch. Soc. London; mem. Nat. Geneal. Soc. (mem. nat. program com. 1988-92, lectr. nat. meetings), Antiquarian Soc. Birmingham (sec., 2d v.p. 1982-84), DAR (regent Cheaha chpt. 1977-78), Daus. Am. Colonists (regent Edward Waters chpt. 1978-79), Nat. League of Am. Penwomen, Phi Kappa Phi (charter mem. Samford U. chpt. 1972). Avocations: reading, research, travel, bridge, chess. Home: PO Box 660562 Birmingham AL 35266-0562

MORTON, PATSY LOU, social worker; b. Columbia, Mo., Sept. 15, 1951; d. Delbert Alan and Patsy J. (Johnson) M.; 1 child, Mike A. Morton BSW, U. Mo., 1977; MSW, Washington U., 1979. Lic. clin. social worker. Recreation therapist St. Louis State Hosp., 1978-79; case mgr. Belleville (Ill.) Mental Health, 1979; social worker/dir. of social svc. St. Francis Hosp., Litchfield, Ill., 1979-81; social worker, supr. day treatment Macoupin County Mental Health, Carlinville, Ill., 1981-83; social worker II Dept. of Children and Family Svcs., Springfield, Ill., 1984-91; sch. social worker Southeastern Spl. Edn. Coop., St. Marie, Ill., 1991-92, West Ctrl. Ill. Spl. Edn. Coop., Macomb, Ill., 1992—; social work cons. McDonough Dist. Hosp., Macomb, Ill., 1996—2002, Carthage (Ill.) Meml. Hosp., 1999—2000. Field internship instr, sch. social worker U. Ill., 1996—97, St. Ambrose U., 2002—03; adv. bd. School Social Work Jour., 2003—. Advisor Explorer Post, St. Louis State Hosp., 1978—79; coord. Fulton County Next Steps Team, 1995—97; host family Youth for Understanding, 1995—98; mem. Cuba Ch. of Nazarene, 2000—, Sunday sch. tchr. pre-teens, 2001—02, primary class, 2003—, bd. dir., 2004—, sec. ch. bd., 2005—. Recipient Social Worker of Yr., Ill. Assn. Sch. Social Workers, 2005. Mem.: Ill. Assn. Sch. Social Worker (com. mem. 1991—92, conf. com. 1994—97, regional rep. 1994—98, sec. 1998—99, webmaster 1999—2001, pres.-elect 2001—02, pres. 2002—03, past pres. 2003—04, bd. manual revisions 2004—05, regional rep. 2004—, conf. chair 2005—), Phi Delta Kappa (membership com. 1994—95). Avocations: cross stitch, computers, reading, rubber stamping, scrapbooks. Home: 401 North llinois St Apt 206 Lewistown IL 61542 Office: WCISEC 130 S Lafayette St Macomb IL 61455-2230 Personal E-mail: plmorton@sbcglobal.net.

MORTON, SAMANTHA, actress; b. Nottingham, Eng., May 13, 1977; d. Peter and Pamela; 1 child, Esme. Actor: (TV miniseries) Band of Gold, 1995, The History of Tom Jones, a Foundling, 1997; (TV series) Soldier Soldier, 1991, Max and Ruby, 2002; (TV films) The Token King, 1993, Emma, 1996, Jane Eyre, 1997; (films) The Future Lasts a Long Time, 1996, Under the Skin, 1997, This is the Sea, 1998, Sweet and Lowdown, 1999 (Acad. award nomination for best supporting actress, 2000), Jesus' Son, 1999, The Last Yellow, 1999, Eden, 2001, Morvern Callar, 2002, Minority Report, 2002, In America, 2002 (Acad. award nomination for best actress, 2004), Code 46, 2003, The Libertine, 2004, River Queen, 2005, Lassie, 2005. Mailing: c/o Creative Artists Agy 9830 Wilshire Blvd Beverly Hills CA 90212*

MORTON, SANDRA JORGENSEN, retired school librarian; b. Balt., Apr. 23, 1947; d. Woodrow Wilson and Evelyn Waters Jorgensen; m. William Alexander, JR Morton, Feb. 12, 1972; children: Cassandra Lee Butt, W. Alexander, III(dec.), Ian Andrew. BS, Madison Coll., 1965—69; MS, Towson U., 1987—92. Libr. Balt. County Pub. Schs., Balt., Md., 1993—94; asst. dir. libraries/mid. sch. libr. Friends Sch. of Balt., 1994—2006. Sec./mem. Roland Pk. Libr. Friends Group, Balt., 1993—98; presenter in field. Reviewer (critical rev.) Tech. Connection, Libr. Talk, Book Rev., Libr. Media Connection. Mem./pres. Episcopal Social Ministries, Balt., 1976—81; pres. Mt. Wash. Clin. Practice, Balt., 1980—. Mem.: ALA, Assoc. Supervision and Curriculum Devel., Md. Ednl. Media Orgn., Internat. Assn. Sch. Librs., Religious Soc. of Friends, Nat. Trust Hist. Preservation, People for Ethical Treatment of Animals, Humane Soc. U.S. Avocations: reading, dogs, knitting, music, opera. Home: 101 Longwood Rd Baltimore MD 21210-2119 Office: Friends Sch of Balt 5114 N Charles St Baltimore MD 21210 Office Phone: 410-649-3244. Business E-Mail: smorton@mail.friendsbalt.org.

MORTON-YOUNG, TOMMIE, psychology professor, writer; b. Nashville; BA cum laude, Tenn. State U., 1951; MA, Peabody Vanderbilt U., 1955; PhD, Duke U., 1977; postgrad., U. Okla., 1967, U. Nebr., 1968. Coord. Young Adult Program Lucy Thurman br. YWCA, 1951-52; instr. edn. Tenn. State U., Nashville, 1956-59; instr. coord. media program Prairie View Coll. (Tex.), 1959-61; asst. prof. edn., assoc. prof. English, dir. IMC Ctr. U. Ark., Pine Bluff, 1965-69; asst. prof. English and edn., dir. learning lab N.C. Central U., Durham, 1969-74; prof., dir./chairperson libr. /dir. Afro-Am. Family Project, prof. philosophy sociol. found. N.C. Agrl. and Tech. State U., Greensboro, 1975—92; adj. prof. langs., lit. and philosophy, dir. schs. history project Tenn. State U., Nashville, 1994—. Dir. workshops, grants; pres., dir. Ednl. Cons. Svcs.; owner Historic Black Nashville Tours. Author: Afro-Am. Genealogy Sourcebook, 1987, Oral Histories of Former All-Black Public Schs., 1991, After School Program for At-Risk Youth and Their Families, 1997, Sable Scenes, 1996, Genealogist's Guide to Discovering Your African Ancestors, 1997, A Sister Speaks, 1998, Nashville, Tennessee, 2000, Fabulous You: Women Celebrating the Fabulous Self, 2005; contbr. poem to Poetry: American Heritage; contbr. rsch. papers, articles to profl. jours. Nat. chmn. Com. to Re-Elect the Pres.; past sec. Fedn. Colored Women's Clubs; bd. dirs. Southwestern div. ARC, Nashville area, 1994-, dir. Volun-Teens; chairperson schs. div. Durham County Unit Am. Cancer Soc.; past mem. adv. bd., bd. dirs. YMCA, Atlanta; chair Guilford County Commn. on Needs of Children; bd. advisors NIH, N.C. Coun. of the Arts; mem. Guilford County Involvement Coun.; chmn. N.C. adv. com. U.S. Civil Rights Com.; mem. exec. planning com. Greensboro; hon. staff mem. 54th Legis. Dist., Nashville, 1996; pres. Davidson County Dem. Women, 2003-04; rep. dist. I exec. com. Davidson County Dem. Party; chair resolutions com. Nat. Fedn. Dem. Women. Recipient awards ARC, 1968, 73, NAACP, 1973, HEW, 1978, U.S. Commn. on Civil Rights, 1982, cert. of Accomplishement Contributing to Youth Devel. Bus. and Profl. Women, 2000, Extraordinary Cmty. Svc. award Tenn. Coun. Women, 2005, Athena Internat. award CABLE, 2006, Civil Rights Leadership award Tenn. Dem. Party, 2006, others; named Disting. Alumni Tenn. State U., 1994, Peabody Colls. Gift to the World. Mem. AAUW (honor award 1983, pres. Greensboro br., chairperson internat. rels. com.), ALA (divsn. coll. and rsch. librs., past chair), NAACP (life, 1st v.p. Durham br., exec. bd. Greensboro br. dir. parent edn./child advocacy program, chair exec. com. Nashville, Woman of Yr. 1992, Dedicated Svc. to Civil Rights, 2005, President's award Nashville br. 2006), NEA, LWV (bd. dirs. Nashville), Assn. Childhood Ednl. Internat., Comperative and Internat. Edn. Assn., Archives Assoc., Internat. Platform Assn., Nat. Hist. Soc., Greenboro Jr. League (community adv. bd. 1991—), African Am. Gen. Soc. Tenn. (founder 1994), Zeta Phi Beta (chairperson polit. action com. eastern region, nat. grammateus, Polit. and Civic Svc. award 1974, Outstanding Social-Polit. Svc. award 1982, Woman of Yr. 1977), Comm. on Status of Women (Woman of Achievement 1991), Phi Kappa Phi (Disting. Alumni award Tenn. State U. 1994, Disting. Alumni NAFEO award, 1995, Carl Rowan-Oprah Winfrey lectr. Tenn. State U., 1995, Excellence in Journlism award SPJ, 1995, Tenn. Outstanding Achievement award, 1997), 100 Black Women, Steering Com., Tenn. Trust for Historic Preservation, 1999 (named Woman of Distinction Top Ladies, 2001, named Peabody/Vanderbilt Jnin Great, 2005, nominee Athena award 2005). Achievements include being the first African American to graduate from Peabody College (Vanderbilt University) 2006; having a community Service award named in her honor by Vanderbilt University, 2006. Home: PO Box 281613 Nashville TN 37228-8506

MORVANT, BARBARA L., nursing administrator; Exec. dir. La. State Bd. Nursing, Metairie. Recipient R. Louise McManus award, Nat. Coun. State Bds. Nursing, 2005. Office: La State Bd Of Nursing 5207 Essen Ln Ste 6 Baton Rouge LA 70809-3565 Office Phone: 504-838-5332. Office Fax: 504-838-5433. E-mail: norvant@lsbn.state.la.us.

MOSBACHER, GEORGETTE PAULSIN, cosmetics executive; b. Hammond, Ind., Jan. 16, 1947; d. George Michael and Dorothy (Bell) Paulsin; m. Robert Mosbacher Sr., Mar. 1, 1985. BS, Ind. U., 1969; DFA (hon.), Internat. Fine Arts Coll., 1990; DBA (hon.), Bryant U., 1992. V.p. lic. Faberge, Inc.; CEO La Prairie, Inc., NYC, 1987—95; pres., CEO Borghese, NYC; chair, CEO Georgette Mosbacher Enterprises. Author: Feminine Force, It Takes Money Honey. Bd. dirs. Houston Gran Opera Exec. Com., Am. Hosp. in Paris, Ind. U. Found., Statute of Liberty/Ellis Island Commn., Am. Art Alliance, M.D. Anderson Hosp., United Negro Coll. Fund, Child Help U.S.A., Hudson River Park Trust; mem. adv. bd. Ctr. Strategic Internat. Studies; presdl. appointment Advocate Com. for Trade and Internat. Negotiations; Republican Nat. Committeewomen, State NY. Mem. Women's Econ. Alliance. Avocations: scuba diving, sailing. Office: Borghese 10 E 34th St New York NY 10016*

MOSBY GNADER, NORA JANE, music educator; b. El Paso, Tex., June 9, 1970; d. Knox Wesley and Bettie Mae Mosby. BS, U. Tex., Tyler, 1995, MA, 1997; MEd, No. Ariz. U., Flagstaff, 2005. Chair dept. fine arts Higley H.S., Gilbert, Ariz., 2000—05; band dir. Florence Unified Sch. Dist., Ariz., 2005—. Recipient Reacher of Month, Higley Unified Sch. Dist., 2005. Mem.: Ariz. Music Educator's Assn., Soc. for Ethnomusicology, Internat. Clarinet Assn., Ariz. Band and Orch. Dirs. Assn., Phi Kappa Phi. Home: 2110 E Spruce Dr Chandler AZ 85249 Office: Florence Unified Sch Dist 250 S Main St Florence AZ 85232 Office Phone: 520-866-3500. Home Fax: 480-664-3071. Personal E-mail: muzik77@cox.net.

MOSCATT, ANGELINE ALICE, librarian; b. Bklyn., Nov. 9, 1926; d. Joseph and Giovanna (Napoli) M. BA, Hunter Coll.; M.L.S., Pratt Inst. Cert. librarian, N.Y. Librarian N.Y. Pub. Library, N.Y.C., 1957—. Vice pres., mem. exec. bd. N.Y. Pub. Library Guild, Local 1930, AFSCME, N.Y.C., 1968—. Mem. ALA, N.Y. Library Assn., Women's Nat. Book Assn., U.S. Bd. Books for Young People Democrat. Roman Catholic. Avocations: travel; opera. Home: 290 9th Ave # 6 New York NY 10001-5704 Office: Donnell Library Ctr Central Childrens Room 20 W 53rd St New York NY 10019-6185

MOSCRIPT, BARBARA ANN, science educator; b. Chanute, Kans. d. Kenneth and Ann Stilwell; m. James Tracy Moscript, Aug. 10, 1968; children: Stacy Caliguiro, Sarah. AA, Pratt Jr. Coll., Kans., 1966; BA, Emporia State U., Kans., 1968; MA, Wichita State U., Kans., 1985. Tchr. 5th grade United Sch. Dist. 470, Arkansas City, Kans., 1969—2004, tchr. 6th grade sci., 2004—. Cons. aerospace edn. Civil Air Patrol, Kans., 1980—, Kans. Commn. Aerospace Edn., 1992—. Mem. disaster team, head vols. ARC, Arkansas City, 1996—2002. Mem.: NEA, Nat. Sci. Tchrs. Assn. Home: 27165 43d Rd Arkansas City KS 67005

MOSELEY, CAROL JUNE, security supervisor, small business owner; b. Portland, Oreg., Apr. 20, 1952; d. David Palmore Moseley and Patricia Ann (Goar) Craig. AS in Criminal Justice, Portland C.C., 1985; degree in psychology, Portland State U., 1985-88. Cert. in pvt. security Oreg. Bd. on Pub. Safety Stds. and Tng. Security supr. Burns Internat. Security Svcs., Portland, 1991—; owner Tomorrows Star Natural Health. Cons. on security Bethlehem Ch., Lake Oswego, 1993-94, Tech. Design and Constrn., Portland, 1996. Vol. case asst. Clackamas (Oreg.) Parole & Probation, 1984, State of Oreg. Parole & Probation, Portland, 1985-88; lifeguard, swim instr. City of Portland Pks. and Recreation, 1990-95; chief of peace officers Bethlehem Ch.-Coffeehouse, Lake Oswego, Oreg., 1992; deaconess Bethlehem Ch., Lake Oswego, 1990-94; supporter Right to Life, Portland, 1994—; 1st lt. CAP Aux., USAF, 1986-88. Named Outstanding Security Officer, Portland Trailblazers NBA, 1988. Mem. Internat. Platform Assn., Internat. Soc. of Poets (disting. mem., life mem.), Ofcl. Centennial Olympic Games Club, Elks (ladies aux.), Fraternal Order of Eagles (patron, ladies aux.). Avocations: swimming, crocheting, painting, beachcombing.

MOSELEY, CHRIS ROSSER, marketing executive; b. Balt., Apr. 13, 1950; d. Thomas Earl and Fern Elaine (Coleman) Rosser; m. Thomas Kenneth Moseley. BA with honors, The Coll. of Wooster, 1972. Asst. dir. advt. and promotion Sta. WBAL-TV, Balt., 1972-74; dir. pub. rels. Mintz & Hoke Advt. Inc., Hartford, Conn., 1974-75; promotion mgr. Sta. WFSB-TV, Hartford, 1975-77; audience promotion mgr. Sta. WTVJ-TV, Miami, Fla., 1977-78; pres. CMA Mktg. Cons., Hyde Park, NY, 1979-82; promotion mgr. Ind. Network News-Sta. WPIX-TV, N.Y.C., 1982-84; sr. v.p., mgmt. supr. Christopher Thomas Muller Jordan Weiss, N.Y.C., 1984-89, Earle Palmer Brown/N.Y., N.Y.C., 1989-90; sr. v.p. advt., promotion Discovery Networks, U.S., Bethesda, Md., 1990-99; exec. v.p. mktg. ABC, Inc., N.Y.C., 1999—2000; exec, v.p., chief mktg. officer Hallmark Channel, Studio City, Calif., 2000—. Bd. dirs. Promax/BDA, Cable Positive, WICT, CTAM. Recipient Best Bus.-to-Bus. award Art Direction mag., 1984, achievement award in media rels. and edn. Nat. Resources Coun. Am., 1991, Best Editorial Excellence award Mag. Age, 1992, Best Overall Mktg. Campaign award MIP/MIPCOM, 1994, 1st Place Print award: Media Promotion, London Internat. Advt. awards, 1993, Gold award Broadcast Designers, 1993, Mktg. 100 award Ad Age, 1995, Cable Marketer of Yr. award Ad Age, 1995. Mem.: Advt. Women N.Y., Nat. Cable TV Assn. (conv. com. 1995, 1996, named one of Multichannel News' Wonderwomen of Yr. 2002, Vanguard award 1996), Cable and Telecom. Assn. Mktg. (chair Mark award 1995, bd. dir. 1996, co-chair 1997, bd. dir. 1997). Avocations: horticulture, travel. Home: 5224 Los Encantos Way Los Angeles CA 90027 Office: Hallmark Channel 12700 Ventura Blvd Ste 100 Studio City CA 91604-6201 Office Phone: 818-755-2587. E-mail: chrismoseley@hallmarkchannel.com.

MOSELEY, JULIA W., music educator, preservationist; b. Tampa, Fla., Mar. 21, 1919; d. Hallock Preston and Ruby Winifred Moseley. BA, Agnes Scott Coll., Decatur, Ga., 1940. Nat. cert. music tchr. Asst. food and fashion editor Atlanta Constn., 1940-41; credit report typist, publicist, fund raiser Mchts. Assn. Tampa, 1942-43; teletype operator, writer/editor, commodities marketer USDA, Atlanta, 1943-47; self-employed music tchr. Atlanta, 1945-47; hist. rschr. New Orleans, 1947—48; self-employed music tchr. Fla., 1948—; also cattle raiser, citrus grower; preservationist Moseley Homestead, Brandon, Fla., 1948—. Author, editor: Come to My Sunland, 1997; co-author: Internet Lake Atlas, 1999, Recipes and Remembrances, 1999-2004; composer song Brandon, Brandon. Mem. Brandon Citizens Adv. Com.; established Timberly Trust, Inc., 1994; worked with Historic Tampa/Hillsborough Cunty Preservation Bd., 1983-92; spokesperson to Hillsborough County Bd. Commrs. on land use and preservation, 1966-99; mem. Brandon Task Force involved with county devel. issues; mem. hist. com. Brandon Centennial Celebration, 1990. Elizabeth Ordaway Dunn Found. grantee, 1998. Mem.: Fla. State Music Tchrs. Assn. (past officer), Limona Acad. Arts, Letters and Scis. (past officer and dir.), Art Publ. Soc. (Guild tchr.), Nat. Fedn. Music Clubs, Nat. Guild Piano Tchrs., Music Tchrs. Nat. Assn., Tampa Music Tchrs. Assn. (officer), Fla. Breeding Bird Atlas, Tampa Preservation, Inc., Nature Conservancy, Fla. Trust for Historic Preservation, Nat. Trust for Historic Preservation, Friday Morning Musicale Club. Avocations: bird watching, reading, walking, photography, star gazing. Personal E-mail: ttland@hotmail.com.

MOSELEY, KAREN FRANCES FLANIGAN, educational consultant, retired school system administrator, educator; b. Oneonta, N.Y., Sept. 18, 1944; d. Albert Francis and Dorothy (Brown) Flanigan; m. David Michael McLaud, Sept. 8, 1962 (div. Dec. 1966); m. Harry R. Lasalle, Dec. 24, 1970 (dec. Feb. 1990); 1 child, Christopher Michael; m. Kel Moseley, Jan. 22, 1994. BA, SUNY, Oneonta, 1969; MS, SUNY and Hockerill Coll., Eng., 1970. Cert. secondary edn. tchr., Fla., Mass., NY. Tchr. Hanover (Mass.) Pub. Schs., 1970-80; lobbyist Mass. Fed. Nursing Homes, Boston, 1980-84; tchr., dept. chair Palm Beach County Schs., Jupiter, Fla., 1985-95; ret., 1996; chair of accredidation Jupiter H.S., 1990-91. Fulbright tchr., Denmark, 1994-95. Author: How to Teach About King, 1978, 10 Year Study, 1991. Mem., spkr. PBC chpt. ARC; disaster team vol. Palm Beach County Red Cross; vol. Pace Ctr. for Girls, PACE Ctr. for Girls; del. Dem. Conv., Mass., 1976-84; campaign mgr. Kennedy for Senate, NY, 1966, Tsongas for Senate, Boston, 1978; dir. Plymouth County Dems., Marshfield, Mass., 1978-84; mem. Sch. Accountability Com., 1991-95; polit. cons. Paul Tsongas U.S. Senate, Boston, 1978-84, Michael Dukakis for Gov., Boston, 1978-84. Mem. AAUW (North Palm Beach County, officer, Ednl. Found. Honor award 2003), NEA (life), Nat. Honor Soc. Polit. Scientists, Classroom Tchrs. Assn., Palm Beach County Classroom Tchrs. Assn., Mass. Coun. Social Studies (bd. dirs. Boston chpt. 1970-80), Mass. Tchrs. Assn. (chair human rels. com. Boston chpt. 1976-80), Plymouth County Social Studies (bd. dirs. 1970-80), Mass. Hosp. Assn. (bd. dirs. Boston chpt. 1980-84), Nat. Coun. for Social Studies, Fulbright Alumni Assn., Prologue Soc., Forum Club of the Palm Beaches, Fla. History Ctr., Marine Life Ctr., Norton Mus. Art. Roman Catholic. Avocations: reading, fishing, travel, art collector, snorkeling. Home: 369 River Edge Rd Jupiter FL 33477-9350 Office Phone: 561-744-6286. Personal E-mail: karenmoseley@adelphia.net.

MOSELEY, LAURICE CULP, small business owner; b. Chilton County, Ala., Feb. 15, 1927; d. John Curtis and Alma Roma (Hand) Foshee; student Air U. Extension Course Inst., 1951-57; m. Charles W. Culp, Oct. 23, 1946; children— Randall D., Robert C.; m. 2d Ernest B. Moseley, Jr. May 21, 1966. Auditor, personnel clk. fed. govt., 1949-55; founder, chmn. bd. Culp Piano & Organ Co. Co. (doing bus. as Fairview Piano Co., Inc., Electronics Organ Service Co., Moseley Piano Co., Crown Gems Internat., Culp Internat. Inc.), Montgomery, Ala., 1955—, also dir.; dir. Dimensions Inc., Montgomery. Mem. Nat. Assn. Music Mchts., Am. Music Conf. Republican. Club: Soroptimist. Author: (with A.T. Thomas) 6 Lessons Toward Keyboard Mastery, 1978; creator Music Home Study Course; composer 32 songs. Office: Culp Piano & Organ Co 1214 Madison Ave Montgomery AL 36107-1830

MOSELY, ELAINE W., school librarian; b. Tuscaloosa, Ala. d. Ollie and Minnie S. Washington; m. Willard Mosely, Dec. 29, 1973; children: Taimon, Erin. BA in Psychology, Coe Coll., 1973; postgrad., U. Mo., 1976—78; MS in Libr & Info. Sci., U. N.Tex., 2000. Cert. tchr. Iowa, Tex., libr. Tex. Tchr. Cedar Rapids (Iowa) Cmty. Schs., 1973—76; journalist various radio, TV and newspapers, Houston, 1979—85; pub. rels. practitioner City of Houston, 1985—88, Am. Heart Assn., Houston, 1988—89; pub. rels. cons. Coop. Ventures, Houston, 1989—91; tchr. Fort Bend Indep. Sch. Dist., Missouri City, Tex., libr. media specialist, 1994—2002. Adv. bd. Fort Bend County Librs., Richmond, Tex., 1999—2002. Mem. project blueprint United Way, Houston, 1990; charter mem. Fort Bend Lit. League, Sugar Land, Tex., 2000. Grantee, Viburnam Found. & ALA, 1992. Mem.: ALA, Tex. Libr. Assn., Houston Assn. Black Journalists (past bd. pres.), Alpha Kappa Alpha. Avocations: antiques, books.

MOSER, BARBARA JO, elementary school educator; b. Jacksonville, Fla., Jan. 12, 1947; d. Paul N. and Georgia J. Baldwin; m. Max L. Moser, Nov. 2, 1968; children: Max L. II, Robert P. Student, DePauw U., 1965—66; BS in Edn., Ball State U., 1969; MS in Edn., Ind. U., Indpls., 1974—74. English/journalism instr. Stonybrook Mid. Sch., Indpls., 1982—96, computer instr., 1996—. Tchr. leadership acad. Ctrl. Ind. Edn. Ctr., Indpls., 1998. Precinct worker Rep. Party, Indpls., 1969—2003. Recipient Golden Apple award, Indpls. Power and Light Co., 1998, Hon. Life Memebrship, Ind. PTA, Stonybrook PTA. Mem.: NEA (2nd vice-president 1993—98), Assn. for the Supervision of Curriculum Devel., Phi Delta Kappa. Avocations: reading, music, history. Home: 1625 Fogelson Dr Indianapolis IN 46229 Office: Stonybrook Middle Sch 11300 Stonybrook Dr Indianapolis IN 46229 Personal E-mail: barbmoser2@aol.com.

MOSER, GLENDA FAYE, media specialist; b. Fairview, Okla., May 27, 1944; d. Leon Lyle Hunt and Faye Gladys Hunt (Gooch); m. James Calvin Moser; children: Bruce Wayne Brinson, Bret Orin Brinson, James Lee Huckaby, Darla Durree Brinson, Dianna Leigh Fisher. B in Edn., Brinson U., 1978; M in Libr. Edn. (hon.), SW Okla. State U., 1982. 3rd gr. tchr., libr. Verden (Okla.) Pub. Sch., 1990—91; humanities 8th gr. tchr., k-12 libr. media specialist Davenport (Okla.) Pub. Sch., 1992—98; libr. media specialist Tecumseh (Okla.) Mid. Sch., 1998—. Author (illustrator): (children's book) Mancestor (Writer's award at NWOSU, 1980). Writer marionette play Lincoln County Children's Mus., Chandler, Okla., 1994—2006. Recipient Overall Best Show for History Day, S.W. Okla. State U., 1982—84. Mem.: NEA, ALA (assoc. Pres. 1985). Independent. Achievements include research in teach the 8 parts of speech for middle School, I called it NAPVAPIC' IT'S MAGIC!. Avocations: cake decorating, sewing, farm animals, reading, writing. Home: RR #1 Box 27 Sparks OK 74869 Office: Tecumseh Mid Sch 315 W Park St Tecumseh OK 74873 Office Phone: 405-598-2067. Office Fax: 405-598-1948. Personal E-mail: jgmosaic@yahoo.com. Business E-Mail: moserg@tecumseh.k12.ok.us.

MOSER, TERI, literature educator; d. Alma Porter and Kay Squires Moser; m. Harry Andrew Ziegler; children: Jason Moser Ziegler, Austin Moser Ziegler, Kaitlin Moser Ziegler. BA, Utah State U., Logan, 1983, MA, 1986; PhD, Ariz. State U., Tempe, 1999. Adj. faculty English Maricopa Cmty. Colls., Tempe, 1994—2001; residential faculty English Chandler-Gilbert CC, 2001—. Svc. learning faculty liaison Chandler-Gilbert CC, 2003—06. Recipient Sterling Scholar award in English, State of Utah, 1979, Svc. Learning award, Chandler-Gilbert C.C., 2003; Dissertation Rsch. fellow, Ariz. State U., 1994—95, Academic scholar, Utah State U., 1979—83. Mem.: MLA (assoc.), Rocky Mountain MLA (assoc.), Coll. Composition and Communication (assoc.), Nat. Coun. Tchrs. English (assoc.), Assn. Study Lit. and Environment (assoc.), Phi Kappa Phi, Sigma Tau Delta, Lambda Iota Tau, Alpha Lambda Delta. Office: Chandler-Gilbert Community College 2626 E Pecos Rd Chandler AZ 85225 Office Phone: 480-857-5120.

MOSES, ANICE N., elementary school educator, minister; b. Bogalusa, La., Sept. 5, 1956; d. Llewellyn and Lucille Nichols; m. Rodney Arness Moses, Feb. 16, 1985; children: Keavina R. Nichols, Tenisha C. Dyson-Foster, Shannon A. Dyso. BA, Southeastern La. U., 2001; MA, Interdenominational Theology Ctr., 2004. Asst. mgr. Show Town, Bogalusa, 1995—96; teller Hancock Bank, Bogalusa, 1996—98; pastor United Meth. Ch., Baston, La., 1998—; tchr. Wesley Ray Elem. Sch., Angel, La., 2005—. Mem. conf. bd. discipleship La. Conf. United Meth. Ch., 2004, mem. strengthen black ch. task force, 1998. Mem.: Gammon Fellowship. Avocations: reading, music, sewing, basketball. Mailing: PO Box 265 Angie LA 70467

MOSES, BONNIE SMITH, lawyer, educator; b. Phila., Jan. 20, 1955; d. D. Ralph (dec.) and Mercedes McKinley (Harrison) S.; m. Richard Moses, July 8, 1978; children: Michelle Irene, Jacquelyn Elyse. BS in Psychology summa cum laude, Pa. State U., 1975; JD, Temple U., 1978, LLM in Taxation, 1981. Bar: Pa. 1978, U.S. Dist. Ct. (ea. dist.) Pa. 1978, U.S. Ct. Appeals (3d cir.) 1980, U.S. Tax Ct. 1981, U.S. Supreme Ct. 1986. Law clk. Ct. Common Pleas, Phila., 1978-79; assoc. Leonard M. Sagot Assocs., Phila., 1979-80, mng. assoc. Jenkintown, Pa., 1980-84; ptnr. Dessen, Moses & Sheinoff, Phila., 1984—2004, Dessen Moses & Rossitto, Willow Grove, 2005—. Adj. prof. bus. law Arcadia U., Glenside, Pa., 1982—. Co-author The Physician's Guide to Medical Practice, 2003; mem. staff Temple U. Law Rev., 1976-78; contbr. articles to profl. jours. Bd. dirs., v.p., chair pers. com. Phila. Jewish Archives; bd. dirs., chair pers. Girls Inc. Greater Phila.; bd. dirs. Thymic Cancer Found.; mem. Leadership Coun. Phila.; vol. Lawyers for the Arts; mentor Women's Law Caucus, Temple U. Law Sch. Fellow Pa. Bar Assn.; mem. ABA, AAUW, NAFE, Pa. Bar Assn., Montgomery County Bar Assn., Am. Prepaid Legal Svcs. Inst. (chmn. conf. com. 2001—), Temple Law Alumni Assn. (exec. com.), Ogontz Campus Alumni Assn., Phi Beta Kappa, Phi Kappa Phi (Woman of Vision award 1997). Office: Dessen Moses & Rossitto 600 Easton Rd Willow Grove PA 19090 Office Phone: 215-564-5600. Business E-Mail: bmoses@dms-lawyer.com.

MOSES, CATHERINE, political science professor; d. Edwin Davis and Barbara O'Shields Moses; m. Kenneth Gregory Dobson; children: Eleanor, Brigid. BA, Rice U., Houston, 1987; MA, U. Ga., Athens, Ga., 1989, PhD, 2004. Fgn. svc. officer USIA, Washington, 1989—96; instr. U. Ga., Athens, 1998—2000; asst. prof. polit. sci. Ga. Coll. and State U., Milledgeville, 2001—. Author: Real Life in Castro's Cuba, 2000. Office: Ga Coll and State U Dept Govt and Sociology Milledgeville GA 31061

MOSES, CYNTHIA GLASS, realtor; b. Kittery, Maine, Jan. 27, 1954; d. Park Roy Jr. and Mintie Jane (Eberhart) Glass; m. Robert William Moses, Nov. 26, 1983. BA, U. Md., 1975; MA, U. Va., 1976; postgrad., U. Conn., 1976-79. Cert. residential specialist; cert. relocation profl.; accredited buyer's rep. e-Pro, grad. Realtors Inst. Owner Cynthia Glass Antiques, Alexandria, Va., 1981-83; assoc. Shannon and Luchs, Bethesda, Md., 1983-89; assoc. broker Re/Max 2000, Rockville, Md., 1990-2000; broker Broker Residential Referrals Direct, 1994—; assoc. broker Keller Williams Md. Realtors, Gaithershurg, 2000—04; broker, owner Keller Williams Metro Realty, Rockville, 2004—. Docent Nat. Mus. African Art, Washington, 1979-83. Recipient Rsch. grant U. Conn., Storrs, 1978. Mem. Nat. Assn. Realtors (gov. residential sales coun. 1993-96, dist. v.p. Montgomery County, 2006), Md./D.C. CRS Chpt. (pres. 1991-92, Diamond award 1992), Real Estate Buyers Agy. Coun., Montgomery County Assn. Realtors (life), Rotary Internat. Avocations: skiing, roller blading, scuba diving. Home: 26301 Mullinix Mill Rd Mount Airy MD 21771-4301 Office: Keller Williams Metro Realty Ste 100 11333 Woodglen Dr Rockville MD 20852 Office Phone: 240-514-1510. E-mail: cindy@moseshometeam.com.

MOSES, GAYE ANITA, elementary school educator; m. Curtis TeeArtur Moses, Dec. 29, 1990; children: Curtis TeeArtur Moses Jr., Precious Gaye Anita Moses II. BS, Loyola Marymount U., L.A., 1981—85. Cert. Tchr. Calif. Dept. Edn., 1989. Tchr. Hesperia Unified Sch. Dist., Hesperia, Calif., 1989—90, Victor Elem. Sch. Dist., Victorville, 1990—. Office: Victor Elem Sch Dist 15579 8th St Victorville CA 92395 Office Phone: 760-243-2012. Office Fax: 760-243-1291. Personal E-mail: gmoses@vesd.net. E-mail: gmoses@veds.net.

MOSES, MARCIA SWARTZ, artist; b. Canton, Ohio, Oct. 3, 1947; d. Elmer John Swartz and Marguerite Mary Welsh; m. Frederick Oscar Moses, June 7, 1969; children: Frederick, Angela Parker, John. Student, Kent State U., 1965—67, BFA, 1987; student, Ohio State U., 1984—86. Artist Watercolor Originals, Canton, 1991—. Author: (watercolor book) Untitled, 2002, Easy Watercolor, Learn to Express Yourself; prin. works include Vessels of Antiquity, 2000 (Best of Show award, 2000). Bd. dirs. Canton Artists League, 2001. Home and Office: Watercolor Originals 5101 Summitview Cir Canton OH 44708 E-mail: mosesart@neo.rr.com.

MOSES, SHEILA JOHNSON, nurse, bookkeeper; b. Darlington, SC, June 22, 1965; d. Elijah Johnson Jr. and Inez Williams Johnson; m. Donnie Moses, June 5, 1993; 1 child, Donte Jevon. A in Acctg. and Data Processing, Sumter Tech. Coll., SC, 1985; A in Health Sci. in Nursing, Ctrl. Carolina Tech. Coll., Sumter, 1997. EMT SC. Bd. EMS; RN State Bd. Nursing for SC Dept. of Labor, Licensing and Regulations. Nurse Tuomey Hosp., Sumter, SC, 1997—99; nurse supr. Springdale Nursing Home, Camden, SC, 1999—2003; dialysis nurse Lee County Dialysis, Bishopville, SC, 2002—; bookkeeper Johnson and Johnson Constrn., Camden, 1988—; sch. nurse Lee county Sch. Dist., Bishopville, 2003—. EMT Lee Rescue Squad, Bishopville, 1989—95; com. mem. Lee County Health Connection for Sch. Success, SC; team capt. Lee County Cancer Soc.; bd. mem. Lee County First Steps, Bishopville; rep. Avon, 1987—, unit leader, 2004—. Notary pub., 1988—. Recipient Mem. of the Future Bus. Leaders, Lee County Vocat., 1981-1882, Honors Soc., Bishopville. Mem.: Nat. Assn. of Sch. Nurse, Lee County Health Ministry, Lee County First Step. Baptist. Avocations: meeting people, travel, cooking, basketball. Office Phone: 803-484-5386.

MOSES, SHELIA P., writer, poet, playwright, producer; b. Rich Square, NC, 1961; Author: So They Burned the Black Churches, 1996, One More River to Cross, The Legend of Buddy Bush, 2004 (Nat. Book Award finalist, 2004), I, Dred Scott, 2005; co-author (with Dick Gregory): Callus on My Soul: A Memoir, 2000; co-author: (plays) Ain't No God in Hollywood. Recipient Coretta Scott King Honor Book award, 2005.

MOSES BROWN, BRENDA GENE, elementary school educator; b. Precious Plains, Jamaica, Feb. 25, 1946; arrived in U.S., 1977; d. Wilfred Samuel and Joyce May (Unicie) Moses; m. Esric C.A. Brown, Dec. 16, 1972 (div.); 1 child, Kimberley C. Brown. Cert. tchr., Shortwood Tchrs. Coll., Jamaica, 1969; BS in Early Childhood Edn. summa cum laude, CUNY, NYC, 1984, MS in Elem. Edn., 1986. Cert. tchr. NY. Tchr. Harbour View Primary Sch., Kingston, Jamaica, 1969—77; substitute tchr. All Soul's Nursery Sch., NYC, 1984; sci. tchr. Pub. Sch. 399, Bklyn., 1984—. Mem. Cambria Heights Gospel Chpt., NY, 1991—, chmn. coll. prayer group, 1997—; mem. Unity Caucus, NYC, 1996—; mem., mentor Congl. Youth Leadership Coun.; mem. So. Poverty Ctr. for Law and Justice, 1996—. Mem.: NSTA, Alumni Assn. CUNY (bd. dirs. edn. group 1984—), Am. Fedn. Tchrs. (traveling del. 2000—), United Fedn. Tchrs. (chpt. leader, del. 1988—). Democrat. Mem. Christian Brethren. Avocations: reading, gardening, travel, Scrabble, crafts. Home: 218-91 99th Ave Queens Village NY 11429 Office: Stanley Eugene Clark Sch 2707 Albemarle Rd Brooklyn NY 11226

MOSHER, DONNA PRESCOTT, retired secondary school educator; b. Sublette, Ill., Dec. 19, 1929; d. Francis Green Prescott and Ruth Viola Carver; m. William V. Mosher, Oct. 3, 1954; children: Jane Ellen Turley, Jacog Jeffery Turley, James Francis Turley. BA, U. Nebr., Lincoln, 1952; MS, No. Ill. U., DeKalb, 1962. Dir. health edn. YWCA, Lincoln, Nebr., 1952—54; tchr. phys. edn., counselor LaSalle-Peru HS, Ill., 1959—63; counselor Sterling HS, Ill., 1963—66; tchr. spl. edn., counselor unit 4 Centennial HS, Champaign, Ill., 1967—85; ret., 1985. Com. chair unit 4 Centennial H.S., Champaign, 1971—84, head spl. edn. unit 4, 1980—83. Bd. dirs. ARC, Champaign County and Shelby County, Ill., 1970—96, chair bd. Shelby County, Ill., 1996—2000; bd. dirs. Urban League, Champaign County, 1979—85; water safety chmn. ARC, Champaign County and Shelby County, Ill., 1969—2000. Recipient 50 Yrs. Vol. award, ARC, 2002. Republican. Presbyterian. Home: 2803 Stratford Ct Bloomington IL 61704

MOSHER, JANET A., counselor; d. Robert Ernest and Hildreth Lelia Allard; m. Pasquale Alosa (div.); children: Judith Ann Alosa, Matthew Robert Alosa; m. Rodney Daniel Mosher, Dec. 30, 1994. A, Colby Jr. Coll., New London, NH, 1957; BA, U. NH, Durham, 1959; M in Counseling Psychology, Antioch New Eng., Keene, NH, 1979. Lic. mental health counselor NH, cert. sports counselor, family life educator, HIV pre-post test counselor. English tchr. Concord (NH) Sr. HS, 1959—62; vol. Concord Mental Health, 1970—76; intern Greater Manchester Mental Health, 1978—79; counselor, cmty. edn. coord. Manchester Family Planning, 1979—89; social worker, counselor, case mgr. Elliott Hosp. Prenatal Program, Manchester, 1989—92, exec. dir., 1992—93; family cmty. health coord. Manchester Cmty. Health Ctr., 1993—99; counselor Dartmouth-Hitchcock Med. Ctr., Manchester, 1999—. Adj. faculty U. NH, 1988. Chair Manchester Area Interdisciplinary Team on Child Abuse and Neglect, 1985—86, United Way Cmty. Task Force on AIDS, Manchester, 1988—90; mem. adv. bd. Parent-Baby Adventure, Manchester, 1980—, Manchester Office of Youth Svcs., 1990—2000, Homeless Cmty. Health Svcs., Manchester, 1995—; commr. NH Commn. on Status of Women, 1987—90. Mem.: Am. Assn. Counselors, NH Assn. Counselors, Nat. Inst. Sports. Avocation: photography. Home: 633 Canal St at Amos Keng Pl Manchester NH 03101 Office: Dartmouth-Hitchcock Med Ctr 100 Hitchcock Way Manchester NH 03104 Office Phone: 603-695-2937. Office Fax: 603-695-2919. E-mail: janet.a.mosher@hitchcock.org.

MOSHER, SALLY EKENBERG, lawyer, musician; b. N.Y.C., July 26, 1934; d. Leslie Joseph and Frances Josephine (McArdle) Ekenberg; m. James Kimberly Mosher, Aug. 13, 1960 (dec. Aug. 1982). MusB, Manhattanville Coll., 1956; postgrad., Hofstra U., 1958-60, U. So. Calif., 1971-73, JD, 1981. Bar: Calif., 1982. Musician, pianist, tchr., 1957-74; music critic Pasadena Star-News, 1967-72; mgr. Contrasts Concerts, Pasadena Art Mus., 1971-72; rep. Occidental Life Ins. Co., Pasadena, 1975-78; v.p. James K. Mosher Co., Pasadena, 1961-82, pres., 1982—, Oakhill Enterprises, Pasadena, 1984—; assoc. White-Howell, Inc., Pasadena, 1984-94; real estate broker, 1984-96. Harpsichordist, lectr., composer, 1994—; pub. Silver Wheels Pub., ASCAP. Musician (CD recs.) William Byrd: Songs, Dances, Battles, Games, 1995, From Now On: New Directions For Harpsichord, 1998, Sally Mosher Plays English Renaissance Harpsichord Music, Images and Moods, (with Patrick Lindley, Scott Frasier, Justin Weaver) Towards the Light; author: People and Their Contexts: A Chronology of the 16th Century World; contbr. articles to various publs. Bd. dirs. Jr. League Pasadena, 1966-67, Encounters Concerts, Pasadena, 1966-72, U. So. Calif. Friends of Music, L.A., 1973-76, Calif. Music Theatre, 1988-90, Pasadena Hist. Soc., 1989-91, I Cantori, 1989-91; bd. dirs. Pasadena Arts Coun., 1986-92, pres., 1989-92, chair adv. bd., 1992-93; v.p., bd. dirs. Pasadena Chamber Orch., 1986-88, pres., 1987-88; mem. Calif. 200 Coun. for Bicentennial of U.S. Constn., 1987-90; mem. Endowment Adv. Commn., Pasadena, 1988-90; bd. dirs. Foothill Area Cmty. Svcs., 1990-95, treas., 1991, vice chair, 1992-94, chair, 1994-95; sec., bd. dirs. Piano Spheres, 2001-02, pres., 2002—. Manhattanville Coll. hon. scholar, 1952-56. Mem. ABA, Calif. Bar Assn., Assocs. of Calif. Inst. Tech., So. Calif. Baroque Assn. (bd. dirs., 2004—), Athenaeum, Kappa Gamma Pi, Mu Phi Epsilon, Phi Alpha Delta. Home: 1260 Rancheros Rd Pasadena CA 91103-2759 Fax: 626-795-3146. E-mail: sally@cyberverse.com.

MOSIER, CHERYL ANGELINE, secondary school educator, consultant; b. Longmont, Colo., Mar. 31, 1968; d. Douglas and Evangeline Martfeld; m. Christopher R. Mosier, July 4, 1997; 1 child, Ryan Matthew. Diploma in Earth Sci. Edn., diploma in Phys. Sci. Edn., U. No. Colo., Greeley, 1992; MA in tchg., Grand Canyon U., Phoenix, 2003. Lic. Profl. Tchr. Colo., 2006. Sci. tchr. Columbine HS, Littleton, Colo., 1997—. Cons. It's About Time Pub., Herrf Jones Edn. Divsn., Armonk, NY, 2005—, Am. Geol. Inst., 2005—; bldg. liaison for gifted/talented students Columbine HS; presenter Colo. Sci. Conv., Denver, 2005—. Founding mem. Am. Geological Inst. Geosci. Tchrs. Acad. Recipient Math and Sci. medal of achievement, Colo. Sch. Mines, 1986, Departmental Scholar in Earth Sci., U. No. Colo., 1990, Excellence in Tchg. of Earth Scis. award, Rocky Mountain Assn. Geologists Found., 2005; grantee Lockheed Martin Columbine Meml. scholarship, 2002. Mem.: NSTA, Colo. Assn. Sci. Tchrs., Nat. Earth Sci. Tchrs. Assn. Office: Columbine HS 6201 S Pierce St Littleton CO 80123 Office Phone: 303-982-4474. Business E-Mail: camosier@jeffco.k12.co.us.

MOSKOVITZ, ELISA MCMILLAN, music educator, musician; b. Columbia, S.C., Nov. 29, 1953; d. William Gooding and Elizabeth Anne McMillan; m. Barry L. Moskovitz, Apr. 5, 1980 (div. Dec. 1982); m. Finnbarr T. Dunphy, Nov. 19, 2000. B of Music Edn., Winthrop U., 1976, MMus, 1977; D of Musical Arts, U. S.C., 1989. Tchr. gen. music and chorus Lexington (S.C.) Sch. Dist. 1, 1977—89, program specialist for fine arts; tchr. music theory Lexington H.S., 1990—2002; choral dir. White Knoll H.S., 2002—06. Organist, choirmaster St. Timothy's Episcopal Ch., Columbia, 1985—2002; pianist So. Arts Trio, Columbia, 1994—; adj. prof. U. S.C., Columbia, 1990—2004, Limestone Coll., Columbia, 1990, Columbia, 96; coord. music Tri-Dist. Arts Consortium, Columbia, 1997—99; organist, choirmaster Centennial Presbyn. Ch., Columbia, 2004—, Centennial Assoc. Reformed Presbyn., 2004—; coord. SC State Choral Festival, 2004—. Author: The American Music Teacher, 1990, Yemassee, 2001, JRME, 0992. Coord. A Little Summer Music concert series St. Timothy's Ch., Columbia, 1995—; mem. People to People Ambassadorial Program, 2003—. Fellow, NEH, 1992; grantee, Nat. Music Edn. Project, 1991. Mem.: S.C. Music Educators Assn., Am. Guild Organists, Pi Kappa Lambda, Delta Kappa Gamma. Episcopalian. Avocations: golf, poetry, literature. Office Phone: 803-996-4558. Office Fax: 803-996-4558.

MOSKOWITZ, RANDI ZUCKER, nurse; b. N.Y.C., Oct. 19, 1948; d. Seymour and Gertrude (Levy) Zucker; m. Marc N. Moskowitz, July 11, 1976. RN, Jewish Hosp. and Med. Ctr., 1969; BA, Marymount Manhattan Coll., 1975; MS, Hunter Coll., 1979; MBA, Columbia U., 1990. Gen. staff nurse neurosurgery unit N.Y. Hosp., N.Y.C., 1969—71, sr. staff nurse recovery rm., 1971—76, nurse coord. utilization rev., 1976—79; health educator Office of Cancer Commn. Meml. Sloan-Kettering Cancer Ctr., N.Y.C., 1979—81, adminstr. Surg. Day Hosp., 1990—98; adminstrv. nurse oncologist Bklyn. Cmty. Hosp. and Meth. Hosp., 1981—83, grants coord. radiotherapy dept., 1983—86; adminstr. Ambulatory Oncology Ctr. Columbia-Presbyn. Med. Ctr., N.Y.C., 1986—89; mgr. Oncology Svcs., St. Vincent Cath. Med. Ctrs., Jamaica, NY, 1999—2006; adminstr. pediat. oncology Columbia U. Med. Ctr., N.Y.C., 2006—. Masters prof. oncology Columbia U. Sch. Nursing. Co-editor Oncology Nursing: Advances, Treatments and Trends into the Twenty-first Century; contbr. articles to profl. jours. Mem. N.Y. Assn. Ambulatory Care, Oncology Nursing Soc. (sec. N.Y.C. chpt. 1983-87, pres. 1988-89). Home: 446 E 86th St Apt 5F New York NY 10028-6474 Office: Columbia Univ Med Ctr 161 Ft Washington Ave New York NY 10032 Office Phone: 212-342-3455. Personal E-mail: rm2505@columbia.edu.

MOSLAK, JUDITH, retired music educator; b. New Kensington, Pa., Sept. 16, 1942; d. Michael B. and Edith V. Moslak. MusB, Marygrove College, Detroit, Mich., 1964; MA, University of Detroit, 1967; student internat. piano workshops, France, 1998, Austria, 2000, student internat. piano workshops, 2004, Norway, 2002. Cert. Orff-Schulwerk Levels 1, 2, 3 1973. Assistant organist Archdiocese of Detroit, Mich., 1957—67; organist/choir director Immaculate Heart of Mary Ch., Detroit, 1964—65; elem. vocal music tchr. Detroit Pub. Schs., 1964—69; elem. vocal music cons. Farmington (Mich.) Pub. Schs., 1969—97; pvt. piano tchr. Piano Studio of Judith Moslak, West Bloomfield, Mich., 1997—. Adj. asst. prof. music Madonna U., Livonia, Mich., 2003—. Founder Pebble Creek Chamber Orch. Mem.: Orchard Lake Philharmonic Soc. (founder, pres.), Oakland Piano Tchrs. Forum, Mich. Assn. Calligraphers, Livonia Area Piano Tchrs. Forum, Music Tchrs. Nat. Assn., Am. Guild Organists (Detroit chpt.), Am. Orff-Schulwerk Assn. (treas. 1973—75), Friends of Four Hands (charter bd. mem. 1981), Delta Kappa Gamma (treas. 1994—96). Roman Catholic. Avocations: calligraphy, travel, ensemble piano performance, digital photography. Personal E-mail: kmoslak@comcast.net.

MOSLEY, ELAINE CHRISTIAN SAVAGE, principal, consultant; b. St. Louis, Mo., Mar. 4, 1941; d. John W. Savage and Mabel (Mahone) Christian; m. Melvin Ronell Mosley, Aug. 7, 1966; children: Dawn Edith, Melanie Denise, Dana Jean, John Melvin. BS, Lincoln U., 1964, MEd, 1973; EdD, Okla. State U., 1982. Tchr. St. Louis Pub. Sch. System, 1964-70, Immaculate Conception Sch., Jefferson City, 1970-73; counselor Bartlesville (Okla.) Sch. System, 1973-75, elem. prin., 1975-83, Bartlesville Pub. Sch. System, 1983-85, Oak Park (Ill.) Pub. Sch. System, 1985-87; founder, prin., chief edn. officer Corp. Cmty. Schs. of Am., Chgo., 1987—. Adj. instr. Langston U. Urban Ctr., Tulsa, Okla., 1983; edn. cons. pub. speaking, workshops, seminars, nat., 1985—; bd. regents Rogers State Coll., Okla., 1978-85; adv. bd. First Nat. Bank, Okla., 1982-85; nat. edn. adv. bd. Channel One, Whittle Communications, 1989-91. Freelance writer in field. Active Westside Assn. Community Action, Chgo., mem. nat. adv. bd. Marwen Found., mem. early childhood adv. bd. North Ctrl. Regional Ednl. Lab. Named Citizen of the Day for contbns. to edn. Bartlesville Area C. of C., 1976; numerous other awards, citations. Mem. League of Black Women (Black Rose award for Edn. 1990), Assn. Supervision and Curriculum Devel., Nat. Assn. Edn. Young Children, Nat. Black Child Devel. Inst., Delta Sigma Theta (West Suburban chpt.), Jack & Jill of Am., Inc. (West Suburban chpt.). Democrat. Baptist. Avocations: writing, poetry reading (oral), singing, travel, cooking. Home: 5666 Cascade Dr Lisle IL 60532-2047 Office: Corp Community Schs of Am 751 S Sacramento Blvd Chicago IL 60612-3365

MOSLEY, JESSIE BRYANT, retired science educator; b. Houston, Nov. 30, 1903; d. William and Emma Bryant; m. Charles Clint Mosley (dec.); children: Charles Mosley, Jr., Gene Lavell, Wilma Emma Clopton. LHD, BS, Jarvis Christian Coll.; LHD (hon.), Tougaloo Coll.; lifetime tchr.'s cert. Cert. libr. sci. Teen cons. YWCA, Jackson, Miss., 1950—60; bank teller State Mut. Fed. Savs. and Loan, Jackson, Miss., 1960—65; tchr. Jackson Pub. Schs., Jackson, Miss., 1965—70; founder Smith Robertson Mus. and Cultural Ctr., Jackson, Miss., 1970, dir., 1970—90, mus. dir., 1970—90. Author: The Negro In Mississippi History, 1950, The History of the Women's Movement in Mississippi, 1978. State convener Nat. Coun. Negro Women, Jackson, 1977—2001; mem. LeFleur's Bluff Links, Jackson, 1970, 100 Black Women, Jackson, 1990, Miss. Humanities Coun., Jackson, 1990; founder Farish St. Dist. Neighborhood Found., Jackson, 1980; mem. Jackson Urban League, 1967, Nat. Bus. League, Jackson, 1968, Integrated Ch. Women United, Jackson, 1960, Fedn. of Colored Women's Clubs, Jackson, 1950; chmn. Iwy, Jackson, 1977; chaperone Y-Teens, Jackson, 1950. Named Dr. Jessie B. Mosley Health and Human Services Bldg., Hinds County, 1990, Dr.Jessie B. Mosley St., City of Jackson, 1990, Disting. Black Citizen, U. Miss., 1990, Mary McCleod Bethune Living Legend, NCNW, 1998; recipient Carter G. Woodson award, NEA, Outstanding and Dedicated Svc. award, NCNW, 1978, Disting. Svc. to Religious and Civic Orgn. award, United Christian Ch., 1984, Oustanding Leadership award, NCNW, 1996, Outstanding Achievement-Civics, Arts and Culture award, NOBW, 1998-1999, Years of Endearing and Committed Svc. award, Nat. Coun. of Negro Women, 2000, Resolution for Life-Long Svc. award, NCNW, 2000, Cmty. Partners award, State Instns. Higher Learning bd. trustees, 2000. Mem.: AAUW, Alpha Kappa Alpha (hon. Dedicated Svc. to Cmty. 1986). Home: 1968 Wingfield Cir Jackson MS 39209-7101

MOSLEY, KAREN D., retired elementary school educator; b. St. Louis, Feb. 13, 1952; d. Leola Rollins Mason; m. Kem G. Mosley, July 22, 1978. BA, MacMurray Coll., 1974; ME, Washington U., St. Louis, 1979. Cert. tchr. Mo. Elem. vocal music tchr. Furguson-Florissant Sch. Dist., Florissant, Mo., 1974—2002, ret., 2002. Adminstrv. dir. SPROG, Inc., Kirkwood, Mo., 1983—96, sec., 1989—, also bd. dirs. Contbr. articles to profl. jours. Min. music Kirkwood Ch. of God, 1990—. Mem. Church Of God. Avocations: theater productions, travel, computers, reading quotes. Home: 1319 Grant Rd Webster Groves MO 63119

MOSLEY, MARY MAC, retired librarian; b. Rome, Ga., Nov. 11, 1926; d. William McKinley and Mary (Caldwell) H.; m. Samuel A. Mosley, June 12, 1946 (div. 1964); children: Samuel A. Jr., Pamela Ann, James Irwin. Student, Ga. State Coll. for Women, 1943-45; BS, Auburn U., 1947; cert. in teaching, Athens Coll., 1963; M in Library, Emory U., 1968. Tchr. sci. Rome City Schs., 1964-66; extension libr. Tri-County Regional Libr., 1966-67; libr. Shorter Coll., 1967-68, assoc. prof. libr. sci., 1968-76, dir. libr. svcs., 1968-93. Ch. libr., Decaon, historian Christian Women's Fellowship, 1st Christian Ch., 1998—; corr. sec. Rome Symphony Women's Assn., v.p., 1996-99, pres., 1999-2001; vol. Good Neighbor Ministry, Rome Floyd County Libr. Mem.

ALA, AAUW (pres. Rome br. 1974-1976, v.p. 2002-2004, 2006), Delta Kappa Gamma. Democrat. Mem. Christian Ch. Avocations: piano, reading, gardening, bridge. Home: 205 Benton Dr Rome GA 30165-1703 E-mail: marymacmo@earthlink.net.

MOSLEY, SHERRY JO, athletic trainer; d. James A. and Sharon Ann Seddon; m. Alan F. Mosley, July 24. BS, Ohio U., 1997, U. Charleston, 1999; MS, Marshall U., 2000. Cert. athletic trainer The Athletic Tng. Ctr. Nat. Athletic Trainers Assn. Bd. Office mgr. Prestera Health, Huntington, W.Va.; asst. prof. Marshall U., Huntington, W.Va., 2000, grad. asst., 1999; cert. athletic trainer Frazier Rehab. Inst., Scottsburg, Ind., 2001—. Employee com. sec. Scott Meml. Hosp., Scottsburg, Ind., 2004—, kids fest com., 2006. Mem.: Nat. Athletic Trainers Assn. (sec. employee com. 2004—). Avocations: sports, reading. Office: Frazier Rehab Inst 1473 N Gardner St Scottsburg IN 47170 Personal E-mail: sherryseddon@hotmail.com.

MOSLEY-MCCALL, JERALDINE, funeral director; b. Chgo., June 3, 1944; d. James and Artra Nell Mosley; m. John Sullivan McCall, Dec. 16, 1984. Cert. in Auto Mechanics, Wilson Tech. Coll., 1971; degree in Mortuary Sci., Worsham Coll. Mortuary Sci., 1971. Lic. embalmer Ill., 1971. Preparation mgr. Leak Funeral Home, Chgo., 1973—2004; co-owner Paradise Garden Funeral Home, Chgo., 2004—. Mem. adv. bd. So. Ill. U., Carbondale, Ill., 1995—, Worsham Coll., Wheeling, Ill., 1998—; ednl. dir. Ill. Selected Morticians, Chgo., 1990—92, 2002—. Mem. Ill. Rep. Committeewoman's Roundtable, 0858. Recipient Cert. of Achievement, Ill. Select Morticians. Mem.: Acad. Profl. Funeral Svc. Practice (cert. funeral svc. practitioner 2004), Epsilon Nu Delta (pres. 1987—88, treas. 2001—, Soldier award 2003). Republican. Baptist. Avocation: reading. Home: 8913 So Laflin St Chicago IL 60620 Office: 300 E 115th St Chicago IL 60628

MOSNER, ANN L., music educator; b. Buffalo, July 27, 1956; d. Salvatore Michael and Josephine Francis La Russo; m. James L. Mosner, June 27, 1980. BA Music Edn., Rosary Hill Coll., 1978; M Elem. Edn., SUNY, Buffalo, 1982. Vocal music tchr. Buffalo Pub. Schs., 1978—98, Maryvale UFSD, Cheektowaga, NY, 1998—. Recipient BPO award for Musical Excellence. Mem.: MENC, NY State Sch. Music Assn. (state chair for musical theatre 2000—), Maryvale Tchrs. Assn. (VOTE/COPE chair 2000—), Am. Choral Dirs. (N.Y. chpt.) (sec. 1998—), Erie County Music Educators (bd. dirs. 1982—, adv. to bd. 2000—). Home: S-5349 Dennis Rd Orchard Park NY 14127 Personal E-mail: panno88@msn.com.

MOSQUERA, ZOILA BIANCA, social worker; b. Rockland County, NY, Feb. 7, 1960; d. José M. and Cynthia M. Mosquera. BSW in Social Work with honors, LI U., 2003. Vol. St. Marks Sr. Ctr., Bklyn.; vol. adv. City Hall, Manhattan, 1980—91; adv. Altro Mentally Disabled, Manhattan, 1985—87. Recipient Adv. award, Fed. Employment Guidance Svs., 1991. Democrat. Methodist. Avocations: bowling, fencing, basketball, pottery, softball.

MOSS, BARBARA GAE, education educator; b. Akron, Ohio, Apr. 7, 1950; d. Bruce E. and Gae C. (Caldren) Kesselring; m. Patrick L. Moss, June 25, 1988; 1 child, Brian Singleton. BEd, Ohio State U., 1971; MEd, Kent State U., 1975, PhD, 1988. Cert. educator, Ohio. Tchr. Crestwood Schs., Mantua, Ohio, 1971-81; elem. cons. Portage County Bd. Edn., Ravenna, Ohio, 1981-88; asst. prof. U. Akron, Ohio, 1988-94, assoc. prof. Ohio, 1994-99, prof. Ohio, 1999—2001; Comprehensive Assessment Sys. for Adult Students prof. San Diego State U., 2001—. Profl. devel. editor; reading tchr.; cons. Assoc. editor Reading Tchr., 1992-94; contbr. articles to profl. jours. Co-pres. Literacy Educators and Advocates, Columbus, Ohio. Recipient scholarship Delta Kappa Gamma, 1987. Mem. Nat. Coun. on Rsch. in English, Internat. Reading Assn., Coll. Reading Assn., Nat. Coun. Tchrs. English, Phi Delta Kappa (co-editor newsletter 1994). Avocations: reading, travel. Home: 4327 Goldfinch St San Diego CA 92103-1315 Personal E-mail: bmoss4327@cox.net. Business E-Mail: bmass@mail.sdsu.edu.

MOSS, BETTY HARRIS, secondary education educator; b. Little Rock, Sept. 6, 1946; d. Alfred Jefferson and Carolyn Vernon (Dobson) M.; m. John Harrison Keech, Aug. 20, 1966 (div. Apr. 1972); m. John Duffy Jr., Apr. 20, 1974 (div. 1983); m. James Nathan Pruitt, Aug. 13, 1986. BA in English, U. Iowa, 1968; MA in English, Ark. State U., 1972; PhD in English, La. State U., 1981. Cert. tchr., Tex. English tchr. Jonesboro (Ark.) Pub. Schs., 1968-72, West Baton Rouge Pub. Schs., Brusly, La., 1982-86; tchg. asst. La. State U., Baton Rouge, 1972-77, instr., 1978-81; English tchr. Alamo Heights Ind. Sch. Dist., San Antonio, 1986—2004; AP strategies cons. dept. English, San Antonio Coll. Cons. advanced placement English, Coll. Bd., 1992—; cons. in curriculum planning and textbook adoption State of Tex., 1990-93; mem. adj. faculty San Antonio Coll., 1994—. Recipient edn. award State Times-Morning Advocate Newspapers, 1985, Tchg. Excellence award So. Meth. U., 1991, Advanced Placement English Spl. Recognition award S.W. Region Coll. Bd., 1995, Tex. Excellence award U. Tex. Ex-Students Assn. and Coll. Edn., 1996; grantee NEH, 1987. Mem. NEA, Tex. Edn. Assn., Nat. Coun. Tchrs. English, Tex. Coun. Tchrs. English, San Antonio Coun. Tchrs. English, Alamo Heights Tchrs. Assn. Avocations: reading, travel, pets. Home: 444 Sheraton Dr San Antonio TX 78209-5436 Office Phone: 210-820-8850. E-mail: mbulls6@yahoo.com.

MOSS, DAVID, music company executive; Cert., Musician's Inst. in Hollywood, 1985; B of commerce in mktg and fin., Concordia U., 1989. Dir., sch. of fine arts Saidye Bronfman Ctr. for the Arts, 1994—96, exec. dir., 1996—2003; gen. dir. Montreal Opera, 2003—. Founding mem., mem. exec. com. Culture Montreal; apptd. to Groupe Conseil pour la Politique Culturelle de Montreal, 2002; appt. to bd. La Vitrine Culturelle de Montreal, 2003. Office: L'Opera de Montreal 260 Maisonneuve Blvd W Montreal PQ H2X 1Y9 Canada Office Phone: 514-985-2222.

MOSS, JOY FOLKMAN, elementary school educator; b. Grand Rapids, Mich., Feb. 2, 1937; d. Jerome Daniel and Bessie Schomer Folkman; m. Arthur Jay Moss, June 23, 1957; children: Katherine Moss Lowengrub, Deborah Rose Moss Somers, David Abraham. BA, Wellesley Coll., Mass., 1958; MEd, U. Rochester, NY, 1969. Cert. Elem. Sch. Tchr. NY, 1969, Reading Tchr. NY, 1977. Dir. Cmty. Tchr. Ctr., Rochester, NY, 1973—78; asst. lectr. U. Rochester, 1974—76, assoc. lectr., 1976—78, adj. asst. prof., 1978—88; tchr. second grade Harley Sch., Rochester, NY, 1969—71, lit. tchr. k-4th, 1971—. Adj. prof. U. Rochester, 1988—; cons., guest speaker in field, 1970—. Author: Focus Units in Literature, 1984, Focus on Literature: A Context for Literacy Learning, 1990, Using Literature in the Middle Grades, 1994, Teaching Literature in the Elementary School, 1996, Teaching Literature in the Middle Grades: A Thematic Approach, 2000, From Literature to Literacy, 2002, Literary Discussion in the Elementary School, 2002, Literature, Literacy and comprehension Strategies in the Elementary School, 2005; contbr. articles to profl. jour. Mem. interfaith edn. com. Temple B'rith Kodesh, Rochester, 1961—70. Curriculum Devel. and Evaluation grant, Cummings Found., 2003. Mem.: Internat. Reading Assn., Nat., Coun. Tchrs. English. Avocations: reading, travel. Office: Harley Sch 1981 Clover St Rochester NY 14618

MOSS, JUDITH DOROTHY, lawyer, consultant, lecturer; b. Indpls., June 2, 1945; d. Frank Maxwell and Dorothy Grace (Wisnofske) M.; A in Computer Sci., Electronic Computer Programming Inst., Columbus, Ohio, 1969; BSBA, Ohio State U., 1975, JD, 1977. Bar: Ohio 1978, U.S. Dist. Ct. (so. dist.) Ohio 1978. Organic chemistry research technician O.M. Scott and Sons, Marysville, Ohio, 1965-68; computer programmer/systems analyst State of Ohio, Columbus, 1969-75; pvt. practice, Columbus, 1978-81; pres. Barrett and Barrett Co., L.P.A., Columbus, 1982-85; pres. Barrett & Moss Co., L.P.A., 1985-86; ptnr. Brownfield, Cramer & Lewis, Columbus, 1986—; cons. to Pres. U.S. and Congress, Nat. Adv. Council on Women's Ednl. Programs, chmn. civil rights com., 1983-84, 86—; pub. speaker and guest lectr. on constl. integrity. Coordinator Ohio Eagle Forum, 1982, gen. counsel, 1978-82, 83—; mem. Ohio Gov.'s Coordinating Commn. for Ohio, White House Conf. on Families, 1980, also nat. task force, 1980; del. Central Regional White House Conf. on Families, 1980; ofcl. observer Internat. Women's Yr. Conf., Houston, 1977; adv. bd. Franklin County (Ohio) Extension Service, Area Soil Conservation Service, 1980—; trustee United Conservatives of Ohio, 1984—, 1st v.p. 1985—; mem. Chmn.'s Club, Franklin County Ohio Republican Com., 1981—; active leadership program Pvt. Industry Council of Columbus and Franklin County, Inc., 1985-86; adv. commn. Columbus Area Cable TV, 1985—, Ohio Elections Commn., 1986—; past pres., chmn. planning com. Ravine Condominium Unit Owners Assn.; trustee Friends of 4-H, Area Soil Conservation Service, Cen. Ohio Lung Assn., Crossroads Counseling; bd. dirs. Pvt. INdustry Council Columbus and Franklin County; mem. adv. council Columbus Area Cable TV. Recipient Eagle award Phyllis Schlafly and Eagle Forum, 1980, cert. appreciation Pres. Carter, White House Conf. on Families Nat. Task Force, 1980. Mem. Ohio Bar Assn., Columbus Bar Assn., Alpha Xi Delta. Author various positions papers, pamphlets on constl. integrity. Home and Office: 275 Dogwood Ln Westerville OH 43082-9525

MOSS, KELLY ANNE, assistant principal; b. Tampa, Fla., May 19, 1967; d. William J. and Judy R. Moss. BA, U. Fla., Gainesville, 1990, MEd, 1991; EdS, U. Ga., Athens, 1996. Cert. Profl. Educator State of Fla., 2005. Tchr. Dacula H.S., Ga., 1991—95, asst. prin., 1995—2005, Freedom H.S., Orlando, Fla., 2005—. Office: Freedom High School 2500 Taft-Vineland Rd Orlando FL 32837

MOSS, LINDA ELAINE, science educator; d. Howard Adkins and Reva Helen Barnes Tribble; m. Leonard Joe Moss, July 25, 1980; children: Gayle Lynne Nichols, Cheryl Diane Zeiss. BS Agr., U. of Mo., 1972; BS in Chemistry Edn., Ark. State U., 1991, MS in Chemistry Edn., 1991, Specialist in C.C. Tchg., Biology, 1993, D of Ednl. Leadership, 2000. Lic. tchr. Ark. Acctg. clk. Empire Gas, Lebanon, Mo., 1972—73; sci. and fgn. lang. tchr. Poughkeepsie H.S., Ark., 1987—89, Evening Shade H.S., Ark., 1987—95; sci. instr. Ozarka Tech. Coll., Melbourne, Ark., 1993—95, Black River Tech. Coll., Pocahontas, Ark., 1995—. Beta delta phi chpt. adv. Phi Theta Kappa Internat. Honor Soc., Pocahontas, Ark., 2000—; sci. club adv. Black River Tech. Coll., Pocahontas, Ark., 1995—, north ctrl. accreditation steering com., 1998—2003, north ctrl. accreditation instl. integrity com. chair, 1998—2003; pres. black river coll. edn. assn. Ark. Edn. Assn., 1995—; chair, hazards identification com. Black River Tech. Coll., Pocahontas, 2003—. Mem. Keep Randolph County Beautiful, Pocahontas, Ark., 1998—2006. Recipient Ark. Acad. of Sci. Best Grad. Student Presentation, Ark. Acad. of Sci., 1995, Student Body Choice Tchr., Black River Tech. Coll. Student Coun., 1997, Phi Theta Kappa Faculty Scholar, Phi Theta Kappa Internat. Honor Soc., 2002, Most Disting. Faculty Advisor, Okla./Ark. Region Phi Theta Kappa Internat. Honor Soc., 2006, Empire Who's Who Registry of Executives and Professionals, 2005, Appreciation of Outstanding Svc., Okla./Ark. Region Phi Theta Kappa Internat. Honor Soc., 2006. Mem.: NEA, Ark. Edn. Assn. (assoc.; pres. local chpt. 1995—2006), Okla./Ark. Region Assn. of Chpt. Advisors Phi Theta Kappa Internat. Honor Soc., Phi Theta Kappa Internat. Honor Soc., Kappa Delta Phi Internat. Edn. Honor Soc. Home: 314 Elmont Road Maynard AR 72444 Office: Black River Tech Coll Highway 304 East Pocahontas AR 72455 Office Phone: 870-248-4000 4136. Office Fax: 870-248-4100. E-mail: lindam@blackrivertech.org.

MOSS, LYNDA BOURQUE, museum director; Dir. Western Heritage Ctr., Billings, Mont.

MOSS, MARCIA LYNN, retired biochemist; d. Frank and Loretta Moss; m. Fred Harold Rasmussen; 1 child, Alden Rasmussen. PhD, U. Wis., 1989. Organic chemist U. Mich., Ann Arbor, 1980—84; postdoctoral U. Wis. Sch. Pharmacy, Madison, 1990—92; postdoctoral dept. physiology U. Wis., Madison, Wis., 1989—90; rsch. investigator I and II Glaxo, Research Triangle Park, NC, 1992—99, ret., 1999; sr. project leader Cognosci, Research Triangle Park, NC, 2001—02; dir. rsch. BioZyme Inc., Apex, NC, 2003—04. Author (primary investigator): (identification of novel metalloprotease) Cloning of a disintegrin metalloproteinase that processes precursor tumour-necrosis factor-alpha; author: (graduate student) (mechanism of enzyme) The role of S-adenosylmethionine in the lysine 2, 3-aminomutase reaction; author: (co-investigator) (mechanistic studies on finasteride) Mechanism of time-dependent inhibition of 5 alpha-reductases by delta 1-4-azasteroids: toward perfection of rates of time-dependent inhibition by using ligand-binding energies; author: (senior investigator) (phage display) Substrate specificity of human collagenase-3 assessed using a phage display library, (novel enzyme in tgf alpha processing) Multiple Metalloproteinases Process ProTransforming Growth Factor- (ProTGF-; prin. author: rev. articles Shedding Membrane Proteins by ADAM Family Proteases, Therapeutic Benefits from Targeting of ADAM Family Members; contbr. articles to profl. jours. Ch. mem. New Horizons, Apex, NC. Grantee, NIH, 2001, 2002, 2002-2005, 2004—; Procter and Gamble fellowship, U. Wis., 1988, 1989, Fellowship grant, NIH, 1989, 1990. Mem.: ACS, Internat. Proteolysis Soc., Jour. Biol. Chemistry. Achievements include patents pending for Assays to measure matrix metalloproteinases. Home: 1513 Old White Oak Church Rd Apex NC 27523 Office: Duke Univ Research Dr 242 Nanaline Durham NC 27710 Office Phone: 919-668-5376. Personal E-mail: mmoss@biozyme-inc.com. E-mail: moss120@bellsouth.net.

MOSS, MYRA ELLEN (MYRA MOSS ROLLE), philosophy educator; b. LA, Mar. 22, 1937; m. Andrew Rolle, Nov. 5, 1983. BA, Pomona Coll., 1958; PhD, The Johns Hopkins U., 1965. Asst. prof. Santa Clara (Calif.) U., 1968-74; prof. Claremont McKenna Coll., 1975—, chmn. dept. philosophy, 1992-95. Assoc. dir. Gould Ctr. for Humanities, Claremont, Calif., 1993-94; adv. coun. Milton S. Eisenhower Libr./Johns Hopkins U., 1994-96, 2001—; vis. scholar Am. Acad. Rome, 2005. Author: Benedetto Croce Reconsidered, 1987, Mussolini's Fascist Philosopher: Giovanni Gentile Reconsidered, 2004, Italian edit., 2006; translator: Benedetto Croce's Essays on Literature & Literary Criticism, 1990; co-author: Values and Education, 1998; assoc. editor Special Issues; Journal of Value Inquiry, 1990-95 (Honorable Mention, Phoenix award); cons. editor Jour. Social Philosophy, 1988—; assoc. editor: Value Enquiry Book Series, 1990-95; editor: The Philosophy of José Gaos, by Pio Colonnello, Value Inquiry Book Series, 1997. Bogliasco fellow, Liguria, Italy, 2000; vis. scholar Am. Acad. Rome, 2005. Mem. Am. Philos. Assn., Am. and Internat. Soc. for Value Inquiry, Soc. for Aesthetics, Internat. Ctr. for the Arts, Humanities and Value Inquiry (assoc.), Collingwood Soc. (life), Phi Beta Kappa. Avocations: gardening, horseback riding. Office: Claremont McKenna Coll 850 Columbia Ave Claremont CA 91711-3901

MOSS, NANCY EVANS, nurse midwife, women's health nurse; b. Louisville, Sept. 20, 1944; d. Howard Heath and Emily Trimble (Muir) Evans; m. Edward Jewell Moss Jr., Dec. 21, 1984; children: Catherine Howard Rehm, Keith Hayes Rehm. Diploma, Norton Meml. Infirmary, Louisville, 1967; BSN, U. Pitts., 1973; MS in Nursing, U. Ky., 1975; PhD in Health Edn., U. Utah, 1991. Cert. Am. Coll. Nurse Midwives. Mem. clin. faculty dept. ob-gyn. U. Utah Coll. Medicine, Salt Lake City; asst. prof. U. Ky. Coll. Nursing, Lexington; asst. prof., dir. nurse midwifery ednl. program East Carolina U., Greenville, N.C.; prof., dir. nurse-midwifery ednl. program U. Cin. Mem. Am. Coll. Nurse-Midwives (bd. dirs.), Sigma Theta Tau. Home: 518 Fawn Run Dr Highland Heights KY 41076-3790 Office Phone: 513-558-5282.

MOSS, PATRICIA L., bank executive; m. Greg Moss; children: Jennifer, Jeffrey. BS in bus. adminstrn., Linfield Coll., Oreg.; masters studies Portland State U.; certification ABA Comml. Banking Sch., U. Okla. From mem. staff to pres., CEO Cascade Bancorp, Bend, Oreg., 1977—99, pres., CEO, 1998—; CEO Bank of the Cascades, Bend, Oreg., 1998—. Bd. dirs. Cascade Bancorp, Bank of the Cascades, Aquilla Tax-Free Trust of Oreg., Ctrl. Oreg. Ind. Health Svcs., MDU Resources Group Inc., 2003—. Adv. bd. Oreg. State U. Cascade Campus. Named Disting. Citizen of Yr., Bend C. of C., Ctrl. Oreg. Bus. Woman of Yr. Mem.: Ind. Cmty. Bankers Assn. Am., Oreg. Bankers Assn. (bd. dir.), Oreg. Women's Forum. Office: Cascade Bancorp 1100 NW Wall St Bend OR 97701*

MOSS, PRINCESS RENAI, elementary school educator; b. Fredericksburg, Va., Apr. 26, 1961; d. Ernest and Hazel Jeanette Moss. BA, Mary Washington Coll., Fredericksburg, 1983; MEd, U. Va., Charlettesville, 1986. Tchr. Louisa (Va.) County Pub. Sch., 1983—. Apptd. mem. P-16 edn. coun., Richmond, Va., 2005—. Mem.: NEA (bd. dirs. 2006—), Va. Educators Assn. (pres. 2004—). Baptist. Home: 13001 Chimney Stone Ct Richmond VA 23233 Office: Va Edn Asn 116 S 3rd St Richmond VA 23219 Office Phone: 804-648-5801. Office Fax: 904-775-8399. Business E-Mail: pmoss@veanea.org.

MOSS, SARA E., delivery service executive, lawyer; b. NYC, Nov. 13, 1946; BA magna cum laude, U. Mass., 1968; JD, NYU, 1974. Bar: N.Y. 1975, U.S. Dist. Ct. (so. dist.) N.Y. 1976, U.S. Ct. Appeals (2d cir.) 1975, U.S. Tax Ct. 1983, U.S. Supreme Ct. 1983. Law clk. to Hon. Constance Baker Motley U.S. Dist. Ct. (so. dist.) N.Y., 1974-75, asst. U.S. atty., 1978-81; law clk. Davis Polk & Wardell, 1975-78, 80-84; ptnr. Howard Smith & Levin, 1984-96; v.p., gen. counsel Pitney Bowes, Inc., Stamford, Conn., 1996—2003; sr. v.p., gen. counsel, sec. Estée Lauder, NYC, 2003—. Instr. Nat. Inst. Trial Advocacy. Contbr. articles to profl. jours. Mem. ABA, Fed. Bar Coun. (trustee 1996—), Am. Arbitration Assn. (bd. dirs.), N.Y. Coun. Def. Lawyers (bd. dirs. 1994-96), Assn. Bar City of N.Y. (mem. fed. cts. com., mem. litig. com.), Phi Beta Kappa. Office: Estee Lauder 767 Fifth Ave New York NY 10153 Home: 325 Central Park W Apt 3N New York NY 10025-7686 Office Phone: 212-572-4200. Business E-Mail: emoss@estee.com.

MOSS, SUSAN, nurse, small business owner; b. Youngstown, Ohio, Aug. 17, 1940; d. Jarlath G. and Sara G. (Curley) Carney; divorced; children: John P., Jerri Ann Moss Winn. Lic. nurse, Choffin Sch., 1973; AS in Am. Bus. Mgmt., Youngstown State U., 1992. Surg. scrub nurse St. Elizabeth Hosp., Youngstown, 1972-78; office mgr. Moss Equipment Co., North Jackson, Ohio, 1978-83; pvt. duty nurse Salem, Ohio, 1979—; night nurse supr. Gateways for Better Living, Youngstown, 1982-84; owner Laura's Bride and Formal Wear, Salem, 1987—; CEO Strawberry Sunshine Svcs. Co., Salem, 1994—; co-owner McCollough Retirement Home for Ladies, 1998—. Cons. Edith R. Nolf, Inc., Salem. Author: (novelette) Turlaleen, (novels) The Document Box, Her Other Life, The Energy Makers. Water therapy aide Easter Seal Soc., Youngstown, 1970-75, bd. trustees, 1973-75; mem. Hear, Now, Denver, 1989; mem. regional bd. rev. Selective Svcs. Mem. LPN Assn. Ohio, Bus. and Profl. Women, Youngstown State U. Alumni Club, Short Hills Lit. Soc., Beta Sigma Phi (v.p., Silver Circle award 1986, Order of the Rose 1987). Democrat. Roman Catholic. Avocations: writing, painting, music, public speaking, travel.

MOSS, SUSAN HECHT, artist, writer; b. Chgo., May 6, 1944; d. Benjamin Franklin and Amy (Hecht) Moss; m. Glen Galloway, Jan. 15, 1964 (div. Sept. 1974). BA in Art/Psychology with honors, U. Nev., 1966; MFA, Otis Art Inst., 1970. Spkr. World Conf. on Breast Cancer, Canada. Author: Keep Your Breasts! Preventing Breast Cancer the Natural Way (in German, Dutch and English), 1994, 6th edit., 2002; contbr. poetry to profl. publs.; exhibitions include David Findlay Jr. Gallery, N.Y., Albright-Knox Mus., Forum Gallery, N.Y., Represented in permanent collections L.A. County Mus. Art, Skirtball Mus., L.A., Laguna Mus. Art. Mem.: Cancer Ctrl. Soc. (spkr. 1996, 2002, 2003). Democrat. Jewish. Avocations: swimming, weightlifting, hiking, filmmaking. Studio: 4767 York Blvd Los Angeles CA 90042-1648 Home: 1879 Montiflora Ave Los Angeles CA 90041-2016 Office Phone: 323-255-3382. Personal E-mail: susanbc@aol.com.

MOSS, SUSAN P., biology professor; d. Daniel and Mary Anne Moss; life ptnr. Scott Bailey. BA, Mercer U., Macon, Ga., 1987; MS, U. Okla., Norman, 1991; MS in Tchg., U. Fla., Gainesville, 1998. Adj. biology prof. Santa Fe C.C., Gainesville, 1998—99, Valencia C.C., Orlando, Fla., 2002—03; asst. prof. biology Madisonville C.C., Madisonville, Ky., 2003—. Dir. Audubon ecology workshop Nat. Audubon Soc., Greenwich, Conn., 1999—2000. Mem.: Assn. Coll. and U. Biology Educators. Office: Madisonville CC 2000 College Dr Madisonville KY 42431 Office Phone: 270-824-1837. Business E-Mail: susan.moss@kctcs.edu.

MOSSMAN, KAROLYN R., elementary school educator; b. Casper, Wyo., Sept. 19, 1957; d. Robert Louis and Theresa Veronica (Cravalho) Browning; m. Leonard James Habersham, July 23, 2002; children: Lenora Habersham, Leonard Habersham Jr., Shae Habersham, Kyle Habersham; m. Chris S. Mossman (div.); children: Ryan, Krislii. BA, U. No. Colo., Greeley, 1979; MA in Intermediate Edn., U. Hawaii, Honolulu, 1999. Tchr. Kahului Elem. Sch., Hawaii, 1979—80, Maui H.S., 1980—81, 1985—98, Baldwin H.S., Wailuku, 1981—85, Kalama Intermediate Sch., Makawao, 1998—. Mailing: 3359 Lower Kula Rd Kula HI 96790-8733

MOSS-SALENTIJN, LETTY (ALEIDA MOSS-SALENTIJN), anatomist, educator; b. Amsterdam, The Netherlands, Apr. 14, 1943; arrived in U.S., 1968; d. Ewoud and Johanna Maria (Schoonhoven) Salentijn; m. Melvin Lionel Moss, Apr. 17, 1970. DDS, State U. Utrecht, Netherlands, 1967, PhD, 1976. Asst. prof. histology State U. Utrecht, 1967-68; asst. prof. Columbia U., N.Y.C., 1968-74, assoc. prof., 1974-86, prof., 1986—, Edwin S. Robinson prof., 1999—, dir. dental radiology, 1980-86, dir. grad. program dental sci., 1986—, dir. postdoctoral affairs, 1987-90, asst. dean postdoctoral programs, 1990-94, assoc. dean acad. affairs, 1994—2005, sr. assoc. dean acad. affairs, 2005—. Author: Orofacial Histology & Embryology, 1972; Dental and Oral Tissues, 1980, 2d edit., 1984, 3d edit., 1990; contbr. chpts. to books, articles to profl. jours. Fellow Royal Microscopical Soc., Am. Coll. Dentists, NY Acad. Dentistry; mem. Am. Assn. Anatomists, Internat. Assn. Dental Rsch., Am. Soc. Biomechs., Sigma Xi (chpt. sec. 1980-87, pres. 1987-89, 98-99), Omicron Kappa Upsilon (pres. local chpt. 1987). Avocation: stained glass art. Home: 560 Riverside Dr Apt 20K New York NY 10027-3239 Office: Columbia Univ Coll Dental Medicine Sr Assoc Dean Acad Affairs 630 W 168th St New York NY 10032-3702 Office Phone: 212-305-8334. Business E-Mail: lm23@columbia.edu.

MOSS-VREELAND, PATRICIA ELLEN, artist; b. N.Y.C., July 26, 1951; m. Robert Moss-Vreeland. BFA, Phila. Coll. Art, 1974; postgrad., Tyler Sch. Art, Rome, 1972-73. Artist, Phila., 1975—. One-woman shows include Marian Locks Gallery, Phila., 1979, 83, 88, Ptnrs. Gallery, Bethesda, Md., 1988, Penn State Gallery, Harrisburg, 1988, Arronson Gallery, U. of Arts, Phila., 1993, 99-2000, Univ. City Sci. Ctr., Esther Klein Gallery, Phila.; exhibited in group shows at Marian Locks Gallery, Phila., 1975, 77, 81, Inst. Contemporary Art, U. Pa., Phila., 1976, Cheltenham Art Ctr., Pa., 1977, 85, Squib Gallery, Princeton, N.J., 1977, Glassboro (N.J.) State Coll., 1977, Freedman Gallery, Albright Coll., Reading, Pa., 1978, Pa. Acad. Fine Arts, Phila., The Bklyn. Mus. Art, N.Y., 1980, Am. Cultural Ctr., Brussels,; commd. to design and fabricare Meml. Rm., Holocaust Mus. Houston, 1995-96. Recipient Drucker Painting prize Cheltenham Art Ctr., 1977, Phila. Mus. Art Purchase award Phila. Mus. Art, 1985, Purchase award Beaver Coll. Collection, 1985, Winning Design award Holocaust Edn. Ctr. and Meml. Mus., 1993. Mem. Am. Edn. Rsch. Assn., Coll. Art Assn. Home and Office: 2229 Bainbridge St Philadelphia PA 19146-1130 E-mail: mossvreelands@earthlink.net.

MOSTER, MARY CLARE, public relations executive; b. Morristown, NJ, Apr. 7, 1950; d. Clarence R. and Ruth M. Moster; m. Louis C. Williams, Jr., Oct. 4, 1987. BA in English with honors, Douglass Coll., 1972; MA in English Lit., Univ. Chgo., 1973. Accredited pub. rels. counselor. Editor No. Trust Bank, Chgo., 1973-75, advt. supr., 1975-77, communications officer, 1977-78; account exec. Hill & Knowlton, Inc., Chgo., 1978-80, v.p., 1980-83, sr. v.p., 1983-87, sr. v.p., mng. dir., 1987-88; staff v.p. comms. Navistar Internat. Corp., Chgo., 1988-93; v.p. corp. comms. Comdisco, Inc., Rosemont, Ill., 1993—2002; sr. v.p. L.C. Williams and Assocs., Chgo., 2002—. Adj. prof. Integrated Mktg. Comm. Medill Sch., Northwestern U., 2000-05 Author poetry, poetry translation. Bd. govs. Met. Planning Coun., Chgo., 1988-94; fellow Leadership Greater Chgo., 1989-90; bd. dirs. New City

YMCA, Chgo., 1986-92; corp. devel. bd. Steppenwolf Theatre Co., Chgo., 1988-90; active Chgo. Network, 1994—, bd. dirs., 1996-99. Mem. Nat. Investor Rels. Inst. (bd. dirs. 1988-89, 90-99, pres. Chgo. chpt. 1998-99), Arthur W. Page Soc., Pub. Rels. Soc. Am., Internat. Women's Forum. Avocations: sailing, cross country skiing, book groups, biking. Office: L C Williams & Assocs 150 N Michigan Ave Ste 3800 Chicago IL 60601

MOTCH, MARJORIE MCCULLOUGH, service organization executive; b. Cin., July 12, 1923; d. Robert Stedman and Mildred (Rogers) McCullough; m. Homer E. Lunken, Apr. 15, 1944 (dec. 1970); children: Karen Lunken- (dec.), Kathryn Lunken Summers, Margo Lunken Yesner; m. William McLeod Ittmann, Mar. 17, 1972 (dec. 1982); m. Harold Hiatt, Apr. 14, 1984 (dec. 1999); m. Graham E. Marx, Jan. 4, 2003 (dec. 2003); m. Arthur E. Motch Jr., Sept. 18, 2004 (dec. 2005). Student, U. Cin., Ohio, 1941—43, DFA (hon.), 2003. Active Girl Scouts U.S., 1962—, chmn. conv. com., 1972, del. world convs., 1969, 72, 75, 78, 81, 84, 87, 93, chmn. pub. relations com., 1963-66, mem. nat. exec. com., 1963-75, mem. nat. bd., 1962—, 4th v.p., 1966-69, 1st v.p., 1969-72, nat. pres., 1972-75, chmn. nat. adv. council, 1975-82, mem. birthplace adv. com., 1980-97. Vice chmn. world conf., Orleans, France, 1981; world com. World Assn. Girl Guides and Girl Scouts, 1978-87, vice chmn., 1984-87; trustee emeritus U. Cin. Found. Regional dir. Assn. Jr. Leagues Am., 1958—60, nat. pres., 1960—62; mem. br. Nat. Assembly for Social Policy and Devel., 1968—71; mem. exec. com. Coun. Nat. Orgns. for Children and Youth, 1960—62, 1968—72; mem. br. Jr. League Cin., 1944—58, Nat. Tng. Labs., 1963—66; mem. policy com. Ctr. Vol. Soc., 1971—72; mem. Ohio Citizens Coun., 1956—58; mem. bd. advisors U. Cin. Coll. Nursing, 2000—; bd. dirs. 7th Presbyn. Ch., 1967—74, 1985—, ruling elder, 1976—78, 2000—, chmn. bd. trustees, 1992—94; sr. warden St. Martin's in the Field, Biddeford Pool, Maine; bd. dirs. United Way Am., 1962—67, sec., 1965—66, v.p., 1966—67, 1989—; bd. dirs. Fine Arts Fund, 2002—, Coll. Prep. Sch., Cin., 1962—69, pres., 1964—69; bd. dirs. Cin. Speech and Hearing Ctr., 1955—66, v.p., 1958—62, pres., 1963—66, trustee emeritus, 1966—; mem. bd. Children's Theatre, Cin., 1948—58, pres., 1948—50; bd. dirs. Cmty. Health and Welfare Coun. Cin., 1957—63, Hamilton County (Ohio) Rsch. Found., 1963—65, Cancer Family Care, Cin., 1971—72, Boys Clubs Greater Cin., Marjorie P. Lee Home for the Aged, Ctrl. Psychiat. Clinic, Music Hall Assn., Cin. Symphony Orch., Beechwood Home for Incurables, 1975—87, St. Margaret Hall, 1991—, Cin. Civic Garden Ctr., 1992—95, Greater Cin. Found., 1979—87, Ctrl. Clinic, 2000—, YWCA, 1998—, Fine Arts Fund, 2002—. Recipient Mary Herriman award, 2000, Mardee Wachs Vol. Svc. award, Hearing, Speech, and Deaf Ctrs., 2006. Mem. Olave Baden-Powell Soc. (v.p. 1991-93, pres. 1993-97), World Found. for Girl Guides and Girl Scouts (v.p. 1989—), Garden Club Am. (vice chmn. founder's fund 1991-92), Am. Psychiat. Assn. Aux. (bd. dirs., rec. sec. 1991-92). Home: 2353 Bedford Ave Cincinnati OH 45208-2656

MOTEN, DARLENE, elementary school educator; d. Spencer and Arlishie Moten; children: Nichole Antoinette, Ana Lisa, Candy Sue, Sandy Darlene, Micah Jeremiah, Ann Marie, Taheerah Janiece, Donald Vance, Ebonee Lashey, Aleizah Janae. BS in Bus. Edn., U. Ariz., Tucson, 1975; MEd, U. Ariz., 1981. Sec. U. Ariz., Tucson, 1972—76; tchr. bus. edn. Amphitheater Pub. Schs., Tucson, 1977—. Libr. rev. com. Amphitheater Pub. Schs., Tucson, 1995—99; poetry contest judge Amphitheater Mid. Sch., Tucson, 2004—. Dir. of children's ministry Mt. Olive Ch. Of God In Christ, Tucson, 1975; state children's dir. Ch. Of God In Christ, Phoenix, 1986. Recipient Cmty. Svc. award, Mayor City of Tucson, 2000, Pima County Supr. Dan Eckstrom, 2000. Mem.: NEA (assoc.), Amphitheater Edn. Assn. (assoc.). Penecostal. Avocations: reading, travel, writing, home remodeling. Office: Amphitheater Public Schools 315 E Prince Rd Tucson AZ 85705 Office Phone: 520-696-6305. E-mail: dmoten@amphi.com.

MOTEN, SARAH ELIZABETH, federal agency administrator, educator; b. Norfolk, Va., Dec. 9, 1941; d. Woodrow Wilson and Mary Elizabeth (Peelich) Price; 1 child, Michele Denise Moten. B.S., Hampton U., 1964; M.A., George Washington U., 1970; Ed.D., Atlanta U., 1979. Tchr. D.C. Pub. Schs., Washington, 1964-67, tchr. reading, 1967-70, counselor, 1970-74, asst. prin., 1974-80; adminstr. research Howard U., Washington, 1980-82; country dir. U.S. Peace Corps, Swaziland, 1982; deputy asst. sec. refugee programs, Dept. State; coord, Edn. Devel. Democracy Initiative; edn. div. chief, Office Sustainable Devel., US Agency Internat. Develop.; lectr. Spelman Coll., Atlanta, 1977-78; asst. to pres. Morehouse Coll., Atlanta, 1978-79; chairperson Nat. Council for Accreditation Tchr. Edn., Washington, 1970-82. Speaker Nat. Black Republicans, San Francisco, 1980; mem. Coalition for Social and Econ. Change, San Francisco, 1980; mem. U.S. del. UN Conf. for Women, Nairobi, Kenya, 1985. Rockefeller Found. fellow, 1977. Episcopalian. Avocations: reading; bowling; playing cards. Office: Ronald Reagan Bldg 1300 Pennsylvania Ave NW Romm 4 07 105 Washington DC 20523-4600

MOTT, MARY ELIZABETH, retired computer educator; b. West Hartford, Conn., July 10, 1931; d. Marshall Amos and Mary Herman Mott. BA, Conn. Coll. for Women, 1953; MA, Western Res. U., 1963. Cert. tchr., Ohio; cert. computer tchr., Ohio. Mgr. sales promotion Cleve. Electric Illuminating Co., 1953-60; tchr. Newbury Bd. Edn., Ohio, 1960-67, West Geauga Bd. Edn., Chesterland, Ohio, 1967—97, ret., 1997. Chmn. state certification com. in computers ECCO, Mayfield, Ohio, 1983—, exec. bd., 1980—. Asst. dir. West Geauga Day Camp, Chesterland, 1968. Mem. Ednl. Computer Consortium Ohio, West Geauga Edn. Assn. (exec. bd. 1975-97), Delta Kappa Gamma. E-mail: pci238@aol.com.

MOTTRAM-DOSS, RENÉE, corporate financial executive; b. Erie, Pa., Apr. 7, 1939; d. Robert Harlan and Anita Gray; m. Arden Doss Jr., Mar. 7, 1986; children from previous marriage: Lisa Marie Mottram, Jeffrey Scott Mottram. Student, Barry U., 1968-70, Vt. State Coll., 1975-76. Various positions D.W.G. Corp., Royal Crown Cola, Arby's, Victor Posner Affiliated Cos., Miami Beach, Fla., 1972-90, sr. v.p., 1989—; chmn. Renar Devel. Co., St. Lucie West, Fla., 1990—. Bd. dirs. Coconut Grove Playhouse, Miami, Barry U., Miami. Recipient Twin award YWCA, 1984; named Outstanding Woman of Yr. Dade County Fla., 1983. Office: Renar Development Co 7500 Reserve Blvd Port Saint Lucie FL 34986-3237

MOTYKA, SUSANNE VICTORIA, music educator; b. Manhattan, N.Y., May 29, 1949; d. John Szenher and Anna Victoria Galluccio; m. William Joseph Motyka, Aug. 29, 1976; children: Matthew, Caroline, Eric. B in Music Edn., Coll. Misericordia, 1971. Cert. secondary tchg. Tchr., Tunkhannock, Pa., 1971—73, 1976—80; head music dept. Wyoming Sem., Kingston, Pa., 1973—76; choral dir. Dallas (Pa.) H.S., 1990; tchr. Gate of Heaven Sch., Dallas, 1991—2002. Orch. dir. Bishop O'Reilly, Kingston, 2000—02; choir dir., organist Gate of Heaven Ch., Dallas, 2000—02; counselor Jr. Mozart, Wilkes-Barre, Pa., 1976—2002. Recipient Paderewski award, Nat. Coll. Musicians, Washington, 1997—2001. Mem.: NCTA, Music Educators Nat. Conf., Nat. Guild Piano Tchrs. Home: 3 Laselle Ave Shavertown PA 18708

MOTZ, DIANA GRIBBON, federal judge; b. Washington, July 15, 1943; d. Daniel McNamara and Jane (Retzler) Gribbon; m. John Frederick Motz, Sept. 20, 1968; children: Catherine Jane, Daniel Gribbon. BA, Vassar Coll., 1965; LLB, U. Va., 1968. Bar: U.S. Dist. Ct. Md. 1969, U.S. Ct. Appeals (4th cir.) 1969, U.S. Supreme Ct. 1980. Assoc. Piper & Marbury, Balt., 1968—71; asst. atty. gen. State of Md., Balt., 1972—81, chief of litigation, 1981—86; ptnr. Frank, Bernstein, Conaway & Goldman, Balt., 1986—91; judge Md. Ct. of Special Appeals, 1991—94, U.S. Ct. Appeals (4th Cir.), 1994—. Mem.: ABA, Fed. Cts. Study Com., Lawyers Round Table, Md. Bar Found., Am. Bar Found., Am. Law Inst., Balt. City Bar Assn. (exec. com. 1988), Md. Bar Assn., Wranglers Law Club. Roman Catholic. Office: 920 US Courthouse 101 W Lombard St Ste 920 Baltimore MD 21201-2611

MOTZKIN, JUDITH E., artist; b. Mar. 20, 1954; d. Arthur and Marilyn M.; m. Richard Mandel; children: Sasha, Jamin. BA, Cornell U., 1976. Artist Clay Dragon Studios, Cambridge, Mass., 1977-85; owner, artist Judy Motzkin Studio, Cambridge, 1985—. Founder Cambridgeport Artists Open Studios. One-woman shows include Gallery 57, Cambridge, Mass., 1998, Grohe Gallery, Boston, 2000, An Am. Craftsman, N.Y.C., 2000, Zeitgeist Gallery, Cambridge, 2001, Left Bank Gallery, Wellfleet, Mass., 2001.

MOUDY, LINDA ANN, elementary school educator; d. Shag and Mattie Ruth Moudy. BS, Tex. Tech U., Lubbock, 1970; MEd, West Tex. A&M U., Canyon, 1984. Tchr. Hobbs Ind. Sch. Dist., N.Mex., 1970—85, Frenship Ind. Sch. Dist., Wolfforth, Tex., 1985—. Head dept. social studies Frenship Mid. Sch., 2006—. Mem.: NEA (life). Office Phone: 806-866-4443.

MOULEDOUS, PIERRETTE MARIE, music educator; d. Roland Marie Robert Palasset and Marthe Germaine Normand; children: Alfred Eugene III, Laurie Michele Farris, Daniel Walter. Studied with Paul Kovalov, Russian Conservatory; studied with Isabelle Poncin and Reine Gianoll, Ecole Normale de Musique; MusM, So. Meth. U., Dallas, Tex., 1970. Head Dept. Piano El Centro Coll., Dallas, 1966—70, Eastfield Coll., Mesquite, Tex., 1970—. Staff pianist Am. Inst. Musical Studies, Graz, Austria, 1972—77; co-founder, co-dir. French Organ Seminar, Paris, 1985—91; founder Eastfield Metroplex East Piano Festival, Mesquite, 2004—. Musician (founder): Trio Accord, 1984—91, Elysee Piano Quartet, 1994—2006. Cons. Mesquite Symphony Orch. Bd., 2001—05. Recipient Excellence in Tchg. award, Nat. Inst. Staff and Orgnl. Devel., 1990. Office Phone: 972-860-7136. Business E-Mail: pxm4433@dcccd.edu.

MOULES, DEBORAH ANN, not-for-profit developer; b. Milton, Mass., Nov. 11, 1955; m. Brandon Thomas Boyd, Sept. 7, 1987; 1 child, Sienna Nicole Boyd. BFA, U. Mass., 1980; MFA cum laude, SUNY, New Paltz, 1984. Instr. Middlesex C.C., Burlington, Mass., 1988, North Shore C.C., Beverly, Mass., 1989; art program coord. Inst. Family, Danvers, Mass., 1985-96; art expressive cons. Women's Crisis Ctr., Newburyport, Mass., 1995-97, Cape Ann Families, Gloucester, Mass., 1998; founder, exec. dir., pres. S.A.F.E. Studio, Ipswich, Mass., 1993—. Mem. workshop com. North Shore Clay Works, Ipswich, 1989—96; art cons. Merrimack Sch., Chelmsford, Mass., 1990—96. Exhibitions include Harvard U., 1992, Ipswich, 1995, Radclift, Mass., 1995. Mem. adv. bd. Montessori Sch., Topsfield, Mass., 1997—99; mem. Cultural Coun., Ipswich, 1992—98; mem. edn. com. Domestic Violence Roundtable, Ipswich, 1998—99. Grantee Oper., McCarthy Family Found., 1996—98, Forest Found., 1997—98, Dolphin Trust, 1997. Mem.: Ipswich Bus. Assn., Assn. Granmakers Mass. Avocations: reading, dance, performance art, walking.

MOULIN, LINDA LONG, science educator; d. Larry E. and Willa G. Long; children: Brett Richard, Jackson Jeffrey. BS in Biology, U. Kans., Lawrence, 1990—94; M in Ednl. Leadership, Emporia State U., Kans., 2003—06. K-12 Bldg. Leadership Kans., 2006, cert. Tchr. Kans. Dept. Edn. Sci. tchr. Blue Valley West HS, Overland Park, 2001—, Blue Valley West H.S., Overland Park, 2003—06. Freshman transition coord. Blue Valley West, Overland Park, 2003—06. Grantee Goals 200, U.S. Govt., 1997, Servive Learning grant, Blue Valley Edn. Found., 2004. Office: Blue Valley West HS 16200 Antioch Overland Park KS 66085 Office Phone: 913-239-3700. Personal E-mail: lndmoulin@yahoo.com.

MOULTON, GRACE CHARBONNET, retired physicist; b. New Orleans, Nov. 1, 1923; d. Wilfred J. and Louise A. (Hellmers) Charbonnet; m. William Gates Moulton, June 1, 1947; children: Paul Charbonnet Moulton, Nancy Gates Moulton. BA, Tulane U., 1944; MS, U. Ill., 1948; PhD, U. Ala., 1962. Asst. prof. physics U. Ala., Tuscaloosa, 1962-65, Fla. State U., Tallahassee, 1965-74, assoc. prof. physics, 1974-80, prof. physics, 1980-91, prof. emerita, 1991. Cons. State Bd. Regents, Fla., 1985-90, Fla. Univ. System, 1985, 90. Referee jour. articles Jour. Chem. Physics, Radiation Rsch.; contbr. many sci. rsch. articles to profl. jours. Scholar, U. Ill.; Four Yr. Undergrad. scholar, Tulane U., rsch. grantee, NIH. Mem. Am. Phys. Soc., (mem. coun. southeastern sect. 1988-92). Avocations: gardening, music (classical and folk), birding. Office: Fla State U Dept Physics Tallahassee FL 32306 Business E-Mail: gmoulton@phy.fsu.edu.

MOULTON, MARY E., secondary school educator; d. George Michael Menzik and Monica Cecilia (Mellen) Mellen Menzik; 1 child, Samantha Morgan Moulton Burgess. BS in Pol Sci., Idaho State U., Pocatello, 1989; MS in Edn., Utah State U., Vernal, 2006. Cert. tchr. Idaho, ESL tchr. Utah. Tchr. social studies Marsh Valley HS, McCammon, Idaho, 1990—93, Uintah HS, Vernal, Utah, 1993—. Accreditation team State Office of Edn., Salt Lake City, 2003—; adj. prof. Utah State U., Vernal, 2004—. Registrar for voting Uintah County Clerk's Office, Vernal, 1994—2006; vol. Com. to Elect Ronald Regan, Pocatello, Idaho, 1979—80; edn. instr. St. James Cath. Ch., Vernal, 1994—97. Named Tchr. of Yr., Uintah HS, 1999—2000; recipient Heart of Uintah award, 1999—2000. Mem.: Nat. Profl. Bus. Women's Assn. (assoc.), Utah Edn. Assn. (assoc.), Uintah Edn. Assn. (assoc.; bldg. rep. 2000—06). Democrat. Roman Catholic. Avocations: travel, sewing, walking, knitting. Office: Uintah High Sch 1880 West 500 North Vernal UT 84078 Office Phone: 435-781-3110 ext 2691. Business E-Mail: mary.moulton@uintah.net.

MOULTON, SARA, chef, magazine editor; m. Bill Moulton; children: Ruth, Sam. Grad., U. Mich., 1974, Culinary Inst. Am., 1977; postgrad. stagaire with a master chef, Chartres, France, 1979. With Julia Child and More Co., 1979; mem. test kitchen Gourmet mag., 1984—88, exec. chef, 1988—, Good Morning Am., food corr., 1997, food editor; sous chef La Tulipe, NY; instr. Peter Kump's NY Cooking Sch. Co-founder NY Women's Culinary Alliance. Host Cooking Live, Food Network, 1996—2002, Sara's Secrets, 2002—; co-author (with Jean Anderson): (cookbooks) Good Morning America Cut the Calories Cookbook, 2000; author: Sara Moulton Cooks at Home, 2002, Sara's Secrets for Weeknight Meals, 2005. Office: Sara Moulton Enterprises Inc 130 W 24th St 3B New York NY 10011 Business E-Mail: sara@saramoulton.com.*

MOUNT, CINDY KAY, small business owner; b. Inglewood, Calif., Aug. 30, 1960; d. Barry Allen and Valora Zell (Dorsey) Pirtle; m. Ross Keenan Mount, Apr. 14, 1984; children: Kelly Ann, Christopher Ross, Cody James. AA, Glendale Community Coll., 1980. Sr. exec. sec. Bank Am., Newport Beach, Calif., 1979-84; office mgr. McGuinness & Assocs., Newport Beach, Calif., 1984-86; adminstrv. mgr. Bank Am., Laguna Niguel, Calif., 1986-90; owner Ribbons, Ruffles & Lace, Costa Mesa, Calif., 1988—. Skincare cons. Arbonne Internat. Organizer Mom & Tot Sunshine Playgroup, Costa Mesa, 1990—. Republican. Home and Office: 16195 Mount Nimbus St Fountain Valley CA 92708-1743

MOUNT, WILLIE LANDRY, state legislator; b. Lake Charles, La., Aug. 25, 1949; d. Lee Robert and Willie Veatrice (McCullor) Landry; m. Benjamin Wakefield Mount, Aug. 19, 1976. BS, McNeese State U., 1971. Geophys. asst. La. Land and Exploration, Lake Charles, La., 1971-76; pharm. rep. Lederle, Lake Charles, 1976-80; realtor May Kay Hopkins, Lake Charles, 1976-87; co-owner Paper Place, Lake Charles, 1991-95; mayor City of Lake Charles, 1993—2000; mem. La. State Senate, 2000—, mem. select com. on consumer protection, mem. jud. C, health and welfare, legis. audit adv. commn., bond commn., mem. state tch. adv. commn., joint juvenile justice commn., millennium port com., sch. fin. rev. commn., mem. edn. com., vice chair joint legis. com. on capital outlay, chmn. revenue and fiscal affairs com. Gov. Violent Crime & Homicide Task Force, Baton Rouge, 1993—95; mem. steering com. La. conf. Mayors bd. pres. La. Asset Mgmt. Pool Bd., 1997. Guest condr. Lake Charles Symphony, 1992; active La. Mcpl. Assn., Baton Rouge, 1995-98; pres. Jr. League of Lake Charles; mem. state interagy. coordinating coun. Dyslexia Study Com.; mem. adv. bd. S.W. La. Literacy Coalition; mem. adv. coun. Pet Overpopulation; active First United Meth. Ch., La. Meth. Conf., McNeese State U. Found., Prevent Child Abuse bd. Micro-Enterprise Devel. Alliance of La. Bd., McNeese State U. Found. Bd., St. Patrick Hosp. Bd. Councillors, Coastal Plain Conservancy Bd., United Way, Children's Miracle Network; exec. com. Coun. for a Better La. Recipient Spiritual Aims award Kiwanis Club, 1991, Cmty. Svc. award, 1995, Citizen of Yr. 1996-97, Dorthea Combre award NAACP, 1994, La. Mcpl. Assn. Cmty. Achievement award, 1995-97, Disting. Citizen award Boy Scouts Am., 1999, Patron Architecture, 2000, Disting. Alumni award McNeese State U., 2000, Golden Apple award Delta Kappa Gamma, 2002, Disting. Svc. award La. Restaurant Assn., 2002, Spl. Friend of La. Mcpl. Assn. award, 2003, Wilton Bellard Jr. award S.W. La. Ctr. for Health Svcs., Ron Schroeder award MEDAL; named Woman of Yr., Quota Club, 1991, Citizen of Yr., Women's com. S.W. La., 1992, Woman of Yr., Pub. Ofcl. of Yr. Msgr. Cramers KC, Pub. Ofcl. of Yr., NASW, 1997, Legislator of Yr., La. Orthopaedic Assn., Champion for Children, Prevent Child Abuse. Mem.: LWV, S.W. La. Mayor's Assn. (chmn. 1993—94). Home: 205 Shell Beach Dr Lake Charles LA 70601-5933 Office: PO Box 3004 Lake Charles LA 70602-3004 Business E-Mail: lasen27@legis.state.la.us.

MOUNTAIN, JANET, foundation administrator, former computer company executive; BBA, U. Tex., Austin; MBA, Harvard Bus. Sch. Former sr. consultant Andersen Consulting, Houston; v.p. & gen. mgr., US consumer div. Dell, Inc., 1993—2003; exec. dir. Michael & Susan Dell Found., 2003—. Named a Young Global Leader, Forum of Young Global Leaders, 2006. Office: Michael & Susan Dell Found One Dell Way Round Rock TX 78682*

MOUNTFORD, ALISON LEIGH, psychologist; b. Orange, N.J., Oct. 6, 1959; d. Donald Franklin and Lura Allen Mountford; m. Peter Wood DiIanni, Oct. 11, 1997; children: Jackson Mountford DiIanni, Emma Mountford DiIanni. BA with honors, Trinity Coll., 1981; MAT, Brown U., 1982; PsyD, Rutgers U., 1993. Lic. psychologist Mass., 1995. Clin. intern, fellow psychology McLean Hosp./Harvard Med. Sch., Belmont, Mass., 1990—91; sch. psychologist Wellesley (Mass.) H.S., 1991—. Asst. attending psychologist McLean Hosp., Belmont, 1995—97; adj. faculty U. Mass., Boston, 1997; pvt. practice, Brookline, Mass., 1995—; bd. mem. Polaris Found., Jaffrey, NH. Mem.: APA. Avocations: swimming, reading. Office: Ste 4B 1180 Beacon St Brookline MA 02446 Office Phone: 617-738-7660. E-mail: alison_mountford@wellesley.mcc.edu.

MOUNTS, KRISTI LYNN, personal trainer; b. Clyde, Ohio, Oct. 8, 1980; d. Stanley and Cynthia Mounts. BS, Defiance Coll., Ohio, 2002; MS, Ga. State U., Atlanta, 2004. Cert. athletic trainer Nat. Athletic Trainers Assn., Ga. Bd. Athletic Trainers, CPR for Profl. Rescuer ARC, Ga., CPR ARC, Ga. Grad. asst. athletic trainer Westminster Sch., Atlanta, 2002—04; head cert. athletic trainer Whitefield Acad., Mableton, Ga., 2004—. Mem.: Nat. Strength and Conditioning Assn. Office: Whitefield Acad One Whitefield Dr Mableton GA 30126 Office Phone: 321-206-9821. E-mail: kristim@whitefieldacademy.com.

MOUNTS, NANCY, secondary school educator; Tchr. home econs. North High Sch., Sioux City, Iowa; tech. prep. specialist Cen. Campus, Sioux City, 1995—; dir. Northwest Iowa Ctr. Teaching and Learning Morningside Coll. Recipient State Tchr. of Yr. Home Econs. award Iowa, 1992. Office: Cen Campus 1121 Jackson St Sioux City IA 51105-1434

MOUSSATOS, MARTHA ANN TYREE, librarian; b. Parris Island, S.C., Sept. 18, 1936; d. Frank La Prade and Vireen Florrie (Varn) Tyree; m. Apostolos Harilaos Moussatos, June 27, 1959; children— Vasiliana Vireen, Harilaos Apostolos. B.A., Columbia Coll., 1958; M.L.S., U. Ariz., 1974. Asst. reference librarian U. S.C., Columbia, 1958-59; librarian Fulton High Sch., Atlanta, 1962; substitute tchr. pub. schs., Sierra Vista, Ariz., 1967-68; librarian Naco Elem. Sch. (Ariz.), 1968-70, Benson High Sch. (Ariz.), 1970-75; head librarian Depot Library, Parris Island, S.C., 1975—99. Author: Young Eliza (play), 1958; Hagar (play), 1980; Marshgrass and Muscadines (poetry), 1980; Scuppernong Wine at Room Temperature (poetry), 1984, (cookbook) The Sandlappers' Salvation Cookbook, 1988; editor: No More Blues Now (poetry), 1990; editor, contbr.: Port Royal Sound (poetry), 1995; contbr. articles to profl. jours. and popular mags. Mem. Historic Port Royal Found. (S.C.), 1976—, bd. dirs., 1981—; active Carteret St. United Meth. Ch. Recipient award as head of outstanding single parent family Beaufort County Homebuilders Assn. (S.C.), 1980. Mem. ALA, Library Assn. Beaufort County, S.C. Library Assn. (editoral com. 1979—), Poetry Soc. S.C. (bd. dirs. 1980-83), Beaufort Writers, Parris Island Poets (founder), Grey Blades, Lydia McAfee Cir. Home: 3011 Hickory St Beaufort SC 29906-6831

MOUTTET, JANE ELIZABETH, school librarian, educator; b. Grand Rapids, Mich., Mar. 23, 1961; d. Roger Willis and Celia Driesens; m. David Frederick Mouttet, June 4, 1988; 3 children. BA, Calvin Coll., 1983. Cert. elem. tchr. ACSI. Tchr., libr. Hilltop Christian Sch., Window Rock, Ariz., 1983—2004. Contbr. column to Christian Libr. Jour., 2002. Mem.: ALA, Soc. Children's Book Writers and Illustrators, Nat. Coun. Tchrs. English, N.Mex. Libr. Assn. E-mail: jane@mouttetfamily.com.

MOUZON, MARGARET WALKER, information services executive; b. Durham, N.C., Aug. 22, 1940; d. James Carlisle and Elizabeth (Walker) M.; m. Wayne T. VanWagoner, 1959 (div. 1971); children: William Thomas VanWagoner, Margaret Michelle Hallgren. BA, U. Mich., 1975, MA in Libr. Sci., 1982. Tchr. Monroe County Sch., Key West, Fla., 1975-79, Grace Luth., Key West, Fla., 1979-80; tchr. math. Ann Arbor (Mich.) Adult Edn., 1984-88; pres. Mouzon Info. Svcs., Ann Arbor, 1983—; editor in chief Am. Disability Evaluation Rsch. Inst., Ann Arbor, 1989—91. Author: (bibliography) Child Passenger Restraint System, 1982, Medical Legal Aspects Of DCE's, 1989, Stress and Disability, 1989. Bd. dirs. LWV. Mem. Nat. Safety Coun., Soc. Automotive Engrs., Assn. Ind. Info. Profls., Mich. Libr. Consortium, Beta Phi Mu, Phi Kappi Phi, Pi Lambda Theta. Home: 2687 Appleway St Ann Arbor MI 48104-1801 Office Phone: 734-662-9227. E-mail: mouzon@mouzon.info.

MOUZON, THELMA P., retired elementary school educator; b. Sumter, SC; d. John and Carrie Mouzon; divorced; children: Ossietta D. Pinkney, Howard O. Pinkney. Student, Morris Coll., 1961, SC State U., 1963, Marywood Coll., 1978, Temple U., 1993. Cert. tchr. SC, Pa. Tchr. Lamar Elem., Latta, SC, 1961—63, West Lee Elem., Bishopvile, SC, 1963—65; tchr. early childhood Blankenburg Child Care, Phila., 1966—72, Harrity Child Care, Phila., 1973—89, Whittier Child Care, Phila., 1989—93; tchr. K-2 John Barry Elem., Phila., 1993—2001; ret., 2001. Treas. 900 Block Assn.; mother Overbrook Gospel Choir, 1990—95; youth dir. 59th St Bapt. Ch., Phila., 1993—, youth usher supr., 1993—, scholarship treas., 1993—, youth ministry, sr. usher, fin. sec. Named Kindergarden Tchr. of Yr., John Barry Elem., 1996, William Ross Honoree Tchr., 2000; recipient Black Hertigate award, 59th St. Bapt. Ch., 2001. Baptist. Avocation: reading. Home: 938 S 58th St Philadelphia PA 19143

MOWRER-REYNOLDS, ELIZABETH LOUISE, educational psychology educator; b. Camden, N.J., Jan. 5, 1955; d. Philip Aubrey and Louise Jamison (Koykka) M.; 1 child, Cali Jo., m. James O. Reynolds. BA, Trenton State U., 1977; MEd, Rutgers U., 1982, EdD, 1990. Rschr. assit. for dyslexia reading grant Rutgers U., New Brunswick, NJ, 1979-84; co-adj. prof. Rutgers Univ., New Brunswick, 1989—90; assoc. prof. U. Idaho, 1990—. Faculty in residence housemother for farmhouse Fraternity, Univ. of Idaho; progam coord. Univ. of Idaho Gifted & Talented. Author: (book) Study Guide for Good and Brophy, 1995, Contemporary Educational Psychology;Study Guides for Woolfolk, 1998, 2001; contbr. articles prof. jour. Recipient Evelyn Headley Award, Rutgers Univ., 1991, Coll. of End. tchg., public service, and advising award, Univ. of Idaho, 1993, Pi Beta Tchg. Excellance Award, 1995, Faculty Tchg. Excellance Award, Univ. of Idaho, 1994, 1995, 2001. Mem. Phi Delta Kappa (rsch. coord. 1991—, chmn. 1991—), Psi Chi, Am. edn. rsch. assoc., 1991—,Northwest Assoc. of Tchr. Educators, 1991—, (state rep., 1992), Am. Assoc. of Univ. Women, 1993, Acad. of Science, 1994—. Lutheran. Avocations: horseback riding, backpacking, camping, fishing, hunting.

MOWREY, CORINNE RUTH, secondary school educator; b. Niles, Mich., Aug. 12, 1950; d. Henry Christian and Alice Mary Kass; m. Frank Arthur Mowrey, June 9, 2001; m. Patrick Jay Hillard (div.); children: Jacqueline Hillard-Conn, Angela Mercy Hillard, Jay Patrick Hillard, Christina Hillard-

Kimble. BA in Psychologhy, Edn. and Math., U. Mich., Ann Arbor, 1972; M of Math. Edn., Ferris State U., Big Rapids, Mich., 2004. Tchr. secondary math. Cadillac Area Pub. Schs., Mich., 1974—. Ajd. faculty math. Baker Coll., Cadillac, 1991—99, Northwestern Mich. Coll., 1994—95. Precinct del. Wexford Rep. Party, Mich., 1980—84, 2004—. Recipient Heart and Soul award, Ctrl. Mich. Tech Prep Partnership Region 7, 2001. Mem.: Mich. Coun. Tchrs. Math., Nat. Coun. Tchrs. Math., Mensa. Avocations: scuba diving, skiing, bridge. Home: 610 Oak St Cadillac MI 49601 Office: Cadillac Jr High Sch 500 Chestnut St Cadillac MI 49601

MOY, AUDREY, retired retail buyer; b. Bronx, N.Y., May 6, 1942; d. Ferdinand Walter Melkert and Stella (Factorow) Schroff; m. Edward Moy, Aug. 16, 1974. BA in Biology, Hunter Coll., 1964, MA in Biology, 1966. Asst. buyer Bonwit Teller, N.Y.C., 1961-68; dept. mgr. Franklin Simon, N.Y.C., 1968; asst. buyer Saks Fifth Ave, N.Y.C., 1968-73; buyer Martins, Bklyn., 1973, Belk Store Svcs, N.Y.C., 1974-97. Mem.: AAUW. Avocations: cooking, antique collecting, gardening.

MOYA, EVA M., health services executive; b. El Paso Ciudad Juarez; BA, MS, U. Tex. Exec. dir. U.S.-Mex. Border Health Commn. Sr. program coord. U.S.-Mex. Border health collaborative outreach project U. Ariz., 1995—2001, assoc. dir. health career occupation program; project dir. Cmty. Health Worker's Evaluation Tool Kit Project, 1998—2001; co-dir. Cmty. Access Program for Ariz.; pres. U.S.-Mex. Border Health Assn., 1999—2000. Contbr. articles to profl. jours. Named one of Top 10 Latinos in Healthcare, LatinoLeaders mag., 2004; recipient Adelante Mujer Hispana: Cmty. Involvement award, Tex. Cmty. Health Program award, 1990, Award for Excellence, U.S. Dept. Health & Human Services, Human Svcs. Nat. Health Program award. Office: US Mex Border Health Commn 201 E Main Ste 1616 El Paso TX 79901 E-mail: emoya@borderhealth.net.*

MOYA, MARCIA TEWKSBURY, director; b. Indpls., Mar. 29, 1953; d. Richard Lee and Helen Maxine Tewksbury; m. Ernest Escalante Moya, Aug. 14, 1982; children: Eric Scott, Ryan Christopher. BA summa cum laude, DePauw U., 1975; MA, Ball State U., Muncie, Ind., 1977. Cert. tchr. Calif., tchr. in spl. edn., phys. edn., health Calif., English lang. devel. Calif. Adaptive phys. edn. tchr. Santa Clara County Office Edn., San Jose, Calif., 1977—85; classrooom tchr. developmentally disabled Santa Clara Office Edn., San Jose, 1985—90; resource specialist El Dorado Union HS Dist., El Dorado Hills, Calif., 1990—2002; student activities dir. Oak Ridge HS, El Dorado Hills, 2002—. Sec. Santa Clara County Spl. Olympics, San Jose, 1985—90. Recipient Svc. award, Santa Clara County Spl. Olympics. Mem.: Calif. Activities Dirs. Assn. Office: Oak Ridge HS 1120 Harvard Way El Dorado Hills CA 95762 Office Phone: 916-933-6980 1046. Office Fax: 916-933-6987. Business E-Mail: mmoya@eduhsd.k12.ca.us.

MOYA, ROSEMARY MERCEDES, mental health administrator; b. Santa Fe, Aug. 11, 1957; d. Willie and Mercedes Sadie Ramona (Rivera) Padilla; m. Raymond Anthony Moya, Aug. 9, 1980; children: Joslyn Monique, Alyssa Nichole. BS in Edn., U. N.Mex., 1979, MPA, 1990. Adminstrv. asst. Hubbard Broadcasting, Albuquerque, 1980; staff asst. N.Mex. Mcpl. League, Santa Fe, 1980-81, Div. Mental Health/Dept. of Health, Santa Fe, 1981-82, pers. adminstr., 1982-84, planner, 1981-88, health program mgr., 1988-91, chief community programs bur., 1991—97, chief enhancement bur., 1997—. Parent vol. St. Francis Cath. Sch., 1990-2000; vol. Am. Cancer Soc., 1993, Easter Seals, Santa Fe, 1991; sec. liturgy com. Santa Maria de la Paz Cath. Com., 1991-94, chair liturgy com., 1994-97, mem. bldg. com., 1991-94, mem. art selection com., 1992-94, mem. fin. coun., 2001-03, chmn. fin. coun., 2003—, mem. pastoral coun., 2003—; chmn. acad. com. St. Michael's H.S., mem. parent coun. exec. com., 2001-, mem. alumni assn., 2000-. N.Mex. Mcpl. League scholar, 1987-90; named Woman of Yr., Girls Club, Santa Fe, 1987. Mem. NAFE, Nat. Orgn. for Victim Assistance, Pi Alpha Alpha, Phi Kappa Phi. Democrat. Roman Catholic. Avocations: volleyball, skiing, tennis, camping, reading. Office: Dept Health/Behavioral Health Svcs Divsn 1190 S Saint Francis Dr Santa Fe NM 87505-4182

MOYARS-JOHNSON, MARY ANNIS, retired history professor; b. Lafayette, Ind., July 19, 1938; d. Edward Raymond and Veronica Marie (Quigg) Moyars; m. Raymond Leon Molter, Aug. 1, 1959 (div. 1970); children: Marilyn Eileen Molter Davis, William Raymond Molter Johnson, Ann Marie Molter Guentert; m. Thomas Elmer Johnson, May 25, 1973 (div. 1989); children: Thomas Edward, John Alan, Barbara Suzanne. BS, Purdue U., 1960; MA, Purdue U., West Lafayette, Ind., 1991, postgrad., 1985—. Grader great issues Purdue U., West Lafayette, 1960-63, writer ednl. films, 1962-65, publicity dir. convocations and lectures, 1969-74, devel. officer Sch. Humanities, 1979-88, asst. to dir. Optoelectronics Rsch. Ctr., 1989-90, mgr. indsl. rels. Sch. Elec. and Computer Engring., 1990—2002, assoc. v.p. for info. tech., for comm., 2002—04; tchr. English and math. Benton Cmty. Schs., Fowler, Ind., 1966-69, ret., 1969; pub. rels. dir. Sycamore Girl Scout Coun., Lafayette, Ind., 1974-78; dir. pub. info. Ind. Senate, Majority Caucus, Indpls., 1977-78; sr. script writer Walters & Steinberg, Lafayette, 1988-89; ret., 2004. Adj. faculty Ivy Tech State Univ., 2005. Author: Colonial Potpourri, 1975, Ouiatanon--The French Post Among the Ouia, 2000; co-author: Historic Colonial French Dress, 1982, 2nd edit., 1998; contbr. articles to profl. jours. Bd. govs. Tippecanoe County Hist. Assn., Lafayette, 1981-97. Mem. Women in Comms., Inc. (Pres. award 1983, pres. Lafayette chpt. 2004-05), Ctr. for French Colonial Rsch. (dir. 1986-89, 2006-, editor 1988-89), Palatines to Am., Ind. History Assn., Ind. Hist. Soc., French Colonial Hist. Soc. Roman Catholic. Avocations: history, genealogy, embroidery. Home: 924 Elm Dr West Lafayette IN 47906-2246 Personal E-mail: mamoyars@indy.net.

MOYE, ALANA NICOLE, pre-school educator; b. Pitts., Mar. 1, 1982; d. Richard Greg Sr. and Carol Ann Moye. Student, Shippensburg U., 2000—02, U. Pitts., 2003—05. Reading tchr. Ozanion Cultural Ctr., Pitts., 2001; asst. tchr. Jewish Cmty. Ctr., Pitts., 2002—. Author: (play) True Beauty, 2005. Mem.: Children Inc., Amnesty Internat., People for Ethical Treatment of Animals. Avocations: writing, music, computers.

MOYE, SIDLEY ANDREA, lobbyist; b. Elizabeth, NJ, Dec. 30, 1968; d. Leonard Joseph and Sheila (McBreen) Moye. BA in Polit. Sci., Stockton Coll., 1991; MA in Am. Govt., George Washington U., 1995; JD, Cath. U., 2005. Bar: Md. 2005. Suprr. regulatory dept. Dept. Legislature, Washington, 1995—97; dir. spl. projects Nat. Assn. State Aviation Ofcls., Silver Spring, Md., 1997—99; sr. mgr. govt. rels. Smith Bucklin Corp., Washington, 1999—. Student atty. Elder Law Clinic, Washington, 2003—04, Innocence Project, Washington, 2004—05. Nat. co-chmn. Young Women's Caucus, Washington, 1994—95; vol. Women Empowered Against Violence, Washington, 2000—01; bd. dirs. Women's Info. Network, Washington, 1997—98. Mem.: Women in Govt. Rels. Avocations: politics, guitar, writing. Home: 1810 California St NW # 106 Washington DC 20009 Office: Smith Bucklin 202 S M St NW # 808 Washington DC 20036

MOYER, DIANNA KAY, social studies educator; b. Lancaster, Pa., Feb. 5, 1963; d. Larry Goodman and Verna Marie Snyder; m. Mitchel Ray Moyer, Dec. 27, 1958; children: Alexandra Lynn, Hanna Grace, Austin Mitchel. Masters, Kennesaw State U., Ga., 2006. Cert. tchr. Ga. Social studies dept. chair Hiram H.S., Ga., 2001—. Advanced placement coord. Hiram H.S., Ga., 2004—06. Named STAR Tchr., PA Ga. Educators, 2004, Character Tchr. of Yr., Hiram H.S., 2005, Outstanding Grad. Student - Edn. Leadership, Kennesaw State U., 2006. Mem.: PAGE (assoc.). Avocations: RMP class, weight training. Home: 141 Mill Point Ct Dallas GA 30157 Office: Hiram High School 702 Ballentine Dr Hiram GA 30141 Office Phone: 770-443-1182. Personal E-mail: dmoyer@paulding.k12.ga.us.

MOYER, GENEVIEVE J., counselor; b. Toledo, Ohio, Mar. 19, 1949; d. John Thomas and Genevieve Mary Bork; m. Thomas Eugene Moyer (dec.); 1 child, Eugene Thomas. BA, U. Toledo, 1977, MEd in Counseling, 1983, EdS in Counseling, 1986. Lic. counselor Mich., 1990, registered technologist Am. Registry Radiol. Tech., 1969. Student radiol. tech. St. Vincent Med. Ctr., Toledo, 1967—69; radiol. tech. Toledo (Ohio) Hosp., 1969—70, Flower Meml. Hosp., Sylvania, Ohio, 1970—88; vocat. counselor State of Mich., Adrian, 1988—95, Saginaw, 1995—. Adj. tchr. Monroe (Mich.) C.C., 1989—95; breeder Alpaca Registry Inc., Midland, Mich., 2003—05. Represented in permanent collections Toledo (Ohio) Art Mus. Bd. dirs. Cath. Social Svcs., Monroe, Mich. Mem.: Lions Club (bd. dirs. 1998—2005, officer, 3d v.p. 2004, 2d v.p. 2005). Republican. Roman Cath. Avocations: sewing, hand spinning fleece, needlecrafts, painting, drawing. Home: 4114 N Ehlers Rd Midland MI 48642 Office: Michigan Rehabilitation Svcs 3875 Bay Rd Ste 7 Saginaw MI 48603

MOYER, LINDA LEE, artist, educator, author; b. Niles, Mich, Feb. 11, 1942; d. Roy Delbert and Estelle Leona (Beaty) Moyer; m. Brock David Williams Dec. 3, 1994; 1 child from previous marriage, Metin Ata Gunsay. Student, Occidental Coll., 1959-61; BA, UCLA, 1964; MA, Calif. State U., Long Beach, 1977, MFA, 1980. Cert. tchr. secondary edn., cert. computer graphics, Calif. Instr. art. Huntington Beach Union HS, Calif., 1967-81, Calif. State U., Long Beach, 1981-85, Saddleback Coll., Mission Viejo, Calif., 1986-88, Fullerton Coll., Calif., 1990, 94, Goldenwest Coll., Huntington Beach, 1990. Artist-in-residence St. Margaret's Episc. Sch., San Juan Capistrano, 1993; lectr., workshop presenter Santa Barbara C.C., Calif., 1992; series lectr. Rancho Santiago Coll., 1985, 90; lectr. Cypress Coll., 1986, Watercolor West, 1987, others; methods and materials show instr. Am. Artist Mag., 1996, 97, 98, 99, 99, 2000, 01, 03; juror fine art exhbns; presenter workshops in field; website co-founder watercolor-online.com. One-woman shows include Orange County Ctr. Contemporary Art, 1982, 1985, Laguna Beach Mus. Art, Calif., 1982, Orlando Gallery, Sherman Oaks, Calif., 1983, Orange County Ctr. Contemporary Art, 1985, Cerritos Coll., Norwalk, Calif., 1986, Louis Newman Galleries, Beverly Hills, 1986, 1988, 1990, Westmont Coll., Santa Barbara, 1992, Maturango Mus., Ridgecrest, Calif., 1996, exhibited in group shows at Owensboro, Mus. Fine Arts, Ky., 1979, Newport Harbor Art Mus., Newport Beach, Calif., 1981, Burpee Art Mus., Rockford, Ill., 1981, Nat. Acad. Galleries, NYC, 1982, Leslie Levy Gallery, Scottsdale, Ariz., 1983, Art Inst. So. Calif., 1984, Saddleback Coll., Mission Viejo, Calif., 1988, Ch. of Jesus Christ of LDS Mus. Art and History, Salt Lake City, 1988, Ch. of Jesus Christ of LDS Mus. Art and Riverside (Calif.) Art Mus., 1989, Ch. of Jesus Christ of LDS Mus., Calif., 1996, Springville History, Salt Lake City, 1991, Mt. San Antonio Coll., Calif., 1996, Springville Art Mus., Utah, 1999, Kimball Art Ctr., Park City, Utah, 2003, Springville Art Mus., Utah, 2000, others, Represented in permanent collections Springville Mus. Art, Home Savs. Bank of Am., Nat. Bank of La Jolla, Greenburg Deposit Bank, Ashland, Ky., INMA Gallery, Saudi Arabia, pvt. collectors; author: Light Up Your Watercolors Layer by Layer, 2003; included in: The Watercolorists Answer Book, 2005; Mid So. Watercolorists, 2006. Recipient Gold Medal of Honor, Am. Watercolor Soc., 1982, Walser S. Greathouse medal, 1988, Gold Medal of Honor for Watercolor Allied Artists Am., 1982, cash merit award Ch. of Jesus Christ Latter Day Saints Mus. Art and History, 1991, Best of Show award Utah Watercolor Soc., 2000, 2d award, Religious and Spiritual Art of Utah Exhbn., 2d award, 1998, 3d award, 1999, Best of Show, Challenge of Champions, Watercolor Art Soc. Houston, 2003. Signature mem. Nat. Watercolor Soc., Watercolor West (1st award 1984, N.W.S. award 1999, pres. 1999-2001), Watercolor West (life), Utah Watercolor Soc. Mem. Lds Ch. Avocations: reading, playing piano, genealogy. Home and Office: 22 Lakeview Stansbury Park UT 84074 Office Phone: 435-843-1611. E-mail: lindamoyer@watercolor-online.com.

MOYERS, JUDITH DAVIDSON, television producer; b. Dallas, May 12, 1935; d. Henry Joseph and Eula E. (Dendy) Davidson; m. Bill D. Moyers; children: William Cope, Suzanne, John. BS, U. Tex., 1956; LittD (hon.), L.I. U., 1989, SUNY, 1990. Pres., exec. prodr. Pub. Affairs TV, N.Y.C., 1987—; exec. editor NOW, 2001—05. Exec. prodr. TV documentaries (Emmy 1980, 93, 98, 2001,03, DuPont 1999, Christopher 1990, Parker 1992, Gold Hugo 1991, Humanitas prize 1995); exec. editor Now with Bill Moyers, 2001-; contbr. articles to profl. jours., newspapers, mags. Trustee SUNY, 1976-90; commr. U.S. Commn. UNESCO, Washington, 1977-80, White House commn. Internat. Yr. of Child, Washington, 1978-80; mem. jud. selection com. State N.Y., 1992-93; dir. Pub. Agenda Found. Recipient Christopher award, 2004. Mem. Acad. TV Arts and Scis., Century Club. Mem. Congregational Ch. Office: Pub Affairs TV Inc 450 W 33rd St Fl 7 New York NY 10001-2603

MOYERS, KELLI R., psychotherapist; b. Knoxville, Tenn., Sept. 8, 1961; d. Rayburn Neal and Vonnie Rae (Corley) M. BS in Edn., No. Tex. State U., 1988; MS in Edn., U. No. Tex., 1992. Lic. profl. counselor, Tex. Edn. cons. Adolescent Resource Corp., Kansas City, Mo., 1990-92; group home dir. Crittenton Ctr., Kansas City, Mo., 1992-94; adj. faculty Park Coll., Kansas City, Mo., 1994; program dir. STOP: Teen Outpatient Svc., Kansas City, 1994-96; supr. crisis ctr. Denton Co. MHMR, Denton, Tex., 1996-97; intake therapist Charter Hosp., Grapevine, Tex., 1997-98; psychotherapist pvt. practice, Grapevine, 1998—. Cons. and training, Devel. Sys., K.C., Mo., 1995-96. Vol. Kaufman Found., K.C., 1995-96; coord. Teen Pregnancy Coun., K.C., Mo., 1991-92. Recipient Outstanding Licensing Rep. award, State Tex. Dept. Human Resources, 1989. Mem. Tex. Counseling Assn. Democrat. Avocations: running, bicycling, home improvement.

MOYERS, SYLVIA DEAN, retired medical librarian; b. Independence, W.Va., Oct. 22, 1936; d. Wilkie Russell and Ina Laura (Watkins) Collins; m. Paul Franklin Moyers, June 29, 1957; children: Tammy Jeanne, Thomas Paul, Tara Sue. Student, Am. Med. Record Assn., 1977—79. Sec. Teets Lumber Co., Terra Alta, W.Va., 1954-58, Preston County News, 1958-60; med. record clk. med. record dept. Hopemont (W.Va.) Hosp., W.Va., 1960-75, dir., 1975-88; sec. The Terra Alta Bank, 1990-95; ret., 1995. Charter mem., past mother advisor Order of Rainbow Girls (Terra Alta Assembly No. 26), past grand editor Mountain Echoes; vol. Preston Meml. Hosp., ARC, Salvation Army, Am. Cancer Soc., Boy Scouts Am., Muscular Dystrophy Assn.; active Kingwood Fire Dept. Aux. Mem.: Preston County Hist. Soc., Kingwood Red Hat Mamas (charter), Preston Meml. Hosp. Aux., Kingwood Civic Club. Republican. Methodist. Home: 120 Miller Rd Kingwood WV 26537-1321

MOYNAHAN, BRIDGET (KATHRYN BRIDGET MOYNAHAN), actress; b. Binghamton, NY, USA, Sept. 21, 1970; d. Brad M. Trained as actress, Caymichael Patten Studio, NYC. Actor: (TV series) Sex and the City, 1999—2001, Going to California, 2001, The Late Show with Craig Kilborn, 2004, Six Degrees, 2006; (films) Row Your Boat, 2000, In the Weeds, 2000, Trifling with Fate, 2000, Coyote Ugly, 2000, Whipped, 2000, Serendipity, 2001, The Sum of All Fears, 2002, The Recruit, 2003, I, Robot, 2004, Gray Matters, 2005, Lord of War, 2005. Office: c/o Endeavor Talent Agy 9601 Wilshire Blvd 10th Fl Beverly Hills CA 90212*

MOYNAHAN, KAREN PEELER, performing arts association administrator; b. Balt., May 12, 1957; d. Richard N. and Frances A. (Signorelli) P.; m. J. Patrick Moynahan, Aug. 11, 1979. MusB, St. Mary's Coll., Notre Dame, Ind., 1979; MBA, Loyola Coll., Balt., 1987. Assoc. dir. various assns. various assns., Reston, Va., 1981—. Orchestral mgr. Prince William Symphony Orch., Woodbridge, Va., 1981-84. Mem. Percussive Arts Soc. Republican. Roman Catholic. Avocations: sailing, bicycling.

MRAMOR, MARTI, engineer, linguist; b. Indpls., Apr. 17, 1971; d. Joseph Thomas Mramor and Nancy Ann Clark Mramor. BA in Biology and Chemistry, Spring Arbor U., Mich., 1994; Paralegal Cert. in Gen. Law with highest honors, Nat. Ctr. for Paralegal Tng., Ga., 1995; AA in Russian, Def. Lang. Inst., Calif., 1998; AAS in Comm. Tech., C.C. of the Air Force, Ala., 2001; MS in Geosciences, Miss. State U., 2005. Engr. L-3 Comm., Bellevue, Nebr., 2004—. Vol. Fontenelle Nature Assn., Bellevue, 2002—06, Katherine and Fred Buffett Forest Learning Ctr., Bellevue, 2002—06, Neale Woods Nature Ctr./Obs., Omaha, 2002—06, Creighton U. Med. Ctr., Omaha, 2006—06; vol. tutor and transl. Staff sgt. USAF, 1997—2001, Okinawa, Japan, master sgt. USAFR, 2001—. Decorated Good Conduct medal USAF, Longevity Svc. medal, Overseas Long Tour ribbon, Aerial Achievement medals, Achievement medals, Noncommissioned Officer Grad. ribbon, Armed Forces Expeditionary medal, Global War on Terrorism Expeditionary medal, Iraq Campaign medal, Afghanistan Campaign medal, Air Force Expeditionary Svc. medal, Air medals, Meritorious Unit award, Commendation medal; named Airman of the Yr., 1999; recipient Martin J. Kellogg award for Excellence, Def. Lang. Inst., 1998; Academic Athlete scholar, Spring Arbor U., 1990—94. Mem.: VFW (life), Air Force Sgts. Assn., Nat. Weather Assn., Am. Meteorol. Soc., Am. Math. Soc., Am. Phys. Soc., Am. Mensa Soc. Avocations: swimming, running, writing, art, astronomy.

MUCH, KATHLEEN, editor, publishing executive, consultant; b. Houston, Apr. 30, 1942; d. Frederick and Ortrud V. (Lefevre) Much; m. W. Robert Murfin, Aug. 17, 1963 (div. 1981); children: Brian C. Murfin, Glen M. Murfin; m. Paul Stanley Peters, Jr., Jan. 1, 1988. BA, Rice U., 1963, MA, 1971, postgrad., 1978. Tchr. Kinkaid H.S., Houston, 1964—66; editor Rice U., 1969—81; freelance editor and writer Calif., 1971—; dir. info. Meth. Hosp., Houston, 1981—84; sr. editor Addison-Wesley Pub. Co., Menlo Park, Calif., 1984—86; editor Ctr. Advanced Study Behavioral Scis., Stanford, Calif., 1986—2005. Dir. Tex. Wordworks, Inc. Editor; contbr. articles to profl. jours. Bd. dirs. Friends Stanford String Quartet, Assn. Rice Alumni. Mem.: Soc. Scholarly Pub., Internat. Assn. Bus. Communicators, Phi Beta Kappa. Office: Book Doctor 128 Hillside Ave Menlo Park CA 94028 E-mail: much.bookdr@gmail.com.

MUCHA, MARY ANN K., quality assurance professional; b. Cleve., Dec. 31, 1961; d. Benedict Joseph and Irene Mary (Neecywinski) Mucha; 1 child, Clarisse Gates. BS in Allied Health Professions, Eastern Mich. U., 1985; cert. in Secondary Edn., Cleve. State U., 1986; MA in Counseling and Human Svc., John Carroll U., 1990. Staff occupational therapist Cleve. Clin. Found., 1986—89, sr. occupational therapist, 1989; lectr., faculty intern Cleve. State U., 1989—90; individual and family therapist Dr. Todd Gates, Beachwood, Ohio, 1989—90; clin. specialist Hudson (Ohio) Youth Devel. Ctr., 1990—92; coord. activity therapy Windsor Hosp., Chagrin Falls, Ohio, 1990—92; itinerant supr. Cleve. State U., 1995, itinerate supr. allied health dept.; occupational therapist Cleve. Clin. Found., 1995—2005, Sundance Rehab. Corp., 1996—99, GNA & Assoc., Grand Haven, Mich., 1998—99, Nextstep Healthcare, Eastlake, Ohio, 2000—03, Light of Hearts Villas, Bedford, Ohio, 2001—02; Quality Assurance Clinician Visiting Nurse Assn. of Cleve., 2003—. Vol. Ypsilanti Regional Psychiatric Hosp., Mich., Manor Care Willoughby, Ohio, St. Vincent Charity Hosp., Cleve, El Centro Clinica de Rehabilitacion, Morelos, Mexico; mental health liaison Ohio Occupational Therapy Assn., 1993—94; ad hoc com. chairperson Cleve. Dist. Ohio Occupational Therapy Assn., 1992—93; treas. Cleve. Clin. Coun., 1991—95. Recipient Svc. award, Ohio Occupational Therapy Assn., 1994, Cleve. Dist. Ohio Occupational Therapy Assn., 1993, Recognition award, Cleve. State U., 1989, 1990. Mem.: MENSA, Am. Occupational Therapy Assn., Sigma Delta Pi, Chi Sigma Iota. Avocations: travel, vintage jewelry. Home: 3305 Green Rd Beachwood OH 44122-4050 Office: Visiting Nurse Assn E 22nd St Cleveland OH

MUCHNIC, SUZANNE, art writer, educator, lecturer; b. Kearney, Nebr., May 16, 1940; d. Walter Marian Ely and Erva Nell Liston; m. Paul D. Muchnic, 1963. BA, Scripps Coll., 1962; MA, Claremont Grad. Sch., 1963. Art instr. Weber State Coll., Ogden, Utah, 1972—73; art history instr. LA City Coll., 1974—82; editor for So. Calif., Artweek, 1976—78; art writer LA Times, 1978—. Art criticism instr. Claremont Grad. Sch., 1984; LA corr. Arthews mag., 1990—2003. Author: (catalogues) Tim Nordin retrospective catalogue, 1982, Martha Alf retrospective catalogue, 1984, Mark Lere catalogue, 1986, (catalogue essay) Taiwan Mus. of Art, 1988, (art essay) The World Book Yr. Book, 1993—95, Odd Man In: Norton Simon and the Pursuit of Culture, 1998. Recipient Disting. Alumna award, Claremont Grad. Sch., 1982, Scripps Coll., 1987, 1st prize for Arts and Entertainment Reporting, Greater LA Press Club, 1993, Donald H. Pflueger History award, Hist. Soc. Southern Calif., 2002. Mem.: Internat. Assn. Art Critics, Coll. Art Assn. Office: LA Times 202 W 1st St Los Angeles CA 90012

MUDD, ANNE CHESTNEY, mediator, law educator, real estate broker; b. Macon, Ga., June 30, 1944; d. Bard Sherman Chestney and Betty (Bartow) Houston; children: Charles Lee Jr., Richard Chestney, Robert Jason. BA, U. Louisville, 1966, MA, 1976; JD cum laude, John Marshall Law Sch., 1998. Math statistician U.S. Bur. Census, Jeffersonville, Ind., 1966-70; instr. math. U. Louisville, 1975-77, Coll. DuPage, Glen Ellyn, Ill., 1978-85, 92; tchr. math and substitute tchr. Lyons Twp. High Sch., La Grange, Ill., 1986-91; realtor First United Realtors, Western Springs, Ill., 1989-92; owner, mgr. retail bus., 1992—2000; lawyer Mudd Law Offices, 1998—. Adj. prof. law. Editor: Mathematics Textbook, 1991-92. Steering com. Village Western Springs, 1986-87; bd. dirs. Children's Theater, 1987-91; sec. Collaborative Law Inst. of Ill., Leave a Legacy N.E. Ill. Outreach Com.; major gift task force Am. Cancer Soc. DuPage County. Mem.: LWV (pres. 1983—85, bd. dirs.), DuPage Assn. Women Lawyers, DuPage County Bar Assn., West Suburban Bar Assn., Ill. State Bar Assn., ABA, Collaborative Law Inst. Ill. (sec. bd. dir.), Suburban Chgo. Planned Giving Assn., Nat. Assn. Women Bus. Owners, Nat. Assn. Women Entrepreneurs (pres.), Assn. for Conflict Resolution, Mediation Coun. Ill. Avocations: gardening, politics, local govt. Office: Mudd Law Offices 3344 North Albany Ave Chicago IL 60618 Office Phone: 773-588-5410. Office Fax: 773-588-5440. E-mail: amudd@muddlawoffices.com.

MUDD, MARY CORDELIA, historian; b. Oak Park, Ill., July 24, 1948; d. Edward Lee and Audrey Sack Michaels; m. John Edward Mudd, Sept. 4, 1976 (dec.); 1 child, Andrew. BA in English cum laude, U. Houston, 1969, BS in Math., 1969; MA in History, Rutgers U., New Brunswick, NJ, 1974, PhD in History, 1984. Ind. scholar Roman and Byzantine History, Wall, NJ, 1984—; med. sec. Lakewood Pathology Assoc., NJ, 1996—99, Olsten Staffing Svcs., Tinton Falls, NJ, 1999—2004; physician credentials coord. Meridian Health, Wall, 2004—. Freelance lectr. archaeology and Roman history, 1978—95. Author: I, Livia: The Counterfeit Criminal, 2005, Studies in Reign of Constantius II, 1989; contbr. articles to scholarly publs. Recording sec. Freedom Theatre Parents Group, Phila., 1993—95; environ. activist Clean Ocean Action, Highlands, NJ, 1984—. Mem.: Nat. Assn. Med. Staff Svcs., Am. Hist. Assn., PEO Sisterhood, NJ Environ. Fedn., Earthjustice. Avocations: bicycling, swimming, theater, ballet, cooking, archaeology, cats. Office: Mary Mudd PhD PO Box 1275 Wall NJ 07719 Office Phone: 732-299-8608.

MUDLOCK, LAURA, athletic trainer; d. Stephen and Christine Mudlock. BS in athletic tng. and sports medicine, West Chester U., Pa., 2000. Lic. athletic trainer Pa., 2000. Assoc. Ruane & Regan Funeral Home, Pittston, Pa., 1998—; head athletic trainer Wyo. Area Sch. Dist., Exeter, 2000—. Mem.: Pa. Athletic Trainers Soc. (licentiate), Ea. Athletic Trainers Assn. (licentiate), Nat. Athletic Trainers Assn. (licentiate), Am. Coll. Sports Medicine (hon.). Mem. Biblicist. Avocations: sports, fishing, volunteer work. Office: Wyo Area Sch Dist 20 Meml St Exeter PA 18643 Office Phone: 570-655-2836. E-mail: lmudlock@wyomingarea.org.

MUEHL, LOIS BAKER, writer, retired language educator; b. Oak Park, Ill., Apr. 29, 1920; d. Arthur Franklin and Mary Hull Baker; m. Siegmar Muehl, Apr. 15, 1944; children: Erika, Sigrid, Torsten, Brian. BA in English, Oberlin Coll., 1941; MA in English Edn., U. Iowa, 1966. English tchr., drama coach Upper Sandusky (Ohio) H.S., 1941—42; TV sta. camera operator, actress W9XBK, Chgo., 1942—43; news anchor WIS Radio Sta., Columbia, SC, 1944; freelance writer, 1959—; dir. reading lab., assoc. prof. rhetoric U. Iowa, Iowa City, 1964—66, 1968—85; reading specialist Johnson C. Smith U., Charlotte, NC, 1966—68; English tchr. Hehei U., Nanjing, China, 1987—88. Tchr. creative writing, adult edn. Iowa City Pub. Schs., 1961—63; tchr. ESL adult edn. Merced (Calif.) Pub. Schs., 1984, 86, Kyungnam U., Masan, Republic of Korea, 1985. Author: My Name is ____, 1959 (Jr. Lit. Guild choice), Worst Room in the School, 1961 (N.Y. Times 100 Best List, 1961), The Hidden Year of Devlin Bates, 1967, Winter Holiday Brainteasers, 1979, A Reading Approach to Rhetoric, 1983, Talkable Tales, 1993; co-author: Trading Cultures in the Classroom, 1993; contbr. poetry to: New Adventures of Mother Goose, 1993, Golf, It's Just a Game, 1996,: Phonics Through Poetry, 1998; contbr. also numerous jours., mags. Vol. tchr. writing Sr. Ctr.,

Iowa City, 1991—93; co-founder, sustainer wild flower pk. Neighborhood Assn., Iowa City, 1998—2003; vol. tchr. refugee camps Internat. Rescue Com., Thailand, 1980, 1982. Recipient Cmty. Svc. commendation, Merced County, Calif., 1984, award, Lucidity, Midwest Poetry Rev., Lyrical Iowa, Grand prize, The Poetry Guild, 1997; fellow Old Gold Creative fellowship, U. Iowa, 1980. Mem.: Univ. Club Writers' Group, Iowa Poetry Assn. (area rep. 1990—, poetry prizes), Nat. League Am. PEN Women (treas. 1990—2003, prizes for poetry and craft work), Phi Beta Kappa. Avocations: folk art, gardening, swimming, beachcombing, yoga.

MUELLER, ANITA LAVONNE, special education educator; b. Apr. 7, 1961; d. Clifford Lavon and Verna Mae (Hahn) L. BA in Edn., Wayne State U., 1984. Cert. secondary tchr. Spl. edn. and chpt. I reading/math Exeter (Nebr.) Pub. Sch., 1984—. Mem. Sch. and Community Internat. Program, Exeter, 1988—. Mem. at-large Exeter Community Improvement Coun., 1991-93, scrapbook com., 1990, treas., 1993—. Mem. NEA, Exeter Edn. Assn. (sec., treas., pres., pres.-elect), Nebr. Edn. Assn. Republican. Lutheran. Avocations: reading, cross stitching, camping, water-skiing, swimming.

MUELLER, BARBARA STEWART (BOBBIE MUELLER), alcohol/drug abuse services professional, volunteer; b. Weslaco, Tex., Oct. 5, 1934; d. Roy Wesley Stewart and Marjorie Eleanor (Crossley) Willis; m. Charles Paul Mueller, Sept. 5, 1957 (div. 1985); children: Kathryn Anne Bencomo, John Stewart. BA, U. Tex., 1957. Owner Kid Puppets and Co., San Antonio. Cons. Parent Music Resource Ctr., Washington, 1986; drug edn. prevention chmn. U.S. Attys. Office, San Antonio, 1989-90; prevention chmn. Mayor's Alcohol and Drug Task Force, San Antonio, 1986-88. Author: (childrens TV): Henry Blue Shoe KONO-TV San Antonio, 1957; contbr. articles to profl. publs. Sec. Alamo Heights Recreation Coun., Tex., 1977-78; pres. San Antonio Petroleum Aux., 1978-79; founder, pres. Community Families in Action, 1980-89; trustee Youth Alternatives, Inc., 1983-85; allocation panel United Way, 1988-90; mem. alcolol and drug adv. com. N.E. Ind. Sch. Dist., 1986-91; drug free schs. com. S.W. Ind. Sch. Dist., 1991-92; regional coord. Texans War on Drugs, 1988-92; vol. U.S. Dept. Justice, San Antonio, 1984-88; proclamation com. Stop Tex. Epidemic, 1982 Recipient Yr. award Drug Awareness Ctr., San Antonio, 1984, Bexar Co. Med. Soc. Aux., San Antonio, 1984, Gov.'s Cert., Texans War on Drugs, Austin, 1982, Commendation U.S. Pres. Child Safety Partnership, Washington, 1986. Mem. Women in Communications, Inc. (hon.) (Pub. Awareness award 1984), Zeta Tau Alpha (sec., v.p., pres. San Antonio chpt. 1969-77, Nat. Merit award 1980). Avocations: genealogy, puppetry, hand embroidery, creative writing. Office Phone: 210-822-5437. Personal E-mail: barbsmueller@ev1.net.

MUELLER, BETTY JEANNE, social work educator; b. Wichita, Kans., July 7, 1925; d. Bert C. and Clara A. (Pelton) Judkins; children— Michael J., Madelynn J. MSSW, U. Wis., Madison, 1964, PhD, 1969. Asst. prof. U. Wis., Madison, 1969-72; vis. asso. prof. Bryn Mawr (Pa.) Coll., 1971-72; asso. prof., dir. social work Cornell U., Ithaca, NY, 1972-78, prof. human svcs. studies, 1979-96, prof. policy and mgmt., 1996-98, prof. emeritus, 1998—. Nat. cons. Head Start, Follow Through, Appalachian Regional Commn., N.Y. State Office Planning Svcs., N.Y. State Dept. Social Svcs., N.Y. State Divsn. Mental Hygiene, Nat. Congress PTA, ILO; mem. internat. adv. com. Family Resources Tng. Ctr., Singapore, 1999—. Author: (with H. Morgan) Social Services in Early Education, 1974, (with R. Reinoehl) Computers in Human Service Education, 1989, Determinants of Human Behavior, 1995; contbr. articles to profl. jours. Recipient Fulbright Rsch. award, 1990; grantee, HEW, 1974—76, 1979—80, State of N.Y., 1975—95, Israeli Jewish Agy., 1985—87. Mem. Leadership Am., Chi Omega. Democrat. Unitarian Universalist. Home: 412 Highland Rd Ithaca NY 14850-2216 Office: Cornell U Policy and Mgmt 108 MVR Hall Ithaca NY 14853 Personal E-mail: bjm5@cornell.edu.

MUELLER, CHERONE, religious organization administrator, writer, minister; b. The Dalles, Oreg. Diploma in Acctg., Chemeketa Coll., Oreg., 1984, diploma in Bus. Mgmt., 1984; DD (hon.), World Christianship Ministries, Calif., 2002. Ordained minister World Christianship Ministries, 2002, cert. counselor World Christianship Ministries, 2002. Founder Cherone Faith Ministry, Jacksonville, 1999—, pres., CEO, 2000—. Ordained min. A Call to Worship Ch., Jacksonville, 2001—. Author: (book) At San Jose Make a Left, Dancing Around the Throne, of numerous poems. V.p. singles group Salem UPC, 1983—91, choir Salem, 1982—91, treas. ladies aux., 1984—90, v.p. Singles Group, 1983—91; nursery caregiver First UPC, Jacksonville, 1995—97; Sunday sch. tchr. Christ Ch. Jacksonville, 1997—98, praise singer, fellowship coord., 1997—2001; dir. Daughters of Zion (praying for our children) UPC Internat., Jacksonville, 1999—2001. Named Pastor of the Month, Radio WAYR, Jacksonville, Fla. June, 2003; recipient Editor's Choice award, Internat. Libr. Poetry, 2001, 2002, 2003, 2004, 2005, 2006. Master: World Christianship Ministries (licentiate; rev. 2002). Avocations: sewing, cooking, crocheting, sign language, designing clothes. Office: Cherone Faith Ministry PO Box 47077 Jacksonville FL 32247-7077 Personal E-mail: cheronefaith@mail.com.

MUELLER, DOROTHY ANN, university official; b. Feb. 10, 1938; d. George Henry and Caroline (Schoettlin) M. AB, Birmingham So. Coll., 1959; MA, George Peabody Coll., 1961. Intern med. librarian UCLA, 1961-62; reference librarian Duke U. Med. Ctr. Library, Durham, N.C., 1962-65; circulation librarian U. Ala. Med. Ctr. Library, Birmingham, 1965-66; trainee Nat. Library Medicine, Bethesda, Md., 1966-67; chief searcher Ala. MEDLARS Ctr., Birmingham, 1967-70; assoc. dir. Lister Hill Library, Birmingham, 1970-76; assoc. dir. instnl. study program U. Ala., Birmingham, 1972-73, asst. dean adminstrn., 1976-77, asst. to v.p. research and grad. studies, 1977-83, asst. v.p. research and instl. advancement, 1983-88, asst. v.p. for research devel., 1988-91, asst. v.p. for univ. affairs, 1991-95, asst. provost for faculty affairs, 1995—2001. Spkr. at profl. meetings. Contbr. articles to profl. publs. Loaned exec. United Way of Ctrl. Ala., 1987, mem. agy. review com. and vis. allocation teams, 1990—, mem. ctrl. allocations com., 1997-2001; trustee St. John's Evang. Ch., Birmingham, 1983-85, 92-93; treas. The Women's Network, Birmingham, 1995-97, pres., 2000; bd. mem. YWCA of Ctrl. Ala., 1989-2004, v.p. programs, 1989-2004, v.p. planning, 1992-95, 2001-02. Mem. Ala. Assn. Univ. Adminstrs., Ala. Assn. Women Deans, Adminstrs. and Counselors (pres. 1984-86), Med. Librs. Assn. (So. Regional Group chmn. 1973-74), AAUW (Birmingham br. exec. bd. 1981-2000), Zonta (pres., 1986-1988, 2003-06, svc. chmn. dist. XI 1988-90, 92-94, chmn. dist. conf. 1991). Avocations: photography, travel. Home: 3236 Georgetown Pl Birmingham AL 35216-5112 Office: YWCA Ctrl Ala 309 N 23rd Rd St Birmingham AL 35203 Office Phone: 205-322-9922. E-mail: dmueller@ywcabham.org.

MUELLER, JEAN MARGARET, nursing consultant; b. Huntington, N.Y., June 3, 1951; Diploma in Nursing, Pilgrim State Hosp., 1973; BSN, SUNY, Stony Brook, 1979; M in Profl. Studies, New Sch. for Social Rsch., 1986. RN, N.Y. Nurses aide Huntington Hosp., N.Y., 1971, LPN N.Y., 1972, RN, charge ICU/CCU, MICU/SICU, telemetry N.Y., 1973-77; charge nurse, MICU North Shore U. Hosp, Manhasset, N.Y., 1977-78; private duty cases, Holter monitor scanning, 1978-84; dir. nursing svcs., assoc. dir. nursing svcs. Nesconset (N.Y.) Nursing Ctr., 1984-86; nursing edn. instr. St. Charles Hosp., Port Jefferson, N.Y.; labor and delivery nurse SUNY, Stony Brook; teaching and rsch. nurse II Diabetes Ctr., SUNY, Stony Brook; tchg. hosp. insvc. educator I SUNY, Stony Brook, 1990-94; hosp. nursing svcs. cons. Office Health Sys. Mgmt., N.Y. State Dept. Health, Hauppauge, N.Y., 1994—; team leader cross functional team pub. health edn. and info. N.Y. State Commr. Health, 1998—. Mem. adj. faculty Sch. of Nursing SUNY, Stony Brook, 1992—, St. Joseph's Coll., 1994; rsch. com. dept. family medicine with E. Stark, E.A.P.; hosp. nursing svcs. cons. office health sys. mgmt. N.Y. State Dept. Health, 1994—; lectr. Med., Emotional and Psychol. Indicators of Family Violence. Contbr. articles to profl. jours. Active Mothers Against Drunk Driving; mem. Suffolk County Family Violence Task Force. Recipient President's award for leadership tng. programs SUNY, 1993, for spl. needs of elderly tng. programs and humanistic approach to health care tng. programs, 1994. Mem. Nat. Nurses Assn., Sigma Theta Tau. Home: 234 Hallock Rd Stony Brook NY 11790-3026

MUELLER, JENA LYNN, athletic trainer; b. Pitts., June 10, 1978; d. Donald Joseph and Deborah Armstrong Mueller. BS in Health Sci., Lock Haven U., Pa.; MS in Health Adminstrn. and Health Edn., St. Joseph's U., Phila. Cert. Nat. Athletic Trainers. Childcare provider, Pitts.; water ski instr. Pine Forest Camp, Greeley, Pa.; athletic trainer Grandview Sports Medicine, Sellersville, Pa., Healthsouth/North Allegheny HS, Wexford, Pa., Pain Relief and Phys. Therapy, Havertown, Pa. Home: 906 N 63d St Philadelphia PA 19151-4510

MUELLER, LISA MARIA, chemical engineer; b. Macedonia, Ohio, Aug. 29, 1966; d. Dieter Hermann and Hannelore (Habeck) Mueller. BSChE, U. Akron, 1988, postgrad., 1988—89, Kent State U., 1993; MSChE, Lamar U., 1999. Newspaper delivery The Bull./Newsleader, 1979—80; dry cleaner Nordonia Dry Cleaners & Coin Laundromat, 1980—87; sys. adminstr. Engring. and Computer Graphics Facility, 1985—87; rschr. Process Engring. Computer Catalyst Controls, Akron, 1986—88; devel. engr. chem. divsn. Goodyear, Akron, 1988—90; engr. AcroMed Corp., Cleve., 1990; engr. process design NorPro, Akron, 1991—93; engr. contract and assoc. BF Goodrich Co., Akron, 1994—95; engr. contract BASF, Taco Bell, Kingfish Restaurant, Louisville, 1996; sr. engr. process ExxonMobil, Beaumont, Tex., 1996—97; cons. engr. Matrix Engring., Beaumont, 1998, Labor Ready, 2006. Recipient Gold Key Nat. Art Scholastic Merit award, 2006. Mem.: NOW, Cum Laude Latin Club, United Way Keel Club, Tau Beta Pi, Nat. Honor Soc. Avocations: music, computers, stamp collecting/philately. Home: Apt 12 4025 Crow Rd Beaumont TX 77706-7032 Personal E-mail: mueller-lisa@sbcglobal.net.

MUELLER, LISEL, writer, poet; b. Hamburg, Germany, Feb. 8, 1924; BA in Sociology, U. Evansville; postgrad., Ind. U. Vis. faculty Goddard Coll., 1977-80, Warren Wilson Coll., 1983, 85-86; vis. lectr. U. Chgo., 1984; disting. writer-in-residence Wichita State U., 1981. Author: Dependencies, 1965, 2d edit. 1998, Life of a Queen, 1970, The Private Life, 1976, Voices from the Forest, 1977, The Need to Hold Still, 1980, Waving from Shore, 1989, Second Language, 1986, Learning to Play by Ear, 1990, Alive Together: New & Selected Poems, 1996 (Pulitzer prize). Recipient Pulitzer prize for poetry, Nat. Book award for poetry, Carl Sandburg award, Ruth Lilly Poetry prize, 2002, Jacob Glatstein Meml. prize, Eunice Tietjens Meml. prize; NEA fellow. Mem.: Poetry Ctr. Chgo. (founding mem.). Office: La State U Press PO Box 25053 Baton Rouge LA 10894-5053

MUELLER, LOIS M., psychologist; b. Milw., Nov. 30, 1943; d. Herman Gregor and Ora Emma (Dettmann) M. BS, U. Wis., Milw., 1965; MA, U. Tex., 1966, PhD, 1969. Cert. family mediator; lic. psychologist, Ill., Fla. Postdoctoral intern VA Hosp., Wood, Wis., 1969-71; counselor, asst. prof. So. Ill. U. Counseling Ctr. and dept. psychology, Carbondale, 1971-72, coord. personal counseling, asst. prof., 1972-74, counselor, asst. prof., 1974-76; individual practice clin. psychology Carbondale, 1972-76, Clearwater, Fla., 1977-90, Port Richey, Fla., 1990—. Family mediator, 1995—; mem. profl. adv. com. Mental Health Assn. Pinellas County, 1978, Alt. Human Services, 1979-80; cons. Face Learning Center, Hotline Crisis Phone Service, 1977-87; advice columnist Clearwater Sun newspaper, 1983-90; pub. speaker local TV and radio stas., 1978, 79; talk show host WPLP Radio Sta., Clearwater, 1980-83, WTKN Radio Sta., Tampa Bay, 1988-89, WPSO Radio Sta., New Port Richey, 1991. Contbr. articles to profl. jours. Campaign worker for Sen. George McGovern presdl. race, 1972; sec. bd. dirs. PACE Ctr. for Girls of Pasco; bd. dirs. Suncoast Girl Scout Coun. Mem. APA, Fla. Psychol. Assn., Pinellas Psychol. Assn. (founder, pres. 1978), Am. Soc. Clin. Hypnosis, Fla. Soc. Clin. Hypnosis, Calusa Bus. & Profl. Women (pres., Woman of Yr. 1999), West Pasco C. of C., Cmty. Svc. Coun. Office: 6709 Ridge Rd Ste 109 Port Richey FL 34668-6851

MUELLER, MARYLIN, graphic supply company executive; Pres., CEO Mueller Graphic Supply Co. Office: 11475 W Theodore Trecker Way Milwaukee WI 53214-1138

MUELLER, NANCY SCHNEIDER, retired biology professor; b. Wooster, Ohio, Mar. 8, 1933; d. Gilbert Daniel and Winifred (Porter) Schneider; m. Helmut Charles Mueller, Jan. 27, 1959; 1 child, Karl Gilbert. AB in Biology, Coll. of Wooster, Ohio, 1955; MS in Zoology, U. Wis., Madison, 1957, PhD in Zoology, 1962. Instr. zoology U. Wis., Madison, 1966; asst. prof. poultry sci. and zoology N.C. State U., Raleigh, 1968-71; vis. prof. biology N.C. Ctrl. U., Durham, 1971-73, assoc. prof., 1973-79, prof., 1979-93; ret., 1993. Vis. scientist U. Vienna, Austria, 1975. Contbr. articles, abstracts to profl. publs. Mem. Soc. for Integrative and Comparative Biology, Wis. Acad. Sci., Arts and Letters, N.C. Acad. Sci., LWV, Sigma Xi. Avocations: bird migration, conservation and environmental issues. Home: 409 Moonridge Rd Chapel Hill NC 27516-5576 E-mail: hmuelle@earthlink.net.

MUELLER, PAULA DEUTSCH, retired music educator; b. Chgo., Mar. 27, 1950; d. Zoltan (Bud) Robert Deutsch and Eleanor Esther Tomaszewski/Deutsch; m. Martin F. Mueller, May 5, 1973. MusB in Edn., VanderCook Coll. of Music, 1972. Cert. music tchr. Music Educators National Conference. Fine arts tchr. Elem. Sch. Dist. 2, Bensenville, Ill., 1973—2005. Handchime ensemble dir. Elem. Sch. Dist. 2, 1980—2005, fine arts dept. coord. gen. music, instrumental music, visual art, chorus, drama, 1993—; freelance handchime ensemble clinician, bassoon player, Ill., 1980—. Contbr.: gen. music chpt. Music Resource Manual for Curriculum Planning, 1993. Mem. fine arts content-area stds. panel Ill. State Bd. of Edn., Springfield, 1990, 2003—04; rep. Bensenville (Ill.) Arts Coun.; bd. dirs. Glen Ellyn (Ill.) Children's Chorus, 1993—2003, pres. bd. dirs., 1996—2002. Recipient Founder's Award for enduring contributions of exceptional quality and for sustained commitment to the educatiional well-being of the children in Bens. Elem. Sch. Dist. #2, 1990. Mem.: PTA (life), Chorus Am., Bensenville (Ill.) Edn. Assn. (pres. 1984—91, 1997—2004), Ill. Edn. Assn. (bd. dirs., chmn. region 58 1998—2005, exec. com. 2001—03), Ill. Music Educators Assn. (assoc.), Music Educators Nat. Conf. (assoc.; chmn., jr. h.s., elem. music coun. Dist. 9). Democrat. Presbyterian. Avocations: gardening, cooking, crafts. Personal E-mail: paula.mueller@ieanea.org.

MUELLER, PEGGY JEAN, dance educator, choreographer, rancher; b. Austin, Tex., June 14, 1952; d. Rudolph George Jr. and Margaret Jean (Locke) M.; m. John Yerby Tarlton, June 24, 1972 (div. June 1983). BS in Home Econs., Child Devel., U. Tex., Austin, 1974. Dance tchr. Shirley McPhail Sch. Dance, Austin, 1972-75, Jean Tarlton Sch. Dance, Alpine, Tex., 1975-77, College Station, Tex., 1977-80, Sul Ross State U., Alpine, 1975-77, Tex. A&M U., College Station, 1977-80, A&M Consol. Community Edn., Coll. Station, 1977-78, Jean Mueller Sch. Dance, Austin, 1980—, U. Tex., Austin, 1980—. Dancer, contest judge Gt. Tex. Dance-Off, Austin, 1985—86; mem. equestrian com. Austin Travis County Livestock Show and Rodeo, 1980—92, chmn. trail ride, 1986—, Star Tex. Fair and PRCA Rodeo, 2000—; trial boss, pres. Austin Founders Trail Ride, 1986—; trail boss Bandera Longhorn Cattle Dr. and Trail Ride, 1990, 91; choreographer, head cheerleader Austin Texans Pro Football Team, 1981; dance tchr. Austin Ballroom Dancers, 1988, the Austin Club, 1997, 98; dancer, agt. George Strait/Bud Light Comml. Auditions, 1990; head contest judge Am.'s Ultimate Dance Contest, Austin, 1994; contest judge Two-Stepping Across Am., Austin, 1994; hon. trial boss Dream Catcher Ranch Trail Ride, Franklin, Tex., 1995, 96, Grapevine/Housgon Country Donkey, Mule and Horse Trail Ride, 1997, 2000. Dancer Oklahoma, Austin, 1969, Kiss Me Kate, Austin, 1970; choreographer, lead role Cabaret, Alpine, 1976, (mini-series) True Women, 1997. Active Women's Symphony League Austin, 1972—, Settlement Club, Austin, 1987—; recreation chmn. St. Martin's Evang. Luth. Ch., Austin, 1972—; hon. trail boss St. Jude Children's Rsch. Hosp. Trail Ride, Austin and Kyle, Tex., 1991. Recipient Outstanding Trail Rider of Yr. award Wild Horse Trail Ride, Okla., 1984; named Tex. First Lady Trail Boss, Gov. Mark White, Mayor Frank Cooksey, Austin City Coun., 1986, Judge Bill Aleshire, Travis County Commrs., 1989, Outstanding Intramural Sports Team Mgr.-Player, Tex. A&M U., 1978-79. Mem. Tex Assn. Tchrs. of Dancing, Inc., U.S. Twirling and Gymnastics Assn., Univ. Tex. Ex-Students Assn., Tex. Execs. in Home Econs., Am. Vet. Med. Assn. Aux. (v.p. 1978-79, pres. 1979-80), Am. Horse Shows Assn., Internat. Arabian Horse Assn., Austin Women's Tennis Assn. (v.p. 1985-86, pres. 1986-90, spl. events chmn. 1990-92, advisor 1990—, winner 2d ann. Harriet Crosson Outstanding Player & Community Svc. award), Women's Team Tennis of Austin Assn. (pres.-elect 1992-93, pres. 1993-94), Capital Area Tennis Assn. (membership com. 1991, 92), Houston Salt Grass Trail Ride Assn., San Antonio Alamo Trail Ride Assn., Ft. Worth Chisholm Trail Ride Assn., U. Tex. Longhorn Alumni Band, Austin C. of C., Am. Bus. Women's Assn., Austin Alumnae Panhellenic Assn. (1st v.p. 1989-90, rush forum chmn. 1990, pres. 1990-91, parliamentarian 1991-92), Lone Grove Cmty. Club (treas. 199697, v.p. 1997-99, pres. 1999—, exec. trustee 1997-99, exec. dir. 1999-2000), Omicron Nu (v.p. 1973-74), Jr. Austin Woman's Club (historian 1990-91), Austin Country Club (team tennis captain 1994-95, player 1994—, dance tchr. 1993-96), Zeta Tau Alpha (Austin Alumnae Chpt., alumnae photographer, social advisor 1982-87, treas. 1987-89, publicity chmn. 1989, Easter Seals fundraiser, Honor Cup winner 1990, pres. 1991-92, internat. convention official del. 1988, 91, nominating chmn. 1992-93, mem. yearbook com. 1992-94, 2d v.p. 1993-94). Clubs: Cen. Tex. Arabian Horse, Capitol Area Quarter Horse Assn., Jr. Austin Woman's, Austin Country. Republican. Avocations: theater, piano, drums, sports, travel. Home and Office: PO Box 5868 Austin TX 78763-5868 E-mail: aftr@USATrailRides.com.

MUENCH, DEBBY S., elementary school educator; b. Trenton, N.J., Aug. 8, 1953; d. Bruce C. Lyons and Edith A. Breth; m. Alan R. Muench; children: Eric, Kelli. BS in Early Childhood Edn., Elizabethtown Coll., 1975. Lic. elem. tchr. N.J., nursery tchr. N.J. Tchr. Washington Twp. Bd. Edn., Robbinsville, NJ, 1977—. Sci. faciliator Washington Twp. Bd. Edn., Robbinsville, 2004—, workshop presenter, 1990—, team leader curriculum devel., 1990—. Mem.: N.J. Sci. Tchrs. Assn., N.J. Edn. Assn., Washington Twp. Edn. Assn. (pres. 1990—94). Avocations: reading, home renovation. Home: 415 Church St Trenton NJ 08620 Office: Sharon Sch 234 Sharon Rd Robbinsville NJ 08691

MUFFOLETTO, MARY LU, retired educational association administrator, editor; b. Chgo., May 25, 1932; d. Anthony Joseph and Lucile (Di Giacomo) Muffoletto. PhB in Philosophy, DePaul U., 1959; ME, U. Ill., 1967. Tchr. elem. edn. Community Cons., Palatine, Ill., 1959-65; tchr. gifted children Sch. Dist. 15, Palatine, 1965-67, curriculum supr., 1967-75, dir. gifted edn. program, 1972-95, coord. state and fed. programs, 1975-95, asst. prin., 1975-95, retired, 1995; assoc. prof. Nat. Coll. Edn., Evanston, Ill., 1979-95; editor Tchg. Ink, Inc., 1995—. Chairperson State Bd. of Edn. Adv. Com. on Gifted Edn., Springfield, Ill., 1977-85; pres. No. Ill. Planning Commn. for Gifted, 1978-80. Editor: (tchr. activity books) Teaching Ink, 1995—. Mem. Nat. Coun. for Social Studies, Assn. for Curriculum and Supervision, Coun. for Exceptional Children, U. Ill. Alumni Assn. (pres. Champaign chpt. 1982-85, Loyalty award), Kiwanis, Phi Delta Kappa (sec. 1985-87). Home: 21302 W Brandon Rd Kildeer IL 60047-8618

MUHAMMAD, AVA, minister and national spokesperson for the Nation of Islam; b. Columbus, Ohio, 1951; m. Darius Muhammad, 1988. JD, Georgetown U., 1975. Bar: NY 1976. Asst. DA Borough of Queens, NY; defense atty. NYC; joined Nation of Islam, 1981, min., 1985—, so. regional min., 1998, head Muhammad Mosque No. 15 Atlanta, 1998, nat. spokesperson, 2000—. Author: Queen of the Planet Earth, The Rebirth, Rise of the Original Woman. Achievements include first woman in Islam to be given authority over a Mosque; successfully sued the NY Post for defamation of Louis Farrakhan's character, 1994. Office: Nation of Islam 734 W 79th St Chicago IL 60620

MUHAMMAD, CLAUDETTE MARIE, religious organization administrator; d. Travis and Ernestine Johnson; 1 child, Anthony L. Pinkins. Student, U. Abidjan, 1978—79; BA, Am. U., 1982; postgrad., UN, Geneva, 1982, U. Geneva, 1982, Johns Hopkins Sch. Advanced Internat. Studies, 1982. Tech. libr. Gen. Dynamics Astronautics, 1960—62; sec. to Congressman Lionel Van Deerlin U.S. Congress, Washington, 1963—68; spl. asst. to commrs. Pres.'s Commn. on Civil Disorders, Washington, 1968—69; dir. cmty. affairs Fed. City Coll., Washington, 1973—75; dir. of mayor's call program Dep. Mayor Econ. Devel., Washington; dir. mktg. Manara Travel Agy., Washington, 1987—88; enrollment mgmt./recruitment counselor U. D.C., Washington, 1988; chief protocol to Hon. Min. Louis Farrakhan Nation of Islam, 1989—2005; commr. commn. discrimination and hate crimes Gov. Ill., 2005—. Contbr. articles to profl. jours. Model Ebony Fashion Model, 1963; pres. Jimmy Carter's Inauguration Com. Protocol; exec. bd. Millions More Movement, Inc., 2005; nat. dep. dir. Million Man March, Washington, 1995, Million Family March, Washington, 2000. Finalist 3d runner-up Miss Bronze California, 1958; recipient Women in History award, Urban League, 2002, Jerusalem 2000 Unity Day Conf. award, 2000, Jr. Achievement award, 1961—62.

MUHAMMAD, GHOLNECSA EUSHENA, elementary school educator; b. Gary, Ill., June 5, 1981; d. Maria Muhammad. BA in Elem. Edn., So. Ill. U., Edwardsville, 2003; MA in Edn. Adminstrn., Lindenwood U., Mo., 2006. Cert. Tchr. Type 03 Ill., 2003, Administration type 75 Ilinois, 2006. Tchr. Wirth Parks Mid. Sch., Cahokia, Ill., 2003—. Tchr. advisor MEECA, Belleville, Ill., 2005—. Recipient Thirst for Knowledge Tchg. award, Coca Cola, 2003; fellow, Nat. Endowment for Humanities, 2006; grantee Youth Svc. Am. Learning Grant, State Farm Ins., 2006. Office Phone: 618-332-3722.

MUHAMMAD, LATONJA WALKER, control engineer; b. Detroit, June 19, 1966; d. Harold Walker and Doris Barksdale Dandridge; m. Derick Muhammad, Nov. 24, 1994 (div.); children: Sultan A., Tariq L. BSME, Tuskegee U., 1989. Structural design engr. LTV Aircraft Products Group, Dallas, 1989—94; dimensional validation engr. Epcom (contracted to GM), Warren, Mich., 1999—2001; dimensional engring. project mgr. Craft Line Inc., Hazel Park, Mich., 2001—02; sr. dimensional control engr. Aerotek (contracted to Lear Corp.), Dearborn, Mich., 2002—; owner, agt Globehoppers Travel & Cruises. Site leader, VIS trainer Ford divsn. Dimensional Mgmt., Dearborn, 2002—03. Contbr. newsletter Future Leaders of Detroit, 2000—03. Campaign vol. Mich. Dem. Party, 2002, mem., 2002—; site mgr. Democratic Caucus Voting, 2004; precinct del. Wayne County, Mich., 2002—; vol. Detroit Exec. Svc. Corps., 2001—, Black Alliance for Ednl. Options, 2002—03, A.C.E.S. Mem.: Future Leaders of Detroit, Jim Dandy Ski Club. Democrat. Avocations: golf, skiing, writing, travel, mentoring. Personal E-mail: globehopping@yahoo.com.

MUHLENFELD, ELISABETH S., academic administrator, literature educator, writer; b. Washington, Nov. 12, 1944; d. Merle Roberts and Cornelia Elizabeth (Herring) Showalter; m. Edward F. Muhlenfeld, Sept. 10, 1966 (div. 1975); children: Allison Elisabeth Finch, David Edward; m. Laurin A. Wollan, Jr., June 5, 1982; stepchildren: Ann Louise Wollan Westberg, Laurin A. Wollan III. BA in Philosophy, Goucher Coll., 1966; MA in English, U. Tex., Arlington, 1973; PhD, U. S.C., 1978. With U. S.C., Columbia, 1975-78; asst. prof. English Fla. State U., Tallahassee, 1978-82, assoc. prof., 1982-87, prof. English, 1987-96, dean undergrad. studies, 1984—96; pres. Sweet Briar (Va.) Coll., 1996—. Mem. ABA Commn. on Coll. and Univ. Legal Studies, 1991—94; mem. adv. com. US Com. UN Devel. Fund for Women; bd. dirs. Employee Assistance of Ctrl. Va., United Way Ctrl. Va., chair, 2003. Author: Mary Boykin Chesnut: A Biography, 1981; editor: William Faulkner's Absolom, Absolom: A Critical Casebook, 1984, The Private Mary Chesnut: The Unpublished Civil War Diaries, 1984, Two Novels By Mary Chestnut, 2002; contbr. chpts. to books and articles to publs. Chair Coun. Ind. Colls. in Va., 2001—02; mem. exec. com. Va. Found. Ind. Colls.; mem. commn. on colls. So. Assn. Colls. and Schs., 2001—, mem. exec. com., 2003—05, vice chair, 2005—; bd. dirs. Employment Assistance of Ctrl. Va., United Way of Ctrl. Va., chair, 2003; bd. dirs. Am. Civil War Ctr. at Tredegar. NEH Dir.'s grantee, 1983-84. Mem. MLA, St. George Tucker Soc. (charter fellow), So. Assn. Women Historians, William Faulkner Soc. (charter mem; sec.-treas. 1991-94), Phi Kappa Phi (exec. bd., pres. 1992-93). Office: Sweet Briar Coll Pres's Office Box C Sweet Briar VA 24595 Office Phone: 434-381-6210. Business E-Mail: muhlenfeld@sbc.edu.

MUHLERT, JAN KEENE, art museum director; b. Oak Park, Ill., Oct. 4, 1942; d. William Henry and Isabel Janette (Cole) Keene; m. Christopher Layton Muhlert, Jan. 1, 1966; 1 son, Michael Keene. BA in Art and French, Albion Coll., Mich., 1964; MA in Art History, Oberlin Coll., Ohio, 1967; student, Neuchatel U., Switzerland, Inst. European Studies, Paris, Inst. de Phonetique, Acad. Grande Chaumiere. Asst. curator Allen Meml. Art Mus., Oberlin, 1967-68; asst. curator 20th Century painting and sculpture Nat. Collection Fine Arts, Smithsonian Instn., Washington, 1968-73, assoc. curator, 1974-75; dir. U. Iowa Mus. Art, 1975-79, Amon Carter Mus., Ft. Worth, 1980-95, Palmer Museum of Art, University Park, Pa., 1996—. Author museum brochures, catalogues. Mem. Nat. Mus. Act. Adv. Coun., 1980—83; vis. com. Allen Meml. Art Mus. Oberlin Coll., Ohio, 1992—2003; chair adv. com. North Tex. Inst. Educators on the Visual Arts, U. North Tex., 1992—95. Grantee Nat. Endowment Arts-Donner Found., 1979; recipient Friend of Art Edn. award Tex. Art Edn. Assn., 1994. Mem. Assn. Art Mus. Dirs. (trustee 1981-82, 84-86, 92-93, chmn. govt. and art com. 1982-84, chmn. profl. practices com. 1990-92), Western Assn. Art Mus. (regional rep. 1978-79), Am. Assn. Mus. (commn. for new century 1981-84, gen. co-chair 1993 ann. meeting), Am. Arts Alliance (dir. 1980-86, vice-chmn. 1982-84). Office: Palmer Museum of Art Pa State U Curtin Rd University Park PA 16802-2507 Office Phone: 814-865-7673.

MUHN, JUDY ANN, psychologist, genealogist, trainer; b. Detroit, Dec. 29, 1952; d. Wilbur William and Dolores Eleanor (Sutinen) Nimer; m. Dennis James Muhn, June 6, 1975. BS, Mich. State U., East Lansing, 1975; MEd, Boston U., Mass., 1992; MA in Counseling, U. San Francisco, Calif., 1997. Lic. psychologist Mich. Legis. aide press sec. to Calif. state senator, 1982—84; dir. pub. rels. Tierra del Oro coun. Girl Scouts U.S., 1984—86, mgr. mem. devel. San Antonio area coun., 1986—90; adj. faculty U. Md. Germany, 1992—94; ind. cons. Capital Enquiry, Sacramento, 1994—96; counselor Yuba City Indian Health Ctr., 1997; intervention counselor Sutter-Yuba Mental Health, 1997—98; counselor, intern White Ho. Cmty. Counseling Ctr., 1998; pvt. practice Wixom, Mich., 1998—; dep. exec. dir. U. Santo Tomas Alumni Assn., 1998—2000; therapist Brighton Hosp., 2000—01; dir. adult devel. and vol. svcs. Girl Scouts Metro Detroit, 2002—. Adj. faculty Henry Ford CC, 1998—2001, Oakland CC, 1998—2001; therapist Brighton Hosp., 2000—01, Advanced Counseling Svcs., Brighton, 2001—03; spkr. in field. Columnist: Press-Republican, 1995—98. Bd. dirs., chmn. pub. affairs com. Planned Parenthood Clinton County, NY, 1980—81; bd. dirs. Family Planning Advs., Albany, 1981, Planned Parenthood San Antonio, 1987—89; founder Women's Roundtable, Plattsburgh, 1981; pres. Planned Parenthood Assn. Sacramento Valley, 1982—84; sec. San Antonio Coun. Native Ams., 1986—89; co-founder Womanspirit Rising, 1987—89; mem. Metis Cmty. Ea. Can. Named Bd. Mem. of Yr., Planned Parenthood Sacramento Valley, 1982; recipient Human Rights award, Sacramento Fair Housing Commn., 1983, Woman of Yr. award-Nonprofit, YWCA, Sacramento, 1984. Mem.: ASTD, Nat. Geneal. Soc., Assn. Prof. Genealogists, Metis Cmty. Ea. Can., Assn. Vol. Adminstrs., Met. Detroit Vol. Adminstrs., Assn. Univ. Women, Amnesty Internat., Greenpeace, San Antonio Women's C. of C. (bd. dirs. 1989), Assn. Girl Scout Exec. Staff. Personal E-mail: jmuhn@aol.com. Business E-Mail: jmuhn@gsofmd.org.

MUHR, SYLVIA ANNE, elementary school educator; b. Bridgeport, Nebr., July 28, 1952; d. Donald E. and Verna Mae Muhr; 1 foster child, Shannon Hicken. BS in Edn., Chadron State Coll., Nebr., 1974. Tchr. McGrew Pub. Schs., Nebr., 1974—86, Bayard Pub. Schs., 1986—. Curriculum specialist sci. Curriculum Com., Bayard, 1998—; mem. Lang. Arts Curriculum Com., Bayard, 1994—, Math. Curriculum Com., Bayard, 1996—. Mem.: NEA, Bayard Edn. Assn. (pres. elect, pres., sec., treas.), Nebr. State Edn. Assn., Nat. Sci. Tchrs. Assn., Nat. Coun. Tchrs. Math. Republican. Methodist. Avocations: reading, gardening, crafts. Home: 646 E 5th Box 146 Bayard NE 69334 Office: Bayard Pub Schs East 8th Box 607 Bayard NE 69334

MUIR, LINDA ANN, music educator, director; b. Hartford, Conn., Sept. 22, 1966; d. Neil Wellington and Louise Ellen Brouder; m. Scott Hastings (div.); m. Adrian Stuart Muir, June 12, 1994; children: Sarah Elizabeth, Haley Rose, Abigail-Lynn. MusB cum laude, Keene State Coll., NH, 1989. Intern Goodspeed Opera House, East Haddam, Conn., 1991; dir. edn. Clavier Music, Old Saybrook, Conn., 1992—94; pvt. practice Lees Summit, Mo., 1994—; dir. edn. Jenkins Music, Kansas City, Mo., 1994—98, Schmitt Music, Kansas City, 1999—2000, Falke Hi Music, Shrewsbury, Mass., 2000—01; accompanist Blue Springs Sch. Dist., Md., 2005—. Singer: (CD) Americana: in Perspective, 2002, An American Christmas, 2002, Americana: Sea to Shining Sea, 2005, (Operas) Conn. Opera Chorus, 1991, Brattleboro Opera Theater, 1989—90. Active Kansas City Singers, 2002—04. Mem.: Am. Choral Dirs. Assn., Music Educators Nat. Conf. Democrat. Home: 120 SE Carolina Dr Lees Summit MO 64063 Office: Moreland Ridge Mid Sch 900 SW Bishop Dr Blue Springs MO 64015

MUIR, PATRICIA ALLEN, professional association administrator; b. Dallas, Nov. 4, 1929; d. Jack Charleton Allen and Anna Patricia (Hovis) Allen Atchison; m. Lester Doyle Rader, Jr., Aug. 4, 1950 (dec. Sept. 1950); 1 child, Lester Doyle III; m. Perren James Muir, June 2, 1956 (div.); children: Edward John, Patricia Jane. Grad., Our Lady of Victory Coll., 1948; student, George Washington U., 1948-49, Washington Sch. for Sec., 1949-50. Traffic mgr. Am. Storage Co., Washington, 1960-69; asst. sec. Ind. Tele. Pioneer Assn., Washington, 1969-76; adminstrv. asst. ALA, Washington, 1977-98, staff liaison to Fed. Libr. Round Table, 1991-98, staff liaison to Armed Forces Libr. Round Table, 1991-98, staff liaison to Govt. Documents Round Table, 1991-98; office mgr. Fed. Documents Clearing House, Washington, 1998-2000; cons., 2000—. Columnist, contbr. The Ind. Pioneer, 1969-76. V.p. Friendship House Child Devel. Ctr. Parents, Washington, 1978, pres., 1979—83; mem. parish coun. St. Peter's Cath. Ch., 1987—91, mem. edn. and spiritual devel. com., 1986—, chair, 1988—91, coord. Bible study, 1999—2003; vol. St. Peter's Interparish Sch. Reading Program, 2001—02. Mem. Ladies Ancient Order of Hibernians (state pres. 1991-97, nat. budget com. 1996-98, nat. elections com. 1998—, nat. constn. com. 1998-02, nat. rules of order com. 2000-02). Avocations: travel, genealogy, reading, writing.

MUIR, PATTY K., special education educator; d. Gene Earl and Beverly Elaine Hogen; children: Bonnie, Amy, Kelly. BS in Edn., Mont. State U., Billings, 1979, MS in Edn., 1997. Tchr. kindergarten, spl. edn. Broodvich Pub. Schs., Mont., 1979—81; tchr. kindergarten Billings Cath. Sch. Dist., 1981—84; tchr. elem. sch. Broadview Pub. Schs., 1984—89; tchr. elem. sch., spl. edn. Laurel Pub. Schs., 1989—. Mem. adv. coun. Comprehensive Sys. Personnel Devel., Billings, 2004—; mem. OPI Statewide Mentor Task Force, 2004—. Mem. Laural Dem. Club, 2003—. Recipient Outstanding Educator of Yr., Laurel Mid. Sch., 2005. Mem.: ASCD, Laurel Unified Edn. Assn. (pres. 2002—), Mont. Edn. Assn. (bd. dirs. 1979—2006). Democrat. Lutheran. Avocations: travel, reading, sports.

MUIR, RUTH BROOKS, alcohol/drug abuse services professional, consultant; b. Washington, Nov. 27, 1924; d. Charles and Adelaide Chenery (Masters) B.; m. Robert Mathew Muir, Nov. 26, 1947 (dec. Feb. 20, 1996); children: Robert Brooks, Martha Louise, Heather Sue. BA in Art, Rollins Coll., Winter Park, Fla., 1947; MA in Rehab. Counseling, U. Iowa, 1979. Cert. substance abuse counselor, Iowa. Program advisor Iowa Meml. Union, Iowa City, 1959-66; counselor, coord. Mid Eastern Coun. on Chem. Abuse, Iowa City, 1976-81; patient rep. Univ. Hosp., Iowa City, 1982-85; rsch. project interviewer dept. psychiatry U. Iowa Coll. Medicine, 1985-88; pvt. practice family counselor, 1984—. Docent U. Iowa Mus. of Art, 1999—. Art exhibited at Iowa City Sr. Ctr., 1987, 92, Iowa City Art Ctr., 1989, U. Iowa Hosp., 1991, Great Midwestern Ice Cream Co., 1991, Summit St. Gallery, 1995, Iowa City C. of C., 2001, Iowa City's First Art Walk March, 2003; creator, coord. therapeutic series Taking Control, Iowa City Sr. Ctr., 1986-87, Art Walk Lorenz Boot Shop, 2003. Vol. coord. art exhibits Sr. Ctr., Iowa City, 1992-94, Iowa City Arts Exhbn. Com., 1996, Arrowmont Sch. Art, 1996—, Arrowmont Amb., 1996-98; treas. bd. dirs. Crisis Ctr., Iowa City, 1976-77; sec. coun. elders Sr. Citizens Ctr., Iowa City, 1976-78; pres. Unitarian-Universalist Iowa City Women's Fedn., 1985, mem. pastoral com., 2006; friend U. Iowa Mus. Art, docent, 1999—; active Opera Supers, Iowa City Unitarian U.N. Envoy; fgn. rels. coun., bd. dirs. annual changing family conf. U. Iowa, 1986-92; non-govtl. rep. Earth Summit Global Forum, 1992; care review bd. Mental Health Homes, 1997-99; bd. dirs., exhbn. chair Arts Iowa City, 2002—. Mem.: AAUW (state cultural rep. 1990—92, Iowa City chpt. co-chair for programs 1998—99), Health Care: Health Svcs., Nat. League Am. PEN Women (membership chair 2002—04, v.p. 2004—), Iowa City Unitarian Soc. (adult program com. 1993—94, unitarian care com. 1993—, membership com.), Nat. Soc. Colonial Dames, U. Iowa Retirees Assn. (bd. mem. 2004—, chair membership 2005—, membership chair), U. Iowa Print and Drawing Study Club (bd. dirs. 2003—04, pres. elect 2005), Pi Beta Phi (pres. alumnae club 1995—97). Home and Office: 6 Glendale Ct Iowa City IA 52245-4430 Office Phone: 319-337-7287. Business E-Mail: ruthmuir2989@inavia.net.

MUJA, KATHLEEN ANN, state official, consultant; b. Denver, June 24, 1965; d. Thomas Raymond and Bridget Catherine (Hirschfeld) Cramer; m. Adrian Constantin Muja, June 4, 1988 (div. Apr. 1991); 1 child, Thomas Constantin. BBA, U. Denver, 1995. Employment specialist Dept. of Labor and Employment, Colo., 1991—98, Colo., 2000—02; office mgr. Colo. Dept. Labor, Denver, 1999-2000, bus. analyst, 2002—. Contbr. poems to various publs. Vol. Mus. Natural History, Denver, 1987—; home visitor Cmty. Caring Project, Denver, 1996-2001. Mem. AAUW, U. Denver Alumni Assn. Roman Catholic. Avocations: hiking, biking, canvas cross-stitch, writing, reading. Home: 460 Washington St Denver CO 80203-3810 Office: Colo Dept Labor 251 E 12th Ave Denver CO 80203-2272 Office Phone: 303-318-9091. E-mail: katmuja@hotmail.com.

MUJICA, BARBARA LOUISE, language educator, writer; d. Louis and Frieda (Kline) Kaminar; m. Mauro E. Mujica, Dec. 26, 1966; children: Lillian Louise, Mariana Ximena, Mauro Eduardo Ignacio. AB, UCLA, 1964; MA, Middlebury Coll., 1965; PhD, NYU, 1974. Instr. French UCLA, 1963-64; assoc. editor modern langs. Harcourt Brace Jovanovich, N.Y.C., 1966-73; instr., asst. prof. Romance langs. CUNY, 1973-74; prof. Spanish Georgetown U., Washington, 1974—. Mem. faculty NEH Summer Inst., 1980. Author: (book) A-LM Spanish, Levels I-IV, 1969—74, Readings in Spanish Literature, 1975, Calderon's Characters: An Existential Point of View, 1980, Pasaporte, 1980, rev. edit., 1984, Aqui y ahora, 1979, Entrevista, 1982, Iberian Pastoral Characters, 1986, Texto y Espectáculo, 1987, Et in Arcadia Ego, 1990, Texto y Vida: Introduccion a la Literature Española, 1990, Antología de la Literatura Española: La Edad Media, 1991, Renacimiento y Siglo de Oro, 1991, Siglos XVII y XIX, 1999, Texto y Vida: Introduccion a la Literature Hispano-Americana, 1992, Looking at the Comedia in the Year of the Quincentennial, 1993, Premio Nobel, 1997, Books of the Americas, 1997, El Texto Puesto en Escena, 2000, (novels) Sanchez Across the Street, 1997, The Deaths of Don Bernardo, 1990, Far From My Mother's Home, 1999, Frida: A Novel, 2001, (book) Teresa de Jesus: Espiritualidad y feminismo, Milenio, 2002, Sister Teresa, 2006; editor: Comedia Performance Jour.; editor, pub. Verbena: Bilingual Rev. of Arts, 1979—85, sr. assoc. editor, bd. dirs. Washington Rev., mem. editl. bd. Bull. of Comediantes Hispana; editor: (book) Women Writers of Early Modern Spain: Sophia's Daughters, 2004, (jour.) Comedia Performance. Named winner, E.L. Doctorow Internat. Fiction Competition, 1992; named one of 50 Best Op Eds of Decade, N.Y. Times, 1990; recipient Pangolin prize best short story, 1998, Hoepner award for fiction, 2002, Trailblazers award, 2004; grantee, Spanish Govt., 1987, Poets and Writers of N.Y., Georgetown U., 2005—06; Penfield fellow, 1971. Mem.: MLA (pres. Golden Age sect.), Assn. Hispanic Classical Theater (pres.). Office: Georgetown U Dept Spanish Washington DC 20057-1039 Office Phone: 202-687-5778. Business E-Mail: mujica@georgetown.edu.

MUKAI, CHIAKI, astronaut; b. Tatebayasha, Japan, May 6, 1952; MD, Keio U., 1977, D Physiology, 1988. Cert. cardiovascular surgeon Japan Surg. Soc. Resident in gen. surgery Keio U. Hosp., Tokyo, 1977—78, resident in cardiovascular surgery, 1980, chief resident cardiovascular surgery, 1983; mem. med. staff gen. surgery Shimizu Gen. Hosp., Japan, 1978; mem. med. staff in emergency surgery Saiseikai Kanagawa Hosp., Japan, 1979; mem. med. staff in cardiovascular surgery Saiseikai Utsunomiya Hosp., Tochigi, Japan, 1982; astronaut, payload specialist Nat. Space Devel. Agy. Japan, 1985—, mem. STS-65 Columbia mission, 1994, mem. STS-95 Discovery mission, 1998. Contbr. over 60 articles to profl. publs. Named hon. pres., Tatebayashi Children's Sci. Exploratorium, 1995; recipient Outstanding Svc. award, Nat. Space Devel. Agy. Japan, 1992, 1994, commendation, Min. State Sci. and Tech., 1992, 1994, award for disting. accomplishments, Tokyo Women's Found., 1994, cert. of appreciation, People of Gunma Prefecture, 1994, Spl. Congl. Recognition award, U.S. Congress, 1995, Happy Hands award, Satte Jr. C. of C., 1995, De La Vaux medal, Fedn. Aeronautique Internationale, 1995, award for disting. svc. in advancement of space biology, Japanese Soc. Biol. Scis. in Space, 1995, Outstanding svc. award, Soc. Japanese Women Scientists, 1996. Mem.: Japan Surg. Soc., Japanese Soc. Cardiovascular and Thoracic Surgery, Japan Soc. Aerospace and Environ. Medicine (commendation for tech. award 1993), Japan Soc. Microgravity Applications, Am. Aerospace Med. Assn. Office: c/o Astronaut Office/CB NASA/Johnson Space Ctr Houston TX 77058

MUKHERJEE, BHARATI (MRS. CLARK BLAISE), writer, language educator; b. Calcutta, India, July 27, 1940; d. Sudhir Lal and Bina (Banerjee) M.; m. Clark L. Blaise, Sept. 19, 1963; children: Bart Anand, Bernard Sudhir. BA, U. Calcutta, 1959; MA, U. Baroda, India, 1961; MFA, U. Iowa, 1963, PhD, 1969. Instr. in English Marquette U., Milw., 1964-65; instr. U. Wis., Milw., 1965; lectr. McGill U., Montreal, Que., Can., 1966-69, asst. prof. English, 1969-73, assoc. prof., 1973-78, prof., 1978-79, Skidmore Coll., Saratoga Springs, N.Y., 1979-84; assoc. prof. Montclair (N.J.) State College, 1984-87; prof. CUNY, 1987-89, U. Calif., Berkeley. Vis. prof. of writing U. Iowa, Iowa City, 1979, 82; vis. prof. Emory U., Atlanta, 1983. Author: The Tiger's Daughter, 1972, Wife, 1975, (with Clark Blaise) Days and Nights in Calcutta, 1977, Darkness, 1985, The Middleman and Other Stories, 1988 (Nat. Book Critics Circle award 1989), (with Clark Blaise) The Sorrow and the Terror, 1988, Jasmine, 1989, The Holder of the World, 1993, Leave It to Me, 1997, Desirable Daughters, 2002, The Tree Bride, 2004; contbr. short stories, essays and book revs. to several jours. Grantee McGill U., 1968, 70, Can. Arts Coun., 1973-74, 77, Shastri Indo-Can. Inst., 1976-77, Guggenheim Found., 1978-79, Can. Govt., 1982; recipient 1st prize Periodical Distbn. Assn., 1980, NEA award, 1986. Mem. PEN. Hindu. Office: U Calif Dept English 322 Wheeler Hall Berkeley CA 94720-1030

MUKHERJEE, GOPA, psychiatrist, educator; d. Gourhari and Swapnarekha Mukherjee; 1 child, Raka Sen. MS in Microbiology, Brigham Young U., 1991; MD, U. Colo., Denver, 1998. Diplomate Am. Bd. Psychiatry and Neurology. Asst. prof. U. Colo. Health Scis. Ctr., Denver, 1998—2000; staff psychiatrist Mental Health Ctr. of Denver, 2002—. Mem.: Colo. Psychiat. Soc., Am. Psychiat. Assn. Hindu. Office: Mental Health Corp of Denver 4353 E Colfax Ave Denver CO 80220-1115 Office Phone: 303-504-1238. Office Fax: 303-504-1815. E-mail: gopa.mukherjee@mhcd.org.

MULCAHY, ANNE MARIE, printing company executive; b. Rockville Centre, N.Y., Oct. 21, 1952; d. Thomas and Anne Dolan; m. Joe Mulcahy; 2 children. BA in English & Journalism, Marymount Coll., 1974. With Chase Manhattan Bank, 1974—76; various mgmt. positions Xerox Corp., 1976—88, v.p. regional gen. mgr., 1988—91, v.p. worldwide mktg. ops. planning, 1991, dir. corp. human resources, 1991—92, v.p. human resources, 1992-95, v.p., staff officer customer ops. worldwide, 1996-97, sr. v.p., chief staff officer, 1998, pres. gen. mkts. ops. Stamford, Conn., 1999—2000, COO, 2000—01, pres., 2000—02, CEO, 2001—, chmn., 2002—. Bd. dirs. Xerox Corp., 2000—, Fannie Mae, 2000—, Catalyst, Citigroup Inc., 2004—, Fuji-Xerox Co. Ltd., Target Corp. Named one of Most Powerful Women, Forbes mag., 2005, World's Best CEO, Barron's Mag., 2006, The TIME 100-The People Who Shape Our World, 2006, 100 Most Powerful Women, Forbes Mag., 2006, 50 Most Powerful Women in Bus., Fortune mag., 2006. Mem.: Bus. Coun. Office: Xerox Corp 800 Long Ridge Rd Stamford CT 06904-1227 Office Fax: 203-968-3218.*

MULCAHY, LUCILLE BURNETT, freelance writer; b. Albuquerque, Nov. 10, 1918; d. Harry Leland and Grace Ruth (Lomax) Burnett; m. Clemons David Mulcahy Jr., Sept. 1, 1939 (div. May 1957); children: Burnette Anne, DeeAnn Eileen Student, N.Mex. State U., 1947, U. Albuquerque, 1975. Freelance writer, 1953—; procurement officer Albuquerque Pub. Libr., 1963—76. Tchr. Raja yoga Manzano Mesa Multigenerational Ctr., Albuquerque. Author: (childrens books) Dark Arrow, 1953, reprint 95, Pita, 1954, Magic Fingers, 1958, 95 (Jr. Lit. Guild award), Blue Marshmallow Mountains, 1959, Natoto, 1960, Fire on Big Lonesome, 1967, (under pseudonym) Dale Evans and Danger in Crooked Canyon, 1958 Storyteller various schs. Recipient Zia award N.Mex. Press Women, 1967 Avocation: yoga. Home: 505 Doe Ln SE Albuquerque NM 87123-3530 Personal E-mail: lucille@hubwest.com.

MULDAUR, DIANA CHARLTON, actress; b. N.Y.C., Aug. 19, 1938; d. Charles Edward Arrowsmith and Alice Patricia (Jones) M.; m. James Mitchell Vickery, July 26, 1969 (dec. 1979); m. Robert J. Dozier, Oct. 11, 1981. BA, Sweet Briar Coll., 1960. Actress appearing in: Off-Broadway theatrical prodns., summer stock, Broadway plays including A Very Rich Woman, 1963-68; guest appearances on TV in maj. dramatic shows; appeared on: TV series Survivors, 1970-71, McCloud, 1971-73, Tony Randall Show, 1976, Black Beauty, 1978; star: TV series Born Free, 1974, Hizzoner, 1979, Fitz & Bones, 1980, Star Trek: The Next Generation, 1988-89; NBC miniseries and TV series A Year in the Life, 1986; TV movie Murder in Three Acts, The Return of Sam McCloud, 1989; TV series L.A. Law, 1989-91; motion picture credits include McQ, The Lawyer, The Other, One More Train to Rob, Mati, etc. Bd. dirs. Los Angeles chpt. Asthma and Allergy Found. Am.; bd. advisors Nat. Ctr. Film and Video Preservation, John F. Kennedy Ctr. Performing Arts, 1986. Recipient 13th Ann. Commendation award Am. Women in Radio and TV, 1988, Disting. Alumnae award Sweet Briar Coll., 1988. Mem. Acad. Motion Picture Arts and Scis., Screen Actors Guild (dir. 1978), Acad. TV Arts and Scis. (exec. bd., dir., pres. 1983-85), Conservation Soc. Martha's Vineyard Island. Office: Bauman Bedanty & Shaul 5757 Wilshire Blvd Ste 473 Los Angeles CA 90036 Office Phone: 310-454-2241.

MULDER, MICHELLE KAY, music educator; b. Granite Falls, Minn., Feb. 16, 1957; d. Loyis and Beulah Esther Eekhoff; m. Kevin Ross Mulder, Aug. 13, 1977; children: Ryan Christopher, Lisa Michelle, Jennifer Lynn. BA in Music Edn., Concordia Coll., Moorhead, Minn., 1979. Cert. music educator State of Minn., 2005. Music tchr. Casselton Pub. Sch., ND, 1979—80; piano instr. The Music Store, Greeley, Colo., 1980—81; music tchr. Renville County West, Minn., 1982—2000, Ctrl. Minn. Christian Sch., Prinsburg, 2000—. Organist Emden Christian Ref. Ch., Renville, Minn., 1982—, choir dir., 1982—, youth leader, 1995—2001, musician and praise team, 2000—. Conservative. Avocations: piano, water-skiing, gardening, fishing, reading. Home: 513 East Park Ave Renville MN 56284 Office: Ctrl Minn Christian Sch 204 Sch St Prinsburg MN 56281 Office Fax: 320-978-6797. Business E-Mail: mmulder@willmarnet.com.

MULDER, SUSAN ELIZABETH, special education educator; b. Grand Rapids, Mich., June 23, 1956; d. Frank Nick and Frances Elizabeth Budnick; m. Michael Jon Mulder, Feb. 3, 1978; 1 child, Michael Jon. BA, Ctrl. Mich. U., 1978; MEd, Grand Valley U., 1984, MA in Adminstrn., 2002. Tchr. spl. edn. Kent City (Mich.) Schs., 1978—98, spl. edn. adminstr., supr., 1998—. Named Tchr. of Yr., Region I Parent Adv. for Spl. Edn., 1982. Avocations: travel, camping, reading. Home: 680 Indian Lakes Sparta MI 49345 Office: Kent City Cmty Schs 35 E Muskegon Kent City MI 49330

MULDROW, ELIZABETH SMITH, retired secondary school educator, minister; b. Phila., Oct. 25, 1931; d. I. Willison, Jr. Smith and Elizabeth Madison Kennedy; m. William Fulton Muldrow, June 7, 1957; children: Margaret Elizabeth, Mark Ellison, David Drummond. BA in History, Wheaton Coll., Ill., 1953; MA in U.S. History, U. Pa., Phila., 1956; MA in English Edn., U. Colo., Denver, 1987. Ordained clergywoman Ohio Valley Presbytery, 1976; lic. secondary tchr. Pa., Colo. Tchr. Norristown (Pa.) Sr. HS, 1954—57, United Presbyn. Ch., Ethiopia, 1963—71, Denver Pub. Schs., 1973—74, Jefferson County Pub. Schs., Golden, Colo., 1974—94; ret., 1994. Author: Marmalade Stories, 2004; contbr. articles to publs. Asst. pastor Ctrl. Presbyn. Ch., Denver, 1972—73; program interpretation Presbyn. Ch., 1957—71; chair, mem. numerous coms. Presbytery of Denver. Recipient tribute, Colo. State Senate, 1983. Mem.: Soc. Hist. Preservation, Internat. Dyslexia Soc. Democrat. Avocation: travel. Home: 13631 E Marina Dr # 507 Aurora CO 80014

MULÉ, ANN C., oil industry executive; b. Phila., Oct. 22, 1956; BA magna cum laude, St. Joseph's U., 1978; JD cum laude, Villanova U., 1981. Bar: Pa. 1981, U.S. Supreme Ct. 1988. From atty. to chief governance officer Sunoco Inc., Phila., 1980—2002, chief governance officer, 2002—. Bd. dirs. Phila. Zoo; mem. adv. bd. Ctr. Corp. Governance, U. Del. Mem.: ABA, Am. Corp. Counsel Assn. (vice chmn. exec. counsel, mem. corp. and securities law com.), Phila. Bar Assn., Pa. Bar Assn. (chmn. bus. law sect., mem. bd. govs., chmn. com. securities regulation, mem. title 15 task force), Am. Soc. Corp. Secs. (bd. dir., mem. exec. steering com., mem. nat. conf. com., mem. corp. practices com.). Office: Sunoco Inc Mellon Bank Ctr 1735 Market St Ste LL Philadelphia PA 19103

MULGREW, KATHERINE KIERNAN (KATE MULGREW), actress; b. Dubuque, Iowa, Apr. 29, 1955; d. Thomas James and Joan Virginia (Kiernan) M.; m. Robert Harry Egan; children: Ian Thomas, Alexander James. Student, Northwestern U., U. Iowa; AA, NYU, 1976; studies with Stella Adler; trained at, Tyrone Guthrie Theater, Mpls. Formerly waitress and model. Actor: (TV films) Alien Lover, 1975, The American Woman: Portraits of Courage, 1976, Kate Loves a Mystery, 1979, Jennifer: A Woman's Story, 1979, A Time for Miracles, 1980, Carly Mills, 1986, My Town, 1986, Roses Are for the Rich, 1987, Heartbeat, 1988, Roots: The Gift, 1988, Daddy, 1991, Fatal Friendship, 1991, For Love and Glory, 1993, Star Trek: Voyager - Caretaker, 1995, Riddler's Moon, 1998; (TV series) Ryan's Hope, 1975—78, 1983, 1986, 1989, Mrs. Columbo, 1979, Jessie, 1984, (voice) Pirates of Darkwater, 1991, Gargoyles, 1994, Star Trek: Voyager, 1995; (TV miniseries) The Word, 1978, The Manions of America, 1981; (films) Lovespell, 1981, A Stranger Is Watching, 1982, Remo Williams: The Adventure Begins, 1985, Throw Momma from the Train, 1987, Round Numbers, 1992, Camp Nowhere, 1994, Captain Nuke and the Bomber Boys, 1995, Star Trek: Nemesis, 2002, (voice) Lords of Everquest, 2003, Star Trek: The Experience - Borg Invasion 4D, 2004, Perception, 2005. Address: care Star Trek Voyager Paramount Pictures 5555 Melrose Ave West Hollywood CA 90038-3197

MULHALL, KIMBERLY A., business manager; b. Evanston, Ill., Dec. 26, 1967; d. Michael J. and Karen A. Mulhall, Mary M. Mulhall (Stepmother). B in Bus. Adminstrn., Roosevelt U., Chgo., 1990, MBA, 1996. Asst. Network Svcs. Co., Mount Prospect, Ill., 1990—95, sr. acct., 1995—97; asst. payroll supr. Underwriters Labs. Inc., Northbrook, Ill., 1997—98, payroll supr., 1998—2000, bus. analyst, 2000—01, sr. mktg. analyst, 2001—05, US regional bus. mgr., 2005—. Vol. Children's Advocacy Ctr. N.W. Cook County. Named Vol. of Yr., Children's Advocacy Ctr. N.W. Cook County, 2003. Mem.: Am. Mktg. Assn. Roman Catholic.

MULHOLLAND, NANCY W., state agency administrator; BA, Vassar Coll. Various info. tech. mgmt. and tech. positions GE; dir. NY State Project Mgmt. Office Office Tech.; dep. exec. dir. and chief info. officer NY State Workers' Compensation Bd., Albany, 2002—. Named one of Premier 100 IT Leaders,

Computerworld, 2005; recipient Award for Excellence in Govt. Info. Services, NYS Forum, 2005. Office: NY State Workers Compensation Bd 20 Park St Albany NY 12207 Office Phone: 518-474-6670.

MULKEY, SHARON RENEE, gerontology nurse; b. Miles City, Mont., Apr. 14, 1954; d. Otto and Elvera Marie (Haglof) Neuhardt; m. Monty W. Mulkey, Oct. 9, 1976; children: Levi, Candice, Shane. BS in Nursing, Mont. State U., 1976. RN, Calif.; nat. cert. gerontol. nursing. Staff nurse, charge nurse VA Hosp., Miles City, Mont., 1976-77; staff nurse obstetrics labor and delivery Munster (Ind.) Cmty. Hosp., 1982-83; nurse mgr. Thousand Oaks Health Care, 1986-88; unit mgr. rehab. Semi Valley (Calif.) Adventist Hosp., 1988-89, DON TCU, 1989-91; DON Pleasant Valley Hosp. Extended Care Vacility and Neuro Ctr., 1991-93, Victoria Care Ctr., Ventura, Calif., 1993—; clin. supr. Procare Home Health, Oxnard, Calif., 1996-97; staff nurse acute rehab. Los Robles East Campus Rehab. Unit, Westlake, Calif., 1998, clin. coord., 1998—2004; founder, CEO Internat. Womens Conf. Spkr. for Spiritual Growth and Devel., 2000—, Women of Destiny. Internat. conf. spkr. WCCD, 1991—. Mem. ANA, Nat. Gerontol. Nursing Assn., Internat. Platform Assn., Alpha Tau Delta (pres. 1973-75), Phi Kappa Phi. Home: 3461 Pembridge St Thousand Oaks CA 91360-4565 Office Phone: 805-444-1727. Personal E-mail: smulkey1@aol.com.

MULL, BETH A., counseling educator; b. Reading, Pa., Oct. 30, 1961; d. Edward William and Anna Catherine (Pazdrick) M. BA in Psychology, Alvernia Coll., 1994; MA in Counseling Psychology, Immaculata Coll., 1997, postgrad., 1998—. Therapist Progressions Health Sys., Reading, Pa., 1996—; adj. faculty Alvernia Coll., Reading, 1998. Psychology award for Clin. Excellence, Alvernia Coll., 1994. Mem. APA, ACA, Psi Chi, Chi Sigma Iota (past chpt. treas.). Roman Catholic. Avocations: aerobics, music.

MULL, MICHELLE RACHAEL, secondary school educator; b. Phila., June 16, 1978; d. Alfred Sergeant and Marcia Ellen Mull. BS in Edn., Pa. State U., State College, 2000; MEd, Arcadia U., Glenside, Pa., 2004. Cert. social studies 7-12 Pa., spl. edn. Pa. Tchr. homebound Coun. Rock Sch. Dist., Newtown, Pa., 2000—; tchr. Centennial Sch. Dist., Warminster, Pa., 2001—. 9th grade advisor Centennial Sch. Dist., Warminster, 2005—. Office: Centennial Sch Dist 333 Centennial Rd Warminster PA 18974 Office Phone: 215-441-6181 2091. Business E-Mail: mullmi@centennialsd.org.

MULLALLY, MEGAN, actress; b. LA, Nov. 12, 1958; d. Carter and Martha Mullally; m. Michael A. Katcher, 1992 (div. 1996); m. Nick Offerman, Sept. 20, 2003. Student, Northwestern U. Actor: (TV films) Rainbow Drive, 1990, Winchell, 1998, Everything Put Together, 2000, Lifetime, The Pact, 2002; (TV series) My Life and Times, 1991, Ellen Burstyn Show, 1986, Fish Police, 1992, Rachel Gunn, RN, 1992, Will and Grace, 1998—2006 (Emmy Award Supporting Actress in a Comedy, 2000, Outstanding Comedy Series award, 2000, Am. Comedy Award, 2001, Outstanding Female Actor Award, 2001, Screen Actors Guild award Outstanding Actress in a Comedy Series, 2001, 2002, 2003, Emmy award for Outstanding Supporting Actress in a Comedy Series, 2006); (Broadway plays) Grease, 1994, How to Succeed in Business Without Really Trying, 1995—96; host (talk show) Megan Mullally Show, 2006—; actor: (films) Once Bitten, 1985, Last Resort, 1986, About Last Night, 1986, Anywhere But Here, 1999, Best Man in Grass Creek, 1999, Everything Put Together, 2000, Monkey Bone, 2001, Stealing Harvard, 2002; actor, actor: (films) Speaking of Sex, 2001, (voice) Teacher's Pet, 2004, Rebound, 2005, (guest appearance): (TV series) Murder, She Wrote, 1988, China Beach, 1989, Wings, 1990, Herman's Head, 1991, Seinfeld, 1993, Frasier, 1997, Mad About You, 1997, Caroline in the City, 1997, Just Shoot Me!, 1998, 3rd Rock from the Sun, 2000; (TV series, voice) King of the Hill, 2002. Office: The Gersh Agency PO Box 5617 Beverly Hills CA 90210*

MULLANE, JEANETTE LESLIE, artist, educator; b. Chgo., Oct. 7, 1938; d. Clarence Leslie and Marion Janet Shumaker; m. Richard Michael Mullane, Apr. 16, 1977. Degree, Am. Acad. Art, 1966; BS in Art Edn., U. Wis., 1973. Painting tchr. in Wis. & Oreg., Bergen, Norway. Exhibitions include Cider Painters Am. Ann. Internat. Miniature Art Exhbns. (Best of Show award, 1996, Judge's award, 1997, Excellence in Watercolor awards, 1998, 2000, 2001, 2002, 2003, 2004), Miniature Painters, Sculptors and Gravers Soc. Washington D.C. (3rd pl. still life, 1992, 2d pl. watermedia, 2002), exhibited in group shows at Miniature Art Soc. Fla. Ann. Internat. Miniature Art Show, 1990—2004 (7 awards transparent watercolor including 1st Pl. award, 2004, 3 awards human figure), Portland Audubon Soc. Wild Arts Festival, 1990—94, Rose Festival Art Show, 1990, 1991 (Portland Rose Soc. award), 1992, 1993, El Dorado Gallery, 1992 (1st pl. watercolor), exhibitions include Miniature Art Soc. N.J., 1993 (2nd pl. florals), World Fedn. Miniaturists Internat. Exhbn., London, Eng., 1995, one-woman shows include Trent Hughes Gallery, Portland, 1995, Artspace Gallery, Bay City, Oreg., 1995, 1996, exhibited in group shows at Irving Shapiro Meml. Nat. Watercolor Competition, Chgo., 1995, 1996, Antoinette Hatfield Gallery, Portland, Oreg., 1996—99, exhibitions include Paper Mill Playhouse Internat. Miniature Art Exhbn., 1996—2002, Snow Goose Gallery, Bethlehem, Pa., 1996, 1998, 2000, 2002, Watercolor Soc. Oreg. Exhbn., 1997, 2001, 2002, 1st Tone Internat. Miniature Exhbn., Dhaka, Bangladesh, 1998 (1st pl. florals), Hilliard Soc. Exhbns., Eng., 2000, 2002, World Fedn. Miniaturists Internat. Exhbn., Tasmania, 2000, Fine Art Miniature Internat. Exhbn., Smithsonian Inst., 2004; curator (internat. minature art show) Lake Oswego Festival of Arts, Oreg., 2001—02; Exhibited in group shows at Lawrence Gallery, Portland, Oreg., 2002. Mem.: Watercolor Soc. of Oreg., Miniature Painters, Sculptors and Gravers Soc., Miniature Art Soc. Fla., Miniature Artists Am. (signature mem.), Cider Painters Am. (signature mem.), Phi Kappa Phi. Home: 8240 SW Ridgeway Dr Portland OR 97225 Office Phone: 503-292-0032. Personal E-mail: jmullane3@comcast.net.

MULLARKEY, JILL, secondary school educator; b. Iowa; d. Dennis and Barb Mullarkey. BS in Chemistry, Truman State U., Kirksville, Mo., 2000, MA in Edn., 2001. Lic. tchr. Colo., 2003. Chemistry tchr. Littleton H.S., Colo., 2001—, head girls cross country and track and field coach, 2001—. Named Track and Field Coach of Yr., Continental League Track Coaches, 2005. Mem.: NSTA, Colo. H.S. Coaches Assn. Office: Littleton High School 199 E Littleton Blvd Littleton CO 80121 Office Phone: 303-347-7744. Personal E-mail: jmullarkey@lps.k12.co.us.

MULLARKEY, MARY J., state supreme court chief justice; b. New London, Wis., Sept. 28, 1943; d. John Clifford and Isabelle A. (Steffes) M.; m. Thomas E. Korson, July 24, 1971; 1 child, Andrew Steffes Korson. BA, St. Norbert Coll., 1965, LLD (hon.), 1989; LLB, Harvard U., 1968. Bar: Wis. 1968, Colo. 1974. Atty.-advisor U.S. Dept. Interior, Washington, 1968-73; asst. regional atty. EEOC, Denver, 1973-75; 1st atty. gen. Colo. Dept. Law, Denver, 1975-79, solicitor gen., 1979-82; legal advisor to Gov. Lamm State of Colo., Denver, 1982-85; ptnr. Mullarkey & Seymour, Denver, 1985-87; justice Colo. Supreme Ct., Denver, 1987—, chief justice, 1998—. Fellow: Colo. Bar Found., ABA Found.; mem.: ABA, Denver Bar Assn. (Jud. Excellence award 2003), Colo. Women's Bar Assn. (Mary Lathrop award 2002), Colo. Bar Assn., Thompson G. Marsh Inn of Ct. (pres. 1993—94). Office: Supreme Ct Colo Jud Bldg 2 E 14th Ave Denver CO 80203-2115*

MULLARKEY, MAUREEN T., game company executive; BS, U. Tex., 1980; MBA, U. Nev., 1988. From fin. analyst to CFO Internat. Game Tech., Reno, 1989—2001, CFO, 2001—, exec. v.p., 2003—, treas., 2003—; CFO Zoho Corp., 2000—01. Office: International Game Technology 9295 Prototype Dr Reno NV 89521

MULLEN, DEBORAH W., elementary school educator; b. Muskogee, Okla., Aug. 9, 1955; d. William Hoile and Helen Lorene Withrow; m. Jon David Withrow, May 9, 1986; children: Alisa Suzanne, Jonny Buck. M, Northeastern State U., Tahlequah, Okla., 1985. Tchr. Inola Pub. Schs., Okla., 1983—; prof. Rogers State U., Claremore, 2003—06. Dept. head Pub. Edn., Inola, 1992—2006. Democrat. Baptist. Avocations: ranching, horseback riding, travel. Home: 8729 S 427 Inola OK 74036 Office: Inola Public School 801 E Commercial Inola OK 74036 Office Fax: 918-543-2345. Personal E-mail: dmullen@inola.k12.ok.us.

MULLEN, EILEEN ANNE, human resources executive; b. Phila., Feb. 14, 1943; d. Joseph Gregory and Helen Rita (Kane) M.; m. William John Raschiatore (dec.). BS in English, St. Joseph's U., 1967; MA in English, Villanova U., 1978. Cert. tchr., Pa. Tchr. St. Anastasia Sch., Newtown Square, 1960-67, West Cath. Girls H.S., 1967-74; mgr. staff tng. and devel. ASTM, Phila., 1974-96, dir. human resources, 1996—. Instr. lit., speech and communications Widener U., Chester, Pa. and Wilmington, Del. Contbg. author articles on comms. tng. programs; contbr. articles to profl. jours. Mem. ASTD (pres. Phila./Del. Valley chpt. 1980-81, Outstanding Leadership as Pres. award 1981), Soc. for Human Resource Mgmt. Democrat. Roman Catholic. Office: ASTM 100 Barr Harbor Dr West Conshohocken PA 19428-0700 Office Phone: 610-832-9766. Business E-Mail: emullen@astm.org.

MULLEN, LISA CAITLIN, elementary school educator; b. Chgo., Oct. 3, 1964; d. Patricia Anne Dobler; m. Kevin Russell Mullen, Dec. 19, 1992; children: Griffin Thomas, Cade Michael. BS, U. Pitts., 1988; MA, Coll. Notre Dame, Balt., 1996. Cert. elem. tchr. Pa. Mid. sch. English tchr. Balt. County Pub. Schs., Towson, 1988—92; 8th grade English tchr. North Harford Mid. Sch., Pylesville, Md., 1992—. Cooperating tchr. for student tchrs. Towson (Md.) U., 1992—93, cooperating tchr., 1999—2000. Finalist Harford County Tchr. of Yr., 2004—05; recipient Student Leadership award, U. Pitts., 1988, Academic Achievement award, Coll. Notre Dame, 1992. Lutheran. Avocations: dance, reading, puzzles. Office: North Harford Mid Sch 112 Pylesville Rd Pylesville MD 21132 Office Phone: 410-638-3658. Business E-Mail: lisa.mullen@hcps.org.

MULLEN, M. DENISE, art educator, higher education administrator, photographer, artist; b. Lawton, Okla., July 25; BA, Sweet Briar Coll., 1970; MFA, Pratt Inst., 1973. Asst. prof. art Sweet Briar (Va.) Coll., 1974-75; instr. art County Coll. of Morris, Dover, N.J., 1977-78, adj. instr. art, 1977, 78, NJ City U., 1977-86; asst. prof. art, coord. photography Jersey City State Coll., 1986-93, chair dept. art, assoc. prof., 1994—2000; vice dean Corcoran Coll. Art and Design, Washington, 2000—04; dean Purchase Coll., SUNY, Sch. Art and Design, 2004—. Vis. evaluator Nat. Assn. Schs. Art and Design, Reston, Va., 1994—, bd. mem. 2004-, comm. on accreditation, 1999-2004; mem. exec. bd., art dir. Printmaking Coun. N.J., Sommerville, 1986-89, mem. adv. bd., 1985, 90; bd. dirs. Nat. Coun. Arts Adminstr., 1999-2005. Solo exhbns. include Jersey City Mus., 1996, Mednick Gallery, U. of the Arts, Phila., 1996; exhibited works in group shows at ARTspace Gallery, Richmond, Va., 1994, Ctr. for Book Arts, N.Y.C., 1994, Galerie Mesa, 1995. Trustee N.J. Ctr. for the Visual Arts, Summit, 1996-98. Recipient various merit and purchase awards. Mem. Ctr. for Book Arts, Dieu Donne Paper Mill, Coll. Art Assn., Soc. Am. Graphic Artists, Guild of Bookworkers. Office: Purchase Coll SUNY 735 Anderson Hill Rd Purchase NY 10577

MULLEN, MAUREEN ANN, social worker; b. Chgo., Mar. 22, 1949; d. Robert Vincent and Mary Geraldine M. BA, U. Ill., 1971; MEd, Coll. of William and Mary, 1974; MSW, Univ. Ill., 1990; postgrad., U. Chgo., 1985, 86. Programmer Computer Task Group, N.Y.C., 1980-81; analyst, programmer Guy Carpenter, N.Y.C., 1981-82; analyst C.N.A. Ins., Chgo., 1982-84; analyst, programmer Lakeshore Nat. Bank, Chgo., 1984-85; sales support Sterling Software, Chgo., 1986; owner Mullen Designs, Chgo., 1987; dir. of social svcs. Vista Health, Fayetteville, Ark., 2002—03; employee assistance counselor Ark. Employee Assistance Program, Fayetteville, 2003—06. Prodr., host (TV show) Ozarks Live!, 2003—06. Vol. Samaritans Hotline, Chgo., 1986; adv. bd. Lakeview Mental Health Ctr., Chgo., 1986; active Chgo. Coun. on Fgn. Rels., 1986—87; chmn. fundraiser Habitat for Humanity, 1987; vol. Manic Depressive and Depressive Assn. and Nat. Alliance for Rsch. into Schizophrenia and Depression, 1988, Wilmette Sch. Bd. Caucus, 1997, endowment fund com., 1996—97; vol. Chgo. Bot. Garden, 1999; spkrs. chmn. Fayetteville Freedom Festival, 2003; nominating com. ACLU, 2005—06; vol. Thomas Hynes campaign, Chgo., 1987, New Trier Dem. Orgn., 2000; alderman candidate, 2004; bd. dirs. ACLU N.W. Ark., 2005—06, N.W. Ark. Mental Health Assn., 2002—04, chmn. sch. libr. book project, 2002, 2003; bd. dirs. Cmty. Access TV, Fayetteville, 2003—. Recipient Fat Cat award, Cmty. Access TV, Fayetteville, 2003—05; Ill. State scholar, 1971. Mem.: ACLU (bd. dirs. NW Ark. chpt. 2005—06), NOW, Nature Conservancy, Sierra Club, Dem. Nat. Com., So. Poverty Law Ctr. Avocations: painting, poetry, backpacking, photography, acting. Home: 51 Grove Hill Ave Newton MA 02460 Office Phone: 617-678-3773. Personal E-mail: momoses2002@yahoo.com.

MULLEN, REGINA MARIE, lawyer; b. Cambridge, Mass., Apr. 22, 1948; d. Robert G. and Elizabeth R. (McHugh) M. BA, Newton Coll. Sacred Heart, 1970; JD, U. Va., 1973. Bar: Pa., Del., U.S. Dist. Ct. Del., U.S. Ct. Appeals (3d cir.), U.S. Supreme Ct. Dep. atty. gen. State Del. Dept. Justice, Wilmington, 1973—79, state solicitor, 1979—83, chief fin. unit, 1983—88; v.p., counsel MBNA Am. Bank, N.A., Wilmington, Del., 1988—91, 1st v.p., sr. v.p., counsel, 1991—98, exec. v.p., sr. counsel, 1998—2005. Bd. profl. responsibility State of Del., 1996-99. Bd. dirs. Wilmington Music Festival, 1992-98, New Castle Hist. Soc., 1999—, World Affairs Coun. Wilmington, 2002—; fin. com. Girl Scouts Chesapeake Bay Coun., Newark, Del., 1985-94, bd. dirs., 1988-94, v.p., 1990-94, cmty. devel. com., 1994-96, 99—2003, chair pers. com., 1996-99; bd. dirs. Cmty. Legal Aid Soc., 1994-99, treas., 1995-97. Mem. ABA, Del. State Bar Assn. (chair adminstrv. law sect. 1983-85), U. Va. Law Sch. Alumni Assn. (mem. alumni coun.). Democrat. Roman Catholic. Office: PO Box 335 New Castle DE 19720-0335

MULLENIX, LINDA SUSAN, law educator; b. N.Y.C., Oct. 16, 1950; d. Andrew Michael and Roslyn Marasco; children: Robert Bartholomew, John Theodore, William Joseph. BA, CCNY, 1971; M Philosophy, Columbia U., 1974; PhD Pres.'s fellow, 1977; JD, Georgetown U., 1980. Bar: D.C. 1981, U.S. Dist. Ct. D.C. 1981, U.S. Ct. Appeals (D.C. cir.) 1981, U.S. Supreme Ct. 1986, Tex. 1991, U.S. Ct. Appeals (5th cir.) 1995. U. Md. European divsn., Ramstein, Germany, 1974; adj. instr. Fordham U., N.Y.C., 1975—76, adj. asst. prof., 1977; instr. N.Y. Inst. Tech., N.Y.C., 1976; assoc. prof., lectr. George Washington U., Washington, 1977-80; asst. prof. Am. U., Washington, 1979; assoc. Pierson, Ball & Dowd, Washington, 1980-81; clin. prof. Loyola U. Law Sch., L.A., 1981-82; asst. prof. Cath. U. Law Sch., Washington, 1984-86; assoc. prof., 1986-90; prof., 1990; Reuschlein disting. vis. chair Villanova Law Sch., 2000. Vis. asst. prof. CCNY, 1977, Cooper Union Advancement Sci., Art, N.Y.C., 1977, Loyola U. Law Sch., L.A., 1982-83, Cath. U. Law Sch., Washington, 1983-84; jud. fellow U.S. Supreme ct. and fed. Jud. Ctr., 1989-90; Bernard J. Ward Centennial prof. U. Tex., 1991-2001, Morris and Rita Atlas chair in advocacy, 2001—; vis. prof. Harvard Law Sch., 1994-95, Mich. Law Sch., 1996; resident scholar Rockefeller Found. Bellagio (Italy) Study Ctr., 2002. Author: Mass Tort Litigation: Cases and Materials, 1996, Civil Procedure Roadmap, 1997, Casenotes: Federal Courts, 1997, ExamPro: Civil Procedure, 1998, State Class Actions: Practice and Procedure, 2000, Civil Procedure, 2004; co-author: Understanding Federal Courts, 1998, Federal Courts in the Twenty-First Century, 1996, 2d edit., 2002; Moore's Federal Practice and Procedure, 1991, 97, and annual updates; editor bibliographies Polit. Theory, A. Jour. Polit. Philosophy, 1972-74, The Tax Lawyer Jour., 1978-80; columnist The National Law Jour., 1998—; contbr. editor preview of U.S. Supreme Ct. Cases; co-reporter Report and Plan of Civil Justice Reform Act Adv. Group, S.d., Tex., 1991; assoc. reporter ALI, Restatement of the Law Governing Lawyers; contbr. articles to profl. jours. Alt. del. Dem. State Conv., 1980. Fellow NDEA, 1971-74; N.Y. State Regents Scholar, 1967-71. Fellow Tex. Bar Found.; mem. ABA (reporter task force on class actions 1995-97), Internat. Assn. Procedural Law, Am. Law Inst., DC Bar Assn. (com. on ethics, CLE and the Model Rules 1987), Am. Assn. Law Schs. (exec. com. sect. on civil proc. 1987-88, exec. com. sec. on conflicts of law 1991-92, chair prof. devel. com. 1991-93), Jour. Legal Edn. (editl. bd. 1997-1999), Phi Beta Kappa. Home: 722 Crystal Creek Dr Austin TX 78746-4730 Office: U Tex Sch Law 727 E Dean Keeton St Austin TX 78705-3224 Office Phone: 512-232-1375. Business E-Mail: lmullenix@law.utexas.edu.

MULLER, CAROL BLUE, former academic administrator, nonprofit organization executive, consultant; b. Bethesda, Md., Mar. 9, 1955; d. Ragnwald and Myree (Blue) M.; m. Albert Karl Henning, Sept. 4, 1977; children: Kaethe Blue Henning, Scott Anders Henning. AB in Philosophy and English, Dartmouth Coll., 1977; AM in Edn. Adminstrn. and Policy Analysis, Stanford U., 1981, PhD in Edn. Adminstrn. and Policy Analysis, 1986. Asst. to dir. admissions Dartmouth Coll., Hanover, NH, 1977-79, asst. dean Thayer Sch. Engring., 1987-92, assoc. dean, 1992-96; rsch. asst. Stanford U., Calif., 1979-82, resident dir. Calif., 1982-85, project coord. Calif., 1985-87, cons. assoc. prof. mech. engring. Calif.; pres. Blue Sky Consulting, 1996—97; founder, pres., CEO MentorNet, San Jose, Calif., 1997—. State coord. Am. Coun. Edn. Nat. Identification Program, Washington, 1994-96; co-founder, designer Women in Sci. Project, 1990-, Dartmouth U.; designer, dir. Engring. Concepts in H.S. Classroom, 1990—; exec. dir. Dartmouth Project for Tchg. Engring. Problem Solving, 1990-; spkr. in field. Authored or co-authored (conferences and jour. articles). Sch. dir. Norwich (Vt.) Sch. Bd. Sch. Dist., 1994-96; trustee Am. Dresden Precision Mus., Windsor, Vt., 1993-95; bd. dirs. Women in Engring. Program Advocates Network, 1995—; adv. bd. Internat. Sci. Camp: The Earth We Share, Houston, 1995—. Recipient Exemplary Model Adminstrv. Leadership award Am. Assn. Univ. Adminstrs., 1993, Anita Borg award Anita Borg Inst. Women and Tech. & Assn. Computing Machinery, 2006; grantee NSF, 1993-96, Alfred P. Sloan Found., 1993. Mem. Am. Assn. Higher Edn., Am. Soc. Engring. Edn., Nat. Assn. Women in Edn. (state liaison 1993-96), N.H. Assn. Women in Edn. Avocations: hiking, cooking, gardening, reading. Office: MentorNet 1275 S Winchester Blvd Ste E San Jose CA 95128-3910 Office Phone: 408-296-4405. Business E-Mail: cbmuller@mentornet.net.*

MULLER, CAROLYN BUE, physical therapist, volunteer; b. Crosby, N.D., Feb. 24; d. Sigurd Christian and Eleanor (Rushfeldt) Bue; m. Willard Chester Muller, Jan. 27, 1945; children: Marolyn Jean, Barbara Anne, Nancy Eleanor. BA, St. Olaf Coll., 1940; cert. in phys. therapy, Harvard U., 1944. Assoc. dir. younger girls and phys. edn. sect. YWCA, Syracuse, N.Y., 1940-43; phys. therapist Valley Forge Hosp., Phoenixville, Pa., 1944-45; med. records libr. Trust Territory of Pacific Islands, Truk, Caroline Islands, 1951-52. Founder, prin. organizer Am. Cmty. Sch., Truk, 1952, Lincoln Sch., Katmandu, Nepal, 1956, Am. Cmty. Sch., Mogadiscio, Somali Republic, 1958, Kampala, Uganda, 1966; panelist workshop Wash. Commn. for Humanities, Yakima, 1996. Author: Living in Uganda, 1967; cartographer: Maudie - An Oregon Trail Childhood, 1993. Charter registrar Clallam County Mus. and Hist. Soc., Port Angeles, Wash., 1977-87; vol. reading tutor Port Angeles Sch. Dist., 1980—; cmty. coord. UNICEF, Port Angeles, 1982-85; rep. Target Wash. Seminar, Seattle, 1984; rep. Asia-Can. Women in Mgmt. Conf., Victoria, B.C., Can., 1985; regional judge Wash. State Nat. History Day Contest, Port Angeles, 1985-2002; selection judge Wash. State Inquiring Mind Lecture Series, Seattle, 1989, 90, 96, organizer/coord., Inquiring Mind Lecture Series 1983-2002; Wash. state judge Nat. History Day Contest, Ellensburg, Wash., 1993-2003; bd. dirs. Wash. State Friends of the Humanities, 1991-94; trustee Wash. Commn. for the Humanities, 1995-97; pres. Am. Women's Club, Katmandu, 1957-58, Mogadiscio, 1959-60; v.p. Internat. Women's Club, Saigon, South Vietnam, 1971; mem. selection com. Evergreen State Soc. Awards, 1998, 99. Recipient Women Making a Difference award Soroptimist Internat., 1984, Outstanding Vol. award Citizens' Ednl. Ctr. N.W., 1988, Evergreen award Evergreen State Soc., 1992. Mem. AAUW (br. pres. 1980-84, Edn. Found. scholarship in her name 1996). PEO (rec. sec. 1984-85, v.p. 1985-86, pres. 1987-89, chaplain 1994, Internat. Peace scholarship in her name 1990, state chmn. Internat. Peace scholarship 1989-90), Washington Athletic Club. Avocations: growing flowers, cross-country walking, painting, reading, travel. Home: 3624 S Mount Angeles Rd Port Angeles WA 98362-8910 E-mail: muller@tenforward.com.

MULLER, FREDERICA DANIELA, psychology educator; d. Leopold and Elena; m. Dr. L. Muller; children: Daniela, Adrian. Grad., Med. Inst. Radiology, Romania, 1962, PsyD in Clin. Psychology, 1965, M in Internat. Law and Bus., 1966; specialization courses in Psychodrama, Moreno Inst., Vienna, 1969; grad., Inst. Rsch. in Aging, Rome, 1970, Miami Inst. Psychology, 1987. Diplomate Am. Bd. Forensic Medicine, Am. Bd. Forensic Examiners; lic. psychologist, Fla., Pa.; lic. psychotherapist, Fla.; cert. family mediator, Fla. Supreme Ct. continuing edn. units provider psych. Prof. Sch. Continuing Edn. Barry U., North Miami, Fla. Instr. advanced courses in psychology, psychodrama, med. ethics, social manners; guest speaker Colloque Internat., Bucharest, Romania, 1989-93; guest lectr. U. Arboga, Sweden 1968-72; founder Internat. Studies for Biopsychosocial Issues, 1991; cons. dept. of marriage, family and child devel. systemic studies, Nova U., 1992; founder Euro Am. Exch. Co., 1980; with Santé Internat., Switzerland, 1982-85; dir. Ctr. Biopsychosocial Medicine, 1995. Conducted rsch. on stress and aging with Dr. Anna Aslan, world renowned author; developed 45 minute stress reduction program for use in the work place. Author: The Management of Occupational Stress and Its Linkage to Social Pressures; contbr. articles to profl. jours. Mem. APA, Medicins du Monde (hon.), Am. Soc. Group Psychotherapy and Psychodrama, Soc. Psychol., Studies Social of Issues, World Fedn. for Mental Health.

MULLER, JANICE ELAINE, secondary school educator; b. Littlefield, Tex., Oct. 23, 1955; d. Calvin Roy and Hazel Louise Stevens; m. Mark C. Muller, Aug. 24, 1973; 1 child, Amanda Marie Thompson. BS, Tex. Tech U., Lubbock, 1977, MEd, 1995. Cert. tchr. Tex., 1977, mid mgmt./ednl. adminstrn. Tex., 1995. Tchr. Littlefield H.S., Tex., 1984—. Mem. reading com. ETS/TEA, Austin, 1996—99; mem. site based com. on edn. Littlefield H.S., 1998—, TAKS com. chmn., 2000—04; academic coord. U. Interscholastic League, Littlefield, 1999—. Founder Friends of the Libr., Littlefield, 1978—84; mem. adminstrv. bd. First United Meth. Ch., Littlefield, 2003—06; bd. dirs. Meals on Wheels, Littlefield, 1978—90. Named Outstanding Tex. H.S. Tchr., U. Tex., 1992, Tchr. of Yr., Tex. Assn. of Future Educators, 1997, 2005; fellow Caprock Area Writing Project, Tex. Tech. U., 1992. Mem.: Tex. Classroom Tchrs. Assn. (assoc.), Golden Key Nat. Honor Soc. (assoc.), Delta Kappa Gamma (assoc.; sec. 2000—02, Achievement award 2003). Democrat. Methodist. Avocations: golf, travel, writing. Home: 136 E 23rd St Littlefield TX 79339 Office: Littlefield HS 1100 Waylon Jennings Blvd Littlefield TX 79339 Office Phone: 806-385-5683. Personal E-mail: jmu1952672@aol.com.

MULLER, JENNIFER, choreographer, dancer; b. Yonkers, NY, Oct. 16, 1944; d. Don Medford and Lynette (Heldman) Muller. BS, Juilliard Sch. Music, 1967. Instr. in dance H.S. Performing Arts, 1967-72, Sarah Lawrence Coll., 1968-72, The Juilliard Sch., 1969-70, Nederlands Dans Theater, 1971-76, Utah rep., 1973-74, Centre Nat. de la Dance, Paris, 1998, Acad. Isola Danzo, Venice, 1999-2001, Atelier de Paris, 1999, Institut del Teatre de Barcelona, 2001, Centro Andaluz de Danza-Seville, 2003-05; commns.: Alvin Ailey Am. Dance Theatre, N.Y.C., 1977, 85, 2005, Festival d'Avignon, France, 1980, Lyon Opera Ballet, France, 1984, Aterballetto, 1988, Ballet Stagium, 1991, Dansgroep Krisztina de Chatel, 1992, Tanz-Forum Staatsoper Koln, Sachsische Staatopera-Dresden, ARTSCAPE-Balt., 1991, 95, Aterballetto, Italy, 1993, Les Ballet Jazz de Montreal, 1994, Ballet du Nord, France, 1995, White Wave Rising, 1996, Bat Dor Dance Co., Israel, Nederlands Dans Theatre 3, Ballet Contemporaneo, Argentina, Ohio Ballet, 2000, Dance Inst. U. Akron, 2003; cons. Met. Mus. Art, 1971-72. Mem. Pearl Lang Dance Co., N.Y.C., 1959-63, prin. dance, Jose Limon Dance Co., N.Y.C., 1963-71, assoc. dir., choreographer, prin. dancer, Louis Falco Dance Co., N.Y.C., 1968-74; founder, dir., choreographer: Jennifer Muller/The Works, N.Y.C., 1974-; choreographic works include: Nostalgia, 1971, Rust, 1971, Cantata, 1972, Tub, 1973, An American Beauty Rose, 1974, Biography, 1974, Speeds, 1974, Winter Pieces, 1974, Clown, 1974, Four Chairs, 1974, Wyeth, 1974, White, 1975, Strangers, 1975, Beach, 1976, Crossword, 1977, Predicaments for Five, 1977, Mondriaan, 1977, Lovers, 1978, Solo, 1979, Conversations, 1979, Chant, 1980, Terrain, 1981, Shed, 1982, Kite, 1983, Souls, 1984, The Enigma,

1986, Fields, 1986, Couches, 1986, Life/Times, 1986, Darkness and Light, 1986, Interrupted River, 1987, Occasional Encounters, 1988, City, 1988, The Flight of a Predatory Bird, 1989, Refracted Light, 1990, RIGHTeous About Passing (on the LEFT), 1990, Woman with Visitors at 3am, 1991, Regards, 1991, arm in arm in arm., 1991, Thesaurus, 1991, Glass Houses, 1991, 2-1-1/Attic, 1992, Momentary Gathering, 1992, The Waiting Room, 1993, The Politician/Peeling the Onion, 1993, Orbs, Spheres and Other Circular Bodies, 1993, HUMAN/NATURE-A Response to the Longhouse Gardens, 1993, Pierrot, 1993, Desire-That DNA Urge, 1994, Point of View (A Case of Persimmons and Picasso), 1994, The Spotted Owl, 1995, Some Days are Like That, 1995, Promontory, 1996, Fruit, 1996, The Dinner Party, 1996, A Broken Wing, 1996, Ricochet, 1997, Degas Revisited, 1998, Dialectics Part I, 1998, Spores, Solitude & Summer Humming, 1999, Beethoven-Not Four Naught, 2000, aSOlo, 2000, Hymn for Her, 2000, Time Treading, 2000, China Project: Sagone; Suk Road; Dancing Waves, 2001, The Door, 2001, Never in The Same Room, 2002, To Live Alone., 2002, Moon, 2002, It's a c#!* City, 2002, Prayer, 2003, Bounce, 2003, Footprints, 2003, Flowers, 2004, Ecstatic Poems, 2004, A Candle at Both Ends, 2004, Island, 2005, Sunlight and Shadow, 2005, Momentum, 2005; choreographer for theatrical prodns.: Frimbo, 1980, The Death of von Richthofen., 1982, Fame, The Musical, 1988, Up Against It, 1989, The Seven Deadly Sins, 1990, Signature, 1990, Esther, 1993, Once Around the City, 1998, 01; dir. Le Jongleur, 2000. Recipient Best Performance award Berlin Festival, 1977, Acad. award Juilliard Sch. Music, 1967, Carbonell award, 1989; grantee Nat. Endowment for Arts, 1971-77, 80-85, 86-87, 87-88, Creative Artists Pub. Svc., 1976-77, NY State Coun. on Arts, 1976-77, 78-79, 85-93, NYC Dept. Cultural Affairs, 1978-79, 94-06, NYC Dept. Youth and Cmty. Devel., 2001-05. Mem. Am. Guild Mus. Artists, Soc. Stage Dirs. and Choreographers, World Arts Coun. (founding mem.). Home and Office: The Muller Works Found Inc 131 W 24th St New York NY 10011-1942 Office Phone: 212-691-3803. Business E-Mail: jmuller@jmtw.org, twinfo@jmtw.org.

MULLER, JENNY HELEN, physician, psychiatrist; b. Johannesburg, Dec. 21, 1953; d. Eric and Lily Muller; 1 child, Jonathan Meshekow. MD, U. Witwatersrand, South Africa, 1977. Diplomate Am. Bd. Psychiatry and Neurology. Intern in internal medicine, surgery, orthop., Johannesburg, 1978; intern in internal medicine and psychiatry Va. Med. Ctr., Sepulveda, Calif., 1986—87, resident in psychiatry, 1987—90, Calif. and Olive View Hosp. Child and Adolescent Rotation UCLA, 1987—90; pvt. practice LA, 1990—. Mem.: APA, So. Calif. Psychiat. Soc. Avocation: horseback riding. Office: 9808 Venice Blvd Ste 505 Culver City CA 90232-6818 Office Phone: 310-204-1057. Office Fax: 310-204-1006. Personal E-mail: phy1@sbcglobal.net.

MULLER, KATHERINE LYNN, clinical psychologist; b. Point Pleasant, NJ, Nov. 22, 1973; d. Barbara Jean (Mahlschnee) Morey Hahn and Charles Muller; m. Simon Alexander Rego, May 18, 2003. BA, Douglass Coll., 1992—96; M in Psychology, Rutgers U., 1999, D in Psychology, 2001. Lic. psychologist State of NY, 2003, State of Pa., 2004. Rsch. asst. Rutgers U., New Brunswick, NY, 1996—2000; psychology intern Montefiore Med. Ctr., Bronx, NY, 2000—01; clinician/rschr. U. of Pa., Ctr. for the Treatment and Study of Anxiety, 2001—03; assoc. dir. of psychology tng./dir., cognitive behavior therapy program Montefiore Med. Ctr., Bronx, 2003—; asst. prof. of psychiatry and behavioral sciences Albert Einstein Coll. of Medicine, Bronx, 2003—. Curriculum dir., cognitive behavior therapy program Montefiore Med. Ctr., Bronx, 2003—; cons. Healthcare Coun., NY, 2004—. Contbg. editor: Einstein Journal of Biology and Medicine. V.p. Fairmount Tenants Assn., Phila., 2002—03; mental health provider NY Project Liberty 9-11 Program, Bronx, 2003—04. Grad. Excellence fellowship, Rutgers U. Grad. Sch. of Applied and Profl. Psychology, 1996—2000, Agnes McDede Murray fellowship, Douglass Coll., 1996, Ocean County C. of C. scholarship, Toms River, NJ, 1996. Mem.: Assn. for Advancement of Behavior Therapy, Nat. Assn. of Cognitive Behavioral Therapists, Am. Psychol. Assn., Phi Beta Kappa. Avocations: music, theater. Office: Montefiore Med Ctr 111 East 210th St Bronx NY 10467 Office Phone: 718-920-5024. Office Fax: 718-920-6538. Business E-Mail: kmuller@montefiore.org.

MULLER, MARCIA, writer; b. Detroit, 1944; m. Bill Pronzini. BA in English, Univ. Mich., MA in Journalism. Writer Sunset Mag. Author: (novels) Edwin of the Iron Shoes, 1977, Ask the Cards a Question, 1982, The Cheshire Cat's Eye, 1983, The Tree of Death, 1983, Games to Keep the Dark Away, 1984, Leave a message for Willie, 1984, Legend of the Slain Soldiers, 1985, Thre's Nothing to Be Afraid Of, 1985, The Cavalier in White, 1986, Eye of the Storm, 1988, There Hangs the Knife, 1988, There's Something in a Sunday, 1989, Dark Star, 1989, Shape of Dread, 1989, Trophies and Dead Things, 1990, Where Echoes Live, 1991, Pennies on a Dead Woman's Eyes, 1992, Wolf in the Shadows, 1993 (Edgar Allan Poe award nominee for Best Crime Novel, 1994, recipient Anthony Boucher award), Till the Butchers Cut Him Down, 1994, A Wild and Lonely Place, 1995, The Broken Promise Land, 1996, Both Ends of the Night, 1997, While Other People Sleep, 1998, A Walk Through the Fire, 1999, Listen to the Silence, 2000, Point Deception, 2001, Dead Midnight, 2002, Cyanide Wells, 2003, The Dangerous Hour, 2004, Cape Perdido, 2005, Vanishing Point, 2006, (with Bill Pronzini) Double, 1984, Beyond the Grave, 1986, The Lighthouse, 1987; (short story collections) Deceptions, 1991, McCone and Friends, 2000, Time of the Wolves, 2003, (with Bill Pronzini) Duo, 1998; (non-fiction) 1001 Midnights: An Aficionado's Guide to Mystery and Detective Fiction, 1986. Recipient Private Eye Writers of Am. Life Achievement award, 1993, Romantic Times Lifetime Achievement in Suspense award, 1999, Ridley award, Grand Master award, Mystery Writers of Am., 2005. Avocation: flying. Address: c/o Warner Books 1271 Ave of the Americas New York NY 10020

MULLER, NANCY HRDLICKA, elementary school educator; b. St. Louis, Aug. 10, 1945; d. Charles Joseph, Sr. and Mary Mikesch Hrdlicka; m. John Michael Muller, June 27, 1969; children: Laura Goddard, Joseph, Michael. BA, St. Louis U., 1967. Tchr., drama dir. St. Mary's HS, St. Louis, 1968—73; clk. bd. edn. Kirkwood Sch. Dist., Mo., 1984—86; tchr., social studies coord. St. Peter Sch., Kirkwood, 1986—. Steering com., bd. dirs. Mo. Coun. for History Edn., St. Louis, 1998—. Named St. Peter Sch. Tchr. of Yr., Rotary, Kirkwood, 1999. Mem.: Nat. Cath. Edn. Assn., Mo. Coun. for Social Studies (Mid. Sch. Tchr. of Yr. 2005), Nat. Coun. for Social Studies (Outstanding Mid. Sch. Tchr. of Yr. 2005), Mo. Hist. Soc. (bd. dirs. 2005—, curriculum team 2003—). Roman Catholic. Avocations: singing, reading, gardening, travel. Office: St Peter Sch 215 N Clay Kirkwood MO 63122

MULLER, PATRICIA ANN, nursing administrator, educator; b. N.Y.C., July 22, 1943; d. Joseph H. and Rosanne (Bautz) Felter; m. David G. Smith, Mar. 19, 1988; children: Frank M. Muller III, Kimberly M. Muller. BSN, Georgetown U., 1965; MA, U. Tulsa, 1978, EdD, 1983. RN. Coord. staff devel. St. Francis Hosp., Tulsa, 1978—79, asst. dir. for nursing svc., nursing edn., 1979—82, dir. dept. edn., 1982—98, St. Francis Health Sys., 1998—2002, cons., 2002—. Mem. faculty Okla. U., Northeastern U., Tulsa U.; presenter at confs. and convs. Contbg. editor JOPAN, 1992-2001; contbr. articles to profl. jours. Mem. Leadership Tulsa, 1991; bd. dirs. Am. Heart Assn., Ronald McDonald House. Mem. ANA, Nat. League for Nursing, Am. Soc. for Nursing Svc. Adminstrs., Am. Soc. for Health Manpower Edn. and Tng., Okla. Nurses Assn., Okla. Orgn. of Nurse Execs. (pres. 1992-93), Sigma Theta Tau. Home and Office: 6203 W Utica Ct Broken Arrow OK 74011 Office Phone: 918-671-7767. E-mail: mullsmi@aol.com.

MULLER, RIANA RICCI, musician, educator; b. Orange, Calif., July 14, 1943; d. Ruggerio Ricci and Ruth (Ricci) (Rink) Mairs; m. William Paul Muller, Aug. 17, 1968; 1 child, Christine Rae. BM with Distinction, Eastman Sch. of Music, Rochester, N.Y., 1965; MM Performance, Music Lit., 1969. Instr. Amarillo Coll, Tex., 1973—76; asst. prof. Coll. St. Benedict, St. Joseph, Minn., 1976—78; violinist Puerto Rico Symphony, San Juan, 1978—79; music tchr. (orch.) Hendrick Hudson Pub. Sch., Montrose, NY, 1984—2004; violinist freelance, Greater NY Area, 1984—2004, Pa., 2004—, Muller Duo, Lewisburg, Pa., 1979—; instr. Lycoming Coll., Williamsport, Pa. Violin study with Carrol Glenn, Joseph Knitzer, Louis Persinger and Ruggerio Ricci (my father). Author (and violinist): (DVD) Classical composers in the Foreign Language Classes, 2005; author: Ear Training Exercises for Violin Students, 2006. Decorated with medal and Diplome d'Honneur Eugene Ysaÿe Found., Brussels; recipient Cert. of Commendation for Chamber Music Tchg., Chamber Music Am., 1993. Mem.: Sigma Alpha Iota. Achievements include world premiere performance of Ysaÿe Violin Concerto No.8 (1977). Home: 1119 W Market St Lewisburg PA 17837

MULLER, SUSAN MARIE, physician; b. Holyoke, Mass., Jan. 18, 1964; d. Robert Eugene and Antoinette Irene (Riccio) Muller. BS in Biology, SUNY, Albany, 1986; MD, Albany Med. Coll., 1991. Commd. ensign USN, 1988, advanced through grades to lt. comdr., 1997; internship Nat. Naval Med. Ctr., Bethesda, Md., 1992; gen. med. officer USS Emory S. Land, Norfolk, Va., 1992—94, Naval Air Sta. Oceana, Virginia Beach, Va., 1994—97, med. dir. acute care dept., 1994—97; family practice residency program Family Practice Med. Group, Inc., U. of Fla., 1997—99; family practitioner Benedict Family Health, Ballston Spa, NY, 1999—2001, Saratoga Family Health, Saratoga Springs, NY, 2001—. Med. dir. Saratoga Care Family Health Care Ctrs., Saratoga Springs, NY, 2000—. Recipient Achievement award, UpJohn, 1991, Physician's Recognition award, Am. Med. Assocs., 2002, Ams. Top Family Doctor's award, 2002—03, Med. medal of Honor, 2000,. Avocations: equestrian sports, painting, photography, drawing, sculpting. Office: Saratoga Family Health 119 Lawrence St Saratoga Springs NY 12866 Office Phone: 518-584-7361.

MULLETT, JENNIFER ANNE, lawyer; b. Md., Oct. 14, 1978; BA in Psychology, Hollins U., Roanoke, Va., 1999; JD, George Mason U., Arlington, Va., 2002. Bar: Va. 2002. Atty. Betty A. Thompson, Ltd., Arlington, 2002—. Mem. Jaycees, Alexandria, Va., 2006—. Mem.: Arlington County Bar Assn. (chmn. family law sect. 2006—), Va. Bar Assn., Va. Trial Lawyers Assn. Avocations: travel, English bulldog rescue. Office: Betty A Thompson Ltd 1800 N Kent St Ste 1001 Arlington VA 22209 Office Phone: 703-522-8100. Office Fax: 703-522-3770.

MULLETTE, JULIENNE PATRICIA, health facility administrator; b. Sydney, Australia, Nov. 19, 1940; came to U.S., 1953; d. Ronald Stanley Lewis and Sheila Rosalind Blunden (Phillips) M.; m. Fred Gillette Sturm, Nov. 24, 1964 (div. Dec. 1969); m. Kenneth Walter Gillman, Dec. 28, 1971 (div. Dec. 1978); children: Noah Khristoff Mullette-Gillman, O'Dhaniel Alexander Mullette-Gillman. BA, Western Coll. for Women, Oxford, Ohio, 1961; postgrad., Harvard U., 1964, U. Sao Paulo, Brazil, 1965, Inst. Philosophy, Sao Paulo, 1965, Miami U., Oxford, 1967—69. Tchr. English, High Mowing Sch., Wilton, N.H., 1962-64, Stoneleigh-Prospect Hill Sch., Greenfield, Mass., 1964; seminar dir. Western Coll. for Women, 1967-69; pres. Family Tree, Home U., Montclair, NJ, 1978—88; dir. Pleroma Holistic Health Ctr., Montclair, 1980—. Dir. Astrological Rsch. Ctr., Sydney, Australia, 1983; founder Spiritual Devel. Rsch. Group, 1986—; pvt. counselor, 1962—; guest on radio & TV shows, 1962—; lectr. worldwide, 1963—; founder Pleroma Found. for Astrological Rsch. & Studies, 1990; breeder, trainer exotic animals; mem. Woodstock Pub. Access Com., 1993—. Author: The Moon-Understanding the Subconscious, 1973; contbg. columnist: mags; contbr. articles to profl. jours.; editor (founding): KOSMOS Mag., 1968—78, Jour. Astrological Studies, 1970—; hostess (radio talk shows) The Julienne Mullette Show, 1985—, You and the Cosmos, Binghamton, N.Y., others, (TV series) You and the Cosmos, Woodstock, NY, 1992—, The Julienne Mullette Show Connections TV, Newark, NJ, 1985—, (radio) You and The Cosmos, WHRW, Binghamton, NY, 2006—. Founder local chpt. La Leche League, Montclair, 1974; founding pres. The Internat. Astrology Forum, 2000. Mem. AAUW (chmn. cultural affairs Montclair chpt. 1987—), NAFE, Spiritual Devel. Group (founder), Internat. Soc. Astrological Rsch. (founding pres. 1968-78), Cosmos Hyperspace Astrological Origins and Supergravity Studies (founder), Am. Fedn. Astrologers (cert.), Belgian Soc. Astrology, Am. Assn. Humanistic Psychology, Internat. Llamas Assn., Internat. Soc. Astrological Studies and Rsch. (founder 2002). Avocations: tennis, local theatre, singing. E-mail: julienne@nep.net.

MULLIGAN, DANA MATHEWS, assistant principal; b. Flemington, NJ, Feb. 19, 1974; d. Ronald Frederick and Nancy Elizabeth Mathews; m. Donald Philip Mulligan, July 12, 2003; 1 child, Donald Philip Jr. BA, Fairfield U., Conn., 1996; MA in Tchg., Sacred Heart U., Fairfield, 1998; Sixth Yr. in Ednl. Leadership, So. Conn. State U., New Haven, 2004. Cert. adminstr. Conn., 2004. Asst. women's basketball coach Sacred Heart U., Fairfield, 1996—98; social studies tchr. Hamden H.S., Conn., 1999—2005, asst. prin., 2005—. Recipient Student Motivation award, Hamden Rotary CLub, 2003, 2004, 2005. Mem.: Assn. Hamden Pub. Sch. Adminstrs. (treas. 2005—06). Democrat. Roman Catholic. Office: Hamden Public Schools 2040 Dixwell Ave Hamden CT 06514 Office Phone: 203-407-2089. Business E-Mail: dmulligan@hamden.org.

MULLIGAN, ELINOR PATTERSON, lawyer; d. Frank Clark and Agnes (Murphy) Patterson; m. John C. O'Connor; children: Christine Fulena, Valerie Clark, Amy O'Connor, Christopher Criffan O'Connor; m. William G. Mulligan, Dec. 6, 1975. BA, U. Mich.; JD, Seton Hall U., 1970. Bar: N.J. 1970. Assoc., Springfield and Newark, 1970—72; pvt. practice Hackettstown, NJ, 1972; ptnr. Mulligan & Jacobson, N.Y.C., 1973—91, Mulligan & Mulligan, Hackettstown, 1976—. Atty. Hackettstown Planning Bd., 1973-86, Blairstown Bd. Adjustment, 1973-95; sec. Warren County Ethics Com., 1976-78, sec. Dist. X and XIII Fee Arbitration Com., 1979-87, mem. and chair, 1987-91, mem. dist. ethics com. XIII, 1992—; mem. spl. com. on atty. disciplinary structure N.J. Supreme Ct., 1981—; lectr. Nat. Assn. Women Judges, 1979, N.J. Inst. Continuing Legal Edn., 1988—. Contbr. articles to profl. jours. Named Vol. of Yr., Attys. Vols. in Parole Program, 1978. Fellow Am. Acad. Matrimonial Lawyers (1st woman pres. N.J. chpt. 1995-96); mem. ABA, Warren County Bar Assn. (1st woman pres. 1987-88), N.J. State Bar ASsn., N.J. Women Lawyers Assn. (v.p. 1985—), Am. Mensa Soc., Union League Club (N.Y.C.), Baltusrol Golf Club (Springfield, N.J.), Panther Valley Golf and Country Club (Allamuchy, N.J.), Kappa Alpha Theta. Republican. Home: 12 Goldfinch Way Hackettstown NJ 07840-3007 Office: 933 County Road 517 Hackettstown NJ 07840-4654 Office Phone: 908-852-0202. Personal E-mail: llp-nj@mindspring.com. Business E-Mail: elinormulligan@mulliganmulligan.com.

MULLIGAN, ERIN LEAH, lawyer; b. Harrisburg, Pa., Dec. 5, 1974; d. James Reid and Kathie Eileen Mulligan; m. Peter T. Graber, May 20, 2006. BS, U. Pitts., 1997; JD, Loyola U., New Orleans, 2003. Bar: NC 2004. Clk. New Orleans Legal Assistance, New Orleans, 2002—03; law clk. U.S. Dist. Ct., Raleigh, 2004—05; atty. Law Offices James R. Ansley, Raleigh. Atty. Vol. Lawyers Program, Raleigh, 2004—, Project Together, Raleigh, 2004—. Mem.: Assn. Trial Attys., NC Bar Assn., Wake Women Attys. Democrat.

MULLIGAN, ERLINDA RITA, medical/surgical nurse; b. Gallup, N.Mex., June 11, 1954; d. Reginaldo Fred and M. Maggie (Apodaca) Gallegos; m. Michael Joseph Mulligan,; children: Raymond Fredrick, Margaret Rose, Erin Pablo, Kimberly Edel. ADN, U. N.Mex., Gallup, 1988. RN, N.Mex., Ariz.; cert. med.-surg. nurse Am. Nurses Credentialing Ctr. Nurse Rehoboth McKinley Christian Hosp., Gallup, 1988-89, nurse I, 1989-90, nurse II, rep. med.-surg. and pediat. units, 1990-91, nurse III, 1991-92, nurse IV, 1992-95, surg./med. specialist, 1993—, home health nurse, 1994-97, psychiatric nurse, 1993-94; clin. nurse dept. ob-gyn. Gallup (N.Mex.) Indian Med. Ctr. Indian Health Svc., 1997—. Active St. Francis Ch., Gallup, 1954—, mem. choir, 1991-94; active St. Francis Sch. PTO, Gallup, 1982-92; mem. Right to Life Com. of N.Mex., 1992-94, sec. Gallup chpt., 1993-94. Roman Catholic. Avocations: reading, exercise, sewing, gardening. Home: 205 E Logan Ave Gallup NM 87301-6133

MULLIKIN, SANDRA MARIE, music educator; b. Louisville, May 11, 1960; d. James Edward Stewart Sr. and Mary Angela Stewart; m. Douglas Lee Mullikin, June 15, 1991; children: Tiffany Marie Nicole, Emily Elizabeth Ludmila. MusB in Ch. Music magna cum laude, Ky. Wesleyan Coll., 1982, MusB Edn. with honors, 1982; MA in Elem. Edn. summa cum laude, We. Ky. U., 1986. Office asst. Dr. Alan Bornstein, Louisville, 1977—78; youth dir. Kirk Meml. United Meth., Owensboro, Ky., 1978—79; travel counselor Am. Auto. Assn., Owensboro, 1980—82; choir dir. Breckenridge St. United Meth., Owensboro, 1982—86; music tchr. Owensboro City Schs., 1982—85; sales mgr. Cottonwood Sales, Evansville, Ind., 1985—89; music tchr., band dir. Cloverport Ind. Schs., Ky., 1989—96; tchr. music Ohio County Bd. Edn., Hartford, Ky., 1996—. Realtor L. Steve Castlen Realtors, Owensboro, 1990—92; mem. arts and humanities com. Fordsville and Wayland Alexander Elem., Ky., 1998—2004. Active Civitan, Owensboro, 1980; co-leader brownies Girl Scouts Am., Owensboro, 2001—02; precinct co-capt. Rep. Party, Owensboro, Ky., 1996, 2000, del. to state conv. Louisville, 1996; choir dir. Thruston United Meth. Ch., Maceo, Ky., 1986—94. Scholar, Kappa Kappa Iota, 2001, Ky. Orff-Schulwerk Assn., 1995. Mem.: Ky. Orff-Schulwerk Assn., Am. Orff-Schulwerk Assn., Ky. Music Educators Assn., Music Educators Nat. Conf., Gideons Aux. (pres.), Kappa Kappa Iota (past state music chair), Delta Omicron (Outstanding Svc. award 1982). Republican. Methodist. Avocations: travel, reading, singing, photography. Home: 2417 Whirlaway Dr Owensboro KY 42301 Personal E-mail: musicteach7@aol.com.

MULLIN, NORMA ROSE, psychotherapist; b. Edon, Ohio, July 17, 1933; d. Howard Harrison and Mary Esther Myers; divorced; children: David Farris(dec.), Sarah Esther. BA in Econs. cum laude, Hillsdale Coll., Mich., 1955; MA in Counseling, Oakland U., Rochester, Mich., 1989; Cert. secondary tchr., sec. sci., Hillsdale Coll. Cert. secondary tchr. secretrial sci., lic. profl. counselor Mich. Contract counselor Luth. Social Svcs. of Mich., Oak Park, Mich., 1989—91; profl. counselor Pvt. Practice, Rochester, Mich., 1991—96; contract counselor Macomb Family Svcs., Shelby Township, Mich., 1996—2000, Oakland Psychol. Clinic, Lake Orion, Mich., 2000—03, Advanced Counseling Svcs., Clarkson, Mich., 2003—05; pvt. practice Rochester, 2005—. Mem.: Mich. Counseling Assn., Am. Counseling Assn. Avocations: reading, writing, remodeling. Office: Rochester MI

MULLINS, ANGELA, lawyer; d. Peter and Harriet Mullins. BA, U. San Diego, 1996; MA, St. Xavier U., 1997; JD, U. San Diego, 2002. Juris Doctor: U. Of San Diego, Sch. Of Law 2002; Master Of Arts St. Xavier U., 1997. Commd. ensign USN, 2002, mil. atty. Judge Adv. Gen. Corps San Diego, 2002—06; with Neil Dymott Attys., San Diego, 2006—. Decorated Gold Star USN. Mem.: Lawyer's Club San Diego. Liberal. Office: Neil Dymott Attys 1010 Second Ave Ste 2500 San Diego CA 92101 Office Phone: 619-556-2483, 619-238-1712.

MULLINS, BARBARA J., financial executive; b. Day, Fla., Aug. 29, 1938; d. James Eli and Bessie Geraldine (Johnson) Grantham; m. Mike B. Mullins, Dec. 20, 1956; children: Ronald Lee, Richard Bryan, Mikel Duane. Acctg. Cert., Longview C.C., Lee's Summit, Mo., 1978; AS, Johnson County C.C., Overland Park, Kans., 1980; student, Avila Coll., Kansas City, Mo., 1980-84. Contr., v.p. Bride Co., Leawood, Kans., 1970-82; mgr., cons. Price Waterhouse, Atlanta, 1984-92; owner, cons. Sys. Adv. Svcs., Kansas City, Mo., 1992—99; CFO Memphis Brooks Mus. Art, 1999—. Mem. Inst. Mgmt. Accts. (chpt. pres., nat. dir., regional dir.). Avocations: reading, interior decorating, sewing.

MULLINS, DIANE LOUISE, dermatologist; b. Ravenna, Ohio, Aug. 21, 1955; d. Austin and Bernice Heritage; m. Marshall Mullins; children: Amanda, April, Sarah. BS, Kent State U., Ohioa, 1987; MD, NEOUCOM, Rootstown, Ohio, 1987. Cert. anatomic and clin. pathology, dermatopathology. Resident Akron City Hosp., Ohio, 1987—92; fellow U. Ala., Birmingham, 1992—93; assoc. prof. U. Fla., Gainesville, 1993—98; ptnr. PML, Asheville, NC, 1998—. Office: 55 Sharon Rd Fairview NC 28730-8789

MULLINS, JANE COMPTON, investment manager; d. Homer Barry Compton and Edith Dixon Witt; children: Laura Mullins Nolen, John Ellsworth. BA in Math. and English, Emory and Henry Coll., Emory, Va., 1966. Collegiate profl. tchg. cert. Va., tchr.'s profl. tchg. cert. Ga. Tchr. math. Marion H.S., Va., 1966—67, Fairfield Mid. Sch., Richmond, Va., 1967—70, Athens Acad., Ga., 1981—82; prin. investment mgr. Athens, 1985—. Mem. Jr. League Athens, 1981—2006; mem., treas. Athens Cancer Aux., 1977—81; aux. mem. YWCO, Athens, 1979—81; chairman ball fundraising St. Mary's Hosp. Aux., Athens, 1979; mem. Athens Regional Hosp. Aux., 1977—85; mem., treas. Crawford Long Med. Aux., Athens, 1997—2004; docent Ga. Mus. Art, Athens, 1977—2006; pres., mem. Friends of Ga. Mus. Art, Athens, 1977—2006; chmn., bd. advisers Ga. Mus. Art, Athens, 1996—99; bd. trustees Emory and Henry Coll., 2001—; govtl. appointee Ga. Coun. for Arts, Atlanta, 2001—04. Named Patron of Yr., Ga. Assn. Mus. and Galleries, 2000. Avocations: tennis, bridge, gardening, golf.

MULLINS, PATTY, artist; MFA, Ctr. for Emerging Visual Artists, 2001. Exhibitions include New Arts Gallery, Litchfield Hills, Ct., Main. St. Art Festival, 2005, Whitney Mus. Invitational, Whitney Mus. Am. Arts, 2006; author: (book) The Best Work of Your Life. Office: New Arts Gallery 513 Maple St Litchfield CT 06759*

MULLINS BERG, RUTH GLADYS, nurse; b. Westville, N.S., Can., Aug. 25, 1943; came to U.S., 1949, naturalized, 1955; d. William G. and Gladys H.; m. Leonard E. Mullins, Aug. 27, 1963 (dec.); children: Deborah R. Jenkins, Catherine M., Leonard III; m. Berknard J. Berg, June 19, 2004 BS in Nursing, Calif. State U., Long Beach, 1966; MSN, UCLA, 1973; PhD, Columbia Pacific U. Cert. pediatric nurse practitioner. Pub. health nurse Los Angeles County Health Dept., 1967-68; nure Meml. Hosp. Med. Ctr., Long Beach, 1968-72; dir. pediatric nurse practitioner program Calif. State U., Long Beach, 1973-97, asst. prof., 1975-80, assoc. prof., 1980-85, prof., 1985—, coord. accelerated BSN program, 2003—. Health svc. credential coord. Sch. Nursing Calif. State U., Long Beach, chmn., 1979-81, coord. grad. programs, 1985-92; mem. Calif. Maternal, Child and Adolescent Health Bd., 1977-84; vice chair Long Beach/Orange County Health Consortium, 1984-85, chair 1985-86. Author: (with B. Nelms) Growth and Development: A Primary Health Care Approach; contbg. author: Quick Reference to Pediatric Nursing, 1984; assoc. editor Jour. Pediatric Health Care, 1985—. Tng. grantee HHS, Divsn. Nursing Calif. Dept. Health. Fellow Nat. Assn. Pediatric Nurse Assocs. and Practitioners (exec. bd., pres. 1990-91), Nat. Fedn. Nursing Splty. Orgns. (sec. 1991-93); mem. APHA, Nat. Alliance Nurse Practitioners (governing body 1990-92), Assn. Faculties Pediatric Nurse Practitioner Programs. L.A. and Orange County Assn. Pediatric Nurse Practitioners and Assocs. (treas. 1998—), Am. Assn. Univ. Faculty. Democrat. Methodist. Home: 13240 Eldorado Dr #187A Seal Beach CA 90740 Office: Calif State U Dept Nursing 1250 N Bellflower Blvd Long Beach CA 90840-0001 Office Phone: 562-985-4476. Personal E-mail: rgmullins@sprintmail.com. Business E-Mail: rmullins@csulb.edu.

MULLIS, REBECCA, education educator, department chairman; d. Wiley Emmett and Carrie Taylor McNeill; m. David Mullis; children: Meredith children: Megan. PhD, U. Tenn., Knoxville, 1976. Registered dietitian. Exec. dir. U. Minn. Ctr. for Partnerships with Industry, Mpls., 1988—89; asst. dir. program devel. Centers for Disease Control, Atlanta, 1989—94; prof., chair Ga. State U., Atlanta, 1994; prof., dept. head U. Ga., Athens, 1999—. Adj. assoc. prof. Emory U., Atlanta, 1990—; sci. adv. panel Shape Up Am. Campaign, Washington, 1994—; food certification team Am. Heart Assn., Dallas, 2002—; nat. adv. panel winner's cir. healthy restaurant program U. NC, Chapel Hill, 2002—. Nat. spokesperson food certification program Am. Heart Assn., 2000, task force on nutrition counseling needs, 1991. Grantee, Healthcare Ga. Found., 2005, Atlanta Falcons Youth Found., 2005, Ga. State U./Healthcare Ga. Found., 2004—05, Wash. Mills Meml. Hosp., 2004, Ga. State U., 2002—05. Mem.: Ga. Coalition for Nutrition Edn. (bd. dirs. 1997), Ga. Dietetic Assn. (bd. dirs. 1995). Office: Univ Ga Rm 280 Dawson Hall 305 Sanford Dr Athens GA 30602-3632 Office Phone: 706-542-4875. Business E-Mail: rmm@fcs.uga.edu.

MULLOY, JEAN MARIE, psychologist, human services administrator; b. L.A., Apr. 20, 1964; d. Charles Sullivan and Ann (Ahern) M.; m. Edward Joseph Steinborn, Dec. 31, 1987 (div. Apr. 11, 2001); children: Lauren Steinborn, Ryne Steinborn, Matthew Steinborn. BA magna cum laude, Coll. Mt. St. Vincent, Bronx, N.Y., 1986; MA, Fordham U., Bronx, N.Y., 1987, PhD, 1994. Lic. psychologist Fla., 1996. Rehab. specialist Easter Seal Rehab. Ctr., Stamford, Conn., 1989—92; psychology intern James A. Haley V.A. Hosp., Tampa, Fla., 1993—94; clin. coord. ACTS/Juvenile Justice Program, Tampa, 1995—96; asst. prof. Fla. Sch. Profl. Psychology, Tampa, 1996—98; psychologist Rehab.Ctr., Stamford, 1998—99; pvt. practice Tampa, 1999—2003; exec. dir., bd. pres. Kathy's Place Ctr. Grieving Children, Tampa, 2000—. Presenter, CEO Feminist Family Therapy, 2003. Contbr. articles. Mem. West Shore Alliance, Tampa, 2001. Mem.: APA, Tampa Bay Assn. Women Psychotherapists (sec.), Fla. Psychol. Assn. Avocations: jetskiing, flower arranging, home design. Office: 2504 W Azeele St Tampa FL 33609 Home: 4205 W Watrous Ave Tampa FL 33629-4914

MULRYAN, LENORE HOAG, art curator, writer; b. Lompoc, Calif., Aug. 25, 1927; d. William Thomas and Lois Lorraine (Fratis) Hoag; m. Henry Trist Mulryan; children: Patricia Trist (dec.), James William, Carrie M. Neal. BA in Art History, UCLA, 1979, postgrad., 1979—81; Cert., Am. Inst. Fgn. Trade, Glendale, Ariz., 1949. Vis. art curator UCLA Fowler Mus. Cultural History, 1982—2004; art curator, editor, cons. Internat. Exec. Svc. Corps, 1998—2004. Dir. fine art print calendars for Chapin Sch., Princeton, NJ, 1971-73; co-chair Fine Arts Tours, Princeton, 1973; cons. Internat. Exec. Svc. Corp., Zimbabwe, 1998, Romania, 1998. Author, art curator, editor: (books/exhbns.) Mexican Figural Ceramists and Their Works, 1982, Nagual in the Garden: Fantastic Animals in Mexican Ceramics, 1996, Ceramic Trees of Life: Popular Art from Mexico, 2003-04, UCLA Fowler Mus. Cultural History, 2003—; curator Wilmot Collection of Mexican Art, 1982-91. Mem. Eisenhauer Disting. Fgn. Leader Program U. So. Calif. Mem. Exec. Svc. Corps, Delphians (pres. 1963-64), Westwood Village Rotary Club (chair amb. scholarship selection com. 2000-2005). Avocations: music, art, yoga, travel.

MULVANEY, LOIS, French, English educator; d. William and Arlene Alley; m. Rex D. Mulvaney, Jan. 25, 1954; children: Michele Stainbrook, Dana. BA, Upper Iowa U., Fayette; MA in Edn., Viterbo U., Madison, Wis., 2003. Cert. Master Gardener Benton County, Iowa, 2005. French/English tchr. Vinton/Shellsburg Cmty. Schs., Vinton, Iowa, 1985—. Fellow, NEH. Mem.: Am. Assn. Tchrs. French, ACLU, NOW. Office: Washington HS Vinton/Shellsburg CSD 212 W 15th St Vinton IA 52349

MULVANEY, MARY FREDERICA, systems analyst; b. NY, Nov. 27, 1945; d. Michael Joseph and Mary Catherine (Clapper) Mulvaney. BA, Marymount Coll., 1967; MA, U. Va., 1968; MS in Computer Sci., Marymount U., 1999. Cert. data processor Inst. Cert. Computer Profls. Computer systems analyst Dept. of Def., Ft. Meade, Md., 1968-74; sr. programmer analyst Planning Rsch. Corp., McLean, Va., 1974-83; mem. tech. staff Fed. Systems Group TRW, Inc., Fairfax, Va., 1983-90, engr., scientist, 1994—2002; sr. mem. tech. staff GTE Govt. Sys. Corp., Rockville, Md., 1990-94; software engr. Northrop Grumman, Fairfax, 2003—. Mem.: IEEE, Cath. Assn. Scientists and Engrs., Computer Measurement Group, Data Processing Mgmt. Assn. Roman Catholic. Office: Northrop Grumman Mission Sys 12900 Federal Sys Park Dr Fairfax VA 22033

MULVANEY, MARY JEAN, retired physical education educator; b. Omaha, Jan. 6, 1927; d. Marion Fowler and Blanche Gibons (McKee) M. BS, U. Nebr., 1948; MS, Wellesley Coll., 1951; LHD (hon.), U. Nebr., 1986. Instr. Kans. State U., Manhattan, 1948-50, U. Nebr., Lincoln, 1951-57, asst. prof., 1957-62, U. Kans., Lawrence, 1962-66; assoc. prof. U. Chgo., 1966-76, prof., 1976-90, prof. emeritus, 1990—, chmn. women's divsn., 1966-76, chmn. dept. phys. edn. and athletics, 1976-90; mem. vis. com. on athletics MIT, 1978-81, Wellesley Coll., 1978-79. Dir. athletics U. Chgo., 1980—90; mem. selection com. U. Chgo. Athletics Hall of Fame, 2004—. Recipient Honor award Nebr. Assn. Health, Phys. Edn. and Recreation, 1962, U. Nebr. Alumni Achievement award, 1998; named to U. Chgo. Athletics Hall of Fame, 2003; Office of Dir. Athletics, U. Chgo., named in honor, 2003. Mem.: AAHPERD, Univ. Athletic Assn. (sec. 1986—90, exec. com. 1986—90, dels. com. 1986—90, chmn. athletic adminstrs. com. 1986—88), Ill. Assn. Intercollegiate Athletics for Women (chmn. 1978—80), Nat. Assn. Collegiate Dirs. of Athletics (exec. com. 1976—80, Hall of Fame 1990), Midwest Assn. Intercollegiate Athletics for Women (chmn. 1979—81), Nat. Collegiate Assn. Women Athletic Adminstrs. (Lifetime Achievement award 2006), Nat. Collegiate Athletic Assn. (coun. 1983—87), Alpha Chi Omega, Mortar Bd. Home: 5821 Kennelley Ct Lincoln NE 68516-3799 Personal E-mail: maryjeanmulvany@aol.com.

MULVEY, ELIZABETH N., lawyer; b. NYC, Apr. 7, 1958; BA, Harvard U., 1979; JD, Suffolk U., 1983. Bar: Mass., Maine, Conn., N.H., R.I., U.S. Dist Ct. Dist Mass., U.S. Dist. Ct. Dist. N.H., U.S. Ct. Appeals First Cir. Founding ptnr. Crowe & Mulvey, Boston. Prof. Mass. Continuing Legal Edn., Harvard Law Sch., Nat. Inst. Trial Advocacy; appointed by Supreme Judicial Ct. to 4 yr. term Bd. Bar Overseers. Contbr. chapters to books Expert Witnesses, Mass. Tort Law Manual, articles to profl. jours. Named one of top Boston lawyers, 2004. Fellow: Internat. Acad. Trial Lawyers, Am. Coll. Trial Lawyers (chairperson state com., Mass. 2003—); mem.: Am. Bd. Trial Adv. (adv.), Mass. Bar Assn.-Civil Litig. Sect. (bench bar com.), N.H. State Bar Assn., R.I. State Bar Assn., Maine State Bar Assn. Office: Crowe & Mulvey 141 Tremont St Boston MA 02111 Office Phone: 617-426-4488. Office Fax: 617-426-5511. Business E-Mail: emulvey@croweandmulvey.com.

MULVIHILL, MAUREEN ESTHER, writer, educator; b. Detroit; d. Charles James and Esther (Byrne) M.; m. Daniel R. Harris, June 18, 1983. PhD, U. Wis., 1983; postgrad., Columbia U., Met. Mus. Art, Yale U. Instr. U. Detroit, 1968-70, Wayne State U., Detroit, 1969-70, Penn Valley C.C., Kansas City, Mo., 1970-71; project writer Office of Gov., State of Wis., Madison, 1972-82; chief mktg. and sales writer Gruntal & Co., Inc. Wall St., N.Y.C., 1983-85; vis. asst. prof. Hunter Coll. CUNY, 1984; assoc. fellow Inst. for Rsch. in History, N.Y.C., 1984-89; vis. asst. prof. Touro Coll., N.Y.C., 1985; mem. Princeton (N.J.) Rsch. Forum, 1991—; cons. writer-editor Securities Industry Automated Corp./NYSE, N.Y.C., 1986-94. Proposal evaluator NEH, Washington, 1989—; juror Clifford Com. Am. Soc. for 18th Century Studies, 1991; vis. faculty NYU, 1983-85, 93, Marymount Manhattan Coll., 1993-94, Nyack Coll., N.Y.C., 2004; vis. assoc. prof. Fordham U.-Lincoln Ctr., 1994-96; vis. prof. English, St. Joseph Coll., Bklyn., 1997, Berkeley Coll., N.Y.C., 2000-1, Mercy Coll., N.Y.C., 2002, Met. Coll. N.Y., 2004, St. John's U., Manhattan, 2005-2006; guest spkr. Bklyn. Mus., Bklyn. Pub. Libr., NYU, Princeton U., Utah State U., S.W. Tex. State U., Am. Irish Hist. Soc., N.Y.C.; corp. liaison Irish Art Exhbn., U.S., U.K.; writer mktg. com. Saatchi & Saatchi, N.Y.C., 1998-99; cons. book devel., book proposal evaluator MLA, N.Y.C., 1998—; cons. writer in field. Editor: Poems by Ephelia (ca. 1679), 1992, 1993, Ephelia, 2003; author: Thumbprints of Ephelia: An Online Multimedia Archive, 2001—; contbr. articles to profl. jours.; adv. editor: ABC-CLIO Encyclopedia of Irish-American Relations, 3 vols., 2006—. Recipient scholarships and awards Wayne State U., 1966, 67-68, U. Wis., 1971-81, Inst. Rsch. History, N.Y.C., 1984-89; NEH fellow, John's Hopkins U., 1990, Princeton Rsch. Forum, N.J., 1992, 95, 97, Honors List of Scholars & Tchrs, Women's Caucus, Am. Soc. Eighteenth-Century Stds, 2001. Democrat. Roman Catholic. Avocation: rare book collecting.

MUMMANENI, PADMAJA, research scientist, educator; d. Ram Mohan Rao and Lakshmiswaramma Mummaneni. BSc in Life Scis., Delhi U., India, 1980, MSc, 1982, PhD, 1989. Postdoctoral rsch. fellow U. Ky., Lexington, 1989—96; staff fellow NIH, Bethesda, Md., 1996—2000; scientist Neuralstem Inc., Gaithersburg, Md., 2000—03; vol. consult dir. Neuronascent Inc., Md., 2004; contract RSR fellow CDER, FDA, Rockville, Md., 2004—05; adj. prof. microbiology Marymount U., Va., 2005. Guest lectr. Found. for Advanced Edn. in the Scis. NIH, Bethesda, Md., 1998—2000, juror, 1998—2000. Contbr. articles to profl./peer-reviewed jours. Fellow: AAAS, Am. Soc. of Cellular and Molecular Biology, N.Y. Acad. Scis.; mem.: Am. Women In Sci. Hindu. Avocations: painting, art. Home: 10513 Montrose Ave Bethesda MD 20814 Office: FDA 1451 Rockville Pike Rockville MD 20852 Personal E-mail: pmummaneni@aol.com.

MUMTAZ, **See GIFFORD, NANCY**

MUND, GERALDINE, judge; b. LA, July 7, 1943; d. Charles J. and Pearl M. BA, Brandeis U., 1965; MS, Smith Coll., 1967; JD, Loyola U., 1977. Bar: Calif. 1977. Bankruptcy judge U.S. Ctrl. Dist. Calif., 1984—, bankruptcy chief judge, 1997—2002. Past pres. Temple Israel, Hollywood, Calif.; past mem. Bd. Jewish Fedn. Coun. of Greater L.A. Mem. ABA, L.A. County Bar Assn. Office: 21041 Burbank Blvd Woodland Hills CA 91367-6606 Office Phone: 818-587-2840.

MUNDELL, SUSAN BELLE, special education educator; b. Denver, July 15, 1950; d. Robert James and Hazel F. (Foster) Hermes; m. James Lee Mundell; children: Jeffrey, Jenna. BS, Colo. State U., 1973; MA, U. No. Colo., 1979; cert. endorsement Ednly. Handicapped, U. Colo., Denver, 1984. Lic. tchr. Colo; K-12 spl. edn., 7-12 occupl. home econs. Tchr. Jefferson County Pub. Schs., Arvada, Colo., 1979—; libr. info. specialist Stotl Elem., 2003—05; ret. Co-author: (book) Practical Portfolios: Reading, Writing, Math. and Life Skills, 1994. Flutist Cmty. Concert Band, Arvada, 1990—. Mem. Colo. Coun. Internat. Reading Assn. (Star Grant award 1994), Coun. Learning Disabilities (1 of 8 Nat. Tchrs. of Yr. 1993, Colo. Tchr. of Yr. 1993) Avocations: writing, reading, hiking, flutist.

MUNDINE, RACHEL QUINN, music educator; b. Newport, NC, Aug. 14, 1935; d. Raymond Thomas and Ada Elizabeth (Quinn) M. Student, East Carolina U., Greenville, N.C., 1953—54. Music dir. Program Search For a Star WNCT-TV, Greenville, NC, 1954—55, pianist various programs, 1954—55; soprano soloist Santa Monica (Calif.) Civic Opera, 1968—71; music tchr. piano, voice, organ Melody Haven Studio, Newport, NC, 1972—; 19organist First United Meth. Ch., Morehead City, NC, 1984—; guest piano soloist N.C. Symphony, Morehead City, 1981. Organist, pianist, vocalist in field; pres., founder La Musique Club of Carteret County, NC, 1975—; dir. Miss La Musique Pageant, Morehead City, 1993-2005; area and state chmn. music festivals NC Fedn. Music Clubs, Greenville and Chapel Hill, 1984-94. Composer: Our Majestic Mountains, 1986. Active Carteret County Social Svcs. Bd., 2002—; contbns. chmn. NC Symphony Carteret County chpt., Morehead City, 1993—2002, pres., 1981; entertainment chmn. Festival of the Trees, Hospice, Morehead City, 1997—2005; adv. bd. Civic Ctr., Morehead City, 1999—2001. Named Woman of Yr. in Arts Carteret County Coun. Women, Morehead City, 1990, 92. Mem. Nat. Guild Piano Tchrs. (adjudicator 2003, 2005), NC Music Tchrs. Assn., Order Eastern Star (worthy matron 1977-78, grand organist 1981-82), NC Music Assn. (founder, pres. 1995-2005), Lions. Methodist. Avocations: hiking, sailing, skiing, swimming. Home and Office: Melody Haven Studio 580 Lake Rd Newport NC 28570-6956

MUNDINGER, MARY O'NEIL, nursing educator; b. Fredonia, N.Y., Apr. 27, 1937; d. Thomas Lewis and Dorothy (Hanselman) O'Neil; m. Paul C. Mundinger, Aug. 23, 1958; children: Paul Jr., Ann Mundinger Schimenti, Thomas, Elizabeth. BS, U. Mich., 1959; MA, Columbia U., 1974, PhD, 1981; LHD (hon.), Hamilton Coll., 1996. Adminstr., instr. Tchrs. Coll. Columbia U., NYC, 1975; adj. instr. Pace U., NYC, 1975-77, asst. prof., 1977-82; asst. prof. nursing, dir. grad. program Columbia U. Sch. Nursing, NYC, 1982-83, assoc. prof. nursing, dir. grad. program, 1983-84, assoc. prof., assoc. dean adminstrv. affairs, 1984-85, assoc. prof., asst. dean faculty of medicine, 1986, dean, Centennial prof. health policy, 1986—. Bd. dirs. Conn. Hospice, Branford, UnitedHealth Group, 1997-, Cell Therapeutics, Inc., 1997-, Gentiva Health Services, 2002-, Welch Allyn Inc., 2002-; adv. group steering com. N.Y. Acad. Medicine, N.Y.C., 1992—; regional adv. com. Nat. Network Librs. of Medicine, N.Y.C., 1992—; Robert Wood Johnson health policy fellows bd. Inst. Medicine, Washington, 1990—, Health Svcs. Improvement Fund, NYC, 1992—, health policy adv. com. Sen. Edward Kennedy, Washington, 1985—, med. adv. bd. Walt Disney Imagineering (Wonders of Life), Orlando, Fla., 1988-89; charter mem. health care tech., Inst. Medicine, NAS, 1985-. Author: Home Care Controversy: Too Little, Too Late, Too Costly, 1983 (Book of Yr. 1984), Autonomy in Nursing, 1980 (Book of Yr. 1981). Recipient grant W.K. Kellogg Found., 1989, grant Katzenbach Found., 1986; Nurse Practitioner Year award, The Nurse Practitioner Journal, 1998. Fellow: Am. Acad. Nursing, NY Acad. Medicine; mem.: Inst. Medicine. Avocations: skiing, reading. Office: Office of Dean of Nursing 630 W 168th St Box 6 New York NY 10032-3702 Fax: (212) 305-1116.*

MUNDORFF SHRESTHA, SHEILA ANN, dental educator; b. Rochester, N.Y., Dec. 14, 1945; d. Karl Mundorff and Elizabeth Mary (Braun) Ross; m. Buddhi Man Shrestha, June 18, 1988. BS in Biology, Nazareth Coll., Rochester, 1967; MS in Microbiology, U. Rochester, 1984. Lab. technician Eastman Dental Ctr. U. Rochester, 1967-69; rsch. asst. Eastman Dental Ctr., 1969-71, rsch. assoc., 1971-92, small animal expt. coord., 1984-92, sect. head animal/microbiol. rsch., 1987—, chmn. Instl. Animal Care and Use Com., 1990-97, vivarium dir., 1990-97, mem. emergency program dir., 1991-92, asst. prof., 1992-97; assoc. prof. U. Rochester Eastman Dept. Dentistry, 1997—. Mem. univ. com. on animal resources U. Rochester, 1997-2003; mem. animal resource group ADA Health Found., Chgo., 1981-83; cons. working group Sci. Consensus Conf.-Assessment Cariogenic Potential of Foods, San Antonio, 1985; participant, reactor, co-chair animal caries models working groups Conf. on Clin. Aspects of Demineralization of Teeth, Rochester, N.Y., 1994; invited session chair symposium 2000, Univ. Leeds, 2000. Patentee in field. CPR instr. ARC, Rochester, 1978-94, cert. 1st responder, N.Y.S., 1992-95. NIH, Nat. Inst. Dental Rsch. grantee, 1986, 87, 88. Mem. Am. Assn. Dental Rsch. (sec.-treas. Rochester sect. 1977-92). Roman Catholic. Avocations: dance, sewing, swimming, flower arranging, painting on silk. Office Phone: 585-704-5020. Personal E-mail: bshrestha@rochester.rr.com.

MUNFORD-CLARK, CENELL RENEA, healthcare educator, athletic trainer; d. Dan Defred and Bertha Lee Munford; m. Fendrich Randall Clark, Sept. 4, 1999; children: Fendrich Randall Clark Jr., Daniel Lee Clark. BS, Mt. Union Coll., Alliance, Ohio, 1993; MS, U. Akron, Ohio, 1995; postgrad., Ohio State U., Columbus, 1995—98. Lic. and cert. athletic trainer Ohio. Grad. assoc. Ohio State U., Columbus, 1995—98, instr. health edn., 1999; dir. residence halls Mt. Union Coll., Alliance, 1999—, instr., athletic trainer, 2000—. Presenter in field. Contbr. articles to profl. jours. Mem. GALA fundraiser com. Am. Heart Assn., 2005—, mem. Sister Steps program for African Am. women, 2005—, mem. minority outreach com., 2002—. Nominee YWCA Women's Hall of Fame, 2006; named Mrs. Fitness Ohio Am., 2005; named one of Top 10 Mrs. Ohio Am., 2006; recipient Cert. Appreciation, Am. Heart Assn., 2005, 2006. Mem.: Nat. Exercise Trainers Assn., Ohio Athletic Trainers Assn., Nat. Athletic Trainers Assn., Delta Sigma Theta (chair phys. and mental health com. 1999—2002). Office: Mt Union Coll 1972 Clark Ave Alliance OH 44601

MUNGAS, ANDREA MARIE, elementary school educator; b. Butte, Mont., Mar. 12, 1949; d. Peter August and Mary Theresa (Andrews) Malyevac; m. Charles Robert Mungas, June 12, 1971; children: Nicholas, Jeannette. Degree in Elem. Edn., U. Mont., 1971. Cert. edn. Tchr. grades 1, 2 La Motte Sch., Bozeman, Mont., 1972-76; tchr. kindergarten St. Matthew's Sch., Kalispell, Mont., 1980-81; lib. aide Sch. dist. #5, Kalispell, Mont., 1981-83; tchr. grades 1, 2 Fair-Mont-Egan Sch., Kalispell, Mont., 1984-90; tchr. grades 1, 2, 4 Rainbow Am. Elem. Sch., Ansbach, Germany, 1990-95, tchr. kindergarten, 2006—; math. coord. Dept. Def. Edn. Activities Wuertzburg Dist., Bavaria, Germany, 1995—96; tchr. grade 1 Kitzingen Elem. Sch., 1996—99; reading recovery, tchr. grade 1 Kitzingen, Wuerzburg Elem Schs., 1999—2006. Mem. math-sci. CIRC Dept. Def. Edn. Activities Worldwide, 1992—, math. leadership course, 1994, Early Childhood task force, Nuernberg/Wuertzburg, 1993—, Math. task force, Wuertzburg dist., 1994-; presenter in field. V.p. PTSA Rainbow Sch., Ansbach, Germany, 1993-94, 94-95; mem. choir, prayer and study groups Ansbach Chapel, Germany, 1990—. Recipient Presidential award for Excellence Nat. Sci. Found., 1994, Phoebe Apperson Hearst Outstanding Educator award, PTSA Rainbow Sch., 1995. Mem. Nat. Coun. Tchrs. of Math., Coun. of Presidential Awardees in Math. Roman Catholic. Office: Ansbach High Sch CMR 454 Box 2764 APO AE 09250

MUNGUIA, GAY YEAGER, retired elementary school educator, retired secondary school educator; b. Tyler, Tex., Aug. 17, 1934; d. George Allen and Alice Rhoda (Sanders) Yeager; m. Douglas A. Thibodeaux, June 10, 1955 (div. Nov. 1979); children: Lane David, Lynn Alice, Lee Douglas; m. Jeffrey Joe Wheeler, Sept. 25, 1982 (div. June 1992); m. Michael Anthony Munguia, June, 1995. BA in History and English, Lamar U., 1955; MEd, Sam Houston State U., 1995; M in Ednl. Adminstrn., Sam Houston State U., Huntsville, Tex., 1995. Cert. tchr., Tex., ESL cert., 2004, accredited jewelry profl., diamond and diamond grading Gemological Inst. of Am., 2005. Tchr. Ball High Sch., Galveston, 1955-58; high schs. tutor Mich., La., Tex., 1958—88; coll. tutor Tex., 1971—77; receptionist Theatre Under the Stars, Houston, 1978; asst. mgr. Heavenly Body Health Spa, Houston, 1979-80; salesperson Carbondale, Colo., 1980-82; dept. supr. Glenwood Med. Assoc., Glenwood Springs, Colo., 1983-88; tutor Colo. Mt. Coll., Glenwood Springs, 1988—2004; ladies mgr., aerobics instr. Tex. Lady-Texan Spa, Houston, 1988-89; tchr., curriculum devel. Inter-Faith Child Devel. Ctr., The Woodlands, Tex., 1989—97; kindergarten tchr. Couroe Indept. Sch. System, 1997—2004; ret., 2004. Curriculum devel. cons. St. Barnabas Ch., Glenwood Springs, 1983-85, St. Christopher's Pre-Sch., Houston, 1968-70; text book cons. Galveston schs., 1957. Author weekly coll. activity column, essays, poems, children's stories; acted, directed and produced local dramas including Truman Capote's A Christmas Memory; acted in several movies and TV commls. Century Casting, 1978-81. Vol. St. Barnabas Ch. Thrift Gift Sale, 1983-85, St. Christopher's Thrift Shop, 1960-69; outreach chmn. St. Barnabas Ch. Vestry, 1983-86; active Walden Cmty. Ch., 1988—. Recipient Humanitarian of Yr., Conroe Ind. Sch. Dist., 2002, Tchr. of Yr., 2003. Mem. Alpha Chi Omega, Pi Kappa Phi. Episcopalian. Avocations: writing, drama, Bible, dance, camping.

MUNIZ, DIANE VIRGINIA, psychologist; b. Jersey City, Aug. 7, 1962; d. Adolph Edward and Florence Mary (Desmond) Stewart; children: Christopher, Sean; m. Emmanuel M. Ramirez, April 16, 2005. BS in Psychology, Barry U., Miami Shores, Fla., 1985, MS in Clin. Psychology, 1987; PhD in Clin. Psychology, Nova Southeastern U., Ft. Lauderdale, Fla., 1995. Lic. psychologist, 1999. Ednl. cons., Miami Shores, 1987—; intern psychology Bayview Ctr. for Mental Health, North Miami, Fla., 1994-95, clin. specialist, 1995-96; quality improvement dir. Behavioral Health Network, Miami, Fla., 1998—99; sch. psychologist Miami Dade County Pub. Schs., 2000—. Roman Catholic. Avocations: swimming, reading. Office: 1515 NW 167th St Miami FL 33169-5100 E-mail: ramirezdoc@comcast.net.

MUNN, POLLY, retired elementary school educator; b. Kans. City, Kans., Feb. 13, 1931; d. Virgil Dwight and Veta Elizabeth Wood; Bachelor's, Emporia State U., Kans., 1952, Master's, 1963; postgrad., various schs., 1963—67. Tchr. 1st grade Miles Elem. Sch., Tucson, 1952—54, Oak Grove Sch., Wyandotte County, Kans., 1954—55; tchr. 2d and 3rd grades Maplewood Chouteau Sch., North Kans. City, 1955—59; tchr. grades 7-12 Kendall, Kans., 1959—61; tchr. grades 7-9 Harvey Vernon Washington Sch., Kenosha, Wis., 1961—90; ret., 1990. Pres. Kenosha Sr. Citizens, 1993—96; mem. Kenosha Sch. Bd., 1996—2005; chair adminstrv. bd. trustees 1st Congl. Ch. Named on plaque four dist. schs. Mem.: Kenosha County Retired Tchrs. (pres. 1995—96), Kenosha Women's Club. Democrat. Congregationalist. Achievements include Polly Munn Scholarship Fund named in her honor. Avocation: bridge.

MUNNELL, ALICIA HAYDOCK, economist; b. NYC, Dec. 6, 1942; d. Walter Howe Haydock and Alicia (Wildman) Haydock Roux; m. Thomas Clark Munnell (div.); children: Thomas Clark Jr., Hamilton Haydock; m. Henry Scanlon Healy, Feb. 2, 1980. BA in Econs., Wellesley, 1964; MA in Econs., Boston U., 1966; PhD in Econs., Harvard U., 1973. Staff asst. bus. rsch. div. New Eng. Tel. Co., Boston, 1964-65; teaching fellow econs. dept. Boston U., 1965-66; rsch. asst. for dir. econ. studies program Brookings Instn., Washington, 1966-68; teaching fellow Harvard U., Cambridge, Mass., 1971-73; asst. prof. econs. Wellesley Coll., Mass., 1974; economist Fed. Res. Bank Boston, 1973-76, asst. v.p., economist, 1976-78, v.p., economist, 1979-84, sr. v.p., dir. rsch., 1984-93; asst. sec. for econ. policy Dept. Treasury, Washington, 1993-95; mem. Coun. of Econ. Advisors, 1995—97; prof. Carroll Sch. Mgmt., Boston Coll., 1997—; dir. Ctr. for Retirement Rsch., Boston Coll., 2006—. Mem. Gov.'s Task Force on Unemployment Compensation, Mass., 1975; mem. spl. funding adv. com. for Mass. pensions, 1976; mem. Mass. Retirement Law Commn., 1976-82; staff dir. joint com. on pub. pensions Nat. Planning Assn., 1978; mem. adv. com. for urban inst. HUD grant on state-local pensions, 1978-81; mem. pension rsch. council Wharton Sch. Fin. and Commerce, U. Pa., 1979—; mem. adv. group Nat. Commn. for Employment Policy, 1980-81; mem. adv. bd. Nat. Aging Policy Ctr. in Income Maintenance, Brandeis U., 1980-84; participant pvt. sector retirement security and U.S. tax policy roundtable discussions Govt. Rsch. Corp., 1984; mem. supervisory panel Forum Inst. of Villers Found., 1984; mem. Medicare working group, div. of health policy rsch. and edn. Harvard U., 1984-87; mem. Commn. on Coll. Retirement, 1984-86; mem. com. to plan major study of nat. long term care policies Inst. Medicine, Nat. Acad. Scis., 1984-87; mem. steering com. Am. Assn. Ret. Persons, 1987—; mem. adv. coun. Am. Enterprise Inst., 1987—; com. mem. Inst. Medicine, Nat. Acad. Scis. Human Rights Com., 1987—; co-founder, pres. Nat. Acad. Social Ins., 1986—; bd. dirs. Pension Rights Ctr.; mem. program rev. com. Brigham and Women's Hosp., 1988—; mem. Commn. to Rev. Mass. Anti-Takeover Laws, 1988-89; mem. econs. vis. com. MIT, 1989—. Author: The Impact of Social Security on Personal Saving, 1974, Future of Social Security, 1977 (various awards), Pensions for Public Employees, 1979, The Economics of Private Pensions, 1982; co-author: Options for Fiscal Structure Reform in Massachusetts, 1975; editor: Lessons from the Income Maintenance Experiments, 1987, Is There a Shortfall in Public Capital Investment?, 1991, (conf. proc.) Retirement and Public Policy, 1991, Pensions and the Economy: Sources, Uses, and Limitations of Data, 1992, Framing the Social Security Debate: Values, Politics and Dollars: The Role of Gifts and Bequests in America, 2003, Coming Up Short: The Challenge of 401(K) Plans, 2004, Oxford Handbook of Pensions and Retirement Income, 2006, others; co-editor: Pensions and the Economy: Sources, Uses, and Limitations of Data; contbr. articles to profl. jours., chpts. to books. Mem. Inst. Medicine of NAS, Nat. Acad. Pub. Adminstrn. Office: c/o Boston College 140 Commonwealth Ave Chestnut Hill MA 02467

MUÑOZ, CALISE I., federal agency administrator; Grad., U. So. Calif.; JD, Georgetown U., 1995. Bar: Calif. White House intern Bush Adminstrn., Washington; law clk. Office Atty. Gen. State Wash.; legal clk., legis. asst. fed. affairs health team Am. Assn. Ret. Persons, Washington; legis. policy cons. Calif. State Senator Ken Maddy; legis. adv.; dep. dir. policy Office Intergovernmental Affairs U.S. Dept. Health and Human Svcs., 2001—04, regional rep. Region IX San Francisco, 2004—. Office: US Dept HHS Fed Office Bldg Rm 431 50 United Nations Plaza San Francisco CA 94102

MUNOZ, CELIA ALVAREZ, artist; b. El Paso, Tex., Aug. 15, 1937; d. Frank P. and Enriqueta (Limon) Alvarez; m. Andres Munoz, July 27, 1965; children: Anna Celia, Andres III. BA, U. Tex., 1964; MFA, U. North Tex., 1982. Fashion illustrator White House Dept. Store, El Paso, Tex., 1961; art instr. El Paso Pub. Schs., 1964-74, Bauder Fashion Coll., Arlington, Tex., 1984-88; lectr. U. Tex., Arlington, 1984-89. Adv. bd. Arlington Mus. Art, 1993—; mem. design team Sky Harbor Internat. Airport, 1993, N.Y. Percent for Art, P.S. 8, 1995—, Henry B. Gonzalez Convention Ctr. Expansion Project, 1995-98, Dallas Area Rapid Transit, 1998, Dallas Dept. Cultural Affairs Commn. Latino Cultural Ctr., 1999. Author: If Walls Could Speak, 1991, 95, Biennial Whitney Mus. of Am. Art.; one woman shows include Irving Arts Ctr., 1999; group shows include Arlington Mus. Art, Handley-

Hicks Gallery, Tex. Tech U. NEA fellow, 1988, 91; recipient Outstanding Achievement in the Arts award Women's Caucus. Avocations: bicycling, walking, cinema, music, photography. Home: 5815 Arbor Valley Dr Arlington TX 76016-1522*

MUNOZ, CHERYL ANN, portfolio manager; d. Roy D. and Karen Gene Willis; m. Rick Munoz, Sept. 6, 1998. MusB, Calif. State U., 1997; postgrad., Pepperdine's Graziadio Sch. Bus., 2003—06. CFA, various certs. NASD. Gen. office clk. Marine & Roubidoux, Inc., Westlake Village, Calif., 1996—97, adminstrv. asst., 1998—99, portfolio adminstr., 1999—2002, portfolio mgr., strategist, 2002—05; portfolio mgr., v.p. Zephyr Investment Mgmt., Westlake Village, 2006—. Named Nat. Essay Writing Competition Winner, Big Bros./Big Sisters Orgn., 1987; Music scholar, Calif. State U. Northridge, 1991. Mem.: CFA Soc. LA, CFA Inst., Beta Gamma Sigma, Golden Key Honor Soc. Achievements include researching and creating various proprietary investment management models with the goal of reducing risk and enhancing returns. Avocations: horseback riding, skiing, clarinet, reading. Office Phone: 805-496-6810. Personal E-mail: chermunoz@yahoo.com.

MUNOZ, CHRISTINE, systems analyst; children: Paul, Nicole, Daniel. Mac/pc sys. adminstr. NASA, Moffett Field, Calif., 1986—. Avocations: guitar, singing, dance. Office: NASA Ames Rsch Ctr Bldg 204 Moffett Field CA 94035

MUÑOZ DONES DE CARRASCAL, ELOISA (ELOISE MUNOZ DONES), hospital administrator, pediatrician, educator; b. San Lorenzo, P.R., Oct. 25, 1922; d. Pedro and Maria (Dones) Muñoz; m. José D. Carrascal, Dec. 7, 1962; children: Lilia, Maria. BA in Edn. cum laude, BS in Chemistry cum laude, U. P.R., Rio Piedras, 1943; MD, Tulane U., 1948. Diplomate Am. Bd. Pediatrics. Intern Arecibo Charity Dist. Hosp., 1948-49; resident in pediatrics San Juan (P.R.) City Hosp., 1949-51, chief newborn svc., attending pediatrician, 1951—, dir. neonatal-perinatal medicine, 1965—, dir. fellowship tng. program, 1972—; from instr. to assoc. prof. clin. pediatrics sch. medicine U. P.R., 1951-89, prof., 1989—. Courtesy pediatrician neonatologist Tchrs. Hosp., Hato Rey, P.R., 1951-76, Ashford Presbyn. Drs. Hosp., Santurce, P.R., 1951-76, San Jorge H. H. Pavia Fernandez, Santurce, 1951-76; cons. pediatrician neonatologist Tchrs. H. Auxilio Mutuo H., Hato Rey, 1976—, Drs. H. San Jorge H. Ashford, San Juan, 1976—; mem. exec. com. San Juan City Hosp., 1976—, pres. med. faculty, 1976-77, 87-89, mem. instl. rev. bd., mem. ednl. rev. bd., mem. various coms.; lectr. in field. Contbr. articles to profl. jours. U.S. del. Care Orgn. Latin Am., 1962-63. Recipient Bronze medal Brazilian Acad. Human Scis., 1975, Hon. Cert. Internat. Yr. Women, City Mayor Lodo Carlos Romero Barceló, 1975, Hon. Cert. Disting. Svc. to Cmty., Julio Sellés Solá Elem. Sch., 1976, Pioneer Pediatrician award P.R. Pediat. Sect. Convention, 1993, Pioneer in Neonatology award P.R. Pediat. Sect. Convention, 1995, Pioneer Pidiat. Critical Care award Pediat. Critical Care Assn., 1996; grantee NIH, 1962. Fellow Am. Acad. Pediatrics (neonatal perinatal sect., mem. com. fetus and newborn P.R. chpt. 1956—, sec.-treas. 1962-64, mem. com. history perinatal sect. 1992—, Plaque in Recognition Disting. Pediatrician and Tchr. 1985), Pan Am. Pediatrics; mem. Am. Med. Women Assn., P.R. Med. Assn. (pediat. sect., mem. chamber of dels. 1962-63, Bronze plaque 1967, 91, Gold Pin 1980), P.R. Med. Women Assn. (sec.-treas. 1957-60, pres. 1960-64), Pan Am. Med. Women Assn. (pres. P.R. chpt. 1960-64, P.R. del. VIII Congress Manizales Colombia 1962), Pan Am. Med. Women Alliance (vis. lectr. 1962), Tulane Med. Alumni, London Royal Soc. Health, Colegio de Químicos, Soc. Dominicana de Pediatría (hon., vis. lectr. 1971), Dominican Rep. Soc. (hon.). Avocation: poetry.

MUÑOZ FERNÁNDEZ, MICHELA, electrical engineer, researcher; arrived in US, 2000; d. Juan and Alicia. Diploma summa cum laude in Elec. Engring., Escuela Politécnica, U.A.H., Madrid, Spain, 1998; MS in Space Studies, Internat. Space U., Strasbourg, France, 2000; MSEE, Calif. Inst. Tech., 2001, PhD in Elec. Engring., 2005; MSEE, U. Complutense, Madrid, 2004. Registered profl. engr., Spain, 1998. Database mgmt. engr. SEMA Group Alcatel Formacion y Consultoria, Madrid, 1996; elec. engr. European Space Agy. ROSETTA mission Nat. Aerospace Inst. of Spain, Madrid, 1997—99; telecom. engr. Jet Propulsion Lab. NASA, Pasadena, Calif., 1999, rschr. Jet Propulsion Lab., 2000—06, project sys. engr. Jet Propulsion Lab., 2006—. Organizer politechnical congress Escuela Politécnica, U.A.H., Madrid, 1994—95. Contbr. articles to profl. jours. (Best paper Advanced Systems for Satellite Comm. Category award). Recipient award, Caltech/JPL, 2004; fellow, U. Politécnica, 1999, Divsn. Sci. and Engring., Calif. Inst. of Tech., 2000—01; grantee, NASA, 2002—05; scholar, European Space Agy., 1999—2000; Calvo Rodés fellowship, Nat. Aerospace Inst., 1997, Amelia Earhart fellowship, Zonta Internat. Found., 2002, 2004. Mem.: IEEE, The Internat. Soc. Optical Engring., Athenaeum-Caltech Club. Achievements include first to new technology for high-rate coherent optical communications for deep space. Mailing: 158 S Madison Ave No 209 Pasadena CA 91101 Office Phone: 818-219-9306. Personal E-mail: michela@caltech.edu. Business E-Mail: michela.munoz.fernandez@jpl.nasa.gov.

MUÑOZ-SOLÁ, HAYDEÉ SOCORRO, library administrator; b. Caguas, PR, Dec. 27, 1943; d. Gilberto Muñoz and Carmen Haydeé (Solá) de Muñoz; m. Juan M. Masini-Soler, Jan. 8, 1966 (div. 1979); children: Juan Martín Masini-Muñoz, Haydeé Milagros Masini-Muñoz. BA in Psychology, U. P.R., Río Piedras, 1965, MLS, 1970; D in Libr. Sci., Columbia U., 1985. Asst. libr. U. P.R., Río Piedras, 1964-67; dir. libr. Interam. U., Aguadilla, PR, 1974-75; head svcs. to pub. U. P.R., Aguadilla, 1975-76; cataloguer Cath. U., Ponce, PR, 1976-79, U. P.R., Río Piedras, 1982-84, head libr. and info. sci. libr., 1984-85, prof. grad. libr. sch., 1986, 99, dir. libr. sys., 1986-93, coord. external resources libr. sys., 1994-97, dir. of libr. Ponce, PR, 1997, collection devel. officer Rio Piedras, 1998, sabbatical leave, 2000-01; compiler, editor Puerto Rican Bibliography, 2001—. Dir. P.R. Newspaper Project, Río Piedras, 1986-90; mem. Adv. Com. on Pub. Librs., San Juan, 1987-93; proposal reviewer NEH, 1990—; chmn. Puerto Rican Del. to Nat. White House Conf. on Libr. and Info. Svcs., 1991. Author: La Información y la Documentación Educativa/Informe Sobre la Situación Actual en Puerto Rico, 1991, Memorias: Sequnda Pre-Conferencia de Casa Blanca Sobre Bibliotecas y Servicios de Información en Puerto Rico, 1991, Lineamientos para Colecciones Bibliograficas Nacionales, 1997, Premio por Excelencia en Investigación Aplicada y Publicación, 1997; contbr. articles to profl. jours. Mem. Ponce Sport Club, 1976—83, ARC, Ponce, 1978. Recipient plaque White House Pre-Conf. on Libr. and Info. Sci., 1990, others, Leccion Magistral Josefina del Toro Fulladosa, 2002; French Alps Study Tour scholar Assn. Caribbean Univ. Rsch. and Instl. Libr., 1989, Germany Study Tour scholar Fgn. Rels. Office, Germany, 1991, coord. So. area 1974, Lauro award 1989, Leccion Magistral Josefina del Toro Fulladosa award, 2002. Mem. ALA, Am. Mgmt. Assn., Grad. Sch. Libr. and Info. Sci. Alumni Assn. (pres. 1988-90), Seminar for Acquisitions L.Am. Libr. Materials, Iberoamerican Nat. Libr. Assn. (pres. 1992-93), Puerto Rican Libr. Soc., Assn. Caribbean U. Rsch. and Instnl. Libr. (Parchment award 1988), Asoc. para las Comunicaciones y Tecnología Educativa, Mid. States Assn. Coll. and Sch. (collaborator), Am. Women Assn., Nat. Commn. P.R. Women, Phi Delta Kappa (chair P.R. com. 1988-90, Kappan of Yr. 1990), Eta Gamma Delta. Roman Catholic. Avocations: reading, crewel work, embroidery, knitting, movies. Office: PO Box 23302 San Juan PR 00931-2302 Office Phone: 787-764-0000 x2707. Business E-Mail: hmunoz@uprrp.edu.

MUNRO, ALICE, writer; b. Wingham, Ont., Can., July 10, 1931; d. Robert Eric and Anne Clarke (Chamney) Laidlaw; m. James Armstrong Munro, 1951 (div. 1976); children: Sheila, Jenny, Andrea; m. Gerald Fremlin, 1976 BA, U. Western Ont., 1952, DLitt (hon.), 1976. Established Munro Books bookstore, 1963; writer in residence U. BC & U. Queensland, 1980. Author: (first short story) The Dimensions of a Shadow, 1950, (short story collections) Dance of the Happy Shades, 1968 (Gov. Gen.'s Lit. Award, Can. Coun. Arts, 1968), Something I've Been Meaning to Tell You, 1974, Who Do You Think You Are? (pub. outside Can. as Beggar Maid: Stories of Flo and Rose), 1978 (Gov. Gen.'s Lit. Award, Can. Coun. Arts, 1978), The Moons of Jupiter, 1982, The Progress of Love, 1986 (Gov. Gen.'s Lit. Award, Can. Coun. Arts, 1986), Friend of My Youth, 1990 (Trillium Book Award, 1991, Commonwealth Writers' Prize, 1991), Open Secrets, 1994 (WH Smith Award, 1995), Selected Stories, 1996, The Love of a Good Woman, 1998 (Giller Prize, 1998, Nat. Book Critics Circle Fiction Award, 1998, Named Fiction Book of Yr., Can. Booksellers Assn. Ex Libris Awards, 1999), Hateship, Friendship, Courtship, Loveship, Marriage, 2001, Runaway, 2004 (Giller Prize, 2004), (novels) Lives of Girls and Women, 1971 (Can. Booksellers Assn. Internat. Book Yr. Award, 1972). Recipient Can.-Australia Lit. Prize 1977, Marian Engel Award, 1986, Rea Award for the Short Story, 2001; Named one of Time Mag. 100 Most Influential People, 2005. Office: William Morris Agy 16th Fl 1325 Avenue of the Americas New York NY 10019

MUNRO, BARBARA HAZARD, nursing educator, dean, researcher; b. Wakefield, RI, Nov. 28, 1938; d. Robert J. and Honore (Egan) Hazard; children: Karen Aimee, Craig Michael, Stephanie Anne. BS, MS, U. RI, Kingston; PhD, U. Conn. RN, Conn. Asst. prof. U. RI Coll. Nursing, Kingston; assoc. prof., chmn. program in nursing rsch. Yale U., New Haven; assoc. prof., asst. dir. Ctr. for Nursing Rsch. U. Pa., Phila.; dean, prof. Boston Coll. Sch. Nursing, 1991—. Presenter and workshop leader various nursing confs. and seminars in U.S. Contbr. articles and rsch. to profl. pubs. Trustee St. Elizabeth's Med. Ctr. Boston, 1994—. Recipient Nat. Rsch. Svc. award. Fellow Am. Acad. Nursing; mem. ANA, Golden Key, Sigma Theta Tau, Pi Lambda Theta, Phi Kappa Phi. Office: Boston Coll Sch Nursing Cushing Hall Chestnut Hill MA 02467-3812 Office Phone: 617-552-1710. Business E-Mail: barbara.hazard.1@bc.edu.

MUNRO, ELEANOR, writer, lecturer; b. Bklyn., Mar. 28, 1928; d. Thomas and Lucile (Nadler) Munro; m. Alfred Frankfurter (dec. 1965); children: David, Alexander (dec.); m. E.J. Kahn, Jr. (dec.). BA, Smith Coll., Northampton, Mass., 1949; MA, Columbia U., N.Y.C., 1968. Staff writer, editor Art News Mag., N.Y.C., 1952-59; freelance writer, art critic, lectr. N.Y.C., 1960—. Vis. fellow Woodrow Wilson Nat. Fellowship Fedn., Princeton, N.J., 1990—; cons., juror Bush Fdn., St. Paul, 1994; resident fellow Bellagio Study Ctr., Lake Como, Italy, 1991, Yaddo, Saratoga Springs, N.Y., 1984. Author: Encyclopedia of Art, 1961, Through the Vermilion Gates, 1971, Originals: American Women Artists, 1979 (a N.Y. Times Notable Book of Yr.), Memoir of a Modernist's Daughter, 1988, On Glory Roads: A Pilgrim's Book about Pilgrimage, 1987 (N.Y. Times Notable Book of Yr.); author articles, criticism, fiction and poetry. Bd. dirs. Truro (Mass.) Ctr. for Arts, 1979—, The Living Theater, N.Y.C., 1989—, Nat. Alliance Rsch. into Schizophrenia and Depression, N.Y.C., 1995-2000. Recipient Cleve. Arts prize, 1988, medal of honor Smith Coll., 1990, Nat. Lifetime Achievement award Women's Caucus for Art, 2003. Mem. PEN Am., Am. Internat. Assn. Art Critics, Authors Guild. Home: 176 E 71st St # 3B New York NY 10021-5159

MUNROE, MARY LOU SCHWARZ (MRS. ROBERT E. MUNROE), educational administrator; b. Denver, Nov. 18, 1927; d. John Anthony and Lutie A. (Benefiel) Schwarz; m. Robert E. Munroe; children: Robert M., Carol E., John E. Dir. Jr. and Collegiate Great Books Program, Archdiocese of Denver, 1961-71, leader tng. staff, 1963-71, archdiocesan dir. grade and high sch., 1966-71; undergrad. counselor Sch. Edn. U. Denver, 1971-74; adminstrv. dir., ednl. coord. child and adolescent prog. Mt. Airy Psychiat. Ctr., Denver, 1975-90; supr. Cath. Community Svcs., Denver, 1990-91, assoc. dir., 1992—. Feature writer Register, Denver, 1963-71; lectr., workshop dir. Loretto Heights Coll., 1966. Author: Counseling the Parishoner, 1967. Mem. steering com. Cinema Critique Series of Denver, 1967; mem.-at-large Bd. Cath. Edn. of Denver Met. Area, 1969—, pres., 1974-75; mem. Denver Met. Adv. Com. Cath. Edn., 1968-69, Juvenile Ct. Task Force, 1969; supr. family and children svcs. Denver Cath. Charities and Community Svcs., 1990; assoc. dir. Cath. Charities, 1992—. Named Woman of Yr., Archdiocese of Denver Edn. Assn., 1971; named to Denver Post Gallery of Fame, 1975; recipient papal medal Pro Ecclesia et Pontifice, 1975; Dr. Mary Lou Munroe Learning Ctr. dedicated in her honor, 1985. Mem. Cath. Edn. Guild, Mortar Bd., Ednl. Forum Colo. (charter), Phi Beta Kappa, Kappa Delta Pi, Delta Kappa Gamma, Phi Delta Kappa, Delta Gamma.

MUNSELL, ELSIE LOUISE, retired lawyer; b. N.Y.C., Feb. 15, 1939; d. Elmer Stanley and Eleanor Harriet (Dickinson) M.; m. George P. Williams, July 14, 1979. AB, Marietta Coll., 1960; JD, Marshall-Wythe Coll. William and Mary, 1972. Bar: Va. 1972, U.S. Dist. Ct. (ea. dist.) Va. 1974, U.S. Ct. Appeals (4th cir.) 1976, U.S. Supreme Ct. 1980. Tchr. Norview High Sch., Norfolk, Va., 1964-69; asst. Commonwealth atty. Commonwealth Atty.'s Office, Alexandria, Va., 1972-73; asst. U.S. atty. Alexandria, 1974-79; U.S. magistrate U.S. Dist. Ct. (ea. dist.) Va., Alexandria, 1979-81; U.S. atty. Dept. Justice, Alexandria, 1981-86; sr. trial atty. Office of Gen. Counsel, Dept. Navy, Washington, 1986-89, asst. gen. counsel installations and environ. law, 1989-91; dep. asst. environ. and safety Sec. Navy, 1991-2001, ret., 2001. Mem. USEPA Clean Air Act Adv. Com., 1997—; bd. dirs. BMT Designers & Planners. Active Va. Commn. on Status of Women, 1966-74; bd. vistors Coll. William and Mary, 1972-76; active Atty. Gen.'s Adv. Com. U.S. Attys., 1981-83; bd. dirs. Carpenter's Shelter, Inc., 1990-93; vestry St. Alban's Ch., Annandale, Va., 1996-99, 2003; fed. preservation officer Dept. Navy, 1999. Presdl. Meritorious Exec., 1999; recipient Spl. Achievement award Nat. Mil. Fish and Wildlife Assn., 2001, Disting. Civilian Svc. award, 2001. Mem. Sr. Execs. Assn., Chi Omega. Episcopalian.

MUNSEN, RENEE LYNN, music educator; d. William Theodore and Donna Mae Pederson; m. Paul Edwin Munsen, Dec. 19, 1998; children: Keah, Chloe, Kirstie. B in Music Edn., No. State U., Aberdeen, SD, 1992. Elem. music tchr. Canby Pub. Sch., Minn., 1992—93, band tchr. 7-12, 1993—95; vocal music tchr. 7-12 Chamberlain Sch., SD, 1995—97; tchr. band 4-12, gen. music 3d grade White Lake Sch., SD, 1997—. Dir. White Lake Cmty. Band, 2002—. Mem.: SD Educators Assn. (local pres.), SD Bandmasters, SD Music Educators. Office: White Lake Pub Sch 502 E Division White Lake SD 57383 Office Phone: 605-249-2251.

MUNSHI, NALINI BHAT, elementary school educator; b. Jammu, India, Jan. 15, 1967; d. Choni Lal and Leela Sadhu Bhat; m. Raja Raman Munshi, Nov. 24, 1993; children: Yashasvee, Vinayak. PhD, Kanpur U., India, 1994. Cert. tchr. Conn. Tchr. Kendriya Vidyalaya, Jabalpur, M.P, India, 2002—03, New Britain (Conn.) Schs., 2003—. Achievements include research in phsiology of hormones in birds; effects of light and hormones on the plumage pigmentation of finches. Home: 224 Plainville Ave Unionville CT 06085 Office: Roosevelt Mid Sch 40 Goodwin St New Britain CT 06051 Office Phone: 860-612-3334. Business E-Mail: munshi@csdnb.org.

MUNSON, NANCY K., lawyer; b. Huntington, NY, June 22, 1936; d. Howard H. and Edna M. (Keenan) Munson. Student, Hofstra U., 1959—62; JD, Bklyn. Law Sch., 1965. Bar: NY 1966, U.S. Dist. Ct. (ea. and so. dists.) NY 1968, U.S. Supreme Ct. 1970, U.S. Ct. Appeals (2d cir.) 1971. Law clk. to Hon. E. Merritt Weidner, Huntington, NY, 1959—66; pvt. practice, 1966. Legal adv. bd. Chgo. Title Ins. Co., Riverhead, NY, 1981—; bd. dirs., legal officer Thomas Munson Found. Trustee Huntington Fire Dept. Death Benefit Fund; pres., trustee, chmn. bd. dirs. Bklyn. Home Aged Men Found.; bd. dirs. Huntington Rural Cemetery Assn., Inc.; trustee Noyac Harbor Property Owners Assn. Mem.: DAR (trustee, treas. Ketewamoke chpt.), NRA, ABA, Federalist Soc. for Law and Pub. Policy Studies, Bklyn. Bar Assn., Suffolk County Bar Assn., N.Y. State Bar Assn., Soroptimists (past pres.). Republican. Christian Scientist. Office: 197 New York Ave Huntington NY 11743-2711 Office Phone: 631-271-8161.

MUNSTERMAN, INGRID ANITA, assistant principal; b. The Hague, The Netherlands, Dec. 10, 1957; d. Theodorus and Hendrica Doesburg; m. Patrick Dean Munsterman. AA, Chaffey Coll., 1977; BA, Calif. State U., 1979; MA, Calif. State U., 1990. From elem. tchr. to asst. prin. Colton Joint Unified Sch. Dist., Calif., 1980—. Adj. faculty U. Redlands, Calif., 2000—, Nat. U., Calif., 2001—.

MUNT, JANET STAPLES, state senator; b. NYC, June 14, 1923; m. Plummer Coldwell Munt (dec.); 4 children. BA, Sweet Briar Coll., 1944; MS, Columbia U., 1948. Bd. cert. diplomate. Dir. maternal and child health divsn. Visiting Nurse Assn. Chittenden County, 1978—95; pvt. practice clin. social worker, 1995—2005. Trustee Burlington Coll. Sgt. WAC, WWII. Fellow Am. Orthopsychiat. Assn., Inc.; mem. NASW, Acad. Cert. Social Workers. Democrat.

MÜNTER, LEILANI MAAJA, race car driver; b. Rochester, Minn. d. Manfred and Doris Munter. MS in Biology, U. Calif., San Diego. Lic. stock car driver Nat. Assn. Stock Car Auto Racing. Former tchg. asst. cellular biology U. Calif., San Diego; race car driver Nascar Elite divsn., 2004—; competed in ROMCO Super Late Model Series, Allison Legacy Series. Spl. corr. Nascar.com, 2004—. Photo double (for Catherine Zeta-Jones films) in Traffic and America's Sweethearts. Avocations: scuba diving, snowboarding. Office: PO Box 3335 Mooresville NC 28117 also: 5315 Highgate Dr Ste 204 Durham NC 27713 Business E-Mail: marketing@leilanimunter.com.

MUNZER, ANNETTE ELIZABETH, cultural affairs consultant; b. Washington, Aug. 19, 1944; d. Edward Norman and Mary Elizabeth (Snider) Munzer; children: Edward Van Riper, Aaron Erkin. BA, Syracuse U., 1966; MA, U. Okla., 1970. Head libr. art libr. U. Okla., Norman, 1968-70; prof. anthropology U. Alaska, College, 1970-93, anthropologist College and Anchorage, 1973-77; rsch. libr. Phoenix Art Mus., 1978-80; curator of edn., collections, hist. sites, hispanic culture Tucson Mus. Art, spl. events and pub. program coord., 1980-85; exec. dir. Tucson Festival Soc., 1985-93; dir. cultural affairs City of Savannah, Ga., 1993; cons. El Centro Cultural de Las Americas, Tucson, 1994—2001, 2006—. Cons. Cultural Olympiad, Savannah, 1993—94, Amigos de la Danza, Tucson, 1995—96, Bus. Expo, Tucson Bus. Coalition, Tucson, 1996—97, Mujer 2000, Tucson, 1996—2000; tour planner, dir. Grayline Tours/Citizen's Autostage; instr. Austin C.C., 2002—. Author: Olaf Wieghorst, 1984; author, editor: Contact, 1972; author text (portfolio) Alaskan Eskimo Masks, 1973. Panelist Ariz. Commn. on Arts, Phoenix, 1995-96, Tucson/Pima Arts Commn., 1994-2001. Mem. Am. Assn. State and Local History, Am. Assn. Museums, Internat. Festival and Spl. Events Assn. (cert. festival exec.). Avocation: training service/assistance dogs. Home and Office: 17213 Sandwick Dr Pflugerville TX 78660 Office Phone: 520-203-7941. Personal E-mail: amunzer@cox.net.

MURAKANE, CHARLEEN, elementary school educator; B in Natural Scis., U. of Hawaii, Hilo, 1995. Cert. secondary sci. edn. U. Phoenix, Hawaii, 2000. Tchr. Honokaa H.S., Hawaii, 2000—01; tchr. intermediate sch. Kealakehe Intermediate Sch., Kailua-Kona, Hawaii, 2001—. Office Phone: 808-327-4314.

MURANO, ELSA A., academic administrator, former federal agency administrator; b. Havana, Cuba; BS in Biol. Sci., Fla. Internat. U.; MS in Anaerobic Microbiology, Va. Polytechnic Inst.; PhD in Food Sci. and Tech., Va. State U. Asst. prof. Iowa State U., Ames, 1990—92, prof. in charge rsch. programs linear accelertor facility, 1992—95; various positions including dir. food safety Tex. A&M U., College Station, Tex., 1995—2001, assoc. prof. animal sci., 1995—2000, prof. dept. animal sci., 2000—01, vice chancellor, 2005—, dean agrl. & life sciences, 2005—; dir. Tex. Agrl. Experiment Station, College Station, Tex., 2005—; under sec. for food safety USDA, Washington, 2001—04. Chair food safety state initiative com. Tex. Agr. Ext. Sta., 1999—2001; nat. adv. com. meat and poultry inspection USDA, 2001; mem. Nat. Alliance for Food Safety Ops. Com., 1998—2001, chair, 2000—01; bd. dirs. Hormel Foods Corp., 2006—. Mem.: Intenat. Assn. Food Protection, Poultry Sci. Assn., Inst. Food Technologists, Assn. Meat Sci., Am. Soc. Microbiology. Office: Tex A&M U 109 Kleberg Bldg 2042 TAMU College Station TX 77843

MURASHIMA, KUMIKO, artist, educator; arrived in US, 1967; d. Minoru and Michiko (Nagashima) M. BFA in Fiber Arts, Women's Coll. Fine Arts, Tokyo, 1962; MFA in Fiber Arts, Ind. U., 1970. Craftsman apprentice Serizawa Dyed Paper Inst., Tokyo, 1963-65; freelance textile designer Izumi Archtl. Design Co., Tokyo, 1965-67, Saphier, Lerner, Schindler Environetics, Inc., Chgo., 1970-71; asst. prof. art dept. Rowan U., 1971—, assoc. prof. art dept., 1974—. Artistic dir. Trio Creations, Sewell, 1987—. Author: Katazome in Contemporary Use, 1994. Recipient Malcolm Koch Mus. Purchase, Evansville (Ind.) Mus. Art, 1969, Wilber D. Peat Meml. award, 1970, Mr. and Mrs. Paul Arnold Merit award Herron Mus. Art, 1971; Craftsman's fellow N.J. State Coun. on Arts, 1985. Mem. Am. Crafts Coun., Artists Equity Assn. (Dorothy Grafly Meml. award 1981), Coll. Art Assn. Am., N.J. Designer and Craftsmen, Inc. (chairperson 1985-87), Am. Fedn. Tchrs. Avocations: reading, theater, classical music, gourmet foods, walking. Home: PO Box 515 Williamstown NJ 08094-0515 Office: Rowan Univ 201 Mullica Hill Rd Glassboro NJ 08028 Office Phone: 856-256-4023. Business E-Mail: murashima@rowan.edu.

MURCOTT, SUSAN, civil and environmental engineer, lecturer, consultant; BA, Wellesley Coll., 1990; BS, MIT, 1990, MS, 1992. Sr. lecturer and prin. investigator, dept. civil and environ. engring. MIT. Established a program at MIT, Clean Water for 1 Billion People; co-chair, Implementation Working Group WHO, Internat. Network to Promote Household Drinking Water Treatment and Safe Storage; tchr. Water and Sanitation in Developing Countries; Dissemination: Implementing Innovations for the Common Good; co-tchr. with Peter Guthrie and Carl Martland, Sustainable Develop. for Large Infrastructure Projects Cambridge U.; spkr. in field. Author: (book) First Buddhist Women: Songs and Stories from the Therigatha, 2nd edit., 2006, profl. papers. Recipient Wall Street Jour. Tech. Innovation award, Environ. category, 2005. Achievements include research and development of inexpensive water treatment systems for drinking water quality and treatment in developing countries like Nepal, Ghana, and Nicaragua; researching innovative wastewater treatment technology in Brazil; researching arsenic remediation technologies and sustainable development. Office: MIT Civil and Environ Engring Rm 1-138 77 Massachusetts Ave Cambridge MA 02139 Business E-Mail: murcott@mit.edu.*

MURDOCH, AMELIA CLARA, educational association administrator; d. Thomas Jerome and Viola Scanlan Murdoch. AB with honors, U. Pa., 1945, PhD, 1952. Instr. Juniata Coll., Huntingdon, Pa., 1950—51; linguist Nat. Security Agy., Ft. George Meade, Md., 1951—82, 1985—94; pres. and founder Nat. Mus. Lang., College Park, Md., 1998—. Mem. Tree and Landscape Bd., College Park, 1991—; chair Com. for a Better Environment, College Park, 1983—97, Vets. Meml. Improvement Com., College Park, 1991—2003. Am. Coun. Learned Socs. and Jusserand study and travel fellow, U. Pa., 1948—49. Mem.: MLA, Medieval Acad. Am., Internat. Arthurian Soc., Phi Beta Kappa (Mary Isabel Sibley fellow 1947—48). Avocations: reading, gardening. Office: Nat Museum of Language 7100 Baltimore Ave Ste 202 College Park MD 20740 Office Phone: 301-864-7071. Business E-Mail: acmurdoch@languagemuseum.org.

MURDOCK, DORIS DEAN, special education educator, program developer; b. Pacific Junction, Iowa, Feb. 7, 1913; m. Myron J. Murdock, June 28, 1933; 1 child, John Timothy. BS in Elem. Edn., So. Oreg. U., 1964; MS in Remedial Edn., U. Oreg., 1968. Primary tchr. Days Creek Elem. Sch., Oreg., 1962—66, Grants Pass Dist., 1966—67, Riddle Elem., Riddle, Oreg., 1968—71; founder, dir. Plowshare Sch., Rogue River, Oreg., 1972—78, Child Life Sanctuary, Rogue River, 1978—88; founder, dir., special education program developer Ctr. for Habilitation Living, Grants Pass, 1989—2006. Author: No Thank You! No Ritalin for Me Today!, 2003. Vol. Peace Corp., 1978—80. Mem.: Coun. for Exceptional Children (life). Republican. Seventh Day Adventist. Office: Ctr for Habilitative Living Inc 4493 Jerome Prairie Grants Pass OR 97527

MURDOCK, PAMELA ERVILLA, travel and advertising company executive; b. L.A., Dec. 3, 1940; d. John James and Chloe Conger (Keefe) M.; children: Cheryl (dec.), Kim. BA, U. Colo., 1962. Pres. Dolphin Travel,

Denver, 1972-87; owner, pres. Mile Hi Tours, Denver, 1973—, MH Internat., 1987—, Mile Hi Advt. Agy., 1986—. Bd. dirs. Rocky Mountain chpt. Juvenile Diabetes Found. Internat., 1994-2000; exec. bd. Rocky Mountain Father's Day Coun., 1998, 99. Named Wholesaler of Yr., Las Vegas Conv. and Visitors Authority, 1984; recipient Leadership award Nat. Multiple Sclerosis Soc., 1996. Mem.: NAFE, Nat. Fedn. Ind. Businessmen, Am. Soc. Travel Agts. Republican. Personal E-mail: pamelaemurdock@aol.com. Business E-Mail: pamm@milehitours.com.

MURDOCK, ROSAMOND LOUISE, retired pediatrician; b. Brockton, Mass., May 27, 1931; d. Frederick William Murdock and Louise Moulton Peck; m. Robert Nielson Pilon (div.); children: Aprile L. Pilon, Craig S. Pilon, Jeffrey S. Pilon. BS, Tufts U., Medford, Mass., 1953, MD, 1958. Diplomate Nat. Bd. Med. Examiners. Intern in pediats. Boston City Hosp., 1958—59; resident in psychiatry Boston Vets. Hosp., Jamaica Plane, Mass., 1959—60; physician Hanover Med. Clinic, Mass., 1960—66; pediatrician Well Child Clinics for Pembroke, Hanover and Halifax, Mass., 1961—66; sch. physician Hanover, 1964—65; pediat. fgn. OPD Severance Hosp., Seoul, Republic of Korea, 1966—67; vis. physician Yonseii U. Sch. Medicine, Seoul, 1966—67; fellow in clin. genetics Children's Hosp. Med. Ctr., Boston, 1969—70, asst. in clin. genetics, 1970—77; fellow in child devel. and clin. genetics Boston Floating Hosp., New England Med. Ctr., 1970—71; pediatrician Paul A. Dever State Sch., Taunton, Mass., 1979—81, Laconia State Sch., NH, 1982—85; asst. clin. prof. Tufts U. Med. Sch., 1971—83; clin. instr. pediats. SUNY, Buffalo, 1981—82; asst. adj. prof. maternal and child health Dartmouth Med. Sch., Hanover, NH, 1982—85; ret. Rsch. asst. in genetics LI Biol. Lab., Cold Spring Harbor, NY, 1953—54; fellow clin. genetics Children's Hosp. Med. Ctr., Boston, 1969—70, attending physician, genetics counselor Inborn Errors of Metabolism Clinic, 1971—75; fellow in birth defects and child devel. New England Med. Ctr., 1970—71, part-time physician Birth Defects and Child Devel. Clinic, 1972—79; sr. fellow in human genetics Buffalo Children's Hosp., 1981—82; sr. fellow medicine and pediats. and med. genetics Buffalo Gen. Hosp., Erie County Med. Ctr., Buffalo VA Hosp., 1982. Mem. Cataumet Civic Assn., 1990—, bd. dirs., pres.; adminstrv. officer Scraggy Neck Recreation Assn. Mem.: Mass. Med. Soc. Home: PO Box 371 Cataumet MA 02534-0371

MURDOCK, TULLISSE ANTOINETTE (TONI MURDOCK), academic administrator; BS, MA, N. Mex. State U.; PhD, U. Ariz.; grad. HERS, Bryn Mawr Inst. Women in Higher Edn., 1988. Adminstr. Western Wyo. Coll., faculty; asst. dean coll. arts and scis. U. Ariz.; assoc. provost of programs Seattle U., 1989—97; pres. Antioch U., Seattle, 1997—. Office: Antioch U 2326 Sixth Ave Seattle WA 98121-1814

MURGUIA, JANET, non-profit organization administrator; BS in Journalism, Kans. U., 1982, BA in Spanish, 1982, JD, 1985. Legis. coun. to Rep. Jim Slattery US Ho. Reps., Washington, 1987—94; various postions including dep. asst. to Pres. Clinton, dep. dir. legis. affairs, sr. liaison to Congress Washington, 1994—2000; exec. vice. chancellor univ. rels. U. Kans., 2001—04; exec. dir., COO Nat. Coun. La Raza, Washington, 2004, pres., CEO, 2005—. Bd. trustees YouthFriends. Named one of 100 Top Latinas, Hispanic mag., 100 Most Influential Hispanics, Hispanic Bus. mag., 80 Elite Hispanic Women. Office: Nat Coun La Raza 1111 19th St NW Ste 1000 Washington DC 20036 Office Phone: 202-785-1670.

MURILLO, CAROL ANN, secondary school educator; b. Portland, Oreg., Mar. 1, 1948; d. Carl Harvey and Frances Berniece Bryan; children: Michelle Frances, Adam Carlos Bryan. BA, Seattle Pacific U., 1970. Multiple subjects tchg. credential Calif., reading specialist credential Calif., secondary tchg. credential Calif. Exec. sec. Sybron Corp. - Heritage Laboratories, Inc., Seattle, 1971—72; elem. tchr. Highlands Acad., Daly City, Calif., 1973—74; dir. of childrens' ministries Resurrection City Ch., Berkeley and Oakland, Calif., 1980—82; interim prin. and tchr. Hilltop Christian Sch., Vallejo, Calif., 1982—93; cfo, ceo asst., event planner Mario Murillo Ministries, Inc., San Ramon, Calif., 1993—98; elem. sch. tchr. Vallejo City Unified Sch. Dist., Calif., 1998—2002. Mem. Falconette Academic Honors Club, Seattle, 1968—70. Editor (contributor): (book) Religious - Inspirational, 2000; editor: I'm the Christian the Devil Warned You About, 1996, Love Letters to Dangerous Christians, 1996; contbr. articles to religious magazines. Spkr. Lay Leadership conf.; worship leader religious retreats; corp. sec., trustee bd. mem. First Assembly of God, Inc., Ch. on the Hill, Vallejo, Calif., 1998—2002; mem. bd. dirs. Hilltop Christian Sch., Vallejo, 1997—2002. Mem.: Delta Kappa Gamma (grantee 1999). Avocation: travel. Home: 3008 Georgia St Vallejo CA 94591 Personal E-mail: carolannmurillo@msn.com.

MURILLO-ROHDE, ILDAURA MARIA, marriage and family therapist, consultant, educator, retired dean; b. Garachine, Panama; came to U.S., 1945; d. Amalio Murillo and Ana E. (Diaz) de Murillo; m. Erling Rohde, Sept. 19, 1959. BS, Columbia U., 1951, MA, 1953; diploma (hon.), Escuela Nat. de Enfermeria, Guatemala, 1964; MEd, Columbia U., 1969; PhD, NYU, 1971; diploma (hon.), Centro Estudios Naturista, Barcelona, Spain, 1992. RN; lic. marriage and family therapist, N.J.; cert. mental health-psychiat. nursing, ANA; lic. sex. therapist, N.J. Instr., supr. Bellevue Psychiat. Hosp., N.Y.C., 1950-54; asst. dir., dir. psychiat. div. Wayne County Gen. Hosp., Eloise, Mich., 1954-56; chief nurse psychiat. div. Elmhurst Gen. Hosp., Queens, N.Y., 1956-58, Met. Hosp. Med. Ctr., N.Y.C., 1961-63; psychiat. cons. to govt. of Guatemala WHO, UN, Guatemala, 1963-64; assoc. prof., chmn. psychiat. dept. N.Y. Med. Coll. Grad. Sch. Nursing, N.Y.C., 1964-69; dir. mental health-psychiatry, asst. prof. NYU, N.Y.C., 1970-72; assoc. prof. Hostos Coll., CUNY, N.Y.C., 1972-76; assoc. dean. acad. affairs, prof. U. Wash., Seattle, 1976-81; prof., dean Coll. of Nursing SUNY, Downstate Med. Ctr., Bklyn., 1981-85; dean and prof. emeritus SUNY, Bklyn., 1985—. Bd. dirs. Puerto Rican Family Inst., N.Y.C., 1983—96; dir. Latin Am. Oncological Nurses Fuld Fellowships, 1989-90; psychiat. cons. Sch. Nursing, U. Antioquia, Medellin, Colombia, 1972-73, WHO; psychiat./rsch. cons. for master program Sch. Nursing, U. Panama, Project Hope, 1986; dir., leader mental-psychiat. interdisciplinary group to study the Chinese family after 30 yrs. of communism People to People Amb. Program, 1985. Editor: National Directory of Hispanic Nurses, 1981, 2d edit., 1986, 3d edit., 1994; contbr. numerous articles to profl. nat. and internat. jours., chpts. to books in field. Bd. dirs. Nat. Coalition of Hispanic Mental Health and Human Svcs. Orgns., 1974-84, chmn. bd., 1980-84; mem. Wash. State adv. com. U.S. Commn. on Civil Rights, Seattle, 1971-81; nat. adv. com. White House Conf. on Families, Washington, D.C., 1979-81; pres. King County Health Planning Coun., Seattle, 1979-81; exec. com. Puget Sound Health Systems Agy., Seattle, 1979-81; mem. bd. advisors Marquis Who's Who, 1983-91; mem. Mosby Consumer Health's Hispanic adv. bd., 1996. Univ. Honors scholar NYU, 1972; named Citizen of the Day, Radio Sta. KIXI and N.W. Airlines, Seattle, 1979, Disting. lectr. Sigma Theta Tau, 1988-89, Woman of Yr., N.Y. Gotham Club Bus. and Profl. Women, 1989; recipient 1st Nat. Intercultural Nursing award Coun. of Intercultural Nursing, ANA, New Orleans, 1984, Women's Honors in Pub. Svc. award Minority Fellowship Programs and Cabinet Human Rights, ANA, 1986, Disting. Alumna award Divsn. Nursing, NYU Alumni Assn., 1989, 1st Nat. Dr. Hildegard Peplau award for outstanding svcs. in mental health, psychiat. nursing, edn., rsch. and practice, Las Vegas conv. ANA, 1992, Practice award Tchrs. Coll., Columbia U. Nursing Edn. Alumni, 1994; designated Living Legend for leadership in practice, edn. and rsch. Am. Acad. Nursing, 1994; inducted into Nursing Hall of Fame, Columbia U., 1999; bd. advisors Marquis Who's Who, 1991-99. Fellow Am. Assn. Marriage and Family Therapy; mem. ANA (affirmative action task force 1974-84, commn. human rights, cabinet human rights, rep. ANA at ICN Cong. Tokyo 1977, spokesperson Nat. Health Ins., conceived and designed Coun. Intercultural Nursing), Am. Orthopsychiat. Assn. (bd. dirs. 1976-79, treas. 1986-89, Presdl. nominee 1980, 93), N.Y. Assn. Marriage and Family Therapy (pres. 1973-76), Nat. Assn. Hispanic Nurses (founder, 1st pres. 1976-80), Internat. Fedn. Bus. and Profl. Women (UN rep. to UNICEF London, 1987—, del. to World UN Summit for Children N.Y.C. 1990, UN N.Y. Com. for Internat. Yr. of Family 1994, Hall of Fame for Outstanding Achievements in Field of Sci., Rsch., Mental Health-Psychiatry, 4th edit., 1995), Am. Rsch. Inst. (dep. govt. 1987), NYU Club, Gotham Bus. and Profl. Women's Club. Democrat. Avocations: travel, reading, music, stamp collecting/philately, skiing. Home: 300 W 108th St Apt 12A New York NY 10025-2704 Office: SUNY Bklyn Coll Nursing Box 22 450 Clarkson Ave Brooklyn NY 11203-2056 E-mail: murillorohde@aol.com.

MURKOWSKI, LISA ANN, senator; b. Ketchikan, Alaska, May 22, 1957; d. Frank Hughes Murkowski & Nancy 9Gore); m. Verne Martell, Aug. 22, 1987; children: Nicholas, Matthew. BA in Economics, Georgetown U., 1980; JD, Willamette Coll., 1985. Dist. coun. atty., Anchorage, 1987-89; comml. atty. Hoge and Lekisch, 1989-96; pvt. law practice, 1989—96; mem. Alaska Ho. of Reps., Anchorage, 1999—2002, majority leader, 2002; U.S. Senator from Alaska, 2002—. Dir. First Bank; mem. Mayor's Task Force Homeless, 1990-91; state ctrl. com. Dist. 14 Rep. chair, 1993-98; commr. Anchorage Equal Rights Commn., 1997-2002; citizens adv. bd. Joint Com. Mil. Bases in Alaska, 1998—. Trustee Cath. Svcs.; pres. Govt. Hill Elem. PTA; dir. Alaskan Drug Free Youth; mem. YWCA, Arctic Power. Recipient Comunity Leadership award, FBI Dir., 1993, Outstanding Volunteer award, Alaska Sch. Dist., 1998, 2000, Food Safety award, Nat. Food Processors Assn., 2003. Mem. Alaska Bar Assn., Anchorage Bar Assn., Alaska Fedn. Rep. Women (bd. dirs.), Anchorage Rep. Womens Club, Midnight Sun Rep. Women. Republican. Roman Catholic. Address: 510 L St # 550 Anchorage AK 99501 Office: US Senate 709 Hart Senate Office Bldg Washington DC 20510 Office Phone: 202-224-6665.*

MURLEY, SUSAN W., lawyer; b. 1959; BA summa cum laude, Tufts Univ., 1981; JD, Univ. Va., 1986. Bar: Mass. 1986. Assoc. to ptnr., Corp. dept., mem. mgmt. com. Wilmer Cutler Pickering Hale & Dorr, Boston, 1986—. Named a Mass. Super Lawyer, Boston Mag., 2004. Mem.: Mass. Bar Assn., Boston Bar Assn., Phi Beta Kappa. Office: Wilmer Cutler Pickering Hale & Dorr 60 State St Boston MA 02109 Office Phone: 617-526-6832. Office Fax: 617-526-5000. Business E-Mail: susan.murley@wilmerhale.com.

MURNANE, MARGARET MARY, engineering and physics educator; b. Limerick, Ireland, Jan. 23, 1959; d. Matthew and Helen (Bourke) M.; m. Henry Cornelius Kapteyn, Mar. 26, 1987. MSc, U. Coll. Cork, Ireland, 1983; PhD, U. Calif., Berkeley, 1989. Postdoctoral researcher U. Calif., Berkeley, 1990; asst. prof. Wash. State U., Pullman, 1990-95; assoc. prof. U. Mich., Ann Arbor, 1996—99; prof. physics U. Colo., 1999—, fellow, Joint Inst. Lab. Astrophysics. Presdl. Young Investigator awardee NSF, 1991, Sloan Found. fellow, 1992, Presdl. faculty fellow NSF, 1993, John D. and Catherine T. MacArthur fellow, 2000. Mem. NAS, Am. Phys. Soc. (Simon Ramo award 1990, Maria Goeppert-Mayer award 1997), Optical Soc. Am., Soc. Photo-Optical Instrumentation Engrs., Assn. Women in Sci.; Fellow Am. Acad. Arts & Sciences Office: Univ Colo Joint Inst Lab Astrophysics 440 UCB Boulder CO 80309-7789*

MURNEY, JULIA, actress; d. Christopher Murney. Grad., Syracuse U. Actress (plays) Funny Girl, 2002, Chess, 2003, Hair, 2004, Ragtime, (NYC theatre plays) The Wild Party, The Vagina Monologues, Crimes of the Heart, A Class Act, Time and Again, Cloud 9, Snapshots, Mata Hari, First Lady Suite, Broadway By the Year 1953, (plays) Into The Woods, (NYC theatre plays) Broadway By the Year 1963, (Broadway plays) Lennon, 2005, Wicked, 2006, (TV appearances) Ed, Sex and the City, NYPD Blue, Law & Order, One Life to Live. Mailing: c/o Broadhurst Theatre 235 W 44th St New York NY 10036*

MURNIEKS, KIMBERLY ANN, educational administrator; b. Marietta, Ohio, May 3, 1971; d. William Charles West and Sarah Sue Schafer; 3 children. BA suma cum laude, Marietta Coll., Ohio, 1993; MPA, Ohio State U., Columbus, 1995. Mgmt. analyst Ohio EPA, Columbus, 1995—96; budget and mgmt. analyst edn. policy Ohio Office Budget & Mgmt., Columbus, 1996—2000; policy advisor info. tech. office Ohio Dept. Edn., Columbus, 2000—02, dep. chief of staff, 2002—05, chief program officer ednl. choice scholarship, 2005—. Active St. Paul Luth. Ch., Westerville, Ohio, 1999; student pen pal for adopt-a-school program McGuffey Elem. Sch., Columbus. Recipient Writing Cert. with Distinction, Marietta Coll., 1993; fellow, Ohio State U. Grad. Sch., 1993—94. Mem.: Columbus Mothers of Twins Club, Am. Mensa, Phi Alpha Theta, Phi Beta Kappa. Lutheran. Avocations: travel, reading, writing. Office: Ohio Dept Edn 25 S Front St Columbus OH 43215-4183 Office Phone: 614-995-9936. Business E-Mail: kim.murnieks@ode.state.oh.us.

MURNIGHAN, MARY E., elementary school educator; d. David F. and Mary M. Murnighan. BS in Edn., Ctrl. Mich. U., Mount Pleasant, 1974, MA in Edn., 1981. Tchr. Birch Run Pub. Schs., Mich., 1974—80, Howell Pub. Schs., Mich., 1980—82, Lemon Bay H.S., Englewood, Fla., 1982—85, L. A. Ainger Mid. Sch., Rotonda West, Fla., 1985—, chmn. lang. arts dept., 2004—06, profl. learning cmty. chmn., 2004—, chmn. reading dept. Asst. forensics coach Birch Run H.S., 1978—80; forensics coach Howell Pub. Schs., 1981—82; asst. band dir. Lemon Bay H.S., 1983—84. Named Tchr. of Yr., VFW Post 10476, 2006, Mid. Sch. Social Studies Tchr. of Yr., Charlotte County Pub. Schs., 1998; Strategic Grantmaking in Edn. grantee, Gulf Coast Cmty. Found. Venice, 2004—06. Roman Catholic. Office: L A Ainger Mid Sch 245 Cougar Way Rotonda West FL 33947 Office Phone: 941-697-5800 ext. 280.

MURO-TORRES, ROSALITA, elementary school educator; b. Villalba, P.R., July 15, 1971; d. Neftali Torres-Suarez and Victoria López-Hernández; m. Ernest Baron Muro, Apr. 25, 1996; children: Eric Muro, Baronessa Muro, Contessa Muro. A in Bus. Adminstrn., Bernardino Cordero Bernard, Ponce, P.R., 1990. Tchr. asst. Clairmont Sch., Dumfries, Va., 2002; ESL tutor D. F. Walker Elem., Edenton, NC, 2003—. Mem. tchr. asst. learning team S.E.R.V.E., 2003—; host Spanish club D. F. Walker Elem., Edenton, 2005—06. Mem. Arbor Day Found. Recipient Excellence in Acctg., Bernardino Cordero Bernard, 1990. Office: D F Walker Elem 125 Sandy Ridge Rd Edenton NC 27932

MUROW, CHRISTINE, music educator; b. Chgo., Feb. 19, 1945; d. David R. and Dorothy B. Groth; m. Raymond J. Murow, Oct. 10, 1966. B. Susquehanna U., 1967. Budget analyst U.S. Dept. H.E.W., Washington, 1967-69, pub. info. specialist, 1969-72; tchr. piano Potomac, Md., 1972—; dir. KITS, Potomac, Md., 1985—. Author: KITS Music Theory Course, 1989-98; contbr. articles to profl. jours.; composer Sounds for One Hand, 1986, Voices of Invention, 1987; contbg. composer: Allison Contemporary Piano Collection, 1993, 96. Mem. Nat. Guild Piano Tchrs., Potomac Area Music Tchrs. (sec. 1989—). Avocations: gardening, bird watching. Office: KITS 9732 Corral Dr Potomac MD 20854-1510 Personal E-mail: musictheory@earthlink.net.

MURPH, ROXANE COHEN, writer, researcher; b. Bklyn., June 8, 1928; d. Joseph Nathaniel and Lee Nagler Cohen; m. Adrian Franklin Murph, Jan. 28, 1948; children: Mary Bader, Joseph Franklin, Taylor Campbell. Author: (books) Richard III: Making of a Legend, 1977, The Wars of the Roses in Fiction, 1995, The English Civil War Through the Restoration, 2000, Rewriting the Wars of the Roses: The 17th Century Royalist Histories of John Trussell, Sir Francis Biondi and William Habington, 2006. Mem.: Medieval Acad. Am., Richard III Soc. (chmn. 1986—89, Dickon award 1990). Democrat. Unitarian. Avocations: reading, needlecrafts, travel. Home: 3501 Medina Ave Fort Worth TX 76133

MURPHEY, JEANNETTE WINDHAM, psychology professor; b. Indianola, Miss., Jan. 1, 1956; d. Sidney and Helen Windham; m. Joey Murphey, June 29, 1975; children: Jay, Justin. AA, Miss. Delta C.C., Moorhead, 1975; BS, Miss. State U., Starkville, 1977, MEd, 1978, PhD, 1986. Nat. cert. sch. psychology Nat. Assn. Sch. Psychologists, 1989. Ednl. resources staff mem. Coll. Vet. Medicine, Miss. State U., Starkville, 1978—79; mental health cons. State of Miss., Starkville, 1979—80; assoc. psychologist State Dept. Edn., Newton (Miss.) Ctr., 1980—82; psychology prof. Clarke Coll., Newton, 1982—89, Meridian (Miss.) C.C., 1989—. Author: (test bank) Test bank for Psychology, A Journey, 2nd edit., Test bank for Psychology, A Modular Approach, Test bank for Personal Adjustment, Test Bank for Psychology, Gateways Medicine; contbr. articles to profl. jours. Active Newton United Meth. Ch., 1979—2006; coord. psychology vols. Meridian C.C., 1991—2006. Named Tchr. of Yr., Meridian C.C., 1995, Young Woman of Yr., Meridian Jaycees, 1995; recipient Lamplighter award, Miss. Cmty. Colleges, 1994. Mem.: Phi Delta Kappa (assoc.). Methodist. Avocations: swimming, travel, reading, pets, gardening. Office: Meridian Community College 910 Highway 19 North Meridian MS 39307 Office Phone: 601-484-8655. Business E-Mail: jmurphey@mcc.cc.ms.us.

MURPHEY, MARGARET JANICE, retired marriage and family counselor; d. Glen Roosevelt Wurster and Lucile Mildred Lopez; m. Russell Warren Murphey, June 20, 1959; children: Lucinda Huff, Rochelle Scott, Janice Sorenson. BA in Social Sci., Calif. State U., Chico, 1986, MA in Psychology, 1989; postgrad., La Salle U. Sec. Folson State Prison, Calif., 1963-66; tchr. Desert Sands Unified Schs., Indio, Calif., 1969-72; claims determiner Employment Development Dept., Redding, Calif., 1976-78; sec. Shasta County Pers., Redding, 1978-79; welfare worker Shasta County Welfare Office, Redding, 1979-85; therapy intern Counseling Ctr. Calif. State U., Chico, 1989-90; therapist Family Svc. Assn., Chico, 1987-90, Butte County Drug and Alcohol Abuse Ctr., Chico, 1989-90; mental health counselor Cibecue (Ariz.) Indian Health Clinic, 1990-98; sch. counselor Cibecue Apache H.S. and Elem. Sch., 1998—2006; ret. Mem. Kinisba Child Abuse Com., 1994—98. Vol. Pacheco Sch., Redding, 1972-76; Sunday sch. tchr., dir. vacation Bible sch. Nazarene Ch., Sacramento, Indio and Redding, 1958-85. Recipient Sch. Bell award Pacheco Sch., Indian Health Svc. Dirs. award excellence, 1997. Mem. ACA, Am. Assn. Christian Counselors, Am. Acad. Bereavement Facilitators, Ariz. Sch. Counselors Assn. Avocations: study of american indian history, sewing, crafts, travel, bluegrass music. Office: Cibecue Apache HS PO Box 80068 Cibecue AZ 85911-0068

MURPHEY, SHEILA ANN, infectious diseases physician, educator, researcher; b. Phila., July 10, 1943; d. William Joseph and Sara Esther (Mallon) M. AB, Chestnut Hill Coll., 1965; MD, Women's Med. Coll. of Pa., 1969. Diplomate Am. Bd. Internal Medicine, Am. Bd. Infectious Diseases. Intern in internal medicine Mt. Sinai Hosp. of NY, 1969—70, resident in internal medicine, 1970—72, instr. internal medicine, 1971—72; fellow infectious diseases U. Pa. Sch. Medicine, Phila., 1972—74, instr. dept. medicine, 1974—75, asst. prof. dept. medicine, 1975—77; chief infectious diseases sect. Phila. Gen. Hosp., 1974—77; attending physician Hosp. U. Pa., Phila. Gen. Hosp., 1974—77; dir. divsn. infectious diseases, asst. prof. medicine Jefferson Med. Coll., Phila., 1977—80, clin. assoc. prof. medicine, 1980—2003; dir. divsn. infectious diseases Thomas Jefferson U., Phila., 1977—88; infection control officer, attending physician Thomas Jefferson U. Hosp., Phila., 1977—2003; br. chief infection control devices br., Office Device Evaluation Ctr. for Devices and Radiologic Health, FDA, Rockville, Md., 2005—. Contbr. articles to profl. jours. Fellow Coll. Physicians Phila.; mem. ACP, Am. Soc. Microbiology, Soc. Healthcare Epidemiology of Am., Infectious Diseases Soc. Am., Alpha Omega Alpha. Democrat. Roman Catholic.

MURPHREE, A. LINN, ophthalmologist; b. Houston, Miss., June 6, 1945; d. John Alan and Maxine (Linn) M. BS, U. Miss., 1967; MD, Baylor Coll., 1972. Cert. Am. Bd. Ophthalmology. Resident affiliated hosps., 1973-76, chief resident ophthalmology, 1975-76; fellow ophthalmic genetics and pediatrics The Wilmer Inst., Johns Hopkins U. Hosp., 1976-77; asst. prof. ophthalmology and pediatrics U. So. Calif., Los Angeles, 1978-83, assoc. prof., 1983—91, prof., 1991—, dir. pediatric and devel. ophthalmology Los Angeles, 1978—; head, div. ophthalmology Children's Hosp. Los Angeles, 1978—, dir. Clayton Found. Ctr. Ocular Oncology, 1978—; chief med. ops. Childrens Hosp. of Los Angeles, 1986-87. Profl. adv. com. Blind Children's Ctr., Los Angeles, 1980—; med. adv. bd. Nat. Assn. Visually Handicapped, 1980—. Contbr. numerous articles to profl. jours. Served to capt. med. corps., USAR, 1972-80. Dolly Green scholar Research to Prevent Blindness, 1984, Fulbright scholar U. Copenhagen, 1967-68; Medical Genetics fellow Baylor Col. of Med. Affiliated Hosps., 1972-73. Mem. Calif. Assn. Ophthalmology, Calif. Med. Assn., Los Angeles County Med. Assn., Los Angeles Ophthalmol. Soc., Los Angeles Pediatric Soc., Ophthalmology Research Study Club Los Angeles, Pacific Coast Oto-Ophthalmol. Soc., Salerni Collegium, Am. Acad. Ophthalmology (honor award 1983), Am. Assn. Pediatric Ophthalmology and Strabismus, Am. Orthoptic Council, Assn. Research in Vision and Ophthalmology, Ophthalmic Genetics Study Club, Am. Bd. Ophthalmology (assoc. examiner), Internat. Soc. Genetic Eye Disease (sec. 1986—). Office: Childrens Hosp Los Angeles 4650 Sunset Blvd Mailstop 88 Los Angeles CA 90027-6016

MURPHREY, ELIZABETH HOBGOOD, history professor, librarian; b. Rocky Mount, N.C., Mar. 22, 1947; d. Isaac Green and Ernestine Ragsdale (Hobgood) Murphrey. BA, U. N.C., Greensboro, 1969; MA, Duke U., 1971, PhD, 1976; postgrad., U. Fla., 1984; MLS, U. N.C., Chapel Hill, 1993. Vis. instr. history Wake Forest U., Winston-Salem, NC, 1976; asst. prof. history N.C. A&T State U., Greensboro, 1977—81; intelligence rsch. specialist U.S. Army, Fayetteville, NC, 1982—89; adj. prof. history Fayetteville State U., 1989—90; adj. instr. history Fla. Met. U. South Campus, Orlando, 2000—03, adj. history, instr. Columbia Coll. Orlando divsn., 2005, rsch. libr., 1998—. Vis. asst. prof. of history Elizabeth City State U., NC, 1993—96; adj. instr. history Colmbia Coll., 2005. Editor (guidebook): Socialist Party of America Papers, microfilm edit., 2 vols., 1973—77. Apptd. Seminole County Disiability Adv. Coun., 2005. Recipient award, NEH, 1994, 1996, 2000. Mem.: LWV (bd. dirs. Seminole County chpt. 2001—, bd. dirs. Guilford County chpt. 1978—82), ALA, Fla. Libr. Assn., Am. Hist. Assn. Home: 424 Windmeadows St Altamonte Springs FL 32701 Office: Fla Met U South Orlando Campus 9200 Southpark Center Loop Orlando FL 32819 Office Phone: 407-851-2525. Personal E-mail: emurphrey@hotmail.com.

MURPHY, ANDRA BROWN, theater arts director, educator; b. Atlanta, Nov. 13, 1973; d. James Warren and Debra Brock Brown; m. Robert Murphy, June 16, 2001. BFA, U. Tex., Austin, 1996. Tchr. James Madison HS, San Antonio, 1996—2006, theater arts dir., 2006—. Home: 4802 Aspen View San Antonio TX 78217 Office: James Madison High Sch 5005 Stahl Rd San Antonio TX 78247 Office Phone: 210-637-4400 293. Personal E-mail: amurph@neisd.net.

MURPHY, BETTY JAGODA, small business owner; b. Washington, July 30, 1947; d. Harry Earl and Flory (Kabilio) Jagoda; m. Gregory James Murphy, Mar. 18, 1972; 1 child, Joshua. BA in Dance, Adelphi U., 1969. Cert. psychomotor therapy N.Y. Med. Ctr., 1970. Market research coord. Lee Creative Research, Fairfield, NJ, 1972-73; dir. new product test ctr. Lehn & Fink (Sterling Drug), Montvale, NJ, 1973-75; cons. new products Montclair, NJ, 1975-79; co-founder, pres. Creative Products Resource Assn., Fairfield, NJ, 1979—99; v.p. Jagoda Labs., Inc., Clifton, NJ, 1986—; pres., mng. mem. ReGenesis LLC, Montclair, NJ. Inventor, patentee household cleaning products and health & beauty aids. Adv. bd. Dress for Success, NY. Mem.: N.J. Assn. Women Bus. Owners, N.Y. Women in Comm. (membership com.). Democrat. Jewish. Office: ReGenesis LLC 31 S Fullerton Ave Montclair NJ 07042 Office Phone: 973-233-1064. E-mail: bjm@regenesisllc.com.

MURPHY, BETTY SOUTHARD (MRS. CORNELIUS F. MURPHY), lawyer; b. East Orange, N.J. d. Floyd Theodore and Thelma (Casto) Southard; m. Cornelius F. Murphy, May 1, 1965; children: Cornelius Francis Jr., Ann Southard Murphy; m. H. Leland Hernly, Apr. 26, 2003. AB, Ohio State U.; student, Alliance Française and U. Sorbonne, Paris; JD, Am. U. Washington Coll. Law, Washington, DC; LLD (hon.), Ea. Mich. U., Ypsilanti, 1975, Capital U., Columbus, Ohio, 1976, U. Puget Sound (now Seattle U.), 1986; LHD (hon.), Tusculum Coll., Greenville, Tenn., 1987. Bar: D.C. Corr., free lance journalist, Europe and Asia, UPI, Washington; practiced in Washington DC, 1960—74; mem. firm McInnis, Wilson, Munson & Woods (and predecessor firm Roberts & McInnis); dep. asst. sec., adminstr. Wage and Hour Divsn. Dept. Labor, 1974-75; chmn. and mem. NLRB, 1975-79; ptnr.

firm Baker & Hostetler, LLP, 1980—. Adj. prof. law Am. U., 1972-80, 99—; mem. adv. com. on rights and responsibilities of women to Sec. HHS; mem. panel conciliators Internat. Ctr. Settlement Investment Disputes, 1974-85; mem. Adminstrv. Conf. U.S., 1976-80, Pub. Svc. Adv. Bd., 1976-79; mem. human resouces com. Nat. Ctr. for Productivity and Quality of Working Life, 1976-80; mem. Presdl. Commn. on Exec. Exch., 1981-85, Ctr. for Study of the Presidency, 1998—. Trustee Mary Baldwin Coll., Staunton, Va., 1977—85, Am. U., Washington, 1980—99, George Mason U. Found., Inc., Fairfax, Va., 1993—2000, 2001—; US Constn. mem. exec com. Commn. on Bicentennial; chmn. internat. adv. com. Commn. on Bicentennial of US Constn., 1985—92; vice chmn. James Madison Meml. Fellowship Found., 1969—96; trustee Friends of Congl. Law Libr., 1992—, Friends of Dept. of Labor, 1984—; mediator World Intellectual Property Orgn., 1996—; nat. bd. dirs. Med. Coll. Pa., Phila., bd. corporators, 1976—85; bd. dirs. Ctr. for Women in Medicine, Phila., 1980—86, Meridian Internat. Ctr., 1992—98; bd. mem. Summer Opera Theatre, 2006—; bd. govs. St. Agnes Sch., Alexandria, Va., 1981—87. Recipient Ohio Gov.'s award, 1980, fellow award, 1981, Outstanding Pub. Service award U.S. Info. Service, 1987; named Disting. Fellow John Sherman Myers Soc., 1986, 96; fellow Nat. Acad. Human Resources, 1998. Fellow: ABA (chmn. labor law com. 1980—83, chmn. internat. and comparative law adminstrv. law sect. 1983—88, chmn. customs, tariff and trade com. 1988—90, employment law sect. 1990—2004, chmn. internat. com. dispute resolution sect. 1995—); mem.: Am. Inns of Ct. (Professionalism award 2006), US-Mex. Bar Assn. (US chair, com. on labor and employment law 2006—), Nat. Acad. Human Resources, Nat. Assn. Women Lawyers, Women's Bar Assn., Internat Bar Assn., Am. U. Alumni Assn. (Women's Leadership Award 2004), Supreme Ct. Hist. Soc., Union Internat. des Advocats (gov. bd. 1997—2000, 2003—), Rep. Nat. Lawyers Assn. (nat. v.p. 1990—95, nat. vice chmn. 1996—2000, 2001—03, co-chmn. 2003—, mem. exec. bd. 2003—, Rep. Lawyer of Yr. 2005), Am. Arbitration Assn. (bd. dirs. 1985—2000, mem. editl. bd. 1992, mem. exec. com. 1995—2000, mem. internat. arbitration com. 1997—, steering com. lawyers for Bush 2000, mem. exec. com. 2002—, bd. dirs. 2004—, trustee summer opera 2006—, mem. exec. com. 2006—, bd. dirs. 2006—, 2001—), Bar Assn. D.C., Inter-Am. Bar Assn. (co-chmn. labor law com. 1975—83, editor newsletter, Silver medal 1967), FBA, World Peace Through Law Ctr., Mortar Bd., Kappa Beta Pi. Republican. Office: Baker & Hostetler LLP Ste 1100 1050 Connecticut Ave NW Washington DC 20036-5304 Office Phone: 202-861-1500. Office Fax: 202-861-1783. Business E-Mail: bsmurphy@bakerlaw.com.

MURPHY, BRITTANY, actress; b. Atlanta, Nov. 10, 1977; Actor: (films) Clueless, 1995, Freeway, 1996, Drive, 1997, The Prophecy II, 1998, Bongwater, 1998, Phoenix, 1998, Zack and Reba, 1998, Falling Sky, 1998, Drop Dead Gorgeous, 1999, Girl, Interrupted, 1999, Trixie, 2000, Angels!, 2000, Cherry Falls, 2000, The Audition, 2000, Sidewalks of NY, 2001, Summer Catch, 2001, Don't Say a Word, 2001, Riding in Cars with Boys, 2001, Spun, 2002, 8 Mile, 2002, Just Married, 2003, Uptown Girls, 2003, (voice) Good Boy!, 2003, Little Black Book, 2004, Sin City, 2005; (TV films) Double Jeopardy, 1996, David and Lisa, 1998, The Devil's Arithmetic, 1999, Common Ground, 2000; (TV series) Drexell's Class, 1991, Almost Home, 1993, Sister, Sister, 1994, (voice) King of the Hill, 1997, Pepper Ann, 1997; TV appearances include: Murphy Brown, 1991; Kids Incorporated, 1992; Parker Lewis Can't Lose, 1992; Blossom, 1993; Frasier, 1994; Party of Five, 1994; Boy Meets World, 1995; Murder One, 1995; The Marshal, 1995; SeaQuest DSV, 1995; Nash Bridges, 1996; Clueless, 1996.

MURPHY, CARLA M., secondary school educator; b. Wallace, Idaho, June 27, 1949; d. Carl Franklin Conner and Marzell Stella Thompson-Conner; m. Bill Brummet (div.); children: Amy Brummet, Dwayne Brummet; m. Ron Gene Murphy, May 18, 1997; 1 child, Angie. AA, Northeaster Okla. A&M Coll., 1969; BS, Pitts. State U., 1980, MS, 1995. Cert. edn. specialist Pitts. State U., 1998. Tchr. reading and English Fairland (Okla.) Schs., 1981—91, tchr. family and consumer scis., 2001—; tchr. Northeaster Okla. A&M Coll., Miami, 1991—2001. Chmn., advisory bd. Fairland Enrichment Found., 2004—. Mem. Fairland Sch. Bd., 1993—95; sec., treas. Standing Rock Ministries, Miami, 2004—. Mem.: Assn. Career and Tech. Edn., Back Road Cloggers, Phi Upsilon Omicron, Omicron Delta Kappa. Democrat. Avocations: clog dancing, reading, fishing, sewing. Home: PO Box 669 Miami OK 74355 Office Phone: 918-676-3246.

MURPHY, CAROLINE PATRICIA, historian, writer; b. Taplow, Eng., Oct. 10, 1969; arrived in U.S., 1988; d. Brian Dermot Murphy and Olwen Hazel Hufton; m. Henry Dietrich Fernandez. BA, U. Coll., London, 1990, PhD, 1996. Assoc. prof. modern European art, gender and culture U. Calif., Riverside, 1998—. Author: (biography) Lavinia Fontana; A Painter and Her Patrons in Sixteenth Century Bologna, The Pope's Daughter; The Extraordinary Life of Felice della Rovere. John Paul Getty postdoctoral fellow, John Paul Getty Found., 2001—02, Villa I Tatti fellow, Harvard U., 2001—02. Mem.: Renaissance Soc. Am. Office: U Calif Riverside CA 92521

MURPHY, CAROLYN, model; b. Walton Bch., Fla., Aug. 11, 1975; m. Jake Schroeder; 1 child. Model IMG Agy.; spokesperson Estee Lauder, 2001—. Actor: (films) Liberty Heights, 1999. Named Model Yr., VH1 Fashion Awards, 1998. Achievements include appeared on numerous mag. covers including Vogue, Harper's Bazaar, W, Elle, Marie Claire; one of the models to appear on the cover of Vogue's "Model of the Millennium" issue; starred in Calvin Klein's "Contradiction" comml. and print ads. Mailing: 420 W 45th ST New York NY 10036

MURPHY, CAROLYN J. MANCINI, secondary school educator; b. Providence, R.I., May 27, 1941; d. Anthony and Constance (Sullo) M.; m. Grayson Paul Murphy, Aug. 18, 1961; children: Chrisopher, Pamela, Colin. BE, R.I. Coll., 1962, masters equivalency, 1964. Tchr. math. Park View Jr. H.S., Cranston, R.I., 1962-63; tchr. French George J. West Jr. H.S., Providence, 1963-66; tchr. math Lincoln (R.I.) Jr.-Sr. H.S., 1973—. Mentor, resource cons. State of R.I., Providence, 1995—; judge nat. selection com. Presdl. Awards, Washington, 1993. Appeared in (film) Dreams Count, 1995. Recipient Presdl. award Excellence in Tchg. Maths., 1993; named Tchr. of the Year Cumberland Sch. Sys., 1992. Mem. R.I. Math Tchrs. Assn., Nat. Edn. Assn., Nat. Coun. Tchrs. Maths., Assn. Tchrs. Maths. New Eng., Coun. Prsdl. Awareness in Maths., Habitat for Humanity, Amnesty Internat., R.I. Coll. Assn., Greenpeace. Democrat. Home: 3249 Diamond Hill Rd Cumberland RI 02864-2922

MURPHY, CARYLE MARIE, foreign correspondent; b. Hartford, Conn., Nov. 16, 1946; d. Thomas Joseph and Muriel Kathryn (McCarthy) Murphy. BA cum laude, Trinity Coll., 1968; M in Internat. Pub. Policy, Johns Hopkins U., 1987. Tchr. English, history St. Cecilia Tchr. Tng. Coll., Nyeri, Kenya, 1968—71; reporter Brockton (Mass.) Enterprise, 1972—73; freelance corr. Washington Post, Newsweek, Sunday Times of London, et al, Luanda, Angola, 1974—76; reporter Fairfax County Washington Post, 1976—77, fgn. corr. in South Africa, 1977—82, reporter immigration issues, 1982—85, bur. chief Alexandria, Va., 1985—89, fgn. corr. Mid. East Cairo, 1989—94, religion corr. Vol. ARC, Washington, 1984, Whitman-Walker Found., Washington, 1988—89. Recipient Courage in Journalism award, Internat. Women's Media Found., 1990, George Polk award, L.I. U., 1991, Edward Weintal Journalism award, Sch. Fgn. Svc., Georgetown U., 1991, Pulitzer Prize for internat. reporting, 1991, Edward R. Murrow fellow, Coun. on Fgn. Rels., N.Y., 1994—95. Roman Catholic. Avocations: foreign languages, hiking. Office: Washington Post Fgn Desk 1150 15th St NW Washington DC 20071-0002

MURPHY, CATHERINE, painter; b. Cambridge, Mass., 1946; BFA, Pratt Inst., 1967; student, Skowhegan Sch. Painting and Sculpture, 1966. One-woman shows First Street Gallery, N.Y.C., 1972, Piper Gallery, Mass., 1972, Fourcade, Droll, Inc., N.Y.C., 1975, Phillips Collection, Washington, 1976, Xavier Fourcade, Inc., N.Y.C., 1979, 85, J. Rosenthal Fine Arts, Ltd., Chgo., 1988, Lennon, Weinberg, Inc., N.Y.C., 1989, 92, 95, 97, 2001; exhibited in group shows at Whitney Mus. Am. Art, N.Y.C., 1972, 73, Indpls. Mus., 1974, Inst. Contemporary Art, Boston, 1976, Mus. Contemporary Art, Chgo., 1977, Am. Acad. and Inst. Arts and Letters, N.Y.C., 1979, 87, 89, 90, 92, Xavier Fourcade, Inc., N.Y.C., 1977, 80, 83, 87, 93, (traveling exhbn.) San Francisco Mus. Modern Art, 1985, Daniel Weinberg Gallery, L.A., 1989, (traveling exhbn.) Cin. Art Mus., 1989, Lennon Weinberg, Inc., N.Y.C., 1989, 90, 91, 93, 94, 97, 98, 2000, 2003, (traveling exhbn.) Miyaqi Mus. Art, Sendai, Japan, 1991-92, Forum Gallery, N.Y.C., 1993, Koplin Gallery, Santa Monica, Calif., 1993, Tibor de Nagy Gallery, N.Y.C., 1994, Apex Art Curatorial Program, NYC, 1997, DC Moore Gallery, NYC, 1999; permanent collections Chase Manhattan Bank, N.Y.C., Hirshhorn Mus. & Sculpture Garden, Washington, Met. Mus. Art, N.Y.C., Newark Mus., N.J. Art Mus., Trenton, Phillips Collection, Washington, Va. Mus. Fine Arts, Richmond, Weatherspoon Art Gallery, Greensboro, N.C., Whitney, Mus. Am. Art, N.Y.C. Grantee NEA, 1979, 89, Ingram Merrill Found., 1986; Guggenheim fellow, 1982; recipient AAIAL award, 1990. Mem.: NAD (academician). Mailing: c/o Lennon Weinberg Inc 514 W 25th St New York NY 10001

MURPHY, CATHY EMILY, photographer, educator, journalist; b. Bay City, Mich., Jan. 27, 1943; d. Douglas Patrick and Grace Anna Churchfield; m. Denis Michael Murphy, Mar. 1964 (div. 1974); 1 child, Paul. AA journalism, Diablo Valley Coll., Pleasant Hill, Calif., 1963; BA, Calif. State Univ.-Chico, Chico, Calif., 1992. ESL tchg. credential Univ. Zagreb, Yugoslavia, 1966, Brooks Inst. of Photo, Santa Barbara, Calif., 1975, Univ. Calif., 1964, tchg. credetial photography Ariz., Calif., Washington. Staff photographer Cesar Chavez and UFW, Keene, Calif., 1974—75, So. Ariz. Discovery, Tucson, 1977—78; photo instr. Clover Pk. Vocat. Tech Inst., Tacoma, 1980—84; photographic stringer US/Mex. Ariz. Rep., Phoenix, 1985—87; photo instr. Seattle Ctrl. C.C., 1989—90; photo journalist Bisbee Observer, Bisbee news, Ariz., 1996—2000, Bisbee Daily Rev., Ariz., 2001—03. Photo instr. Butte Coll., Oroville, Calif., 1990—94, Cochise Coll., Douglas, Ariz., 1978, Douglas, 1980—87, Douglas, 1995—; photographer/tour guide Mex. Geronimo Ednl. Travel Studies, Bisbee, Ariz., 1997—2003; judge Profl. Photographers of Wash., Spokane, Wash., 1998. Author (photographer): (traveling photo essay) From the Califorina Fields, 1976, (photo documentary) Living on the Edge- The Tarahumara of Copper Canyon, 2000; photographer (exhibitions) Tang Gallery, Nat. Chaveny Ctr., Keene, Calif., 2006, U. Ariz., Tucson, Ariz., 2006, Pasadena City Coll., Calif., 2006. Friends Copper Queen Libr., Bisbee, Ariz., 2002—03; mem. Nat. Mus. Women in Arts, Washington, 1998; bd. dirs. Cochise Fine Arts, Bisbee, Ariz., 1978. Grantee, Woody Guthrie Found., N.Y., 1976, Ariz. Arts. Commn., Phoenix, Ariz., 1978—79; scholarship award, Brooks Inst. of Photography, Santa Barbara, Calif., 1974. Mem.: Ariz. Newspaper Assn. (numerous state awards for photography and writing), Nat. Press Assn. Democrat. Achievements include photographs from Cesar Chavez days in PBS documentary 1999; Nat. merit awards from Profl. Photographers of Am. in fashion, fine art and archl. photography, state awards profl. photographers of Oreg. and Wash; 5 photographs of Tarahumara women in archives of the inst. nat. de las Mujeres, Mex. City, Mex. Avocations: photography, swimming, studying Spanish, documenting lifestyles native peoples of Mex. Home: 31 Temby, PO Box 67 Bisbee AZ 85603 Office: Cochise Coll Art Dept 4190W Hwy 80 Douglas AZ 85607

MURPHY, CLAIRE RUDOLF, author, consultant; b. Spokane, Wash., Mar. 9, 1951; d. Kermit Max and Frances Claire (Collins) R.; m. Robert Patrick Murphy, June 9, 1979; children: Conor, Megan. BA in History, Santa Clara U., 1973; MFA in Creative Writing, U. Alaska, 1988. Cert. tchr., Calif., Alaska, Wash. Tchr. secondary lang. arts St. Mary's (Alaska) Sch., 1974-77; tchr. lang. arts North Pole H.S., Fairbanks, Alaska, 1977-82, Ryan Mid. Sch., Fairbanks, 1982-83; instr. adult learning programs Fairbanks Correctional Ctr., 1983-89; adj. prof. U. Alaska, Fairbanks, 1989-90; dir. Young Writers Inst., Fairbanks, 1993-98; writing cons. Alaska State Writing Consortium, 1983-98; freelance writer Spokane, 1998—; instr. writing Eastern Wash. U., Spokane, 1999—. Mem. curriculum adv. bd. Fairbanks Sch. Dist., 1997-98. Author: Friendship Across Arctic Waters: Alaskan Cub Scouts Meet Their Soviet Neighbors, 1991, To the Summit, 1992, The Prince and the Salmon People, 1993, Gold Star Sister, 1994, A Child's Alaska, 1994 (Parents Coun. selection, Sequoyah Children's Book award 1996-97, Caribou Girl, 1998, Gold Rush Winter, 2000, Daughters of the Desert, 2003, I am Sacajawea, I am York: OUr Journey West with Lewis and Clark, 2005, Chilren of Alcatraz: Growing up on the Rock, 2006; co-author: (with Jane Haigh) Gold Rush Women, 1997, (with Jan Haigh) Children of Gold Rush, 1999, Gold Rush Dogs, 2001. Recipient Contbrn. to Literacy in Alaska award Alaska Ctr. for the Book, Anchorage, 1998. Mem. Soc. Children's Book Writers and Illustrators, Author's Guild. Democrat. Roman Catholic. Avocations: sports, music. Home: 1514 E 19th Ave Spokane WA 99203-3714

MURPHY, DIANA E., federal judge; b. Faribault, Minn., Jan. 4, 1934; d. Albert W. and Adleyne (Heiker) Kuske; m. Joseph Murphy, July 24, 1958; children: Michael, John E. BA magna cum laude, U. Minn., 1954, JD magna cum laude, 1974; postgrad., Johannes Gutenberg U., 1954—55, U. Minn., 1955—58; LLD, St. Johns U., 2000, U. St. Thomas, 2003. Bar: Minn. 1974, U.S. Supreme Ct. 1980. Assoc. Lindquist & Vennum, 1974—76; mcpl. judge Hennepin County, 1976—78, Minn. State dist. judge, 1978—80; judge U.S. Dist. Ct. for Minn., Mpls., 1980—94, chief judge, 1992—94; judge U.S. Ct. of Appeals (8th cir.), Mpls., 1994—. Chair U.S. Sentencing Commn., 1999—2004. Bd. editors: Minn. Law Rev., Georgetown U. Jour. on Cts., Health Scis. and the Law, 1989—92. Bd. dirs. Nat. Assn. Pub. Interest Law Fellowships for Equal Justice, 1992—95, Mpls. United Way, 1985—2001, treas., 1990—94, vice-chmn., 1996—97, chmn. bd. dirs., 1997—98; bd. dirs. Bush Found., 1982—2006, chmn. bd. dirs., 1986—91; organizer, 1st chmn. adv. coun. Amicus, bd. dirs., 1976—80; chair Mpls. Charter Commn., 1973—76; bd. dirs. Ops. De Novo, 1971—76, chmn. bd. dirs., 1974—75; mem., chmn. bill of rights com. Minn. Constl. Study Commn., 1971—73; regent St. Johns U., 1978—87, 1988—98, chmn. bd., 1995—98, bd. overseers sch. theology, 1998—2001; mem. Minn. Bicentennial Commn., 1987—88; trustee Twin Cities Pub. TV, 1985—94, chmn. bd., 1990—92; trustee U. Minn. Found., 1990—, chmn. of bd., 2003—05; bd. dirs. Sci. Mus. Minn., 1988—94, vice-chmn., 1991—94; trustee U. St. Thomas, 1991—, chair exec. com., 2006—; vice chair bd. govs. U. St. Thomas Law Sch., 2001—04, chair, 2004—06; bd. dirs. Spring Hill Conf. Ctr., 1978—84; bd. govs. Hill Mus. and Manuscript Libr., 2005—; bd. dirs. Minn. Opera, 1998—2004, 2005—. Recipient Amicus Founders' award, 1980, Outstanding Achievement award, U. Minn., 1983, YWCA, 1981, Disting. Citizen award, Alpha Gamma Delta, 1985, Devitt Disting. Svc. to Justice award, 2001, Disting. Alumnus award, U. Minn. Law Sch., 2002, Woman Who Makes a Difference award, Internat. Women's Forum, 2003, Iustitia et Lex award, 2006; scholar Fulbright. Fellow: Am. Bar Found.; mem.: ABA (ethics and profl. responsibility judges adv. com. 1981—88, standing com. on jud. selection, tenure and compensation 1991—94, standing com. on fed. jud. improvements 1994—97, Appellate Judges conf. exec. com. 1996—99, chmn. ethics and profl. responsibility judges adv. com. 1997—2000), Fed. Jud. Ctr. (bd. dirs. 1990—94, 8th cir. jud. coun. 1992—94, 1992—94, convener gender fairness task force 1993, U.S. jud. conf. com. on ct. adminstrn. and case mgmt. 1994—99, chair gender fairness implementation com. 1997—98), Hist. Soc. for 8th Cir. (bd. dirs. 1988—91), Fed. Judges Assn. (bd. dirs. 1982—2003, v.p. 1984—89, pres. 1989—91), U. Minn. Alumni Assn. (bd. dirs. 1975—83, nat. pres. 1981—82), Minn. Women Lawyers (Myra Bradwell award 1996), Nat. Assn. Women Judges (Leadership Judges Jud. Adminstrn. award 1998, Honoree of Yr. 2002), Nat. Assn. Governing Bds. Univs. Colls. (dir. 1998—, vice chair 2006—), Am. Judicature Soc. (bd. dirs. 1982—93, v.p. 1985—88, treas. 1988—89, chmn. bd. 1989—91), Am. Law Inst., Hennepin County Bar Assn. (gov. coun. 1976—81), Minn. Bar Assn. (bd. govs. 1977—81), Order of Coif, Phi Beta Kappa. Office: 11 E US Courthouse 300 S 4th St Minneapolis MN 55415-1320

MURPHY, DONNA, actress; b. Corona, N.Y., Mar. 7, 1959; m. Shawn Elliott, 1990. Student, NYU Sch. of the Arts. Actor: (Broadway plays) They're Playing Our Song, The Human Comedy, The Mystery of Edwin Drood, Passion (Tony award best actress in a musical, 1994, Drama Desk award, Drama League award), The King and I, 1996 (Tony award best actress in a musical, 1996, Drama League award), Wonderful Town, 2003—04 (Tony nom. best actress in a musical, 2004, Drama Desk award best actress in a musical, 2004, Drama League award, 2004); (plays) Song of Singapore, Privates on Parade, Showing Off, Birds of Paradise, Little Shop of Horrors, A.My Name Is Alice, Twelve Dreams, 1995, Hello Again, 1994; (TV series) Murder One, 1995—96, Law & Order, 1993, 1997, 2000, The Practice, 1998, Ally McBeal, 1998, What About Joan, 2001, Hack, 2002—03; (TV miniseries) LIBERTY! The American Revolution, 1997; (TV films) Tales from the Hollywood Hills: A Table at Ciro's, 1987, Power, Passion and Murder, 1987, Passion, 1996, Someone Had to Be Benny, 1996 (Cable ACE award, 1996, Daytime Emmy, 1996), The Day Lincoln Was Shot, 1998, The Last Debate, 2000; (films) Jade, 1995, October 22, 1998, Star Trek: Insurrection, 1998, The Astronaut's Wife, 1999, Center Stage, 2001, The Door in the Floor, 2004, Spiderman 2, 2004, Ira and Abby, 2006, World Trade Center, 2006. Office: Innovative Artists 235 Park Ave S New York NY 10003*

MURPHY, EDRIE LEE, laboratory administrator; b. Redwood Falls, Minn., Dec. 4, 1953; d. Melvin Arthur and Betty Lou (Wenholz) Timm; m. David Joseph Murphy, July 28, 1984; children: Michael David, Scott Christopher. BS in Med. Tech. summa cum laude, Mankato State U., 1976; MBA, U. St. Thomas, 1984. Registered med. technologist. Med. technologist Children's Hosps. and Clinics, St. Paul, 1976-81, chemistry supr., 1981-85, lab. mgr., 1985-95, dir. lab. sys. Mpls., St. Paul's Campus, 1995-99; lab. mgr. Fairview Health Sys., Mpls., 2000—. Contbr. articles to profl. jours. Charles H. Cooper scholar, 1975. Mem.: Minn. Soc. Clin. Lab. Mgmt. Assn. (sec.-treas. Minn. chpt. 1994—96, bd. dirs. 1996—, pres.-elect 1998—2000, pres. 2000—02), Am. Soc. Clin. Lab. Scis., Elan Vital Ski Club (v.p. membership 1981—82), Phi Kappa Phi. Avocations: photography, sailing, skiing, tennis, travel. Office: 2450 Riverside Ave S W1-505 Minneapolis MN 55454 Office Phone: 612-672-4185. E-mail: emurphy2@fairview.org.

MURPHY, EILEEN BRIDGET, retired mathematics professor; b. Newport, RI, Dec. 28, 1940; d. Henry Timothy and Mary Anne (Lyne) M. BA in Teaching Math., Elms Coll., 1969; MAT in Math., Purdue U., 1971; MSA in Adminstrn., U. Notre Dame, 1981; postgrad., Nova Southeastern U., 1992—96. Cert. secondary edn., math. and adminstrn., Mass. Tchr. math. Cathedral H.S., Springfield, Mass., 1961-71; tchr. Holyoke Cath. H.S., Mass., 1971-84, dept. chair, 1975-84; asst. prof., lectr. Elms Coll., Chicopee, 1984—2006, dept. chair math. scis., 1985-90, div. chair math. and sci., 1987-89; ret., 1989. Steering com. Accreditations New Eng. Assn. Secondary Schs. and Colls., Chicopee, 1991-92. Mem. Sisters of St. Joseph of Springfield, Sisters of St. Joseph Fin. Team; co-treas. Sisters of St. Joseph Festival, 1984-86; bd. dirs. Mont Marie Health Care Ctr., 1999-2005; vol. computer tchr. Hampden County Dept. Corrections; vol. tchr. math. and computer applications Elms Coll., 2006—. Recipient Econs. of Pvt. Enterprise grant Strathmore Paper Co., Springfield Coll., Mass., 1978. Mem. Math. Assn. Am., Nat. Coun. Tchrs. Math., Assn. Computing Machinery (Western Mass. chpt. pub. rels. com. 1985-86, sec. 1986-91). Democrat. Roman Catholic. Avocations: peer support for multiple sclerosis groups, knitting, puzzle solving. Home: 414 Chestnut St Apt 1204 Springfield MA 01104-3442 Personal E-mail: murphye@elms.edu.

MURPHY, ELISABETH MARIA, physical design engineer, consultant; b. Cleve., Nov. 9, 1956; d. Thomas Jerome and Dolores Dorothy (Bost) M. AAS, Ctrl. Ohio Tech. Coll., 1990; student, Ohio State U., 1991-92, Franklin U., 1992-94. Jewelry designer P.J. Rone Co., Reading, Pa., 1983-87; registrar Office Continuing Edn., Ctrl. Ohio Tech. Coll., Newark, 1987-88; civil engring. designer dist. 5, Ohio Dept. Transp., Newark, 1988-90; phys. design engr. Bell Labs./Lucent Techs., Columbus, Ohio, 1990—, safety coord., 1990-92, Ams. with Disabilities Act Disability adv. and archtl. cons., 1993—, edn. and resource developer, disability spokesperson, 1993—. Freelance writer, 1977—; portrait artist, 1983—; freelance math. tutor, Columbus, 1990-93, Ohio State U. and Ctrl. Ohio Tech. Coll., 1988-90; disability rights cons. Contbr. articles to profl. publs., poetry to newspaper. Mem. NOW, Instrument Soc. Am. (Outstanding Tech. Paper award 1989), Soc. Mfg. Engrs., Nat. Woodcarvers Assn., Nat. Mus. Women in Arts. Avocation: research on pre-modern women sculptors. E-mail: elisabethmurphy@lucent.com.

MURPHY, ELVA GLENN, executive assistant; b. Chickasha, Okla., Aug. 21, 1934; d. Elsie Lee (Murphy) Sommer and Maynard F. Glenn; m. Calvin E. Morgan, Mar. 11, 1972 (dec. Dec. 1976); m. C. Gordon Murphy, Oct. 17, 1981. Student, UCLA, 1954—55, Columbia U., 1973. Various secretarial positions, Calif., 1956-67; fgn. svc. sec. U.S. Dept. State, Paris, 1967-69; exec. asst. to Cyrus R. Vance Simpson Thacher & Bartlett, N.Y.C., 1969-77, 80-98, U.S. Dept. State, Washington, 1977-80; asst. to pres. Coun. on Fgn. Rels., Inc., N.Y.C., 1997—2003; asst. social medicine and pub. policy program Weill Med. Coll. Cornell U., N.Y.C., 2003—. Mem. Seraphic Soc. (pres. 1990-92), Women's City Club N.Y. Avocations: sailing, skiing, cooking, reading, theater. Office: Weill Med Coll Cornell Univ 525 E 68th St Box 171 New York NY 10021 Home: 315 E 70th St Apt 1j New York NY 10021-8689 Business E-Mail: egm2003@med.cornell.edu.

MURPHY, ERIN MELISSA, art educator; b. Fon du Lac, Wis., Feb. 21, 1978; adopted d. Kristin Sue and John William Murphy. A of Sci. and Fine Art, U. Wisc., Waukesha, 1996—98; BFA, U. Wisc., Milwaukee, 1999—2003. Pre-K-12 Art Wis. Bd. Edn., 2003. Tchr. aide Grandma's Ho. Daycare Worker, Brookfield, Wis., 1997—2003; foster parent edn. program child care worker/arts and crafts St. Aemilin Lakeside, Milwaukee, 2000—03; tchr. Artist's Working in Edn., Inc, Milwaukee, 2003; elem. art tchr. Three Lakes Sch. Dist., Wis., 2003—; waitress Bonnie's Lakeside, Three Lakes, 2004—. Artist in residency com. Three Lakes Sch. Dist., 2004—05, citizenship com., 2004—05; judge Artarama, Eagle River, 2005—. Vol., arts activities Three Lakes Info. Bur.: Pk. Week, Three Lakes, 2004; art activities planner Three Lakes Arts Coun./Faith Luth. Ch., 2004. Mem.: Wis. Edn. Assn. Coun., Doris Day Animal League, Ducks Unlimited. Avocations: boating, fishing, hiking. Office: Three Lakes Sch Dist 6930 W School St Three Lakes WI 54562 Office Phone: 715-546-3323. Home Fax: 715-546-2156. Personal E-mail: erinartist@earthlink.net.

MURPHY, EVELYN FRANCES, economist; b. Panama Canal Zone, May 14, 1940; d. Clement Bernard and Dorothy Eloise (Jackson) M. AB, Duke U., 1961, PhD, 1965; MA, Columbia U., 1963; degree (hon.), Regis Coll., 1978, Curry Coll., Northeastern U., Simmons Coll., Wheaton Coll., Anna Maria Coll., Bridgewater State Coll., Salem State Coll., Emmanuel Coll., Suffolk U. Pres. Ancon Assocs., Boston, 1971-72; ptnr. Llewelyn-Davies, Weeks, Forrester-Walker & Bor, London, 1973-74; sec. environ. affairs Commonwealth of Mass., Boston, 1975-79, sec. econ. affairs, 1983-86, lt. gov., 1987-91; mng. dir. Brown Rudnick Freed and Gesmer, Boston, 1991-93; exec. v.p. Blue Cross/Blue Shield of Mass., Boston, 1994-98; also bd. dirs. Blue Cross Blue Shield Mass., Boston; resident scholar Brandeis U. Women's Studies Rsch. Ctr., 1999—; founder, pres. The Wage Project, Inc., 2003—. Vice-chmn., chmn. Nat. Adv. Com. on Oceans and Atmosphere, 1979-80; bd. dirs. Citizens Energy Corp., The Commonwealth Inst., Polaris Project, Nat. Ctr. on Women and Aging, chair, 1998-2002, chmn. emeritus, 2002; pres. Health Care and Policy Inst., 1997-98; resident scholar Brandeis U., 1998—; bd. trustees Regis Coll., 2003—; vice chair SBLI USA Mut. Life Ins. Author: (books) Getting Even: Why Women Don't Get Paid Like Men & What to Do About It, 2005. Recipient Dist. Svc. award New Eng. Coun., 1996, Nat. Sierra Club, 1978, Nat. Bd. Govs. Assn., 1978, Outstanding Citizen award Mass. Audobon Soc., 1978; Harvard U. fellow, 1979-80. Mem. Women Execs. in State Govt. (chair 1987), Internat. Women's Forum, 1993—. Democrat. Avocation: jogging. Personal E-mail: evmurphy1@aol.com.

MURPHY, FRANCES LOUISE, II, retired newspaper publisher; b. Balt., Oct. 8, 1922; d. Carl James and L. Vashti (Turley) M.; m. James E. Wood (div.); children: Frances Murphy Wood Draper, James E. Jr., Susan Wood Barnes, David Lloyd Campbell. BA, U. Wis., 1944; BS, Coppin State Coll., Balt., 1958; MEd, Johns Hopkins U., 1963. City editor Balt. Afro-Am., 1956-57; dir. News Bur., Morgan State Coll., Balt., 1964-71; chmn. bd. dirs.

Afro-Am. Newspapers, Balt., 1971-74; assoc. prof. journalism State Univ. Coll., Buffalo, 1975-85, Howard U., Washington, 1985-91; editor Washington Afro-Am., 1951-56, pub., 1987-99; editl. page editor Afro-Am. Newspapers, Balt., 1999—. Contbr. columns in newspapers. Treas. African Am. Civil War Meml. Freedom Found.; trustee State Colls. Md., 1971-76, U. D.C., 1994-99; bd. dirs. Delta Rsch. and Ednl. Found., 1993-95; nat. bd. dirs. NACCP, 1971-76; vestry St. James' Episcopal Ch. Named one of 100 Most Influential Black Ams., Ebony mag., 1973, 74, Disting. Marylander, Gov. State of Md., 1975; recipient Ida B. Wells award Congl. Black Caucus, 1989, Public Svc. award African Methodist Episcopal Ch., 1991, Invaluable Svc. award Martin L. King Jr. Found., 1992, Black Women of Courage award Nat. Fedn. Black Women Bus. Owners, 1993, Black Awareness Ach. award Holy Redeemer Catholic Ch., 1993, Bus. of the Yr. award Bus. and Profl. Women's League, 1993, Oustanding Svc. award Capital Press Club, 1993, Black Conscious Commitment trophy Unity Nation, 1993, Dedicated Cmty. Svc. award Ward I Cmty. and DC Pub. Schs., 1994, Women of Strength award Nat. Black Media Coalition, 1994-95, Outstanding Woman of Yr. award Alpha Gamma chpt. Iota Phi Lambda, 1994, Art Carter Excellence award Capital Press Club, 1994, Excellence in Comm. award Washington Inter-Alumni Coun. United Negro Coll. Fund, 1994, 95, Disting. Cmty. Svc. award The Questers, Inc., 1995, Outstanding Journalist award Masons, 1995, Outstanding Achievement award Beta Zeta chpt. Zeta Phi Beta, 1996, award in recognition of outstanding contbns. made to youth The Soc., 1996, Disting. Black Women award BISA, 1996, Woman of 20th Century award Nat. Pol. Congress Black Women, 1999. Mem. Nat. Newspaper Pubs. Assn. (editl. com. 1987—, Merit award 1987, 89-97, First Pl. editl. writing 2003), Soc. Profl. Journalists (Disting. Svc. in local journalism award Washington chpt. 1994), Links (pres. Balt. chpt. 2004—), Capital Press Club (exec. bd. 1987-98, Outstanding Svc. award 1993, Art Carter award 1994), Delta Sigma Theta (Frances L. Murphy II Comm. award Fed. City Alumnae chpt. 1993, Fortitude Image award Prince George's County chpt. 1994, Ethel L. Payne award 1996-97), Kiwanis Club (first woman hon. 1995), Iota Phi Lambda (hon.) Democrat. Avocation: bridge. Office: Baltimore 2519 N Charles St Baltimore MD 21218-4602 Address: 2406 Overland Ave Baltimore MD 21214-2440 Office Phone: 410-554-8200. Personal E-mail: frankielou@aol.com.

MURPHY, FRANCES M., federal agency administrator; MD with honors, Georgetown U., Washington, 1979; MPH, Uniformed Svcs. U. of the Health Scis., 1993. Diplomate Am. Coll. Psychiatry and Neurology. Resident in neurology Georgetown U., Washington; staff neurologist Andrews AFB, Md., 1983—87; chief cons. occupl. and environ. medicine US Dept. Veterans Affairs, Washington, dep. under-sec. for health, 1999—2002, acting under sec. for health, 2002, dep. under sec. for health policy coord., 2002—. Adj. assoc. prof. neurology Uniformed Svcs. U. of the Health Scis. Contbr. articles to profl. jours. With USAF. Office: US Dept Veterans Affairs 810 Vermont Ave NW Washington DC 20420*

MURPHY, HELEN, recording industry executive; b. Glasgow, Scotland, Oct. 2, 1962; came to U.S., 1990; d. Francis and Kathleen (Gallagher) M.; m. Michael Christopher Luksha, Apr. 1, 1989. BA in Econs. with honors, U. Guelph, Can., 1982; MBA, U. Western Ontario, Can., 1984. CFA. Asst. mgr. securities rsch. Confederation Life, Toronto, Can., 1984-86; sr. analyst entertainment & merchandising Prudential Bache Securities, Toronto, Can., 1986-89; v.p. rsch. Richardson Greenshields Can., Toronto, 1989-90; v.p. investor rels. Polygram Holding, Inc., N.Y.C., 1990-91; v.p., treas. Polygram Records Inc., N.Y.C., 1991-92, sr. v.p. corp. fin., treas., 1992-95; sr. v.p. investor rels. PolyGram Internat. Ltd., N.Y.C., 1995-97; sr. v.p. mergers and acquisitions PolyGram Holding, Inc., N.Y.C., 1995-97, CFO, 1997-99, Westvaco Corp., 1999; CFO & chief adminstrv. office Martha Stewart Living Omnimedia, Inc., N.Y.C., 1999—2001; exec. v.p., CFO Warner Music Group, 2001—. Lectr. U. Guelph, 1982-90. Fellow Nat. Investor Rels. Inst., N.Y. Soc. Security Analysts, N.Y. Treas. Group. Office: Warner Music Group 75 Rockefeller Plz New York NY 10019

MURPHY, JEANNE M., science educator; d. Ben Harrison Banta and Marilyn Francois; m. Dan Murphy; children: Patricia, James, Hannah. BA in Biology, U. Calif., Santa Cruz, 1992. Sci. tchr. James Weldon Johnson Coll. Prep. Mid. Sch., 1988—; tchr. sci. So. Bapt. Acad., Jacksonville, Fla., 1989—90; adj. lab. tchr. U. North Fla., Jacksonville, 1989—90; sci. tchr. Duval County, Jacksonville, 1990—93, 1998—. Mem.: Nat. Assn. Sci. Tchrs. Avocations: cooking, photography. Home: 519 Sapela Rd Jacksonville FL 32216 Office: James W Johnson Mid Sch 1840 W 9th St Jacksonville FL 32209 Office Phone: 904-630-6640 ext 130. E-mail: murphyj@educationcentral.org.

MURPHY, JENNIFER, elementary school educator; d. Ronald and Barbara Murphy. BS, U. W. Ala., 1997; M in Elem. Edn., Samford U. Cert. Tchg. Standards Nat. Bd. Profl. Tchrs. Tchr. 3rd grade Center Point Elem. Jefferson County Bd. Edn., Birmingham, Ala., 1998—99, tchr. 3rd grade Erwin Elem., 1999—2006, tchr. 3d grade Bryan Elem., 2006—. Finalist Tchr. of Yr., Jefferson County Bd. Edn., Jefferson County Found., 2005. Mem.: Phi Kappa Phi. Office: Bryan Elem 600 Kimberly Rd Morris AL 35116

MURPHY, JOANNE BECKER, writer; b. Detroit; d. Louis Norman and Gertrude Margaret (Kornmeier) Becker; m. Joseph A. Murphy, Jr., June 24, 1961; children: Michael Ellis, Joseph A. III. BA in Journalism, Mich. State U., 1958; MA in Humanities, Wayne State U., 1975. With pub. rels. dept. WBZ TV, Boston, 1958-60, The Jam Handy Orgn., Detroit, 1960-62, Detroit Symphony Orch., 1969-70; freelance writer, editor Detroit, 1978—90, Washington, 1990—. Contbg. writer: Affecting Change, 1986, Glass: State of the Art, 1989; editor: As Parents We Will, 1985 (1st Pl. award Pub. Svc. Nat. Found. for Alcoholism Comm.); writer, editor publs. for arts and human svcs. orgns.; contbr. articles to mags., newspapers. Program bd. Grosse Pointe (Mich.) War Meml., 1987—90; bd. dirs. Detroit Artists Market, 1982—90, Mich. Metro coun. Girl Scouts USA, 1971—78, Family Svcs. Detroit and Wayne County, 1970—76, All Hallows Guild Grounds Oversight Bd., Washington Nat. Cathedral, 1993—; bd. canvassers Grosse Pointe Sch. Sys., 1986—90; DC regional bd. Nat. Capital Area United Way, Washington, 1999—. Mem.: Washington Ind. Writers, Am. News Women's Club (Washington, bd. dirs. 1996—2001), Kappa Alpha Theta. Home and Office: 2717 O St NW Washington DC 20007-3128 Office Phone: 202-337-7856. E-mail: murphy.joanne@verizon.net.

MURPHY, JUDITH CHISHOLM, trust company executive; b. Chippewa Falls, Wis., Jan. 26, 1942; d. John David and Bernice A. (Hartman) Chisholm. BA, Manhattanville Coll., 1964; postgrad., New Sch. for Social Research, 1965-68, Nat. Grad. Trust Sch., 1975. Asst. portfolio mgr. Chase Manhattan Bank, N.A., N.Y.C., 1964-68; trust investment officer Marshall & Ilsley Bank, Milw., 1968-72, asst. v.p., 1972-74, v.p., 1974-75; v.p., treas. Marshall & Ilsley Invesmtent Mgmt. Corp., Milw., 1975-94; v.p. Marshall & Ilsley Trust Co., Phoenix, 1982—, Marshall & Ilsley Trust Co., Fla., Naples, 1985—; v.p., dir. instnl. sales Marshall & Ilsley Trust Co., Milw., 1994-97, sr. v.p., 1997-98, M&I Investment Mgmt. Corp., 1998—. Coun. mem. Am. Bankers Assn., Washington, 1984-86; govt. relations com. Wis. Bankers Assn., Madison, 1982-88. Contbr. articles to profl. jours. Chmn. Milw. City Plan Commn., 1986—97; commr. Milw. County Commn. on Handicapped, 1988—90; bd. dirs. Cardinal Stritch Coll., Milw., 1980—89, Children's Hosp. Wis., Milw., 1989—98, Milw. Ballet Co., 1996—2001, Milw. Ctr. for Independence, 1999—2004, Girl Scouts Milw. Area, 2002—, Milw. Symphony Orch., 2002—. Recipient Outstanding Achievement award YWCA Greater Milw., 1985, Sacajawea award Profl. Dimensions, Milw., 1988, Pro Urbe award Mt. Mary Coll., 1988, Vol. award Milw. Found., 1992; named Disting. Woman in Banking, Comml. West Mag., 1988. Mem. Milw. Analysts Soc. (sec. 1974-77, bd. dirs. 1977-80), Fin. Women Internat. (bd. dirs., v.p. 1976-80), Am. Inst. Banking (instr. 1975-78), TEMPO (charter), Profl. Dimensions (hon.), University Club, Woman's Club Wis., Rotary. Democrat. Roman Catholic. Home: 3622 N Lake Dr Milwaukee WI 53211-2644 Office: M&I Investment Mgmt Corp 111 E Kilbourn Ave Milwaukee WI 53202-3197 Business E-Mail: judith.murphy@micorp.com.

MURPHY, KAREN, sports association executive; b. 1971; With Ernst & Young, Chgo., Walt Disney Co.; contr. Chgo. Bears Football Club Inc., Lake Forest, Ill., 1999—2002, CFO & treas., 2002—. Named one of 40 Under 40, Crain's Chgo. Bus., 2006. Office: Chgo Bears Football Club Inc 1000 Football Dr Lake Forest IL 60045*

MURPHY, KATHLEEN ANNE FOLEY, communications executive; b. Fresh Meadows, NY, Oct. 15, 1952; d. Thomas J. and Audrey L. Finn; m. Timothy Sean Murphy, Sept. 26, 1992; 1 child, G. David. BA, Marymount Coll., 1974; postgrad., Smith Coll., 1985. V.p. acct. supr., sr. v.p. mgmt. supr., sr. v.p. group dir. Ogilvy & Mather Inc., NYC, 1974-90; sr. v.p., worldwide account dir. Young & Rubicam, San Francisco, 1990-92, sr. v.p., dir. account svcs., 1992-95, exec. v.p., dir. acct. svcs., 1995-97, exec. v.p., gen. mgr., 1997—2002, COO, 2002—03; dir. network devel. WPP, San Francisco, 2003—. Mem. Family Caregivers Alliance. Roman Catholic. Home: One Brookside Ave Berkeley CA 94705 Office: WPP 303 Second St S Tower 9th Fl San Francisco CA 94107

MURPHY, KATHLEEN M., lawyer; b. Evergreen Park, Ill. BA, St. Xavier Coll., 1980; MA, Loyola U., Chgo., 1982, JD, 1985. Bar: Ill. 1985, US Ct. Appeals, 7th Cir., US Ct. Appeals, Fed. Cir., US Ct. Internat. Trade, US Dist. Ct., No. Dist Ill. Ptnr., nat. chair Customs and Internat. Trade Dept. and Global Trade Adv. Group Katten Muchin Zavis Rosenman, Chgo. Mem.: ABA, Women in Internat. Trade, Midwest Importers Trade Assn., Joint Industry Group, Customs and Internat. Trade Bar Assn., Am. Assn. of Exporters and Importers. Office: Katten Muchin Zavis Rosenman 525 W Monroe St Chicago IL 60661 Office Phone: 312-902-5364. Office Fax: 312-577-8849. E-mail: kathleen.murphy@kmzr.com.

MURPHY, KATHLEEN MARY, former law firm executive, alternative healing professional; b. Bklyn., Dec. 16, 1945; d. Raymond Joseph and Catherine Elizabeth (Kearney) Murphy. BA in Edn., Molloy Coll., 1971; MS in Edn., Bklyn. Coll., 1975. Ordained minister Ch. of the Loving Servant; cert. hypnotherapist; cert. elem. sch. tchr., N.Y. Elem. sch. tchr. various parochial schs., L.I., Bklyn., Queens, N.Y., 1969-80; from asst. prin. to prin. parochial sch. Queens, 1980-82; supr.-trainer Davis, Polk, Wardwell law firm, N.Y.C., 1982-88; mgr. Schulte Roth & Zabel, N.Y.C., 1988-95; Reiki master (alternative healing profl.), 1996—. Trainer program for new employees, 1984; speaker edn. topics, Bklyn., Queens, 1979-81. Mem.: NAFE, Reiki Alliance. Democrat. Roman Catholic. Avocations: psychic phenomenon, workings of mind, ancient histories, crossword puzzles, museums. Home: 290 14th St Brooklyn NY 11215

MURPHY, KATHLEEN S., science educator; b. Cleve., July 16, 1956; d. Janice Lee and Raymond L Maher; children: James L. Globokar, Leo F., Kristine E. BS, Cleve. State U., 1978; MEd, Ashland U., Ohio, 1995. Lic. sci., health and phys. edn. tchr. Ohio, 1978, class I umpire Ohio HS Athletic Assn., 1978. Tchr. Twinsburg (Ohio) Sch. Dist., 1993—. Umpire, Cleve., NCAA Divsn. II Nat. Tournament, 1999, 2000, Ohio Athletic Conf., 2004, 05, 06; bd. dirs. Suburban Umpires Assn., Berea, Ohio, 2002—. Recipient Exemplary Tchr. award, Summit County Ednl. Assn., 1998—99. Mem.: NEA, Ohio Edn. Assn., Ohio H.S. Assn., World Wildlife Fedn. Roman Catholic. Avocations: golf, travel. Home: 5126 E 131st St Garfield Heights OH 44125 Office: Twinsburg High Sch 10084 Ravenna Rd Twinsburg OH 44087 Office Phone: 330-486-2400.

MURPHY, KATHRYN J., lawyer; b. Moorhead, Minn., Dec. 28, 1961; BA with honors, Univ. Tex., Tyler, Tex., 1986; JD, So. Meth. Univ., Dallas, 1989. Bar: Tex. 1989. Ptnr. Koons Fuller Vanden Eykel & Robertson PC, Plano, Tex., 1995—. Named a Tex. Super Lawyer, Tex. Monthly mag., 2003, 2004; named one of the Best Lawyers in Dallas, D Mag., 2005. Fellow: Am. Acad. Matrimonial Lawyers, Collin County Bench Bar Found.; mem.: Coll. State Bar Tex., J. Reuben Clark Law Soc. (bd. dir. 1997—99), Intern. Acad. Collaborative Profl., Dallas Alliance Collaborative Law Inst. Tex., Tex. Acad. Family Law Specialists, Collin County Bar Assn., Dallas Bar Assn., ABA. Office: Koons Fuller Vanden Eykel & Robertson PC 2311 Cedar Springs Rd Suite 300 Dallas TX 75201 Office Phone: 214-871-2727. Office Fax: 214-871-0196. E-mail: Kathryn@koonsfuller.com.

MURPHY, KELLY ANN, psychologist; b. Smithtown, N.Y., Dec. 8, 1978; d. William G. Murphy and Kathleen Ann Millus. BA cum laude in Psychology, Hofstra U., Hempstead, N.Y., 2000, MS in Psychology, 2001, PhD in Psychology, 2004. Lic. psychologist N.Y., cert. sch. psychologist N.Y. With Options For Cmty. Living, Smithtown, NY, 2000—01; family educator L.I. (N.Y.) Head Start, Patehogue, NY, 2001—02; counselor Adults and Children with Learning Disabilities, Melville, NY, 2002; therapist early childhood Bilinguals Inc. Child and Parent Svcs., Huntington, NY, 2003—04; psychologist PCA Jefferson Sch. Dist., Port Jefferson, NY, 2004, Dr. Sabarese & Assocs., Amityville, NY, 2004—, Bay Shore (N.Y.) Union Free Sch. Dist., 2004—. Intern psychologist South Nassau Cmty. Hosp., Oceanside, NY, 2003—04; ind. evaluator BOCES East Suffolk, Patehogue, NY, 2004; substitue SCOPE, Smithtown, NY, 2001—03. Recipient Bovennan award, Hofstra U., 1999; grantee, Camelot, 2003. Mem.: APA, N.Y. State United Tchrs., Assn. Advancement Behavior Therapy, Nat. Assn. Sch. Psychologists, Suffolk County Psychol. Assn., Psi Chi, Phi Eta Sigma. Office: Bay Shore Sch Dist 155 Third Ave Bay Shore NY 11706

MURPHY, LISA M., primary school educator; b. Cambridge, Mass., Jan. 1972; d. Gerald and Carol Mottdo; m. Michael W. Murphy, Apr. 18, 1999; children: Siobhain, Aidan. BSc, Salem Sate Coll., Salem., Mass., 1994; MEd, Salem State Coll., 1999. K-tchr. Boutwell Sch., Wilmington, Mass., 1994—98; 3 grade tchr. Abbott Sch., Westford, Mass., 1994—98; K-tchr. St. Francis of Assi, Medford, Mass., 1998—99, St. Raphael Sch., Medford, Mass., 1999—.

MURPHY, MADELEINE, literature educator; MLitt, Edinburgh U., Scotland, 1990. Instr. Coll. San Mateo, Calif., 1993—.

MURPHY, MARGARETTE CELESTINE EVANS, educator, writer; b. Chgo., June 25, 1926; d. Crawford and Ethel Hazel (Cartman) Evans. Ph.B., U. Chgo., 1945, M.A., 1949, postgrad., 1950-79, Ph.D., Colo. Christian Coll., 1972; m. Robert H. Murphy, Sept. 25, 1949; children: Linda, Michelle. Tchr. English, Spanish and French Willard Elem. Sch., 1950-52, McKinley High Sch., 1952-60, chmn. fgn. langs. dept. Crane High Sch., 1960-64, Harlan High Sch., Chgo., 1967-94; tchr. TESL, Chgo. City Jr. Colls., 1976-94. Min. of Praise St. Clotilde Cath. Ch. Mem. Women's Share in Pub. Svc., Brazilian Soc. Chgo., Am. Security Council (nat. adv. bd.), U. Chgo. Alumni Assn., AAUW, Esperanto Soc. Chgo., Alpha Kappa Alpha. Republican. Roman Catholic. Club: 1200 of Chgo. Author: Notes on Martinez Zuviria, Argentinian Novelist, 1949. Home: 907 Polk Ave Memphis TN 38104-6034 Office: care Mrs Eva C Martin and Linda M Murphy 907 Polk Ave Memphis TN 38104-6034

MURPHY, MARY LEIGH, artist; d. Terence John and Mary Stuart Murphy. BFA in Graphic Design, U. Fla., Gainesville, 1988. Artist-in-residence Duval County Pub. Schs., Jacksonville, Fla., 1999—2000. Watercolor paintings, oil paintings, stone and bronze sculpture, mosaics, acrylic, mixed medica paintings; contbr. articles to profl. jours. and mags. Recipient Grumbacher Silver medal winner, Best of Show award, Cummer Mus. Art, Julington Creek Plantation Art Exhbn., 1999, Fabulous Fla. Exhibn., 2002, Jacksonville Watercolor Soc., 2004, FCCJ Wilson Ctr. for Arts, 2005, Ponte Vedra Cultural Ctr., 2005, Karpeles Mus., 2006, First Pl. Watercolor award, Coconut Grove Arts Fest, 2000, Meml. award, Appleton Mus. Art, Fla. Watercolor Soc. Exhbn., 2000, 1st Pl. award, Jacksonville Coalition Visual Arts, 2003, Region 1 winner, Nat. Parks Acad. Arts, 2003, Mus. Dirs. award, Cornell Museum Arts, 2003; Individual Artist fellow, Cultural Coun. of Jacksonvile, 2001, 2004. Mem.: St. Augustine Art Assn. (corr.), Jacksonvile Coalition Visual Arts (assoc.), Fla. Watercolor Soc. (life Am. Artist Mags. Honor award 2002, Meml. award 2006), Jacksonville Watercolor Soc. (corr.; pres. 1999—2001, Artist Yr. award 1998), Jacksonville Shell Club (assoc.). Personal E-mail: leighmurphyart@yahoo.com.

MURPHY, MARY PATRICIA, elementary school educator; b. Buffalo, Mar. 5, 1950; d. Anthony Ralph and Lena (Tirone) Scime; m. Dennis Patrick Murphy, May 4, 1973; children: Gregory Raymond, Daniel Anthony. BS, Damien Coll., 1972; MS in Elem. Edn., SUNY, Buffalo, 1975. Cert. elem. and secondary tchr., N.Y., Nat. Bd. Profl. Tchg. Stds., 2002. Tchr. grade 4 North Tonwanda Sch. Dist., NY, 1972—75; staff devel. specialist Shenendehowa Ctrl. Sch. Dist., Clifton Park, NY, 2002—03, instr., effective tchg. program, 2003—, acad. intervention support specialist, 2005—. Assistance tchr. mentor program Shenendehowa Sch. Dist., 1993—; presenter in field. Active PTA (life mem. award, 1998), Am. Diabetes Assn., Juvenile Diabetes Found., part. Mentor/Intern program. Shenendehowa Ctrl. Sch. Dist. grantee, 1988-90. Mem. ASCD, Am. Fedn. Tchrs., N.Y. United Tchrs., N.Y. Coun. Tchrs. English, Intergenerational Writers' Conf., Internat. Women's Writing Guild (staff devel. 2002-2004 Avocations: reading, cross country skiing. Home: 120 East Ave Saratoga Springs NY 12866-8743 Office: Shenendehowa Central School District Csd 5 Chelsea Pl Clifton Park NY 12065-3200 Office Phone: 518-881-0530. Personal E-mail: murprimary@shenet.com. Business E-Mail: mdmurphy3@msn.com.

MURPHY, MICHELLE ZICK, special education educator; d. Christine Hayduk and Albert Adam Zick; m. John Michael Murphy, Aug. 17, 2002. BS in spl. edn., U. of Scranton, 1997—2003. Cert. Mental and/or Physical Handicapped, Bus. Computer Info. Tech. K-12 Commonwealth of PA, 2003. Tchr. Scranton Sch. Dist., Scranton, Pa., 2003—. Assistant editor (newsletter) The Theory and Practice Newsletter, Challenges. Recipient Academic Excellence in Spl. Edn., U. of Scranton, 2003, Outstanding Coop. Edn. Student, Lackawanna Trail H.S.; Lit. scholarship, Charlotte Newcomb, 2000—02, Peckville Profl. Women's Club, 2001—02, Scranton Profl. Women's Club, 2001—02. Mem.: Coun. for Exceptional Children, Kappa Delta Pi. D-Conservative. Roman Catholic. Avocations: kick boxing, power walking, travel, reading, fine dinning. Personal E-mail: zanderzk@aol.com.

MURPHY, MOLLY ANN, investment company executive; d. Charles William and Joan (Saul) Murphy. BS, Miami U., Oxford, Ohio, 1989; MBA, Xavier U., Cin., 1994. Chartered fin. analyst, Ohio. Mutual funds sales rep. Fidelity Investments, Cin., 1989—90; brokerage rep., fixed income specialist Fidelity Brokerage Svcs., Cin., 1990—93; portfolio mgr., officer Fifth Third Bank, Cin., 1993—2000; chief investment officer, v.p. Seasongood Asset Mgmt., Cin., 2000—. Bus. cons. Art League of Cin., 1999—2002; educator Ctr. for Pub. Investment Mgmt., Columbus, Ohio, 2000—02; presenter in field. Active Jr. League of Cin., 1998; com. mem. ann. workshop Ohio Assn. Sch. Bus. Ofcls., Columbus, 2000—. Mem.: Cin. Soc. Fin. Analysts, Assn. Investment Mgmt. and Rsch., Queen City Mcpl. Bond Club, Mensa. Office: Seasongood Asset Mgmt 414 Walnut St Cincinnati OH 45202-3910

MURPHY, PAMELA ANN, music educator, actress, musician; b. Cooperstown, NY, June 8, 1962; d. William John and Mary Kathryn Barrett; m. Michael Francis Murphy, II, July 11, 1987; children: Michael Francis III, Sean Patrick, Timothy Andrew. MusB, SUNY, Potsdam, 1984; MS, Western Conn. State U., 1990. Permanent tchg. lic. N.Y., cert. adjudicator NYSSMA. Music tchr. Valley Ctrl. Mid. Sch., Montgomery, NY, 1984—89, Valley Ctr. Mid. Sch., Montgomery, 1999—, Valley Ctrl. H.S., Montgomery, 1991—94, Kinry Rd. Elem. Sch., Poughkeepsie, NY, 1994—97. Guest condr. for all-county chorus Dutchess County (N.Y.) Music Educators Assn., 1994; owner, music dir. Hudson Valley Conservatory Fine Arts, Walden, NY, 1995—; profl. vocalist and keyboard player for various radio commls., weddings and bands; adjudicator state and local vocal competitions. Composer: (songs) My Love, 2002; actor: New Rose Theatre, 1996—. Facilitator fundraising activities Am. Heart Assn., Otego, NY, 1995; artistic dir. Hudson Valley Parents Performing Students, Walden, 1997—; fundraiser Muscular Dystrophy Assn., Newburgh, NY, 2003. Mem.: Orange County Music Educators Assn. (guest condr. for all-county chorus 1986, 1989, 2002, govt. rels. officer), N.Y. State Sch. Assn., Music Educators Nat. Conf., Nat. Write Your Congressman. Roman Catholic. Avocations: singing, dance, acting, flute, painting. Home: 30 Browns Rd Walden NY 12586 Office: Hudson Valley Conservatory Fine Arts PO Box 704 35 E Main St Walden NY 12586 Office Phone: 845-778-2478. Personal E-mail: murphhvc@yahoo.com.

MURPHY, PATRICE ANN (PAT MURPHY), writer; b. Spokane, Wash., Mar. 9, 1955; m. Dave Wright, Feb. 14, 1999. BA in Biology, U. Calif., Santa Cruz, 1976. Sr. rsch. writer ednl. graphics dept. Sea World, 1978—82. Former instr. Clarion Speculative Fiction Workshop, Mich. State U.; former tchr. sci. fiction U. Calif., Santa Cruz; tchr. sci. fiction writing Creative Writing Program, Stanford U., 1995, 96, 97, 98. Author: The Shadow Hunter, 1982, The Falling Woman, 1987 (Nebula award 1987), Adventures in Time and Space with Max Merriwell, 2002, (novelette) Rachel in Love (Nebula award 1987, Isaac Asimov Reader's award 1987, Theodore Sturgeon Meml. award 1987), (short story collection) Points of Departure, 1990 (Philip K. Dick award 1990), (novella) Bones, 1991 (World Fantasy award 1991), (novelette) An American Childhood, Nadya-The Wolf Chronicles, There and Back Again, The City, Not Long After, 1984, By Nature's Design, The Color of Nature, 1996, The Science Explorer, 1996, Explorabook Bat Science, The Science Explorer, Out and About. Avocation: Karate. Office: c/o Tor Books 14th Fl 175 5th Ave Fl 14 New York NY 10010-7703 also: c/o Exploratorium 3601 Lyon St San Francisco CA 94123

MURPHY, PATRICIA, English educator; BA, Ind. U., Bloomington, 1973; MA, Northwestern U., Evanston, Ill., 1991, U. Iowa, Iowa City, 1995; PhD, U. Iowa, 1997. Editor H.H. Bucker Assoc., 1974—92; vis. asst. prof. U. Iowa, 1997—99; from asst. to assoc. prof. Mo. So. State U., Joplin, 1999—. Author: Time Is of the Essence: Temporality, Gender, and the New Woman, 2001, In Science's Shadow: Literary Constructions of Late Victorian Women, 2006; contbr. articles to profl. jours. Mem.: Phi Beta Kappa. Office: Missouri Southern State University 3950 E Newman Rd Joplin MO 64801

MURPHY, PATRICIA ANN, physician, otolaryngologist; b. N.Y.C., Oct. 22, 1951; d. John Francis and Teresa (Whitney) M. BS, Wagner Coll., S.I., N.Y., 1974; MD, Virgen Milagrosa, The Philippines, 1981. Biochemist N.Y.C. Dept. Health, 1976-77; internist L.I. Coll. Hosp., Bklyn., 1981-82; surgeon St. Francis Hosp. and Med. Ctr., Trenton, N.J., 1982-83; clin. asst. instr., fellow otolaryngology SUNY Health Sci. Ctr. of Bklyn., 1984-87; fellow otolaryngology SUNY Health Sci. Ctr. of Bklyn., Brookdale Hosp. Med. Ctr., 1986-87; physician Family Health Plan, Fountain Valley, Calif., 1989-90; pvt. practice Santa Cruz, Calif., 1990-98, Elkins, W.Va., 1998—; clin. asst. instr. Otolarynology dept. W.Va. U., 1998—. Bd. dirs. W.Va. Acad. Otolaryngology, 2000—; clin. instr. W.Va. U. Dept. Otolaryngology, 1999—; physician Hearing, Edn. and Awareness for Rockers, San Francisco; physician rock medicine Haight Ashbury Free Clin., San Francisco; clin. instr. W.Va. U., 1990—; bd. dir. W.Va. Otolaryngology Soc. Author: (with others) Ears, Nose, Throat Emergency Treatment, 1986. Fed. Rsch. grantee N.Y.C. Dept. Health, 1976-77. Mem. Am. Women's Med. Assn. (sec. 1990—), Women in Otolaryngology, Am. Acad. Otolaryngology, Am. Acad. Otolaryngic Allergy, W.Va. Acad. Otolaryngology (bd.dirs.), Am. Acad. Facial Plastic and Reconstructive Surgery. Liberal. Roman Catholic. Avocations: reading, skiing, trekking. Office: Patricia Murphy Md 1 Pleasant Ave Ste 202 Elkins WV 26241-4610 Office Phone: 304-637-0400. Personal E-mail: drnose@mountain.net.

MURPHY, PEARL MARIE, medical and surgical nurse; b. Portsmouth, Ohio, Feb. 9, 1954; d. Chester Eugene and Eunice Jean (Windsor) M. LPN, Scioto Tech. Coll., Lucasville, Ohio, 1973; ADN, Hocking Tech. Coll., Nelsonville, Ohio, 1980; BSN, Ohio U., 1989. Cert. med./surg. nurse, Am. Nursing Credentialing Ctr. Staff nurse med.-surg. unit So. Hills Hosp., Portsmouth, 1973-75, staff nurse psychiat.-alcohol unit, 1975-79, staff nurse psychiat. unit, 1980-87, Mercy Hosp., Portsmouth, 1987-88; staff nurse diabetic unit Scioto Meml. Hosp., Portsmouth, 1988-89; staff nurse med.-surg. unit Women's Ctr., So. Ohio Med. Ctr., Portsmouth, 1989—. Nursing asst. program coord., instr. Scioto Tech. Coll., 1991-92. Mem. Ohio Nurses Assn., Order Ea. Star. Baptist. Avocations: camping, hiking, fishing, working in church. Home: 905 Stoney Run Rd West Portsmouth OH 45663-8959 Office: So Ohio Med Ctr Portsmouth OH 45662 Office Phone: 740-356-8121. Personal E-mail: pearlmurphyrn@yahoo.com.

MURPHY, ROSEMARY, actress; b. Munich; came to U.S., 1939; d. Robert D. and Mildred (Taylor) M. Student, Paris, France and Kansas City, Mo. Broadway appearances include Look Homeward Angel, 1958, Night of the Iguana, World premier at Spoleto (Italy) Festival of Two Worlds, 1959, Period of Adjustment, 1961, King Lear, 1963, Any Wednesday, 1964-66, Delicate Balance, 1966, Weekend, 1968, Butterflies are Free, 1970, Lady Macbeth, Stratford, Conn., 1973, Ladies of the Alamo, 1977, John Gabriel Borkman, 1980, Learned Ladies, 1982, Coastal Disturbances, 1987, The Devil's Disciple, 1988, A Delicate Balance, 1996, Waiting in the Wings, 1999; motion picture appearances include To Kill a Mockingbird, 1962, Any Wednesday, 1966, Ben, 1972, Walking Tall, 1972, You'll Like My Mother, 1972, Forty Carats, 1973, Julia, 1976, September, 1987, For the Boys, 1991, And The Band Played On, 1993, The Tuskegee Airmen, 1995, Message in a Bottle, 1998, Dust, 2001, The Savages, 2006; TV appearance Eleanor and Franklin, 1975 (Emmy award for best supporting actress 1976), George Washington, 1983 (Tony award nominations 1961, 64, 67, award Motion Picture Arts Club 1966), E-Z Streets, 1996, The Unicorn's Secret, 1998, Frasier, 1997, 99. Recipient Variety Poll award, 1961, 67. Address: 220 E 73rd St New York NY 10021-4319 Office Phone: 213-713-5294.

MURPHY, SANDRA FERGUSON, elementary school educator; b. Cambridge, Mass., June 14, 1952; d. Charles Wright and Ruth Bryant (Miller) Ferguson; m. Kevin James Murphy, Sept. 4, 1971; children: Galen, Joshua. BA, U. N.H., 1974; MEd, Antioch Grad. Sch., 1984. Cert. elem. edn., N.H. Tchr. Milford (N.H.) Elem. Sch., 1974-77, 92—, 1984-90; dir. Great Beginning Kindergarten, Milford, 1977-84; tchr. Halvorsen Elem. Sch., Frankfurt, Germany, 1990-92. Trustee Wadleigh Libr., Milford, 1987-90. Recipient Presdl. award for excellence in math. NSF, 1994. Mem. Nat. Coun. for Tchrs. Math., NEA, N.H. Assn. Tchrs. Math. in New Eng. (Excellence in Edn. award 1995). Avocations: exercising, skiing, gardening. Home: 52 Federal Hill Rd Milford NH 03055-3542 Office: Milford Elem Schs 5 Elm St Milford NH 03055-4810

MURPHY, SANDRA ROBISON, lawyer; b. Detroit, July 28, 1949; m. Richard Robin. BA, Northwestern U., 1971; JD, Loyola U., Chgo., 1976. Bar: U.S. Dist. Ct. (no. dist.) Ill. 1976. Assoc. Notz, Craven, Mead, Maloney & Price, Chgo., 1976-78; ptnr. McDermott, Will & Emery, Chgo., 1978—. Mem. ABA (family law sect.), Ill. Bar Assn. (chair sect. family law coun. 1987-88), Chgo. Bar Assn. (chair matrimonial law com. 1985-86), Am. Acad. Matrimonial Lawyers (sec. 1990-91, v.p. 1991-92, pres. Ill. chpt. 1992-93, pres.-elect 1994-95, pres. 1995-96), Legal Club Chgo. Business E-Mail: smurphy@mwe.com.

MURPHY, SHARON MARGARET, retired communications educator; b. Milw., Aug. 2, 1940; d. Adolph Leonard and Margaret Ann (Hirtz) Feyen; m. James Emmett Murphy, June 28, 1969 (dec. May 1983); children: Shannon Lynn, Erin Ann; m. Bradley B. Niemcek, Aug. 7, 1999. BA, Marquette U., 1965; MA, U. Iowa, 1970, PhD, 1973. Cert. K-14 tchr., Iowa. Tchr. elem. and secondary schs., Wis., 1959-69; dir. publs. Kirkwood C.C., Cedar Rapids, Iowa, 1969-71; instr. journalism U. Iowa, Iowa City, 1971-73; asst. prof. U. Wis., Milw., 1973-79; assoc. prof. So. Ill. U., Carbondale, 1979-84; dean, prof. Marquette U., Milw., 1984-94; prof. Bradley U., Peoria, Ill., 1994—2006, provost, v.p. acad. affairs, 1994-97, pres. Cmty. Career and Tech. Ctr., 1997-98, prof. emeritus, 2006. Pub. rels. dir., editor Worldwide mag., Milw., 1965—68; reporter Milw. Sentinel, 1967; Fulbright sr. lectr. U. Nigeria, Nsukka, 1977—78; Fulbright sr. scholar U. Ljubljana, Slovenia, 2002. Author: Other Voices: Black, Chicano & American Indian Press, 1971; (with Murphy) (with Wigal) Screen Experience: An Approach to Film, 1968; (with Murphy) Let My People Know: American Indian Journalism, 1981; (with Schilpp) Great Women of the Press, 1983; editor: (with others) International Perspectives on News, 1982. Mem. Peoria Riverfront Commn., 1995—2000; co-chair Peoria Race Rels. Com., 1999—2000; mem. NCA Higher Learning Commn.; bd. dirs. Dirksen Congl. Leadership Ctr., 1994—2000, Dow Jones Newspaper Fund, NY, 1986—95, Peoria Symphony, 1996—2002. Recipient Merit medal Journalism Edn. Assn., 1976, Tchg. Excellence award Amoco, 1977, Outstanding Achievement award Greater Milw. YWCA, 1989, Paul Snider Tchg. Excellence award Bradley U., 2005; named Knight of Golden Quill, Milw. Press Club, 1977; Nat. headliner Women in Comm., Inc., 1985. Mem. Assn. Edn. in Journalism and Mass Comm. (pres. 1986-87), Soc. Profl. Journalists, Nat. Press Club, Accrediting Coun.on Edn. in Journalism and Mass Comm. (v.p. 1983-86). Democrat. Roman Catholic. Office: Bradley U Global Comm Ctr Peoria IL 61625-0001 Business E-Mail: smm@bradley.edu.

MURPHY, STACIA, health service association executive; BA, Talladega Coll. With Cmty. Service Soc., N.Y. City Mission Soc., NY State Divsn. Youth, Alcoholism Coun. of N.Y.; exec. dir. NYC affiliate Nat. Coun. on Alcoholism and Drug Dependence, Inc., 1990-99, pres. NYC, 1999—2005. Office: Nat Coun Alcoholism and Drug Dependence 22 Cortlandt St Ste 801 New York NY 10007-3128 Office Phone: 212-269-7797. Business E-Mail: president@ncadd.org.

MURPHY, SUSAN (JANE MURPHY), small business owner, real estate broker; b. Williamsport, Pa., Dec. 26, 1950; d. Jack W. and Edythe J. (Grier) M.; m. Michael J. Sanchez, Dec. 30, 1979. BBA, Pa. State U., 1978. Gen. mgr. Murphy Swift Homes, Hummelstown, Pa., 1970-75; owner, operator Murphy's Home Ctr., Hummelstown, 1975-79, 85-91; mgr. Builder's Emporium, San Diego, 1979-80; entrepreneur Castle in the Sand, San Diego, 1980-83; adminstr. Sohio Constrn., Prudhoe Bay, Alaska, 1983-85; fin. systems analyst Blue Shield, San Francisco, 1991-93; pres. San Francisco Mgmt. Svcs., Inc., San Francisco, 1993-99; entrepreneur Blue Skies Inn and Island Place of Olde Key West, Key West, Fla., 1999—; prin., owner Realty Execs. Advantage, Vero Beach, Fla., 2004—. Cons. in field; dealer Servistar Home Ctrs. Photographs displayed at San Diego Art Inst. Vol. Hershey (Pa.) Free Ch. Donald MacIntyre scholar, 1979, Class of 1920 scholar, 1979, Congressman Kunkel scholar, 1979. Mem.: Mem. Pa. Hardware Assn., Hummelstown C. of C., Better Bus. Bur. Evangelical Christian. Avocations: sailing, scuba diving, photography. Office: 5055 N Hwy A1A Vero Beach FL 32963 Office Phone: 772-231-5823. Personal E-mail: suzyqq@earthlink.net.

MURPHY, SUSAN RYAN, literature and language educator; English tchr. Oneonta H.S., NY, 1985—. Staff devel. Catskill Regional Tchr. Ctr., Oneonta, 2002—. Office: Oneonta City Sch Dist 130 East St Oneonta NY 13820 Office Phone: 607-433-8200.

MURPHY, THELMA ARABELLA, elementary school educator, photographer; b. Cardston, Alta., Can., June 12, 1947; arrived in U.S., 1986; d. Raymond and Isabella (Many Feathers) King; m. Laurence Patrick Murphy, May 12, 1971. EdB, U. Lethbridge, Alta., 1976. Cert. tchr. Hawaii, grad. Profl. Devel. and Svc. Program 2004. Tchr. Dept. Indian Affairs, Edmonton, Alta., 1971—80, Edmonton Pub. Sch. Bd., 1980—86; tchr. spl. edn. Highlands Intermediate Sch., Pearl City, Hawaii, 1986—87; tchr. St. Theresa Sch., Honolulu, 1987—. Profl. wedding photographer, 1980—. Author poetry. Recipient scholarship, U. Lethbridge, 1967; scholar, Dept. Indian Affairs, 1967—71. Mem.: Nat. Cath. Edn. Assn., Indian Rights for Indian Women (sec. 1971—85). Roman Catholic. Avocations: photography, writing, reading, beading, sewing. Business E-Mail: murphyf008@hawaii.rr.com.

MURRAH, ANN RALLS FREEMAN, historical association executive; b. Gadsden, Ala., June 23, 1932; d. Oscar William Freeman, Sr. and Annie Collier (Ralls) Freeman; m. Robert Leland Murrah, Aug. 9, 1952; children: Frances Ralls Murrah Lovett, Robert Leland Murrah Jr. Grad., Brenau U., 1954. Pres. Gen. Descendants of the Signers of the Constn., Orlando, Fla., 1991—. Rep. Fla. 8th congl. dist. Congl. Sr. Intern Program, Wash., 1998; keynote spkr. Feminist Summit for Global Peace, Taipei, Taiwan, 1995; mem. protocol & hospitality coms. for equestrian events 1996 Olympics; mem. Am. com. Ball des Rosenkavaliers, Vienna, 1989—90; bd. dir. Arnold Palmer Hosp. Bd., Orlando, Fla.; founder Nat. Constn. Ctr., Phila., 2003—; spkr. in field. Mem. women's com. N.Y. U. Downtown Hosp., 1996—99; gala chmn. Winter Pk. Health Found., Winter Pk., Fla., 1996; ball chmn. Arnold Palmer Hosp. for Women & Children, Orlando, Fla., 1997—99, 2001; mem. Orlando Regional Healthcare Found., Orlando; active Coun. of 101-Orlando Mus. Art; v. chmn. dinner com. fundraiser March of Dimes, 1998. Named First Woman Knighted in her own right, Order of St. John of Jerusalem, 1992; named to Brenau U. Alumni Hall of Fame, 2001; recipient Meritorious Svc. award, Sons of the Am. Revolution, 1986, Martha Washington medal, 1988, The Rallye Saintogeais Hunt award, Foret De La Coubre, France, 1988. Mem.: DAR (first vice-regent), Nat. Soc. So. Dames Am., Met. Opera Guild, Plantagenet Soc., Washington Soc., Gavel Soc., Fla. Opera Guild, Nat. Steeplechase Assn., Shakerag Hunt Club (awarded colors), Nat. Soc. of Colonial Dames, Daus. of the Cin., Sovereign Colonial Soc. Am. of Royal Descent, Sonsand Daus. of the Pilgrims (gov. in Ga. 1992—94, historian gen. of the U.S. 1994—97, first vice-gov.), Descs. of Knights of the Garter, Colonial Dames of Am., Colonial Order of the Crown, Magna Charta Dames (herald and courier), Alpha Delta Pi (province pres., dir. ritual and paraphernalia). Home and Office: Soc of Descendants of Signers of Constitiution 903 Sussex Close Orlando FL 32804

MURRAY, ABBY DARLINGTON BOYD, psychiatric clinical specialist, educator; b. Johnstown, Pa., Mar. 1, 1928; d. Frank Reynolds Boyd and Marion Gasson Allen; m. Joseph Christopher Murray, Sept. 16, 1950; children: Anne, Joseph Jr., Mary, John, James. BSN, Georgetown U., 1950; MS Edn. in Guidance and Counseling, L.I. Univ., Brookville, N.Y., 1976; MEd Psychiat. Clin. Specialist, Columbia U., 1977; postgrad., Ctr. for Family Learning, New Rochelle, N.Y., 1981-82. Lic. marriage and family counselor; provisional cert. sch. counselor, N.Y. Sch. nurse Huntington (N.Y.) Pub. Schs.; with VA Med. Ctr., Northport, Va., 1973-76; prof. U. Md., Balt., 1978-79, L.I. Univ., Brookville, 1979-81; psychiat. clin. specialist VA Med. Ctr., Brooklyn, Va., 1984-87, East Orange, N.J., 1987-89; nurse educator Ft. Monmouth, N.J., 1989—; ret., 1996. Family therapist Family & Cmty. Counseling Agy., Red Bank, N.J., 1989—; program planner, Ft. Monmouth; adj. prof. Monmouth U., 1997-98; lic. profl. marriage and family counselor, N.J., 1996-99. Mem.: DAR. Republican. Roman Catholic. Avocation: tennis. Address: 207 William St Red Bank NJ 07701-2462

MURRAY, AMANDA KAY, elementary school educator; b. Franklin, Ala., Jan. 23, 1971; d. William Thomas and Linda Kay Green; m. Richard Lee Murray, Jan. 18, 1990; children: Mason Hunter, Kylie Laken. Degree in Elem. Edn., Athens State U., Ala., 2003. Title I math tchr. k-6 Vina H.S., Ala., 2003—. Office Phone: 256-331-2260.

MURRAY, CARLA MARY, sound effects artist, artist; b. North Bay, Ont., Can., Apr. 3, 1957; d. Thomas Joseph and Laura Catherine Murray; life ptnr. Paula Kathleen Fairfield. BFA, N.S. Coll. Art and Design, Halifax, Can., 1982; MFA, York U., Toronto, Ont., 1996. Cofounder, adminstrv. dir. Women's Art Resource Ctr., Toronto, 1984—91; contract art adminstr., writer, rschr. various clients Toronto, 1992—94; sound designer, sound effects editor MHz Sound Design Inc., L.A., 1997—. Ways and means com., adminstr. Trinity Sq. Video, Toronto, 1987; author, exhbn. co-coord. Graphic Feminism: Graphic Art of the Ont. Women's Movement 1970-1986, (catalogue) Women's Movement Archives, Toronto, 1986; founding mem. Power Up, L.A., 2000, vol. sound designer, sound effects editor, 2001—03. One-woman shows include Gallery 940, Toronto, Stride Gallery, Calgary, IDA Gallery, Toronto, exhibitions include Out of the Frame, Advocate Gallery, LA; sound designer, sound effects editor (films) A Rumour of Angels; sound designer, sound effects editor: (films) Spy Kids 3D: Game Over; Terminator 3: Rise of the Machines; The Adventures of Shark Boy and Lava Girl in 3D; Assault on Precinct 13; Sin City; Lucky Number Slevin; The Black Dahlia; founding mem. editl. bd.: Matriart: A Can. Feminist Art Jour., 1990—91. Bd. dirs. A Space Gallery, Toronto, 1984; jury mem. Ont. Arts Coun., Toronto, 1994. Grantee, Ont. Arts Coun., 1984—91; Explorations grantee, Can. Coun., 1984, Photography grant, 1992. Mem.: Am. Film Inst., Nat. Mus. Women in Arts, Internat. Alliance Theatrical Stage Employees, Moving Picture Technicians, Artists and Allied Crafts of the US, Its Territories and Can., Motion Picture Editor's Guild. Office Phone: 818-980-0306.

MURRAY, CAROL ANNE, chemistry educator; d. Frederick Peter and Geraldine McKinnon Murray. BA, Salve Regina Coll., Newport, R.I., 1963; MA, U. Scranton, Pa., 1968. Joined Religious Sisters of Mercy, 1957. Tchr. St. Xavier's Acad., Providence, 1964—70; tchr. and vice prin. Our Lady of Providence H.S., 1971—88; tchr. Bishop Hendricken H.S., Warwick, 1989—. Named Chemistry Tchr. of Yr., Am. Chem. Soc., 2006. Mem.: Nat. Assn. Sci. Tchrs. Home: 64 East Ave North Providence RI 02911 Office Fax: 401-739-3450. E-mail: Kobiecd@Juno.com.

MURRAY, CATHERINE MARY MURPHY, retired accountant; b. Severn, Md., July 7, 1940; d. George William Murphy and Emma May Rodgers; m. Rudolph Chesley Stanley, Dec. 21, 1963 (dec. Oct. 31, 1978); children: Kenneth Michael Stanley, Mary Ellen Stanley Fahlstrom; m. Charles Edward Murray, Nov. 22, 1988 (dec. Dec. 13, 2001). Student in Early Childhood Edn., U. Maine, 1981. Classroom asst. to coord. Coastal Econ. Devel. Corp., Boothbay Harbor/Bath, Maine, 1969—81; acct. Pvt. Contractor Constrn., 1984—89; project acct. Chesapeake Sprinkler Co., Odenton, Md., 1990—2006; ret., 2006. Proofreader, asst., editor David W. Webster FSA Scot, Livingston, Scotland, 1998—; presenter in field. Author: Through the Generations, 1999, To Honor Thy Family, 1999; co-author: The Family True, 2001. Contbr. genealogy material Ch. of Jesus Christ of LDS, Salt Lake City; sponsor Anne Arundel County Scottish Festival, Inc., Crownsville, Md.; contbr. genealogy material Amesbury (Mass.) Pub. Libr. With USN, 1958—59. Avocations: genealogy, history, reading, travel, music. Personal E-mail: catherinemmurray@comcast.net.

MURRAY, DANA L., state legislator; b. Harrisburg, Ill., Jan. 18, 1946; m. Dennis Murray; children: Timothy, Kevin, Dennis, Sean. Sch. bus driver Spl. Sch. Dist. of St. Louis County; rep., Dist. 69 Mo. Ho. of Reps., 1993—2002. Volunteer Neighborhood Watch, Ferguson Cmty. Non-Conflict Resolution Program. Mem.: Nat. Orgn. Women Legislators, Women Legislators of Mo. (pres.), North County Exposure, Halls Ferry Democratic Club, Norwood Democratic Club, Ferguson Democratic Club. Democrat. Catholic. Office: Mo House Repr 201 West Capitol Ave Rm 313-2 Jefferson City MO 65101 Home: 2259 Lakeshore Dr Cuba MO 65453-9624 Office Phone: 573-751-5538, 314-388-0417. Office Fax: 573-526-0572, 314-868-1169.

MURRAY, DIANE ELIZABETH, librarian; b. Detroit, Oct. 15, 1942; d. Gordon Lisle and Dorothy Anne (Steketee) LaBoueff; m. Donald Edgar Murray, Apr. 22, 1968. AB, Hope Coll., 1964; postgrad., Mich. State U., East Lansing, 1964-66; MLS, Western Mich. U., 1968; MM, Aquinas Coll., 1982. Catalog libr., asst. head acquisitions sect. Mich. State U. Librs., East Lansing, 1968-77; libr. tech. and automated svcs. Hope Coll., Holland, Mich., 1977-88; dir. librs. DePauw U., Greencastle, Ind., 1988-91; acquisitions libr. Grand Valley State U., Allendale, Mich., 1991—. Sec., vice chair, chairperson bd. trustees Mich. Libr. Consortium, Lansing, 1981—85. V.p. Humane Soc. Putnam County, Greencastle, 1990—91; bd. dirs. Loutit Dist. Libr., 1999—. Mem.: ALA. Methodist. Avocations: dog breeding and showing, handbell ringing. Office: Grand Valley State U Zumberge Libr Allendale MI 49401 Business E-Mail: murrayd@gvsu.edu.

MURRAY, EILEEN K., investment company executive; BSc in acctg., Manhattan Coll., 1980. Formerly with Peat Marwick; with Morgan Stanley, 1984—2002; v.p. Morgan Stanley Group Inc., 1988—91, prin., 1991—94, mng. dir., 1994, controller and treas.; chief adminstrv. officer, instl. securities group Morgan Stanley Dean Witter & Co., 1999—2002; head of global tech, ops. & product control Credit Suisse First Boston, NYC, 2002—05; head global ops. & tech., mem. mgmt. com. Morgan Stanley, NYC, 2005—. Bd. dirs. Omgeo LLC, 2001—. Office: Morgan Stanley 1585 Broadway New York NY 10036*

MURRAY, ELIZABETH, artist; b. Chgo., 1940; married; 1 child, Dakota Sunseri. B.F.A., Art Inst., Chgo., 1962; M.F.A., Mills Coll., Oakland, Calif., 1964; D (hon.), Art Inst., Chgo., 1992; degree (hon.), RI School Design, 1993; D (hon.), New School U., 2001. Vis. instr. Wayne State U., 1975, Calif. Inst. Arts, 1975-76, Chgo. Art Inst., 1975-76; instr. Bard Coll., Annandale on Hudson, NY, 1974-75, 76-77, Princeton U., 1977, Yale U., 1978-79. One-woman shows, Jacobs Ladder Gallery, Washington, 1974, Paula Cooper Gallery, N.Y.C., 1975, 76, 78, 81, 83, 88, 89, Jared Sable Gallery, 1975, Ohio State U., Columbus, 1978, Phyllis Kind Gallery, Chgo., 1978, Galerie Mukai, Tokyo, 1980, Susanne Hilberry Gallery, Birmingham, Mich., 1980, Smith Coll. Art Gallery, Northampton, Mass., 1982, Daniel Weinberg Gallery, Los Angeles, 1982, Portland Ctr. Visual Arts, Oreg., 1983, Knight Gallery, Charlotte, N.C., 1984, San Francisco Mus. Modern Art, 1988, Mayor Rowen Gallery, London, 1989, Barbara Krakow Gallery, Boston, 1990, Gallery Mukai, Tokyo, 1990, John Berggruen Gallery, San Francisco, 1990, Wexner Center for the Arts, 1991, 92, Jaffe-Friede Strauss Galleries, Hanover, N.H., 2005, Mus. Modern Art, N.Y.C., 2005, Maier Mus. Art, Lynchburg, Va, 2005; group shows include, Whitney Mus. Am. Art, N.Y.C., 1972, 73, 77, 79, 81, 82, 84, John Doyle Gallery Cologne, Ger., 1974, Paula Cooper Gallery, 1974, 76, 77, 78, 79, 81, 82, 83, 84, Michael Walls Gallery, N.Y., 1975, Middlebury (Vt.) Coll., 1976, Gallery of July and August, Brockport, N.Y., 1976, Susanne Hilberry Gallery, Detroit, 1976, Guggenheim Mus., N.Y.C., 1977, Sarah Lawrence Coll. Gallery, Bronxville, N.Y., 1977, Lowe Art Gallery Syracuse U., 1977, Mus. Contemporary Art, Chgo., 1977, Inst. Contemporary Art, U. Pa., 1978, Tampa Bay Art Center, Fla., 1978, Phyllis Kind Gallery, Chgo., 1979, William Patterson Coll., Wayne, N.J., 1979, Susan Caldwell Gallery, N.Y., 1979, U. N.C. Weatherspoon Art Gallery, Greensboro, 1979, Galerie Yvon Lambert, Paris, 1980, Bklyn. Mus., 1980, Dart Gallery, Chgo., 1981, Contemporary Arts Center, Cin., 1981, High Mus. Art, Atlanta, 1981, 82, Galerie Mukai, Tokyo, 1981, Va. Mus., Richmond, 1981, Boston Mus. Fine Arts, 1982, Milw. Art Mus., 1982, Art Inst. Chgo., 1982, Daniel Weinberg Gallery, Los Angeles and San Francisco, 1983, Hirshhorn Mus., Washington, 1983, Hobart and William Smith Colls., Geneva, N.Y., 1983, Mus. Art, Ft. Lauderdale, Fla., 1986, 40th Biennial Exhbn. Comtemp. Am. Paintings Corcoran Gallery of Art, 1988, Mus. Modern Art, 1990, 91, numerous others; artist and curator Elizabeth Murray: Modern Art N.Y., Mus. Modern Art, N.Y., 1995; represented in permanent collections: Whitney Mus. Am. Art, N.Y.C., Guggenheim Mus., Hirshhorn Mus. and Sculpture Garden, Washington, H.H.K. Found., Milw., St. Louis Art Mus., Detroit Inst. Arts, Albright-Knox Art Gallery, Buffalo, N.Y., Allen Meml. Art Mus., Oberlin Coll., Art Inst. Chgo., Baltimore Mus. Art, Carnegie Mus. Art, Pittsburgh, Pa, Cleveland Mus. Art, Dallas Mus. Art, High Mus. Art, Atlanta, Met. Mus. Art, N.Y.C., Nat. Gallery Art, Washington, Mus. Contemporary Art, L.A., Mus. Fine Arts, Boston, Nelson-Atkins Mus. Art, Kansas City, Phila. Mus. Art, Va. Mus. Fine Arts, Walker Center, Minn., Yale U. Art Gallery. Recipient Walter M. Campana award Art Inst. of Chgo., 1982, Am. Academy & Inst. of Arts & Letters award, 1984, Skowhegan prize for painting, 1986, Larry Aldrich prize in contemporary art, 1993, John D. & Catherine T. MacArthur Found. award, 1999, Nat. Artist award Anderson Ranch Art Ctr., 2002; honored by Artists Space, NYC, 2001. Mem. Am. Acad and Inst. of Arts and Letters, 1992, NAD (academician). Office: Pace Wildenstein Gallery 32 E 57 St New York NY 10001

MURRAY, HARRIET JOHNSON, secondary school educator; b. Gadsden, Ala., Oct. 31, 1956; d. Robert Greenwood and Charlie Nell (Shropshire) Johnson; m. Dwight Keith Murray, Mar. 5, 1983; 1 child, Hannah Johnson. BS in Home Econs. Edn., U. Ala., Tuscaloosa, 1979, M Home Econs. Edn., 1981, AA cert. in home econs. edn., 1982. Cert. home economist. Tchr. vocat. home econs. Emma Sansom H.S., Gadsden, 1979—. Sec. adminstrv. bd. 1st United Meth. Ch., 1991-94, 99-1000, mem. bldg. com., 1997-99. Named Tchr. of Yr., Emma Sansom H.S., 1989. Mem. NEA, Ala. Edn. Assn., Am. Vocat. Assn., Gadsden Assn. Profl. Educators (faculty rep. 1985-88), Gadsden Svc. Guild, Alpha Delta Kappa (parliamentarian 1992-93), Zeta Tau Alpha. Avocations: baseball, tennis, sports. Office: Emma Sansom HS 2210 W Meighan Blvd Gadsden AL 35904-1706 Home: 216 Lakewood Dr Gadsden AL 35901-5342 Office Phone: 256-549-2979. E-mail: hjmurray1956@yahoo.com.

MURRAY, HEIDI MAGDALENA, secondary school educator; b. Chgo., Ill., Sept. 16, 1966; d. James Roy and Leontine Fidalia Murray. BEd cum laude, Northeastern U., Chgo., 1994; M in Curriculum and Instrn., Olivet Nazarene U., Bourbonnais, Ill., 2006; M in Math. Edn., Nat. Louis U., Wheaton, Ill., 2000. Tchr. 6th-8th grade reading Frederick Von Schiller, Chgo., 1995—96; tchr. 6th grade math. River Trails Mid. Sch., Mt. Prospect, Ill., 1996—. Mem.: Nat. Coun. Tchrs. of Math. Home: 518 S Louis St Mount Prospect IL 60056

MURRAY, JEANNE See STAPLETON, JEAN

MURRAY, JENNIFER ADAMS, music educator, musician; b. Fairfield, Calif., Nov. 27, 1975; d. Kevin MacGregor Adams and Claire Gagnon Ward; m. Christopher Ryan Murray, July 25, 1999. MusB, Old Dominion U., Norfolk, Va., 1998. Cert. tchr. Va. Music tchr. Oceanair Elem. Sch., Nofolk Pub. Schs., Norfolk, Va., 1998—2000, Langley Elem. Sch., Hampton City Schs., Va., 2000—. Profl. singer Va. Opera Assn., Norfolk, 1996—2005. Dir.: (play) The Wizard of Oz, 2005. Named Tchr. of Jr., Langley Elem. Sch., 2005. Episcopalian. Home: 912 Pine Mill Ct Newport News VA 23602 Office: Langley Elem Sch 16 Rockwell Rd Hampton VA 23669 Office Phone: 757-850-5138.

MURRAY, JUDITH, artist; b. N.Y.C., Feb. 22, 1941; BFA, Pratt Inst., 1962, MFA, 1964; postgrad., Acad. Bellas Artes San Fernando, Madrid, 1963. Tchr. L.I. U., N.Y. Inst. Tech., Westbury, U. Hawaii, Honolulu, Pratt Inst., Bklyn.; artist-in-residence U.S. Info. Agy., Warsaw, Krakow & Szczecin, Poland. Lectr. in field. One woman shows include Parson-Truman Gallery, N.Y.C., 1976, The Clocktower Inst. for Art and Urban Resources, N.Y.C., 1978, Pam Alder Gallery, N.Y.C., 1979, 80, 86, Betsy Rosenfield Gallery, Chgo., 1981, Janus Gallery, L.A., 1982, Dallas Mus. Fine Arts, Tex., 1982, Hillwood Art Gallery L.I.U., N.Y., 1985, Jan Turner Gallery, Inc., L.A., 1987; group shows include Susan Caldwell Gallery, N.Y.C., 1977, Moore Coll. Art Gallery, Phila., 1977, The Whitney Mus. Am. Art, N.Y., 1979, John Weber Gallery, N.Y.C., 1979, Pam Alder Galler, N.Y.C., 1980, 85, Artists Space, N.Y.C., 1980, 84, Miami Dade Coll., Miami, 1981, Delahunty Gallery, Dallas, 1982, Moody Gallery Art, 1983, Weatherspoon Art Gallery, Greensboro, N.C., 1983, Westbeth Gallery, N.Y.C., 1984, Washington County Mus. Art, Md., 1985, The Bronx Mus. of the Arts, N.Y.C., 1986, 88, 1996, City Gallery N.Y.C., 1987, 55 Mercer Street Gallery, N.Y.C., 1989, Neuberger Mus., Purchase, N.Y., 1989, Stephen Solovy Fine Arts, Chgo., 1991, 1997, Schmidt/Dean Gallery, Phila., 1999, 2001 Trans Hudson GALLERY, 1999, Mitchell Algus Gallery, 2000, Newhouse Ctr. for Contemporary Art, 2003-2004, Am. Acad. Arts and Letters, 2005, Whitney Mus. Am. Art, 2006; pub. comms. Lincoln Ctr. for the Performing Arts, 1981, Fisher Hall Mostly Mozart Festival, N.Y.C., 1986; numerous permanent collections including The Mus. Modern Art, The Met. Mus. Art, The Guggenheim Mus., The Brit. Mus., The Bronx Mus. Art, Chase Manhattan Bank, First Nat. Bank, Shearman and Sterling; works also in mumerous pvt. collections. NEA fellow, 1983-84. Mem. Am. Abstract Artists, Fine Arts Fedn. Studio: 429 W Broadway New York NY 10012-3766

MURRAY, JULIA KAORU (MRS. JOSEPH E. MURRAY), occupational therapist; b. Wahiawa, Oahu, Hawaii, 1934; d. Gijun and Edna Tsuruko (Taba) Funakoshi; m. Joseph Edward Murray, 1961; children: Michael, Susan, Leslie. BA, U. Hawaii, 1956; cert. occupl. therapy, U. Puget Sound, 1958.

Therapist Inst. Logopedics, Wichita, Kans., 1958; sr. therapist Hawaii State Hosp., Kaneohe, 1959; part-time therapist Centre County Ctr. for Crippled Children and Adults, State College, Pa., 1963; vice chmn. adv. bd. Hosp. Improvement Program East Oreg. State Hosp., Pendleton, 1974; v.p. Ind. Living, Inc., 1976—79; instr. job search; mem. adv. com. Oreg. Ednl. Coordinating Commn., 1979—82; mem. Oreg. Bd. Engring. Examiners, 1979—87; supr., occupl. therapist Fairview Tng. Ctr., Salem, Oreg., 1984—94; occupl. therapist U.S. Naval Hosp., Okinawa, Japan, 1994—99, Yokosuka, Japan, 1999—. Rep. from Umatilla County Commrs. to Blue Mountain Econ. Devel. Council, 1976-78; mem. Ashland Park and Recreation Bd., 1972-73; vice chmn. adv. bd. LINC, 1978; mem. exec. bd. Liberty-Boone Neighborhood Assn., 1979-83. Decorated Meritorious Civilian Svc. medal USN. Mem. Am. Occupational Therapy Assn., Oreg. Occupational Therapy Assn., Hawaii Occupational Therapy Assn. (sec. 1960, LWV (bd. dirs. Pendleton 1974, 77-78, pres. 1975-77; bd. dirs. Oreg. 1979-81, Ashland, Wis., 1967-71, Wis. v.p. 1970). Personal E-mail: jkfmurray@hotmail.com.

MURRAY, KAY, lawyer; b. Cinn. BA, Xavier U., 1985; JD, Northwestern U., 1988. Comml. litigator Clifford Chance (formerly Rogers & Wells), NYC, 1988—92; with Kornstein, Veisz & Wexler, 1992—94; staff atty. Author's Guild, NYC, 1994—96, asst. dir., 1997—, gen. counsel, 1999—; exec. editor Author's Guild Bulletin. Exec. dir. Author's Guild Found. Co-author (with Tad Crawford): The Writer's Legal Guide, 2002.

MURRAY, MARIAN SELENA, medical/surgical nurse; d. Haddon Benjamin and Beatrice Anderson Murray; 1 child, Damio Lamar. A in Nursing, J. Sargent Reynolds C.C., Richmond, Va., 1993; LPN, Richmond Pub. Sch. Practical Nursing, 1997; degree in parish nurse ministry, Union Theol. Sem. and Presbyn. Sch. of Christian Edn., Richmond, 1998. RN Va., 1994. Icu staff nurse Retreat for The Sick Hosp., Richmond, 1979—85; emergency dept. night charge nurse Richmond Cmty. Hosp., 1997—99, Retreat Hosp., Richmond, 1985—2005; recovery rm. staff nurse Retreat Hca Hosp., Richmond, 2005—. Parish nurse Union Theol. Sem., Richmond, 1998—. Mem. Retreat Ethic com., Richmond, 1995—2006. With USAR, 1976—81. Named Employee of Yr., Retreat Hosp., 1999; recipient Golden Poet award, World of Poetry, 1988, Silver Poet award, 1990, Frist Humanitarian award, Columbia/HCA Hosp., 1999; scholar, Columbia /Hca Hosp., 1998. Mem.: Parish Nurse Ministry (corr.). Avocations: art, poetry, gardening, travel. Office: Columbia/Hca Retreat Hosp 2621 Grove Ave Richmond VA 23220 Office Phone: 804-254-5100. Personal E-mail: bless7msm@aol.com.

MURRAY, MARY A., transportation executive; b. Savannah, Ga., June 17, 1950; d. James Buck and Dorothy Lee M.; m. Earnest Jackson Jr., Jan., 1978 (div. Jan. 1984); children: Chandra R. McKinney, Antony LaTroy Jackson, Earnesha J. Jackson. BS in Bus. Adminstrn., Savannah State U., 1968-71, 90-91. cert. key-punch, typing. Sales J.C. Pennys, Valdosta, Ga., 1973-75, Savannah, 1975-76; switchboard operator Savannah Fire Dept., 1976-80; a/c mechanic Gulfstream Aerospace, Savannah, 1982-94, engr. adminstr., 1994-95; exec. adminstr. Gulfstream Flight Test, Savannah, 1995—; resident mgr. Sihes Apt. Complex. Democrat. Avocations: bowling, photography. Home: 133 Bradford Ct Savannah GA 31406-4122 E-mail: amurra11@bellsouth.net.

MURRAY, MARY ROSE, securities regulation investigator; d. John Gregory and Mary Helen Murray. BA, Cath. U. Am., Washington, 1975; MBA, George Washington U., Washington, 1981. SIPC clk. Nat. Assn. Securities Dealers, Washington, 1975—78, fin. reporting coord., 1978—80, market surveillance analyst, 1980—83, market surveillance investigator Rockville, Md., 1983—. Mem. oats competency team Nat. Assn. Securities Dealers, Rockville, 1996—98, com. mem. Series 55 exam., 2002—. Bd. dirs. Cath. U. Aluni Bd. of Govt., Washington, 2003—; coord., participant food delivery Lord's Table, St. Martin Ch., Gaithersburg, Md., 2003—. Recipient Excellence in Svc. award, Nat. Assn. Securities Dealers, 1987. Roman Catholic. Avocations: jazzercise, travel. Office: Nat Assn Securities Dealers 9509 Key West Ave Rockville MD 20850

MURRAY, NANCY JEAN, language educator, humanities educator; d. David Joseph and Irene Cecelia Murray; children: Katelyn Irene Miller, Lindsay Jean Murray-Miller, Colin David Miller. MEd, St. Michael's Coll., Colchester, Vt., 2006. Prof. English and Humanities Vt. Tech. Coll., Rancolph Center, 2005—. Instr. gen. edn. Woodstock Festival Project Vt. Tech. Coll., 2006. Recipient Tchg. Excellence award, Vt. Tech. Coll., 2006. Home: 277 Dr Barry Rd Brookfield VT 05036 Office: Vermont Technical College Ridge Rd Randolph Center VT 05061 Business E-Mail: nmurray@vtc.edu.

MURRAY, PATRICIA, electronics company executive; b. Detroit; BA, Michigan St. U.; BS, St. Louis U.; JD, U. Mich., 1986. Nurse, intensive care unit, nursing adminstr. U. Mich. Hospitals; employment litigator Morrison & Foerster, Palo Alto, Calif., until 1990; atty. human resources legal staff Intel Corp., 1990—91, mgr. human resources legal staff, 1992—95, dir., v.p. human resources Santa Clara, 1996—97, sr. v.p., 1997—. Chmn. Intel Found. Office: Intel Corp PO Box 58119 2200 Mission College Blvd Santa Clara CA 95052-8119 E-mail: patricia.murray@intel.com.

MURRAY, PATTY (PATRICIA J. MURRAY), senator; b. Bothell, Wash., Oct. 10, 1950; d. David L. and Beverly A. (McLaughlin) Johns; m. Robert R. Murray, June 2, 1972; children: Randy P., Sara A. BA, Wash. State U., 1972. Sec. various cos., Seattle, 1972-76; citizen lobbyist various ednl. groups, Seattle, 1983-88; legis. lobbyist Orgn. for Parent Edn., Seattle, 1977-84; instr. Shoreline Community Coll., Seattle, 1984-88; mem. Wash. State Senate, Seattle, 1989-92; US Senator from Wash., 1993—. Mem. com. appropriations US Senate, com. budget, com. health, edn., labor and pensions, com. veterans affairs. Author (with Catherine Whitney): Nine and Counting: The Women of the Senate, 2000. Mem. bd. Shoreline Sch., Seattle, 1985-89; mem. steering com. Demonstration for Edn., Seattle, 1987; founder, chmn. Orgn. for Parent Edn., Wash., 1981-85; 1st Congl. rep. Wash. Women United, 1983-85. Recipient Outstanding award Washing. Women United, 1986, Recognition of Svc. to Children award Shoreline PTA Coun., 1986, Golden Acorn Svc. award, 1989; Outstanding Svc. award Wash. Women United, 1986, Outstanding Svc. to Pub. Edn. award Citizens Ednl. Ctr. NW, Seattle, 1987, Wash. State Legis. of Yr., 1990, George Falcon Spike award Nat. Assn. Railroad Passengers, 2003, Person of Yr. award Wash. State VFW, 2004. Democrat. Roman Catholic. Office: US Senate 173 Russell Senate Office Bldg Washington DC 20510-0001 also: Henry M Jackson Federal Bldg Ste 2988 915 Second Ave Seattle WA 98174-4067 Office Phone: 202-224-2621, 206-553-5545. Office Fax: 202-224-0238, 206-553-0891.*

MURRAY, RENEE LOGSDON, educational association administrator, consultant; b. Hart County, Ky., June 1, 1951; d. Roy Edward Logsdon, Jr. and Myra Jean Logsdon; children: John Michael, Jared Logsdon. BS, Murray State U., Ky., 1973, MS, 1974. Instr. Ctrl. Mo. State U., Warrensburg, Mo., 1974—76; v.p. Beverly Norman Pub. Rels., Kans. City, 1976—82; editor Hart County Herald, Horse Cave, Ky., 1982—86; tchr. Caverna Schs., Horse Cave, 1986—91, Hart County Schs., Manfordville, Ky., 1991—96; br. mgr. Ky. Dept. Edn., Frankfort, Ky., 1996—2001; cons. sch. improvement So. Regional Edn. Bd., Atlanta, 2001—. Co-author: Literacy Across the Curriculum, 2004, Getting Ready for College Prep/Honors English, 2004, Improving Reading Achievement in Middle Grades Rural Schools, 2005. Mem.: Am. Soc. Curriculum Devel., Internat. Reading Assn. (officer Ky. chpt. 1997—2001, bd. dirs. Ky. chpt. 1997—2001). Office: Southern Regional Edn Bd 592 10th St NW Atlanta GA 30318 Business E-Mail: renee.murray@sreb.org.

MURRAY, STEPHANIE LYNN, special education educator, consultant; b. Harvey, Ill., Oct. 20, 1979; d. Ernest Thomas Langbeen and Donna Jean Logan; m. Bryon Jonn Murray, Dec. 20, 2003; 1 child, Logan Michael. B in Special Edn., Ball State U., Muncie, Ind., 2002; M in Special Edn., Ball State U., 2005. Cert. Learning Impairments, Ednl. Behavoir Disorders, Learning Disabilities. Tchr. Storer Elem., Muncie, Ind., 2003, Yorktown HS, Yortown, Ind., 2003—. Sr. class sponsor Yorktown HS, 2003—, softball coach jr. varsity, 2006. Vol. Am. Breast Cancer Soc. Avocations: running, weightlifting, reading. Office: Yorktown HS 1100 S Tiger Dr Yorktown IN 47396

MURRAY-NORMAN, NATASHA J., political science professor, pastor; b. Forrest City, Ark., Mar. 2, 1976; d. Nathaniel and Chaney Murray; m. Mark Norman, July 25, 1998; children: Kelly J., Mylas C. BA in Polit. Sci., Harding U., Searcy, Ark., 1997; MA in Polit. Sci., Ark. State U., Jonesboro, 1998. Adj. prof. U. Ark. at Pine Bluff-North Campus, North Little Rock, 2000—01; dept. chair polit. sci. Philander Smith Coll., Little Rock, 2000—; adj. prof. Pulaski Tech. Coll., North Little Rock, 2004—06; local pastor United Meth. Ch., Little Rock, 2006—. Lay spkr. St. Paul United Meth. Ch.-Maumelle, Little Rock, 2005, co-coord. children's worship, 2005—06; Area II instr. Ark. Gov.'s Sch., Conway, 2006. Home: 9803 Pinnacle Valley Rd Little Rock AR 72223 Office Phone: 501-370-5319. Personal E-mail: njmurraynorman@sbcglobal.net.

MURRELL, MONICA LYNN, personal trainer; d. Richard L. and Mamie L. Murrell. BA, U. N.C., Chapel Hill, 1999; MEd, U. Va., Charlottesville, 2002. Cert. athletic trainer Nat. Athletic Trainers Assn., 2000; performance enhancement specialist Nat. Acad. Sports Medicine, 2004. Head athletic trainer U. S.C. Upstate, Spartanburg, 2002—04; atheltic trainer IMG Acads., Bradenton, Fla., 2004—05; asst. athletic trainer U. N.C., Charlotte, 2005—06; head athletic trainer Charlotte Sting WNBA, 2006—. V.p. Young Adult Coun., Parkwood Instl. CME Ch., Charlotte, 2005. Mem.: Nat. Athletic Trainers Assn. Avocation: travel. Office Phone: 704-688-8429.

MURRELL, SUSAN DEBRECHT, librarian; b. St. Louis, Aug. 10, 1951; d. Edward August and Edith (Keeney) DeB.; children: Brian, Katherine. BA in History, U. Ky., 1973; MLS, U. Mo., 1976. Children's libr. Louisville Free Pub. Libr., 1974-76, talking book libr. head, 1976-83; lower/mid. sch. libr. Ky. Country Day Sch., Louisville, 1983-84; children's libr. Emmet O'Neal Libr., Mountain Brook, Ala., 1984-86, asst. dir., 1986-89, dir., 1989—. Active Jefferson County Pub. Libr.; mem. admissions com. United Way; exec. bd. Jefferson County Libr. Bd.; bd. dirs. Mountain Brook Libr. Found., 1993—, Ala. Ctr. for Book. Mem. ALA, Ala. Libr. Assn. (mem. publicity com. 1992-93, pub. libr. chair 1995-96), Rotary Internat. Roman Catholic. Office: Emmet O'Neal Libr 50 Oak St Birmingham AL 35213-4295 Office Phone: 205-879-0492.

MURTHY, PADMINI, physician; b. Madras, India, Jan. 2, 1961; d. Kashinath Mokshagundam and Krishna Kashinath; m. S. Murthy Narasimhadevara, May 25, 1987; 1 child, Aishu. MB BS, Siodhartha Med. Coll., Vijaydwada, India, 1987; DGO, Gulbarga Med. Coll., 1992; MS in Mgmt., NYU, 1999. Cert. health edn. specialist. Resident Govt. Gen. Hosp., Gulbarga, India, 1990-92; physician in pvt. practice Hyderabad, India, 1992-93; ob-gyn. Al-Arda Hosp., Saudi Arabia, 1993-95; physician UN Population Fund, N.Y.C., 1996-97. Cons. London Sch. Tropical Medicine; parent vol. Pub. Sch. 209, N.Y.C., 1996—. Healthy Mothers & Children: A Guide for Health Care Workers in Developing Countries. Vol. Internat. Health Awareness Network, 1998—. Recipient Cert. of Appreciation, Min. of Health, Kingdom of Saudi Arabia, 1996. Mem. APHA, Soc. Adolescent Medicine, Jacobs Women's Inst., Nat. Coun. Women (exec. com. 1999—), Am. Med. Women's Assn. (N.Y.C. chpt. bd. dirs., mem. exec. com. 1999—), Am. Reproductive Health Profls., Indian Med. Coun., Pi Theta Lambda. Home: 27 Skidmore Rd Pleasant Valley NY 12569-5000 E-mail: aishu@aol.com.

MUSACCHIO, MARILYN JEAN, nurse midwife, educator; b. Louisville, Dec. 7, 1938; d. Robert William and Loretta C. (Liebert) Poulter; m. David Edward Musacchio, May 13, 1961; children: Richard Peter, Michelle Marie. BSN cum laude, Spalding Coll., 1968; MSN, U. Ky., 1972, cert. in nurse-midwifery, 1976; PhD, Case Western Res U., 1993. RN; cert. nurse-midwife; advanced registered nurse practitioner; registered nurse-midwife. Staff nurse gynecol. unit St. Joseph Infirmary, Louisville, 1959-60, staff nurse male gen. surgery unit, 1960; instr. St. Joseph Infirmary Sch. Nursing, Louisville, 1960-71; from asst. prof. to assoc. prof., dir. dept. nursing edn. Ky. State U., Frankfort, 1972-75; asst. prof. U. Ky. Coll. Nursing, Lexington, 1976-79, assoc. prof., coord., 1979-92, acting coordinator nurse-midwifery, 1982-84, coordinator for nurse-midwifery, 1987-92; assoc. prof., dir. nurse-midwifery U. Ala., Birmingham, 1992-96, assoc. prof., 1997-98; dean, prof. Tenn. Technol. U., Cookeville, 1998—2005; prof. Spalding U., Louisville, 2006—, chmn., 2006—. Cons. in field. Mem. editorial bd. Jour. Obstet., Gynecol. and Neonatal Nursing, 1976-82; author pamphlet; contbr. articles to profl. jours. Mem.Louisville Safety Coun., 1973-80. Brig. Gen. Army Nurse Corps, USAR, 1992-95. Recipient Disting. Citizen award City of Louisville, 1977, Jefferson Cup award Jefferson County, Ky., 1991; named Outstanding Alumna, Mercy Acad., 1993; named to Hall of Disting. Alumni, U. Ky., 1995; recipient scholarships and fellowships, other awards. Fellow Am. Acad. Nursing; mem. AWHONN, NAFE, ANA, Nurse Assn. Am. Coll. Ob-Gyn. (charter; nat. sec. 1970-72, chmn. dist. V 1969), Am. Coll. Nurse-Midwives, Res. Officers Assn., Assn. Mil. Surgeons U.S., Sr. Army Res. Comdr. Assn., Assn. U.S. Army, Army Nurse Corps. Assn., Army War Coll. Alumni Assn. (life). Roman Catholic. Avocations: reading, candy making, cake decorating, cooking, sewing. Home: PO Box 4907 Louisville KY 40204-4907 Office Phone: 502-585-7125. Office Fax: 502-588-7175. Business E-Mail: mmusacchio@spalding.edu.

MUSANTE, LINDA, psychologist; b. Cambridge, Mass., Apr. 20, 1954; d. Robert and Louise Musante; m. Lynn Bryan, Mar. 30, 1991. PhD, U. NC, Chapel Hill, 1981. Dana prof. psychology U. Tampa, Fla., 1981—. Office: U Tampa 401 W Kennedy Blvd Tampa FL 33606 Office Phone: 813-253-3333. Business E-Mail: lmusante@ut.edu.

MUSANTE, PATRICIA W., library director; b. Pitts., June 15, 1944; d. Edward Anthony and Katherine (Webber) Wagner; m. Guido J. Musante, Ap4. BA, Carlow Coll., Pitts., 1967; MA, Carnegie Mellon U., 1970; MLS, U. Pitts., 1991. Tchr. Canevin H.S., Pitts., 1967-69; flight attendant Capitol Internat. Airways, Nashville, 1971-79; adj. prof. Carlow Coll., 1990-91; pub./editor Ft. Covington (N.Y.) Sun, 1982-89; asst. dir. Potsdam (N.Y.) Pub. Libr., 1991-99, dir., 1999—. Bd. dirs. North Country Dist. PTA, Potsdam, 1996—; founding trustee Ft. Covington Reading Ctr., 1984-89. Recipient Jos. Schubert Moving Toward Excellence award N.Y. State Libr., Albany, 1997, North Country Reference and Rsch. Resources award for excellence in libr. svcs., 2001. Mem. AAUW (chair book discussion group 1993—), Beta Phi Mu. Home: 871 River Rd Norwood NY 13668-3155

MUSAT, KATHERINE GADUS, retired music educator; b. Cleve., Feb. 6, 1944; d. William Martin Gadus and Catherine Ruth Salmon; m. John George Musat, July 5, 1969; children: John William, Mary Katherine Smith, Danielle Eleanor. MusB in Edn., Baldwin-Wallace Coll., Berea, Ohio, 1966; MSc in Edn., Coll. Mt. St. Joseph, Cin., Ohio, 1988. Cert. tchr. Ohio, 1966. Dir. instrumental music Parma (Ohio) City Schs., 1967—2004; ret., 2004. Studio brass tchr. Baldwin-Wallace Coll., 1985—; prin. trumpet Parma Symphony Orch., 1967—, Hermit Club Orch., 1985—. Vol. church musician various chs., 1964—. Home: 2141 Jacqueline Dr Parma OH 44134-6858 Personal E-mail: kagy@cox.net.

MUSCHAL, JUDITH ANN, health facility administrator; b. Newark, Apr. 14, 1948; d. Charles Simons and Viola Catherine (Lange) Freeman; m. Michael Donald Muschal, June 12, 1983. BA in Edn., Newark State Coll., Union, N.J., 1970. Asst. dir. purchasing Clara Maass Meml. Hosp., Belleville, N.J., 1966-74; corp. dir. purchasing CentraState Healthcare System, Freehold, N.J., 1975-96; dir. univ. and healthcare svcs. Internat. Schs. Svcs., Princeton, N.J., 1996—. Chairperson adv. coun. Hamilton (N.J.) Twp. Sch. for Adult Edn., 1981-84. Mem. Am. Soc. Healthcare Materials Mgmt. (cert. sr.), Healthcare Materials Mgmt. Soc. N.J. (past pres. 1980-81), N.J. Hosp. Assn. Group Purchasing Program (vice chairperson 1986-89). Republican. Episcopalian. Avocations: reading, crossword puzzles, sailing, volleyball, touring historic sites. Home: 5 Burholme Dr Trenton NJ 08691-3331

MUSE, MARTHA TWITCHELL, foundation executive; b. Dallas, Sept. 1, 1926; d. John Blackburn Muse and Kathryn (Poole) M. BA, Barnard Coll., 1948; MA, Columbia U., 1955; D.H.L., Georgetown U., 1981. Exec. dir. Tinker Found., NYC, 1965-68, pres., 1968-95, chmn., 1975—. Bd. dirs. Americas Found., Americas Soc. Inc., Coun. of the Ams.; trustee emeritus Columbia U., N.Y.C.; vice chmn., bd. dirs. Spanish Inst.; bd. visitors Edmund A. Walsh Sch. Fgn. Svc., Georgetown U., 1973—; bd. dir. Am. Portuguese Soc.; mem. Wilson coun. Woodrow Wilson Internat. Ctr. for Scholars; mem. coun. Internat. Exec. Svc. Corps; mem. adv. coun. Luso-Am. Devel. Found. Decorated Comdr. Orden del Sol del Peru, Comdr. Ordem Nacional do Cruzeiro Do Sul (Brazil), Comdr. Order of Bernardo O'Higgins (Chile), Comdr. Orden de Mayo al Merito (Argentina), Lazo de Dama de la Orden de Merito Civil (Spain), Assoc. Dame Orde St. John Jerusalem (Great Britain); recipient Alumni award for excellence Columbia U. Grad. Faculties, 1987. Mem. Huguenot Soc., Nat. Soc. Colonial Dames. Clubs: Colony (N.Y.C.), Met (N.Y.C.). Episcopalian. Home: 3664 SE Fairway E Stuart FL 34997-6116 Office: Tinker Found Inc 55 E 59th St Rm 2102 New York NY 10022-1187

MUSETTI, MYRTLE JANE HOLT, clinical nurse specialist, community health nurse; b. Phila. d. Herbert Spencer and Janet Muir (Bald) Holt; m. Carl Francis Musetti, Sept. 17, 1960 (div. Oct. 1980); children: Mary, Janet Carpenter, Rachel Morgan, Carl, Andrew. BSN, Thomas Jefferson U., 1981; MSN, U. Pa., 1987. Cert. in oncology; cert. clin. specialist advanced oncology; clin. nurse specialist. Staff nurse Hosp. of U. Pa., Phila., 1981-84; pub. health nurse Cmty. Nursing Svc. Delaware County, Lansdowne, Pa., 1984-86; staff nurse U. Pa.-Presbyn. Med. Ctr., Phila., 1986-89; community health nurse Cmty. Health Affiliates, Ardmore, Pa., 1989—; clin. nurse specialist W. Jersey Hosp., Camden, NJ, 1987-93; oncology clin. nurse specialist Chester County Hosp., W. Chester, Pa., 1993—2002; nurse supr. HCR Manor Care King of Prussia, Phila., 2002—04, clinical nurse liaison In Home Program, 2004—06; clinical nurse liaison Milennium HomeCare, 2006—. Bd. dirs. N.J. div. Am. Cancer Soc., 1989—, chmn. svc. and rehab., 1989-92; bd. dirs. Upper Merion unit Am. Cancer Soc., 1989-90, chmn. pub. edn., 1989-92; bd. dirs. Camden County unit. Am. Cancer Soc.; chmn. nurses edn. com. Chester County unit Am. Cancer Soc.; bd. dirs. Upper Merion Park and Hist. Found., King of Prussia, Pa., 1981—, pres., 1988-93. Recipient Profl. Edn. award and Svc. and Rehab. award Camden County unit Am. Cancer Soc., Commendation awrd for excellence in advanced practice N.J. Dept. Health, 1990. Mem. Oncology Nursing Soc., Penns Wood Chpt. Oncology Nursing Soc. (pres. 1996-97), Wayne Woods Garden Club (Silver award 1977, Staging award 1985). Republican. Episcopalian. Avocations: nature, gardening, reading. Home: 379 Heritage Ln King Of Prussia PA 19406-2205 Office Phone: 610-717-2738. Personal E-mail: mmusetti@earthlink.net.

MUSGNUG, KRISTIN A., art educator, artist; b. Buffalo, Nov. 10, 1959; MFA in Painting, Ind. U., 1988. Recipient Glassell Sch. Core fellowship, Mus. of Fine Arts, Houston, 1988; Ark. Individual Artist fellowship, 2002. Office: Univ of Ark Art Dept Fnar 116 Fayetteville AR 72701 Office Phone: 479-575-6295. Business E-Mail: kmusgnug@uark.edu.

MUSGRAVE, EVA MAE, innkeeper, educator; d. Archie Higgins and Medora Adelma Gifford; m. Frank Webster Musgrave, Oct. 15, 1960; children: Scott Kenneth, Marcia Carol. Nursing degree, Jersey City Med. Ctr., 1960; degree in history, Ithaca Coll., NY, 1976. RN NJ, NY; cert. Life Underwriter Tng. Coun., Tompkins County, N.Y. Pediat., surg., and emergency rm. nurse Point Pleasant Hosp., 1960—68; tchr. kindergarten and 1st grade Ithaca Sch., 1968—70; nurse counselor Ithaca Coll., 1970—76; fin. counselor Luth. Brotherhood and Mass. Mut., NY, 1976—93; inn keeper, owner The Edge of Thyme, Candor, NY, 1984—; tchr. bed and breakfast course and high tea course Broom C.C., Binghamton, NY, 1996—. Pres. Life Underwriters, Ithaca, 1989—93; treas. Finger Lakes (N.Y.) Tourism Alliance. Author: (cookbook) Tastes at the Edge of Thyme, 1999. Co-founder, bd. dirs., pres. Human Svc. Coalition, Ithaca, 1977—84; 1st pres., bd. dirs. Tompkins County Youth Bd., Ithaca, 1978—84; chair, bd. dirs. Tioga County Red Cross, 1984—92; sec. Local Devel. Corp. Tioga County, Owego, 2002—; awards recognition chair N.Y. State Red Cross, Syracuse, 1998—2005; bd. dirs. Comprehensive Health Planning Coun., Ithaca, 1978—83; mem. United Way Tioga County, Owego, 2003—. Recipient Ruth Pettingill Youth award, Tompkins County Youth Bd., 1984, Paul Harris fellowship, Rotary Club Tioga County, 2006. Mem.: Empire State Bed and Breakfast Assn., Profl. Inn Keepers Assn., Finger Lakes Bed and Breakfast Assn. (various positions 1984—). Republican. Lutheran. Avocations: reading, travel, counted cross stitch. Home and Office: 6 Main St PO Box 48 Candor NY 13743 E-mail: innthyme@twcny.rr.com.

MUSGRAVE, MARILYN N., congresswoman; b. Greeley, Colo., Jan. 27, 1949; m. Steven Musgrave, 4 children. BA, Colo. State U., 1972. Co-owner Musgrave Bale Stacking; mem. Colo. Ho. Reps., 1995—99, Colo. Senate, Dist. 1, Denver, 1998—2003; chmn. transp. com.; mem. health, environment, welfare and instns. com.; mem. state, vets. and mil. affairs com.; mem. US Congress from 4th Colo. dist., 2003—; mem. Agriculture com., Edn. & Workforce com., Resources com. & Small Bus. com. Past pres. Morgan County Rep. Women; former bd. mem. RE-3 Sch. Dist. Republican. Office: US Ho Reps 1507 Longworth Ho Office Bldg Washington DC 20515-0604

MUSGRAVE, THEA, composer, conductor; b. Edinburgh, Scotland, May 27, 1928; m. Peter Mark, 1971. Student MusBac, Edinburgh U.; student, Paris Conservatory. Composer: (opera) The Abbot of Drimock, 1955, The Decision, 1964-65, The Voice of Ariadne, 1972-73, Mary, Queen of Scots, 1975-77, (first performed Scottish Opera) A Christmas Carol, 1978-79 (first performed Va. Opera Assn., 1979), An Occurrence at Owl Creek Bridge, 1981, Harriet, The Woman Called Moses, 1981-84 (first performed Va. Opera 1985), Simon Bolivar, Pontalba, New Orleans Opera, 2001-03, (ballet) Beauty and the Beast, 1969, (symphony and orchestral music) Obliques, 1958, Nocturnes and Arias, 1966, Concerto for Orch., 1967, Clarinet Concerto, 1968, Night Music, 1969, Scottish Dance Suite, 1969, Memento Vitae, 1969-70, Orfeo II, 1975, Soliloquy II and III, 1980, From One to Another, 1980, Peripeteia, 1981, The Seasons, 1988, (marimba concerto) Journey through a Japanese Landscape, (bass-clarinet concerto) Autumn Sonata, (oboe concerto) Helios, Phoenix Rising, 1997, (chamber and instrumental music) String Quartet, 1958, Trio for flute, oboe and piano, 1960, Monologue, 1960, Serenade, 1961, Chamber concerto No. 1, 1962, Chamber Concerto No. 2, 1966, Chamber Concerto No. 3, 1966, Music for horn and piano, 1967, Impromptu No. 1, 1967, Soliloquy I, 1969, Elegy, 1970, Impromptu No. 2, 1970, Space Play, 1974, Orfeo I, 1975, Fanfare, 1982, Pierrot, 1985, Narcissus, 1987, Niobe, 1987, (vocal and choral music) Two Songs, 1951, Four Madrigals, 1953, Six Songs: Two Early English Poems, 1953, A Suite O'Bairnsangs, 1953, Cantata for a Summer's Day, 1954, Song of the Burn, 1954, Five Love Songs, 1955, Four Portraits, 1956, A Song for Christmas, 1958, Triptych, 1959, Sir Patrick Spens, 1961, Make Ye Merry for Him That Is to Come, 1962, Two Christmas Carols in Traditional Style, 1963, John Cook, 1963, Five Ages of Man, 1963-64, Memento Creatoris, 1967, Primavera, 1971, Rorate Coeli, 1973, Monologues of Mary, Queen of Scots, 1977-86, O Caro M'e Il Sonno, 1978, The Last Twilight, 1980, Black Tambourine, 1985, For the Time Being, 1986, Echoes Through Time, 1988, Wild Winter for Viols & Voices, 1993, On the Underground Sets 1, 2 & 3, 1994, 95, (Robert Burns' poems for soprano & orch.) Songs for a Winter's Evening, 1995, (for orch.) Phoenix Rising, 1996-97, (for 3 flutes and percussion) Voices from the Ancient World, 1998, (for chorus and orch.) Celebration Day, 1998-99, (for 8 instruments) Lamenting With Ariadne, 1999, (orchestral work) Turbulent Landscapes, Boston Symphony, 2004, Journey into Light (soprano and orch.), 2004-05, Going North (childrens chorus and 2 clarinets), 2004. Office: Va Opera Assn PO Box 2580 Norfolk VA 23501-2580

MUSHINSKY, JANE MARLA, humanities educator, writer; b. New Haven, Conn. d. Edward Steven Mushinsky and Rita O'Leary; m. Eric Kuniholm; m. Dana Barry Carter (dec.). BA, U. Mass., Amherst, 1985; MA, U. Va., Charlottesville, 1989. Adj. faculty Piedmont Va. C.C., Charlottesville, 1989—91; prof. MiraCosta Coll., Oceanside, Calif., 1991—. Author: (short story) You Tell Me What You Want (Finalist, New Fiction Competition, Glimmertrain Press, 2005), (poetry) Assaying (Calif. State Poetry Soc. competition, 2004), (poem) You Should Think Seriously About Quitting Your Job. Mem.: Shakespeare Oxford Soc., C.C. Humanities Assn., The Skeptics Soc., Calif. Nature Conservancy, Nature Conservancy, Phi Theta Kappa (advisor 2005). Green Party. Zen Buddhist. Office: MiraCosta College One Barnard Drive Oceanside CA 92056 E-mail: jmush@miracosta.edu.

MUSHINSKY, MARY M., state legislator; b. New Haven; m. Martin J. Waters; children: Martin Waters, Edward Waters. BA, So. Conn. State U., 1973; postgrad., Fla. Atlantic U.; MA, Wesleyan U., Middletown, Conn., 1993. Mem. Conn. Ho. of Reps., Hartford, Conn., 1981—, mem. environ., fin. revenue and bonding com., mem. select com. on children, asst. majority leader. Democrat. Home: 188 S Cherry St Wallingford CT 06492-4016 Office: Conn House of Reps Capitol Ave Hartford CT 06106 Office Phone: 860-240-8585.

MUSICK, MARILYN IRENE, retired secondary school educator; b. Springfield, Ill., Mar. 20, 1950; d. Kenneth Ray and Ida May Sampson; m. David Neil Musick, Aug. 19, 1972; children: John David, Allison Renee. B in Music Edn., Ill. Wesleyan U., 1972. Vocal music tchr. grades 5-12 El Paso-Gridley Unit II, Ill., 1972—2005; ret., 2005. Music advisor Ill. Elem. Sch. Assn., Bloomington, 2000—03; music cons. Immanuel Bible Found., Bloomington, 1996—2001. Choir dir. Evang. Free Ch., Bloomington, 1984—. Recipient Those Who Excel award of recognition, Ill. State Bd. of Edn., Springfield, 1993. Mem.: Am. Choral Dirs. Assn., Music Educators Nat. Conf. Avocation: rose gardening. Home: 217 Reitan Rd Normal IL 61761 E-mail: marilynim@yahoo.com.

MUSICK, PAT, artist; b. LA, Sept. 14, 1926; d. Mark Melvin and Emma Lucille (Ferguson) Tapscott; m. John Elmore Musick, Aug. 18, 1946 (dec. Nov. 1977); children: Cathleen M. Goebel, Melinda M. King, Laura M. Wright; m. Gerald Paul Carr, Sept. 14, 1979. MA, Cornell U., 1972, PhD, 1974. Rsch. asst. Cornell U., Ithaca, N.Y., 1971-73; prof. SUNY, Oswego, 1974-76, U. Houston, 1976-85; postdoct. fellow Med. Sch. U. Tex., Galveston, 1978. Adj. prof. Syracuse (N.Y.) U., 1974-76, U. Ark., Fayetteville, 1986—; mem. bd, dirs. Alumni Cornell U., 1996-97; mem. com. site integrated art planning, art selection com. Walton Arts Ctr., Fayetteville, Ark., 1988-90; pres. CAMUS, Inc., Huntsville, Ark., 1995—. One-woman exhbns. Huntsville (Ala.) Mus. Art, 1992, Springfield (Mo.) Mus. Art, 1992, Ark. Arts Ctr., Little Rock, 1992, Walton Arts Ctr., Fayetteville, Ark., 1992, 95, Amarillo (Tex.) Mus. Art, 1995, Trail of Tears Traveling Exhibit to 11 midwestern/so. museums, 2002-06, Charles B. Goddard Ctr., Ardmore, Okla., 1997, U. Ark., Little Rock, 1997, Albrecht Kemper Mus., 1998, tour of 7 Tex. museums, 1998—; group exhibns. include Senator David Pryor's Offices, Washington, 1991-93, Ark. Art Ctr., Little Rock, 1994, Walton Arts Ctr., 1994, So. Vt. Art Ctr., 2004, travelling show 2003-06, Sculpture Fest, Woodstock, Vt., 2006; permanent collections Jewish Theol. U., Ark. Aerospace Edn. ctr., Ark. Arts Ctr., Dartmouth Coll., Huntsville (Ala.) Mus. Art, Internat. Ctr. Transp. Studies, Promus Hotels, U. Houston, Springfield (Mo.) Art Mus., U. Ozarks, Walton Arts Ctr., U. Ark., Morrilton, Washington Regional Hosp., Fayetteville, Ark., Cornell U., Fine Arts scholar U. So. Calif., 1944; fellow in sculpture, Ark. Arts Coun. Touring grantee Ark. Arts Coun., NEA, 1987-88, Assistance grantee Ark. Arts Coun., 1997; Connemara Found. fellow, 1998; recipient Gold Medal Pizzo Calabro (Italy) Internat. Invitational, 1983, Gold Medal Southeastern Mus. Conf., 1993, Richard A. Florsheim Art Fund award, 1997; winner 9th Ann. Outdoor Sculpture Competition, Miami U., Ohio, 1998, Tour of Six Tex. Mus., 1998-99, Irving (Tex.) Art Ctr., 2000, Ozarks Woodland Sculpture Garden, 2000, Monarch Sculpture Garden, 2001, Buffalo Bayou Artpark, Houston, 2002, Ark. Art Ctr., 2003. Avocations: cooking, swimming, reading, poetry. Office: CAMUS Inc PO Box 919 Huntsville AR 72740-0919 Home: 49 Maple St 123 Manchester Center VT 05255 Office Phone: 479-559-2966.

MUSKOPF, BETH A., supervisor; b. Hicksville, Ohio, July 25, 1943; d. Claron Lavon Laub and Florence Elizabeth Laub; m. David Earl Muskopf, June 26, 1965; children: Richard, Stephen. BS in Edn., Miami U., Oxford, Ohio, 1965, MEd, 1973, PhD, 1998. Tchr. Mason (Ohio) Local Schs., 1967-68, Mason Local/City Schs., 1982-95; asst. prof. Cin. Bible Coll., 1996-98; supr. curriculum Clermont County Edn. Svc. Ctr., Batavia, Ohio, 1999—. Recipient Excellence in Tchg. award Warren County (Ohio) Area Progress Coun., 1990; Morrison scholar Dept. Edn. Leadership, Miami U., Oxford, 1997. Mem. ASCD, Internat. Reading Assn., Nat. Coun. Tchrs. English, Ohio Coun. Internat. Reading Assn., Phi Delta Kappa (rsch. chair 1999-2001, treas. 2001—). Avocations: reading, hiking, travel. Home: 8060 Crest Acres Dr Mason OH 45040-9656 Office: Clermont County Ednl Svc Ctr 2400 Clermont Center Dr Batavia OH 45103-1957 Business E-Mail: muskopf_b@ccesc.org.

MUSKOPF, MARGARET ROSE, elementary school educator; b. Saint Louis, July 18, 1942; d. George Oliver and Providence Pearl Knittel; m. Donald R. Muskopf, Mar. 29, 1969. AA, Chaffey Jr. Coll., Alta Loma, Calif., 1962; BA, San Diego State U., 1964; Qigong cert., Xiyuan Hosp., Beijing, China, 1999; Reiki master, 1991; cert., Holos Inst., 1998. Cert. elem. tchr., remedial reading K-12. Elem. tchr. LaMesa-Spring Valley Sch., 1964-70; jr. h.s. tchr. state operated schs., Adak, Alaska, 1970-73; remedial reading tchr. Ritnour Dist., Overland, Mo., 1973-77; dir. Sch. Metaphysics, 1978-79; Tai Chi tchr. Rockhaven, House Springs, Mo., 1988—2000; energy tchr. Sisters of St. Benedict Kordes, Ferdinand, Ind., 1998-99. Co-owner Passport to Wellness, Webster Groves, Mo., 2001—. Foster parent Bur. Indian Affairs, Alaska, 1970-73; hospice vol. St. Anthony's Hosp., St. Louis, 1989-92; vol. tchr. Maria Ctr. Sch. Sisters Notre Dame, St. Louis, 1987-91; vol. Mercy Ctr., Sisters of Mercy, St. Louis. Mem. Greenpeace, Amnesty Internat., Children Internat., Women's Connection Network. Avocations: tai chi, qigong, volunteering, reading.

MUSSEHL, PEGGY ANN, nurse; b. Atlantic, Iowa, July 16, 1933; d. William Leroy and Frances Ellen (Berry) Kelso; m. Thomas Wolff Mussehl (div.); children: Marsha Ann, Judy Marie Mussehl-Aziz. RN diploma, U. Iowa, Iowa City, 1954; BSN, Mont. State U., Bozeman, 1968; MSN, Mont. State U., 1990. Registered nurse. RN St. Joseph Hosp., Lewistown, Mont., 1958—61; staff RN Marcus Daly Meml. Hosp., Hamilton, Mont., 1962—66; coord., staff RN Mont. State U., 1966—95; office allergy RN Heetderks Clin., Bozeman, Mont., 1970—72; staff RN Gallatin Co., Bozeman, 1970—72; clin. mgr. student health U. Colo., Boulder, 1995—98; telehealth RN McKesson Health Care, Broomfield, Colo., 1998—2005. Mem.: ANA (bd. dirs. 1990—98), Mont. Nurses Assn. (pres. 1986—90, Peggy Mussehl CE award 1982). Democrat. Presbyn. Avocations: reading, golf, travel. Home: 10191 Green Ct A Westminster CO 80031-6794 Personal E-mail: pmucolorado@yahoo.com.

MUSSER, CHERRI M., information technology executive; m. Jack Musser. BA in Math., Miss. State Univ., 1973; MBA, Southern Methodist Univ. Various positions from programmer to dir. bus. sys. Texas Instruments, 1973—94, v.p. R&D, TI software, 1994—96; process information officer, bus. svcs. GM, 1996; acting chief information officer GM Europe; chief information officer GMAC, Detroit, 2003—. Recipient Coll. of Arts & Scis. Alumnus of Yr., Miss. State Univ., 1999. Mem.: Mich. Coun. Women in Tech. (pres. 2005—).

MUSTARD, MARY CAROLYN, financial executive; b. North Bend, Nebr., Sept. 21, 1948; d. Joseph Louis and Rosalie Margaret (Emanuel) Smaus; m. Ronald L. Mustard, Apr. 19, 1969 (div. 1988); children: Joel Jonathan, Dana Marie. Student, Creighton U., 1966—67, C.E. Sch. Commerce, 1967—68, Coll. of St. Mary, 1983—84, Met. C.C., Omaha, 1988—90, Bellevue U., 1991—92. With Platte County Dept. Pub. Welfare, Columbus, Nebr., 1968-69; sec. to plant mgr. B.L. Montague Steel Co., Sumter, SC, 1969-70; property disposal technician Property Disposal Office, Shaw AFB, SC, 1970-71; libr. technician Hdqs. Strategic Air Command Libr., Offutt AFB, Nebr., 1971-76; sec.-steno Hdqs. Strategic Air Command Comm./Frequency Mgmt., Offutt AFB, 1976-79; security specialist/program analyst Hdqs. Strategic Air Command Security Police, Offutt AFB, 1979-88; budget analyst Hdqs. Strategic Air Command Fin. Mgmt., Offutt AFB, 1988-92; funds control analyst Hdqs. Air Mobility Command, Scott AFB, Ill., 1992-93, chief hdqs. and comm. account, 1993-94, chief hdqs. relocation, transition assistance/comm. programs, 1994-95; chief base realignment and closure program Air Mobility Command, Scott AFB, 1995-96; sys. adminstr. Def. Fin. and Acctg. Svc., Kansas City, Mo., 1996-2000, fin. sys. mgmt., 2000—02, fin. ops. analyst, bus. mgmt. office, 2002—. Mem. Am. Soc. Mil. Comptrs. (SAC Budget Analyst of Yr. 1990). Democrat. Roman Catholic. Avocations: walking, reading, biking. Home: 7137 Aminda St Shawnee Mission KS 66227-2117 Office: DFAS-KC/ADB 1500 E Bannister Rd Kansas City MO 64197-0001

MUSTELIER, ALINA OLGA, travel consultant, music educator; b. Havana, Cuba, Sept. 28, 1949; d. Carlos Enrique and Olga Castellanos Mustelier; children: Antonio Freire, Ana Freire. MusB, U. Miami, 1971; MS, Fla. Internat. U.,, 1982. Cert. ednl. leadership. Customer care rep. So. Bell, Miami, Fla., 1973—74; music tchr. Shenandoah Elem., Miami, Fla., 1974—75; music tchr. Coral Way Elem., Miami, Fla., 1975—78, Fairlawn Elem., Miami, Fla., 1979—88; tchr. Whispering Pines Elem., Miami, Fla., 1988—93; music tchr. Claude Pepper Elem. Sch., Miami, Fla., 1998—2001. Singer: Miami Opera Guild Chorus, 1970, Church By the Sea Choir, 1979. Recipient Sword of Honor, Sigma Alpha Iota, 1968-1971. Office: Claude Pepper Elem Sch 14550 SW 96 St Miami FL 33186 Office Phone: (305) 386-5244. Office Fax: (305) 382-7150. Personal E-mail: musteliera@aol.com.

MUSTOKOFF, HENRIETTA M., music educator; b. Phila., Feb. 28, 1946; d. Simon and Goldye (Love) Mustokoff. MusB in Bassoon, U. of the Arts, Phila., 1968. Cert. tchr. Pa., N.J. Elem. music tchr. Atlantic City Bd. Edn., 1968—69; elem. vocal and instrumental music tchr. Willingboro Bd. Edn., NJ, 1969—2001; pvt. music tchr. Burlington, NJ, 1965—. Workshop leader New Sch. Am. Music, Paradise, Calif., 2001—; mem. Wind Symphony So. N.J., Golden Eagle Band, Pastorial Woodwind Quintet, Warminster Symphony Orch. Mem.: Burlington (N.J.) Union, Double Reed Soc., Phila. (Pa.) Musician's Union, Music Educators Nat. Conf. Home and Office: 1139 Kaye Ct Burlington NJ 08016 Personal E-mail: hmustokoff@comcast.net.

MUSZYNSKA, AGNIESZKA (AGNES MUSZYNSKA), mechanical engineering researcher, consultant; b. Warsaw, Oct. 10, 1935; came to U.S., 1980; d. Zdzislaw E. and Wida-Wanda (Jellinek) Galinowski; m. Jerzy Muszynski, Dec. 2, 1954 (div. July 1974); 1 child, Roman. MSME, Warsaw Tech. U., Poland, 1960; PhD Tech. Scis., Polish Acad. Scis., Warsaw, 1966, habilitation, 1977. Designer Machine Tool Design Co., Warsaw, 1960—61; asst. prof. Inst. Fundamental Tech. Rsch., Polish Acad. Scis., 1961—78, assoc. prof., 1978—82; sr. rsch. scientist Bently Nev. Corp., Minden, 1981—82; rsch. mgr. Bently Rotor Dynamics Rsch. Corp., Minden, 1982—99; cons. A.M. Cons., Minden, 1999—. Vis. prof. Inst. Nat. Scis., Lyon, France, 1975—77; vis. rsch. scientist U. Dayton, Ohio, 1980—81; mem. faculty U. Nev., Reno, 1984—89; vis. prof. Swiss Fed. Inst. Tech., Zurich, 2000—01, U. Franche Comte, Besancon, France, 2001; co-sponsor Bently-Muszynska Found. Rotordynamics Cleve. U., 2003; co-sponsor Bently Muszynska Found. Energy Korean Advanced Inst. Sci. Tech., 2004; co-sponsor Bently-Muszynska Found. Life Scis. Korea U., Seoul, 2004. Editor 7 books; sci. editor: Dynamics of Machines (in Polish), 1974, Dynamics of Machines: Vibration Control in Machines (in Polish and English), 1978, (with D. E. Bently, R.C. Hendricks) Instability of Rotating Machinery, 1985, (with J.C. Simonis) Rotating Machinery Dynamics, 1987, Don Bently Through the Eyes of Others, 1995, Procs. of 7th Internat. Symposium on Transport Phenomena and Dynamics of Rotating Machinery, 1998, Internat. Symposium Stability Control Rotating Machinery, 2003; editor Internat. Jour. Rotating Machines, 1994—; contbr. articles to profl. jours. Co-sponsor Bentley-Muszynska Found. in Roterdynamics, 2003, Bentley-Muszynska Found. in Energy, Kaist, Republic of Korea, 2004, Bentley-Muszynska Found. in Life Scis., Seoul, Republic of Korea, 2004. Recipient Gold Cross Merit Polish Acad. Scis., 1975, Innovation award NASA, 1990, Outstanding Rsch. award Pacific Ctr. Thermal Fluids Engring., 1996; titled Prof. Tech. Scis., Pres. Poland, 1998 Fellow ASME (assoc. editor Trans. 1988-94); mem. NAFE, Am. Acad. Scis Achievements include rsch. in mechanical engineering, vibrational diagnostics of rotating machines. Office Phone: 775-782-7229. Personal E-mail: agnesm@charter.net.

MUTH, JILL, elementary school educator; b. Huron, SD, Mar. 1, 1978; d. Tom and Cindy Schlimgen; m. Brady Muth, Aug. 27, 1977; children: Colin, Hannah. BS in Math. Edn., Mt. Marty Coll., Yankton, SD, 2001. Tchr. 8th grade math. Yankton Mid. Sch., SD, 2001—. Grantee, SD Dept. Edn., 2004. Office: Yankton Middle School 2000 Mulberry Yankton SD 57078 Office Phone: 605-665-2419.

MUTO, SUSAN ANNETTE, theology studies educator, academic administrator; b. Pitts., Dec. 11, 1942; d. Frank and Helen (Scardamalia) M. BA in Journalism and English, Duquesne U., 1964; MA, U. Pitts., 1967, PhD in English Lit., 1970. Asst. dir. Inst. of Formative Spirituality Duquesne U., Pitts., 1965—80, dir., 1980—88, faculty coord. grad. programs in foundational formation, 1979—88, prof., 1981—2004. Guest lectr. formative reading various colls. and cmty. orgns., 1970—. Author: Catholic Spirituality from A to Z: An Inspirational Dictionary, 2000, Deep Into the Thicket: Soul Searching Meditations Inspired by the Spiritual Canticle of Saint John of the Cross, Praying the Lord's Prayer with Mary; author: (with Adrian van Kaam) Growing Through the Stress of Ministry, 2005, Christian Articulation of the Mystery. Formation Theology, 2004, Christian Articulation of the Mystery, revised edit., 2005; co-author: Foundations of Christian Formation, vol. 1, Formation Theology Series, Epiphany Manual on the Art and Discipline of Formation-in-Common, revised edit., 2004; contbr. Mem.: Ephinany Acad. of Formative Spirituality (dean), Epiphany Assn. (exec. dir. 1998—), Soc. for Sci. Study of Religion, Phi Kappa Phi. Office: 820 Crane Ave Pittsburgh PA 15216-3050 Office Phone: 412-341-7494. Business E-Mail: samuto@epiphanyassociation.org.

MUTTER, JENNIE, secondary school educator, artist; b. Pikeville, Ky., May 20, 1956; d. Ruey and Delois Jean Mutter; children: Ruey Thomas Bentley, Kelley Michelle Faster. BS in Secondary Edn., Pikeville Coll., 1991; MS, Morehead State U., Ky., 1996, AP cert. U.S. history, 2002; Army cert. marksmanship tng., Fort Campbell, Ky., 2005. Headstart tchr. Lookout Grade Sch., Ky., 1977—78; subsitute tchr. Pike County Bd. Edn., Ky., 1979—96; history/art educator Feds Creek H.S., Ky., 1996—2002, East Ridge H.S., Lick Creek, Ky., 2002—. Mem. Coalfield Edn. Endeavor, Grundy, Va., 2000—, pres., 2000—03, v.p., 2003—. Coord. Goals 2000, 1996—99; capt. Civil Air Patrol, Grundy, 2002—; marksmanship coach Warrior Battalion JROTC, Lick Creek, 2004—; camp photographer Sons of Confederate Vets.-Camp 1863, Grundy, Va., 1999—2003; conductress Order Ea. Star Pine Mountain Chpt. #247, Jenkins, Ky., 1990, 1994, assoc. matron, 1991, 1995, worthy matron, 1992, 1996. Cedar grantee, Cedar Coal Group, 1996—2002. Mem.: Pike County Edn. Assn. (sec. 1996—97, rep. 1996—2003), Ea. Ky. Edn. Assn., Ky. Edn. Assn. Avocations: drawing, painting, photography, motorcycling, dance. Home: 380 Upper Chloe Creek Pikeville KY 41501

MUTTON, HOLLY BETH, psychiatrist; b. Kenmore, N.Y., Jan. 6, 1966; d. David Kenneth and Susan Kathleen Mutton; life ptnr. Gregory F. Smith. BFA in Applied Media Arts, Edinboro U., Pa., 1988; postgrad., Canisius Coll., 1996; DO, NY Coll. Osteo. Medicine, 2002. Freelance graphic artist HB Graphics, East Amherst, NY, 1982—; resident asst. Edinboro U., 1984—88; salesperson The Ltd. Stores, Inc., Buffalo, 1988—91; art dir., account exec. RQC Ltd., Williamsville, NY, 1990—92; sales rep. Azerty Inc., Orchard Park, NY, 1992—97; nat. account mgr. McGregor Supplies Divsn., Elma, NY, 1997—98; resident pediats. U. Buffalo Med. Sch. Hosp. Consortiums, 2002—03, resident psychiatry, 2003—05, fellow child psychiatry, 2005—. Anatomy and embryology artist, tchg. asst., student amb. N.Y. Coll. Osteo. Medicine, Old Westbury, 1999—2000; vol. Sisters Hosp. Emergency Rm., Buffalo, 1993—95. Named Hon. Letter Carrier/cert. of appreciation, U.S. Postal Svc., 1990, winner Marilyn Monroe Lookalike Contest, Bon Ton Dept. Store and Warners, 1997; recipient Humanism and Excellence in Tchg. award, Arnold P. Gold Found., 2004. Mem.: Am. Acad. Pediat. (life), Western N.Y. Osteo. Med. Soc. (life), Am. Psychiatry Assn. (life), Am. Acad. Child and Adolescent Psychiatry (life). Office: Univ at Buffalo Med Sch Hosps Buffalo NY Office Phone: 716-887-5800.

MUZYKA-MCGUIRE, AMY, marketing professional, nutritionist, consultant; b. Chgo., Sept. 24, 1953; d. Basil Bohdan and Amelia (Rand) Muzyka; m. Patrick J. McGuire, June 3, 1977; children: Jonathan, Elizabeth. BS, Iowa State U., 1975, postgrad., 1978—; registered dietitian, St. Louis U., 1980. Cert. dietitian. Home economist Nat. Livestock and Meat Bd., Chgo., 1975-77; dietary cons. various hosps. and nursing homes, Iowa, 1978-79; supr. foodsvc. Am. Egg Bd., Park Ridge, Ill., 1980-83; assoc. dir., mgr. foodsvc. Cole & Weber Advt., Seattle, 1984-85; prin., owner Food and Nutrition Comms., Federal Way, Wash., 1986—. Co-author: Turkey Foodservice Manual, 1987; editor: (newsletter) Home Economists in Business, 1975-77, Dietitians in Business and Industry, 1982-85; Food Net on Internet, 1995, Food and Culinary Profls. Newsletter, 1999-2001; contbr. articles to profl. jours. Named Outstanding Dietitian of Yr. North Suburban Dietetic Assn., 1983, Tastemaker of the Month, 2001, 02, 03. Mem. Am. Dietetic Assn., Internat. Foodsvc. Editl. Coun., Cons. Nutritionists, Internat. Assn. Culinary Profls. (CCP; chair nutritional food scis. group 2003-05). Avocations: gardening, travel, music, food and beverage tastings. Home: 5340 SW 315th St Federal Way WA 98023-2034

MYATT, SUE HENSHAW, nursing home administrator; b. Little Rock, Aug. 16, 1956; d. Bobby Eugene and Janett Lanell (Ahart) Henshaw; m. Tommy Wayne Myatt; children: James Andrew, Thomas Ryan. BS in Psychology, Old Dominion U., 1978, MS in Ednl. Counseling, 1982. Cert. activity cons. Nat. Cert. Coun. of Activity Profls., gerontol. activity therapy cons., Va. Dir. activity Manning Convalescent, Portsmouth, Va., 1983—84, Camelot Hall, Norfolk, Va., 1984—86; coord. activities Beverly Manor, Portsmouth, 1986—87, Georgian Manor Assisted Living Facility, 1989—90; dir. activities Huntington Convalescent Ctr., Newsport News, Va., 1990—91; nursing home adminstr.-in-tng. Bayview Healthcare Ctr., Newport News, 1991—92; adminstr. Evangeline of Gates, Gatesville, NC, 1992—95, Mary Washington Health Ctr., Colonial Beach, Va., 1993—95, Brian Ctr. Health & Rehab., Lawrenceville, Va., 1995—97; social worker, admissions/mktg. dir. Thornton Hall Nursing Home, 1997—98; adminstr. Arcadia Nursing and Rehab. Ctr., 2000—. Instr. Tidewater Community Coll., 1990. Mem. Nat. Assn. Activity Profl. (cert. legis. com.), Va. Assn. Activity Profl. (v.p. 1986-87, creator logo), Hampton Roads Activity Profls. Assn. (sec. 1985-86, pres. 1986-87, v.p. 1987-88). Avocations: crafts, aerobics. Home: 824 Tahoe Trl Williamsburg VA 23188-9420

MYER, CHERYL JO, music educator; d. Raymond Edward O'Brien and Anna J. Moore; m. Joel Reynolds Myer, Mar. 20, 1970; children: Christopher Joel, Cyndra Jill Whiddon. MusB in Edn., Wichita State U., Kans., 1971, MusM, 1973. Tchr. strings & orch. Wichita Pub. Schs., 1973—, tchg. specialist strings, 1987—. Profl. violinist Wichita Symphony Orch., 1968—; rehearsal asst. Wichita Symphony Youth Orch./Chamber Players, 1998—. Named Outstanding Tchr., Robinson Mid. Sch., 1998—99; recipient, Mid-West Band and Orch. Clinic, 1999, 2004. Mem.: Am. String Tchrs. Assn. (Kans. chpt. pres. 1984—86). Conservative. Mem. Ch. Christ. Office: USD 259 Wichita Public Schools 201 North Water Wichita KS 67202 Office Phone: 1-316-973-4440.

MYERBERG, MARCIA, investment banker; b. Boston, Mar. 25, 1945; d. George and Evelyn (Lewis) Katz; m. Jonathan Gene Myerberg, June 4, 1967 (div. Mar. 1994); 1 child, Gillian Michelle. BS, U. Wis., 1966. Corp. trust adminstr. Chase Manhattan Bank, N.Y.C., 1966-67; asst. cashier Glore Forgan, Wm. R. Staats, Phoenix, 1967-68; bond portfolio analyst Trust Co. of Ga., Atlanta, 1969-72; asst. v.p. 1st Union Nat. Bank, Charlotte, N.C., 1973-78; dir. cash mgmt. Carolina Power & Light Co., Raleigh, N.C., 1978-79; sr. v.p., treas. Fed Home Loan Mortgage Corp., Washington, 1979-85; dir. Salomon Bros. Inc., N.Y.C., 1985-89; sr. mng. dir. Bear, Stearns & Co. Inc., N.Y.C., 1989-93; mng. dir. Bear, Stearns Home Loans, London, 1989-93; chief exec. Myerberg & Co., L.P., N.Y.C., 1994—. Home: 37 W 12th St Apt 6K New York NY 10011-3205 Office: 780 3rd Ave New York NY 10017-2024

MYERS, ADRIENNE CELESTE, assistant principal; b. Longview, Tex., Mar. 11, 1955; d. Charles Edward and Frankie Lorraine Gray; m. Kenneth P. Myers (div.); 1 child, Kern P. BS in Edn., Stephen F. Austin State U., Nacogdoches, Tex., 1977; MEd, East Tex. State U., Commerce, 1986. Tchr. Hailsville schs., Tex., 1977—78, Longview schs., Tex., 1978—82; tchr. kindergarten Pleasant Run Elem., Lancaster, Tex., 1982—85; tchr. 2d, 5th and 7th grades Redwater Elem./Jr. H.S., Tex., 1985—88; tchr. 4th grade Plummer Elem., Cedar Hill, Tex., 1988—91; tchr. reading, English, Permenter Mid. Sch., Cedar Hill, Tex., 1991—94; tchr. English, lang. arts Foster Mid. Sch., Longview, Tex., 1994—2001; asst. prin. Bramlette Elem., Longview, Tex., 2001—03, Judson Mid. Sch., Longview, Tex., 2003—. Cons. Region X, XI, Dallas/Ft. Worth area, 1990—94, McDougal, Littell, Dallas, 1999; asst. prin. elem. summer sch. Longview Ind. Sch. Dist., 2001. Pres. Foster Mid. Sch. PTA, Longview, Tex., 1995—96; weekend obituary writer Longview News Jour., 1999—2005; cmty. awareness task force Ctr. for Profl. Devel. Tchrs., U. Tex., Tyler, 2000—01; Welcome Ctr. greeter First United Meth. Ch., Longview, 2002—04. Recipient Master Tchr. Recognition award, Gov. Ann Richards, Tex., 1992. Mem.: Tex. Elem. Prins. and Suprs. Assn., Tex. Assn. Secondary Sch. Prins. (Asst. Prin. of Yr. 2005—06), Nat. Assn. Secondary Sch. Prins., Kappa Delta Pi. Avocations: reading, dance, drawing, needlepoint. Office: Judson Mid Sch 5745 Judson Rd Longview TX 75604 Office Phone: 903-663-0206. Office Fax: 903-663-0275. E-mail: amyers@lisd.org.

MYERS, ANGELA MICHELLE, music educator, department chairman; b. Kokomo, Ind., Nov. 29, 1978; d. Ronald Wayne Myers and Sandra Jane Myers Gaiser. BS in Instrumental Music Edn., Ball State U., Muncie, Ind., 2001. Band dir. Prince William County Sch., Stonewall Jackson HS, Manassas, Va., 2002; band dir., dept. chair Prince William County Sch., Bull Run Mid. Sch., Gainesville, Va., 2002—. Fine arts rep. Bull Run Mid. Sch. Adv. Council, Gainesville, Va., 2004—; curriculum cons. Prince William County Sch., Manassas, Va., 2004—, camp dir., instr., 2004—; presenter in field. Band pres. Ball State U., Sch. of Music, Muncie, Ind., 2000—01, 2000—01; presenter Prince William County Schs., 2004—, music literacy com. mem., 2006—, music syllabus com. mem., 2006—. Recipient Richard L. Dunham Band award, Ball State U. Marching Band, 2000, John R. Emens Leadership award, Ball State U. Sch. Music. Mem.: Sigma Alpha Iota, Va. Music Educators Assn., Music Educators Nat. Conf. Achievements include founding staff mem. Bull Run Mid. Sch., 2002.

MYERS, CAROL MCCLARY, retired sales administrator, editor; b. Dawson, N.Mex. d. Joseph Franklin and Alberta Lenore (McGarvey) McClary; m. Dwight Andrew Myers, Sept. 16, 1950 (dec. Sept. 1995); children: Robert Andrew, Debra Ann, James Allen. MusB, U. Redlands, 1950. Cert. tchr., Calif. Tchr. music Barstow (Calif.) Pub. Schs., 1950-52; sec., acct. U.S. Army, Columbus, Ga., 1952-54; part-time sec. Robert Lafollette, Atty., Albuquerque, 1954-57; sec., acct. Midland Specialty Co., Albuquerque, 1957-60; pvt. tchr. piano Oakland, N.J., 1960-70; organist, choir dir., ch. sec. Ramapo Valley Bapt., Oakland, N.J., 1965-70; order fulfillment/invoicing U. N.Mex. Press, Albuquerque, 1974-76, sales mgr., 1976-88, ret., 1988. Editor (mag.) Book Talk, 1971-2001; (7 books) In Celebration of the Book: Literary New Mexico, 1982, Literary New Mexico: Essays From Book Talk, 1998. Recipient Edgar Lee Hewett award Hist. Soc. N.Mex., 1985, Paso Por Aquí award Rio Grande Hist. Collections, 1990. Mem. N.Mex. Libr. Assn. (hon. life, treas. 1989-91, bd. dirs. 1992-94), Rocky Mountain Book Pubs. Assn. (Jack D. Rittenhouse award 1994), Mountains and Plains Booksellers Assn. Republican. Avocation: piano. Home: 8632 Horacio Pl NE Albuquerque NM 87111-3218

MYERS, CHARLOTTE, secondary educator; Tchr. Lowell (Ind.) Sr. High Sch. Named Outstanding High Sch. Tchr. Inland Steel Ryerson Found., 1992. Office: Lowell Sr High Sch 2051 E Commercial Ave Lowell IN 46356-2115

MYERS, DEBRA TAYLOR, elementary school educator, writer; b. Balt., Feb. 5, 1953; d. James Zachary and Gene Elizabeth (Blubaugh) Taylor; m. Kenneth Lee Myers Jr., June 18, 1977; children: Kenneth Andrew, Katherine Elizabeth. BS in Elem. Edn., Towson State U., 1975, MEd, 1983. Cert. tchr., Md. 5th grade tchr. N.W. Mid. Sch., Taneytown, Md., 1975-80; home and hosp. sch. tchr. Balt. County Schs., 1992-93; tchr. educator in elem. edn. dept. Towson (Md.) State U., 1993—94; 2d grade tchr. Balt. County Pub. Schs., 1994—. Tchr. Dept. Elem. Edn. Towson (Md.) U.; workshop leader in field; lectr. in field. Contbr. articles to children's mags. and jours. Mem. Fieldstone Hist. Com., A Randallstown Cmty. Group Assn., Balt., 1993—; bd. dirs. Child Devel. Ctr., Milford Mill United Meth. Ch., 1992—; coord. Jr. Fieldstone Garden Club. Recipient Outstanding Vol. award Balt. County PTA, 1992, 93, 94; named N.W. Area Educator of Yr., 1999. Mem. Kappa Delta Pi. Avocations: travel, reading, writing for children, volunteering, spending time with family. Home: 3607 Blackstone Rd Randallstown MD 21133-4213 Office: Office of Gifted and Talented Edn and Magnet Programs 6019 Charles St Towson MD 21204

MYERS, DOROTHY ROATZ, artist; b. Detroit, Mar. 24, 1921; d. Harry Agustus and Lola May (Kelly) Roats; children: Bruce, Leslie Ann, Douglas. Student, Antioch Coll., 1941, Corcoran Gallery Art Sch., 1943, Art Students League, 1965—. Asst. to design dir. Harper & Row Pub., N.Y.C., 1981-87. Lectr. and writer on art-related affairs. Contbr. revs. to profl. publs.; exhibited in numerous shows including N.Y. ArtExpo, 1992, Art Miami, 1992, Cornell Med. Libr. Ann., 1992, Hellenic Art Inst. Exhbn., 1991, Vt. Inst. Natural Sci., 1983, Montserrat Gallery Internat. Exhbn. (hon. mention 1993); represented in permanent collection Ward-Nasse Gallery, N.Y.C. Recipient 1st place award for drawing Brookdale Coll., 1994, 2d place award for sculpture, 1993, Bronze medal for animal art, 1986, 20th Century award for Achievement Internat. Biog. Ctr.; apptd. Acad. Ofcl. Knight Acad. Internazionale Dept. Arts, Italy. Mem.: Academia del Verbano, Italy, N.Y. Artists Equity, Garrison Art Ctr., Hellenic Art Inst., League Sci. et Edn. Sociale, Arts, Scis., Lettres; Soc. Academique de Edn. et Encouragement, Art Students League (life), Acad. Am. Poets.

MYERS, ELISSA MATULIS, publishing executive, professional society administrator; b. Munich, Aug. 4, 1950; (parents Am. citizens); d. Raymond George and Anne Constance (Moley) Matulis; m. John Wake Myers, Sept. 13, 1967 (div. 1972); 1 child, Jennifer Anne Myers Bick. BA in English Lit., George Mason U., 1972, MA in English Lit., 1982. Dir. rsch. and info. Am. Soc. Assn. Execs., Washington, 1972-80, dir. mem. svcs., 1980-88, v.p., pub. Assn. Mgmt. mag., 1988-97; pres., CEO Nat. Informercial Mktg. Assn., Washington, 1997—2004, Electronic Retailing Assn., Washington, 1998—2003; chmn. Assn. Internet Radio Network. Chmn. Assn. Internet Radio Network, 2004; host weekly radio show Assn. Nation, Assn. Power and Politics. Pub. Principles of Association Management, 1976, 3d edit., 1996; columnist Footnotes, 1988-97. Bd. dirs. Ethics Resource Ctr., Washington, 1982-86; mem. Universal Postal Union Adv. Group 2000-; mem. Fed. Adv. Commn. on e-commerce; appointee DofC 1fac-4 Ecommerce, 2001-. Mem. Am. Soc. Assn. Execs. (cert.), Assn. Conv. Mktg. Execs., Greater Washington Soc. Assn. Execs. (bd. dirs. 2000—), Nat. Assn. Hispanic Mktg. Profls. (adv. bd.), Soc. Nat. Assn. Publs., Com. of 100 U.S. C. of C., Soc. Scholarly Pubs. Roman Catholic. Avocations: running, scuba diving. Home: 5315 Moultrie Rd Springfield VA 22151-1915 Office: AIR 5673 Ravnel Ln Springfield VA 22151 Office Phone: 703-626-9087. E-mail: elissa@elissamyers.com.

MYERS, ELLEN HOWELL, historian, educator; b. Bryan, Tex., Feb. 16, 1941; d. Douglas Wister and Ann Olive (Emory) Howell; m. William Allen Myers, Dec. 23, 1967; 1 child, William Webb. Student, Mt. Vernon Jr. Coll., 1959—61, U. Madrid, 1961—62; BA, Sophie Newcomb Coll. of Tulane U., 1963; MA, U. Va., 1965, PhD, 1970. Lectr. U. Houston, 1966—67; instr. Okla. State U., Stillwater, 1967—70; asst. prof. San Antonio Coll., 1970—73, assoc. prof., 1973—77, prof. history, 1977—. Author: (student's rev. manuals, instrs. manuals) The American Nation, 1975, 1977, 1979, 1983, 1987, Test Bank for the West Transformed, 2000; contbr. articles to profl. jours. Mem. S.W. Conf. Commn. on Higher Edn. and Campus Ministry Meth. Ch., 1978—81; bd. dirs. Family Svc. Assn., 1978—85, pres., 1983—84; bd. dirs. San Antonio Area Red Cross, 1979—85, Laurel Heights Weekday Sch., 1980—83, chmn., 1982—83. Mem.: AAUP (exec. com. San Antonio Coll. 1973—74), Conf. on L.Am. History, S.W. Conf. on L.Am. Studies (exec. com. 1974—75), Tex. C.C. Tchrs. Assn., Tues. Musical Club, Jr. League of San Antonio (bd. dirs. 1977—79), Kappa Alpha Theta, Phi Alpha Theta. Democrat. Methodist. Home: 307 Arcadia Pl San Antonio TX 78209-5950 Office: 1300 San Pedro Ave San Antonio TX 78212-4201

MYERS, FRANCES J., artist; b. Racine, Wis., Apr. 16, 1938; d. Stephen George and Bernadette Marie (Gales) M.; m. Warrington Colescott, Mar. 15, 1971. BA, U. Wis., 1959, MA, 1960, MFA, 1965. Lectr. St. Martin's Sch. Art, London, 1967; disting. prof. printmaking Mills Coll., Oakland, Calif., 1979; vis. lectr. U. Calif., Berkeley, 1982; asst. prof. art U. Wis., Madison, 1988-90, assoc. prof. art, 1990-. One-woman shows include Horwich Gallery, Chgo., 1977, 81, Haslem Gallery, Washington, 1981, 88, Madison Art Center, 1981, Carnegie Inst., Pitts., 1982, Wis. Acad. Arts, 1985, Perimeter Gallery, Chgo., 1986, 88, 91, 93, 97, Natasha Nicholson Works of Art, 1989, Dittmar Gallery, Northwestern U., Evanston, Ill., 1989, Peltz Gallery, Milw., 1990, 91, 94, 99, Wis. Acad. Gallery, 1997; group shows include U.S. Pavilion, World's Fair, Osaka, Japan, 1970, Biennale of Prints Musée d'Art Moderne, Paris, 1970, Bklyn. Mus. 20th Biennale Exhbns. of Prints, 1976, 23d Biennale, 1982, 14th and 16th Internat. Biennial Graphic Arts, Ljubljana, Yugoslavia, 1981, 85, Am. Biennial Graphic Arts, Cali, Colombia, 1981, Brit. Internat. Print Biennale, Bradford, Eng., 1984, Bklyn. Mus. 25th Print Biennale, 1986, prints displayed in Am. Consulate, Leningrad, USSR, 1987, USIA, Yugoslavia, 1989-90, Pace Gallery, N.Y.C., 1990, Figurative Graphics, Amerikahaus, Cologne, Fed. Rep. Germany, 1991, Portland (Oreg.) Art Mus., 1992, Milw. Mus. Art, 1990, Nat. Mus. Am. Art, Washington, 1991, Duke U. Mus. Art, Durham, N.C., 1993, Internat. Biennial of Prints, Bhopal, India, 1995, Madison Art Cen., Wis. Triennial, 1990, 92, 94, 99; represented in permanent collections Met. Mus. of Art, Victoria and Albert Mus., London, Chgo. Art Inst., Library of Congress, Phila. Mus. Art, Mus. Fine Arts, Boston. Nat. Endowment for the Arts fellow, 1974-75, 85-86, Stuart M. Egnal award, 1988, Purchase award, 22nd Bradley Nat. Print & Drawing Exhbn., 1989, H.I. Romnes fellow U. Wis., 1991. Mem. NAD (academician), Am. Print Alliance. Office: 6641d Humanities Building Univ Wisconsin 455 North Park St Madison WI 53706 Office Phone: 608-262-0719. Business E-Mail: fjmyers@facstaff.wisc.edu.

MYERS, GERALDINE RUTH, special education educator, consultant; b. Massillon, Ohio, Apr. 22, 1924; d. Clinton Alvin and Edna Frances (Piper) Koontz; m. Ralph Richards; children: Beth (Richards) Herthel, Robyn; m. Gerald Thomas Myers. BA, Heidelberg Coll., Tiffin, Ohio, 1946; MA, Wayne State U., Detroit, 1962. Tchr. South Rockwood H.S., Mich., 1946-48; secondary sch. tchr. Riverview Cmnty. Schs., Mich., 1953-59, secondary counselor Mich., 1959-63; social worker Washoe County Welfare Dept., Reno, 1963-64; tchr. Washoe County Sch. Dist., Reno, 1964-66, s.e. transitional counselor, 1966-90; ednl. cons., 1990—. Summer relief case worker Washoe County Welfare Dept., 1964-66; guest lectr. U. Nev., Reno, 1967-75, supr. student tchrs., 1990—; lectr. Truckee Meadows C.C., Reno, 1979-88. Editor: (newsletter sch. dist. s.e.) Of Special Note, 1969-90. Mem. Nev. Gov.'s Com. on Employment of Handicapped, 1990. Nev. winner for School-Work Experience Program, Nat. Sch. Adminstrs., 1989; inducted in Lake Hall of Fame, Hartville, Ohio, 1996. Mem. Coun. for Exceptional Children (pres. 1986-87, newsletter editor 1983-89, Frank South award 1987), Washoe County Tchrs. Assn. (disting. svc. award 1977), Phi Delta Kappa (educator of yr. 1984). Republican. Home: 12160 Georgian Cir Reno NV 89511-9211

MYERS, IONA RAYMER, real estate property manager; b. Guymon, Okla., Sept. 18, 1931; m. Harold Rudolph Myers, Mar. 28, 1953 (dec. Apr. 13, 2003); children: Richard Galen, Sandra Dawn, Paula Colleen. BS magna cum laude, So. Nazarene U., 1952; MEd, U. Okla., 1959; postgrad., McNeese State U., 1970. Tchr. home econs. Can. County Pub. Schs., Mustang, Okla., 1952-53; tchr. elem. Oklahoma City Pub. Schs., 1955-61, Transylvania County Pub. Schs., Brevard, N.C., 1961-67; elem. tchr., student tchr. supr. Allen Parish Pub. Schs., Oakdale, La., 1967-71; mgr. DeRidder Tracts and Comml. Property, Metairie, 1968-94; tchr. elem. and jr. high history Lafourche Parish Pub. Schs., Raceland and Lockport, La., 1974-76; tchr. elem. sci. Jefferson Parish Pub. Schs., Metairie, 1976-80; treas. Harold R. Myers Engrng. (divsn. Harold R. Myers, Inc.), Metairie, 1993—2003; mgr. Harion Properties, L.L.C., Metairie, 1980—. Vol. founding bd. dirs. Jefferson Performing Arts Soc., Metairie, 1977-83; vol. founding mem. community adv. coun. East Jefferson Gen. Hosp., Metairie, 1980-87. Vol. scout leader S.E. La. Girl Scouts U.S. coun., Metairie, 1977-89, fund raising com., 1992-93, spl. contbr., 2001-05; vol. tchr. music Harold Keller Elem. Sch., Metairie, 1981-83; life mem. Rep. Nat. Com., Washington, 1980-91, mem. fin. com., 1988; jubilee chmn., fundraiser Jefferson Performing Arts Soc., Metairie, 1987; candidate La. Ho. of Reps. Dist. 88, Baton Rouge, 1991; com. YWCA New Orleans Role Model Luncheon, 1994-95; financier Bus. and Profl. Women USA Found., 1990-95, Golden Circle donor, 1996-2005; sec. East Jefferson Rep. Parish Coun., 1998-99; parlimentarian Nat. Women's Polit. Caucus Greater New Orleans Region, 1998-99, pres., 1999-2000, v.p. polit. activity, 2000-01. New Orleans Mus. of Art fellow, 1984-94, So. Nazarene U. fellow, 1985-94; recipient Rice in the Ear award S.E. La. Girl Scouts U.S., 1982, Great Lady/Great Gentleman award Ladies Aux. East Jefferson Gen. Hosp., 1987, Commendation award Jefferson Performing Arts Soc., 1988, Women as Winners award YWCA New Orleans, 1993; honoree City Business Woman of the Year, 2001. Mem.: AAUW (del. 5 nat. and 5 regional convs. 1987—94, pres. 1988—90, corr. sec. La. chpt. 1989—91, vol. coord. Metairie chpt. 1990—91, Magnolia editor 1991—96, chair nominating com. 1992—93, Magnolia co-editor 1996—97, program v.p. Metairie br. 1997—99, del. 5 nat. and 5 regional convs. 1998, chair nominating com. 1998—99, sec. 1998—2000, del. 5 nat. and 5 regional convs. 1999, Parliamentarian br. 1999—2000, state parliamentarian 2000—01, chmn. fin. 2000—01, state pres. 2002—04, pres. Metairie chpt. 2002—06, state sec. 2004—06, scholar and grantee 1989, grant honoree 1994), Jefferson Twenty-Five Bd. (sec. 2003—04, pres. 2005, Patty Strong award 1997), Nat. Women's Polit. Caucus (del. nat. conv. 1997, 1999, New Orleans region pres. 1999—2000, v.p. polit. activity 2000—01, del. nat. conv. 2001, br. pres. 2002—, del. nat. conv. 2003), E. Jefferson Parish Rep. Coun., La. Assn. Parliamentarians (2d v.p., edn. chair 1997—2001, state 1st v.p. 2001—05), La. Landmarks Soc. (life), Jefferson Hist. Soc. (life), Nat. Assn. Parliamentarians (pres. Metairie unit 1996—97, del. nat. conv. 1997—99, pres. Metairie unit 1998—99, v.p. program chair 1999—2000, parliamentarian 2000—01, pres. 2002—03, sec. 2003—04, treas. 2004—05, parliamentarian 2005—06), New Orleans Mus. Art (fellow 1984—94), Metairie Woman's Club (corr. sec. 1994—96, parliamentarian 2002—03), La. Fedn. Bus. Profl. Women's Clubs, Inc. (pres. Jefferson Parish chpt. 1980—82, auditor, legis. chmn. 1990—91, rec. sec. 1991—92, membership v.p. 1992—93, 1st v.p. 1993—94, program v.p. 1993—94, Vision editor 1993—96, Jefferson Parish Voice editor 1993—, pres.-elect 1994—95, state pres. 1995—96, state newsletter Pelican editor 1995—2000, sec. 1998—99, parliamentarian 1999—2001, pres. 2001—02, state historian 2001—05, state treas. 2006—, Outstanding Dist. Dir. award 1985, Nike award 1991, Higher Mem. honor 1992—93, Best Membership Recruiter 1993—94). Methodist. Avocations: plate collector, gardening, lobbyist. Home: 4701 Chastant St Metairie LA 70006-2059 E-mail: ionaloumyers@aol.com.

MYERS, JANIS MARIE, secondary school educator; b. Waterloo, Iowa; d. William H. and M. Burdine Bartling; m. Mel H. Myers, Jan. 1, 1977. BA, U. No. Iowa, Cedar Falls, 1974, MA, 1993. Tchr. Spencer H.S., Iowa, 1975—. Dist. chmn. Nat. Forensics League We. Iowa, 1990—92; adj. prof. Iowa Lakes C.C., Spencer, Iowa, 1990—; dir. talented and gifted program Spencer H.S., 1994—; pres. Lakeland Talented and Gifted, 2004; presenter Internat. Comparative Edn. Conf., Stanford, Calif., 2005. Balin fellow, U. Iowa Balin Ctr., 1995. Mem.: Iowa Talented and Gifted Assn. (Gifted Educators award 2006). Avocation: reading. Home: 1400 13th Ave W Spencer IA 51301 Office: Spencer HS Box 200 Spencer IA 51301

MYERS, JULIE L., federal agency administrator; b. Shawnee, KS, 1969; m. John Wood, 2005. BA, Baylor U.; JD, Cornell U., 1994. Law clk. to Hon. C. Arlen Beam US Ct. Appeals (8th cir.); assoc. Mayer, Brown & Platt, Chgo., 1993—97; assoc. ind. counsel Office of Ind. Counsel Kenneth Starr, Washington, 1998—99; asst. U.S. atty. (ea. dist.) N.Y. US Dept. Justice, Bklyn., 1999—2001, chief of staff to asst. atty. gen. criminal divsn. Washington, 2003; dept. asst. sec. for money laundering and fin. crimes US Dept. Treasury, Washington, 2001—03; asst. sec. for export enforcement, Bur. Industry & Security US Dept. Commerce, Washington, 2003—05; spl. asst. to the Pres. for presdl. personnel The White House, Washington, 2005—06; asst. sec. US Immigration & Customs Enforcement US Dept. Homeland Security, Washington, 2006—. Office: US Dept Homeland Security US Immigration & Customs Enforcement 425 Eye St NW Rm 7100 Washington DC 20528*

MYERS, LEE ANN, accountant; b. Loveland, Colo., Apr. 7, 1965; d. Henry Lee and Maria Lenore Klump. BSBA, Bowling Green State U., 1987. CPA. Auditor Deloitte & Touche, Toledo, 1987-90, sr. health care auditor Detroit, 1990-92; reimbursement specialist Mercy Svcs. Aging, Farmington Hills, Mich., 1992-95, reimbursement mgr. Novi, Mich., 1995-99, mgr. third party contracting, 1998-99, dir. reimbursement and compliance, 1999—. Mem. com. Nat. Subacute Care Reimbursement, 1998—. Mem. Healthcare Fin. Mgmt. Assn., Mich. Assn. CPAs, Mich. Assn. Homes Svcs. Aging. Avocations: reading, golf, hiking. Home: 765 Burlington Rd Canton MI 48188-1501 Office: Mercy Continuing Care 39500 Orchard Hill Pl Novi MI 48375-5370

MYERS, LIBBY ANN, retired medical/surgical nurse; b. Hutchinson, Kans., July 22, 1936; d. Edwin Eugene and Verna Maxine (Craig) Schroëder; m. William Wayne Osborne, Apr. 1950 (div. 1960); m. William Andrew Myers III, June 21, 1962; children: Linda Kay, Lloyd Lee, Diana Gaye, Joe Lyle, Delbert Matthew. MSN, Okla. Bapt. U., 1958. RN, Okla. Nurse Bapt. Meml. Hosp., Oklahoma City, 1967-70, Doctors Gen. Hosp., Oklahoma City, 1970-73, Mercy Hosp., Oklahoma City, 1973-79; nurse, team leader PICU Hutchinson (Kans.) Hosp., 1979-87; pvt. practice pvt. duty nurse Oklahoma City, 1987-93; ret., 1993. Owner, operator Day Care Facility, Oklahoma City, 1977-79. Precinct poll inspector Precinct 238 Oklahoma City Election Bd., 1988-96, precinct com. chair Precinct 238 Oklahoma City Rep., 1992-96; exec. com. Oklahoma County Rep. Hdqrs., Oklahoma City, 1994-96; pres., former block capt. Epworth Neighborhood Assn., Oklahoma City, 1991-96; counselor Homicide Survivors Support Group, Oklahoma City, 1991-96, lobbyist for victims bills, 1992-96; Sunday sch. tchr., Bible sch. tchr. Crestwood Bapt. Ch., Oklahoma City; rescue worker during Oklahoma City bombing aftermath, also mem. survivor notifcation team, 1st Christian Ch., and victim advocate, Save Haven, Oklahoma City, during trials; candidate for Okla. Ho. of Reps., Dist. 88, 1998. Mem. Tri-City Rep. Women. Bapt. Women. Avocations: reading, poetry writing, watching ball games, cooking, crafts.

MYERS, MARGARET JANE (DEE DEE MYERS), television personality, editor; b. Quonset Pt., R.I., Sept. 1, 1961; d. Stephen George and Judith Ann (Burleigh) M. BS, U. Santa Clara, 1983. Press asst. Mondale for Pres., L.A., 1984; deputy Senator Art Torres, L.A., 1985; dep. press sec. to press sec. Mayor Tom Bradley, L.A., 1985-87; deputy press sec. Tom Bradley For Gov., L.A., 1986; Calif. press sec. Dukakis for Pres., L.A., 1988; press sec. Feinstein for Gov., L.A. and San Francisco, 1989-90; campaign dir. Jordan for Mayor, San Francisco, 1991; comm. cons. DeeDee Myers Assocs., Valencia, Calif., 1991—; press sec. Clinton for Pres., Little Rock, 1991-92, White House, Washington, 1993-94; co-host Equal Time, CNBC, Washington, 1995-97; contbg. editor Vanity Fair, Washington, 1995—. Mem. bd. of trustees, Calif. State U.,1999— Recipient Robert F. Kennedy award Emerson Coll., Boston, 1993. Democrat. Roman Catholic. Avocations: running, bicycling, music, major league baseball.

MYERS, MARILYN GLADYS, pediatric hematologist, oncologist; b. Lyons, Nebr., July 17, 1930; d. Leonard Clarence and Marian N. (Manning) M.; m. Paul Frederick Motzkus, July 24, 1957 (dec. Aug. 1982). BA cum laude, U. Omaha, 1954; MD, U. Nebr., 1959. Diplomate Am. Bd. Pediat. Intern Orange County Gen. Hosp., Orange, Calif., 1959-60, resident, 1960-62; fellow in hematology/oncology Orange County Gen. Hosp./Children's Hosp. L.A., 1962-64; assoc. in rsch., chief dept. hematology/oncology Children's Hosp., Orange, 1964-80, dir. outpatient dept., 1964-73, assoc. dir. leukapheresis unit, 1971-80; clin. practice hematology, oncology, rheumatology Orange, 1964-80; instr. Coll. Medicine U. Calif., Irvine, 1968-71, asst. clin. prof. pediatrics, 1971—; pvt. practice hematology, oncology, rheumatology Santa Ana, Calif., 1980—. Clin. rschr. exptl. drugs. Contbr. articles to med. jours. Med. adv. com. Orange County Blood Bank Hemophiliac Found. Grantee Am. Leukemia Soc., 1963, Am. Heart Assn., 1964. Fellow Am. Acad. Pediat.; mem. AMA, Calif. Med. Assn., LA County Med. Assn., Orange County Med. Assn., Orange County Pediat. Soc., Southwestern Pediat. Soc., LA Pediat. Soc., Internat. Coll. Pediat., Orange County Oncologic Soc., Am. Heart Assn. (Cardiopulmonary Coun.). Republican. Methodist. Avocation: reading. Office: 2220 E Fruit St Ste 217 Santa Ana CA 92701-4459 Office Phone: 714-541-3393.

MYERS, MARY KATHLEEN, publishing executive; b. Cedar Rapids, Iowa, Aug. 19, 1945; d. Joseph Bernard and Marjorie Helen (Huntsman) Weaver; m. David F. Myers, Dec. 30, 1967; children: Mindy, James. BA in English and Psychology, U. Iowa, 1967. Tchr. Lincoln HS, Des Moines, 1967-80; editor Perfection Learning Corp., Des Moines, 1980-87, v.p., editor-in-chief, 1987-93; pres., founding ptnr. orgn. to promote Edward de Bono Advanced Practical Thinking Tng., Des Moines, 1992—; founder Myers House LLC, 2002. Pres. Innova Tng. & Comns., Inc., 2000-05. Editor: Six Thinking Hats, 1991, Lateral Thinking, 1993, Direct Attention Thinking Tools, 1997, Total Creativity, 1997 Focus on Facilitation, 2004, Simplicity, 2005; pub. A Disgrace to the Profession, 2002. Adv. bd. Sch. Bus., Econs. and Acctg., Simpson Coll., 1998—. Mem. ASTD, Am. Creativity Assn. (bd. dirs. 1997-2000, pres. 1999), Instrnl. Systems Assn. (mem. bd. dirs. 2002-04). Home: 813 56th St West Des Moines IA 50266-6314 Office: de Bono Thinking Systems 2570 106th St # A Des Moines IA 50322-3771 Office Phone: 515-334-2687. Business E-Mail: kmyers@debonosystems.com.

MYERS, MICHELE TOLELA, academic administrator; b. Rabat, Morocco, Sept. 25, 1941; arrived in U.S., 1964; d. Albert and Lillie (Abecassis) Tolela; m. Pierre Vajda, Sept. 12, 1962 (div. Jan. 1965); m. Gail E. Myers, Dec. 20, 1968 (div. Oct. 2003); children: Erika, David. Diploma, Inst. Polit. Studies, U. Paris, 1962; MA, U. Denver, 1966, PhD, 1967; MA, Trinity U., 1977; LHD, Wittenberg U., 1994, Denison U., 1998, U. Denver, 1999. Asst. prof. speech Manchester Coll., North Manchester, Ind., 1967—68; asst. prof. speech and sociology Monticello Coll., Godfrey, Ill., 1968—71; asst. prof. communication Trinity U., San Antonio, 1975—80, assoc. prof., 1980—86, asst. v.p. for acad. affairs, 1982—85, assoc. v.p., 1985—86; assoc. prof. sociology, dean Undergrad. Coll. Bryn Mawr Coll., Pa., 1986—89; pres. Denison U., Granville, Ohio, 1989—98, Sarah Lawrence Coll., Bronxville, NY, 1998—. Comm. analyst Psychology and Commn., San Antonio, 1974—83; bd. dirs. Sherman Fairchild Found., 1992—; mem. Fed. Res. Bank Cleve., 1995—98; pres.'s commn. Nat. Collegiate Athletic Assn., 1993—97, JSTOR, 1999—, ARTSTOR, 2003—. Co-author (with Gail Myers): The Dynamics of Human Communication, 1973, The Dynamics of Human Communication, 6th and internat. edits., 1992, The Dynamics of Human Communication, French transl., 1984, Communicating When We Speak, 1975, Communicating When We Speak, 2d edit., 1978, Communication for the Urban Professional, 1977, Managing by Communicaton: An Organizational Approach, 1982, Managing by Communicaton: An Organizational Approach, Spanish transl., 1983, Managing by Communicaton: An Organizational Approach, internat. edit., 1982. Trustee Phila. Child Guidance Clinic, 1988—89; trustee assoc. The Bryn Mawr Sch., Balt., 1987—89; v.p., bd. dirs. San Antonio Cmty. Guidance Ctr., 1979—83, Bank One, Columbus, 1990—94. Fellow in acad. adminstrn., Am. Coun. Edn., 1981—82. Mem.: Am. Coun. Edn. (commn. on women in higher edn. 1990—92, bd. dirs. 1993—99, chmn. 1997—98). Home: 272 W 107th St #6B New York NY 10025 Office: Sarah Lawrence Coll One Mead Way Bronxville NY 10708 Office Phone: 914-395-2201. Business E-Mail: mmyers@sarahlawrence.edu.

MYERS, MICHELLE, publishing executive; Group advt. mgr. Mode mag., Girl mag.; advt. dir. Shape mag., 1999—2000, v.p., assoc. pub., 2000—01, Allure mag., 2001—04; v.p., pub. Star mag., 2004—. Office: 1 Park Ave 3d Fl New York NY 10016

MYERS, MICHELLE E., education educator, consultant; d. John David and Mary Ann Myers. BA, Western Ky. U., 1985; MEd, U. of Ark., 1989, EdD, 1990. Myers-Briggs Type Indicator CAPTA, 1999, Wellness Tech. Trainer Polar-HealthFirst, 2002. Elem. tchr. Thomas Jefferson Elem. Sch., Bentonville, Ark., 1990—91; asst. prof. SE Mo. State U., Cape Girardeau, 1991—97; assoc. prof. Ctrl. Mo. State U., Warrensburg, 1997—2003; interium assoc. dean Coll. Edn. and Human Svcs., Ctrl. Mo. State U., Warrensburg, 2003—04; acting asst. dean Divsn. Edn. Queens Coll./CUNY, Flushing, 2004—. Curriculum cons. Mo. Assn. of Health, Phys. Edn., Recreation and Dance, Mo., 1994—; task force chair Goals 2000 SW Mo. Health/Phys. Edn. Consortium, Springfield, 1998—2001; cons., trainer Polar-HealthFirst, Albuquerque, 2002—. Co-author: (jour. articles) Mo. Jour. of Health, Phys. Edn., Recreation and Dance, 1998—99; reviewer (assessment series) Assessing Heart Rates in Phys. Edn., 2000, assoc. editor, reviewer Phys. Edn. Index, 1993—2000. Vol. ARC, Cape Girardeau, Mo., 1993—95, Warrensburg Cmty., Mo., 2002—03. Mem.: Am. AAHPERD, Ctrl. Dist. Assn. for Health, Phys. Edn., Recreation and Dance (rsch. divsn. chair 2002—03), Mo. Assn. for Health, Phys. Edn., Recreation and Dance (coll. divsn. chair 1994—96, Presdl. Appreciation 1997), Phi Kappa Phi (life). Avocations: physical activity, youth sport coach volunteer, gardening, woodworking, reading.

MYERS, NANCY ELIZABETH, education educator; b. Berkeley, Calif., July 2, 1949; d. Victor and Frances Winifred Myers; BA, U. Calif., Davis, 1971; teaching credential Calif. State U., 1977; MA, Pepperdine U., 1984, adminstrv. credential, 1984, pupil personnel services credential, Calif. Luth. U., 1986. Tchr., Los Angeles Unified Sch. Dist., 1973-86, coordinator ESL/bilingual program, 1975-77, 80-81, coordinator attendance, 1982-84, dean students, 1984-86, counselor, Yuba City (Calif.) Unified Sch. Dist., 1986—; master tchr. Calif. State U., Northridge, 1974-77. Am. Driving Soc. ("r" rated judge). Republican. Office: Yuba City High Sch 850 B St Yuba City CA 95991-4926

MYERS, PRISCILLA A., insurance company executive; BS in Polit. Sci. and Econs., U. Mass., 1973; MBA, Suffolk U., 1978. Staff auditor The Prudential Ins. Co. Am., Boston, 1976-95, sr. v.p. and auditor, 1995-98, sr. v.p. demutualization, 1998—2002; sr. v.p., chief mktg. officer Prudential Fin., Inc., Newark, 2002—. Mem. Auditing Com. Mcpl. Excess Liability Joint Ins. Fund; trustee Inst. Internal Auditors Profl. Rsch. Found. Trustee St. Peter's Coll. Office: Prudential Fin Inc Chief Mktg Officer 213 Washington St 18th Fl Newark NJ 07102-2992

MYERS, ROSE (TONI) A., art educator; b. Wilkinsburg, Pa., Mar. 31, 1953; d. Biagio and Messalina Feliciani; m. Donald Scott Myers, Sept. 30, 1978; children: Adam, Victor, Ross. BA in Art Edn., Seton Hill Coll., Greensburg, Pa., 1976. Tng. and comm. specialist Volkswagon of Am., Inc., New Stanton, Pa.; tchr. art Garden Spot H.S., New Holland, Pa. Home: PO Box 809 115 Oak Leaf Ct Bowmansville PA 17507 Personal E-mail: myers01@ptd.net.

MYERS, SARA A., research scientist; b. Aurora, Nebr., Apr. 26, 1983; d. Marvin Joseph and Teresa A. Fagan, Anne Louise Daly; m. Matt A. Myers, Mar. 14, 2003; children: Jackson Lee children: Jacey Lynn. EdB in Exercise Sci., U. Nebr., Omaha, 2004. Grad. tchg. and rsch. asst. biomechanics lab. U. Nebr., Omaha, 2004—. Vol. Race for the Cure, Omaha, 2001—04, Girls Inc., Omaha, 2001—03, Read Across Am., Omaha, 2002—03. Recipient Dean's award, Coll. Edn. U. Nebr., Omaha, 2003, U. Honors Convocation, dept. health, phys. edn., and recreation U. Nebr., Omaha, 2004, Outstanding Undergraduate award, Coll. Edn. U. Nebr., Omaha, 2004; Regional scholar, York Elks Club, 2001, James M. Cox scholar, Hamilton Cmty. Found., 2001, Frank and Alice Farr scholar, 2001, Hamiton County scholar, 2002, Emley scholar, U. Nebr., Omaha, 2002—04, Helen B Hewitt scholar, 2003—04. Mem.: AAHPERD, N.Am. Soc. Psychology of Sport and Phys. Activity, Am. Soc. Biomechanics, Alliance Fitness Profls. Office: University of Nebraska at Omaha 6001 Dodge St Omaha NE 68182-2000 Office Phone: 402-554-3225. Business E-Mail: sfagan@mail.unomaha.edu.

MYERS, SHARON DIANE, auditor; b. Lawrence, Kans., Sept. 18, 1955; d. Richard Paul and Helen Carol (Overbey) M. AA, Mt. San Antonio Coll., Walnut, Calif., 1981; BSBA, Calif. State U., Pomona, 1983, MBA, 1986. Cert. fraud examiner; cert. govt. fin. mgr. Revenue agt. IRS, Glendale, Calif., 1984-85; auditor Def. Contract Audit Agy., L.A., 1985-92; auditor Office Inspector Gen. FDIC, Newport Beach, 1992—2002; auditor officer Inspector Gen., USPS, Portland, Oreg., 2002—. Instr. Azusa (Calif.) Pacific U., 1987, 88, West Coast U., San Diego, 1992. Musician, Sunday sch. supt. Covina (Calif.) Bapt. Temple, 1975-95, Liberty Bapt. Ch., Irvine, Calif., 1995-2002, Landmark Bapt. Ch., Olympia, Wash., 2002—. Mem. Assn. Govt. Accts. Republican. Avocations: piano, travel. Home: 2702 44th Ave NW Olympia WA 98502-3692

MYERS, SUE BARTLEY, artist; b. Norfolk, Va., Aug. 22, 1930; d. Louis and Rena M. Bartley; m. Bertram J. Myers, Nov. 24, 1949; children: Beth R., Mark F., Alyson S. Student, Stephens Coll., Va. Wesleyan. V.p. Jamson Realty Inc., Myers Realty Inc. Ltd. ptnr. Downtown Plaza Shopping Ctr., Warwick Village Shopping Ctr., Suburban Park Assocs. Solo shows at Village Gallery, Newport News, 1988, Artist at Work Gallery, Virginia Beach, Va., 1991, Va. Wesleyan U., Virginia Beach, 1991, 92, Will Richardson Gallery, Norfolk, Va., 1993, 94, Ctrl. Fidelity Bank, Norfolk, Va., 1995. Pres. adv. coun. Va. Wesleyan U., 1982-94; mayor's del. Sister Cities, Norwich, Eng., 1984, Kidikushu, Japan, 1982, Edinburgh, Scotland, 1991, Toulon, France, 1992; mem. entertainment com. Azalea Festival Norfolk, 1984; founder art scholarship Va. Wesleyan; bd. dirs. corp. campaign Va. Zool. Soc., 1996; trustee Guardian Angels, Jackson Meml. Hosp., Miami. Mem. Tidewater Artists Assn., Art Odyssey, Harbor Club, Bayville Golf Club. Jewish. Avocations: travel, physical fitness, reading, golf.

MYERS, SUSAN MARIE, language educator; b. Salem, NJ, Aug. 1, 1963; d. Robert Harvey and Betty Jane Jordan; m. William Allen Myers, July 17, 1993; 1 child, Caitlin Marie; 1 child, Sarah Elizabeth. BA, Houghton Coll., NY, 1984; MA, Bowling Green State U., Ohio, 1986; PhD, Ind. U., 1994. Prof. French William Jewell Coll., Liberty, Mo., 1995—. Mem.: MLA, Am. Assn. Tchrs. of French. Office: William Jewell Coll 500 College Hill Liberty MO 64068 Office Phone: 816-781-7700 ext 5713. E-mail: myerss@william.jewell.edu.

MYERS, TOBY MILLICENT, advocate; b. St. Louis, May 4, 1937; d. Joseph Lyle and Lillian (Lake) M.; children: Nancy, Philip, Jordan; life ptnr. M.G. Yoes Jr. BS, U. Tex., 1959, MEd, 1965; EdD, U. Houston, 1976. Lic. social worker, Tex. Rsch. specialist TV Rsch. Inst. Mental Scis., Houston, 1965-79; assoc. prof. Tex. Woman's U., Houston, 1979-83; dir. staff devel. and continuing edn. Houston Internat. Hosp., 1983-85; dir. The PIVOT Group, 1985—. Mem. adj. faculty U. Tex. Sch. Pub. Health, Houston, 1978-98, U. Houston, Clear Lake, Tex., 1983-89. Chair, bd. dirs., founder Tex. Coun. on Family Violence, Austin, 1978-81, Aid to Victims of Domestic Abuse, Houston, 1980-90; chair, bd. dirs. Greate Houston Area Coun. on Family Violence, 1983-84; bd. dirs. Nat. Coalition Against Domestic Violence, Washington, 1982-85; life bd. dirs. Tex. Coun. on Family Violence, 1991. Recipient Hannah G. Solomon award Nat. Coun. Jewish Women, 1986, Spotlight award Nat. Coun. Crime Prevention, 1989, Spl. Commendation, Tex. Dept. Human Svcs., 1988. Mem. Am. Group Psychotherapy Assn., Am. Assn. for Counseling and Devel. Democrat. Jewish.

MYERS, VALERIE HARWELL, psychologist; d. Ilene and Jim Walker; m. Shane Myers, July 11, 2003. BS, La. State U., 1995; MA, Hahnemann U., 2001; PhD, Drexel U., 2003. Psychology intern W.Va. U., Sch. Medicine, Charleston, 2002—03; fellow Pennington Biomedical Rsch. Ctr., Baton Rouge, 2003—05, instr., 2005—; therapist La. State U. Health Sci. Ctr., Adult Psychology Clinic, Earl K. Long Med. Ctr., Baton Rouge, 2004—. Patient svcs. chair ALS La. Friends Group, Baton Rouge, 2004. Mem.: APA (assoc.), Soc. Behavioral Medicine (assoc.), Soc. for Sci. Clin. Psychology (assoc.), Assn. Behavioral and Cognitive Therapies (assoc.). Office: Pennington Biomed Rsch Ctr 6400 Perkins Rd Baton Rouge LA 70808-4124 Office Phone: 225-763-3085. E-mail: myersvh@pbrc.edu.

MYERS, VIRGINIA LOU, education educator; b. Indpls., July 18, 1940; d. John Rentschler and Bonnie Mae (Powell) Jones; m. James W. Rose, Jr., Aug. 2, 1966 (div. Nov. 1986); m. Byron P. Myers, Sept. 11, 1987. BS in Edn., U. Indpls., 1966; MS in Edn., Butler U., 1971; PhD in Edn. Psychology, U. South Fla., 1991. Cert. elem. tchr., reading specialist and prin. Ind. Tchr. Indpls. Pub. Schs., 1966-72; pvt. tutor Self, Indpls., 1972-74; tchr.'s tchr. Urban/Rural Sch. Devel. Project, Indpls, 1974-77; reading tchr. Met. sch. dist. Pike Twp., Indpls., 1977-80; curriculum specialist Met. sch. Dist. Washington Twp., Indpls., 1980-82; tchr. chpt. I Noblesville (Ind.) Pub. Schs., 1982-83; instr. social scis. Manatee C.C., Venice, Fla., 1983-87; asst. prof. edn. Mo. So. State Coll., Joplin, 1990-91, East Carolina U., Greenville, NC, 1992-96; ednl. cons. Cath. Diocese of Venice, 1996-99; program mgr. child devel. and edn. Manatee C.C., 1999—2001; sr. rsch. assoc. Fla. Inst. Edn., 2001—02; ind. early childhood cons., 2002—. Cons. Bertie County Schs., Windsor, NC, 1994—96; lead coach early literacy and learning model project Fla. Inst. Edn., 2001—02; cons. Early Learning Accelerates Total Edn. Treas. Smart Start Initiative, Greenville, 1993—96; chair Birth Through Kindergarten Higher Edn. Consortium, 1994—96; mem. Fla. C.C. Early Childhood Network, 1999—, Manatee County Early Childhood Trainers Adv. Coun., 2000—, Sch. Readiness Coalition of Sarasota County, Inc., 2001—, exec. dir., 2002; mem. adv. coun. Children First, 2004—. Mem.: ASCD, Assn. Childhood Edn. Internat., Nat. Assn. Edn. Young Children, Venice Area C. of C. (mem. edn. com. 2001—02), Phi Theta Kappa (advisor 2000—01). Presbyterian. Avocations: needle work, reading. Home: PO Box 22 Osprey FL 34229 Office Phone: 941-468-2938. Personal E-mail: drvmyers@comcast.net.

MYERS BROWN, JOAN, performing company executive; b. Phila., Dec. 25, 1931; d. Julius Thomas Myers and Nellie (Woods) Lewis Myers; m. Frederick Johnson, 1951 (div.); m. Max Brown, Nov. 18, 1967 (div.); children: Dannielle C. Brown, Marlisa J. Brown-Saint. D (hon.), U. Arts, 1994. Dancer various prodns. U.S, Can., Caribbean, 1950—61, Pearl Bailey Prodns., nat. tour, 1961—66; choreographer Harlem Prodns., Atlantic City, 1958—67; dir., choreographer, tchr. Phila. Sch. of Dance Arts, 1960—; founder, exec. dir. Phila. Dance Co., 1970—. Bd. dirs. Univ. City Coun., 2000—. Arts and Bus. Coun., 1999—; hon. chair, founder Internat. Assn. Blacks in Dance; cons. Nat. Endowment for Arts, 1970—84, panelist, 1970—82, Ohio State Arts Coun, 1981—84, Mich. State Arts Coun., 1981—84; dance panel Pa. State Arts Coun., 1987, Md. State Arts Coun., 1990, Arts Presenters, 1995, NJ/Del. State Coun. on The Arts, 1994, The Kennedy Ctr. AAEP, 1996; advisor Nat. Dance Project, 1999—2004; dir. Wade Comm., 1983—. Mem. Mayor's Cultural Adv. Coun., 1984—; bd. dirs. Greater Phila. Cultural Alliance, Dance/USA, Citizens for Arts in Pa., Coalition of African-Am. Culture Inst., Spruce Family Planning Clinic. Named one of 50 Most Influential Women award, 1995; recipient award, Nat. Council Negro Women, 1983, Award of Merit, West Phila. C. of C., 1983, Arts and Humanities Cultural award, Phila. chpt. Continentals Socs., 1979, Philadelphians for Pub. Awareness award, 1984, Womens Way award, 1986, Theodore L. Hazlett Meml. award for excellence in the arts in Pa., 1986, Kool Achiever award, 1989, Black United Fund Arts award, 1989, Phila. Arts and Cultural award, 1989, Stella Moore Dance award, 1990, Black Unite Fund award, 1990, UNCF award, 1990, YWCA-Pioneer award, 1990, Excellence in Arts award, 1995, Arts and Business Coun. award, 1996, Chisolm award NPCBW, 1996, Keeper of the Flame award, 2003, mayoral award, Alpha Kappa Alpha, 2004, Phila. Black Profls., 2004, Theater Co. Interact, 2004, Frontiers Internat., 2004; Nat. Endowment Arts Choreographic fellow, 1979. Democrat. Office: Phila Dance Co 9 N Preston St Philadelphia PA 19104-2299 Office Phone: 215-387-8200. Business E-Mail: jmb@philadanco.org.

MYHAND, CHERYL, minister, educator; d. Jack and Ora Williams; children: Kenyana children: Anjela, Patrick, Bernadette, Nikita. DD (hon.), Solomon's Temple of The World, 1984. Licensed Pastor United Meth. Ch., Mich., 1990; Certified Prevention Specialist Detroit Pub. Schools, Mich., 2000. Pres. Myhand & Associates Pub. Rels. Co., Detroit, 1977—89; site coord. Detroit Coun. of the Arts, Detroit, 1987—89; pastor North Detroit United Meth. Ch., Detroit, 1990—94; adminstrator Non-Profit Sector, Detroit, 1989—2001; prevention specialist Detroit Pub. Schools, 2000—; pastor John Wesley United Meth. Ch., River Rouge, Mich., 2000—. Youth commr. Detroit City Coun., 1987—90; mem. bio ethics com. Aurora Youth & Adolescent Hosp., Detroit, 1994—99; mem. exec. team Faith Base Initiative, Wayne County, Detroit, 2000—02; mem. bd. of global ministries United Meth. Detroit Ann. Conf., 2000—. Prodr.: (plays) What You Believe You Can Achieve - The Ron Milner; prodn. asst. (films) One In A Million - The Ron LeFleur Story, 1980, associate producer (albums) Lord We Need A Miracle, 1983, production assisant (TV films) United Negro College Fund - Lou Rawls Telethon, mng. editor Detroit Life Magazine, assoc. editor-writer (newspaper) For My People, contributing editor (magazine) Tribe Magazine. Goodwill amb. Sarvodaya Shramadana Movement Sri Lanka, 2004; planning com. Gov. Jennifer Granholm Inaugural, Detroit, 2002—03, Mayor Dennis Archer Inaugural, Detroit, 1994, 1998; transition team Mayor Kilpartick, Detroit, 2000; chair Hunger Action Coalition, Detroit, 1994; bd. dirs. Empowerment Zone, Detroit, 1998; cmty. adv. panel Pub. TV-56, Detroit, 1999. Recipient Disting. Citizen award, Detroit City Clerk's Office, 1981, Cmty. Leader award, Wayne County C.C., 1992, Outstanding Cmty. Leadership and Spirit of Detroit award, Mayor City of Detroit, 1994, Outstanding Clergy Leadership, Wayne County Commn., 1997, Crescent award - Outstanding Spiritual Leadership, Nation of Islam, 1998, Proclamation for Outstanding Leadership, United State Congl., 2000, Outstanding Leadership award, Detroit 300 Com., 2001, Outstanding Svc. award, Wayne County Commn. and NAACP, 2002, Human Svc. award, NAACP, 2002, Peace award, Denby H.S., Detroit, 2003; fellow, Eureka Communities, 1994, Golden Inst. for Internat. Partnership and Peace, 2002. Mem.: Inkster Ministerial Alliance (polit. action chairperson 1999), Nat. Assn. for Advancement of Colored People (life). Democrat. Methodist. Avocations: travel, writing, reading, collecting dolls. Office: John Wesley United Methodist Church 555 Beechwood River Rouge MI 48218 Office Phone: 313-928-0043.

MYKLEBY, KATHY, newscaster, reporter; Degree, U. Iowa, 1976. With KRNA-FM Radio, Iowa City, 1976, WKY-Radio, Oklahoma City, 1976—80, WVTV-TV Channel 18, Milw., 1980; reporter, anchor WISN, Milw., 1980—. Active telethon Children's Miracle Network; co-chmn. Briggs and Stratton Run/Walk for Children's Hosp. of Wis. Recipient Regional award for best TV feature, UP Internat., 1984, Best Single Report Contbg. to Cmty. Welfare award, Milw. Press Club, 1987, Press Club award, 1992, Best Spot News award, Wis. Broadcasters Assn., 1997. Office: WISN PO Box 402 Milwaukee WI 53201-0402 Office Phone: 414-937-3331.

MYLES, MARGARET JEAN, real estate appraiser; b. Detroit, Oct. 26, 1952; d. William Thompson and Patricia M.; 1 child, Tessa Marie. Student, Western Mich. U., 1973, Oakland U., 1974; AA, Coastline C.C., 1986. Unit sec. Hoag Meml. Hosp., Newport Beach, Calif., 1976-80, buyer, 1981-86; real estate appraiser P.M. Myles & Assocs., Irvine, Calif., 1986—, MJM Appraisal Svc., Irvine, Calif. Home: 4531 Wyngate Cir Irvine CA 92604-2345 Office: MJM Appraisal Svc Irvine CA 92604 E-mail: mylbon@cox.net.

MYLLYMAKI, MELANIE KAYE, operating room nurse; b. Great Falls, Mont., Jan. 10, 1953; d. G. W. and Joyce Marie (Strouf) Clark; children: Echo Lyn, Summer Dawn. Lic. practical nurse, Great Falls Vo-Tech, 1977; BA in Social Work, U. Mont., 1987; ADN, SUNY, 1989. Practical nurse Columbus Hosp., Great Falls, 1978-84; staff nurse St. Patrick Hosp., Missoula, 1987-91; charge nurse extended care facility Village Health Care, Missoula, Mont., 1991-92; staff nurse oper. room Barrett Meml. Hosp., Dillon, Mont., 1992-95; nurse Oper. Rm. Central Montana Hosp., Lewistown, Mont., 1996-98, Enumclaw Meml. Hosp., Enumclaw, 1997, nurse Oper. Rm., chemotherapy, 1999—; nurse Oper. Rm. Pullman Meml. Hosp., Wash., 2000—01; charge nurse Marion Wood Rehab. Unit, Issaquan, Wash., 2002; circulating nurse day surgery Polyclinic, Seattle, 2003; charge nurse Pacific Regents Rehab. Unit, Bellevue, Wash., 2003—04; mgr. clin. care Am. Healthways, 2005—.

MYRDAL, ROSEMARIE CARYLE, state official, former state legislator; b. Minot, North Dakota, May 20, 1929; d. Harry Dirk and Olga Jean (Dragge) Lohse; m. B. John Myrdal, (dec.) June 21, 1952; children: Jan, Mark, Harold, Paul, Amy. BS, N.D. State U., 1951. first grade tchr., N.D. Tchr., ND, 1951-71; bus. mgr. Edinburg Sch. Dist., ND, 1974-81; mem. N.D. Ho. of Reps., Bismarck, ND, 1984-92, mem. appropriations com., 1991-92; lt. gov. State of N.D., Bismarck, 1993—2001. Sch. evaluator Walsh County Sch. Bd. Assn., Grafton, N.D., 1983-84; evaluator, work presenter N.D. Sch. Bd. Assn., Bismarck, 1983-84; mem. sch. bd. Edinburg Sch. Dist., 1981-90; adv. com. Red River Trade Corridor, Inc., 1989-2001. Co-editor: Heritage '76, 1976, Heritage '89, 1989. Precinct committeewoman Gardar Twp. Rep. Com., 1980-86; leader Hummingbirds 4-H Club, Edinburg, 1980-83; bd. dir. Camp Sioux Diabetic Children, Grand Forks, N.D., 1980-90; N.D. affiliate Am. Diabetes Assn., Families First-Child Welfare Reform Initiative, Region IV, 1989-92; dir. N.D. Diabetes Assn., 1989-91; chmn. N.D. Ednl. Telecom. Coun., 1989-90; vice chmn. N.D. Legis. Interim Jobs Devel. Commn., 1989-90. Mem. AAUW (pres. 1982-84 Pembina County area), Pembina County Hist. Soc. (historian 1976-84); Northeastern N.D. Heritage Assn. (pres. 1986-92), Red River Valley Heritage Soc. (bd. dir. 1985-92); N.D. Sch. to Work Mgmt. Team chair-person Clubs: Agassiz Garden (Park River) (pres. 1968-69). Republican. Lutheran. Avocations: gardening, architecture, ethnic foods, history, cultural preservation. Home: 12987 80th St NE Edinburg ND 58227-9635

MYRICK, SUE WILKINS, congresswoman, former mayor; b. Tiffin, Ohio, Aug. 1, 1941; d. William Henry and Margaret Ellen (Roby) Wilkins; m. Jim Forest (div.); children: Greg, Dan; m. Wilbur Edward Myrick Jr., Sept. 11, 1977. Student, Heidelberg Coll., 1959-60, LLD (hon.), 1995. Exec. sec. to mayor and city mgr., Alliance, Ohio, 1962-63; dir. br. office Stark County Ct. of Juvenile and Domestic Rels., Alliance, Ohio, 1963-65; pres. Myrick Advt. and Pub. Rels., Charlotte, NC, 1971-95; at-large mem. City Coun., Charlotte, NC, 1983—85; mayor Charlotte, NC, 1987-91; pres. Myrick Enterprises, 1992—94; mem. US Congress from 9th NC Dist., 1995—. Candidate for US Senate, NC, 1992; mem. energy and commerce com. US Congress, dep. majority whip, 2003—, co-chair cancer caucus. Active Heart Fund, Multiple Sclerosis, March of Dimes, Arts and Scis. Fund Dr.; bd. dirs. NC Inst. Politics; v.p. Sister Cities Internat.; mem. Pres. Bush's Affordable Housing Commn.; founder, coord. Charlotte vol. tornado relief effort; lay leader, Sunday sch. tchr. 1st United Meth. Ch.; treas. Mecklenburg Ministries. Recipient Woman of Yr. award Harrisonburg, Va., 1968; named one of Outstanding Young Women of Am., 1968, Senator George L. Murphy award, 1998, Yr. of the Sr. award, 2000, Sr. Legis. Achievement award, 2000, Small Grain Leadership award, 2000, Pub. Leadership in Tech. award, 2002, Pub. Svc. Leadership award, 2002, Small Bus. Survival Com. award, 2004, Oncology Medal of Honor award, 2005. Mem. Women's Polit. Caucus, Beta Sigma Phi. Republican. Methodist. also: US House of Reps 230 Cannon Ho Office Bldg Washington DC 20515-0001 Home and Office: 8437 Olde Troon Dr Charlotte NC 28277 Office Phone: 202-225-1976. E-mail: myrick@mail.house.gov.

MYRICK, TANA SHEY, medical/surgical nurse, educator; b. Salem, Ky., Dec. 14, 1957; d. Cecil Jerome and Marjorie Ella M. Student, Paducah (Ky.) Community Coll., 1979; BSN, Western Ky. U., 1981; MSN, U. Evansville, 1988; postgrad., U. Ky. Primary care clin. nurse City of Faith, Tulsa; staff nurse in critical care Lourdes Hosp., Paducah, Ky.; med.-surg. staff nurse Livingston County Hosp., Salem, Ky.; adult health, edn. specialization, asst. prof. nursing Paducah (Ky.) Community Coll. Mem. ANA (polit. action coun.), AAUW, Nat. League Nursing, Ky. League for Nuring, Christian Nurses Fellowship, Ky. State Nurses Assn., Sigma Theta Tau.

MYRTH, JUDY G., editor; d. James Douglas and Ruth Evelyn Sheeran; children: Susanne, Evelyn. BA, SUNY Albany and U. Würzburg, Germany, 1968; MA, SUNY, Albany, 1969; postgrad., Ind. U., Bloomington, 1969—70, Free U., Berlin, 1970—71; MLS, SUNY, Albany, 1988. Cert. pub. libr. N.Y., permanent tchg. cert. in German N.Y. Tchr. English Gymnasium Landau a.d. Isar, Germany, 1971—73, Realschule Niederviehbach, 1973—76; editor Bibliography of the History of Art J. Paul Getty Trust, Williamstown, Mass., 1989—2000, L.A., 2001—. Mem.: Coll. Art Assn. Avocations: travel, reading. Office: J Paul Getty Trust 1200 Getty Center Dr Los Angeles CA 90049 Office Phone: 310-440-6362.

MYSKINA, ANASTASIA, professional tennis player; b. Moscow, July 8, 1981; d. Andrey and Galina Myskina. Profl. tennis player WTA Tour, 1998—. Recipient Commitment to Cmty Award, Fla. Times-Union, 2005. Achievements include Winner 10 WTA Tour singles titles; Winner 1 WTA Tour doubles title; Winner 3 ITF Women's Circuit singles titles; Winner 3 ITF Women's Circuit doubles titles; Member Russian Olympic Team 2000, 2004. Office: c/o WTA Tour Corp Hdqs One Progress Plz Ste 1500 Saint Petersburg FL 33701

MYSZKA, JUDITH ANNE, nurse; b. Newton, N.J., Nov. 27, 1957; d. Edward Albert and Barbara Anne (Noe) F. Diploma, Buffalo Gen. Sch. Nursing, 1979; BSN, Daemen Coll., 1999. RN, N.Y.; cert. oper. rm. nurse. Nurses aid Buffalo Gen. Hosp., 1978, acute care tech., 1978, LPN, 1978-79, RN, 1979-81, asst. head nurse, 1981-83, oper. rm. nurse, 1983—, charge nurse, 1998—. Preceptor oper. rm. Buffalo Gen. Hosp., 1991—, quality assurance, 1991-94. Mem. adv. bd. Niagara C.C.s, Niagara Fall, NY, 1991—94, 1994—; eucharist minister St. Edwards Ch., Tonawanda, NY. Named Western N.Y. Nurse of Distinction, 2001. Mem.: N.Y. State Nurses Assn. (dist I 1996—, leg com. 1996—, bd. dirs. 2003—05, mem. perioperative task team 2004—), Assn. Operating Rm. Nurses of Western N.Y. (bd. dirs. 1988—90, pres.-elect 1990—91, pres. 1991—92), Assn. Operating Rm. Nurses (coun. N.Y. state chairperson 1994—96, cert., orthop. splty. assembly), Buffalo Gen. Sch. Nursing Alumnae, Sigma Theta Tau. Democrat. Roman Catholic. Avocations: travel, reading, walking, sailing, skiing. Home: 695 Evergreen Dr Tonawanda NY 14150-4644 Office: Kaleida Health Buffalo Gen Hosp A 3 Surgery 100 High St Buffalo NY 14203-1154

NABEL, ELIZABETH G., cardiologist, researcher; BA summa cum laude, St. Olaf Coll., Northfield, Minn., 1974; postgrad., Union Theol. Sem., 1974—75, Columbia U., N.Y.C., 1975—77; MD, Cornell U., Ithaca, N.Y., 1981; DHC (hon.), Katholik U. Leuven, 2001. Diplomate Am. Bd. Internal Medicine and cardiovascular diseases. Intern & resident in internal medicine Brigham and Women's Hosp.-Harvard Med. Sch., Boston, 1981—84, clin. and rsch. fellow cardiovasc. divsn., 1984-87; asst. prof. internal medicine U. Mich., Ann Arbor, 1987-91, assoc. prof. internal medicine, 1991-94, prof. internal medicine, 1994—99, dir. Cardiovasc. Rsch. Ctr., 1992—99, prof. physiology, 1995—, chief divsn. cardiology, 1997-99; sci. dir. clin. rsch. Nat. Heart, Lung, and Blood Inst. NIH, Bethesda, Md., 1999—2005, dir. Nat. Heart, Lung, and Blood Inst., 2005—. Mem. sci. adv. bd. Vical Inc., San Diego, 1992-96; mem. arteriosclerosis, hypertension, and lipid metabolism adv. com. NHLBI, NIH, 1991-93, parent program project grant rev. com., 1995—, mem. task force on human gene therapy, 1992, mem. cardiology adv. com., 1993-94, mem. spl. emphasis panel arterial thrombosis, 1996; chair sci. pub. com. Am. Heart Assn., 1996-98, bd. of dir., 1996-98; chair Atherosclerosis Thrombosis and Vascular Biology Coun., 2002—, Gordon Conf. on Vascular Cell Biology, 1996; pres. N.Am. Vascular Biology Orgn., 1996-97; sci. adv.bd. Keystone Symposia, 1999—, bd. of dir. 2001—; mem. com. on space medicine Inst. of Medicine, 1991-2001; councilor and sec.-treas. Am. Soc. of Clin. Investigation, 2001—; lectr. Mayo Clinic, 1996, Yale Univ., 1997, Univ. of Texas, 1997, Womens Hosp., 1997, 2001, Univ. of Hawaii, 1980, Temple Univ., 1999, John Hopkins, 1999, 2000, 2002, Am. Heart Assn., 1999, Univ. of Mich., 2001, Vanderbilt Univ., 2001, Univ, of Va., 2002, among many others. Assoc. editor Jour. of Clin. Investigation, 1997—2002, mem. editl. bd., 2002—05, mem. bd. reviewing editors Science, 1998—2005, mem. editl. bd. New Eng. Jour. Medicine, 2001—; editor: Trends in Cardiovascular Medicine, 2001; cons. editor Circulation, Circulation Rsch., Atherial Thrombosis and Vascular Biology, 2000—05. Fellow Am. Coll. Cardiology, Am. Heart Assn. (basic sci. coun., clin. cardiology coun., circulation coun., atherosclerosis coun., bd. dirs. 1996-97, sci. adv. and coord. com. 1996-97, chair sci. pub. com. 1996-97, sci. pub. com. 1994-96, sci. sessions program com. 1994-95; rsch. fellowship com. Mich. chpt. 1993-95, rsch. grant-in-aid com. 1994-96, vice chair rsch. grant-in-aid com. 1995-96, rsch. exec. com. 1995-96, rsch. com. 1995-96, chair peer rev. rsch. com. 1996-97); mem. AAAS, ACP, Am. Soc. for Biochemistry and Molecular Biology (Amgen Sci. award 1996), Am. Fedn. Clin. Rsch., Am. Soc. Investigative Pathology, Am. Soc. Clin. Investigation, N.Y. Acad. Scis., Am. Soc. Gene Therapy (bd. dirs. 1996), Assn. Am. Physicians, N.Am. Vascular Biology Orgn. (councillor 1994-95, sec., treas. 1994-95, pres. 1996-97), Inst. of Medicine, Ctrl. Soc. Clin. Rsch., Phi Beta Kappa, Alpha Omega Alpha. Office: NIH/NHLBI 31 Center Dr Bldg 31 Rm 5A52 Bethesda MD 20892

NABER, FAITH, retired librarian, educator; b. Miltonvale, Kans., Sept. 27, 1920; d. Peter Gombert and Mary Orilla (Grise) N.; m. Frank E. Robinson, Sept. 5, 1943 (div. July 1976); children: Paul David, Mary Martha Howard, John Timothy, Faith Ann, Frank Eric. AA, Kendall Coll., 1942; AB, Otterbein Coll., 1944; postgrad., Hartford (Conn.) Sem. Found., 1949-50; MLS, Ball State U., 1970; postgrad., Chgo. State U., 1979-83. Cert. sch. librarian K-12, Ill. Edn. missionary Meth. Ch., Philippines, 1950-55; tchr. Mississinewa Valley Sch., Union City, Ohio, 1957-60; librarian numerous secondary schs., Ohio, 1962-70, Bluffton (Ohio) Pub. Library, 1970-71, H.H. Conrady Jr. High Sch., Hickory Hills, Ill., 1971-86. Cons. Chgo. State U., 1976-80, Orchard Hill Farm Sch., Tinley Park, Ill., 1976—. Author: Philippine Dialect Primers. Leader Buckeye Trails council Girl Scouts U.S. 1955-56, Wapahani council, 1957-62; mem. Commn. on Status and Role of Women, No. Ill. Conf. United Meth. Ch., 1978-94. Mem. AAUW (program chmn. 1987-94, legis. chair 1987-91), Coalition Labor Union Women. Avocations: flowers, storytelling, world travel, children photography. Home: 21697 McClung Ave Southfield MI 48075-7804

NABITY, CYNTHIA DAWN, music educator; b. Blair, Nebr., July 26, 1953; d. Earl Martin Pace and Charlotte Maurine Hunsche; m. Gregory Lee Nabity, July 23, 1988; children: Caroline Elisabeth, Joseph Anton. BA, Midland Luth. Coll., Nebr., 1975; MusM, U. Nebr., 1978. Choral music dir. Millard Pub. Schs., Omaha, 1975—. Choir dir. Trinity United Meth. Ch., Ralston, Nebr., 1981—96, Wahoo First United Meth. Ch., Nebr., 2005—. Mem.: Nebr. Music Educators, NEA, Music Educators Nat. Conf., Nebr. Choral Dirs., Am. Choral Dirs., Phi Delta Kappa. Methodist. Home: 1719 Sunrise Cir Wahoo NE 68066 Office: Millard North HS 1010 S 144th St Omaha NE 68154

NABORS, MARION CARROLL, retired English educator; b. Marshall, Tex., Mar. 12, 1948; d. Aldon Edgar and Iola Hall; 1 child, Inetha Iola Sheffield. MS, U. Dallas, Irving, Tex., 1993; PhD, U. North Tex., Denton, 2006. Cert. supt. Tex. Edn. Agy., 2001, prin.-EC-12 Tex. Edn. Agy., 2000, tchr. English, French Tex. Edn. Agy., 1976. English tchr. Lincoln Humanities and Comm. Magnet, Dallas, 1983—98; adminstr. Yvonne Ewell Townview Ctr., Dallas, 1998—2005; adj. prof. ElCentro CC, Dallas, 1993—98, Cedar Valley C.C., Lancaster, Tex., 2002—04; coll. prof. adj. Eastfield Coll., Mesquite, Tex., 2005—; adj. prof. Paul Quinn Coll., Dallas, 2006—; co-owner Izanhour and Nabors Tutoring Co., Dallas, 2006—. Cons. Paul Quinn Coll., Dallas, 2006—. Tutor Dallas Ind. Sch. Dist., 1986—2004. Named Tchr. of the Yr., Lincoln H.S. and Acad. Evening Sch., 1987, 1988, 1990, 1995, 1996. Mem.: Nat. Alliance of Black Sch. Educators (life). Independent. Roman Catholic. Avocations: reading, baking, cooking, chess. Home and Office: Izanhova and Nabors Tutoring Co 1438 Mirage Canyon Dr Dallas TX 75232 Office Phone: 972-228-6770.

NABOZNY, HEATHER, professional sports team groundskeeper; b. Milford, Mich., 1970; Grad. Turf Mgmt. Prog., Mich. State U., 1993. Groundskeeper Toronto Blue Jays spring tng. camp, Dunedin, Fla.; head groundskeeper Class A West Mich. Whitecaps, 1994, Detroit Tigers, 1999—. Named one of 40 Under 40, Crain's Detroit Bus., 2006. Achievements include becoming first female goundskeeper in Major League Baseball and World Series game. Office: c/o Detroit Tigers Comerica Park 2100 Woodward Ave Detroit MI 48201*

NABUDA, JANICE ANN, social studies educator; d. Kenneth Max Lowery and Irene Elizabeth Lucas; m. David Joseph Nabuda, Nov. 22, 1980; children: Daniel James, James David. BS in Home Econs./Dietetics, Seton Hill Coll., Greensburg, Pa., 1976; Cert. in Edn., Seton Hill Coll., 2003; MA in Curriculum and Edn., Gannon U., Erie, Pa., 2006. Staff dietitian John Kane Hosp., Pitts., 1980—91; dietitian West Allegheny Hosp., Oakdale, Pa., 1981—83; spl. edn. asst. North Allegheny Sch. Dist., Pitts., 1994—2004; social studies tchr. Penn-Trafford Sch. Dist., Harrison City, Pa., 2004—. Mem. student assistance team Penn-Trafford Sch. Dist.; counselor People to People Internat., Seattle, 2005; social studies tchr. Neighborhood Acad., Pitts., 2003, Pitts., 04. Sec. Tiger Pride Football, Pitts., 1989—96; mem. Ptnrs. in Prevention, Pitts.; pres. Ctrl. Cath., Pitts., 1998—2003; CCD tchr., ch. vol., mentor; mem. St. John Neumann Parish Coun., 2006—. Recipient Dwight R. Troutman award, Seton Hill U., 2003. Mem.: Nat. Ski Patrol (patroller/instr.), Nat. Coun. for Social Studies. Avocations: reading, dance, rowing, skiing.

NACCACH-HOFF, SELMA, language educator; b. Manchester, N.H., Jan. 5, 1950; d. Elias G. and Wady (Elhady) Naccach; m. Paul W. Hoff, July 23, 1983. BA, U. N.H., 1972; MA, Boston Coll., 1974. Tchr. English, Manchester H.S. Ctrl., NH, 1975—, chmn. dept., 1997—. Instr. speech Hesser Coll., Manchester; instr. classics St. Anselm Coll., Goffstown, N.H.; mem. Disco, Manchester, 1988—. Author: History of First Congregational Church, 1976. Bd. trustees First Congregational Ch., Manchester, 1994—, Elliot Hosp., 1998—; chair Mary and John Elliot Charitable Found., 2002—; chair bd. trustees VNA, 2005—. Named Tchr. of Yr., NH VFW, 2004; recipient Pastoral Counseling award for excellence in edn., 2004. Mem. N.H. Classical Assn. (pres. 1994-96, 2003-05), N.H. Humanities Coun. (bd. dirs. 2004—), Alpha Delta Kappa (sec. 1994—, chaplain 2002-04), Phi Beta Kappa. Avocation: travel. Office: Manchester HS Ctrl 207 Lowell St Manchester NH 03104-4912

NACHTIGAL, PATRICIA, lawyer; b. 1946; BA, Montclair State U.; JD, Rutgers U.; LLM, NYU. Corporate atty. Ingersoll-Rand Co., Ltd., Hamilton, Bermuda, 1979—83, dir. taxes and legal, 1983—88, sec., mng. atty., 1988—91, v.p., gen. counsel, 1991—2000, sr. v.p., gen. counsel, 2000—, bd. dirs., 2002—. Gov., trustee Rutgers, State U. N.J., 1996—, chair, 2003—04. Office: Ingersoll-Rand Co Ltd 155 Chestnut Ridge Rd Montvale NJ 07645 Office Phone: 201-573-0123.

NACOL, MAE, lawyer; b. Beaumont, Tex., June 15, 1944; d. William Samuel and Ethel (Bowman) N.; children: Shawn Alexander Nacol, Catherine Regina Nacol. BA, Rice U., Houston, 1965; postgrad., South Tex. Coll. Law, 1966. Bar: Tex. 1969, U.S. Dist. Ct. (so. dist.) Tex. 1969, U.S. Supreme Ct., U.S. Dist. Ct. (we. dist.), U.S. Ct. Appeals (5th cir.). Pvt. practice law, Houston, 1969—; escrow officer Land Am./Commonwealth Land Title Co., Houston; mem. bd. devel. Prosperity Bank, Houston. Author, editor ednl. materials on multiple sclerosis, 1981-85. Nat. dir. A.R.M.S. of Am. Ltd., Houston, 1984-85. Recipient Mayor's Recognition award City of Houston, 1972. Mem. Fed. Bar Assn., Houston Bar Assn. (chmn. candidate com. 1970, membership com. 1971, chmn. lawyers referral com. 1972), Assn. Trial Lawyers Am., Tex. Trial Lawyers Assn., Am. Judicature Soc. (sustaining), Houston Fin. Coun. Women, Houston Trial Lawyers Assn. Presbyterian. Office: 600 Jefferson St Ste 750 Houston TX 77002 also: 2600 S Gessner Ste 120 Houston TX 77063 E-mail: wmnacol@sbcblobal.net.

NADELSON, CAROL COOPERMAN, psychiatrist, educator; b. Bklyn., Oct. 13, 1936; m. Theodore Nadelson, July 16, 1965; children: Robert, Jennifer. BA magna cum laude, Bklyn. Coll., 1957; MD with honors, U. Rochester, N.Y., 1961. Dir. med. student edn. Beth Israel Hosp., Boston, 1974-79, psychiatrist, 1977; assoc. prof. psychiatry Harvard U. Med. Sch., Boston, 1976-79; rsch. scholar Radcliffe Coll., Cambridge, Mass., 1979-80; prof. psychiatry Tufts Med. Sch., Boston, 1979-95; vice-chmn., dir. tng. and edn. dept. psychiatry Tufts-New Eng. Med. Ctr., Boston, 1979-93; clin. prof. psychiatry Harvard Med. Sch., Boston, 1995—; psychiatrist dept. medicine, divsn. psychiatry Brigham and Women's Hosp., Boston, 1998, dir., ptnr. office for women's careers, 1998. Cons. Peace Corps, 2000. Editor: The Woman Patient, Vols. 1, 2 and 3, 1978, 82; Treatment Interventions in Human Sexuality, 1983; Marriage and Divorce: A Contemporary Perspective, 1984, Women Physicians in Leadership Roles, 1986, Training Psychiatrists for the '90s, 1987, Treating Chronically Mentally Ill Women, 1988, Family Violence, 1988, Women and Men: New Perspectives on Gender Differences, 1990, International Review of Psychiatry Vols. 1 & 2, 1993, 96, Major Psychiatric Disorders, 1982, The Challenge of Change: Perspectives on Family, Work and Education, 1983; editor-in-chief Am. Psychiatric Press, Inc., 1986—, pres., CEO, 1995—; contbr. over 217 articles to profl. jours. Trustee Menninger Found., 1988—. Recipient Gold Medal award Mt. Airy Psychiat. Ctr., 1981, award Case Western Res. U., 1983, Elizabeth Blackwell award Am. Med. Women's Assn., 1985, Women in Medicine Leadership Devel. award Am. Assn. Med. Colls., 1999, Alexandra Symonds award 2002; Picker Found. grant, 1982-83. Fellow: Am. Psychiat. Assn. (pres. 1985—86, Seymour D. Vestermark award 1992, Disting. Svc. award 1995), Ctr. Advanced Study Behavioral Scos.; mem.: AMA (impaired physicians com. 1984, Sidney Cohen award 1988), Group for Advancement of Psychiatry (bd. dirs. 1984), Am. Coll. Psychiatrists (bd. regents 1991—94, Disting. Svc. award 1989), Phi Beta Kappa, Alpha Omega Alpha. Avocation: travel. Office: Brigham and Women's Hosp 75 Francis St PB502 Boston MA 02119 Home: 50 Longwood Ave 1114 Brookline MA 02446 Business E-Mail: carol_nadelson@hms.harvard.edu.

NADELSON, SANDRA G., nursing educator; m. Louis Nadelson. MSN, MEd, Calif. State U., LA, 1990; student, U. Nev. Las Vegas. RN Calif., 1984. Faculty mem. CC of S. Nev., Las Vegas, 2002—04, U. Nev. Las Vegas, 2005—. Mem.: MENSA, Sigma Theta Tau (assoc.; sec. 2005—06). Office: Univ Nev Las Vegas 4505 Maryland Pkwy Las Vegas NV 89154 Office Phone: 702-895-4696. Business E-Mail: sandra.nadelson@unlv.edu.

NADER, KATHLEEN OLYMPIA, psychotherapist, consultant in childhood trauma; b. La. d. S. and E. Nader. BA, Duke U., 1970; MSW, Tulane U., 1974, DSW, 1989. Lic. clin. social worker; bd. cert. clin. social worker. Psychotherapist Youth Svcs. Program, Fountain Valley, Calif., 1976-82; pvt. practice psychotherapy Two Suns, Laguna Hills, Calif., 1978—; program dir., cons. UCLA, 1985-94. Appeared in films and videotapes; contbr. books and numerous articles to profl. jours. Mem. bd. advisors Gift from Within. Mem. Nat. Registry of Social Workers, Internat. Soc. for Traumatic Stress Studies, Trauma Grief and Mourning Interest Group. Address: # 102 2809 Rathlin Dr Cedar Park TX 78613-5730

NADER, LAURA, anthropologist, educator; b. Winsted, Conn., Sept. 30, 1930; m. Norman Milleron, Sept. 1, 1962; 3 children BA, Wells Coll., 1952; PhD, Radcliffe Coll., 1961. Faculty mem. U. Calif., Berkeley, 1960—, prof. anthropology; vis. prof. Yale Law Sch., New Haven, fall 1971; Henry R. Luce prof. Sch. Law Harvard Wellesley Coll., Mass., 1983-84; Henry R. Luce prof. Sch. Law Stanford U. Law Sch., 1987-89. Field work in Mex., Lebanon, Morocco and US; mem. adv. com. NSF, 1971-75; mem. cultural anthropology com. NIMH, 1968—, chmn. to 1971, chmn. social scis. rsch. tng. rev. com., 1976-78; mem. NAS-NRC assembly behavioral and social scis., 1969-71, 73-75, 75—; mem. com. Nuclear and Alternative Energy Forms, NAS, 1976-80. Editor: Law in Culture and Society, 1969, The Disputing Process, 1978, No Access to Law-Alternatives to the American Judicial System, 1980, Harmony Ideology, 1990, Naked Science, 1996, The Life of the Law, 2000; contbr. articles to profl. jours.; author ednl. films, mem. editl. com. Law and Soc. Rev., 1967—. Mem. Calif. Coun. for the Humanities, 1975—79, Carnegie Coun. on Children, 1972—77; active Coun. Librs. at Libr. of Congress, Washington, 1988—. Radcliffe Coll. grantee, 1954-59; Thaw fellow Harvard U., 1955-56, 58-59; Peabody Mus. grantee, 1954-59; Am. Philos. Assn. grantee, 1955; Mexican Govt. grantee, 1957-58; Milton Fund grantee, 1959-60, Wellness Found. grantee, 1993-96; fellow Ctr. Advanced Study in Behavioral Scis., Stanford, Calif., 1963-64; NSF grantee, 1966-68; Wenner Gren Found. grantee, 1964, 66, 73; Carnegie Corp. grantee, 1975; Woodrow Wilson fellow, 1979-80; Wells Coll. Alumnae award, 1980; Radcliffe Coll. Alumnae award, 1984. Mem.: AAAS, Soc. Women Geographers (Outstanding Achievement award 1990), Am. Acad. Arts and Scis., Ctr. for Study of Responsive Law (trustee 1968—), Law and Soc. Assn. (trustee 1967—72, Harry Kalven prize 1995), Social Sci. Rsch. Coun., Am. Anthrop. Assn. (planning and devel. com. 1968—71, 1975—76), Am. Acad. Arts and Scis. Office: U Calif Dept Anthropology 313 Kroeber Hl Berkeley CA 94720-0001 Office Phone: 510-643-1218.

NADINE, CLAUDIA, French language educator; b. Oakland, Calif., July 13, 1960; d. Ernest Theodore and Nancy Jane Fickas; m. Kurt O. Fosso, May 26, 1991. AA, Stephens Coll., 1980; BS in Bio. Sci., Univ. Calif., Irvine, 1983, BA in French, 1984, MA in French, 1987; PhD, U. Calif., Irvine, 1994. Asst. prof. French Westminster Coll., New Wilmington, Pa., 1992-95, U. Ala., Tuscaloosa, 1995—2000, Pacific Luth. U., 2000—02, Reed Coll., 2003, Lewis and Clark Coll., 2005—. Mem. MLA. Office: U Ala Dept Modern Langs Classics Tuscaloosa AL 35487-0001

NADLER, JUDITH, school librarian; BA in English and Romance Studies, U. Jerusalem; MLS, Israel Grad. Sch. With U. Chgo. Libr., from cataloger to dir., 2004—. Office: Joseph Regenstein Libr U Chgo 1100 E 57 St Chicago IL 60637 Office Phone: 773-702-8743. Office Fax: 773-702-6623. E-mail: judi@uchicago.edu.

NADLER-HURVICH, HEDDA CAROL, public relations executive; b. Bronx, N.Y., June 15, 1944; d. Julius Louis and Julia Cohen; m. David George Nadler, Oct. 3, 1965 (div. 1979); 1 child, Laura Lee Nadler; m. Burton Earl Hurvich, Dec. 8, 1984. BBA, Baruch Coll., 1965. V.p., sec. Irving L. Straus Assocs., Inc., N.Y.C., 1965-80; pres. Mount & Nadler Inc., N.Y.C., 1999—. Avocations: aerobics, yoga. Office: Mount & Nadler 425 Madison Ave New York NY 10017-1110 Office Phone: 212-759-4440. E-mail: Hedda615@aol.com.

NADZICK, JUDITH ANN, accountant; b. Paterson, NJ, Mar. 6, 1948; d. John and Ethel (McDonald) N. BBA in Acctg., U. Miami, 1971. CPA, N.J. Staff acct., mgr. Ernst & Whinney, C.P.A.s, N.Y.C., 1971-78; asst. treas. Gulf & We. Industries, Inc., N.Y.C., 1979-83; asst. v.p., 1980-82; v.p., 1982-83; v.p., corp. contr. United Mchts. and Mfrs. Inc., N.Y.C., 1983-85; sr. v.p., 1985-86; exec. v.p., CFO, 1986-97; pres., 1997—; also bd. dir. Mem. U. Miami Alumni Assn., Delta Delta Delta. Roman Catholic. Home: 280 Lincoln Ave Elmwood Park NJ 07407-2824 E-mail: judenadz@aol.com.

NAEGLE, LADAWN, lawyer; BA, U. San Diego, 1981; JD, George Washington U., 1984. Bar: DC 1984. Ptnr., group dep. Corp. Fin. and Securties Bryan Cave LLP, Washington, DC. Office: Bryan Cave LLP 700 Thirteenth St NW Washington DC 20005 Office Phone: 202-508-6046. Fax: 202-508-6200. E-mail: lnaegle@bryancave.com.

NAESER, NANCY DEARIEN, geologist, researcher; b. Morgantown, W.Va., Apr. 15, 1944; d. William Harold and Katherine Elizabeth (Dearien) Cozad; m. Charles Wilbur Naeser, Feb. 6, 1982. BS, U. Ariz., 1966; PhD, Victoria U., Wellington, New Zealand, 1973. Geol. field asst. U.S. Geol. Survey, Flagstaff, Ariz., 1966; sci. editor New Zealand Jour. Geology and Geophysics, New Zealand Dept. Sci. and Indsl. Rsch., Wellington, 1974-76; postdoctoral rsch. assoc. U. Toronto, 1976-79, U.S. Geol. Survey, Denver, 1979-81, geologist, 1981—2006, scientist emeritus, 2006—. Adj. prof. Dartmouth Coll., Hanover, NH, 1985—97, U. Wyo., Laramie, 1984—91. Editor: Thermal History of Sedimentary Basins--Methods and Case Histories, 1989, Debris-Flow Hazards - Mechanics, Prediction and Assessment, 2000; contbr. articles on fission-track analysis to profl. jours. Docent, Denver Zoo, 1991-99. Fulbright fellow, New Zealand, 1967-68. Fellow Geol. Soc. Am.; mem. Geol. Soc. New Zealand, Mortar Board, Phi Kappa Phi. Methodist. Office: US Geol Survey Mail Stop 926 A 12201 Sunrise Valley Dr Reston VA 20192-0002 Office Phone: 703-648-5328. Business E-Mail: nnaeser@usgs.gov.

NAFISI, AZAR, humanities educator; b. 1950; arrived in US, 1997; d. Ahmad and Nezhat Nafisi; m. Bijan Naderi; children: Negar, Dara. PhD in English Lit., Okla. U. Prof. Tehran U., Allemeh Tabatabai U.; vis. fellow Oxford U.; prof. Johns Hopkins U., Sch. Advanced Internat. Studies, Washington. Author: Eye of the Storm: Women in Post-Revolutionary Iran, 1992, Anti-Terra: A Critical Study of Vladimir Nabakov's Novels, 1994, Muslim Women and Politics of Participation, 1997, Religious Fundamentalism and the Human Rights of Women, 1999, Reading Lolita in Tehran: A Memoir in Books, 2003; contbr. Home: 12026 Gatewater Dr Potomac MD 20854-2875 Office: c/o Random House 1745 Broadway New York NY 10019

NAGDIMON, ELLEN TARA, artist, educator; b. N.Y.C., Dec. 13, 1957; d. Jeoash Morris and Evelyn (Uretzky) Nagdimon; m. J. Martin Kahn, June 7, 1994. BA, CUNY, 1981; cert. legal asst., Adelphi U., 1982. Studio liaison N.Y. Feminist Art Inst., N.Y.C., 1985-88; gallery asst. Studio K Gallery, Long Island City, NY, 1986-88; instr., cons. Children's Art Carnival, N.Y.C., 1990-92; instr. Forest Hills (N.Y.) Adult Edn., 1988-95. Chair, treas. Arts Anon Tools, Forest Hills, 1993—94. Exhibitions include Ceres Gallery, N.Y.C., 1985—87, NYU, 1985, 1988, Emerging Collector, N.Y.C., 1986—, Uptown Mpls. Calhoun Sq., 2002. Support provider Common Link, St. Paul, 2002—; mem. visual arts focus group Twin Cities, Minn., 2003—. Recipient exhbn. support, Artists' Space, 1985, Minn. Work Force Ctr., 2002, assistanceships, DCA, 1985; fellow, Vt. Studio Ctr., 1991. Mem.: Minn. Artist Orgn., Art Initiatives, Orgn. Ind. Artists. Avocations: travel, photography, cooking. Home: 4861 Grenwich Way N Oakdale MN 55128-

NAGLE, JEAN SUSAN KARABACZ, retired sociologist, psychologist; b. Detroit, 1936; d. Peter and Hedy (Grusczynski) Karabacz; m. Robert D. Nagle, Nov. 20, 1956; children: Carl A., Sonya L., Paula E. BS in Sociology, Wayne State U., 1956; postgrad., U. Chgo., 1953-55; MA, N.Mex. Highlands U., 1960; PhD, Union Grad. Sch., 1977; postgrad., Bryn Mawr. Inst., 1981. Diagnostic technician Vocat. Counseling Inst., Detroit, 1952; rsch. technician United Auto Workers-CIO, Detroit, 1958; clin. psychology intern N.Mex. State Hosp., Las Vegas, 1962-63; clin. psychology trainee VA Hosp., Omah and Lincoln, Nebr., 1963-64; instr. sociology N.W. Mo. State U., Maryville, 1965-70, prof. sociology and psychology, 1971-92, ret., 1992. Bd. dirs. Inst. Discourse. Grantee N.W. Mo. State U., 1981, 82. Mem. APA, Am. Sociol. Assn., Am. Psychol. Soc., Midwest Sociol. Soc., Psychology/Sociology Club, Mo. Psychol. Assn., World Federalists, Psi Chi, Pi Gamma Mu. also: 3106 E 80th St Kansas City MO 64132-3638

NAGORKA, STEFANIE, artist; b. Munich, Mar. 26, 1954; d. Henry Jozef and Diane Helen (Suchoff) N; children: Adam, Michelle. BFA, Pratt Inst., 1974, MFA, 1979. Bd. dirs. Visual AIDS, N.Y.C. Exhibits include The Drawing Ctr., N.Y.C., 1991, Information Gallery, N.Y.C., 1993-94, N.J. State Mus., Trenton, 1994, Sculpture Ctr. Gallery, N.Y.C., 1995, Addison Gallery Am. Art, 1997, Debs & Co., N.Y.C., 2002; works in permanent collections Bklyn. Mus., Fogg Art Mus., Yale U. Art Gallery, Fields Sculpture Pack, Ghent, N.Y., Ark. Art Ctr., Little Rock, N.J. State Mus., Treuton. Mem. Mus. Modern Art. Recipient Excellence award David Adler Cultural Ctr., 1992; grantee Artists Space. Home: 22 Saint Lukes Pl Apt 37 Montclair NJ 07042-2159

NAGRA, PARMINDER, actress; b. Leicester, England, Oct. 5, 1975; Actor: (films) Bend It Like Beckham, 2002, Ella Enchanted, 2004; (TV series) Turning World, 1996, Always and Everyone, 1999, ER, 2003—; (TV films) King Girl, 1996, Donovan Quick, 1999, Twelfth Night, 2003, Second Generation, 2003.

NAGY, DONNA M., dean, law educator; BA, Vassar Coll., 1986; JD cum laude, NYU Sch. Law, 1989. Assoc. Debevoise & Plimpton, Washington, DC, 1989—94; asst. prof. U. Cin. Sch. Law, 1994—98, assoc. prof., 1998—99, prof., 1999—2001, Charles Hartsock Prof. Law, 2001—, assoc. dean faculty devel., 2002—04, interim dean, 2004—. Vis. prof. law U. Ill. Coll. Law, Urbana-Champaign, 2001; vis. scholar U. Canterbury Sch. Law, New Zealand, 2002. Co-author: Ferrara on Insider Trading and the Wall, 1995, 2002, Securities Litigation and Enforcement: Cases and Materials, 2003; contbr. articles to law jours. Recipient Howard C. Schott Publ. Prize, 2002, 2003; Order of Coif. Mem.: ABA (mem. sec. Bus. Law), Am. Assn. Law Schs. (sec. Bus. Assns., Securties Regulation, and Women in Legal Edn.), Soc. Am. Law Tchrs., ACLU, Vassar Club of Cin. (Alumni Appointments Chair 1995—99). Office: U Cin Coll Law Clifton Ave & Calhoun St Cincinnati OH 45221-0040 Office Phone: 513-556-0113. E-mail: donna.nagy@law.uc.edu.

NAGY, ELIZABETH GARVER, artist; b. Martinsville, Ill., Jan. 14, 1928; d. Ralph Tibbs and Evelyn Fasig Garver; m. William Roger Achleman (dec.); children: Shelly Marth, Todd Jeffrey; m. Stephen Michael Nagy (dec.); children: Stephanie Nagy-Agren, Patricia Nagy Adelman. Degree in art, Studio Sch. Advt. Art, Cin., 1948. Illustrator Wolf & Dessauer, Ft. Wayne, Ind., 1949—51; freelance illustrator Ft. Wayne, 1951—; art instr. Springfield (Ohio) Art Ctr., 1968—77, Fine Line Creative Arts Ctr., St. Charles, Ill., 1986—92. Presenter in field. One-woman shows include Mountainlair Gallery, W.Va. U., Morgantown, W.Va., 1974, Clay N Caboodle Cadence, Geneva, Ill., 1993, 1993, Transylvania County Arts Ctr., Brevard, N.C., 1999, many others, numerous group shows including most recently, exhibited in group shows at Schumacher Gallery, Columbus, Ohio, 1975, Old State Capitol Galleries, Baton Rouge, La., 1976, 1978, 1979, Greenhill, Woodmere Gallery, 1976—90, Phila. Civic Ctr., 1976—90, Port History Mus., Phila., 1976—90, Tweed Mus., Duluth, Minn., 1978, Bahr-West Mus., Manitowoe, Wis., 1979, Davenport Art Mus., Iowa, 1983, Transylvania County Arts Coun. Gallery 7, Brevard, 1996, 1997, Transylvania County Arts Ctr., Brevard, 1999—2005, many others, Represented in permanent collections Time Temporary, Ft. Wayne, Kane County Jud. Ctr., Geneva, Bankers Club Worldwide Ho., Taipei, Taiwan, Springfield (Ohio) Art Mus., many others. Sec., bd. dirs. Springfield Art Ctr., 1969—76; mem. visual arts com. Dellora A. Norris Cultural Arts Ctr., St. Charles, 1980—88. Recipient award of excellence, Midwest Watercolor Soc., 1983, 3d award, 41st Ann. Artists Guild of Chgo., 1983, award of merit, The Anderson (Ind.) Fine Arts Ctr., 1988. Mem.: Phila. Water Color Soc. (hon. life), Transparent Watercolor Soc. Am. (signature), Watercolor West (signature), Western Ohio Watercolor Soc. (founder, 1st pres.). Avocations: creating wearable art, knitting, weaving, sewing, embroidery.

NAGY-HARTNACK, LOIS ANN, art educator; b. Elizabeth, N.J., June 12, 1949; d. Charles and Helen (Kosztyn) Nagy; children: Rebecca Ann, Amanda Noelle. BA Art Edn., Wagner Coll., 1971; MA Art Edn., Kean U., 1977; MA Counseling Psychology Art Therapy Specialization, Caldwell Coll., 2004. Cert. elem. tchr., art tchr., lic. assoc.counselor, NJ. Art educator Kingsway Regional H.S., Swedesboro, NJ, 1971—72, Woodbridge Twp. Bd. Edn., NJ, 1972—. Sea scout Boy Scouts Am. Mem. AAUW, NATE, Am. Art Therapy Assn., N.J. Art Therapy Assn., Art Educators N.J., N.J. Counseling Assn., N.J. Edn. Assn., Woodbridge Edn. Assn., Morris Mus., Newark Mus., Inst. Arts and Scis., Coun. Arts and Humanities S.I, Edison Soc. for the Arts. Avocations: painting, gardening, cooking, boating, making jewelry. Home: 39 Wick Dr Fords NJ 08863-1406 Office: Woodbridge Twp Bd Edn School St Woodbridge NJ 07095 E-mail: lois2524@verizon.net.

NAGYS, ELIZABETH ANN, environmental services administrator, educator; b. St. Louis; d. Dallas and Miriam (Miller) Nichols; m. Sigi Nagys, Feb. 7, 1970; children: Eric M., Jennifer R., Alex E. BS., So. Ill. U. Extenstion, Edwardsville, 1970. Cert. tchr., Mo., Ill. Announcer Sta. KMTY, Clovis, N.Mex., 1970-71; substitue tchr. Ritneour Sch. Dist., Overland, Mo., 1977-78; instr. biology, environ. issues Southwestern Mich. Coll., Dowagiac, Mich., 1988-92; exec. v.p. Profl. Sound Designers, Goshen, Ind., 1994-96; customer svc. coord. Meijer, Inc., 1995-96; constrn. adminstr. Trans Eastern Homes, Weston, Fla., 1997—98, Trafalger Assocs., 1998—99. Reviewer textbooks Harcourt, Brace & Co., 1993; notary pub. State of Fla., 1999—. Active Nat. Arbor Day Found.; hazardous waste com. Elkhart County, Ind., 1991—94; asst. dir. South Fla. Folk Festival, 1998—2003, dir., 2003—04; bd. dirs. United Meth. Ch., Marvin Park, 1979—84; coord. United Meth. Women, 1980—87; bd. dirs., corr. sec. Broward Folk Club, 1998—2004; charter mem. Holocaust Meml. Mus.; assoc. mem. Art Inst. Chgo. Mem. AAUW (v.p. Goshen 1994-96), Nat. Audubon Soc., Nat. Women's History Mus. (charter mem.), Sierra Club, Welcome Wagon Club. Avocations: reading, gardening.

NAHRA, LYNDA, bank executive; Gard., Calf. Western U., Pacific Coast Banking School. Various positions Bank of America; management Community West Bank, Goleta, Calif., 1997—, pres., CEO, 2000—. Dir. Women's Economic Ventures. Office: c/o Community West Bank 5827 Hollister Avenue Goleta CA 93117*

NAIL, KATHY SUE See CAPSHAW, KATE

NAIMAN, ADELINE LUBELL, educational administrator; b. Boston, Oct. 27, 1925; d. Joseph and Jennie Rachel (Samuel) Lubell; m. Mark Lewis Naiman, July 3, 1947; children: Joris, Alaric, P. Kieron. BA, Radcliffe Coll., 1946. Editor Little, Brown Co., Boston, 1945-48; freelance script writer Coronet Films, Chgo., 1948-51; freelance editor J.B. Lippincott Co., Phila., 1954-57, Beacon Press, Boston, 1964-65; editor-in-chief Elem. Sci. Study, Newton, Mass., 1964-71; dir. publs., asst. to pres. Edn. Devel. Ctr., Newton, 1970-79; mng. dir. Tech. Edn. Rsch. Ctrs., Cambridge, Mass., 1979-82; software dir. Human Rels. Media, Pleasantville, N.Y., 1982-88; dir. publs. Nat. Scis. Resources Ctr., Washington, 1988; dir. edn. The Computer Mus., Boston, 1988-90; acad. dir. Mass. Corp. for Edn. Telecommunications, Cambridge, 1990-94. Trustee Lesley Coll., Cambridge, Mass., 1975—; vice-chair Mass. Ednl. Tech. Adv. Coun.; editl. bd. Science Education and Technology. Co-author: Practical Guide to Computers for Administrators, 1985; author: Microcomputers in Education: An Introduction, 1981; contbg. editor BCS Update, Personal Computing; contbr. articles to profl. jours. Mem. Mass. Bilingual Adv. Coun., 1971—83; bd. mem. Lincoln Disabilities Commn.; bd. dir. Mus. Inst. Teaching Sci.; bd. dirs. Met. Boston YWCA, 1977—82; mem. Radcliffe Alumnae Recogntion Awards Com. Home: 1 Moccasin Hl Lincoln MA 01773-4508 E-mail: adeline@nalman.net.

NAIR, LAURA, music educator; d. John Henry and Elizabeth Richards Nair. MusB, Ohio Wesleyan U., Delaware, 1973. Music tchr. Saratoga Springs City Schs., NY, 1973—; coord. music ministries Shenendehowa United Meth. Ch., Clifton Park, NY, 1979—. Music camp dir. Skye Farm Camps, Warrensburg, NY, 1976—2006. Nominating com. mem. Troy Ann. Conf., United Meth.

Ch., Saratoga Springs. Mem.: NY State United Tchrs., Choristers' Guild, Fellowship of United Methodists in Music and Worship Arts, Am. Choral Dirs.' Assn., Music Educators' Nat. Conf., Chi Omega (rush chairperson 1972—73). Methodist. Avocations: travel, golf, swimming. Home: 10A Greensboro Blvd Clifton Park NY 12065 Office: Greenfield Elementary School 3180 Route 9N Greenfield Center NY 12065 Office Phone: 518-893-7402. Office Fax: 518-893-7408. Business E-Mail: lnair@saratogaschools.org.

NAIR, MIRA, film director, film producer; b. Bhubaneshwar, Orissa, India, Oct. 15, 1957; m. Mahmood Mamdani; 1 child, Zohran. Student, U. New Delhi, Harvard U. Dir., prodr. (films) Salaam Bombay, 1988 (Camera d'Or and Prix du Publique, Cannes Film Festival, Acad. Award nominee for Best Fgn. Lang. Film), Mississippi Masala, 1991 (three awards at Venice Film Festival), Kama Sutra: A Tale of Love, 1996, Monsoon Wedding, 2001 (Golden Lion Award, Venice Film Festival); dir. only (films) Jama Masjid Street Journal, 1979, So Far From India, 1982, The Perez Family, 1995, September 11, 2002, Vanity Fair, 2004; prodr. only (films) Still, the Children Are Here, 2004; dir. (TV movies) India Cabaret, 1985 (American Film Festival Award for Best Documentary of 1985), Children of a Desired Sex, 1987, My Own Country, 1998, The Laughing Club of India, 1999, Hysterical Blindness, 2002. Office: Mirabi Films Inc 5 E 16th St 12th Fl New York NY 10003

NAJARIAN, CHERYL ANN, exercise physiology educator; b. Lawrence, Mass., Nov. 23, 1959; d. Peggy and Harry Najarian. BS, Plymouth State Coll., 1981; A in Fitness Tech., NH Tech. Coll., 1991; MS, Northeastern U., Boston, 1997. Educator Mt. St. Mary H.S., Nashua, NH, 1985—92, Bishop Guertin H.S., Nashua, NH, 1992—; adj. faculty Middlesex C.C., Lowell, Mass., 1999—. Athletic dir. Mt. St. Mary H.S., Nashua, NH, 1987—92; health & fitness dept. head Bishop Guertin H.S., Nashua, NH, 1993—. Mem.: Am. Coll. of Sports Medicine. Achievements include Completed 17 Marathons. Home: 11 Bowman Ln Pelham NH 03076 Office: Bishop Guertin HS 194 Lund Rd Nashua NH 03060-4398 Office Phone: 1.603.889.4107. Office Fax: 1.603.889.0701. E-mail: najarianc@bghs.org.

NAJIMY, KATHY, actress; Actress theater The Kathy and Mo Show, 1985-89 (also writer)(Obie award, 1989), Afterbirth: Kathy and Mo's Greatest Hits, 2004; Broadway shows Dirty Blonde, 2001; films Topsy and Bunker, Other People's Money, 1991, The Hard Way, 1991, The Fisher King, 1991, Soapdish, 1991, This Is My Life, 1992, Sister Act, 1992, Hocus Pocus, 1993, Sister Act 2: Back in the Habit, 1993, It's Pat, 1994, Jeffrey, 1995, Cats Dont' Dance, 1997, Nevada, 1997, Woman Without Implants, 1997, Hope Floats, 1998, Zack and Reba, 1998, Bride of Chucky, 1998, Attention Shoppers, 2000, Leaving Peoria, 2000, The Wedding Planner, 2001, Rat Race, 2001; TV: King of the Hill (voice), 1997-, Veronica's Closet, 1997-2001; TV movies: If These Walls Could Talk II, 2000, The Scream Team, 2002. Office: Creative Arts Agy 9830 Wilshire Blvd Beverly Hills CA 90212-1804

NAJJAR, DIANA, elementary school educator; d. Carl and Mary Snider; children: David, Mark. BS in Elem. Edn., Ball State U., 1970; MS in Edn. with concentration in Spl. Edn., Ind. U.-Purdue U., Indpls., 1977; postgrad. in gifted edn., Purdue U., 1981—83. Cert. elem. edn. tchr. Ind. Dept. Edn. Tchr. Indpls. Pub. Schs., 1970—72, The Orchard Sch., Indpls., 1984—. Gov.'s sch. task group State Dept. of Ind., 1984—86; creator dance curriculum; dance instr., choreographer sch. musicals, plays, operettas; screenwriter, actress Factor Blocks math video, 1999. Author: (book and math. kit) Namagram, 1997; author, actress: video Factor Blocks, 1999. Catechism coach St. George Ch., Indpls., 1989—95, 2005—06. Mem.: Ind. Assn. for the Gifted (legis. team 2005—05, legis. chmn. 1979—88, Svc. award 1985). Achievements include discovery of 4 set Venn diagram; created test to measure conceptual understanding of mathematical concepts through constructions; copywright Namagram book and design. Office: The Orchard Sch 615 W 64th St Indianapolis IN 46260

NAJM, TAMI LYNN, music educator; b. Cairo, Nasr City, Egypt, June 16, 1981; d. Ahmad Shafik and Joy Dennis Najm. MusB, Barry U., 2003. Cert. K-12 music tchr. Fla. Music instr. Carol City (Fla.) Elem. Sch., 2004, North County Elem. Sch., Miami Gardens, Fla., 2004—. Musician: (concert) Carnegie Hall, 2006. Named Rookie Tchr. of Yr., North County Elem. Sch., 2005. Mem.: NEA, Am. Fedn. of Teachers, Fla. Music Edn. Assn. Baptist. Avocations: travel, volleyball, choral performances. Office: Mirror Lake Elem Sch 1200 NW 72nd Ave Plantation FL 33313 Office Phone: 305-624-9648. Home Fax: NA; Office Fax: 305-620-2372, 754-322-7140. Personal E-mail: prncez637@comcast.net. Business E-Mail: tami.najm@browardschools.com.

NAKAI, TANYA B., music educator; b. Lewiston, N.Y., Apr. 6, 1975; d. Gerald W. and Sandra F. Iulg; m. Ryan A. Nakai, July 8, 2000; children: Lindsay R., Drew T. MusB, Houghton Coll., N.Y., 1997. Cert. tchr. N.J., 1997. Asst. band dir. and substitute music tchr. Cumberland Regional H.S., Seabrook, NJ, 1997—98; music tchr. Upper Deerfield Twp Schs., 1997—. Named Tchr. of Yr., Upper Deerfield Twp Schs., 2003. Mem.: Music Educators Nat. Conf. Home: 7 Amy Ct Millville NJ 08332 Office: Upper Deerfield Twp Schs 1373 State Hwy 77 Seabrook NJ 08302 Office Phone: 856-455-2267. E-mail: nakait@udts.org.

NAKAMURA, KIMIKO, language educator; b. Fukui-Ken, Japan, Feb. 11, 1945; arrived in USA, 1966; d. Toshiji and Emiko Matsumura; m. Takamitsu Nakamura, Jan. 22, 1966; children: Takashi, Yoko. BM, Osaka Coll. Music, Japan, 1966; MusB, DePaul U., 1993; MusM, Valparaiso U., 1996. Japanese tchr. Inland/EastPack Co., Ea. Chgo., 1987—. Piano instr. O'Day Music Sch., Highland, Ind., 1999—. Mem.: Nat. Guild Piano Tchrs., Japan-Am. Soc. (Japanese lang. tchr. 1996—). Office: Japan America Soc Chgo 20 N Clark St Ste 750 Chicago IL 60602

NAKASHIMA, JOANNE PUMPHREY, retired education administrator; b. Broseley, Mo., Feb. 3, 1937; d. Walter and Ola A. (Keener) Pumphrey; m. Christian A. Tirre, Aug. 15, 1959 (div. 1983); 1 foster child, Gary L. Wycuff; m. Masao Nakashima, Dec. 31, 1983; stepchildren: Cathy Reando, Lisa Nakashima. BS in Edn., S. E. Mo. U., Cape Girardeau, 1959; MEd, Miami U., Oxford, Ohio, 1963. Elem Tchr., Sch. Counselor, Sch. Adminstr. Tchr. Green Valley Sch., Ind., 1959-60, Shawnee Sch. System, Camden, Ohio, 1960-62; tchr./counselor Columbus Pub. Sch., Columbus, Ohio, 1962—70; tchr. Eleele Elem. Sch., Eleele, Hawaii, 1970-71, Kaumakani Elem. Sch., Kaumakani, Hawaii, 1971-76; coun. vice prin. Kauai High and Waimea High, Lihue, Waimea, Hawaii, 1976-79; prin. Eleele Elem. Sch., Eleele, HI, 1983-86; dist. ednl. specialist Kauai Dist., Lihue, Hawaii, 1979-83, 1986—2000, dir. sch. based mental health svcs., 2000—03; ret. Part time instr. U. Hawaii, Kauai Site, 1972-75; trainer of facilitative leadership, Dept. of Edn., Kauai, 1990-96; edn. cons. for Hawaii State Sen. Gary Hooser, 2003—. Author: Baptist Materials, International Christian Endea. Dem. party chair County of Kauai, Hawaii, 1982-84; v.p. Kauai Chorale; co-chairperson Com. to Elect Senator Akaka, Kauai, 1990-91; pres. Hawaii Conf. United Ch. of Christ, 1984-85. Recipient Adminstr. of Year, High Sch. Counselors Assn., Top Ten Freshman, S.E. Mo. U. Mem. Hawaii Govt. Employee Assn., Hawaii Sch. Counselors Assn., Child and Family Svc., Kauai Concert Assn. (bd. dirs., sec.), Delta Kappa Gamma (pres. Eta chpt., 2d v.p. Beta Beta state, pres.).Kauai Concert Assn. (bd. mem.), Storybook Theatre (bd. sec., trea.). Democrat. Avocations: singing, piano, reading, computers. Home: PO Box 965 Kalaheo HI 96741-0965

NAKAYAMA, PAULA AIKO, state supreme court justice; b. Honolulu, Oct. 19, 1953; m. Charles W. Totto; children: Elizabeth Murakami, Alexander Totto. BS, U. Calif., Davis, 1975; JD, U. Calif., 1979. Bar: Hawaii 1979. Dep. pros. atty. City and County of Honolulu, 1979-82; ptnr. Shim, Tam & Kirimitsu, Honolulu, 1982-92; judge 1st Cir. Ct. State of Hawaii, Oahu, 1992-93; assoc. justice Hawaii Supreme Ct., Honolulu, 1993—. Mem. Am. Judicature Soc., Hawaii Bar Assn., Sons and Daughters of 442. Office: Hawaii Supreme Ct Ali'iolani Hale 417 S King St Honolulu HI 96813-2902*

NAKER, MARY LESLIE, legal firm executive; b. Elgin, Ill., July 6, 1954; d. Robert George and Marilyn Jane (Swain). BS in Edn., No. Ill. U., 1976, MS in Edn., 1978, postgrad., 1980, Coll. Fin. Planning, 1990. Cert. tchr., Ill., fin. paraplanner. Retail sales clk. Fin'n Feather Farm, Dundee, Ill., 1972-75; pvt. practice tchr. South Elgin, Ill., 1974-78; tchg. asst. Sch. Dist #13, Bloomingdale, Ill., 1976-78, substitute tchr.; office mgr. Tempo 21, Carol Stream, Ill., 1978-82, LaGrange, Ill., 1982-85; sales coord. K&R Delivery, Hinsdale, Ill., 1986-89; fin. planner coord. Elite Adv. Svcs., Inc., Schaumburg, Ill., 1989-90; adminstrv. coord. Export Transports, Inc., Elk Grove Village, Ill., 1990-98; adminstrn. mgr. SBS Worldwide Chgo. Inc., Bensenville, Ill., 1998-99; office adminstr. DiMonte & Lizak, Attys. at Law, Park Ridge, Ill., 2000—. Leader Girl Scouts U.S.A., 1972—77, camp counselor, 1972—79; Sunday sch. tchr., 1999—. Music Scholar PTA, U. Wis., 1967, PTA, U. Iowa, 1968-69. Mem. Nat. Geographic Soc., Smithsonian Assn. Lutheran. Avocations: ceramics, bowling, knitting, camping, sewing. Home: 2020 Clearwater Way Elgin IL 60123-2588 Office: DiMonte & Lizak 216 Higgins Rd Park Ridge IL 60068-5706

NAKHIMOVSKY, ALICE STONE, foreign language educator; b. Bklyn., Mar. 19, 1950; d. Morton Dramin and Dorothy (Hershkowitz) Stone; m. Alexander David Nakhimovsky, Aug. 27, 1974; children: Isaac, Sharon. AB, Cornell U., 1971, PhD, 1975. Asst. prof. Russian Colgate U., Hamilton, N.Y., 1976-82, assoc. prof. Russian, 1982-91, prof. Russian, 1991—, chair dept., 1989—. Author: Laughter in the Void, 1981, Russian-Jewish Literature and Identity, 1992; co-author: Beginning Russian Vol. I, 1981, Vol. II, 1982, 2d edit., 1991; editor: The Semiotics of Russian Cultural History, 1985. Fellow NEH, 1986-87, 95, Meml. Found. for Jewish Culture, 1988-89; Internat. Rsch. and Exch. Bd. grantee, 1988, 94. Mem. Am. Assn. Advancement of Slavic Studies, Am. Assn. Tchrs. Slavic and East European Langs., Nat. Assn. Scholars. Office: Modern Lang Dept Colgate U Hamilton NY 13346

NAKHLE, DJENANE, psychologist; b. Cairo, Oct. 9, 1945; came to U.S., 1981; children: Joëlle, Sabrina. BA in Psychology cum laude, NYU, 1988, MA in Psychology, 1992, PhD in Child and Sch. Psychology, 1995. Lic. psychologist, N.Y.; cert. sch. psychologist, N.Y. Staff psychologist Special Needs Clinic Columbia-Presbyn. Med. Ctr., 1994-95, supervising staff psychologist Special Needs Clinic, 1995-97, dir. therapeutics, 1997-98, supervising psychologist dept. pediatric psychiatry, 1998, 1998—; supervising psychologist N.Y. Hosp.-Cornell Med. Ctr., 1998; cons. St. Luke's-Roosevelt Hosp. Ctr., Global Comm. Svcs., Inc., N.Y. Devel. Cons.; asst. clin. prof. med. psychology in psychiatry Columbia U. Coll. of Physicians and Surgeons. Adj. asst. clin. prof. applied psychology NYU Sch. of Edn. Contbr. articles to profl. jours. Rsch. fellowship Dept. of Health and Human Svcs., 1992. Mem. Soc. of Practitioners of the Columbia-Presbyn. Med. Ctr., Am. Psychol. Assn., Nat. Assn. of Sch. Psychologists, N.Y. Assn. of Sch. Psychologists, Internat. Soc. for Prevention of Child Abuse and Neglect, Am. Profl. Soc. on the Abuse of Children. Office: 815 Park Ave New York NY 10021-3276 E-mail: NakhleD@aol.com.

NAKONECZNYJ, NADIA, marketing professional; b. Cleve., Dec. 22, 1976; d. Gene and Brenda Jane Nakoneczny. BA, Hiram Coll., Ohio, 1999. Legis. intern Legis. Svc. Commn., Columbus, Ohio, 1999—2000; admissions counselor Coll. Wooster, Ohio, 2000—02; mktg., recruiting specialist Lorain County C.C., Elyria, Ohio, 2002—. Coach volleyball Lorain County C.C., 2002—; coach Sokol Ceska Sin Gymnastics, Cleve, 2002—; mem. Westshore Chorale, Cleve, 2002—. Mem.: Ohio Assn. Coll. Admissions Counselors (chair Govt. Rels. Com. 2005—), Am. Sokol Orgn. (dir. edn. 2004—06, dir. women 2005—). Avocations: volleyball, gymnastics, music. Office: Lorain County Cmty Coll 1005 N Abbe Rd Elyria OH 44035 E-mail: nakoneczny j@hotmail.com.

NAMBIAR, PRABHA, science educator; b. Tellicherry, Kerala, India, Dec. 10, 1945; arrived in U.S., 1984; d. Narayan and Rukminkamma Nambiar; m. Efrain Molina, Mar. 21, 2003; children: Alex Papali, Harry Papali, Fred Papali. BSc, Nirmala Coll., Coimbature, India; BEd, Bhopal U., India; EdM, Harvard U., Boston; MA, Tufts U., Boston. Tchr. Ctrl. Sch. Mumbai, India; tchr. sci./math. Park Sch., Brookline, Mass., head sci. dept., tchr. sci. Grantee Horizon grant, Park Sch., 2003. Mem.: NSTA. Catholic. Avocations: travel, reading, gardening. Home: 3 Roundhill St Jamaica Plain MA 02130 Business E-Mail: prabha_nambiar@parkschool.org.

NANAGAS, MARIA TERESITA CRUZ, pediatrician, educator; b. Manila, Jan. 21, 1946; arrived in U.S., 1970; d. Ambrosio and Maria (Pasamonte) Cruz; m. Victor N. Nanagas, Jr.; children: Victor III, Valerie, Vivian. BS, U. of the Philippines, 1965, MD, 1970. Diplomate Am. Bd. Pediat. Intern, resident St. Elizabeth's Hosp., Boston, 1971-74; fellow in ambulatory pediat. North Shore Children's Hosp., Salem, Mass., 1974-75; active staff medicine Children's Med. Ctr., Dayton, Ohio, 1976—, head divsn. gen. pediat., 1988-90, 95-97, co-interim head ambulatory pediat., 1989-90, med. dir. ambulatory pediat., 1990—. Clin. asst. prof. pediat. Wright State U., Dayton, 1977-83, clin. assoc. prof. pediat., 1983—, selective dir., 1989—, assoc. prof. pediat., 2000—; clin. asst. prof. family practice Wright State U., Dayton, 1999—; dir., preceptor Wright State U. residents continuing clinic Children's Med. Ctr., 1989—, attending physician family practice programs, 1978—. Active Miami Valley Lead Poisoning Prevention Coalition, 19926. Fellow Am. Acad. Pediat.; mem. Western Ohio Pediat. Soc., Ambulatory Pediat. Assn. Office: Children's Med Ctr Health Clinic 1 Childrens Plz Dayton OH 45404-1898 Office Phone: 937-641-3500.

NANCE, BETTY LOVE, librarian; b. Nashville, Oct. 29, 1923; d. Granville Scott and Clara (Mills) N. BA in English magna cum laude, Trinity U., 1957; MLS, U. Mich., 1958. Head dept. acquisitions Stephen F. Austin U. Libr., Nacogdoches, Tex., 1958-59; libr. 1st Nat. Bank, Ft. Worth, 1959-61; head catalog dept. Trinity U., San Antonio, 1961-63; head tech. processes U. Tex. Law Libr., Austin, 1963-66; head catalog dept. Tex. A&M U. Libr., College Station, 1966-69; chief bibliographic svcs. Washington U. Libr., St. Louis, 1970; head dept. acquisitions Va. Commonwealth U. Libr., Richmond, 1971-73; head tech. processes Howard Payne U. Libr., Brownwood, Tex., 1974-79; libr. dir. Edinburg (Tex.) Pub. Libr., 1980-91. Pres. Edinburg Com. Salvation Army. Mem. ALA, Pub. Libr. Assn., Tex. Libr. Assn., Hidalgo County Libr. Assn. (v.p. 1980-81, pres. 1981-82), Pan Am. Round Table Edinburg (corr. sec. 1986-88, assoc. dir. 1989-90), Edinburg Bus. and Profl. Womens Club (founding bd. dirs., pres. 1986-87, bd. dirs. 1987-88), Zonta (bd. dirs. West Hidalgo Club, 1986-88, San Antonio 1996-97), Alpha Lambda Delta, Alpha Chi. Methodist. Home: The Forum at Lincoln Heights 311 Nottingham W Apt 301 San Antonio TX 78209-1828

NANCE, MARIONE E., biology educator; b. Tuscaloosa, Ala., May 27, 1951; d. Francis Elmond and Ella Lucinda (Dunning) Evans; m. Thomas Stanley Nance; children: Gwen Lucinda, Frances Marione. M in Biology, Samford U., Homewood, Ala., 1977. Instr. biology dept. Samford U., 1973—. Senate chmn., faculty pres., com. mem. numerous univ., coll. and departmental coms. Samford U. Vol. spokesman, asst. to veterinarian Birmingham (Ala.) Zoo, 1980—82; vol. tchr. microbiology and dissection local elem. and high schs., Homewood, Mountain Brook, and Bessemer, Ala., 1991—95; club pres., dist. sgt.-at-arms Toastmaster's Internat., Birmingham, 1981—82. Mem.: DNA Methylation Soc., Ala. Acad. Sci., Am. Bryological and Lichenological Soc., Am. Soc. Microbiology, Beta Beta Beta. Achievements include first bio-disaster drill resulting in written protocols for first responders. Avocations: reading, travel, singing, speaking. Office: Samford U Biology Dept 800 Lakeshore Dr Homewood AL 35209-2234 Office Phone: 205-726-2303. E-mail: menance@samford.edu.

NANCE, MARY JOE, retired secondary school educator; b. Carthage, Tex., Aug. 7, 1921; d. F.F. and Mary Elizabeth (Knight) Born; m. Earl C. Nance, July 12, 1946; 1 child, David Earl. BBA, North Tex. State U., 1953; postgrad., Northwestern State U. La., 1974; ME, Antioch U., Seattle, 1978. Cert. bus. educator. Tchr. Port Isabel (Tex.) Ind. Sch. Dist., 1953-79; tchr. English Tex., 1965, Splendora (Tex.) H.S., 1979-80, McLeod, Tex., 1980-81, Bremond, Tex., 1981-84; ret., 1985. Vol. tchr. for Indian students, 1964—65; vol. tutor, tchr. ESL; active WAAC, 1942—43, WAC, 1945. Recipient Image Maker award Carthage C. of C., 1984; named on Meml. for Women, Washington. Mem. NEA, Tex. Tchrs. Assn., Tex. Bus. Tchrs. Assn. (Cert. of Appreciation 1978), Nat. Women's Army Corps Vets. Assn., Air Force Assn. (life), Gwinnett Hist. Soc., Hist. Soc. Panola County, Panola County Hist. & Geneal. Assn., Nat. Hist. Soc. Baptist.

NANCE, STARLYNN R., academic counselor; d. Charles Edwin Nance and Linda Wilson. AAS, Rose State Coll., Midwest City, Okla., 1994; EdB, U. Ctrl. Okla., Edmond, 1998; EdM, U. Okla., Norman, 2005. Dance tchr. Connie's Sch. Dance, Moore, Okla., 1991—; optometry asst. Dr. Jon E. Painter, Moore, 1994—2005; tchr. Noble H.S., Okla., 1998—2005; academic counselor U. Okla., Norman, 2006—. Named Tchr. of Yr., Noble H.S., 2005. Mem.: NACADA/OCADA. Republican. Episcopalian. Avocations: reading, travel, dance. Office: University of Oklahoma Rm 100 650 Parrington Oval Norman OK 73071 Office Phone: 405-325-3521.

NAND, SUCHA, medical educator; b. Thiriewal, Punjab, India, Feb. 3, 1948; d. Narsingh Dass and Swaran Devi; m. Surinder S. Nand, June 15, 1973; children: Ranveer, Rahul. Pre-med. student, Dayanand Ayur Vedic Coll., Amritsar, India, 1966; MB, BS, Med. Coll., Amritsar, India, 1971. Diplomate Am. Bd. Internal Medicine, Am. Bd. Hemotology, Am. Bd. Med. Oncology. Asst. prof. Stritch Sch. Medicine Loyola U., Maywood, Ill., 1981-88, assoc. prof. Stritch Sch. Medicine, 1989-95; prof. medicine, 1996—. Editor Jour. of Med. Coll., 1969-71; contbr. articles to profl. jours. Clin. fellow Am. Cancer Soc., 1981; Brilliant Student scholarships, 1962-71. Mem. Am. Soc. Hematology, Am. Soc. Clin. Oncology, S.W. Oncology Group (mem. leukemia com. 1988—). Avocations: chess, reading, running. Office: Loyola Univ Med Ctr 2160 S 1st Ave Maywood IL 60153-3304 Office Phone: 708-327-3182.

NANKERVIS, MEDORA B., artist; b. L.A., Oct. 5, 1925; d. Granville Harrison and Sylvia (Tolman) Pierson; m. William Melvin Nankervis, May 9, 1957 (dec. 1995); children: Craig Melvin, Sylvia Kay, Michael Scott. Grad. high sch., Ashland, Oreg. Bookkeeper Pierson Prodn., Lynwood, South Gate, Calif., 1940-50's, Map Brass Products, Lynwood, South Gate, 1940-50's; co-operator Pierson Brass Foundry, South Gate, 1950's, Sunset Beach Airport, Huntington Beach, Calif., 1955-57; bookkeeper Wm. Nankervis Bldg. Contractors, Garden Grove, Calif., 1958-67; operator, owner Sunnyside Cattle and Guest Ranch, Rogue River, Oreg., 1968-76, May Hill Tree and Art Farm, Rogue River, 1987—2000. Workshop instr., so. Oreg., 1970's-80's. One-woman shows include Kunes Gallery, San Francisco, Calif., 2001, Grants Pass Mus. Art, 2002. Founder Woodville Fine Arts Assn. and Gallery, Rogue River, 1968-88; mem. founding bd. Grants Pass (Oreg.) Mus. Art, 1979—, chair bd., 2001—; founder Women Artists Cascades, Oreg., 1982—, Hillary Rodham Clinton Fan Club, 1995-2000, Great We Artists Retreats; mem. Josephine County, Cultural Trust. Named Champion of Arts, Rogue Valley Women's Caucus, 2002; recipient award, So. Oreg. Arts Coun., 1996, ACLU, 1999; grantee, Art Mall So. Oreg., 2000—04. Mem. Inst. Noetic Scis., Watercolor Soc. Oreg. Independent. Mem. Soc. Of Friends.

NAPADENSKY, HYLA SARANE, engineering consultant; b. Chgo., Nov. 12, 1929; d. Morris and Minnie (Litz) Siegel; m. Arnaldo I. Napadensky; children: Lita, Yafa. BS in Math., MS in Math., U. Chgo. Design analysis engineer Internat. Harvester Co., Chgo., 1952-57; dir. rsch. Ill. Inst. Tech. Rsch. Inst., Chgo., 1957-88; v.p. Napadensky Energetics Inc., Evanston, Ill., 1988-94; engrng. cons., Lutsen, Minn., 1994-98. Contbr. numerous articles to profl. jours. Bd. overseers Armour Coll. Engring. Ill. Inst. Tech., 1988-93. Mem. NAE, Sigma Xi. Home and Office: 3284 W Highway 61 Grand Marais MN 55604-7537

NAPIER, CAMERON MAYSON FREEMAN, historic preservationist; b. Shanghai, Dec. 5, 1931; d. Hamner Garland and Cameron Middleton (Brame) Freeman; m. John Hawkins Napier III, Sept. 11, 1964. Student, L'Ecole des Artes Municipale, Paris, 1950-51, Westhampton Coll./U. Richmond, 1951—53; BA, U. Ala., 1955. Photographer's asst. Scott, Demott & Perry, Montgomery, Ala., 1951; art dir. WCOV-TV, Montgomery, 1955; self-employed graphic designer Dallas, 1956-64; self-employed designer Alexandria, Va., 1965-71; restoration chmn. White House Assn. Ala., Montgomery, 1973-76, 1st vice regent, 1976-80, regent, 1980—. Co-founder Friends of Stratford Hall for No. Va., Alexandria, late 1960s; docent chmn. Lee's Boyhood Home, late 1960s; bd. dirs. Landmarks Found., Montgomery, 1971-75; advisor Conde Charlotte House, Mobile, Ala., 1994-95. Author, designer booklet: The First White House of the Confederacy, 1978 (nat. printers award 1979), The Struggle to Preserve the First White House of the Confederacy, 1982; contbr. to Ency. of So. Culture, 1989, Ency. of Ala.-online, 2006. Bd. dirs. English Speaking Union, Montgomery, 1980-83. Named Hon. First Lady, by the Gov.'s wife, Montgomery, Ala., 1985; recipient Awards of Excellence, Advt. Artists Assn., Dallas, 1960, 1961, 1962, disting. svc. award, Ala. Hist. Commn., Montgomery, 1977, Cert. of Commendation, Gov. Ala., 1986, So. Patriot award, 1997, Lifetime Achievement award, Ala. Preservation Alliance, 2001, Jefferson Davis award, 1984, Winnie Davis award, United Daus. of Confederacy, 1985. Mem.: Antiquarian Soc. (pres. 1981—82), Sojourners Lit. Club (pres.), Order of the Crown in Am., Soc. Descs. of Colonial Clergy, Am. Soc. Most Venerable Order of the Hosp. St. John of Jerusalem (assoc. officer sister 1995, named Comdr. Sister 2002), Nat. Soc. Colonial Dames in Am. (hist. properties com. 1994—95, state bd. mgrs. 1998—2000, ctr. vice chmn. 1998—2000), Daus. of Barons Runnymede, Militi Templi Scotia, Kappa Delta. Episcopalian. Avocations: jumbles, cryptoquotes, crossword puzzles, afternoon tea. Office: First White House Confed 644 Washington St Montgomery AL 36130-3057 Office Phone: 334-242-1861.

NAPIER, LISA BRIGGS, maternal/child health nurse; b. Boulder, Colo., Sept. 6, 1963; d. Thomas David Briggs and Ramona June (Miles) Sheftel; m. David Napier, 1993; children: Alden, Dolan, Rowan. BA in Philosophy, George Mason U., 1989, BSN, 1991; MS in Nursing and Midwifery, Georgetown U., 2003. Staff nurse Washington Hosp. Ctr., 1991-92, Hospice Care of D.C., Washington, 1992-93; occupational health nurse Washington Area Met. Transit Authority, 1993-94; ind. childbirth educator, 1988—2001; instr. anatomy and physiology Fairfax County Adult Edn., 1993-99. Birthing asst., 1994—2001; home sch. group leader Lee Dist. Coop., 2004—, Mt. Vernon, 1998—2004. Vol. Alexandria (Va.) Red Cross, United Cmty. Ministries. Mem. Sigma Theta Tau (Epsilon Zeta chpt.). Avocations: reading, hiking, camping. Home: 6842 Deer Run Dr Alexandria VA 22306-1123

NAPLES, MARY CECILIA, mental health services professional, health facility administrator; b. Ocana, Colombia, Oct. 31, 1954; d. Efrain and Olga (Rodriguez) Pineres; m. Anthony Louis Naples Jr., May 30, 1981; children: Marina Nicole, Alysia Marie. BA, Coll. of Comm. and Fine Arts, 1992, MEd in Counselor Edn., 1994; PhD in Family Therapy, Nova Southeastern U., 2003. Lic. mental health counselor; bd. cert. clin. hypnotherapist; bd. cert sex therapist. Owner, CEO Every Woman's Place, Boca Raton, Fla., 1997-99, Family Life Counseling Ctr., Boca Raton, Fla., 1999—. Mem. ACA (profl.). Roman Catholic. Avocations: movies, connecting with family and friends. Office: Family Life Counseling Ctr 400 S Dixie Hwy Ste 100 Boca Raton FL 33432 E-mail: napleslmhc@aol.com.

NAPOLI, DONNA JO, linguistics educator, writer; b. Miami, Fla., Feb. 28, 1948; d. Vincent Robert and Helen Gloria Napoli; m. Barry Ray Furrow, Dec. 29, 1968; children: Elena, Michael Enzo, Nicholas Umberto, Eva, Robert Emilio. BA in Math., Harvard U., 1970, MA in Italian Lit., 1971, PhD in Gen. and Romance Linguistics, 1973. Instr. Italian Berlitz, Seattle, 1970, Concord (Mass.) Pub. Schs., 1970-72; tchg. fellow dept. linguistics, math. and romance langs. Harvard U., 1970-73; lectr. dept. philosophy, dept. romance langs. and lit. Smith Coll., Northampton, Mass., 1973-74; lectr. dept. math. and dept. romance langs. and lit. U. N.C., Chapel Hill, 1974-75; asst. prof. linguistics Georgetown U., 1975-80, U. Mich., Ann Arbor, 1980-82, assoc. prof., 1982-84, prof., 1984-87; prof., dir. linguistics Swarthmore (Pa.) Coll.,

1987—. Linguistics cons. Ednl. Testing Svc., Princeton, N.J., 1971-72; S.W. Brooks vis. lectr. dept. English U. Queensland, St. Lucia, Australia, summer 1992; instr. First Australian Linguistic Inst., U. Sydney, Australia, 1992, U. Geneva, 1993; vis. prof. English dept. San Francisco State U., summer 1994; vis. lectr. linguistics U. Witwatersrand, Johannesburg, South Africa, summer 1995; prof. Coll. English Tchr. Tng. Inst., summer 1997. Author: The Two si's of Italian: An Analysis of Reflexive, Inchoative, and Indefinite Subject Sentences in Modern Standard Italian, 1976, (with E. Rando) Syntactic Argumentation, 1979, Predication Theory: A Case Study for Indexing Theory, 1989, Syntax: Theory and Problems, 1993, (with S. Davis) Phonological Factors in Historical Change: The Passage of the Latin Second Conjugation into Romance, Linguistics: Theory and Problems, 1996, over 40 fiction books for children; editor: Elements of Tone, Stress, and Intonation, 1978; co-editor: (with J. Kegl) Bridges Between Psychology and Linguistics: A Swarthmore festschrift for Lila Gleitman, 1991; contbr. articles to profl. jours. Recipient Briggs award Radcliffe Coll., 1970; Fulbright-Hays Jr. lectr. in linguistics, Italy, 1974-75, Fulbright-Hays sr. lectr. in linguistics, Italy, 1975-76; NEH fellow, 1979-80, 90-91, Eugene Lang Faculty fellow, 1994-95; grantee Radcliffe Inst., 1970, 72, Nederlandse Organisatie voor Zuiverwetenschappelijk Onderzoek, Amsterdam, 1976, NSF, 1981-83, Rackham Faculty grantee, 1983-84, Sloan Found. grantee, 1988, Curricular Devel. grantee Swarthmore, 1989; scholar Radcliffe Coll., 1966-70. Office: Linguistics Dept Pearson 116 Swarthmore Coll Swarthmore PA 19081 Office Phone: 610-328-8422. E-mail: dnapoli1@swarthmore.edu.*

NAPOLI, MARY, education educator; b. Dover, N.J., Jan. 4, 1969; d. Patrick and Josephine N. BS in Elem. Edn., East Stroudsbourg (Pa.) U., 1991; MS in Reading, Marywood U., 1997; postgrad., Pa. State U. Tchr. K-1st grade Pocono Mountain Sch. Dist., Swiftwater, Pa., 1987-98; asst. prof. dept. edn. Elizabeth Town Coll., 2001—03; asst. prof. Sch. Edn., Pa. State U., Harrisburg, 2003—. Recipient Nat. Writing Project fellow, 1994. Mem. NBGS com., Children's Lit. Assn., Internat. Reading Assn., Nat. Coun. of Tchrs. of English, Kappa Delta Pi., Omicron Delta Kappa. Roman Catholic. Avocations: basketball, reading. Office Phone: 717-948-6725. Business E-Mail: mxn130@psu.edu.

NAPOLITANO, GRACE F., congresswoman; b. Brownsville, Tex., Dec. 4, 1936; d. Miguel and Maria Alicia Ledezma Flores; m. Frank Napolitano, 1982; 1 child, Yolando M., Fred Musquiz Jr., Edward M., Michael M., Cynthia M. Student, Cerritos Coll., L.A. Trade Tech, Tec Southwest Coll. Mem. Calif. Assembly, 1993-98, U.S. Congress from 38th Calif. dist., Washington, 1999—; mem. resources com., sml. bus. com. U.S. Ho. Reps.; mem. Ho. Com. on Internat. Relations. Councilwoman City of Norwalk, Calif., 1986-92, mayor, 1989-90; active Cmty. Family Guidance. Mem. Cerritos Coll. Found., Lions Club. Democrat. Roman Catholic. Office: US Ho Reps 1609 Longworth Ho Office Bldg Washington DC 20515-0538

NAPOLITANO, JANET ANN, governor; b. NYC, Nov. 29, 1957; d. Leonard Michael and Jane Marie (Winer) Napolitano. BS summa cum laude, U. Santa Clara, Calif., 1979; JD, U. Va., 1983. Bar: Ariz. 1984, U.S. Dist. Ct. Ariz. 1984, U.S. Ct. Appeals (9th cir.) 1984, U.S. Ct. Appeals (10th cir.) 1988, U.S. Ct. Appeals (5th cir.), U.S. Ct. Appeals, U.S. Ct. Appeals (7th cir.), U.S. Ct. Appeals (8th cir.). Law clk. to Hon. Mary Schroeder U.S Ct. Appeals 9th Cir., 1983—84; assoc. Lewis & Roca, Phoenix, 1984—89, ptnr., 1989—93; U.S. atty. Dist. Ariz., Phoenix, 1993—97; atty. Lewis and Roca, Phoenix, 1997—98; atty. gen. State of Ariz., Phoenix, 1999—2002, gov., 2003—. Mem. Atty. Gen.'s Adv. Com., 1983—, chair, 1995—96; chair victims rights subcom. Ariz. Criminal Justice Commn.; chair Ariz. High Intensity Drug Traficking Area; mem. Ariz. Peace Officer Stds. and Tng. Bd., Ariz. Pros. Attys.' Adv. Coun.; past com. to study civil litigation abuse, cost and delay Ariz. Supreme Ct.; past pres. Ariz. Cmty. Legal Svcs. Corp.; past judge pro tem Ariz. Ct. Appeals. Contbr. articles to profl. jours. Chmn. Nucleus, 1989—91; active Phoenix Design Stds. Rev. Com., 1989—91, Ariz. Women's Forum, Charter 100; hon. chmn. Camp Fire Boys and Girls, 1999; 1st vice-chmn. Ariz. Dem. Com., 1990—92; active Dem. Nat. Com., 1990—92; chmn. Ariz. del. Dem. Nat. Conv., 1992, chmn., 2000; active Ariz. Bd. Tech. Registration, 1989—92; bd. dirs. Ariz. Fire Fighters and Emergency Paramedics Meml., Phoenix Children's Hosp., Actors' Lab Ariz., Inc., Ariz. Peace Officers Meml.; bd. regents Santa Clara U., 1992—. Named Ariz. Dem. of Yr., 1989; recipient Leader of Distinction award, Anti-Defamation League, Human Betterment award, Roots and Wings, Golden Apple award, West Valley NOW, Nat. Network To End Domestic Violence award, Woman of Distinction award, Crohns and Colitis Disease Found., Women Making History award, Nat. Mus. Women's History, Tribute to Women award, YWCA; fellow Dillard fellow; scholar, Truman Scholarship Found, 1977. Fellow: Ariz. Bar Found.; mem.: ABA, Raven Soc., Sandra Day O'Connor Inn of Ct. (barrister), Ariz. Women Lawyers Assn., Ariz. State Bar (chmn. civil practice and procedure com. 1991—92), Am. Judicature Soc., Maricopa County Bar Assn. (past long range planning com.), Ariz. Bar Assn. (past com. on minorities in law, past chmn. civil practice and procedure com.), Nat. Assn. Attys. Gen. (exec. com., tobacco bankruptcy working group, health care fraud group, co-chmn. civil rights com., stop underage smoking com., exec. working group on prosecutorial rels.), Am. Law Inst., Alpha Sigma Nu, Phi Beta Kappa. Democrat. Avocations: hiking, walking, travel, reading, films. Office: Office of Gov 1700 W Washington Phoenix AZ 85007 Office Phone: 602-542-4331. Office Fax: 602-542-7601.*

NAPP, GUDRUN F., artist; b. Kiel, Germany, Aug. 14, 1929; arrived in U.S., 1986; d. Walter Alexander and Erika Elisabeth (Burchard) Rode; m. Edmund Carl Napp, Dec. 29, 1951 (dec. Dec. 2001); children: Helenita F., Johann Christian, Anneke J., Florian D. Student, Art Sch., Kiel, 1949, Escuela Artes Plastias, Caracas, Venezuela, 1950, Toronto Coll. Art, Can., 1950—51. Assoc. dir. One Ear Soc., 1999—2001. Exhibited in group shows at Miami Beach Conv. Ctr., 1997, Art Expo LA, 1997, 98, Art Expo NY, 1998, Art Expo Fla., 2000, FIA Caracas Internat. Art Fair, 2003; one-woman shows include Art Am., 1997. Recipient cert. of excellence Art Horizon, NYC, 1988, hon. mention Royal Poinciana Fiesta, Miami, 1993, The Fla. Mus. of Hispanic and L.Am. Art, Miami, 1994, Miami Watercolor Soc. exhibit, 1999, One Ear Soc. exhibit. Mem. Am. Soc. Interior Design (industry ptnr. 2005), Nat. Collage Soc., Internat. Soc. Exptl. Artists (signature mem.), Miami Watercolor Soc. (signature mem., pres. 1995-96, trustee 1997, publicity chair 1998-99, 3rd place 1990), Art Expo Fla. Lutheran. Avocation: painting. Home and Studio: Studio Gallery Napp Inc An ASID Industry Ptnr 1034 Waterside Cir Weston FL 33327-2022 Office Phone: 954-217-1722. Personal E-mail: art1100@aol.com.

NAPPIER, DENISE L., state official; BA, Va. State U., 1973; MA in Cmty. Planning, U. Cin., 1975. Analyst Office Hartford (Conn.) City Mgr.; cons. Conn. Office of Policy and Mgmt.; dir. instnl. rels. U. Conn. Health Ctr.; city treas. City of Hartford, 1989—98; treas. State of Conn., Hartford, 1999—. Exec. dir. Riverfront Recapture, Inc. Office: Office of State Treas 55 Elm St Hartford CT 06106-1746

NAQUIN, DEBORAH ANN, humanities educator; d. William Clarence and Elizabeth Beshada Stewart; m. Douglas Joseph Naquin, Dec. 18, 1976; children: Kaely Maria, Julie Vanessa. EdB, Old Dominion U., 1976; EdM, U. So. Calif. L.A., 1982; MA applied linguistics, Nova/Southeastern U., 1993; EdD higher edn. adminstrn./tech., George Washington U., 2001. Prof. English/reading No. Va. C.C., Sterling, 1976—; tchr. English Fairfax County Pub. Schs., Va., 1976—80; instr. English U. Md., Okinawa, Japan, 1980—82; instr. ESL Thammasat U., Bangkok, 1982—84, Panama Canal Coll., 1987—89; ednl. counselor Fulbright Commn., Nicosia, Cyprus, 1991—92; dir. writing program Fgn. Broadcast Info. Svcs., Reston, Va., 1995—2001. Webmaster No. Va. C.C., Sterling, Va., 1997—99, chair, tchg. and learning tech. roundtable, 2000—, English dept. coord., 2001—02, tech. applications ctr. liaison, Annandale, Va., 2001—. Grantee Funded devel. of a web-based course, The Sloan Found., 1998, Funded web publ. of a faculty tech. manual, Va. C.C. Sys., 1999, Funded rsch. into the diffusion of ednl. tech., No. Va. C.C., 2000. Mem.: Va. Assn. Devel. Educators. Home: 21240 Rosetta Place Ashburn VA 20147 Office: No Virginia Cmty Coll 1000 Harry Byrd Highway Sterling VA 20164 Office Phone: 703-450-2519. Business E-Mail: dnaquin@nvcc.edu.

NARASAKI, KAREN KEIKO, advocate, lawyer; b. Seattle, Apr. 4, 1958; d. Richard and Dorothy Narasaki. BA magna cum laude, Yale U., 1980; JD, UCLA, 1985. Bar: Calif. 1985, Wash. 1986, admitted to practice: US Supreme Ct., US Ct. Appeals (9th Cir.). Law clk. to Judge Harry Pregerson US Ct. Appeals (9th Cir.), LA, 1985-86; sr. assoc. Perkins Coie, Seattle, 1986-92; Washington Rep. Japanese Am. Citizens League, 1992-94; pres. and exec. dir. Nat. Asian Pacific Am. Legal Consortium, Washington. Chairperson Nat. Council of Asian Pacific Americans, Asian Pacific Am. Media Coalition, Nat. Network Against Anti-Asian Violence, Washington, 1993—; chairperson, compliance/enforcement com. Leadership Conf. on Civil Rights, Washington, 1995—. Named one of 100 Most Powerful Women, Washingtonian Mag., 2001; recipient Community Award, Asian Pacific Am. Labor Alliance, 1999, Citizen Vol. Svc. Award, US Dept. Justice, 2000, Ruth Standish Baldwin Award, Greater Sacramento Urban League, 2004, We the People Award, Internat. Channel, 2004, Spirit of Excellence Award, ABA, 2005. Mem.: Nat. Assn. Pacific Am. Women's Forum, Nat. Asian Pacific Am. Bar Assn. (founding mem., bd. dir., Trailblazers Award 1994). Office: Nat Asian Pacific Am Legal Consortium 1140 Connecticut Ave NW Washington DC 20036-4001

NARASIMHAN, PADMA MANDYAM, physician; b. Bangalore, India; came to U.S., 1976; d. Alasingracher Mandyam and Alamela Mandyam Narasimhan; 1 child, Ravi. MD, Maulana Azad Med. Coll., New Delhi, 1970. Diplomate Am. Bd. Internal Medicine. Intern in internal medicine Flushing Hosp., N.Y.C., 1976-77; resident in internal medicine Luth. Med. Ctr., N.Y.C., 1977-79; fellow hematology, oncology Beth-Israel Med. Ctr., N.Y.C., 1979-81; asst. prof. King Drew Med. Ctr., L.A., 1983-87, Harbor UCLA, Torrance, 1987—2000, USC, 2003—. Mem. editorial bd. Jour. Internal Medicine, 1986—. Mem. ACP, AAPI, Am. Soc. Clin. Oncology, So. Calif. Acad. Clin. Oncology. Hindu. Avocations: travel, reading, meeting people, music, walking. Home: 6604 Madeline Cove Dr Palos Verdes Peninsula CA 90275-4608 Office Phone: 310-377-9555. Personal E-mail: padmanarasim@yahoo.com.

NARAYAN, ASH, lawyer; b. 1965; BS in acctg., Valparaiso U.; JD, Loyola Law Sch. Mng. ptnr. RGT Capital Mgmt., Irvine, Calif. Editor: Loyola Law Sch. Law Review. Mem.: Sports Lawyers Assn. (bd. dirs.), Inst. Cert. Fin. Planners, several State Bar Assn. and CPA Soc. Office: RGI Capital Mgmt 1 Park Plz #970 Irvine CA 92614 Office Phone: 949-955-5525. Business E-Mail: anaryan@rgtnet.com.

NARAYANAN, RADHA, chemist, researcher; b. Savannah, Ga., July 15, 1978; d. Venkataraman Ananthanarayanan and Ananthanarayanan Jayalakshmi. BS summa cum laude, Armstrong Atlantic State U., 2000; PhD, Ga. Inst. Tech., 2005. Media asst. Armstrong Atlantic State U., Savannah, 1998—99, undergrad. lab. asst., 1999—2000; grad. rsch. asst. Ga. Inst. Tech., Atlanta, 2000—05; postdoctoral rsch. assoc. Iowa State U., Ames, 2005—06, Ariz. State U., Tempe, 2006—. Contbr. articles to profl. jours. Cherry Emerson fellow, Ga. Inst. Tech., 2004—05, Boyd scholar, Armstrong Atlantic State U., 1998—2000, Gov.'s scholar, Ga. State Govt., 1996—2000, HOPE scholar, 1996—2000, Minority Academic Achievement Scholars scholar, Armstrong Atlantic State U., 1999, Hodge scholar, 1996—98, Kids Who Care scholar, Jr. League, 1996—97, Presdl. fellow, Ga. Inst. of Tech., 2000—04, Grad. Assistance to Areas of Nat. Need fellow, 2000—01. Mem.: Assn. Women in Sci., Materials Rsch. Soc., Am. Chem. Soc. (reviewer Nano Letters 2004—, grant reviewer 2005—, reviewer Jour. Phys. Chemistry B 2003—, Most Highly Accessed Paper award 2005), Am. Mensa. Avocations: reading, computer games, puzzles, travel, internet. Home: 500 N Metro Blve Apt 1293 Chandler AZ 85226 Office: Ariz State U Biodesign Inst Tempe AZ 85287-6401 E-mail: Radha.Narayanan@asu.edu.

NARBIT, HEATHER ALYCE, not-for-profit developer, writer; b. Lake Charles, La., Apr. 7, 1981; d. Thomas Samuel Jr. and Vickie Ann Narbit. BS in Mass. Comms., McNeese State U., Lake Charles, 2000. Religion and food editor Am. Press, Lake Charles, 1999—2003; dir. of devel. Our Lady of Good Counsel Cath. Ch., Lake Charles, La., 2003—04; dir. comm. and ann. giving Dominican Sisters of Houston, Tex., Inc., Houston, 2004—. Group coord. Amnesty Internat., Houston, 2006; bd. dirs. Human Rights Radio Show, Houston, 2005—06. Recipient Second Pl. Headline Writing award, La. Press Assn., 2001, First Pl. Family News Coverage award, 2000; Ad and Press Club SW La., 2000. Mem.: Mensa (assoc.), Alpha Lambda Delta (assoc.), Phi Kappa Phi (assoc.), Pi Sigma Alpha (assoc.), Epsilon Alpha Epsilon (assoc.), Lambda Pi Eta (assoc.). Roman Catholic. Avocations: triathlon, Francophone activities. Personal E-mail: heather@heathernarbit.com. Business E-Mail: hnarbit@domhou.org.

NARDI, GLEN, publishing executive; Grad., US Naval Acad.; M in Personnel Mgmt., George Wash. U. Joined Knight Ridder, 1980; production mgr. Miami Herald, 1980—84; with Philadelphia newspapers Knight Ridder, 1984—87; various positions to v.p. ops. The State, Columbia, SC, 1987—2004; sr. v.p. ops., IT and circulation San Jose Mercury News, San Jose, 2004—. Office: San Jose Mercury News 750 Ridder Park Drive San Jose CA 95190

NARDI RIDDLE, CLARINE, chief of staff; b. Clinton, Ind., Apr. 23, 1949; d. Frank Jr. and Alice (Mattioda) Nardi; children: Carl Nardi, Julia Nardi. AB in Math with honors, Ind. U., 1971, JD, 1974; LHD (hon.), St. Joseph Coll., 1991. Bar: Ind. 1974, U.S. Dist. Ct. (so. dist.) Ind. 1974, Conn. 1979, Fed. Dist. Ct. Conn. 1980, U.S. Supreme Ct. 1980, U.S. Ct. Appeals (2d cir.) 1986, U.S. Ct. Appeals (D.C. cir.) 1994. Staff atty. Ind. Legis. Svc. Agy., Indpls., 1974-78, legal counsel, 1978-79; dep. corp. counsel City of New Haven, 1980-83; counsel to atty. gen. State of Conn., Hartford, 1983-86, dep. atty. gen., 1986-89, acting atty. gen., 1989, atty. gen., 1989-91, judge Superior Ct., 1991-93; assn. exec., sr. v.p., gen. counsel Nat. Multi-Housing Coun., Nat. Apartment Assn., 1995—2003; chief of staff Senator Joseph I. Lieberman, Washington, 2003—. Asst. counsel state majority Conn. Gen. Assembly, Hartford, 1979, legal rsch. asst. to prof. Yale U., New Haven, 1979; legal counsel com. on law revision Indpls. State Bar Assn., 1979; mem. Chief Justice's Task Force on Gender Bias, Hartford, 1988-90; mem. ethics and values com. Ind. Sector, Washington, 1988-90; co-organizer Ind. Continuing Legal Edn. Forum Inst. Legal Drafting Legislature and Pvt. Practice; Internat. Women's Yr. panelist Credit Laws and Their Enforcement; mem. Atty. Gen.'s Blue Ribbon Commn., Chief Justice's Com. Study Publs. Policy Conn. Law. Jour., Law Revision Commn. Adminstrv. Law Study, Chief Justice's Task Force Gender, Justice and Cts., Gov.'s Task Force Fed. Revenue Enhancements; mem. exec. com. Jud. Dept.; mem. panel arbitrators Am. Arbitration Assn., 1994; gen. counsel Nat. Multi Housing Coun.; lectr. in field. Author: (with F.R. Rembusch) Drafting Manual for the Indiana General Assembly, 1976; sr. editor Ind. U. Law Sch. Interdisciplinary Law Jour.; contbr. articles to profl. jours. Bd. visitors Ind. U., Bloomington, 1974-92; mem. Gov.'s Missing Children Com., Hartford, Conn. Child Support Guidelines Com., Gov.'s Task Force on Justice for Abused Children, Hartford, 1988-90; mem. Mayor's City of New Haven Task Force Reorganization Corp. Counsel's Office, Gov.'s Child Support Commn., Mayor of New Haven's Blue Ribbon Commn.; former bd. dirs. New Haven Neighborhood Music Sch.; bd. dirs., mem. youth adv. com. Gov.'s Partnership Prevent Substance Abuse Workforce-Drugs Don't Work; mem. Blue Ribbon Com. Army War Coll., 2006. Recipient Women in Leadership Recognition award Hartford Region YWCA, 1986, Award of Merit, Women & Law Sect. Conn. Bar Assn., 1989, Fellowship award South End Ladies Dem. Club, 1989, Woman of Yr. award Greater Hartford Fedn. of Bus. & Profl. Women's Clubs, 1990, Conn. Original award Somers-Mabelle B. Avery Sch., 1990, Cert. of Recognition, Consortium Law-Related Edn., 1990, Citizen award Conn. Task Force Children's Constl. Rights, 1991, Ann. award Hartford Assn. Women Attys., 1993; named Conn. History Maker, U.S. Dept. Labor, Women's Bur. & Permanent Commn. Status Women, 1989, Impact Player, The Conn. Law Tribune, 1992; inductee Ind. U. Sch. Law Alumni Acad. Fellow, 1999. Mem. ABA, Conn. Bar Assn. (chair com. on gender bias, Citation of Merit women and law sect. 1989), Nat. Assn. Attys. Gen. (chair charitable trusts and solicitation 1988-90), New Haven Neighborhood Music Sch. (bd. dirs.), Am. Arbitration Assn. (arbitration panel 1994), Ind. Bar Assn., Conn. Bar Assn. (chair com. gender bias legal profession), Indpls. Bar Assn., Ind. Civil Liberties Union (bd. dirs., mem. exec. com., chair long range planning com., mem. women's rights project, membership v.p., Disting. Svc. award), Conn. Consortium Law and Citizenship Edn., Inc. (bd. dirs.), Conn. Judges Assn. (mem. legislation com.), Ind. U. Law Sch. Alumni Assn. (bd. dirs.), Enomene Hon. Soc., Pleiades Hon. Soc., Mortar Bd. (nat. fellow), Alpha Lambda Delta. Democrat. Presbyterian. Office: Nat Multi Housing Coun 1850 M St NW Ste 450 Washington DC 20036-5803 Office Phone: 202-224-4041. Business E-Mail: clarine_nardi_riddle@lieberman.senate.gov.

NAREY, MARTHA ADELE CATHERINE, biomedical equipment technician, geography educator; b. Little Rock, Aug. 5, 1946; life ptnr. Josephine Rose. PhD in Climatology, U. Denver, 1999. Cert. biomed. equipment technician Assn. for Advancement of Med. Instrumentation. Health scis. maintenance technician US Army Med. Svc. Corps, 1978—97; asst. prof. geography U. Nebr., Kearney, 1997—2000; adj. asst. prof. Women's Coll. and geography U. Denver, 2000—. Chief warrant officer US Army Med. Svc. Corps, 1965—97. Mem.: Colo. Assn. Biomed. Equipment Technicians, Assn. Am. Geographers, Am. Indian Sci. and Engring. Soc., Sigma Xi. Green Party. Wiccan. Achievements include being first woman in North America to be certified biomedical equipment technician. Avocations: hiking, snowshoeing, travel, acoustic music, botanical and scientific illustration. Home: 132 W Irvington Pl Denver CO 80223 Office: U DenverGeography and GIS 2050 E Iliff Ave Denver CO 80208 Office Phone: 303-871-2513. Office Fax: 303-871-2201. E-mail: mnarey@du.edu.

NARMONEVA, DARIA, engineering educator; PhD, Duke U., Durham, N.C., 2000. Rsch. assoc. MIT, Boston, 2001—03, Brigham & Women's Hosp., Boston, 2002—04; asst. prof. in tissue engring. U. Cin., 2005—. Mem.: Am. Heart Assn. (fellowship 2002—04), BMES. Achievements include patents pending for Novel scaffold for capillary formation and growth. Office: Univ Cin Dept Biomed Engring ML 0048 Cincinnati OH 45221 Office Phone: 513-556-3997. Office Fax: 513-556-4162.

NARRETT, CARLA MARIE, university administrator; b. Iron Mountain, Mich., June 26, 1956; d. Peter Michael and Lucille Ann (Beitel) Belpedio; m. Walter Richard Ott, May. 27, 2000. BS, No. Mich. U., 1978; MS, Syracuse U., 1981, PhD, 1982. Lic. psychologist, N.Y.; permanent cert. sch. psychologist, N.Y.; nat. cert. sch. psychologist. Sch. psychologist East Syracuse (N.Y.)-Minoa Cen. Sch. Dist., 1981-82; from asst. prof. to assoc. prof. to prof. psychology Alfred (N.Y.) U., 1982-96, chairperson divsn. sch. psychology, 1985-96, assoc. dean Coll. Engring. and Profl. Studies, 1995-96; dean Grad. Sch. and Rsch. Montclair State U., Upper Montclair, NJ, 1996—2004. Program dir. Crisis Intervention Svcs., Alfred, 1985-90; dir. The Child and Family Svcs. Ctr., Alfred, 1986-89; sr. rsch. fellow Oreg. Social Learning Ctr., Eugene, 1989-90. Contbr. articles to profl. jours. Bd. dirs. Child Devel. Ctr., Bloomfield, NJ. Grantee U.S. Dept. Edn., 1991-96, A&L Powell Found., 1994-96, N.Y. State Office of Mental Retardation and Developmental Disabilities, 1985-90. Mem. Nat. Assn. Sch. Psychologists (co-chair accreditation credentialling and tng. 1994-97, exec. bd. program approval bd. 1995-99), Sch. Psychology Educators Coun. (pres. 1988-89, 91-92), Nat. Coun. for Accreditation of Tchr. Edn., Mid. State Assn. (mem. accreditation team 1999-2004). Avocations: reading, opera. Home: 26039 Seminole Lakes Blvd Punta Gorda FL 33955 Office Phone: 973-736-5779. Personal E-mail: cmn@predictiveedge.com.

NARSAVAGE, GEORGIA ROBERTS, nursing educator, researcher; b. Pittston, Pa., Jan. 1, 1948; d. George H. Roberts and Betty (Smith) Brown; m. Peter P. Narsavage, Oct. 26, 1968; children: Peter A., Paul J., Marea L. BSN, U. Md., Washington DC, 1969; MSN, Coll. Misericordia, 1984; PhD in Nursing, U. Pa., Phila., 1990. RN, Ga.; cert. adult nurse practitioner, Ohio, Ga. Staff nurse Mercy Hosp., Scranton, Pa., 1970-72; pvt. duty nursing Pa., 1972-79; pvt. duty nurse Community Med. Ctr., Scranton, Pa., 1979; clinical instr. Lackawanna County Vo-Tech Practical Nursing Program, Dunmore, Pa., 1979-82; clinical and theoretical instr. Mercy Hosp. Sch. of Nursing, Scranton, Pa., 1982-84; asst. prof. nursing dept. nursing U. Scranton, Pa., 1984-93, assoc. prof., 1993—99, chmn. dept., 1991-94, dir. RN program dept. nursing, 1990-92, assoc. dean Panuska Coll. Profl. Studies, 1998—99; assoc. prof. Case Western Res. U., Cleve., 1999—2005, dir. MSN program Sch. Nursing, 1999—2004, assoc. dean Academic Programs, 2003—05; prof. and assoc. dean academic affairs Med. Coll. Ga., 2005—. Postdoctoral fellow U. Pa., Phila., 1995-97; cons. in field. Contbr. articles to profl. jours. Gifted program mentor Scranton Sch. Dist.; active in ch. and civic choirs. Grantee U. Scranton, 1989, 91, 94-98, NIH NRSA, 1995-97, Health Resources and Svcs. Adminstrn. Divsn. Nursing, 2004—; recipient Rsch. award European Respiratory Soc., 2002, Ednl. Rsch. award Midwest Nursing Rsch. Soc., 2004; Alumni award Nursing Edn. Coll. Misericordia, 2005. Fellow Am. Acad. Nursing; mem. ANA, APHA, Am. Thoracic Soc./Am. Lung Assn. (chmn. nursing assembly 2004—, bd. dirs., Abstract award 2002), Pa. Nurses Assn. (bd. dirs., chmn. com., conv. del., Excellence award 1996), Lackawanna Nurses Assn. (bd. dirs., com. chmn., dist. pres.), Nat. League for Nursing, Coun. Nursing Informatics (chair nominating com. 1993-95), Pa. League for Nursing (chair nominating com.), Ohio Nurses Assn. (chmn. practice com.), Midwest Nursing Rsch. Soc. (chmn. membership com., vice chmn. conf. com.), U. Md. Nurses Alumnae Assn., Ea. Nursing Rsch. Soc. (mem.-at-large bd. dirs., interim treas., rsch. grantee 1994), Theta Phi, Sigma Theta Tau (Rsch. award 1994), Iota Omega (Mentor award 2002). Lutheran. Office: Med Coll of Ga Son 997 St Sebastian Way Augusta GA 30912 Office Phone: 706-721-2787. Personal E-mail: narsavageg1@hotmail.com. Business E-Mail: gnarsavage@mcg.edu.

NARVAEZ, BERNICE WILLIAMS, process engineer, consultant; b. Houston, June 7, 1956; d. Ella Mae Williams; 1 child, Alexis Appollonia; m. Raymond Narvaez, June 5, 1999. BS in Mech. Engring., MIT, 1978; MS-MIS, George Washington U., 1994. Engr. Shell Oil Co., Houston, Sacramento, 1977-81; programmer U. Tex., Houston, 1985-89; cons. Ciber/MCI, Arlington, Tyson's Corner, Va., 1989-90; system analyst MCI Comm., Arlington, 1990-94; sr. cons. Comsys. Tech. Svcs. Network MCI, Arlington, 1994-97; tech. staff IBM Global Svcs., Tampa, 1997-99; sr. cons. Comsys/Metamor Tech. Svcs., 1999-2000; sr. bus. process cons. Sci. Applications Internat. Corp., Balt., 2000—04, sr. process engr., 2003—. Pres. ALEXIS Enterprises, Tampa, 1994—; co-founder of All4Less distbr., 2001; cons. in field. Vol. industry adv. bd. Pub. Schs., Balt.; process improvement com. Darfur Relief Fund, active Care, Watchtower soc., Internat. Relief Fund, Habitat Internat., Internat. Coun. Sys. Engring., 2003-2005; sr. bus. process engr., process mgr. Scis. Apps. Internat. Corp. Avocations: tennis, piano, parenting, art collecting, travel. Office: 7125 Columbia Gateway Dr Ste 300 Columbia MD 21046 Business E-Mail: bernice.w.narvaez@saic.com.

NASCIMENTO, ANA PAULA, entrepreneur, food service executive; b. Brasilia, Brazil, July 11, 1970; arrived in U.S., 1989; d. Eliseu Botani and Elizete de Freitas Nascimento; m. Christopher Noel Kellon, Feb. 7, 1993 (div. Sept. 27, 1997). Student, Brasilia U., No. Va. Coll. Au parir, Arlington, Va., 1989—91; flyer girl Focaccia Fiorentina, N.Y.C., 1991, hostess, gen. mgr., 1999; owner Nascimento Restaurant, N.Y.C., 1999; entrepreneur Nascimento Sauces and Dressings, N.Y.C., 2001—. Contbr. Kennedy Child Study Ctr., March of Dimes, Parents Assn. Internat. Pre-Schs., Joey di Poglo AIDS Found., Art of Am., Ricardo O'Gorman Garden Sch., City Harvest, Meals-on-Wheels, QSAC-Autism, Share our Strength, The Charles Dickens Found., Builders of a Better World. Mem.: Nat. Restaurant Assn. (Outstanding Cmty. Involvement award 2001), Jewish Found., Holocaust Found. Avocations: volunteering, reading, running marathons, travel, inspirational speaking. Office: 1068 1st Ave New York NY 10022-2202

NASH, ALICIA, application developer, physicist; b. San Salvador, Jan. 1, 1933; came to U.S., 1944; d. Carlos Roberto and Alicia (Lopez-Harrison) Larde; m. John Forbes Nash, Jr., Feb. 16, 1957; children: John Charles Martin Nash. BS in Physics, MIT, 1955, postgrad., 1959. Physicist Nuclear Devel. Corp. of Am., White Plains, NY, 1956-57, Tech. Ops., Burlington, Mass., 1957-58; rsch. assoc. MIT Computation Ctr., Cambridge, Mass., 1958-59; physicist, aerospace engr. R.C.A. Astro Divsn., Hightstown, NJ, 1960-66; programmer, analyst Mgmt. Data Processing, N.Y.C., 1972-74, Con Edison, N.Y.C., 1974-80, Blue Cross Blue Shield of N.Y., N.Y.C., 1980-82; systems/analyst programmer specialist N.J. Transit, Newark, 1983—. Mem. AAUW, MIT Club of Princeton (past pres., bd. dirs.), Soc. of Women Engring. Achievements include being the subject for the role of Alicia Nash in the movie "A Beautiful Mind". Home: 932 Alexander Rd Princeton Junction NJ 08550-1002 Office: NJ Transit One Penn Plaza East Newark NJ 07105 E-mail: alroad932@hotmail.com.

NASH, CATHY L., meeting planner; b. Washington, Nov. 27, 1956; d. Robert E. Weeks and Marjorie A. Earnest; m. Martin J. Nash, Aug. 4, 1989; 1 child, Jason T. Earnest; stepchildren: Bryan S., Kevin P. Cert. meeting planner Conv. Industry Coun., Va., 2004. Budget asst. US Bur. of Census, Suitland, Md., 1974—78; coord. continuing med. edn. course Am. Psychiat. Assn., Arlington, Va., 1979—83, assoc. dir., office to coordinate ann. meetings, 1984—85, dir., ann. meetings dept., 1985—. Mem.: Am. Soc. of Assn. Execs., Solomons Island Yacht Club. Office: Am Psychiat Assn 1000 Wilson Blvd Ste 1825 Arlington VA Office Phone: 703-907-7822.

NASH, CYNTHIA JEANNE, journalist; b. Detroit, Dec. 24, 1947; d. Frederick Copp and Carolyn (Coffin) N.; 1 child, Lydia Anne Maza; m. Richard Zahler, July 22, 1994. BA, U. Mich., 1969. Reporter Detroit News, 1970-75, sports columnist, 1975-77, Life Style columnist 1977-79, Life Style editor, 1979-82; news features editor Seattle Times, 1983; asst. mng. editor Sunday Seattle Times, 1983-86, assoc. mng. editor, 1986-97, dir. content devel., 1986-2000, dir., brand and content devel., 2000—. Mem. Harbor Sq. Club. Office: Seattle Times PO Box 70 Fairview Ave N & John St Seattle WA 98111-0070 E-mail: cnash@seattletimes.com.

NASH, JESSIE MADELEINE, journalist, science writer; b. Elizabeth City, N.C., Sept. 11, 1943; d. John V. and Jessie B.; m. E. Thomas Nash, June 9, 1970. AB in History magna cum laude, Bryn Mawr Coll., 1965. Clip girl to sec. Time Mag., N.Y.C., 1965-66, reporter rschr., 1966-70, stringer Bonn, Germany and Chgo., 1970-74, staff corr. Chgo., 1974-87, sr. sci. corr., 1987—. Mem. adv. com. on pub. infor. Am. Inst. of Physics, 1993-95. Contbr. articles to mags. Recipient Page One award Newspaper Guild of N.Y., 1981, award Leukemia Soc. Am., 1994, Popular Sci. Writing award, Am. Astronomical Soc., 1997. Mem. AAAS (Westinghouse award 1987, 90, Sci. Journalism award 1987, 91, 96,), Nat. Assn. Sci. Writers, Author's Guild, Sigma Xi (hon. mem). Avocation: travel. Office: Time Mag 303 E Ohio St Chicago IL 60611-3373*

NASH, JUDITH KLUCK, mathematics professor; b. Manchester, Conn., Dec. 26, 1946; d. Erwin John and Eleanor May (Starke) Kluck; m. Stephen T. Nash, Apr. 7, 1990. BS, So. Conn. State U., 1969, MS, 1976. Math. tchr. Cheshire (Conn.) Pub. Schs., 1969-93; instr. math. Tunxis CC, Farmington, Conn., 1994—. Home: 72 Tunxis Path Plantsville CT 06479-1348 Office: Tunxis CC 271 Scott Swamp Rd Farmington CT 06032-3324

NASH, LINDA KAY, music educator; b. Fort Worth, Tex., Feb. 23, 1946; d. Charles Edwin and Mary Ella Webb; m. Hollis Westbrook Nash, Aug. 26, 1965; children: Stephen Hollis, Sean Michael. BMusEd magna cum laude, Tex. Christian U., Ft. Worth, 1968, MMusEd, 1974. Cert. elem. tchr. Tex., 1969, vocal music tchr. Tex., 1969, music tchr. K-12 Fla., 1995, early, mid. music tchr. Nat. Bd. of Profl. Tchg. Standards, 2002, Level III Orff Am. Orff Schulwerk Assn., 1999. Grad. tchg. asst. Tex. Christian U., Fort Worth, 1968—69; elem. tchr., grade 5 and music Ft. Worth Ind. Sch. Dist., 1969—71; first grade tchr. Spaulding/Griffin Co. Schs., Griffin, Ga., 1973—74; dir. music Winterfield United Meth. Ch., Longview, Tex., 1974—77; adj. voice instr. East Tex. Bapt. Coll., Marshall, 1975—76; elem. music tchr. Immaculate Conception Cath. Sch., Laurel, Miss., 1977—87, Va. Beach City Pub. Schs., Va., 1991—95, Sch. Dist. of Lee County, Ft. Myers, Fla., 1995—. Bd. dirs. Windamere Sch., Longview, Tex., 1976—77; mem. unified arts coun. Sch. Dist. of Lee County, Ft. Myers, Fla., 2005—, coord. of all county elem. chorus, 2003—05; mem., pre-sch. insvc. tng. cadre Sch. Bd. of Lee County, Ft. Myers, Fla., 2006—. Named Elem. Music Tchr. of the Yr., Sch. Dist. of Lee County, 1998, Subject Area Tchr. of the Yr., 1998; grantee World Music Resources, Found. for Lee County Schs., 2001; scholar Tchg. Assistantship, Tex. Christian U., 1968—69. Mem.: Lee County Network of Nat. Bd. Cert. Tchrs. (bd. mem. 2005—06), S.W.Fla. Orff (pres. 2006—), Am. Orff Schulwek Assn., NEA, Fla. Elem. Music Edn. Assn., Fla. Music Edn. Assn., Music Educators Nat. Conf. Avocations: swimming, boating, fishing, collecting owl art.

NASH, RUTH S., foundation administrator; b. Westfield, Mass., May 7, 1916; d. George Whitney and Marguerite (Mueller) Searle; m. Clayton Richmond Nash, Sept. 7, 1940 (dec. 1990); children: Roberta Marie, Marguerite Louise, Gail Winifred; m. Charles Williams, Mar. 13, 2002 (dec. 2004) Student, Simmons Coll., 1935-37; Diploma, Sch. Handicraft and Occupl. Therapy, 1937-39; B in Liberal Studies, Fla. So. Coll., 1996. Leader Girl Scouts, Winthrop, Mass., 1934-40, field dir., exec. dir. Greater Lynn (Mass.), 1940-43; leader, bd. mem. Reading, Mass., 1940-60; field dir., exec. dir. Naumkeag Area Girl Scouts, Salem, Mass., 1949-56, field dir., tng. dir. Greater Lawrence (Mass.), 1958-63; leader Mystick Side Medford, Mass., 1960-63; field dir., pub. rels., tng. dir., camping svcs. dir. Merrimack River Coun., Andover, Mass., 1963-78. Author: High Seas to High Stakes, 2000, Tales & Tails From Stagecoach Lodge, 2002, Monah: Adventures By Stagecoach in New Hampshire Mid 1800's; editor: Monthly Civic Newspaper Beacon, 1984-99; contbr. articles to profl. jours. Vol. Meals on Wheels, 1991-96, Cmty. Svc., 1978-98; sec., mem. choir, handbell ringer Harbour Heights (Fla.) United Meth. Ch., 1991—; mem., founder H.H. Kitchen Band, 1990—; trail guide Charotte Harbor Environ. Ctr., Punta Gorda, Fla., 1997-2000; leader disadvantaged girls Girl Scouts USA, 1998—, study ptnr. for disadvantaged children, 1998-2000 Mem. AAUW (sec. 1998-2003), Learning in Retirement (sec. bd.), Alzheimers Assn. (support leader, bd. dirs. 1992-97, local environ. com. 2004—), Friends Camp Runels Republican. Methodist. Avocations: writing, watercolors, canoeing, golf, camping. Home: 3524 Peace River Dr Harbour Heights FL 33983-3523 also: 99 Stage Coach Rd Punta Gorda NH 03809-9719

NASH, SYLVIA DOTSETH, management consultant; b. Montevedio, Minn., Apr. 25, 1945; d. Owen Donald and Selma A. (Tollefson) Dotseth; married; 1 child, Elizabeth Louise. Grad., Calif. Luth. Bible Sch., 1965; doctorate (hon.), Pilgrims Theol. Seminary, 1994. Office mgr. First Congl. Ch., Pasadena, Calif., 1968-75; pastoral asst. Pasadena Presbyn. Ch., 1975-78; dir. adminstrv. svcs. Fuller Theol. Sem., Pasadena, 1978-81; CEO Christian Mgmt. Assn., Diamond Bar, Calif., 1981-94; pres. Christian Healthcare Network, La Mirada, Calif., 1994-95; sr. cons. Lillestrand and Assocs., Chino Hills, Calif., 1996—. Cons. various orgns., 1985—. Author: Inspirational Management, 1992 (Your Church Mag. award 1992); editor: The Clarion, 1975-78, The Christian Mgmt. Report, 1981-94; mem. editl./adv. bd. Your Church Mag.; mem. editl. bd. Jour. Ministry Mktg. and Mtmg.; contbr. articles to profl. jours. Bd. dirs. Nat. Network of Youth Ministries, The Mustard Seed, Inc., Nat. Assn. of Ch. Bus. Adminstrn., Found. for His Ministry, Lamb's Players, Gospel Lit. Internat., Evang. Coun. for Fin. Accountability, Campus Crusade for Christ Internat. Sch. Theology. Mem. NAFE, Nat. Assn. Ch. Adminstrs. (sec. 1979-81), Am. Soc. Assn. Execs., So. Calif. Soc. Assn. Execs. Office: Lillestrand & Assocs 2729 Brookside Drive Chino Hills CA 91709

NASO, VALERIE JOAN, automobile dealership executive, travel company operator, artist, photographer, writer; b. Stockton, Calif., Aug. 19, 1941; d. Alan Robert and Natalie Grace (Gardner) McKittrick Naso; m. Peter Joralemon, May 31, 1971 (div.). Student pub. schs., Piedmont, Calif. Cert. graphoanalyst. Pres., Naso Motor Co. (formerly Broadway Cadillacs, Oakland, Calif.) Bishop, Calif., 1964—; freelance artist, 1965—; owner, operator Wooden Horse Antiques, Bishop, 1970-82; editor, writer, photographer Sierra Life Mag., Bishop, 1980-83; freelance writer, photographer, 1972—; owner, operator Boredom Tours, Bishop, 1981—; owner, sole photographer, Renaissance Photography, N.Y.C. and Bishop, Calif., 1982—, Keyboard Colors, 1986; cons. graphoanalyst, 1976—. Fiction, non-fiction work pub. in Horse and Horseman, Am. Horseman, Horse & Rider Mag., Cameo Mag., Desert Mag., Sierra Life Mag. Mem. Nat. Assn. Female Execs., Authors Guild, Inc., Authors League Am., Am. Film Inst., Archives of Am. Art, Lalique Soc. Am., Musical Box Soc. Internat., Alliance Francaise (N.Y. chpt.), Bishop C. of C., Victorian Soc. Am., Nat. Trust for Hist. Preservation, Am. Craft Coun., Nat. Rifle Assn. Clubs: Cadillac LaSalle (nat. and so. calif. chpts.); Wagner Soc. (N.Y.C.). Office: 783 N Main St Bishop CA 93514-2427 also: PO Box 1625 Bishop CA 93515-1625

NASON, DOLORES IRENE, computer company executive, social welfare administrator, minister; b. Seattle; d. William Joseph and Ruby Irene Lockinger; m. George Malcolm Nason, Jr.; children: George Malcolm III, Scott James, Lance William, Natalie Joan. Student, Long Beach (Calif.) City Coll.; cert. in Religious Edn. for elem tchrs., Immaculate Heart Coll., cert. teaching, cert. secondary teaching; attended, Salesian Sem. Buyer J. C. Penney Co., Barstow, Calif.; prin. St. Cyprian Confraternity of Christian Doctrine Elem. Sch., Long Beach; prin. summer sch. St. Cyprian Confraternity of Christian Doctrine Elem. Sch., Long Beach; pres. St. Cyprian Confraternity Orgn., Long Beach; dist. co-chmn. L.A. Diocese; v.p. Nason & Assocs., Inc., Long Beach, 1978—; pres. L.A. County Commn. on Obscenity & Pornography, 1984—; eucharistic minister St. Cyprian Ch., Long Beach, 1985—; bd. dirs. L.A. County Children's Svcs., 1988—; assoc. dir. social svcs. Disabled Resources Ctr., Inc., Long Beach, 1992—. Mem. scholarship com. Long Beach City Coll., 1984—90, Calif. State U., Long Beach, 1984—90; bd. dirs. County Access Svc. Inc., 2004—. Active Long Beach Civic Light Opera, 1973—96, Assitance League Long Beach, 1976—; vol. Meml. Children's Hosp., Long Beach, 1977—; pres. St. Cyprian's Parish Coun., 1962—. Mem.: KC (Family of Month award 1988), U. Pacific Club. Roman Catholic. Avocations: physical fitness, theater, choir, travel.

NASON, NICOLE R., federal agency administrator; married; children: Alexandra, Abigail. Grad., Am. U., Washington, 1992; JD, Case Western Res. U., Cleve., 1995. Counsel House Judiciary Subcom. on Crime, Washington; govt. affairs counsel Met. Life Ins. Co., 1999—2000; comm. dir., counsel to US Rep. Porter J. Goss US Congress, 2000—02; asst. commr. Office of Congl. Affairs, U.S. Customs Svc., Washington, 2002—03; asst. sec. for govtl. affairs US Dept. Transp., Washington, 2003—06, adminstr., Nat. Hwy. Traffic Safety Adminstrn., 2006—. Office: Nat Hwy Traffic Safety Adminstrn US Dept Transp 400 7th St Washington DC 20590

NASON, ROCHELLE, conservation organization administrator; b. Oakland, Calif., May 21, 1959; d. Milton and Ann Frances (Reed) Nason. BA, U. Calif., Berkeley, 1984; JD, U. Calif., San Francisco, 1987. Bar: Calif. 1987. Law clk. to Chief Justice Malcolm Lucas Supreme Ct. of Calif., San Francisco, 1987-88; litigation assoc. Morrison & Foerster, San Francisco, 1988-92; staff lawyer League to Save Lake Tahoe, South Lake Tahoe, Calif., 1992-93, exec. dir., 1993—. Adj. instr. Sierra Nev. Coll., Incline Village, 1992—94, Lake Tahoe C.C., 1992—96. Editor: The Traynor Reader, 1987; sr. rev. editor: Hastings Law Jour., 1986—87; editor: (jour.) Keep Tahoe Blue, 1992—; columnist: newspaper Tahoe Daily Tribune; contbr. articles to profl. jours. Mem. leadership coun. Tahoe-Truckee Regional Econ. Coalition, Stateline, Nev., 1992—94; v.p., bd. dirs. Jewish Cmty. South Lake Tahoe/Temple Bat Yam, 1992—99; bd. dirs. Tahoe Ctr. Sustainable Future, Glenbrook, Nev., 1995—98, Earthshare Calif., 2002—. Mem.: Thurston Soc., Order of Coif. Jewish. Avocations: backpacking, skiing. Office: League to Save Lake Tahoe 955 Emerald Bay Rd South Lake Tahoe CA 96150-6410

NASRALLAH, JUNE, plant pathologist, department chairman; PhD in Genetics, Cornell U. Prof. plant biology, chair plant genomics Cornell U., Ithaca, NY. Contbr. articles to profl. jours. Mem.: NAS. Office: Cornell U 218 Plant Sciences Ithaca NY 14853 Business E-Mail: jbn2@cornell.edu.

NASS, DEANNA ROSE, counselor, professor; b. NYC, June 30, 1939; d. Nat. and Jean (Mark) Spitzer. BFA, U. Chgo., 1961, MFA, 1964; MA, NYU, 1969; MPhil, PhD, Columbia U., 1979. Art tchr. N.Y.C. Bd. Edn., 1964-68; assoc. prof., counselor Dept. Student Svcs., CUNY, 1968-95; dir. counseling svcs. Coll. of S.I./CUNY, 1992-95; assoc. prof. emeritus CUNY, 1998—. Cons. to pvt. art investors, 1995—. Editor: The Rape Victim, 1977; contbr. articles to profl. jours. Recipient Full Tuition Scholarship U. Chgo., 1964; Grantee Drug Edn. Program, 1970-71; recipient Cert. Recognition U.S. Dept. Labor, 1976. Mem. Am. Assn. U. Profs., Phi Delta Kappa, CUNY Acad. for Humanities & Scis. Avocations: drawing, painting, graphic arts, writing, reading. Home: 225 E 73rd St New York NY 10021-3654 Personal E-mail: deanna.nass@comcast.net.

NASS, RUTH, pediatric neurologist; b. N.Y.C., Apr. 14, 1947; d. Samuel and Edna (Kadin) N.; m. Theodore Gross, Aug. 28, 1977; 1 child, Nora Gross. BA, Brandeis U., 1969; postgrad., MIT, 1969-70, Brandeis U., 1970-72; MD, Einstein Coll. Medicine, 1975. Diplomate Nat. Bd. Med. Examiners, Am. Bd. Pediatrics, Am. Bd. Psychiatry and Neurology with spl. competence in child neurology; lic. physician, N.Y. Resident pediatrics N.Y. Hosp., N.Y.C., 1975-77; resident neurology Columbia Presbyn. Hosp., N.Y.C., 1977-80; clin. rsch. fellow in neurology/neuropsychology Cornell U. Med. Coll., N.Y.C., 1980-82, instr. pediatrics, 1981-82, asst. prof., 1982-88, asst. prof. neurology, 1982-89; asst. attending pediatrics and neurology N.Y. Hosp., N.Y.C., 1982-89; divsn. chief pediatric neurology N.Y. Hosp., Cornell Med. Ctr., N.Y.C., 1986-89, assoc. attending pediatrician, 1988-91; assoc. prof. clin. pediatrics Cornell Med. Coll., N.Y.C., 1988-89, assoc. prof. neurology and pediatrics, 1989-91; assoc. attending neurologist N.Y. Hosp., N.Y.C., 1989-91; assoc. prof. neurology and pediatrics NYU Med. Ctr., N.Y.C., 1991—; assoc. attending pediatrician, neurologist Tisch Hosp., Bellevue Hosp., N.Y. U. Med. Ctr., 1991—; dir. learning diagnostics program NYU Med. Ctr., 1991—. Neurologic cons. N.Y. Foundling Hosp., N.Y.C., 1980-83; dir. Learning Disability Ctr. N.Y. Hosp.-Cornell Med. Ctr., 1983-91; neurologic cons. St. Mary's Hosp., Bklyn., 1984-86, Englewood (N.J.) Hosp., 1986, Hosp. for Spl. Surgery, N.Y.C., 1987-91; acting chief divsn. pediatric neurology N.Y. Hosp.-Cornell Med. Ctr., 1985-86; chief neurology Blythedale Children's Hosp., 1989-91; adj. assoc. prof. pediatrics N.Y. Hosp.-Cornell U. Med. Ctr., 1991—; NIH ad hoc site com. Nosology of Learning Disabilities, Washington, Isabelle Rapin, P.I., 1987, N.Y.C., 1988; external rev. panel Child Neurology Soc. Nosology Project in Presch. Child, 1989; ad hoc NIH site com. at Boston Children's Hosp. Program Project on Learning in At Risk Groups, 1990, ad hoc NIH site com. for Ctr. and Program Project on Neurobiology of Dyslexia, 1992; mem. written bds. com. Am. Acad. Psychiatry and Neurology, 1992-93; mem. NIH Consensus Com. on Early Identificaiton of Hearing Impairment, 1993; lectr. univs., hosps, orgns., workshops and symposiums. Ad hoc reviewer Neurology, Annals of Neurology, Cognitive Neurosci., Psychol. Bull., Pediatrics, Psychoneuroendocrinology, Jour. Neuro-oncology, Epilepsia; contbr. articles to profl. jours., chpts. to books. Mary Putnam Jacobie fellow, 1981; grantee NIH Nat. Rsch. Svc., 1980-83, NIH Biomed. Rsch., Cornell U. Med. Coll., 1983-84, March of Dimes, 1984-95, United Cerebral Palsy, 1984-87, Rita G. Rudel Found., 1986-88, NIH Ctr., 1991—; recipient Rockefeller Bros. Clin. Scholarship N.Y. Hosp.-Cornell Med. Coll., 1983-84. Mem. Am. Neurol. Assn., Am. Acad. Neurology, Am. Acad. Pediatrics (develop. disabilities com. 1992-93), Assn. for Rsch. in Nervous and Mental Diseases, Child Neurology Soc. (sci. selection com. 1988-89, 91-93, clin. practice com. 1991-93, award com. 1990-92), Internat. Child Neurology Soc., Am. Epilepsy Soc., Am. Acad. Cerebral Palsy, N.Y. Acad. Sci., Orton Dyslexia Soc., Soc. for Children with Attention Deficit Disorder. Office: NYU Med Ctr Rusk Rsch 212 550 1st Ave New York NY 10016-6402

NATALE, BARBARA GUSTAFSON, retired librarian; b. Hartford, Conn., Jan. 12, 1938; d. Carl William and Gertrude Fallon Gustafson; m. John Charles Natale, Sept. 12, 1959; children: Linda Skehan, John A., Mary Ellen. BA, U. Conn., 1959; MLS, So. Conn. State U., 1977. Libr. media specialist Windsor (Conn.) Pub. Schs., 1976—82; pub. svcs. libr. Manchester (Conn.) C.C., 1982—90, dir. libr. svcs., 1990—98, ret., 1998. Vice chmn. campus master planning com. Manchester (Conn.) C.C., 1992—98; mem. coun. librs. Conn. C.C.s, Hartford, Conn., 1992—98, chmn. coun. librs., 1993—95; evaluator New Eng. Assn. Schs. and Colls., Bedford, Mass., 1994—95; bd. dirs. Sea Call Supporters, Inc., sec., 2003—. Vol. Snow Libr., Orleans, Mass., 2003—05; sec. Friends of N.W. Park, 1981—87, vice chair, 1988—89; Windsor mayor's rep. Riverfront Recapture, Hartford, 1992—96; dist. capt., campaign coord. Windsor (Conn.) Dem. Com., 1978—92. Recipient Ednl. Excellence and Disting. Svc. award, Conn. C.C., 1994, Leadership Women award, Women's Caucus, Manchester (Conn.) C.C., 1994. Fellow: LWV, Wellfleet Garden Club; mem.: Conn. Libr. Assn. (bd. coll. and univ. sect. 1984—86, mem. ref. and adult svcs. com. 1986—90, chmn. 1989—90). Democrat. Avocations: travel, reading, gardening, bicycling, photography. Home: PO Box 1467 11 Pleasant View Dr East Orleans MA 02643

NATALICIO, DIANA SIEDHOFF, academic administrator; b. St. Louis, Aug. 25, 1939; d. William and Eleanor J. (Biermann) Siedhoff. BS in Spanish summa cum laude, St. Louis U., 1961; MA in Portuguese lang., U. Tex., 1964, PhD in Linguistics, 1969. Chmn. dept. modern langs. U. Tex., El Paso, 1973-77, assoc. dean liberal arts, 1977-79, acting dean liberal arts, 1979-80, dean Coll. Liberal Arts, 1980-84, v.p. acad. affairs, 1984-88, pres., 1988—. Bd. dirs. El Paso br. Fed. Res. Bd. Dallas, chmn., 1989; mem. Presdl. Adv. Commn. on Ednl. Excellence for Hispanic Ams., 1991; bd. dirs. Sandia Corp., Trinity Industries; bd. dirs. Nat. Action Coun. for Minorities in Engring., 1993—; mem. Nat. Sci. Bd. 1994-2000; mem. NASA Adv. Coun., 1994-96; bd. mem. Fund for Improvement of Post-Secondary Edn., 1993-97; bd. dirs. Fogarty Internat. Ctr. of NIH, 1993-96; bd. chair Am. Assn. Higher Edn., 1995-96; bd. dirs. U.S.-Mexico Commn. for Ednl. and Cultural Exch., 1994—. Co-author: Sounds of Children, 1977; contbr. articles to profl. jours. Bd. dirs. United Way El Paso, 1990-93, chmn. needs survey com., 1990-91, chmn. edn. divsn., 1989; chmn. Quality Edn. for Minorities Network in Math. Sci. and Engring., 1991-92; chairperson Leadership El Paso, Class 12, 1989-90, mem. adv. coun., 1987-90, participant, 1980-81; mem. Historically Black Colls. and Univs./Minority Instns. Consortium on Environ. Tech. chairperson, 1991-93; trustee Rockefeller Found. Recipient Harold W. McGraw. Jr. prize in edn., 1997, Torch of Liberty award Anti-Defamation League B'nai B'rith, 1991, Conquistador award City of El Paso, 1990, Humanitarian award El Paso chpt. NCCJ, 1990; named to El Paso Women's Hall of Fame, 1990, Tex. Women's Hall of Fame, 1998. Mem. Philos. Soc. Tex. Avocations: hiking, bicycling, skiing, skating. Office: U Tex at El Paso Office of the Pres 500 W University Ave El Paso TX 79968-0001*

NATALUCCI-HALL, CARLA, psychologist; b. Manhasset, N.Y., Mar. 24, 1964; d. John and Mary (Amisano) Natalucci; m. Dwight Avery Hall, June 12, 1994. BA, Fordham U., N.Y.C., 1986; MA, Columbia U., 1987, L.I. U., 1992, PsyD, 1994. Psychology extern L.I. Jewish Hosp., Glen Oaks, N.Y., 1990-93; psychology intern St. Mary's Children and Family Svcs., Syosset, N.Y., 1993-94; therapist Profl. Svc. Ctrs., Astoria, N.Y., 1994-96; psychologist Behavioral Medicine Assocs., Great Neck, N.Y., 1996—; pvt. practice Great Neck, 1996—. Mem. APA, N.Y. State Psychol. Assn., Nassau County Psychol. Assn. Republican. Episcopalian. Office: 8 Barstow Rd Ste 1C Great Neck NY 11021-3502

NATARAJAN, UMA, mathematician, educator; b. Toronto, Can., Feb. 22, 1979; d. Raja and Mallika Natarajan. MEd in Sch. Adminstrn. and Supervision, Tenn. State U., Nashville, 1999; BS in Math and Secondary Edn., Vanderbilt U., Nashville, Tenn., 2001. Math. tchr. Williamson County Schs., Franklin, Tenn., 2001—. Nominee Tchr. of Yr., Centennial H.S., 2006, Shining Apple award, 2006; Career and Tech. 1 grant-Using Tech. to Enhance Learning Achievement, State of Tenn., 2005—.

NATHAN, JOAN, cookbook author, freelance writer, lecturer; b. Providence, Jan. 26, 1943; d. Ernest Nathan and Pearl (Gluck) N.; m. Allan Gerson, Oct. 20, 1974; children: Daniela Gerson, Merissa Gerson, David Gerson. BA with honors, U. Mich., 1965, MA in French Lit., 1966; MPA, Harvard U., 1976. Cons. Smithsonian Inst., Office of Mayor, City of N.Y.; fgn. press attache Mayor of Jerusalem, Israel, 1970-72; pub. rels. profl. Inst. Internat. Edn., N.Y.C.; adminstrv. asst. Embassy of Malagasy Republic, N.Y.C. Author: (cookbooks) Flavor of Jerusalem, 1975, Jewish Holiday Kitchen, 1979, 1989, An American Folklife Cookbook, 1984, Children's Jewish Holiday Kit, 1985, 1995, Jewish Cooking in America, 1994, The New American Cooking, 2005; sr. prodr. Passover: Traditions of Freedom, 1994, guest curator Food Culture U.S.A., Smithsonian Folklife Festival. Recipient Golda award Am. Jewish Congress, Chris award Columbus Film Festival, 1994, 2d Place award Houston Internat. Film Festival, 1994, Best Cookbook in Am. award IACP/Julia award, 1994, James Beard Best Cookbook of Ams., 1994. Mem. Les Dames d'Escoffier (founding mem.), Am. Inst. Wine and Food, Internat. Assn. Culinary Profls., James Beard Assn. Democrat. Jewish. Avocations: tennis, swimming, gardening. Home: 4221 Lenore Ln NW Washington DC 20008-3835*

NATHANSON, BARBARA A., painter, artist; d. Laurence Washington and Alma Ruth Pence; m. Weston Nathanson, July 13, 1958; children: Eric F., Tasha. BA, Calif. State U., Northridge, 1980; MA, Calif. State U., 1985. Mem. LA chpt. Artist's Equity, 1985—88; artist in residence Akiba Acad., LA, 1987; gallery mgr. Seeing It Through Exhibition, LA, 1992—94, bd. dir., 1992—95; mem. LA Artcore, 1997—99. Painter: art book An American Album, 1985; exhibitions include UN Conf. Women, Nairobi, Kenya, 1985, Korea Internat. Free Art Festival, South Korea, 2004, Lantern of East Internat. Art Festival, Bangkok, 2005, ASTO Mus. of Art, LA, 1997, Represented in permanent collections Nat. Mus. Women in Arts, one-woman shows include, Cracow, Poland, 2002, exhibitions include Ken Ritsu Mus., Nagasaki, Japan, 2004, Gwang Hua Moon Internat. Art Ctr., Seoul, 2004, one-woman shows include L.A. Artcore, 1997. Reader Northridge, Porter Ranch br., LA Pub. libr., 1994—. Recipient Art Achievement award, Artists Soc. Internat. Gallery, San Francisco, 1987. Mem.: Gallery 825, LA Art Assn., Group Nine Art Collaborators, Lantern of the East L.A. Br. Methodist. Avocations: reading, hiking, theater, music, films.

NATHANSON, LINDA SUE, publishing executive, writer; b. Washington, Aug. 11, 1946; d. Nat and Edith (Weinstein) N.; m. James F. Barrett. BS, U. Md., 1969; MA, UCLA, 1970, PhD, 1975. Tng. dir. Rockland Rsch. Inst., Orangeburg, NY, 1975—77; asst. prof. psychology SUNY, 1978—79; pres. Cabri Prodns., Inc., Ft. Lee, NJ, 1979—81; rsch. supr. Darcy, McManus & Masius, St. Louis, 1981—83; mgr. software tng., documentation On-Line Software Internat., Ft. Lee, 1983—85; pvt. practice Ft. Lee, 1985—87; founder, exec. dir. Edin. Group, Inc., Gillette, NJ, 1987—98; founder, pres. Edin Books, Inc., Gillette, 1994—. Author: (with others) Psychological Testing: An Introduction to Tests and Measurements, 1988; (with S.J. Thayer) Interview with an Angel, 1997, The Heart of Interview with an Angel, 1998; publ. A Funny Thing Happened at the Interview (G.F. Farrell), 1996, Angel Talk (R. Crystal), 1996; (audiobook with W. Barnes) I Built the Titanic: Past-Life Memories of a Master Shipbuilder, 1999, Thomas Andrews, Voyage into History, 2000; (audio book on CD with W. Barnes and F. Baranowski) My Life and Death: A Past-Life Interview with Titanic's Designer, 2005. Recipient Rsch. Svc. award 1978; Rsch. fellow Albert Einstein Coll. Medicine, 1978-79. Jewish. Home and Office: 102 Sunrise Dr Gillette NJ 07933-1944 Business E-Mail: edinbooks@patmedia.net.

NATHANSON, MARJORIE ANN, clinical psychologist; b. Boston, Sept. 3, 1942; d. George B. and Sylvia (Dane) N.; m. Theodore Edwin Keeler, Aug. 29, 1982; 1 child, Daniel Christopher. AB, Vassar Coll., 1964; PhD, U. Calif.-Berkeley, 1974; candidate San Francisco Jung Inst., 1980-85, mem., 1985—. Lic. psychologist, Calif. Pvt. practice psychologist, Berkeley, Calif., 1976—; supr. Psychotherapy Inst., 1976-86. Margaret Floy Washburn fellow, 1964. Mem. C.J. Jung Inst. San Francisco (chair nominating com. 1998-1999, chair certifying com. 1998-1999, mem. exec. com. 1994-1998, 2000—06, pres.-elect, 2000-02, pres., 2002-04, bd. govs., 1998-1999, 2000—), Internat. Assn. Analytical Psychologists (exec. com. 2004—), Calif. State Psychol. Assn. Democrat. Office: 921 The Alameda Berkeley CA 94707-2311 Office Phone: 415-524-8075. E-mail: marjorie.nathanson@comcast.net.

NATION, PAMELA GRACE, secondary school educator; b. Louisville, Apr. 15, 1964; d. Oscar Thomas and Helen (Scrogham) N. BS, U. Louisville, 1986, MA in Teaching, 1988. Cert. tchr., Ky. Substitute tchr. Jefferson County Pub. Schs., Louisville, 1988-90, math. and sci. tchr., 1990—. Mem. NEA, Nat. Coun. Tchrs. Math., Jefferson County Tchrs. Assn., Ky. Edn. Assn., Ky. Sci. Tchrs. Assn., Louisville Biology Tchr. Alliance (coach sci. olympiad, coord.). Avocations: poetry, painting, entomology, reading, gardening. Home: 3108 Bobolink Rd Louisville KY 40213-1206

NATION, SAMIE BOWMAN, retired elementary and special education educator; b. Ringgold, Ga., Dec. 8, 1925; d. Samuel Joshua and Mamie (Tallant) Bowman; m. Harold Lloyd Nation, June 14, 1984; children: Frank La Prade Padgett, Therese Padgett. BS in Elementary Edn. cum laude, Tift Coll., Forsyth, Ga., 1971; MEd, Mercer U., Macon, Ga., 1973. Resource tchr. McMinn County Bd. Edn., Athens, Tenn.; math tchr. Title I, Catoosa County Bd. Edn.; tchr. 2d and 5th grades Boynton Elementary Sch., Catoosa County Bd. Edn., Ringgold, Ga. Mem.: Ga. Ret. Educators Assn., Nat. Ret. Tchrs. Assn., Catoosa County Ret. Educators Assn. (past pres.). Home: 4615 Old Mission Rd Chattanooga TN 37411-3812 E-mail: samiebn@earthlink.net.

NATIVIDAD, IRENE, women's rights advocate; b. Manila, Philippines, Sept. 14, 1948; m. Andrea Cortese; 1 child, Carlo Natividad Cortese. Graduate, Long Island Univ., 1971; LHD (hon.), Marymount Coll., 1994, Long Island Univ. Pres. Globe Women, Inc., Washington, Nat. Women's Political Caucus, 1985—89; chmn. Nat. Commn. on Working Women. Dep. vice chair Dem. Party Asian Caucus, 1982—84; pres. Global Summit of Women; co-chair Corp. Women Dir. Internat.; exec. dir. Philippine Am. Found.; bd. dir. Nat. Mus. Women in Arts, Nat. Assn. Corp. Dir., Sallie Mae; adv. bd. Cigna, Wyndham Internat. Exec. editor Asian American Almanac, 1995, frequent commentator, panelist on TV news shows; contbr. columns in newspapers. Named one of 100 Most Power Women in Am., Ladies Home Jour., 1988, 74 Women Changing Am. Politics, Campaigns & Elections Mag., 1993, 25 Most Influential Working Mothers, Working Mother Mag., 1997, 21 Leaders for the 21st Century, Women's eNews, 2004, Top 25 Influental Asian Americans, A. Mag.; recipient Women Making History award, Women's Congl. Caucus, 1985, Magnificent 7 award, Bus. & Profl. Women/USA, 1995, Women of Genius award, Trinity Coll., Washington, DC, 2001. Office: Natividad Assn 504 1211 Connecticut Ave NW Washington DC 20036 Business E-Mail: president@globewomen.com.

NATIVIDAD, LISALINDA SALAS, health facility administrator; b. AAFB, Guam, Mar. 31, 1971; d. Paul Castillo and Concepcion Quichocho Natividad; 1 child, Atdao-mami Paul. BA, U. Hawaii, 1993, MSW, 1996. Cert. marriage and family therapist Guam. Caseworker Sanctuary, Inc., Mangilao, Guam, 1993—94, cons., 1993—, dep. dir., 1998—2001; outreach counselor Key Project, Kahaluu, Hawaii, 1995; clinician Waianae (Hawaii) Mental Health Ctr., 1996; adj. prof. U. Guam, Mangilao, guam, 1998—; individual marriage and family therapist Marianas Clinic, Tamuning, 2001—. Contbr. chpt. Culturally Competitent Practice with Pacific Islanders, 1998. Recipient Pulama Project award, State of Hawaii, 1994—96, Women's Studies scholarship, U. Hawaii, 1993. Mem.: NASW (pres. bd. dirs. Guam chpt. 2001—), Guam Assn. Social Workers (v.p. 1999—2000). Avocations: hiking, the beach.

NATORI, JOSIE CRUZ (JOSEFINA ALMEDA CRUZ NATORI), apparel executive; b. Manila, Philippines, May 9, 1947; arrived in NYC, 1964; d. Felipe F. and Angelita A. (Almeda) Cruz; m. Kenneth R. Natori, May 20, 1972; 1 child, Kenneth E.F. BA in Econs., Manhattanville Coll., 1968; Degree (hon.), Acad. Art Coll., San Francisco, 2003. With Bache Securities, N.Y.C.; joined Merrill-Lynch Co. as an investment banker, 1971; v.p., 1976—77; owner, CEO The Natori Co., N.Y.C., 1977—. Bd. dirs. The Alltel Corp., 1995—. Bd. dirs. Philippine Am. Found., Jr. Achievement, Inc., 1992, Ednl. Found. for Fashion Industries; trustee Manhattanville Coll., Asian Cultural Coun.; commr. White House Conf. on Small Bus., 1993. Recipient Human Relations award Am. Jewish Com., N.Y.C., 1986, Harriet Alger award Working Woman, N.Y., 1987, Castle award Manhattanville Coll., Purchase, 1988, Galleon award Pres. Philippines, 1988, N.Y.C. Asian-Am. award, Friendship award Philippine-Am. Found., Hall of Fame award Mega Mags., Salute to Am. Fashion Designers award Dept. of Commerce, Ellis Island medal of Honor, 1994, Presdl. Awards for Filipino Individuals and Orgns. Overseas, Pamana ng Pilipino award Philippine Consulate Gen., 2002; named Bus. Woman of Yr. N.Y.C. Partnership and C. of C., 1998. Mem. CFDA, Young Pres.'s Orgn., Fashion Group, Com. of 200. Avocations: pianist, tennis player. Home: 45 E 62nd St New York NY 10021-8025 Office: The Natori Company 180 Madison Ave # 19 New York NY 10016-5267

NATOUR, NAHILLE I., obstetrician, gynecologist; b. Midland, Tex., Oct. 18, 1974; d. I. J. and Janet I. Natour. MD, Tex. A&M U. Health Sci. Ctr., College Station, 2001. Intern Baylor U. Med. Ctr., Dallas, 2001—02, resident, 2001—05; physician Women's Health Ptnrs., Health Tex. Provider Network, Irving, 2005—. Mem.: AMA, Tex. Assn. Ob-gyn., Dallas County Med. Soc., Tex. Med. Assn., Am. Coll. Ob-gyn. Office: Women's Health Partners 2021 N MacArthur Blvd Suite 500 Irving TX 75061 Office Phone: 972-251-2200.

NATSUYAMA, HARRIET HATSUNE KAGIWADA, mathematician, educator; b. Honolulu, Sept. 2, 1937; d. Kenjiro and Yakue Natsuyama; children: Julia, Conan. BA, U. Hawaii, 1959, MS, 1960; PhD, Kyoto U., 1965. Math. Rand Corp., Santa Monica, Calif., 1961—68, cons., 1968-77; adj. assoc. prof. U. So. Calif., L.A., 1974-79; sr. scientist Hughes Aircraft Co., El Segundo, 1979-87; chief engr. Infotec Devel. Inc., Camarillo, 1987-89; prof. systems engring. Calif. State U., Fullerton, 1990-96; co-founder Planet Aura, Inc., 2002—. Fgn. spl. vis. prof. Oita U., 1995, Kyoto Sch. of Computer Sci., 1997—2000; vis. prof. Sci. U., Tokyo, 1998; co-founder Planet Aura, Inc., 2002—; sec. Yeru Bon Ctr., L.A., Calif., 2005; founder U. Hawaii, Kenjiro and Yakue Natsuyama Scholarship, 2006. Author: Invariant Imbedding and Time-Dependent Transport Processes, 1963, System Identification: Methods and Applications, 1974, Integral Equations via Imbedding Methods, 1974, Multiple Scattering Processes: Inverse and Direct, 1975, Numerical Derivatives and Nonlinear Analysis, 1986, Terrestrial Radiative Transfer: Modeling, Computation, Data Analysis, 1998. Recipient Disting. Alumna, U. Hawaii, 1991. Mem. Inst. Noetic Scis., Grad. Women in Sci. (pres. 1990-91), Phi Beta Kappa, Phi Kappa Phi.

NAUGHTON, EILEEN, Internet company executive; d. Patrick J. Naughton; m. Craig Allen Chesley, Aug. 29, 1987; 3 children. BA in Internat. Rels., Univ. Pa., 1979, MBA, 1987; MA, Lauder Inst. Internat. Studies, 1987. Joined Time Inc., 1989, gen. mgr., Fortune mag. NYC, 1993—97, v.p., dir. fin., 1997—99; pres. Time Inc. Interactive, 1999—2000; v.p. investor rels. AOL Time Warner, 2000—02; pres., Time mag. Time Inc., 2002—05; head, advt. sales Google, NYC, 2006—. Bd. dirs. The Knot, Inc., 2006—. Bd. dir. Volunteers of Am. of NY, Fragile X Rsch. Found. (FRAXA). Office: Google Advt Sales Fl 8 437 5th Ave New York NY 10016 Office Phone: 212-624-9600.*

NAUGHTON, GAIL K., biomedical researcher, academic administrator; 3 children. BS, St. Francis Coll., NYC, 1976; MS, NYU, 1978, PhD med. sci., 1981, postdoctoral, dept. dermatology, 1982; MBA, UCLA, 2001. Asst. rsch. prof. NYU Med. Ctr., 1983—85; asst. prof. biology Queensborough Cmty. Coll., NYC, 1985—87; co-founder, dir. Advanced Tissue Sciences, 1987—2002, prin. scientist, 1987—89, sr. v.p., chief sci. officer, 1989—91, exec. v.p., COO, 1991—95, pres., COO, 1995—2000, vice chmn., 2000—02; dean, Coll. Bus. Adminstrn. San Diego State Univ., 2002—. Bd. dir. Calif Health Inst., San Diego World Trade Ctr., San Diego Corp. Governance Inst.; mem. sci. adv. bd. Johns Hopkins Univ., Ga. Inst. Tech., Univ. Calif. San Diego, Univ. Wash., MIT. Mem. San Diego Sci. & Tech. Council, UCSD Connect Leadership Council. Named Inventor of the Yr., Intellectual Property Owners Assn., 2000. Mem.: Rotary Internat. Achievements include holding over 75 U.S. & fgn. patents in tissue engring. Office: Coll Bus Adminstrn San Diego State Univ 5500 Campanile Dr San Diego CA 92182-8230*

NAUGHTON, MARGARET MARY, elementary school educator; b. Phila., May 5, 1976; d. Charles Wayne and Margaret Mary Waldron; m. Denis Anthony Naughton, July 18, 2003. BS in Elem. Edn., U. Scranton, Pa., 1998; MA in Elem. Edn., Villanova U., Pa., 2002. 3d gr. tchr. Maternity BVM Sch., Phila., 1998—2001, Cmty. Acad. Phila., 2001—03; 4th gr. tchr. Bayonne (N.J.) Sch. Dist., 2003—. Mem.: Phi Kappa Phi. Personal E-mail: marglenaughton@yahoo.com.

NAUGHTON, NOREEN KALE, art educator, artist; b. Schenectady, N.Y., Oct. 30, 1945; d. John Joseph and Eleanor Jane (Kale) N.; m. Joseph Allen Hansen, Dec. 28, 1968 (div. May 1975); children: Christina Noreen, Catharine Anne. BA, U. Hawaii, 1967, MEd, 1974, MFA, 1979. Violoncellist Honolulu Symphony Orch., 1965-68; lectureship in art Leeward C.C., Pearl City, Hawaii, 1970-77, Univ. Hawaii, 1977-85; asst. prof. art Kapiolani C.C., Honolulu, 1985-94, leader study abroad tours to Italy, 1989—, coord. art adv. bd., 1990—; assoc. prof. art, 1994—. Art curriculum coord. Community Coll. System, State of Hawaii, 1989—. Numerous one-woman shows, Hawaii, 1979—. Coord. Ho-omaluhia (Hawaii) Artist Group, 1985—. Staff devel. grantee Kapiolani C.C., 1991, 94. Mem. Founds. in Art Theory and Edn., Coll. art Assn., Univ. Hawaii Profl. Assembly. Roman Catholic. Office: Kapiolani Community College 4304 Diamond Head Rd Honolulu HI 96816-4422 Home: 45-527 Puoni Pl Kaneohe HI 96744-5923

NAUGHTON, PAMELA J., lawyer; BA summa cum laude, St. Olaf Coll., 1976; JD, Yale U., 1979. Bar: DC 1980, Minn. 1980, Calif. 1981, US Ct. Appeals (9th cir.). Atty. advisor Office Legis. Affairs, US Dept. Justice, 1979—81; asst. US atty. So. Dist. Calif., San Diego, 1981—87; assoc. counsel US Ho. of Reps. (select com. to investigate covert arms transactions with Iran), 1987; assoc. spl. counsel for impeachment US House Judiciary Com., 1988—89; ptnr. White Collar Criminal and Civil Fraud Practice Group Sheppard, Mullin, Richter & Hampton LLP, San Diego. Instr. US Atty. Gen.'s Advocacy Inst., 1985, Nat. Inst. of Trial Advocacy Depositions, 1992; trial practice judge San Diego Inns of Ct., 1990; lawyer delegate Ninth Cir. Judicial Conf.; commentator MSNBC, KFMB-TV, 1998—2002. Mem.: Assn. Bus. Trial Lawyers, Fed. Bar Assn., State Bar Calif., San Diego County Bar Assn. (mem. Judicial Evaluation Com.), Am. Inns Ct. (barrister William B. Enright Chap.), Phi Beta Kappa. Office: Sheppard, Mullin, Richter & Hampton LLP Ste 300 12544 High Bluff Dr San Diego CA 92130 Office Phone: 858-720-8984. Office Fax: 858-509-3691. E-mail: pnaughton@sheppardmullin.com.

NAULTY, SUSAN LOUISE, archivist; b. Abington, Pa., May 28, 1944; d. Charles J. and Ruth E. (Schick) N. BA, Whittier Coll., 1967; MA, Loyola U., L.A., 1972. Tchr. history and English, Whittier (Calif.) H.S., 1968-70; from libr. asst. to asst. curator Huntington Libr., San Marino, Calif., 1972-91; archivist Richard Nixon Libr. and Birthplace, Yorba Linda, Calif., 1991—.

NAUMAN, ANN KEITH, education educator; b. Greensboro, N.C., Aug. 2, 1931; d. Erle Almon and Santa Maria Keith; m. William Logan Nauman, Sept. 15, 1951; children: Richard Logan, Gerald Keith. BA, La. State U., 1961, MA, 1965, BS, 1966, MS, 1969, PhD, 1974; postgrad., Southeastern La. U., 1976-78, Cath. U., Santiago, Chile. Sch. libr. Parish Sch. Sys., Baton Rouge, 1966-76; asst. prof. ednl. founds. Southeastern La. U., Hammond, 1976-80, assoc. prof., 1986-89, prof., 1989—; prof., head dept. St. Joseph Sem. Coll., St. Benedict, La., 1980—. Author: Biographic Handbook of Educators, 1981, Guide to Latin American Archives, 1982, Time Management for Librarians, 1991, Inés de Suarez, Conquistadora, 2002. Fellow La. State U., 1972, OAS, Santiago de Chile, 1973; Mellon grantee Tulane U. Office: Southeastern La U PO Box 659 Hammond LA 70402-0001

NAUMER, CAROLA, art historian, educator; d. Helmuth and Tomee Naumer. BA, San Francisco State U., 1983, MA, 1987; PhD, Fla. State U., 1998. Instr. Fla. A&M U., Tallahassee, 1989—95, Bainbridge Coll., Ga., 1995—96, Tallahassee C.C., 1995—98; grad. tchg. asst. Fla. State U., Tallahassee, 1998—98; prof. Truckee Meadows C.C., Reno, 1999—. Participant NEH Summer Seminar, Naples, Italy, 2000. Contbr. articles to profl. jours. Mem.: Coll. Art Assn., Archaeol. Inst. Am. Office Phone: 775-673-8269. Office Fax: 775-674-4853. Business E-Mail: cnaumer@tmcc.edu.

NAVA, CARMEN P., communications executive; Degree in Bus. Adminstrn., U. So. Calif., 1984. Joined gen. mgmt. devel. program Pacific Bell, 1984, v.p., gen. mgr. Diverse Markets Group; regional pres. L.A. SBC Comm., L.A., 1997—99, pres. SBC Ctr. for Learning, 1999, pres. SBC West Consumer Markets San Antonio, 1999—. Bd. govs. U. So. Calif. Alumni Assn. Office: SBC Comm Inc 175 E Houston San Antonio TX 78205-2233

NAVA, MARY MARGARET, secondary school educator; b. Thomas, Okla., June 29, 1965; d. Russell Milson and Mary Lou Preston; m. J. Luis Nava, July 17, 1993; children: Elaine Marie, Marianna Elise. BS, S.W. Okla. State U., Weatherford, 1987, M in Edn., 1991. Cert. Okla., 1987, Tex., 1987. Tchr. Pampa Ind. Sch. Dist., Tex., 1987—. Choir mem. First Bapt. Ch., Pampa, Tex., 1990—99. Home: 2418 Christine Pampa TX 79065 Office: Pampa Ind Sch Dist 321 W Albert Pampa TX 79065 Office Phone: 806-669-4800.

NAVAB, APHRODITE DESIREE, artist, educator, writer; b. Esfahan, Iran, Oct. 31, 1971; arrived in U.S., 1980; d. Ali and Katina Navab; m. Richard C. Foltz, Aug. 21, 1994; children: Shahrzad Foltz-Navab, Bijan Foltz-Navab. BA magna cum laude, Harvard U., 1993; MA, EdM, Columbia U., 2000, EdD, 2004. Asst. prof. U. Fla., Gainesville, 2004—. Adj. asst. prof. U. Fla., 2000—02, grad. faculty supr., 2000—, faculty minority mentor, 2001—02, vis. asst. prof., 2002—04, faculty advisor undergrad. photography, 2002—, chair photography Sch. Arts & Art History, 2003—04. Contbr. articles to profl. jours.; one-woman shows include Bernice Steinbaum Gallery, Miami, Brown Gallery, Duke U., Durham, N.C., Charles Culpeper Photography Gallery, NYC. Recipient David McCord prize Outstanding Visual Artist, Harvard U., Cambridge, Mass., 1993. Mem.: Soc. Internat. Studies, Nat. Art Edn. Assn., Coll. Art Assn. Avocations: travel, languages, literature. Office: U Fla Coll Fine Arts PO Box 115801 Gainesville FL 32611 E-mail: dnavab@ufl.edu.

NAVARRA, TOVA, writer; b. Newark, July 10, 1948; d. Joe and Rose Leslie Treihart; m. John G. Navarra Jr., Aug. 26, 1967 (div. 1998); children: Yolanda, John G. III; m. Robert B. Kern, July 10, 2004. BA magna cum laude, Seton Hall Univ., 1974; AAS, Brookdale C.C., Lincroft, N.J., 1984; postgrad., Fairleigh Dickinson U. Elem. sch. tchr., Jersey City, 1967-69; corr. Village Times, Long Island, NY, 1974-75; tchr. music, humanities, German, art, art history Seton Hall Prep. Sch., South Orange, NJ, 1975-78; entertainment, feature writer, press corr. Asbury Park Press, Neptune, NJ, 1978-85, feature writer, art critic, family writer, 1985-92; feature writer, art columnist Two River Times, Red Bank, NJ, 1993-94. Psychiatric charge nurse, 1985; supr. grant rsch. Vis. Nurse Assn. Ctrl. Jersey, Red Bank, N.J., 1993-94; art coord. Monmouth Players, Navesink, N.J.; lectr. at writing confs; instr. Bayshore fitness and Wellness Ctr., Hazlet, N.J., 2005. Author: The New Jersey Shore: A Vanishing Splendor, 1985, Jim Gary: His Life and Art, 1987, Your Body: Highlights of Human Anatomy, 1990, Playing It Smart: What to Do When You're on Your Own, 1989, also, pub. On My Own: Helping Kids Help Themselves, (translated into Italian, Portuguese and Hebrew) 1994, 2d edit., 2003, An Insider's Guide to Home Health Care: An Interdisciplinary Approach (with Margaret Lundrigan), 1995, Wisdom for Caregivers, 1995; (staged readings) Through the Kunai Grass with Dad, 1988, Don't Cry, Pandora, 1989; (with Myron A. Lipkowitz and John G. Navarra) Therapeutic Communication: A Guide to Effective Interpersonal Skills for Health Care Professionals, 1990, Encyclopedia of Vitamins, Minerals, and Supplements, 1995, 2d edit., 2004; (with Lipkowitz), Allergies A-Z, 1994; Images of America: Howell and Farmingdale 1996; (with Lundrigan) Image of America: Levittown: The First Fifty Years, 1997, Staten Island, 1997, Staten Island II, 1998, Levittown II, 1998; Toward Painless Writing, 1998; The American Century: Staten Island (with Lundrigan), 1999; Seton Hall University: A Photographic History, 1999, Monmouth University, 2001, Encyclopedia of Asthma and Respiratory Disorders, 2003, Young People/Tough Problems, 2003, Encyclopedia of Allergies 2d edit., 2004, Encyclopedia of Complementary and Alternative Medicine, 2004; illustrator Drugs and Man, 1973; editor in chief Shore Affinity, 1979-81; contbg. editor Am. Jour. Nursing, 1990-94; staff writer, illustrator, photographer N.J. Music and Arts, 1978-81; editor Associated Univ. Presses, 1981-82; copywriter, photographer Jersey Shore Med. Ctr., 1985; feature writer, columnist Copley News Svc., 1988-93; health trend columnist Personal Fitness, 1989-90; assoc. editor The Courier, Middletown, N.J., May-Dec. 1998; lifestyle editor The Two River Times, Red Bank, N.G. May 1999-2000; contr. to Nursing Spectrum Magazine; photography exhbns. in N.Y., N.J., Pa. Mid-Atlantic Riviera Magazine, 2005; guest various radio and TV programs; contbr. photographs to books, articles and photogs. to mags., newspapers; solo exhibits include Atlantic City Art Ctr., 1982, O.K. Harris Works of Art, N.Y.C., 1990, Gallery Axiom, Phila., 1991, Monmouth U., 1991, M. Thomson Kravetz Gallery, Bay Head, N.J., Oceanic Pub. Libr., 2000, Navesink Libr. Theater, 2004, 05; group shows at Art Forms, Red Bank, 1991, Moravian Coll., Bethlehem, Pa., 1992. Mem. Gov.'s Coun. on Alcoholism and Drug Abuse Prevention, co-chair Later Childhood subcom., 1992 Mem. N.J. Playwrights Workshop (charter), N.J. State Nurses Assn. Avocations: singing, guitar, piano, dance, crafts. Office: Sanford J Greenburger Assocs care Faith H Hamlin 55 5th Ave New York NY 10003-4301

NAVARRO, BJ, federal agency administrator; married, 1980; children: Mark, Manuel. B, San Jose State U. With Space Life Scis. Projects Office NASA Ames Rsch. Ctr., Moffett Field, Calif., with leadership program, stowage mgr. Musician (trumpet player): Milpitas Cmty. Concert Band. Avocations: sports, theater. Office: NASA Ames Rsch Ctr Bldg 240 Rm 206, Mail Stop 240-10 Moffett Field CA 94035 Business E-Mail: bjnavarro@mail.arc.nasa.gov.

NAVARRO, LYDIA, language educator; b. Yabucoa, P.R., Oct. 20, 1949; d. José Navarro and Juana Crespo; m. Arnaldo Rivera; children: Arnaldo Jr., Miguel Angel, Jorge Luis, José Antonio. BA in english, U. P.R., 1986; MS in TESOL, Nova Southeastern U., 1997; D in edn., U. Ctrl. Fla., 2004. Cert. profl. educator in english, TESOL. Tchr. P.R. Pub. Schs., Mayaguez, PR, 1986—90, Volusia County Schs., Deltona, Fla., 1990—2000, dist. translator, 2000—02, tchr. on assignment, 2002—. Foreign lang. dept. chmn. Deltona (Fla.) HS, 1996—2000; dist. ESOL trainer ESOL Program, Deland, Fla., 1996—; clin. edn. Volusia County Schs., 1997—. Mem.: Assn. TESOL, Assn. Supr. and Curriculum Devel., Leadership West Volusia, C of C West Volusia, Nat. Rep. Party, Kappa Delta Pi. Avocations: dance, gardening, swimming, landscaping, interior decorating. Home: 1640 Humphrey Ct Deltona FL 32738 Office: Volusia County Schs 200 N Clara Ave Deland FL 32720

NAVARRO, MONICA, lawyer; b. 1967; arrived in US, 1984; m. Mark Crane. BA in Polit. Sci. and Internat. Rels., Fla. Internat. U., 1990; JD, U. Mich. Law Sch., 1993. Bar: Ill., Mich., US Supreme Ct., US Ct. of Appeals Sixth Cir., US Dist. Ct. Eastern Dist. Mich., US Dist. Ct. Western Dist. Mich. Judicial clerk Hon. Julian Abele Cook, Jr., US Dist. Ct., Eastern Dist. Mich.; atty. Frank, Haron; prin. mem., ptnr. Frank, Haron, Weiner and Navarro, 2004—. Mem., HIPAA Compliance Com. Troy Chamber of Commerce; trustee Mich. Psychoanalytic Found. Guest Hospitals and Physicians: Friends and Foes, Bloomfield Cmty. TV, 2006. Named one of Top 10 Qui Tam Lawyers in Country, Corp. Crime Reporter, 40 Under 40, Crain's Detroit Bus., 2006; recipient Am. Jurisprudence award in Adminstrv. Law, Best Oralist award. Fellow: Oakland County Bar Found.; mem.: State of Mich. Bd. Psych., Mich. Trial Lawyers Assn., Assn. Trial Lawyers Am., Oakland County Women's Bar Assn. (Work Life balance award 2006), Oakland County Bar Assn. (Med./Legal Com.), Mich. Assn. Health Lawyers (mem. Tech. Subcommittee), Hispanic Bar Assn. Mich., Am. Health Lawyers Assn. Office: Frank, Haron, Weiner and Navarro 5435 Corporate Dr Ste 225 Troy MI 48098 Office Phone: 248-952-0400. Office Fax: 248-952-0890. Business E-Mail: mnavarro@fhwnlaw.com.*

NAVARRO-STEINEL, CATHERINE A., municipal official; Degree in Bus. Mgmt., ICS Newport Pacific, 1995; BSc in Criminal Justice Mgmt., La Salle U., 1997; student, Rutgers U., Thomas Edison State Coll. Cert. Pub. Supr. Mgmt. N.J. Dept. Personnel, 99, registered Mpl. Clk. State Dept. Cmty. Affairs, cert. pub.mgr. 2003. Supr. fire dispatcher N. Hudson Regional Comm. Ctr., West N.Y., NJ, 1985—91; prin. tech. aid to supt. Twp. Teaneck, Teaneck, NJ, 1992; fire comm. dispatcher N. Hudson Regional Comm. Ctr., 1992—94; police records clk. Twp. Teaneck, 1994—95, fire dept. sr. clk., 1995—99; dep. mcpl. clk. City of Orange, Orange, NJ, 1999—2000; mcpl. clk. Borough of Fairview, NJ, 2000—02; borough adminstr. Borough of Little Ferry, NJ, 2002—. Mem.: Internat. Inst. Mcpl. Clk., Am. Soc. Notary Pub., Internat. Soc. Cert. Employee Benefits Assn., Am. Acaed. Cert. Pub. Mgrs., Cert. Pub. Mgr. Soc. N.J., Bergen County Clk. Assn., Mcpl. Clk. Assn. N.J. Home: 16 Ann Street Bergenfield NJ 07621-1602 Office: Borough of Little Ferry 215-217 Liberty St Little Ferry NJ 07643

NAVE, PAMELA J., music educator; b. Anderson, Ind., Apr. 10, 1968; d. Robert W. and Trudy J. Nave; life ptnr. Courtney L. Kennedy, Aug. 20, 1982. MusB, Ball State U., Muncie, Ind., 1991, BS, MA, Ball State U., Muncie, Ind., 1996; D in Musical Arts, Ohio State U., Columbus, 2001. Pvt. instr. Nave's Percussion Studio, Noblesville, Ind., 1991—95; prof. percussion Ball State U., Muncie, 1996—97; assoc. prof. bands and percussion Purdue U., Lafayette, Ind., 1999—. Recipient Undergraduate Concerto Competition winner, Ball State U., 1990, Grad. Concerto Competition winner, 1996, Grad. Tchg. Award, Ohio State U., 1999, Grad. Concerto Competition winner, 1999; scholar, Ball State U., 1995, Ohio State U., 1997. Master: Yamaha Drum Co. (assoc.; clinician 1999), Kori Marimbas (assoc.; clinician 2004), Remo Drum Head Co. (assoc.; clinician 1999), Zildjian Cymbals Co. (assoc.; clinician 2005); fellow: Tau Beta Sigma (hon.; advisor 1999); mem.: Ind. Music Educators Assn. (assoc.; asst. dir. 2001), Percussive Arts Soc. (assoc.; v.p. 2005), Lafayette Symphony Orch. (assoc.; percussion sect. leader 2005), Lafayette Citizens Band (assoc.; percussion sect. leader 1999), Pi Kappa Lambda, Phi Kappa Phi. Liberal. Methodist. Avocations: European travel, museums, camping, hiking, fishing. Home: 16 Coldbrook Dr Lafayette IN 47909 Office: Purdue Univ 712 Third St West Lafayette IN 47907-2005 Office Phone: 765-494-4689. Home Fax: 765-496-2822; Office Fax: 765-496-2822. E-mail: pjnave@purdue.edu.

NAVIAUX, LAREE DEVEE, psychologist; b. Lewellen, Nebr., Aug. 18, 1937; d. Prosper Leo and Dorothy DeVee (Walters) N.; m. Frank Anthony D'Abreo, June 16, 1973. B.S., U. Nebr., 1959; M.S., Iowa State U., 1963; Ph.D., Duquesne U., 1973. Instr. Iowa State U., Ames, 1963-65; asst. prof. Kans. State U., Manhattan, 1965-66; grad. faculty part-time assoc. Margaret Morrison Coll. Carnegie-Mellon U., Pitts., 1966-69; asst. prof. West Ga. Coll., Carrollton, 1969-72; regional dir. Children's Mental Health, Charleston, W.Va., 1973-80; therapist, educator Community Mental Health Ctr., Charleston, 1980-82; pvt. practice, 1982—2004; ret., 2004; assoc. spiritual dir. W.Va. Inst. Spirituality, 2004—; asst. clin. prof. W.Va. U., 1977-87. bd. dirs. Creative Arts Clinic, 1981-83, Parents Anonymous of W.Va., 1979-82, YWCA, 1991-97, Charleston Chamber Music, 2004, W.Va. Pub. TV Friends,

2004; mem. Charleston Chamber Music Bd., 2004, W.Va. Pub. TV Friends Bd., 2004-. Grantee Humanities Found. W.Va., 1978, 79, 81, 82, 2005. Mem. U. Nebr. Alumni (life), Iowa State U. Alumni (life), Am. Psychol. Assn. (life), Mental Health Assn. (life). Democrat. Clubs: Gourmet, Indian Assn., Avampato Mus. Art Collectors Club. Contbr. articles to profl. jours. and books.

NAVRATILOVA, MARTINA, professional tennis player; b. Prague, Czech Republic, Oct. 18, 1956; came to US, 1975, naturalized, 1981; d. Miroslav Navratil and Jana Navratilova. Student, schs. in Czechoslovakia; Hon. doctorate, George Washington U., 1996. Tennis commentator/broadcaster HBO Sports, 1995-99; Profl. tennis player, 1973-94, 2003—06. Player Czech Fed. Cup Team, 1975, U.S. Fed Cup Team, 1982, 86, 89, 95, 2003; mem. World Team Tennis, 1990—. Author: (with George Vecsey) Martina, 1985; (with Liz Nickles) The Total Zone, 1995, Breaking Point, 1996, Killer Instinct, 1997, Shape Your Self: My 6-Step Diet and Fitness Plan to Achieve the Best Shape of Your Life, 2006; columnist. Co-founder Rainbow Card. Winner Czechoslovak Nat. singles, 1972-74, U.S. Open singles, 1983, 84, 86, 87, U.S. Open doubles, 1977, 78, 80, 83, 84, 87, 90, U.S. Open mixed doubles, 1987, 2006, Va. Slims Championsips, 1978, 83, 84, 85, 86, Va. Slims Championships, 1991, Wimbledon singles, 1978, 79, 82, 83, 84, 85, 86, 87, 90, Wimbledon women's doubles, 1976, 79, 81, 82, 83, 84, 86, Wimbledon mixed doubles, 1985, 93, 95, 2003, French Open singles, 1982, 84, Australian Open singles, 1981, 83, 85, Australian Doubles (with Betsy Nagelsen) 1980, (with Pam Shriver), 1982, 84, 85, 87, 88, 89, Australian Mixed Doubles, 2003, Roland Garros (with Pam Shriver), 1985, 87, 89, Italian Open doubles (with Gabriela Sabatini), 1987, (with Pam Shriver) COREL WTA Tour doubles team of yr., 1981-89, triple Crown at U.S. Open, 1987; recipient Women's Sports Found. Flo Hyman award, 1987, BBC Lifetime Achievement Award, 2003; named Female Athlete of the Decade (1980s) The Nat. Sports Review, UPI, and AP, WTA Player of Yr., 1978-79, 82-86, Women's Sports Found. Sportswoman of Yr., 1982-84, Hon. Citizen of Dallas, AP Female Athlete of Yr., 1983; named to Internat. Tennis Hall of Fame, 2000; Martina Navratilova Day proclaimed in Chgo., 1992 Mem. Women's Tennis Assn. (dir., exec. com., pres.), Women's Tennis Assn. Tour Player's Assn. (pres. 1979-80, 83-84, 94-95). Achievements include being the holder of 167 singles titles and 173 doubles titles; holder of record of singles-match wins (1,309), 1991; holds record for 109 consecutive doubles matches won (with Pam Shriver).*

NAWARA, LUCILLE PROCTER, artist, educator; b. Oklahoma City, Okla., June 26, 1941; d. Leland Herrick and Alice McElroy Procter; m. James Edward Nawara, Dec. 15, 1968; children: Juliet Glinski, Stephen Procter; 1 child, Todd Keenan (dec.). BA, Smith Coll., Northampton, Mass., 1962; BFA equivalent, Boston U., 1967; MFA, U. Ill., Champaign, 1969. Asst. prof. drawing Wayne State U., Detroit, 1969—76; instr. painting and drawing Macomb C.C., Mt. Clemens, Mich., 1977—84; instr. watercolor Ctr. for Creative Studies, Detroit, 1982—84; artist-in-residence Fraser Pub. Schs., 1983—86; instr. painting and drawing Macomb C.C., Mt. Clemens, Mich., 1991; vis. artist painting Cranbrook Acad. Art, Bloomfield Hills, Mich., 1992; art instr. Birmingham (Mich.)-Bloomfield Art Ctr., 2003—. Asst. Inst. Contemporary Art, Boston, 1965; exhbn. coord. Detroit Focus Gallery, Detroit, 1980; dir. Nawara Art Gallery, Walled Lake, Mich., 1986—88; owner, designer, installer Nawara Landscapes, 1992—; concert-mistress Bach Soc. Orch., Cambridge, Mass., 1966—67; artist-in-the-parks resident Nat. Park Svc. at Sleeping Bear Dunes, Empire, Mich., 1998; artist-in-the-schs. resident Fraser Pub. Sch.-Mich. Coun. for Arts, 1983—86; adj. instr. watercolor Ctr. Creative Studies, Detroit. Violinist: Detroit Sinfonia, Detroit Chamber Orch., Princeton Symphony. Co-pres. bd. Detroit Focus Gallery, 1991—92; founder, chairperson Present for the Arts in Detroit, Detroit, 1980—86, Wayne Park Com., Detroit, 1978—83; co-founder, co-chairperson Project Retree, Detroit, 1977—79. Recipient individual artist grants, Mich. Coun. for Arts, 1981, 1983. Democrat. Episcopalian. Avocations: gardening, landscaping, cooking, violin, knitting. Home: 30585 Vernon Dr Beverly Hills MI 48025

NAWROCKI, SUSAN JEAN, librarian; b. Aurora, Ill., Mar. 3, 1942; d. David John and Sarah (Willoughby) Calvert; m. Thomas Dennis Nawrocki, June 25, 1966; children: Selena, Steffan. BA, Coe Coll., Cedar Rapids, Iowa, 1964; MS in Art, Milw., 1965. Cert. Tchr. Iowa, 1966, Wis., 1967. Libr. Milw. Pub. Libr. Main Br., 1966—67; reference libr. Columbus/Lowndes County Libr., Columbus, Miss., 1986—. Exhibitions include 57 competitive: Watercolor Wis., Weston Mus. Fine Arts, Milw., 1966, exhibitions include Ann. San Antonio Artists' Exhbn., 1968 ($200 award, 1969), Witte Meml. Mus., San Antonio, 1969, Exhbn. Southwest Prints and Drawings, Dallas Mus. Fine Arts, 1969 (award, 1969), Ann. Festival of Arts 8-State Exhbn. Paintings and Graphics, Fort Smith Art Ctr., Ark., 1971 (award, 1971), Ann. Print and Drawing Competition, 1972, Ann. U. Wis. Art Competition, U. Wis., Milw., 1976, 1977, 1979, 1982, Bi-State Competition, Meridian (Miss.) Mus. of Art, 1976 (purchase award, 1987), 1978, 1980, 1987, Nat. Arts Festival, Tupelo, Miss., 1980 (Purchase award, 1980, 2 Purchase awards, Top Graphics award, 1981, Purchase award and Graphics award, 1983), 1981, 1983, Ann. Miss. Arts Exhbn., Univ. So. Miss., Hattiesburg, 1982, Ann. Miss. Arts Exhbn. Juried, 1987, 1988 (Purchase award, 1987); contbg. editor (art editor): (Coll. Mag.) Acorn, 1962—64; co-editor, 1964; contbg. editor: Caravan Literary Mag., 1963—64. Home: 147 Shane Cir Columbus MS 39702 Business E-Mail: refer@lowndes.lib.ms.us.

NAY, PATRICIA TOMSKO, medical association administrator; b. Cumberland, Md., Apr. 4, 1964; d. Robert and Shirley Tomsko; m. Gordon Allan Nay, Mar. 17, 1954. MD, Ohio State U., Columbus, 1994. Cert. med. dir. Am. Med. Dirs. Assn., 1998. Dep. med. examiner Office of the Chief Med. Exam., Balt., 1998—; med. dir. Shady Grove Adventist Hosp., Rockville, Md., 2005—. Fellow: Am. Assn. Family Practice. Office: Rockville Geriatrics & Palliative Med Ste G-100 11119 Rockville Pike Rockville MD 20852 Office Phone: 301-294-1864. Home Fax: 301-349-5177; Office Fax: 301-349-5177. Personal E-mail: tricianay@comcast.net.

NAYLIS, STEPHANIE ANNE, music educator; b. Teaneck, NJ, Mar. 27, 1982; d. Gerard James and Nancy Lucille Naylis. MusB, Rider U., 2004. Vocal music tchr. Newton (NJ) Pub. Schs., 2004—. Mem. Masterworks Chorus, Morristown, NJ, 2004—05. Office: Newton HS 44 Ryerson Ave Newton NJ 07860

NAYLOR, MAGDALENA RACZKOWSKA, psychiatrist, educator; b. Warsaw, Aug. 4, 1950; arrived in U.S., 1981; d. Wlodzimierz Raczkowski and Urszula Raczkowska-Cieslik; m. Thomas Herbert Naylor, Dec. 14, 1985; 1 child, Alexander Watkins. MD, Warsaw Med. U., Poland, 1976, PhD, 1987. Diplomate psychiatry and neurology Nat. Bd. Certification in Psychiatry and Neurology, 1994. Asst. prof. Warsaw Med. U., 1977—83; rsch. assoc. Med. Coll. Va., Richmond, 1981—82; resident psychiatry Duke U., Durham, NC, 1984—88; pvt. practice psychiatry Richmond, Va., 1988—93; attending physician psychiatry Fletcher Allen Health Care, Burlington, Vt., 1993—; asst. prof. U. Vt., Burlington, 1993—99, assoc. prof., 1999—. Rsch. assoc. Med. Coll. Va., Richmond, Va., 1981—82; med. dir. women's program Psychiat. Inst. Richmond, Va., 1991—92; med. dir. partial hospitalization program Charter Westbrook Hosp., 1992—93; med. dir. psychiat. unit Flecher Allen Health Care, Burlington, Vt., 1994—97; dir. mindbody medicine clinic U. Vt. Med./Flecher Allen Health Care, 1998—; assoc. dir. clin. neuroscience rsch. unit U. Vt. Med.; spkr. on search for meaning and integration of mind, body and spirit into med. practice. Author (with Thomas Naylor and William Willimon): The Search for Meaning, 1994, The Search for Meaning Workbook, 1994; contbr. articles to profl. jours. Com. mem. Vt. Pain & Symptom Mgmt. Com.; mem. Gailer Sch., Shelburn, Vt., 2001—03. Recipient Best Tchr. of Yr. Dept. of Psychiatry, U. Vt. Med. Sch., 1996, 1998; grantee, NIH, 2002, 2004, 2005, U. Vt. Med. Sch., 2004. Mem.: Am. Pain Soc., Vt. Med. Assn. Achievements include research in coping skills training for patients in chronic pain, obesity and chemical dependence. Home: 202 Stockbridge Rd Charlotte VT 05445 Office: U Vt UHC 1 S Prospect St Burlington VT 05401 Office Phone: 802-847-2673. Business E-Mail: magdalena.naylor@vtmednet.org.

NAYLOR, MARY D., medical professor, director; BSN, Villanova U.; PhD, MSN, U. Penn. Assoc. dean, dir. undergrad. studies U. Penn. Sch. Nursing, Philadelphia, 1986—98, founder, dir. Living Independently for Elders (LIFE) program, 1998—, Marian S. Ware prof. gerontology; dir. RAND/Hartford Ctr. Inderdisciplinary Geriatric Health Care Rsch. U. Penn., Philadelphia. Named to Nat. Honor Soc. Nursing; recipient Lenore Williams award, U. Penn., Outstanding Alumni award, U. Penn. Sch. Nursing., Claire Fagin Disting. Rsch. award, U. Penn. Sch. Nursing, 2003, Disting. Lectr. award, Sigma Theta Tau, Pa. Nurses Assn. Nursing Rsch. award, Nightingale Award of Pa., McCann Scholar award, Joy McCann Found., 2004; Nat. Leadership Fellowship, W.K. Kellogg Found. Fellow: Leonard Davis Inst. Health Economics, Am. Heart Assn.; mem.: Inst. Medicine. Office: UPenn Sch Nursing Rm 364 NEB 420 Guardian Dr Philadelphia PA 19104-6069 Office Phone: 215-898-6088. E-mail: naylor@nursing.upenn.edu.*

NAYLOR, PHYLLIS REYNOLDS, writer; b. Anderson, Ind., Jan. 4, 1933; d. Eugene Spencer and Lura Mae (Schield) Reynolds; m. Thomas A. Tedesco, Jr., Sept. 9, 1951 (div. 1960); m. Rex V. Naylor, May 26, 1960; children: Jeffrey, Michael. Diploma, Joliet Jr. Coll., 1953; BA, Am. U., 1963. Author more than 125 books including Crazy Love: An Autobiographical Account of Marriage and Madness, 1977, Revelations, 1979, A String of Chances, 1982 (ALA notable book), The Agony of Alice, 1985 (ALA notable book), The Keeper, 1986 (ALA notable book), Unexpected Pleasures, 1986, Send No Blessings, 1990 (YASD best book for young adults), Shiloh, 1991 (ALA notable book, John Newbery medal 1992), The Fear of Place, 1994, Sang Spell, 1998, Walker's Crossing, 1999, Blizzard's Wake, 2002, After, 2003. Recipient Golden Kite award Soc. Children's Book Writers Am., 1985, Child Study award Bank St. Coll., 1983, Edgar Allan Poe award Mystery Writers Am., 1985, 2004, Internat. book award Soc. Sch. Librs., 1988, Christopher award, 1989, Newbery award ALA, 1992, Nat. Endowment of Arts Creative Writing fellow, 1987. Mem.: PEN, Authors Guild, Soc. Children's Book Writers, Children's Book Guild of Washington (pres. 1974—75, 1983—84), Amnesty Internat., Physicians for Social Responsibility, Coun. for a Livable World. Unitarian Universalist. Avocations: theater, swimming. Home and Office: 9910 Holmhurst Rd Bethesda MD 20817-1618 Office Phone: 301-530-2340.

NAYLOR, SUSAN EMBRY, music educator; b. Huntington Park, Calif., Feb. 21, 1951; d. Hollie J. and Sara Mozelle (Maddox) E. MusB in piano performance, Converse Coll., Spartanburg, S.C., 1973; MusM, Ga. State U., Atlanta, 1975. Cert. music tchr. Ga. Prof. piano and music theory Reinhardt Coll., Waleska, Ga., 1975—, music program coord., 1995-2000. Pvt. piano tchr. Waleska, Marietta, and Kennesaw, Ga., 1973—. Performer solo piano and ensemble recitals colls., chs. and profl. orgns., 1973—; pianist Spartanburg (S.C.) Symphony Orch., 1970-73, featured soloist, 1972; guest pianist Nat. Pub. Radio, 1988. Ch. pianist Bapt., Meth. Churches in Marietta, Dallas, and Kennesaw, 1973—. Recipient Cobb County Young Artist Award; Cobb County Arts Coun. Parks and Recreation and Jr. League, 1983, 86. Mem. Ga. Music Tchr. Assn. (adjudicator 1976—, coll. faculty chair 1996-98, cert. credentials chair 1997-99, pres.-elect 1998-2000, pres. 2000-2002, fin. advisory com., 2000—), Ga. Fedn. Music Clubs (adjudicator 1976—), Cherokee Music Tchr. Assn. (pres. 1988-91, 1st v.p. program 1997-99), Cherokee County Arts Coun. (exec. bd., v.p. 1993-95), Music Tchr. Nat. Assn. (nat. coll. faculty cert., nat. cert. evaluation team 1993-96, ho. dels. 2000-2002). Baptist. Avocations: antiques, reading. Home: 109 Myrtle Ct Waleska GA 30183-4202 Office: Reinhardt Coll 7300 Reinhardt Coll Cir Waleska GA 30183-2981 Business E-Mail: sen@reinhardt.edu.

NAZARETH, ANNETTE LAPORTE, commissioner, lawyer; b. Providence, Jan. 27, 1956; d. George Robert and Dolores (LaPorte) Nazareth; m. Roger Walton Fergunson, May 3, 1986; 2 children. AB magna cum laude, Brown U., 1978; JD, Columbia U., 1981. Assoc. Davis Polk & Wardwell, NYC, 1981-86; gen. ptnr., gen. counsel Mabon, Nugent & Co., NYC, 1986-91; mng. dir., gen. counsel Mabon Securities Corp., NYC, 1991—94; sr. v.p. Lehman Brothers, Inc., NYC, 1994—97; mng. dir., dep. head Salomon Smith Barney, NYC, 1997—98; sr. counsel to chmn. SEC, Washington, 1998—99, acting dir., Divsn. Investment Mgmt., dir., Divsn. Mkt. Regulation, 1999—2005, commr., 2005—. Mem.: Securities Industry Assn., Phi Beta Kappa. Office: SEC 100 F St NE Washington DC 20549 Office Phone: 202-551-6551.

NAZARIO, SONIA, reporter; b. Madison, Wis., Sept. 8, 1960; m. William Regensburger. BA in History, Williams Coll., Williamstown, Mass., 1982; MA in Latin Am. studies, U. Calif., Berkeley, 1988. Freelance reporter El Pais, Madrid, 1980; staff reporter Wall St. Jour., Atlanta, 1982—84, Miami, 1984—86, LA, 1988—93; urban affairs writer L.A. Times, 1993—94, projects and urban affairs reporter, 1994—. Author: Enrique's Journey: The Story of a Boy's Dangerous Odyssey to Reunite with His Mother, 2006 (Pulitzer Prize for feature writing for original articles in LA Times, 2003). Recipient Pulitzer prize finalist for pub. svc., 1998, Nat. Coun. on Crime and Delinquency PASS award, 1998, Commendation for outstanding reporting on psychiat. issues, Am. Psychiat. Assn., 1998, Life-Time award, Inst. for Suicide Prevention, 1997, Guillermo Martinez-Marquez award for overall excellence, Nat. Assn. Hispanic Journalists, 1995, George Polk award for local reporting, 1994, Cameron R. Duncan World Hunger Media award, 1994, George Polk award for internat. reporting, 2003, Robert F. Kennedy Journalism award, 2003, Overseas Press Club award, 2003, award, Nat. Assn. Hispanic Journalists Guillermo Martinez-Marquez, 2003. Mailing: Author Mail Random House 1745 Broadway New York NY 10019 Business E-Mail: sonia.nazario@latimes.com.*

NAZEMETZ, PATRICIA, human resources specialist; BA, MA, Fordham U. Benefits analyst W.R. Grace and Co.; various positions in human resources including benefits ops. mgr. Xerox Corp., Stamford, Conn., 1979—99, v.p. human resources, 1999—. Bd. dirs., chair human resources com. Nat. Bus. Group Health and Human Svcs., Long Island; trustee, vice-chmn. bd. Fordham U. Office: Xerox Corp 800 Long Ridge Rd Stamford CT 06904 Office Phone: 203-968-3000. Office Fax: 203-968-3218.

NDIAYE, MARIE, writer, playwright; b. Pithiviers, France; m. Jean-Yves Cendrey; 3 children. Author: (novels) As For the Rich Future, 1985, Classical comedy, 1987, The Women Turned into a Log, 1989, A Time of the Year, 1994, The Witch, 1996, Among Family, 1997, Rosie Carpe, 2001, Daddy Must Eat, 2003, (plays) Hilda, 1999 (Grand Prix de la Critique, 2001), Providence, 2001, The Serpents, 2004, Nothing Human, 2004, (short stories) All My Friends, 2004, (autobiography) Self-Portrait in Green, 2005. Home: Barie Normandy France

NEAGA KHAYT, ANGELA, music educator; b. Moscow, May 12, 1947; arrived in U.S., 1997; d. Gheorghe Neaga and Lily Nyaga; m. Yury Khayt, Oct. 1, 1999. M in Piano, Acad. Music, Kishinev, USSR, 1974. Piano tchr., mgr. Conservatory Music, Kishinev, 1976—92, Spl. Music Sch., Kishinev, Moldova, 1992—97, Angela's Piano Studio, Arlington, Tex., 1998—. Accompanist Grace Luth. Ch., Arlington, 2001—; substitute accompanist U. Tex., Arlington, 2001—. Mgr., participant charity recitals Jewish Cmty. Ctr., Echad and Golden Acres Ctrs., Dallas, 1997—. Mem.: Nat. Assn. Self Employed, Music Tchrs. Nat. Assn. Avocations: literature, art, movies, computers, cooking. Home: 3508 Raynorwood Ct Arlington TX 76015 E-mail: aneaga@hotmail.com.

NEAGOY, MONICA MARIA MARTHA, mathematician, consultant; d. George Daniel and Angela Hrissetta Neagoy; m. Didier Rousselet, Dec. 27, 1997; 1 child, Nicolas Rousselet. BS in Math., MA in Math.; PhD, U. Md., College Park, 1995. Math. instr. Georgetown U., Washington, 1980—85; program dir. NSF, Arlington, Va., 2001—04. Cons. in field, 1987—. Tchr. Enhancement grantee, NSF. Mem.: Math. Assn. Am. Personal E-mail: monicaneagoy@earthlink.net.

NEAL, ANN PARKER See PARKER, ANN

NEAL, BONNIE JEAN, real estate agent; b. Kansas City, Mo. d. David Ira and Juanita Mae (Duncan) Johnson; m. Howard Stranton Neal, July 24, 1948 (div. Oct. 1972); children: Randall Stranton, William Scott, Douglas Kelly. Student, U. Omaha, 1980-86, Londay Sch. Real Estate, Omaha, 1987. Lic. real estate broker. Data processing supr. Enron Corp., Omaha, 1980-85, adminstrv. support analyst, 1985-86; real estate sales agt. Allen, Young Assocs., Omaha, 1987, Home Real Estate (merger Allen Young Assocs. and Wurdeman & Maenner), Omaha, 1988; with Coldwell Banker Action Real Estate, 1988-91, Coldwell Banker BJ Brown, La Vista, Nebr., 1991-92. Active PTA, Council Bluffs, Iowa, 1957-59; vol. March of Dimes, Council Bluffs, 1963; mem. Realtors Polit. Action Com.; mem. pub. rels. com. Bd. Realtors, 1994-2000, mem. forms com., 1995-96. Fellow Omaha Bd. Realtors, Women's Bowling Assn., Order Ea. Star (25-Yr. award 1980, 50 Yr. award 2005); mem. Women's Coun. Realtors. Democrat. Baptist. Avocations: music, piano, water sports, bicycling, motor sports. Office: CBSHome Real Estate 14250 W Maple Rd Omaha NE 68164-2436 Office Phone: 402-680-7893. E-mail: bonnie.neal@cbshome.come.

NEAL, DARWINA LEE, federal agency administrator; b. Mansfield, Pa., Mar. 31, 1942; d. Darwin Leonard and Ina Belle (Cooke) N. BS, Pa. State U., 1965; postgrad., Cath. U, 1968-70. Registered landscape architect. Landscape architect nat. capital region Nat. Pk. Svc., 1965-69, office of White House liaison, 1969-71, office of profl. services, 1971-74, div. design svcs., 1974-89, chief design svcs., 1989-95, chief landscape arch. office of stewardship and partnership Washington, 1996-98, chief cultural resource preservation svcs. nat. capital reg., 1998—. Judge numerous award juries. Contbr. articles to profl. jours.; co-author sects. of profl. bull., mag.; author introduction to book Women, Design and the Cambridge School; columnist: Land monthly, 1975-79. Recipient Merit award Landscape Contractors Met. Washington; recipient hon. mention Les Floralies Internat. Montreal, 1980 Alumni Achievement award Pa. State U. Arts and Architecture Alumni Soc., 1981 Fellow Am. Soc. Landscape Architects (v.p. 1979-81, pres. elect 1982-83, pres. 1983-84, trustee 1976-77, nat. treas. 1977-79, legis. coord. 1975-79, sec. Coun. Fellows 1988-90, del. to Internat. Fedn. Landscape Architects 1989-92, 00-03, ex-officio rep. to U.S./internat. coun. on monuments and sites 1985-98, liaison to historically black coll. and univ. program Dept. Interior, chair internat. task force 1999-00, Pres.' medal 1987), U.S. Internat. Coun. on Monuments and Sites (treas. 1998-04, trustee 2004—), Internat. Fed. Landscape Architects (sec. West Region, 2003-06, v.p. West Region 20060); mem. Landscape Archtl. Accreditation Bd. (roster vis. evaluators), Nat. Recreation and Parks Assn., Nat. Soc. Park Resources (bd. dirs. 1978-80), Nat. Trust Hist. Preservation, Pa. State U. Alumni Assn. (Washington met. chpt. trustee 1972-74), Am. Arbitration Assn. (nat. panel arbitrators), Com. 100 for the Fed. City, Preservation Action, Nat. Assn. Olmsted Parks, Beekman Pl. Condominium Assn. (bd. dirs. 1985-91, archtl. control com. 1977-00, landscape com. 2000-02), Alliance for Historic Preservation, Garden Conservancy, Scenic Am., Preservation Action, Preservation Roundtable, Hist. Soc. Washington Office: Nat Park Svc/Nat Capital Region Off Lands Resources & Plan 1100 Ohio Dr SW Washington DC 20242-0001

NEAL, DIANE L., retail executive; BS in Retailing, Mich. State U., 1979. Various positions to pres. of Target subs. Mervyn's Target Corp., 1985—2001, pres. Mervyn's, 2001—04; sr. v.p. merchandising Gap Inc., 2004—05, pres. Gap Inc. Outlet, 2005—06; pres., COO Bath and Body Works Limited Brands Inc., 2006—. Bd. dirs. Nautilus Inc., 2004—. Mem. corp. fundraising com. San Francisco Museum Modern Art. Office: Bath and Body Works Inc Seven Limited Pkwy Reynoldsburg OH 43068*

NEAL, ELAINE ZIRLI, health products executive; Cert. Coun. Certification IRB Profls., 2000; film N.Y.U., 1994. Sec. dept. physiology and biophysics Weill Med. Coll., Cornell U., N.Y.C., 1982—88; asst. to pres., CEO Bio-Technology Gen. Corp. (Savient Pharmaceuticals, Inc.), 1988—93; spl. projects coord., grants adminstrn. & rsch. svcs. N.Y.U. Sch. Medicine, 1994—95; asst. instl. rev. bd. North Shore-Long Island Health Sys., Manhasset, 1996—99, mgr. instl. rev. bd., 1999—2000, asst. dir. instl. rev. bd. Lake Success, 2001—. Awards steering com. Health Improvement Inst./U.S. HHS Office Human Rsch. Protections Award Excellence Human Rsch. Protection Program, Bethesda, 2003—, award panel judge, best practice, 2002—03, award criteria reviewer, 2002—03; moderator U.S. DHHS Office Rsch. Protections/U.S. FDA/Dept. VA/North Shore-LIJ Health Sys. Nat. Workshop Protecting Human Subjects: Whose Responsibility is it, Anyway?, Garden City, NY, 2002. Contbr. chapters to books. Bd. mem. Cmty. Bd. No. 11, Coun. of City of NY, 1996—98; mem. Little Neck/Douglaston Meml. Day Parade Com., 1995—96; mentor ARENA, 2005—. Andreas Zahler scholar Advanced Filmmaking Studies, N.Y.U., 1994. Mem.: AAAS, Soc Rsch. Adminstrs., Applied Rsch. Ethics Nat. Assn., Pub. Responsibility Medicine and Rsch., Am. Soc. Bioethics and Humanities, Soc. Clin. Rsch. Assocs., Assn. Clin. Rsch. Profls., Am. Soc. Law, Medicine and Ethics, N.Y. Acad. Scis. Conservative. Achievements include research in NIH Natl. Ctr. for Research Resources Grant Awards for Improvements in Human Research Protections: IRB Oversight and Educational Enhancement Program (2002), Human Subjects Enhancement Program (2003). Office: North Shore-LIJ Health Sys 5 Dakota Dr Ste 307 New Hyde Park NY 11042 E-mail: elaine@nshs.edu.

NEAL, GAIL FALLON, physical therapist, educator; b. New Haven, May 6, 1938; d. Edward Francis and Ruth Alexina (Hutchinson) Fallon; m. Marcus Pinson Neal Jr.; children: Sandra Neal Dawson, Marcus Pinson III, Ruth-Catherine Neal Perkins. Student, Mary Washington Coll., 1955-57; BS in Phys. Therapy, Med. Coll. Va., 1959. Lic. phys. therapist. Staff phys. therpist Univ. Hosps., U. Wis., Madison, 1959-61; chief phys. therapy Stoughton (Wis.) Cmty. Hosp., 1961-63; vol. phys. therapy Cerebral Palsy Ctr., Richmond, Va., 1963-64; pvt. practice Richmond, 1965—68; interim dir. Stuart Cir. Hosp., Richmond, 1968-69; phys. therpist on call St. Mary's Hosp., Richmond, 1968-74; pres., owner Capital Phys. Therapy Assocs., Richmond, 1989—. Phys. therapist St. Mary's Hosp., Richmond, 1975-88; lectr. Med. Coll. Va., Richmond, 1992-93, John Tyler C.C., Richmond, 1992-94; adv. bd. phys. therapy Va. State Bd. Medicine, 1990-96, vice chmn., 1992-93, chmn. 1995-96. Adv. bd. Va. Opera, 1979—; bd. visitors Mary Washington Coll., Fredericksburg, Va., 1980-82, rector bd. visitors, 1982-84; pres. Richmond Symphony Orch. League, 1986-88. Named Clubwoman of Yr., Richmond Newsleader, 1972. Mem. Am. Phys. Therapy Assn., Richmond Acad. Medicine Aux. (pres. 1967-68), Med. Soc. Va. Alliance (pres. 1980-81), Med. Coll. Va. Hosps. Aux. (pres. 1973-75), Va. Cultural Laureate Soc. Avocations: reading, music, skiing, indian folklore. Home: Pony Bluffs 7301 Riverside Dr Richmond VA 23225-1066 Office: Capital Phys Therapy Assocs Stratford Hills Pony Bluffs Richmond VA 23225 Office Phone: 804-330-2440. Personal E-mail: gfncpta@hotmail.com.

NEAL, LEORA LOUISE HASKETT, social services administrator; b. NYC, Feb. 23, 1943; d. Melvin Elias and Miriam Emily (Johnson) Haskett; m. Robert A. Neal, Apr. 23, 1966; children: Marla Patrice, Johnathan Robert. BA in Psychology and Sociology, City Coll. N.Y., 1965; MS in Social Work, Columbia U., 1970, cert. adoption specialist, 1977; IBM cert. community exec. tng. program, N.Y., 1982. Cert. master social worker N.Y., lic. clin. social worker, lic. master social worker, N.Y.; cert. social worker, N.Y. Caseworker N.Y.C. Dept. Social Service, 1965-67, Windham Child Care, N.Y.C., 1967-73; exec. dir., founder Assn. Black Social Workers Child Adoption Counseling and Referral Service, N.Y.C., 1975-96; adoption tng. specialist Ctr. for Devel. Human Svcs., SUNY-N.Y. State Office Children and Family Svcs., Yonkers, 1996—. Cons. in field; founder Haskett-Neal Publs., Bronx, N.Y., 1993. Co-author: Transracial Adoptive Parenting: A Black/White Community Issue, 1993; contbr. articles to profl. jours. Pres. bd. dirs. Fountain Ave. Cmty. Devel. Corp.; bd. dirs. Grandparents Advocacy Project, 2000—. Child Welfare League Am. fellow, 1976; recipient No Time to Lose cert. NY State Dept. Social Svcs., 1989, Pyramid award NY Assn Black Social Workers, 2005. Mem. NAFE, Nat. Assn. Black Social Workers (co-chair task force on foster care and adoption 1994—, Outstanding Cmty. Svc. award 1994), Columbia U. Alumni Assn., CCNY Alumni Assn., Missionary Com. Revival Team (outreach chair 1982-88). Democrat. Avocations: writing, religious studies, travel, cultural activities, history. Office: NY State Office of Children and Family Svcs SUNY 525 Nepperhan Ave Yonkers NY 10703-2857 Office Phone: 914-377-2079.

NEAL, MARIETHA MAE, primary school educator; m. Anderson Neal, Jr., Aug. 2, 1956; children: Miranda Ty, Mylia Denise. BS in Elem. Edn., Ark. State U., Jonesboro, 1979; MEd, Ark. State U., Fayetteville, 1983. Lic. tchr. Ark. Dept. of Edn., elem. prin. Ark. Dept. of Edn. Reading tchr. Wheatley Elem. Sch., Ark., 1979—80; tchr. 1st grade Ft. Smith Pub. Sch., Ark., 1980—86; tchr. 2d grade Texarkana Ark. Sch. Dist., 1986—88, reading tchr., 1988—89, math tchr., 1989—97, instr. alt. learning edn. and in-sch. suspension instr., 1997—. Recipient award, NAACP, Internat. Paper grant, Internat. Paper Co., Texarkana Mill, 1999, Recondition for Superior Leadership as Pres. award, Texarkana Classroom Tchrs. Assn., 1998, Recondition for Outstanding Achievement of Collaborative Advocacy award, Ark. Edn. Assn., 1997. Mem.: Delta Sigma Theta. Office Phone: 870-774-9691 139.

NEAL, MARILYN YOUNG, librarian; b. Bartlesville, Okla., Oct. 11, 1949; d. Robert Earl and Mary Ann (Martin) Young; m. Everett Gilbert Neal, Apr. 7, 1978; children: Daniel Young, Anna Beth. BA in Elem. Edn., U. Tulsa, 1971; MLS, U. Okla., Tulsa, 1996. Assoc. libr. Tulsa City Co. Libr., 1971—78, children's libr., 1999, branch mgr., 1999—; libr. Monte Cassino Sch., Tulsa, 1987—99. Performer: Am. Theatre Co., 1970—. Vol., sec. Susan Wade Roberson Rally, Tulsa, 1999—. Mem.: ALA, Okla. Libr. Assn. Avocations: acting, singing. Office: Maxwell Park Libr 1313 N Canton Ave Tulsa OK 74115

NEAL, MELINDA K., science educator; d. James David and Judith Kay McCall; m. Melvin D. Young (div.); children: Clayton Young, Kristopher Young; m. Marcus L. Neal, July 1, 2000. BA, Southwestern Coll., Winfield, Kans., 1981, MEd, 1990. Tchr. sci. Dexter (Kans.) H.S., 1986—2002; instr. natural sci. Cowley Coll., Arkansas City, Kans., 2002—. Adviser Phi Theta Kappa, Arkansas City, 2006. Mem.: Cowley Coll. Edn. Assn. (sec. 2004—06), Delta Chi (sec. 2006). Office: Cowley Coll 125 S 2d Arkansas City KS 67005

NEAL, TERESA, school counselor, educator; d. Michael Preuss and Barbara Thomas; m. Anthony James Neal. BA, Purdue U., West Lafayette, Ind., 1999; MS, Ind. U., Bloomington, 2001, EdS, 2003. Lic. sch. counselor Ga. Counselor CrossRoads HS and Mid. Sch., Holly Springs, Ga., 2001—; adj. instr. Fla. CC, Jacksonville, 2004—. Adj. instr. U. Phoenix Online, 2003—. Office: CrossRoads HS/MS 3921 Holly Springs Pkwy Holly Springs GA 30142 Office Phone: 770-345-2005.

NEAL, TERESA SCHREIBEIS, secondary school educator; b. Wheatland, Wyo., Mar. 19, 1956; d. Gene L. and Bonnie Marie (Reed) Schreibeis; m. Michael R. Neal, Apr. 7, 1990; 1 child, Rianna Michele. BA in Am. Studies and English Edn., U. Wyo., 1978; MA in History, U. So. Calif., 1989, PhD, 1994, Cert. Studies of Women/Men in Soc., 1995. Cert. secondary edn. tchr., Wyo., Colo. Tchr. lang. arts and social studies, asst. coach Carbon County Sch. Dist. 1, Rawlins, Wyo., 1978-86; asst. lectr. freshmen writing program U. So. Calif., L.A., 1986-90; adj. prof. history Palomar (Calif.) C.C., San Diego, 1991; software support specialist Dynamic Data Systems, Westminster, Colo., 1992-93; tchr. humanities gifted and talented classes Arvada (Colo.) West H.S., 1993-98; tchr., program developer New Montessori Mid. Sch., 1998-00, Mountain Shadows Mid. Sch., Boulder, Colo., 1998-2000; adj. prof. history, humanities and English composition Red Rocks C.C., Lakewood and Arvada, Colo., 2002—04; tchr. English and Internat. Baccalaureate Program, Lakewood (Colo.) HS, 2004—. Participant critical thinking and humanities secondary edn. project NEH, Wyo., 1985-86; adj. prof. English Composition, Front Range C.C., Westminster, Colo., 2000-03; presenter Nat. Women's Hist. Project Fall Conf., 2005-06. Author: Evolution Toward Equality: Equality for Woman of the American West, 2006. Mem., chmn. Reading Is Fundamental Program, Rawlins, 1983-85, Women of the West Mus., 2001—; tchr., sponsor Denver-Metro YMCA Youth and Govt., 1994-97, Close Up, Washington, 1984-86, 97; tchr., advisor Nat. History Day Contest, 1995—2001; tchr., sponsor World Affairs Challenge, Denver U., 1998; vol. math. tutor Foothills Acad., Wheat Ridge, Colo., 2001-02. Mem. AAUW (Project Renew fellow 1987-88), Western Assn. Women Historians, G. Autrey Mus. Western Art, Denver Art Mus., Buffalo Bill Western Heritage Ctr., Phi Beta Kappa. Avocations: travel, fine arts, reading, crafts. E-mail: tneal@javakats.com.

NEAL-PARKER, SHIRLEY ANITA, obstetrician, gynecologist; b. Washington, Aug. 28, 1949; d. Leon Walker and Pearl Anita (Shelton) Neal; m. Andre Cowan Dasent, June 21, 1971 (div. Feb. 1978); 1 child, Erika Michelle Dasent; m. James Carl Parker, Feb. 11, 1979; 1 child, Amirah Nabeehah. BS in Biology, Am. U., 1971; MD, Hahnemann U., 1979. Lic. Md., Calif., Wash., Oreg. Intern Howard U. Hosp., 1979-80, resident, 1980-84; physician Nat. Health Svc. Corp., Charleston, W. Va., 1984-86; clin. instr. W.Va. U., Charleston, 1985-86; pvt. practice ob./gyn. Sacramento, 1986-95; pvt. practice Chehalis, Wash., 1995—2004; chair dept. perinatology Providence Centralia Hosp., 1999-2000; group practice Tulane County Health and Human Svcs., 2004—. Bd. dirs. Ruth Rosenberg Dance Ensemble, Sacramento, 1992-95, Human Response Network, Chehalis, 1995-97. Mem.: Wash. State Obstet. Assn., Lewis County Med. Soc., Wash. State Med. Assn., Am. Med. Women's Assn. (comty. svc. award Mother Hale br. 1994), Nat. Med. Assn., Am. Reproductive Health Profls., Am. Assn. Gynecologic Laparoscopists, Soroptomist Internat. Avocations: travel, reading, crocheting, collecting ethnic dolls, magnets. Home: 6614 Harrington Ct Chino CA 91710 Office: Ste 3 5450 Jefferson Ave Chino CA 91710 Office Phone: 909-464-8980. Personal E-mail: drsanp@earthlink.net.

NEAL-WALDEN, TRACY A., psychologist; d. Gloria Adell and Robert Larry Neal; m. Jeffrey T. Walden, July 23, 1993; 1 child, Collin Alexander Walden. BA, Ind. U. of Pa., 1989; PhD, Hahnemann U., 1996. Lic. psychologist Am. Psychol. Assn., 1996. Commd. USAF, 1993, advanced through grades to maj., 2001; psychology resident Wilford Hall USAF Med. Ctr., Lackland AFB, Tex., 1993—94; staff psychologist Malcolm Grow USAF Med. Ctr., Andrews AFB, Md., 1994—96, asst. dir., psychology residency program, 1996—98; asst. prof. dept. behavioral sci. USAF Acad., Colo., 1998—99, chief sexual assault svc., asst. prof. Cadet Counseling Ctr. Colo., 1999—2001; dir. mental health svcs. 51st Med. Group, Osan Air Base, Republic of Korea, 2001—02; dir. life skills support ctr. 21st Med. Group, Peterson AFB, Colo., 2002—05, postdoctoral fellow clin. health psychology, 2005—. Cons. Nat. Capital Area Mental Health Alliance Sys. Access Team, Walter Reed Army Medical Center, DC, 1994—95; cons. hostage negotiations team Security Forces, Andrews AFB, Md., 1994—98; clin. asst. prof. Uniformed U. Health Sci., Bethesda, Md., 1999—2001; adj. prof. U. Colo., Colorado Springs, 1999—2001; mem. Integrated Delivery Sys., Peterson AFB, Colo., 2001—; chief critical incident stress mgmt. team, Osan Air Base, Republic of Korea, 2001—02; instl. rev. bd. USAF Acad., Colo., 2003—05; exec. dir. Cmty. Action Info. Bd., Peterson AFB, Colo., 2003—05; govt. cons., Brooks City Base, Tex., 2004—04. Contbr. articles to profl. jours. Bd. mem. Colo. Coalition Against Sexual Assault, Denver, 1999—2001. Named Psychologist of Yr., Air Force Space Command, 2004; recipient Cir. of Excellence, GlaxoSmithKline, 2003; grantee, Hahnemann U. Grad. Sch., 1991; scholar, 1990. Mem.: Soc. Air Force Psychologists (sec. 1999—2004), APA, Assn. Advancement of Behavior Therapy. Avocation: travel. Office: 59 MDOS/MMCP 2200 Bergquist Dr Ste 1 Lackland Afb TX 78236 Office Phone: 210-292-5968. Personal E-mail: tracywalden@yahoo.com.

NEARING, VIVIENNE W., lawyer; b. NYC; d. Abraham M. and Edith Eunice (Webster) N. BA, Queens Coll.; MA, JD, Columbia U. Bar: N.Y., D.C., U.S. Dist. Ct. (so. and ea. dists.) N.Y., U.S. Ct. Appeals (2d cir.), U.S. Claims Ct. Ptnr. Stroock & Stroock & Lavan, N.Y.C. gen. counsel Plays for Living, 1998—2002, gen. co-counsel, 2002—. Mem. editorial bd. Communications and the Law, 1978-82, adv. bd. 1982—; mem. editorial bd. U.S. Trademark Reporter, 1982-86. Bd. dirs. Light Opera of Manhattan, 1981-82, Lyric Opera N.Y., 1984-90, Concert Artists Guild, 1989-91, Plays for Living, 1998—. Mem. ABA, Fed. Bar Coun., N.Y. State Bar Assn., U.S. Trademark Assn., Copyright Soc. U.S.A., N.Y. Lawyers for Pub. Interest (bd. dirs. 1983-87), Am. Arbitration Assn., Commn. for Law and Social Justice, Carnegie Coun., Women's City Club, Respect for Law Alliance. Office: Stroock Stroock & Lavan 180 Maiden Ln New York NY 10038-4982 Business E-Mail: vnearing@stroock.com.

NEARY, PATRICIA ELINOR, ballet director; b. Miami, Fla. d. James Elliott and Elinor (Mitsitz) N. Corps de ballet Nat. Ballet of Can., Toronto, Ont., 1957-60; prin. dancer N.Y.C. Ballet, 1960-68; ballerina Geneva Ballet, Switzerland, 1968-70, ballet dir., 1973-78; guest artist Stuttgart Ballet, Germany, 1968-70; asst. ballet dir., ballerina West Berlin Ballet, 1970-73; ballet dir. Zurich Ballet, Switzerland, 1978-86, La Scala di Milano ballet co., Italy, 1986-88; tchr. Balanchine ballets, Balanchine Trust, 1987—.

NEASE, JUDITH ALLGOOD, marriage and family therapist; b. Arlington, Mass., Nov. 15, 1930; d. Dwight Maurice Allgood and Sophie Wolf Allgood Morris; m. Theron Stanford Nease, Sept. 1, 1962; children: Susan Elizabeth, Alison Allgood. Student, Rockford Coll., 1949-50; BA, NYU, 1953, MA, 1954; MS, Columbia U. Sch. Social Work, 1956. Lic. clin. social worker, marriage and family therapist. Psychiat. social worker Bellevue Psychiat. Hosp., N.Y.C., 1956-59, St. Luke's Hosp., N.Y.C., 1959-62; asst. psychiat. social work supr. N.J. Neuropsychiat. Inst., Princeton, 1962-64; group co-leader Ctr. for Advancement of Personal and Social Growth, Atlanta, 1973-76; asst. dir., social work supr., group co-leader Druid Hills Counseling Ctr., Columbia Theol. Sem., 1973-82; marriage and family therapist Cath. Social Svcs., Atlanta, 1978-87; chief Cmty. Mental Health Svc., Ft. McPherson, Atlanta, 1987-92; master's level clinician Ctr. for Psychiatry, Smyrna, Ga., 1990-92; pvt. practice Grayson, Ga., 1992—. Mem.: Am. Psychotherapy Assn. (diplomate). Democrat. Episcopalian. Home and Office: 3030 Hollywood Dr Decatur GA 30033-5126 Office Phone: 770-982-9590. E-mail: judynease@yahoo.com.

NEASMAN, ANNIE RUTH, health facility administrator; b. Moore Haven, Fla., Oct. 24, 1947; d. Nathan and Daisy Mae Miles; children: Beatrice Daizine, Barry Anthony. BSN, Fla. A&M U., 1969; MS, Fla. Internat. U., 1976. Registered Nurse, Fla. Dept. Health, Bd. Nursing. Staff nurse Jackson Meml. Hosp., Miami, 1969—71, adminstr., nursing R&D, 1976—84; adminstr. Jackson Meml. Health Sys., North Dade Health Ctr., Miami, 1984—90; adminstr., dept. health Fla. Dept. Health, Rehabilitative Svcs., Miami, 1990—92, dep. dist. adminstr., 1992—96; adminstr. Fla. Dept. Health, Miami, 1996—99, divsn. dir., family health svc. Tallahassee, 1999—2001, dep. sec., state nursing dir., 2001—04; pres., CEO Econ. Opportunity Health Ctr., Miami, 2004—. Bd. mem. Fla. Am. Lung Assn., Jacksonville, 2004—06; mem. Mt. Hermon AME Ch., Miami Gardens, Fla., 2004—06; bd. mem. Fla. Ctr. for Nursing, Orlando, 2002—04; mem. Fla. Nurses Assn., Orlando, 1976—2006, Black Nurses Assn., Miami, 2004—06. Named to Nursing Hall of Fame, Fla. A&M, 1996; recipient Woman of Yr., Pub. Health, 1994, Sr. Mgmt. Svc. award, Health and Rehab. Svcs., 1996. Mem.: Black Nurses Assn., Fla. Nurses Assn., Chi Eta Phi Nursing Sorority (Humanitarian award 1994), Delta Sigma Theta Sorority. Democrat-Npl. Ame. Avocations: travel, walking, reading. Home: 6799 Brookline Dr Miami FL 33015 Office: Econ Opportortunity Family Health Ctr Inc 700 S Royal Poinciana Blvd Ste 300 Miami Springs FL 33166 Office Phone: 305-805-1710. Office Fax: 305-805-1715. Personal E-mail: aruthmg47@aol.com. Business E-Mail: aneasman@hcnetwork.org.

NEATHERY, CHERYL ALISSA, secondary school educator; m. Robert Mark Neathery, June 1, 1996; children: Sara Dries, Laci Lauren Bills Newhouse. BS cum laude in Edn., Abilene Christian U., Tex., 1976. Cert. ESL Tex., 1998. English tchr. Whitewright H.S., Sherman, Tex., 1976—78; English, ESL, speech and health tchr. Douglass Learning Ctr. H.S., Sherman, 1995—. Cardiac rehab. technician David F. Davis MD, Sherman, 1986—87. Sec., historian PTA, 1984—90; vol. Loveland HS, Piner Mid. Sch., Perin Elem. Sch., 1984—95; Sunday sch. tchr. Western Heights Ch. of Christ, 1976—. Named Tchr. of Yr., Douglas Sch., Sherman Ind. School Dist., 1999—2000. Mem.: Tex. Classroom Tchr. Assn. (assoc.), Tex. Alt. Sch. Assn. (assoc.). Avocation: stained glass. Office: Fred Douglass Learning Ctr 505 E College Sherman TX 75090 Office Phone: 903-891-6545.

NEBLETT, CAROL, soprano; b. Modesto, Calif., Feb. 1, 1946; m. Philip R. Akre; 3 children. Studies with, William Vennard, Roger Wagner, Esther Andreas, Ernest St. John Metz, Lotte Lehmann, Pierre Bernac, Rosa Ponselle, George London, Jascha Heifetz, Norman Treigle, Sol Hurak, Dorothy Kirsten, Maestros Julius Rudel, Claudio Abbado, Daniel Barenboin, Erich Leinsdorf, James Levine, others. Soloist with Roger Wagner Chorale; performed in U.S. and abroad with various symphonies; debut with Carnegie Hall, 1966, N.Y.C. Opera, 1969, Met. Opera, 1979; sung with maj. opera cos. including Met. Opera, N.Y.C., Lyric Opera Chgo., Balt. Opera, Pitts. Opera, Houston Grand Opera, San Francisco Opera, Boston Opera Co., Milw. Florentine Opera, Washington Opera Soc., Covent Garden, Cologne Opera, Vienna (Austria) Staatsoper, Paris Opera, Teatro Regio, Turin, Italy, Teatro San Carlo, Naples, Italy, Teatro Massimo, Palermo, Italy, Gran Teatro del Liceo, Barcelona, Spain, Kirov Opera Theatre, Leningrad, USSR, Dubrovnik (Yugoslavia) Summer Festival, Salzberg Festival, others; rec. artist RCA, DGG, EMI; appearances with symphony orchs., also solo recitals, (film) La Clemenza di Tito; filmed and recorded live performance with Placido Domingo, La Fancuilla del West; numerous TV appearances.

NECCO, EDNA JOANNE, school psychologist; b. Klamath Falls, Oreg., June 23, 1941; d. Joseph Rogers and Lillian Laura (Owings) Painter; m. Jon F. Puryear, Aug. 25, 1963 (div. Oct. 1987); children: Laura L., Douglas F.; m. A. David Necco, July 1, 1989. BS, Ctrl. State U., 1978, MEd, 1985; PhD in Applied Behavioral Studies, Okla. State U., 1993. Med.-surg. asst. Oklahoma City Clinic, 1961-68; spl. edn. tchr. Oklahoma City Pub. Schs., 1978-79, Edmond (Okla.) Pub. Schs., 1979-83; co-founder, owner Learning Devel. Clinic, Edmond, 1983-93; asst. prof. profl. tchr. edn. U. Ctrl. Okla., Edmond, 1993-97, assoc. prof., 1998—2001, prof. profl. tchr. edn., 2002—. Adj. instr. Ctrl. State U., Edmond, 1989-93, Oklahoma City U., 1991-93; rsch. group Okla. State U., Stillwater, 1991-93; faculty senator U. Ctrl. Okla., 1998-2000; tri-coord. Am. Democracy project, 2003-05, campus exec. dir. U. Ctrl. Okla., 2005—; Coll. Edn. rep. AAUP, 2000-01; presenter in field Contbr. articles to profl. jours. Com. mem. Boy Scouts Am., SCUBA Post 604, Oklahoma City, 1981-86; mem. Edmond Task Force for Youth, 1983-87, Edmond C. of C., 1984-87; evaluator for Even Start Literacy Program, 1994-96, reviewer Okla. Even Start applicants, 1997 Named to State of Okla. Outstanding Profs.' Acad., 2003; recipient Provost award, 2004. Mem. AAUP, ASCD, PEO, Am. Psychol. Soc., Nat. Assn. for Sch. Psychologists, Am. Bus Women's Assn., Coun. for Exceptional Children, Learning Disabilities Assn., Am. Assn. for Gifted Underachieving Students, Am. Tchr. Educators, Okla. Learning Disabilities Assn., Okla. Ctr. Neurosci., Okla. Assn. for Counseling and Devel., Okla. Psychol. Soc., U. Ctrl. Okla. Golden Key Nat. Honor Soc., Internat. Soc. for Sci. Study of Subjectivity, Am. Coun. on Rural Spl. Edn., Ctrl. State U. (Okla., life), Phi Delta Kappa. Republican. Avocations: scuba diving, underwater photography, water-skiing, travel, golf. Home: 3624 Equestrian Ct Edmond OK 73034-5871 Office: U Ctrl Okla Coll Edn 100 N University Dr Edmond OK 73034-5207 Business E-Mail: jnecco@ucok.edu. E-mail: jnecco@cox.net.

NECHAS, EILEEN TUCKER, retired writer; b. Phila., June 24, 1944; d. Louis and Freda (Neidorf) Tucker; m. Marshall Robert Mazer, June 21, 1964 (div. 1981); children: Dale Michelle, Julie Rachelle; m. James William Nechas, Oct. 15, 1982; stepchildren: Alexander David Nechas, Jonathan Philip Nechas. BS in Med. Tech. summa cum laude, Kutztown U., 1978. Rsch. assoc., writer Prevention mag., Emmaus, Pa., 1980, assoc. editor, 1980-81, sr. editor, 1981-86; exec editor Children mag., Emmaus, 1986-89; media spokesperson TV shows including Hour mag., Regis and Kathie Lee, 1987—2004; freelance writer, 1989—2004. Co-author: (books) The Women's Encyclopedia of Health and Emotional Healing, 1992, What Do I Do Now?, Parent-Tested, Expert Approved, Solutions to 100 Common and Uncommon Parenting Problems, 1992, The Doctor's Book of Home Remedies for Children, 1994, Unequal Treatment: What You Don't Know About How Women Are Mistreated by the Medical Community, 1994; co-author: (columns) Children's Health Bulletin, 1990—, Women's Health News, 1994—, Good Times Health NEWS, 1996; contbg. writer: Mayo Clinic Women's HealthSource, 1997, various mag. articles. Recipient Health Info. Silver award, 1993. Home and Office: 218 Hummels Hill Rd Kutztown PA 19530-9297

NECTOWAK, TILLIAN, small business owner; b. Portland, Aug. 26, 1950; d. David and Abigail Nectowak; m. Adam Charles Hartcliff, June 19, 1970 (div. 1981); children: Adam Charles Hartcliff Jr., Emily Hartcliff; m. David Hobes, June 3, 1981 (div. 1995); children: Lily Hobes, Rebecca Hobes. Degree in Nursing, Central Maine Med. Ctr. Sch. Nursing, Lewiston, 1966; BA in Anthropology, U. Maine, 1970. Exec. asst. Bayside Products, Portland, Maine, 1976—80; classroom asst. Early Start Charter Sch., Windham, Maine, 1980—82; children's program coord. Windham YMCA, Maine, 1982—86; florist Posy Petals, Westbrook, Maine, 1986—95, The Corner Shop, Westbrook, 1995—97; founder, co-owner, mgr. Meriks Flowers, Portland, Maine, 1997—. Avocations: gardening, flower arranging, photography. Office: Meriks Flowers 135 Marginal Way #300 Portland ME 04104-5015

NEDDER, JANET MARIE, elementary school educator; b. Lowell, Mass., June 17, 1943; d. Arthur T. and Mary M. (Kennedy) DeAngelo; m. Robert S. Nedder, Apr. 23, 1966; children: Joseph A., Robert S. Jr., Arthur P. BA in Math., Regis Coll., 1965, MA, cert. elem., 1973, MA, cert. reading, 1983, MA, cert. math., 1991. Cert. in elem. edn., reading, math., Mass. Mathematician Regis Coll. Math. Project, Weston, Mass., 1962-65; rsch. mathematician Air Force Cambridge Labs., Waltham, Mass., summer 1964; math. analyst Rust Craft Greeting Cards, Dedham, Mass., summer 1965; elem. tchr. St. Pius X Sch., Milton, Mass., 1965-66; mathematician Space Physics Lab., Hanscom AFB, Bedford, Mass., 1966-67; Title I tchr. Dedham Pub. Schs., 1978—. Campaign aide local rep., Hyde Park, 1961, Selectman, Dedham, 1989. Grantee in biostats. Lemuel Shattuck Hosp./Harvard U., 1965. Mem. Internat. Reading Assn., Exec. Female, Mass. Reading Tchrs. Assn., Dedham Title I Tchrs. Assn. (bargaining com. 1989, treas. 1989-90, v.p. 1990—, sec. 2000—), Dartmouth Women's Club. Democrat. Roman Catholic. Avocations: reading, travel, writing, piano. Home: 43 High St Medfield MA 02052-3119

NEDZA, SANDRA LOUISE, manufacturing executive; b. Chgo., Aug. 20, 1951; d. Thomas and Ina Louise (Wilson) Ingle; m. James Owen Earnest, May 5, 1973 (div. Nov. 1984); m. Ronald Edward Nedza, Nov. 22, 1986; 1 child, Thomas Edward. Student acctg., Met. Sch. Bus., Chgo., 1970. Acctg. clk. Gane Bros. & Lane, Inc., Chgo., 1967-72; advanced from expeditor to buyer Hammond Organ Co., Chgo., 1972-84; purchasing/prodn. control supr. IRP-Profl. Sound Products, Addison, Ill., 1984-2000; purchasing agt. ANI Safety and Supply, Inc., Lincolnwood, Ill., 2000; adminstrv. asst. to v.p. mktg. svcs. and mktg. The Willy Wonka Candy Factory divsn. Nestle, Itasca, Ill., 2001—03; adminstrv. asst. to v.p. of internat. buying D.M. Merchandising Inc., Elmhurst, Ill., 2004—. Mem. Jobs Daughters, 1967—. Mem. Lions (pres. 2000-04), Alpha Iota (scholarship key 1970). Clubs: Juke Box Sno-Riders (sec. 1986-87) (Fox Lake, Ill.), Lakeview Sno-Riders. Lodges: Lioness (pres. 1988-89) (Chgo.). Lutheran. Office: Dm Merchandising Inc 835 N Church Ct Elmhurst IL 60126-1005 Personal E-mail: buzzylion@juno.com.

NEECE, OLIVIA HELENE ERNST, investment company executive, consultant; b. LA, Jan. 3, 1948; d. Robert and Beatrice Pearl Ernst; m. Huntley Lee Bluestein, 1967 (div. 1974); children: Melissa Dawn, Brendon Wade; m. Anthony Ray Neece, Mar. 20, 1976. Cert. interior design, UCLA, 1975, MBA, 1993; BSBA, U. So. Calif., 1990; postgrad., Claremont U., 1998—. Cert. interior designer Calif. Coun. for Interior Design; lic. gen. contractor, real estate broker, Calif. Staff designer Frances Lux Designs, LA, 1974; project designer Yates Silverman Inc., LA, 1974-77; owner Olivia Neece Planning & Design, Tarzana, Calif., 1977-86; v.p. project devel. Design Svc. /Aircoa, Englewood, Colo., 1986-87; v.p. project adminstrn. Hirsch-Bedner Assoc., Santa Monica, Calif., 1987—; treas.-sec. EON Corp., LA, 1980—87; owner Olivia Neece Planning & Design, Tarzana, 1980—88; dir. ops. The Ernst Group, LA, 1988—2005; pres. Neece Assocs., 2003—. Instr. ext. program UCLA, 1981—83; part-time prof. Calif. State U., Northridge, 1994—99; acad. rschr. Jet Propulsion Lab., 2000—02; spkr. in field. Co-author: A Step by Step Approach to Hotel Devel., 1988; contbr. chapters to books, articles to profl. jours. Co-chair LA Master Chorale Gala; mem. Hollywood Bowl Soc.; charter mem. L.A. County Mus. Art; vol. restoration of San Diego R.R. Mus., 1985—92; patron LA Philharm., LA Opera Soc.; Found. of Music Ctr. of Los Angeles; fellow circle Ctr. Theatre Group; Patron and charter mem. of LA Country Mus. of Art; bd. dir.,historian Master Choral Assoc. Recipient Holiday Inn Devel. award, Foster City, Calif., 1986, Warwick, R.I., 1988, 1st and 2d pl. awards, Lodging Hospitality Designers Cir., 1987, Gold Key award, Russell St. Inn, 1986, Best Paper award, Am. Conf. on Info. Systems, 2002. Mem. Am. Soc. Interior Designers (1st pl. portfolio competition 1974), Acad. of Mgmt. (Best Paper award 2002), Fin. Mgmt. Assn., Internat. Inst. Designers & Arch. (profl., v.p., bd. dir.), We. Acad. Mgmt., Assn. Info. Sys., Inst. Ops. Rsch. and Mgmt. Sci, Beta Gamma Sigma. Office: Neece Assoc 18200 Rosita St Tarzana CA 91356-4622

NEEDHAM, KATHLEEN ANN, gerontology educator, consultant; b. Saginaw, Mich., Aug. 30, 1944; d. George Whitcomb and Ann (Drensky) N.; m. Kenneth Edward Cassady, June 19, 1982. BA, Olivet (Mich.) Coll., 1967; MA, Mich. State U., 1970, postgrad., 1972-76, 90—; cert., U. Mich., 1977. Cert. tchr., Mich. HS tchr. Pontiac (Mich.) schs., 1968-72; grad. asst. Mich. State U., East Lansing, 1972-76; assoc. prof., chmn. dept. gerontology Madonna U., Livonia, Mich., 1981-90, mem. faculty, 1991—2000. Grant project dir. Adminstrn. on Aging, Washington, 1977-83, Mich. Dept. Labor, Lansing, 1985-86; grant project supr. NIMH, Washington, 1981-83; cons. in field. Producer tapes and articles in field. Del. Mich. White House Conf. on Aging, Dearborn, 1981; mem. com. Mich. Office Svcs. to Aging, Lansing, 1983-92; bd. dirs. United Cmty. Svcs., 1985-94, mem. health svcs. com., 1991—; chmn. Mich. Minimum Stds. for Aging, 1987; vol. Focus Hope, Detroit, Mich. Lupus Found.; chair Mich. Myositis Assn. dir. Gov.'s Task Force on Older Worker, Lansing, 1987, 88, Mich. Exec. Commn. on Older Learner Summit, 1990-93; chair Mich. Gov.'s Conf. on Aging, 1991; cons. to bd. Mich. Assoc. Svc. Orgns., 1991-93; Mich. regional facilitator and del. White House Conf., 1994; mem. ann. conf. planning com. Mich. Soc. Gerontology, 1994, 95, 96, 98. Recipient Svc. award Internat. Healthcare Assn., 1988, 89, 90, 91, Harry J. Kelly award Mich. Soc. Gerontology, Lifetime Achievement award Agency on Aging. Mem. Gerontol. Soc. Am., Mich. Soc. Gerontology (bd. dirs. 1987, 99,), Assn. Gerontology in Higher Edn. (membership com. 1982, pub. policy com. 1988, pub. rels. and fund raising 1992, 93), Am. Soc. Aging, Myositis Assn. (state rep.), Sigma Phi Omega. Presbyterian. Home: 22760 Clear Lake Dr Farmington MI 48335-3834 Office: Madonna Univ Gerontology Dept 36600 Schoolcraft Rd Livonia MI 48150-1176

NEEL, BARBARA ANNE SPIESS, elementary school educator, artist; b. Alexandria, Va., Feb. 19, 1945; d. Philip Daniel and Dorothy Elaine (Goepp) Spiess; m. William Barton Neel, June 6, 1966; children: Jennifer Lloyd, Elizabeth Barton. BFA, BS in Edn., U. Cin., 1967. Cert. tchr. NJ, Va. Elem. art tchr. Hamilton Twp. (N.J.) Schs., 1967-68; vol. to art tchr. Arlington (Va.) County Pub. Schs., 1977-81, elem. art tchr., 1983—2006, drawing and painting fine arts tchr., 1986-90, summer laureate art tchr., 1991; World Village tchr., Common Ground on the Hill McDaniel Coll., Westminster, Md., 2003—06. Tapestry weaver; water color and acrylic painter. One-woman shows include Ellipse Gallery, Arlington, Va., 2001, exhibitions include Common Ground on the Hill, 2003—06. Mem. NEA, Nat. Art Edn. Assn., No. Va. Art Edn. Assn., Va. Art Edn. Assn. (quilter convention 2004), Arlington Edn. Assn., Va. Edn. Assn., Arlington Visual Artists Coalition, Springwater Fibers Workshop (Tapestry 1st prize 1992). Presbyterian. Avocations: knitting, folk music, piano, singing, quilting. Home: 2308 N Upton St Arlington VA 22207-4045 Office: Key Elem Sch 2300 Key Blvd Arlington VA 22201-3415 Office Phone: 703-228-4210. E-mail: barbara_neel@apsva.us.

NEEL, JUDY MURPHY, management consultant; b. Rhome, Tex. d. James W. and Linna B. (Vess) Neel; m. Ellis F. Murphy, Jr., Dec. 30, 1975; children from previous marriage: Mary B. Schmidt, Janet E. Hollingsworth, Susan E. Salinas. BS, Northwestern U., 1977; MBA, Roosevelt U., 1983. V.p. Murphy, Tashjian & Assocs., Chgo., 1960-73; exec. dir. Automotive Affiliated Rep. Assn., Chgo., 1973-78; mgr. Automotive Svc. Ind. Assn., Chgo., 1978-80; exec. dir. Am. Soc. Safety Engrs., Des Plaines, Ill., 1980-98, Am. Assn. Diabetes Educators, 1999—2003; mgmt. cons., 2003—. Recipient Assn. Leadership Award Bus. Women's Network/Assn. Trends Mag., 1998. Mem. Chgo. Soc. Assn. Execs. (bd. dirs. 1979—, pres. 1985—, Shapiro award 1991), Am. Soc. Assn. Execs. (sec.-treas. 1994, found. dir. 1986-90, bd. dirs. 1990-95, Key award 1986). Republican. E-mail: jneelcae@aol.com.

NEELEY, BEVERLY EVON, sociologist, consultant; b. Oakland, Calif., June 14, 1947; d. Chester Arthur Neeley Jr. and Thalia Evon Neeley-Littlefield; m. Niles Bruce, Sept. 13, 1970 (div. Aug. 1977); 1 child, Autumn Yvonne Curd BA, U. Calif., Berkeley, 1970, MPH, 1972; PhD, U. Calif., San Diego, 1983. Eligibility supr. W. Oakland Health Ctr., 1970-72; health edn. supr. San Diego County Drug Edn., 1972-74; proposal writer, cons. Cmty. Crisis Ctr., San Diego, 1974-77; sociologist, dir., sec., treas. Image Mind, Inc., Oakland, 1993—. Instr. Calif. State U., San Diego, 1976; health planner Health Sys. Agy., San Diego, 1978; mem. adv. bd. Help Other People Evole Inst., Oakland, 2000—; sr. acad. cons. Hercules NAACP Saturday Sch., 2002; tchrs., rschr. Oakland Pub. Schs., 1983—. Author: The Ethiopian Grail: On the Origin of Cultural Excellence, 1994, Ancient Ethiopian Egyptian Cultural Excellence, 2003. Founder S.E. Drug Coalition, San Diego, 1974, Nu-Way Youth Svc. Ctr., San Diego, 1976. Mem. NAACP, Sojourner Truth Tenants Assn., Nat. Assn. Negro Bus. and Profl. Women's Clubs Inc. Avocations: reading, walking, cooking. Home and Office: 5915 Martin Luther King Jr Way B10 Oakland CA 94609 Office Phone: 510-653-7561. E-mail: drbneeley3@hotmail.com.

NEELEY, JANET MEIGS, surgical nurse; b. Wichita, Kans., Oct. 20, 1955; d. Donald Keith and Yvonne Hammond (Newman) Meigs; children: James Donald, William Keith. BSN, U. Ala., 1977. Bus. mgr. Huntsville (Ala.) Hosp. Vol. Healthy Cmty. Initiative. Mem. Assn. Oper. Rm. Nurses, Sigma Theta Tau, Phi Kappa Phi, Alpha Lambda Delta. Home: 2100 Twist Cir SW Huntsville AL 35803-2004

NEELEY, KATHLEEN LOUISE, librarian; b. Pitts., Feb. 22, 1946; d. George Edward Jr. and Mildred Jane (Snellbacher) Kratt; m. James Dalton Neeley, July 20, 1968; children: Laura Elizabeth, Alan Dalton. BS in Chemistry, Chatham Coll., Pitts., 1968; MS in LS, Syracuse U., 1972. Analytical chemist U.S. Plant, Soil and Nutrition Lab., Cornell U., Ithaca, N.Y., 1968-69, libr. asst. Olin Libr., 1969-70; libr. Syracuse (N.Y.) U. Sch. Nursing Libr., 1971; libr. Logan Lewis Libr., Carrier Corp., Syracuse, 1971-72; med. libr. Health Sci. Libr., U. Minn., Duluth, 1973-74; tech. libr. Nuclear Energy Sys. Libr., Westinghouse Electric Corp., Pitts., 1974-77; asst. sci. libr. U. Kans. Librs., Lawrence, 1977-85, acting head sci. librs., 1985-86, head sci. librs., 1986—. Mem. access to health info. task force Kans. Libr. Network Bd. Contbr. articles to profl. jours. Mem. ALA (programming planning com. sci. and tech. sect.), Am. Chem. Soc., Assn. Coll. and Rsch. Librs., Beta Phi Mu. Avocations: reading, gardening, travel.

NEELEY, SHIRLEY, school system administrator; 1 child, Brandy. BA, U. Houston, EdD in Curriculum and Instrn.; MA, Prarie View A&M U. Supt. Galena Park Independent Sch. Dist., Tex., 1995—2004; commr. Tex. Edn. Agency, 2004—. Former pres. Tex. Assn. of Suburban and Mid-Urban Schs.; mem. So. Regional Edn. Bd., 2003; supt. Tex. Assn. of Sch. Bd.'s, 2003. Bd. mem. Harris County Youth Program, Tex. Academic Decathlon; bd. dirs. North Channel Area C. of C. Mem.: Houston Livestock Show (life; com. mem.), Rotary Club. Office: Tex Edn Agency 1701 N Congress Ave Austin TX 78701-1494 Office Phone: 512-463-8985. E-mail: commissioner@tea.state.tx.us.

NEELON, ANN MARIE, literature educator; b. Boston, Sept. 1, 1955; d. William Raphael and Evelyn Rose Neelon; m. Richard Harry Parker, July 25, 1992; children: Liam Alexander Parker, Brendan Raphael Parker. MFA, U. Mass., Amherst, 1982. Jones lectr. in poetry Stanford (Calif.) U., 1989—92; prof. Murray (Ky.) State U., 1992—. Vis. writer Murray City Schs., 2000—06. Author: (poetry book) Easter Vigil (Anhinga Prize for Poetry, 1995). Al Smith fellow, Ky. Arts Coun., 1998, Wallace Stegner fellow, Stanford U., 1988—99. Mem.: Associated Writing Programs (life). Home: 507 Broad St Murray KY 42071 Office: Murray State University 7C Faculty Hall Murray KY 42071-3341 Office Phone: 270 8090 4713. Office Fax: 270-809-4545.

NEELY, ELLEN J., lawyer; b. 1964; BA in Govt. and History, U. Tex.; JD, U. Chgo. Assoc. Wildman, Harrold, Allen & Dixon; asst. gen. counsel Chgo. Mercantile Exchange, 1995—99; v.p., gen. counsel Chgo. Stock Exchange, 1999—2001, sr. v.p. legal and market regulation, gen. counsel, corp. sec., 2001—05, pres. & gen. counsel, 2005—. Office: Chgo Stock Exchange One Financial Pl 440 S LaSalle St Chicago IL 60605

NEELY, HILARIE, dancer, educator; b. LA, Nov. 22, 1955; d. Alfred W. and Eloise L. Neely; m. Steven E. Job, Aug. 28, 1982; children: Matt Job, Travis Job. BFA, So. Meth. U., Dallas, 1977. Registered dance educator. Dancer Portland (Oreg.) Dance Theater, 1977—79; sch. dir., instr. Portland Dance Theater, 1977—80; dancer Cirque, Portland, 1979—80, Idaho Dance Ensemble, Sun Valley, 1980—85; sch. dir., instr. Ballet Sch. Found., Sun Valley, 1980—84; sch. dir., instr., owner Footlight Dance Ctr., Ketchum, 1984—; dance specialist, instr. Cmty. Sch., Sun Valley, 1990—; dance instr. Wood River Mid. Sch./HS, Hailey, Idaho, 2000—. Cons. State Bd. Edn., Boise, 1982—2001. Choreographer children's dance performance tours, 1984—. Treas., edn. chair Wood River Arts Alliance, Ketchum, 1994—; exec. bd., chmn. Idaho Alliance Arts Edn., Boise, 1998—2003. Named Arts Adv. of the Yr., Sun Valley C. of C., 1999; grantee, Idaho Commn. Arts, 1990. Mem.: AAHPERD (NW Dist. Dance Educator of Yr. 2005), Nat. Dance Edn. Orgn., Idaho Dance Arts Alliance, Cecchetti Coun. Am. (licentiate). Avocations: hiking, camping, gardening. Home and Office: Box 3593 Ketchum ID 83340

NEELY, SALLY SCHULTZ, lawyer; b. LA, Mar. 2, 1948; BA, Stanford U., 1970, JD, 1971. Bar: Ariz. 1972, Calif. 1977. Law clk. to judge U.S. Ct. Appeals (9th cir.), Phoenix, 1971-72; assoc. Lewis and Roca, Phoenix, 1972-75; asst. prof. Law Sch. Harvard U., Cambridge, Mass., 1975-77; assoc. Shutan & Trost, P.C., LA, 1977-79; ptnr., sr. counsel Sidley Austin LLP, LA, 1980—. Co-chair Am. Law Inst.-ABA Chpt. 11 Bus. Reorgns., 1989-95, 97—, Banking and Comml. Lending Law, 1997-99, Nat. Conf. Bankruptcy Judges, 1988, 90, 95, 96, 97, 99, 02, 06, Fed. Jud. Ctr., 1989, 90, 94-95, Southeast Bankruptcy Law Inst., 2002, 06, Workshop Bankruptcy and Bus. Reorgn. NYU, 1992—; rep. 9th cir. jud. conf., 1989-91; mem. Nat. Bankruptcy Conf., 1993—, co-chair com. on legis., 2001—, mem. exec. com. Chair Stanford U. Law Sch. Reunion Giving, 1996; bd. vis. Stanford U. Law Sch., 1990-92. Mem.: ABA, Calif. Bar Assn., Am. Coll. Bankruptcy (mem. bd. regents 1998—2003, chair ednl. programs com. 2003—, bd. dirs. 2003—05, v.p. 2005—). Office: Sidley Austin LLP 555 W 5th St Ste 4000 Los Angeles CA 90013-3000 Office Phone: 213-896-6024. Business E-Mail: sneely@sidley.com.

NEERKEN, JULIE P., lawyer; b. Denver, Nov. 26, 1949; BS cum laude, U. Mich., 1971; MA, U. Wis., 1974; JD cum laude, U. Mich., 1979. Bar: Ill. 1979, N.Mex. 1981, Tex. 2000. Ptnr. Rodey, Dickason, Sloan, Akin & Robb PA, Albuquerque. Author: Med. Plans Involve Many Choices, 1993, Reviewing Actuarial Report, 1984. Named one of best lawyers in Am., 2003—04. Mem.: State Bar N. Mex., ABA. Office: Rodey Dickason Sloan Akin & Robb PA 201 Third St NW Ste 2200 PO Box 1888 Albuquerque NM 87103 Office Phone: 505-766-7557. Office Fax: 505-768-7395. Business E-Mail: jneerken@rodey.com.

NEFF, AMY HANCOCK, elementary school educator; b. Phila., Dec. 1, 1961; d. Vance and Doris (Kroesser) Hancock; m. Ernest William Neff, July 18, 1987; 1 child, Kaylee. BS in Edn., Bloomsburg U., 1983; MEd, Beaver Coll., 1990. Elem. tchr. Archdiocese of Phila., 1983-85; contract specialist GSA, 1985-86; elem. tchr. Neshaminy Sch. Dist., Langhorne, Pa., 1987—. Bldg. sci. rep. K-12 Sci. Adv. Com., Langhorne, 1987-99, 2001-2002; mem. Sci. Textbook Selection Com., Langhorne, 1991; sch. sci. fair coord., 1992-94; participant NASA Ednl. Workshop for Elem. Sch. Tchrs., Kennedy Space Ctr., Fla., 1990, Johnson Space Ctr., Houston, 1991; Project LABS participant Rohm and Haas Corp., summer, 1994, presenter Delaware Valley Sci. Week; presenter dist.-wide space and physics workshops, 1990-94; participant Sci. Lesson Study, 2004-2005; mem. Grade 4 Curriculum Devel. Com. for Social Studies, sci. program pilot tchr., 2006-. Rider Am. Cancer Soc., Bike-a-Thons, 1989-92, MS 150 Bike Tour, 1992; vol. Action Team, Langhorne, 1991. Mem. Am. Fedn. Tchrs., Nat. Sci. Tchrs. Assn. (dist. rep. nat. conv. 1991-93), Bucks County Sci. Tchrs. Assn., Phila. Area Elem. Sci. Tchrs. Assn., Kappa Delta Pi (v.p. 1981-82). Avocations: guitar, bicycling, singing, aerobics, yoga. Home: 12 Amaryllis Ln Newtown PA 18940-1246 Office: Oliver Heckman Elem Sch Cherry St Langhorne PA 19047

NEFF, CAROLE CUKELL, lawyer; b. Geneva, NY, Aug. 3, 1951; d. Samuel and Hannah (Schoenfeld) C.; m. Richard Theodore Neff, Dec. 28, 1976; children: Alex Ryan, Hilary Shayna. BS magna cum laude, SUNY, Buffalo, 1973; JD, Tulane U., 1977. Bar: La. 1977. Law clk. La. State Supreme Ct., New Orleans, 1977—78; assoc. Session & Fishman, New Orleans, 1978—83; ptnr. Session, Fishman & Nathan, LLP, New Orleans, 1983—. Co-author: (with Max Nathan) Louisiana Estate Planning, Will Drafting and Estate Administration 2nd ed., 2000; mem. bd. editors Tulane U. Law Rev. Bd. dirs., pres. Jewish Endowment Found., New Orleans, 2006—. Named Achiever, Am. Coun. for Career Women, 1990, Woman of Yr., New Orleans Bus. and Profl. Women, 1991, YWCA Role Model, 1992; recipient Young Family Profl. Excellence award Jewish Endowment Found., 1989. Fellow Am. Coll. Trust and Estate Counsel; mem. NCJW, La. Bar Assn., New Orleans Bar Assn. (CLE chair 1987-89, 3d v.p. 1989-90, probate chair 1991-2000), Women's Profl. Coun. (bd. dirs., 1st v.p. 1989-90, pres. 1990-91), Profl. Fin. Planners of Greater New Orleans (sec. 1982-83, pres. 1983-84), New Orleans Estate Planning Coun. (pres. 2002-03), Order of Coif, Rotary Internat. (bd. dirs. 1994-96), Hadassah, Sisterhood Shir Chadash (v.p. 2006—). Democrat. Jewish. Avocations: cooking, piano playing, travel. Office: Session Fishman & Nathan LLP 201 Saint Charles Ave Ste 3500 New Orleans LA 70170-3500 Office Phone: 504-582-1500. Business E-Mail: cneff@sessions-law.com.

NEFF, DIANAH L., information technology executive; BA in Mktg. and Economics, San Jose State Univ.; MBA with concentration in ops. rsch., U. Calif. Berkeley. Chief info. officer City of Phila., 2001—06; sr. ptnr. Civitium, LLC, Alpharetta, Ga., 2006—. Guest prof., pub. adminstrn. progra Hayward State Univ., U. Washington; spkr. in field. Named Chief of Yr., Innovations and Influencers category, Information Week, 2005; named one of Top 25 Women of Distinction in Phila., 2005, Premier 100 IT Leaders, Computerworld, 2006; recipient Tech. Leadership award, Pub. Tech. Inst., 2004. Achievements include playing a leading role in making City of Palo Alto the first city in the US to have a website; working with San Bernardino County businesses and School District to develop a joint venture, Enterprise for Economy Excellence; developing and implementing the City of Bellevue, Washington Y2K compliance; identifying and mapping the 70,000 miles of fiber underneath the city's streets in effort to attract businesses downtown in San Diego in conjunction with City Center Development Corporation; leading the biggest and most controversial city-wide wireless project in the US, by building a 135-square-mile wireless network to cover the city for public and commercial use. Office: Civitium LLC 12850 Hwy 9 Ste 600 PMB-306 Alpharetta GA 30004 Fax: 215-686-8258.*

NEFF, DIANE IRENE, university administrator; b. Cedar Rapids, Iowa, Apr. 26, 1954; d. Robert Mariner and Adeline Emma (Zach) N BA Psychology and Home Econs., U. Iowa, 1976; MA Sociology, U. Mo., 1978; MEd Ednl. Leadership, U. West Fla., 1990; EdD Ednl. Leadership, U. Ctrl. Fla., 2003. Contract compliance officer, dir. EEO, City of Cedar Rapids, 1979—81; commd. ensign USN, 1981, advanced through grades to lt. comdr.; asst. legal officer Naval Comm. Area Master Sta., Guam, 1982—83; comm. security plans and requirements officer Comdr.-in-Chief U.S. Naval Forces in Europe, London, 1983—85; dir. stds. and evaluation dept. Recruit Tng. Command, Orlando, Fla., 1985—89; rsch. and analysis officer Naval Res. Officers Tng. Corps Office Chief Naval Edn. and Tng., Pensacola, Fla., 1989—91; tech. tng. officer Recruit Tng. Command, Great Lakes, Ill., 1991—92, mil. tng. officer, 1992—93, dir. apprentice tng., 1993—95; coord. ednl. and tng. programs U. Ctrl. Fla., Orlando, 1995—. Founding mem. Unity of Gulf Breeze, Fla., 1990; performer various benefits for chs., mus., others, Orlando, 1988, 91, 95, 96, 97 Fellow Adminstrn. on Aging, 1977 Unitarian Universalist. Avocation: piano. Business E-Mail: dneff@mail.ucf.edu.

NEFF, JEANNE HENRY, academic administrator; b. Fairmont, W. Va., Oct. 5, 1942; d. Percy Byron Henry and Rebecca Jacqueline Ridgely; m. Richard E. Kammer, Aug. 6, 1966 (div. July 1978); 1 child, Brian S. Kammer; m. Edward W.S. Neff II, Dec. 19, 1982; stepchildren: Larrie A., Edward W.S. III. BA, Wheeling Coll., 1964; MA, Rice U., 1966; ArtsD, Carnegie-Mellon U., 1976; postdoct., Harvard U., 1984. Instr. English Carlow Coll., Pitts., 1966-69; from asst. prof. to assoc. prof. English Wheeling (W. Va.) Coll., 1970-77, from assoc. dean to dean, 1977-80, academic v.p., 1980-86; v.p. academic affairs Susquehanna U., Selingsgrove, Pa., 1986-95; pres. The Sage Colls., Troy and Albany, N.Y., 1995—. Bd. dirs. Capital Bank & Trust Co., Albany. Trustee Albany Acad., 1996—; mem. Waterfront Commn., Troy, N.Y., 1996—; dir., v.p. Troy Redevel. Found., 1996—. Mem. Am. Coun. Edn. (fellow 1978-79, mem. commn. leadership devel. 1995—), Assn. New Am. Colls. (mem. pres.'s coun. 1997—), Assn. Am. Colls. and Univs. (dir. 1984-88, chair Am. Conf. Academic Deans, 1987), Univ. Heights Assn. (dir., v.p. 1996—). Home: 46 1st St Troy NY 12180-3811 Office: The Sage Colls 45 Ferry St Troy NY 12180-4115

NEFF, JENNIFER ELLEN, painter, artist; b. Kingston, NY, July 16, 1973; d. Wilfred Henry Neff and Susan Jean Foster. BFA, SUNY, New Paltz, NY. Sr. support staff and analysis Philliber Rsch. Assocs., Accord, NY, 1989—; freelance artist Jennifer Neff Studios, Kingston, 1999—; pres., owner Off the Wall Studios, Inc., Kingston, 1999—2001. Bd. dirs. Marbletown Arts Assn., 2003—. Office Phone: 845-340-8613. Personal E-mail: jnefferart@yahoo.com.

NEFF, KARLA SUE, secondary school educator; b. Harrisonville, Mo., Jan. 7, 1972; d. Gary Eugene Burchett and Gayla Sue Hampshire; m. Eric Frederick Neff, June 23, 2001; children: Michael Paul Norris, Alexander Paul Norris, Whitney Monica Norris, Riley Ryne Morgan. BA in Biology, Avila U., Kansas City, Mo., 1997; MA in Tchg., Webster U., Kansas City, Mo., 2004. Cert. tchr. Mo. Tchr. Raytown (Mo.) Sch. Dist., 1998—2001, Blue Springs (Mo.) Sch. Dist., 2002—. Named Family of Yr., Blue Springs, 2005; recipient Tchr. of Yr. award, Hall McCarter Edn. Ctr. Mem.: NEA (assoc.). Independent. Avocations: sports, travel. Home: 1217 SW Persels Rd Lees Summit MO 64081 Office: Valley View HS 5000 NW Valley View Rd Blue Springs MO 64015 Office Phone: 816-224-4388. Personal E-mail: kneff@bssd.net.

NEFF, MARIE TAYLOR, museum director, artist; d. James Arthur Taylor and Pearl Jackson; m. Edward Lewis Neff, June 24, 1946 (dec. July 1, 1994); children: James Edward, Charles Lewis(dec.). Degree in art and photography, Western Tex. Coll., 1985. Studio artist, Post, 1943—; art instr. Neff Art Sch., Post, 1963—78; co-owner retail bus. Post, 1963—88; art instr. Post Art Guild, Kids n Art, Post, 1975—85; dir. OS Ranch Found. Mus., Post, 1991—. Represented in permanent collections, pvt. collections. Pres., bd. dirs. Post Commerce and Tourism Bur., 1994—2002; dir., coord. Tex. Plains Trail Region, 2002—04, treas., 2004—. Named Queen Panhandle South Plains, Mrs. Tex. Sr. Pageant, 1999. Mem.: North Tex. Mus. Assn. (pres. 2001—04), Tex. Assn. Mus. (planning bd. state conv. 1997—2001, trustee-sec. 2000—05), Post C. of C. (designer commemorative coin 1976, Woman of Yr. 1972), Post Art Guild (pres., founding mem. 1974—2003), Rotary. Avocations: archaeology, photography, reading, travel. Office: OS Ranch Found Mus Ste 3 201 E Main St Post TX 79356 E-mail: mtneff@caprock-spur.com.

NEFF, MARILYN LEE, nursing consultant; b. Lancaster, Pa., Nov. 12, 1942; d. Norman Booth and F. Irene (Fridy) N. RN, U. Pa., 1963, BA, 1974; MBA, Widener U., 1988. Cert. nephrology nurse, nurse adminstr. advanced. Staff nurse Hosp. of U. Pa., Phila., 1963-64, asst. head nurse, 1964-68, staff nurse, 1968-71, asst. head nurse, 1971-75, head nurse, 1975-77, nursing supr., 1977-84; adminstr. Out-patient Dialysis Unit U. Pa., Phila., 1984-86; v.p. ops. Renal Care Cts. Corp., Wilmington, Del., 1986-88, Renal Treatment Ctrs., Inc., Berwyn, Pa., 1988-91; cons. MLN Cons., Wallingford, Pa., 1991-92; v.p. bus. devel. Healthdyne Home Nutritional Svcs., Inc., Marietta, Ga., 1992-94; cons. MLN Enterprises, Marietta, Ga., 1994—. Contbr. articles to profl. jours. Pres. Women's Fellowship, Calvary Presbyn. Ch., Media, Pa., 1982-86. Mem. ANA, Nat. Renal Adminstrs. Assn., Nat. Kidney Found. (del. 1990-91, Disting. Vol. Svc. award, 1990), Am. Nephrology Nurses Assn. (pres. 1991-92, Shiley Mgmt. award 1988, rsch. grant 1989). Avocations: teaching Sunday School, choir, reading, motorsports. Home and Office: 5222 Pikes Peak Ct Marietta GA 30062-6550

NEFF, MARY ELLEN ANDRE, retired elementary school educator; b. Indiana, Pa., July 6, 1943; d. Frank Vincent and Marie Isabel (Elrick) Andre; children: Gary V. Jr., Traci Dawn. BS, Indiana U. Pa., 1965, MEd, 1971. Elem. sch. tchr. Blairsville (Pa.)-Saltsburg Sch. Dist., Derry (Pa.) Area Sch. Dist.; ret., 2002. Zone chmn. Lions Dist. 14E; bd. mem. Ind. County Tourist Bur. Mem.: PTA, NEA, Pa. State Edn. Assn., Derry Area Hist. Soc. (bd. dirs.), Saltsburg Hist. Soc. (pres.), Nat. Soc. DAR (vice regent), Westmoreland County Hist. Soc. (bd. dirs., sec.), Latrobe Lions Club (pres.), Delta Kappa Gamma (pres. 1986—90, treas. 1992—2000). Home: 17 Carriage Rd Greensburg PA 15601-9014 E-mail: meneff@infionline.net.

NEGA, NANCY KAWECKI, middle school science educator; b. Chgo., Mar. 16, 1946; d. John Sebastian and Irene M. (Wantuch) Kawecki; m. Lance J. Nega, Feb. 24, 1968 (div. 1997); children: Sandi Kawecka Nenga, Todd J. BA Biology, Ill. Coll., 1968; MS Elem. Math., U. Ill., Chgo., 1991. Nat. bd. cert. early adolescent sci. tchr. 1999. Rschr. Morton-Norwich, Inc., Woodstock, Ill., 1968—72; tchr. Elmhurst Unit Dist. 205, Ill., 1986—; master tchr. Dept. Energy pre-svc. tchr. program Argonne Nat. Lab., Ill., 2001—. Trainer Globe Program, Washington, 1995-99; Internet trainer Argonne Nat. Lab., 1996-2000 Recipient Presdl. Excellence in Sci. and Math. Tchg. award NSF, 1995, Paul DeHart Hurd award, NMLSTA, 1999 Mem. NSTA, Ill. Sci. Tchrs. Assn. (Excellence award 1994), Nat. Mid Level Sci. Tchrs. Assn., Mid Level Sci. Tchrs. Network Office: Churchville Mid Sch 155 Victory Pkwy Elmhurst IL 60126-1215 Office Phone: 630-832-8682. E-mail: n.nega@comcast.net, nnega@elmhurst.k12.il.us.

NEHEZ, SUSAN SPRINGMAN, elementary school educator; b. Beech Grove, Ind., Aug. 10, 1957; d. LeRoy Albert and Theresa E. (Roembke) Springman; m. Casper Michael Nehez III, June 2, 1984. BS in edn., Ind. U., 1980; MS in edn., Butler U., 1984. Cert. reading recovery Purdue U., 1994. Tchr. Indpls. (Ind.) Pub. Sch., 1980—81, M. S. D. Warren Twp., Indpls., 1981—. Reading recovery, literacy support, and literacy coach Moorhead Elem. Warren Arts and Edn. grant, Warren Arts and Edn. Found., 1996, 1999, 2001, At Risk, Desegregation grant, Warren Twp., 1994, 1995, 2001. Mem.: Assn. for Supr. and Curriculum, Reading Recovery Coun. of No. Am., Internat. Reading Assn., Alpha Delta Kappa (pres. 2004—). Cath. Achievements include development of literacy learning at the sch. and dist. level. Avocations: reading, travel, sports. Office: Moorhead Elem Sch 8400 E 10th St Indianapolis IN 46219 Office Phone: 317-532-3885. Business E-Mail: snehez@warren.k12.in.us.

NEIBERT, BETSY LYN, psychologist; b. Harrisburg, Pa., Sept. 24, 1973; d. Jack Eugene and Lynne Elizabeth Neibert. BS, Susquehanna U., 1995; MSEd, Bucknell U., 1997. Cert. sch. psychologist, elem. guidance counselor Pa. Sch. psychologist Mecklenburg County Pub. Schs., Boydton, Va., 1997—2004, Wake County Pub. Schs., Raleigh, NC, 2004—. Coord. Spl. Olympics, Boydton, 2003—05. Mem.: NASP. Personal E-mail: bneibert@nc.rr.com.

NEIDICH, BROOKE GARBER, foundation administrator, art patron; m. Daniel Neidich. BA, NYU. Founder, chmn. NYU Child Study Ctr. Trustee Chapin Sch., Mt. Sinai - NYU Health Care Sys., NYU Med. Sch. Found.; bd. dir. Lincoln Ctr. Theater, Lubovitch Dance Co.; adv. coun. Children's Defense Fund - NY; vice chmn. Whitney Mus. Am. Art. Recipient Health Care Leadership Award distinguished cmty. svc., United Hosp. Fund., 1999. Mailing: c/o Whitney Mus Am Art 945 Madison Ave New York NY 10021

NEILL, REBECCA ANNE, middle school educator; b. Bryan, Tex., Jan. 6, 1960; d. Walter and Marilyn Goff; m. Travis L. Neill, June 11, 1994; children: Shannon, Darby. BS, Tex. A&M U., 1982, Master of Edn. Curriculum and Instrn., 1992. Cert. elem. tchr., Tex. Tchr. sci. Klein Ind. Sch. Dist., Houston, 1989—2004; ESST collaborative TXBESS; tchr. sci. Aldine Ind. Sch. Dist., Spring Ind. Sch. Dist. Mem. Nat. Coalition Coun., 1990—96; computer workshop facilitator, 2000—; presenter in field, 2000—. Contbr. rsch. to profl. jours. Recipient award, Honors Inst. Elem. Tchrs., 1987, Thanks to Tchrs. award, 1990; grantee technology grants. Mem. NSTA, Coun. Elem. Sci. Internat., Tex. Coun. Elem. Sci., Sci. Tchrs. Assn. Tex., Met. Area Tchrs. Sci. Home: 4719 Marywood Dr Spring TX 77388-4977

NEILL-GREEN, TERESA, art therapist, social worker, educator; b. Marietta, Ohio; d. Harold and Evelyn Neill; m. Daniel Green; children: Daniel, Courtney. BFA, Columbus Coll. Art and Design, Ohio, 1982; MAT, Wright State U., Dayton, Ohio, 1984. LSW Ohio, bd. cert. art therapist Ohio. Art therapist Homereach Hospice, Riverside Meth. Hosp., 1991—. Part-time instr. Columbus Coll Art and Design, Columbus, 1990—; art therapist and coord. St. Joseph Residential Ctr., 1983—85. Author short stories; contbr. articles to profl. jours. Recipient Ptnr. of Yr. award, Riverside Meth. Hosp., 2006. Mem.: Buckeye Art Therapy Assn., Am. Art Therapy Assn. (past by-laws chair). Office: Liberal Arts Divsn Columbus Coll Art and Design 107 N 9th St Columbus OH 43215-1700

NEILSON, JANE SCOTT, mathematics educator; b. Oakland, Calif., July 29, 1919; d. George Robert and Ethel Genevive (Smith) Scott; m. James Drake Neilson II, Sept. 24, 1955 (dec.). Student in engring., U. Mich., 1937, student in lit. and art, 1938-40; BA in Elem Edn., Calif. State U., Northridge, 1960; postgrad. in secondary edn., UCLA, 1966-67. Process engr. Brigs Mfg. Co., Detroit, 1941-43; mathematician dept. purchasing Detroit GM, 1943-44; mathematician Chrysler Corp., Highland Pk., Mich., 1944-45; dir. recreation ARC, Europe and Korea, 1945-54; assoc. engr. Dr. Betando, Santa Monica, Calif., 1954-56; tchr. math. Las Virgines Unified Sch. Dist., Calabasas, Calif., 1961-79, subs. tchr., 1984-93. Docent Getty Mus., Malibu, Calif., 1982-94. Avocations: sno-skiing, biking, painting, piano, photography. Home: 4624 Eastbourne Bay Oxnard CA 93035-3703

NEIMARK, EDITH DEBORAH, psychologist, educator; b. Long Branch, N.J., May 24, 1928; d. Solomon J. and Regina (Stein) N. BA, Skidmore Coll., 1949; MA, Ind. U., 1952, PhD, 1953. Instr. Tulane U., New Orleans, La., 1953-55; asst. prof. Goucher Coll., Towson, Md., 1955-56; rsch. psychologist AFP & TRC, USAF, Lackland AFB, Tex., 1956-58; from asst. to assoc. prof. NYU, 1958-64; from assoc. prof. to prof. Rutgers U., New Bruswick, N.J., 1964-91; prof. emeritus, 1992—; vis. prof. dept. psychology U. N.Mex., Albuquerque, 1992-92. Author: Adventures in Thinking, 1987; editor: Stimulus Sampling Theory, 1967, Moderators of Competence, 1985. Fellow AAAS, Am. Psychol Assn., Soc. for Res. Child Devel., N.Y. Acad. Sci. Address: 17 Boxwood Dr Princeton NJ 08540-9455 E-mail: neimark@rci.rutgers.edu.

NEISLER, OTHERINE JOHNSON, education educator, consultant; b. St. Louis, Apr. 27, 1954; d. Robert Louis and Ruth (Wilson) Johnson; m. Anton Ross Neisler, Sr. (div. 1988); children: Maiya Rose Neisler Benda, Anton Ross Jr. BA, Brandeis U., 1972; MA, Fairfield U., 1991; PhD, Syracuse U., 1994. Tchr. social studies Warren H.S., Newton, Mass., 1974-76; mktg. mgr./analyst IBM, White Plains, N.Y., 1976-88; asst. prof. instrnl. tech. Boston Coll., Chestnut Hill, Mass., 1994-2000; assoc. dir. tchr. preparation program Yale U., New Haven, 2000—04; dean edn. St. Joseph Coll., West Hartford, Conn., 2004—. Curriculum cons. numerous schs., 1994—. Contbr. articles to profl. jours. Pres. bd. dirs. Erie County (Pa.) Domestic Abuse Agy., 1978-80; bd. dirs. The Multicultural Resource Ctr., Phila., 1996—, Primary Source, Inc., Boston, 1996-98. Mem. ASCD, Am. Edn. Rsch. Assn. (equity com. 1992—), Nat. Coun. Social Studies (citizenship com. 1992—), Links, Inc. Avocations: hiking, tennis. Office: Saint Joseph Coll 1678 Asylum Ave West Hartford CT 06117 Business E-Mail: otherine.neisler@yale.edu, oneister@sjc.edu.

NEITA, MARGUERITE ELAINE, science educator; d. Vernon Carl and Gloria Arabell Neita; life ptnr. Rufus Rosser; children: Natalie Denise Kaye Rosser, Erica Nicole Rosser, Renee Yolande Rosser, Jennifer Alexis Rosser. AA in Med. Microbiology, Inst. Med. Lab. Scis., London, 1971; BSc cum laude in Med. Tech., Howard U., Washington DC, 1977, MSc in Microbiology, 1981, PhD in Nutritional Sci., 1996. Med. technologist dept. microbiology U. WI, Kingston, 1968—69, sr. technologist in charge of tchg. and rsch. dept. microbiology, 1973—74; med. technologist St. George's Hosp. Group, Pub. Health Lab., London, 1969—72, The Jamaica Govt. Svcs., The Pub. Health Lab., Kingston, 1972—73, Howard U. Hosp., Washington, 1976—79; assoc. prof. Howard U., Washington, 1981—. Exec. sec. Caribbean Soc. Med. Technologists, Kingston, 1972—74; chairperson, program dir. dept. clin. lab. sci. Howard U., 2004. Contbr. chapters to books. Avocations: gardening, reading, embroidery. Office: Howard U Annex 1 6th & Bryant Sts NW Washington DC 20059 Office Phone: 202-806-5632. Office Fax: 202-806-7918. E-mail: mneita@howard.edu.

NELIPOVICH, SANDRA GRASSI, artist; b. Oak Park, Ill., Nov. 22, 1939; d. Alessandro and Lena Mary (Ascareggi) Grassi; m. John Nelipovich Jr., Aug. 19, 1973. BFA in Art Edn., U. Ill., Champaign/Urbana, 1961; postgrad., Northwestern U., Evanston, Ill., 1963, Gonzaga U., Florence, Italy, 1966, Art Inst. Chgo., 1968; diploma (hon.), Accademia Universale Alessandro Magno, Prato, Italy, 1983. Tchr. art Edgewood Jr. High Sch., Highland Park, Ill., 1961-62, Emerson Sch. Jr. High Sch., Oak Park, 1962-77; batik artist Calif., 1977—; illustrator Jolly Robin Publ. Co., Anaheim, Calif., 1988—2001, Assistance League of Anaheim, Calif., 2000—. Supr. student tchrs., Oak Park, 1970-75; adult edn. tchr. ESL, ceramics, Medinah, Ill., 1974; mem. curriculum action group on human dignity, EEO workshop demonstration, Oak Park, 1975-76; guest lectr. Muckenthaler Ctr., Fullerton, Calif., 1980, 92, Niguel Art Group, Dana Point, Calif., 1989, Carlsbad A.A., 1990, ARt League, Oceanside Art Group, 1992; 2d v.p. Anaheim Hills Women's Club, 1990-91, rec. sec. 1991-92; fabric designer for fashion designer Barbara Jax, 1987; illustrator Assistance League Anaheim (Calif.), 2000—, muralist Lincoln Sch. Ill., 2002-2003. One-Woman shows include Lawry's Calif. Ctr., L.A., 1981-83, Whittier (Calif.) Mus., 1985-86, Anaheim Cultural Ctr., 1986-88, Ill. Inst. Tech., Chgo., 1989, Muckenthaler Cultural Ctr., Fullerton, 1990; also gallery exhibits in Oak Brook, 1982, La Habra, Calif., 1983, Millard Sheets Gallery, Pomona, Calif., 1996; represented in permanent collections McDonald's Corp., Oak Brook, Glenkirk Sch., Deerfield, Ill., Emerson Sch., Oak Park, Calif.; poster designer Saratoga Fine Arts. Active Assistance League, Anaheim, Calif., 1992—, 2d v.p. ways and means com., 1995—96, 1997—98, 2d v.p. ways and means, 2004—05, 2005—, historian, 2002—03, Anaheim Arts Coun., 2002—, 2004—06; chairwoman Toscanini Guild Orange County Performing Arts Ctr., 2006—. Recipient numerous awards, purchase prizes, 1979—; featured in Calif. Art Rev., Artists of So. Calif., Vol. II, Nat. Artists' Network, 1992, Batik for Artists and Quilters, 2001. Mem. AAUW (hospitality chmn. 1984-85), Soc. Children's Book Writers and Illustrators, Assistance League Anaheim, Orange Art Assn. (jury chmn. 1980). Roman Catholic. Avocations: cooking, gardening, travel. Home and Office: 5922 E Calle Cedro Anaheim CA 92807-3207 Personal E-mail: sgneli@adelphia.net.

NELKIN MILLER, CATHY, hotel executive; Pres., gen. mgr. The Garden City (N.Y.) Hotel, NY. Bd. dirs. Alzheimer's Found., Long Island; mem. dinner com. Tilles Ctr.; bd. dirs. Famil and Children's Assn. Office: The Garden City Hotel 45 7th St Garden City NY 11530

NELLIGAN, ANNETTE FRANCES, social worker; b. Bangor, Maine, Sept. 20, 1954; d. Paul James and Laura Jenny (Sumner) N.; m. Peter Jamie Smith, June 22, 1985 (dec. June, 1997); children: Angelica Grace Nelligan-Smith, Acatia Faith Nelligan-Smith. AA, U. Maine, Bangor, 1974; BS, U. Maine, 1977, MEd, 1978, EdD, 1995. Lic. clin. profl. counselor; lic. marriage and family counselor; lic. social worker; cert. secondary sch. tchr., Maine, sch. counselor, Maine. Tchr. Bangor H.S., 1978, Etna (Maine)-Dixmont Sch., 1979-80; residential advisor Penobscot Job Corps, Bangor, 1980-84; group life worker St. Andre's Home, Bangor, 1984; caseworker, supr. Maine Dept. Human Svcs., Bangor, 1984-96; clin. coord. Old Town Regional Program, Bangor, 1996—. Mem. Homeless Edn. Adv. Bd., Bangor, 1992-95; instr. counselor edn. U. Maine, 1996—. Mem. ACA, Assn. for Specialists in Group Work. Roman Catholic. Avocations: doll collecting, camping, skiing, sailing. Home: 24 Albert Ln Glenburn ME 04401-5505 Office: Jefferson St Old Town ME 04468 E-mail: annettenelligan@unit.maine.edu.

NELLIGAN, GLORIA JEAN, science educator; b. Milford, Del., Nov. 21, 1947; d. Alvin Chipman and Mabel Elizabeth Donophan; m. James Patrick Nelligan, July 31, 1966; children: Richard Neil Kratsas, James Patrick, Tina Michelle. BS, Del. State U., Dover, 1996; MS, Western Md. Coll., Westminster, 2001. Cert. tchr. Md., 2002. Tchr. sci., spl. edn. Woodbridge Sch. Dist., Bridgeville, Del., 1996—98; tchr. sci. Caroline County Schs., Denton, Md., 1998—. Master gardener Del. Dept. of Agr., Dover, 1990. Avocations: gardening, writing poetry. Office: Lockerman Mid Sch 410 Lockerman St Denton MD 21629 Office Phone: 410-479-2760.

NELLIGAN, KATE (PATRICIA COLLEEN NELLIGAN), actress; b. London, Ont., Can., Mar. 16, 1951; d. Patrick Joseph and Alice (Dier) N. Attended, York U., Toronto, Ctrl. Sch. Speech and Drama, London. Appeared in plays in Bristol, London, and New York: Barefoot in the Park, 1972, Misalliance, A Streetcar Named Desire, The Playboy of the Western World, London Assurance, Lulu, Private Lives, Knuckle, 1974, Heartbreak House, 1975, Plenty, 1975, As You Like It, A Moon for the Misbegotten, 1984, Virginia, 1985, Serious Money, 1988, Spoils of War, 1988, Bad Habits; films include: The Count of Monte Cristo, 1979, The Romantic Englishwoman, 1979, Dracula, 1979, Mr. Patman, 1980, Eye of the Needle, 1980, Agent, 1980, Without a Trace, 1983, Eleni, 1985, White Room, 1990, Bethune: The Making of a Hero, 1990, Frankie and Johnnie, 1991 (BAFTA Film award, 1992), The Prince of Tides, 1991, Shadows and Fog, 1992, Fatal Instinct, 1993, Wolf, 1994, Into the Deep, 1994, How to Make an American Quilt, 1995, Margaret's Museum, 1995, Up Close and Personal, 1996, U.S. Marshals, 1998, (voice) Stolen Moments, 1998 Boy Meets Girl, 1998, The Cider House Rules, 1999; TV appearances include: The Arcata Promise, 1974, The Onedin Line, The Lady of the Camellias, Licking Hitler, Measure for Measure, Therese Raquin, 1980, Forgive Our Foolish Ways, 1980, Kojak: The Price of Justice, 1987, Control, 1987, Love and Hate: A Marriage Made in Hell, 1990, Terror Strikes the Class Reunion, 1992, The Diamond Fleece, 1992, Liar Liar, 1993, Shattered Trust: The Shari Karney Story, 1993, Spoils of War, 1994, Million Dollar Babies, 1994, A Mother's Prayer, 1995, Captive Heart: The James Mink Story, 1996, Calm at Sunset, Calm at Dawn, 1996, Love Is Strange, 1998, Swing Vote, 1999, Blessed Stranger: After Flight 111, 2000, Walter and Henry, 2001, A Wrinkle in Time, 2002; TV guest appearance Road to Avonlea, 1990. Recipient Best Actress award Evening Standard, 1978. Avocations: reading, cooking.

NELLIS, NORA LAJOY, special education educator, writer; b. Glens Falls, NY, July 2, 1938; d. William Thomas LaJoy and Pauline Elizabeth LaPlanche; m. Robert Selmser Nellis, June 7, 1980 (dec.); m. Warren Merritt Cole, Sept. 11, 1964 (div. Apr. 30, 1970); 1 child, Stephen Merritt Cole. AA in English, Adirondack C.C., Queensbury, N.Y., 1987; BA in English, Skidmore Coll., Saratoga Springs, N.Y., 1990; MA in Creative Writing and Women's Studies, Vt. Coll. of Norwich U., Montpelier, 1993. Editor internat. trade mag. Glens Falls Continental Ins., Glens Falls, NY, 1958—62; advt. mktg. specialist Radio Sta. WSET, Glens Falls, 1962—63; libr. Bklyn. Pub. Libr. Ft. Hamilton, Bklyn., 1964—66; Title I instr. spl. needs Glens Falls City Schs., 1971—97; freelance writer and workshop leader, 1998—. Mentor - facilitator children's writing Bd. of Coop. Ednl. Svcs., Saratoga Springs, 1998—2000; founding com. mem. and tchr. Intergenerational Writing, Glens Falls, 1995—2000. Contbr. Linking Roots, 1993, Unbearable Uncertainty, 2000; author and co-editor: From the Listening Pl., 1999. Founder Nat. Cystic Fibrosis Found. (Adirondack chpt.), Glens Falls, 1990, Support Group Single Parents, Glens Falls, 1995. Grantee DfSCA SPOKES, 1997, Troy Arts Coun., 1999; Golub Found. scholarship, 1991. Mem.: Nat. Assn. of Poetry Therapy, Am. Cancer Soc. (breast cancer resource), Wiawaka Women's Creative Orgn. (founding com. mem., facilitator 1995—). Liberal. Lutheran. Avocations: photography, recitation, health and fitness. Home: PO Box 564 Lake George NY 12845 Office: Poemweavers at Mohawk Mountain 2204 Luzerne Rd Lake George NY 12845 E-mail: nnellis@capital.net.

NELSEN, EVELYN RIGSBEE SEATON, retired secondary school educator; b. Jonesboro, Ark., Nov. 9, 1930; d. Glen Brown and Ruby Beatrice (Minton) Rigsbee; m. Frank W. Seaton, Apr. 19, 1952 (div. Aug. 1980); children: Susanna, Frank, Caroline, Rebecca, Elizabeth; m. David Allen Nelsen, July 25, 1981. BS in Edn., Ark. State U., 1968, MS in Edn., 1976; postgrad., U. Miss., 1968, U. Ark., Little Rock, 1989-90, U. Ctrl. Ark., 1990-92. Cert. English, French and gifted edn. tchr., adminstrn., secondary prin., Ark. Saleswoman Fan-Craft, Inc., Plainville, Conn., 1955-61; pers. dir. St. Bernard's Hosp., Jonesboro, 1961-68; tchr. Jonesboro Pub. Schs., 1968-81, Hazen (Ark.) Schs., 1985-92; remodeler, Little Rock, 1981-85, Hazen and Jonesboro, 1992—. Tchr. Gov.'s Sch. for Gifted, summer 1983; former mem. English Planning Commn., State of Ark, former mem. Gifted Edn. Commn. Author: (novel) Tori; contbr. numerous articles to trade jours., essays to newspaper. Vol. various Dem. polit. campaigns, Ark., 1968—, Clinton Presdl. Campaign, Little Rock, 1992, Dem. Nat. Com. Grantee U. Miss., summer 1968. Mem. Am. Assn. Ret. Persons, Ark. Assn. Ret. Tchrs., AAUW, MENSA, Royal Trust, Nat. Trust, Phi Delta Kappa, Delta Kappa Gamma, Lambda Iota Tau. Avocations: reading, gardening, wallpapering, writing, house painting. Home: 1007 W Washington Ave Jonesboro AR 72401-2676

NELSON, ALICE CARLSTEDT, retired nursing educator; b. Strandquist, Minn., May 25, 1921; d. Peter Gustaf and Florence Olivia (Berg) Carlstedt; m. Armour Halstead Nelson June 5, 1954 (dec. Dec. 1993). RN, Bethesda Hosp., St. Paul, 1944; BS, Augustana Coll., 1948; MA, U. Chgo., 1954. RN, Minn., Ill., N.D., Iowa, Calif.; cert. lactation educator, cert. lifetime cmty. coll. tchr. Ob nurse Moline Luth. Hosp., Ill., 1943—44; asst. night supr. Bethesda Hosp., St. Paul, 1944—45; with Army Nurse Corps, 1945—46; ob nurse Miller Hosp., St. Paul, 1947; nurse intermediate grade Wadsworth VA Hosp., L.A., 1947—48; head nurse Crippled Children's Sch., Jamestown, ND, 1948—50; head nurse Sch. Handicapped Children U. Iowa, Iowa City, 1950—51; clin. instr. Chgo. Lying-In Hosp., 1951—54, St. Luke's Hosp., Fargo, ND, 1954—60; tchr., supr. lab. pre-sch. N.D. State U., Fargo, 1962—64; coll. health svc. Calif. Luth. U., Thousand Oaks, 1968—74, faculty dept. nursing, 1982—85; pvt. duty nurse Thousand Oaks, 1976—81; ret., 1990. State sec. League for Nursing, N.D., 1956-64; team mem. preparation Nat. Achievement Test in Nursing of Children, N.Y., 1959 Author: Post-War Europe Through The Eyes of Youth, 2002; editor: The Conquest of Chicago, 2004; contbr. articles to profl. jours. Various offices including Ch. Coun. Holy Trinity Luth. Ch., Thousand Oaks, 1964-90; founding bd. dirs. Honey Tree Pre-Sch., Thousand Oaks, 1972; mem. task force on aging S.W. Pacific Luth. Synod Office, L.A., 1979; parent-aide, hotline, etc. Child Abuse & Neglect, Ventura County, Calif., 1979-82; bd. dirs. La Serena Retirement Ctr., Thousand Oaks, 1985-88; mem. ch. choir Salemsborg Luth. Ch., Smolan, Kans., 1990-2000, mem. ch. coun., 1996-2000, tchr. adult classes, 1996-99 Recipient award writing contests Am. Jour. Nursing, 1969, Calif. Nurse, 1987, Outstanding Vol. award Ventura County Child Abuse & Neglect, 1982. Mem. Bethany Bibliophiles Book Club, Writer's Cramp Group Democrat. Avocations: travel, reading, writing.

NELSON, ALISON, food products executive; Founder, owner, CEO Chocolate Bar, NYC, 2002—. Co-author (with Matt Lewis): (cookbook) Chocolate Bar, 2004. Named one of 40 Under 40, Crain's NY Bus., 2006. Mailing: Chocolate Bar 48 8th Ave New York NY 10014 Office Phone: 212-366-1541.*

NELSON, ALONDRA R., social sciences educator; b. Bethesda, Md., Apr. 22, 1968; d. Robert Samuel and Delores Yvonne Nelson; m. Benjamin D. Williams, Oct. 21, 2000. BA magna cum laude, U. Calif., San Diego, 1994; PhD, NYU, 2003. Trustee dissertation fellow Skidmore Coll., Saratoga Springs, NY, 2000—01; Ann E. Plato fellow Trinity Coll., Hartford, Conn., 2001—02; lectr. Yale U., New Haven, 2002—03, asst. prof. sociology and African Am. studies, 2003—. Co-editor: Technicolor: Race, Technology and Everyday Life, 2001. Fellow W.E.B. DuBois Inst., Harvard U., 2006; Career Enhancement fellowship, Woodrow Wilson Nat. Fellowship Found., Andrew S. Mellon and Found., 2006—. Mem.: Soc. for the Social Studies of Sci., Am. Studies Assn., Am. Sociol. Assn., Phi Beta Kappa. Office: Yale U Dept African Am Studies PO Box 203388 New Haven CT 06520-3388 Office Phone: 203-432-1170. Business E-Mail: alondra.nelson@yale.edu.

NELSON, ANNA M., elementary school educator, administrative assistant; b. Dallas, Oct. 2, 1944; d. Jack Walter and Maria Mitchell; m. B. S. Nelson, June 19, 1965. Student, St. Peter's Acad., Dallas, 1961—63; A in Mgmt., El Centro Coll., 2001, postgrad., 2004—05. Cert. nurses aide. Patient care staff St. Paul Hosp., Dallas, 1965—66; nurses asst. Parkland Hosp., Dallas, 1967—72; respiratory therapy technician, pulmonary technician supr. Meth. Hosp., Dallas, 1973—75; mgr. G.W. JR's Restaurant, Dallas, 1981—83; substitute tchr. Highland Park Ind. Sch. Dist., Dallas, 2003—05; nurses asst. technician Tech. Stat. Nat. Health Care, Dallas, 2005; data entry US Small Bus. Adminstrn., Ft. Worth, 2005—. Planning bd. Dallas Area Rapid Transit; precinct judge, clk. Dallas County Election Dept., 1991—2004. Mem.: Soc. for Advancement Mgmt., Students in Free Enterprise (Outstanding Job Performance medal 2001). Home: PO Box 225940 Dallas TX 75222

NELSON, ANNE, playwright, former reporter; married; 2 children. BA, Yale U. War corr. LA Times, NY Times, El Salvador, 1980—83, Guatemala, 1980—83; prof. journalism Columbia U., NYC, dir. Internat. Programs, Grad. Sch. Journalism, adj. assoc. prof. Sch. Internat. and Pub. Affairs. Author: (screenplays) The Guys, 2002, (plays) The Anglo-American Alliance, 2005, Savages, 2006. Guggenheim fellow, 2005—06, New Harmony Dramatists fellow. Mailing: c/o Internat Creative Mgmt 40 West 57th St New York NY 10019 Office: Sch Internat and Public Affairs Internat Affairs Bldg 13th Floor 420 West 118th St Mailcode 3323 New York NY 10027 Office Phone: 212-854-3239. E-mail: an115@columbia.edu.*

NELSON, ANTONYA, writer; b. Wichita, Kans., 1961; m. Robert Boswell; children: Jade, Noah. BA, U. Kans., 1984; MFA, U. Ariz., 1986. Prof. Warren Wilson MFA program, N.Mex. State U. Author: The Expendables (Flannery O'Connor award, 1990), In the Land of Men, Family Terrorists, Talking in Bed (Heartland award, 1996), Nobody's Girl, Living to Tell; contbr. stories to mags. Named one of N.Y. Times Notable Books, 1992, 1996, 1998, 2000; fellow, Guggenheim Found., 2000—01; grantee, NEA, 2000—01. Office: New Mexico State Univ Dept English Dept 3E Las Cruces NM 88003

NELSON, ARLEEN BRUCE, social worker; b. Loma Linda, Calif., Oct. 25, 1926; d. Delbert Francis and Sarah Enns Bruce; m. A. Gordon Nelson, Oct. 29, 1948 (div. Sept. 1976); children: Gregory Bruce, Mark Andrew, Heidi, Scott Bradford. BA, UCLA, 1948; MSW, U. Wash., 1975. Cert. ACSW 1979, BCSW 1987, MSW Wash., 1989, LCSW Wash., 2001. Case worker L.A. County DPSS, L.A., 1949—50, 1958—61, child protective Svc. Supr., 1966—69; dir. Manson Migrant Daycare Ctr., Manson, Wash., 1970—72; I and A coord. Sr. Svc., Seattle, 1975—78; co-dir., psychotherapist Soc. Workers N. W., Seattle, 1979—95; coord., HIV-AIDS Seattle Counseling Svc. for Sexual Minorities, 1986—94, psychotherapist, supr., 1994—2000, intern supr., 1993—96; aux. faculty U. Wash., 1995—2001; clin. cons. Seattle Counseling Svcs., 2000—; intern supr. Seattle Counseling Svc. for Sexual Minorities, 2002—. Edn. com. Wash. Soc. of Clin. Soc. Work, Seattle, 1986. Co-founder Nat. Parents and Friends of Gays and Lesbians; dir. PNU / Mountain Region Nat. PFLAG, multi states, 1981—83, v.p., 1983—89; gay and lesbian advocate multiple T.V. appearances, 1978—85; task force for gays and lesbians Ch. Coun. of Greater Seattle, 1977—80; bd. mem. The Dorian Group, Seattle, 1980; co-founder Seattle Chap. Parents and Friends of Lesbians and Gays, Seattle, 1979; pres. Seattle Chap. PFLAG, 1993—94; Bd. Ch. and soc. PNW Conf. United Meth. Ch., Wash., 1970—82, commn. of race and religion Wash., 1982—88. Recipient The Dorian Award, Dorian Group, 1982, 1998 Cmty. Leadership Award, Greater Seattle Bus. Assn., 1999, Founders Award, Seattle PFLAG, 1989, Nat. PFLAG, 1991, Award for Dedication and Svc., Seattle Gay Clinic, 1994, Award of Merit for long Svc. to the Trans - gendered Cmty., The Trans-gendered Group, 2000. Mem.: Nat Assn. of Soc. Workers, Wash. Chap. NASW. Democrat. Methodist. Avocations: travel, reading. Office: Seattle Counseling Svc 1216 Pine St Seattle WA 98101 Office Phone: 206-323-1768.

NELSON, BARBARA ANNE, judge; b. Mineola, N.Y., Jan. 16, 1951; d. Richard William and Dorothee Helen (Thorne) Nelson. BA, Inter Am. U. P.R., 1072; JD, New Eng. Sch. Law, 1975. Legal editor Prentice Hall Pub. Co., Englewood Cliffs, N.J., 1976-77; assoc. Antonio C. Martinez Law Firm, N.Y.C., 1977-79, Pollack & Kramer, N.Y.C., 1979-83; pvt. practice N.Y.C., 1983-95; immigration judge U.S., N.Y.C., 1995—. Author, spkr., tng. film. Mem. ACLU, Legal Aid Soc. N.Y., Amnesty Internat., Asia Soc., Internat. Assn. Refugee Judges. Avocations: travel, yoga, foreign languages. Home: 324 W 14th St Apt 5A New York NY 10014-5003 Office: 26 Federal Plz New York NY 10278-0004 Personal E-mail: nelsonferrets@yahoo.com.

NELSON, BARBARA J., dean; b. Ohio; d. Bernard James and Betty-Jane (James) N. BA in Polit. Sci., Ohio State U., 1971, MA in Polit. Sci., 1975, PhD in Polit. Sci., 1976. Policy rsch. assoc. Mershon Ctr. Pub. Policy, Columbus, Ohio, 1974-76; asst. prof. Princeton (N.J.) U., 1976-83; assoc. prof. Hubert H. Humphrey Inst. U. Minn., Mpls., 1983-89, program dir. MA program, 1987-90, dir. ctr. women & pub. policy, 1984-94, prof. Hubert H.Humphrey Inst., 1983-94; v.p., disting. prof. Radcliffe Coll., Cambridge, Mass., 1994-96; dean UCLA Sch. Pub. Policy & Social Rsch., L.A., 1996—. Bd. trustees Ctr. Women in Pub., Mpls., 1984-98. Author: Making an Issue of Child Abuse, 1984, American Women in Politics, 1984; co-editor: Wage Justice, 1989, Women and Politics Worldwide, 1995. Bd. trustees Radcliffe Coll., 1994-96; mem. Minn. Supreme Ct.'s Commn., 1987-88; advisor Govt. of Sweden Parliamentary Commn. Women & Democracy. W.K. Kellogg Found. grantee, 1994-97, Ford Found. grantee, 1993-97, Hewlett Ctr. Conflict Resolution grantee, 1988, 93. Mem. Am. Polit. Sci. Assn. (bd. trustees 1988-98), Assn. Pub. Policy Analysis & Mgmt. Office: UCLA Sch Pub Policy/Social Rsch 3284 Pub Policy Bldg Los Angeles CA 90095-0001

NELSON, BARBARA KASZTAN, marketing professional; d. Eugeniusz and Danuta Kasztan; m. Kelley Nelson, June 26, 2004. B in Mktg., Seton Hall U., 1998, MBA magna cum laude, 2004. Mktg. rsch. assoc. Schering Plough Pharms., Kenilworth, NJ, 1997—99, analyst, mktg. rsch., 1999—2001; sr. analyst, mktg. rsch. Novartis Pharms., East Hanover, NJ, 2001—03, mgr., mktg. rsch., 2003—05, assoc. dir. mktg. rsch., 2005—. Participant Habitat For Humanity, NJ, 2003—05. Mem.: Healthcare Businesswomens Assn., Am. Mktg. Assn., Beta Gamma Sigma, Panhellenic Coun. (pres. 1996—97), Alpha Sigma Tau. Office: Novartis Pharms One Health Pl East Hanover NJ 07936 E-mail: barbara.nelson@novartis.com.

NELSON, BEATRICE RUTH, cultural organization administrator, artist; b. Newport, Vt., Oct. 29, 1944; d. Ira Hastings Aldrich and Beatrice Rosella Coutts; m. Roger Arthur Nelson, Oct. 12, 1969; children: William Bradley, Rebecca Jean. BEd in Secondary Edn., Keene State Coll., NH, 1966. Lic. tchr. N.H. Tchr. Colebrook (N.H.) Acad., 1967—73, Morgan (Vt.) Elem. Sch., 1975—76; prin., owner Bea's Hive Studio, Derby Line, Vt., 1975—; tchr. Sacred Heart Mid. Sch., Newport, Vt., 1981—83; networker Alnobak Nebesakiak, Derby Line, 1995—2002; mgr. cultural resource Alnebak Heritage Preservation, Derby, Vt., 1999—. Teller Cmty. Nat. Bank, Derby Line, 1989—92; adminstrv. adv. Vt. Folklife Ctr., Middlebury, Vt., 1997—99; cons. in field. Author (illustrator): Country Nostalgia, 1975, Around Lake Memphremagog, 2003; editor (pub.): Nebasak News, 1995—2003; co-author: Holland and Its Neighbors, 2004; contbr. columns to jours. Badge counselor pack 880 Green Mountain Coun., Derby, Vt., 2001—; adv. panel Office Minority Health Vt. Dept. Health, 1998—99. Mem.: Memphrenagog Hist. Soc. (dir. 1998—), Vt. Archaeol. Soc., Holland Hist. Soc. (officer 1981—), Merrybrook Assn. (bd. dirs. 2000—). Avocations: archaeology, writing, painting, history, gardening. Office: Alnobak Heritage Preservation Center PO Box 201 Derby Line VT 05830

NELSON, BETSY S., association administrator; b. St. Louis, Mar. 10, 1950; m. David Nelson; children: Sara, Stephanie, Jennifer. BA, Boston U., 1972; MSW, Washington U., 1973; postgrad., St. Louis Psychoanalytic Inst., 1977. Social worker Planned Parenthood, St. Louis, 1973—79; therapist Women's Care Group, 1979—83; exec. dir. Assn. Balt. Area Grantmakers, 1986—. Bd. dirs., pres. comms. and tech. com. chair Forum of Regional Assns. of Grantmakers, 1998—. Pres. Parents Assn., chair maj. fundraising events, capital campaign com. Bryn Mawr Sch., 1983—; bd. dirs., chair vol. Cen. Fundraising Com., 2000—; adv. com. Live Balt. Mktg. Ctr., 1998—; bd. dirs., chair cmty. initiatives com. United Way Cen. Md., 1999—; adv. com. Balt. Chesapeake Bay Outward Bound Program, 1985—99; mem. Balt. adv. com. Enterprise Forum, 1999—; mem. Greater Balt. Com.'s Leadership program, 1996; bd. dirs. Hurricane Island Outward Bound Sch., 1994—98, Parks and People Found., 1985—2000. Mem.: Balt. Equitable Ins. Assn. (bd. dirs. 1998—), Md. Assn. Nonprofit Orgns. (bd. dirs., vice-chair 1995—). Office: 8th Fl 2 E Read St Baltimore MD 21202

NELSON, BONNIE KAY, elementary school educator; b. Paso Robles, Calif., Aug. 3, 1950; d. Vernon Carroll and Hilda Marie (Engelke) N. Degree in standard elem. edn., Calif. Poly. State U., San Luis Obispo, 1973, cert. early childhood edn., 1976. Tchr. kindergarten Paso Robles Union Elem. Sch. Dist., 1973—. Sch. improvement project coordinator Paso Robles Union Elem. Sch. Dist., 1980-83, sch. site council chmn., 1981-82, k-1 mentor, tchr., 1988-91. Recipient Svc. award, Paso Robles PTA, 1983; named Outstanding Young Educator for Paso Robles, 1985, Outstanding Young Educator for State Calif., 1986. Mem. Paso Robles Tchrs. Assn. (pres. 1980-82), North County Athletic Assn. (exec. bd. 1987-95), Phi Delta Kappa, Delta Kappa Gamma (treas. 1992-93). Republican. Avocations: skiing, photography, sports, travel. Home: 124 21st St Paso Robles CA 93446

NELSON, BRANDY RENÉ, assistant principal; d. Harold and Sandra Nelson. BS, Salem Coll., Winston-Salem, N.C., 1997; M in Sch. Adminstrn., U. NC, Greensboro, 2002. Cert. CPR and First Aid ARC. Math. tchr. NYC Bd. Edn., Bronx, 1997—99, Salem Acad., Winston-Salem, 1999—2003, profl. devel. coord., 2001—02; sch. dir. Teach for Am., Houston, 2002, assoc. inst. dir., 2003; asst. prin. Brighton HS, Wake County Pub. Schs., Raleigh,

NC, 2003—. Chairwoman Salem St. svcs. Salem Coll., Winston-Salem, 1999—2001. Facilitator study cirs. YWCA, Raleigh, 2004—05. Recipient Young Alumnae award, Salem Coll., 2001, Joel Weston award for faculty excellence, Salem Acad., 2002. Mem.: ASCD. Office: Broughton H S 723 St Mary's St Raleigh NC 27605

NELSON, CAROL EVELYN, retired pre-school educator; b. Grand Meadow, Minn., May 25, 1939; d. Charles Henry and Evelyn Hazel Lockwood; m. Loren Dean Nelson, Feb. 6, 1960; children: Sonia Jayne, Barrett Christopher, Bryce Phillip. BS, U. Minn., 1962. Cert. tchr., Minn. Substitute tchr. mil. schs. Camp Darby, Livorno, Italy, 1960—61; tchr. St. Paul Pub. Schs., 1962-63, Caledonia (Minn.) Pub. Schs., 1963-64, Rochester (Minn.) Pub. Schs., 1964-67, 83-87; early childhood educator Kids' Tree House, Rochester, 1987—2004; owner, mgr. CEN, Inc., Kids' Tree House, Rochester, 1988—99; ret., 2004. Mentor entrepreneurial tng. pilot program Minn. Women's Network, 1990-99. Canvasser, Rochester United Way, 1978-84; mem. climate control com., Elton Hills PTA, Rochester, 1983-85; leader Northwest Notables 4-H Club, Rochester, 1977-86. Mem. AAUW (Rochester, Minn. br. pres. 2002-04, chair Upper Midwest Regional Conf. Biannual Conf. 2004), Women Ind. Bus. Owners, Rochester Edn. Assn., S.E. Minn. Assn. for Edn. of Young Children, Rochester Civic Music Guild, Stock Club. Republican. Lutheran. Avocations: singing, reading. Personal E-mail: cenelson60@msn.com.

NELSON, CAROL GRETCHEN, music educator; b. Bend, Oreg., Jan. 16, 1944; d. Charles Clyde and Marion Burgess Corkett; m. Donald P. Nelson, Dec. 29, 1968 (dec.); children: Sara, Scott, Andrew. B of Mus. Edn., U. Oreg., 1966, M of Music Edn., 1975. Tchr. El Monte Sch. Dist., Calif., 1967—71; tchr. music Corvallis Sch. Dist., Oreg., 1971—2006. Exec. dir. Heart of the Valley Children's Choir, Corvallis, Oreg., 1984—. Finalist Oreg. Music Tchr. of Yr., 2004; named Honored Pub. Servant, LDS Ch., Corvallis, Oreg., 2004; recipient Meritorious Svc. award, Benton County Found., Oreg., 2004. Mem.: Music Edn. Ventures, Music Educator's Nat. Conf., Am. Choral Dirs. Assn. Christian Scientist. Achievements include founder and director of children's choir organizations for over 20 years. Home: 1502 NW Dixon St Corvallis OR 97330 Office: Heart of Valley Childrens Choir 260 SW Madison Ste 101 Corvallis OR 97333 Office Phone: 541-738-7888.

NELSON, CAROL KOBUKE, bank executive; m. Ken Nelson; 2 children. BA in fin. magna cum laude, Seattle U., Wash., 1978, MBA, 1984; attended grad. sch. Credit & Fin. Mgmt., Santa Clara U., Calif. With SeaFirst Bank (now Bank of Am.); sr. v.p., No. regional consumer exec. Bank of Am.; pres., COO Cascade Fin. Corp., Everett, Wash., 2001—02, pres., CEO, 2002—, Cascade Bank, Everett, Wash., 2001—. Exec. adv. bd. Albers Sch. Bus. and Economics Seattle U. Chair bd. dirs. United Way, Snohomish County; bd. dirs. Boys and Girls Club, Snohomish County, Econ. Devel. Coun., Snohomish County; adv. bd. Leadership Snohomish County; bd. pub. facilities dist. Washington States Baseball Stadium. Named One of 25 Women to Watch, U.S. Banker Mag., 2003; named one of The 25 Most Powerful Women in Banking, 2004, 2005. Mem.: Wash. Bankers Assn. (bd. dirs.), Wash. Fin. League (bd. dirs.). Office: Cascade Financial Corp 2828 Colby Ave Everett WA 98201

NELSON, CAROLYN, state legislator; b. Madison, Wis., Oct. 8, 1937; m. Gilbert W. Nelson; children: Paul, John, Karla. BS, N.D. State U., 1959, MS, 1960. Sr. lectr. emeritus N.D. State U., 1968—; mem. N.D. Ho. of Reps., 1986-88, 92-94, N.D. Senate from 21st dist., 1994—; mem. judiciary com., vet. affairs com. N.D. Senate, minority caucus leader, 2000—. Mem. N.D. State Investment Bd., 1989-92. Mem. Bd. Edn., Fargo, N.D., 1985-91, pres., 1989-90; trustee N.D. Tchrs. Fund for Retirement, 1985-92, pres., 1990-92; mem. N.D. PTA, pres., 1978-81, N.D. Women's and Children's Caucus. Recipient Merit Svc. award Gamma Phi Beta, 1978, 90, Legis. Voices award Children's Caucus, 1995; named Legislator of Yr., N.D. Bar Assn., 2000, N.D. Student Assn., 2001. Mem. LWV, Am. Guild English Handbell Ringers (area chmn. 1982-84, nat. bd. dirs. 1982-90), Nat. Fedn. Music Clubs (Bd. dirs., legis. chair 2004—), N.D. Fedn. Music Clubs (life, pres. 1997-2001, nat. bd. mem., legis. chair, Rose Fay Thomas fellow 2001), Gamma Phi Beta, Phi Kappa Phi, Sigma Alpha Iota. Office: ND Senate State Capitol Bismarck ND 58505 Address: One 2d St S 5 402 Fargo ND 58103-1959 Business E-Mail: cnelson@state.nd.us.

NELSON, CHARLOTTE BOWERS, public administrator; b. Bristol, Va., June 28, 1931; d. Thaddeus Ray and Ruth Nelson (Moore) Bowers; m. Gustav Carl Nelson, June 1, 1957; children: Ruth Elizabeth, David Carl, Thomas Gustav. BA summa cum laude, Duke U., 1954; MA, Columbia U., 1961; MPA, Drake U., 1983. Instr. Beaver Coll., 1957-58, Drake U., Des Moines, 1975-82; office mgr. LWV of Iowa, Des Moines, 1975-82; exec. asst. Iowa Dept. Human Svcs., Des Moines, 1983-85; exec. dir. Iowa Commn. on Status of Women Dept. Human Rights, Des Moines, 1985; pub. adminstr. State of Iowa, 1983—. Bd. dirs., pres. LWV, Beloit, Wis., 1960-74; bd. dirs. LWV, Des Moines, 1974-82, Westminster House, Des Moines, 1988-97, pres. 1996-97. Recipient Gov.'s Golden Dome award as Leader of the Yr., 2002; named Visionary Woman, Young Women's Resource Ctr., 1994. Mem. Am. Soc. Pub. Adminstrn. (mem. exec. coun. 1984-92, 98-99, past pres., Mem. of Yr. 1993), Phi Beta Kappa, Pi Alpha Alpha. Home: 1141 Cummins Cir Des Moines IA 50311-2113 Office: Human Rights Dept Lucas State Office Bldg Des Moines IA 50319-0001 Office Phone: 515-281-4467. E-mail: charlotte.nelson@iowa.gov, nelson514@aol.com.

NELSON, CYNTHIA J., city official; Re-devel. project mgr. City of Long Beach, Calif., until 1983, City of Santa Ana, Calif., 1983—, exec. dir. Santa Ana Cmty. Devel. Agy. Calif. Mem. Calif. Assn. Local Econ. Devel. (past chairperson Orange County chpt.), Calif. Redevel. Assn. (bd. dirs.)

NELSON, CYNTHIA KAYE, infrastructure security engineer; b. Kearney, Nebr., May 8, 1949; d. LeRoy J. and W. Eileen (Schmidt) Wacker; m. James C. Nelson (div. 1987); children: Alexis Ann, Whitney Eileen. BA, U. No. Iowa, 1971; postgrad., No. Ill. U., 1973. Cert. tchr. Ill., Mo. Tchr. Dixon (Ill.) Pub. Schs., 1972-74, Maplewood (Mo.)-Richmond Heights Sch. Dist., 1974-75; counselor Mo. Bus. Men's Clearing House, St. Louis, 1975-76; dir. edn. Deltex Co., Naperville, Ill., 1982-84; trainer Electronic Data Systems Co., LaGrange, Ill., 1985-86; learning technologist Bellcore Tng. and Edn. Ctr., Lisle, Ill., 1988-90; sr. tech. tng. engr. Fujitsu Network Comm., Raleigh, N.C., 1990-98; sr. network engr. Signal Corp., Raleigh, 1998-2000; network design engr. Nortel Networks, Raleigh, 2000—01; infrastructure security engr. Nat. Info. Sys. Support Ctr., Raleigh, NC, 2002—. Mem. ASTD, AAUW, Internat. Soc. of Performance and Improvement, Alpha Chi Omega, Beta Sigma Phi. Republican. Lutheran. Home: 7404 Rainwater Rd Raleigh NC 27615-3743 E-mail: cknelson@nc.rr.com.

NELSON, DEBORAH D., music educator; d. Bradley V. and Diane K. Grover; m. Mark Alexander Nelson, Mar. 16, 2002; 1 child, Matthew Alexander. BA Music Edn., North Ctrl. Coll., Naperville, Ill., 2001. Mgr. sheet music mgr. Brookdale Music, Naperville, Ill., 2002—03; tchr. gen. music, dir. choral Eagle Pointe Elem. Sch., Plainfield, Ill., 2003—. Pianist and dir. choral Naperville Ch. of the Brethren, Cross of Glory Luth. Ch., Homer Township, Ill.; pianist for new visions North Ctrl. Coll., Naperville, Ill., dir. choral for new visions, 2004—05; pianist Faith Fellowship Ch., Oakbrook, Ill.; accompanist Sch. Performing Arts, Naperville. Mem. music outreach and ministry Proclamacion, Ill. Presdl. Acad. Scholarship, North Ctrl. Coll., 1997—2001, Music Edn. Scholarship, 1997—2001, Vocal Scholarship, 1997—99, Piano Scholarship, 1997—99. Mem.: NEA, Ill. Edn. Assn., Music Educators Nat. Conf. Avocations: piano, singing.

NELSON, DEBORAH JANE, family and consumer science educator; d. Roy Irvin and Jane Maurine Nelson. BS in Vocat. Home Economics Edn., Colo. State U., Fort Collins, 1983; MA in Ednl. Psychology, U. Colo. at Denver, 1991. CFCS Am. Assn. of Family & Consumer Sciences, 1986. Tchr. home econ. Cripple Creek-Victor Sch., Colo., 1983—84; tchr. family and consumer scis. Jefferson H.S., Edgewater, 1984—2000, Alameda H.S., Lakewood, 2000—. Mem. career devel. focus team Jefferson County Pub. Schs., Golden, Colo., 2004—; mem. state stds. rev. team family and consumer scis. Colo. Cmty. Colleges Sys., Denver, 2002—04; state star event chair and evaluator Family, Career & Cmty. Leaders Am., 1983—. Contbr. articles to profl. jours. Walkamerica vol. Mar. of Dimes, Denver, 1974—; clarinetist Denver Concert Band, 1986—; supporter 4-H Clubs, El Paso County, 1991—; judge Job's Daughters, Denver, 1995. Named Colo. FACS Profl. of Yr., Colo. Assn. Family and Consumer Scis., 1995; named an Outstanding Tchr., Colo. Tchr. Awards, 1996. Mem.: NEA, Internat. Fedn. Home Econ., Assn. Career and Tech. Edn. (sec. Colo. divsn. 1999—2001, CATFACS Outstanding Tchr. 2003), Am. Assn. Family and Consumer Scis. (v.p. svcs. 2003—05). Avocations: swimming, scrapbooks, travel, clarinet, piano. Office: Alameda HS 1255 S Wadsworth Blvd Lakewood CO 80232-5406

NELSON, DEBRA J., dancer, educator, choreographer; d. Roy O. and Joan C. Nelson. BA in Edn., U. Ill., Champaign-Urbana, 1974; MS in Edn., Chgo. State U., 1988; postgrad., No. Ill. U., DeKalb, 2000—. Dance Master Chgo. Nat. Assn. Dance Masters, 2003, group exercise instrn. Chgo. State U., 1998. Profl. dancer Miller-Reich Prodns., Miami, Fla., 1979—95, co. mgr., 1995—98; prof. Chgo. State U., 1998—. Lectr. and presenter in field. Recipient Univ. Faculty Excellence award, Coll. Edn. Disting. Educator award, Dean's Profl. Devel. Initiative award. Mem.: Black Coll. Dance Exch., Chgo. Nat. Assn. Dance Masters, Ill. Dance Assn., Ill. Assn. for Health, Phys. Edn., Recreation and Dance, Am. AAHPERD, Kappa Delta Pi, Alpha Chi Omega (life). Avocations: dance, travel, theater. Office Phone: 773-821-2827.

NELSON, DEBRA L., non-profit organization consultant; b. Williston, N.D., Sept. 14, 1953; d. Duane Robert Leroy and Ida M. (Lester) Evanson; m. Kenneth E. Nelson, Nov. 8, 1975; children: Brian Paul, Brent Allen. BS in Secondary Edn., Minot State U., 1975. Classroom instr. Donnybrook (N.D.) H.S., 1976-82, Dickinson (N.D.) H.S., 1982-83; mgr. B. Dalton Bookseller, Dickinson, 1983-88; traffic safety coord. City of Dickinson, 1988-93; prevention and traffic safety coord. Cmty. Action and Devel., Dickinson, 1993-98; state and fed. hwy. safety cons. State N.D. Dept. Transp./Nat. Hwy. Traffic Safety Adminstrn., Bismarck, N.D. and Denver, 1998—; owner, mgr. DLN Consulting, Inc., Dickinson, N.D. Editor: (manuals) N.D. Cmty. Traffic Safety Program Manual, 1996, N.D. Safe Cmtys. Coords. Handbook, 1998, 2000. Adult coord. Teen Action Group, 1990-2000; bd. dirs. children's svcs. coord. com., Dickinson, 1993-99, Sunrise Youth Bur., Dickinson, 1998-99; mem. City of Dickinson Traffic Commn., 1994-97, N.D. Safety Belt Coalition, 1989-93, N.D. Children's Caucus, 1996—. Named to ND Traffic Safety Hall of Fame, 2006; recipient Gold Belt award, ND Safety Belt Coalition, 1993, ND Gov.'s Hwy. Safety award, Bismarck, 1998. Mem. AAUW, Roughrider Country Kiwanis (fellow, bd. dirs. 1992-97, pres. 2001, chmn. orientation com. 1989-2001, Builders award 1996). Avocations: volunteering with Boy Scouts Am., reading, gardening, concerts, plays, sporting events. Home: 130 7th Ave W Dickinson ND 58601-5013 Office: 2493 4th Ave W Ste G Dickinson ND 58601 Office Phone: 701-483-2801. Business E-Mail: deb@dlnconsulting.com.

NELSON, DIANE W., broadcast executive; BS in Comm., Syracuse U. Dir. nat. promotions Walt Disney Records; dir. worldwide corp. promotions Warner Brothers Pictures, 1996—98, v.p. worldwide corp. promotions, 1998—2001, sr. v.p. family entertainment, 2001—02, exec. v.p. domestic mktg., 2002—04, exec. v.p. global brand mgmt., 2004—. Mailing: Warner Bros Pictures 4000 Warner Blvd Burbank CA 91522 Office Phone: 818-954-6000.*

NELSON, DONNA GAYLE, state representative; b. Paducah, Tex., June 13, 1943; d. Jack Harold Williams and Hazel Louise (Cooper Moss) Stephens; m. Douglas Caldwell Nelson, June 24, 1966 (div. 1976); children: Kellye Lou Fetters, Robert Kreg Nelson, J. Graigory. AB, South Plains Coll., Levelland, Tex., 1963; BBA, West Tex. A&M U., Canyon, 1965, MBA, 1967. Founder Evergreen Mut., McMinnville, Oreg., 1975; co-founder Evergreen Life Line, McMinnville, 1978—; founder, corp. dir. AAA Profl. Promotions, McMinnville, 1977—; pres. Evergreen Bus. Mgmt. Co., McMinnville, 1978—; sr. v.p. Evergreen Helicopters, Inc., McMinnville, 1978—, Evergreen Internat. Aviation, Inc., McMinnville, 1978—; mem. Oreg. State Ho. of Reps., 2000—, chair veterans commn., vice chair edn. bus. com., vice chair govt. com., vice chair agr. com. Bd. dirs. Evergreen Air Ctr., Inc., Marana, Ariz., Evergreen Aircraft Sales & Leasing Co., Evergreen Aviation Ground Logistics Enterprises, Inc.; sr. v.p., bd. dirs. Evergreen Internat. Aviation, Inc., McMinnville; speaker Nat. Speakers' Assn., Phoenix, 1986—; mem. adv. bd. Chemeketa Community Coll., McMinnville, 1984-85; owner 3N & Assocs. Inc., Donna G. Nelson Auctions, LLC; founder Yamhill Co. Market; teacher Tex., Calif., and Oregon; author, journalist. Poet World's Most Beloved Poetry, 1985 (Silver poet); writer Aviation/Space Writers' Assn., 1989-90; columnist It Takes Grit. Mem. Team 100 Rep. party, Washington, 1989; co-founder Poyama Land Treatment Ctr., Independence, Oreg., 1973; den mother, sustained membership chmn. Boy Scouts Am., McMinnville, 1977-79; dr. mem. March of Dimes, Heart Fund, McMinnville, 1973-75; sr. transportation com., Yamhill Co. Budget Parks, Elks Lions, Red Cross, NRA, N1IB Farm Bur.; founder Newcomers Club, Fund for Hope, Free Enterprise Fund for Kids; bd. dirs. Humane Soc., Linfield Chamber Orch., Salvation Army. Named Woman of Excellence, Portland, Oreg., 1985. Mem. DAR, C. of C., McMinnville Duplicate Bridge Assn. (founder), Soroptimists Club, Elks, Lions, Beta Sigma Phi (pres. 1974-75, Woman of Yr. 1990). Republican. Baptist. Avocations: music, sports, bridge, writing, fishing, speaking, travel, fishing, computers, charity auctioneer. Home and Office: 2150 St Andrews Dr Mcminnville OR 97128-2436 Office Phone: 503-472-8015. Business E-Mail: donnanelson@state.or.us.

NELSON, DONNA JEAN, chemistry educator, researcher; b. Eufaula, Okla., Aug. 29, 1952; d. John Howard Jr. and Dorotha (Eckelkamp) Baker; 1 child, Christopher Brammer. BS in Chemistry, U. Okla., 1974; PhD, U. Tex., 1979. Robert A. Welch pre-doctoral fellow, 1977, 78, 79; Robert A. Welch postdoctoral fellow, 1980; asst. prof. U. Okla., Norman, 1983-89, assoc. prof., faculty adminstrv. fellow Provost's Office, 1989—. Jr. faculty rsch. fellow Okla. U., 1984, assocs. disting. lectr., 1985-86; vis. prof. MIT, 2003. Asst. editor: Progress Mag., 2002—, assoc editor: AWIS Mag., 2002—03. Recipient Sooner Spotlight award U. Okla., 1986, Sequoyah medal Am. Indians in Sci. and Engring. Soc., 2003, Nat. Woman of Courage award NOW, 2004, Nat. Woman of Courage award, Nat. Orgn. for Women, 2004, Okla. Outstanding Prof., 2005; named Woman of Achievement, USBE and Info. Tech. Mag., 2003, Okla. Outstanding Prof., 2005; Robert A. Welch grantee, 1979; A.P. Sloan Found. travel awardee, 2003; Ford Found. fellow, 2003-04; Guggenheim awardee, 2003-04. Mem. Am. Chem. Soc. (women chemists com. 1988—, James Flack award com. 1987-90), Phi Lambda Upsilon, Alpha Chi Sigma, Iota Sigma Pi, Sigma Xi (nat. diversity com. 2001—). Home: 1700 Winding Ridge Rd Norman OK 73072-3149 Office: U Okla Dept of Chemistry Norman OK 73072 Office Phone: 405-325-2288. Business E-Mail: djnelson@ou.edu.

NELSON, DOREEN KAE, mental health counselor, educator, reserve military officer; b. Duluth, Minn., Oct. 18, 1957; d. Norman G. Nelson and Carola Gerene (Sunneli) Cooper. B Applied Scis., U. Minn., 1983; MS in Human Resources Mgmt. Devel., Chapman U., 1988; MAEd in Mental Health Counseling, Western Ky. U., 1995. Commd. 2nd lt. U.S. Army, 1983, advanced through grades to lt. col., 2001, pers. officer 62nd Med. Group Ft. Lewis, Wash., 1987—88, med. pers. officer Acad. Health Scis. Ft. Sam Houston, Tex., 1989, chief adminstrv. svcs. div. Med. Dept. Ctr. and Sch., 1989—92; med. advisor Readiness Group Knox, Ft. Knox, Ky., 1992—94; counselor intern Ireland Army Hosp., Ft. Knox, 1995; mental health counselor IV Meridian Behavioral HealthCare, Inc., Gainesville, Fla., 1995—97; substitute tchr. Ind. Sch. Dist. #381, Silver Bay, Minn., 1997—2001, Title I tchr., 2001—. Lutheran. Avocation: family genealogy.

NELSON, DOROTHY WRIGHT (MRS. JAMES F. NELSON), federal judge; b. San Pedro, Calif., Sept. 30, 1928; d. Harry Earl and Lorna Amy Wright; m. James Frank Nelson, Dec. 27, 1950; children: Franklin Wright, Lorna Jean. BA, UCLA, 1950, JD, 1953; LLM, U. So. Calif., 1956; LLD (hon.), Western State U. Coll. Law, 1980, U. So. Calif., 1983, Georgetown U., 1988, Whittier U., 1989, U. Santa Clara, 1990, U. San Diego, 1997, Pepperdine U. Sch. of Law, 2003. Bar: Calif. 1954. Rsch. assoc. fellow U. So. Calif., 1953—56, instr., 1957, asst. prof., 1958—61, assoc. prof., 1961—67, prof., 1967—, assoc. dean., 1965—67, dean., 1967—80; judge U.S. Ct. Appeals 9th Cir., 1979—95, sr. judge, 1995—. Com. to consider stds. for admission to practice in fed. cts. Jud. Conf. U.S., 1976—79; cons. project STAR Law Enforcement Assistance Adminstrn.; select com. on internal procedures Calif. Supreme Ct., 1987—; co-chair Sino-Am. Seminar on Mediation and Arbitration, Beijing, 1992. Contbr. articles to profl. jours.; author: Judicial Adminstration and The Administration of Justice, 1973; author: (with Christopher Goelz and Meredith Watts) Federal Ninth Circuit Civil Appellate Practice, 1995. Co-chair Confronting Myths in Edn. for Pres. Nixon's White House Conf. on Children, Pres. Carter's Commn. for Pension Policy, 1974—80; pres. Reagon's Madison Trust; mem. Nat. Spiritual Assembly of Bahais of U.S., 1967—; bd. dirs. Dialogue on Transition to a Global Soc., Weinacht, Switzerland, 1992; bd. vis. U.S. Air Force Acad., 1978; bd. dirs. Coun. on Legal Edn. for Profl. Responsibility, 1971—80, Constl. Right Found., Am. Nat. Inst. for Social Advancement; adv. bd. Nat. Ctr. for State Cts., 1971—76; adv. com. to promote equality for woman and men in cts. Nat. Jud. Edn. Program; bd. dirs. Pacific Oaks Coll., Childrens Sch. & Rsch. Ctr., 1996—98; adv. bd. World Law Inst., 1997—, Tahirih Justice Inst., Washington, 1998—; chmn. bd. Western Justice Ctr., 1986—; chair 9th Cir. Standing Com. on Alternative Dispute Resolution, 1998—. Named Law Alumnus of Yr., UCLA, 1967, Woman of Yr., Times, 1968, Disting. Jurist, Ind. U. Law, 1994; recipient Profl. Achievement award, 1969, AWARE Internat. award, 1970, Ernestine Stalhut Outstanding Woman Lawyer award, 1972, Humanitarian award, U. Judaism, 1973, Pax Orbis ex Jure medal, World Peace thru Law Ctr., 1975, Pub. Svc. award, Coro Found., 1978, Hollzer Human Rights award, Jewish Fedn. Coun., 1988, Medal of Honor, UCLA, 1993, Emil Gumpert Jud. ADR Recognition award, L.A. County Bar Assn., 1996, Julia Morgan award, YWCA, 1997, Samuel E. Gates Litigation award, Am. Coll. Trial Lawyers, 1999, Bernard E. Witkin award, State Bar Assn. Calif., 2000, Judge of the Year award, Pasadena Bar Assn., 2002, Thurgood Marshall Career Achievement award, 2005, Harry Sheldon award, Pasadena Human Relations Comm., 2006; fellow, Davenport Coll.; Lustman fellow, Yale U., 1977. Fellow: Davenport Coll., Am. Bar Found.; mem.: ABA (sect. on jud. adminstrn., chmn. com. on edn. in jud. adminstrn. 1973—89, D'Alemberte/Raven award 2000), Assn. Am. Law Schs. (chmn. com. edn. in jud. adminstrn.), Am. Judicature Soc. (bd. dirs., Justice award 1985), Bar Calif. (bd. dirs. continuing edn. bar commn. 1967—74), Order of Coif (nat. v.p. 1974—76), Phi Beta Kappa. Office: US Ct Appeals Cir 125 S Grand Ave Ste 303 Pasadena CA 91105-1621 Office Phone: 626-229-7400. Business E-Mail: dorothy-nelson@ca9.uscourt.gov.

NELSON, ELAINE EDWARDS, lawyer; b. Waco, Tex., Sept. 16, 1947; d. Bedford Duncan and Joyce (Harlan) Edwards; m. David A. Nelson, Apr. 12, 1969; children: Carol Christine, Harlan Claire. BA, Baylor U., 1969, JD, 1978. Bar: Tex. 1978. Gen. counsel Austin Industries, Inc., Dallas, 1978—. Office: Austin Industries Inc 3535 Travis St Ste 300 Dallas TX 75204-1466 also: PO Box 2879 Dallas TX 75221-2879

NELSON, ETHELYN BARNETT, civic worker; b. Bessemer, Ala., Jan. 16, 1925; d. Laurence McBride and Ethel Victoria Fortesque (King) Barnett; m. Stuart David Nelson, May 6, 1949; children: Terryl Lynn, Cynthia Dianne, Jacqueline Margo. Student, Huntingdon Coll., 1943, U. Ala., 1948, George Washington U., 1948—49, student, 1974. Sec. U.S. Air Force, Montgomery, Ala. and Panama Canal Zone, 1944—49; sec. to dep. undersec. U.S. Dept. State, Washington, 1951—53, U.S. Ho. of Reps. and U.S. Senate, 1959—60; adminstrv. asst. editl. divsn. Nat. Geog. Soc., Washington, 1962—65; rec. sec. Dist. IV Nat. Capital Area Fedn. Garden Clubs, Inc., Washington, 1981—83. Mem. Women's Com. Nat. Symphony Orch. Mem.: Nat. Trust for Historic Preservation, Salvation Army Aux., Am. Scandinavian Assn., Landon Woods Garden Club (pres. 1978—80), Congl. Country Club. Republican. Methodist. Achievements include patentee. Home: 6410 Maiden Ln Bethesda MD 20817-5612

NELSON, FREDA NELL HEIN, librarian; b. Trenton, Mo., Dec. 16, 1929; d. Fred Albert and Mable Carman (Doan) Hein; m. Robert John Nelson, Nov. 1, 1957 (div. Apr. 1984); children: Thor, Hope. Nursing diploma, Trinity Luth. Hosp., Kansas City, Mo., 1950; B. Philosophy, Northwestern U., 1961; MS in Info. and Libr. Sci., U. Ill., 1986. RN. Operating rm. nurse Trinity Luth. Hosp., Kansas City, Mo., 1950-52, Johns Hopkins Hosp., Balt., 1952, Wesley Meml. Hosp., Chgo., 1952-58, Tacoma Gen. Hosp., 1958-59, Chgo. Wesley Hosp., 1959-61; libr. asst. Maple Woods Campus Met. Community Colls., Kansas City, 1987-89, libr., libr. mgr. Blue Springs Campus, 1989-96; ret., 1996. Co-founder Coll. for Kids, Knox Coll., Galesburg, Ill., 1982. Nurses scholar Edgar Bergen Found., 1947; recipient Award of Merit, Chgo. Bd. Health, 1952. Avocations: swimming, walking, cross-word puzzles. Home: 5708 N Polk Dr Kansas City MO 64151

NELSON, GLENDA KAY, special education educator; b. Crosby, Miss., Oct. 11, 1942; d. John and Nellie (McDonald) Jackson; m. Ralph Gordon Nelson, Nov. 26, 1964; children: Karl Christian, Andrew Jon. BS, U. Houston, 1964; MEd, Incarnate Word Coll., San Antonio, 1985. Cert. sch. counselor. Tchr. history Houston Ind. Sch. Dist., 1964-70; tchr. spl. edn. San Antonio Ind. Sch. Dist., 1985—. Vol. counselor Bexar County Women's Ctr.; coach Spl. Olympics, 1987-92; mem. San Antonio Conservation Soc., 1983—. Mem. AAUW, UDC, Delta Kappa Gamma. Avocations: tennis, swimming, reading, ballet, symphony. Home: 13403 Southwalk St San Antonio TX 78232-4867

NELSON, HEATHER M., elementary school educator; b. Heppner, Oreg., June 29, 1977; d. Danonne R. Smith and Jim A. Nelson. BS Edn., We. Oreg. U., Monmouth, 2000. Tchr. Hillsboro Sch. Dist., Oreg., 2001—. Avocations: golf, running, travel. Office: Evergreen Middle School 29850 NW Evergreen Road Hillsboro OR 97124 E-mail: nelsonh@hsd.k12.or.us.

NELSON, JANIE RISH, health facility administrator; b. Mar. 1, 1941; d. William Hubert and Essie Dell (Davis) Rish; m. John Preston Nelson, Aug. 19, 1984. Student, S.W. Miss. Jr. Coll., 1959—61, Stephens Coll., 1981—. Accredited record tech. Admissions clk. Field Hosp., Centreville, Miss., 1963—68, asst. dir. med. records, 1968—73; dir. med. records West Feliciana Parish Hosp., St. Francisville, La., 1976—2000; ret., 2000. Med. records cons. Beverly Enterprises & Centreville Health Care, 1983—84. Mem. U.S. Congl. Adv. Bd. for La., 1985; fund raiser Rep. Com., 1984; mem. nat. adv. bd. Am. Security Coun., 1984—85. Mem.: NAFE, Tumor Registration Assn. La., La. Med. Records Assn., Am. Med. Records Assn., Miss. Sheriffs Assn. (hon.), Civic Club. Republican. Presbyterian. Avocations: reading, public speaking, gardening. Home: PO Box 374 Centreville MS 39631-0374

NELSON, JOANN, secondary school educator, educational consultant; b. Little Rock, Arkansas, July 11, 1943; d. Lucinda Nelson. BA cum laude (hon.), Philander Smith Coll., Little Rock, 1962—66; EdM, Cleveland State U., 1977—79. Cert. tchg. Ark., 1966; Ohio, 1966, 1987. English tchr. Cleve. Pub. Sch., 1966—78, dept. chmn., English, reading, and language arts, 1978—96. Cons., Cleve., 1996—. Rec. sec. Neighborhood St. Club, Cleve., 1978—96. Mem.: Greater Cleve. Roundtable, Metro Cleve. Alliance of Black Sch. Educators, Nat. Coun. of Negro Women, Nat. Coun. of Teachers of English. Democrat. Baptist. Achievements include city wide lesson plans, Cleve. Pub. Sch., 2002; students' performance and reading tests, Cleve. Pub. Sch., 1986; proficiency test coord.,Cleve. Pub. Sch., 1994. Avocations: reading, theater, photography, travel, collecting brass and crystal. E-mail: njoann1@aol.com.

NELSON, JOELLE GRACE KENNEY, lawyer; b. Augusta, Maine, Dec. 4, 1973; d. Meylon Grant and Lois Marie Kenney; m. Christopher Caldwell Nelson, May 6, 2006. BS, U. So. Maine, Portland, 1996; JD, South Tex. Coll. Law, Houston, 2000. Bar: Tex. 2001. Law clk. Justice Eric Andell First Dist. Ct. Appeals, State of Tex., Houston, 1999—2000; briefing atty. for Justice John S. Anderson 14th Dist. Ct. Appeals, State of Tex., Houston, 2000—01; med. malpractice assoc. McGehee & Pianelli, LLP, Houston, 2001—03; comml. litig. assoc. Johnson DeLuca Kennedy & Kurisky, P.C., Houston, 2003—. Author law seminar South Tex. Coll. Law, 2003, U. Houston Law Ctr., 2003; spkr. in field. Vol. Spl. Olympics, Houston, 1999—2006; participant bike tour Nat. Multiple Sclerosis Soc., Houston, 2005—06. Student advocacy scholar, South Tex. Coll. Law, 1998—2000. Mem.: Houston Young Lawyers Assn., Houston Bar Assn., Tex. Trial Lawyers Assn. (adv. 2001—06). Democrat. Rman Catholic. Avocations: marathon running, cycling, camping, travel. Office: Johnson DeLuca Kennedy & Kurisky PC 1221 Lamar St Ste 1000 Houston TX 77010 Office Phone: 713-652-2525. Office Fax: 713-652-5130. Business E-Mail: jnelson@jdkklaw.com.

NELSON, JOYCE M., medical association administrator; d. Wesley and Margaret N.; m. John Hansell. BA In English, Secondary Edn., North Park Univ., 1972. Devel. mgr., No. Calif. Chpt. Nat. Multiple Sclerosis Soc., exec. dir., Mid-Am. Chpt. Kansas City, 1985—91, nat. dir. campaign devel. Denver, 1991—94, v.p. chpt. programs, 1994—2000, v.p. field ops., 2000—05, pres., CEO NYC & Denver, 2005—. Office: Nat Multiple Sclerosis Soc 733 Third Ave New York NY 10017*

NELSON, JULIE LOFTUS, lawyer; b. Milw., Jan. 14, 1967; BA, U. Wis., Madison, 1996; JD cum laude, Hamline U., 2002. Bar: Minn. 2002, US Ct. Appeals (8th cir.) 2004, US Dist. Ct. (dist. Minn.) 2005. Jud. clk. to Judge R.A. Randall Minn. Ct. Appeals; jud. clk. to Judge P. Hunter Anderson Dist. Ct.; assoc. Frederic Bruno & Assocs., Mpls. Named a Rising Star, Minn. Super Lawyers mag., 2006. Mem.: Minn. Assn. Criminal Def. Attys., Minn. State Bar Assn. (sec. criminal law sect.). Office: Frederic Bruno & Assocs 5500 Wayzata Blvd Ste 1450 Minneapolis MN 55416 Office Phone: 763-545-7900. E-mail: julie@brunolaw.com.*

NELSON, JUNE LUSK, music educator; d. William Thomas and Gwendolyn Reeves Lusk; m. Keith Warren Nelson, June 25, 1961. AA, San Bernardino Valley Coll.; MusB, U. So. Calif., 1954, MusM, 1955. Prof. El Camino Coll., Torrance, Calif., 1956—. Founding mem., treas. Wildwood Music Assn. Inc.; tchr. Pvt. Studio, Irvine. Performer numerous recitals. Recipient Excellenc in Art award, City of Torrance, 2002; Fulbright grantee, Cologne, Germany, 1955—56. Mem.: Music Tchrs. Nat. Assn., MENC, Music Tchrs. Assn. Calif., Mu Phi Epsilon (v.p.). Avocations: gardening, quilting, travel. Home: 15 Lexington Irvine CA 92620

NELSON, K. BONITA, literary agent; b. Austin, Minn., July 5, 1945; d. Wallace Arthur and Opal Rebecca (Lastine) N. BA, Hunter Coll., 1969; B in laws, LaSalle U., 1982. Lit. agt. Am. Play Co., Inc., N.Y.C., 1970-75; legal sec., reviewer Eastman & DaSilva, Esqs., N.Y.C., 1975-79; founder, pres. BK Nelson Literary Agy., N.Y.C., 1983—, BK Nelson Lect. Bureau, N.Y.C., 1994—; pres., publ. Internat. Media Comm., Inc., 1998. Bd. dirs. Dynaray, N.Y.; founder BK Nelson, Inc., 1995; founder Literacy Inst. for Edn. (Life) Inc., 1996. Collaborator: Looking for Canterbury, 1994; author: My Literary Agent, 1998; co-prodr. (movies) Dancing Dan's Christmas, 2006, (musical) Packed Full of Miracles, 2006. Mem. Authors Guild (assoc.), NAFE (assoc.), Nat. Assn. Campus Activities (assoc.), AAUW, (assoc.), Dramatists Guild (assoc.), Minority and Woman Owned Businesses. Avocations: yoga, stamp collecting/philately, automobiles. Home and Office: 1565 Paseo Vida Palm Springs CA 92264 Office: Bk Nelson Lecture Bureau 1565 Paseo Vida Palm Springs CA 92264-9508 Office Phone: 760-778-8800. E-mail: bknelson4@cs.com.

NELSON, KAREN ANN, lab administrator, director, immunologist, educator; b. Spokane, Wash., Feb. 16, 1948; d. John Andrew and Ruth Louise (Kennedy) Schermer; m. Randall Paul Nelson, Aug. 7, 1971; children: Siri Oranda, Peder Andreas. BSs in Microbiology, U. Wash., 1970, PhD in Pathology, 1975. Rsch. asst. dept. microbiology U. Wash., Seattle, 1970-75, rsch. asst. prof. dept. pathology, 1983—; postdoctoral fellow div. tumor immunology U. Lund, Sweden, 1975-77, rsch. assoc., 1977-78; rsch. assoc. div. tumor immunology Fred Hutchinson Cancer Rsch. Ctr., Seattle, 1978-84; rsch. mgr. Genetic Systems Corp., Seattle, 1984-88; assoc. dir. Puget Sound Blood Ctr., Seattle, 1988—89, dir., 1989—. Bd. dirs. NW Girlchoir, Seattle, 1988—94. Mem. Am. Soc. for Histocompatibility and Immunogenetics, Am. Assn. Immunologists, Clin. Immunology Soc., Transplantation Soc., Am. Soc. Transplantation. Democrat. Office: Puget Sound Blood Ctr 921 Terry Ave Seattle WA 98104-1256 Office Phone: 206-292-6549. Business E-Mail: knelson@psbc.org.

NELSON, KATHY, broadcast executive; Sr. v.p., gen. mgr. MCA Records Inc.; pres. film music The Walt Disney Motion Picture Group, 1996—2001, Universal Music Group & Universal Pictures, 2001—. Bd. dir. Women in Film. Office: Universal Music Group 1755 Broadway New York NY 10019*

NELSON, KIMBERLY TERESE, computer software company executive, former federal agency administrator; b. Phila., July 15, 1956; B, Shippensburg U.; M, U. Pa. Spl. asst. to sec., spl. asst. to deputy sec. adminstrn., spl. asst. deputy sec. field ops. Pa. Dept. Environ. Resources, 1987—95; dir. program integration and effectiveness then chief info. officer Pa. Dept. Environ. Protection, 1999—2001; asst. adminstr. for environ. info. EPA, Washington, 2001—05; exec. dir. e-govt. Microsoft Corp., Redmond, Wash., 2006—.*

NELSON, KIRSTEN CIGLER, language educator; d. Allan James and Beth Ellen Cigler; m. Kyle Evan Nelson; 1 child, Cade William. BA, U. Kans., Lawrence, 1995; Masters, Washburn U., Topeka, Kans., 2001. Tchr. English, Topeka Pub. Schs., 1997—. Editor Spl. Connection, Lawrence, Kans., 2005—06. Mem.: Internat. Reading Assn., Nat. Coun. Tchrs. of English, Phi Delta Kappa. Office Phone: 785-295-3376.

NELSON, LAUREN KATHRYN, education educator; b. Escanaba, Mich., July 24, 1955; d. Harry Roy and Kathryn Johanna (McCarthy) N. BS, No. Mich. U., 1977; MA, Ctrl. Mich. U., 1978; PhD, Memphis State U., 1984. Cert. Clin. Competence Speech Pathology. Speech lang. clinicial No. Trails Area Edn. Agy., Clear Lake, Iowa, 1978-80; grad. asst. Memphis State U., 1980-84; asst. prof. The Ohio State U., Columbus, 1984-88, U. No. Iowa, Cedar Falls, 1989-93, assoc. prof., 1993—. Contbr. articles to profl. jour. Mem. Am. Speech Language Hearing Assn., Linguistic Soc. Am., Am. Phonetics Soc., Iowa Speech and Hearing Assn.

NELSON, LINDA J., state legislator; b. Plentywood, Mont., June 12, 1942; m. Roger Nelson. Grad., Medicine Lake H.S. Farmer, rancher; mem. Mont. Ho. of Reps., 1989-94, Mont. Senate, Dist. 49, Helena, 1994—2004; mem. ethics com., mem. rules com., mem. fin. and claims com.; mem. agr., livestock and irrigation com.; mem. jt. appropriations subcom. natural resources/commerce; minority whip Mont. Senate, 1999—2002, dean of senate, 2003—04. Mem. Medicine Lake (Mont.) Sch. Bd., 1981-88, chair, 1984-88; active Mont. Dem. Party; dir. Nemont Tel. Coop.; bd. mem., chair Mont. Oil and Gas Conservation; mem. Mont. ELCA Synod Coun. Mem. N.E. Mont. Land and Mineral Owners Assn., Sheridan County Dem. Women. Democrat. Lutheran. Home: 469 Griffin Medicine Lake MT 59247-9708

NELSON, LOIS NADINE, retired special education educator; b. Albuquerque, Oct. 16, 1937; d. O. D. Clark and Lillian Esther Large-Clark; children: Jeanine Rasco, Katherine White, William D. BS, U. N.Mex., 1973, student. Cert. tchr. N.Mex., 1973. Tchr. spl. edn. Bernalillo (N.Mex.) Pub. Schs., 1973—95, ret., 1995. Tchr. Sunday Sch. So. Bapt. Ch., 1955—; clk. Agape Cmty. Ch., 2002—. Recipient 40 Yr. Tchg. cert., So. Bapt. Conv., 1995, Appreciation cert., Sandoval County Hist. Soc., 2001. Mem.: S.W. Writers, Phi Kappa Phi. Republican. Bapt. Avocation: writing.

NELSON, LORAINE PRATT, principal; b. Charleston, S.C., Sept. 11, 1949; d. John W.S. and Kathryn Pratt; m. David K. Nelson, Apr. 14, 1992; m. Troy Lee Long, III (dec.); 1 child, Troy Lee (Trip) Long III. BS, Ga. So. Coll., Statesboro, 1971; MEd in Adminstrn. and Supervision, U. North Fla., Jacksonville, 1977. Cert. elem. edn. K-6 Fla., 1971, ednl. leadership K-12 Fla., 1971. Tchr. Heritage Christian Sch., Gainesville, Fla., 1971—74, Hyde Park Elem., Jacksonville, 1974—83; asst. prin. Woodland Acres Elem., 1983—84, Pine Forest 5th and 6th Grade Ctr., 1984—85, Jacksonville Heights Elem., 1985—87; prin. Justina Rd. Elem., 1987—92, Oak Hill Elem., Fla., 1992—. Mem. Full Svc. Sch. Oversight Com., Prin.'s Crisis Support Team; co-owner "A" Wise Choice - Edn. Solutions, 2005—. Contbr. articles to profl. jours. Mem. Mayor's Intensive Care Neighborhood, Freedom Found., Jacksonville, Ed White HS Booster Club, 1992—95; sponsor Ed White HS Golddiggers, 1993—95; vol. Ronald McDonald Ho., Saturday Scholars, Salvation Army Kans Kids, Toys Tots; elder St. Andrew's Presbyn. Ch. Nominee Nat. Disting. Prin., 2006; named Tchr. of Yr., 1981—82, Outstanding Prin., Duval Tchrs. United, 1987, 1988, 1989, 1992, 1993, Prin. of Yr., Coun. Exceptional Children, 1988, Hon. Life Mem. Svc. to Children, PTA, 1989; recipient Golden Sch. award, 1987—2006, recognition, Am. Sch. Bd. and Exec. Educator, 1988—89, Patriotic Emphasis in the Schs. award, Freedom Found., 1987—89, Little Red Schoolhouse awards, 1987—89, Fla. Model Sch. award, 1987, Excellence in Edn. merit cert., U.S. Dept. Edn., 1987—88, Fla. Disting. Sch. Drug Prevention Edn., 1987—88, Commr.'s Prin. Achievement award, Commr. Betty Castor, 1989, Mayor's Edn. Excellence award, Hon. Tommy Hazouri, Supt.'s Leadership award, 1993, Am.'s Best Sch. Project, Redbook, 1993, Ednl. Leadership award, Westside Bus. Leader, 1993, Multicultural Edn. Innovation Program award, U.S. Dept. Edn., 1993, STARS award, 1994, Prin. of Yr. Art Edn. award, 2001—02, JAX-PRIDE award, 1996, 2002, Nat. Learning for Life award, 2003—05, F.A.S.T. recognition, 2003, 2005. Mem.: Fla. Assn. Elem. and Mid. Sch. Prins. (dist. III dir. 1994—, dist. III rep. 1997—), Fla. Assn. Sch. Adminstrs. (state officer 1994—), Duval Elem. Prin. Assn. (bd. mem.), Duval County Reading Coun., Nat. Assn. Elem. Sch. Prins. (Excellence in Edn. award 1991—92), Alliance World Class Edn., Jacksonville C. of C., Westside Bus. Leaders, Kappa Delta Pi (pres. 1995—97, counselor 1997—, chaplain, treas.), Alpha Delta Kappa (pres. 1988—90, pres. Jacksonville chpt. 1990—92, sec. Jacksonville chpt. 2004—06). Avocation: travel. Home: 6327 Ortega Farms Blvd Jacksonville FL 32244 Office Phone: 904-573-1030.

NELSON, MARCELLA MAY, volunteer; b. Schaunavon, Sask., Can., Oct. 11, 1928; d. Ilmer Alexander and Zylpha May (Geier) Madson; m. William Robert Nelson, June 12, 1951 (dec. Nov. 2000). Stenographer Idaho Employment Security, Bonners Ferry, 1947—50, interviewer, 1950—51, mgr., 1951—63; supr., asst. mgr. Employment Security Agy., Sandpoint, Idaho, 1963—83, program supr. Coeur d'Alene, Idaho, 1983—84; ret., 1984. Tutor illiteracy program NIC Coll., Coeur d'Alene, 1985-91; v.p. solicitations Festival at Sandpoint, 1988—, pres., 2005-. Mem. Cmty. Assistance League, 1994—; citizens adv. mem. Com. on Hwy Bypass in Sandpoint, 2000—; mem. com. Leadership Sandpoint, 2000—; mem. Sandpoint Centennial Commn., 2001; mem. com. Ponderay Cmty. Devel. Corp., 2003—; mem. Ponderay (Idaho) Cmty. Devel. Corp., 2003—, Bonner County Area Transp. Team Com., 2004—; membership com. Bonner County Econ. Devel. Corp., 2004—; chmn. Ponderay Days Cmty. Devel., 2004; chmn. fundraising auction Sandpoint C. of C., 2001—02, One Festival, Sandpoint, 2002, Winter Carnival, Sandpoint C. of C., 2003; mem. centennial com. Bonner County, 2006—; campaign mgr. state rep. candidate for Vi Sims, Sandpoint and Bonners Ferry, 1984; mem. Bonner County Republican Women's Group, 2005—; bd. dirs. Clean Air Coalition, Nat. Festival of Wooden Boats, 2003; bd. dirs. fundraising com. Panida Theatre; pres. Pend Oreille Arts Coun., 1993—95, bd. dirs.; chmn. fundraising auction The Festival at Sandpoint, 2003, v.p. bd. dirs., 2003, pres. bd., 2004. Named Vol. of the Month, Sandpoint C. of C., 1987, 2000, Citizen of Yr., 1990, Retiree of Yr. Idaho chpt. 1985, Internat. Assn. Personel in Employment Security, Woman of Wisdom Women Honoring Women, 2000, Cmty Star of Yr., 2004; recipient Woman of Distinction award, sr. category, Women's Forum Inc. of N. Idaho, 1999. Mem. Employment Security Agy. Rets., Internat. Pers. in Employment Security (sec., treas. 1970, Retiree of Yr. award 2003), Idaho State Employees Assn. (v.p. 1977, pres. elect 1978, pres. 1979, Employee of the Yr. 1968), North Idaho C. of C., Sandpoint C. of C. (events asst. 1984—, membership coord. 1984—, chmn. auction fundraiser 2001, 02, chmn. winter carnival 2003, v.p. bd. dirs. 2003, leadership com. 2000—), Rotary Club (Ponderay centennial). Republican. Avocations: dressmaking, skiing, swimming, aerobics, reading. Home: PO Box 54 Sandpoint ID 83864-0054 Office: Ponderay Cmty Devel Corp PO Box 615 Ponderay ID 83852 Office Phone: 208-255-2414.

NELSON, MARGUERITE HANSEN, special education educator; b. S.I., NY, June 23, 1947; d. Arthur Clayton and Marguerite Mary (Hansen) Nelson. AB magna cum laude, Boston Coll., 1969; MS in Edn., SUNY, Plattsburgh, 1973; cert. in gerontology, Yeshiva U., 1982; PhD, Fordham U., NYC, 1995. Cert. elem. and spl. edn. tchr. NY. Pre-primary tchr. Pub. Sch. 22R S.I., 1969—70; primary tchr. Oak Street Sch., Plattsburgh, 1971—73, Laurel Plains Sch., New City, NY, 1973—78; primary tchr. resource rm. Lakewood Sch., Congers, NY, 1978—2002; assoc. prof. St. Thomas Aquinas Coll., Sparkill, NY, 2002—. Adj. faculty St. Thomas Aquinas Coll., Sparkill, 1985—89, 1995—2002, Fordham U., 1990; presenter in field. Author: Teacher Stories, 1993, Research on Teacher Thinking, 1993, Metaphor as a Mode of Instruction, 1995; contbr. articles to profl. jours. Recipient Impact II Tchr. Recognition award, 1984; grantee, Chpt. II, 1983—84, Clarkstown Ctrl. Schs., 1986—91, Office Spl. Edn., 1992, 1995, NY Assn. Comprehensive Edn., 1997. Mem.: APA, AAUW, Coun. for Exceptional Children, Am. Ednl. Rsch. Assn., NY State Congress Parents and Tchrs. (hon.). Avocations: reading, poetry, ballet, gardening, flower arranging. Home: PO Box 395 Valley Cottage NY 10989-0395 Office: Saint Thomas Aquinas Coll Rt 340 Sparkill NY 10976 Business E-Mail: mnelson@stac.edu.

NELSON, MARILYN CARLSON, hotel executive, travel company executive; b. Mpls. m. Glen Nelson; children: Diana, Curtis C., Wendy. Student, U. Sorbonne, Paris, Inst. Hautes Etudes Econ., Geneva; degree in internat. econs. with honors, Smith Coll., 1961; DBA (hon.), Johnson & Wales U.; DHL (hon.), Coll. St. Catherine, Gustavus Adolphus Coll. Securities analyst Paine Webber, Mpls.; pres., COO Carlson Cos., Inc., Mpls., 1998—2003, CEO, chmn., 1998—, also bd. dirs. Co-chair Carlson Holdings, Inc., 2000—; co-chair Carlson Wagonlit Travel, 1994-2003; disting. vis. prof. Johnson & Wales U.; bd. dirs. Exxonmobil Corp., Mayo Clinic Found., Com. to Encourage Corp. Philanthropy; chmn. Nat. Women's Bus. Coun., 2002-05; vice chair U.S. Travel and Tourism Adv. Bd.; bd. mem. Singapore Tourism Bur. Pres. United Way Mpls., campaign chair, 1984; bd. dirs. United Way Am., 1984-90, U.S. Nat. Tourism Orgn., 1996-98, Ctr. for Internat. Leadership, 1989-2003; mem. disting. adv. coun. Coll. of St. Catherine, 1991-94; hon. bd. dirs. Svenska Inst., Stockholm, 1993—; mem. adv. bd. Hubert H. Humphrey Inst. Pub. Affairs, 1992-96; co-founder Minn. Women's Econ. Roundtable, 1974—; chair Minn. Super Bowl Task Force, 1984-92; chair, founder Midsummer Internat. Festival of Music, 1992; co-chair New Sweden '88; past bd. dirs. Guthrie Theatre, Greater Mpls. Girl Scout Coun., Jr. Achievement, Jr. League Mpls., KTCA Pub. TV, Minn. Econ. Assn., Minn. Congl. Award, Minn. Opera Co., Women's' Assn. Minn. Symphony Orch.; trustee Smith Coll., Northampton, Mass., 1980-85, Macalester Coll., St. Paul, 1974-80; mem. adv. bd. Minn. Women's Yearbook; trustee Curtis L. Carlson Family Found. Named Sales Exec. of Yr., Sales and Mktg. Exec. of Mpls., Outstanding Individual in Tourism, Minn. Office of Tourism, 1992, Woman of Yr., Roundtable for Women in Foodsvc., 1995, Woman of Yr., Minn. Exec. Women in Tourism, 1991—92, Swedish Am. of Yr., King and Queen of Sweden, 2003, Minnesotan of Yr., Minn. Monthly mag., 2003, Businesswoman of Yr., U.S. Commerce Dept. Small Bus. Adminstrn., 2005; named one of The Top 25 Execs. Yr., Bus. Week, 1999, Exec. Yr. Corp. Report Minn., 1999, 100 Most Powerful Women, Forbes mag., 2004—06, 25 Most Influential People in Mktg. Industry, Meeting News mag., 2005, Forbes Richest Americans, 2006; named to Sales and Mktg. Execs. Hall of Fame, 2003; recipient Minn. Congl. award for initiative and svc. to cmty., cert. of commendation State of Minn., Cmty. Svc. award, YWCA, Independence award, Vinland Nat. Ctr., Cmty. Svc. award, Park-Nicollet Med. Ctr., Outstanding Mktg. Exec. of Yr. award, Minn. Distributive Edn. Club Am., Career Achievement award, Sales and Mktg. Execs. Mpls., Outstanding Achievement award, United Way Mpls., Extraordinary Leadership award, Greater Mpls. C. of C., Disting. Svc. award, United Way of Am., 1984—90, Nat. Caring award, Caring Inst., 1995, Outstanding Bus. Leader award, Northwood U., 1995, The 50 Most Powerful Women award in Am. Bus., Fortune, 1998—2003, United Way Minn. Disting. Svc. award, United Way's highest vol. honor, 1998, Good Neighbor award, WCCO Radio, 1999, Caring Heart award charitable contbns. by Larry King Cardiac Found., 1999, Am.'s 100 Most Important Women award, Ladies' Home Jr., 1999, The Most Powerful Women in Travel #1, Travel Agent Mag., 1997—2003, Svc. Above Self award, The Rotary Club Downtown, Minn., 1999, The Top 500 Women-Owned Bus.'s award, Working Woman, 1999—2001, The 25 Most Influential Executives award, Leisure Travel News, 2000, Northwest Airlines Disting. World Traveler award, Hospitality Sales and Mktg. Assn. Internat., 2000, Responsible Capitalism award, FIRST mag., 2001, Businesswoman of World, Bus. Women's Network, 2001, Glass Ceiling award, Minn. Women's Consortium, 2001, Great Swedish Heritage award, Swedish Coun. Am., 2002, Lifetime Achievement award, Internat. Investment Forum, 2002, Athena award, Athena Found., 2004, Lifetime Achievement award, Hospitality Sales and Mktg. Assn. Internat., 2004, 18th Ann. Lucia Travel award, 2005, many others. Mem. World Econ. Forum, World Travel and Tourism Coun., Travel Industry Assn. Am. (bd. dirs.), Hennepin County Med. Soc. Aux., Bus. Roundtable, Smith Coll. Alumni Assn., Smith Club Mpls., Woodhill Country Club, Mpls. Club, N.W. Tennis Club, Nat. Ctr. Social Entrepreneurs, Com. of 200, Hospitality Sales and Mktg. Assn. Internat. (Lifetime Achievement award 2004), Minn. Orchestral Assn., Orphei Dranger, Alpha Kappa Psi. Office: Carlson Cos Inc 701 Carlson Pkwy Minnetonka MN 55305 Office Phone: 763-212-5000.*

NELSON, MARTHA JANE, magazine editor; b. Pierre, SD, Aug. 13, 1952; d. Bernard Anton and Pauline Isabel (Noren) Nelson. BA, Barnard Coll., 1976. Mng. editor Signs: Jour. of Women in Culture, NYC, 1976—80; staff editor Ms. Mag., NYC, 1980—85; editor-in-chief Women's Sports and Fitness Mag., San Francisco, 1985—87; exec. editor Savvy, NYC, 1988—89, editor-in-chief, 1989—91; asst. mng. editor People, 1993; founding editor In Style Mag., NYC, 1993—2002, exec. prodr. TV program Celebrity Weddings, 1997—2002, exec. prodr. TV programs Celebrity Moms, Celebrity Homes, 2001; mng. editor People Mag., NYC, 2002—06; editor, People group Time Inc., NYC, 2006—. Editor: Women in the American City, 1980; editor: (cons. editor) Who Weekly, 1992; contbr. articles to profl. jours. Bd. dirs. Painting Space 122, NYC, 1982—85, 1995—96, Urban Athletic Assn., 1986, ACRIA, Comm. Rsch. Inst. on AIDS, Am. Soc. Mag Editors, Accessories Coun., 1999—2001, Athletic and Swim Club, 2000—; adv. bd. NYU Grad. Sch., 2000—03. Named One of the Top 25 Most Influential People in Media, Brill's Content, 1999; named one of 100 Most Powerful Women, Forbes Mag., 2004—06; recipient Child Victimization in the News award, Nat. Ctr. for Missing and Exploited Children, 2003, Achiever award, Cosmetic Exec. Women, 2000, Inspiration award, Women's Step Up Network, 2004, Matrix award, NY Women in Comm., Inc., 2004. Mem.: NY Women in Comm., Women in Film, Am. Soc. Mag. Editors.*

NELSON, MARTINE LEVY, mathematics professor; b. Brussels, Nov. 16, 1955; arrived in U.S., 1969; d. Benjamin and Francine Fernande Levy; 1 child, Natalie Genevieve. BSEE, Fla. Atlantic U., Boca Raton, 1977; MS in Math. Edn., Nova Southeastern U., Orlando, 1997. Jr. engr., assoc. engr. IBM, Boca Raton, Fla., 1977—80; elec. field engr. Nat. bus. Equipment Co., St. Maarten, Netherlands Antilles, 1980—81; field engr. Fla. Power & Light Co., Miami, 1981—83; mgr., elec. engr. Wintel Svc. Corp., Longwood, 1984—85; ops. engr., elec. engr. Orlando Utilities Commn., 1985—89; pres., computer programmer Powercomp Internat. Corp., 1989—90; prof. math. Valencia C.C., 1998—, Seminole C.C., Sanford, 2001, Fla. Met. U., Orlando, 2002, Nova Southeastern U., 2002—03. Tutor Seminole C.C., 1997. Mem.: Nat. Coun. Tchrs. Math., Math. Assn. Am., Am. Math. Assn. Two-Yr. Colls. Baha'I.

NELSON, MARY CARROLL, artist, writer; b. Bryan, Tex., Apr. 24, 1929; d. James Vincent and Mary Elizabeth (Langton) Carroll; m. Edwin Blakeley Nelson, June 27, 1950; children: Patricia Ann, Edwin Blakely. BA in Fine Arts, Barnard Coll., 1950; MA, U. N.Mex., 1963. Juror Am. Artist Golden Anniversary Competition, 1987. Guest instr. continuing edn. U. N.Mex., 1991; conf. co-organizer Affirming Wholeness, The Art and Healing Experience, San Antonio, 1992, Artists of the Spirit Symposium, 1994. Group shows include N.Mex. Mus., 1987, Art is for Healing, The Universal Link, San Antonio, 1992, Fuller Lodge Art Ctr. Los Alamos, N.Mex., 1993, Layering, Albuquerque, 1993, Crossings, Bradford, Mass., 1994, The Layered Perspective, Fayetteville, Ark., 1994, Tree of Life, San Miguel de Allende, Mex., 1996, (honoree Magnifico, Albuquerque, 1997, Bravos award Excellence in Arts 2004, Achievement award Masterworks, 2005), Guardian Spirits, Marlborough, Eng., 1997, Memories in Multi-Media, Columbus, Ohio, 1998, Agora Gallery, NYC, 1998, Celtic Connections, Mass., 1998, Bridging Time and Space, Calif., 1999, Musings on the Millennium, Ohio, 2000, Layerists in Multi-Media/Affirming Wholeness, Albuquerque, 2000, The Birth of Wisdom, N.M.and Gordes, France, 2000, Tides of Change, Tex., 2001, Earth-Spirit, Ohio, 2001, Shadow & Light, Albuquerque, 2001, Landscape and Memory, Sedona, Ariz., 2002, dsg Gallery, Albuquerque, 2002, Albuquerque Mus., 2003, Fire in the Heart, Ashland, Oreg., 2003, Layered Images, Albuquerque, 2003, Masterworks Miniatures, 2004 (1st award Mixed Media, Juror Masterworks award 2005), Get the Lead Out, Los Alamos U., 2005, Weynich Gallery, Alburquerque, 2006, N.Mex. State U., Las Cruces, 2006, Soul Shrines, Las Cruces, 2006, Mus. Fine Arts, Las Cruces, 2006, Rock, Paper, Scissors, Los Alamos, N.Mex., 2006, Masterwork Miniatures, Albuquerque, 2006, Connections: We Are All One, Lexington, Ky., 2006, Art of Space, Las Cruces, 2006; represented in pvt. collections in U.S., Germany, Eng. and Australia; author: American Indian Biography Series, 1971-76, (with Robert E. Wood) Watercolor Workshop, 1974; (with Ramon Kelley) Ramon Kelley Paints Portraits and Figures, 1977, The Legendary Artists of Taos, 1980, (catalog) American Art in Peking, 1981, Masters of Western Art, 1982, Connecting, The Art of Beth Ames Swartz, 1984, Artists of the Spirit, 1994, Doris Steider, A Vision of Silence, 1997, Beyond Fear, A Toltec's Guide to Freedom and Joy, 1997, Layering, An Art of Time and Space, 1985, (catalog) Layering/Connecting, 1987; contbg. editor Am. Artist, 1976-91, Southwest Art, 1987-91; editor (video) Layering, 1990; arts corr. Albuquerque Jour., 1991-93; contbr. One Source Sacred Journeys, 1997, Lightstream, 2003; co-author: Bridging Time and Space, Essays on Layered Art, 1998, Toltec Prophecies of Don Miguel Ruiz, 2003; co-editor The Art of Layering: Making Connections, 2004 Mem. Albuquerque Arts Bd., 1984—88. Mem. Soc. Layerists in Multi-Media (founder 1982). Home: 1408 Georgia St NE Albuquerque NM 87110-6861 Personal E-mail: mcn50@comcast.net.

NELSON, MARY ELLEN GENEVIEVE, adult education educator; b. Milw., Sept. 13, 1948; d. William Paul and Evelyn Marie (Saduske) Naber; m. Kenneth Arthur Nelson, July 22, 1972; children: William Norris, Victoria Marie. BS in Edn., Mt. Mary Coll., 1970; MEd, Carroll Coll., 1994. Cert. tchr., Wis.; cert. in math., computers, careers Wis. Tech. Coll. Sys., ABE/GOAL basic edn.; lic. math computer careers, reading and writing. Clk. Oldline Life Ins., Milw., 1967-70; math. tchr. Menomonee Falls East HS, Wis., 1970-76; math. and adult basic edn. tchr. Waukesha County Tech. Coll., Pewaukee, Wis., 1978-82, math. tchr., goal instr., 1982-88, lead adult basic edn. tchr. and goal instr. Menomonee Falls, 1988—2005; ret., 2004. Co-chair Tech. Acad. Edn., 1995; initiator adult ESL pilot program Wis. Tech. Coll., 2001; mgr. adult ESL pilot program Menomonee Falls Sch. Dist., 2003—04, mgr. study program, 2003—04; established Tech. Coll. Naber Carpentry Classes, Dominican Republic, 2005—; presenter in field. Contbr. papers to prof. jour. Dir. presch. program St. Agnes Cath. Ch., Butler, Wis., 1979-82, presch. tchr., 1977-79; den mother cub scout Pack 72, Boy Scouts Am., Butler, 1983-84, candy fundraiser chmn., 1985, 86; mem. Menomonee Falls Edn. Com., 1987-97; initiator and chair yearly student advancement fundraiser, Waukesha County. Tech. Coll., 1993-2004; mem. Leadership Menomonee Falls, 1995-96, mem. bd. govs., 1997-2000; initiator Families Learning Together, 2001-02, 02-03; mem. Com. Expansion Menomonee Falls Cmty. Ctr., 2001-02. Nominee Gold Alumnus, Carroll Coll., 2004; recipient Outstanding Svc. pin, Menomonee Falls Cmty. Sch. Dist., 1994, recognition mktg. efforts to improve ednl. opportunities in cmty., 2004, 35 Yr. Svc. Friend of Edn. award, 2006, award, Wis. Math. Coun., 1995, YWCA, 1996, cert., U. Wis. Coop. Ext. Program, 2002, Mentor award, Leadership Menomonee Falls Orgn., 2004. Mem. Wis. Math. Coun., Wis. Adult and Continuing Edn. Assn., Menomonee Falls C. of C. (Waukesha County Tech. Coll. rep. 1993-2004, edn. com. 1986-2004), Rotary (partnership). Roman Catholic. Achievements include development of Luncheon Symposium format for Wis. Tech. Coll. Sys. Avocations: crafts, golf, travel, reading, stained glass art. Home: N54W15485 Northway Dr Menomonee Falls WI 53051-6716 Personal E-mail: menelson72@sbcglobal.net.

NELSON, MARY KATHRYN, bilingual counselor, small business owner, real estate agent, artist, singer; b. Chgo., May 28, 1954; d. James C. Nelson and Leila R. Cooke. BS in Social Work, So. Ill. U., 1978; MS in Rehab. Counseling, U. Ariz., 1982. Cert. rehab. counselor, substance abuse counselor, profl. counselor, Ariz.; nat. cert. counselor; lic. real estate agt., Ariz., lic. ins. agent Allstate, Ariz., 2006. Bilingual counselor Ill. Migrant Council, 1975-76; social worker Child Protective Svcs., 1980-85; bilingual clinician pvt. nonprofit agys., 1985-96; bilingual counselor contractor, counselor Suprme Ct. Ariz., Phoenix, 1995—; owner, mgr. Bilingual Svcs., LLC, Phoenix, 1985—, owner Peoria, Ariz., 1994—; real estate agt. Liberty Properties, Inc., 2003—05, Ken Meade Realty, Sun City, Ariz., 2005—06; bilingual agent Am. Farmer's Ins., Peoria, Ariz., 2006—, Weinstein-Fehris Realty, Scottsdale, Ariz., 2006—. Exhibited in group shows at Franciscan Renewal Ctr., Scottsdale, 2001, exhibitions include Artareas.com, 2001—; performer: Talent Show at Crossroads, 1999—2001; singer: Franciscan Renewal Ctr., 2000—01; exhibitions include Fountain Hills Ariz. Art Exhibit, 1995, Channel 22 Phoenix Cable Amateur Hr., Spanish Songs, 1996, Iberoamericana Internat. Art Exhibit, Miami, Fla., 1997, Phoenix K Lite Radio TV Commn., 1997, Peoria Sportscomplex Art Fair, Ariz., 1998, Franciscan Renewal Ctr. Art Fair, Scottsdale, Ariz., 1999, 2001, ArtAreas.com. Vol. Big Bros.-Big Sisters, Tucson, 1999; family advocate Cesar Chavez Farmworkers Union Labor Movement; art donor Ariz. Foster Care Assn., Paradise Valley, Ariz., 2001, donor original oil painting with World Trade Ctr. motif, 2001; founder Morris Dee's Ctr. for Justice/Civil Rights Mtml. Ctr.; mem. So. Poverty Law Ctr.; vol. campaign worker Jon Kyle for Senator, Phoenix, 1996—2006; fundraiser John Shadeg for Congressman, Ariz., 2002, Women Reps. for Kyl, 1996—2006; choir mem. Franciscan Renewal Ctr., Paradise Valley, Ariz., 1999—2002. Recipient humanitarian award Inst. Arts Plastiques, 1997; named to Martin Luther King Meml. Wall of Tolerance, 2003. Mem. Drama Beat Acting Club. Republican. Avocations: singing, comedy, acting. Home: 12667 W Maya Way Peoria AZ 85383-2829 E-mail: marynelsonsc@aol.com.

NELSON, MEREDITH GAFFNEY, counselor, educator; b. Shreveport, La., Oct. 25, 1973; d. Joseph Peter and Charlotte Coleman Gaffney; m. Clay Harry Nelson, Apr. 15, 2000; 1 child, Grace Nelson Gaffney. BA, Southwestern U., Georgetown, Tex., 1994; MS, U. Houston, Clark Lake, Tex., 1998; PhD, U. New Orleans, 2001. Nat. cert. counselor Nat. Bd. Cert. Counseling, lic. profl. counselor La. Lic. Profl. Counseling Bd., supr. La. Lic. Profl. Counseling Bd., marriage/family therapist La. Permanent substitute tchr. spl. edn. Clear Lake H.S., Houston, 1997—98; grad. asst., fellowship U. New Orleans, 1998—2000; mental health counselor Acorn Adoption Agy., New Orleans, 2001—02; therapist Cmty. Support Programs, Shreveport, 2003—; asst. prof. La. State U., Shreveport, 2001—. Pres., bd. dirs. Acorn Adoption Agy., New Orleans, 2000—01; pro bono mental health counselor Pool of Siloam Med. Ministry, Shreveport, 2006—; vol. mental health counselor ARC, Shreveport, 2005—. Named Outstanding Doctoral Role Model, U. New Orleans, 2001; recipient Best Conf. Presentation award, La. Counseling Assn., 2000. Mem.: ACA, Assn. Marriage and Family Therapists (clin. mem.), Coun. Young Profls., N.W. La. Counseling Assn. (v.p. 2003—07), Psi Chi, Chi Sigma Iota. Episcopalian. Avocations: horseback riding, cooking, reading, fishing, wine. Office: La State U 1 University Pl Shreveport LA 71115

NELSON, MURIEL YVETTE, elementary school educator; b. Fort Valley, Ga., Nov. 5, 1957; d. Susie Pearl Johnson; m. Willie L. Appling, June 8, 2001; children: Jared L. Blassingame, Millicent Yvette Shannon, Johnathan Appling Shannon. BS, Ft. Valley State U., Ga., 1975. Cert. tchr. Ga. Tchr. Taylor County Bd. Edn., Butler, Ga., 1979—82, Macon County Bd. Edn., Marshallville, Ga., 1982—83, Griffin (Ga.)-Spalding Bd. Edn., 1983—. Active Shiloh Bapt. Ch., Fort Valley, Ga., 1964—2006; pianist Oak Grove Bapt. Ch., Griffin, 1998—. Democrat. Baptist. Avocations: reading, travel. Home: 5489 Shirewick Ln Lithonia GA 30058 Office: Jordan Hill Elem Sch 75 Jordan Hill Rd Griffin GA 30058 Office Phone: 770-229-3777. Personal E-mail: wnelson311@aol.com. Business E-Mail: mshannon@spalding.k12.ga.us.

NELSON, NANCY ELEANOR, pediatrician, educator; b. El Paso, Apr. 4, 1933; d. Harry Hamilton and Helen Maude (Murphy) N. BA magna cum laude, U. Colo., 1955, MD, 1959. Intern, Case Western Res. U. Hosp., 1959-60, resident, 1960-63; pvt. practice medicine specializing in pediats., Denver, 1963-70; clin. prof. U. Colo. Sch. Medicine, Denver, 1988-2002, assoc. dean student affairs U. Colo. Sch. Medicine, 1988—. Mem. Am. Acad. Pediats., AMA (sect. med. schs. governing coun. 1994-96), Denver Med. Soc. (pres. 1983-84), Colo. Med. Soc. (bd. dirs. 1985-88, mem. jud. coun. 1992—, mem. liason com. med. edn. 1995—).

NELSON, PAMELA HUDSON, artist, educator; b. Oklahoma City, Mar. 25, 1947; d. Charles Howard and Maurine Lanell (Curtis) Hudson; m. William Nelson, Feb. 18, 1968; children: Keith, Charles. BFA, So. Meth. U., Dallas, 1974. Artist, 1979—. Instr. Artlington Mus. Art, 1991; juror DART Garland (Tex.) Bus Transit Ctr., 1992, Site Sculpture Competition, Mcpl. Ctr., Plano, Tex., 1993; created, produced award for Leadership Tex., 1993, Girls Club Am., Dallas, 1987, 89; guest lectr. Dallas Mus. Art, 1993; supr. studio assts. in mentor program, 1988-91; pvt. art tutor, 1987-93; co-curator Theatre Gallery, Dallas, 1985; workshops Dallas Mus. Art, 1982, 85. One-woman shows include Toni Jones Gallery, Houston, 1980, 500 Exposition Gallery, Dallas, 1981, Clifford Gallery, Dallas, 1983, 85, Peregrine Gallery at the Crescent, Dallas, 1987, 91, Studio Gallery, Brookhaven Coll., Dallas, 1992, Artisana Gallery, Dallas, 1993; two and three person shows include Clifford Gallery, Dallas, 1979, Forum Gallery, Brookhaven Coll., 1988, Galveston Art Ctr., Galveston, Tex., 1992, Nat. Arts Club, N.Y.C., 2002; exhibited in group show at U. Houston, 1979, Toni Jones Gallery, Houston, 1979, Clifford Gallery, Dallas, 1984, DW Gallery, 1984, Mus. of Art of the Am. West, Houston, 1985, Adolphus Hotel, Dallas, 1985, Tex. Christian U., Ft. Worth, 1986, Frito-Lay Corp., Plano, Tex., 1986, Caroline Lee Gallery, 1986, Cullen Ctr., Houston, 1987, LTV Ctr., Dallas, 1987, Laguna Gloria Art Mus., Austin, Tex., 1987, Dallas Pub. Libr., 1987, Tex. Commerce Tower, Dallas, 1988, Amarillo (Tex.) Art Ctr., 1988, Belo Mansion, Dallas, 1988, Nat. Mus. Women in the Arts, Washington, 1988, Ctr. Rsch. Contemporary Art, U. Tex., Arlington, 1988, The Gallery, So. Meth. U., Dallas, 1989, Dallas Mus. of Art, 1989, Hall-Barnett Gallery, New Orleans, 1989, X Art Gallery, New Orleans, 1990, Peregrine Gallery at the Crescent, Dallas, 1990, Ark. Arts Ctr., Little Rock, 1990, Very Spl. Arts Gallery, Washington, 1991, Cullen Ctr., Houston, 1991, Lubbock (Tex.) Arts Ctr., 1991, Arlington (Tex.) Art Mus., 1992, Collin County C.C., Plano, 1992, Ida Green Gallery, Austin Coll., Sherman, Tex., 1992; represented in permanent collections Corp. Hdqrs. Steak and Ale Corp., Dallas, M-TV Collection, N.Y.C.; prin. works include sculptures at Mississippi County Ct. House, Blytheville, Ark., 1986, Dallas Zoo, 1988, DFW Airport, 2002. Presdl. appointee U.S. Commn. Fine Arts, Washington, 2001—, vice chair, 2005—; bd. dirs. Tex. Sculpture Assn., 1987-89, Dallas Artists Rsch. and Exbn., 1989-91; mem. adv. coun. Dallas Arts Resource System, 1991; mem. steering com. Emergency Artists Support League, Dallas, 1992; exhbn. cons. SPCA and Dallas Zoo, 1993; participant, Dallas City Ctr. TIF Streetscape Project (recipient City of Dallas Urban Design award); dir. Open Art Project, Stewpot Shelter, Dallas; mem. Pub. Art Com., City of Dallas. Recipient award Laguna Art Mus., 1982, Merit award Tex. Christian U., 1984, Crystal award Dallas Cable System, 1985, Merit award Crescent Gallery, 1986, Merit award Alexandria Mus., 1987, Patrick Media Billboard award, 1988, Excellence '88 award Plz. of Ams., 1988, Hon. Mention award Longview Mus. and Arts Ctr., 1990, Legend award, Dallas Visual Art Ctr., Merit award, AIA; named Artist-in-Residence, Connemara Conservancy, 1993. Home: 312 S Harwood St Dallas TX 75201-5602 E-mail: pamelaandbill@hotmail.com.

NELSON, PATRICIA JOAN PINGENOT, retired language educator; b. Boulder, Colo., Nov. 12, 1930; d. Elmer Louis and Elizabeth Isabelle (Madden) Pingenot; children: Gail Jo Gardner, Marvin D. Jr., Stephen Michael. BA, Hastings Coll., 1942; MA in English, U. Nebr., 1964; postgrad., U. Minn. Cert. elem. tchr. 1-6, english/lang. arts 7-12, devel./remedial reading 7-12, reading specialist/cons. K-12. Freshman composition writing lab instr. Hastings (Nebr.) Coll.; tchr. Edina (Minn.) Schs.; English tchr., reading specialist Woodbury (Minn.) HS, South Washington County Schs.; ret., 1991. Mem.: ASCD, NEA, Minn. ASCD, Minn. Acad. Reading (pres., v.p.), Minn. Reading Assn. (chair publs. com., editor MRA Highlights, mem. newspaper edn. com.), Twin City Area Reading Coun., Nat. Coun. Tchrs. English, Minn. Coun. Tchrs. English, Minn. Edn. Assn., Capitol Uniserv (v.p., comm. chair), S. Washington Edn. Assn. (v.p., treas., IPD co-chair), Delta Kappa Gamma (Alpha Omega chpt.). Home: 5524 Warden Ave Edina MN 55436-2241

NELSON, PAULA MORRISON BRONSON, reading specialist; b. Memphis, Mar. 26, 1944; d. Fred Ford and Julia (Morrison) Bronson: m. Jack Marvin Nelson, July 13, 1968; children: Eric Allen, Kelly Susan BS, U. N.Mex., 1967; MA, U. Colo., Denver, 1985. Tchr. phys. edn. Grant Union Sch. Dist., Sacramento, 1967—68, Denver Pub. Schs., 1968—74, with program for pupil assistance, 1974—80; tchr. ESL Douglas County Pub. Schs., Parker, Colo., 1982—83; Chpt. 1 reading specialist Denver Pub. Schs., 1983—96, computer/reading specialist, 1996—98, reading specialist, tchr. gifted and talented, 1998—99, lead tchr. in charge instrn., 1999—2001, edn. cons., 2001—02. Demonstration tchr. Colo. Edn. Assn., 1970-72; mem. curriculum com. Denver Pub. Schs., 1970-72; mem. Douglas County Accountability Com., Castle Rock, Colo., 1986-92; mem. educators rev. panel Edn. for Freedom; computer trainer Denver Pub. Schs. Tech. Team, 1992-02; bd. dirs. Obie Harrington-Howes Found., 2005-. Co-author: Gymnastics Teacher's Guide Elementary Physical Education, 1973, Applauding Our Constitution, 1989; editl. reviewer G is for Geography, Children's Literature and the Five Themes, 1993; prodr. slide shows Brotherhood, 1986, We the People.Our Dream Lives On, 1987, Celebration of Cultures, 1988 Named Pub. Edn. Coalition grantee, Denver, 1987, 88, 89, 90, grantee Rocky Mountain Global Edn. Project, 1987, Wake Forest Law Sch., Winston-Salem, N.C., 1988, 89, 90, 92, Read to Achieve grantee Colo. State Dept. Edn., 2000, Chpt. II grant, 1991, Tech. grant, 1993, Title VI Reading grant, 1999, 2000; recipient Three R's of Freedom award State Dept. Edn., 1987, Nat. Recognition award Commn. on Bicentennial of Constn., 1987, Disting. Tchr. award City of Denver, 1994 Mem.: Denver Fedn. Tchrs., Am. Fedn. Tchrs., Tech. in Edn. Republican. Methodist. Avocations: snow and water skiing, tennis, sailing. Home: 18 Covewood Dr Norwalk CT 06853

NELSON, SANDRA E., information technology executive; d. Samual Aaron and Nelia Mary Aronson; children: Ryan Dagen, Kyle Degn. Mgmt. of Tech., Kennedy Western U., Thousand Oaks, CA, 2000—02. Career & Tech. Edn. Wash., 2005. Curriculum devel. asst. SW Regional Sch. Dist., Dillingham, Alaska, 1985—89; media specialist Sumner Sch. Dist., Wash., 1989—95; dir. of its Fed. Way Pub. Schs., Federal Way, Wash., 1995—. Cons. in field, 1999—2005; prin., cons. Leadership upward, Tacoma, 1999—2005; trainer Aha Process, Baytown, Tex., 2000—05. Master: Assn. Computer Profls. in Edn. (pres. 2002—03); fellow: Wash. Assn. Sch. Administrs. (presenter 2002—05); mem.: Advancing Leadership (presenter 2003—05), Fed. Way C of C. Office Phone: 253-945-2111. E-mail: snelson@fwps.org.

NELSON, SARA, editor; With Bookreporter.com, Oxygen TV network, BP Report, Self Mag.; founding books editor Inside.com; sr. contbg. editor Glamour Mag.; pub. columnist NY Observer; pub. columnist, books editor NY Post; editor-in-chief Publisher's Weekly Mag., 2005—. Author: So Many Books, So Little Time: A Year of Passionate Reading, 2003. Office: Publishers Weekly 360 Park Ave S New York NY 10010 Office Phone: 646-746-6758. Office Fax: 646-746-6631.

NELSON, SARAH MILLEDGE, archaeology educator; b. Miami, Fla., Nov. 29, 1931; d. Stanley and Sarah Woodman (Franklin) M.; m. Harold Stanley Nelson, July 25, 1953; children: Erik Harold, Mark Milledge, Stanley Franklin. BA, Wellesley Coll., 1953; MA, U. Mich., 1969, PhD, 1973. Instr. archaeology U. Md. extension, Seoul, Republic Korea, 1970-71; asst. prof. U. Denver, 1974-79, assoc. prof., 1979-85, prof. archaeology, 1985—2004, rsch. prof., 2004—, chair dept. anthropology, 1985-95, dir. women's studies program, 1985-87, John Evans prof., dir. Asian studies, 1996, vice provost for rsch., 1998—2002, interim vice provost grad. studies and rsch., 2001—02. Vis. asst. prof. U. Colo., Boulder, 1974; resident Rockefeller Ctr. in Bellagio, Italy, 1996. Author: Archaeology of Korea, 1993, Gender in Archaeology: Analyzing Power and Prestige, 1997, 2d revised edit., 2004, (novel) Spirit Bird Journey, 1999, Ancient Queens: Archaelogical Perspectives, 2003, Jade Dragon, 2004, co-author: Denver: An Archaeological History, 2001; editor: The Archaeology of Northeast China, 1995, Ancestors for the Pigs: Pigs in Prehistory, 1998, Handbook of Gender in Archeology, 2006; co-editor: Powers of Observation, 1990, Equity Issues for Women in Archaeology, 1994, Archaeology of the Russian Far East, 2005, In Pursuit of Gender: Worldwide Archaeological Perspectives, 2001, Korean Social Archaeology, 2005, Archeology of the Russian Far East, 2006, Integrating the Diversity of the 21st Century Anthropology, 2006. Active Earthwatch, 1989. Recipient Outstanding Scholar award U. Denver, 1989; grantee S.W. Inst. Rsch. on Women, 1981, Acad. Korean Studies, Seoul, 1983, Internat. Cultural Soc. Korea, 1986, Colo. Hist. Fund, 1995-97, Rockefeller Found. Residency, Bellagio, Italy, Wenner-Gren Found., 2000-02, Nat. Geographic Soc., 2000—. Fellow Am. Anthrop. Assn.; mem. Soc. Am. Archaeology, Assn. Asian Studies, Royal Asiatic Soc., Sigma Xi (sec.-treas. 1978-79), Phi Beta Kappa. Democrat. Avocations: travel, gardening. Home: 5878 S Dry Creek Ct Littleton CO 80121-1709 Office: U Denver Dept Anthropology Denver CO 80208-0001 Office Phone: 303-871-2682. Business E-Mail: snelson@du.edu.

NELSON, SHIRLEY W., bank executive; From jr. teller to v.p., sr. mgr. Ctrl. Bank Med. Ctr. branch, Oakland, Calif., 1966—82; founder, chmn., CEO, pres. Summit Bank, Oakland, Calif., 1982—90, chmn., CEO, 1982—, Summit Bancshares Inc. Chmn. bd. Summit Bank Found., 1998—, No. Calif. Women's Leadership Forum. Co-chmn. No. Calif. Women's League Coun.; bd. dirs. Cal State Hayward Ednl. Found. Named One of 25 Most Powerful Women in Banking, U.S. Banker Mag., 2003. Office: Summit Bancshares Inc 2969 Broadway Oakland CA 94611-5710

NELSON, SUE GRODSKY, humanities educator, consultant; b. Bklyn., Apr. 1, 1943; d. Juliette Dorfman and Louis Grodsky; m. Michael R. Nelson, Nov. 23, 1968; children: Andrew Robert, John Samuel. BA, Allegheny Coll., Meadville, Pa., 1964; EdM, John Carroll U., University Heights, Ohio, 1995. Cert. tchr. Ohio, 1988. Asst. prodn. mgr. CBS, NYC, 1964—65; tchr./dept. chair of English, honors English, reading, journalism, French Cleve. Bd. of Edn., 1965—71; group home foster parent Jewish Children's Bur., Shaker Heights, Ohio, 1971—75; tchr. of English, inclusion English/learning cmty., career edn., journalism East Cleve. Bd. of Edn., 1972—98; adj. instr., reading cons. Cuyahoga CC, Cleve. Mem. tchr. rev. panel McDougal, Littell & Co., Evanston, Ill., 1990—92; presenter Cons. - Multiple Intelligences Workshops, Ohio, 1994—99; mem. adv. com. John Carroll U., University Heights, Ohio, 1995—97; mem. Newbury Bd. of Edn., Ohio, 2000—04, past pres. Author: (instruction manual) Getting Elected to Public Office; contbr. anthology Humanities Programs Today; co-author/editor (instruction manual) Multiple Intelligences at Work!; editor: (inspirational lessons) Zen Shin Talks. Chairperson Social Action Coun., 2005—, People for Polensek, Cleve., 1977—90; vice chairperson and sec. Cuyahoga County Dem. Party, Cuyahoga County, Ohio, 1982—89; vol. coord. Boyle for Senate, Cleveland, Ohio, 1997—98; trustee Suburban Temple-Kol Ami, 2005—. Recipient Ashland Achievement award, Ashland Oil, Inc., 1992; Coach of State Champion - Oratorical Interpretation, Ohio H.S. Speech League, 1986. Mem.: NEA (life), East Cleve. Edn. Assn. (pres. 1982—83), Ohio Sch. Bd. Assn., Ohio Edn. Assn. (life; chairperson svc. coun. 1980—81). Democrat. Jewish. Avocations: reading, exercising, interior decorating, political activism, travel. Home: 10450 Bell St Newbury OH 44065 Office: Cuyahoga CC 2900 Community College Avenue Cleveland OH 44114 E-mail: m.s.nelson@juno.com.

NELSON, SUSAN JOY, nurse; b. Dallas, Dec. 3, 1951; d. Roy Charles and Joyce Elma (Stirling) Nelson; life ptnr. Dennis K. Kline. AA, Los Angeles Pierce Coll., 1975; BSPA, St. Joseph's Coll., North Windham, Maine, 1983; MN, UCLA, 1989. RN, Calif.; cert. critical care nurse; cert. ACLS; sr. med. rev. analyst, Blue Shield of Calif. Head RN, asst. head RN UCLA Hosp. and Clinics; cardiovascular CNS Lancaster (Calif.) Community Hosp.; head RN Valley Hosp. Med. Ctr., Van Nuys, Calif. Guest speaker undergrad. critical care course UCLA Sch. Nursing, 1985; inservice educator hemodynamic monitoring and chest X-ray interpretation UCLA. Contbr. articles to profl. jours. Elder, Parish MInistry, Orangevale Seventh-day Adventist Ch. Mem. AACN (past sec., study guide chair, symposium chair San Fernando Valley chpt.), Am. Heart Assn., Sigma Theta Tau.

NELSON, SUSAN RHODES, media specialist, educator; b. Birmingham, Ala., June 27, 1948; d. Horace and Evelyn Vines Rhodes; m. Roger Hudson Nelson, Dec. 19, 1970; children: Jay Matthew, Jon Bradley. BS, Auburn U., 1970; MA, U. Ala., Birmingham, 1973, EdS, 1985; MLIS, U. Ala., Tuscaloosa, 1997, EdD, 2001. Cert. tchr. Ala. Tchr. Jefferson County Bd. of Edn., Birmingham, 1970—94, media specialist, 1994—; adj. prof. U. Ala., Tuscaloosa, 2001—. Adv. bd. Jefferson County Librarians, Birmingham, 2001—; chmn. Jefferson County Elem. Librarians, Birmingham, 2003—; mem. bldg. leadership team Hueytown (Ala.) Elem. Sch., 1994—, tech. coord., 1994—; cons., rschr. Learning Through Sports, Birmingham, 2003—; leader People to People Ambassador Program, Birmingham, 2004—; online facilitator Ala. State Dept. Edn. Bd. dirs. Daycare, Bessemer, Ala., 2000—05. Named Leader of the Yr., Jefferson County 4-H, 1975, Tchr. of Yr., Hueytown Elem. Sch., 2003; recipient Exemplary Libr. Program award, Libr. and Media Professionals, 1999, 2003, Most Exemplary Elem. Libr. award, Jefferson County Libr. Links for Success, 2004. Mem.: ALA (assoc.), NEA (assoc.), Ala. Libr. Assn. (assoc.), Alpha Delta Kappa (treas. 2002—), Kappa Delta Pi (assoc.), Kappa Delta Epsilon (assoc.). Republican. Avocations: travel, music, reading, sports. Home: 11227 Apple Valley Rd Mc Calla AL 35111-2448 Office: Hueytown Elem Sch 112 Forest Rd Hueytown AL 35023 Office Phone: 205-379-4123. Personal E-mail: nelsonsr2@bellsouth.net. E-mail: snelson@jefcoed.com.

NELSON, VITA JOY, editor, publisher; b. N.Y.C., Dec. 9, 1937; d. Leon Abraham and Bertha (Sher) Reiner; m. Lester Nelson, Aug. 27, 1961; children: Lee Reiner, Clifford Samuel, Cara Ritchie. BA, Boston U., 1959. Promotion copywriter Street & Smith, N.Y.C., 1958-59; asst. to mng. editor Mademoiselle Mag., N.Y.C., 1959-60; mcpl. bond trader Granger & Co., N.Y.C., 1960-63; founder, editor, pub. Westchester Mag., Mamaroneck, NY, 1968-80, L.I. Mag., 1973-78; founder, editor, pub., pres. Moneypaper, 1981—. Pub. The Guide to Dividend Reinvestment Plans, Direct Investing; founder MP63 Fund; pres. Moneypaper Advisor Inc., 1999—. Author: (with Donald Korn) Create and Manage Your Own Mutual Fund, 1994. Bd. dirs. United Way of Westchester/Putnam County, 1998—2002; bd. govs., v.p. Am. Jewish Com., Westchester, 1979—89. Recipient citation Coun. Arts, 1972, Media award Pub. Rels. Soc. Am., 1974. Mem. Women in Comms. (Outstanding Communicator award 1983). Democrat. Home: Pleasant Ridge Rd Harrison NY 10528-1004 Office: The Moneypaper Inc 555 Theodore Frend Ave Rye NY 10580 Office Phone: 914-925-0022. E-mail: vitajoy@aol.com.

NELSON-KAUFFMAN, WENDY, history educator; b. Evanston, Ill., Mar. 7, 1961; d. Wayne Keith Nelson and Jane Van Dellen; m. Matthew William Kauffman, Oct. 5, 1961; children: David Alexander Nelson Kauffman, Sam VanDellen Nelson Kauffman. BS, Dartmouth Coll., Hanover, NH, 1983; MS, Northwestern U., Evanston, IL, 1984; MS in History, So. Conn. State U., New Haven, 1990. Cert. tchr. Conn., 1990. Tv news anchor, reporter WAOW-TV, Wausau, Wis., 1984—86; tv reporter WTNH-TV, New Haven, 1986—88; adult educator New Haven and Hartford Adult Edn., 1990—96; tchr., chair dept. Bloomfield H.S., 1996—2004; history educator Met. Learning Ctr., 2004—. Mem. closing achievement gap task force Conn. Dept. Edn., Hartford, 2003—04; advisor Student Abolitionists Stopping Slavery, Bloomfield, 2004—06; mem. conn. task force revise state social studies stds. Conn. Dept. Edn., 2005—06; tchr. adv. bd. Unitarian Universalist Ch., West Hartford, 2005—06. Recipient Conn. Tchr. of Yr. award, 2003, All-Star Tchg. Team awaqrd, USA Today, 2004, Kidger award for outstanding history tchr. in New Eng., 2004, Conn. History Tchr. of Yr., 2005. Mem.: Nat. Coun. History Edn., Nat. Coun. Social Studies, Conn. Coun. Social Studies (assoc.; bd. mem. 2004—06). Unitarian Universalist. Avocations: travel, reading, gardening, physical fitness. Home: 101 Four Mile Rd West Hartford CT 06107 Office: Metropolitan Learning Center 1551 Blue Hills Ave Bloomfield CT 06002 Office Phone: 860-242-7834. Personal E-mail: wnkauffman@yahoo.com. E-mail: wnelson-kauffman@crec.org.

NELSON-SARGEANT, SUSAN MARIE, speech pathology professional; b. Washington, Oct. 21, 1953; d. Boyce Gerald and Mary (Murphy) Nelson; children: Rachel Marie Sargeant, Rebekah Ann Sargeant. BS, James Madison U., 1976; MS, Vanderbilt U., Nashville, 1979. Cert. tchr. Va. Dept. Edn. Speech therapist Danville Pub. Schs., Va., 1976; spl. edn. tchr. early childhood Rockingham County Pub. Schs., Harrisonburg, Va., 1979—80; program coord. in early intervention Rappahannock Area Cmty. Svcs. Bd., Fredericksburg, Va., 1980—86; cons. in early intervention, 1986—92; speech therapist Spotsylvania County Pub. Schs., Va., 1992—. Cons. Parent Ednl. Advocacy Tng. Ctr., Alexandria, Va., 1982; co-sponsor Future Educators of Am. Club Chancellor H.S., 2002—; presenter, session leader at profl. workshops and confs. Puppeteer Kids on the Block, Va., 1988—98; bd. dirs. Stagedoor Cmty. Theater, 2000—, Piedmont Group Home, 2003—; catechist St. Jude Ch.; rep. Va. Easter Seal Soc., 1980—82. Recipient Outstanding Child Advocate award Va. Div. Children, 1982; named one of Ten Outstanding Young Women of Am., 1986. Mem.: NEA (del. 1976—80, 1998—), TASH Advocacy, Coun. for Exceptional Children (local arrangements chair internat. conv. 1988, Va. pres. 1997), Internat. Assn. Infant Massage Instrs. (cert.,), Assn. Retarded Citizens (bd. dirs.), Speech and Hearing Assn. Va., Va. Divsn. for Early Childhood, Va. Divsn. Mental Retardation/Coun. Exceptional Children (sec., del., gov.-at-large, pres. 1990—93, Kuhn-Barnett award, Jennie Brewer award). Democrat. Roman Catholic. Avocation: volunteering for community activites. Home: 458 Laurel Ave Fredericksburg VA 22408 Office: Chancellor HS 6400 Harrison Rd Fredericksburg VA 22407

NELSON-SMALL, KATHY ANN, foundation administrator; b. Williamsport, Pa., Sept. 21, 1954; d. Dan LeRoy and Shirley Joann (Klein) Hoover; m. Robert Joseph Small, Feb. 14, 1996. BS in German Edn., Ind. U. of Pa., 1976; postgrad., Pa. State U., 1978-83. Tchr. German Hollidaysburg (Pa.) Area Sch. Dist., 1977-85; adminstr. Carlisle (Pa.) Project, 1985; dir. fin. devel. and pub. rels. Am. Lung Assn., York, Pa., 1986; chief profl. officer Adams County United Way, Gettysburg, Pa., 1987—. Press sec. Nancy Kulp's campaign for 9th Congl. Dist., Pa., 1984; mem. Main Street Gettysburg, 1987—, mem. pub. rels. com., 1996-98, 125th Battle of Gettysburg Anniversary Commn., 1988; treas. Adams County Coun. Cmty. Svcs., 1987-89, sec. 1995-99, Pa. State Club of Adams County, 1989—; mem. adv. bd. Adams County Job Ctr., 1989-91, Minority Youth Ednl. Inst., 1988-91, Intercultural Resource Ctr., Gettysburg Coll., 1989-91; mem. Adams Area Postal Customer Coun., 1987-89; dir. Adams Cmty. TV, 1988-89; mem. profl. adv. coun., chmn. small cities task force United Way Pa., 1990—, mem. network com., 1992-94, now mem. pub. sector impact com. and pers. com.; mem. planning com. United Way Leaders' Conf., 1995, also participant; mem. collaborative bd. Family Svc. Sys. Reform Initiative; bd. dirs. Adams County Interfaith Housing Corp., Adams County Coop. Ext., bd. dirs., 1996—, v.p., 2001—, sec., 1999-2000, strategic planning com. chair, 1999—; bd. dirs. Adams County Partnership for Cmty. Health, 1996—. Fulbright/Goethe Haus scholar, Stuttgart, Germany, 1982; named citizen of yr. Gettysburg-Adams County Area C. of C., 2000. Mem. Ctrl. Pa. Assn. Women Execs. (charter), Kiwanis (pres. Hist. Gettysburg chpt. 1989-95, chmn. dist. conv. Pa. chpt. 1992, dist. maj. emphasis program chairperson 1992-93), Gettysburg Rotary (club svc. chair 1998-2000, sec. 2000—), Pa. State Alumni Assn. (life), Gettysburg-Adams County Area C. of C. (pub. rels. com. 1989-98, strategic planning com. 1998—), Alpha Omicron Pi (endowment com. 1993—). Democrat. Lutheran. Avocations: travel, skiing, antiques, sewing, gardening. Home: 2566 Old Route 30 Orrtanna PA 17353-9417 Office: Adams County United Way PO Box 3545 Gettysburg PA 17325-0545 Office Phone: 717-334-5809. E-mail: uwaccares@planetcable.net.

NELSONWILLIAMS, CECELIA ELAINE, dietician, nutritionist; d. Henry Austin Williams and Geraldine Jackson; m. Reverend John Alexander Nelson, Aug. 26, 1995. MS, CUNY, 1982. Registered dietitian-nutritionist SUNY Edn. Dept., 1996. Food svc. dir., clin. nutritionist Sheepshead Nursing Home, Bklyn., 1987—93; nutrition cons. Met. Jewish Hospice Greater NY, 1994—; correctional health care nutritionist, 2002—. Adj. lectr. NYU Sch. Contunining Edn., NYC, 1992—96. Trustee N.Y. ann. conf. United Meth. Ch., White Plains, 1999—. Recipient Devoted and Loyal Svc. award, John Wesley United Meth. Ch., 1994, Vol. Am. Heart Assn. Recognition award, 1997. Mem.: Am. Dietetic Assn. (assoc.). Democrat. Methodist. Avocations: swimming, tennis, antique buyer, reading, travel. Home: PO Box 415 Mount Vernon NY 10552 Office: Health Edn Inst 100 Stevens Ave Mount Vernon NY 10550 Office Fax: 914-664-4797. Personal E-mail: ceceliard@aol.com.

NELUND, MARTHA, secondary school educator; b. Quito, Ecuador, May 15; m. John W. Nelund; 1 child, Brittany. BS in Comm. Disorders, Andrews U., Berrien Springs, Mich., 1985. Girls dean Ind. Acad., Cicero, Ind., 1988—91; tchr. Forest Lake Acad., Apopka, Fla., 1991—, head fgn. lang. dept., 2004—06. Sophomore sponsor Forest Lake Acad., Apopka, 2005—06. Mem.: ASCD, Spanish and Portuguese Tchrs. of SDA. Republican. Home: 2519 Walnut Heights Rd Apopka FL 32712 Office: Forest Lake Acad 3909 E Semoran Blvd Apopka FL 32712

NEMARA, VANESSA ANNE, federal official; b. Middle Village, N.Y., Aug. 24, 1953; d. Frank Joseph and Ann Margaret (O'Mara) Nemara; 1 child, Sophia Marie. BS in Police Sci., John Jay Coll., 1975, MA in Criminal Justice, 1980; MA in Nat. Security and Strategic Studies, Coll. of Naval Warfare, 2003. Salesperson Lane Bryant Dept. Store, N.Y.C., 1973-74; purchasing agt. Gen. Svc. Adminstrn., N.Y.C., 1973—78, bldg. mgmt. specialist, 1978—81, supr. contract specialist, 1982—85, U.S. Dept. Agr., Orient Point, NY, 1985-86, USCG, Governor's Island, NY, 1988—97, Norfolk, Va., 1996—. Roman Catholic. Avocation: baseball. Home: 1446 Shortleaf Ln Chesapeake VA 23320-0656 Office: 300 E Main St Ste 600 Norfolk VA 23510-9102 Office Phone: 757-628-4634. E-mail: vnemara@mlca.uscg.mil.

NEMECEK, GEORGINA MARIE, molecular pharmacologist; b. Mineola, N.Y., Aug. 27, 1946; d. George and Frances Valerie (Masaryk) N. AB, Mt. Holyoke Coll., 1968; PhD, U. Pa., 1972; Master's cert. in Project Mgmt., George Washington U., 2000. Cert. project mgmt. profl. Project Mgmt. Inst., 2005. Rsch. assoc. dept. biochemistry U. Mass. Med. Sch., Worcester, 1972-73, postdoctoral fellow of Am. Heart Assn., dept. biochemistry, 1974, asst. prof., 1974-80, assoc. prof., 1981-83; sr. scientist platelet dept. Sandoz Pharm. Corp., East Hanover, NJ, 1983-85, mem. sr. sci. staff, platelet dept., 1986, fellow, sect. head molecular biology, 1987-91, fellow diabetes, 1991-93, study dir. regulatory toxicology, 1993-96; team rep. internat. project preclin. safety Novartis Pharm. Corp., East Hanover, 1997, assoc. dir. project mgmt., 1997-2000, dir. project mgmt., 2000—02, dir. integrative compound and product profiling, 2002—03, dir. project review, biomarker devel., 2003—04, dir. neurosci. project mgmt., biomarker devel., 2004—. Vis. scientist dept. molecular biology, Princeton (N.J.) U., 1987, Sea Pharm. Inc., 1985, NATO, U. Libre, Brussels, 1979, biotechnology dept. Sandoz AG, Basel, Switzerland, 1988. Contbr. articles to profl. jours. Named Nat. Heart, Lung, and Blood Inst. Young Investigator, NIH, 1977-81. Mem. Am. Soc. Pharmacol. Exptl. Therapeutics, N.Y. Acad. Scis. (chmn. biochem. sect. 1992-94), Project Mgmt. Inst., Sigma Xi. Avocations: boating, gardening, riding, needlecrafts. Office: Novartis Pharm Corp 1 Health Plz East Hanover NJ 07936-1005 Office Phone: 862-778-2342. Business E-Mail: georgina.nemecek@novatis.com.

NEMEROWICZ, GLORIA, academic administrator; 2 children. BA, MA, Rutgers U., PhD in Sociology. Assoc. prof. sociology Monmouth Coll., NJ, provost NJ; exec. dir. Women's Leadership Inst. Wells Coll., Aurora, NY, 1993—96; pres. Pine Manor Coll., Chestnut Hill, Mass., 1996—. Author: (books) Children's Perceptions of Gender and Work Roles; co-author (with Eugene Rosi): Professionalism in Unpaid Work; contbr. op-ed pieces to newspapers. Office: Pine Manor Coll 400 Health St Chestnut Hill MA 02467

NEMETH, CHARLAN JEANNE, psychology educator; b. St. Louis, Dec. 29, 1941; d. Joseph Frank and Loretto Julia (Linkul) N.; children: Brendan Gibbs Nemeth-Brown, Lauren Loretto Nemeth-Brown. BA, Washington U., 1963; MA, U. Wis., 1965; postgrad., Oxford U., Eng., 1965-66; PhD, Cornell U., 1968. Fellow in law and psychology Battelle Seattle Rsch. Ctr., 1974-75; asst. prof. dept. psychology U. Chgo., 1968-73, U. Va., Charlottesville, 1973-75, U. B.C., Can., 1975-77, U. Calif., Berkeley, 1977—. Vis. prof. U. Bristol, Eng., 1969-70, Ecole des Hautes Etudes, Paris, 1969-70, U. Mannheim, Fed. Republic of Germany, summer, 1977, Ecole des Hautes Etudes en Sciences Sociale, 1984, 89; cons. in psychology and law. Author: Social Psychology: Classic and Contemporary Integrations, 1974, Differential Contributions of Majority and Minority Influence, 1986; contbr. chpts. to books, articles to profl. jours. Grantee NIMH, 1970-81, NSF, 1986-89; Hon. Woodrow Wilson fellow, 1963. Fellow Am. Psychol. Assn., Am. Psychol. Soc.; mem. Soc. for Exptl. Social Psychology, European Assn. Soc. Psychology (affiliate), Phi Beta Kappa. Democrat. Roman Catholic. Office: U Calif Dept Psychology Berkeley CA 94720-0001

NEMETH, DIAN JEAN, secondary school educator; b. Lakewood, Ohio, Mar. 5, 1949; d. Alex Ray and Doris Jean (Sakach) N.; 1 child, Kymberlee Marie. BS, Kent State U., 1971, MEd, 1994. Cert. home econs. tchr., vocat. consumer-homemaking tchr., Ohio. Tchr. vocat. family and consumer scis. Cleve. Bd. Edn., 1972—2002. Piloted modern design fine arts course Cleve. Bd. Edn., 1989-90; writer course of study for hospitality and facility care svcs. Active Tchrs.-Leader Inst., 1994-97, Urban Task Force. Mem. Greater Cleve. Assn. Family and Consumer Sci. (auditor 1994-95, treas. 1995-98, 2002-), Ohio Hotel and Motel Assn., Sigma Sigma Sigma (chpt. adv. bd. 1992, chpt. housing coord. 1992), Omicron Tau Theta. Democrat. Roman Catholic. Home: 12640 Sabal Park Dr Apt 106 Pineville NC 28134-7513

NEMETZ MILLS, PATRICIA LOUISE, engineering educator; b. Bethlehem, Pa., June 10, 1956; d. Stephen Andrew N. and Anna Julia Schadl; m. Alyn James Mills, June 18, 1983; 1 child, Andrea. BS in Mech. Engring., Pa. State U., 1979; MBA, Gonzaga U., 1985; PhD in Bus. Adminstrn., U. Wash., 1989. Project engr. Air Products and Chems., Trexlertown, Pa., 1979-83; instr. Gonzaga U., Spokane, Wash., 1984-85; prof. Ea. Washington U., Spokane, 1989—. Cons. Spokane Auto Transport, Auburn, Wash., 1985-95, Boeing, Seattle, 1988-89, Eldec, Seattle, 1988; instr., seminar leader Bulgaria, 1990, EWU/Montenegro U., 1991. Contbr. articles to profl. jours. Office: Ea Washington U 668 N Riverpoint Blvd Ste A Spokane WA 99202-1677

NEMIRO, BEVERLY MIRIUM ANDERSON, author, educator; b. St. Paul, May 29, 1925; d. Martin and Anna Mae Anderson; m. Jerome Morton Nemiro, Feb. 10, 1951-75; children: Guy Samuel, Lee Anna, Dee Martin. Student, Reed Coll., 1943-44; BA, U. Colo., 1947; postgrad., U. Denver. Tchr. Seattle Pub. Sch., 1945-46; fashion coord., dir. Denver Dry Goods Co., 1948-51; fashion dir. Denver Market Week Assn., 1952-53; free-lance writer Denver, 1958—. Moderator TV program Your Presch. Child, Denver, 1955-56; instr. writing and comm. U. Colo. Denver Ctr., 1970—, U. Calif., San Diego, 1976-78, Met. State Coll., 1985; dir. pub. rels. Fairmont Hotel, Denver, 1979-80; freelance fashion and TV model. Author, co-author: The Complete Book of High Altitude Baking, 1961, Colorado a la Carte, 1963, Colorado a la Carte, Series II, 1966, (with Donna Hamilton) The High Altitude Cookbook, 1969, The Busy People's Cookbook, 1971 (Better Homes and Gardens Book Club selection 1971), Where to Eat in Colorado, 1967, Lunch Box Cookbook, 1965, Complete Book of High Altitude Baking, 1961, (under name Beverly Anderson) Single After 50, 1978, The New High Altitude Cookbook, 1980. Co-founder, pres. Jr. Symphony Guild, Denver, 1959-60; active Friends of Denver Libr., Opera Colo.; mem. Friends of Painting and Sculpture, Denver Art Mus. Recipient Top Hand award Colo. Authors' League, 1969, 72, 79-82, 100 Best Books of Yr. award NY Times, 1969, 71; named one of Colo. Women of Yr., Denver Post, 1964. Mem. Am. Soc. Journalists and Authors, Colo. Authors League (dir. 1969-79), Authors Guild, Friends Denver Libr., Denver Women's Press Club, Kappa Alpha Theta. Address: Park Towers 1299 Gilpin St Apt 15W Denver CO 80218-2556

NEMIROFF, MAXINE CELIA, small business owner, art historian; b. Chgo., Feb. 11, 1935; d. Oscar Bernard and Martha (Mann) Kessler; m. Paul Rubenstein, June 26, 1955 (div. 1974); children: Daniel, Peter, Anthony; m. Allan Nemiroff, Dec. 24, 1979. BA, U. So. Calif., 1955; MA, UCLA, 1974. Sr. instr. UCLA, 1974-92; dir., curator art gallery Doolittle Theater, Los Angeles, 1985-86; owner Nemiroff Deutsch Fine Art, Santa Monica, Calif. Leader of worldwide art tours; cons. L'Ermitage Hotel Group, Beverly Hills, Calif., 1982—, Broadway Dept. Stores, So. Calif., 1979—, Security Pacific Bank, Calif., 1978—, Am. Airlines, Calif. Pizza Kitchen Restaurants; art chmn. UCLA Thieves Market, Century City, 1960—, L.A. Music Ctr. Mercado, 1982—; lectr. in field. Apptd. bd. dirs. Dublin (Calif.) Fine Arts Found., 1989; mem. Calif. Govs. Adv. Coun. for Women, 1992; mem. art selection com. Calif. State Office Bldgs., 1997—. Named Woman of Yr. UCLA Panhellenic Council, 1982, Instr. of Yr. UCLA Dept. Arts, 1984; recipient Woman of Achievement award Friends of Sheba Med. Ctr., 2003; elected to Fashion Circle of the Costume Coun., L.A. County Mus. Art, 1997—; honoree L.A. Art Core 15th Ann. Awards Benefit, 2003. Mem. L.A. County Mus. Art Coun., UCLA Art Coun., UCLA Art Coun. Docents, Alpha Epsilon Phi (alumnus of yr. 1983). Avocations: tennis, horseback riding, skiing, piano and guitar. Personal E-mail: mumseyart@aol.com.

NEMYIER, MARGARET GERTRUDE, sales executive; b. Herkimer, NY, Dec. 23, 1930; d. Franklin Clark and Reba Louise (Jones) Culver; m. Charles Henry Nemyier, July 22, 1978. BS, SUNY Oneonta, 1953; MS in Edn., SUNY Geneseo, 1973. Cert. elem. tchr. N.Y. Elem. tchr. Richfield Springs Ctrl. Sch., NY, 1953—54, Ilion Ctrl. Sch., NY, 1954—57, Webster Ctrl. Sch., NY, 1957—76; sales rep. Equitable Ins. Co., Perfield, NY, 1976—77; sales clk. Fuelihan's Dress Store, East Rochester, NY, 1977—79; with Projansky Furier & Dress Shop, Victor, NY, 1979—81; sales rep. Avon Products, 1977—. Sec.-treas. Webster Plank North PTA, 1959; vol. cemetery tours Mt. Hope Cemetery Orgn., Rochester, NY, 1978—83; vol. fundraiser at various PBA's, 1977—79; reach for recovery vol. Am. Cancer Soc., Rochester, 1981—86; vol. Gen. Herkimer's Homesite, Ilion Little Theatre Club, 2004; mem. planning com. Chester Gilette-Grace Brown Ann., 2005—06; cert. disaster team vol. ARC, 2005—06; election insp. Monroe & Herkimer Counties, NY, 1990—; coord. Ilion HS Mega Reunion Com., 2002. Recipient Cert. of Appreciation, Dept. of Recreation and Parks, Rochester, 1980. Mem.: NEA (life), Red Hat Soc. Democrat. Methodist. Avocations: latch hook rugs, embroidery, traveling to historic places, collectibles, Scherenschnitte (German scissor cuttings). Home: 236 E Main St Ilion NY 13357

NEOS, PERI FITCH, small business owner; b. San Pedro, Calif., Apr. 27, 1938; d. William Roosevelt Fitch and Adele (Russell) Kane; m. Thomas Harold Holston, May 27, 1957 (div. 1969); children: Kevin T. Russell, Kelly J. Russell, Adele H. Phillips; m. Konstantinos Demetrios Neos, July 3, 1981 (dec. March 28, 2001). BSL, Western State U. Coll. Law, 1975, JD, 1976. Process piping designer The Fluor Corp., L.A., 1965-68; sr. designer CF Braun, L.A., 1968-70; sr. designer, contractor various enginr./constrn. firms L.A., 1970-81; painting contractor, owner El Greco Painting, Hanford, Calif., 1981—2002; substitute tchr. Kings and Fresno County Sch. Dists., 1992—2003; self empolyed notary public Hanford, Calif. Mem. citizens adv. bd. alcohol and other drug programs, Kings County, Hanford, 1991-2003; mem. City of Hanford Hist. Resources Commn., 1994-2002; mem. Kings County Mental Health Bd., 2004—, chair, 2005; mem. st. tree commn., Hartford, 2004— With USN, 1956-58. Mem. AAUW, Hanford C. of C., Mensa. Avocations: iconography, reading, camping, choral singing. Home and Office: 426 N Redington St Hanford CA 93230-4452 Office Phone: 559-584-2329. Personal E-mail: peri1@sbcglobal.net.

NERENG, LINDA RAE, elementary school educator; b. Eau Claire, Wis., Feb. 21, 1957; d. Lloyd Eugene and Bernice Ruth (Peterson) Nicolet; m. Kenneth R. Nereng, June 23, 1947; children: TJ, Ashley. Bachelor's degree, U. Wis., Eau Claire, 1978, MEd, 1983. Tchr. St. Charles (Minn.) Pub. Sch., 1978—79, Blair-Taylor Sch. Dist., Blair, 1979—; summer recreation dir. City of Blair, 2002—. Chmn. kiddie parade Blaire Cheese Fest, 1986—; v.p. ch. coun. 1st Luth. Ch., Blair, 1996—2000. Recipient John and Ellie Ellison scholarship, U. Wis.-LaCrosse, 1999, Civic award, Blair Cheese Fest, 2003. Mem.: Blair-Taylor United Educators Assn. (negotiator for tchrs. union 2001—). Avocations: sewing, quilting.

NERO, MOLLY JOANNA, elementary school educator; b. Cin., Aug. 25, 1965; d. George E. and Vernie E. Costen; m. Bernard D. Nero, Apr. 20, 1991; children: Claire Nicole, Nicolas Joseph. BA, U. Tex., Austin, 1989. Cert. Tchr. Pre-K thru 6th Tex. State Bd. of Edn., 1995. Office mgr. Three Ring Svc., Austin, 1989—91; tchr. Brushy Creek Elem., Round Rock, Tex., 1993—. Peer mediation mentor Brushy Creek Elem., Round Rock, Tex., 1995—98, team leader, 1997—98. Dir.(choreographer): (six school musical prodns. yearly); singer (female lead): (musical prodn.) Carousel, My Fair Lady; singer: (2d female lead) West Side Story; singer: Annie. Home: 1705 Cedar Bend Dr Austin TX 78758 Office: Brushy Creek Elem - Round Rock ISD 3800 Stonebridge Dr Round Rock TX 78681 Office Phone: 512-428-3049. Personal E-mail: mobenero@sbcglobal.net. Business E-Mail: molly_nero@roundrockisd.org.

NERONI, JANE KESSLER, art educator; b. Bklyn., Aug. 12, 1940; d. Henry M. and Lillian (Horowitz) Kessler; m. Delmont P. Neroni, Aug. 28, 1966; children: Hilary, Nico. BA, U. Mich., 1962; MA, CCNY, 1968; cert. in sci. and tech. illustration, RISD, 1986. Cert. tchr., N.Y., R.I. Art tchr. N.Y.C. Pub. Schs., 1966-68; art tchr., adminstr. adult edn. YWCA, Kingston, N.Y., 1973-77; art tchr. youth programs RISD, Providence, 1987—; art tchr., chair dept. Alternate Learning Project, Providence, 1987-90; art tchr. Ctrl. HS, Providence, 1990—; art dept. chair Feinstein HS, Providence, 1994—; dir. nat. sci. illustration program, children's book illustration program, drawing painting studies R.I. Sch. Design, continuing edn. instr. drawing. Critic tchr. R.I. Sch. Design, 1990—; freelance Nat. Sci. Illustrator, Providence, 1986—. Grantee Pub. Edn. Fund, 1988, 90, 91-92, 93, R.I. State Coun. on Arts, 1992. Mem. Nat. Art Edn. Assn., R.I. Art Tchrs. Assn., Guild of Natural Sci. Illustrators.

NESBIT, LYNN, literary agent; BA in Speech, Northwestern U. Asst. to agent Sterling Lord; head literary dept. Internat. Creative Mgmt.; ptnr. Janklow & Nesbit Assocs., N.Y.C., 1989—. Achievements include representing leading authors, among others, Tom Wolfe, Toni Morrison. John LeCarre, Jimmy and Rosalynn Carter, Anne Rice, Nora Ephron, Michael Crichton and Gail Sheehy.

NESBIT, MELANIE ANN, athletic trainer; b. Salt Lake City, June 15, 1979; d. Dennis and Patricia Nesbit. AAS, Ricks Coll., Rexburg, Idaho, 1999; BS, Brigham Young U., Provo, Utah, 2001; MS, Ea. Ill. U., Charleston, 2004. Cert. athletic trainer NATA: Nebr., 2002, lic. Ill., 2003. Athletic trainer South Mountain Sports Medicine, Draper, Utah, 2002—03; head athletic trainer Alta H.S., Sandy, Utah, 2002—03, Lake Land Coll., Mattoon, Ill., 2003—, adj. faculty, 2004—, aerobic fitness ctr. co-supervisor, 2005—. Tchr. LDS Ch., Mattoon, Ill., 2004—06, family history cons., 2004—06. Named Acad. All Am., 1999; scholar Hart scholar, Brigham Young U., 2001, acad. scholar, 1999—2000, Ricks Coll., 1997—99. Mem.: Nat. Athletic Trainer's Assn., LDS Student Assn. (pres. 2003—04), Phi Theta Kappa. Mem. Lds Ch. Avocations: running, reading, softball, travel. Office Phone: 217-234-5374.

NESBITT, DEETTE DUPREE, small business owner, investor; b. Houston, May 5, 1941; d. Raymond Benjamin DuPree and Alice Lula (Cade) Foster; children: Alice L., Charles S. Massey Nesbitt; m. Ernest V. Nesbitt, Aug. 20, 1971. Student, Sam Houston State U., 1960-61, U. Houston, 1961-62, 81-83. Lic. real estate, Tex. Contbr. articles to various publs. Former trustee Pace Soc. Am., Inc., 1992-95, Ladies Oriental Shrine N.Am., Inc.; bd. dirs. Evergreen Friends, Inc., 1991-92; dir., sec. competitive swim team Dad's Club YMCA, Houston, 1981-83; vol. adminstrv. asst. numerous orgns., Houston; patron Houston Jr. League. Recipient Varina Howell Davis medal Mil. Order Stars and Bars, 1992, Silver Good Citizenship medal SAR, 1992, Honor award Tex. SCV, 1992; featured on Eyes of Texas, NBC, 1992, Nat. Honor award Hereditary Soc. Cmty., 2003; Ky. Col. Mem.: Nat. Soc. Colonial Dames Am. in Commonwealth of Va., Harris County Hist. Commn., Nat. Soc. Sons and Daus. Antebellum Planters 1607-1861, Freedoms Found. Valley Forge (George Washington Honor medal 1994), United Daus. Confederacy (Confederate Ball com. 1985—95, co-chmn. ball 1988, adv. to chmn. 1989, 1990, hon. chmn. Houston's confederate ball 1995, Charleston chpt. #4, So. Heritage Hall com. 2005—, Jefferson Davis Hist. award, Winnie Davis medal, Spl. Recognition award), Daus. Rep. Tex. (Appreciation award 1996), Nat. Gavel Soc., Nat. Jamestown Soc. (mem. coun. 1993—95, auditor gen. 1995—97, lt. gov. gen. 1997—98, gov. gen. 1998—2000, Resolution of Appreciation, Outstanding Leadership 2000), Plantagenet Soc., Soc. First Families of S.C. 1670-1700 (life; 3rd v.p.), Order of First Families of Va. 1607-1624 (life; mem. coun. 2001—, rec. sec. 2005—), Order of First Families of Miss. 1699-1817 (life), Nat. Soc. DAR, Huguenot Soc., S.C. Soc. Descs. of Colonial Clergy, Nat. Soc. Magna Charta Dames (Houston colony historian 1992—95), Am. Royal Descent, First Tex. Co. Jamestowne Soc. (lt. gov., gov. 1985—93, hon. gov. emerita), Dames of Colonial Cavaliers 1640-1660 (organizing dep. gov. gen. 2001—03, gov. gen. 2003—05, life hon. gov. gen. emerita), Colonial Dames Am. (pres. chpt. VIII 1995—97), Sons and Daus. of Pilgrims (nat. com. 1993—97), Galveston Yacht Club, Petroleum Club Houston. Republican. Episcopalian. Home: 15411 Old Stone Trail Houston TX 77079-4206

NESBITT, VERONICA A., program support analyst; b. Henderson, Tenn., June 10, 1959; d. Hiawatha Daniel and Laura Mae (Green) Thompson; divorced; children: Shemenya A. Davis, Maleka L. Cert. stenographer, Miller-Hawkins B. Coll., 1979; Cert. data transcriber, IRS, Memphis, Tenn., 1981; Cert. computer operator, U.S. Army, Newport News, Va., 1985, Cert. computer programmer, 1987; postgrad., Columbia Coll., 1990. Cert. computer opr. Stenographer Memphis & Shelby County Health Dept., Memphis, 1979-80; cash clk./data transcriber IRS, Memphis, 1980-82; data transcriber U.S. Army, Fort Sheridan, Ill., 1982-83, work order clk., 1984-85, quality control clk., 1985-89; mgmt. asst. HQ USAREC, Fort Sheridan, Ill., 1989-92; data transcriber Selective Svc., North Chicago, Ill., 1983-84; telemarketer Allstate Ins. Co., Northbrook, Ill., 1986-88, unit supr. Glenview, Ill., 1988-92; employee coun., 1994; total quality facilitator Allstate Ins. Co., Glenview, Ill., 1992; mgmt. asst. Hdqs. US Army Recruiting Command, Ft. Knox, Ky., 1992-94, 233d Base Support Bn., Darmstadt, Germany, 1994-97; staffing specialist Snelling Staffing Network, Columbia, Md., 1997-99; exec. adminstrv. asst. GSE Sys., Inc., Columbia, Md., 1999; mgmt. analyst Navy Internat. Programs/INS, Inc., 1999-2001; internat. jr. analyst/adminstr. Jil Info. Sys., Inc., 2001—03; program support analyst AT&T Govt. Solutions, 2003—. Mgmt. analyst INS, Inc., Washington, 1999—2001; chmn. task force Allstate, Glenview, 1990; interviewer Mathematica Policy Rsch., Inc., Columbia, Md., 1998—99, supr., 1999—; sr. cons. Mary Kay, 2004. Mem. Am. Heart Disease Found., 1991-92, Easter Seal Soc., 1991-92, March of Dimes, 1991—, Nat. Heart Rsch., 1991-95; mem. Nat. Cancer Rsch., 1991-95, fed. women's program mgr., 1995-97; treas. Second Glance Thrift Store, 1996-97; welfare com., continuing edn. grants Darmstadt Women's Club, 1995-96, chmn. Second Glance Thrift Store; counselor Equal Employment Opportunity, 1995-97; mem. Equal Opportunity Adv. Action Team, 1995-97; asst. supt. ch. schs. Asbury Town Neck United Meth. Ch., Severna Park, Md. Mem. NAFE, Am. Cancer Soc., Am. Heart Disease Prevention Found., Jack Anderson Internat. Platform Assn., Order Ea. Star (assoc. matron 1997). Baptist. Avocations: reading, knitting, drama, bicycling, sewing. Office: Naval Sea Systems Command 1333 Isaac Hull Ave Washington DC 20376 Office Phone: 410-872-7476. Business E-Mail: vnesbittself@marykay.com.

NESBITT, VIRGINIA, retired special education educator, poet; b. Blackwell, Okla., Nov. 22, 1944; d. Earl Raymond and Myrtle Iva Combs; m. Raymond Lee Delaney, Dec. 24, 1964 (div. Sept. 1977); m. Emmanuel William Benjamin Nesbitt, June 20, 1992 (div. Feb. 1997). BS in Spl. Edn., Ctrl. Okla. State U., 1975. Cert. tchr. Tex., Pa. Tchr. 5-County Coop, McAlester, Okla., 1985—86, Cotton-Comanche Coop, Faxon, Okla., 1986—88; tchr., cons. Vision Guest Sch., Franklin, Pa., 1990—92; tchr. Houston Ind. Sch. Dist., 1996—98, Mrs. Wagner's Pvt. Sch., Houston, 2000—01. Contbr. articles to profl. jours., poetry to anthologies. Bd. dirs. Ch. Daycare, Oklahoma City, 1973—75, dir., 1975—78. With U.S. Army, 1963—65. Mem.: Internat. Soc. Poets. Avocations: dance, reading, cooking, sewing, baking. Home: 3814 Lyons Ave Apt 335 Houston TX 77020-8354

NESBITT, WANDA L., ambassador; b. Phila., Dec. 1956; married. BA in Internat. Rels. and French, U. Pa., 1978; postgrad., Nat. War Coll., 1996—97. Vice-consul Dept. State, Port-au-Prince, Haiti, 1982—83, Paris, 1983—85, with Bur. L.Am., 1986—88, regional consular officer Kinshasa, Zaire, 1990—92, with consular affairs Kinshasa, Zaire, 1992—93, with legis. affairs, 1995—96, dep. chief of mission Kigali, Rwanda, 1997—99, Dar es Salaam, Tanzania, 1999—2001, U.S. amb. to Madagascar, 2002—. Office: DOS Amb 607 Braxton Pl Alexandria VA 22301 E-mail: nesbittwl@state.gov.

NESHYBA, MONICA VASQUEZ, language educator; b. Austin, Tex., May 12, 1974; d. Phillip Ramirez Vasquez and Caroline Reyna-Davis; m. Victor Peter Neshyba III, May 26, 2001. BA in Spanish Lang., U. Tex., Austin, 1999; MEd in Elem. Edn., SW Tex. State U., San Marcos, 2001. Std. classroom tchg. cert. bilingual/ESL Gr.1-8 Tex. Bilingual tchr. Del Valle Ind. Sch. Dist., Tex., 1999—2005; tchg. asst. U. Tex., Austin, 2005; bilingual tchr. Austin Ind. Sch. Dist., Tex., 2005—06; program specialist Tex. Edn. Agy., Austin, 2006—. Contract curriculum developer and instr. Austin C.C., 2003—05. Grantee Polaroid Corp., 2004. Mem.: ASCD, NEA, Pi Lambda Theta, Kappa Delta Pi. Personal E-mail: mneshyba@mail.utexas.edu.

NESS, BERNICE HAGIE, retired music educator; b. Mpls., Sept. 4, 1926; d. John Leonard and Mathilda Caroline Hagie; m. Elmo Vernon Ness, Aug. 3, 1974. BS, U. Minn., Mpls., 1948, MEd, 1950. Elem. music supr. Lake Co. Schs., Two Harbors, Minn., 1950—51, Mounds View Dist. #621, New Brighton, Minn., 1951—54; tchr., choral music & music theory Mounds View H.S., New Brighton, Minn., 1954—81, tchr., choral music & French, 1981—83; ret., 1983. Mem. adv. bd. U. Minn. Alumni Band, Mpls., 1949—51, coun. mem., 1996—98; dir., arranger Mounds View Alumni Choir, New Brighton, Minn., 1996—2006. Chair, music com. Abiding Savior Ch., Mounds View, Minn., 1985—94; mem., music com. Christ the King Ch., New Brighton, Minn., 1995—97. Recipient Pillar award, Mounds View H.S., 2005.

NESS, SHARON L., social studies educator, coach; b. Boston, Feb. 25, 1970; d. Bruce A. and Arlene M. Fleming; m. William H. Ness, July 12, 2003; 1 child, Zachary P. BA in History, North Adams State Coll., Mass., 1992; MA in Tchg. History, Bridgewater State Coll., Mass., 1999. Lic. tchr. Dept. Edn., Mass., 1997, cert. Dept. Edn., Fla., 2004. Tchr. social studies Abington HS, Mass., 1997—2004, Lemon Bay HS, Englewood, Fla., 2004—; ind. beauty cons. Mary Kay Cosmetics, North Port, Fla., 2002—. Head coach girls cross country and track & field Abington HS, 1997—2004, sr. class advisor, 1999—2000; head coach girls track & field Lemon Bay HS, 2004—05, head coach girls cross country, 2004—. Author: (lesson plans) Making Freedom II Sourcebook. Vol. San Pedro Cath. Ch., North Port, Fla., 2006. Mem.: NEA (assoc.), Fla. Edn. Assn. (assoc.), Mass. Tchrs. Assn. (assoc.), Charlotte County Edn. Assn. (assoc.), Abington Edn. Assn. (assoc.; v.p. 2003—04). Avocations: running, reading, travel. Office: Lemon Bay HS 2201 Placida Rd Englewood FL 34224 Office Phone: 941-474-7702. Business E-Mail: sharon_ness@ccps.k12.fl.us.

NESS, SUSAN, federal official; married; 2 children. BA, Rutgers U., 1970; JD cum laude, Boston Coll.; MBA, U. Pa. Asst. counsel com. banking, currency and housing U.S. House of Reps.; founder, dir. jud. appointments project Nat. Women's Polit. Caucus; commr. FCC, Washington, 1994—2001. Chair Charter Rev. Commn., Montgomery County, Md.; vice chair Montgomery County Task Force on Cmty. Access TV; pres. Montgomery County Commn. for Women. Named one of 12 to Watch, Electronic Media, 1997. Mem. Nat. Assn. Regulatory Utility Commrs. (com. comm.), Leadership Washington, Fed. Comm. Bar Assn.

NESS MARINEAU, BRENDA L., language educator; b. Lodi, Wis., June 29, 1960; d. Dale Royal and Alice Audrey (Gasser) Ness; m. Stephen C. Marineau, June 29, 1985. BS in Social Studies and History, U. W. Madison, 1982; MS, U. W. Milw., 1989. Cert. secondary edn. with history, econ. and BFSS and ESL. History tchr. Waukesha North HS, Wis., 1982—89; econ. tchr. Waukesha South HS, Wis., 1990—96, bilingual/ESL tchr., 1996—. Exec. dir. Waukesha Area Sister City Assn., 1998—; grant coord. exchange projects: youth, law enforcement, domestic violence, community wide, etc. Recipient Wis. Global Educator, Freidns of Internat. Edn., 2002, Herb Kohl Tchg. award, Herb Vohl, Senator Found., 2003. Democrat. Avocations: exercise, reading, pet care, diving, travel, Spanish study. Office: Waukesha South HS 401 E Roberta Ave Waukesha WI 53186 Office Phone: 262-970-3837. Business E-Mail: bness@waukesha.k12.wi.us.

NESTLE, MARION, nutritionist, educator; BA in Bacteriology, U. Calif., Berkeley, 1959, PhD in Molecular Biology, 1968, MPH in Pub. Health Nutirition, 1986. Lab. technician, rsch. asst., Encephalitis Rsch. Lab. Sch. Pub. Health, U. Calif. Berkeley, 1959—61; postdoctoral trainee, dept. molecular biology U. Calif., Berkeley, 1963—68; postdoctoral fellow, dept. biology, biochemistry Brandeis U., 1968—70, postdoctoral fellow, dept. biology, develop. biology, 1970—71, lectr., biology Waltham, Mass., 1971—73, asst. prof. biology, 1974—76; lectr. biochemistry and biophysics U. Calif., Sch. Medicine, San Francisco, 1976—84, lectr. medicine, 1979—84, associated faculty, Inst. for Health Policy Studies and Inst. for Aging Health Policy, 1983—86, lectr. family medicine and cmty. medicine, 1984—85, adj. assoc. prof., family and cmty. medicine, 1985—86, assoc. dean, human biology programs, adminstrv. dir., med. scientist tng. program, acting dir., 1983—84, dir., John Tung/Am. Cancer Soc. Clin. Nutrition Edn. Ctr., 1984—86; sr. nutrition policy advisor, staff dir. for nutrition policy Office of Disease Prevention and Health Promotion, Dept. Health and Human Services, Washington, 1986—88, mng. editor, Surgeon General's Report on Nutrition and Health, 1988; prof., chair NYU, Steinhardt Sch. Edn., Dept. Nutrition, Food Studies & Pub. Health, 1988—2003, prof., dir., pub. health initiatives, 2003—04, Paulette Goddard prof., 2004—. Former bd. dir. Ctr. for Sci. in the Pub. Interest; mem. Calif. nutrition coun. State of Calif., Interdepartmental Coun. on Food and Nutrition, 1976—86; William Evans vis. fellow, physiology dept. U. Otago Sch. Medicine, 1983; faculty, US-Nicaragua Health Colloquium Health Ministry of Nicaragua and the Com. for Health Rights in Ctrl. Am., 1984; faculty, Sino-US workshop on edn. and culture Shanghai Mcpl. Health Dept., People's Republic of China, 1986; staff dir., nutrition policy bd. US Dept. Health and Human Services, 1986—88, staff liason Task Force on the 1990 Nutrition Objectives, 1986—88, mem. Task Force on the Homeless, 1986—88, staff liason NIH Nutrition, 1986—88, liason, USDA Dietary Guidance Working Group, 1986—88; dietetic intern Veterans Adminstrn. Med. Ctr., Bronx, NY, 1988—95; mem. Project LEAN NYC Health Dept., 1989—94; mem. external peer reviewed com. Univ. Medicine and Dentistry NJ, 1992—93; mem. expert advisory panel on changing the Am. diet Assn. of State and Territorial Health Officers, 1993; mem. external advisory com., WHELS trial U. Calif. San Diego Cancer Ctr., 1994—2000, mem. data mgmt. com., WHELS trial, 2000—; mem. vis. com., nutrition dept. Lehman Coll., 1996, Hunter Coll., 1996; ad hoc reviewer USDA grant awards, 1996; judge, final examinations French Culinary Inst., 1996—97; mem. com. on nutrition and food habits Internat. Union Nutritional Sci., 1997; mem. internat. jury Grande Covian award (Barcelona), 1997—2002; mem. Research!America! Nat. Advisory Com. on Prevention Rsch., 2000—; ad hoc grant reviewr NSF, 2001; mem. exec. com. World Health Policy Forum, Lausanne, 2002; mem. external advisory bd. Hunter Coll. Urban Pub. Health Program, 2002—; mem. internat. jury Slow Food award for Def. Biodiversity, 2002; chair NY State Health Dept. Heart Prevention Plan, 2002; mem. selection com. USDA Helios award for Communication Excellence, 2005; mem. Pediatric Pulmonary Ctr., Mt. Sinai Med. Ctr., 1990—92, Nat. Cancer Inst. Ethnic and Law Literacy Materials Project, 1991—93, Vis. Com., Nutrition Dept., NY Med. Coll., 1991, HRSA/NIH Resource Com. on Nutrition Edn. for Physicians, 1992, FDA Food Adv. Com., 1992—95, NY State Commn. on Dietetics and Nutrition, 1993—97, US Dept. Health and Human Services/USDA Dietary Guidelines Adv. Com., 1994—95, Private and Pub., Scientific, Academic and Consumer Food Policy Com., Harvard Bus. Sch., 1995—, Dept. Health and Human Services/PHS editl. adv. bd. for the Surgeon General;s Report on Dietary Fats and Health, 1998—99, Nat. Cancer Inst. Nutrition Implementation Com., 1998—2000, FDA Sci. Adv. Bd., 1998—2001, Expert Panel on Dietary Supplementation for Food Stamp Recipients, Life Sciences Rsch. Office, 1998; cons. US Agy. for Internat. Develop., Bangkok and Jakarta, 1986, Fed. Trade Commn., 1988—91, 1996—97, Nutrition Counseling Sect., US Preventative Services Task Force, 1988—89, Hungarian Ministry of Health and Social Welfare, Budapest, 1989, N.Am.-Cuban Scientific Exchange, Ministry of Health, Havana, 1990, NYC Human Resources Adminstrn., 1990—91, NYC Dept. Health, 1990—91, Iowa State Atty. General's Office, 1990—91, Nat. Cancer Inst., Multi-Ethnic Nutrition Project, 1991—93, WHO Regional Office for Europe, Health Ministry of Mauritus, 1991, Consumer Reports, Zillions TV Project, 1992, U. Calif. San Diego, Cancer Rsch. inst., 1992, Scribner's/Simon & Schuster, The Joy of Cooking, 1996, WHO Regional Office for Europe, Copenhagen, 1995, Hunter Coll. Sch. Health Sciences, 1996, World Bank, 2002, WHO, Geneva, 2002—; invited presenter in field; conference spkr. Pub. Health Advocacy Inst.; mem. adv. com., Wagner Sch. Pub. Svc., Advanced Mgmt. Program for Clinicians NYU, 1988—92, mem., faculty resource network planning com., 1991—92, mem. curriculum challenge grant review com., 1991—98, mem., middle state organizational profile com.: internat. edn. and rsch., 1993, mem. adv. com., biology core curriculum, 1996—97, mem. review com., Whitehead faculty fellowship, 1995—98, mem., com. on promotion and tenure, sch. edn., 1996—98, chair, com. on promotion and tenure, sch. edn., 1998, mem. steering com., Internat. MPH program develop., 2003—, mem. adv. com., faculty collections, Bobst Libr., 2004—, mem. com. on promotion and tenure, Steinhardt Sch. Edn., 2004—; chair to all the following committees at U. Calif. San Francisco, Sch. Medicine: Women's Faculty Assn., Med. Scientist Tng. Program Coun., Human Biology adv. coun., curriculum subcommittee on nutrition, Chancellor's Task Force on the Child Care/Study Ctr., Chancellor's Com. on the Status of Women, Biochemistry med./pharmacy course com., admissions com. med. scientist panel, 1976—86; mem. of the following committees at Brandeis U. Adv. Com. to the Health and Mental Health Services, adv. com. minority spl. services bd. of premedical advisors, com. on admissions and financial aid, & program planning com., women's studies, 1971—76. Contbr. articles to profl. jours., chapters to books, to editorials, commentaries, encyclopedias, proceedings and reports; author: Nutrition in Clinical Practice, 1985, 1986, 1987, Food Politics: How the Food Industry Influences Nutrition and Health, 2002 (World Hunger Year Harry Chapin Media award, 2003, Assn. of American Publishers, Outstanding Profl. and Scholoarly Titles of 2002 (Category: Nursing and Allied Health), 2003, James Beard Found. Book award (category: Literary), 2003), 2004, 2005, Safe Food: Bacteria, Biotechnology, and Bioterrorism, 2003 (San Francisco Chronical Best Books of 2003, Daniel E. Griffiths Rsch. award, NYU Steinhardt Sch. Edn., 2004), 2004, 2005, What to Eat, 2006; co-editor: Taking Side: Clashing Views on Controversial Issues in Food and Nutrition, 2004; mem. adv. bd. Botany of Desire (PBS), 2002—, mem. editl. adv. bd. Nutrition Week, Gastronomica, and Jour. of Pub. Health Policy, Pub. Health Nutrition (UK), Jour. Culinary Sci. & Tech. (Dublin), Food and Foodways (UK) and European Jour. Pub. Health, editl. cons. The Lancet, former mem. editl. bd. Nutrition Reviews, Jour. Nutrition Edn., Eating Well, Cambridge World History of Food and Nutrition, Longevity Mag., Am. Health Mag., Nutrition Action Healthletter, frequent guest appearances and interviews ABC News, Boston Globe, British Medical Journal, Business Week, CNN, CBS News, Der Spiegel, Die Zeit, Financial Times, Fortune, Lancet, London Times, LA Times, Newsday, Newsweek, NY Observer, NY Times, People, Phila. Inquirer, Portland Oregonian, San Francisco Chronicle, TIME, USA Today, US News & World Report, Wall Street Journal, Washington Post, and others. Bd. dir. Ctr. for Cuban Studies, 1995—2002; mem. Commonwealth Policy Adv. Com., 1976—86, Episcopal Sanctuary Adv. Bd., 1976—86, East Harlem Healthy Heart Program, 1988—93; bd. dir. Ctr. for Sci. in Pub. Interest, 1988—93, mem. Citizens' Commn. on Sch. Nutrition, 1989—91; mem., Task Force on Nutrition Edn. Am. Heart Assn., NY, 1990—91; mem., Coun. on Sports Medicine and Sci., Nutrition Subcommittee US Olympic Com., 1990—91; chair, expert panel on children's food guidelines Ctr. for Sci. in Pub. Interest, 1990—92; mem. adv. bd. World Food Mus., 1992—98; mem., food adv. bd. Food and Hunger Hotline, 1993—94; grant reviewer Am. Cancer Soc., 1992—93, chair, prevention subcommittee on nutrition; dietary guidelines com., 1995—96, mem. nutrition and physical activity adv. com., 1995—2002; mem. adv. bd. NY Restaurant Sch., 1998—2002; disting. sci. sponsor NY Hall of Sci., 1998—; mem. scientific adv. com. Union of Concerned Scientists, 2001—; mem. scientific advisor Calif. Ctr. for Pub. Health Advocacy, 2002—; bd. dir. Slow Food, U.S.A., 2003—04; mem. adv. bd. Chez Panisse Found., 2005—. Named Nutrition Educator of Yr., Eating Well Mag., 1997, Food Influential, Self Mag., 1999, Pacesetter Educator of Yr., Roundtable for Women in Food Service, 1999, Women Who Change the Way We Eat, Health Mag., 2001, The Saveur 100 Favorites, Saveur Mag., 2004, Alumni of Yr., U. Calif. Berkeley, Sch. Pub. health, 2004, Obesity Warrior, Time Mag., 2004; named one of 100 Women Who Shape Our City, NY Daily News, 2004, Organic Style Environ. Power 50 List -Guardian of Good Eating, 2004; recipient Health Quality award, Nat. Com. for Quality Assurance, 2005; UCLA Ctr. for Soc., the Individual, and Genetics Fellow, 2004. Fellow: Soc. for Nutrition Edn. (mem. jour. policy advisory com. 1986—88), AAAS; mem.: Am. Dietetic Assn. (mem. com. on legislation and pub. policy 1986—88), Soc. for Epidemiological Rsch., NY Acad. Pub. Edn., NY Acad. Sciences, NY Acad. Medicne (mem. com. on pub. health 1988—94, mem. NY-NJ Regional Ctr. for Clin. Nutrition 1989—92, chair, subcommittee on nutrition edn. 1992—93), Pub. Health Assn. NYC, Nat. Assn. for Pub. Health Policy (vice-chair, coun. on food policy 1991—93), James Beard Found. (judge, journalism awards 1993—96, judge, book awards 1996—2002, Lifetime Achievement, Who's Who in Food and Beverage in America 2003), Internat. Assn. of Culinary Profls., Ctr. for Sci. in the Pub. Interest, Assn. for the Study of Food and Soc., Am. Soc. for Nutrition Sci., Am. Soc. for Clin. Nutrition (mem. awards com. 2000—02), Am. Pub. Health Assn. (mem. food and nutrition sect. coun. 1997—98, Food and Nutrition Sect., Excellence in Dietary Guidance award 1994, David P. Rall award for Advocacy in Pub. Health 2004), Les Amis D'Escoffier, Am .Inst. Wine and Food, Women Chefs and Restaurateurs, Les Dames d'Escffier. Office: Dept Nutrition Food Studies & Pub Health NYU 35 W 4th St 12th Fl New York NY 10012-1172 Office Phone: 212-998-5595. Office Fax: 212-995-4192. Business E-Mail: marion.nestle@nyu.edu.*

NESTOR CASTELLANO, BRENDA DIANA, real estate company executive; b. Palm Beach, Fla., Nov. 10, 1948; d. John Joseph and Marion O'Connor Nestor; m. Robert Castellano. Student, U. Miami, Fla., 1978. Lic. real estate broker, Fla. Salesman Oscar E Dooley, Inc., Miami, Fla., 1978-80; prin. Brenda Nestor Assocs, Inc., Miami Beach, Fla., 1980—. Exec. v.p., bd. dirs. D.W.G. Corp., 1988-94, N.V.F. Corp., Salem Corp., 1988-97, Southeastern Pub. Svc., Graniteville Corp., 1988-94, Essex Ins., Chesapeake Ins.; exec. v.p., dir. Security Mgmt. Bd. dirs. Vizcayan Mus.; dir. Miami's Jackson Meml. Found. Named Ms. Charity, City of Miami, 1985, Lady Comdr., State of Fla. Mem. Miami Beach Bd. Realtors (bd. dirs. 1984—), Real Estate Securities and Exch. Com., Knights of Malta, Doubles Club (N.Y.C.), La Gorce Country Club, Fisher Island Club, Surf Club, Ocean Reef Club, Carnegie Abbey (R.I.) Espicopalian. Avocations: golf, tennis, boating. Home and Office: 39 Palm Ave Miami FL 33139-3263 E-mail: ladybnestor@aol.com.

NETTELS, ELSA, English language educator; b. Madison, Wis., May 25, 1931; d. Curtis Putnam and Elsie (Patterson) Nettels. BA, Cornell U., 1953; MA, U. Wis., 1955, PhD, 1960. From instr. to asst. prof. English Mt. Holyoke Coll., South Hadley, Mass., 1959-67; from asst. prof. to prof. English Coll. William and Mary, Williamsburg, Va., 1967-97, prof. emeritus, 1997—. Author: James and Conrad, 1977 (South Atlantic MLA award, 1975), Language, Race and Social Class in Howells' America, 1988, Language and Gender in American Fiction: Howells, James, Wharton, and Cather, 1997; contbr. articles to profl. jours. Fellow, NEH, 1984—85. Mem.: MLA, South Atlantic MLA (mem. editl. bdl. 1977—83), Henry James Soc. (mem. editl. bd. 1983—). Office: Coll William and Mary Dept English Williamsburg VA 23187 Office Phone: 757-221-3905. Business E-Mail: exnett@wm.edu.

NETTLES, JENNIFER, singer; b. Atlanta, Ga., Sept. 12, 1974; BA, Agnes Scott Coll., Decatur, Ga. Lead singer Soul Miner's Daughter, 1996, Jennifer Nettles band, Sugarland, 2002—. Signed to Mercury Records. Singer: (albums) (solo albums) Story of Your Bones, 2000, (with Sugarland) Twice the Speed of Life, 2004. Recipient Ind. Musician of Yr. award, 2001, New Duo/Group award, Acad. Country Music, 2006. Office: Gail Gellman Mgmt 23852 PCH 920 Malibu CA 90265 Office Phone: 310-456-2620. Office Fax: 310-456-1415. E-mail: gellmanmgmt@aol.com, sugarlandmail@aol.com.*

NETTLES, KATHRYN CHAPPELL, visual artist, educator; b. Clarksville, Va., Nov. 4, 1938; d. Robert Harvey and Edna Kathryn (Lumpkin) Chappell; m. Edwin Carter Nettles Jr., July 19, 1958; children: Bryar Chappell, Kathryn Carter, Edwin Carter III. BA, Coll. William & Mary, 1984. Art instr. K-12 Tidewater Acad., Wakefield, Va., 1985-89; art instr. Rawls Mus. Arts, Courtland, Va., 1985—. One woman shows include Va. State U., Petersburg, 1984, Coll. William & Mary, Williamsburg, Va., 1984. Sr. warden Christ Episcopal Ch., Waverly, Va., 1996, jr. warden, 1997; mem. County Dem. Com., Sussex, Va., 1980-90; bd. dirs. Petersburg (Va.) Art League, 1980-81, Wakefield (Va.) Found., 1985-88; commr. Va. Commn. Arts, Richmond, 1988-93; bd. trustees Walter C. Rawls Libr. & Mus., Courtland, 1994—. Recipient Disting. Svc. award Va. Alliance Art Edn., 1994. Mem. Am. Watercolor Soc. (assoc.), Va. Watercolor Soc. (signature mem.), Va. Mus. Fine Arts, Rawls Mus. Arts, Perterburg Area Art League. Avocations: gardening, boxwood propagation, reading, needlecrafts. Home and Office: 323 E Church St Wakefield VA 23888-2739

NETTLES, SAUNDRA R. MURRAY, psychologist, writer, educator; b. Atlanta, Ga., Jan. 6, 1947; d. Edna Lewis and George Halbert Rice; m. Donald Gaines Murray, Mar. 14, 1972 (div.); m. Reginald Nettles (div.); children: Alana Denise Murray, Kali Nicole Murray. BA, Howard U., 1963—67; MS, U. of Ill. Grad. Sch. of Libr. and Info. Sci., 1967—68, Howard U., 1972—74, PhD, 1972—76. Prof. and dept. chair Coll. of Edn., Ga. So. U., 2004—; assoc. prof. of human devel. U. of Md., 1994—2003; prin. rsch. scientist Johns Hopkins U. Ctr. for Social Orgn. of Schools, Balt., 1988—99; dir., office of field services United Planning Orgn., Washington, 1983—87; sr. rsch. scientist Am. Inst. for Rsch., Washington, 1978—82. Contbr. articles to profl. jours. Mem. Jack and Jill of Am., Columbia, Md., 1989—92; rsch. scholars panel Pathways to Coll. Network, Boston, 2001—04. Mem.: APA, APA Sect. on the Psychology of Black Women (pres. 1986—87), Environ. Design Rsch. Assn., Am. Ednl. Rsch. Assn. Office: Georgia Southern Univ Po B 8144 Statesboro GA 30460-8144 Office Phone: 912-681-0672. Office Fax: 912-681-5091. E-mail: snettles@georgiasouthern.edu.

NETZ, DEBORAH RUDDER, psychologist; b. Freeport, Tex., July 4, 1953; d. Leroy Brooks and Lois Carol (Mann) Rudder; m. Charles E. Netz, Dec. 30, 1977 (div. 1990); children: Elizabeth Anne, Andrew Charles. BFA, U. North Tex., 1975; MS, Angelo State U., 1992. Employment spl. Concho Resource Ctr., San Angelo, Tex., 1991-93; assoc. psychologist Denton (Tex.) State Sch., 1993-96; spl. edn. counselor Lewisville (Tex.) Ind. Sch. Dist., Tex., 1996—2006. Children's counselor Ann's Haven Hospice Bereavement Group, Denton, 1993-96; counselor Hospice of San Angelo (Tex.) Children's Bereavement Group, 1991-93. Mem. Pi Gamma Mu. Democratic. Methodist. Avocation: astrology. Office: 400 W Main St Lewisville TX 75057 Office Phone: 817-591-3613, 972-219-3892. Business E-Mail: dnetz@cebridge.net.

NETZER, LANORE A(GNES), retired educational administration educator; b. Laona, Wis., Aug. 27, 1916; d. Henry N. and Julia M. (Niquette) Netzer; m. Glen G. Eye, 1979. Diploma, Oconto County Normal Sch., 1935; BS, State Tchrs. Coll., Oshkosh, Wis., 1943; MS, U. Wis., 1948, PhD, 1951. Tchr. Goldhorn Rural Sch., Pound, Wis., 1935-36, Goldfield Sch., Pound, 1936-37, tchr., acting prin., 1937-39; tchr., prin. Spruce (Wis.) Grade Sch., 1939-41; tchr. pub. schs. Neenah, Wis., 1943-46; demonstration and critic tchr. Campus Sch. State Tchrs. Coll., Oshkosh, 1946-48, supr. student tchrs.' coll. instrn. Milw., 1950-55; teaching asst. U. Wis., Madison, 1948-50, assoc. prof. edn. Milw., 1955-63, prof. edn. adminstrn. Madison, 1963-77, emeritus prof., 1977—. Rsch. assoc. U.S. Office Edn., 1963-66; supr. student tchrs. coll. instrn. State Tchrs. Coll., Milw., 1950-55; mem. curriculum adminstrn. com. Wis. Coop. Curriculum Planning Program, 1945-52; mem. Wis. Joint Com. on Edn., 1957-59, E.B. Fred Fellowship Com., U. Wis., 1966—; ednl. cons. Educators Progress Svc., 1970—. Author: The Use of Industry Aids in Schools, 1952, (with Glen G. Eye) Supervision of Instruction: A Phase of Administration, 1965, 2d. edit., 1971, (with others) Interdisciplinary Foundations of Supervision, 1969, (with G. Eye) School Administrators and Instruction, 1969, (with others) Education Administration and Change, 1970, (with others) Supervision of Instruction, 1971, Strategies for Instructional Management, 1977; contbr. articles to profl. jours. Rsch. grantee Hill & Knowlton, Inc., N.Y.C., 1949; grantee Wis. Mfrs. Assn., 1954; recipient award of Distinction Nat. Coun. of Adminstrv. Women in Edn., 1975. Mem. AAUP, Wis. Edn. Assn. (life), So. Wis. Edn. Assn., Nat. Assn. Supervision and Curriculum Devel., Wis. Assn. Supervision and Curriculum Devel., Southwestern Assn. Supervision and Curriculum Devel., Wis. Elem. Sch. Prins. Assn., Am. Assn. Sch. Adminstrs., Wis. Assn. Sch. Dist. Adminstrs., Am. Edn. Rsch. Assn., Wis. Edn. Rsch. Assn., Univ. Coun. Ednl. Adminstrn., U. Wis. Alumni Assn. (life), U. Wis. Meml. Union (life), Phi Beta Sigma, Kappa Delta Pi, Pi Lambda Theta, Phi Delta Kappa. Office: U Wis Dept Ednl Adminstrn 1025 W Johnson St Madison WI 53706-1706

NETZER, NANCY, museum director, art historian, educator; b. Pitts., July 25, 1951; m. Robert A.S. Silberman, Nov. 10, 1974. MA, Harvard U., 1978, PhD, 1986; LittD (hon.), U. Ulster, No. Ireland, 2000. Asst. curator Mus. Fine Arts, Boston, 1982-90; prof. art history Boston Coll., 1990—; dir. McMullen Mus. Art, 1990—. Bd. advs. Internat. Ctr. Medieval Art., N.Y.C., 1990-94; dir. Internat. Ctr. Medieval Art, 1995-2000 Author: Medieval Objects in the Museum of Fine Arts, 1986, vol. II, 1991, Cultural Interplay in the Eighth Century, 1994, Memory and the Middle Ages, 1995, Fragmented Devotion, 2000, Secular Sacred, 2006. Bd. advisors Woodrow Wilson Nat. Fellowship Found.; gov. appointee bd. dirs. Mass. Found. Humanities; bd. dirs. ICMA, 1995. Fellow: Soc. Antiquaries. Office: McMullen Mus Devlin Hall #423 140 Commonwealth Ave Chestnut Hill MA 02467-3800 Business E-Mail: netzer@bc.edu.

NEU, JENNIFER ELIZABETH, music educator; b. Los Gatos, Calif., Mar. 27, 1972; d. Gerald Dean and Elizabeth Ann Goetsch; m. Gregg Eugene Neu, Aug. 11, 2000; 1 child, Nathan Eugene. B in Music Edn., No. State U., 1995. Pvt. vocal/piano instr., 1995—; mid. sch. music and drama tchr. Huron (S.D.) Pub. Schs., 1996—99; H.S. vocal tchr., musical dir. Aberdeen (S.D.) Pub. Schs., 1999—2001; mid. sch. vocal tchr. St. Michael (Minn.)-Albertville Schs., 2001—; ch. choral dir. Immaculate Conception Ch., Becker, Minn., 2002—. Showchoir/jazz dir. Aberdeen Pub. Schs., 1999—2001. Mem. cmty. builders St. Michael Mid. Sch., 2001—. Mem.: NEA (student coun. advisor 1997—99), Music Educators Nat. Conf., Am. Choral Dirs. Assn., Kappa Delta Phi (life), Sigma Alpha Iota (life Nat. scholar 1992). Republican. Roman Catholic. Avocations: music, fishing, theater, scrapbooks.

NEUBAUER, ANTONIA, educational association administrator; MA in French Lit., EdD in Ednl. Adminstrn. Lang. tchr. & researcher; co-chmn. Phila. Urban Affairs Coalition; founder, pres, CEO & chmn. Myths & Mountains, Inc., 1988—; founder & chmn. READ (Rural Edn. & Devel.) Global, 1991—. Bd. dirs. Phila. Futures, White Williams Found., Internat. House; cons. Lilly Endowment, US Dept. Edn. Recipient Friend of Nepal award, Assn. Nepalis in the Americas, Walk the Talk Global Citizen award, 2006. Achievements include READ Nepal received the Bill & Melinda Gates Found. Access to Learning award, 2006. Office: READ Global/Myths & Mountains Inc 976 Tee Ct Incline Village NV 89451 Office Phone: 800-670-6984, 775-832-5454, 775-832-5032. Office Fax: 775-832-4454. E-mail: info@readglobal.org, travel@mythsandmountains.com.*

NEUBAUER, LISA S., lawyer; b. Mpls., July 21, 1957; BA polit. sci., U. Wis., 1979; JD with honors, U. Chgo., 1987. Bar: Wis. 1987. Legis. aide to Fred Risser pres. Wis. State Senate, 1979—82; staff mem. U.S. Senate, 1982—84; law clk. to Hon. Barbara B. Crabb chief judge, U.S. Dist. Ct., We. Dist. Wis.; ptnr. Foley & Lardner LLP, Milw., chairperson recruiting com.-Milw. office, chairperson ins. dispute resolution practice group. Mem.: State Bar Wis., ABA, Racine Bar Assn., Milw. Bar Assn., Order Coif. Office: Foley & Lardner LLP 777 E Wisconsin Ave Milwaukee WI 53202-5306 Office Phone: 414-297-5507. Office Fax: 414-297-4900. Business E-Mail: lneubauer@foley.com.

NEUBURGER, JANE, education educator; d. Robert and Phyllis Marie (Amori) Laurenson; m. Louis David Neuburger, May 20, 1972; children: Louis, Thomas, Michael, Elizabeth. BA in English, Coll. of Mount Saint Vincent, N.Y.; MS, Western Conn. State Coll. Cert. tchr. Conn. Instr., lectr. Syracuse U., NY, 1985—92, freshman seminar coord., 1989—90, tutor, reading/writing specialist, 1985—2002, adj. asst. prof. writing, reading, 1992—2002, title IV student support svcs. program writing specialist, 1992—97, HEOP writing specialist, 1995—99, tutor coord., profl. and peer tutors, 1995—99, tutor coord., interim reading coord., 1999—2000, reading coord., tutor coord., 2000—02, dir. tutoring and study ctr., 2002—. Writing across the curriculum com. Cazenovia Coll., 1989—, task force outcomes measures, middle states evaluation, 1990, task force institutional program assessment, 1996—97, council bus. affairs., 1996—98, task force on academic program assessment, 1996—97, institutional review bd., 1996—2000, faculty forum sec., 1997—98, program assessment com., 1997—99, 2000—02, continuous quality assurance think tank team, 1998—99, faculty council sec., 1998—99, faculty council rep., 1998—99, council on enrollment mgmt., 1998, rank and tenure com., 1999—2000, faculty bd. trustees, 2000—01, chair, 2000—01, sec., campus liaison, 2001—02; adv. bd. SUNY, Delhi, 1998—2003; cons. Lumina Found., 2003. Reviewer (book) Improving Student Learning Skills, 1999; editor: (newsletter for) NYCLSA, 1996—99. Mem.: Math. Assn. Am., Nat. Coll. Learning Ctr. Assn., Assn. Tutoring Profls., Nat. Tutoring Assn., Coll. Reading and Learning, Nat. Council Tchrs. English, Am. Assn. Univ. Women, N.Y. Learning Skills Assn. (chair 1994—96, bd. position 1996—99, pres. elect 1999—2000, pres. 2000—01, immediate past pres. 2001—02, chair 2002, co-chair assessment and evaluation 2002—05, political action chair 2002—05, political liaison 2001—05), Nat. Assn. Developmental Educators (cert. bd. publs. 1999—2001, program proposal review com. 1999—2002, profl. devel. com. 2000—02, monograph review com. 2000—02, tng. coord. 2001—02, chair 2002—). Avocations: swimming, skiing, reading. Office: Syracuse Univ 111 Waverly Ave Ste 220 Syracuse NY 13244 Personal E-mail: jneuburg@syr.edu.

NEUERBURG-DENZER, URSULA, theater director, educator, actress; b. Bonn, Germany, May 18, 1962; U.S., 1990; d. Helmut Neuerburg, Doris Neuerburg-Heusler; m. Ralph Denzer; children: Clara Louise Denzer, Emil Jakob Denzer. Acting cert., Arne Baur-Worch Acting Sch., Berlin, 1987; BA, Freie U. Berlin, 1990; MA, NYU, 1992; postgrad., Freie U., 2003. Cert. midwife. Vis. asst. prof. U. Calif., Santa Cruz, Calif., 1996—99; resident dir. Swarthmore (Pa.) Coll., 1999—. V.p. Theater Zerbrochene Fenster, Berlin, 1985—90; pres. East Coast Artists, N.Y.C., 1992—96. Dir.: (Shakespeare) Macbeth, 1995, (Seneca) Trojan Women, 1997, (Brecht) Mother Courage, 1998, (Tretyakov) I Want a Baby, 2002. Named Outstanding Artist Visa, Internal Naturalization Svs., 1994, 1995; grantee, Arts Internat., 1992, Goethe Inst., 1992—94. Mem.: Theatre Comm. Group.

NEUFELD, ELIZABETH FONDAL, biochemist, educator; b. Paris, Sept. 27, 1928; married, 1951. PhD, U. Calif., Berkeley, 1956; DHc (hon.), U. Rene Descartes, Paris, 1978; DSc (hon.), Russell Sage Coll., Troy, N.Y., 1981; DSc (hon.), Hahnemann U. Sch. Medicine, 1984; DSc (hon.), Queens Coll., 1996. Asst. rsch. biochemist U. Calif., Berkeley, 1957—63; with Nat. Inst. Arthritis, Metabolism and Digestive Diseases, Bethesda, Md., 1963—84, research biochemist, 1963—73, chief sect. human biochem. genetics, 1973—79, chief genetics and biochem. br., 1979—84; prof. Dept. Biol. Chemistry Sch. Medicine U. Calif., 1984—, chmn. Dept. Biol. Chemistry Sch. Medicine, 1984—2004. Named Passano Found. sr. laureate, 1982, Calif. Scientist of Yr., 1990; recipient Dickson prize, U. Pitts., 1974, Hillenbrand award, 1975, Gairdner Found. award, 1981, Albert Lasker Clin. Med. Rsch. award, 1982, William Allan award, 1982, Elliott Cresson medal, 1984, Wolf Found. prize, 1988, Christopher Columbus Discovery award for biomed. rsch., 1992, Nat. Medal of Sci., 1994. Fellow: Fellow AAAS; mem.: NAS, Am. Soc. Gene Therapy, Am. Soc. Clin. Investigation, Am. Soc. Cell Biology, Am. Soc. Biochemistry and Molecular Biology (pres. 1992—93), Am. Chem. Soc., Am. Soc. Human Genetics, Am. Philos. Soc., Am. Acad. Arts and Scis, Inst. Medicine of NAS. Office: UCLA David Geffen Sch Medicine Dept Biol Chemistry 33-257 CHS 33-355 CH Box 951737 Los Angeles CA 90095-1737 Business E-Mail: eneufeld@mednet.ucla.edu.

NEUFELD, MAUREEN PATRICIA, elementary school educator; b. Phila., Sept. 27, 1955; d. John Little and Evelyn Pauline (Schimek) Forrest; m. Bradley John Neufeld, Jan. 1, 2004; 1 child, Matthew Dean Forrest; 1 child, Sarah Nicole McComb. BS in Elem. Edn., U. Nev., Las Vegas, 1977; postgrad., Weber State U., Utah. Cert. tchr. Utah. Tchr. 4-5th grade Webster Elem., Salt Lake City, 1978—79; tchr. 3rd grade Stansbury Elem., Stansbury Park, Utah, 1982—83; resource tchr. East Elem., Tooele, Utah, 1983—84, Stansbury Park Elem., 1984—87; tchr. 1st grade Bob Hope Primary Sch., Okinawa, Japan, 1987—88; resource tchr. 4th and 6th grade Monroe Elem., Utah, 1988—2001; tchr. math. Hunter Jr. High, Utah, 2001—02, Matheson Jr. High, Magna, Utah, 2002—. Grantee, Utah Edn. Assn., 2003, 305 Credit Union, 2005. Mem.: Granite Edn. Assn. (rep. 2003—05). Lds. Avocations: swimming, reading.

NEUFELD, NAOMI DAS, endocrinologist; b. Butte, Mont., June 13, 1947; d. Dilip Kumar and Maya (Chaliha) Das; m. Timothy Lee Neufeld, Nov. 27, 1971; children: Pamela Anne, Katherine Louise. AB, Pembroke Coll., 1969; M. in Med. Sci., Brown U., 1971; MD, Tufts U., 1973. Diplomate Am. Bd. Pediatrics, Am. Bd. Endocrinology. Intern R.I. Hosp., Providence, 1973-74, resident in pediatrics, 1974-75; fellow in pediatric endocrinology UCLA, 1975-78; staff endocrinologist Cedars-Sinai Med. Ctr., Los Angeles, 1978-79, chief pediatric endocrinology sect., 1979-85, dir. pediatric endocrinology, 1985—. Asst. research pediatrician UCLA, 1978-79, asst. prof.-in-residence pediatrics, 1979-85, assoc. prof.-in-residence, 1985—; med. dir. Kidshape Program Children's Weight Control, 1986—; pres. Neufeld Med. Group, Inc., 1996—; consulting physician Ventura County Med. Ctr., 1989—; attending physician Cedars Sinai Med. Ctr., 1995—; clin. prof. pediatrics Sch. Med. UCLA, 1995—; med. dir., owner, founder Kidshape, 1986—; cons. physician Pasadena Diabetes & Endoscopy Med. Group, 1998-2002 Contbr. articles to profl. jours. Mem. bd. deacons Pacific Palisades Presbyn. ch. 1988—. Named Clin. Investigator, NIH, 1978; grantee United Cerebral Palsy Soc., 1979, March of Dimes, 1981, NIH, 1983-88. Fellow Am. Coll. Endocrinology; mem. Am. Diabetes Assn., Soc. Pediatric Research, Endocrine Soc., Juvenile Diabetes Found. (research grantee 1980). Presbyterian. Avocations: sailing, reading, sewing, cooking. Home: 16821 Charmel Ln Pacific Palisades CA 90272-2218 Office: 8635 W 3rd St Ste 295 Los Angeles CA 90048-6113

NEUGEBAUER, CYNTHIA A., lawyer; b. Queens, NY, Apr. 26, 1964; BA, SUNY, Buffalo, 1986; MA, SUNY, Stony Brook, 1987; JD, Touro Coll., 1994. Bar: NJ 1995, NY 1996, US Dist. Ct. Ea. Dist. NY, US Dist. Ct. No. Dist. NY, US Dist. Ct. So. Dist. NY. Ptnr. Wilson, Elser, Moskowitz, Edelman & Dicker LLP, NYC. Mem. appellate courts com. State of NY. Mem.: ABA. Office: Wilson Elser Moskowitz Edelman & Dicker LLP 23rd Fl 150 E 42nd St New York NY 10017-5639 Office Phone: 212-490-3000 ext. 2496. Office Fax: 212-490-3038. Business E-Mail: neugebauerc@wemed.com.

NEUGEBAUER, MARCIA, physicist, researcher; b. NYC, Sept. 27, 1932; d. Howard Graeme MacDonald and Frances (Townsend) Marshall; m. Gerry Neugebauer, Aug. 25, 1956; children: Carol, Lee. BS, Cornell U., 1954; MS, U. Ill., 1956; D of Physics (hon.), U. New Hampshire, 1998. Grad. asst. U. Ill., Urbana, 1954-56; vis. fellow Clare Hall Coll., Cambridge, Eng., 1975; sr. research scientist Jet Propulsion Lab. Calif. Inst. Tech., Pasadena, 1956-96, disting. vis. scientist, 1996—2003; vis. prof. planetary sci. Calif. Inst. Tech., Pasadena, 1986-87. Mem. com. NASA, Washington, 1960-96, NAS, Washington, 1981-94; Regents lectr. UCLA, 1990-91; adj. sr. rsch. sci. Lunar & Planetary Lab., U. Ariz., 2002-; bd. dirs. Acad. Svcs. Corp., Ariz. Sr. Acad., pres., 2004—. Contbr. numerous articles on physics to profl. jours. Named Calif. Woman Scientist of Yr. Calif., Mus. Sci. and Industry, 1967, to Women in Tech. Internat. Hall of Fame, 1997; recipient Exceptional Sci. Achievement medal NASA, 1970, Outstanding Leadership medal NASA, 1993, Disting. Svc. medal NASA, 1997, COSPAR award for space sci., 1998. Fellow Am. Geophys. Union (sec., pres. solar planetary relationships sect. 1979-84, editor-in-chief Rev. Geophysics 1988-92, pres.-elect 1992-94, pres. 1994-96) mem. governing bd. Amer. Inst. Physics, 1995-97. Democrat. Home: 7519 S Eliot Ln Tucson AZ 85747-9627 Office: U Ariz Lunar & Planetary Lab 1629 E Univ Blvd Tucson AZ 85721 Business E-Mail: nmeugeb@lpl.Arizona.edu.

NEUMAN, ISABEL, mathematics educator; b. N.Y.C., Dec. 3, 1939; d. J. Morton and Irene Finke; m. David Wagner Neuman, June 18, 1960; children: Randi Levin, Leslie Spillman, Andrea Malkin. BS, Syracuse U., 1960; MA, Ariz. State U., 1978. Cert. Edn. Specialist Ariz. State U., 1980, in Elem. Edn. Ariz. Dept. Edn. Tchr. Westwood Sch., Park Forest, Ill., 1960—62, Little Friends, N.Y.C., 1968—70, Holiday Park, Phoenix, 1976—2002, math coach, tchr., 2002—. Pres. Hadassah, Phoenix, 1980—82. Named Tchr. of Yr., Walmart, Tempe, Ariz., 2002; recipient Vol. award, 4-H, 2003, Urban Forest award, Phoeniz Pk. and Recreation, 2003; grantee, Wells Fargo, 1999, 2001. Mem.: Nat. Coun. Tchrs. Math. Avocations: reading, music box collecting, travel, music. Home: 15806 W Acapulco Ln Surprise AZ 85379

NEUMAN, LINDA KINNEY, retired state supreme court justice, lawyer; b. Chgo., June 18, 1948; d. Harold S. and Mary E. Kinney; m. Henry G. Neuman; children: Emily, Lindsey. BA, U. Colo., 1970, JD, 1973; LLM, U. Va., 1998. Ptnr. Betty, Neuman, McMahon, Hellstrom & Bittner, 1973-79; v.p., trust officer Bettendorf Bank & Trust Co., 1979-80; dist. ct. judge, 1982-86; supreme ct. justice State of Iowa, 1986—2003; ptnr. Betty Neuman & McMahon. L.L.P., Davenport, Iowa, 2003—05. Mem. adj. faculty U. Iowa Law Sch., 2003-; part-time jud. magistrate Scott County, 1980-82; mem. Supreme Ct. continuing legal edn. commn.; chair Iowa Supreme Ct. commn. planning 21st Century; mem. bd. counselors Drake Law Sch., time on appeal adv. com. Nat. Ctr. State Cts.; mem. Uniform State Laws Commn., 2004. Trustee St. Ambrose U. Recipient Regents scholarship, U. Colo. award for disting. svc. Fellow ABA (life; chair appellate judges conf., mem. appellate standards com., JAD exec. coun.); mem. Am. Judicature Soc., Iowa Bar Assn., Iowa Judges Assn., Scott County Bar Assn., Nat. Assn. Woman Judges (bd. dirs.), Dillon Am. Inn of Ct. (pres. 2003-04), US Assn. Constl. Law, Am. Acad. ADR Attys. (pres. 2006), Nat. Uniform Laws Comm. (commnr., 2004). Office Phone: 563-289-3255. Business E-Mail: lkn@neumanadr.com.

NEUMAN, NANCY ADAMS MOSSHAMMER, civic leader; b. Greenwich, Conn., July 24, 1936; d. Alden Smith and Margaret (Mevis) Mosshammer; m. Mark Donald Neuman, Dec. 23, 1958; children: Deborah Adams, Jennifer Fuller, Jeffrey Abbott. BA, Pomona Coll., 1957; LLD, 1983; MA, U. Calif., Berkeley, 1961; LHD, Westminster Coll., 1987. Disting. lectr. Am. govt. Pomona Coll., 1990; disting. vis. prof. Washington and Jefferson Coll., 1991, 94, Bucknell U., 1992. Editor: A Voice of Our Own: Leading American Women Celebrate the Right to Vote, 1996, True to Ourselves: A Celebration of Women Making a Difference, 1998. Pres. Lewisburg (Pa.) LWV, 1967-70; bd. dirs. LWV Pa., 1970-77, pres., 1975-77; bd. dirs. LWV U.S., 1977-90, 2nd v.p., 1978-80, 1st v.p., 1982-84, pres., 1986-90; mem. Pa. Gov.'s Commn. on Mortgage and Interest Rates, 1973, Pa. Commonwealth Child Devel. com., 1974-75, Nat. Commn. on Pub. Svc., 1987-90; bd. dirs. Housing Assistance Coun., Inc., Washington, 1974—2003, pres., 1978-80; bd. dirs. Nat. Coun. Agrl. Life and Labor, 1974-79, Nat. Rural Housing Coalition, 1975-95, Pa. Housing Fin. Agy., 1975-80, Jud. Inquiry and Rev. Bd. Pa., 1989-93; disciplinary bd. Supreme Ct. Pa., 1980-85; mem. Pa. Gov.'s Task Force on Voter Registration, 1975-76, Nat. Task Force for Implementation Equal Rights Amendment, 1975-77; mem. adv. com. Pa. Gov.'s Interdepartmental Coun. on Seasonal Farmworkers, 1975-77; mem. Appellate Ct. Nominating Commn. Pa., 1976-79; mem. Fed. Jud. Nominating Commn. Pa., 1977-85, chmn., 1978-81, 82-83; mem. Pa. Gov.'s Study Commn. on Pub. Employee rels., 1976-78; del. Internat. Women's Yr. Conf., 1977; bd. dirs. ERAmerica, Inc., 1st v.p., 1977-79, Nat. Low Income Housing Coalition, 1979-82; Rural Am., 1979-81, Fed. Home Loan Bank Pitts., 1979-82; mem. Nat. adv. Com. Women, 1978-79; mem. nat. adv. com. Pa. Neighborhood Preservation Support Sys., 1976-77; bd. dirs. Pa. Women's Campaign fund, 1984-86, 92-2002, pres., 1992-96, 2001-02, Rural coalition, Washington, 1984-90, Com. on the Constitutional Sys., 1988-90, Am. Judicature Soc., 1989-93; exec. com. Leadership Conf. Civil Rights, 1986-90; bd. dirs. Pennsylvanians for Modern Cts., 1986—; trustee Citizen's Rsch. Found., 1989-99; mem. mid. dist. Pa. adv. com. judicial and U.S. atty. nominations, 1993-94; bd. dirs. Pathmakers, 1993-97, pres. 1993-95; bd. dirs. Capital Concerts, 1997—. Virginia Travis lectureship Bucknell U., 1982; Woodrow Wilson vis. fellow, 1993-2000; recipient Disting. Alumna Award MacDuffie Sch. Girls, 1979, Liberty Bell award Pa. Bar Assn., 1983, Barrows Alumni Award Pomona Coll., 1987, Disting. Daus. of Pa. award, 1987, Thomas P. O'Neill Jr. award for Exemplary Pub. Svc., 1989. Mem. ABA (com. election law and voter participation 1986-90, accreditation com. 1990-96, coun. sect. legal edn. 1997-03), Disting. Daughters Pa. (pres. 2005, Disting. Daughters Pa. award 1987), Cosmos Club. Home: 190 Verna Rd Lewisburg PA 17837-8747 Business E-Mail: neuman@bucknell.edu.

NEUMAN, PAULA ANNE YOUNG, cultural organization administrator; b. Tiffin, Ohio, Sept. 15, 1960; d. Paul Everett and Mary Virginia (Brocious) Young; children: Nichole Adele, Jessica Theresa, Samantha Rebekah, Mary Elizabeth; m. Russell M. Neuman, Aug. 19, 2000. BS in Psychology, Heidelberg Coll., 1982; MA in Polit. Sci., Bowling Green (Ohio) State U., 1987; MA in Adult Edn., Ball State U., 1996; EdD, Nova Southeastern U., Ft. Lauderdale, Fla., 2000; cert. in fundraising mgmt., Ind. U., 1997; postgrad., Adler Sch. Profl. Psychology, 2004—, MA in Counseling Psychology, 2006. Cert. tng. cons. CTC; Ball State U., 2003, human performance improvement IUPUI, 2004. Child therapist Sandusky (Ohio) Youth Referral Svc., 1982-83; parole officer State of Ohio, Columbus, 1983-86; dep. dir. Seneca, Sandusky and Wyandot Commn. Mental Health Bd., Tiffin, 1987-88; program dir. WSOS Cmty. Action Commn., Fremont, Ohio, 1988-90; exec. dir. Tiffin Area C. of C./Seneca Indsl. & Econ. Devel. Corp., Tiffin, 1988-90; pres. Chapman Cmty. Devel. Cons., Tiffin, 1990—93; dir. devel. St. Francis Health Care Ctr., Green Springs, Ohio, 1993-94, St. Francis Coll., Fort Wayne, Ind., 1994-95; dir. of fund devel. Girl Scout Coun., Inc., Fort Wayne, 1995-97; exec. dir., CEO McMillen Ctr. for Health Edn., Fort Wayne, 1997-2000; pres., owner edn. and devel. cons., 2000—. Adj. prof. econs. Tiffin U., 1987—94; adj. prof. non-profit mgmt. Ivy Tech. State Coll., 1999—2000; mem. edn. adv. bd. Vanguard/Sentinel Vocat Sch., Fremont, 1989—90; chmn. Tiffin Fair Housing Bd., 1985—90; bd. dirs. Ohio Indsl. Tng. Program, Sandusky, 1988—90, Pvt. Industry Coun., Fremont, Seneca County Revolving Loan Fund, Tiffin; chair adv. bd. WSOS; cons. in field. Candidate Seneca County Commr., 1992; mem. Grad. Ft. Wayne Leadership Works, 1994; bd. dirs. Purdue U. Ext., 2000-02; founder, bd. dirs. Children of Divorce & Broken Relationships. Mem. Nat. Soc. Fundraising Execs. (bd. dirs. Ind. chpt. 1999-2002), Bus. and Profl. Women's Assn. (Young Career Woman of Yr. 1987, 89), Glens of Liberty Mills Assn. (bd. dirs., sec., 2002-03, 2005-, pres. 2003-2005). Avocations: philanthropic studies, childrens rights issues. Home: 6217 Spy Glass Run Fort Wayne IN 46804 Office Phone: 260-436-7137. Personal E-mail: neumans2000@yahoo.com.

NEUMANN, EVA, information technology executive; BS, Univ. Md. Sr. mgmt. positions Nat. Trade Productions, Govt. Tech. Services Inc.; founder & pres. ENC Mktg. & Communications, McLean, Va. Bd. mem. Fed. Info. Resources Mgmt. Assn.; pres. Women in Tech.; bd. mem. Mid-Atlantic region Make-A-Wish, Capital Speakers Club; mem. exec. bd. AFFIRM. Named a Heroine in Tech., March of Dimes & Women in Tech., 2005. Office: ENC Mktg & Communications Ste 401 1420 Spring Hill Rd Mc Lean VA 22102*

NEUMANN, IRMA WANDA, musician, educator; b. L.A., Apr. 9, 1916; d. William and Wanda Gisella Neumann. Studied with, Carmon Luboviski and Felix Slatkin. First violin Hancock Ensemble, L.A., 1943, L.A. Philharm. Orch., 1944—45, 20th Century Fox film Orch., L.A., 1946—58; free lance musician L.A., 1958—. Tchr. violin, L.A.

NEUMANN, LISELOTTE, professional golfer; b. Finspang, Sweden, May 20, 1966; With LPGA, 1987—. Mem. European Solheim Cup Team, 1990, 92, 94, 96, 98. Named Golf Digest Rolex Rookie of Year, 1988, Swedish Golfer of Year, 1994, GolfWorld's Most Improved Golfer, 1994. Achievements in LPGA victories include: U.S. Women's Open, 1988, Mazda Japan Classic, 1991, Minn. LPGA Classic, 1994, Weetabix Women's Brit. Open, 1994, GHP Heartland Classic, 1994, Chrysler-Plymouth Tournament of Champions, 1996, PING/Welch's Championship, 1996, First Bank-Edina Realty Classic, 1996, Welch's Champsionship, 1997, Toray Japan Queens Cup, 1997, Standard Register Ping, 1998, Chick-fil-A Charity Championship, 1998; other victories include: European Open, 1985, German Open, 1986-88, French Open, 1987, Solheim Cup, 1998. Office: LPGA 100 International Golf Dr Daytona Beach FL 32124-1092

NEUMANN, LUCI, rehabilitation center executive; Joined as physical therapist then to mgmt. positions Baylor Inst. for Rehabilitation, Dallas, 1987—, pres., 2003—. Bd. dir. N Tex. Health Care Laundry. Office: Baylor Inst for Rehabilitation 3505 Gaston Ave Dallas TX 75246-2018*

NEUMANN, NANCY RUTH, private school educator; b. L.A., Feb. 1, 1948; d. Robert Thomas and Frances Andersen; m. Bernd Fritz Dietmar Neumann, June 26, 1971; children: Peter, Christina, Linda, Christoph, Karin. BA, U. Calif., Riverside, 1969; MA, Sorbonne U., Paris, 1971; credentials, Calif. State U., San Bernardino, 1985. Cert. community coll. tchr., various subjects, Calif., studio tchr., Calif. Missionary, reading instr., Maroua, Cameroon, Africa, 1971-73; instr. Pasadena (Calif.) City Coll., 1974-75; secondary tchr. Riverside (Calif.) Christian Sch., 1985-86; studio tchr. Vista Films, Culver City, 1986, Hollywood (Calif.) Studios, 1986-88, Paramount Studios, Hollywood, Calif., 1986—2006, MGM - Lorimar Prodns., Culver City, Calif., 1986-91, Universal Studios, Universal City, Calif., 1986-90, R.J. Louis Prodns., Burbank, Calif., 1987, Michael Landon Prodns., Culver City, 1987-88, Carsey-Werner Prodns., L.A., 1988; instr. Riverside Community Coll., 1988; studio tchr. Bob Booker Prodns., Hollywood, 1988-90, Walt Disney Prodns., Burbank, 1992—; exec. producer Am. Pictures, Riverside, 1989—; studio tchr. NBC Prodns., Burbank, 1990—2003, New Line Cinema, 1991—2006, 20th Century Fox, 1993—2004, Warner Bros., 1996—2004, CBS, 2005—06. Pvt. tutor, Riverside, L.A., 1987—; drama coach Grace Ch., Riverside, 1981-82, Magnolia Ave. Bapt. Ch. Riverside, 1986-89. Author: several plays, 1981-89; writer 80 songs, 1968—2004; pub. access TV prodr. Nancy Norway Presents: Windmills, L.A. and Riverside, 1994-2004; TV prodr., 1994-2006. Coach mock trial Riverside Christian H.S., 1985-86; choir dir. Riverside Christian Sch., 1985-86; Sunday Sch. tchr. Grace Bapt. Ch., Harvest Christian Fellowship, Riverside, Magnolia Ave. Bapt. Ch., 1968-92, Wheat, Oil and Wine Christian Fellowship, Riverside, Sunday sch. supt., 1992-93; children's choir dir. Grace Bapt. Ch., 1981-82; Christian edn. coord., Sunday sch. tchr., and vacation Bible sch. dir. First United Meth. Ch., Riverside, 2002-03. Recipient Golden Star Halo award, Star Sapphire Halo award, Jeanie Golden Halo award for acting and teaching So. Calif. Motion Picture Coun., 1994. Mem. Nat. Assn. Christian Educators, Internat. Alliance of Theatre and Stage Employees, Internat. Platform Assn., Greater L.A. World Trade Ctr. Assn., Sons of Norway (study scholar 1967), Delta Phi Alpha. Democrat. Avocations: photography, music, travel, production of films and videos. Office: Walt Disney Studios 500 S Buena Vista St Burbank CA 91521-0006 Home: 1244 SE Seaport Cir Corvallis OR 97333-3110 E-mail: nrneumann@yahoo.com.

NEUMANN, SERINA ANN LOUISE, psychologist, researcher; b. Fitchburg, Mass., Dec. 29, 1970; d. James Martin Neumann and Annette Marie Rooney; m. Mark Cardiff, Feb. 19, 1973. BS in Psychology and Bus. cum laude, U. Pitts., 1992; MA in Clin. Psychology and Behavioral Medicine, U. Md., Balt., 1999, PhD in Clin. Psychology and Behavioral Medicine, 2001. Lic. Psychologist Bur. Profl. Occupl. Affairs, Pa., 2003. Postdoctoral scholar, cardiovasc. behavioral medicine rsch. tng. program U. Pitts., 2001—04, rsch. asst. prof., 2004—05; ast. prof. psychiatry and behavioral scis. Eastern Va. Med. Sch., 2006—. Author articles and papers in field. Fellow Ruth L. Kirschstein Nat. Rsch. Svc. award, NIH, Nat. Heart, Lung, and Blood Inst., 2001-2004; Loan Repayment Program grant, NIH, 2002—, Grant (NIMH) Kiosk award, 2005—. Mem.: APA (mem. Health Psychology Divsn. 38), Internat. Soc. Behavioral Medicine, Soc. Behavioral Medicine, Am. Psychosomatic Soc. (program com. student mem. 2000—01, Citation award 2005), Phi Kappa Phi. Achievements include discovery of preliminary evidence of an association between genetic variation in the choline transporter gene and parasympathetic-cardiac function, depressive symptomatology; corticolimbic reactivity and subclinical measures of atherosclerosis. Office: Eastern Va Med Sch Dept Psychiatry 825 Fairfax Ave Norfolk VA 23501 Office Phone: 757-446-5888. Business E-Mail: neumansa@evms.edu.

NEUMANN, STEPHANIE TOWER, retired librarian; b. N.Y.C., Jan. 26, 1947; d. George Francis and Mary Corbet Neumann; m. Charles Donald Dukes, Mar. 21, 1994; 1 stepchild, Jonathan Andrew Dukes. BA, Ea. Wash. U., 1973; MLS, Western Mich. U., 1975. Svc. rep. Mountain Bell (now U.S. West), Albuquerque, 1970—74; reference libr. City of Littleton, Colo., 1977—90, econ. intelligence specialist, 1990—98. Mem.: Rocky Mountain Spl. Libr. Assn., Spl. Libr. Assn. (presenter 1991, 1995), Beta Phi Mu. Home: 53 W Ranch Trl Morrison CO 80465 E-mail: stnm@earthlink.net.

NEUMARK, GERTRUDE FANNY, materials science educator; b. Nuremberg, Germany, Apr. 29, 1927; came to U.S., 1939; d. Siegmund and Bertha (Forchheimer) N.; m. Henry Rothschild, Mar. 18, 1950. BA, Barnard Coll., 1948; MA, Radcliffe Coll., 1949; PhD, Columbia U., 1951. Advanced rsch. physicist Sylvania Rsch. Labs., Bayside, N.Y., 1952-60; sr. mem. tech. staff Philips Labs., Briarcliff Manor, N.Y., 1960-85; prof. materials sci. Columbia U., N.Y.C., 1985-99, Howe prof. materials sci. and engring., 1999—. Cons. Am. Inst. Physics, N.Y.C., 1968-69; NSF vis. prof., 1982; panelist NRC; panelist, reviewer NSF. Contbr. Encyclopedia of Advanced Materials, numerous articles to sci. jours., chpt. to books; inventor in field. Rice fellow, 1948, Dana fellow, 1948, AAUW Anderson fellow, 1951. Fellow Am. Phys. Soc. (Goeppert-Meyer award com. 1987-89); mem. Materials Rsch. Soc., Soc. Women Engrs. (sr.), Am. Chem. Soc.

NEUNER, LYNN K., lawyer; b. Providence, July 15, 1967; BA summa cum laude, Williams Coll., 1989; JD, Yale U., 1992. CLU U.S. Supreme Ct., 2001; bar: Conn. 1992, N.Y. 1994, U.S. Dist. Ct. (so. dist.) NY 1996, U.S. Dist. Ct. Conn. 2001, US Dist. Ct. (ea. dist.), NY 2001, U.S. Ct. Appeals (2nd cir.) 2004. Law clk. Hon. H. Lee Sarokin, U.S. Dist. Ct., Dist. N.J., 1992—93, Hon. John M. Walker Jr., U.S. Ct. Appeals, second cir., 1993—94; ptnr. Simpson Thacher & Bartlett LLP, N.Y.C., 1994—, co-chmn. recruiting com., litig. training com. & diversity com. Mem. bd. editors, co-author Ins. Coverage News Bull. Mem.: Yale Law Sch. Alumni Fund (mem. bd. dirs.), Conn. Bar Assn., ABA (co-chmn. property ins. sub-com.), N.Y. State Bar Assn., Assn. Bar City N.Y. (fed. ct. com. 2003—). Office: Simpson Thacher & Bartlett LLP 425 Lexington Ave New York NY 10017-3954 Office Phone: 212-455-2696. Office Fax: 212-455-2502. Business E-Mail: lneuner@stblaw.com.*

NEURATH, RACHEL, mathematics educator; b. Omaha, Nebr., Sept. 13, 1974; d. Richard E. and Nancy E. Moreland; m. Jason W. Neurath, Aug. 8, 2001. BS in Math., Coll. St. Mary, Omaha Nebr., 1996; MA in Tchg. Math., U. Nebr., Omaha Nebr., 2002. Cert. secondary edn. Nebr. Dept. Edn., 1996. Tchr. Omaha Pub. Schs., 1997—. Adj. instr. Met. C.C., Omaha, 2002—. Personal E-mail: rachel.neurath@ops.org.

NEURAUTER, ELIZABETH STRAIN, secondary school educator; b. Indpls., Mar. 7, 1959; d. Edward Richard Strain and Elizabeth Meyer (Strain) Gunn; m. Ronald Otto Neurauter, July 7, 1984; children: Stacy Marie, Ronald Paul, Beatrice Grace, Clara Helen. BA, Elmhurst Coll., Ill., 1981; EdM, Nat. Louis U., Wheeling, Ill., 2004; cert. advanced studies edn. leadership, Nat. Louis U., 2005. Cert. tchr. English, ESL and psychology Ill. Staff asst. for vol. affairs ESL/ABE dept. Coll. DuPage, Glen Ellyn, Ill., 1991—94, ESL tchr. H.S. summer credit program, 2002—; tutor English lang. learner, asst. dir. student activities Glenbard South H.S., Glen Ellyn, 1994—. Presenter in field; adj. faculty adult and family svcs. Joliet Jr. Coll., Ill., 2006—. Legis. apptd. mem. Ill. Literacy Coun., 1998. Nominee Golden Apple award, 2000; named Person of Character, Glen Ellyn Character Counts Coalition, 2004. Mem.: ASCD, Nat. Assn. Realtors, Ill. Assn. Realtors, Ill. Assn. Tchrs. English, Nat. Coun. Tchrs. English, Archaeol. Conservancy. Republican. Avocations: archaeology, real estate. Home: 22W521 Burr Oak Dr Glen Ellyn IL 60137 Office: Glenbard South HS 23W200 Butterfield Rd Glen Ellyn IL 60137 Office Phone: 630-469-6500.

NEUROHR, SHIRLEY ANN, retired special education educator; b. Chgo., Nov. 18, 1936; d. Anton and Anna (Ludvik) Sedlak; m. Joseph Henry Neurohr, Apr. 7, 1956 (dec. 1995); children: Debora Neurohr-Wearne, Kathleen Neurohr Rodenhauser, Jacqueline Neurohr Rueden; m. James Brennan, 2001. AA in Edn., Morton Coll., 1955; BA Psychology/Sociology summa cum laude, Mundelein Coll., 1977; MS in Edn. Adminstrn. with dept. honors, Winona State U., 1983. Cert. elem. edn. tchr., learning disabilities edn., behavioral disorders edn., elem. adminstrn. Elem. tchr. St. Mary's Cath. Sch., Tomah, Wis., 1978-80, elem. prin., 1980-85; secondary tchr. behaviorally disordered Sparta (Wis.) Sr. H.S., 1985-86, 86—; elem. tchr. behaviorally disordered Tomah Area Sch. Dist., 1986-87, secondary tchr. behaviorally disordered, 1987-90, secondary tchr. learning disabled, 1990—2001; ret., 2001. Mem. Edn. for Employment Coun., Tomah, 1990-95, Spl. Edn. Transition Task Force, Tomah, 1988-93, Sch. to Work Task Force, Tomah, 1990-95. Troop leader, program cons., v.p. coun. Girl Scouts DuPage County Coun., DuPage, Ill., 1963-77; lay min. Diocese of LaCrosse, Wis., 1985; mem. St. Mary's Coun. Cath. Women, 1977—. Recipient Thanks Badge, DuPage County coun. Girl Scouts U.S., 1976; named Woman of Yr., St. Joseph's Coun. of Cath. Women, 1977. Mem. AAUW (Tomah br. 1977-95, v.p., past sec.-treas.), ASCD, Nat. Coun. Tchrs. English, Midwest Reading Coun., Tomah Edn. Assn. (bldg. rep. 1986, asst. v.p., pres. 2000), Sierra Club Nat. Wildlife Found., Crane Found., Monroe County Ret. Tchrs. Assn (pres.

2006), Delta Kappa Gamma (sec. Alpha Upsilon chpt., pres. 2006), Master Gardeners Assn. Democrat. Roman Catholic. Avocations: travel, gardening, birding. Home: 23584 Emblem Ave Tomah WI 54660-9731 Personal E-mail: shirlgym@charter.net.

NEUVEL, MELISSA, secondary school educator; BA in History, Va. Tech, Blacksburg, 2000, MEd in Curriculum and Instrn., 2001. Tchr. Spotsylvania Schs., Va., 2001—03, Hawaii Pub. Schs., Waimea, 2003—06.

NEUWIRTH, BEBE (BEATRICE NEUWIRTH), dancer, actress; b. Newark, Dec. 31, 1958; d. Lee Paul and Sydney Anne Neuwirth; m. Paul Dorman, 1984 (div.); m. Michael Danek. Student, Juilliard Sch., 1976-77. Appeared: (on Broadway) A Chorus Line (as Sheila), 1975-90, Dancin', 1978-82, Little Me, 1982, Sweet Charity, 1986-87 (Tony award for best featured actress in a musical, 1986), Damn Yankees, 1994-95, Chicago, 1996 (Tony award for best actress in a musical, 1997, Outer Critics Circle award for best actress in a musical, 1997, Drama League Award for disting. performance, 1997, Drama Desk Award for outstanding actress in a musical, 1997, Astaire Award for best female dancer, 1997), Fosse, 1999-2001, Funny Girl, 2002, Here Lies Jenny, 2004; (off Broadway) include West Side Story, 1981, Upstairs at O'Neal's, 1982-83, The Road to Hollywood, 1984, Just So, 1985, Waiting in the Wings: The Night the Understudies Take the Stage, 1986, Showing Off, 1989, Kiss of the Spider Woman (London), 1993, Pal Joey, 1995, Here Lies Jenny, 2004. Prin. dancer on Broadway Dancin', 1982; leading dance role Kicks, 1984. Actor: (TV series) The Edge of Night, 1981, Cheers, 1986-93 (Emmy award for Best Supporting Actress in a Comedy Series 1990, 91), (voice) Aladdin, 1993, (voice) All Dogs Go to Heaven: The Series, 1996, Deadline, 2000-01; (TV series guest appearances) Frasier, 1994-2003; (TV miniseries) Wild Palms, 1993; (TV films) Without Her Consent, 1990, Unspeakable Acts, 1990, Dash and Lilly, 1999, Cupid & Cate, 2000, Sounds From a Town I Love, 2001; (films) Say Anything, 1989, Green Card, 1990, Bugsy, 1991, The Paint Job, 1992, Malice, 1993, Jumanji, 1995, (voice) All Dogs Go to Heaven 2, 1996, The Adventures of Pinocchio, 1996, The Associate, 1996, Dear Diary, 1996, Celebrity, 1998, The Faculty, 1998, (voice) An All Dogs Christmas Carol, 1998, Summer of Sam, 1999, Liberty Heights, 1999, Getting to Know You, 1999, Tadpole, 2002, How to Lose a Guy in 10 Days, 2003, Le Divorce, 2003, The Big Bounce, 2004. Vol. performances for March of Dimes Telethon, 1986, Cystic Fibrosis Benefit Children's Ball, 1986, Ensemble Studio Theater Benefit, 1986, Circle Repertory Co. Benefit, 1986, all in N.Y.C. Democrat.

NEUZIL, AMY REED, physician, entrepreneur; b. Peterborough, Ont., Can., Apr. 4, 1977; arrived in US, 1991; d. Ivo Jan and Bonnie Elaine Neuzil. BA in Psychology, U. Va., Charlottesville, 1998; D of Naturopathy, SW Coll. Naturopathy Medicine, Tempe, Ariz., 2003. Pvt. practice, Austin, Tex., 2004—; owner Excelon Health LLC, Austin, 2005—. Cmty. outreach cons. People's Pharmacy, Austin, 2005—. Mem.: Nat. Ctr. for Homeopathy, Tex. Assn. Naturopathic Physicians, Am. Assn. Naturopathic Physicians. Avocations: piano, writing, hiking, travel. Office: Excelon Health 5524 Bee Cave Rd Ste B-1 Austin TX 78746

NEVANS, LAUREL S., rehabilitation counselor; b. NYC, Aug. 1, 1964; d. Roy N. and Virginia (Place) Nevans; m. Russell Baird Palmer III, Oct. 12, 1991 (div. Jan. 2001). BA in English, Secondary Edn. cum laude, U. Richmond, 1986, postgrad., 1989-92; MA in Edn. and Human Devel., George Washington U., 1991, cert. in job devel. and placement, 1992. Group leader S.E. Consortium for Spl. Svcs., Larchmont, NY, 1980—85; vocat. instr. Assn. for Retarded Citizens Montgomery County, Rockville, Md., 1986—89; edn. specialist George Washington U. Out of Sch. Work Experience Program, Washington, 1989—90; rsch. asst. George Washington U. Dept. Tchr. Prep. & Spl. Edn., Washington, 1989—91; employability skills tchr., rsch. intern Nat. Rehab. Hosp. Rehab. Engring. Dept., Washington, 1991; vocat./ind. living skills specialist The Independence Ctr., Rockville, Md., 1991—93; leadership team mgr. Career Choice project The Endependence Ctr. of No. Va., Arlington, 1993—94; program dir. United Cerebral Palsy of D.C. and No. Va., Washington, 1994—97; sr. assistive tech. specialist Tech., Automation & Mgmt., Inc., Greenbelt, Md., 1997—98; owner WebLaurels Designs, Silver Spring, Md., 1998—, ArtistCrafts, 2001—. Clayers with Disabilities Listserv (electronic discussion list), 2002—, Artist Crafts, Silver Spring, 2001—. Teaching asst. Rehab. Counseling Program, George Washington U., 1991; moderator FPList Electronic Discussion List, 2000—; owner Clayers with Disabilities Electronic Discussion List, 2002-, webmaster, St. Pete Polymer Clay Guild, 2005-, bd. mem. webmaster, Nat. Polymer Clay Guild, 2005-. Bd. mem., newsletter editor Cameron Hill Owners Assn., 2002—. Recipient traineeship GWU Counseling Dept., 1990, 91. Mem. Nat. Rehab. Assn., Nat. Rehab. Counselors Assn., D.C. Met. Area Assn. Person's in Supported Employment (editor newsletter 1995-97), Nat. Career Devel. Assn., Nat. Employment Counseling Assn., Nat. Assn. Ind. Living, Am. Assn. Counseling and Devel., Am. Rehab. Counseling Assn., Nat. Polymer Clay Guild. Democrat. Avocations: writing, photography, music, travel, jewelry making. Home: 6250 Holmes Blvd Unit 23 Holmes Beach FL 34217-1668 Business E-Mail: laurel@artistcrafts.com.

NEVE, VICTORIA J., music educator; b. Watseka, Ill., Apr. 25, 1950; d. Frank J and Florence M Rider; m. Patrick M Neve, Aug. 30, 1970; 1 child, Branwyn. B in music, Ill. Wesleyan, 1972; M in music, U. of Kans., 1975, Mus D, 1979. Prof. of music San Francisco State U., 1975—; dir. San Francisco Young Pianists Competition, 1983—. Adj. MTNA, MTAC et al., 1984—. Office: San Francisco State U Dept of Music 1600 Holloway Ave San Francisco CA 94132 Business E-Mail: docvic@sfsu.edu.

NEVILLE, ELIZABETH EGAN, artist, educator; b. Albany, N.Y., May 16, 1937; d. Philip Sidney and Harriet Rust Egan; m. Robert Cummings Neville, June 8, 1963; children: Naomi Louise, Leonora Alice. BA, Smith Coll., 1959; MA in Tchg., Harvard U., 1961. Dir. Neville Art Enterprises, Milton, Mass., 1969—. Art instr. Town of Huntington, NY, 1982—88, Adelphi U., Garden City, NY, 1983—85; dir. Milton Art Mus., 1993—97, art instr., 1998—2006; lectr. in field. Art critic: Art N.Eng., 1998—2006; Represented in permanent collections Heckscher Mus., Huntington, L.I., Fine Arts Mus. L.I., Hempstead, N.Y., Maritime Mus., State U. N.Y., Throgs Neck, Katonah Gallery, N.Y., Hudson-Athens Lighthouse Preservation Soc., Symbols of Jesus, 2001, Boston Confucianism, 2000, The God Who Beckons, 1999, The Cosmology of Freedom, 1995, Creativity and God, 1995, God the Creator, 1992, Eternity and Times Flow, 1993, A Theology Primer, 1991, Behind the Masks of God, 1991, Recovery of the Measure, 1989, The Butterfly as Companion, 1989, The Puritan Smile, 1987, solo exhbns., Neville Gallery, 2004, Boston U. Sch. Theology, 1998, Claremont Sch. Theology, Calif., 1997, 1995, 1991, Sturdy Meml. Hosp. Gallery, Attleboro, Mass., 1997, Weston Theol. Inst., Mass., 1995, U. Mass. Med. Ctr. Gallery, Worcester, 1994, Kaaterskill Gallery, Columbia-Greene C.C., Hudson, N.Y., 1992, Milton Art Mus, Mass., 1990, NoHo Gallery, NYC, 1981, 1983. Mem. Newport Mus., RI, 2006—, Capt. Robert Forbes Mus., Milton, 1989—2006; pres. bd. trustees Milton Art Mus., 2001—06, 2003. Grantee, Henry Luce Found., 1990, Milton Cultural Arts Coun., 1995, 1996, 1997, 2006. Mem.: Nat. Mus. Women in Art (charter mem.), Women's Caucus for Art, Harvard Club Boston (adv. bd. fine arts com. 1998—2006), Smith Coll. Club Boston, Milton Garden Club (chair Smithsonian garden history 2001—06), Alpha Kappa XI. Democrat. Avocations: landscape architecture, photography, history, citrus horticulture.

NEVILLE, MARGARET COBB, physiologist, educator; b. Greenville, SC, Nov. 4, 1934; d. Henry Van Zandt and Florence Ruth (Crozier) Cobb; m. Hans E. Neville, Dec. 27, 1957; children: Michel Paul, Brian Douglas. BA, Pomona Coll., 1956; PhD, U. Pa., 1962. Asst. prof. physiology U. Colo. Med. Sch., Denver, 1968-75, assoc. prof., 1975-82, prof., 1982—, dir. med. scientist tng. program, 1985-94, prof. ob-gyn., 2002—, chief sect. basic reprodn. sci., 2002—. Editor: Lactation: Physiology, Nutrition, Breast Feeding, 1983 (Am. Pubs. award 1984), Human Lactation I, 1985, The Mammary Gland, 1987, Jour. Mammary Gland Biology and Neoplasia, 1995-2001; contbr. numerous articles to profl. jours. Recipient Rsch. Career Devel. award NIH, 1975, NIH merit award, 1993. Mem. AAAS, Am. Physiol. Soc., Am. Soc. Cell Biology, Internat. Soc. Rsch. in Human Milk and Lactation, Soc. Gynecol. Investigation, Phi Beta Kappa. Office: U Colo Divsn Basic Reprodn Sci PO Box 6511 Mail Stop 6511 Aurora CO 80045 Office Phone: 303-724-3506. E-mail: peggy.neville@uchsc.edu.

NEVILLE, PHOEBE, choreographer, dancer, educator; b. Swarthmore, Pa., Sept. 28, 1941; d. Kennith R. and Marion (Eberbach) Balsley; m. Philip E. Hipwell, June 21, 1969 (dissolved Sept. 1978); m. Philip Corner, Nov. 3, 1996. Student, Wilson Coll., 1959-61. Cert. practitioner body mind centering, registered somatic movement therapist. Instr. Bennington (Vt.) Coll., 1981-84, 87-88; vis. lectr. UCLA, 1984-86. Dancer, choreographer Judson Meml. Ch., N.Y.C., 1966—70, Dance Uptown Series, 1969, Cubiculo Theatre, 1972—75, Delacorte Dance Festival, 1976, Dance Umbrella Series, 1977, Riverside Dance Festival, 1976, 1978, N.Y. Seasons, 1979—, dancer, artistic dir. Phoebe Neville Dance Co., N.Y.C., 1975—, Jacob's Pillow Splash! Festival, 1988—, Dance Theater Workshop Winter Events, 1988—, Mersdith Wonk Benefit, 1994, performances with Philip Corner: Venice, Genoa, San Michele al' Adige, 1996—, BBB Festival, Thailand, Genoa, Salso Maggiore, Terme, 1997—, Seoul NY Max Festival, N.Y.C., 1998, Malpartida de Caseras, Spain, Caserano, Italy, 1998, Besancon, France, 1998, Paris, Lyon, 1999, Saluggia, Italy, 1999, Performance Festival, Odense, Denmark, 1999, 2001, Bassano del Grappa, Genoa, Italy, 2000, 2001, 2002, Novarra, Italy, 2002—; performances with, Ghent, Belgium, 2002—; performances with: Castelvetro di Modena, 2003; Argos Festival, 2003. Recipient Creative Artist Public Svc. award, 1975; Nat. Endowment for Arts fellow, 1975, 79, 80, 85-87, 92-94, Choreographic fellow N.Y. Found. for Arts, 1989. Mem.: Internat. Assn. Healthcare Practitioners, Internat. Somatic Movement Edn. and Therapy Assn. (registered), Body-Mind Centering Assn. (cert. practitioner and tchr.). Buddhist.

NEVIN, JEAN SHAW, artist; b. Bklyn., Dec. 21, 1934; d. Marshall Robert and Dorothy Frances (Brown) Shaw; m. Robert Stephen Nevin, Dec. 9, l955. BA in English, SUNY, Albany, 1956. Textbook and freelance editor, 1959—74; printmaker, papermaker Jean Nevin Graphics, Indpls., 1969—84; owner, mgr., knitwear designer Chameleon, Indpls., 1985—88; pres., knitwear designer Knitting Machine Shop, Inc., Indpls., 1988—91; owner Knitwearables, Albuquerque, 1991—97; painter Albuquerque, 1995—. Instr. print and paper making Indpls. Art League, 1974-83, exhibits coord., 1969, 73, edn. coord., 1979-80, editor Artifacts, 1968-69, 72-73; editor, pub. Swatchnotes, 1987-91; owner, gallery dir. Kokopelli Gallery, 2000-01. Exhibited to nat. group shows and galleries prints and handmade paper, 1970-84, garments and jewelry, 1992-97, Relief Paintings, 1999-2001, Digital Paintings, 2002-05, Florence Biennale, Florence, Italy, 2003; painter, sculptor, mixed media artist, 1998-2001; digital painter, 2001—, collages and handmade books, 2006-; mixed media artist. Mem.: Book Artists Guild, N.Mex. Book Arts Guild, Soc. Layerists in MultiMedia (signature mem.). Home and Studio: 9641 Mendoza Ave NE Albuquerque NM 87109-6614 Office Phone: 505-823-9364. E-mail: jean@nevinart.com.

NEVIN, LAURA JEAN, music educator; b. Denver, Colo., Apr. 30, 1981; d. Richard Lee and Lynn Marie Nevin. MusB in Edn, Colo. Christian U., Lakewood, 2004. Music educator Foothills Elem. Sch., Lakewood, Colo., 2004—. Office Phone: 303-982-9287.

NEVINS, FRANCES (FRANKIE) RUSH, tourism professional; b. Kansas City, Mo., Dec. 15, 1932; d. George Herbert and Bertha Emmaline (Hyne) Rush; m. Warren Griffith Nevins, Feb. 17, 1952 (div. Mar. 2002); children: Ronald Douglas(dec.), Deborah Lynn, Philip Rush. Grad., Baker U., 1954; cert. tourism industry specialist, Ind. U.-Purdue U., 1990. Personnel adminstr. Man-Wood, 1974—81; relocation dir. Gallery of Homes, 1982—84; tourism develop. mgr. N.J. Divsn. Tourism, Trenton, 1984—98; ret., 1998. Co-editor: N.J. State Guide, 1984—98. Mem. Somerset County (N.J.) Hist. Commn., 1987—98; active various civic and charity coms., Augusta, Ga.; mem. Daus. of the King, Episcopal Ch. Women. Mem.: DAR, Am. Bus. Assn. (panel mem. 1984—98, conf. planning com., edn./scholarship com.), Nat. Tour Assn. (panel mem. 1984—98, conf. planning com.), Federated Women's Club (past pres.), Delta Delta Delta (past pres.). Republican. Episcopalian. Home: 3753 Boulder Tr Augusta GA 30907-5124

NEVINS, LYN (CAROLYN A. NEVINS), school disciplinarian; b. Chelsea, Mass., June 9, 1948; d. Samuel Joseph and Stella Theresa (Maronski) N.; m. John Edward Herbert, Jr., May 1, 1979; children: Chrissy, Johnny. BA in Sociology, Edn., U. Mass., 1970; MA in Women's Studies, George Washington U., 1975. Cert. tchr., trainer. Tchr. social studies Greenwich (Conn.) Pub. Schs., 1970-74; rschr. career/vocat. edn. Conn. State Dept. Edn., Hartford, 1975-76; rschr., career/vocat. edn. Area Coop. Edn. Svcs., Hamden, Conn., 1976-77; program mgr., trainer career edn. and gender equity Coop. Ednl. Svcs., Norwalk, Conn., 1977-83, trainer, mgr., devel., Beginning Educator Support and Tng. program Trumbull, Conn., 1987—; state coord. career edn. Conn. State Dept. Edn., Hartford, 1982-83; supr. Sacred Heart U., Fairfield, 1992—. Bias com. Conn. State Dept. Edn., Hartford, 1981—; vision com. Middlesex Mid. Sch., Darien, Conn., 1993-95; ednl. quality and diversity com. Town of Darien, 1993-95; cons., trainer career devel./pre-retirement planning Cohen and Assocs., Fairfield, 1981—, Farren Assocs., Annandale, Va., 1992—, Tracey Robert Assocs., Fairfield, 1994—; freelance cons., trainer, Darien, 1983-87; presenter Nat. Conf. GE, 1980, Career Edn., 1983, Am. Edn. Rsch. Assn., 1991, Nat. Conf. New Tchr. Induction, 2006; mem. statewide B.E.S.T. adv.com., 2006; lectr. in field. Tennis coach Spl. Olympics, 1993—, Darien (Conn.) Girls' Softball League, 1992-96, tennis coord. Spl. Olympics Summer Games, 1997—; tennis coach Unified Ptnr. Spl. Olympics Nat. Games, 2005-06; tennis coach, Conn. delegation Nat. Games for Spl. Olympics, 2005—06; bldg. com. Darien HS, 1999—. Mem. NOW (founder, state coord. edn. 1972-74), ASCD. Avocations: tennis, running, walking, golf, travel. Home: 4 Hollister Ln Darien CT 06820-5404 Office: Coop Ednl Svcs 40 Lindeman Drive Trumbull CT 06611-4723 Business E-Mail: nevinsl@ces.k12.ct.us.

NEVINS, SHEILA, television producer; b. NYC; d. Benjamin and Stella Nevins; m. Sidney Koch, 1972; 1 child, David Andrew. BA, Barnard Coll.; MFA, Yale U. TV prodr. Great Am. Dream Machine, NET, 1971-73, The Reasoner Report, ABC, 1973, Feeling Good, Children's TV Workshop, 1975-76, Who's Who, CBS, 1977-78; dir. documentary and family programming HBO, N.Y.C., 1978-82; v.p. documentary programming Home Box Office, N.Y.C., 1986-95, sr. v.p. original programming, 1998-99; exec. v.p. original programming HBO, N.Y.C., 1999—2003, pres. documentary and family, 2004—. Bd. dirs. Film Forum, Creative Capital, Ind. Feature Project. Bd. dirs. Women's Action Alliance. Named Woman of Achievement YMCA, 1991, Top 25 Women in TV, Emmy mag., 1996, Top 25 Smartest Women Am., Mirabella Mag., 1999; named one of Top 50 Women in TV, Hollywood Reporter Mag., 2005; named to Broadcasting and Cable Hall of Fame, 2000; recipient Peabody award, 1986, 1992, 1995, 1996, 1997, 1999, 2000, 2003, 2004, Glaad Media award, 1989, Acad. Award for Documentary, 1993, 1996, 1998, 1999, 2000, 2001, 2003, Emmy award, 1994, 1995, 1996, 1997, 1998, 1999, 2000, 2002, 2003, 2004, Media award Mental Health Assn. N.Y.C., 1996, Personal Peabody award, 1999, NATAS Silver Cir., 2000, Wellness Cmty. award, 2001, Humanitarian award, Nat. Bd. Rev., 2002, Lucy award, Women in Film, 2003, Three Arts award. Mem.: Internt. Documentary Assn. (Vision award 1998), N.Y. Women in Film (Muse award 1998), Writers Guild Am.*

NEVINS, TRACY ANNE, elementary school educator; d. Janet V. Sinusas; m. John J. Nevins, Sept. 7, 1991; children: Emily R., Laura R. BA cum laude, CUNY, N.Y.C., N.Y., 1992, MS magna cum laude in Edn., 1995. Cert. tchr. N.Y., 1994, perminent 6-8 English extention N.Y., 1995, profl. educator Conn., 2003, lic. tchr. highly qualified K-5 elem. Conn., 2006, tchr. highly qualified 6-12 sci. Conn., 2006. Tchr. mid. sch. St. Anselm's Sch., Bronx, NY, 1992—94; tchr. Elizabeth Blackwell Mid. Sch., South Ozone Park, NY, 1993—96, Schaghticoke Mid. Sch., New Milford, Conn., 1996—. Mem. bldg. com. H.S. New Milford (Conn.) Pub. Schs., 1997—98; team leader Schaghticoke Mid. Sch., 1999—2000, head tchr. summer sch., 1998—99. Contbr. chapters to books. Vol. Rep. Party, New Milford, 2004. Scholar, Local 721 Unionf Licensed Practical Nurses, 1987, Regents Com. N.Y. State, 1987. Master: Kappa Delta Pi (life; pres. 1990—91); mem.: Conn. Educator Assn. (licentiate), Conn. Sci. Educator Assn. (assoc.), Elem. Sci. Assn. (life), Golden Key Honor Soc. (life). Republican. Roman Catholic. Achievements include Nomination for Teacher of the Year 2004. Avocations: reading, gardening, crafts, bargain hunting, flying. Office Phone: 860-354-2204. Business E-Mail: nevinst@new-milford.k12.ct.us.

NEVIUS, JANET DRYDEN, real estate company executive, government agency administrator; b. Verona, Nj, Jan. 17, 1926; d. Harold Clifford and Marian Longstreth Dryden; m. Robert Foster Nevius, Oct. 11, 1958; children: Janet, Carolyn. BA, Barnard Coll., 1949; MA, Seton Hall U., 1970; PhD, NYU, 1975. Cert. tchr. in French, Spanish and secondary edn. NJ. Liaison officer-interpreter U.S. Dept., Washington, 1955—61; secondary sch. tchr. Montclair H.S., Montclair, NJ, 1961—68; dir. Am. Inst. for Fgn. Study, Greenwich, Conn., 1968—76; mgr. Citibank, New York, NY, 1977—82; v.p. dir. of mktg. J. Henry Schroder bank & Trust Co., New York, NY, 1982—87; real estate exec. UN, New York, NY, 2002—. Trustee NJ Hist. Soc., Newark; exec. v.p. UN Delegations Hospitality Com., New York, NY; sponsor Orpheus Chamber Orch., NY. Mem.: The Met. Club, The Mus. of Natural History, The Met. Opera Guild, The Met. Mus. of Art, The Essex Fells Country Club, President's Cir. R-Conservative. Episcopalian. Avocations: music, golf, book club discussions, theater, literary history. Home: PO box 175 Essex Fells NJ 07021

NEW, MARIA IANDOLO, pediatrician, educator; b. N.Y.C. d. Loris J. and Esther B. (Giglio) Iandolo; m. Bertrand L. New, 1949 (dec. 1990); children: Erica, Daniel, Antonia. BA, Cornell U., 1950; MD, U. Pa., 1954; degree in medicine (hon.), U. degli Studi di Roma, Rome, 1999, U. di Parma, Italy, 2000. Diplomate Am. Bd. Pediat. Med. intern Bellevue Hosp., N.Y.C., 1954-55; resident in pediat. N.Y. Hosp., 1955-57; fellow NIH, 1957-58, 61-64; practice medicine specializing in pediat. N.Y.C., 1955—; mem. staff N.Y. Hosp., dir. Pediatric Endocrine and Metabolism Clinic, 1964—2004, attending pediatrician, 1971-80; pediatrician-in-chief N.Y.-Presbyn. Hosp., 1980—2002, dir. pediatric endocrinology, 1998—2002; prof. pediat. Mt. Sinai Sch. Medicine, N.Y.C. Asst. prof. dept. pediat. Joan and Sanford Weill Med. Coll. of Cornell U., N.Y.C., 1963-68, assoc. prof., 1968-71, prof., 1971-2004, Harold and Percy Uris prof. pediatric endocrinology, 1978-2004, prof., 1980-2004, chmn. dept. pediat., 1980-2002; program dir. Childrens Clin. Rsch. Ctr., 1996-2002; assoc. dir. Pediatric Clin. Rsch. Ctr., 1980-88; adj. faculty prof. Rockefeller U., 1981—; career scientist N.Y.C. Health Rsch. Coun., 1966-75; adj. attending pediatrician dept. pediat. Meml. Sloan-Kettering Cancer Ctr., 1979-93; cons. United Hosp., Port Chester, N.Y., 1977—, North Shore Univ. Hosp., 1982-97, dept. pediat. Cath. Med. Ctr. Bklyn. and Queens, N.Y., 1987—; vis. physician Rockefeller U. Hosp., N.Y.C., 1973-87; mem. endocrine study sect. NIH, 1977-80, Gen. Clin. Rsch. Ctrs. Adv. Com.; chmn. Divsn. Rsch. Resources Gen. Clin. Rsch. Ctrs. Com. NIH, 1987-88; bd. dirs. Robert Wood Johnson Clin. Scholars Program; mem. N.Y. State Gov.'s Task Force on Life and Law, 1985—; mem. NIH Reviewers Res.; mem. FDA endocrinology and metabolism drug adv. com., 1994—; panelist ACGME bd. appeals, 1994—; cons. Meml. Sloan-Kettering Cancer Ctr., 1993—, Meml. Hosp. for the Cancer and Allied Diseases, 1993—; hon. mem. pediat. dept. Blythedale Children's Hosp., Valhalla, N.Y., 1992—; mem. rsch. adv. com. Population Coun. Ctr. for Biomed. Rsch., 1991-97. Editor-in-chief Jour. Clin. Endocrinology and Metabolism, 1994-99; mem. editl. adv. coun. Jour. Endocrinological Investigation, 1995—; mem. editl. bd. Jour. Women's Health, 1993, Endotext; corr. editor Jour. Steroid Biochemistry, 1985; mem. adv. bd. pediatric anns., assoc. editor Metabolism. Trustee Irma T. Hirschl Trust. Recipient Mary Jane Kugel award Juvenile Diabetes Found., 1977, Katharine D. McCormick Disting. Lectureship, 1981, Robert H. Williams Disting. Leadership award, 1988, Albion O. Bernstein award Med. Soc. State N.Y., 1988, medal N.Y. Acad. Medicine, 1991, Disting. Grad. award U. Pa. Sch. Medicine, 1991, Optimate Recognition award Assn. Student-Profl. Italian-Ams., 1991, Outstanding Woman Scientist award N.Y. chpt. Am. Women in Sci., 1986, Maurice R. Greenberg Disting. Svc. award, 1994, Humanitarian award Juvenile Diabetes Found., 1994, Rhône Poulenc Rorer Clin. Investigator Lecture award, 1994, Dale medal Brit. Endocrine Soc., 1996, MERIT award USPHS, NIHCHD, 1998, 11th Ann. award for excellence in clin. rsch. USPHS, NIH, 1998; grantee; named to Hall of Honor, NICHD, 2003. Fellow AAAS, Italian Soc. Endocrinology (hon.); mem. NAS (sr. mem. Inst. Medicine), AAAS, APHA, Am. Soc. Human Genetics, Am. Acad. Pediat., Soc. for Pediatric Rsch., Harvey Soc., Endocrine Soc. (mem. coun. 1981-84, pres. 1991-92, Fred Conrad Koch award 2003), Lawson Wilkins Pediatric Endocrine Soc. (pres. 1985-86), Am. Soc. Nephrology, Am. Soc. Pediatric Nephrology, Am. Pediatric Soc., Am. Fedn. Clin. Rsch., Am. Diabetes Assn., European Soc. Pediatric Endocrinology, Soc. for the Advancement of Women's Health Rsch. (basic sci. award 1996), Am. Coll. Clin. Pharmacology, Am. Clin. and Climatol. Assn., N.Y. Acad. Scis., Pan Am. Med. Assn., Assn. Am. Physicians, Am. Fertility Soc., U.S. Pharmacopeial Conv. (elected), Am. Acad. of Arts and Scis. (elected 1992), Alpha Omega Alpha. Office: Mt Sinai Sch Medicine Box 1198 1 Gustav L Levy Pl New York NY 10029 Office Phone: 212-241-7847. E-mail: maria.new@mssm.edu.

NEW, ROSETTA HOLBROCK, retired secondary school educator, retired department chairman, retired nutrition consultant; b. Aug. 26, 1921; d. Edward F. and Mabel (Kohler) Holbrock; m. John Lorton New, Sept. 3, 1943; 1 child, John Lorton Jr. BS, Miami U., Oxford, Ohio, 1943; MA, U. No. Colo., 1971; PhD, Ohio State U., 1974; student, Kantcentrum, Brugge, Belgium, 1992, Lesage Sch. Embroidery, Paris, 1995, Kent State U., 1998. Cert. tchr. Colo. Tchr. English and sci. Monahans (Tex.) H.S., 1943—44; emergency war food asst. USDA, College Station, Tex., 1945—46; dept. chmn. home econs., adult edn. Hamilton (Ohio) Pub. Schs., 1946—47; tchr., dept. chmn. home econs. East H.S., Denver, 1948—59, Thomas Jefferson H.S., Denver, 1959—83; ret., 1983. Exec. bd. Denver Pub. Schs.; lectr. in field; exec. dir. Ctr. Nutrition Info. U.S. Office Edn. Grantee, Ohio State U., 1971—73. Mem.: Internat. Platform Assn., Fairfield (Ohio) Hist. Soc., Ohio State Home Econs. Alumni Assn., Ohio State U. Assn., Hamilton Hist. Soc., Am. Vocat. Assn., Am. Home Econs. Assn., Nat. Trust for Hist. Preservation, Cin. Art Mus., Internat. Old Lacers, Embroiders Guild Am., Rep. Club Denver, Order White Shrine of Jerusalem, Daus. of the Nile, Masons, Order of Ea. Star, Phi Upsilon Omicron. Presbyterian. Office Phone: 513-863-2252.

NEWBERG, ESTHER, literary agent; d. Marion Newberg. MA, Wheaton Coll., Norton, Mass., 1963, degree, 2003. Worked with Gov. Ella Grasso, Conn., Robert F. Kennedy, Bella Abzug, Morris Udall Presdl. Campaign, 1976; joined Internat. Creative Mgmt., N.Y.C., 1976, v.p., co-dir. lit. dept., 1988, sr. v.p., co-dir. lit. dept. Recipient Matrix Award, N.Y. Women in Comm., 1997. Office: Internat Creative Mgmt 40 W 57th St New York NY 10019 E-mail: enewberg@icmtalent.com.*

NEWBERN, DIANNA J., management consultant, educator; d. Albert Virgil and Devota Delcine Goodpasture; 1 child, Natalie de la Giraudiere. BS, Philips U., Enid, Okla., 1985; MS, Tex. Christian U., Ft. Worth, 1992, PhD, 1996. Prof. profl. practice Tex. Christian U., Ft. Worth, 1994—; owner-operator Self Mgmt. Sys., 1999—. Assoc. rsch. scientist Inst. Behavioral Rsch. Tex. Christian U., Ft. Worth, 1994—98. Contbr. chapters to books, articles to profl. jours. Mem.: Acad. Mgmt. Office: Tex Christian Univ TCU Box 298920 Fort Worth TX 76129 Office Phone: 817-257-6438. Business E-Mail: d.newbern@tcu.edu.

NEWBERRY, ELIZABETH CARTER, greenhouse and floral company owner; b. Blackwell, Tex., Nov. 25, 1921; m. Weldon Omar Newberry, Sept. 24, 1950 (dec. Nov. 1984); 1 child. Student Hardin Simmons U., 1938-39. Office mgr. F. W. Woolworth, Abilene, Tex., 1939-50; acct. Western Devel. & Investment Corp., Englewood, Colo., 1968-72; owner, operator Newberry Bros. Greenhouse and Florist, Denver, 1972—; bd. dirs. Western Devel. and Investment Corp. Englewood, Colo., 1979-87. Pres. Ellsworth Elem. Sch. PTA, Denver, 1961-62; v.p. Hill Jr. High Sch. PTA, Denver. Home: 201 Monroe St Denver CO 80206-5505 Office Phone: 303-322-0443.

NEWBERRY, PAULA ANITA, singer, music educator; b. Memphis, Tenn. d. Fred Allen and Doris Louise Howell; m. Ray Charles Newberry, June 3, 1989. BA, Oberlin Coll., Ohio, 1985. Certificate in Italian Voice Internat. Sommacademie Universitat, Salzburg, Austria, 2000, Spoleto Vocal Arts Symposium, Italy, 2001. Opera singer/server Braun Ristorante, Memphis, 1992—95; opera singer Romano's Macaroni Grill, Memphis, 1995, Ctrl. Fla. Lyric Opera, Orlando, 1995—96; concert artist (classic vocal) Ebony Diva Enterprises, San Francisco Bay Area, 1997—99; tchr. music Oakhaven Cherokee Elem. Sch., Memphis, 1999—2000, Dunbar Elem. Sch., Memphis, 2000—01, Immaculate Conception Elem. Sch., Memphis, 2002—03; opera/concert artist Ebony Diva Enterprises, Memphis and San Francisco Bay Area, 1997—; classical radio announcer KASU, Jonesboro, Ark., 2004—05. Author: (book) Someone Noticed, 2005; author: (poet) Didn't matter to me what dry sed, 2001. Recipient award, Bagby Musical Found., N.Y.C., 2004; grantee, Change, Inc., N.Y.C., 1998, MusiCrues, Nashville, 2001, 2004, Actor's Fund, Chgo., 2001. Mem.: Am. Guild Musical Artists. Avocations: jogging, weightlifting. Office: Ebony Diva Enterprises PO Box 753446 Memphis TN 38175 Office Phone: 901-216-6593. E-mail: nudraof2005@yahoo.com.

NEWBERY, ILSE SOFIE MAGDALENE, German language educator; b. Darmstadt, Germany, Nov. 15, 1928; came to U.S., 1965; d. Otto and Charlotte (Brill) Brusius; m. A.C.R. Newbery, Dec. 28, 1954; children: Martin Roger, Frances Janet. Diplom akad. gepr. Übersetzer, U. Mainz, Germany, 1949; Staatsexamen Höh. Lehrfach, U. Frankfurt, Germany, 1954; PhD, U. B.C., Vancouver, Can., 1964. Part-time lectr. Queen's U., Belfast, Ireland, 1955-56; grad. asst. U. B.C., 1958-62; lectr. U. Calgary, Can., 1964-65; asst. prof. Georgetown (Ky.) Coll., 1965-67, assoc. prof., 1968-83, prof. German, 1983-94, chair langs. dept., 1989-94, prof. emeritus, 1994—. Examiner Goethe Inst., 1983-87; oral proficiency tester ACTFL, 1985-87; rsch. in German exile lit. Author software in field, 1989—. Founding mem. internat. folk ensemble Singing Hons, Lexington, 1977—. Recipient KCTFL Project award, Ky. Coun., 1994, Rollie Graves Tech. Excellence award, 1993. Mem. Am. Assn. Tchrs. German (v.p. Ky. chpt. 1979-81, pres. 1981-83), Am. Coun. Tchrs. Fgn. Langs., Ky. Coun. Tchrs. Fgn. Langs. (bd. dirs. 1979-83). Avocations: music, tennis, squash, skiing, climbing. E-mail: ilsebrusius@yahoo.com.

NEWBILL, KAREN MARGARET, elementary school educator, education educator; b. East Orange, N.J., Oct. 6, 1945; d. Richard Oliver and Edna Mae (Crook) Jacobson; m. Gary C. Newbill, Aug. 18, 1965; children: Kari L., Erick D. BA, Seattle Pacific U., 1968; MEd, City U., Bellevue, Wash., 1993. Cert. tchr., Wash. Tchr. Shoreline Pub. Schs., Seattle, 1969-71, Northshore Sch. Dist., Bothell, Wash., 1971-74; tutor, substitute tchr. Issaquah (Wash.) Sch. Dist., 1980-89, tchr., 1989—, tech. and curriculum integration cons., 1991—. Adj. prof. N.W. Coll., Kirkland, Wash., 1994—, mem. prof. edn. adv. bd., 1994—; adj. prof. Seattle Pacific U., 1994—; student tchr. supr. U. Wash., Seattle, 1991—, guest lectr., 1996—98, City U., 1998—; presenter Nat. Brain Expo, 2000—03. Mem. ASCD, NEA, Wash. Edn. Assn., Internat. Reading Assn. Avocations: decorative painting, reading, travel, music. Home: 420 Kalmia Pl NW Issaquah WA 98027-2619 Office: Issaquah Sch Dist 565 NW Holly St Issaquah WA 98027-2899 E-mail: newbillk@aol.com.

NEWBURG, ANNE COLBY, writer; b. Paris, Dec. 24, 1957; d. Andre W.G. and Ellen French (Vanderbilt) N.; m. Jeffrey Andrew Wasserman, Jan. 2, 1990; children: Jane Olga, Hugo Joseph. BA, Trent U., Peterborough, Ont., 1977; MA in Philosophy, McGill U., Montreal, Que., 1987. Contbr. short stories to The Antioch Rev., Other Voices, American Short Fiction, Turnstile. Teaching fellow McGill U., 1985-87; McDowell Colony fellow, Peterborough, 1992. Democrat.

NEWBURY, KIRSTEN RAE, computer scientist, educator; b. Inglewood, Calif., July 20, 1946; d. Ray Selmer and Ella Louise (Carter) Newbury. BS, U. Wis., Oshkosh, 1971; MS, U. Colo., 1980; postgrad., Army War Coll., 1987; EdD in Adult and Higher Edn., Mont. State U., 1998, EdD, 1998. Cert. Java Instr., Cisco, project mgmt. profl. Project Mgmt. Inst., 2005; flight instr. FAA. Chief info. svc. Mont. State Dept. Labor and Industry, Helena; dir., personal property and bus. lic. div. County of Fairfax, Va.; analyst officer U.S. Army Pentagon, Washington; battalion commdr. U.S. Army, Frankfurt, Germany, assoc. prof. West Point, NY; adj. tchr. computer tech. Helena Coll. Tech., U. Mont., chmn. computer electronics tech. dept., 2002—03; computer cons., 2004—. Adj. prof. Western Mont. Coll., U. Mont.; del. People-to-People Women Computer Sci. Profls. program, China; coord. 1st statewide program for instrs. new to 2-yr. coll. sys.; faculty practitioner U. Phoenix; faculty fellow for svc. learning Mont. Campus Compact, 1999—2000, mentoring fellow, 2001—03. Del. to China Citizen's Amb. Program, 1993. Lt. col. U.S. Army, 1964—88. Mem.: Women in Mil. Svc. Am., Project Mgmt. Inst., Assn. Computing Machinery. Business E-Mail: krgraham@acm.org.

NEWBY, TERRICA LEE, elementary school educator; d. Larry Wilson and Delores Ann Smith; m. Roger Antonio Newby, June 21, 1997; children: Toni, Tyrell. BS in Elem. Edn., Campbell U., NC, 1995; MEd in Adminstrn. and Supvn., Va. Tech., Blacksburg, 2003. Cert. tchr. Tchr. 3rd grade Gentry Primary Sch., Erwin, NC, 1995—97; tchr. 6th grade L.P. Jackson Mid. Sch., Surry, Va., 1997—2000, 2004—05, tchr. 5th grade, 2004—05; tchr. 2d grade Surry Elem., 2005—. Auditor chair Surry Elem. PTA, 2004—; asst. youth adv. Cypress Bapt. Ch., Derdron, Va., 2000—, praise dance coord., 2003—. Named Tchr. of Yr., L.P. Jackson Mid. Sch./Surry County Pub. Schs., 2002. Mem.: ASCD, NEA, Associated Women's Club (asst. sec. 2005—). Democrat. Baptist. Avocations: singing, shopping. Home: 124 Mullet Dr Ivor VA 23866

NEWBY TYNES, DENISE J., elementary school educator, secondary school educator; b. Nansemond County, Va., Mar. 25, 1957; d. Lee A. and Elizabeth Joe Newby; m. J. Adrian Tynes; 1 child, Asten L. BS, Norfolk (Va.) State U., 1980; MA, Hampton (Va.) U., 1986. Tchr. Charles City (Va.) County Pub. Schs., Isle of Wight (Va.) County Pub. Schs. Chairperson We. Tidewater Cmty. Svcs. Bd. Mem. NEA, Internat. Coun. for Computers in Edn., Va. Edni. Computer Assn., Va. Edn. Assn., Pilot Internat., Pilot Club IOW. Home: PO Box 735 Smithfield VA 23431-0735

NEWCOMB, BETTY LOU ATKINSON, retired mathematics educator; b. Roanoke, Va., Apr. 25, 1938; d. Robert Clayton and Hazel (Cox) Atkinson; m. Frederick Lee Newcomb, Sept. 12, 1959; children: Frederick Jr., Laurie Anne Wilson, Joseph Gary. BA, Randolph-Macon Woman's Coll., 1959; MEd, U. NC, 1986. Cert. adminstr., supr., mentor NC. Interim math. tchr. J.T. Williams Jr. HS, Charlotte, NC, 1983; math. tchr. Wilson Jr. HS, Charlotte, NC, 1978-83, West Mecklenburg Sr. HS, Charlotte, NC, 1983-95, tchr. leadership I and II, 1989-93; asst. site adminstr. summer sch. Myers Pk. Sr. HS, Charlotte, NC, 1989; asst. prin. Shamrock Gardens Elem. Sch., Charlotte, NC, 1995-98, Rama Rd Elem. Sch., Charlotte, NC, 1998—2000; ret. CMS, 2005. Advisor student govt., 1984—93; mem. interclub coun., 1984—93; mem. Order of Feather, 1985—95; advisor Randolph-Macon Women's Coll., 1992—94; fellow Inst. Govt. U. NC, Charlotte, 1991; participant NC Ctr. Advancement Tchg., 1991, NC Math. Algebra I Project, 1992; asst. to prin. West Mecklenburg, 1993—95. Officer Montclaire Elem. Sch. PTA, Charlotte, 1967—77; life mem. NC PTA. Mem.: Symphony Guild (sch. concerts chair 2002—03, lollipops concert chair 2003—04, v.p. enrichment 2004—05, show house com. seminars chair 2004, mem. renewal chair, showhouse com. landscape liaison grounds chair 2006), Nat. Assn. Students (activities advisor), Randolph-Macon Women's Coll.-Charlotte Alumnae Assn. (pres. 1964—65, dist. dir. Nat. Assn. 1974—76, pres. 1990—92), Phi Delta Kappa (social chmn. 1991—92, svc. project chmn. 1992—93, pub. info. chmn. 1993—94, v.p. programs 1994—95, pres. 1995—97, advisor 1997, alt. chpt. del. 1994—95, Outstanding Com. Contbn. to Chpt. award 1992, Outstanding Com. Recognition award 1993, Kappan of Yr. award 1994—95, Outstanding Chpt. award 1996—97, Gerald Howard Read Internat. Seminar scholar 1996), Alpha Delta Kappa (treas. 1988—90, sgt. at arms 1992—94). Avocations: travel, tennis. Home: 1817 Delchester Dr Charlotte NC 28210-4533

NEWCOMB, RACHEL, anthropologist, educator; d. Wilburn Newcomb and Lorraine Gorrell; m. Nour Bennani, Apr. 19, 2001. BA, Davidson Coll., N.C., 1995; MA, Johns Hopkins U., Balt., 1997; MA, PhD, Princeton U., N.J., 2004. Asst. prof. of anthropology Rollins Coll., Winter Park, Fla., 2004—. Contbr. articles and short stories to profl. jours. Faculty fellow - cmty. engagement Rollins Coll., Winter Park, Fla., 2005—06. Recipient First Award - Fiction, Soc. for Humanistic Anthropology, 2005, Vereen Bell First Award for Creative Writing, Davidson Coll., 1994—95; fellow Fulbright fellow, Fulbright Found., 2001—02, Thomas J. Watson fellow, Thomas J. Watson Found., 1995—96, Reginald Tickner Writing fellow, Gilman Sch. of Balt., 1997—98; grantee Cornell grantee, Rollins Coll., 2005; scholar Full Grad. scholar, Princeton U., 1998—2003, Full Grad. Tchg. scholar, Johns Hopkins U., 1996—97. Mem.: Am. Anthrop. Assn., Omicron Delta Kappa. Avocations: writing, running, travel, cooking. Office Phone: 407-691-1703.

NEWCOMBE, NORA, psychology professor; BA in Psychology, Antioch Coll., Ohio, 1972; PhD in Psychology and Social Relations, Harvard U., 1976. Asst. prof. Dept. Psychology Pa. State U., 1976—81; assoc. prof. Dept. Psychology Temple U., 1981—87, prof., 1987—, dir. undergrad. studies, 1981—86, assoc. chair Dept. Psychology, 1986—89, dir. Cognitive Divsn., 1995—99, James H. Glackin Disting. faculty fellow, 2003—. Vis. scholar U. Pa., 1986—87, 1993—94, Princeton U., 1999—2000; vis. scholar Spatial Cognition Group Wissenschaftskolleg, Berlin, 2003—04; editor Jour. Exptl. Psychology: Gen., 1996—2001; guest editor spl. issues on early memory Jour. Exptl. Child Psychology, 1993—94; assoc. editor Psychological Bull., 1990—94; cons. editor Child Develop., 1982—96, Developmental Psychology, 1981—87, Jour. Cognition and Develop., 2002—, Psychological Sci., 2004—; reviewer Behavioral and Brain Sciences, Jour. Exptl. Psychology: Learning, Memory, and Cognition, Psychological Rev., Psychonomic Bull. and Rev., Science. Co-editor (with L.S. Liben and A.H. Patterson): (book) Spatial representation and behavior across the life span, 1981; author: Child development: Change over time, 1996; co-author (with J. Huttenlocher): Making space: The development of spatial representation and reasoning, 2000; contbr. articles to profl. journals, chapters to books. Adv. bd. Cornell Inst. Rsch. on Children, 2003—. Recipient Paul W. Eberman Faculty Rsch. award, Temple U., 2004; fellow James McKeen Cattell, 1999—2000. Fellow: Am. Psychological Soc., APA (early career award com. 1995, publications and comm. bd. 1998—2000, chair coun. elders 1999—2000, exec. com. divsn. 1 1999—2000, pres. divsn. 7 2001—02, com. scientific awards 2004—06, George A. Miller award 2004), AAAS (sec. sect. psychology 2002—06), Am. Acad. Arts and Sciences; mem.: Soc. Rsch. Child Develop. (program com. 1993—99, co-chair program com. 1995—97), Sigma Xi, Psychonomic Soc. (governing bd. 2002—06), Jean Piaget Soc., Internat. Soc. Study of Behavioral Develop., Internat. Soc. Infant Studies, Cognitive Neuroscience Soc., Cognitive Develop. Soc. (bd. dirs. 2003—). Office: Dept Psychology Temple Univ 1701 N 13th St Rm 565 Philadelphia PA 19122-6085 Office Phone: 215-204-6944. Office Fax: 215-204-8100. E-mail: newcombe@temple.edu.*

NEWDIGGER, CARRRIE, secondary school educator; m. Glenn Newdigger; 1 child, Cali. AA, Coffeyville CC, Kans.; BS in Edn., Mo. So. State, Joplin; MS in Biology, Emporia State U., Kans. Sci. tchr. Hartford (Kans.) HS, 1994—95, Macksville (Kans.) HS, 1995—.

NEWELL, ANN MARIE, music educator; b. Fargo, N.D., Feb. 19, 1948; d. Orlando J. and Merriam Melroe Dahl; m. Norman Charles Newell, June 12, 1971; children: Eric, Marc, David. BA in Music Edn., Concordia Coll., Moorhead, Minn., 1970. Elem. music tchr. Ind. Sch. Dist. 191, Cottage Grove, Minn., 1970—72, Ind. Sch. Dist., Chatfield, Minn., 1973—74, Our Lady of Victory Sch., Fergus Falls, Minn., 1985—86, Ind. Sch. Dist. 544, Fergus Falls, Minn., 1989—. Grant chmn. Ctr. for the Arts, Fergus Falls, Minn., 2002—05. Dir., music Grace United Methodist Ch., Fergus Falls, Minn., 1980—93, ch. organist, 1993—. Recipient Human Rights Award, City of Fergus Falls, Minn., 2003. Mem.: Fergus Falls Edn. Assn. (Tchr. of Yr. 2003), Music Educators Nat. Conf. Avocations: bridge, exercise. Office Phone: 218-998-0544.

NEWELL, BARBARA ANN, coatings company executive; b. Portland, Oreg., Mar. 20, 1945; d. John Wesley and Marion Josephine (Hill) Clausen; children: Shamaz, Hukam (dec.), Mardana. BA, Lindenwood Coll. for Women, 1968; MA, Portland State U., 1972; PhD, Summit U., 2000. Owner Shamaz Trading Co., Ukiah, Calif., 1974-77; mgr. small bus. dept. Ernst & Ernst, Portland, 1977-78; CFO All Heart Lumber Co., Ukiah, 1978-83; CFO, CEO Performance Coatings Inc., Ukiah, 1983—, chmn. bd. dirs., 1992—. Chmn. bd. dirs. Rural Visions Found.; treas. chmn. fin. com. Mendocino County Health Clinic, chmn. bd. dirs., 2001-03; CEO, chmn. bd. dirs. Dusky Rose & Assoc., Botanics of Calif.; founder Potter Valley Cafe, 2000; owner Hukam Maj Arabian Horse Ranch, 1998—. Founder, chair Penofin Jazz Festival; chmn. bd. dirs. Mendocino Ballet Co.; bd. dirs. Potter Valley Youth and Cmty. Ctr. Mem. Nat. Paint and Coatings Assn., Golden State Paint and Coatings Assn., Ukiah C. of C. (mem. econ. devel. com. 1993-94), Women in Coatings (Leadership award 1994), Leadership Mendocino. Avocations: showing Arabian horses, reading, children, organic gardening, dance. Office: Penofin-Performance Coatings Inc PO Box 1569 Ukiah CA 95482-1569 Office Phone: 707-462-3023. Business E-Mail: ceo@penofin.com.

NEWELL, CHARLDEAN, public administration educator; b. Ft. Worth, Oct. 14, 1939; d. Charles Thurlow and Mildred Dean (Looney) Newell. BA, U. North Tex., 1960, MA, 1962; PhD, U. Tex., 1968; cert., Harvard U., 1988. Instr. U. North Tex., Denton, 1965-68, asst. prof., 1968-72; assoc. prof., dir. Fedn. North Tex. Area Univs., Denton, Dallas, 1972-74; assoc. prof., assoc. v.p. acad. affairs U. North Tex., Denton, 1974-76, assoc. prof., chair dept. polit. sci., 1976-80, prof. polit. sci., 1980-92, assoc. v.p., spl. asst. to chancellor, 1982-92, regents prof. pub. adminstrn., 1992—2002, prof. emerita, 2002—. Cons. Miss. Bd. Trustees State Instns. Higher Learning, Jackson, 1983—84, Ednl. Testing Svc., Princeton, NJ, 1980, Princeton, 82, Princeton, 85, Spear Down & Judin, Dallas, 1994—95, North Tex. Inst. Edn. Visual Arts, Denton, 1993—94; bd. regents Internat. City/County Mgmt. Assn., Washington, 1994—98, vol. credentialing adv. bd., 2002—; trainer Emergency Leaders Program, 2005—. Author (with others): City Executives: Leadership Roles, Work Characteristics and Time Management, 1989, The Effective Local Govt. Mgr., 2004, Essentials of Tex. Politics, 2004, Texas Politics, 2005; contbr. articles to profl. jours. Chmn. Denton Charter Rev. Com., 1978—79; mem. Denton CSC, 1989—97, chmn., 1992—97; active Denton Blue Ribbon Capital Improvements Com., 1995—96; mem. Denton Devel. Plan Com., 1996—97, Denton Pub. Utilities Bd., 1997—, chmn., 2002—; v.p. Denton Christian Pre-Sch. Bd., 2001—02, pres., 2002—05, mem., 2005—, City Coun. Ethics Com., 2004; v.p. Our Daily Bread, 2005—, vice-chair, 2005—; mem. exec. coun. Episcopal Diocese Dallas, 1985—88. Recipient Elmer Staats Career Pub. Svc. award, Nat. Assn. Sch. Pub. Affairs Adminstrn., 1993. Fellow: Nat. Acad. Pub. Adminstrn.; mem.: Am. Soc. for Pub. Adminstrn. (sect. chmn. 1982—83, mem. editl. bd. 1985—88, Donald C. Stone award 2004), Internat. City/County Mgmt. Assn. (hon.), Pi Alpha Alpha (exec. coun. 1995—99), Pi Sigma Alpha (exec. coun. 1988—92). Democrat. Avocations: spectator sports, reading. Home: 2008 Tremont Cir Denton TX 76205-7408 Business E-Mail: cn0003@unt.edu.

NEWELL, CHARLENE A, music educator; b. Price, Utah, July 21, 1938; d. Gerald James and Thelma McKinnon Anderson; m. Ray Newell, May 13, 1966; children: Mark, Gerald, Daniel, David, Stephen, Darin Douglas, Barbara, Becky, Boni, Joseph, Tina. BA, Brigham Young U., 1960. Choral music tchr. Granite Sch. Dist., 1988—. Recipient Outstanding Gold Medal Svc. award, Carlson Coll., 1956. Mem.: Nat. Music Edn., Utah Music Educators Assn. Republican. Latter Day Saints. Home: 605 East 2000 South Draper UT 84020

NEWELL, CHRISTEL, music educator; d. Terry William and Sharon Kay Dill; children: Chelsey Lynn, Mazie. BEd in Music, SE Mo. State U., Cape Girardeau, 1992. Gen. music tchr. Columbia Unit Sch. Dist., Ill., 1992—. Mem.: Music Educators Nat. Assn. Office: Parkview Elem Sch 1 Parkview Dr Columbia IL 62236-1147

NEWELL, ELIZABETH CAROLYN, retired secondary school educator; b. Georgetown, Ky., Mar. 26, 1940; d. George M. Newell, Sr. and Pearl Carlton Newell. BA in Speech and Drama, Georgetown Coll., 1961; student in Speech, Hist. and Theater, U. Ky., 1963—64; MA magna cum laude in Secondary Guidance and Counseling, Georgetown Coll., 1971. Tchr. Jefferson County Pub. Sch. Sys., 1961—97, ret., 1997, substitute tchr., 1997—; mutuel clk. Keeneland Downs, 2005—; clk. Churchill Downs, 2005—. Coach championship debate club Butler HS, dir. championship drama club, coach championship future problem-solving club. Editor: History of Butler Traditional High School: 50 Years of Excellence, 2004. Co-coord. crisis team JCTA, 1976. Named Tchr. of Yr., Ky. H.S. Speech League, 1965, Elizabeth C. Newell Day, JC Judge Exec. David Armstrong, 1997; recipient Tchr. Recognition award, Butler H.S., 1968; grantee, Capitol Holding, WAVE TV, 1992. Mem.: Svc. Employees Internat. Union, Jefferson County Tchrs. Assn. Retired, Ky. Edn. Assn. Avocations: horses, cats, U.K. ballgames, travel, genealogy. Home: 12001 Running Creek Rd Louisville KY 40243-1932

NEWELL, KARIN BARNES, small business owner; b. Oklahoma City, June 24, 1951; d. Lynn Carl Barnes and Donna-Jean Berry; m. Michael Roy Jackson, Dec. 30, 1970 (div. Sept. 1988); children: Micah Roy Jackson, Aaron Lynn Jackson; m. Gary Lynn Newell, Nov. 26, 1994 (div. Dec. 2003). A in Bus., Tarrant County Jr. Coll., Ft. Worth, 1983. Group One ins. lic.; Series 6 and 63 securities lic. Mktg. officer Bank of Arlington, Tex., 1984-90; event coord. March of Dimes, Ft. Worth, 1990-91; bank mgr. Bank One Tex., Arlington, 1991-96; personal banking officer Compass Bank, Dallas, 1996-97; br. mgr., v.p. Bank of Commerce, Southlake, Tex., 1997-99; v.p. Frost Nat. Bank, Southlake, 1999—2001; with Adminstaff, Dallas, 2002—03; pres. ARTSNET, 2003—, KarinNewell.com, 2004—. Mem. city coun. City of Bedford, Tex., 1998-2001, mayor pro-tem, 1999-2001; liaison Bedford Hotel/Motel Assn., 1999-2000, Regional Transp. Authority, 2000-2001, North Tex. Coun. Govts., 2000-2001; bd. dirs. Arts Coun. of N.E. Tarrant County, gala chair, 1998, Am. Heart Assn., Childrens Ctr. for Self Esteem, ARK Program, Am. Cancer Soc.; bd. sec. Supporters of the Shelter, 2003; mem. Leadership Colleyville, 2001. Mem. Bedford Citizens Police Acad. Alumni Assn., Bedford Citizens Fire Acad. Alumni Assn., N.E. Leadership Forum, Southlake C. of C. (chair Southlake bus. expo 1999), Hurst-Euless-Beford C. of C. (chair HEB econ. devel. found. 1999-2000), Grapevine C. of C., Irving (Tex.) C. of C., N.E. Tarrant County Women in Govt., Rotary, North Tex. USAFA Acad. Parents Club (publicity chair 2000-01, sgt. at arms 2001-02, pres. 2002-03), Ams. for the Arts, Texans for the Arts, Fort Worth Children's Charities, Assn. of Fund Raising Profls. Avocations: volunteering, public speaking, travel. Office: PO Box 211792 Bedford TX 76095-8792 E-mail: karin@karinnewell.com.

NEWELL, RACHEL PIERCE, music educator; b. Salisbury, Md., Nov. 22, 1949; d. Hersie Beale and Ann Howell Pierce; m. Wayne Linwood Newell, June 6, 1992; children: Margaret Davis Price, Mary Darden Price. MusB, Westhampton Coll., 1972; MME, Shenandoah U., 1990. Music tchr. Louisa County Pub. Sch., Mineral, Va., 1972—74, Loudoun County Pub. Sch., Leesburg, Va., 1974—76, 1977—79, 1984—; tchr. Dales Sch. Lang., Cambridge, England, 1976—77; choir dir. St. James Episcopal Ch., Leesburg, Va., 1981—84. Mem. adv. coun. Shenandoah U., Leesburg, Va.; Summer in the Arts coord. Loudoun County Pub. Schs. Named Tchr. of Year, Shenandoah U., 1999, Agnes Meyer Tchr. of Year, Washington Post, 2003; Fulbright fellow, Japan. Mem.: NEA, Va. Edn. Assn., Music Educators Nat. Conf., Va. Music Educators Assn. Episcopalian. Avocations: reading, water sports, music, travel. Home: 101 Liberty St NW Leesburg VA 20176 Office: Loudoun County Pub Sch Hillside Elem Sch 43000 Ellzey Dr Ashburn VA 20148 Office Phone: 571-252-1622. Personal E-mail: rachnewell@aol.com.

NEWELL, SHIRLEY ANN CECIL, retired art dealer, artist; d. Francis M. and Ora A. Cherry, Sr.; m. Richard A. Cecil (div.); children: David B., Valerie A., Vicki E.; m. David B. Newell (div.). Student, U. Tenn., 1958—61, Calif. Luth. Coll., 1970, U. Calif., 1971, Ga. State U., 1977. Pvt. practice art instr., Atlanta, 1970; prin., owner Collectors Art, Atlanta, 1979—85, Cecil B. Day Investment Co., Ga., 1986—95, adminstrv. asst. Ga.; adminstrv. asst. Siemens Energy and Automation, 1998—2006. Exhibitions include Oxnard Art Club Festival of Art, Hilton Head Art League, Garden Club of Ga., Habitat Atlanta. Mem. Nat. Mus. Women of the Arts, Washington, Roswell Cultural Arts; charter mem. High Mus. Art, Atlanta; mem. Americans for the Arts Action Fund, Washington; bd. dirs. DeKalb Coun. Arts, 2005—; bd. dirs. Peachtree Arts Atlanta (Ga.) High Mus. Art, 1998—99, sec. suburban art com., 1982—83; mem. individual arts com. coalition Olympics '96, Atlanta, 1996. Recipient award, WSB Radio, Civic Svc. award, Boys Club Am., 1971. Mem.: Roswell Cultured Arts, Nat. Women Arts. Methodist. Avocations: reading, dance, art.

NEWGENT, REBECCA ANN, counselor, educator; b. Ohio; BA in Psychology, Kent (Ohio) State U., Kent, OH, 1986; MEd in Cmty. Counseling, Kent (Ohio) State U., 1993; PhD in Guidance and Counseling, U. Akron, 2001. Cert. family and divorce mediator. Case mgr. II/counselor trainee Cmty. Support Svcs., Inc., Akron, Ohio, 1988—93; counselor, family life edn. coord., vol. coord., divorce mediator Jewish Family Svc., Akron, 1993—95; counselor Cath. Svc. League, Akron, 1995—96; divorce mediator Domestic Rels. Divsn. Summit County Ct. Common Pleas, Akron, 1995—99; pvt. practice counselor, divorce mediator Akron Psychol. Assocs., 1995—98; counselor, sch.-based counselor, divorce mediator Cath. Social Svcs. of Summit County, Inc., Akron, 1997—99; emergency clinician Portage Path Behavioral Health-Psychiat. Emergency Svcs., Akron, 1997—2000; grad. asst. dept. counseling and spl. edn. U. Akron, 1998—2000, mem. adj. faculty dept. ednl. founds. and leadership, 2000, mem. ad hoc temporary grad. faculty, doctoral intern dept. counseling and spl. edn., 2000—01; asst. prof. counselor edn. U. Ark., Fayetteville, 2001—06, assoc. prof., 2006—. Bd. advisors The Clinic for Child Study and Family Therapy U. Akron, 1998—2001. Mem. mental health trauma action team Summit County Red Cross Disaster Svcs., Akron, 1998—2000. Mem.: ACA, AAUP, Ark. Assn. Assessment in Counseling, Ark. Assn. Counselor Edn. and Supervision, Ark. Counseling Assn., Assn. Counselor Edn. and Supervision, Chi Sigma Iota (Outstanding Doctoral Student award 2001). Office: U Ark 236 Graduate Education Bldg Fayetteville AR 72701 Office Phone: 479-575-7311. Business E-Mail: rnewgent@uark.edu.

NEWHALL, BARBARA FALCONER, writer, journalist; b. Mich. d. David Bishop and Catherine Ann Falconer; m. Jonathan Newhall, Mar. 5, 1977; children: Peter Falconer, Christina Falconer. BA, U. Mich.; Cert. in German Lang. and Culture, U. Heidelberg, Germany. Copy editor, reporter San Francisco Chronicle, 1972-80; feature writer, columnist Oakland (Calif.) Tribune, 1980-92; religion reporter Contra Costa Times, Walnut Creek, Calif., 1992-96; writer, journalist freelance, Oakland, 1997—. Recipient 1st Place award for humor San Francisco Press Club, 1990. Mem. Religion Newswriters Assn., East Bay Press Club, Delta Delta Delta. Episcopalian. Avocations: photography, travel, swimming, hiking.

NEWHALL, EDITH ALLERTON, writer; b. Phila., Feb. 13, 1951; d. John Allerton and Dorothy (Todd) N.; m. David Walters, May 29, 1988. BA in Art History, Moore Coll., 1973; MFA, Art Inst. Chgo., 1979. Asst. editor Phila. Bulletin, 1974-76, Harry N. Abrams Publ., N.Y.C., 1979-81; writer N.Y. Mag., N.Y.C., 1981—.

NEWHOUSE, SHERRI FRANCE, elementary school educator; b. Columbus, Ohio, Nov. 22, 1966; d. John Richard and Patricia Jean France; m. Timothy Wayne Newhouse, Dec. 23, 1971; children: Samuel John, Tyler Brice, Franklin Abbott, Evelyn Rose; m. Timothy Wayne Newhouse, Dec. 18,

1993. BS, U. NC, Greensboro, 1989; MSA, NC State U., Raleigh, 2003. Tchr. Durham Pub. Schs., NC, Wake County Pub. Schs., Raleigh, 1997—. Tchr. Sunday, worship leader Garner Christian Ch., NC, 2005—06. Mem.: Phi Kappa Phi. Home: 97 Black Angus Dr Garner NC 27529 Office: Wake County Public Schools Wake Forest Rd Raleigh NC 27601 Personal E-mail: newhousesherri@wmconnect.com. E-mail: snewhouse@wcpss.net.

NEWKIRK, INGRID, animal rights activist; b. Surrey, Eng., July 11, 1949; m. Steve Newkirk, 1967 (div. 1980). Former animal protection officer and dep. sheriff, Md.; poundmaster Washington, 1978; former chief of animal disease control Commn. on Public Health, Washington; dir. cruelty investigations Washington Humane Soc., Washington, 1978-80; pres., co-founder (with Alex Pacheco) People for the Ethical Treatment of Animals, Washington, 1980—. Author: Save the Animals! 101 Easy Things You Can Do, 1990, Kids Can Save the Animals! 101 Easy Things you Can Do, The Compassionate Cook, 250 Things You Can Do to Make Your Cat Adore You, You Can Save the Animals: 251 Simple Ways to Stop Thoughtless Cruelty, Making Kind Choices; TV appearances include The Today Show, The Oprah Winfrey Show, Nightline, 20/20. Office: PETA 501 Front St Norfolk VA 23510

NEWKIRK, TRIXIE DARNELL, family nurse practitioner; b. Sault St. Marie, Mich., July 22; d. Mitchell and Lois I. (Johnston) Darnell; m. Shane P. Newkirk, July 19, 1986; 1 child, Breana Alysha. BSN, Southwestern Okla. State U., 1986; MS, Tex. Woman's U., 1994, cert. family nurse practitioner, 1997. RN, Okla., Tex.; cert. nurse practitioner, Tex.; cert. BCLS, instr. ACLS, CCRN, FNP. Staff nurse St. Francis Hosp., Tulsa; asst. nurse mgr. CCU Humana MCD Hosp., Dallas; staff nurse Baylor U. Med. Ctr., Dallas, supr. nurse educator critical care unit, 1991-95; clin. nurse specialist for cardiovasc. svcs., 1995-98; family nurse practitioner BG Mills Clinic Assn., Mesquite, Tex., 1997-98; nurse practitioner Heart Place Cardiology, Dallas, 1998-2000, St. Paul U. Hosp. Cardiovasc. Inst., Dallas, 2000—05, Newkirk Family Practice Clinic, Mesquite, Tex., 2005—. Mem. ANA, Am. Acad. Nurse Practitioners, Tex. Nurses Assn., AACN, Sigma Theta Tau. Home: PO Box 465 Scurry TX 75158 Office Phone: 972-279-6767. Personal E-mail: trixienewkirknp@yahoo.com.

NEWLAND, CHEYRL MARIE, music educator; b. Kirksville, Mo., Sept. 8, 1955; d. Charles Stafford and Oreta Marie Walker; m. Billy Joe Newland, July 3, 1982; children: Marie Elizabeth, Emily Angeline, Charles Eugene, John William. B of Music Edn., Truman State U., Kirksville, Mo., 1977. Tchr. 7-12 vocal music Lincoln Co R-III, Troy, Mo., 1977—79; tchr. 4-12 vocal music Putnam Co R-I, Unionville, Mo., 1979—81; tchr. 5-12 instrumental, 7-12 vocal music Moulton-Udell Schs., Iowa, 1981—84; music dir./organist First Bapt. Ch., Kirksville, Mo., 1985—2005; tchr. k-2 music Kirksville R-III, Mo., 2001—03; tchr. pre-kindergarten-12 vocal music Moulton-Udell Schs., Iowa, 2003—06; pvt. music tchr. Moulton, 2006—. Music dir. First Bapt. Ch., Kirksville, Mo., 1985—2005. Mem.: Iowa Bandmasters (assoc.), Am. Choral Dirs. (assoc.), Music Educators (assoc.), Sigma Alpha Iota (life). Nazarene. Home: 3209 N Lincoln St Kirksville MO 63501

NEWLAND, RUTH LAURA, small business owner; b. Ellensburg, Wash., June 4, 1949; d. George J. and Ruth Marjorie (Porter) N. BA, Cen. Wash. State Coll., 1970, MEd, 1972; EdS, Vanderbilt U., 1973; PhD, Columbia Pacific U., 1981. Tchr. Union Gap (Wash.) Sch., 1970-71; owner Newland Ranch Gravel Co., Yakima, Wash., 1998; ptnr. Arnold Artificial Limb, Yakima, 1981-86, owner, pres. Yakima and Richland, Wash., 1986—. Owner Newland Ranch, Yakima, 1969—. Contbg. mem. Nat. Dem. Com., Irish Nat. Caucus Found.; mem. Pub. Citizen, We The People, Nat. Humane Edn. Soc.; charter mem. Nat. Mus. Am. Indian. George Washington scholar Masons, Yakima, 1967. Mem. NAFE, NOW, Am. Orthotic and Prosthetic Assn., Internat. Platform Assn., Nat. Antivisection Soc. (life), Vanderbilt U. Alumni Assn., Peabody Coll. Alumni Assn., Columbia Pacific U. Alumni Assn., World Wildlife Fund, Nat. Audubon Soc., Greenpeace, Mus. Fine Arts, Humane Soc. U.S., Wilderness Soc., Nature Conservancy, People for Ethical Treatment of Animals, Amnesty Internat., The Windstar Found., Rodale Inst., Sierra Club (life), Emily's List. Democrat. Avocations: reading, gardening, sewing, handcrafts. Home: 2004 Riverside Rd Yakima WA 98901-8540 Office: Arnold Artificial Limb 9 S 12th Ave Yakima WA 98902-3106

NEWMAN, BARBARA MAE, retired special education educator; b. Rockford, Ill., July 16, 1932; d. Greene Adam and Emma Lorene (Fields) N. BS Edn., No. Ill. U., 1973. Cert. elem. edn. K-8 tchr., spl. edn. (blind and p.s.) K-12 tchr. Exec. sec. Rockford Art Assn., 1961-70; tchr. Title 1 Rockford Pub. Sch. Dist. #205, 1975-76, tchr. vision impaired, 1977-91. Feature editor (Rock Valley Coll. newpaper) The Valley Forge, 1970; contbg. writer (Rockford Coll. history) A Retrospective Look, 1980. St. Bernadette adult choir, 1958-95, Cathedral Chorale, 1995—; holder 5 offices Am. Bus. Women's Assn., Forest City chpt., 1963-70; vol. Winnebago Ctr. for the Blind, Rockford, 1965-70; mem. Rockford Diocesan Chorale, 1969—. Named Woman of Yr., Am. Bus. Women's Assn., Forest City chpt., Rockford, 1966; scholar Ill. State Scholarship Commn., No. Ill. U., 1970-73. Mem. Ill. Ret. Tchrs. Assn., Cath. Woman's League. Roman Catholic. Avocations: writing, swimming.

NEWMAN, BARBARA MILLER, psychologist, educator; b. Chgo., Sept. 6, 1944; d. Irving George and Florence (Levy) Miller; m. Philip R. Newman, June 12, 1966; children: Samuel Asher, Abraham Levy, Rachel Florence. Student, Bryn Mawr Coll.; AB with honors in Psychology, U. Mich., 1966, PhD in Devel. Psychology, 1971. Undergrad. research asst. in psychology U. Mich., 1963-64, research asst. in psychology, 1964-69, teaching fellow, 1965-71, asst. project dir. Inst. for Social Research, 1971-72, univ. lectr. in psychology and research assoc., 1971-72; asst. prof. psychology Russell Sage Coll., 1972-76, assoc. prof., 1977-78; assoc. prof. and chair dept. family rels. and human devel. Ohio State U., 1978-83, prof. and chair, 1983-86, assoc. provost for faculty recruitment and devel., 1987-92, prof., 1992-2000; prof. and chair dept. human devel. and family studies U. R.I., 2000—. Author: Development Through Life, 1975, 9th edit., 2006; author: (with P. Newman) Living: The Process of Adjustment, 1981, Understanding Adulthood, 1983; author: Adolescent Development, 1986, When Kids Go to College, 1992, Childhood and Adolescence, 1997; author: (with P. Newman, L. Landry-Meyer and B. Lohman) Life Span Development: A Case Book, 2003; contbr. articles to profl. jours. Mem.: AAAS, APA, Soc. Rsch. in Child Devel., Am. Psychol. Soc., Nat. Coun. Family Rels., Groves Conf. on Marriage and Family, Soc. for Rsch. on Adolescence. Office: U RI Human Devel and Family Studies 112 Transition Ctr Kingston RI 02881 Office Phone: 401-874-7135. Business E-Mail: bnewman@uri.edu.

NEWMAN, BARBARA TATE, retired social studies educator; b. Spartanburg, S.C., Apr. 9, 1950; d. Clester Hurd and Frances Louise Tate; life ptnr. Isaac Vastyne McJimpsey; children: Charlene Yvette Wiggleton, Clester Charles Wiggleton. BS in Social Sci., Barber-Scotia Coll., Concord, N.C., 1972; MEd, Converse Coll., 1980. Cert. tchr. mid. and secondary edn. State Dept. of SC, 1972. Social studies tchr. Fairforest Mid. Sch., Spartanburg, SC, 1972—2006, social studies dept. chairperson, 1978—81, student coun. sponsor, 1980—2006; ret., 2006. Ch. trustee Friendship Bapt. Ch., Spartanburg, 2006, sr. missionary aux., 1995—2006, sr./gospel choir, 2005—06; vol. Spartanburg Regional Healthcare Hospice, 1996—98, Best Chance Network, Spartanburg/ Union Counties, 1995—96. Mem.: NEA (assoc.), SC. Edn. Assn. (assoc.). D-Liberal. Baptist. Avocation: travel. Home: 105 Old Farm Rd Moore SC 29369 Office: Fairforest Middle School 4120 N Blackstock Rd Spartanburg SC 29301 Office Phone: 864-576-9778.

NEWMAN, CAROL L., lawyer; b. Yonkers, NY, Aug. 7, 1949; d. Richard J. and Pauline Frances (Stoll) N. AB/MA summa cum laude, Brown U., 1971; postgrad., Harvard U. Law Sch., 1972-73; JD cum laude, George Washington U., 1977. Bar: D.C. 1977, Calif. 1979. With antitrust divsn. U.S. Dept. Justice, Washington and L.A., 1977-80; assoc. Alschuler, Grossman & Pines, L.A., 1980-82, Costello & Walcher, L.A., 1982-85, Rosen, Wachtell & Gilbert, L.A., 1985-88, ptnr., 1988-90, Keck, Mahin & Cate, L.A., 1990-94; pvt. practice L.A., 1994—. Adj. prof. Sch. Bus., Golden Gate U., spring 1982. Commr. L.A. Bd. Transp. Commrs., 1993—98, v.p., 1995—96; pres. Bd. Taxicab Commrs., 1999—2001; candidate for State Atty. Gen., 1986; bd. dirs. Women's Progress Alliance, 1996—98. Mem. ABA, State Bar Calif., L.A. County Bar Assn., Ventura County Bar Assn., L.A. Lawyers for Human Rights (co. pres. 1991-92), Log Cabin (bd. dirs. 1992-97, 2003—, pres. 1996-97), Calif. Women Lawyers (bd. govs. 1991-94), Order of Coif, Phi Beta Kappa. Office Phone: 818-225-0056. E-mail: cnewman540@aol.com.

NEWMAN, CONSTANCE BERRY, federal agency administrator; b. Chgo., July 8, 1935; d. Joseph Alonzo and Ernestine (Siggers) B.; m. Theodore Roosevelt Newman, July 25, 1959 (div. 1980). AB, Bates Coll., 1956; BSL, U. Minn., 1959; JD (hon.), Bates Coll., 1972, Amherst Coll., 1980; LHD (hon.), Central State U., 1991. Dir. VISTA, Washington, 1971-73; commr. Consumer Product Safety Commn., Washington, 1973-76; asst. sec. U.S. HUD, Washington, 1976-77; pres. The Newman & Hermanson Co., Washington, 1977-82; cons. Govt. of Lesotho, 1987-88; dir. nat. voter coalition Bush-Quayle '88, Washington, 1988; dir. Office Pers. Mgmt., Washington, 1989-92; under sec. Smithsonian Instn., Washington, 1992-2000; vice chair D.C. Fin. Responsiblity and Mgmt. Assistance Authority, 1994—2000; ptnr. Upstart Ptnrs., 2000—01; asst. adminr. bur. for Africa USAID, Washington, 2001—04; asst. sec. for African affairs US Dept. State, 2004—. Mem. adj. faculty John F. Kennedy Sch. Govt., Harvard U., Cambridge, Mass., 1979-82. Contbr. articles to profl. jours. Mem. Adminstrn. Conf. U.S., Washington, 1973-76, 1989—; commr. M.L. King Fed. Holiday Commn., Washington, 1989; chmn. Def. Adv. Com. on Women in the Svcs., Washington, 1985-86; trustee Community Coll. Balt., 1985-89; adv. to chmn. 1988 Rep. Nat. Conv., New Orleans, 1988; bd. overseers Morehouse Coll. Sch. Medicine, Atlanta, 1976-77; bd. dirs. Brookings Instn., Aspen Inst., Coun. for Excellence in Govt. Recipient Pub. Svc. award Ohio State U., 1991. Mem. NAACP, Exec. Women in Govt. (founding mem.), Internat. Repub. Inst., 1998-2000. Republican. Avocation: photography. E-mail: newmancb@state.gov.

NEWMAN, DAVA JEAN, aerospace engineering educator, director; b. Helena, Mont., Aug. 11, 1964; d. Daniel L. Newman and Deanna A. (Mack) Elliott. BS in Aerospace Engring., U. Notre Dame, 1986; MS in Tech. and Policy, MIT, 1989, MS in Aeronautics and Astronautics, 1989, PhD in Aerospace Biomed. Engring., 1992. Engr. Boeing Co., Seattle, 1986; cons., lectr. Internat. Space U., Strasbourg, France, 1987—; rsch. fellow NASA Ames Rsch. Ctr., Mountain View, Calif., 1989-92; asst. prof. U. Houston, 1992-93; C.S. Draper asst. prof. aerospace engring. MIT, Cambridge, Mass., 1993-95, prof. aeronautics, astronautics and engring. sys., 1998—2004, full prof. aeronautics, astronautics and engring. sys., 2004—, dir. Tech. and Policy Program, 2003—. Bd. dirs. Aeronautics and Space Engring. Nat. Acad.; cons. NASA Hdqs., Washington, 1995-96, Trotti and Assocs., Inc., Boston, 1996—, Nascent Technologies, Inc., 1999; affiliate faculty Health, Scis. and Tech. Harvard/MIT. Author: Interactive Aerospace Engineering and Design, 2002; contbr. author: Fundamentals of Space Life Sciences, 1997; contbr. over 100 articles to profl. jours.; author, prodr. U.S./Russian Astronaut Training Video, 1996. Bd. dirs. OMNISport 2001, 1990-2004; advisor KEYS To Empowring Youth, Cambridge, 1995—. Named Prof. of Yr., U. Houston, Soc. Automotive Engrs., 1993; recipient Manned Space Flight award NASA, 1995, Nat. Aerospace Educator award Women in Aerospace, 2001; numerous rsch. grants NASA, 1993—. Fellow AIAA (assoc.); mem. Am. Soc. for Engring. Edn., Internat. Soc. Biomechanics, Union Concerned Scientists, NY Acad. Scis., Soc. Women Engrs. Democrat. Achievements include rsch. in astronaut biomechanics and energetics for space flight and on the moon and Mars; world record holder of women's human-powered hydrofoil speed record. Office: MIT Rm 33-307 77 Massachusetts Ave Cambridge MA 02139-4307 Business E-Mail: dnewman@mit.edu.

NEWMAN, DEBORAH RAE, minister; b. Gainesville, Fla., Dec. 27, 1961; d. Robert Thomas and Norma Bess Bowles; m. Brian Kevin Newman, Jan. 5, 1985; children: Rachel Mae, Benjamin Kevin. BA, Bryan Coll., 1983; MA, Grace Theol. Sem., 1984; DPhil, Oxford Grad. Sch., 1991. Lic. counselor, marriage and family therapist, Tex. Counselor Liberty Bible Ch., Valparaiso, Ind., 1984-85; psychotherapist Meier New Life Clinic, P.A., Richardson, Tex., 1985—2003; women's min. Christ Ch., Plano, Tex., 2003—. Author: Passages of Marriage, 1991, Love Is a Choice Workbook, 1991, Day by Day Love Is a Choice, 1991, Thin Disguise, 1992, Then God Created Woman, 1997, Loving Your Body, 2002, A Womans Search for Worth, 2002, Passion on Purpose, 2003, How to Really Love God as Your Father, 2005. Bd. dirs. Collin County Women's Shelter, Plano, Tex., 1990—94. Republican. Anglican. Office: Christ Ch Plano 4550 Legacy Rd Plano TX 75024

NEWMAN, DIANA S., foundation administrator, consultant; b. Toledo, June 15, 1943; d. Fred Andrew and Thelma Elizabeth (Hewitt) Smith; m. Dennis Ryan Newman, Feb. 15, 1964; children: Barbara Lynn Newman LaBine, John Ryan, Elizabeth Anne. Student, Oberlin Coll., 1961-64. Asst. treas. Marble Cliff Quarries Co., 1964-68; cmty. vol., 1968-83; dir. Ohio Hist. Found., Columbus, 1983-90; v.p. advancement The Columbus (Ohio) Found., 1990-95; pres. Philanthropic Resource Group, Columbus, 1995—. Author: Opening Doors: Pathways to Diverse Donors, 2002 (AFP/Skystone Ryan prize for rsch., 2003), Nonprofit Essentials: Endowment Building, 2005. Bd. dirs. Leader Inst., Inc., 2001-04; mem. governing bd. First Cmty. Ch., 1983-88, chair, 1987-88; bd. dirs. LWV Ctrl. Ohio, 1968-72, Ohio Mus. Assn., 1985-90, Crittenton Family Svcs., Columbus, 1992-95; founder Franklin County Com. on Criminal Justice, Columbus, 1972; pres. Jr. League Columbus, 1980-81. Mem. Assn. Fundraising Profls. (bd. dirs. Ctrl. Ohio chpt. 1985-88, 2004-, nat. rsch. coun. 2003—, Outstanding Profl. Fundraiser 2004), Ctrl. Ohio Planned Giving Coun. (bd. dirs. 1990-2001, pres. 1998), Columbus Female Benevolent Soc. (bd. dirs. 1984—). Home: 1944 Chatfield Rd Columbus OH 43221-3702 Office: Philanthropic Resource Group 926 Augusta Glen Dr Columbus OH 43235 Office Phone: 614-486-4787. Business E-Mail: diana@diananewman.com.

NEWMAN, GAYLE JOANN, elementary school educator; b. Belleville, Ill., Oct. 4, 1949; d. Charles Elza and Marcella Adelia Augusta Caldwell; m. James Russell Newman, Aug. 28, 1971; children: Bridget Elaine, Jason Russell; m. James Russell Newman, Aug. 28, 1971. BS, Ctrl. Mo. State U., Warrensburg, 1971, MS, 1974. 2d gr. tchr. Raytown (Mo.) Sch. Dist., 1971—74; reading specialist Blue Valley Sch. Dist., Overland Park, Kans., 1975. Contbr. articles to profl. jours. Chmn. banquet Kans. Tchr. of Yr. Region 3, 2002—; chmn. children's Christmas program Christ Luth. Ch., Overland Park, 1979—; co-chair after prom Blue Valley H.S. PTO, Stilwell, Kans., 1993—98. Named Master Tchr., Indian Valley Elem., 1998, Tchr. of Yr., Blue Valley Sch. Dist., 1999, Kans. Region 3, 2000. Mem.: Internat. Reading Assn., Kans. Reading Assn., Kans. Nat. Edn. Assn., Phi Delta Kappa. Home: 15436 Iron Horse Cir Leawood KS 66224 Office: Indian Valley Elem 11600 Knox Overland Park KS 66210 Office Phone: 913-239-6400. Personal E-mail: newjo@hotmail.com.

NEWMAN, GERALDINE ANNE, advertising executive; b. Boston, Apr. 01; d. Joseph M. and Clara (Bistry) N. BS, UCLA; postgrad., Alliance Francaise, Paris, Los Angeles Sch. Fine Arts, NYU. Writer Tinker Dodge and Delano, N.Y.C., 1970-72, Ketchum Advt., N.Y.C., 1972-75, Advt. to Women, N.Y.C., 1975-78; v.p., creative supr. Young and Rubicam, N.Y.C., 1978-83; v.p., assoc. creative dir. Backer Spielvogel Bates Worldwide Internat. Div., N.Y.C., 1983-90; pres. Geraldine Newman Comm., Inc., N.Y.C., 1990—. County committeewoman Dem. Party, N.Y.C., 1972; advt. adviser Youth at Risk, Breakthrough Found., Food Bank, Food for All, Gifts that Give Back. Featured in Adweek Mag., 1986, Response Mag., 2003; winner Andy award 1975, 78, 82, 84, Clio award 1982, ERA award, 1998, 2004, Astrid award Mercomm Internat., 2002, numerous others. Mem.: Ad Club N.Y., Electronic Retailing Assn., Ad-net (bd. dirs. 1984—89, creative dir. 1986—89, Pres.'s award 1988), N.Y. Women in Film. Avocations: travel, painting. Home and Office: 315 E 72nd St New York NY 10021-4625 Office Phone: 212-988-3395. E-mail: advertisingmuse@aol.com.

NEWMAN, GWILL LINDERME, volunteer; b. Cleve., July 9, 1932; d. Frederick William Linderme and Sara Louise (Lindquist) Petrequin; m. Scott R. York, Sept. 11, 1954 (div. Apr. 1980); children: Gwill Elaine, Frederick William (dec.); m. Bruce L. Newman, Apr. 11, 1980. BA in French, Vassar Coll., 1954. Tchr. French, Spanish Laurel Sch., 1954-62; staff dept. lang. rsch. Harvard U., 1956-57; vol. cons. Action Agy., Washington, 1977-78; pres., bd. dirs. Nat. Alliance for Rsch. on Schizophrenia and Depression, 1983-89; pres. bd. trustees Brain Rsch. Found. U. Chgo., 1985-89, vice chmn., pres. emeritus, 1989—. Ohio rep. Carter's 51.3 % Com., 1975-76; mem. planning com. nat. conf. Coun. on Founds. Trustee Chgo. Horticultural Soc., 1981—, Ill. Facilities Fund, 1989—, Lake Forest Coll., 1990—; vice chmn. Cleve. Found., 1970-78, Chgo. Urban League, 1981-91; pres. Recreation League Cleve., 1977-78; chmn. Cleve. Congress Internat. Women's Yr., 1975; mem. exec. com. Downtown Cleve. Corp., 1975-78; co-founder, v.p. Playhouse Sq. Assocs., 1972-78; pres. Cleve. Music Sch. Settlement, 1966-78; chmn. community involvement rev. bd. Lake Erie Regional Transit Authority, 1974-77, numerous other civic activities. Recipient Disting. Alumna award Laurel Sch., Shaker Heights, Ohio, 1989, Ruth T. Lucas award for Outstanding Vol. Svc., 1973; named Hon. Trustee Cleve. Music Sch. Settlement, 1977, Cleve. Woman of Yr. Cleve. Plain Dealer, 1975, Hon. Mem. Jr. League Cleve., Inc., 1972; named to Hon. Order Ky. Cols., 1989; Gwill Newman fellowship established in her honor Nat. Alliance for Rsch. on Schizophrenia and Depression, 1989. Mem. Phi Beta Kappa.

NEWMAN, J. BONNIE, academic administrator, former government official; b. Lawrence, Mass., June 2, 1945; d. William Michael and Louise Catherine (Casey) Newman BA, St. Joseph's Coll., Maine, 1967; MEdn, Pa. State U., 1969; LHD (hon.), Rivier Coll., Nashua, NH, 1983; LLD (hon.), Notre Dame Coll., Manchester, NH, 1984, Keene State Coll., NH, 1987; LHD (hon.), St. Joseph's Coll., Standish, Maine, 1990. Exec. dir. Forum on NH's Future, 1978-80, dir, 1980-82; asst. dean students U. NH, Durham, 1969—72, dean of students, 1972-78, interim dean Whittemore Sch. of Bus. and Econs., 1998—99, interim pres., 2006—; chief of staff Congressman Judd Gregg, 1981-82; assoc. dir. Office Presdl. Pers. The White House, Washington, 1982-84, asst. sec. commerce for econ. devel., 1984-85, asst. to the Pres. for Mgmt. and Adminstrn., 1989—91; exec. dean Kennedy Sch. Govt., Harvard U., 2000—05. Bd. dirs. NH Charitable Found., Citizens Advisors, Lumina Found., Markem Corp.; chmn. US Navy Acad. Bd. of Visitors. Bd. dirs. Gov.'s Econ. Devel. & Land Use Com., 1979-80. Named Alumni Fellow, Pa. State U.; recipient Granite State Award, Yankee Award, Pub. Rels. Soc., Lifetime Achievement Award, Bus. and Industry Assn. of NH, New England Coun.'s Leadership Award, Abigail Adams Award, Mass. Women's Polit. Caucus, 2005. Mem.: Bus. and Industry Assn. NH (pres. 1985—88), Econ. Club of NY. Republican. Roman Catholic. Office: Office of Pres / U NH Thompson Hall 105 Main St Durham NH 03824 Office Phone: 603-862-2450. Office Fax: 603-862-3060.*

NEWMAN, JOAN MESKIEL, lawyer; b. Youngstown, Ohio, Dec. 12, 1947; d. John F. and Rosemary (Scarmuzzi) Meskiel; children: Anne R., Elyse S. BA in Polit. Sci., Case-Western Reserve U., 1969; JD, Washington U., St. Louis, 1972, LLM in Taxation, 1973. Bar: Mo. 1972. Assoc. Lewis & Rice, St. Louis, 1973-80, ptnr., 1981-90, Thompson Coburn, St. Louis, 1990—2005. Adj. prof. law Washington U. Sch. Law, St. Louis, 1975-92; past pres. St. Louis chpt., mem. Midwest Pension Conf. Mem. nat. coun. Washington U. Sch. Law, 1988—91; chmn. bd. dir. Great St. Louis coun. Girl Scouts USA, 1975—92, officer, 1978—92; mem. cmty. wide youth svcs. panel United Way Greater St. Louis, 1992—96; fin. futures task force Kiwanis Camp Wyman, 1992—93; chmn. staff blue ribbon fin. com. Sch. Dist., Clayton, 1986—87; vol. Women's Self Help Ctr.; bd. dirs. Parents as Teachers, 2001—04; bd. dir., exec. com. Girl Scouts USA, 1993—99, nat. treas., 1996—99; bd. dirs. Met. Employment and Rehab. Svcs., 1980—2001, chmn. bd. dir., 1994—96; bd. dirs. Jewish Ctr. Aged, 1990—92, bd. dir., 1999—2001, Jewish Fedn. St. Louis, 1991—96, City Mus., 1998—2001, Parents as Tchrs., 2000—; chmn. bd. dir. Women of Achievement, 1993—96; bd. dir. United Way Greater St. Louis, 2000—, Oasis, 1999—2001; bd. dirs. MERS/Goodwill Industries, 2001—, Walker Scottish Rite Ctr., 2002—. Named Woman of Achievement St. Louis, 1991. Mem. Mo. Bar Assn. (staff pension and benefits com. 1991—), Bar Met. St. Louis (past chmn. taxation sect.), St. Louis Forum, Order of Coif (hon.). Office Phone: 314-645-5001. Business E-Mail: joan@joannewmanassociates.com.

NEWMAN, LESLÉA, writer; b. Bklyn., Nov. 5, 1955; d. Edward and Florence Newman; m. Mary Vazquez. BS in Edn., U. Vt., 1977; cert. in poetics, Naropa Inst., Boulder, Colo., 1980. Author: A Letter to Harvey Milk, 1988, Heather Has Two Mommies, 1989, In Every Laugh a Tear, 1992, Fat Chance, 1994, Too Far Away to Touch, 1995, Remember That, 1996, Still Life with Buddy, 1997, Out of the Closet and Nothing to Wear, 1997, Matzo Ball Moon, 1998, Girls Will Be Girls, 2000, Signs of Love, 2001, Cats, Cats, Cats!, 2001, Dogs, Dogs, Dogs!, 2002, Runaway Dreidel, 2002;: She Loves Me, She Loves Me Not, 2002, Felicia's Favorite Story, 2002, Pigs, Pigs, Pigs!, 2003, Best Short Stories of Leslea Newman, 2003, The Best Cat in the World, 2004 (Muse Medallion Best Children's Book award Cat Writers Assn., awards), The Boy Who Cried Fabulous, 2004, A Fire Engine for Ruthie, 2004, Where is Bear?, 2004, Hachiko Waits, 2004 (Henry Bergh Children's Book Honor award), Jailbait, 2005, The Eight Nights of Chanukah, 2005. Recipient fiction award Highlights for Children, 1992; fellow Mass. Artists Fellowship, 1989, NEA, 1997. Mem. Author's Guild, Poets and Writers, Soc. Children's Book Writers and Illustrators, Pub. Triangle. Jewish. Avocations: crossword puzzles, bowling, collage-making. Address: PO Box 815 Northampton MA 01061-0815

NEWMAN, LIBBY, painter, printmaker, curator; b. Rockland Del., Nov. 17, 1925; d. Hyman and Dora (Horowitz) Goldberg; children— Don, Andrea Newman Orsher. BFA U. Arts; postgrad. U. Pa., Villanova U. Mem. visual arts panel Pa. Council on Arts, 1971-76; artist-in-residence/curator exhbns. University City Sci. Ctr., Phila., 1975—; co-curator sculpture Gov.'s Mansion, Harrisburg, Pa., 1979—88; one-woman shows Phila. Art Alliance, 1971, 2003, Mangel Gallery, Phila., 1972, 75, 78, 84, 88, 92, 95, 99, 2004, 05, University City Sci. Ctr. Gallery, Phila., Tianjin Fine Arts Coll., China, 1988, 89; group shows include Mangel Gallery, 1972-2000, Pa. Acad. Fine Arts, Phila., Peale Galleries of Pa. Acad. Fine Arts, Woodmere Art Mus., Chestnut Hill, Pa., Moore Coll. Art, Phila., Fritz Miller Gallery, N.Y.C., William Penn State Mus., Harrisburg, Pa., Fountain Gallery, Portland, Oreg., Del. Art Mus., Wilmington, Phila. Mus. Art, Circle Gallery, N.Y.C., Chgo., So. Alleghenies Mus. Art, Loretto, Pa., Mus. Phila. Civic Ctr., Moore Coll. Art, Phila., 1982, Sichuan Fine Arts Inst., Changging, People's Republic China, 1985, Tianjin Fine Arts Coll., People's Republic China, 1986, Art in City Hall, Phila., 1986, King St. Mus., Szekesherva, Hungary; represented in permanent collections Phila. Mus. Art, Nat. Mus. Belgrade (Yugoslavia), Mus. Modern Art, Buenos Aires, Argentina, U. Pa. Law Sch., Mus. Phila. Civic Ctr., Temple U. Law Sch., Phila., Glassboro State Coll. (N.J.), Free Library Phila., University City Sci. Ctr., Phila., St. Joseph's Coll., Phila., St. Charles Borromeo Sem., Overbrook, Pa., Temple U. Health and Sci. Ctr., Phila., Nationalities Service Ctr., Phila., Phila. Assn. Clin. Trials., Mus. Andropologico, Guayagui, Equador, Indus Valley Sch. Arts and Architecture, Karachi, Pakistan, 2006, Biblioteca Alexandrina and International Biennale, 2006; Editor: R. Buckminster Fuller Sketchbook, 1981; A City Sketched: A Guide to the Art and History of Philadelphia, 1976. Mem. Mayor's Com. for Sci. and Tech., 1979-82. Recipient Fleischer Art Meml. award; Cheltenham Nat. Graphic award; Best Pictures of the Yr. award Phila. Art Alliance; Carl Zigrosser Nat. Meml. award Am. Color Print Exhbn., Disting. Daus. Pa. award, 1992; chosen for vis. artist project Brandywine Graphics, 1984; Nat. Endowment grantee, 1973; fellowship of the Pa. Acad. of Fine Arts, Perry Owens award, Mayor's citation City of Phila., 1995. Mem. Artists Equity Assn. (pres. Phila. chpt. 1969-71), Am. Color Print Assn., Phila. Art Alliance, Phila. Watercolor Club. Home: 2401 Pennsylvania Ave Apt 7b34 Philadelphia PA 19130-3029 Office Phone: 215-765-4555. Personal E-mail: libby2401@aol.com.

NEWMAN, MALANE L., computer graphics designer, cartoonist, illustrator, computer graphics designer, educator; b. San Diego, Aug. 6, 1955; d. Charles L. and Marlene A. (Walker) Newman. Cert., Art Instrn. Schs., Mpls., 1972; BA, U.S. Internat. U., San Diego, 1975. Graphic artist La Jolla (Calif.) Advt., 1972; lead illustrator PS Mag., Perspective Corp., San Diego, 1983; art dir. CBT Courseware, Inc., San Diego, 1986; owner, creator animated cards Imagination Enterprises, San Diego, 1986; creative dir., lead designer websites, WBT, electronic design Accenture Corp., 1989; owner Malane Newman Designs, Ramona, Calif., 2001; tchr. computer applications, computer art and design, multimedia Ramona H.S., 2004. Guest lectr. cartooning, self pub., copyright, mail order; cons. corp. graphics, bus. presentations. Mem.: So. Calif. Cartoonist Soc., Nat. Computer Graphics Assn., Nat. Cartoon Soc. Home: 16765 Daza Dr Ramona CA 92065-4613 Office Phone: 760-789-4583. Personal E-mail: malanenewman@cox.net.

NEWMAN, MARGARET ANN, nursing educator, department chairman; b. Memphis, Oct. 10, 1933; d. Ivo Mathias and Mamie Love (Donald) N. BSHE, Baylor U., 1954; BSN, U. Tenn., Memphis, 1962; MS, U. Calif., San Francisco, 1964; PhD, NYU, 1971. DON, asst. prof. nursing Clin. Rsch. Ctr., U. Tenn., 1964-67; asst. prof. NYU, 1971-75, assoc. prof., 1975-77; prof. in charge grad. program and rsch. dept. nursing Pa. State U., 1977-80, prof. nursing, 1977-84, U. Minn., 1984-96, prof. emeritus, 1996—. Disting. resident Westminster Coll., Salt Lake City Utah, 1991. Author: Theory Development in Nursing, 1979, Health as Expanding Consciousness, 1986, 2nd edit., 1994, A Developing Discipline, 1995; editor: (with others) Source Book of Nursing Research, 1973, 2d edit., 1977. Travelling fellow New Zealand Nursing Ednl. and Rsch. Fund, 1985; Am. Jour. Nursing scholar, 1979-80; recipient Outstanding Alumnus award U. Tenn. Coll. Nursing, 1975, Disting. Alumnus award NYU Divsn. Nursing award NYU Divsn. Nursing, 1992, Sigma Theta Tau Founders Rsch. award, 1993, Nursing Scholar award St. Xavier U., 1994, E. Louise grant award for nursing excellence U. Minn., 1996, Margaret Newman scholar award Zeta chpt. Sigma Theta Tau, 1996—. Fellow Am. Acad. Nursing. Achievements include research on patterns of person-environment interaction as indices of health as expanding consciousness; also models of professional practice.

NEWMAN, MARJORIE YOSPIN, psychiatrist; b. NYC, July 8, 1945; d. Toby and Audrey (Kreinik) Yospin; children: Eric, David. Student, Smith Coll., 1963-64; AB, Barnard Coll./Columbia U., 1967; MD, Med. Coll. Pa., 1971. Diplomate Am. Bd. Psychiatry and Neurology. Psychiatry intern, resident Albert Einstein Coll. Medicine, N.Y.C., 1971-75; asst. prof. psychiatry U. Tex. Health Sci. Ctr., San Antonio, 1975-77, UCLA Sch. Medicine, 1977-80; dir. residency tng. in psychiatry Harbor-UCLA Med. Ctr., 1977-79; asst. clin. prof. psychiatry UCLA Sch. Medicine, 1980—; pvt. practice Pasadena, Calif., 1983—. Mem. admissions com. UCLA Med. Sch., 1995—. NSF grantee, London, Eng., 1969; Am. Field Svc. Internat. scholar, Argentina, 63. Fellow Am. Psychiat. Assn., Smith Coll. Alumna Assn., Barnard Coll. Alumnae Assn., Columbia U. Alumni Assn., L.A. (Calif.) Acad. Medicine (bd. govs. 2000—, sec. 2002-03, v.p. 2003-04, pres. 2004-05); mem. So. Calif. Psychiat. Soc. (regional coun. 2001-04). Avocations: travel, music, art, swimming, bicycling. Office: Cotton Med Ctr South 50 Alessandro Pl Ste 340 Pasadena CA 91105-3149 Office Phone: 626-564-1750.

NEWMAN, MIRIAM See **DEHORITY, MIRIAM**

NEWMAN, MURIEL KALLIS STEINBERG, art collector; b. Chgo., Feb. 25, 1914; d. Maurice and Ida (Nudelman) Kallis; m. Albert H. Newman, May 14, 1955; 1 son by previous marriage, Glenn D. Steinberg. Student, Art Inst. Chgo., 1932-36, Ill. Inst. Tech., 1947-50, U. Chgo., 1958-65. Hon. life trustee, benefactor Met. Mus. Art, N.Y.C., vis. com. dept. 20th Century Art, acquisitions com., 1981—, decorative arts com., 1989, Costume Inst. Dir., 20th Century Painting and Sculpture Com., Art Inst. Chgo., 1955-80, governing mem. inst., 1955—; pioneer collector Am. abstract expressionist art, 1949—, major show of collection, Met. Mus. Art, N.Y.C., 1981, personal collection of costumes and jewelry, 1981. Bd. govs. Landmarks Preservation Council, Chgo., 1966-78; woman's bd. U. Chgo., 1960-81, Art Inst. Chgo., 1953—, 20th century com., Asian com.; trustee Mus. Contemporary Art, 1970, benefactor, 1970; trustee Chgo. Sch. of Architecture Found., 1971, Archives Am. Art, 1976; bd. dirs. Bright New City Urban Affairs Lecture Series, 1966—; trustee Art Inst. Chgo., mem. African and American art com. Recipient Scroll Recognition of Pub. Svc., U.S. Dept. State, 1958; named Disting. Benefactor, Art Inst. Chgo., 1998. Mem. Antiquarian Soc. of Art Inst. Chgo., Chgo. Hist. Soc. (mem. guild 1958—), Arts Club Chgo., Casino Club Chgo., Arts Club (Chgo.), Casino Club (Chgo.)

NEWMAN, NANCY MARILYN, ophthalmologist, educator; b. San Francisco, Mar. 16, 1941; BA in Psychology magna cum laude, Stanford U., 1962, MD, 1967. Diplomate Am. Bd. Ophthalmology. NIH trainee neurophysiology Inst. Visual Scis., San Francisco, 1964-65; clin. clk. Nat. Hosp. for Nervous and Mental Disease, London, 1966-67; intern Mount Auburn Hosp., Cambridge, Mass., 1967-68; NIH trainee neuro-ophthalmology, from jr. asst. resident to sr. asst. resident to assoc. resident dept. ophthalmology sch. medicine Washington U., St. Louis, 1968-71; NIH spl. fellow in neuro-ophthalmology depts. ophthalmology and neurol. surgery sch. medicine U. Calif., San Francisco, 1971-72, clin. asst. prof. ophthalmology sch. medicine, 1972; asst. prof., chief divsn. neuro-ophthalmology Pacific Med. Ctr., San Francisco, 1972-73, assoc. prof., chief, 1973-88; physician, cons. dept. neurology sch. medicine U. Calif., VA Med. Ctr., Martinez, Calif., 1978—. Prof. dept. spl. edn. Calif. State U., San Francisco, 1974-79; vis. prof. Centre Nat. D'Ophtalmologie des Quinze-Vingts, Paris, 1980; clin. assoc. prof. sch. optometry U. Calif., Berkeley, 1990—; bd. dirs., adv. bd. Frank B. Walsh Soc., 1974-91, Rose Resnick Ctr. for the Blind and Handicapped, 1988-92, Fifer St. Fitness, Larkspur, 1990-92; Internat. Soc. for Orbital Disorders, 1983—, North Calif. Soc. Prevention of Blindness, 1978-88, North African Ctr. for Sight, Tunis, Tunisia, 1988—; pres., CEO Minerva Medica; cons. in field. Author: Eye Movement Disorders; Neuro-ophthalmology: A Practical Text, 1992; mem. editoral bd. Jour. of Clin. Neuro-ophthalmology, Am. Jour. Opthalmology, 1980-92, Soc. Francaise d'Ophtalmogie, Ophthalmology Practice, 1993—; contbr. numerous articles to profl. jours. Recipient NSPI award Self Instrnl. Materials Ophthalmology, Merit award Internat. Eye Found., fellow 1971; Smith-Kettlewell Inst. Vis. Scis. fellow, 1971-72. Mem. AMA (leader Calif. del. continuing med. edn. 1982, 83), San Francisco Med. Soc., Calif. Med. Assn. (sub com. med. policy coms. 1984—, chair com. on accreditation continuing med. edn. 1981-88, chair quality care rev. commn. 1984), Assn. for Rsch. in Vision and Ophthalmology, Pan Am. Assn. of Ophthalmology, Soc. of Heed Fellows, Pacific Coast Oto-Ophthalmology Soc., Lane Medical Soc. (v.p. 1975-76), Internat. Soc. of Neuro-Ophthalmology (founder), Cordes Soc., Am. Soc. Ophthalmic Ultrasound (charter), Orbital Soc. (founder), West Bay Health Systems Agy., Oxford Opthalmology Soc., Pacific Physician Assocs., Soc. Francaise D'Ophtalmologie (mem. editorial bd. jour.). Home: 819 Spring Dr Mill Valley CA 94941-3924

NEWMAN, PAULINE, federal judge; b. NYC, June 20, 1927; d. Maxwell Henry and Rosella Newman. BA, Vassar Coll., 1947; MA, Columbia U., 1948; PhD, Yale U., 1952; LLB, NYU, 1958. Bar: N.Y. 1958, U.S. Supreme Ct. 1972, U.S. Ct. Customs and Patent Appeals 1978, Pa. 1979, U.S. Ct. Appeals (3d cir.) 1981, U.S. Ct. Appeals (fed. cir.) 1982. Research chemist Am. Cyanamid Co., Bound Brook, NJ, 1951—54; mem. patent staff FMC Corp., N.Y.C., 1954—75, Phila., 1975—84, dir. dept. patent and licensing, 1969—84; judge U.S. Ct. Appeals (fed. cir.), Washington, 1984—; Disting. prof. George Mason Law Sch., 1995—. Program specialist Dept. Natural Scis. UNESCO, Paris, 1961—62; mem. State Dept. Adv. Com. on Internat. Indsl. Property, 1974—84; lectr. in field. Contbr. articles to profl. jours. Trustee Phila. Coll. Pharmacy and Sci., 1983—84; bd. dirs. Med. Coll. Pa., 1975—84, Midgard Found., 1973—84. Mem.: ABA (coun. sect. patent trademark and copyright 1983—84), Coun. Fgn. Rels., U.S. Trademark Assn. (bd. dirs. 1975—79, v.p. 1978—79), Pacific Indsl. Property Assn. (pres. 1979—80), Am. Inst. Chemists (bd. dirs. 1960—66, 1970—76), Am. Chem. Soc. (bd. dirs. 1972—81), Am. Patent Law Assn. (bd. dirs. 1981—84), Yale Club, Vassar Club, Cosmos Club. Office: US Ct Appeals Nat Cts Bldg 717 Madison Pl Washington DC 20439-0002*

NEWMAN, PHYLLIS, counselor, therapist, hypnotist; b. NYC, Aug. 20, 1933; d. Max and Frieda Yetta (Pechter) Hershkowitz; BS, Mercy Coll., 1977; MS, LIU, 1979; m. Milton Newman, Dec. 28, 1952; children: Renee Holly, Eileen Sharon, Jeffrey Mark. Pvt. practice hypnosis and therapy, Peekskill, NY, 1977—89; lectr. Pepsico Fitness Ctr., Purchase, NY, 1984, Purdue U., 1986, 88, Girl Scouts' Council, local radio; dir. counseling Hypnosis Group, 1979—89; featured local TV, 2004, 60 Minutes 2, 2004, Ivanhoe Broadcasting Co., 2005, Purdue Alumnus Mag., 2005. Mem. parents exec. bd. Purdue U., 1978-83, mem. pres.' council, 1982—89; bd. dirs. Hand to Mouth Players, Garrison, NY, Yorktown Cmty. Players, NY, 1988-89; v.p. bd. dirs. Temple Emanuel Tempe, Ariz., 1996-; chair Beit Am. (Ho. of People), 2003-, healing svc. 2005-; active for Normal Pressure Hydrocephalus awareness Barrows Neurol. Inst., Phoenix, 2005, Hydrocephalus Assn., San Francisco, 2005; lectr. Ahwautukee Cancer Assn., 2002; leader meditation JCC, 1994-2001; liaison coun. Jewish Family Concerns, 2006—. Mem. Am. Assn. Counseling and Devel., Am. Mental Health Counselors Assn., NY Soc. Ericksonian Hypnosis, Am. Assn. Profl. Hypnotherapists. Contbr. articles to profl. jours. Address: 4333 W Walton Way Chandler AZ 85226 Personal E-mail: phylnew820@cox.net.

NEWMAN, RACHEL, editor; b. Malden, Mass., May 1, 1938; d. Maurice and Edythe Brenda (Tichell) Newman; m. Herbert Bleiweiss, Apr. 6, 1973 (div. Apr. 1989); m. Michael Lucas, Feb. 24, 2004. BA, Pa. State U., 1960; cert., N.Y. Sch. Interior Design, 1963. Accessories editor Women's Wear Daily, N.Y.C., 1964—65; designer, publicist Grandoe Glove Corp., N.Y.C., 1965—67; assoc. editor McCall's Sportswear and Dress Merchandiser mag., N.Y.C., 1967; mng. editor McCall's You-Do-It Home Decorating, 1968—70, Ladies Home Jour. Needle and Craft mag., N.Y.C., 1970—72; editor-in-chief Am. Home Crafts mag., N.Y.C., 1972—77; fashion dir. Good Housekeeping mag., N.Y.C., 1977—78, home bldg. and decorating dir., 1978—82; editor-in-chief Country Living mag., N.Y.C., 1978—98; founding editor Country Cooking mag., 1985—90, Dream Homes mag., 1989—2000, Country Kitchens mag., 1990—93, Country Living Gardener Mag., 1993—2000, Healthy Living mag., 1996—2000. Bd. dirs. Mothers and Others for a Livable Planet. Named Disting. Alumna, Pa. State U., 1988; recipient Cir. of Excellence award, Internat. Furnishings and Design Assn., 1992, YMCA Hall of Fame, 1992; Pa. State U. Alumni fellow, 1986. Mem.: Am. Soc. Mag. Editors, Am. Soc. Interior Designers, Nat. Home Fashions League, N.Y. Fashion Group. E-mail: Rachelsfree@earthlink.net.

NEWMAN, RUTH GALLERT, psychologist; b. N.Y.C., June 16, 1914; d. Ernest Ezra and Belle (Cohen) Gallert; m. James R. Newman (July 27, 1940 (dec.); children: Jeffrey Frederick, Brooke Anne. BA, Rtugers U., 1937; MA, George Washington U., 1942; PhD, U. Md., 1950. Tchr. Emerson Sch., N.Y.C., 1938-40; remedial tutor Remedial Edn. Ctr., Washington, 1942-45; remedial tchr. Geroge Wahsington Day Sch., Washington, 1948-51; clin. tchr., supr. Children's Hosp., Washington, 1955-60; pvt. practice group therapy Washington Sch. Psychiatry, 1960—. Mem. AKPice Group Rels.; speaker in field; cons. in field. NIMH grantee. Democrat. Address: c/o Brooke Newman 273 Roaring Fork Dr Aspen CO 81611-2238 Personal E-mail: thelittletern@hotmail.com.

NEWMAN, SANDRA SCHULTZ, state supreme court justice; BS, Drexel U., 1959; MA, Temple U., 1969; JD, Villanova U., 1972; D (hon.), Gannon U., 1996, Widener U., 1996, Clarion U., 2000, Drexel U., 2001. Bar: Pa., U.S. Dist. Ct. (ea. dist.) Pa., U.S. Ct. Appeals (3d cir.), U.S. Supreme Ct. Asst. dist. atty. Montgomery County, Pa., 1972—74; pvt. practice, 1974—93; judge Commonwealth Ct. of Pa., 1993—95; justice Pa. Supreme Ct., 1995—. Past chair bd. consultors Villanova U. Law Sch.; mem. jud. coun. Supreme Ct. of Pa., liaison to the 3rd cir. task force on mgmt. of death penalty litigation, liaison to Pa. lawyers fund for client security bd., liaison to domestic rels. procedural rules com.; liaison Pa. Bar Inst.; jud. work group HHS; mem. adv. com. Nat. Ctr. for State Cts., Am. Law Inst.; mem. Drexel U. Coll. Bus. and Adminstrn.; lectr. and spkr. in field. Author: Alimony, Child Support and Counsel Fees, 1988; contbr. articles to profl. jours. Named named Disting. Daughter of Pa.; recipient Phila. award for Super Achiever, Pediatric Juvenile Colitis Found. Jefferson Med. Coll. and Hosp, 1979, award for Dedicated Leadership and Outstanding Contbns. to the Cmty. and Law Employment, Drexel 100 award, Police Chiefs Assn. of Southeastern Pa., 1993, Medallion of Achievement award, Villanova U., 1993, Susan B. Anthony award, Women's Bar Assn. Western Pa., 1996, award, Justinian Soc., 1996, Tau Epsilon Law Soc., 1996, Legion of Honor Gold Medallion award, Chapel of Four Chaplain, 1997, honored by, Women of Greater Phila., 1996, Person of Yr. award, Shomrim of Phila., 1998, Women of Distinction award, Greater Phila. Council of Jewish Women Internat., 2005, Person of Yr. award, Pa. State Constables Assoc., 2005. Fellow: Pa. Bar Found., Am. Bar Found.; mem.: Montgomery Bar Assn., Nat. Assn. Women Judges, Am. Law Inst. Office: Supreme Ct Pa Ste 400 100 Four Falls Corporate Ctr West Conshohocken PA 19428-2950*

NEWMAN, SHERRYL HOBBS, former district secretary; BA in Chemistry, Rutgers U., 1986, BA in Economics, 1986; MBA in Management, Lubin Graduate Sch. of Bus. Pace Univ., White Plains, NY, 1992. Exec. sec.-Tax Operation Bureau NYC-Dept. of Finance, 1986, special projects coordinator-Program Devel. Divsn., 1986—87, special property coordinator-Program Devel. Divsn., 1986—87, asst. to dir.-Taxpayer Assistance Divsn., 1987—89, unit mgr.-Taxpayer Corr., 1989—90, unit mgr.-Real Estate Tax Assistance, 1990—92, acting dep. dir.-Taxpayer Assistance Divsn., 1992—93, city collector-Property Bureau, 1993—96; dir. Customer Svc. Adminstrn.-Office of Tax and Revenue, Washington, 1997—99, Citywide Customer Svc. Adminstrn.-Office of the City Adminstr., Washington, 1999, Dept. of Motor Vehicles, Washington, 1999—2003; sec. dist. DC Govt., 2003—05, dep. CFO, Office Tax & Revenue, 2005—. Democrat. Office: John A Wilson Bldg 1350 Pennsylvania Ave NW Rm 419 Washington DC 20004 Business E-Mail: shnewman@dc.gov.*

NEWMAN, STACEY CLARFIELD, artist, curator; b. N.Y.C., July 21, 1956; d. Wallace J. Clarfield and Elinor (Kandel) Clarfield-Toberoff; m. Fredric Alan Newman, Nov. 27, 1983; children: Benjamin Clarfield, Marissa Paige, Alexandra Brooke Student, Franklin & Marshall, 1974—76; BS Labor Rels. and Mgmt., U. Bridgeport, 1978. Dir. ops. Nat. Rec. and Video Studios, N.Y.C., 1978—80; dir. tech. ops. VCA/Teletronics, N.Y.C., 1980—82, cons., client rep./MTV, 1981—83, exec. prodr., 1982—85, dir. tech ops. prodr.; artist, art curator Stacey Clarfield Newman Studios, Scarsdale, NY, 1986—. Merchandise cons. Tahari Fashions, N.Y.C., 1985—86; artist mem., jury com. You Gotta Have Art program White Plains Hosp. Ctr., NY, 1990—92; art tchr. collage Scarsdale Adult Edn. Program, 1993—95; artist in residence Scarsdale Elem. Schs., 1995—97; art cons., curator Manhattan Transfer, Inc., N.Y.C., 1997—2000; mem. faculty Young at Art enrichment program, Scarsdale, 2002—; juror Figure and Form Edward Hopper House Mus., N.Y.C., 2004. One-person shows include Quogue Gallery, N.Y., 1986, Piermont Fine Arts Gallery, N.Y., 1997-98, 2001, Manhattan Transfer, Inc., 1997, J&W Gallery, New Hope, Pa., 1999, Studio 4 West, 1999, 93 South Gallery, 2000, Adele Greenberg Salon, Cambridge, Mass., 2000, Amb. Galleries, Palm Beach, Fla., 2001, Viridian Gallery, N.Y.C., 2001, 02, 05, Viridian Gallery @ Chelsea, 2002, 04, 05; exhibited in juried group shows: Piermont Fine Art Gallery, 1995, 96, 98, 99, 2000, 01, Anaya Gallery, Scarsdale, 1986, Katonah Gallery, N.Y., 1986, Gallery at Jamaica, Stratton Mountain, Vt., 1987, CDS Contemporary Art, Albuquerque, 1989, Mari Galleries, Mamaroneck, N.Y., 1992, Manhattan Transfer, Inc., 1993, 98, 93 South Gallery, Nyack, N.Y., 1998-99, Bibro Fine Arts Gallery, Chelsea, N.Y., 1998, Weber Fine Art, Scarsdale, 1998, 2000, J&W Gallery, New Hope, 1998, 99, 2001, 02, Studio 4 West, Hewlett Mus., 2000, Amb. Gallery, Palm Beach, 2000, Viridian Gallery, N.Y.C., 2000-04, Adele Greenberg Salon, 2000, 01, A Pirate Space, Denver, 2001, Contemporary Art Oasis, Denver, 2001, Manhattanville Coll. Gallery, 2002, Nat. Assn. Women Artists, N.Y.C., 2003, Chgo. Fine Arts Bldg. Gallery, 2003, Inklings, Viridian Artists, Chelsea, 2005, 06, News Art, Virdian Artists, 2005, John Jay Coll. Pres.'s Gallery, 2005, Fountain St. Gallery, Cape Girardeau, Mo., 2006, Veridian Artists Inc., N.Y.C., 2006; commd. Am. Soc. Plastic and Reconstructive Surgeons, L.A. Conv. Ctr., 1988, White Plains Hosp. Ctr., 1989, 90, Cystic Fibrosis Found., N.Y.C., 1990, Joan Kroc Found., Calif., 1989-91 1st v.p., bd. dirs. Internat. Coll. Surgeons Aux., Chgo., 1988—90; mem. Gala com. Juvenile Diabetes Found., 2000; Regional v.p. Am. Cancer Soc., White Plains, 1986—88; bd. dirs. White Plains Hosp. Ctr. Aux.; fund raiser, event planner Holocaust Commn., N.Y.C., 1998; active Scarsdale Tremont Synagogue Gala, 2001, 2002; fund-raiser Alternative Arts and Music Events, Scarsdale Teen Ctr., 2003—; liaison Scarsdale H.S. PTA, Alternative Art and Music Events, Scarsdale Teen Ctr., 2003—05; bd. dirs. com. on spl. edn. Scarsdale Sch. Dist. Mem. Internat. Platform Assn., Nat. Mus. Women in Contemporary Arts, Nat. Assn. Women Artists, Inc., Katonah Mus., Nat. Mus. Women in Arts (artist), Nat. Arts Club Avocations: piano, photography, tennis, kayaking, skiing. Studio: 21 Wayside Ln Scarsdale NY 10583-2911 Personal E-mail: StaceySCN21@aol.com.

NEWMAN, SUZANNE DINKES, web site design company executive; b. Bklyn., Apr. 28, 1949; d. Philip and Natalie (Hollander) Dinkes; m. Ralph Michael Newman, Mar. 9, 1975. Student, Cooper Union, 1967—71, Sch. Visual Arts, NYC, 1971—72. Asst. art dir. Lincoln Ctr. Art Programs, NYC, 1973-74; art dir. BimBamBoom Mag., Yonkers, NY, 1974; with Fairfax Advt., NYC, 1974-75; dir. ops. TBE Advt., NYC, 1975-87, CEO Yonkers, NY, 1987-94; art dir. Timer Barrier Express, Yonkers, 1975-80; CEO R.S. Newman Assocs., Yonkers, 1994-98; ptnr. WWW.Dott-Comm.com, 1997—. Concert coord. Classic Harmony Prodns., NYC, 1975; apl. event planner, The Left Bank, Mt. Vernon, NY, 1980-81; apl. event cons. Glen Island Casino, New Rochelle, NY, 1984-85; event coord., Top Brass, Yonkers, 1986-87; art dir., cons. various music publs., 1974-80. Editor: Rockin' in the Fourth Estate, 1979-80, Chamber News, 1998—; art dir.: White and Still All Right!, 1977, Sun Records, 1980, The Buddy Holly Story, 1979. Mem. Yonkers Citizen's Adv. Grp., Yonkers Mayorial Transition Com., 1991-92, Alliance Devel. Com., Yonkers Sch. and Bus. Alliance, 1991-94, program com., 1991-94; mem. Yonkers Coun. Pres.'s Citizens Adv., Group, 1992, Yonkers Dem. Com., dist. leader, 1991-93; jour. chair gala com. Hudson River Mus., 1992; mem. Yonkers Local Bus. Adv. Coun., 1992-94; mem. Yonkers Pvt. Industry Coun., 1992-94, sec. 1993-94; promotion chair Yonkers Hudson Riverfest, 1992-93; bus. adv. com. Yonkers Econ. Devel. Zone, 1993-94; active Yonkers Waterfront Task Force, 1993-94; bd. dirs. Youth Theater Interaction, 1994—; bd. dirs. Westchester divsn. Jewish Guild for Blind, 1994-97, gala chair, 1994; events coord. Mayor's Inaugural Ball, 1996; leader Jr. Girl Scouts, Southwest Yonkers, 1996—. Recipient Disting. Leadership and Svc. award, Westchester County C. of C., 1985, Westchester award, Westchester Small Bus. Coun., 1989, Outstanding Leader award Girl Scouts U.S., 2000. Mem. Westchester Small Bus. Coun. (comm. chmn. 1984-85, Westchester winner, 1989), Yonkers C. of C. (bd. dirs. 1996—, comm. chair 1996-97), Coun. for Arts Westchester. Democrat. Jewish. Avocations: reading, antiques, gardening. E-mail: snewman@dott-comm.com.

NEWMAN, TERRY E., lawyer; b. Chgo., Jan. 15, 1947; BA, Loyola U., Ill., 1969; JD, DePaul U., 1977. Bar: Ill. 1977, U.S. Dist. Ct. (no. dist.) Ill. 1977, D.C. 1991. Asst. states atty. Cook County, 1977-78; ptnr. Katten Muchin Zavis Rosenman, Chgo. Sec. bd. trustees City Coll. Chgo., 1989. Mem. ABA, Ill. State Bar, D.C. Bar, Chgo. Bar Assn. (real estate tax sect.). Office: Katten Muchin Zavis Rosenman 525 W Monroe St Ste 1600 Chicago IL 60661-3649 Office Fax: 317-577-8781.

NEWMAN-GORDON, PAULINE, French language and literature educator; b. NYC, Aug. 5, 1925; d. Bernard and Eva Newman; m. Sydney A. Gordon, Sept. 13, 1959 (dec.); m. Richard Yellin, Feb. 9, 1997. BA, Hunter Coll., 1947; MA, Columbia U., 1948; PhD, Sorbonne U., Paris, 1951. Instr. French Wellesley (Mass.) Coll., 1952-53; mem. faculty Stanford (Calif.) U., 1953—, prof. French lit., 1969-93, prof. emerita, 1994—. Author: Marcel Proust, 1953, Eugene Le Roy, 1957, Corbiere, Laforgue and Apollinaire, 1964, Helen of Troy Myth, 1968, (poetry) Mooring to France, (prose poem) Sydney: editor: Dictionary of Ideas in Marcel Proust, 1968, also articles in field; contbr. articles to profl. jours. Scholar Internat. Inst. Edn., 1948-51, MLA, 1956-57, AAUW, 1962-63, Am. Philos. Soc., 1970-71, NEH, 1989; elected to Hall of Fame, Alumni Assn. Hunter Coll. of CUNY, 1990 Mem. MLA, Am. Assn. Tchrs. French, Soc. Friends Marcel Proust. Office: Stanford U Dept French Italian Stanford CA 94305

NEWMARK, MARILYN, sculptor; b. NYC, July 20, 1928; d. Edward Ellis and Mabel (Davies) Newmark; m. Leonard J. Meiselman, Mar. 15, 1952. Student, Adelphi Coll., 1945—47, Alfred U., N.Y., 1949. Sculpture specializing in horses, equestrian figures, dogs, foxes. Exhibited in group shows Derby Mus., Fleischer Mus., Scottsdale, Leigh Yawkey Woodson Art Mus., Wis., Bennington Ctr. for Arts, Vt., NAD, NYC, Nat. Arts Club, NYC, Smithsonian Instn., Washington, Mus. of Horse, Ky., Port of History Mus., Pa., Marietta/Cobb Mus. Art, Wildlife Experience, Denver, Nat. Geog. Soc., Washington, Allegheny Colls. Galleries, Butler Inst. Am. Art; represented in permanent collections Nat. Mus. Racing, Saratoga, NY, Internat. Mus. Horse, Ky. Horse Park, Brookgreen Gardens, S.C., also pvt. collections. Recipient Anna Hyatt Huntington award, 1970-72, 75, 78, 80-83, 86, 88, 90, 97, 2002, Gold medal, 1973, award Coun. Am. Artists Socs., 1972, 73, 79, 80, Hudson Valley John Newington award, 1973, 77, Gold medal, 1979, Elliot Liskin Meml. award, 1989, 96, Academician NAD Ellin P. Speyer award, 1974, 93, 99, Artist Fund award, 1982, Michael Gressel award, 2006. Fellow Nat. Sculpture Soc. (coun. 1973-75, rec. sec. 1976, sec. 1977-79, coun. 1981-83, 92-97, 2006-, Bronze medal 1986, Mildred Victor Meml. award 1996, Leonard Meiselman Meml. award 2003), Audubon Artists (Elliott Liskin Meml. award 2000, 02), Am. Artists Profl. League (Gold medal 1974, 77, medal of hon. 1987), Allied Artists Am. (Gold medal 1981, 93, In Memorium award 1994), Pen & Brush Club (Gold medal 1977, Salmagundi Club award 1982, 83, 91, C. Dunwiddie Meml. award 1999, 2004), Soc. Animal Artists (jury of admissions 1972-75, 90—, bd. dirs. 1991—, v.p. 1998—, Legacy award 2002), Am. Acad. Equine Art (founding mem., dir. sculpture 1980—), Nassau Suffolk Horsemans Assn. (dir. 1968-82), Catherine Lorillard Wolfe Art Club, Smithtown Hunt Club, Meadowbrook Hunt Club. Address: 22 Woodhollow Rd Roslyn Heights NY 11577-2217 Office Phone: 516-621-5914.

NEWPORT, ELISSA L., psychology professor; b. St. Louis, July 3, 1947; d. Eugene and Anita Evelyn (Ginsberg) N.; m. Theodore Supalla, Oct. 12, 1980; children: Susanna, Zachary. Student, Wellesley Coll., 1965-67; BA, Barnard Coll., 1969; MA, U. Pa., 1974, PhD, 1975. Asst. prof. U. Calif. San Diego, La Jolla, 1974-79; assoc. prof., prof. U. Ill., Champaign, 1979-88; prof. U. Rochester, NY, 1988—, George Eastman prof. brain an cognitive sciences and linguistics NY, chair Dept. Brain and Cognitive Sciences NY. Mem. editorial bd. Cognitive Psychology, 1981—, Language Acquisition, 1989—. Editor: (book series) MIT Press, 1982—; contbr. articles to profl. jours. Alfred P. Sloan Found. fellow MIT, 1981, U. Pa., 1982; NIH rsch. grantee, 1980—; recipient Arnold O. Bediman Rsch. award U. Ill., 1982-83, William Bonsall Vis. Chair in Humanities Stanford U., 1984, Claude Pepper award of excellence, NIH. Fellow Am. Acad. Arts and Scis.; mem. AAAS, NAS, Am. Psychol. Assn., Soc. Rsch. in Child Devel., Linguistic Soc. Am., Cognitive Sci. Soc. Office: Univ Rochester Dept Psychology Meliora Hall 414 Rochester NY 14627-0268 Office Phone: 585-275-8689. E-mail: newport@bcs.rochester.edu.*

NEWPORT, L. JOAN, retired social worker; b. Newkirk, Okla., July 5, 1932; d. Crawford Earl and Lillian Pearl (Peden) Irvine; m. Don E. Newport, July 9, 1954 (div. 1971, dec. 1999); children: Alan Keith, Lili Kim. BA cum laude, Wichita State U., 1955; MSW, U. Okla., 1977. Diplomate Acad. Cert. Social Workers; lic. clin. social worker, Okla. Dir. children's work Wesley United Meth. Ch., Oklahoma City, 1969-71; social worker Dept. Human Svcs., Newkirk, Okla., 1972-77; in-sch. suspension counselor Kay County Youth Svcs., Ponca City, Okla., 1977; med. social worker St. Joseph Med.

Ctr., Ponca City, 1977-78, dir. social work, 1978-83; pvt. practice, Ponca City, 1979-97; med. social worker Healthcare Svcs., Ponca City, 1983-84; pvt. practice Newkirk, 1997—2005; ret., 2005. Sponsor, organizer Kay County Parents Anonymous, Ponca City, 1976-83; vice chair Okla. State Bd. Lic. Social Workers, Oklahoma City, 1988-90; supr. students Okla. U. Sch. Social Work, Okla. State U., No. Okla. Coll., Okla. Christian Coll., 1977-85; supr. for clin. social workers working toward lic. in Okla., 1985-2005; cons., presenter, lectr. in field Mem. Okla. Women's Network, 1989-96; adv. bd. Displaced Homemakers, Ponca City, 1985-89; adv. bd. Kay County Home Health, 1979-83, chair, 1979-81; Sunday sch. tchr. Newkirk United Meth. Ch.; mem. Newkirk Main St., 1999-2000. Named Hon. State Life Mem. Burbank PTA, Oklahoma City, 1971; scholar Wichita (Kans.) Press and Radio Women, 1953, Conoco, Inc., Houston, 1951-54. Mem. NASW (Okla. del. Del. Assembly Washington 1987, chmn. vendorship com. 1985-87, pres. Okla. chpt. 1988-90, Social Worker of Yr. 1987), Child Abuse Prevention Task Force (pres. dist. 17 1986-88, mem. grant evaluation com. 1986-96), Zeta Phi Eta. Democrat. Methodist.

NEWSOM, CAROLYN CARDALL, management consultant; b. South Weymouth, Mass., Feb. 27, 1941; d. Alfred James and Bertha Virginia (Roy) Cardall; m. John Harlan Newsom, Feb. 4, 1967; children: John Cardall, James Harlan. AB, Brown U., Providence, R.I., 1962; MBA, Wharton Sch., 1978; PhD, U. Pa., 1985. Systems engr. IBM, Seattle, 1964-70, Newsom S.E. Services, Seattle, 1970-76; instr. U. Pa. Wharton Sch., Phila., 1978-81; v.p., prin. sr. cons. PA Cons. Group, Princeton, NJ, 1981-88; pres. Newsom Assocs., Yardley, Pa., 1988; ptnr. Bus. Strategy Implementation, Princeton, NJ, 1989-90; pres. Strategy Implementation Solutions, Yardley, Pa., 1990—. Examiner N.J. Gov.'s Performance Excellence Award, 1993, sr. examiner, 1994—2002, judge, 2003—06; examiner Malcolm Baldrige Nat. Quality Award, 2003—05. Trustee St. Mary Hosp., Langhorne, Pa., 1986—94; sec. bd. dir. Gordonstown Am. Found., 1999—2005; bd. dir. Chandler Hall, 1980—87. Mem.: Quality N.J. (vice chair 1998—99), Am. Soc. for Quality, Am. Acad. Mgmt., Brown Alumni Assn. (pres.-elect 1993—95, pres. 1995—97). Office: Strategy Implementation Solutions 1588 Woodside Rd Yardley PA 19067-2611

NEWSOM, DOUGLAS ANN JOHNSON, author, journalism educator; b. Dallas, Jan. 16, 1934; d. J. Douglas and R. Grace (Dickson) Johnson; m. L. Mack Newsom, Jr., Oct. 27, 1956 (dec.); children: Michael Douglas, Kevin Jackson, Nancy Elizabeth, William Macklemore; m. Bob J. Carrell, 1993. BJ cum laude, U. Tex., 1954, BFA summa cum laude, 1955, M in Journalism 1956, PhD, 1978. Gen. publicity State Fair Tex., 1955; advt. and promotion Newsom's Women's Wear, 1956-57; publicist Auto Market Show, 1961; lab. instr. radio-tv news-writing course U. Tex., 1961-62; local publicist Tex. Boys Choir, 1964-69, nat. publicist, 1967-69; pub. rels. dir. Gt. S.W. Boat Show Dallas, 1966-72, Family Fun Show, 1970-71, Horace Ainsworth Co., Dallas, 1966-76; pres. Profl. Devel. Cons., Inc., 1976-89; faculty Tex. Christian U., Ft. Worth, 1969—, prof. dept. journalism, chmn. dept., 1979-86, adviser yearbook and mag., 1969-79; dir. ONEOK Inc., diversified energy co., 1980—; Fulbright lectr. in India, 1988. Author: (with Alan Scott) This is PR, 1976, 3d edit., 1984, (with Alan Scott and Judy Van Slyke Turk) 4th edit., 1989, 6th edit., 1995, (with Judy Van Slyke Turk and Dean Kruckeberg), 1996, (with Bob Carrell) Writing for Public Relations Practice, 4th edit., 1994, (with Jim Wollert) Media Writing, 1984, 2d edit., 1988; editor (with Carrell) Silent Voices, 1995; mem. editorial bd. Pub. Rels. Rev., 1978—. Sec.-treas. Pub. Rels. Found. Tex., 1979-80, also trustee; pub. rels. chmn. local Am. Heart Assn., 1973-76, state pub. rels. com. 1974-82, chmn., 1980-82; trustee Inst. for Pub. Rels. Rsch. and Edn., 1985-89; mem. Gas Rsch. Adv. Coun., 1981—. Fellow Pub. Rels. Soc. Am. (chmn. Coll. Fellows 1992, nat. edn. com. 1975, chmn. 1978, nat. faculty adviser, chmn. edn. sect.); mem. Assn. Edn. in Journalism and Mass Communication (pres. pub. rels. div. 1974-75, nat. pres. 1984-85), Women in Communications (nat. conv. treas. 1967, nat. pub. rels. chmn. 1969-71), Tex. Pub. Rels. Assn. (dir. 1976-84, v.p. 1980-82, pres. 1982-83), Mortar Bd. Alumnae (adviser Tex. Christian U. 1974-75), Phi Kappa Phi, Kappa Tau Alpha, Phi Beta Delta. Episcopalian. Home: 4237 Shannon Dr Fort Worth TX 76116-8043 Office: Tex Christian U Dept Journalism PO Box 298060 Fort Worth TX 76129-0001

NEWSTEAD, JENNIFER G., lawyer; b. 1969; AB, Harvard U., 1991; JD, Yale Law Sch., 1994. Mng. editor Yale Law Jour.; editor Yale Jour. Internat. Law; law clk. to Hon. Laurence H. Silberman US Ct. Appeals (DC Cir.), 1994—95; law clk. to Justice Stephen G. Breyer US Supreme Ct., 1995—96; assoc. Davis Polk & Wardwell LLP, NYC, 1997—2001, 2005—06, ptnr., 2006—; dep. asst. atty. gen., Office of Legal Policy US Dept. Justice, Washington, 2001—02, prin. dep. asst. atty. gen., Office of Legal Policy, 2002; assoc. gen. counsel Office Mgmt. & Budget, Exec. Office of the President, Washington, 2002—03, gen. counsel, 2003—05. Adj. prof. law, national security law Georgetown U. Law Ctr., 2002; exec. branch liaison to ABA section on Adminstrv. Law & Regulatory Practice The White House, 2004—05. Office: Davis Polk & Wardwell LLP 450 Lexington Ave New York NY 10017 Office Phone: 202-395-5044. Office Fax: 202-395-7289. E-mail: jennifer.newstead@dpw.com.*

NEWTON, CHERYL KAY, music educator; b. Arlington, Va., May 16, 1953; d. Andren Earl and Alberta Christine Newton. B Music Edn., E. Carolina U., 1975; MS, U. Ill., 1981; EdD, Va. Tech, 1988. Lic. tchr. K-12 music Va., secondary prin. Va. Dir. band Fairmont City Schs., NC, 1975—80, Thomas Jefferson H.S., Alexandria, Va., 1980—84, Oakton H.S., Vienna, Va., 1984—. Democrat. Presbyterian. Avocations: sailing, gardening. Home: 67 McPherson Cir Sterling VA 20165 Office Phone: 703-319-2746. Personal E-mail: NEWT53@aol.com.

NEWTON, ELIZABETH DEANE, music educator; b. Chattanooga, Sept. 29, 1951; d. Talbert Swanson and Grace Stryker Deane; m. Ronald Steve Gallimore (div.); 1 child, Grace Medora Stryker; m. Scott Howard Newton, July 22, 1989. B in Music Edn., Greensboro Coll., 1973; MA, Trenton State U., 1975. Cert. music tchr. grades K-12 Va. Tchr. adult basic edn. U.S. Army, Ft. Dix, NJ, 1974—78; tchr. adult basic edn., GED, ESL Richmond (Va.) Pub. Schs., 1979—86, elem. music tchr., 1986—87, Chesterfield County (Va.) Pub. Schs., 1987—, elem. summer sch. site coord., 2004, 2005. Pvt. voice and piano tchr., Richmond, 1979—; dir. Crestwood Celebration Singers, 1990—2005. Choir mem., soloist Forest Hill Presbyn. Ch., Richmond, 1957—2005, from deacon to elder, 1980—90, early svc. music dir., 1998—2001. Recipient Spl. Ch. Stewardship award, Forest Hill Presbyn. Ch., 1998;, Golden Rule Found., 1999. Mem.: NEA, Va. Music Educators Assn., Music Educators Nat. Conf., Va. Edn. Assn. Avocations: breeding and raising registered yellow labrador retrievers, gardening, boating, fishing, reading. Home: 151 Duncan Store Rd Columbia VA 23038 Office: Crestwood Elem Sch 7600 Whittington Dr Richmond VA 23225

NEWTON, ELIZABETH PURCELL, counselor, consultant, author; b. Madison, N.C., June 3, 1925; d. Charles Augustus and Anna Meta (Buchanan) P.; m. William Edward Newton, June 11, 1949; children— James Purcell, Betsy Newton Hein, Christina Newton Harwood. A.A., Peace Coll., 1944; B.A., U. N.C., 1946; M.Ed., Ga. State U., 1969; Ed.S., West Ga. Coll., 1981. Tchr., counselor S. Cobb High Sch., Austell, Ga., 1965-69; counselor, dept. head Wheeler High Sch., Marietta, Ga., 1969-76; counselor, div. head guidance services Walton High Sch., Marietta, Ga., 1976—90; ret., 1990; sch. rep. Coll. Bd., Princeton, N.J., 1981—90, panelist, presenter S.E. region, Atlanta, 1983-85; presenter Ga. Sch. Counselors Assn., Atlanta, 1980—90; cons. Panhandle Area Edn. Coop., Chipley, Fla., 1985. Author: Steps to College Admissions, 1978; Student's Guide to College Admissions, 1981; Student's Guide to Career Preparation, 1982. Sch. rep. Citizens Adv. Council, Marietta, 1981, 82, 85. Ga. Dept. Edn. grantee, 1981; named Outstanding Woman in Edn., Atlanta Jour., 1985. Mem. Cobb Counselor Assn. (organizer, chmn. nominations com. 1985), Ga. Sch. Counselors Assn. (Secondary Counselor of Yr. 1983), Am. Sch. Counselors Assn. (Nat. Secondary Counselor of Yr. 1984), Phi Delta Kappa. Presbyterian.

NEWTON, ESTHER MARY, anthropologist, educator; b. NYC, Nov. 28, 1940; d. Saul B. and Virginia Newton. BA, U. Mich., 1962; MA, U. Chgo., 1964, PhD, 1968. Asst. prof. CUNY, Queens, 1968-71; from asst. prof. to assoc. prof. anthropology SUNY, Purchase, 1971-92, prof. anthropology, 1992—, Kempner disting. professorship, 1999; adj. prof. Am. culture and women's studies U. Mich., Ann Arbor, 2004—. Coord. women's studies program SUNY, Purchase, 1984-86; vis. prof. Yale U., 1970, U. Amsterdam, 1993; affiliated scholar CUNY, 1992-93; scholar in residence U. Calif., Santa Cruz, 1993; curator exhbn. Gay and Lesbian Cmty. Svcs. Ctr., 1993. Author: Mother Camp: Female Impersonators in America, 1972, reprinted with new introduction, 1979, Cherry Grove, Fire Island: Sixty years in America's First Gay and Lesbian Town, 1993, Margaret Meade May Me Gay, 2000; co-author: (with Shirley Walton) Womanfriends, 1976; contbr. to anthologies including The Lesbian Issue: Essays from Signs, 1985, Hidden from History: Reclaiming the Gay and Lesbian Past, 1989, International Gay Studies: The Amsterdam Conference, 1994, History of Homosexuality in Europe and America, 1994, Writing Lesbian and Gay Culture, 1995; mem. editl. bd. The Cutting Edge: Lesbian Life and Literature Series, Between men, Between Women: Lesbian and Gay Studies Series, GLQ: Jour. of Queer Studies, Jour. of Homosexuality, Jour. Sexuality in History; contbr. to books including Amazon Expedition, 1973, Anthropology and American Life, 1974, Symbolic Anthropology: A Reader in the Study of Symbols and Meaning, 1977, Strategies des femmes, 1984, Pleasure and Danger: Exploring Female Sexuality, 1984, Homosexuality, Which Homosexuality? Vol. 2, 1987, The Lesbian and Gay Studies Reader, 1993; contbr. articles to mags. and jours. La Verne Noyes scholar U. Chgo., 1962-63; training grantee NIH, 1963-65, faculty support grantee SUNY, Purchase, 1987, 92; pre-doctoral fellow NIMH, 1965-67; recipient experienced faculty travel award SUNY, 1987, 91; Rockefeller Humanities fellow, 1999. Mem. Am. Anthrop. Assn. (cochair commn. lesbian and gay issues, 1994-96). Avocation: dog training. Office: Divsn Social Sci SUNY Purchase NY 10577

NEWTON, JANET GAIL, office manager; b. Florence, Ala., Sept. 10, 1956; d. Gardis Dowell and Effie Mae (White) N. Student, J.C. Calhoun Community Coll., Decatur, 1976, J.C. Calhoun Community Coll., 1975. Office mgr. Johnson and Feigley CPA, Athens, Ala., 1975—. Mem. Civitan Club. Democrat. Methodist. Home: PO Box 33 Athens AL 35612-0033 Office: Johnson & Feigley CPA 105 W Washington St Athens AL 35611-2659

NEWTON, JO ANN GODDARD, corporate financial executive; BA in Math., Smith Coll., 1975; JD, NY Law Sch., 1978. Mgr. treasury dept. Pacific Telesis Group, mgr. wholesale fins. and regulatory support Pacific Bell subs., dir. fed. regulatory rels. Washington, dir. investor rels. San Francisco; dir. investor rels. and shareholder svcs. So. Calif. Edison; with Edison Internat., Rosemead, Calif., 1996—, v.p. investor rels. Office: Edison Internat 2244 Walnut Grove Ave Rosemead CA 91770

NEWTON, JUANITA, social worker, educator; b. LaGrange, Ga., Sept. 16, 1931; d. Limus Lee Newton and Lillia Bertha Baugh; children: Marcellette A. Reynolds, Lymus Dannerro(dec.), De'Juan, Sharold Lynn, Lydia. AA, Wayne County C.C., 1976; B in Social Work, Wayne State U., 1978, MSW in Social Work, 1979. Cert. in elem.edn. 1988. Social worker local ctrs. and schs., Hamtramck, Mich., 1979—80; dir. social work Brent Gen. Hosp., 1980—81, Sidney A. Sumby Hosp., 1981—83; tchr. Detroit Pub. Schs., 1985—91; v.p. Detroit Gen. Hosp., 1972—81; chair proposal rev. com. Detroit Wayne County Mental Health Bd., 1972—75; adminstr. The Haven Mission 138, 1990—93; instr. genealogy rsch. Wayne County C.C., 1994—97; ret. Mem. exec. com. 4th precinct Police Cmty. Rels. Coun., 1998—; cmty. rels. chairperson Friends of Duffield Br. Pub. Libr., 2001; pres. Concerned Citizens of N.W. Goldberg Cmty., Inc., 1995—; urban coord. 4H, 1995—; del. county rels. Citywide Police. Named Angel for Caring for Children, Blue Cross/Blue Shield Network, 2002—03; recipient 8th Spirit of Detroit award for Cmty. Svcs., Gov.'s award for Cmty. Svcs., Gov. William Milligen. Mem.: NASW, SCLC, NAACP (life), FH Williams Geneaol. Soc., Elks Club (life). Democrat.

NEWTON, LISA HAENLEIN, philosopher, educator; b. Orange, N.J., Sept. 17, 1939; d. Wallen Joseph and Carol Bigelow (Cypiot) Haenlein; m. Victor Joseph Newton, June 3, 1972; children: Tracey, Kit, Cynthia Perkins, Daniel Perkins, Laura Perkins. Student, Swarthmore Coll., 1957-59; BS in Philosophy with honors, Columbia U., 1962, PhD, 1967. Asst. prof. philosophy Hofstra U., Hempstead, NY, 1967-69; from asst. prof. to assoc. prof. Fairfield (Conn.) U., 1969—78, prof., 1978—, dir. program applied ethics, 1983—, dir. program environ. studies, 1986—; lectr. in medicine Yale U., 1984—. Lectr., cons. in field. Author: Ethics and Sustainability, 2002, Ethics in Am., Study Guide, 2d edit., 2003, Ethics in Am. Source Reader, 2d edit., 2003, Business Ethics and the National Environment, 2004, Permission to Steal, 2006; co-author: Watersheds, 1994, 4th edit., 2005; author, 2004; co-author: Wake-Up Calls, 2d edit., 2003; co-editor: Taking Sides: Controversial Issues Bus. Ethics, 8th edit., 2004, Taking Sides: Controversial Issues Bus. Ethics, 9th edit., 2006; contbr. articles to profl. jours. Mem. exec. bd. Conn. Humanities Coun., 1979—83. Mem.: Internat. Soc. Environ. Ethics (mem. exec. bd.), Assn. Practical Prof. Ethics (exec. bd.), Soc. Bus. Ethics (past pres.), Am. Soc. Bioethics and Humanities, Soc. Ethics Across Curriculum, Am. Soc. Polit. and Legal Philosophy, Am. Philos. Assn., Am. Soc. Value Inquiry (past pres.), Phi Beta Kappa (local sec.). Home: 1870 Redding Rd Fairfield CT 06824 Office: Fairfield U Program Applied Ethics Fairfield CT 06824 Office Phone: 203-254-4128. Business E-Mail: lhnewton@mail.fairfield.edu.

NEWTON, MICHELLE MARIE, sales executive; b. Orange, Calif., May 27, 1971; d. Wayne Clair and Maria Palmar Newton; 1 child, Jazmyn Victoria Wallington. BA in Comm., Calif. State U., Fullerton, 1994; MBA, Pepperdine U., 2000. Mktg. adminstr. Ingram Micro, Santa Ana, Calif., 1994—96, internat. mktg. adminstr., 1995; sales support rep. APL, Ltd., Costa Mesa, Calif., 1996—97, inside sales rep., 1997—98, acct. exec., 1998—2000, sr. acct. exec., 2000—02; child care owner Michelle's Child Care, Rancho Santa Margarita, Calif., 2002—03; internat. sales Oakley, Inc., Foothill Ranch, Calif., 2003—. Roman Catholic. Avocations: motorcycling, skiing, rollerblading, walking, yoga. Home: 1 Spinel Ct Rancho Santa Margarita CA 92688 Office Phone: 949-829-6462.

NEWTON, NELL JESSUP, dean, law educator; b. St. Louis, Apr. 30, 1944; d. Robert Edward and Marcella (Boehm) Mier. BA, U. Calif., Berkeley, 1973; JD, U. Calif., Hastings, 1976. Bar: Calif., Washington, U.S. Ct. Appeals (9th crct.), U.S. Supreme Ct. Prof. Cath. U. Sch. Law, 1976-92; prof. Washington Coll. Law Am. U., Washington, 1992—98; dean U. Denver Law Sch., 1998—2000, U. Conn. Sch. Law, Hartford, 2000—06, U. Calif. Hastings Coll. Law, San Francisco, 2006—. Lectr. Internat. Law Inst., Washington, 1984-89; prof. Pre-Law Summer Inst. for Native Am. Students, U. N.Mex. Law Sch., Albuquerque, 1990, 91, 93; panelist, speaker NEH, 1981; presenter S.W. Intertribal Ct. of Appeals, 1990; panelist Orgn. Am. Historians, 1991; vis. prof. Boston Coll. Law Sch., Hastings Law Sch. Co-author: American Indian Law, 3d edit., 1991; contbr. articles to profl. jours. NEH fellow Harvard Law Sch., 1980. Mem. Assn. Am. Law Schs. (Native Am. rights sect., mem. exec. com. 1987—, chair 1987-88, oral argument newsletter editor 1987—, mem. women in legal edn. sect. 1987—, chair profl. devel. workshop com. 1992, sec. 1993), Balt.-Washington-Va. Women Law Tchrs. Group (planning com. Symposium on Scholarship I 1985, II 1986), Thurston Soc., Order of Coif. Office: U Calif Hastings Coll Law 200 McAllister St San Francisco CA 94102 Office Phone: 415-565-4700. E-mail: newtonn@uchastings.edu.*

NEWTON, NILES RUMELY, psychologist, educator; b. N.Y.C., Jan. 19, 1923; d. Edward and Fanny (Scott) Rumely; m. Michael Newton, Mar. 27, 1943; children: E. Willow Reed, Frances Lees Stuntz, Edward Robson, Warren Polk. BA, Bryn Mawr Coll., 1945; PhD, Columbia U., 1952. Research assoc. obstetrics Sch. Medicine, U. Pa., Phila., 1952-55; mem. faculty (part-time) Sch. Medicine, U. Miss., Jackson, 1955-66; asst. prof. dept. psychiatry, div. psychology Northwestern U. Med. Sch., Chgo., 1966-68, assoc. prof., 1968-73, prof., 1973-80, prof. dept. psychiatry and behavioral scis., 1980—. Mem. bd. cons. Am. Found. for Maternal and Child Health, N.Y.C., 1978—, v.p., 1981—; sr. cons. Am. Coll. Nurse-Midwives Found., 1984-86; mem. sci. group on physiology of lactation WHO, 1963 Author: Maternal Emotions, 1955, Family Book of Childcare, 1957; contbr. numerous articles on psychosomatic obstetrics to profl. jours.; columnist: Chicago Tribune, 1973-74; mem. editorial bd. Child and Family, 1962-67, Jour. Psychosomatic Ob-Gyn, 1982-93, Birth, 1975—. Jour. Qualitative Health Rsch., 1990—; contbg. editor: Baby Talk, 1965-74. Mem. adv. bd. Nat. Childbirth Trust, Eng., 1966-84; bd. dirs. Family Focus, Chgo., 1977—; trustee Children's Home and Aid Soc. of Ill., 1979—. USPHS research fellow, 1949-51; recipient spl. award Miss. Psychol. Assn., 1966, hon. plaque Internat. Childbirth Edn. Assn., 1968, Outstanding Achievement award Internat. Lactation Cons. Assn., 1987. Fellow Am. Psychol. Assn., Am. Psychol. Soc.; mem. Midwestern Psychol. Assn., Soc. Behavioral Medicine, Internat. Soc. Psychosomatic Ob-Gyn (founding mem., exec. sec. 1974-80, v.p. 1980-83, exec. com. 1983-86, 89-92, founding fellow 1986—), Chgo. Network, La Leche League Internat. (mem. profl. adv. bd. 1972—, Outstanding Contbn. award 1989), Internat. Acad. Sex Rsch., Sigma Xi.

NEWTON, RHONWEN LEONARD, writer, data processing executive, consultant; b. Lexington, N.C., Nov. 13, 1940; d. Jacob Calvin and Mary Louise (Moffitt) Leonard; children: Blair Armistead Newton Jones, Allison Page, William Brockenbrough III. AB, Duke U., Durham, N.C., 1962; MS in Edn., Old Dominion U., Norfolk, Va., 1968. French tchr. Hampton Pub. Schs., Va., 1962-65, Va. Beach Pub. Schs., 1965-66; instr. foreign lang. various colls. and univs., 1967-75; foreign lang. cons. Portsmouth Pub. Schs., Va., 1973-75; dir. The Computer Inst., Inc., Columbia, S.C., 1983; pres., founder The Computer Experience, Inc., Columbia, 1983-88, RN Enterprises, Columbia, 1991—. Author: WordPerfect, 1988, All About Computers, 1989, Microsoft Excel for the Mac, 1989, Introduction to the Mac, 1989, Introduction to DOS, 1989, Introduction to Lotus 1-2-3, 1989, Advanced Lotus 1-2-3, 1989, Introduction to WordPerfect, 1989, Advanced WordPerfect, 1989, Introduction to Display/Write 4, 1989, WordPerfect for the Mac, 1989, Introduction to Microsoft Works for the Mac, 1990, Accountant, Inc for the Mac, 1992, Introduction to Filemaker Pro, 1992, Quicken for the MAC, 1993, Quicken for Windows, 1993, WordPerfect for Windows, 1993, Advanced WordPerfect for Windows, 1993, Lotus 1-2-3 for Windows, 1993, Introduction to Quick Books, 1994, Quick Book for Windows, 1994, Introduction to Word for Windows, 1995, Introduction to File Maker Pro 4.0, 1998, Introduction to Microsoft Word, 1999, Introduction to Microsoft Excel, 1999, Introduction to AOL, 1999, Introduction to Excel, 1999, Using America OnLine, 1999. Mem. Columbia Planning Commn., 1980-87; bd. dirs. United Way Midlands, Columbia, 1983-86, Assn. Jr. Leagues, NYC, 1980-82, SC Wildlife Fedn., 1997-98; trustee Heathwood Hall Episcopal Sch., Columbia, 1979-85; active SC Episcopal Home Bd., 1999-2005, chmn., 2001-2003; vestry Trinity Cathedral, 1999-02; active SC Real Estate Appraisers Bd., 2000, sec., 2002—. Mem. Investment Club (pres. 1995-97, regional coun.), Nat. Assn. Investors Corp. (dir. S.C. Midlands regional coun. 1998-02). Republican. Episcopalian. Avocations: golf, walking. Home and Office: 1635 Kathwood Dr Columbia SC 29206-4509 Personal E-mail: rhonwenln@yahoo.com.

NEWTON, VIRGINIA, archivist, historian, librarian; d. John Walter and Reba Catherine Newton; m. Alvin E. Schmid, 2003. Student, Inst. Tecnológico y de Estudios Superiores de Monterrey, Nuevo Leon, Mex., 1957; AA in Bus. Adminstrn., Stephens Coll., 1958; BA in History, Okla. State U., 1960; M of Librarianship, U. Wash., 1963; cert. in libr. sci., U. Tex., 1968, MA in Latin Am. Studies, History, Archives and Libr. Sci., 1975, PhD in Latin Am. Studies, History, Archives and Libr. Sci., 1983. Libr. Inst. Pub. Affairs U. Tex., Austin, 1963-65, libr. Art Libr., 1965-67; coord. Sr. Cmty. Svcs. Program Econ. Opportunities Devel. Corp., San Antonio, 1968-69; archivist, spl. collections libr. Trinity U., San Antonio, 1969-73; spl. collections and reference libr. Pan Am. U., Edinburg, Tex., 1974-77; archivist, records analyst Alaska State Archives and Records Svc., 1983-84, dep. state archivist, 1984-87; state archivist Alaska State Archives & Records Mgmt. Svcs., 1988-93; dir. Columbus Meml. Libr. OAS, Washington, 1993—2001. Archives cons. Ford Found. for Brazilian Archivists Assn., 1976, Soc. for Ibero-Latin Thought, 1980, Project for a Notarial Archives Computerized Guide, 1980; chair Alaska State Hist. Records Adv. Bd., 1988-93, coords. steering com., 1991-93; cons. Puerto Rican Hist. Records Adv. Bd., 1997-99. Author: An Archivists' Guide to the Catholic Church in Mexico, 1979; contbr. articles to profl. publs. Founder jail libr. Bexar County Jail, San Antonio; hon. dep. sheriff Bexar County, 1972-75; mem. Dem. party; chair Dems. Abroad in Mex., 1979-81; mem. Dems. Abroad Del. The Dem. Nat. Conv., N.Y., 1980; vice- chair Bill Egan Forum Greater Juneau Dem. Precinct, 1986-88 Recipient Commendation award Gov. of Alaska William Sheffield, 1985, Disting. Alumnae award U. Tex. Sch. Libr. and Info. Sci., 1998; Masonic Scholarship for internat. rels. George Washington U., 1960-61; univ. fellow U. Tex.-Austin, 1982-83, post masters fellow U.S. Dept. Edn.-U. Tex., Austin, 1967-68; scholar Orgn. Am. States, 1980, 81, Fulbright-Hays scholar, 1979, 80, scholar Nat. Def. Fgn. Lang.-U. Tex., Austin, 1978-79, scholar Calif. State Libr., 1962-63. Mem. AAUW (bd. dirs. 1983-86, scholar 1983), Nat. Assn. Govt. Archives and Records Adminstrs. (bd. dirs. 1989-93, chair membership com. 1989-93), Alaska Hist. Soc. (bd. treas. 1988-94), Alaska Libr. Assn., Acad. Cert. Archivists (cert. 1989), Rotary, Phi Kappa Phi. Democrat. Unitarian Universalist. Avocations: skiing, dance, researching, reading, hiking. Office: 206 Laurel Heights Place San Antonio TX 78212

NEWTON-JOHN, OLIVIA, singer, actress; b. Cambridge, Eng., Sept. 26, 1948; arrived in Australia, 1954, arrived in England, 1964, arrived in Am., 1975; d. Brin and Irene (Born) Newton-John; m. Matt Lattanzi, Dec. 1984 (div. 1995); 1 child, Chloe Rose Lattanzi. Student pub. schs. Co-owner Koala Blue, 1982—. Singer, actress in Australia, Eng. and US, 1965—; actress: (films) Funny Things Happen Down Under, 1965, Tomorrow, 1970, Grease, 1978, Xanadu, 1980, Two of a Kind, 1983, It's My Party, 1996, Sordid Lives, 2000; (TV) Timeless Tales from Hallmark, 1990, A Mom for Christmas, 1990, A Christmas Romance, 1994, Snowden on Ice (voice), 1997, The Christmas Angel: A Story on Ice, 1998, The Wilde Girls, 2001; singer: (albums) If Not for You, 1971, Let Me Be There, 1973, If You Love Me Let Me Know, 1974, Long Live Love, 1974, First Impressions, 1974, Have You Ever Been Mellow, 1975, Clearly Love, 1975, Come on Over, 1976, Don't Stop Believin', 1976, Making a Good Thing Better, 1977, Greatest Hits, 1977, Totally Hot, 1978, Grease, 1978, Xanadu, 1980, Physical, 1981, Greatest Hits, 1982, (with John Travolta) Two of a Kind, 1984, Soul Kiss, 1985, The Rumour, 1988, Warm And Tender, 1989, Back To Basics-The Essential Collection, 1992, Gaia, 1994, Heathcliff, 1995, Back With A Heart, 1998, The Main Event, 1998, Two, 2002, Indigo-Women of Song, 2004, Stronger Than Before, 2005; TV prodn. In Australia, 1988. Decorated as Officer, Order Brit. Empire, 1979, Order of Australia, 2006; named one of 50 Most Beautiful People in the World, People mag., 1998, one of 100 Greatest Women of Rock N Roll, VH1.; recipient Acad. Country Music, 1973, Country Music Assn. U.K., 1974-75, Country Music Assn. award, 1974, Grammy award, 1973-74, AGVA award, 1974, Billboard Mag. award, 1974-75, People's Choice award 1974, 1976, 1979, Record World award, 1974-76, 1978, Nat. Assn. Retail Merchandisers/Cashbox, 1974-75, Am. Music award 1974-76, Nat. Juke Box award, 1980, Lifetime Achievement award, Australian Record Industry Assn., 2002. Address: PO Box 2710 Malibu CA 90265-7710 Office: MCA 70 Universal City Plz North Hollywood CA 91608-1011

NEY, RHONDA G., elementary school educator; b. Lake Charles, La., Sept. 4, 1971; d. Lorraine G. and Stanley T. Eisiliones; m. John Robert Ney, Dec. 30, 1997; children: Christian J., Cameron A. BA in Elem. Edn., McNeese State U., 1996. Cert. early childhood edn. La., 2000. Elem. tchr. Rice Consol. Ind. Sch. Dist., Eagle Lake, Tex., 1996—97, Acadia Parish Sch., Rayne, La., 1997—98, Calcasieu Parish Sch. Bd., Lake Charles, La., 1998—. Dancer in ministry feet of fire Christian World Ministries, Lake Charles, 2003—06. Mem.: Calcasieu Parish Reading Coun. (pres., treas. 2001—06), Assoc. Profl. Educators La. (mem. at large 2004—06), Delta Kappa Gamma (officer scholarships 2003—04). Office Phone: 337-625-3396.

NEYMAN, PAULA, pediatrician; b. Breslau, Germany, Apr. 1, 1927; arrived in US, 1947; d. George and Lisa Getzowitz; m. Daniel Neyman, May 5, 1950; children: Sarena, Freyda. BA, Hunter Coll., NYC, 1953; MD, NYU, 1957. Diplomate Am. Bd. Pediat. Lectr. on Holocaust pub. schs., Orange County, NY, 1991—. Fellow: Soc. Ambulatory Pediat.; mem.: Am. Acad. Pediat. Avocations: civic work, tennis, reading. Office: Ramapo Valley Pediat Central Valley NY 10917 Office Phone: 845-728-2544. Fax: 845-782-9518.

NEZIRI, MARIA G. DE LUCIA, elementary school educator; b. Mineola, N.Y., Dec. 27, 1967; d. Salvatore and Alfonsina DeL.; m. Lulzim Neziri, Aug. 20, 1995; children: Noah, Olivia. BS Edn., Adelphi U., 1990; MS in Edn., Queens U., 1994; MS in Reading and Spl. Edn., Hofstra U., 1999. Cert. tchr. reading, spl. edn. K-12. Elem. tchr. Westbury (N.Y.) Pub. Schs., 1990—. Creator, coord The Write View, The Writing Club after school club; creator, instr. inservice courses Reading and Writing Workshop; mentor for new tchrs.; 5th grade grad. coord. Mem. Nat. Coun. Tchrs. Maths., Nat. Coun. Tchrs. English, Internat. Reading Assn. Avocations: gardening, cooking, reading.

NG, KIM (KIMBERLY J. NG), professional sports team executive; b. Wu Peiqin, China, Nov. 17, 1968; m. Tony Markward. BA in Pub. Policy, U. Chgo., 1990. Front office arbitration intern Chgo. White Sox, 1990, spl. projects analyst, 1991, asst. dir., baseball ops., 1991—95; dir. waivers, player records MLB Am. League, 1995—97; asst. gen. mgr. NY Yankees, 1998—2001; asst. gen. mgr., v.p. baseball ops. LA Dodgers, 2001—. Office: Los Angeles Dodgers 1000 Elysian Park Ave Los Angeles CA 90012-1199*

NG, MING T., psychologist; came to U.S., 1967; BA, Mt. Holyoke Coll., 1985; Profl. diploma, Fordham U., 1989; PsyD, Yeshiva U., 1999. Lic. psychologist. Mem. APA.

NGUYEN, CHRISTAL, personal trainer; d. Rusty and Debbie Henderson; m. Tony Nguyen, June 22, 2000; 1 child, Sydney. Diploma in Human Performance and Athletic Tng., U. So. Miss., 2000. Cert. Atc NATABOC, 2001. Atc Bapt. Healthcare, Pensacola, 2000—. Mem.: NATA.

NGUYEN, HUONG TRAN, former elementary and secondary language educator, former district office administrator; b. Haiphong, Vietnam, Nov. 16, 1953; came to the U.S., 1971; d. Joe (Quang) Trong Tran and Therese (Nguyet-Anh) (Do) Dotran; m. Tony (Phu) The Nguyen; children: Long Tran Nguyen, Ty Tran Nguyen. B in Liberal Studies, San Diego State U., 1976, tchg. credential grades K-12, 1977; M in Curriculum Devel., Point Loma Coll., 1984; lang. devel. specialist cert., Calif. Commn. Credentialing, 1991; PhD in Edn., Curriculum & Instrn., U. Calif. Riverside, 2004. ESL tchr. San Diego (Calif.) Job Corps, 1978-80; resource tchr. grades K-12 San Diego (Calif.) Unified Sch. Dist., 1980-82; resource tchr. SEAL project grades K-12 Long Beach (Calif.) Unified Sch. Dist., 1982-83, ESL specialist, 1983-85, 85-92, English lang. devel. tchr., chair, 1992-95; adminstr., 1996-98; sr. fellow officer U.S. Dept. Edn., Office Bilingual & Minority Lang. Affairs, Washington, 1995-96; from disting. tchr.-in-residence to asst. prof. Calif. State U., Long Beach, 1998—2004, asst. prof., 2003—. Instr. curriculum PhD Program Calif. State U., 2004. Named Outstanding Tchr. of 1994, Disney Co. Am. Tchr. Awards, Washington, 1994, Outstanding Tchr. in Fgn. Lang./ESL, Disney Co. Am. Tchr. Awards, Washington, 1994. Mem.: Pacific Am. Edn., Calif. Assn. Asian Pacific Bilingual Edn., Calif. Coun. Tchr. Edn., Am. Ednl. Rsch. Assn., Nat. Coun. Tchrs. English. Avocations: reading, travel, gardening, meditation, yoga. Office: Calif State U Coll Edn Dept Tchr Edn 1250 N Bellflower Blvd Long Beach CA 90840-0001 Office Phone: 562-985-4536. Business E-Mail: hnguye10@csulb.edu.

NGUYEN, LAN THI HOANG, physician, educator; b. Hai-Duong, Vietnam, July 18, 1950; came to U.S., 1975; d. Thua Nang and Niem Thi (Do) N.; m. Khanh Vinh Quoc, Oct. 15, 1981. MD, U. Kans., 1983. Intern St. Mary Med. Ctr./UCLA, Long Beach, Calif., 1983-84; resident City of Faith Med. Rsch. Ctr.-Oral Roberts Sch. Medicine, Tulsa, 1986-88; fellow VA Med. Ctr.-Wadsworth-UCLA, 1988-90; physician Santa Ana (Calif.) Med. Ctr., Doctors Hosp. Santa Ana, Fountain Valley (Calif.) Regional Med. Ctr. Clin. assoc. prof. family medicine Keck Sch. Medicine U. So. Calif., L.A., 2002—. Contbr. articles to profl. jours. V.p. Vietnamese Am. Med. Rsch. Found. Kans. Med. scholar, 1979-81. Fellow: ACP, Am. Coll. Endocrinology, Am. Coll. Nutrition; mem.: Am. Assn. Clin. Endocrinologists (charter). Office: 14971 Brookhurst St Westminster CA 92683-5556 Office Phone: 714-839-5898.

NGUYEN, MAI (MAI TUYET NGUYEN), writer; b. Saigon, Vietnam, Nov. 18, 1936; arrived in U.S.A., 1983; d. Tu Van Mai and Hiep Thi Doan; m. Tony Tung Quoc, Sept. 30, 1967; 1 child, Kevin Duy. Degree, Dai Hoc Van Khoa, Saigon, Vietnam, 1960. Sec. Soc. Gen. de Surveillance, Belgium Consulate, Saigon, Vietnam, 1954—57; adminstrv. mgr. Connell Bros. Co., Saigon, 1959—75; adminstrv. asst. Tandon Corp., Calif., 1983—86; freelance writer Calif., 1986—. Author: God's Will, 1996, Little Daisy, 1998, 10 books, 1996—2001, Shadow of Hapiness, 2002. Mem.: Independent Scholars Asia, Nat. Writers Assn. Avocations: reading, art, music, travel, landscaping.

NGUYEN-POOLE, MARY, physician; MD. Chmn. family medicine dept. Southwest Methodist Hosp. Clinical asst. prof. U. Tex. Health Sci. Ctr., San Antonio. Team physician Medina Valley Middle Sch. & HS. Recipient Leadership award (Young Physicians), AMA Found., 2005. Mem.: Am. Acad. Family Physicians, Bexar County Med. Soc., Tex. Med. Assn., AMA, Tex. Acad. of Family Physicians (pres. Alamo Chpt.). Mailing: PO Box 960 Castroville TX 78009 Office Phone: 830-538-2254.*

NICASTRI, ANN GILBERT, science educator; b. N.Y.C., May 26, 1934; d. Ralph and Ruth Gilbert; m. Anthony D. Nicastri, July 2, 1960; children: RuthAnn, Christina, Catherine, Daniel. BA magna cum laude, Bklyn. Coll., 1954; MA, Columbia U., N.Y.C., 1956. Tchg. asst. Barnard Coll., N.Y.C., 1954—55; tchr. Balt. Jr. H.S., 1960—61, Balt. Jr. Coll., 1961—62, Julia Richman H.S., N.Y.C., 1962—63, Midwood H.S., Bklyn., 1955—60, tchr. biology, AP biology, rsch., 1986—2004; adj. faculty fellows program Bklyn. Coll., 2004—. Judge NYCSEF Sci. Contest, 2002—06; rsch. coord. student projects Midwood H.S., Bklyn., 2003—04. Recipient ISEF Mentor award, USAF, 2004; NSF fellow, Harvard U., Boston, 1957—58, Columbia U., 1959. Mem.: N.Y. Acad. Sci., Kappa Delta Pi, Phi Beta Kappa. Home: 164 Beach 143rd St Neponsit NY 11694 Personal E-mail: agnicastri@aol.com.

NICASTRO, TRACEY A., lawyer; b. 1969; BA, U. Ill., 1991; JD, Valparaiso U., 1994. Bar: Ill. 1994. With Sidley Austin Brown & Wood, Chgo., 1996—, ptnr., 2002—. Mem.: ABA, Chgo. Bar Assn. Office: Sidley Austin Brown and Wood Bank One Plz 10 S Dearborn St Chicago IL 60603

NICCOLINI, DIANORA, photographer; b. Florence, Italy, Oct. 3, 1936; arrived in U.S., 1945, naturalized, 1960; d. George and Elaine (Augsbury) N. Student, Hunter Coll., 1955—82, Art Students League, 1960, Germain Sch. Photography, 1962; BA magna cum laude, Marymount Manhattan Coll., 1995. Med. photographer Manhattan Eye, Ear and Throat Hosp., 1963—65; organizer med. photography dept. Lenox Hill Hosp., 1965—67, 1st chief med. photographer, 1965—67; organizer, head dept. med. and audio visual edn. St. Clare's Hosp., N.Y.C., 1967—76; mem. Third Eye Gallery, N.Y.C., 1974—76; owner Dianora Niccolini Creations, 1976—. Instr. photography Camera Club N.Y., 1978-79, Germain Sch. Photography, 1978-79, N.Y. Inst. Photography, 1981-83; instr. comml. photography N.Y. Inst. Tech., 1996-97. One-woman shows include 209 Photo Gallery, Top of the Stairs Gallery, Third Eye Gallery, 1974, 75, 77, Photographics Unltd. Gallery, N.Y.C., 1981, West Broadway Gallery, N.Y.C., 1981, Camera Club N.Y., 1982, Overseas Press Club, N.Y.C., 1983, Impulse Gallery, Provincetown, Mass., 1983, Throckmorton Fine Art Gallery, N.Y.C., 1998, 2001; exhibited in group shows at Photography Over 65, N.Y.C., 1978, Jacob Javits Fed. Bldg., N.Y.C., 1992, Neikrug Gallery, N.Y.C., 1993, Ward-Nasse Gallery, N.Y.C., 1996, Internat. Salon, N.Y.C., 1996, Curcio-Spector Gallery, N.Y.C., 1996, Throckmorton Fine Art, Inc., 1997, 2001; pub. portfolios; author: Women of Vision, 1982, Men in Focus, 1983, Big Fun with Billy, 2001; editor: P.W.P. Times, 1981-82; contbr. to photog. books; designer greeting cards Flashcards, Inc., 1988-90; contbg. editor Functional Photography, 1979-80, N.Y. Photo Dist. News, 1980. Mem. Women Photographers N.Y. (founder 1974), Biol. Photog. Assn., Internat. Ctr. Photography, Am. Soc. Mag. Photographers, Am. Soc. Picture Profls., Profl. Women Photographers (pres. 1980-84). Home: 356 E 78th St New York NY 10021-2239 Personal E-mail: dianoran@aol.com.

NICE, KATHARINE ANNE, mathematics educator, music educator; b. Norristown, Pa., Sept. 17, 1977; d. Edward Howard Creesman and Nancy Jean Cressman; m. Matthew Anthony Nice, Nov. 1, 2003; 1 child, Josephine Eve. MA in Math. and Music, Bucknell U., Lewisburg, Pa., 1999; Mus M in Edn., Immaculata U., Immaculata, Pa., 2003. Cert. tchg. Math, Music level 2 Pa. Tchr. Phoenixville Area Sch. Dist., Phoenixville, Pa., 1999—. Tchr. dir. Old Goshenhopper UCC, Woxall, Pa., 1999—. Recipient Outstanding Supporting Actor, Forge Theatre, 2005. Avocations: horseback riding, acting, running, singing. Office: Phoenixville Area HS 1200 Gay St Phoenixville PA 19460

NICHOLAS, CAROLINE JEAN, retired nurse, consultant; b. Lansing, Mich., Feb. 11, 1935; d. Homer Paul and Lucinda Rachel (McDonald) Anderson; m. William C. Nicholas (div.); children: Jan Marie, David Craig, Jill Elizabeth. BSN, Mich. State U., East Lansing, 1956, MA, 1969. RN Mich. Staff nurse Med. Hosp., East Lansing, 1956—57, clin. instr., 1957—62; nurse, 1962—86; nursing instr. Lansing CC, 1967—79; nurse cons. Mich. Dept. and Pub. Health, 1979—90, ret., 1990. Docent Women's Hist. Soc. and Hall of Fame, Lansing, 1980—; elder, deacon Presbyn. Ch. Mem.: Phi Kappa Phi, Sigma Theta Tau, Alpha Omicron Pi. Avocations: reading, sewing, cross stitch. Home: 2734 Trudy Ln Lansing MI 48910-3826

NICHOLAS, LYNN B., medical association administrator; b. Tenn. BS in med. tech., Tenn. Wesleyan Coll.; M in mgmt., Cent. Mich. U., 1983. Bd. cert. fellow Am. Coll. Healthcare Exec. (ACHE). Med. technologist to sr. v.p. clinical and ambulatory svc. Morristown Meml. Hosp., NJ; exec. v.p., COO NJ Hosp. Assn., 1995—2000; pres., CEO La. Hosp. Assn., 2000—04; CEO Am. Diabetes Assn., Alexandria, Va., 2004—. Mem. bd. gov. Am. Coll. Healthcare Exec.; chair La. Health Works Commn.; mem. La. Health Care Commn.; rep. La. hosp. Am,. Hosp. Assn. Recipient Early Career Healthcare Exec. award (first recipient in NJ), Am. Coll. Healthcare Exec. Office: Am Diabetes Assn 1701 N Beauregard St Alexandria VA 22311 Office Phone: 703-549-1500, 800-342-2383. Office Fax: 703-739-9346.*

NICHOLAS, LYNN HOLMAN, historian, researcher, writer; b. New London, Conn., Nov. 11, 1939; d. William Grizzard Holman and Carol (Ackiss) Wakelin; m. Robert Carter Nicholas III, Dec. 20, 1965; children: William C., R. Carter, Philip H. Student, Radcliffe Coll., 1957-59; diploma, U. Madrid, 1960; BA, Oxford (Eng.) U., 1964. Mem. adv. panel Presdl. Commn. on Holocaust Assets in the U.S., 1999. Author: The Rape of Europa: The Fate of Europe's Treasures in the Third Reich and the Second World War, 1994 (Nat. Book Critics Circle award 1995), Cruel World: The Children of Europe in the Nazi Web, 2005. Decorated chevalier Légion d'Honneur (France); named Amicus Poloniae, Govt. of Poland, 2003. Personal E-mail: lynnick105@aol.com.

NICHOLS, CAROL D., real estate professional; BA, U. Pitts., 1964; cert. in advanced mgmt., U. Chgo. From mgmt. trainee to buyer May Dept. Stores Co., Pitts., 1964-70; various mgmt. positions, then mng. dir. mortgage/real estate Tchrs. Ins. and Annuity Assn. Am., NYC, 1970-97; sr. mng. dir. Insignia/ESG Capital Advisors, NYC, 1997. Instr. real estate div. continuing edn. Marymount Manhattan Coll., N.Y.C., 1975-76, Woman's Sch. Adult Edn. Ctr., N.Y.C., 1976-77; Real Estate Bd. N.Y., past chmn. fin. com. Recipient Nat. Humanitarian award, Arthur B. Lorber award Nat. Jewish Med. and Rsch. Ctr., Nat. Brotherhood award NCCJ. Mem. Assn. Real Estate Women (past pres.), Urban Land Inst. (trustee, past chmn. urban devel. and mixed use coun., past chmn. awards for excellence jury). Office: Insignia/ESG Capital Advisors 200 Park Ave New York NY 10166-0005 Home: 9208 Hillside Dr Ne Mineral City OH 44656-9727 E-mail: carol.nichols@iesg.com.

NICHOLS, CAROL-LEE, real estate broker, property manager; b. Middletown, N.Y., Aug. 1, 1964; d. Donald Larry Powell and Malia Kaipolani Gullette; m. Albert Emile Nichols, Mar. 21, 2003; children: Gerry Donald Pinson, David Bradford Powell, Sean Paul Clarke King. Diploma, Framingham Tech. Ctr., Mass., 1984; cert. in bookkeeping, CCD Tech. Ctr., Denver, 1991. Real estate brokers lic. J. Y. Monk. Dancer Dandy Dans, Denver, 1986—97; asst. deli mgr. Safeway, Denver, 1997—99; salesperson, broker Bob Vurno Real Estate, Fayetteville, NC, 1999—2002; broker N.C. Properties Unlimited, Fayetteville, 2002, Abode Real Estate, Fayetteville, 2002; owner CL's Real Estate, Fayetteville, 2002—. Realtor Fayetteville Assoc. Realtors, 2002—. Deacon Mountain Christian Ch., Lakewood, Colo., 1997; svc. dir. 1st Christian Ch., Fayetteville, 2002—. Office: CLs Real Estate PO Box 71357 Fort Bragg NC 28307 Home: 203 Winding Ridge Rd Sanford NC 27332 Office Phone: 910-391-0243. Personal E-mail: CLsRE64@aol.com. E-mail: clsreine@alltel.net.

NICHOLS, CHERIE L., composer; b. Portsmouth, Va., Apr. 4, 1955; d. Conley Ray and Ann Lanease (Holderfield) Edwards; m. Harold Eugene Nichols, 1971 (div. 1975); life partner Chloe S. Burke. Art sales Poster Art-N-Graphics, Tarzana, Calif., 1982—84; art cons. Martin Lawrence Galleries, L.A., 1984—86; mgr. print rm. Circle Fine Art Corp., L.A., 1986—93; driver United Cerebral Palsy, Sacramento, 1997—98; owner Morning Dove Pub., Sacramento, 1997—. Art dir. Lavender Libr., Archives and Cultural Exch., Sacramento, 1999-2002; artist, rep. and product devel. plush toys Milk Buds, 1999; assoc. Frames Unlimited, Mich., Ohio, Ind. Songwriter Time Doesn't Play, 2003, Reckless, 2003, If Only, 2004, What's There To Say, 2004; songwriter: Nothing Like You, 2005. Avocations: music, guitar, golf. Office Phone: 916-599-4870. Personal E-mail: cnik55@yahoo.com.

NICHOLS, CHRISTINA R., music educator; b. Joliet, Ill., June 26, 1963; d. Gerald E. and Henrietta Lyday; m. Kenneth W. Nichols, Dec. 28, 1984; 1 child, Kaleb W. B of Music Edn., Ouachita Bapt. U., Arkadelphia, Ark., 1985. Cert. tchr. Tenn., 1988. Tchr. music Bismark Sch. Dist., Ark., 1987—88, Fayette County Sch., Somerville, Tenn., 1988—96; choral dir. Collierville Mid. Sch., Tenn., 1996—99, Schilling Farms Mid. Sch., Collierville, Tenn., 1999—. Music in-svc. com. Shelby County Schs., Memphis, 1998—2005; mentor for non-tenured tchrs. Schilling Farms Mid. Sch., Collierville, Tenn., 1999—2004, specialist chmn., 1999—, sch. improvement plan part 1 chmn., 2000—02, curriculum mapping expanded site coun., 2000—01; chmn. steering com. Southern Accredidation Colleges and Schools, 2006—. Bd. mem. Former Student Assn. of Ouachita Bapt. U., Arkadelphia, Tenn., 2004—; v.p. Bubba Conlee Nat. Jr. Golf Tournament, Olive Branch, Miss., 2004. Nominee Premier Player, Memphis chpt. NARAS, 2003; recipient Tchr. of Yr. award, Schilling Farms Mid. Sch., 2001-2002, Shelby County Schs., 2002-2003; grantee, Collierville Edn. Found., 2000 & 2003, 20th Century Club of Collierville, 2006. Mem.: Tenn. Music Educators Assn., Music Educators Nat. Conf., West Tenn. Vocal Educators Assn. (treas. 2004). Office: Schilling Farms Mid Sch 935 S Colbert St Collierville TN 38017 Office Phone: 901-854-2345. Personal E-mail: hushyall3@aol.com. E-mail: cnichols@scsk12.org.

NICHOLS, CHRISTINE CAROLYN, science educator; d. Guy H. and Christine R. Nichols. AB, Bryn Mawr Coll., Pa., 1970; MAT, Harvard U., Cambridge, Mass., 1971; MS, Pa. State U., University Park, 1984. Lic. tchr. secondary level Colo. Physics tchr., k-12 sci. coord. State Coll. Area Sch. Dist., Pa., 1971—83; velocity modeler, geophys. interpreter Exxon Co. USA, Englewood, Colo., 1983—85; sci. tchr. Kent Denver Country Day, Englewood, 1985—87; sci. tchr., dept. chair Englewood HS, 1988—. Cons. Physics Tchr. Edn. Collaborative, 2000—02; toyota tchr. leader Looking at the Environ. Curriculum, Evanston, Ill., 2001—05; cohort A NsnoLeap Project, Denver, 2005—; tchr.-in-residence Colo. State U., Ft. Collins, 1996—97. Asst. dir., head counselor, health care supr. C Bar T Trail Ranch, Idledale, Colo., 1986—2004. Recipient Tchr. Recognition award, Boettcher Found., 1992, St. Lynn Ednl. Excellence award, EHS Faculty & Staff, 1997—98. Mem.: DAPT, CAST, NEA, Nat. Sci. Tchrs. Assn., Am. Assn. Physics Tchrs., Colo. Edn. Assn., Phi Delta Kappa. Independent. Avocations: horseback riding, gardening, quilting.

NICHOLS, DEBRA, bank executive; Sr. v.p. and dir. women's fin. adv. svcs. Wachovia Bank, Charlotte, NC, 1997—. Office: Wachovia Corp 301 South College St Charlotte NC 28288-0570

NICHOLS, DIANE COLLEEN, historian, retired municipal official; b. Oconto, Wis., Apr. 4, 1943; d. Earl Frank and Betty Florence (Ingram) Kamke; m. Lyle Richard Nichols, Aug. 14, 1965; children: Lara Jeanne, Brett William. BS, U. Wis., Madison, 1965; MS, U. Wis., Green Bay, 1976. Tchr. Ashwaubenon H.S., Green BaY, Wis., 1965—69; advsor U. Without Walls, Green Bay, 1977—79; small bus. owner A Nichol's Worth, Oconto, Wis., 1985—2000; devel. coord. Oconto Hosp. Found., 1999—2000; program mgr. Revitalize Gillett, Wis., 2002—04. Pres. Oconto County Hist. Soc., 1994—2000. Author: A History of Oconto Falls: 1839-1900, Vol. I, 2004; editor: John and Almira Volk, 1996, From the McCauslin to Jabswitch, 1998, The Oconto River Sackers, 2000, A Wisconsin Farm Woman, 2005. Methodist. Home: 4295 County J Oconto WI 54153 E-mail: n4c2d95@ez-net.com.

NICHOLS, DONNA MARDELL, nurse anesthetist; b. Mpls., Mar. 24, 1936; d. Donald Burma and Lucille Elvera Nichols. Diploma, Northwestern Hosp. Sch. Nursing, Mpls., 1957, Mpls Sch. Anesthesia, 1959; BS in Nurse Anesthesia, U. Minn., 1977. RN Minn., 1957. Nurse anesthetist Hennepin County Med. Ctr., Mpls., 1959—60, Eden Twp. Hosp., Castro Valley, Calif., 1960—63, Bethesda Hosp., St. Paul, 1963—64, Meml. Bapt. Hosp., Houston, 1964—67, St. Joseph's Hosp., St. Paul, 1967—95; ret., 1995. Mem.: Minn. Assn. Nurse Anesthetists (bd. dirs. 1975—77), Am. Assn. Nurse Anesthetists (emeritus, cert. anesthetists). Avocations: golf, gardening, antiques. Home: 10427 Upton Ave S Bloomington MN 55431

NICHOLS, EDIE DIANE, real estate broker; b. Grahamstown, Eastern Cape Province, Republic of South Africa, Mar. 28, 1939; arrived in U.S., 1963; d. Cyril Doughtry and Dorothy Ethel (Nottingham) Tyson; m. John F. Nichols, Dec. 16, 1962 (div. Dec. 1978); 1 child, Ian Tyson. Adminstrv. asst. Am. Acad. Medicine, N.Y.C., 1963-64, Jack Lenor Larsen, Inc., N.Y.C., 1964-70; v.p. John Scott Fones, Inc., N.Y.C., 1971-76, Howard J. Rubenstein Assocs. Inc., N.Y.C., 1976-80; dir. comm. Carl Byoir & Assocs., N.Y.C., 1981-83; account supr. Hill and Knowlton, N.Y.C., 1983-85; broker Cross & Brown Co., N.Y.C., 1986-88; v.p. Marc Nichols Assocs., Inc., N.Y.C., 1989-95; mng. ptnr. Nichols Brown Internat., N.Y.C., 1995—2004; real estate broker Citi-Habitats, N.Y.C., 2005—. Trustee Ctrl. Pk. Hist. Soc., N.Y.C., 1978-80. Mem. NOW, Internat. Assn. Corp. and Profl. Recruitment, N.Y. Women in Comm. (pub. rels. chair 1980-81, v.p., programs bd. dirs. 1985-87), Fin. Women's Assn. of N.Y. (bd. dirs. 1997-98), City Club of N.Y. (trustee, v.p., fin. and devel. 1987-89). Democrat. Episcopalian. Office: Citi-Habitats 118 Perry St New York NY 10014 Home: 16 Stuyvesant Oval Apt 10F New York NY 10009 Office Phone: 212-561-0690. E-mail: ednny@aol.com.

NICHOLS, ELIZABETH GRACE, nursing educator, dean; b. Tehran, Iran, Feb. 1, 1943; d. Terence and Eleanor Denny (Payne) Quilliam; m. Gerald Ray Nichols, Nov. 20, 1965; children: Tina Lynn, Jeffrey David. BSN, San Francisco State U., 1969; MS, U. Calif., San Francisco, 1970, D of Nursing Sci., 1974; MA, Idaho State U., Pocatello, 1989. Staff nurse Peninsula Hosp., Burlingame, Calif., 1966-72; asst. prof. U. Calif.-San Francisco Sch. Nursing, 1974-82; chmn. dept. nursing Idaho State U., Pocatello, 1982-85; assoc. dean Coll. Health Scis. Sch. Nursing U. Wyo., Laramie, 1985-91, asst. to pres. for program revs., 1991-95; dean Coll. Nursing U. N.D., 1995—2004, Mont. State U., Bozeman, 2004—. Cons. U. Rochester, NY, 1979, Carroll Coll., Mont., 1980, divsn. Nursing Dept. HHS, Washington, U. Maine, Ft. Kent, 1992, Stanford Hosp. Nursing Svc., Calif., 1981—82, Ea. N.Mex. U., 1988, Met. State U., Minn., 1998, U. Nev.-Reno, 2003; cons. evaluator Higher Learning Commn., 1993—2004; site visitor CCNE, 1998—; mem. accreditation review com. The Higher Learning Commn., 2001—04, budget com. Contbr. articles to profl. jours. Mem. adv. bd. dir. U. Calif. Home Care Svc., San Francisco, 1975—82, Ombudsman Svc. of Contra Costa Calif., 1979—82, Free Clin. of Pocatello, 1984; mem. bd. of rev. coun. baccalaureate & higher degree programs, 1990—92; mem bd. dirs. United Way of Grand Forks/East Grand Forks, 2000—04. Recipient Jo Eleanor Elliott award, 1994; fellow ACE, U. Maine Sys., 1990—91. Fellow: Am. Acad. Nursing, Gerontol. Soc. Am. (chmn. clin. medicine sect. 1987, sec. 1990—93); mem.: ANA, Western Inst. Nursing (chmn. 1990—92, bd. govs., bd. dir. mid-west alliance), Idaho Nurses Assn. (dist. 51 adv. bd. dir. 1982—84), ND Nurses Assn. (pres. 2003—04), Oakland Ski Club. (1st v.p. 1981—82), Sigma Theta Tau. Democrat. Office Phone: 406-994-3784. Business E-Mail: egnichols@montana.edu.

NICHOLS, GRACE A., retail executive; b. 1946; married; 2 children. Degree, UCLA. With Weinstock's, Sacramento, 1971—78; mgr. gen. merchandise The Broadway, Calif., 1978—86; v.p., mgr. gen. merchandise Victoria's Secret Stores, 1986—88, exec. v.p., mgr. gen. merchandise, 1989—91, pres., CEO, 1991—. Office: Victorias Secret Stores Inc Four Ltd Pkwy Reynoldsburg OH 43068

NICHOLS, IRIS JEAN, retired illustrator; b. Yakima, Wash., Aug. 2, 1938; d. Charles Frederick and Velma Irene (Hacker) Beisner; (div. June 1963); children: Reid William, Amy Jo; m. David Gary Nichols, Sept. 21, 1966. BFA in Art, U. Wash., 1978. Freelance illustrator, graphic designer, Seattle, 1966—2004; med. illustrator, head dept. illustration Swedish Hosp. Med. Ctr., Seattle, 1981-86; owner, med. and sci. illustrator Art for Medicine, Seattle, 1986—2003; ret., 2003. Med. illustrator U. Wash., Seattle, 1966-67; part-time med. illustrator, graphic coord. dept. art The Mason Clinic, 1968-78; instr. advanced illustration Cornish Coll. Arts, Seattle, 1988-90; organized, coordinated and gifted the artwork of Prof. Glen E. Alps of U. Wash. after his death in 1996 Illustrator various books including Bryophytes of Pacific Northwest, 1966, Microbiology, 1973, 78, 82, 94, 98, Introduction to Human Physiology, 1980, Understanding Human Anatomy and Physiology, 1983, Human Anatomy, 1984 Regional Anesthesia, 1990, many other med. and sci. books, and children's books on various subjects; exhibited in group shows at Seattle Pacific Sci. Ctr., summer 1979, 82, Am. Coll. Surgeons (1st prize 1974), N.W. Urology Conf. (1st prize 1974, 76, 2d prize 1975); pub. illustrations Constellation Pk. and Marine Res., City Seattle Pk., 1999, Whale Tail Park, Seattle. Pres. ArtsWest (formerly West Seattle Arts Coun.), 1983; chmn. West Seattle (Wash.) H.S. Art Acquisition Com., 2003—. Named to West Seattle H.S. Alumni Hall of Fame, 1986, Matrix Table, 1986-96. Mem. Assn. Med. Illustrators (Murial McLatchie Fine Arts award 1981), Nat. Mus. Women in the Arts (Wash. state com., bd. dirs. 1987-95, pres. 1993-94), Women Painters of Wash. (pres. 1987-89), U. Wash. Alumni Assn., Lambda Rho (pres. alumni assn. 1995-98, treas. 2002-04) Avocations: artwork, printmaking, small books.

NICHOLS, JANET HILDRETH, elementary school educator, childbirth and parenting educator; b. Glenwood Springs, Colo., July 1, 1948; d. Pershing Loveland and Myrna Jean Nichols; children: Carrie Christine Schultz, Taylor James Pruss. BA, U. N.Colo., 1971, MA, 1973. Lic. childbirth educator Lamaze Internat., 1982, cert. prenatal parenting instr. Prenatal Parenting, 2003. Spl. edn. tchr., kindergarten tchr. Ouray Pub. Schs., Colo., 1971—72; spl. edn. tchr. Jefferson County Schs., Lakewood, Colo., 1973—74; child find evaluator St. Vrain Pub. Schs., Longmont, Colo., 1979—80, tchr. physically handicapped, 1985—87; lead tchr. Mountain View Presch., Boulder, Colo., 1983—84; pre-acad. tchr. Boulder Valley Schs., 1987—92; kindergarten tchr. Douglass Elem. Sch., 1992—2006; tchr. Rocky Mt. Sch. for Gifted and Creative, 2006—. Childbirth & parenting instr. Boulder Cmty. Hosp., 1990—.

Contbr. Head Start, Boulder, 1988—89. Grantee Math Edn. grant, Found. Boulder Valley Schs., 1995, Reading Comprehension grant, 2002, Map Making grant, 2003. Mem.: Lamaze Internat. (assoc.). Home: 1775 Holeman Dr Erie CO 80516 Business E-Mail: jan.nichols@bvsd.org. E-mail: jannichols548@yahoo.com.

NICHOLS, JOANIE MAE, science educator; b. Maysville, Ky., Apr. 5, 1976; d. Gary and Dorothy Phillips; m. Bradley Allen Nichols, July 3, 1997; 1 child, Bret Tyler. B in Biology and Secondary Edn., Shawnee State U., Portsmouth, Ohio, 2000. Cert. Ky. Dept. Edn., 2002. Sci. tchr. Fleming County Sch., Flemingsburg, Ky., 2002—. Mem. Cmty. Bible Ch., Aberdeen, Ohio, 1998—2006. Mem.: ARSI (assoc.). R-Consevative. Avocations: sports, travel, exercise. Home: 8883 Elizaville Rd Ewing KY 41039 Office Phone: 606-845-6601. Personal E-mail: jmnich01@moreheadstate.edu.

NICHOLS, KATIE, investment company executive; b. Des Moines, May 19, 1940; d. Gardner (Mike) and Lois (Thornburg) Cowles; m. Julian Strauss, June 11, 1960 (div. 1971); children: Elizabeth Lois Strauss Grossi, Gwen Beatrix Strauss Jenkins, Kate Anne Strauss Long; m. Roger Marvin Nichols, Sept. 1, 1973 (div. 1981); m. H.E. Rummel, Mar. 27, 1983 (div. 1994). Student, Cornell U., 1957—61. Ptnr., v.p. The Rummel Group, Inc., St. Petersburg, Fla., 1985—2003, chmn., 2003—, pres., 2003—, CEO, 2003—. Trustee Cowles Charitable Trust, NYC, 1985—. Vol. Hosp. Albert Schweitzer, Deschapelles, Haiti, 1961-63; vice chmn. Fla. Human Rels. Commn., Tallahassee, 1974-75; Dem. candidate Fla. Pub. Svc. Commn., 1976; commr. Fla. Pub. Svc. Commn., 1981-89, chmn., 1987-89; vice chmn. Fla. Corrections Commn., 1994-98; bd. dirs. Nat. Coun. on Crime and Delinquency, San Francisco, 1990—, chmn. 1997-98; bd. dirs. HAS2000 Campaign for Hosp. Albert Schweitzer, Haiti; trustee Cowles Charitable Trust, 1985—. Recipient Honor award, Fla. Human Rels. Commn., 1985. Mem. NOW, Emily's List, League of Women Voters of Fla. Democrat. Episcopalian. Avocations: reading, needlepoint. Home: 1682 Oceanview Dr Tierra Verde FL 33715-2500 Office: The Rummel Group Inc 1641 1st Ave N Saint Petersburg FL 33713-8935

NICHOLS, KYRA, ballerina; b. Berkeley, Calif., July 2, 1958; Studied with Alan Howard, Pacific Ballet, Sch. Am. Ballet, N.Y.C. With N.Y.C. Ballet, 1974—, prin. dancer, 1979—. Created roles in Tricolore, 1978, A Sketch Book, 1978, Jerome Robbins' Four Seasons, 1979, John Taras' Concerto for Piano and Wind Instruments, Stravinsky Centennial Celebration, 1982, Jacques d'Amboise's Celebration, 1983; performed in N.Y.C. Ballet's Balanchine Celebration, 1993. Ford Found. scholar; recipient Dance Mag. award, 1988. Office: NYC Ballet Inc NY State Theater Lincoln Ctr Pla New York NY 10023

NICHOLS, LEEANN, library media specialist; b. Denver, Apr. 27, 1946; d. Bernard Anthony and Margaret Mary (Pughes) Wilhelm; m. Robert Joseph Nichols, July 12, 1975; children: Rachel, Steven, Sarah. BS in Edn., St. Mary of the Plains, Dodge City, Kans., 1968; MA in Edn., Colo. U., 1978. Cert. type B profl. tchr., Colo. Tchr. So. Tama Sch. Dist. Montour, Iowa, Iowa, 1968-70, Strasburg (Colo.) Sch. Dist., 1970-73; svc. rep. Montain Bell, Denver, 1973-75; libr., tchr. Simla (Colo). Sch. Dist., 1976-78; dir. Simla Br. Libr., 1978-81; dir. Christian edn. St. Anthony's Ch/, Sterling, Colo., 1983-84; libr. cons. Rel Valley Sch., Iliff, Colo., 1984-98, Plateau Sch. Dist., Peetz, Colo., 1986-99; dir. Fleming Cmty. Libr., Colo., 1997—. Mem. Colo. Coun. for Libr. Devel., Denver, 1986-92, chmn. 1991; instr. Northeastern Jr. Coll., Sterling; del. Gov.'s Conf. on Libr. and Info. Scis., 1990. Author: Computers 101.in a Nutshell, 2002; contbr. articles to profl. jours. Active Sterling Arts Coun., sec., 1982-85, v.p., 1985, pres., 1986-87; chair Northeastern Jr. Coll. Found., Sterling, 1983-87, mem. 1981-91; mem. community adv. coun. Northeastern Jr. Coll., 1991-93, chair, 1993; bd. dirs. Wagon Wheel chpt. Girl Scouts Am., 1975-78. Mem. ALA, Am. Assn. Sch. Librs., Assn. Libr. Svcs. to Children, Colo. Ednl. Media Assn., Colo. Libr. Coun., Internat. Reading Assn. (Colo. Coun.). Avocations: reading, sewing. Home: 12288 County Road 370 Sterling CO 80751-8494 Office: Fleming Cmty Libr 506 N Fremont Ave Fleming CO 80728-9520

NICHOLS, M. KATHLEEN, therapist, educator; b. Balt., Sept. 23, 1936; d. Edward Bernard and Mary Elizabeth Quirk; m. Joseph Howard Nichols, Oct. 27, 1955; children: Donald James, Stephen Paul, John Robert. MA, Bowie State U., 1984; PhD, Union Grad. Sch., 1987. Diplomate forensic psychology, hypnotherapy; cert. drug and alcohol counselor. Program dir. Turnabout Counseling Ctr., Georgetown, Del., 1992—93; clin. dir. therapeutic cmty. Correction Med. Sys., Georgetown, 1993—94; prof. Wilmington Coll., Georgetown, 1995—2005; ret., 2005. Mem. adv. bd. Del. Tech. C.C., Dover, RSVP-Sr. Retirees, Georgetown, Del Drug and Alcohol Bd., Wilmington; mem. task force Atty. Gen., Dover. Editor (hist. articles, jours.). Bd. dirs. Del. Drug and Alcohol Coun., 2001—; v.p. Ret. Citizen Adv. Coun., 2000—; mem. Sussex County Interacy Coun., 1991—; active Rep. Party Sen.'s Campaign, Sussex County, Del. Mem.: North Atlantic Assn. for Counselor Edn. Republican. Avocations: travel, the beach. Home: 15 E Stony Run Selbyville DE 19975 Office: Wilmington Coll Georgetown DE 19947

NICHOLS, MARGARET IRBY, librarian, educator, library and information scientist; b. Maud, Tex., July 9, 1924; d. James Rainwater and Winnie (Pride) Irby; m. Irby Coghill Nichols Jr., Apr. 18, 1953 (div. Jan. 1992); children: Nina Nichols Austin, Irby C. Nichols III. BA, U. North Tex., 1945; MLS, U. Tex., 1957. Libr. Mercedes (Tex.) H.S., 1945-46; cataloger Bethany (W.Va.) Coll., 1946; chief reference libr. Tex. Tech U., Lubbock, 1946-48; ref. libr. El Paso Pl., 1949-51; chief reference libr. N.Mex. Mil. Inst., Roswell, 1951-53; sch. libr. South Jr. H.S., Roswell, 1954-55; acad. dean Selwyn Sch., Denton, Tex., 1965-67; prof. Sch. Libr. and Info. Scis. U. North Tex., Denton, 1968-91, assoc. dean Sch. Libr. and Info. Scis., 1989-91, emeritus prof., 1996. Cons. in field, 1991—; exec. bd. North Tex. Regional Libr. Sys., 1996—, chair, 1997-99; chmn. exec. bd. Libr. Ptnrs., 2003— Author: Core Reference Collections, 1986, 2d edit., 1993, Guide to Reference Sources, 4th edit., 1992, Reference Sources for Small and Medium Libraries, 1988, 2d edit., 1994, Texas Information Sources, 1996, Building And Using A Core Reference Collection, 4th edit., 2004; contbr. articles to profl. jours. Named one of 100 Libr. Champions of 20th Century, Tex. Libr. Assn., 2001; recipient Margaret Irby Nichols award (named in her honor), North Tex. Regional Libr. Sys., 2004; Margaret Irby Nichols scholar, U. North Tex., 1992. Mem. ALA (mem. coun. 1988-92), Tex. Libr. Assn. (exec. bd. 1983-86, 88-92, pres. 1984-85, Disting. Svc. award 1990, Lois Bebout Outstanding Svc. award Ref. Roundtable 1995, Tex. Libr. Champion 2001, recipient Elizabeth Crabb Disting. Svc. award 2003). Home: 2514 Royal Ln Denton TX 76209-2244 E-mail: nichols2514@charter.net.

NICHOLS, NANCY RUTH, elementary school educator; b. Boston, Mar. 11, 1949; d. Anthony and Ruth Grace (Fino) DiNicola; m. Raymond C. Nichols Jr., Aug. 20, 1988. BS, Boston State Coll., 1971, MEd, 1974; MA + 60, Curry Coll., Salem State Coll., 1998. Tchr. Dexter Elem. Sch., Dedham, Mass., 1972-82, Riverdale Elem. Sch., Dedham, Mass., 1982—84, 1996—2004, Avery Elem. Sch., 1984-96, Oakdale Elem. Sch., Dedham, Mass., 2004—. Recipient Golden Apple award, 1994. Mem. ASCD, Dedham Edn. Assn., Norfolk County Tchrs. Assn., Whole Lang. Tchrs. Assn., Internat. Reading Assn. Republican. Avocations: reading, gardening. Home: PO Box 751 Walpole MA 02081-0751 Office: Oakdale Elem Sch 147 Cedar St Dedham MA 02026-7012

NICHOLS, SALLY JO, geriatrics nurse; b. Coldwater, Mich., Jan. 28, 1965; d. Leo Arnold and Charlotte (Ferguson) N.; m. Lorenzo Evander Perryman, Sr., Jan. 3, 1998. LPN, Pasco-Hernando C.C., 1985, AA, 1986, ASN, 1992; student, U. South Fla., 1990-91, 94-96. RN, LPN, Fla. LPN All Cmty. Walk-In Clinic, Spring Hill, Fla., 1986; office mgr. Internat. Clerical Labs., Crystal River, Fla., 1986; LPN, charge nurse Eastbrooke Health Care Ctr., Brooksville, Fla., 1987-91; pvt. duty LPN Nursefinders, Inverness, Fla., 1991; med.-surg. LPN Oak Hill Hosp., Spring Hill, 1991; LPN charge nurse, then RN supr. Avante at Inverness, 1991—, resident assessment coord., care plan asst. coord., 1993-95, care plan coord., 1995-96, utilization rev./Medicare rev. coord., 1995-96, nurse mgr., 1996-97, asst. dir. of nurses, 1997-98, staff nurse, 1998—99, nurse mgr., 1999—. Relief ch. pianist Grace Tabernacle Ind. Bapt. Ch., Brooksville, 1983-91. Mem. Golden Key Honor Soc. Democrat. Avocations: piano, reading, travel, education. Office: Avante of Inverness 304 N Citrus Ave Inverness FL 34450-4157

NICHOLS, VICKI ANNE, financial consultant, librarian; b. Denver, June 10, 1949; d. Glenn Warner and Loretta Irene (Chalender) Adams; m. Robert H. Nichols, Oct. 28, 1972 (div.); children: Christopher Travis, Lindsay Meredith. BA, Colo. Coll., 1972; postgrad., U. Denver, 1976-77. Treas., controller, dir. Polaris Resources, Inc., Denver, 1972-86; controller InterCap Devel. Corp., 1986-87; treas., controller, dir. Transnat. Cons., Ltd., 1986-91; web coord. Jefferson County (Colo.) Pub. Libr., 1986—. Dir., owner Nichols Bus. Services. Home: 4305 Brentwood St Wheat Ridge CO 80033-4412 Office: 10200 W 20th Ave Lakewood CO 80215 Business E-Mail: vnichols@jefferson.lib.co.us.

NICHOLS, VIRGINIA VIOLET, independent insurance agent, accountant; b. Monroe County, Mo., Oct. 26, 1928; d. Elmer W. and Frances L. (McKinney) N. Student, Belleville Jr. Coll., Ill., 1959-60, Rockhurst Coll., 1964-65, Avila Coll., Kansas City, Mo., 1981-84. Sec. Panhandle Eastern Pipeline Co., Kansas City, Mo., 1964-65, St. Louis County Dept. Revenue, 1965-69, Forest Park Community Coll., 1969-71, Nooney Co., St. Louis, 1971-77, J. A. Baer Enterprises, St. Louis, 1979; acct. Panhandle Eastern Pipe Line Co., Kansas City, Mo., 1979-85. Vol. ARC, 1965—. Mem. Profl. Secs. Internat. (Sec. of Year 1979, sec. Mo. div. 1975-76), Jr. Women's C. of C. (Girl of Yr. 1975, pres. 1974-75), Soroptimist's Internat. (treas. Kansas City chpt. 1990-91), Desk and Derrick Club Kansas City (pres. 1999). Republican. Mem. United Ch. of Christ. Home: PO Box 33076 Kansas City MO 64114-0076 Office Phone: 816-941-8328.

NICHOLSON, AMBER SHAY, music educator; d. Ronald Homer and Darlene Vivian Shay; m. Jeremy Paul Nicholson, Aug. 13, 2005. BMus in Piano, Eastman Sch. Music, 1999, MMus in Piano, 2001; D in Musical Arts, Eastman Sch. Music, Rochester, NY, 2004. Asst. prof. piano U. So. Miss., Hattiesburg, 2004—. Liberace scholar, Liberace Found., Las Vegas, 1996—2004. Mem.: Music Tchrs. Nat. Assn. (nat. cert. tchr. music in piano). Office: Univ So Miss 118 College Dr #5081 Hattiesburg MS 39406-0001 Office Phone: 601-266-6932. Business E-Mail: amber.shay@usm.edu.

NICHOLSON, BERNICE LOUGHRAN, art educator; b. Newark, June 8, 1919; d. Harvey Whitfield and Carolyn (Augenstein) Bingham; m. Joseph S. Loughran, Mar. 31, 1947 (dec. 1977); children: Kevin, Mary Ann Loughran Rundell; m. Loren Lee Nicholson, Feb. 26, 1983. BS in Art Edn., Kean Coll., 1940; MA in Art, Ohio State U., 1946; EdD in Art and Edn., Stanford U., 1958. Art tchr. elem. sch., Irvington, N.J., 1940-43; instr. Johnson (Vt.) State Coll., 1943-47; tchr. elem. sch. Redwood City, Calif., 1954-56; prof. art Calif. Poly. State U., San Luis Obispo, 1958-88, emeritus prof. art, 1988—. Co-dir. Integrated Arts for the Classroom Workshops, 1991—. Author: Art Experiences: An Experimental Approach, 1963, Experiences in Twentieth Century Art, 1970, revision, 1990. Mem. com. state curriculum visual and performing arts, 1980-82. Recipient Award of Excellence, Calif. State Fair "Calif. Works", 1989, Bernice Loughran Nicholson Endowment for Arts Edn. Cal Poly State U., 2005. Mem. Calif. Humanities Assn. (state pres. 1978-80), Inst. Noetic Sci. (leader local study group 1992—). Congregationalist. Avocations: travel, dance. Home and Office: 156 Del Norte Way San Luis Obispo CA 93405-1508

NICHOLSON, CIE (CYNTHIA NICHOLSON), marketing executive, beverage company executive; b. Chgo. With R.J. Reynolds; dir. innovation Pepsi Cola N. Am., 1997; dir. Mountain Dew, 2000; v.p. Mountain Dew Pepsi Cola N. Am., v.p. flavors, 2002, v.p. carbonated soft drink flavors, v.p. non-carbonated beverages, 2004—05, chief mktg. officer, exec. v.p., 2005—. Named a Marketer of the Year, Brandweek, 2002. Avocation: golf. Office: Pepsi North America 700 Anderson Hill Rd Purchase NY 10577*

NICHOLSON, DIANE M., special education educator; BS in Psychology, Ga. Coll., 1977; MEd in Behavior Disorders, West Ga. Coll., 1989, EDs in behavior disorders, 1993. Cert. K-12 in behavior disorders, learning disabilities, mental retardation and inter-related TSS, early childhood edn. 2005. Behavior disorder/learning disability resource room instr. Whitesburg Elem. Sch., Carroll County Bd. Edn., 1980—87, 1988—91; academic therapist Burwell Psychoeducational Ctr., Carrollton, Ga., 1987—88; behavior disordered program instr. Ctrl. Mid. Sch. Carroll County Bd. Edn., 1991—92; grad. asst., tchg. asst. spl. edn. dept. West Ga. Coll., Carrollton, 1992—93, tchng. asst. for seminar for pre-tchrs., 1993, adj. instr., 1993—95, instr., 1994, adj. instr., 1995; resource tchr. for emotional and behavior disorders/learning disabled/mildly mentally handicapped Carroll County Bd. Edn., Ga., 1993—. Consultant, team mem. (book) Language Movement Strategies, 1983. Mem.: Phi Delta Kappa. Avocations: reading, computers. Home: 25 Agean Way Whitesburg GA 30185

NICHOLSON, DOROTHY NELIS, retired pre-school educator; b. Piqua, Ohio, Mar. 26, 1923; d. Frank Allen and Elsie Mamie Nelis; m. Robert Arthur Nicholson, June 17, 1944; children: Paul M., Gary A. BS, Anderson U., Ind., 1946, LittD (hon.), 2006; MS in Edn., Ind. U., Bloomington, 1977. Dir. children's work Nat. Bd. Christian Edn. Ch. of God, Anderson, 1947—48, children's dir. Park Pl., 1948—51; tchr. Park Pl. Nursery Sch., Anderson, 1965—67; dir. Park Pl. Children's Ctr., Anderson, 1967—78; ret., 1978. Curriculum writer, advisor Warner Press, Anderson, 1950—65. Editor: Egermeier's Favorite Bible Stories, 1965; author: Toward Effective Teaching - Young Children, 1970, I Can Choose, 1974, Lord It's Late But I Can't Sleep, 1984, The Cookery Collection, 1989. Bd. dirs. Anderson YWCA, 1984—86; bd. dirs., chair Park Pl. Ch., Anderson, 1984—85. Recipient Lifetime Achievement award, Anderson U., 2001. Mem.: AAUW, Charissa Club (chair, treas. 1950—). Avocations: travel, needlepoint, exercise. Home: 2727 Crown Pointe Cir Apt 127 Anderson IN 46012

NICHOLSON, ELLEN ELLIS, clinical social worker; b. Boston, Apr. 1, 1940; d. George Letham and Mary Stirling (Money) McIver; divorced; 1 child, Matthew Norman Ellis. Dental Hygienist, Forsyth Coll., 1959; BS, Northeastern U., 1973, MEd in Counseling, 1974; MSW, Boston U., 1984. Registered dental hygienist, Mass. Dental hygienist, 1959—66; clin. coord., pvt. dental practice Forsyth Dental Ctr., Boston, 1966—70; dir. vol. counseling Solomon Mental Health Ctr., Lowell, Mass., 1974—75; social worker East Boston Social Ctrs., Inc., 1976—77, dir. youth family counseling, 1977—79; supr. family svc. Boston Housing Authority, 1979—81; social worker Mass. Soc. Prevention Cruelty to Children, Hyannis, 1984—86, supr., 1986—93, clinic dir., 1993—95; dir. profl. svcs. Child and Family Svc. of Cape Cod, Hyannis, 1995—98, dir., 1998—2005, dir. Abuse Prevention Svcs., 1995—96, dir., 1995—2005; cons., therapist Child & Family Svcs. Cape Cod, 2005—. Psychotherapist Riverview Sch., Sandwich, Mass., 1989-93. Advisor youth group Christ Episcopal Ch., Needham, Mass., 1960-64, St. Paul's Ch., Newburyport, Mass., 1964-65; vol. counselor Solomon Mental Health Ctr., Lowell, 1972-74; chair Barnstable County Children's Task Force, 1994-96; chmn. adv. com. Barnstable County Sexual Abuse Intervention Network, 1994-96; mem. task force Barnstable County Juvenile Firesetters, 1995-96, mem. steering com., 1996—; mem. adv. bd. Cape and Islands Child Advocacy Ctr.; mem. Cape & Islands Domestic Violence Coun. Bd., 1998—. Mem. NASW, Am. Profl. Soc. on Abuse of Children, Assn. for Treatment of Sexual Abusers, Sigma Phi Alpha, Sigma Epsilon Rho, Kappa Delta Pi. Avocations: travel, ballroom dancing, skiing. Office: Child and Family Svc Cape Cod 1019 Rt 132 Hyannis MA 02601-1839

NICHOLSON, JUNE CONSTANCE DANIELS, retired speech pathologist; b. Augusta, Maine, Dec. 28, 1938; d. Sumner T. and Bernadette (Dulac) Daniels; m. Kenneth E. Nicholson, June 27, 1964; children: Jeffrey Scott, Daren Patrick. BS, Abilene Christian U., 1963; MS, U. Vt., 1980. Cert. ASHA CCC Vt. Dept. Edn., tchr. Vt. Speech pathologist grades K-12 Arlington (Vt.) Pub. Sch., ret., 1996. Vol. Peace Corp., Shumen, Bulgaria, 2001—03, St. Lucia, West Indies, 1971—73. Recipient Outstanding Vt. Tchr. award, U. Vt., 1992. Mem.: NEA, Bennington County Ret. Tchrs. Assn. (pres. 2004—06), Vt. Ret. Tchrs. Assn., Vt. Edn. Assn., Vt. Speech/Hearing Assn., Am. Speech/Hearing Assn., Ret. Tchrs. Assn. of NEA.

NICHOLSON, MARILYN LEE, arts administrator; b. San Jose, Calif., Feb. 7, 1949; d. John Hart Nicholson and Betty Ann (Price) Shepardson; m. Neal Luit Evenhuis. BA in English and History, U. Ariz., 1972; BFA in Studio, U. Hawaii-Manoa, Honolulu, 1977, MA in English, 1977, AS, 1984. Edn. coord., dir. Bishop Mus. Arts and Crafts Sch., Honolulu, 1977-79; owner Fiber Arts Store, Kailua, Hawaii, 1978-82; field coord. Hawaii State Found. on Culture and Arts, Honolulu, 1981-85; exec. dir. Sedona (Ariz.) Arts Ctr., 1986-92, Volcano (Hawaii) Art Ctr., 1992—. Mem. bd. artist selection com. Ariz. Indian Living Treasures, 1988-92; bd. dirs., treas. Sedona Cultural Arts Ctr., 1987-92; conf. speaker Nat. Assembly Arts Agys., 1988. Founding Chmn. Sedona Gallery Assn., 1990-92; mem. com. Sedona Acad., 1986-92; mem. steering com. community plan City of Sedona, 1989-91; commr. Arts & Cultural Ctr., Sedona, 1989-91; mem. exec. com. planning Volcano Community Assn., 1993-96. Recipient Mayor's award for Disting. Svc., Sedona City Coun., 1992. Mem. Hawaii Mus. Assn. (bd. dirs. 1995-00), Cooper Ctr. Coun. (bd. dirs. 1992—), Aloha Festivals-Hawaii Islands (bd. dirs. 1992-99). Office: Volcano Art Ctr PO Box 129 Volcano HI 96785

NICHOLSON, ROSANN, gifted and talented educator; b. Chgo., Ill., Nov. 2, 1955; d. Anthony James and Rose Cicchetti; m. James W. Nicholson, Aug. 5, 1978. Degree, Ill. State U., Normal, 1977. Tchr. jr. h.s. St. Frances of Rome Sch., Cicero, Ill., 1977—95, South Berwyn Sch. Dist. 100, Berwyn, Ill., 1995—97, tchr. gifted edn., 1997—. Coord. performing arts South Berwyn Sch. Dist., Berwyn, 1997—. Mem.: NEA. Avocations: theater, travel. Office: South Berwyn Sch Dist 100 3400 S Gunderson Berwyn IL 60402

NICHOLSON, VIRGINIA MAE, retired elementary school educator; BS in Elem. Edn., Shippensburg U., 1962; postgrad., Indiana U. Pa., 1962, 63, No. Ariz. U., 1982. Cert. tchr. Pa., Ariz. Tchr. Rockwood (Pa.) Area Sch. Dist., 1962-68, 73-80; substitute tchr. Lake Havasu City (Ariz.) Sch. Dist., 1980-83, tchr., 1983-84, Shanksville -Stonycreek Sch. Dist., Pa., 1984—2006, ret., 2006. Mem. NEA, Pa. State Edn. Assn, Delta Kappa Gamma. Home: 428 S Columbia Ave Somerset PA 15501-1901

NICHOLSON, YVETTE RENEE, science educator; b. Mobile, Ala., Oct. 14, 1974; d. Matthew Gulley Jr. and Ernestine Elizabeth Gulley; m. Larry Wayne Nicholson, Dec. 22, 1999; children: Larry Wayne Jr., Michael Jerome, Imani Renee. BS in Biology, Prairie View A&M U., Tex., 1997. Cert. secondary sci. educator Ala. Rsch. technologist II U. South Ala., Mobile, 1998—99; sci. tchr. Mobile County Pub. Sch. Sys., Ala., 1999—. Mem.: Nat. Sci. Tchrs. Assn., Ala. Sci. Tchrs. Assn., Nat. Educators Assn., Ala. Educators Assn., Mobile County Educators Assn., Delta Sigma Theta (Mobile Alumnae chpt. nominating com., various other coms. 2004). Democrat. Baptist. Avocations: travel, reading, tennis, medical research. Office: Jeremiah A Denton Mid Sch 3800 Pleasant Valley Rd Mobile AL 36609 Office Phone: 251-221-2148. Fax: 251-221-2152. Personal E-mail: yrenee31@gmail.com. E-mail: ynicholson@mcpss.com.

NICHTER, RHODA SAMUELS, writer, educator; b. Bklyn., June 22, 1926; d. Joseph and Celia Samuels; m. Murray Nichter, June 26, 1948; children: Shelli Binder, Judith Morris. Student, Bklyn. Coll., 1943-47. Cert. smoking cessation specialist. Smoking cessation specialist St. Francis Hosp., Roslyn, NY, 1975—, Dept. of Drug and Alcohol Addiction, Hempstead, NY, 1978—; nonsmokers rights coord. Am. Lung Assn., Hauppauge, NY, 1978—81. Author: Yes, I Do Mind if You Smoke, 1978, How to Stop Smoking Once and For All, 1980; prodr., host Smoking and Your Health, WHPC-FM-Radio, 1980—. Pres., founder, activist Group Against Smoking Pollution of NY, Plainview, 1971—; past pres. Women's Am. Orgn. for Rehab. through Tng.; pres. YJCC In Between Couples Club. Recipient Nonsmokers' Rights award Am. Lung Assn., 1980. Avocations: lap swimming, painting, art and antique collecting, bridge. Home: 7 Maxine Ave Plainview NY 11803-3606 Office Phone: 516-938-0080.

NICKA, BETTY LOU, secondary school educator; b. Madison, Wis., June 2, 1937; d. Marvin J. and Tilla S. (Haakinson) Lindberg; m. John George Nicka, June 27, 1970; 1 child, Karyn Theresa. BS, U. Wis., LaCrosse, 1959. Tchr. Mitchell Jr. High Sch., Racine, Wis., 1959-63, Cherokee Jr. High Sch., Madison, Wis., 1963-65, East High Sch., Madison, Wis., 1965-92. Coach tennis, volleyball, basketball & track Madison East High Sch., 1965-73, dir. dance, performing arts, 1965-92, choreographer theatre plays and musicals, 1970-73. Coord. com. performing arts in dance Tower Twirler Dancers, Wis., 1978-92. Mem. NEA, Am. Assn. Health, Phys. Edn., Recreation and Dance, Wis. Edn. Assn. (coun. 1959—), Wis. Assn. Health, Phys. Edn., Recreation and Dance, So. Wis. Edn. Insvc. Orgn. (chair phys. sec. 1966-67), Madison Area Retired Educators Assn. Democrat. Lutheran. Home: 2105 Sheridan Dr Madison WI 53704-3844

NICKEL, JANET MARLENE MILTON, retired geriatrics nurse; b. Manitowoc, Wis., June 9, 1940; d. Ashley and Pearl Milton; m. Curtis A. Nickel, July 29, 1961; children: Cassie, Debra, Susan. Diploma, Milw. Inst., 1961; ADN, N.D. State U., 1988. Nurse Milw. VA, Wood, Wis., 1961-62; supervising nurse Park Lawn Convalescent Hosp., Manitowoc, 1964-65; newsletter editor Fargo (N.D.) Model Cities Program, 1970-73; supervising night nurse Rosewood on Broadway, Luth. Hosps. and Homes, Fargo, 1973-92; assoc. dir. nursing Elim Care Ctr., Fargo, 1992-94, night nurse, 1994—2005; ret., 2005. Mem. Phi Eta Sigma.

NICKELS, RUTH ELIZABETH, band director; b. Warsaw, Ind., Nov. 21, 1955; d. Marjorie Jane Shipley; m. David Brent Nickels, July 7, 2001. MusB in Performance, DePauw U., 1978; MusM in Performance, Ithaca Coll., 1980; cert. in edn., Grace Coll., 1986; post-master credits, Ind. U., 1986. Profl. tchg. lic. music edn. Dir. bands Fairfield Jr.-Sr. H.S., Goshen, Ind., 1986—92; H.S. band dir. Yorktown (Ind.) H.S., 1992—93; dir. bands Orleans (Ind.) Jr.-Sr. H.S., 1993—97, Southwestern Mid., H.S., Hanover, Ind., 1997—. Music judge Ind. State Music Assn., Indpls. Mem.: NEA, Ind. State Tchrs. Assn., Ind. Bandmasters Assn., Music Educator's Nat. Conf., Women Band Dirs. Assn., Nat. Band Assn. Avocations: reading, travel, cooking, walking. Home: 31665 River Bluff Dr Hanover IN 47243 Office: Southwestern Mid and HS 167 S Main Cross St Hanover IN 47243 Personal E-mail: nickels@aol.com. Business E-Mail: rnickels@swjcs.k12.in.us.

NICKELSON, KIM RENÉ, internist; b. Chgo., Feb. 13, 1956; d. Robert William and Carolynn Lucille (Marts) N.; m. Louis Peter Sguros; children: Brian Louis, Justin Robert Peter. BS in Chemistry, U. Ill., 1978; MD, Loyola U., Maywood, Ill., 1981. Diplomate Am. Bd. Internal Medicine. Intern and resident in internal medicine Luth. Gen. Hosp., Park Ridge, Ill., 1981-84; pvt. practice Oakbrook, Ill., 1984-87, Plantation, Fla., 1987—. Adj. attending staff Rush-Presbyn. St. Luke's Med. Ctr., Chgo., 1984-87; assoc. attending staff Hinsdale (Ill.) Hosp., 1984-87, Westside Regional Med. Ctr., Plantation, Plantation Gen. Hosp., Fla. Med. Ctr., Lauderhill, Fla. Musician Elk Grove (Ill.) Cmty. Band, 1978-87, Sunrise (Fla.) Pops Symphony, 1987—. Mem. ACP, Internat. Horn Soc. Office: Internal Medicine Assocs 499 NW 70th Ave Ste 200 Plantation FL 33317-7578 Office Phone: 954-581-1900.

NICKELSON, PAMELA SUE, music educator; b. Berwyn, Ill., Apr. 16, 1955; d. William Clayton and Mae Amanda Barber; m. Dwayne Edward Nickelson, Aug. 30, 1986; 1 child, Thomas Alexander. MusB in Edn., Aquinas Coll., Grand Rapids, Mich., 1976. Cert. tchr. Mich. Bd. Edn., 1976. Tchr. music K-12 Mancelona Pub. Schs., Mich., 1976—79; tchr. music K-8, choir dir. Immaculate Heart of Mary Ch., Grand Rapids, 1979—81; music dir. Holy Redeemer Cath. Ch., Jenison, Mich., 1981—86; tchr. grades 4 and 6 St.

Patrick's Cath. Sch., Portland, Mich., 1986—99; tchr. music K-6 East Lansing Pub. Schs., Mich., 1999—. Music curricular chair East Lansing Pub. Schs., 2003—; assn. rep. East Lansing Edn. Assn., 2004—. Mem. Right To Life, Portland, Mich., 1988—92. Grantee, East Lansing Edn. Found., 2004, 2006. Mem.: Mid Mich. Orff Schulwerk Assn. (v.p. 2005—). Liberal. Catholic. Avocations: swimming, reading, children's drama productions, scouting. Office: East Lansing Pub Schs 841 Timberlane East Lansing MI 48823 Office Phone: 517-333-7424.

NICKENS, CATHERINE ARLENE, retired nurse, freelance writer; b. Litchfield, Ill., Oct. 30, 1932; d. Harley Lloyd Moore and Ida Mae Reynolds; m. Carl Roland Nickens, Sept. 4, 1954 (div. Apr. 1975); children: Linda Dianne, Carl Roland Jr., Karen Patricia, Eric Moore. Nursing diploma, St. Joseph's Hosp., 1954. RN, Calif. Staff nurse St. Joseph's Hosp., Alton, Ill., 1954-55, St. Mary's Hosp., Streator, Ill., 1962-68, supr., acting dir., 1968-70; nursing supr. Illini Hosp., Silvis, Ill., 1970-74; office nurse pediatrician's office Silvis, 1974-75; staff nurse telemetry/drug abuse North Miami Gen. Hosp., Miami, Fla., 1975-80; staff nurse, relief supr. Petaluma (Calif.) Valley Hosp., 1981-97. Participant women's health study Brigham and Women's Hosp., Boston, 1994-2004. Author: (hist. fiction) The Thoroughly Compromised Bride, 1991 (award 1992), The Highwayman, 1993 (award 1994). Mem. ACLU, N.Y.C., 1995, Parents, Families and Friends of Lesbians and Gays, Washington, 1994-99, Nat. Mus. of Am. Indian/Smithsonian Instn., Washington, 1996-97; friend of the quilt NAMES Project Meml. Quilt, San Francisco, 1992-99; mem. friendship cir. Am. Found. for AIDS Rsch., Washington, 1994—; vol. Santa Rosa Police Dept., 1997-2000. Mem. Romance Writers of Am. (mentor to unpublished writers 1995-99). Avocations: reading, travel, needlecrafts, doll-making. Home and Office: 105 Olive St Santa Rosa CA 95401-6241

NICKLEBY, KATHE JO ANNE, assistant principal; d. Robert Raymond and Geraldine Iris McArdell; m. John David NIckleby, Jan. 1, 2002; children: Emily Laura Decker-Steele, Amy Michelle Decker. M in Edn. Leadership, St. Mary's U., Minn., 2001. Cert. adminstrv. specialist Minn., 2001. Tchr. chemistry and physics Mahtomedi H.S., Minn., 1995—2005, asst. prin., 2005—. Office: Mahtomedi HS 8000 75th St N Mahtomedi MN 55015 Office Phone: 651-407-2102.

NICKLES-MURRAY, ELIZABETH, advertising executive, writer; b. Miami Beach, Fla., May 29, 1948; d. Arnold C. and Audrey (Reid) Nelson. BS, Northwestern U., 1968; MA, DePaul U., 1970. Creative supr. Esquire Inc., Chgo., 1975—76; copy supr. Marsteller Inc., Chgo., 1976—77; assoc. creative dir. J. Walter Thompson, Chgo., 1977—80; sr. v.p. D'Arcy MacManus Masius, Chgo., 1980; exec. v.p., creative dir. Warwick Advt., NYC, 1990; exec. v.p., exec. creative dir. Ketchum Advt., NY, 1990—. Cons. ptnr. Nickles & Ashcraft, Chgo., 1978—; founder, dir. Update: Women, 1980—. Author: The Coming Matriarchy, 1982, Girls in High Places, 1986, Hype, 1989; contbr. articles to popular mags. Named Outstanding Young Woman Achiever, Nat. Coun. Women US, 1982, All Time Top 10 Working Women, Glamour Mag., 1984, Chgo. Advt. Woman of Yr., 1982.

NICKLESS, BARBARA A., primary school educator; b. Clark AFB, Philippines, 1960; d. Anthony and Ruby Borzymowski; m. Geoffrey G. Nickless, Jan. 1999. BA in Social Work and Criminal Justice, Colo. State U., Ft. Collins, 1983; postgrad. in MA in Edn. program, Calif. State U., Sacramento, 2003. Cert. tchr. Calif. Mid. sch. educator Winters (Calif.) Mid. Sch., 1994—98; h.s. educator Natomas H.S., Sacramento, 1998—99; mid. sch. educator Leroy F. Greene Mid. Sch., Sacramento, 1999—2002; primary sch. educator Two Rivers Elem. Sch., Sacramento, 2002—. Ind. contractor The Coll. Bd., Western Regional Office, San Jose, Calif., 2002—; master tchr. Intel Teach to the Future Program, Sacramento, 2000—03; tchr.-cons. Area 3 Writing Project U. Calif., Davis, 1996—. Mem.: Calif. Teachers Assn., Nat. Teachers Assn., Porsche Club Am. (sec. SVR region 1996—97, v.p. 1997—98), Italian Cultural Soc. Roman Catholic. Avocations: travel, competitive go-cart racing, Italian. Office: Natomas Unified Sch Dist TR 1901 Arena Blvd Sacramento CA 95834

NICKLIN, EMILY, lawyer; b. Cooperstown, N.Y., June 24, 1953; d. George Leslie Jr. and Katherine Mildred (Aronson) N.; m. Jay Schleusener, Dec. 28, 1974; children: Max, Lucas, Anna. BA, U. Chgo., 1975, JD, 1977. Bar: Ill. 1977, U.S. Dist. Ct. (no. dist.) Ill. 1979, U.S. Ct. Appeals (7th cir.) 1979. Law clk. to judge U.S. Dist. Ct. (no. dist.) Ill., Chgo., 1977-79; assoc. Kirkland & Ellis, Chgo., 1979-83, ptnr., 1983—, mem. firm mgmt. com., 1995—. Tchr. Ill. Continuing Legal Edn. Bar Program, Chgo., 1983—; fellow Salzburg Seminar, Austria, 1983; dep. corp. counsel City of Chgo., 1989-91; mem. bd. trustees, Univ. Chgo.; lectr. law, Univ. Chgo., 2001. Named one of Am. Top 50 Women Litigators, Nat. Law. Jour., 2001, 30 Tough Lawyers, Chgo. Mag. Mem. Nat. Inst. Trial Advocacy (tchr., team leader 1982—), Order of Coif, Phi Beta Kappa. Office: Kirkland & Ellis LLP 200 E Randolph St Fl 54 Chicago IL 60601-6636 Office Phone: 312-861-2387. Office Fax: 312-861-2200. Business E-Mail: enicklin@kirkland.com.

NICKOLS, MARCIA LYNN, retired art educator; b. Eau Claire, Wis., Feb. 28, 1948; d. Charles Lewis and Juanita Grace (Claflin) Riggin; m. Thomas Carl Nickols, June 16, 1973; children: Joshua Charles, Sara Jeanette. BA in Art Edn., U. Wis., Eau Claire, 1970; M Art Edn., U. Wis., Madison, 1990. Art tchr. Schaumburg (Ill.) Dist., 1970-73, Parkview Sch. Dist., Orfordville, Wis., 1973—2005. Mem. Nat. Art Edn. Assn., Wis. Art Edn. Assn.

NICKS, STEVIE (STEPHANIE LYNN NICKS), singer, songwriter; b. Phoenix, May 26, 1948; Joined Fleetwood Mac, 1974. Albums include: (with Lindsey Buckingham) Buckingham Nicks, 1973, (with Fleetwood Mac) Fleetwood Mac, 1975, Rumours, 1977 (co-winner, Billboard award for Album of the Year, Group of Year 1977), Tusk, 1979, Fleetwood Mac Live, 1980, Mirage, 1982, Tango in the Night, 1987, Greatest Hits, 1989, Behind The Mask, 1990, 25 Years-The Chain, 1992, The Dance, 1997, Say You Will, 2004; (solo) Bella Donna, 1981, The Wild Heart, 1983, Rock a Little, 1985, The Other Side of the Mirror, 1989, Time Space, 1991, Street Angel, 1994, Enchanted: The Works of Stevie Nicks, 1998, Trouble in Shangri-La, 2001, The Divine, 2001; composer songs Rhiannon, 1975, Landslide, 1975 (Most Performed Country Song of the Year, BMI Awards 2003), Leather and Lace, 1975, Dreams, 1977, Sara, 1979, Edge of Seventeen, 1981, If Anyone Falls (with Sandy Stewart), 1982, Stand Back (with Prince Rogers Nelson), 1983, I Can't Wait (with others), 1985, Seven Wonders (with Sandy Stewart), and others.

NICODEMUS, EMILY HULSIZER, technology educator; b. Orange, N.J., Jan. 12, 1945; d. James England and Elisabeth S. (Peck) Hulsizer; m. Robert Evans Nicodemus, July 29, 1967; children: Aaron, Todd, Wendy. BA, Wilson Coll., 1967; MEd, U. Md., 1970. Tech. coord. N. Attleboro (Mass.) Pub. Schs., 1993—. Mem. Norfolk (Mass.) Sch. Com., 1979-82, sec. 1980, v.p. 1982, rep. to Mass. Assn. Sch. Coms., 1979-82. Editor: King Philip Parents' Network Newsletter, Wrentham, Mass., 1990-94. Mem. Internat. Soc. Tech. in Edn., Mass. Computer-Using Educators (southeastern SIG leader). Avocations: gardening, computers. Home: 7 Diamond St Norfolk MA 02056-1517 Office: Technology Office Community Sch North Attleboro MA 02760 E-mail: enicodemus@naschools.net.

NICOL, NANCY J., lawyer; b. Middletown, Ohio, Aug. 1, 1949; BS, Univ. Dayton, 1971; JD, DePaul Univ., 1978. Bar: Ill. 1978. Law clerk, Hon. Helen F. McGillicuddy Ill. Appellate Ct.; ptnr., civil litig., appellate law The Sullivan Firm, Ltd., Rolling Meadows, Ill. Adj. law faculty Loyola Univ., Chgo. Note and comment editor DePaul Law Rev. Mem.: Nat. Assn. Women Lawyers (v.p. 2004), Women's Bar Assn. Ill. (pres. 1992—93). Office: The Sullivan Firm Ltd Ste 101 Medows Corp Ctr E Tower 2550 W Golf Rd Rolling Meadows IL 60008-4501 Office Phone: 847-228-1100. Office Fax: 847-228-5199. Business E-Mail: njn96@aol.com.

NICOLAIDES, MARY, lawyer; b. N.Y.C., June 7, 1927; d. George and Dorothy Nicolaides. BCE, CUNY, 1947; MBA with distinction, DePaul U., 1975, JD, 1981. Bar: Ill. 1982, U.S. Dist. Ct. (no. dist.) Ill. 1982, U.S. Patent Office 1983. Sr. design engr. cement subs. U.S. Steel Corp., N.Y.C., then Pitts., 1948-71; sole practice Chgo., 1982—. Republican. Greek Orthodox. Address: 233 E Erie St Apt 1804 Chicago IL 60611-2903

NICOLL, GAYLE, chemistry educator; b. Ind., Aug. 23, 1973; d. James D and Linda R Wozniewski; m. Alex Nicoll, Aug. 13, 1994; children: Serena, Lyta. BS in chemistry, Ind. U., 1991—94, BS in physics, 1991—94; MS, Purdue U., 1994—97, PhD, 1994—2000. Asst. prof. Tex. Tech U., Lubbock, 1999—2000; lectr. U. of Nebraska-Lincoln, 2000—. Contbr. articles to profl. jours. Sci. fair judge Internat. Sci. & Engring. Fair, 1999—2003; judge 4-H, Omaha, Nebr., 2000—01; host of chemistry edn. workshop NSF, Lincoln, Nebr., 2003—03. Nebr. Women in Sci., EPSCoR Small Grant Program, 2003. Mem.: Nat. Assn. of Rsch. in Sci. Tchg., AAAS, Iota Sigma Pi (outreach coord. 1997—99), Am. Chem. Soc., Phi Lambda Upsilon. Office: University of Nebraska-Lincoln Dept of Chemistry Hamilton Hall Lincoln NE 68583

NICOLOSI, GIANNA RUTH, marketing professional; b. Birmingham, Ala., July 3, 1977; d. Robert Joseph and Karen Bristley Nicolosi. Degree in Mktg., U. Ky., 1999. From field mktg. rep. to acct. exec. Black and Decker, NJ, 1999—2002, acct. exec. Tampa, Fla., 2002—03, mgr. comml. ter., 2004—. Recruiter Black and Decker, N.Y.C., NY, 1999—, Tampa, 1999—, mem. mentor com., 1999—, N.Y.C., 1999—. Office: Black and Decker 701 E Joppa Rd Towson MD 21286

NICOLS, ANGELA C., software engineer, consultant; b. Jamaica, N.Y., Apr. 15, 1940; d. Henry Ralph and Josephine Sadie (Zarcone) Grieco; m. Otto John Nicols, May 21, 1960; children: Annemarie Nicols-Grinenko, Elizabeth Marie Crevani, John Joseph, William Joseph, Richard Joseph. BS in Math., Hofstra U., 1979; MS in Math. and Computer Sci., Adelphi U., 1985. Supr. programs/project leader Book Clubs Info. Sys. Doubleday and Co. Inc., Garden City, N.Y., 1979-87; mgr. software engring. Martin Marietta Info. Sys., Orlando, Fla., 1987-94; with Apopka Hist. Soc., 1994—, pres., 2005—; computer cons. and trainer, owner Nicols Cons., Apopka, 1995—. Vol. Apopka H.S. Adv. Coun., 1994-97; sec. Bd. Edn.: Bishop Moore H.S., Orlando, 1995-98. Mem. St. Francis Disabilities Com., 1995—; mem. pastoral coun. St. Francis of Assisi Ch., mem. social action commn., 2000-03; chair helping hands Errol Estates Property Owners Assn., 2005—. Mem. AAUW, IEEE Computer Soc., Assn. for Computing Machinery, Math. Assn. Am., Nat. Assn. Women in Computing, Am. Math. Soc., Coun. Cath. Women, Gray Panthers, Foliage Garden Club of Apopka (2d v.p. 1996-2001, 2005—), Errol Estates Country Club (comms. com. 1998-2000), Henry Nehrling Soc. (bd. dirs. 2006—), Golfside Village Homeowners Assn. (exec. v.p. 1999—), Kappa Mu Epsilon. Office Phone: 407-886-2057. E-mail: angenic@cfl.rr.com.

NICOLSON, CHRISTINA CARRELL, elementary school educator; b. Akron, Ohio, Apr. 13, 1945; d. William Buford and Virginia (Andrews) Carrell; m. James Shelley Nicolson, Aug. 20, 1977. BA, Vassar Coll., Poughkeepsie, N.Y., 1967; postgrad., Columbia Tchrs. Coll., N.Y.C., 1968-70, Lesley Coll., Cambridge, Mass., 1994—. Tchr. 4th grade Riverbank Elem. Sch., Stamford, Conn., 1967-68; tchr. 3d grade Greenwich (Conn.) Country Day Sch., 1968-70; mkt. rsch. cons. Rath & Strong Inc., Lexington, Mass., 1970-73; 4th grade tchr. The Park Sch., Brookline, Mass., 1973-79; mgr. Galeria de Christina, Belmont, Mass., 1979-83; project dir. Stage One Mktg. Rsch., Cambridge, Mass., 1982-85; mkt. rsch. analyst Polaroid Corp., Cambridge, 1982-85; tchr. 3d and 4th grade The Pike Sch., Andover, Mass., 1985—. Pvt. math. tutor, Boston area, 1988—; spkr. Nat. Coun. Tchrs. Math., 1987—, Nat. Coun. Tchrs. English, 1985—. Editor math curricula, SRA/McGraw Hill, 1994. Co-chair anewcomers and grant com. Follen Cmty. Ch., Lexington, Mass., 1995—, com. mem. of Hopi Exch., 1994—. Recipient Presdl. Award for Excellence in Teaching Sci. and Math., NSF, 1993-94. Mem. Nat. Mus. of the Am. Indian, New Eng. Women Bus. Owners (events coord. 1980-83). Unitarian Universalist. Avocations: computers, singing, swimming. Home: 400 Pleasant St Belmont MA 02478-3242 Office: The Pike School Sunset Rock Rd Andover MA 01810

NICOTRA, MARY, health facility administrator, consultant; b. Evanston, Ill., June 29, 1966; d. William Thomas and Mary Louise (Jackson) Hofstetter; m. Paul Anthony Nicotra, July 4, 1993; 1 child, Jacob Arthur. BA in Bus., Columbia Coll., Chgo., 1990. Acct. terr. rep. injectable pharms. Bristol Meyers, Downers Grove, Ill., 1991-93; acct. mgr. outsourcing OME equipment mgmt. Universal Hosp. Svcs., 1993-96; acct. exec. Matria Healthcare, 1996—99; acct. mgr. Accredo Therapeutics. Regional trainer Matria Healthcare Inc. Avocations: gardening, aerobics, boating, scuba diving. Home: 1428 Keats Ave Naperville IL 60564-4119

NICOVICH, MARY C., medical/surgical nurse; b. Hattiesburg, Miss., Apr. 6, 1956; d. Marco W. and Mary D. (Pfleging) N. BS in Psychology, U. So. Miss., 1979; BSN, William Carey Coll., 1981. Psychiat. technician Forrest Gen. Hosp., Hattiesburg, 1978-79; nursing technician So. Bapt. Hosp., New Orleans, 1980-81; staff and charge nurse Meth Hosp., Hattiesburg, 1981-86, Forrest Gen. Hosp., Hattiesburg, 1986-92; nurse South Cen. Regional Med. Ctr., Laurel, Miss., 1992—2001; nurse, donor care specialist III United Blood Svcs., Hattiesburg, 2001—06; nurse Oxford Health & Rehab. Ctr., Lumberton, Miss., 2006—. With Forrest Gen. Hosp., 1986—. Vol. Make a Wish Found., Sacred Heart Cath. Ch. Home: 1811 Brooklane Dr Hattiesburg MS 39401-7411

NIDIFFER, SHERI LYNN, medical/surgical nurse; b. Mohave Desert, Calif., July 29, 1964; d. Kenneth Eugene and Mary Emma (Walsh) N. BSN, Davis and Elkins Coll., 1987; MBA, MSN, George Mason U., 1998; grad. nurse practitioner, George Washington U., 1999. RN; cert. med./surg. nurse, nurse practitioner. From aide to charge nurse Fairfax Nursing Home, Va., 1983-87; floor nurse Fairfax Hosp., Falls Church, Va., 1987-88, asst. nursing coord., 1988-92, nurse trauma med.-surg. ICU, 1992—; HIV clin. specialist INOVA Home Infusion, 1994-95; nurse practitioner adminstr. Medic 1, Fredericksburg, Va., 2000—. Nurse practitioner adminstr. Medic One, Fredericksburg, Va., 2000—. Home: 8819 Aquary Ct Springfield VA 22153-1255 Office: 3429 Jefferson Davis Hwy Fredericksburg VA 22408-4170

NIDZGORSKI, BARBARA HELEN, gifted and talented educator, puppeteer; b. Wilmington, Del., July 15, 1951; d. Joseph Edward and Angela Victoria (Palczewski) N. BFA, U. Del., Newark, 1973; MA, U. Conn., 1980; MFA, Conn. Coll., New London, 1989. Cert. tchr., Conn, art tchr. K-12, Conn. Tchr. grade 4, grade 7/8 algebra Woodland Country Day Sch., Jericho, N.J., 1974-78; tchr. gifted and talented Greenwich (Conn.) Pub. Schs., 1979-80, New London Pub. Schs., 1987-94; tchr. gifted and talented, grades 6-12 Dist. 18 Lyme/Old Lyme, Conn., 1994—2002; tchr. gifted and talented secondary sch. Dist. 4, Deep River, Conn., 2002—. Gen. mgr. nat. puppetry conf. Eugene O'Neill Theatre, Waterford, Conn., 1990—; instr. U. Conn., Storrs, 1982-98. Co-author: (cards for classroom) Mission Possible, 1981-82. Recipient Mark Shedd Excellence award Conn. Consortium for Law and Citizenship in Edn; named to Outstanding Young Women of Am., 1985; named Conn. Tchr.-In-Space, NASA, 1985. Mem. Delta Kappa Gamma (art chair 1991-98, state chair 1994-97), Phi Delta Gamma. Avocations: theater, kayaking, mountain biking, musical instruments, pottery. Home: 41 White Birch Cir Niantic CT 06357-1610 Office: Regional Dist 4 1 Winthrop Rd Deep River CT 06417 Office Phone: 860-526-9546. Personal E-mail: oneillpupconf@aol.com.

NIEBYL, JENNIFER ROBINSON, obstetrician, gynecologist, educator; BSc, McGill U., Mont., 1963; MD, Yale U., 1967. Diplomate Am. Bd. Ob-Gyn., Am. Bd. Maternal and Fetal Medicine. Intern in Internal Medicine N.Y. Hosp.-Cornell Med. Ctr., 1967-68, resident in ob-gyn., 1968-70, Johns Hopkins Hosp., Balt., 1970-73, fellow in maternal and fetal medicine, 1976-78, mem. staff, 1973—88, U. Iowa Hosps. and Clinics, Iowa City, 1988—; prof., head ob-gyn. dept. U. Iowa Sch. Medicine, Iowa City, 1988—. Mem. ACOG, Am. Gynecol. and Obstetrical Soc., Soc. Gynecol. Investigation, Soc. Maternal Fetal Medicine, Inst. Medicine of NAS. Office: U Iowa Hosps & Clinics 200 Hawkins Dr Iowa City IA 52242 Office Phone: 319-356-1976.

NIEDERBERGER, JANE, information technology executive; m. Mark Niederberger; children: Amy, Sarah. BS in nutrition, Simmons Coll., 1982; MBA in health care adminstrn., Northeastern U. Various mgmt. positions Harvard Pilgrim Health Care, Boston, 1983—96; with IT divsn. Anthem, Inc., Indpls., 1997, acting chief info. officer, 1998—99, sr. v.p., chief info. officer, 1999—. Bd. dir. Managed Care Exec. Group. Bd. mem. Jr. Achievement, Indpls. Recipient Women and Hi Tech Leading Light award, 2002. Office: Anthem Inc 120 Monument Cir Indianapolis IN 46204

NIEDERER, MARLA LEE, special education educator; b. N.Y.C., May 9, 1956; d. David Carl and Francesca Juran; m. Robert Hans Niederer, Aug. 26, 1990; 1 child, Jason A. BS magna cum laude, SUNY, Cortland, 1984; MS in Edn., SUNY, Binghamton, 1990. Pub. sch. tchrs. cert. N.Y. Admissions/discharge coord. Highgate Manor Nursing Home, Cortland, NY, 1985—88; spl. edn. tchr. Oxford (N.Y.) Acad. Mid. Sch., 1990—96; transition tchr. St. Lawrence Lewis BOCES, Canton, 1999—. Com. mem. Keys for Your Future Conf., Canton, 2003—; thcr. rep. shared decision com. St. Lawrence Lewis BOCES, Canton, 2002—. Empire State Challenger fellow, SUNY Binghamton, 1988, 1989. Mem.: Empire State Assn. Persons Supported Employment, Phi Kappa Phi. Democrat. Avocations: doll making, beading, gardening, reading, painting. Office: Saint Lawrence Lewis BOCES Washington Ednl Ctr 616 Rensselaer Ave Ogdensburg NY 13669

NIEDERMEIER, MARY B., retired nutritionist; b. Webster Groves, Mo., Oct. 20, 1914; d. Albertus and Daisey May (Christman) Wickersham; m. Walter H. Niedermeier, Sept. 9, 1939; children: Gail Santarelli, Bart. BS, Mich. State U., 1937; MA, Columbia U., 1957, profl. diploma, 1959. Cert. in dietetics Ohio, 1938. Dist. nutritionist N.J. State Dept. of Health, Newark; instr. nutrition edn. Sch. of Dentistry Fairleigh Dickinson U., Teaneck, NJ; instr. nutrition edn. Sch. of Nursing St. Louis U. Pres. Oradell (N.J.) Pub. Sch. PTA, 1954—57; bd. dirs. Rancho Bernardo (Calif.) Oaks N. Cmty. Ctr., 1974—76; treas. PEO-TV chpt., Rancho Bernardo, 1990; bd. deacons Rancho Bernardo Presbyn. Ch., 1975—76. Grace McCloud fellow, Columbia U., 1957—59. Mem.: AAUP, AAUW, N.J. Dietetic Assn., Calif. Dietetic Assn., Am. Dietetic Assn., Alpha Omicron Pi. Republican. Avocations: electronic organ music, painting, golf, lawn and indoor bowling. Home: 16925 Hierba Dr # 430 San Diego CA 92128-2223

NIEHAUS, MARY C., lawyer; b. 1961; BA with honors, Grinnell Coll., 1985; JD cum laude, Northwestern U., 1988. Bar: Ill. 1988, U.S. Dist. Ct. (no. dist.) Ill. 1988, U.S. Tax Ct. 1989. With Sidley & Austin, Chgo., 1988—, ptnr., 1996—. Mem. editl. staff Northwestern U. Law Rev., 1987-88. Mem. Order of Coif, Phi Beta Kappa. Office: Sidley & Austin Bank One Plz 10 S Dearborn St Chicago IL 60603 Fax: 312-83-7036. E-mail: mniehaus@sidley.com.

NIEHOFF, KARISSA L., principal; b. St. Louis, Nov. 24, 1965; d. Randall and Marilyn Niehoff. BS in Phys. Edn., U. Mass., 1988; MS in Health Edn., So. Conn. State U., 1997; student in Ednl. Leadership, U. Conn., 2003—. Cert. supt. schs. Conn., in sch. adminstrn. Conn., tchr. phys. edn. and health Conn., Mass. Tchr. Joel Barlow H.S., Redding, Conn., 1990—92, Bethel (Conn.) Mid. Sch., 1992—93; tchr., dir. athletics, chmn. dept. Litchfield (Conn.) H.S., 1993—99; tchr. Newington (Conn.) H.S., 1999—2000; asst. prin. Har-Bur Mid. Sch., Burlington, Conn., 2000—04; prin. Lewis S. Mills H.S., Burlington, 2004—. Mem. edn. com. U.S. Olympics Com., Colo. Springs, Colo., 1995—2001; mem. sportsmanship com. Conn. Interscholastic Athletic Conf., Inc., Cheshire, Conn., 2005—, bd. controls, 2005—; cons. edn. Capitol Region Edn. Coun., Hartford, Conn., 1998—; spkr. in field. Author: Olympic Day In the Schools, 1999; contbr. articles to profl. jours. Dean youth sport leadership Nat. Olympic Acad., 1995—2000, del.; program leader Internat. Olympic Youth Camp, 1996; bd. dirs. Private Victories Mag., 1994—98. Mem.: Conn. Assn. Schs. (mem. profl. studies com. 2004—), Harwinton Women's Club (active cmty. svcs. 2003—), Region 10 Adminstrs. Union (pres. 2000—), Phi Delta Kappa. Democrat. Avocations: fitness, horseback riding, violin, cooking, travel. Home: 172 Burlington Rd Harwinton CT 06791 Office: Lewis Mills High School 26 Lyon Rd Burlington CT 06013

NIEKAMP, CYNTHIA ANN, automotive executive; b. Dayton, Ohio, May 13, 1959; arrived in France, 1986; d. Andrew Joseph and Janet (Willke) N. BS in Indsl. Engring., Purdue U., 1981; MBA, Harvard U., 1983. Sr. ptnr. B-Sch. Travel, Inc., Boston, 1983-84; planning analyst Gen. Motors Corp., Detroit, 1983; sr. indsl. engr. Delco-Moraine Divsn. Gen. Motors Corp., Dayton, 1984-85, gen. mfg. supr., 1985-86; ops. mgr. Gen. Motors France, Paris, 1988-89; plant mgr. Delco Moraine NDH Divsn., General Motors Co., Dayton, 1989—90; v.p. TRW Engine and After Market Group, 1990—92; dir. ops. TRW Technar, Inc., 1992—93; mng. dir. TRW Transportation Systems, 1993—95; v.p., corp. strategy and planning Mead Corp., 1995—98; pres. Mead Specialty Papers, 1998—2003; sr. v.p., CFO MeadWestvaco Corp., 2003—04; pres., gen. mgr., TorqTransfer Systems BorgWarner, Inc., Auburn Hills, Mich., 2004—, v.p., 2004—. Bd. dir. Delphi Corp., 2003—05, Rockwood Holdings, Inc., 2006—. Named one of 100 Leading Women in N.Am. Auto Industry, Automotive News; recipient Outstanding Indsl. Engring. award, Purdue U., 1998, Disting. Engring. Alumnus award, 2005. Office: BorgWarner Inc Powertrain Technical Ctr 3800 Automation Ave Ste 300 Auburn Hills MI 48326-1784*

NIELSEN, DIANE KAY, music educator; b. Albert Lea, Minn., May 28, 1954; d. Dwaine M. and Mavis C. Abbe; m. Dan Allen Nielsen, June 19, 1976; children: Jennifer Kay, Jared Allen. MusB Edn. (hon.), Wartburg Coll., Waverly, Iowa, 1976; MA in Music Edn., U. St. Thomas, St. Paul, 1992. Tchr. Weaver Lake Elem. Sch., Maple Grove, Minn., 1987—. Co-dir. children's chorus Dist. 279, Maple Grove, 1993—. Contbr. articles to profl. jours. Mem.: Am. Choral Dirs. Assn. (assoc.), Minn. Music Educators (assoc.). Dfl. Lutheran. Avocations: travel, running, quilting, golf. Home: 18381 87th Ave North Maple Grove MN 55311 Office: Weaver Lake Elem Sch 15900 Weaver Lake Rd Maple Grove MN 55311 Office Phone: 763-420-3337. Personal E-mail: danddnielsen@comcast.net. Business E-Mail: nielsend@district279.org.

NIELSEN, JENNIFER LEE, molecular ecologist, researcher; b. Balt., Mar. 21, 1946; d. Leo Jay and Mary Marriott (Mules) N.; divorced; children: Nadja Wilson, Allisha Ochs MFA, Ecole des Beaux Arts, Paris, 1968; BS, Evergreen State Coll., 1987; MS, U. Calif., Berkeley, 1990, PhD, 1994. Artist, Seattle, 1969-78; fish biologist Weyerhaeuser Co., Tacoma, 1978-89; resource cons. Berkeley, 1989-90; rsch. biologist USDA-Forest Svc., Albany, Calif., 1990-99; vis. scientist Stanford U., Pacific Grove, Calif., 1994-99; supr. fisheries Alaska Sci. Ctr., Anchorage, 1999—. Rsch. assoc. Calif. State U. Mossland-ing Marie Sta., 1995-99; adj. prof. integrated biology U. Calif., Berkeley, 1998; adj. prof. U. Alaska, Fairbanks, 1999—, U. Alaska Anchorage, 2001-; supervisory rsch. fishery biologist U.S. Geol. Svc., Alaska Sci. Ctr., Anchorage, 1999—. Editor-in-chief: Reviews in Fish Biology and Fisheries, 1999—; editor: Evolution and the Aquatic Ecosystem, 1995, Advisory Editor Environment Biology of Fishes, 1998—; contbr. over 100 articles to profl. jours.; paintings exhibited at Metro. Mus. Modern Art, 1966; represented in numerous pvt. collections, U.S. and Europe. Mem. Am. Fisheries Soc. (pres. chpt. 1993-94, genetics sect. pres. 1999-2001, pres.-elect of society 2005, pres. 2006-), Molecular Marine Biology and Biotech. (regional editor 1995), Animal Behaviour Soc. (policy com. 1993-94). Avocations: painting, cooking, gardening, skijoring. Office: USGS Alaska Sci Ctr 1011 E Tudor Rd Anchorage AK 99503-6119 Office Phone: 907-786-3670. E-mail: jennifer_nielsen@usgs.gov.

NIELSEN, LINDA MILLER, councilman; b. Cedar Falls, Iowa, Apr. 13, 1948; d. Donald Hugh and Mary I. (Hansen) Miller; m. Kenneth Andrew Nielsen, Aug. 22, 1970; children: Annette Marie, Kirsten Viola. BS in Home Econs., Iowa State U., 1970, MS in Food Sci., 1972. Rsch. asst. Iowa State U., Ames, 1970-72, rsch. assoc., 1972-74, instr., 1975-76; city councilwoman City of Charleston, W.Va., 1988—; minority leader Charleston City Coun., 2003—; asst. dir. continuing edn. and cmty. svc. W.Va. State Cmty. and Tech. Coll., 1998—. Leader Girl Scouts U.S.A., 1978-96; chair environ. and recycling com. of Charleston, 1991-2003, realignment com. of Charleston, 1992-94, 2002, mcpl. planning com., 1988—, fin. com., 1995—, storm water com., 1997-99, 2003—, parks and recreation com., 1988-95; classroom vol. Kanawha County Schs., Charleston, 1978-90; mem., officer Forest Hills Comm. Assn., Charleston, 1983-87. Contbr. articles to profl. publs. Mem. NICS (bd. dirs. 1994—), Sigma Xi, Iota Sigma Pi, Omicron Nu. Republican. Avocations: hiking, camping, reading, sewing, cooking. Personal E-mail: nielsen413@charter.net.

NIELSEN, LOUISA AUGUSTA, broadcast executive; b. Balt., Dec. 14, 1950; d. William Alexander and Louisa Augusta N. BA, Coll. Notre Dame Md., Balt., 1972; MA, Antioch U., 1975. Coord. Assn. Ind. Md. Schools, 1972-75; chair theater dept. Maryvale Coll. Prep. Sch., 1972-75; coord. Balt. Cable Planning Ctr., 1974-75; proj. founder/dir. Mayor's Office Manpower Resources Sidewalk Theater, Balt., 1975; documentary dir. Wash. Cmty. Video Access Ctr., D.C., 1975; adj. asst. prof. Antioch Coll., Balt. and D.C., 1976-79; asst. prof. Howard U., D.C., 1976-77; dir. ednl. programming svcs. Nat. Publ. Radio, D.C., 1976-79; humanities adminstr. media programs Nat. Endowment Humanities, D.C., 1979-82; dir. cable TV, asst. dir. broadcast TV Nat. Captioning Inst., D.C., 1982-83; vis. asst. prof. George Wash. U., D.C., 1983-1985, dir., prodr. ednl. programming, 1985-87; exec. dir., CEO Broadcast Edn. Assn., D.C., 1987-96; pub. Jour. Broadcasting & Electronic Media, Feedback mag., Jour. Radio Studies, others. Spl. invitee/fellow, Harvard Law Sch., 1987—; trustee, Brit. Broadcasting Corp., Nat. Univ., 1999—; bd. dirs. George Foster Peabody Awards, Ohio State Awards; bd. advisors, FCC; video conf. moderator, Nat. U.; judge, ACE Awards, NCTA, Corp. Publ. Broadcasting Programming Awards; presenter, AT&T, Publ. Svc. Satellite Consortium; invited panelist, Internat. Inst. Astronautics, Annenberg Wash. HDTV workshop; reviewer, Annenberg/CPB Project prog. Editl. advisory bd. Simon & Schuster Communications Dictionary; appeared as guest, PBS Nat. Narrowcast Svc. Telecommunication and Distance Learning. Chair, Soc. Satellite Profls. Internat., mid-atlantic region. Office: Broadcast Education Assn World Hdqs 1771 N St NW Washington DC 20036-2812 Home: 604 Gittings Ave Baltimore MD 21212-2603 E-mail: lnielsen@nab.org.

NIELSEN, NANCY H., health organization executive; m. Don Nielsen; 5 children. BA, W.Va. U., 1964; MS in Microbiology, Cath. U., 1967, PhD in Microbiology, 1969; MD, SUNY, Buffalo, 1967. Past chief med. officer N.Y. State Dept. Health Western Region; former pres. med. staff Buffalo Gen. Hosp.; asst. dean med. edn., clin. prof. medicine U. Buffalo Sch. Medicine and Biomed. Sci., Buffalo; sec. US Dept. Health and Human Svcs. Adv. Com. on Regulatory Reform, 2002; assoc. med. dir. for quality, interim chief med. officer Independent Health Assn., NY. Bd. dirs. Med. Liability Mut. Ins. Co.; assoc. med. dir. for quality Ind. Health Assn. N.Y. Bd. dirs. Nat. Patient Safety Found. Recipient Samuel P. Capen award, U. Buffalo Alumni Assn., 1996. Fellow: ACP; mem.: AMA (vice speaker Ho. of Dels. 2000—03, speaker Ho. of Dels. 2003—, bd. trustees, Coun. on Sci. Affairs), Med. Soc. State of N.Y. (spkr. ho. dels. 1995—2000), Erie County Med. Soc. (former pres.). Office: Independant Health Assn 511 Farber Lakes Dr Buffalo NY 14221 also: AMA 515 N State St Chicago IL 60610 Business E-Mail: nielse@buffalo.edu.*

NIELSON, ALYCE MAE, poet; b. Saugerties, NY, Feb. 27, 1943; d. George John Wodischeck and Martha Elizabeth Casler; m. David Bruce Nielson, Oct. 5, 1963; children: Kenneth David, Nancy Lynn Nielson Nowicki. AS in Food, SUNY, Cobleskill, N.Y., 1963. Sch. lunch mgr. Bklyn. Pub. Sch. #61, 1963-64; clk. stock and bond dividend dept. First Nat. City Bank, N.Y.C., 1966—69; lectr., trainee, group leader, ctr. mgr. Weight Watchers, N.Y.C., Bklyn., S.I., 1979—97. Contbr. poetry to anthologies. Vol. Warm up Am., Kingston, N.Y., 1999-2002, Busy Bees Kingston, N.Y., knitting and crochet for needy, 2003— Named to Internat. Poetry Hall of Fame, 1996—; recipient numerous Editors Choice awards, 1995—2003. Mem. Internat. Soc. of Poets. Avocations: tae kwon do (2d degree black belt), tai chi, music, needlecrafts, cooking.

NIELSON, CONSTANCE JO, psychologist, educator; b. Kansas City, Mo., Oct. 21, 1950; d. Elrod Pierce and Emily Jorene (Bullock) Wilson; m. Dennis Thomas Joe, Aug. 5, 1972 (div. 1982); m. Gary Francis Nielson, Aug. 17, 1984; 1 child, Garrett Joseph; stepchildren: Heather Marie, Adam Stevens. BS, U. Houston, 1972, MEd, 1978; postgrad., U. Mo., 1982-93, Cen. Mo. State U., 1968-70. Cert. elem. edn. and kindergarten tchr.; cert. in mental retardation all level, generic spl. edn., Mo., Tex. Resource tchr. Houston Ind. Sch. Dist., 1972-78, spl. edn. supr., 1978-79, staff devel., 1979-81; sch. psychol. examiner North Kansas City Schs., Kansas City, Mo., 1981—. Mem. faculty, prof. Avila Coll., Kansas City, 1983-85; adj. prof. U. Mo., Kansas City, 2001—, Rockhurst U., 2005-. Coord. North Kansas City Kids on the Block Troupe, 1982-1995. Named Vol. of the Yr., Easter Seals Soc., 1984, Puppetter of the Yr., 1984. Mem. Coun. for Exceptional Children (officer (2002—), Coun. for Edn. Diagnostic Svcs., Mo. Coun. Ednl. Diagnostic Svcs. (v.p. 1996-97, treas., 1997—). Avocations: zoos, travel, reading, movies. Home: 3504 NE 56th Ter Kansas City MO 64119-2341 Office: North Kansas City Schs 2000 NE 46th St Kansas City MO 64116-2042

NIELSON, KRISTY ANN, psychology educator, researcher; b. Inglewood, Calif., Dec. 11, 1964; d. Alfred M. Nielson Jr. and Dolores M. (Gattuso) Hetland. BA, Calif. State U., Long Beach, 1987; MA in Exptl. Psychology, So. Ill. U., 1990, PhD in Biopsychology, 1992. Instr. Learning Ctr., Santa Ana, Calif., 1985-86; rsch. asst. psychology So. Ill. U., Carbondale, 1988-92, lectr. in psychology, 1991-92; neuropsychology intern U. Calif., Irvine, 1992-95, postdoctoral rsch. fellow, 1992-96, lectr. in psychobiology, 1996; asst. prof. psychology Marquette U., Milw., 1996—2002, assoc. prof. psychology, 2002—; asst. clin. prof. psychiatry Med. Coll. Wis., Milw., 1998—, dir. Foley Ctr. for Aging and Devel., 1998—. Bd. dirs., vice chair Clement Manor, Inc., Greenfield, Wis. Contbr. articles to profl. jours. Block watch capt. City of Wauwatosa, Wis., 1996—; sci. adv. bd. Alzheimer's Assn. S.E. Wis., Milw., 1996- Grantee Nat. Inst. Aging, 1995-96, 2003—, Med. Coll. Wis., 1998—, Epilepsy Found. Am., 1999. Fellow APA; mem. AAAS, AAUP, Soc. for Neurosci., Assn. Psychol. Sci., Sigma Xi. Avocations: volleyball, softball, golf. Office: Marquette U Dept Psychology PO Box 1881 Milwaukee WI 53201-1881 E-mail: kristy.nielson@marquette.edu.

NIEMAN, VALERIE GAIL, language educator, journalist; b. Jamestown, N.Y., July 6, 1955; d. Warner Ernest and Eleanor A. (Aiken); m. Jack Hobbs Student, Jamestown C.C., 1975-76; BS in Journalism, W.Va. U., 1978; postgrad., Queens U. of Charlotte. Staff writer W.Va. U News Svc., Morgantown, W.Va., 1978; reporter Dominion Post, Morgantown, 1978, Times West Virginian, Fairmont, W.Va., 1979-92, city editor, 1992-95, exec. editor, 1995-97; asst. city/state editor News & Record, Greensboro, NC, 1997—2004. Tchr. basic newswriting W.Va. U., Morgantown, 1990, tchr. sci. fiction writing, 1995; instr. dept. journalism and mass comm. N.C. A&T State U., 2000-04, asst. prof. English and journalism, 2004—; lectr., vis. writer tri-state area, 1988-1997; founding co-editor Kestrel lit. jour., Fairmont, 1992-1997; co-founder, co-dir. Kestrel Writers Conf., Fairmont, 1993-97; dir. HBCU Nat. Newspaper conf., 2006. Author: (novel) Neena Gathering, 1988, Survivors, 2000, (short story collection) Fidelities, 2004, (poetry chpts.) How We Live, 1996, Slipping Out of Old Eve, 1988, (poetry collection) Wake Wake Wake, 2006. W.Va. cir. writer W.Va. Humanities Commn., 1994; mem. Leadership Marion, Fairmont, 1995-96. Recipient award in letters Fairmont Arts and Humanities, 1988, 94, Elizabeth Simpson Smith prize, 1998, 2002, Greg Grummer award in poetry George Mason U., 1999, others; fellow in poetry NEA, 1991, fellow in fiction Ky. Found. for Women, 1991, fellow in fiction W.Va. Commn. on Arts, 1992. Democrat. United Ch. Of Christ. Avocations: gardening, hiking, travel, sailing. Office: NC AT&T State U 1601 E Market St Greensboro NC 27411 Office Phone: 336-334-7223 4011. Business E-Mail: vgneiman@ncat.edu.

NIEMANN, PATRICIA, nurse; b. Montrose, S.D., June 30, 1941; d. Alfred Hagen and Alvina Margaret Johnson; m. Marvin Carl Niemann, July 2, 1960; children: Charlotte Niemann Crisp, Paula Niemann Nussbaum, John, Jill Niemann Brown, Julie (dec.). LPN, S.E. Area Sch. Practical, 1977; student, U. Sioux Falls, 1989-91. Nurse Good Samaritan Ctr., Sioux Falls, 1977, VA, Sioux Falls, 1977—2002. Bd. dirs. ARC, Sioux Falls, 1987-88; union pres. Orgn. Grievance Negotiations Local Contract, 1981. Mem. NOW, AIC, Am. Inst. Cancer Rsch., Am. Fedn. Govt. Employees (local union pres.), LPN Assn. (local). Democrat. Lutheran. Avocations: reading, swimming, music, snowmobiling. Home: 5605 W 14th St Sioux Falls SD 57106-0207

NIEMELA, APRIL JOY, secondary school educator; d. David and Patti Harrison; m. Shane Niemela, July 28, 2001. BA, Lewis-Clark State Coll., Lewiston, Idaho, 1999; MEd, U. Idaho, Moscow, 2006. Tchr. Homedale Jr. Sch. Dist., Idaho, 1999—2001, Craigmont, Idaho, 2001—. Adv. bd. chair NW Inland Writing Project, Moscow, 2004—. Pres. Highland Edn. Assn., Craigmont, 2003—. Mem.: Kappa Delta Pi (assoc.). Christian. Avocations: travel, music, literature. Office: Highland HS PO Box 130 Craigmont ID 83523 Personal E-mail: shanarra_76@hotmail.com.

NIEMI, JANICE, retired lawyer, retired state legislator; b. Flint, Mich., Sept. 18, 1928; d. Richard Jesse and Norma (Bell) Bailey; m. Preston Niemi, Feb. 4, 1953 (div. 1987); children: Ries, Patricia. BA, U. Wash., 1950, LLB, 1967; postgrad., U. Mich., 1950-52; cert., Hague Acad. Internat. Law, The Netherlands, 1954. Bar: Wash. 1968. Assoc. firm Powell, Livengood, Dunlap & Silverdale, Kirkland, Wash., 1968; staff atty. Legal Svc. Ctr., Seattle, 1968-70; judge Seattle Dist. Ct., 1971-72, King County Superior Ct., Seattle, 1973-78; acting gen. counsel, dep. gen. counsel SBA, Washington, 1979-81; mem. Wash. State Ho. of Reps., Olympia, 1983-87, chmn. com. on state govt., 1984; mem. Wash. State Senate, 1987-95; sole practice Seattle, 1981-94; superior ct. judge King County, 1995-2000; chief criminal judge, 1997-2000; ret., 2000; mem. Wash. State Gambling Commn., 2002—. Mem. White Ho. Fellows Regional Selection Panel, Seattle, 1974—77, chmn., 1976, 77; incorporator Soudn Savs. & Loan, Seattle, 1975; bd. dirs. Artists Trust; mem. panel Am. Arbitration Assn., 2003—. Bd. visitors dept. psychology U. Wash., Seattle, 1983—87, bd. visitors dept. sociology, 1988—98; mem. adv. bd. Tacoma Art Mus., 1987—; mem. Wash. State Gender and Justice Commn., 1987—89; Bd. dirs. Allied Arts, Seattle, 1971—78, Ctr. Contemporary Art, Seattle, 1981—83, Women's Network, Seattle, 1981—84, Pub. Defender Assn., Seattle, 1982—84, Artist's Trust, 2002—. Named Woman of Yr. in Law, Past Pres.'s Assn., Seattle, 1971, Woman of Yr., Matrix Table, Seattle, 1973, Capitol Hill Bus. and Profl. Women, 1975. Mem. Wash. State Bar Assn., Wash. Women Lawyers, Am. Arbitration Assn. (panel 2003—). Democrat. Home: PO Box 20516 Seattle WA 98102-1516 Personal E-mail: janicen@aol.com.

NIENSTADT, JEAN E. (JEAN E. SULLIVAN), physician; b. Taft, Calif., Mar. 24, 1925; d. Willard Edward and Mildred Louise (Beall) Sullivan; children: Myles, Felix, Linus, Laura. BA, Pomona Coll., Claremont, Calif., 1947; MD, Woman's Med. Coll. Pa., Phila., 1954. Bd. cert. family practice. Dir. Redbud Clinic, Hyden, Ky., 1994. Mem.: Ky. Med. Assn. Avocations: watercolor, gardening. Office: Redbud Clinic PO Box 950 Hyden KY 41749-0950 Home: 611 Thousandsticks Br Rd Hyden KY 41749 Office Phone: 606-672-3846.

NIETO, SHIRLEY L., science educator; b. S.C., June 11, 1951; d. Lester Conread and Ann L. Bridgman; m. Ralph A. Nieto, 1985; 1 child, Chris. BS, U. Ctrl. Fla., Orlando, 1974; MSc, Nova U., Fort Lauderdale, Fla., 1990. Cert. tchr. Fla. Tchr. adult edn. and GED Orange County Dist. Sch., Orlando, Fla., 1972—79; tchr. biology Maynard Evans H.S., Orlando, Fla., 1974—75; tchr. biosciences, human anatomy and physiology Lake Brantley H.S., Altamonte Springs, 1975—, chmn. sci. dept., 1977—. Mailing: 562 W Springtree Way Lake Mary FL 32746-6007 Office: Lake Brantley HS Altamonte Springs FL 32714

NIETO, SONIA MARY, retired education educator; b. N.Y.C., Sept. 25, 1943; d. Federico and Esther (Mercado) Cortes; m. Angel Nieto, Jan. 4, 1967; children: Alicia, Marisa. BS, St. Johns U., 1965; MA, NYU, 1966; EdD, U. Mass., 1979. Cert. elem. tchr. Prof. edn. U. Mass., Amherst, 1980—2005, prof. emerita, 2005—, mem. emerita lang. literacy and culture. Instr. Bklyn. Coll., CUNY, 1972-75; speaker, author on multicultural and bilingual edn. and curriculum renewal, workshop leader. Author: Affirming Diversity: The Sociopolitical Context of Multicultural Education, 1992, 4th edit., 2004, The Light in Their Eyes, 1999, Puerto Rican Students in U.S. Schools, 2000, What Keeps Teachers Going?, 2003; editor: Why We Teach, 2005; co-editor (with Ralph Rivera): The Education of Latinos in Massachusetts: Research and Policy Considerations, 1993. Mem.: Am. Edn. Rsch. Assn., Nat. Assn. Bilingual Edn., Phi Delta Kappa. E-mail: snieto@educ.umass.edu.

NIEVES, JOSEPHINE, federal agency administrator; BBA, CUNY; MS, Columbia U.; PhD, Union Grad. Sch. Assoc. asst. sec. employment and tng. Dept. of Labor, 1994-96; exec. dir. Nat. Assn. Social Workers, 1996-01. Recipient Lifetime Achievement award Nat. P.R. Forum, Disting. Achievement Human Svcs. award Boricua Coll., Martin Luther King Jr. medal Freedom; named Acad. Women Achievers YWCA, N.Y.C. Home: 7900 Radnor Rd Bethesda MD 20817 E-mail: josephinenieves@msn.com.

NIEVIEDGAL, CAROL BELMARCE, elementary school educator; b. New Bedford, Mass., Sept. 4, 1948; d. Palmira Ferreira Belmarce and Baldomar Chaves Ferreira; m. John Theodore Nieviedgal, May 24, 2003; children: Derek Carl Araujo, John T. IV. BS Elem. Edn., Bridgewater State Coll., Bridgewater, Mass., 1970; MA in Counseling Psychology, Lesley U., Cambridge, Mass., 2005. Cert. Elem. Tchr. Mass. Bd. of Edn., 1970, Prin./Asst. Prin. K-8 Mass. Bd. of Edn., 1982. Second grade tchr. Cushman Sch., Dartmouth, Mass., 1970—82, acting prin., 1973—83, kindergarten tchr., 1982—83, DeMello Sch., Dartmouth, Mass., 1983—. Sec. Bristol County Educators Assn., Raynham, Mass., 2001—03; first v.p. Delta Kappa Gamma Psi Chpt., New Bedford, Mass., 2001—03, second v.p., 1999—2001. Ch. lector St. Bernard's Ch., Assonet, Mass., 1985—2001. Mem.: AAUW (assoc.), Dartmouth Educators Assn. (assoc.), Mass. Tchrs. Assn. (assoc.), Nat. Educators Assn. (assoc.), Bridgewater State Coll. Alumni Assn. (assoc.), Coll. Club of New Bedford (assoc.; corr. sec. 1996—98), Nat. Kindergarten Alliance (assoc.), Mass. Sch. Counselors Assn. (assoc.), Harvard-Radcliffe Club (assoc.). Independent. Non-Denom. Achievements include Bristol County Educators Assn. Disting. Svc. Award; Bristol County Educators Assn. Human Rels.Award. Avocations: travel, dance, music, cooking, reading. Home: 11 Joaquin Ave Assonet MA 02702-1568 Office: DeMello Sch 654 Dartmouth St Dartmouth MA 02748 Office Phone: 508-996-6759. Office Fax: 508-990-2519. Personal E-mail: carolbelmarce@aol.com. Business E-Mail: cbelmarce@dartmouthps.org.

NIEWIAROSKI, TRUDI OSMERS (GERTRUDE NIEWIAROSKI), social studies educator; b. Jersey City, Apr. 30, 1935; d. Albert John and Margaret (Niemeyer) Osmers; m. Donald H. Niewiaroski, June 8, 1957; children: Donald H., Donna, Margaret Anne, Nancy Noel. AB in History and German, Upsala Coll., East Orange, N.J., 1957; MEd, Montgomery County Pub. Schs., Rockville, Md., 1992. Cert. tchr. Md. Tchr. geography Colego Americano, Quito, Ecuador, 1964-66; bd. dirs. Cotopaxi Acad., Quito, 1964-65; tchr. speed reading Escuela Lincoln, Buenos Aires, Argentina, 1966-67; substitute thcr. Montgomery County Pub. Schs., Rockville, 1978-83, tchr. social studies, 1984—. Del. Eisenhower People to People Educators' Del. Vietnam, 1993; pres. Fulbright Meml. Fund Program, 1997; resident tchg. fellow Russia-Ukraine Excellence in Tchg. Program, 1997; resident scholar in Korea, The Korea Soc., 1999. Author curricula; contbr. chpts. to books, articles to profl. jours.; lectr. at workshops. Bd. dirs. Cotopaxi Acad., Quito, 1964-65; pres. Citizens Assn., Potomac, Md., 1977-81; leader Girl Scouts U.S., 1975-76; adv. coun. Milken Found; pres. Fulbright Meml. Fund Program Japan Alumni, 1999—. Recipient Md. Tchr. of Yr. award State of Md. Edn. Dept., 1993, finalist nat. Tchr. of Yr., 1993, Disting. Alumni award Upsala Coll., 1993, Nat. Educator award Milken Found., 1994, Summer Fellowship Korean Studies Program, 1999, Joseph Malone fellowship Sultanate of Oman, 2003, Goethe Inst. fellowship, Germany, 2003; Fulbright fellow, India, 1985, China, 1990, Japan Keizai Koho Ctr. fellow, 1992, Fulbright Meml. Fund Tchr. Program fellow, Japan, 1997, Fulbright fellow, South Africa, 2001, Malone fellow, Oman, 2003, U. Tex. Mideast Inst. fellow, 2005; UMBC-U. Mex. Art and Culture scholar, 1995; mem. Cuba Study Tour, 2004, Dar Al Islam Study Tour, Iran, 2004; fellow U. Pitts. and Freeman Found., China, 2004; Fulbright fellow, China, 2004; Egypt fellow U. Tex. Middle East Inst., 2005. Mem. AAUW, ASCD, Nat. Coun. Social Studies, Md. Coun. for Social Studies, Asia Soc., Smithsonian Instn., Montgomery County Hist. Soc., Spl. Interest Groups-China, Japan and Korea, Md. Bus. Roundtable for Edn., Nat. Social Studies Suprs. Assn., Kappa Delta Pi. Avocations: cake and cookie decorating, travel. Office: R Montgomery High Sch Rockville MD 20852 Office Phone: 301-279-8442. Personal E-mail: niewiaroski.dandt@aol.com. Business E-Mail: trudi_niewiaroski@fc.mcps.k12.md.us.

NIFFENEGGER, AUDREY ANNE, artist, writer; b. June 13, 1963; BFA, Sch. of the Art Inst. of Chgo., 1985; MFA, Northwestern U., Evanston, Ill., 1991. Asst. prof., art, printmaking Columbia Coll. Chgo. Ctr. for Book and Paper Arts, 1995—; on sabbatical, 2004—05. Author: (novels) The Time Traveler's Wife, 2003 (Publishers Weekly paperback bestseller, NY Times bestseller), The Three Incestuous Sisters: An Illustrated Novel, 2005. E-mail: aniffenegger@popmail.colum.edu.

NIFFENEGGER, TAMMIE JEAN, secondary school educator, science educator; b. Neenah, Wis., Dec. 18, 1964; d. Robert John and Shirley May Mattson; m. Fred Niffenegger, June 8, 1985; children: Robert John, Kelsie Ann, Randall William. BS in Biology, U. Wis., 1990, BS in Edn., 1990, BS in Broad Field Sci., 1990, MS in Sch. Psychology, 1999. Cert. tchr. Nat. Bd. Profl. Tchg. Standards, 2002. Tchr. sci. Port Wash. (Wis.) H.S., 1990—, chmn. Dept. Sci., 1990—. Reviewer devel. and lab safety Holt, Rinehart, and Winston Pub. Co., Austin, Tex., 2001—05, pub., 2001—05. Mem. exec. bd. Sheboygan (Wis.) County 4-H, 2005—06. 1st lt. U.S. Army, 1983—92. Recipient Vol. of Yr. Hon. Mention award, Sheboygan (Wis.) County, 2002, Excellence in Sci. Edn. award, Wis. State Soc. Sci. Tchrs., 2004. Mem.: Nat. Sci. Tchrs. Assn., Wis. State Sci. Tchrs. Assn. (assoc.; membership com. 2002—06). Republican. Office: Port Washington High School 427 W Jackson St Port Washington WI 53074 Office Phone: 262-268-5653. Office Fax: 262-268-5520. Business E-Mail: tammie.niffenegger@pwssd.k12.wi.us.

NIGGEMAN, KIMBERLY SUPPLEE, medical nurse; b. Bryn Mawr, Pa., Jan. 14, 1965; d. Robert Samuel and Nancy Jeanne (Neilson) Supplee; m. Stephen John Niggeman, June 22, 1991. BSN, Widener U., 1988; postgrad., West Chester U., 1993—. RN, BLS, ACLS. Nurse Grad. Hosp., Phila., 1988-90, Bryn Mawr (Pa.) Hosp., 1990-95; sr. staff nurse Paoli (Pa.) Meml. Hosp., 1992—. Mem. Assn. Advanced Critical Care Nurses, Southeastern Pa. chpt. Republican. Methodist. Avocations: water-skiing, skiing, golf, roller-blading, stained glass. Home: 8 Houndstooth Ln Chester Springs PA 19425-3130

NIGHSWONGER, LINDA, science educator; b. Kans. BS, Bethany Coll., Lindsborg. Sci. tchr. Lenora HS, Kans., 1985—99, Logan HS, Kans., 1999—2006, Longfellow Mid. Sch., Hill City, Kans.

NIGHTINGALE, ELENA OTTOLENGHI, pediatric geneticist, academic administrator, educator; b. Livorno, Italy, Nov. 1, 1932; arrived in U.S., 1939, naturalized; d. Mario Lazzaro and Elisa Vittoria (Levi) Ottolenghi; m. Stuart L. Nightingale, July 1, 1965; children: Elizabeth, Marisa. AB summa cum laude, Barnard Coll., 1954; PhD, Rockefeller U., 1961; MD, NYU, 1964. Asst. prof. Cornell U. Med. Coll., N.Y.C., 1965—70, Johns Hopkins U., Balt., 1970—73; fellow in clin. genetics and pediat. Georgetown U. Hosp., Washington, 1973—74; sr. staff officer NAS, Washington, 1975—79, sr. program officer Inst. Medicine, 1979—82, sr. scholar-in-residence, 1982—83; spl. advisor to pres. Carnegie Corp. N.Y., N.Y.C., 1983—94, sr. program officer, 1989—94; scholar-in-residence Inst. of Medicine, NAS, Washington, 1995—. Vis. assoc. prof. Harvard Med. Sch., Boston, 1980—84, vis. lectr., 1984—95; adj. prof. pediat. Georgetown U. Med. Ctr., 1984—, George Washington U. Med. Ctr., 1994—; mem. recombinant DNA adv. com. NIH, Bethesda, Md., 1979—83. Editor: The Breaking of Bodies and Minds: Torture, Psychiatric Abuses and the Health Professions, 1985, Prenatal Screening, Policies and Values: The Example of Neural Tube Defects, 1987, Promoting the Health of Adolescents: New Directions for the 21st Century, 1993, Adolescent Risk and Vulnerability: Concepts and Measurement, 2001; co-author: Before Birth: Prenatal Screening for Genetic Disease, 1990; contbr. numerous sci. articles to profl. publs. Bd. dirs. Amnesty Internat., U.S.A., Washington, 1989—91, Ctr. for Youth Svcs., Washington, 1980—84, Sci. Svc., Inc., Washington, 1985—96. Fellow: AAAS (chmn. com. on sci. freedom and responsibility 1985—88), N.Y. Acad. Scis.; mem.: Inst. Medicine of NAS (chmn. com. on health and human rights 1987—90), Genetics Soc. Am., Am. Soc. Human Genetics (social issues com. 1982—85), Am. Soc. Microbiology, Sigma Xi, Phi Beta Kappa. Office: NAS 500 5th St NW Washington DC 20001 Business E-Mail: enightin@nas.edu.

NIGHTINGALE, SUZANNE M., management consultant; d. Stanley Wren and Ann Mary Nightingale; m. Kathleen P. Clementson, May 20, 2004. BA in Econ., U. San Francisco, 1985. Cert. sys. engr. Microsoft Corp., Redmond WA, 2000; spiritual healer Okla. City, Okla., 1985; lic. pvt. pilot, single engine land FAA, 1989. Project mgr. Lockheed Missiles and Space Co., Sunnyvale, Calif., 1982—89. Constrn. project mgr. Nightingale Assoc., The Sea Ranch, Calif., 1983—89, prin., Cape Coral, Calif., 1989—; data base analyst Lockheed Missiles and Space, Sunnyvale, Calif., 1987—89; corr. Door County Adv., Sturgeon Bay, Wis., 1991—94. Dir. Interfaith Events to Promote Cmty. Unity, Fort Myers, 1997—2002, Quality Life Acad., Fort Myers, 2004—05; founder Wash. Island Aviation Libr., Washington Island, Wis., 1990—94. Achievements include invention of purifier for diesel fuel using magnetic technology; design of major contribution to data base dictionary of first national security project employing artificial intelligence for intelligence analysis. Avocations: writer, artist, pilot. Home and Office: Nightingale Assocs 309 Cape Coral Pky W #206 Cape Coral FL 33914-5973 Office Phone: 239-945-2579.

NIGN, STACIE MARIE, secondary school educator; d. John L. and Blanche M. Nign. BA in Biol. Scis., Ohio U., Athens, Ohio, 1998; MA, Nova Southeastern U., Fort Lauderdale, Fla., 2002. Cert. tchr. Ohio, 2002. Tchr. phys. sci., biology Meigs H.S., Pomeroy, Ohio, 1998—99; tchr. biology Dover (Ohio) H.S., 1999—. Coach jr. varsity softball Dover (Ohio) City Schs., 1999—2001, advisor scholar challenge academic team, 2002—. Named Coach of Yr., East Cen. Ohio League, 2002—03, 2005. Office: Dover City Schools Dover High School 520 North Walnut Street Dover OH 44622 Office Phone: 330-364-7148. Office Fax: 330-364-7142. Business E-Mail: snign@dover.k12.oh.us.

NIGREVILLE, CARRIE CHRISTOPHER, principal; d. Frank Eugene and Judith Ellen Lalli; m. John Frank Nigreville, June 4, 2004; children: Jayci Lalli, Jaden Range. BS, N.Mex. State U., Las Cruces, 1994; MEd, Ea. N.Mex. U., Portales, 2001. Tchr. Clovis (N.Mex.) Mcpl. Schs., 1995—2001, assessment program coord., 2001—02, prin., 2002—. Mem. fund com. United Way, Clovis, 2005—06; mem. Clovis Jr. Women's Club, 1995—2004. Mem.: ASCD, Nat. Assn. Elem. Sch. Prins. Avocations: reading, travel. Office: Clovis Mcpl Schs 1600 Cameo St Clovis NM 88101

NIGUIDULA, KATHLEEN ANN, music educator, musician; b. Upper Darby, Pa., Apr. 5, 1972; d. Faustino Nazario Niguidula and Brenda Marie Maybury; m. Christopher Jordan O'Neill, Aug. 30, 2004; 1 child, Luke O'Neill. B in Music Edn., Eastman Sch. Music, 1994; MusM in Piano Performance, Boston Conservatory, 1998. Cert. K-12 music tchr. N.Y., Tex., Mass. Music tchr., choir dir. grades 6-8 Aldine Ind. Sch. Dist., Houston, 1994—95; music tchr., choir dir. grades 7-8 Norwood Pub. Schs., Mass., 1998—99; music tchr. K-8 Music On The Move, Chelsea, Mass., 1999—2001; piano tchr. Timeline Music, Wakefield, Mass., 1998—2001; music tchr. Wolf Sch., Providence, 2001—05; piano tchr. Music Sch. R.I. Philharm., Providence, 2001—, registrar, 2005—. Freelance accompanist, Boston, 1996—; choir dir. K-5 after-school programs Wolf Sch., Providence, 2001—05; coord. early childhood music Music Sch. R.I. Philharmonic, 2002—04. Music dir., organist Islington Cmty. Ch., Westwood, Mass., 1999—2004. Finalist piano, Florida Concerto Competition, 1989; recipient Excellence in Music award, Sarasota Visual and Performing Arts, 1990, 1st prize Composition, Women's Soc. Sarasota, 1990, 1st prize Music Performance, Shriner's Club, 1990; scholar, Eastman Sch. Music, 1990—94. Mem.: Orff-Schuwerk Assn., Music Educators Nat. Conf., Music Tchrs. Nat. Assn., New Eng. Piano Tchrs. Assn., Chopin Club. Personal E-mail: kathleen-o@cox.net.

NII, YUKO, artist; b. Tokyo, Toshima-ku, Japan, Oct. 22, 1942; arrived in US, 1963; d. Satoshi and Chieko Nii. BFA, Macalester Coll., St. Paul, Minn., 1965; MFA, Pratt Inst., Bklyn., 1969. Residency Yaddo, Saratoga Springs, NY, 1980, 1982; artist (painter); founder, dir. Williamsburg Art and Hist. Ctr., Bklyn., 1996—. Costume and stage set designer Chiang Ching Dance Company, N.Y.C., 1977—78, Zignal I at La-Mama, 1978—79; contbr. N.Y. Jour., Japan, 1982—83, NY Arts Mag., 2002, 11211 mag., 2004, Friends and Mentors Art Show catalog, 2001. One-woman shows include Elaine Benson Gallery, L.I., 1977, 1986, 1994, Fairleigh Dickenson U., N.J., 1978, Berkshire Mus., Mass., 1979, Monique Lnowlton Gallery, N.Y.C., 1979, Vered Internat. Gallery, L.I., 1979, Haber Theodore Gallery, N.Y.C., 1980, Internat. Monetary Fund, Washington, 1980. Recipient Woman of Yr., Office of Bklyn Borough Pres. Howard Golden, 1998, Office of Gov. of N.Y. State George Pataki, 2001, Office of Bklyn Borough Pres. Marty Markowitz, 2003, Outstanding Citizen award, N.Y.C. Coun., 2003; fellow, Pratt Inst., Bklyn., 1966—69; scholar, Macalester Coll., St. Paul, Minn., 1963—65. Home: 385 Clinton Ave Brooklyn NY 11238 Office: Williamsburg Art & Hist Ctr 135 Broadway Brooklyn NY 11211 Office Phone: 718-486-7372. Home Fax: 718-486-6012. Personal E-mail: wahcenter@earthlink.net.

NIJINSKY, TAMARA, actress, puppeteer, author, librarian, educator; b. Vienna; arrived in U.S., 1961; d. Waslaw and Romola (de Pulszky) Nijinsky; widowed; 1 child, Kinga Maria Szakats-Gaspers. Student, Europe; postgrad. studies in U.S. Mem., actress Nat. Theater of Budapest; owner, tchr. Tamara Nijinsky Performing Art Studio, Montreal; tchr. speech/drama, French and German, libr. Cath. H.S., Phoenix; established non-profit internat. orgn. The Waslaw and Romola Nijinsky Found., Inc., 1991, exec. dir., 1991—. Lectr. in field. Author: Nijinsky and Romola, 1991. Decorated chevalier de l'Ordre des Arts et des Lettres, officier de l'Ordre des Arts et des Lettres (France); recipient Nijinsky medal, Pagart, Poland, Polish Order of Arts and Letters, 1997, La Medaille Vermeil de Paris, 2000. Roman Catholic. Avocations: reading, computer, swimming. Office: Nijinsky Foundation Inc PO Box # 15981 Phoenix AZ 85060-5981 Fax: 602-840-9605.

NIJMAN, JENNIFER T., lawyer, department chairman; b. Aug. 27, 1962; BA, U. Ill., 1984; JD, U. Chgo., 1987. Bar: Ill. 1987, US Dist. Ct. (no. dist.) Ill. 1987. Assoc. to ptnr. Winston & Strawn LLP, Chgo., 1994—, co-chmn. environ. dept. Bd. dirs. Pub. Interest Law Initiative, Ctr. Conflict Resolution; chair Ill. Legal Needs Study, Ill. Coalition Equal Justice. Contbr. articles to profl. jours. Mem.: ABA (mem. environ. litigation com.), Economic Club Chgo., Ill. State Bar Assn., Chgo. Bar Assn. (pres. 2002—03). Office: Winston & Strawn LLP 35 W Wacker Dr Chicago IL 60601-9703 Office Phone: 312-558-5771. Office Fax: 312-558-5700. Business E-Mail: jnijman@winston.com.

NIKIRK, (SILVA) SUSAN, minister, writer, dancer; b. NYC, Mar. 13, 1947; d. Victor and Lina Silva; m. Gerald Eugene Nikirk, Jan. 29, 1988. English, City Coll. of N.Y., N.Y., 1966; fashion mktg., Fashion Inst. Tech., N.Y., 1967; Biblical studies, Heart to Heart Internat., Norwich, Conn., 1993. Rev. Ordination Kingsway Fellowship Internat., Iowa, 1992; cert. Dance Tchg. Nat. Dance Tchrs. of Am., 1985. Profl. dancer Broadway, Off Broadway Theatre & TV, N.Y., 1964—72; dir. fashion merchandising sch. Barbizon Sch. of Queens, Rego Pk., Queens, NY, 1973—75; mgmt. cons. RTW Mgmt., N.Y., 1975—77; profl. ballroom tchr. Fred Astaire, Arthur Murray, various ind. dance studios, 1977—89, profl. ballroom dancer, 1977—86, theatrical, exhbn., Am. smooth ballroom dance champion, 1982—85; night club act Hamilton & Silva, 1980—85; profl. ballroom adjudicator Nat. Dance Coun. of Am., Arthur Murray Internat., Nat. Dance Tchrs. Assn., N.Am. Dance Tchrs. Assn., 1986—; profl. ballroom adjudictor Nat. Dance Coun. of Am., Arthur Murray Internat., 2006—; choreographer Ind. Dance Teams, 1977—89; author & mktg. cons. Arthur Murray Internat., Coral Gables, Fla., 1985—89; cosmetic cons. Estee Lauder, Inc., Conn., 1989—91; co-founder, ordained min., v.p. bd. dirs. Nikirk Ministries, Colchester, Conn., 1992—. Ordained min., nat. & internat. speaker inter Denom. chs. and confs., USA, Holland, Belgium, Switerland, Germany, Iceland, 1992—; pastor VINE Tng. and Worship Ctr., 1997—2005; dir. founder Watchmen Sch. of Prayer, Colchester, Conn., 1998—. Co-host (TV series) Voice In New Eng. T.V. Broadcast, 1996—; dancer (discotheque) Beatles Tour, 1965; author: (tchg. video, manual) Arthur Murray Bronze Theatrical Ballroom Syllabus, 1986—88, (tchg. video) Watchmen Sch. of Prayer, 2002; contbr. articles pub. to profl. jour. Mem.: Nat. Dance Tchrs. Coun. Am., N.Am. Dance Tchrs. Assn. (adjudicator 2006—), Nat. Dance Tchrs. Assn. (master tchr. and adjudicator 2006—), Assn. Jewish and Christian Believers, Kingsway Fellowship Internat. Messianic Jew. Avocation: gardening. Office: Nikirk Ministries PO Box 211 Colchester CT 06415 Office Phone: 860-537-5881. Business E-Mail: snikirk@nikirkvoice.org.

NIKLES, JACQUELINE AMINE, chemistry professor; d. Gerald A. and Mary Werstler; m. David E. Nikles, June 16, 1979; children: Sarah M., Daniel E. BS in Chemistry, Marietta Coll., Ohio, 1977; PhD, Case Western Res. U., 1985. Asst. prof. chemistry U. Ala., 2001—. Grantee, Ala. Commn. Higher Edn., 2005—06; Advance grantee, NSF, 2004—05. Mem.: Am. Chem. Soc. (treas. Ala. sect. 2005—). Office: U Ala Birmingham Dept Chemistry 901 14th St S Birmingham AL 35294 Office Phone: 205-934-8130. Business E-Mail: nikles@uab.edu.

NIKODINOV, ANGELA, professional figure skater, Olympic athlete; b. Spartanburg, S.C., May 9, 1980; Competitive history includes 2nd place Pacific Coast Jr., 1994, 3rd place Southwest Pacific Jr., 1994, 5th place U.S. Championships Jr., 1994, 2nd place Pacific Coast Jr., 1995, 3rd place Southwest Pacific Jr., 1995, 5th place U.S. Championships Jr., 1995, 6th place World Jr. Selections Competition, 1996, 2d place Pacific Coast Sr., 1996, 5th place U.S. Olympic Festival, 1995, 1st place Southwest Pacific Sr., 1996, 3rd place O. Nepela Meml., 1996, 1st place Pacific Coast Sr., 1997, 3rd place World Jr. Selection Competition, 1997, 2nd place Pokal Der Blauen Scwerter, 1996, 4th place U.S. Championships, 1997, 4th place Skate America, 1997, 5th place U.S. Championships, 1998, 11th place World Jr. Championships, 1998, 4th place Goodwill Games, 1998, 2nd place Keri Lotion Figure Skating Classic, 1998, 3rd place Four Continents Championships, 1999, 3rd place Skate America, 1998, 3d place U.S. Championships, 1999, 12th place World Championships, 1999, 7th place Skate America, 1999, 5th place Keri Lotion Figure Skating Classic, 1999, 4th place Cup of Russia, 1999, 4th place U.S. Championships, 2000, 1st place Four Continents, 2000, 9th place World Championships, 2000, 3d place Cup of Russia, 2001, 3rd place Nations Cup, 2001, 3rd place, U.S. Championships, 2001, 2nd place, Great American Figure Skating Challenge, 2001, 5th place Workd Championships, 2001, 4th place, U.S. Championships, 2002, 1st place, Pacific Coast Sectionals, 2004, 5th place, U.S. Championships, 2004. Avocations: water-skiing, skiing, rollerblading, jet skiing. Office: USFSA 20 1st St Colorado Springs CO 80906-3624

NIKSIC, GWEN M., biology professor; d. Thomas and Kathleen Niksic; m. Lucian Babiarz, Aug. 28, 2006. BS in Animal Sci., U. Ill., Urbana, 1990; MS in Animal Sci., U. Nev., Reno, 1993; postgrad. in Animal Sci., U. NH, Durham, 1996; PhD, U. ND, Grand Forks, 2005—. Tutor hearing impaired program Whitney Young Magnet HS, Chgo., 1985—86; grad. asst. U. Nev., Reno, 1991—93; tchg. and rsch. asst. U. NH, Durham, 1993—96; clk. Melroe, Bismarck, ND, 1997—2001; profl. math. and sci. tutor and lab instr. U. of Mary, Bismarck, 2001—04, asst. prof., 2004—. Recipient Quality Cost/Improvement award, Melroe, 1998. Mem.: Riverside Readers, Sigma Xi. Avocation: reading. Office: U of Mary 7500 University Dr Bismarck ND 58504 Office Phone: 701-355-8198.

NILES, BARBARA ELLIOTT, psychoanalyst; b. Boston, Jan. 31, 1939; d. Byron Kauffman and Helen Alice (Heissler) Elliott; m. John Denison, June 25, 1960 (div. 1981); children: Catherine Elliott, Andrew Elliott. AA, Briarcliff Coll., 1958; BA, SUNY, 1984; MSW, Hunter Coll. Sch. of Social Work, 1986. Cert. psychotherapy and psychoanalysis Inst. Contemporary Psychotherapy; social worker N.Y. Exec. com. Legal Aid Soc. Women's Aux., N.Y.C., 1965-67; sec. Water Quality Task Force Scientists' Com. for Pub. Info., N.Y.C., 1970-77; dir. devel. Consumer Action Now's Council Environ., N.Y.C., 1976-77; dir. 170 Tenants Corp., N.Y.C., 1979-81; mem. pub. interest com. Cosmopolitan Club, N.Y.C., 1979-82; dir. INFORM Inc., N.Y.C., 1978-84; pvt. practice psychotherapy and psychoanalysis N.Y.C., 1986—2005. Mem. adj. faculty metro ctr. Empire State Coll., N.Y.C., NY, 1987—96. Editor: (biography) Off the Beaten Track, 1984. Bd. trustees Salisbury Assn., 2001—; active Land Trust Bd., 2001—; bd. dirs. Salisbury Housing Trust, 2001—, Salisbury Vis. Nurse Assn., 2001—. Mem.: NASW, Salisbury Vis. Nurse Assn., St Botolph Club (Boston), Vincent Club (Boston), Cosmopolitan Club (NYC). Avocations: wilderness camping, travel, literature.

NILES, JOYCE LYNN, writer, editor, consultant; b. San Diego, Dec. 8, 1941; d. Thomas Elwood Niles and Opal Murl Alexander; m. Fouad Salameh Abu Jassar, Nov. 12, 1962 (div. Jan. 12, 1989); children: Aliya, Rula, Omar, Marianne, Tarik. BS, U. San Francisco, 1994. Fin. mgr. Tyrrell Jewelers, Oakland, Calif., 1959—62; reporter Jordan Times, Amman, Jordan, 1977—79; corr. Reed-Elsevier Bus. Pub., Guildford, United Kingdom, 1979—88; columnist Jerusalem Star, Amman, 1982—85; mng. editor Jordan Med. Jour., Amman, 1984—87; exec. sec. Ednl. Testing Svc., Emeryville, Calif., 1987—91; freelance writer Internal Medicine World Report, Old Bridge, NJ, 1989—92; editor Kaiser Found. Rsch. Inst., Oakland, 1992—96; writer and editor Health Info. Network, San Ramon, Calif., 1996—97. Cons. Joyce Niles Comm., Stockton, Calif., 1997—. Author short stories. Bd. deacons St. John's Presbyn. Ch., Berkeley, Calif., 1994—2000. Mem.: Nat. Mus. Women in Arts, Lodi Writers Assn. (v.p. 2003—04, pres. 2004—06), Am. Med. Writers Assn. (pres. 2003—04, newsletter editor 2004—06). Avocations: reading, photography, painting, crocheting, knitting. Home and Office: Joyce Niles Comms 1625 Knickerbocker Ct Stockton CA 95210 Office Phone: 510-333-7929. Office Fax: 209-951-2868. Business E-Mail: medmaam@netzero.net.

NILES, NANCY L., endocrinologist; b. Portland, Oreg., Sept. 9, 1952; d. Nelson R. and Esther D. Niles; m. Scott J. McCorkell, July 24, 1982; children: Jack Thomas McCorkell, Peter Niles McCorkell, Kathleen Lindsay McCorkell. AB, Princeton U., 1974; MD, U. Rochester, 1978. Diplomate Am. Bd. Internal Medicine, Am. Bd. Endocrinology. Intern, resident U. Wash., Seattle, 1982, endocrinology fellow, 1982—85, King Faisal Specialist Hosp. and Rsch. Ctr., Riyadh, Saudi Arabia, 1982—85; pvt. practice endocrinology Seattle, 1987—. Mem.: ACP, Am. Assn. Clin. Endocrinologists, Am. Coll. Endocrinology, Am. Diabetes Assn. Avocations: walking, reading. Office: 1530 N 115th # 208 Seattle WA 98133 Office Phone: 206-362-0035.

NILSON, PATRICIA, clinical psychologist; b. Boulder, Colo., Oct. 22, 1929; d. James William and Vera Maude (Peacock) Broxon; m. Eric Walter Nilson, Dec. 23, 1950; children: Stephen Daniel, Eric Jon, Christopher Lawrence. Registered Phys. Therapist, Med. Coll. Va., 1951; MA in Clin. Psychology, L.I. U., 1972, PhD, 1973. Cert. psychologist N.Y. Clin. psychologist Court Cons. Unit, Hauppauge, NY, 1972-92, Three Village Counseling Svc., Setauket, NY, 1974-75, Farmingville (N.Y.) Mental Health Ctr., NY, 1992-95; pvt. practice Commack, NY, 1975—. Adj. asst. prof. C.W. Post Coll., Brookdale, 1974-80; cons., supr. psychologist Wayside Sch. for Girls, Valley Stream, 1975-85; cons. L.I. Lighting Co., 1980; lectr. in field. Author children's therapeutic stories; author therapeutic games: The Road to Problem Mastery; contbr. articles to profl. jours. Mem.: Soc. for Clin. and Exptl. Hypnosis (life). Office: 11 Montrose Dr Commack NY 11725-1312 Office Phone: 631-864-2393. Personal E-mail: drpat11@optonline.net.

NILSSON, ANNIE, singer, music educator; b. Fairbanks, Alaska, Nov. 19, 1973; d. Don Ian Gray and Malie Carolyn Burgin Gray; m. Levi S Nilsson, Sept. 17, 1993. BA in Music, U. Oreg., Eugene, 1994—97; MS in Edn. & Info. Tech., Western Oreg. U., Monmouth, 1999—2001. Cert. Tchr., K-12 Music Oreg. Dept. Edn., 1998, Alaska Dept. Edn., 1998. Tchr. Anchorage Sch. Dist., 1998—. Singer: (opera, musical theater, jazz, choral) Bel Canto. Recipient Excellence in Tchg. Spl. Ed Students award, Wendler Mid. Sch., 2000. Mem.: Music Educators Nat. Conf. Democrat. Office: Chugiak Elem Sch 19932 Old Glenn Hwy Chugiak AK 99508 Office Phone: 561-9766.

NILSSON, MARY ANN, music educator; b. NYC, Jan. 5, 1944; d. Gerhard Eugene and Selma Christine (Landy) N.; m. June 19, 1988. BS with honors, New Paltz State U., 1965; MA, NYU, 1983; MM, Meredith Coll., Raleigh, N.C., 2000; student, The Christian U., 2003. LPN, NY. Piano tchr. New Paltz (N.Y.) State U. Coll., 1983-85, Ulster County C.C., Stone Ridge, N.Y., 1983-85; music instr. Piedmont C.C., Roxboro, N.C., 1999, Durham Tech. Coll., 1999, Durham (N.C.) C.C., 2000—02; coll. instr. Vance-Granville C.C., Henderson, NC, 2002, Mt. Olive Coll., Research Triangle Park, NC, 2002—, Wake Tech. C. C., Raleigh, 2006—. Music history tchr. Family of Ellenville, NY, 1990-91; tchr. music appreciation Long Meml. Music Acad., Roxboro, NC, 2001, tchr. music course continuing edn., 2001; tchr. medieval and renaissance music Duke U., Durham, 2005, Independence Village, Raleigh, NC, 2005; music instr. Mt. Olive Coll., Research Triangle Park, NC, 2002, creative artist in residence, Durham and Orange County Pub. Schools, 2004; lectr. in field. Musician (Performances): New Paltz State U., 1992, Town of Lumberland, N.Y., 1993, Lunch & Listen series, 1994, Hudson Valley Sr. Residence, 1995, South Winds Sr. Residence, 1995, Forest at Duke, 1997, Long Meml. Ch., 1997, others; musician: (pianist competition) Meredith Coll., 1999; musician: (master class) Walter Hautzig Meredith Coll., 1999; musician: (recital) Meredith Coll., Durham Regents, 2001, Forest at Duke, Carolina House, 2001, Carol Woods, Croasdale, Chapel Heill Sr. Ctr., 2003, Donnell Pub. Libr., 2005; contbr. articles to profl. jours.; musician: (piano performance) Independence Village Retirement, 2005, No. H.S., 2005, So. Mid. Sch., 2005, Carrboro Town Hall, 2005, Riverside H.S., 2005, Glennaire Retirment, 2005, Carolina Meadows Retirement, 2005, Creasdaille Retirement, 2005, Cart Woods Retirement, 2005, Springmoor Retirement, 2006, Hillside H.S., 2006, Forest at Duke Retirement, 2006, Windsor Point Retirement, 2006, Brighton Gardens Retirement, 2006. Choir dir., organist First Presbyn. Ch., Monticello, N.Y., 1985-86; vol. Durham (N.C.) Hosp., 1996—. Named one of 12 winners, Van Cliburn Tchrs. program, Ft. Worth Tex., 2003; recipient Tchr. Excellence award, Piedmont C.C., 2003, Excellence in Tchg. award, Durham Tech. CC, 2004; grantee, Ulster County Office of Aging, 1983, Sullivan County Office of Aging, Nat. Music Tchrs. Assn., 2001, Music Tchrs. Nat. Assn., 2001. Mem. Nat. Guild Piano Tchrs. (adjudicator 1983—, chmn. piano audition ctr. 1988-95), Durham Music Tchrs. Assn., Pi Kappa Lambda. Avocations: reading german, walking, exercise. Home and Office: 214 Equestrian Chase Rougemont NC 27572-9351 Office Phone: 919-479-7020. Personal E-mail: missmnilsson@aol.com.

NIMMO, CHARLENE, minister; b. Hamilton, Ontario, Can., May 21, 1938; d. Robert Ernst and Marie Esther LeMon; m. Del Wayne Roy Nimmo, May 27, 1960; children: Christina Brooke Clapp, Charity Anne Chapman. BS, Evangel U., 1960; MDiv, Denver Sem., 1986; D in Ministry cum laude, Fuller Sem., 2002. Ordained minister Disciples of Christ, Rocky Mountain Region, 1986. Min. Disciples of Christ, Colo.; sr. min. Park Hill Christian Ch., Pueblo, Colo. Instr. Disciples of Christ, Rocky Mountain Region, Denver, 1998—2002. Chmn. Larimer County Colorado Citizen's Budget Com., Ft. Collins, Colo., 1982—85. Mem.: Colo. 14rs. Avocation: high altitude climbing. Home: 245 S Montecito Drive Pueblo West CO 81007 Office: Park Hill Christian Church 1401 E 7th Street Pueblo CO 81001 Office Phone: 719-544-6349. E-mail: revdoc@aculink.net.

NIPERT, DONNA ANN See BARRETT, JESSICA

NIPPER, CHRISTINA JOY, music educator; b. Bartow, Fla., Sept. 16, 1975; d. Merle Hart and Ella Marie Bishop; m. John Andrew Nipper, July 11, 2003. BS in Music Edn., U. S. Fla., Tampa, 1999. Elem. music tchr. Jesse Keen Elem., Lakeland, Fla., 1999—2000, Pinewood Elem., Eagle Lake, Fla., 2000—. Named Tchr. of the Yr., Pinewood Elem., 2004—05. Mem.: Fla. Music Educators Assn., Jr. League Greater Winter Haven.

NIPPERT, CAROLYN COCHRANE, academic administrator, information scientist; b. Bklyn., Mar. 14, 1946; d. Fredrick and Astrid (Bergh) Cochrane; m. Charles Raymond Nippert Jr., Nov. 11, 1972; children: Andrew, Philip, Collin, Corinne. BA, Adelphi Suffolk Coll. (now Dowling Coll.), 1968; MLS, U. Pitts., 1971. Sci. and engrng. cataloger Lehigh U., Bethlehem, Pa., 1971-74; dir. libr. Lehigh Valley Hosp. Ctr., Allentown, Pa., 1974-88; reference libr. Cedar Crest Coll., Allentown, Pa., 1988-93, head info. and instrnl. svcs., 1994—. Conf. presenter Nat. Online Meeting, 1985. Mem. Cooperating Hosp. Lehigh Valley, 1974-88, mem. adv. bd., 1979-85. Mem. Med. Libr. Assn., Acad. Health Profls. (sr.). Home: 222 Pleasantview Rd Pottstown PA 19464 Office: Cedar Crest Coll Cressman Libr 100 College Dr Allentown PA 18104-6132

NIQUETTE, GERALDINE NORMA, marriage and family therapist; b. Kansas City, Mo., Apr. 27, 1924; d. Glenn Nesbit Niquette and Naomi Ruth Wilson-Niquette; m. Brigham Julius Lundquist, Feb. 28, 1946 (div. June 1, 1966); children: Gerre Niquette Lundquist, Lorenn Ruth Lundquist, Philip Julian Lundquist, John Brigg Lundquist. AA, Contra Costa Coll., San Pablo, Calif., 1966; BA, Calif. State U. Sonoma, Cotati, 1976; MPH, Loma Linda U., Calif., 1978; PhD in Counseling Psychology, Prof. Sch. Psychol. Studies, San Diego, 1984. RN Calif., 1966; cert. Marriage Family Therapist Calif. Bd. Behavioral Sci., 1987. Clin. dir./program mgr. Dual Diagnosis Extended Care, San Marcos and Palm Springs, Calif., 1987—93; pvt. practice therapist, supr., educator Rancho Mirage, Del., 1988—93; cons. Splty. Hosp., Redding, Calif., 1994—94; clinician/treatment planner Consol. Tribal Health, Ukiah, Calif., 1996—99; clinician/childrens' team leader Lake County Mental Health, Lakeport, Calif., 2000—03; pvt. clinician Lakeport, Calif., 2001—. Pub. health extern WHO, Geneva, 1977; continuing edn. provider Ca Bd. Registered Nursing, Sacramento, 1990—94; adv. bd. Canyon Springs Psychiat. Hosp., Cathedral City, Calif., 1992—93; lectr. and mem. Nat. Coun. of Alcoholism, San Diego, 1984—93. Vol./developmentally delayed Los Lomas Sch., Lafayette, Calif., 1958—60; nursing aux. Seattle Well Baby Clinics, Seattle, 1953—57; vol. support person various drug and alcohol programs, Calif., 1972—. Mem.: Am. Assn. Family Therapists (licentiate), Calif. Assn. Marriage Family Therapists (licentiate), Lake County Women's Club. Avocations: acquiring new knowledge, travel, gardening, needlecrafts. Home: 1240 N Pine St Apt 21 Ukiah CA 95482-3848

NIRMALANI, ANJALI, psychiatrist; b. Washington, Feb. 13, 1977; d. Hiro and Punam Nirmalani. BS, Va. Commonwealth U., Richmond, 1999; MD, Med. Coll. Va., Richmond, 2003. Resident U. South Fla., Tampa, 2003—. Resident rep. Greater Tampa Bay Psychiat. Soc., 2005—. V.p. Class of 2003, Med. Coll. Va., 2000—03, sec. student govt., 2001—02. Presdl. scholar, Va. Commonwealth U., 1995—99, med. scholar, Alumni Assn. of Med. Coll. Va., 2002—03, travel grantee, Am. Acad. Child and Adolescent Psychiatry, 2004. Mem.: Fla. Psychiat. Soc. (assoc.; resident rep. 2004—, advocate 2003—, Tom and Donna Buchanan grantee 2004, 2005), Am. Acad. Child and Adolescent Psychiatry (assoc.), Am. Psychiat. Assn. (assoc.), Am. Assn. Physicians of Indian Origin (assoc.; sec. med. student, resident and fellow sect. 2005—06), Alpha Phi Omega (life; sec. 1997—98). Office: 3315 E Fletcher Ave Tampa FL 33613 E-mail: anirmala@hsc.usf.edu.

NIRO, CHERYL, lawyer; b. Feb. 19, 1950; d. Samuel James and Nancy (Canezaro) Ippolito; m. William Luciano Niro, July 1, 1979; children: Christopher William, Melissa Leigh. BS with highest honors, U. Ill., 1972; JD, No. Ill. U., 1980. Bar: Ill. 1981, U.S. Dist. Ct. (no. dist.) Ill. 1981, U.S. Ct. Appeals (7th cir.) 1990, U.S. Supreme Ct. 1999, cert.: negotiator, mediator, facilitator, arbitrator. Ptnr. Quinlan & Carroll, Chgo.; pres. Judicial Dispute Resolution, Inc., Chgo.; exec. dir. commn. on professionalism. Ill. Supreme Ct. Spl. counsel to Atty. Gen., 1996—99; tchg. asst. program instrn. lawyers mediation and negotiation workshops and guest lectr. Harvard Law Sch. Program of Instrn. for Lawyers Harvard U.; mem. appt. panel U.S. Ct. Appeals (7th cir.); found. dir. Nat. Ctr. for Conflict Resolution Edn.; mem. copyright arbitration royalty panel U.S. Libr. of Congress, 2000—05; mem. London Ct. of Internat. Arbitation. Named 100 Women Making A Difference, 2001; named one of Ten Most Influential Women Lawyers in Ill, Am Lawyer Media, 2000; named to Today's Chgo. Woman Mag. Hall of Fame, 2002. Mem.: ATLA, ABA (comn multijurisdictional practice, standing comt bar servs, dispute resolution sect coun, house delegs), Nat. Caucus State Bar Assns. (pres.-elect), Internat. Ctr. for Healing the Law (mem. bd. adv.), Internat. Bar Assn., Ill. State Bar Assn. (mem assembly 1993, bd govs 1994—97, treas 1995—96, 2d vpres 1997—98, pres 1999—2000, standing comt legal-related educ pub), Ill Trial Lawyers Asn. Home: 633 N East Ave Oak Park IL 60302-1715 Office: Quinlan & Carroll 30 N Lasalle St Ste 2900 Chicago IL 60602-2590 Office Phone: 312-917-8839. Business E-Mail: cherylniro@qclaw.com.

NISHIMOTO, ALICE KEIKO, elementary school educator, consultant; d. Tom and Shizuye Nishimoto. BA in Home Econ., Whittier Coll., Calif., 1978; MEd, Calif. State U., LA, 2004. Textile analyst U.S. Testing Co., L.A., 1983—92; adminstr. Keiro Svcs., L.A., 1993—98; tchr. Rice Elem., Garvey Sch. Dist., Rosemead, Calif., 1998—. Monterey Pk. commr. Comm. on Aging, Monterey Pk., Calif., 1997—99; docent Monterey Pk. Hist. Mus., 1983—. Mem.: Whittier Home Economists in Home and Cmty., Optimist Club. Avocations: travel, sewing, cooking, photography. Office: Rice Sch 2150 N Angeles Ave Rosemead CA 91770

NISLY, LORETTA LYNN, obstetrical nurse, geriatrics nurse; b. Cheverly, Md., Jan. 26, 1967; d. Mart and Mary (Miller) Overholt; m. Timothy Daniel Nisly, July 18, 1987; children: Michael Jeffrey, Russell Benjamin. AD, Germanna Community Coll., Locust Grove, Va., 1994; LPN, Piedmont Tech. Edn. Ctr., Culpeper, Va., 1989. LPN, RN, Va. Med.-surg. charge nurse Culpeper Regional Hosp., 1989—90, 1995—2002; RN Family Birth Ctr./Culpeper Regional Hosp., 2002—; charge nurse Mt. View Nursing Home, Aroda, Va., 1990-92, Orange County Nursing Home, Orange, Va., 1992-94. Recipient Florence Nightengale award Germanna Cmty. Coll., 1995. Mem. Mennonite. Avocations: horseback riding, reading, sports, gardening. Home: 732 Tom Johnston Rd Aroda VA 22709-9703

NISSENSON, NORMA, clinical psychologist; b. Frankfort, Ky., Nov. 18, 1917; d. Jacob and Pearl (Klass) Rosen; m. Marc Nissenson, July 6, 1940 (dec. 2000); children: Carol, Mary; m. Mayer S. Gunther, 2006. BS, Northwestern U., 1938, MA, 1948. Cert. clin. psychologist, Ill. Exec. dir.

Guidance Agy. Adolecents, Chgo., 1946-52; assoc prof. Roosevelt U., Chgo., 1962-70; gen. practice psychology Nissenson Assocs. Ltd., Chgo., 1962—. Bd. dirs. Moraine council Girl Scouts USA, Moraine PTA, Operation Higher Edn. Pays; pres. N. Shore Film Soc.; lectr., participant TV talk shows, Chgo., 1962—. Fellow Am. Orthopsychiat. Assn., Internat. Coun. Sex Edn. and Parenthood; mem. Am. Psychol. Assn., Ill. Psychol. Assn., Chgo. Psychol. Assn. (pres. 1982), Am. Assn. Counseling and Devel. (life), Am. Assn. Marriage and Family Therapist, Ill. Commn. Human Rels. (state adv. coun.). Home: 222 E Chestnut St Apt 6b Chicago IL 60611-2355

NISSL, COLLEEN KAYE, lawyer; b. McMinnville, Oreg., June 3, 1950; d. Anton Arthur and Luella Elaine (Kerr) N.; m. Roger Philip Sugarman; children: Jordan Elizabeth, Zachary Max. BA, Ohio Wesleyan U., 1972; JD, U. Toledo, 1975. Bar: Ohio 1975, U.S. Dist. Ct. (so. dist.) Ohio 1977, U.S. Supreme Ct. 1980. Litigation sect. chief Atty. Gen. Ohio, Columbus, 1976-82; sr. counsel Battelle Meml. Inst., Columbus, 1982-84; v.p., asst. gen. counsel Borden Chemical, Inc., Columbus, 1984—. Mem. ABA, Ohio Bar Assn., Columbus Bar Assn. (chmn. alt. dispute resolution com.). Democrat. Roman Catholic. Avocations: skiing, bicycling, antiques. Office: Borden Inc 180 E Broad St 27th Fl Columbus OH 43215

NISSON, MARY, elementary school educator; b. Berkeley, Calif., May 19, 1960; d. Peter Fenn Samuelson and Jeanne Francis Mulligan. BA in Econs., U. Calif., Davis, 1984; multiple subjects credential, Calif. State U., 1994. ESL/parent literacy tchr. Old Marshall Sch., Susan B. Anthony Elem. Sch., Sacramento, 1996—; bus. English educator Blue Diamond Almond Co., Sacramento, 1998; reading remediation instr. River Oaks Elem. Sch., Galt, Calif., 1999—. Co-founding adult educator Twilight Program, Elk Grove Sch. Dist. Prairie Elem. Site, Sacramento, 1995-97; elem. tchr. Feickert Elem., Elk Grove, Calif., 1995. Co-author: (ESL handbook) Curricular Reference, 1996; editor (cookbook) The Melting Pot, 1999; contbr. articles to profl. jours. Founding coord. Natomas Mothers Group, Sacramento, Calif., 1988; co-founder, mem. AUTASTICS, San Francisco, 1996—; mem. Graffiti Busters, Autism Soc. Am. Recipient Recognition certificate Natomas Mothers Group, Sacramento, 1998. Mem. Calif. Tchrs. Assn., Calif. Tchrs. of English to Speakers of Other Langs. Roman Catholic. Avocations: reading, birdwatching, bicycling, cross country skiing. Office: Old Marshall Adult Edn Ctr 2718 G St Sacramento CA 95816-3720 E-mail: mdsong@earthlink.net.

NITSCHE, LINDA, gifted and talented educator; d. Richard and Virginia Ludwick; m. John Nitsche, June 19, 1976; children: Jessica, Todd. BA, Muhlenberg Coll., Allentown, Pa., 1974; EdM, Temple U., Phila., 1990. Cert. instrnl. II Pa., 1977. Gifted support tchr. Owen J. Roberts Sch. Dist., Pottstown, Pa., 1974—. Keystone tech. integrator Pa. Dept. Edn., Harrisburg, 2005—. Mem.: ASCD (assoc.), Pa. Assn. Gifted Edn. (assoc.), Pa. Assn. Ednl. Comm. and Tech. (assoc.), Internat. Reading Assn. (assoc.), Nat. Coun. Tchrs. English (assoc.), Nat. Coun. Tchrs. Math. (assoc.). Office: Owen J Robers School District 901 Ridge Rd Pottstown PA 19465

NITTLER, JESSICA RAE, psychiatrist; b. Kans. City, Mo., May 8, 1976; d. Leslie Kent and Karen Craft Lampe; m. Tom Bernard Nittler, May 29, 1999; 1 child, Lila Grace. BA, U. Mo., 1999, MD, 2000. Residency Karl Mennings Sch., Topeka, 2000—01; second yr. residency Western USA Mental Health Ctr., Kans. City, 2001—02; third yr. residency Baylor Coll. Medicne, Houston, 2002—04; staff psychiatrist Harry S. Truman H.S., Columbia, Mo., 2004—. Assoc. residency dir. U. Mo., Columbia, 2005—06. Mem.: APA. Home: 1809 S Fairview Rd Columbia MO 65203 Office: Harry S Truman Va Hosp 800 Hospital Dr Columbia MO 65201 Office Phone: 573-814-6486.

NIX, BARBARA LOIS, real estate broker; b. Sept. 25, 1929; d. Martin Clayton and Norma (Gunter) Westfield; m. B. H. Nix, July 12, 1968; children: William Martin Dahl, Theresa Irene Dahl stepchildren: Dennis Leon, Denise Lynn. Student, St. Elizabeths Sch. Nursing, Yakima, Wash., 1949-50; AA, Sierra Coll., 1978; student, Calif. State U., Sacramento, 1984. Bookkeeper, office mgr. Lakeport (Calif.) Tire Svc., 1966-69, Dr. K. J. Absher, Grass Valley, Calif., 1972-75; real estate sales and office mgr. Rough and Ready Land Co., Penn Valley, Calif., 1976-77, co-owner, v.p., sec., 1978—, Wildwood West Real Estate, Gateway Real Estate. Co-owner Nix's Antiques, 1996—. Youth and welfare chmn. Yakima Federated Jr. Women's Club, 1957; den mother Cub Scouts, 1959—60; leader Girls Scouts U.S., 1961—62; mem. Friends of Hospice, Sierra, Nev. Meml. Hosp. Found.; adv. bd. dirs., v.p. Roots and Wings Ednl. Found., 1991—95; mem. Nevada County Sch. Dist. Redistricting Bd. Recipient Pres.'s award, Sierra Coll., 1973, others. Mem.: Am. Assn. Univ. Women, Sierra Nev. Meml. Hosp. Aux., Penn Valley (founder, pres. 1978), Lake Wildwood Women's Club, Job's Daus. (life). Republican. Roman Catholic. Home: 19365 Wildflower Dr Penn Valley CA 95946-9735 Office: POBox 191 Penn Valley CA 95946

NIX, KATHERINE JEAN, medical case manager; d. Samuel Watson and Dorothy Lee (Woods) Lewis; m. Robert Milton Nix, May 5, 1963 (div. Feb. 1988); children: Araina Catrice, Cynthia Lathier. AA in Safety and Health, Merritt Coll., 1976; AA in Nursing, Chabot Coll., 1974; BSN, U. San Francisco, 1979. RN Calif. Staff nurse Highland Hosp., Oakland, Calif., 1961-73; nurse cmty. health Alameda County, Oakland, Calif., 1973-75; nurse occupational health Caterpiller Tractor Co., San Leandro, Calif., 1975-77, inspector safety hygiene, 1981-84; nurse cons. occupational health Intel Corp., Livermore, Calif., 1981-84; cons. health & safety Quaker Oats Co., Oakland, 1984-86; nurse cons. occupational health Rawson Drug & Sundry Co., San Leandro, 1986-89; rehab. nurse Continental Rehab. Resources, Pleasanton, Calif., 1989-91; rehab. nurse cons. GAB, Campbell, Calif., 1991-93; med. case mgr. Conservco Travelers Ins. Co., Walnut Creek, Calif., 1993-95, Olsten Kimberly Quality Care, San Leandro, Calif., 1995—. Health advisor Black Women Organized for Polit. Action, Oakland, 1979—, Alameda (Calif.) Coll., 1982-86. Fellow Nat. Safety Coun., Rehab. Nurses Group. Democrat. Avocations: skiing, reading, stage plays. Home: PO Box 5834 Oakland CA 94605-0834 Office: St Marys Hosp 450 Stanyan St San Francisco CA 94117-1079

NIX, LINDA ANNE BEAN, public relations executive; b. Sept. 20, 1943; d. Norman Arthur and Gladys Mae (Charlton) Bean, Jr.; m. Henry Taylor Betts, Jr., Sept. 5, 1964 (div. 1970); m. John Asa Nix, Nov. 24, 1971 (div. 1990). Student, Syracuse U., 1961-64; BA, Scarritt Coll., 1965; postgrad., Middle Tenn. State U., 9171-73. Mobile coord. Children's Mus., Nashville, 1967-69; promotion dir. Sta. WDCN-TV/8, Nashville, 1969-82; dir. pub. info. Sta. WYES-TV/12, New Orleans, 1982—; mktg. dir. Sta. KOFY-TV Radio San Francisco, 1989-91, Sta. KUSI-TV, San Diego, 1992-93; self-employed in pub. rels., 1992—. Mem. pub. info. adv. com. Pub. Broadcasting Service, Washington, 1977-80, chmn. 1979-80, mem. festival task force, 1979-80. Author, editor: (tchr. workbook) Yellow Submarine, 1968; contbr. Great Chefs, 2001—; contbr. articles to profl. jours. Bd. dirs. Nashville League for Hearing Impaired, 1973-76, Tennessee Williams/New Orleans Literacy Festival, 1995–; chmn. membership com. Coun. Cmty. Svcs., Nashville, 1978-80; mem. allocation panel United Way Greater Nashville, 1979-81, United Way Greater New Orleans, 1982-86. Mem. Pub. Rels. Soc. Am. (chmn. accreditation com. 1985, pres. New Orleans chpt. 1988), Broadcast Promotion and Mktg. Execs., Inc. (Promax) (bd. dirs. 1982-91, pres. 1989-90). Avocations: flying, sewing. Home and Office: PO Box 7068 Metairie LA 70010-7068 Office Phone: 504-581-5000. E-mail: lagator@mindspring.com.

NIX, PATRICIA, artist; d. Nobe Astin Briggs and Lela Mae (Lucas) Rockstrom; m. (dec.); children: Pandora Nix Shaw, William Riley Jr., John Houston. BA, NYU, 1982. One-woman shows include Tower Gallery, Southampton, N.Y., 1978—82, 1985, NYU, 1980, Sutton Gallery, N.Y.C., 1982—83, Baumgartner Gallery, Washington, 1984, S.I. (N.Y.) Mus., 1986, Andre Zarre Gallery, N.Y.C., 1987, S.I. (N.Y.) Mus., 1988, Nerlino Gallery, N.Y.C., 1988, Andre Zarre Gallery, 1991, U. Windsor (Ont., Can.) Mus., Griffin McGear Modern Gallery, N.Y.C., 1989, San Angelo (Tex.) Mus. of Art, 1991, Hurlbutt Gallery, Greenwich, Conn., 1990, Galerie Donguy, Paris, 1994, Dillon Gallery, N.Y.C., 1994—98, numerous group shows including most recently, exhibited in group shows at Merill Chase Galleries, Chgo., 1999, Am. Embassy, Rome, Italy, 1999, Hilligoss Galleries, 2000—03, Tex. Tech. Mus., Lubbock, 2000; represented in numerous permanent collections, designer sets and costumes (ballets) Petrushka, Pulcinella, Jeu de Cartes, 2002, Totem Altar, Saint Peters Ch., N.Y.C., 2004, Gallerie Mary Claude Goinnard, Paris, France, 2005, Totem Altar, St. John the Devine Cathedral., N.Y.C., 2005, Mary Claude Goinnard, Paris, France, 2005. Office Phone: 212-686-3512.

NIX, PATRICIA PERRY, retired librarian; b. LaCrosse, Kans., July 16, 1932; d. William Jarold and Sara Ruth (Gray) Perry; m. Stephen Daniel Nix, June 20, 1994 (dec.). AA, Ft. Smith Jr. Coll., Ark., 1957; BA, Tulsa U., Okla., 1959; MLS, La. State U., Baton Rouge, 1962. Tchr. elem. sch. Irvington (Calif.) Sch., 1959—60; libr. elem. sch. Tulsa, 1960—61; libr. trainee La. State U., Baton Rouge, 1961—62; libr. catalog supr. Bklyn. Pub. Libr., 1963—65; libr. comty. U.S. Army Spl. Svcs., 1965—82; libr. engring. and law U.S. Army Corps Engrs., Seattle, 1982—94; ret., 1994. Author: (poetry) No Stone Unturned, 1968. Bd. dirs. Master Gardeners Found., Sequim, Wash., 1997—2002, Port Angeles (Wash.) Symphony Orch., Port Angeles, 1996—2006, pres., 2002—03; bd. dirs. Olympic Theater Arts, Sequim, 1997—99; pres. Sequim Arts, 2002—. Mem.: Olympic Peninsula Enol. Soc. (bd. dirs. 2002—), Mensa, Audubon Soc. Democrat. Avocations: painting, collage, drawing, creative writing.

NIX, RACHEL ANN HACKMANN, science educator; b. Royal Oak, Mich., Oct. 1, 1975; d. Renata Leslie and Larry Fenton Hackmann; m. Brad Nix, June 11, 2004. B in Biology, U. Mich., Ann Arbor, 1997; B in Mid. Grades Edn., Kennesaw State U., Ga., 2003. Cert. mid. sch. math and sci. Ga., 2003. Sci. educator Cobb County Sch, Marietta, Ga., 2003—. Recipient Outstanding Sr. award, Kennesaw State U., 2003. Office Phone: 770-578-2710.

NIX, SHARON J., principal; MEd, Liberty U., Lynchburg, Va., 1994, EdS, 2004. Acad. prin. Altamonte Christian Sch., Altamonte Springs, Fla., 1987—. Tchr. Sunday sch. 1st Bapt. of DeBary, Fla. Office Phone: 407-831-0950.

NIXON, BRENDA JOYCE, elementary school educator, small business owner; b. Hazlehurst, Miss., Feb. 6, 1949; d. Archie C. Ashley, Sr. and Joyce B. Ashley; m. W.B. (Benny) Nixon, Jr. (div.); children: Ashley Michelle Nixon Rogers, Christopher Jarrett. BA, William Carey Coll., Hattiesburg, Miss, 1971; post grad., 1987—. CPA; lic. educator Miss. Group leader Ga. Bapt. Children's Home, Palmetto, Ga.; tchr. grade 6 Union Academy, Georgetown, Miss., 1987—95, Windsor Academy, Macon, Ga., 1993—2000, Crystal Springs Mid. Sch., Crystal Springs, Miss., 2000—. Tchr. participant So. Regional Edn. Bd.; pres. club rep. Avon, 2001—. Vol. fund raiser Bethel Vol. Fire Dept., Hazlehurst, 2004; state level judge Pre Teen Am. Program, 1994—96; music dir. Bethel Bapt. Ch., Hazlehurst, 2000—, mission action dir., 2003—. Named Tchr. of Yr., Macon/Bibb County Fire Dept., 1997—98, Macon Sheriff's Dept., 1998—99. Nat. Honor Roll Outstanding Am. Tchr., 2006. Avocations: reading, painting, music. Office: Crystal Springs Mid Sch 2092 S Pat Harrison Dr Crystal Springs MS 39059-3038 Home: 8157 Hwy 472 Hazlehurst MS 39083 Office Phone: 601-892-2789. Personal E-mail: abcnixon@aol.com.

NIXON, CYNTHIA, actress; b. NYC, Apr. 9, 1966; d. Walter and Anne Nixon; children: Samantha Mozes, Charles Ezekiel Mozes. BA in English, Barnard Coll., 1988. Founding member The Drama Dept., 1996. Actor: (plays) The Philadelphia Story, 1980 (Theatre World Award, 1981), The Real Thing, 1984, Hurly Burly, 1984, Indiscretions, 1996 (Tony Award nom., 1996, Tony award, best performance by leading actress in a play, 2006), Rabbit Hole, 2006, The Prime of Miss Jean Brodie, 2006; (films) Little Darlings, 1980, Prince of the City, 1981, Tattoo, 1981, I Am the Cheese, 1983, Amadeus, 1984, The Manhattan Project, 1986, O.C. and Stiggs, 1987, Let It Ride, 1989, Through an Open Window, 1992, The Pelican Brief, 1993, Addams Family Values, 1993, Baby's Day Out, 1994, The Cottonwood, 1996, 'M' Word, 1996, Marvin's Room, 1996, Advice From a Caterpillar, 1999, The Out-of-Towners, 1999, Igby Goes Down, 2002, The Paper Mache Chase, 2003; (TV series) Sex and the City, 1998—2004 (Emmy nom. for Outstanding Supporting Actress in a comedy series, 2002, Emmy award Outstanding Supporting Actress in a Comedy Series, 2004); (TV miniseries) Tanner '88, 1988; (TV films) The Seven Wishes of a Rich Kid, 1979, The Private History of a Campaign That Failed, 1981, Rascals and Robbers: The Secret Adventures of Tom Sawyer and Huck Finn, 1982, My Body, My Child, 1982, Fifth of July, 1982, The Murder of Mary Phagan, 1988, Women & Wallace, 1990, Love She Sought, The, 1990, Face of a Stranger, 1991, Love, Lies and Murder, 1991, Kiss-Kiss, Dahlings!, 1992, Sex and the Matrix, 2000, Papa's Angels, 2000, Stage on Screen: The Women, 2002, Tanner on Tanner, 2004, Warm Springs, 2005. Office: William Morris Agency One William Morris Place Beverly Hills CA 90212*

NIXON, JUANA LYNN WHITLEY, advertising executive; b. LaGrange, Ga., Aug. 11, 1964; d. John Hamilton and Lena Pearl (Knight) Whitley. BA in Math. and Bus. magna cum laude, LaGrange Coll., 1986. Gen. mgr. Unique Advt. Specialties, LaGrange, 1985—. Neighborhood capt. Am. Cancer Soc.; active La Fayette Singers, Rep. Presdl. Task Force; mem. choir 1st Bapt. Ch., 3 yr.-old choir dir., 4 yr.-old Sunday sch. tchr., co-dir., mem. adult choir; active Troup County Hist. Soc. Scholar Ty Cobb, 1985, 1986. Mem.: NAFE, NASE, Alpha Omicron Pi (chair philanthropy com.), Omicron Delta Kappa. Home: 811 Wisteria Way Lagrange GA 30240-1639 Office: Unique Advt Specialties 818 N Greenwood St Lagrange GA 30240-1705 Office Phone: 706-882-7178. E-mail: lynnwhitleynixon@charter.net.

NIXON, JUDITH MAY, librarian; b. Gary, Ind., June 14, 1945; d. Louis Robert Sr. and Mable Sophia (Reiner) Vician; m. Cleon Robert Nixon III, Aug. 20, 1967; 1 child, Elizabeth Marie. BS in Edn., Valparaiso U., 1967; MA in LS, U. Iowa, 1974. Tchr. U.S. Peace Corps, Tonga, 1968—69; popular books libr. Lincoln Libr., Springfield, Ill., 1971—73; ref. libr. Cedar Rapids (Iowa) Pub. Libr., 1974—76; ref.coord. U. Wis., Platteville, 1976—82; bus. libr. U. Ariz., Tucson, 1982—84; consumer and family sci. libr. Purdue U., West Lafayette, La., 1984—93, Krannert mgmt. and econs. libr., 1993—2005, humanities, social sci. and edn. head libr., 2005—. Editor: Industry and Company Information, 1991, Organization Charts, 1992, 2d edit., 1996, Hotel and Restaurant Industries, 1993; editor quar. serial Lodging and Restaurant Index, 1985-93. Leader Girl Scouts U.S., Lafayette, 1985—. Recipient John H. Moriarty award Purdue U. Librs., 1989. Mem. ALA (chair bus. reference and svcs. sect. 1995-96, GALE Rsch. award for excellence in bus. librarianship 1994). Home: 2375 N 23rd St Lafayette IN 47904-1242 Office: Purdue U Libraries Humanities Social Sci Edn Libr 504 W State St West Lafayette IN 47907-2058 Office Phone: 765-494-2927. Business E-Mail: jnixon@purdue.edu.

NIXON, MARNI, singer; b. Altadena, Calif., Feb. 22, 1930; d. Charles and Margaret (Wittke) McEathron; m. Ernest Gold, May 22, 1950 (div. 1969); m. Lajos Frederick Fenster, July 23, 1971 (div. July 1975); m. Albert David Block, Apr. 11, 1983. Student, L.A. City Coll., UCLA, U. So. Calif., Tanglewood, Mass. Dir. vocal faculty Calif. Inst. Arts, Valencia, 1970-72; pvt. tchr., vocal coach, condr. master classes, 1970—; pvt. voice tchr., coach, condr. master classes, 1970—; head apprentice divsn. Santa Barbara Music Acad. of West, 1980; formerly dir. opera workshop Cornish Inst. Arts, Seattle. Tchr. in field; judge Met. Opera Internat. Am. Music Awards, Nat. Inst. Music Theatre, 1984—87; dialect dir., opera recs. Actor: (musicals) Pasadena (Calif.) Playhouse, 1940—45; (films) Sound of Music, 1964, I Think I Do, 1996; (TV series) Boomerang, 1975; (plays) My Fair Lady, 1964, Taking My Turn, 1983, Opal, 1992—94, Cabaret, 1998, Ballymore, 1999, Follies, 2000—01, James Joyce's The Dead, 1999—2001, Nine, 2003; singer (soloist): Roger Wagner chorale, 1947—53; singer: (Operas) New Eng. Opera Co., LA Opera Co., Ford Found. TV Opera, 1948—63, San Francisco Spring Opera, 1966, Seattle Opera, 1971—73, classical recitals and appearances with symphony orchs. throughout U.S., Can., Eng., Israel, Ireland; voice dub: (films) My Fair Lady; The King and I; An Affair to Remember; West Side Story; Disney's Mulan; others; singer: (albums) Columbia, Mus. Heritage Records, Capital, RCA Victor, Ednl. Records, Reference Recs., Varese-Sarabande, Nonesuch; author: I Could Have Sung All Night: My Story, 2006. Nominee Drama Desk award, 2 Grammy award, NARAS; recipient 4 Emmy awards for best actress, 2 Action for Childrens TV awards, 1977, Chgo. Film Festival award, 1977, 2 Gold Records for Songs from Mary Poppins and Mulan. Mem.: Nat. Assn. Tchrs. Singing (pres. N.Y. chpt. 1994—97, panelist new music).

NIXON, RONDA LYNN, paralegal; b. Ashland, Ky., Jan. 9, 1971; d. Ronnie Dewey and Sadie Francis Bishop; m. Norman Brian Nixon, May 1, 2004; children: Darren Connors, Shelby Connors, Roni Nixon. AAS in Paralegal Tech., Miller Motte Bus. Coll., Clarksville, Tenn., 1995; student, Kaplon U., Chgo. Cert. Paralegal Nat. Assn. of Legal Asst., 2005. Paralegal Pruitt & Thorner, Catlettsburg, Ky., 2003—; legal sec. Robinson & Rice, Ashland, Ky., 2003. Advocate CASA, Ashland, Ky., 2004—06. Mem.: Nat. Assn. of Legal Assistants, Assn. of Trial Lawyers of Am. Home: 102Township Rd 286 Chesapeake OH 45619 Office: Pruitt & Thorner P O Box 352 Catlettsburg KY 41129

NIXON, SUNNY JEANNE, lawyer; b. Saratoga, Wyo., Sept. 8, 1948; BA with honors, U. Wyo., 1970, JD, 1973. Bar: Wyo. 1974, N.Mex. 1977, Colo. 1988, U.S. Claims Ct., U.S. Ct. Appeals Fed Cir., U.S. Ct. Appeals Tenth Cir., U.S. Dist. Ct. Dist. N. Mex. Legis. asst. U.S. Senator's Office, Washington; ptnr. Rodey, Dickason, Sloan, Akin & Robb PA, Santa Fe. Mem.: ABA-pub. utility, comm. & transportation law sect., State Bar N. Mex., First Judicial Dist. Bar Assn., Wyo. State Bar Assn., Colo. State Bar Assn. Office: Rodey Dickason Sloan Akin & Robb PA 315 Paseo de Peralta Santa Fe NM 87501 Office Phone: 505-954-3900. Office Fax: 505-954-3942. Business E-Mail: snixon@rodey.com.

NIYEKAWA, AGNES MITSUE, foreign language professor; b. Tokyo, May 9, 1924; came to U.S., 1949, naturalized; d. Basil Zensaku and Irene (Kano) N.; m. Roy C. Calogeras (div. 1964); children: Erik, Meagan. BA in English, Tokyo Women's U., 1945; BA in Sociology, U. Hawaii, 1952; MA in Psychology, Bryn Mawr Coll., 1954; PhD in Psychology, NYU, 1960. Rsch. assoc. psychology dept. NYU, 1959-61; asst. prof. ednl. psychology U. Hawaii, Honolulu, 1964-67, from prof. human devel. to chmn. East Asian langs., 1971-81, prof. East Asian langs. and lit., 1973-91, prof. emeritus, 1992—; assoc. prof. ednl. psychology Northeastern U., Boston, 1968-69; from sr. specialist Inst. Advanced Rsch. to assoc. dir. Culture Learning Inst. East West Ctr., Honolulu, 1969-71. Vis. scholar Columbia U., N.Y.C., 1961-63, MIT, Cambridge, 1967-68, Harvard U., Cambridge, 1987, U. Tokyo, 1982, U. Vienna, Austria, 1986-87. Author: Minimum Essential Politeness, 1992, (with others) Cross-Cultural Learning, 1977, Design for Cross-Cultural Leaning, 1987; contbr. numerous articles to profl. publs., 1952—. USPHS fellow, 1961-63; grantee U.S. Office Edn., 1965-67, Am. Coun. Learned Socs., 1962, 67-68, Fulbright, 1981-82, Social Sci. Rsch. Coun. Mem. Chamber Music Hawaii, Austrian Assn. of Hawaii. Home: 500 University Ave Apt 2003 Honolulu HI 96826-4941 Personal E-mail: agnesmn@hawaiiantel.net.

NIZNIK, CAROL ANN, electrical engineer, educator, consultant; b. Saratoga Springs, NY, Nov. 10, 1942; d. John Arthur Niznik and Rosalia Sopko; m. Donald H. Walter, Jan. 11, 1964. AAS in Engring. Sci., Alfred (NY) State Coll., 1962; BSEE, U. Rochester, NY, 1969, MSEE, 1972; PhD in Elec. Engring., SUNY, Buffalo, 1978. Technician Taylor Instrument Corp., Rochester, 1962-64; sr. technician IBM Corp., Poughkeepsie, NY, 1964-68; rsch. scientist Eastman Kodak Corp., Rochester, 1969-70; sr. engr. Xerox Corp., Webster, NY, 1971-74; rsch. asst. prof. SUNY, Buffalo, 1979-80; assoc. prof. elec. engring. U. Pitts., Pitts., 1980-83; pres., cons. NW Sys. Function: Software Theoretical Protocol Devel. and Performance Evaluation, Rochester, 1975—. Adj. prof. math. Rochester Inst. Tech., 1993-94; faculty fellow Battelle/Rit/White Sands Missile Range, 1994-97; vis. assoc. prof. Ctr. Brain Rsch., Sch. Medicine, U. Rochester, dept. math., 1983-84 Author tech. monograph on cerebellum prosthesis component, monograph missile def. to homeland def. and security software R & D; contbr. some 80 articles to profl. confs. and jours., 32 conf. publs. presentations; patentee in field. Recipient fellowships, grants and 16 US govt. contracts, Irmgard Flugge-Lotz award outstanding tchg. and academic achievement, 1983, Engr. of Yr. award SUNY Buffalo Engring. Alumni Assn., 2004, Star Wars Strat. Def. Initiative Orgn. (SDIO) Phase I SDIO/SBIR Contract Def. Nuc. Agy., 1986, Congestion Controlled Sequential Contention Resolution Protocol award Rockwell Internat. Corp. Thousand Oaks Patriot Missile Software. Mem. IEEE (sr.), Sigma Xi, Eta Kappa Nu, Tau Beta Pi. Roman Catholic. Avocations: doll collecting, gardening. Office: NW Sys PO Box 18133 Rochester NY 14618-0133 Personal E-mail: dr_carol_niznik@yahoo.com.

NJAVRO, E. RANDELLE, science educator; b. Fullerton, Calif., Nov. 9, 1949; d. Arthur Fredrick and June Pressel; m. Jerry Arthur Njavro, May 8, 1982; children: Shannon Nicole, Jerry Ryan. BS in Physical Edn., Health and Biol. Scis., UCLA, Calif., 1972; Masters in Edn. Adminstrn., Azusa Pacific Coll., Calif., 1979. Cert. tchg. credential UCLA. Swim instr. City of Anaheim, Calif., 1962—77; tchg. asst. UCLA Med. Ctr., Los Angeles, 1972—73; tchr. Katella HS, Anaheim, 1973—76, Crescent Jr. HS, Anaheim, 1976—79, Trident and Pine Jr. HS, Anaheim, 1979—80, Los Alamitos (Calif.) HS, 1980—83, Oak Mid. Sch., Los Alamitos, 1983—85, McAuliffe Mid. Sch., Los Alamitos, 1985—. Volleyball, basketball, swim coach various schs., Calif., 1973—; coach sci. club, sci. olympiad McAuliffe Mid. Sch., 1995—, sch. advisory com., 2003—. Candelighters Loma Linda Hosp., Calif., 2002—. Recipient Honorary Svc. award, McAuliffe Mid. Sch., 2002, Dorothy Shaw Leadership award, Alpha Delta Pi Sorority, 1972, Chancelor's award, UCLA, 1972, Sci. Coaching award, Sci. Olympiad Countywide Competition. Mem.: Nat. Tchrs. Sci. Assn., Nat. Educators Assn., Los Alamitos Edn. Assn., Moose Lodge, Alpha Delta Pi. Avocations: swimming, crafts. Office: McAuliffe Mid Sch 4112 Cerritos Ave Los Alamitos CA 90720 E-mail: r_njavro@losal.org.

NJIE, VERONICA P.S., clinical nurse, educator; d. Edward G. Njie and Grace B.S. Daniels-Njie. BSN, Howard U., Washington, 1992; MSN, The Cath. U. Am., Washington, 1996. RN Washington, clin. specialist in med.-surg. nursing. Tchr. Dept. Edn., Banjul, Gambia, The Gambia, 1980—82; state registered nurse (SRN) Royal Victoria Hosp., Banjul, 1985—86; rsch./field asst. Med. Rsch. Coun., Fajara, 1986—87; nurse technician Howard U. Hosp., Washington, 1988—90, clin. nurse II, 1990—96; clin. nurse N.W. Health Care Ctr. Beverly Enterprise, 1990—98; clin. instr. Montgomery Coll., Tacoma Park, Md., 1996; asst. prof. nursing Balt. City C. C., Balt., 1997. Contbr. articles to profl. jours. Recipient Intramural Rsch. Tng. award, NIH, 2000. Mem.: Md. Assn. Higher Edn., ANA, Nat. League Nursing, Sigma Theta Tau. Democrat. Roman Catholic. Avocations: reading, travel, theater, dance, movies. Office: Johns Hopkins U Sch Nursing 525 N Wolfe St Baltimore MD 21205 Office Phone: 410-502-2606. Personal E-mail: vpnjie@aol.com. Business E-Mail: vnjiel@son.jhmi.edu.

NJOKU, SCHOLASTICA IBARI, retired college librarian, writer; d. David Mgbahuruike Njoku and Elizabeth Ekeoma Ukaegbu; divorced; children: Anthony, Emelia, Martina, Iheanyi, Chinedu, Onyekachi. BA cum laude in English, Wiley Coll., 1963; MLS, U. Oreg., 1965, MS in Edn., 1967, PhD in Edn., 1969; diploma in writing for children and teenagers, Inst. Children's Lit., Conn., 1996. Ref. libr. Knapp Libr. Project, Portland, Oreg., 1965—66; asst. edn. libr. Portland State U., 1969—70; assoc. prof. edn. Miss. Valley State Coll., Itta Bena, 1970—72; ref. cons. Oreg. State Libr., Salem, 1974—81, on-line cataloger, 1981—86; ref. libr. Portland C.C., 1986—2003; ret., 2003. Multicultural mentoring com. Portland C.C., 1996—2003, ednl. adv. coun. com., 1999—2003, women history planning com., 1999—2003. Author: The Miracle of A Christmas Doll, 1986, Dog What?, 1989; contbr. poems to poetry anthologies. Recipient 3d prize Poetry award, Ann. Reader's Digest, United Negro Coll. Fund, 1963. Mem.: ALA, The Willamette Writers,

Pacific NW Libr. Assn., Oreg. State Poetry Assn., Am. Assn. Higher Edn., Oreg. Libr. Assn., Delta Sigma Theta (Sisterhood award 2006). Democrat. Roman Catholic. Avocations: gardening, story telling, reading, writing. Home: 307 NE Holland St Portland OR 97211

NNADI, EUCHARIA E., academic administrator; BS in Pharmacy, Creighton U., 1977; MS in Hosp. Pharmacy, U. Minn., 1978, PhD in Social and Adminstrv. Pharmacy, 1982; JD with high honors, Fla. State U., 1993. Lic. pharmacist. Asst. prof. pharmacy adminstrn. Coll. Pharmacy and Pharm. Scis. Fla. A&M U., Tallahassee, 1981—89, prof., 1989—94, dean, 1994; former dean Coll. Pharmacy and Pharm. Scis. Howard U.; v.p. acad. affairs U. Md. Ea. Shore, Princess Anne. Reviewer health affairs divsn. Tex. Higher Edn. Coordinating Bd. Contbr. articles to profl. jours., chpts. to books. Recipient Pharmacist award, Md. Pharm. Soc., 1996. Mem.: Nat. Assn. Bds. Pharmacy (item writer), Am. Coun. on Pharm. Edn. (accreditation site visits team for colls. and schs. pharmacy), Nat. Assn. State Univs. and Land-Grant Colls. (coun. acad. affairs), Order of Coif, Rho Chi.

NNAEMEKA, OBIOMA GRACE, French language and women's studies educator, consultant, researcher; b. Agulu, Anambra, Nigeria; came to U.S., 1974; d. Christopher Egbunike and Jessie Ifemelue (Ogbuefi) Obidiegwu; children: Ike, Uchenna. BA with honors, U. Nigeria, Nsukka, 1972; MA, U. Minn., 1977, PhD with distinction, 1989. Rsch. fellow U. Nigeria, 1972-74, lectr., 1982-87; asst. prof. Concordia Coll., Minn., 1988-89, Coll. Wooster, Ohio, 1989-91; assoc. prof. Ind. U., Indpls., 1991—2000, prof., 2000—. Cons. Govt. Senegal, Dakar, 1990-92; commentator Internat. Svc. Radio Netherlands, Hilversum, 1990—; Edith Kreeger Wolf Disting. prof. Northwestern U., 1992. Author: Agrippa d'Aubigné: The Poetics of Power and Change, 1998; editor: The Politics of Mothering, 1996, Sisterhood, Feminisms, & Power, 1997; contbr. articles to profl. jours. Founder, pres. Assn. African Women's Scholars, 1995; convener, organizer First Internat. Conf. Women in Africa & African Diaspora, 1992. Named Achiever of Yr. Leadership Nigeria Network, 1994; grantee from McArthur Found, Rockefeller Found., Swedish Internat. Devel. Agy., Swedish Agy. for Rsch. Cooperation with Developing Countries, 1991-92. Mem. Am. Assn. Tchrs. French, Ind. Fgn. Lang. Tchrs. Assn., Modern Langs. Assn., African Studies Assn., African Lit. Assn. Avocations: reading, travel. Office: Ind U Dept Fgn Langs Cultrs 425 University Blvd Indianapolis IN 46202-5148 E-mail: waad@iupui.edu.

NOAH, JULIA JEANINE, retired librarian; b. Craig, Mo., July 14, 1932; d. Hiram Curtis and Eloise Julia (Puckett) True; m. Raymond Laverne Noah, Sept. 5, 1954; children: David Scott, Danny Ray, Deborah Jill, Douglas True. BS, U. Ill., 1953; MA in Library Sci., U. South Fla., 1983. Asst. rsch. librarian Parke, Davis & Co., Detroit, 1953-55; cataloging librarian U. Mo., Columbia, 1955-57; sch. librarian High Point Elem. Sch., Clearwater, Fla., 1968; library aide Clearwater High Sch., 1973-78; reference asst. Dunedin (Fla.) Pub. Library, 1978-84, dir. info. svcs., 1984-88, library dir., 1988-94; ret. Mem. DAR, Fla. Libr. Assn., Pinellas Genealogy Soc., Nat. Soc. Colonial Dames XVII Century, Daus. of Union Vets. of the Civil War 1861-1865, Nat. Soc. Magna Charta Dames, Nat. Soc. Women Descendants of the Ancient and Hon. Artillery Co., Nat. Soc. Daus. of Founders and Patriots of Am., Phi Kappa Phi, Beta Phi Mu Republican. Presbyterian. Avocations: antiques, genealogy.

NOAKES, BETTY LAVONNE, retired elementary school educator; b. Oklahoma City, Aug. 28, 1938; d. Webster L. and Willie Ruth (Johnson) Hawkins; m. Richard E. Noakes, Apr. 22, 1962 (dec.); 1 child, Michele Monique. Student, Oklahoma City U., MEd, 1971; BS, Cen. State U., 1962; postgrad., Cen. State U., Okla. State U. Elem. tchr. Merced (Calif.) Pub. Schs., 1966-67, Oklahoma City Schs., 1971-73, Mid-Del Schs., Midwest City, Okla., 1973-95; founder, owner Noakes-I Care Day Care, 1995—2002. 2d v.p. PTA, Pleasant Hill, 1991, cert. recognition, 1992-93; active Nat. PTA, 1991-92; charter mem. Nat. Mus. of Am. Indian-Smithsonian Instn.; chmn. stewardship com. Quayle U. Meth. Ch., 1997—; mem. Wesley Found. bd. Langston U.; mem. Urban League, Urban League Guild, YWCA, Nat. Law Enforcement Mus.; judge for Miss Black Oklahoma City Contest. Recipient Cert. Appreciation YMCA, 1992-92, Disting. Svc. award Mid-Del PTA, 1992. Mem. NEA, AAUW, NAACP, NAFE, LWV, Okla. Edn. Assn., Nat. Ret. Tchrs. Assn., Okla. Ret. Tchrs. Assn., Smithsonian Instn., Oklahoma City U. Alumni Assn., United Meth. Women Assn., Ctrl. State U. Alumni Assn., Okla. Order Ea. Star, Order of the Golden Cir. (aux. of Great We. Consistory 34 Dorcas-LL Golden Ci. assembly 41, Standard Bearer), Daus. of Isis (outside spy), Queen Alaraf Ct. 69 (dau. Isis Gala Day 2006), Masonic Ensemble Chantress Choir Alaraf Court 69, Phi Delta Kappa (Dean of Pledges, Soror of Yr., Gamma Epsilon chpt. 2005, Regional Soror of Yr. 2005), Zeta Phi Beta (1st v.p., Zeta of Yr., Chi Zeta chpt. 2000-01). Avocations: aerobics, singing, piano, clarinet, folk dancing. Home: 5956 N Coltrane Rd Oklahoma City OK 73121-3409 E-mail: nblnzeta@sbcglobal.net.

NOBERT, FRANCES, music educator; b. Winston-Salem, N.C., Dec. 12, 1936; d. Henry Carrington and Frances Mozelle (Harrison) Cuningham; m. Jon Marshall Nobert (div. Jan. 1980). BM in Music Edn., Salem Coll., 1959; Fulbright Cert. in Organ, Conservatory of Music, Frankfurt am Main, Germany, 1961; MM in Organ, Syracuse U., 1963; DMA in Choral Music, U. So. Calif., 1980. Organist, choir dir. United Ch., Fayetteville, N.Y., 1961-67; choral, gen. music tchr. Fayetteville Manlius Sch. Dist., 1963-67; vocal music tchr. U.S. Grant HS, Van Nuys, Calif., 1967-80; organist United Ch. Christ Congregational, Claremont, Calif., 1981-83; organist, choir dir. St. Matthias Episc. Ch., Whittier, Calif., 1983-94; organist First United Meth. Ch., Pasadena, Calif., 2000—03; prof. music, coll. organist Whittier Coll., 1982-98, coord. women's studies, 1995-98, disting. svc. prof. music, 1998—99, prof. emerita, 1999—. Singer L.A. Master Chorale, 1972-86; vis. instr. of key bd. theory, L.A. Valley Coll., Van Nuys, 1980-81, spring 1982; bd. dirs., program chair, sub-dean, dean Pasadena chpt. Am. Guild of Organists, Calif., 1991-95, dean, 1998-99, south coast dist. convenor, 1999-2004, Region IX councillor, 2004—; v.p. Mader Corp., 2005-; resident dir. for Denmark's Internat. Study Program, Whittier Coll., 1994. Faculty Rsch. grantee Whittier Coll., 1984, devel. grantee, 1986, 88, 90, 91, 93. 96, 97, Irvine grantee, 1995. Mem. NOW, Internat. Alliance for Women in Music (treas. 1997-2000, v.p. 2000-03), Am. Guild Organists, Organ Hist. Soc., Rio Hondo Symphony Guild, Whittier Cultural Arts Found., Mader Corp., Feminist Majority, Pi Kappa Lambda, Mu Phi Epsilon. Episcopalian. Avocations: travel, languages. Personal E-mail: fnobert99organ@aol.com.

NOBLE, KARYN SUE, elementary school educator; b. Merrillville, Ind., Nov. 10, 1977; d. David Lee Hodges and Sally Jean Collins, Robert Collins (Stepfather) and Gail Hodges (Stepmother); m. Gregory Elliot Noble, June 2, 2001 (div. Apr. 18, 2006). BA in Elem. Edn., Purdue U., Hammond, Ind., 2002; MA in Literacy Edn., Concordia U., 2005. Cert. tchr. Nebr. Dept. Edn., 2002, Ind. Dept. Edn., 2002, reading specialist endorsement Nebr. Dept. Edn., 2004. Tchr. reading Ralston (Nebr.) Pub. Schs., 2002—05; tchr. elem. sch. Elkhorn (Nebr.) Pub. Schs., 2005—. Instr. coll. for kids Metropolitan C.C., Omaha, 2005—; instr. summer sch. Ralston (Nebr.) Pub. Schs., 2003—04. Mem.: Internat. Reading Assn. Democrat. Achievements include development of intervention program for struggling readers; design of a series of guided reading workshops for in-service days with classroom teachers. Avocations: reading, exercise, travel, music, dance. Home: 18642 O Street Omaha NE 68135

NOBLE, PAMELA LEE, primatologist; b. Honolulu, Aug. 9, 1968; d. Charles Clifford and Patrica Lee (Hammond) Noble; children: Amanda Lee, Griffin Earl. OAS, Pima C.C., 1995; BA in Anthropology and Psychology with honors, U. Ariz., 1999; postgrad., Ga. Inst. Tech., 1999—2000; MBA postgrad, Univ. Phoenix, 2005. Tutor Pima C.C., Tucson, 1993-96; intern, rschr. Jane Goodall Inst., 1996-98, Dian Fossey Gorilla Fund, 1997—; rsch. assoc. TECHLAB, Zoo Atlanta, 1999—2000; sr. rsch. specialist, psychol. Yerkes Primate Center, 2000—03; projects mgr., neurobiology NIMH Intramural Rsch. Program, 2003—. Guest lectr. grad. level animal behavior U. Ariz., 1997. Contbg. author The Scholastic Tradition, 1993, The Jane Goodall Institute World Report, 1997, Ark Animals online mag.; asst. editor ChimpanZoo Newsletter, 1996, 97, asst. editor conf. procs., 1995, 96; contbr. articles to profl. jours. Spkr. Casa Niños Montessori Sch., Tucson, 1996-97. Ariz. State Champion Women's Flying 200 Meter and Women's 500 Meter Track Racing, 1999. Mem. So. Ariz. Mountain Biking Assn., Golden Key Nat. Honor Soc. Avocations: mountain biking, wine tasting, cooking. Office: NIHAC Bldg 110 Rm 119 16701 Elmer School Rd Poolesville MD 20837 Home: 5035 St Simon Terr Frederick MD 21703 Office Phone: 301-451-2195. Business E-Mail: noblep@mail.gov.

NOBLE, SUNNY A., business owner; b. Moorhead, Minn., May 22, 1940; m. Eric Scott Noble, Apr. 11, 1980. MBA, U. Calif., Berkeley, 1960; qualified parapsychologist, U. Minn., 1979. Mgr. Spear & Hill Attys., N.Y.C., 1969-70; mgr. exec. property mgmt. May Co. Dept. Stores, La Jolla, Calif., 1981-82; owner, pres. The Computer Tutor, L.A., 1984—94; freelance portrait artist. Columnist: That Computes, 1984-88, The Storyteller, 1987-91, Chit-Chat, The Westside Examiner, 1996-97; author stage plays: The Garlic Eater (Writer's Digest Mag. nat. writing competition award 1998), Mother's Day (Writer's Digest Mag. nat. writing competition award 1998); (screen play) The Tangled Web; editor: From Book Signing to Best Seller. Recipient Short Story award, Palm Springs Writer's Guild, 2001. Mem.: DAR, Internat. Platform Assn., Dramatists Guild, Safe Harbor Writers Workshop, Mensa, Toastmasters Internat. (ednl. v.p. 1988), Beta Sigma Phi. Home and Office: 4152 W Ave L-2 Quartz Hill CA 93536 Personal E-mail: syber.snob@verizon.net.

NOBLITT, NANCY ANNE, aerospace engineer; b. Roanoke, Va., Aug. 14, 1959; d. Jerry Spencer and Mary Louise (Jerrell) N. BA, Mills Coll., Oakland, Calif., 1982; MS in Indsl. Engring., Northeastern U., 1990; JD, Coll. William and Mary, 2003. Data red specialist Universal Energy Sys., Beaver Creek, Ohio, 1981; aerospace engr. turbine engine divsn. components br. turbine group aero-propulsion lab. Wright-Patterson AFB, Ohio, 1982-84, engine assessment br. spl. engines group, 1984-87; lead analyst cycle methods computer aided engr. GE, Lynn, Mass., 1987-90, Lynn PACES project coord., 1990-91; software sys. analyst Sci. Applications Internat. Corp., with artificial intelligence McLean, Va., 1991-92, software engring. mgr., intelligence applications integration Hampton, Va., 1992-93, mgr. test engring. and sys. support, 1993-94, mgr. configuration mgmt., 1994, mgmt. asst. to TBMCS program mgr., 1994-95; sr. simulation engr. Chem Demil, 1995-98; supervisory engr. Analytical Mechanics Assocs., Hampton, 1998-99; sr. project engr. Newport News (Va.) Shipbuilding Inc., 1999-00; quality assurance mgr. Sci. Applications Internat. Corp., 2005—. Tutor math. and sci. Centerville Sch. Bd., Ohio, 1982-86; tutor math. and physics Marblehead Sch. Bd., Mass., 1988-90; tutor math., chemistry and physics Poquoson Sch. Bd., Va., 1994—; rep. alumnae admissions Boston area Mills Coll., 1987-91, trustee, bd. govs., 1995-98; mem. Citizens for Hilton Area Revitalization, 1994—. Math. and sci. tutor Centerville Sch. Bd., Ohio, 1982-86, math. and physics tutor Marblehead (Mass.) Sch. Bd., 1988-90; tutor math., chemistry and physics Poquoson Sch. Bd., Va., 1994—; rep. alumnae admissions Mills Coll., Boston area, 1987-91, trustee/bd. govs., 1995-98; mem. Citizens for Hilton Area Revitalization, 1994—. Recipient Notable Achievement award USAF, 1984, Spl. award Fed. Lab. Consortium, 1987. Mem. Soc. Mfg. Engrs., Sports and Entertainment Law Soc., Phi Alpha Delta. Avocation: book collecting. Home: 58 Hopkins St Newport News VA 23601-4034 Office: SAIC Suffolk VA 23535 Office Phone: 757-686-9815.

NOBUMOTO, KAREN S., prosecutor; BA, U. Hartford, 1973; JD Southwestern U., 1989. Dep. dist. atty. County of L.A. Named Unsung Hero, KFWB Radio, 1997, Prosecutor of Yr., Century City Bar Assn., 1998, Person of Yr., Met. News-Enterprise, 2001, Lawyer of Yr., Calif. Lawyer Mag., 2003, Alumna of Yr., Southwestern U., 2003, Super Lawyer, L.A. mag., 2004. Mem.: L.A. County Bar Assn., Calif. Assn. Black Lawyers, Assn. Dep. Dist. Attys., Black Women Lawyers L.A., Women Lawyers Assn. L.A., John M. Langston Bar Assn. (pres. 1997), State Bar Calif. (pres. 2001—02), Coalition 100 Black Women, Breakfast Club, Chancery Club. Office: LA Dist Attys Office 210 W Temple St Ste 18000 Los Angeles CA 90012-3210 Office Phone: 310-288-1246. E-mail: karennobu@aol.com.

NOCE, DONNA, retail executive; With Petrie Stores, Lerner NY; merchandising v.p. separates, dresses and suits Ann Taylor Stores, 1996—2000; v.p. merchandising and planning AnnTaylor.com, 2000—02; v.p. Ann Taylor Factory Stores, 2002, sr. v.p.; exec. v.p. merchandising and design Ann Taylor LOFT, 2006—. Office: Ann Taylor Stores Corp 7 Times Square 15th Fl New York NY 10036*

NOCHLIN, LINDA, art history educator; b. NYC, Jan. 30, 1931; d. Jules and Elka (Heller) Weinberg; m. Philip Nochlin (dec. 1960); 1 child, Jessica; m. Richard Pommer, June 3, 1968; 1 child, Daisy. BA in philosophy, Vassar Coll., 1951; MA in English, Columbia U., 1952; PhD in art history, NYU Inst. Fine Arts, 1963; doctorate (hon.), Mass. Coll. Art, Parsons Sch. Design, Colgate U., 1987; LittD (hon.), Harvard U., 2003. Instr. Vassar Coll., Poughkeepsie, NY, 1952-63, asst. prof., 1963-66, assoc. prof., 1966-69, prof., 1969-71, Mary Conover Mellon Prof. Art History, 1971-79; disting. prof. art history CUNY, 1980—90; prof. art history and humanities Yale U., 1990—92, Robert Lehman Prof. Art History; Lila Acheson Wallace Prof. Modern Art NYU Inst. Fine Arts, NYC, 1993—. Vis. prof. Columbia U., NYC, 1967-68, 75-76, Hunter Coll., NYC, 1970, Stanford U., 1971, CUNY Grad. Ctr., NYC, 1975-76; mem. editl. bd. Yale Jour. Criticism, Vassar Quarterly. Author: (essay) Why Have There Been No Great Women Artists?, 1971, (books) Realism and Tradition in Art, 1948-1900, 1966, Realism, 1971, 1993, Women as Sex Object: Studies in Erotic Art, 1730-1970, 1972, Women, Art and Power and Other Essays, 1988, The Politics of Vision: Essays on Nineteenth-Century Art and Society, 1989, The Body in Pieces: The Fragment as Metaphor of Modernity, 1994, Representing Women, 1999; co-editor: The Jew in Text: Modernity and Construction of Identity, 1995; Co-curator/co-author (with Anne Sutherland Harris) (exhibition and catalogue) Women Artists: 1550-1950, LA County Mus. Art, 1976. Named Scholar of Yr., NY State Coun. for Humanities, 1997; recipient Harbison Award for gifted teaching, Danforth Found., 1972, Woman of Yr. Award, Mademoiselle Mag., 1977, Disting. Svc. to the Visual Arts Award, ArtTable, 2003; Fulbright Fellowship, 1958—59, Fels Fellowship, 1962—63, Am. Coun. Learned Societies Fellowship, 1972—73, NEH Fellowship, 1977—78, Guggenheim Fellowship, 1984—85, Inst. Advanced Studies Fellowship, 1985, Resident Fellowship Bellagio Study and Conf. Ctr., Rockefeller Found., 1999, Self and History: A Symposium in Honor of Linda Nochlin presented at NYU, 1999. Fellow: Am. Philos. Soc., Am. Acad. Arts and Sciences; mem.: Am. Assn. Univ. Professors, Coll. Art Assn. (Arthur Kingsley Porter Prize for article Gustave Courbet's Meeting: A Portrait as a Wandering Jew 1968, Frank Jewett Mather Prize 1978, Ann. Recognition Award, Com. on Women and the Arts 1998), NOW, Phi Beta Kappa. Office: NYU Inst Fine Arts James B Duke House 1 E 78th St New York NY 10021

NOCHMAN, LOIS WOOD KIVI (MRS. MARVIN NOCHMAN), retired literature educator; b. Detroit, Nov. 5, 1924; d. Peter K. and Annetta Lois (Wood) Kivi; m. Harold I. Pitchford, Sept. 6, 1944 (div. May 1949); children: Jean Wood Pitchford Scott, Joyce Lynn Pitchford Undiano; m. Marvin A. Nochman, Aug. 15, 1953; 1 child, Joseph Asa. AB, U. Mich., 1946, AM, 1949. Tchr. adult edn., Honolulu, 1947, Ypsilanti (Mich.) H.S., 1951—52; spl. instr. English Wayne State U., Detroit, 1953—54; tchr. Highland Park (Mich.) Coll., 1950—51, instr. English, 1954—83; ret., 1983. Mem. exec. bd. Highland Park Fedn. Tchrs., 1963—66, 1973, del. to nat. conv., 64, 1971—74; rep. higher edn. Mich. Fedn. Tchrs. Exec. Com., 1972—76; mem. faculty adv. com. Gov's Commn. Higher Edn., 1973—. Contbr. articles to profl. jours. Tchr. Baha'i Schs., Davison, Mich., 1954—55, 1958—59, 1963—66, Beaulac, Que., Canada, 1960, Greenacre, Maine, 1965; sec. local spiritual assembly Baha'is, Ann Arbor, Mich., 1953, sec. Detroit, 1954, chmn., 1955; mem. nat. com. Baha'is U.S., 1955—58; sec. com. and coun. Baha'i Schs., Davison, Mich., 1956, 1958, 1963—68; Baha'i lectr. subject of local TV show Senior Focus, 1992. Recipient Women's Movement plaque, Women Lawyers Assn. Mich., 1975. Mem.: MLA, NOW, Nat. Soc. Lit. and Arts, Am. Fedn. Tchrs., Mich. Coll. English Assn., Nat. Coun. Tchrs. English, Women's Equity and Action League (sec. Mich. chpt. 1975—79), Alpha Gamma Delta, Alpha Lambda Delta. Avocation: U.S. Swimming Master Champion.

NODDINGS, NEL, education educator, writer; b. Irvington, N.J., Jan. 19, 1929; d. Edward A. Rieth and Nellie A. (Connors) Walter; m. James A. Noddings, Aug. 20, 1949; children: Chris, Howard, Laurie, James, Nancy, William, Sharon, Edward, Vicky, Timothy. BA in Math., Montclair State Coll., 1949; MA in Math., Rutgers U., 1964; PhD in Edn., Stanford U., 1973; PhD (hon.), Columbia Coll., S.C., 1995; LLD (hon.), Queen's U., Can., 2006; LHD (hon.), Montclair State U., 2006. Cert. tchr. Calif., NJ. Tchr. Woodbury (N.J.) Pub. Schs., 1949-52; tchr. math. dept. Matawan (N.J.) High Sch., 1958-62, chair, asst. prin., 1964-69; curriculum supr. Montgomery Twp. Pub. Schs., Skillman, NJ, 1970-72; dir. precollegiate edn. U. Chgo., 1975-76; asst. prof. Pa. State U., State College, 1973; from asst. prof. to assoc. prof. Stanford (Calif.) U., 1977-86, prof., 1986—, assoc. dean, 1990-92, acting dean, 1992-94, Lee L. Jacks prof. child edn., 1992-98, prof. emeritus, 1998—; prof. philosophy and edn. Columbia U., N.Y.C., 1998—. Bd. dirs. Ctr. for Human Caring Sch. Nursing, Denver, 1986-92; cons. NIE, NSF and various other sch. dists. Author: Caring: A Feminine Approach to Ethics and Moral Education, 1984, Women and Evil, 1989; author: (with W. Paul Shore) Awakening the Inner Eye: Intuition in Education, 1984; author: (with Carol Witherell) Stories Lives Tell, 1991; author: The Challenge to Care in Schools, 1992, Educating for Intelligent Belief or Unbelief, 1993, Philosophy of Education, 1995, Starting at Home: Caring and Social Policy, 2002, Educating Moral People, 2002, Happiness and Education, 2003; editor (with Suzanne Gordon and Patricia Benner): Caregiving, 1996; editor: (with Michael Katz and Kenneth Strike) Justice and Caring, 1999; editor: Educating Citizens for Global Awareness, 2005, Critical Lessons: What Our Schools Should Teach, 2006. Mem. disting. women's adv. bd. Coll. St. Catherine. Recipient Anne Roe award for Contbns. to Profl. Devel. of Women, Harvard Grad. Sch. Edn., 1993, medal for disting. svc. Tchrs. Coll. Columbia, 1994, Willystine Goodsell award, 1997, Laureate chpt. Kappa Delta Pi, Pi Lambda Theta award, 1999, award for disting. leadership in edn. Rutgers U., 2004; Spencer Mentor grantee, Spencer Found., 1995-97. Fellow Philosophy of Edn. Soc. (pres. 1991-92); mem. Am. Ednl. Rsch. Assn. (Div B, 2000, Lifetime achievment award), Am. Philos. Assn., Nat. Acad. Edn. (pres. 2001—), John Dewey Soc. (pres. 1994-96), Phi Beta Kappa (vis. scholar). Avocation: gardening. Office Phone: 732-988-9695. Business E-Mail: noddings@stanford.edu.

NODDINGS, SARAH ELLEN, lawyer; b. Matawan, NJ; d. William Clayton and Sarah Stephenson (Cox) Noddings; children: Christopher, Aaron. BA in Math., Rutgers U., New Brunswick, N.J., 1965, MSW, 1968; JD cum laude, Seton Hall U., Newark, 1975; postgrad., UCLA, 1979. Bar: Calif. 1976, Nev. 1976, N.J. 1975, U.S. Dist. Ct. (ctrl. dist.) Calif. 1976, U.S. Dist. Ct. N.J. 1975. Social worker Carteret (N.J.) Bd. Edn., 1970-75; law clk. Hon. Howard W. Babcock, 8th Jud. Dist. Ct., Las Vegas, Nev., 1975-76; assoc. O'Melveny & Myers, L.A., 1976-78; atty. Internat. Creative Mgmt., Beverly Hills, Calif., 1978-81, Russell & Glickman, Century City, Calif., 1981-83; from atty to v.p. Lorimar Prodns., Culver City and Burbank, Calif., 1983—93; atty., v.p. Warner Bros. TV, Burbank, Calif., 1993—2001, sr. atty., 1999-2001; pvt. practice, 2001—. Dir. county youth program, rsch. analyst Sonoma County People for Econ. Opportunity, Santa Rosa, Calif., 1968-69; VISTA vol. Kings County Cmty. Action Orgn., Hanford, Calif., 1965-66; officer, PTA bd. West H.S., Casimir Mid. Sch. and Arlington Elem. Sch. Mem.: USTA (capt.), Media Dist. Intellectual Property Bar Assn. (bd. dir. 1999—2001), L.A. County Bar Assn. (intellectual property sect.), Women Entertainment Lawyers, Acad. TV Arts and Scis. (nat. awards com. 1994—96), L.A. Copyright Soc. (trustee 1990—91), Women in Film, South Bay Marine League (B-2 rep.). Avocations: travel, tennis, skiing, bicycling, swimming.

NODEEN, JANEY PRICE, information technology executive; b. Scotland Neck, NC, Nov. 7, 1959; d. Wade Hampton and Joyce Ann (Councill) P.; m. Thomas Nodeen. BS in Info. Sci., Christopher Newport Coll., 1987; grad., Def. Sys. Mgmt. Coll., 1994; grad. advanced mgmt. program, Nat. Def. U., 1995. Engring. analyst Newport News (Va.) Shipbldg., 1978-86; mgr. submarine info. resources and computer ops. Dept. of the Navy, Washington, 1986-93, mem. exec. devel. program, 1993-96, sr. staff Navy Acquisition Reform Exec., 1995, dep. program exec. officer Submarines for Acquisition, 1996-97; prin. Burke Consortium, Inc., Springfield, Va., 1997—. Mil. legis. fellow for Congressman Sam Gejdenson, 1994; sr. exec. fellow John F. Kennedy Sch. Govt. Harvard U., class officer, 1994. Home: 6915 Ashbury Dr Springfield VA 22152-3221 Office: Burke Consortium Inc Ste 510 5500 Cherokee Ave Alexandria VA 22312

NOE, ADRIANNE, museum administrator; PhD in History, U. Del. Assoc. dir. Armed Forces Inst. Pathology; dir. Nat. Mus. Health and Medicine, Washington. Adj. prof. computational biosciences George Mason U., Fairfax County, Va.; v.p. bd. dirs. Nat. Health Sci. Consortium. Fellow, Guggenheim Found.; History fellow, USAF. Mem.: Med. Mus. Assn. (past pres.), Washington Soc. for the History of Medicine (pres.), Acad. Medicine. Office: Nat Mus Health and Medicine Bldg 54 6825 16th St NW Washington DC 20306-6000

NOE, ELIZABETH HARDY, lawyer; b. Albertville, Ala., Sept. 24, 1964; d. John William and Nancy Jo (Luther) Hardy; m. George McRae Noe, Nov. 6, 1993. BA, Agnes Scott Coll., 1986; JD, U. Va., 1989. Bar: La. 1989, Ga. 1996. Assoc. Jones, Walker, Waechter, Poitevent, Carrere & Denegre, New Orleans, 1989-94; of counsel Paul, Hastings, Janofsky & Walker, Atlanta, 1995—, mem. policy com., co-chmn. atty. devel., ptnr., 2001—. Mem. ABA, La. Bar Assn., Ga. Bar Assn. Office: Paul Hastings Janofsky & Walker 600 Peachtree St NE Ste 2400 Atlanta GA 30308-2265 Office Phone: 404-815-2287. Business E-Mail: elizabethnoe@paulhastings.com.

NOE, ELNORA (ELLIE NOE), retired chemicals executive; b. Evansville, Ind., Aug. 23, 1928; d. Thomas Noe and Evelyn (West) Dieter. Student, Ind. U.-Purdue U., Indpls. Sec. Pitman Moore Co., Indpls., 1946—60; with Dow Chem. Co., Indpls., 1960-90, pub. rels. asst. then mgr. employee comm., 1970-87, mgr. cmty. rels., 1987-90, DowBrands, Inc., Indpls., 1986-90, vice chmn. Indpls. C. of C. corp. affairs discussion group, 1988—89, chmn., 1989-90; mem. steering com. Learn About Bus. Recipient 2d pl. award as Businesswoman of Yr., Indpls. Bus. and Profl. Women's Assn., 1980, Indpls. Profl. Woman of Yr. award Zonta, Altrusa, Soroptomist & Pilot Svc. Clubs, 1985, DowBrands Great Things Cmty. Svc. award, 1991. Mem. Am. Bus. Women Assn. (Woman of Yr. award 1965, past pres.), Ind. Assn. Bus. Communicators (hon., Communicator of Yr. 1977), Assn. Women in Comm. (Louise Eleanor Kleinhenz award 1984), Zonta (dist. pub. rels. chmn. 1978-80, area dir. 1980-82, pres. Indpls. club 1977-79, bd. dirs. 1993-95, 2000-02, 04-06, v.p. 2006—), Dow Indpls. Retiree Group (pres. 1995—). Personal E-mail: elenoe@aol.com.

NOE, JOYCE M., architecture educator; BArch, U. Ill., 1964; M in Design Studies with distinction, Harvard U., 1998. Lic. arch., Hawaii. Assoc. prof. Arch. Sch. U. Hawaii, Honolulu, 1982—, assoc. dean, prof., practice program dir. Mem. City and County of Honolulu Bldg. Bd. Appeals, chair, 1983; mem. preservation rev. com. hist. structures Historic Hawaii Found.; mem. Mayor's Vision 2000 Team. Mem.: AIA (Honolulu chpt. urban design and profl. devel. coms., Honolulu chpt. Design award 1980, Nat. Educator award 1997), AIA Students, Gargoyle Archs. Honor Soc. Office: Univ Hawaii Sch Arch 2410 Campus Rd Honolulu HI 96822

NOEL, BARBARA HUGHES MCMURTRY, retired music educator; b. Mt. Vernon, Wash., Feb. 27, 1929; d. Lowell Robinson and Mary Evelyn (Hayton) Hughes; children: Sarah Kathleen, Martha Elizabeth. BM, U. Ky., 1951, MM, 1952; PhD, U. Ill., 1972; student, Oberlin Conservatory, 1947-49. Instr. music Union Coll., Barbourville, Ky., 1952-54; instr. music and fine arts Annie Wright Sem., Tacoma, 1957-63; organist, choirmaster Episc. churches,

Calif., Wash., 1954-66; chmn. music dept. U. Richmond (Va.), 1971-76, Mankato (Minn.) State U., 1976-78; dean coll. humanities and fine arts Tex. Woman's U., Denton, 1978-81; dean coll. visual and performing arts U. Mass. Dartmouth, North Dartmouth, 1981-89; prof. music U. Mass., Dartmouth, 1990—96, ret., 1996. Cons. for various music orgns. and univs., 1976—, textbook pubs., 1980—; reviewer Nat. Endowment for the Humanities. Book reviewer Providence Sunday Jour., 1984—; contbr. articles to music jours.; contbr. New Grove Dictionary of Music, 1974. Bd. dirs. Community Symphony Orchs., Mankato, 1976-78, New Bedford, Mass., 1981-87. Grad. fellow Danforth Found., U. Ill., 1966-71. Mem. Coll. Music Soc. (treas. 1983-87, v.p. 1979-83, coun. mem.), Nat. Assn. Schs. Music (undergrad. commr. 1978-81). Episcopalian. Avocations: reading, travel, hiking. Home: 301 Linden Ponds Way BC 521 Hingham MA 02043

NOEL, CAROL ADELE, music educator, opera singer; d. Albert Edgar and Adelaide L. Noel. MusB, Boston Conservation of Music, 1962; MusM, Northwestern U., Ill., 1970. Cert. K-12 tchr. Ill., Tex., music and elem. edn. K-9th grade. Opera singer State Opera House of Rendsburg & Hagen Germany, 1965—67; music tchr. Chgo. Pub. Schs., 1971—; wind ensemble Chgo. Wind Ensemble, 1977; soloist Southwest Allied Arts Assn., Chgo., 1982; opera singer Lyric Opera of Chgo., 1989. Choir dir. Posen Sch. Choir, Ill., 1982; music dir. Grant Cmty. Acad., Chgo., 1995—98; chorus dir. Thorp Elem. Sch., Chgo., 2005—. Recipient Alderman Pacini award, First Pl. in vocal; grantee Voice Scholarship, Roary Coll. Mem.: AARP, Chgo. Tchrs. Union, Music Educators Nat. Conf., German Theatre Union, Actors Equity Assn., Am. Guild of Musical Artists. Avocations: travel, theater, dance, concerts, museums. Home: 6629 S Whipple St Chicago IL 60629-2925 Personal E-mail: cancatlady11@aol.com.

NOEL, CHERYL ELAINE, artist, poet; b. Syracuse, N.Y., Oct. 1, 1954; d. Arthur Raymond and Alice Thane N. BA in Philosophy, Randolph-Macon Women's Coll., 1978; postgrad., Lynchburg Coll. Rehab. counselor Hudson House, Lynchburg, Va.; waitress The Ground Round, Lynchburg; tchr. modern dance Campbell County Dept. Recreation, Lynchburg; asst. mgr. Burgerette, Inc., Lynchburg; staff counselor Camp Zarahemela, Clintwood, Va.; inventory counter GE, Lynchburg, copper plating processor. Author: poems; dancer traveling dance theater, Randolph-Macon; exhibitions include Leagett at Randolph-Macon, featured, Randolph-Macon Alumnae Bull., 1978.

NOEL, KAREN ANN, science educator; d. Beverly Ann and Gary Joseph Narewski; m. John Harrison Noel, June 24, 1995; children: Paige Marie, Nicholas Mahlon. MS, SUNY, Oswego, 2001. Cert. sci. tchr. K-9 N.Y., 1993. 3d grade tchr. Fulton City Sch., NY, 1993—94, sci. tchr., 1997, sci. facilitator, 1998—, facilatator. Roman Catholic. Avocations: camping, baseball. Home: 1117 Utica St Fulton NY 13069 Office: Fulton City Sch 129 Curtis St Fulton NY 13069 Office Phone: 315-593-5440.

NOEL, MARY MARGARET, nutritionist, educator; b. Tacoma, July 13, 1948; d. Webster Young and Mary Leize Barth; m. George W. Noel, June 30, 1973; children: Katherine Mary, Joseph William. BS in Dietetics, Mich. State U., 1969; MPH, U. Mich., 1973; PhD in Family Ecology, Mich. Sate U., 1988. Registered dietitian. Intern in dietetics Barnes Med. Ctr., St. Louis, 1970; nutrition cons. Vis. Nurse Assn., St. Louis, 1970-72; clin. nutritionist U. Mich., Ann Arbor, 1973-76; instr. dietetics Mich. State U., East Lansing, 1975-76; cons. in nutrition East Lansing, 1976-86; exec. dir. Dairy Coun. of Mich., Okemos, 1986-88; asst. prof. dept. family practice, Coll. Human Medicine Mich. State U., East Lansing, 1988-93, assoc. prof., 1993—2000, prof., 2000—, assoc. chair dept., 1997—. Vol. Neighborhood Assn., East Lansing, 1983-97; bd. dirs., treas. Downtown Devel. Authority, East Lansing, 1986-96; vol. East Lansing Pub. Schs., 1982-98. Grantee, NIH, 1997—2001. Mem. Am. Dietetic Assn. (sect. sec. 1970—), Mich. Dietetic Assn. (parliamentarian 1972—, nominating com., Recognized Young Dietitian 1977), Soc. for Tchrs. of Family Medicine, Vis. Nurses of Lansing (vice chair, then chair 1987-91) Office: Mich State U Dept Family Practice Coll Human Medicin B101 Clin Ctr East Lansing MI 48824 Business E-Mail: noel@msu.edu.

NOËLDECHEN, JOAN MARGUERITE, writer; b. West Islip, NY, May 20, 1963; d. Warren G. Noëldechen and Joan Marguerite Walter. BA in English and Drama, Flagler Coll., St. Augustine, Fla., 1985. Author: (novel) Dreamers Out of Step, 1995, 00, (poetry) Ashes and Embers, 1996, (poetry) Ashes & Embers: Complete Poems, 2000, (poetry) Following Angels and Wolves, 1997, (novella) Eve's Song, 1997, 00,(anthologies) Bedside Prayers, 1997, Bless the Day, 1998, Trinity Poems, 1999, (screenplays) Takoma Blue, 2003, (screenplays) Borrowed Starling, 2004, (poetry) House Blessings, 2004, (poetry) Everyday Blessings, 2005, 06, (poetry) Beyond Katrina, 2005, (poetry) Pocket Prayers, 2006, (poetry) Forever in Love, 2006; co-author (with Silvi M. Richardson): And the Angels Sing, 1995, Shadowdance, 1996, Pasaquan Daze, 1996, (play) And the Angels Sing, 1996. Mem. Thomas Wolfe Soc. Avocations: reading, cooking, gardening, hiking, photography.

NOELDNER-WENIGER, LISA ANN, music educator; b. Watertown, S.D., Dec. 25, 1969; d. Eugene Wayne and Leone Annette Noeldner; m. Ronald Weniger, June 17, 1995. BS in Instrumental Music, S.W. State U., Marshall, Minn., 1993; MA in Instrumental Music, U. S.D., Vermillion, 1999. Dir. of bands Verndale Pub. Sch., Minn., 1993—98; dir. mid. sch. band Gibbon-Fairfax-Winthrop, Fairfax, 1999—2006; dir. of bands Wadena-Deer Creek, 2006—. Chairperson Prairie Winds Band, Willmar, Minn., 2001—04. Mem.: NEA, Edn. Minn., Minn. Band Dirs. Assoc., Minn. Music Edn. Assoc.

NOESEN, DARLENE DOROTHY, mathematics educator; b. Chgo., July 9, 1947; d. Leonard Michael and Mary Anna Noesen. BA Sociology, Loyola U., 1970; MA Math., Northeastern U., Chgo., 1985. Secondary Tchg.6-12 Ill. State Tchr. Certification Bd., 1985, Elem. Tchg. K-9 Ill. State Tchr. Certification Bd., 1970. Tchr. first grade St. Simeon, Bellwood, Ill., 1970—74; tchr. elem. sch. St. Benedict Elem. Sch., Chgo., 1974—87; math. educator St. Benedict H.S., 1987—90; chair math. dept. St. Hilary Sch., Chgo., 1990—98, St. Gregory H.S., Chgo., 1998—. Regional program dir. Sch. Sisters of St. Francis Assoc. Relationship. Dir. nat. office Women-Ch. Convergence, 1995—2001; coord. Chgo. Cath. Women, Chgo., 1982—94; founding mem. Chgo. Women-Ch., 1994—2007. Master: Nat. Honor Soc. (advisor 1987—2007). Roman Catholic. Avocations: photography, handbells & choir, reading, travel, camping, hiking, bicycling, skiing, swimming. Home: 2572 W Argyle St Chicago IL 60625

NOETH, CAROLYN FRANCES, speech and language pathologist; b. Cleve., July 21, 1924; d. Sam Falco and Barbara Serafina (Loparo) Armaro; m. Lawrence Andrew Noeth Sr., June 29, 1946; children: Lawrence Andrew Jr. (dec.), Barbara Marie. AB magna cum laude, Case Western Res. U., 1963; MEd, U. Ill., 1972; postgrad., Nat. Coll. Edn., 1975—. Lic. speech and lang. pathologist, Ill. Speech therapist Chgo. Pub. Schs., 1965; speech, lang. and hearing clinician J. Sterling Morton High Schs., Cicero and Berwyn, Ill., 1965-82, tchr. learning disabilities/behavior disorders, 1982, dist. ednl. diagnostician, 1982-84, Title I Project tchr., summers 1966-67, lang. disabilities cons., summers 1968-69, in-svc. tng. cons., summer 1970, dir. Title I Project, summers 1973-74; learning disabilities tchr. West Campus of Morton, 1971-75; chmn. Educable-Mentally Handicapped Opportunities Tchrs. Com., 1967-68; spl. edn. area and in-sch. tchrs. workshops, 1967—. Chmn. in compiling and publishing Student Handbook, Cleve. Coll., 1962; contbr. lyric parodies and music programs J. Sterling Morton H.S. West Retirement Teas, 1972-83. Precinct elections judge, 1953-55; block capt. Mothers March of Dimes and Heart Fund, 1949-60; St. Agatha's rep. Nat. Cath. Women's League, 1952-53; collector various charities, 1967, 93-94, 98, 99, 2000, 2001, 2002; mem. exec. bd. Morton Scholarship League, 1981-84, corr. sec., 1981-83; vol. Am. Cancer Soc., 1985—; vol. judge Ill. Acad. Decathlon, 1988—. First recipient Virda L. Stewart award for Speech, Western Res. U., 1963, Outstanding Sr. award, 1963. Mem. Am. Speech, Lang. and Hearing Assn. (life, cert.), Ill. Speech, Lang. and Hearing Assn. (life), Coun. Exceptional Children (divsn. for learning disabilities, pioneers divsn., chpt. spl. projects chmn., exec. bd. 1976-81, chpt. pres. 1979-80), Coun. for Learning Disabilities, Profls. in Learning Disabilities, Kappa Delta Pi, Delta Kappa Gamma (chmn., co-chmn. chpt. music com. 1979—, state program com. 1981-83, chpt. music rep. to state 1982—, chmn. chpt. promotion com. 1993-94, 96—), St. Norbert's Women's Club (Northbrook, Ill.), Case-Western Res. U., U. Ill. Alumni Assns., Lions (vol. Northbrook 1966-93). Roman Catholic. Home and Office: 1849 Walnut Cir Northbrook IL 60062-1245

NOFFSINGER, NANCY LEIGH, special education educator; b. Princeton, Ky., Oct. 20, 1948; d. Charlie H. and Margaree (Oates) N. BS, Murray (Ky.) State U., 1980, masters equivalent, 1982, postgrad., 1987. LPN, 1974. Sch. nurse, then spl. edn. tchr. Dawson Springs (Ky.) Bd. Edn., 1980-83; spl. edn. substitute tchr. various counties, Ky., 1983-85; spl. edn. tchr. Critten County Bd. Edn., Marion, Ky., 1985—98, Christian County Bd. Edn., Hopkinsville, Ky., 1998—2003; ret., 2003; sub. tchr., 2004—. Mem. NEA, ACLU, Ky. Edn. Assn. (1st dist. pres. 1996-97, human and civil rights state com. 1994—, chair 1997-98), Crittenden County Edn. Assn. (pres. 1992-95, 97-98, chair KePAC legis. chair 1995-97), Christian County Edn. Assn. (bldg. rep. 1998-2003), Nature Conservancy, World Wildlife Fund, Sierra Club, Nat. Wildlife Fedn. Democrat. Office Phone: 270-619-1117. Personal E-mail: nancy@noffsinger.net.

NOFZIGER, KAREN FAE, elementary school educator; b. Norristown, Pa., Mar. 12, 1959; d. Dean Edward and Janeth Rose Nofziger. BA in Middle Sch. Edn., Goshen Coll., 1981; MEd in Math., Beaver Coll., 1989. Middle sch. math tchr. Penn View Christian Sch., Souderton, Pa., 1981—. Mem. Nat. Coun. Tchrs. Math. Mennonite. Avocations: reading, sports, crafts. Home: 112 Wheatsheaf Ln Telford PA 18969-1800

NOGUERE, SUZANNE, trade association executive, poet; b. Bklyn., Dec. 1, 1947; d. Eugene R. and Virginia Helene (Braun) N.; m. Henry Grinberg, June 5, 1983. BA in Philosophy magna cum laude with honors, Columbia U., N.Y.C., 1969. Classified ad. mgr. Printing News, Melville, NY, 1973—2006, sr. acct. exec., 1999—2006; sr. dir. mem. svcs. Nat. Assn. for Printing Leadership, Paramus, NJ, 2006—. Author: (children's books) Little Koala, 1979, Little Raccoon, 1981, (poetry collection) Whirling Round the Sun, 1996; poet (with artist Miriam Adams): (exhibitions) Leaf Lines, 1998, poet (with artist Lesley Nishigawara): (exhibitions) Left Out, 2003; co-author (with James V. Hatch): The Stone House, A Blues Legend, 2000; co-author: (plays) Klub Ka, The Blues Legend, U. Iowa, 2002, La MaMa E.T.C., 2004, U. Md., 2006. Recipient Discovery award The 92nd St. Y Unterberg Poetry Ctr. and The Nation mag., 1996. Mem. Acad. Am. Poets, Poetry Soc. Am. (Gertrude B. Claytor Meml. award 1989), Poets House, Dramatists Guild Am., Authors Guild. Home: 27 W 96th St Apt 12B New York NY 10025-6614 Office: Nat Assn for Printing Leadership 75 W Century Rd Paramus NJ 07652 Office Phone: 800-642-6275 ext. 6304. Personal E-mail: snoguere@napl.org.

NOLAN, JOAN T., elementary school educator; b. Bklyn., Jan. 31, 1942; d. Thomas Louis and Vivian LaForte; m. Gerard Thomas Nolan, Nov. 19, 1996 (div. Oct. 1994); children: Kenneth, Andrew. BA, Bklyn. Coll., 1963; MS, Hunter Coll., 1968. Classrm. tchr. Bd. Edn., City of N.Y., Bklyn., 1963-68, Richardson (Tex.) Ind. Sch. Dist., 1981—. Cooperating tchr. for student tchrs. Forestridge Elem. Sch., Richardson, 1993, 97, sci. fair coord., 1995-99, initiator sci. club, 1999—. Mem. AAUW (cultural rep., Ednl. Found. Gift given in her name 1999), Assn. Tex. Profl. Educators, Sci. Tchrs. Assn. Tex., Sierra Club. Roman Catholic. Avocations: reading, needlecrafts, exercising, travel, cooking.

NOLAN, LESLIE MARIAN, artist; b. Portland, Mar. 11, 1948; d. John Edward Nolan and Marion May Lindseth; m. K. Steven Halter, May 30, 1979; children: Ryan, Edward, Douglas. BA in French, Portland State U., 1970; MS in spl. studies, George Washington U., Washington, D.C., 1975; MS in nat. security, Nat. Def. U., Washington, D.C., 1997. Chief fgn. activities U.S. Info. Agy., Washington, 1979—82, dep. chief physical security, 1982—87, chief overseas support, 1987—93, chief security svc., 1993—96, resource analyst, 1997—99; chief attestation officer of U.S. U.S. Dept. of State, Washington, 1999—2004; artist self-employed, Herndon, Va., 2004—. V.p. programs Fairfax Art League, Va., 2000—04; co-chair hanging Art League, Alexandria, Va., 2005—06. Logo, Fairfax Art League, 2003. Mem.: League of Reston Artists, Potomac Valley Watercolorists, So. Watercolor Soc., League of Women Voters. Avocations: reading, travel, hiking. Home: 11660 Gilman Ln Herndon VA 20170

NOLAN, MARILYN ANN, health facility administrator; b. Brighton, Mass., July 17, 1935; d. Anthony Henry and Anne Claire Nikiel; m. George Francis Nolan; 2 children. BA, Trinity Coll., Washington, 1957; MSS in Social Wk., Boston U., 1959. Diplomate Am. Inst. of Hypnotherapy; LCSW. Med. social worker Peter Bent Brigham Hosp., Boston, 1959—60; geriatric and psychiat. social worker Modesto State Hosp., Calif., 1960—63; psychiat. social worker, geriatric med. substance abuse therapist, visual impairment svc. coord. VA Med. Ctr., Bedford, Mass., 1966—87, psychiat. social worker, substance abuse therapist, 1989—91, visual impairment svc. team coord. Long Beach, Calif., 1987—89, St. Petersburg, Fla., 1991—2004; pvt. practice guided imagery, visualization and stress mgmt. St. Petersburg, 2004—. Chmn. disabled people's program Bay Pines VA Med. Ctr., St. Petersburg, 1991—94; field work instr. Boston Coll., 1972—86, Boston U., 1972—86. Recipient Outstanding Contrbn. award, Am. Legion, 1990, Tampa Bay Fed. Equal Employment Opportunity, 1993, Blinded Vets. Assn., 2002. Mem.: NASW (bd. cert. diplomate), Nat. Guild of Hypnotists (cert.), Acad. Cert. Social Workers. Roman Catholic. Avocations: reading, piano, accordion. Home and Studio: 63 Edgewater Dr Wareham MA 02571 Office Phone: 727-399-0258. Personal E-mail: magenol@aol.com.

NOLAN, SUSAN MARIE, mathematics educator; b. Erie, Pa., Oct. 15, 1952; d. Raymond Ellis and Dorothy Mary Guthrie; 1 child, Patrick Ray. Student, Edinboro State Coll., Pa, 1970—74; BS in Math., Edinboro U., 1987; M Curriculum and Instrn., Gannon U., Erie, Pa., 2001. Cert. math. tchr. Pa., libr. Pa., in curriculum and instrn. Pa. Substitute tchr. Wattsburg Sch. Dist., Erie, 1974—87, math tchr., 1987—. Race horse trainer Pa. Horse Racing, Erie, 1975—86. Coord. fair queen contest Erie County Fair, Wattsburg, Pa., 2002—06. Recipient Yearbook Dedication, Seneca HS, 1998, 2001. Mem.: Nat. Coun. Tchrs. Math., Pa. State Edn. Assn., Pa. Assn. Student Couns. (dist. 1 dir. 2005—06, Dist. 1 Advisor of Yr. 2000, 2003, 2006), Phi Delta Kappa. Home: 8050W Platz Rd Fairview PA 16415 Office: Wattsburg Sch Dist 10770 Wattsburg Rd Erie PA 16509 Office Phone: 814-824-3400. Home Fax: 814-825-2262; Office Fax: 814-825-2262. Business E-Mail: snolan@wasd.iu5.org.

NOLAN, THERESA A., retired judge, mediator, arbitrator; b. Washington, Dec. 10, 1930; d. Peter James Sr. and Mary Dorothea (Gerhardt) Hagan; m. Bernard A. Nolan, Jr. (dec.); children: Patrick, Theresa Davis, Mary Ellen Purcell, Joanne Kowalczyk, Frances McKeever, Bernard, Christine, Thomas, Barbara Kristek, William, Kathleen, Joseph; m. Walter G. Planet (dec.). BA, U. Balt., 1973; LLB, U. Balt. Sch. Law, 1975. Bar: Md. 1976. Legal sec. Law & Sinclair, Upper Marlboro, Md., 1961—68, McGrane, Casey, Miller, Lanham, 1968—72; legis. asst. Prince George's County Office Law, Upper Marlboro, 1972—76; ptnr. Sherry, Boyer & Nolan, Bowie, 1977—79; sole practitioner, 1979—80; master domestic rels. causes 7th Jud. Cir. Ct. Md., Upper Marlboro, 1981—85; judge 4th Dist. Ct. Md., 1985—97, civil coordinating judge, 1991—2000; judge 7th Jud. Cir. Ct. Md., 1997—2000; mediator Md. Ct. Sys., 2000—. Instr. paralegal program Prince George's Cmty. Coll., 1980—88, USDA, 1980—88, U. Md. U. Coll., 1985—2000; family law sect. coun. Md. State Bar Assn., 1982—85; mem. Gov.'s Coun. Child Support Enforcement, 1983—86; mem. adv. bd. Dist. Pub. Defender, Upper Marlboro, 1984—; bd. govs. Md. State Bar Assn., 1985—87, 1989—91, local bar liaison, 1986—88; com. on criminal law procedure Md. Jud. Conf., 1987—88, dist. ct. edn. com., 1988—89, exec. com., 1990—91, chair dist. ct. edn. com., 1990—91, faculty, 1990—2000, vice chair, 1991—92, chair, 1992—93, civil law and procedures com., 1992—94, adminstrv. judges com., 1995—96, pub. rels. com., 1996—2000; pres. Prince George's County Women Lawyers Caucus, 1979—80, treas., 1981—82, exec. com., 1989—91; mem. Commn. Future of Md. Cts., 1995—96, chair criminal, juvenile and family matters sub-com. Charter mem. Law Found. Prince George's County; chmn. Prince George's County Cable Television Commn., 1978; mem. sodality Sacred Heart Parish; bd. dir. Prince George's Hosp., Cheverly, Md., 2000—03, Md. Vol. Lawyers Svcs., Inc., 1986—93; adv. bd. Family Crisis Ctr., Prince George's County Hotline and Suicide Prevention Ctr. Named a Woman of History, 1990, Woman of Achievement, Prince George's County, 1994; named one of Md. Top 100 Woment, 1998; named to Women's Hall of Fame, Prince George's County, 1993; recipient Fabulous Forties award, Prince George's Cmty. Coll., 1998, Disting. Svc. award, Prince George's County, 2000, Salute to Women award, Gtr. Bowie C. of C., 2000. Mem.: Am. Judges Assn., Inns of Ct., Md. Cir. Judges Assn., Women's Bar Assn. Md. (pres.-elect 1994—95, treas. 1981—82, bd. dir. 1982—94, nominating com. 1985—87, chmn. elections 1986, exec. com. 1989—90, chmn. awards com. 1989—93, Rita Davidson award 1993), Nat. Assn. Women Judges (sec. 4th dist. 1991—92, treas. 1993—94, pres. 1995—97, chair women in prison com. 2000, women in prison com. 2000—, ret. mem.), Prince George's County Bar Assn. (criminal liaison com. 1978, bd. dir. 1978—90, domestic rels. com. 1980—90, treas. 1981—82, sec. 1982—83, pres.-elect 1983—84, pres. 1984—85, budget com. 1984—86, chair social com. 1985—98, chmn. ABA-MSBA liaison com. 1986, nominating com. 1989—90). Democrat. Roman Catholic. Avocations: dance, golf, theater, book club, travel. Home: 2802 Berth Ter Annapolis MD 21401-7103

NOLAN, VICTORIA, theater director; b. Portland, Maine, June 15, 1952; d. Herbert Wallace and Diane Katharine (Kremm) N.; m. Clarkson Newell Crolius, Aug. 30, 1980; children: Covey Emmeline, Wilhelmina Adams. BA magna cum laude, U. Maine, 1976. Publicity asst. Loeb Drama Ctr. Harvard U., Cambridge, Mass., 1975; pub. rels. asst. to dir. Sch. Arts Boston U., 1975-76; mgmt. asst. TAG Found., N.Y.C., 1976-77; mng. dir. Ram Island Dance Co., Portland, 1977-78; dir. devel. Ctr. Stage, Balt., 1979-81, assoc. mng. dir., 1981-87; mng. dir. Ind. Repertory Theatre, Indpls., 1988-93; dep. dean, mng. dir. and prof. Yale Sch. Drama Yale Repertory Theatre, New Haven, 1993—. Program evaluator Nat. Endowment Arts, Washington, 1988—, panelist, 1991—; mem. Indpls. Cultural Consortium, v.p., 1991-93; bd. dir. Greater Indpls. Progress Com., Indpls. Urban League, Arts Coun. Indpls.; mem. nat. bd. Theatre Comm. Group, N.Y.C., treas., 1995-99; bd. dir. New Haven Arts Industry Coalition, co-chair, 1997-99, treas., 1999-2002. Mem. exec. com. League Resident Profl. Theatres, 2000-04. Nat. Performing Arts Mgmt. fellow Exxon, Doner Fedn. and NEA, 1978; Elizabeth L. Mahaffey arts adminstrn. fellow Conn. Commn. on the Arts, 2000; recipient SetonElm Ivy award Yale U. and City of New Haven, 2005. Home: 120 Rimmon Rd Woodbridge CT 06525-1915 Office: Yale Repertory Theater PO Box 208244 Yale Station 222 York St New Haven CT 06520-8244

NOLAND, CHRISTINE A., judge; b. 1945; BA, JD, La. State Univ. Law clk. to Hon. John V. Parker U.S. Dist. Ct. (La. mid. dist.), 5th circuit, magistrate judge Baton Rouge, 1987—. Mem. ABA, La. State Bar, La. trial Lawyers Assn., Baton Rouge Bar Assn., Dean Henry George McMahon Inn of Ct. (counselor 1995-97). Office: Russell B Long Fed Bldg & Courthouse 777 Florida St Rm 278 Baton Rouge LA 70801-1717 Office Phone: 225-389-3592.

NOLAND, MARY RICHERSON, retired management consultant; b. Lebanon, Ky., Aug. 6, 1925; d. Thomas Wesley and Mary Suda Richerson; m. James Russell Noland, Jr., Dec. 22, 1945; children: James Russell III, Ellen Gay, Mary Elise. BA in Sociology and Psychology, U. Louisville, Ky.; student in Sociology and Psychology, New Haven State U., Conn., 1946—47; student, U. Houston, 1969—70. Exec. dir. vol. svcs. Meml. City Hosp., Houston, 1971—73; exec. cons. Mgmt. Techs., Inc., Houston, 1975—78, pres., CEO; chmn. Personalysis Corp., Houston. Editor: Real Estate Focused Newsletter, 1973—75. Organizer, dir. Heart of Houston, 1965—66. Methodist. Avocations: reading, history, politics, music, piano. Home: 13303 Havershire Houston TX 77079 Office: Personalysis Corp 5847 San Felipe 650 Houston TX 77079

NOLD, AURORA RAMIREZ, finance company executive; b. Honolulu, Apr. 21, 1958; m. Allan Jeffrey Nold, Aug. 1, 1995. BSBA cum laude, St. Louis U., 1969, MS in Bus. Adminstrn. magna cum laude, 1975, PhD summa cum laude, 1986. Exch. prof., dept. chairperson mgmt. St. Louis U., Baguio City, Philippines, 1980-86, dean Coll. Bus., 1980—86; rsch. asst. East/West Ctr. for Am. Studies, Honolulu, 1986-87; dir. Am. studies USIS, Washington, 1987-89; fin. cons. Shadow Hill Samaritan, Long Beach, Calif., 1989-93; dir. A&A Edu Care Consultancy Programs, Inc., Las Vegas, Nev., 1993—; prin., owner Felocor Diversified Funding, Las Vegas, Nev., 2005—. Bd. advisors Am. Biog. Inst., Raleigh, N.C., 1995—, Internat. Biog. Ctr., Cambridge, Eng., 1995—; rschr. S.H.S. Inc., Las Vegas, 1995—; prof. econs., bus and mgmt. C.C. So. Nev.; prof. stats. U. Nev., Las Vegas; tutor C.C. So. Nev.; pres., founder Felocor Diversified Funding Co Author: Business Education in the Philippines, 1986; contbr. articles to profl. jours. Pres. Rep. Presdl. Task Force, Las Vegas, 1995—. Cultural Exch. grant Fulbright Am. Studies, 1987, scholarship grant St. Louis U., 1979-86; recipient Appreciation award Nat. Humane Edn. Soc., 1996, Nat. Park Trust, 1996, Nat. Law Enforcement Officers Meml. Fund, 1997, Oustanding Cmty. and Profl. Achievement Commemorative medal Am. Biog. Inst., 1997, internat. cultural diploma of honor, 2000. Mem. AAUW, NAFE, Asian Am. Studies Assn., U.S. Profl. Bookkeepers Assn., Am. Cash Flow Assn., Las Vegas C. of C., Nev. Faculty Alliance Republican. Mem. Lds Ch. Avocations: collecting rare coins, writing, reading, music and coin collecting. Office Phone: 702-242-6020. Personal E-mail: auroranold@aol.com.

NOLD, LISA MARIE, athletic trainer; b. Evergreen Park, Ill., Mar. 14, 1979; d. Edward Graham and Lucinda Jane Nold. BA in Bus. Adminstrn., Augustana Coll., Rock Island, Ill., 2001; MA in Edn., U. Ala., Birmingham, 2004. Cert. athletic trainer Nat. Athletic Tng. Assn. Bd. of Certification. Cert. athletic trainer Jevitz Chiropractic Clinic, Elmhurst, Ill., 2002; cert. athletic trainer grad. asst. Samford U., Birmigham, Ala., 2002—04; cert. athletic trainer HealthSouth Sports Medicine and Rehab. Ctr., Birmigham, 2004—05, Accelerated Rehab. Ctrs., Chgo., 2005—. Contbr. articles to profl. jours. Mem.: Nat. Strength and Conditioning Assn., Ill. Atheltic Tng. Assn., Nat. Athletic Tng. Assn., Alpha Phi Omega. R-Consevative. Avocations: baking, reading, travel, exercise, bicycling. Office: Accelerated Rehabiliation Centers 205 Wacker Ste 820 Chicago IL 60606

NOLEN, DARLENE ELIZABETH, small business owner; b. Beaumont, Tex., Aug. 7, 1947; d. Louis Joseph and Audrey Elizabeth Wheeler; m. C. E. Page, Aug. 1965 (div. 1976); children: Dwayne Edward, Brett Louis stepchildren: Rochelle, Mark; m. E. E. "Butch" Nolen, Feb. 14, 1977. H.s. grad., Sour Lake, Tex., 1965. Acct. Beaumont Coca-Cola Bottling Co., Beaumont, Tex., 1974—76, Beaumont 7-Up Bottling Co., Beaumont, Tex., 1976—77, Kirby Forest Industries, Silsbee, Tex., 1978—82; substitute tchr. aide Silsbee Sch. Dist., Silsbee, Tex., 1982—84; owner, mgr. Klothes Kloset Inc., Jasper, Tex., 1987—. CEO Cir. of Peace Found., Jasper, Tex., 2000—; bd. dirs. Mayor's Task Force on the Arts, Jasper, Tex., 2001—, Mayor's Task Force on Cmty. Businesses, Jasper, Tex., 1999—, Jasper/Lake Sam Rayburn C. of C., Jasper, Tex., 1996—, Jasper Main St., Jasper, Tex., 1993—, Jasper Walk of Hope-Breast Cancer Awareness, Jasper, Tex., 2001—. Mem.: Nat. Trust Hist. Preservation, Jasper Lion Club (cmty. activities com.). Avocation: community fundraisers. Home: PO Box 1228 Jasper TX 75951-0013 Business E-Mail: darlene@klotheskloset.com.

NOLAN, JEANADA H., retired state agency administrator, social worker, educator; b. Fresno, Calif., Aug. 6, 1915; d. John Andrew and Lucille Wallace Hamilton; children: Jay Hamilton, Thomas Joseph. BA, Fresno State Coll., Calif., 1938; MA, Sacramento State Coll., Calif., 1953; PhD, Union Grad. Sch., Cin., 1977. Social worker Fresno County Welfare Dept., Calif., 1935—42; social welfare agt. State Dept. Social Welfare, Sacramento, 1942—45; coord. parent and preschool edn. Sacramento City Unified Sch. Dist., 1951—66, coord. Project Head Start, 1965; chief bur. preschool edn. programs Calif. State Dept. Edn., 1966—72, asst. to assoc. supt. early childhood edn., 1972—74; ret., 1974. Mem. Gov.'s Adv. Commn. Children and Youth, Sacramento, 1959—65; exec. sec. Gov.'s Adv. Com. Child Devel. Programs, 1966—72; parent involvement specialist Nat. Head Start, 1966—69; adv. bd. Parent Participation Preschools Internat., 1966—70; co-chmn., leader child devel. com. Wilson Riles Early Childhood Edn. Program, 1972; vis. lectr. in orgn., mgmt. and adminstrn. preschool and child care programs U. Calif. Ext., 1974—79; prodr. radio series Families are Our Bus., 1954; mem. State Bd. Mgrs. Calif. Congress Parents and Tchr. Contbr. articles to profl. jours. Mem.: Sacramento Mental Health Assn. (charter mem.), Calif. Assn. Edn. Young Children, Nat. Assn. Young Children, UN-USA, Ret. Tchrs. Assn., Soroptimist Internat.

NOLFF, SUSAN D., web site designer, small business owner; b. Highland Park, Mich., Oct. 31, 1963; d. Kenneth A. and Georgia A. Blodick; m. Shawn R. Nolff, Aug. 25, 1984; children: Joshua L., Sheryl L. Slovinski, Daniele J. AAS in Visual Comm., Northwestern Mich. Coll., Traverse City, Mich., 2004; Webmaster Cert. (Level II), Northwestern Mich. Coll., 2005. Registered Gen. Contr., Mich., 1993. Archtl. draftsperson Cmty. Design, Inc., Traverse City, 1988—92; property mgmt./mortgage originator First of Am. Bank, Traverse City, Mich., 1992—95; real estate closer Corp. Title, Traverse City, 1995—97; gen. ptnr./ops. mgr. Countryside Constrn., Grawn, 1995—; paraprofessional-visual imaging tech. dept. Traverse Bay Area Intermediate Sch. Dist., Traverse City, 2003—05; web designer Byte Prodns., LLC, Traverse City, 2005—. Spkr., presenter, mentor Zonta Club, Traverse City, 2006; spreaker, presenter, mentor GirlTech, Traverse City, 2004—05. Recipient Adult Student of Yr. award, Northwestern C.C., 2003, Webmaster Departmental Award, Computer Info. Systems Dept. - Northwestern Mich. Coll., 2005; scholar Women's Coun. Scholarship, Home Builders Assn. Grand Traverse Area - Women's Coun., 2002—04, Edn. Scolarship, Home Builder's Assn. of the Grand Traverse Area, 2003, Home-In-A-Day Scholarship, 2002—04, Honors Scholarship, Northwestern Mich. Coll., 2003. Mem.: Visual Comm. Adv. Bd. (assoc.), Visual Imaging Tech. Adv. Bd. (assoc.), Mensa Soc. - NW Mich. Chpt. (assoc.), Phi Theta Kappa (life). Lutheran.

NOLL, AMY, secondary educator; b. Madison, Wis., Sept. 12, 1956; d. David John and Eva Joyce (Tappen) N. BA, Milton (Wis.) Coll., 1978; MA, L.I. U., 1990. Tchr. orch. Sun Prairie (Wis.) Pub. Schs., 1979-85; freelance violinist N.Y.C., 1985—; tchr. orch. Hicksville (N.Y.) Pub. Schs., 1987—. Violinist Akron (Ohio) Symphony Orch., 1979-80, Canton (Ohio) Symphony Orch., 1979-80, Madison (Wis.) Symphony Orch., 1980-85; conducting debut Lincoln Ctr., 1999; violnist Nepethe Ensemble, 1994—. Recipient Tchr. Excellence award, Hicksville Pub. Schs, 1989, PTSA Founders Day award, 1994—95, Paul Vetrano Tchr. of the Yr. award, 2000. Mem. Nat. Sch. Orch. Assn., Am. String Tchrs. Assn., Music Educators Nat. Conf., Nassau Music Educators Assn. Avocations: chamber music, jogging, travel, reading, printmaking. Office: Hicksville Pub Schs Division Ave Hicksville NY 11801 Home: 5 Dorchester St Huntington Station NY 11746-8407

NOLL, JEANNE C., retired music educator; b. Reading, Pa., Aug. 12, 1935; d. Carl Foreman and Barbara Rebecca (Mengel) Winter; m. Clair W. Noll; children: Eric W., Douglas C. BS Music Edn., Lebanon Valley Coll., Annville, Pa., 1957; music student, West Chester U., Milligan U., Lehigh U., MIT. Cert. tchr. Pa., 1961. Tchr. elem. music North Coventry Elem. Sch., Chester County, Pa., Yokohama Army Sch., Japan, 1957—58; tchr. vocal jr. H.S. Reading Sch. Dist., Pa., 1959—61; organist, choir dir. St. Paul's United Ch. of Christ, Fleetwood, Pa., 1967—2001, organist/choir dir. emerita, 2002—; tchr. vocal music elem., jr. and sr. H.S. Kutztown Area Sch. Dist., Pa., 1981—94. Dir. show choir Kutztown Area Sch. Dist., 1981—94; accompanist Kutztown Cmty. Choir, 1999—2001, organist, mem., 2001—. Del. 17th congl. dist. Rep. Nat. Conv., NY, 2004, del. 6th congl. dist. Phila., 2000; com. mem. Berks County Rep. Com., Fleetwood, 1982—, vice chmn.; committee-woman Pa. Rep. state com., Harrisburg, 1998—; active Berks Area Muhlenberg Coun. Rep. Women, 1996, 2d v.p., 2005; vice chair Berk County Rep. Com., 2005—. Mem.: East Penn Valley Kiwanis Club (Dir., Key Club Advisor 1994—, Kiwanian of the Year 2000). Mem. United Ch. Of Christ. Avocations: travel, music, reading, politics.

NOLL, LAURIE JANE, secondary school educator; b. Alton, Ill., Aug. 27, 1961; d. David Richard and Shirley Ann Bliven; m. Tim Joseph Noll, Mar. 22, 1982; children: Emily, Ian, Eileen. BA, MacMurry Coll., Jacksonville, Ill., 1982; MA, Western Ill. U., 1994. Tchr. Davenport Schs., Iowa, 1982—85, AEA, Bettendorf, Iowa, 1985—92; spl. svc. tchr., dept. chmn. Burlington Cmty. Schs., Iowa, 1992—, dept. chmn., 1997—, interpreter, 1984—92. Bd. dirs. Players Workshop, 2000—, Burlington Steamboat Days, 2005—; interpreter Players Workshop, Burlington, 1999—, City of Burlington, 1998—. Named Local Tchr. of Yr., Wal-Mart, 2002. Mem.: PEO, Nat. Assn. Secondary Sch. Prins., Phi Kappa Phi, Pi Lambda Theta. Home: 1639 Madison Ave Burlington IA 52601 Office: Burlington Community Schs 421 Terrace Dr Burlington IA 52601 Office Phone: 319-753-2211. E-mail: noll1982@burlington.k12.ia.us.

NOLLER, RUTH BRENDEL, retired education educator, consultant, researcher; b. Buffalo, Oct. 6, 1922; d. John Michael and Ellen (Bement) Brendel; m. David Conrad Noller, June 7, 1947; children: David Carl, Paul John. BA, U. Buffalo, 1942, EdM, 1944, EdD, 1952. Inst. math. U. Buffalo, 1942-52; professorial lectr. math. SUNY, Buffalo, 1957-71, rsch. asst. in creativity, lectr., 1964-69; assoc. prof. creative studies State U. Coll. Buffalo, 1969-78, prof., 1978-82, disting. svc. prof. emeritus, 1982—. Alex F. Osborn vis. prof. State U. Coll., Buffalo, 1992-93; cons. in field. Author 12 books; contbr. articles to profl. jours. Lt. (j.g.) W.A.V.E.S., USNR, 1944-46. Mem. AAUW (edn. chmn. 1985-93, endowment honoree edn. found. program 1988), United U. Professions, Creative Edn. Found. (colleague, disting. leader exceptional svc. award 1988, svc. and commitment award 1987), N.Y. Tchrs., Sch. Vols. of Sarasota County, Delta Kappa Gamma. Democrat. Episcopalian. Avocations: travel, bell collecting, gardening, photography. Home: 1040 Sylvan Dr Sarasota FL 34234-8333

NOLPH, GEORGIA BOWER, physician; b. Appleton, Minn., Jan. 26, 1938; d. Clarence Walter and Gladys Mae (Hanson) Bower; m. Karl David Nolph, July 26, 1961; children: Erika Lynn, Kristoper Karl. BA, St. Olaf Coll., 1960; MD, Woman's Med. Coll. Pa., 1964. Pvt. practice with G.H. Ferguson MD, Bala-Cynwyd, Pa., 1965-67; civil service Walter Reed Army Med. Ctr., Washington, 1967-69; instr. community health and med. practice U. Mo., Columbia, 1969-70; asst. prof. U. Mo. Med. Sch., Columbia, 1970-77, assoc. prof. family and community medicine, 1977—. Acting med. dir. Family Med. Care Ctr., U. Mo. Hosp. and Clinics, Columbia, 1980—87; med. dir. NBA Lenoir Retirement Cmty., 1987—99, Lenoir bd. dirs., 2000—05, v.p., 2001—03, pres., 2003—05. Assoc. editor. (profl. jour.) Continuing Education for the Family Physician, 1972-73. V.p. Parents for Drug Free Youth, Columbia, Mo., 1985-86, 86-87, pres. 1987-88, 88-89; bd. dir. Columbia Civic Orch., 2003—, sec., 2004—. Mem.: Boone County Med. Soc., Mo. State Med. Assn., Am. Bus. Women's Assn. (pres. Boone Belles chpt. 2004—06), Am. Med. Women's Assn. (state dir. 1975—2003, region VII gov. 1996—2003), Am. Legion Aux. Republican. Methodist. Avocations: music, reading, travel, needlecrafts. Home: 908 Hickory Hill Dr Columbia MO 65203-2320 Office: U Mo Med Sch Dept Family and Cmty Medicine 1 Hospital Dr Columbia MO 65201-5276

NOLT, JANELLE, athletic trainer; d. A. Ray and Nancy L. Nolt. BA in Athletic Tng., Messiah Coll., Grantham, Pa., 2002. Cert. athletic trainer Nat. Athletic Trainers' Assn. Bd. Cert., 2002; strength and conditioning specialist Nat. Strength and Conditioning Assn., 2002. Asst. athletic trainer Dickinson Coll., Carlisle, Pa., 2002—. Health and phys. edn. instr. Dickinson Coll., Carlisle, Pa., 2003—04. Active Christ Cmty. Ch., Camp Hill, Pa., planning com. young adults, 2004—06. Mem.: Nat. Strength and Conditioning Assn., Nat. Athletic Trainers' Assn. Avocations: fastpitch softball, reading, music, outdoor activities. Office: Dickinson Coll Kline Ctr PO Box 1773 Carlisle PA 17013

NOONAN, JACQUELINE ANNE, pediatrician, educator; b. Burlington, Vt., Oct. 28, 1928; BA, Albertus Magnus Coll., 1950; MD, U. Vt., 1954, DSc (hon.), 1980. Diplomate Am. Bd. Pediatrics, Am. Bd. Pediatric Cardiology. Intern N.C. Meml. Hosp., Chapel Hill, 1954-55; resident in pediatrics Children's Hosp., Cin., 1955-57; rsch. fellow Children's Med. Ctr., Boston, 1957-59; asst. prof. pediatrics State U. Iowa Sch. Medicine, 1959-61; asst. prof. pediatrics cardiology U. Ky. Coll. Medicine, Lexington, 1961-64, assoc. prof., 1964-69, prof., 1969-99, chmn. dept. pediatrics, 1974-92, emeritus prof., 1999—. Mem. embryology and human devel. study sect. NIH, 1973-78; mem. U.S.-USSR Symposium on Congenital Heart Disease, 1975; mem. sub. bd. pediatric cardiology Am. Bd. Pediatrics, 1977-82; examiner, mem. test. com. Nat. Bd. Med. Examiners, 1984-90, exec. com., 1991-95; participant various confs. in field; vis. prof. Vanderbilt U., Nashville, 1987; spkr. in field. Contbr. articles, revs. to med. publs.; mem. editl. bd. Am. Jour. Diseases Children, 1970-80, Am. Jour. Med. Edn., 1975-78, Pediatric Cardiology, 1978-90, Am. Heart Jour., 1994-96, Clin. Pediatrics, 1990-99. Fellow: Royal Coll. Irish Physicians (hon.); mem.: AMA, So. Soc. Pediat. Rsch. (pres. 1972), Soc. Pediat. Rsch., NIH Alumni Assn., Ky. State Med. Assn., Irish-Am. Pediat. Soc. (pres. 1999—2001), Fayette County Pediat. Soc., Am. Pediat. Soc., Assn. Med. Sch. Pediatrics (dept. chmn. exec. com. 1978—81), Am. Coll. Cardiology (gov. Ky. chpt. 1989—92), Am. Acad. Pediatrics (chmn. cardiol. sect. 1972—74). Office Phone: 859-257-4679.

NOONAN, JOSETTE MARIE, music educator; b. Melrose Park, Ill., Mar. 6, 1955; d. Frank Eugene and Barbara Ann Noonan. ADN, Waubonsee Coll., Ill., 1984; MusB, DePaul U., 1990. Registered Profl. Nurse, Ill., 1984; cert. musikgarten educator 1999, dir. music ministries 2005. Music dir. St. Mary's Ch., West Chgo., Ill.; RN surg. resource team Children's Meml. Med. Ctr., Chgo., 1985—90; singer Grant Pk. Symphony Chorus, 1985—90; artist in residence Coll. of DuPage, Glen Ellyn, Ill., 1987—88; asst. dir. Light Opera Works, Evanston, Ill., 1990—91; RN rehab. Oak Pk. Hosp., Ill., 1992—97; soprano soloist and sect. leader First United Meth. Ch. at Chgo. Temple, Chgo., 1993—2004, children's choir dir., 1999—2003; voice tchr. No. Ill. U. Cmty. Sch. of Music, DeKalb, Ill., 1999—2002; music and movement tchr. No. Ill. U. Suzuki Sch., DeKalb, 1999—2002; tchr. voice and strings Countryside Music Sch., Elburn, Ill., 1999—; music tchr. Creative Beginning Presch., 2005—06. Violist Celebration String Quartet, Arlington Heights, Ill., 2000—04; dir. Countryside Players, Elburn, Ill., 2002—, Kindechor and Angeli Musicali Children's Choirs St. Mary's, West Chgo., Ill., 2005—06; founder and adminstr. Patrick Edgar Triplett Meml. Scholarship Program; rehabilitative music specialist Healing Harps, DeKalb, Ill., 2000—03; guest artist German Song Text Workshop, Vienna, 2004—, Assisi Music Festival, Italy, 2005—06, Mladi Fest, Medjugorje, Bosnia-Herzegovina, 2005, Accademia Voci d'Estate, Verona, Italy, 2006, Art Song Festival, 2006. Composer: (songs) Songs for Children's Worship; arranger (musical) From Mozart to Moulin Rouge; singer: (improvisatory music for dance troupe) The Death of the King, author of poems. Past pres. Ill. Collegiate Music Educators, Mokena, Ill., 2000—01; canvas voters to encourage passage of referendum for schs. Save our Schs., West Chgo., Ill., 1970; fed and clothed homeless people First United Meth. Ch. at Chgo., Chgo., 2000—02; care and concern ministry First United Meth. Ch. at Chgo. Temple, Chgo., 2002—04; mem. Pax Christi, 2005—06, Christian Peacemaker Team, 2005—06, Kairos Retreat Leadership Team, 2006. Recipient Invitation to sing for Martin Katz, DePaul U., 1987, Invited to sing for John Wustman, 1988, Invitation to sing Honors Recitals, 1985—88, Invited to sing and speak at a meml. concert honoring composer, Moses Hogan, Abyssinian Bapt. Ch. NY, 2002, First prize, Italian Cultural Soc. Voice Competition, 1988. Mem.: Nat. Assn. Pastoral Musicians, Nat. Guild Hypnotists (assoc.), Am. Choral Dirs. Assn. (assoc.; treas. local chpt. 1999—2001), Music Educator's Nat. Conf. (assoc.; pres. of ill. collegiate assn. 2000—01), Healing Harps (assoc.). Independent. Achievements include Specialist in German Lied interpretation; development of music program for autistic children at Northern Illinois University; Set up music and movement program for local preschool; Planned, executed and evaluated a weekend workshop for music education students in the state of Illinois entitled, What I didn't learn in music school. Avocations: backpacking, german language and culture, scuba diving, fiddling, hypnosis. Home: 324 Church St West Chicago IL 60185 Office: St Mary's Church 140 North Oakwood Avenue West Chicago IL 60185 Office Phone: 630-231-0013. Office Fax: 630-293-2671. E-mail: scotchdiva@aol.com.

NOONAN, NORINE ELIZABETH, academic administrator, researcher; b. Phila., Oct. 5, 1948; d. Alaric Edwin and Norine (Radford) Freeman. BA summa cum laude, U. Vt., 1970; MA, Princeton U., 1972, PhD, 1976. Asst. prof. Coll. Vet. Medicine, U. Fla., Gainesville, 1976-81, assoc. prof., 1981; rsch. assoc. prof. Georgetown U., Washington, 1981-82; A. Chem. Soc. sci. fellow U.S. Senate Commerce Com., Washington, 1982-83; program and budget analyst Office Mgmt. and Budget, Washington, 1983-87, acting br. chief sci. and space programs, 1987-88, br. chief, 1988-92; v.p. rsch. Fla. Inst. Tech., Melbourne, 1992—, dean grad. sch., 1993—. Mem. bd. advisors U.S. Found. for the Internat. Space U., 1989-90; disting. lectr. MITRE Corp. Inst., 1991; vis. faculty Exec. Seminar Ctrs., Office Pers. Mgmt.; cons. com. chem. and pub. affairs Am. Chem. Soc.; mem. space sci. adv. com. NASA; mem. com. Antarctiv policy and sci. NRC; mem. future of space sci. DOE environ. mgmt. sci. program NRC; councilor Oak Ridge Assn. Univs.; trustee S.E. Univs. Rsch. Assn., also chair fin. com. Mem. editl. bd. Fla. Today, 1997; contbr. articles to sci. jours. Vol. Balt. City Fair, 1982-91; bd. dirs. Brevard Symphony Orch., 1993-96, Wolf Trap Farm Pk. Assocs.; bd. dirs. Wolf Trap Farm Pk. for the Performing Arts, 1988-92, mem. exec. com., 1990-92, exec. vice chmn., 1991-92, treas., 1992; mem. adv. coun. Brookings Instn. Ctr. for Pub. Policy Edn., 1989-93; treas. White House Athletic Ctr., 1990-92, Potomac Basset Hound Club, Space Coast Tiger Bay Club. Recipient Spl. Performance award OMB, 1987, 88; grantee Fla. divsn. Am. Cancer Soc., 1977, NIH, 1979, NSF, 1979. Fellow AAAS (mem. at large sect. gen. interest in sci. and tech. 1994-97, chair elect 1997—, mem. sci., engring. and pub. policy com.); mem. Am. Soc. Cell Biology, Sigma Xi, Phi Beta Kappa (pres. Fla. chpt. 1980-81). Mem. United Ch. of Christ. Avocations: running, purebred dogs, fishing, cooking, aerobics. Office: EPA/ORD 401 M St SW Washington DC 20460-0002 Home: 1337 Wynbrook Trce Mount Pleasant SC 29466-6726

NOONAN, PEGGY, writer; b. Bklyn., Sept. 7, 1950; d. Jim and Mary Jane (Byrne) N.; m. Richard Kahn, Nov. 27, 1985 (div. 1990); 1 child, Will. BA in English Literature & Journalism, Fairleigh Dickinson U., Rutherford, N.J., 1974, PhD in Humane Letters (hon.), 1990. Premium adjuster Aetna Ins. Co., Newark, 1968-70; student Antiwar Protester of Vietnam; temp. agency sec. N.Y.C., 1974; news staffer WEEI Radio (CBS station), Boston, 1974, editl. dir., 1975-77; writer, editor CBS News, N.Y.C., 1977-80, commentary for Walter Cronkite and Dan Rather, 1980-81, full time commentary writer for Dan Rather, 1981-84; White House speech writing tech. Ronald Reagan, Washington, 1984-86; White House speech writer George Bush, Washington, 1988-89; contbg. editor The Wall St. Jour., Time, Good Housekeeping. Bd. dir. The Manhattan Inst. Author: What I Saw at the Revolution: A Political Life in the Reagan Era, 1990, Life, Liberty, & the Pursuit of Happiness, 1995, Simply Speaking: How to Communicate Your Ideas With Style, Substance, and Clarity, 1998, The Case Against Hillary Clinton, 2000, When Character was King: A Story of Ronald Reagan, 2001, A Heart, a Cross and a Flag, 2003, John Paul the Great: Remembering a Spiritual Father, 2005; contbr. articles to Forbes, Mirabella, Newsweek, N.Y. Times, O Mag., Time, Wash. Post. Coll. Guest Editor Mademoiselle, 1990; Mother of Yr. award, 1990; Nat. Mother's Day Com., 1990. Mem. Judson Welliver Soc. Republican. Roman Catholic. also: ICM 40 W 57th St Fl 16 New York NY 10019-4001*

NOONAN, SHAUNA GAY, petroleum engineer; b. Edmonton, Alta., Apr. 11, 1969; came to U.S., 1997; d. Duane Thomas and Edna Irene (Carlson) Freeman; m. Michael James Noonan, Aug. 3, 1996; children: Heather Gwendolyn, Lisa Danielle. BS in Petroleum Engring., U. Alta., Edmonton, 1993. Prodn. engr. Chevron Can. Resources, Edmonton, 1993-94, Fox Creek, Alta., 1994-96, petroleum engr. Calgary, Alta., 1996-97; prodn. engr. artificial lift Chevron Petroleum Tech. Co., Houston, 1997—2004; staff prodn. engr. ConocoPhillips Upstream Tech. Co., Houston, 2004—. Mem. adv. panel La. State U. Downhole Water Separation Initiative, Baton Rouge, 1998, Baton Rouge, 2001, U. Tulsa Sand Monitoring Project, 1998; chmn. working group Am. Petroleum Inst., Houston, 1998—. Mem.: ASME (chmn. gas lift workshop 2003), Soc. Petroleum Engrs. (electric submersible pump adv. panel 1997—, mem. progressive cavity pump steering com. 2002, chmn. electric submersible pump adv. panel 2003—, chair PCP workshop 2004, Outstanding Achievement award 1998—2005), Montgomery County Alumnae Delta Gamma Sorority (publicity officer 2000—02). Office: Conoco Phillips 600 N Dairy Ashford Houston TX 77079 E-mail: shauna.g.noonan@conocophillips.com.

NOONAN, SUSAN ABERT, public relations executive; b. Lancaster, Pa., May 10, 1960; d. James Goodear and Carole (Althouse) Abert; m. David Lindsay Noonan, July 28, 1986; children: Caroline du Pont, Elizabeth Augusta. BA, Mt. Holyoke Coll., 1982. Account exec. Merill Lynch, N.Y.C., 1982-83; sr. v.p. Cameron Assocs., N.Y.C., 1983-88; pres., founder Noonan/Russo Comm. (now Euro RSCG Life NRP), N.Y.C., 1988—. Mem. Nat. Investor Rels. Inst.

NOONE, LAURA PALMER, academic administrator, lawyer; BBA, U. Dubuque; MBA, JD, U. Iowa; PhD in higher edn. adminstrn., Union Inst. Atty gen. civil practice, Iowa, Ariz.; judge City of Chandler, Ariz.; faculty mem. U. Phoenix, 1987—91, dir. acad affairs, 1991—94, provost, sr. v.p. acad. affairs, 1994—2000, pres., 2002—. Adj. faculty Grand Canyon Univ., Chandler-Gilbert Cmty. Coll.; mem. Ariz. State Bd. for pvt. postsecondary edn.; trustee Phoenix Internat. Sch. Law. Mem.: ABA, Ariz. State Bar Assn., Maricopa County Bar Assn. Office: University of Phoenix 4615 E Elwood St Phoenix AZ 85040

NOOYI, INDRA K., food products executive; b. Madras, India, Oct. 28, 1955; m. Raj K. Nooyi; 2 children. BS, Madras Christian Coll., India, 1976; MBA, Indian Inst. Mgmt., Calcutta, 1978; M Pub. and Pvt. Mgmt., Yale U., 1980. Product mgr. Johnson & Johnson, India, Mettur Beardsell, Ltd., India; dir. internat. corp. strategy projects Boston Cons. Group, 1980—86; bus. devel. exec. Motorola, Inc., v.p., dir. corp. strategy and planning, 1986—90; sr. v.p. strategy, planning and strategic mktg. Asea Brown Boveri, 1990—94; sr. v.p. strategic planning PepsiCo, Inc., Purchase, NY, 1994-2000, sr. v.p., CFO, 2000-01, pres., CFO, 2001—, pres., CEO, 2006—. Bd. dir. Phoenix Home Life Mut. Ins. Co. Bd. dir. PepsiCo Found.; trustee Convent of Sacred Heart Sch., Greenwich, Conn. Named one of Most Powerful Women, Forbes mag., 2005, 50 Women to Watch, Wall St. Jour., 2005, 100 Most Powerful Women, Forbes Mag., 2006, 50 Most Powerful Women in Bus., Fortune mag., 2006. Achievements include being the first women CEO for PepsiCo, Inc. Office: PepsiCo, Inc 700 Anderson Hill Rd Purchase NY 10577-1444*

NORA, AUDREY HART, physician; b. Picayune, Miss., Dec. 5, 1936; d. Allen Joshua and Vera Lee (Ballard) H.; m. James Jackson Nora, Apr. 9, 1966; children: James Jackson Jr., Elizabeth Hart. BS, U. Miss., 1958, MD, 1961; MPH, U. Calif., 1978. Diplomate Am. Bd. Pediat., Am. Bd. Hematology and Oncology. Resident in pediat. U. Wis. Hosp., Madison, 1961-64; fellow in hematology/oncology Baylor U., Tex. Childrens Hosp., Houston, 1964-66, asst. prof. pediat., 1966-70; assoc. clin. prof. pediat. U. Colo. Sch. Medicine, Denver, 1970—; dir. genetics Denver Childrens Hosp., 1970-78; commd. med. officer USPHS, 1978, advanced through grades to asst. surgeon gen., 1983, cons. maternal and child health Denver, 1978-83, asst. surgeon gen. regional health adminstr., 1983-92, dir. maternal & child health bur., health resources and svc. adminstrn., 1992-99. Mem. adv. com. NIH, Bethesda, 1975-77; mem. adv. bd. Metronet Health, Inc., Denver, 1986-92; mem. adv. bd. Colo. Assn. Commerce and Industry, Denver, 1985-92, WIC program USDA, 1989-99; mem. adv. coun. NICHD, 1992-99; bd. mem. RMC for Health Promotion and Edn., pres., 2004-05. Author: (with J.J. Nora) Genetics and Counseling in Cardiovascular Diseases, 1978, (with others) Blakiston's Medical Dictionary, 1980, Birth Defects Encyclopedia, 1990, (with J.J. Nora and K. Berg) Cardiovascular Diseases: Genetics, Epidemiology and Prevention, 1991; contbr. articles to profl. jours. Recipient Virginia Apgar award Nat. Found., 1976. Fellow Am. Acad. Pediat.; mem. Am. Pub. Health Assn. (governing coun. 1990-92, coun. mem. maternal and child health 1990—), Commd. Officers Assn., Am. Soc. Human Genetics, Teratology Soc., Western Soc. Pediatric Rsch. Presbyterian. Avocations: cooking, hiking, quilting. Office: 1973 S Kenton Ct Aurora CO 80014-4709

NORA, LOIS MARGARET, neurologist, educator, academic administrator, dean; BS in Biology with honors, U. Ill., 1976; MD, Rush Med. Coll., Chgo., 1979; JD, U. Chgo., 1987; MBA, U. Ky., 2002. Fellow Am. Bd. Neurology, Am. Bd. Electrodiagnostic Medicine; bar: Ill. 1988, D.C. 1988. Intern in family medicine Cmty. Meml. Gen. Hosp., LaGrange, Ill., 1980; resident in neurology Rush-Presbyn.-St. Luke's Med. Ctr., Chgo., 1981-84, chief resident in neurology, 1983-84, fellow electromyography and neuromuscular disease, 1984-85; asst. prof. dept. neurology, asst. dean clin. curriculum Rush Med. Coll., Chgo., 1987-94, assoc. prof. dept. neurology, 1994-95; fellow Ctr. for Clin. Med. Ethics U. Chgo., 1993-95; assoc. dean acad. affairs, assoc. prof. dept. neurology U. Ky. Coll. Medicine, 1995—2002; prof. neurology U. Ky. Coll. Law, 1996—2002; pres. Northeastern Ohio Univ. Coll. of Med., 2002—, dean, 2002—. Spkr. in field. Contbr. articles to profl. jours., chpts. to books. Vice chair Epilepsy Found. of Greater Chgo., 1988-90, chair, 1991, chair strategic planning com. 1990-91, bd. dirs., 1987-94; bd. dirs. Epilepsy Found. of Am., 1992-95, co-chair quality standards com. 1992-94; mem. needs assessment com. United Way of Chgo., 1989-90; camp physician children's summer camp program Muscular Dystrophy Assn., 1984-86; vol. tchr. Christ the King Elem. Sch., 1996—2002. Mem. AMA (mem. dean's com. on family violence curriculum 1993, mem. report and resolutions subcom. for reference com. C 1997), Am. Acad. Neurology (mem. ethics com. 1997—2002), Am. Assn. Electrodiagnostic Medicine (chair profl. practice com. 1991—97, sec., treas., 1999-2002, pres.-elect, 2002-03, pres. 2003-04), Soc. Clin. Neurologists. Office: Northeastern Ohio U Coll Med PO Box 95 4209 St Rt 44 Rootstown OH 44272

NORAH, PATRICIA ANN, music educator; b. Columbus, Ga., Sept. 1, 1946; d. Tommy T. and Mary Farley Norah; 1 child, Terrence D. Murphy. Student, Spelman Coll., 1964—65, U. Fla., 1972; B Music Edn., Columbus State U., 1971, MEd, 1978. Cert. tchr. Ga. Gen. music tchr. South Columbus Elem. Sch., 1971—78, Matthew Elem. Sch./Ft. Benning Pub. Schs., Columbus, 1986—87; choral dir. Ft. Middle Sch., Columbus, 1978—84, Baker H.S., Columbus, 1987—91, Carver H.S., Columbus, 1991—. Vocal coach, Columbus, 1995—; asst. min. music St. Benedict Cath. Ch., Columbus, 1999—; dir., cons. Franchise Ch., Phenix City, Ala., 2004. Performer Columbus Consol. Gov. One Columbus, 2003; active Keep Columbus Beautiful. Named to Most Outstanding Women Am., 1974; recipient Outstanding Ga. Citizen award, Sec. of State Cathy Cox, 2000, Outstanding African-Am. award, Carver H.S. Fellow: Ga. Music Educators Assn. (mem.-at-large elem. coun. 1974); mem.: NEA, Nat. Music Educators Assn., Ga. Assn. Educators. Avocations: reading, travel, music. Home: 2700 Double Churches Rd # 151 Columbus GA 31909 Office: Carver HS 3100 8th St Columbus GA 31906 E-mail: pnorah@mscdga.net.

NORBECK, JANE S., retired nursing educator; b. Redfield, SD, Feb. 20, 1942; d. Sterling M. and Helen L. (Williamson) N.; m. Paul J. Gorman, June 28, 1970. BA in Psychology, U. Minn., 1965, BSN, 1965; MS, U. Calif., San Francisco, 1971, DSN, 1975. Psychiat. nurse Colo. Psychiat. Hosp., Denver, 1965-66, Langley Porter Hosp., San Francisco, 1966-67; pub. health nurse San Francisco Health Dept., 1968-69; prof. U. Calif. Sch. of Nursing, San Francisco, 1975—2003, dean, 1989-99, dept. chair, 1984-89, prof. and dean emeritus, 2003. Chair study sect. Nat. Inst. of Nursing Rsch., 1990-93, mem.

editl. bd. Archives of Psychiat. Nursing, 1985-95, Rsch. in Nursing and Health, 1987-2003. Co-editor: Annual Review of Nursing Research, 1996-97; contbr. articles to profl. jours. Mem. ANA, Am. Acad. Nursing, Inst. of Medicine, Sigma Theta Tau.

NORBY, RENA FAYE, science educator; b. Atlanta, July 7, 1942; d. William Milton Ritchey and Willie Kathleen Blair; m. William G. Smith, Aug. 15, 1963 (div. Sept. 1971); children: Eric P. Etheridge, Kathleen C. Wilker, William H. Smith; m. John Arthur Norby, June 10, 1989. BA, Emory U., 1965; MS, MEd, Ga. State U., 1978, PhD, 1983. Asst. prof. North Ga. Coll., Dahlonega, 1984-85, Fla. Atlantic U., Davie, 1995-96, Black Hills State U., Spearfish, SD, 1997—2004; computer programmer Internat. Soc. for Telecomms., College Park, Ga., 1985-86; computer ops. mgr. Spence, Moriarity et al, Jackson, Wyo., 1990-93; grad. tchg. asst. U. Wyo., Laramie, 1993-95; Fulbright scholar Instructional Tech. and Design, Saratov, Russia, 2004—05; asst. prof. Mercer U., McDonough, Ga., 2005—. Computer cons. Buffalo Software, Pinedale, Wyo, 1987-90; reviewer gender rsch. proposals, NSF, 2000. Contbr. articles to profl. jours. Nat. Merit scholar, 1959. Mem. Nat. Sci. Tchrs. Assn., Nat. Assn. Rsch. in Sch. Tchg., Am. Assn. Physics Tchrs., Ga. Sci. Tchrs. Assn., Ga. Assn. Marine Edn., Sigma Xi, Sigma Pi Sigma, Phi Delta Kappa. Episcopalian. Avocations: whitewater boating, hiking, knitting, travel. Home: 98 Floresta Dr Mcdonough GA 30252 Office Phone: 678-547-6555.

NORCROSS, BARBARA BREEDEN, retired educator; b. Stanardsville, Va., Mar. 11, 1934; d. John Ray and Orphia Virginia (Caldwell) Breeden; m. George M. Norcross, Jr., Dec. 18, 1954; children: Teresa Rea Norcross Bibb, Angelea Caldwell Norcross Foster. BS, U. Va., 1955. Cert. tchr., Va. Sec. to asst. dir. U. Va. Hosp., Charlottesville, 1955-56; tchr. Greene County Schs., Stanardsville, 1956-61, Charlottesville Pub. Schs., 1962-91; retired, 1991. Writer, organizer, tchr. self-paced instr. for at-risk students Charlottesville High Sch., 1989. Author: (with others) Individualized Progress in Driver Education, 1966. Exec. mgr. Joe Wright for State Senate, Va., 1984; dir., chmn. Va. Student Aid Found., 1987-88. Mem. Va. Assn. Driver Edn. and Traffic Safety, Assn. Driver Tng. and Safety Educators Am. (exec. bd.), Va. Basketball Club (sec. 1980-85), U. Va. Women's Basketball Club (pres. 1987-88). Avocations: gardening, sports, music, sewing. Home: 2608 Northfield Rd Charlottesville VA 22901-1233

NORD, MYRTLE SELMA, writer, researcher; b. Lane, SD, Mar. 13, 1918; d. Carl Frederick Schaefer and Minna Anna (Meyer) Scandrett; m. Warren E. Nord, Aug. 10, 1938. BA, Fort Lewis Coll., 1972. Sec. Anaconda Mining, Robeau, SD, 1935; waitress Rapid City, SD, 1935-38; office mgr. Farmers Ins. Group, Durango, Colo., 1947-62, ret., 1962. Author: Tell Me a Story, 1956, Inspiring Stories, 1975, Prospectives on Mass Communications, 1982, Main Currents in Communications, 1986, Leadville's Chicken Bill, 1977, The Searcher, 1993-94, Hot Flashes From Writing, 2005, Sestina and Haiku, Observations, 2006, To Kill A Bird, Murder 101, 2006; (plays) Five Under Cover 6, 1983, Celebrations 6, 1986, Virtue of Necessity, 1982, (stage plays) Tomorrow = X2,19, 1968, Sound Another Trumpet, 1976, (serials) Children's Friend, Missing Red Envelope, 1950-51, The Blue Triangle, 1952-53, (musicals) Getting It 2-Gether, 1982, No Patsy Like a Dame, 1985, High Blonde Pressure, 1986, Katie's Capers in the Mining Camp, 1989, (poetry) Hold Dear a Long Time Love, 1998, Story, Out-Guessing Ourselves, 1999 (Palomar Showcase); contbr. (book) Multiculture Theater, 1996, The King and the Apostle, 2002, (anthology) A Way With Murder, 2004, (essays) Ariz. Ozark Sr. News mag., Good Old Days, Writer's Jour., 2003, 04, 05, 06, (short stories) Visions, 2006. Mem. Nat. League of Am. Pen Women (state pres. 1966-68), Mystery Writers of Am. Avocations: herbs, music, outdoors. Home: Apt 213 11 E Orange Grove Rd Tucson AZ 85704-5555 E-mail: myrtle.nord747@comcast.net.

NORDGREN, KATHY See NORDGREN, MARY

NORDGREN, MARY KATHLEEN (KATHY NORDGREN), secondary school educator; b. Minn. d. Robert J. and Ihla L. Ellingson; m. Richard B. Nordgren; children: Stephanie, Erik. BS in Home Econ., U. Minn., Mpls., 1973, MEd, 1987. Home econ. educator Lake Superior Sch. Dist., Silver Bay, Minn., 1973—82; banker Union State Bank, Hazen, ND, 1982—92; family & consumer sci. educator Golden Valley (N.D.) H.S., 1992—. Del. leader People to People Student Ambassadors, 2001. Advisor Kids on the Block; bd. dirs. English Luth. Ch., fin. sec., tchr. Sunday sch.; Sunday sch. tchr. Recipient Prevention Through Edn. award, Mental Health Assn., 2001, 2002. Mem.: Hazen Lions Club, Jaycees, Lioness Club (charter pres.), Phi Upsilon Omicron, Alpha Delta Kappa. Office: Golden Valley High Sch 10 3rd St NW Golden Valley ND 58541

NORDQUIST, SONYA LYNN, information technology executive; b. Syracuse, N.Y., Nov. 7, 1969; d. Fred James and Mary Jo Nordquist; m. Hans F. Altenbach, Apr. 20, 2003. Student, Geneva Coll., 1987—89; BS in Bus. Adminstrn., SUNY, Oswego, 1989—91. Mortgage credit processor Commonwealth Info. Svcs., Charleston, SC, 1992—93; asst. to v.p. mktg. Dynapower/Stratopower, Charleston, 1993—95; telecom. cons. TTE, Inc., Charleston, 1995—96; sales mgr. Enterprise Network Svcs., Charleston, 1996—2002; CEO, tech. cons. C3 Technology, Inc., Charleston, 2002—. Fundraiser Happy Days and Spl. Times, Charleston, 1996—2002, Girl Scouts Carolina Low Country, Charleston, 2003—. Mem.: C. of C. (CEO Roundtable 2003—), Trident Bus. Assn., Young Profl. Kiwanis Club Charleston. Top Informed Profl. Sales Club (pres. 1995—2000), Toastmasters Daniel Island Club (v.p. pub. rels. 2003—). Republican. Achievements include patents pending in field. Avocations: tennis, running, travel. Home and Office: C3 Tech Inc PO Box 22081 Charleston SC 29413 Office Phone: 843-881-9503.

NORDSTRAND, NATHALIE ELIZABETH JOHNSON, artist; b. Woburn, Mass., Nov. 6, 1932; d. Edward N. and Ruth Peterson Johnson; m. Robert I. Nordstrand, Jan. 12, 1962. AA, Bradford Jr. Coll., 1952; BA, Columbia U., 1954; studied with Jay Connaway, Don Stone, Roger Curtis, Paul Strisik. Rsch. assoc. Gerontology Age Ctr. of New Eng., Boston, 1955-64; clk. corp. dir. Johnson Bros. Greenhouses, Inc., Woburn, 1958-84; owner Nordstrand Gallery, Rockport, Mass., 1970-99. Exhibited at Nat. Acad. Galleries, NYC, Springfield Mus. Fine Arts, Hammond Mus., North Salem, NYC, Bhulabha Meml. Inst., Bombay, India, Copley Soc. at Boston Symphony Hall, Hermann Fine Arts Ctr., Marietta, Ohio, Am. C. of C., Hong Kong, 1975-76, Silvermine Guild, Conn., 1976, Wall of Fame, Balt. Watercolor Soc., 1976, Ann. Copley Masters Exhbn. Boston, others; one woman shows include Rockport (Mass.) Art Assn., 1969, Laura Knotts Art Gallery, Bradford Coll., 1982, Reading Pub. Libr. Found., 1997; paintings in Nat. Mus. Am. Art, Smithsonian Inst., 1994, Best of Watercolors, 1995, Best of Oil Painting, 1996, Landscape Inspirations, 1997, Gallery of Marine Art, 1998. Planning bd. North Suburban Art Festival, 1963—68; chair. planned giving Barnard Coll., NYC, 2003—04. Named Citizen of Yr., Reading chpt. Am. Cancer Soc., 1983; recipient Louis E. Seley award, Salmagundi Art Club, 1974, Excellence in Watercolor award, Rockport Art Assn., 1997, Philip Isenberg Meml. award, Salmagundi Club, 1997, more than 180 awards in nat. and regional competition, 1960—, Joseph Santoro Meml. award, Rockport Art Assn., 2005, Ogden Pleissner Meml. award, Salmagundi Art Club, 2006. Fellow Am. Artist Profl. League (Gold medal 1971, 75, award 1978-79); mem. Acad. Artists Assn. (Watercolor awards 1973-74, 76-77, New Eng. Heritage award 1993), Copley Soc. Boston (master artist), Hudson Valley, North Shore (bd. dirs. 1964-67, 86-95), Rockport Art Assn. (Lifetime Dedication to Promotion of Art award 1999, Joseph Santoro Meml. award 2005), Affiliated Art Assn. Mass. (v.p. 1980), Reading Art Assn. (charter, program chmn. 1960-86, Pres.'s awards 1973-80), Am. Watercolor Soc. (juror internat. exhbn. 1992), Allied Artists Am. (Watercolor Gold medals 1973-74), New Eng. Watercolor Soc. (2d v.p. 1984-90), Boston Watercolor Soc. (award 1975), Guild Boston Artists (bd. dirs. 1986-99, A. Lassall Ripley award 1993), Reading Assn. Fine and Performing Arts (charter, bd. dirs. 1993), Nat. Mus. Women in Arts (charter mem.), Salmagundi Art Club (40 awards including MacGowin Tuttle Meml. award 1976, 78-79, Elliot Liskin Meml. award 1988, Steven Blackman award 1988, Joseph Hartley award 1989, 2001, 2002, Mortimer Freehof Meml. award 1991, Bruce Crane award 1994, Rita Duis Meml. award 2001, Margery Saroka Meml. award 2003, Thomas Moran award 2004, Ogden Pleissner Meml. award 2006). Methodist. Address: 384 Franklin St Reading MA 01867-1036 Personal E-mail: nordstrands@aol.com.

NORDSTROM, DONNA OLENE, language educator; b. LaCrosse, Wis., July 19, 1936; d. Orion A. and Dena N. (Mathison) Tostrud; m. Charles W. Nordstrom, June 28, 1958; children: Carl R., Colin J., Marc J. BS, LaCrosse U., 1958. Kindergarten tchr. Cashton (Wis.) Pub. Schs., 1958-62, Viroqua (Wis.) Pub. Schs., 1966-70; 1st grade tchr. Westby Area Schs., Coon Valley, Wis., 1970-80, jr. high sch. English tchr., 1980—97; ret. Contbr. poems to profl. publs. (Golden Poet award 1990, 91). Organist Coon Valley Luth. Ch., 1973-84. Home: PO Box 216 Coon Valley WI 54623-0216

NORELL, DIANE MARIE, social worker, occupational therapist, educator; b. Maddock, ND, Sept. 28, 1952; d. Marvin LeRoy and Delores Lorraine Norell; m. Craig Donald Bader, Nov. 6, 1951; children: Amanda Justine Norell Bader, Seth Christopher Norell Bader. B in Occupl. Therapy, U. ND, Grand Forks, 1974; MSW, Ea. Wash. U., Cheney, 1982. Cert. psychiatric rehab practitioner U.S. Psychosocial Rehab., 2003, registered occuptional therapist Nat. Bd. Occupl. Therapy, 1975, lic. Dept. Health, Wash., 1985. Occupl. therapist ND State Hosp., Jamestown, 1975—77, Tri-County Mental Health Ctr., Reedsburg, Wis., 1977—78, State of Idaho, Coeurd'Alene, 1978—80; social worker Dept. Social and Health Svcs., Medical Lake, Wash., 1984—87; dir. rehab. svcs. Dept. Social and Health Svcs., Ea. State Hosp., 1987—88; quality mgmt. specialist Ea. State Hosp., Dept. Social and Health Svcs., 1988—2001; rsch. assoc. Wash. Inst. Mental Illness Rsch. and Tng., Spokane, 2001—. Adj. faculty Ea. Wash. U., Sch. Social Work and Human Svcs., Cheney, 1994—, Ea. Wash. U., Dept. Occupl. Therapy, 2005—. Contbr. articles to profl. jours. Sponsor ch. youth group Unity Chruch Truth, 2003—06; bd. mem. Nat. Alliance Mentally Ill, Spokane, 1995—2002. Mem.: U.S. Psychiat. Rehab. Assn. Democrat. Avocations: music, travel, art. Office: Wash Inst Mental Illness/Rsch WSU/PO Box 1495 Spokane WA 99210-1495 Office Phone: 509-358-7625.

NORELL, JUDITH REGINA, small business owner, musician, political administrator; b. N.Y.C. d. Sandor and Sylvia (Duchin) Hirsch; m. Ian Strasfogel, Feb. 15, 1973; children: Daniella, Gabrielle. MM, Juilliard Sch., 1971. Artistic dir. Bach Gesselschaft N.Y., N.Y.C., 1984-86, Opera Antica, Palm Beach, Fla., 1987-93; exec. dir. Women's Campaign Sch. Yale U., New Haven, 1996—; prin., owner Silver Moon Bakery, N.Y.C., 2000—; ptnr. PicNic Market and Cafe, 2004. Ford Found. fellow, 1970; recipient medal Mayor of City of N.Y., 1995. Mem. LWV, NWPC (legis. dir. N.Y. state chpt. 1995—). Office: Silver Moon Bakery 2740 Broadway New York NY 10025

NORELLI, TERIE THOMPSON, state legislator; b. Orange, N.J., July 7, 1952; d. George Russell and Iverna C. (Weber) Thompson; m. Allen M. Norelli, Dec. 31, 1973; children: Gina Marie, Daniel Thompson. BS in Math. summa cum laude, U. NH, 1985. Tchr. math. Winnacunnet H.S., Hampton, NH, 1985—95; mem. NH Ho. of Reps., Concord, 1996—, sci., tech. and energy com., 1996—2003, telecomm. oversight com., 1997—2003, ho. Dem. leadership, 1998—, asst. Dem. whip, 2002—04, asst. Dem. leader, 2005—, chair clean air subcom., 1998—2003, electric utility restructuring oversight com., 1998—2003, pub. works and hwys. com., 2003—05, rules com., 2003—05, co-chair reproductive rights caucus, 1996—, mem. legis. caucus for children, 1997—2002, mem. fin. com., 2005—. Participant in devel. series geometry insvc. workshops U. NH, 1986-89. Area team Nat. Abortion Rights Action League of NH, Portsmouth, 1990-94, bd. dirs., Concord, 1996-2000; chair Naral-Prochoice NH Pac, 2001-; bd. dirs. Sexual Assault Support Svcs., Portsmouth, 1992-96, pres. bd., 1993-95; del. to Joint US-China Conf. on Women's Issues, Beijing, 1995; organizing com. Bringing Back Beijing '95, Statewide Women's Conf., Concord, 1996, Beijing +5 Tri-State Preperation Conf., 1999; adv. bd. Feminist Health Ctr. Ports, Portsmouth, 1996-97; mem. Leadership Seacoast, 1995. Recipient NH Women's Lobby Meritorious Svc. award, 2002, Naral Pro-Choice N.H. Champion for Choice award, 2003, NASW-NH Legislator of Yr. award, 2004. Mem. Phi Beta Kappa, Phi Kappa Phi, Pi Mu Epsilon. Avocations: travel, arts and culture, running. Office: Rm 210 LOB State St Concord NH 03301 Office Phone: 603-271-2136.

NORFLUS, FRAN, biology professor; b. Bklyn., Mar. 29, 1964; AB in Chemistry, Duke U., Durham, NC, 1985; PhD, George Washington U., Washington, 1999. Biologist NIH, Bethesda, Md., 1991—93; adj. asst. prof. Columbia Union Coll., Takoma Park, Md., 1998—99; adj. instr. J. Sargeant Reynolds CC, Richmond, Va., George Washington U., Washington, 1999, Bunker Hill CC, Charlestown, Mass., 2002, U. Md., College Park, 2002—05, Capella U., Mpls., 2005—06; postdoctoral rsch. assoc. Emory U., Atlanta, 2000—01, Mass. Gen. Hosp., Boston, 2001—05; asst. prof. Clayton State U., Atlanta, 2005—. Contbr. articles to profl. jours. Postdoctoral fellow, Hereditary Disease Found., 2001—03. Mem.: Soc. Neuroscience. Office Phone: 678-466-4852. Business E-Mail: francinenorflus@clayton.edu.

NORGAARD, VERONICA R., real estate lawyer; b. Everett, Wash., Feb. 21, 1978; d. Robert Norgaard and Roberta C. Smith. BA, U. Wash., Seattle, 2000; JD, Syracuse U., 2003. Law clk. Hon. Joseph Foster, Toms River, NJ, 2003—04; assoc. atty. Bathgate, Wegenet & Wolf, Lakewood, NJ, 2004—05; ptnr. Koufaos & Norgaard, Brick, NJ, 2005—06. Treas. Letip, Brick, NJ, 2005—06. Pro bono atty. NAACP, Edison, NJ, 2005—06. Mem.: ABA, Assn. of Trial Lawers, Phi Alpha Delta. Avocations: soccer, softball. Office: Koufos & Norgaard 826 Mantoloking Rd Brick NJ 08723

NORKIN, CYNTHIA CLAIR, retired physical therapist; b. Boston, May 6, 1932; d. Miles Nelson and Carolyn (Green) Clair; m. Stanislav A Norkin, Feb. 19, 1955 (dec. 1970); 1 child, Alexandra. BS in Edn., Tufts U., 1954; cert. phys. therapist, Bouve Boston Coll., 1954; MS, Boston U., 1973, EdD, 1984. Instr. Bouve Boston Coll., 1954—55; staff phys. therapist New Eng. Med. Ctr., Boston, 1954—55, Abington (Pa.) Meml. Hosp., 1965—70, Ea. Montgomery Country Vis. Nurse Assn., 1970—72; asst. prof. phys. therapy Sargent Coll./Boston U., 1973—84; assoc. prof. phys. therapy, dir., founder Ohio U. Sch. Phys. Therapy, Athens, 1984—95, ret., 1995. Consult Boston Ctr Independent Living, Cambridge Vis Nurse Asn, Mass Medicaid Cost Effectiveness Project, 1978; secy Health Planning Coun Greater Boston, 1976—78; book, manuscript reviewer F A Davis Co, 1986—; arthritis adv comt Ohio Dept Health. Author (with P Levangie and C Norkin): Joint Structure and Function: A Comprehensive Analysis, 1983, 4th edit., 2005; author: (with D J White) Joint Measurement: A Guide to Goniometry, 1985; author: 3d edit., 2003. Trustee Brimmer and May Sch, 1980. Mem.: APHA, AAAS, Athens County Vis Nurse Asn (secy adv coun 1984—95), Mass Asn Mental health, Mass Physical Therapy Asn (chair quality assurance comt 1980—83), Am Physical Therapy Asn (on site evaluator comn on accreditation 1986—95). Episcopalian.

NORMAN, CHARLENE WILSON, secondary school educator; b. Ft. Campbell, Ky., Apr. 19, 1949; d. Charles B. and Mary (Powe) Wilson; m. John D. Norman, Mar. 21, 1971; children: David, Mary Katharine. AS, Mid. Ga. Coll., 1969; BS in Edn., Ga. So. U., 1971; MEd in Math., Ga. Coll., 1979. Cert. tchr., Ky., Ga. Tchr. Tabor Jr. H.S., Warner Robbins, Ga., 1971-72, Windsor Acad., Macon, Ga., 1972-78, North Cobb H.S., Acworth, Ga., 1978-79, Campbell H.S., Smyrna, Ga., 1979-81, U. Ky., Lexington, 1981—, Bryan Sta. H.S., Lexington, 1982—. Insvcs. presenter Fayette County Bd. Edn., Lexington, 1988—; presider Nat. Coun. Tchrs. Math., Paducah, Ky., 1993; state conf. presider Ky. Coun. Tchrs. Math., Lexington. Asst. Sunday sch. tchr. First United Meth. Ch., Paris, Ky., 1989-96. Named Outstanding Tchr., Tandy Corp., 1991-92, FAME Outstanding tTchr., Nat. City Bank and Fayette County Schs., 1994, 96, Star Tchr., 1978, Math. Edn. Svc. and Achievement award, 2004. Mem. Nat. Coun. Tchrs. Math., Ky. Coun. Tchrs. Math., Lexington Coun. Tchrs. Math. (pres. 1990). Avocations: reading, crafts. Home: 173 Northland Dr Paris KY 40361-9133 Office: Bryan Sta HS 1866 Edgeworth Dr Lexington KY 40505-2010 E-mail: cnorman@fayette.k12.ky.us.

NORMAN, CHRISTINA, broadcast executive; b. July 30, 1963; m. Charles Hunt; children: Zoe, Asha. BA, Boston U. Freelance prodn. coord MTV, 1986—91, prodn. mgr., 1991—93, supervising prodr., on-air promotions, 1993—94, dir., on-air promotions, 1994—95, v.p., on-air promotions, 1995—97, sr. v.p., on-air promotions, 1997—99, sr. v.p., mktg. and on-air promotion, 1999—2002; exec. v.p. and gen. mgr. VH1, 2002—04, pres., 2004—05, MTV, 2005—. Named one of 10 Most Powerful Blacks in TV, Ebony mag., 2002; named to 100 Most Powerful Women in Hollywood list, Hollywood Reporter, 2003, 40 under 40 list, Crain's N.Y. Bus., 2003; recipient Nat. Pub. Svc. award, Television Acad. Emmy Awards, 2002, Namiq Qasar Vision award, 2003. Office: VH1 20th Fl 1515 Broadway New York NY 10036*

NORMAN, E. GLADYS, retired finance educator, management consultant; b. Oklahoma City, June 13, 1933; d. Joseph Eldon and Mildred Lou (Truitt) Biggs; m. Joseph R.R. Radeck, Mar. 1, 1953 (div. Aug. 1962); children: Jody Norman, Ray Norman, Warren Norman (dec. May 1993), Dana Norman; m. Leslie P. Norman, Aug. 26, 1963 (dec. Feb. 1964); 1 child, Elayne Pearce. Student, Fresno (Calif.) State Coll., 1951-52, UCLA, 1956-59, Linfield Coll., 1986-95. Lic. tax preparer Oreg., 2005. Math. aid U.S. Naval Weapons Ctr., China Lake, Calif., 1952-56, computing systems specialist, 1957-68; systems programmer Oreg. Motor Vehicles Dept., Salem, 1968-69; instr. in data processing, dir. Computer Programming Ctr., Salem, 1969-72; instr. in data processing Merritt-Davis Bus. Coll., Salem, 1972-73; sr. programmer, analyst Teledyne Wah Chang, Albany, Oreg., 1973-79; sr. systems analyst Oreg. Dept. Vets. Affairs, Albany, 1979-80; instr. in bus. computers Linn-Benton C.C., Albany, 1980-95; ret., 1995. Computer cons. for LBCC Ret. Sr. Vol. Program, 1995-2002; presenter computer software seminars State of Oreg., 1991-93, Oreg. Credit Assoc. Conf., 1991, Oreg. Regional Users Group Conf., 1992; computer tchr. Linn-Benton C.C., 1999-2001; computer cons. Oremet-Wah Chang, 1996-2002, Oreg. State Yr. 2000 Project, 1997-98; adj. prof. Chemeketa C.C., 2000-02; computer cons. in field. Mem.: Assn. Info. Tech. Profls. (bd. dirs. 1977—84, assoc. v.p. 1988, bd. dirs. 1989—95, region sec. 1995—96, region treas. 1999, region sec. 2000—04, 2002—04, region treas. 2005, Diamond Individual Performance award 1985). Democrat. Avocations: drawing, painting, gardening.

NORMAN, ELAINE MITCHELL, information technology executive; Chief info. officer United Way of Met. Atlanta; sr. dir. info. tech. strategy and planning Ga. Pacific; v.p. info. tech. Am. Cancer Soc. Mem.: Women in Tech. (Named Woman of Yr. Tech. (not for profit/public sector) 2005), Tech. Assn. Ga., Ga. Chief Info. Officer Leadership Assn. (chair membership com. 2005, Ga. Chief Info. Officer of Yr. 2002). Office: American Cancer Society 1599 Clifton Rd NE Atlanta GA 30329-4251*

NORMAN, JESSYE, soprano; b. Augusta, Ga., Sept. 15, 1945; d. Silas Sr. and Janie (King) N. B.M. cum laude, Howard U., 1967; postgrad., Peabody Conservatory, 1967; M.Mus., U. Mich., 1968; MusD (hon.), U. South, 1984, Boston Conservatory, 1984, U. Mich., 1987, U. Edinburgh, 1989, Cambridge U., 1989. Debut, Deutsche Oper, Berlin, 1969, Italy, 1970; appeared: in operas Die Walküre, Idomeneo, L'Africaine, Marriage of Figaro, Aida, Don Giovanni, Tannhauser, Gotterdammerung, Ariadne auf Naxos, Les Troyens, Dido and Aeneas, Oedipus Rex, Hérodiade, Les Contes d'Hoffmann; debut in operas, La Scala, Milan, Italy, 1972, Salzburg Festival, 1977, U.S. debut, Hollywood Bowl, 1972, appeared with, Tanglewood Festival, Mass., also Edinburgh (Scotland) Festival, debut, Covent Garden, 1972; appeared in 1st Great Performers recital, Lincoln Center, N.Y.C., 1973—; other guest performances include, L.A. Philharm. Orch., Boston Symphony Orch., Am. Symphony Orch., Chgo. Symphony Orch., San Francisco Symphony Orch., Cleve. Orch., Detroit Symphony, N.Y. Philharm. Orch., London Symphony Orch., London Philharm. Orch., BBC Orch., Israel Philharm. Orch., Orchestre de Paris, Nat. Symphony Orch., English Chamber Orch., Royal Philharm., London Phila. Orch., Milw. Symphony Orch., Stockholm Philharm. Orch., Vienna Philharm. Orch., Berlin Philharm. Orch.; tours, Europe, S. Am., Australia, numerous recs., Columbia, EMI, Philips Records; PBS TV spcls. include Kathleen Battle and Jessye Norman Sing Spirituals, 1991, Concert at Avery Fisher Hall, 1994; recordings include Amazing Grace, Brava, Jessye!, Jessye Norman at Notre Dame (Cable Ace award), Lucky to Be Me, Sacred Songs, With a Song in My Heart, In The Spirit. Nat. spokesperson Partnership for the Homeless, Lupus Found.; bd. mem. Ms. Found., Nat. Music Found., City-Meals-on-Wheels, N.Y.C., N.Y. Bot. Garden, Paine Coll., Augusta, Ga. Recipient 1st prize Bavarian Radio Corp. Internat. Music Competition, 1968, Grand Prix du Disque, Acad. du Disque Francais, 1973, 76, 77, 82, 84, Deutsche Schallplatten, Preis, 1975, 81, Alumni award U. Mich., 1982, Outstanding Musician of Yr. award Musical Am., 1982, Grand Prix du Disque Academie Charles Cros, 1983, Commandeur de l'Ordre des Arts et des Lettres, France, 1984, Grammy awards, 1980, 82, 85, Legion d'Honneur, France, 1989, Radcliffe medal Radcliffe Coll. Alumnae Assn., 1997, numerous other awards; named hon. life mem. Girl Scouts U.S., 1987; inductee Am. Classical Music Hall of Fame, 2002. Mem. Royal Acad. Music (hon.), Alpha Kappa Alpha, Gamma Sigma Sigma, Sigma Alpha Iota, Pi Kappa Lambda. Clubs: Friday Morning Music (Washington). Office: L'Orchidee PO Box S Crugers NY 10521-0710

NORMAN, MARY JO, education educator; b. Savannah, Tenn., Dec. 5, 1943; d. Henry Landon Faubion and Mary Jewel (Patterson) Davidson; m. Charles George Norman, July 4, 1964; children: Carolyn Lee Ronco, Charles Landon Norman. BS in Elem. Edn., Tenn. Temple U., 1984; MS in Elem. Edn., U. Tenn., Chattanooga, 1988. Tchr. City Bd. Edn., Adult Edn., Huntsville, Ala., 1974-76, Triana Village Christian Sch., Huntsville, Ala., 1976-78; supr., tchr. Tenn. Temple U., Chatanooga, 1980-90, asst. prof., 1990—98, Grace Bapt. Acad., 1998—. Presenter workshops Am. Assn. Christian Schs., in eastern and southern states, 1985—, Assn. Christian Schs. Internat., Ohio, Ind., Calif., 1991—. Bd. dirs. Jr. Achievement, 1995-97. Mem. Nat. Coun. Tchrs. of Math., Tenn. Assn. Tchr. Educators (sec. 1993-96), Kappa Delta Pi. Avocations: travel, decorating, entertaining. Home: 1043 Shady Fork Rd Chattanooga TN 37421-4536

NORMAN, MARY MARSHALL, academic administrator, alcohol/drug abuse services professional, educator; b. Auburn, NY, Jan. 10, 1937; d. Anthony John and Zita Norman. BS cum laude, LeMoyne Coll., 1958; MA, Marquette U., 1960; EdD, Pa. State U., 1971. Cert. alcoholism counselor. Tchr. St. Cecilia's Elem. Sch., Theinsville, Wis., 1959-60; vocat. counselor Marquette U., Milw., 1959-60; dir. testing and counseling U. Rochester (N.Y.), NY, 1960-62; dir. testing and counseling, dean women, assoc. dean coll. Corning (N.Y.) C.C., Corning (N.Y.) C.C., 1962-68, asst. dean students, dir. student activities, asst. prof. ps University Park, 1962-68; rsch. asst. Ctr. for Study Higher Edn. Pa. State U., University Park, Pa., 1969-71; dean faculty South Campus C.C. Allegheny County, West Mifflin, Pa., 1971-72, campus pres., coll. v.p., 1972-82; pres. Orange County C.C., 1982-86; alcohol counselor Sullivan County Alcohol Drug Abuse Svc., 1985-90; sr. counselor Horton Family Program, 1990-96, ednl. cons., writer, 1996—. Cons. Boricua Coll., N.Y.C., 1976-77; reader NSF, 1977-78; govtl. commn. com. Am. Assn. Cmty. and Jr. Colls., 1976-79, bd. dirs., 1982—; chmn. middle state accreditation teams; chmn. Ernest Boyer, pres. Carnegie Found., 1987. Contbr. articles to profl. jours. Active Econ. Devel. Seneca County, Seneca County Tourism Bd.; com. to redefine the Liberal Arts degree Carnegie Found., 1982; mem. planning bd. Town of Seneca Falls, 2006—; active St. Patrick's Ch.; bd. dirs. Orange County United Way, Orange County Alcoholism and Drug Abuse Coun., 1993—96, Seneca County Hist. Soc., 1997—, Guild and Altar Soc., 1999. Mem. Nat. Women's Hall of Fame. Mem.: Pa. Coun. on Higher Edn., Nat. Am. Coun. on Edn. (Pa. rep. identification women for adminstrn. 1978—82, pres. 1980—96, bd. dirs.), Pitts. Coun. Women Execs. (charter), Pa. Assn. Acad. Deans, Pa. Assn. Two-Yr. Colls., Am. Assn. Women in Cmty. and Jr. Colls. (charter, Woman of the Yr. 1981), Nat. Assn. Women Deans and Counselors, Am. Assn. Higher Edn., Seneca County C. of C. (bd. dirs., mem. tourism com.), Orange County C. of C. (bd. dirs.), Amnesty Internat. (charter mem. women's coun. 2000—), Concerned Citizens for Good Govt. (charter), Kiwanis (planning bd. Seneca Falls 2006), Gamma Pi Epsilon. Home: 9 S Park St Seneca Falls NY 13148-1423

NORMAN, SHERI HANNA, artist, educator, cartographer; b. Chgo., Dec. 15, 1940; d. L. J. and Margaret Maxine (Kuyper Fleischer) Hanna; m. Donald Lloyd Norman, Feb. 28, 1963 (div. 1996); 1 child, Ronald Wayne. BA, U. Wyo., Laramie, 1963; postgrad., Dayton Art Inst., 1975; MFA, San Francisco Art Inst., 1993. Substitute tchr. Arlington, Va. and Yellow Springs, Ohio Pub. Sch. Dists., 1965-71; tech. illustrator, draftsperson U. Tex. Austin, Geotek, Inc., Denver, 1976-85; cartographer British Petroleum, San Francisco, 1985-87; draftsperson Earth Scis. Assocs., Palo Alto, Calif., 1988-92; intern, printmaking asst. Crown Point Press, San Francisco, 1991-92; freelance cartographer San Francisco and Napa, 1993—2004; sr. designer Bergin Glass Impressions, Napa, Calif., 2002—. Leader pub. nature/women's ceremony-ritual, San Francisco, 1991—93; artist in residence Villa Montalvo Ctr. Arts, Saratoga, Calif., 1996, Dorland Mountain Arts Colony, Temecula, Calif., 1996; adj. faculty Art Inst. Boston, 2002—; tchr. Napa Valley Adult Sch., 1999—2001; workshop leader, demonstrator in field. Author, illustrator: Envisioning An Unbroken Arc, vol. I, 1992, vol. II, 1992; designer (book) Garden Haven Reminiscences, a Collection, 2002, participating artist San Francisco Bay Area Presses; Visual Arts Ctr., Bluffton (Ohio) Coll., 1996, Bay Area Art II, 1999, Created Spaces, Nature as a Point of Departure, 2002, Napa Valley Coll. Art Gallery, 2002, Florence Crittenton Svcs., San Francisco, 1995, San Francisco Women Artists Gallery, 1995—97, Visual Aid's BIG DEAL, San Francisco, 1996—98, Napa Artists for People with AIDS, The Art of Giving, The Giving Art, Calistoga, 1999, 2000, St. Helena, Calif., 2001, Flying Fish of the Napa River, Copia Arts Ctr., 2005; curator, participating book artist A Display of Contemporary Book Arts Main Libr., Napa, 2000. Mem. Arts Coun. Napa Valley, Land Trust Napa County. Grantee, North Coast Calif. Coun. Adult Edn., 2000. Mem.: Calif. Soc. Printmakers (exhbn. com. 1995). Avocations: ongoing nature studies and nature advocacy, early mythologies and meditative practice. Home: 423 Cross St Napa CA 94559-3335 Personal E-mail: inklings@napanet.net.

NORMAN, THERESA J.C., philosophy professor; b. Tucson, Jan. 6, 1956; d. Martin Luther Dotson and Elizabeth Sue Marie Brouillette; m. Kenneth Lee Buckman, May 1, 1982. BA, So. Ill. U., Edwardsville, 1984, MA, 1986; postgrad., So. Ill. U., Carbondale, 1986—90. Vis. asst. prof. U. Tex., Arlington, 1990—91, Southwestern U., Georgetown, Tex., 1991—92; adj. prof. U. Tex.-Pan Am., Edinburg, 1992—2004; prof. philosophy South Tex. Coll., McAllen, 2004—. Home: 2012 Anacua Cir Edinburg TX 78539-5906

NORMANN, MARGARET ELLA, deacon, educator; b. Providence, Jan. 13, 1931; d. Parker Edward and Margaret Millard (McDowell) Monroe; m. Conrad Neil Normann, July 17, 1953; children: Andrea Kristin Mudge, Margaret Ingrid Wierdsma, Conrad Neil, Parker Monroe. BA in Drama, Vassar Coll., 1952; MA in English, NYU, 1966; MS in Recreation and Leisure, So. Conn. State U., 1978. Ordained deacon Protestant Episcopal Ch., 1993. Human svc. officer, dir. recreation programs Town of Bedford, NY, 1975—83; cmty. edn. coord., writer Cmty. Residences Info. Svc. Program, White Plains, NY, 1983—91; initiator, exec. dir. Apropes Housing Opportunities and Mgmt. Enterprises, Inc., Bedford, 1985—93; deacon Ch. of the Holy Communion, Mahopac, NY, 1993—99; chaplain Four Winds Hosp., Cross River, NY, 1993—99. Writing instr., tutor, evaluator SUNY Empire State Coll., Hartsdale, NY, 1984—99. Recipient Disting. Svc. Alumnae award, Lincoln Sch., Providence, 1988, Cert. of Merit, State of N.Y., Albany, 1991, Mickey Leland Home for the Homless award, 1991. Republican.

NORMENT, RACHEL GOBBEL, artist, educator, writer; b. Durham, NC, Apr. 3, 1934; d. Luther Lafayette and Marcia (Russell) Gobbel; m. Owen Lennon Norment, Jr., Dec. 21, 1957; children: Marcia Lynnette, Russell Owen. AB in English, Rhodes Coll., 1955; MA in Art Edn., Vanderbilt U., 1956. Tchr. arts and crafts Bainbridge Jr. High Sch., Richmond, Va., 1956—57; tchr. 3d grade E.S.H. Greene Sch., Chesterfield County, Va., 1957—59; tchr. 2d & 3d grade Cameron Park Sch., Hillsborough, NC, 1962—64; art instr. Southside Va. C.C., various locations, 1972—82. Instr. watercolor painting Southside Va. C.C., Keysville, 1989, Keysville, 91, Keysville, 95, Reynolds Homestead, Critz, Va., 1989, Critz, 91, Ctrl. Va. Watercolor Guild, Charlottesville, Va., 1998, Buckingham Arts Ctr., Va., 1991, Fluvanna Art Assn., Fork Union, Va., 1985, Fork Union, 97; lectr. in field. One-woman shows include Hampden-Sydney Coll., Va., 1968, 1969, 1970, 1971, 1972, 1974, 1977, 1980, 1981, 1984, 1986, 1994, Va. Nat. Bank, Farmville, 1968, 1969, 1971, 1973, Southside Cmty. Hosp., 1970, 1971, 1973, 1975, Southside Va. C.C., Keysville, 1972, 1979, Citizens Savs. and Loan, Farmville, 1973, 1974, 1975, 1976, 1982, The Palette Gallery, Christiansburg, Va., 1974, Fortnightly Club, Chase City, Va., 1975, Fidelity Am. Bank, Centerville, Va., 1977, Farmville, 1979, Ctrl. Fidelity Bank, 1981, Westminster-Canterbury House, Richmond, Va., 1981, 1987, Piedmont Geriatric Hosp., Crewe, Va., 1982, U. Va. Hosp., Charlottesville, 1983, Greensboro C. of C., 1990, Shenandoah Valley Art Ctr., Va., 1990, Fluvanna County Libr., 1998, Thomas Jefferson Meml. Ch., Charlottesville, Va., 1999, Westminster-Canterbury of the Blue Ridge, Charlottesville, 2000, numerous invitational and juried group exhbns., Represented in permanent collections Hampden-Sydney Coll., Longwood U., Greensboro Coll., Va. Episc. Sch., Westtown Sch., Ethyl Corp.; author: Guided by Dreams: Breast Cancer, Dreams, and Transformation; contbr. articles to area newspapers. Group facilitator Dreamwork, 1994—. Mem.: Ctrl. Va. Watercolor Guild, Miss. Watercolor Soc., So. Watercolor Soc., Ky. Watercolor Soc., Va. Watercolor Soc. (v.p. 1994—95, pres. 1996—97), Internat. Assn. Study of Dreams, Zeta Tau Alpha. Home: 1247 Courtyard Dr Charlottesville VA 22903-7881 E-mail: r.g.norment@earthlink.net.

NORMINGTON, NORMA SHOTWELL, secretary; b. Lakewood, Ohio, Apr. 7, 1924; d. Phillip Bassett and Alice Mae (Teed) Shotwell; m. Joshua James Normington, July 18, 1944; children: Peter Jay, Patricia Jean Normington Zieher. BS in English, U. Wis., 1948. Cert. tchr., Wis. Tchr. Madison (Wis.) East High Sch., 1948-50, Belmont (Calif.) Primary Grades, 1951; sec.-treas., now CEO Saddle Mound Cranberry Co., Inc., City Point, Wis., 1975—. Mem. AAUW (sec. 1953, pres. 1954), Marshfield Women's Club (v.p.), Wood County Rep. Women's Club, Sigma Alpha Iota, Kappa Delta. Avocations: travel, cooking, playing organ, needlepoint, reading. Home and Office: 7848 Shotwell Rd Pittsville WI 54466

NORRANDER, BARBARA, political science professor; PhD, Ohio State U., Columbus. Prof. U. Ariz., Tucson, 1990—. Author: (textbook) American Government: Using MicroCase ExplorIt, 9th edition; editor: (book) Understanding Public Opinion, 2nd edition. Mem.: Western Polit. Sci. Assn. (pres. 2004—05). Office: U Ariz Dept Polit Sci Tucson AZ 85721

NORRELL, MARY PATRICIA, nursing educator; b. Seymour, Ind., Jan. 03; d. William C. and Mary Elizabeth (Elkins) Ulrey; m. Robert Gerald Norrell, Aug. 17, 1974; children: Shannan, Richard, Trisha. BSN, Ball State U., Muncie, Ind., 1971; MS, Ind. U., Bloomington, 1996. Cert. inpatient obstetrics, TB and CPR instr. Team leader Mt. Sinai Med. Ctr., Miami Beach, Fla., 1971—73; charge nurse Jackson County Schneck Meml. Hosp., Seymour, Ind., 1971, 1973—74; nurse Camp Matoaka, Oakland, Maine, 1973; prof. Ivy Tech. C.C. Ind., Columbus, Ind., 1974—. Item writer Nat. Coun. Licensure Exam. Practical Nurses, 1992; participant Acad. Instrl. Excellence, Ivy Tech. C.C. Ind., 2001-02; practical nursing program chair Ivy Tech. C.C. Ind., 2003-06. Textbook reviewer, cons.: Saunders, 1990—97, textbook reviewer: Prentice-Hall, 2005; textbook reviewer F.A. Davis, 2005—. Bd. dirs. Sr. Ctr., Columbus, Ind., 2005—. Recipient Pres.'s award for instrnl. excellence, 2003. Home: 572 Shawnee Ct Seymour IN 47274-1956 Business E-Mail: mnorrell@ivytech.edu.

NORRIS, ANDREA SPAULDING, art museum director; b. Apr. 2, 1945; d. Edwin Baker and Mary Gretchen (Brendle) Spaulding. BA, Wellesley Coll., 1967; MA, NYU, 1969, PhD, 1977. Intern dept. western European arts Met. Mus. Art, N.Y.C., 1970, 72; rsch. and editorial asst. Inst. Fine Arts NYU, 1971, lectr. Washington Sq. Coll., 1976-77; lectr. Queens Coll. CUNY, 1973-74; asst. to dir. Art Gallery Yale U., New Haven, 1977-80, lectr. art history, 1979-80; chief curator Archer M. Huntington Art Gallery, Austin, Tex., 1980-88; lectr. art history Dept. Art U. Tex., Austin, 1984-88; dir. Spencer Mus. Art U. Kans., Lawrence, 1988—2004. Co-author: (catalogue) Medals and Plaquettes from the Molinari Collection at Bowdoin College, 1976; author: (exhbn. catalogues) Jackson Pollock: New-Found Works, 1978, Vanished Voices, The Legacy of the Northeast Kansas Indians, 2004; exhbn. The Sforza Court: Milan in the Renaissance 1450-1535, 1988-89, Am. Indian Traditions Transformed, 2000. Mem.: Mus. Loan Network (adv. bd. 2002—04), Assn. Art Mus. Dir., Coll. Art Assn. (bd. dir. 2000—05, v.p. for coms. 2002—04, v.p. for ann. conf. 2004—05), Renaissance Soc. Am., Phi Beta Kappa. Office: Spencer Mus Art U Kans 1301 Mississippi St Lawrence KS 66045-7500 E-mail: asnorris@earthlink.net.

NORRIS, CAROLYN SUE, artist; b. Martinsurg, W.Va., Apr. 23, 1946; d. James R. and Roberta Norris; children: Vicky, Jacqueline, Janet, Ricky, Cynthia. Cons. in field. One-woman shows include C&G, Greenville, Miss., 1994, Mostly African Market, Natciez, Miss., 1994, exhibited in group shows at Delta Axis, Memphis, 1994, Delta State U., Cleve., Miss., Crosstie Arts Festival, 1993, 1994, 1995, 1996, 1997, 1998, 2000 (First in Painting award, 1998, First in Drawing award, 1998, Best in Show award, 1998, Third in Painting award, 1997, First in Painting award, 1996, 1995), exhibitions include Miss. Valley State U. Johnston Gallery, 1998, exhibited in group shows at First St. Gallery, Grenada, Miss., 2001, Guachoya Cultural Art Ctr., Lake Village, Ark., 2001, Delta State U., Cleve., Miss., 2002, Cathead Gallery, Clarksdale, Miss., 2004, others. Mem.: Nat. Mus. Women. Home: 200 North Andrew Cleveland MS 38732 Office Phone: 662-843-7484.

NORRIS, JEANNIE, headmaster; Head of sch. Miss Hall's Sch., Pittsfield, Mass., 1996—. Mem. bd. dirs. Secondary Sch. Admission Test Bd., 2004—05. Mem.: Nat. Assn. of Principals of Schs. for Girls. Office: Miss Hall's Sch PO Box 1166 492 Holmes Rd Pittsfield MA 01202-1166

NORRIS, JOAN CLAFETTE HAGOOD, retired assistant principal; b. Pelzer, SC, June 26, 1951; d. William Emerson and Sarah (Thompson) Hagood; divorced; 1 child, Javiere Sajorah. BA in History and Secondary Edn., Spelman Coll., 1973; MA in Teaching in Edn., Northwestern U., 1974; MA in Adminstrn. and Supervision, Furman U., 1984. Cert. elem. edn. tchr., elem. prin., social studies tchr., elem. supr., S.C.; notary pub., S.C. Clk. typist Fiber Industry, Greenville, SC, 1970, Spelman Coll. Alumni Office, Atlanta, 1970-73; tchr. Chgo. Bd. Edn., 1973-74, Greenville County Pub. Schs., Greenville, S.C., 1974-97, Hollis Acad., Greenville, S.C., 1996-97; asst. prin. Nevitt Forest Elem. Sch., Anderson, SC, 1997—2002; ret., 2002. Dir. elem. summer sch. Anderson Sch. Dist. 5, 1998, asst. prin. acad., 2001—02; mem. steering com. N.W. area Greenville County Sch. Dist., 1994—95, chmn. elem. steering com., 1996, participant Curriculum Leadership I, 96, participant potential adminstrs. internship program, 1997—; participant Asst. Prins. Inst. Furman U., summer, 1999; flagship status application reader S.C. Sch., 2000. Contbr. articles to profl. jours. Staff devel. com. summer sch. program Anderson County Elem. Sch. Dist. 5, 2000—02; bd. dirs. Girl Scouts of Old 96 Coun. Inc., 2001—, mem. scholarship com., 2001—05, mem. nominating com., 2002—05, chairperson nominating com., 2004—05, sec., personnel com., exec. com., 2005—; sec. Webette's Temple 1312, Greenville, 1985, parliamentarian, 1986; bus. ptnr. contact person Nevitt Forest Elem. Sch., 1997—2000, comm. contact person, 1997—2000, after-sch. site dir., 2000—01. Selected to Potential Adminstrs. Acad., Furman U., 1991; named Tchr. of Yr., Armstrong Elem. Sch., 1982, 91; grantee Alliance of Quality Edn., 1989-90, 97-98, Chick-A-Fil-A extended day program in math and reading, 1998; grantee Publix Charities Media Ctr. Books, 2000. Mem. AAUW (exec. bd. cmty. rep. Greenville br. 1993-94, v.p. programs 1994-96, pres.-elect. 1996-97, pres. 1997-98, nominating com., gift honoree, 5 Star Recognition award 1998), Ret. NEA, S.C. Edn. Assn., S.C. Assn. Sch. Adminstrs. (nom. Disting. Asst. Prin. 2000, Sch. of Promise application reader 2000), Northwestern Alumni Assn., Am. Assn. Ret. Persons, S.C. Educator's Ret. Assn., Phi Delta Kappa (chpt. alt. del. 1992-93, sec. chpt. 1993-94, v.p. membership 996-97). Democrat. Baptist. Avocations: reading, talking to older people, listening to blues music, travel, watching old black and white movies. Home: 219 Barrett Dr Mauldin SC 29662-2030 Personal E-mail: jhagoodnorris1@yahoo.com.

NORRIS, KAREN W., grants specialist; b. Washington, Mar. 5, 1950; d. Jerome J. and Lillian (Pittle) N.; children: Elysa, Mindy. BA, George Washington U., 1972; MBA, Hood Coll., 1994. Tchr. journalism, TV and English Montgomery County Pub. Schs., Rockville, Md., 1972-80; broadcast engr. CBS TV-WDVM-TV, Washington, 1980-83; pvt. practice comm. cons. Washington, 1983-88; grants specialist Prince George's County Pub. Schs., Upper Marlboro, Md., 1988—. Mem. cultural arts adv. com. Montgomery County Govt., Rockville, 1975; mem. performing arts adv. com. Prince George's County Pub. Schs., Upper Marlboro, 1994-98; panel chair U.S. Dept. Edn. 21st Century Sch., 2001 Bd. dirs. Journalism Edn. Assn., Balt., 1972-75. Recipient Excellence in H.S. Journalism award Montgomery County C. of C., Rockville, 1978; named Md. Journalism Tchr. of Yr., Md. Journalism Edn. Assn., Rockville, 1972. Mem. AAUW (mem. pub. policy com. 1998). Office: Baltimore City Pub Sch Grants Adminstrn 200 E North Ave Baltimore MD 21202

NORRIS, LAURIE, secondary mathematics educator; b. Seattle, June 10, 1960; d. Lyman F. and Beverly J. (Lusk) Bush; m. Scott C. Norris, Aug. 15, 1986; 1 child, Michael. BA, Washington State U., Pullman, 1982; MA, Pacific Luth. U., Tacoma, 1991. Tchr. math. Steilacoom Hist. Sch. Dist., Tacoma, Wash., 1983—. Participant Applied Math. Consortium, Wash., 1989—, Tech. in Edn., Seattle, 1989-92. Recipient various excellence in edn. awards. Mem. ASCD, Nat. Coun. Tchrs. Math., Math. Assn. Am., N.W. Coun. Computer Educators, Wash. State Math. Coun. Office: 54 Sentinel Dr Steilacoom WA 98388-1663

NORRIS, LOIS ANN, retired elementary school educator; b. Detroit, May 13, 1937; d. Joseph Peter and Marguerite Iola (Gourley) Giroux; m. Max Norris, Feb. 9, 1962 (div. 1981); children: John Henry, Jeanne Marie, Joseph Peter. BS in Social Sci., Ea. Mich. U., 1960, MA, 1960; cert. adminstr., Calif. State U., Bakersfield, 1983. Kindergarten tchr. Norwalk-LaMirada Unified Sch. Dist., 1960-62; tchr. various grades Rialto Unified Sch. Dist., 1962-66; kindergarten tchr. Inyokern (Calif.) Sch., 1969-82; 1st grade tchr. Vieweg Basic Sch, 1982-92, kindergarten tchr., 1992-96; ret., 1996. Head tchr. Sierra Sands Elem. Summer Sch.; adminstrv. intern Sierra Sands Adult Sch., master tchr., head tchr., counselor. Ofcl. scorekeeper, team mother, snack bar coord. China Lake Little League; team mother, statistician Indian Wells Valley Youth Football; bd. mem. PTA; pres. Sch. Site Coun.; treas. Inyokem Parents Club; run coord. City of Hope; timekeeper, coord. Jr. Olympics; mem. planning com. Sunshine Festival; active Burros Booster Club; docent Maturango Mus.; mem. Pink Lady orgn., mem. hosp. corp. bd. Ridgecrest Regional Hosp.; mem. Women's Aux. for Commd. Officers Mess; mem. civilian svc. unit Sheriff Dept., Altrusa, Calif.; bd. mem. Indian Wells Valley Concert Assn. Recipient Hon. Svc. award PTA, 1994. Mem. NEA, AAUW, Calif. Tchr. Assn., Desert Area Tchr. Assn., Assn. Calif. Sch. Adminstr., Inyokern C. of C. (sec.), Am. Motorcycle Assn., NRA, AOPA, Altrusa, Civilian Svc. Unit Kern County Sheriff Dept., Bakersfield Coll. Diamond Club, Inyokern Rotary, Indian Wells Valley Concert Assn.(bd. mem.), Beta Sigma Phi. Republican. Mem. Lds Ch. Avocations: swimming, physical fitness, music, American history, gardening. Home: PO Box 163 201 N Brown Rd Inyokern CA 93527 E-mail: annnorris@verizon.net.

NORRIS, MACKIE LYVONNE HARPER, registered nurse, health care consultant; b. Bivins, Tex., Dec. 10, 1940; d. McNoble and Corine Rosetta (Collins) Harper; m. Alfred L. Norris Sr., Sept. 9, 1961; children: Alfred, Lisa, Tyrone, Angela. BSN, Dillard U., 1960; MN, Emory U., 1971, PhD, 1996. RN, N.Mex., La., Ga. Asst. prof. Dillard U., New Orleans, 1977-84; assoc. prof. Woodruff Sch. Nursing Emory U., Atlanta, 1985-92. Cons. Aftercare, Ltd., Atlanta, 1991-92, United Meth. Ch., N.Y.C., 1996—, Not Even One Project, N.Mex., 1997; mem. faculty U. Phoenix Nursing Dept. Mem. Presbyn. Hosp. IRB, Albuquerque, 1993—; treas. N.Mex. Sickle Cell Coun., Albuguerque, 1994—. Mem. ANA, APHA, Nat. League Nursing, N.Mex. Pub. Health Assn., Omichron Delta Kappa, Sigma Theta Tau.

NORRIS, RUTH ANN, social worker; b. Leavenworth, Kans., Oct. 29, 1955; d. Ival Eugene and Maxine Barbara (Ripper) Scholtz; m. V.W. Rusty Norris, May 21, 1977 (div. 2005) BA, Graceland Coll., 1978; MSW, U. Kans., 1988. LCSW. Social worker Okla. Dept. Human Svcs., Miami, 1979-82, Mo. Div. Family Svcs., Kansas City, Mo., 1982-87; clin. social worker Western Mo. Mental Health Ctr., Kansas City, 1988-97; exec. dir., pres. Ctr. for Wholeness Concepts, Independence, Mo., 1992-93; with Norris Counseling Svcs., Independence, 1993—2001; sr. social worker Truman Behavioral Health Network, Kansas City, Mo., 1997—2001; group home dir. Western Mo. Mental Health Ctr., Kansas City, Mo., 2001—. Named one of Outstanding Young Women Am., 1991. Mem. NASW, Acad. Cert. Social Workers. Avocations: travel, reading. Office: Western Mo Mental Health Ctr Esperanza House 1000 E 24th St Kansas City MO 64108 Personal E-mail: norrismsu@comcast.net. Business E-Mail: ruth.norris@clmh.mo.gov.

NORRIS, SANDRA LOVE, occupational therapist; b. East St. Louis, Ill., Jan. 6, 1956; d. Morrison Love and Sarah (Cameron) Miller; m. Frank Rex Norris, Aug. 15, 1987. AAS, Ill. Ctrl. Coll., 1979. Lic. occupl. therapy asst. Ill. Tchr. asst. Mamie O Stookey Sch., Belleville, Ill., 1980—83; activity therapy asst. Belleville Meml. Hosp., 1983—90, occupl. therapy asst., 1990—95, Good Samaritan Hosp., Mt. Vernon, Ill., 1995—97, Eden Village Therapy Ctr., Glen Carbon, Ill., 1997—2001, Select Therapies, Lebanon Greenville, Highland, Ill., 2002—, So. Ill. Specialized Healthcare Assocs./Anderson Hosp., Maryville, Ill., 2003—, Staffing Concepts Nat., Inc., Edwardsville, Ill., 2004—. Clin. instr. Eden Village Therapy Ctr., Glen Carbon, 1997—99. Radio reader for blind Radio Info. Svc. Shrine Lady Snows, Belleville, 1984—; vol., Buddy Program Bethany Pl. AIDS Svc. Orgn., Belleville, 1995—96. Avocations: reading, Bingo. Home: 814 N Douglas Ave Belleville IL 62220 Office: Univ Nursing Home 1095 University Dr Edwardsville IL 62025 Office Phone: 618-656-1081.

NORRIS, SUSAN ELIZABETH, social worker; b. Lubbock, Tex., Oct. 8, 1952; d. William Oxford and Katherine Burton (Sydnor) N. BA, U. Tex., Arlington, 1974; MSW, U. Conn., 1987. Child protective svcs. social worker Tex. Dept. Human Resources, Ft. Worth, 1978-82; temp. word processor various cos., 1983-85; rsch. cons. Hartford, Conn., 1986-89; dir. child care svcs. United Way Conn., Hartford, 1987-92, dir. program svcs., 1992-93; faculty/assoc. dir. child and family studies, pediatrics U. Conn. Health Ctr., Farmington, 1993-94, dir., 1994-96; program mgr. Work/Family Directions, Boston, 1996-97; dir. child care svcs. Maximus, 1997-98, deputy project mgr., 1998-2000, project mgr., 2000—02, dir., 2002—03, v.p., 2003—. Mem. adj. faculty sch. social work U. Conn., 2000—. Bd. dirs., sec. Hartford Interval House, 1989-93; pres. bd. dirs. Hartford Area Child Collaborative, 1992-94. Democrat. Avocations: travel, reading, exercise. Office: 11419 Sunset Hills Rd Reston VA 20190

NORRIS, VIRGINIA OAKLEY, secondary school educator; b. L.A., Jan. 14, 1928; d. Earl James Taylor Oakley and Florence Marian (Ashley) Guthrie; m. Robert Matheson Norris, Jan. 5, 1952; children: Donald Oakley Norris, James Matheson Norris, Elizabeth Anne-Norris Dodson. AA, UCLA, 1946, BA, 1948. Cert. secondary tchr., Calif. Tchr., art dept. chmn. Anaheim Union H.S., Calif., 1949—51; engring. draftsman Hughes Aircraft, L.A., 1951; tchr. Santa Barbara City Schs. and H.S., Santa Barbara, 1963—79; tchr./spinning U. Calif. Santa Barbara Ext., 1973; instr./fiber arts adult edn. Santa Barbara City Coll., 1972—84; demonstrator various schs., mus., chs., confs. and fairs, Calif., 1972—. Workshop for fiberarts groups presenter, Calif., New Zealand, Norfolk Island and Faroe Islands, 1973—. Contbr. articles to profl. jours. Bd. dirs., pres. Arboleda Park Improvement Assn., Santa Barbara, 1960-81; mem. Santa Barbara County Libr. Adv. Com., 1964-72, Goleta Valley Gen. Plan Adv. Com., Santa Barbara, 1973-81. Recipient Best Handspun Wool award Nat. Handcrafted Wool Showcase, 1978. Mem. Wellington Handweavers and Spinners Guild, Santa Barbara Fiber Arts Guild (pres. 1977-79), New Zealand Spinners, Weavers and Woolcraft Soc., Tawa Spinners Guild, UCLA Alumni Assn., U. Calif. Santa Barbara Faculty Women's Club (pres. 1984-86), Chi Omega. Congregationalist. Home: 4424 Nueces Dr Santa Barbara CA 93110-2006

NORRIS, WANDA PAYNE, science educator; b. Richlands, Va., Dec. 1, 1942; d. Orbin Chester and DeMarcy Mae Payne; m. P. J. Giampocaro (div.); children: Marcus Joe, Marshall Lee; m. Howard Marvin Norris Jr. BS, Radford U., Va., 1964, MS, 1967. Tchr. Dublin Elem. Sch., Va., 1964—65, Conehurst Elem. Sch., Salem, 1965—66, Cave Spring Elem. Sch., Roanoke, 1965—70; tchr. sci. Esser H.S., Tappahannock, 1970—96, Plainview Elem Sch., Dunn, NC, 1996—98, Midway Mid. Sch., Dunn, NC, 1998—. Grantee, Midway Mid. Sch., 1998—2005. Mem.: NEA, NC Edn. Assn. Republican. Presbyterian. Home: 681 Ernest Williams Rd Roseboro NC 28382 Office: Midway Mid Sch 1115 Roberts Grove Rd Dunn NC 28334

NORSTRAND, IRIS FLETCHER, psychiatrist, neurologist, educator; b. Bklyn., Nov. 21, 1915; d. Matthew Emerson and Violet Marie (Anderson) Fletcher; m. Severin Anton Norstrand, May 20, 1941; children: Virginia Helene Norstrand Villano, Thomas Fletcher, Lucille Joyce. BA, Bklyn. Coll., 1937, MA in Biochemistry, 1965, PhD in Biochemistry, 1972; MD, L.I. Coll. Medicine, 1941. Diplomate Am. Bd. Psychiatry and Neurology, cert. geriat. psychiatry. Intern Montefiore Hosp., Bronx, NY, 1941-42; asst. resident in neurology N.Y. Neurol. Inst.-Columbia-Presbyn. Med. Ctr., N.Y.C., 1944-45; pvt. practice Bklyn., 1947-52; resident in psychiatry Bklyn. VA Med. Ctr., 1952-54, resident in neurology, 1954-55, staff neurologist, 1955-81, asst. chief neurol. svc., 1981-91, staff psychiatrist, 1991-95. Neurol. cons. Indsl. Home for Blind, Bklyn., 1948-51; clin. prof. neurology SUNY Health Sci. Ctr., Bklyn., 1981—; attending neurologist Kings County Hosp., Bklyn., State U. Hosp., Bklyn.; cons. in field. Contbr. articles to profl. jours. Mem. Nat. Rep. Congl. Com., Rep. Senatorial Inner Circle. Recipient Spl. plaque Mil. Order Purple Heart, 1986, Spl. Achievement award PhD Alumni Assn. of CUNY, 1993, Lifetime Achievement award Bklyn. Coll., 1995, others. Fellow Am. Psychiat. Assn., Am. Acad. Neurology, Internat. Soc. Neurochemistry, Am. Assn. U. Profs. Neurology, Am. Med. EEG Soc. (pres. 1987-88), Nat. Assn. VA Physicians (pres. 1989-91, James O'Connor award 1987), N.Y. Acad. Scis., Sigma Xi. Republican. Presbyterian. Avocations: writing, piano, travel, reading. Home: 7624 10th Ave Brooklyn NY 11228-2309

NORTH, HELEN FLORENCE, classicist, educator; b. Utica, NY; d. James H. and Catherine (Debbold) N. AB, Cornell U., 1942, MA, 1943, PhD, 1945; LLD (hon.), Rosary Coll., 1982; DLitt (hon.), Trinity Coll., Dublin, 1984, Fordham U., 1999; LHD (hon.), La Salle U., 1985, Yale U., 1986. Instr. classical lang. Rosary Coll., River Forest, Ill., 1946-48; faculty Swarthmore Coll., 1948—91, prof. classics, 1961-91, chmn. dept., 1959-91, emerita, 1991—, Centennial prof. classics, 1966-73, 78-91, Kenan prof., 1973-78, sr. rsch. scholar, 2003—. Vis. asst. prof. Cornell U., 1952—; vis. assoc. prof. Barnard Coll., 1954—55; vis. prof. LaSalle Coll., Phila., 1965, Am. Sch. Classical Studies, Athens, 1975, Athens, 87; Blegen disting. vis. rsch. prof. Vassar Coll., 1979. Author: Sophrosyne: Self-Knowledge and Self-Restraint in Greek Literature, 1966, From Myth to Icon: Reflections of Greek Ethical Doctrine in Literature and Art, 1979, (with Mary C. North) The West of Ireland: A Megalithic Primer, 1999, Cork and the Rest of Ireland: A Megalithic Primer II, 2003; translator: John Milton's Second Defense of the English People, 1966; editor: Interpretations of Plato: A Swarthmore Symposium, 1977; co-editor: Of Eloquence, 1970; editor Jour. History of Ideas; mem. editl. bd. Catalogus Translationum et Commentariorum, 1979. Bd. dirs. Am. Coun. Learned Socs., 1977-85; trustee LaSalle U., 1972-2003, chmn. bd. trustees, 1991-93; trustee King's Coll., Am. Acad. in Rome; chmn. com. on Classical Sch. Recipient Harbison prize Danforth Found., 1969, Centennial medal Am. Acad. Rome, 1995; named Distinguished Daughter of Pa., 1989, del. of Am. Philological Assn. to Am. Coun. Learned Socs., 1991-95; grantee Am. Coun. Learned Socs., 1943-45, 73, fellow, 1971-72, 87-88; Mary Isabel Sibley fellow Phi Beta Kappa Found., 1945-46, Ford Fund Advancement Edn. fellow, Fulbright fellow Rome, 1953-54, Guggenheim fellow, 1958-59, 75-76, AAUW, 1963-64; grantee Danforth Found., 1962, Lindbach Found., 1966; Sr. fellow NEH, 1967-68; NEH Coll. Tchrs. fellow, 1983-84; Martin classical lectr. Oberlin Coll., 1972. Mem. Am. Philol. Assn. (dir. 1968—, pres.

1976—, Charles J. Goodwin award 1969, Disting. Svc. medal 1996), Classical Assn. Atlantic States, Catholic Commn. Intellectual and Cultural Affairs (chmn. 1968-69), Am. Acad. Arts and Scis., Am. Philos. Soc., Soc. Religion Higher Edn., Phi Beta Kappa (bd. vis. scholars 1975-76, senate 1991—2003), Phi Kappa Phi. Home: 604 Ogden Ave Swarthmore PA 19081-1131 Personal E-mail: hnorth1@swarthmore.edu.

NORTH, JULIE A., lawyer; b. Canberra, Australia, Mar. 20, 1962; BA cum laude, Hamilton Coll., NY, 1984; JD magna cum laude, Syracuse Univ., 1989. Bar: NY 1990. Assoc. Cravath Swaine & Moore LLP, NYC, 1989—97, ptnr., litig., 1997—. Notes, comments editor Syracuse Law Rev. Bd. trustees Hamilton Coll., Clinton, NY; bd. visitors Syracuse Univ. Coll. of Law. Office: Cravath Swaine & Moore LLP Worldwide Plz 825 Eighth Ave New York NY 10019-7475 Office Phone: 212-474-1752. Office Fax: 212-474-3700. Business E-Mail: jnorth@cravath.com.

NORTH, KATHRYN E. KEESEY (MRS. EUGENE C. NORTH), retired music educator; b. Columbia, Pa., Jan. 25, 1916; d. Isaac and Elizabeth (French) Keesey; m. Eugene C. North, Aug. 18, 1938. BS, Ithaca Coll., N.Y., 1938; MA, NYU, 1950. Dir. music Cairo (N.Y.) Ctrl. Sch. Dist., 1938; music edn. cons. Argyle (N.Y.) Ctrl. Sch. Dist., 1939; dir. gen. music curriculum Hartford (N.Y.) Ctrl. Sch. Dist., 1939; mem. staff Del. Pub. Instrn., Dover, 1943; dir. music edn. Herricks (N.Y.) Pub. Schs., 1944—71; ret., 1971. Vis. lectr. Ithaca Coll., 1959—60, 1962—65, Fairleigh-Dickinson U., Rutherford, NJ, 1966, Albertus Magnus Coll., New Haven, 1968; instr. Adelphi Coll., 1954—55, Sch. Edn., NYU, 1964—65. Mem.: NEA, Herricks Tchrs. Assn. (pres. 1948), N.Y. State Coun. Adminstrs. Music Edn. (chpt. v.p. 1967—68), Nassau Music Educators Assn. (exec. bd. 1947—58), N.Y. State Tchrs. Assn., N.Y. State Sch. Music Assn., Music Educators Nat. Conf., Order of Eastern Star, Sigma Alpha Iota. Home: 1645 Calle Camille La Jolla CA 92037-7107

NORTH, MARJORIE MARY, columnist; b. Mt. Clemens, Mich., Oct. 21, 1945; d. Robert Haller and Hilla Beryl (Willard) Wright; m. William B. Hirons; children: Laura, Christina, Angela. Student, Wayne State U., 1963—66. Features editor Elizabeth City (N.C.) Daily Advance, 1966-69; news/mng. editor Brandon (Fla.) News, 1977-78; city editor Leesburg (Fla.) Comml., 1978-79; metro editor Sarasota (Fla.) Herald Tribune, 1979-80, Fla. West editor, 1980-85, daily columnist, 1985—. Host Weekly Interview Show, SNN-TV, 1997—. Author: Sarasota: A City For All Seasons, 1994, (plays) With the Best Intentions, 1994, Back in the Game, 1998. Recipient Layout, Creativity and Overall Publ. awards Fla. Press Assn., numerous comty. awards and citations; winner Fla. shorts competition Fla. Studio Theater New Play Festival, 1994, 98; Paul Harris fellow. Avocations: tennis, entertaining, theater. Office: Sarasota Herald-Tribune PO Box 1719 Sarasota FL 34230-1719 E-mail: mnorth10@comcast.net.

NORTH, MICHELLE, mortgage broker; b. Rochester, N.Y. d. Jack Meyer; m. Russell F. North, July 26, 1997; children: Holley Evans Esmay, Heidi Evans Megginson. BA in Bus. Adminstrn. Owner, broker Beachline Mortgage, Pt. Hueneme, Calif., 1998—2004, Mission Adobe Realty, Oxnard, Calif., 1998—, 101 Mortgage, Oxnard, Calif., 2004—; owner, oper. North Mortgage Tng., Oxnard, Calif., 1998—. Author, editor: Home Buyer's Guide, 2002, Practical Guide to Mortgage, 2000. Mem.: Calif. Assn. Mortgage Brokers (mem. edn. com. 2003—), Mensa. Office: 101 Mortgage 3655 W 5th St Oxnard CA 93030

NORTH, TRICIA A., secondary school educator; BA in English and History, Ft. Hays State U., 1996; MA in History, Emporia State U., Kans., 1998. Summer sch. tchr.'s asst. St. Teresa's Home for Children, Ft. Worth, 1995; grad. tchg. asst. Dept. Social Scis. Emporia State U., 1996—98; mus. coord. Korean War Vets. Nat. Mus. and Libr., Tuscola, Ill., 1998—99; serials libr. asst. Forsyth Libr. Ft. Hays State U., Hays, 1999—2001, libr. asst. II, 2001—03; tchr. Wallace County H.S., 2003—. Apprentice Ellis County Hist. Soc., Hays, 1995; intern Nat. Archives and Records Adminstrn., Kansas City, Mo., 1998; guest lectr., commentator Dept. Social Scis. Emporia State U., 1998. Author: (video script) Remembering the Forgotten War: The Korean War in American History, 1998. Home: 218 N Palmer Sharon Springs KS 67758-9769

NORTHCUTT, ORA BEATRICE, author; b. Jan. 6, 1928; Student, Independence C.C., 1966, 78. Owner Bill & Bea's Home Furnishings, Cherryvale, Kans., 1961-77; sales and health cons. Dodson's Nutritional Food Ctr., Norman, Okla., 1983-97. Writer Maguire Jour. Newspaper, Noble, Okla. Author: Tomorrow Will Be Better, 2001.

NORTHEN, HELEN E., retired social work educator, consultant; b. Butte, Mont. d. John Alfred and Amelia Sigred (Anderson) N. BA, U. Wash., 1939; MSW, U. Pitts., 1944; PhD, Bryn Mawr Coll., 1953. Lic. social worker, Calif. Field instr. YWCA-U. Pitts., 1945-49; rsch. asst. Bryn Mawr (Pa.) Coll., 1949-51; assoc. prof. U. Hawaii, Honolulu, 1951-53, U. So. Calif., L.A., 1953-59, prof. social work, 1959-86, prof. emerita, 1986—, disting. prof. emerita, 1999—. Cons. to numerous local and nat. social welfare orgns. Author: Clinical Social Work, 1982, 2d edit., 1995, Social Work With Groups, 1969, 2d edit., 1988, 3d edit., 2001; co-author: Child, Family, Neighborhood, 1982, Families and Health Care, 1990; co-editor: Theories of Social Work With Groups, 1976; mem. editorial bds. several profl. jours., 1985-88; cons. editor Jour. Social Work Edn., 1989—; contbr. articles to profl. jours. Mem. nat. bd. Camp Fire Girls, Inc., N.Y.C., 1961-70; bd. dirs. Portals House, L.A., 1968-76. Mem. Nat. Acads. Practice (Disting. Practitioner award 1983), NASW (Nat. Coun. on Clin. Social Work 1987—, award for Outstanding Achievement in Health/Mental Health Policy 1998), Assn. for Advancement Social Work with Groups (exec. com. 1985-88, cert. honor 1979), Coun. on Social Work Edn., Am. Friends of London Sch. Econs., AAUP, AAUW, LWV, Phi Kappa Phi. Democrat. Avocations: travel, contemporary literature, beach combing. Home: 1325 N Allen Pl Apt 136 Seattle WA 98103-7555 E-mail: hnorthen@earthlink.net.

NORTHERN, ERNESTINE, gifted and talented educator; d. Ella and Ernest Northern; children: Imoni Unique, Dana Ferron. M in ednl. adminstrn., U. of So., 2002—03. Tchr. Atlanta Pub. Schools, Atlanta, Ga., 1994—; site leader Ga. Reading Challenge, Atlanta, Ga., 2000—01. Author: Language Arts Handbook Strategy for Success, 2000. Recipient Coun. for Exceptional Children Classroom award, Coun. for Exceptional Children, 2001—02. Mem.: Coun. for Exceptional Children (assoc.). Non-Denominational. Achievements include development of Project Friends, an intergenerational group of students and community residents.

NORTHRUP, CHRISTIANE, obstetrician, gynecologist; b. Buffalo, Oct. 4, 1949; d. George Wilbur and Edna (Zwilling) N.; children: Ann Christiane, Kate Northrup. BA, Case Western Res., 1971; MD, Dartmouth Coll., 1975. Diplomate Am. Bd. Ob-Gyn. Intern Tufts New Eng. Med. Ctr. Affiliated Hosps., Boston, 1975; intern then resident Tufts New Eng. Med. Ctr., Boston, 1976-79; assoc. clin. prof. ob-gyn Tufts U. Sch. Medicine, Boston, 1979-80; clin. instr. ob-gyn U. Vt. Coll. Med., Portland, Maine, 1980—82, asst. clin. prof. ob-gyn, 1982—2001; practice medicine specializing in ob-gyn Gynecol. Assocs., South Portland, 1979-85, Women's Health Care Orgn. Women to Women, Yarmouth, Maine, 1985—96; private practice ob-gyn, Yarmouth, Maine, 1979—. Mem. high risk perinatal group Maine Med. Ctr., Portland, 1981-83. Author: Mother-Daughter Wisdom, 2005, The Wisdom of Menopause, 2001, Women's Bodies, Women's Wisdom, 1998; contbr. various articles on women's health to profl. jours. Fellow Am. Coll. Ob-Gyn; mem. Am. Holistic Med. Assn. (sec. 1986-88, pres. 1988-90), Am. Holistic Med. Found. (pres. 1986-88). Avocations: music, harpist, skiing, movies, yoga. Office: PO Box 199 Yarmouth ME 04096

NORTHRUP, REBECCA LYNN, athletic trainer; b. Oak Lawn, Ill., Jan. 24, 1978; d. Robert D. and Susan A. Northrup. BS magna cum laude, Ill. State U., Normal, 2001; MS, U. Ill., Champaign/Urbana, 2003. Contract athletic trainer Healthsouth/Advanced Occupl. Medicine Specialists, Bellwood, Ill., 2003—04; asst. athletic trainer Lewis U., Romeoville, Ill., 2005—. Approved clin. instr. U. Ill., Champaign, 2001—03, Lewis U., 2005—. Mem. St. Panteleimon's Ch. Sisterhood, Summit, Ill., 2006. Mem.: Ill. Athletic Trainers Assn., Gt. Lakes Athletic Trainers Assn., Nat. Athletic Trainers Assn. (cert.). Avocations: travel, hiking, bicycling, sports. Office: One University Pkwy Romeoville IL 60446

NORTHUP, ANNE MEAGHER, congresswoman; b. Louisville, Jan. 22, 1948; d. James L. and Floy Gates (Terstegge) Meagher; m. Robert Wood Northup, Apr. 12, 1969; children: David, Katherine, Joshua, Kevin, Erin, Mark. BA in Econs. and Bus., St. Mary's Coll. Notre Dame, South Bend, Ind., 1970. Mem. Ky. Ho. of Reps., Frankfort, 1987-96, U.S. Congress from 3d Ky. Dist., 1997—; mem. house appropriations com.; founder House Reading Caucus, 1998; mem. speaker's drug free task force, 1998; chair speaker's task force on education, 1998; mem. World Trade Org. congl. advisory group, 1999, free trade working group, 2000, comm. on educational accountability, 1993—95, economic development task force, 1991—92, task force to study highway needs, 1990—91, state debt capacity task force. Mem. fin. adv. bd. EPA, 1989-93; mem. home econs. adv. bd. U. Ky. Coll. Agr., 1992— Appeared on Meet the Press, Fox News Sunday, Larry King Live, CNN & Co., Hardball with Chris Matthews. Mem. exec. com. Partnership Ky. Sch. Reform, 1990—; bd. dirs. Greater Louisville Pub. Radio, 1993—, Hospice Louisville, 1994—, Ky. Cancer Consortium, 1992—; mem. cmty. adv. bd. Jr. League Louisville, 1993—; active Holy Spirit Cath. Ch. Named Outstanding Woman of Achievement St. Matthews BPW, 1990; recipient Cath. Schs. Disting. Alumni award, 1991, U. Notre Dame award of the yr. Ky. Alumni Assn., 1991, Clearing the Air award Am. Lung Assn. of Ky., 1991, Svc. Above Self award St. Matthews Rotary Club, 1992, Pub. Svc. award Am. Heart Assn., 1992, Sacred Heart Acad. Alumna award, 1994, Nat. Fedn. of Ind. Bus./Guardian of Small Bus. award, 1996, 97, 98, Legislator of Yr. award Environ. Industry Assn., 1997, Outstanding Freshman Mem. of Congress award Nat. Industries for Blind, 1997, Spirit of Enterprise award U.S. C. of C., 1997, Bulldog award Watchdogs of Treasury, 1998, Jefferson award Citizens for Sound Economy, 1998, Outstanding Support award Am. Printing House for Blind, 1998, Legislator of Yr. award Assn. Equipment Distbrs., 1999, Cmty. Healthcare Champion award Nat. Assn. Cmty. Health Ctrs., Inc., 1999, Spirit of Enterprise award C. of C., 1999, Susan B. Anthony Congl. award, 1999, Pub. Policy Adv. of Yr. award Nat. Assn. Women Bus. Owners, 1999, Honor Roll of Legis. Achievement in Econ. Devel. award So. Econ. Devel. Coun., Inc., 1999, Legislator of Yr. award Nat. Beer Whoesalers Assn., 1999. Mem. Nat. Order Women Legislators, Nat. Conf. State Legislators, Nat. Rep. Legis. Conf., Inst. Rep. Women, So. Legis. Conf. (alternate from Ky. to fiscal affairs and govtl. com.), Nat. Fedn. Ind. Bus. Republican. Roman Catholic. Office: US Ho Reps 2459 Rayburn Ho Office Bldg Washington DC 20515-1703 also: Dist Office 600 Martin Luther King Jr Pl #216 Louisville KY 40202

NORTHUP, MARIE L., music educator; d. Donald P. and Constance R. Pilsner; m. Greg L. Northup, Nov. 22, 1989; children: Brian E., Nathan D. MusB, Viterbo U., 1996; MusM, Vandercook Coll. Music, 2004. Music tchr. Westby (Wis.) Area Sch. Dist., 1997—2000, Sch. Dist. LaCrosse, Wis. Choir dir. United Ch. Christ, LaCrosse, 1995—2000. Bldg. rep. LaCrosse Edn. Assn., 2004—06. Mem.: Music Educator's Nat. Conf. Independent-Republican. Roman Cath. Avocations: travel, gardening, music theater. Office Phone: 608-789-7690.

NORTHUP, NANCY JEAN, lawyer; b. 1959; BA magna cum laude, Brown Univ.; JD, Columbia Univ. Law clk. U.S. Ct. Appeals Fifth cir.; asst. U.S. atty. so. dist. N.Y., 1989—96; cons. atty. ACLU Reproductive Freedom Project; dir. Democracy Program, Brennan Ctr. Justice, N.Y.U., 1996—2002; pres. Ctr. for Reproductive Rights, N.Y., 2003—. Adj. prof. N.Y. Univ. Editor (mng.): Columbia Law Rev. Kent Scholar. Office: Center for Reproductive Rights 120 Wall St New York NY 10005

NORTHWAY, WANDA I., real estate company executive; b. Columbia, Mo., July 11, 1942; d. Herman W. and Goldie M. (Wood) Proctor; m. Donald H. Northway, June 12, 1965; 1 child, Michelle D. RN, U. Mo. Lic. real estate agt. Mo., grad. Realtors Inst. Realtor, 1970—81; co-owner, pres., realtor, ptnr. House of Brokers Realty, Inc., Columbia, 1981—. Pres., organizer Realtor-Assoc. Sales Club, Columbia, 1975; pres. Columbia Bd. Realtors, 1982. Contbr. articles to realty mags. Vol. ARS, local hosp.; mem. allocation com. United Way; active vol. Am. Cancer Soc. and Heart Assn.; campaign worker for various legislators; Sunday sch. tchr., girls' aux. leader Bapt. Ch. Named Realtor Assoc. of Yr., Columbia Bd. Realtors, 1974, Realtor of Yr., 1980. Mem.: Nat. Assn. Realtors (nat. dir. 1977), Realtors Nat. Mktg. Inst. (cert. residential specialist 1978), Mo. Assn. Realtors (state dir. 1974—77, Realtor Assoc. of Yr. 1977), Epsilon Sigma Alpha (state corr. sec., local pres.). Baptist. Office: House of Brokers Realty Inc 1515 Chapel Hill Rd Columbia MO 65203-5457 Office Phone: 573-446-6507. Business E-Mail: wnorthway@houseofbrokers.com.

NORTON, CHERYL J., academic administrator; m. Henry Norton; children: Joel, Aaron. B in Phys. Edn. and Recreation with honors, Denison U., 1971; EdM, Columbia U., M in Applied Physiology, EdD in Applied Physiology, 1980. From temp. faculty mem. to full prof. Met. State U., Denver, 1976, chair dept. human performance, sport and leisure studies, 1992—96, interim assoc. dean Sch. Profl. Studies, 1996—97, provost, v.p. for acad. affairs, 1997—2004; pres. So. Conn. State U., New Haven, 2004—. Pres. Colo. Assn. for Health, Phys. Edn., Recreation and Dance; pres. Ctrl. dist. Am. Alliance Health, Phys. Edn., Recreation and Dance. Author 2 books; contbr. articles to profl. jours. Fellow: Am. Coll. Sports Medicine (past pres. regional chpt.). Office: So Conn State Univ 501 Crescent St New Haven CT 06515

NORTON, ELEANOR HOLMES, congresswoman, lawyer, educator; b. Washington, June 13, 1937; d. Coleman and Vela (Lynch) Holmes; m. Edward W. Norton (div.); children: Katherine Felicia, John Holmes. BA, Antioch Coll., 1960; MA in Am. Studies, Yale U., 1963, LLB, 1964. Bar: Pa., 1965, U.S. Supreme Ct., 1968. Law clk. to Judge A. Leon Higginbotham Fed. Dist. Ct., 1964-65; asst. legal dir. ACLU, 1965-70; exec. asst. to mayor City of N.Y., 1971-74; chmn. N.Y.C. Commn. on Human Rights, 1970-77, EEOC, Washington, 1977-81; sr. fellow Urban Inst., Washington, 1981-82; prof. law Georgetown U., Washington, 1982—; del. (at large) US Congress from DC, 1990—; mem. coms. on govt. reform and transp./infrastructure. Named one of 100 Most Influential Black Americans, Ebony mag., 2006. Democrat. Office: US Ho of Reps 2136 RayburnHo Office Bldg Washington DC 20515-0001 Office Phone: 202-225-8050. Office Fax: 202-225-3002.*

NORTON, ELIZABETH WYCHGEL, lawyer; b. Cleve., Mar. 25, 1933; d. James Nicolas and Ruth Elizabeth (Cannell) Wychgel; m. Henry Wacks Norton Jr., July 16, 1954 (div. 1971); children: James, Henry, Peter, Fred; m. James Cory Ferguson, Dec. 14, 1985 (div. Apr. 1988). BA in Math., Wellesley Coll., 1954; JD cum laude, U. Minn., 1974. Bar: Minn. 1974. Summer intern Minn. Atty. Gen.'s Office, St. Paul, 1972; with U.S. Dept. Treasury, St. Paul, 1973; assoc. Gray, Plant, Mooty, Mooty & Bennett, P.A., Mpls., 1974-79, prin., 1980-94, of counsel, 1995-96. Mem. Minn. Lawyers Bd. Profl. Responsibility, 1984-89; mem. U. Minn. Law Sch. Bd. Visitors, 1987-92. Trustee YWCA, Mpls., 1979-84, 89-91, co-chmn. deferred giving com., 1980-81, chmn. by-laws com., bd. dirs., 1976-77, lectr.; treas. Minn. Women's Campaign Fund, 1985, guarantor, 1982-83, budget and fin. com. bd. dirs., 1984-87; trustee Ripley Meml. Found., 1980-84; treas. Jones-Harrison Home, 1967, bd. dirs., 1962-69, 2d v.p., chmn. fin., 1968-69; mem. Sen. David Durenberger's Women's Network, 1983-88. Durant scholar. Fellow Am. Bar Found.; mem. ABA (mediation task force family law sect. 1983-84), Minn. Bar Assn. (human rights com. family law sect., task force uniform marital property act 1984-85), Minn. Bar Found. (dir. 1991-94), Hennepin County Bar Assn. (pres. 1987-88, chmn. task force on pub. edn. 1984, chmn., mem. exec. com. family law sect. 1979-94), Minn. Inst. Legal Edn., Minn. Women's Lawyers (exec. com.), Hemlock Soc. of S.W. Fla. (co-chmn. 1999-2001), U. Minn. Law Sch. Alumni Assn. (dir. 1975-81, exec. com. 1981-83), Wellesley Club (Naples, pres. 2002-04), Phi Beta Kappa. Home: 26 Water Oaks Way Naples FL 34105-7157 Personal E-mail: betsynorton@swfla.rr.com.

NORTON, GALE ANN, former secretary of the interior; b. Wichita, Mar. 11, 1954; d. Dale Bentsen and Anna Jacqueline (Lansdowne) N.; m. John Goethe Hughes, Mar. 26, 1990. BA, U. Denver, 1975, JD, 1978. Bar: Colo. 1978, U.S. Supreme Ct. 1981. Jud. clk. Colo. Ct. of Appeals, Denver, 1978-79; sr. atty. Mountain States Legal Found., Denver, 1979-83; nat. fellow Hoover Instn. Stanford (Calif.) U., 1983-84; asst. to dep. sec. USDA, Washington, 1984-85; assoc. solicitor US Dept. Interior, Washington, 1985-87; pvt. practice law Denver, 1987-90; atty. gen. State of Colo., Denver, 1991—99; sr. counsel Brownstein, Hyatt & Farber, P.C., 1999—2000; sec. US Dept. Interior, Washington, 2001—06. Lectr. U. Denver Law Sch., 1989; transp. law program dir. U. Denver, 1978-79. Contbr. chpts. to books, articles to profl. jours. Past chair Nat. Assn. Attys. Gen. Environ. Com.; co-chair Nat. Policy Forum Environ. Coun.; candidate for 1996 election to U.S. Senate; chair environ. commn. Rep. Nat. Lawyers Assn. Named Young Career Woman Bus. and Profl. Women, 1981, Young Lawyer of Yr., 1991, Mary Lathrop Trailblazer award Colo. Women's Bar Assn., 1999. Mem. Federalist Soc., Colo. Women's Forum, Order of St. Ives. Republican. Methodist. Avocation: skiing.

NORTON, JANE E. (JANE BERGMAN), lieutenant governor; b. Grand Junction, Colo. d. Walter F. and Elinor (Pitman) Bergman; m. Mike Norton; children: Lacee, Tyler. BS in Health Sci., with distinction, Colo. State U., 1976; MS in Mgmt., Regis U. With Med. Group Mgmt. Assn., Englewood, Colo.; mem. Colo. Ho. Reps., 1986—87; regional dir. U.S. Dept. Health and Human Svcs.; exec. dir. Colo. Dept. Pub. Health Environment, 1999—2002; lt. gov. State of Colo., Denver, 2003—. Chair Colo. Commn. on Indian Affairs; del. Aerospace State Assn., Edn. Commn. of States; co-chair Colo. Space Coalition; Colo. spokesperson Go Red for Women Campaign Am. Heart Assn.; hon. chair Prematurity Campaign Colo. March of Dimes; hon. chair Colo. Freedom Meml. Bd. dirs. Internat. Found. Electronic Systems, Am. Coun. Young Polit. Leaders; nat. bd. adv. Inst. Sci. and Space Studies; adv. bd. women's health U. Colo.; bd. adv. Colo. History Day; co-chair Colo. Health Disparities Commn. Named Woman of Distinction, Girls Scouts, 2005, Public Servant of Yr., Rocky Mt. Family Coun.; recipient Disting. Veterans Advocate award, United Veterans Com. Colo., Legislator of Yr. award, Persons Living with HIV Action Network of Colo., David M. Clark, S.J. Innovative Leadership award, Regis U., Family Values award, State of Colo., Honor Alumna award, Colo. State U. Coll. Applied Human Sci., US Public Health Svc. award outstanding accomplishment increasing childhood immunization rates, Outstanding Svc. to Seniors award, US Adminstrn. on Aging. Mem.: Nat. Lt. Governors Assn. (chair-elect 2006), Omicron Kappa Upsilon (hon.). Republican. Avocations: hiking, skiing. Office: Office Lt Governor 130 State Capitol Denver CO 80203*

NORTON, KAREN ANN, accountant; b. Nov. 1, 1950; d. Dale Francis and Ruby Grace (Gehlhar) N. BA, U. Minn., 1972; postgrad., U. Md., 1978; MBA, Calif. State Poly. U., Pomona, 1989. CPA Md. Securities transactions analyst Bur. of Pub. Debt, Washington, 1972-79, internal auditor, 1979-81, IRS, Washington, 1981; sr. acct. World Vision Internat., Monrovia, Calif., 1981-83, acctg. supr., 1983-87; sr. sys. liaison coord. Home Savs. Am. (name changed to Washington Mut.), 1987-97, sys. auditor, 1997-2000, sect. mgr., 2000—02, group mgr., v.p., 2003—04, v.p., 2005—; project mgr. II Indy Mac Bank, 2004—05, v.p. to pres., 2005—. Author: (poetry) Ode to Joyce, 1985 (Golden Poet award 1985). 2d v.p. chpt. Nat. Treasury Employees Union, Washington, 1978, editor chpt. newsletter; mem. M-2 Prisoners Sponsorship Program, Chino, Calif., 1984-86. Recipient Spl. Achievement award Dept. Treasury, 1976, Superior Performance award Dept. Treasury, 1977-78; Charles and Ellora Alliss scholar, 1968. Mem. Angel Flight, Flying Samaritans, Habitat for Humanity. Avocations: flying, chess, tennis. E-mail: skypilot@pacbell.net.

NORTON, LINDA LEE, pharmacist, educator; b. Vallejo, Calif., Aug. 12, 1953; d. Don Leroy and Pearl Etta (Cain) Hartzell; m. Lawrence Henry Norton, Aug. 19, 1972; children: Joshua David, Gabriel Aaron. PharmD, U. Pacific, 1991. Lic. pharmacist, Calif., Nev. Pharmacy resident St. Joseph's Med. Ctr., Stockton, Calif., 1991-92, U. Ariz., Tucson, 1992-93; fellow in pain rsch. and drug info. U. of Pacific and Am. Acad. Pain Mgmt., Stockton, 1993-95; asst. prof. pharmacy practice U. of Pacific, Stockton, 1995-99, assoc. coord. postgrad. profl. edn., 1995-99, assoc. prof., dir. postgrad. profl. edn., 1999—. Mng. editor Enjoying Good Health, 1997-99; contbr. articles to profl. jours. Mem. shared governance com. Liberty Union H.S., Brentwood, Calif., 1995-97, health careers acad. com., 1995-97; bd. dirs. SMART Coalition, Sacramento, 1998-2000. Recipient Award for outstanding article in pain mgmt. Am. Jour. Pain Mgmt., 1997; grantee Valley Mountain Reg. Ctr., 1998-2000, Diagnostek, 1994; Thomas J. Long Faculty fellow, 1997, 98, 2000-03. Mem. Am. Assn. Colls. Pharmacy (chmn. CPE sect. 2001-2003), Am. Soc. Health-Sys. Pharmacists, Calif. Soc. Health-Sys. Pharmacists (co-chair C.E. Focus '98), Rho Chi. Avocations: small-scale farming and ranching, horse shoe pitching, fishing. Office: Univ Pacific Sch Pharmacy 751 Brookside Rd Stockton CA 95211-0001

NORTON, MARGARET SARAH, retired insurance company executive; d. William Leander Norton and Mattie Rice Reed. BA in Speech, Birmingham So. Coll., 1953; postgrad. in speech therapy, Emory U., 1953—54. Registered rep. Nat. Assn. Securities Dealers, 1973. Asst. to dean women Finch Coll., NYC, 1960—64; agent The Equitable Life Assurance Soc. US, Mobile, Ala., 1968—76; asst. dir. Historic Blakeley State Pk., Spanish Ft., Ala., 1978—94; ret., 1994. Pres. Ea. Shore Rep. Women, Fairhope, Ala., 1999—2004; mem. steering com. Baldwin County Rep. Party, Ala., 1999—, mem. exec. com., 1999—, Ala. Rep. Party, 2003—; founding bd. mem. Mobile Ballet; bd. mem. Baldwin County Humane Soc.; dir. Dist. 1, Ala. Fedn. Rep. Women; bd. dirs., ho. & hospitality chmn. Mobile Assn. Life Underwriters, 1970—74; bd. dirs., govs. appointee Historic Blakeley Auth., 2003—. Recipient Woman of Yr., Am. Bus. Women's Assn., 1992, resolutions of commendation, Ala. Senate and Ho. of Reps., 2004, day proclaimed in her honor, Gov. Ala. and also Fairhope, Ala., 2004. Mem.: Nat. Assn. Life Underwriters (life). Republican. Methodist. Avocations: piano, politics, art, public speaking. Home: 402 Fairwood Blvd Fairhope AL 36532

NORTON, MARY BETH, history educator, writer; b. Ann Arbor, Mich., Mar. 25, 1943; d. Clark Frederic and Mary Elizabeth (Lunny) N. BA, U. Mich., 1964; MA, Harvard U., 1965, PhD, 1969; DHL (hon.), Siena Coll., 1983, Marymount Manhattan Coll., 1984, De Pauw U., 1989; DLitt (hon.), Ill. Wesleyan U., 1992. Asst. prof. history U. Conn., Storrs, 1969-71; from asst. prof. to prof. Cornell U., Ithaca, NY, 1971-87, Mary Donlon Alger prof. Am. history, 1987—. Pitt prof. Am. history and instn. U. Cambridge, 2005—06. Author: The British-Americans: The Loyalist Exiles in England, 1774-1789, 1972, Liberty's Daughters: The Revolutionary Experience of American Women, 1750-1800, 1980 (Berkshire prize for Best Book Woman Historian 1980), Founding Mothers and Fathers: Gendered Power and the Forming of American Society, 1996 (finalist Pulitzer prize in history 1997), In the Devil's Snare: The Salem Witchcraft Crisis of 1692, 2002 (Amb. Book award of English-Speaking Union 2003); co-author: A People and A Nation, 1982, 7th rev. edit., 2004; editor: AHA Guide to Hist. Literature, 3d rev. edit., 1995; co-editor: Women of America: A History, 1979, To Toil the Livelong Day: America's Women at Work, 1790-1980, 1987, Major Problems in American Women's History, 1989, 3d rev. edit., 2003; contbr. articles to profl. jours. Trustee Cornell U., 1973-75, 83-88; mem. Nat. Coun. Humanities, Washington, 1979-84. Woodrow Wilson Found. fellow, 1964-65, NEH fellow, 1974-75, Shelby Cullom Davis Ctr. fellow Princeton U., 1977-78, Rockefeller Found. fellow, 1986-87, Soc. for Humanities fellow Cornell U., 1989-90, John Simon Guggenheim Meml. Found. fellow, 1993-94, Starr Found. fellow Lady Margaret Hall, Oxford U., 2000, Mellon postdoctoral fellow Huntington Libr., 2001. Fellow Soc. Am. Hist. (exec. bd. 1974-87, 2003—, Allan Nevins prize 1970); mem. Am. Hist. Assn. (v.p. for rsch. 1985-87), Am. Acad. Arts and Sci., Orgn. Am. Hist. (exec. bd. 1983-86), Berkshire Conf. Women Hist. (pres. 1983-85) Democrat. Methodist. Office: Cornell U Dept History 325 Mcgraw Hall Ithaca NY 14853-4601 E-mail: mbn1@cornell.edu.

NORTWEN, PATRICIA HARMAN, music educator; b. New Ulm, Minn., Mar. 6, 1930; d. Joseph Absolom and Viola Maureen (Stroud) Harman; m. Dallas Ernest Andrew Nortwen, Dec. 22, 1956; children: Laura Lee, Daniel Harman. BA magna cum laude, U. Minn., 1952, BS in Edn., 1956, MA, 1956. Tchr. music N.W. Sch., U. Minn., Crookston, 1952-54; instr. music S.D. State U., Brookings, 1954-56; tchr. music Robbinsdale (Minn.) Jr. H.S., 1956-57; music dir. Bethlehem Luth. Ch., Mpls., 1957-67; instr. music Golden Valley Luth. Coll., Mpls., 1967-85; ind. music tchr., Mpls., 1957—2000. Performer Early Music Consort, also others; prodr. (cable TV series) Women/Music, 1984-85; author, mng. editor: Music Theory Workbook, Vols. 1-6, 1993-96. Bd. dirs., sec., pres. Civic Orch. Mpls., 1989-94; cmty. adv. bd. U. Minn. Sch. Music, 1998—. Mem.: Thursday Mus. (pres. 1988—92, various offices 1992—97, devel. chair 1997—2004, treas. 2004—05), Young Peoples Symphony Concert Assn. (v.p. 1992—2000), U. Minn. Sch. Music Alumni Coun. (chair 1997—99), Minn. Music Tchrs. Assn. (chair edn. found. 1995—97, pres.-elect 1997—99, pres. 1999—2001, found. bd. dirs. 2000—02, found. treas. 2002, edn. coun. 2002—), Frederic Chopin Soc. (sec. 1992—96, bd. dirs. 1992—), Music Tchrs. Nat. Assn., Phi Beta Kappa, Sigma Alpha Iota (province officer 1975—85, nat. dir. 1975—89, 1998—2003, Nat. Leadership award 1952, Ring of Excellence award 1990). Avocations: reading, singing, hiking, fishing, knitting. Home: 210 W Grant St Apt 313 Minneapolis MN 55403-2244 E-mail: pdnortwen@juno.com.

NORVILLE, DEBORAH ANNE, news correspondent; b. Aug. 8, 1958; d. Zachary S. and Merle Olson Norville; m. Karl G. Wellner Dec. 12, 1987; children: Karl Nikolai, Kyle Maximilian, Mikaela Katharina. ABJ summa cum laude, U. Ga., 1979. Reporter Sta. WAGA-TV, Atlanta, 1978-79, anchor, reporter, 1979-81, Sta. WMAQ-TV, Chgo., 1982-86; anchor NBC News, NYC, 1987-89; news anchor Today Show, NBC, NYC, 1989, co-anchor, 1990-92; corr. Street Stories, CBS, NYC, 1992-94; co-anchor America Tonight, CBS, NYC, 1994; anchor Inside Edition, King World Prodns., 1994—; contbg. editor McCall's, NYC; host Deborah Norville Tonight MSNBC, NYC, 2004—05. Author: Back on Track: How to Straighten Out Your Life When it Throws You a Curve, 1997, I Don't Want To Sleep Tonight, 1999, I Can Fly, 2001. Bd. dirs. Greater N.Y. coun. Girl Scouts U.S., 1989-, Broadcaster's Found.; mem. steering com. Rita Hayworth Gala Alzheimer's Assn; nat. celebrity spokesperson Mother's March of Dimes, 2001, 02. Recipient Outstanding Young Alumni award Sch. Journalism, U. Ga., Emmy award, 1985-86, 89, Gracie Award, Am. Women in Radio and TV; named Person of Yr., Chgo. Broadcast Advt. Club, 1989, 91, Anchor of Yr. 2000, Washington Journalism Rev., 1989. Mem. Soc. Profl. Journalists. Office: Inside Edition 555 W 57th St Ste 1300 New York NY 10019-2925

NORWALK, LESLIE V., federal agency administrator; b. Dayton, Ohio, 1966; B in Economics and Internat. Rels. cum laude, Wellesley Coll.; JD, George Mason U. Atty. Epstein Becker & Green, P.C.; acting dep. adminstr. Ctrs. for Medicare & Medicaid Svcs. (CMS), 2003—04, dep. adminstr., 2004—06, acting adminstr., 2006—. Office: Ctrs Medicare and Medicaid Svcs 200 Independence Ave SW Washington DC 20201*

NORWARD, JOSEPHINE NORMA, social work educator, consultant; b. Johannesburg, Jan. 8, 1949; arrived in U.S., 1980; d. Henry and Florence Nxumalo; m. Howard Norward, Sept. 22, 1984 (div. June 1996); children: Nontuthuzelo, Mandisa. Diploma in Social Work, U. Zululand, Empargeri, South Africa, 1972; MSW, U. N.C., Chapel Hill, 1982; PhD, Atlanta U., 1989. Social worker City Coun. Johannesburg, 1972—80; asst. prof. Tampa U., Fla., 1987—89; sch. social worker Hillsborough County Bd. Edn., Tampa, 1989—91; assoc. prof. Kean U., Union, NJ, 1991—. Cons. Resources for Change, Phila., 1999—2005, Camden City Youth Svc. Commn., NJ, 2004—; faculty mentor N.J. Undergrad. Minority Academic Career Program. Contbg. author: book Social Work and Social Activism in South AFrica, 2006. Vol. Edn. Law Ctr., Camden, 2005—. Mem.: Coun. Social Work Edn. Episcopalian. Avocations: travel, yoga, theater, pilates. Office: Kean Univ 1000 Morris Ave Union NJ 07083 E-mail: jnorward@aol.com.

NORWOOD, BRANDY RAYANA (BRANDY), singer, actress; b. McComb, Miss., Feb. 11, 1979; d. Willie and Sonia Norwood; m. Robert Smith, 2001 (div. 2003); 1 child, Sy'rai. Student, Pepperdine U. Singer: (albums) Brandy, 1994 (NAACP Image Award: Best New Artist, 1996), De Falda Cortita, 1995, Never S-A-Y Never, 1998, Full Moon, 2002, Afrodisiac, 2004; actor: (TV series) Thea, 1996, Moesha, 1995—2001 (NAACP Image Award: Best Youth Actor/Actress, 1997), Brandy: Special Delivery, 2002; (TV films) Cinderella, 1997; actor, exec. prodr.: (TV films) Double Platinum, 1999; actor: (films) I Still Know What You Did Last Summer, 1998; voice Osmosis Jones, 2001, judge (TV series) America's Got Talent, 2006—. Named Favorite New Artist, Am. Music Awards, 1996; recipient Grammy award (with Monica) Best R&B Performance By A Duo Or Group With Vocal for song "That Boy Is Mine", 1998. Office: 15030 Ventura Blvd 710 Sherman Oaks CA 91403

NORWOOD, DEBORAH ANNE, law librarian; b. Honolulu, Nov. 12, 1950; d. Alfred Freeman and Helen G. Norwood; 1 child, Nicholas Evans. BA, U. Wash., 1972, M in Law Librarianship, 1979; JD, Willamette U., 1974. Bar: Wash., U.S. Dist. Ct. (we. dist.) 1975, U.S. Ct. Appeals (9th cir.) 1980. Ptnr. Evans and Norwood, Seattle, 1975-79; law libr. U.S. Courts Libr., Seattle, 1980-89; state law libr. Wash. State Law Libr., Olympia, 1989—2002, reporter of decisions, 1994-2001; asst. dir. pub. svcs. Jacob Burns Law Libr. George Washington U., Washington, 2002—. Mem. Freedom to Read Found. Mem. Am. Assn. Law Librs. (chmn. state, ct. and county spl. interest sect. 1995-96, chair legal info. svcs. to pub. spl. interest sect. 2001-02). Office: Jacob Burns Law Libr George Washington U 716-20th St NW Washington DC 20052 Office Phone: 202-994-7338. E-mail: dnorwood@law.gwu.edu.

NORWOOD, JANET LIPPE, economist; b. Newark, Dec. 11, 1923; d. M. Turner and Thelma (Levinson) Lippe; m. Bernard Norwood, June 25, 1943; children: Stephen Harlan, Peter Carlton. BA, Douglass Coll., 1945; MA, Tufts U., Medford, Mass., 1946; PhD, Fletcher Sch. Law and Diplomacy, 1949; LLD (hon.), Fla. Internat. U., 1979, Carnegie Mellon U., Phila., 1984, Harvard U., Cambridge, Mass., 1997, Rutgers U., 2003. Instr. Wellesley Coll., 1948-49; economist William L. Clayton Ctr., Tufts U., 1953-58; with Bur. Labor Stats., U.S. Dept. Labor, Washington, 1963-91; dep. commr., then acting commr. Bur. Labor Stats. Dept. Labor, Washington, 1975-79, commr. labor stats., 1979-92; sr. fellow The Urban Inst., Washington, 1992-99; counselor, sr. fellow N.Y. Conf. Bd., 2001—. Dir. Nat. Opinion Rsch. Ctr., chair adv. coun. unemployment compensation, 1993—96; pres. COSSA, 2001—02; mem. bd. sci. counselors Nat. Ctr. Health Stats.; chair panel on food insecurity NAS, 2004—05; mem. adv. bd. Bur. Transp. Stats., 2005; chair panel on offshoring Nat. Acad. Pub. Adminstrn., 2005—; chair panel to evaluate Title VI and Fulbright-Hayes programs NAS, 2006—. Author: Organizing to Count: Change in the Federal Statistical System, 1995; contbr. Named Hall Disting. Alumni, Rutgers U., 1987; recipient Disting. Achievement award, Dept. Labor, 1972, Spl. Commendation award, 1977, Philip Arnow award, 1979, Elmer Staats award, 1982, Pub. Svc. award, 1984, Presdl. Disting. Exec. Rank, 1988, Elizabeth Scott award, Com. Pres.'s Statis. Assns., 2002. Fellow: AAAS, Nat. Assn. Bus. Economists, Royal Statis. Soc., Am. Statis. Assn. (pres. 1989, Founder's award 1997); mem.: Nat. Inst. Statis. Sci. (bd. trustees 1991—2000), Nat. Acad. Sci. (assoc.), Nat. Acad. Pub. Adminstrn., Internat. Assn. Ofcls. Stats., Internat. Statis. Inst., Douglass Coll. Soc. Disting. Achievement, Cosmos Club (pres. 1995—96). Home: 5610 Wisconsin Ave Ph 21-d Chevy Chase MD 20815-4444 Personal E-mail: janetnor@aol.com.

NORWOOD, PHYLLIS KATHERENE, director, educator; d. E. Terrell Holloway and Emily Jane Gray; m. John M. Norwood (div. May 26, 1984); children: Gregory, Denetra. BS, Jackson State U., 1964; MA in English, Calif. State U., Dominguez Hills, 1981. English tchr. Burgland H.S., McComb, Miss., 1963—64; libr. J.E. Johnson H.S., Prentis, Miss., 1964—66; English prof. L.A. C.C. Dist., 1966—; dir. workforce edn. L.A. C.C., 1987—. Bd. mem. Eureka Arts Soc., L.A., 1989—95, NETWORK, Washington, 1992—96. Recipient Commendation/Citation, Excellence for Econ. Devel. Excellence, L.A. County Excellence in Welfare to Work Program. Mem.: Nat. Coun. English (assoc.), Top Ladies Distinction (assoc.), Alpha Kappa Alpha (assoc. Honored by Mu Bega Omega Chpt. for establishing Partnership in Math and Sci. for disadvantaged youth). Office: Los Angeles Cmty Coll Dist 1600 West Imperial Hwy Los Angeles CA 90047 Business E-Mail: norwoopk@lasc.cc.ca.us.

NOSANOW, BARBARA SHISSLER, museum program director, curator; b. Roanoke, Va. d. Willis Morton and Kathryn Sabin (Bradford) Johnson; m. John Lewis Shissler Jr., July 28, 1957 (dec. May 1972); children: John Lewis Shissler III, Ada Holland Shissler; m. Lewis Harold Nosanow, Oct. 15, 1973. AB, Smith Coll., 1957; MA, Case Western Res. U., 1958. Asst. mng. editor Jour. Aesthetics and Art Criticism, Cleve. Mus. Art, 1958-63; dir. publs. and rsch. Mpls. Inst. Arts, 1963-72; dir. U. Minn. Art Mus., Mpls., 1972-76; dir. exhbns. and edn. Nat. Archives, Washington, 1976-79; curator Smithsonian Instn., Washington, 1979-82; asst. dir. Nat. Mus. Am. Art, Smithsonian Instn., 1982-88; dir. Portland (Maine) Mus. Art, 1988-93, Art Spaces, 1993—; study leader, lecturer Smithsonian Study Tours of France and Russia, 1997—. Lectr. in field. Past mem. various rev. panels NEH, Washington. Bd. dirs. Md. Com. for Humanities, Balt., 1980-83. Mem. Internat. Women's Forum. Avocation: travel. Office: Art Spaces 3386 Piperfife Ct Keswick VA 22947-9142 Office Phone: 434-923-0019.

NOSSAMAN, MARIAN ALECIA, manufacturing engineering executive; b. Kansas City, Mo., Apr. 26, 1961; d. M.A. and Ellen Ardena (Hume) Nossaman; m. Michael Keith Taylor, July 26, 1986 (div.); children: Alecia Ellen, Nathaniel Alexander. AA, Johnson County C.C., 1989; BSME, BS in Bus., U. Kans., 1993; MS in Theology, SMU, 2002. Dental asst. SE Brotherson DDS, Kansas City, Kans., 1983-85; dental instr. Kansas City Coll. of Med. and Dental Careers, Overland Park, 1985-86; math tutor Overland Park, 1988-91; tech. writer ArComm, Lenexa, Kans., 1991-92; total quality mgmt. rschr. U. Kans., Lawrence, 1992-93; process engr. Symbios Logic Inc., Ft. Collins, Colo., 1993-95; mfg. devel. engr. Hewlett Packard, Loveland, Colo., 1995-97, mech. engring. mgr., 1998-99, support engring. sect. mgr., 1999—2001, strategic support program mgr. Houston, 2001—02, customer adv., mktg., 2002—; owner Alyse Sagen, Houston. Sec. Hilltop Child Devel. Ctr., Lawrence, 1991-93. Contbr. articles to profl. jours. Student senator U. Kans. Student Senate, Lawrence, 1992-93; com. mem. Kans. U. Child Care Com., Lawrence, 1991-93, work and family com., 1991-92; mem. libr. bd. City of Loveland, 1999—. Recipient U. Kans. Hilltopper award, 1993. Mem. ASME (treas. 1992-93), Oaks Nontraditional Students Orgn. (pres. 1991-92, treas. 1990-91, editor 1990-92), Tau Beta Pi, Pi Tau Sigma. Avocations: reading, sports events, music, hiking, puzzles. Office: Hewlett Packard Loveland Mfg Ctr 815 14th St SW Loveland CO 80537-6330 Home: 12906 Oakwood Manor Dr Cypress TX 77429-4900 Office Phone: 281-518-4882.

NOTHDURFT, DONNA JEAN, occupational therapist; b. Aug. 12, 1952; BS in Occupl. Therapy, U. Kans., 1974; MS in Health Scis. Instrn., Tex. Woman's U., 1985. Cert. in hand therapy. Chief occupl. therapist U. Tex. Health Sci. Ctr., Dallas, 1980-86; mgr. upper extremity rehab. Fondren Orthop. Group, Houston, 1987-94; dir. occupl. therapy Suncoast Rehab., Naples, Fla., 1994-97; rehab. specialist hand/upper extremity Nova Care/ProActive therapy, Hickory, NC, 1997—2000. Cons. NASA, Houston, 1993; lectr. in field. Co-author chpt. in book: Comprehensive Rehabilitation of Burns, 1984. Home: 1167 E Lake Dr Tarpon Springs FL 34688-8140 Office Phone: 727-786-1996.

NOTLEY, THELMA A., retired librarian, educator; b. Ogbomosho, Nigeria, Feb. 7, 1928; came to U.S., 1931; d. John Spurgeon and Della (Black) Richardson; m. Loren Spencer Notley, June 16, 1946 (dec.); children: Dan, Kathleen, R. Steven, Laura. BS in Lang. Arts, Okla. State U., Stillwater, 1961; MS in LS, Okla. U., 1972. Tchr. English, Helena (Okla.) Pub. Schs., 1962-64, Skiatook (Okla.) Pub. Schs., 1964-66, Tulsa Pub. Schs., 1966-67, sch. libr., 1967-86; tchr. ESL Dongbi U. Fin. and Edn., Dalian, China, 1988-90; tchr. English, libr. Anglican Internat. Sch., Jerusalem, Israel, 1994-96. Author: China Bound, 1999; contbr. articles to profl. jours. Republican. Episcopalian. Avocations: writing, quilting, travel.

NOTTI, DONNA BETTS, special education educator; b. Manassas, Va., Sept. 4, 1968; d. William Jackson and Christine Joan (Fant) B.; m. David L. Notti, Oct. 14, 1995. BS in Spl. Edn., Old Dominion U., Norfolk, Va., 1990. Tchr., counselor Southeastern Cooperative Ednl. Programs, Norfolk, Va., 1991—2004; vol. tutor Tonelson Teaching and Learning Ctr., Norfolk, Va., 1989; secondary spl. edn. tchr. Chesapeake City Schs., Va., 2004—. Chair child study com. Oscar Smith HS, Chesapeake, Va., 2006—. Mem. Coun. for Exceptional Children (v.p. 1989-90), Coun. for Children With Behavior Disorders, Coun. for Exceptional Children-Mental Retardation, Am. Re-ED Assn., Va. State Reading Assn., Chesapeake Reading Coun. Lutheran. Office: 1994 Tiger Dr Chesapeake VA 23320 Personal E-mail: dbnotti@yahoo.com.

NOTTINGHAM, JUANITA C., medical/surgical nurse; b. Bozeman, Mont., Dec. 24, 1916; d. Lyman L. Crockett and Gussie Kienast; m. Armond L. Bean, Oct. 29, 1939 (dec. apr. 1985); children: Linda Davis, Shirley Pomeroy, Timothy Bean; m. Charles E. Nottingham, Sept. 18, 1992. Diploma in nursing, Mont. Deaconess Hosp., Gt. Falls, 1939; BSN, Mont. State U., 1971, MSN, 1973. Lic. RN Mont., Ind., pub. health nurse Alaska. Head nurse St. John's Hosp., Linny, Mont., 1970—72; asst. prof. Anderson (Ind.) U., 1974—77; pub. health nurse State of Alaska, Fairbanks, Alaska, 1977—83; counselor North Slope Borough, Anaktuwk Pass, Alaska, 1984—85. Adv. bd. Patient Hostel-Tanana Chiefs, Fairbanks, 1974—77; counselor Crisis Counseling., Fairbanks, 1980, Rescue Mission, Fairbanks; vis. counselor Fairbanks Correctional Ctr., 1985—2001. Author: Tundra Tales, 2001; contbr. articles to profl. jours. Named a clinic after, North Slope Borough Adminstrn., Anakturuk Pass, 1980; recipient Social Svc. Worker of Yr., State of Alaska, 1984. Mem.: Alpha Beta Tau. Republican. Avocations: music, writing. Home: PO Box 80946 Fairbanks AK 99708

NOUR, NAWAL M., obstetrician, gynecologist, health facility administrator; arrived in US, 1980; BA, Brown U, 1984; MD, Harvard U., 1994; MPH, Harvard U, 1999. Chief residency Brigham and Women's Hosp., Boston, 1998; instr. dept of Obstetrics, Gynecology and Reproductive Biology Harvard Sch. of Medicine; dir. obstetric resident practice Brigham and Women's Hosp., Boston; founder African Women's Health Practice, 1999—. Recipient Commonwealth Fund Harvard U., 1999; fellow H. Rchard Nesson Fellowship, Brigham and Women's Hosp., 1999, MacArthur Found., 2003. Office: Brigham and Women's Hosp 75 Francis St Boston MA 02115

NOVAK, BARBARA, art history educator; b. NYC; d. Joseph and Sadie (Kaufman) N.; m. Brian O'Doherty, July 5, 1960. BA, Barnard Coll., 1951; MA, Radcliffe Coll., 1953, PhD, 1957. TV instr. Mus. Fine Arts, Boston, 1957-58; mem. faculty Barnard Coll., Columbia U., N.Y.C., 1958-98, prof. art history, 1970—, Helen G. Altschul prof., 1984-98, prof. emeritus, 1998—. Vis. Mellon prof. U. Pitts., 1971; mem. adv. coun. Archives of Am. Art, NAD Author: American Painting of the 19th Century, 1969, revised edit., 1979, Nature and Culture, 1980, rev. edit., 1995, Voyages of the Self, 2006, The Thyssen-Bornemisza Collection 19th Century American Painting, 1986, Alice's Neck, 1987, The Margaret-Ghost, 2003, (novels) The Ape and the Whale, 1995, (play) The Ape and the Whale: Darwin and Melville in Their Own Words, 1987 (performed at Symphony Space 1987), Dreams and Shadows: Thomas H. Hotchkiss in 19th Century Italy, 1993; co-editor: Next to Nature, 1980; mem. editorial bd. Am. Art Jour. Commr. Nat. Portrait Gallery. Recipient disting. tchg. award, Coll. Art Assn., 1997, Lawrence Fleishman award for outstanding scholarship, Archives Am. Art, 1999, medal of distinction, Barnard Coll., 2002; Fulbright fellow, Belgium, 1953—54, Guggenheim fellow, 1974, Nat. Book Critics nominee, 1980, L.A. Times Book Award nominee, 1980, Am. Book Award paperback nominee, 1981. Fellow Soc. Am. Historians, Phila. Atheneum; mem. Soc. Am. Historians, Am. Antiquarian Soc., Coll. Art Assn. (dir. 1974-77, Disting. Tchg. of Art History award 1997); PEN. Achievements include honored with Barbara Novak professorship in art history at Barnard Coll. and Columbia U., 2004; Barbara Novak Acquisition Fund at Nat. Portrait Gallery.

NOVAK, CAMILLE, small business owner, consultant; d. Edward Sherrill Arnold, Sr. and Nila Ruth (Grow) Arnold; m. Robert Novak, Nov. 1, 1975. AA, St. Louis C.C., St. Louis, Mo., 1996; BA in Media Comm., Webster U., St. Louis, Mo., 1998, BA in History, 1998, MA in Media Comm., 2000. Paralegal Cert.: Nat. Acad. of Paralegals 1991; Leadership Devel. Cert. Phi Theta Kappa Internat. Honor Soc., 2001. Exec. adminstrn. Christian Appalachian Project, Lancaster, Ky., 1974—77, St. William's Cath. Ch., Lancaster, 1974—77; comm. adminstr. First Bapt. Ch. of St. John, St. Louis, 1978—82; writer: features, film/theatre rev., oped, edn. The Montage Newspaper, 1993—98; adminstrn. mgmt. Lyss Fine Arts, 1993—2003; adminstr. social and behavioral scis.,history and govt. tutor program St. Louis C.C., 1996—2000; intern Ky. filmmakers collection U. of Ky. Spl. Collections and Archives, Lexington, 1998—98; adminstrn. support ARC, 1999—2004; bus. mgr. St. Louis Assn. Retarded Citizens, 2005—; adminstrv. support Meramec Global Studies Program St. Louis C.C. Dist., 2000—01; instr. St. Louis C.C. Dist., 2000—02; bus. mgr. Tower Hills Claims Mgmt. Inc., St. Louis, 2004—05. Owner Novak Enterprises, St. Louis, 1982—. Actor: (A World of Their Own), (The Big Brass Ring), (King of the Hill), (Soul of the Game); prodr.: (graphic design) The New Millennium (The Eichling Yearbook Internat. Award, 2000); dir.(editor, cinemtographer): (film) The Star-True life acctg. about an Appalachian African Am. youth with cognitive & phys. disabilities who taught the true meaning of life to a class of misfits (Mind over TV Best of Camille show 1997, Meramec Classic Film Festival, 1997, various U.S. film and video festivals, 1997); author: (journalistic writing) Body of Work (Internat. Bus. Communicators Assn. Award, 1996, The Press Club of Met. St. Louis Milton Ferman Meml. Award, 1997), (novels) The Stewart Chronicles, (pub.) Film Hist.:The Age of Aquarius: The Dawning of The New Hollywood., (The Liguorian Mag.) The Star, Lights, Camera, Propaganda Starring American Film as Propaganda Tool: 1938-1945; prodr.(animator): (animated film emphasizing global unity) Scarlet Ribbons (Presented at Meramec Classic Film Festival and Mind Over TV Best of Camille show, 1997), (editor) (documentary) Psalm 23-an alternative reading of 20th Century hist. as filtered through post- modern media. Founder/prodr./dir./steering com. Meramec Classic Film Festival, St. Louis, 1999—2000; founder/prodr./dir. Dollars for Scholars Scholarship programming, St. Louis, 1997—2002, Petey K. Bear Says Reading is FUN! state-wide literacy project, St. Louis, 1998—99. Nominee Presidents Merit Award for Excellence in Academics, SLCC-Meramec Campus Pres., 1996; recipient Most Disting. Chpt. Advisor, Mo. Phi Theta Kappa, 2002, ALL-USA TODAY Academic Team Scholar Campus Representative, St. Louis C.C., 1997, Mo. State All-Academic First Team, Mo. C.C. Assn., 1997, US Achievement Acad. All-American Scholar, 1997, Meramec Honors Program Honors Grad. (and Scholarship Recipient), 1993-2000; Graduate in 1996, 1997, Commencement Spkr., SLCC-Meramec Coll., 1996, Horizon Award for Advisors, Mo. Phi Theta Kappa, 2002, Paralegal Student of Mo., Nat. Acad. of Paralegal Studies, 1992, Nat. Acad. for Paralegal Studies Scholarly Distinction of Merit, NAPS, 1992, West Ednl. Pub. Paralegal Student Award, West Ednl. Pub. Co., 1992, Nat. Deans List, 1996, 1997, 1998, 1999, 2000, Campus Deans List, SLCC and Webster U., 1993-2000, Phi Theta Kappa Internat. Paragon Award for New Advisors Nominee, Phi Theta Kappa Internat., 2002, Honors Program Instr. Recognition Award, Forest Pk. C.C. Honors Program, 2002, Rotary Internat. Amb. of Goodwill Alt., Rotary Internat. of Mo., 1997, Phi Theta Kappa Internat. Disting. Regional Officer Award, 1999, Phi Theta Kappa Internat. Disting. Chpt. Pres. Award, 1997; scholar Guistwhite Scholar, Phi Theta Kappa Internat., 1997, Hites Scholar, St. Louis C.C., 1997, Am. Bus. Women's Assn. Scholar, ABA, 1996, St. Louis Journalism Found. Scholar, 1996-1997-1998-only 3 time awardee, Phi Theta Kappa Transfer Scholar, Webster U., 1996-1998, A. E. Hotchner Scholar, Scholarship Found. of St. Louis, 1996—2002, Alpha Kappa Alpha, 1997. Master: The Spirit of St. Louis Alumni Assn. (life; assn. advisor 2002—03); mem.: Phi Theta Kappa (life; chpt. & regional pres. 1996—99, chpt. advisor 2000—02, Internat. Disting. Regional Officer Award (99) & Internat. Disting. Chpt. Pres. Award (97) 1999, 1997 respectively, Mo. Region Disting. Chpt. & Regional Pres., Advisor 1996—99). Home: 9930 Carlyle Ave Saint Louis MO 63114-1305 Office Phone: 314-569-2492 268.

NOVAK, DONNA BURNETT, secondary school educator; b. Phila., Dec. 8, 1947; d. Verlin Theodore and Betty Elaine (Knopf) Burnett; m. John Charles Novak, Mar. 21, 1970 (div. July 1989); children: Andrew John, Justin Theodore, Christopher Ian, Jonathan Patrick; m. Russell U. Biondo, Apr. 3, 1994. BS in Secondary Edn., History, Govt., East Stroudsburg U., 1969; MEd in Reading, Towson State U., 1983; AA in Criminal Justice, Essex Community Coll., 1992. Cert. secondary edn., social studies, reading specialist. Educator Mitchell Sch., Haverford, Pa., 1969-72; rsch. asst. Govt. Cons. Svc., Fels Inst., Phila., 1970; jr. evaluator Govt. Studies and Systems, Phila., 1973; pvt. reading specialist Balt., 1981-83; educator Balt. County Pub. Schs., Towson, Md., 1983—. Lawyer mentor rep. Balt. County Schs., 1989—, police-sch. liaison, 1989—; presenter, dir. WAC, Perry Hall H.S., Balt., 1986—; presenter Coun. Econ. Edn. Md., Balt., 1986—, Constitutional Rights Found., Chgo., 1991—, Citizenship & Law Related Edn. Program in Md., Balt., 1990—. Author, cons. Juveniles & Law: Maryland Perspective, 1990, Crime & Justice: Maryland Perspective, 1991. Mem. Nat. Coun. Social Studies, Tchr.'s Assn. Balt. County, Md. State Tchrs. Assn. Nat. Edn. Assn., Md. Coun. Social Studies. Republican. Methodist. Avocations: car racing, tennis, photography. Home: 11126 Old Carriage Rd Glen Arm MD 21057-9416 Office: Perry Hall High Sch 4601 Ebenezer Rd Baltimore MD 21236-1999

NOVAK, JANICE ELAINE, pre-school educator; b. McKeesport, Pa., May 14, 1951; d. Howard Madeira and Jean Evelyn Martin; m. J. Lawrence McCormley; children: Matthew Steven McCormley, Katherine Lane McCormley; m. William A. Novak, July 23, 1992. BA in Elem. Edn., Ariz. State U., Tempe, 1978; MEd, No. Ariz. U., Flagstaff, 1997. Tchr. kindergarten Paradise Valley Sch. Dist., Scottsdale, 1987—. Avocations: hiking, bicycling. Home: 5526 E Janice Way Scottsdale AZ 85254

NOVAK, JOYCE KEEN, artist, secondary school educator; d. Clifford Patrick and Mildred Ella Keen; m. Jack Janis, Dec. 15, 1950 (div. July 16, 1954); m. William John Moore, Oct. 28, 1955 (div. Feb. 26, 1965); children: Robert John, William Keen, Marilyn Joyce, James Clifford; m. Robert Novak, May 7, 1966; stepchildren: Susan Grace, Nina Louise. BS of Bus. Edn., U. Mich., 1954, MS of Bus. Edn., 1950. Tchr. H.S. Southfield H.S., Highland Pk., Mich., 1950, Wayne Meml. H. S., 1955—57, Dist. 214, Wheeling, Ill., 1964—66; profl. fine artist Arlington Heights, Ill., 1968—89, Palatine, Ill., 1989—95, Nokomis, Fla., 1995—. Pres. Contemporary Art Ctr., Arlington Heights, Ill., 1984—86; adv. bd. Space 900, Chgo., 1992—95. 40 solo exhbns. Pres. N.W. Suburban Panhellenic Assn., Chgo.; sister city emissary Village Arlington Heights, Zoazhuang, China, 1989. Recipient numerous nat., regional and local art awards. Mem.: Nat. League Am. Pen Women Inc., Fla. Artists Group (v.p. 2003—05, pres. 2005—), Women's Contemporary Artists (life), Chi Omega Alumni Assn. (chpt. advisor 1970—73). Presbyterian. Avocations: swimming, hiking. Home: 1066 Truman St Nokomis FL 34275 Personal E-mail: jnart@comcast.net.

NOVAK, RANDI RUTH, systems engineer, computer scientist; b. Chgo., July 10, 1954; d. Bernard Richard and Shirley Ann (Fiedorczyk) Novak; children: Rona Rachel Reich, Bonnie Shaina Reich. BS in Math., U. Calif., Santa Cruz, 1976, BA in Econs. with honors, 1976; postgrad., U. Rochester, 1976-78. Rsch. asst. U. Calif., Santa Cruz, 1974-76; Russian translator U. Chgo., 1977—78; intern economist Congl. Budget Office, Washington, 1977; engr. Lockheed MSC, Sunnyvale, Calif., 1978-82; software engr. contractor Silicon Valley Systems, Belmont, Calif., 1982, 83-84, Data Encore (subs. of

Verbatim), Sunnyvale, 1982-83; systems programmer CompuPro/Viasyn Corp., Hayward, Calif., 1984-87; mem. tech. staff Network Equipment Techs., Redwood City, Calif., 1987-89; v.p. engring., founder Segue Setups, Burlingame, Calif., 1989-92, ptnr., 1992—; sr. tech. staff NEC Am., San Jose, Calif., 1992—94; sr. systems engr. Hitachi Computer Products, Santa Clara, Calif., 1994-96; prin. engr. Rapid-City Comms./Bay Networks/Nortel Networks, Santa Clara, Calif., 1996—2002, Trapeze Networks, Pleasanton, Calif., 2002—04; prin. engr. tech. staff Foundry Networks, San Jose, 2004—. Fellow Dept. Treasury, 1974-76, NSF, 1977-78, U. Rochester, Rush Rhees fellow. Mem. IEEE Computer Soc., Am. Math. Assn., Computer Profls. for Social Responsibility, Soc. for Computing and Info. Processing, Internat. Platform Assn., Calif. Scholarship Fedn. (life). Avocations: piano, oboe, music, photography, mathematics. Home: 4166 School St Pleasanton CA 94566-6218 Office Phone: 408-207-1528. Personal E-mail: rrnovak@comcast.net.

NOVAK, RYNELL STIFF, retired university official; b. Collin County, Tex., May 24, 1929; d. Roy Odus and Wilma (Vermillion) Stiff; m. Joseph Robert Novak, May 11, 1954; children: Robert David, Daniel Allan, Timothy Criswell, Rebekah Novak Proctor, Elisabeth Novak Richards. BA, U. North Tex., Denton, 1949, cert. in libr. studies, 1965, MA, 1973, PhD, 1975, postdoctoral studies, 1975-78, Tex. A&M U., College Station, 1987; MRE, S.W. Bapt. Theol. Sem., 1953. cert. profl. in human resources. Tchr. Plainview (Tex.) Ind. Sch. Dist., 1949-50; draftsman Convair, Ft. Worth, 1951-52; rsch. assoc. U. North Tex., Denton, 1974-79; text editor Home Mission Bd. So. Bapt. Conv., Atlanta, 1979-83; staff assoc. Tex. A&M U. System, College Station, 1984—94. Instr. in speech Blinn Coll., Brenham, Tex., 1988-95. Author: The Novak Connection, 1983. Dist. officer Tex. PTA, 1966—71; active local Bapt. Ch.; mem. exec. bd. Bapt. Gen. Conv. Tex., 1974—79. Mem.: Hist. Park Found. of Denton County (pres.), Denton County Hist. Commn., Descs. of Washington's Army at Valley Forge (brigade comdr. 1991—95, comdr.-in-chief 2004—06), Tex. Brigade, Mensa, United Daus. of the Confederacy, Tex. Soc. DAR (regent La Villita chpt. 1990—92, 1994—95, regent Benjamin Lyon chpt. 2000—01), Nat. Soc. US Daus. 1812 (treas. 2003—06), Tex. Soc. US Daus. 1812 (hon. state pres.). Avocation: genealogy. Home: 624 W University Dr #241 Denton TX 76201-1889

NOVELLI, KATHERINE ANNE, art educator; BS in Art Edn., Pa. State U., University Park, 1999. Cert. instrnl. II art K-12 Pa. Art educator Northgate Sch. Dist., Pitts., 2000—, Pine-Richland Sch. Dist., Gibsonia, Pa., 2001. Mem. fine arts com. Northgate Sch. Dist., Pitts., 2000—, liaison arts edn. collaborative, 2002—. Fundraiser dance marathon Delta Delta Delta, Pa. State U., University Park, 1996—99. Mem.: Golden Key Internat. Honor Soc. Republican. Roman Catholic. Avocations: walking, painting, photography, knitting, skiing. Office: Bellevue Elem 435 Lincoln Ave Pittsburgh PA 15202

NOVELLO, ANTONIA COELLO, state health commissioner, pediatric nephrologist, former Surgeon General of the United States; b. Fajardo, P.R., Aug. 23, 1944; d. Antonio and Ana D. (Flores) Coello; m. Joseph R. Novello, May 30, 1970. BS, U. P.R., Rio Piedras, 1965; MD, U. P.R., San Juan, 1970; MPH, Johns Hopkins Sch. Hygiene, 1982; DrPh (hon.), Johns Hopkins U., 2000; DSc (hon.), Med. Coll. Ohio, 1990, U. Ctrl. Caribe, Cayey, P.R., 1990, Lehigh U., 1992, Hood Coll., 1992, U. Notre Dame, Ind., 1991, N.Y. Med. Coll., 1992, U. Mass., 1992, Fla. Internat. U., 1992, Cath. U., 1993, Washington Coll., 1993, St. Mary's Coll., 1993, Ea. Va. Med. Sch., 1993, Ctrl. Conn. State U., 1993, Georgetown U., 1993, U. Mich., 1994, Mt. Sinai Sch. Medicine, 1995; LHD (hon.), Alvernia Coll., 1996; HHD (hon.), Kings Coll., 1996; D in Health Sci. (hon.), Ponce Sch. of Medicine, 1996; D in Law (hon.), Gannon U., 1997; LHD (hon.), Loyola U., 1997; DSc (hon.), U. North Tex., Ft. Worth, 2002, Howard U., 2003, NYU, 2003, Pace U., 2003, others. Diplomate Am. Bd. Pediatrics. Intern in pediatrics U. Mich. Med. Ctr., Ann Arbor, 1970-71, resident in pediatrics, 1971-73, pediatric nephrology fellow, 1973-74, Georgetown U. Hosp., Washington, 1974-75; project officer Nat. Inst. Arthritis, Metabolism and Digestive Diseases NIH, Bethesda, Md., 1978-79, staff physician, 1979-80; exec. sec. gen. medicine B study sect., div. of rsch. grants NIH, Bethesda, 1981-86; dep. dir. Nat. Inst. Child Health & Human Devel., NIH, Bethesda, 1986-90; surgeon gen. US Dept. Health & Human Services, Washington, 1990-93; spl. rep. for health and nutrition UNICEF, NYC, 1993—96; vis. prof. health policy and mgmt. Johns Hopkins U. Sch. of Hygiene and Pub. Health, 1996—99; commr. of health State of NY, 1999—. Clin. prof. pediatrics Georgetown U. Hosp., Washington, 1986, 89, Uniformed Svcs. U. of Health Scis., 1989; adj. prof. pediatrics and communicable diseases U. Mich. Med. Sch., 1993; adj. prof. internat. health Sch. Hygiene and Pub. Health, Johns Hopkins U., Balt.; prof. dept. health policy mgmt. and behavior SUNY, 1999—; clin. prof. pediats. U. Rochester, N.Y., 1999—; mem. Georgetown Med. Ctr. Interdepartmental Rsch. Group; legis. fellow U.S. Senate Com. on Labor and Human Resources, Washington, 1982-83; mem. Com. on Rsch. in Pediatric Nephrology, Washington; participant grants assoc. program seminars Nat. Inst. Arthritis, Diabetes and Digestive and Kidney Diseases, NIH, Bethesda, 1980-81; pediatric cons. Adolescent Medicine Svc., Psychiat. Inst., Washington, 1979-83; nephrology cons. Met. Washington Renal Dialysis Ctr. affiliate Georgetown U. Hosp., Washington, 1975-78; phys. diagnosis class instr. U. Mich. Med. Ctr., Ann Arbor, 1973-74; chair Sec.'s Work Group on Pediatric HIV Infection and Diseases, DHHS, 1988; cons. WHO, Geneva, 1989; mem. Johns Hopkins Soc. Scholars, 1991. Contbr. numerous articles to profl. jours. and chpts. to books in field; mem. editorial bd. Internat. Jour Artificial Organs, Jour. Mexican Nephrology. Served in USPHS, 1978-99. Recipient Intern of Yr. award U. Mich. Dept. Pediatrics, 1971, Woman of Yr. award Disting. Grads. Pub. Sch. Systems, San Juan, 1980, PHS Commendation medal HHS, 1983, PHS Citation award HHS, 1984, Cert. of Recognition, Divsn. Rsch. Grants, NIH, 1985, PHS Outstanding medal HHS, 1988, PHS Unit Commendation, 1988, PHS Surgeon Gen.'s Exemplary Svc. medal, 1989, PHS Outstanding Unit citation, 1989, DHHS Asst. Sec. for Health Cert. of Commendation, 1989, Surgeon Gen. Medallion award, 1990, Alumni award U. Mich. Med. Ctr., 1991, Elizabeth Blackwell award, 1991, Woodrow Wilson award for disting. govt. svc., 1991, Congl. Hispanic Caucus medal, 1991, Order of Mil. Med. Merit, 1992, Washington Times Freedom award, 1992, Charles C. Shepard Sci. award, 1992, Golden Plate award, 1992, Elizabeth Ann Seton award, 1992, Ellis Island Congl. Medal of Honor, 1993, Legion of Merit medal, 1993, Athena award Alumnae Coun., 1993, Nat. Citation award Mortar Bd., 1993, Disting. Pub. Svc. award, 1993, Healthy Am. Fitness Leaders award, 1994, Pub. Leadership Edn. Network Mentor award, 1994, Disting. Svc. award Nat. Coun. Cath. Women, 1995, James E. Van Zandt Citizenship award, 1995, Ronald McDonald Children's Charities Excellence award, 1995, Hispanic Heritage Leadership award, 1998, Disting. Alumnus award Am. Assn. of State Colls. and Univs., 1997, Humanitarian award Am. Cancer Soc., 2001, James Smithson Bicentenial medal Smithsonian Inst., 2002; named Health Leader of Yr., COA, 1992; inductee Nat. Women's Hall of Fame, 1994, Internat. Pediatric Hall of Fame Miami Children's Hosp., 1996, Am. Med. Women Assn. Hall of Fame, 2002. Fellow Am. Acad. Pediatrics (Excellence Pub. Svc. award 1993); mem. AMA (Nathan Davis award 1993, Meritorious Svc. award 1993, Luther L. Terry award, 2000), Inst. Medicine, Internat. Soc. Nephrology, Am. Soc. Nephrology, Latin Am. Soc. Nephrology, Soc. for Pediatric Rsch., Am. Pediatric Soc., Assn. Mil. Surgeons U.S., Am. Soc. Pediatric Nephrology, Pan Am. Med. and Dental Soc. (pres.-elect, sec. 1984), D.C. Med. Soc. (assoc.), Johns Hopkins U. Soc. Scholars, Alpha Omega Alpha. Avocation: collecting antique furniture. Office: NY State Health Commr Corning Tower Empire State Plz Albany NY 12237 Office Phone: 518-474-2011.*

NOVETZKE, SALLY JOHNSON, former ambassador; b. Stillwater, Minn, Jan. 12, 1932; married; 4 children. Student, Carleton Coll., 1950-52; PhD (hon.), Mt. Mercy Coll., 1991. Amb. to Malta, Am. Embassy, Valletta, 1989-93. Past mem., legis. rep. Nat. Coun. on Vocat. Edn.; past mem. adv. coun. for career edn., past mem. planning coun. Kirkwood C.C.; bd. dir., life trustee Cedar Rapids Cmty. Theater, Cedar Rapids; past bd. dir. James Baker III Pub. Policy Inst., Rice U.; past trustee, v.p. bd. dir. Shattuck-St. Mary's Sch., Faribault, Minn., Mt. Mercy Coll., Cedar Rapids; vice chmn., life trustee, mem. exec. com. Hoover Presdl. Libr., 1982—, v.p. Hoover trustees; mem. Coun. Am. Amb.; trustee 4-Oaks Juvenile Facility; chmn. Nat. Coun. Youth Leadership; adv. coun. Shattuck-St. Mary's Sch., Faribault, Minn.; state chmn. Iowa Rep. Ctrl. Com., 1984—86; co-chair rep. Ctrl. Com.; chmn. Linn County Rep. Com., 1980—83; mem. adv. bd. Nat. Rep. Women, 1987—89; co-chmn. V.P. Bush Inauguration, 1980; Iowa co-chmn. George Bush for Pres.; trustee Am. U. in Rome, 2001—; bd. dir. Amb. Forum. Decorated dame Order of Knights of Malta; recipient Disting. Alumnus award Stillwater High Sch., 1991; Disting. Alumni award for outstanding achievement Carleton Coll., 1994. Republican.

NOVICK, CARA D., pediatric orthopedic surgeon; d. Sam and Anita Novick. MD, NYU, 1995. Diplomate Am. Bd. Orthop. Surgery. Orthop. surgeon Shriners Hosp., Tampa, Fla., 2001—. Office: Shriners Hosp 12502 Pine Dr Tampa FL 33612 Office Phone: 813-972-2250.

NOVIK, YELENA, oncologist, hematologist; b. June 29, 1959; MD, Sch. Medicine and Dentistry, Moscow, 1988. Asst. prof. medicine Albert Einstein Coll. Medicine, N.Y.C., 1996—, N.Y. Med. Coll., N.Y.C., 1980—2000, 2003—; attending phys. Comprehensive Cancer Ctr., N.Y.C., 1998—2000; attending physician Beth Israel Cancer Ctr., N.Y.C., 2001—. Mem. Ea. Coop. Oncology Group. Contbr. articles to med. jours. Fellow ACP; mem. Am. Cancer Soc., Am. Soc. Clin. Oncology, Am. Soc. Hematology. Office Phone: 212-731-5350. Business E-Mail: yelena.novik@med.nyu.edu.

NOVO, NIETA R., education educator; children: Dustin, Darcy. BA, Chico State Coll., Calif., 1964; MA, Simpson Coll., Redding, Calif., 1996; EdD, St. Mary's Coll. Calif., Moraga, 2005. Tchr. elem. sch. Morgan Hill Sch. Dist., Calif., 1964—66, Pittsburg Sch. Dist., Pittsburg, 1966—70; tchr. music Ft. Jones Sch. Dist., 1978—89, Big Spring Sch. Dist., 1983—96; facilitator Success for All U. Balt., 1996—98; asst. prof. edn. Simpson U., 2000—. Mem.: Internat. Reading Assn. Avocations: music, writing. Office: Simpson U 2211 College View Dr Redding CA 96003

NOVOGROD, NANCY GERSTEIN, editor; b. NYC, Jan. 30, 1949; d. Max and Hilda (Kirschbaum) Gerstein; m. John Campner Novogrod, Nov. 7, 1976; children: James Campner, Caroline Anne. AB, Mt. Holyoke Coll., 1971. Sec. fiction dept. The New Yorker, NYC, 1971-73, reader, 1973-76; asst. editor Clarkson Potter/Pubs., NYC, 1977-78, assoc. editor, 1978-80, editor, 1980-83, sr. editor, 1984-86, exec. editor, 1987; sr. editor HG (House & Garden mag.), NYC, 1987-88, editor-in-chief, 1988-93, Travel + Leisure, NYC, 1993—; editl. dir. Am. Express Pub., NYC, 2000—. Bd. dirs. Am. Soc. Mag. Editors. Bd. dirs. NY Bot. Garden, 1991—; exec. com., bd. dirs. Mount Holyoke Coll., 1992—97; adv. bd. Breast Cancer Rsch. Found., 1993; bd. dirs. Children's Advocacy Ctr. Manhattan, 2003. Office: Travel + Leisure 1120 Avenue of the Americas New York NY 10036-6700 Personal E-mail: nancy.g.novogrod@aexp.com.

NOVOTNA, JANA, retired professional tennis player; b. Brno, Czech Republic, Oct. 2, 1968; Profl. tennis player, 1993—; winner four Grand Slam doubles titles Australian Open and Wimbledon, 1995; winner Grand Slam singles title Wimbledon, 1998; retired, 1999.

NOWAK, CAROL ANN, city official; b. Buffalo, Mar. 5, 1950; d. Walter S. and Stella M. (Gurowski) N. AAS in Bus. Adminstrn., Erie Community Coll., Buffalo, 1986; BS in Bus. Mgmt., SUNY, Buffalo, 1991. With Liberty Nat. Bank/Norstar, Buffalo, 1968-70, City of Buffalo, 1970-74, asst. adminstrn. and fin., 1974-82, pension clk., adminstr. city police and fire pension fund, city clk., 1982-90, sr. coun. clk., city clk., 1990—. Artist, designer holiday greeting cards, 1984—. Mem. Nat. Notary Assn., SUNY Alumni Assn., Golden Key, Alpha Sigma Lambda. Avocations: fashion design, art, writing. Home: 422 Dingens St Buffalo NY 14206-2321 Business E-Mail: cnowak@ci-buffalo.ny.us.

NOWAK, CAROL LEE, retired art educator; b. Bryan, Ohio, Aug. 31, 1946; d. Otho Byron and Martha Lee (Hall) Stockman; children: Lisa Michelle Dickey, Travis Christian, Matthew Jay. BS in Art Edn., Bowling Green State U., 1968. Spl. cert. in art, K-12, Ohio. Art tchr. North Central (N.Y.) H.S., 1968-69, Hilltop H.S., West Unity, Ohio, 1972-74, Bryan (Ohio) City Schs., 1987—2003; adminstr., head tchr. Headstart, Bryan, 1970-71; LD tutor Bryan City Schs., 1974-75, LD tutor, tchr. K-5, 1975-77; tchr. Edgerton (Ohio) Elem. Schs., 1977-83, Edgerton and Bryan City Schs., 1988—2002. Hot glass asst. Sauder FarmCraft Village, Archbold, Ohio, 1989-98; insight facilitator Williams County Probation Schs., Bryan, 1988-94; adv. Hi Art Assn., 1987-2000; tchr. N.W. State C.C., 2001-2002. V.p. Tri State Artists Club, Angola, Ind., 1994-95; mem. Assn. Recognizing Talented Students. Jennings scholar, 1991; recipient Art Appreciation award Northwest State Cmty. Coll., 2001. Mem. Toledo Art Mus., Black Swamp Art Guild, Motherlode, Artlink. Avocations: art history, reading, travel, writing, collecting art. Home: 315 N Walnut St Bryan OH 43506-1355

NOWAK, JUDITH ANN, psychiatrist; b. Albany, N.Y., Feb. 18, 1948; d. Jacob Frank and Anne Patricia Nowak. BA, Cornell U., 1970, MD, 1974. Diplomate in psychiatry Am. Bd. Psychiatry and Neurology. Resident U. Va. Hosp., Charlottesville, 1974-77; fellow in psychiatry Westchester divsn. Cornell U. Med. Coll. Westchester Div., White Plains, N.Y., 1977-78; clin. affiliate Cornell U. Med. Coll., White Plains, N.Y., 1978-79; staff psychiatrist Chestnut Lodge Hosp., Rockville, Md., 1979-81; med. officer in psychiatry St. Elizabeths Hosp., Washington, 1981; pvt. practice Washington, 1981—. Clin. asst. prof. of psychiatry, George Washington U., Washington, 1981-89; clin. assoc. prof. psychiatry, George Washington U. 1989-94, clin. prof. psychiatry, 1994—. Mem. Am. Psychiat. Soc. (pub. affairs rep. 1995), Am. Psychoanalytic Soc., Washington Psychiat. Soc. (sec. 1989-90, 2001-2003, pres. 1991-92), D.C. Med. Soc. (speaker ho. of dels. 1996-98, chair coun. med. specialty socs. 1998-2000). Office Phone: 202-887-5495.

NOWAK (JAROSZ), LINDA THERESE, special education educator, consultant; b. Buffalo, Nov. 25, 1954; d. Joseph John Sr. and Theresa E. Jarosz; m. Raymond John Nowak, Sr., June 18, 1982; 1 child, Raymond John Jr. BS in Edn., Buffalo State Coll., 1988, MEd, 1994, Niagara U., N.Y., 1998. Cert. sch. dist. adminstr. N.Y., sch. adminstrn. and supervision N.Y., spl. edn. tchr. N.Y., elem. edn. tchr. N.Y. Spl. edn. cons. tchr. West St. Elem. Sch. Niagara Wheatfield Cen. Sch. Dist., Sanborn, NY, 1989—, prin. summer sch., 1999—2000, head tchr. summer sch., 2001—04. Adj. prof. edn. Niagara U., 2004—. Fundraiser, supporter United Spinal Assn., Milford, NH, 2003—05; vol. Am. Cancer Soc., Amherst, NY, 2001—03; bd. dirs., mem. devel. com. Niagara Frontier Ctr. for Ind. Living, Niagara Falls, 2002—05. Orleans/Niagara Tchr. Ctr. grantee, 2002—04. Mem.: ASCD (assoc.), Am. Fedn. Tchrs., NY State United Tchrs., Coun. for Exceptional Children, Delta Kappa Gamma (assoc.). Democrat. Roman Catholic. Avocation: collecting antiques. Home: 5761 Dunnigan Rd Lockport NY 14094 Office: West St Elem Sch 5700 West St Sanborn NY 14132 Office Phone: 716-215-3200. Personal E-mail: ltnowak82@adelphia.net. Business E-Mail: lnowak@nwcsd.org.

NOWAK, LISA M., astronaut, military officer; b. Washington, D.C., May 10, 1963; d. Alfredo and Jane Caputo; m. Richard T. Nowak; 3 children. BS in Aerospace Engring., USN Acad., Annapolis, Md., 1985; MS in Aeronautical Engring., USN Postgrad. Sch., Monterey, Calif., 1992, degree in Aeronautical Engring., 1992. Commd. ensign U.S. Navy, Annapolis, 1985, advanced through grades to cmmdr.; Temporary duty NASA Johnson Space Ctr., Houston, 1985; student pilot USN Flight Sch., 1986; trainee Electronic Warfare Sch., Corry Sta., Fla., 1988; pilot Electronic Warfare Aggressor Squadron 34, Point Magu, Calif., 1989—90; grad. student USN Postgrad. Sch., Monterey, Calif., 1990—92; engr. Systems Engring. Test Directorate, Pauxent River, Md., 1993; student test pilot U.S. Navy Test Pilot Sch., Pauxent River, Md., 1993—94; aircraft systems project officer Strike Aircraft Test Squadron, Pauxent River, 1994—95; acquistion project USN Air Systems Command, 1995—96; astronaut NASA Johnson Space Ctr., Houston, 1996—. Mission specialist STS-121 (Discovery), a return-to-flight test mission and assembly flight to the International Space Station, 2006. Recipient Navy Commendation medal, Navy Achievement medal. Mem.: AIAA, USN Acad. Alumni Assn., Tau Beta Pi. Achievements include 0ver 1,100 flight hours using 30 different aircraft. Avocations: bicycling, crossword puzzles, gourmet cooking, running, rubber stamps, skeet shooting, piano. Office: Astronaut Office/CB Johnson Space Ctr Houston TX 77058*

NOWELL, LINDA GAIL, not-for-profit executive; b. Ft. Worth, Apr. 24, 1949; d. Jesse Wayne and Bennie Dale (Flint) Stallings. BA in English, North Tex. State U., 1970. Cert. secondary edn. tchr. Tex. Ind. sales rep. Jostens Printing & Pub. Div., Owatona, Minn., 1980—84; v.p. Nowell Equipment Co., Cranfils Gap, Tex., 1984—89; edn. coord. Tex. Farm Bur., Waco, Tex., 1987—90; account exec. MAC Printing, Las Vegas, 1991—94; mgr. frontier health outreach program Nev. Rural Health Ctrs., Inc., 1994—97; state coord. Nev. 5-A-Day Coalition, 1995—96; exec. dir. No To Abuse, Pahrump, Nev., 1999—2005; v.p. cmty. devel. United Way So. Nev., Las Vegas, 2005—. Active Landmark Edn., Inc.; bd. dirs. United Way of Pioneer Terr., 1999—2004. Mem.: NAFE. Office Phone: 702-892-2319. Personal E-mail: graymare@viawestdu.net. E-mail: lindan@euwsn.org.

NOWIK, DOROTHY ADAM, medical equipment company executive; b. Chgo., July 25, 1944; d. Adam Harry and Helen (Kichkaylo) Wanaski; m. Eugene Nicholas Nowik, Aug. 9, 1978; children: George Eugene, Helen Eugene. AA, Columbia Coll., 1980. Cert. lactation counselor, lactation educator, consultant. Sec., adminstrv. asst. to pres. Zenco Engring. Corp., Chgo., 1970—71; sales rep. Medizenco USA Ltd., Chgo., 1971—73; ptnr. Pacific Med. Systems, Inc., Bellevue, Wash., 1973—76, pres., 1976—. Mem.: NAFE, Wash. Assn. Lactation Cons. (treas. 1994—2005), Pacific Mothers Support Inc. (pres. 1991—). Orthodox Ch. Am. Home: 303 126th Ave NE Bellevue WA 98005-3217 Office: 1407 132nd Ave NE # 10 Bellevue WA 98005-2259 Office Phone: 425-462-0577.

NOWLIN, CONNIE BLACKWELL, artist; b. Jacksonville, Fla., Oct. 1, 1948; d. Joseph Earl Blackwell and Harryet Hazel Stewart Blackwell; m. Phillip Neil Nowlin, Aug. 22, 1970; children: Stewart Andrew, Erin Blake. BS, East Tenn. State U., 1970; postgrad., Arrowmont Sch. Crafts, 1973—78; EdM, U. N.C., Charlotte, 1979. Art tchr. West Charlotte High, 1970—86, Myers Park H.S., Charlotte, 1986—2006. Mem. tchr. adv. bd. Mint Mus. Craft and Design, Charlotte, 1998—. Home: 100 Emory Pl Huntersville NC 28078 Personal E-mail: cnowlin@adelphia.net.

NOZIGLIA, CARLA MILLER, forensic scientist; b. Erie, Pa., Oct. 11, 1941; d. Earnest Carl and Eileen (Murphy) Miller; m. Keith William Noziglia, Nov. 21, 1969; children: Pama Noziglia Cook, Kathryn Noziglia Volpi. BS, Villa Maria Coll., 1963; MS, Lindenwood Coll., 1984. Registered med. technologist, Am. Soc. Clin. Pathologists. Med. technologist Monmouth Gen. Hosp., NJ, 1963—64; spl. chem. med. technologist Hamot Hosp. Med. Ctr., Erie, 1965—69; pathologists' assoc. Galion Cmty. Hosp., Ohio, 1969—75; dir. Richland County Crime Lab. Mansfield Police Dept., Ohio, 1978—81; crime lab. supr. St. Louis County Police, Clayton, Mo., 1981—84; dir. crime lab. Las Vegas Met. Police, Nev., 1984—88, dir. lab. svcs., 1988—93, dir., cons. forensic scis., 1993—95; dir. Forensic Lab. Tulsa Police Dept., 1995—2000, cons. forensic sci., 2000—; forensic advisor US Dept. of Justice/Internat. Criminal Investigative Tng. Assistance Program, Tbilisi, Georgia, 2002, sr. forensic advisor Dar es Salaam, Tanzania, 2002—. Tech. abstracts editor Jour. Police Sci. and Adminstrn., 1983-91; mem. editl. bd. Jour. Forensic Identification, 1988—; editor chpt. in Drug Facilitated Sexual Assault: A Forensic Handbook, 2001; co-editor The Real Crime Lab, 2005, The Forensic Laboratory Handbook, 2006; contbg author: Journal of Police Science, 1989, Encyclopedia of Police Science, 1989. Mem. Gov.'s Com. on Testing for Intoxication, Las Vegas, 1984-93; mem. adv. bd. Nev. Bd. Pharmacy, 1988-93; recruiter United Blood Svcs., Las Vegas, 1986-93; bd. dirs., pres. Cmty. Action Against Rape, Las Vegas, 1987-94; co-founder So. Nev. Sexual Assault Protocol, 1986; adv. bd. Tulsa C.C., 1999-2000, Tulsa Tech. Ctr., 1997-2000; chmn. bd. trustees Forensic Sci. Found., 2000—06; vol. Named Outstanding Cath. Erie Diocese N.W. Pa., 1988, Woman of Achievement, Las Vegas C. of C., 1989, Outstanding Alumni, Villa Maria Acad., 2001, Disting. Alumna Sci., Gannon U., 2004; recipient award, Ohio Ho. of Reps., 1981, Alumni of Yr. award, Villa Maria Coll., 1981. Am. Acad. Forensic Scis. (dist. fellow, 2003, bd. dirs. 1988-91, sec. Criminalistics sect. 1986, sect. chmn. 1987, Outstanding Svc. award 1995, Paul L. Kirk award 1998); mem. Am. Coll. Emergency Physicians (nat. sexual assault task force 1999), Am. Soc. Crime Lab Dirs. (emeritus, bd. dirs. 1980-87, treas. 1981-82, 88-91, pres. 1986-87), Internat. Homicide Investigator's Assn.(charter), Internat. Police Assn., Internat. Assn. for Identification (life), S.W. Assn. Forensic Scientists (emeritus), Am. Bus. Women's Assn. (Woman of Yr. 1988, one of Nat. Top Bus. Women 1993), Alzheimer's Assn. (Okla. chpt. bd. dirs. 1997-2000, exec. bd. sec. 1999). Republican. Roman Catholic. Avocations: avid reader, knitting, sewing, needlepoint, swimming. Office Phone: 803-649-9803. Personal E-mail: skipncar@gforcecable.com.

NUBEL, MARIANNE KUNZ, cultural organization administrator, writer, composer; b. Cin., Sept. 14, 1966; d. Walter Charles and Marjorie (Larson) Kunz; m. Christopher Robert Nubel, Aug. 12, 1989. BS in Cmty. Arts Mgmt., East Carolina U., 1989. Exec. dir. Cmty. Arts Ctr., Wilmington, N.C., 1989-94; dir. film and media svcs. and cultural arts coord. City of Wilmington, 1994—. Founding mem., v.p. 5 & Dime Cultural Prodns., Wilmington, 1992-96,Big Dawg Productions, 1995; bd. dirs. Arts Coun. of the Lower Cape Fear, Wilmington, 1991-95, sec., 1994-95; pres. prodn. bd. Cape Fear Shakespeare, Wilmington, 1994—, music dir., coord., 1994—; pres. adv. bd. Journey Prodn. Performance Edn. Theatre, 2000—; mem. adv. bd. Big Dawg Theatre Co, 2001—. Composer for children's theatre. Music dir. Pied Piper Theatre, Jr. League, Wilmington, 1989-95; mem. co. Bessie's Underground Mole Players, Wilmington, 1995-99; mem. Arts Coun. Lower Cape Fear, Opera House Theatre Co. Recipient Arts and Humanities award N.C. Recreation and Parks Soc., 1993, 94, Cmty. Svc. award Thalian Assn. Cmty. Theatre, 1993, 94. Mem. Theatre N.O.W., Blues Soc. of the Lower Cape Fear (bd. dirs. 1990-92, 1st woman dir.), Big Dawg Theatre Co., Lower Cape Fear Hist. Soc., Opera House Theater Co., Wilmington Choral Soc. Avocations: writing, composing, community theatre, children's theatre, travel.

NUCCI, SUNNI LYNN, social studies educator; b. Denver, Aug. 19, 1971; d. Allan Nucci and Patricia Martin. BA in Social Scis., Colo. State U., Ft. Collins, 1989—93; MA in Curriculum & Pedagogy, U. Colo., Denver, 1994—97. Profl. Tchg. Lic. Colo. Dept. Edn., 1998. Adolescent direct care worker Gemini Treatment Facility, Lakewood, Colo., 1994—96; social studies tchr. Northglenn HS, Colo., 1997—. Cons. Ctr. Law & Democracy, Denver, 1999—, Constl. Rights Found., Chgo., 1999—2000. Lobbyist/union rep. Dist. Twelve Edn. Assn., Thornton, 2004—06. Recipient Norse Choice award, Northglenn HS, 2001. Mem.: NEA (assoc.). Office: Northglenn HS 601 W 100th Pl Northglenn CO 80211 Office Phone: 720-972-4642. Business E-Mail: sunni.nucci@adams12.org.

NUGENT, MARY KATHERINE, elementary school educator; b. Terre Haute, Ind., Aug. 15, 1953; d. Thomas Patrick and Jeanne (Butts) N. BS, Ind. State U., Terre Haute, 1975, MS, 1978. Cert. in elem. edn., spl. edn., Ind. Tchr. 6th grade Cloverdale (Ind.) Sch. Corp., 1976-79; tchr. 4th-6th grades Glenwood Sch., Richardson, Tex., 1986-88; tchr. intermediate mentally handicapped class Meadows Elem. Sch., Terre Haute, 1988-89, tchr. 5th grade, 1989-90, tchr. 4th grade, 1990-93; tchr. 6th grade lang. arts and reading Woodrow Wilson Mid. Sch., Terre Haute, 1993—, team leader, 1997—99, 2001—04, lang. arts co-chair, n. ctrl. com., 2004—06, bldg. rep. Vigo County Tchrs Assn., 2005—06, exec. bd., mid. sch. rep., 2004—06. Avocations: reading, gardening, computers. Office: Vigo County Sch Corp 961 Lafayette Ave Terre Haute IN 47804-2929 Business E-Mail: mknugent@joink.com.

NUGENT, NELLE, theater, film and television producer; b. Jersey City, May 24, 1939; d. John Patrick and Evelyn Adelaide (Stern) N.; m. Donald G. Baker, June 6, 1960 (div. 1962); m. Benjamin Janney, June 22, 1969 (div. Apr., 1980); m. Jolyon Fox Stern, Apr. 7, 1982; 1 child, Alexandra Fox Stern.

BS, Skidmore Coll., 1960, DHL (hon.), 1981. Chmn. bd. McCann & Nugent, Prodns. Inc., NYC, 1976-86; pres. Foxboro Prodns., Inc., NYC, 1985-94; pres., CEO Foxboro Entertainment, 1990-94; pres. The Foxboro Co., Inc.; co-prin. Golden Fox Films, Inc. Adj. faculty NYU, N.Y.C., 2003—. Stage mgr. various off-Broadway shows, 1960-64; stage mgr. Broadways plays Any Wednesday, 1963-64, Dylan, 1964, Ben Franklin in Paris, 1964-65; prodn. supr., then gen. mgr., 1969-76, assoc. mng. dir. Nederlander Corp., operating theaters and producing plays in NYC and on tour, 1970-76; co-founder McCam & Nugent Prodns., Inc., 1976; prodr.: Dracula, 1977 (Tony award), The Gin Game (Tony nom.), The Elephant Man, 1978 (Tony award, Drama Critics award), Morning's at Seven, 1980 (Tony award), Home, 1980 (Tony nomination), Amadeus, 1981 (Tony award); also produced: Rose and Piaf, 1980, Otherwise Engaged, The Life and Adventures of Nicholas Nickleby, 1981 (Tony award, Drama Critics award), The Dresser (Tony award nominee), 1981, Mass Appeal, 1981; The Lady & The Clarinet, 1982; The Glass Menagerie (revival), 1983; Painting Churches (Obie award), 1983; Total Abandon, 1983; All's Well That End's Well, 1983 (Tony nominee); Pilobolus Dance Company, 1983; Pacific Overtures (revival), 1984; Much Ado about Nothing/Cyrano de Bergerac (repertory) (Tony award nominees), 1984; Leader of the Pack (Tony award nominee), 1985, The Life and Adventures of Nicholas Nickleby (revival) (Tony award nominee), 1986; prodr.: TV spls.: Morning's At Seven, Piaf; Pilobolus; prodr. A Fighting Choice, 1986-88, A Conspiracy of Love, 1987, The Final Verdict, 1990 (Cable Ace award nominee Best Picture); exec. prodr. (TV pilot) Morning Maggie, 1987, Dick Clark Prodns., 1988-90, (feature films) Student Body, 1993, Getting In, 1994, Jane Doe, 1996; (TV films) In the Presence of Mine Enemies, 1995-96 (Houston Festival Silver Star award), A Town Has Turned to Dust, 1997 (World Festival Silver medal 1998), After the Storm (Best Feature Film NY Internat. Independent Film & Video Festival, 2000), Angelciti Festival (Best Feature 2001), Houston Worldfest (Platinum award, Best Film Made for TV 2001), (Broadway prodn.) The Smell of the Kill, 2002, Sly Fox, 2004, A Mother, A Daughter and a Gun, 2005, And Then There Were None, London, West End, 2005. Mem.: Prodrs. Guild Am. East (exec. bd.), League Am. Theaters. Office: 222 E 44th St 4th Fl New York NY 10017

NUGENT, S. GEORGIA, academic administrator; m. Thomas J Scherer. B cum laude, Princeton U., 1973; PhD in classics, Cornell U. Instr. Swarthmore Coll.; assoc. prof. Brown U., 1985; asst. prof. Princeton U., 1979, dean, Harold McGraw Jr. Ctr. for tchg. and learning, asst. to pres., 1992—95; assoc. provost, 1995; pres. Kenyon Coll., 2003—. Author books. Recipient Wriston award for excellence in tchg. Office: President Ransom Hall Kenyon Coll Gambier OH 43022 Office Phone: 740-427-5111. Office Fax: 740-427-2335. Business E-Mail: nugent@kenyon.edu.*

NULAND, VICTORIA, US permanent representative to NATO; m. Robert Kagan. BA, Brown U., RI. Chief of staff to dep. sec. of state US Dept. State, 1993—96, dep. dir. former Soviet Union affairs, 1997—99, US dep. permanent rep. to NATO in Brussels, 2000—03, US permanent rep. to NATO, 2005—; prin. dep. nat. security adv. to US v.p. Cheney Office of the V.P., 2003—05. "Next Generation" fellow Coun. Fgn. Rels., 1999—2000, state dept. fellow, 1996—97; speaks Russian, French and some Chinese. Recipient Disting. Civilian Svc. medal, US Sec. Def. Office: US Mission NATO Blvd Leopold III 1110 Brussels Belgium*

NULL, ELISABETH HIGGINS, librarian, editor; b. Worcester, Mass., Dec. 1, 1942; d. Carter Chapin Higgins and Katharine Huntington (Bigelow) Doman; m. Henry Harrison Null IV, July 13, 1963 (div. 1970); children: John Higgins, Jacob Van Vechten. BA, Sarah Lawrence Coll., Bronxville, N.Y., 1983; MA, Yale U., 1985, MPhil in Am. History, 1989; MA in Folklore, U. Pa., 1987; M Libr. and Info. Sci., Cath. U. Am., 1995. V.p. Abington Pub. Co., Clark's Summit, Pa., 1966-70; CEO Green Linnet Records, Danbury, Conn., 1971-81; vis. lectr. Am. Musical Life, Georgetown U., 1991-98; libr. and conversion specialist nat. digital libr. program Libr. of Congress, Washington, 1996-98, expert cons., 1995; writer on edn. issues Rural Sch. and Cmty. Trust, 1999—2004; rsch. coord. congl. campaign Janine Selendy (Dem.) N.Y. Dist. 17, 2002, 2004; freelance editor, writer Null Editl. Svcs., 2005—; rsch. assoc. for Journalist John Dickerson, 2005—. Bd. dirs. Maine Folklife Ctr.; program co-chair Washington Folk Festival, 1999-2000; program chair Folklore Soc. Greater Washington, 1993-94; humanities scholar-in-residence Conn. Coun. for Humanities and Conn. Dept. for the Arts, Waterbury, Conn., 1986-87; fieldworker in folklore Waterbury Ethnic Music Project, 1986-87. Singer 2 recordings: The Feathered Maiden, 1977, American Primitive, 1981; performance career with guitarist Bill Shute included 6 appearances with Garrison Keillor's A Prairie Home Companion; major venues include Phila. Folk Festival, Bklyn. Mus., Mus. Natural History. Incorporator John Woodman Higgins Armory, Worcester, Mass., 1966—; sec. Stanton Park Neighborhood Assn., Washington, 1990; bd. dirs. John and Clara Higgins Found., 1999—, Horizon Internat., 1980-2006. Folger Shakespeare Libr. Seminar fellow, 1989-91. Mem. ALA, Am. Folklore Soc. Democrat. Episcopalian. Avocations: folk music performer, song writer. Home and Office: 706 Bonifant St Silver Spring MD 20910-5534 Office Phone: 301-587-2286. Personal E-mail: enul@starpower.net.

NULTY, COLLEEN M., counseling administrator; d. Carl Thomas and Phyllis Jean Nulty. BSE, John Brown U., 1989, MS, 1997. Cert. elem. sch. prin. U. Ark., 2001. 1st grade tchr. Bentonville (Iowa) Pub. Schs., 1989—98, 2d grade tchr., 1998—2000, sch. counselor, 2000—. Named Tchr. of Yr., Bentonville Pub. Schs., 1998—99. Mem.: Ark. Counseling Assn. (mem. human rights governing bd. 2004—, Ark. Elem. Counselor of Yr. 1998—99), Ark. Sch. Counselors Assn., N.W. Ark. Sch. Counselors Assn. (pres. 2002—03, pres. elect 2001—02, past pres. 2003—04). Office: Apple Glen Elem 1801 NE Brave Ln Bentonville AR 72712 Office Phone: 479-254-5588.

NUMANN, PATRICIA JOY, surgeon, educator; b. Bronx, N.Y., Apr. 6, 1941; BA, U. Rochester, 1962; MD, SUNY Health Sci. Ctr., Syracuse, 1965. Intern, resident SUNY Health Sci. Ctr., Syracuse, 1970, from asst. prof. to assoc. prof. surgery, 1970-89, assoc. dean Coll. Medicine, 1978-84, assoc. dean Coll. Medicine Clin. Affairs, prof. surgery, 1989—, Lloyd S. Rogers prof. of surgery, med. dir., 1997—. Dir. breast care program SUNY Health Sci. Ctr., Syracuse, 1986—; presenter in field. Contbr. chpts. to books, articles to profl. jours. Found. bd. dirs. Vera House, Syracuse, 1993-94; hon. bd. dirs. F.A.C.T., Syracuse, 1994. Named one of Women of Distinction, N.Y. State Gov. Mario Cuomo, 1994, Disting. Tchg. Prof. SUNY, 1994, Disting. Svc. Prof.; recipient Disting. Surgeon award Assn. Women Surgeons, 1991. Mem. AMA (coun. sci. affairs), ACS (com. on cancer grad. med. edn. com., 2nd v.p. 1999, 2d v.p. 1999-2000), Am. Bd. Surgeons (bd. dirs. 1994—, chair 2001), Am. Assn. Endocrine Surgeons (v.p. 1992), Assn. for Surg. Edn. (pres. 1985), Corinthian Club. Office: SUNY Health Sci Ctr 750 E Adams St Syracuse NY 13210-1834 Office Phone: 315-464-6365. Business E-Mail: numannp@upstate.edu.

NUNAMAKER, SUSAN SUN, mathematics professor; d. Chin-tse and Jean Hwei-Lan Sun; m. Michael Edward Nunamaker; 1 child, Marina. BS in Math., U. Ill., Urbana-Champaign, 1982, BS in Civil Engring., 1982, MS in Applied Math., 1984. Rsch. asst. Ill. State Water Survey, 1979—81; tchg. and rsch. asst. U. Ill., 1982—86; math. prof. DeVry U., Addison, Ill., 1997—2006; math instr. Triton Coll., River Grove, Ill., 1997, Waubonsee CC, Sugar Grove, Ill., 2005—, Coll. DuPage, Glen Ellyn, Ill., 2006—; owner Sunflower Bear R & D, Urbana-Champaign, 1993—96, cons., 2006—. Computing analyst Minnow Bear Computers, Urbana-Champaign, 1984—93; engring. technician US Corps Engring. Rsch. Lab, Urbana-Champaign, 1979—80; instr. Waubimsee C.C., Sugar Grove, Ill., 2006—. Recipient Book award, Harvard U., 1976, Lazarus Human Rels. award, Am. Jewish Cmty., 1977; Engring. scholarships, U. Ill., 1977, Math scholarships, 1978. Mem.: Ill. Math. Assn. CC, Math. Assn. Am., Am. Math. Soc. (assoc.). Home: 5 South 370 Vest Naperville IL 60563 Office: Coll DuPage 425 Fawell Blvd Glen Ellyn IL 60137 also: Waubonsee CC Route 47 at Waubonsee Dr Sugar Grove IL 60554 Office Phone: 630-942-2800 ext. 51498, 630-466-7900 ext. 3587, 312-671-9340. Personal E-mail: susan@nunamaker.com. Business E-Mail: nunama@cdnet.cod.edu.

NUNES, WINIFRED O., minister, educator; d. Jacob Albert Oliver and Katherine Collis Champion; children: Katherine Taylor, Julius Harper. A, U. Hartford, 1978. Ordained to ministry Pentecostal Assemblies of World, 1977. Paraprofl. Sch. Readiness, Hartford, Conn., 1966—67, tchr. presch., 1967—80; assoc. pastor Zion Apostolic Ch., Hartford, 1970—75; pastor New Testament Tabernacle, Bloomfield, 1988—. Author: Born & Bred in the Apostolic Way, 2004; contbr. articles to profl. jours. Mem.: Internat. Missionary & Christian Women's Aux. (pres. 1998—2004). Avocations: reading, travel, writing. Personal E-mail: pwnunes@aol.com.

NUNLEY, CYNTHIA ANN, special education educator; b. Sheridan, Wyo., June 26, 1953; d. John Franklin, Jr. and Virginia Houx Nunley. BA in Elem. Edn./Spl. Edn., U. Wyo., 1977; MEd in Ednl. Tech., Lesley U., 2000. Cert. administrv. endorsement Wyo. Profl. Tchg. Stds. Bd. Spl. edn. tchr. Fremont County Sch. Dist. #1, Lander, Wyo., 1977—. Chair agrl. com. Lander 2020 Visioning Group, 1995—98; mem. Lander Econ. Devel. Assn., 1992—2000; mem. state bd., sec. Wyo. Very Spl. Arts, 2002—; Fremont County state comitteewoman Wyo. State Dems., 1994—2003; committee woman Dem. Nat. Com., Wyo., 2004—; mem. rsch., rev. and priorities com. U. Wyo., Water Resources Ctr., Laramie, 1995—97. Named Wyo. Dem. Partybuilder of the Yr., Wyo. Dems., 1996; Mid-Career, Spl. Edn. scholar, Wyo. Assn. Spl. Edn. Dirs., 2003. Mem.: ASCD, Wyo. Schools Univ. Partnership (chair staff devel. task force 1999—2002), Wyo. Edn. Assn. Avocation: music. Home: 864 N 4th Lander WY 82520 Office: Fremont County Sch Dist #1 400 Baldwin Creek Rd Lander WY 82520 Personal E-mail: cnunle@hotmail.com.

NUNN, CAROLYN M., principal, speech pathology/audiology services professional; b. Kankakee, Ill., Mar. 24, 1954; d. Edwin William and Jane Ellen Meyer; m. Edward Joseph Nunn, Nov. 10, 1979; children: Julia, Meredith, Laura. BSc, Bradley U., Peoria, Ill., 1976; MSc, Bradley U., 1977. Cert. Clin. Competence. Speech lang. pathologist Peoria Assn. Retarded Citizens, Peoria, Ill., 1977—78, Peoria Pub. Sch., Peoria, Ill., 1978—91, speech lang. supr., 1991—95, asst. prin., 1995—2005, prin., 2005; with Tyng Primary Sch., Peoria, 2006—. Speech pathologist Rosewood Ctr., Peoria, 2003—; health bd. Peoria County, Peoria, 2006—; inst. com. Peoria Pub. Sch., Peoria, 1991. Contbr. articles to profl. jour. Charter mem. Boys Scouts Am., 1998—2006. Mem.: Am. Speech Lang Hearing Assn., Assn. for Supr. & Curriculum Devel., Phi Delta Kappa. Avocations: reading, baking, gardening, travel. Office: Tyng Primary Sch 809 Frye Ave Peoria IL 61603

NUNN, CYNTHIA S., history educator; b. Reymolds, Ga., June 3, 1953; d. C. Hugh and Eugenia H. Sawyer; m. Wesley E. Nunn; children: Natalie, Lisa. BS, La. State U., 1974; MEd, Ga. State U., 1982. Tchr. East Coweta High Sch., Senora, Ga., 1976—88, Early Years Sch., Fayetteville, 1992—97, John Milledge Acad., Milledgeville, 1997—. Chair edn. com. Milledgeville First United Meth. Ch., 2004—. Named STAR Tchr., John Milledge Acad., 2005; recipient Tchr. of Yr., East Coweta High Sch., 1982. Mem.: Ga. Coun. Social Studies, Ga. Coun. Econ. Edn., Nat. Coun. Social Studies. Republican. Methodist. Avocations: gardening, gourmet cooking, reading. Office: John Milledge Acad 197 Log Cabin Rd Milledgeville GA 31061

NUNN, PATARICA DIAN, poet; b. Arkadelphia, Ark., Aug. 10, 1951; m. Freddie Lee Nunn, Mar. 16, 1979; children: Katarica Lakisha, Roshonda Lanae, Ophelia Lorraine, Opal Laverne. Student, Ouachita Bapt. U., 1971—72. Dir. assistance operator Southwestern Bell Tel. Co., Hot Springs, Ark., 1978—2003; ret., 2003. Songwriter My Moment of Miles, Time, 1998, Mellow Drifting, 2002, Sassy Sassy Lady, 2003; author: (poetry) Sacred Memories, 1996, A True Mother's Love, 1997, A True Father's Love, 1998, Out in Left Field, 1998, A Breathe of Fresh Air, 2002. Bd. dirs., mem. adv. com. Nat. Libr. Poetry. Named to Internat. Poetry Hall of Fame, 1997, Internat. Hall of Fames's Mus. Mem.: Poetry Guild, Nat. Author's Registry. Democrat. Home: 4 Stillman Dr Little Rock AR 72209

NUOVO, BETTY A., state representative; b. Englewood, NJ, Dec. 10, 1931; m. Victor L. Nuovo, 1953; two children. BS, Bucknell U., 1953. State rep. Vt. Ho. of Reps., Middleury, 1981-90, 96—; pvt. law practice Middleury, 1974—94. Jud. com. Ho. of Reps., 1981-88, chmn. 1985-88, chmn. jud. rules com. 1985-86, adminstrv. rules com. 1985-88, vice-chmn. 1987-88, ways and means com. 1989-90, Middlebury natural resources and energy com., 1996-2000, jud. com., 2001-02, agr. com., 2003-04, ways and means com., 2004—. Chair Vt. State Dem. Platform Com., Middlebury Charter Comn., Vt., Addison County Dem. Com.; bd. dirs., exec. bd. Addison County Regional Planning Com; bd. selectmen Middlebury; bd. dirs. Vt. YMCA; mem. Middlebury LWV. Office: PO Box 1113 Middlebury VT 05753-0347 E-mail: bnuovo@leg.state.vt.us.

NURIK, CINDY BUNIN, educational consultant, marriage and family therapist; b. Bronx, N.Y., May 24, 1952; d. Murray and Kitty Bunin; m. Marc Steven Nurik, Sept. 16, 1978; 1 child, Kacey Leigh. D of Early Childhood and Devel., Nova Southeastern U., 1981; MusM in Therapy and Edn., U. Miami, 1977; BA, Ithaca Coll., 1975. Lic. marriage and family therapist Fla. Dept. of Health, 2003, registered Music Therapist Nat. Assn. of Music Therapy, 1977. Music therapist Seagull Sch. For The Handicapped, Ft. Lauderdale, Fla., 1978—80; founder, child devel. specialist, chairwoman bd. Mommy and Me Enterprises, Inc., Ft. Lauderdale, 1993—2004; child devel. cons., dir. of content Mommy and Me Co., Burbank, Calif., 2002—; founder, dir. of edn., tchr. Parent Child Enrichment Ctr., Coral Springs, Fla., 1980—87; founder, dir. of progarm, clinician Cancer Wellness Program, Ft. Lauderdale, 1988—90; marriage and family therapist, crisis counselor Cimineo and Assocs., Miami and Ft. Lauderdale, 1991—97. V.p. Y-Me Breast Cancer Program, Ft. Lauderdale, 1987—92; child devel. specialist Moms Online/Oxygen Media, New York, 1997—2001. Author: (book) Fun With Mommy and Me; contbr. children's videos Fun and Friends, Splish Splash, and Lullabye and Goodnight (Dr. Toy Award for best activity product in 2001); author and ednl. cons.: Mommy and Me Playgroup Favorites and More Playgroup Favorites, 2003. Chairwoman Mommy and Me Holding Co., Ft. Lauderdale, 1998—. Recipient Hall of Gt. Grads., Lindenhurst H.S. Student Coun., 2002, Discovery Award of Excellence for Fun With Mommy and Me, Discovery Channel, 2001, Best Parenting Book, Parents Choice Awards, 2001, Top 10 Parenting Books, Amazon.com, 2001, Editor's Choice award, Parenting Publ. Am. award, 2001. Fellow: Am. Assn. Of Marriage and Family Therapists. Achievements include first to A pioneer of the Mommy and Me class movement. Created her unique curriculum and has taught thousands of families throughout the years. Avocations: singing, painting, animal advocate. Office: Mommy and Me Company 4100 W Alameda Ave Burbank CA 91505 Office Phone: 954-472-2052.

NUSBACHER, GLORIA WEINBERG, lawyer; b. NYC, July 22, 1951; d. Murray and Doris (Togman) Weinberg; m. Burton Nusbacher, Aug. 4, 1974; 1 child, Shoshana. BA magna cum laude, Barnard Coll., 1972; JD with hons., Columbia U., 1975. Bar: N.Y. 1976. Assoc. Hughes Hubbard & Reed LLP, NYC, 1975-83, counsel, 1983-91, ptnr., 1991—. Lectr. in field. Mem. Columbia Law Rev.; contbr. articles to profl. jours. Troop leader, leader trainer Girl Scouts USA, 1991-97. Mem. ABA (employee benefits and exec. compensation com. 1987—, fed. regulation securities com., subcom. employee benefits, exec. compensation and sect. 16, 1983—, task force Sect. 16, 1991-97, vice-chair com. employee benefits and exec. compensation 2001-03, chair subcom. fed. and state securities laws of com. employee benefits and exec. compensation 1994-2001, 03-, mem. task force exec. compensation 1992-94). Office: Hughes Hubbard & Reed LLP 1 Battery Park Plz New York NY 10004-1482 Office Phone: 212-837-6719. Business E-Mail: nusbache@hugheshubbard.com.

NUSBAUM, CANDACE ANN, elementary school educator; b. Abington, Pa., Apr. 29, 1950; d. Milton Horace and Mary Elizabeth Heuberger; m. Bruce Maximilian Nusbaum, Nov. 8, 1969; children: Lara Brice Baum, Danielle Renee, Nicholas Bruce, Max Andrew, Abigail Marie McGuire. BS, Millersville U., Pa., 1991. Cert. instrnl. II tchg. Pa., 1996. Tchr. Ctrl. York Sch. Dist., Pa., 1992—. Planetarium dir. Ctrl. York Sch. Dist., 1992—. Contbr. writing curriculum. Tchr. St. Philip the Apostle Ch., Millersville, Pa., 1977—84, children's liturgy dir., 1980—85; den mother Cub Scout Pack 268, Millersville, 1980—84; costumer Lancaster Cath. H.S., Lancaster, Pa., 1985—91; pres. Sacred Heart Sch., Lancaster, Pa., 1981—83. Recipient Tchr. of Yr., York chpt. Phi Delta Kappa, 2003. Mem.: Nat. Honor Soc. (life; v.p. 1967—68). Democrat. Roman Catholic. Avocation: travel. Home: 321 N Prince St Millersville PA 17551 Office: Central York HS 601 Mundis Mill Rd York PA 17402 Office Phone: 717-846-6789.

NUSS, BARBARA GOUGH, artist; b. Washington, Apr. 11, 1939; d. Gaines Homer Gough and Edwerta Barbara (Beyer) Barber; m. Frederick A. Johnson, Sept. 30, 1968 (div. 1975); 1 child, Mark Eugene; m. Fred Dean Nuss, Dec. 18, 1982. BFA, Syracuse U., 1960; postgrad., Schuler Sch. Fine Arts, Balt., 1986—87. Art dir. Chappell's Dept. Store, Syracuse, NY, 1960-62, 66; mgr., illustrator Holman Anderson & Moore, Washington, 1967-70; art dir., advt. mgr. Ad-Media & Howard Advt. Assocs., Columbia, Md., 1970-75; acct. exec. Graphic Arts Inc., Alexandria, Va., 1975-77; sales mgr. The Jour. Newspapers, Washington, 1977-82; tchr., adult edn. Montgomery Coll., Rockville, Md., 1984-85; pvt. tchr. fine arts, Woodbine, Md., 1982-96; instr. Plein air painting workshop, 1998—2005. Chmn. Montgomery County Juried Art Exhibit, Rockville, 1988, Mid-Atlantic Regional Watercolor Exhibit, 1998—99; pres. Nuss Fine Arts, Inc., 1992—; judge Am. Landscape Show Art League Torpedo Factory, Alexandria, Va., 2002; judge Mountain State Forest Festival Fine Art Exhibition, Elkins, W.Va., 2002, Potomac Valley Watercolorists Ann. Juried Show, 2004, Mont. County Art Assn. Ann. Show, 2001, 04, 05. One-woman shows include Pa. State U., 1986, NIH, Bethesda, Md., 1989—90, Md. Nat. Capital Pk. and Planning Commn., 1991, Art League Gallery, Alexandria, 1992, Bendann Art Galleries, Towson, Md., 1999—2000, Troika Gallery, Easton, Md., 2004, Strathmore Hall Art Ctr., Bethesda, Md., 2004, Washington County Arts Coun. Gallery, Hagerstown, Md., 2004, Grand Style Gallery, Balt., 2004, Andrei Kushnir / Michele Taylor Gallery, N.Y.C, 2005, exhibited in group shows at Art League at the Torpedo Factory, 1987—92, 2002, Mid-Atlantic Regional Watercolor Exhbn., 1989 (Holbein award, 2006), Heritage Gallery Classical Realism, 1989—90, Art Barn Gallery, Washington, 1990, Carmen's Gallery, 1991—2000, Art Showcase 100 Md. Artists, 1991—92, Assn. pour la Promotion du Patrimoine Artistique Francais, Galerie Jean Lammelin, Argenteuil, France, 1991, Salmagundi Club 14th Ann. Exhbn., 1991, 18th Annual Exhbn., 1995, Thumb Box Exhbn., 2005, Atrium Gallery Georgetown U., Washington, 1991, 18th Ann. Exhbn., 1995, State House, Annapolis, 1996, World Trade Ctr., Balt., 1996, Bendann's Art Gallery, Towson, 1997—2002, Principle Gallery, Alexandria, 1998—2005, Miniature Painters, Sculptors and Gravers Soc. Washington, 1999, Addison/Ripley Fine Art Gallery, Washington, 1999, Rock Creek Gallery, 1999, 2001, Main St. Gallery, Annapolis, 1999—2000, Miniature Art Soc. Fla., 2000, Oil Painters Am., 2000—01, Troika Gallery, Easton, 2001—05, Washington County Arts Coun. Gallery, Hagerstown, 2001—04, Brazier Fine Art, Richmond, Va., 2002, Grand Style Gallery, Balt., 2002—04, Black Rock Ctr. for the Arts, Germantown, Md., 2003—04, Andrei Kushnir / Michele Taylor Gallery, Ellicott City, Md., and N.Y.C., 2003, MD Hall, Annapolis, Md., 2004, 2005, 2006, Washington County Mus. Fine Arts, Hagerstown, Md., 2006, Represented in permanent collections Am. Coun. Edn., NIH, Bell Atlantic, Kiplinger Washington Editors, Fairhaven Retirement Cmty., Md. State Treas.'s Office, NIH; work represented in: Art from the Parks, How Did You Paint That?, 2000; author: 14 Formulas for Painting Fabulous Landscapes, 2004. Finalist still life competition, Artist's mag., 1996, landscape competition, 2003; recipient 1st prize for watercolor, C&O Canal Show, 1987, 1st prize for oil painting, Rockville Art League, 1987, Montgomery County Art Assn., 1983, 1989, Gaithersburg Fine Arts Assn., 1983, 1989, grand champion award for oil painting, Howard County Fair, 1989, Top 100 award for oil painting, Nat. Arts for Parks, 1989, 1991, 1992, 2001, 2006, Top 200, 1990, 1993, 1996, 2006, award of excellence, Washington Soc. Landscape Painters, 1999, 2005, Best in Show award, Nat. League Am. Pen Women, Md. Biennial Conv., 1999, 2003, 1st Prize Watercolor, 1st Prize Oils award, MAPAPA Paint Annapolis, 2003, Award of Excellence, 2004. Mem. Nat. League Am. Pen Women (sec. Bethesda, Md. 1989, treas. 2000-06, state treas. 2006), Balt. Watercolor Soc. (bd. dirs. 1997-99), Washington Soc. Landscape Painters (sec. 1999, pres. 2000-03), Salmagundi Club (NYC), Oil Painters Am. (assoc.). Avocations: crossword puzzles, quilting. Home: 3132 Cabin Run Woodbine MD 21797-7933 E-mail: barbara@barbaranuss.com.

NUSS, JOANNE RUTH, artist; b. Gt. Bend, Kans., May 2, 1951; d. Melvin Oliver and Ruth Helen (Brauer) Nuss. Student, Valparaiso U., Ind., 1969—71, U. Kans., 1972—73, U. Copenhagen, 1974; BA, Ft. Hays State U., 1975; MFA, Santa Fe Inst. Fine Arts, 1991. Lectr. Noon Edition Sta. KCMO-TV, Kansas City, 1981, Menoriah Hosp., Brookridge Elem. Sch., Jill Shurin Show Telecable 10, Kansas City, 1982, Barton County CC, Gt. Bend, Nelson-Atkins Mus., Kansas City, Mo., 1984; artist-in-residence Helen Wurlitzer Found., Taos, N.Mex., 1984, Taos, 90. One-woman shows include Bette Moses Gallery, Great Bend, 1980, Art Expo Ctr., San Francisco, 1981, Univ. Gall., Ft. Hays State U., 1985, Am. Legation Mus., Tangiers, Morocco, 1986, Inma Gallery, Dhahran, Saudi Arabia, 1994, Bab Rouah Gallery, Rabat, Morocco, 1996, Agora Gallery, Soho, New York, 2001, Amsterdam Whitney Internat. Fine Art Gallery, N.Y.C., 2003, others, exhibited in group shows at Second Internat. Sculpture Fair, Boston, 1980, Joan Cooke Gallery, Kansas City, Mo., 1983, Batz Lawrence Gallery, Kansas City, 1984, Galerie de Rond Point des Champs Elyssees, Paris, 1989, Tetouan & La Kabila Gallery, Tetouan, Morocco, 1991, N.Mex. Sculptors Guild, Fuller Lodge Art Gallery, Los Alamos, 1992, Hermosas Fine Arts Gallery, Durango, Colo., 1995, Tanjah Flandria Art Gallery, Tangiers, 1997—99, Shidoni Gallery, Tesuque, N.Mex., 1999—2002, Birger Sandzen Gallery, Lindsborg, Kans., 2000, Nat. Assn. Women Artists, Sarasota Visual Arts Ctr., 2000, U. No. Iowa, Cedar Falls, 2001 (1st pl., 2001, 1st Pl. award Period Gallery, Omaha, Nebr., 2002), Coplan Gallery, Boca Raton, Fla., 2002, Attleboro (Mass.) Mus., 2002, Jeanette Hare Art Gallery, West Palm Beach, Fla., 2002, Attleboro (Mass.) Mus., 2003, Nat. Assn. Women Artists Fifth Ave. Gallery, NYC, 2003, Baker Arts Ctr., 2004, McDowell Arts and Crafts Assn., Shelby Arts, 2004—05, exhibitions include Nat. Assn. Women Artists, 2003, Baker Arts Ctr., 2004, 2005, Nat. Assn. Women Artists Travelling the Carolinas, Ashe County Arts, 2004—05, Pen & Brush 59th Annual Sculpture exhbn., N.Y.C., The Lawrence-Arnott Art Gallery, Marrakech, Morocco, 2005, 2006, Upstream People Gallery, Omaha, 2006, prin. works include archtl. project, Tangiers, 1988—90; featured artist Artist Spectrum Mag. Named 1st female fgn. artist commd. for archtl. major project, Tangiers, 1988—90, Internat. Profl. of Yr., Internat. Biog. Ctr., Cambridge, Eng., 2005; recipient Best 3-D Works award, Wichita Art Assn, 1983, 1st Kans. Artist Purchase award, Ft. Hays State U., 1985, 1st Pl. award, Nat. Exhbn., U. No. Iowa, 2001, Women of Achievement award, Am. Biog. Inst., Inc., 2004—05, Award of Excellence, 7th Annual All Media Internat. Juried Online Exhbn., Lipstream People Gallery, Omaha, 2005, Spl. Recognition award, Upstream People Gallery, 2006. Mem.: Kans. Sculptors Assn., Internat. Sculpture Ctr., Nat. Sculpture Soc., Nat. Assn. Women Artists, Internat. Platform Assn., N.Mex Women in Arts, Nat. Mus. Women in Arts. Avocations: travel, working with other artists, developing private sculpture garden. Office Phone: 505-988-2758.

NUSSBAUM, PAUL M., lawyer; b. Bklyn., 1959; BA, Fairleigh Dickinson U., 1980; JD cum laude, Calif. Western Sch. Law, 1984. EIT; bar: U.S. Ct. Appeals, U.S. Dist. Ct., U.S. Bankruptcy Ct., Md., NY, NJ. Law clerk to Hon. Prudence B. Abram U.S. Bankruptcy Ct., So. Dist. N.Y., 1984—85; ptnr. Whiteford, Taylor & Preston, head Debtor/Creditor Rights and Bankruptcy Dept. Named one of Best Lawyers in Am., 2000; recipient Am. Jurisprudence Award in Bankruptcy, Contracts and Remedies. Mem.: ABA, Md. Inst. Continuing Profl. Edn. Lawyers, Bankruptcy Bar Assn. Office: Whiteford, Taylor & Preston Seven Saint Paul St Baltimore MD 21202 Office Phone: 410-347-8974. E-mail: pnussbaum@wtplaw.com.

NUSSBAUMER, MELANY HAMILTON, program director; b. Huntsville, Ala., Aug. 18, 1956; d. Douglas Wayne and Barbara (Reid) Hamilton; m. Bernard Joseph Nussbaumer, Jan. 26, 1980; children: Nicholas Lang, Elizabeth Reid. BS, Presbyn. Coll., Clinton, S.C., 1983; MA, U. S.C., 1989, MEd,

1998. Tchr. Bell Street Mid. Sch., Clinton, 1983-84, Saluda (S.C.) Elem. Sch., 1984-87, Riverside Mid. Sch., Saluda, 1987-94; dir. Upper Savannah Sci. and Math. Hub Lander U., Greenwood, S.C., 1994-95; curriculum dir., tchr. Salude (S.C.) H.S., 1995—. Adj. prof. U. S.C., Columbia, 1990; cons. S.C. Dept. Edn., 1988-90; conf. presenter in field. Author: OceanSCope, 1989. Recipient Outstanding Earth-Sci. Tchr. award Nat. Assn. Geology Tchrs., 1992; grantee S.D. Dept. Edn., 1987-93. Mem. NSTA (Presdl. award for excellence in sci. and math 1991), S.C. Assn. for Children's Sci. (pres.-elect 1990-91), S.C. Sci. Coun., Marine Educators Assn. Roman Catholic. Avocations: collecting antiques, sewing, reading.

NUSZ, PHYLLIS JANE, not-for-profit fundraiser, consultant, educational consultant; b. Lodi, Calif., Dec. 16, 1941; d. Fred Henry and Esther Emma (Enzminger) Nusz. BA, U. Pacific, 1963, MA, 1965; EdD, Nova Southeastern U., 1987. Cert. fund raising exec. Prof. speech comm. Bakersfield (Calif.) Coll., 1965-86; from asst. dir. student activites to found. exec. dir. Bakersfield (Calif) Coll., 1965-86; mgmt. seminar dir. Delta Kappa Gamma Soc. Internat., Austin, 1983-86; loaned exec. United Way San Joaquin County, Stockton, Calif., 1990; meeting planning, fundraising and edn. cons. PJ Enterprises, Lodi, 1987—. Bd. dirs. U. Calif. Sch. Medicine Surg. Found., San Francisco, 1989—92; mem. Heritage Cir. and Chancellor's Assn. U. Calif., San Francisco, 1987—. Recipient Archives award of merit, Evang. Luth Ch. Am., 1988; fellow, Calif. Luth. U., 1985—. Mem.: NEA, World Affairs N. Am. Coun., Nat. Assn. Parliamentarians, Nat. Soc. Fund Raising Execs. (bd. dirs. 1988—91, chmn. mentor program Calif. Capital chpt. 1991, chmn. acad. fund raising 1991, chmn. mentor program Golden Gate chpt. 1991, founding pres. San Joaquin chpt. 1992—93, Pres.'s award for Meritorious Svc., Golden Gate chpt. 1991), U. Pacific Alumni Assn. (bd. dirs. 1974—82), Rotary Internat. (North Stockton bd. dir. 1993—99, treas. 1994—96, dist. 5220 North Stockton pres. 1997—98, dist. 5220 membership devel. com. 1997—98, membership task force 1998—99, dist. 5220 membership chair 1999—2000, mem. Far West PETS planning com. 2000—06, dist. 5220 gov. 2001—02, mem. internat. Afghan refugee relief com. 2001—02, avoidable blindness task force zone coord. 2002—03, conv. promotion com. zone coord. 2002—03, zones 23 and 24 inst. program chair 2003, alleviation poverty task force coord. 2003—04, centennial com. mem. 2003—05, team 1 found. permanent fund nat. advisor 2003—05, chair Far West PETS 2004, mem. internat. North Am. affairs com. 2004—05, dist. 5220 chair Paul Harris Soc. 2004—05, mem. zones 23 and 24 inst. exec. com. 2004—05, Romanian centennial group study exch. team leader 2004—05, mem. fellowships com. 2005—, Far West PETS instr. 2005—06, found. major gifts advisor 2005—06, zone 24 coord. avoidable blindness task force, Svc. Above Self Lifetime Humanitarian award 2004—, multiple Paul Harris fellow, RI Found. Bequest Soc., RI Found. major donor benefactor, Svc. Above Self award 2005—06), Delta Kappa Gamma (chpt. pres. 1976—78, Chi State parliamentarian 1979—81, chair Internat. Golden Gift Fund 1982—86, sec. 1985—87). Republican. Lutheran. Avocations: photography, travel, swimming, walking, fishing. Office: PJ Enterprises 5250 Claremont Ave Ste 123 Stockton CA 95207 Personal E-mail: pjnusz@aol.com.

NUTT, AMY ELLIS, journalist; BA in English and Philosophy, Smith Coll., Mass.; MS in Philosophy, MIT; MS in Journalism, Columbia U. Feature writer The Star-Ledger, 1997—. Recipient non-deadline writing award, Am. Soc. Newspaper Editors, 2003, Science Journalism award, AAAS, 2004; Nieman Fellow, Harvard U., 2005. Office: Star-Ledger 1 Star Ledger Plz Newark NJ 07102-1200 Office Phone: 973-392-1794. Business E-Mail: anutt@starledger.com.

NUTTER, CAROL ANGELL, academic librarian; b. Hinton, W.Va., Aug. 13, 1948; d. Woodrow Wilson and Sadie Eileen (Yancey) Angell; m. David Henan Nutter, May 31, 1969; children: Jon David, Matthew Jay. MS in Libr. Sci., Univ. Ky., 1978; MA, Morehead State Univ., 1984. Interlibr. loan librarian Camden-Carroll Libr. Morehead State Univ., Morehead, Ky., 1976-78, coord. reg. libr. svcs., 1978-86, reference librarian, 1986-89, head, reference dept., 1989—, asst. dir. pub. svcs., 2001—05, asst. dean for pub. svcs., 2005—. Mem. Am. Libr. Assn., Ky. Libr. Assn. (pres. 2004), Ky. Libr. Assn. Acad. Libr. Sect. (chair 2000-01), Ky. Libr. Assn. Libr. Instruction Roundtable (chair 1991-92). Avocations: singing, song writer. Office: Camden Carroll Libr Morehead State Univ Morehead KY 40351 Office Phone: 606-783-5110. Business E-Mail: c.nutter@moreheadstate.edu.

NUTTER, SUSAN K., librarian, academic administrator; b. Boston, Aug. 9, 1944; m. Joe Hewitt, 1982; stepchildren: Kirsten Elizabeth Hewitt(dec.), Stephen A. Hewitt. BS, Colby Coll., 1966; MLIS, Simmons Coll., 1968. Libr. intern to libr. Project INTREX MIT, 1966—73, assoc. head engring. libraries, assoc. dir. libraries collection mgmt. and technol. services, 1980—87; Coun. on Libr. Resources Academic Libr. Mgmt. Intern U. NC, Chapel Hill, 1979—80; dir. libraries NC State U., Raleigh, 1987—, vice provost, 1995—. Mem. steering com. NC Libraries for Virtual Edn. (NC LIVE); mem. exec. com., governing bd. Triangle Rsch. Libraries Network. Named Libr. of Yr., Libr. Jour., 2005; recipient Alumni Achievement Award, Simmons Coll., 1995, Hugh C. Atkinson Meml. Medal, Assn. College & Rsch. Libraries, 1999. Mem.: Assn. Rsch. Libraries (pres. 1993). Office: DH Hill Libr NC State U Campus Box 7111 Raleigh NC 27695-7111 Office Phone: 919-515-7188. Business E-Mail: susan_nutter@ncsu.edu.*

NUTTER, ZOE DELL LANTIS, retired public relations executive; b. Yamhill, Oreg., June 14, 1915; d. Arthur Lee Lantis and Olive Adelaide (Reed) Lantis-Hilton; m. Richard S. West, Apr. 30, 1941 (div. Nov. 1964); m. Ervin John Nutter, Dec. 30, 1965. Assoc. in Bus., Santa Ana Jr. Coll., 1944. Cert. spl. emergency secondary tchr., Calif.; FAA cert. lic. commercial, instrument, single/multi engine land airplanes pilot. Promoter World's Fair & Comml. Airlines Golden Gate Internat. Expn., San Francisco, 1937-39; pirate theme girl, official hostess Treasure Island's World Fair, San Francisco, 1939-40; prin. dancer San Francisco Ballet, 1937-41; artist, 1941-45; program dir. Glenn County H.S., Willows, Calif., 1952-58; pub. rels. Monarch Piper Aviation Co., Monterey, Calif., 1963-65; pilot, pub. rels. Elano Corp., Xenia, Ohio, 1968-85. Bd. dirs. Nat. Aviation Hall of Fame, Dayton, Ohio, pres., chmn., 1989-92, bd. trustees, 1976—, chmn. bd. nominations, 1992—; bd. trustees Ford's Theatre, Washington, Treasure Island Mus., San Francisco; charter mem. Friends of First Ladies, Smithsonian, Washington, 1990-93. Assoc. editor KYH mag. of Shikar Safari Internat., 1985-87; contbg. columnist Scripps Howard San Francisco News, 1938. Bd. dirs. Cin. May Festival, 1976-80, San Francisco Aero. Soc., 1997-; cen. com. Glenn County Rep. Party, Willows, 1960-64; state cen. com. Rep. Party, 1962-64; adv. bd. Women's Air & Space Mus., Dayton, 1987-94. Warrant officer, Civil Air Patrol, 1967-69. Recipient Civic Contbn. Honor award Big Brothers/Big Sisters, 1991, John Collier Nat. award Camp Fire Girls & Boys, 1988, Tambourine award Salvation Army, 1982, State of Ohio Gov.'s award for Volunteerism, 1992, Spirit of Innovation award Wright State U., 2001, Amb. award Wright Bros. Heritage Benefit, 2001, East Ann. Zoe Dell Nutter Dayton Air Show award, 2003, In grateful appreciation of contbn. 1909 Wright Flyer Monument award Inventing Flight (orgn. charted by Congress), 2003, Deeds-Kettering award Outstanding Contbn., Engrs. CLub Dayton, 2004; named Most Photographed Girl in World, News Burs. & Clipping Svcs., 1938-39. Mem., founder Dancers Over 40, NYC; Fellow Pres.'s Club U. Ky., Ohio State U., Wright State U.; mem. 99's Internat. Women Pilots Orgn. (life, hospitality chmn. 1968), San Francisco Aeronaut. Soc. (bd. dirs. 1997—), Monterey Bay Chapter 99's (mem. chmn. 1964-65), Walnut Grove Country Club, Rotary (Paul Harris fellow 1987), Shikar Safari Internat. (host com. 1976), Country Club of the North. Achievements include established ann. Zoe Dell Nutter Dayton Air Show award, 2003. Avocations: aviation, flying, horseback riding, hunting, shooting, fashion. Home: 986 Trebein Rd Xenia OH 45385-9534

NWOSU, VERONICA C., microbiologist, science educator, medical researcher; d. Peter E. and Elizabeth E. Dike; m. Basil Derrick Nwosu, Apr. 23, 1983; children: Ijeoma Yvonne, Arinze Clement, Nkem Derrick, Jr., Chiedu Victor. BS in biol. sciences, U. of Ill., 1972—76; MS in microbiology, Roosevelt U., 1976—78; PhD in microbiology, Wayne State U., 1986—92. Quality control scientist Fearn Food Inc., Franklin Pk., Ill., 1978—81; sr. lectr. in microbiology Anambra State U. of Tech., Enugu and Awka, Nigeria, 1981—86; rsch. scientist Apex Bioscis., Inc., Research Triangle Park, NC, 1992—94; assoc. prof. NC Ctrl. U., Durham, NC, 1994—. Vis. rsch. fellow Nat. Inst. of Environ. Health Scis., Research Triangle Park, NC, 1998—; cons. DNA Scis., Morrisville, NC, 2000—01. Contbr. articles to profl. jours. Eucharistic min. St. Raphael Cath. Ch., Raleigh, NC, 1994—2003; sch. bd. mem. St. Raphael Cath. Sch., Raleigh, NC, 2003—; dir. of biology grad. program NC Ctrl. U., Durham, NC, 1998—2003, chairperson, biology faculty evaluation com., 2001—03. Recipient Best Biology Tchr. award, Kano State, Nigeria, 1978—79; Academic Merit scholarship, U. of Ill., 1974—76, B. Haley fellowship, Wayne State U., 1991, Faculty fellowship, Am. Soc. for Microbiology, 1997, Rsch. Grant award, Nat. Inst. of Gen. Med. Sciences, 2002—, Provost's Enhancement Rsch. fellowship, Wayne State U., 1990—91, Travel grant, NRC/NAS in conjunction with IUMS, 1999, HMU Ednl. Grant award, NC Biotechnology Ctr., 1994—96, Student Traineeship award, EPA, 2001—. Mem.: NC Acad. of Sci., Inst. of food Tech., Am. Soc. for Microbiology. Achievements include research in antibiotic resistance mechanisms; mechanism of benzene induction of leukemia in bone marrow cells; prevalence of e. coli in meats; characterization of recombinant hemoglobin; isolation, purification, and characterization of D-3-phosphoglycerate mutase enzyme. Avocations: travel, reading, writing, music, dance. Home: 1409 Shadyside Dr Raleigh NC 27612 Office: NC Central Univ 1801 Fayetteville St Durham NC 27707 Office Phone: 919-530-6170. Business E-Mail: vcnwosu@nccu.edu.

NYBORG, VANESSA MARIE, psychologist, researcher, educator; b. San Francisco, Mar. 1, 1972; d. Milton and Beatrice Nyborg. BA, UCLA, 1995; PhD, Duke U., 2001. Postdoctoral rsch. fellow Brown Med. Sch., Providence, 2001—03; rschr. Ctr. for Sch. Based Youth Devel., U. Calif., Santa Barbara, 2003, asst. rschr., adj. prof. Gevirtz Sch. Edn., 2003—. Grantee, NIH, 2003—. Mem.: APA, Psi Chi. Office: U Calif Gevirtz Grad Sch Edn Santa Barbara CA 93106 Home: 233 Fernwood Dr Pleasant Hill CA 94523

NYCUM, SUSAN HUBBELL, lawyer; BA, Ohio Wesleyan U., 1956; JD, Duquesne U., 1960; postgrad., Stanford U., Calif. Bar: Pa. 1962, Calif. 1964, U.S. Supreme Ct. 1967. Pvt. practice, Pitts., 1962—65; designer, adminstr. legal rsch. sys. U. Pitts., Aspen Sys. Corp., Pitts., 1965-68; mgr. ops. Computer Ctr., Carnegie Mellon U., Pitts., 1968-69; dir. computer facility Computer Ctr., Stanford U., 1969-72, Stanford Law and Computer fellow, 1972-73; cons. in computers and law, 1973-74; sr. assoc. MacLeod, Fuller, Muir & Godwin, Los Altos, LA and London, 1974-75; ptnr. Chickering & Gregory, San Francisco, 1975-80; ptnr.-in-charge high tech. group Gaston Snow & Ely Bartlett, Boston, NYC, Phoenix, San Francisco, 1980-86; mng. ptnr. Palo Alto office Kadison, Pfaelzer, Woodard, Quinn & Rossi, LA, Washington, Newport Beach, Palo Alto, Calif., 1986-87; sr. ptnr., chmn. U.S. intellectual property/info. tech. practice group Baker & McKenzie, Palo Alto, 1987—2002, mem. U.S. leadership team, 1987-97, mem. Asia Pacific regional coun., 1995—2002. Founder Tech. Disputes Resolution Svcs., Inc., 2002—; trustee EDUCOM, 1978-81; mem. adv. com. for high tech. Ariz. State U. Law Sch., Santa Clara U. Law Sch., Stanford Law Sch., U. So. Calif. Law Ctr., Harvard U. Law Sch., U. Calif.; U.S. State Dept. del. OECD Conf. on Nat. Vulnerabilities, Spain, 1981; invited spkr. Telecom., Geneva, 1983; lectr. N.Y. Law Jour., 1975—, Law & Bus., 1975—, Practicing Law Inst., 1975—; chmn. Office of Tech. Assessment Task Force on Nat. Info. Sys., 1979-80. Author:(with Bigelow) Your Computer and the Law, 1975, (with Bosworth) Legal Protection for Software, 1985, (with Collins and Gilbert) Women Leading, 1987; contbr. monographs, articles to profl. publs. Fellow Am. Bar Found.; mem. Town of Portola Valley Open Space Acquisition Com., Calif., 1977; mem. Jr. League of Palo Alto, chmn. evening div., 1975-76 NSF and Dept. Justice grantee for studies on computer abuse, 1972-. Fellow Am. Bar Found., Assn. Computer Machinery (mem. at large of coun. 1976-80, nat. lectr. 1977—, chmn. standing com. on legal issues 1975—, mem. blue ribbon com. on rationalization of internat. propr. rights protection on info. processing devel. in the '90s 1990—, Hall of Fame 2004), Coll. Law Practice Mgmt. (trustee 2002—), Coll. Comml. Arbitration; mem. ABA (chmn. sect. on sci. and tech. 1979-80), Computer Law Assn. (v.p. 1983-85, pres. 1986—, bd. dirs. 1975—), Calif. State Bar Assn. (founder first chmn. econs. of law sect., vice chmn. law and computers com.), Internat. Bar Assn. (U.S. mem. computer com. of corps. sect.), Nat. Conf. Lawyers and Scientists (rep. ABA), Strategic Forum on Intellectual Property Issues in Software of NAS, Internat. Coun. for Computer Comm. (gov. 1998). Office: 35 Granada Ct Portola Valley CA 94028-7736 Office Phone: 650-851-3304. Business E-Mail: susan@nycum.net.

NYE, DOROTHY MAE, freelance journalist, educator; d. Robert Nathan and Marinda Josephine Nye; m. Joseph Arlo Westby, Nov. 20, 1955 (div.); children: Timothy Scott Westby, Pamela Kay Westby, Lisa Maureen Westby Peltier, Thomas Oscar Westby, Theodore Edward Westby, Erik Charles Westby. BA, U. Denver, 1999—2001, Combined Licensure & Master's Program, 2002—03. Administrator's Credential Nat. Assn. Edn. of Young Children (NAEYC) & Red Cross, 1993, Montessori Certification Nat. Ctr. for Montessori Edn., 1992. Asst. to v.p. of sales Morton Buildings, Morton, Ill., 1971—83; assoc. dir. of admissions Parks Coll., Denver, 1984—86; dir. of admissions Denver Tech. Coll., 1986—90; primary tchr. Montessori Inst., Houston, 1991—93; sales team mgr. Time Warner, Denver, 1993—96; counselor Open Door, Valley City, ND, 1996—99; communicatons specialist Theodore Roosevelt Medora Found., Medora, ND, 1999—2000; ednl. specialist for elderly Life Care of Am., Aurora, Colo., 2001—04; h.s. english tchr. Life Skills Charter Sch. of Colo. Springs, 2004—. Coord. for internat. program U. of ND & Mexican Universities, Valley City, ND, 1997—99. Com. monitor Majority Caucus Colo. Ho. of Representatives, Denver, 1993—95. Mem.: Pi Lambda Phi, Sigma Tau Delta. Office Phone: 719-471-0684. Business E-Mail: dnye@mylsc.net, dorothy.nye@lifeskillscenters.com. E-mail: grand_ma10@msn.com.

NYE, JENI HIATT, music educator; b. Payson, Ariz., Feb. 2, 1959; d. Reid Moore and Susette Vilate (Cardon) Hiatt; m. David James Nye, Aug. 22, 1980; children: David James Jr., Deric Hiatt, Dexton Hiatt, Chelsi. At, Brigham Young U.; MusB, Utah State U., 1984; M in Edn. Leadership, No. Ariz. U., 2002. Music tchr. Peoria Sch. Dist., Ariz., 1994—98; choir tchr. Mesa Sch. Dist., Ariz., 1998—. Office Phone: 480-472-2974. Business E-Mail: jnnye@mpsaz.org.

NYE, MARY JANE LOVE, pediatrician, educator; b. Charlotte, Oct. 22, 1925; d. Walter Erdman Love and Annie Lola Arnold; m. Charles Byers Nye, June 22, 1951 (dec.); children: Charles Howard, Rosemary Love. BA, Queens Coll., Charlotte, 1947; MD, Duke U., Durham, NC, 1961. Pediatrician London, Watson & Nye, Durham, 1963—68, pvt. practice, 1969—79, Rice, Neal Group, 1980—85, Kaiser Permanente, 1985—89. Staff pediatrician Durham County Regional Hosp., 1965—85, Duke Hosp., Durham, Cerebral Palsy Hosp., Durham. Mem.: AMA, Hope Valley Country Club. Presbyterian. Home: 1919 Wilshire Dr Durham NC 27707

NYIEN, PATRICIA, music educator; b. Kenosha, Wis., May 16, 1953; d. David Arne and Sarah Viola (Molgaard) Dissmore; m. Phillip Dwayne Nelson, Aug. 16, 1973 (div. Oct. 1995); children: Phillip Kirk Nelson, Kindra Lynn Nelson; m. Harvey David Nyien, Apr. 20, 1996; 1 child, Kevin Patrick Nelson. Student, LaSalle Extension U., 1971; B Music Edn., Belmont U., 1977. Pvt. piano tchr., Avilla, Mo., 1973—75, Hendersonville, Tenn., 1975—77, Clarksville, Tenn., 1977—79, Hinsdale, Ill., 1979—86, Westmont, Ill., 1986—; choral dir. Greenwood Annex/Jr. H.S., Clarksville, 1977—79; presch. music/jr. choir dir. Oak Brook (Ill.) Christian Sch., 1981—95. Mem.: The Internat. Cat Assn., Am. Choral Dirs. Assn., Music Tchrs. Nat. Assn. (theory chmn. 2001—03, cert.), Salt Creek Music Tchrs. Assn. (publicity com. 1990—94, membership com. 1994—98, treas. 1998—2000, theory chmn. 2001—, pres. 2003—), Internat. Bengal Cat Assn., Ill. state music tchr. assoc. (treas. 1998—2000). Republican. Mem. Assemblies Of God. Avocations: needlepoint, skiing, singing, knitting, breeding Bengal cats. Home: 830 Franklin St Westmont IL 60559

NYLANDER, JANE LOUISE, museum director, educator, writer; b. Cleve., Jan. 27, 1938; d. James Merritt and Jeannette Cayford; m. Daniel Harris Giffen, 1963 (div. 1970); children: Sarah Louise, Thomas Harris; m. Richard Conrad Nylander, 1972: 1 child, Timothy Frost. AB, Brown U., Providence, R.I., 1959; MA, U. Del., Newark, 1961; postgrad., Attingham Summer Sch., Eng., 1970; PhD (hon.), New Eng. Coll., Henniker, N.H., 1994. Curator Hist. Soc. York County, Pa., 1961-62, N.H. Hist. Soc., Concord, 1962-69; instr. New Eng. Coll., Henniker, NH, 1964-65, Monadnock C.C., Peterborough, NH, 1966-69; curator of textiles and ceramics Old Sturbridge Village, Mass., 1969-85; adj. assoc. prof. Boston U., 1978-85; sr. curator Old Sturbridge Village, 1985-86; dir. Strawbery Banke Mus., Portsmouth, NH, 1986-92, Soc. for Preservation of New Eng. Antiquities, Boston, 1992-93, pres., 1993—2002, pres. emerita, 2002—. Adj. prof. art history and Am. studies Boston U., 1993—96; mem. adv. bd. Concord (Mass.) Mus., 1986—94, Wentworth-Coolidge Commn., 1991—96, mem. adv. com., 1996—2004; mem. adv. bd. John Nicholas Brown Ctr. for Am. Studies, Providence, 1995—2003; mem. adv. bd. dept. Am. decorative arts Mus. Fine Arts, Boston, 1971—99, Art of the Ams., 1999—2000; mem. adv. com. Lakes Region Conservation Trust, 2002—04, Charles S. Parsons Fund, 2004—; advisor house com. Moffatt Ladd House, 1973—; mem. adv. bd. Strawbery Banke Mus., 2004—, mem. steering com. Ctr. for Study of Cmty., 2004—05; cons. in field. Author: Fabrics for Historic Buildings, 4th edit., 1990, Our Own Snug Fireside: Images of the New England Home 1760-1860, 1993, paperback edit., 1994, Windows on the Past, 2000, The Art of Family, 2002; author: (with Richard C. Nylander) Fabrics and Wallpaper for Historic Buildings, 2005; mem. editl. bd.: Hist. N.H., 1993—, The Dublin Seminar, 1984—; contbr. numerous articles to profl. jours. Trustee Worcester (Mass.) Hist. Mus., 1978—84, Hist. Deerfield (Mass.) Inc., 1981—94, 2003—, chair strategic planning com., 2003—, hon. trustee, 1994—2003, Hist. Mass., Inc., 1991—93, Decorative Arts Trust, 1991—, Portsmouth Athenaeum, 1988—90, Japan Soc. N.H., 1988—92, Fort Ticonderoga, 2000—02; mem. adv. bd. New Eng. Heritage Ctr., 1993—2002; active State Ho. Adv. Com., Boston, 1984—85, Gov.'s Coun. for Wentworth Coolidge Mansion, Concord, 1964—66; mem. Com. for Preservation of N.H. State Flags, 1989—92; mem. H.F. duPont award com. Winterthur Mus., 1993—, mem. Mt. Vernon adv. com. for 1999, 1996—99; designator The Henderson Found., 1992—2004. Recipient Charles F. Montgomery prize, Decorative Arts Soc., 1985, Disting. Sophomore Book prize, Boston U., 1993, (with Richard C. Nylander) The Anne and Roger Webb award, Historic Mass., Inc., 1996, John F. Ayer award, The Bay State League, 2002, Boston History award, Bostonian Soc., 2003, award for outstanding contbn. to decorative arts, Iris Found., 2005, Lifetime Achievement award (with Richard C. Nylander), Victorian Soc. Am., 2005, Roll of Honor, Nat. Soc. Colonial Dames of Am., N.H., 2006. Mem.: N.H. Hist. Soc. (interpretation com. 2003—05, mem. exbns. and pubs. com. 2005—), Costume Soc. Am. (bd. dirs. 1977—83), New Eng. Hist. Geneal. Soc., N.H. Humanities Coun., Soc. Preservation of N.H. Forests, Soc. Winterthur Fellows, Mass. Hist. Soc., Portsmouth Athenaeum, Royal Oak Assn., Nat. Trust for Hist. Preservation, Am. Assn. for State and Local History (Cert. of Commendation 2001), Am. Antiquarian Soc., Castle Preservation Soc. (bd. dirs. 2004—, v.p. 2004—, vice chair 2004—), Colonial Soc. Mass., Nat. Soc. Colonial Dames in N.H. (bd. dirs. 1967—73, program chair 2002—, Roll of Honor 2006), Friends of Hist. Deerfield, Friends of the Moffatt Ladd House, Lakes Region Conservation Trust, Brown Club N.H. (trustee 1988—93). Episcopalian. Home: 17 Franklin St Portsmouth NH 03801-4501 Personal E-mail: jane.nylander@verizon.net.

NYLANDER, PATRICIA MARIE, pilot; d. Mary Ellen Weise and Lawrence William Schweitzer; m. Ryan George Nylander, Mar. 18, 2000; children: Morgan Elizabeth children: Madeline Marie. BS, No. Ariz. U., 1987. Cert. airline transport pilot FAA, 1992, flight instr. FAA, 1993, sea plane pilot FAA, 1993, flight engr. rating FAA, 1998. Pilot Grand Canyon Airlines, Ariz., 1992—93, Doss Aviation, Hondo, Tex., 1993—94, Minn. Air N.G., St. Paul, 1994—2001, N.W. Airlines, St. Paul, 1998—. Mem. Christ's Ch. Of The Valley, Phoenix, 1996—2003, Mountain Life Ch., Park City, Utah. Decorated Commendation Medal USAF, Achievement Medal. Mem.: Airline Pilots Assn. (licentiate), Delta Delta Delta (life; panhellenic v.p. 1986—87, highest sorority mem. grade point average 1985, 1986, 1987). R-Consevative. Avocations: running, travel, skiing, hiking, water-skiing. Office: Northwest Airlines 5101 Northwest Dr Saint Paul MN 55111

NYMAN, TERRI RUFFIN, special education educator, director; b. New Augusta, Miss., Mar. 8, 1959; d. John Charles Ruffin and Judith Darlene Bosarge; m. Michael A. Nyman, June 8, 2000; children: Jason Elliot Tomlin, Jr., Jessica Tomlin Welford. BSc, U. Tex., Tyler, 1980, MEd, 1997; PhD in Ednl. Adminstrn., U. So. Miss., Hattisburg, Miss., 2006. Tchr. Lindale Ind. Sch. Dist., 1986—90, Whitehouse Ind. Sch. Dist., 1990—98, George County Schs., Lucedale, Miss., 1998—2003, dir. spl. edn., 2003—06, dir. fed. programs, 2006—. Mem. governing body Headstart, Lucedale, 2005—. Coord. tutoring program First United Meth. Ch., Lucedale, 1998—2005. Mem.: ASCD. Avocations: reading, golf, travel, walking. Office: George County Schs 5152 Main St Lucedale MS 39452 Home: 128 Nyman Rd Lucedale MS 39452

NYOKKA, SUZETTE, artist, natural health educator; b. Meadowbrook, Pa., June 10, 1961; d. adopted d. Walter H. Schmitz; children: Thomas Ziembа children: Gaelen Ishi Nyokka Morrell, Emily Luna Rose Nyokka Morrell. BA, Calif. Inst. Integral Studies, 2001. Advanced Massage Therapies, Natural Health Educator Inst. of Ednl. Therapy, Heartwood Inst., 1988, cert. in Jin Shin Jyutsu 2005. Founder Heartwood Garden, Garberville, Calif., 1984—89; creator/artist Island Mt. Basketry, Garberville, 1986—; massage therapist/educator Advanced Massage Therapies, Woodside, Menlo Park, Calif., 1989—2005, massage therapist/educator Garberville/Novato, 2005—; ednl. activist So. Humboldt Cmty. Sch. Dist., Garberville, 1984—; dir. Skyfish Sch. Permaculture Program, Garberville, 1997—2005; artistic dir. Teen's Radio, Redway, Calif., 2005—; instr. permacuture design, adj. advisor Skyfish Sch., Briceland, 1997—. Prodr.: (storytelling festivals) Live Performances; co-creator (cd) All Spirits Sing (Best Native Am. Rec., 1998). Co-coord. Arts and Ecology Ctr., Garberville, Calif., 2005—; developmennt coord. KMUD Teen's Cmty. Radio, Garberville, Calif., 2004—05; vp So. Humboldt Youth and Cmty. Ctr., Garberville, Calif.; pres. Trees Found., Garberville, Calif., 1996—98; participant in a cross cultural sharing Nat. Storytelling Assn., San Francisco, 2002, China, 2002. Grant, Music For Little People Found., 2002, Humboldt Area Found., 2004, Calif. Inst. of Integral Studies, 2000. Mem.: So. Humboldt Cmty. Parks and Garden Club (life). Democrat-Npl. Avocations: reading, photography, language, film, travel. Home: 352 Meadowview Rd Garberville CA 95542 Office Phone: 415-250-1733. Personal E-mail: suzette@asis.com.

NYQUIST, CORINNE ELAINE, librarian; b. Minnesota Falls, Minn., Nov. 1, 1935; d. Clair Francis and Ebba Ingeborg Johnson; m. Thomas Eugene Nyquist, Dec. 22, 1956; children: Jonathan Eugene, Lynn Marie. BA (cum laude), Macalester Coll., 1956; MALS, U. Minn., 1971; PhD (hon.), U. Albany, 2004. Asst. librarian U. Minn., Mpls., 1959-60, Evanston (Ill.) Pub. Library, 1962-64, Skokie (Ill.) Pub. Library, 1965-66; asst. librarian, research asst. Rhodes U., Grahamstown, Republic of South Africa, 1967; asst. librarian to librarian SUNY, New Paltz, 1968—, ombudsman, 1983-85. Co-project dir. human rights documentation project Ford Found., 1986-88; cons. N.Y. State Edn. Dept., Albany, 1980-82; chmn. internat. librs. com. SUNY, 1984-86. Contbr. articles to profl. jours. Chmn. Town Dem. Com., New Paltz, 1984-86; mem. SUNY adv. com. on awards, 1989-94. Recipient Chancellor's award, 1986; grantee SUNY Research Found., 1975, 84-86, Ford Found., 1986. Mem. ALA (chmn. human rights task force 1989-91, exec. internat. rels. task force 1987-92, interlibr. loan code revision com. 2006—), African Studies Assn., NY African Studies Assn. (co-editor newsletter 1974-99, v.p. 1991-92, pres. 1992-93), Ulster County Librs. Assn. (exec. com. 1984-94), Sojourner Truth Inst. (bd. (1997-2001), SUNY Librs. Assn., Beta Phi Mu. Avocations: reading, hiking, cross country skiing, travel. Office: SUNY Sojourner Truth Libr New Paltz NY 12561-2493 Home: 140 Huguenot St New Paltz NY 12561-1018 Office Phone: 845-257-3681. E-mail: nyquistc@newpaltz.edu.

NYSETH, ELIZABETH ANN, retired secondary school educator; b. St. Paul, Nov. 4, 1948; d. Herbert John and Dagna Mabel (Eimon) Borgert; m. Gary Lynn Nyseth, Dec. 7, 1988; children: Robert, Catherine, Mark; stepchildren: Jeff, Amy, Pete, Christopher. BS in Home Econs. Edn., U. Wis.-Stout, Menomonie, 1970, MS in Clothing, Textiles and Related Art, 1984. Cert. home econs. tchr., Wis. Tchr. Chippewa Falls (Wis.) Schs., 1970—, student tchr. supr. with U. Wis.-Stout, 1973—, curriculum asst. for family/consumer edn., bus. and mktg., 1990—2004, ret., 2004. Advisor Future Homemakers of Am., 1972—; mem. curriculum devel. pilot project Wis. Dept. Pub. Instrn., Madison, 1983-91, workshop facilitator, 1985-91; curriculum cons., 1989-91; adj. instr. U. Wis., Stout, 2004—. Contbg. mem.: Wis. Mid. Sch. Curriculum Guide for Family and Consumer Edn., 1983—91; author: Sewing Tech., 2001. Recipient Cert. of Appreciation Wis. Dept. Pub. Instrn., 1991, U. Wis.-Stout, 1992, 93. Mem.: ASCD, Chippewa Falls Fedn. Tchrs. (v.p. 1993—, bldg. steward), Wis. Family and Consumer Edn. (State award for Dedicated Svc. 2004), N.W. Wis.Edn. Assn. Lutheran. Avocations: sewing, crafts, boating, fishing. Home: N7890 555th St Menomonie WI 54751-5903 Personal E-mail: boatnsew@charter.net.

NYSTROM, TAMMY C., elementary school educator, consultant; b. Chgo., Aug. 2, 1957; d. Coy Kirts Ellison and Maybelle Andrews; m. John Charles Nystrom, Dec. 20, 1982; children: Kevin Coy, Andrew Charles. BA in Bible/Greek, William Tyndale Coll., 1980; MA in Linguistics, U. Tex.-Arlington, 1985. Lic. tchg. South Bend, Ind., 1993. Linguist/translator Wycliffe Bible Translators, Dallas, 1980—88; tchr. English Austin Peay State U., Clarksville, Tenn., 1989—91, Bethel Coll., Mishawaka, Tenn., 1993—96; tchr. grade 6 St. Charles Borromeo Sch., Peru, Ind., 2000—. Mem.: Feminist for Life, NRA. Republican. Avocations: reading, woodworking. Office: St Charles Borromeo Sch 80 W 5th St Peru IN 46970 Business E-Mail: tnystrom@stcharlesperu.org.

OAKES, ELLEN RUTH, psychotherapist, health facility administrator; b. Bartlesville, Okla., Aug. 19, 1919; d. John Isaac and Eva Ruth (Engle) Harboldt; m. Paul Otis Oakes Sr., June 12, 1937 (div. April 1974); children: Paul Otis Jr., Deborah Ellen, Nancy Elaine Masters; m. Siegmar Johann Knopp, Nov. 24, 1975 (div. Feb. 1998). BA in Sociology, Psychology summa cum laude, Oklahoma City U., 1961; MS in Clin. Psychology, U. Okla., 1963, PhD, 1967. Lic. clin. psychologist, Okla. Chief psychometrist Okla. U. Guidance Ctr., Norman, 1962; psychology trainee VA Hosp., Oklahoma City, 1962-64, Cerebral Palsy Ctr., Norman, Okla., 1964-65; psychology intern Guidance Service, Norman, 1965-66, staff psychologist, 1966-67; asst. prof. psychology Okla. U. Med. Sch., Oklahoma City, 1967-70; supr. psychology interns Okla. Univ. Health Scis. Ctr., 1967-80; founder, dir. Timberridge Inst., Oklahoma City, 1970-90, pres., 1980-90; pvt. practice clin. psychologist Oklahoma City, 1970-92. Instr. Okla. U. extension course, Tinker AFB, Oklahoma City, 1963, U. Okla., 1965-66; discussion leader Inst. for Tchrs. of Disadvantaged Child Oklahoma City Sch. System, 1966; leader group therapy sessions Asbury Meth. and Westminster Presbyn. Chs., Oklahoma City, 1966; mem. psychology team confs. for hearing disorders, Okla. U. Med. Sch., 1967-70; cons. Oklahoma City Pub. Schs., 1970-72; cons., group leader halfway house, 1972; mem. Okla. State Bd. Examiners Psychologist, 1974, 75; lectr. chs., PTAs, hosps.; reviewer Am. Psychol. Assn. Civilian Health and Med. Program of the Uniformed Svcs., 1978-89. Workshop conductor on Shame & Sexuality, Zurick Jungian Inst. winter seminar, 1992; attended Européen Congrés de Gestalt Thérapie in Paris, 1992; contbr. articles to profl. jours. Speaker Okla. County Mental Health Assn. Annual Worry Clinic, St. Luke's Ch., Oklahoma City, 1968-92, psychology dept. Sorosis Club, St. Luke's Ch.; charter mem. English spkg. Christian Congregation mission outreach Pauluskirche, Bochum, Germany, 1993-97, exec. coun., 1996-97. Mem. APA (peer rev. project with CHAMPUS, 1978-89), Okla. Psychol. Assn. (life, pres. 1975-76, named Pioneer Psychologist of Okla. by exec. com. 1998). Avocations: art, travel, poetry, photography, walking.

OAKES, JENNIFER SHARYL, physical education educator, athletic director, coach; b. Worcester, Mass., July 27, 1950; d. Nancy H. Oakes. M in Edn., Lesley Coll., Cambridge, Mass., 1997. Phys. educator, coach Williston Ctrl. Sch., Vt., 1972—. Named to Athletic Hall Of Fame, U. Vt., 2002, New Agenda Hall of Fame for Women in Sport, 2004; recipient Charles Christensen award for excellence in tchg. phys. edn., U. Vt., 2006. Office: Williston Ctrl Sch 195 Central School Dr Williston VT 05495 Office Phone: 802-879-5826.

OAKES, MARIA SPACHNER, medical/surgical nurse; d. William Spachner and Roberta Mae (Linville) Stephens; m. John Culwell Oakes; children: John Culwell II, Laura Suzann. Diploma, King's Daus.' Hosp. Cert. med./surg. nurse. Staff nurse Ohio State U. Hosp., Columbus, Lawrence County, Ironton; head nurse, neonatal intensive care King's Daus.' Med. Ctr., Ashland, Ky. Bd. dirs. Am. Cancer Soc.; v.p. West Ironton Parent-Tchr. Group; pres. Kingsbury Parents Better Schs.; mem. strategic planning com. Ironton City Sch. Dist., Acad. Boosers Assn., HS Band Boosters Team, band nurse; deacon bd. sessions, pres. Women's Assn. 1st Presbyn. Ch.; past pres. Kings Daus. Hosp. Sch. Nursing Alumni Assn. Mem.: ANA, Cabell Lincoln County (work camp project co-dir., camp nurse), Ky. Nurses Assn. (state offices nursing practice com., legis. com., state nominating com., nurse practice commn., past pres., v.p., treas. Dist. 4, program chmn., seminar planner, continuing edn. coord, current v.p. Dist. 4, mem. ad hoc com. health care reform), Ironton Coop. Club (past pres.). Home: 2210 N 3rd Ave Ironton OH 45638-1068 Personal E-mail: mariaoakes@adelphia.net.

OAKES-HALL, NANCY ANNE, artist, ski instructor; b. Aspen, Colo., Aug. 10, 1957; d. John Morgan and Bette Daniels Oakes; m. Garry Jay Hall, Sept. 25, 2003. AA, Bradford Coll, 1977; BFA, U. Colo., 1980; MA in Tchg., RI Sch. Design, 1985; MFA, Kendall Coll. Arts and Design, 2004. Ski instr. Aspen Skiing Co., Colo., 1975—88, Sun Valley Ski Sch., Ketchum, Idaho, 1989—96, Aspen Ski and Snowboard Schs., 1998—2003; artist Grand Rapids, Mich., 2000—; adj. prof. Kendall Coll. Art and Design, 2005—. Knitwear, outerwear designer Serac Ski Clothing, Sandpoint, Idaho, 1986—89, Perigrine Ski Clothing, Ketchum, Idaho, 1990—92; knitwear designer, Ketchum, 1992—96; Alpine demonstration team Profl. Ski Instrs. Am., Lakewood, Colo., 1992—96; Alpine skiing examiner Profl. Ski Instrs. Am. No. Intermountain, Burley, Idaho, 1993—96, Alpine skiing clinician, 1993—95, Profl. Ski Instrs. Am. Ctrl., 1998—2000. Exhibited in group shows at Lowell 16th Ann. Regional Show, 2002 (2d place award). Mem.: Profl. Ski Instrs. Am. (cert. level III). Avocations: bicycling, hiking, windsurfing, knitting. Personal E-mail: nancyohski@comcast.net.

OAKLEY, CAROLYN LE, state legislator, city manager, director; b. Portland, Oreg., June 28, 1942; d. George Thomas and Ruth Alveta Victoria (Engberg) Penketh; children: Christine, Michelle. BS in Edn., Oreg. State U., 1965. Educator Linn County (Oreg.) Schs., 1965-76; owner Linn County Tractor, 1965-90; mem. Oreg. Legis. Assembly, Salem, 1989—, asst. majority leader, 1993—, majority whip, 1994; apptd. regional dir. region 10 Dept. Health and Human Svcs., Seattle, 2002—. Mem. exec. bd. Oreg. Retail Coun., 1987-90. Chmn. Linn County Rep. Ctrl. Com., 1982-84; chmn. bd. dirs. North Albany Svc. Dist., 1988-90; chair Salvation Army, Linn and Benton Counties, 1987—; vice chmn. bd. trustees Linn-Benton C.C. Found., 1987—; pres. Women for Agr., Linn and Benton Counties, 1984-86; mem. STRIDE Leadership Round Table, 1991—; state chair Am. Legis. Exch. Coun., 1991-96; nat. bd. dirs., 199-99, exec. com., 1995, 1st vice chair, 1998; mem. Edn. Commn. of the States, 1991—, com. policies and priorities, 1993—, steering com., 1998—, exec. com., 1998; mem. Leadership Coun. on Higher Edn., 1995—; mem. nat. policy bd. Danforth Found., 1995—; state dir., Women in Govt., 1996—; state dir., Nat. Order Women Legislators, 1993—; hon. mem. Linn-Benton Compact Bd., 1993—; active Linn County Criminal Justice Coun., 1994—; vol. Good Samaritan Hosp. Found., State Land Trust for Affordable Housing, Majestic Theater. Named Woman of Yr. Albany chpt. Beta Sigma Phi, 1970. Mem. Nat Conf. State Legislators (chmn. edn. com. 1992—), Albany C. of C. (bd. dirs. 1986-93, 96—), Linn County Rep. Women (legis. chmn. 1982-91), Greater Corvallis Rotary Club (bd. dirs.). Republican. Methodist. Avocations: gardening, camping, volunteering. Home: 3197 NW Crest Loop Albany OR 97321-9627 Office Phone: 541-928-7745. Personal E-mail: cloakley@juno.com.

OAKLEY, DEBORAH JANE, public health service officer, nursing educator; b. Jan. 31, 1937; d. George F. and Kathryn (Willson) Hacker; m. Bruce Oakley, June 16, 1958; children: Ingrid Andrea, Brian Benjamin. BA, Swarthmore Coll., 1958; MA, Brown U., 1960; MPH, U. Mich., 1969, PhD, 1977. Dir. teenage and adult programs YWCA, Providence, 1959-63; editl. asst. Stockholm U., 1963-64; rsch. investigator, lectr. dept. population planning U. Mich., 1971-77, asst. prof. cmty. health programs Ann Arbor, 1977-79, asst. prof. nursing rsch., 1979-81, assoc. prof., 1981-89, prof., 1989—2002, interim dir. Ctr. Nursing Rsch., 1988-90, acting dir. Ctr. Nursing Rsch., 1998, prof. emeritus, 2002—, interim dir. Health Asian Ams. program, 2005. Vis. prof. Beijing Med. U., 1996-2002; prin. investigator NIH, CDC and pvt. found. funded rsch. grants and contracts on family planning, women's health and health care in China, mem. nat. adv. com. nursing rsch., 1993-97; mem. adv. workshop on Nat. Survey on Family Growth, 1994-97; co-chair Mich. Initiative for Women's Health, 1993-95. Author: (with Leslie Corsa) Population Planning, 1979; contbr. articles to profl. jours. Bd. dirs. Planned Parenthood Fedn. Am., 1975-80. Recipient Margaret Sanger award Washtenaw County Planned Parenthood, 1975, Outstanding Young Woman of Ann Arbor award Jaycees, 1970, Dist. Faculty award Mich. Assn. Gov. Bds., 1992, Blue Cross Blue Shield Found. of Mich. award for Excellence in Health Policy, 1996. Mem. APHA (chmn. population sect. coun.), Internat. Union Sci. Study Population, Midwest Nursing Rsch. Soc., Population Assn. Am., Delta Omega, Sigma Theta Tau (hon.). Democrat. Home: 5200 S Lake Dr Chelsea MI 48118-9481 Office: U Mich Sch Nursing Ann Arbor MI 48109-0482 Office Phone: 743-763-6730. E-mail: doakley@umich.edu.

OAKLEY, MARY ANN BRYANT, lawyer; b. Buckhannon, W.Va., June 22, 1940; d. Hubert Herndon and Mary F. (Deeds) Bryant; m. Godfrey P. Oakley, Jr., Sept. 2, 1961; children: Martha, Susan, Robert. AB, Duke U., 1962; MA, Emory U., 1970, JD, 1974. Tchr. Winston-Salem/Forsyth County Schs., NC, 1961-65; assoc. Margie Pitts Hames, Atlanta, 1974-80; ptnr. Stagg Hoy & Oakley, Atlanta, 1980-83, Oakley & Bonner, Atlanta, 1984-90; pvt. practice, 1990-96; ptnr. Holland & Knight LLP, Atlanta, 1996—. Adj. prof. trial practice Ga. State U., 1986-95; adj. prof. pretrial Emory U. Law Sch., 1991, 95; bd. dirs. Nat. Employment Lawyers Assn., 1989-94; founding coord. NELA, Ga.; mem. Ga. Supreme Ct. Commn. on Racial and Ethnic Bias, 1994-95; mem. Ga. Bd. Bar Examiners, 1990-94, chmn., 1994. Author: Elizabeth Cady Stanton, 1972; mem. editl. rev. bd.: The Ga. Labor Letter, 1997—2001, notes and comments editor: Emory Law Jour., 1973—74; contbr. articles to law jours. Bd. dirs. Holland & Knight Charitable Found. Bd., 2002—, Atlanta Met. YWCA, 1975—79, 1st v.p., 1978—79; mem. Leadership Atlanta, 1979; bd. dirs. Ga. chpt. ACLU, 1981—83; bd. dirs. Ga. Legal Svcs. Program, 1991—98, Planned Parenthood Ga., 2006—; trustee Unitarian Universalist Congregation Atlanta, 1977—80, pres., 1979—80; mem. Unitarian Universalist Commn. Appraisal, 1980—85; bd. dirs. Unitarian Universalist Svc. Com., 1984—90, v.p., 1986—88, pres., 1988—90. Recipient Lifetime Commitment to Pub. Svc. award, Emory U. Sch. Law, 2005, Shining Star award, Atlanta Women's Found., 2006, Randolph Thrower award, Emory U. Sch. Law, 2005; Nat. Merit scholar, 1958. Fellow: Ga. Bar Found., Am. Bar Found.; mem.: ABA, Atlantic Vol. Lawyers Found. (adv. bd. 2006—), Ga. State Bar Disciplinary Bd. (investigative panel 1985—88, chmn. 1987—88), Ga. Assn. Women Lawyers (Kathleen Kessler award 1998), Atlanta Bar Assn., State Bar Ga. (chmn. individual rights sect. 1979—81, H. Sol Clark Pro Bono award 1996, Disting. Svc. award 1998), Am. Judicature Soc., Order of Coif, Phi Beta Kappa, Bleckley Inn of Ct. (pres. 1996—99). Home: 2224 Kodiak Dr NE Atlanta GA 30345-4152 Office: 1201 W Peachtree St One Atlantic Ctr Ste 2000 Atlanta GA 30309-3400 Office Phone: 404-817-8507. Business E-Mail: maryann.oakley@hklaw.com.

OAKS, LUCY MOBERLEY, retired social worker; b. Lexington, Ky., May 10, 1935; d. Shelton Neville Moberley and Jane Emison (Roberts) Meadors; m. William Bryant Oaks, Nov. 10, 1956; children: Bryant, Michael, Kevin, Richard, Deborah. BA in Social Work, U. Ky., 1957; MA in Counseling Psychology, Bowie State Coll., Md., 1979. Lic. mental health counselor, Wash. Youth dir. Calvary Bapt. Ch., Renton, Wash., 1960-64, ch. tng. dir., 1980-87; youth dir. Temple Bapt. Ch., Redlands, Calif., 1965-68, Calvary Bapt. Ch., Morgantown, W.Va., 1971-73; cmty. coll. parent educator Bellevue C.C., Wash., 1980-89; pvt. counselor Renton, 1980-90; Christians social svcs. dir. Puget Sound Bapt. Assn., Federal Way, Wash., 1984-87; therapeutic program dir. ACAP Child and Family Svcs., Auburn, Wash., 1984—94, assoc. dir., 1994—96; ret., 1996. Parent instr. APPLE Parenting, Auburn, 1990-92; seminar presenter, Puget Sound, Wash., 1980-95; dir. social svc. ministries ACAP Child and Family Svcs., 1996-98; cons. Mary Kay Cosmetics, 1996—; file supr. Year 2000 Dept. of Commerce/Census Bur., Bellevue (Wash.) br., 1999-2000; product advisor Advocare, 2003—04. Bd. trustees Valley Cmty. Players, Renton, 1995; featured spkr. parent edn. Puget Sound Area, 1988—96; bd. dirs. Calvary Bapt. Ch., Renton, 1981—87. Mem. Puget Sound Adlerian Soc. (bd. dirs. 1981-83), Kiwanis (chmn. interclub com., membership chmn. 1994-95). Democrat. Avocations: drama, reading, walking, travel, bowling. Home: 2218 177th Pl NE Redmond WA 98052-6071 Office Phone: 425-241-0264.

OATES, JOYCE CAROL, writer; b. Lockport, NY, June 16, 1938; d. Frederic James and Caroline (Bush) O.; m. Raymond Joseph Smith, Jan. 23, 1961. BA, Syracuse U., 1960; MA, U. Wis., 1961. Instr. English U. Detroit, 1961-65, asst. prof., 1965-67; prof. English U. Windsor, Ont., Canada, 1967-87; writer-in-residence Princeton (N.J.) U., 1978-81, prof., 1987—. Author: (short story collections) By the North Gate, 1963, Upon the Sweeping Flood, 1966, The Wheel of Love, 1970, Marriages and Infidelities, 1972, The Hungry Ghosts, 1974, The Goddess and Other Women, 1974, Where Are You Going, Where Have You Been?: Stories of Young America, 1974, The Poisoned Kiss and Other Stories From the Portuguese, 1975, The Seduction and Other Stories, 1975, Crossing the Border, 1976, Night-Side, 1977, All the Good People I've Left Behind, 1978, The Lamb of Abyssalia, 1980, A Sentimental Education: Stories, 1981, Last Days: Stories, 1984, Wild Nights, 1985, Raven's Wing: Stories, 1986, The Assignation, 1988, Heat: And Other Stories, 1991, Where is Here?: Stories, 1992, Haunted: Tales of the Grotesque, 1994, Will You Always Love Me? and Other Stories, 1995, The Collector of Hearts: New Tales of the Grotesque, 1996, Faithless: Tales of Transgressions, 2001, Small Avalanches: And Other Stories, 2003, I Am No One You Know, 2004, High Lonesome: Stories 1966-2006, 2006; (novels) With Shuddering Fall, 1964, A Garden of Earthly Delights, 1967 (Nat. Book award nomination 1968), Expensive People, 1967 (Nat. Book award nomination 1969), them, 1969 (Nat. Book award for fiction 1970), Wonderland, 1971, Do With Me What You Will, 1973, The Assassins, 1975, Childwold, 1976, The Triumph of the Spider Monkey, 1976, Son of the Morning, 1978, Unholy Loves, 1979, Cybele, 1979, Bellefleur, 1980 (LA Times Book award nomination 1980), A Sentimental Education, 1981, Angel of Light, 1981, A Bloodsmoor Romance, 1982, Mysteries of Winterthorn, 1984, Solstice, 1985, Marya, 1986, You Must Remember This, 1987, (as Rosamond Smith) The Lives of the Twins, 1987, American Appetites, 1989, (as Rosamond Smith) Soul-Mate, 1989, Because It Is Bitter, and Because It Is My Heart, 1990, (as Rosamond Smith) Nemesis, 1990, I Lock My Door Upon Myself, 1990, The Rise of Life on Earth, 1991, Black Water, 1992, (as Rosamond Smith) Snake Eyes, 1992, Foxfire: Confessions of a Girl Gang, 1993, What I Lived For, 1994 (PEN/Faulkner award nomination 1995), Zombie, 1995, First Love, 1996, We Were the Mulvaneys, 1996, Man Crazy, 1997, Devil's Half Acre, 1997, Come Meet Muffin!, 1998, My Heart Laid Bare, 1998, Broke Heart Blues, 1999, Starr Bright Will Be With You Soon, 1999, Blonde, 2000, The Barrens, 2001, Faithless: Tails of Transgression, 2001, Middle Age: A Romance, 2001, Big Mouth and Ugly Girl, 2002, I'll Take You There, 2002, Freaky Green Eyes, 2003, Rape: A Love Story, 2003, Where Is Little Reynard, 2003, The Tattooed Girl, 2003, Sexy, 2005, Missing Mom, 2005, The Female of the Species, 2006, (as Lauren Kelly) The Stolen Heart, 2005, Blood Mask, 2006, Black Girl/White Girl, 2006; (non-fiction) The Faith of a Writer: Life, Craft, Art, 2003; (poetry collections) Women in Love, 1968, Expensive People, 1968, Anonymous Sins, 1969, Love and Its Derangements, 1970, Angel Fire, 1973, Dreaming America, 1973, The Fabulous Beasts, 1975, Season of Peril, 1977, Women Whose Lives are Food, Men Whose Lives are Money: Poems, 1978, The Stepfather, 1978, Celestial Timepiece, 1981, Invisible Women: New and Selected Poems, 1970-1972, 1982, Luxury of Sin, 1983, The Time Traveller, 1987; (plays) The Sweet Enemy, 1965, Sunday Dinner, 1970, Ontological Proof of My Existence, 1970, Miracle Play, 1974, Three Plays, 1980, Daisy, 1980, Presque Isle, 1984, Triumph of the Spider Monkey, 1985, In Darkest America, 1990, I Stand Before You Naked, 1990, The Perfectionist and Other Plays, 1995; (essays) The Edge of Impossibility, 1972, The Hostile Sun: The Poetry of D.H. Lawrence, 1973, New Heaven, New Earth, 1974, Contraries: Essays, 1981, The Profane Art, 1984, On Boxing, 1987, (Woman) Writer: Occasions and Opportunities, 1988; editor, compiler: Scenes from American Life: Contemporary Short Fiction, 1973, (with Shannon Ravenel) Best American Short Stories of 1979, 1979, Night Walks, 1982, First Person Singular: Writer's on Their Craft, 1983, (with Boyd Litzinger) Story: Fictions Past and Present, 1985, (with Daniel Halpern) Reading and Fights, 1988, The Oxford Book ofAmerican Short Stories, 1992, The Sophisticated Cat: An Anthology, 1992,(editor)The Best American Mystery Stories 2005; editor (with Raymond Smith) Ontario Rev.; contbr. to nat. mags. including NY Times Book Rev., Mich. Quarterly Rev., Mademoiselle, Vogue, North Am. Rev., Hudson Rev., Paris Rev., Grand Street, Atlantic, Poetry, Esquire. Recipient O. Henry award, 1967, 73, Rosenthal award Nat. Inst. Arts and Letters, 1968, O. Henry Spl. award continuing achievement, 1970, 86, Award of Merit Lotos Club, 1975, St. Louis Lit. award, 1988, Rea award for the Short Story, 1990, Alan Swallow award for fiction, 1990, Nobel Prize in Lit. nomination, 1993; Guggenheim fellow, 1967-68, Nat. Endowment for the Arts grantee, 1966, 68. Mem. Am. Acad. and Inst. Arts and Letters. Office: care John Hawkins Agy 71 W 23rd St Ste 1600 New York NY 10010-4102 also: Princeton U Dept Creative Writing 117 185 Nassau St Princeton NJ 08544-0001*

OATESS, JANET SUE, language educator; b. Peru, Ind., Apr. 29, 1945; d. Lloyd Roscoe and Rheva Lucille Slusher; m. Stephen Paul Oatess, Mar. 7, 1964; children: Diana Lynn Barry, Stephanie Jean Oatess-Imbler, Kristen Lee Taylor. BS in Edn., Ind. U., Bloomington, 1972. English dept. head Maconaquah H.S., Bunker Hill, Ind., 1974—; adj. lectr. English Ind. U., Kokomo, 1978—. R-Liberal. Protestant. Avocations: gardening, restoring furniture. Home: 202 S Madison St Converse IN 46919

OAXACA, SUSAN RENNA, secondary school educator; b. Lubbock, Tex., Feb. 26, 1956; d. Horace Oscar and Betty Sue Abbott; m. Francisco Javier Oaxaca, Dec. 17, 1973 (div. Dec. 12, 1983); children: Fransicso Javier Oaxaca, Jr., Richard Abbott. BBA, McMurry U., Abilene, Tex., 1974—78. Cert. Math. Tchr. Tex. Bd. Edn., 1983. 7th grade math tchr. Sweetwater Ind. Sch. Dist., Tex., 1984—85; 8th grade math tchr. Levelland Ind. Sch. Dist., 1985—86; 8th algebra/math. tchr. Clyde Ind. Sch. Dist., 1986—2001; 8th algebra i tchr. Ft. Worth Ind. Sch. Dist., 2001—04; HS algebra i tchr. Tyler Ind. Sch. Dist., 2004—. Sponsor Jr. Beta Sponsor, Clyde, 1986—2001, Cheerleaders, Clyde, 1986—2001; mem. Campus Improvement, Clyde, 1990—92, Site Base Com., Clyde, 1992—93, Ins. Com., Clyde, 1994—98; coach Volleyball, Ft. Worth. Mem. Pollard United Meth. Ch., Tyler, 2004. Recipient Golden Apple award for Edn., CBS19 News, 2006. Mem.: ATPE (assoc.). Methodist. Home: 5207 Hollytree Dr #721 Tyler TX 75703 Office: John Tyler HS Loop 323 Tyler TX 75704 Office Phone: 903-262-2850. Personal E-mail: oaxaca.s@sbcglobal.net.

O'BAIRE-KARK, MARIKA, nurse, educator, poet, writer; b. Manila, Oct. 3, 1947; d. Gerald John and Giovanna (BelForti) Barry; m. Pieter Kark, Oct. 3, 2004; children from previous marriage: Matthew Plocharczyk, Alexei Plocharczyk, Rita Higgins, D. Patrick Higgins. Student, U. Conn., 1964—65; diploma, Ellis Hosp. Sch. Nursing, 1977; BSN, Russell Sage Coll., 1980, postgrad., 1983, postgrad., 1994; grad. ontological design, Logonet Inc. ODC-J, 1993; postgrad. humanities, Calif. State U., Dominguez Hills, 1995; postgrad., U. Dundee, 2000; postgrad. in Disaster and Emergency Mgmt., Touro U., 2005—; postgrad. in Writing, Stanford U., 2006—. RN NY, Calif.; lic. avatar master/wizard Star's Edge Internat. Tchr. English Lang. Inst., Taipei, Taiwan, 1971—73; team leader, staff nurse acute psychiatry Samaritan Hosp., Troy, NY, 1978—80; staff nurse pediat. ICU Albany Med. Ctr., NY, 1980—84, 1997—; rsch. nurse Commn. on Quality Care for Mentally Disabled, Albany, 1984; staff nurse Columbia-Greene Med. Ctr., Catskill, NY, 1984—89; night charge nurse Conifer Park, Scotia, NY, 1991—92; nursing educator St. Clare's Hosp., Schenectady, NY, 1992—96; adj clin. educator Albany Med. Ctr. So. Vt. Coll., Bennington, 1997—2001; nurse, specialized surg. pre-ICU, Stanford U. Hosp., 2005—. On-call nurse Cmty. Hospice Saratoga, NY, 1998—2004; founder Future Design: Create What You Prefer, Avatar Tech. & Skills, 2000, Favorite Nurses, Colonie, NY, 2002—; cons. Author: (novels) Dragon, 2002, Future Joyous, 2002, (short stories) About Love, (screenplays) Syin; contbr. articles to Echo Mag. Past vol. curriculum designer gifted and talented programs; firefighter Cazenovia, NY. Mem.: Ontological Design Cmty., Upstate Ind. Filmakers/Screenwriters, Childreach Plan Internat., Toastmasters Internat. Personal E-mail: mobaire@yahoo.com.

OBAMOGIE, MERCY A., physician; b. Lagos, Nigeria, Jan. 18, 1954; d. Godwin I and Janet E. (Amiolemen) O.; m. Abiodun O. Odunmbaku, June 20, 1980 (div. 1995); children: Abisola, Adenike, Abiodun. BS, Columbia U., 1980; MD, U. Medicine and Dentistry N.J., Piscataway, 1984; MPH, Johns Hopkins U., 1987; MBA, U. Calif., Irvine, 2000. Diplomate Am. Bd. Family Practice, Nat. Bd. Med. Examiners. Intern in internal medicine Muhlenberg Hosp., Plainfield, NJ, 1984-85; resident in gen. preventive medicine Johns Hopkins U., Balt., 1985-86; resident in family practice Georgetown U./Providence Hosp., Washington, 1986-89; pvt. practice Washington, Greenbelt, Md., 1989—; med. dir. Doctors Slim and Fitness Ctr., Greenbelt, 1996-98. Med. adv. bd. Metra Health Ins. Co., 1992-94; utilization com. Aetna Ins. Co., 1993-95, credentialing com., 1996; med. adv. com. United HealthCare, 1997; mem. planning com. Providence Hosp., Washington, 1996-98; with Prince George's Hosp. Ctr., Cheverly, Md., Howard U. Hosp., Washington, Doctors Cmty. Hosp., Lanham, Md., Providence Hosp., Washington; pres., med. dir. Mercy Med. Ctr., Benin City, Nigeria, 1996—; pres., CEO ASAKI Corp., Greenbelt, Md., 2000—. Contbr. articles to profl. jours. Home: 25 Atwood Ct Silver Spring MD 20906-2089 Office: 7323 Hanover Pkwy Ste A Greenbelt MD 20770-3617 Office Phone: 301-345-5900. E-mail: aimmercy@aol.com.

OBED, LEONORA RITA VILLEGAS, writer; b. Manila, Philippines, May 22, 1971; arrived in US, 1973; d. Reynaldo Nera and Josefina Kalaw (Villegas) Obed. BA, St. Joseph's U., 1993; MA, U. Toronto, 1994; postgrad. in English Lit., U. Edinburgh. Spkr. in field. Author: The Invention of Candles, 2001, I Won't Send Roses, 2001, (plays) Epitome, 2003; contbr. articles to profl. jours. Mem.: Hopkins Soc., Yeats Soc., Oscar Wilde Soc. Home: 10 Michelle Ct Trenton NJ 08628-2924 Office Phone: 609-575-4959. Personal E-mail: leonora.obed@hotmail.com.

OBER, JANE FINLEY, career planning administrator; b. Rochester, Pa., Jan. 30, 1955; d. John Martin and Frances Welborn Finley; m. Keith Edward Ober, Dec. 23, 1976; 1 child, Courtney Ann. BS in Edn., Shippensburg State Coll., Pa., 1976; MS in Edn., Shippensburg U., Pa., 1981. Cert. Nat. Bd. for Cert. Counselors, 1984, lic. profl. counselor State Bd. Social Workers, Marriage and Family Therapists and Profl. Counselors Pa., 2002. Summer tchr. intern Quaker Oats Co., Shiremanstown, Pa., 1978; h.s. bus. tchr. Cumberland Valley Sch. Dist., Mechanicsburg, Pa., 1976—81; bus. divsn. counselor, asst. prof. Harrisburg (Pa.) Area C.C., 1981—85, dir. admissions, 1985—87, coll. admissions counselor, 1988—92; pvt. practice counselor Pa. Counseling Svcs., Carlisle, Mechanicsburg, 1992—93; h.s. counselor Carlisle Area Sch. Dist., 1993—. Mktg. cons. Harrisburg Area C.C., 1988; faculty coun. mem. Carlisle H.S. chpt. - Nat. Honor Soc., 2003—. Actor: (videotape) The Teacher Summer Intern Program. Vol. Project SHARE Food Bank, Carlisle, 1991—2006; Sunday sch. tchr. - jr. and sr. h.s. class Trinity United Meth. Sunday Sch., New Kingstown, Pa., 1986—2006; Sunday sch. supt. Trinity United Meth. Ch. Sunday Sch., New Kingstown, 2000—06; adv. bd.

mem. Carlisle Victory Cir., 1994—2000; treas., edn. chair Internat. Mgmt. Coun., Carlisle, 1978—87; reporter to local media Carlisle H.S. Girls' Lacrosse Team, 2003—05. Nominee Excellence in Edn. award, Carlisle Area Sch. Dist., 2005. Mem.: ACA, Pa. Sch. Counselors' Assn., Greenpeace, Natural Resources Def. Coun., The Sierra Club, Environ. Def. Fund, Delta Kappa Gamma Soc. Internat. (life; pres. 1984—86, Outstanding Woman Educator Beta Iota chpt. 2003). Democrat. Methodist. Avocations: golf, reading, travel, gardening, exercise. Office: Carlisle Area School District 623 West Penn St Carlisle PA 17013 Office Phone: 717-240-6800 26806.

OBERFIELD, SHARON ELEFANT, pediatric endocrinologist; b. NYC, Aug. 14, 1950; d. Nicholas and Anna (Weiss) Elefant; m. Richard A. Oberfield; 2 children. AB in Biology, Cornell U., 1970, MD, 1974. Diplomate in pediatrics and pediatric endocrinology Am. Bd. Pediatrics. Intern in pediatrics The N.Y. Hosp., 1974-75, resident in pediatrics, 1975-76, fellow in pediatric endocrinology, 1976-79, asst. attending pediatrician, 1979-84; asst. attending pediatrian endocrinology Meml. Sloan Kettering Cancer Ctr., N.Y.C., 1986—2001. Provisional pediatrician to outpatient dept. N.Y. Hosp., 1976-79; assoc. attending pediatrician St. Luke's-Roosevelt Hosp. Ctr., N.Y.C., 1984-91, Presbyn. Hosp., N.Y.C., 1991, Tisch Hosp., Bellevue Hosp., N.Y.C., 1992—; attending pediatrician Children's Hosp. of N.Y.-Presbyn. Hosp., 1998—; asst. attending pediatrician Meml. Sloan Kettering Cancer Ctr., 1979-84; asst. prof. pediatrics Cornell U. Med. Coll., N.Y.C., 1979-84, Columbia U. Coll. Physicians & Surgeons, N.Y.C., 1984-91, assoc. prof. clin. pediatrics, 1991, prof., 1998—, dir. pediat. endocrinology, 2004—. Grantee NIH, 1978-84, 2005-, Hoffman-LaRoche, 1985-89, Eli Lilly, 1986-92. Children's Brain Tumor Found., 1995-98; recipient Mitchell Spivak Meml. prize in pediatrics, 1974. Mem. Am. Med. Women's Assn. (citation 1974), N.Y. Acad. Scis., N.Y. Pediatric Soc., Soc. Pediatric Rsch., Endocrine Soc., Lawson Wilkins Soc., Pediatric Endocrinology, Alpha Omega Alpha. Office: Divsn Pediat Endocrinology 630 W 168th St PH-5E-522 New York NY 10032 Office Phone: 212-305-6559. Business E-Mail: seo8@columbia.edu.

OBERLANDER, ERYN L., psychiatrist, preventive medicine physician; d. Melvyn S. and Norma Oberlander; children: Sage Mandel, Tristyn Mandel, Graelin Mandel. BA, Amherst Coll., Mass., 1984, degree (hon.) summa cum laude, 1987; MD, Albert Einstein Coll. Medicine, Bronx, N.Y., 1988; post grad., Columbia U. Coll. Physicians and Surgeons, N.Y.C., 1992. Diplomate Am. Bd. Psychiatry and Neurology, 1993. Resident psychiatry Yale U. Sch. Medicine, New Haven, 1990; pvt. practice N.Y.C., NY, 1992—; asst. clin. prof. dept. psychiatry Columbia U. Coll. Physicians and Surgeons; asst. attending dept. psychiatry N.Y. Presbyn. Hosp., North Shore- Manhasset Hosp, NY. Fulbright scholar, Amherst Coll., 1987. Mem.: AMA, Nassau County Med. Soc., Med. Soc. State of N.Y., Am. Coll. Health Assn., Am. Med. Women's Assn., Am. Psychiatric Assn., Phi Beta Kappa. Office: Ste 1D 41 Park Ave New York NY 10016 Office Phone: 212-725-8111.

OBERLY, KATHRYN ANNE, lawyer, diversified financial services company executive; b. Chgo., May 22, 1950; d. James Richard and Lucille Mary (Kraus) Oberly; 1 child, Michael W. Goelzer; m. Haynes B. Johnson, June 29, 2002. Student, Vassar Coll., 1967—69; BA, U. Wis., 1971, JD, 1973. Bar: Wis. 1973, D.C. 1981, N.Y. 1995. Law clk. U.S. Ct. Appeals, Omaha, 1973-74; trial atty. U.S. Dept. Justice, Washington, 1974-77, spl. asst., 1977-81, spl. litig. counsel, 1981-82, asst. to Solicitor Gen., 1982-86; ptnr. Mayer, Brown & Platt, Washington, 1986-91; assoc. gen. counsel Ernst & Young LLP, Washington, 1991-94, vice-chair, gen. counsel N.Y.C., 1994—. Bd. dirs. Appleseed Found., 2003—04. Named one of 50 Most Influential Women Lawyers in Am., Nat. Law Jour., 1998. Mem. ABA, Am. Law Inst. (coun. mem.), Am. Acad. Appellate Lawyers, Wis. Bar Assn., D.C. Bar Assn., NY Bar Assn. Democrat. Office: Ernst & Young LLP 5 Times Sq New York NY 10036 Office Phone: 212-773-2500. Business E-Mail: kathryn.oberly@ey.com.

OBERMARK, SARAH MARIE, English educator; b. St. Louis, May 17, 1980; d. Christopher David Obermark and Leah I. Diamandis. BA in English, U. Ill., Champaign-Urbana, 2002, MA in Edn., 2005. Mid. sch. tchr. Columbia Ctr. Alternative, Champaign, 2002—05; tchr. English Danville H.S., Danville, Ill., 2005—; mid. sch. sci. tchr. Kingswood Sch., Urbana, Ill., 2003—; prof. Parkland Coll., Champaign, 2006—. Mem. curriculum team Danville Dist. 118, 2005—; bldg. leader lang. arts Champaign Unit Sch. Dist., 2003—05. Named Am. Smart Educator, Am. IP, Urbana, 2002, 2004, 2005; recipient Beginning Educator award, U. Ill. Alumni Assn., 2006; grantee Am. Power Up grantee, Am. IP, Urbana, 2006; scholar, Golden Apple Orgn., 2005—. Mem.: NEA. Methodist. Avocations: reading, bicycling. Office: Kingswood School PO Box 834 Urbana IL 61803-0834

OBERMEYER, THERESA NANGLE, sociology educator; b. St. Louis, July 25, 1945; d. James Francis and Harriet Clare (Shafer) Nangle; m. Thomas S. Obermeyer, Dec. 23, 1977; children: Thomas Jr., James, Margaret, Matthew. BA, Maryville U., St. Louis, 1967; MEd, St. Louis U., 1970, PhD, 1975. Lic. real estate broker Alaska, 1979, cert. Type A teacher Alaska, 1979. Dir. student activities Lindenwood U., St. Charles, Mo., 1969—70; asst. dean of students Loyola Coll., Balt., 1972—73; asst. dir. student activities St. Louis C.C., Florissant Valley, 1973—78; dir. student activities U. Alaska, Anchorage, 1978—79; instr. sociology Chapman U., Anchorage, 1981—93; tchr. secondary McLaughlin Youth Ctr. for Juvenile Delinquents, 1984—90. Mem Anchorage Munic Health Commn., 1980—81; elected alt. coun. urban bd edn. Nat Sch. Bds. Assn., 1994; maj. party nominee US Senate Gen. Election, 1996; founder, mem. Alaska Women's Polit. Caucus, 1979—; elected Anchorage Sch. Bd., 1990—94, treas., 1993. Recipient Fed Women's Equity Act, US Dept Educ Univ Alaska, 1978—79; fellow Fulbright, Project India, 1974, Project Jordan, 1977; grantee Title I, Univ Md and Loyola Col, 1972—73; scholar NDEA, 1968—70. Mem.: AAUW (bd. dirs. Anchorage br. 1980—81), DAR (regent col. John Mitchell chpt. 1992—94), Am. Soc. Pub. Adminstrn. (pres., bd. dirs. south ctrl. chpt. 1981). Avocations: athletics, swimming, horseback riding, skiing, running. Home and Office: 3000 Dartmouth Dr Anchorage AK 99508-4413 Office Phone: 907-278-9455. E-mail: tobermeyer@gci.net.

OBERN, VIVIAN MARIE, volunteer; b. Park Ridge, Ill., May 26, 1921; d. Vaughn Webber and Beatrice Beckwith Hapeman; m. Earl George Obern, Dec. 4, 1942; children: George Vaughn, Dale Marie, Reade Webber. BA, Principia Coll., Elsah, Ill., 1942. Co-chmn. Am. Revolutionary Bicentennial Com., 1974—77; chmn. County Christopher Columbus Quincentennial, 1992; pres. Santa Barbara Trust for Hist. Preservation, 1989—91; leader Girl Scouts Am., 1960—66; mem. Calif. Recreational Trails Com., Sacramento, 1971—76; vol. Hope House, 1986; mem. adv. com. to suprs. Santa Barbara County Riding and Hiking Trails, Calif., 1967—2006; mem. Santa Barbara Courthouse Docents Coun., 1974—2006. Named Woman of Yr., Santa Barbara Advt. Club, 1989; recipient Hon. Life Svc. award, PTA, 1968, 1976, Disting. Alumna award, Principia Coll., 1996, Lifetime Achievement award, Calif. Recreational Trails, 1997, Environ. award, Santa Barbara County Trails Coun., 1997, Pearl Chase Hist. Preseravation award, Santa Barbara Trust for Hist. Preservation, 1998, Wildlife Sanctuary award, 2002, Obern Bikeway/Trail named in her honor, 2004, Environ. Studies Cmty. Svc. award, 2006. Mem.: Calif. Recreational Trails, Daus. of Union Vets. (pres. Calif. dept.). Christian Scientist. Avocation: equestrian activities. Home: 4140 Marina Dr Santa Barbara CA 93110

OBERNDORF, MEYERA E., mayor; m. Roger L. Oberndorf; children: Marcie, Heide. BS in Elem. Edn., Old Dominion U., 1964. Broadcaster Sta. WNIS, Norfolk, Va.; chair Pub. Libr. bd., Va.; mem. city coun. City of Virginia Beach, Va., 1976—, vice-mayor Va., 1986—88, mayor Va., 1988—. Mem. exec. bd. Tidewater coun. Boys Scouts Am.; bd. dirs. Va.Beach Pub. Libr., 1966-76, chmn. bd., 1967-76; past pres. Va. Muncipal League; bd. dir. Hampton Roads Partnership; Econ. Develop. Alliance; adv. com. Va. Inst. of Gov. Named 25 Most Dynamic Mayors in the US, Newsweek. Mem. AAUW, U.S. Conf. Mayors (trustee), Va. Mcpl. League (exec. bd.), Nat. League Cities (vice-chmn., mem. adv. bd., past chair Energy, Environ., and Natural Resources Steering Com.), Princess Anne Women's Club; chair Standing Com. on Internat. Affairs. Jewish. Home: 5404 Challedon Dr Virginia Beach VA 23462-4112 Office: 2401 Courthouse Drive City Hall Bldg 1 Municipal Ctr Virginia Beach VA 23456 Office Phone: 757-427-4581. Office Fax: 757-426-5669. E-mail: mobernd o@VBgov.com.*

OBERSTAR, HELEN ELIZABETH, retired cosmetics company executive; b. Ottawa, Ill. d. Milton Edward and Helen (Herrick) Weiss; m. Edward Charles Oberstar, Feb. 3, 1945 (dec. 1984). BS in Chemistry, Monmouth (Ill.) Coll., 1943; postgrad., Northwestern U., Chgo., 1947-49; LLD (hon.), Monmouth Coll., 1987. Asst. food technologist Standard Brands, Inc., Bklyn., 1943-45; chemist Miner Labs., Midwest div., Arthur D. Little, Chgo., 1946-50; rsch. chemist/rsch. supr. Toni Co., div. Gillette Co., Chgo., 1951-65; group leader rsch. and devel. Shulton, Inc., Clifton, N.J., 1965-72; sect. leader rsch. and devel. Am. Cyanamid, Clifton, 1972-75; mgr. rsch. and devel. Clairol Bristol Myers Internat., Stamford, Conn., 1975-82; dir. tech. Clairol Bristol Myers Squibb Consumer Products Group Internat., Stamford, 1982-93; dir. technology internat. group Clairol, Inc. divsn. Bristol-Myers Squibb, Stamford, 1993-95; ret. Wilton, Conn., 1995. Patentee in field. Recipient Disting. Alumni award Monmouth Coll., 1986, Hall of Achievement award Monmouth Coll., 1995. Mem. Soc. Cosmetic Chemists (house chmn. 1963-64), Cosmetic Toiletries Fragrance Assn. (internat. com. 1985-95). Episcopalian. Avocations: rughooking, gardening, travel. Home and Office: 512 Belden Hill Rd Wilton CT 06897-4221

OBERSTEIN, MARYDALE, geriatric specialist; b. Red Wing, Minn., Dec. 30; d. Dale Robert and Jean Ebba-Marie (Holmquist) Johnson; children: Kirk Robert, Mark Paul, MaryJean. Student, U. Oreg., 1961-62, Portland State U., 1962-64, Long Beach State U., 1974-76. Cert. geriatric specialist, Calif. Florist, owner Sunshine Flowers, Santa Ana, Calif., 1982—; pvt. duty nurse Aides in Action, Costa Mesa, Calif., 1985-87; owner, activity dir., adminstr. Lovelight Christian Home for the Elderly, Santa Ana, 1987—; activity dir. Bristol Care Nursing Home, Santa Ana, 1985-88; evangelist, speaker radio show Sta. KPRZ-FM, Anaheim, Calif., 1985-88; adminstr. Leisure Lodge Resort Care for Elderly in Lake Forest, Lake Forest, Calif., 1996—. Nursing home activist in reforming laws to eliminate bad homes, 1984-90; founder, tchr. hugging classes/laughter therapy terminally ill patients, 1987—; founder healing and touch therapy laughter therapy Merry Sunshine, 1991-93; bd. dirs. Performing Arts Ctr.; speaker for enlightenment and healing. Author (rewrite) Title 22 Nursing Home Reform Law, Little Hoover Commn.; model, actress and voiceovers. Bd. dirs. Orange County Coun. on Aging, 1984—; chairperson Helping Hands, 1985—, Pat Robertson Com., 1988, George Bush Presdl. Campaign, Orange County, 1988; bd. dirs., v.p. Women Aglow Orange County, 1985—; evanglist, pub. spkr., v.p. Women Aglow Huntington Beach; active with laughter therapy and hugging classes for terminally ill; helped write AB 180 Nursing Home Reform Bill and revised title 22. Recipient Carnation Silver Bowl, Carnation Svc. Co., 1984-85, Gold medal Pres. Clinton, 1994; named Woman of Yr., Kiwanis, 1985, ABI, 1990, Woman of Decade, Am. Biog. Soc., 1995, Little Hoover Commn., 1995; honored AM L.A. TV Show, Lt. Gov. McCarthy, 1984. Mem. Calif. Assn. Residential Care Homes, Orange County Epilepsy Soc. (bd. dirs. 1986—), Calif. Assn. Long Term Facilities. Home: 2050 Oak St Santa Ana CA 92707-2921

OBERT, MARY ELLEN NEWTON, retired internist; b. Ellwood City, Pa., Apr. 12, 1926; d. J. Holliday and Jeanetta Newton; m. Gerard J. Obert, July 11, 1927 (dec.); children: David, John, Clare, Anne, Barbara. BS, Westminster Coll., New Wilmington, Pa., 1946; MD, Temple U., Phila., 1950. Intern Mercy Hosp., Pitts., 1950—52; resident Presbyn. Hosp., 1952—55; pvt. practice internist Rochester, Minn., 1955—60, Grand Forks, ND, 1961—63; internist VA Hosp., Fargo, 1964—76, Concordia Coll., Moorhead, Minn., 1977—91; ret., 1991. Vol. physician Salvation Army Free Clinic, Fargo, 1991—98. Avocations: reading, needlecrafts, swimming.

OBLER, GERI, small business owner, artist, educator; b. N.Y., May 1, 1942; m. Arnold Obler, June 30, 1963; children: Nancy, Gary. BFA, Pratt Inst., 1963; MA, Hunter Coll., 1966; EdD, T.C. Columbia U., 1974. Tchr. art John Bowne H.S., Flushing, NY, 1963—74; prin., owner Geri Obler Fine Arts, N.Y., 1985—. Assoc. website Sotheby's Auction Ho., N.Y., 2000—03. Author: (catalogue introduction) Mel Ramos: His Graphic Work, 2002; exhibitions include Geri Obler Fine Arts. Mem.: Nat. Assn. Women Artists. Home: 26 Brokaw Ln Great Neck NY 11023 Office: Geri Obler Fine Arts 153 E 57th St New York NY 10022 Office Phone: 917-913-4244. Personal E-mail: oblerart@aol.com.

OBLINGER, JESSICA MARIE, health facility administrator; d. Duane Fredrick and JoAnn Oblinger. BSc, Duquesne U., Pitts., 2000; MSc, La. State U., Baton Rouge, 2002. Cert. athletic trainer NATABOC, 2000. Grad. asst. athletic trainer La. State U., Baton Rouge, 2000—02; clin. asst. Ortho Rx, Baton Rouge, 2002—03, site supr., 2003—06; area mgr. Orthor Rx, Baton Rouge, 2006—. Recipient People's Choice award, Baton Rouge Market, 2003, 2004. Mem.: La. Athletic Trainers Assn., Nat. Athletic Trainers Assn. Catholic. Avocations: strength training, running, skiing, travel. Office Phone: 225-763-9757.

OBOLENSKY, MARILYN WALL (MRS. SERGE OBOLENSKY), metals company executive; b. Detroit, Aug. 13, 1929; d. Albert Fraser and Christine (Frischkorn) Wall; m. Serge Obolensky, June 3, 1971. Student, Duschesne Jr. Coll., 1947. Chmn. bd. Wall-Colmondy Corp., Detroit, 1959-61, exec. sec., 1961—. Chmn. bd. Wall-Gases Inc., Morrisville, Pa., 1959-61; pres. Serge Obolensky Assocs. Bd. dirs. Heart and Lung Assn. N.Y.C., 1963—. Mem.: Bathing Corp. (Southampton, N.Y.), Southampton. Republican. Roman Catholic. Address: 45 Preston Pl Grosse Pointe Farms MI 48236-3035

O'BOYLE, MAUREEN, television show host; News prodr., anchor Sta. KREM-TV, Spokane, Wash.; reporter, prodr., writer, co-anchor Sta. WMAZ-TV, Macon, Ga.; nightside reporter, anchor Sta. WECT-TV, Wilmington, N.C.; morning news anchor Sta. WITN-TV, Washington, N.C.; anchor A Current Affair; anchor, sr. corr. Extra, Glendale, Calif., 1995-96, co-host, 1997—; host In Person With Maureen O'Boyle, 1996-97.

OBRAMS, GUNTA IRIS, clinical research administrator; b. Düsseldorf, Germany, Sept. 2, 1953; came to U.S., 1961; d. Robert and Olga (Baltins) O.; m. Malcolm DeWitt Patterson, Dec. 22, 1975; 1 child, Andrew McDougal Patterson. BS in Biology cum laude, Rensselaer Poly. Inst., 1977; MD, Union U., Albany, N.Y., 1977; MPH, Johns Hopkins U., 1982, PhD, 1988. Resident in obstetrics and gynecology Ea. Va. Grad. Sch. Medicine, Norfolk, 1977-78; community physician Southampton Meml. Hosp., Franklin, Va., 1978-81; resident in gen. preventive medicine sch. hygiene and pub. health Johns Hopkins U., Balt., 1981-84, project dir., 1983-85, med. dir., 1985-86; med. officer divsn. cancer etiology Nat. Cancer Inst., Bethesda, Md., 1986-89, dep. chief, 1989-90, chief, 1990-96, dir. extramural epidemiology & genetics program, 1996-2001; mgmt. US Coast Guard Health Svcs., 2001—05; med. officer divsn. clin. resources NIH, Bethesda, 2005—. Editor: (with M. Potter): The Epidemiology and Biology of Multiple Myeloma, 1991; contbr. articles to profl. jours. With USPHS, 1987—. Recipient Nat. Cancer Inst. Nat. Rsch. Svc. award, 1981, Rsch. Career award Nat. Inst. Occupational Safety & Health; scholar Am. Med. Women's Assn., 1977. Mem. Phi Beta Kappa, Delta Omega, Alpha Omega Alpha. Office: DCRR NCRR NIH 6701 Democracy Blvd MSC-4874 Bethesda MD 20892

O'BRIEN, ADRIENNE GRATIA, communications educator; b. NYC, Nov. 19, 1935; d. John Robert and Regina C. (Murphy) O'B.; m. David G. Salten, Dec. 21, 1987. AB, Hunter Coll., NYC; MA, MA, Villanova (Pa.) U.; PhD, Syracuse U. Faculty Cabrini Coll., Radnor, Pa., 1962-68, dir. R & D, 1971-72; prof., chair MA program NY Inst. Tech., Old Westbury, 1974-78, dean Sch. Media and Arts, 1979-91, prof. comm. arts, 1992—. Pres. AID Assocs., NYC, 1972-74, Creative Cons., Port Washington, NY, 1992—; reviewer Nat. Coun. Humanities, Washington, 1981; pres. Women in Instrnl. Tech., Washington, 1981. Editor: Computer Based Training Today, 1987; prodr., dir. (video) Then and Now, 1995 (Communicator award, 1996), Legacy of Mother Ursula, 1996 (Communicator award, 1997), Maritime Mus. of L.I., founder, exec. prodr. L.I. News tonight, 1984; reviewer: Jour. Staff Devel., 1990. Mem. project steering com. Where Are the Women?, 2002; bd. dirs. Girl Scouts of Nassau County, 2002—. Named one of 90 Women for 90 Yrs., Girl Scouts of Nassau County; recipient Instrnl. Nat. Leadership award, Assn. Ednl. Comm. and Tech., Washington, 1989, Comm. award, Maritime Mus. L.I., 2001, L.I. Top 50 Women award, L.I. Bus. News, 2002, Lifetime Achievement award, Pub. Rels. Profls. L.I., 2005, Cmty. Svc. award, Patron of the Arts, NY, 2005, Women on the Job Achievement in Edn. award, 2005. Mem.: Women on the Job (v.p. 1995—2004), Alpha Epsilon Rho (hon.). Avocation: tennis. Office: NY Inst Tech Old Westbury NY 11568 Business E-Mail: aobrien@nyit.edu.

O'BRIEN, AMY V., apparel designer; b. Santa Rosa, Calif., Nov. 30, 1961; d. Kenneth and Arleen Elizabeth (Hill) O'B.; divorced. AA, Fashion Inst. Design and Merchandise, L.A., 1983. Designer Faris Bros., L.A., 1983-86, Tosca, L.A., 1986-92; tech. product mgr. MAST, Andover, Mass., 1992-95; quality control Nap, N.Y.C., 1995-96; designer Deena, L.A., 1994-96, Jezebel, L.A., 1996-99, On Gossamer, Miami, Fla., 1999—. Owner Marvelous Mayhem, L.A., 1996-2000. Mem. Underfashion Club, Ultimate Apparel Sq. Club. Democrat.

O'BRIEN, BEA JAE, artist; b. Oshkosh, Wis., Dec. 4, 1940; d. Harry A. and Mammie Anna (Smith) Mac Farlane; m. John Walsh O'Brien, July 27, 1965; 1 child, John Christian. BA, U. Wis. Profl. artist B.J.'s Fine Arts, Moraga, Calif. Art included in various art publs.; exhibitions include Dennos Mus., Calif. Art & Wine Festival, 2001, Internat. Art Show, 2001, Valley Art Gallery, Calif., 2001—03, Calif. Art (3 awards), Internat. Art Show, Chgo., First Cyberspace Art Exhibit, New Zealand, Internat. Collage Constrn. Mus., Mexico City, one-woman shows include, Moraga, Calif., 1996—2001. Vol. children's art publ. Moraga Sch. Sys.; vol. local sch. projects Calif. Open Art Exhbits, 2003; vol. organizer Cmty. Art Gallery, Moraga Gallery, 2000—01; donated, vol. Outreach Art Funds and Scholarships, Calif. Recipient 1st pl. award, Calif. Art and Wine Festival, 1999, Bay Area Art Festival, 1999, 2000. Mem.: Digital Image Art Career, Intuitive Layering Art Group, Valley Arts Ctr., Collage Artists Am., Nat. Collage Soc. (award 1997—99, 2004, signature), Internat. Soc. Exptl. Artists (Nautilus award 2003, signature), Lamorinda Arts Alliance, Coll. Art Am., Women in Arts Mus. (honor roll). Avocations: reading, volunteering. Office: BJs Fine Arts 34 Sea Pines Moraga CA 94556-1029 Office Phone: 925-376-8018. Personal E-mail: dancincollag7@yahoo.com.

O'BRIEN, BONNIE JEANNE, counseling administrator; b. Winsted, Conn., Oct. 10, 1970; d. Charles Joseph and Jeannette Grace O'Brien. BA in Psychology, Ctrl. Conn. State U., 1993, MSc, 2000; student, Sacred Heart U., 2004—. Cert. elem. edn. tchr. 1997. Child devel. counselor Kaburne Sch., New Marlborough, Mass., 1990—92; pre-sch. tchr. Kindercare, Conn., 1992—95; tchr. Lake Tahoe (Calif) Elem., 1996—97; learning specialist Ctrl. Conn. State U., New Britain, Conn., 1997—2000; sch. counselor intern Avon (Conn.) Pub. Schs., 1996—2000; sch. counselor Woodbury (Conn.) Mid. Sch., 2000—. Cheerleading & field hockey coach Woodbury Mid. Sch., 2000—. Mem.: Am. Sch. Counselor Assn., Conn. Counseling Assn., Conn. Sch. Counselor Assn. (Sch. Counselor award 2004), Phi Delta Kappa. Avocations: travel, kayaking, dance. Office: Woodbury Mid Sch 67 Washington Ave Woodbury CT 06798

O'BRIEN, CATHERINE LOUISE, museum administrator; b. N.Y.C., July 21, 1930; d. Edward Denmark and Catherine Louise (Browne) O'B.; m. Philip R. James (div.); m. Sterling Noel (div.). BA, Finch Coll., 1952; postgrad, Williams Coll., 1954, Marymount Coll., 1954. Reprodn. mgr. Met. Mus. Art, N.Y.C., 1975—; dir. sales Simon Pearce Gallery, N.Y.C. Exhibited in group shows at Parrish Art Mus., Southampton, NY, 1965-70, Met. Mus. Art, NYC, 1975-85, Guild Hall Exhibit, East Hampton, NY, 1965-85. Mem. aux. Southampton Hosp., 1970-85; founder East Hampton Horse Show, Ladies Village Improvement Soc., East Hampton, 1970—; fair coms. St. James Ch., NYC, St. Luke's Ch., East Hampton, 1970-85; alumnae adv. bd. Marymount Coll., NYC, 1984-86, chmn. alumnae event, 1994; active Women's Nat. Rep. Club, NYC, John Drew Theater Co., Guild Hall, 1956-59; chmn. Landmark and Tree Planting Com. for Madison Ave. Assn., NYC, 1994—; mem. founding com. Internat. Debutante Ball, Waldorf Astoria, NYC, 1955; founding mem. Williamstown (Mass.) Theater, 1955; founder Parrish Art Mus. Players, Southampton, NY, 1955. Mem. DAR (founding; vice regent East Hampton chpt. 1974-85), Colonial Dames Am. (archives com. 1980-85), Daus. Brit. Empire (historian 1978-85), United Daus. Confederacy (state historian 1970-85), Daus. Colonial Wars (corr. sec. 1983-85), Sons and Daus. of Pilgrims (corr. sec. 1983-85), Victorian Soc., Soc. Mayflower Descs. (life), English Speaking Union, New Eng. Soc. (mem. ball com. 1983-86), Daus. of Cin. (historian 1979-85), Squadron "A", Devon Yacht, Maidstone, Southampton Yacht, Metropolitan Club (women's com., chmn. debutante ball 1980-84), Reciprocal/India House, St. Anthony Union League. Republican. Episopalian. Avocations: show horses, dogs. Home: 605 Park Ave New York NY 10021-7016 also: Seacote PO Box 1488 East Hampton NY 11937-0711 Office: Met Mus of Art 5th Ave New York NY 10028 also: Simon Pierce Gallery 500 Park Ave New York NY 10022-1606

O'BRIEN, CINDY, chemistry educator; b. Pitts., Sept. 04; d. Alan and Judith Pazin; m. John Thomas O'Brien, Aug. 20, 2000; 1 child, Kristin Michelle. Cert. Nat. Bd. Profl. Tchg. Stds. Tchr. chemstry Deerfield Beach H.S., Fla., 1988—. Mem.: Nat. Sci. Tchrs. Am. Office: Deerfield Beach HS 910 SW 15th St Deerfield Beach FL 33441 Office Phone: 754-322-0650. Office Fax: 754-322-0780. E-mail: cindy.o'brien@browardschools.com.

O'BRIEN, CLARE, lawyer; b. Ireland, 1961; children: Una, Lucy. BA summa cum laude, Trinity Coll., 1982. Bar: Ireland, NY 1986, U.S. Dist. Ct. NY (so. dist.) 1987. Atty. Eugene F. Collins & Son, Brady & Tarpey, 1987—88, Shearman & Sterling LLP, NYC, 1988—95, mem., mergers & acquisitions group, 1989—, ptnr., 1995—. Bd. dirs. Am. Assn. Internat. Commn. Jurists. Named Dealmaker of Yr., Am. Lawyer mag., 2006. Office: Shearman & Sterling LLP 599 Lexington Ave New York NY 10022-6069 Office Phone: 212-848-8966. Office Fax: 212-848-7179. E-mail: cobrien@shearman.com.*

O'BRIEN, DONNA M., public health service officer; Degree, Coll. Holy Cross; MA, St. Louis U. Former adminstrv. resident Tulane U. Med. Ctr., New Orleans; former asst. adminstr. M.D. Anderson Cancer Ctr., U. Tex.; former assoc. dir. human svcs. Archdiocese of N.Y.; former assoc. dir. Alliance for Cath. Health; former dir. health svcs. Chat. Charities; former exec. dir. Cath. Healthcare Network, Long Island; exec. v.p., chief adminstrv. officer Cath. Health Svcs. Long Island, Melville, NY, 1997—. Fellow, sr. fellow Accrediting Commn. Edn. for Health Svcs. Adminstrn. Fellow: Am. Coll. Healthcare Execs. Office: Cath Health Service of Long Island 992 N Village Avenue Rockville Centre NY 11570

O'BRIEN, EILEEN KATHRYN, art educator; b. Hudson Falls, N.Y., June 4, 1961; d. James Michael and Lorraine Catherine O'Brien; children: Ashley Gatto, Krista Gatto, Michelle Gatto. AAS in Fine Arts, Jr. Coll. Albany, NY, 1981; BS in Art Edn., SUNY, New Paltz, 1983, MS in Elem. Edn., 1995. Cert. tchr. N.Y., N.C. Tchr. art/recreation McQuade Children's Svcs., New Windsor, NY, 1984—87; tchr. art Goshen Secure Ctr., NY, 1992—95, Jeffersonville-Youngsville C.S., NY, 1989—95; tchr. 3d grade St. Casimir's Cath. Sch., Albany, NY, 1996—97; tchr. visual arts Western Harnett Mid. Sch., Lillington, NC, 1997—. Mgr. Rite-Aid, Monticello, NY, 1993—94; swing shift mgr. McDonalds, Lillington, NC, 2003—. Tchr., leader People to People Orgn., Raleigh, NC, 2006; mem. Boonetrail Elem. PTO, 2001—06. Mem.: Profl. Educators of N.C. Avocations: gardening, painting, sewing, reading. Home: 485 Ray Byrd Rd Lillington NC 27546 Office: Western Harnett Mid Sch 11135 NC Hwy 27 W Lillington NC 27546 Office Phone: 919-499-4497. Office Fax: 919-499-1788. E-mail: eobrien_61@msn.com.

O'BRIEN, ELVY SETTERQVIST, art historian, educator, editor; b. Bklyn., Dec. 12, 1925; d. Ernst Adolf and Astrid Sofia Vilhelmina (Setterqvist) Carlson; m. Charles Harold O'Brien, Dec. 21, 1964. Degree, Frans Schartaus Handelsinstitut, Sweden, 1946; BA, Wittenberg U., 1969; student, U. Basel, 1968—71; MA, Ohio State U., 1974; PhD, U. Iowa, 1982. Purchasing agent Ericsson Telephone Sales, NYC, 1950—52; sec. Remington Rand, Stockholm, 1952—55, Ford Motor Co., 1955—60; exec. sec. Svenska Fotografernas Förbund, Stockholm, 1960—61; asst. Meet Modern Sweden, Stockholm, 1961—64; instr. Monmouth (Ill.) Coll., 1974; asst. prof. art history We. Ill. U., Macomb, Ill., 1974—88; editor Bibliography of History of Art, Williamstown, Mass., 1988—92. Contbr. articles to profl. jours. Vol. ARC, Williamstown, 1998—; vol. fund drive WAMC Radio, Albany, NY, 1993—. Grantee, Sam Kress Found., 1978, Gustaf VI Adolf Found., 1985. Mem.: Swedish Am. Hist. Soc., Soc. Advancement Scandinavian Studies, Berkshire Internat. Club. Democrat. Lutheran. Avocations: travel, languages, photography. Home: 738 Simonds Rd Williamstown MA 01267

O'BRIEN, JANE, special education educator; b. Garfield Heights, Ohio, June 24, 1954; d. Harry Edward and Helen Lena Sykora; m. Fred Eugene Yoak, Oct. 3, 1981 (div. Oct. 1998); children: Helen Alexis Yoak, Evan Edward Yoak, Trevor Franklin Yoak; m. Russell O'Brien, Aug. 31, 2002. BS in Edn., Bowling Green State U., 1976; MS in Edn., U. Akron, 1981; postgrad., Kent State U., 1994-96. Cert. tchr. Ohio. Spl. edn. tchr. Cleve. Pub. Schs., 1976, Marshall (Ill.) Schs., 1976-78, Stow (Ohio) City Schs., 1978-94, Ravenna (Ohio) City Schs., 1996—. Instr. childbirth Childbirth Edn. Assn., Akron, 1984—86; instr. parenting Cath. Svc. League, 1994; student tchr. supr., grad. asst. Kent (Ohio) State U., 1994—96; rep. Ravenna City Schs. Portage County Tchr. Adv. Coun., 1997—99; workshop presenter, 1996—99. Mem. PTA, Stow Players Theater Group. Recipient Apple Tchr. award, Ashland Oil, 1997, Friend of Children award, 1995; Martha Holden Jennings scholar, 2000. Mem.: NEA, Coun. Exceptional Children, Ravenna Edn. Assn., Ohio Edn. Assn. Avocations: storytelling, vocal and instrumental music, gardening, acting. Office: Ravenna City Schs West Park 1076 Jones Ave Ravenna OH 44266-3558

O'BRIEN, JANE MARGARET, academic administrator; b. Washington, Nov. 17, 1953; d. Thomas and Edith (Pedersen) O'B; m. James A. Grube, June 28, 1975; children: William Howard Grube-O'Brien, Harold Thomas Grube O'Brien. BS in Biochemistry, Vassar Coll., 1975; PhD in Chemistry, U. Del., 1981. Rsch. asst. U. Vt., Burlington, 1978-79; asst. prof. chemistry Middlebury (Vt.) Coll., 1980-88, assoc. provost, 1988-89, assoc. prof. chemistry, 1988-91, dean of faculty, 1989-91; pres. Hollins Coll., Roanoke, Va., 1991—96, St. Mary's Coll., Md., 1996—. Ednl. chmn. biology task force New Eng. Consortium Undergraduate Sci., 1988-91; project mgr. H. Hughes Med. Inst. Instl. Awards, 1988-91; mem. steering com. Sloan New Liberal Arts Initiative, 1988-91; bd. dir. Norfolk Southern Corp., So. Md. Navy Alliance, Nat. Outdoor Leadership Sch.; mem. NCAA Div. III Pres. Council. Implementation com. Vermont EPSCoR, 1989-91; bd. dirs. Coun. Ind. Colls. in Va., 1991-96, Va. Found. for Ind. Colls., 1991-96; ednl. adv. com. Rainforest All, 1991—; bd. dir. Md. Citizens for the Arts Found., Univ. Mobility. Grad. fellow U. Del., 1975-76, Kellogg fellow W.K. Kellogg Found., 1989-92, Internat. fellow Assoc. Am. Colls., 1990-91, Regional fellow finalist White House Fellowship, 1991; Eisenhower Fellow, 1999. Mem.: Phi Beta Kappa, Sigma Xi. Office: St Mary's College Office of the President 18952 E Fisher Rd Saint Marys City MD 20686-3001

O'BRIEN, JOAN SUSAN, lawyer, educator; b. NYC, Apr. 14, 1946; d. Edward Vincent O'Brien and Joan Therese (Kramer) Quinn; m. Michael P. Wilpan, May 27, 1979; children: Edward B. Wilpan, Anabel T. Wilpan. BA, NYU, 1967; JD, Georgetown U., 1970. Bar: N.Y. 1971, Mass. 1971, U.S. Dist. Ct. (so. and ea. dist.) N.Y. 1972, U.S. Ct. Appeals (2d cir.) 1971. Law clk. to Hon. Frank J. Murray U.S. Dist. Ct. Mass., Boston, 1970-71; asst. U.S. atty. Office of U.S. Atty. U.S. Dist. Ct. (ea. dist.) N.Y., Bklyn., 1972-76; pvt. practice N.Y.C., 1976-79; trial atty. Mendes & Mount, N.Y.C., 1979-84; asst. prof. St. Johns U., Jamaica, N.Y., 1984-90; adminstrv. law judge N.Y. State Workers Compensation Bd., Hempstead, N.Y., 1990-93; appellate atty. Scheine, Fusco, Brandenstein & Rada, Woodbury, N.Y., 1993-97; trial atty. Grey & Grey, L.L.P., Farmingdale, N.Y., 1997—. Editor: Georgetown Law Jour., 1968-70. Pres. Nassau County Dem. Com. Women's Caucus, Westbury, N.Y., 1988-90; leader Girl Scouts Nassau County, 1990-93. Unitarian-Universalist. Office: Grey & Grey LLP 360 Main St Farmingdale NY 11735-3592 Office Phone: 516-249-1342.

O'BRIEN, K. PATRICIA, product development engineer; b. Cin., Feb. 13, 1970; d. John Edward and Carolyn Ann (Hufler) O'Brien; m. Robert J. Novak, July 1, 1995. BS in Mech. Engring., U. Cin., 1993. Grad. Ford Coll. Ford Motor Co., Livonia, Mich., 1993-95, product devel. engr., 1995—. Bus. mentor Jr. Achievement, Livonia, 1994; mem. adv. bd. Univ. Cinn.-Detroit. Mem. Soc. Women Engrs. (chair golf outing, fundraising and publicity 1993—). Avocations: scrapbooking, reading, biking, hiking, travel.

O'BRIEN, KATHLEEN ANNE, science educator; b. Brussels, Dec. 16, 1976; d. Robert C. (Stepfather) and Constance Kay Barker, Kenneth Allen O'Brien; m. Jason Scott Crippen, Oct. 13, 2001. BS in Animal Sci. and Industry, Kans. State U., Manhattan, 1999. Cert. in Project Wild Kans. Dept. Wildlife and Parks, 1997, in Project Learning Tree Kans. Dept. Wildlife and Parks, 1997, tchr. Kans. Dept. Edn., 2002. Sci. tchr. SE HS, Wichita, 2002—04, Derby Alternative HS, Kans., 2004—. Zookeeper Sedgwick County Zoo, Wichita, 2000—01; grad. tchg. asst. Wichita State U., 2000—01. Vol. Sedgwick County Zoo, 2000—06; vol. oboe instr. SE HS, 2002—04; vol. Derby Hist. Soc., 2005—06; with choir and music performance St. Andrew's Episcopal Ch., Derby, 2005—06. Gwendlyn Hawley Trust scholar, Kans. Sch. for Blind, 1997, 1998, Flower Bulb grantee, Dutch Bulb Growers Assn., 2005. Mem.: NEA (assoc.), NSTA (assoc.), Am. Fedn. Tchrs. (assoc.), Wichita Fedn. Tchrs. (assoc.), Kans. Edn. Assn. (assoc.), Kans. Assn. Conservation and Environ. Educators (assoc.), Kans. State U. Alumni Assn. (corr.). Avocations: swimming, reading, horseback riding, gardening, outdoor activities. Office Phone: 316-788-8515.

O'BRIEN, KATHLEEN L., special education educator; b. Oneida, NY, Aug. 31, 1975; d. Neal Patrick and Teresa Joan O'Brien. BS in Psychology, LeMoyne Coll., Syracuse, NY, 1997; MA of Edn., Cambridge Coll., Mass., 2006. Behavior specialist May Ctr., May Inst., Chatham, NJ, 1997—98; spl. edn. tchr. Albien Pub. Schs., NY, 1999—2000, Barnstable Pub. Schs., Hyannis, Mass., 2000—. Mentor Health Adventures Cape Cod Hosp., Hyannis, 2003—04. Mem. Barnstable Rep. Com., Hyanis, 2001—02. Republican. Roman Catholic. Avocations: tennis, volleyball, softball, music, reading. Home: 415 Cedar St West Barnstable MA 02668 Office: Barnstable Mid Sch 895 Falmouth Rd Hyannis MA 02601

O'BRIEN, KENDRA ALLEN, psychologist, researcher; b. Tachikawa, Japan, July 25, 1959; (parents Am. citizens); d. Jerry Eugene and Beverly Ann Allen; m. Daniel Kehaulani O'Brien, Apr. 19, 2002; 1 child, Pierce Keahi Aualii. BA, Colo. U., 1982; MA, Calif. Sch. Profl. Psychology, 1990, PhD in Clin. Psychology, 1997. Adolescent unit coord. Castle Med. Ctr., Kailua, Hawaii, 1983—88; addiction recovery aftercare coord. Vista Hill Hosp., San Diego, 1991—94; clin. rsch. coord. Damluji Bari Clinic, 1993—95; VA program specialist Nat. Ctr. Post Traumatic Stress, Honolulu, 1997—98; individual, family therapist C.A.R.E. Hawaii Inc., 1998—. With athletics dept. drug edn. San Diego State U., 1993—96; drug edn. addiction cons. Atlantic Richfield Co. Olympic Tng. Ctr., Chula Vista, Calif., 1994; adj. faculty Nat. U., San Diego, 1994—96. Named Most Innovative Intern, Met. Correctional Ctr. Fed. Bur. Prisons, San Diego, 1992. Mem.: APA, Hawaii Psychol. Assn., Gen. Soc. Mayflower Descs. (sec. 2001—03). Democrat. Methodist. Achievements include development of a drug education and consulting program that was used as a national model for effective education and intervention at an athletics conference in 1995. Avocations: photography, reading, scuba diving, running. Home: 485 Wana'ao Rd Kailua HI 96734 Office: CARE Hawaii Inc Ste 1003 677 Ala Moana Blvd Honolulu HI 96813-5417

O'BRIEN, LISA ANNE, middle school educator; b. Kingston, Pa., Dec. 9, 1969; d. Robert John and Irene Mary Cardillo; m. Kenneth O'Brien, July 5, 1999. BS in Engring. Mgmt., Wilkes U., 1992; MS in Elem. Edn., U. Scranton, 1995, MS in Instrnl. Tech., 2005. Quality control mgr. Diamond Mfg. co., West Wyoming, Pa., 1992-95; tchr. Wyoming Valley West Sch., Kingston, Pa., 1995—2006, Dana St. Elem. Ctr., Wyoming Valley West Sch. Dist., Forty Fort, Pa., 2006—. Mem. NSTA, Pa. Sci. Tchr. Assn., Luzerne County Sci. Tchr. Assn. Avocations: gardening, playing the piano. Home: 262 Kessler Hollow Rd Benton PA 17814

O'BRIEN, MARY DEVON, communications executive, consultant; b. Buenos Aires, Feb. 13, 1944; came to U.S., 1949, naturalized, 1962; d. George Earle and Margaret Frances (Richards) Owen; m. Gordon Covert O'Brien, Feb. 16, 1962 (div. Aug. 1982); children: Christopher Covert, Devon Elizabeth; m. Christopher Gerard Smith, May 28, 1983 BA, Rutgers U., 1975, MBA, 1976. Project mgmt. cert., 1989. Contr. manpower Def. Comm. divsn. ITT, Nutley, NJ, 1977-80, adminstr. program, 1977-78, mgr. cost, schedule control, 1978-79, voice processing project, 1979-80; mgr. project Avionics divsn. ITT, Nutley, 1980-81, sr. mgr. projects, 1981-93, cons. strategic planning, 1983-95; pres. Anamex, Inc., 1995—. Bd. trustees South Mountain Counseling Ctr., 1987-98, chmn. bd. trustees, 1994—; bd. dir. N.J. Eye Inst.; session leader Internet Conf., Florence, Italy, 1992; session moderator, panel mem. MES Conf., Cairo, Egypt, 1993, spkr., session leader Vancouver, 1994, keynote spkr. New Zealand, 1995; lectr. in field Author: Pace: System Manual, 1979, Voices, 1982; contbr. articles to profl. jours. and Maplewood Community calendar. Chmn. Citizens Budget Adv. Com., Maplewood, N.J., 1984-87, chmn. recreation, libr., pub. svcs., 1982-83, 94-96, chmn. pub. safety, emergency svcs., 1983-84, chmn. schs. and edn., 1984-85, chmn. gen. gov. and fin., 1998-2000; first v.p. Maplewood Civic Assn., 1987-89, pres., 1989-91, 2000—, sec. 1993-94, bd. dirs., officer, 1984—; chmn. Maple Leaf Svc. award Com., 1987-89, 94—, Community Svc. Coun. of Oranges and Maplewood Homelessness, Affordable Housing, Shelter Com., 1988—; chmn. speaker's bur. United Way, 1989-93; bd. trustees United Way Essex and West Hudson Cmty. Svc. Coun., 1988—; v.p. mktg. United Way Community Svc. Coun. of Oranges and Maplewood, 1990-93, v.p. 1994; mem. Maplewood Zoning Bd. of Adjustment, 1983-95; officer, mem. exec. bd. N.J. Project Mgmt. Inst., 1985—, pres., 1987-88, 95-2000, v.p. adminstrn., 1994-95; bd. dirs. Performance Mgmt. Assn.; chmn. Charter Com.; chmn. Internat. Project Mgmt. Inst. Jour. and Membership survey, 1986-87, mktg. com., 1986-89, long range planning and steering com., 1987—; bd. dir., vice chmn. Coun. Chpt. Pres. Interaction Com., 1986-90, chmn., 1991—, pres. Internat. Project Mgmt. Inst., 1991, chmn., 1992, v.p. Region II, 1989-90; adv. bd. Project Mgmt. Jour., 1987-90, N.J. PMI Ednl., 1987—; liaison officer, PMI internat. liaison to Australian Inst. of Project Mgmt. and Western Australia Project Mgmt. Assn.; apptd. fellow Leadership N.J., 1993—, Internat. Project Mgmt. Inst. and Performance Mgmt. Assocs.; mem. MCA/N.J. Blood Bank Drive; chmn. Maplewood Community Calendar, 1990-98; trustee community svc. coun. and edn. program United Way Essex and West Hudson, 1988—, also, chmn. leadership div., chmn. speakers bur., 1991— and mem. communications com.; mem. bd. dirs. Governing Inst. N.J.; chmn. Maplewood Rep. County Com., 1996—; chair, sec. Essex County Rep. County Com. Recipient Spl. commendation for Cmty. Svc. Twp. Maplewood, 1987; First Place award Anti-Shoplifting Program for Distributive Edn. Club Am., 1981, N.J. Fedn. of Women's Clubs, 1981, 82, Retail Mchts. Assn., 1981, 82; Commendation and Merit awards Air Force Inst. Tech., 1981; Pres.'s Safety award ITT, 1983; State award 1st Pl. N.J. Fedn. of Women's Clubs Garden Show, 1982; Cert. Spl. Merit award N.J. Fedn. of Women's Clubs, 1982, Disting. Contbn. award United Way, 1990, Pursuit of Exellence Cost Savs. Achievement award ITT Avionics, 1990, Maple Leaf award outstanding cmty. svc., 1992, Phoebe and Benjamin Shackelford award United Way, 1992, U.S. Ho. Reps. citation, 1992, N.H. Gen. Assembly Senate resolution Cmty. Leadership and Svc., 1992, resolution of Appreciation Township of Maplewood, Maplewood C. of C. Disting. Svc. award, 2005; N.J. Leadership fellow, 1993, awarded fellow of Internat. Project Mgmt. Inst., 1995. Mem. NAFE, Internat. Platform Speakers Assn., Grand Jury Assn., Telecomms. Group and Aerospace Industries Assn., Women's Career Network Assn., Nat. Security Indsl. Assn., Assn. for Info. and Image Mgmt., Internat. Project Mgmt. Inst. (liaison officer pres. 1991—, Outstanding Svc. and Contbrn. award 1986-87, Outstanding Pres. award 1988, Meritorious Svc. Recognition award 1989-1990), Performance Mgmt. Assn, Indsl. Rels. Rsch. Assn., ITT Mgmt. Assn., Rutgers Grad. Sch. Bus. Mgmt. Alumni Assn., Maplewood LWV (chair women and family issues com., voter registration bd. dir.), Maplewood Women's Evening Membership Div. (pres. 1980-82), Lions (Maplewood dir. 1992-95, program chmn. 1991-92, treas. 1994-95, N.J. dist. 16E zone gov., chmn. 1992-93, 95-96, cabinet sec. internat. dist., region chmn. 1993-94, 96-98, trustee Eye Bank N.J., internat. dist. 16-E cabinet sec. 1994-95, dist. 16-E chmn. peace poster contest 1995-99, pres. Newark 1995-97, sec. 1997—, N.J. State chmn. youth outreach and quest 1995-98, internat. dist. 16-E gov., 1999—, dist. MD16 treas., 1999—, youth oppportunities chmn. N.J dist. MD-16, coun. chmn. 2003-2004, state advisor 2004-, trustee Eye Bank of Delaware Valley, sec.-treas. 2003-05, 3d vice chmn. 2005-). Home: 594 Valley St Maplewood NJ 07040-2616 Office: 21 Madison Plz Ste 152 Madison NJ 07940-2354

O'BRIEN, MARY KATHLEEN, state legislator, lawyer; b. Kankakee, Ill., June 4, 1965; d. Donald Lawrence and Norma Margaret O'Brien. BS, Western Ill. U., 1986; JD, U. Ill., 1994. Bar: Ill. 1994. Asst., advocate Ill. Atty. Gens. Office, Kankakee, 1987-91; asst. state's atty. Grundy County State's Atty., Morris, Ill., 1993-94; lawyer Cortina, Mueller & O'Brien, Coal City, Ill., 1994-99; pvt. practice Coal City, 1999—; state rep. Ill. Gen. Assembly, Coal City, 1997—. Bd. dirs. Trailways Girl Scouts, Joliet, 1998—, Breaking Award Domestic Violence, Morris, 1997—, Ill. Valley Ctr. for Ind. Living, LaSalle, Ill., 1998—; precinct com. Kankakee County Dems., 1988-90, Grundy County Dems., Morris, 1996—. Named Legis. of Yr. Advocates United, 1999, Cmty. Behavioral Assn. of Ill., 1998; recipient William Morgan Meml. award Kankakee County Mental Health Coun., 1998, Activator award Ill. Farm Bur., 1998. Mem. Kiwanis Club of Ill. Roman Catholic. Avocations: gardening, reading, cooking. Office: 760 E Division St Coal City IL 60416-1367

O'BRIEN, NANCY MARIE (MEYER), secondary school educator; b. Buffalo, N.Y., Dec. 31, 1960; d. John Nicholas Meyer and Joan Ann Bachman; m. Kevin Patrick O'Brien, Aug. 20, 1983; children: Timothy Patrick, Kelly Marie, Sean Francis. BA in Biology, SUNY Coll., Buffalo, 1980—82; MBA, Canisius Coll., Buffalo, 1984—87; MS in Edn., Niagara U., Lewiston, NY, 2002—03. Secondary Edn. N.Y. Edn. Dept., 2003. Budget analyst LTV - Sierra Rsch. Divsn., Cheektowaga, 1982—89; tchr. Cleve. Hill Mid. Sch., Cheektowaga, NY, 2003—. Catechist St. Teresa's Roman Cath. Ch., Niagara Falls, NY, 1990—97. Recipient Catechist of Yr., Diocese of Buffalo, St. Teresa's R.C. Ch., 1995, Outstanding Grad. Student in Tchr. Edn., Niagara U., 2003. Mem.: NSTA, Kappa Delta Pi. Office: Cleveland Hill Mid Sch 105 Mapleview Rd Cheektowaga NY 14225 Office Phone: 716-836-7200. Personal E-mail: nobrien@clevehill.org.

O'BRIEN, NANCY PATRICIA, librarian, educator; b. Galesburg, Ill., Mar. 17, 1955; d. Leo Frederick O'Brien and Yvonne Blanche (Uhlmann) O'Brien Tabb; 1 child, Nicole Pamela. AB in English, U. Ill., 1976, MS in LS, 1977. Vis. instr. U. Ill., Urbana, 1977-78, asst. prof. libr. adminstrn., 1978-84, assoc. prof., 1984-91, prof., 1991—, serials bibliographer, 1977-78, social sci. bibliographer collection devel. div., 1979-81, project dir. Title II-C grant, 1987-88, acting libr. and info. sci. libr., 1989-90, head Edn. and Social Sci. Libr., 1994—, coord. social scis. divsn., 1996—2003, edn. subject specialist, 1981—. Discussion leader Ill. White House Conf. on Libr. and Info. svcs., 1990; mem. nat. adv. bd. Office Ednl. Rsch. and Improvement, U.S. Dept. Edn., 1989-91; grant proposal reviewer NEH, 1991; mem. adv. bd. Ctr. for Children's Books, 1992-97; cons. Ark. Coll., 1989; chmn. rev. team Instrnl. Materials Ctr., U. Wis., Madison, 1989; chair exec. com. Nat. Edn. Network Nat. Libr. Edn. U.S. Dept. Edn., 1998—2002; presenter in field. Author: Test Construction: A Bibliography of Resources, 1988, (with Emily Fabiano) Core List of Books and Journals in Education, 1991; Education: A Guide to Reference and Information Sources, 2d edit., 2000, (with John Collins III) Greenwood Dictionary of Edn., 2003; co-editor Media/Microforms column Serials Rev., 1979-82; mem. editl. bd. Bull. Bibliography, 1982-90; asst. editor Libr. Hi Tech., 1983-85; editor EBSS Newsletter, 1990-91; contbr. articles to profl. jours., chpts. to books. Mem. ALA (Whitney-Carnegie grantee 1990-91), Am. Ednl. Rsch. Assn. (spl. interest group on libr. resources and info. tech.), Assn. Coll. and Rsch. Librs. (access policy guidelines task force 1990-95, vice chmn., chmn.-elect edn. and behavioral scis. sect. 1993-94, chmn. 1994-95, acad. status com. 1996—2000, Disting. Edn. and Behavioral Scis. Libr. 1997), Libr. Adminstrn. and Mgmt. Assn. (edn. and tng. com. pub. rels. sect. 1990-95), Resources and Tech. Svcs. Divsn.(micropub. com. 1982-85, chmn. 1983-85, cons. 1985-87). Office: U Ill Edn & Social Sci Libr 100 Main Libr 1408 W Gregory Dr Urbana IL 61801-3607 Office Phone: 217-333-2408. Business E-Mail: npobrien@uiuc.edu.

O'BRIEN, ODESSA LOUISE, protective services official; m. John Daniels O'Brien, May 30, 1964; children: James John, Jeanne Jacqueline, Kevin Raymond. B.Elective Studies, St. Cloud State U., 1975. Lic. pilot. Stewardess Northwest Airlines, St. Paul. Area rep. Youth for Understanding, Brainerd, Minn., 1979—82; v.p. Christian Women's Club, Brainerd, 1976—80; chmn. St. Francis Ch. Women's Guild, Brainerd, Minn., 1978—79; chmn. bd. St. Francis Parochial Sch. Bd., Brainerd, Minn., 1979—80; mem. coun. St. Francis Ch., Brainerd, Minn., 1979—80; adv. bd. Pine County Vo-Tech Sch., Pine City, Minn., 1967—71. Lt. col. USAF. Recipient Outstanding Woman of Collier County, Am. Bus. Women's Assn., 1983—85, Comdrs. Commendation, Naples Sr. Squadron, Civil Air Patrol, 1983, Grover Loening award, Minn. Wing Civil Air Patrol, Air Force Aux., Paul E. Garber award, Civil Air Patrol, 2003, Gill Robb Wilson award, 2004. Mem.: AAUW (life; pres. Naples br. 1983—85), Collier Automotive Mus. (sec. of vol. docents), Naples Woman's Club (internat. chmn.), Phi Theta Kappa (life). Roman Catholic. Avocations: bridge (Bronze Life Master), flying, travel, tennis, reading.

O'BRIEN, ORIN YNEZ, musician, educator; b. Hollywood, Calif., June 7, 1935; d. George Joseph and Marguerite Graham (Churchill) O'Brien. Studied with Frederick Zimmermann, Milton Kestenbaum and Herman Reinshagen; diploma, The Juilliard Sch., 1957. Double bassist N.Y.C. Ballet Orch., 1956—66, Saidenberg Little Symphony, Music Aeterna, Am. Symphony (with Stokowski), N.Y. Philharm., N.Y.C., 1966—; faculty Manhattan Sch. Music, N.Y.C., 1969—, Mannes Coll. Music, N.Y.C., 1988—, The Juilliard Sch., N.Y.C., 1990—, co-chair double bass dept., 1992—2002. Participant numerous chamber music festivals, including Marlboro; featured in 1st performances of Gunther Schuller Quartet for 4 double basses; artist for GM, CBS and RCA Recording cos. Mem.: Internat. Soc. Bassists, Am. Fedn. Musicians, The Bohemians. Avocations: reading, writing, cooking.

O'BRIEN, ROSANNE P., corporate financial executive; d. Rosalie Theresa O'Brien; m. Donald Anderson, May 20, 1985. BS in Bus. Adminstrn., U. Redlands, Calif., 1972. Dir. corp. comm. Tiger Internat./Flying Tiger, 1972—83; sr. v.p., dir. corp. comm. Glendale Fed. Bank, 1983—92; v.p., corp. rels. Teledyne, Inc./Allegheny Teledyne, 1993—99; corp. v.p., comm. Northrop Grumman Corp., L.A., 1999—. Bd. mem. Calif. Sci. Ctr., L.A., L.A. Ednl. Partnership; trustee San Francisco Acad. Mem.: Nat. Investor Rels. Inst. Office: Northrop Grumman Corp 1840 Century Park E Los Angeles CA 90067 Business E-Mail: rosanne.obrien@ngc.com.

O'BRIEN, SALLY NAHAS, special education educator, consultant; b. Willimantic, Conn., Feb. 9, 1954; d. Nicholas Joseph and Mary Lasnier Nahas; m. Peter Christopher O'Brien, Aug. 12, 1978; children: Nicholas, James, Elyse. BS, So. Conn. State Univ., New Haven, Conn., 1975; MEd, Univ. Hartford, Hartford, Conn., 1983. Cert. profl. educator pre-K-8, comprehensive special edn. pre-K-12 Conn. Primary special edn. Avalon Sch., Monterey, Mass., 1975—76, Regional Edn. Sernts Ctr., Litchfield, Conn., 1976—92; kindergarten, resource tchr. Sandisfield Pub. Sch., Sandsfield, Mass., 1982—91; pre-kindergarten, resource tchr. Farmington River Regional, OtisOtis, Mass., 1981—99; inclusion special edn. pre-K thru 8 Breakthrough Magnet Sch., Hartford, Conn., 1999—. Headstart cons. Regional Edn. Seminar Ctr. (RESCU), Litchfield, Conn., 1978; early childhood coord. Sandsfield & Farmington Reg., Sandsfield, Mass., 1991—99; mentor State Conn. Support Tng. Program, Hartford, Conn., 2000—. Recording artist: CD Passion, 2006. Field asst. Girl Scouts, Norfolk, Conn., 1995—2004; lectr., mem. Immaculate Conception Ch., Norfolk, Conn., 1978—; mem. Bd. Edn., Norfolk, Conn., 1983—89. Avocations: singing, cooking, reading, gardening. Home: 41 Greenwoods Rd E Norfolk CT 06058-0352 Office: Breakthrough Magnet Sch 121 Cornwell St Hartford CT 06112

O'BRIEN, SOLEDAD, news anchor; m. Brad Raymond; children: Sofia, Cecilia, Charlie, Jackson. Student, Harvard U. Prodr. Second Opinion, reporter Health Week in Review Sta. KISS-FM, Boston; assoc. prodr., newswriter Sta. WBZ-TV, Boston; prodr. NBC News, 1991—93; co-host The Know Zone Discovery Channel; chief East Bay bur. Sta. KRON-TV, San Francisco, reporter, 1993—96; co-host The Site, Nightly News, Weekend Today MSNBC, 1996—99; anchor, Weekend Today NBC, 1999—2003; co-anchor, American Morning CNN, 2003—. Recipient Emmy. Office: CNN 820 1st St NE Washington DC 20002-4243

O'BRYAN, C. JILL, visual artist, writer; b. Chgo., June 13, 1956; d. Robert Louis and Connie Clair (Johnson) O'B. BA, Macalaster Coll., St. Paul, 1978; student, Marchutz Sch. Painting, Aix-en-Provence, France, 1976-77, 81-82; MFA, San Francisco Art Inst., 1990; PhD, NYU, 1993-00. Freelance theatre set and costume designer, Boston, San Francisco, Aix-en-Provence, 1980-87; art instr. painting and drawing Exploratorium, San Francisco, 1984-85, San Francisco Art Inst. Extension Sch., 1988-90; graphic artist Jamison, Cawdrey, Benjamin Advt., San Francisco, 1984-90, N.Y. Observer, N.Y.C., 1991-92; art dir. Terry Pimsleur & Co., San Francisco, 1992-93; tchg. asst. art history, painting and drawing NYU, N.Y.C., 1993-95; documentarian, achivist Star Axis, N.Y.C., 1995—; adj. prof. women's studies NJCU, 2001. Exhibited works in shows at Jan Holloway Gallery, San Francisco, 1989, 91, Gallerie Annick Ketelle, Antwerp, 1993, 450 Broadway Gallery, N.Y.C., 1995, ABC No Rio Gallery, N.Y.C., 1998, 2000, 02, 04, 06, Rosenberg Gallery, N.Y.C., 1999, Lyon Bienelle, 2000, Ace Gallery, N.Y.C., 2001, Sideshow Gallery, Bklyn., 2003, 04, Kramarsky Found., N.Y.C., 2005-06; author: Carnal Art: Orlan's Refacing, 2005; contbr. articles to profl. jours. including N. Paradoxa Art Jour., Women/Performance, 2002; drawings published in Jáime la Vie, Artists to Artist, ABC No Rio Catalogue, N. Paradoxa', Time Capsule: A Concise Ency. by Women Artists. Office: 383 W Broadway New York NY 10012-4377 Business E-Mail: cjobryan@hotmail.com.

O'BRYANT, CATHY, retired social worker, evangelist; b. Camden, N.J., Jan. 5, 1941; d. James Hearl and Ruth Virginia Jackson; children: Wendell, Penny, Terence, George, Ramona. AA Liberal Arts, Camden County Coll., Blackwood, N.J., 1972; BA Psychology, Glassboro State Coll., N.J., 1976. Dir. Nat. Congress of Neighborhoods, Washington, 1980—82; social worker Dept. Human Svcs., Phila., 1989—94; ret., 1994. Coord. internat. housing conf. Alternatives for Women and UN, Camden, 1987; workshop leader Black Women's Health Project, Nairobi, Kenya, 1985; welfare caucus leader Women, Work and Welfare, Houston, 1978; motivational spkr.; workshop developer Welfare, IWY Conf., Houston, 1978. Author: (book) If My People, 1996; editor: (newsletters) Christian Voices, 2002—, (newletters) Grassroots Women Speak, 1980—82. Asst. state chairperson N.J. Welfare Rights Orgn., Camden, 1974—77; mem. D.C. Women's Polit. Caucus, 1981—82; bd. dirs. Ctr. Ind. Living South Jersey, 2004—05; cert. mem. Juvenile Conf. Com. of Camden County, NJ, 1976—77. Recipient Bronze Star Outstanding Achievement award, Nat. Hook-Up of Black Women, 1992. Mem.: Poetic Ministries (founder, dir. 1998—), Parade of Poets (founder, coord. 1996—), Sketches of Abundant Life (founder, pres. 2001—). Democrat. Seventh Day Adventist. Avocations: travel, nature walks, logic puzzles. Home: 231 N Evergreen Ave Apt 34B Woodbury NJ 08096

O'BRYON, LINDA ELIZABETH, broadcast executive; b. Washington, Sept. 1, 1949; d. Walter Mason Ormes and Iva Genevieve (Batrus) Ranney; m. Dennis Michael O'Bryon, Sept. 8, 1973; 1 child, Jennifer Elizabeth BA in Journalism cum laude, U. Miami. News reporter Sta. KCPX (now KTVX), Salt Lake City, 1971-73; documentary and pub. affairs prodr. Sta. WPLG-TV, Miami, Fla., 1974-76; producer, reporter, anchor, news dir. then v.p. for news and pub. affairs, exec. editor, sr. v.p. Nightly Business Report Sta. WPBT (PBS), Miami, 1976—. Recipient award Fla. Bar, Tallahasse, 1977, 2 awards Ohio State U., 1976, 79, award Corp. for Pub. Broadcasting, 1978, Econ. Understanding award Dartmouth Coll., 1980, award Fla. AP, 1981, 1st prize Nat. Assn. Realtors, 1986, Bus. News Luminary award TJFR, 1990, Am. Women in Radio and TV award, 1995, 98, Disting. Achievement award Soc. Am. Bus. Editors and Writers, 2004; named Most Influential Woman Bus. News Exec., TJFR, 2001. Mem. NATAS (past bd. dirs. So. Fla. chpt., regional Emmy award), Radio-TV News Dirs. Assn. (past trustee). Republican. Roman Catholic. Avocations: aerobics, tennis, golf. Office: Sta WPBT 14901 NE 20th Ave Miami FL 33181-1121 Office Phone: 305-424-4050.

O'BYRNE, ELIZABETH MILIKIN, retired pharmacologist; b. Miami, Fla., May 19, 1944; d. Richard Mershon and Anne (Smith) Milikin; m. Brian Kenneth O'Byrne, July 1, 1972; children: Lucy Milikin, Kenneth Daniel. AB in Chemistry, Emory U., 1965, MS in Biochemistry, 1968; PhD in Biochemistry, N.Y. Med. Coll., 1985. Assoc. scientist Eli Lilly Rsch. Labs., Indpls., 1968-70; sr. rsch. scientist CIBA-GEIGY Pharms., Summit, NJ, 1970-96; rsch. fellow Novartis Pharms., East Hanover, NJ, 1997—2004; vis. scientist dept. animal sci. Rutgers U., NJ, 2005—. Co-founder CIBA-GEIGY Partnership in Sci. Contbr. articles to profl. jours. Mem. AAAS, N.Y. Acad. Sci., Inflammation Rsch. Assn., Osteoarthritis Rsch. Soc. Achievements include isolation, characterization and development of radioimmunoassay for hormone relaxin to monitor production and secretion, of assays of cytokine and enzyme degradation of cartilage in vitro and in vivo, of proton and sodium magnetic resonance properties of cartilage; demonstration of therapeutic efficacy of matrix metalloprotease inhibitors to retard tissue damage in animal models of diseases; investigation of autologous bone marrow-derived mesechymal stem cells to repair osteoarthritic lesions in cartilage and bone. Home: 234 Sagamore Rd Millburn NJ 07041-2136 Personal E-mail: lizobyrne@yahoo.com.

OCCHETTI, DIANNE, psychologist, writer; b. Henderson, N.C., Aug. 27, 1951; d. Archie W. and Lillie J. Reavis; m. Armand Occhetti, June 10, 1979. MSW, Univ. N.C., Chapel Hill, N.C., 1974; PhD, Fielding Grad. Inst., Santa Barbara, Calif., 1988. AAMFT approved Supr. and Clin. Mem. Am. Assn. for Marriage & Family Therapy, cert. Group Psychotherapists. Pres., ptnr. Pembroke Psychological Svc. L.L.P., Raleigh, NC, 1983—. Author: Do I Stay or Do I Go? How To Make a Wise Decision About Your Relationship, 2000, transl. into Spanish, 2002; contbr. articles to profl. jour. Human svc. bd. appt. by Wake County Commr., Raleigh, NC, 1996—; bd. mem. Good Shepard Pre-Sch., Raleigh, NC, 2000—. Mem.: Raliegh Profl. Women's Forum. Office: Pembroke Psychol Svc LLP 6512 Six Forks Rd Ste 202A Raleigh NC 27615 E-mail: d.occhetti@aol.com.

OCCHIOGROSSO, MALLAY BARCLAY, psychiatrist; b. N.Y.C., N.Y., June 16, 1967; d. Samuel Barclay and Ann Danberg Charters; m. Glenn Arthur Occhiogrosso, Aug. 26, 2001. BA, Harvard-Radcliffe, Cambridge, Mass., 1990; MD, Cornell U., N.Y.C., 2003. Lic. physician N.Y. Trainee, sales asst. Simon & Schuster, N.Y.C., 1990—91; editl. asst. Random House, N.Y.C., 1992—94; journalist various locations, 1994—2000; psychiatry resident N.Y. Presbyn. Hosp., N.Y.C., 2003—. Fellow: Group for Advancement of Psychiatry; mem.: Am. Psychiat. Assn. Office Phone: 212-746-3797.

OCHESKEY, ELIZABETH R. BLOOM, theater director, educator; d. Charles A. Miner and Carole Ruth Miner Bloom; m. Eddie Ocheskey, Oct. 5, 2002; children: Charles A. Paquet-Ocheskey, Caroline J. BE, Mo. State U., Springfield, 1992—94. Cert. secondary theater tchr. Mo., 2005. Dir. edn. & outreach Kans. City Repertory Theater, 1999—2002; theater tchr. Westport HS, Kansas City, 2003—. Chmn. Kans. City Cappies, 2002—06. Dir.: (theater) Everyman, How The West Was Fun, The Musical Comedy Murders of 1940, Crimes Of The Heart, Leader Of The Pack, A Raisin In The Sun, A Little Night Music, Servant Of Two Masters, Little Women. Drama ministry First Christian Ch. Grandview, Mo., 1998—2006. Mem.: Speech & Theater Assn. Mo. (corr.), Internat. Thespians (life), Nat. Forensics League (corr.). D-Conservative. Avocations: theater, travel, reading.

OCHMAN, JANET, psychology professor; b. Mpls., Minn. d. Armand and Jeanne Ochman. PhD, Murdoch U., Perth, Australia, 1991. Coll. prof. Inver Hills C.C., Inver Grove Heights, Minn., 1992—. Contbr. articles to profl. jours. Vol. parrot rescue groups, Mpls. and St. Paul, 1999—2006. Avocations: travel, reading, nature. Home: 1960 Hamline Ave N Roseville MN 55113 Office: Inver Hills CC 2500 80th St Inver Grove Heights MN 55076 Office Phone: 651-450-8602. E-mail: jochman@inverhills.edu.

OCHOA, ELLEN, astronaut; b. L.A., May 10, 1958; d. Roseanne Ochoa; m. Coe Fulmer Miles; one son. BS in Physics, San Diego State U., 1980; MSEE, Stanford U., 1981, PhD in EE, 1985. Rsch. engr. Sandia Nat. Labs., Livermore, Calif., 1985—88; chief intelligent systems tech. br. NASA/Ames Rsch. Ctr./Moffet Field Naval Air Sta., Mountain View, Calif.; Astronaut NASA, Houston, 1991—, dep. dir., flight crew ops. Recipient two Space Act Tech Brief Awards, 1992, Space Flight Medals 1993, 1994, 1999, 2002; Outstanding Leadership Medal, 1995, Exceptional Svc. Medal, 1997, Women in Aerospace Outstanding Achievement Award, the Hispanic Engr. Albert Baez Award for Outstanding Tech. Contribution to Humanity, the Hispanic Heritage Leadership Award, San Diego State U. Alumna of the Year. Mem. Optical Soc. Am., Am. Inst. Aeronautics and Astronautics, Phi Beta Kappa, Sigma Xi, Pres. Commn. on the Celebration of Women in Am. History. Achievements include being the first female Hispanic astronaut chosen for Space Shuttle program. Office: NASA Johnson Space Ctr Astronaut Office Houston TX 77058

OCHOA, LORENA, professional golfer; b. Guadalajara, Mex., Jan. 15, 1981; d. Javier and Marcela. Attened, U. Ariz., 2000—02. Winner Franklin Am. Mortgage Championship, 2004, Wachovia LPGA Classic, 2004. Five-time U.S. 8-12 Jr. World Championship winner; NCAA Player of Yr., 2001; NCAA Freshman of Yr., 01; finished second NCAA Championships, 2001; finished first place Futures Tour money list, 2002. Recipient Nancy Lopez Award for outstanding amateur accomplishments, 2002, Louise Suggs Rolex Rookie of Yr., 2003, Nat. Sports Award, Mex., 2001. Achievements include Topped $1 million in earnings in 2002 and 2005. Avocations: triathalons, marathons, mountain climbing, tennis, basketball, accordion. Office: c/o LPGA 100 International Golf Dr Daytona Beach FL 32124-1092

OCHOA-BECKER, ANNA S., education educator; b. Windsor, Ont., Can., Oct. 5, 1933; came to U.S., 1953; d. David and Vera (Makaroff) Sultanoff. BS, Wayne State U., Detroit, 1955; MA, U. Mich., Ann Arbor, 1963; PhD, U. Wash., Seattle, 1970. Cert. secondary social studies educator, Mich., Calif. Elem. tchr. Bendle Schs., Flint, Mich., 1955-57; secondary social studies tchr., dept. chmn. Grand Blanc Schs., Mich., 1961—67; elem. tchr. Fremont Unified Schs., Calif., 1967-68; project asst., tri-univ. project U. Wash., Seattle, 1968-70; asst. prof., asst. dept. chmn. Fla. State U., Tallahassee, 1971-76, assoc. prof., 1974—75; assoc. prof. social studies Ind. U., Bloomington, 1987—, full prof., 1988-91, prof. Edn., 1991—. Cons. Global Perspectives in Edn., 1980-83, Fgn. Policy Assn., 1984-86, Indpls. Children's Mus., 1984-86; chmn. adv. bd. social studies panel Nat. Assessment for Edn. Progress, 1980-83; dir. undergrad. edn., dir. tchr. edn., co-chair dept. curriculum and tchr. edn. Ind. U., 1976-97. Co-author: Education for a Democracy, 1988; also author 4th grade text, 1978; contbr. articles to profl. jours. Grantee NSF, 1981-82, U.S. Dept. Edn., 1983-86, 85-86. Mem. Nat. Coun. for Social Studies (v.p. 1976, pres. 1978, bd. dirs. 1972), Ind. Coun. for Social Studies. Democrat. Avocations: photography, theater, reading, walking, cooking. Office: Ind U 3218 Education Bloomington IN 47406 Business E-Mail: ochoa@indiana.edu.

OCHOA-BRILLEMBOURG, HILDA MARGARITA, investment banker; b. July 8, 1944; BS in Econs., U. Catolica Andres Bello, Caracas, Venezuela; MPA, Harvard U.; postgrad. in fin., Harvard Bus. Sch. Chief investment officer, pension investment div. World Bank, 1976—87; mng. dir. Emerging Markets Investment Corp.; founder, pres., CEO Strategic Investment Group, 1987—. Bd. dirs. Harvard Mgmt. Co., Bank Fund Staff Fed. Credit Union, Gen. Mills, Inc., McGraw-Hill Inc.; treas. C.A. Luz Electrica de Venezuela, Caracas, 1967—71; lectr. U. Catolica Andres Bello, 1970; ind. cons. in econs. and fin. Published articles in Fin. Analyst Jour. and Pensions & Investments. Bd. dirs. Nat. Symphony Orch., Washington Nat. Opera, Cath. Charities Found.; chmn. bd. dirs. Youth Orch. of the Americas; mem. investment com. Rockefeller Family Fund; vice chair, Group of 50 Carnegie Endowment for Internat. Peace; mem. adv. com. Rockefeller Ctr. for Latin Am. Studies, The Hauser Ctr. at Harvard U., Small Enterprise Asst. Funds. Fulbright-Hays fellow. Office: 1001 19th St N 16th Fl Arlington VA 22209-1722 Office Phone: 703-243-4433.

OCHS, CAROL REBECCA, theologian, writer, theology studies educator, philosopher; b. N.Y.C., May 7, 1939; d. Herman and Clara Florence (Michaels) Blumenthal; m. Michael Ochs, Sept. 27, 1959; children: Elisabeth Amy, Miriam Adina. BA, CUNY, 1960, MA, 1964; PhD, Brandeis U., 1968. Philosophy lectr. CUNY, 1964-65; from asst. prof. to prof. philosophy Simmons Coll., Boston, 1967-92, prof. emerita, 1992—. Adj. faculty Grad. Sch. Union Inst., Cin., 1992—97, Hebrew Union Coll.-Jewish Inst. Religion, N.Y.C., 1994—97, dir. grad. studies, vis. prof. philosophy, 1997—2001, dir. grad. studies, adj. prof. Jewish Religious Thought, 2001—; cons. Inst. for Svc. to Higher Edn., Chestnut Hill, Mass., 1972, St. Mary's Coll., South Bend, Ind., 1980; scholar-in-residence Hollins Coll., Roanoke, Va., 1987, numerous temples and synagogues; mem. selection com. Kent Postdoctoral Fellowships Bunting Inst., Radcliffe Coll.; lectr. in field. Author: Behind the Sex of God: Toward a New Consciousness Transcending Matriarchy and Patriarchy, 1977, Women and Spirituality, 1983, 2d edit., 1997, An Ascent to Joy: Transforming Deadness of Spirit, 1989, The Noah Paradox: Time as Burden, Time as Blessing, 1991, Song of the Self: Biblical Spirituality and Human Holiness, 1994, Jewish Spiritual Guidance, 1997, Our Lives as Torah: Finding God in Our Own Stories, 2001, Reaching Godward: Voices from Jewish Spiritual Guidance, 2004; contbr. articles to profl. jours. Mem. Jewish-Cath. Dialogue, Boston, 1989-93; mem. Cath.-Jewish com. Archdiocese of Boston, 1989-93. Fellow NEH, 1976, 88, Nat. Humanities Inst., U. Chgo., 1978-79, Danforth Found., 1981-86, Coolidge Rsch., Colloquium, 1985, Resource Theologian, 1995-99. Fellow Soc. for Values in Higher Edn. (bd. dirs. 1982-88, chair ctrl. com. 1985-87, 2003—, v.p. 2004-), Assn. for Religion and Intellectual Life (mem. editl. bd. 1986—). Office: Hebrew Union Coll 1 W 4th St New York NY 10012 Office Phone: 212-824-2267. Personal E-mail: cochs@earthlink.net.

OCHSNER, CAROL M., science educator; b. 1971; d. John and Rosi Ochsner. BS in Sci. Edn., U. Wis., Whitewater, 1994. Cert. tchr. Wis. Tchr. sci. Monroe H.S., Wis., 1996—. Track and field coach - throws Monroe H.S., 1996—. Asst. camp dir. Girls Scouts U.S., Duluth, Minn., 1994—. Mem.: Am. Chem. Soc., Nat. Sci. Tchrs. Assn., Wis. Soc. of Sci. Tchrs. Avocations: travel, camping, walking. Business E-Mail: carol.ochsner@monroe.k12.wi.us.

OCKER, DEBRA LYNN, secondary school educator; b. Greenfield, Ind., Oct. 18, 1961; d. Francis Lee and Beverly Ann Ocker. BA in Phys. Edn./Bus. Edn., Huron U., S.D., 1980—84; MS in Counseling Psychology, Nova Southeastern U., Ft. Lauderdale, Fla.; D in Health Scis., Union Inst. & U., Cin., Ohio, 1995—2004. Nat. tchg. cert., cert. state & nat. massage therapy cert. Bus./phys. edn. instr. Cocoa HS, Fla.; owner Heartrest Health Ctr., Merritt Island. Author: (book) Massage Therapy: Is It Just For The Body, 2004. Vol. Nat. Kidney Found., Orlando, 1995—, adv. bd., 2006; vol. Am. Cancer Soc., Cocoa, 2003—. Named Ms. Merritt Island, Ms. U.S. Continental Pageant, 2000, 2003; recipient Sports Massage Therapist of Yr., Brevard County, 1998. Mem.: NEA, Fla. Tchr. Edn. Assn., Brevard Found. Tchrs. Assn., Fla. State Massage Therapists Assn. Republican. Avocations: walking, reading, fishing, going to the beach. Home: 319 Fillmore Ave Cape Canaveral FL 32920 Office: Heartrest Health Ctr 1395 N Courtenay Pkwy Ste 206 Merritt Island FL 32953

OCKO, STEPHANIE, writer, journalist; b. Newport, R.I. d. Howard Webster and Irma Coffin (Richardson) Goss; m. Stephen Ocko (div. 1993); 1 child, Peter Jeffrey. BA in Anthropology, Boston U., 1972; grad. diploma in comm., Simmons Coll., 1978; MA in Fine Arts, Harvard U., 1986. English instr. Inst. Pedagogique Nat., Kinshasa, Zaire, 1965-66, Stonehill Coll., North Easton, Mass., 1985-89. Author: Environmental Vacations, 1990, 2d edit., 1991 (Best Travel Book, Am. Book Assn. 1990-91), Water, Almost Enough for Everyone, 1995, Adventure Vacations, 1995, Doomsday Denied, 1997, Spiritual Adventures, 2003, Fantasy Vacations, 2003, Adventure Vacations for Animal Lovers, 2004. Mem. Nat. Writers Union, Soc. Environ. Journalists. Avocations: photography, sailing. Home: PO Box 51959 Boston MA 02205-1959 Personal E-mail: ocko2000@att.net.

O'CONNELL, CARMELA DIGRISTINA, appraisal executive, consultant; b. Johnstown, Pa., Nov. 8, 1925; d. Salvatore and Josephine (Riggio) Digristina; m. Maurice F. O'Connell, Sept. 21, 1974 (dec. Feb. 1984); children: Geraldine, John, Bernard. Diploma, Eastern Secretarial Sch., N.Y.C., Sch. Interior Design. From typist to sec.-treas. Philip P. Masterson Co., N.Y.C., 1942-72; exec. v.p., bd. dirs. Masterson & O'Connell Inc., N.Y.C., 1972-80, cons., 1981—; founder, pres. N.Y. Appraisal Corp., N.Y.C., 1971-80; co-founder, pres. Park Ave. Appraisal, N.Y.C., 1981—. Mem. N.Y. Rep. Com., 1974—, Met. Opera Guild, N.Y.C., 1986; chmn. Ch. of Our Saviour, N.Y.C., 1986; mem. Ladies of Charity, Cath. Charities Archdiocese of N.Y., 1990; bd. dirs. 80 Park Avenue Condominiums, 1997—. Recipient Amita award for Bus. Woman of Yr., 1977, Lena Madesin Phillips award N.Y. League/Fortune 500 Bus. and Profl. Women, 1989. Mem. Nat. Fedn. Bus. and Profl. Women's Clubs Inc. (2d v.p. 1964, 1st v.p. 1966). Roman Catholic. Home: 2421 Old Collier Rd Land O Lakes FL 34639 Office Phone: 813-948-8941.

O'CONNELL, MARY ITA, psychotherapist; b. Balt., July 3, 1929; d. Richard Charles and Ona (Buchness) O'C.; m. Leon Jack Greenbaum, Dec. 28, 1962 (div. Jan. 1986); children: Jessie A., Elizabeth K. BA, U. Md., 1956; postgrad., Am. U., 1960—; M in Creative Arts in Therapy, Hahnemann Med. Coll., 1978. Registered Acad. Dance Therapists. Tchr. Robert Cohan Sch. Dance, Boston, 1958-61; instr., choreographer Wheaton Coll., Norton, Mass., 1959-60, Harvard/Radcliffe Colls., Boston, 1960-62; tchr., performer, choreographer Profl. Studios, Washington, 1962-69; asst. prof., adminstr. Fed. City Coll., Washington, 1969-74; movement psychotherapist Woodburn Ctr. for Community Mental Health, Fairfax, Va., 1975-76, Gundry Hosp., Balt., 1976-77, Prince Georges' Community Mental Health Dept., Capitol Heights, Md., 1978-80; lectr. George Washington U., D.C., 1981-85; pvt. practice psychotherapy specializing in stress mgmt., anger mgmt. and internal energy, Silver Spring, Md., 1977—. Sr. movement psychotherapist Regional Inst. for Children and Adolescents, Rockville, Md., 1980-82; movement cons. Ctr. for Youth Svcs., Washington, 1981-83; movement psychotherapist D.C. Mental Health Ctrs., Washington, 1985-87, 90-99, Community for Creative Non-Violence Women's Shelter, Washington, 1986, LICSW, Washington, 1989. Choreographer, soloist (dance performance) The Artist: A Theatre Happening, 1963; choreographer, co-dir. (outdoor dance event) Tree Sculpting, 1974; choreographer (dance performance) Excitations, 1967, A Dance Event, 1974; choreographer (dance performance) Excitations, 1967, A Dance Event, 1974; choreographer New England Opera, 1961; performer, choreographer WGBM soloist, New England Opera, 1961; performer, CBS-TV/Erika Thimey TV/Laboratory Concert Series, 1961; performer, CBS-TV/Erika Thimey Dance Theatre, 1965; guest artist, Harford Coll. Art Festival, 1967. U. Md. scholar, 1955-56. Mem. Dance Circle of Boston (life, pres. 1959-61), Modern Dance Council of Washington (exec. bd dirs., editor 1965-69), Am. Dance Therapy Assn. (treas. metro chpt. 1977-81), Assn. Humanistic Psychology, Family Therapy Network, Am. Dance Guild, NIH (movement specialist 1978-79). Democrat. Avocations: sailing, lacrosse, stone collecting, collage making. Home and Office: 1400 East West Hwy # 523 Silver Spring MD 20910

O'CONNELL, MARY-KATHLEEN, lawyer; BA cum laude, Yale Univ., 1977; JD, NYU, 1981. Bar: Mass. 1981. With Goodwin Procter LLP, Boston, 1981—, ptnr., chair, trusts & estate planning practice, mem., investment com. Staff NYU Law Rev. Mem.: ABA, Estate Planning Coun., Women's Bar Assn., Mass Bar Assn., Boston Bar Assn. Office: Goodwin Procter LLP Exchange Pl 53 State St Boston MA 02109 Office Phone: 617-570-1391. Office Fax: 617-523-1231. Business E-Mail: moconnell@goodwinprocter.com.

O'CONNELL, MAUREEN C., county official, former state legislator; m. Donald O'Connell; 1 child, Donald. BS in Health Care Adminstrn., St. Josephs Coll.; JD, St. John's U.; RN, Flushing Hosp. Med. Ctr. Mem. NY State Assembly, Dist. 17, 1998—2006; clk. Nassau Co., NY, 2006—. Mem. adv. bd. Nassau Cmty. Coll., Molloy Coll. Sch. of Nuring. Recipient Am. Jurisprudence award. Mem.: Oncology Nursing Soc., Nassau Co. Bar Assn., Am. Cancer Soc. Republican. Office: Nassau County Clk 1 West St Mineola NY 11501*

O'CONNELL, PATRICIA ELLEN, music educator, musician; b. Endicott, N.Y., Jan. 12, 1955; d. Harold Seymour Arnold and Sylvia Patricia Russell; m. William Harry O'Connell, July 1, 2006; children: Jennifer Lynn Kotski, William Hancock Ellis, Matthew Charles Ellis. Regents diploma, Owego Free Acad., N.Y., 1973; MusB, Crane Sch. of Music, Potsdam, N.Y., 1977; MusM, Ithaca Coll. Sch. Music, N.Y., 1983. Cert. music edn. K - 12 N.Y. State. Band dir. LaFargeville (N.Y.) Cen. Sch., 1977—78, Newark Valley (N.Y.) Mid. Sch., 1978—90, Vestal (N.Y.) Jr. H.S., 1990—92; band and chorus dir. Vestal Sr. H.S., Vestal, 1992—97, band dir., 1977—; dir. Vestal Marching Band, 1992—2002, co-dir., 2004—. French horn performer Binghamton (N.Y.) Philharm. Orch., 1978—. Tri Cities Opera Orch., Binghamton, 1978—, Glimmerglass Opera Orch., Cooperstown, NY, 1979—; guest condr. Band Festival, Sullivan County, Pa., 1990, Sullivan County, 98; founder So. Tier Comty. Band Workshops; former condr. The Kirby Band. Contbr. sch. band and orch. mag. Warden St. Paul's Episcopal Ch., Owego, 2004; bd. dirs. Spectrum Drum and Bugle Corps, Corning and Owego, NY, 1994—98. Recipient Solo Performer award1995, Binghamton Cmty. Orch., 1995, Midi Sta. grant, Vestal Schools Found., 1996. Mem.: N.Y. State Sch. Music Assn., Am. Fedn. Musicians (orch. rep. 1998), N.Y. State Band Dirs, Assn., Music Educators Nat. Conf. Episcopalian. Avocations: ferrets, needlework, yardwork, walking, small ensemble performance. Home: 132 Southside Dr Owego NY 13827 Office: Vestal H S 205 Woodlawn Dr Vestal NY 13850 Office Phone: 607-757-2286. Personal E-mail: pea522@stny.rr.com.

O'CONNELL, TAAFFE CANNON, actress, publishing executive; b. Providence; d. Joseph Ceril and Edith Ethelyn (Dent) O'C. BA, MFA, U. Miss., University. Regional supr. Gloria Marshall Figure Salons, SC; v.p., co-founder Doc Sox Inc., Pacific Palisades, Calif., 1988-90; pres., founder Canoco Pub., L.A., 1991—, 1-800-266-DYNE, L.A., 1992-93. Founder Rising Star Distbn., Yes I Can Actor's Workshops, 2001—, Get Inside the Agent's Head Seminars, 2003, Actors Acing Hollywood Seminars, 2006; exec. prodr. Beanie/Twigg 1999—, Canoco Prodn. Appeared in films, including Men Without Dates, Dangerous, Hot Chili, Cheech & Chong Nice Dreams, Rocky II, Galaxy of Terror, New Years Evil, Rich Man Poor Man Book I, Caged Fury; TV appearances include Malubu Branch, General Hospital, Dangerous Women, Dallas, Knight and Daye, The New Gidget, Knight Rider, Three's Company, Dr. Joyce Brothers Show, Blansky's Beauties, Peter Lupus Show, Fix-It City, Happy Days, Laverne & Shirley, Wonder Woman, The Incredible Hulk; theater appearances include Too True to be Good, Damn Yankees, Anastasia, Star Spangled Girl, The Beaux Stratagem, The Canterbury Tales; founder, pub. The Caster, 1991, Power Agent, 1993; Jan. founder Rising Star Distbn. and Canoco Prodns., 1999—, Get Inside the Agents' Head Seminars, Yes I Can Actors Workshops, Actors Acing Hollywood Seminars, 2005—; exec prodr.: Beanie & Twigg, Paranormal Private Eyes, Inside the Industry, 2000. Mem. Screen Actors' Guild, Am. Fedn. TV Radio Artists, Actor's Equity, Actor's Forum (bd. dirs. 1985-94). Avocations: singing, spinning, sailing, travel. Office: Canoco Pub 11611 Chenault St Ste 118 Los Angeles CA 90049-4574 Office Phone: 310-471-2287. Personal E-mail: industryedge@adelphia.net.

O'CONNELL, VALERIE BETH, finance educator; b. Omaha, Nebr., Feb. 24, 1980; d. Daniel T. and Debbie A. O'Connell. Vocat. Bus. Edn. and Diversified Occupations, U. Nebr., Kearney, 2002, MA in Instrnl. Tech., 2003. Tchr. informationl tech. Omaha NW H.S., 2004—. Coach varsity volleyball Omaha NW H.S., 2004—. Office: Omaha NW HS 8204 Crown Point Ave Omaha NE 68134 Office Phone: 402-557-3500. Business E-Mail: valerie.oconnell@ops.org.

O'CONNOR, BETTY LOU, retired hotel executive, food service executive; b. Phoenix, Oct. 29, 1927; d. Georg Eliot and Tillie Edith Miller; m. William Spoeri O'Connor, Oct. 10, 1948 (dec. Feb. 1994); children: Thomas W., William K. (dec.), Kelli Anne. Student, U. So. Calif., 1946-48, Calif. State U., Los Angeles, 1949-50. V.p. O'Connor Food Svcs., Inc., Jack in the Box Restaurants, Granada Hills, Calif., 1983-93; pres. O'Connor Food Svcs., Inc., Granada Hills, Calif., 1994—, C.E.O. Foods, Inc., Victorville, Calif. Recipient Frannie award Foodmaker, Inc., Northridge, Calif., 1984, First Rate award, 1992. Mem. Jack in the Box Franchisee Assn., Spurs Hon. (sec. U. So. Calif. 1947-48), Associated Women Students (sec. U. So. Calif. 1946-47), Gamma Alpha Chi (v.p. 1947-48), Chi Omega. Republican. Roman Catholic. Avocation: sewing. Personal E-mail: clmocon@aol.com.

O'CONNOR, BRIDGET, labor union administrator, lawyer; b. 1966; AB, Mount Holyoke Coll.; JD, Univ. Chgo. Atty. NLRB; staff counsel Internat. Union Bricklayers and Allied Craftworkers, Washington. Office: Internat Union Bricklayers 1776 Eye St Washington DC 20006 Office Phone: 202-783-3788. Office Fax: 202-393-0219.

O'CONNOR, CATHERINE MARIE, music educator; b. Oakland, Calif., Dec. 26, 1959; d. Jack Wilbur and Arlene Mary O'Connor. BA, Calif. State U., Hayward, 1982. Pvt. piano instr., Hayward, Calif., 1982—. Musician: (chamber music /accompanist /performances) Solo and ensemble performances, 2000—. Mem.: Music Tchrs. Nat. Assn., Chamber Musicians of No. Calif., Music Tchrs. Assn. Calif. (pres. 1996—98, chmn. Friends of Today's Music Project 2001). Avocation: golf. Personal E-mail: cathoc@aol.com.

O'CONNOR, DORIS JULIA, not-for-profit fundraiser, consultant; b. Apr. 30, 1930; 1 child: Kim C. BA cum laude in Econs., U. Houston, 1975. Adminstrv. asst. Shell Cos. Found. Inc., N.Y.C., 1966-71, asst. sec. Houston, 1971-73, sec., 1973-76, sr. v.p., dir., mem. exec. com., 1976-93; prin. Doris O'Connor & Co., 1993—. Corp. assoc. United Way of Am., Washington, 1976-93; corp. advisor Bus. Com. of Arts, N.Y.C., 1976-91, del., 1982-87; dir. Ind. Sector, Washington, 1981-89, vice chmn., 1983-87; mem. contbns. coun. Conf. Bd., N.Y.C., 1976-93; advisor Coun. of Better Bus. Burs., Washington, 1975-94, vice chmn., 1983-87; commr. adv. commn. on work-based learning, Dept. Labor, 1991-93; mem. Houston/Harris County Arts Task Force, 1991-93, Houston Ind. Sch. Dist. Task Force, 1991-93; trustee Houston Grand Opera, 1993-99, Houston Symphony Soc., 1993-99, Soc. Performing Arts, 1993-99, Cultural Arts Coun., 1993-96, Greater Houston Coalition Edn. Excellence, 1993-96; mem. adv. bd. Houston Zool. Soc., 1993-99; mem. Mus. Fine Arts, Houston. Mem. Houston Com. Fgn. Rels., Houston World Affairs Coun., Houston Philos. Soc., Plaza Club (bd. givs. 1987-89), Omicron Delta Epsilon. Office Phone: 713-522-3278.

O'CONNOR, EILEEN J., federal agency administrator; Grad., Columbus State U., Cath. U. Corp. tax law specialist IRS; ptnr. Office Fed. Tax Svcs. Grant Thornton, 1984—99; officer for tax svcs. Aronson, Fetridge and Weigle, 1999—2002; asst. atty. gen. tax divsn. U.S. Dept. Justice, Washington, 2002—. Disting. adj. prof. law George Mason U. Law Sch.; adj. prof. law Georgetown U. Law Sch.; former tax cons. various acctg. firms. Mem.: Am. Inst. Cert. Pub. Accountants (past mem. tax. exec. com.), Fed. Bar Assn., DC Bar Assn. Office: US Dept Justice Tax Divsn 950 Pennsylvania Ave NW Washington DC 20530-0001

O'CONNOR, ELIZABETH HILL, elementary school educator; d. William Shaw Blalock and Barbara Hill Maass; m. Christopher Sean Deigh O'Connor, Dec. 12, 1987. BS in Acctg., U. Fla., Gainesville, 1987; MA in K-12 Edn., Tusculum Coll., Greeneville, Tenn., 2002; EdS in Instrnl. Leadership, Tenn. Tech. U., Cookeville, 2005. Lic. profl. tchr. Tenn. Dept. Edn. Field audit specialist Wausau Ins., Beaverton, Oreg., 1988—95; tchr. sci Hixson Mid. Sch. Hamilton County Dept. Edn., Tenn., 1998—. Golf coach Hixson Mid. Sch., Hixson, Tenn., 2001—03, chair sci. dept., 2001—03; chartered property casualty underwriter Soc. Chartered Property Casualty Underwriter, 1988—95. Contbr. articles to periodicals. Hike leader Sierra Club, 1994—95; co-leader support group Crohn's and Colitis Found., 1997—2000. Recipient Assoc. in Premium Auditing award, Soc. of Chartered Property Casualty Underwriters, 1990; Nat. Merit scholar, U. Fla., 1983—87, Tchr. scholar, Target Stores, 2001. Mem.: Chattanooga Hiking Club (outings chair). Avocations: mountaineering, backpacking, bicycling, travel journals. Office: Hixson Mid Sch 5401 Sch Dr Hixson TN 37343

O'CONNOR, GENEVIEVE, marketing executive; b. Cortland, N.Y., Mar. 5, 1975; d. Sean Gary and Sharon Anne O'Connor; m. Brian Patrick Faulk. BS, Villanova U., 1997; postgrad., Fordham U. Events coord. Rainbow Pormotions, Landsdowne, Pa., 1993—95, World Class Promotions, Balt., 1994—95; fgn. exch. traders asst. The Asahi Bank, Ltd., N.Y.C., 1998—99; pharm. sales rep. 3M Pharm., St. Paul, 1999—2000, profl. instl. sales rep., 2000—01, sr. profl. instl. sales rep., 2001—04; cert. surg. specialist US Surg. Auto Suture, Norwalk, Conn., 2004—05. Regional trainer 3M Pharm., St. Paul, 2002—04, intranet adv. bd., West Coldwell, NJ, 2001—02, computer trainer, 2002—05. Mem.: Alpha Chi Omega (chi connections coord. 1994—96). Avocations: skiing, tennis, travel, art, writing. Home: 75 Ellis St Haddonfield NJ 08033-1826 Office: 10 Lake Ctr 401 Rte 73N #205-10 Marlton NJ 08035 E-mail: vievefaulk@yahoo.com.

O'CONNOR, SISTER GEORGE AQUIN (MARGARET M. O'CONNOR), academic administrator, educator; b. Astoria, N.Y., Mar. 5, 1921; d. George M. and Joana T. (Loughlin) O'C. BA, Hunter Coll., 1943; MA, Catholic U. Am., 1947; PhD (NIMH fellow), NYU, 1964; LL.D. Manhattan Coll., 1983; D of Pedagogy (hon.), Dowling Coll., 1997; DHL, St. Francis Coll., 1997, St. Joseph's Coll., 1997. Mem. faculty St. Joseph's Coll., Bklyn., 1946—, prof. sociology and anthropology, 1966—, chmn. social sci. dept., 1966-69, pres., 1969-97; pres. emeritus. Fellow African Studies Assn., Am. Anthrop. Assn.; Bklyn. C. of C. (dir. 1973-97), Alpha Kappa Delta, Delta Epsilon Sigma. Author: The Status and Role of West African Women: A Study in Cultural Change, 1964. Named one of N.Y. State Senate's Women of Distinction. Office: Saint Joseph's Coll 245 Clinton Ave Brooklyn NY 11205-3602 Office Phone: 718-636-6800. Business E-Mail: goconnor@sjcny.edu.

O'CONNOR, KAREN, political science professor, researcher, writer; b. Buffalo, Feb. 15, 1952; d. Robert J. and Norma (Wilton) O'Connor; m. Allen McDonogh, June 7, 1974 (div. 1986); 1 child, Meghan; m. Richard Cupitt, July 31, 1992. BA, SUNY, Buffalo, 1973, JD, 1977, PhD, 1979. Bar: Ga. 1978. Instr. polit. sci. Emory U., Atlanta, 1977—78, asst. prof., 1978—83, assoc. prof., 1983—88, prof., 1988—95, Am. U., Washington, 1995—2006, Jonathan N. Halfat disting. prof., 2006—. Editor Women & Politics, 1999—2004, Law & Policy, 1982—2005, Jour. of Politics, 1984—87, Am. Politics Quar., 1987—90; founder and dir. Women& Politics Inst., 1999. Author: Women's Organization's Use of the Courts, 1980; author: (with N.E. McGlen) Women's Rights, 1983; editor: Women and Congress, 2002; co-author (with McGlem): Women, Politics and American Society, 2004; co-author: (with L. Sabato) American Government, 9th edit., 2005; co-editor (with S. Brewer and M. Fisher): Gendering Politics, 2005; mem. editl. bd. Women, Politics & Public Policy; contbr. articles to profl. jours. Mem.: Nat. Capitol Area Polit. Sci. Assn. (pres. 2001—02), So. Polit. Sci. Assn. (pres. 2000—01), Women and Politics (pres. elect organized sect. 2005—), Am. Polit. Sci. Assn. (exec. coun. 1985—87), Cosmos Club. Home: 4383 Westover Pl NW Washington DC 20016-5555 Office: Dept of Govt American Univ 4400 Massachusetts Ave NW Washington DC 20016 Office Phone: 202-885-6237. Business E-Mail: oconn@american.edu.

O'CONNOR, KAREN LENDE, Olympic athlete, sports association administrator; b. Feb. 17, 1958; m. David O'Connor, 1993. Mem. US Equestrian Olympic Team, Seoul, Korea, 1988, Atlanta, 1996, Sydney, Australia, 2000, US Equestrian Team, Pan Am. Games, 2003. Co-chmn. instr. cert. prog. US Eventing Assn.; bd. dir. US Equestrian Fedn.; mem. athlete adv. bd. US Olympic Comm. Winner CCI, Boekelo (Holland), 1984, CCI, Chesterland (Pa.), 1985, placed 1st Role/Kentucky Internat. CCI Three Day Event, 1991, 1st Tetbury (Eng.) Horse Trials, 1991, 1st Fair Hill (Md.) Horse Trials, 1991, 3rd Burghley Three Day Event CCI (Eng.), 1991, 6th World Three Day Event Rider Rankings L'Annee Hippique, 1991, 3rd CCI, Loughanmore (Ireland), 1992, 6th Blenheim Audi Internat. Horse Trials (Eng.), 1993, 1st CCI, Punchestown (Ireland), 1993, 10th CCI Internat. de Saumur, 1994; recipient Silver medal, Olympic Games, Atlanta, 1996, Team Bronze medal, Olympic Games, 2000, Silver medal, Pan Am. Games, 2003; winner Foxhall Cup, 2001; named U.S. Combined Tng. Assn. Lady Rider of the Year, 1989, 90, 91, 95, 96, 97, 98, Female Equestrian Athlete of the Year Olympic Com., 1993, USET spring champion, winning Kentucky CCI, USET FAll Reserve champion, 2nd Fair Hill, 1999, World Equestrian Games Bronze Medal Team, 1998, USET spring champion, winner Kentucky CCI, 1997; grantee USET, 1991. Office: OCET PO Box D The Plains VA 20198

O'CONNOR, KATHLEEN MARY, lawyer; b. Camden, Jan. 14, 1949; d. John A. and Marie V. (Flynn) O'C. BA, U. Fla., 1971, JD, 1981. Bar: Fla. 1981, U.S. Ct. Appeals (11th cir.) 1982, U.S. Supreme Ct. 1987. Atty. Walton, Lantaff, Schroeder & Carson, Miami, Fla., 1981-84, Thornton, Davis & Murray PA, Miami, 1984-98, Thornton, Davis & Fein, P.A., Miami, 2002—. Exec. editor U. Fla. Law Rev., 1981; contbr. articles to profl. jours. Legal advocate Miami Project to Cure Paralysis, 1992-97. Mem. ABA, Dade County Bar Assn. (chmn. appellate cts. com. 2004—), Def. Rsch. Inst., Fla. Def. Lawyers Assn., Fla. Assn. for Women Lawyers (bd. dirs. Miami-Dade County chpt. 2002—), Fla. Bar (mem. appellate rules com. 2002—, cert. 1995—). Office: Thornton Davis & Fein PA 80 SW 8th St Ste 2900 Miami FL 33130 Home: 7445 SW 147 St Coral Gables FL 33158 Office Phone: 305-446-2646. E-mail: oconnor@tdflaw.com.

O'CONNOR, KIM CLAIRE, chemical engineering and biotechnology educator, researcher; BS magna cum laude, Rice U., Houston, 1982; PhD, Calif. Inst. Tech., Pasadena, 1987. Postdoctoral rsch. fellow chemistry dept. Calif. Inst. Tech., Pasadena, 1987-88; postdoctoral rsch. fellow chem. engring., biochemistry, molecular biology, and cell biology depts. Northwestern U., Evanston, Ill., 1988-90; asst. prof. chem. engring. Tulane U., New Orleans, 1990-96, mem. faculty molecular and cellular biology grad. program, 1991—, assoc. prof. chem. engring., 1996—2002, prof. chem. engring., 2002—03, prof. chem. and biomolecular engring., 2003—, co-dir. molecular and cellular biology grad. program, 1996-99, interim dir. molecular and cellular biology grad. program, 1997. Mem. Tulane Cancer Ctr., 1994—; adj. assoc. prof. dept. surgery Tulane U. Sch. Medicine, 1999—; vis. prof. Ctr. for Cell and Gene Therapy, Baylor Coll. Medicine, Houston, 2005; cons. in field including NASA, NSF, NRC. Mem. editl. bd. Jour. Cellular and Molecular Medicine; contbr. articles to profl. jours. Recipient Space Act award NASA, 1994-96, Outstanding Engring. Student award Tex. Soc. Profl. Engrs., 1982, Tulane award for excellence in undergrad. tchg., 1999, Lee H. Johnson award, 2001, Tulane Interdisciplinary Tchg. award, 2001, Tulane Health Scis. award for Leadership and Excellence in Intercampus Collaborative Rsch., 2005; Robert A. Welch Merit scholar, 1978-82, Brown Engring. Merit scholar, 1980-82, Roy Merit scholar, 1981-82; Weyerhaeuser Co. Found. fellow, 1982-83. Mem.: AIChE, Biomed. Engring. Soc., Tissue Engring. Soc., Soc. Women Engrs., Soc. In Vitro Biology, European Soc. Animal Cell Tech., Am. Assn. for Cancer Rsch., Phi Lambda Upsilon, Tau Beta Pi, Sigma Xi. Achievements include patents in field; research in engring. and biological sciences. Office: Tulane U Dept Chem Engring Lindy Boggs Ctr Rm 300 New Orleans LA 70118 Business E-Mail: koc@tulane.edu.

O'CONNOR, MAUREEN, state supreme court justice; b. Washington, Aug. 7, 1951; d. Patrick and Mary E. O'Connor; children: Alex, Ed. BA, Seton Hill Coll., 1973; postgrad., SUNY, 1975-76; JD, Cleve. State U., 1980. Pvt. practice, 1981-85; magistrate Summit County Probate Ct., 1985-93; judge Summit County Ct. of Common Pleas, 1993-95; prosecuting atty. Summit County, 1995-99; lt. gov., dir. Dept. Pub. Safety State of Ohio, 1999—2003; justice Ohio Supreme Ct., Ohio, 2003—. Dir. Summit County Child Support Enforcement Agy.; former chair Ohio Security Task Force, Building Security Review Com.; spkr. in field. Parishioner St. Vincent's Ch.; vol. Comty. Drug Bd., Am. Cancer Soc., bd. dirs.; bd. dirs. Victim Assistance, St. Edward Home, Fairlawn, Furnace St. Mission. Recipient MADD Law Enforcement award, 1997, Cleve. State Disting. Alumnae award for Civic Achievement, 1997. Mem. MADD, Nat. Dist. Attys. Assn., Nat. Child Support Enforcement Assn., Nat. Coll. Dist. Attys. Assn., Ohio Prosecuting Attys. Assn. (exec. com.), Ohio Family Support Assn., Atty. Gen.'s Prosecutor Liaison Com., Summit County Police Chiefs Assn., Summit Forum, Summit County Child Mortality. Republican. Office: Ohio Supreme Ct 65 S Front St Columbus OH 43215*

O'CONNOR, NAN G., social worker; b. Chgo., Apr. 27, 1952; d. Joseph Daniel and Donna Marguerite (Birmingham) O'C. BSW, U. Ill., 1975, MSW, 1978. Med. social worker Schaumburg (Ill.) Elem. Sch. Dist., 1978-79, Ingalls Meml. Hosp., Harvey, Ill., 1979-84; case mgmt. supr. United Charities of Chgo., 1984-85; social worker Village of Skokie, Ill., 1990-97. Sec. Mental Health Coalition So.-Suburban, Oak Forest, Ill., 1980-83; co-chair Social Workers in Home Care, Chgo., 1981-83; founder, chairperson Niles Twp Inter-Agy. Network, Skokie, 1993-96. Bd. dirs. CEDA/Neighbors at Work, Evanston, Ill., 1995-96. Recipient Timothy J. Nugent award Delta Sigma Omicron, U. Ill., Champaign, 1974. Mem. NASW, Niles Twp. InterAgency Network (chairperson 1993-96). Avocations: poetry, short stories. Home: 1747 W Crystal Ln Apt 102 Mount Prospect IL 60056-5439 E-mail: nanoconnor@aol.com.

O'CONNOR, SANDRA DAY, retired United States Supreme Court Justice; b. El Paso, Tex., Mar. 26, 1930; d. Harry A. and Ada Mae (Wilkey) Day; m. John Jay O'Connor, III, 1952; children: Scott, Brian, Jay. BA with great distinction, Stanford U., 1950, LLB, 1952. Bar: Calif., Ariz. Dep. county atty., San Mateo, Calif., 1952—53; civilian atty. Q.M. Market Ctr., Frankfurt am Main, Germany, 1954—57; pvt. law practice Maryvale, 1958—60; asst. atty. gen. State of Ariz., 1965—69, state senator, 1969—75; chmn. com. on state, county and mcpl. affairs, 1972—73; senate majority leader, 1972—75; judge Maricopa County Superior Ct., Phoenix, 1975—79, Ariz. Ct. Appeals, 1979—81; assoc. justice US Supreme Ct., Washington, 1981—2006; vis. judge US Ct. Appeals (2nd Cir.), NYC, 2006—. Mem. Maricopa County Bd. Adjustments and Appeals, 1963—64, Ariz. Criminal Code Commn., 1974—76, Nat. Defense Adv. Com. on Women in Svcs., 1974—76; chmn. vis. bd. Maricopa County Juvenile Detention Home, 1963—64; chmn. Ariz. Supreme Ct. Com. to Reorganize Lower Cts., 1974—75, Maricopa County Superior Ct. Judges Tng. and Edn. Com., 1977—79; vice chmn. Ariz. Select Law Enforcement Review Commn., 1979—80; served on Legis. Coun., Probate Code Commn., Ariz. Adv. Coun. on Intergovernmental Relations. Mem. bd. editors: Stanford (Calif.) U. Law Rev.; co-author (with H. Alan Day): (memoir) Lazy B: Growing Up on a Cattle Ranch in the American Southwest, 2002; author (with Dan Andreasen, illustrator): (children's books) Chico: A True Story from the Childhood of the First Woman Supreme Court Justice, 2005. Trustee Rockefeller Found.; mem. adv. bd. Smithsonian Nat. Mus. Natural History, 2006—; mem., selection com. Okla. City Nat. Meml. and Mus., 2005—; co-chair nat. adv. coun. Campaign for Civic Mission of Schs., 2005—; mem. Cathedral Chpt. Wash. Nat. Cathedral, 1991—99. Named Woman of Yr., Phoenix Advt. Club, 1972, National Women's Hall of Fame, 1995; named one of Most Powerful Women, Forbes mag., 2005; recipient Ann. award, NCCJ, 1975, Disting. Achievement award, Ariz. State U., 1980, Gimble Nat. award, Gimble Phila. awards Com., 1982, Elizabeth Blackwell award, Hobart & William Smith Coll., 1985, award of Merit, Stanford Law Sch., 1990, OH State Law award, OH State U., 1992, Fordham Stein prize, Fordham U., 1992, Sara Lee Frontrunner award, 1997, ABA medal, 1997, Thomas Jefferson award of Law, U. Va., 1987, William Green award for Profl. Excellence, U. Richmond, 1990. Mem.: Anglo-Am. Exchange, Ariz. State Personnel Commn., Stanford Ctr. Ethics (adv. bd. 2005—), Am. Soc. Internat. Law (adv. com. 2001—), Ariz. Women Lawyer's Assn., Nat. Assn. Women Judges, Ariz. Judges' Assn., Calif. Bar Assn., Maricopa County Bar Assn. (chmn. Lawyer Referral Svc. 1960—62), Ariz. Bar Assn. (former mem. Com. Legal Aid, former mem. Com. Public Relations, former mem. Com. Lower Ct. Reorganization, former mem. Com. Continuing Legal Edn.), ABA (exec. bd. Ctrl. European and Eurasian Law Initiative 1990—, exec. com. Mus. Law 2000—, adv. commn. Standing Com. on Law Library of Congress 2002—, mem. Commn. on Civic Edn. and Seperation of Powers 2005—), Adv. Com. for Judiciary Leadership Devel. Coun. (hon.). Office: US Ct Appeals 500 Pearl St New York NY 10007

O'CONNOR, SHEILA ANNE, freelance writer; b. Paisley, Scotland, Jan. 20, 1960; came to the U.S., 1988; d. Brian Aubrey Witham and Margaret Kirk (Reid) Davies; m. Frank Donal O'Connor, Aug. 9, 1986; children: David Michael, Andrew James, Christine Charlotte. BA in French and German, Strathclyde U., 1980, postgrad. diploma in office studies, 1981, MBA, 1992. Office asst. BBC, London, 1982-83; asst. to mng. dir. Unimatic Engrs. Ltd., London, 1983-84; freelance word processing operator London, 1984-88; staff asst. Internat. Monetary Fund, Washington, 1988-94; prin. Internat. Media Assn., Washington, 1988—. Co-author: Chocolate for a Woman's Spirit, 1999; contbr. articles to profl. jours. Mem. Am. Mktg. Assn., Bay Area Travel Writers Assn., Calif. Writers Club. Avocations: animals, travel. Home and Office: 1974 46th Ave San Francisco CA 94116-1005 E-mail: sheila.oconnor@juno.com.

O'CONNOR, SHERYL BRODERICK, literature and language educator; b. Macon, Ga., Apr. 14, 1943; d. Charles Robert and Gloria Broderick; children: Kimberly O'Connor Biss, Broderick Jeffrey. BA, Mt. Holyoke Coll., South Hadley, Mass., 1965; MA in Tchg. English, Smith Coll., Northampton, Mass., 1965. Cert. tchr. English Mass., tchr. secondary English N.J. Tchr. Sweeney Meml., Chicopee, Mass., 1966—69; tchr., jr. sch. chair MacDuffie Sch., Springfield, Mass., 1969—72; instr. critical reading Camden County Coll., Blackwood, NJ, 1987—90; tchr. East Camden Mid. Sch., Camden, NJ, 1984—. Mem. curriculum adv. com. Camden Bd. Edn., 1996; mem., v.p. Bd. Edn., Medford, NJ, 1979—89. Contbr. poetry to mags. Fellow: Rotary Found. of Rotary Internat.; mem.: Camden Edn. Assn. (rep. 2000—), Mensa, Cherry Hill Rotary (pres. 2000—). Republican. Anglican. Home: 2 Andover Ct Southampton NJ 08088

O'CONNOR VOS, LYNN, healthcare group executive; b. NY; BS, Alfred U. CEO, pres. Grey Healthcare Group, Inc., NY. Mem.: Am. Skin. Assn., Healthcare Businesswomen's Assn., Multiple Myeloma Rsch. Found. Office: Grey Healthcare Group Inc 114 Fifth Ave New York NY 10011 Office Phone: 212-886-3000. Office Fax: 212-886-3097. E-mail: voc@ghgroup.com.

O'DAY, ANITA BELLE COLTON, entertainer, musician, vocalist; b. Chgo., Dec. 18, 1919; d. James and Gladys (Gill) C. Singer, entertainer various Chgo. music clubs, 1939—41; singer with Gene Krupa's Orch., 1941—45, with Stan Kenton Orch., 1944, with Woody Herman Orch., 1945, Benny Goodman Orch., 1959; singing tours in US and abroad, 1947—; rec. artist Polygram, Capitol, Emily Records, Verve, GNP Crescendo, Columbia, London, Signature, DRG, Pablo. Million-seller songs include Let Me Off Uptown, 1941, And Her Tears Flowed Like Wine, 1944, Boogie Blues, 1945; appeared in (films) Gene Krupa Story, 1959, Jazz on a Summer's Day, 1960, Zigzag, 1970, Outfit, 1974, (TV shows) 60 Minutes, 1980, Tonight Show, Dick Cavett Show, Today Show, Big Band Bash, CBS Sunday Morning, CNN Showbiz Today, (documentary) Indestructable, 2006; author: High Times, Hard Times, 1981, rev. edit., 1989; performer 50 yr. Anniversary Concert Carnegie Hall, 1985, Avery Fisher Hall, 1989, Tanglewood, 1990, JVC Festival Town Hall, 1993, Rainbow and Stars, 1995, JVC Festival Carnegie Hall, 1996, JVC Festival Avery Fisher Hall, 1999, Hollywood Palladium, 1999, Blue Note, NYC, 2000, Atlas Supper Club, LA, 2000, Fez, NYC, 2001, Plush Room, San Francisco, 2002, Iridium, NYC, 2003-05, Blue Note, NYC, Jazz Alley, Seattle, 2003, Pizza-in-the-Park, London, 2004, New Paltz State Coll, NY, 2005; albums include Drummer Man, Kenton Era, Anita, Anita Sings The Most, Pick Yourself Up, Lady is a Tramp, An Evening with Anita O'Day, At Mr. Kelly's, Swings Cole Porter, Travelin' Light, All the Sad Young Men, Waiter Make Mine Blues, With the Three Sounds, I Told Ya I Love Ya Now Get Out, Uptown, My Ship, Live in Tokyo, Anita Sings the Winners, Incomparable, Anita 1975, Live at Mingos, Anita O'Day/The Big Band Sessions, Swings Rodgers and Hart, Time for Two, Tea for Two, In a Mellowtone (Grammy nomination 1990), At Vine St. Live, Mello'Day, Live at the City, Angel Eyes, The Night Has a Thousand Eyes, The Rules of the Road, Jazz Masters, Skylark, Swingtime in Hawaii, SS 'Wonderful (Carnegie Hall), Jazz Past Midnight, Compact Jazz, Let Me Off Uptown, The Complete Verve/Cleff Sessions, Ultimate Anita O'Day, After Midnight, Hi-Ho Trailus Bootwhip, Legends of the Swing Era, The Legacy Lives On, Finest Hour, Complete Signature and London Recordings, The Young Anita, Still Swinging, Indestructible, Live at Basin St. West. Jazz Masters fellow Nat. Endowment for Arts, 1997, Nat. Endowment fellowship; inductee Jazz Hall of Fame, Tampa, 1997. Mem. AFTRA, BMI, Screen Actors Guild. Office: 1010 Hillcroft Rd Glendale CA 91207-1542 Office Phone: 818-507-8918. E-mail: aeichler@earthlink.net.

O'DAY, KATHLEEN M., federal official, lawyer; Assoc. to dep. gen. counsel Fed. Res. Sys., Washington. Office: Fed Res Sys Bd Mems Office 20th & C Sts NW Ofc Washington DC 20551-0001

ODDI, MARIE CAPORALE, educational administrator; b. New Haven, July 27, 1927; d. Michael and Rose (Monaco) Caporale; B.A. cum laude, Brown U., 1949; M.S., So. Conn. State U., 1968, postgrad., 1974—; m. Frank Oddi, Apr. 2, 1951; children— Laura, Frank, Elissa. Service rep. So. New Eng. Tel. Co., New Haven, 1949-54; tchr. Hamden (Conn.) Public Schs., 1964-73, prin. Hamden Public Schs., 1973-87; prin. Beecher Rd. Sch., Woodbridge, Conn. 1987—92; mem. consortium for study for sch. needs of children from one-parent families Charles Kettering Found. and Nat. Assn. Elem. Sch. Prins.; grant reader NEH; curriculum adv. and developer. Mem. Elem. and Middle Sch. Prins. Assn. of Conn. (recipient Joseph J. Formica Disting. Service award 1980, Pres.'s award 1978, 79, 81, 82, 84), Nat. Assn. Elem. Sch. Prins., Assn. Hamden Public Sch. Adminstrs., Adminstrn. and Supervision Assn. of So. Conn. State Colls., LWV Phi Delta Kappa (pres. So. Conn. State Coll. chpt. 1981-82), Delta Kappa Gamma. Author: (with Gilbert Rebhun) Looking in on an Open Space Classroom; contbr. articles in field to profl. jours.; editor Elem. and Middle Sch. Prins. Assn. of Conn. News Forum, 1978-82. Home: 26 Parmalee Dr Hamden CT 06514-2008

O'DEA, SUZANNE DORES, author; b. Sioux City, Iowa, Jan. 1, 1950; d. William Joseph and Lois Darlene (Riediger) O'Dea; children: William O'Dea Schenken, Marguerite-Louise O'Dea Schenken. BA, Upper Iowa U., Fayette, 1978; MA, Iowa State U., 1987, PhD, 1992. Lobbyist, Petroleum Marketers of Iowa, Des Moines, 1985; adj. faculty Simpson Coll., 2002-04; mem. adv. com. Inst. Women's Policy Rsch., pres., 2001-02. Author: Citizen Lobbying in Iowa, 1981, Legislators and Politicians, 1995, Iowa Women of Achievement, 1996, From Suffrage to the Senate, 1999; columnist Sioux City Jour., 1984. Vol. coord. Iowa ERA Coalition, 1980; campaign mgr. ERA Iowa, 1992; cons. ERA Com., Iowa, 1998; bd. dirs. The White House Project, 1998-2004. Recipient Christine Wilson medal, Iowa Commn.on the Status of Women. Mem. Friends of the Iowa Commn. on the Status of Women (pres. 1995-2004, Christine Wilson medal for Equality and Justice, 2000). Republican. Lutheran. Avocation: gardening. Home: 567 Cape Rd Mckinleyville CA 95519 E-mail: suzodea@mac.com.

ODELBO, CATHERINE G., publishing executive; BA in Am. History with gen. honors, U. Chgo., 1985, MBA with honors, 2000. Mut. fund analyst Morningstar, Inc., Chgo., 1988-91, editor closed-end funds, 1991-95, pub. equities group, 1995-97, v.p. retail markets, 1997-98, sr. v.p. content devel., 1998-99; pres. Morningstar.com., 2000—. Mem. Phi Beta Kappa. Avocations: bridge, movies, reading. Office: Morningstar Inc 225 W Wacker Dr Chicago IL 60606-1224

O'DELL, JOAN ELIZABETH, lawyer, mediator, consumer products company executive, educator; b. East Dubuque, Ill., May 3, 1932; d. Peter Emerson and Olive (Bonnet) O'Dell; children: Dominique R., Nicole L. BA cum laude, U. Miami, 1956, JD, 1958. Bar: Fla. 1958, D.C. 1974, Ill. 1978, Va. 1987, U.S. Supreme Ct. 1972; lic. real estate broker Ill., Va., W.Va., cert. D.C. Trial atty. SEC, Washington, 1959-60; asst. state atty. Office State Atty., Miami, Fla., 1960-64; asst. county atty. Dade County Atty.'s Office, Miami, 1964-70; county atty. Palm Beach County Atty.'s Office, West Palm Beach, Fla., 1970-71; regional gen. counsel Region IV EPA, Atlanta, 1971-73, assoc. gen. counsel Washington, 1973-77; sr. counsel Nalco Chem. Co., Oakbrook, Ill., 1977-78; v.p., gen. counsel Angel Mining, Washington and Tenn., 1979-96; pres. S.W. Land Investments, Miami, 1979-88; v.p. Events U.S.A., Washington, 1990—. Mem. Exec. Women's Coun., Tucson, 1982—85; co-chmn. sch. improvement coun. Harpers Ferry Jr. HS, 2000—04; bd. dirs. Tucson Women's Found., 1982—84, U. Ariz. Bus. and Profl. Women's Club, Tucson, 1981—85, LWV, Tucson, 1981—85, pres., 1984—85, chmn. nat. security study, bd. dirs. Palm Beach County, Fla., 1990—92, Jefferson County Visitors and Conv. Bur., Harpers Ferry, W.Va., 2001—. Mem.: Ill. Bar Assn., Va. State Bar Assn., DC Bar Assn., Fla. Bar Assn. Avocations: camping, hiking, skiing. Office Phone: 304-724-1763. Personal E-mail: treetopsjodell@adelphia.net.

O'DELL, LISA A., elementary school educator; b. Galesburg, Ill., May 10, 1961; d. Edward Andrew and Una Arillis Bowman; m. Craig Warren O'Dell, July 5, 1986; 1 child, Michael Craig. BS in Edn., Ill. State U., Normal, 1983, MS in Ednl. Adminstrn., 2003. Spl. edn. tchr., K-12 Lee Ctr. Dist. 271, Paw Paw, Ill., 1983—86; mid. sch. and spl. edn. tchr. Dimmick Dist. # 175, Peru, Ill., 1986—90; tchr. 4th grade McLean County Unit # 5, Normal, Ill., 1992—. Co-chmn. sch. inclusion com., Normal, 2001—04; mem. sch. dist. evaluation com., Normal, 1998—2001; mem. spl. edn. assessment com., Normal, 2000—04; presenter workshops, 1998—2001; chmn. sch. edn. com. McLean County Unit #5, 2002—05. Grantee Beyond the Books Found., Normal, 1996, 1997, 2000, 2005. Mem.: NEA, Alpah Delta Kappa. Office: Fairview Elem Sch 416 Fairview St Normal IL 61761 Office Phone: 309-452-4491. E-mail: odellla@unit5.org.

O'DELL, NANCY, television personality; b. Myrtle Beach, SC; d. Leonard and Betty Humphries; m. Richard O'Dell (separated). Grad, Clemson U. Reporter, anchor WPDE-TV, Myrtle Beach, SC; morning news anchor, crime reporter WCBD-TV, Charleston; co-anchor, investigative reporter WTVJ-TV, Miami; entertainment reporter A Current Affair, 1995—96; weekend coanchor, weekday corr. Access Hollywood, 1996—99, co-anchor, 1999—; host Nashville Star, USA Network, 2003—. Contbr. reports NBC News's The Today Show and Dateline; host Emmys Pre-Show, Fox, 1999, Emmys Pre-Show, ABC, 2000; co-host Emmys Post Show, NBC, 2002, Hollywood Christmas Parade, 1999, 2000, 02, Tournament of Roses Parade coverage, NBC, 2001, 02, 03, 04, Golden Globes Arrivals Show, NBC, 2002, 03, 04, Miss USA, 2004. Actress (films) Scream 2, 1997, The Adventures of Ragtime, 1998, The Bachelor, 1999, Scream 3, 2000, Outta Time, 2002, (TV series) General Hospital, 1998, Days of Our Lives, 2002—03. Mem. Nat. Celebrity

Cabinet, Am. Red Cross, 2002—; internat. bd. mem Best Buddies; Celebrity Amb. Childhelp USA; spokesperson March of Dimes. Named State SC Hall of Fame, 1998; recipient 2 AP Awards, 2 Soc. Profl. Journalists Awards, Spirit of Leadership Award, Best Buddies, 2002. Office: Access Hollywood NBC Studios 3000 W Alameda Ave Burbank CA 91523

O'DELL, PATSY JUNE, art gallery director; b. Wenatchee, Wash., June 27, 1936; d. Claude Woodrow Martin and Ethel Edna Boyd-Martin; m. Robert F. O'Dell, Mar. 24, 1956; children: Cathy J. Hogan, Cindy J. Wilken, Carol O'Dell-Forgey. BA in Art Edn., Ctrl. Wash. Coll. Edn., Ellensburg, 1958. Mem. office staff Renton (Wash.) Sch. Dist., 1966—69, Kent (Wash.) United Meth. Ch., 1974—79; mem. dist. office staff Boy Scouts Am., Walla Walla, Wash., 1969—72, Camp Fire Orgn. King County, Seattle, 1972—73; bd. dirs. Vols. South King County United Way, Seattle, 1979—89; treas., bd. dirs., pres. Seahurst Art Gallery, Burien, Wash., 1989—. Bd. dirs., coord. Renton River Artists Area, 1972—2005; active Girl Scouts, PTA; fundraiser various orgns.; active Discover Burien Assn., 2000—. Recipient Outstanding Svc. award, Renton River Days, 2005, Charlotte Joy Fansworth award, Seattle/King County Camp Fire, 1973. Mem.: Olde Burien Merchants Assn. (treas./sec. 2003—), Renton Creative Arts (treas. 1972—). Avocations: community arts functions, pets. Home and Office: 15775 118th Pl SE Renton WA 98058-4658

O'DELL, TONJA RENEE, primary school educator; b. Sevierville, Tenn., May 5, 1970; d. H. Burnett O'Dell and Freda Louise Hodges, Kenneth Watson Hodges (Stepfather). BS, East Tenn. State U., Johnson City, 1992; MEd, Carson-Newman Coll., Jefferson City, Tenn., 1996; EdS, Lincoln Meml. U., Harrogate, Tenn., 1996. Tchr. Pigeon Forge Primary Sch., Sevierville, 1993—. Dir. Vacation Bible Sch., Kodak, Tenn., 2002—04; vol. Alzheimer's Memory Walk, Pigeon Forge, 2002—05. Mem.: NEA, Internat. Reading Assn. Methodist. Avocation: scrapbooks. Office: Pigeon Forge Primary Sch 1766 Waldens Creek Rd Sevierville TN 37862

ODEM, JOYCE MARIE, human resources specialist; b. Des Moines, Mar. 21, 1936; d. Robert Gibson and Minnie Anna (Godown) Hague; m. Phillip Wayne Odem, May 23, 1954; children: Vickie, Phillip, Beth, Amy, Keith. Student, Merced C.C., 1976-78. Legal sec. C. Ray Robinson, Merced, Calif., 1959-60; office mgr., legal aid Kane & Canelo, Merced, Calif., 1960-65; recorder disciplinary control bd. U.S. Army Civil Svc., Okinawa, Japan, 1965-69; legal aid, office mgr. Courtney & Sharrow, Merced, 1969-72; adminstr. USAF Civil Svc., Okinawa, 1972-75; asst. indsl. rels. mgr. Maracay Mills Divsn. Mohasco, Merced, 1975-78; safety dir., personnel mgr. Keller Industries, Merced, 1978-83; mgr. employee rels. McLane Pacific, Merced, 1983-85; corp. dir. human resources McLane Co., Inc., Temple, Tex., 1983—2002; v.p. people dept. McLane Foodservice, Carrollton, Tex., 2002—. Mem. adv. bd. Pvt. Industry Coun., Merced, 1980-85. Mem. Cen. Tex. Human Resource Mgrs. Assn. (adv. coun.), Soc. Human Resource Mgrs. Avocations: sporting clays, golf, hunting. Office: McLane Foodservice Inc 2085 Midway Rd Carrollton TX 75006 Office Phone: 972-364-2078.

ODEN, GLORIA, language educator, poet; b. Yonkers, N.Y., Oct. 30, 1923; d. Redmond Stanley and Ethel (Kincaid) Oden. BA in History, Howard U., 1944, JD, 1948. Faculty New Sch. for Social Rsch., N.Y.C., 1966; vis. lectr. dept. English SUNY, Stony Brook, 1969-70; asst. prof. English U. Md., Balt., 1971—75, assoc. prof., 1975—83, prof., 1983—96. Sr. editor IEEE proc. and tech. mags., 1966—67; supr. math./sci. books Appleton-Century-Crofts, 1967—68; project dir. lang. arts books Hold, Rinehart and Winston, 1968—72, sr. editor coll. dept., 1968—71; editor Am. Inst. Physics/Am. Jour. Physics, 1961—66; lectr. in field; condr. numerous poetry readings; juror fiction panel Mass. Cultural Coun., 1994; juror poetry panel N.J. State Coun., 1993, 94; numerous others; cons. Reel Deal Prodns. Co., NEH, 1984, 87. Author: (poems) Resurrections, 1978, The Tie that Binds, 1980, Appearances, 2003; contbr. poetry to mags., newspapers, audio, anthologies, articles to profl. jours. Recipient Disting. Black Women's award, Towson U., 1984; NEH Summer grantee, 1974, Breadloaf Writers scholar, 1960, Creative Writing fellow, John Hay Whitney Found., 1955—56, Yaddo fellow, 1956. Mem.: PEN Am. Ctr., Poetry Soc. Am. (bd. govs. 1981—82, v.p. 1983—84). Home: 707 Maiden Choice Ln Apt 8119 Catonsville MD 21228-4185

O'DESKY, ILYSE HOPE, psychologist, educator; b. Newark, Oct. 27, 1964; d. Sheldon O'Desky and Leona Brenner; m. Leonard Brian Garber, June 28, 1992. D of Clin. Psychology, Yeshiva U., Bronx, 1992. Asst. prof. Kean U., Union, NJ, 2001—; pediatric neuropsychologist Neuropsychological Testing Ctr., Springfield, 2003—. Med. staff St. Barnabas Med. Ctr., Livingston, NJ, 1997—. Invited spkr. Nat. NLD Orgn., San Francisco, 2006. Recipient Rschr. Yr. award, NJ Psychol. Assn., 2003; grantee, Kean U., 2001—02, 2005—06. Mem.: APA, NJ Psychol. Assn. (sec. to academic and sci. affairs com. 2003—06), NJ Neuropsychological Soc. (exec. bd. 2002—04), Nat. Acad. Neuropsychology. Achievements include patents for Thinking Board Game Line by Line; Board Game Boxed In; research in Overdiagnosis of Attention Deficit/Hyperactivity Disorder; Misdiagnosis of ADHD and NLD. Office: 26 Linden Avenue Springfield NJ 07081 Office Phone: 973-376-5511.

ODNOPOSOFF, BERTHE HUBERMAN, musician; b. Paris; m. Adolfo Odnoposoff (dec.). MusB, Ministry Edn. Music tchr. U. Puerto Rico; piano faculty U. North Tex., 1976—. Musician (pianist): UNT Summer Music Inst., Beetoven's Tripple Concerto, 1987. Named an hon. Citizen Goodwill Ambassador, City of Houston, 1980. Mem.: Denton Music Tchrs. Assn. (Collegiate Tchr. Year 2000), Nat. Guild of Piano (hon. Tchr. Hall of Fame 1987), Phi Beta Delta. Home: 1012 Longridge Dr Denton TX 76205

O'DOHERTY, KATHLEEN MARIE, library director; b. May 25, 1950; d. Thomas and Elizabeth Theresa (Keleher) O'D; m. Shaheen Mozaffar, Dec. 7, 1991. BA, Northeastern U., 1973; MS, Simmons Coll., 1979. Asst. reference libr., asst. cataloguer Woburn Pub. Libr., 1977-79; cataloguer Bradford (Mass.) Coll., 1979-81, libr. dir., 1981-83, Brooks Sch., North Andover, Mass., 1983-85, Woburn Pub. Libr., 1986—. Vol. mem. Woburn Mcpl. Fed. Credit Union, 1996—. Author: Images of America, 2000. Mem. Cable Adv. Com. Woburn, 1997—, Violence Prevention Task Force, Woburn, 1994—; judge Pub. Speaking contest, Woburn H.S., 1987-95. Mem. ALA, Minuteman Libr. Network (sec. 1996-97, exec. bd. 1998-99), Friends of Woburn Pub. Libr. (founder), Rotary Club of Woburn (sec. 1996-99). Home: 3 Lewis Rd Apt 5 Winchester MA 01890-2533 Office: Woburn Pub Libr 45 Pleasant St Woburn MA 01801-4135

ODOM, JANET LYNN, post-anesthesia nurse; b. Columbia, Miss., Sept. 21, 1952; BSN, Miss. Coll., 1975; MS in Nursing Svc. Adminstrn., U. So. Miss., 1989. Lic. nurse, Miss., Ky.; cert. post-anesthesia nurse; cert. instr. ACLS, BLS, Am. Heart Assn. Staff nurse med.-surg. unit Marion County Gen. Hosp., Columbia, Miss., 1975; staff nurse intensive care nursery Humana Hosp.-Audubon (formerly St. Joseph Infirmary), Louisville, 1975-77, head nurse intensive care nursery, 1977-80, staff nurse intensive care nursery, 1982-83, nurse mgr. recovery rm., 1983-86; staff nurse newborn nursery Gulf Coast Community Hosp., Panama City, Fla., 1980-81; staff nurse intensive care nursery, pediatrics Forrest Gen. Hosp., Hattiesburg, Miss., 1986, staff nurse cardiovascular recovery rm., 1987, staff nurse pre and post-anesthesia care, outpatient surgery facility, 1988-89, clin. dir. ob-gyn. post partum, pediatrics, L&D, L&D PACU, WBN, ICN, 1989-90, clin. nurse specialist surg. svcs., 1990—, mem. nurse practice coun., 1990—. Nat. spkr., presenter in field; cons. Nursing Solutions ASPAN Lecture Series, 1992—. Contbr. chpts. to several books; editl. cons. Jour. Post Anesthesia Nursing, 1990, 1994-95; revision reviewer, contbr. articles to profl. jours. Com. mem. United Way Humana Hosp.-Audubon, Louisville, 1984, 85; mem. health care adv. bd. to Congressman Gene Taylor, 1992-94; trustee ASPAN Found., 1993-94, pres., 1995— Mem. ANA, AORN, Am. Soc. of Post Anesthesia Nurses (pres. 1992-93, chair membership com. 1989-90, chair pub. rels./mktg. com. 1990-91, liaison to Am. Soc. Anesthesiologists 1992-93, nat. conf. com. 1990—, ad hoc editor search com. 1992-93, v.p./present elect 1991-92, liaison to Nat. Fedn. for Nursing Specialty Orgns. 1991-92, adminstrv. rep. long range planning com. 1991-92, rep. to ANA task force on standards and guidelines 1991-92, ad hoc exhibit contract com. 1991-92, mem. rsch. com. 1994—), Miss. Nurses Assn. (nominating com. 1990-91, Clin. Nurse Specialist of Yr. 1993), Ky. Soc. of Post Anesthesia Nurses, Miss. Soc. of Post Anesthesia Nurses (mem. com. 1989-90, nat. dir. ASPAN 1988-91), Sigma Theta Tau (Gamma Lambda chpt.), Phi Kappa Phi, Miss. Coll. Alumni Assn. (Hattiesburg area chpt. v.p. 1988-89, pres. 1989-90). Office: Forrest County Gen Hosp PO Box 16389 6051 U S Highway 49 Hattiesburg MS 39401-7200

ODOM, JUDY, software company executive; b. 1952; BBA in Acctg., Tex. Tech. U., 1974. CPA. With Coopers & Lybrand, Dallas, 1974-76, Grant Thornton, Dallas, 1976-85; co-founder, owner Software Spectrum, 1983—2002, CEO, 1988—2002. Bd. dirs. Storage Tek, Leggett & Platt Inc., Harte-Hanks Inc. Named to, Computer Reseller News Industry Hall of Fame, 2003.

ODOM, MARSHA MCCLELLAND, elementary school educator; d. Elizabeth Moren and Edward Lee McClelland; m. Larry Von Odom, Oct. 19, 1973; children: Justin Larry, Ryan Hunter. A in Music Edn., Chowan Coll., Murfreesboro, NC, 1973; B in Music Edn., Coll. William and Mary, Williamsburg, Va., 1976; M in Elem. Edn., Old Dominion U., Norfolk, Va., 1986. Cert. tchr. Va. Music tchr. Walsingham Acad., Williamsburg, 1976—80, Poquoson (Va.) Mid./HS, 1980—81, Southwestern Elem. Sch., Suffolk, Va., 1989—95, Smithfield (Va.) HS, 1995—2005, Westside Elem. Sch., Smithfield, 2005—. Choir dir. Benn's United Meth. Ch., Smithfield, 1990, Hilton Christian Ch., Newport News, Va. Avocations: swimming, reading, singing. Home: 208 Wainwright Dr Smithfield VA 23430 Office: Westside Elem Sch 800 Main St Smithfield VA 23430 Office Phone: 757-357-3021.

ODOM, MARY E. (LIBBY ODOM), musician, educator; b. Mobile, Ala., Dec. 18, 1928; d. Frederick and Bertha (Summers) Yost; m. Gerald Stuart Odom, Sept. 3, 1947 (dec. Oct. 1997); 1 child, Maria Renee. BS cum laude, U. Ala., 1980, MA in Edn., 1982. Voice tchr., accompanist Madame Rose Palmai Studio, Mobile, Ala., 1944-50; voice and piano tchr. Birmingham, Ala., 1954-64; music therapist State Sch. for Girls, Springville, Ala., 1951-57; voice and theory tchr. Meridian (Miss.) Jr. Coll., 1964-68; voice and piano tchr. Birmingham, 1968-88. Performer Mobile Opera Guild, Mobile Opera Workshop, 1943-53, Carnegie Hall, 1947, Met. Opera, N.Y.C., 1950-52, Boris Goldovsky Opera, W.Va., 1952-53, Town and Gown Little Theatre, Birmingham, 1953-73. Co-founder Mobile Opera Guild, 1943, Birmingham Civic Opera, 1955, Birmingham Civic Chorus, 1964; choir soloist Govt. St. Meth. Ch., Ctrl. Presbyn. Ch., Mobile, 1943-49, choir soloist, children's choir Ind. Presbyn. Ch., Birmingham, 1953-64; soloist, youth choir dir. Mountain Brook Presbyn. Ch., Birmingham, 1968-78; ch. organist Riverchase Presbyn. Ch., Birmingham, 1980-84, co-founder Active Elders, 1983; chmn., v.p. Birmingham Opera Guild, 1958—; mem. Salvation Army Women's Aux., 1989—; chorus dir. Shades Valley Music Club, 1980—. Recipient Cert. Appreciation Presbytery of Sheppards and Lapsley, Presbyn. Ch. USA, 1991, Riverchase Presbyn. Ch., 1999. Mem. AAUW, Ala. Fedn. Music Club (officer 1953—, Odom scholarship 1999, parliamentarian, past state pres.), Shades Valley Music Club (2d v.p. for programs), Birmingham Music Club Guild (publicity chmn., bd. dirs. 1964-68, guest artist 1953—), Delta Omicron, Kappa Delta Pi. Avocations: gardening, reading, programs for senior citizens, cooking. Home: 3804 Briar Oak Dr Birmingham AL 35243-4834

ODOM, MARYANN BELL, secondary school educator; b. Greenwood, Miss., Apr. 26, 1928; d. Van Amintus and Fannie Tennyson Bell; m. Troy Lee Odom, Mar. 5, 1949 (dec.); children: Ellen Odom Rogers, Troy Lee Jr. BS in Edn., Delta State U., Cleve., Miss., 1949. English tchr. Margaret Green Jr. HS, Cleveland, Miss., 1960—65, Cleveland HS, 1965—70, Bayou Acad., Boyle, Miss., 1970—. Contbr. poetry, articles to profl. publs. Leader Bible study Boliver County Correctional Ctr., 2006. Named Queen, Cleveland Jr. Aux. Charity Ball, 1989, Star Tchr., Cleveland's Favorite Tchr.; recipient People's Choice award, 2006. Mem.: DAR, Cleveland Woman's Club. Baptist. Home: 612 Odom Rd Cleveland MS 38732 Office: Bayou Acad Crosby Rd Cleveland MS 38732

ODOM, TERI WANG, chemist; BS in chemistry, Stanford U., 1996; AM in chemistry, Harvard U., 1999, PhD in chemical physics, 2001, postdoctoral rsch., 2001—02. Asst. prof. dept. chemistry Northwestern U. Contbr. articles in profl. jours. Named one of Top 100 Young Innovators, MIT Tech. Review, 2004; recipient Prize for Young Chemists, IUPAC, 2001, Top Prize, Australian Jour. Chemistry, 2001, Victor K. LaMer award, ACS, 2003, Career award, NSF, 2004, NUE award, 2004; fellow, David and Lucille Packard, 2003; postdoctoral fellowship, NIH NRSA, 2001, Searle fellow, 2003. Mem.: Phi Beta Kappa. Office: Northwestern U Dept Chemistry 2145 Sheridan Rd Evanston IL 60208 Business E-Mail: todom@northwestern.edu.

O'DONNELL, ANGELA GINA, literature and language professor, writer; b. Wilkes-Barre, Pa., Apr. 13, 1960; d. Charles Francis Alaimo and Marian Mary Salvi; m. Brennan Patrick O'Donnell; children: Charles Brennan, Patrick Aloysius, William Michael. BA, Pa. State U., State College, 1981; MA, U. NC, Chapel Hill, 1987. Affililiate faculty English dept, Loyola Coll., Balt., 1987—2005, dir. affiliate faculty, 2003—05; asst. to v.p. academic affairs for academic programming Fordham U., Bronx, NY, 2005—06, affiliate faculty English dept., 2005—. Author: (poetry) Jesuits (finalist Foley Poetry award, 2004), The Net, Elegy for the Mother of a Nameless Child, Grandmother's Pears, Dante in the Kitchen, Sixth Grade Dance, Druscilla's Dance, Waking the Children, Fool's Art, Lost and Found, TWIN, The First Art, The Oldest Art, LIES, On Reading Anne Sexton, Other Mothers, Saints' Lives, Glitter Makes Everything Better, Tattoo, Falling for Texas, Breaker, Northern Nights, The Conversation, Oberammergau at Dusk, Kind Ground, Waiting for Ecstacy, Late Elegy, December Roll Call, New Years' Poem, Welcome to Baltimore, Hon, At Mass with Emily, Grandma's Hands, The Price of Poetry, Nuns in the Zone, Hopkins in Ireland, Home Geometrics, Coming and Going, Manet's Oranges, The Last Dance; contbr. articles to profl. jours. Participant inaugural JustFaith seminar St. Francis of Assisi, Balt., 2003—04. Grantee, Loyola Coll. Ctr. for the Humanities, 1999, 2001, 2002, 2004. Democrat. Roman Catholic. Office: Fordham U Dept English 441 E Fordham Rd Bronx NY 10458 Business E-Mail: aodonnell@fordham.edu.

O'DONNELL, ANNE U., dietician; d. William Marion and Marion Arnold McManus; m. Robert O'Donnell, Oct. 10, 1981; children: Emily, Kate. BA in Math., U. Calif., Santa Cruz, 1974; MPH, U. Calif., Berkeley, 1983, MS in Nutrition, 1984. Registered dietitian. Nutrition cons., Santa Rosa, Calif., 1986—90; faculty Santa Rosa Jr. Coll., 1988—. Adj. instr. City Coll. San Francisco, 1984—86, U. Calif., Berkeley, 1985—87. Contbr. articles to profl. jours. Mem.: Am. Dietetic Assn., Calif. Dietetic Assn. (mem. edn. coun. 2003—). Office: Santa Rosa Jr Coll 1501 Mendocino Ave Santa Rosa CA 95401

O'DONNELL, DENISE ELLEN, lawyer, former prosecutor; BS in Polit. Sci., Canisius Coll., 1968; MSW, SUNY, Buffalo, 1973, JD summa cum laude, 1982. Bar: NY 1983, U.S. Dist. Ct. (we., no., ea. and so. dists.) NY, U.S. Ct. Appeals (2d cir.), U.S. Supreme Ct. Law clk. to Hon. M. Dolores Denman NY Appellate Divsn. 4th Dept., Buffalo, 1982-85; asst. U.S. atty. (we. dist.) NY, US Dept Justice, Buffalo, 1985-90, appellate chief, 1990-93, 1st asst. U.S. atty., 1993—97, U.S. atty., 1997-2001; ptnr. Gen. Litigation Practice Group, Hodgson, Russ, LLP, Buffalo, 2001—. Part-time instr. trial technique program SUNY, 1990—2002; lectr. ethics, evidence and trial practice Office Legal Edn.U.S. Dept. Justice, 1988—2000; lectr. NITA seminar Western NY Trial Acad., 1994, 98; mem. Atty. Gen.'s Adv. Com., 1999—2001, vice-chair, 2000—01; trustee SUNY Buffalo Found. Mem. Vol. Lawyers Program, 1997—2001; bd. dirs. NCCJ, 2000—; trustee SUNY Buffalo Found., 2004—; sec. Nat. Women's Hall of Fame, 2001—04, bd. dirs., 2001—. Fellow: N.Y. State Bar Found.; mem.: ABA, Nat. Assn. Former U.S. Attys. (bd. dirs.), Western NY Trial Lawyers Assn., Women's Bar Assn. State NY (founding mem. Western NY chpt. 1985), Bar Assn. Erie County (dep. treas. 1992—93, treas. 1993—94), West Side Rowing Club. Office: Hodgson Russ LLP One M&T Plz Ste 2000 Buffalo NY 14203-2931 Office Phone: 716-848-1314. Business E-Mail: dodonnel@hodgsonruss.com.

O'DONNELL, DUCK HEE, cellist, music teacher; b. Seoul, Korea, Dec. 30, 1938; came to U.S., 1963; d. Kap Cho and Hei Sun (Kim) Lee; m. Edward O'Donnell, Aug. 31, 1968; children: Edward, Helen, Nancy. BS in Music, Seoul Nat. U., 1960; Diploma, U. Cin., 1968. Cellist Fla. Gulf Coast Symphony Orch., Tampa, 1968-71; pvt. music tchr. Rockville, Md., 1976—; cellist Friday Morning Music Club, Washington, 1976—. Recipient Tchr. of Yr. award Md. String Tchrs. Assn., 1998. Mem. Music Tchrs. Assn. Am., Md. Music Tchrs. Assn., Friday Morning Music Club. Home: 6 Cleveland Ct Rockville MD 20850-3719

O'DONNELL, ELISABETH PALLANT, social studies educator; b. Cleve., May 17, 1947; d. Kenyon Allen and Elisabeth Horvath Pallant; m. Paul Regis O'Donnell, Feb. 3, 1984; 1 child, Thomas Paul Theodore. MA, John Carroll U., University Heights, Ohio, 1975. Cert. Fla. Dept. Edn., 2006. Tchr. A. Philip Randolph Academies, Jacksonville, Fla., 1984—. Involved with voter registeration drives, Jacksonville, 2003—. Named Tchr. of Yr., A. Philip Randolph Academies, 2004. Mem.: Fla. Social Studies Tchrs. Home: 6831 Cartegena Ct Jacksonville FL 32210 Office: A Philip Randolph Academies 1157 Golfair Blvd Jacksonville FL 32208 Office Phone: 904-924-3011. Business E-Mail: odonnelle@educationcentral.org.

O'DONNELL, ELIZABETH D., music educator; b. Ames, Iowa, Mar. 7, 1980; d. David and Judy Eggers; m. Joseph O'Donnell. BS in Instrumental Music Edn., NW Mo. State U., Maryville, 2002; MEd, Mid Am. Nazarene U., Olathe, Kans., 2005. Cert. K-12 instrumental music tchr. Kans., 2002. Band tchr. Westridge Mid. Sch., Overland Park, Kans., 2002—. Pvt. music tchr. Mem.: Music Educator's Nat. Conf., Kans. Music Educators Assn., Sigma Alpha Iota, Kappa Kappa Psi. Office Phone: 913-993-1279.

O'DONNELL, JANET COSTA, secondary school educator; b. Bridgeport, Conn., June 25, 1955; d. Shirley Wells Dearstyne and Anthony Costa; m. Thomas Edward O'Donnell, Apr. 12, 1987; children: Sean Matthew, Mary Kathryn. BS, Fairfield U., Conn., 1977, MEd, 1980; postgrad., SCSU, New Haven, Conn., 1999—2000. Cert. edn. profl. Conn., 1993. Dir. Bushy Hill Nature Ctr., Ivoryton, Conn., 1981—83; tchr., naturalist Conn. Audubon Soc., Fairfield, Conn., 1983—88; sci., math instrnl. aide Middlesex Mid. Sch., Darien, Conn., 1990—94; tchr. Amity Regional Dist. #5, Woodbridge, Conn., 1994—. Vestry mem. St. Paul's Episcopal Ch., Fairfield, 2002—05. Mem.: Conn. Edn. Assn. (assoc.). D-Liberal. Episcopalian. Avocations: reading, swimming. Home: 37 Hemlock Tr Trumbull CT 06611 Office: Amity High Sch Newton Rd Woodbridge CT 06545 Office Phone: 203-397-4178.

O'DONNELL, KATHLEEN C., artist; b. Clifton, N.J., Nov. 15, 1919; d. George Francis and Alvina Rose (Munzell) Denzel; m. John Joseph O'Donnell, Feb. 17, 1942; children: John Joseph, Sharon Rose. BA cum laude, Montclair (N.J.) State Coll. Designer Denzell Mfg. Co., Passaic, NJ, 1937—38, clk., 1939—41; sec. Marschalk Ins., Clifton, NJ, 1941—42; clk. The Fair, Passaic, 1968—69; designer Arise Ministry, Lakewood, NJ, 1983—91; assoc. N.J. Bell, Clifton & Totowa, NJ, 1969—85. One-woman shows include Dwight Eisenhower Libr., Totowa, 1982, No. Lights Art Gallery, Clifton, 1985, YWHA, 1988, Fine Arts Ctr., Passaic, 1988, Denville Libr., 2003, Roxbury Pub. Libr., 2005, exhibited in group shows at Fine Arts Ctr., Passaic, 1983, 1988, Willowbrook Mall, Wayne, N.J., 1984, YWHA, Clifton, 1985, Clifton Libr., 1988, The Nathan's Art Gallery, West Paterson, N.J., 1994, Montclair Country Club, 1994, Montclair State U., 1995, 1998, Westbeth Gallery, N.Y.C., 1996, Caldwell (N.J.) Women's Club, 1999, Botto House, Haledon, N.J., 1999, Clifton Arts Ctr., N.J., 2001, Hamilton House, Clifton, 2002, Clifton Arts Ctr., 2003, 2004, Pub. Libr. Twp. of Roxbury, 2005, Roxbury Township Pub. Libr., 2005, 2006, The Atrium Gallery, Morris County Adminstrn. and Records Bldg., 2006, represented in numerous pvt. collections. Mem.: Roxbury Assn. Art, Clifton Assn. Artists, Bell Atlantic Pioneers. Roman Catholic.

O'DONNELL, KATHLEEN MARIE, lawyer; b. Methuen, Mass., Dec. 16, 1955; d. John Joseph and Helen Miriam (McCormack) O'D. BA magna cum laude, Wheaton Coll., Norton, Mass., 1977; JD cum laude, Suffolk U., 1980. Bar: Mass. 1981, U.S. Dist. Ct. Mass. 1982, U.S. Ct. Appeals (1st cir.) 1982. Instr. Suffolk U., Boston, 1980-82; assoc. Law Office Albert J. Marcotte, Lowell, Mass., 1982—. Bd. dirs. Greater Lowell Pastoral Gounseling Ctr., 1987—, Greater Lowell Rape Crisis Ctr., Sohier Park Com., York, Maine, 1989—, co-chair, 1991—; bd. govs. Mass. Acad. Trial Attys. Mem. ABA, Mass. Bar Assn. (v.p. 2001, treas. 2002, pres.-elect 2003, pres. 2004), Mass. Acad. Trial Attys.(treas. 1995, pres. 1996), Greater Lowell Bar Assn. (treas. 1987, sec. 1988, v.p. 1989, pres. 1990), Assn. of Trial Lawyers of Am., Am. Bd. Trial Advocates, Phi Delta Phi. Democrat. Roman Catholic. Office: Law Office Albert Marcotte 45 Merrimack St Lowell MA 01852-1729

O'DONNELL, KATHLEEN MARIE, lawyer; b. San Diego, Jan. 2, 1952; d. James Joseph and Patricia Ann (Dunne) O'D. AB, Boston Coll., 1974; JD, U. Miami, 1977. Bar: Mass. 1978. Title atty. Lawyers Title Ins. Corp., Boston, 1979-85; assoc. Hay & Dailey, Boston, 1985-86, DiCara, Selig, Sawyer & Holt, Boston, 1986-87, Ropes & Gray, Boston, 1987-92; ptnr. Dillingham & O'Donnell, Boston, 1992-97, Kopelman & Paige, P.C., Boston, 1997—. Adj. prof. Boston U., 1995-97. Editor: Handling Residential Real Estate In Mass., 1996. Mem.: Mass. Bar Assn. (chair property law sect. 2005—06), Real Estate Bar Assn. Mass. (bd. dirs. 1995—2003, pres. 2001), New Eng. Women in Real Estate, Dedham (Mass.) Choral Soc. (pres.), Cohasset Yacht Club, The Abstract Club, Larchmont Yacht Club. Roman Catholic. Home: 12 Belcher Cir Milton MA 02186-5105 Office: Kopelman & Paige PC 101 Arch St Boston MA 02110 Office Phone: 617-556-0007.

O'DONNELL, RHONDA, software company executive; M in Innovation and Svc. Mgmt. Mng. dir. Global Customer Solutions, Cambridge Tech. Ptnrs.; pres. Asia Pacific Novell, Inc., 2001—, also mem. worldwide mgmt. com. Mem. Victorian Govt. Innovation Economy Bd., Victorian Govt. Purchasing Bd., Australian Inst. Co. Dirs. Recipient Victorian Bus. Women of Yr. award. Fellow: Inst. Mgmt.; mem.: Nat. Coun. Australian Inst. Customer Svc. (founding mem.), Customer Svc. Inst. Australia. Office: Novell inc 404 Wyman Ste 500 Waltham MA 02451*

O'DONNELL, ROSIE, television personality, actress, comedienne; b. Commack, NY, Mar. 21, 1962; m. Kelli Carpenter, Feb. 26, 2004; children: Parker Jaren, Chelsea Belle, Blake Christopher, Vivienne Rose. Attended, Dickinson Coll., Boston Univ. Appearances include (TV series) Gimme A Break, 1986-87, Stand By Your Man, 1992, Women Aloud, 1992, Stand-up Spotlight, VH-1 (American Comedy award nomination best female performer in a TV special 1994, Cable ACE award nomination best entertainment host 1994); (TV) host The Rosie O'Donnell Show, 1995-2002 (Daytime Emmy awards 1997, 98, 99, 2000, 2001); (TV) co-host The View, 2006-; (TV films) The Twilight of the Golds, 1997; (films) A League of Their Own, 1992, Sleepless in Seattle, 1993 (American Comedy award nomination best supporting female in a motion picture 1994), Another Stakeout, 1993 (American Comedy award nomination best actress in a motion picture 1994), Car 54, Where Are You?, 1994, I'll Do Anything, 1994, The Flintstones, 1994, Exit to Eden, 1994, Now and Then, 1995, Beautiful Girls, 1996, Harriet the Spy, 1996, A Very Brady Sequel, 1996 (uncredited), Wide Awake, 1996, Get Bruce, 1999, Jackie's Back, 1999, Tarzan, 1999 (voice), Flintstones in Viva Rock Vegas, 2000; Broadway shows include Grease, 1994, Seussical the Musical, 2001, Fiddler on the Roof, 2005; author: Find Me, 2002; editor: Rosie mag., 2000-2002; prodr.: Taboo (Broadway) 2003-2004; exec. prodr. (TV films) Kids are Punny, 1998, (films) Mina & the Family Treasure, 2004; actor, exec. prodr. (TV films) Riding the Bus with My Sister, 2005; guest appearances Ally McBeal, 1999, Third Watch, 2000, The Practice, 2000, Will & Grace, 2002, Judging Amy, 2003, Queer as Folk, 2005.

O'DONNELL RICH, DOROTHY JUANITA, small business owner; b. Midland, Pa., Aug. 31, 1934; d. William Theodore and Jennie Cecilia (Forrest) Verzella; m. Hugh Terrence O'Donnell, Aug. 9, 1958 (dec. Jan. 1987); children: Kathleen Denise O'Donnell, Suzanne Lynn O'Donnell; m. Hugh B. Rich, IV, Nov. 12, 1988. Ch. organist Blessed Virgin Mary Ch., Midland, 1948-59; sec. E.W. Bliss Co., Midland, 1952-59; tchr. piano Beaver, Pa., 1962-81; owner, bus. mgr. H.B. Rich, Media, Pa., 1988—. Mem. ways and means com. Jr. Women's Club, Midland, 1954—56; counselor Cath. Daus. Am., Midland, 1952—54; program chmn. Sr. Cath. Daus. Am., Beaver, 1958—68; mem. Midland Cath. Sodality, Italian Sons and Daus. Am., Sewickley, Pa., 1954—60. Named Jr. of the Yr., Jr. Cath. Daus., 1948. Mem.: NAFE, Red Hat Soc. Roman Catholic. Avocations: piano, walking, reading, chess, bicycling. E-mail: dot310@comcast.net.

ODORIZZI, MICHELE L., lawyer; b. Chgo., July 12, 1952; BA, Northwestern U., 1973; JD cum laude, U. Chgo., 1976. Bar: Ill. 1976, U.S. Ct. Appeals (7th cir.) 1976, U.S. Dist. Ct. (no. dist.) Ill. 1977, U.S. Supreme Ct. 1980, U.S. Ct. Appeals (4th, 9th, 10th cirs.). Ptnr. Mayer, Brown & Platt, Chgo. Office: Mayer Brown & Platt 190 S La Salle St Ste 3100 Chicago IL 60603-3441

O'DOWD, SARAH A., lawyer; b. Manchester, NH, Sept. 7, 1949; AB, Immaculata Coll., 1971; MA, Stanford U., 1973, JD, 1977. Bar: Calif. 1978. Atty. Heller, Ehrman, White & McAuliffe, Palo Alto, Calif., 1978—, managing shareholder, Silicon Valley Office, 1995—99, firmwide practice chair, mem. exec. comm., 1999—2002. Mem. ABA.

OE, EMILY NORENE, counselor, play therapist; b. Dickinson, N.D., Nov. 12, 1942; d. Nicholas George and Eunice Norene (Wilson) O. BEd, U. Alaska, Fairbanks, 1977; MA, Gonzaga U., 1978; PhD, U. North Tex., 1989. Lic. clin. profl. counselor, Idaho; registered play therapist and play therapy supr.; nat. cert. counselor. Child care worker Home of Good Shepherd, St. Paul, 1972-73; counselor Emmaus Sch. for Girls, King George, Va., 1973-74; guidance counselor Immaculate Conception Sch., Fairbanks, 1974-76, 78-80; child counselor Fairbanks Counseling and Adoption Agy., 1978-80; elem. counselor Fairbanks North Star Borough Sch. Dist., 1980-86; assoc. prof., counselor edn. Sam Houston State U., Huntsville, 1989-96; pvt. practice Huntsville, 1991-96; pvt. practice, play therapist, cons. Houston, 1995—98, Pharr, Tex., 1998—2000; agy. counselor, elem. counselor Dickinson, ND, 2000—04; agy. counselor, play therapist The Children's Ctr., Idaho Falls, Idaho, 2004—. Co-author: Counseling Program Handbook, 1993; co-editor: Kaleidoscope of Play Therapy Stories, 1996; guest editor Internat. Newsletter, 1991; contbr. articles to profl. jours. Named Counselor Educator of Yr., Tex., 1995. Mem. Am. Counseling Assn., Assn. for Play Therapy (bd. dirs. 1989-99, sec. 1989-96, 97-99), Tex. Assn. Play Therapy (Nancy Guillory award 1997), Sam Houston Assn. Play Therapy, Idaho Assn. for Play Therapy. Roman Catholic. Home: 2755 Hallon St Idaho Falls ID 83402-3868 Office Phone: 208-529-4300.

OEHLER, JUDITH JANE MOODY, retired counselor; b. Farner, Tenn., Mar. 5, 1942; d. William Henry and Peggy (Lindsey) Moody; m. Carl Bailey Oehler, June 1, 1963; children: David W., Paul E. BS in Elem. Edn., U. Tex., 1964; MEd, Tex. Christian U., 1976. Lic. profl. counselor. Elem. tchr. Arlington (Tex.) Ind. Sch. Dist., 1965-78, elem. counselor, 1979—96, ret., 1996. Mem. Arlington Women's Club. Fellow AACD; mem. DAR (regent 2000-04), Tex. Assn. Counseling and Devel., North Ctrl. Tex. Assn. Counseling and Devel. (sec. 1995-96, Caring award 1995), Tex. State Tchrs. Assn., Arlington Assn. Tex. Profl. Educators (sec. 1994—95), Aux. Tex. Soc. Profl. Engrs. (pres. Mid-Cities chpt. 1992-94, state sec. 1993-94, v.p. Region V 1994-95, state pres. 1997-98), Encore Club (1st v.p. 2004-05), Arlington Woman's Club (antique dept. chmn. 2004-05, club photographer 2005—), Nat. Soc. U.S. Daus 1812, Daus. Am. Colonists, Arlington Women Rotary, Phi Delta Kappa. Methodist. Avocations: travel, reading, swimming, gardening, walking. Home: 2408 Westwood Dr Arlington TX 76012-2905

OELKE, ANITA JEAN, special education educator; b. Beloit, Kans., July 6, 1948; d. John William and Virginia Lee Severance; m. Jimmie Dean Oelke, Mar. 16, 1997; 1 child, Eva Lee Gavin. B.S. in Elem. Edn., Ft. Hays State U., Kans., 1970. Cert. early childhood spl. educator Kans. Tchr. Grinnell (Kans.) Unified Sch. Dist., 1970—76, Hoxie (Kans.) Unified Sch. Dist., 1976—2002; tchr. early childhood spl. edn. Oakley (Kans.) Unified Sch. Dist., 2002—, tchr., 2002—. Bd. mem. High Plains Mental Health. Mem.: Coun. for Exceptional Children (state v.p.), Phi Delta Kappa (treas. 1986—90). Avocation: reading. Home: 1425 15th PO Box 751 Hoxie KS 67740 Office: NW Kans Ednl Svc Ctr 703 W 2nd Oakley KS 67748

OERTEL, YOLANDA CASTILLO, pathologist, educator; b. Lima, Peru, Dec. 14, 1938; came to U.S., 1966; d. Leonardo A. and Dalila (Ramirez) C.; m. James E. Oertel, Sept. 24, 1969. MD, Cayetano Heredia, Lima, 1964; Dr. honoris causa, U. Peruana Cayetano Heredia, 1999. Diplomate Am. Bd. Pathology (mem. test com. for cytopathology 1988-94). Internat. postdoctoral fellowship NIH, Bethesda, Md., 1966-68; asst. prof. pathology Sch. Medicine George Washington U., Washington, 1975-78, assoc. prof., 1978-84, prof., 1984-98, prof. emerita, 1998—. Adj. prof. pathology and lab. medicine MCP Hahnemann U. Sch. Medicine; cons. Registry Cytology Armed Forces Inst. Pathology, Washington, 1981—. Author: Fine Needle Aspiration of the Breast, 1987; contbr. chpts. to books, articles to profl. jours. Decorated comendador de la Orden Cayetano Heredia, 1999; recipient Francisco A. Camino prize Peruvian Med. Assn., 1965, cert. Meritorious Svc. Armed Forces Inst. Pathology, 1974; named Disting. Alumna Cayetano Heredia Med. Sch., 1989. Mem. Assn. Mil. Surgeons (hon.), Colombian Soc. Pathology (hon.), Argentinian Soc. Pathology (hon.), Peruvian Soc. Pathologists (hon.), Argentinian Soc. Cytopathology, (hon.), Am. Soc. Cytopathology, Internat. Acad. Pathology, Soc. Latinoamericana Patologia, Am. Soc. Clin. Pathologists (coun. on cytopathology 1982-88), Coll. Am. Pathologists, Arthur Purdy Stout Soc. Surg. Pathologists, Am. Thyroid Assn., L.Am. Thyroid Soc. Avocations: reading, opera. Office: Washington Hosp Ctr Pathology Dept Washington Cancer Inst 110 Irving St NW Washington DC 20010-2975 Office Phone: 202-877-2740. Office Fax: 202-877-0197. Business E-Mail: Yolanda.C.Oertel@medstar.net.

OERTER, CYNTHIA LYNN, medical technologist; b. Waupaca, Wis., Mar. 8, 1948; d. Lavern Charles and Geraldine Mae (Huffcutt) Trinrud; m. Gregory Van Oerter, June 8, 1968; children: Nathan, Justin. BS, U. Wis., Oshkosh, 1971; MS, Cardinal Stritch Coll., 1993. Cert. Am. Soc. Clin. Pathologists. Med. technologist Mercy Med. Ctr., Oshkosh, Wis., 1970-76, Iola (Wis.) Hosp., 1978-86, wellness cons., 1985-86, Riverside Med. Ctr., Waupaca, Wis., 1986—95, med. technologist, hematology supr., insvc. coord., cons., 1987-95; pres. Pro Health Consul, Inc., Waupaca, Wis., 1994—; bus. ptnr., adminstr. Garden Park House, 1994—2000, owner, adminstr., 2000—; owner Back Door Bakery, 2003—, Secret Garden Cafe, 2003—. Tchr. Fox Valley Coll., Appleton, Wis., 1986, 87; organizer Overeaters Anonymous, Iola, 1985-89; owner Green Fountain Inn, 1995—. Mem. parent's com. for gifted and talented Waupaca Sch. Sys., 1984, charter mem. edn. employment coun., 1989-92, mem. adv. com. guidance program K-12, 1992; vol. Nat. Wellness Inst., 1986-97, Am. Lung Assn., 1986-87; tchr. smokeless program Am. Inst. Preventative Medicine, 1988-93; com. mem. Main St. Design, 1999-2001. Mem. NAFE, Nat. Platform Assn., Am. Sch. Health Assn. (com. mem.), Waupace C. of C. (mem. tourism com. 2002—), Rotary (sec. 1996-98, bd. dirs. 1995-2004, pres. elect 1999-2000, pres. 2000-2001). Republican. Lutheran. Avocations: gardening, gourmet cooking, sailing, bible study, hobby farm. Business E-Mail: greenfountain@gglbbs.com.

OESTERLIN, LOVYE GWENDOLYN, retired chemist, educator, retired educational consultant; b. Cheraw, S.C., Aug. 26, 1932; d. John Eliot Davis and Lucile Monica (Davis) McIver; m. Rudolf Oesterlin, Dec. 29, 1956; children: Monika Oesterlin Wiltshire, Barbara Oesterlin Heath, Michael, Margrete Oesterlin Jean-Louis. BS, Bennett Coll., Greensboro, N.C., 1953; MS, N.Mex. Highlands U., Las Vegas, 1966. Chem. technician Sloan-Kettering Inst., N.Y.C., 1953; rsch. chemist sanitary engring. U. Calif., Berkeley, 1955—59; phys. sci. tchr. Hamilton Jr. H.S., Oakland, Calif., 1960—63; tchr. chemistry Columbia H.S., East Greenbush, NY, 1967—93, SUNY, Albany, 1988—93, ret., 1993; field supr. of student tchrs. Cabrini Coll., Radner, Pa., 1994—2001. Cons. State Edn. Dept., N.Y. State, Albany, NY, 1973—93. Recipient Belle Tobias award, Bennett Coll., 1949; grantee, NSF, 1960, 1962, 1981; Fulbright grant, State Dept., Washington, 1953. Mem.: NSTA (evaluator), Am. Chem. Soc., East Greenbush Tchrs. Assn., State Tchrs. Assn. N.Y. State (Sci. Fair dir.), Nat. Assn. Biology Tchrs. (dir.), Sci. Tchrs. Assn. N.Y. (rep. to bd. regents, Svc. award), The Links, Inc., Delta Sigma Theta. Democrat. United Methodist. Avocations: reading, piano, quilting, travel, opera. Home Fax: 610-469-1057. E-mail: loveBBS@aol.com.

OETTING, MILDRED KATHERINE See SQUAZZO, MILDRED

O'FARRILL, MARLINE STABILE, director; b. Birmingham, Ala., Sept. 14, 1946; d. Benard Leonard and Mada Pauline (King) Stabile; m. Alan John O'Farrill, Aug. 18, 1970; children: John Michael, Christopher Benard. MusB, Univ. Ala., Tusculoora, Ala., 1968; MA Mental retardation, Univ. S.C., Columbia, S.C., 1973; specialist preschool handicap, Fla. Atlantic Univ., Boca Raton, Fla., 1991. Cert. tchg. Fla. Mentally handicapped tchr. The Quest Ctr., Hollywood, Fla., 1971—81; chorus tchr. Plantation Md., Ft. Lauderdale, Fla., 1981—82; music tchr. Croissant Pk. Elem., Ft. Lauderdale, Fla., 1982—83; tchr. preschool devel. delay Sheridan Hill Elem., Hollywood, Fla., 1982—83; band dir. Bethune Elem. Sch., Dania, Fla., 1992—95, Attucks Mid. Sch., Dania, Fla., 1995—98; music tchr. Embassy Creek Elem. Sch., Cooper City, Fla., 1998—99; band dir. HD Perry Mid. Sch., Miramar, Fla., 1999—2002, Everglads H.S., Miramar, 2002—, chair music dept. Organizer All State Trip. Composer: (ednl. program) On The Move with Virgil, 1991, workshops. Trumpet player Sheriden Hill Bapt. Ch., 1990—2000. Recipient Tchr. of Yr., Coun. for Exceptional Children, 1994. Office Phone: 754-323-0528.

OFFIELD, CAROL JEAN DUBBERLY, elementary school educator; b. Houston, Sept. 19, 1954; d. Emmett Orinza and Mary Rebekah (Lane) Dubberly; children: Ryan Michael, Whitney Lane. BS in Edn., Stephen F. Austin State U., 1977. Cert. tchr., Tex. Tchr. aide Nacogdoches (Tex.) Ind. Sch. Dist., 1977-78; tchr. elem. Hudson (Tex.) Ind. Sch. Dist., 1978-81, Nacogdoches (Tex.) Ind. Sch. Dist., 1981-87, tchr. third grade, 1987-95. Chmn. ch. sch. adv. bd. First United Meth. Ch., Nacogdoches. Recipient Tchr. Who Makes a Difference award, 1992, Runner-up Young Educator award Jaycees, 1989. Mem. Tex. Assn. for Supervision and Curriculum Devel. (sci. curriculum writing fellow), Assn. Tex. Profl. Educators. Methodist. Office: Fredonia Elem Sch 1326 N Fredonia St Nacogdoches TX 75961-4021 Home: 5109 Northway Dr Apt 904 Nacogdoches TX 75965-1439

OFFUTT, REBECCA SUE, business and sales executive; b. Wheeling, W.Va., Jan. 20, 1951; d. John Howard and Mary Concetta (Lanzuisi) Warden; m. Denver C. Offutt, Apr. 13, 1970 (div. 1990); children: Kimberly Dawn, Jody Monroe. Student, W.Va. U., 1968-70, W.Va. State Coll., 1973-75. Founder, pres. Marabec Designs, Inc., Charleston, W.Va., 1980-82; realtor, sales assoc. McQuire Realty Co., Huntington, 1988-89; sales assoc. Focus Mktg. Consultants, Charleston, 1987-90; ter. mgr. Quorum Corp., Hurricane, W.Va., 1990—96; network sales specialist Danka Office Imaging, Charleston, 1996—99; founding ptnr. Komax Bus. Sys., LLC, South Charleston, W.Va., 1999—. Developer five-yr. plan Jr. League, Charleston and Huntington, 1984; docent Huntington Galleries; pres. Pea Ridge Elem. PTA, Huntington, 1986-87; del.-at-large Ohio Valley Tennis Assn., 1986-87; mem. South Charleston Area Devel. Coun., 2004-; South Charleston Conv. and Visitors Bur., 2000-02, bd. dirs., 2004—; chmn. U.S. Congl. Bus. Adv. Coun., 2004; bd. dirs. Appalachian Children's Chorus, 2004-05. Finalist Nat. award, Ricoh Corp., 1994; named Businessman of Yr. in W.Va., 2004; recipient Local, Dist. and Regional awards, Ricoh Corp., 1993. Mem.: Putnam County Rotary (charter mem., Disting. West Virginian 2004). Home: 318 Southpointe Dr Charleston WV 25314 Office Phone: 304-744-7440. Personal E-mail: obecks1@aol.com. Business E-Mail: boffutt@komaxbusinesssystems.com.

OFRI, DANIELLE, internist; b. N.Y.C., Aug. 22, 1965; d. Zacharia and Marcia Kashdan Ofri; m. Benjamin Akman, Nov. 7, 1999; children: Naava Ofri-Akman, Noah Ofri-Akman, Ariel Ofri-Akman. BSc, McGill U., Montreal, Que., Can., 1986; MS, NYU, 1990, PhD, 1992, MD, 1993. Lic. physician N.Y. State. Resident physician Bellevue Hosp., N.Y.C., 1993—96; attending physician Bellevue Hosp./NYU Sch. Medicine, N.Y.C., 1998—. Dir. Anticoagulation Clinic Bellevue Hosp., N.Y.C., 2002—. Editor-in-chief, co-founder: lit. mag. Bellevue Lit. Rev., 2000—; author: (memoir) Singular Intimacies, 2003, (songs) (non-fiction) Incidental Findings: Lessons from My Patients in the Art of Medicine, 2005; assoc. chief editor: med. textbook Bellevue Guide to Outpatient Medicine, 2001 (AMWA Best Med. Textbook, 2002). Recipient Editors Prize for nonfiction, Mo. Rev., 2001, award, Best Am. Essays, 2001, 2005, Pushcart Prize nomination, 2002, award, Best Am. Sci. Writing, 2003, McGovern award, Am. Med. Writers Assn., 2005. Jewish. Avocations: writing, music, piano, literature. Office: Bellevue Hosp Md Clinic 462 1st Ave New York NY 10016 E-mail: danielle.ofri@nyu.edu.

OFSTAD, EVELYN LARSEN BOYL, retired primary school educator, radio personality, film producer; b. Laurel, Oreg., Sept. 11, 1918; d. Walter Winfred and Nellie Lyle (Gellatly) Larsen; m. Robert Morris Boyl (dec.); children: Kathleen Roberta Boyl, Robert Morris Boyl Jr., Shannon Gae Boyl, Brian Larsen Boyl; m. Olaf Ofstad, Nov. 15, 1988. BS, Oreg. State U., 1940; MS in Tchg., Portland State U., 1968. Cert. learning specialist. Radio announcer Sta. KOAC, Corvallis, Oreg., 1939-40; announcer, script writer Sta. KWIL, Albany, Oreg., 1940-42, operator, announcer, 1941-42; sec. Higgins Ship Bldg., New Orleans, 1943-44; elem. tchr. Portland Pub. Schs., 1968-71; learning specialist North Clackamas Schs., Milw., Ore., 1972-85, home instr. Milwaukie, Oreg., 1985-86. Prodr., actor (video travelogues) Portland Cable Access, 1987—; actor: Oreg. Sr. Theater, 1987—95, Plz. Players, 1999—. Co-leader Girl Scouts Am., Oak Grove, Oreg., 1954—55, Webelos Boy Scouts Am., 1956—57, 1970—71; videographer Ptnrs. Ams., Oreg., Costa Rica, 1990—91; head video prodn. Channel 29 In-House TV Ret., 1999—2004; prodr. biweekly travel show, 1999—; mem. synchronized swim team Holladay Park Plz., 2003—04. Mem.: AAUW (pres. Albany chpt.). Avocations: painting, video production, travel, narration, script writing.

O'GARDEN, IRENE, writer, actress; b. Mpls., Dec. 23, 1951; d. Donald Edward and Betty O'Brien; m. John Leonard Pielmeier, Oct. 9, 1982. BA in Theatre and English, U. Minn., 1974; grad. student, State Coll. Pa., 1996. Actress Guthrie Theatre, Mpls., 1975—76; freelance actress N.Y., 1976—80. Bd. dirs. Philipstown Performing Arts, Garrison, NY, sec.; founder, host Art Garden Seasonal Peforming Literary Mag., 1987—; co-creator Inner Girl/Outer Girl, a writing workshop addressing self-injurious behavior in adolescent girls. Author (illustrator): Fat Girl: One Woman's Way Out, 1993; author: Maybe My Baby, 1995, The Scrubbly Bubbly Carwash, 2003 (Best Book award, 2004), (plays) Women On Fire, 2003—04 (nominee Lucille Lortel award, 2004), Little Heart, 2006; performer (poetry): Nuyoncan Poet's Cafe, Bowery Poetry Club, Hudson Valley Poet's Festival; contbr. poetry to jours. Grantee, Poets and Writers, N.Y., 1984, 1985, 1997, 2003, 2005; Berilla Kerr Playwrighting fellow, Millay Colony Arts, 2004, New Harmony Play Project fellow, 2005. Mem.: Soc. of Scribes, The Authors Guild, The Dramatists Guild, Actors Equity Assn. Avocations: calligraphy, bookbinding, gardening.

OGATA, CAROLEE KIMI, school system administrator; b. LA, Jan. 15, 1967; d. Masami and Patsy Kiyomi Ogata. EdD, U. So. Calif., 2005. Cert. tchr. Calif. Tchr. Ocean View Sch. Dist., Huntington Beach, Calif., 1992—98; prin. Garden Grove (Calif.) Unified Sch. Dist., 2000—03, dir., 2003—. Named Tchr. of Yr., Ocean View Sch. Dist., 1994. Office: Garden Grove Unified Sch Dist 10331 Stanford Ave Garden Grove CA 92840 Office Phone: 714-663-6427. Personal E-mail: cogata@aol.com.

OGATA, SUSAN NAOMI, psychologist; b. N.Y.C., Mar. 13, 1957; d. Kenneth Kenji and Misako (Koshiyama) Ogata; m. Lawrence Joseph Ledesma, Aug. 3, 1985; children: Evan Sadao, Jason Satoru. BA cum laude, UCLA, 1978; MEd, Harvard U., 1980; PhD, U. Minn., 1988. Clin. psychologist Healthcare Ptnrs. Med. group, Inc., Redondo Beach, Calif., 1988—. Contbr. articles to profl. jours. Mem. APA, Calif. Psychol. Assn. Avocations: movies, ballet, aerobics, reading, piano. Home: 9051 Colbreggan Dr Huntington Beach CA 92646-5813

OGBURN, JOYCE, library director; Libr. Old Dominion U., Yale U., Pa. State U.; assoc. dir. resources and collection mgmt. svcs. U. Wash. Librs., 1999—2005; dir. J. Willard Marriott Library U. Utah, Salt Lake City, 2005—. Mem.: ALA. Office: J Willard Marriott Libr 295 S 1500 E Salt Lake City UT 84112-0860 Office Phone: 801-585-9521. E-mail: joyce.ogburn@utah.edu.*

OGDEN, LYDIA LEE, government agency administrator; b. Murfreesboro, Tenn., July 17, 1960; d. Alfred Edwin and June (McCarter) O.; m. Kenneth Roland Askew, Nov. 15, 1986 (div. Dec. 1994); m. James Walter Buehler, Mar. 27, 1997; children: Philip, Lauren, Branch, Guthrie. BS summa cum laude, Middle Tenn. State U., 1981; MA, Vanderbilt U., 1984; MPP, Harvard U., 1998. Editor Am. Health Cons., Atlanta, 1984-86; strategic comms. cons. Words' Worth, Atlanta, 1986-89; account exec. Pringle Dixon Pringle, Atlanta, 1988; cmty. liaison Agy. for Toxic Substances & Disease Registry, Atlanta, 1989-92; comms. specialist Divsn. of HIV/AIDS Prevention Ctrs. for Disease Control & Prevention, Atlanta, 1992—96; sr. policy analyst Nat. Ctr. HIV, STD and TB Prevention, 1998—2001, dir. policy and planning Global AIDS Program, 2001—04; dep. chief of staff Ctrs. Disease Ctrl. and Prevention, 2004—. Mem. Atlanta Episcopal Diocese Commn. on AIDS, 1995—. Author: Applying Prevention Marketing, 1995; editor: Hosp. Risk Mgmt., 1984-86, The Public Health Implications of Medical Waste: A Report to Congress, 1989. Democrat. Episcopalian. Office: Ctrs for Disease Control & Prevention 1600 Clifton Rd NE # E7 Atlanta GA 30329-4018

OGDEN, MAUREEN BLACK, retired state legislator; b. Vancouver, B.C., Nov. 1, 1928; came to U.S., 1930; d. William Moore and Margaret Hunter (Leitch) Black; m. Robert Moore Ogden, June 23, 1956; children: Thomas, Henry, Peter. BA, Smith Coll., 1950; MA, Columbia U., 1963; M in City and Regional Planning, Rutgers U., 1977. Researcher, staff asst. Ford Found., N.Y.C., 1951-56; staff assoc. Fgn. Policy Assn., N.Y.C., 1956-58; mem. Millburn (N.J.) Twp. Com., 1976-81; mayor Twp. of Millburn, N.J., 1979-81; mem. N.J. Gen. Assembly, Trenton, 1982-96. Chmn. Assembly Environment Com., N.J. Gen. Assembly; chmn. Energy and Pub. Utilities Com., Coun. State Govts., 1991-92; mem. adv. bd. Sch. Policy and Planning, Rutgers Univ., New Brunswick, N.J., 1992-96, vice chair Nat. Affairs and Legis. Com. Energy Sources. Author: Natural Resources Inventory, Township of Millburn, 1974. Bd. govs. N.J. Hist. Soc., Newark, 1992-2000; trustee N.J. chpt. The Nature Conservancy, 1994-99; hon. trustee Paper Mill Playhouse, Millburn, 1990—; former trustee St. Barnabas Med. Ctr., Livingston, N.J.; former pres. N.J. Drug Abuse Adv. Coun.; chair Gov.'s Coun. on N.J. Outdoors, 1996-99; mem. Palisades Interstate Park Commn., 1996-99; chair Garden State Preservation Trust, 1999—; co-chair policy com. N.J. Conservation Found., 2000—; mem. steering com. Highlands Coalition of NJ-NY-Conn. Recipient citation Nat. Assn. State Outdoors Recreation Liaison Officers, 1987, cert. appreciation John F. Kennedy Ctr. for the Performing Arts, The Alliance for Art Edn., 1987, disting. svc. award Art Educators N.J., 1987, ann. environ. quality award EPA Region II, 1988, citation Humane Soc. U.S., 1989, award N.J. Hist. Sites Coun., 1989, N.J. Sch. Conservation, 1990, pres.'s award The Nature Conservancy, 1995, pub. policy award Nat. Trust for Hist. Preservation, 1995. Mem.: Garden Club Am. (vice chair). Republican. Episcopalian. Home: 59 Lakeview Ave Short Hills NJ 07078-2240 E-mail: mrogden@worldnet.att.net.

OGDEN, PEGGY A., retired personnel director; b. N.Y.C., Mar. 21, 1932; d. Stephen Arnold and Margaret (Stern) O. BA with honors, Brown U., 1953; MA, Trinity Coll., Hartford, Conn., 1955. Asst. dir. YMCA Counseling Svc., Hartford, 1953-55; employment interviewer R.H. Macy & Co., N.Y.C., 1955; asst. pers. dir. Inst. Internat. Edn., N.Y.C., 1956-59; pers. advisor Girl Scouts U.S.A., N.Y.C., 1959-61; store and pers. mgr. Ohrbachs, Inc., N.Y.C., 1961-74; dir. pers. N.Y.C. Coll. Tech., CUNY, Bkyn., 1974-2000, ret., 2000. Arbitrator, mediator Better Bus. Bur., N.Y.C., 1988—; cons. Girl Scout Coun. N.Y., N.Y.C., 1988-89. Advocate Am. Diabetes Assn., 1999-2003; bd. dir. Project Eye to Eye, 2006—. Mem APA, AAAS, Am. Assn. U. Adminstrs., Women in Human Resources, N.Y. Pers. Mgmt. Assn. Home: 1100 Park Ave New York NY 10128-1202

OGDEN, VALERIA MUNSON, management consultant, state representative; b. Okanogan, Wash., Feb. 11, 1924; d. Ivan Bodwell and Pearle (Wilson) Munson; m. Daniel Miller Ogden Jr., Dec. 28, 1946; children: Janeth Lee Ogden Martin, Patricia Jo Ogden Hunter, Daniel Munson Ogden. BA magna cum laude, Wash. State U., 1946. Exec. dir. Potomac Coun. Camp Fire, Washington, 1964-68, Ft. Collins (Colo.) United Way, 1969-73, Designing Tomorrow Today, Ft. Collins, 1973-74, Poudre Valley Community Edn. Assn., Ft. Collins, 1977-78; pres. Valeria M. Ogden, Inc., Kensington, Md., 1978-81; nat. field cons. Camp Fire, Inc., Kansas City, Mo., 1980-81; exec. dir. Nat. Capital Area YWCA, Washington, 1981-84, Clark County YWCA, Vancouver, Wash., 1985-89; pvt. practice mgmt. cons. Vancouver, 1989—; mem. Wash. Ho. of Reps., 1991—2002, spkr. pro tempore, 1999—2002. Mem. adj. faculty pub. adminstrn. program Lewis and Clark Coll., Portland (Oreg.) State U., 1979-94; mem. Pvt. Industry Coun., Vancouver, 1986-95; mem. regional Svcs. Network Bd. Mental Health, 1993-03. Author: Camp Fire Membership, 1980. Mem. Wash. State Coun. Vol. Action, Olympia, 1986—90; county vice-chair Larimer County Dems., Ft. Collins, 1974—75; spkr. pro tem Wash. Ho. of Reps., 1999—2002; rep. Gov. Chris Gregoire S.W. Wash., 2005; mem. precinct com. Clark County Dems., Vancouver, 1986—88; treas. Mortar Bd. Nat. Found., Vancouver, 1987—96; bd. dirs. Clark County Coun. for Homeless, Vancouver, 1989—2004, chmn., 1994; bd. dirs. Wash. Wild Life and Recreation Coalition, 1995—2002, Human Svcs. Coun., 1996—2002, State Legis. Leaders Found., 2001—02; mem. adv. bd. Wash. State U., Vancouver, 2002—; chair arts and tourism com. Nat. Conf. State Legis., 1996—97, mem. exec. com., 2000—02; bd. dirs. Wash. State Hist. Soc., 1996—2006, Affordable Cmty. Environments, 1998—, Columbia Springs Environ. Edn. Ctr. Found., 2003—; pres. Nat. Order of Women Legislators, 1999—2001; chair Wash. State Interagy. Com. for Outdoor Recreation, 2003—, Wash. State Historic Preservation Fund, 2003—06, S.W. Wash. Ctr. for the Arts, 2003—; bd. dirs. Clark County Skill Ctr. Found., 2003, S.W. Wash. Child Care Consortium, 2003—. Named Citizen of Yr. Ft. Collins Bd. of Realtors, 1975, State Legislator of Yr., Wash. State Labor Coun., 2000, Citizen of Yr., Vancouver, Wash., 2002, First Citizen, Clark County, 2006; recipient Gulick award Camp Fire Inc., 1956, Alumna Achievement award Wash. State U. Alumni Assn., 1988; named YWCA Woman of Achievement, 1991. Mem. AAUW, Internat. Assn. Vol. Adminstrs. (pres. Boulder 1989-90), Nat. Assn. YWCA Exec. Dirs. (nat. bd. nominating com. 1988-90), Sci. and Soc. Assn. (bd. dirs. 1993-97), Women in Action, Philanthropic and Ednl. Orgn., Soroptimists, Phi Beta Kappa. Democrat. Avocations: hiking, travel. Home and Office: 3118 NE Royal Oak Dr Vancouver WA 98662-7435 Office Phone: 360-254-8886. Personal E-mail: repval@comcast.net.

OGILVIE, DONNA LEE, retired marketing professional, retired journalist; b. Saint Louis, Sept. 19, 1930; d. Carl Nolan D. Dunkeson and Helen Margaret Sanford; m. Thomas W. Ogilvie, Apr. 2, 1974 (dec.); children from previous marriage: Michael Harry Jennings, Steven Andrew Jennings. BA, Western Res. U., Cleve., 1965. Reporter Cleve. News, 1948—50; libr. Akron Beacon Jour., Ohio, 1950—52; reporter Women's Wear Daily, Cleve., 1952—57; reporter, news editor Farmington Daily Tides, N.Mex., 1967—78; pub. rels. dir. San Juan Med. Ctr., Farmington, 1978—81; mktg. dir. San Juan Coll., Farmington, 1981—95. Owner Media Prodn., Farmington, 1993—2000. Author: Roots and Wings of San Juan College, 2003. Tchr. Project Read; mem., pub. rels. dir. Dem. Party, Farmington; bd. dirs. Civic Ctr. Found., 2003—; bd. dirs., pres. Anasari Found., 1985—, San Juan Animal

League, 2005—; actor, dir., bd. dirs. Cmty. Theater. Named Woman of Yr., Women's Leadership, Farmington, 1992; named to San Juan Coll. Hall of Fame, 1995; Paul Harris fellow, Rotary, Farmington, 2000. Presbyterian. Home: 3327 Santa Fe Ct Farmington NM 87401 E-mail: donnadonnanoel@aol.com.

OGILVIE, MARILYN BAILEY, natural science eduator, historian, writer, bibliographer; b. Duncan, Okla., Mar. 22, 1936; d. William T. and Mildred (Pate) Bailey; m. Philip W. Ogilvie, June, 1959 (div. 1975); children: Martha, William, Kristen. AB in Biology, Baker U., 1957; MA in Zoology, U. Kans., 1959; PhD in History of Sci., U. Okla., 1973, MLS, 1983. Asst. prof. history of sci. Portland (Oreg.) State U., 1971-75; adj. instr. in Am. history Oscar Rose Jr. Coll., Midwest City, Okla., 1975-76; vis. asst. prof. history of sci. U. Okla., Norman, 1977-83, adj. asst. prof. history of sci., 1987; with Okla. Bapt. U., Shawnee, 1979—, asst. prof. natural sci., 1980-85, chair div. nat. sci. and maths., assoc. prof. natural sci., 1985-91; curator history of sci collections, assoc prof. bibliography U. Okla., Norman, 1991-94, prof. history sci., 1994—. Adj. assoc. prof. history of sci. U. Okla., Norman, 1991—. Author: Women in Science: Antiquity through the Nineteenth Century, 1986, (with others) Proceedings of the American Philosophical Society, 1981; contbg. author: Uneasy Careers and Intimate Lives: Women in Science, 1789-1979, 1987, The Expansion of American Biology: The Interwar Years, 1991. Mem. History of Sci. Soc., AAUP (sec., treas. local chpt., v.p., pres. 1981—), Brit. Soc. for the History of Sci., ALA, Assn. Coll. and Rsch. Librs., Phi Sigma, Beta Phi Mu, Sigma Xi, Omicron Delta Kappa. Democrat. Methodist. Home: 1629 Franklin Dr Norman OK 73072-6355 Office: U Okla Librs History of Sci Collections 401 W Brooks St Norman OK 73069-8824

OGILVIE, TAMARA A., rancher, elementary school educator; d. Hugh Lynn Anderson and Marjorie Ada McKinney; m. David W. Ogilvie Jr.; children: Ryan, Andrew, Erin. BS in Agrl., U. Ariz., Tucson, 1979. Intern Ariz. State Senate, Phoenix, 1980; livestock prodr. Ogilvie Cattle Co., Flagstaff, Ariz., 1987—, Silver City, N.Mex., 1987—; tchr. Silver Consolidated Sch., 1996—. Chair Ariz. Cattle Growers Rsch. & Edn. Com., Phoenix, 1988—98. Mem.: Internat. Dyslexia Assn., N.Mex. Cattle Growers, N.Mex. Beef Coun. (chair 2006—).

OGLE, AMANDA MCKIBBIN, music educator, theater educator, director; b. Grinnell, Iowa, Oct. 8, 1973; d. Gary James and Vicki Lynne McKibbin; m. Scott T. Ogle, Dec. 31, 1996. MusM in Edn., U. Colo., Boulder, 2000. Lic. profl. tchr. Colo. Dept. of Edn., 1997. Music tchr. Bergen Valley and Bergen Meadow Elem. Schs., Evergreen, Colo., 2002—. Artistic dir. Evergreen Players Drama Camp, Colo., 2006—. Performer: (musical theater) Into the Woods, The Secret Garden, The Music Man. Participant ednl. outreach Evergreen Arts Coun., Colo., 2001—05; vol. drama camp dir. Evergreen Players, Evergreen, Colo., 2005—06; sec. Crest at Sun Creek Homeowners Assn., Evergreen, Colo., 2001—03. Mem.: NEA, Music Educators Nat. Conf. Avocations: travel, writing, reading, yoga, bicycling. Office: Evergreen Players PO Box 1271 Evergreen CO 80437 Office Phone: 720-953-1136. E-mail: mogle@jeffco.k12.co.us.

OGLE, ROBBIN SUE, criminal justice educator; b. North Kansas City, Mo., Aug. 28, 1960; d. Robert Lee and Carol Sue (Gray) O. BS, Ctrl. Mo. State U., 1982; MS, U. Mo., 1990; PhD, Pa. State U., 1995. State probation and parole officer Mo. Dept. Corrections, Kansas City, 1982-92; collector J.C. Penney Co., Mission, Kans., 1990-92; instr. U. Mo., Kansas City, 1990-92; grad. lectr. Pa. State U., University Park, 1992-95; prof. criminal justice dept. U. Nebr., Omaha, 1995—. Author: Battered Women Who Kill: A New Framework, 2002, The Wienie Dog Adventure Series: The Great Ham Heist, 2005; contbr. articles to profl. jours. Athletic scholar Ctrl. Mo. State U., Warrensburg, 1978-82. Mem. AAUW, ACLU, NOW, Am. Soc. Criminology, Acad. Criminal Justice Scis., Am. Correctional Assn., Phi Kappa Phi. Avocations: reading, watching basketball, walking dog. Office: U Nebr Dept Criminal Justice 1100 Neihardt Lincoln NE 68588-0630 Home: 2410 N 99th St Omaha NE 68134-5642 Office Phone: 402-472-3677. Personal E-mail: rsogle@cox.net. Business E-Mail: rogle@mail.unomaka.edu.

OGLE, SARAH J., assistant principal; d. Henry Albert and Myra Jane Smith; m. Melvin David Ogle, May 27, 1972; children: Melvin Keith, Lynnette J. Ogle Davidson. BA, Belmont U., 1967; student in Edn. Adminstrn., U. Tex., Arlington, Tex., 2000—; student, Baylor U., Tex. Wesleyan U. Cert. tchr. Tex., 1992, tchr. ESL Tex., 1995, mid-mgmt. adminstr. Tex., 1999. Adminstrv. asst. Weldon Aston & Co. CPA, Ft. Worth, 1973—90; tchr. South Hills Elem. Sch., Ft. Worth, 1990—97; instrl. specialist Briscoe Elem. Sch., Ft. Worth, 1997—98; asst. prin. Greenbriar Elem., Ft. Worth, 1998—2001; prin. Souder Elem. Sch., Everman, Tex., 2001—04; asst. prin. Hubbard Heights Elem. Sch., Ft. Worth, 2004—. Exchange tchr. Japan Sister Citites Ft. Worth; team officer Ft. Worth (Tex.) Reading Coun.; presenter in field. Pres. Adolescent Pregnancy Prevention, Ft. Worth, 1988—89; deacon U. Bapt. Ch., Ft. Worth, tchr. Named Tchr. of Week, Dillards. Mem.: Delta Kappa Gamma. Home: 5504 Winifred Dr Fort Worth TX 76133 Office: Hubbard Heights Elem Sch 1333 W Spurgeon Fort Worth TX 76115

OGLESBY, ELAINE SUE, elementary school educator; b. Rensselaer, Ind., Dec. 11, 1958; d. Richard E. and Lois I. Oglesby. BS in Natural Resources and Environ. Sci., Purdue U., 1981; MEd, Ind. U., 1988, MLS, 2005. Tchr. Indpls. Pub. Schs., 1986—2004, digital coach, 2004—. Recipient Shining Star, Indpls. Pub. Schs., 1993—94, Spirit of Harshman, Harshman Mid. Sch., 1998, Tchr. of the Yr. award, 2003, Top Ten Tchr. award, Indpls. Pub. Schs., 2003; grantee, Eli Lily Found., 1993. Mem.: Ind. Mid. Level Educators (assoc.), Nat. Mid. Sch. Assn. (assoc.), Ind. Libr. Fedn. (assoc.), Assn. Curriculum and Devel. (assoc.). Office Phone: 317-226-4030.

OGLESBY, GEORGANN HEDLESTEN, lawyer; b. London, Ohio, Apr. 24, 1973; d. James Rudolph and Diane Marie Hedlesten; m. Stephen Wofford Oglesby, May 6, 2000; 1 child, Alexandra Maria. BA in History, Southwest Tex. State U., 1997; JD, Tex. Southern U., 2003. Sr. sales assoc. Intercall Commn., Dallas, 1998—2000; internship Harris County Dist. Atty. Office, Houston, 2001—03; law clk. Law Offices of Philip Accer, Houston, 2000—02, Law Offices of James R. Hedlesten, Houston, 2002—04; atty. Hedlesten & Oglesby, LLP, Houston, 2004—. Vol. atty. Legal Lines, Houston; fundraiser Cerebral Palsy Found., 1985—. Mem.: Tex. Trial Lawyers Assn., Am. Trial Lawyers Assn., Susan G. Komen Found. Presbyn. Home: 7030 Blandford Lane Houston TX 77055 Office: Hedlesten & Oglesby LLP 2000 Smith St Houston TX 77082

OGUNKOYA, ANDREA, marketing executive; BA in Law, Thames Valley Univ., Ealing, London. Retail, wholesale, sales, mktg. AT&T Wireless, Mount Vernon, NY, 1993—96; sr. mktg. specialist Nortel Networks, Tarrytown, NY, 1996—99; dir. mktg. Technotel Data Svcs., NYC, 1999—2001; sr. acct. dir. MSCO Mktg., NYC, 2001—05; v.p. ops., sales, mktg. Storage Deluxe, NYC, 2005—. Vol. Arthritis Found., Child Abuse Prevention Ctr. Office: Storage Deluxe 2887 Atlantic Ave Brooklyn NY 11207*

OGUT, BILGE AYSE, investment advisor; arrived in U.S., 1990; m. Haro Cumbusyan, July 20, 2002. BA, U. Pa., 1994, BS in Econs., 1994; MBA, Harvard U., 1998. Fin. analyst Goldman Sachs Internat., London, 1994—96; summer intern McKinsey & Co, Istanbul, Turkey, 1995; mng. dir. Warburg Pincus, NYC, 1998—. Office: Warburg Pincus 466 Lexington Ave 10th Floor New York NY 10017

OH, ANGELA E., lawyer; b. LA, Sept. 8, 1955; BA, UCLA, 1977, MPH, 1981; JD, U. Calif., Davis, 1986. Bar: Calif. 1986. Lawyer, 1987—. Lawyer del. 9th Cir. Jud. Conf., 1995-96, lawyer rep.; mem. Senator Boxer's Jud. Noms. Com. for Ctrl. Dist. Calif., 1994-95; bd. dirs. Calif. Women's Law Ctr., Lawyers Mut. Ins. Co.; mem. cmty. adv. bd. First Interstate Bank Calif.; spkr. in field. Contbr. articles to profl. jours. and newspapers. Spl. counsel to the Assembly Spl. Com. on the L.A. Crisis. Mem. ABA, State Bar Calif., Korean-Am. Bar Assn. So. Calif. (pres.), L.A. County Bar Assn. Office: 8th Fl 601 W Fifth St Los Angeles CA 90071 Office Phone: 213-225-5825.

OH, SANDRA, actress; b. Nepean, Ont., Can., July 20, 1971; m. Alexander Payne, Jan. 1, 2003. Actor: (films) Double Happiness, 1994, Bean, 1997, The Princess Diaries, 2001, Big Fat Liar, 2002, Full Frontal, 2002, Long Life, Happiness & Prosperity, 2002, Rick, 2003, Under the Tuscan Sun, 2003, Break a Leg, 2003, Wilby Wonderful, 2004, Sideways, 2004 (Screen Actors Guild Award, outstanding performance by cast in motion picture, 2005), 8 Minutes to Love, 2004, Hard Candy, 2005, Break a Leg, 2005, Cake, 2005, 3 Needles, 2005, Sorry, Haters, 2005, The Night Listener, 2006; (TV series) Arli$$, 1996—2002 (CableACE Award, 1997), Grey's Anatomy, 2005— (Best Performance by an Actress in a Supporting Role in a Series, Mini-Series or Motion Picture Made for TV, Hollywood Fgn. Press Assn. (Golden Globe), 2006, Outstanding Performance by a Female Actor in a Drama Series, Screen Actors Guild award, 2006); (TV miniseries) Further Tales of the City, 2001.*

OH, SOOJIN SUSAN, elementary school educator; b. Seoul, Republic of Korea, July 7, 1980; d. Hyun Kyung and Eunsim Oh. BA summa cum laude, U. Pa., 2003, MS in Edn., 2004. Cert. tchr. elem. edn. Pa. Info. tech. asst. mgr. Coll. Ho. Computing, U. Pa., Phila., 1999—2003; acad. and career advisor U. Pa., Phila., 2000—03; product mgmt. intern Chubb Group of Ins. Cos., Washington, 2001; pub. svc. intern Korean Am. Coalition, Washington, 2001; tchg. asst. Wharton Sch., U. Pa., Phila., 2002—03; strategic mktg. intern Toyota Motor Corp., Torrance, Calif., 2002; rsch. analyst U. Pa. Grad. Sch. Edn., Phila., 2004; head tchr. grade 1 Abington Friends Sch., Jenkintown, Pa., 2004—; ednl. cons. Laurus Enterprise, 2005. Mem. math curriculum planning and devel. com. Abington Friends Sch., Jenkintown, Pa., 2004—, mem. acad. planning com., 2004—, internat. intern liaison; ethnographer Hist. Soc. Pa., Phila., 2004; transl., interpreter interviews, press confs., articles; fellow Klingenstein Summer Inst., Columbia U., 2006; presenter in field. Editor rev. bd.: Urban Edn. Jour.; editl. bd. Dear Theopilus Newsletter; contbr. articles to profl. jours. Local area coord. Habitat for Humanity, Reseda, Calif., 1995—99; liaison Tree People, Beverly Hills, 1995—99; chpt. mem. UNICEF, Phila., 2003—; curriculum developer Quo Vadis West Philly Edn. Outreach Program, Phila., 2004—; vol. nursery, maternity, oncology, pediat., newborn ICU Valley Presbyn. Hosp., Van Nuys, Calif., 1993—99; liaison Salvation Army, Canoga Park, Calif., 1995—99; pub. svc. intern Korean Am. Coaltion, Washington, 2001—; women's ministry, small group ministry leader Emmanuel Ch. in Phila., 1999—; pianist, ministry dir., youth group pres. Calvary Presbyn. Ch., Granada Hills, Calif., 1992—99. Recipient rsch. grant, Samuel S. Fels Fund, 2004, Penn Alumni scholarship, U. Pa., 1999—2003, Korean Ambassadorial scholarship, Embassy of Republic of Korea, 2003, Nat. Merit Commended scholar, Edn. Testing Svcs., 1999, Nat. AP scholar, 1999, Nat. Leadership and Svc. award, USAA Ednl. Found., 1997, rsch. grant, U. Pa. Grad. Sch. of Edn., 2004, All Am. scholarship, USAA Ednl. Found., 1996, Nat. Math. award, U.S. Acade. Achievement, 1997, UCLA Chancellor's scholarship, 1999, UCLA Alumni Assn. scholarship, 1999, U. Calif. Berkeley Regent's scholarship, 1999, Trustees' Scholarship, Boston U., 1999, Nat. Prudential Leadership Award, Prudential Fin., 1998, Toyota Cmty. scholarship, Toyota Motor U.S.A., 1999—2003, Tylenol Cmty. scholarship, Johnson & Johnson, 1999, Korean Am. scholarship, Korean Am. Scholarship Found., 2000, 2001, 2002, 2003, 2004, Ca. Golden State Scholar, Central Daily News scholar, 2001, Scott Kyungmo Kim Scholarship, 2004; scholar Korean Am. Student Leader of the Yr. award, Korean Heritage Found., Leadership award, Korean Sr. Citizens Mut. Club, 2001;, Korea Times Scholarship, 2000, 2002, Klingenstein Summer Inst. fellow, Columbia U. Tchrs. Coll., 2000. Mem.: North Am. Reggio Emilia Alliance (assoc.), Nat. Assn. for Edn. of Young Children (assoc.), Key Club Internat. (life; pres., v.p., dist. rep. 1995—99, Kiwanis Internat. Cmty. Leadership award 1999, Disting. Leader of the Yr. award 1995), Kiwanis (pres. local chpt. Key Club 1995—99), Pi Gamma Mu (life), Ephebian Honor Soc. (life), Golden Key Internat. Honor Soc. (life; pres. 2002—03), Psi Chi (life; pres., v.p., fin. dir. 2000—03). Achievements include research in educational policy, research and practice across K-12 schools and higher education institutions in China; key factors that facilitate effortless recall, accuracy and memory retention for simple multiplication; historical, cultural, and sociopolitical forces that have shaped the West Philadelphia neighborhood; featured in various newspapers such as: LA Times, Korea Times, Dong-A Daily News, Central Daily News. Avocations: photography, travel, interior design, literature, classical concerts. Office: Abington Friends Sch 575 Washington Ln Jenkintown PA 19046 Office Phone: 215-886-4350.

O'HAGAN, DENISE MARIE, physical therapist, personal trainer; b. Phila., Feb. 5, 1976; d. William John and Nancy Jean O'Hagan. BS in Psychology, Sacred Heart U., Fairfield, Conn., 1998, MS in Phys. Therapy, 2001. Cert. MSPT, ATC Calif. Phys. therapist Dynamic Phys. Therapy, El Centro, Calif., 2001—06, Care South Home Health, El Cajon, Calif., 2006—, Integrated Phys. Therapy, San Diego, 2006—. Mem.: Am. Coun. Sports Medicine, Calif. Athletic Tng. Assn., Nat. Athletic Tng. Assn. Republican. Avocations: running, hiking, travel.

OHANJANIAN, RUZANNA, clinical psychologist; d. Vladimir and Nina Ohanjanian; 1 child, Irene Gyulnazarian. BA in Linguistics & Lit. with honors, Leninakan Ednl. Inst., 1977; MA in Psychology, Yerevan P. State U., 1981; PhD, Moscow Acad. Scis., 1985; postdoctoral, U. San Francisco Med. Ctr., 1996. Cert. trauma specialist, Traumatic Incident Reduction Calif., 1991, lic. clin. psychologist Bd. Psychology, Calif., 1999. Clin. psychologist Dept. Pub. Health, San Francisco, 1998—2002, Family Svcs., Palo Alto, Calif., 1998—2002, Multilingual Psychology Cons., Mountain View, Calif., 1996—98, UCSF Med. Ctr., Mt. Zion Hosp., San Francisco. Nat. disaster team mem. Min. Health, Armenia, 1989—91; assoc. prof. Yerevan State U., Armenia, 1990—92, vis. prof., 1992; presenter State of World Forum, San Francisco, 1997; crisis mgmt. team mem. Family Enterprise Internat. Behavioral Health, 1999—. Contbr. over 30 publs. and presentations in field. Chmn. Irene Gyulnazarian Ednl. Fund for Armenia, Los Gatos, Calif., 2003—. Named Hon. Dr., Yerevay State U., 2005; recipient Appreciation award, FEI Behavioral Health, 2000, Alaska Airlines, 2000, Make a Difference award, Total Employee Assistance and Mgmt. Inc., 2002, Employee Assistance Program Appreciation award, Pacific Care Behavioral Health. Mem.: APA, Armenian Profl. Soc. Avocations: painting, piano. Office: Ohanjanian Ruzanna POBox 320652 Los Gatos CA 95032 Personal E-mail: irachka2@hotmail.com.

O'HANLON, CAROL ANN, minister; b. Jacksonville, Fla. d. Oscar Lee Miller and Elsie (Beecher) Simpson; m. Arthur Francis, July 16, 1963; 1 child, Arthur Patrick. BA, Montreat, 1956; M of Religious Edn., Union Sem., 1959, MDiv, 1963; MS in Counseling, L.I. U., 1977, Profl. Diploma, 1980. Ordained to ministry United Meth. Ch., 1965; cert. Christian edn. min., expert in traumatic stress; nat. cert. counselor; cert. hypnotherapist; registered behavioral therapist. Asst. pastor, minister edn. Kings Hwy. United Meth. Ch., Bklyn., 1961-63; asst. pastor Bellmore (L.I.) United Meth. Ch., 1964-66; assoc. pastor Farmingdale (L.I.) United Meth. Ch., 1966-80; assoc. pastor, coord. food pantry Babylon (N.Y.) United Meth. Ch., 1980-95; pastor United Meth. Ch., Bellmore, NY, 1995—98; interim pastor Bridgehampton United Ch., 1999; counselor Mental Health Faculty Mercy Haven Inc., 2000—. Coord. children's work United Meth. Ch., L.I., 1966-78, chmn. dist. edn., 1978-85, 87-91, dist. dir. Sch. Faith and Life, 1980-92, coord. adult ministries, 1983-85, founder dist. edn. com, 1979-93, dist. bd. ministry, 1990-95, dist. nominating com., 1983-91, dist. coun. on ministries, 1966-93. Author: The Knockout Punch - Facets and Ways of Coping with a Sudden Death, 1999. Mem.: Am. Acad. ExpertsTraumatic Stress, Am. Assn. Profl. Hypnotherapists, N.Y. Mental Health Counselors Assn., Suffolk Coalition. Home: 25 Barry Rd Amity Harbor NY 11701-4001

O'HARA, DEE, medical/surgical nurse; Nurse USAF, Patrick AFB, 1959; nurse to astronauts NASA, Houston, 1959—83; nurse NASA Ames Rsch. Ctr., Moffett Field, Calif., 1983—. Office: NASA Ames Rsch Ctr Bldg 243 Rm 120 Moffett Field CA 94035 Business E-Mail: dohara@mail.arc.nasa.gov.

O'HARA, MAUREEN (MAUREEN FITZSIMONS), actress; b. Dublin, Aug. 17, 1920; d. Charles and Marguerite (Liburn) FitzSimons; m. George Hanley Brown (annulled), Will Price, Dec. 29, 1941 (div. 1952); 1 child, Bronwyn Bridget Fitzsimons; m. Charles Blair, 1967. Pres. Antilles Air Boats, St. Croix, V.I., 1978-81, chief exec. officer, 1978-79; owner, columnist The Virgin Islander, 1975-80. Actress in numerous prodns. including: (movies) Jamaica Inn, Hunchback of Notre Dame, 1939, A Bill of Divorcement, Dance, Girls, Dance, 1940, They Met in Argentina, How Green Was My Valley, 1941, To the Shores of Tripoli, 1942, Ten Gentlemen from West Point, 1942, The Black Swan, 1942, This Land is Mine, 1943, Immortal Sergeant, 1943, The Fallen Sparrow, 1943, Buffalo Bill, 1944, The Spanish Main, 1945, Do You Love Me?, 1946, Rio Grande, At Sword's Point, 1952, Kangaroo, 1952, Flame of Araby, 1952, The Quiet Man, 1952, Against All Flags, 1952, Redhead from Wyoming, 1953, War Arrow, 1953, Sinbad the Sailor, 1947, Miracle on 34th St., 1947, Lady Godiva, 1955, Wings of Eagles, 1957, Our Man in Havana, 1960, The Parent Trap, 1961, The Deadly Companions, 1961, Mr. Hobbs Takes a Vacation, 1962, McClintock, 1963, Spencer's Mountain, 1963, The Rare Breed, 1966, The Battle of the Villa Fiorita, 1965, How Do I Love Thee, 1970, Big Jake, 1971, Only the Lonely, 1991; (TV film) The Christmas Box, 1995, Cab to Canada, 1998, The Last Dance, 2000; (play) Christine, 1960; (TV) The Red Pony, Mrs. Miniver, Scarlet Pimpernel, Spellbound, High Button Shoes, Who's Afraid of Mother Goose. Recipient Heritage award, Am. Ireland Fund, 1991.

O'HARA, PATRICIA ANNE, dean, law educator; BA summa cum laude, Santa Clara U., 1971; JD summa cum laude, Notre Dame, 1974. Bar: Calif. 1974. Assoc. Brobeck, Phleger & Harrison, 1974—79, 1980—81; assoc. prof. law Notre Dame Law Sch., 1981, prof., 1990, v.p. student affairs, 1990—99, Joseph A. Matson dean, law educator, 1999—. Contbr. chapters to books, articles to law jours. Office: U Notre Dame 203 Law Sch PO Box 780 Notre Dame IN 46556-0780 Office Phone: 574-631-6789. Office Fax: 574-631-8400. E-mail: Patricia.A.O'Hara.3@nd.edu.

O'HARA, SABINE U., academic administrator, dean, economist, educator; b. Ludwigsburg, W. Germany, Oct. 29, 1955; d. Wolfgang E. and Margarete Maier; m. Philip O'Hara, Mar. 17, 1983; children: Daniel, David, Dennis. Doctorate, U. Gottingen, Germany, 1984. Dir. pub. policy N.Y. State Coun. Chs., Albany, 1990—93; asst. prof. econs. Rensselaer Poly. Inst., Troy, NY, 1994—99, dir. grad. studies in econs., 1996—99; provost and prof. econs. Green Mountain Coll., Poultney, Vt., 1999—2002; v.p. acad. affairs and dean Concordia Coll., Moorhead, Minn., 2002—04; pres. Roanoke Coll., Salem, Va., 2004—. Lectr. in field. Author: (books) Economic Theory for Environmentalists, 1996; contbr. articles to profl. jours. Steering com. Downtown Revitalization Initiative, Poultney, 2001—02; bd. dirs. Girls Inc. of the Greater Capital Dist., Albany, NY, 1998—2000, Employee Ownership Project, Albany, 1997—2000; vice chair Schenectady Econ. Devel. Initiative, NY, 1994—97. Recipient Outstanding Paper award for excellence, Internat. Jour. Social Econs., 1996, 2000, Outstanding Svc. award, N.Y. State Coun. Chs., 1997; grantee Rsch. grantee, Hewlett Found., Froehlich Found., Sloan Found. Mem.: Am. Econ. Assn., Internat. Assn. Feminist Econs., Assn. Social Econs., Internat. Soc. Ecol. Econs. Business E-Mail: ohara@roanoke.edu.

O'HARE, VIRGINIA LEWIS, human resources administrator; b. Pitts., May 2, 1951; d. Robert Edward and Ellen Marie (Saylor) Lewis; m. John Francis O'Hare, Sept. 17, 1994; 1 child, Merit Elisabeth. BS in Edn., U. Pitts., 1973; MS in Human Resources Mgmt., Laroche Coll., 1984. Legal asst. Meyer, Darragh, Buckler, Bebenek & Eck, Pitts., 1973-85; legal office mgr. Rockwell Internat., Pitts., 1985-86; pers. mgr. Rose, Schmidt, Hasley & DiSalle, Pitts., 1986-88; legal adminstr. Duquesne Light Co., Pitts., 1988-99; mgr. human resources Klett Lieber Rooney & Schorling, Pitts., 1999—. Mem. Assn. Legal Adminstrs., Pitts. Legal Adminstrn. Assn. (sec. 1989-93, membership chair 1993-97, edn. chair 1997-2000, pres.-elect 2000-2001), Pa. Bar Assn., Allegheny Bar Assn., Pitts. Human Resources Assn. Republican. Avocations: horseback riding, target shooting, walking, biking.

O'HERN, JANE SUSAN, psychologist, educator; b. Winthrop, Mass., Mar. 21, 1933; d. Joseph Francis and Mona (Garvey) O'H. BS, Boston U., 1954, EdD, 1962; MA, Mich. State U., 1956. Instr. Mercyhurst Coll., 1954-55, Hofstra Coll., 1956-57, State Coll., Salem and Boston, 1957-60; asst. prof. Boston U., 1962-67, assoc. prof., 1967-75, prof. edn. and psychiat. (psychology), 1975-95, prof. emeritus, 1995—, chmn. dept. counseling psychology, 1972-75, 88-89, dir. mental health edn. program, 1975-81, dir. internat. edn., 1978-81, asst. v.p. internat. edn., 1981; prof. emeritus mental health and behavioral medicine program Boston U. Sch. Medicine, 2001—. Pres. ASSIST Internat., Inc., 1989—98; adv. bd, Internat. Study Cons., 1994—98; founder BettyBoston LLC, 2002—. Contbr. articles to profl. jours. Trustee Boston Ctr. Modern Psychoanalytic Studies, 1980-92. Recipient grants U.S. Office Edn., NIMH, Dept. of Def. Mem. Assn. Counselor Edn. and Suprs., Am. Counseling Assn., North Atlantic Assn. Counselor Edn. and Supervision (past pres.), Mass. Psychol. Assn., Am. Psychol. Assn., Mortar Bd., Pi Lamda Theta, Sigma Kappa, Phi Delta Kappa, Phi Beta Delta. Home: 111 Perkins St Apt 287 Boston MA 02130-4324 Office Phone: 617-414-2325. Personal E-mail: assistint@aol.com. E-mail: johern@bu.edu.

OHL, JOAN ESCHENBACH, federal agency administrator; b. Harrisburg, Pa. m. Ronald E. Ohl. Grad., U. Del., 1967; EdM, SUNY, Buffalo, 1969; post grad., Pa. State U. Dir. women's housing Colo. Coll., Colo. Springs, 1969; positions at U. Ark., Pa. State U.; asst. to v.p. Fairleigh Dickinson U., Rutherford, NJ, 1975—82; v.p. Independent Coll. Fund of NJ; cons. to C.E. "Jim" Compton of FIVE-J Energy Inc. & Grafton Coal Co., 1984—93; sec. Dept. Health and Human Resources, W.Va., 1997—2001; commr. Adminstrn. Children, Youth and Families Adminstrn. Children and Families, HHS, Washington, 2002—. Bd. mem. W.Va. Health Care Cost Rev. Authority, 1993—97. Recipient Disting. West Virginian award, 2000, Joan E. Ohl Rural Health Leadership award, W.Va. Rural Health Assn., 2000, Leadership Award, Multi-CAP, Inc., 2000, Bateman Award, W.Va. Hosp. Assoc., 2000, Leadership Award, W.Va. Pub. Health Assoc., 2000. Office: HHS Adminstrn Children and Families 370 L'Enfant Promenade SW Washington DC 20447

OHST, WENDY JOAN, government agency administrator, educator; b. Muskegon, Mich., Feb. 20, 1949; d. Edward John Barron, Jr. and Mable Barron; m. Terrence Duane Ohst, Oct. 21, 1972; children: Heather Lynn Reyes, Holly Ann Garratt. AA, Muskegon CC, Mich., 1969; BS, Calif. Coast U., 1994; BBA, Baker Coll., 1998; MPA, Grand Valley State U., 2001. Contract asst. Teledyne Continental Motors, Muskegon, 1968; bookkeeper, teller FMB Lumberman's Bank, Muskegon, 1969—72; adminstrv. svcs. supr. Muskegon (Mich.) County Dept. of Employment & Tng., 1972—94, dep. dir., 1994—. Adj. prof. Baker Coll., Muskegon, Mich., 2002—; cons., presenter in field. Pres. local chpt. Nat. Fedn. of Bus. & Profl. Women, Muskegon, 1990—91; campaign coord. United Way, 1990—2001; bd. dir. Muskegon (Mich.) Schs. Health & Human Svcs. Adv. Bd., 2002—03, Baker Corp. Svcs. Adv. Bd., 1999—. Mem.: Muskegon (Mich.) C.of C., Mich. Works Assn., Nat. Assn. Workforce Devel. Profls., Pi Alpha Alpha, Phi Kappa Phi, Delta Mu Delta. Lutheran. Avocations: travel, reading. Office: Department of Employment & Training 1611 Oak Avenue Muskegon MI 49442 Office Phone: 231-724-6381. Business E-Mail: ohst@co.muskegon.mi.us.

OJEDA, ANA MARIA, therapist, clinical caseworker; b. Miami, Feb. 1, 1980; d. Juan Bruno and Daisy Irene Ojeda. BSc in Psychology and Elem. Edn., U. Miami, Coral Gables, Fla., 2002, MSc in Mental Health Counseling, 2004; MA in Clin. Psychology, Regent U., 2006. Milieu therapist Miami Children's Hosp., 2001—03; therapist Psychsolutions, Miami, 2002; psychotherapist Miami Children's Hosp., 2003—04; residential counselor The Pines

Residential Treatment Ctr., Portsmouth, Va., 2004—05, therapist/clin. caseworker, 2005—06. Assoc. tchr. U. Miami, Hialeati, 2002, rsch. asst., Coral Gables, 03. Nominee Excellence award, Miami Children's Hosp., 2003; named to Provost's Honor Roll, U. Miami, 2001—02, Dean's List, 2001—02; recipient academic merit, 2004, certificate of appreciation, Miami Children's Hosp., 2003. Mem.: APA, Pi Lambda Theta. Republican. Catholic. Avocations: travel, bicycling, running, reading. Office: The Pines Residential Treatment Ctr 825 Crawford Pkwy Portsmouth VA 23704 Personal E-mail: anamojeda@aol.com.

OJI, PAULINE E., secondary school educator; b. Ozuitem, Nigeria; arrived in U.S., 1995; d. Shedrack N. and Mercy O. Udah; m. Madumere Oji, June 1, 1995; children: Mercy A., Victoria O. BS in Chemistry, Univ. Port Harcourt, 1987; MEd Spl. Edn., Coppin State Coll., 1999. Cert. spl. educator. Sub. tchr. Balt. City Pub. Sch., Balt., 1997—99; math. tchr. Woodbourne Ctr. Inc., Balt., 1997; sci. tchr. Strawbridge Sch., Balt., 2001—04, Woodlawn H.S., Balt., 2004—. Dept. chair Strawbridge Sch., Balt., 2001—02; mem. adv. com. John Hopkins Univ., 2003—. Facilitator (presentation) Picoturbine Windmills, 2001. Vol. Girl Scouts of Am. Troop 1536, Balt., 2003—; presenter Md. Assn. of Non Pub. Spl. Edn. Facilities, 2002, Md. Assn. of Non Pub. Spl. Edn. Facilitier, 2003; supporter Spl. Olympics, 2000—. Nominee Educator of the Yr., Ten Conf., 2001; recipient Gov. Citation, Md. Gov., 2000. Mem.: NEA, ASCD, Nat. Sci. Tchrs. Assn., Internat. Reading Assn., Coun. Exceptional Children (vol.), Md. State Tchrs. Assn. (vol.), Nat. Coun. for Tchrs. of Math., Md. State Coun. for Tchrs. of Math. Achievements include participated in Md. Educators Summer Rsch. Program. Avocations: reading, travel, dance, basketball, tennis. Home: 12 Hickory Nut Ct Baltimore MD 21236 Office: Balt County Pub Sch Woodlawn H S 1801 Woodlawn Dr Baltimore MD 21207 Office Phone: 410-887-1310. Personal E-mail: mvpeo@juno.com.

OJINNAKA, BECKY, publishing executive; b. Orlu, Nigeria, July 27, 1956; d. Kevin and Felicia Anasott. BSBA, Southeastern U., Washington, 1978, MBA, 1980; PhD, Fell Sem., Calif., 1996; DBA, Calif. Coast U., 1999. Youth svc. ACB-Bank, Lagos, Nigeria, 1981-82; with Fin. Merchant Bank, Lagos, 1982-86; sr. mgr. CCB Bank, Lagos, 1986-92; asst. gen. mgr. Winggold Savings, Lagos, 1992-96; pres. World Achievers, Lagos, 1994—, Jireh Shammah, Lagos, 1998—. Author: Be You Own Cosmetics, 1985, Cosmetician, 1990, Part 1 and 2. Cons. to First Lady of Nigeria, 1996-98. Mem. DBA Execs., Nigerian Assn. Female Execs. (cons. 1994). Home: 6703 Kerman Ct Lanham Seabrook MD 20706-2186

O'KANE, BARBARA LYNN, research psychologist; b. Jersey City, Sept. 7, 1950; d. Herbert and Pearl Clair Sandick; m. David Dean O'Kane, June 25, 1988; 1 child, Nathan Sean. BS, Suffolk U., 1976; PhD, Brandeis U., 1982. Rsch. psychologist U.S. Army Natick R&D Ctr., Natick, Mass., 1979-85; R&D insp. U.S. Army Material Command, Alexandria, Va., 1985-89; engring. rsch. psychologist U.S. Army Night Vision and Electronic Sensors Directorate, Ft. Belvoir, Va., 1985—. Author: (chpt.) Vision Models for Target Detection and Recognition, 1995; contbr. articles to profl. jours. Avocations: music, public speaking, creation science, skiing. Home: 6117 Burnett St Alexandria VA 22310-2662 Office: US Army Night Vision Lab Burbeck Rd Fort Belvoir VA 22060 Business E-Mail: okane@nvl.army.mil.

O'KANE, MARGARET E., non-profit organization executive; children: Katie, Beth. BA in French, Fordham U., 1969; MHS in Health Adminstrn. and Planning, Johns Hopkins U. Sch. Hygiene and Public Health. Second grade tchr. St. Ambrose Sch., Bklyn., 1970-72; neurology rsch. asst. Children's Hosp., Boston, 1972-73; respiratory therapist St. Elizabeth's Hosp., Boston, U. Va. Med. Ctr., Charlottesville, Va., Children's Hosp., Washington, DC, 1973-78; program analyst office of planning, evaluation, legislation health svcs. adminstrn. U.S. Dept. Health and Human Svcs., Washington, 1979-81; rsch. assoc. intergovermental health policy project (IHPP) The George Washington U., Washington, 1981-83; public health svc. fellow U.S. Dept. Health and Human Svcs. Nat. Ctr. for Health Svcs. Rsch., Washington, 1983-84, special asst. to dir., 1985-86; dir. med. dirs. divsn. Am. Assn. Health Plans (formerly Group Health Assn. of Am., Inc.), Washington, 1986-89; dir. quality mgmt. Group Health Assn., Inc., Washington, 1989-90; pres. Nat. Com. Quality Assurance, Washington, 1990—. Elected mem. Inst. of Medicine, 1999. Named Health Person of Yr. Medicine & Health Jour., 1996; recipient Founder's award Am. Coll. Med. Quality, 1997. Office: Nat Com for Quality Assurance 2000 L St NW Ste 500 Washington DC 20036-4918

O'KEEFE, BEVERLY DISBROW, state official, federal official; b. Wilton, Conn., Sept. 1, 1946; d. Harry Harbs and Jane Corrine (Young) Disbrow; children: Marcia Corrine, Jennifer Lynn; m. John Patrick O'Keefe, Aug. l981 (div. 1985). AA, Berkshire Community Coll., 1973; BA in Psychology, U. Mass., 1975; MPA, U. S.C., 1979; cert. master gardener, U. R.I., 1999. Lic. social worker, S.C., 1989. Statis. clk. U. S.C., Columbia, 1976-78; pub. adminstr. employment and tng. Office of Gov., State of S.C., Columbia, 1976-78, 88—; project coord. Trident Tech. Coll., Charleston, S.C., 1981-82; office mgr. Med. U. S.C., Charleston, 1983-85; coord. bus. svcs. AMI East Cooper Community Hosp., Mt. Pleasant, S.C., 1985-87; mktg. rep. R.L. Bryan Co., Columbia, 1987; pub. adminstr. S.C. Dept. Social Svcs., Columbia, 1988; pub. adminstr., employment and tng. Office Gov. State S.C., Columbia, 1988-89; mem. employment and tng. staff City of Norfolk (Va.) Div. Soc. Svcs., 1990-91; social sci. analyst Naval Edn. and Tng. Ctr. Family Svc. Ctr., Newport, R.I., 1992-96; program coord. Naval Edn. and Tng. Ctr. Family Svc. Ctr., Newport, R.I., 1996—; rsch. assoc. U. R.I., Kingston, 1999; project dir. U. R.I. Family Resource Partnership, Providence, 1999; marine rsch. specialist Sea Grant Coll. Program, U. R.I. Narragansett Bay Campus, 2002—03; supervising planner RI Water Resources Bd., Providence, 2003—. Editor newsletter Friends of Library, 1982-84. Sec. Friends of Charleston County Libr., 1981-82, pres. 1982-84; bd. dirs. Wando High Sch. Local Adv. Coun., Mt. Pleasant, 1981-84, Newport Armed Svcs. YMCA, 1996-98; pres. Wando High Sch. PTA, 1982-83, editor newsletter, 1982-85; vol. Navy-Marine Corps Relief Soc., 1993-96; mem. Newport County Coun. Cmty. Svcs., 1996-98; publicity chmn. Navy-Marine Corps Relief Soc., Newport, 1993-94; asst. dir., fin. U. R.I. Sea Grant Program, 2002; supr. planner R.I. Water Resources Bd., Providence, 2003—. Grantee Marine Rsch. Specialist Sea Grant Coll. Program, U. R.I., Narragansett, 2002—03. Mem. Am. Soc. Pub. Adminstrs.,R.I. Orchid Soc. (sec. 2000), Ocean State Orchid Soc. (sec. 2003), Nat. Marine Educators Assn., U. RI (coop. ext. cert. master gardener, 1999-, mem. exec. bd. adv. edn. coord, 2005-). Democrat. Roman Catholic. Avocations: writing fiction, water colors, gardening. Home: 472 Gardiner Rd West Kingston RI 02892-1068 Office: RI Water Resources Bd 100 N Main St 5th Flr Providence RI 02903 E-mail: ladyslip1@mindspring.com.

O'KEEFE, KATHERINE PATRICIA, elementary school educator; b. Long Beach, N.Y., Mar. 6, 1971; d. Raymond John and Therese Marie (Lederman) O'K. Student, U. Fribourg (Switzerland), 1991-92; BA, Providence College, 1993; postgrad. Instrnl. Technology, N.Y. Inst. Tech. Lic. FCC; provisional cert. tchr., N.Y., 2003. Journalist Merrick Life, NY, 1993; adminstrv. asst. Grey Entertainment, NYC, 1994-95, acct. coord., 1995-97; acct. exec. Rabasca & Co., Melville, NY, 1997—98; elem. sch. tchr. in art Pub. Sch. 151, Bklyn., 1998—2001, tchr. 2d grade, 2001—05; elem. sch. sci. tchr. Pub. Sch. 150, Queens, NY, 2005—. Prodn., script and continuity asst. Piccoli and Piccoli Prodns., N.Y.C., 1995. Exhibitions include N.Y.C. Artist/Tchr. Exhbn., 2006. Mem.: Internat. Soc. for Tech. in Edn., Sierra Club. Roman Catholic. Avocations: guitar, scuba diving, art, songwriting, voice acting. Home: 1992 Debra Ct North Merrick NY 11566-1732 Office: Pub Sch 150! 40-01 43rd Ave Sunnyside NY 11104

O'KEEFE, KATHLEEN MARY, state official; b. Butte, Mont., Mar. 25, 1933; d. Hugh I. and Kathleen Mary (Harris) O'Keefe; m. Nick M. Baker, Sept. 18, 1954 (div. 1970); children: Patrick, Susan, Michael, Cynthia, Hugh, Mardeen. BA in Comm., St. Mary Coll., Xavier, Kans., 1954. Profl. singer, mem. Kathie Baker Quartet, 1962-72; rsch. cons. Wash. Ho. of Reps., Olympia, 1972-73; info. officer Wash. Employment Security Commn., Seattle, 1973-81, dir. pub. affairs, 1981-90, video dir., 1990-95, ret., 1995. Freelance writer, composer, producer, 1973—. Author: Job Finding In the Nineties, The Third Alternative, handbook on TV prodn., (children: So You Want to be President, 1995; composer numerous songs, also writer, dir., prodr. numerous spots. Founder, pres. bd. Eden, Inc., visual and performing arts, 1975—; pub. rels. chmn. Nat. Women's Dem. Conv., Seattle, 1979, Wash. Dem. Women, 1976-85; bd. dirs., composer, prodr., dir. N.Y. Film Festival, 1979; Dem. candidate Wash. State Senate, 1968. Recipient Silver medal Seattle Creative Awards Show for composing, directing and producing Rent A Kid, TV Pub. Svc. spot, 1979. Mem. Wash. Press Women. Roman Catholic. Home: 11225 19th Ave SE C104 Everett WA 98208 Office Phone: 425-337-0356. E-mail: kathie@nwrain.com.

O'KEEFE, KERRY ANN, elementary school educator; b. Great Bend, Kans., Feb. 15, 1951; d. Everett Lee and Margaret Holland Borron; m. Michael Dennis O'Keefe, June 2, 1973; 1 child, Tomas Michael. BS, Ea. Conn. State U., Willimantic, Conn., 1973; MA, U. R.I., Kingston, R.I., 1979. Tchr. Ledyard Bd. Edn., Conn., 1973—. Tchr. Three Rivers Cmty. Coll., Norwich, Conn., 1984. Grantee, Conn. and Mohegan Tribe, 2005, Ledyard Edn. Found., 2005, 2006. Mem.: AAUW, NEA, Ledyard Edn. Assn. Avocations: travel, reading, gardening. Office: Ledyard Ctr Sch 740 Col Ledyard Hwy Ledyard CT 06339

O'KEEFE, LINDA LEE, physical education educator; b. Mojave, Calif., Apr. 28, 1947; d. Edward and Betty June O'Keefe. BS in Phys. Edn., U. Dayton, Ohio, 1971, MS in Phys. Edn., 1976. Tchr. Bellehaven Elem. Sch., Dayton, 1971—72, Meadowdale HS, Dayton, 1972—78; prof. Sinclair CC, Dayton, 1979—, coach, 1979—2003. Spkr., event organizer Am. Cancer Soc., Dayton, 2000—. Named Coach of Yr., Sinclair CC, 1979—2003; named one of Ohio's Top Educators, Ohio Mag., 2003; named to Hall of Fame, Dayton Tennis Commn., 1987, Nat. Jr. Coll. Athletic Assn., 1996; recipient Excellence in Tchg. award, Nat. Inst. Staff Devel., 2003, Faculty Excellence and Innovation award, Southwestern Ohio Coun. Higher Edn., 2003. Mem.: AAHPERD, Am. Assn. Health Educators, Ohio Assn. Health, Phys. Edn., Recreation and Dance. Avocations: reading, bicycling, tennis, hiking, gardening. Home: 1100 Stanwick Beavercreek OH 45430 Office: Sinclair CC 444 W 3d St Dayton OH 45430 Fax: 937-512-3056. Office Phone: 937-512-2287. Business E-Mail: linda.okeefe@sinclair.edu.

O'KEEFE-HARDY, LEE MARILYN, psychotherapist; b. Orange, Calif., May 17, 1946; d. Darrel Dean Wilson and Laverne Rasmussen Winifred; m. Michael Edward O'Keefe; 1 child, Christopher Michael O'Keefe; m. William James Hardy, Dec. 23, 1978; 1 child, Jennifer Michelle Hardy. AA, Orange Coast Coll., Calif., 1966; undergrad. in Psychology, Calif. State U., Long Beach, 1967; BS in Psychology, U. Calif., LA, 1971; AA in Human Svcs., Psychiat. Tech., Golden West Coll., Calif., 1975; MS in Counseling, Calif. State U., Fullerton, 1978. Cert. marriage and family counseling Malibu Counseling Ctr., Calif., Hypnosis Cross Creek Counseling. Psychiat. tech. Huntington Hosp., Huntington Beach, Calif., 1976, Hoag Hosp., Newport, Calif., 1976—78; sch. counselor Irvine (Calif.) Unified Sch. Dist., 1978—79; counselor Malibu Counseling Ctr., 1981—83; owner, counselor Cross Creek Counseling, Malibu, 1983—. Exhibitions include Western Colo. Watercolor Soc., 11th Nat. Exhibit, 2001, San Diego Watercolor Soc., 21st Internat. Exhibit, 2001, Realism, Va., 2002, Watercolor West, Cherry Valley Exhibit, 2002, Grey Whale, 2002, Montrose/Verdugo City Exhibit, 2003, Malibu Art Assn. Juried Show, 2003, Woman Painters West Pacific Palisades, 2004, Allied Artists Nature's Preserve Show, 2005, Palm Springs Mus. 37th Annual Juried Exhibit, 2006. Recipient Top 100 award, Arts for the Parks, 1991, 2004, Judges award in painting, 2004, Carson award, Palm Springs Art Mus., 2006. Mem.: San Diego Art Inst., San Dieog Mus. Art, LA Mus. Art, Nat. Mus. Women in Arts, Woman Painters West, Western Colo. Watercolor Soc. (painter 1990—), Watercolor West (painter 1980—), San Diego Watercolor Soc., Nat. Watercolor Soc., Malibu Art Assn. (HS student liason 1979—), Am. Watercolor Soc., Allied Artists of Santa Monica Mts. and Seashore, Books @ the Beach (sec. 2004—). Democrat. Avocations: reading, skiing. Personal E-mail: crosscreek@aol.com.

O'KELLY, CRYSTAL KATHLEEN, secondary school educator, television producer; b. Pomona, Calif., Dec. 10, 1957; d. Guy Lewis and Doris Lowell (Schmidt) O. BS in Comm., Calif. Poly. U., 1984. Cert. tchr. Calif. Trainer, server CNC Orgn., Rancho Cucamonga, Calif., 1977-84; cons. Grubb & Ellis, Ontario, Calif., 1985; salesperson Nordstrom, Montclair, Calif., 1986; sr. analyst Gen. Dynamics, Pomona, 1986-90; asst. dir. Crystal Cathedral, Garden Grove, Calif., 1996; prodr., on-air talent Claremont (Calif.) Pub. Access TV, 1991—; substitute tchr. Claremont Unified Sch. Dist., 1993—2005; English tchr. H.S. Porrona Unified Sch. Dist., 2005—. Staff writer Poly Post, Pomona, 1981-82; chmn. bd., 1995-97, bd. mem. Claremont Pub. Access TV, 1994—; summer sch. tchr., Webb Pvt. Sch., 2000-05. Ind. prodr., dir., host, writer, editor, TV show People to Know, a show dedicated to excellence in TV and the arts, 1994—; creator, producer Miss O'Kelly's Story Time, 1999. Vol., co-host fundraiser Claremont Pub. Access TV, 1991—, Sta. CPAT and The Prodrs. Club, Claremont, 1991-93; various other cmty. and mun. projects. Recipient Calif. State scholar, 1976, Basic Edn. Opportunity grantee, 1978. Mem. Toastmasters (v.p. 1997, pres. 1999—), Toastmasters Club 12, Pomona Valley Art Assn., Claremont Tennis Club. Protestant. Avocations: painting, dance, acting, art collecting, photography. Office: People to Know PO Box 992 Claremont CA 91711-0992

OKERLUND, ARLENE NAYLOR, academic administrator, writer; b. Emmitsburg, Md., Oct. 13, 1938; d. George Wilbur and Ruth Opal (Sensenbaugh) Naylor; m. Michael Dennis Okerlund, June 6, 1959 (div. Apr. 1983); 1 dau., Linda Susan. BA, U. Md., 1960; PhD, U. Calif.-San Diego, 1969. Instr. sci. Mercy Hosp. Nursing Sch., Balt., 1959-63; prof. English San Jose (Calif.) State U., 1969—2005, dean humanities and arts, 1980-86, acad. v.p., 1986-93. Cons. Ednl. Testing Svc., Berkeley, Calif., 1976—80. Author: Elizabeth Wydeville: The Slandered Queen, 2005; editor San Jose Studies, 1975—80; contbr. articles on the humanities to profl. jours. Bd. dirs. World Forum Silicon Valley, Peninsula Banjo Band. Grantee NEH, 1979; grantee San Jose State U., 1971-72. Mem.: MLA (del. to assembly, west coast rep. 1976—77), Am. Beethoven Soc. (v.p. bd. dirs.), Calif. Coun. Fine Arts Deans (pres. 1984—86), Internat. Coun. Fine Arts Deans, Philol. Assn. Pacific Coast (sec.-treas. 1975—78). Democrat. Office: San Jose State U Dept English Washington Sq San Jose CA 95192-0090 Office Phone: 408-924-4425. Business E-Mail: okerlund@email.sjsu.edu.

OKERSON, ANN SHUMELDA LILLIAN, librarian; d. Jacob and Alexandra Tereshtshenko Shumelda. MLS, U. Calif. Libr. Simon Fraser U., Vancouver, B.C., Canada, 1970—85; dir. libr. svcs. Jerry Alper Inc., Eastchester, N.Y., 1985-90; sr. program officer Assn. of Rsch. Librs., Washington, 1990-95; assoc. dir. librs. Yale U., New Haven, 1995—. Editor numerous books; contbr. articles to profl. publs. Named Alumni of Yr. Mt. View Acad., 1995; recipient Best Article Am. Libr. Assn., 1988, 93, Excellence in Libr. Tech., 2000; numerous grants. Avocations: chocolate, travel, reading. Office: Yale U Libr PO Box 208240 New Haven CT 06520-8240

OKOLSKI, CYNTHIA ANTONIA, psychotherapist, social worker; b. N.Y.C., July 26, 1954; d. Augusto and Valerie (Toffolo) Zaccari; m. Andrzej L. Okolski, Jan. 8, 1983; children: Gabriel, Christian. BA, Hofstra U., 1976; MA, Columbia U., 1978, MSW, 1983; cert. psychoanalytic psychotherapy, Advanced Ctr. Analytic Therapy, 1986. Counselor, instr. Hofstra U., Hempstead, N.Y., 1975-76; recreational dir. Residence for Young Adults Hostel, Hempstead, 1976-78; rsch. asst. Ctr. Policy Rsch., N.Y.C., 1978-79, Ctr. Psychosocial Studies, N.Y.C., 1979-81; group leader Fidel Sch., Glen Cove, N.Y., 1981; rsch. asst. Assn. of Jr. League, N.Y.C., 1982; social worker Children's Aid Soc., N.Y.C., 1983-84, Manhattan Psychiat. Ctr., N.Y.C., 1984-85; psychotherapist Advanced Inst. Analytic Psychotherapy, Jamaica, N.Y., 1986—. Supervising psychotherapist in therapeutic foster care program St. Christopher-Ottillie, 1994—. Mem. NASW, Acad. Cert. Social Workers, Alpha Kappa Delta.

OKONEDO, SOPHIE, actress; b. London, Jan. 1, 1969; 1 child, Aoife. Grad., Cambridge U. Actor: (films) Young Soul Rebels, 1991, Go Now, 1995, Ace Ventura: When Nature Calls, 1995, The Jackel, 1997, This Year's Love, 1999, Mad Cows, 1999, Peaches, 2000, Once Seen, 2001, Dirty Pretty Things, 2002, Cross My Heart, 2003, Hotel Rwanda, 2004 (Oscar Nominee for Best Performance by an Actress in a Supporting Role, 2005, Nominee Image award for Outstanding Supporting Actress in a Motion Picture, 2005), Aeon Flux, 2005; (TV films) Age of Treason, 1993, Deep Secrets, 1996, Never Never, 2000, Sweet Revenge, 2001, Dead Casual, 2002, The Inspector Lynley Mysteries: In the Presence of the Enemy, 2003, Alibi, 2003, Whose Baby?, 2004, Born with two Mothers, 2005; (TV miniseries) Doctor Who: Scream of the Shalka, 2003; (TV series) Staying Alive, 1996, The Governor, 1996, In Defiance, 2000, Clocking Off, 2000.*

OKONIEWSKI, LISA ANNE, psychologist; BA in Psychology and Studio Art, Coll. William and Mary, 1975; MS in Clin. Psychology, Hahnemann U., 1978; PhD in Counseling Psychology, Temple U., 1984. Lic. psychologist. Counselor Eastern State Hosp., Va., 1974-75; staff psychologist Main Line Day Sch., Pa., 1978-79, Jewish Employment Vocat. Svc., Pa., 1981-82; rsch. asst. Dr. Zygmunt Piotrowski, Pa., 1980-85; staff psychologist Plymouth Healthcare Assocs., Pa., 1984-87; pvt. practice Phila., 1987—. Home: 4951 Mckean Ave Philadelphia PA 19144-4160 Office: 4953 Mckean Ave Philadelphia PA 19144-4160 Office Phone: 215-842-9399.

O'KONSKI, MARJORIE KATHERINE, music educator; d. Robert Thomas and Katherine Josephine Kilbride; m. James Edward O'Konski, July 15, 1972; children: Mary Elizabeth, Katherine Helena, Robert Michael, Brian James, Richard Joseph. MusB in Piano Performance, U. Mo., Kansas City, 1968; MusM in Piano Performance, U. Mich., Ann Arbor, 1970; MusM in Edn. and Music Therapy, U. Kans., Lawrence, 1996. Tchg. asst. U. Mich., Ann Arbor, 1968—70; instr. piano Wash. State U., Pullman, 1970—71, Southwestern Coll., Winfield, Kans., 1971—72, O'Konski Piano Studio, Bradenton, Fla., 1973—79, Olathe, Kans., 1979—89, Lawrence, 1990—97; music therapist Wichita Falls State Hosp., Tex., 1996—97; instr. piano O'Konski Piano Studio, Topeka, 1997—2003; dir. music therapy clin. tng. and activities Midwest Health Svcs., 1997—2003; music therapist O'Konski Music Therapy Contract Svcs., 2002—03; dir. music therapy program Wartburg Coll., Waverly, Iowa. Advisor music therapy majors Wartburg Coll. Music Therapy Program, Waverly, Iowa, 2003—; mem. Wartburg Coll. Human and Animal Rsch. Com., 2004—06, Wartburg Coll. Faculty Interest Group, 2006—, Wartburg Coll. Instrnl. Resources Com., 2006—; advisor Southwestern Coll. Female Athletes, Winfield, Kans., 1971—72; coord. quality assurance Lexington Pk. Nursing and Post-Acute Care Facility, Topeka, 2001—03; mem. practice analysis com. Certification Bd. Music Therapists, Kansas City, Mo., 2003—03; advisor Wartburg Coll. Cath. Knights, 2003—, Wartburg Music Therapy Student Assn., 2003—; adj. faculty Washburn U., Tokepa, 1998—2003; presenter, spkr. in field. Performer: (soloist) Kansas City Philharmonic, Bach Concerto for Four Harpsichords, (piano accompanist) Washburn U. Faculty Recital, Saxophone, Graduate Recital, Saxophone, Washburn U. Student Recital, voice, Washburn U. Studio Recital, Violin, Violin Music for Memorial Service, Washburn University Faculty Recital, Voice, Senior Recital, Violincello, Senior Recital, Trumpet, Senior Recital, Percussion, Auditions for Washburn Univ.Honors Recital, (soloist) Kansas City Youth Symphony, Symphonic Variations, C. Frank, (piano accompanist) Honors Recital, Washburn University, Studio Recital, Trumpet, Student Recital, Washburn University, Washburn University Senior Recital, Voice, Washburn University Faculty Recital, Voice, Senior Recital, Violincello, Student Recital, Washburn University, Regional Voice Competition, NATS, Washburn University Joint Faculty Recital, Opera Selections, (soloist) Concerto in A Minor, R. Schumann, (piano accompanist) Studio Recital, Violin, Washburn University Student Recital, Opera Selections, Topeka Opera Society (KS), Masterclass, Violincello, Student Recital, Washburn University, Senior Recital, Viola, Wartburg College Faculty Recital, Voice, Benefit Concert, Violincello, (piano soloist) Fundraiser (Dinner), Wartburg Symphony, (piano accompanist) Wartburg College Scholarship Auditions, (soloist) Southwestern Coll. Orch., Concerto in A Major, W. A. Mozart, (piano accompanist) Wartburg College Senior Recital, Bassoon, Wartburg College Junior Recital, Voice, Student Recitals, Wartburg College, Voice Audition, Wartburg Faculty Position, (symphony pianist) Topeka Symphony Orchestra Concerts, Wartburg Community Symphony Concerts; piano adjudicator (performance evaluation) Student Day Auditions, FSMTA (Florida), Student Day Auditions, KMTA (Kansas); performer: (piano) Chorale Fantasy, L. van Beethoven, (piano soloist) Salon Music at Lexington Park, (piano accompanist) University of Kansas Faculty Recital, Trombone, Violin Studio Recital (KS), University of Kansas Senior Recital, Student Compositions. Mem. Lawrence Civic Choir, Kans., 1991—94; sec., mem. Wartburg Cmty. Symphony, Waverly, 2003—06. Recipient Activity Dir. Yr., Kans. Health Care Assn., 1999, Aging Rsch. Devel. Support award, Wartburg Coll., 2005; fellow, Robert F. Unkefer Acad. Neurologic Music Therapy, Colo. State U., 2005; grantee, Midwest Health Svcs., Kans., 2000, 2002, Wartburg Coll., 2005. Mem.: AAUW (assoc.), AAUP (assoc.), Topeka Activity Dirs. Assn. (sec. 1999—2000, pres. 2000—01, sec., treas. 2001—03), Am. Music Therapy Assn. (assoc.; mem. rep. midwestern region 2003—06), Pi Kappa Lambda, Mu Phi Epsilon (life; pres., Alpha Kappa chpt. 1966—68, Outstanding Sr. 1968). Conservative. Roman Catholic. Achievements include development of comprehensive music therapy program for long-term care, Midwest Health Services (Kansas); six-month national roster music therapy internship program at Midwest Health Services (KS); Tone Bar Chimes Performing Ensemble For Long-Term Care Residents; Performances Within Facility, Local Community, And Adjoining Communities; Uniform Concert Attire; Compact Discs And Videos Produced; intergenerational performing ensemble; choreography, singing, playing instrument, spoken dialogue included; costumes, set designs, original scripts; music arranged by Marjorie O'Konski. Avocations: reading, travel, hiking, cryptography, solving sudoku puzzles. Home: 1209 Charlene Street Waverly IA 50677-9631 Office: Wartburg College 100 Wartburg Boulevard Waverly IA 50677-0903 Office Phone: 319-352-8401. Office Fax: 319-352-8501. E-mail: marj.okonski@wartburg.edu.

OKOS, MILDRED, city manager; b. L.I., N.Y., July 17, 1913; d. William Fohs and Estelle Solomon; 1 child. Grad. H.S., N.Y.; student, Birds Bus. Sch. Model, sec., sales and mktg. staff Macy's Dept. Stores & Lord & Taylor, N.Y.C., 1940-44; with Floyd Bennett Airport, Bklyn., 1944-48; mgr. sales boutique L.I., N.Y., 1994; exec. dir. Town Village Aircraft Safety & Noise Abatement Gov. Town of Hempstead, N.Y., 1985-99. Office: Town Village Aircraft Safety & Noise Abatement Com 196 Central Ave Lawrence NY 11559-1438

OKOSHI-MUKAI, SUMIYE, artist; b. Seattle; One-woman shows include Gallery Internat., N.Y.C., 1970, Miami Mus. Modern Art, 1972, Galerie Saison, Tokyo, 1982, St. Peter's Ch., Living Room Gallery, N.Y.C., 1987, Viridian Gallery, 1987, 1992, 1996, 1999, Port Washington (N.Y.) Pub. Libr., 1985, NAS, Washington, 1991—92, exhibited in group shows at Bergen Mus. Art and Scis., 1983, Am. Acad. Arts and Scis., 1984, Port Washington Pub. Libr., 1985, Hudson River Mus., 1985, Sao Paulo and N.Y. Culture Exch., 1988, Hyundai Gallery, Pusan, Korea, 1988, Gary Snyder Fine Art, N.Y.C., 2002, Represented in permanent collections The Mitsui & Co., N.Y., Hotel Nikko, Atlanta, Bank of Nagoya, N.Y., Palace Hotel, Guam Island, Port Washington Pub. Libr., Lowe Gallery-U. Miami, Miami Mus. Modern Art, Nat. Women's Edn. Ctr., Saitama-ken, Japan, NAS, Hammond Mus., North Salem, N.Y., The Jane Voorhees Zimmerli Art Mus., N.J., Asian Traditions Modern Expressions; included in Collage-Techniques, 1994. Mem. Nat. Women Artists Assn. (Belle Cramer award Zluta and Joseph Fund award, Ralph Mayer Meml. award, Doris Kreindler Meml. award 2002), Nat. Mus. Women in the Arts (charter mem. 1994).

OKOUCHI, CARLA HO'NOA HIGDON, music educator; b. Honolulu, July 18, 1974; d. Charles William and Faye S. Higdon. BA in Music Edn., Auburn U., Ala., 1997. Lic. K-12 Va. Dept. Edn., 2005, Ala. Dept. Edn., 1997. Music educator Fairfax County Pub. Sch, Alexandria, Va., 1997—, Hayfield

Elem. Sch., Alexandria, 2004—. Choir dir. Mt. Vernon Presbyn. Ch., Alexandria, 2001—; dir. Kids Creation Camp. Musician (french horn): Fairfax Wind Symphony. Help the homeless walker Fannie Mae Found., Washington, 1999—2006; crop walk- walker Ch. World Services, Alexandria, Va., 1999—2005; elder Mt. Vernon Presbyn. Ch., Alexandria, 2000—06, worship coun. chair, 2000—06, youth leader, 2002—06, choir dir., interim pastor nominating com., 2005—06, pastor nominating com., 2005—. Mem.: Fairfax Gen. Music Educators Assn. (newsletter editor 2005—, all county choral festival co-chair 2006—), Fairfax Educators Assn. (bldg. rep. 2005—06), Va. Educators Assn., Auburn Women of Music (life; founding pres. 1994—96), Kappa Kappa Gamma (life; activities chair 1994—96). Presbyterian. Avocations: hiking, horseback riding, billiards, travel, crafts. Office Phone: 703-924-4535. E-mail: carla.okouchi@fcps.edu.

OKSAS, JOAN KAY, economist, educator; b. Chgo., Feb. 21, 1927; d. John Joseph and Antoinette (Pestinick) Kazanauskas; m. Casimir G. Oksas, Nov. 3, 1956; children: Stephen, Mary. BS, Northwestern U., 1944; MS in Edn., Chgo. State U., 1975, Northern Ill. U., 1981; EdD, Loyola U., Chgo., 1986. From instr. to assoc. prof. Chgo. State U., 1976-89, prof., 1989-93; ret., 1993; chair dept. libr. sci. and communication Chgo. State U., 1986-88. Judge Am. Film and Video Festival, N.Y., Chgo., 1980-93, Chicagoland History Fairs, 1986—; mem. vis. com. North Ctrl. Assn. Accreditation, Chgo., 1980-93; cons. Adopt-a-Sch. program, 1984; bd. dirs. Mut. Fedn. Savs. and Loan, Chgo. Contbr. articles, revs. to profl. jours. Recipient Faculty Excellence award Chgo. State U., 1991. Mem. Ill. Libr. Assn., Phi Delta Kappa, Delta Kappa Gamma (Ill. Gamma Alpha chpt.) (bd. dirs. 1982—, pres. 1986-88). Republican. Roman Catholic.

OKSILOFF, CHRISTA, technologist, educator; b. Berlin, Dec. 6, 1926; arrived in U.S., 1947, naturalized, 1952; d. Gustav Otto Uecker and Elisabeth Schulzek; m. Assen Oksiloff, 1953; 1 child, Assenka. Degree for kindergarden tchr., State Kindergarten Seminar, Berlin; degree for med. technologist, Norwegian Drs. Home and Hosp., Bkly. Dental asst. pvt. office, Berlin; medical technologist Shoregate Shopping Ctr., pvt. office; med. asst. Assen Oksiloff, MD, Willoughby, Ohio. Author: Art and Writing Exhbn., Passing on "Senior Wisdom", Frau Holle, Berlin in Crisis, 1945, The Journey of the Wedding Cake, 1996, Morris the Cat, 1996, Stigma, 1996, Seniors Childhood Memories of Christmas in Berlin, 1996, The Birthday Cake Surprise, 1997, Mt. St. Michel, 1997, Parents' Anguish, 1997, Teenage Carefree Summer Days, 1997, The Emigrants, 1998, The Gift Dogs Are, and Bring, 1998, Dedicated Teachers, 1998, Understanding in More Depth, 1998, The Remote Risk of Gardening, 1998, Floppy the Therapist, 1999, A Just Person, 1999, Blunder, 1999, The Inheritance, 1999, Albania Kosovo, 1999, Bulgaria One of the Balkans, 1999, Light Healing, 1999, The Cleanup, 1999, Grandpa, 1999, A Late Response, 1999, Renewal and Restoration, 2000, The Lure and Healing of the Sea, 2000, Spook, 2000. Mem.: Cleve. Mus. Art., Epworth United Meth. Ch. Univ. Cir., Cleve. Coll. Club. Avocations: writing, classical music, opera, travel, theater. Office Phone: 440-942-4342.

OKTAVEC, EILEEN M., anthropologist, artist; b. Apr. 9, 1942; d. Albert W. and Margaret (O'Reilley) O. Student, Cooper Union, N.Y.C., 1960-61; BA in Anthropology, SUNY, Stony Brook, 1973; MA in Anthropology, U. Ariz., 1975. Instr. anthropology White Pines Coll., Chester, NH, 1975-76; art dir. Great Walks, Inc., Goffstown, NH, 1989—. Author: Answered Prayers: Miracles and Milagros Along the Border, 1995; photographs in: Great Walks of Acadia National Park and Mount Desert, 1990, Great Walks of Southern Arizona, 1991, Great Walks of Big Bend National Park, 1991, Great Walks of the Great Smokies, 1992, Great Walks of Yosemite National Park, 1993, Great Walks of Sequoia and Kings Canyon National Parks, 1994, Great Walks of Acadia National Park and Mount Desert Island, 1994, Great Walks of the Olympic Peninsula, 1999, The Woodland Garden, 1996; exhibited in group shows at Rockport (Mass.) Art Festival, 1977, 78, Berkshire Art Assn., Pittsfield, Mass., 1979, The Ogunquit (Maine) Art Ctr., 1982, 83, N.H. Art Assn., Manchester, 1985, Concord (Mass.) Art Assn., 1988, 91, 92, 96-98, Sharon (N.H.) Art Ctr., 1998. Winner Southwest Book award for Answered Prayers, 1997. Mem. Concord Art Assn., Sharon Arts Ctr. Home: 3151 Hazens Notch Rd Montgomery Center VT 05471-4408 Office Phone: 603-497-8020.

OKUN, BARBARA FRANK, psychologist, educator; b. Phila., July 17, 1936; d. James and Auguste Lenson (Sachs) Frank; m. Sherman Kenneth Okun, Nov. 24, 1960; children: Marcia Lorraine, Jeffrey Michael, Douglas Howard. BA, Wellesley Coll., 1957; MA, U. Mich., 1966; PhD, Northwestern U., 1970. Lic. psychologist, Mass. Sales corr. Harcourt, Brace & Co., Inc., N.Y.C., 1957-58; personnel mgr. McCall Corp., N.Y.C., 1958-60; psychologist Counseling Center, Northwestern U., Evanston, Ill., 1968-70, Mundelein Counseling Center for Women, Chgo., 1970; instr. psychology Coll. of Lake County, Grayslake, Ill., 1970; asst. prof. dept. counselor edn. Northeastern U., Boston, 1970-75, chmn., prof. dept. counselor edn., 1975-82, prof. dept. counseling psychology, spl. edn. and rehab., 1982—. Clin. instr. dept. psychiatry Harvard Med. Sch. and Cambridge Hosp, 1989—; hpvt. practice cons. and psychotherapy. Author: Effective Helping: Interviewing and Counseling Techniques, 1976, 3d edit., 1987, 4th edit., 1992, Working with Families: An Introduction to Family Therapy, 1980, Working with Adults: Individual, Family and Career Development, 1984, Seeking Connections in Psychotherapy, 1990; editor: Vol. 9 of The Family Therapy Collections, 1984, ERIC Searchlight on Marriage and Family Counseling, 1984; co-editor: Intimate Environments: Sex, Intimacy and Gender in Families, 1989 Bd. dirs. Met. Boston YWCA, 1976-80, v.p., 1979-80. Mem. Am. Psychol. Assn., Am. Assn. Counseling and Devel., Am. Orthopsychiatric Assn., Am. Family Therapy Assn.

OKUN, DEANNA TANNER, federal official; m. Bob Okun; children: Rachel, Kelsi. BA in Polit. Sci., Utah State U.; JD, Duke U. Sch. of Law. Research assoc. Competitive Enterprise Inst., Washington; assoc. attorney and mem. of Internat. Trade Group Hogan & Hartson law firm, Washington; legis. asst. to Senator Frank Murkowski US Senate, counsel for internat. affairs to Sen. Frank Murkowski, 1993—99; commr. U.S. Internat. Trade Comm., 1999—, vice chmn., 2000—02, 2004—06, chmn, 2002—04. Office: US Internat Trade Commission 500 E Street SW Washington DC 20436

OLAYAN, LUBNA S., finance company executive; b. Saudi Arabia; d. Suliman S. Olayan. BS in Agr., Cornell U.; MBA, Ind. U. With Morgan Guaranty, NYC, 1979—81; joined Olayan Grp., Riyadh, Saudi Arabia, 1983—; CEO Olayan Financing Co., Riyadh, Saudi Arabia. Bd. dirs. Olayan Investments Co. Establishment, Egyptian Fin. Co., Capital Union, Dubai, United Arab Emirates; non-exec. dir. Chelsfield, UK, WPP, UK; bd. trustees Arab Thought Found.; pres. Suliman S. Olayan Found. Named one of 100 Most Influential People, Time mag., 2005, 50 Most Powerful Women, Fortune mag., 2005, 100 Most Powerful Women, Forbes mag., 2006; recipient Achievement award, Arab Bankers Assn. of N.Am., 2004. Mem.: World Econ. Forum (Women Leadership Initiative, Arab Bus. Coun. Exec. Com.), World Bank (World Links Adv. Coun.), INSEAD Internat. Coun. Office: Olayan Financing Co PO Box 8772 Riyadh 11492 Saudi Arabia*

OLDENBURG, CHLOE WARNER, performing arts association administrator, educator; d. Wilbert Charles and Elizabeth Rowe Warner; m. Frederick A. Oldenburg (dec.); children: Frederick Alan Jr., Chloe Rankin, Warner Andrew. BA, Case Western Res. U., 1942, MA, 1969. V.p. Cleve. Play House, pres., 1982—85; pres. bd. Cleve. Sch. of the Arts, v.p. bd. Author: Leaps of Faith, 1985. V.p. Jr. League of Cleve.; women's coun. Cleve. Mus. Art, 1975—; bd. dirs. St. Lukes Hosp. Recipient Frances Payne Bolton award, Jr. League of Cleve., 1998. Unitarian. Avocations: tutoring, theater going around the world. Home: 31699 Trillium Tr Pepper Pike OH 44124

OLDFIELD, JOY MALEK, lawyer; b. Akron, Ohio, Nov. 9, 1975; d. Danny N and Amelia Ann Malek; m. Charles W. Oldfield, Aug. 31, 2002. BA, John Carroll U., 1997; JD, U. Akron, 2000. Bar: Ohio 2000. Assoc. Scanlon & Gearinger Co., LPA, Akron, Ohio, 2000—06; prin. Hill Co., LLC, Akron, Ohio, 2006—. Arbitrator BBB, Akron, 2000—. Contbr. articles to profl. jours. Mem. Cmty. Legal Aid Svcs., Akron, 2003—06. Scholar Judge Oscar A. Hunsicker scholar, U. Akron, Sch. Law, 1999—2000. Mem.: ATLA, Summit County Trial Lawyers Assn. (scholar 1999), U. Akron Alumni Assn., Ohio Acad. Trial Lawyers (bd. trustees 2006), Akron Bar Assn., Ohio State Bar Assn. (bd. gov. new lawyers divsn. 2003—05). Office: Hill /Co LLC One Cascade Plaza Ste 2000 Akron OH 44308 Office Phone: 330-253-4000. Office Fax: 330-253-3840. E-mail: joldfield@hillcompanyllc.com.

OLDHAM, MAXINE JERNIGAN, real estate broker; b. Whittier, Calif., Oct. 13, 1923; d. John K. and Lela Hessie (Mears) Jernigan; m. Laurance Montgomery Oldham, Oct. 28, 1941; 1 child, John Laurence. AA, San Diego City Coll., 1973; student Western State U. Law, San Diego, 1976-77, LaSalle U., 1977-78; grad. Realtors Inst., Sacramento, 1978. Mgr. Edin Harig Realty, LaMesa, Calif., 1966-70; tchr. Bd. Edn., San Diego, 1959-66; mgr. Julia Cave Real Estate, San Diego, 1970-73; salesman Computer Realty, San Diego, 1973-74; owner Shelter Island Realty, San Diego, 1974—. Author: Jernigan History, 1982, Mears Geneology, 1985, Fustons of Colonial America, 1988, Sissoms. Mem. Civl Svc. Commn., San Diego, 1957-58. Recipient Outstanding Speaker award Dale Carnegie. Mem. Nat. Assn. Realtors, Calif. Assn. Realtors, San Diego Bd. Realtors, San Diego Apt. Assn., Internationale des Professions Immobilieres (internat. platform speaker), DAR (vice regent Linares chpt.), Colonial Dames 17th Century, Internat. Fedn. Univ. Women. Republican. Roman Catholic. Avocations: music, theater, painting, genealogy, continuing edn. Home: 3348 Lowell St San Diego CA 92106-1713 E-mail: lilyham@coxs.com.

OLDMAN, MARTHA JEANE, retired medical missionary; b. DesMoines, Iowa, Aug. 23, 1923; d. Charles Leslie and Honora Fleming Shaw; m. Melvin Edward Oldman, Nov. 20, 1999; m. Robert Greenhill Cochrane. BA, Maryville Coll., 1945; DO, Phila. Coll. of Osteopathic Medicine, 1949. Med. missionary Africa Inland Mission Internat., Tanzania, 1952—72; pvt. practice Norristown, Pa., 1972—88. Author: Biblical Leprosy, 2004, (autobiography) Aurora Lea, 2006. Republican. Bapt. Avocations: gardening, reading, sewing. Home: 350 Yonside Dr P O Box 147 Pleasant Hill TN 38578

OLDS, JACQUELINE, psychiatrist, educator; b. Springfield, Mass., Jan. 4, 1947; d. James and Marianne (Ejier) O.; m. Richard Stanton Schwartz, Aug. 26, 1978; children: Nathaniel Leland, Sarah Elizabeth. BA, Radcliffe Coll., 1967; MD, Tufts U., 1971. Diplomate Am. Bd. Psychiatry and Neurology. Resident in adult psychiatry Mass. Mental Health Ctr., Boston, 1974; resident in child psychiatry McLean Hosp., Belmont, Mass., 1976, assoc. attending child psychiatrist, 1979—; psychiatrist-in-charge inpatient unit McLean Hall-Mercer Children's Ctr., Belmont, 1976-79; assoc. child psychiatry Beth Israel Hosp., Boston, 1979—; cons. in child psychiatry Mass. Gen. Hosp., Boston, 1994—. Instr. psychiatry Harvard U. Med. Sch, Boston, 1976-86; asst. prof. clin. psychiatry, 1986-2000, assoc. clin. prof. psychiatry, 2000—; cons. North Shore Mental Health Ctr., Salem, 1981-82. Author: Overcoming Loneliness in Every Day Life, 1996, Marriage in Motion, 2000, editor Clin. Challenges column in Harvard Rev. of Psychiatry; contbr. articles to profl. jours.; author (translator into Spanish): Matrimonio in Moviemento. Recipient Mentoring award Mass. Gen. Hosp. Dept. Child Psychiatry, 1998. Disting. fellow, Am. Psychiat. Assn.; mem. Mass. Psychiat. Soc. (ethics com. 1988-93, mem. pub. affairs com. 1992—), Am. Acad. Child Psychiatry, Am. Psychoanalytic Assn., New England Coun. Child and Adolescent Psychiatry (bd. dirs.). Democrat. Avocations: piano, writing, cooking, watercolors. Office Phone: 617-547-5920.

OLDS, SHARON, poet; b. San Francisco, Nov. 19, 1942; BA, Stanford U., 1964; PhD in English, Columbia U., 1972. Lectr.-in-residence on poetry Theodor Herzl Inst., 1976-80; Fanny Hurst chair Brandeis U., Waltham, Mass., 1986-87; dir. grad. program in creative writing NYU, 1988-91, assoc. prof. English, 1992—. Vis. tchr. poetry Manhattan Theater Club, 1982, Poetry Ctr. for YMCA of N.Y.C., 1982, Poetry Soc. of Am., 1983, NYU, 1983, 85, Sarah Lawrence Coll., 1984, Goldwater Hosp., Roosevelt Island, N.Y., 1983-95, Columbia U., 1986, SUNY, Purchase, 1986; adj. prof. grad. program in creative writing NYU, 1983-92. Author: Satan Says, 1980 (San Francisco Poetry Ctr. award 1981), The Dead and Living, 1984 (Lamont Poetry Selection of the Am. Acad. Poets 1984, Nat. Book Critics Circle award 1985), The Gold Cell, 1987, The Matter of This World, 1987, The Sign of Saturn, 1991, The Father, 1992, The Wellspring, 1996, Blood, Tin, Straw, 1999, The Unswept Room, 2002, Strike Sparks: Selected Poems, 2004; contbr. poetry to numerous anthologies. Guggenheim fellow, 1981-82; Nat. Endowment for Arts grantee, 1982-83; recipient Madeline Sadin award N.Y. Quar., 1978, Poetry Miscellany Younger Poets award, 1979. Fellow: Am. Acad. Arts & Sci. Office: NYU Grad Program in Creative Writing 19 University Pl Rm 200 New York NY 10003-4556

O'LEARY, COLLEEN ALISON, counselor; b. Nashua, NH, June 2, 1979; BA, Keene State Coll., 2002; MA, Arcadia U., 2005. Grad. asst. Arcadia U., Glenside, Pa., 2002—04; cons. Ken-Crest Cons., Plymouth Meeting, Pa., 2003—; counselor, intern Lincoln Ctr. Family and Youth, Bridgeport, Pa., 2004—. Mem.: ACA, APA, Pa. Counseling Assn., Alpha Epsilon Lambda. Home: 1026 Oak Knoll Dr Harrisburg PA 17111-4673

O'LEARY, HAZEL R., academic administrator, retired federal official, lawyer; b. Newport News, Va., May 17, 1937; d. Russell E. and Hazel (Palleman) Reid; m. John F. O'Leary, Apr. 23, 1980 (dec.); 1 child, Carl G. Rollins. BA, Fisk U., Nashville, 1959; JD, Rutgers U., Newark, 1966. Bar: N.J. 1967, D.C. 1985; cert. fin. planner. V.p., gen. counsel O'Leary & Assocs., Inc., Washington, 1981-89; pres. O'Leary & Assocs., Chevy Chase, Md., 1997—; exec. v.p. corp. affairs No. States Power Co., Mpls., 1989-93; adminstr., dep. adminstr. econ. regulatory commn. U.S. Dept. Energy, Washington, 1977—81, sec., 1993-97; COO Blaylock & Ptnrs., N.Y.C., 1997—2002; dir. Scottish Re Group Ltd., 2001—; pres. Fisk U., 2004—. Trustee AES Copr., ICF Kaiser, Inc. Trustee Morehouse Coll., Africare, Ctr. Democracy, Keystone Ctr. Mem. Phi Beta Kappa. Office: Fisk Univ 1000 17th Ave N Nashville TN 37208-3051 also: Scottish Re Group Ltd Crown House 3d Fl 4 Par la Ville Rd Hamilton HM 12 Bermuda

O'LEARY, KATHLEEN ANN, nonfiction writer; b. Washington, Dec. 17, 1946; d. Patrick Christopher and Hilda Elizabeth (Gobrecht) O'Leary; children: Kara Ann Topper, Scott Patrick Thompson, Ryan Arthur Thompson, Kelly Marie Shifflett. Student, Montgomery Jr. Coll., 1964-66, Colo. State U., 1973-74; BS in Bus. Adminstrn., U. Md., 1975. Acct. exec. Sta. WSBT-AM-FM-TV, South Bend, Ind., 1972-74; mgr. advt. and promotion Sta. WGHP-TV, High Point, N.C., 1978-83, Am. Women in Radio and T.V., 1978—84; acct. exec. Wheat, First Securities, Greensboro, N.C., 1983-85; investment broker Legg Mason Wood Walker, Greensboro, 1985-88; investment exec. Ferris, Baker Watts, Inc., Bethesda, Md., 1988-90. Legal sec., paralegal complex civil and criminal investigation and def. practice Washington, 1988-94; legal staffer Morgan, Lewis & Bockius LLP, Washington; lectr. in investment field, 1986-2002. Exec. prodr. TV documentary Classic Memories, 1985. Founder, 1st pres., bd. dirs. Big Brothers/Big Sisters of High Point, 1981-85; founder, sec.-treas. Furniture City Classic, Inc., High Point, 1981-88; founder, bd. dirs. Henredon Classic LPGA Golf Tourament, High Point, 1981-88; mem. Leadership High Point, 1987-89; Challenge: High Point grad. and steering com. mem. High Point C. of C., 1984-85; bd. dirs. met. bd. YMCA of High Point, 1981. 82, Adams Meml. YWCA, High Point, 1985-87, Salvation Army Boys Club, 1980-81, Vols. to Ct., Guilford County, 1980-81; Sunday sch. tchr. Immaculate Heart of Mary Ch., High Point, 1980-87; exec. bd. mem. Greater Washington Open LPGA Golf Tourament, 1980-90. Democrat. Roman Catholic. Avocations: creative writing, classical piano.

OLEISKY, DEBORAH FISCHER, elementary school educator; d. Doris Peters Fischer Malesardi; m. Jonathan Marc Oleisky, July 12, 1992; children: Sarah Elizabeth, Emily Rebecca. BA in Chemistry and Computer Sci., Sweet Briar Coll., 1985; MS in Edn., Johns Hopkins U., 1990. Tchr. Garrison Forest Sch., Owings Mills, Md., 1985—, mem. residential life faculty, 1990—. Mem. Jr. League Balt., 1986—2004. Mem.: NSTA, Iota Sigma Pi. Avocations: travel, gardening, reading. Office: Garrison Forest Sch 300 Garrison Forest Rd Owings Mills MD 21117 Office Phone: 410-559-3151. Business E-Mail: debbie_oleisky@gfs.org.

OLESEN, CAROLYN MCDONALD, dance educator, choreographer; b. Blytheville, Ark., Aug. 27, 1963; d. Travis Eugene and Barbara Jean (Myers) McDonald; m. Donald John Olesen Jr., Nov. 3, 2001. BA in Dance, U. Calif., Irvine, 1987; MA in Edn., U. Iowa, 1998; choreographer, Coe Coll., 1998. Instr. dance Kirkwood C.C., Cedar Rapids, Iowa, 1987-90, choreographer, 1987—2001, artistic dir., 1990—2001; owner, pres. McDonald Arts Ctr., Marion, Iowa, 1988—2001; instr. dance Coe Coll., Cedar Rapids, 1989—2001; choreographer color guard dance ensemble Washington H.S., Cedar Rapids, 1996-97; choreographer show choir All Saints Mid. Sch., Marion, Iowa, 1998-2000; choreographer The Lofte Theatre, Manley, Nebr., 2002; instr. fitness, gourmet cooking S.E. C.C., Lincoln, Nebr., 2002—, instr., 2002—. Cons. Jane Boyd Cmty. House, Cedar Rapids, 1993—94; instr. S.E. C.C., 2002—04; dir. Auburn Dance Team, 2003—04; dir. dance program Wellness Ctr. of Nemaha County, 2004—. Singer/songwriter Rockit Science, 2000-01, Split Decision, 2001, Dark Horse, 2001-04, Enigma, 2005-; CD (with Enigma) Juxtaposition, 2006. Avocations: wine tasting, gourmet cooking, gardening, song writing.

OLESKOWICZ, JEANETTE, physician; b. N.Y.C., Oct. 10, 1956; d. John Francis and Helen (Zielinski) Oleskowicz. BA, NYU, 1977; D Chiropractic, N.Y. Chiropractic Coll., 1982; MS, U. Bridgeport, 1984; MD, U. Medicine and Dentistry N.J., 1990. Diplomate Am. Bd. Psychiatry and Neurology, cert. in addiction psychiatry. U.S. immigration officer U.S. Dept. Justice, N.Y.C., 1977; commd. med. officer USAR, 1983, advanced through grades to maj., 1990; resident and intern Eisenhower Army Med. Ctr., Ft. Gordon, Ga., 1990-94; chief psychiatry U.S. Army Hosp., Vicenza, Italy, 1994-95; cons.-liaison psychiatrist Brooke Army Med. Ctr., Tex., 1995-98; staff psychiatrist Value Options, Phoenix, 1998—2001; hospitalist VA Med. Ctr., Roseburg, Oreg., 2001—. Supporter Am. Leprosy Missions, India, Children Internat.; visited leprosy projects in ctrl. India. Mem.: AMA, Am. Psychiat. Assn. Home: 2515 NW Edenbower 20 Roseburg OR 97470 Office: Dept VA Affairs 913 Garden Valley Blvd Roseburg OR 97470 Office Phone: 541-440-1000 44662.

OLESON, SARAH ELIZABETH, elementary school educator; b. Lima, Ohio, Dec. 12, 1947; d. Olin T. and Mary Elizabeth (Wright) Zurfluh; m. William D. Oleson, June 12, 1971; children: Amanda Marie, Joshua Seth. BS, Wittenberg U., 1970; MS, Marygrove U., 1994. 5th grade tchr. Lima City Schs., 1970—71; 4th grade tchr. Elida (Ohio) Local Schs., 1971—81, 3rd grade tchr., 1988—. V.p. St. Luke's Luth. Ch. Coun., 1996—2002; bd. mem. YWCA, Lima, 1984—87. Democrat. Avocations: yoga, reading, tennis. Home: 4261 Sunnydale Elida OH 45807 Office: Elida Local Schs 300 Pioneer Rd Elida OH 45807

OLESZKIEWICZ-PERALBA, MALGORZATA, Latin American literature and culture studies educator; b. Warsaw; came to U.S., 1977; d. Eliquiusz and Kazimiera Oleszkiewicz. Magister in Iberian and L.Am. Studies, Warsaw U., 1981; MA, CUNY, 1981; MPhil in Latin Am. Lit. & Culture, NYU, 1986, PhD, 1991. Lang. instr. CUNY, Flushing, 1979-81; instr. Spanish NYU, N.Y.C., 1981-87, 90-91; tchr. Spanish UN, N.Y.C., 1982; instr. Spanish CUNY, Bklyn., 1983-84, Rutgers U., Newark, 1987; lang. instr. SUNY, New Paltz, 1988; asst. prof. Bard Coll., Annandale-on-Hudson, N.Y., 1991-95, U. Tex., San Antonio, 1995—2001, assoc. prof., 2001—. Presenter XI Internat. Symposium Lit., Montevideo, Uruguay, 1993, II Internat. Conf. Ibero Am. and Argentine Theater, Buenos Aires, 1993; 48th Internat. Congress of Americanists, Stockholm, 1994; cultural meeting, The Birth of the Two Natures: The Creole and the Mestizo in Spanish America, Mérida, 1996, Afro-Latin Am. Rsch. Assn. Conf., Salvador, Brazil, 1996, others. Author: Teatro popular peruano: del precolombino al siglo XX, 1995; contbr. articles to profl. jours. Univ. fellow NYU, 1986-87, 89-90, Penfield fellow NYU, 1987-88, Dean's dissertation fellow NYU, 1988-89, Asher Edelman Released Time fellow Bard Coll., 1992; recipient CONCYTEC grant, Lima, 1988-89, Faculty Rsch. award U. Tex. San Antonio, 1995-96, 1998-1999, 2003-2004. Mem. MLA, LASA, Inst. Internat. Lit. Iberoamericana, Inst. Lit. Cultural Hispánico. Avocations: theater, dance, music, cinema. Home: 13311 Deer Falls Dr San Antonio TX 78249-3691 Office: U Tex San Antonio Divsn Fgn Langs 6900 N Loop 1604 W San Antonio TX 78249-1130

OLIAN, JOANNE CONSTANCE, curator, art historian; b. N.Y.C. d. Richard Edward and Dorothy (Singer) Wahrman; m. Howard Olian; children: Jane Wendy, Patricia Ann Student, Syracuse U.; BA, Hofstra U., 1969; MA, NYU Inst. Fine Arts, 1972. Grad. internship Met. Mus., N.Y.C., 1973; asst. curator Mus. City of N.Y., 1974, curator costume collection, 1975—91; cons. curator Costume Collection, 1992—95, curator emeritus, 1995—. Lectr. Parsons Sch. Design; vis. lectr. Musée des Arts Decoratifs, Paris, summers, 1983—85; co-curator Art and Fashion Nassau County Mus. Art, 2006. Author: The House of Worth: The Gilded Age, 1860-1918, 1982; editor: Authentic French Fashions of the Twenties, 1990, Everyday Fashions of the Forties, 1992, Children's Fashions from Mode Illustrée 1860-1914, 1994, Wedding Fashions, 1862-1912, 1994, Everyday Fashions, 1909-1920, 1995, La Mode Illustrée, 1997, Victorian and Edwardian Fashions, 1998, 80 Godey's Full-Color Fashions Plates, 1838-1880, 1998, Full-Color Victorian Fashion, 1870-1893, 1999, Everyday Fashions of the Sixties, 1999, Parisian Fashions of the Teens, 2002, Everyday Fashions of the Fifties, 2002, Children's Fashions, 1900-1950, 2003; contbr. articles to profl. jours., chpts. to books Mem. Internat. Coun. Mus. (costume com.), Costume Soc. Am. (dir. 1976-79, 83-86), Fashion Group (bd. dirs. 1985-86), Centre Internat. d'Etude des Textiles Anciens, Cosmopolitan Club N.Y.C Home and Office: 2 Shepherds Ln Sands Point NY 11050 Personal E-mail: joanneolian1@aol.com.

OLIAN, JUDY D., dean; b. Australia; BS in psychology, Hebrew U., 1974; MS in indsl. rels., U. Wis., 1977, PhD in indsl. rels., 1980. Lectr. to full prof. mgmt. and orgn. Robert H. Smith Sch. Bus., U. Md., 1979—2000, sr. assoc. dean, 1999—2000; fellow Am. Coun. Edn. Fellow to pres., U. Md., 1990—91, special asst. to pres., 1991—92, founder, dir. IBM-TQ Project, 1991—92; dean, prof. mgmt. Smeal Coll. Bus., Pa. State U., 2000—; dean-elect UCLA Anderson Sch. Mgmt., 2005—. Exec. com. Personnel and Human Resources divsn. Acad. Mgmt., 1984—87, 1991—94; exec. com. bd. dirs. Assn. to Advance Collegiate Sch. Bus., 2000—01. Author: (syndicated weekly column) About Business; past mem. editl. bd.: Jour. Quality and Mgmt., Acad. Mgmt. Review. Bd. dirs. The Second Mile, Penn State Found. Recipient award for curriculum innovation, Md. Assn. for Higher Edn., 1996. Office: Dean's Office Smeal Coll Bus Adminstrn Pa State Univ 801-H Bus Adminstrn Bldg University Park PA 16802 Office Phone: 814-863-0448. Office Fax: 814-865-7064. Business E-Mail: jdo10@psu.edu.

OLIMPIO, SUZANNE M., psychologist; b. Kearny, N.J., May 10, 1963; d. John and Arlene Onnembo; m. Edward Olimpio; children: Alyssa, Alexander. BA, Villanova U., Pa.; MA in Counseling, Dider Coll.; diploma in Sch. Psychology, Jersey City U., NJ; cert. in Supr., Seton Hall U. Psychologist Monteville (N.J.) Bd. Edn., 1992—95; dir. Spl. Edn. Boonton (N.J.) Bd. Edn., 1995—97; psychologist Mi Arlington (N.J.) Bd. Edn., 2001—. Coach Girls Travel Soccer, Montville, 2004—. Mem.: N.J. Sch. Psychology Assn., Nat. Assn. Sch. Psychologists, Morris County (N.J.) Psychol. Assn. (v.p. 1992—95), Valhalla Civic Assn. (v.p. 2003—05, bd. dirs. 2001—03). Home: 43 Abbott Rd Towaco NJ 07082

OLIN, LENA MARIA JONNA, actress; b. Stockholm, Mar. 22, 1956; d. Britta Alice Holmberg; m. Orjan Ramberg (div.), 1 child, August; m. Lasse Hallstrom, Mar. 18, 1994, 1 child, Tora. Actress Royal Dramatic Theatre, Stockholm, Bklyn. Acad. Music; performances include (theater) The Alchemist, Paradisbarnen, Juno and the Peacock, Gross and Klein, Servitore Di Due Padrone, Restoration, King Lear, Nattvarden, Summer, A Dream Play, The

Master and Margerita, Miss Julie; (films) The Adventures of Picasso, 1978, Karleken, 1980, Fanny and Alexander, 1982, Grasanklingar, 1982, After the Rehersal, 1984, Friends, 1988, The Unbearable Lightness of Being, 1988, Enemies, A Love Story, 1989, Havana, 1990, Mr. Jones, 1993, Romeo is Bleeding, 1994, The Night and the Moment, 1994, Lumiere et Compagnie, 1995, The Golden Hour, 1996, Polish Wedding, 1997, Hamilton, 1997, Night Falls on Manhattan, 1997, Planet 16, 1998, The Ninth Gate, 1999, Mystery Men, 1999, The Ninth Gate, 2000, Chocolat, 2000, Ignition, 2001, Queen of the Damned, 2002, Darkness, 2002, The United States of Leland, 2003, Hollywood Homicide, 2003, Casanova, 2005, Bang Bang Orangutang, 2005; (TV films) Gypsy Woman, 1977, After the Rehearsal, 1984, Wallenberg: A Hero's Story, 1985, Lady with dog, 1986, Komediianter, 1987, Hebriana, 1990, Hamilton, 2001; (TV series) Alias, 2002-03.*

OLIN, MARILYN, secondary school educator; b. Rochester, N.Y. BA in English, Nazareth Coll. Rochester, 1965; MS in English Edn., SUNY, Brockport, 1971. Nat. bd. cert. tchr. 1999. Tchr. Rochester Diocese Cath. Schs., 1965—68, Rochester Pub. Schs., Duval County (Fla.) Pub. Schs., 1972—, Paxon Sch. for Advanced Studies, Jacksonville, Fla., 1996—. Mem.: Nat. Forensic League, Nat. Bd. for Profl. Tchg. Stds. Office: Paxon Sch for Advanced Studies 3239 Norman E Thagard Blvd Jacksonville FL 32254 Office Phone: 904-693-7583 ext 161.

OLINGER, CARLA D(RAGAN), medical advertising executive; b. Cin., Oct. 8, 1947; d. Carl Edward and Selene Ethel (Neal) Dragan; m. Chauncey Greene Olinger, Jr., May 30, 1981. BA, Douglass Coll., 1975. Mgr. info. retrieval services Frank J. Corbett, Inc., N.Y.C., 1976—77; editor, proofreader, prodn. asst. Rolf W. Rosenthal, Inc., N.Y.C., 1977—78, copywriter, 1978—80, copy supr., 1980—82, v.p. copy dept., 1982—83; v.p., group copy supr., adminstrv. copy supr. Rolf W. Rosenthal, Inc., divsn. Ogilvy & Mather, 1984—89; v.p., assoc. creative dir. RWR Advt., 1989; v.p., copy supr. Barnum & Souza, N.Y.C., 1990—92, Botto, Roessner, Horne & Messinger, Ketchum Comm., N.Y.C., 1992—95, Lyons Lavey Nickel Swift, N.Y.C., 1995—. Editor: Antimicrobial Prescribing (Harold Neu), 1979. Mem.: Nat. Inst. Social Scis., St. George's Soc. N.Y., Church Club N.Y. Office: Lyons Lavey Nickel Swift 220 E 42nd St New York NY 10017-5806

OLIN ZIMMERMAN, SARA JANE, education educator; b. Lawrence, Kans., Jan. 3, 1953; d. William Medill and Jeannette Pearl (Perkins) Olin; m. Ward Brian Zimmerman, Aug. 3, 1975; children: Ward Alexander, Brian Nathaniel, Zachary Skywarrior, Elizabeth Briana Jane. BGS in Human Devel. and Psychology, U. Kans., 1974, BS in Edn., 1976, MS in Edn., 1979, PhD in Spl. Edn. and Adminstrn., 1986. Presch. and kindergarten tchr. Child Devel. Ctr., Topeka State Hosp., 1975-76; 2d grade tchr. Topeka Pub. Schs., 1976-77, learning disabilities tchr., 1977-79, Lawrence Pub. Schs., Kans., 1979-88; rsch. assoc. Kans. Inst. for Rsch. in Learning Disabilities, 1987-88; asst. prof. psychology and spl. edn. Emporia State U., Kans., 1988; asst. prof. spl. edn. Murray State U., Kans., 1988-90; prof. curriculum and instrn. Appalachian State U., Boone, NC, 1992—. Cons. Western Ky. Ednl. Coop., Murray, 1988-90. Contbr. articles to profl. publs. Den leader Boy Scouts Am., Boone, 1991-92. Grantee Coun. for Learning Disabilities, 1987, Murray State U., 1989, 90. Mem. ASCD, Am. Ednl. Rsch. Assn., Internat. Reading Assn., Coun. for Exceptional Children, Coun. for Learning Disabilities, Learning Disabilities Assn., Phi Delta Kappa. Avocations: scuba diving, travel. Office: Appalachian State U Coll Edn Curriculum & Instruction Boone NC 28607

OLIPHANT, MARTHA CARMICHAEL, civic worker; b. Providence, Sept. 17, 1935; d. Leonard and Pearl (Kidston) Carmichael; m. S. Parker Oliphant, June 2, 1962 (dec. Jan. 2001); children: Leonard Carmichael, Samuel Duncan. BA, Wellesley Coll., 1957. Lab. asst. NIMH, Bethesda, Md., 1957-63; chmn. DC Com. for Stratford Hall, Robert E. Meml. Assn., 2004—06. Bd. govs. Washington Home and Hospice, 1976—. Bd. dirs., past pres. All Hallows Guild, Washington Cathedral, 1971-93; mem. bd. lady visitors Childrens Nat. Med. Ctr., 1971-93, Children's Hosp. Found., 1974-90; mem. Com. of 100 of Fed. City, 1977-86; bd. dirs. Washington Home and Hospice, 1976—, also past pres.; past bd. dirs., v.p. Jr. League Washington; mem. Smithsonian Women's Com., Washington, 1993—. Recipient voluntarism award Jr. League Washington, 1988. Mem. Sulgrave Club (bd. dirs. 1985-88), Evergreen Garden Club (pres. 1989-91). Republican. Episcopalian. Home: 4977 Glenbrook Rd NW Washington DC 20016-3222

OLIVEIRA, THERESA RAZZANO, secondary school educator; b. Queens, N.Y., Apr. 3, 1952; d. Pasquale A. and Agnes M. Razzano; m. Antonio M. Oliveira, Aug. 6, 1978; children: Antonio Razzano, Francesca Razzano. BA magna cum laude, Ladycliff Coll., 1973; MA, William Paterson State Coll., 1978. Cert. secondary edn. teaching, student personnel svcs., N.J. High sch. math. tchr. Randolph (N.J.) Twp. Bd Edn. Recipient Non Art Educator award Art Educators N.J., 1989, mini grant N.J. State, 1979-80. Mem. Randolph Edn. Assn. (pres. 2002-, negotiations chair, 1990-2002), N.J. Edn. Assn. (state budget com. 2002-), Nat. Edn. Assn. Rep. Assembly (delegate NEA-RA 1999-), Phi Delta Kappa. Home: 64 Lawrence Rd Randolph NJ 07869-3105

OLIVER, ANN BREEDING, secondary school educator, art dealer; b. Hollywood, Fla., Sept. 21, 1945; d. Harvey James and Ruth (Lige) Breeding; 1 child, Anna Liege; m. Ted J. Oliver, June 29, 1996. BA in Fgn. Lang., U. Ky., 1967; MA in History of Art, Ohio State U., 1971. Curatorial intern Lowe Art Mus., Coral Gables, Fla., 1972; adj. faculty Fla. Atlantic U., Boca Raton, Fla., 1972-73, 78; lectr. Miami (Fla.) Dade C.C., 1974, with art-music workshop, 1980-81, lectr.-cons., 1972—, adj. faculty music dept., 1991; curator of edn. Ctr. for the Fine Arts, Miami, 1987-92, High Mus. of Art, Atlanta, Ga., 1992-96; Spanish tchr. Sprayberry H.S., Cobb County Bd. Edn., Marietta, Ga., 1997—. Mem. Artists in Edn. Panel, Ga. Coun. for Arts, 1994; field reviewer Inst. Mus. Svcs., 1994; adj. faculty in art history Kennesaw State U., Marietta, Ga., 1996—; Spanish tchr. Cobb County Bd. Edn., Atlanta, Spray H.S., Marietta, Ga.; collector, dealer, historial so. folk art & outsider culture. Contbg. editor African Art: An Essay for Teachers, 1993; project mgr. and contbg. author: Rings: Five Passions in World Art: Multicultural Curriculum Handbook, 1996. Mem. Cobb County Com. for Fgn. Lang. Curriculum Alignment. Recipient Nat. award for graphics Mead Paper Co., 1989, Gold Medal of Honor publication design S.E. Mus. Educators Publ. Design, 1994. Mem. Am. Assn. of Mus., Inst. Mus. Svcs., Nat. Art Edn. Assn., Am. Coun. Tchrs. Fgn. Langs., Fla. Art Edn. Assn. (dir. mus. divsn.), Ga. Art Edn. Assn. (dir. mus. divsn., Mus. Educator of Yr. 1993), Fgn. Lang. Assn. of Ga. Home: PO Box 1032 Flat Rock NC 28731 Personal E-mail: oliverta@bellsouth.net.

OLIVER, BARBARA ANN, retired apparel executive; b. Coffeeville, Miss., July 1, 1936; d. Raymond Victor Branum, Georgia Rae Caver; m. Collie Oliver, July 17, 1956 (dec. Jan. 1994); children: Mitchell Caver, Susan Annelle. Student, Memphis Art Acad. Cutting supr. Normandie Mills, Coffeeville, 1960—63, FormFit Rogers, McMinnville, Tenn., 1963—91, Alamo Mills, Alamo, Tenn., 1991—93, FormFit Apparel, Lafayette, Tenn., 1993—2001; ret., 2001. Owner gift shop, McMinnville, Tenn., 1993—94; owner antique mall, McMinnville, 1994—98; cons. in field. Active various charitable orgns. Named Congeniality Winner, Ms. Sr. Macon County, 2002; recipient 4-Star award, Tenn. Divsn. Am. Cancer Soc., 1990, Award of Appreciation for Cmty. Svc., WalMart, 2002, numerous other cmty. svc. awards. Mem.: AARP, Am. Legion, Nat. Garden Club, Women of Moose, Ladies Aux. of VFW (nat. info. com. chmn. 89th conv. 2001—02, sec. and treas. 2002—03, pres. 2003—, Mary B. Cochran award Dept. Tenn. 2001—02, Bronze medallion Outstanding Pres. 2001—02). Methodist. Avocations: painting, fishing, dance, gardening, cooking. Home: 1003 Ellington Dr Lafayette TN 37083

OLIVER, BARBARA LYNN, special education educator; b. Charleston, W.Va., Oct. 11, 1957; d. Merle Loidley Oliver, Jr. and Martha Faye Oliver; 1 child, Clifford. BS in Music Edn., W.Va. Inst. Tech., Montgomery, 1984; MA in Spl. Edn., W.Va. U., Institute, 1991. Cert. national health cons. Washington, 2003, instrumental and vocal music K-12, learning disabilities K-12, mental impairment K-12, behavior disorders K-12 tchr. W.Va. Tchr. Sissonville H.S., Charleston, W.Va., 1986—, mem. informational studies com., 2004—. Mem.: Ams. for the Arts, Internat. Reading Assn., Nat. Coun. Tchrs. English, Nature Conservancy, Alpha Delta Kappa. Avocations: camping, reading, hiking, natural alternatives in health treatment. Office: Sissonville HS 6100 Sissonville Dr Charleston WV 25312

OLIVER, DANIELLE MICHELLE, special education educator, recreational therapist; b. Rockville Center, N.Y., July 1, 1975; d. Gary James and Patti Lynn Gardiner; m. Edward Jason Oliver, July 10, 2005. AAS, Nassau CC, Garden City, N.Y., 1996; BS, SUNY, Fredonia, 2000; MS, LI U., 2003. Bd. cert. music therapist. Music therapist, activities dir. ACLD, Bethpage, NY, 2000—03, respite provider, 2001—; spl. edn. tchr. All About Kids, Plainview, NY, 2004—, BOCES, Plainview, NY, 2005, Valley Stream (N.Y.) Sch. Dist., 2005—. Drama instr. OBAY Gap Program, Massapequa, NY, 2004—05. Breast cancer fundraiser; nat. autism awareness rsch. fundraiser. Mem.: Am. Music Therapy Assn., Coun. Exceptional Children. Home: 114 Park Ln Massapequa NY 11758

OLIVER, DARLA DEANE, elementary school educator; d. Leroy Joseph Elsass and Beth Inez Clapsaddle; m. Patrick Steven Oliver, Sept. 20, 1974; children: Derek Andrew, Joe Oliver Casey. BS, Boise State U., Idaho, 1973. Cert. std. secondary edn. Idaho Dept. Edn., 1973. Tchr., coach Kuna H.S., Idaho, 1974—75; tchr., dept. head, head coach Meridian Sch. District-Lowell Scott Mid. Sch., Idaho, 1975—99, tchr., dept. head, coach, 2000—. Named Tchr. of Yr., Meridian Sch. Dist., 1988, 2006; recipient Pulling for Kids award, Lewis and Clark Mid. Sch., 2000—01. Home: 2056 N Cool Creek Ave Meridian ID 83646 Office: Lewis and Clark Middle School 4141 E Pine Meridian ID 83642 Office Phone: 208-377-1353. Office Fax: 208-377-3718. Business E-Mail: oliver.darla@meridianschools.org.

OLIVER, DEBBIE EDGE, elementary school educator; b. Houston, Jan. 8, 1953; d. John Orval and Charlotte (Laird) Edge; m. Lawrence Allen Oliver, July 21, 1973; 1 child, Kelly Dawn. BA in Tchg., Sam Houston State U., 1975, kindergarten cert., 1975. Cert. elem. tchr., Tex. Tchr. computer lab Big Sandy Ind. Sch. Dist., Dallardsville, Tex., 1975—. Mem. site-based decision group, mem. textbook com., tech. com., gifted and talented com., Univ. Interscholastic League sponsor Big Sandy Ind. Sch. Dist., 1989—; H.E.B. Edn. 2000 rep., 1993—; mem. grant writing com. Telecomms. Infrastructure Fund, 1997; univ. interscholastic league sponsor; rep. H.E.B. Grocery Store Edn., 1993-2000. Hon. mem. Future Farmers Am., Livingston, 1987; rodeo sec. Polk County Youth Rodeo Assn., Livingston, 1984—; adult leader 4-H, Livingston, 1984—; rodeo sec. Coldspring Lions Rodeo, 1997, 98. Recipient Disting. Svc. award Future Farmers Am., 1989; Title II math./sci. minigrantee Edn. Svc. Ctr., Huntsville, Tex., 1992. Mem. Ch. of Christ. Office: Big Sandy Ind Sch Dist PO Box 188 Dallardsville TX 77332 Home: 186 Highland Dr Livingston TX 77351-6311 Business E-Mail: doliver@livingston.net.

OLIVER, DIANA CLOUTIER, elementary school educator; b. Waterville, Maine, Apr. 10, 1938; d. Basil Anthony and Era Bessie (Horan) Cloutier; m. Robert Henery Oliver Jr., July 11, 1959; children: Michael, Janet, Beth, Sandra. BS, Farmington Tchrs. Coll., 1989; MEd, U. Maine, 1991. Cert. tchr., Maine. Tchr. North Jay (Maine) Sch., 1959-62, Augusta, Maine, 1962-64, North Belgrade (Maine) Sch., 1966-69, Maine Sch. Dist. # 9, Farmington, 1969—2001; libr. New Sharon Jim Ditzler Meml. Libr., 2001—. Active Human Rights Com., Farmington, 1991-94; vol. Literacy Vols. Am., Farmington, 1991—, Spl. Olympics, Maine, 1983; coord. Stroy Camp, Farmington, 1991—. Mem. NEA, ASCD, Maine Tchrs. Assn., Western Maine Assn. for Retarded Citizens (bd. dirs., pres. 1982-92), Emblem Club (pres. 1988-89, chmn. 1991-93), Maine State Assn. Emblem Clubs (1st trustee 1994-95, chmn. meml. svc. 1993, drug awareness chmn. 1993), Sandy River Edn. Assn. (chmn. libr. com. 1991-93, staff devel. com. 1991-93, bldg. rep. 1992-95, tech. com. 1994-95). Democrat. Roman Catholic. Avocations: reading, camping, handmade crafts. Home: 132 Gushman Dr Farmington ME 04938

OLIVER, DONNA H., academic administrator, secondary school educator; AB, Elon Coll.; MEd, U. NC, Greensboro; MS, NC Agrl. and Tech. State U.; PhD, U. NC. Tchr. biology Hugh M. Cummings High Sch., Burlington, NC; v.p. academic affairs Bennett Coll., Greensboro, NC, 1989—. Office: Bennett College 900 E Washington St Greensboro NC 27401

OLIVER, ELIZABETH KIMBALL, historian, writer; b. Saginaw, Mich., May 21, 1918; d. Chester Benjamin and Margaret Eva (Allison) Kimball; m. James Arthur Oliver, May 3, 1941 (div. July 1967); children: Patricia Allison (dec.), Dexter Kimball. BA, U. Mich., 1940. Tchr. Dexter (Mich.) High Sch., 1940-41; libr. Sherman (Conn.) Libr. Assn., 1966-75; pres. Sherman (Conn.) Libr. Assn., 1983-84; writer, historian, 1976—. Reporter Sherman Sentinel, 1965-70; editor newsletter Sherman Hist. Soc., 1977-78; columnist Citizen News, Fairfield County, Conn., 1981-83. Author: History of Staff Wives-AMNH, 1961, Background and History of the Palisades Nature Association, 1964, History and Architecture of Grace United Methodist Church, 1990, Legacy to St. Augustine, 1993, Franklin W. Smith and His Casa Monica Hotel, 2000, Viewpoint of a St. Augustine Columnist, 2004; guest columnist Mandarin News, 1995-97; columnist St. Augustine Record, 1998-2005, Viewpoint of St. Augustine, 2004, Florida Impact--8 Biographical Sketches, 2004. Vol. N.Y. Hist. Soc., N.Y.C., 1961-65; treas. Coburn Cemetery Assn., Sherman, 1976-82; historian Greenbrook-Palisades Nature Assn., Tenafly, N.J., 1962-64; mem. St. Augustine Hist. Soc., Naromi Land Trust (life), Cedar Key Hist. Soc.; adv. bd. IBC (Eng.). Mem. AAUW, Friends of Libr. (life), Inst. Am. Indian Studies, Marjorie Kinnan Rawlings Soc. (charter), St. Augustine Woman's Club (archivist, cert. of appreciation 1990), Sherman Hist. Soc., Mandarin Hist. Soc., Smithsonian Nat. Mus. of the Am. Indian (charter). Republican. Congregationalist. Avocations: reading, piano, botany, dulcimer playing. Home: 2292 Commodores Club Blvd Saint Augustine FL 32080-9161

OLIVER, KERRYN HINRICHS, music educator, religious studies educator; b. Webster City, Iowa, Dec. 1, 1954; d. Lowell K and Kathryn Rosa Hinrichs; m. Michael L. Oliver, Dec. 16, 1978; children: Erin Michelle Bandow, Mark Michael. AA, Ellsworth Coll., Iowa Falls, 1985; MusB, U. No. Iowa, Cedar Falls, 1997. Lic. pastor NE Assn. UCC/Iowa, 2005, NW Assn. UCC/Iowa, 2005; cert. Level I in Kodaly Drake U., Iowa, 2003. Pvt. piano/vocal tchr., Alden, Iowa, 1980—; music dir. Immanuel Meml. United Ch. of Christ, Alden, Iowa, 1985—; vocal music tchr. Alden Elem./Iowa Falls-Alden Schs., Alden and Iowa Falls, 1999—; adj. vocal instr. Ellsworth Coll., Iowa Falls, 2003—05; parish assoc./christian educator/pastor Immanuel Meml. United Ch. of Christ and Jewell United Ch. of Christ, Alden and Jewell, Iowa, 2005—. Workshop leader/cons. Nebr. Conf. United Ch. of Christ, Lincoln, 2003—05, Iowa Conf. United Ch. of Christ, Des Moines, 2005—; ptnr. in edn. United Ch. of Christ, Cleve. and Des Moines, 1997—. Contbr. article/workshop. Vol. music tchr. Alden Cmty. Presch., Iowa, 2001. Mem.: Iowa State Edn. Assn., NEA, Iowa Choral Dirs. Assn., Am. Choral Dirs. Assn., Alden Edn. Assn. (membership chair 2003—04), Phi Theta Kappa, Pi Kappa Lambda Music, Kappa Delta Pi Edn., Golden Key, Omicron Delta Kappa, Sigma Alpha Iota. United Church Of Christ. Avocations: reading, perennial gardens, backyard bird watching/feeding, travel. Home: P O Box 63 712 Hardin St Alden IA 50006-0063 Office Phone: 515-859-7259. Personal E-mail: olivers@iowatelecom.net.

OLIVER, KIMBERLY, Teacher of the Year; b. Wilmington, Del. BA in English Arts, Hampton U.; MEd in elem. edn., Wilmington Coll. Cert. Nat. Bd. Profl. Teaching Standards, 2004. Kindergarten teacher Broad Acres Elem., Silver Spring, Md., 2000—. Named Md. Teacher of the Year, 2006, Teacher of the Year, Coun. Chief State Sch. Officers, 2006; recipient Greenblatt Excellence Teaching award, Greenblatt Edn. Fund. Office: Broad Acres Elem Sch 13313 Old Columbia Pike Silver Spring MD 20903*

OLIVER, LOUISE V., ambassador; m. Daniel Oliver; 5 children. BA with distinction, Smith Coll. Apptd. commr. Nat. Commn. on Children, 1989; pres. Oliver Mgmt. Consultants; permanent US rep. UNESCO, Paris, 2004—. Chmn. Philanthropy Roundtable, Washington, Intercollegiate Studies Inst.; co-founder New Atlantic Initiative; bd. dirs. Independent Women's Forum. Office: UNESCO 7 Place de Fontenoy 75352 Paris France Office Phone: 33-1-4524-7416. E-mail: parisunesco@state.gov.

OLIVER, MARY, poet; b. Maple Heights, Ohio, Sept. 10, 1935; d. Edward William and Helen Mary (Vlasak) O. Student, Ohio State U., 1955—56, Vassar Coll., 1956—57. Chmn. writing dept. Fine Arts Work Ctr., Provincetown, Mass., 1972-73, mem. writing com., 1984; Banister poet-in-residence Sweet Briar Coll., 1991-95. William Blackburn vis. prof. creative writing Duke U., 1995; Catharine Osgood Foster prof. Bennington Coll., 1996-2001. Author: No Voyage and Other Poems, 1963, enlarged edit., 1965, The River Styx, Ohio, 1972, The Night Traveler, 1978, Twelve Moons, 1979, American Primitive, 1983, Dream Work, 1986, House of Light, 1990, New and Selected Poems, 1992, Vol. 2, 2005, A Poetry Handbook, 1994, White Pine, 1994, Blue Pastures, 1995, West Wind, 1997, Rules for the Dance, 1998, Winter Hours, 1999, The Leaf and the Cloud, 2000, What Do We Know, 2002, Owls and Other Fantasies, 2003, Why I Wake Early, 2004, Long Life, 2004, Blue Iris, 2004, New and Selected Poems, Vol. 2, 2005, Thirst, 2006; contbr. to Yale U. Rev., Kenyon Rev., Poetry, Atlantic, Harvard mag., others. Recipient Shelley Meml. award, 1970, Alice Fay di Castagnola award, 1973, Cleve. Arts prize for lits., 1979, Achievement award Am. Acad. and Inst. Arts and Letters, 1983, Pulitzer prize for poetry, 1984, Christopher award, 1991, L.L. Winship award, 1991, Nat. Book award, 1992, Lannan award, 1998; Nat. Endowment fellow, 1972-73; Guggenheim fellow, 1980-81. Mem. PEN. Home: PO Box 619 Provincetown MA 02657-0619

OLIVER, NANCY LEBKICHER, artist, retired elementary school educator; b. Stockton, Calif., 1939; d. John B. and Marjorie Lebkicher; m. Douglas C. Oliver, 1963; children: Charles, Elaine. BA with honors, San Jose State U., 1961. Summer playground dir. Recreation Dept., Redwood City, Calif., 1956-61; 1st grade tchr. Redwood City (Calif.) Elem. Sch. Dist., 1961-63; kindergarten tchr. Ukiah (Calif.) Unified Sch. Dist., 1963-67; assoc. tchr. kindergarten San Carlos (Calif.) Elem. Sch. Dist., 1976-81. Dept. store shopper Macy's, San Francisco, 1975-82; asst. hist. rsch., 2000—. Active White Oaks PTA, San Carlos, 1973-81, newsletter editor, 1978-81; leader Girl Scouts U.S.A., San Carlos, 1978-81; bd. dirs. Sequoia H.S. Ednl. Found., co-chmn., 2002-05, sec., 2005-; bd. dirs. San Mateo County Hist. Resources Adv. Bd., 2000-; Sunday sch. dir. St. Peter's Episcopal Ch., Redwood City, 1973-78; mem. San Mateo County Sesquicentennial Com., 2005-06. Mem.: AAUW (pres. Willits br. 1966—67, San Carlos br. newsletter editor 1972—74, chmn. historic preservation sect. 1979—, editor historic tour booklet 1981, editor historic resources booklet 1989, co-pres. San Carlos br. 2002—04, dir.-at-large 2004—06, parliamentarian 2004—, Gift honoree 1976), SeriPrinters (serigrapher 1986—), San Carlos Heritage Assn. (founder and dir. 1995—), Sequoia H.S. Alumni Assn. (founding sec. and membership chmn 1985—, centennial coord. 1992—95, pres. 1996—98, sec. 2002—, newsletter editor 2003—, Unsung Hero award 1998), Internat. Order Rainbow Girls (grand officer Calif. 1957—58, mother advisor Redwood City 1987—89, quilt com. 1989—). Democrat. Episcopalian. Avocations: needlecrafts, historic preservation activities, walking, calligraphy, classical music. Home: 147 Belvedere Ave San Carlos CA 94070-4818

OLIVER, NURIA, computer scientist; b. Spain; BS, Tech. U. Madrid, 1992, MS, 1994; PhD in Media Arts & Scis., MIT, 2000. Rsch. asst. engr. Siemens F&E, 1992—93; software engr. Telefonica R&D, Spain, 1994—95; rsch. asst. Media Lab, MIT, 1995—2000; rschr. adaptive systems & interaction group Microsoft Rsch., 2000—. Named one of 40 Most Promising Young Spanish Persons, El Pais, 1999, Top 100 Young Innovators, MIT Tech. Review, 2004; fellow, La Caixa Found., 1995; Motorola fellow, 1997. Avocation: ballet. Office: Microsoft Rsch One Microsoft Way Redmond WA 98052-6399

OLIVER, PATRICIA, physician assistant; b. Atwater, Calif., July 30, 1954; d. Robert and Helen Raye Wilson; m. Alonzo Charles Oliver, May 1, 1974. AA in Social Sci., Coll. of Sequoias, Visalia, Calif., 1996, AS in Math., Sci. and Engring., 1997, AS in Nursing, 1999. RN, Calif. Supr. data entry Huntington Computing, Corcoran, Calif., 1980-83; data enterer, biller Hillman Health Ctr., Tulare, Calif., 1983-85, lab. asst., 1995—; dep. sheriff, bailiff Tulare County Sheriff's Office, Visalia, 1985-95; med. asst. Visalia Walk-In Med. Clinic, 1995—. Rschr. chemistry dept. Coll. of Sequoias, 1997—; sci. nursing tutor, 1995—. Mem. NAFE, Am. Chem. Soc., Math., Sci. and Engring. Achievement Assn. Avocations: aerobics, softball, reading, Karate, relating at home. Home: 23434 5 1/2 Ave Corcoran CA 93212

OLIVER, PATRICIA, lawyer; b. Erie; m. Jim Oliver. BA in Polit. sci., Allegheny Collge; JD, Case Western Reserve U. Sch. Law, Cleve. Atty. Squire, Sanders & Dempsey, Cleve.; gen. counsel BB&T Corp, Winston-Salem, NC, 2004—. Recipient Rainmaker (community svc.), No. Ohio Live Magazine, 2003, Profl. Woman of Excellence, Cleve. YMCA. Achievements include founder of Cleve.'s "Women in Family Bus." seminar series; pres. Children's Aid Soc. Office: BB&T Corp 200 W 2nd St Winston Salem NC 27101

OLIVER, SUSAN, history professor, writer, consultant; b. Helena, Mont., Mar. 25, 1945; d. Lloyd G. and June (Norfleet) Oliver; m. Richard Meyer, Feb. 13, 1965 (div. Nov. 1, 1990); children: Mark Meyer, David Meyer, Lisa Meyer; m. Russell Storkan, May 3, 2003. BA, George Wash. U., Washington, 1979; MA, PhD, UCLA, 1995. Dir. rsch. SW region Grubb & Ellis Comml Real Estate, Irvine, Calif., 1984—86; tchg. fellow UCLA, 1989—92; guest lectr., tchg. fellow Koc U., Istanbul, Turkey, 1993—94; prof. history Cerritos Coll., Norwalk, Calif., 1995—; instr. history Santa Monica C.C., Calif., 1997—99. Coord. women's studies program Cerritos Coll., 1996—2000; project dir. Cerritos Coll. Regional Ctr., New Media Classroom, CUNY, 2000—04; campus coord. Cerritos Coll., Visible Knowledge Project, Georgetown U., Washington, 2001—05. Author: (ednl. website) Dorothea Lange: Photographer of the People. Recipient Most Outstanding Faculty award, Cerritos Coll., 1997—98, Best Tchg. Practices award, Nat. Inst. Staff and Orgnl. Devel., 1999, Outstanding Leadership award, Chair Acad., 2001. Mem.: Western Assn. Women Historians (corr.), Am. Hist. Assn. (corr.), Orgn. Am. Historians (corr.), Am. Studies Assn. (corr.). Avocations: photography, writing, travel. Office: Cerritos Coll 11110 Alondra Blvd Norwalk CA 90650 Office Phone: 562-860-2451. E-mail: soliver@cerritos.edu.

OLIVER, SUSAN M., air transportation executive; b. Des Moines, Iowa, July 6, 1947; married; 3 children. BS, George Washington U., 1970; JD, U. Denver, 1980. Atty. Kempell, Huffman and Ginder, 1983—84; asst. counsel Wein Airlines, 1984—85; labor rels. cons. City of Reno, 1985—86; counsel employee rels. Am. Airlines, 1986—90, mng. dir. flight svcs., 1990—96, mng. dir. strategic planning, 1996—97, v.p. employee rels., 1997—2000, sr. v.p. human resources, 2000—. Office: AMR Corp 4333 Amon Carter Blvd Fort Worth TX 76155

OLIVER LEAHY TINEN KAEHLER, JEANNETTE See LEAHY, JEANNETTE

OLIVER-SIMON, GLORIA CRAIG, human resources advisor, consultant, lawyer; b. Chester, Pa., Sept. 19, 1947; d. Jesse Harper and Lavinia Craig Cuff; m. James Russell Norwood, Sept. 1970 (div.); 1 child, James Russell Jr.; m. Joseph M. Simon, Jan. 1993. BS, U. Md., 1987; JD, Am. U., 1990, MS, 1992. Bar: Pa. 1991, U.S. Ct. Appeals (fed. cir.) 1994, D.C. 1997. Pers. specialist VA Med. Ctr., Phila., 1974-80; pers./human resources specialist VA Ctrl. Office, Washington, 1980-90, human resources mgr., 1990-97; atty./adviser human resource mgmt./sr. human resources cons. VACO. Mem. VA Work Group on Minority Initiatives, 1990, 93—; VA coord., rep. Coun. for Excellence in Govts. Spkrs. Bur. Project, 1991-92, Pub. Employees Roundtable for Pub. Svc. Recognition Week, 1991-92; subcom. chair Student

Employee Programs, Office of Pers. Mgmt. Work Group, 1993; coord. VA Caring and Courtesy Campaign Focus Group, 1993; mem. VA Veterans Health Adminstrn. Nursing Shortage Task Group, 1987, 93, VA Work Group on the Nat. and Cmty. Svc. Program, 1993-94, 95-96, Veterans Health Adminstrn. Healthcare Reform Work Group on Customer Svc., 1993-94; VA's Nat. Com. on Employment of Disabled Vets. and People with Disabilities, 1992-93; VA Office Human Resources Mgmt. coord. Pres.'s Com. on Employment of Persons with Disabilities/Dept. of Def. Student Employment Initiative, 1994-95; VA Office of Human Resources Mgmt. steering com. 1994-96; mem. Dept. of Energy Student Employment Task Group, 1994-96; VACO coord. Welfare to Work Initiative, 1997—; VACO coun. mem. VA Early Mediation Program, 1999—; mem. VACO Workgroup on Position Sensitivity and Suitability Adjudication, 1999—; mentor VA VACO Fed. Women's Program, 1999—. Bd. dirs. So. PG County Cmty. Charities, Inc., 1999—, pres., CEO, 2000. Mem. ABA, Fed. Bar Assn., Nat. Bar Assn., Fed. Cir. Bar Assn., D.C. Bar Assn., Bar Assn. of D.C., Phi Delta Phi, U. Md. Alumni Assn. (mentor program), Am. U. Alumni Assn. (admissions com., mentor program for grad. and law students), Leadership VA Alumni Assn. (chair promotions com. 1997-2000), AKA Sorority Inc., DAV Aux. (fed. unit 1), Zonta Internat., Am. Legion Aux. Avocations: reading, travel. Home: 809 Braeburn Dr Fort Washington MD 20744-6022 Office: Dept Vets Affairs 810 Vermont Ave NW Washington DC 20420-0001

OLIVER-WARREN, MARY ELIZABETH, retired library science educator, library and information scientist; b. Hamlet, N.C., Feb. 23, 1924; d. Washington and Carolyn Belle (Middlebrooks) Terry; m. David Oliver, 1947 (div. 1971); children: Donald D., Carolyn L.; m. Arthur Warren, Sept. 14, 1990 (dec. Feb. 1995). BS, Bluefield State U., 1948; MS, South Conn. State U., 1958; student, U. Conn., 1977. Cert. tchr., adminstr. and supr., Conn.; cert. pub. sch. substitute tchr., K-12, N.J. Media specialist Hartford Pub. Schs., Conn., 1952—86; with So. Conn. State U., New Haven, 1972—, asst. prof. Sch. Libr. Sci. and Instructional Tech., 1987—95, ret., 1995; substitute tchr. K-12 Windsor, Conn., 1999—2004, Grady County Pub. Schs., Cairo, Ga., 2004—. Mem. dept. curriculum com. So. Conn. State U., 1987-95, adj. prof., 1995—; cert. substitute tchr. Somerset County Pub. Schs., 1997—; cert. substitute tchr. Windsor, Conn. Sch. Sys., 1999-. Author: My Golden Moments, 1988, The Elementary School Media Center, 1990, Text Book Elementary School Media Center, 1991, I Must Fight Alone, 1991, (textbook) I Must Fight Alone, 1994. Mem. ALA, Conn. Ednl. Media Assn., Black Librs. Network N.J. Inc., Assn. Ret. Tchrs. Conn., Black and Hispanic Consortium, So. Conn. State U. Women's Assn., Cicuso Club (v.p.), Friends Club (v.p.), Delta Kappa Gamma, Alpha Kappa Alpha. Avocations: reading, music, piano, walking. Home: 1710 S Broad St Apt 35 Cairo GA 39828-3574

OLIVIER, JEANNE C., lawyer; b. New Orleans, 1953; BA magna cum laude, Tulane U., 1975; JD, U. Pa., 1979. Bar: NY 1980, La. 1982. Assoc. Shearman & Sterling LLP, NYC, 1980—88, ptnr., 1988—, mem. project devel. and fin. group. Office: Shearman & Sterling LLP 599 Lexington Ave New York NY 10022-6069 Office Phone: 212-848-8593. Office Fax: 212-848-7179. E-mail: jolivier@shearman.com.

OLIVIER, SAMARA LYNN, music educator; b. Redwood City, Calif., Feb. 12, 1978; d. Rufus and Vida Lynne Olivier. AA in Fine Arts, Ohlone Coll., Fremont, Calif., 1998; BA in Music, Calif. State U., Hayward, 2000, MA in Music. Music min., team mem. Celebration Fellowship, Redwood City, Calif., 1990—2003; asst. dir. Golden Gate Boys Choir, Hayward, 1996—2001; music tchr. k-8 St. John Cath. Sch., San Lorenzo, Calif., 2000; 4th grade handbell dir. All Saints Sch., Hayward, 2000—01; choral dir. Patten U., Oakland, Calif., 2002—05; recruitment dir. Golden Gate Boys Choir and Bellringers, Hayward, 2005—. Worship team mem. Santa Rosa (Calif.) Christian Ch., 2001; vol. counselor Pregnancy Choices, Union City, Calif., 1997—2001. Avocations: travel, singing, studying psychology profiling, piano. Office: St John Catholic School 270 E Lewlling Blvd San Lorenzo CA 94580 Office Phone: 510-276-6632. Personal E-mail: smarlynn@netzero.net.

OLIVOS, CLAUDIA, artist, educator; d. Luis Olivos Olivos and Ximena Quiroga; 1 child, Julian. BFA in Painting, George Mason U., 1991, BA in Psychology, 1991; MFA, Vt. Coll., 2001. Counselor to adolescents Rappahanock Cmty. Svcs., Fredericksburg, Va., 1989—91, mental health counselor, 1991—97; housing counselor No. Va. Family Svc., Arlington, 1998—2000; faculty The Art League Alexandria, 1998—; owner Olivos ARt Studio LLC. Co-owner, dir. Internat. Visions Gallery, Washington, 1997—99; artist in residence Rappahanock Falls Acad., Fredericksburg, 1997—98, Key Elem. Sch., Arlington, 1999—; faculty Art Inst. Washington, Arlington; bd. mem. Teatro de la Luna, Arlington; guest artist various schs., 2001—. Cover of book, Coming Home, 1998, painting on cover, Anthology of Latin American Poetry, 2006, CD cover, Silence Beyond Octaves, 2000, numerous exhbns. Cmty. artist Streets of Arlington, 2000—, Cultural Affairs Dept., Arlington, Va., 2000. Office Phone: 703-237-7562. Business E-Mail: claudia@claudiaolivos.com.

OLIX-ANDERSON, SUSAN, music educator; d. Carolyn and George Olix; m. John Anderson, Aug. 13, 1994 (dec. Jan. 1, 1999); children: Carolyn Anderson, Erin Anderson. B, SUNY, Potsdam, 1989; M, Northwestern U., Evanston, Ill., 1990; postgrad., U. NC, Greensboro, 1990—92. Lic. music tchr. K-12 NY State Dept. Edn., 1992. Elem. music tchr. Alfred Almond Ctrl. Sch., NY, 2000—. Adj. lectr. Alfred U., 2005—, adj. music instr., 2004—06. Contbr. articles to profl. jours. Prin. saxophonist Hornell Area Wind Ensemble, NY, 1984—2006; coach Alfred-Almond Softball League, NY, 2002—06; leader Girl Scout of Am., Almond, 2002—06; mem. bd. assessment rev. Town of Almond, 2004—06. Fellow, U. N.C., 1990—92; Eckenstein scholar, Northwestern U., 1989—90. Mem.: NY State Band Dirs. Assn. (assoc.), North Am. Saxophone Alliance (assoc.; pres. Crane Sch. Music chpt. 1986—89), Music Educators Nat. Conf. (assoc.), NY State Sch. Music Assn. (assoc.; adjudicator 1998—), Gamma Sigma Sigma (assoc.), Sigma Alpha Iota (assoc.). Roman Catholic. Office: Alfred Almond Ctrl Sch Rt 21 Almond NY 14804 Office Phone: 607-276-2171. Personal E-mail: solix@aacs.wnyric.org.

OLKERIIL, LORENZA, English language educator; b. Koror, Palau, Oct. 10, 1948; d. Ngiratewid and Modekngei Olkeriil; children: Kevin O. Chin, Renee Chin. BA in Elem. Edn., U. Guam, 1982; MA in Instnl. Tech. in Edn., San Jose State U., 1989. Classroom tchr. Ministry of Edn., Koror, 1972-76, 78—, curriculum specialist, 1976-78, edn. trainer, 1988—, coord. bilingual program, 1988—; chair English dept. Palau High Sch.; elem. sch. prin. Ngiwal Elem. Sch., 1999—. Tng. dir. Peace Corp, Palau, summer 1987; GED instr., Palauan lang. instr. Micronesian Coll., Koror; cons. to pvt. sch., Koror. Speaker Ngiwal State Legis., Koror, 1992, 98; mem. Ngiwal State Constitution, 1983. San Jose State U. fellow, 1987. Mem. Didil Belau (pres. 1992-93), Ngaraboes (treas.-sec. 1980—). Avocations: farming, fishing, softball, weaving, dance. Home: PO Box 966 Palau PW 96940-0843 Office: PO Box 159 Palau PW 96940-0159

OLLIE, PEARL LYNN, artist, singer, lyricist; b. Highland Park, Mich., Oct. 15, 1953; d. Sam and Estelle Theresa Ollie; m. Christopher John Keyes, Nov. 29, 1975 (div. Nov. 1978); 1 child, Shane Michael Fiondella. Student, Henry Ford C.C., Dearborn, Mich., 1988—89, Soc. Arts and Crafts Coll., 1971—74, Ctr. for Creative Study, 1980—81. Tchr. ceramics Detroit Head Start, Mt. Zion, Mich., 1973; logo designer, platemaker, printer and painter Island Art Ctr., St. Simons Island, Ga., 1976—79; sec., receptionist High Performance Tube Inc., St. Simons Island, 1976—79; personal legal sec. State Senator Bill Littlefield, St. Simons Island, 1979; art coord., booking agt. Club Savoy Tivoli, San Francisco, 1979; tchr. art Redmond Hall, Skamokawa, Wash., 1980; artist Hollywood Costumes, Dearborn, 1980—90; account mgr. ins. Dr. Sheryl A. Ollie, Lynn, Mass., 1990; tchr. art Art in Nahant, Mass., 1991—97; staff artist, acting, costumes Creative Currents, Ferndale, Mich., 1990—. Make-up artist Paramount Costumes (was Hollywood Costumes), Dearborn; tchr. art and music St. Lukes Montessori Sch., Detroit; artist Mich. Art and Design, Detroit, Dearborn Awnings, Lincoln Park, Mich.; instr. Aups, Provence, France, 1997 Make-up artist TV commls. and shows, movies, commd. portrait artist, illustrator, guest (TV program) All Star Kids. Co-pres. Nahant PTO, Johnson Sch., 1991-92; tchr. 8th grade religious edn., vocalist area ch. chorus, choir dir. St. Anselms; vocal instr. Axis Music Musicians Inst.; instr. art, music and drama Hope of Detroit Acad Roman Catholic. Avocations: paint, sculpting, singing, writing, piano. Home and Office: The Cultured Pearl 840 Brevard Ave Rockledge FL 32955 Office Phone: 321-536-3523. Personal E-mail: pearlollieartist@yahoo.com.

OLMSTEAD, MARJORIE ANN, physics professor; b. Glen Ridge, NJ, Aug. 18, 1958; d. Blair E. and Elizabeth (Dempwolf) Olmstead. BA in Physics, Swarthmore Coll., 1979; MA in Physics, U. Calif., Berkeley, 1982, PhD, 1985. Rsch. staff Palo Alto (Calif.) Rsch. Ctr. Xerox Corp., 1985-86; asst. prof. physics U. Calif., Berkeley, 1986-90, U. Wash., Seattle, 1991-93, assoc. prof., 1993-97, prof., 1997—, dir. nanotech. PhD program, 2004—. Prin. investigator sci. materials divsn. Lawrence Berkeley Lab., 1988—93. Contbr. articles to profl. jours. Named Presdl. Young Investigator, NSF, 1987; recipient Devel. award, IBM, 1986, 1987, Rsch. award, A. von Humboldt Found., 2000. Fellow: Am. Phys. Soc. (chair com. on status of women in physics 1999, Maria Goeppart-Mayer award 1996), Am. Vacuum Soc. (Peter Mark Meml. award 1994). Office: U Washington Dept Physics PO Box 351560 Seattle WA 98195-1560 Office Phone: 206-685-3031. E-mail: olmstd@u.washington.edu.

OLMSTED, AUDREY JUNE, communications educator, department chairman; b. Sioux Falls, SD, June 5, 1940; d. Leslie Thomas and Dorothy Lucille (Else) Perryman; m. Richard Raymond Olmsted; 1 child, Quenby Anne. BA, U. No. Iowa, 1961, MA, 1963; PhD, Ind. U., 1971. Comm. instr. Boston U., 1964-71, acting chair comm., 1972-73, asst. prof. comm., 1971-74; debate coach RI Coll., Providence, 1978-92, asst. prof. comm., 1987—, chmn. dept. of comm., 1999—2005, internat. student advisor, 1980—. Text editor Prentice-Hall Pub., 1986-88. Recipient Faculty award R.I. Coll. Alumni Assn., 1987. Mem. Nat. Assn. Fgn. Student Advisors, Eastern Comm. Assn., Nat. Comm. Assn. Democrat. Office: RI Coll Dept Comm 600 Mount Pleasant Ave Providence RI 02908-1924 Office Phone: 401-456-8645.

OLNESS, KAREN NORMA, medical educator; b. Rushford, Minn., Aug. 28, 1936; d. Norman Theodore and Karen Agnes (Gunderson) O.; m. Hakon Daniel Torjesen, 1962. BA, U. Minn., 1958, BS, MD, 1961. Diplomate Am. Bd. Pediat., Am. Bd. Med. Hypnosis, Develop. & Behavioral Pediatrics. Intern Harbor Gen. Hosp., Torrance, Calif.; resident Nat. Children's Hosp. Med. Ctr., Washington; asst. prof. George Washington U., Washington, 1970-74; assoc. prof. U. Minn., Mpls., 1974-87; prof. pediat., family medicine and internat. health Case Western Res. U., Cleve., 1987—. Named Outstanding Woman Physician, Minn. Assn. Women Physicians, 1987; recipient Christopherson award Am. Acad. Pediat., 1998, Aldrich award, Am. Acad. Pediat., 1999, Ann. award Soc. Devel. and Behavioral Pediat., 2003; named to Cleve. Med. Hall of Fame, 2000. Fellow Am. Acad. Pediat. (chair internat. health sect. 2001), Am. Acad. Family Physicians, Am. Soc. Clin. Hypnosis (pres. 1984-86), Soc. Clin. and Exptl. Hypnosis (pres. 1991-93); mem. Soc. for Devel. and Behavioral Pediat. (pres. 1991-92), Northwestern Pediat. Soc. (pres. 1977), Internat. Hypnosis Soc. (pres. 2003—). Office: Case Western Res U 11100 Euclid Ave Cleveland OH 44106-6038 Office Phone: 216-368-4368. Business E-Mail: karen.olness@case.edu.

O'LOONEY, PATRICIA ANNE, medical association administrator; b. Bridgeport, Conn., Dec. 2, 1954; d. John Joseph and Marjorie Ellen (Curran) O'L. BA in Molecular Biology, Regis Coll., 1976; MS in Biochemistry, George Washington U., 1978, PhD in Biochemistry, 1982. Rsch. asst. biochemistry dept. George Washington Med. Sch., Washington, 1976-82, teaching asst., 1978-81, rsch. assoc., 1982-84, sr. rsch. scientist, 1984-86, asst. prof. medicine and biochemistry, 1986-88; asst. dir. The Nat. Multiple Sclerosis Soc., N.Y.C., 1988-90, assoc. dir. rsch. and med. programs, 1990-91, dir. rsch. and med. programs, 1991—. Vis. lectr. George Washington Med. Sch., 1988—. Author: Lipoprotein Lipase, 1987; contbr. articles to profl. jours. Recipient New Investigator Rsch. award NIH, 1985. Mem. Am. Soc. for Biochemistry and Molecular Biology, N.Y. Acad. Scis., Assn. for Women in Sci., The Mid-Atlantic Lipid Soc., Sigma Xi, Beta Beta Beta. Republican. Roman Catholic. Avocations: tennis, golf. Office: Nat Multiple Sclerosis Soc 733 3rd Ave New York NY 10017-3204 Office Phone: 212-476-0413. E-mail: patricia.olooney@nmss.org.

OLOPADE, OLUFUNMILAYO FALUSI (FUNMI OLOPADE), geneticist, educator, oncologist, hematologist; b. Nigeria, Apr. 29, 1957; m. Christopher Sola Olopade; 3 children. MD with distinction, U. Ibadan, Nigeria, 1980. Diplomate Am. Bd. Internal Medicine, Am. Bd. Med. Oncology, Am. Bd. Hematology; lic. MD Ill., Ind. Med. officer Nigerian Navy Hosp.; intern in medicine, surgery, pediatrics, ob-gyn. Univ. Coll. Hosp., Ibadan, 1980—81; intern in internal medicine Cook County Hosp., Chgo., 1983—84, resident in internal medicine, 1984—86, chief resident in medicine, 1986; clin. instr. U. Ill. Abraham Lincoln Sch. Medicine, Chgo., 1986—87; postdoctoral fellow jt. sect. hematology/oncology U. Chgo., 1987—91, asst. prof. hematology/oncology, Pritzker Sch. Medicine, 1991—2002, mem. Cancer Rsch. Ctr., 1991—, mem. Cancer Biology com., 1994—, mem. Genetics com., 1996—, assoc. prof. medicine, prof. medicine and human genetics Ill., 2002—, dir. Ctr. for Clinical Cancer Genetics, Cancer Risk Clinic Ill., 1992—, dir. Hematology/Oncology Fellowship Program Ill., 1998—. Attending physician Cook County Hosp., Chgo., 1987; mem. steering com., cooperative family registry for breast cancer studies, Nat. Cancer Inst., also mem. adv. com. Cancer Genetics Network and bd. scientific counselors; mem. adv. bd. Cancerandcareers.org; lectr. in field. Ad hoc reviewer Jour. AMA, Genes, Chromosomes and Cancer, Genomics, Human Molecular Genetics, Cancer Rsch., Blood, Molecular Carcinogenesis, Jour. Clin. Oncology, New Eng. Jour. Medicine; contbr. articles to profl. jours.; contbr. to book chpts. and abstracts on topics including genetics of cancer. Mem. med. adv. bd. Young Survival Coalition. Named a Top Doctor, Chicago Mag., 1997; recipient Sir Samuel Manuwa Gold medal for Excellence in Clin. Sciences, 1980, Scholar award, James S. McDonnell Found., 1992, Doris Duke Disting. Clin. Scientist award, 2000, Phenomenal Women award, 2003, People Are Today's Heroes (PATH), Gov. Rod R. Blagojevich, presented by First Lady Patti Blagojevich, State Ill., 2005, Heroes In Healthcare award, Access Cmty. Network, 2005, Am. Assn. Cancer Rsch. (AACR)-Minorities in Cancer Rsch. Jane Cooke Wright Lectureship, 2006; Ellen Ruth Lebow Fellowship, Assn. for Brain Tumor Rsch., 1990, MacArthur "Genius Grant" Fellow, John D. and Catherine T. MacArthur Found., 2005. Mem. AAAS, Am. Assn. Cancer Rsch. (membership credentialing com. 1994-95, program com. carcinogenesis subcom. 1993), Am. Soc. Clin. Oncology (mem. program com. subcom. tumor biology and genetics 1997, Young Investigator award, 1991), Am. Assn. Preventive Oncology, Women in Cancer Rsch., Am. Soc. Hematology, Am. Coll. Physicians, Am. Soc. Breast Disease, Am. Soc. Hematology, Assn. Am. Professors, Nigerian Med. Assn., Am. Cancer Soc. (adv. com. cancer control investigations, epidemiology, diagnosis, therapy 1994-97). Office: U Chgo Med Ctr 5841 S Maryland Ave # MC2115 Chicago IL 60637-1463 Office Phone: 773-702-1632, 773-702-6149. Office Fax: 773-702-0963. Business E-Mail: folopade@medicine.bsd.uchicago.edu.*

O'LOUGHLIN, KATIE EILEEN BRIDGET, poet; m. Scott Koblish, July 26, 2003; 1 child, Violet Ophelia Koblish-O'Loughlin. AA in Theater and Early Childhood Edn., Palomar Coll., San Marcos, Calif., 1984; BS in Computer and Info. Sci., Coleman Coll., La Mesa, Calif., 1986. Poetic License Poetry Slam Inc., 2001. Ind. creator, prodr., host 6 Women Revealed and 6 Men Revealed, Hollywood, Calif., 1999—2000. Poet in the schs. mid. sch. and HS, East Los Angeles, Calif., 2001—. Author: (book of poetry) I Can't Pull it Together Enough to Look Like My Poster; author: (performer) (spoken word poetry slam performance) Unknown Man with Soft, Soft skin (1st Pl. (tie) BBC Radio Scotland Internat. Poetry Slam, Edinburgh/Glasgow, Scotland, 2002), They Always Said You're Gonna be Like Your Momma When You Grow Up (3rd Pl. Bristol Poetry Festival 2002 Internat. Poetry Slam in Bristol, Eng., 2002), Skinny be Damned, Concave Bellies Don't Bear Babies, Compassion, Being Tempted to Fall from Grace (3rd Pl. Bristol Internat. Poetry 2000 Slam, 2000), They Always Said You're Gonna be Like Your Momma, Snow Globe, Compassion (2nd Pl. Urban Grind San Diego Poetry Slam, 2003), Snow Globe, They Always Said Your Gonna be Like Your Momma, Being Tempted to Fall from Grace (1st Pl. Orange County Big Damn Poetry Slam, 2003), Compassion, Exact Shade, Skinny be Damned, Concave Bellies Don't Bear Babies (1st Pl. Long Beach Big Damn Poetry Slam, 2002), Being Tempted to Fall From Grace, Exact Shade, Skinny be Damned, Concave Bellies Don't Bear Babies (1st Pl. Urban Grind San Diego Poetry Slam, 2002), Exact Shade, Compassion, Being Tempted to Fall from Grace (2nd Pl. Los Feliz Pig Slam, 2002), Being Tempted to Fall from Grace, Compassion, Exact Shade (1st Pl. Long Beach Big Damn Poetry Slam, 2001); author: (book of poetry) For My Sisters; author: (performer) (spoken word poetry slam performance) Skinny be Damned, Concave Bellies Don't Bear Babies, Compassion, Being Tempted to Fall From Grace (2nd Pl. Urban Grind San Diego Poetry Slam, 2001), (spoken word poetry performance) A Woman Revealed (Acceptance into the LA Women's Theatre Festival 2001, 2001). Performer for benefit show Sojourner Ho. for Abused Women and Children, L.A., Calif., 2001. Mem.: Poetry Slam Inc. Avocations: travel, scuba diving. Office Phone: 310-410-8051. Personal E-mail: katieo@performancekatieo.com.

O'LOUGHLIN, SANDRA S., lawyer; b. Buffalo, Jan. 15, 1942; BA summa cum laude, Rosary Hill Coll., 1973; JD cum laude, U. Buffalo, 1978. Bar: N.Y. 1979. Atty. Hiscock & Barclay, LLP, Buffalo, 1978-79, ptnr., 1990—. Chmn. character and fitness com. appellate divsn. 4th dept. 8th jud. dist. N.Y. Supreme Ct., 1986—2006; adj. prof. SUNY Law Sch., Buffalo. Note editor Buffalo Law Rev., 1977-78. Mem. Erie County Legis. Task Force Mental Health, 1979-81; mem. adv. bd. Congregation of Sisters of St. Joseph, 1987—. Mem. ABA (bus. law com. on securities), Nat. Assn. Bond Lawyers, N.Y. State Bar Assn. (ethics com. 1984-94, 2000-03, vice chmn. 1987-92, unauthorized practice of law com. 1998-2002, mem. com. on securities regulation 1999—, com. standards atty. conduct 2004—), Erie County Bar Assn. (ethics com. 1984-87, chmn. 1987-89, corp. law com. 1984, grievance com. 1993—). Office: Hiscock & Barclay LLP 1100 M&T Ctr 3 Fountain Plaza Buffalo NY 14203-1414 Business E-Mail: sologhlin@hiscockbarclay.com.

OLSEN, ASHLEY FULLER, actress; b. Sherman Oaks, Calif., June 13, 1986; d. David and Jarnette Olsen, Mackenzie Olsen (Stepmother). Student, NYU, 2004—. Co-founder, prin. Dualstar Entertainment, Calif., 1993—; co-editor-in-chief Mary-Kate and Ashley Mag. Launched clothing line with sister Mary-Kate, 2002. Actor: (films) To Grandmother's House We Go, 1992, Double, Double, Toil and Trouble, 1993, The Little Rascals, 1994, How the West Was Fun, 1994, It Takes Two, 1995, The Challenge, 2003, Charlie's Angles: Full Throttle, 2003; (TV films) Billboard Dad, 1998; (TV series) Full House, 1987—95, Two of a Kind, 1998; actor, prodr.: So Little Time, 2001; Mary-Kate and Ashley in Action!, 2001; actor, prodr., prodr.: (films) Switching Goals, 1999; actor, prodr. Passport to Paris, 1999; Our Lips are Sealed, 2000; Winning London, 2001; Holiday in the Sun, 2001; Getting There, 2002; When In Rome, 2002; New York Minute, 2004; (video series) The Adventures of Mary-Kate and Ashley; You're Invited to Mary-Kate and Ashleys; prodr.: (TV series) Tough Cookie, 2002, Fashion Forward: Spring 2001, 2001. Named one of 100 Most Powerful Women in Hollywood, Hollywood (Calif.) Reporter, 2003. Office: Dualstar Entertainment Group 1801 Century Park East Los Angeles CA 90067*

OLSEN, BARBARA ANN, music educator; b. Fullerton, Calif., May 28, 1947; d. W. M. Ledbelter and Lavone Louise Scott; m. David Eugene, June 28, 1968; adopted children: Brandon, Michael, Andrew children: Todd, Amber, Heather. Grad., Simpson U., San Francisco, 1968. Pre-sch. tchr. Home Day Care, Redlands, Calif., 1970—80; para profl. Rolling Ridge Sch., Olathe, Kans., Staples High Sch., Minn.; music tchr. K-8 St. Paul's Cath. Sch., Olathe, 2002—. Concert music tchr. St. Paul's Sch., Olathe, 2002—. Author: (children's book) Lorenza and the Secret, 1983, God's Critters, 1990. Mem.: Nat. Cath. Edn. Assn. Republican. Independent. Avocations: piano, volleyball, reading, decorating, cooking. Home: 1101 W Elm St Olathe KS 66061

OLSEN, FRANCES ELISABETH, law educator, theorist; b. Chgo., Feb. 4, 1945; d. Holger and Ruth Mathilda (Pfeifer) O.; m. Harold Irving Porter, June 8, 1984. Cert., Roskilde (Denmark) Højskole, 1967; BA, Goddard Coll., 1968; JD, U. Colo., 1971; SJD, Harvard U., 1984. Bar: Colo. 1972, U.S. Dist. Ct. Colo. 1972. Law clk. hon. Arraj U.S. Dist. Ct. Colo., Denver, 1972; lawyer Am. Indian Movement, Wounded Knee, S.D., 1973; pvt. practice Denver, 1973-74; law prof. U. Puget Sound, Tacoma, Wash., 1975-79, St. John's U., Jamaica, N.Y., 1982-83, UCLA, 1984—. Vis. fellow New Coll., Oxford (Eng.) U., 1987; vis. prof. U. Mich., Ann Arbor, 1988, Harvard U., Cambridge, Mass., 1990-91, U. Berlin, Germany, 1995, Ochanomizu U., Tokyo, 1997, U. Tokyo, 1997, Cornell U., 1997, French U. Reunion, 2000, Hebrew U. Jerusalem, 2001, Haifa U., 2001, Tel Aviv U., 2001, 2002, Addis Ababa U., 2002, Bar Ilan U., 2002, Alberto Hurtado U., Santiago, Chile, 2004; sr. Fulbright prof. U. Frankfurt, Germany, 1991-92; overseas fellow Churchill Coll., Cambridge, Eng., 1997-99; mem. faculty law Cambridge U., 1997-99; del. UN 4th World Conf. on Women, Beijing, China, 1995, NGO Forum, Huairou, China, 1995. Co-author: Cases and Materials on Family Law: Legal Concepts and Changing Human Relationships, 1994; editor: Feminist Legal Theory I: Foundations and Outlooks, 1995, Feminist Legal Theory II: Positioning Feminist Theory Within the Law, 1995; contbr. articles to law revs. Named Outstanding Alumnus U. Colo., 1989. Mem. Assn. Am. Law Schs. (chair jurisprudence sect. 1987-88, chair women in law tchg. sect. 1995-96), Conf. on Critical Legal Studies, European Conf. Critical Legal Studies, Internat. Bar Assn. Avocations: scuba diving, kayaking, hiking. Office: UCLA Sch Law 405 Hilgard Ave Los Angeles CA 90095-1476 Office Phone: 310-825-6083. E-mail: olsen@law.ucla.edu.

OLSEN, JODY (JOSEPHINE K. OLSEN), federal agency administrator; B, U. Utah; MSW, PhD, U. Md. Vol. Peace Corps, Tunisia, 1966—68, various positions including chief of staff, regional dir. North Africa, Near East, Asia and the Pscific, country dir. Togo, 1979—84, 1989—92; exed. dirs. Coun. Internat. Exch. of Scholars, 1992—97; sr. v.p., dir. Peace Corps, Washington, 1997—2002, dep. dir., 2002—, acting dir., 2006. Office: Peace Corps 1111 20th St NW Washington DC 20526-0001*

OLSEN, JUDITH JOHNSON, reference librarian; b. Manitowoc, Wis., May 13, 1948; d. Gordon Frank Johnson and Ellen Jeanette Knutson; m. Axel K. Olsen (div. 1999); children: Maren, Kristina; m. Charles Andrew Jones, 2006. BA, Luther Coll., 1970; ML, U. S.C., 1976; MA, Villanova (Pa.) U., 1996. Reader's svcs. libr. Cabrini Coll., Radnor, Pa., 1977-88; ref. and publs. libr. Villanova (Pa.) U., 1988—. Mem. MLA, ALA, Assn. of Colls. and Rsch. Librs. Democrat. Office: Villanova U 800 Lancaster Ave Villanova PA 19085 Office Phone: 610-519-5183. E-mail: judith.olsen@villanova.edu.

OLSEN, KATHIE LYNN, science foundation director; b. Portland, Oreg., Aug. 3, 1952; d. Roland Berg and Gladys Elizabeth (Eldreth) O. BS, Chatham Coll., 1974; PhD, U. Calif., Irvine, 1979. Postdoct. fellow Harvard Med. Sch., Boston, 1979-80; rsch. scientist Long Island Rsch. Inst., Stony Brook, N.Y., 1980-83; rsch. asst. prof. SUNY, Stony Brook, 1982-85, asst. prof., 1985-89; assoc. program dir. NSF, Washington, 1984-86, program dir., 1988, leader neurosci., 1991; legis. fellow Brookings Instn., Washington, 1996—97; chief scientist NASA, 1999—2002; acting assoc. adminstr. Enterprise in Biological and Physical Research, 2000—02; assoc. director, tech. Off. Science & Tech. Policy, Washington, 2002—05; dep. dir. NSF, Washington, 2005—. Adj. assoc. prof. George Washington U., Washington, 1989—; cons. editor Hormones and Behavior, 1988—. Contbr. articles to profl. jours, chapters to books. Recipient Dir. Superior Accomplishmentaward, NSF, Barry M. Goldwater Educator award, Am. Inst. of Aeronautics & Astronautics -Nat. Capital Section, Outstanding Leadership medal, NASA, Internat. Behavioral Neuroscience Soc. award, Soc. for Behavioral Endocrinology award, Barnard medal of Distinction. Mem. Soc. Neurosci., Endocrine Soc., Women in Neurosci., Sod. Study of Reproduction, Internat. Acad. Sex Rsch. Office: NSF 4201 Wilson Blvd Arlington VA 22230

OLSEN, MARIA TERESA, middle school educator; b. North Miami Beach, Fla., June 23, 1956; d. Elmer Glynn Wolfe and Marianne Patricia (Morgan) Donahay; m. Svend Peter Olsen, Sept. 4, 1989. AA, U. Fla., 1975, BA, 1977, MEd, 1979. Bd. cert. profl. tchr. in early adolescent math. 2003. Tchr. math. Union County (Fla.) High Sch., 1978, Lake Weir Mid. Sch., Ocala, Fla., 1978-79, Hawthorne (Fla.) High Sch., 1979-83; tchr. math., team leader Lincoln Mid. Sch., Gainesville, Fla., 1983-92; tchr. math. Westwood Mid. Sch., Gainesville, 1992-96, Kanapaha Mid. Sch., Gainesville, 1997—, chair dept. math. Mem. Alachua County Tchrs. Math. (pres. 1990-91, sec. 1992-94, treas. 1997—). Avocations: gardening, houseplants, bicycling, fish. Office: Kanapaha Mid Sch 5005 SW 75th St Gainesville FL 32608-4491 Office Phone: 352-955-6960.

OLSEN, MARY-KATE, actress; b. Sherman Oaks, Calif., June 13, 1986; d. David and Jarnette Olsen, Mackenzie Olsen (Stepmother). Student, NYU, 2004—05. Co-founder, prin. Dualstar Entertainment, LA, 1993—; co-editor-in-chief Mary-Kate and Ashley Mag. Launched clothing line with sister Ashley, 2002. Actor: (films) To Grandmother's House We Go, 1992, Double, Double, Toil and Trouble, 1993, The Little Rascals, 1994, How the West Was Fun, 1994, It Takes Two, 1995, The Challenge, 2003, Charlie's Angels: Full Throttle, 2003; (TV films) Billboard Dad, 1998; (TV series) Full House, 1987—95, Two of a Kind, 1998; actor, prodr.: (films) Switching Goals, 1999; Passport to Paris, 1999; Our Lips are Sealed, 2000; Winning London, 2001; Holiday in the Sun, 2001; Getting There, 2002; When In Rome, 2002; New York Minute, 2004; (TV series) So Little Time, 2001; Mary-Kate and Ashley in Action!, 2001; (video series) The Adventures of Mary-Kate and Ashley; You're Invited to Mary-Kate and Ashley's; prodr.: (TV series) Tough Cookie, 2002, Fashion Forward: Spring 2001, 2001. Named one of 100 Most Powerful Women in Hollywood, Hollywood (Calif.) Reporter, 2003. Office: Dualstar Entertainment Group 1801 Century Park East Los Angeles CA 90007*

OLSEN, TAVA MARYANNE LENNON, industrial and operations engineering educator; b. Aarhus, Denmark, Dec. 20, 1969; came to U.S., 1990; d. Michael James and Jennifer Anne Lennon; m. Timothy Robert Olsen, Dec. 30, 1995. BSc in Math. with honors, U. Auckland, New Zealand, 1989; MS in Stats., Stanford (Calif.) U., 1992, PhD in Ops. Rsch., 1994. Summer intern Tiwai Aluminum Smelters, Invercargill, New Zealand, 1987—88; vacation scholar Australia Nat. U., Canberra, 1988—89; summer intern, Dept. Ops. Rsch. AT&T, Holmdel, NJ, 1991; rsch. and teaching asst., Dept. Ops. Rsch. Stanford U., 1990—94; asst. prof., Dept. Indsl. and Ops. Engring. U. Mich., 1994—2001; visiting lectr., Engring. Sci. Dept. U. Auckland, New Zealand, 2000; assoc. prof., Olin Sch. Bus. Wash. U., 2001—. Assoc. editor Management Sci., 1999—, Ops. Rsch., 2003—, editl. bd. mem. M&SOM, 2003—, sr. editor Prodn. and Ops. Mgmt., 2004—. Recipient Meritorious Svc. award, Ops. Rsch., 1998, 2002, 2004. Mem. Inst. Ops. Rsch. and Mgmt. Sci., Sigma Xi. Office: John M Olin Sch Bus Campus Box 1133 Washington Univ in St Louis Saint Louis MO 63130-4899 Office Phone: 314-935-4732. Office Fax: 314-935-6359. E-mail: olsen@olin.wustl.edu.*

OLSEN, TILLIE LERNER, author; b. Omaha, Nebr., Jan. 14, 1912; d. Samuel and Ida (Beber) Lerner; m. Jack Olsen; children: Karla, Julie, Kathie, Laurie. LittD (hon.), U. Nebr., 1979, Knox Coll., 1982, Hobart and William Smith Coll., 1984, Clark U., 1985, Albright Coll., 1986, Wooster Coll., 1991, Mills Coll., 1995, Amherst Coll., 1998. Writer-in-residence Amherst Coll., 1969-70; vis. faculty Stanford U., 1972; Writer-in-residence, vis. faculty English M.I.T., 1973-74, U. Mass., Boston, 1974; internat. vis. scholar Norway, 1980; Hill prof. U. Minn., spring 1986; writer-in-residence Kenyon Coll., 1987—. Regents lectr. U. Calif. at San Diego, 1977—, UCLA, 1987; commencement spkr. English dept. U. Calif., Berkeley, 1983, Hobart and William Smith Coll., 1984 Bennington Coll., 1986. Author: Tell Me A Riddle, 1961 (title story received First prize O'Henry award 1961), Rebecca Harding Davis: Life in the Iron Mills, 1972, Yonnondio: From the Thirties, 1974, Silences, 1978, The Word Made Flesh, 1984; editor: Mother to Daughter, Daughter to Mother, 1984; Preface Mothers and Daughters, That Special Quality: A Exploration in Photographs, 1987, 95, Essay Afterword: Saxton's Bright Web in the Darkness, 1998; short fiction published in over 200 anthologies; books translated in 11 langs. Pres. women's aux. Calif. CIO, 1941-43, dir. war relief, 1944-45. Recipient Am. Acad. and Nat. Inst. of Arts and Letters award, 1975, Ministry to Women award Unitarian Universalist Fedn., 1980, Brit. Post Office and B.P.W. award, 1980, Mari Sandoz award Nebr. Libr. Assn., 1991, REA award Dungannon Found., 1994, Disting. Achievement award Western Lit. Assn., 1996; Grantee Ford Found., 1959, NEA, 1968; Stanford Univ. Creative Writing fellow, 1962-64, Guggenheim fellow, 1975-76, Bunting Inst. Radcliffe Coll. fellow, 1985; Tillie Olsen Day designated in San Francisco, 1981. Mem. Authors Guild, PEN, Writers Union. Address: c/o Elaine Markson Agency 44 Greenwich Ave New York NY 10011-8347*

OLSEN, V. BETH KUSER, science educator; d. Edmund Rutherford and Ann S. Kuser; children: Hiller, Brant. BS, Towson U., 1974; MS, Johns Hopkins U., 2001; doctoral student, U. Md., 2004—. Cert. wildlife biologist and recreational devel. specialist Pa. Dept. Environ. Resources. Instr. Harford C.C., Bel Air, Md., 1987—90; environ. educator Conowingo (Md.) Visitors Ctr., 1991—95; biology lab specialist Cecil C.C., North East, Md., 1995—2002, asst. prof., 2002—03, assoc. prof., 2003—. Advisor S.E. Sch. Dist. Adv. Com., York County, Pa., 1984—91, Healthy York County Coalition, 1997—98; pvt. practice wildlife landscape design, Md., 1990—98, Pa., 1990—98; sci. lectr. Harford C.C., Bel Air, 2001. Author: (lab manual) Scientific Method: The Process of Science, 2000, 2003, 2004, 2005, 2006. Instr. Chesapeake Bay Found., Smith Island, Md., 1984—88; VIP instr. S.E. Sch. Dist., York County, 1989—90. Md. Senatorial scholar, Md. Senate, 1970—74, Darwin scholar, U. Md., College Park, 2004—05, Travel grant, NSF, 2005. Mem.: Ecol. Soc. Am., Md. Ornithological Soc. (field trip leader 1982—2002, Helen Miller scholar 1989), Drum Point Club (past pres.). Office: Cecil Community College One Seahawk Dr North East MD 21901

OLSEN, VIRGINIA, human services manager; b. L.A., Mar. 6, 1920; d. Alva Millard and Pearl Ann Smith; m. Ralph Orlando Olsen, Feb. 22, 1941; children: Bonnie Lee, Greg Millard. AA, Orange Coast Coll., 1962; MPH, Loma Linda U., 1993. RN. Nurse Co. Hosp., Orange, Calif., 1962—64; nurse supr. Palm Harbor Hosp., Garden Grove, Calif., 1964—68; pediat. nurse Childrens Hosp., Orange, 1968—75; pediat. supr. Cmty. Hosp., Huntington Beach, 1976—80; head nurse pediat. John F. Kennedy Hosp., 1982—84; nurse med. surg. Eisenhower Med. Ctr., Rancho Mirage, Calif., 1984—88; case mgr. Hemet Hosp., Calif., 1988—96. Author: (book) Wethew, Withee, 1977. Nurse bd. Cmty. Hosp., Huntington Beach; circle leader Congregational Ch., Hemet; regent DAR, 1976—; mem. Womens Rep. Party, 1979-82. Mem. Calif. Nurses Assn. Avocation: genealogy.

OLSEN-ESTIE, JEANNE LINDELL, golf course owner; b. Everett, Wash., July 17, 1946; d. Carmen David Lindell and Violet Louise (Harrison) Johnson; m. Wayne William Olsen, Dec. 22, 1984 (dec. Apr. 1993); children: Kenda, Justin; m. John Gary Estie, Nov. 5, 1994. Grad., Lee Sch. Cosmetology, 1966, Everett Beauty Sch., 1968, Everett Plz. Sch. Cosmotology, 1987. With Marysville Police Dept., Wash., 1967—72, Durham Transp., 1979—87; owner, mgr. Olsen's Riverside Golf Course and Olsen's Golf Equipment, 1979—. Author of poems. Active Maryfest, Marysville, 1976-78; bd. dirs. Snohomish County Camp Fire Boys and Girls. Recipient Editors Choice award for outstanding achievement in poetry, 1999. Mem. Nat. Granite Ware Collectors, Everett Antique Club, Hummel Club Collectors,Everett Elks (officer lodge #479, Exalted Ruler of Yr. 2004). Achievements include pubished in third book of poetry; second woman Exalted Ruler of Elks Lodge #479 since 1899; Perfect Attendance Award, Elks Lodge, 2004. Avocations: golf, collecting and restoring antiques, singing. Home and Office: PO Box 5609 Everett WA 98206-5609

OLSHAN, REGINA, lawyer; b. Kiev, Ukraine, 1964; m. Yves Cantin; children: Maxime, Gabrielle. AB cum laude, Harvard U., 1985; cert. in European Studies, Coll. d'Europe, 1986; JD, Yale U., 1989. Bar: Conn. 1991, N.Y. 1994. Law clk. Hon. José Cabranes U.S. Dist. Ct. Conn., 1989—90; atty. Skadden, Arps, Slate, Meagher & Flom LLP, N.Y., 1990—98, ptnr., 1998—. Scholar, Fulbright Found. Office: Skadden Arps Slate Meagher & Flom LLP Four Times Square New York NY 10036

OLSON, BARBARA FORD, physician; b. Iowa City, June 15, 1935; d. Leonard A. and Anne (Swanson) Ford; m. Robert Eric Olson, 1959 (div. 1973); children: Katherine Gee, Eric Ford, Julie Marie. BA, Gustavus Adolphus Coll., 1956; MD, U. Minn., 1960. Diplomate Am. Bd. Family Practice, Am. Bd. Geriat. Medicine, added qualification geriat. medicine. Intern St. Paul-Ramsey Med. Ctr., 1960-61; resident in anesthesiology U. Hosp. Cleve., 1961-62, U. Minn. Hosp., Mpls., 1962-63; pvt. practice anesthesiology St. Johns Hosp. and Devine Redeemer Hosp., St. Paul, 1963-67, Mercy Hosp., Coon Rapids, Minn., 1967-74; staff physician Oak Terrace Nursing Home, Minnetonka, Minn., 1974-88; staff physician, med. dir. geriatric evaluation clinic VA Med. Ctr., St. Cloud, Minn., 1988—. Pres. Alpha Epsilon Iota Med. Found., Mpls., 1980—86, bd.dirs., 1980—86, 2003—. Mem. Minn. Med. Assn., Minn. Women Physicians (pres. 1981-82, bd. dirs. 2003—). Office: VA Med Ctr 4801 8th St N Saint Cloud MN 56303-2015 Home: P O Box 27187 Minneapolis MN 55427 Business E-Mail: Barbara.Olson@med.va.gov.

OLSON, BETTYE JOHNSON, artist, retired educator; b. Mpls., Jan. 16, 1923; d. Emil Antonious and Irene Irina (Wandtke) J.; m. Howard Einar Olson, July 16, 1949; children: Martha, Jeffrey, Barbara, Virginia. BS in Art Edn., U. Minn., 1945, MEd in Art Edn., 1949; student, U. N.Mex., Taos, 1947, Cranbrook Summer Art, Mich., 1948. Tchr. art grades 3-12 Summit Sch. for Girls, St. Paul, 1945-47; instr. art U. Minn., Mpls., 1947-49; instr. painting and design Concordia U., St. Paul, 1975-78, 83-84; instr. painting summer sch. Augsburg Coll., Mpls., 1983—89, instr. painting prints, 1988—89; lectr. art Augsburg Coll. of 3rd Age, Mpls., 1984—2006, dir., 1992—98; ret.; instr. painting Elder Learning Inst. U. Minn., 2000—04. Mem. staff Walker Art Ctr., summer 1947; instr. Grunewald Guild, Wash., summer 1990; lectr. women in liturgical arts Luther Northwestern Sem., 1985, lectr. theology and the arts, 1987, 89; lectr. art and lit. series AAUW, 1986-89, 2005-06; artist-in-residence Holden Village Luth. Retreat Ctr., Chelan, Wash., summers 1967-68, 70-71, 73, 78-79, 86-90, 94-96; curriculum bd. Elder Learning Inst., U. Minn., 2000-04. One-woman shows include Unitarian Ch. Gallery, Mpls., 1958, Met. Med. Ctr., Mpls., 1974, Concordia Coll., St. Paul, 1975, St. Olaf Coll., Northfield, Minn., 1977, West Lake Gallery, 1964, 67, 71, 75, 78, 82, Inver Hills Coll., Inver Grove Heights, Minn., 1978-, House of Hope Ch., St. Paul, 1978, 1998, Plymouth Congl. Ch., Mpls., 1978-97, Jerome Gallery, Aspen, Colo., 1978, Osborn Gallery, St. Paul, 1979, Augsburg Coll., 1979, 96, Luther Coll., Decorah, Iowa, 1980, Wilson Libr., U. Minn., 1981, St. Paul Campus Gallery, U. Minn., 1981, Am. Swedish Inst., 1978, 1982, Smaland Mus., Vaxjo, Sweden, 1982, Luth. Brotherhood Co., 1983, Phipps Gallery, Hudson, Wis., 1985, Luther Sem., St. Paul, 1998, Berge Gallery, Stillwater, Minn., 1995, 2001, Johnson Heritage Gallery, Grand Marias, Minn., 2002, Undercroft Gallery St. Matthews Ch., 2005, St. Catherines Coll., 2006; participant juried exhbns., including Walker Art Biennial, 1947, Mpls. Art Inst., 1947, St. Paul Gallery, 1961, Sky Gallery, 1975, Minn. Arts Assn., 1975 (Merit award 1975, 76), 76, Minn. Mus. Art, 1976, Watercolor U.S.A., Springfield, Mo., 1977, Minn. State Fair, 1947, 64, 66-68, 74-79, 90, 93 (Merit award 1976, 3rd prize 1977, 93), Lakewood Coll., White Bear Lake, Minn., 1974-79, 81 (Grand prize 1977, Purchase prize 1977), Butler Inst. Am. Art, Youngstown, Ohio, 1977, W.A.R.M. Gallery, Mpls., 1977, Women Art Registry Minn. Invited Exhbn Group, 1977, Calif. Women's Coll., Pasadena, Calif., 1978, AAUW, Boston U., 1981; exhibited in group shows at Friends of Art Inst., 1979, West Lake Gallery, 1964-83, Kuopio Art Mus., Finland, 1982, St. Paul Co., 1983, Augsburg Coll., 1988, 89, Minn. Mus. Art, 1988, Modena Italy, 1989, Nash Gallery, U. Minn., 1994, Hill Mansion-History Soc., 1995, 96, Sosin and Sosin Gallery, Mpls., 2002, Stillwater Print Show, 2002, Best of Show St. Matthew Comm, 2004-; represented in permanent collections: 3M Co., Minn. History Soc., Minn. Mus. Am. Art, Employers Ins. Co. of Wausau, Concordia Coll., No. States Power Co., Cray Rsch., Pillsbury World Headquaters, Luther Coll., Kuopio Art Mus. Finland, Am. Swedish Inst., Smaland Mus. Sweden, Augsburg Coll., Luther Sem., St. Paul, and many others. Mem. bd. congl. life Evang. Luth. Ch. Am., St. Paul, 1989-91; coop. mem. West Lake Gallery, Mpls., 1963-83; mem. Mpls. Art Inst., 1945—, Minn. Mus. Am. Art, Walker Art Ctr.; juror, Minn. State Fair, 2001. Mentor tchg. scholar Met. Arts Coun. to Woman's Art Registry Minn., St. Paul, 1990-94; grantee liberal arts programs Minn. Humanities Commn., Augsburg Coll Third Age, St. Paul, 1995-96, 97-98. Mem. AAUW (bd. dir. 1992-94), Woman's Art Registry Minn. (bd. dir. 1992-95). Avocations: attending concerts, theater, skiing, hiking, reading. Home: 1721 Fulham St Apt H Saint Paul MN 55113-5251 Personal E-mail: howols@aol.com.

OLSON, CANDY, school system administrator; b. Glen Ridge, N.J., Sept. 3, 1947; d. George Francis and Elizabeth Ehlers Sullivan; m. John Karl Olson, June 26, 1974; children: Elizabeth Ann, Katherine Louise. BA, Newton (Mass.) Coll., 1969; MBA, U. South Fla., Tampa, 1976. Staff Exec. Office Transp. and Constrn., Boston, 1972; registered rep. Josephthal & Co. and Estabrook & Co., Boston, 1972-73; analyst, adminstrv. asst. Endowment Mgmt. & Rsch., Boston, 1973-75; trust investment resource officer Exch. Bank, Tampa, 1976-77; dir. fin. and planning Drug Abuse Comprehensive Coord. Office, Tampa, 1977-80; freelance writer Tampa, 1981-95. Mem. adv. bd. Child Abuse Coun., Tampa, 1990-99, Sch. Enrichment Resource Vols., T ampa, 1994-2000; mem. Hillsborough County Sch. Bd. 1994—, chair 1998-99; bd. dirs. United Way, Tampa, 1994-99, mem. fin. com., 1996—; bd. dirs. Tampa Bay Performing Arts Ctr., 1998—, chair edn. com., 1999—; mem. parent bd. U. Del., 1998-2002, co-pres., 2000-2002. Mem. Jr. League Tampa, Athena Soc., Tiger Bay Club. Roman Catholic. Avocations: gardening, reading. Office: Hillsborough County Sch Bd 901 E Kennedy Blvd Tampa FL 33602-3507 E-mail: candy.olson@sdhc.k12.fl.us.

OLSON, CAROL ANN, retired librarian; b. Chgo., Dec. 16, 1945; d. Kenneth Carlyle and Marion Heath (Barkway) Nygaard; m. Ray Alan Olson, June 15, 1974; children: Eric Robert, Peter Alan. BA in History, Jamestown (N.D.) Coll., 1968; MALS, U. Minn., 1970. Acquisitions libr. Luther Sem. Library, St. Paul, 1971-97; catalog libr. Hamma Libr., Trinity Luth. Sem., Columbus, Ohio, 1998—2006; ret., 2006. Editor: (with others) Landings Across the Ocean, 1997. Chair libr. rsch. roundtable, life mem. Vesterheim Norwegian-Am. Mus., Decorah, Iowa, Vesterheim Geneal. Ctr., Madison, Wis. Mem. Am. Theol. Libr. Assn., Minn. Theol. Libr. Assn., Minn. Libr. Assn., Libr. Rsch. Roundtable Divsn. Minn. Libr. Assn., Ohio Theol. Libr. Assn., Scandinavian Club Columbus, Sons of Norway, Romerike Lag and Landings Lag (editor Landings Lag newsletter 1984-94, genealogist Landings Lag 1995—, Voss Lag 1995-98), Beta Phi Mu (life). Lutheran. Home: 475 Doverwood Dr Reynoldsburg OH 43068-1166 Office: Hamma Libr Trinity Luth Sem 2199 E Main St Columbus OH 43209-3913 E-mail: caolson@copper.net.

OLSON, CAROL HANKINS, occupational therapist, educator; d. Robert E. and Florita Thielen Hankins; m. Thomas A. Olson, July 24, 1982; children: Nicole E., Kyla M. BS, U. N.D., Grand Forks, 1980; MS, Moorhead State U., Minn., 1997; PhD, U. N.D., Grand Forks, 2006. Registered occupl. therapist Nat. Bd. Cert. in Occupl. Therapy, Inc., 1980. Occupl. therapist Immanuel Mental Health Ctr., Omaha, 1980—85, West Fargo Pub. Schs., ND, 1986—89, Moorhead Pub. Schs., 1989—97; asst. prof. U. Mary, Bismarck, ND, 1997—. Aspire cadre mem. Coun. Exceptional Children, Washington, 2000—04. Mem.: ND Occupl. Therapy Assn., Am. Occupl. Therapy Assn. (Svc. award 2004), Pi Theta Epsilon. Avocations: travel, camping, reading. Office: Univ Mary 7500 University Dr Bismarck ND 58504 Office Phone: 701-355-8156.

OLSON, CAROL JOAN, foundation administrator, consultant; b. Cleve., Mar. 3, 1937; d. Edward Andrew Olson and Mildred Mary (Robejsek) Olson. BA in Psychology, Baldwin Wallace Coll., Berea, Ohio, 1975. Adminstrv. asst. United Appeal/Cmty. Fund, Cleve., 1960—71; exec. asst. United Way Svcs., Cleve., 1971—81; cons. George M. Keith and Assocs., Cleve., 1981; exec. dir., sec. Cleve. Zool. Soc., 1982—96, cons., 1997; cons., pres. Carol J. Olson, Inc., Lakewood, Ohio, 1997—. Publ. dir. Exec. Women Internat., Cleve., 1980—81; chmn., resource fund devel. com. Eliza Jennings Corp., Cleve., 1984—86; mem. bd., chmn. com. Samaritan Counseling Ctr., Cleve., 1988—90. Editor: (quar. publ.) Zoo News, 1997 (Merit, 1997), (ann. report) Cleveland Zoological Soc. A.R., 1997 (Gold, 1997); advisor (manuscript by Ralph Brody, PhD and Marcie Goodman) Fund-Raising Events, Strategies and Programs for Success, 1988, (manuscript by Ralph Brody, PhD) Effectively Managing Human Service Organizations, 1993. Recipient Printing Industry Assn. award, North Coast Print Competition, No. Ohio, 1996, Resolution of Appreciation award, Bd. Park Commrs. Cleve. Metroparks, 1996, Comm. Awards Competition, 1997. Mem.: Ohio Coun. Fundraising Execs., Lakewood C. of C., Am. Zoo and Aquarium Assn., Assn. Fundraising Profls., Press Club Cleve. Republican. Lutheran. Avocations: cross country skiing, biking, yoga, antiques, alpine skiing. Home and Office: Carol J Olson Consulting 1478 Bunts Rd Lakewood OH 44107-4518 E-mail: cjo@bge.net.

OLSON, CAROL LEA, photographer; b. Anderson, Ind., June 10, 1929; d. Daniel Ackerman and Marguerite Louise Olson. AB, Anderson Coll., 1952; MA, Ball State U., 1976. Pasteup artist Warner Press, Inc., Anderson, 1952-53, apprentice lithographer stripper, 1953-57, journeyman, 1957-63, lithographic dot etcher, color corrector, 1959-73, prepres coord. art dept., 1973-81, prepres tech. specialist, 1981-83, color film assembler, 1983-96. Part-time photography instr. Anderson Univ.; tchr. photography Anderson Fine Arts Ctr., 1976-79; instr. photography, photographics Anderson U., 1979-2003, Ind. U. East, 2003-054 mag. photographer Bd. Christian Edn. of Ch. of God, Anderson, 1973-86; freelance photographer. One person show Anderson U., 1979; exhibited in group shows Anderson U., 1980—, Purdue U., 1982. Instr. 1st aide ARC, Anderson, 1969-79; sec. volleyball Anderson Sunday Sch. Athletic Assn., 1973-2000. Recipient Hon. mention, Ann Arbor, Mich., 1977, Anderson Fine Arts Ctr., 1977, 78, 83, 1st Pl., 1983, Hon. Mention, 1983, 2d Pl., 1988, Hon. Mention, 1988, 93, Best of Show, 1983, 91, 92, Best Nature Catagory Anderson Fine Arts Ctr., 1994. Mem. AAUW, Associated Photographer Internat., Nat. Inst. Exploration, Profl. Photographers Am. Mem. Ch. of God. Avocations: camping, travel, canoeing. Home: 2604 E 6th St Anderson IN 46012-3725

OLSON, CYNTHIA LOUISE, dermatologist; b. St. Paul, Minn., Oct. 30, 1957; d. Roland Jack Lystad and Edith Mae Amundson; m. Field Daily Olson, Apr. 19, 1986; 1 child, Nicole Meredith. BA in Biology, Macalester Coll., 1979; MD, U. Minn., 1983. Diplomate Am. Bd. Dermatology, 1987. Intern St. Paul-Ramsey Hosp., 1983—84; resident in dermatology U. Minn., Mpls., 1984—87; faculty physician Hennepin Faculty Assocs., Mpls., 1987—. Clin. assoc. prof. Med. Sch. U. Minn., Mpls., 1998—; dermatology rep. adv. com. Medicare Carrier, Mpls., 1999—2005. Del. Minn. Dem. Party, Minnetonka, Minn., 2006. Mem.: Minn. Med. Assn., Am. Acad. Dermatology, Minn. Dermatol. Soc. (exec. com. 1999—2005). Democrat. Office: Hennepin County Med Ctr 701 Park Ave So Minneapolis MN 55415 Office Phone: 612-873-2332. Business E-Mail: olson334@umn.edu.

OLSON, DEBORAH J., psychologist, educator; b. Minot, N.D., Apr. 28, 1954; d. Leonard H. and Beverly C. Olson; m. Lloyd E. Yantes, July 11, 2003. BS in Psychology & Zoology, N.D. State U., Fargo, 1977—81; MS in Psychology, U. Mass., Amherst, 1981—86, PhD in Psychology, 1981—89. Undergraduate rsch. asst. N.D. State U., Fargo, 1979—81; grad. rsch. asst. U. Mass., Amherst, 1981—89, grad. tchg. asst., 1983—88, postdoctoral rsch. assoc., 1989—91, U. Nebr., Lincoln, 1991—95, spl. instr., 1993—95; lectr. Minot State U., ND, 1996—2004, asst. prof., 2004—. Co-chair Expanding Your Horizons Conf. in Math. and Sci., Lincoln, Nebr., 1992—95. Contbr. papers to profl. jours. and pubs. Recipient E.V. Estensen Outstanding Psychology Maj., N.D. State U., 1981. Mem.: Minot Psychol. Assn., Assn. Psychol. Sci. Office: Minot State Univ 500 University Ave W Minot ND 58707 Office Phone: 701-858-4258.

OLSON, DIANA CRAFT, image and etiquette consultant; b. Langley, Va., May 5, 1941; d. Winfred O. and Joyce (Clark) Craft; m. Robert J. Olson, May 30, 1976; stepchildren: Stacey, Kirsten Lowry. BA, U. Tex., 1963; MA, San Francisco State U., 1970; cert. image cons., Fashion Acad., Costa Mesa, Calif., 1980; cert., Protocol Sch. Washington, 1988. Cert. image profl. Assn. Image Consultants Internat., 2002. Tchr. USAF, PR, 1963—64, Long Beach Unified Sch. Dist., Calif., 1964—68, South San Francisco Unified Sch. Dist., 1968—79; founder Diana's Color Collage & Color Collage Inst., Pasadena, Calif., 1979—. Etiquette affiliates Dorthea Johnson and Marjabelle Stewart, Washington, 1988—; cons. Weight Watchers Internat., L.A., Ventura, Calif., 1987-90, Marriott Hotels, Long Beach, 1989, 1st Interstate Bank, L.A., 1990, Ritz Carlton Hotels, 1995. Designer: The Compassionate Friends nat. meml. pin, 1998; prodr. (book, CD and tape) The Secrets of Color and Style, 2001; contbr. articles to mags. Mem.: Assn. Image Consultants Internat. (sec. 1989—90, v.p. 1990—92, 2000—01, v.p. programs 2001—02, pres. So. Calif. chpt. 2002—04, v.p. programs 2004—). Republican. Presbyterian. Avocations: swimming, skiing. Studio: Diana's Color Collage 465 E Union St Ste 100 Pasadena CA 91101-1783 Office Phone: 626-584-9761. Personal E-mail: diana@dianaolson.com.

OLSON, ELIZABETH ANN, small business owner; b. Pomona, Calif., May 2, 1958; d. John Wilfred Corr Jr. and Patricia Warren Corr; m. Norman Everett Olson Jr., Sept. 27, 1986. BA, Ursuline Coll., 1996. Dist. mgr. Jean Nicole, Inc., Richmond, Calif., 1980—85, T. Edwards, Inc., San Francisco, 1985—87; fin. adv. Prudential Securities, Houston, 1987—92; prin., owner Elizabeth Olson Antiques, Houston, 1995—97, Stars & Stripes Antiques, Ft. Lauderdale, Fla., 1997—2000, Valentine Antiques, Kans. City, Mo., 2001—. Vol. hunger ctr. Euclid Ave. Christian Ch., Cleve., 1992—95; vol. Project Exodus, Cleve., 1992—95; mem. altar guild St. Andrew's Episcopal Ch., Kans. City, 2001—. Episcopalian. Home: 5520 Westover Road Kansas City MO 64113 Office: Valentine Antiques 1701 W 45th St Kansas City MO 64111

OLSON, ELLEN JO, elementary school educator; b. Prairie du Chien, Wis., June 3, 1977; d. David Max and Marilyn Ann Nies; m. Aaron Gerard Olson, July 10, 1999; children: Brady David, Carter Brian. Diploma in Elem. Edn., U. Wis., Platteville, 1999; MEd, Olivet Nazarene U., Ill., 2003. Cert. Elem. Edn. DPI, Wis., 2004. 7th grade math tchr. Lomira Sch. Dist., Wis., 2000—. 7th grade girls basketball coach Lomira Basketball Program, Wis., 2000—; student coun. advisor Lomira Mid. Sch., Wis., 2000—. Independent. Roman Catholic. Avocations: running, travel. Office: Lomira Sch Dist 1030 4th St Lomira WI 53048

OLSON, HOLLY LOUISE, obstetrician, gynecologist; b. Cleve., June 9, 1965; d. Charles and Marijean Louise Hagan; m. Robert Leslie Olson (dec.); children: Brittany A., Tyler J. BS, US Mil. Acad., West Point, NY, 1987; MD, Vanderbilt U., Nashville, Tenn., 1992. Commd. 2d lt. U.S. Army, 1992; intern and resident in ob-gyn. Tripler Army Med. Ctr., Honolulu, 1992—96, dir. ambulatory care dept. ob-gyn., 2000—02, program dir. ob-gyn., 2002—; staff physician Keller Army Cmty. Hosp., West Point, 1996—99; chief ob-gyn. svc. Munson Army Cmty. Hosp., Ft. Leavenworth, Kans., 1999—2000. Fellow: ACOG. Home: 95-1067 Alaoki St Mililani HI 96789-4906

OLSON, JEAN LOUNSBURY, social worker; b. Detroit, Feb. 19, 1942; d. James Breckinridge and Vivian Beatrice (Thomen) Lounsbury; children: James Gary Pittman, David Bern Pittman, Patrick Alan Pittman. BS, N.C. State U., Raleigh, 1975, BSW, 1976; MSW, U. N.C., Chapel Hill, 1985. Vol. VISTA, Raleigh, NC, 1977—78; counselor Drug Action, Raleigh, NC, 1978-82; counselor, supr. Juvenile Restitution, Raleigh, 1978-82; clin. social worker Dorothea Dix Hosp., Raleigh, 1984-91. Pvt. practice, Cary and Raleigh, N.C., 1991—. Sunday Sch. tchr. Presbyn. Ch. Mem. NASW, AAUW, Am. Soc. Clin. Hypnosis, N.C. Soc. Clin. Hypnosis, N.C. Soc. Clin. Social Work (program com. 1984-2005, sec. bd.). Democrat. Presbyterian. Avocations: swimming, tennis, oboe, trumpet, basketball. Home: 2901 Day Lily Ln Apex NC 27539-

OLSON, KRYN DACIA, elementary school educator, artist; b. Cleve., May 6, 1958; d. Duane Earl and Joel Catherine Olson; children: Travis Alexander Placke, Sarah Catherine Placke. BA, Sienna Heights Coll., Adrian, Mich., 1986; M in Tchg. Sci. Through the Arts, SUNY, Stony Brook, 2001. Owner Matte Ink Frame Shop, Plano, Tex., 1986—93; art tchr. Sag Harbor Elem., NY, 1994—97, sci. tchr., 1998—. Author, illustrator: children's book Are Pickels Made From Frogs, 2006; exhibitions include Parrish Art Mus., 2003, Guild Hall Mus., 2004, 2005. Grantee, Peconic Tchrs., 2003, 2004, Sag Harbor Found., 2005—06. Avocations: gardening, travel, art. Home: PO Box 1845 Sag Harbor NY 11963

OLSON, LINDA ANN SALMONSON, minister; b. Charleston, Ill., Apr. 12, 1951; d. Kenneth Emmett Salmonson; m. Sheldon Ellis Olson, Sept. 18, 1971; children: Jeffery Ellis, Steven Eric, Ingrid Ann Olson Douglas, Karin Melinda. BSN, Oreg. Health Scis. U., 1973; MDiv, Pacific Luth. Theol. Sem., Berkeley, Calif., 1997. RN Calif., cert. diplomate, Am. Bd. Quality Assurance and Utilization Rev.; ordained Evang. Luth. Ch. in Am., 1997. Intensive care charge nurse St. Vincent Hosp. and Med. Ctr., Portland, Oreg., 1973—75; med. rev. specialist Multnomah Found. Med. Care, Portland, 1975—77; rehab. specialist Internat. Rehab. Assocs., Portland, 1979—81; nursing cons. SAIF Corp., Eugene, Oreg., 1981; med. rev. analyst Blue Cross/Blue Shield of Oreg., Portland, 1981—83; quality assurance mgr. Good Samaritan Hosp. and Med. Ctr., Portland, 1983—84; unit mgr., dist. mgr., nat. product dir. Intracorp, Wayne, Pa., 1984—91; dir. quality svcs. Golden State Rehab. Hosp., San Ramon, Calif., 1991—93; parish pastor Our Savior's Luth. Ch., Ferndale, Calif., 1997—2002; hospice chaplain VITAS Healthcare Corp. of Calif., San Diego, 2002—. Spkr. in field. Contbr. articles to profl. jours. Bd. dirs. Luth. Home for Aging of Humboldt County, Fortuna, Calif., 1998—2002, Newburg Retirement Ctr., Fortuna, 1998—2002, Mt. View Village, Fortuna, 1998—2002; mem. Chaplaincy Svcs. Bd. of John Muir Hosp. and Med. Ctr., Walnut Creek, Calif., 1993—97; chair social concerns com. Resurrection Luth. Ch., Dublin, Calif., 1992—94; pres. bd. dirs. Thirvent Fin. Lutherans, No. San Diego County chpt., 2005—. Recipient 2d pl. nat. photography contest, Luth. Brotherhood, 1986, 1st pl. photography contest, Cat Fanciers Assn., Bend, Oreg., 1991; scholar, Luth. Brotherhood, 1993—97, Aid Assn. for Luths., 1993—97. Republican. Avocations: photography, tennis, poetry. Office: VITAS Healthcare Corp of California 9655 Granite Ridge Ste 300 San Diego CA 92123 Office Phone: 858-499-8901. Office Fax: 858-503-4785.

OLSON, MARGARET SMITH, retired foundation administrator; b. Niagara Falls, NY; d. Andrew Maule and Mary Elizabeth (Hurst) Smith; m. Lou Fletcher Mathews (dec.); children: Kimberly Mathews Harkins, Christopher Scott Mathews; m. Richard Carlson Stevens (div.); 1 child, Andrea Stevens Kraus; m. Richard C. Olson, July 19, 1985; stepchildren: Scott Erik, Katherine Ann. BA cum laude, Niagara U., 1972, MA cum laude, 1977. Instr. Niagara U., Niagara Falls, 1972-79; supr. mfg. Harrison Radiator divsn. GM, Lockport, NY, 1979-85; owner, mgr. Town House Restaurant, Ligonier, Pa., 1985-91; dir. restaurant mgmt., dir. acad. affairs Pa. Inst. Culinary Art, Pitts., 1992-97; sr. mgr. Gen. Cinema, Bridgewater, NJ, 1997-2001; dir. Ctr. for Workforce Excellence in Info. Tech. Middlesex Coll., Edison, NJ, 2001—04; ret., 2004. Advisor: (videos) Food Service Security, 1992, Sexual Harassment, 1994. Bd. dirs., treas. Hist. Soc. Ligonier, 1987-90; com. mem. Ligonier Libr. Arts, 1988-90; bd. dirs. Christian Charities, Ligonier, 1997—; mem. adv. bd. Goodwill Industries, Pitts., 1984-97. Named Hospitality Profl. of Yr., Allegheny County C.C., 1991. Avocations: reading, cross-stitch, crossword puzzles, theater, music.

OLSON, MARIAN KATHERINE, management consultant; b. Tulsa, Okla., Oct. 15, 1933; d. Sherwood Joseph and Katherine M. (Miller) Lahman; m. Ronald Keith Olson, Oct. 27, 1956 (dec. May 1991). BA in Polit. Sci., U. Colo., 1954, MA in Elem. Edn., 1962; EdD in Ednl. Adminstrn., U. Tulsa, 1969. Tchr. pub. schs., Wyo., Colo., Mont., 1956-67; tchg. fellow, adj. instr. edn. U. Tulsa, 1968-69; asst. prof. edn. Eastern Mont. State Coll., 1970; program assoc. rsch. adminstrn. Mont. State U., 1970-75; on leave with Energy Policy Office of White House then with Fed. Energy Adminstrn., 1973-74; with Dept. Energy and predecessor, 1975—, program analyst, 1975-79, chief planning and environ. compliance br., 1979-83; regional dir. Region VIII Fed. Emergency Mgmt. Agy., 1987-93; exec. dir. Search and Rescue Dogs of the U.S., 1993—. Pres. Marian Olson Assocs., Bannack Pub. Co Contbr. articles in field. Bd. dirs. Disaster Preparedness and Emergency Response Assn. Internat.; incorporator Jeffco Citizens League. Grantee Okla. Consortium Higher Edn., 1969, NIMH, 1974. Mem. Internat. Assn. Emergency Mgrs., Am. Soc. for Info. Sci., Am. Assn. Budget and Program Analysis, Assn. of Contingency Planners, Nat. Inst. Urban Search and Rescue (bd. dirs.), Nat. Assn. for Search and Rescue, Colo. Search and Rescue, Search and Rescue Dogs of U.S., Colo. Emergency Mgmt. Assn., Front Range Rescue Dogs, Kappa Delta Pi, Phi Alpha Theta, Kappa Alpha Theta. Republican. Home: 203 Iowa Dr Golden CO 80403-1337 Office: Marian Olson Assocs 203 Iowa Dr Ste B Golden CO 80403-1337 Personal E-mail: mlolson@ix.netcom.com.

OLSON, MARY JANE, elementary school educator; b. Gloucester, Mass., June 1, 1951; d. Richard Shaw and Catherine Blaisdell Burbank; m. John Charles Olson, June 2, 1973; children: Daniel McLean, Jeffrey Charles, Thomas John. BS, Westfield State Coll., Mass., 1973; MEd, Cambridge Coll., Mass., 1995. Tchr. Landmark Sch., Beverly, Mass., 1974—78, 1990—91; asst. mid. sch. Rockport Pub. Schs., Mass., 1973—74; tchr. Rockport Pub. Schools, 1991—. Vol. Holy Family Parish, Gloucester, Mass., 1973—2006; troup leader Girl Scouts U.S.A., Rockport, 1973—90; vol. Rockport Pub. Schs., 1978—90. Named to Who's Who Am. Tchrs., 2004, 2005. Office: Rockport Public Schools Jerden's Lane Rockport MA 01966

OLSON, MYRNA RAYE, education educator; b. Lakota, N.D., Mar. 11, 1947; d. Merlin W. and Ruby A. (Tufte) Munson; children: Nathan, Austin. BS in edn., No. Mont. Coll., 1969; MEd, Mont. State U., 1971; EdD, U. N.D., 1975. Prof. of higher edn. U. N.D.; tchr. Mont. Sch. for the Deaf and Blind, Gt. Falls, Mont., N.D. Sch. for the Blind, Grand Forks, ND. Spkr. in field of higher edn. Author: Collaboration Handbook for Educators, 1995, Women's Journeys Through Crisis, 1988, others. Named Chester Fritz Disting. Prof., U. N.D., 2003; recipient Humanitarian award, N.D. Coun. for Exceptional Children, 1999. Home: 3602 Chestnut St Grand Forks ND 58201-7654 Business E-Mail: myrna_olson@und.nodak.edu.

OLSON, PAMELA FAITH, lawyer, former federal agency administrator; b. Fargo, ND, July 6, 1954; d. Norman Clifford and Inga (Larson) O.; m. Grant Douglas Aldonas, Apr. 12, 1980; children: Nicole Helen, Kirsten Inga, Noah Grant. BA magna cum laude, U. Minn., 1976, JD, 1980, MBA, 1984. Bar: DC 1981. Instr. U. Minn., Coll. Bus. Adminstrn., Mpls., 1979; atty., Office of Chief Counsel, IRS US Dept. Treasury, Washington, 1981—86; assoc. Skadden, Arps, Slate, Meagher & Flom, LLP, Washington, 1986-90, ptnr., 1990—2001, 2004—; dep. asst. sec. for tax policy US Dept. Treasury, Washington, 2001—02, asst. sec. for tax policy, 2002—04. Bd. dirs. Tax Analysts, 2004-, So. Fed. Tax Inst., 2005-. Coun. mem. Resurrection Luth. Ch., Va., 2002-05; trustee Millenium Inst., 1993-99. Fellow Am. Bar Found., Am. Coll. Tax Counsel; mem. ABA (vice chmn. employment taxes com. 1988-90, chair employment tax com. 1990-92, com. on govt. rels. 1992—, com. on coms. 1992—, com. on women and minorities 1993—, com. on membership and mktg. 1993—, coun. dir. sect. on taxation 1993-95, vice chair sect. taxation 1995-98, chair-elect sect. on taxation 1999-00, chair sect. on taxation 2000-01, bd. dirs. retirement funds 2004-), Equipment Leasing Assn., DC Bar Assn. (chmn. legis. and regulations com.), U. Minn. Law Sch. Alumi Assn. (bd. dirs. 1992-97), Phi Beta Kappa. Avocations: children, volunteering, cooking, softball, skiing. Office: Skadden Arps Slate Meagher & Flom LLP 1440 New York Ave NW Ste 600 Washington DC 20005-6000

OLSON, PAULA SUE, director; b. Sabetha, Kans., July 30, 1950; d. Raymond Eugene and Ivena Orene Legler; m. Carl Arthur Olson, Oct. 3, 1986; 1 child, Matthew Wesley Smith. BS in Edn., Troy State U., Ala., 1975; MS in Edn., U. Ariz., 1985, EdS in Adminstrn., 1983. Cert. tchr. K-8 Ariz. ESL tchr. U. Md., Camp Casey, Republic of Korea, 1975—76; tchr. freshman English, Cochise Coll., Ft. Huachuca, Ariz., 1976—77; classroom tchr. Sierra Vista Pub. Schs., Ariz., 1977—85; program facilitator Esperanza Elem. Sch., Tucson, 1989—93; Title I dir. fed. funds for at-risk students Sunnyside Sch. Dist., Tucson, 1993—94; elem. sch. prin. Craycroft Elem. Sch., Tucson, 1994—96; lang. arts and reading instr. Apollo and Challenger Mid. Schs., Tucson, 1996—2003; program facilitator Challenger Mid. Sch., Tucson, 2003—. Author: (interactive textbook) Arizona!. Prayer chaplain Unity of Tucson, 2005. Mem.: Pi Lambda Theta. Achievements include Tchr. of the Yr.- Sierra Vista, Ariz. 1980; Mid. Sch. Educator of the Yr. 1994; Nat. Geographic Tchr. Cons; Outstanding Law-Related Educator of the Yr. 1993. Personal E-mail: psolson@dakotacom.net. Business E-Mail: paulao@susd12.org.

OLSON, RACHEL ANN, performing arts educator, director; b. Wausau, Wis., Nov. 23, 1951; d. Ralph H. and Lucille M. Kresin; children: Jordan E., Kelsey Ann. BA, U. Wis. Milw., 1973. Cert. Tchr. State of Wis. Dept. Pub. Instrn., 1973. Tchr. D.C. Everest Sch. Dist., Weston, Wis., 1996—2001; tchr., dir. theatre Edgar Sch. Dist., Wis., 2001—. Dir. Wausau Cmty. Theatre, Wis., 2000—05. Author: (children's religious plays, book pub.) 'Twas the Night Before (4 plays, 1 book pub. in 1990's). Chair play selection com. Wausau Cmty. Theatre, 2001—05; /bd. mem. Ctrl. Wis. Children's Theatre, Wausau, 1995—99. Named H.S. Tchr. of Yr., Edgar Sch. Dist., 2006; recipient Champion of Youth award, United Way, 2006. Lutheran. Achievements include United Way's Champion of Youth Award, 2006; HS Teacher of the Year 2006 (Edgar School Dist). Avocations: reading, theater. Office: Edgar High School 203 E Birch St Edgar WI 54426-0196 Office Fax: 715-352-3198. E-mail: rachel@edgar.k12.wi.us.

OLSON, REBECCA JANE, special education educator; b. Kankakee, Ill., Aug. 12, 1972; d. Lawrence Edward Rolph and Jane Glenna Cahan; m. Brian David Olson, Dec. 3, 1994; children: Holly Janet, Daniel Edward. BS in Edn., Ea. Ill. U., Charleston, 1994, MS in Edn., 1997. Cert. edn. adminstrn. type 75 Ea. Ill. U., 2001. Elem. resource tchr. Villa Grove Elem. Sch., Ill., 1994—98; resource tchr. Villa Grove Jr. HS, 1998—2002; K-8 prin. Villa Grove Sch. Dist. 302, 2002—04; resource tchr. Villa Grove Jr. HS, 2004—. Summer camp dir. Champaign-Urbana Spl. Recreation, Champaign, Ill., 1998—2000. Mem.: Ill. Prins. Assn., Coun. Exceptional Children. Office: Villa Grove Sch Dist #302 400 N Sycamore Villa Grove IL 61956

OLSON, RUE EILEEN, retired librarian; b. Chgo., Nov. 1, 1928; d. Paul H. and Martha M. (Fick) Meyers; m. Richard L. Olson, July 18, 1964; children: Catherine, Karen. Student, Herzl Coll., 1946-48, Northwestern U., 1948-50, Ill. State U., 1960-64, Middle Mgmt. Inst. Spl. Librs. Assn., 1985-87. Acct. Ill. Farm Supply Co., Chgo., 1948-59; asst. libr. Ill. Agrl. Assn., Bloomington, 1960-66, libr., 1966-86, dir. libr. svcs., 1986-96, ret., 1996. Bd. dirs. Corn Belt Libr. Sys., 1989-94, sec., 1991-94; mem. area com. Nat. Libr. Week, 1971, area steering com., 1972; mem. steering com. Illinet/OCLC, 1985-87; mem. adv. coun. of librs. Grad. Sch. Libr. Sci. U., Ill., 1976-79; mem. Ill. State Libr. Adv. Com. for Interlibr. Cooperation, 1979-80; del. Ill. White Ho. Conf. on Libr. and Info. Svcs., 1978; coord. Vita Income Tax Assistance, Bloomington, Ill., 1986-89, 95-99, preparer, 1978—2002; sec. Hawthorn Village Homeowner's Assn., 1995-2002, v.p., 2002—04; congl. sec. Good Shepherd Luth. Ch., 1999-2001, newsletter editor, 1994-96. Mem. Am., Ill., McLean County (pres. 1970-71), Libr. Assns., Spl. Librs. Assn. (pres. Ill. chpt. 1977-78, first to be named Disting. Mem. food, agr. and nutrition divsn. 1989), Ill. OCLC Users Group (treas. 1988-90, bd. dirs. 1991-92), Internat. Assn. Agrl. Librs. and Documentalists, Am. Soc. Info. Sci., Am. Mgmt. Assn., USIN, Mended Hearts, Inc. (sec. Ill. chpt. 250, 1994-95, v.p. 1995-96, pres. 1996-98), Zonta (pres. 1987-89), Bloomington Club, Am. Heart Assn. (McLean County divsn., midwest affiliate, sec. 1998-2000). Home: 8 Aspen Ct Bloomington IL 61704-2781

OLSON, SANDRA DITTMAN, medical/surgical nurse; b. Duluth, Minn., Mar. 27, 1953; d. Donald Gene and Evelyn Mae (Wilson) Dittman; m. Douglas Bruce Olson, Aug. 10, 1974; 1 child, Perryn Douglas. BSN, S.D. State U., 1974. Cert ACLS; cert. PALS. Staff nurse U.S. Army Hosp., Nurnberg, Fed. Republic Germany, 1975-79; dir. staff devel. Oak Ridge Care Ctr., Mpls., 1979-81; staff nurse med.-surg. Profl. Nursing, Metairie, La., 1982-83; staff nurse, weekend spl. Tulane Med. Ctr., New Orleans, 1982-83; charge nurse Meadowcrest Hosp., Gretna, La., 1983, house supr., 1983-95; utilization rev. risk mgr., and infection control nurse Advance Care, Marrero, La., 1995-99; field based med. case mgr. Concentra Integrated Svcs., 2003—05. Employee activity com. bd. mem. Pharmacy-Nursing Task Force; active numerous workshops on edn., staff devel., coronary and intensive care, infection control, long term care, mgmt. bd. dirs., sec. Bon Temps Homeowners Assn.; chair ct. of honor troop 378 Boy Scouts Am., treas.venturing crew troop 378. Named Spink County Wheat Queen; recipient 1989 LA Great 100 Nurses award; S.D. Gov.'s scholar. Mem. Assn. of Women's Students (chmn. social-publicity), U. Women's Svc. Orgn. (Guidon historian), Sigma Theta Tau, Alpha Xi Delta (chmn. philathropy). Avocations: music, interior design, travel, cooking, animals. Home: 2144 Lasalle Ave Terrytown LA 70056-4515

OLSON, SANDRA FORBES, neurologist; b. East Chicago, Ind., Jan. 8, 1938; MD, Northwestern U., 1963. Diplomate Am. Bd. Psychiatry and Neurology. Intern Chgo. Wesley Meml. Hosp., 1963—64, resident in internal medicine, 1964—65; resident in neurology Northwestern Med. Sch., Chgo., 1965—68, fellow in electroencephalography, 1968—69; pvt. practice neurology Chgo., 1969—2003; assoc. attending physician Northwestern Meml. Hosp., Chgo., 1969—75; attending physician Northwestern Meml. Hosp., Chgo., 1975—; prof. clin. neurology Northwestern U., Chgo. Bd. dirs. Accreditation Coun. for Grad. Med. Edn., 2004. Bd. dirs. Northwestern Meml. Found., 2004. Mem.: AMA (past chair, Coun. on Med. Edn., del., Ill.), Ill. State Med. Soc. (past pres.), CNS, AE, Am. Acad. Neurology (pres.-elect 2002—03, pres. 2003—). Office: Northwestern U Feinberg Sch Medicine Dept Neurology Abbott Hall 11th Fl Room 1419 710 N Lake Shore Dr Chicago IL 60611-3078 Office Phone: 312-503-4658. Fax: 312-503-4649. E-mail: sfolsonnw@aol.com.

OLSON-ARENZ, BARBARA D., chemistry educator; d. William Stacey Cudlip and Andree Petitjean-Cudlip; m. John M. Arenz, Dec. 27, 2002; children: Cory S. Olson, Stacey K. Olson. BS in Microbiology, Calif. Poly. State U., 1983. Cert. Tchr. Credential Secondary Edn. Calif., 1987. Rsch. technologist Dako Inc., Santa Barbara, 1984—85; chemistry tchr. Oak Ridge HS, El Dorado Hills, Calif., 1987—. Grantee Women in Sci. award, Intel, 1997—99. Mem.: Rotary Internat. (hon.; none). Office Phone: 916-933-6980.

OLSON-HELLERUD, LINDA KATHRYN, elementary school educator; b. Wisconsin Rapids, Wis., Aug. 26, 1947; d. Samuel Ellsworth and Lillian (Dvorak) Olson; m. H. A. Hellerud, 1979; 1 child, Sarah Kathryn Hellerud. BS, U. Wis., Stevens Point, 1969, tchg. cert., 1970, MST, 1972; MS, U. Wis., Whitewater, 1975; EdS, U. Wis., Stout, 1978. Cert. K-12 reading tchr., K-12 reading specialist, tech.and computer tng. Clk. U. Counseling Ctr. U. Wis., Stevens Point, 1965—69; elem. sch. tchr. Wisconsin Rapids, 1970—76; sch. counselor, 1976—79; dist. dir. elem. guidance, 1979—82; tchr. elem. and reading, 1982—. Instr. Summer Remedial Reading Program; cons. in field. Advocate Lit. Mentoring Program; adv. Moravian Ch. Sunday Sch. Mem.: NEA, Ctrl. Wis. Reading Assn., Internat. Reading Assn., Wood County Lit. Coun. (cons.), Wis. Reading Assn. Avocations: literacy activities, piano, technology, tennis. Home: 120 11th St N Wisconsin Rapids WI 54494-5371 Office: Howe Elem Sch Wisconsin Rapids WI 54494

OLSSON, ANN-MARGRET See ANN-MARGRET

OLSZEWSKI, JANET, state agency administrator; B sociology, Boston Univ.; MSW, Univ. Mich., 1975. With Mich. Office Svc. to the Aging, 1977—85; mgmt. positions Mich. Dept. Public Health, 1985—91, acting dir. div. svc. for crippled children, 1991—92, dir. managed care quality assessment div., 1992—97, dir. Medicaid quality improvement & customer svc., 1998—2000; v.p. govt. programs & regulation M-CARE, Univ. Mich., 2000—03; dir. Mich. Dept. Cmty. Health, Lansing, 2003—. Office: Dept Cmty Health 7th Fl Capitol View Bldg 201 Townsend St Lansing MI 48913*

OLVER, RUTH CAROL, retired social worker; b. Allentown, Pa., Feb. 16, 1918; d. Isadore and Sarah (Wexler) Prosky; m. John Appley Olver, Dec. 12, 1944; children: Richard, Amy. BS, Hunter Coll., 1939; MSW, Fordham U., 1970. Sr. psychiat. social worker St. Joseph's Hosp., Yonkers, N.Y.; social worker Graham Home for Children, Hastings on Hudson, N.Y., Cath. Charities, Yonkers, Abbott House, Irvington, N.Y.; founder, coord. Women's Justice Coun. Westchester, 1986—95; ret., 1995. Co-founder My Sister's Place Shelter, Westchester; adj. prof. Sch. of Social Svcs. Fordham U., 1988—90; caseworker numerous orgns. in field. Vol. founding com. UN Internat. Sch., N.Y.C., 1948; vol. refugee camp/A Women's Sch. Clothing and Ednl. Materials Depot, Tripoli, Libya, 1951; past bd. dirs. Westchester County Commrs. Mental Health Advs., Yonkers Cmty. Mental Health Adv. Bd. Mem.: LWV, NASW (Westchester Social Worker of Yr. 1990), Mental Health Assn., Acad. Am. Social Workers, Am. Orthopsychiat. Assn., UN Women's Guild (founder Westchester chpt.), Sierra Club. Home: 4208 Thiell Rd Rye NY 10580

OLZEROWICZ, SHARON, information technology executive; Founder Matrix, Rochelle Park, NJ, 1986—. Office: Matrix Info Consulting Inc 365 W Passaic St, 4th Fl Rochelle Park NJ 07662 Business E-Mail: Sharon@matrixcc.com.

O'MALIA, MARY FRANCES, special education educator; d. Horace Emmett Fansler and Frances Fansler Kittle, Robert Blair Kittle (Stepfather); m. William Biff O'Malia, Nov. 8, 1980; children: Nohealani Marie, Shanice Francine. BA, Dominican U. of Calif., San Rafael, 1977; postgrad., Dominican U., 1977—83; postgrad. in Sch. Counseling, U. Nev., 1998—. Lic. tchr. Nev., 1979, cert. alcohol and drug abuse counselor Nev., 1999. Tchg. prin. Mineral County Sch. Dist., Hawthorne, Nev., 1986—88; spl. edn. tchr. Hawaii State Dept. of Edn., Holualoa, 1989—91; HIV/AIDS instr./trainer ARC: Hawaii State Chpt., Honolulu, 1992—97; substance abuse counselor Ctr. Behavioral Health, Reno, 1999—99; grad. tchg. asst. U. Nev., Reno, 1999—2001; spl. edn. diagnostician Washoe County Sch. Dist., Reno, 2001—03; spl. edn. tchr. Silver Stage Mid. Sch., Silver Springs, Nev., 2003—. Contbr. articles to profl. jours. Recipient Vol. of the Quarter, ARC, 1995, Distinguished Svc. award, Mineral County Sch. Dist., 1988. Mem.: Coun. for Exceptional Children. Catholic. Avocations: scuba diving, travel, computers, reading. Office: Silver Spring Mid Sch Silver Springs NV Office Phone: 775-423-6322. Business E-Mail: momalia@lyon.k12.nv.us.

O'MALLEY, DENISE MARGARET, judge; b. Chgo., Mar. 15, 1940; d. Edward O'Malley and Muriel McGuirl; m. Thomas Murphy, Sept. 16, 1961 (div. Apr. 1971); children: Brian Murphy, Brigid Murphy, Patrick Murphy. BA, Mundelein Coll., 1961; MA, U. Chgo., 1971; JD, John Marshall Law Sch., 1981. Bar: Ill. 1981, U.S. Dist. Ct. (no. dist.) Ill. 1982. Sch. social worker Matteson Dist. 162, Ill., 1971—78; with State Atty's Appellate Office, 1981—85; atty. Chgo. Transit Authority, 1985—86, Fasano & Farina, Chgo., 1986—87, O'Connor Schiff and Meyer, Chgo., 1987—89; sr. trial counsel, torts divsn. City of Chgo., 1989—92; trial judge, domestic rels. Chgo., 1992—94; trial judge, law divsn., 1994—2002; appellate ct. judge Ill. Appellate Ct., Chgo., 2002—. Adj. prof. law John Marshall Law Sch., Chgo., 1998—. Home: 160 N La Salle St Fl 15 Chicago IL 60601-3103

O'MALLEY, KATHLEEN M., federal judge; b. 1956; AB magna cum laude, Kenyon Coll., 1979; JD, Case Western Reserve, 1982. Law clk. to Hon. Nathaniel R. Jones U.S. Ct. of Appeals, 6th circuit, 1982-83; with Jones, Day, Reavis & Pogue, Cleve., 1983-84, Porter, Wright, Morris & Arthur, Cleve., 1985-91; chief counsel, first asst. atty. gen., chief of staff Office of Atty. Gen., Columbus, 1991-94; district judge U.S. Dist. Ct. (Ohio no. dist.), 6th circuit, Cleve., 1994—. Vis. prof. Sch. Law Case Western Res. U. Mem.: ABA, FBA, Fed. Cir. Bar Assn., Anthony J. Celebrezze Inn of Ct., Order of Coif, Phi Beta Kappa. Office: US District Ct 801 W Superior Ave Cleveland OH 44113-1840

O'MALLEY, KATHY, radio personality; b. July 22, 1945; children: Patrick, Colleen. Student, No. Ill. Univ. Sec. Chgo. Tribune, 1979—83, reporter to co-writer, Inc. column, 1983—94, features writer, 1994—95; radio talk show host with Judy Markey WGN-AM, Chgo., 1989—. Co-founder Aaron Gold Scholarship Fund, Theater Sch., DePaul Univ.; vol. Open Hand, Chgo.; tutor Fourth Presbyn. Ch. Chgo. Partners in Edn. Named Career Woman of Yr., Ill. Prairie Girl Scout Coun., 1987; named one of 100 Most Influential Women, Crain's Chicago Bus., 2004, 100 Most Important Talk Show Hosts in Am., Talkers Mag., 2005; named to 20th Anniversary Hall of Fame, Today's Chgo. Woman, 2002. Office: WGN Radio 435 N Michigan Ave Chicago IL 60611 Office Phone: 312-222-4700. Office Fax: 312-222-5165. Business E-Mail: kathyomalley@wgnradio.com.

O'MALLEY, MARGARET PARLIN, marketing administrator; b. Cin., Jan. 20, 1940; d. John Andrew and Agnes Sophia (Tietig) Parlin; m. Daniel L. Hutchinson, Nov. 6, 1965 (div. 1986); children: Daniel L., Jr., Agnes Alexina; m. John Patrick O'Malley, June 24, 1989. AB, Bryn Mawr Coll., 1961, postgrad., 1963-65; MBA, Villanova U., 1989. Tchr. The Shipley Sch., Bryn Mawr, Pa., 1961-63; adminstrv. asst. Bryn Mawr Coll., 1963-67, Villanova (Pa.) U., 1976—90; v.p. Winsor Assocs., 1990-91; mgr. mktg. and support svcs. Normandeau Assocs., Inc., 1992—. Mem. women's commn. Univ. Mus., U. Pa., Phila., 1969—76; trustee The Old Eagle Sch., Wayne, Pa., 1997—99; v.p. Phoenixville Area C. of C., 1998—99, commerce bd., 1997—99; bd. trustees The Norfolk Libr., 2001—; bd. dirs. Normandeau Assocs., 2001—02, Phila. Child Guidance Clinic, 1970—76, The Agnes Irwin Sch., 1982—85, Strings for Schs., 1982—89, The West Hill Sch., 1970—87, The Schuylkill River Greenway, Assn., 1993—96. Mem. The Weeders Club, Norfolk Libr. Assocs. Republican. Congregationalist. Office: Normandeau Assocs Inc PO Box 586 Norfolk CT 06058-0586

O'MALLEY, PATRICIA, nurse, researcher; b. Boston, May 13, 1955; d. Peter and Catherine (Dwyer) O'M. BSN, Coll. Mt. St. Joseph, Cin., 1977; MS, Ohio State U., 1984, PhD, 2000. Cert. critical care nurse. Palliative care svcs. Miami Valley Hosp., Dayton, Ohio, critical care nurse, nurse educator, cons., 2005—. Adj. faculty Wright State U., Dayton, Ind. U. East. Contbr. articles to profl. jours., textbooks. Recipient honors Dayton Area Heart Assn., Ohio Ho. of Reps., 1994, Ohio Dept. Health, 1996. Mem. AACN, Soc. Critical Care Medicine, Midwest Nursing Rsch. Soc., Nat. Assn. Clin. Nurse Specialists, Assn. for Death Edn. and Counseling, Sigma Theta Tau. Office: Miami Valley Hosp 1 Wyoming St Dayton OH 45409-2722 Office Phone: 937-208-4518. Business E-Mail: pomalley@mvh.org. E-mail: paomalley@riva.net.

O'MALLEY, SUSAN, professional basketball team executive; d. Peter and Jan O'Malley. BS in Bus. and Finance, Mt. St. Mary's Coll., 1983. With Earl Palmer Brown Advt., 1983—86; dir. advt. Washington Bullets, 1986-87, dir. mktg., 1987-88, exec. v.p., 1988-91, pres., 1991-96, Washington Wizards, 1996—, Washington Sports and Entertainment, 1995—. Recipient Americanism Award, Alexandria-Olympic Boys and Girls Club, 1997, Adj. Prof. of Yr. Award, Georgetown U., 2002. Achievements include becoming first female president of an NBA franchise. Avocations: tennis, vacations. Office: Washington Wizards 718 7th St NW Washington DC 20001-3716

OMAN, DEBORAH SUE, health science facility administrator; b. North Platte, Nebr., Aug. 26, 1948; d. Rex Ardell and Opale Louise (Smith) O. BS, Kearney State Coll., 1970; MA in Journalism and Mass Comm., U. Nebr., 1993. Med. technologist Physicians Pathology Labs., Lincoln, Nebr., 1970-71; med. technologist student health Colo. State U., Ft. Collins, 1971-72; supr. hematology lab. Bryan Meml. Hosp., Lincoln, 1972-76; sect. supr. hematology, hemostasis QUEST Diagnostics, Inc., 1976—. Hemostasis cons. Dade-Behring, Inc., Miami Fla., 1998-2000; clin. cons. Med. Lab. Automation, Inc., Pleasantville, N.Y., 1990-97; adj. prof. Sch. Med. Tech., Nebr. Wesleyan U., Lincoln, 1979-85; clin. instr. Sch. Med. Tech., U. Nebr. Med. Ctr., Omaha, 1990-95. Contbr. articles to profl. jours. Mem. Am. Soc. Clin. Pathologists (cert., affiliate, recognition award 1986), Lancaster Soc. Med. Technologists, Fastbreaker's for Nebr. Women's Basketball (sec. 1995-98), UNL Touchdown Club, Cornhusker Ski Club (pres. 1982-83), Kappa Tau Alpha. Republican. Mem. Christian Ch. Avocations: skiing, golf, tennis, spectator college football and basketball. Office: Quest Diagnostics Inc Ste 100 5925 Adams St Lincoln NE 68507-2229

O'MEARA, ANNA M., lawyer; b. Chgo., Aug. 11, 1947; BS cum laude, Loyola U., 1969, JD cum laude, 1984. Bar: Ill. 1984, U.S. Dist. Ct. (no. dist.) Ill. 1984. Ptnr. Mayer, Brown & Platt, Chgo., 1984—. Mem. ABA, Ill. Bar Assn. Office: Mayer Brown & Platt 190 S La Salle St Ste 3100 Chicago IL 60603-3441

O'MEARA, SARA, non-profit organization executive; b. Knoxville, Tenn., Sept. 09; m. Robert O'Meara (dec.); children: John Hopkins, Charles Hopkins (dec.); m. Robert Sigholtz, Nov. 1986 (dec.); stepchildren: Taryn, Whitney. Attended, Briarcliff Jr. Coll.; BA, The Sorbonne, Paris; D (hon.), Endicott Coll. Co-founder, chmn. bd., CEO CHILDHELP USA (formerly Children's Village USA), Scottsdale, Ariz., 1960—. Bd. dirs. Nat. Soc. for Prevention of Child Abuse and Neglect of Gt. Britain, Children to Children, Inc.; hon. com. mem. The Dyslexia Found., Inc.; mem. Mayor's adv. bd., Defense for Children Internat., Nat. Soc. Prevention Cruelty to Children, World Affairs Coun., Ariz. Found. Women Charter 100; bd. dirs. Internat. Alliance on Child Abuse and Neglect; sustaining mem. Spastic Children's League, past pres.; mem., past recording sec. Assistance League So. Calif. Recipient Cross of Merit, Knightly Order of St. Brigitte, 1967, Victor M. Carter Diamond award Japan-Am. Soc., 1970, Dame Cross of Merit of Order of St. John of Denmark, 1980, Official Seal of 34th Gov. Calif., 1981, Woman of Achievement award Career Guild, 1982, Women Making History award Nat. Fedn. Bus. Profl. Women's Clubs, 1983, Disting. Am. award for svc., 1984, Humanitarian award Nat. Frat. Eagles, 1984, Nat. Recognition award outstanding leadership Am. Heritage Found., 1986, Notable Am. award svc. to Calif., 1986, Dove of Peace award Pacific Southwest and Ctrl. Pacific Regions B'nai B'rith, 1987, Paul Harris fellow award Rotary Found., 1989, Internat. Collaboration to Prevention Child Abuse award HRH Queen of Eng., 1989, Living Legacy award Women's Internat. Ctr., 1989, Love and Help the Children award, 1990, Presdl. award, 1990, Kiwanis World Svc. medal, 1991, Women Who Make a Difference award Family Circle Mag., 1992, Outstanding Woman from Tenn. award Nat. Mus. Women in Arts, 1993, Nat. Caring award Nat. Caring Inst., 1993, Hubert Humphrey award Touchdown Club Washington, 1993, Lifetime Achievement award Nat. Charity Awards Com., 2001, Champions of Children award Nat. Children's Alliance, Sandra Day O'Connor award Ariz. Found. Women, 2004, Nobel Peace Prize nominee, 2005, numerous others. Mem. SAG, AFTRA, Victory Awards (exec. com.), Am. Biographical Inst. (nat. bd. advisors), Alpha Delta Kappa (hon.). Office: Childhelp USA 15757 N 78th St Scottsdale AZ 85260-1629 Office Phone: 480-922-8212.

O'MEARA, VICKI A., lawyer; b. Mpls., May 13, 1957; d. James Michael and Joan Kathleen (Shepers) O'M.; children: Joseph O'Meara Masterman, Nicolas James Reisinger O'Meara. BA in Polit. Sci. cum laude, Cornell U., 1979; JD, Northwestern U., Chgo., 1982; MA in Environment & Natural Resource, George Washington U., Washington, 1987. Bar: Minn. 1982, D.C. 1983, Ill. 1989. Asst. to Army gen. counsel U.S. Army-Pentagon, Washington, 1982-86; spl. asst. to White House Counsel The White House Fellows Program, Washington, 1986-87; dep. exec. sec., domestic policy counsel, cabinet affairs The White House, Washington, 1987; dep. gen. counsel litigation and regional ops. U.S. EPA, Washington, 1987; ptnr. Jones, Day, Reavis & Pogue, Chgo., 1988-92, 93—; asst. atty. gen. U.S. Dept. Justice, 1992; exec. vice-pres., chief corp. ops., gen. counsel Ryder Systems Inc., Miami, Fla., pres. US Supply Chain Sol. Faculty mem. Army Logistics Management Inst., Ft. Lee, Va., 1982—86; guest lctr. Nat. ALI ABA progs., 1984—97; adj. prof. Union Inst., Cin., 1994—95. Author rev. Nat. Wetlands Newsletter, 1990; contbr. articles to profl. jours. Bd. dirs. Northwestern U. Alumni Assn., Chgo., 1988-90, Laidla Inc., 2003-04, Health Management Assn.; dir. Defenders of Property Rights, Zoological Soc. S.Fla.; mem. com. Chgo. Coun. Fgn. Rels, Cornell Pres. Coun. Women, Fla. Coun. Econ. Edn. Mem. Chgo. Econ. Club Chgo. (com. fgn. affairs). Office: Ryder System Inc 11690 NW 105th St Medley FL 33178-1103

OMEIS, LISA MARIE, principal; b. Bklyn., N.Y., Dec. 12, 1966; d. Andrew Joseph Davis and Olga Ferruggia; m. Steven Omeis; children: Kelsey, Steven. AA, Nassau CC, Garden City, NY, 1985; BA, Adelphi U., Garden City, 1991; MA, L.I. U., Greenvale, NY, 1993; SDA, Coll. New Rochelle, NY, 2001. Tchr. Brentwood Union Free Sch. Dist., NY, 1992—2001; asst. prin. Three Village Union Free Sch. Dist., East Setauket, NY, 2001—02; elem. prin. Lindenhurst Union Free Sch. Dist., NY, 2002—. Den leader Cub Scouts Am., Nassau County, NY, 2005—. Recipient JFK scholarship, Nassau C.C., 1986. Mem.: NAESP, Coun. of Adminstrs. and Suprs., Assn. Supr. and Curriculum Developers, Phi Beta Kappa. Avocation: reading. Office: West Gates Ave Elem Sch 175 W Gates Ave Lindenhurst NY 11757 Office Phone: 631-226-6437. Office Fax: 631-226-6428. E-mail: lomeis@optonline.net.

OMEL, JUNE M., elementary school educator; b. Spring Grove, Minn., June 4, 1945; d. Ernest W. Jameson and Norma L. Wiste; m. Alexander A. Omel, July 13, 1968 (dec.); children: Andrei A., Peter E. BA, Luther Coll., Decorah, Iowa, 1967; postgrad., South Conn. State U., New Haven, 1968—95, Cen. Wash. U., Ellensburg, 1968—95, Ea. Wash. U., Cheney, 1968—95, Antioch U., Seattle, 1968—95, Fresno U., Calif., 1968—95, Portland State U., Oreg., 1968—95. Tchr. 2d grade Turkey Hill Sch., Orange, Conn., 1967—69; tchr. 4th grade Kiona-Benton Elem. Sch., Benton City, Wash., 1979—81, tchr. 2d grade, 1981—91, tchr. 3d grade, 1991—. Chmn. Young Aus. Com., Benton City; mem. Safe and Civil Schs. Com., Benton City. Contbr. articles to newspapers. Mem. Yale-New Haven (Conn.) Chorale, 1968, Redeemer Oratorio Choir, New Haven, 1968, Chancel Choir, Richland, Wash., 1996—2000. Mem.: ASCD, NEA, Wash. Tchrs. Assn. Republican. Avocations: music, art, writing, reading, gardening. Office: Kiona-Benton Elem Sch 1107 Grace Ave Benton City WA 99320

OMLAND, JACQUELINE LEIGH-KNUTE, secondary school educator, small business owner; b. Grand Forks, ND, Nov. 19, 1955; d. Denora Muriel and Jerry John Knute; m. Thomas Jay Omland, May 17, 1985; 1 child, Brian. BS in Natural Scis., U. N.D., 1978; MS in Edn., No. State U., 1985. Sci. tchr. Thief River Falls (Minn.) Pub. Schs., 1978—79, Alvarado (Minn.) Pub. Schs., 1979—83; sci. instr. Aberdeen (S.D.) Pub. Schs., 1984—2002; adj. physics instr. Presentation Coll., Aberdeen, 1995—; Matster E-Learning physics tchr. No. State U. Statewide E-learning Ctr., Aberdeen, 2002—. Adj. physics instr. No. State U., Aberdeen, 1994. Police and fire commr. City of Aberdeen, 2001—04, public works commr., 2001—05. Named S.D. Tchr. of Yr. award, Coun. of Chief Sch. Officers, 1996; recipient Presdl. award for Excellence in Sci. and Math. Tchg., NSF, 1995, Walt Disney Am. Tchr. award, The Disney Corp., 1998. Mem.: Nat. Sci. Tchrs. Assn., Aberdeen Edn. Assn. (sec. 1984—85), NEA, Phi Delta Kappa, Am. Legion Auxiliary (pres. 1995—99, 2002—, Legionette of Yr. 2001, Legionette of Yr. 2002), Zonta (pres. 1997—99, Silver Plate), Delta Kappa Gamma (pres. 1996—98). Lutheran. Avocation: travel. Home: Box 1177 Aberdeen SD 57402-1177

ONA, CAROLINE JEAN, history educator; b. Alexandria, Va., Mar. 4, 1980; d. Florentino Garcia and Cecilia Basco Ona. BS in Social Sci. and Mid. Edn., James Madison U., Harrisonburg, Va., 2002; MS in Instrn., U. Va., Charlottesville, 2006. 7th grade U.S. history tchr. Fairfax County Pub. Schs., Springfield, Va., 2002—; social studies dept. chair Washington Irving Middle Sch., Springfield, 2005—. Nominee Disney Tchr. award, 2005—06. Avocations: reading, running, travel. Office: Washington Irving Middle School 8100 Old Keene Mill Rd Springfield VA 22152 Office Phone: 703-912-4500.

O'NEAL, GWENELLE MARINE S., mental health services administrator; b. Atlanta, Dec. 27, 1948; d. Julian English and Jennie Marine (Sims) Styles; m. Rondald A. O'Neal, Apr. 29, 1981; children: Eavvon, Taila. BA, Spelman Coll., 1970; MSW, NYU, 1972; D in Social Welfare, Columbia U., 1981. Asst. dir. alcoholism clinic Bellevue Psychiat. Hosp., N.Y.C., 1973-77; program assoc. Coun. on Social Work Edn., N.Y.C., 1978-85; sole practice social work, cons. N.J., N.Y., 1977-86; researcher Family Svcs. Burlington County, Mt. Holly, N.J., 1986; dir. consultation and edn. CAMcare Mental Health Clinic, Camden, N.J., 1986-87, dir. out patient counseling edn. and prevention, 1988-91; asst. prof. social work dept. Rutgers Univ., Camden, 1991—. Mem. adj. faculty Camden County Coll., 1986—; asst. prof. Rutgers U., 1991. Editor: Primary Prevention Approaches in Ethnic Minority Communities, 1982. Scholar Rockefeller Found., 1966-70, U.S. Dept. HEW, 1970-72; NIMH trainee, 1978-79. Office: Rutgers U Social Work Dept 327 Cooper St Camden NJ 08102-1519

O'NEAL, NELL SELF, retired principal; b. Glenwood, Ark., Feb. 19, 1925; d. Jewell Calvin and Nannie May (Bankston) Self; m. Billie Kenneth O'Neal, Apr. 1, 1943 (div. Jan. 1976); children: Kenneth Dan O'Neal, Rikki Devin O'Neal, Teresa Lynn Severson Gordon. BA, Little Rock U., 1964; MS in Edn., Ark. State Tchrs. Coll., 1965. Cert. tchr. mentally retarded, blind7, elem. sch. prin. Spl. edn. tchr. Little Rock Pub. Schs., 1961-65; prin. exceptional unit Ark. Sch. for the Blind, Little Rock, 1965-95; retired, 1995. Mem. LWV, AARP, NOW, NEA, AAUW, Assn. for the Edn., and Rehab. of Blind and Visually Impaired (J. Max Woolly Superior Svc. award 1990), Ark. Edn. Assn., Ark. Retired Tchrs. Assn., Sierra Club, Alpha Delta Kappa. Democrat. Methodist. Avocations: dance, swimming, gardening, reading, writing. Home: 6513 Cantrell Rd Little Rock AR 72207-4218

O'NEIL, CAROLYN, cable network executive, cable television host; BS in Nutrition and Dietetics cum laude, Fla. State U., MS in Nutrition cum laude. Registered dietitian. Registered dietitian outpatient edn. Peter Bent Bringham Hosp., Boston; consumer reporter Warner Cable TV, Boston; consumer reporter, news anchor WTVX-TV (CBS), West Palm Beach, Fla.; host On The Menu program CNN, Atlanta, 1982—, exec. prodr., sr. corr. food & health unit, 1982—. Recipient Journalistic Excellence awards Am. Heart Assn., James Beard awards, 1995, Outstanding Achievement in Broadcast Journalism award Am. Women in Radio and TV. Mem. Am. Dietetic Assn.

O'NEIL, ROBYN, artist; b. Omaha, 1977; Attended, Kings Coll., London, 1997; BFA, Tex. A & M- Commerce, 2000; attended, U. Ill., 2000—01. One-woman shows include These Are Pictures of Boats & Dinosaurs, Angstrom Gallery, Dallas, 2002, Even If It Shall Break Them: Prelude to a Solid Hope for Something Better, Clementine Gallery, NY, 2003, New Works, ArtPace, San Antonio, 2003, Bodybuilder & Sportsman, Chgo., 2004, Clementine Gallery, NY, 2005, exhibited in group shows at Bad Touch, Ukranian Inst. Modern Art, Chgo., 2002, Drawn II, Barry Whistler Gallery, Dallas, 2002, Summer Drawings, Mixture Gallery, Dallas, 2002, Super Nature, Inman Gallery, Houston, 2002, The Co. We Keep, 2003, Come Forward, Dallas Mus. Art, 2003, Am. Dream, Ronald Feldman Fine Arts, NY, 2003, Whim?, Angstrom Gallery, Dallas, 2003, Young Americans, Galerie Hof & Huyser, Amsterdam, The Netherlands, 2004, The Drawn Page, Aldrich Mus. Contemporary Art, Ridgefield, Conn., 2004, It's a Wonderful Life: Psychodrama in Contemporary Painting, Spaces, Cleve., 2004, Whitney Biennial, Whitney Mus. Am. Art, 2004. Artadia Grant, Fund Art & Dialogue, NY, 2003, Tex. Internat. Artist in Residence, ArtPace Found Contemporary Art, San Antonio, 2003. Mailing: c/o Whitney Museum American Art 945 Madison Ave at 75th St New York NY 10021

O'NEIL, SHARON LUND, educator; b. Spokane, Wash., June 23, 1942; d. Thorvald J. and Lulu B. (Wentland) Lund; m. Roger G. O'Neil, June 6, 1971. BA, Walla Walla (Wash.) Coll., 1964, MA, 1967; PhD, U. Ill., 1976. Instr. U. Ill./Ill. Comml. Coll., Champaign-Urbana, 1971-76; bus. edn. tchr. various pub. schs., 1964-72; dir. pupil pers. New Milford (Conn.) pub. schs., 1976-79; chair, ITEC dept., prof. bus. edn., assoc. vice provost U. Houston, 1979—. Cons. on bus. practices; lectr. and presenter in field. Author: (books) Office Information Systems, 1990, Leadership: Essential Skills Every Manager Needs to Know, 2000, Motivation: An ATM Card for Success, 2003, Your Attitude is Showing!, 2004, 11th edit., 2006; co-author: (book) Supervision Today!, 1995; editor, contbg. author 6 books; contbr. articles to profl. jours. Active various charitable orgns. Recipient numerous grants, Faculty Excellence and Teaching Excellence awards U. Houston and U. Ill., Disting. Alumni award, U. Ill., 2006, others. Mem. Nat. Assn. Tchr. Educators in Bus. Edn. (pres. 1990-92, dist. svc. award), Mountain-Plains Bus. Edn. Assn. (pres. 1990-91, Tchr. of Yr. 1991, Leadership award 1993), Nat. Bus. Edn. Assn. (pres.-elect 2001-02, pres. 2002-03,yearbook editor 1990, exec. bd. dirs. 1991-94, Coll. Educator of Yr. 1993, Gregg Lifetime Achievement award 1995), Policies Commn. for Bus. and Econ. Edn. (chair 1989-90), Am. Voc. Assn. (exec. bd. bus. edn. div., Award of Merit 1991), Nat. Assn. for Bus. Tchr. Educators (rsch. coord. 1991-93), Phi Kappa Phi (U. Houston chpt. pres. 1987-88, Delta Pi Epsilon (nat. v.p. 1992-93, exec. bd. 1992-97, nat. pres. 1994-95), Pi Omega Pi (sponsor 1981—). Avocations: golf, skiing, reading, travel. Home: 2349 Bellefontaine St Houston TX 77030-3203 Office: U Houston Sr VP's Office 4800 Calhoun Rd Houston TX 77004-2610

O'NEILL, BEVERLY LEWIS, mayor, former college president; b. Long Beach, Calif., Sept. 8, 1930; d. Clarence John and Flossie Rachel (Nicholson) Lewis; m. William F. O'Neill, Dec. 21, 1952 AA, Long Beach City Coll., 1950; BA, Calif. State U., Long Beach, 1952, MA, 1956; EdD, U. So. Calif., 1977. Elem. tchr. Long Beach Unified Sch. Dist., 1952-57; instr., counsellor Compton (Calif.) Coll., 1957-60; curriculum supr. Little Lake Sch. Dist., Santa Fe Springs, Calif., 1960-62; women's advisor, campus dean Long Beach City Coll., 1962-71, dir. Continuing Edn. Ctr. for Women, 1969-75, dean student affairs, 1971-77, v.p. student svcs., 1977-88, supt.-pres., 1988—93, exec. dir. LBCC, 1983—; mayor City of Long Beach, Calif., 1994—. Advisor Jr. League, Long Beach, 1976—, Nat. Coun. on Alcoholism, Long Beach, 1979—, Assistance League, Long Beach, 1982—; bd. dirs. NCCJ, Long Beach, 1976—, Meml. Hosp. Found., Long Beach, 1984-92, Met. YMCA, Long Beach, 1986-92, United Way, Long Beach, 1986-92. Named Woman of Yr., Long Beach Human Rels. Commn., 1976, to Hall of Fame, Long Beach City Coll., 1977, Disting. Alumni of Yr., Calif. State U., Long Beach, 1985, Long Beach Woman of Yr. Rick Rackers, 1987, Assistance League Aux., 1987, Woman of Yr., Calif. Legislature 54th Dist., 1995; recipient Hannah Solomon award Nat. Coun. Jewish Women, 1984, Outstanding Colleague award Long Beach City Coll., 1985, NCCJ Humanitarian award, 1991, Woman of Excellence award YWCA, 1990, Community Svc. award Community Svcs. Devel. Corp., 1991, Citizen of Yr. award Exch. Club, 1992, Pacific Regional CEO award Assn. Community Coll. Trustees, 1992, EDDY award, 1999, Long Beach Excellence in Leadership, 1999. Mem. Assn. Calif. Community Coll. Adminstrs. (pres. 1988-90, Harry Buttimer award 1991), Calif. Community Colls. Chief Exec. Officers Assn., Rotary, Soroptimists (Women Helping Women award 1981, Hall of Fame award 1984), U.S. Conf. Mayors (trustee, 2001-), League Calif. Cities (pres. 2002-). Democrat. Office: Office Mayor Civic Ctr Plz 333 W Ocean Blvd Fl 14 Long Beach CA 90802-4604*

O'NEILL, BRIDGET R., lawyer; b. 1963; BSBA, Georgetown U., 1985; JD, U. Wis., 1988. Bar: Wis. 1988, Ill. 1988, N.Y. 1992. With Sidley Austin Brown & Wood, Chgo., ptnr., 1996—. Office: Sidley Austin Brown & Wood Bank One Plz 10 S Dearborn St Chicago IL 60603

O'NEILL, CATHERINE, cultural organization administrator; m. Richard Reeves; children: Colin, Conor, Fiona O'Neill Reeves. BA in History, St. Joseph's Coll., Bklyn.; MS in Social Welfare, Howard U.; MS in Internat. Rels., Columbia U., N.Y.C. Editl. writer KFWB Radio, L.A.; pub. affairs officer Internat. Monetary Fund, Internat. Herald Tribune, Atlantic Inst. for Internat. Affairs, Fgn. Policy Assn. of the U.S.; pub. affairs dir. RCA; dir. UN Info. Ctr., Washington, 1999—. Co-founder Women's Commn. for Refugee Women and Children, chair emeritae. Office: UN Info Ctr 1775 K St NW Ste 400 Washington DC 20006

O'NEILL, ELIZABETH STERLING, trade association administrator; b. NYC, May 30, 1938; d. Theodore and Pauline (Green) Sterling: m. W.B. Smith, June 18, 1968 (div. Aug., 1978); 1 child, Elizabeth S. Kroese; m. Francis James O'Neill, May 19, 1984. BA, Cornell U., 1958; postgrad. studies, Northwestern U., 1959-60. Social sec. Perle Mesta Ambassador Luxembourg, N.Y.C.; spl. asst. Vivian Beaumont Allen, philanthropist, N.Y.C.; rep. Prentice-Hall Pub. Co., Eastern Europe; exec. dir. New Caanan (Conn.) C. of C., 1985-97. Apptd. Commn. Small Bus. State of Conn., 1996; spkr. in field. Pres. Newcomers, New Caanan, Conn.; pub. rels. rep. Girl Scouts of U.S., Fairfield County; bd. dirs. Young Women's Rep. Club; mem. Gov. Weicker's Com. for Curriculum Reform; mem. community bd. Waveny Care Ctr., New Caanan; apptd. mem. Gov. John Roland's Commn. on Small Bus., Conn., 1996—; bd. dirs., trustee Clinton (N.J.) Mus. Art; bd. trustees, Hunterdon Mus. Art, 2000, Tewksbury Women's Club (program chair). Recipient Service awards New Caanan YMCA, N.Y. ASPCA, certs. of appreciation New Caanan Lions Club, President Bush. Mem. AAUW (bd. dirs. New Canaan chpt.), Kiwanis, Woman's Club of Tewksbury Twp. (pres. 2002-03, 2003-04). Christian Scientist. Avocations: tennis, horses, travel. Home: 17 Lance Rd Lebanon NJ 08833-5007

O'NEILL, HARRIET, state supreme court justice; married, 2 children. BA, Converse Coll.; studied, U. Coll., Oxford, England; JD, U. S.C., 1982; PhD (hon.), Converse Coll., 2001. Practice law, Houston; atty. Porter & Clements, Morris & Campbell; pvt. practice, 1982-92; judge 152d Dist. Ct., Houston, 1992—95; justice 14th Ct. Appeals, Houston, 1995—98, Tex. Supreme Ct., Austin, 1998—. Lectr. continuing edn. courses; adv. bd. CLE Inst., 1996; panelist Tex. Ctr. Advanced Jud. Studies., Austin, 1993. Contbr. articles to profl. publs. Mem. U. S.C. academic honors soc.; founder Jud. Outreach for Literacy Training. Named Appellate Justice of Yr., Tex. Assn. of Civil Trial & Appellate Specialists, 2002, 2006. Mem.: Harris County Bar Assn., ABA. Office: Supreme Ct PO Box 12248 Austin TX 78711-2248*

O'NEILL, JUDITH D., lawyer; b. NYC, Dec. 9, 1945; BA in Romance Lang., Am. Univ. and Univ. Madrid, 1966; MA magna cum laude, Am. Univ., 1972; JD summa cum laude, Univ. Balt., 1975. Bar: Md. 1975, DC 1979, NY 2001, US Supreme Ct. 1976. Shareholder tech. media, telecom. Greenberg Traurig LLP, NYC. Founder, dir. Pan Am. Tech. Policy Forum. Contbr. articles to profl. journals. Mem.: ABA, Fed. Comm. Bar Assn., InterAm. Bar Assn. Office: Greenberg Traurig LLP MetLife Bldg 200 Park Ave New York NY 10166-1400 Office Phone: 212-801-9387. Office Fax: 212-801-6400. Business E-Mail: oneillj@gtlaw.com.

O'NEILL, JUDITH JONES, insurance agent; b. Cin., Dec. 24, 1935; d. Charles Haddon Jones and Adelle Geagan; m. Howard Tiel O'Neill, Mar. 27, 1965; children: Samantha Lee, Rebecca Tiel. BA in Polit. Sci., Duke U., 1958. Registered agt. property, casualty, accident and health Pa. Staff asst. TPF&C, Inc., Phila., 1959—66, Martin Ins. Agy., Jenkintown, Pa., 1980—90; account mgr. Posse-Walsh, Inc., Blue Bell, Pa., 1990—92, Ryers Agy./Gembridge, Jenkintown, 1992—98; account exec. Oxford Ins. Agy. Group, Jenkintown, 1998—2004; ret., 2004. Bd. dirs. Jenkintown Urban Mobilization Program, 1985—90; elected mem. Jenkintown Borough Coun., 1978—94, v.p., 1980—85, pres., 1986—90; lay vol. Episcopal Ch. of Our Saviour, vestry mem., 1997—2003, sr. warden, 1998—2002, people's warden, 2002—03. Recipient Cmty. Svc. award, Greater Jenkintown C. of C., 1991, citation, Commonwealth Pa. Ho. Reps., 1994. Republican. Episcopalian.

O'NEILL, JUNE ELLENOFF, economist; b. NYC, June 14, 1934; d. Louis and Matilda (Liebstein) Ellenoff; m. Sam Cohn, 1955 (div. 1961); 1 child, Peter; m. David Michael O'Neill, Dec. 24, 1964; 1 child, Amy. BA, Sarah Lawrence Coll., Bronxville, N.Y., 1955; PhD, Columbia U., 1970. Econs. instr. Temple U., Phila., 1965-68; rsch. assoc. Brookings Instn., Washington, 1968-71; sr. economist Pres.'s Coun. Econ. Advisors, Washington, 1971-76; chief human resources budget Congl. Budget Office, Washington, 1976-79; sr. rsch. assoc. The Urban Inst., Washington, 1979-86; dir. Office Policy and Rsch. U.S. Commn. Civil Rights, Washington, 1986-87; prof. econs. and fin., dir. Ctr. for Study Bus. and Govt. Baruch Coll., CUNY, 1987—; Morton Wollman Prof. Econs. Zicklin Sch. Bus. Baruch Coll., 1999—; dir. Congl. Budget Office U.S. Congress, Washington, 1995-99. Adj. scholar Am. Enterprise Inst., 1994-95, 99—; mem. Nat. Adv. Com., The Poverty Inst., U. Wis., 1988-95; chair bd. sci. counselors Nat. Ctr. for Health Stats., 2003—; mem. Nat. Bur. Econ. Rsch., 2004—. Contbr. articles to profl. jours. Mem. Am. Econs. Assn. (v.p. 1998-99), Nat. Acad. Social Ins. Republican. Jewish. Home: 420 Riverside Dr New York NY 10025-7773 Office: CUNY Baruch Coll Ctr Study of Bus and Govt 17 Lexington Ave New York NY 10010-5518 Office Phone: 646-312-3540. E-mail: june_oneill@baruch.cuny.edu.

O'NEILL, MARGARET E., psychological counselor; b. Youngstown, Ohio, Jan. 23, 1935; d. Julius and Anna (Zakel) Huegel; children: Paul McCann, Kathleen McCann, Kevin McCann; m. Thomas B. O'Neill, Oct. 21, 1971 (div. 1979). BSN, UCLA, 1961, MSN, 1963; MA in Counseling, Calif. Luth. Coll., Thousand Oaks, 1974; PhD in Psychology, U.S. Internat. U., San Diego, 1986. Cert. hypnotherapist Calif., critical incident stress mgmt., trauma specialist. Instr. Ventura (Calif.) Coll., 1965-69, dept. chair, 1969-74, coord. Women's Ctr., 1974-79, counselor, 1979-91; marriage, family and child psychologist Ventura, 1981-92, Morro Bay/San Luis Obispo, 1992—. Trainer; cons. County of Ventura, 1984—90, County of San Luis Obispo, 1991—98. Mem. commn. on the status of women San Luis Obispo County Bd. Suprs. Mem.: Coast Psychol. Assn., Rotary Morro Bay, Morro Bay C.of C. Democrat. Avocations: reading, dance, hiking, walking, travel.

O'NEILL, MARY JANE, not-for-profit administrator, consultant; b. Detroit, Feb. 24, 1923; d. Frank Roger and Kathryn (Rice) Kilcoyne; m. Michael James O'Neill, May 31, 1948; children: Michael, Maureen, Kevin, John(dec.), Kathryn. PhB summa cum laude, U. Detroit, 1944; postgrad., U. Wis., Madison, 1949—50. Editor East Side Shopper, Detroit, 1939—45; club editor Detroit Free Press, 1945—48; reporter UP, Milw. and Madison, 1949; dir. pub. rels. Fairfax-Falls Church Cmty. Chest, Va., 1955—60; copy editor Falls Church Sun-Echo, 1958—60; freelance writer Washington, 1960—63; assoc. editor Med. World News, Washington, 1963—66; dir. publ. rels. Westchester Lighthouse N.Y. Assn. for Blind, 1967—71; dir. pub. edn. The Lighthouse, N.Y.C., 1971—73, dir. pub. rels., 1973—80; exec. dir., CEO Eye-Bank for Sight Restoration, Inc., 1980—2000; ret., 2000. Mem. N.Y. State Transplant Coun., 1991—2002; mem. instl. rsch. rev. bd. Manhattan Eye, Ear and Throat Hosp., 1981—; bd. dirs. N.Y. Organ Donor Network, 1997—2003, Pro Mujer, 1997—2003, mem. adv. coun., 2004—. Named to Top 100 Irish Ams., Irish Am. Mag., 1999. Mem.: Pan Am. Eye Bank Assn. (bd. dir.), Women Execs. in Pub. Rels. (dir. 1982—88, pres. 1986—87, found. bd. dir. 2002—, treas. 2004—), Eye Bank Assn. Am. (lay adv. bd. 1981—83, dir. 1983—86, pres. N.E. Region 1993—96, exec. com. 1994—96, EBAA Heise award 1997), Women in Comm. (pres. NY chpt. 1980—81), Cosmopolitan Club. E-mail: maryjaneoneill@aol.com.

O'NEILL, MAUREEN ANNE, city administrator, arts administrator; b. Seattle, Nov. 11, 1948; d. Robert P. and Barbara F. (Pettinger) O. BA in Sociology cum laude, Wash. State U., 1971; MA, Bowling Green State U., 1972. Grad. asst. dept. coll. student personnel Bowling Green (Ohio) State U., 1971-72; asst. coordinator coll. activities SUNY-Geneseo, 1972-75, acting coordinator coll. activities, 1975-76; regional mgr. northeast Kazuko Hillyer Internat. Agy., N.Y.C., 1976-77; mgr. lectures and concerts Meany Theater U. Wash., Seattle, 1977-81; mgr. performing and visual arts Parks and Recreation City of Seattle, 1981-83, recreation dist. mgr., 1983-92, recreation mgr. north divsn., 1992—97; northeast parks and recreation mgr. Seattle Parks and Recreation, 1997—2004, ops. divsn. north recreation mgr., 2004—. Cons. Nat. Endowment for Arts: Site Evaluator, 1980; interarts panel 1981; multi-music panel 1988, 89, 90; workshop presenter Washington Parks and Recreation, 1989, Washington Recreation and Parks to Washington State Arts Commn., 1988, 89, 90, bd. dirs. liaison; mem. program and edn. com. Seattle Art Mus., 1981—; workshop presenter Nat. Recreation and Parks Assn. Regional Confs., 1985-86; mem. conf. com. Internat. NW Parks and Recreation Assn. Conf., 1986. Bd. dirs. Bumbershoot-Seattle Arts Festival, 1979,

80; bd. dirs. Northwest Folklife Inc., 1982-97, treas., 1985, 86, pres., 1986-89, chmn. edn. com., 1991-94, chair ad hoc com.; cantor Sacred Heart Ch., Seattle, 1982-97; mem. Seattle Art Mus. NEA Advancement Grant, 1994-96. Mem. Phi Beta Kappa, Mu Phi Epsilon, Alpha Delta Pi. Roman Catholic. Home: PO Box 19278 Seattle WA 98109-1278 Office: Seattle Parks and Recreation 8061 Densmore Ave N Seattle WA 98103 Office Phone: 206-684-7096. E-mail: MaureenA.O'Neill@seattle.gov.

O'NEILL, MICHELLE, federal agency administrator; m. Marshall Mills; 1 child. BA, Sweet Briar Coll., 1985; MA, LBJ Sch. Pub. Affairs, 1987. With Office of Antidumping and Countervailing Duty Investigations, 1987—90; mem. internat. econ. policy team White House Office of Policy Develop., 1991—91; exec. asst. to dep. under sec. for internat. trade US Dept. Commerce, Washington, 1992—95, chief of staff to under sec. for internat. trade, 1998—2000, dep. under sec. for tech., 2004—; legis. fellow House Ways and Means Trade Sub-com., Washington, 1995; comml. attache US Mission to Orgn. for Econ. Cooperation and Develop. (OECD), Paris, 1995—98; dep. asst. sec. for info. tech. industries Internat. Trade Adminstrn., Washington, 2000—04. Mem.: Am. C. of C. in France (bd. mem. 1995—98). Office: US Dept Commerce 1401 Constitution Ave, NW Washington DC 20230 Office Phone: 202-482-8242. E-mail: Michelle.ONeill@technology.gov.

O'NEILL, PATRICIA TYDINGS, performing arts educator, language educator; b. Prince Frederick, Md., Dec. 16, 1953; d. James Martin and Mary Evelyn O'Neill, Edward Joseph Pineault (Stepfather); children: Lauren Ann Veneziani, Scott Martin Veneziani. M in English, Pa. State U., State College, 1976; M in Edn., Shenandoah U., Winchester, Va., 2004. Cert. nat. bd. tchr. Nat. Bd. Profl. Tchg. Standards, 2005. Theatre/English tchr. No. H.S., Owings, Md., 1976—. Theatre dir. No. High. Dir. Parks and Recreation Summer Theatre for Children, Owings, 1999—2005. Recipient Tchr. of Yr., No. H.S., 1996, Shakespeare Tchr. of Yr., English Speaking Union Wash. DC Area Br., 2004, Outstanding Sch. in Theatre, Md. H.S. Theatre Assn., 1996, 2000, 2006. Mem.: NEA/CEA (assoc.), Delta Kappa Gamma (life). D-Liberal. Christian. Avocations: travel, directing plays. Office: Northern HS 2950 Chaneyville Rd Owings MD 20736 Office Phone: 410-257-1519. Office Fax: 410-257-1530.

O'NEILL MCGIVERN, DIANE, nursing educator; PhD, NYU, 1972. RN. Head divsn. nursing NYU, N.Y.C., Erline Perkins McGriff prof. nursing, head divsn. nursing, vice chancellor Bd. Regents, 1999—. Fellow AAN. Office: NYU Sch Edn Divsn Nursing 50 W 4th St Rm 429 New York NY 10012-1156

O'NEILL TATE, FRANCES, construction executive; b. Memphis, Aug. 16, 1957; d. Mark Alexander and Luanne (Davis) Harris; m. Keith J. O'Neill, Nov. 21, 1987 (div. Feb. 1990); 1 child, Sean Patrick; m. Charles Daniel Tate, June 15, 1997 (div. June 1999); 1 child, Charles Alexander. BFA in Product Design, Memphis State U., 1980. Lic. contractor, Tenn.; lic. real estate broker N.C. Interior designer J.M. Walton's, Phila., 1982; rsch. asst. Larry King Show, Washington, 1981; space designer, office Desks & Furnishings, Washington, 1983-84; lic. contractor Residential Home Builder, Tenn. and N.C., 1985—; lic. real estate broker Tenn. and N.C., 1987—. Home: 166 Walnut St Collierville TN 38017-2674

O'NEILL WOTANOWSKI, EILEEN MARY, special education educator; b. Livingston, NJ, Dec. 9, 1975; d. Eugene Lawrence and Mary Teresa O'Neill; m. Wotanowski Matthew Thomas, Aug. 9, 2002. BA in sociology, Rutgers U., 1996; MEd in counseling, William Patterson U., 2004; EdD in ednl. leadership, Lehigh U., 2004—. Cert. tchr. of handicapped, sch. counselor, elem. educator U. NC, 2000, instr. of nonviolent crisis intervention CPI Inst., 2004. Support counselor Options, Wilmington, NC, 1998—2000; special edn. tchr. New Hanover County BOE, Wilmington, 1998—2000; spl. edn. tchr. East Orange (NJ) BOE, 2001—02; cmty. support counselor Easterseals, Somerset, NJ, 2000—04; behavior cons. ARC of Morris County, Morristown, NJ, 2002—04; spl. edn. tchr. Lebanon Twp. (N.J.) BOE, 2002—03; sch. counselor Mount Olive BOE, 2003—. Nat. cons. First Step Cons., Livingston, NJ, 2003—; behavior analyst, ABA/VBC cons., social skill therapist, Essex, Hunterton, Warren Counties, NJ, 2000—. Recipient Loyal Heart award for Assisting Disabled Persons, NJ Coalition on Women and Disabilities, 2003. Mem.: Coun. for Exceptional Children, Phi Lambda Theta (Lillian Barry award 2003). Roman Cath. Avocations: running, cooking, gardening, interior decorating, scrapbooks. Office Phone: 973-444-9116. E-mail: merton1275@cs.com.

ONEL, SUZAN, lawyer; b. NYC, Sept. 29, 1964; d. Joseph and Miriam (Spitzer) O.; m. Keith B. Bickel, Sept. 8, 1990. BA with hons., U. Pa., 1986; JD, U. Va., 1990. Bar: Pa. 1990, D.C. 1991. Assoc. Arent, Fox, Kintner, Plotkin & Kahn, Washington, 1990-92, Hyman, Phelps & McNamara, Washington, 1992-94, McKenna & Cuneo, Washington; ptnr. Kirkpatrick & Lockhart Nicholson Graham LLP, Washington. Mem. Food and Drug Law Inst. Notes editor Va. Environ. Law Jour.; contbr. articles to profl. jours. Mem. facilities com. Williamsburg Condominium, 1994—; legal clk./investigator D.C. Pub. Defenders Svcs./Mental Health Divsn., D.C., 1988. Mem. ABA (past co-chmn. tech. assessment com.), Regulatory Affairs Profl. Soc., D.C. Bar Assn. Avocations: travel, photography, aerobics, bicycling, reading. Office: Kirkpatrick & Lockhart Nicholson Graham LLP 2d Fl 1800 Massachusetts Ave Washington DC 20036-1221 Office Phone: 202-778-9134. Office Fax: 202-778-9100. Business E-Mail: sonel@klng.com.

ONES, DENIZ S., psychologist, educator; b. Istanbul, Turkey, Aug. 12, 1965; d. Somer and Ulker (Saime) Ones; m. Ates Haner, July 5, 1993; 1 child, Daria M. Haner. BA, Augustana Coll., 1988; PhD, U. Iowa, 1993. Asst. prof. U. Houston, 1993—96; Hellervik Prof. indsl. psychology U. Minn., Mpls., 1996—; founder Thetametrics LLP, Maple Grove, Minn., 2004—. Author: Handbook of Industrial, Work and Organizational Psychology. Recipient Cattell Award for Outstanding Early Career Contbns., Soc. of Multivariate Exptl. Psychology, 2003, Ernest J. McCormick Award for Disting. Early Career Contbns., Soc. for Indsl. and Orgnl. Psychology, 1998; Fellow of Divsn. 14 (Indsl. and Orgnl. Psychology), APA, 1999, Fellow of Divsn. 5 (Measurement, Stats., and Evaluation), 1998. Achievements include research in meta-analyses of integrity tests, managerial selection, police selection, employment testing. Office: Thetametrics LLP 6427 Ranchview Ln N Maple Grove MN 55311 E-mail: ones@thetametrics.com.

ONG, LAUREEN E., broadcast executive; b. NYC, Sept. 24, 1952; d. Douglas and Marion (Chin) Ong; m. Richard Ong. BA in math. and speech theater arts, Montclair State Coll., N.J., 1974; MA in comm., Columbia U., N.Y.C., 1977. Mgr. sales MTM TV Distbn. Group; acct. exec. WPVI-TV, Phila.; sales mgr. KRON-TV, San Francisco; sr. exec. Rainbow Programming, 1994—96; v.p. and gen. mgr. KSAZ-TV, Phoenix, 1997—98, WTTG-TV, Washington, 1998—2000; pres. and CEO Nat. Geog. Channel, Washington, 2000—. Mem.: Cable TV Adminstrv. and Mktg. Execs., Women in Comm., Women in Cable, Nat. Cable TV Assn. Lutheran. Office: Nat Geog Channel 1145 17th St NW Washington DC 20036

ONLEY, SISTER FRANCESCA, academic administrator; Prin. Nazareth Acad. H.S.; asst. to pres. Holy Family U., Phila., 1980—81, pres., 1981—. Chair Internat. Assn. of U. Pres., UN Commn. on Disarmament Edn., Conflict Resolution and Peace. Office: Holy Family U Grant and Franklin Aves Philadelphia PA 19114

ONO, YOKO, conceptual artist, singer, recording artist; b. Tokyo, Feb. 18, 1933; U.S. citizen; m. Toshi Ichiyanagi, 1956 (div. 1962); m. Tony Cox, Nov. 28, 1962 (annulled March 1, 1963), remarried, June 6, 1963 (div. Feb. 2, 1969) children: Kyoko Chan; m. John Ono Lennon, Mar. 20, 1969 (dec. Dec. 8, 1980); children: Sean Taro; m. Sam Havadtoy, 1981,(separated 2002) Student, Peers' Sch., Gakushuin U., Tokyo, Sarah Lawrence Coll., Harvard U.; PhD (hon.), Art Inst. Of Chicago, 1997, Liverpool U., 2001, Bard College, 2002. One-woman shows include Alchemical Wedding, Albert Hall, London, 1967, Evening with Yoko Ono, Birmingham, 1968, Event, U. Wales, 1969, Everson Mus., Syracuse, N.Y., 1971, Yoko Ono: Objects, Films, Whitney Museum of Amer. Art, 1989, Yoko Ono: A Piece of Sky, Galleria Stefania Miscetti, Rome, 1993, Endangered Species, Wacoal Art Center/Spiral Garden, Tokyo, 1993, Yoko Ono and Fluxus, Royal Festival Hall, South Bank Centre, London, 1997, Have You Seen The Horizon Lately?, Museum Of Modern Art, Oxford, 1997, Open Window, Umm El-Fahem, Israel, 2000, YES Yoko Ono, Japan Society, 2001, My Mommy Was Beautiful, Shoshana Wayne Gallery, Santa Monica, 2002, Yoko Ono Women's Room, Musée d'Art moderne de la Ville de Paris, 2003, Yoko Ono: Odyssey of a Cockroach, Institute of Contemporary Arts, London, 2004; recorded albums: (with John Ono Lennon) Two Virgins, 1968, Life With Lions, 1969, Wedding Album, 1970, Live Peace in Toronto (1969), 1970, Some Time in New York City, 1972, Double Fantasy, 1980 (Grammy award Album of Yr., 1982), Milk and Honey, 1984; solo albums include Yoko Ono Plastic Ono Band, 1970, Fly, 1971, Approximately Infinite Universe, 1973, Feeling the Space, 1973, Welcome: The Many Sides Of Yoko Ono, 1973, Season of Glass, 1981, It's Alright (I See Rainbows), 1982, Every Man Has A Woman, 1984, Starpeace, 1985, Walking On Thin Ice, 1992, Rising, 1995, New York Rock, 1995, Rising Mixes, 1996, Blueprint For A Sunrise, 2001; co-prodr. Gimme Some Truth - The Making Of John Lennon's Imagine Album, 2001 (Grammy award best long form music video, 2001); exec. prodr. Come Together: A Night for John Lennon's Words & Music, 2001; composer numerous songs including Don't Worry Kyoko, Mummy's Only Looking for her Hand in the Snow, Walking on Thin Ice (Grammy award nomination Best Female Rock Performance on Single 1981), Don't Be Sad; author: Grapefruit, 1964, A Hole to See the Sky Through, 1971, Just Me! (Tada No Atashi), 1986, Sometime In New York City, 1995, Acorns, 1996,; author 6 film scripts, Tokyo, 1964, 13 film scores, London, 1967, John & Yoko Calendar, 1970. Recipient Helen Caldicott leadership award, 1987, Skowhegan award, 2002, Lifespire award, 2002, MOCA award, 2003. Office: c/o John Hendricks 488 Greenwich St New York NY 10013-1313

ONOCHIE, FLORENCE N., accountant; b. Lagos, Nigeria, Apr. 27, 1961; arrived in U.S., 1987; d. Francis Wilcock E. and Mary Nwamaka E. Okolo; m. Henry Chuks Onochie; children: Chuks, Chizo, Kosi, Ndo's, Kenn. Degree in Fin., U. Tech. Enugu, Nigeria, 1985; BS in Acctg., U. Indpls., 1991. Reconciler Peoples Bank and Trust Co., Indpls., 1988—92; field examiner Ind. State Bd. Accounts, Indpls., 1992—94; acct., pres. HCO, Inc., Indpls., 1992—2001; auditor RGIS, Indpls., 1993—94; reconciler Bank One, Indpls., 1994; acct., pres. FNO, Inc., Indpls., 2001—. Mem. Inst. Bus. Fin. and Estate Planning. Former v.p. Rotary Club Nigeria; bd. mem. Profl. Womens Adv. Bd., Indpls., 2000. Named Woman of Yr., 2000, 2004. Mem.: NAFE, Greater Indpls. C. of C., Ind. Assn. Black Accts., Nat. Assn. Black Accts. (v.p. 2005—), Ind. Soc. Pub. Accts., Nat. Assn. Pub. Accts. Home: 8836 Worthington Cir Indianapolis IN 46278 Office: FNO Profl Svcs Inc Ste 130 3921 N Meridian St Indianapolis IN 46278 Office Phone: 317-872-3437.

ONTON, ANN LOUISE REUTHER, chemist; b. Bridgeport, Conn., Sept. 29, 1943; m. Aare Onton, 1965; children: Alan David, Daryl John, Julie Ann. BS in Chemistry, Purdue U., 1965. Lab. chemist Great Lakes Chem. Corp., 1965-67; rsch. asst. Geigy Chem. Corp., 1967-70; abstractor Chem. Abstracts Svc., 1970-72; rschr. Cancer Prevention II Study, 1980-90; chemist Prototek Enzyme Sys. Products, 1992-93; rsch. assoc. Applied Biotech Concepts, Inc., 1995-98, Genaissance Pharms., 1999-2000; mgr. rsch. devel. and prodn. AllExcel, Inc., 2000—03; lab. asst. U. San Diego, 2003—05; lab. mgr. TheraCour Pharma, Inc., 2003—05; sr. scientist NanoViricides Inc., 2006—. NIH grantee, 1996, 97. Mem. NAFE, AAUW, Am. Chem. Soc., Assn. for Women in Sci. Achievements include co-inventor on patent pending for solubilization and targeted delivery of drugs with amphilphilic polymers; first to isolate, sequence and clone A Nidulans ahr asparaginase gene; development of novel materials and methods for improved electrophoresis and DNA sequencing technologies, development of methodologies for purification and testing of enzymes, U.S.A. Nat. and world medalist in Masters and Senior Olympic Swimming. Office: NanoViricides Inc 135 Wood St Ste 205 West Haven CT 06516-3700 Office Phone: 203-937-6137. Business E-Mail: annonton@snet.net.

ONUFER, NICOLE HOLDER, music educator; b. Durham, NC, Apr. 19, 1976; d. Raymond and Loretta Holder; m. Michael Onufer, June 23, 2001. MusB, East Carolina U., 1998. Music tchr. Stokes Sch., Greenville, NC, 1998—2001; choral dir. Hunt-Mapp Mid. Sch., Portsmouth, Va., 2001—02; music tchr. H.C. Bellamy Elem. Sch., Wilmington, NC, 2002—. Tchg. fellow, State of NC, 1994—98. Mem.: Music Educators Nat. Conf. Republican. Office: HC Bellamy Elem Sch 70 Sanders Rd Wilmington NC 28411 Office Phone: 910-350-2039.

ONYEKWULUJE, ANNE BERNICE, sociology educator; d. Peter and Nellie Bernice Reese; m. Osi K. Reese; children: Shane LaMont Green, Kanayo Hakeem, Kene' Obiora, Krystal Anne. PhD, U. Nebr., Lincoln, 1995. Sociology instr. U. of Nebr., Lincoln, 1990—95; asst. prof. of sociology Western Ky. U., Bowling Green, 1996—2002, assoc. prof. sociology, 2002—. Author: (manuscript) Women Faculty of Color in the White College Classroom; contbr. articles to profl. jours. Dir. Found. for a Healthy Ky., Louisville, 2003—06; mem. CASA, Bowling Green, 2001—03. Recipient Faculty Scholarship grant, Scholar of Yr. award, Midwest Sociol. Soc., Larson Minority Fellowship award. Mem.: NAACP (life), Am. Sociol. Assn. (life minority fellowship 1993—95). Avocations: reading, writing, travel, cooking, watching football games. Office: Western Ky Univ 1906 College Heights Blvd #11057 Bowling Green KY 42101-1057 Office Phone: 270-745-2190.

OPARIL, SUZANNE, cardiologist, researcher, educator; b. Elmira, N.Y., Apr. 10, 1941; d. Stanley and Anna (Penkova) Oparil. AB, Cornell U., 1961; MD, Columbia U., 1965. Diplomate Am. Bd. Internal Medicine. Intern in medicine Presbyn. Hosp., N.Y.C., 1965—66; sr. asst. resident in medicine Mass. Gen. Hosp., Boston, 1967—68, clin. and rsch. fellow in medicine, cardiac unit, 1968—71; asst. prof. medicine Med. Sch., U. Chgo., 1971—75, assoc. prof., 1975—77; assoc. prof. dept. medicine U. Ala., Birmingham, 1977—81, asst. prof. physiology and biophysics, 1980—81, assoc. prof., 1981—, prof. medicine, 1981—, dir. vascular biology and hypertension program, 1985—, prof. med. physiology and biophysics, 1993—. Mem. vis. faculty Nat. High Blood Pressure Edn. Program, 1974—, Joint Nat. Com. on Detection, Evaluation and Treatment High Blood Pressure, 1991; mem. bd. sci. advisors Sterling Drug, Inc., 1988—91; lectr. in field; Selkurt lectr. Ind. U. Sch. Medicine, 1994; hon. prof. Peking Union Med. Coll., 1994; Louis Gross-Harold Segall lectr. Jewish Gen. Hosp., Montreal, Que., 1995; Joy Goodwin Disting. lectr. Auburn U., 1996; A Ross McIntyre award U. Nebr., 1996. Author books on hypertension; editor: Am. Jour. Med. Scis., 1984—94; assoc. editor: Hpertension, 1979—83, mem. editl. bd.:, 1984—, assoc. editor: Am. Jour. Physiology-Renal, 1989—91, mem. editl. bd.: Jour. Hypertension, 1989—98; contbr. over 450 articles to profl. jours., chapters to books. Recipient Young Investigator award, Internat. Soc. Hypertension, 1979, ann. award, Med. Coll. Pa., 1984; fellow, Am. Coll. Cardiology, 1992. Fellow: Am. Coll. Cardiology; mem.: AAAS, Am. Fedn. for Clin. Rsch. (midwest councillor 1974—75, nat. councillor 1975—78, sec.-treas. 1978—80, pres. 1981—82), Assn. Am. Physicians, So. Soc. for Clin. Investigation (Founder's award 1995), Soc. Exptl. Biology and Medicine (councillor 1993—), Am. Soc. for Clin. Investigation (sec.-treas. 1983—86), Am. Physiol. Soc. (clin. physiology advd. com. 1992—, Carl Ludwig disting. lectr. 2002), Am. Heart Assn. (coun. for high blood pressure rsch. 1973—, coun. on basic scis. 1978—, mem.-at-large, exec. com. 1979—81, chmn. Louis B. Katz Prize com. 1984—86, exec. com. 1985—90, vice chmn. 1986, v.p. Ala. affiliate 1986—87, pres.-elect Ala. affiliate 1987—88, pres. Ala. affiliate 1988—89, chmn. 1988—90, chmn. budget com. 1990—91, mem.-at-large bd. dirs. 1992, Lewis K. Dahl Meml. lectr. 1993, pres.-elect Ala. affiliate 1993—94, nat. pres.-elect 1993—94, nat. pres. 1994—, Arthur C. Corcoran Meml. lectr. 1998, Irving Page-Alva Bradley Lifetime Achievement award 2002), Assn. for Women in Sci., Am. Soc. Hypertension (sci. program com. 1990—92, pub. policy com. 1990—), Inter-Am. Soc. Hypertension, Endocrine Soc., Inst. Medicine of NAS (corr. com. on human rights 1992, chmn. com. adviser Dept. Def. 1993 Breast Cancer Rsch. Program), Phi Kappa Phi, Alpha Omega Alpha (mem. nat. bd. dirs., dir.-at-large 1991, treas. 1993), Sigma Xi, Phi Beta Kappa. Avocations: horseback riding, tennis, hiking, travel. Office: U Ala 703 S 19th St ZRB 1034 Birmingham AL 35294-0007 E-mail: soparil@uab.edu.

OPENSHAW, JENNIFER, finance company executive; BA in comm. studies, MBA in comm. studies, UCLA. Press sec. Calif. State Treas.; dir. media rels. ICN Pharm., 1995; sr. v.p. Bank One; v.p. investment mgmt. svcs. group Bank Am.; dir. investment svcs. Wilshire Assoc., 1999; founder, chmn., CEO, pres. Women's Fin. Network, 1999—2000; vice chmn. Women's Fin. Network at Siebert, 2000—. Fin. commentator Wise Women, Lifetime TV; corr. Money Expert, CBS-TV, LA; columnist Women & Money, CBS MarketWatch; featured on CNBC; featured in Bus. Week publ., Wash. Times publ.; adv. bd. Wyndham Hotels, MuchoInfo. Author: What's Your Net Worth? Click Your Way to Wealth, 2001. Commr. Little Hoover Commn., Calif. Recipient Tribute to Women and Industry award, YWCA, 2001. Mem.: Young Entrepreneurs Orgn. Office: WFN at Seibert 885 Third Ave Ste 1720 New York NY 10022

OPOLKA, JAYME LYN, medical writer, researcher; b. Iron Mountain, Mich., Nov. 8, 1977; d. Frank David and Suzan Ann Opolka. BS in Biol. Scis. summa cum laude, Mich. Technol. U., 1999; MS in Pharmacy Adminstrn. summa cum laude, U. Tex., 2001. Cert. pharmacy technician. Global outcomes profl. intern Pharmacia Corp., Kalamazoo, 2001—02; health outcomes vis. scientist Eli Lilly and Co., Indpls., 2002—03; med. writer Takeda Pharms. N.Am., Lincolnshire, Ill., 2003—04; brand sci. copywriter Corbett Accel Healthcare Group, Chgo., 2004; freelance copywriter, med. writer, med. educator, 2005—. Health outcomes cons. Eli Lilly and Co., Indpls., 1999—2003; adj. faculty Butler U., Indpls., 2003; grad. rsch. asst., cons. Office Quality Assurance for Tex. Long-Term Care Facilities, Tex. Dept. Human Svcs., 2000—03; presenter in field. Contbr. articles to profl. jours. Recipient numerous scholarships. Mem.: Am. Coll. Clin. Pharmacy, Internat. Soc. Pharmacoecons. and Outcomes Rsch. Democrat. Roman Catholic. Achievements include research in neuroscience, diabetes, women's health, ophthalmology. Avocations: travel, outdoor activities, crafts, photography. Home: 4630 River St Quinnesec MI 49876 E-mail: jlopolka@yahoo.com.

OPP, NANCY JEAN SHIFFLER, visual artist, arts volunteer; b. Pitts., Sept. 15, 1954; d. Richard W. and Olive Helms (Griffith) Shiffler; m. Gregory Lynn Opp, June 3, 1978; children: Daniel, Thomas, David. BS in Fashion Design, U. Cin., 1977; postgrad., Danforth Mus. Sch., 1991-93, Framingham State Coll., 1994-98. Freelance artist, Hudson, Mass., 1992—; art instr. Hudson Drama Workshop, 1992—, Worcester Art Mus., Mass., 1994, Danforth Mus. of Art, Framingham, Mass., 1994, Arts Afterschool, Hudson, 1995-98, Assalet Valley C. of C., 2000—04; owner creating custom clothing and art quilts, 2005—. Asst., visual arts and arts after sch. coords. Hudson Area Arts Alliance, 1997-99, Hudson Cultural Coun., 1991-97, 99—. Exhibited in juried and open art shows including Hudson Area Art Alliance, Marlborough Regional Exhibit, Southboro Regional Exhibit, Framingham Artist Guild, 1990-96, Out of the Blue Gallery, Cambridge, Mass. Bd. dirs. Hudson Area Arts Alliance, 1992-94; apptd. Hudson Cultural Coun., 1991-97. Avocations: walking for fitness, pets, gardening, the arts. Home: 109 Fort Meadow Dr Hudson MA 01749-3138

OPPENHEIM, MARTHA KUNKEL, pianist, educator; b. Port Arthur, Tex., June 25, 1935; d. Samuel Adam and Grace (Moncure) Kunkel; m. Russell Edward Oppenheim, June 18, 1960; children: Lauren Susan, Kristin Lee Oppenheim Mortenson. MusB with honors, U. Tex., 1957, MusM, 1959; diploma in piano, Juilliard Sch. Music, 1960; student, Am. Conservatory, Fontainebleau, France, 1956, student, 1958. Soloist Amarillo (Tex.) Symphony, Austin (Tex.) Symphony, U. Tex. Orch., San Antonio Symphony, Dallas Symphony, Heilbronner Kammer Orch., Heilbron, Germany. Solo and chamber music recitals in Tex., N.Y., France; mem. Halcyon Trio, 1974—77; tchg. asst. U. Tex., 1957—59, 1968—69; pvt. piano tchr., San Antonio, 1962—; pianist in duo with cellist Dan Zollars, 1991—. Recipient 1st place award, Internat. Piano Rec. Festival, Nat. Guild Piano Tchrs., 1956, 1956, Tuesday Mus. Club Young Artist Competition, 1956, 1st place award Young Artist Competition, Amarillo Symphony, 1959, 1st place award G.B. Dealey competition, Dallas Symphony and Dallas Morning News, 1959; scholar, U. Tex., Juilliard Sch. Music. Mem.: San Antonio Music Tchrs. Assn., Tex. Music Tchrs. Assn., Music Tchrs. Nat. Assn., Tuesday Musical Club (San Antonio, bd. dirs.), Pi Kappa Lambda, Sigma Alpha Iota. Presbyterian. Home and Office: 9118 E Valley View Ln San Antonio TX 78217-5160 E-mail: moppenheim@satx.rr.com.

OPPENHEIM, SARA E., psychologist; b. NYC, Feb. 7, 1958; d. David and Ellen (Adler) Oppenheim; m. Alfred Boland; children: Julian David Boland, Theodore James Boland. ABL in Psychology, Harvard U., 1984; PhD in Psychology, NYU, 1996. Rsch. scientist dept. neuroscience N.Y. State Psychiat. Inst., 1995—2001; asst. adj. prof. John Jay Coll. of Criminal Justice, 1999—2002; pvt. practice NYC, 1997—. Mem.: APA. Democrat. Jewish. Avocation: flute. Home: Apt 3G 165 Pinehurst Ave New York NY 10033-1814 Office: 159 W 53d St # 33H New York NY 10019 Office Phone: 212-765-7948. E-mail: saraoppenheim@yahoo.com.

OPPENHEIMER, SUZI, state legislator; b. NYC, Dec. 13, 1934; d. Alfred Elihu Rosenhirsch and Blanche (Schoen) O.; m. Martin J. Oppenheimer, July 3, 1960; children: Marcy, Evan, Josh, Alexandra. BA in Econs., Conn. Coll. for Women, 1956; MBA, Columbia U., 1958. Security analyst McDonnell & Co., N.Y.C., 1958-60, L.F. Rothschild Co., N.Y.C., 1960-63; mayor Village of Mamaroneck, NY, 1977-85; mem. N.Y. State Senate, Albany, 1985—. Ranking mem. edn., mem. fin., transp., water resources, health, ethics, environ. conservation and banking com., chmn. N.Y. State Women Legislators' Lobby, chmn. Senate Dem. Task Force on Women's Issues, treas. Legis. Women's Caucus, pres. Senate Club. Former pres. Mamaroneck LWV, Westchester County Mcpl. Ofcls. Assn., Westchester Mcpl. Planning Fedn. Recipient Humanitarian Svc. award Am. Jewish Com., 1988, Legis. Leadership award Young Adult Inst., 1988, Legis. award Westchester Irish Com., 1988, Hon. Svc. award Vis. Nurses Svcs., 1989, Humanitarian Svc. award Project Family, 1990, Meritorious Svc. award N.Y. State Assn. Counties, 1990, Friend of Edn. award N.Y. State United Tchrs., 1991, Assn. Health Care Providers award, 1993, Govtl. award Cmty. Opportunity Program, 1994, Spl. Recognition award Open Door Family Med. Group, 1995, Appreciation award, Careers for People with Disabilities, 1996, Dominican Sisters Family Health Svcs., 1996, Vets. Svc. award JWV, 1997; honoree Windward Sch. Ann. Dinner, 1992, Leadership award Westchester Dem. Com., 2003, Citizen of Yr. award NASW, 2003, Legal Advocacy award PACE Women's Justice Ctr., 2004, Lifetime Achievement award, The Guidance Ctr., 2004, Amigo award Hispanic Resource Ctr., 2005, others; named Legislator of Yr., N.Y. State Women's Press Club, Woman of Yr., Westchester ORT, 1990, Woman of Yr., Woman of the Yr., Bus. and Profl. Women's Club, 2001, Pub. Svc. award cmty. housing, 2002; honoree Wash. Housing Alliance Dinner, 2002, Hope Cmty. Svcs. Club, 2002, Westchester Fedn. Women's Clubs, 2002, Hadassah Westchester Chpt., 2005 Democrat. Jewish. Office: 222 Grace Church St Port Chester NY 10573-5168 Office Phone: 914-934-5250. E-mail: oppenhei@senate.state.ny.us.

OPPERMAN, ROSANNA RESENDEZ, vice principal; b. LA, Apr. 06; d. Victor Thomas and Dolores Resendez Mendez; m. Daniel Charles Opperman, Aug. 3, 1974; children: Joshua Mendez, Timothy Mendez, Laura Mendez. BA in Exptl. Psychology, U. Calif., Santa Barbara, Calif., 1976; degree in Multiple Subject Tchg., Azusa Pacific Coll., 1979; MA in Ednl. Leadership, Calif. State U., Sacramento, 2005. Admin. Svcs. Credential Calif. State U., Sacramento, 2003. From instr. to coord. ABE Program Fremont Sch. for Adults, Sacramento, 1989—2002, coord. ESL Program, 2002—04, Wasc accreditation co-chair, 2002—03; from coord. to vice prin. Winterstein & Bella Vista Adult Ctrs., Sacramento, 2004—; chair Wasc, 2000. Awards chmn. no. sect. Calif. Coun. Adult Edn., Sacramento, 1997—99, pres. no. sect., 1999—2000, v.p. no. sect., 1999—2000. Cmty. adv. co-chair Fremont Sch. for Adults, Sacramento, 1999—2000; caravans dir. Nazarene Ch., Sacramento, 1988—94. Recipient Outstanding Leadership award, Calif. Coun. Adult Edn., 1997—2001, Excellence in Tchg. award, 1998. Mem.: Adult Basic Educators (assoc.), Calif. Assn. Tchrs. English to Spkrs. Other Langs. (assoc.). Office: Winterstein & Sunrise Tech Adult Ctrs 900 Morse Ave Sacramento CA 95864 Office Phone: 916-979-8521.

OPRI, DEBRA A., lawyer; b. Paterson, NJ, June 10, 1960; BFA, NYU, 1982; JD, Whittier Coll., 1987. Bar: Calif. 1989, NJ 1991, DC 1991. Ptnr. Opri & Assoc., 1989—. Legal/polit. analyst and commentator 97.1 FM Talk, LA, Fox News, Inside Edition; columnist The Opri Opinion, www.debraopri.com. Author: Video Rentals and the First Sale Doctrine: The Deficiency of Proposed Legislation, 1986. Mem.: ATLA, Calif. Trial Lawyers Assn., LA Trial Lawyers Assn. Office: 8383 Wilshire Blvd Ste 830 Beverly Hills CA 90211 Office Phone: 213-658-6774. Office Fax: 213-658-5160.

OPRSAL, NANCY UPSHAW, retired elementary school educator; b. Dallas, Tex., July 10, 1931; d. Banks and Catherine Richards (Butler) Upshaw; m. George Oprsal, Apr. 23, 1957 (dec.); 1 child, Paul Oprsal (dec.). BS in elem. edn., No. Tex. State U., 1952; MA in edn., George Peabody Coll. for Teachers, 1953. Pre-sch. music tchr. Greenhill Sch., Dallas, 1948—53; tchr. Denver Pub. Schools, 1953—55; music tchr. Ft. Worth Pub. Schools, Tex., 1955—57; tchr. Dallas Ind. Sch. Dist., 1957—60, Del Paso Heights Sch. Dist., Sacramento, 1960—62, San Juan Sch. Dist., Sacramento, 1966—96; ret. Server Loaves and Fishes; ch. sch. tchr. Unitarian Univeralist Soc. of Sacramento, 1960—; receptionist and docent Effie Yeaw Nature Ctr., Carmichael, Calif., 1980—; sec. Carmichael Garden Club, 1962—66; coord. Family Promise Interfaith Hospitality Network, 2004—. Democrat. Unitarian. Avocations: gardening, hiking. Home: 6235 Vernon Way Carmichael CA 95608 Personal E-mail: noprsal@aol.com.

OPSAL, PAMELA E., music educator; b. Cocoa Beach, Fla., Feb. 4, 1953; d. Phillip M. and Jeannine N. Opsal; children: Michael Jason Stones, Megan Amber Manthos, Logan G. Manthos, Cassandra J. Kremer-Opsal. MusB Edn., Mesa State Coll., Grand Junction, Colo., 1999; postgrad., Lesley U., Grand Junction. Trainer/bartender W.R. Grace Co./ Houlihan's, Denver, 1977—85; ch. music dir. Unity/Meth. chs., Grand Junction/Mesa, 1985—2006; children's ski instr. Powderhorn Ski, Mesa, Colo., 1986—89; beverage dir. Country Jam, Grand Junction, Colo., 1993—96; music tchr. Dos Rios Elem., Grand Junction. Free-lance musician, Grand Junction, Colo., 1963—. Named Educator of Yr., Grand Junction C. of C., 2006. Mem.: CMENC (dist. rep. 2006—), AOSA (treas. 2006). Avocations: reading, gardening, music. Home: 468 W 1st St Palisade CO 81526 Office: Dos Rios Elementary 265 Linden Grand Junction CO 81503 Office Phone: 970-255-8525. Personal E-mail: popsal1@juno.com.

O'QUIN, KAREN, psychology professor, dean; b. Pineville, W.Va., June 29, 1953; d. Floyd Arvil and Lily Nyre O'Quin; m. Mark Charles Stack, May 17, 1985; 1 child, Kathleen Ashley Stack. BS, Ohio State U., Columbus, 1975; PhD, Mich. State U., East Lansing, 1980. Prof. psychology Buffalo State Coll., 1999—2006, assoc. dean, 2001—. Contbr. articles to profl. jours., chapters to books. Recipient Faculty Merit award, Ednl. Opportunity Program, 2001. Mem.: Phi Kappa Phi (life). Office: Buffalo State College 1300 Elmwood Avenue Buffalo NY 14222 Office Phone: 716-878-6434. Office Fax: 716-878-4009. E-mail: oquink@buffalostate.edu.

ORABONE, JOANNE CHRISTINE, accountant, educator; d. William Edward and Elizabeth Christine Merluzzo; m. Steven Henry Orabone, June 17, 1984; children: Kristin Joanne, Jillian Stephanie. BSBA, Bryant Coll., Smithfield, R.I., 1980; grad. level coursework in taxation, Internal Revenue Svc., Providence, 1989; MA in Adult Edn., U. R.I., 2002. Agt. IRS, Providence, 1981—89, fed. women's program mgr., 1984—88; faculty mem. bus. dept. C.C. of RI, Providence, 2001—. Adv. Delta Epsilon Chi, Providence, 2003—; mem. adj. faculty com. C.C. of R.I., Providence, 2002—, faculty mem. student success program, 2004—. Author: (book) Workshop of Time Management Skills. Competition judge Delta Epsilon Chi, Providence, 2003—, R.I. Acad. Decathalon, Warwick, 2001—03. Mem.: Am. Assn. for Adult and Continuing Edn., R.I. Assn. of Acctg. Profs., Phi Delta Kappa, Phi Theta Kappa (Outstanding Faculty Mem. of Yr. 2005), Delta Esilon Chi (True Spirit award 2004). Office: C C of RI 1 Hilton St Providence RI 02905 Office Phone: 401-455-6107. E-mail: jorabone@ccri.edu.

ORAM, FERN AMY, editor-in-chief, director; b. Phila., May 19, 1965; d. Linda Shirley and Stuart Jerome Oram; m. David Adam Riegelhaupt, Oct. 5, 2002. Listings editor TVSM, Horsham, Pa., 1986—87, listings mgr., 1987—97, listings dir., 1997—99; prodn. mgr. Thomson Peterson's, Lawrenceville, Pa., 1999—2003, editl. dir., 2003—. Mem.: So. Poverty Law Ctr., Eta Theta Chpt. of Kappa Delta at Villanova U. (chair 2004—06, chpt. adv. bd.), Phila. Suburban West Alumna Assn. of Kappa Delta (pres. 1997—2004), Kappa Delta. Home: 2223 Woodland Rd Roslyn PA 19001 Office: Thomson Petersons 2000 Lenox Dr Lawrenceville NJ 08648 Office Phone: 800-338-3282. Personal E-mail: thinkpink@zdial.com. Business E-Mail: fern.oram@thomson.com.

ORAN, ELAINE SURICK, physicist; b. Rome, Ga., Apr. 16, 1946; d. Herman E. and Bessye R. (Kolker) Surick; m. Daniel Hirsh Oran, Feb. 1, 1969. AB, Bryn Mawr Coll., 1966; MPh, Yale U., 1968, PhD, 1972. Rsch. physicist Naval Rsch. Lab., Washington, 1972-76, supervisory rsch. physicist, 1976-88, sr. scientist reactive flow physics, 1988—. Head Ctr. for Reactive Flow and Dynamical Systems, 1985-87; mem. adv. bd. NSF; cons. to U.S. govt., agys., NATO.; mem. Aero. Adv. Coun. NASA, 1995-97; adj. prof. dept. aerospace engring. U. Mich., 2005—. Author: Numerical Simulation of Reactive Flow, 1987, 2d edit., 2001, Numerical Approaches to Combustion Modeling, 1991; assoc. editor Jour. Computational Physics, 1992-2002; mem. editl. bd. Prog. Ener. Comb. Sci., 1990-2005; mng. editor Shock Waves, 1998-2002; editor-in-chief AIAA Jour., 2003-; contbr. numerous articles to profl. jours., chpts. to books. Named hon. prof., U. Wales, 2001—; named to Hall of Fame, Women in Tech. Internat., 2002; recipient Arthur S. Flemming award, 1979, Women in Sci. and Engring. award, 1988, Oppenheim prize, 1999, Zeldovich Gold medal, 2000; grantee, USN, NASA, USAF, Def. Advanced Rsch. Projects Agy. Fellow AIAA (pubs. com. 1986—2002, v.p. publs. 1993-97, Dryden Disting. lectr. 2002, editor-in-chief AIAA Jour.), Nat. Acad. Engring., Am. Phys. Soc. (exec. com. fluid dynamics divsn. 1986, 96, exec. com. computational physics 1989—, chair 1991-92); mem. Am. Geophys. Union, Combustion Inst. (bd. dirs. 1990-2002), Inst. Dynamics of Energetic Sys. (bd. dirs. 1989—, pres.), Soc. Indsl. and Applied Math., Soc. Women Engrs., Sigma Xi. Office: Naval Rsch Lab Code 6404 6004 Washington DC 20375 Office Phone: 202-767-6182. Business E-Mail: oran@lcp.nrl.navy.mil.

ORANGE, VALERIE, rehabilitation center executive; Acting CEO Rancho Los Amigos Nat. Rehabilitation Ctr., Downey, Calif., 2004—05, CEO, 2005—. Office: Rancho Los Amigos Nat Rehabilitation Ctr 7601 E Imperial Hwy Downey CA 90242 Office Phone: 562-401-7022. Office Fax: 562-803-0056. Business E-Mail: vorange@ladhs.org.*

ORBAN, KIMBERLIE W., elementary school educator; b. Indpls., June 27, 1968; d. Richard B. and Linda J. Orban; 1 child, Kamren Audrey. A in Early Childhood, IUPUI, Indpls., 1991, B in Elem. Edn., 1994; Endorsement in Spl. Edn., Butler U., Indpls., 2001; Master's, Ind. Weselyan U., Marion, 2004. Tchr. Indpls. Pub. Schs., 1995—. Home: 81 Winterwood Dr Greenwood IN 46143 Office: Indpls Pub Schs 1202 E Troy Ave Indianapolis IN 46203 Office Phone: 317-226-4272. Personal E-mail: tbear10653@netzero.net. Business E-Mail: orbank@ips.k12.in.us.

ORCUTT, BEN AVIS, retired social work educator; b. Falco, Ala., Oct. 17, 1914; d. Benjamin A. and Emily Olive Adams; m. Harry P. Orcutt, 1946 (dec.). AB, U. Ala., 1936; MA, Tulane U., 1939, MSW, 1942; DSW, Columbia U., 1962. Social worker ARC, Lagarde Gen. Hosp., New Orleans; social worker, acting field dir. Fort Benning (Ga.) Regional Hosp., 1942-46; chief social work svc. VA Regional Office, Phoenix, 1946—51; chief social work svc. unit outpatient office VA, Birmingham, Ala., 1954-57, 58; rsch. asst. Rsch. Ctr. Sch. Social Work, Columbia U., N.Y.C., 1960-62, field advisor social work, 1962, assoc. prof. social work, 1965-76, La. State U., Baton Rouge, 1962-65; prof. social work, dir. doctoral program U. Ala., University, 1976-84; ret. Rsch. cons. Tavistock Centre, London, 1972; cons. sch. social work U. Houston, 1990, Troy State System, 1992. Author: Science and Inquiry in Social Work Practice, 1990, (with Harry P. Orcutt) America's Riding Horses, 1958, (with Elizabeth R. Prichard, Jean Collard, Austin H. Kutscher, Irene Seeland, Nathan Lefkowitz) Social Work with the Dying Patient and the Family, 1977, (with others) Social Work and Thanatology, 1980; editor: Poverty and Social Casework Services, 1974; mem. editl. bd. Jour. Social Work, 1982-84; contbr. articles to profl. books and jours. Mem. alumni bd. Sch. Social Work Columbia U., 1985—88, 1991—94. Recipient Centennial award for edn. Columbia U. Sch. Social Work, 1998; named to Ala. Social Work Hall of Fame, 1999; NIMH fellow, 1957-60; Ben Avis Adams Orcutt doctoral scholar in social work named in her honor, U. Ala. Mem. Group for Advancement Doctoral Edn. (steering com., editor newsletter 1980-83). Episcopalian. Office: PO Box 870314 Tuscaloosa AL 35487-0314 Home: 1199 Valley View Dr Andalusia AL 36424

ORD, LINDA BANKS, artist; b. Provo, Utah, May 24, 1947; d. Willis Merrill and Phyllis (Clark) Banks; m. Kenneth Stephen Ord, Sept. 3, 1971; children: Jason, Justin, Kristin. BS, Brigham Young U., 1970; BFA, U. Mich., 1987; MA, Wayne State U., 1990. Asst. prof. Sch. Art U. Mich., Ann Arbor, 1994—. Juror Southeastern Mich. Scholastic Art Award Competition, Pontiac, 1992, Scarab Club Watercolor Exhbn., Detroit, 1991, Women in Art Nat. Exhbn., Farmington Hills, Mich., 1991, U. Mich. Alumni Exhbn., 1989-90; mem. dean's adv. coun. U. Mich. Sch. Art and Design, 2001—. One-woman shows Atrium Gallery, Mich., 1990, 91; group shows include Am. Coll., Bryn Mawr, Pa., Riverside (Calif.) Art Mus., Kirkpatrick Mus., Oklahoma City, Montgomery (Ala.) Mus. Fine Arts, Columbus (Ga.) Mus., Brigham Young U., Provo, Utah, Kresge Art Mus., Lansing, Mich., U. Mich., Ann Arbor, Detroit Inst. Arts, Kirkpatrick Ctr. Mus. Complex, Oklahoma City, 1994, Riverside (Calif.) Art Mus., 1995, San Bernadino County Mus., Redlands, Calif., 1996, Neville Mus., Green Bya, Wis., 1996, Downey Mus. Art, Calif., 1996, Detroit Inst. Arts, 1996, Gallery Contemporary Art, U. Colo., Colorado Springs, 1996, Saginaw (Mich.) Art Mus., 1998, Springfield (Mo.) Art Mus., 1998, Art Inst. So. Calif., Laguna Beach, 1998, San Diego Art Inst., 1998, U. Mich., Dearborn, 1998, Hillsdale (Mich.) Coll., 1998, Ferris State U., Big Rapids, Mich., 1998, Sangre de Cristo Arts Ctr., Pueblo, Colo., 1999; works in many pvt. and pub. collections including Kelly Svcs., Troy, Mich., FHP Internat., Fountain Valley, Calif., Swords Into Plowshares Gallery, Detroit; work included in: (books) The Artistic Touch, 1995, Artistic Touch 2, 1996, Best of Watercolor-Painting Color, 1997, Best of Watercolor-Painting Light; Shadow, 1997, Artistic Touch 3, 1999; (mag.) Watercolor, An Am. Artist, 1996; subject of articles. Chairperson nat. giving fund Sch. Art U. Mich., 1993, Sch. art rep. Coun. Alumni Svcs., 1992—, mem. dean's adv. coun. Sch. Art and Design, 2001—. Recipient 1st Pl. award Swords Into Plowshares Internat. Exhbn., Detroit, 1989, Silver award Ga. Watercolor Soc. Internat. Exhbn., 1991, Pres.'s award Watercolor Okla. Nat. Exhbn., Oklahoma City, 1992, Flint Jour. award Buckham Gallery Nat. Exhbn., 1993, Ochs Meml. award N.E. Watercolor Soc. Nat. Exhbn., Goshen, N.Y., 1993, Color Q award Ga. Watercolor Soc., 1994, St. Cuthberts award Tex. Watercolor Soc., 1996, Daler-Rowney award San Diego Watercolor Soc. Internat. Exhbn., 1998, Hon. Mention award Nat. Watercolor Okla. Exhbn., 1998, Winsor:Newton award N.e. Watercolor Soc., 22d Annual Nat. Exhbn., 1998; many state and nat. painting awards. Mem. U. Mich. Alumni Assn. (bd. dirs. 1992—, Sch. Art rep.), U. Mich. Sch. Art Alumni Soc. (bd. dirs. 1989-91, pres.), Mich. Watercolor Soc. (chairperson 1992-93, bd. dirs. adv. 1993-94). Avocations: music, theater, tennis, golf, reading. Personal E-mail: lbanksord@cox.net.

ORDIN, ANDREA SHERIDAN, lawyer; m. Robert Ordin; 1 child, M. Victoria; stepchildren: Allison, Richard. AB, UCLA, 1962, LLB, 1965. Bar: Calif. 1966. Dep. atty. gen. Calif., 1965-72; So. Calif. legal counsel Fair Employment Practices Commn., 1972-73; asst. dist. atty. L.A. County, 1975-77; U.S. atty. Central Dist. Calif. L.A., 1977-81; adj. prof. UCLA Law Sch., 1982; chief asst. atty. gen. Calif. L.A., 1983-90; sr. counsel Morgan, Lewis & Bockius, LA, 1993—. Mem. L.A. County Bar Assn. (past pres., past exec. dir.). Office: Morgan Lewis & Bockius 300 S Grand Ave Ste 2200 Los Angeles CA 90071-3109 Office Phone: 213-612-1090. Business E-Mail: aordin@morganlewis.com.

ORDWAY, ELLEN, biologist, educator, entomologist, researcher; b. N.Y.C., Nov. 8, 1927; d. Samuel Hanson and Anna (Wheatland) Ordway. BA, Wheaton Coll., Mass., 1950; MS, Cornell U., 1955; PhD, U. Kans., 1965. Field asst. N.Y. Zool. Soc., N.Y.C., 1950-52; rsch. asst. Am. Mus. Natural History, N.Y.C., 1955-57; tchg. asst. U. Kans., Lawrence, 1957-61, rsch. asst., 1959-65; asst. prof. U. Minn., Morris, 1965-70, assoc. prof. biology, 1970-85, prof., 1986-97, prof. emeritus, 1997, acad. advisor, 1997—. Cooperator, cons. USDA Bee Rsch. Lab., Tucson, 1971, Tucson, 83. Contbr. articles to profl. jours. Lectr. Morris area svc. clubs, 1972—2004; mgr. preserves Nature Conservancy, Mpls., 1975—; bd. dirs. county chpt. ARC, 1998—2003; vol. Stevens County Hist. Mus., 2005—; bd. dirs. U. Minn. Morris Retirees Assn., 1997—2003, sec., treas., 1998—2003. Mem.: AAAS, Ecol. Soc. Am., Internat. Bee Rsch. Assn., Kans. Entomol. Soc., Sigma Xi. Episcopalian. Avocations: travel, photography. Office: U Minn Div Sci And Math Morris MN 56267

O'REILLY, HEATHER ANN, Olympic athlete; b. East Brunswick, NJ, Jan. 2, 1985; Student, U.N.C. Mem. U.S. Women's Nat. Soccer Team, 2002—, U.S. Women's Olympic Soccer Team, Athens, 2004. Named National High School Player of the Yr., 2002; named to NCAA All-Tournament Team, 2003. Achievements include being a member of NCAA Champion University of North Carolina Tar Heels Women's Soccer Team, 2003; being a member of gold medal US Women's Soccer Team, Athens Olympic Games, 2004. Office: c/o US Soccer Federation 1801 S Prairie Ave Chicago IL 60616

O'REILLY, MARY, environmental scientist, educator; b. NYC, Aug. 3, 1948; d. Luke Edward and Regina (Mahoney) O'Reilly; m. Jonathan Haney; children: Robert Brophy, Sara Brophy, Lena Reid. Student, Fordham U., 1966—68; BS, U. Mich., 1970, MS, 1972, PhD, 1979. Rsch. asst. prof. Health Sci. Ctr., Syracuse, NY, 1979-84; environ. toxicologist Syracuse Rsch. Corp., 1984-86; pres. ARLS Cons., Inc., Syracuse, 1993—; sr. indsl. hygienist N.Y. State Dept. Labor, Syracuse, 1987—2000; environ. specialist N.Y. State Dept. Transp., Binghamton, 2000—. Adj. asst. prof. SUNY Sch. Pub. Health, Albany, 1990—; dir. Am. Bd. Indsl. Hygiene, Lansing, Mich., 1995—2001; adj. prof. chemistry LeMoyne Coll., 2000; mem. Z10 com. Am. Nat. Stds. Inst., 2001—05; mem. adv. bd. N.Y. State Inst. Health and Environment, 2001—; bd. dirs. Am. Conf. Govt. Indsl. Hygienists, 2006—. Author: An Ergonomics Guide to VDTs, 1994; author: (with others) Occupational Ergonomics, 1996; co-author: ILO's Encyclopedia of Occupational Health and Safety, 1998, Implications of Hormesis for Industrial Hygienists, 2003, Health Risk Assessment at Brownfield Redevelopment Sites, 2003, Groundwater Effects from Highway Tire Shreds, 2004, others; contbr. articles to profl. jours. Mem. Syracuse Peace Coun. Mem.: Hormesis Soc., N.Y. State Assn. Transp. Engrs., Human Factors and Ergonomics Soc., Am. Assn. Govtl. Indsl. Hygienists, Am. Indsl. Hygiene Assn. Avocations: Karate, fly fishing, dance, folk harp. Home: 7705 Farley Ln Manlius NY 13104-9571 Office Phone: 607-721-8138. Personal E-mail: Mary_O'Reilly@sln.suny.edu. Business E-Mail: moreilly@dot.state.ny.us.

O'REILLY, MARY CATHERINE, elementary school educator; b. St. Louis, Nov. 11, 1949; d. James C. and Ada C. (Stevens) Duke; m. Robert J. O'Reilly (div. 1992); children: Jennifer M., Lori C. BS in Edn., Ctrl. Mo. State U., 1973; MA, Maryville U., 1990. Cert. tchr. K-8, Mo. Elem. sch. educator Ritenour Schs., St. Louis, 1973-98, ret., 1998. Councilwoman Hazelwood, Mo., 1996-2005; homecoming coord./alumni, Delta Zeta, 1997; bd. dirs. Ctrl. Mo. State U. Alumni, 1999—2005. Mem. Delta Zeta Alumni Assn. Avocations: gourmet cooking, civic improvement. Home: 5272 Ville Rosa Ln Hazelwood MO 63042-1662

OREILLY, MEAGHAN KELLY, art educator; b. Balt., May 3, 1978; d. Francis Patrick and Susan Carol Kelly; m. Bartholomew Patrick O'Reilly, Apr. 3, 2004. BA, McDaniel Coll. (formerly Western Md. Coll.), Westminster, 2000. Cert. art tchr. Md. Presch. Montessori tchr./arts coord. Rainbow Montessori, Dublin, 2000—02; mid. sch. art tchr. Balt. County Pub. Schs., 2002—04, elem. art tchr., 2004—. Recipient Outstanding Greek Pres. of Yr. award, McDaniel Coll., 2000, Hon. mention Coll. Art Show, 2000, Tchr. of Yr. award, Old Ct. Mid. Sch., 2002. Mem.: Alpha Nu Omega (life; pres. 1999—2000, Outstanding Pres. of Yr. 2000). Avocations: art (ceramics/sculpture), travel. Office: Hawthorne Elem Sch 125 Kingston Rd Baltimore MD 21220 Office Phone: 410-887-0138. Personal E-mail: moreilly@bcps.org.

O'REILLY, SARAH M., sales executive; b. Painsville, Ohio, Nov. 22, 1940; d. John F. and Edna Jamie (A.) Mobry; m. Robert Lee Born (div.); children: Elizabeth A. Born, Amy C. Born; m. Bernard George (B. G.) O'Reilly, July 27, 1996. BA, Mt. Union Coll., 1962. English tchr., Whitehall, Ohio, 1962—65; exec. staff Girl Scouts, Des Plains, Ill., 1970—75; pres. Sales by Sarah, Inc., Ill., 1975—2005. Trustee, bd. chair Harper Cmty. Coll., Palatine, Ill., 1990—96; bd. mem. Chgo. Red Cross, 1996—2004; bd. chair Youth Commission, Arlington Heights, Ill., 1975—90; exec. bd. Ill. Cmty Coll. Trustee Assn., Springfield, Ill., 1993—96. Named Woman of Yr., Old Trail Sch., 1993, BPW, 1989. Mem.: Horticultural Hall, United Way. Achievements include development of miniature furniture Thorne Rooms at Chgo. Art Inst. Home: 3132 Geneva Boy Dr Lake Geneva WI 53147 Office Phone: 262-248-0143. E-mail: oreilly@genevaonline.com.

ORENDER, DONNA, sports association executive; m. M.G. Orender; children: Jacob, Zachary stepchildren: Morgan, Colleen. Grad., Queens Coll. NY, 1978; postgrad., Adelphi U. With ABC Sports, SportsChannel, NBA Entertainment, PGA Tour, 1988—2001, sr. v.p. strategic devel., 2001—05; pres. WNBA, NYC, 2005—. Hon. pres. PGA Am. Prodr.: Inside the PGA Tour. Office: WNBA Olympic Tower 645 Fifth Ave New York NY 10022 Office Phone: 212-688-9622, 212-750-9622.

ORESKES, NAOMI, science historian; b. NYC, Nov. 25, 1958; d. Irwin Oreskes and Susan Eileen Nagin Oreskes; m. Kenneth Belitz, Sept. 28, 1986; children: Hannah Oreskes Belitz, Clara Oreskes Belitz. BSc with honors, Imperial Coll., London, 1981; PhD, Stanford U., 1990. Geologist We. Mining Corp., Adelaide, Australia, 1981—84; rsch. and tng. asst. Stanford U., Calif., 1984—89; vis. asst. prof. Dartmouth Coll., Hanover, NH, 1990—91, asst. prof., 1991—96; assoc. prof. Gallatin Sch. NYU, 1996—98, U. Calif., San Diego, 1998—2005, prof., 2005—. Consulting geologist Western Mining Corp., 1984-90; consulting historian Am. Inst. Physics, N.Y.C., 1990-96. Author: The Rejection of Continental Drift, 1999, Theory and Method in American Earth Science, 1999; editor: Plate Tectonics: An Insider's History of the Modern Theory of the Earth, 2001; contbr. articles to profl. jours. Recipient Lindgren prize Soc. Econ. Geologists, 1993, Young Investigator award NSF, 1994-99, George Sarton Lectr. award AAAS, 2004; fellow NEH, 1993. Mem. Geol. Soc. Am., History Sci. Soc. Jewish. Home: 14174 Bahama Cv Del Mar CA 92014-2901 Office: U Calif San Diego 9500 Gilman Dr La Jolla CA 92093-0104 Office Phone: 858-534-4695. Business E-Mail: noreskes@ucsd.edu.

OREVNA, NELLIE LOU, music educator; b. Salem, Ohio, Oct. 12, 1947; d. Wayne N. and Doris E. Weingart; children: Alicia Marie, David Wayne. B, Youngstown State U., 1970. Music tchr. Western Reserve Local Schools, Berlin Ctr., Ohio, 1970—. Asst. marching band dir. Western Res. Sch. Sys., Berlin Ctr., 1985—. Recipient Sword of Honor, Sigma Alpha Iota Music Soc., Rose of Honor. Mem.: NEA, Ohio Edn. Assn., Music Educators Nat. Conf., Tchrs. of Western Res. Avocations: gardening, travel. Home: 8585 Knauf Rd Canfield OH 44406 Office: Western Res Local Schools 15904 Akron Canfield Rd Berlin Center OH 44401

ORFIELD, ANTONIA MARIE, optometrist, researcher; d. Alfred Anthony and Eva Swenson Stoll; m. Gary Allan Orfield, May 24, 1963; children: Amy Elizabeth, Sonia Marie, Rosanna Antonia. BA in History, Smith Coll., 1963; MAT in History/Social Studies, U. Chgo., 1966; BS in Visual Sci., Ill. Coll. Optometry, 1987, OD, 1989. Lic. Mass. Bd. Optometry. Optometrist Michael Reese HMO, Chgo., 1989—91, Eye Exam 2000, Chgo., 1989—91; behavioral optometrist Harvard U. Health, Cambridge, Mass., 1991—. Asst. prof. New Eng. Coll. Optometry, Boston, 1991—2000, dir., chief investigator, clin. preceptor Mather Sch. Vision and Learning Rsch./Svc. Clinic, 1993—99; pvt. practice behavioral optometrist, Cambridge, 1996—; spkr. in field. Contbr. articles to profl. jours. Parent rep. Kenwood Acad. Sch. Coun., Chgo., 1989—91. Grantee, State Street Bank, N.E. Congress Optometry, Mass. Soc. Optometrists, Am. Found. Vision Awareness, Friends of the Sensorily Deprived. Fellow: Coll. Optometrists in Vision Devel., Am. Acad. Optometry; mem.: Neurooptometric Rehab. Assn. (charter), Internat. Coll. Applied Kinesiology. Democrat. Achievements include research in children in poverty have a great number of vision problems that interefere with learning; near poiint glasses can raise test scores; tracking problems are correlated with reading failures; vision therapy is correlated with improvement in grades. Avocations: study of homeopathic medicine, sports vision training, study of educational kinesiology, study of nutrition and vision, swimming. Office: Harvard Univ Health Svc 75 Mt Auburn St Cambridge MA 02138 also: Ste 205 678 Massachussetts Ave Cambridge MA 02139 Office Phone: 617-868-8742. E-mail: antoniaorfield@yahoo.com.

ORGEBIN-CRIST, MARIE-CLAIRE, retired biology professor, department chairman; b. Vannes, France, Mar. 20, 1936; License Natural Scis., License Biology, Sorbonne, U. Paris, 1957; D. Scis., Lyons U., France, 1961. Stagiaire dept. biochemistry faculty medicine, Paris, 1957—58; stagiaire Centre Nat. de la Recherche Scientifique, Paris, 1958—60, attachee de recherche, 1960—62; research assoc. Population Council (Med. Div.), N.Y.C., 1962—63; research assoc. dept. ob/gyn Vanderbilt Sch. Medicine, 1963—64, research instr., 1964—66, asst. prof., 1966—70, assoc. prof., 1970—73, Lucius E. Burch prof. reproductive biology, 1973—2005, prof. dept. anatomy, 1975—2005; dir. Vanderbilt Sch. Medicine (Center Reproductive Biology Research.), 1973—2005, prof. emeritus, 2005—. Editor-in-Chief Jour. Andrology, 1983-89 Recipient Career Devel. award NIH, 1968-73, NIH Merit award, 1986,; Fogarty Internat. sr. fellow, 1977; Disting. Scientist award Am. Soc. Reproductive Medicine, 1996. Mem. Am. Assn. Anatomists, Am. Soc. Cell Biology, Am. Soc. Andrology (v.p. 1994-95, pres. 1995-96, Disting. Svc. award 1997, Disting. Andrologist award 1990), Internat. Com. on Andrology, Endocrine Soc., Soc. for Study Fertility (Eng.), Soc. for Study Reprodn., N.Y. Acad. Scis. Office: Vanderbilt U Sch Med Ctr Reproductive Biology Rsch Rm C-3306 MCN Nashville TN 37232-0001 E-mail: m-c.orgebin-crist@vanderbilt.edu.

ORGELFINGER, GAIL, literature educator; b. N.Y., Dec. 18, 1951; d. Louis and Caroline Mary Orgelfinger; m. Charles C. Hanna, June 26, 1976. BA with hons. in English, George Washington U., Washington, D.C., 1972; MA in English, U. Chgo., 1973, PhD in English, 1978. Tutor Devel. Edn. Ctr. Anne Arundel C.C., 1980—81, lectr. English, 1980—81; instr. English U. Md., Coll. Pk., Md., 1981—94; instr. English to sr. lectr. U. Md. Balt. County, 1995—; asst. prof. English USN Acad., 1985—86. Editl. cons. Office Vice Chancellor Acad. Affairs U. Md. Sys. Adminstrn., 1989—90, staff writer Office V.P. Academic Affairs and Provost, 1987—90; asst. to v.p. academic affairs U. Md., 1990—94; policy analyst asst. Md. Higher Edn. Commn., 1992; asst. to v.p. academic affairs and student affairs Anne Arundel C.C., 1998; lectr. in field. Contbr. chapters to books, articles to profl. jours. Named Hons. Coll. Tchr. of Yr., U. Md., Balt. County, 1999; grantee, NEH, 1985, U.

Md., 2001—04. Mem.: Internat. Joan of Arc Soc. (founding mem.), Phi Beta Kappa. Office: U Md Balt County Dept English 1000 Hilltop Cir Baltimore MD 21250 Business E-Mail: orgelfin@umbc.edu.

ORGERON, ROCHELLE MARY, secondary school educator; b. Galliano, La., Dec. 10, 1963; d. Rodney Paul Orgeron and Doris Dorothy Vegas. B of Elem. Edn., Nicholls State U., Thiboduax, La., 1985, M of Reading, 1998, postgrad., 2003. Tchr. Lafourche Parish Sch. Bd., Thibodaux, 1985—. 4-H leader Galliano 4-H Club, La., 1986—2006. Recipient 4-H Alumni award, 4-H Youth Devel. Program, 2005. Mem.: La. Fedn. (sec. 2006), Alpha Delta Kappa (historian 1993—2005). Roman Catholic. Avocations: travel, crafts, music, remodeling. Home: 15827 E Main Cut Off LA 70345 Office: Galliano Elem Sch 148 W 158 Galliano LA 70354

O'RILEY, KAREN E., principal; b. L.A. BA, Loyola Marymount U., L.A., 1981; MPA, Calif. State U., 1983. Home: PO Box 261005 Encino CA 91426-1005

ORITSKY, MIMI, artist, educator; b. Reading, Pa., Aug. 14, 1950; d. Herbert and Marcia (Sarna) O. Student, Phila. Coll. Art, 1968-70; BFA, Md. Inst. Coll. Art, 1975; MFA, U. Pa., 1979. Artist, supr. subway mural projects Crisis Intervention Network, Phila., 1978-83; instr. painting U. Arts, 1984, 1989—93, Abington Art Ctr., Jenkintown, 1989—, Main Line Art Ctr., Haverford, 1993—. One-woman shows include Gross McCleaf Gallery, 1980-82, Callowhill Art Gallery, Reading, Pa., Amos Eno Gallery, NYC, 1986, 89, 91, 94, 96, 98, 2001, 03, 06, Hahnemann U. Gallery, Phila., 1988, Kauffman Gallery, Shippensburg, Pa., 1989, 97, Kimberton (Pa.) Gallery, 1990, Rittenhouse Galleries, Phila., 1992-94, A.I.R. Gallery, NYC, 2003, Abington Art Ctr, 2004, U. Arts, Phila., 2006; exhibited in group shows at Current Representational Painting in Phila., 1980, Gross McCleaf Gallery, 1980-82, Yearsley Spring Gallery, Phila., 1998, Phila. Art Alliance, 1998, Coll. Art Gallery, Trenton, NJ, 1996, 98, 2000, Abington Art Ctr., 1999, Brattleboro Mus., TW Wood Mus., Montshire Mus., Phila. Art Alliance, Florence Griswold Mus., 2002-04; pub. in NewAmerican Paintings, 2000, 2005. Recipient Purchase award Pa. Coun. Arts and Arcadia Coll., 1983, Reading Pub. Mus., 1984, Best of Show award Abington Art Ctr. Juried Annual, 1998; fellow Environment Found., 1980, Millay Colony for Arts, 1983. Mem.: Coll. Art Assn. Office Phone: 212-226-5342.

ORLANDO, ANN MARIE, educator; b. Birmingham, Ala., Dec. 18, 1950; d. Elmo Marion McCraw and Georgianna Margaret; m. Joseph Anthony Orlando, Nov. 6, 1982 (dec.). BA in Psychology and Edn., Kean U., Union, N.J., 1972, postgrad. Owner, oper. Miss Ann's Dance Studio, Roselle, NJ, 1965—76; dance instr. Roselle Recreation, 1971; dance tchr. Arthur Murray, Rahway, NJ, 1980—85; substitute tchr. St. Patricks, Elizabeth, NJ, 1971—79; tchr., coord. St. Joseph the Carpenter, Roselle, 1979—; dir., tchr. Rev. John C. Dowling Aftercare, Roselle, 1986—. Mem. adv. bd. Liberty Sci. Ctr., Jersey City, 1993—; bd. dirs., bd. trustees Rev. John C. Dowling Aftercare, Roselle; intern Schering Plough, Kenilworth, NJ, 2003. Mem.: N.J. Sci. Tchrs. Assn., Nat. Sci. Tchrs. Assn., Nat. Cath. Edn. Assn. Avocations: dance, baking, choreography, crafts. Home: 128 Walnut St Roselle NJ 07203 Office: St Joseph the Carpenter 140 E 3d Ave Roselle NJ 07203

ORLANDO, SUSAN (ISADORA), academic administrator, educator; b. Hartford, Conn., Sept. 27, 1946; d. Carl Kivi and Leola Leanette Poch; m. Richard Orlando, Aug. 13, 1972; children: Rebecca, Dara. BS, Skidmore Coll., 1968; MA, Columbia U., 1969. Cert. permanent tchg. cert. N-6 N.Y. Elem. tchr. North Rockland Cen. Sch. Dist., Garnerville, NY, 1969—2002; tchr. Hebrew sch. Temple Beth Shalom, New City, NY, 1978—85, Beth Am Temple, 1978—80, 1992—96; supr. student tchrs. Tchrs. Coll., Columbia U., NYC, 2002—05, St. Thomas Aquinas Coll., Sparkill, NY, 2006—. Tchr. substitute tchrs. North Rockland Ctrl. Sch. Dist., Garnerville, 2002—. Contbr. guidebook North Rockland Central School District English-Language Arts Curriculum, 2000. Pres. Montebello (N.Y.) Jewish Ctr. Sisterhood, 2001—03, bd. trustees, 2003—; rec. sec. Hudson Valley br. Women's League of Conservative Judaism, 2004—. Avocations: travel, reading, knitting. Home: 12 Brook Hollow Ct Chestnut Ridge NY 10977 Personal E-mail: sipo1@aol.com.

ORLANDO, VALERIA, music educator, musician, artist; d. Ross and Mary Orlando. MusB magna cum laude, Hartt Sch. Music, Hartford, Conn., 1972; MA in Music, CUNY, 1974. Tchg. credential K-12 Calif., c.c. instr. credential Calif. Music educator Santa Monica (Calif.) C.C., 1986—96, El Camino C.C., Torrance, Calif., 1986—96, L.A. Valley Coll., Van Nuys, Calif., 1987—95, U. of Redlands, Calif., 1995—97, Moreno Valley (Calif.) Unified Sch. Dist., 1997—2000, Anaheim (Calif.) Union H.S. Dist., 2000—. Bd. dirs. Nat. Assn. Tchrs. of Singing, L.A., 1992—94; music adjudicator numerous orgns.; music cons. YMCA, Anaheim, 2002—. Mem., vol. Anaheim Arts Coun., 2000—. Named winner, Viotti Internat. Voice Competition, Italy, nat. finalist, Lyric Opera of Chgo. Ctr. for Am. Artists, semi-finalist, Young Concert Artists Internat., N.Y.C.; recipient Tchr. Recognition and Talent Search award, Nat. Found. for Advancement of Arts, 1997; Disneyland Arts Partnership Enabling grantee, 2001. Mem.: Tech. Inst. for Music Educators, So. Calif. Vocal Assn., Calif. Music Educators Assn. (bd. dirs., 2d v.p. 2001—), Zurich Opernhaus Studio, Mu Phi Epsilon. Avocations: genealogy, gourmet cooking, reading, gardening. Office: Ball Jr HS 1500 W Ball Rd Anaheim CA 92802 Office Phone: 714-999-3663.

ORLANDO, VALERIE, language educator; BA in French, U. Redlands, Calif., 1985; PhD in French Studies, Brown U., Providence, 1996. Asst. prof. humanities Ea. Mediterranean U., Famagusta, Cyprus, 1996—97; vis. asst. prof. French Purdue U., West Lafayette, Ind., 1997—99; asst. prof., then assoc. prof. French Ill. Wesleyan U., Bloomington, 1999—2006; assoc. prof. French and Francophone studies U. Md., College Park, 2006—. Dir. of women's studies Ill. Wesleyan U., 2005—06. Author: (analytical/literary theory) Nomadic Voices of Exile: Feminine Identity in Francophone Literature of the Maghreb, Of Suffocated Hearts and Tortured Souls: Seeking Subjecthood through Madness in Francophone Women's Writing of Africa and the Caribbean. Fulbright-Hays grantee to Morocco, U.S. Dept. Edn., 2004, Fulbright grantee to Morocco and Tunisia, U.S. Dept. State, 2006—, Summer Seminar grantee to Dakar, Senegal, NEH, 2005. Mem.: African Literatures Assn., Conseil Internat. d'Etudes Francophones, Modern Languages Assn. Democrat. Avocations: running, yoga, weightlifting, bicycling. Office: U Md Dept French and Italian College Park MD 20742 Office Phone: 301-405-4027.

ORLANDO-SPINELLI, JOSEPHINE, gifted and talented educator, educational consultant; b. Phila., Mar. 15, 1958; d. Frank and Rita Orlando; m. Paul F. Spinelli, June 20, 1992; 1 stepchild, Paul A. Spinelli. EdB, Coll. St. Elizabeth, Convent Sta., N.J., 1976—80; M in Holocaust and Genocide Studies, Stockton Coll., Pomona, N.J., 2005. Cert. tchg. N.J., 1980. Tchr. of lang. arts, gifted and talented Atlantic City Bd. of Edn., Atlantic City, 1980—95; tchr. of gifted and talented Brigantine Pub. Sch., Brigantine, NJ, 1995—2002, Upper Twp. Pub. Sch., Petersburg, NJ, 2002—. Attended Lest We Forget Study Tour du Europe, 2003. Founding mem. Red and Gray Gridiron Club, Vineland, NJ, 1999—2003; com. mem. SITE, Upper Twp. Pub. Sch., Petersburg, NJ, 2002—03, Impact, Upper Twp. Pub. Sch., Petersburg, NJ, 2001—03. Recipient to attend Stamm Found., Phila., N.J., 2001. Mem.: N.J. Assn. for Gifted Children, mem., pres. Alpha Delta Kappa, Gamma Chap. Achievements include establishing the Frank Orlando Meml. Gifted Awards in Brigantine Pub. Schools. Avocations: theater, singing, dance, singing the Nat. Anthem at the Atlantic City Surf games, 1999. Home: 2284 Baywood Dr Vineland NJ 08361-6682 Office: Upper Twp Pub Sch 525 Perry Rd Woodbine NJ 08270 Personal E-mail: JosieCatLover@comcast.net.

ORLET, VERONICA LYNNE, secondary school educator; b. Corpus Christi, Tex., Feb. 24, 1969; d. Ralph L. and Mary Lynne Brantley; m. Gerhard Hermann Orlet, July 4, 1992; children: Alexander Gerhard, Ashley Lynne. BA in English, U. Ga., Athens, 1991; MEd in English, Augusta State U., Ga., 1998. Tchr. Evans H.S., Ga., 1994—. Office: Evans HS 4550 Cox Rd Evans GA 30809 Office Phone: 706-863-1198. Business E-Mail: vorlet@ccboe.net.

ORLIK, DAWN, mathematics and computer science educator; m. Joseph Orlik; children: Christopher, Crystal. MA in Secondary Math Edn., SUNY, New Paltz, 1998. Cert. secondary math. tchr. NY, 1998. Assoc. prof. math. Dutchess C.C., Poughkeepsie, NY, 1989—93; tchr. math., computer sci. Arlington H.S., LaGrangeville, NY, 1993—. Office: Arlington HS 1157 Rt 55 Lagrangeville NY 12540 Office Phone: 845-486-4860. E-mail: dorlik@acsdny.org.

ORLIN, KAREN J., lawyer; b. Washington, Apr. 2, 1948; d. Hyman and Lenore O.; 1 child. AB summa cum laude, U. Pa., 1969; JD, Harvard U., 1972. Bar: N.Y. 1973. U.S. Dist. Ct. (so. and ea. dists.) N.Y. 1973, U.S. Ct. Appeals (2d cir.) 1973, Fla. 1982. Assoc. Kronish, Lieb, Weiner & Hellman, N.Y.C., 1972-81; sr. assoc. Valdes-Fauli, Bischoff, Kriss and Mandler, Miami, 1981-82, ptnr., 1982-83; sr. assoc. Ruden, Barnett, McClosky, Smith, Schuster & Russell, P.A., Ft. Lauderdale, Fla., 1983-85, Shea & Gould, N.Y.C. and Miami, 1985-87; of counsel Thomson, Muraro, Razook and Hart P.A., Miami, 1987-88; sr. v.p.-assoc. counsel, asst. sec. Am. Savs. of Fla., F.S.B., Miami, 1988—. Mem. Trustee's Coun. Penn Women, U. Pa., 1987—. Mem. Fla. Bar (corps. and securities com. 1983—), Am. Mensa, Nat. Auctioneers Assn., U. Pa. Dade Alumni Club (pres. 1993—), Greater Miami C. of C. (lawyers com. bus. revitalization group), Zonta Internat. (Downtown Miami chpt. bd. dirs.), Mortar Bd., Sphinx Soc., Nat. Auctioneers Assn., Phi Beta Kappa.

ORLINSKY, DIANE JULIE, dermatologist; d. Stephen Bruce and Marian Joyce Bauer; m. Eric Gustav Orlinsky, May 30, 1993; children: Rachel Celia, Charles Henry, Alexandra Moriah, Sara Daniella. BA cum laude, Columbia Coll., NYC, 1988; MD, Johns Hopkins Sch. Medicine, Balt., 1993. Diplomate Am. Bd. Dermatology. Intern Johns Hopkins Sch. Medicine, Balt., 1993—94, resident in internal medicine, 1994—95, resident in dermatology, 1995—98, asst. prof. dept. dermatology, 2000—, asst. prof. dept. medicine, 2004—; dir. dermatology Union Meml. Hosp., Balt., 1999—2000. Leader's soc. Dermatology Found., Evanston, Ill., 2006—; Maimonides soc. The Associated, Balt., 2005—. Contbr. articles to profl. jours., chapters to books. Fundraiser chair 5th grade class Roland Pk. Country Sch., Balt., 2005—06; bd. trustees Temple Beth El, Balt., 2005—06. Recipient Upjohn Achievement award, Johns Hopkins Sch. Medicine, 1993, America's Cosmetic Doctors and Dentists award, Castle Connolly Med. Ltd, 2005. Fellow: Am. Acad. Dermatology; mem.: Md. Dermatologic Soc., Women's Dermatologic Soc., Am. Soc. for Dermatologic Soc., Hadassah Orgn. (life), Alpha Omega Alpha (councilor 2001—03). Avocations: piano, sports, cooking, travel. Office: Simmons-O'Brien & Orlinsky LLC 8320 Bellona Ste 20 Towson MD 21204 Office Phone: 410-821-7546.

ORLOSKI, SHARON, secondary school educator; b. Taylor, Pa., Aug. 15, 1943; d. Leo Paul and Sophie Ann O. BS, Ctrl. Conn. State U., New Britain, 1965; MS, U. Conn., Storrs, 1970; CAS, Wesleyan U., Middletown, Conn., 1972. Cert. tchr. biology, chemistry and gen. sci., Conn. Gen. sci. tchr. Bridgeport (Conn.) Adult Edn., 1966-68; homebound tchr. Bridgeport Bd. Edn., 1966-67; tchr. biology Ctrl. H.S., Bridgeport Bd. Edn., 1965-82, Ctrl. Magnet H.S., Bridgeport Bd. Edn., 1982—. Master tchr. Bridgeport Bd. Edn., 1974, 2002, tchr. mentor vertical curriculum devel., 2002; leader citywide workshops. Bd. dirs., pres., sec. Madison Gardens Condominium Assn. NSF grantee, 1967-71. Mem. NEA, Nat. Assn. Biology Tchrs., U. Conn. Alumni Assn. (life), Ctrl. Conn. State Alumni Assn. (life), Conn. Edn. Assn., Bridgeport Edn. Assn., Lladro Soc., U.S. Humane Soc. Avocations: N.Y. Yankees, stocks, gardening. Office: Ctrl Magnet HS One Lincoln Blvd Bridgeport CT 06606

ORLOWSKA-WARREN, LENORE ALEXANDRIA, art educator, fiber artist; b. Detroit, May 22, 1951; d. William Leonard and Aloisa Clara (Hrapkiewicz) Orlowski; m. Donald Edward Warren, May 11, 1990. AA, Henry Ford C.C., 1972; BS in Art Edn., Wayne State U., 1974, M in Spl. Edn., 1978; BFA, Ctr. for Creative Studies, 2000. Tchr. arts and crafts Detroit Pub. Schs., 1974—2002; fiber artist Detroit Inst. Arts. Cons. Arts Detroit Cmty. Plan, TRIACO Arts & Crafts, 1996—; instr., demonstrator weaving Detroit Inst. Arts; represented by Gallery Five, Tequesta, Fla., Ann Arbor Art Ctr. One-woman show at Dearborn C. of C., Ctr. for Creative Studies, 2000; exhibited in group shows, including alumni exhibit Henry Ford C.C., 1989, Detroit Artist Market, 1995-2000, Scarab Club, 1996, Lansing Art Gallery, 1997, Ctr. for Creative Studies, 1997, Yr. of the Woman Exhibit, 1998, Tom Thompson Meml. Art Gallery Juried Ontario Artists Exhibit, 1998, 2001, One Focus, Two Worlds Exhibit, 1999, Fashion Exhibit and Felt the Feeling of Fiber, U.245 Gallery, 1999, Ctr. Creative Studies, 2000, Ann Arbor Art Ctr., 2001, Downriver Coun. for the Arts, 2001, Alumni Fiber Artist exhibit Coll. Creative Studies, 2002, Ann Arbor Art Ctr. All Media Exhbn., 2002 (Barbara Dorr Meml. award), Outside The Lines Gallery, 2001, 02, Padziewski Gallery, 2003, Scarab Club, 2003; contbr. to Sch. Arts Mag.; represented in permanent collections Gallery Five, Tequesta, Fla., Ann Arbor Art Ctr. Mem. exec. bd. Springwells Pk. Assn., 1989-99, pres., 1994-96, chairperson youth act workshops; com. mem. Dearborn cmty. art coun. Art on the Ave., 1993-99, Gallery Crawl chairperson, 1998; chair Nat. Woman's History Month workshop, 1995. Mem.: Cranbrook Acad. Art, Am. Tapestry Alliance, Art Inst. of Chgo., Downriver Coun. for Arts, Surface Design Assn., The Textile Mus., The Nat. Mus. Women in Art Williamsburg Burgesses, Met. Mus. Art, Norton Mus. Art (Williamsburg assoc.), Mich. Surface Design, Friends of Fiber Art Internat. Assn., Coll. Art Assn., Birmingham Bloomfield Art Assn., Detroit Inst. Arts-Founders Soc., Am. Craft Coun., Mich. Art Edn. Assn. (presenter art advocacy workshop), Nat. Art Edn. Assn. (electronic gallery coord. 1992—99). Avocations: fiber art, travel, colonial gardening, reading colonial history and biographies.

ORLOWSKI, KARELANN, elementary school educator; b. Fremont, Ohio, Dec. 22, 1949; d. Karl and Angeline Marie (Oudersluys) Kooistra; m. Paul Joseph Orlowski, Apr. 28, 1973; l child, Jennifer Frann. BA in Music Edn., U. Mich., 197l; MS in Elem. Edn., Dowling Coll., Oakdale, N.Y., l978. Cert. tchr., N.Y. Tchr. vocal music Patchogue-Medford Schs., NY, 1971—2005, lead tchr. music dept., 1986—88, 1991—94; dir. musicals Eagle Elem. Sch., 1990—94. Dir. drama dept. River Elem. Sch., Patchogue, 1974-90, Chosen Few show choir South Ocean Mid. Sch., Patchogue, 1984-90, Notation! show choir Eagle Elem. Sch., 1990-94, 1995-2005, A Chords show choir Barton Elem. Sch., 1994-95. Mem. Suffolk County Music Educators Assn. (co-chmn. so. divsn. I chorus 1993-95, divsn. II S.W. chorus 1996-97, asst. v.p. divsn. I festivals 1997-98, exec. v.p. for festivals 1998-2000, standing coms. 1999-2000, co-chmn. membership 2003—04). Republican. Episcopalian. Avocations: reading, renaissance music, vocal jazz, nascar sk class and figure-eight racing. Home: 37 Detmer Rd East Setauket NY 11733-1912

ORM, SALLY S., music educator, consultant; d. Harvey Jacob and Lucille Mae Seyler; children: Jennifer E., Andrea. Student, Eastman Sch. Music. With FBI, Washington, 1970—75; co-owner, ptnr. All Things Music, LLC. Founder keyboard donations Orm Music Studios, Neenah, Wis., 2001—. Treas. Regional Domestic Abuse, Oshkosh, Wis., 1984—86, pres., 1986—88; treas. Audubon Soc., Appleton, 1985—86; Gold award coord. Fox Valley Area Girl Scouts, Appleton, Wis., 1995—99. Named Mem. of the Yr. award, Fox Valley Area Girl Scouts, 1999. Mem.: Wis. Music Tchrs. Assn. (chmn. found. 2006—), Music Tchrs. Nat. Assn., Fox Valley Keyboard Tchrs. (v.p., program dir. 1999—2003, Mem. of the Yr. award 2002), World Piano Pedagogy Conf., Keyboard Music Educators Assn. (adjudicator keyboard competition 2002—). Presbyterian. Avocations: gardening, travel. Office: Orm Music Studios 749 S Commercial St Neenah WI 54956 E-mail: sormusic@aol.com.

ORMAI-BUZA, ILDIKO, soprano, composer, music educator; b. Budapest, Hungary, Dec. 21, 1927; came to U.S., 1949, naturalized, 1955; d. Janos and Margit Ormai; m. George Buza, Oct. 28, 1950; children: George F., Paul L. Student in piano and theory, Hannig Conservatory, Budapest, 1938-44; student, Ecole D'Arts Coll., Freiburg, Germany, 1947-49; studied voice with Carmela Cafarelli; studied composition and orchestration, Janos Kiss. Cert. pvt. voice, piano and organ tchr., Ohio. Organist, soloist St. Raphael Cath. Ch., Bay Village, Ohio, 1957-72; concert soprano Cafarelli Opera Co., Cleve., 1957-67; organist, soloist Holy Spirit Ch., Avon Lake, Ohio, 1972-97, Our Lady of Angels Ch., Cleve., 1998-99; frequent guest, organist, soloist St. Emeric Ch., Cleve. Choir dir. Midnszenty Chamber Choir, Cleve., 1981-84; guest soloist Fatima World Congress, Germany, 1985, Portugal, 1992; guest concert soloist, U.S. and Can., 1960—. Composer: (organ and chorus) Mass of Adoration (Silver medal 1975), (choir and organ) Berzsenyi Poem: Supplication (Gold medal 1986), Piano Solos, 1996; performed solo concert Perpetual Adoration Ch., Budapest, 1989; soprano guest soloist West Suburban Philharm. Orch., Ann. Opera Concert, Cleve., 1980, 82, in concert record, 1981; commd. composer Hymn of Worldwide St. Ladislaus Order, 1989; prodr., announcer NBN weekly classical Hungarian Concert Hall Radio Hour, 1977-85; performer voice and piano Hungarian Assn., 1955—. Recipient Papal Blessing for composition Ave Maria, Pope John Paul II, 1987. Mem. Music Tchrs. Nat. Assn., Am. Guild Organists, Ohio Music Tchrs. Assn. (winner composition contest 1989, publicity com. 1981-97), St. Ladislaus Order (knighted Dame 1983, Cross of Honor 1987), Arpad Acad., Cleve. Piano Tchrs. Club. Avocations: painting, portrait drawing, sewing, dance, poetry.

ORMAN, EVELYN KAY, music educator, consultant; d. Donald Lee Orman and Nancy Vivian Orman - Maiden Name: Morgan. MusB in Edn., Murray State U., Ky., 1983; MEd, U. Ctrl. Fla., Orlando, 1992; EdD, U. Ala., Tuscaloosa, 1995. Grad. student saxophone performance Nationale Conservatoire de Musique, Bordeaux, France, 1983—84; dir. of bands South Fulton H.S., 1984—85; band dir., arts dept. chairperson Westridge Mid. Sch., Orlando, Fla., 1985—92; grad. tchg. asst. U. of Ala., Tuscaloosa, 1992—94, grad. rsch. asst., 1994—95; asst. prof. music The U. West Ala., Livingston, 1995—96; asst. prof. music edn. George Mason U., Fairfax, Va., 1996—99, La. State U., Baton Rouge, 1999—2005, assoc. prof. music edn., 2005—. Cons. music tech.; music edn. rschr. Contbr. articles to profl. jours. Editl. bd. mem. Update: Applications of Rsch. in Music Edn., 2004—. Named Cecil and Ida Green Honors Prof., Tex. Christian U., 2002—03; grantee Curriculum Program grantee, Coll. of Arts and Sci., George Mason U., 1997, Honor Music Festival grantee, Office of Sponsored Program, George Mason U., 1998, Celebration of Learning granee, Small Grants Programs, George Mason U., 1998, Tech. Fee grantee, La. State U., 2001—04, 2002, Summer Rsch. grantee, 2002, Faculty Rsch. grantee, 2004, Summer Rsch. grantee, 2005. Mem.: Music Educators Nat. Conf., Soc. for Rsch. in Music Edn., Gamma Beta Phi (life), Kappa Delta Pi (life). Office: Louisiana State University 102 School of Music Baton Rouge LA 70803 Office Phone: 225-578-9270. Home Fax: 225-578-3333; Office Fax: 225-578-3333. E-mail: eorman1@lsu.edu.

ORMAN, NANETTE HECTOR, psychiatrist; b. Highland Park, Ill., Feb. 1, 1943; d. William Joseph and Agnes (Daly) Hector; m. John Christopher Orman, July 2, 1964; children: Laurel Anne, Nathaniel William. BA in Journalism, U. Calif., Berkeley, 1964; postgrad., Stanford U., 1978-81; MPH in Epidemiology, U. Calif., Berkeley, 1984, MS in Health and Med. Scis., 1985; MD, U. Calif., San Francisco, 1987. Diplomate Am. Bd. Psychiatry and Neurology; lic. physician, Calif. Psychiatrist San Jose (Calif.) State U., 1989-93; pvt. practice Los Altos, Calif., 1991—; staff El Camino Hosp., 1991-94, assoc. staff, 1994—; staff Stanford (Calif.) U. Hosp. and Med. Ctr., 1998—. Asst. clin. prof. Stanford (Calif.) U. Sch. Medicine, 1995—; oral bd. examiner Am. Bd. Psychiatry & Neurology, Deerfield, Ill., 1995—, chief resident in psychiatry, 1991; spkr. and cons. in field. Editor San Mateo County Planned Parenthood Assn. Newsletter, 1968-69. Bd. dirs. Mid-Peninsula Task Force for Integrated Edn., 1972-82, Psychiat. Found. No. Calif., 2001—; consumer mem. San Mateo County Mental Health Adv. Bd., 1987. Fellow Am. Psychiat. Assn. (disting., 2004; pub. info. com. 1989—); mem. No. Calif. Psychiat. Soc. (chair membership com. 1996-2002, pub. info. com., media spokesperson, moderator ann. meetings 1993-94), Nat. Alliance for the Mentally Ill, San Francisco Depressive and Manic Depressive Assn. Office: 851 Fremont Ave Ste 98 Los Altos CA 94024-5602

ORMAN, SUZE, news correspondent, writer; Cert. fin. planner. Account exec. Merrill Lynch, 1980—83; v.p. investments Prudential Bache Securities, 1983—87; dir. Suze Orman Fin. Group, 1987—97. Former fin. contbr. NBC News' Today; host QVC Fin. Freedom hour. Contbr. to Self mag.; author: (PBS spl.) The Road to Wealth; co-prodr.: (PBS spl.) The Road to Wealth; host (PBS spl.) The Road to Wealth; author: (PBS spl.) The Courage to Be Rich; co-prodr.: (PBS spl.) The Courage to Be Rich; host (PBS spl.) The Courage to Be Rich; author: (PBS spl.) The 9 Steps to Financial Freedom; co-prodr.: (PBS spl.) The 9 Steps to Financial Freedom; host (PBS spl.) The 9 Steps to Financial Freedom; contbg. editor: O: The Oprah Mag.; host (nat. syndicated radio talk show) The Suze Orman Show; author: You've Earned It, Don't Lose It, 1995, The 9 Steps to Financial Freedom, 1997 (NY Times bestsellers), The Courage to Be Rich, 1999 (NY Times bestsellers), Motivational book award Books for a Better Life, 1999), The Road to Wealth, 2001 (NY Times bestsellers), The Money Book for the Young, Fabulous & Broke, 2005 (Publishers Weekly Bestseller). Named Top 30 Power Brokers Who Most Influenced Mutual Fund Industry and Affected Money, Smart Money mag., 1999, Outstanding Svc. Show Host for Suze Orman: For the Young, Fabulous & Broke, Nat. Acad. TV Arts and Sciences, Daytime Emmy award, 2006; named to 100th issue as those "who have revolutionized the way Am. thinks about money", Worth mag., 2001. Office: CNBC 2200 Fletcher Ave Ste 5 Fort Lee NJ 07024 Mailing: c/o Amanda Urban ICM 40 W 57th St New York NY 10019 Office Phone: 201-585-2183.

ORMOND, JULIA, actress; b. Surrey, Eng., 1965; m. Rory Edwards (div. 1993); m. Jon Rubin, 1999. Grad., Webber Douglas Acad. Drama Art, 1988. Appeared in films The Baby of Macon, 1992, Legends of the Fall, 1994, Nostradamus, 1994, Captives, 1994, First Knight, 1995, Sabrina, 1995, The Prime Gig, 2000, Resistance, 2003; TV appearances include Traffik, 1990, Young Catherine, 1991, Stalin, 1992, The 67th Annual Academy Awards, 1995, Smilla's Sense of Snow, 1997, Sibirsky Tsiryulnik, 1998, (voice) Animal Farm, 1999, Varian's War, 2001, Iron Jawed Angels, 2004; stage appearances include Faith, Hope and Charity, 1989 (London Critics best newcomer award); producer: Calling the Ghosts, 1996. Recipient Female Star of Tomorrow award Sho West Awards, 1995.

ORNDOFF, BETTY KATHERINE (BETTY KATHERINE MADAGAN), secondary school educator; b. Winchester, Va., Nov. 17, 1934; d. Harold Fred Sr. and Mildred Catherine (Anderson) Madagan; m. Edwin Pifer Orndoff, Dec. 21, 1958; 1 child, Edwina Katherine. BS, James Madison U., 1958. Cert. tchr. Va. Tchr. Robinson Meml. Sch., Winchester, Va., 1958-59, Va. Ave Sch., 1959-61, Kline Sch., 1961-63; substitute tchr. Frederick County Pub. Sch., 1963-86; sales assoc. Bell's Ladies, 1970-80; owner, mgr. Orndoff's Appraisal & Auction Svc., 1973—, appraiser, 1987—. Substitute tchr. Frederick County Pub. Sch., Winchester, 1963-86. Contbr. articles to profl. jours. Active Nat. Trust for Hist. Preservation, Washington, 1992—; fashion show com. The Women's Civic League of Winchester, 1964—89, bd. dirs., 1973—88; vol. Preservation of Hist. Winchester, Winchester-Frederick County Hist. Soc.; active Shenandoah Valley Music Festival, 1986—; libr. chairwoman The Women's Civic League of Winchester; active Shenandoah Arts Coun., 1989—, Friends of Handley Libr., 1980—; auction chair Winchester-Frederick County C. of C., 1983—89; active Shenandoah Apple Blossom Festival, Winchester, 1991—, Belle Grove/Nat. Trust for Hist. Preservation, Middletown, Va., 1993—; charter mem. Va. Quilt Mus., 1995, Glen Burnie Historic Ho., Gardens of Julian Wood glass Jr. Collection; active Dem. Nat. Com., 1988—; v.p. Blue Ridge Dem. Women, charter mem., 1970, publicity chairwoman, 1985—86; active Dem. Party of Va., 1983—, Winchester Dem. Com.; apptd. bd. dirs. Winchester Musica Viva, 2002. Recipient 1st prize in advt. for spl. entry in newspaper category Va. Auctioneer Assn.

Inc., 1990; grant to The Educational Foundation of American Association of University Women in hon. of Betty Orndoff, 1998. Mem.: AAUW (life; treas. 1982—85, bd. dirs. Winchester br. 1982—, membership v.p. 1985—88, 1990—, br. del. to AAUW of Va. and AAUW of W.Va. State Conv. 2006), Blue Ridge Fine Arts League, Inc. (asst. to audio-visual chair 1981—88), Mus. Shenandoah Valley (charter), French and Indian War Found. (charter), The Club Continental (charter). Home and Office: 621 S Stewart St Winchester VA 22601-4022 Office Phone: 540-662-1616.

ORNE, EMILY CAROTA, psychologist, researcher; b. Boston, Sept. 7, 1938; d. Emil and Ruth (Farrell) Carota; m. Martin T. Orne, Feb. 3, 1962; children: Franklin Theodore, Tracy Meredith. BA, Bennington Coll., 1959. Rsch. assoc. Mass. Mental Health Ctr., Boston, 1963-64; rsch. psychologist Unit for Exptl. Psychiatry, Phila., 1964-79, sr. rsch. psychologist, 1979-83, co-dir., 1982—; rsch. assoc. psychology U. Pa. Sch. Medicine, Phila., 1983—. Trustee Inst. Exptl. Psychiatry Rsch. Found., Mass., 1964—, assoc. co-dir., 1987-97, exec. dir., 1998—; bd. dirs. False Memory Syndrome Found., 1995- Contbr. articles to profl. jours.; assoc. editor Internat. Jour. Clin. and Exptl. Hypnosis, 1977- Recipient Benjamin Franklin Gold medal Internat. Soc. Hypnosis, 1982, Roy M. Dorcus award Soc. Clin. and Exptl. Hypnosis, 1985, Bernard B. Raginsky award, 1993, Morton Prince award Soc. Clin. and Exptl. Hypnosis and APA, 1994 Avocations: fishing, swimming, reading. Office: U Pa Sch Medicine 1013 Blockley Hall 423 Guardian Dr Philadelphia PA 19104-6021

ORNER, LINDA PRICE, family therapist, counselor; b. Gettysburg, Pa., June 27, 1943; d. John Robert and Ruby Pearl (Vines) Price; m. Ted Arnold Orner, Mar. 29, 1963; children: Penni Ann, Jennifer Arianna. AA, North Harris Coll., 1991; BA summa cum laude, U. St. Thomas, 1994; MEd in Counseling Psychology, U. Houston, 1997; MA in Family Therapy, U. Houston, Clear Lake, 1999. Lic. profl. counselor. Therapist Houston VA Hosp./Trauma Recovery Program, 1996, U. Houston Counseling and Testing Svcs., 1997, U. Houston-Clear Lake Psychol. Svcs., 1998—99; intern/assoc., family therapist Houston Galveston Inst., 1998—2000; pvt. practice counselor Family Life Svcs., Colorado Springs, 2001—. Vol. Women's Ctr.; vol. seminar instr., counselor Tex. Prison; keynote spkr. Christian Women's Clubs Internat. Mem.: APA, ACA, Am. Assn. Christian Counselors, Am. Psychotherapy Assn., Am. Assn. for Marriage and Family Therapy. Presbyterian. Avocations: travel, scuba diving, hiking, antiques, art. Home: 4684 Stone Manor Hts Colorado Springs CO 80906-8605 Address: 2210 W Dallas # 942 Houston TX 77019 Office Phone: 719-632-4661. Personal E-mail: ornery62@adelphia.net.

ORNT, JEANINE ARDEN, lawyer; b. Apr. 29, 1955; BA, SUNY, 1977; JD, Union U., 1980. Ptnr. Greisberger, Zicari, Rochester, N.Y., 1985-89; gen. counsel med. ctr. U. Rochester, 1989—2003.

OROPEZA, JENNY, state official; b. Montebello, Calif., Sept. 27, 1957; m. Tom Mullins. Mem. Long Beach Unified Sch. Dist. Bd. Edn., 1988—94; coun. mem. Long Beach City Coun., 1994—2000; state assembly mem. Dist. 55 Calif. State Assembly, 2000—. Mem. Latino Caucus. Democrat. Mailing: PO Box 942849 Rm 2148 Sacramento CA 94249 Office: One Civic Plaza Dr Ste 460 Carson CA 90745 Office Phone: 916-319-2055. Business E-Mail: assemblymember.oropeza@assembly.ca.gov.

O'RORK, AIMÉE, music educator, composer; b. Altoona, Pa., Aug. 2, 1973; d. Christine Adele Jarrett; m. Rory O'Rork, June 22, 2002; 1 child, Christiana Renée. BA, West Liberty State Coll., W.Va., 1998. Provisional tchr. cert. Ohio, W.Va., Pa., Ga. Vocal choir dir. grades 3-12 Oberlin (Ohio) City Schs., 1999—2004; music tchr., choir dir. Griffin (Ga.) Spalding City Schs., 2004—. Song writer, poet, composer, musician: albums Example: Diamond. Youth leader Pleasant Grove (Ohio) Pentecostal Ch., 1992—95; children's choir dir. Christian Faith Assembly, Elyria, Ohio, 2001—04. Mem.: Music Educators Nat. Conf. (assoc.).

O'ROURKE, MAUREEN A., dean, law educator; BS summa cum laude, Marist Coll.; JD, Yale Law Sch. With IBM; assoc. prof. Boston U. Sch. Law, 1993—98, prof., 1998—, assoc. dean adminstrn., assoc. dean academic affairs, 2003—04, interim dean, 2004—. Vis. prof. Columbia U. Sch. Law, La Trobe U., Australia, 2002, U. Victoria Law Sch., British Columbia, British Virgin Islands. Co-author: Copyright in a Global Economy; contbr. articles to law jours. Recipient Metcalf Award, 2002. Mailing: Boston U Sch Law 765 Commenwealth Ave Boston MA 02215

OROZCO, EDITH DELL, counselor, special education counselor; b. Stanton, Tex., June 11, 1940; d. Oran Rivers and L. Juanita Nichols; m. Luis Arturo Orozco, Jan. 26, 1963; children: Julia M., Daniel Luis, David Arturo. BS, U. North Tex., 1962, MEd, 1967; ASN, San Antonio Coll., 1984. Lic. profl. counselor, Tex.; cert. sch. counselor, Tex.; cert. spl. edn. counselor, Tex.; cert. bilingual/ESL tchr., Tex.; cert. faith based therapon Belief Therapist, 2000. Elem. tchr. Midland (Tex.) Ind. Sch. Dist., 1962-63, Irving (Tex.) Ind. Sch. Dist., 1963-67, South San Antonio Ind. Sch. Dist., 1975-82, 84-93, sch. counselor, 1993-99, spl. edn. counselor, 1999—. Counselor South Tex. Counseling Svcs., San Antonio, 1998—; co-leader support group Project Heart, Olivares Elem. Sch., San Antonio, 1993-99. Family/sch. coord. counseling Families & Schs. Together, Olivares Elem. Sch., San Antonio, 1997-99; counseling vol. Palo Alto Coll. Returning Adult Ctr., San Antonio, 1996-97; screening vol. Nat. Depression Screening, Palo Alto Coll., San Antonio, 1995, 96. Mem.: Christian Counselors Tex., Am. Assn. Christian Counselors, Tex. Counseling Assn. Baptist. E-mail: eoro@earthlink.net.

ORPHANIDES, NORA CHARLOTTE, ballet educator; b. NYC, June 4, 1951; d. M.T. and Mary Elsie (Tilly) Feffer; m. James Mark Orphanides, July 1, 1972; children: Mark, Elaine Orphanides Mastrosimone, Jennine. BA, CUNY, 1973; student, Joffrey Ballet Sch., N.Y.C., 1970-75; postgrad., Princeton Ballet Sch., 1976-86. Cert. speech and hearing handicapped tchr. With membership dept. M.M.A., N.Y.C., 1987—2002; mem. faculty Princeton (N.J.) Ballet Sch., 1983—, trustee emeritus, 1992—. Master tchr. ballroom dance. Mem. cast Princeton Ballet ann. Nutcracker, 1985-90, now Am. Repertory Ballet Co., 1993—; appeared in Romeo & Juliet, 1995-96, 2000. Fundraising gala chmn. Princeton Ballet, 1985, 86, 91-92, chmn. spl. events, 1987—, trustee, 1986—, chmn. Nutcracker benefit, 1990—, Dracula benefit, 1991, honoree, 1999; dept. chmn. June Fete to benefit Princeton Hosp., 1988, 90-92, 96, 2000, trustee, 1995-99; vol. Nat. Hdqrs. Recording for the Blind, 1991-93; dinner chmn. Nassau Ch. Music Festival, 1992, Handel Festival, Nassau Ch., 1993, Princeton Chamber Symphony, 1993; hon. chmn. Princeton Ballet Gala, 1993, Art First to benefit U. Med. Ctr., 2006; chmn. Christmas Boutique, Princeton Med. Ctr., 1993; trustee, Princeton Med. Ctr. Aux. Bd., 1992-2002, trustee 1995—, pres., 1997-99, past pres., 2000-2002; found. bd. dirs. U. Med. Ctr. Princeton, 2004—; choreographer Stuart Country Day Sch., Princeton, 1996-99, 2001; chmn. benefit dinner Eden Inst., 2000. Named honoree Princeton Ballet, 1999, recipient Edward R. and Irene D. Farley Cmty. Stewardship award Eden Inst. Found., 2003. Democrat. Avocations: piano, skiing, tennis. Office: 301 N Harrison St Princeton NJ 08540-3512

ORR, AMY J., sociologist, educator; d. Jody Ann Klute; m. A. Erik Svec, July 5, 1996; 1 child, Hunter Phoenix. BS with highest distinction, Nebr. Wesleyan U., Lincoln, 1993; MA, U. Notre Dame, 1996, PhD, 2000. Vis. asst. prof. sociology U. Notre Dame, Notre Dame, Ind., 2000—01; asst. prof. sociology Linfield Coll., McMinnville, Oreg., 2001—. Bd. mem. Multicultural Adoption Adv. Program, Inc., McMinnville, Oreg., 2003—05. Contbr. articles to profl. jours. and encys., chapters to books. Founding mem. Nat. Campaign for Tolerance (So. Poverty Law Ctr.), Montgomery, Ala., 2001—03; friend of the Ctr. So. Poverty Law Ctr., Montgomery, Ala., 2003—. Recipient Samuel Graf Faculty Achievement award, 2006; grantee, Carnegie Scholarship of Tchg. Program and the Kaneb Ctr. for Tchg. and Learning, 2000, Nat. Coun. Teachers English, 2001. Mem.: AAUW, NAACP, ACLU, Pacific Sociol. Assn. (mem. program com. 2003—05, mem. membership com. 2005—), Am. Sociol. Assn. (soe nominations com. 1996—97), Nat. Women's History Mus. (charter). Achievements include research on the effects of wealth (net worth) on academic achievement (especially with regard to the black-white test score gap and marital status). Business E-Mail: aorr@linfield.edu.

ORR, BOBETTE KAY, diplomat; b. Oak Park, Ill., Oct. 28, 1941; d. Robert Jay and Neta (Hoobler) Pottle; m. William Rucker Orr, Oct. 11, 1974; step children: Bridgette, Brietta, Alyson, William Jr. BA in Econs., Conn. Coll. for Women, 1963; student auditor Internat. Econs., London Sch. of Econs., 1964; postgrad. studies in Internat. Econs., George Washington U., 1964-65. Rsch. asst. C. of C. USA, Washington, 1965—66; country desk officer for Scandanavia U.S. Dept. Commerce, Washington, 1966—69, country desk officer for France, 1970—72, 1979—81, country desk officer for Belgium, Netherlands, Luxembourg, 1974—77, country desk officer for Japan, 1981—82; mkt. rsch. officer United States Trade Ctr., Stockholm, 1973, trade promotion officer London, 1977—78; asst. comml. attache Am. Embassy, Paris, 1982—87; comml. attache Am. Consulate Gen., Auckland, New Zealand, 1988—92, consul gen. Edinburgh, Scotland, 1992—95; comml. counselor Am. Embassy, London, 1995—99, Cairo, 1999—2002; regional dir. Africa, Near East, South Asia U.S. Dept. Commerce, Washington, 2002—04, 2006, regional dir. for Europe, 2005, regional dir. for Africa, Near East, South Asia, 2006—. Mem. bd. dirs. U.S. Dept. Commerce Fed. Credit Union, Washington, D.C., 1972-77, pres., 1976-77, mem. supervisory com., 1979-81; equal employment opportunity counselor for Greater Washington Met. Area, 1972-75; mission dir. for USDOC's Concrete Constrn. Techniques Seminar Mission to Hong Kong, Singapore, Malaysia, 1980; detailed to Office of Dir. Fgn. Comml. Svc. as evaluator of candidates for Fgn. Comml. Svc., 1981. Author: (with others) 10 pamphlet series, on free enterprise, The Power of Choice, 1966; contbr. to Bus. Am., 1966-81, Overseas Bus. Reports 1966-76 (Dept. Commerce publs.). Mem. Am. Women's Club of Edinburgh, (hon. pres.), The English Speaking Union. Avocations: skiing, bicycle riding. Home: PO Box 63 Great Falls VA 22066-0063 Office: USFCS/ITA Dept Commerce 14th and Constitution Ave NW Rm 2013 Washington DC 20230 Office Phone: 202-482-0368. Business E-Mail: Bobette.Orr@mail.doc.gov.

ORR, CAROLE, artist; b. Alexandria, Ind., June 10, 1933; d. Carl Victor and Marian Martha (Long) Coonse; m. Larry D. Ribble (dec. July 1953); m. Thomas LeRoy Orr, Nov. 10, 1950 (div. Oct. 1979); children: Karen Sue, Terri Ribble, David Thomas; m. Lev C. Hamblet Jr., Feb. 5, 1982 (div. Oct. 1998); stepchildren: James, Jean, Laura, Anne. Cert., Famous Artist Sch., Westport, Conn., 1956, Art Instrn. Schs., Mpls., 1962. Asst. art dir. La Gallerie du Mall, Houston, 1975—78; freelance fine artist Lantern Ln. Gallery, Houston, 1968—81, asst. mgr., design cons., 1979—81; artist Artist Showroom, Houston, 1982—. Participating artist Assistance Guild, Houston, 1968, Beaux Arts, Houston, 1968-70, Houston Gamma Phi Gallery, 1971-72, Houston Delta Gamma Found., 1978-81, Glassell Sch. of Art Houston, 1983; art instr. children's art Houston Park and Recreational Programs, 1964-68. One-woman shows include Nobler Gallery, Houston, 1967, Art Gallery, Pasadena, Tex., 1968, Gallarie La Rue, Austin, Tex., 1971, Gallery 12, Houston, 1972, Main St., Houston, 1974, La Galerie de Mall, Houston, 1976-78, Triumvirate Gallery, Santa Fe, N.Mex., 1980, Houshang's Gallery, Dallas, 1980-82, Battle Horn Galleries Ltd., Santa Fe, 1984, New Trends Inc., Santa Fe, 1985-88, Horizons Galleries, Houston, 1990-93, Houston C.C., 1992, Heinen Theatre, 1992, Windsor Gallery, Ft. Lauderdale, Fla., 1994; exhibited in group shows at Motorola Invitational, Houston, 1964, Assistance Guild Houston, 1968, Am. Gen. Bldg., Houston, 1968, Beaux Arts, Houston, 1968-70, Gamma Phi Gallery, Houston, 1971-72, Lantern Ln. Gallery, Houston, 1971-72, Delta Gamma Found., Houston, 1978-81, Glassell Sch. Art, Houston, 1983, New Trends Gallery Inc., Santa Fe, 1985-88, Pasadena (Tex.) Art Invitational, 1988, Double Tree Hotel, Houston, 1990, Horizons Gallery, Houston, 1990-93, Windsors Gallery, Dania, Fla., 1993, 2003, Magnolias Art Gallery, Town and Country Ctr., Houston, 2003-06, Bakery of the Poets, 2005—; T. Symington & Co. Interiors, Brenham, Tex., 2006. Art instr. adults Ch. of the Advent, Houston, 1968-70; adult edn. instr. arts Ch. Sch. Conf., Dept. Christian Edn., Trinity Ch., Diocese of Tex., Houston, 1969. Recipient Profl. Best Ann. Competition Art Instrn. Schs., Mpls., 1965; named Best-Selling Artist of Yr., 2001, Paintings DIRECT, N.Y.C., 2001, 03, Art on 5th, Austin, 2005, Diamond Domani Galleria, Houston, 2005, T. Sumington & Co. Interiors, Tex., 2006. Avocations: self-study in psychology, music, dance. Home and Office: Artist Showroom DBA 880 Tully Rd Apt 29 Houston TX 77079-5418

ORR, HEATHER MICHELLE, music educator, vocalist; b. Altoona, Pa., Dec. 1, 1969; d. Daniel L. and Annette M. Phipps; m. William Payne Adams Orr, Aug. 28, 1993; children: Carly, Abby, Christopher, Claire. MusB in Voice Performance, Heidelberg Coll., Tiffin, Ohio, 1991; MA in Vocal Pedagogy, Ohio State U., Columbus, 1994. Choir dir. Eisenhower H.S., Houston, 1995—2001, Montgomery H.S., 2001—. Mem.: Am. Choral Dirs. Assn., Tex. Choral Dirs. Assn., Tex. Music Adjudicators Assn., Tex. Music Educators Assn. Republican. Roman Catholic. Home: 11 Balboa Rd Montgomery TX 77356 Office: Montgomery HS 22825 Hwy 105 W Montgomery TX 77356 Office Phone: 936-597-3146.

ORR, JENNIE MARIE (JENNIE THOMAS), family physician; b. Sioux City, Iowa, Feb. 16, 1952; d. J. Allen and Ione B. (Gronlund) O.; m. Daniel Joel Thomas, Aug. 23, 1980; children: Lorraine Marie, Joel Allen. BS in Computer Sci., Mich. State U., 1973, MD, 1976. Diplomate Am. Bd. Family Practice. Sub-intern pediatrics Grad. Med. Edn., Inc., Lansing, Mich., 1977; intern, resident family practice Cedar Rapids (Iowa) Med. Edn. Program, 1977-80; staff Allina Med. Clinic, Hastings, Minn., 1980—, corp. sec., 1984—88. Chmn. dept. obstetrics Regina Meml. Hosp., Hastings, 1986-90. Fellow Am. Acad. Family Practice. Lutheran. Office: Allina Med Clinic 1210 1st St W Hastings MN 55033-1085

ORR, KATHLEEN KAYSER, special education educator; b. Biloxi, Miss., Mar. 2, 1949; d. Thomas Edward Kayser and Clara Bertice Johnson; m. Gary Fremond Orr, Sept. 4, 1971; children: Chad Fremond, Katie Kay. BS in Edn., We. Ill. U., 1972, cert. in spl. edn., 1987. Elem. tchr., 2d and 3d grade Grand Prairie Sch., Plainfield, Ill., 1972—78; tchr. spl. K-5 East Moline (Ill.) Elem. Sch. Dist., 1986—87; tchr. spl. K-12 Annawan (Ill.) Sch. Dist., 1987—88; spl. edn. dir. and tchr., h.s. Erie (Ill.) Sch. Dist. No. 1, 1988—. Bd. mem. Messiah Luth. Ch. Coun., Port Byron, Ill., 1998—2000. Mem.: Coun. for Exceptional Children, Erie Tchrs. Assn. (v.p. 1999—2001, pres. 2002—), Ill. Edn. Assn. (assembly del.), NEA (assembly del.). Avocations: dance, gardening. Office: Erie High Sch 435 6th Ave Erie IL 61250 Business E-Mail: korr@erie1.net.

ORR, MARCIA, pre-school administrator, consultant; b. Anamosa, Iowa, Mar. 2, 1949; d. Harold Edward Eiben and Clara Elizabeth (Hubbard) E.; m. Robert J. Orr, Sept. 6, 1969; 1 child, Jennifer. Student, U. Iowa, 1977; BS, St. Xavier U., Chgo., 1981; MEd in Early Childhood Leadership, Nat. Louis U., 1996. Bookkeeper Monticello State Bank, 1967-69; exec. sec. Davenport Bank and Trust, 1969-73; asst. educator Elisabeth Ludeman Devel. Ctr., Park Forest, Ill., 1979; tchr. Flossmoor Hills (Ill.) Elem. Sch., 1980-1984; exec. dir. Co-Care, Inc., Park Forest, 1984-89; child devel. rschr., Flossmoor, Ill., 1989—; tchr. Nazarene Nursery Sch. and Kindergarten, Chicago Heights, Ill., 1991; child care ctr. cons. Matteson Sch. Dist. 162, Park Forest, 1991—; founder, exec. dir. Before and After Sch. Enrichment, Park Forest, 1991—; adv. mem. project early start Matteson Sch. Dist. 162, Park Forest, 1991—, home-sch. coord., 1992—. Grant writer Matteson Sch. Dist. 162 and Before and After Sch. Enrichment, Inc.; officer Boleo Childcare Ctr., Iowa City, 1975-77; mentor to dirs. child care programs early childhood edn. dept. Nat.-Louis U., Ill, 1994—; co-founder Reaching New Horizons, Inc., 1996—. Contbr. articles pub. to profl. jour. Tchr. religion Infant Jesus of Prague Ch., Flossmoor, Ill., 1982—; mem. Flossmoor PTO, 1987-89; music chmn. Dist. 161 PTO, 1980-90; exec. dir. Before and After Sch. Enrichment, Inc.; parent resource coord. Matteson Sch. Dist. 162. McCormick fellow, 1995—; recipient Golden Achievement award Nat. Sch. Pub. Rels. Assn., 2001; named Best Practices and Rsch. honoree Louis U., Evanston, Ill., 2001. Mem. NAFE, Nat. Assn. for Edn. Young Children (validator), Women Employed Orgn., Internat. Platform Assn., Parent Inst., South Suburban Small Bus. Assn. (charter). Democrat. Roman Catholic. Avocations: piano, classical music, travel. Home: 9411 Fox Run Ct Frankfort IL 60423-1380 Office: Before and After Sch Enrichment 210 Illinois St Park Forest IL 60466-1100 Office Phone: 815-464-8690. Business E-Mail: base@base-inc.net.

ORR, MARGARET, newscaster; b. New Orleans; married; 3 children. Grad. in English, La. State U., 1975; grad. in Broadcast Meteorology, Miss. State U., 1995. Photographer, editor, prodr., reporter, anchor, weathercaster WCIV-TV, Charleston, SC; weathercaster WBRZ-TV, Baton Rouge; from assignment reporter to meteorologist WDSU News Channel 6, New Orleans, 1979—. Mem.: Am. Meteorol. Soc. Avocations: gardening, painting. Office: WDSU News Channel 6 846 Howard Ave New Orleans LA 70113

ORR, NANCY A., educational psychologist; b. Cin., 1952; d. Lowell and Betty Orr. BA, Ind. U., 1974, MS in Edn., 1977; PhD, U. Pa., 1988. Asst. dean of students Coll. Wooster, Ohio, 1977—79; asst. dean Swarthmore Coll., Pa., 1979—84, assoc. dean, 1984—85; rsch. assoc. Nat. Bd. Med. Examiners, Phila., 1985—97, evaluation officer, 1998—2000, sr. assessment officer, 2001—05, dir. client programs, 2006—. Mem. Media (Pa.) Youth Aid Panel, 1999—. Avocations: travel, sports, gardening, quilts, cultural events. Office: Nat Bd Med Examiners 3750 Market St Philadelphia PA 19104 Office Phone: 215-590-9500.

ORR, SANDRA JANE, civic worker, pharmacist; b. Marion, Ohio, June 27, 1930; d. Lawrence Edward and Wanita Izell (Noyes) Schneider; m. Ross Moore Orr, Jr., Aug. 12, 1951; children: Sandra K. Orr Whiston, Sara L. Orr Cochrane. BS in Pharmacy, Med. Coll. Va., 1952. Pharmacist Atkison & Howard, Richmond, Va., 1952-54, Schneider's Walgreen Agy., Kenton, Ohio, 1954-73. Part-time pharmacist Drug Svc., Bethlehem, Pa., 1954-57, Fastchnacts' Drug, Bethlehem, 1954-57. One-woman shows in oils, pastels and watercolors. Chmn. ball St. Luke's Hosp., Bethlehem, 1985, 87; bd. dirs. Hist. Bethlehem, 1988—; dir. liturgical dance 1st Presbyn. Ch., 1968, 78; instr. needlework YMCA, 1980-81; instr. movement Orff tchrs.; instr. ballet Lehigh U. football team, 1966; docent Allentown Art Mus., 1956-68, Art Goes to Sch., 1960-62. Mem. Jr. League Lehigh Valley. Republican. Presbyterian. Avocations: flying, boating, travel, golf, cooking. Home: 405 High St Bethlehem PA 18018-6103

ORR, SUSAN PACKARD, small business owner, foundation administrator; BA in Econs., Stanford U., 1968, MBA, 1970; MS in Computer Sci., N.Mex. Inst. Mining and Tech., 1984. Chmn. David and Lucile Packard Found., Los Altos, Calif.; CEO Telosa Software (formerly Tech. Resource Assistance Ctr.), Palo Alto, Calif., 1986—. Trustee Stanford U., 1998—. Office: The Packard Found 300 2nd St Ste 200 Los Altos CA 94022-3643

ORR, ZELLIE, entrepreneur, educator, writer, researcher; b. Holly Ridge, Miss., May 12, 1951; d. Leonard and Lucille Rainey; m. Foster G. Orr Jr., Feb. 28, 1976 (div. July 14, 1998); children: Kai A., Nia Haley. Student, L.A. City Coll., 1970—71, U. Calif., Northridge, 1971—73; cert., Airline Schs. Pacific, 1974, CMLS Inst., 1979; MA in Human Letters, U. Metaphysics, 1983. Cert. real estate salesperson, Ga., 1979, pub. notary, Ga. 1985. Personal lines underwriter Kemper Ins. Co., L.A., 1976—78, Comml. Union Ins. Co., Atlanta, 1980—82, Moore Group ins. Co., Atlanta, 1982—85; lic. real estate agent Wofford Realty, Riverdale, Ga., 1979—81; owner Traffic Jam Lounge and Restaurant, Sunflower, 1986—89; documentation specialist Windsor Group, Atlanta, 1989—2001, mem. billing and collection mgmt. sys., 1991; pres., founder Comm. Unltd., Austell, Ga., 1995—. Mem. rsch. bd. advisors Am. Biog. Inst., Raleigh, NC, 1992—93. Co-author: Treasured Poems of America, 1989 (Editor's Choice award, 1989), The Best Poems & Poets of the 20th Century, 2000 (Editor's Choice award, 2000), Theatre of The Mind, 2003; author: numerous poems. Co-organizer Sunflower County Civil Rights and Cmty. Reunion, Indianola, 1999; founder Charles E. Scattergood Meml. Found., Marietta, Ga., 2000; mem. So. Poverty Law Ctr., Habitat for Humanity, Feed the Children. Recipient Cert. Appreciation, Superior Ct., Calif., 1976, Cert. Recognition, CME Ch., Indianola, 1999, Disting. Svc. award, Nat. Mus. of Tuskegee Airmen, 2004, Disting. Svc. and Dedication award, Alva N. Temple chpt. Tuskegee Airmen Inc., 2005, Presdl. award, Tuskegee Airmen, Inc., 2006. Mem.: NAACP, NAFE, Am. Metaphys. Drs. Assn., Nat. Trust Hist. Preservation, Nat. Mus. Women in Arts, Internat. Soc. Poets, Nat. Black MBA Assn. Avocations: stamp collecting/philately, reading, coin collecting/numismatics, antiques, chess. Home: 3285 Doyle Ln Marietta GA 30060 Office: Comm Unltd 3999 Austell Rd Ste 303 #158 Austell GA 30106 Personal E-mail: orrs@artsonwheels.com. E-mail: orrz@bellsouth.net.

ORR-CAHALL, ANONA CHRISTINA, museum director, art historian; b. Wilkes-Barre, Pa., June 12, 1947; d. William R.A. and Anona (Snyder) Boben; m. Richard Cahall. BA magna cum laude, Mt. Holyoke Coll., 1969; MA, Yale U., 1974, MPhil, 1975, PhD, 1979. Curator of collections Norton Gallery Art, West Palm Beach, Fla., 1975-77; asst. prof. Calif. Poly. State U., San Luis Obispo, 1978-81, Disting. prof., 1981; dir. art div., chief curator Oakland (Calif.) Mus., 1981-88; chief exec. officer Corcoran Gallery Art, Washington, 1988-90; dir. Norton Mus. Art, West Palm Beach, 1990—. Author: Addison Mizner: Architect of Dreams and Realities, 1974, 2d printing, 1993, Gordon Cook, 1987, Claude Monet: Am Impression, 1993; editor: The Art of California, 1984, The American Collection at the Norton Museum of Art, 1995. Office: Norton Museum of Art 1451 S Olive Ave West Palm Beach FL 33401-7162 Fax: 561-832-6529.

ORRIS-MODUGNO, MICHELE MARIE, public relations, marketing and advertising consultant; b. Norwalk, Conn., Feb. 23, 1958; d. Stephen Joseph and Arcenia (Rodriguez) O. Student, U. N.Mex., Albuquerque, 1976-78; BA with honors, U. Bridgeport, Conn., 1980, postgrad., 1981-83. Tchr. Norwalk Pub. Schs., 1981-83; head tchr. presch. Norwalk YMCA, 1983-84; exec. dir. Norwalk Seaport Assn., 1984-86; cons., 1986-87, Barnum Festival, Bridgeport, Conn., 1987-88, P.T. Barnum Found., Bridgeport, 1987; mgr. communications Human Resources Inc., Stamford, Conn., 1987; owner, mgr. Michele Orris, Norwalk, Conn., 1988—. Dir. pub. rels. YWCA of Stamford (Conn.), 1989-90. Past sec., pres. Marvin Beach Assn., East Norwalk; asst. dir. pub. rels. Conn. Women's Celebration, 1986; chmn. subcom. auditorium com. New City Hall, Norwalk; active numerous other civic orgns.; bd. dirs. Southwestern Conn. coun. Girl Scouts U.S., 1987-88, Cmtys. In Schs. of Norwalk, Inc., 2000-01; gdn. dirs. Levitt Pavilion Performing Arts, Westport, Conn., 1991-93; mgr. Orch. New Eng., 1993-95; mem. Unquowa Parents Assn., 2000-05; pres. Unquowa Parents' Assn., 2002-04. Recipient award City of Norwalk, 1987. Mem. Greens Farms Acad. Alumni Assn. (pres., class sec.), Phi Sigma Iota (life). Democrat. Roman Catholic. Avocations: reading, tennis, bicycling, golf, art museums. Home and Office: 455 Primrose Ln Fairfield CT 06825-2343 Office Phone: 203-259-8232. Business E-Mail: entmom@optonline.net.

ORROCK, NAN, state legislator; children: Jesse, Daniel. BA, U. Va., 1965. Mem. Ga. State Ho. of Reps., Atlanta, 1986—. Mem. Econ. Devel. Com., Indsl. Rels. Com., Ways and Means Com.; pres. Women Legislators' Lobby of WAND; past exec. dir. Fund for So. Cmties; bd. chair Ctr. for Policy Alternatives Exec. dir. Fund for So. Cmties. Mem. Unitarian Ch. Unitarian Ch. Home: 1070 Delaware Ave SE Atlanta GA 30316-2470 Office: Capitol Sq 612 Legislative Office Bldg Atlanta GA 30334 Office Phone: 404-656-0325. Business E-Mail: norrock@legis.state.ga.us.

ORSAK, LISA GAYLE, secondary school educator; b. Borger, Tex., May 27, 1961; d. Royce Douglas and Betty June Porter; m. Ronald Ray Orsak, Aug. 8, 1969; 1 child, Tristan Hunter. BS, U. Tex., Austin, 1983. Cert. tchr. Tex. Edn. Agy., 1983. Mental health worker Mainland Ctr. Psychiat. Unit, Texas City, Tex., 1983—85; h.s. tchr. LaMarque Ind. Sch. Dist., Tex., 1985—96, Newton Unified Sch. Dist., Kans., 1996—2002, Alvin Ind. Sch. Dist., Tex., 2002—. Part-time mental health worker psychiat. ward St. Mary's Hosp., Galveston, Tex., 1987—94; part-time mental health worker Prairie View Psychiat. Unit, Newton, Kans., 1996—2002; human and civl rights commr. KNEA, Newton, Tex., 1999—2000; mem. Newton Diversity Com., Kans., 1999—2000. Active Ch. of Christ, League City, Tex., 2005—06. Named Dec. Tchr. of Month, LaMarque H.S., 1995, Jan. Tchr. of Month, 1996; recipient Outstanding Program award, Galveston County C. of C., 1990—91. Mem.: Alpha Delta Kappa. Republican. Avocations: reading, needlepoint, outdoor activities. Home: 514 Sherwood Forest Dickinson TX 77539 Office: Alvin ISD 802 S Johnson Alvin TX 77511 Office Phone: 821-331-8151. Personal E-mail: lorsak@hotmail.com.

ORSBORN, MARY KAY, school librarian, educator; b. Emmetsburg, Iowa, Nov. 8, 1954; d. Andrew Joseph Gappa II and Mary Elizabeth Moses; children: Maureen, Maxwell. BSc summa cum laude, U. Minn., 1977. Sch. libr. Armstrong-Ringsted Cmty. Schs., Iowa, 1977—84; tchr., libr. West Bend-Mallard Cmty. Schs., Iowa, 1990—2006; libr. Harrisburg Sch. Dist., SD, 2006—. Mem.: Iowa Assn. Sch. Librs., Delta Kappa Gamma (v.p. Chi chpt. 2004—06).

ORSER, JANET CHRISTINE, psychologist; b. Buffalo, Mar. 29, 1953; d. Andrew Christopher and Beulah Rodeghiero; m. Glenn Orser, July 24, 1976; children: Ryan Seth, Shane Michael. MA in Sch. Psychology, Alfred U., 1977—77; BA in Psychology and English, Canisius Coll., Buffalo, 1975. Cert. sch. psychologist NY. Sch. psychologist Springville (NY) -Griffith Inst., 1977—78, Orchard Park (NY) Ctrl. Sch. Dist., 1979—. Bd. dirs. Boys and Girls Club, Orchard Park, 1993—98; mm. med. mission to Honduras The Tabernacle, Orchard Park, 2005—06. Grantee, Spl. Edn. Tng. and Resource Ctr., 1988—89. Mem.: Nat. Assn. Sch. Psychologists. Mem. Assemblies Of God. Avocations: tennis, travel, reading, crafts. Home: 7147 Chestnut Ridge Rd Orchard Park NY 14127 Office: Orchard Park Ctrl Sch Dist 3330 Baker Rd Orchard Park NY 14127

ORSON, BARBARA TUSCHNER, actress; b. N.Y.C., May 19, 1929; d. Jonah Tuschner and Rebecca Traceman; m. Jay M. Orson, June 24, 1956; children: Beth-Diane, Theodore. Student, Dramatic Workshop, N.Y.C., 1948-50. Leading soubrette Am. Savoyards, N.Y.C., 1950-51, 53-55; actress Trinity Repertory, Providence, 1964—2002. Founding mem. Trinity Sq. Repertory Co., Providence, 1964—2001. Actress Edinburgh Festival, Scotland, 1968, Am. Repertory Theatre, Cambridge, Mass., 1981-85, Williamstown (Mass.) Theatre, 1985-89, Dallas Theatre Ctr., 1985, Yale Repertory Co., New Haven, Conn., 1991; appeared in: (films) Mission Hill, Code of Ethics, My One and Only, Swimming Upstream, Mr. North, Strangers in Transit (TV) Theatre in America, Feasting with Panthers, Life Among the Lowly, House of Mirth, Camera Three, RI Demon Murder, Miller's Court, Conflict of Interest (Am. premiere) The Suicide, 1980, (world premiere) Grown Ups, 1981, God's Heart, 1995; founding mem., appeared in over 100 prodns. Trinity Sq. Repertory Co., Providence, 1964—; (radio) House of Mirth, Masterpiece Radio Theatre with Jane Alexander; guest artist (Lady Macbeth), Brown U. Recipient Adrian Hall award, Trinity Repertory Co., RI, 2002. Mem. Am. Fedn. Radio and TV Artists, Screen Actors Guild, Actor's Equity Assn., Trinity Rep. Co. (founder). Home: 281 Hillside Ave Pawtucket RI 02860-6119

ORT, SHANNON, lawyer; b. Appleton, Wis. BA magna cum laude in Criminal Justice and Legal Studies, Hamline U., 1998; JD magna cum laude, William Mitchell Coll. Law, 2001. Bar: Minn. 2001, Wis. 2002. Assoc. Steffens & Rasmussen; assoc. atty. litig. dept. Rider Bennett, L.L.P., Mpls. Named a Rising Star, Minn. Super Lawyers mag., 2006. Mem.: Hennepin County Bar Assn., Minn. State Bar Assn., Edina C. of C. Office: Rider Bennett LLP 33 S 6th St Ste 4900 Minneapolis MN 55402 Office Phone: 612-340-7910. E-mail: sort@riderlaw.com.*

ORTCIGER, LISA MARIE, history educator; d. Robert William Cohenour and Bonnie Jean Diewold; m. Edward Guy Ortciger, Sept. 4, 1999. BA, Western Ill. U., Macomb, Ill., 1993. Cert. Social Sci. 7-12 Standard Tchg. Iowa, 2002, Ill. Type 9 Tchg. Ill., 1993. Tchr. Beacon Therapeutic, Diagnostic, and Treatment Ctr., Chgo., 1998—99; tchr. - kids at coll. Prairie State Coll., Chgo. Heights, Ill., 1999—99; sub. tchr. Infant Jesus of Prague, Flossmoor, Ill., 1999—2000; tchr. St. Benedict Sch., Blue Island, Ill., 2000—02; tchr./head of social studies dept. Holy Trinity Cath. Mid. Sch., West Point, Iowa, 2002—. Photographer (book) Burlington, Iowa: A Souvenir 1996. Mem.: Nat. Cath. Edn. Assn., Iowa Coun. for Social Studies, Des Moines County Geneal. Soc., Nat. Trust for Hist. Preservation. Roman Cath. Avocations: genealogy, gardening, travel, photography, cooking. Office: Holy Trinity Cath Sch 412 Ave C West Point IA 52656

ORTEGA, MELISSA LEE, researcher; d. Christian Patrick and Kathleen Mary Ortega. BA in Sociology, U. Fla., Gainesville, 1999; MA in Clin. Psychology, New Sch. U., N.Y.C., 2003. Rsch. asst. Columbia U., N.Y.C., 2004—. Mem.: APA. Office: Columbia U 1051 Riverside Dr Unit 78 New York NY 10032

ORTEGO, GILDA BAEZA, library director, educator; b. El Paso, Tex., Mar. 29, 1952; d. Efren and Bertha (Singh) Baeza; m. Felipe de Ortego y Gasca, Dec. 21, 1986. BA, Tex. Woman's U., 1974, PhD, 2001; MLS, U. Tex., 1976, postgrad., 1990-93; cert., Hispanic Leadership Inst., 1988. Stack maintenance supr. El Paso Libr. U. Tex., 1974-75; pub. svcs. libr. El Paso Community Coll., 1976-77; ethnic studies libr. U. N.Mex., Albuquerque, 1977-81; br. head El Paso Pub. Libr., 1981-82; dep. head Mex.-Am. Svcs., El Paso Pub. Libr., 1982-84; libr. Mex.-Am. Studies U. Tex. Libr., Austin, 1984—86; libr. Phoenix Pub. Libr., 1987-89; assoc. libr., west campus Ariz. State U., Phoenix, 1989-90; Proyecto Leer libr. Tex. Woman's U., Denton, 1991-92; dean divsn. learning resources Sul Ross State U., Alpine, Tex., 1992—99; dir. univ. libr., Tex. A&M U., Kingsville, 1999—. Speaker and cons. in field. Founding editor jour. La Lista, 1983-84; founding indexer Chicano Periodical Index, 1981-86; reviewer jour. Voices of Youth Advocates, 1988-90; contbr. poetry and articles to books and jours. Recipient Silver award, Nat. Commn. Library and Info. Sci., 1996. Mem. ALA (com. on standing of women in profession, com. on profl. edn.), MLA, Assn. for Libr. and Info. Sci. Edn., Tex. Libr. Assn., Ariz. State Libr. Assn. (pres. svcs. Spanish speaking Roundtable 1988-90), Reforma (pres. El Paso chpt. 1983, pres. Ariz. chpt. 1989-90, nat. v.p. 1993-94, natpres. 1994-95), Unltd. Potential, Inc. (treas. 1988-89), Hispanic Leadership Inst. Alumni Assn.

ORTENBERG, ELISABETH CLAIBORNE See CLAIBORNE, LIZ

ORTH, SUSAN LYNN, judge; b. Evansville, Ind., Nov. 15, 1958; d. Orville William and A. Margaret Orth; m. Terrance D. Becker; 1 child, Brandy L. Orth Becker. BSc, Ind. State U., Terre Haute, 1981; MSc, U. Louisville, Ky., 1982; JD, Salman P. Chase Coll. Law, Ky., 1985. Cert.: (mediator advanced family and civil tng.). Chief dep. prosecutor Floyd County Prosecutor's Office, New Albany, Ind., 1987—2002; sr. prosecutor So. Dist. Ind., 2002—04; judge Floyd County Superior Ct., New Albany, 2004—. Instr. Nat. Dist. Attys. Assn., Columbia, SC, 1998—2002; mem. faculty Ind. Prosecuting Attys. Coun., Indpls., 1998—2002, Ind. Jud. Ctr., Indpls., 2005—; mem. state bd. law examiners com. on character and fitness, local com. on race and gender fairness Ind. Supreme Ct. Atty. New Albany City Coun., 1992—95; mem. judiciary and media com. Ind. Supreme Ct., 2004—; vol. Success by Six Metro United Way, New Albany, 2006; mem. bd. So. Christian Leadership Conf., 1998—, Metro United Way, 2004—; mem. Leadership So. Ind. Class of 2006. Named Citizen of Yr., New Albany Mayor's Office, 2002; recipient Drum Major award, So. Christian Leadership Conf., 1999. Mem.: Sherman Minton Inns of Ct. (pres. exec. bd. 2006—07), Am. Justice Inst. (mem. exec. bd. 2004—), Bus. and Profl. Women. Office: Floyd Superior Ct Room 200 City/G Bldg New Albany IN 47150

ORTIZ, AMY MOFFORD, surgical technologist; b. Port Charlotte, Fla., Sept. 19, 1978; d. Richard Murray Mofford and Ruth Marie Webb; m. Joseph Anthony Ortiz, Sept. 20, 2002. AA, Nat. Sch. Tech., N. Miami Beach, Fla., 2001. Cashier, produce stocker Stop & Shop, New Britain, Colo., 1997—98; caregiver Interim Healthcare, Farmington, Conn., 1991—99; pharmacy tech. CVS Pharmacy, New Britain, Conn., 1998—2002; op. rm. aide Fawcett Meml. Hosp., Pt. Charlotte, Fla., 2000—01; lab. asst. Nat. Sch. Tech., N. Miami Beach, 2003; surgical tehcnologist Meml. Hosp., Colo. Springs, 2005—06. Mem.: Assn. Surg. Tech. Republican. Avocation: bicycling. Home: 1410 Luna Dr Fountain CO 80817

ORTIZ, CHRISTINE E., nursing educator; b. Fresno, Calif., Feb. 20, 1951; d. Jessie J. and Elena L. Ortiz. AA, Fresno City Coll., Calif., 1972; MS, U. Calif., San Francisco, 1992; PhD, U. Calif. Sch. Nursing, San Francisco, 2000. RN Calif., 1977, cert. pub. health nurse, Calif., 1988. Staff nurse pre- and post-op Fresno County, Fresno, 1977—88, staff nurse CCU/MICU, 1980—88; pub. health nurse Fresno County Pub. Health Dept., 1989; per diem nurse Mt. Zion-U. State Calif. Home Care, San Francisco, 1989—91; per diem home health and hospice Vis. Nurses and Hospice, San Francisco, 1994—99; hospice per diem and case mgr. Kaiser Permanente, Oakland Hospice, Oakland, 1998—2000; quality assurance, quality outcome nurse, quality coord. Kaiser Permanente, Oakland, Calif., 2000; asst. prof. Calif. State U., Fresno, 2001—. Author: (article) Jour. Transcultural Nursing. Bd. mem. Fresno Covenant Found., 2000. Mem.: Am. Nurses Assn., Am. Pub. Health Assn., Nat. Assn. Hispanic Nurses, Assn. Cmty. Health Nurse Educators (mem. bylaws com. 2005—), Sigma Theta Tau (Recognition award, Mu Nu chpt. 2005). Office: Calif State Univ 2345 E San Ramon Ave M/S MH25 Fresno CA 93740-8031 Office Fax: 559-278-6360. Business E-Mail: cortiz@csufresno.edu.

ORTIZ, DENISE M., science educator; b. New Braunfels, Tex., July 25, 1973; d. Henry and Eva Diaz; m. Reynaldo Ortiz, Jan. 1, 1999; 1 child, Elizabeth Rae Diaz. BS in Biology, Southwest Tex. State U., San Marcos, 1998. Cert. tchr. biology and composite sci. Tex., 1998. Environ. sci. tchr. New Braunfels Ind. Sch. Dist., Tex., 1998—. Grantee Model Classroom, New Braunfels Ind. Sch. Dist. Mem.: NSTA (assoc.), Tex. Watch (assoc.). Office: New Braunfels HS 2551 N Loop 337 New Braunfels TX 78130 Office Phone: 830-627-6000.

ORTIZ, JONI LYNNE, science educator; b. Hawaii, Feb. 24, 1962; d. John Louis and Evelyn Sandlyn Ortiz; life ptnr. Sharon Diane Ortiz; 1 child, Jack Calvin. AS, Linn Benton CC, Oreg.; BS, MS, Oreg. State U. Ednl. asst. II Crescent Valley HS, Corvallis, Oreg., 2000—02; elem. and physics instr. Pacific U., Forest Grove, Oreg., 2001; sci. tchr. Chiefess Kamakahelei Mid. Sch., Lihue, Hawaii, 2003—. Office: Chiefess Kamakahelei Mid Sch 4431 Nuhou St Lihue HI 96766-8001

ORTIZ, KATHLEEN LUCILLE, travel consultant; b. Las Vegas, Feb. 8, 1942; d. Arthur L. and Anna (Lopez) Ortiz. BA, Loretto Hghts. Coll., 1963; MA, Georgetown U., 1966; cert. in tchg., Highlands U., 1980; cert. in travel, ABQ Travel Sch., 1984. Mgr. Montezuma Sq., Las Vegas, 1966—70; office mgr. Arts Food Market, Las Vegas, 1971-75; tchr. Robertson HS, Las Vegas, 1976-80; registered rep. IDS Fin. Svcs., N.Mex., 1980-84; travel cons. VIP Travel & Tours, Albuquerque, 1985-86, New Horizons Travel, Albuquerque, 1986-87, All World Travel, Albuquerque, 1987-90, Premium Travel Svcs., Albuquerque, 1990-91; travel cons., group tours Going Places Travel, Albuquerque, 1991—2003, All World Travel, Albuquerque, 2003—. Contbr. articles to newspapers. Fundraiser St. Anthony's Hosp., Las Vegas, 1969—75; founding mem. Citizens Com. Hist. Preservation, Las Vegas, 1977—79; mem. Hispanic Geneol. Rsch. Ctr., N.Mex., 1996—. Mem.: LWV (com. mem.), Internat. Airlines Travel Agt. Network, Georgetwon Club N.Mex. (bd. dirs. at large 1991—94, tarahumara task force 2002—03). Avocations: languages, photography, writing, genealogy. Home: 7600 Adele Pl NE Albuquerque NM 87109-5362 Office: All World Travel 5200 Eubank Blvd NE Ste C1 Albuquerque NM 87111 Office Phone: 505-294-5031.

ORTIZ, MAYRA ZOE, psychologist; b. Rio Piedras, Puerto Rico, Feb. 2, 1962; d. Guillermo Ortiz and Mirriam Cruz. PsyD, Yeshiva U., 2002. Lic. Psychologist NY. Psychologist Lincoln Med. Ctr., NY, 2001—02; psychologist, pvt. practice Bronx Lebanon Hosp., NY, 2002—04, Indsl. Medicine Assocs., 2004—. Mem.: NY State APA, APA.

ORTIZ-BUTTON, OLGA, social worker; b. Chgo., July 12, 1953; d. Luis Antonio and Pura (Acevedo) Ortiz; m. Dennis Vesley, Aug. 11, 1973 (div. 1976); m. Randall Russell Button, Nov. 3, 1984 (div. Oct. 1993); children: Josh, Jordan, Eli. BA, U. Ill., 1975; MSW, Western Mich. U., 1981. Cert. social worker, sch. social worker, lic. master social worker, bd. cert. diplomate Am. Bd. Clin. Social Workers, 2005, Am. Bd. Clin. Social Workers, 2006. Social svcs. dir. Champaign County Nursing Home, Urbana, Ill., 1976; social svcs. and activity dir. Lawton (Mich.) Nursing Home, 1977; job developer Southwestern Mich. Indian Ctr., Watervliet, 1977-78; staff asst. New Directions Alcohol Treatment Ctr., Kalamazoo, 1978; counselor, instr. Alcohol Hwy. Safety, Kalamazoo, 1978-79; clin. social worker Mecosta County Community Mental Health, Big Rapids, Mich., 1981-84; program dir. substance abuse Sr. Svcs., Inc., Kalamazoo, 1984-85; sch. social worker Martin (Mich.) Pub. Schs., 1985-96, J.C. Huizenga Charter Schs., Grand Rapids, Mich., 1996—; owner, therapist Plainwell (Mich.) Counseling Ctr., 1989-98; co-dir. Everlasting Covenant Ministry, Kalamazoo, 1997—2003; owner Christian Counseling Ctr. PLC, 2004—. S.W. cons. Med. Pers. Pool, 1993-94; founder, owner Christian Coun. Ctr., 2003—. Vol. social worker Hospice-Wings of Hope, Plainwell, 1984-85; mem. Hospice Quality Rev. Bd., 1993-96; supporter Students Against Aparteid South Africa, Kalamazoo, 1979-81; mem. World Vision and Countertop Ptnr., 1984-90; mem., vol. Christian Life Ctr., Kalamazoo, 1996; sponsor, vol. People for Ethical Treatment of Animals, 1986-91; vol. helper Sparkies for Awana Club Ch., 1989-95; consortium mem. Mich. Post Adoption Svc. System, 1994-97; co-founder Everlasting Covenant Ministry, Kalamazoo, 1997; sch. social worker Nat. Heritage Acads., 1997-2004; founder Christian Counseling Ctr., 2002. Rural Mental Health grantee, NIMH, 1979—81. Mem.: NASW, Nat. Assn. Christian Social Workers, Am. Assn. Christian Counselors, Mich. Assn. Sch. Social Workers. Avocations: walking, gardening, cross country skiing. Home: 1339 Cadet Ln Kalamazoo MI 49009-1838 Office Phone: 269-343-2117. Personal E-mail: obutton@ureach.com. E-mail: 14.obutton@heritageacademies.com.

ORTIZ-WALTERS, ROWENA, management educator; d. Ortiz and Rivera; m. Carl Allan Walters, May 14, 1999; 1 child, Ethan Andrew Walters. BS Chemistry, U. Conn., 1996; MBA, U. New Haven, 1999; PhD Mgmt., U. Conn., 2005. Chemist Uniroyal Chem. Corp., Middlebury, Conn., 1996—99; instr. bus. mgmt. U. Conn., Storrs, 2000—; asst. prof. entrepreneurship Quinnipiac U., 2004—. Asst. dir. Wolff Family Program in Entrepreneurship, Storrs, 2000—; pres. Mgmt. Doctoral Student Assn., 2001—02; advisor Quinnipiac U. Entrepreneurial Success team; presenter in field. Contbr. articles to profl. jours. Named Best Teaching Asst. of Yr., U. Conn., 2002, Best Student Tchr. of Yr., 2003; recipient 40 Under 40 award, Bus. Times; Summer Rsch grant, Quinnipiac U., 2005. Mem.: Mgmt. Doctoral Student Assn., Ea. Acad. Mgmt., Acad. Mgmt. Assn. (chair mentoring com., Best Symposium award 2004). Avocations: hiking, snowshoeing, reading, travel. Personal E-mail: rowena.ortiz-walters@quinnipiac.edu.

ORTLUND, ANNE (ELIZABETH ANNE ORTLUND), writer, musician; b. Wichita, Kans., Dec. 3, 1923; d. Joseph Burton and Mary Elizabeth (Weible) Sweet; m. Raymond Carl Ortlund, Apr. 27, 1946; children: Sherrill Anne, Margot Jeanne, Raymond Carl, Nels Robert. Student, Am. U., 1941—43; AA, Am. Guild Organists, 1944; MusB, U. Redlands, Calif., 1945. Organist Old-Fashioned Revival Hour and Joyful Sound, Radio World-Wide, 1960—75; spkr. Orgn. Renewal Ministries, Newport Beach, Calif., 1980—; composer hymns, anthems N.Y.C., 1963—77. Composer: Macedonia, 1966, 250 hymns; author: Up with Worship, 1975, Disciplines of the Beautiful Woman, 1977, The Gentle Ways of the Beautiful Woman, 1998, How Great Our Joy, 2001, Up With Worship, rev. and updated, 2001, A Fresh Start for Your Friendships, 2001; author: (with Raymond Carl Ortlund) The Best Half of Life, 1976, Discipling One Another, 1979, Children Are Wet Cement, 1981 (Christie award Christian Booksellers Assn., 1982), Joanna: A Story of Renewal, 1982, Building a Great Marriage, 1984; author: (with Raymond C. Ortlund) Staying Power, 1986, Disciplines of the Heart, 1987, Renewal, 1989, Confident in Christ, Disciplines of the Home, 1990, Fix Your Eyes on Jesus, 1991, My Sacrifice His Fire, 1993, In His Presence, 1995, Lord, Make My Life a Miracle, rev. and updated, 2002. Named Profl. Woman of Yr., Pasadena Bus. and Profl. Women, 1975; recipient SESAC award, Gospel Musicians, 1978. Home: 601 Lido Park Dr Apt 6E Newport Beach CA 92663-4403 Office: Renewal Ministries 4500 Campus Dr Ste 662 Newport Beach CA 92660-8828 Office Phone: 949-756-1313. E-mail: anne@ortlund.org.

ORTNER, TONI, language educator; b. Bklyn., Mar. 11, 1941; d. Melvin and Sylvia (Klein) O.; m. Stephen Michael Zimmerman, May 27, 1962 (div. 1988); 1 child, Lisa Lampe. BA, Hofstra U., Hempstead, N.Y., 1962; MA in English, We. Conn. State Coll., Danbury, Conn., 1979. Tchr. English dept. Monroe Coll., Bronx, N.Y. Tchr. Mercy Coll., Bronx C.C., Coll. New Rochelle, U. Conn., Norwalk C.C. Author: Woman in Search of Herself, 1971, To An Imaginary Lover, 1975, Never Stop Dancing, 1976, Entering Another Country, 1976, I Dream Now of the Sun, 1976, Stones, 1976, As If Anything Could Grow Back Perfect, 1979, Requiem, 1991, Real Stories, 2003; contbr. articles to profl. jours. Mem. AAUP, AAUW, Poets and Writers, The Authors Guild, Nat. Coun. Tchrs. English, Two Year Coll. Assn. Avocations: reading, hiking, travel. Home: 20 Sherwood Rd Stamford CT 06905-3601 Personal E-mail: ortnerway@aol.com.

ORULLIAN, B. LARAE, bank executive; b. Salt Lake City, May 15, 1933; d. Alma and Bessie (Bacon) O. Cert., Am. Inst. Banking, 1961, 63, 67; grad. Nat. Mortgage Sch., Ohio State U., 1969-71; DHL (hon.), Whittier Coll., 2004. With Tracy Collins Trust Co., Salt Lake City, 1951-54, Union Nat. Bank, Denver, 1954-57; exec. sec. Guaranty Bank, Denver, 1957-64, asst. cashier, 1964-67, asst. v.p., 1967-70, v.p., 1970-75, exec. v.p., 1975-77, also bd. dirs.; chair, CEO, pres. The Women's Bank N.A., Denver, 1977-97, Colo. Bus. Bankshares, Inc., 1980-97; vice chmn. Guaranty Bank and Trust Co., Denver, 1998—. Pres., bd. dirs. Lange Golf Co., Holladay (Utah) Bank; vice-chmn. bd. dirs. Frontier Airlines; bd. dirs. KBDI Channel 12TV; trustee Delta Dental Colo., 2005—. Treas. Girl Scouts U.S., 1981-87, 1st nat. v.p., chair exec. com., 1987-90, nat. pres., 1990-96; 1st vice chair world bd. World Assn. Girl Guides Girl Scouts, London. Recipient Woman Who Made a Difference award Internat. Women's Forum, 1994, Ultimate Woman of Colo. award, 2005, Women Enterprise award U. Denver, 2005; named to Colo. Women Hall of Fame, 1988; named Colo. Entrepreneur of Yr., Inc. Mag. and Arthyr Young and Co., 1989, Woman of Yr., YWCA, 1989, Citizen of Yr., EMC Lions Club, 1995, laureate Colo. Bus. Hall of Fame, 1999. Mem. Bus. and Profl. Women Colo. (3d Century award 1977, Unique Woman of Colo. 2005, Colo. Woman of Enterprise 2005), Internat. Women's Forum, Com. of 200. Independent. Mem. Lds Ch. Home: 6650 W 10th Pl Denver CO 80214 Office Phone: 303-296-9600.

ORY, MARCIA GAIL, social science researcher; b. Dallas, Feb. 8, 1950; d. Marvin Gilbert and Esther (Levine) O.; m. Raymond James Carroll, Aug. 13, 1972. BA magna cum laude, U. Tex., 1971; MA, Ind. U., 1972; PhD, Purdue U., 1976; MPH, Johns Hopkins U., 1981. Rsch. asst. prof. U. N.C., Chapel Hill, 1976-77, from adj. asst. prof. to assoc. prof. sch. pub. health, 1978-88; rsch. fellow U. Minn., Mpls., 1977-78; asst. prof. Sch. Pub. Health U. Ala., Birmingham, 1978-80; program dir. biosocial aging and health Nat. Inst. on Aging, Bethesda, Md., 1981-86, chief social sci. rsch. on aging, 1987—2001; prof. Sch. Rural Pub. Health Tex A&M U. Sys., College Station, 2001—. Dir. RWJF Nat. Program Office on Increasing Phys. Activity in the 50 Plus, 2001—, Program on Health Promotion and Aging. Contbr. articles, editor vols. to profl. jours. Mem. several nat. task forces on aging and health issues; bd. dirs. Ctr. for Health Improvement. Named Disting. Alumna, Purdue U.; named one of 5 Industry Innovators in Active Aging, Internat. Coun. on Active Aging, 2003; named to McKnights Long Term Care News 100, 1997; recipient Dept. HHS award, 1984, 1985, 1988, Dir.'s award, NIH, 1995, Merit award, 1999, 2001, Dir's Lifetime Achievement award, 2000, Polisher award, Gerontol. Soc. Am., 2001, award for excellence in rsch., Sch. Rural Pub. Health, 2006, Excellence in Program Innovation award, Archstone Found., 2005, Excellence in Rsch. award, Sch. Rural Pub. Health, 2005; fellow, Inst. for Advanced Study, LaTrobe U.,vMelbourne, Australia, 2004. Fellow: Soc. Behavioral Medicine (program chmn. pub. health track 1988—89, program com. 1991—92, program chair lifespan/devel. track 2001—02), Acad. for Behavioral Medicine Rsch., Gerontol. Soc. Am.; mem.: APHA (program chmn. 1986, gov. coun. 1986—88, chmn.-elect 1989—91, chmn. 1992—93, leadership group 1996—, chair older women's interest group), Am. Acad. Health Behavior, Am. Sociol. Assn. (regional reporter 1984—94, program com. 1986, nominations com. 1987, councilor-at-large 1992—93), Omicron Nu, Phi Kappa Phi. Avocations: walking, birding, travel. Office: Sch Rural Pub Health 1266 TAMU College Station TX 77843-1266 Office Phone: 979-458-1373. Business E-Mail: mory@srph.tamhsc.edu.

OSBORN, JANIE DYSON, early childhood education educator; b. Huntsville, Ala., July 25, 1946; d. Coy Wayne and Alice Caledonia (Hill) Dyson; m. D. Keith Osborn, June 21, 1974; 1 dau., Michelle. BS, U. Ala.-Tuscaloosa, 1967, MA, 1969, EdD, 1973. Tchr. Bessemer City (Ala.) Schs., 1967-70; adminstr. Jefferson County Head Start, Birmingham, Ala., 1967; reading specialist Hale County Pub. Schs., Akron, Ala., 1971; assoc. dir. Belser-Parton Reading Ctr., Tuscaloosa, 1972-73; coordinator early childhood edn. Columbus (Ga.) Coll., 1973-75; prof., coordinator early childhood edn. North Ga. Coll., Dahlonega, 1975—; cons. World Book-Childcraft, Inc., Chgo., U.S. Dept. Edn. Child Devel. Assoc. Program, Washington, Ga. Dept. Edn. Author: (with D. Keith Osborn) Cognitive Tasks, 1974, Discipline and Classroom Management, 1981, 3d edit., 1989, Cognition in Early Childhood, 1983; contbr. numerous articles to profl. jours. Cons. Kids on the Block Jr. Service League, Gainesville, Ga., 1983; trustee Gainesville Ind. Sch., 1988-90. Recipient Outstanding New Prof. award Columbus Coll., 1974; fellow NDEA, 1971-73, Edn. Testing Service, 1973. Mem. NEA (del. 1971), Lower Chattahoochee Assn. for Young Children (pres. 1973-74), Ga. Assn. Young Children (pres. 1975-76), So. Assn. Children Under Six (exec. bd. 1975-76), Internat. Reading Assn., Alpha Upsilon Alpha (pres. Northwestern U. chpt. 1989).

OSBORN, JUNE ELAINE, pediatrician, microbiologist, educator, foundation administrator; b. Endicott, NY, May 28, 1937; d. Leslie A. and Dora W. (Wright) Osborn; children: Philip I. Levy, Ellen D. Levy, Laura A. Jana. BA, Oberlin Coll., Ohio, 1957; MD, Western Res. U., 1961; DSc (hon.), U. Med. Dental Sch. N.J., 1990, Emory U., 1993, Oberlin Coll., 1993, Rutgers U., 1994, Case Western Res. U., 1997, SUNY, Stony Brook, 1999, U. Wis., 2004; DMS (hon.), Yale U., 1992; LHD (hon.), Med. Coll. Pa., 1994. Intern, resident in pediatrics Harvard U. Hosp., 1961—64; fellow Johns Hopkins, 1964—65, U. Pitts., 1965—66; prof. med. microbiology and pediat. U. Wis. Med. Sch., Madison, Wis., 1966—84, prof. pediat. and microbiology, 1974—84, assoc. dean Grad. Sch., 1975—84; dean Sch. Pub. Health U. Mich. Sch. Pub. Health, 1984—93; prof. epidemiology, pediat. and communicable diseases U. Mich. Sch. Pub. Health and Med. Sch., 1984—96, prof. emeritus, 1997—. Pres. Josiah Macy, Jr. Found., 1997—; mem. rev. panel viral vaccine efficacy FDA, 1973—79, mem. vaccines and related biol. products adv. com., 1981—85; mem. exptl. virology study sect. Divsn. Rsch. Grants, NIH, 1975—79; mem. med. affairs com. Yale U. Coun., 1981—86; chmn. life scis. associateships rev. panel NRC, 1981—84; mem. U.S. Army Med. R&D Adv. Com., 1983—85; chmn. working group on AIDS and the Nation's Blood Supply NHLBI, 1984—89; chmn. WHO Planning Group on AIDS and the Internat. Blood Supply, 1985—86. Contbr. articles to profl. jours.; mem. editl. bd.: Jour. AMA, 2002—. Active task force in AIDS, Inst. of Medicine, 1986; adv. com. Robert Wood Johnson Found. AIDS Health Svcs. Program, 1986—91; nat. adv. com. on health of pub. program Pew and Rockefeller Founds.; active Global Commn. on AIDS, WHO, 1988—92; chmn. Nat. Commn. on AIDS, 1989—93; trustee Kaiser Found., 1990—98, Case Western Reserve U., Cleve., 1993—97; nat. vaccine adv. com. HHS, 1995—98; adv. coun. Nat. Inst. on Drug Abuse, 1995—98; internat adv. bd. Nat. Acads., 2002—05; bd. dirs. Legal Action Ctr., 1994—2001, Ctr. for Health Care Strategies, 1998—2003, The Mind Inst., 2003—05, US Pharmacoperia Bd.,

2005—. Recipient NIH Pub. Svc. award, 2000, Scientific Freedom and Responsibility award, AAAS, 1994; grantee NIH, 1969, 1972, 1974—75, Nat. Multiple Sclerosis Soc., 1971. Fellow: Infectious Diseases Soc. Am., Am. Acad. Microbiology, Am. Acad. Arts and Scis., Am. Acad. Pediat.; mem.: Inst. Medicine (health promotion and disease prevention bd. 1987—90, coun. mem. 1995—2000), Soc. Pediat. Rsch., Am. Assn. Immunologists. Office: Josiah Macy Jr Found 44 E 64th St New York NY 10021-7306 Office Phone: 212-486-2424.

OSBORN, KRISTY LYNN, elementary school educator; d. Robert Turpin Osborn and Kathryn Judith Castgel. BEd, Ball State U., Muncie, Ind., 1993; MLS, Ind. U. Purdue U., Indpls., 2006. Ind. mentor tchr. Tchr. grade 3 Abraham Lincoln Elem., Indpls., 1993—, tchr. music and art K-2, 2005—06. Pres. Perry Twp. Reading Coun., Indpls., 2003—05. Named Tchr. of Yr., Abraham Lincoln Elem. Sch., Indpls., 2006; grantee, Perry Twp. Sch. Dist., 1994—2001. Office: Abraham Lincoln Elem Sch 5241 Brehob Rd Indianapolis IN 46217 E-mail: kosborn@msdpt.k12.in.us.

OSBORN, MARY JANE MERTEN, biochemist, educator; b. Colorado Springs, Colo., Sept. 24, 1927; d. Arthur John and Vivien Naomi (Morgan) Merten; m. Ralph Kenneth Osborn, Oct. 26, 1950. BA, U. Calif., Berkeley, 1948; PhD, U. Wash., 1958. Postdoctoral fellow, dept. microbiology NYU Sch. Medicine, N.Y.C., 1959-61, instr., 1961-62, asst. prof., 1962-63; asst. prof. dept. molecular biology Albert Einstein Coll. Medicine, Bronx, NY, 1963-66, assoc. prof., 1966-68; prof. dept. microbiology U. Conn. Health Ctr., Farmington, 1968—, dept. head, 1980—2002, prof. dept. molecular, microbial and structural biology, 2003—. Mem. bd. sci. counselors Nat. Heart, Lung and Blood Inst., 1975-79; mem. Nat. Sci. Bd., 1980-86; adv. coun. Nat. Inst. Gen. Med. Sci., 1983-86, divsn. rsch. grants NIH, 1989-94, chair, 1992-94; trustee Biosci. Info. Systems, 1986-91, chair, 1990-91; mem. German Am. Acad. Coun., 1994-97; mem. space scis. bd. NRC, 1994-2000, chair com. space biology and medicine, 1994-2000; cochair com. on indications for waterborne pathogens, 2002-03. Assoc. editor Jour. Biol. Chemistry, 1978-80; contbr. articles in field of biochemistry and molecular biology to profl. jours. Mem. rsch. com. Am. Heart Assn., 1972-77, chair, 1976-77. NIH fellow, 1959-61; NIH grantee, 1962-95; NSF grantee, 1965-68; Am. Heart Assn. grantee, 1968-71 Fellow Am. Acad. Arts and Scis. (coun. 1988-91), NAS (coun. 1990-93, com. sci. engring. and pub. policy 1993-96); mem. Am. Acad. Microbiology (bd. govs. 1994-2000), Am. Fedn. Soc. Exptl. Biology (pres. 1982-83), Am. Soc. Biol. Chemists (pres. 1981-82), Am. Soc. Microbiology. Democrat. Office: U Conn Health Ctr Dept Molec Micro and Struct Biology MC3205 Farmington CT 06030-0001 Office Phone: 860-679-4206.

OSBORN, NANCYJEAN MARIE, principal; b. N.Y., Apr. 29, 1956; d. John A. and Rita M. Smith; m. Douglas E. Osborn, Nov. 27, 1975; children: Laura, Jason, Elizabeth. BA in Psychology, St. John Fisher Coll., Rochester, N.Y., 1980; MS in Edn., Nazareth Coll., Rochester, N.Y., 1989; degree in Ednl. Adminstrn., SUNY, Brockport, 1998. Cert. tchr. elem. edn. N.Y., tchr. spl. edn. N.Y., in edn. adminstrn. N.Y. Tchr. Diocese of Rochester, 1985—88, Churchville Chili Ctrl. Sch. Dist., NY, 1988—90, Rush-Henrietta Ctrl. Sch. Dist., NY, 1991—2000; asst. prin. Grates Chili Ctrl. Sch. Dist., Rochester, 2000—02; prin. elem. sch. Byron-Bergen Ctrl. Sch. Dist., NY, 2002—. Contbr. articles to mags. Vol. Camp Ground Days and Spl. Times, Mendon, NY, 1997—; bd. dirs. Gillam Grant Cmty. Ctr., Bergen, NY, 2005—. Named Educator of Excellence, N.Y. State English Coun., 1999; recipient Econs. award, Mobile Chem., 1984; Empire Challenger fellow, 1985. Mem.: ACSD, Sch. Adminstrs. Assn. N.Y. State, Nat. Assn. Elem. Sch. Prins., Phi Delta Kappa. Avocations: reading, quilting, travel. Office: Byron Bergen CSD 6971 W Bergen Rd Bergen NY 14416

OSBORNE, GAYLE ANN, manufacturing executive; b. Bossier City, La., Feb. 1, 1951; d. Walker Henry and Marjorie Evelyn (Cook) Pyle; m. Paul A. Huelsman, June 28, 1969 (div. Jan. 1976); children: Ginger, Paula; m. Luther L. Osborne, Sept. 10, 1976 (div. Aug. 1989). Sales assoc. Model City Real Estate, Midwest City, Okla., 1972-73; mgr. adminstrn. Equipment Renewal Co., Oklahoma City, 1973-76, Gulfco Industries, Inc., Casper, Wyo., 1976-77; with B&B Tool and Supply Co., Inc., Casper, 1977, 79, 81, v.p., 1983—, pres., 1990—, BOP Repair & Machine, Inc., Casper, 1981—. Owner Osborne Leasing Co. Mem. Casper Petroleum Club, Nat. Skeet Shoot Assn. (All Am. Skeet Team), Amateur Trapshooting Assn. Democrat. Avocations: skeet shooting, hunting, scuba diving. Home: 825 N Robertson Rd Casper WY 82604 Business E-Mail: gosborne@mail.bbtoolbop.com.

OSBORNE, GLENNA JEAN, health facility administrator; b. East Rainelle, W.Va., Jan. 5, 1945; d. B.J. and Jean Ann (Haranac) Osborne; m. Thomas Joseph Ferrante Jr., June 11, 1966 (div. Nov. 1987); 1 child, Thomas Joseph Osborne; m. Brian Mark Popp, Aug. 13, 1988 (div. Oct. 1999). BA cum laude, U. Tampa, 1966; MA, Fairleigh Dickinson U., 1982; cert., Kean Coll., 1983. Cert. English, speech, dramatic arts tchr., prin./supr.; cert. nursing child assessment feeding scale and nursing child assessment tchg. scale, DENVER II cert., HOME cert. Tchr. Raritan H.S., Hazlet, N.J., 1966, Keyport (N.J.) Pub. Schs., 1968-86, coord. elem. reading and lang. arts, 1980-84, supr. curriculum and instrn., 1984-86; prin. Weston Sch., Manville, N.J., 1986-88, The Bartle Sch., Highland Park, N.J., 1988-91, Orange Ave. Sch., Cranford, N.J., 1991-92; dir. The Open Door Youth Shelter, Binghamton, N.Y., 1992-94; child protective investigator supr. Dept. Health and Rehab. Svcs., Orlando, Fla., 1994-95; program supr. Children's Home Soc., Sanford, Fla., 1995; clin. supr. Healthy Families-Orange, Orlando, Fla., 1995-98; dir. program ops. Children's Home Soc., Tavares, Fla., 1998—2004; adminstr. Lifestream Acad., Fla., 2004—. Regional trainer Individualized Lang. Arts, Weehawken, N.J., 1976-86; cons. McDougal/Littel Pubs., Evanston, Ill., 1982-83; chair adv. bd. women's residential program Ctr. for Drug Free Living, Orlando, 1996. Contbr. chpt.: A Resource Guide of Differentiated Learning Experiences for Gifted Elementary Students, 1981. V.p. Sch. Readiness Coalition for Lake County, 1999; mem. adv. coun. Lake Cmty. Action Agy., Head Start, 1999; bd. dir. Mt. Dora Cmty. Trust, 2002—04, Leadership Lake County, 2004; bd. dir., sec. Ctrl. Healthy Start Coalition, 1999—2004; bus. adv. coun. Nat. Rep. Congl. Com., 2005; Sunday sch. tchr. Reformed Ch., Keyport, 1975—80, supt. Sunday sch., 1982—84. Mem.: Elks, Order Ea. Star, Mt. Dora Kiwanis (bd. dirs. 2000, pres. 2002—03, 2002—03, internat. Hixson fellow 2003, hon. chairperson, bus. advisory council, nat. rep. congressional com., Divsn. 9 Lt. Gov.'s award outstanding svc. to club and cmty. 2003), Phi Delta Kappa. Republican. Methodist. Avocation: writing. Office: Lifestream Academy PO Box 491000 Leesburg FL 34749-1000

OSBORNE, HANNAH CHRISTINE, school counselor, social worker; b. Houlton, Maine, Jan. 21, 1951; d. Charles Putnam and Carol Maxine (Gardner) Osborne; m. Kerry Allan Stevens, Jan. 1, 1981 (div. Oct. 1989); 1 child, Nathan Allan. BA in Sociology, U. Maine, 1973, MS in Human Devel. summa cum laude, 2005; basic police cert., Maine Criminal Justice Acad., 1974. LSW Maine Dept. Profl. and Fin. Regulation, 1987-91, 95-. Juvenile officer Waterville Police Dept., 1974-78; youth outreach project dir. YMCA, Waterville, 1979; child welfare caseworker Dept. of Human Svcs., Skowhegan, Maine, 1980-81; victim/witness advocate Office of the Dist. Atty., Skowhegan, 1983-85; child welfare caseworker Dept. of Human Svcs., Skowhegan, 1985-88, institutional abuse program specialist Augusta, Maine, 1988-91; child welfare caseworker Dept. of Family and Children Svcs., Atlanta, 1991-94; sch. social worker Maine Sch. Adminstrv. Dist. 74, North Anson, Maine, 1994—99; family resource coord. Maine Jud. Dept., 1999—2001; sch. counselor Maine Sch. Adminstrv. Dist. 47, Oakland, Maine, 2001—. Trainer, presenter Maine Criminal Justice Acad., Waterville, 1975-77, 84; adv. bd. Crisis and Counseling Ctr., Waterville, 1976-78, Crisis Stabilization Unit, Skowhegan, 1984-85, Youth and Family Svcs., Skowhegan, 1986-88; criminal justice adv. com. North Kennebec Regional Planning Com., 1979; presenter and spkr. in field. Foster Parent adv. com. Dept. of Human Svcs., Augusta, 1988; pre-trial intervention com. Cmty. Justice Project, Waterville, 1975; mem. various Gov.'s and Legis. Task Forces, 1976-77, 84-85, 99-01. Named Police Officer of the Yr. Greater Waterville Area Exch. Club, 1975, Outstanding Child Welfare Caseworker Edmund S. Muskie Inst. Pub. Affairs, 1990; recipient Disting. Svc. award Maine Dept. Human Svcs., 1991, James Handley award Maine Criminal Justice Acad., 1974, Editor's Choice award advanced poetic accomplishment, 2004, Local Hero award The Healthy Maine Partnership, 2006. Mem. MENSA, Phi Kappa Phi. Avocations: dance, hiking, writing. Office: Maine Sch Adminstrv Dist 47 131 Messalonskee High Dr Oakland ME 04963

OSBORNE, JUDITH BARBOUR, artist; b. Winnipeg, Man., Can., Oct. 14, 1950; came to U.S., 1952; d. John Anderson and Laura May (Jones) Barbour; m. Frederick Spring Osborne Jr., Feb. 15, 1986; children: Sheila, Thomas, Sophia, Jessica. BFA, Univ. of Arts, Phila., 1974; student, Vt. Studio Ctr., 1984-89; MFA, Pa. Acad. Fine Arts, Phila., 1997. Prin. Barbour CalliGraphics, Phila., 1976—2002; dir. publs. and publicity Phila. Conf. on Calligraphic Arts, Phila., 1982; mem. faculty Phila. Coll. Art (now U. of Arts), 1982-85, 92, 00, Drexel U., Phila., 1991—2002; faculty Innovations Internat. Calligraphy Conf., N.Y., 1987; exhbns. coord. Calleidoscope Internat. Calligraphy Conf., Trenton, NJ, 1993; guest lectr., workshop instr. Nantucket Island Sch. of Design and Arts, 2004. Guest curator Kamin Gallery, U. Pa., Phila., 1993, 95; exhbn. juror Phila. Calligraphers' Soc., 1989, 91, 94-95, 98, Phila. Sketch Club, 2002; spkr. 19th Internat. Calligraphy Conf., Guilford, Conn., 1999; lectr. in field. One-woman shows include Rourke Art Gallery, Moorhead, Minn., 1999, Phila. Art Alliance, 1999, Artists' House, 1998, 2000, 2002, Living Arts, Tulsa, Okla., 2000, Shipley Sch., Bryn Mawr, Pa., 2000, Delaware Ctr. for Contemporary Arts, 2004, Gallery Siano, Phila., 2004, Alexey von Schlippe Gallery, U. Conn, Avery Point, 2005, DeLong Gallery, Toronto, Can., 2005, West Liberty State Coll., W.Va., 2006, So. Vt. Arts Ctr., Manchester, 2006, Chester Gallery, Conn., 2006; exhibited in group shows at Nat. Arts Club, NYC, 1990, Pa. State Mus., Harrisburg, 1994, 2000-01, Am. Coll., Bryn Mawr, Pa., 1996, Nexus Found. for Today's Art, Phila., 1997, Del. Ctr. for Contemporary Art, 2002, Parallels Gallery, Phila., 2002, Tenri Cultural Inst., NYC, 2002, Shaanxi Mus., Xian, China, 2003, Ice House Gallery, Berkeley Springs, W.Va., 2004, Berman Mus. Art, Collegeville, Pa., 2004, Mobile (Ala.) Mus. Art, 2004, Calligrammes Gallery, Ottawa, Can., 2004-06, NY Hall Sci., Queens, 2005, Gallery One, Old Saybrook, Conn., 2005, Calif. State Polytechnic U., Pomona, Calif., 2006; represented in permanent collections Scripps Coll., Claremont, Calif., Mobile Mus. Art, Ala., Brown U., Providence, RI, Fed. Res. Bank Phila., Blue Cross, Rourke Art Gallery Mus., Moorhead, Barbour/Ladouceur Archs., Mpls.; also pvt. collections; collaborator Sophia Osborne Dance Assocs., 1999-2001, poet Jena Osman, 2001-04; contbr. articles to mags. and newspapers including Art Matters, 1997-2001, Letter Arts Rev., 2003. Recipient Best of Show Abington (Pa.) Art Ctr., 1990; Pa. Acad. Fine Arts fellow, Phila., 1997, Independence Found. fellow, 2001. Mem. Coll. Art Assn., Phila. Calligraphers' Soc. (bd. mem., publs. editor 1980-85), Inst. Noetic Scis. Avocation: metaphysics. Address: PO Box 4023 Old Lyme CT 06371-4023

OSBORNE, MARIE-ANGELA, journalist; b. Detroit, Jan. 20, 1957; d. Angelo Guerino and Domenica Mazzocco; m. John Hampton Osborne, Dec. 10, 1945; children: John Taylor children: Domenique Nicole, Robert Hampton. BA, U. Detroit, 1979. Anchor, reporter WJR Radio-ABC Radio, Detroit, 1994—2004; reporter, anchor WWJ Newsradio 950- CBS Radio, Southfield, Mich., 2004—. Adj. instr. Wayne State U., Detroit, 2000—03. Chmn. Lighthouse Oakland County, Pontiac, Mich., 1992. Recipient Edward R. Murrow award, Radio TV News Dirs. Assn., 1997, 1998, 2000, Clarion award, Women in Comm., 1997, 1998, Headliner award, Atlantic City Press Club, 1998. Mem.: Soc. Profl. Journalists. Office: CBS Radio-WWJ Newsradio 950 26495 American Dr Southfield MI 48034 Office Phone: 248-945-9950.

OSBORNE, MARY POPE, writer; b. Ft. Sill, Okla., May 20, 1949; d. William Perkins and Barnette (Dickens) Pope; m. William R. Osborne, May 16, 1976. BA in Religion, U. N.C., 1971. Author: Run, Run, As Fast As You Can, 1982, Love Always, Blue, 1983, Best Wishes, Joe Brady, 1984, Mo to the Rescue, 1985, Last One Home, 1986, Beauty and the Beast, 1987, Favorite Greek Myths, 1988, American Tall Tales, 1990, The Many Lives of Benjamin Franklin, 1990, Moon Horse, 1991, George Washington, Leader of a New Nation, 1991, Spider Kane Mystery Series, 1992, 1993, Magic Tree House Series, 1992—, Haunted Waters, 1994, Molly and the Prince, 1994, Favorite Norse Myths, 1996, One World, Many Religions, 1996, Rocking Horse Christmas, 1997, Favorite Medieval Tales, 1998, Standing in the Light, 1998, The Life of Jesus, 1998, Adaline Falling Star, 2000, My Brothers Keeper, 2000, My Secret War, 2000, Kate and the Beanstalk, 2000, The Brave Little Seamstress, 2002, After the Rain, 2002, The One-Eyed Giant, 2002, The Land of the Dead, 2002, New York's Bravest, 2002, Tales from the Odyssey, 2002, Happy Birthday, America, 2003, Magic Tree House Research Guides, 2000—, Magic Tree House Merline Missions, 2000—, Sleeping Bobby, 2005, Pompeii: Lost and Found, 2006; co-author (with Will Osborne): A Time to Dance, 2003. Recipient Disting. Alumna award, U. N.C., Chapel Hill, 1994, Distinctive Contbn. to Arts award, N.Y. Carolina Club. Mem.: PEN, Authors League Fund (bd. dirs.), Authors Guild (pres. 1993—97). Office: Brandt & Brandt Lit Agy 1501 Broadway Ste 2310 New York NY 10036-5689

OSBORNE-KAY, TRISHA ANN, elementary school educator; b. New Kingston, Ri, Oct. 5, 1968; d. Raymond Paul and Patricia Elaine Osborne; m. John Edward Kay, Oct. 6, 2001. BA in Humanities, Tex. A&M U., 1993. Cert. tchr. Tex. History tchr. Incarnate Word Mid. Level, Corpus Christi, Tex., 1994—, chmn. history dept., 2000, coach, 2005—. Vol. worker Dem. Party, Corpus Christi, 2000. Mem.: Nat. Coun. Social Studies (assoc.). American Independent. Roman Catholic. Avocations: travel, crafting, photography. Office: Incarnate Word Middle Level 2917 Austin St Corpus Christi TX 78404 Office Phone: 361-883-0857 410. Business E-Mail: osbornet@iwacc.org.

OSBOURNE, KELLY LEE, television personality, singer; b. London, Oct. 27, 1984; d. Ozzy and Sharon Osbourne. Singer: (albums) Shut Up, 2002, Changes, 2003, (songs) Papa Don't Preach, 2002, (concert DVD) Live at the Electric Ballroom, 2004; co-star (TV series) The Osbournes, 2002—, creative cons., 2002—. Office: Sanctuary Records Group Sanctuary House 45-53 Sinclair Rd London W14 ONS England

OSBOURNE, SHARON ARDEN, music manager, television personality; b. London, Oct. 9, 1952; d. Don and Hope Arden; m. Ozzy Osbourne, July 4, 1982; children: Aimee, Kelly, Jack; 2 stepchildren. Mgr. Ozzy Osbourne, 1980—; founder & organizer OzzFest, 1995—; co-star The Osbournes, MTV, 2002—04; host The Sharon Osbourne Show, 2003—04. Actor(voice): (films) Garfield: A Tale of Two Kitties, 2006; author: Sharon Osbourne Extreme, 2006. Founder Sharon Osbourne Colon Cancer Found., 2004—. Named One of People Magazine's 50 Most Beautiful People, 2002. Office: The Osbournes MTV Networks 2600 Colorado Ave Santa Monica CA 90404

OSBURN, ELLA KATHERINE, elementary school educator; b. Waycross, Ga., Nov. 25, 1961; d. William Daniel and Mabelle Irene (Tatum) O. BS in Home and Consumer Econs., Freed-Hardeman Coll., Henderson, Tenn., 1984, MEd in Curriculum and Instrn., 1992. Cert. in elem. edn. K-8, Ga. Tchr. 1st grade South Ga. Christian Acad., Albany, 1986-88; substitute tchr. Gwinnett County Schs., Lawrenceville, Ga., 1988-89; childcare worker The Children's Home, Valdosta, Ga., 1989-90; sec. Ga. Christian, Valdosta, 1990-91; tchr. 1st grade S.W. Elem.-Hancock County Schs., 1994-96. Author: (curriculum guide) Log of Intervention and Curriculum Guides for Reading Difficulties, 1991-92. Mem. NEA, ASCD, Ga. Assn. Educators, Smithsonian Inst. Mem. Ch. of Christ. Avocations: travel, antiques, miniature golf. Home: PO Box 575 Hoschton GA 30548-0575

OSBY, LARISSA GEISS, artist; b. Artemowsk, Russia, June 7, 1928; came to U.S., 1951, naturalized, 1958; d. Andrew Frank and Valentine G. (Pogoreloff) Geiss; m. Howard M. Osby, June 7, 1952; children: Erik Andrew, Karin Marian. Student, U. Goettingen, Germany, 1947, 48, 49, Acad. Art, 1949-50, U. Munich, 1949-50; postgrad., U. Goettingen, Germany, 1951. BA in Philosophy U. Goettingen, Germany, 1950, MA in Philosophy, 1951; rsch. asst., translator, med. illustrator U. Pitts. Med. Sch., 1952-53; art instr. Pitts. Ctr. for Arts, 1961-64, 88-90; pvt. art tchr. Pitts., 1961-64; adv. artist Pitts. Bd. Edn., 1964-66; instr. anatomy, drawing and painting High Sch. for Creative and Performing Arts, Pitts., 1984-96. One woman shows at, AAP Gallery, Pitts., 1960, Pitts. Plan for Art Gallery, 1961, 63, 65, 68, 71, 79, Carnegie Inst., Pitts., 1972, Pa. State U., 1973, Duquesne U., Pitts., 1980, Pitts. Ctr. for Arts, 1983, St. Vincent Coll., 1983, others; exhibited in group shows at, Butler Inst., Youngstown, Ohio, 1958, 59, 79, 86, Chautauqua Nat. Anns., 1964, 73, St. Paul Art Center, 1963, Marietta Coll., 1968, Walker Art Center, Mpls., 67, William Penn Meml. Mus., Harrisburg, Pa., 1971, also museums in Germany, France, Scotland, numerous others; represented in permanent collections at, Carnegie Inst., U. Pitts., Pitts. Bd. Edn., Am. Cancer Soc., Alcoa, U.S. Steel, Westinghouse, Koppers Co., others; commns. include, Koppers Co., First Fed. Savings & Loan Assn., Pitts., U.S. Steelworkers Am., others. Recipient Citation as Woman of Distinction, Gov. Pa., 1972; named Artists of Yr., Pitts. Ctr. for Arts, 1983, award Women in Art, 1995, 96, 20 Jury awards, others. Mem. Abstract Group Pitts. (pres. 1964-65), Associated Artists Pitts. (bd. dirs. 1965-68, 80-83), Pitts. Ctr. for Arts, Concept Gallery. Democrat. Address: 2665 Hunters Point Dr Wexford PA 15090-7992

OSBY, MARY ANN CAROLINE, secondary school educator; b. Chgo., Jan. 12, 1948; m. Don Osby; children: Louise Anne Patterson, Olivia Jacqueline. BA in History, U. NC, Asheville, 1988. Cert. tchr. NC. Tchr. Charles D. Owen H.S., Black Mountain, NC, 1988—. Home: 21 Saw Mill Rd Horse Shoe NC 28742 Office Phone: 828-686-3852. Business E-Mail: maryann.osby@bcsemail.org.

OSEGUERA, PALMA MARIE, retired career officer; b. Kansas City, Mo., Dec. 29, 1946; d. Joseph Edmund and Palma Louise (Utke) O'Donnell; m. Alfonso Oseguera, Jan. 1, 1977; stepchildren: Kristie M. Daniels, Michelle L. Nielson, Lori A. Kelley. BA in Phys. Edn., Marycrest Coll., 1969. Commd. 2d lt. USMC, 1969, advanced through grades to col., 1991; asst. Marine Corps exch. officer Hdqs. and Hdqs. Squadron, Marine Corps Air Sta., Beaufort, SC, 1969; classified material control officer Hdqs. and Svcs. Battalion, Camp S.D. Butler, Okinawa, 1971—73; adminstrv. officer, asst. Marine Corps exch. officer Marine Corps Air Sta., El Toro, Santa Ana, Calif., 1973—76, Marine Corps exch. officer Yuma, Ariz., 1976—77; asst. Marine Corps exch. officer Hdqrs. and Support Bn., Marine Corps Devel. and Edn. Command, Quantico, Va., 1977—79; Marine Corps exch. officer Hqrs. Marine Corps, Washington, 1979—80; adminstrv. officer Marine Air Base Squadon 46, Marine Air Group 46, Marine Corps Air Sta., El Toro, Santa Ana, 1981—83, Hdqs. and Maintanence Squadron 46, Marine Air Group 46, Marine Corps Air Sta., El Toro, Santa Ana, 1983—85, Mobilization Tng. Unit Calif. 53, Landing Force Tng. Command, Pacific, San Diego, 1985—89, 3d Civil Affairs Group, L.A., 1989; dep. asst. chief of staff G-1 I Marine Expeditionary Force, Individual Mobilization Augumentee Detachment, Camp Pendleton, Calif., 1990—91; assoc. mem. Mobilization Tng. Unit Del. 01, Del., 1992—94; adminstrn. officer Mobilization Tng. Unit, CA-53, EWTG Pac, NAB, Coronado, San Diego, 1994—96; exch. officer MWRSPT ACT IMA Det MCB, Camp Pendleton, Calif., 1996—99; ret. from 30 yrs. commissioned svc. USMCR, 1999. Choir St. Elizabeth Seaton, Woodbridge, Va., 1978-80, St. Patricks, Arroyo Grande, Calif., 1990-94; vol. Hospice, San Luis Obispo, 1995-2000; active Los Osos (Calif.) Veteran's Events Com., 1994-2000; lector, Eucharistic min., Martha Min. St. Patrick's Cath. Ch., Arroyo Grande, 2004—. Mem. AAUW (past libr.), Marine Corps Assn., Marine Corps Res. Officer Assn., Marine Corps Aviation Assn. (12 dist. dir. 1987), Women in Mil. Svc. for Am., Woman Marine Assn., Marine Corps League. Republican. Roman Catholic. Avocations: skiing, gardening, reading, horseback riding, genealogy. Home: 728 Scenic Cir Arroyo Grande CA 93420-1617

OSENBAUGH, KIMBERLY W., lawyer; b. Mpls., Nov. 28, 1948; BA, U. Iowa, 1970, JD with distinction, 1973. Bar: Wash. 1973. Ptnr., chair Bankruptcy and Insolvency Practice, mem. exec. com. Preston Gates & Ellis LLP, Seattle. Trustee Seattle Ctr. Found. Mem.: ABA, Fed. Bar Assn., We. Dist. Wash., Am. Bankruptcy Inst., Wash. State Bar Assn., King County Bar Assn., Phi Alpha Delta. Office: Preston Gates & Ellis LLP Ste 2900 925 Fourth Ave Seattle WA 98104-1158 Office Phone: 206-370-8288. Office Fax: 206-370-6147. Business E-Mail: kimo@prestongates.com.

OSER, MARY S., music educator; b. Charlotte, NC, Mar. 28, 1966; d. Seth and Margaret Scott; 1 child, Sidney. MusB in Edn., Fla. State U., Tallahassee, 1988. Dir. bands Wellington H.S., Fla., 1991—. Office: Wellington High School 2101 Greenview Shores Blvd Wellington FL 33414 Office Phone: 561-753-9444. Office Fax: 561-795-4934. E-mail: oserm@palmbeach.k12.fl.us.

OSGOOD, JUDY KAY, clinical psychologist, educator, consultant; b. Rockford, Ill., Sept. 13, 1952; d. Harold Joseph and Dorothy Anne (Beetle) O. BA, U. Ill., 1974, MEd, 1978, PhD, 1985. Teaching asst. U. Ill., Urbana, 1976-78, 80; counselor Univ. High Sch., Urbana, 1979-81; clin. counselor intern U. Ill. Counseling Ctr., Urbana, 1982-83; clin. counselor Prairie Ctr. Substance Abuse, Champaign, Ill., 1983-85; clinician, cons. DuPage County Mental Health Ctr., Wheaton, Ill., 1985-86; instr. Loyola U., Chgo., 1989-90; clin. psychologist Lifeline, Weiss Hosp., Chgo., 1985-90; psychology sect. head Carle Clinic Assn., Urbana, 1990-95; corp. cons. IBM Corp., 1994—95; cons. Cunningham Children's Home, Urbana, 1995—. Clin. instr. Coll. Medicine (Psychiatry) U. Ill., Urbana, 1991—; psychologist cons. Ill. child death rev. team Ill. Dept. Children and Family Svcs., 2005—, pyschol. test conductor, 1999—; consulting psychologist forensic cases pvt. and pub. sectors, 2000-. Mem. APA, Phi Delta Kappa, Phi Kappa Phi. Home: PO Box 3156 Champaign IL 61826-3156 Office Phone: 217-398-4226. Personal E-mail: jko@drjudyosgood.com.

OSGOOD, VIRGINIA M., vocational school educator; b. Oklahoma City, Okla., Dec. 9, 1942; d. John Allen Jr. and Christena Hazel (Grove) Simon; m. O. Emmet Osgood Jr., Jan. 19, 1963; children: Christopher J., Steven J. BS in Edn., Ctrl. State U., Edmond, Okla., 1989; MSEd, U. Ctrl. Okla., 1991; EdD, Okla. State U., 1999. Prodn. artist Lowe Runkle Advert. Oklahoma City, 1960-63; graphic designer Comm. Pub., Oklahoma City, 1963-70; owner, graphic designer Osgood Co., Oklahoma City, 1970-86; instr. Can. Valley Area Tech. Sch., El Reno, Okla., 1986-94; asst. prof. U. Ctrl. Okla., Edmond, 1994—. Rschr. in field. Contbg. editor (CD-rom) Advisor Survivor Kit: ASK, 1999. Com. chair St. Monica Parish, Edmond, 1993-99. Named Woman of Achievement, St. Monica Parish, 2000. Mem. Am. Vocat. Assn. (Region IV Trade & Indsl. Instr. of Yr. 1992, Nat. Trade & Indsl. Instr. of Yr. 1993), Okla. Vocat. Assn. (Okla. Vocat. Tchr. of Yr. 1991), Vocat. Indsl. Clubs of Am. (Nat. Advisor of Yr. 1993). Roman Catholic. Avocations: calligraphy, woodworking, crossword puzzles. Office: U Ctrl Okla 100 N University Dr Edmond OK 73034-5207

O'SHAUGHNESSY, ELLEN CASSELS, writer; b. Columbia, S.C., Oct. 1, 1937; d. Melvin O. and Grace Ellen (Cassels) Hemphill; m. John H. Sloan (dec.); children: John H., Anne H.; m. John F. O'Shaughnessy, Dec. 8, 1979 (div. Mar. 1990). BA, Internat. Coll., L.A., 1977; MA in Counseling Psychology, Fielding Inst., Santa Barbara, Calif., 1980. Tchr.'s aide, art instr. Monterey Peninsula (Calif.) Unified Sch. Dist., 1968-74; tchr. adult sch. Pacific Grove (Calif.) Unified Sch. Dist., 1974-82, spl. edn. cons., 1984-85; sustitute tchr. Monterey County Office Edn., Salinas, Calif., 1983-84; owner, writer, pub. Synthesis, Pacific Grove, Calif., 1984—. Author: Teaching Art to Children, 1974, Synthesis, 1981, You Love to Cook Book, 1983, I Could Ride on the Carousel Longer, 1989, Somebody Called Me A Retard Today.And My Heart Felt Sad, 1992, Walker & Co., N.Y.C. Episcopalian. Home: PO Box 51063 Pacific Grove CA 93950-6063

O'SHAUGHNESSY, NADINE M., science educator; d. Wayne and Georgette Andrea Moody; m. Terry L. O'Shaughnessy, Aug. 15, 1992; 1 child, Sydney Rae. BA, Ithaca Coll., N.Y., 1990; MS, SUNY, Potsdam, 1995; postgrad., SUNY, Oswego, 2005—06. Chemistry instr. Jefferson C.C.,

Watertown, NY, 1999; sci. tchr. Copenhagen (N.Y.) Ctrl. Sch., 1990—. Model sch. tech. instr. Jeff-Lewis and Madison Oneida BOCES, Watertown and Verona, NY, 1998—2005; tech. educator PASCO Sci., Roseville, Calif., 1999—. Author: e-Class Guidebook, Leadership and New Technologies, 2001. Grantee Tchr. Integration award, Model Sch., 1999—2000. Master: Copenhagen Ctrl. Sch. Class of 2011 (advisor 2005—06); mem.: Tech. Com., Profl. Devel. Planning Com. (recorder 1995—97), Compact Com. (facilitator 2000—06). Home: 15 1/2 N Jefferson St Carthage NY 13619 Office: Copenhagen Ctrl Sch 3020 Mechanic St Copenhagen NY 13626 Office Phone: 315-688-4411. Office Fax: 315-688-2001. E-mail: noshaughnessy@ccsknights.org.

O'SHEA, ANNA BELLE MARIE, music educator, liturgy administrator; b. Evergreen Park, Ill., Apr. 9, 1956; d. Joseph Bernard and Anna Belle Marie O'Shea. MusB, De Paul U., 1978; diploma in Pastoral Liturgy, St. Joseph's Coll., 2003, MA in Ch. Music and Liturgy, 2004. Pvt. flut instr., Chgo., 1976—; prin. flutist N.W. Ind. Symphony, Munster, Ind., 1977—88; freelance flutist Chgo., 1978—; founder, pres, dir. music Flutes Unlimited, Chgo., 1997—; dir. liturgy Mother McAuley HS, Chgo., 2005—. Mem. music staff Archdiocese Chgo., 2000—. Co-author: The Liturgical Flutist: A Method Book and More, 2005. Mem.: Nat. Flute Assn. (performer), Nat. Assn. Pastoral Musicians (clinician, bd. dirs. ensemble sect. 1999—). Roman Catholic.

O'SHEA, ELIZABETH THERESE, counselor; d. Richard J. and Kathleen M. O'Shea. BA, Southampton Coll., NY, 1985; MA in Psychol. Counseling, Columbia U., NYC, 2004, EdM, 2004. Cert. provisional sch. counselor NY, 2003, limitied permit mental health counselor NY, 2006. Guidance counselor Pub. Sch. 166, NYC, 2003—04; tchg. asst. childhood and adolescence devel. psychology Tchrs. Coll., Columbia U., 2003—05; mental health counselor intern Psychotechnologies, Patchogue, NY, 2005—06; applied behavioral specialist IGHL, Southampton, NY, 2006—. Treas. World Wings Internat., NYC, 2004—05. Active Oxonian Soc., NYC, 2004—05; active mem., past bd. mem. Women's Nat. Rep. Club, NYC, 1992—2006; active, homeless vol. CRC, NYC, 2003—04; active Young Friends Guggenheim Mus., NYC, 2002—03, NY Hist. Soc., NYC, 1996—97. Mem.: ACA (assoc.). Roman Catholic. Avocation: travel. Home: 225 Central Park West New York NY 10024 E-mail: eto18@columbia.edu.

O'SHEA, ERIN K., biomedical researcher; m. Doug Jeffery O'Shea. AB in biochemistry, Smith Coll., 1988; PhD in chemistry, MIT, 1992. Asst. prof. biochemistry and biophysics U. Calif., San Francisco, 1993—97, assoc. prof. biochemistry and biophysics, 1997—2001, prof., vice chair biochemistry and biophysics, 2001—; asst. investigator Howard Hughes Med. Inst., 2000—. Chair sci. adv. bd. Boston U. Sch. Medicine, Dept. Genetics and Genomics, 2002—; mem. sci. adv. com. Helen Hay Whitney Found., 2002—; chair external review com. Bauer Ctr. Genomics Harvard U., 2004. Pub. Libr. Sci., 2003—. Recipient Promega Early Career Life Sci. award, Am. Soc. Cell Biology, 2000, Irving Sigal Young Investigator award, Protein Soc., 2004; fellow, David and Lucile Packard Found., 1994. Fellow: Am. Acad. Arts and Scis.; mem.: NAS (mem. NTC com. on standards and principles in biol. rsch. 2002—, award in molecular biology 2001). Office: Howard Hughes Med Inst Harvard U Dept Molecular & Cellular Biology Bauer 307 7 Divinity Ave Cambridge MA 02138 Office Phone: 617-495-4328. Office Fax: 617-496-5425. Business E-Mail: Erin_OShea@harvard.edu.*

O'SHEA, LYNNE EDEEN, management consultant, educator; b. Chgo., Oct. 18, 1950; d. Edward Fisk and Mildred (Lessner) O'S. BA, BJ in Polit. Sci. and Journalism, U. Mo., MA in Info. Theory, 1971; PhD in Consumer Cultures, Northwestern U., 1978; postgrad., Sch. Mgmt. and Strategic Studies, U. Calif., 1988. Congl. asst., Washington, 1968—70; brand mgr. Procter & Gamble Co., Cin., 1971-73; v.p. Foote, Cone & Belding, Inc., Chgo., 1973-79; v.p. corp. comms. Internat. Harvester Co., Chgo., 1979-82; dir. mktg. and comms. Arthur Andersen & Co., Chgo., 1983-86; v.p. bus. devel. Gannett Co., Inc., Chgo., 1987-94; pres., chief oper. officer Shalit Place L.L.C., 1995—98; exec. v.p. Mus. Broadcast Comm., Chgo., 1996-97; dir. A.T. Kearney, Chgo., 1998—2005; pres. Ill. Women's Forum, 2005—. Prof. mktg. U. Chgo. Grad. Sch. Bus., 1979—80, Kellogg Grad. Sch. Mgmt., 1983—84, 1994—95; co-chair Fed. Glass Ceiling Commn., 1991—95; exec.-in-residence, prof. Kellstadt Grad. Sch. Bus., DePaul U., 2000—03; bd. dirs. AskRex.com, Clark/Bardes Inc., Motown Snacks, Robison Securities/Fleet Bank, Internat. Leadership Forum. Bd. dirs. Off-the-Street Club, Chgo., 1977-86; adv. bd. U. Ill. Coll. Commerce, 1980-2000, Chgo. Crime Commn., 1987-90, DePaul U., 1989-95, Roosevelt U., 1994-2000, St. Mary's U., 1995-98; co-chair Fed. Glass Ceiling Commn., 1991-95, com. 21st century, 1992—. Recipient numerous Eagle Fin. Advt. awards, Silver medalist Am. Advt. Fedn., 1989; named Advt. Woman of Yr. Chgo. Advt. Club, 1989, One of Top 100 in Tech., 2003; fellow Internat. Leadership Forum, 2005—. Mem. Internat. Women's Forum (v.p. devel., v.p. comms., exec. com., bd. dirs.), Chgo. Network, Women's Forum Chgo., Women's Forum Mich., Social Venture Network, Execs. Club Chgo., Mid-Am. Club (bd. govs. 1990-92), Women's Athletic Club Chgo. Office: 1703 Shoreline Dr Saint Charles IL 60174-5562 Office Phone: 847-778-8411. Personal E-mail: lynneoshea@juno.com.

OSHEROW, JACQUELINE SUE, poet, English language educator; b. Phila., Aug. 15, 1956; d. Aaron and Evelyn (Victor) Osherow; m. Saul Korewa, June 16, 1965 (div. 2003); children: Magda, Dora, Mollie. AB Magna cum laude, Radcliffe Coll., Harvard U., 1978; postgrad., Trinity Coll., Cambridge U., 1978-79; PhD in English and Am. Lit., Princeton U., 1990. Prof. English C. Utah, Salt Lake City, 1989—. Author: (poetry) Looking for Angels in New York, 1988, Conversations with Survivors, 1994, With a Moon in Transit, 1996, Dead Men's Praise, 1999. Recipient Witter Bynner prize Am. Acad. and Inst. Arts and Letters, 1990; Ingram Merrill Found. grantee, 1990; Guggenheim fellow, 1997-98, Nat. Endowment for the Arts fellow, 1999—. Mem. Poetry Soc. Am. (John Masefield Meml. award 1993, Lucille Medwick Meml. award 1995, Cecil Hemley Meml. award 1997). Jewish. Office: U Utah Dept English 255 S Central Campus Dr Rm 3500 Salt Lake City UT 84112-0494 Office Phone: 801-581-7947, 801-581-6168. Business E-Mail: j.osherow@english.utah.edu.

OSKIN, JOELLEN ROSS, special education educator, school librarian; b. McKeesport, Pa., Apr. 26, 1943; d. Clarence Melvin Ross and Ada Mae Oliver; m. David William Oskin, Sept. 5, 1964; children: David William, Steven Ross. BS in Spl. Edn. magna cum laude, 1980, MLS So. Conn. U., 1987. Spl. edn. tchr. Greenwich (Conn.) Bd. Edn., 1980—89, Darien (Conn.) Bd. Edn., 1989—91; libr. Automated Kings Coll. Libr., Kings Coll., Auckland, New Zealand, 1992—94. Bd. dirs. Vis. Nurse/VNC Network, Wilton, Conn.; mem. adv. bd. Kids In Crisis, Greenwich, 2001—02. Mem.: AAUW. Avocations: golf, reading, travel.

OSLAK, MEGAN KATHLEEN, elementary school educator; d. Robert R. and Susan Oslak. BA, Monmouth Coll., Ill., 2000; MS in Edn., No. Ill. U., DeKalb, 2006. 7th grade tchr. Old Quarry Mid. Sch., Lemont, Ill., 2001—. Site dir. Girl Scouts of DuPage, Lisle, Ill. Mem.: ASCD, Ill. Coun. Social Studies, Nat. Coun. Social Studies, Kappa Delta Pi, Kappa Kappa Gamma (registrar 1998—99, panhellenic v.p. 1999—2000).

OSMAN, EDITH GABRIELLA, lawyer; b. NYC, Mar. 18, 1949; d. Arthur Abraham and Judith (Goldman) Udem; children: Jacqueline, Daniel. BA in Spanish, SUNY, Stony Brook, 1970; JD cum laude, U. Miami, 1983. Bar: Fla. 1983, U.S. Dist. Ct. (so. dist.) Fla. 1984, US Dist. Ct. (mid. dist.) Fla. 1988, US Ct. Appeals (11th cir.) 1985, Fla. Supreme Ct. 1987, US Ct. Mil. Appeals 1990; cert. family law mediator Fla. Supreme Ct., civil mediator, Fla. Assoc. Kimbrell & Hamann, PA, Miami, 1984-90, Dunn & Lodish, PA, Miami, 1990-93; pvt. practice Miami, 1993-98; shareholder Carlton Fields, Miami, 1998—, practice group leader, family law divsn. Bd. dirs. Miami City Club, Supreme Ct. Historic Soc., So. Legal Coun., Fla. Women of Achievement (bd. dirs. leading atty). Mem. adv. com. for Implementation of the Victor Posner Judgement to Aid the Homeless, 1986-89. Recipient Breaking the Glass Ceiling award Ziff Mus., 2000, In the Company of Women award Dade County, 2000, Judge Mattie Belle Davis award, 2000, FAWL's Rosemary Barkett Achievement award, 1997, Outstanding Past Vol. Bar Pres.'s award, 1996, Women's Park Founders and Wall of Honor award, 2001; selected for photographic exhibit Florida Women of Achievement, 2000, South Fla.'s Top 250 Lawyers South Fla. Legal Guide, 2001, 02, 03, 04, 05; named 100 Women to Watch MIA Metro Mag., Fla. Trend, 2000, Women's Park Hall of Fame, 2001. Fellow Am. Bar Found., Fla. Bar Found.; mem. ABA (family law, alternate dispute resolution, Ho. of Dels. 1998—, standing com. on independence of judiciary 2000-03, standing com. bar svs. 2003-, house select com., 2004-), The Fla. Bar (budget com. 1989-92, 97-98, voluntary bar liaison com. 1989-90, spl. com. on formation of All-Bar Conf. 1988-89, chair mid-yr. conv. 1989, long range planning com. 1988-90, bd. govs. 1991-98, spl. commn. on delivery of legal svcs. to the indigent 1990-92, bus. law cert. com. 1995-96, practice law mgmt. com. 1995-96, chair program evaluation com., 1993-94, exec. com. 1992-93, 96-2000, rules and bylaws com., 1993-94, vice-chair disciplinary rev. com. 1994-95, investment com. 1994-95, vice-chair rules com. 1994-95, All-Bar Conf. chair 1997, chair grievance mediation com. 1997-99, pres.-elect 1998-99, pres. 1999-2000, exec. coun. family law sect. 2001—, vice-chair legis. 2001-2002, co-chair alternative dispute resolution com. 2003—, chair commn. legal needs of children, 2003-04, spl. commn. on disciplinary rev., 2003—, family law rules procedure com. 2003—,spl. com. succession planning), Dade County Bar Assn. (fed. ct. rules com. 1985-86, chmn. program com. 1988-91, bd. dirs., 1988—, 96-97, exec. com. 1987-88), Fla. Assn. Women's Lawyers Assn. (Dade County chpt. bd. dirs. 1984-85, treas. 1985-86, v.p. 1986-87, pres. 1987-88), Fla. Assn. Women Lawyers (v.p. 1988-89, pres. 1989-90), Fla. Bar Found. (dir. 1998-2001), Nat. Conf. Women's Bar Assn. (dir. nat. conf. 1990-91), Cuban Am. Bar Assn., Fla. Acad. Trial Lawyers, Dade County Trial Lawyers Assn., Nat. Conf. Bar Pres., So. Conf. Bar Pres., Leading Attys. (bd. dirs. 2000—), Iron Arrow Honor Soc., First Family Inns of Ct. Office: Carlton Fields PA 100 SE 2nd St Ste 4000 Miami FL 33131-2148 Office Phone: 305-530-0050. E-mail: eosman@carltonfields.com.

OSMER-MCQUADE, MARGARET, broadcast executive, journalist; b. N.Y.C. d. Herbert Bernard and Margaret Normann (Brunjes) O.; m. Lawrence Carroll McQuade, Mar. 15, 1980; 1 son, Andrew. BA, Cornell U., 1960. Assoc. producer UN Bur., CBS News, N.Y.C., 1962-69; producer 60 Minutes, N.Y.C., 1969-72; reporter, producer Bill Moyer's Jour., Pub. Broadcasting Service, N.Y.C., 1972-73, Reasoner Report, ABC News, N.Y.C., 1973-75; corr., anchor person Good Morning Am., ABC Morning News, Washington, 1975-77; corr. ABC TV News, Washington, 1977-79; v.p., dir. programs Council on Fgn. Relations, 1979-93; pres., CEO Qualitas Internat., N.Y.C., 1994—. Dir. Dime Savs. Bank, 1980—; cons. pub. broadcasting; mem. program com. Ditchley Found. Producer, reporter: TV news shows Come Fly A Kite (Nat. Press Photographer's award 1974), Kissinger, 1970, No Tears for Rachel, 1972, Calder: Master of Mobiles, 1975; moderator, producer World in Focus, publ. TV series for Coun. Fgn. Relations/Sta. WNYC, PBS, Worldnet, 1988-93. Mem. U.S. delegation World Conf. on Cambodian Refugees, Geneva, 1980; mem. Def. Adv. Com. on Women in the Service, 1978-82; trustee Cornell U.; mem. bd. overseers Cornell U. Med. Coll., pres.'s coun. Cornell Women; mem. program com. The Ritchley Found., 1994—, task force N.Y. Sch. Vols., 1994—; vol. Nat. Svc. Learning, 1994—. Recipient Peabody award Staff of 60 Minutes, 1970 Mem. NATAS, Coun. Fgn. Relations, program comm. The Mitching Found., Task Force N.Y. Sch. Vol., Nat. Press Club, Mid. Atlantic Club., vol. Nat. Svc. Learning. Clubs: Cosmopolitan, Century.

OSMOND, MARIE, singer; b. Ogden, Utah, Oct. 13, 1959; d. George and Olive O.; m. Stephen Craig, 1982 (div.) m. Brian Blosil, 1986; children: Stephen James, Jessica Marie, Rachel. Student pub. schs., pvt. tutors. Appeared with The Osmond family singing group from age 7, solo act, 1973—;(TV co-star): Donny & Marie TV show, 1976-79, Donny & Marie Christmas Spl, 1979, Osmond Family Show, 1979, Osmond Family Christmas Show, 1980, Donny & Marie, 1998; (star TV spl.) Marie, 1981; appeared in TV series Maybe This Time, 1995, video Buster & Chauncey's Silent Night, 1998; (record albums) include (with Donny Osmond): Make the World Go Away, I'm Leaving It All Up To You; songs from their TV Show Goin Coconuts; (solo albums) include: Paper Roses, In My Little Corner of the World, Who's Sorry Now?, This Is The Way That I Feel, There's No Stopping Your Heart, 1985, I Only Wanted You, 1987, All In Love, 1988, Steppin' Stone, 1989, Twenty Five Hits-Special Collection, 1995; (#1 singles) include Meet Me in Montana (Best Country Duo of Yr. award with Dan Seals), 1986, You're Still New to Me, 1986, There's No Stoppin' Your Heart, 1986, I Only Wanted You, 1987, The Best Of, 1990; toured with Bob Hope, Persian Gulf, 1991; (co-author): Fun, Fame, and Family, 1973; Marie Osmond's Guide to Beauty, Health, and Style, 1980. Recipient (with Donny Osmond) Georgie award for best vocal team Am. Guild Variety Artists, 1978. Mem. Lds Ch.

OSMUNDSEN, BARBARA ANN, sculptor; b. Jacksonville, NC, Apr. 21, 1945; d. Robert Nygäard and Catherine Ann (Wilent) Osmundsen; m. Baxter Smith Rains III, Sept. 20, 1986; 1 child, Holly Christine Delaney. Student, Vanderbilt U., 1963-64; BS, U. Tenn., Chattanooga, 1967; postgrad., U. Tenn., Knoxville, 1969-70, Va. Mus. of Fine Arts, Richmond, 1988-89. Fashion, accessory designer, Atlanta, 1972—85; ptnr. Bara Designs, Richmond, 1987—88; art instr. Mus. Art and Sci., Melbourne, Fla., 1998—2004, Vero Beach Mus. of Arts, 2000—03; artist in residence Brevard Cultural Alliance, Viera, Fla., 1999—2003. V.p., cons. artist Hope Dragon Found., Indian Harbour Beach, Fla., 1996, 2000. Exhibitions include Arlington Arts Ctr., 1991, Raleigh Gallery, Boca Raton, 1992—97, Gaier Contemporary Gallery, Orlando, 1994—96, Renee Foosaner Ctr., Mus. Art and Sci., Melbourne, 1998—2002, Marine Resources Coun. East Fla., Rockledge, 1999, Ctr. for the Arts, Vero Beach, Fla., 2000—02, Brevard Mus. Arts and Sci., Melbourne, 2001, Astronaut Meml. Planetarium and Obs., Cocoa, Fla., 2005, 2006, exhibited in group shows at Brevard Mus. Art and Sci., 2003, 2005, Astronaut Meml. Planetarium and Observatory, Cocoa, Fla., 2005, one-woman shows include Melbourne Internat. Airport, 2001, Brevard County Govt. Complex, Viera, Fla., 2001—03, Indian River County Court House, Vero Beach, 2004, Vero Beach Mus. Art, 2005, Represented in permanent collections Freedom 7 Cmty. Ctr., Wuesthoff Health Sys. Found., Caron Wills Collection, Killaloe/Bullina, Ireland, Mort Harris Collection, Detroit, Sch. Dist. Brevard County, Viera, Edgar and Alberta Holtz Collection, Vero Beach, Price Collection, Oilville, Va., Brevard Mus. Art and Sci., Fay Richardson Picardi Collection, Grant, Fla., James and Carol Minton Collection, Indialantic, Fla., Diana Holtz Jamieson Collection, Chevy Chase, Md.; co-editor, author: Studio Link newsletter, 1994. Adv. bd. Women's Shelter, Valdosta, Ga., 1987; co-founder bd. govs. Vector Arts Endowment, 1997-2000. Mem.: Internat. Sculpture Assn., Nat. League Am. Pen Women (pres. Cape Canaveral Br., Fla. 2000—02). Avocations: organic gardening, gourmet cooking. Office: PO Box 372628 Satellite Beach FL 32937-0628 Office Phone: 321-536-8426. Business E-Mail: barbaraosmundsen@yahoo.com.

OSOWIEC, DARLENE ANN, clinical psychologist, educator, consultant; b. Chgo., Feb. 16, 1951; d. Stephen Raymond and Estelle Marie Osowiec; m. Barry A. Leska. BS, Loyola U., Chgo., 1973; MA with honors, Roosevelt U., 1980; postgrad. in psychology, Saybrook Inst., San Francisco, 1985—88; PhD in Clin. Psychology, Calif. Inst. Integral Studies, 1992. Lic. clin. psychologist, Mo., Ill., Calif. Mental health therapist Ridgeway Hosp., Chgo., 1978; mem. faculty psychology dept. Coll. Lake County, Grayslake, Ill., 1981; counselor, supr. MA-level interns, chmn. pub. rels. com. Integral Counseling Ctr., San Francisco, 1983—84; clin. psychology intern Chgo.-Read Mental Health Ctr. Ill. Dept. Mental Health, 1985—86; mem. faculty dept. psychology Moraine Valley C.C., Palos Hills, Ill., 1988—89; lectr. psychology Daley Coll., Chgo., 1988-90; cons. Gordon & Assocs., Oak Lawn, Ill., 1989; adolescent, child and family therapist Orland Twp. Youth Svcs., Orland Park, Ill., 1993; psychology fellow Sch. Medicine, St. Louis U., 1994-95; pvt. practice Chgo., Geneva and St. Charles, Ill., 1996—; founder Maximum Potential, Chgo., 1996—. Contbr., author: Transpersonal Hypnosis, 1999. Ill. State scholar, 1969-73; Calif. Inst. Integral Studies scholar, 1983. Mem. APA (chair edn. and tng. com. divsn. 30 1998-2000, chair mem. svcs. 2001-05), Am. Psychol. Soc., Am. Women in Psychology, Ill. Psychol. Assn., Calif. Psychol. Assn., Mo. Psychol. Assn., Fla. Psychol. Assn., Am. Soc. Clin. Hypnosis, Chgo. Soc. Clin. Hypnosis, NOW (chair legal adv. corps, Chgo. 1974-76), Lincoln Park Bus. Devel. Inst. (chair program com. 2003—). Avocations: playing piano, gardening, reading, backpacking, writing. Business E-Mail: dr.osowiec@comcast.net.

OSSANA, DIANA LYNN, author, screenwriter; b. St. Louis, Aug. 24, 1949; d. Livio Aldo and Marian Yvonne O.; 1 child, Sara Maria. Pres. Saria Inc., Tucson, 1993—. Co-author: (novel) Pretty Boy Floyd, 1994, Zeke and Ned, 1996; writer, exec. prodr.: (TV miniseries) Streets of Laredo, 1995, Dead Man's Walk, 1996, Johnson County War, 2002; screenwriter, prodr.: (films) Brokeback Mountain, 2005 (with Larry McMurty, Best Screenplay, Hollywood Fgn. Press Assn. (Golden Globe award), 2006, Theatrical Motion Picture, Producers Guild Am., 2006, Outstanding Film and Adapted Screenplay, British Acad. Film and TV Arts, 2006, Best Feature, Spirit Independent award, 2006, Adapted Screenplay, Acad. Motion Pictures Arts & Sciences, 2006) Recipient Teleplay of Yr. award Cowboy Hall of Fame, 1996, Teleplay of Yr. award Dallas Film Critics Assn., 1996. Mem. Pen Am. West (Tex. affiliation), Am. Acad. Poets, Internat. Crime Writers Assn., Women in Film.

OSSEFORT-RUSSELL, CANDYCE, psychotherapist; b. Ft. Belvoir, Va., Nov. 10, 1961; d. Frederick David and Lois Elaine Shockley; m. Rodney Thompson Russell, May 17, 2003; m. Martin John Ossefort, June 21, 1986 (dec. Feb. 15, 1992); 1 child, Zachary Frederick Ossefort. BS in Computing Sci., Tex. A&M U., College Station, 1983; MA in Counseling Psychology, Pacifica Grad. Inst., Carpinteria, Calif., 2001. Lic. Profl. Counselor Tex., 2003. Computer programmer IBM, Austin, Tex., 1983—89; pvt. practice therapist Austin, Tex., 2001—. Instr. Informal Classes U. Tex., Austin, 2005; newsletter editor Austin Group Psychotherapy Soc., 2004—. Vol. patient and family support Hospice Austin, 1997—2000; newsletter editor Parkside Cmty. Sch., Austin, 1996—98; vol. Women and Their Work Art Gallery, Austin, 1994—98; rsch. asst. Austin Longitudinal Project U. Tex. Austin, 1990; vol. counselor Ctr. for Battered Women, Austin, 1986—87. Mem.: ACA (assoc.), Accelerated Experiential Dynamic Psychotherapy Inst. (corr.), Am. Group Psychotherapy Assn. (assoc.), Austin Group Psychotherapy Soc. (assoc.; bd. mem. 2004—06), Writers' League Tex. (assoc.). Avocations: writing, chocolate dessert creation, gourmet cooking, decorating, assemblage art. Office: 1615 W 6th St Ste C Austin TX 78703 Office Phone: 512-789-6244. Office Fax: 512-474-1237. E-mail: candyce@candycecounseling.com.

OSSELLO, KRISTIE, music educator; d. Carmen Holmes; m. John Ossello, Dec. 11, 1991; children: Bailey, Kiley, Jack. BA, U. St. Mary, Leavenworth, Kans., 1992; postgrad., Emporia State U., 2005—. Band dir. Most Pure Heart of Mary Sch., Topeka, 1996—, Hayden H.S., Topeka, 2003—. Musician: (performance) Coleman Hawkins Jazz Festival; composer: (drum line, handbells) Drum Line Features, Handbell Scores. Educator nominator Nat. Youth Leadership Coun., Washington, 2004—06; judge 4-H, Topeka, 1996—98; band mem. Marshall's Civic Band, Topeka, 1997—2006; summer camp tchr. Camp Polycarp, Topeka, 1998—99, Lion's Band, Baldwin City, Kans., 2000—00; dir. parade band St. Patrick's Day Parade, Topeka, 2002—06; judge Battle of the Bands, Topeka, 2004—06; music dir. Most Pure Heart of Mary Ch., Topeka, 1997—2002. Named Educator of Distinction, Nat. Soc. H.S. Scholars, 2005; recipient Teachers Make a Difference award, Channel 49 TV Sta., 2001. Mem.: Cath. Band Dirs. Assn., Am. Guild English Handbell Ringers, Internat. Assn. Jazz Educators, Nat. Assn. Music Educators, Kappa Gamma Pi. Avocations: range shooting, travel, reading, walking, hiking. Office Phone: 785-272-5210. Personal E-mail: ossellok@haydenhigh.org.

OSSENBERG, HELLA SVETLANA, psychoanalyst; b. June 10, 1930; came to U.S., 1957, naturalized, 1964; d. Anatole E. and Tatiana N. (Dombrovski) Donath; m. Carl H. Ossenberg, June 7, 1958. Diploma langs. and psychology, U. Heidelberg, Germany, 1953; MS, Columbia U., 1968. Cert. Nat. Psychol. Assn. Psychoanalysis, 1977, diplomate Am. Bd. Examiners, lic. psychoanalyst; LCSW. Sr. psychiat. social worker VA Mental Hygiene Clinic, NYC, 1975—88; pvt. practice NYC, 1977—. Mem. Theodor Reik Cons. Center 1978—; field instr. Columbia U., Fordham U. schs. social work. Mem. NASW, Nat. Psychol. Assn. Psychoanalysis, Nat. Assn. Advancement Psychoanalysis, Coun. Psychoanalytic Psychotherapists.

OSSEWAARDE, ANNE WINKLER, real estate company executive; b. Dallas, June 2, 1957; d. Lowell Graves and Ruth Lenore (Lind) Winkler; m. Kirk L Ossewaarde, Apr. 27, 1991. BBA in Fin. with honors, Emory U., 1979; MBA in Acctg. and Fin. with honors, U. Tex., 1983; MS in Real Estate Devel., MIT, 1988. Cert. comml. investment mem., Comml. Investment Real Estate Inst. Mgmt. trainee Citizens & So. Nat. Bank, Atlanta, 1979-81; banking assoc. Continental Ill. Nat. Bank, Chgo. and Dallas, 1983-85; asst. v.p., devel. assoc. Trammell Crow Residential, Dallas, 1985-87, Seattle, 1988-91; devel. mgr. Blackhawk Port Blakeley Cmtys., Seattle, 1991-93; v.p., real estate portfolio mgr. Aegon U.S.A. Realty, Atlanta, 1994-98; dir. UBS Brinson Realty Investors (formerly Allegis Realty Investors), Dallas, 1998—2000; exec. dir. asset mgmt. Morgan Stanley (formerly Lend Lease Real Estate Investments, Inc.), Atlanta, 2000—. Charles Harritt Jr. Presdl. scholar U. Tex., 1982, Alexander Grant scholar, 1982. Mem. Comml. Real Estate Women, MIT Ctr. for Real Estate Alumni Assn., Alpha Epsilon Upsilon. Methodist. Avocations: singing, photography, bicycling, reading. Home: 3170 Windsor Lake Dr Atlanta GA 30319

OSSORIO, PILAR NICOLE, professional association administrator; b. L.A., Nov. 16, 1959; BS in Biology, Stanford U., Calif., 1983, PhD in Microbiology and Immunology, 1990; JD, Stanford U., 1997. ESL tchr. Adult Edn. Program, Palo Alto, Calif., 1979-80; English tchr. Tainan First Girl's H.S., Young Men's Christian Assn., Republic of China, 1980-82; postdoctoral assoc. Yale U. Sch. Medicine, 1990—93; spl. govt. employee, bioethics working group of the healthcare reform task force White House, Washington, 1993; bioethics rsch. assoc., program on ethical, legal and social implications of the human genome project, U.S. Dept. Energy Los Alamos Nat. Lab., 1994; com. on scientific freedom and responsibility AAAS, 1994—; summer assoc. Pillsbury Madison & Sutro, San Francisco, 1995, 1996; law clk., patent law group Morrison and Foerster LLP, Palo Alto, Calif., 1996—97; dir., genetics sect. Inst. for Ethics, AMA, Chgo., 1997—2000; faculty assoc., Ctr. for the Study of Cultural Diversity in Healthcare (previously, Ctr. for the Study of Race and Ethnicity in Medicine) U. Wis., Madison, 2000—02, asst. prof., law & bioethics (apptd. at Law and Med. Schools), 2000—05, program faculty, grad. program in population health, 2004—, assoc. prof. law 7 bioethics, 2006—. Frequent ad hoc reviewer of grant proposals NIH and Dept. Energy, 1992—; mem. internat. bd. advisors Found. for Genetic Medicine, 1998—2000; mem. adv. com. Nat. Ctr. for Bioethics in Rsch. and Healthcare, 1999—; mem. steering com. to the secretary's com. on genetic testing US Dept. HHS, 1999—2000; mem. nat. cancer policy bd. Inst. Medicine, NAS, 1999—2002, liaison to the com. on assessing the sys. for protecting human rsch. subjects, 2000—02; liaison to the com. on intellectual property rights NRC, NAS, 2000—03; advisor, Latino Cmty. Engagement Project Baylor U., 2002—; advisor, Ctr. for Devices and Radiological Health FDA, 2002—; participant Lasker Found. Forum on Ethical Issues in Biomedical Rsch. and Practice, 2003; adv. bd. mem. for Definitions of Merit Boalt Hall Sch. Law, Berkeley, Calif., 2003—; advisor Nat. Libr. Medicine, Bioethics Working Group, 2003—04; mem. institutional review bd. U. Wis. Med. Sch., 2003—; advisor, Ctr. for Excellence in Ethics Rsch. Case Western Reserve U., 2004—; and several others; vis. prof. law U. Calif., Berkeley, 2006—; mem. adv. com. human embryonic stem cell rsch. NRC and Inst. Medicine, 2006—; invited spkr. and participant in study programs in the field. Editl. rev. bd. Microbial and Comparative Genomics, 1996-2000; mem. editl. bd. American Journal of Bioethics, 2002-;contbr. articles to profl. jours. NIH predoctoral fellowship, 1989-90, fellowship Am. Heart Assn., 1990-92, Brown-Coxe, 1990-91, minority scientist fellowship NIH, 1992-93. Fellow AAAS(mem. com. for scientific freedom and responsibility, 1994-2000, co-chair, working group on germ-line genetic intervention, 1998-2000, elected to nat. office as as mem. electorate nominating com., 1998-2001, (nat. office) mem.-at-large representing the sect. on societal impacts of sci. and engring., 2001-04), Am. Assn. of Bioethics, Internat. Assn. of Bioethics., Order of Coif. Office: U Wis law Sch Law Bldg 975 Bascom Mall Rm 9103 Madison WI 53706-1399 Office Phone: 608-263-4387. Office Fax: 608-262-5485. Business E-Mail: pnossorio@wisc.edu.*

OSTENDORF, JOAN DONAHUE, fund raiser, volunteer; b. Boston, Dec. 9, 1933; d. John Stanley and Genevieve Catherine (Morrissey) Donahue; m. Edgar Louis Ostendorf, Feb. 10, 1962; 1 child, Mary Elizabeth. BA, Marymount Coll., Tarrytown, N.Y., 1956; postgrad., Boston U., 1956. Tchr. Boston pub. schs., 1956-57, Waltham (Mass.) pub. schs., 1957-62. Trustee Cleve. Inst. Music, 1984—, mem. trustees coordianting coun., 1989; mem. Jr. League Cleve., 1964, 1st v.p. 1972-73; founder adv. coun. pub. rels. com. Cleve. Orch., 1974, 1st v.p., 1975-76; mem. del. assembly United Way, 1977-87; chmn. benefits Vis. Nurse Assn., 1987-88, March Dimes, 1982; trustee women's com. U. Hosps. Case Western Res. U. Med. Sch., 1974—; mem. nominating com. Inst. Music, 1990-91; 2d v.p. Music and Drama Club, 1991-93 (pres. 2001-2003), corresponding sec., 1993-95; chair Lyric Opera, 1992, Platform Assn., 1992—; pres. bd. trustees Cleve. Inst. Music, 1980-82, pres. women's com., 1980-82; mem. adv. bd. Women's Community Found., 1991—; v.p. Cleve. Internat. Piano Competition, 1994—; women's coun. Cleve. Mus., 1996. Mem. Internat. Platform Assn., Longwood Cricket Club, Intown Club, Chagrin Valley Hunt Club. Republican. Roman Catholic. Address: 3425 Roundwood Rd Chagrin Falls OH 44022-6634

OSTER, ROSE MARIE GUNHILD, foreign language professional, educator; b. Stockholm, Feb. 26, 1934; came to US, 1958; d. Herbert Jonas and Emma Wilhelmina (Johnson) Hagetorn; m. Ludwig F. Oster, May 17, 1956; children: Ulrika, Mattias. Fil. mag., U. Stockholm, 1956; PhD, Kiel U., Germany, 1958. Postdoctoral rsch. fellow linguistics Yale U., 1958-60, rsch. fellow Germanic langs., 1960-64, lectr. Swedish, 1964-66; mem. faculty U. Colo., Boulder, 1966-80, assoc. prof. Germanic langs. and lits., 1970-77, prof., 1977-80, chmn. dept., 1972-75, assoc. dean Grad. Sch., 1975-79, assoc. vice chancellor for grad. affairs Grad. Sch., 1979-80; dean for grad. studies and rsch. U. Md., College Park, 1980-83, prof. Germanic langs. and lits., 1980—, acting chair dept., 1997—2001. Mem. Fulbright Nat. Screening Com., Scandinavia, 1973, 83-87, chair, 1986-87; mem. selection com. Scandinavia Internat. Exch. of Scholars, 1982-86; cons. panelist Nat. Endowment for Humanities, 1975—, mem. bd. cons., 1980—; state coord. Am. Coun. on Edn., Colo., 1978-80, Md., 1981-83, dir. dept. leadership program, 1986-91; mem. exec. com. Assn. Grad. Schs., 1980-83; mem. dean's exec. com. African-Am. Inst., 1981-85; interim dir. Washington Sch. Psychiatry, 1994-95; cons. in field. Contbr. articles and revs. to profl. publs. Bd. dirs. Washington Sch. Psychiatry, Am.-Swedish Hist. Mus., Phila., Open Theatre, Washington; mem. nat. fellowship com. Am.-Scandinavian Found., 1997—, bd. trustees, 2001—. Carnegie fellow, 1974; grantee Swedish Govt., 1977, Am. Scandinavian Found., 1997, German Acad. Exch. Svc., 1983; recipient Translation prize Am.-Scandinavian Found., 1997. Mem. NOW, MLA (mem. Del. Assembly 1995—), AAUP, Soc. Advancement Scandinavian Studies (pres. 1979-80), Am. Scandinavian Assn. of Nat. Capital Area (pres. 1983-86, 95—), Am.-Scandinavian Found., Am. Assn. Higher Edn. Home: 4977 Battery Ln Bethesda MD 20814-4931 Office: U Md Dept Germanic Studies College Park MD 20742-0001 Office Phone: 301-405-4096. Business E-Mail: rmoster@umd.edu.

OSTER, TERRI, lawyer; d. Stephen and Sue Oster; m. Darren Beyer, Oct. 29, 2005. BA in Criminology, U. S.Fla., 1992; JD, Stetson U., Fla., 1995; MBA, U. Fla., 2006. Bar: Fla. 1995, U.S. Dist. Ct. (mid. dist.) Fla. 1997, cert.: Fla. Atty. Gen. (spl. prosecutor designation) 2002. Asst. state atty. State Atty.'s Office, Tampa, Fla., 1996—2000; atty. Gold & Resnick, P.A., Tampa, Fla., 2000—00; asst. atty. gen. Fla. Atty. Gen.'s Office, Orlando, 2000—. Bd. mem. Hillsborough County Civil Svc. Bd., Tampa, Fla., 2001—05; barrister Herbert Goldburg Inn of Ct., Tampa, Fla., 2002—05. Actor: (wedding show) Whose Wedding is it Anyway?. Fundraiser Leukemia and Lymphoma Soc., Tampa, 2001—02; mentor Hillsborough Edn. Found., Take Stock in Children, Tampa, Fla., 2001—03. Mem.: Hillsborough County Bar Assn., ATLA, Fla. Bar (assoc.; mem. practice mgmt., trial lawyers, bus. law sects.), Tampa Bay Peforming Arts (assoc.), Phi Alpha Delta (assoc.). Avocations: marathon running, kickboxing, reading, travel, golf. Office Phone: 407-245-0833.

OSTERGAARD, JONI HAMMERSLA, lawyer; b. Seattle, May 26, 1950; d. William Dudley and Carol Mae (Gillett) Hammersla; m. Gregory Lance Ostergaard, May 22, 1976 (div. 1985); 1 child, Bennett Gillett; m. William Howard Patton, Jan. 1, 1988; 1 child, Morgan Hollis; stepchildren: Colin W., Benjamin C. BS, U. Wash., 1972; MS, Purdue U., 1974; JD, U. Wash., 1980. Bar: Wash. 1980, U.S. Dist. Ct. (we. dist.) Wash. 1980, U.S. Ct. Appeals (9th cir.) 1981, U. S. Ct. Claims 1983. Clin. psychol. intern Yale Med. Sch., 1976-77; law clk. U.S. Ct. Appeals (9th cir.), Seattle, 1980-81; assoc. Roberts & Shefelman, Seattle, 1982-86, ptnr., 1987, Foster Pepper & Shefelman, Seattle, 1988-92; sole practitioner Seattle, 1996—2003; dep. pros. atty. Snohomish County Prosecuting Attys. Office Civil Divsn., Everett, Wash., 2004—. Contbr. articles to profl. jours.; notes and comments editor Wash. Law Rev., 1979-80. Recipient Sophia and Wilbur Albright scholarship U. Wash. Law Sch., 1979-80, law sch. alumni scholarship U. Wash. Law Sch., 1978-79; fellow NIMH. Avocations: gardening, reading. Office: Snohomish County Prosecuting Attys Office Civil Divsn 3000 Rockefeller Ave M/S 504 Everett WA 98201-4046 Office Phone: 425-388-6370. Office Fax: 425-388-6333. Business E-Mail: jostergaard@co.snohomish.wa.us.

OSTERKAMP, DALENE MAY, psychology educator, artist; b. Davenport, Iowa, Dec. 1, 1932; d. James Hiram and Bernice Grace Simmons; m. Donald Edwin Osterkamp, Feb. 11, 1951 (dec. Sept. 1951). BA, San Jose State U., 1959, MA, 1962; PhD, Saybrook Inst., 1989. Lectr. San Jose (Calif.) State U., 1960—65, U. Santa Barbara (Calif.) Ext., 1970-76; prof. Bakersfield (Calif.) Coll., 1961-87, prof. emerita, 1987—; adj. faculty, counselor Calif. State U., Bakersfield, 1990—95. Gallery dir. Bakersfield Coll., 1964-72. Juried group shows include Berkeley (Calif.) Art, Ctr., 1975, Libr. of Congress, 1961, Seattle Art Mus., 1962. Founder Kern Art Edn. Assn., Bakersfield, 1962, Bakersfield Printmakers, 1976. Staff sgt. USAF, 1952-55. Recipient 1st Ann. Svc. to Women award Am. Assn. Women in C.C., 1989. Mem. APA, Assn. for Women in Psychology, Assn. for Humanistic Psychology, Calif. Soc. Printmakers. Home: PO Box 387 Glennville CA 93226-0387 Office: Calif State Univ Stockdale Ave Bakersfield CA 93309

OSTRANDER, ELAINE A., federal agency administrator, geneticist; b. Syracuse, NY; BS, U. Washington, 1981; PhD, Oregon Health Sciences U., 1987. With Lawrence Berkeley Nat. Lab., Berkeley, Calif., 1991—93, Fred Hutchinson Cancer Rsch. Ctr., Seattle, 1993—2004; sr. investigator, chief, cancer genetics branch Nat. Human Genome Rsch. Inst., NIH, Bethesda, Md., 2004—, head, comparative genetics sect., 2004—. Affiliate prof., dept. of genome sci., sch. medicine and dept. biology, coll. arts and scis. U. Wash., Seattle; spkr. in field. Co-author more than 100 peer-reviewed publs. Office: Nat Human Genome Rsch Inst NIH Bldg 50 Rm 5351 50 S Dr MSC 8000 Bethesda MD 20892-8000 Office Phone: 301-594-5284. Office Fax: 301-594-0023. E-mail: eostrand@mail.nih.gov.*

OSTRIKER, ALICIA SUSKIN, poet; b. NYC, Nov. 11, 1937; d. David and Beatrice (Linnick) Suskin; m. Jeremiah P. Ostriker, 1958; children: Rebecca, Eve, Gabriel. BA, Brandeis U., 1959; MA, U. Wis., 1961, PhD, 1964. Asst. prof. Rutgers U., New Brunswick, NJ, 1965—68, assoc. prof., 1968—72, prof. English, 1972—2004; mem. faculty MFA program New Eng. Coll. Poetry, Henniker, NH, 2004—. Author: Vision and Verse in William Blake, 1965, Songs, 1969, Once More Out of Darkness, and Other Poems, 1974, A Dream of Springtime, 1979, The Mother/Child Papers, 1980, A Woman Under the Surface: Poems and Prose Poems, 1982, Writing Like a Woman, 1983, The Imaginary Lover, 1986 (William Carlos Williams prize Poetry Soc. Am. 1986), Stealing the Language: The Emergence of Women's Poetry in America, 1986, Green Age, 1989, Feminist Revision and the Bible, 1993, The Nakedness of the Fathers: Biblical Vision and Revisions, 1994, The Crack in Everything, 1996 (Nat. Book award finalist 1996, Paterson Poetry prize 1996, San Francisco State Poetry Ctr. award 1997), The Little Space: Selected and New Poems, 1998 (Nat. Book award finalist 1998), Dancing at the Devil's Party: Essays on Poetry, Politics, and the Erotic, 2000, The Volcano Sequence, 2002, No Heaven, 2005; editor: William Blake: Complete Poems, 1977. Nat. Coun. on Humanities grantee, 1968; NEA fellow, 1976-77, N.J. Arts Coun. fellow, 1982, Guggenheim Found. fellow, 1984-85, faculty fellow Rutgers Ctr. for Hist. Analysis, 1995-96, Rockefeller Found. fellow, 1982; recipient Strousse Poetry prize Prairie Schooner, 1986, Edward Stanley award Prairie Schooner, 1994, Anna David Rosenberg Poetry award, 1994, Best American Poetry award, 1996, Paterson prize, 1997, San Francisco State Poetry Ctr. award, 1997, Pushcart prize, 1999, Larry Levis prize 2001. E-mail: ostriker@rci.rutgers.edu.

OSTROFF, DAWN T., broadcast executive; b. Miami, Mar. 31, 1960; married. Exec. Kushner Locke; asst. 20th Century Fox, pres. devel.; exec., head programming Lifetime; pres. entertainment UPN. Office: UPN 11800 Wilshire Blvd Los Angeles CA 90025 E-mail: Dawn_Ostroff@upn.com.*

OSTROFF, LESLIE DENISE, elementary school educator; b. Decatur, Ga., Sept. 7, 1973; d. Ronnie Hugh and Torry Jane McDearis, Gail McDearis (Stepmother); m. Joel Morris Ostroff, Oct. 27, 2002; 1 child, Torry Eva. Student, Valdosta State U., Ga., 1992—97; EdM, City U., Bellevue, Wash., 2005. Cert. profl. edn. Wash., 2000, educator Ga. Profl. Stds. Commn., 1998. Mid. sch. math./sci. tchr. Brooks County Mid. Sch., Quitman, Ga., 1998—99; mid. sch. math. tchr. Tyee Mid. Sch., Bellevue, 2000—. Math. tutor, Bellevue, 2003—. Recipient Golden Apple award, Tyee Middle Sch., 2001. Mem.: Wash. Edn. Assn. (assoc.). Achievements include research in computational skills in schools. Home: 4335 2nd Ave NW Seattle WA 98107 Office: Tyee Middle School 13630 SE Allen Rd Bellevue WA 98006 Office Phone: 425-456-6800. Office Fax: 425-456-6801. Personal E-mail: jandlo@comcast.net. Business E-Mail: ostrofl@bsd405.org.

OSTROM, BRIGETTE DAWN, special education educator; b. Wellsboro, Pa., June 1, 1980; BA in Psychology, Pa. State U., 2002; MEd, Mansfield U., 2004. Learning support tchr. Galeton (Pa.) Sch. Dist., Liberty H.S. So. Tioga Sch. Dist., 2006—. Address: PO Box 20 Arnot PA 16911-0020

OSTROM, ELINOR, political science professor, researcher; b. L.A., Aug. 7, 1933; d. Adrian and Leah (Hopkins) Awan; m. Charles Scott, Aug. 8, 1954 (div. 1961); m. Vincent Ostrom, Nov. 23, 1963. AB with honors, UCLA, 1954, MA, 1962, PhD, 1965; D in Economics (hon.), U. Zurich, 1999; D (hon.), Inst. Social Studies, The Hague, 2002, Luleå U. Tech., Sweden, 2005; DHL (hon.), U. Mich., 2006. Vis. asst. prof. dept. gov. Ind. U., Bloomington, 1965-66, asst. prof., grad. advisor, dept. gov., 1966-69, assoc. prof. dept. polit. sci., 1969-74, prof. polit. sci., 1974-91, Arthur F. Bentley prof. polit. sci., 1991—, prof., chmn. dept. polit. sci., 1980—84, acting chair dept. polit. sci., 1989—90, co-dir. workshop in polit. theory and policy analysis, 1973—, co-dir. Ctr. Study Instns., Population and Environ. Change, 1996—2006, prof. part-time Sch. Pub. and Environ. Affairs. Employment interviewer, asst. employee relations mgr., Godfrey L. Cabot, Inc., Boston, 1955-57; personnel analyst III, U. Calif., LA, 1957-61; bd. cons., Internat. Assn. Chiefs Police: Police Discipline Project, 1974-75; adv. bd. Nat. Evaluation Program Law Enforcement Assistance (Adminstrn.), Washington, 1975-76; mem. Nat. Adv. Panel, Nat. Acad. Pub. Adminstrn.; Neighborhood-Oriented Metropolitan Gov., 1975-76, task force on criminal justice rsch. and devel. Nat. Adv. Com. on Criminal Justice Standards and Goals, 1975-76, Nat. Sheriffs Assn.: Study of Contract Law Enforcement, 1975-76; adv. panel Div. Policy Rsch. and Analysis, NSF, Washington, 1977-78, panel on Instl. Develop., 1985; rev. panel Polit. Sci. div. NSF, 1983-84; Interuniversity Consortium for Polit. and Social Rsch. Coun., 1983-85; adv. com. nat. urban policy NAS/NRC, 1985-88, panel on Common Property Resources Mgmt., 1985-86, Scientific Com. on Problems of the Environ., 1995-98; rsch. adv. com. U.S. AID, 1989-91; local gov. rsch. adv. bd., US Adv. Commn. on Intergovernmental Rels., 1985-88; adv. bd., Inst. for Policy Reform, 1993-96; bd. dirs., Beijer Internat. Inst. Ecol. Econs., Royal Swedish Acad. Scis., 1997-; academic adv. bd., Max-Planck-Inst. für Gesellschaftsforschung, 2000-; cons. in field. Co-author: Policing Metropolitan America, 1978, Local Government in the United States, 1988, Institutional Incentives and Sustainable Development: Infrastructure Policies in Perspective, 1993, Rules, Games, and Common-Pool Resources, 1994, The Samaritan's Dilemma, 2005, Seeing the Forest and the Trees, 2005; author: Governing the Commons, 1990, Crafting Institutions for Self-Governing Irrigation Systems, 1992, Understanding Institutional Diversity, 2005; editor: Strategies of Political Inquiry, 1982; co-editor: The Commons in the New Millennium: Challenges and Adaptations, 2003, Trust and Reciprocity: Interdisciplinary Lessons from Experimental Research, 2003, Jour. Theoretical Politics, 1987-95, People and Forests: Communities, Institutions, and Governance, 2000, Protecting the Commons: A Framework for Resource Management in the Americas, 2001, Foundations of Social Capital, 2003; mem. editl. bd. Am. Jour. Polit. Sci., Am. Polit. Sci. Review, Criminal Justice Review, Pub. Productivity Review, Publius, Quarterly Jour. Adminstrn., Sage Urban Affairs Ann. Review, Social Sci. Quarterly, Urban Affairs Quarterly, Ecol. Economics; contbr. articles to profl. jours. Grantee NSF, 1974-85, 87—, NIMH, 1977-81, U.S. Dept. Justice, 1978-82, AID, 1984-94, U.S. Geol. Survey, 1987-89, Ford Found., 1991—, FAO, 1992—, MacArthur Found., 1996-; recipient Frank E. Seidman Disting. award in Polit. Economy, 1997, Johan Skytte prize in Polit. Sci., Upsala University, 1999, Aaron Wildavsky Enduring Contbn. award for Governing the Commons, APSA, Pub. Policy Sect., 2000, John J. Carty award for the Advancement Sci., NAS, 2004, Sustainability Sci. award Ecol. Soc. Am., 2005, James Madison award Am. Polit. Sci. Assn., 2005. Fellow Am. Acad. Arts and Scis. (lifetime achievement award Atlas Econ. Rsch. Found., 2003), AAAS; mem. Pub. Choice Soc. (pres. 1982-84, co-chair, Duncan Black award Com., 1986-87, chair, Duncan Black award Com., 1990, exec. coun., 1982-), Am. Polit. Sci. Assn. (v.p. 1975-76, pres.-elect 1995-96, pres. 1996-97, chmn., several coms., 1978-88, mem., several coms., 1970-2002), Midwest Polit. Sci. Assn. (pres. 1984-85), Internat. Polit. Sci. Assn., Am. Econ. Assn., Internat. Assn. for Study Common Property (pres. 1990-91, program co-chair, 2000), Policy Studies Orgn., (nominating com., 1986-87, Miriam Mills award, 1996, Thomas R. Dye Svc. award, 1997), Am. Philos. Soc., Assn. for Politics and the Life Scis., NAS. Democrat. Home: 5883 E Lampkins Ridge Rd Bloomington IN 47401-9726 Office: Ind Univ Workshop in Polit Theory & Policy Analys 513 N Park Ave Bloomington IN 47408-3895 Office Phone: 812-855-0441. Office Fax: 812-855-3150. Business E-Mail: ostrom@indiana.edu.

OSTROM, KATHERINE (KATE) ELMA, retired secondary school educator; b. L.A., Dec. 30, 1928; d. Charles W. and Mabel M. (Christensen) Shults; m. Carl R. Ostrom, Jan. 29, 1949 (dec.); children: Margaret K. Larson, Carl R. Jr. BA cum laude, U. Wash., 1966, MA in Tchg. English, 1973, EdD, 1994. Std. tchg. cert. grades K-12, Wash.; continuing prin. cert.-secondary, Wash. Substitute tchr. Renton, Kent and South Ctrl. Sch. Dist., 1966; tchr. Foster HS, Tukwila, Wash., 1966-67, 75-76, Showalter Mid.Sch., Tukwila, 1967-79; dept. chair Showalter Mid. Sch., Tukwila, 1968-87, vice prin., 1979-87; tchr., supr. student tchr. U. Wash., Seattle, 1989-91; substitute tchr. Tukwila Sch. Dist., 1999—2005. Tchr. Western Wash. State Coll., Bellingham, 1967-68; liaison, supr. Jr. Achievement, Seattle, 1988-89; cons., trainer Nat. Assn. Elem. Sch. Prins., 1992-98; vol. tchr. Immigrant and Refugee Resources Ctr., Seattle, 1996-2003; dir. Forum on Edn., PDK, Seattle, 1997; mem. Citizen Adv. Com. in Curriculum, Renton, S.D., 2001—, chair, 2002-03. Host del., mem. Tukwila-Ikawa (Japan) Sister Cities, 1980—88, 1997—, chair, 1999—2002; block-watch organizer King County, Wash., 1994—2001; key communicator Renton (Wash.) Sch. Dist., 1996—2003; mem. Friends of Skyway Livr., King County Libr. Sys., 2006—; tutor Skyway Meth. Ch., Seattle, 1997—2000, staff parish com., 1996—2003. Named Vol. of Yr., BPW, Tukwila, Wash., 1990; Coll. scholar U. Puget Sound, Tacoma, Wash., 1946; PBK Pathfinder award, 1997; honored City of Ikawa, 1999, honored by Mayor Ikawa, Japan, 2000, 2005. Mem.: Wash. Physicians Social Responsibility (del. to Mid. East 1994), Assn. Wash. Sch. Prin. (chair state vice prin. conf. 1986, regional dir. 1986—88), Puget Sound Theatre Organ Soc., Key Players Prosser Piano and Organ, Phi Beta Kappa (bd. trustees Puget Sound Assn. 2000—, pres. Puget Sound Assn. 2003—), Phi Delta Kappa (editor newsletter 1988—90, pres. chpt. 1991—95, area coord. 1995—2001, editor newsletter 1995—2003). Democrat. Home: 12817 80th Ave S Seattle WA 98178-4911 E-mail: kateostrom@aol.com.

OSTROM, KRISTINA F., academic administrator, optician; d. David John, Sr. and Sandy Elnor Ostrom. AAS in Opticianry, J. Sargeant Reynolds C.C., Richmond, Va., 1995; BS in Chemistry, Va. Commonwealth U., Richmond, 2000; postgrad., Old Dominion U., Norfolk, Va., 2005—. Diplomate Am. Bd. Opticianry, lic. optician and contact lens technician Va. Optician Nat. Vision Assoc., Midlothian, Va., 1995—97, Walmart Corp. Vision Ctrs., Richmond, 1997—2003, Richmond Eye and Ear Surg. Splty. Ctr., 2002—03; program dir., faculty J. Sargeant Reynolds C.C., Richmond, 2003—. Adj. instr. J. Sargeant Reynolds C.C., Richmond, 1999—2003; spkr. in field. Contbr. articles to profl. jours. Treas., chmn. equipment com. Nat. Fedn. Opticianry Schs., Mountain Home, Ark., 2004—06, v.p., 2006—. Recipient Outstanding Achievement award, J. Sargeant Reynolds Sch. Nursing and Allied Health, 2006; scholar, J. Sargeant Reynolds CC, 2006. Fellow: Contact Lens Soc. Am. (assoc.), Nat. Acad. Opticianry (assoc.); mem.: Opticians Assn. Va. (assoc.). Office: J Sargeant Reynolds Opticianry Dept 700 E Jackson St Rm 507 Richmond VA 23219 Office Phone: 804-523-5415. Office Fax: 804-786-5298. Business E-Mail: kostrom@reynolds.edu.

OSTROW, RONA LYNN, retired librarian, educator; b. NYC, Oct. 21, 1948; d. Morty and Jeane Goldberg; m. Steven A. Ostrow, June 25, 1972; 1 child, Ciné Justine. BA, CCNY, 1969; MSLS, Columbia U., 1970; MA, Hunter Coll., 1975; PhD, Rutgers U., 1998. Cert. libr., N.Y. Br. adult and reference libr. N.Y. Pub. Libr., N.Y.C., 1970-73, rsch. libr., 1973-78; asst. libr. Fashion Inst. Tech., N.Y.C., 1978-80; assoc. dir. Grad. Bus. Resource Ctr., Baruch Coll., CUNY, 1980-90, asst./assoc. prof.; assoc. dean of librs. for pub. svcs. Adelphi U., Garden City, NY, 1990-94; chief libr. Marymount Manhattan Coll., N.Y.C., 1994-98; asst. provost Fairleigh Dickinson U., Teaneck, NJ, 1998-2000; chief libr. Lehman Coll., CUNY, Bronx, 2000—06; ret., 2006. Author: Dictionary of Retailing, 1984, Dictionary of Marketing, 1987; co-author: Cross Reference Index, 1989. Mem.: ALA, Assn. Coll. and Rsch. Librs. Office: CUNY Lehman Coll Libr 250 Bedford Park Blvd W Bronx NY 10468-1589 Business E-Mail: rona.ostrow@lehman.cuny.edu.

OSTROWSKI, STACEY, athletic trainer, educator; b. Detroit, Dec. 2, 1973; d. Harry and Betty Ostrowski. AAS, Henry Ford C.C., Dearborn, Mich., 1995; BSc in Sports Medicine/Athletic Tng., Ea. Mich. U., Ypsilanti, 1998; M in Kinesiology/Biomechanics, U. Tenn., Knoxville, 2000. Grad. asst. athletic trainer U. Tenn., Knoxville, 1998—2000; asst. athletic trainer/lectr. Lander U., Greenwood, SC, 2000—02; cert. athletic trainer No. Mich. Sports Medicine Ctr., Petoskey, Mich., 2002—. Guest lectr. anatomy and physiology U. Tenn., 1999—2001; guest spkr. sports medicine No. Mich. Sports Medicine, 2002—. Author: (case studies, articles) Jour. Athletic Tng., Am. Coll. Sports Medicine. Mem. Am. Red Cross, 1998—; lectr. cmty. edn. on knee injuries Bay St. Orthop., Cheboygan, Mich., 2003; lectr. cmty. soccer injury prevention Mich. Dept. Cmty. Health, Indian River, 2004; facilitator phys. therapy/sports medicine involvement Spl. Riders Program, Cheboygan, 2004—; lectr. H.S./cmty. on sports medicine and athletic tng., 2005—. Recipient academic excellence citation, Ea. Mich. U., 1997, Dr. Youman Academic scholarship, Knoxville, 2000. Mem.: Mich. Athletic Trainers Soc., Nat. Athletic Trainers Assn. Catholic. Avocations: hiking, bicycling, kayaking, ice hockey. Office: No Mich Sports Medicine 11153 N Straits Hwy Cheboygan MI 49721 Personal E-mail: michiganatc@aol.com.

OSTRY, SYLVIA, academic administrator, economist; b. Winnipeg, Man., Can. d. Morris J. and B. (Stoller) Knelman; m. Bernard Ostry; children: Adam, Jonathan. BA in Econs., McGill U., 1948, MA, 1950; PhD in Econs., Cambridge U. and McGill U., 1954; also 19 hon. degrees. Lectr., asst. prof. econs. McGill U.; rsch. officer Inst. Stats., U. Oxford, Eng.; assoc. prof. U. Montreal, Can.; with dept. stats. Econ. Coun. Can., Ottawa, 1964-72, chmn., 1978-79; chief statistician Stats. Can., Ottawa, 1972-75; dep. minister consumer and corp. affairs Govt. Can., Ottawa, 1975-78, dep. minister internat. trade, coordinator internat. econ. relations, 1984-85, ambassador for multilateral trade negotiations, personal rep. of Prime Minister for Econ. Summit, 1985-88; chancellor U. Waterloo, 1991-96; head dept. econs. and stats. OECD, Paris, 1979-83; chmn. Ctr. for Internat. Studies U. Toronto, Ont., Can., 1990-97, disting. rsch. fellow Munk Ctr. for Internat. Studies, 1997—. Lectr. Per Jacobssen Found., 1987; chmn. nat. coun. Can. Inst. Internat. Affairs, 1990-95; western co-chmn. Blue Ribbon Commn. for Hungary's Econ. Recovery, 1990-94; mem. adv. bd. Inst. Internat. Econs., Washington; founding mem. Pacific Coun. on Internat. Policy; Volvo Disting. vis. fellow Coun. on Fgn. Rels., N.Y.C., 1989. Author: Governments and Corporations in a Shrinking World: The Search for Stability, 1990, The Threat of Managed Trade to Transforming Economies, 1993; co-author: (with Richard Nelson) Technonationalism and Technoglobalism: Conflict and Cooperation, 1995; co-editor: (with Karen Knop, Richard Simeon, Katherine Swinton) Rethinking Federalism: Citizens, Markets and Governments in a Changing World, 1995; New Dimensions of Market Access, 1995, (with Gilbert R. Winham) The Halifax G-7 Summit: Issues on the Table, 1995, Who's on First: The Post-Cold War Trading System, 1997, APEC and Regime Creation in the Asia-Pacific: The OECD Model?, 1998, Technology, Productivity and Multinational Enterprise, 1998, Intellectual Property Protection in the World Trade Organization: Major Issues in the Millennium Round, 1999, Globalization Implications for Industrial Relations, 1999, The Future of the World Trading System, 1999, Convergence and Sovereignty: Policy Scope for Compromise?, 2000, Regional Versus Multilateral Trade Strategies, 2000, Making Sense of it All: A Post Mortem on the Meaning of Seattle, 2000; The Uruguay Round North-South Grand Bargain: Implications for Future Negotiations, 2000, Regional Dominos and the WTO: Building Blocks or Boomerang?, 2000, Business, Trade and the Environment, 2000, The Changing Scenario in International Governance, 2000, Looking Back to Look Forward: The Multilateral Trading System after 50 Years, 2000, The WTO: Post Seattle and Chinese Accession, 2001, The WTO and International Governance, 2001, Dominos and the WTO: Building Blocks or Boomerang?, 2000, Business, Trade and the Environment, 2000, The Changing Scenario in International Governance, 2000, Looking Back to Look Forward: The Multilateral Trading System after 50 Years, 2000, The WTO: Post Seattle and Chinese Accession, 2001, The WTO and International Governance, 2001, Global Integration: Currents and Counter Current, 2003, What are the Necessary Ingredients for the World Trading Order?, 2003, External Transparency in Trade Policy, 2004, The World Trading System: In the Fog of Uncertainty, 2004, Summitry and Trade: What Could Sea Island Do for Doha?, 2004, External Transparency: The Policy Process at the National Level of the Two-level game, 2004; contbg. author: China and the Long March to Global Trade, 2003, Between Feast and Famine: Fixing Global Trade, 2004, The Future of the World Trading System: Beyond Doha, 2004, Global Integration: Currents and Counter-Currents, 2005, A Global Perspective on the Multilateral System, 2006, What Are the Necessary Ingredients for the World Trading Order?, 2006, others; contbr. articles on empirical and policy-analytic subjects to more than 90 profl. publs. Decorated companion Order of Can., 1990; recipient Outstanding Achievement award Govt. of Can., 1987, Hon. Assoc. award Conf. Bd. of Can., 1992; Disting. vis. fellow Volvo, 1989-90. Fellow Royal Soc. Can., mem. Group of Thirty, Inst. for Internat. Econs. (adv. bd.). Avocations: films, theater, contemporary reading. Office: Munk Ctr Internat Studies U Toronto 1 Devonshire Pl Toronto ON Canada M5S 3K7 Office Phone: 416-946-8927. Business E-Mail: sylvia.ostry@utoronto.ca.

OSUCH, DEBRA K., materials engineer; b. 1969; married; 3 children. BS in Med. Physics, Oakland U.; MS in Hazardous Waste Mgmt., Wayne State U. Mgr., Devel. Services Soil and Materials Engineers Inc., Shelby Twp. Named one of 40 Under 40, Crain's Detroit Bus., 2006. Mem.: Comml. Real Estate Women (pres., Detroit Chpt.). Office: Soil and Materials Engineers Inc 13019 Pauline Dr Shelby Township MI 48315 Office Phone: 586-731-3100. Office Fax: 586-731-3582.*

O'SULLIVAN, BLYTHE ANN, marketing executive; b. Oak Lawn, Ill., Apr. 2, 1982; d. John Patrick and Joan Francis O'Sullivan. BS in mktg., Bradley U., 2004. Promotions intern Regent Broadcasting, Peoria, Ill., 2002—03; mktg. intern Marsh Affinity, Park Ridge, Ill., 2002—03, Soc. of Actuaries, Schaumburg, Ill., 2003—04; edn. and events coord. Denver Metro BOMA, Denver, 2004—05. Bus. mgr. Alpha Psi Omega, Peoria, Ill., 2003—04. Vol. usher Denver Civic Theatre, Denver, 2004—05. Recipient Student award for Mktg. Excellence, Bradley U., 2004. Mem.: Dog Owner Group, Beta Gamma Sigma, Phi Kappa Phi. Office: Denver Metro BOMA 1600 Broadway Ste 650 Denver CO 80202 Office Phone: 303-383-4870. Office Fax: 303-383-4871. E-mail: blytheo@bomadenver.org.

O'SULLIVAN, CINDY MARIE, mathematics professor; b. Blue Island, Ill., Dec. 22, 1956; d. Donald Edward and Frances Gloria Crawford; children: Michael, Ryan, Shannon. BS, No. Ill. U., 1979; M in Math. Edn., Olgethorpe U., Ga., 2000; M in Leadership, Kennesaw U., Ga., 2004. Cert. gifted edn. High sch. math tchr. Bremen High Sch., Midlothian, Ill., 1979—80, Elida High Sch., Ohio, 1980—81; substitute tchr. Grandville Sch. Dist., Mich., 1981; math tutor Huntington Learning Ctr., Mpls., 1987—88; substitute tchr. South Forsyth High Sch., Cumming, Ga., 1995—96; math tchr. South Forsyth Mid. Sch., 1996—99, Vickery Creed Mid. Sch., 1999—. State trainer Ga. Dept. Edn., Atlanta, 2004—05; math dept. chair Vickery Creek Mid. Sch., Cumming, 2000—; math curriculum trainer Forsyth County Schs., 2000—; featured participant Statewide Ednl. Video by Ga. Dept. Edn., Nat. Video by Phil Schlechty Group. Participant, money raiser Relay for Life, Cumming, 2003—05. Recipient Disney Am. Tchr. award, 2001, Honor Tchr., Atlanta Jour. Constitution, 2002, Tchr. of Year, Forsyth County Middle Sch., 2003. Mem.: Ga. Assn. Ednl. Leaders, Assn. Supervision and Curriculum Devel., Nat. Coun. Tchrs. Math. Avocations: reading, travel, exercise, fundraising, embroidery. Home: 4819 S Victor Ave Tulsa OK 74105

O'SULLIVAN, JUDITH ROBERTA, lawyer, writer, artist; b. Pitts., Jan. 6, 1942; d. Robert Howard and Mary Olive (O'Donnell) Gallick; m. James Paul O'Sullivan, Feb. 1, 1964; children: Kathryn, James. BA, Carlow Coll., 1963; MA, U. Md., 1969, PhD, 1976; JD, Georgetown U., 1996. Editor Am. Film Inst., Washington, 1974—77; assoc. program coord. Smithsonian Resident Assocs., Washington, 1977—78; dir. instl. devel. Nat. Archives, Washington, 1978—79; exec. dir. Md. State Humanities Coun., Balt., 1979—81, 1982—84, Ctr. for the Book, Libr. of Congress, Washington, 1981—82; dep. asst. dir. Nat. Mus. Am. Art, Washington, 1984—87, acting asst. dir., 1987—89; pres., CEO The Mus. at Stony Brook, NY, 1989—92; exec. dir. Nat. Assn. Women Judges, Washington, 1993; clk. Office Legal Adviser US Dept. State, Washington, 1994—96; trial atty. Atty. Gen.'s honors program US Dept. Justice, 1996—, sr. trial atty. Criminal divsn., Domestic Security sect., 2002—; spl. asst. US atty. US Dist. (ea. dist.) Va., 1998—2002; asst. US atty. US Dist. Ariz., Tucson, 1999—2000. Summer assoc. Piper & Marbury, Balt., 1995; chair Smithsonian Women's Coun., Washington, 1988-89. Author: The Art of the Comic Strip, 1971 (Gen. Excellence award Printing Industry Am.); Workers and Allies, 1975; (with Alan Fern) The Complete Prints of Leonard Baskin, 1984, The Great American Comic Strip, 1991; editor Am. Film Inst. Catalogue: Feature Films, 1961-70, 1974-77; mem. editl. bd. Am. Film Inst. Catalog, 1979-1990. Trustee Child Life Ctr., U. Md., College Pk., 1971-74; chair Smithsonian Women's Coun., 1988-89. Univ. fellow, U. Md., 1967—70, Mus. fellow, 1970—71, Smithsonian fellow, Nat. Collection Fine Arts, Washington, 1972—73. Mem.: Mystery Writers of Am. (exec. bd. Mid-Atlantic br. 2003—), D.C. Bar Assn., Md. Bar Assn. Avocations: landscape painting, mystery writing.

O'SULLIVAN, KERRY, educational consultant; d. Patrick J. and Patricia J. O'Sullivan. BS, Binghamton U., 1996; MS in Edn., Fordham U., 2002. Cert. tchg. K-6 NY, sch. counselor NY, sch. adminstrn., supr. NY. Dir. children's summer program Rye Recreation Dept., Rye, NY, 1998—2006; tchr. Resurrection Sch., Rye, 1999—. Ednl. cons. Carver Ctr., Port Chester, NY, 2002—03; sch. guidance asst. Yonkers (NY) City Sch. Dist., 2001—02. Contbr. Providence Ho., New Rochelle, NY, 1996. Mem.: ACA (assoc.), Phi Kappa Phi (life), Alpha Phi. Office: Resurrection Sch 116 Milton Rd Rye NY 10580 Office Phone: 914-967-1218.

O'SULLIVAN, LYNDA TROUTMAN, lawyer; b. Oil City, Pa., Aug. 30, 1952; d. Perry John and Vivian Dorothy (Schreffler) Troutman; m. P. Kevin O'Sullivan, Dec. 15, 1979; children: John Perry, Michael Patrick. BA, Am. U., 1974; JD, Georgetown U., 1978, postgrad., 1982-83. Bar: D.C. 1978. Ptnr. Perkins Coie, Washington, 1985-92, Fried, Frank, Harris, Shriver & Jacobson, Washington, 1993-97, Miller & Chevalier, Washington, 1997—2004; asst. dep. gen. counsel dispute resolution USAF, 2004—. Mem. adv. bd. Fed. Contracts Report, 1991-97, Govt. Contract Costs, Pricing & Acctg. Report, 1997-99; mem. faculty govt. contracts program George Washington U., 1993-99; lectr. in field. Contbg. author: Cost Reimbursement Contracting, 3d edit., 2005. Fellow Am. Bar Found.; mem. ABA (chair truth in negotiations com. 1991-94, chair acctg., cost and pricing com. 1996-2000, coun. sect. pub. contract law 1993-95). Office: 1777 N Kent St Arlington VA 22209 Business E-Mail: lynda.osullivan@pentagon.af.mil.

O'SULLIVAN, STEPHANIE L., federal agency administrator; With Office of Naval Intelligence, CIA, 1995—, assoc. dep. dir. sci. & tech., 2003—05, dep. dir. sci. & tech., 2005—. Office: Directorate of Science & Technology CIA Office Dir of National Intelligence Washington DC 20505*

OSWALD, EVA SUE ADEN, retired insurance company executive; b. Ft. Dodge, Iowa, Feb. 2, 1949; d. Warren Dale Aden and Alice Rae (Gingerich) Aspeslet; m. Bruce Elliott Oswald, Nov. 27, 1976. BBS, U. Iowa, 1972. With Great Am. Ins. Co., 1975—, v.p. mktg. div. Orange, Calif., 1987, v.p. profit ctr., 1988-90; pres. Garden of Eva, Inc., 1990—. Mem. Snelling-Selby Bus. Coun. Mem. Nat. Assn. Ins. Women, State Guarantee Fund (bd. dirs. 1986-87), Exec. Women St. Paul, Midway C. of C. Methodist. Office: 1585 Marshall Ave Saint Paul MN 55104-6222

OSWALD, LEIGH HEITING, counseling administrator; b. Barnwell, S.C., Nov. 19, 1967; d. Arnold Wilfred and Priscilla Ann (Rountree) Heiting; m. Gregory Todd Oswald, Feb. 23, 1991 (div.). BS, Winthrop Coll., 1989; MEd in Elem. Sch. Guidance/Counseling, U. S.C. Cert. spl. edn. and elem. tchr., S.C. Spl. edn. tchr. Ebenezer Ave. Elem. Sch., Rock Hill, S.C., 1989-90, Lexington (S.C.) Intermediate Sch., 1990—. Mem. Union United Meth. Ch., Irmo, S.C., 1979—. Mem. Coun. for Exceptional Children, Omicron Delta Kappa, Delta Omicron, Alpha Delta Pi. Avocations: water-skiing, crafts, gardening, reading. Office: Lexington Intermediate Sch 420 Hendrix St Lexington SC 29072-3300

OSWALT, SALLY HUNDT, small business owner; b. Bangor, Wis., Apr. 17, 1917; d. Peter A. Hundt and Mary Ann Zanter-Hundt; divorced; children: David, Mary Ellen, Jeffrey, Nancy. BS in Polit. Sci., U. Wis., La Crosse, 1991. Owner, mgr. Coiffures by Sally, La Crosse, 1941—. Bd. dirs. Diocese of La Crosse Cemetery Assn., 1995—; pres. Ridge History Pk., Inc., 2001—, treas., 2001—. Bd. dir. La Crosse County, 1974-76, 84-90, 92-94, bd. health, 1986—, mem. regional planning com., 1988—, vice chmn. rep. women, 2003; mem. venture cap. fund com. United Way, 1970-75; mem. pharmacy internship bd. Gov., 1980-85; treas. Ridge History Pk., 2001-05, pres., 2000—. Mem.: Bus. and Profl. Women (pres. 1987—89). Republican. Roman Catholic. Avocations: politics, gardening, golf, bridge, singing. Home and Office: Coiffures by Sally 2116 Pine St La Crosse WI 54601-3811

OTANI, YURIKO L. (CHARKO), artist; b. Pasadena, Calif., Mar. 11, 1931; d. Giichi and Shiki Nakamura; m. Herbert Otani, Nov. 24, 1959 (dec.); children: Diana R. Furhmann, Laura M., Glen K., Julia M. Otani Caruso, David E., Robert K. BFA, The Cooper Union Advancement Sci. and Art, 1976. Cert. tchr. Ramapo Coll., N.J. Graphic artist JJ Michaels, Little Ferry, NJ, 1981; art tchr. No. Valley Old Tappan HS, NJ, 1988—93; with prodn. dept. Cmty. Life, Westwood, NJ, 1993—97; graphic artist The Town Jour., Allendale, NJ, 1998, Rockland County Times, NY, 1998—2006. Guest lectr. WWII Japanese-Am. interment at local elem. & HS. Contbr. articles to newspapers and profl. jour. WWII internee, Tulare, Calif., Gila, Ariz.; guest lectr. WWII Japanese-Am. internments; contr. essays to local newspapers. Recipient Recognition award, Bergen County, 1991, Point of Light award, Pres. George H.W. Bush, 1991, Low Fund prize, Cooper Union, 1976, Tchr. Recognition award, Gov. of NJ. Avocations: art, quilting, swimming.

OTERO, LETTICE MARGARITA, lawyer; b. May 7, 1952; JD, Ind. U., Bloomington, 1977; LLM, U. Calif., Berkeley, 1986. Bar: Ind. 1978, Calif. 1989. Sole practice, Gary, Ind., 1978-85; estate and gift tax atty. IRS, San Jose, Calif., 1988-93; chief legal counsel Ind. Dept. Revenue, Indpls., 1993—, inheritance tax adminstr., 1997—. Vol. Girl Scouts Am., Indpls., 1998; chairwoman Hispanic caucus Ind. Dem. Party, Indpls., 1999; mem. adv. coun. Office of Women's Affairs Ind. U., 1996; mem. Gov.'s Task Force on Election Integrity, 2001. Mem. Calif. Bar Assn. (mem. exec. com. 1992). Office: Ind Dept Revenue 100 N Senate Ave Rm N248 Indianapolis IN 46204-2217

OTERO-SMART, INGRID AMARILLYS, advertising executive; b. Santurce, P.R., Jan. 9, 1959; d. Angel Miguel and Carmen (Prann) Otero; m. Dean Edward Smart, May 4, 1991; 1 child, Jordan. BA in Comm., U. P.R., 1981. Traffic mgr. McCann-Erickson Corp., San Juan, P.R., 1981-82, media analyst, 1982, asst. account exec., 1982-83, account exec., 1983-84, sr. account exec., 1984-85, account dir., 1985-87; account supr. Mendoza-Dillon & Assocs., Newport Beach, Calif., 1987-89, sr. v.p. client svcs., 1989-96, exec. v.p., dir. client svcs., 1996—99; Pres. & COO Mendoza-Dillon & Assoc., Aliso Viejo, Calif., 1999—. Mem. Youth Motivation Task Force, Santa Ana, Calif., 1989—; bd. dirs. Orange County Hispanic C. of C., Santa Ana, 1989-90, U.S. Hispanic Family of Yr.; mem. Santa Ana Project P.R.I.D.E., 1993. Mem. Assn. Hispanic Advt. Agys. (bd. dirs. 1998—, pres. 2002-03). Avocations: reading, writing, antiques, music, theater.

OTHELLO, MARYANN CECLILIA, quality improvement specialist; b. N.Y.C., Oct. 23, 1946; d. Alphonse Reasum and Edith (Atwater) O. BS, St. Paul's Coll., Lawrenceville, Va., 1968; MS, Columbia U., 1972. Cert. adoption specialist. Family therapist crisis intervention Dept. Social Svcs., N.Y.C., 1968-72; dir. treatment team Abbott House, Irvington, N.Y., 1972-73; unit chief Manhattan State Psychiat. Facility, N.Y.C., 1973-75; asst. dir., dir. social svcs. St. Peter's Sch., Peekskill, N.Y., 1975-77; dir. Patchwork Svcs. for Children, Santa Ana, Calif., 1977-78; dir. adult and geriatric svcs. Cen. City Community Mental Health, L.A., 1978-79; trainer, facilitator Lifespring, Inc., San Rafael, Calif., 1978-80; sr. mgmt. cons. Nelson Cons. Group, Inc., Mpls., 1980-92; dep. dir. Div. Family Svcs. Dept. of Svcs. to Children, Youth and Their Families, Wilmington, Del., 1992-93; dir. planning and quality assurance Episcopal Cmty./Diocese of Pa., Phila., 1993-94; dep. exec. dir. Episcopal Cmty. Svcs./Diocese of Pa., Phila., 1994-97; CEO, MCO Cons. Ltd., Wilmington, Del., 1997-99; field svc. mgr. N.Am. Ctr. Consultation and Profl. Devel. Child Welfare League of Am., 1999—. Cons. Calif. Dept. Edn., 1977; field instr. casework Hunter Coll. Sch. Social Work, N.Y.C., 1975-77; adj. instr. U. So. Calif., L.A., 1977-78; specialist career devel. Goal for It, L.A., 1977-82; mgmt. devel. cons. Mgmt. Dynamics, Irvine, Calif., 1980-82; treas. Images of Sisterhood, Crofton, Md., 1994. Contbr. articles to profl. jours.; was interviewed twice on radio talk show As It Is, U. Calif., Irvine. Bd. dirs., presenter humanitarian awards L.A. Commn. on Assaults Against Women, 1985-87, Lettye's Sisters In Session, Wilmington, 1993—; facilitator Ch. of Religious Scis., Huntington Beach, Calif., 1981-83, NAACP, Urban League; founding mem. Kinship Alliance, Pacific Grove and Tustin, Calif., 1992—; mem. Afro-Am. Mus., Phila., 1993—; mem. nat. adv. com. on managed care Child Welfare League Am., 1995—; mem. adv. bd. Nat. Leadership Inst., 1996. Named one of Outstanding Young Women of Am., 1976, 81; N.Y. State Regent scholar, 1968; Marie Antoinette Canon fellow Columbia U., 1972. Fellow Child Welfare League Am. (Adoption Specialist plaque 1976); mem. NAFE, Smithsonian Instn., Nat. Soc. for Historic Preservation, Wadsworth Antheneum, Nat. Trust for Hist. Preservation, Assn. for Female Execs. Avocations: caligraphy, photography, bicycling, photography, travel. Office: Nat Ctr for Consultation and Profl Devel CWLA 440 1st St NW Ste 3 Washington DC 20001-2028 Home: 708 Pebble Beach Dr Elkton MD 21921-6305 Office Phone: 410-398-2712. Personal E-mail: consultmco@aol.com.

OTHERSEN-KHALIFA, CHERYL LEE, insurance agent, realtor; b. Bay City, Mich., Aug. 17, 1948; d. Andrew Julius and Ruth Emma (Jacoby) Houthoofd; m. Wayne Korte Othersen, Sept. 5, 1964 (div.); 1 child, Angela Othersen; m. Imed M. B. Salah Khalifa, Sept. 27, 1997 (div.). Lic. ins., Mich. State U., 1980, lic. realtor, 1981. Owner, operator Glad Rags Boutique, Unionville, Mich., 1976-79; dept. mgr. Gantos, Saginaw, Mich., 1979-80; agt., bookkeeper Othersen Ins. Agy., Inc., Unionville, 1979-81, v.p., 1981—; realtor Osentoski Realty Corp., Unionville, 1981—; benefits specialist AFLAC Ins. Co., 1995—. Active Mich. chpt. Nat. Head Injury Found., Crohn's and Colitis Found. Am., Inc.; active Nat. Mus. in Arts, Nat. Trust Hist. Preservation; assoc. mem. Am. Mus. Natural History; charter supporter U.S. Holocaust Meml. Mus.; mem. Saginaw Bay Symphony Orch., 2004—05, Saginaw Art Mus., 2005; vol. local Rep. campaigns, 1982, 1984, 1986, 2001. Fellow: John F. Kennedy Libr. Found. (hon.); mem.: Saginaw County Homebuilders Assn., Nat. Mus. Women in the Arts, Profl. Ins. Agts., Saginaw Christian Women's Assn., Saginaw County C. of C. (diplomat 2004—05), Saginaw Twp. Bus. Assn. (bd. dirs. 2002—). Avocations: sports, painting, travel, gardening, reading. Home: 2575 Ranier St Saginaw MI 48603-3325 Office: Cheri Othersen Agy 2575 Ranier St Saginaw MI 48603 Office Phone: 989-249-4376.

OTIS, LEE (SARAH) LIBERMAN, lawyer, educator; b. N.Y.C., Aug. 19, 1956; d. James Benjamin and Deen (Freed) L.; m. William Graham Otis, Oct. 24, 1993. BA, Yale U., 1979; JD, U. Chgo., 1983. Bar: N.Y. 1985, D.C. 1994. Law clk. U.S. Ct. Appeals (D.C. cir.), Washington, 1983-84; spl. asst. to asst. atty. gen., civil div. U.S. Dept. Justice, Washington, 1984-86, dep. assoc. atty. gen., 1986, assoc. dep. atty. gen., 1986; law clk. to Justice Antonin Scalia U.S. Supreme Ct., Washington, 1986-87; asst. prof. law George Mason U., Arlington, Va., 1987-89; assoc. counsel to the Pres. Exec. Office of the Pres., Washington, 1989-92; assoc. Jones, Day, Reavis & Pogue, Washington, 1993-94; chief judiciary coun. U.S. Sen. Spence Abraham, 1995-96; chief counsel subcom. on immigration Com. on the Judiciary, U.S. Senate, 1997-2000; gen. counsel U.S. Dept. Energy, 2001—05. Adj. prof. law Georgetown Law Sch., 1995, 96. Mem. Federalist Soc. for Law and Pub. Policy (founder). Republican. Jewish. Avocations: sailing, computers.

O'TOOLE, KATHLEEN M., protective services official; b. 1954; m. Dan O'Toole; 1 child, Meghan. BA, Boston Coll., 1976; JD, New Eng. Sch. Law, 1982. Bar: Mass. 1982. Officer Boston Police Dept., 1979-86; officer, supt. Met. Police Dept., 1986-90; security mgmt. Digital Equipment Corp., 1990-92; lt. col. Mass. State Police, 1992-94; sec. Office Pub. Safety, Boston, 1994—98; commr. Boston Police Dept., 2004—06; chief insp. Ireland's Nat. Police Force, 2006—. Office: Garda Siochana Depot Phoenix Park Dublin Ireland*

O'TOOLE, PATRICIA ELLEN, writer, educator; b. Alpena, Mich., Oct. 10, 1946; d. Gordon Roy and Gertrude (McKenna) O'T. BA, U. Mich., 1968. Adj. asst. prof. Columbia U. Sch. Arts, NYC, 1995—2002, lectr., 2002—03, asst. prof., 2004—05, assoc. prof., 2005—. Author: The Five of Hearts: An Intimate Portrait of Henry Adams and His Friends, 1880-1918, 1990 (finalist, Pulitzer Prize and Nat. Book Critics Circle award), Money & Morals in America, 1998, When Trumpets Call: Theodore Roosevelt After the White House, 2005. MacDowell Colony fellow, 1988. Mem. AAUP, PEN, Am. Hist. Assn., Orgn. Am. Historians. Democrat. Office: Dept Arts Columbia Univ 404 Dodge MC 1804 2960 Broadway New York NY 10027-6902

O'TOOLE, TARA JEANNE, medical educator, former federal agency administrator; b. Newton, Mass., May 3, 1951; d. Harold J. and Jeanne (Whalen) O'T. BA, Vassar Coll., 1974; MD, George Washington U., 1981; MPH, Johns Hopkins U., 1988. Diplomate Am. Bd. Internal Medicine, Am. Bd. Preventive/Occupational Medicine. Rsch. asst. Sloan-Kettering Cancer Inst., N.Y.C., 1974-77; resident in internal medicine Yale New Haven (Conn.) Hosp., 1981-84; physician Balt. Cmty. Health Ctrs., 1984-87; fellow in occupational medicine Johns Hopkins U., Balt., 1987-89; sr. analyst Office Tech. Assessment, Washington, 1989-93; asst. sec. energy for environ., safety and health US Dept. Energy, Washington, 1993-97; dep. dir. Johns Hopkins U. Ctr. Civilian Biodefense Studies, 1998—2001, dir., 2001—03; prof. medicine U. Pitts., 2003—; CEO Ctr. for Bio Security, U. Pitts. Medical Ctr., 2003—. Chmn. Bd. Fedn. Am. Scientists, 2004—. Democrat. Office: Ctr for Biosecurity The Pier IV Bldg 621 E Pratt St Ste 210 Baltimore MD 21202 E-mail: Totoole@upmc-biosecurity.org.

OTREMBA, GERALDINE MARIE, congressional and international relations executive; b. NYC, Apr. 13, 1946; d. Frank Stanley and Beatrice Gloria (O'Malley) O.; m. Stanley F. Turesky, Oct. 26, 1975; children: Sarah, Catherine. BA, St. John's U., 1967; MA, U. N.C., 1969, PhD, 1979. Dep. dir. ops. John F. Kennedy Ctr. for the Performing Arts, Washington, 1984-87, dir. planning, 1987-90, dir. ops., 1990-91, dir. govt. liaison, 1991-92, assoc. mng. dir., 1991-94; dir. congrl. rels. Libr. Congress, Washington, 1994—; exec. dir. Open World Leadership Ctr., Washington, 1999—2002; CEO Ctr. Russian Leadership Devel. (former Russian Leadership Program), Libr. of Congress, Washington, 2002. Chmn. Nat. Conf. Performing Arts Ctrs., 1990-93. Roman Catholic. Office: Congl Rels Office Libr Congress James Madison Meml Bldg 101 Independence Ave SW Washington DC 20540-4000 Office Phone: 202-707-7720.

OTT, ATTIAT FARAG, economist, educator; b. Cairo, June 18, 1935; m. David J. Ott (dec.); 1 child, Dana. BA in Econ. with highest honors, Cairo U., 1956; PhD, U. Mich., Ann Arbor, 1962. Assoc. prof., econ. So. Meth. U., 1965—68; vis. assoc. prof. U. Md., College Park, 1968—69; fiscal economist, office tax analysis U.S. Dept. Treasury, 1969; assoc. prof., econ. Clark U., Worcester, Mass., 1969—71, prof., 1971—; dir. Inst. Econ. Studies, 1980—. Vis. scholar Hoover Instn., Stanford U., 1977—78; adj. scholar Am. Enterprise Inst.; prin. investigator Fund for Pub. Policy Rsch.; mem. nat. com. and tax policy bd. Taxation with Representation, Washington. Author: Macroeconomic Theory, 1975, Federal Budget Policy, 1977, The Public Sector in the Global Economy, 2003; co-author: The Massachusetts Health Plan, 1988, Privatization and Economic Effiency, 1991, Public Sector Budgets: A Competitive Study, 1993; guest columnist Worcester Telegram and Gazette, mem. editl. bd. Jour. Econ. Devel., mem. editl. bd., guest editor Atlantic Econ. Jour.; contbr. articles to numerous profl. jours. Fellow, Olin Found., 1980—92; grantee, Am. Bar Found., 1969—72, Hoover Instn., 1978—79; H.B. Earhart fellow, 1982. Home: 262 Salisbury St Worcester MA 01609-1641 Office: Clark U Dept Econs Worcester MA 01610 Office Phone: 508-793-7447. Business E-Mail: aott@clarku.edu.

OTT, DORIS ANN, librarian; b. Elgin, ND, Sept. 24, 1942; d. Oscar Edward Hirning and Lorraine Wilhelmina Gruebele; m. Richard Donald Ott, Nov. 21, 1998; m. Bernnett Gordon Reinke, Sept. 1961 (div.); 1 child, Scott Bernnett Reinke; m. James Lee Daugherty, June 1974 (div.). BS, Dickinson State U., 1964; MLS, George Peabody Coll., 1965. Lic. Ind. life tchr. Elem. tchr. Mott Pub. Schs., ND, 1963-64; asst. prof. Dickinson State U., ND, 1965-73; media specialist Minot Pub. Schs., ND, 1973-74; head tech. svcs. Bartholomew County Libr., Columbus, Ind., 1974-75; media specialist Rushville Pub. Schs., Ind., 1975-86; head interlibr. loan ND State Libr., Bismarck, 1986-87, asst. state libr., 1987—2001, state libr., 2001—. Image cons. Beauty For All Seasons, 1984—. Mem. Humane Soc. Mem. ALA, N.D. Libr. Assn., Mountain Plains Libr. Assn. Avocation: image consulting. Office: ND State Libr 604 E Boulevard Ave Dept 250 Bismarck ND 58505-0800 Office Phone: 701-328-2492. Business E-Mail: dott@nd.gov.

OTT, SHARON, artistic director; Theatre dir.: The Wash, Yankee Dawy You Die; artistic dir.:Berkeley Repertory Theatre; now artistic dir. Seattle Repertory Theatre. Former bd. dirs. Theatre Comms. Group, v.p. Recipient Obie award, numerous others awards.

OTT, VICTORIA E., history professor; b. Florence, Ala., May 16, 1971; d. Thomas O. and Margaret F. Ott; m. John M. Vanover, May 18, 1996. BA, U. Ctrl. Fla., Orlando, 1994, MA, 1998; PhD, U. Tenn., Knoxville, 2003. Grad. asst. women's studies program U. Ctrl. Fla., 1996—98; grad. asst. U. Tenn., Knoxville, 1998—99, grad. tchg. asst., 1999—2003, lectr., 2003—04; asst. prof. history Birmingham-So. Coll., Ala., 2004—. Contbr. articles to profl. jours. Lee Verstanding scholar, U. Tenn., 1999, 2001, Am. History scholar, Nat. Soc. Colonial Dames Am. in State of Tenn., 2002, Charles O. Jackson fellow, U. Tenn., 2000, Mellon Rsch. fellow, Va. Hist. Soc., 2001. Mem.: So. Hist. Assn., So. Assn. Women Historians, Phi Alpha Theta (scholar 2000). Office: Birmingham-So Coll 900 Arkadelphia Rd Birmingham AL 35254 Office Phone: 205-226-7826. Office Fax: 205-226-3089. Business E-Mail: vott@bsc.edu.

OTTESEN, BODIL BANG, art educator; d. Knud Christian Bang and Ingeborg Marie Kristine Nielsen; 1 child, Peter Eik. BA, Goucher Coll., Towson, Md., 1979; MA, U. Md., College Park, 1980, PhD, 1987. Adj. prof. U. Md., 1982—90, Goucher Coll., 1983—84, Towson U., 1982—89, Johns Hopkins U., Balt., 1982—, U. Md., Balt. County, 1989—91, 2003—. Md. Inst. Art, 2003—. Art educator Balt. Mus. Art, 1984—2003. Contbr. papers to profl. pubs. Bd. mem. Contemporary Mus., Balt., 1996—, Friends of Modern Art, BMA, Balt., 1996—. Mem.: Coll. Art Assn., Phi Beta Kappa. Home: 6104 Bellinham Ct #831 Baltimore MD 21210 Office: Md Inst Coll of Art 1300 Mt Royal Ave Baltimore MD 21250 also: Univ Md Balt County Dept Fine Arts 1000 Hilltop Cir Baltimore MD 21250 Personal E-mail: bottesenl@comcast.net.

OTTINGER, MARY LOUISE, podiatrist; b. Valley City, N.D., July 8, 1956; d. Roy A. and Harriet A. Ottinger. BS, N.D. State U., 1978; D of Podiatric Medicine, Scholl Coll. Podiatric Med., 1983. Diplomate Am. Bd. Podiatric Surgery. Resident in podiatric medicine J.A. Haley VA Hosp., Tampa, Fla., 1983—84; podiatrist Med. Ctr. Podiatry Group, Augusta, Ga., 1984—. Author: (with others) Podiatric Dermatology, 1986. Fellow Am. Coll. Foot Surgeons; mem. Am. Podiatric Med. Assn., Ga. Podiatric Med. Assn., Am. Diabetes Assn. Methodist. Avocation: photography. Office: Foot and Ankle Group PC 1515 Laney Walker Blvd Augusta GA 30904

OTTO, CHARLOTTE R., consumer products company executive; b. Duluth, Minn., Aug. 15, 1953; BS, Purdue U., 1974, MS in Mgmt., 1976. With Procter & Gamble, 1976—, from asst. brand mgr. to brand mgr. various products, 1977-83, assoc. advt. mgr. paper products divsn., 1984-87, assoc. advt. mgr. toilet tissue/towels, paper products div., 1987-89, dir. issues mgmt., pub. affairs divsn., 1989-90, dir. pub. rels., pub. affairs divsn., 1990-91; v.p. pub. rels. Procter & Gamble USA, 1991-93; v.p. corp. comms. Procter & Gamble Worldwide, 1993-95, v.p. pub. affairs, 1995-96; sr. v.p. pub. affairs The Procter & Gamble Co., 1996-99, global pub. affairs officer, 1999—2000, global external rels. officer, 2000—. Dir. Royal Bank Fin. Grou, Canada; adv. bd. Jour. Corp. Pub. Rels., The Medill Sch. Journalism, Northwestern Univ. Mem. nat. bd. Boys & Girls Club Am.; mem. YWCA Acad. Career Women of Acheivement; chair (past pres.) Cin. Playhouse in the Park; chair exec. com. Downtown Cin., Inc.; mem. Riverfront Advisors Commn.; v.p. exec. com. Joy Outdoor Edn. Ctr.; trustee Arts & Cultural Coun. Greater Loveland; bd. mem. Am. Red Cross, Cin. Chpt.; bd. selectors, The Jefferson Awards Am. Inst. Pub. Svc.; vice-chmn. exec. com. Greater Cin. C. of C.; bd. mem. The Port of Greater Cin. Devel. Authority, Good Samaritan Hosp., Cin. Fire Mus.; mem. Leadership Cin. - Class XIV. Recipient YWCA Career Woman of Achievement award, 1993, Woman of Distinction award Gt. Rivers Girl Scouts Coun., Inc., 1998, Purdue "Old Master", 1996; recipient Disting. Alumni, Purdue U., Krannert Sch. Mgmt.; named Cincinnatian of the Yr., 2003, Juvenile Diabetes Rsch. Found., Cin. Enquirer Woman of the Yr., 2005; recipient Human Rels. award, Am. Jewish Com., 2004, Matrix award for public rels., NY Women in Comm., 2005. Mem. Ctr. Quality Leadership

Founders, Vice Pres.'s Forum, Commonwealth Club, Women's Capital Club, Queen City Club (bd. govs.), Club at Harper's Point, Arthur Page Soc., PR Seminar Com., Kenwood Country Club. Office: Procter & Gamble Co 1 Procter And Gamble Plz Cincinnati OH 45202-3393

OTTO, CHRISTINE BARNARD, educational association administrator; b. Ridgecrest, Calif, June 22, 1952; d. John and Elisabeth; m. Andrew P. Otto, June 21; m. Douglas G. Bundy (div.); children: Skylar DePedro, Stephanie Shepherd, Douglas B. AA, Antelope Valley Coll., 1989; BS Human Devel. and Family Studies honors, U. Nev., 2001. Literacy asst. U. Nev., Reno, 2000—01; ind. living skills counselor Choices Alta Regional Ctr., Truckee, Calif., 2001—03; career cons. Truckee, 2001—. Tchr. Tahoe Forest Hosp. Children's Ctr., Truckee, 2002—05; baby sign lang. specialist Sign with Kinders, Truckee, 2003—; early head start family advocate Placer Cmty. Action Coun., Auburn, Calif., 2005—. Pres. Mesa P.T.S.A, Palmdale, Calif., 1992—94; dir. Palmdale High Drill Dance Team, 1993—95; vol. Truckee Rotary, 1996—; mem., sunshine chair Tahoe Forest Hosp. Dist. Aux., Truckee, 1997—. Mem.: Calif. Assn. Edn. Young Children (amb. 2003—), Soroptimist Internat. (pres.-elect, pres. 2006, Women's Opportunity award 2000, Emerging Leaders award 2006). Avocations: sewing, scrapbooks, singing, quilting. Home: PO Box 3604 Truckee CA 96160 Office: Sign with Kinders PO Box 3604 Truckee CA 96160 Office Phone: 530-587-2568. Personal E-mail: christruckee@yahoo.com.

OTTO, ELIZABETH HALL, education educator; b. Florence, S.C., Aug. 5, 1939; d. William Everette and Elizabeth Hines Hall; m. Willmer Jerome Otto, Nov. 26, 1971; children: Teresa, Michael, John. BA, Winthrop Coll., Rock Hill, S.C., 1961; MA, U. N.C., Chapel Hill, 1964. Tchr. Lancaster H.S., SC, 1961—62; instr. Mitchell Coll., Statesville, NC, 1963—65; tchr. Myers Park H.S., Charlotte, 1967—68; instr. Bee County Coll., Beeville, Tex., 1968—72; prof. Fla. C.C., Jacksonville, 1979—. Dept. chair Fla. C.C., 1999—2003. Co-author: (article) Jour. Social Sci., 1990; project dir. (coll. course) Cmty. Econ. Devel., 1983 (2d pl. Joint Coun. Econ. Edn.). Named Outstanding Faculty, Fla. C.C., 1994. Mem.: So. Hist. Assn. Avocations: reading, travel. Home: 3665 Manor Oaks Dr Jacksonville FL 32277 E-mail: eotto@fccj.edu.

OTTO, JEAN HAMMOND, journalist; b. Kenosha, Wis., Aug. 27, 1925; d. Laurence Cyril and Beatrice Jane (Slater) Hammond; m. John A. Otto, Aug. 22, 1946; children: Jane L. Rahman, Mary Ellen Takayama, Peter J.; m. Lee W. Baker, Nov. 23, 1973. Student, Ripon Coll., 1944-46. Women's editor Appleton (Wis.) Post-Crescent, 1960-68; reporter Milw. Jour., 1968-72, editorial writer, 1972-77, editor Op Ed page, 1977-83; editorial page editor Rocky Mountain News, Denver, 1983-89, assoc. editor, 1989-92, reader rep., 1992-99; endowed chair U. Denver, 1992-97. Founder, chmn. bd. trustees First Amendment Congress, 1979-85, chmn. exec. com., 1985-88, 89-91, pres. 1991-96, mem. bd. trustees, 1979-96; founding mem. Wis. Freedom of Info. Council. Recipient Headliner award Wis. Women in Communications, 1974; Outstanding Woman in Journalism award YWCA, Milw., 1977; Knight of Golden Quill Milw. Press Club, 1979; spl. citation in Journalism Ball State U., 1980; James Madison award Nat. Broadcast Editorial Assn., 1981; spl. citation for contbn. to journalism Nat. Press Photographers Assn., 1981; Ralph D. Casey award U. Minn., 1984; U. Colo. Regents award, 1985; John Peter Zenger award U. Ariz., 1988; Paul Miller Medallion award Okla. State U., 1990; Colo. SPJ Lowell Thomas award, 1990, Disting. Alumna award Ripon Coll., 1992, Hugh M. Hefner First Amendment Lifetime Achievement award Playboy Found., 1994; named to Milw. Press Club Hall of Fame, 1993, Freedom of Info. Hall of Fame, 1996. Mem.: Soc. Profl. Journalists (nat. treas. 1975, nat. sec. 1977, pres.-elect 1978, pres. 1979—80, pres. Sigma Delta Chi Found. 1989—92, chair Found. 1992—94, First Amendment award 1981, Wells Key 1984), Am. Soc. Newspaper Editors (bd. dirs. 1987—92), Colo. Press Assn. (chmn. freedom of info. com. 1983—89), Assn. Edn. in Journalism and Mass Communications (Disting. Svc. award 1984), Milw. Press Club (Hall of Fame 1993). Home: 2462 N Prospect #311 Milwaukee WI 53211 Personal E-mail: jottofirst@aol.com.

OTTO, MARGARET AMELIA, librarian; b. Boston, Oct. 22, 1937; d. Henry Earlen and Mary (McLennan) O.; children— Christopher, Peter. AB, Boston U., 1960; MS, Simmons Coll., 1963, MA, 1970; MA (hon.), Dartmouth Coll., 1981. Asst. sci. librarian M.I.T., Cambridge, 1963, Lindgren librarian, 1964-67, acting sci. librarian, 1967-69, asst. dir., 1969-75, assoc. dir., 1976-79; librarian of coll. Dartmouth Coll., Hanover, N.H., 1979—. Pres., chmn. bd. Universal Serials and Book Exch., Inc., 1980-81; bd. dirs. Rsch. Libr. Group; trustee Howe Libr., Hanover, 1988—, chmn., 1992—; mem. Brown Libr. Com., rsch. lbirs. adv. com. OCLC, 1991—, ARL; editl. com. Univ. Press New Eng., 1993—. Council on Library Resources fellow, 1974; elected to Collegium of Disting. Alumnus Boston U., 1980 Mem. ALA (task force on assn. membership issues 1993—, ad hoc working group on copyright issues), Assn. Rsch. Librs. (chair preservation com. 1983-85, bd. dirs. 1985-88, mem. stats. com., chair membership com. 1992—), Coun. on Libr. Resources (proposal rev. com. 1992—), Dartmouth Club (N.Y.C.), St. Botolph Club (Boston), Sloane Club (London). Home: 2 Berrill Farms Ln Hanover NH 03755-3205 Office: Dartmouth Coll 115 Baker Meml Libr Hanover NH 03755

OTTO, TAMMY, author, poet, playwright; b. Buffalo, Oct. 16, 1960; BA summa cum laude, SUNY, Buffalo. Free-lance fiction and poetry writer, Buffalo, 1983—. Instr. Literacy Vols., Buffalo, 1992—. Author: (prose) MUR, (stories) Catch Can, Smaller, Julia A Cote De La Boue, (collections) Bird Laughter, Gulls Crying Over Water, Renwls, Over Rock Lake Erie, Remembering & Forgetting, (novels) Rat City, (plays) Sleep, Perdition; contbr. of poetry and prose to various anthologies and periodicals. Poetry reader spring award ceremony SUNY, 1987, 89; contbg. mem. Greenpeace, 1987; asst. Buffalo Hist. Soc., 1992—; creator Stay Smart Stay Safe Abduction Prevention Seminar; vol. asst. Buffalo and Eirie County Historical Soc., 1992. Recipient Arthur Axelrod Meml. award, 1989, Scribbler's Club of Buffalo prize, 1989, Gregory Capasso Creative Writing award, 1990; Sarah Helen Kish Meml. Found. grantee, 1988. Mem.: Arts Council Buffalo and Erie County, Acad. Am. Poets, Golden Key Soc. (life). Home: 36 Wren Ave Lancaster NY 14086

OTTOMBRINO, LOIS KATHRYN, lawyer; b. Bklyn., June 23, 1948; d. Louis Joseph and Kathryn Rosemary (Slevin) O. RN, Sch. Nursing Queens (N.Y.) Hosp. Ctr., 1968; Cert. RN Anesthetist, Sch. Anesthesia Fairfax Hosp., Falls Church, Va., 1974; BS, George Washington U., 1978; JD, Hofstra U., 1981. Bar: NY 1982, US Dist. Ct. (ea. and so. dists.) NY 1982. From assoc. to ptnr. Bower & Gardner, NYC, 1981-94; ptnr. Wilson, Elser, Moskowitz, Edelman & Dicker LLP, NYC, 1994—. Lectr. Nat. Law & Seminar Press, NYC, Risk Mgmt. Groups, NYC, NJ Ins. Exchange, Princeton. Mem. ABA, NY State Bar Assn., Assn. Bar City NY, Bklyn. Bar Assn., NY County Bar Assn., NY State Soc. Anesthesiologists, Am. Assn. of Nurse Anesthetists. Roman Catholic. Home: 40 Remsen St Brooklyn NY 11201-7121 Office: Wilson Elser Moskowitz Edelman & Dicker 150 E 42nd St New York NY 10017-5612 Office Phone: 212-490-3000 2222. Office Fax: 212-490-3038. E-mail: ottombrinol@wemed.com.

OTTOSON, CAROL J., literature and language educator; b. Hoven, SD, Apr. 1, 1950; d. Dwight V. and Mary M. Dixon; m. Keith E. Ottoson, June 10, 1973; children: Heather V. Zehnder, Andrew D. BS, U. Minn., Mpls., 1972; MS, Minn. State U., Mankato, 1976. Sr. high English tchr. Olivia Pub. Schs., Minn., 1980—86, Prior Lake-Savage Dist. 719, Minn., 1986—. Theater dir., speech coach, Guthrie Schs. on Stage advisor, Spirit Players advisor Prior Lake Schs., 1986—, mem. staff devel. com., 2004—. Dir.: (world premiere) Island of Doctor Moreau, Hard Times. SPR chair, Sunday sch. tchr., drama dir. Holy Trinity United Meth. Ch., Prior Lake; bd. dirs. Girl Scout Coun. of Cannon Valley, Northfield, Minn., 1995—2000. Named Prior Lake Advisor of Yr., Prior Lake HS, 1994, 2002, Prior Lake Tchr. of Yr., Prior Lake Edn. Assn., 1999—2000; recipient Prior Lake Tchr. of Excellence, Prior Lake Sch. Bd., 2002; grantee Mass Media and Democracy Conf., Harvard U., 1998. Mem.: Edn. Minn. (licentiate Minn. Honor Roll Tchr. 2000). Home: 16399 Itasca Ave SE Prior Lake MN 55372 Office: Prior Lake HS 7575 150th St W Savage MN 55378 Office Phone: 952-226-8737. E-mail: cottoson@priorlake-savage.k12.mn.us.

OUALLINE, VIOLA JACKSON, psychologist, consultant; b. Edna, Tex., Oct. 17, 1927; d. S.R. Jackson and Myrtle Mae Wood; m. Charles M. Oualline Jr., Sept. 3, 1949; children: Stephen, Susan, Shari. BS, U. Houston, 1949; MS, North Tex. State U., 1962, PhD, 1975. Phys. therapist Hermann Hosp., Houston, 1948-49; pvt. practice Austin, Tex., 1949-54; Miller Orthopedic Clinic, Charlotte, N.C., 1956-57; psychologist Dallas Easter Seal Soc., 1963-81, dir. psychology dept., 1981-93; pvt. practice, 1993—. Psychol. cons. Mesquite Ind. Sch. Dist., Tex., 1974—, Duncanville Sch. Dist., Tex., 1974-76, Grand Prarie Ind. Sch. Dist., Tex., 1976-79. Mem. Am. Psychol. Assn., Tex. Psychol. Assn., Dallas Psychol. Assn., Am. Assn. Counseling Devel., Coun. for Exceptional Children, Chi Omega Mother's Club. Baptist. Avocations: reading, bicycle riding. Office: Ste 208 11311 N Central Expy Dallas TX 75243-6729 Office Phone: 214-696-1079.

OUELLETTE, DEBRA LEE, administrative assistant, consultant; b. Butte, Mont., Aug. 1, 1962; d. Eugene George and Avonne Gail (Smeltzer) O.; m. Anthony Lee Jaeger, Aug. 27, 1994 (div.). BA in Soc. and Tech., Mont. Coll. Mineral Sci. and Tech., 1985. Photographer, trainer Mountain States Energy, Butte, 1984-85; lab. asst. Western Energy, Butte, 1985-86, receptionist, 1986; acctg. data entry clk. N.Am. Resources, Butte, 1986, lease and oil data entry clk., 1986-87; data entry clk. Spl. Resource Mgmt., Butte, 1987-89; adminstrv. asst. N.Am. Indian Alliance, Butte, 1989-97, asst. dir., 1998-99; dir. Butte Parent-Aide Program, 1999; adminstrv. asst. Human Resources Coun. Dist. XII, 2000—01; site coord. Continental Gardens Housing Corp., 1999—. Designer chem. dependency forms. Mem.-at-large Vol. Ctr., Butte, 1995-96; vol. CPR first aid instr. ARC, 1999. Outstanding Pub. Svc. award Soc. Security Adminstrn., Proctective Payee Program.Personnal Invitation to Pres. Inaugration. Mem. VFW Ladies Aux. (sr. v.p. 1994-96, jr. vice trustee 1998—, 3 yr. trustee dist. 4 State of Mont. 1999—, pres. dist. 4 2001-02). Avocations: reading, assisting urban indian programs with policy and procedures, travel. Office: Continental Gardens 100 Gardens Way Butte MT 59701-2840

OUELLETTE, EILEEN MARIE, neurologist, consultant; b. Cambridge, Mass., Aug. 10, 1936; d. Leo A. and Audna M. (La Fortune) O. AB cum laude, Smith Coll., 1958; MD, Harvard U., 1962; JD, Suffolk Univ., Boston. Diplomate Am. Bd. Pediatrics, Am. Bd. Psychiatry and Neurology. Intern in pediatrics Mass. Gen. Hosp., Boston, 1962-63, asst. resident in pediatrics, 1963-64, clin. fellow in pediatrics, 1964-66, asst. resident in neurology, 1968, clin. and research fellow in neuropathology, 1968-69, clin. and research fellow in neurology, 1968-70, acting asst. resident in neuropathology, 1968-69, acting asst. resident in neurology, 1968-70, asst. neurologist, 1976—, asst. pediatrician, 1978—; teaching fellow in pediatrics Harvard U. Med. Sch., Boston, 1963-64, research fellow in neurology, 1968, research fellow in neuropathology, 1968-69, clin. fellow in neurology, 1969-70, asst. in pediatrics, 1965-70, instr. pediatrics, 1967-68, instr. neurology, 1971-76, asst. prof., 1976—; spl. fellow in neurology Nat. Insts. Neurol. Diseases and Stroke, NIH, 1968-70; asst. prof. pediatrics Boston U. Sch. Medicine, 1971-75, asst. prof. neurology, 1971-76, assoc. prof. pediatrics, 1975-76, assoc. prof. neurology, 1975-76; pediatric neurologist Emerson Hosp., Concord, Mass., 1975—; dir. pediatrics Eunice Kennedy Shriver Ctr. Hosp., Waltham, Mass., 1976-79; assoc. dir. univ. affiliated program Eunice Kennedy Shriver Ctr./Mass. Gen. Hosp., Waltham and Boston, 1976-82, dir. univ. affiliated program, 1982-86; assoc. attending pediatric neurologist McLean Hosp., Belmont, Mass., 1981—; pediatric encephalographer Emerson Hosp., Concord, Mass., 1975—. Examiner in child neurology Am. Bd. Psychiatry and Neurology, 1978—; vis. prof. child neurology Children's Hosp. of D.C., George Washington U. Med. Sch., 1975, 76, La. State U., 1983; mem. exec. com. Mass. Devel. Disabilities Council, 1984—; mem. other profl. coms.; lectr. in field. Contbr. chpts. to books, articles to profl. publs.; mem. editorial bd. Jour. Am. Assn. on Mental Deficiency, 1977-80 Bd. dirs. Greater Waltham Assn. for Retarded Citizens, 1983—, Project Pact, Program for Alcoholic Women, 1984—, Newton Hist. Soc., Mass., 1983— Nielson Scholar Smith Coll., 1954-58 Fellow Am. Acad. Pediatrics (alt. chmn. Mass. chpt. 1984—, mem. exec. com. New Eng. chpt. 1984—, nat. pres. 2005-2006); mem. Mass. Med. Soc., New Eng. Pediatric Soc., Am. Soc. Human Genetics, Child Neurology Soc. (nominating com. 1975-76, membership com. 1976-77, devel. disabilities com. 1980-81, jr. membership com. 1981—), Internat. Child Neurology Assn., Am. Acad. Neurology, Am. Epilepsy Soc.; Mass. Bar Assn., ABA. Office: Massachusetts General Hosp Fruit St Boston MA 02114*

OUELLETTE, JAMI, art educator; d. James Louis Geraci, Sr. and Helen M. Geraci; m. Michael F. Ouellette, July 14, 1959; children: Melissa Renae, Christopher Michael. AA, San Jacinto Coll., Pasadena, Tex., 1979—82; BFA, U. N.Tex., Denton, 1981—85. Cert. Secondary Art Edn. Tex. Edn. Agy., 1998. Art tchr. Copperas Cove Jr. High, Tex., 1997—2002, Mayde Creek Jr. High, Houston, 2002—. Mem.: Assn. Tex. Profl. Educators. Home: 3311 Mulberry Hill Ln Houston TX 77084 Office: Katy Ind Sch Dist 2700 Greenhouse Houston TX 77084 Office Phone: 281-237-4914. Office Fax: 281-644-1650. Personal E-mail: jamiouellette@katyisd.org.

OURADNIK, TONI KRISTIN, elementary school educator; b. Fargo, ND, Nov. 30, 1971; d. Gary Calvin and Mary Ann Ouradnik. BA, U. Minn., Mpls., 1996; MA in Tchg., U. San Francisco, 2003. Cert. wilderness first responder Wilderness Med. Inst.; tchr. Calif. Adminstr. and outreach Inst. for Fisheries Resources, San Francisco, 1997—2000; youth program guide Sea Trek Kayak Co., Sausalito, Calif., 1998—; sci. intern tchr. Town Sch. for Boys, San Francisco, 2000—02; kayaking educator and guide Blue Waters Kayak Co., Inverness, Calif., 2001—; sci. and math specialist Keys Sch., Palo Alto, Calif., 2003—; youth camp guide Half Moon Bay Kayak, Half Moon Bay, Calif., 2005—. Wilderness medicine educator Foster Calm Wildnerness Medicine, Nevada City, Calif., 2002—. Restoration vol. Hands On Network, Biloxi, Miss., 2006; vol. Glide Meml. Meth. Ch., San Francisco, 1997—2000; mentor Big Bros. Big Sisters, Mpls., 1993—94; night shift vol. Mpls. Homeless Shelter, 1993—94; food collection and distbn. Second Harvest, Mpls., 1991—93; educator YMCA Point Bonita Outdoor Sch., Sausalito, Calif., 1998—; garden vol. Peace and Justice Ctr., Chico, Calif., 2002—03; team fundraiser, mentor Leukemia and Lymphoma Soc., San Francisco, 2004—06; natural resources restoration and edn. Watershed Stewards project AmeriCorps, Fortuna, Calif., 1995—98; treas. student dormitory U. Salzburg, Austria, 1994—95. Named Top Fundraiser, Leukemia and Lymphoma Soc., 2004; recipient 1st pl., Bear Valley Cross Country Ski Resort 10km Cross-Country Ski Race, 2006; grantee, Calif. Dept. Edn., 2003; scholar, Luth. Brotherhood, 1991—95. Mem.: Assn. Environ. and Outdoor Educators, Calif. Sci. Tchrs. Assn., Keys Sch. Cmty. Leaders Club (founder, faculty adv. 2004—). Avocations: travel, yoga, writing, soccer, photography. Office Phone: 650-328-1711.

OUSLEY, AMY MICHELLE, science educator; b. Ardmore, Okla., Sept. 29, 1977; d. Lonnie William and Angela Sue Norton; m. Mikel Blake Ousley, July 7, 2001; 1 child, Zander Brighton. BS in Health and Sport Scis., U. Okla., Norman, 2000. Tchr. Choctaw (Okla.) Jr. HS, 2003—, coach, 2003—. Named Tchr. of Yr., Choctaw Jr. HS, 2005—06. Home: 612 SW 38th Pl Oklahoma City OK 73160 Office Phone: 405-390-2206.

OUTHWAITE, LUCILLE CONRAD, ballerina, educator; b. Peoria, Ill., Feb. 26, 1909; d. Frederick ALbert and Della (Cornett) C.; m. Leonard Outhwaite, Mar. 1, 1936 (dec. 1978); children: Ann Outhwaite Maurer, Lynn Outhwaite Pulsifer. Student, U. Nebr., 1929-30, Mills Coll., 1931-32; student piano, Paris, 1933-35, Legat Sch., London, 1934, N.Y.C. Ballet, 1936-41, Royal Ballet Sch., London, 1957-59. Tchr. ballet Perry Mansfield, Steamboat Springs, Colo., 1932; toured with Am. Amb. Ballet, Europe and S.Am., 1933-35; tchr. ballet Cape Playhouse, Dennis, Mass., 1937-41, Jr. League, N.Y.C., 1937-41, King Coit Sch., N.Y.C., 1937-41; owner, tchr. dance sch. Oyster Bay, N.Y., 1949-57. Prodr., choreographer ballets Alice in Wonderland, 1951, Pied Piper of Hamlin, 1952. Author: Birds in Flight, 1992, Flowers in the Wind, 1994, To the Ends of the Earth, 1997, Night Wind Whispers (A Glimpse Down Memory Lane), 1999, Far Suns and Open Seas, 2001, The Spice of Life, 2003. Mem. English Speaking Union, Preservation Soc., Alliance Française, Mill Coll. Club, Spouting Rock Beach Club, Clambake Club, Delta Gamma. Republican. Methodist. Office: 26 Elm St Topsham ME 04086-1426

OUTLAW, WANDA CECELIA, priest; b. Washington, Oct. 17, 1954; d. Augustus King and Mary Lena (Booze) Brown; 1 child, Stephen Thomas Jr. Ordained priest 2002. Tng. mgr. Bur. ATF, Washington, 1989—; leadership, women's retreat leader African-Am. Cath. Congregation, Washington, 1993—, priest, 2002—. Preacher Women Uplifting Women Ministries, Washington, 2003—; designer, trainer LJR Group, Inc., Dallas, 2005—. Author: Woven Baskets on the Baobab Tree, In The Fulfillment. Active socks and sandwiches for the homeless Dynamic Crossroads, Washington, 2005; motivational spkr. Execs. of FEW, Balt., 2003—04. Mem.: NAACP (assoc.), NAFE (assoc.). Office: Imani Temple on Capitol Hill 609-611 Maryland Ave NE Washington DC 20002 Office Phone: 202-388-8155. Personal E-mail: wanda.outlaw@atf.gov. Business E-Mail: noni.crowmother@verizon.net.

OUTT, HELEN MAY, retired elementary school educator, psychologist; d. Spurgeon Eugene Weir and Edna May Kling; m. Terry Franklin Outt, May 25, 1960; children: Daina, Holly. BS, West Chester U., Pa., 1964, MEd, 1971. Cert. tchr. Ind., 1987, sch. counselor Ind., 1988, psychologist Assn. Masters in Psychology, 1999, lic. mental health counselor Ind., 2000, psychologist Ind., 2002. Tchr. Interboro Sch. Dist., Prospect Pk., Pa., 1966—69; counselor mid. sch. Chester (Pa.) Sch. Dist., 1969—70; tchr. elem. sch. Cin. (Ohio) Sch. Dist., 1974—85; tchr., counselor Indpls. (Ind.) Sch. Dist., 1986—2005, ret., 2005. Actor: (plays) Little Theater. Vol. food and clothing drive Indpls. (Ind.) Pub. Schs., 1986—2005; vol. polls Cin. (Ohio) Rep., 1975. Recipient Above and Beyond Call of Duty award, Indpls. (Ind.) Pub. Schs., 1993. Mem.: NEA (lic. adminstrn. and supr. 1987), Ind. Mental Health Counselors Assn., N.Am. Masters Psychology, Ind. Sch. Counseling Assn., Ind. Counseling Assn., Ind. State Tchrs. Assn., Indpls. (Ind.) Edn. Assn. (dir. region 1986—2000, dir. dist. 1986—2000, bldg. rep. 1986—2005, chmn. profl. devel. com. 1990—98, nat. rep.), Phi Delta Kappa. Republican. Meth. Avocations: photography, making greeting cards.

OUYANG, NORMA M., psychologist; arrived in U.S., 1985; m. Steve C. Ouyang, Jan. 1, 1970; children: Francis, Luke. BA, Nat. Taiwan Normal U., 1970; MBA, Pacific State U., 1988; MA, Azusa Pacific U., 1998, D of Psychology, 2003. Clin. psychologist Calif. Bd. Psychology. Founder, cons. Family Enrichment, Irvine, Calif., 1988—; with Orange County Health Care Agy., Westminster, 1999; intern U. Calif., Riverside, 2002—03; clin. psychologist Calif. State U., Fullerton, 2004—. Sr. group coord. Orange County Chimes Cath. Assn., Anaheim, Calif., 1989—93; asst. gen. mgr. Valone Computer Co., Irvine, 1988—93. Fellow, Calif. State U., Fullerton, 2003—04. Mem.: APA, Asian Faculty/Staff Assn., Am. Coll. Personnel Assn. Democrat. Roman Catholic. Avocations: reading, music, writing, travel.

OVADIAH, JANICE, not-for-profit developer, cultural organization administrator; m. Isaac Ovadiah; children: Meir Benjamin, Simha Victoria Miriam. BA, Washington U., St. Louis, 1965; MA, Columbia U., 1967, PhD, 1978. Dir. profl. study tours Am. Odysseys, Inc., 1973-84; escort, interpreter in French U.S. Dept. State, 1978-84; asst. to exec. dir. Meml. Found. for Jewish Culture, 1984-87; exec. dir. Congregation Shearith Israel/The Spanish & Portuguese Syn., N.Y.C., 1987—, Sephardic House, N.Y.C., 1987—2003; freelance cons., 2003—. Instr. French Rutgers U., New Brunswick, N.J., 1978-79; asst. to dir. of The Maison Franclase, Columbia U., 1970-72; instr. French Columbia U., 1968-70; lectr. in field. Author: (books) Toward a Concept of Cinematic Literature: An Analysis of Hiroshima, Mon Amour, 1983, The Far Away Island of the Grey Lady, 1979, others; contbr. articles to profl. jours. E-mail: jovadiah@aol.com.

OVERALL, THERESA LYNNE, elementary school educator; d. Edsel and Patricia Overall. AB Divisional Scis., Math. and Stats., Hollins U., Roanoke, Va., 1978; MS Computer Edn. and Cognitive Systems, U. North Tex., Denton, 2000; PhD in Ednl. Computing, U. N.Tex., Denton, 2006. Cert. provisional elem. gen. tchr. Tex. Edn. Assn., 1978, provisional tchr. young children Tex. Edn. Assn., 1978, NK-3 endorsement - gen. Commonwealth Va. State Bd. Edn., 1978. Classroom tchr., tech. coord. The Lamplighter Sch., Dallas, 1978—99; rsch. asst. Inst. for Integration Tech. into Tchg. and Learning, Denton, Tex., 1999—2006. Founder, pres. The Logo Opportunity, Richardson, Tex., 1980—. Author: (curriculum guide) TI Logo Curriculum Guide, (manual) On the Road to Silver and Gold-A Leader's Guide to Helping Girls Earn Preliminary Silver and Gold Award Recognitions: Studio 2B Edition; contbr. articles to profl. jours. Vol. Girl Scouts of the USA, Dallas, 1974—. Named Outstanding Young Women of Am., 1981, 1984, 1985, Outstanding Student of Yr., Computer Edn. and Cognitive Systems Dept., U. North Tex., 2001; recipient Presdl. award for Excellence in Math. Tchg., The Lamplighter Sch., Dallas, 1990, 1991, Outstanding Vol. award, Girl Scouts Tejas Coun., 1995, Green Angel, 1996, Appreciation Pin, 1998, Honor Pin, 2000, Heart of Gold Award, 2005, Tejas award, 2006; Toulouse Sch. Grad. Studies scholar, U. North Tex., Denton, 1999, Alumnae Dau. scholar, Hollins Coll. Alumnae Assn., 1974, 1975, 1976, 1977. Mem.: Am. Ednl. Rsch. Assn., Internat. Soc. for Tech. Edn., Nat. Coun. Tchrs. Math., Leadership Richardson, Kaligrafos, The Dallas Calligraphy Soc. Home: 423 Marilu Richardson TX 75080-4533

OVERBAUGH, MARYANNE W., elementary school educator; b. Bklyn., Sept. 8, 1958; d. George Allen and Doris Virginia (Cusic) Wiseman; m. Mark Charles Overbaugh, Aug. 2, 1980; 1 child, Jeremiah Alden Mark. AA, SUNY, Cobleskill, 1978; BS, Coll. of St. Rose, 1980, MS, 1984. Cert. tchr. N-6, 7-12 English, N.Y. Elem. educator Greenville (N.Y.) Ctrl. Sch., 1980—. Mem., treas. Medusa (N.Y.) Vol. Fire Co., 1984—, EMT Rensselaerville Vol. Ambulance, Medusa, N.Y., 1981-92; Sunday sch. tchr. Greenville Norton Hill (N.Y.) Methodist Ch., 1985—. Mem. United Methodist Women, Norton Hill, N.Y., Delta Kappa Gamma. Avocations: calligraphy, cross stitch, walking, reading. Home: PO Box 46 Medusa NY 12120-0046 Office: Greenville Ctrl Sch SR 32 Greenville NY 12083

OVERBEY, GAIL ANN URHAHN, psychology professor; d. Marvin Zeno and Ruth Ann Urhahn; m. Daniel Leon Overbey, Jan. 5, 1974; children: Jeffrey Leonard, Douglas Marvin. BS, S.E. Mo. State U., 1973; PhD, U. Tex., Austin, 1979. Lic. Psychologist Mo., 1980, cert. Health Svc. Provider Mo., 1993. Instr. in med. psychology in child psychiatry Wash. U. Sch. Medicine, St. Louis, 1979—82; psychologist Pvt. Practice, 1982—84; asst. prof., psychology dept. S.E. Mo. State U., Cape Girardeau, Mo., 1989—98, assoc. prof., psychology dept., 1998—2005, prof., 2005—. Faculty cons. Psi Chi; presenter in field. Supervised prodn. (2 videos); contbr. articles to profl. jours. Vol. Project Charlie, Cape Girardeau, Mo., 1990—. Recipient Project Charlie Facilitator Yr., Excelsior Optimist Club, 2000; grants, Grants and Rsch. Funding Com. of SE Mo. State U., 1990, 1991, 1992, 1998, 2003. Mem.: Coun. Tchrs. Undergrad. Psychology, Am. Psychol. Soc. Roman Catholic. Avocations: reading, sewing. Office: SE Mo State Univ One University Plaza MS 5700 Cape Girardeau MO 63701 Personal E-mail: goverbey@semo.edu.

OVERBEY, SUSAN J., history educator; b. Northampton, Mass., July 21, 1951; d. Frank Joseph Kovalski and Jane Ann Malinowski; m. James Randall Overbey, Nov. 25, 1971; children: Joseph Frank, Katharine Jane, Jacob Thomas. BA, Westfield State Coll., Mass., 1989. Cert. hist. tchr. NH, 2004. Tchr. Dover H.S., NH, 1989—. Advisor Nat. Honor Soc., Dover, 2000—06. Mem.: NEA. Avocation: sailing. Office: Dover High School 25 Alumni Dr Dover NH 03820 Office Phone: 603-516-6971.

OVERCASH, SHELIA ANN, nurse; b. Columbia, Mo., Dec. 17, 1962; d. William Edgar and Lea Rosalee (Pilotte) Bacon; m. Stephen Harry Overcash, July 20, 1990; children: Kari Heller, Julie Keehnast. Diploma, Spoon River Coll., 1992. Cert. in intravenous therapy. Charge nurse Lindenwood Health

Ctr., Peoria, Ill., 1992—93, Havana (Ill.) Health Care, 1993—94; staff nurse Graham Hosp, Canton, Ill., 1994—95, Pekin (Ill.) Hosp., 1995—97, Meth. Med. Ctr., Peoria, Ill., 2000—. Mem. AACN, Critical Care Nurses Assn., Phi Theta Kappa. Avocations: gardening, continuing education.

OVERCAST, VICKIE L., librarian; b. Casper, Wyo., Jan. 28, 1957; d. Peter Bernard Fowler and Mabel Louise Mayland; m. Ronald Lynn Overcast, June 26, 1981; children: Erin, Stacey, Bryan, Bryce. BA, U. Wyo., Laramie, 1979, MA, 1995. HS libr. Washakie County Sch. Dist., Worland, Wyo., 1979—; volleyball coach Worland HS, 1980—2000; career edn. tchr. Worland Migrant Sch., 1980—86, mid. sch. tchr., 2002—. Swimming coach Spl. Olympics, Worland, 2004—. Named Volleyball Coach of Yr., 2000, 2002. Mem.: Worland Edn. Assn. (v.p., pres. 1990—92), Worland Reading Assn. (v.p., pres. 1982—86), Wyo. LIbr. Assn. (sec. 1991—93), Wyo. Edn. Assn. (state bd. dirs. 1993—95), Delta Kappa Gamma (v.p., pres. 2002—03, 2006—). Avocations: counted cross stitch, reading, camping, skiing, swimming. Office: Washakie County Sch Dist 801 S 17th St Worland WY 82401

OVERMYER, JANET ELAINE, counselor; b. Allentown, Pa., July 3, 1951; d. Harold Romig and Amanda Babb Fegely; m. Warren Reichert, June 9, 1973 (div. Sept. 1987); children: Nathan, Rebekah, Matthew; m. Michael Steven Overmyer, May 23, 1997. BA in Psychology, Muhlenberg Coll., 1973; MA in Clin. Counseling, Heidelberg Coll., 2000. Lic. Profl. Clin. Counselor Ohio, cert. Chemical Dependency Counselor Ohio. Dir. social svc. Glanzman Colonial Nursing Home, Toledo, 1994—98; cmty. svc. provider Zepf Cmty. Mental Health Ctr., Toledo, 1999—2001; primary therapist Focus Healthcare of Ohio, Maumee, Ohio, 2000—01; dir. women's outpatient program Behavioral Connections of Wood County, Perrysburg, Ohio, 2001—02; clin. svc. dir. Vol. of Am., N.W. Ohio, Toledo, 2002—03; assessment clinician Behavioral Connections of Wood County, Perrysburg, 2003—. Bd. trustees Huntingdon Cmty. Ctr., Sylvania, Ohio, 1992. Mem.: Nat. Coun. Alcoholism & Drug Dependency (intervention specialist 2001—), Mental Health Counselors Assn., Am. Counseling Assn. Lutheran. Avocations: reading, piano, travel. Home: 4501 Luann Ave Toledo OH 43623

OVERSTREET, KAREN A., federal bankruptcy judge; BA cum laude, Univ. of Wash., 1977; JD, Univ. of Oregon, 1982. Assoc. Duane, Morris & Heckscher, Phila., 1983-86; ptnr. Davis Wright Tremaine, Seattle, 1986-93; bankruptcy judge U.S. Bankruptcy Ct. (we. dist.) Wash., Seattle, 1994—. Assoc. editor Oregon Law Review; dir. People's Law Sch.; mem. advisory com. U.S. Bankruptcy Ct. (we. dist.) Wash. Mem. Nat. Conf. of Bankruptcy Judges, Wash. State Bar Assn. (creditor-debtor sec.), Seattle-King County Bar Assn. (bankruptcy sec.), Am. Bar Assn., Wash. Women Lawyers Assn. Office: US Bankruptcy Ct 700 Stewart St Rm 7216 Seattle WA 98101 Office Phone: 206-370-5330.

OVERSTREET, REGINA NIX, mathematics educator; b. Dawsonville, Ga., Feb. 13, 1946; d. Vernon Stancel and Jewell Fouts Nix; m. James Edward Overstreet, Sr., June 27, 1970; children: Jennifer Overstreet Flacke, James Edward Jr. BS in Edn., U. of Ga., Athens, 1968; MEd, Ga. State U., Athens, 1979. Math. tchr. Clayton County Schs., Jonesboro, Ga., 1968—70, Marietta City Schs., Ga., 1970—71, Cobb County Schs., Marietta, 1971—81; adj. math instr. Kennesaw State U., Ga., 1986—99; math. instr. Chattahoochee Tech. Coll., Marietta, 2004—. Pres. bd. of edn. Transfiguration Cath. Ch., Marietta, 1983—84. Named Tchr. of the Yr., Sprayberry H.S. Key Club, 1979. Mem.: Am. Math. Assn. of 2-Yr. Colls., Ga. Assn. for Devel. Edn., Nat. Assn. for Devel. Edn. Roman Catholic. Avocation: tennis. Office: Chattahoochee Tech Coll 980 S Cobb Dr Marietta GA 30060 Office Phone: 770-528-4566. Home Fax: 770-528-4584; Office Fax: 770-528-4584. Business E-Mail: roverstreet@chattcollege.com.

OVERSTREET-GOODE, JANWIN GAIL, secondary school educator, music educator, director; d. Winfred Hulus Overstreet and Janice Dell Burnett; m. John Paul Goode, June 26, 1982; 1 child, Catherine Gail. MusB in Edn., Murray State U., 1979, MusB, 1979; MusM, U. Ky., 1981. Choir dir. New Washington (Ind.) H.S., 1981—82; tchr. music Anderson County Schs., Lawrenceburg, Ky., 1982—84; choir dir. J. Frank Dobie H.S., Houston, 1984—92, Langham Creek H.S., Houston, 1992—94, Sam Rayburn H.S., Pasadena, Tex., 1994—2004, Friendswood (Tex.) H.S., 2004—. Mem.: Tex. Music Adjudicators Assn., Am. Choral Dirs. Assn., Tex. Choral Dirs. Assn., Tex. Music Educators Assn. (area chmn. 1997—2001, regional chmn. 1997—2001, organizer All State Choir 2004—05). Home: 1406 Frontier Ln Friendswood TX 77546 Office: Friendswood High Sch 702 Greenbriar Friendswood TX 77546 Office Phone: 281-482-3413. E-mail: joversreet-goode@fisdk12.net.

OVERTON, JANE VINCENT HARPER, biology professor; b. Chgo., Jan. 17, 1919; d. Paul Vincent and Isabel (Vincent) Harper; m. George W. Overton, Jr., Sept. 1, 1941; children: Samuel, Peter, Ann. AB, Bryn Mawr Coll., 1941; PhD, U. Chgo., 1950. Rsch. asst. U. Chgo., 1950-52, mem. faculty, 1952-89, prof. biology, 1972-89; prof. emeritus, 1989. Author articles embryology, cell biology; artist exhibitions at Fine Arts Bldg. Gallery, Chgo., 1992-95 NIH, NSF research grantee, 1965-87. Avocations: painting, ceramics. Home: 5550 S South Shore Dr Apt 505 Chicago IL 60637-5061

OVERTON, NICOLE YOLANDA, program analyst; b. Buffalo, Feb. 24, 1973; d. Dewitt David and Mary Lee Overton. BS, Buffalo State Coll., 1996. EDI programmer, analyst Ingram Micro, Buffalo, 1996—; cashier supr. Quality Markets, Buffalo, 1991-96. Tchg. asst., tutor for computers Buffalo State Coll., application designer, career dept. Troop leader Girl Scouts Buffalo and Erie County, 1996—, trip dir., treas., axcct., 1999—. Gir Scout Coun. Delegate 2002-. Democrat. Baptist. Avocations: drawing, dance, reading novels, music, movies. Office: Ingram Micro 1759 Wehrle Dr Buffalo NY 14221-7032

OVERTON, ROSILYN GAY HOFFMAN, finance company executive; b. Corsicana, Tex., July 10, 1942; d. Billy Clarence and Irma Elise (Gay) Hoffman; m. Aaron Lewis Overton Jr., July 2, 1960 (div. Mar. 1975); children: Aaron Lewis III, Adam Jerome; m. Mardiros Hatsakorzian, 1991. BS in Math., Wright State U., Dayton, Ohio, 1972, MS in Applied Econs., 1973; postgrad., NYU, 1974—76. CFP. Rsch. analyst dept. def. Nat. Security Agy., 1962—67; bus. reporter Dayton Jour.-Herald, 1973—74; economist First Nat. City Bank, NYC, 1974, AT&T Co., 1974—75; broker Merrill Lynch, NYC, 1975—80; asst. v.p. E.F. Hutton & co., NYC, 1980—84; v.p., nat. mktg. dir. investment products Manhattan Nat. Corp., 1984—86; pres. R.H. Overton Co., NYC, 1986—; ptnr. Brown & Overton Fin. Svcs., 1987—. Named Businesswoman of Yr., NYC, 1976; fellow, Wright State U. Mem.: Internat. Assn. Fin. Planning (pres. NY chpt.), Inst. Cert. Planners, Mensa, Wright State U. Alumni Assn., Gotham Bus. and Profl. Womens Club, Zonta, Rotary Internat. Methodist. Office: 25418 Northern Blvd Ste 5 Little Neck NY 11362-1451

OVERTON, SHARON FAYE, elementary school educator; b. Tell City, Ind., Oct. 20, 1949; d. Albert John Dauby and Anna Catherine Harpenau; m. Ron Overton, Apr. 14, 1973; children: Jennifer, Jeff. BS cum laude, Ind. State U., 1970, MS, 1972. Cert. elem. tchr., mid. sch. endorsement math. 3d grade tchr. Tell City-Troy Twp. Sch. Corp., 1970-73; 2d grade tchr. E.V.S.C., Evansville, Ind., 1973-74, math. tchr., 1974-84, tchr. 5th grade, 1984—. Mem. PTA. Mem.: Gamma Phi Beta (rituals chairperson). Roman Catholic. Avocations: travel, sewing, golf. Home: 3725 Aspen Dr Evansville IN 47711-3011 Office: Scott School 14 940 Old State Rd Evansville IN 47711

OWEN, AMY, library director; b. Brigham City, Utah, June 26, 1944; d. John Wallace and Bertha (Jensen) Owen. BA, Brigham Young U., 1966, MLS, 1968. Sys. libr. Utah State Libr., Salt Lake City, 1968—72, dir. reference svcs., 1972—74, dir. tech. svcs., 1974—81, dep. dir., 1981—87, dir., 1987—2003. Serials com. chmn. Utah Coll. Libr. Coun., Salt Lake City, 1975—77, exec. sec., 1978—84, mem. coun., 1987—2003; mem. staff Gov.'s Utah Sys. Planning Task Force, Salt Lake City, 1982; staff liaison Utah Gov.'s Conf. on Libr. and Info. Svcs., 1977—79, chmn. exec. planning com., 1990—91; mem. pres.'s adv. panel Baker & Taylor Co., Somerville, NJ, 1977—78; panelist U.S. Dept. Edn., 1992; mem. rsch. project adv. com. U. Wis. Sch. Libr. and Info., Madison, 1992—94; mem. adv. panel Nat. Commn. Libr. and INfo. Svcs., 1985; Alumni Honor lectr. Coll. Humanities Brigham Young U., 1990; cons., trainer in field. Contbr. chpts. to books; contbg. author: various manuals. Presdl. apptd. mem. Nat. Mus. and Libr. Svcs. Bd., 2004; mem. coun. Utah Endowment for Humanities, 1986—91, vice chmn., 1987—88, chmn., 1988—90; trustee Bibliographic Ctr. for Rsch., 1987—2003, mem. pers. com., 1988—89, chmn. person com., 1989—90, mem. nominating com., 1984, v.p. bd. trustees, 1989—91, pres., 1991—93; active Chief Officers of State Libr. Agys., 1987—2003, mem. stats. com., 1988—93, mem. network com., 1993—97, mem. state info. policy workshop com., 1988, bd. dirs., 1992—96; mem. conf. program com. Fedn. of State Humanities Couns., 1988; mem. coop. pub. libr. data sys. task force Nat. Commn. on Libr. and Info. Svcs., 1988—90; grant rev. panelist NEH, 1988, 1992, panel mem. reading and discussion groups, 1988; regional project mgmt. bd. mem. Intermountain Cmty. Learning and INfo. Ctr. Project, 1987—90; mem. midcontinental regional adv. com. Nat. Libr. Medicine, 1991—94; mem. adv. com. Brigham Young U. Sch. Libr. and Info. Svcs., 1989—92. Named Libr. of Yr., Libr. Jour., 1990. Mem.: ALA (planning, orgn. and bylaws com. 1981—85, LITA divsn. Satellite Conf. Task Force mem. 1982, bd. dirs. ASCLA divsn. 1984—86, clene roundtable mem. com. 1984—86, fin. com. 1984—86, SLAS program com. 1984—86, ALA Office for Rsch. coop. pub. libr. data sys. adv. com. 1985—89, pres. program com. 1986, nominations com. 1986—87, PLA divsn. editor column 1987—89, PLA divsn. goals, guidelines and stds. com. 1987—90, nat. adv. bd. office comms. svcs., voices and visions project 1988—89, exec. bd. mem. 1988—90, PLA pub. libr. data svc. adv. com. 1988—91, fin. com. 1989—92, chair 1990—91, PLA non MLS involvement com. 1990—91, PLA Kellogg Phase III EIC project adv. com. chmn. 1990—92, PLA strategic issues and directions com. 1991—92, exec. bd. mem. 1993—94, bd. dirs. ASCLA divsn. 1993—96, fin. com. 1993—96, pres. ASCLA divsn. 1994—95, ASCLA Divsn. Profl. Achievement award 2004), Utah Partnership Edn. and Econ. Devel. (rsch. com. 1995—95), Utah Edn. Network (steering com. 1996—2003), Dynix Snowbird Leadership Inst. (nat. adv. bd. 1990—2002), Mountain Plains Libr. Assn. (rec. sec. 1979—80, fin. com. 1982—84, Disting. Svc. award 1989), Utah Libr. Assn. (exec. bd. 1976—80, pres. 1978—79, Disting. Svc. award 2003, Spl. Svc. award 1989), Alpha Lambda Alpha, Phi Kappa Phi. Home: 4786 Naniloa Dr Salt Lake City UT 84117-5547

OWEN, ANGIE D., elementary school educator; b. Knoxville, Feb. 3, 1968; d. D. Sam and Dianna L. Byrd; m. Jack C. Owen, July 20, 1992; 1 child, Brody Aiden. BA in Psychology, U. Tenn., Knoxville, 1991; MAT, Carson Newman Coll., Jefferson City, Tenn., 1996. Dir. Kiddie Kottage Learning Ctr., Knoxville, 1991—96; tchr. Karns Mid. Sch., 1996—. Office: Karns Middle School 2925 Gray Hendrix Knoxville TN 37931 Office Phone: 865-539-7732.

OWEN, CAROL THOMPSON, artist, educator, writer; b. Pasadena, Calif., May 10, 1944; d. Sumner Comer and Cordelia (Whittemore) Thompson; m. James Eugene Owen, July 19, 1975; children: Kevin Christopher, Christine Celese. Student, Pasadena City Coll., 1963; BA with distinction, U. Redlands, 1966; MA, Calif. State U., L.A., 1967; MFA, Claremont Grad. Sch., 1969. Cert. cmty. coll. instr., Calif. Head resident Pitzer Coll., Claremont, Calif., 1967-70; instr. art Mt. San Antonio Coll., Walnut, Calif., 1968-96, prof. art, 1996—, 1996-97, prof. emeritus, 1997, dir. coll. art gallery, 1972-73. Group shows include Covina Pub. Libr., 1971, U. Redlands, 1964, 65, 66, 70, 78, 88, 92, Am. Ceramic Soc., 1969, 97, 99, 2000, Mt. San Antonio Coll., 1991, The Aesthetic Process, 1993, Separate Realities, 1995, Sequence 1, 2001, San Bernardino County Mus., 1996, 97, 98, 99, Tampa Fla. Black, White & Gray, Artists Unltd., 1998, Current Clay VII, La Jolla, Calif., 1998, Westmoreland Art Nat., 1998, 99, Riverside Art Mus., 1998, Fine Art Inst. Juried Show, San Bernardino, 1998, 99, 2000, Parham Gallery, L.A., 1998, 99, Angels Gate Cultural Ctr., San Pedro, Calif., 1998, Los Angeles County Fair, Pomona, Calif., 1998, Monrovia, Arts Festival, 1998, Art for Heavens Sake Festival, 1998, 99, Riverside Art Mus., 1998, 99, 2000, Birger Sandzen Meml.Gallery McPherson, Kans., 1998, 2000, Earthen Art Works Gallery, LA, 1999, State Polytechnic U., Pomona, 1999, 2001, Mo. State U., Warrensburg, 1999, City, of Brea Gallery, 1999, 2000, All Media Exhibit, Chico, Calif. 1999, Period Gallery, Omaha, 1999, 2000, 01, 02, Mixed Media, Period Gallery, 2002, Franklin Square Gallery, Southpoet, NC, 1999, 2000, Judson Gallery, LA, 1999, San Angelo (Tex.) Mus. Fine Arts, 2000, So. Calif. Juried Art Exhbn., San Bernardino, Calif., 2000, Gallery 212, Ann Arbor, Mich., 2000, Judson Gallery, LA, 2000, Artists Unltd., Inc., Tampa, Fla., 2000, Urban Inst. Contemporary Arts, Grand Rapids, Mich., 2000, Tri-Lakes Ctr. for Arts, Palmer Lake, Colo., 2000, Santa Cruz Art League, Calif., 2000, Fine Arts Inst., San Bernardino County Mus., Redlands Calif. 2000, Vermont Artisan Designs, Brattleboro, 2000, USA Craft, 1999, New Caanan, Cons., 1999, Keith Gallery, Dexter, Mich., 1999, Claremont Forum Gallery, 1999, Parham Gallery, Santa Monica, Calif., 1999 (Grand prize 1999), City of Brea Galleries, Calif., 2000, 01, Chiarosouro Galleries, Chgo., 2000, TLD Design Ctr. and Gallery, Westmont, Ill., 2000, 2001, North Tahoe Art Ctr., Calif., 2000, Palos Verdes Art Ctr., Rancho Palos Verdes, Calif., 2000, Peck Gallery, Providence, 2000, Alder Gallery, Oreg., 2001, Rocky Mt. Arts Ctr., NC, 2001, Esmay Fine Art Gallery, Rochester NY, 2001, Hillcrest Festival, 2001, Dysfunctional, Business of Art Ctr., Manitou Springs, Colo., 2001, Nat. Juried Exhbn., Gallery 214, Montclair, NJ, 2002, Mt. San Antonio Coll., Walnut, Calif., 2001, Gallery Mia Tyson, Wilmington, NC, 2002, Millard Sheets Gallery, Pomona, Calif., 2002 (Honorable mention), Period Gallery, "Abstraction", Omaha, 2002, Rocky Mount Art Ctrs., Rocky Mount, NC, 2003, Kellogg U. Art Gallery, Calif. State Poly. U., Pomona, 2003, 05, Period Gallery, Omaha, 2003, Feats of Clay XVI Lincoln (Calif.) Arts, 2003, Sanchez Art Ctr., Pacifica, Calif., 2003, "Containment", SKH, Great Barrington, Mass., 2003, Multi-Media Mini Show, San Bernardino County Mus., 2004, Fine Arts Acad., 2004, City of Brea Gallery, 2004, Ink adn Clay 31 Exhbhs., Kellogg U. Art Gallery, Claif. State Poly U., Pomona, 2005, XIEM Gallery, Pasadena, 2005, numerous others; one woman show United Meth. Ch., Redlands, 2006; ceramic mural commd. U. Redlands, 1991; represented in permanent collections Redlands Art Assn Gallery, Redlands; artwork in (book) Collectible Teapots, 2000; Group Internat. Exhbn. Internationale Wertbewerb Salzbrand Keramic, 2002, der Handwerks Kammer Koblenz, Galerie Handwerk, Germany, 2002. Recipient San Bernardino County Mus., 1996, Hon. Mention, 1998, 1999,; Past Pres. Monetary award, 1997, Jack L. Conte Design Cons. Purchase award Westmoreland Art Nat., 1998, 3rd Pl. Monetary award All Calif. City of Brea Galleries, 2000, Honorarium for teapots Urban Inst. Contemporary Arts, Grand Rapids, Mich., 2000. Mem. Am. Ceramic Soc. (design divsn., Design chpt. monetary award 1999), Calif. Scholarship Fedn., Coll. Art Assn. Am., Friends of Huntington Library, L.A. County Mus. Art, Redlands Art Assn., Fine Arts Inst., Sigma Tau Delta. Republican. Presbyterian.

OWEN, CAROLYN TRENT, education educator; b. Kingsport, Tenn., July 26, 1951; d. Clyde, Jr. and Gladys Trent; m. Joseph Charles Owen, Mar. 22, 1975; children: Brian Christopher, Robert Trent, John Miller. BA in History, East Carolina U., Greenville, N.C., 1972; MA in Psychology, Pepperdine U., Malibu, Calif., 1987. Part-time instr. Coll. of Lake County, Grayslake, Ill., 1996—2004; adj. prof. Oakton C.C., Des Plaines, Ill., 1996—2004; instr. Wake Tech. C.C., Raleigh, NC, 2005—. Capt. USAF, 1974—77, Griffiss Air Force Base, N.Y. Recipient Ray Hartstein award for Academic Excellence, Oakton C.C., 1999. Republican. Presbyterian. Avocations: cross stitch, scrapbooks. Home: 613 Charleston Dr Clayton NC 27527 Office: Wake Technical CC 9101 Fayetteville Rd Raleigh NC 27603 Office Phone: 919-212-3279.

OWEN, CYNTHIA CAROL, sales executive; b. Ft. Worth, Oct. 16, 1943; d. Charlie Bounds and Bernice Vera (Nunley) Rhoads; m. Franklin Earl Owen, Oct. 20, 1961 (div. Jan. 1987); children: Jeffrey Wayne, Valeria Ann, Carol Darlena, Pamela Kay; m. John Edward White, Jan. 1, 1988 (div. Sept. 1991). Cert. Keypuncher, Comml. Coll., 1963; student, Tarrant County Jr. Coll., 1974-77; BBA in Mgmt., U. Tex., Arlington, 1981. Keypunch operator Can-Tex. Industries, Mineral-Wells, 1966-67; sec. Electro-Midland Corp., Mineral-Wells, 1967-68; exec. sec. to v.p. sales Pangburn Co., Inc., Ft. Worth, 1972-78; bookkeeper, sec. CB Svc., Ft. Worth, 1978-82; project mgr. Square D Co., Ft. Worth, 1982—. Mem.: NAFE, NOW, AAUW. Baptist. Avocations: miniature golf, volleyball. Home: 1221 Pine Ridge Rd Roanoke TX 76262 Office: Square D Co 204 Airline Dr Ste 300 Coppell TX 75019-4663 Business E-Mail: cindy.owen@us.schneider-electric.com.

OWEN, JANE DALE, non-profit organization executive; d. Kenneth Dale and Jane Blaffer Owen; m. Per Arneberg; children: Ingrid Arneberg, Erik Arneberg. Attended, Bennington Coll., Vt. Founder, pres. Citizens' League for Environ. Action Now (CLEAN), Houston, 2000—. Bd. dir. Fedn. Am. Scientists; dealt with govt. agencies EPA, Harris County Pollution Control, Sierra Club, Citizen Environ. Coalition. Former exec. com. mem. Blaffer Gallery, mem. adv. bd., U. Houston; former exec. com. mem. Moores Sch. of Music Soc., U. Houston; recommended and funded the popular children's film program called "Family Flicks" Mus. Fine Arts, Houston; served on Mus. Fine Arts Film Com., Houston; avid supporter Houston SPCA, Planned Parenthood, Houston. Office: CLEAN 5120 Woodway Dr Ste 9004 Houston TX 77056 Office Phone: 713-524-3000.

OWEN, KAREN MICHELLE, manufacturing executive; b. Garden City, Mich., Aug. 22, 1952; d. Leonard Arthur and Katrena Pickford (Floyd) Leonard; divorced; children: Joseph Paul, Nina Bloom. Student, Mich. State U., 1970-73, Eastern Mich. U., 1976-78; BBA, Western Mich. U., 1983. Dept. mgr. Meijer's Thrifty Acres Retail, East Lansing, Mich., 1973-74, Canton Ctr., Mich., 1974-75; insp. hydramatic Gen. Motors, Ypsilanti, Mich., 1975-76, specialized clk., 1976-77, supr. quality, 1977-79, gen. supr. quality, 1979, Three Rivers, Mich., 1979-84, asst. supt. mfg., 1984-87, supt. quality, 1987-94; quality mgr. Am. Axle & Mfg., Three Rivers, Mich., 1994-95, corp. mgr. platforms and quality adminstrn. Detroit, 1995—. Leader Girl Scouts Am., Three Rivers, 1988-92. Mem. NAFE, C. of C., Toastmasters, Beta Gamma Sigma. Republican. Home: 11439 Cloverlawn Dr Brighton MI 48114-8130 Office: Am Axle & Mfg One Dauch Dr Detroit MI 48211-1115 Office Phone: 313-758-4556.

OWEN, LAURI J., lawyer; b. Camp Pendleton, Calif., May 23, 1967; d. Larry H. Owen and Lois L. Allen. BS in Social Scis. summa cum laude, Boise State U., 1998, MA in Comm. summa cum laude, 2001; JD, U. Calif. Boalt Sch. Law, Berkeley, 2006. Cert. peace officers stds. and tng. level III Idaho. Sr. commd. dep. sheriff Ada County Sheriff's Office, Boise, 1990—2003; law clk. Bay Area Legal Aid, San Mateo, Calif., 2005; advocate Internat. Inst. of the East Bay, Oakland, Calif., 2005—06. Presenter workshops on domestic violence; cmty. activist. Contbr. scientific papers to profl. confs. Pres. STOP Domestic Violence U. Calif. Berkeley, Calif., 2004—06; mem. VAWA Task Force, Bay Area, Calif., 2004—06, human Trafficking Task Force, Bay Area, 2006—. Recipient Team award, Ada County Sheriff's Office. Mem.: Alaska Bar Assn., Phi Kappa Phi. Democrat. Office: PO Box 924 Bethel AK 99559

OWEN, MOLLY JACKSON, music educator; b. Corpus Christi, Tex., Nov. 19, 1955; d. James Barton and Mary Elizabeth (Gilbert) Jackson; m. John Brooks Owen, June 6, 1981; 1 child, John Frederick. AA, Del Mar Coll., Corpus Christi, 1976; B Music Edn., Corpus Christi State U., 1978; M Choral Conducting, West Tex. State U., Canyon, 1983. Choir dir. Wynn Scale Jr. HS, Corpus Christi, 1979, Strack Intermediate Sch., Spring, Tex., 1979—81, Rockport-Fulton Mid. Sch., Rockport, Tex., 2000—; office mgr. Steeplechase Pediat. Ctr., Houston, 1986—2000. Clnician various choirs, Tex. Mem. choir St. Peter's Episcopal Ch., Rockport, 2005—. Mem.: Am. Choral Dirs. Assn. (Nat. Student award 1982), Tex. Music Educators Assn. (judge All State process 2000—), Tex. Choral Dirs. Assn. Democrat. Episcopalian. Avocations: reading, gardening, dogs. Home: 121 N Santa Clara Rockport TX 78382 Office: Aransas County Ind Sch Dist 1701 Colorado St Rockport TX 78382

OWEN, PRISCILLA RICHMAN, federal judge, former state supreme court justice; b. Palacios, Tex., Oct. 4, 1954; BA, Baylor U., 1975; JD, Baylor U. Sch. of Law, 1977. Bar: Tex. 1978, U.S. Ct. Appeals (4th, 5th, 8th and 11th cirs.). Law clerk Sheehy, Lovelace & Mayfield, 1976—77; assoc. Andrews, Kurth, Campbell & Jones, 1978—85, ptnr., 1985—94; justice Supreme Ct. Tex., Austin, 1995—2005; judge US Ct. Appeals (5th cir.), New Orleans, 2005—. Liaison to Tex. Legal Svcs. for Poor Spl. Supreme Ct. Tex., Supreme Ct. Adv. Com. on Ct.-Annexed Mediations. Bd. mem. Tex. Hearing & Service Dogs, A.A. White Dispute Resolution Inst.; advisory bd. mem. Federalist Soc. (Houston & Austin Chapter). Named Young Lawyer of Yr., Baylor U., Outstanding Young Alumna. Mem.: ABA, Am. Judicature Soc., Am. Law Inst. Office: US Courthouse 903 San Jacinto Blvd Rm 310 Austin TX 78701-2450*

OWEN, SARAH-KATHARINE, language educator; b. Charlottesville, Va. d. William Davis and Carole Anne (Bradshaw) Owen. AA, Piedmont Va. C.C., Charlottesville, 1992; BA, James Madison U., 1995; MEd, U. Va., 2001, postgrad., Va. Polytech. Inst. Tchr. Spanish and French We. Albemarle H.S., Charlottesville, 1995—96; tchr. Spanish and French, activities dir. Miller Sch. of Albemarle, Charlottesville, 1996—97; tchr. Spanish and French We. Albemarle H.S., Charlottesville, 1997—98, Monticello H.S., Charlottesville, 1998—2006; tchr. Spanish James Madison H.S. Fairfax County Pub. Schs., 2006—. Tchr. Spanish Crozet Elem. Sch., Charlottesville, 1997—98; instr. Spanish Piedmont Va. C.C., Charlottesville, 2002, 06. Author: Spanish Advanced Placement Examination Reader, 2003, 2004. Grantee, Fulbright Found., 2004—05. Avocations: reading, singing, travel, exercising, dogs. Home: 711 N Wayne St 103 Arlington VA 22201 Office Phone: 703-319-2300.

OWEN, SHAUN SONIA, elementary school educator, small business owner, consultant; d. Rose Marie Owen. Degree in Mid. Grades Edn., Augusta State U., Ga., 1995; M in Ednl. Leadership, Troy State U., Augusta, Ga., 2002; Specialist Degree in Ednl. Leadership, Lincoln Meml. U., Cleve., Tenn., 2003. Cert. tchr. Ga. State Dept. Edn., 2000. Tchr. 7th grade Hephzibah Mid. Sch., Ga., 1995—2000; tchr. 6th, 7th, 8th grades Greenbrier Mid. Sch., Evans, Ga., 2000—. Owner Shaun Owen (My Ednl. Co.), Martinez, Ga., 2005—; presenter Ga. Assn. Curriculum and Instrnl. Suprs.' Ann. Conf., Athens, Ga., 2005, Ga. Coun. for Social Studies, Athens, 2005, DeKalb County Sch. Sys., Decatur, Ga., 2005; travel team mem. Ga. Dept. Edn. Excellence Recognition, Atlanta, 2006; com. mem. Ga. Gov. Sonny Perdue's Master Tchr. and Academic Coach Implementation Com., Atlanta, 2005—06, Ga. State Sch. Supt. Kathy Cox's Tchr. Adv. Com., Atlanta, 2005—; framework rev. com. mem. Ga. Assessment for the Certification of Educators, Atlanta, 2005—; presenter ASCD Ann. Conf., Chgo., 2006, Mid. Ga. Regional Ednl. Svc. Agy., Macon, 2006, Lowndes Mid. Sch., Valdosta, Ga., 2006, Discovery Educator Network, Atlanta, 2006. Camp counselor for deaf and hard-of-hearing children Camp Julienna, Winder, Ga., 1993—95; vol. Red Cross Disaster Relief Emergency Team, Valdosta, Ga., 1990, Spinal Cord Rehab. Ctr. at Veterans' Hosp., Augusta, 1992, Safe Kids of Augusta, 1998; vol./ mentor Girl's Home of Augusta, Augusta, 1998; mistress of ceremonies Lakeside HS Scholarship Pageant, Evans, Ga., 2005. Finalist Top Ten for Ga. Tchr. of Yr., Ga. Dept. Edn. Excellence Recognition, 2006; recipient Sallie Mae First Class Tchr. award, Richmond County Bd. Edn., 1995—96, Tchr. of Quarter, Greenbrier Mid. Sch., 2002—03, Tchr. of Yr., 2003—04, Columbia County Tchr. of Yr., Columbia County Bd. Edn., 2004—05. Mem.: Nat. Mid. Sch. Assn., Nat. Coun. for Social Studies, Ga. Mid. Sch. Assn., Ga. Coun. for Social Studies, Ga. Coun. o Econ. Edn., Alpha Kappa Delta Internat. Sociology Honor Soc., ASCD, PA of Ga. Educators, Ga. Tchr. of Yr. Assn. Achievements include presenting in Canada and Chicago, asked by companies interested in marketing the unique teaching strategies I have developed in my classroom over the past 11 years. Office: Greenbrier Middle Sch 5120 Riverwood Pkwy Evans GA 30809 Office Phone: 606-267-2631. Office Fax: 706-650-6085. Personal E-mail: loveoflearning@knology.net.

OWEN, SYLVIA, interior design executive; d. Manfred and Maria Curry; grad. in Interior Design, U. Munich, 1963, N.Y. Sch. Interior Design, 1965; m. Christopher Owen, Oct. 9, 1965; 1 dau., Tjasa. With Internat. Knoll Planning Unit, N.Y.C., 1968-71; sr. interior designer, assoc. John Carl Warnecke and Assocs., N.Y.C., 1971-78; ptnr. Innerplan, N.Y.C., 1978-82; founder, operator Owen & Mandolfo, Inc., 1982—. Mem. Am. Soc. Interior Designers, AIA (assoc.). Projects include Chase Manhattan Bank, Chemical Bank, Republic Nat. Bank, AT&T Hdqrs., Bedminster, N.J., Sun Co. Hdqrs., Radnor, Pa., Globtik Tankers' exec. offices, N.Y.C. (first prize for corp. interiors Interior Design mag. 1976), Am. Hosp. in Paris expansion, CCNY, Commerzbank, N.Y.C., Restoration Villard Houses for Capital Cities Communications, Inc., N.Y.C., Beneficial Mgmt. Corp., Peapack, N.J., David Murdock Assocs., N.Y.C.; developing Gen. Telephone Electric hdqrs. bldg., Stamford, Conn., Dime Savings Banks, L.I., Christian Dior stores, N.Y.C. and Bal Harbour, Fla., tower stes. Waldorf Astoria Hotel, Trump Tower stores, design of N.Y. offices of Continental Airlines, Disney offices in N.Y.C., Belgian Consulate, German-Am. C. of C., Nat. Ctr. Found., Merrill Lynch, Goldman Sachs, numerous others; redesigning Neiman-Marcus store, San Francisco; developing new image Charles Jourdan stores, Davidoff of Geneva, L.A.; designing numerous pvt. residences. Works pub. in Archtl. Record, Interior Design, Interiors, N.Y. Mag., N.Y. Times, Archtl. Digest. Named one of 100 Best Interior Designers Worldwide, Archtl. Digest; recipient Outstanding Achievement award and 1st prize best of competition by Inst. Bus. Designers and Interior Design Mag., 1992, 1st prize for best design Am. Soc. Interior Designers, 1992; featured in Women of Design by Rizzoli. Office: Owen & Mandolfo Inc 192 Lexington Ave Fl 17 New York NY 10016-9598 E-mail: S-Owen@owenandmandolfo.com.

OWENBY, S. DIANE, elementary school educator; d. John and Deloris Smith; m. Jeff Owenby, May 21; children: Adam, Amy, Aaron. BSc, U. Montevallo, Ala.; cert. in Elem. Edn., U. Ala., Birmingham. Cert. tchr. elem. edn., tchr. spl. edn. Tchr. Trinity Christian Sch., Birmingham, Ala., 1981—82, Flint Hill Christian, Bessemer, Ala., 1983—96, Brookwood Elem. Sch., Ala., 1997—2001, Brookwood Mid. Sch., 2002—. Office: Brookwood Middle School 17021 Brookwood Pkwy Vance AL 35490

OWENS, BIRDIE MURPHY, retired music educator; d. Jesse and Emily Murphy; m. Eddie Lee Owens, July 1, 1969; children: Birdette, Eddie Jr., Heather. BS in Choral Music, SC State Coll., 1968, BS in Instrumental Music, 1968; MusM, Winthrop U., 1975. Chorus tchr. Guinyard Butler HS, Barnwell, SC, 1969—70, Rock Hill Sch. Dist. #3, SC, 1977—2004; gen. music tchr. Southside Elem. Sch., Lancaster, SC, 1970—73; music edn. work study tchr. Winthrop U., Rock Hill, SC, 1974—75; piano, voice, chorus tchr. OASIS Performing Arts Sch., Charlotte, NC, 2004—; ret., 2004. Vol. World Vision Activities, Food for the Hungry Activities, Worldwide Christian Ministries; min. music Silver Mt. Baptist Ch., Charlotte, 1970—, husband and wife founder Bone of My Bone Flesh of My Flesh Marriage Ministry, 2003—. Mem.: Music Edn. Nat. Conf., Delta Sigma Theta. Democrat. Baptist. Avocations: reading, walking, jogging, singing, piano.

OWENS, CHRISTINE CLAIRE, art educator, graphics designer; d. John H. and Mary B. Aikens; m. Joseph F. Owens, Oct. 6, 1973; children: Meaghan B., Graham P., Connor T. BA, Clarke Coll., Dubuque, Iowa, 1971; MA, U. Wis., Madison, 1978. Art instr. Madison Area Tech. Coll., Watertown, Wis., 1988—, St. Jerome Parish Sch., Oconomowoc, Wis., 1988—. Graphic designer Patchanna Press, Oconomowoc. Fellow, WCATY, 2002. Mem.: AFT (assoc.).

OWENS, DANA ELAINE See QUEEN LATIFAH

OWENS, DEBORAH, artist, writer; b. Columbus, Ga., Mar. 10, 1951; d. Donald Owens and Diane Stewart Hobbs; m. Jon Gordon Graber, Mar. 24, 1990; children: Edith Hall, Renee Peete. BS, Columbus State U., 1982; postgrad., U. Ga., 1982-83, Auburn U., 1993. Tchr. kindergarten, Columbus; substitute elem. tchr. Fayetteville, N.C.; coll. recruiter Fla. Inst. Sci. and Tech.; self-employed writer and painter Columbus. Tchr. liquid acrylics. Author: (novel) Sacred Cypress, 1995, Between Light and Shadow, 1997, Stonegate of the Braveheart, 1998, Chocolate Secrets to a Dear Friend, Chattahoochee Chicken, Muffin Mallarkey and Wee Bitty Cakes; contbr. to fine art mags.; paintings, drawings, pen and inks are represented in pvt. collections. Women's counsleor, counselor Crisis Intervention Ctr.; hosp. and ARC vol. Recipient award Nat. Mus. of Women in Arts, 1999. Mem. Nat. Watercolor Soc. (assoc.), Am. Watercolor Soc., So. Watercolor Soc., Ga. Watercolor Soc., Watercolor Soc. Ala., N.C. Watercolor Soc. Methodist. Avocations: gardening, painting, drawing, sculpting, photography. Home: 6843 Lorna Dr Columbus GA 31909-3162 E-mail: deborahowens2000@aol.com.

OWENS, DENISE, judge; b. Jackson, Miss. d. Dennis and Grace (Britton) Sweet; m. Bob Owens; children: Selika, Bobby, Brittany, Jason. BA in Polit. Sci., Tougaloo Coll., Miss., 1976; JD, George Washington U., Washington, 1979. Staff atty. Ctrl. Miss. Legal Svcs., Jackson, 1979—82; asst. city prosecutor City of Jackson, 1983; assoc. Owens & Byrd, Jackson, 1983—86; ptnr., mng. atty. Owens & Owens, Jackson, 1986—89; chancery judge Hinds County, Jackson, 1989—. Instr. bus. law Jackson State U.; instr. legal writing Tougaloo (Miss.) Coll., Hinds CC, Jackson. Active Links, Inc., Jackson; bd. dirs. Cath. Charities, Jackson, 1990—92. Mem.: ABA, Nat. Bar Assn., Am. Trial Lawyers, Miss. Bar Assn. (gender bias task force, race and ethics bias task force, delivery legal svcs. com., vice-chair family law sect., facilitator law sch. professionalism orientation program). Home: 3474 Jones Loop Terry MS 39170 Office: Hinds County Chancery Ct 316 S President St Jackson MS 39205

OWENS, DIANE DOBRAY, music educator; b. Galveston, Tex., Mar. 7, 1948; d. Irving Leslie and Sylvia Marie Dobray; m. Ronald Wayne Owens, May 3, 1969. BS in Edn., U. North Tex., 1976; MEd, Tex. A&M, Commerce, 1987. Cert. tchr. Sec. Philco-Ford Corp. - NASA, Houston, 1966—69; piano tchr. First Bapt. Ch. Sch., Carrollton, Tex., 1971—76; substitute tchr. Richardson (Tex.) Ind. Sch. Dist., 1976—77; pre-sch. dir. First Bapt. Ch. - North, Carrollton, 1977—79; pvt. practice Richardson, 1979—92, Coleman, Tex., 1994—99; music instr. City of Richardson, 1988—92; adj. faculty, pre-coll. music dir. Howard Payne U., Brownwood, Tex., 1994—2000, piano instr., pre-coll. music dir., 2001—. Active Coleman County Hist. Hist. Commn., Coleman, 1994—; bd. dirs. Cmty. Concert Series, Brownwood, Tex., 2000—03. Mem.: Am. Coll. Musicians, Kindermusik Internat., Heart of Tex. Music Tchrs. Assn., Tex. Music Tchrs. Assn., Music Tchrs. Nat. Assn., Nat. Fedn. Music Clubs (chmn. dist. 7-A jr. festival). Republican. Baptist. Avocations: cooking, travel, reading. Home: 213 West Pecan St Coleman TX 76834-4005 Office: Howard Payne Univ 1000 Fisk Ave Brownwood TX 76801-2794 Office Phone: 325-649-8501. Business E-Mail: dowens@hputx.edu.

OWENS, DONNA LEE, small business owner, consultant; b. Buffalo, Aug. 19, 1939; d. Millard Douglas and Arlene Josephine (Schalk) Shriver; m. Perry B. Owens, Dec. 31, 1960 (div.); children: Brandon Joseph, Kimberly Ann, Devney, Megan. Student, Mundelein Coll., Chgo., 1957-59, 66-67, Harper Coll., Rolling Meadows, Ill., 1972-73. Cost acct. Signode Steel Strapping, Glenview, Ill., 1960-63; travel cons. Ask Mr. Foster, Barrington, Ill., 1978-83; pres. C-Chgo., Barrington, 1978-83; dir. corp. sales Ill. Corp. Travel, Schaumburg, 1983—. Pres. Sprotours, Inc., Barrington Hills, Ill., 1983—92. Benefit chmn. The Cradle Soc., Evanston, Ill., 1965-67; vol. Chgo. Mental Health Assn., 1970-72, Goodman Theater Women's Bd.; steering com. Alzheimers Assn., 1998—. Mem.: The Meadow. Republican. Roman Catholic. Avocations: cooking, tennis, embroidery, gardening. Home and Office: 615 Melrose Ave Kenilworth IL 60043-1004

OWENS, GEORGIA KATHERINE, social sciences educator, consultant; d. Kenneth Boyd Chapman and Leila Katherine Zollner; children: Lena Gwynn Anderson, Colin Stuart. BS in history and polit. sci., Portland State U., 1979. Staff asst. civil rights City of Portland/Multnomah County, Oreg., 1989—90; asst. dir. affirmative action Portland State U., 1990—96; profl. human resources diversity PacifiCorp, Portland; mgr. nat. employment & compensation AmeriCold Logistics, Atlanta, 1999—2002; recruiter PNM, Albuquerque, 2003—04; part-time faculty U. N.Mex., Albuquerque, 2002—. Nw adv. bd. mem. Ctr. for Dem. Renewal, Seattle, 1989—92; chair Bias Crimes Alert Network, Portland, 1992—93; cons. Ga. Owens Diversity Cons. Facilitator Trainer, Albuquerque, 1990—2003. Civil rights adv., sch. events organizer Met. Human Rights Commn., Portland, 1990—96; civil rights commn. employee Youth Gangs Task Force, Portland, 1990—94; nw adv. bd. Ctr. for Dem. Renewal, Seattle, 1989—92; co-chair, sec., bd. mem. Refugee Immigrant Consortium of Oreg. and SW Wash., Portland, 1990—2003. Mem.: Am. Ex-Prisoners of War, Dept. of N.Mex, Bataan Veterans Orgn. Next of Kin (life). Democrat-Npl. Episcopalian. Avocations: art, painting, ceramics. Home: 902 Edith Blvd NE Albuquerque NM 87102 Personal E-mail: owensgk@hotmail.com.

OWENS, JANA JAE, entertainer; b. Great Falls, Mont., Aug. 30, 1943; d. Jacob G. Meyer and Bette P. (Sprague) Hopper; m. Sidney Greif (div.); children: Matthew N., Sydni C.; m. Buck Owens. Student, Interlochen Music Camp, 1959, Internat. String Congress, 1960, Vienna Acad. Music, 1963—64; BA magna cum laude, MusB magna cum laude, Colo. Womens Coll., 1965. Tchr. music Ontario Pub. Schs., Oreg., 1965—67, Redding Pub. Schs., Calif., 1969—74; entertainer Buck Owens Enterprises, Bakersfield, Calif., 1974—78, Tulsa, 1979—. Concertmistress Boise Philharm., Idaho, 1965—67, Shasta Symphony, Redding, 1969—74; founder Grand Lake Festivals, Inc., Tulsa, 1996—. Rec. artist (violinist, vocalist) Lark Records, 1978—. Avocations: skiing, tennis, swimming. Office: Jana Jae Enterprises Lark Record Prodns Inc PO Box 35726 Tulsa OK 74153-0726 Business E-Mail: janajae@janajae.com.

OWENS, KATE A., registrar; m. John E. Owens, Mar. 1, 1997. BS, Frostburg State U., Md., 1989. Asst. mgr. Friendly Ice Cream Corp., Crofton/Annapolis, Md., 1983—93; dir. HR Wheaton Plaza, Wheaton, Md., 1993—96; adminstrv. asst. Chicora Realty, Myrtle Beach, SC, 1997—99; asst. registrar Keystone Coll., La Plume, Pa., 1999—2004, registrar, 2004—. Mem.: Middle States Assn. of Collegiate Registrars and Admissions Officers, Am. Assn. Collegiate Registrar and Admission Officers. Avocation: sports. Office: Keystone Coll One College Green La Plume PA 18440 Office Phone: 570-945-8222. Office Fax: 570-945-8970. E-mail: kate.owens@keystone.edu.

OWENS, KATHLEEN C., academic administrator; married; 2 children. BS in Biology, Loyola U., Chgo.; MS in Edn. Biol. Scis., DePaul U., Chgo.; EdD in Curriculum and Instr., Loyola U., Chgo. Dean Lewis U., Romeoville, Ill., 1986—92; v.p. academic affairs St. Francis U., Loretta, Pa., 1992—2002; pres. Gwynedd-Mercy Coll., Gwynedd Valley, Pa., 2002—. Office: Gwynedd-Mercy Coll PO Box 901 1325 Sumneytown Pike Gwynedd Valley PA 19437-0901

OWENS, LAURA, painter; b. Euclid, Ohio, 1970; BFA, RI Sch. Design, 1992; MFA, Calif. Inst. Arts, Valencia, Calif., 1994; attended, Sch. Painting & Sculpture, Skowhegan, Maine, 1994. Represented in permanent collections, Guggenheim, NY, Centre Georges Pompidou, Paris, exhibitions include, Rosamund Felsen, Santa Monica, Calif., 1995, Painting Show, Regen Projects, LA, 1995, Palace, Beret Internat. Gallery, Chgo., 1997, Sadie Cole's Headquarters, London, 1997, Young Americans II, Saatchi Collection London, 1998, Gavin Brown's Enterprise, NY, 1998, Galerie Gisela Capitain Köln, Germany, 1999, Examining Pictures, Whitechapel Art Gallery, London, 1999, Original Language, Mus. Contemporary Art, Chgo., 2001, New Work, Isabella Stewart Gardner Mus., Boston, 2001, Urgent Painting, Musée d'Art Moderne de la Ville de Paris, 2002, Laura Owens, Milw. Art Mus., 2003, the undiscovered country, UCLA Hammer Museum, LA, 2004, Whitney Biennial, Whitney Mus. Am. Art, 2004. Mailing: c/o ACME 6150 Wilshire Blvd #1 Los Angeles CA 90048

OWENS, LAURA LEWIS, lawyer; b. Atlanta, Sept. 27, 1960; BA cum laude, Furman U., 1982; JD cum laude, U. Ga., 1985. Bar: Ga. 1985. Ptnr., leader, product liability group Alston & Bird L.L.P., Atlanta. Mem. editl. bd. Ga. Jour. Internat. and Comparative Law, 1983-85, editor-in-chief, 1984-85; author: Annual Survey of Developments in International Trade Law, 1983. Mem. Atlanta Bar Assn., State Bar of Ga. Office: Alston & Bird 1 Atlantic Ctr 1201 W Peachtree St NW Atlanta GA 30309-3424 Office Phone: 404-881-7363. Office Fax: 404-881-7777. Business E-Mail: lowens@alston.com.

OWENS, MARGARET ALMA, educational administrator, naturopathic physician; b. Houston, Mar. 10, 1938; d. Leon Edgar and Velma Rotha (Miller) Owen; m. Robert Harvey Owens, May 28, 1958 (div. 1975); children: Robert Stephen, Keith Randall. BS, Mary-Hardin Baylor U., 1960; MEd, Tex. Woman's U., 1972; supervision cert., 1975; postgrad., 1979-82. Cert. midmgmt. adminstr. Tex. Vocat., Trinity Coll. Nat. Health, ND, 2001, home economist Tex. A&M U., Bryan, Tex., 1960-64; substitute tchr. Dallas Ind. Sch. Dist., 1965-67, permanent substitute tchr. in home econs. and sci., 1968-69, tchr. spl. edn., 1969-71; jr. acct. Burgess Manning Co., Dallas, 1967-68; asst. dir. Camp Nerby, Oak Cliff YMCA, Dallas, 1968; tchr. spl. edn. Austin Ind. Sch. Dist., Tex., 1972-74, supr. secondary spl. edn., 1974—; adminstrv. intern SW Tex. State U., San Marcos, 1973; owner Allergy Elimination Clin., cons. San Marcos Bapt. Acad., Tex., 1976; student tchr. adv. com. U. Tex., Austin, 1984-1994; lectr. in field; citizen ambassador of edn. to China, 1986. Author, editor, advisor various profl. tng. materials. Active Tex. councils Boy Scouts Am., 1968—; mem. Pres.'s Com. on Employment of People with Disabilities, 1987—. Recipient Golden Measure Achievement award Grand Prairie YMCA, 1968, Haskew award for outstanding contbn. to edn., 1990, Outstanding Leadership award Boy Scouts Am., 1971; Fed. edn. grantee, 1971-72. Mem. AAUW, Nat. Coun. for Exceptional Children (pioneer divsn., v.p. 1971), NARF, Tex. Edn. Agy. (com. to revise EXCET test), Austin Assn. Pub. Sch. Adminstrs. (chmn. task force, pres. cen. div. 1989-90), Paramount Theatre Club, World-Wide Vacation Club, Candlelight Dance Club, Demolay (pres. Mother's Aux. 1977-78), Alpha Delta Kappa (former officer), Phi Delta Kappa (sec. Austin 1987-89, found. rep. 1989-91), Pi Lambda Theta. Baptist. Avocations: reading, travel, art collecting, theatre, gourmet cooking Home: 1777 Cricket Hollow Dr Austin TX 78758-4254 Office: Allergy Elimination Clin 4105 Med Pky 202 Austin TX 78756 Office Phone: 512-206-4158. Personal E-mail: mowens3108@msn.com.

OWENS, MARY BENTLEY, science educator, mathematics educator; d. Dwight Allison and Hazel Katrina Bentley; m. Donald William Owens; children: Donald Allison, Jason James. M Edn. Curriculum and Tech., U. Ctrl. Fla., Orlando, 1991. Gifted Endorsement Fla., 1995. Health educator/facilitator/spokesperson/program mgmt. Brevard County Teen Health Coalition, Rockledge, Fla., 1991—95; tchr. coordinating sci. and math. State of Fla., Melbourne, 1995—. Robotics program mgmt. LEGO Robotics Tournaments, Melbourne, 2000—05. Author: Pre-GED Sci. Curriculum. Chairperson Brevard County Teen Health Coalition, Rockledge, 1991—95. Named Exemplenary Sci. Tchr., 2004; recipient Fla. Blue Key Leadership award, U. Fla., 1986—91. Master: Forensics Assn. (assoc.; judge/trainer 1986—91, 1st Pl. in Nat. Competition 1987). R-Liberal. Episcopal. Achievements include first to I developed an organization that taught teens to research political and health issues, trained them in public speaking and helped them network to become advocates.

OWENS, SUSAN, state supreme court justice; b. Kinston, NC, Aug. 19, 1949; d. Frank and Hazel Owens; children: Sunny Roloff, Owen Golden. BA, Duke U., 1971; JD, U. N.C., Chapel Hill, 1975. Bar: Oreg. 1975, Wash. 1976. Judge Dist. Ct., Western Clallam County, 1981—2001; chief judge Quileute Tribe, Lower Elwha S'Klallam Tribe; justice Wash. Supreme Ct., 2001—. Co-founder, chair Rural Courts Com., 1990; lecturer Jud. Coll., Nat. Coll. of Prosecuting Attorneys' Domestic Violence Conference. Co-author: Northwest Tribal Judges Domestic Violence Manual. Mem.: Dist. and Mcpl. Ct. Judges' Assn. (bd. dirs., sec.-treas., v.p., pres.-elect). Avocation: baseball. Office: Wash Supreme Ct PO Box 40929 Olympia WA 98504-0929

OWENS, SUSAN ELIZABETH, realtor; b. Providence, Nov. 22, 1957; d. Lee Edward and Nancy Elizabeth Norton; m. George Ray Bunch Jr., Aug. 15, 1980 (div. Jan. 1986); children: Michael, Melissa, George Ray III; m. Joseph Craig Owens, Oct. 16, 1987. Cert. ct. reporter, Reporting Acad. Va., 1993; study real estate, Tidewater C.C., Chesapeake, Va., 2001. Sec. capital campaign United Way, Norfolk, Va., 1985—86; med. transcriptionist Humana Hosp. Bayside, Virginia Beach, Va., 1986—90; property mgr. Kamla Condominium Assn., Virginia Beach, 1990—93; ct. reporter Adams, Harris & Martin, Norfolk, 1993—94; office mgr. Slone Chiropractic Clinic, Norfolk, 1994—99, Riddle Assoc. Inc., Chesapeake, Va., 1999—2003, comml. real estate agt., 2001—. Pres. So. Bass'n Gal, 1998—; sec. Va. Bassmasters, Inc., 1997—. Avocations: bass fishing, bowling, writing children's stories. Office: Riddle Assoc Inc Ste 100 530 Woodlake Cir Chesapeake VA 23320 Office Phone: 757-523-1900. E-mail: sowens@riddleassociates.com.

OWENS, TERESA GAIL, elementary school educator; d. Louie and Wanda Morton; m. Jerome Owens; children: Jessie, Jordan, Jonathan. BS, U. Ala., Birmingham, 1980, MA, 1984. Cert. tchr. Ala., 2001. Tchr. gifted edn. Blount County Bd. of Edn., Oneonta, Ala., 1982—92; tchr. 5th grade Susan Moore Elem. Sch., Blountsville, Ala., 1992—2006; specialist gifted edn. Blountsville Elem. Sch., 2006—. Author: Acquiring and Utilizing Technology Devices in the Elementary Classroom, 2003. Various coms. Snead Bapt. Ch., Ala., 2000—06. Finalist Jacksonville State Regional Tchr. Hall of Fame, Jacksonville State U., Ala., 2001-02; recipient Unsung Heroes award, Ing, Inc., 2003, Tchr. of Yr. award, Blount County Bd. of Edn., 2005; grantee, Blount County Edn. Found., 1999-2004; SMARTer Kids Connections grant, SMART Techs., 2001-2004, One Class At A Time grant, Channel 42 WIAT, 2002. Mem.: NEA, Nat. Bd. of Profl. Tchrs. Local Assn., Nat. Tchrs. of Sci. Office: Susan Moore Elem Sch 3996 Susan Moore Rd Blountsville AL 35031-7038 Office Phone: 205-466-5844.

OWEN-TOWLE, CAROLYN SHEETS, clergywoman; b. Upland, Calif., July 27, 1935; d. Millard Owen and Mary (Baskerville) Sheets; m. Charles Russell Chapman, June 29, 1957 (div. 1973); children: Christopher Charles, Jennifer Anne, Russell Owen; m. Thomas Allan Owen-Towle, Nov. 16, 1973. BS in Art and Art History, Scripps Coll., 1957; postgrad. in religion, U. Iowa, 1977; DD, Meadville/Lombard Theol. Sch., Chgo., 1994. Ordained to ministry Unitarian-Universalist Ch., 1978. Minister 1st Unitarian Universalist Ch., San Diego, 1978—2004. Pres. Ministerial Sisterhood, Unitarian Universalist Ch., 1980-82; mem. Unitarian Universalist Svc. Com., 1979-85, pres., 1983-85. Bd. dirs. Planned Parenthood, San Diego, 1980-86; mem. clergy adv. com. to Hospice, San Diego, 1980-83; mem. U.S. Rep. Jim Bates Hunger Adv. Com., San Diego, 1983-87; chaplain Interfaith AIDS Task Force, San Diego, 1988—. Mem. Unitarian Universalist Ministers Assn. (exec. com. 1988, pres. 1989-91, African Am. minister's action com. 1995-98). Avocations: reading, walking, promoting human rights.

OWINGS, ALISON JUNE, writer, journalist; b. Pasadena, Calif., June 17, 1944; d. Kenneth Brown and Alice Case (Roberts) O.; m. Jonathan Brittain Perdue, May 1, 1993 Student, Freiburg U., Germany, 1964—65; BA, Am. U., 1966. Writer, rschr. Congl. Quar., Washington, 1966; rschr. Dem. Nat. Com., Washington, 1966—67; news asst. ABC, Washington, 1967—69; assoc. prodr. documentary series WRC, Washington, 1969—71; assoc. prodr. WNBC TV, N.Y.C., 1971—73; TV newswriter CBS TV, N.Y.C., 1973—77, 1980—85; freelance TV newswriter Mill Valley, Calif., 1982—99; freelance editor, 1999—. Author: Wander Women's Phrasebook, 1987, Frauen: German Women Recall the Third Reich, 1993 (NY Times Notable Books of Yr., 94), Hey, Waitress! The USA from the Other Side of the Tray, 2002. Founder Don't Tear It Down (now D.C. Preservation League), Washington, 1971 Democrat. Avocations: theater, American antiques. Home and Office: 111 Inez Pl Mill Valley CA 94941

OWINGS, ANNE MARIE, counselor; d. Henry Leonard and Kathleen Rafferty Pearlberg; m. David D. Owings, July 8, 1995. BEd, West Chester U., 1988; MA in Counseling, Rider U., 1994. Tchr. Council Rock Sch. Dist., Newtown, Pa., 1988—2004, elem. guidance counselor, 2004—. Chairperson Edn. Adv. Com., Bucks County, Pa., 2001—. Mem.: NEA, Penn. Sch. Coun. Assn., Am. Sch. Counselor Assn., Council Rock Edn. Assn. (legis. chairperson 1999—), Penn. State Edn. Assn. Democrat. Avocations: golf, travel, reading.

OWINGS, THALIA KELLEY, elementary school educator; b. Franklin, N.H., Apr. 11, 1948; d. James Warren and Elizabeth Louise (Chadwick) Kelley; m. Alan Morritt, June 25, 1966 (div. June 25, 1990); children: Manderlee, Tiffany, Brooke; m. Frederick Richard Owings, Dec. 31, 1994; children: Jennifer, Lisa. AA, Harvard U. Ext., 1982, BA, 1989; student, Calif. State U., San Bernardino, 1996—2000. Cert. tchr., Calif., emergency tchr. Instr. CEA Internat., Providence, 1971-77; adminstrv. asst. Gulf Oil/Cumberland Farms, Norwood, Mass., 1989-91, So. Calif. Edison Co., Rosemead, Calif., 1991-96; substitute tchr. Palm Springs (Calif.) Unified Sch. Dist., 1996—2000. Tutor Calif. for Literacy!, Pasadena, Chino, and Palm Springs, Calif., 1991-96; applicant interviewer Harvard U.; mem. edn. com. Shelter From the Storm, 2000-03, tutor com. chair, 2000-03, vol. coord., 2002-03; leader Girl Scout jr. troops, 2004—. Mem. So. Calif. Harvard/Radcliff Club, Toastmasters Internat. (v.p. pub. rels. 1995-96), Edison's Roundtable. Avocations: screenplay writing, photography, bicycling, golf. Home: 78075 Ravencrest Cir Palm Desert CA 92211

OWSLEY, TINA KATHLEEN, special education educator; b. Ponca City, Okla., Apr. 3, 1953; d. Lindsey C. Jr. and Nina Jane (Lotts) O. BA in Edn., Northeastern Okla. State U., 1975, MS in Edn., 1978; cert. in deaf edn., Tex. Woman's U., 1981; cert. in spl. edn. adminstrn., Gallaudet U., Washington, 1984. Cert. speech correction, learning disabilities, Mo., speech therapy, learning disabilites, deaf edn., Okla., speech pathology, learning disabilities, deaf edn., educable mentally handicapped, physically impaired, Kans. Tchr. learning disabilities, speech pathologist Perry County Schs., Perryville, Mo., 1975-77; tchr. learning disabilities Vinita (Okla.) Pub. Schs., 1977-78; cons. hearing impaired Sequoyah County Spl. Edn. Coop., Sallisaw, Okla., 1978-80; tchr. hearing impaired Ft. Gibson (Okla.) Pub. Schs., 1980-83; asst. to the v.p. Gallaudet U., 1983-84; coord., tchr. hearing impaired Shawnee County Spl. Edn. Coop., Topeka, 1984—. Parent advisor Project ECHO, Okla. Dept. Edn., Oklahoma City, 1978-83; early interventionist Hearing Cons., Topeka, 1989—. Co-author: Curriculum Guide - Presch. Hearing Impaired Children, 1991. Bd. dirs. Florence Crittendon, 1995—2000. Mem. AAUW (corr. sec. 1998—2002, vice pres. membership 2003-05), Nat. Assn. for Edn. of Young Children (Kans. chpt., pres. Topeka Assn. 1988-89), NEA (Kans. chpt., mem. Topeka spl. edn. com. 1991—, polit. action com. 1991—2001, bldg. rep. 1993-95), Coun. for Exceptional Children (pres. Chpt. 204 1989—2000, v.p. Kans. Fedn. 1991-92, pres.-elect Kans. Fedn. 1992-93, pres. 1993-94, immediate past pres. 1994-95, chmn. Spl. Edn. Day at the Legis. Kans. Coun. 1991, 95), Kans. Divsn. Early Childhood (pres. 1989-90, mem. chair 1993—2000), Kans. Educators of Hearing Impaired (pres. 1989-90, Kans. Educator of the Yr.-Deaf/Hard of Hearing 1996), Kans. Commn. for Deaf and Hearing Impaired (chair Early Identification and Intervention Coun. 1990-95), Soroptimist Internat. Am. (corr. sec. local chpt. 1991-92, cmty. svc. chair 1991-95, del. 1992-94, bd. dirs. 1992-93, 95-97, rec. sec. 1993-94, chair Youth Citizenship Award/Tng. Award Program 1995—99, growth and devel. co-chair 1996—2000, v.p. 1998—2000, Soroptimist of the Yr. 1993, 97, Soroptimist Woman of Distinction, 2000), Sertoma Internat. (publicity chair 1992-94), Topeka Tots Team (sec. 1991-97), Jr. Deaf Club (sponsor 1992-96), Camp Fire Coun. (bd. dirs. 1993-96, chair program/membership 1993-96). Republican. Mem. Christian Ch. (Disciples Of Christ). Avocations: counted cross-stitch, reading, gardening. Home: 2806 SW Engler Ct Topeka KS 66614-4317 Office: Shawnee County Spl Edn Coop 1725 SW Arnold Ave Topeka KS 66604-3306

OXELL, LOIE GWENDOLYN, fashion and beauty educator, consultant, columnist; b. Sioux City, Iowa, Nov. 17, 1917; d. Lyman Stanley and Loie Erma (Crill) Barton; m. Eugene Edwin Eschenbrenner, Aug. 8, 1936 (dec. 1954); children: Patricia Gene, Eugene Edward (dec. Feb. 1994); m. Henry J. Oxell, Nov. 3, 1956 (dec. July 1994) AS Fashion Merchandising, Broward C.C., Davie, Fla., 1978. Fashion rep. Crestmoor Suit & Coat Co., St. Louis, 1951—56; appeared on "To the Ladies" weekly TV show KSD-TV, St. Louis, 1950—58; cons./instr. Miami-Herald Newspaper Glamor Clinic, Fla., 1957—71; pres./owner Loie's (Loy's) Inc., Miami, 1958—71; pres., owner West Coast East Talent Agy.; instr./lectr. Charron-Williams Coll., Miami, 1973—77; instr. Fashion Inst. Ft. Lauderdale, Fla., 1977—86; pres./owner Image Power Unltd., Plantation, Fla., 1992—. Lectr. in field; columnist Sr. Life and Boomer Times, Fla., 1993-97, Sr. Life, 1997-98, The Entertainer, 1997-98 Author: I'd Like You to Meet My Wife, 1964, Executive Wives, A.C. Sparkplug Co., So! We're in Our 60's, 70's, 80's Plus; regularly appeared in comedy skits, fashion segments, commentary, and TV commls. Del Russo Beauty Show, 1960s; actress Red Skelton TV show, Miami, Fla., also fashion show prodns., TV commls Lectr., instr. Work Force, AARP Sr. Cmty. Svc. Employment Program, Ft. Lauderdale and Hollywood, 1987—, keynote spkr. nat. conv., Charlestown, S.C., 1986; life mem. women's com. Miami Children's Hosp. Aux.; faculty adv. Nu Tau Sigma Charron Williams Coll., 1973-77; pres. Venice Am. chpt. Am. Bus. Women's Assn., 1975-76 Recipient Cert. Appreciation Dade County Welfare Dept. Youth Hall, Miami, 1966, Cmty. TV Found., Miami, 1966, 71, Woman of Yr. award Am. Bus. Women's Assn., 1976-77, Award for Svc. AARP Sr. Cmty. Svc. Program, 1993 Mem. The Fashion Group Internat Avocations: bridge, golf.

OXLEY, MARGARET CAROLYN STEWART, elementary school educator; b. Petaluma, Calif., Apr. 1, 1930; d. James Calhoun Stewart and Clara Thornton (Whiting) Bomboy; m. Joseph Hubbard Oxley, Aug. 25, 1951; children: Linda Margaret, Carolyn Blair Oxley Greiner, Joan Claire Oxley Willis, Joseph Stewart, James Harmon, Laura Marie Oxley Brechbill. Student, U. Calif., Berkeley, 1949—51; BS summa cum laude, Ohio State U., 1973, MA, 1984, student, 1985, student, 1988, student, 1992, student, 2003—06. Cert. tchr., Ohio. 2d grade tchr. St. Paul Sch., Westerville, Ohio, 1973—. Presenter in field. Mem. editl. bd. Reading Tchr., vol. 47-48, 1993-94, Jour. Children's Lit., 1996—, Lang. Arts, 2006-; co-author: Reading and Writing, Where it All Begins, 1991, Teaching with Children's Books: Path to Literature-Based Instruction, 1995, Adventuring With Books, vol. 12, 2000, vol. 13, 2002, Children's Literature Remembered: Issues, Trends, and Favorite Books, 2004. Active Akita Child Conservation League, Columbus, Ohio, 1968-70. Named Columbus Diocesan Tchr. of Yr., 1988; Phoebe A. Hearst scholar, 1951, Rose Sterheim Meml. scholar, 1951; recipient Mary Karrer award Ohio State U., 1994. Mem. Nat. Coun. Tchrs. English (Notable Children's Books in the Lang. Arts com. 1993-94, chair 1995-96, treas. Children's Literature Assembly bd. dirs. 1996-99, co-chair fall breakfast children's lit. assembly, 2000-03, co-chair excellence in poetry for children com. 2003-06), Internat. Reading Assn. (Exemplary Svc. in Promotion of Literacy award 1991), Ohio Coun. Internat. Reading Assn., Literacy Connection (pres.), Children's Lit. Assembly, Ohio Coun. Tchrs. English Lang. Arts (Outstanding Educator 1990), Phi Kappa Phi, Pi Lambda Theta (hon., Outstanding Work in Literacy Edn. citation 2004). Democrat. Roman Catholic. Avocations: reading, writing, travel, gardening, working with children. Home: 298 Brevoort Rd Columbus OH 43214-3826

OYEYIPO, BOLANLE T., geriatrician; b. LA, Sept. 15, 1976; d. Tunde S. and Adeline O. Oyeyipo; m. Ademale B. Ajumobe, Sept. 19, 2002. MD, U. Ilorin, Nigeria, 2000. Diplomate Am. Bd. Family Medicine, 2006. Resident in family medicine Pomona Valley Hosp., Calif., 2003—06; fellow in geriatrics UCLA, 2006—. Mem.: Am. Med. Dirs. Assn., Am. Geriatrics Soc., Am. Acad. Family Physicians. Office: UCLA Dept Geriatrics 10945 Le Conte Ave Los Angeles CA 90095-3000

OYLER, AMY ELIZABETH, medical/surgical nurse; b. Roanoke, Va., Aug. 20, 1971; d. James Thomas and Vivian Yvonne (Mills) O. AS, Va. Western C.C., 1991; BSNB, Radford U., 1993. RN, Va.; cert. med. surg. nurse. Nursing asst. Roanoke Meml. Hosp., 1989-93, med.-surg. nurse in diabetic care and renal transplants, 1993—. Avocations: reading, aerobics, family. Home: 950 John Arthur Rd Boones Mill VA 24065-4072

OZAKI, NANCY JUNKO, performance artist, performing arts educator; b. Denver, Feb. 14, 1951; d. Joe Motoichi and Tamiye (Saki) O.; m. Gary Steven Tsujimoto, Nov. 12, 1989. BS in Edn., U. Colo., 1973; postgrad., U. Colo., Denver, 1977, Metro State Coll., 1982, Red Rocks C.C., 1982-83, U. No. Colo., 1982, U. N.Mex., 1985, U. No. Colo., 1988. Elem. tchr. Bur. Indian Affairs, Bloomfield, N.Mex., 1973—75, Aurora Pub. Schs., Colo., 1977—83, Albuquerque Pub. Schs., 1983—84, Denver Pub. Schs., 1984—87, Oak Grove Sch. Dist., San Jose, Calif., 1988—89, San Mateo City Elem. Dist., Calif., 1990—92; performing artist Japanese drums Young Audiences, San Francisco, 1992—93, Denver, 1994—97; performing artist Japanese drums Epcot Ctr. Walt Disney World, Orlando, Fla., 1993—97; co-dir., mgr., performer One World Taiko Japanese Drum Troupe, Denver, 1997—2001, Seattle, 2001—; artist-in-residence Washington States Arts Commn., 2003—. Mem. Touring Arts Roster, King County. Vol. worker with young Navajo children; co-sponsor girl's sewing and camping groups. Mem. Kappa Delta Pi (Theta chpt.). Avocations: reading, sewing, skiing, hiking, snorkeling. Office: PO Box 80158 Seattle WA 98108 E-mail: oneworldtaiko@earthlink.net.

OZANICH, RUTH SHULTZ, artist, poet, retired elementary school educator; b. Calif., Feb. 12, 1915; d. Charles Andrew Shultz and Martha Viola Boring; m. Anton M. Ozanich, Nov. 1931; children: Antom M., Saralen Elaine, Marc Charles Dee. BEd, Fresno (Calif.) State U., 1956. Life cert. tchr. credential, Calif. Tchr. Beardsley Elem. Sch., Oildale, Calif., 1954-65, Sierra Vista Elem. Sch., Arvin, Calif., 1965-70; ret., 1970. Exhibited in group shows Bakersfield Art Assn. Gallery, Cunningham Gallery, Bakersfield, Kern County Fair, Calif. (numerous blue ribbons); contbr. poetry to anthologies. Elder Paiute Coun., Lake Isabella Calif.; treas. Mexican Am. Srs. Mem. Internat. Poetry Hall of Fame (life), Calif. Tchrs. Assn., Kern River Valley Poets and Writers Club (founder, past pres.), Bakersfield Art Assn. (founder, past treas.), Ladies Moose. Avocations: arts and crafts, reading, poetry, writing. Home: 5631 Caranor Rd Kent OH 44240-4206

OZAWA, CONNIE PATRICIA, science educator; d. Edna Y. Ozawa; m. Gerald Sussman, Aug. 25, 1979; children: Daniel Ozawa Sussman, Jacqueline Ozawa Sussman. AB in Environ. Studies, U. Calif., Berkeley, 1976; MA in Geography, U. Hawaii, 1978; PhD, MIT, Cambridge, Mass., 1988. Assoc. Program on Negotiation, Cambridge, 1988—92; lectr. M.I.T., Cambridge, 1992—94; prof. Portland (Oreg.) State U., 1994—. Author: (book) Recasting Science: Consensus Based Procedures in Public Policy Making; editor: The Portland Edge: Challenges and Successes in Growing Communities. Mem.: Phi Kappa Phi (assoc.), Phi Beta Kappa (assoc.). Office: Portland State University 506 SW Mill St Portland OR 97207 Office Phone: 503-725-5126. Business E-Mail: ozawac@pdx.edu.

OZAWA, MARTHA NAOKO, social work educator; b. Ashikaga, Tochigi, Japan, Sept. 30, 1933; arrived in US, 1963; d. Tokuichi and Fumi (Kawashima) O.; m. May 1959 (div. May 1966). BA in Econs., Aoyama Gakuin U., 1956; MS in Social Work, U. Wis., 1966, PhD in Social Welfare, 1969. Asst. prof. social work Portland (Oreg.) State U., 1969-70, assoc. prof. social work, 1970-72; assoc. rsch. prof. social work NYU, 1972-75; assoc. prof. social work Portland State U., 1975-76; prof. social work Washington U., St. Louis, 1976-85, Bettie Bofinger Brown prof. social policy, 1985—2003, Bettie Bofinger Brown Disting. prof. social policy, 2003—; dir. Martin N. Ozawa Ctr. Social Policy Studies, 2005—. Author: Income Maintenance and Work Incentives, 1982; editor: Women's Life Cycle: Japan-U.S. Comparison in Income Maintenance, 1989, Women's Life Cycle and Economic Insecurity: Problems and Proposals, 1989; editl. bd. Social Work, Silver Spring, Md., 1972-75, 85-88, New Eng. Jour. Human Svcs., Boston, 1987-95, Ency. of Social Work, Silver Spring, 1974-77, 91-95, 99-2003, Jour. Social Svc. Rsch., 1977-97, Children and Youth Svcs. Rev., 1991—, Social Work Rsch., 1994-97, Jour. Poverty, 1997-2004; co-editor-in-chief Asian Social Work and Policy Rev., 2005—. Grantee Adminstrn. on Aging, Washington, 1979, 84, NIMH, 1990-93. Mem. Nat. Assn. Social Workers (presdl. award 1999), Nat. Acad. Social Ins., Nat. Conf. on Social Welfare (bd. dirs. 1981-87), The Gerontol. Soc. Am., Soc. for Social Work and Rsch., Washington U. Faculty Club (bd. dirs. 1986-91). Avocations: photography, tennis, swimming, gardening. Home: 13018 Tiger Lily Ct Saint Louis MO 63146-4339 Office: PO Box 1196 Saint Louis MO 63130-4899 Office Phone: 314-935-6615. Business E-Mail: ozawa@wustl.edu.

OZEREKO-DECOEN, MARY T., therapeutic recreation specialist and therapist; b. Salem, Mass., Oct. 4, 1961; d. Domenic S. and Monica M. (Gesek) Ozereko; m. Jeffrey G. deCoen, Nov. 21, 1987. BS, U. Mass., 1982; MEd, Springfield Coll., 1987. Cert. therapeutic recreation specialist, Pa.; cert. golf club maker. Dir. promotions and ops. Wheat Thins mayors cup race Nabisco, Salem, 1984-86; conf. planner Pioneer Valley Conv. and Visitors Bur., Springfield, Mass., 1986-87; dir. tennis and recreation Village of Smugglers Notch, Vt., 1987-88; mental health profl., therapeutic recreation specialist Hoffman Homes for Youth, Gettysburg, Pa., 1988-89; therapeutic recreation aide Chambersburg (Pa.) Hosp., 1990; caseworker, therapeutic recreation specialist Tressler Wilderness Sch., Boiling Springs, Pa., 1989-92, Harrisburg, Pa., 1993-98; behavior specialist cons. Harrisburg, Pa., 1998-99; health edn. specialist Automated Health Sys., 2000—03; behavior specialist Youth Adv. Program, 2004—. Owner Golf Augusta Pro Shops, Hershey, Pa., 1995—2004; cons. clin. seminars on recreational therapy for mental health profls.; adj. asst. prof. York (Pa.) Coll., 1997—; health edn. specialist Automated Health Sys., Pitts., 1999-2003; autistic specialist, youth advocate program, 2003—04. Mem. Hershey Partnership, 1995—2004, Pa. Children's Panel, Harrisburg, 1992-2003. Mem. NAFE, Nat. Recreation and Parks Assn., Pa. Mental Health Providers Assn., Pa. Parks and Recreation Assn., Ctrl. Pa. C. of C. (golf planner ea. amputee spl. olympics 1996—), U.S. Golf Assn., Cert. Golfmakers Assn., Nat. Coun. for Therapeutic Recreation Cert., U. Mass.-Keystone Alumni Assn. (pres. 1994—), Harrisburg Exec. Womens Com. Democrat. Roman Catholic. Avocations: sports, exercise, golf, collecting old toys and antiques, clubmaking. Office: 744 E Chocolate Ave Hershey PA 17033-1211 E-mail: gaps@prodigy.net.

OZICK, CYNTHIA, writer; b. NYC, Apr. 17, 1928; d. William and Celia (Regelson) O.; m. Bernard Hallote, Sept. 7, 1952; 1 dau., Rachel Sarah. BA cum laude with honors in English, NYU, 1949; MA, Ohio State U., 1950; LHD (hon.), Yeshiva U., 1984, Hebrew Union Coll., 1984, Williams Coll., 1986, Hunter Coll., 1987, Jewish Theol. Sem. Am., 1988, Adelphi U., 1988, SUNY, 1989, Brandeis U., 1990, Bard Coll., 1991, Spertus Coll., 1991, Skidmore Coll., 1992, Seton Hall U., 1999, Rutgers U., 1999, U. N.C., Asheville, 2000, NYU, 2001, Bar-Ilan U., Israel, 2002, Balt Hebrew U., 2004. Author: Trust, 1966, reissued, 2004, The Pagan Rabbi and Other Stories, 1971, Bloodshed and Three Novellas, 1976, Levitation: Five Fictions, 1982, Art and Ardor: Essays, 1983, The Cannibal Galaxy, 1983, The Messiah of Stockholm, 1987, Metaphor & Memory: Essays, 1989, The Shawl, 1989, Epodes: First Poems, 1992, What Henry James Knew, and Other Essays on Writers, 1994, Portrait of the Artist as a Bad Character, 1996, The Cynthia Ozick Reader, 1996, Fame & Folly, 1996, The Puttermesser Papers, 1997, (novel) Heir to the Glimmering World, 2004, The Din the Head: Essays, 2006; (plays) Blue Light, 1994, The Shawl, 1996; guest editor Best Am. Essays, 1998, Quarrel & Quandary: Essays, 2000, Collected Stories, 2006; also poetry, criticism, revs., translations, essays and fictions in numerous periodicals and anthologies. Phi Beta Kappa orator, Harvard U., 1985. Recipient Mildred and Harold Strauss Living award Am. Acad. Arts and Letters, 1983, Rea award for short story, 1986, PEN/Spiegel-Diamonstein award for the Art of the Essay, 1997, Harold Washington Literary award City of Chgo., 1997, John Cheever award, 1999, Lannan Found. award for fiction, 2000, Koret Found. award for lit. studies, 2001, Nat. Book Critics Circle award for nonfiction, 2001; Lucy Martin Donnelly fellow, Bryn Mawr Coll., 1992, Guggenheim fellow, 1982. Mem. PEN, Authors League, Am. Acad. of Arts and Scis., Am. Acad. of Arts and Letters, Dramatists Guild, Académie Universelle des Cultures (Paris), Phi Beta Kappa.

OZKAN, UMIT SIVRIOGLU, chemical engineering professor; b. Manisa, Turkey, Apr. 11, 1954; came to U.S., 1980; d. Alim and Emine (Ilgaz) Sivrioglu; m. H. Erdal Ozkan, Aug. 13, 1983. BS, Mid. East Tech. U., Ankara, Turkey, 1978, MS, 1980; PhD, Iowa State U., 1984. Registered profl. engr., Ohio. Grad. rsch. assoc. Ames Lab. U.S. Dept. Energy, 1980-84; asst. prof. Ohio State U., Columbus, 1985-90, assoc. prof. chem. engring., 1990-94, prof., 1994—, assoc. dean for rsch. Coll. Engring., 2000—05. Contbr. articles to profl. jours. French Ctr. NAt. Rsch. Sci. fellow, 1994-95; recipient Women of Achievement award YWCA, Columbus, 1991, Outstanding Engring. Educator Ohio award Soc. Profl. Engrs., 1991, Union Carbide Innovation Recognition award, 1991-92, NSF Woman Faculty award in sci. and engring., 1991, Engring. Tchg. Excellence award Keck Found., 1994, Ctrl. Ohio Outstanding Woman in Sci. & Tech., 1996, Pitts.-Cleve. Catalysis Soc. Outstanding Rsch. award, 1998, Achievement award Soc. Women Engring., 2002, Columbus Outstanding Rsch. award ACS, 2002. Fellow Am. Inst. Chemists; mem. NSPE, N.Am. Catalysis Soc., Am. Inst. Chem. Engring., Am. Soc. Engring. Edn., Am. Chem. Soc., Combustion Inst., Sigma Xi. Achievements include research in selective oxidation; electrocatalysis; in-situ spectroscopy; fuel reformulation; hydrodenitrogenation; hydrodeoxygenation; hydrodesulfurization; NO reduction; hydrogenation. Office: Ohio State U Chem Engring 140 W 19th Ave Columbus OH 43210-1110 Office Phone: 614-292-6623. E-mail: ozkan.1@usa.edu.

OZOG, DIANE L., allergist; b. Chgo., July 28, 1955; MD, U. Health Scis., Chgo. Med. Sch., 1982. Cert. allergy and immunology 1987, pediat. 1987. Resident Cook County Hosp., Ill., 1982—85; fellowship Children's Meml. Hosp., Ill., 1985—87; allergist Good Samaritan Hosp. Mem.: Children's Comm. Physicians Assn. Office: 3825 Highland Ave Tower 2 Ste 204 Downers Grove IL 60515 Address: 636 Raymond Naperville IL 60563

PACE, CAROL REBECCA, elementary school educator; b. Tokyo, Mar. 9, 1960; d. John Lawrence and Melba Johnson Greene; m. George Swanson Pace, Mar. 12, 1988. AA, Jones County Jr. Coll., Ellisville, Miss., 1980; BA in Edn., U. Miss., Oxford, 1982; MEd, Miss. Coll., Clinton, 1998. Lic. educator Miss. Tchr. 1st, 4th, 5th and 6th grades Pine Hills Acad., Gloster, Miss., 1983—85; 4th grade tchr. St. Patrick's Episcopal Day Sch., Zachary, Miss., 1985—86; 5th grade tchr. Vicksburg (Miss.) Mid. Sch., 1986—89; tchr. 1st, 2d and 5th grades Grove St. Elem., Vicksburg, 1989—99; 1st grade tchr. Sherman Ave. Elem., Vicksburg, 1999—2003; instnl. lead tchr. Dana Rd. Elem., Vicksburg, 2003—, AmeriCorps site supr., 2004—. Named Tchr. of yr., Sherman Ave. Elem., 2000—01. Mem.: NEA, Internat. Reading Assn., Nat. Coun. Tchrs. English, Miss. Assn. Educators, Ole Miss Alumni Assn. Republican. Methodist. Avocations: reading, arts and crafts, metal detecting, antiques, jogging. Home: 8023 Oak Ridge Rd Vicksburg MS 39183 Office: Dana Rd Elem 1247 Dana Rd Vicksburg MS 39180 Office Phone: 601-619-2340. Office Fax: 601-619-2343. E-mail: bpace@vwsd.k12.ms.us.

PACE, DIANE MARIE, elementary school educator; b. Rockville Ctr., NY, July 30, 1950; d. Ulys Antoine and Evelyn Ceceila Besnette; m. Donald R. Pace, Jr., Mar. 25, 1972; children: Donald Roy III, Julianne Pace Camacho. Student, Tex. Tech. U., 1968—72; BSc in Interdisciplinary Studies, U. Tex., El Paso, Tex., 1991. Sec., bookkeeper, El Paso, Tex., 1979—89; tchr. Eastwood Heights Elem. Sch., El Paso, 1989—, Ysleta Ind. Sch. Dist. 6th Grade, 2006—. Bookkeeper Thermal Control, Inc. Mem.: Assn. Tex. Profl. Educators. Office: Eastwood Heights Elem Sch 10530 Janway El Paso TX 79925 Personal E-mail: dpace@yisd.net.

PACE, SANDRA MCMILLEN, science educator; b. Louisville, Feb. 14, 1950; d. Gilbert Milton and Macie Ivle (White) McMillen; m. Walter Edward Wendler, Jan. 24, 1969 (div.); m. Warren Lee Pace, Sept. 3, 1977. AA, U. Louisville, 1977; BS in Sci., Va. State U., 1979; MS in Edn., Va. State U./Va. Commonwealth, 1981; postgrad., U. Ga., 1986—. Cert. tchr., Ga. Rsch. tech. Brown and Williamson Tobacco Corp., Louisville, 1969-77; tchr. sci. Matoaca HS, Chesterfield, Va., 1980-85, Southwest HS, Macon, Ga., 1985-88, 1988—; prof. biology Macon Coll., 1986-89; prof. edn. Wesleyan Coll., Macon, 1988—; tchr. sci. Rappahannock C.C., 1996—. Lobbyist Va. Legislature, Richmond, 1980-85, Ga. Legislature, Atlanta, 1985; active legis. contact team U.S. SEnate, Washington, 1984-85; mgr. campaign for state rep., Chesterfield County, Va., 1983; Sunday sch. tchr. Bapt. Ch. Mem. AAUW (chmn. edn. 1987-88), Bibb Assn. Educators (pres. 1989-90), Ga. Sci. Tchr.'s Assn. (state sec. 1989-91, dist. sci. tchr. 1988-89), Ladies' Civic Club. Avocation: travel. Home: 7617 Compromise Hill Rd Gloucester VA 23061-5334

PACECCA, ANDREA LEIGH, mathematics educator; b. Denville, N.J., Nov. 29, 1973; d. Frank George and Diana Jane Schimmenti; m. Robert Theodore Pacecca, Jr., July 11, 1998; children: Brianna Rose, Taylor Dean. BA Math., Cedarville U., Ohio, 1996. Tchr., chmn. Dept. Math. Indian Rocks Christian Sch., Largo, Fla., 1996—99, 2002—; tchr. math. Hermitage H.S., Richmond, Va., 1999—2000, Calvary Christian Sch., Columbus, Ga., 2000—01. Leader youth group Grove Ave. Bapt. Ch., Richmond, 1999—2000, Calvary Bapt. Ch., Columbus, 2000—01, First Bapt. Indian Rocks, Largo, 2001—. Office Phone: 727-596-4321. Personal E-mail: apacecca@tampabay.rr.com.

PACHA, MELINDA JANE, performing arts educator; b. Washinton, Iowa, Dec. 13, 1955; d. Walter Paul Pacha and Helen Darlene Wikoff/Pacha; m. Blair Vaughn Anderson, Aug. 17, 1985; 1 child, Miranda Pacha Anderson. BA, U. of No. Iowa, Cedar Falls, 1979; MFA, Wayne State U., Detroit, 1981. Asst. prof. of theatre U. of Detroit Mercy, Detroit, 1981—; freelance scenic/costume designer various metro theatres, Detroit, 1985—. Theatrical design, Five Women Wearing the Same Dress (Detroit News Award for Best Costume Design, 1995), The Wayside Motor I nn (Detroit Free press Award for Excellance in Scenic Design, 1999). Lector Guardian Angels Cath. Ch., Clawson, Mich., 1995—2006. Mem.: Am. Theatre in Higher Edn. Avocations: gardening, cooking. Office: University of Detroit Mercy 4001 W McNichols Detroit MI 48221 Office Phone: 313-993-3268.

PACHA-GUYOT, DEBRA L., forensic scientist; b. Nov. 22, 1956; Student, Miami Dade Coll., 1975-77; Cert. Radiologic Technologist, U. Ctrl. Fla., Orlando, 1981. Diplomate Am. Bd. Forensic Examiners; cert. profl. coder; cert. technologist instr. Radiographic technologist, office mgr. Physician's Office, South Miami, Fla., 1974-81; pres., founder Review Co. Med. Tech. Cons., Inc., Longwood, Fla.; educator med. forensic rev. NHR, Inc., Longwood. Examination radiol. technologist U. Ctrl. Fla. State Bd., 1981; cons. ins. industry, ins. def., Dept. Ins. Fraud, FBI; guest spkr. seminars, lectures, presentations.; mem. Fla. Health Care Cost Containment Bd., 1991—; arbitrator med. coding, med. technol. issues. Mem. Am. Acad. Thermology (affiliate), Assn. Clin. Thermography Technologist (founder, past pres.), Am. Acad. Neuro-Muscular Thermography (pres. technologist divsn. 1987-88), Fla. Soc. Radiologic Technologists, Ctrl. Fla. Soc. Radiologic Technologists, Am. Acad. Pain Mgmt. (clin. affiliate), Reflex Sympathetic Dystrophy Syndrome Assn. (pres. 1992-93), Assn. Rehab. Profls. in Pvt. Sector, Fla. Assn. Quality Assurance Profls., Nat. Assn. for Healthcare Quality, Am. Coll. Forensic Examiners, Am. Acad. Profl. Coders.

PACHECO, JILL, language educator; m. David A. Ferrie, June 9, 2006; children from previous marriage: Charlie, Lydia, Nicolas, Emily. MAEE, U. PR, Mayaguez, 2000. Cert. tchr. Mo. Ednl. cons./trainer Universal Conceptions, LLC, Ballwin, Mo., 2000—05; asst. prof. St. Louis CC, Kirkwood, Mo., 2005—. Developer University City Sch. Dist., Mo., 2002—06. Recipient Excellence in Edn., U. PR, 1998; scholar, Bus. and Profl. Women's Found., 1997. Mem.: NEA (assoc.). Home: 3690 318th Ave Harmony MN 55939 Office: St Louis CC 11333 Big Bend Blvd Kirkwood MO 63122 Office Phone: 314-984-7266. Personal E-mail: jilpacheco@sbcglobal.net. Business E-Mail: jpacheco@stlcc.edu.

PACHECO, SUSAN, automotive executive; d. Jorge Pacheco; married; children: Alex, Adam. MBA, U. Detroit, 1989. Ford grad. tng. program Ford Motor Co., 1984—86, product design engr., 1986—89, supr. steering column and shiftsystem design and devel., 1989—92, program mgr. Ford Explorer special studies, 1992, chief program engr., pres. Ford Unlimited, dir. Mercury programs. Named one of 50 Most Important Hispanics in Bus. and Tech., Hispanic Engr. & Info. Tech. mag., 2003.

PACHER, NANCY A., real estate company executive; Grad. cum laude, Georgetown U.; JD, Northwestern U. Atty. Katten Muchin Rosenman LLP, Chgo., 1975; sr. v.p., prin. Howard Ecker & Co.; pres., COO US Equities Realty, Chgo., 1993—. Commr. City of Chgo. Plan Commn. Mem. editl. adv. bd.: Ill. Real Estate Jour. Named Broker of the Yr., Chgo. Sun-Times, 1986, 2004; named one of 100 Most Influential Women in Chgo., Crain's Chgo. Bus., 1996; named to Who's Who in Chgo. Bus., 2002, 20th Ann. Hall of Fame, Today's Chgo. Women. Mem.: ABA, Comml. Real Estate Orgn., Comml. Real Estate Exec. Women, The Chgo. Network (bd. chair 2005—06), Chgo. Bar Assn., Econ. Club Chgo., Phi Beta Kappa. Office: US Equities Realty Ste 400 20 N Michigan Ave Chicago IL 60602

PACI, RUTH A., freelance/self-employed writer; b. West New York, N.J., Mar. 7, 1928; d. Joseph Frederick and Theresa Becker Paci. BA in History and Polit. Sci., Fordham U., 1984; MA in Journalism, NYU, 1987. Adminstrv. officer, press officer U.S. Info. Agy., Washington and N.Y.C., 1951—86, dep. dir. Fgn. Press Ctr. N.Y.C., 1985—86; ret., 1986; freelance writer. Author: Down By the River and Under the Cliff, 1994, Dearest Friends, 2004, short stories and essays. V.p., trustee Edgewater Pub. Libr., 1995—; mem., founder Cultural and Hist. Commn. Edgewater, 2000—; hist. preservation advisory bd. Bergen County, 2004. Recipient Cert. of Commendation, Bergen County Bd. Chosen Freeholders, 2003, Hist. Preservation resolution, NJ Gen. Assembly, 2003, Career Achievement award, US Info. Agy., 1986. Roman Catholic. Avocations: travel, gardening, reading. Home: 24 Valley Pl Edgewater NJ 07020

PACK, SANDRA L., federal agency administrator; BS, Notre Dame Coll. CPA. Dir. treasury Phil Gramm for Pres., Inc., Washington, 1995; dep. dir. treasury Bob Dole for Pres., Inc., Washington, 1996; dir. planning and ops. MicroProse divsn. Spectrum Holobyte, Inc., Hunt Valley, Md., 1994—95; dir. small bus. cons. and acctg. svcs. Ernst & Young, Balt., dir. microcomputer consulting and acctg. svcs. Atlanta; dir. of treasury Bush for Pres., Inc., Bush-Cheney 2000, Inc.; asst. sec. for fin. mgmt., comptr., Dept. Army US Dept. Def., Washington, 2001—04; CFO Bush-Cheney Re-Election Campaign, 2004; asst. sec. for mgmt. US Dept. Treasury, Washington, 2005—. Office: US Dept Treasury 1500 Pennsylvania Ave NW Rm 1308 Washington DC 20220

PACK, SUSAN JOAN, writer; b. N.Y.C., June 15, 1951; d. Howard Meade and Nancy (Buckley) P. BA summa cum laude, Princeton U., 1973. Copywriter Laurence Charles & Free, N.Y.C., 1978-83, Warwick Advt., N.Y.C., 1983-85; sr. copywriter Saatchi & Saatchi Compton, N.Y.C., 1985-88; pres. The Pack Collection, 1989—. Author: Film Posters of the Russian Avant-Garde, 1995. Mem. Princeton (N.J.) U. Libr. Coun., 1985-93; trustee Pack Found. for Med. Rsch., N.Y., 1983—; bd. dirs. The Poster Soc., N.Y., 1985-87. Recipient 4 Clio awards, 1981, 1 Clio award, 1982, Kitchen of Yr. award San Diego mag., 2003, Bathroom of Yr. award San Diego Home and Garden mag., 2003; named one of top art collectors and 40 Art and Antiques Mag., 1985, one of top 100 collectors in U.S., 1996. Mem. Phi Beta Kappa. E-mail: puredesign100@gmail.com.

PACK, SUZANNE CHRISTINA, elementary school educator; b. Pendleton, Oreg., Apr. 5, 1940; d. Stanley Maxfield and Christina Doris (Fleming) Day; m. Ward Lynn Pack, Apr. 14, 1962; children: Stacey, Camille, Dennis. BA in Elem. Edn., Idaho State U., 1962, MEd, 1994. Tchr. Sch. Dist. 25, Pocatello, Idaho, 1962-64, Coll. So. Idaho, Twin Falls, 1968-77; dir., co-owner Kids' Club Presch. and Daycare, Twin Falls, 1988—90; tchr. Sch. Dist. 411, Twin

Falls, 1977—2000, Kimberly (Idaho) Sch. Dist., 2000—. Leader Twin Falls Sch. Dist. Math. Network, 1988—; nat. math. cons. Math. Perspectives, 1990—. Mem. Internat. Reading Assn., Nat. Coun. Tchrs. Math., Nat. Coun. Suprs. Math. Home: 739 Rim View Dr W Twin Falls ID 83301-3012 Office: Kimberly Elem Sch 141 Center St West Kimberly ID 83341

PACKARD, BETTY JANE, journalist, consultant; b. Indpls., Oct. 1, 1937; d. Raymond Roy and Juanita Doris Reed; m. James R. Packard Jr., Nov. 28, 1958 (dec.); children: Lisa Lynn Packard Beaudry, James R. III; m. Stephen M. Voris, Sept. 26, 1975. BA, Franklin Coll., 1967. Editor R&R/Newkirk, Indpls., 1969—75; tchr. English and journalism, head journalism dept. Ben Davis H.S., Indpls., 1967—69; pres., owner Packard Cons., 1975—. Dir. Calif. H.S. Journalism Contest, 1982—; columnist, feature writer Franklin Evening Star, Ind.; reporter Indpls. Star, Indpls., Indpls. Times, Indpls. Mem. Ballot Simplification Commn., San Francisco, 1997—, chmn., 2003—; staffing dir. open rehearsals San Francisco Symphony Store, 1990—; mem. Symphony Store vol. coun. San Francisco Symphony; mem. emergency response team ARC, 1992—98, dist. vol. coord., 1980—82, chmn. vols. Ft. Ord, Calif., 1980—82; bd. dirs. Presidio Officers Wives Club, 1982—92; apptd. Ind. Addiction Svcs. Com., 1974—80; U.S. rep. World Conf. Women Journalists, Seoul, Republic of Korea, 1979; apptd. Nat. Security Forum, 1975; prin. lobbyist Equal Rights Amendment ratification, Ind., 1972—79; U.S. rep. USA/USSR meetings with journalists, politicians and educators, 1973. Recipient various citations for speeches, 1973—, 118 writing awards, Calif. Press Women, Women's Press Club Ind., Pub. Rels. Soc. Am., Disting. Svc. award, Gov. of Tex., 1992, Ky. Col. award, 1976. Mem.: Am. Assn. Auto Racing Writers and Broadcasters (editor ann. awards dinner mag 1990—92), Pi Beta Phi (membership chmn., yearbook editor, ways and means chmn., Disting. Nat. Alumnae award 1992), Calif. Press Women (exec. dir. 1995—), Nat. Fedn. Press Women (nat. bd. dirs. 1980—, Individual Achievement in Print Journalism award 1999, 16 writing awards), Indpls. 500 Ladies Oldtimers (yearbook editor, chmn. membership com. 1988—), San Francisco Garden Club (newsletter editor 2004—). Presbyterian. Office Phone: 415-285-1551. Personal E-mail: bettypackard@comcast.net.

PACKARD, JENNIFER ELLEN, music educator; b. Lexington, Ky., Oct. 22, 1978; d. Teresa Ann and Keith Steven House; m. Eric Douglas Packard, Jan. 4, 2003; 1 child, Dylan Douglas. BA in History, Mo. State U., Springfield, 1997—2002. Musician: (yuma civic orchestra) Oboe Player. Democrat. Protestant. Office: Sunrise Elem 9943 E 28th St Yuma AZ 85365 Office Phone: 9285028800 ext 8783. Personal E-mail: jpackard@yumaed.org.

PACKARD, JOYCE HORNADAY, retired counselor; b. Fordyce, Ark., June 21, 1925; d. John Wesley and Nora (Wright) Hornaday; m. Robert G. Packard, Apr. 15, 1954. BA, Baylor U., 1952, MS, 1957; postgrad., Columbia U., 1966, Baylor U., 1980. Lic. counselor Tex. Office mgr./tchr. Western Union Telegraph Co., Crossett, Ark., 1944-48; asst. dean of women Baylor U., Wace, 1952-54, 57-61; tchr. Edison High Sch., Stockton, Calif., 1954-55, Clinton (Miss.) High Sch., 1955-56; tchr. Am. history/govt. Richfield High Sch., Waco, 1963-66, counselor, 1966—81, 1982—86; lectr. Baylor U., Waco, 1981-82, supr. practice tchrs., 1986—90. Tchr. English, U. Calif. Team Arlangga U., Sarabaja, Indonesia, 1961-62; tchr. cons. U. Sci., Penang, Malaysia, summer 1976; mem. Internat. Del. Citizen Ambassador, China, 1990. Mem. team Greater Asian Evangelism Team, Taiwan, 1970; bd. dirs. Brazos Forum, Waco, 1989—, pres., 1997; bd. dirs. Waco Historic Found., 1988—, pres., 1995-96; reg. facilitator Tex. Hospitality Course, 1987—; mem., chair Waco Conv. and Visitors Adv. Bd., 1987-2006; mem. Ind. Sch. Dist. Ednl. Bd., 1996—; bd. dirs. Brazos Higher Edn., Brazos Performing Arts; pres. Baptist Southern Deans, 1958-59. Recipient Woman of Achievement award, 1972, Waco Hospitality award Convention and Tourism Adv. Bd., 1990, Pathfinder award Waco YWCA, 1990, Cert. award Vol. Svcs. Waco City Coun., 1991, Leadership Waco C. of C. Alumnus award, 1994, Athena award, 1995, DAR Cmty. Svc. award Elizabeth Gordon Bardley Chpt., 1997, Madison Cooper award cmty. leadership Madison Cooper Found. Trustees, 1999, Woman of Distinction award Bluebonnet Girl Scouts, 2003, Disting. Faculty award Waco Ind. Sch. Dist., 2004. Mem. Greater Waco Beautification Assn., Baylor Round Table (pres. 1988-89), Baylor Alumni Assn., Leadership Waco Alumni Assn., Epsilon Chi (achievement award 1984, pres. 1976-78), Delta Kappa Gamma (achievement award 1984, corres. sec. 1987-89). Baptist. Avocations: cooking, travel. Home: 69 Sugar Creek Pl Woodway TX 76712-3407

PACKARD, JULIE, aquarium administrator; b. Los Altos Hills; d. David and Lucile Packard. Co-founder & exec. dir. Monterey Bay Aquarium, Monterey, Calif., 1984—, vice chair, bd of trustees, 1984—. Mem. Pew Oceans Commn. Bd. dirs. David and Lucile Packard Found., Monterey Bay Aquarium Rsch. Inst., Calif. Nature Conservancy. Recipient Audubon Medal for Conservation, 1998, Ted Danson Ocean Hero award, 2004. Office: Monterey Bay Aquarium 886 Cannery Row Monterey CA 93940-1023

PACKARD, KERRI SHANNON, theater educator; d. Adrain Wayne and Judith Arlene Bradley; m. Raymond Dean Packard, May 18, 1992; children: Sean Bradley, Cassandra Ashley. BFA, Ariz. State U., 1989; MFA, U. Iowa, 1992. Asst. prof. Kans. State U., Manhattan, Kans., 1992—93; adj. assoc. prof. U. Mo., Columbia, Mo., 1993—. Mng. dir. Summer Repertory Theatre U. Mo., 2002—. Costume designer (plays) The Fool's Journey, U. Mo., 2004—05 (commendation Am. Coll. Theatre Festival Kennedy Ctr., 2005); costumer designer: Leaving Hannibal, York Theatre and Arc Light Theatre, 2005. Asst. leader Girl Scouts, Columbia, 2004—06. Nominee Costume Design Faculty fellow, Kennedy Ctr. Am. Coll. Theatre Festival, 2005. Mem.: Costume Soc. Am., U.S. Inst. Theatre Tech. Office: University of Missouri 129 Fine Arts Building Columbia MO 65211 Office Phone: 573-882-4750. Office Fax: 573-884-4034.

PACKARD, ROCHELLE SYBIL, elementary school educator; b. June 25, 1951; d. Dave Wallace and Jeanette (Goddy) P. BA in Early Childhood Edn., Point Park Coll., 1973; MEd in Elem. Edn., U. Pitts., 1975. Instrnl. II permanent tchg. cert., Pa. Substitute tchr. Pitts. Pub. Bd. Edn., 1973-77, tchr. kindergarten, 1st grade, 2d grade, 1977—92, tchr. kindergarten, 1992—. Chair Israel Day Parade, Pitts., 1981; mem. Hadassah, Pitts., 1983—, Pioneer Women, Pitts., 1982—, ORT, Pitts., 1975—. Mem. Pitts. Fedn. Tchrs., Pitts. State Edn. Agy. Democrat. Jewish. Home: 4100 Lydia St Pittsburgh PA 15207-1135 Business E-Mail: rpackard@pghboe.net.

PACKARD, SANDRA PODOLIN, education educator, consultant; b. Buffalo, Sept. 13, 1942; d. Mathew and Ethel (Zolte) P.; m. Martin Packard, Aug. 2, 1964; children: Dawn Esther, Shana Fanny BFA, Syracuse U., 1964; MSEd, Ind. U., 1966, EdD, 1973. Cert. tchr. art K-12, N.Y. Asst. prof. art SUNY-Buffalo, 1972-74; assoc. prof. art Miami U., Oxford, Ohio, 1974-81, spl. asst. to provost, 1979-80, assoc. provost, spl. programs, 1980-81; dean Coll. Edn. Bowling Green State U., Ohio, 1981-85; provost and vice chancellor for acad. affairs U. Tenn., Chattanooga, 1985-92; pres. Oakland U., Rochester, Mich., 1992-95, prof. edn., 1995—, dir. higher edn. doc. cognate; sr. fellow, dir. tech. in edn. Am. Assn. State Colls. and Univs., 1995; coord. Nat. Coun. for Accreditation of Tchr. Edn., Washington, 1995—2001; acting dir. PhD program in end. leadership Oakland U., 2003—04. Cons. Butler County Health Ctr., Hamilton, Ohio, 1976-78, Univ. of the North, South Africa Project of the Am. Coun. on Edn., 1995; vis. prof. art therapy Simmons Coll., 1979, Mary Mount Coll., Milw., 1981; corp. adv. com. Corp. Detroit Mag., 1994-95. Sr. editor Studies in Art Edn. jour., 1979-81; mem. editl. adv. bd. Jour. Aesthetic Edn., 1984-90; editor: The Leading Edge, 1986; contbr. articles to profl. jours., chpts. to conf. papers Chmn. com. Commn. on Edn. Excellence, Ohio, 1982-83, Tenn. State Peformance Funding Task Force, 1988, Tenn. State Task Force on Minority Tchrs., 1988; reviewer art curriculum NY Bd. Edn., 1985; supt. search com. Chattanooga Pub. Schs., 1987-88; mem. Chattanooga Met. Coun., 1987-88, Chattanooga Ballet Bd., 1986-88, Fund for Excellence in Pub. Edn., 1986-90, Tenn. Aquarium Bd. Advisors, 1989-92, Team Evaluation Ctr. Bd., 1988-90; strategic planning action team Chattanooga City Schs., 1987-88, Siskin Hosp. Bd., 1989-92, Blue Ribbon Task Force Pontiac 2010: A New Reality, City of Pontiac Planning Divsn., 1992—; steering com., cultural action bd. Chattanooga, planning com United Way, 1987; Jewish Fedn. Bd., 1986-91; mem. coun. for policy studies Art Edn. Adv. Bd., 1982-91; ex-officio mem. Meadow Brook Theatre Guild, 1992-95; bd. chair Meadow Brook Performing Arts Co., 1992-95; chair World Cup Soccer Edn. Com./Mich. Host Com. 1993-95; bd. dirs. Ptnrs. for Preferred Future, Rochester Cmty. Schs., 1992-95, Traffic Improvement Assn. Oakland County, 1992-95, Oakland County Bus. Roundtable, 1993-95; Rochester C. of C. host com. chair on edn. World Cup, 1992-95; fin. adv. com. Jewish Fedn. Detroit, 1995-97; bd. dirs. United Way Southeastern Mich., 1992-95: bd. dirs. United Way Oakland County, 1992-95, Pontiac 2010: A New Reality, mayor's transition team city/sch. rels. task force: team evaluation leader Dept of State Am. U. Bulgaria, 1995; bd. trustees Cohn's & Colitis Found., 1996-97; trustee Nat. Art Edn. Found., 2004—, chair fin. com.; steering com. Nat. Forum Access to Democracy Project, 2004. Am. Coun. on Edn. and Mellon fellow Miami U., 1978-79; recipient Cracking the Glass Ceiling award Pontiac Area Urban League, 1992. Fellow Nat. Art Edn. Assn. (disting.); mem. Nat. Coun. Profs. of Ednl. Adminstrn. (technology com., 2000-03), Am. Assn. Colls. for Tchr. Edn. (com. chair 1982-85), Am. Art Therapy Assn. (registered), Nat. Art Edn. Assn. Women's Caucus (founder, pres. 1976-78, McFee award 1986), Am. Assn. State Colls. and Univs. (com. profl. devel. 1993-95, state rep. 1994-95), Econ. Club Detroit (bd. dirs. 1992-95), Rotary Club, Great Lakes Yacht Club (social chmn. 1996-97, ground chmn., bd. dirs. 1997-98), Phi Delta Kappa (Leadership award 1985), Nat. Assn. Profs. of Edn. Adminstrn. (com. chair 1998-), Great Lakes Yacht Club, 1995 (bd. dir. 1996-1998). Avocation: sailing. Home: 10471 Scout Trail White Lake MI 48386 Office: Oakland U 475 Education Bldg Rochester MI 48309-4423 Business E-Mail: packard@oakland.edu.

PACKARD, SOPHIE S., elementary school educator; b. Anacoco, La., Dec. 15, 1935; d. Willie Cranford and Lorea Grace (Dixon) Snell; m. Hyland D. Packard; children: Lajuan Michelle Packard Chopin, Michael Harry. BA in Elem. Tchg. and Reading, MA in Elem. Tchg. and Reading, Northwestern State U., Natchitoches, La. Cert. Gesell devel. examiner Gesell Inst. Human Growth and Devel. Tchr./supr. Northwestern State U., Natchitoches. Vol. Lov'n Care, co-dir., 1997—2006. Recipient Dist. Tchr. of Yr. award, Natchitoches, 1985, Outstanding Elem Cooperating Tchr. of Year, Northwestern State U., 1994—95, Disting. Clinician Yr., La. Assn. Tchr. Edn., 1996, Presdl. Point of Light award, 2000, Tchr. of the Yr. award, Weaver Elem. Sch. Mem.: Retired Tchrs. La., Lions Club (pres. 2004—05), Order of Eastern Star (worthy matron 2003—04, organist 2005, grand rep. to Idaho from La. 2005—), Phi Delta Kappa (past pres.), Delta Gamma Kappa (past pres.). Baptist. Avocations: piano, gardening, handwork.

PACKARD BURNETT, NANCY, biologist; d. David Packard; m. Robin Burnett. BS in Biology, Stanford U., 1965; MS, San Francisco State. Former marine biologist Hopkins Marine Station; founder, marine biologist Monterey Bay Aquarium. Exec. prodr.: (TV films) The Shape of Life, 2002. Bd. dirs. Monterey Bay Aquarium Rsch. Inst.; adv. Whatcom Community Found.; vice chmn. David and Lucile Packard Found.; chmn. Sea Studios Found. Office: Sea Studios Found 810 Cannery Row Monterey CA 93940*

PACKER, DIANA, retired reference librarian; b. Cleve., Sept. 04; d. Herman and Sabina (Hochman) Reich; m. Herbert Packer, June 21, 1964 (dec.); children: Cynthia, Jeremy, Todd. BA, Case Western Res. U., 1951, MLS, 1952. Libr. Horizons Rsch. Inc., Cleve., 1952-64, Cleveland Heights (Ohio) University Heights Pub. Libr., 1969-98, ret., 1998. Officer Cleveland Heights PTA, 1971-84; bd. dirs. LWV, Cleveland Heights, 1974—; officer Spl. Librs. Assn., 1952-64. Mem. Ohio Libr. Assn. Avocations: travel, theater, art, music, reading. Home: 2201 Acacia Park Dr Apt 522 Lyndhurst OH 44124-3841

PACKER, KAREN GILLILAND, cancer patient educator, researcher; b. Washington, Apr. 27, 1940; d. Theodore Redmond and Evelyn Alice (Johnson) Gilliland; m. Allan Richard Packer, Sept. 27, 1962; 1 child, Charles Allan. Student, Duke U., 1957-59, U. Ky., 1959-60, 61-62, U. P.R. Sch. Medicine, 1960-61. Genetics researcher U. Ky., Lexington, 1959-60, 61-62; biologist Melpar Inc., Nat. Cancer Inst., Springfield, Va., 1964-66; rsch. assoc., epidemiology rsch. ctr. U. Iowa Coll. Medicine, Iowa City, 1981-85; founder, dir. Marshalltown (Iowa) Cancer Support Group, 1987—. Mem. County Health Planning Commn., Marshalltown, 1989-96; mem. adv. bd. Cmty. Nursing Svc., Marshalltown, 1990—; v.p. Cmty. Svcs. Coun., Marshalltown, 1992-96, pres. 1996-97; mem. Marshall County Bd. of Health, 1996—2001; mem. dir.'s consumer liaison group Nat. Cancer Inst., 2001-04; mem. Iowa Comprehensive Cancer Control Consortium, 2002—. Editor The Group Gazette, 1988—. Bd. dirs. 1st United Ch. Christ, Hampton, Va., 1973-75; corr. sec. DAR, Marshalltown, 1988-92; chmn. cancer and rsch. aux. VFW, Marshalltown, 1990—; chmn. Marshall County Commn. Aging, 1999—, sec., 2000—03. Recipient Leadership award Marshalltown Area C. of C., 1988, Spl. recognition Nat. Coalition for Cancer Survivorship, 1990, Iowa Senate 1995, 1st place in state award Cmty. Cancer Edn. VFW Aux., 1990-2004, Nat. Vol. Hero of Yr. award Coping Mag., 1995; Genetics Rsch. grantee NSF, 1959-60, NIH, 1961-62. Mem. AAAS, Nat. Guard Bur. Officers Wives Club (publ. editor 1965-68), Iowa Cancer Registrars Assn., N.Y. Acad. Scis. Mem. Congregational Ch. Achievements include establishment of regional orgn. for cancer info. and edn. Home and Office: 1401 Fairway Dr Marshalltown IA 50158-3825

PACKER, ZZ (ZUWENA), writer, literature educator; b. Chgo., Jan. 12, 1973; d. Rose; m. Michael Boros, 2001. BA, Yale U., 1994; MA in Creative Writing, Johns Hopkins U., 1995; MFA, U. Iowa, 1999. Tchr. various pub. schs., Balt.; Jones lectr. Stanford U.; vis. asst. prof. Writers' Workshop U. Iowa, 2003—04. Author: (short stories) Drinking Coffee Elsewhere, 2003. Recipient Ms. Giles Whiting award, 1999, Bellingham Rev. award, 1999; grantee, Rona Jaffe Writers Found., 1997; Wallace Stegner and Truman Capote fellow, Stanford U. Office: Univ Iowa Writers Workshop 102 Dey House 507 N Clinton St Iowa City IA 52242-1000

PACKERT, G(AYLA) BETH, retired lawyer; b. Corpus Christi, Tex., Sept. 25, 1953; d. Gilbert Norris and Virginia Elizabeth (Pearce) P.; m. James Michael Hall, Jan. 1, 1974 (div. 1985); m. Richard Christopher Burke, July 18, 1987; children: Christopher Geoffrey Makepeace Burke Packert, Jeremy Eliot Marvell Packert Burke. BA, La. Tech. U., 1973; postgrad., U. Ill., 1975—81, JD, 1985; MA, U. Ark., 1976. Bar: Ill. 1985, U.S. Dist. Ct. (no. dist.) Ill. 1985, U.S. Ct. Appeals (7th cir.) 1987, Va. 1988, U.S. Dist. Ct. (we. dist.) Va. 1989. Assoc. Jenner & Block, Chgo., 1985—88; law clk. U.S. Dist. Ct. Va. (we. dist.), Danville, 1988—89; asst. commonwealth atty. Commonwealth of Va., Lynchburg, 1989—95; pvt. practice Lynchburg, 1995—2002; English tchr. Paul Laurence Dunbar Middle Sch. for Innovation, Lynchburg, 2004—06. Notes and comments editor U. Ill. Law Rev., 1984-85. Mem. Phi Beta Kappa. Home: 3900 Faculty Dr Lynchburg VA 24501-3110 Office Phone: 434-522-3740.

PACKERT, GINGER E., social studies educator, education educator; BS in Edn., Bowling Green State U., Ohio, 1978—82; MA in History, U. Toledo, Ohio, 1993—99. Cert. Tchr., Secondary Social Studies Ohio Dept. Edn., 1999. Adj. instr. Bowling Green State U.-Firelands Coll., Huron, Ohio, 2002—, Grad., mem. bd. dirs. LEADSandusky, Erie County, 1988. Grantee, James Madison Meml. Fellowship Found., 1993. Mem.: NEA (exec. com. 1985), EHOVE Edn. Assn., Ohio Edn. Assn. Avocation: travel. Office Phone: 419-499-4663.

PACKHAM, MARIAN AITCHISON, biochemistry professor; b. Toronto, Ont., Can., Dec. 13, 1927; d. James and Clara Louise (Campbell) A.; m. James Lennox Packham, June 25, 1949; children: Neil Lennox, Janet Melissa. BA, U. Toronto, 1949, PhD, 1954; DSc honoris causa, Ryerson Poly. U., 1997. Sr. fellow dept. biochemistry U. Toronto, 1954-58, lectr. dept. biochemistry, 1958-63, 66-67; rsch. assoc. dept. physiol. scis. Ont. Vet. Coll., U. Guelph, 1963-65; rsch. assoc. blood and cardiovascular disease rsch. unit U. Toronto, 1965-66, asst. prof. dept. biochemistry, 1967-72, assoc. prof., 1972-75, prof., 1975—, acting chmn. dept. biochemistry, 1983. Contbr. articles to profl. jours. Royal Soc. Can. fellow, 1991; recipient Lt. Govs. Silver medal Victoria Coll., 1949; co-recipient J. Allyn Taylor Internat. prize in Medicine, 1988. Mem.: Can. Soc. Biochemistry and Molecular and Cellular Biology, Can. Atherosclerosis Soc., Internat. Soc. Thrombosis and Haemostasis, Can. Soc. Hematology, Am. Soc. Hematology. Office: U Toronto Dept Biochemistry Toronto ON Canada M5S 1A8

PACUSKA, M. ABBEGAEL, lawyer; b. Wilkes-Barre, Pa., Sept. 4, 1979; d. Joseph Thomas and Mary Elizabeth Pacuska. JD, Widener U., Harrisburg, Pa., 2004. Bar: Pa. 2004. Legal clk. Dept. Gen. Svcs. Office Chief Counsel Commonwealth Pa., Harrisburg, 2003—04; lawyer Robinson & Geraldo, Harrisburg, 2004—. Bd. dirs. Heinz-Menaker Sr. Ctr., Harrisburg. Mem.: ABA, Am. Trial Lawyers Assn., Pa. Bar Assn., Dauphin County Bar Assn. Republican. Roman Catholic. Avocations: travel, reading, drawing. Office: Robinson & Geraldo 4407 N Front Street Harrisburg PA 17110 Office Phone: 717-232-8525. Home Fax: 717-232-5098; Office Fax: 717-232-5098. Business E-Mail: apacuska@robinson-geraldo.com.

PADBERG, HARRIET ANN, mathematician, educator; b. St. Louis, Nov. 13, 1922; d. Harry J. and Marie L. (Kilgen) P. AB with honors, Maryville Coll., St. Louis, 1943; MMus, U. Cin., 1949; MA, St. Louis U., 1956, PhD, 1964. Registered music therapist, cert. tchr. math. and music La., Mo. Tchr. elem. math. and music Kenwood Acad., Albany, N.Y., 1944-46; tchr. secondary math. Acad. of Sacred Heart, Cin., 1946-47; instr. math. and music Acad. and Coll. of Sacred Heart, Grand Coteau, La., 1947-48; secondary tchr. music Acad. Sacred Heart, St. Charles, Mo., 1948-50; instr. math. and music Acad. and Coll. Sacred Heart, Grand Coteau, 1950-55, Maryville Coll., St. Louis, 1955-56; tchr. elem. and secondary math. and music Acad. Sacred Heart, St. Louis, 1956-57; asst. prof. Maryville Coll., St. Louis, 1957-64, assoc. prof., 1964-68, prof. math., 1968-92, prof. emeritus, 1992—; music therapist Emmaus Homes, Marthasville, Mo., 1992—. Recipient Alumni Centennial award Maryville Coll., St. Louis, 1986; grantee Danforth Found., Colorado Springs, 1970, Tallahassee, 1970, Edn. Devel. Ctr., Mass., 1975, U. Kans., 1980. Mem. Assn. Women in Math., Am. Math. Soc., Math. Assn. Am., Nat. Coun. Tchr. Math., Mo. Acad. Sci., Delta Epsilon Sigma (sec. local chpt. 1962), Pi Mu Epsilon (sec. local chpt. 1958), Sigma Xi. Avocations: computer music, organist, knitting. E-mail: hpadberg@rscj.org.

PADDOCK, SANDRA CONSTANCE, music educator; b. Buffalo, Sept. 20, 1972; d. Walter Robert and Susan Elizabeth Wloch; m. Darren Ennis Paddock, July 20, 1996; children: Leanne Kristine, Robert Duane. B in Music Edn. cum laude, SUNY, Buffalo, 1994, M in Arts and Humanities, 1997. Cert. tchr. N.Y. Music tchr. Niagara Wheatfield (N.Y.) Schs., 1995—96; orchestra dir. Kenmore-Tonawanda Schs., 1996—2000; orch. dir., string tchr. Orchard Park (N.Y.) Mid. Sch., 2000—. String adjudicator Erie County Elem. and Jr. High Festivals, 1998, 2002; co-chairperson Erie County (N.Y.) Jr. High Music Festivals, 2001, 02. Musician (solo violinist): faculty recital, 2001. 1st violin Amherst Symphony Orch., 1997—. Mem.: Erie County Music Educator's Assn., Music Educator's Nat. Conf. Avocations: reading, attending concerts.

PADGETT, CYNTHIA S., artist; b. Kansas City, Mo., Mar. 4, 1948; m. Charles Allen Padgett, June 10, 1967; children: Claire Padgett-Doane, Charles Alexander. BA, Goucher Coll., 1972; MA in Liberal Arts, Johns Hopkins U., 1983. Cert. instrument pilot. Docent The Walters Art Gallery, Balt., 1986-89; alumni bd. mem. Goucher Coll., Balt., 1993-95. One-woman show: A. Jain Marunouchi Gallery, NY, 1998, 99, 2000, 01, 03, 04; works exhibited at A. Jain Marunouchi Gallery, NYC, 1993—, Artshowcase, Balt., 1993, Internat. Contemporary Art Festival (NICAF), Yokohama, Japan, 1995, Tokyo, 1997, LINEART, Gent, Belgium, 2000, 01, Europ'art, Geneva, 2001, Art Phil., 2003; slide registries: Maryland Art Place, Nat. Mus. of Women in the Arts. Bd. mem. LWV, St. Petersburg, Fla., 1980-81, Balt., 1981-83; guide Nat. Aquarium, Balt., 1995—; bd. mem., pres. women's com. Historic Hampton, Inc., Towson, Md., 1995-97; chmn. Dulaney Valley, Md. Ho. and Garden Pilgrimage, 1996, 99; Mission Ch., 1992-95. Mem. Johns Hopkins Club, Goucher Club, DAR, Hamilton St. Club. Republican. Episc. Avocations: sailing, travel.

PADGETT, KATHRYN ANN WEINER, medical association administrator, special education educator; b. Denver, July 21, 1949; d. Jerry E. and Mildred G. (Jenson) Padgett; m. Richard S. Weiner, Aug. 25, 1985; 1 child, Rebecca. BA, Ariz. State U., 1971, MA, 1976; PhD, Walden U., 1993. Cert. basic elem., LH specialist, adminstrn. and supervision, resource specialist. Program specialist Stanislaus County Dept. Edn., Modesto, Calif.; coord. spl. edn. Modesto (Calif.) City Schs.; exec. dir. Am. Acad. of Pain Mgmt., Modesto; supr. spl. edn. Modesto (Calif.) City Schs.; founder, exec. dir. Am. Acad. Pain Mgmt., Sonora, Calif. Mem. Assn. Calif. Sch. Adminstrs. (dir.), Soroptimist Internat. (pres.), Mental Health Adv. Bd. (chair), Children's Svcs. Com. (chair). Office: Am Acad Pain Mgmt 13947 Mono Way # A Sonora CA 95370-2807 Business E-Mail: kathryn@aapainmanage.org.*

PADGETT, NANCY WEEKS, law librarian, consultant, lawyer; b. Newberry, S.C., June 3, 1932; d. Price John and Caroline (Weeks) P.; m. David Lazar, Aug. 6, 1953 (dec. May 19, 2002). BS, Northwestern U., 1953; MLS, U. Md., 1972; JD, Georgetown U., 1977. Bar: D.C. 1977. Asst. law libr. U.S. Ct. Appeals for D.C., Washington, 1972—74, supervisory law libr., 1974—84, circuit libr., 1984—. Mem. ALA, D.C. Bar Assn., Am. Assn. Law Librs. Home: 5301 Duvall Dr Bethesda MD 20816-1873 Office: US Ct Appeals for DC Cir Judges' Libr 5518 US Court House Washington DC 20001-5618 Office Phone: 202-216-7400.

PADIAN, NANCY, medical educator, epidemiologist; BA cum laude, Colgate U., 1974; MS in Reading Edn., Syracuse U., 1974; MPH, U. Calif., Berkeley, 1983, PhD in Epidemiology, 1987. Co-founder UZ-U. Calif. San Francisco Collaborative Rsch. Programme Women's Health, Zimbabwe, 1994; founder Women's Global Health Imperative, 2001; assoc. dir. rsch. U. Calif. San Francisco Global Health Scis., 2004; dir. AIDS Rsch. Inst. U. Calif. San Francisco; with Ob.-gyn. dept. U. Calif. San Francisco, co-dir. Ctr. Reproductive Health Rsch. and Policy, internat. expert heterosexual transmission HIV and other sexually transmitted infections, prof. dept. Ob.gyn. and reproductive scis., 2005—; with epidemiology dept. U. Calif. Berkeley. Mem.: Inst. Medicine. Achievements include research in developing and evaluating female-controlled methods for disease prevention, such as the diaphram and microbicides, along with alternative strategies for fostering young women's economic independence; thus reducing their susceptibility to HIV, STIs, and unwanted pregnancies.

PADILLA, REBECCA LYNN, special education educator; b. Washington, Nov. 13, 1978; d. David Joseph and Kathryn Elizabeth Padilla. BS in Psychology, Coll. William and Mary, 2001; MS in Elem. Edn., U. Pa., 2002; MEd in Sch. Counseling, George Mason U., 2006. Lic. tchr. pre-K-6 Va., sch. counselor K-12 Va. Spl. edn. tchr. Oakwood Sch., Annandale, Va., 2002—05; curriculum specialist Ednl. Options, Inc., Arlington, Va., 2005—. Recipient Dean's Urban Tchr. Edn. scholarship, U. Pa., 2001—02. Mem.: Va. Sch. Counselor Assn., Va. Counselor Assn., Am. Sch. Counselor Assn., Am. Counselor Assn. Avocations: music, dance, exercise, reading, dogs. Personal E-mail: padillabecky@hotmail.com.

PADILLA, SARAI RAMONA, health facility administrator, psychologist; b. N.Y., Nov. 30, 1956; d. Joseph Peter and Rosaura Padilla; 1 child, Kassandra Bond. BA, NYU, 1982; MEd, CUNY, 1985; D Psychology, Pace U., 1993. Lic. psychologist N.Y., Fla.; cert. sch. psychologist N.Y. Sr. psychologist child and adolescent unit Gouverneur Hosp., 1992—97; adj. prof. Alliance Grad. Sch. of Counseling, 2001—03, St. Lukes Roosevelt Hosp., 2001—03, supt. psychologist NJ, 1999—2002, dir., 2002—. Chair Ctrl. Bapt. Ch., 1993—97, Sunday sch. tchr., 1999—2002. Mem.: APA, Internat. AIDS Soc. Avocations: reading, movies, exercise, music. Office Phone: 212-523-3847. E-mail: spadilla@chpnet.org.

PADULA, WANDA JEAN, secondary school educator; b. Niagara Falls, N.Y., Oct. 21, 1960; d. Sylvester Richard and Mary Ann Szymanski; m. Charles David Padula, Oct. 15, 1988; children: David, Nicholas, Andrew. BS in Secondary Sci., SUNY, Oswego, 1982, MS in Secondary Sci., 1986. Cert. physics tchr., 7-12 gen. sci. tchr. Earth sci. tchr. St. Mary's H.S., Lancaster, NY, 1982—83; earth sci., physics tchr. Auburn Schs., NY, 1983—87; phys. and earth sci. tchr. Hillsborough County Schs., Tampa, Fla., 1987—89; physics, earth sci. tchr. Hannibal Schs., NY, 1989—90; physics tchr. Liverpool Ctrl. Schs., Liverpool, NY, 1990—91, 1994—; earth sci. tchr. Oswego Ctrl. Schs., Oswego, NY, 1991—94. Mem. conf. com. STANYS, Ellenville, NY; coach Sci. Olympiad, Liverpool, judge. Grantee, NSF, NASA, 1988. Mem.: Nat. Bd. Profl. Tchr. Stds., Nat. Sci. Tchrs. Assn., Sci. Tchrs. Assn. of N.Y. Roman Catholic. Avocations: camping, exercise, skiing, hiking, crossword puzzles. Home: 6 Mapleview Dr E Pennellville NY 13132 Office: Liverpool High School 4338 Wetzel Rd Liverpool NY 13090 Office Phone: 315-453-1500.

PAEZ, CAROLYN JEAN, secondary school educator; b. Wapanucka, Okla., Dec. 14, 1946; d. John Franklin and Etna Ethel (King) Eacret; m. Rudy R. Paez, Nov. 25, 1977; 1 child, Eric Richard. BA, Western N.Mex. U., 1970, MA, 1984. Tchr. Mountainair (N.Mex.) Pub. Schs., 1970-73, St. Mary's Acad., Silver City, N.Mex., 1973-74, Deming (N.Mex.) Pub. Schs., 1974-78, Silver Consolidated Schs., Silver City, N.Mex., 1978—. Bd. dirs., v.p. N.Mex. Teen Coalition, 1988-91; mentor Future Homemakers Am., 1989-93; cons. So. Area Health Edn. Ctr., Las Cruces, N.Mex., 1989-91. Named champion Future Homemakers Am., 1990; recipient Thanks to Tchr. award Applle Computers, 1990, Tchr. of Yr. award N.Mex. State, 1991, Home Econs. Exemplary Program award, 1989-90, Exemplary Tchrs program Burger King. Mem. NEA, SCEA (bldg. rep. 1987-89, 93), N.Mex. Am. Home Econ. Assn. (bd. dirs. 1989-93), N.Mex. Vocat. Assn., Nat. Assn. Vocat. Home Econs. Tchrs., Home Econ. Edn. Assn., Am. Home Econ. Assn., N.Mex. Vocat. Home Econs. Tchrs. Assn. (2d v.p. 1991, 1st v.p. 1992, pres. 1993), Silver Consol. Edn. Assn. Democrat. Avocations: camping, reading, needlecrafts, irish blessings, cooking. Home: 61 Coleman Dr Silver City NM 88061-8954 Office: Silver High Sch 3200 N Silver St Silver City NM 88061-7259

PAGANO, ALICIA I., education educator; b. Sidney, N.Y., June 29, 1929; d. Neil Gadsby Leonard and Norma (Carr) Collins; m. Thomas McNutt, Feb. 20, 1954 (div. Nov. 1962); m. LeRoy Pagano, Feb. 26, 1963 (div. Oct. 1985); children: Janice, Daniel, Jack, Pier. BA in Music, Barrington Coll., 1952; MAT in Music, Rollins Coll., 1964; EdD in Edn. Adminstrn., Am. U., 1972. Tchr. music Prince Georges County Pub. Schs., Beltsville, Md., 1966-69; asst. prof. Medgar Evers Coll., Bklyn., 1973-78; nat. program dir. Girl Scouts USA, N.Y.C., 1978-83; nat. dir. vol. development U.S. Com. UNICEF, N.Y.C., 1983-84; pres. Pagano Consulting Internat., Unadilla, NY, 1984—; asst. prof. mgmt. Coll. Staten Island, CUNY, 1985-89; adj. prof. museum studies NYU, N.Y.C., 1986-91; assoc. exec. dir. Louis August Jonas Found., Red Hook, N.Y., 1988-89; assoc. prof. edn. N.J. City U., 1990—2005. Chair Wingspread Nat. Conf./Nat. Collaboration for Youth, Washington, 1982; adv. bd. dirs. Early Childhood Ctr.; rschr., cons. in early childhood edn. in West Africa, 1988—; vis. prof. Queen Rambha Rajabat U., Chantaburi, Thailand, 2004; curator Girl Scouting in Umadilla exhibit Umadilla Hist. Mus., 2006. Author, editor: Social Studies in Early Childhood, 1979; author: The Future of American Business, 1985, (with others) Learning Opportunities Beyond School, 1987; co-editor: International Early Childhood Teacher Education, 1999; contbr. articles to profl. jours. Judge annual awards Girls, Inc., N.Y.C., 1985-90; reader Jersey City Spelling Bee, 1991; vol. Girl Scouts USA, Essex/Hudson Counties, N.J., 1995—, Boys & Girls Clubs, Hudson County, N.J., 1995—. Mem. ASCD, AAUW, Am. Ednl. Rsch. Assn., Nat. Assn. Early Childhood Tchr. Edn. (bd. dirs. 1995—), N.J. Assn. Early Childhood Tchr. Educators (v.p. 1994-97, pres. 1997-99), Orgn. Mondiale pour l'Edn. Prescolaire (N.J. regional dir. 1996-98, 2005—), Unadilla Hist. Assn., Unadilla Women's Club (bd. dirs. 2006—). Avocations: hiking, swimming, international travel. Home: PO Box 313 Unadilla NY 13849-0313 Office: Pagano Cons Internat PO Box 313 Unadilla NY 13849 Personal E-mail: apagano29@yahoo.com.

PAGANO, JO ANNE, education educator; b. Rochester, N.Y., Dec. 30, 1946; d. John Richard and Marlyn Margaret (Mull) P.; m. William Arnold Gietz, Sept. 30, 1977 (div. May 1983); m. Bruce Peter Berlind, Jan. 17, 1985. BA, U. Rochester, 1973, MS, 1980, PhD, 1982. Assoc. prof. edn. Colgate U., Hamilton, N.Y., 1981—. Co-author: Preparing Teachers as Professionals, 1989; author: Exiles and Communities, 1990; mem. editl. rev. bd. Ednl. Theory, 1988-93; editor-in-chief JCT: Interdisciplinary Jour. Curriculum Studies, 1990—; contbr. articles to ednl. jours., chpts. to books. Grantee Ford Found., 1986. Mem. Am. Ednl. Rsch Assn., Philosophy of edn. Soc., Am. Ednl. Studies Assn. (exec. bd. dirs. 1994, exec. coun. 1993—), Profs. of Curriculum, Nat. Women's Studies Assn. Home: PO Box 237 Hamilton NY 13346-0237 Office: Colgate U Edn Dept 13 Oak Dr Hamilton NY 13346-1383 Office Phone: 315-824-7253. E-mail: jpagano@mail.colgate.edu.

PAGANO, MICHELINA OLIMPIA, art director, consultant, writer, scriptwriter; d. Domenico and Mary Pagano; m. Anthony Jude Parente. Grad. h.s., Floral Pk., N.Y. Dir. art Lintas Worldwide Advt., N.Y.C., 1986—88; dir. sr. art Wells, Rich, Greene, N.Y.C., 1988—93, N.W. Ayer & Ptnrs. Advt., N.Y.C., 1993—95; sr. v.p., group creative dir. D'Arcy Worldwide Advt., N.Y.C., 1996—2000; freelance creative dir., cons., 2000—. Instr. advt. Sch. Visual Arts, N.Y.C., 1989—90. Author: (novel) The Road To Jude, 2004, Grace of the Clouds, 2002, (children's book) The Magic Paint Box, 1990; co-author: (screenplay) The Blood Orange, 2006; writer and co-prodr. (short film) Two Shoes, dir., co-writer and co-prodr. Wishful Thinking, co-creator, dir., writer and co-prodr. Return of the Masterminds, dir., co-prodr. Mini Happy Returns, co-dir., co-writer, co-prodr. (music video) Suit for Jesus. Recipient Cannes Bronze Lion, Cannes Internat. Festival, 1988, Bronze medal, N.Y. Festivals Internat., 1991, Bronze Effie, Effie Awards, 1994, Golden Trailer award, 1999, Internat. Advt. award, London, 1991, award, Hollywood Spiritual Film and Book Festival, 2005. Mem.: Ind. Film Project (assoc.). E-mail: mickipagano@yahoo.com.

PAGE, AMY LYNN, special education educator; d. Darrel Ray and Linda Jean Page. BS in Tchg. Summa cum laude, Winona State U., Minn., 2000. Cert. learning disabilities tchr., crisis prevention intervention. Tchr. spl. edn. Kenyon (Minn.) Wanamingo Pub. Schs., 2001—. Dir. Kenyon Wanamingo Edn. Found., 2002—06; mid. sch. rep. Goodhue County Edn. Distinct Transition Team, Cannon Falls, Minn., 2003—06; adviser Kenyon Wanamingo Family, Career, and Comty. Leaders of Am., 2005—06. Mem.: NEA, Edn. Minn. Avocations: scrapbooks, camping, cross stitch, travel. Office: Kenyon Wanamingo Pub Sch 400 6th St Kenyon MN 55946

PAGE, ANNE EICHELBERGER, violinist; b. Chattanooga, Mar. 5, 1953; d. Edward Lee and Martha Nell (Douthitt) Eichelberger; m. Joseph Thomas Page, June 10, 1978; children: Andrew Joseph, Hannah Carol. MusB, Fla. State U., 1975; MusM, Yale U., 1977, M in Mus. Arts, 1978. Violinist Atlanta Chamber Players, 1978—, Atlanta Opera Orch., 1980—, Atlanta Virtuosi, 1984—, Lullwater String Quartet, Atlanta, 1984—; concertmaster Atlanta Pops Orch., 1984-88; violin teaching affiliate Emory U., Atlanta, 1978-79; music history faculty affiliate Mercer U., Atlanta, 1978-79. Performer Eastern Music Festival, Greensboro, N.C., 1976, 77, numerous recordings and TV programs, 1978—; performed with Atlanta New Music Ensemble, Carnegie Hall, N.Y.C., 1982; toured Spain, Italy and Mexico with Atlanta Virtuosi, 1988, 89; substitute violinist Atlanta Symphony Orch. Mem. Ch. of Christ. Address: 1136 Gunnison Ct Clarkston GA 30021-2833

PAGE, ANNE RUTH, gifted and talented educator, education specialist; b. Norfolk, Va., Apr. 13, 1949; d. Amos Purnell and Ruth Martin (Hill) Bailey; m. Peter Smith Page, Apr. 24, 1971; children: Edgar Bailey, Emmett McBrannon. BA, N.C. Wesleyan Coll., Rocky Mount; student, Fgn. Lang. League; postgrad., N.C. State U., Raleigh; student, Overseas Linguistic Studies, France, Spain, Eng., 1978, 85, 86. Cert. tchr., N.C. Tchr. Cary Sr. H.S., NC, 1971-72; tchr., head dept. Daniels Mid. Sch., Raleigh, NC, 1978-83; chmn. fgn. lang. dept. Martin Mid. Gifted and Talented, Raleigh, 1983—2006; ret., 2006. Leadership team Senate Bill 2 Core co-chair; dir. student group Overseas Studies, Am. Coun. for Internat. Studies, France, Spain, Eng., 1982, 84, 86, 88; bd. dirs. N.T.H., Inc., Washington; cert. mentor tchr. Wake County Pub. Schs., 1989; dir. student exchs. between Martin Mid. Sch. and Sevigné Inst. of Compiegne, France. Sunday sch. tchr. Fairmont United Meth. Ch., Raleigh, 1983-85. Mem. Alpha Delta Kappa. Democrat. Home: 349 Wilmot Dr Raleigh NC 27606-1232

PAGE, CAROLINE JANE, social worker; b. Decatur, Ala., Dec. 29, 1950; d. Charles David and Martha C. (Hancock) P. BS in Edn., Athens Coll., 1973; MSW, U. Tenn., 1975. Cert. social worker, Ala.; diplomate in clin. social work, 1990—; cert. pub. mgr.; qualified clin. social worker NASW. Dir. Athens (Ala.)-Limestone Retired Sr. Vol. Program, 1975-78; social worker III dept. pensions & security Limestone County, Athens, 1978-86, welfare supr. II dept. human resources, 1986-93; county dir. dept. human resources, 1993—. Bd. dirs. ARC, Athens; mem. adv. coun. Ala. Children's Trust Fund, Montgomery, 1988—; adv. bd. mem. Boys & Girls Clubs of Limestone County. Mem. Am. Pub. Welfare Assn., Optimist, Zeta Tau Alpha (pres. Athens alumnae chpt. 1999—). Home: 11997 Page Rd Tanner AL 35671-3805 Office: Limestone County Dept Human Resources PO Box 830 Athens AL 35612-0830 Office Phone: 256-216-6405.

PAGE, CHERYL MILLER, elementary school educator; BS in Social Sciences, Calif. Polytechnic State Univ., San Luis Obispo, Calif., 1975. Cert. health edn. specialist Nat. Commn. for Health Edn. Credentialing, 1993, Edn. Certification Program Calif. Polytechnic State Univ., San Luis Obispo, Calif., 1976. Elem. educator The Dalles Pub. Schs., The Dalles, Oreg., 1980—86, Salem-Keizer Pub. Schs., Salem, Oreg., 1986—95, middle sch. health educator, 1995—2002, health educator; prevention curriculum resource specialist Salem-Keizer Pub. Schs. Mid Valley Partnership. Named Oreg. Outstanding Elementary Health Educator, 1991, Oreg. Outstanding Secondary Health Educator of Yr., 1996, Vol. of Yr., Am. Cancer Soc., 1996; recipient Tambrands award, Am. Assn. Health Edn., 1996, Health and Safety Educator of Year, NW Divsn. AAHPERD, 1996. Mem.: Oreg. Alliance Health, Phys. Edn., Recreation and Dance (treas. 1992—96, pres. 2001—02), Oreg. Assn. for the Advancement of Health Edn. (sec./treas. 1990—92), Nat. Bd. for Profl. Tchg. Stds. (bd. mem.). Avocations: running, reading. Office: Salem-Keizer Sch Dist PO Box 12024 Salem OR 97309 Office Phone: 503-399-3101. E-mail: page_cheryl@salkerz.k12.or.us.

PAGE, JANET LOUISE, accountant; b. Monterey Park, Calif., Feb. 4, 1944; d. John Lester and Maxine (Clift) Page. BS, Brigham Young U., 1966. CPA Calif. Auditor Peat, Marwick, Mitchell & Co., LA, 1966—71; from contr. to v.p., contr. H.F. Ahmanson & Co., LA, 1971—87, contr., 1987—; contr., sr. v.p. Home Savs. Am., Irwindale, Calif., 1987—. Mem.: AICPA, Calif. Soc. CPAs, Fin. Execs. Inst., Am. Mgmt. Assn. Republican. Mormon.

PAGE, LINDA KAY, bank executive; b. Wadsworth, Ohio, Oct. 4, 1943; d. Frederick Meredith and Martha Irene (Vance) P. Student, Ohio U., 1976-77; grad. banking program, U. Wis., 1982-84; BA, Capital U. Asst. v.p., gen. mgr. Bancohio Corp., Columbus, 1975-78, v.p., dist. mgr., 1979-80, v.p., mgr. employee rels., 1980-81, v.p., divsn. mgr., 1982-83; commr. of banks State of Ohio, Columbus, 1983-87, dir. Dept. Commerce, 1988-90; pres., CEO Star Bank Ctrl. Ohio, Columbus, 1990—92; state dir. Rural Devel/USDA, 1993-2000; pub. svc. dir. City of Columbus, 2000—04; mgr. Nationwide Fed. Credit Union, 2004—. Bd. dirs. Clark County Mental Health Bd., Springfield, Ohio, 1982-83, Springfield Met. Housing, 1982-83, Pvt. Industry Coun. Franklin County, 1990-2000—, Ohio Higher Edn. Facilities Commn., 1990-93, Ohio Devel. Corp., 1995—; bd. advisers Orgn. Indsl. Standards, Springfield, 1982-83; trustee League Against Child Abuse, 1986-90; treas. Ohio Housing Fin. Agy., 1980-90; vice chair Fed. Res. Bd. Consumer Adv. Coun., 1989-91; trustee, treas. Columbus State C.C. Found., 1990-00, pres., 1997-99; bd. dirs. Columbus Urban League, 1992-98; mem. CompDrug Bd., 1998-00; mem. Mid Ohio Regional Planning Commn., 2000-04; devel. chair Ohio Coun. Econ. Edn., 2003-. Recipient Leadership Columbus award Sta. WTVN and Columbus Leadership Program, 1975, 82, Outstanding Svc. award Clark County Mental Health Bd., 1983, Giles Mitchell Housing award, 1996. Mem.: LWV (treas. edn. fund 1992—2000), Ohio Coun. Econ. Edn. (devel. chair 2004—), Womens Fund Ctrl. Ohio (grant reader 2003—05), Risk Mgmt. Assn., Women in Transp. (bd. trustees Ohio chpt. 2000, bd. dirs. 2002), Internat. Womens Forum, Am. Pub. Works Assn. (treas. Ohio chpt. 2000—04, govt. affairs com. 2002—03, treas. 2002—04), Ohio Mortgage Bankers Assn. (legis. commn. 1998), Ohio Devel. Assn., Ohio Bankers Assn. (bd. dirs. 1982—83, 1991—92), Conf. State Bank Suprs. (dist. chmn. 1984—85, sec.-treas. 1985—90, bd. dirs.), Women Execs. in State Govt., Am. Bankers Assn. (govt. rels. coun. 1990—92, cert.), Nat. Assn. Bank Women (pres. 1980—81), Rotary. Democrat. Avocations: reading, cultural arts, travel. Home: 1477 Sedgefield Dr New Albany OH 43054-9431 Personal E-mail: lpage@insight.rr.com.

PAGE, PATRICIA (PATTY) NEWTON, real estate broker, real estate company executive; b. Nashville, Tenn., May 16, 1963; d. James Kelton and Alice (Clement) Cuff. Grad., Realtor Inst., 1999. Cert. affiliate broker North Ctrl. Inst., 1993, accredited credit buyer rep. Nat. Assn. Realtors, 2001, lic. real estate broker, cert. residential specialist. Sr. customer svc. rep. Comdata Corp., Brentwood, Tenn., 1981—92; realtor Century 21 ABC, Clarksville, Tenn., 1993—94, Lakeland Properties, Dover, Tenn., 1994—96; designated realtor Cherry Properties, Dover, Tenn., 1996—2003; owner, broker Patty Page Properties, LLC, 2004—. Mem.: Nat. Assn. Realtors (coun. residential specialist 2002). Methodist. Avocations: Continued Education, travel. Office Phone: 931-232-5082. Personal E-mail: PattyPage2000@aol.com.

PAGE, SALLY JACQUELYN, university official, management educator; b. Saginaw, Mich., 1943; d. William Henry and Doris Effie (Knippel) P. BA, U. Iowa, 1965; MBA, So. Ill. U., 1973. Copy editor C.V. Mosby Co., St. Louis, 1965-69; editl. cons. Editl. Assocs., Edwardsville, Ill., 1969-70; rsch. administr. So. Ill. U., 1970-74, asst. to pres., affirmative action officer, 1974-77; officer of instn. U. N.D., Grand Forks, 1977—, lectr. mgmt., 1978—. Polit. comentator Sta. KFJM, Nat. Public Radio affiliate, 1981-90; mem. mayor's com. Employment of People With Disabilities, 1980-97. Contbr. articles to profl. jours. Chmn. N.D. Equal Opportunity Affirmative Action Officers, 1987-2003; chmn. NDUS Diversity Coun.; pres. Pine to Prairie coun. Girl Scouts U.S., 1980-85; mem. employment com. Ill. Commn. on Status of Women, 1976-77; mem. Bicentennial Com., Edwardsville, 1976, Bikeway Task Force, Edwardsville, 1975-77, Greater Grand Forks (N.D.) Bus. Leadership Network; bd. dirs. Grand Forks Homes, 1985—2003, pres., 1996-2001; mem. Civil Svc. Rev. Task Force, Grand Forks, 1982, civil svc. commr., 1983-98, chmn., 1984, 86, 88, 92, 96; ruling elder 1st Presbyn.; mem. Grand Forks Mayor's Adv. Cabinet, 1998-2000. Mem. AAUW (dir. Ill. 1975-77), PEO, Coll. and Univ. Pers. Assn. (rsch. and publs. bd. 1982-84), Soc. Human Resource Mgmt., Am. Assn. Affirmative Action, ADA Coords. Democrat. Presbyterian. Home: 3121 Cherry St Grand Forks ND 58201-7461 Office: U ND Grand Forks ND 58202 Business E-Mail: Sally-Page@mail.und.nodak.edu.

PAGE, STEPHANIE, lawyer; b. 1948; BA, Vassar Coll.; JD, Northeastern U. Bar: Mass. 1978. Sr. trial counsel Com. Pub. Counsel Svc.-Commonwealth Mass., Boston, 1978—. Named one of top Boston lawyers, Boston Mag., 2004. Mem.: Am. Coll. Trial Lawyers.

PAGELS, CARRIE FANCETT, psychologist; b. Newberry, Mich., Jan. 5, 1958; d. William Henry and Ruby Evelyn (Skidmore) F.; m. Jeffrey D. Pagels; children: Cassandra Rose, Clark Jeffrey. BA in Psychology, Lake Superior State Coll., 1978; MA in Sch. Psychology, U. S.C., 1981, PhD in Sch. Psychology, 1984. Lic. psychologist; cert. sch. psychologist. Rsch. asst. U. S.C., Columbia, 1979-80, 81-83, instr., 1983, Lake Superior State Coll., Sault Ste. Marie, Mich., summer 1981; mental health cons. Head Start Program, Columbia, 1983-86, Charleston, S.C., 1987-95; child psychotherapist Counseling and Readjustment Svcs., Columbia, 1985-86; psychologist Richland Meml. Children's Hosp., Columbia, 1983-86; clin. asst. prof. U. S.C. Sch. Medicine, Columbia, 1984-87; sch. psychologist Berkeley County Schs., 1986-87; pvt. sch. psychologist North Charleston, 1987-94; sch. psychologist Erie 1 Boces Presch., Depew, N.Y., 1995-96; asst. prof. Valdosta (Ga.) State U., 1996-98; sch. psychologist Williamsburg James City County Schs., Va., 1998—2001; clin. psychologist Christian Psychotherapy Svcs., Newport News, Va., 1999-2001, Beacon Counseling and Cons., Williamsburg, 2001—. Learning disability diagnostician spl. svcs. program, 1996-98; pvt. practice Midtown Psychol. Assocs., Valdosta, 1996-98; cons. Richland Meml. Hosp., Columbia, 1983, Divorce Mediation Project, Columbia, 1982, Life Satisfaction Grant, Columbia, 1979-81. Book reviewer Contemporary Psychology, 1998; contbr. chpt. to book. Campaign aide Dem. Party, U.S. Senate race, Sault Ste. Marie, Mich., 1978. Stephenson scholar, 1978, NIMH fellow, 1980-81. Mem.: Children and Adults with Attention Deficit Disorder. Baptist. Avocations: writing, computers, crafts, walking. Home: 200 Grafton District Rd Yorktown VA 23692-4045 Office Phone: 757-564-3100. Personal E-mail: cfpagels@aol.com.

PAGELS, ELAINE HIESEY, theology studies educator, writer; b. Palo Alto, Calif. d. William McKinley and Louise Sophia (van Druten) Hiesey; m. Heinz R. Pagels, June 7, 1969 (dec. July 1988); children: Sarah Marie, David van Druten. BA, Stanford U., 1964, MA, 1965; PhD, Harvard U., 1970. Asst. prof. history religion Barnard Coll., Columbia, 1970—74, from assoc. prof. to prof., chair dept. religion, 1974—82; Harrington Spear Paine prof. religion Princeton U., 1982—. Author: The Johannine Gospel in Gnostic Exegesis, 1973, The Gnostic Paul, 1975, The Gnostic Gospels, 1979 (Nat. Book award and Nat. Book Critics Cir. award), Adam, Eve and The Serpent, 1988, Beyond Belief: The Secret Gospel of Thomas, 2003. Grantee, NEH, 1973; Mellon fellow, Aspen Inst. Humanistic Studies, 1974, Hazen fellow, 1975, Rockefeller fellow, 1978—79, Guggenheim fellow, 1979—80, MacArthur prize fellow, 1981—87. Mem.: Am. Acad. Religion., Soc. Bibl. Lit., Bibl. Theologians Club. Episcopalian.

PAGLIA, CAMILLE, writer, humanities educator; b. Endicott, N.Y., 1947; d. Pasquale John and Lydia (Colapietro) P. BA in English summa cum laude with highest honors, SUNY, Binghamton, 1968; MPhil, Yale U., 1971, PhD in English, 1974. Mem. faculty Bennington (Vt.) Coll., 1972-80; vis. lectr. Wesleyan U., 1980, Yale U., New Haven, 1980-84; asst. prof. humanities Phila. Coll. Performing Arts U. Arts, 1984—86, assoc. prof. humanities, 1987—91, prof. humanities, 1991—2000; Univ. prof. humanities and media studies U. Arts, Phila., 2000—. Spkr. in field. Author: Sexual Personae: Art and Decadence from Nefertiti to Emily Dickinson, 1990, Sex, Art, and American Culture, 1992, Vamps and Tramps: New Essays, 1994, Alfred Hitchcock's "The Birds", 1998, Break, Blow, Burn: Camille Paglia Reads Forty-Three of the World's Best Poems, 2005; columnist: Salon.com, 1995—2001; contbg. editor: Interview Magazine, 2001—. Mailing: Univ of the Arts 320 S Broad St Philadelphia PA 19102-4994 Office Phone: 215-717-6265.

PAGON, ROBERTA ANDERSON, pediatrician, educator; b. Boston, Oct. 4, 1945; d. Donald Grigg and Erna Louise (Goettsch) Anderson; m. Garrett Dunn Pagon Jr., July 1, 1967; children: Katharine Blye, Garrett Dunn III, Alyssa Grigg, Alexander Goettsch. BA, Stanford U., 1967; MD, Harvard U., 1972. Diplomate Am. Bd. Pediat., Am. Bd. Med. Genetics. Pediatric intern U. Wash. Affiliated Hosp., Seattle, 1972-73, resident in pediat., 1973-75; fellow in med. genetics U. Wash. Sch. Medicine, Seattle, 1976-79, asst. prof. pediat., 1979-84, assoc. prof., 1984-92, prof., 1992—. Prin. investigator, editor in chief GeneTests (www.genetests.org), Seattle, 1992—; pres. Am. Bd. Med. Genetics, 2002, 03; bd. sci. counselors Nat. Human Genome Rsch. Inst., NIH, 2000—04. Sponsor N.W. region U.S. Pony Club, 1985-94. Mem. Am. Soc. Human Genetics (bd. dirs. 2005—, Excellence award 2006), Am. Coll. Med. Genetics, Western Soc. Pediat. Rsch., Phi Beta Kappa. Avocations: hiking, backpacking, horseback riding. Office: Gene Tests 9725 Third Ave NE Ste 602 Seattle WA 98115 Office Phone: 206-221-4674.

PAGOTTO, SARAH LOUISE, retired library and information scientist; b. Lehighton, Pa., May 11, 1948; d. Peter and Elizabeth Alvesta (Smith) P. BS in Libr. Sci., Kutztown State Coll., 1970, MS, 1977. Clk. Northampton (Pa.) Pub. Libr., 1968-69, head librarian, 1969-70; elem. librarian Northampton Area Sch. Dist., 1970—2005, ret., 2005. Mem. ALA, NEA, Pa. State Educators Assn. Avocations: reading, travel, antiques, music, pennsylvania dutch language. Home: 3622 Mountain View Dr Danielsville PA 18038-9580

PAHL, LAURA E., finance educator; b. Missoula, Mont., Apr. 23, 1942; d. Adolph and Emily Pahl. BA Edn., U. Mont., Missoula, 1968; MA Bus. Edn., U. Mont., 1978, cert. adminstrn. and curriculum, 1980. Tchr. bus. edn. Troy H.S., Mont., 1969, Libby H.S., Mont., 1969—70, Missoula County Pub. Schs., 1970—. Mem. numerous coms. Missoula County Pub. Schs., 1970—. Recipient Disting. Svc. award, Mont. Coun. Adminstrs. Spl. Edn., 1997. Mem.: Mont. Edn. Assn., Am. Fedn. Tchrs. Home: 114 Black Pine Trl Missoula MT 59803

PAIGE, DOROTHY BILLIARD, retired secondary school educator, educational consultant; d. Webb Billiard and Doretha Billiard-Johnson; 1 child, Rochelle Denise Paige-Jones. AA in polit. sci., LA Harbor Jr. Coll., Wilmington, Calif., 1978; BA in polit. sci., Calif. State U. Dominguez Hills, Carson, 1979, MA in pub. adminstrn., 1981. Tchr. Calif. Commn. on Tchg., 1982, cert. Bilingual Edn. Calif. Commn. on Tchg., 2002. History tchr. Compton Unified Sch. Dist., Calif., 1979—2002, resource tchr., program coord., 2002—05; edn. cons. Paige-Schwartz & Assoc., Inc., Carson, Calif., 2005. Fin. sec., scholarship chair Nat. Assn. U. Women, Compton, 2001; christian edn. dir., fin. dir. Mt. Pilgrim Missionary Bapt. Ch., Compton, 1987—95; del. NEA, Orlando, 1999. Mem.: Compton Edn. Assn. (CTA pres. 1982—, segment dir. mid. sch. 1997—99), Boys & Girls Club Am. (sponsor 2001). Democrat. Baptist. Avocations: reading, surfing the net, travel. Home: 21621 Villa Pacifica Cir Carson CA 90745 Office: Paige-Schwartz & Assoc Inc 21621 Villa Pacifica Cir Carson CA 90745 Office Phone: 310-518-7575. Home Fax: 310-427-0279; Office Fax: 310-427-0279. Personal E-mail: dotpaige47@aol.com.

PAIGE, VIVIAN JO-ANN, accountant; b. Memphis, May 7, 1960; d. Charles Thomas and Mary Elizabeth (Manning) P. BS, Old Dominion U., 1981, MBA, 1994. CPA, Va. With IRS, Norfolk, Va., 1980-85; pres. Individual Returns Svcs. Inc., Norfolk, 1991-95; prin. Vivian J. Paige, CPA, P.C., 1986—; adj. instr. acctg. Old Dominion U., 2000—, mem. adv. coun., dept. acctg., 2000—. Bd. dirs. St. Columba Ecumenical Ministries, Inc., 1989-93, v.p. bd. dirs., 1990-91, pres. bd. dirs., 1992-93, Neighborhood Network steering com., 1996-2000, sec. Real Estate Bd. of Equalization, 1999-2001, bd. dirs. 2001-04, pres., 2002-05; co-founder Norfolk United Facing Race, bd. dirs., 2001-04; mem. NAACP, Urban League. With USAR, 1979-81. Mem. AICPA, NAFE, AAUW, NAACP, Urban League, Va. Soc. CPAs. Avocations: music, singing, computers. Business E-Mail: vivian@vjpcpa.com.

PAIN, BETSY M., lawyer; b. Albertville, Ala., Aug. 29, 1950; d. Charles Riley and Jean Faye (Rains) Stone; m. William F. Pain, Nov. 18, 1977 (div. July 30, 2003); children: Taylor Holland, Emily Anne Pain. AA, Northeastern Okla. A&M, Miami, 1970; BA, U. Okla., 1974, JD, 1976. Bar: Okla. 1977; U.S. Dist. Ct. (we. dist.) 1979. Staff atty. Okla. Dept. Corrections, Oklahoma City, 1978-79; gen. counsel Okla. Pardon and Parole Bd., Oklahoma City, 1979-84, exec. dir., 1983—88; corp. counsel Roberts, Schornick & Assocs., Inc., Norman, Okla., 1990-2000, Atkins Benham, Inc., 2002; chief legal officer The Benham Cos., LLC, Oklahoma City, 2002—. Editor: (newsletter) RSA Environ. Report, 1991—. With extended family program Juvenile Svcs., Inc. Cleveland County, Okla., 1983-91. Mem. NAFE, Okla. Bar Assn., Assn.

Corp. Counsel, Phi Alpha Delta. Democrat. Methodist. Avocations: reading, needlecrafts, church activities. Office: The Benham Cos LLC 9400 N Broadway Oklahoma City OK 73114 Office Phone: 405-478-5353. E-mail: betsy.pain@benham.com.

PAINE, LYNN, academic administrator; m. Tom Paine; 3 children. Grad Summa Cum Laude, Smith Coll.; PhD in moral philosophy, Oxford U.; law degree, Harvard Law Sch. Lawyer Hill & Barlow, Boston; asst. prof. Georgetown U. Bus. Sch; prof. U. Va., Darden Sch., Nat. Cheng Chi U., Taiwan; John G. McLean prof. Harvard Bus. Sch., course head, MBA ethics module Leadership, Values, and Decision Making, 1996—2002, co-leader, MBA course: Leadership and Corporate Accountability, 2004—. Permanent mem. Luce Scholar Selection Panel, 1987—. Author: Leadership, Ethics, and Organizational Integrity, 1997, Value Shift: Why Companies Must Merge Social and Financial Imperatives to Achieve Superior Performance, 2002 (Best Bus. Books, 2002, Library Journal, 2002). Mem. adv. bd. Leadership Forum Internat.; mem. Conference Bd. Blue-Ribbon Commn. on Public Trust and Private Enterprise. Named Luce Scholar, 1976—77. Mem.: Mass. Bar Assn, Phi Beta Kappa. Office: Harvard Bus Sch Soldiers Field Boston MA 02163

PAINTER, DIANA JEAN, urban planner, artist, historian; b. Seattle, Dec. 29, 1953; d. Robert Cook and Nancy Marie (Chivers) P.; m. John Hazen McKean, Aug. 10, 1973 (div. Feb. 1975). BA, Western Wash. U., 1977; MUP, U. Wash., 1984; postgrad., U. Pa., 1987; PhD, U. Sheffield, England, 1990. Cert. planner. Designer Cope Linder Assn., Phila., 1987-88, Dagit-Saylor Architects, Phila., 1988; urban designer WRT, Phila., 1989; designer Edwin Schlossberg Inc., N.Y.C., 1989-90; urban designer The SWA Group, Laguna Beach, Calif., 1990-91; assoc. planner City of Tukwila, Wash., 1993-97; project mgr. Sound Transit, Seattle, 1997—2000. Cons. Painter Preservation and Planning, Petaluma, Calif., 2002—; instr. U. Wash., Seattle, 1986, 2000; printmaking instr. Sev Shoon Arts Ctr.; instr. Sonoma State U., 2004, 06; presenter in field. Exhibited prints throughout West Coast; contbr. articles to profl. jours. Active Allied Arts of Seattle Downtown Com., 1984-85; bd. dirs. Greystone Found., Pullman, Wash., 1992-93; chmn. landmark commn. Sonoma County, 2006. Fellow Northwest Inst. Architecture & Urban Studies in Italy; mem. Am. Inst. Cert. Planners, Am. Assn. Planning (head mentoring program 1995—, vice-chmn. urban design divsn.), Am. Inst. Architects L.A. (urban design com. 1990-91). Avocations: painting, rowing.

PAINTER, LORENE HUFFMAN, retired education educator, psychologist; b. Hickory, NC, Aug. 16, 1932; d. Horace Clifton and Jennie Ozelle (Lineberger) Huffman; m. Hanley Hayes Painter, June 11, 1950; children: Charles Nathan, Janet Fern. AB, Lenoir-Rhyne Coll., Hickory, 1953; MA, Appalachian State U., Boone, N.C., 1959; EdD, U. N.C., Greensboro, 1980. Tchr. English and French, Taylorsville H.S., NC, 1953-54; tchr. English and social studies College Park Jr. H.S., Hickory, 1954-59; instr. edn. Lenoir-Rhyne Coll., 1959-62, asst. prof., 1962-69, assoc. prof., 1969-80, prof., 1980—2000, chmn. dept., 1989-94, dir. Curriculum Lab., 1960—2000; ret., 2003. Evaluator sch. programs So. Assn., Piedmont, N.C., 1970—; edn. cons. Catawaba,Burke, Caldwell, Alexander and Iredell counties, N.C., 1970—; mem. career devel. team Catawba County Schs., 1986—. Author: Student Teaching Guidebook, 1968—, Elective English in Secondary Schools, 1980. Scholar Luth. Ch. in Am., 1976, 78. Mem. AAUP, Nat. Coun. for Accrediation Tchr. Edn., N.C. Assn. Tchr. Educators, Delta Kappa Gamma (officer 1963—, state scholar 1977-78), Mu Sigma Epsilon. Advent Christian. Avocations: reading, travel, needlecrafts, gardening, family recreation. Home: 1137 11th Street Cir NW Hickory NC 28601-2254

PAINTER, NELL IRVIN, historian, educator, writer; b. Houston, Aug. 2, 1942; BA, U. Calif., Berkeley, 1964; student, U. Bordeaux, France, 1962-63, U. Ghana, 1965-66; MA, UCLA, 1967; PhD, Harvard U., 1974. Teaching fellow Harvard U., Cambridge, Mass., 1969-70, 72-74; asst. prof. history U. Pa., Phila., 1974-77, assoc. prof., 1977-80; prof. history U. N.C., Chapel Hill, 1980-88, Princeton (N.J.) U., 1988-91, acting dir. Afro-Am. Studies Program, 1990-91, Edwards Prof. Am. History, 1991—. Russell Sage vis. prof. history Hunter Coll., CUNY, N.Y.C., 1985-86. Author: Exodusters: Black Migration to Kansas After Reconstruction, 1976, The Narrative of Hosea Hudson: His Life as a Negro Communist in the South, 1979, Standing at Armageddon: The United States 1877-1919, 1987, Sojourner Truth: A Life, A Symbol, 1996, Southern History Across the Color Line, 2002, Creating Black Americans, 2005; editor: Gender and Am. Culture Series; mem. editl. bd. Jour. Women's History, Ency. Americana; contbr. articles to profl. jours. Ford Found. fellow, 1971-72, Am. Coun. Learned Soc. fellow, 1976-77, Charles Warren Ctr. Studies in Am. History fellow, 1976-77, Radcliffe/Bunting Inst. fellow, 1976-77, Nat. Humanities Ctr. fellow, 1978-79, Guggenheim fellow, 1982-83, Ctr. Advanced Study in Behavioral Scis. fellow, 1988-89, Kate B. and Hall J. Peterson fellow Am. Antiquarian Soc., 1991, NEH fellow, 1992-93; recipient Ccoretta Scott King award AAUW, 1969-70, Grad. Soc. medal Radcliffe Coll. Alumnae, 1984, Candace award Nat. Coalition One Hundred Black Women, 1986; named U. Calif. at Berkeley Alumnae of Yr., 1989. Mem. Am. Coun. Learned Soc., Am. Antiquarian Soc., Am. Hist. Assn. (mem. program com. 1976-78, J. Franklin Jameson fellowship com. 1978-79, Beveridge and Dunning prizes com. 1985-87, mem. coun. 1991-93, Roelker Mentorship award 2001), Am. Studies Assn. (mem. internat. com. 1983-88, mem. nat. coun. 1989-92, mem. adv. coun. 1991-92), Assn. Study Afro-Am. Life and History (mem. program com. 1976, Carter G. Woodson award 2004), Assn. Black Women Historians (mem. rsch. com. 1980—, nat. dir. 1982-84, chair Brown pub. prize com. 1983-86, 88-91), Berkshire Conf. Women Historians (mem. program com. 1976), Inst. So. Studies (mem. exec. com. 1987-88), Orgn. Am. Historians (mem. com. status women 1975-77, mem. program com. 1977-79, 83-85, Frederick Jackson Turner award com. 1983, mem. exec. bd. 1984-87, chair ad hoc com. on minority historians 1985-87, chair Avery O. Craven award 1994-95), Nat. Book Found. (chair non-fiction jury, Nat. Book awards 1994), Social Sci. Rsch. Coun. (mem. com. social sci. pers. 1977-78), So. Hist. Assn. (chair Syndor prize com. 1991-92), So. Regional Coun. (mem. Lillian Smith Book prize com. 1986, mem. exec. com. 1987), Soc. Am. Historians (chair Parkman prize com. 1993—). Office: Princeton U History Dept Princeton NJ 08544-0001*

PAINTER, PAMELA, writer, educator; b. Pitts., Aug. 30, 1941; d. Millard and Irene (Lusebrink) P.; children: Wayne, Katherine, Derek. BA, Pa. State U., 1963; MA, U. Ill., 1979. Tchr. Harvard Extension, Cambridge, Mass., 1980—2001, prof., 2001—. Writer-in-residence Emerson Coll., Boston, 1989—; faculty mem. Vt. Coll., Montpelier, 1987—; bd. dirs. CCLM Coord. Coun. Lit. Mags., N.Y.C., 1978-82, Fine Arts Work Ctr., Provincetown, Mass., 1989-1996, Castle Hill Truro, Mass., 2001—, Grub St., Boston, 2002—. Author: Getting To Know the Weather, 1985; co-author: What If?, 1990, textbook edit., 1994, 2004, Long and Short of It, 1997; contbr. short stories to mags. Fellow Mass. Arts Coun., 1985, NEA, 1987. Home: 65 Marlborough St Boston MA 02116-2018

PAIR, MARCI HOLT, secondary school educator; d. Layton and Melba (Ward) Holt; m. Morris A. Pair, Dec. 28, 1974; children: Mitsi, Matthew, Melanie. BS in Edn., U. Tex., Austin; MEd, Hardin Simmons Coll., Abilene, Tex. Tchr. Abilene Sch. Dist., Tex., 1991—. Reading, writing coach Cooper HS, Abilene, 1996—. UIL coord., 2002—. Mem.: TCTA. Home: 828 Bluebonnet Clyde TX 79510

PAJAK, LOUISE BEARS, music educator, musician; b. Summit, NJ, July 31, 1956; d. Isaac Bruce and Sally Lawson Bears; m. James Alan Pajak, Dec. 28, 1979; 1 child, Johanna Nancy. B in Music magna cum laude, Hartt Sch., 1978; MA, U. NH, 1990. Music tchr. Timberlane Regional Sch. Dist., Plaistow, NH, 1978—. Freelance cellist Mostly Baroque, Portsmouth, NH, 1990—, Granite State Symphony, Concord, 1994—. Chair all state orch. NH Music Educators, 1995—; libr. trustee Sandown Pub. Libr., NH, 2000—. Achievements include development of Timberlane school district's string program in 1983; instituted annual high school musical with other production staff members. Home: 17 Hawkwood Rd Sandown NH 03873 Office Phone: 603-382-6541 ext. 285.

PAJUNEN, GRAZYNA ANNA, electrical engineer, educator; b. Warsaw, Dec. 15, 1951; d. Romuald and Danuta (Trzaskowska) Pyffel; m. Veikko J. Pajunen (div. 1990); children: Tony, Thomas, Sebastian. MSc, Warsaw Tech. U., 1975; PhD in Elec. Engring., Helsinki (Finland) U., 1984. Grad. engr. Oy Stromberg Ab, Helsinki, 1974, design engr., 1975-79; teaching/rsch. asst. Helsinki U. Tech., 1979-85; vis. asst. prof. dept. elec. and computer engring. Fla. Atlantic U., 1985-86, asst. prof. elec. and computer engring., 1986-90, assoc. prof. elec. engring., 1990—; vis. asst. prof. dept elec. engring. UCLA, 1988-89. Cons. Motorola; lectr. in field. Author: Adaptive Systems - Identification and Control, 1986; contbr. articles to profl. jours.; holder 14 patents in field. Grantee Found. Tech. in Finland, Ahlstrom Found., 1982, Wihuri Found., 1982, Foun.d Tech. in Finland, 1983, Acad. Finland, 1984, EIES Seed grantee, 1986, Finnish Ministry Edn., 1985, NSF, 1988-89, 93-94, State of Fla. High Tech. and Industry Coun., 1989. Mem. IEEE, Control Sys. Soci., N.Y. Acad. Sci., AAUW, SIAM, Control and Sys. Theory Group. Roman Catholic. Avocations: jazz, ballet, piano, jogging, skiing. Office: Fla Atlantic U Dept Elec Engring Boca Raton FL 33431 Office Phone: 561-297-3496. Personal E-mail: graz@grazyna.us. E-mail: pajuneng@fau.edu.

PAK, SE RI, professional golfer; b. Daejeon, Korea, Sept. 28, 1977; Professional golfer LPGA Tour, 1997—. Mem. KLPGA, 1996, 97. Recipient Rolex Rookie of Yr. award, South Korea Order of Merit 1998, Golf Writers Assn. of America Player of the Year, 1998, Vare Trophy 2003. Winner of 23 LPGA events including four Grand Slam titles. Won the LPGA championship 1998, 2002, 2006; won the U.S. Open 1998; won the du Maurier Classic 2001; first woman in 58 years to make cut in men's golf tournament, SBS Super Tournament on Korean tour (finished 10th overall); qualified for LPGA Hall of Fame, 2004. Address: LPGA 100 International Golf Dr Daytona Beach FL 32124-1082 Office Phone: 386-274-6200. Office Fax: 386-274-1099.

PAKENHAM, ROSALIE MULLER WRIGHT, magazine and newspaper editor; b. Newark, June 20, 1942; d. Charles and Angela (Fortunata) Muller; m. Lynn Wright, Jan. 13, 1962; children: James Anthony Meador, Geoffrey Shepard; m. E. Michael Pakenham, Sept. 29, 2001. BA in English, Temple U., 1965. Mng. editor Suburban Life mag., Orange, NJ, 1960-62; assoc. editor Phila. mag., 1962-64, mng. editor, 1969-73; founding editor Womensports mag., San Mateo, Calif., 1973-75; editor scene sect. San Francisco Examiner, 1975-77; exec. editor New West mag., San Francisco and Beverly Hills, Calif., 1977-81; features and Sunday editor San Francisco Chronicle, 1981-87, asst. mng. editor features, 1987-96; v.p. and editor-in-chief Sunset Mag, Menlo Park, Calif., 1996—2001. Editl. cons., 2002—; tchr. mag. writing U. Calif., Berkeley, 1975—76; participant pub. procs. course Stanford U., 1977—79; chmn. mag. judges at conf. Coun. Advancement and Support of Edn., 1980, judge, 84, Nat. Mag. Awards, 1998, 99, 2005. Contbr. numerous mag. articles, critiques, revs., Compton's Ency. Mem.: Internat. Assn. Culinary Profls., Am. Soc. Mag. Editors (nat. mag. awards judge, 1998, 99, 2005), Am. Newspaper Pubs. Assn. (Chronicle minority recruiter 1987—94, pub. task force on minorities in newspaper bus. 1988—89), Am. Assn. Sunday and Feature Editors (treas. 1984, sec. 1985, 1st v.p. 1986, pres. 1987, Hall of Fame 1999), Washington D.C. Women's Forum, Women's Forum West (bd. dirs. 1993—, sec. 1994), Internat. Women's Forum. Office Phone: 717-292-6969. Personal E-mail: RosalieMPakenham@aol.com.

PAKTER, JEAN, maternal and child health consultant; b. N.Y.C., Jan. 1, 1911; d. David and Lillian (Kunitz) P.; m. Arnold L. Bachman, Sept. 17, 1939 (dec. Dec. 1992); children: Ellen Bachman Mendelson, Donald M. Bachman. BS, NYU, 1931, MD, 1934; MPH, Columbia U., 1955. Diplomate Am. Bd. Pediat. Intern Mt. Sinai Hosp., N.Y.C., 1934-36, resident in pediat., 1937-39; pvt. practice, N.Y.C., 1939-43; dir. Bur. Dept. Health, Maternity, Newborn and Family Planning, N.Y.C., 1950-82; cons., lectr. maternity, child health Columbia U. Sch. Pub. Health, N.Y.C., 1984—, dep. dir. maternal and child health program, 1984-94, lectr. maternity, child health, 1970—. Contbr. numerous articles to profl. med. jours. Advisor March of Dimes, N.Y.C., 1975—. Recipient Fund for City of N.Y. Pub. Svc. award, 1974, Jacobi medal Mt. Sinai Hosp., 1975, N.Y. State Med. Soc. award, 2006. Fellow APHA (Martha May Eliot award 1990), Am. Acad. Pediatrics, N.Y. Acad. Medicine (trustee 1979-83), N.Y. Obstet. Soc. (assoc.); mem. Pub. Health Assn. N.Y.C. (bd. dirs. 1992-96, The Haven Emerson award 2006), Women's City Club, Alpha Omega Alpha. Avocations: concerts, opera, theater, reading. Home: 1175 Park Ave New York NY 10128-1211

PAKULA, ANITA SUSAN, dermatologist; b. LA, Nov. 20, 1961; BA, Pomona Coll., 1983; BS, Calif. Luth. Coll., 1985; MD, U. Calif., Irvine, 1988. Diplomat Am. Bd. Dermatology, NAt. Bd. Med. Examiners. Intern Evanston (Ill.) Hosp., 1988-89; resident Northwestern U. Med. Sch., Chgo., 1989-92; asst. clin. prof. dermatology UCLA MEd. Ctr., 1993—. Presenter in field. Contbr. articles to profl. jours. Fellow Am. Acad. Dermatology; mem. Soc. Pediatric Dermatology. Office: 267 W Hillcrest Dr Thousand Oaks CA 91360-4923

PALACIO, JUNE ROSE PAYNE, nutritional science educator; b. Hove, Sussex, Eng., June 14, 1940; came to U.S., 1949; d. Alfred and Doris Winifred (Payne) P.; m. Moki Moses Palacio, Nov. 30, 1968 (wid. June 1999); m. Cliff Duboff, Dec. 22, 2002. AA, Orange Coast Coll., Costa Mesa, Calif., 1960; BS, U. Calif., Berkeley, 1963; PhD, Kans. State U., 1984. Registered dietitian. Asst. dir. food svc. and res. halls Mills Coll., Oakland, Calif., 1964-66; staff dietitian Servomation Bay Cities, Oakland, 1966-67; commissary mgr. Host Internat., Inc., Honolulu, 1967-73; dir. dietetics Straub Clinic and Hosp., Honolulu, 1973-80; instr. Kans. State U., Manhattan, 1980-84; prof. and program dir. Calif. State U., L.A., 1984-85; prof., asst. dean Pepperdine U., Malibu, Calif., 1985—. Instr. Kapiolani C.C., Honolulu, 1973-79, U. Hawaii, Honolulu, 1975-80, Ctr. for Dietetic Edn., Woodland Hills, Calif., 1986—; cons. Clevenger Nutritional Svcs., Calabasas, Calif., 1985—, Calif. Mus. Sci. and Industry, L.A., 1989—, Calif. State Dept. Edn., Sacramento, 1985—. Author: Foodservice in Institutions, 1988, Introduction to Foodservice, 1992, 97, 2001, 05, The Profession of Dietetics, 1996, 2000, 05. Mem. Am. Dietetic Assn. (del. 1977-80, 86-89, commr. Commn. for Accreditation of Dietic Edn. 1997—), Calif. Dietetic Assn. (pres. 1992-93), L.A. Dist. Dietetic Assn., Foodsvc. Systems Mgmt. Edn. Coun., Dietetic Educators of Practitioners, Gamma Sigma Delta, Omicron Nu, Phi Upsilon Omicron. Republican. Episcopalian. Avocations: tennis, running, reading, travel. Office: Pepperdine U 24255 Pacific Coast Hwy Malibu CA 90263-0002 Business E-Mail: june.palacio@pepperdine.edu.

PALADINO, JEANNETTE E., advertising executive, public relations executive; b. Bklyn., 1935; d. Albert E. and Jennie Paladino; m. Charles Antin, July 5, 1976. BA, Hofstra U., 1962. Reporter L.I. Comml. Rev., 1961—63; pub. rels. acct. supr. Batten, Barton, Durstine & Osborn, Inc., 1963—68; pub. rels. dir., advt. acct. exec. Warwick, Advt., 1968—72; pub. rels. officer Econ. Devel. Adminstrn. Commonwealth P.R., NYC, 1972—76; pub. rels. mgr. Anaconda Co., NYC, 1976—78; sr. v.p. corp. comm. Marsh & McLennan, Inc., NYC, 1978—83; sr. v.p., dir. comm. Bowery Savs. Bank, NYC, 1984—. Mem.: Pub. Rels. Soc. Am., NY Women in Comm. (Matrix award 1982), Women's Forum. Office: Paladino Co 50 E 89th St New York NY 10128-1225

PALANCA, TERILYN, software industry analyst; b. Chicago Heights, Ill., Aug. 15, 1957; d. Raymond Anthony and Barbara Jean (Schweizer) P. BA, Coll. William and Mary, 1979; MBA, Rutgers U., 1983. Chief auditor, mgr. Williamsburg (Va.) Hilton, 1979-81; corp. auditor RCA, Princeton, N.J., 1982-83; EDP cons. Price Waterhouse & Co., N.Y.C., 1983-84; data base adminstr. Chubb & Son, Inc., Warren, N.J., 1984-85; cons., tech. mgr. Applied Data Rsch., Inc., Princeton, 1985-88; mgr. bus. devel. and product Oracle Corp., Belmont, Calif., 1988-91; mgr. market analysis Sybase, Inc., Emeryville, 1991-92, dir. product mgmt., 1993-95, sr. dir. corp. mtkg., 1996-99; rsch. dir. Giga Info. Group, Cambridge, Mass., 1999—2002; pvt. practice, 2002—04; dir. analyst rels. SeeBeyond Tech. Corp., Monrovia, Calif., 2004—05, Sun Microsys., 2005—. Mem. All Saints Coventry Choir. Mem. NAFE, Assn. of Inst. for Cert. Computer Profls. (cert. in data processing) Avocations: music, literature, outdoor activities, conservation. Office: 42 Diana Dr Savannah GA 31406

PALERMO, BARBARA KELLY, health facility administrator; b. Jackson, Miss., Apr. 15, 1955; d. E. Kenneth and Luna L. Kelly; m. Daniel R. Palermo, Apr. 15, 1994. AA, Young Harris Coll., 1975; BS, Med. Coll. Ga., 1978. Dir. quality improvement Wesley Woods Geriatric Hosp., Atlanta, 1988-91; personnel dir. Ctrl. Vly. Rehab. Hosp., Modesto, Calif., 1991-92; quality improvement dir. Brawner Psychiat. Inst., Smyrna, Ga., 1992-94; quality assurance coord. Bapt. North Hosp., Cumming, Ga., 1994-95, Atlanta Med. Clinic, 1995-96; clin. data specialist Northside Hosp., Atlanta, 1996-97; dir. quality improvement Tenet Physician Svcs., Alpharetta, Ga., 1997—. Vol. Muscular Dystrophy Assn., New Haven, 1983-84. Mem. Ga. Assn. Healthcare Quality. Avocations: reading, travel. Home: 9285 Bluejack Ln Roswell GA 30076-3609

PALERMO, JUDY HANCOCK, retired elementary school educator; b. Longview, Tex., Sept. 7, 1938; d. Joseph Curtis and Bennie Lee (Deason) Hancock; m. Donald Charles Palermo, Apr. 1, 1961; 1 child, Donald Charles Jr. (dec.). BS in Secondary Edn., 1960. Cert. secondary and elem. edn. tchr., Tex. Art tchr. Dallas Ind. Sch. Dist., 1960-62, 65-67; asst. dir. freshmen orientation program North Tex. State U., Denton, summer 1969, dormitory dir. Oak St. Hall, 1968-71, tchr. part-time, 1970-77; substitute tchr. Denton Ind. Sch. Dist., 1975-78, tchr. 5th grade, 1979-87, art tchr., 1987—89; tchr. kindergarten Kiddie Korral Pre-Sch., Denton, 1978-79; ret. Hodge Elem., 1999. Trained gifted tchr. Woodrow Wilson Elem. Sch., Denton, 1980, grade level chmn., 1980; grade level chmn. Eva S. Hodge Elem. Sch., Denton, 1988-89, 92-93; mem. rsch. bd. advisors Am. Biog. Inst., 1991—. Active Denton Humane Soc., Humane Soc. U.S., 1982—, Denton Educators Polit. Action Com., 1984—85; Eva S. Hodge historian PTA, 1992—99. Mem. NEA, NAFE, Tex. State Tchrs. Assn., Denton Classroom Tchrs. Assn. (faculty rep. 1984-85), Denton Edn. Assn., Denton Area Art Edn. Assn. (program chmn. 1990-91), Greater Denton Arts Coun., Denton Ret. Sch. Pers. Assn., Numismatic Assn. (sec. Greater Denton chpt.), Denton Sq. Athletic Club, Denton Greater Univ. Dames Club (treas. 1970), Bus. and Profl. Women's Assn. (treas. 1990-91, chair audit com. 1992-93, chmn. 1993—), Friends of the Libr., Humane Soc. U.S., Delta Kappa Gamma (treas. 1986-88, comm. com. 1994—). Democrat. Avocations: painting, ceramics, drawing, calligraphy, photography. Home: 3405 Nottingham Dr Denton TX 76209-1281 E-mail: doubleeagle55@aol.com.

PALESKY, CAROL EAST, tax accountant; b. Orange, N.J., May 13, 1940; d. Neil Norell and Marie R. Reiss; m. Jacob Palesky; children: Donna, Lewis. AB, Am. Inst., Pleasantville, N.J., 1973; postgrad., Am. Inst., Portland, Maine, 1980; student, Atlantic C.C., Mays Landing, N.J., 1971-73. With mgmt. First Nat. Bank of South Jersey (now First Fidelity), Pleasantville, NJ, 1967-74; loan officer Maine Savs. Bank, Portland, 1980-81; acct., owner East Acctg. Assocs., Topsham, Maine, 1985—. Pres. Sensible Tax Limits Coalition, 1995—. Treas., bd. dirs. Congl. Term Limits Coalition, Topsham, 1993—; bd. dirs. Maine Citizens Rev. Bd., Portland, 1993—. Scholar Nat. Taxpayer Union, 1992, 94; recipient United to Serve Am. award, 1992. Mem. Nat. Assn. Small Business Owners, Maine Taxpayers Action Network (pres. 1990—), Topsham Taxpayer Assn. (pres. 1991—). Roman Catholic. Home and Office: 24 Sokokis Cir Topsham ME 04086-1615 Office Phone: 207-725-4539. E-mail: carol@clinic.net.

PALEY, GRACE, author, educator; b. NYC, Dec. 11, 1922; d. Isaac and Mary (Ridnyik) Goodside; m. Jess Paley, June 20, 1942; children: Nora, Dan.; m. Robert Nichols, 1972. Student, Hunter Coll., NYU. Formerly tchr. Columbia, Syracuse U.; ret. mem. lit. faculty Sarah Lawrence Coll., Stanford, Johns Hopkins, Dartmouth, CUNY. Author: The Little Disturbances of Man, 1959, Enormous Changes at the Last Minute, 1974, Leaning Forward, 1985, Later the Same Day, 1985, Long Walks and Intimate Talks, 1991, New and Collected Poems, 1992, The Collected Stories, 1994 (Nat. Book award nomination, 1994), Just As I Thought, 1998, Begin Again Collected Poems, 2000; contbr. stories to Atlantic, New Yorker, Ikon, Genesis West, others. Sec. N.Y. Greenwich Village Peace Center. Recipient Literary award for short story writing Nat. Inst. Arts and Letters, 1970, Edith Wharton award N.Y. State, 1988, 89, Rea award for short story, 1993, Vt. Gov.'s award for Excellence in the Arts, 1993, award for contbn. to Jewish culture Nat. Found. Jewish Culture; Guggenheim fellow; apptd. Vt. Poet Laureate, 2003—. Mem. Am. Acad. and Inst. Arts and Letters, Am. Acad. Arts and Scis. Office: PO Box 620 Thetford VT 05074-0620

PALI, JENNIFER ROCHELLE, language educator; b. Houston, Oct. 27, 1967; d. John Edward and Thelma Lee Pali. BS in Edn. and Instrn., Tex. A&M U., 1991; MEd in Ednl. Adminstrn., Stephen F. Austin State U., Tex., 2002; postgrad., Oral Roberts U., Tulsa, 2005—. Cert.: Tex. Sch. Bus. (paralegal) 1994; tchr. Tex., 1991. 6th grade tchr. Our Redeemer Lutheran Sch., Houston, 1991—92; pre-k tchr. Camelot for Kids, College Station, Tex., 1992—93, St. Matthews Sch., Houston, 1993—94; paraglegal, adminstrv. asst. MDL 926 Settlement Fund, Houston, 1994—96; 7th grade lang. arts tchr. Galena Park (Tex.) Mid. Sch., 1996—; 3d grade tchr. Houston Ind. Sch. Dist., 2001—02; tchr. Lee Coll., Baytown, Tex., 2004; afterschool. program coord. 3d-5th grades Purple Sage Elem. Sch., 2005—. Mem. PTA, Galena Pk., 1996—. Mem.: ASCD, Am. Fedn. Tchrs. Republican. Avocations: reading, writing, poetry, doll collecting, stamp collecting/philately. Office: Purple Sage Elem Sch 6500 Purple Sage Houston TX 77049 Office Phone: 832-386-3124. Personal E-mail: japplebee67@aol.com.

PALIATKA, JEANNE THERESE, literature and language educator, department chairman; m. Olaf G. Nelson, June 21, 2003; 1 child, Greta A. Nelson. MA in Social Scis., U. Chgo., 2002. English tchr., English dept. chair Nazareth Acad., LaGrange Park, Ill., 1993—. Office: Nazareth Acad 1209 W Ogden Ave La Grange Park IL 60526 Office Phone: 708-354-0061.

PALIYENKO, ADRIANNA MARIA, foreign language educator; b. Kingston, Ont., Can., Feb. 28, 1956; came to U.S., 1958; d. Paul and Alexandra (Sawka) P.; m. Levering B. Sherman Jr., Mar. 14, 1986. AB in French Edn., U. N.C., 1977, PhD in French Lit., 1988; MA in French Lit., Boston U., 1983. Tchr. French, dept. head Northwood High Sch., Pittsboro, N.C., 1977-80; asst. d'anglais Lycée Honoré de Balzac, Paris, 1982-83; vis. instr. N.C. State U., Raleigh, 1987-88; lectr. in French U. N.C., Chapel Hill, 1988-89; asst. prof. Colby Coll., Waterville, Maine, 1989—. Lectr. and researcher in field. Author: Mis-Reading the Creative Impulse: The Poetic Subject in Rimbaud and Calaudel, Restaged, 1997, Segalas, Anais Recits des Antilles: Le Bois de la Soufriere, suivis d'un choix de poemes, 2004; contbr. chapters to books, articles to profl. jours.; mem. editl. bd.: Women in French Studies, 1997—; libr. circulation: Women in French Studies, 1998. Boston U. fellow, 1980-82; Fulbright-Hays scholar, 1982-83; grantee Colby Coll. Humanities, 1991, 92, 96, 2000, Dept. of Edn., 1999-2001 Mem. MLA (regional del. 2006—), New Eng. MLA, South Atlantic MLA, Am. Assn. Tchrs. of French, Internat. Assn. Multidisciplinary Approach and Compartive Studies, Phi Beta Kappa. Avocations: gardening, jogging, creative writing. Office: Colby Coll Dept French and Italian Waterville ME 04901 Office Phone: 207-859-4656. Business E-Mail: ampaliye@colby.edu.

PALKA, TAMARA, psychiatrist; b. Wilkes Barre, Pa., Aug. 24, 1977; d. Edward and Judith (Bezdziecki) Palka. BA, U. Zarogoza, Spain, 1998; BS, Stonehill Coll., Easton, Mass., 1999; MD, Saba U., Netherland Antilles, 2004. Resident U. Md., Balt., 2004—. Chair Plato Symposium, Balt., 2005—; rschr. in field. Vol. Ctrl. Am. Relief Efford, Peru, 1998. Recipient Cmty. award, Saba U. Sch. Medicine, 2002. Mem.: Creative Alliance, Am. Psychiat. Assn., Lambda Epsilon Sigma, Sigma Zeta. Avocations: scuba diving, jewelry making, running, travel, drawing. Office: U Md Hosp 701 W Pratt St Baltimore MD 21201

PALL, ELLEN JANE, writer; b. NYC, Mar. 28, 1952; d. David B. and Josephine H. (Blatt) P.; m. Richard Holmes Dicker, July 12, 1986; 1 child, Benjamin. BA, U. Calif., Santa Barbara, 1973. Freelance writer for several jours., 1987—. Staff assoc. Bread Loaf Writers Conf., Middlebury, Vt., 1986; instr. UCLA-Ext., 1980-83; adj. asst. prof. Fordham U./Coll. at Lincoln Ctr., N.Y.C., 1990-93. Author (under pen name Fiona Hill): The Trellised Lane, The Wedding Portrait, The Practical Heart, Love in a Major Key, Sweet's Folly, The Autumn Rose, The Love Child, The Stanbroke Girls, 1981, The Country Gentleman, 1987; author: (as Ellen Pall) Back East, 1983, Among the Ginzburgs, 1996, Corpse de Ballet, 2001, Slightly Abridged, 2003; contbr. articles to N.Y.Times Mag., N.Y. Times Arts & Leisure, New Yorker mag., Chgo. Tribune, Washington Post; book reviewer. Shane Stevens fellow, Bread Loaf Writer's Conf., Vt., 1983. Mem. Am. PEN (freedom to write com.). Office: care Mary Evans Inc 242 E 5th St New York NY 10003-8501 Business E-Mail: ellen@ellenpall.com.

PALLADINO, ROSANNE C., music educator; b. New Castle, Pa., Dec. 19, 1951; d. Nicholas M. and Constance L. Maiorano; m. Michael A. Palladino. MusB, Dana Sch. of Music of Youngstown State U., 1973; MusM, Dana Sch. of Music of Younstown State U., 1977; Diploma, U. Sienna, 1985. Instructional I Teaching Certificate Pa., 1973, Instructional I Pa., 1973. Elem. music tchr. New Castle Area Sch. Dist., New Castle, Pa., 1973—2001, h.s. choir dir. Mem.: Am. Fedn. of Teachers, New Castle Music Club (pres.). Home: 407 W Clayton Street New Castle PA 16102 Office: New Castle High Sch 300 E Lincoln Ave New Castle PA 16101 Office Phone: 724-656-4700. Personal E-mail: sopclar1@msn.com.

PALLADINO-CRAIG, ALLYS, museum director, educator; b. Pontiac, Mich., Mar. 23, 1947; d. Stephan Vincent and Mary (Anderson) Palladino; m. Malcolm Arnold Craig, Aug. 20, 1967; children— Ansel, Reed, Nicholas. BA in English, Fla. State U., 1967; grad., U. Toronto, Ont., Can., 1969; MFA, Fla. State U., 1978, PhD in Humanities, 1996. Editorial asst. project U. Va. Press, Charlottesville, 1970-76; instr. English Inst. Franco American, Rennes, France, 1974; adj. instr. Fla. State U., Tallahassee, 1978-79, dir. Four Arts Ctr., 1979-82, dir. U. Mus. of Fine Arts, 1982—, prof. mus. studies. Mem. grad faculty Mus. Studies Cert. Program Fla. State U. Curator, contbg. editor: Nocturnes and Nightmares, Monochrome/Polychrome, Chroma, High Roads & Low Roads-Anthems, Dirges, Myths; contbg. editor: Body Language; guest curator, author: Mark Messersmith: New Mythologies; curator, editor Albert Paley--Sculpture, Drawings, Graphics and Decorative Arts, Trevor Bell: A British Painter in America, and Trial by Fire: Contemporary Glass; curator, author: The Abridged Walmsley--Selections from the Career of William Aubrey Walmsley, co-curator, contbg. author: Terrestrial Forces; author: Jack Nichelson: Micro-Theatres, Alexa Kleinbard: Talking Leaves, Jake Fernandez--Ethereal Journeyman, Jim Roche-Sense of Place; editor: Athanor I-XXV, 1980—; Represented in permanent collections Fla. Ho. of Reps., Barnett Bank, IBM. Individual artist fellow Fla. Arts Coun., 1979 Mem. Am. Assn. Mus., Fla. Art Mus. Dirs. Assn. (sec. 1989-91), Phi Beta Kappa. Democrat. Avocation: antiques. Home: 1410 Grape St Tallahassee FL 32303-5636 Office: Fla State U Mus of Fine Arts 250 Fine Arts Bldg Tallahassee FL 32306-1140 Business E-Mail: apcraig@fsu.edu.

PALLAS, ARLENE MARY, elementary school educator; b. Bklyn., May 6, 1938; d. Henry and Kathleen Villa; m. William Joseph Pallas, July 20, 1968; children: William, Marianne. BA, St. Joseph's Coll., 1960; MA, L.I. U., 1963. Tchr. NYC Pub. Schs., 1960—69, Mt. Sinai Pub. Schs., 1977—98. Vol. Atria and Port Jefferson Nursing Homes; lectr., vol. Woodhaven Nursing Home, Port Jefferson Sta., NY, 1998—. Mem.: Miller Pl. Mt. Sinai Hist. Soc., Port Jefferson Country Club. Independent. Cath. Avocations: golf, ballroom dancing, tennis, travel.

PALLASCH, MAGDALENA HELENA (MRS. BERNHARD MICHAEL PALLASCH), artist; b. Chgo., Sept. 6, 1908; d. Frank and Anna (Meier) Fixari; m. Bernhard Pallasch, Nov. 26, 1931 (dec. Nov. 1977); children: Bernhard Michael, Diana Pallasch Miller Student, Art Inst. Chgo., Chgo. Acad. Fine Arts, 1922-26, Am. Acad. Fine Arts, 1926-30; studied with Joseph Allworthy, 1935-38; student, U. Chgo., 1960; doctorate (hon.), 1985. Contbr. two murals and ten life size figures for Woman's World Fair, Chgo., 1928, Century of Progress Exhbn., Chgo., 1933-34; portrait artist, subjects include Cardinal Cody, Chgo., 1980—, Cardinal Francis George, Chgo., 1998, Carlotta Ames, Boston, Mrs. Timothy Kingston, Arlington Heights, Ill., Dr. Neal Coleman, Hinsdale, Ill., Catherine Eardley Murphy, Lake Forest, Ill., Anita Mangels, Sao Paulo, Brazil, Canon Regis Barwig, Oshkosh, Wis., 2000, Dr. Dale King Phelps, Pittsford, NY, Laurel Cummings, Palm Beach Fla.,2001, Barbara and Robert Pendergast, Lake Forest, Ill., Mara Pallasch, Chgo., 2003, Lois Kay Simanton, Northfield Ill., 2004, Bernhard Anthony Miller, Chgo., 2004; mural St. Mary of the Lake Ch., Chgo., 1987; exhbn. at Montifiori Estate, 1992, 93, 94, Hinsdale Art Ctr., 1995, 96, 97; represented in pvt. and pub. collections Loyola U., Chgo., Barat Coll., Lake Forest, Ill., Internat. Coll. Surgeons, Chgo., Med. Library, Columbus Hosp and others.h Recipient first award for still life Arts Club, NYC, 1960, First award Nat. League Am. Pen Women, 1972, 1st place and best of show State Exhibit, Springfield, Ill., 1973, 1st award Chgo. Woman's Club, 1978, hon. mention for portrait Italian Cultural Ctr., hon. alumna award Loyola U., Chgo., 1983, award of excellence for portrait of author Gail Brook Burket, Wheaton Hist. Mus., 1987, Gold Medal of Honor for disting. lifelong achievements, 1987, award of honor for portrait of sculptor Lisa Gengler, 1989, medallion from Archduke Markus Habsburg of Austria, 2003, first award for still life Vanderpoel Gallery, 2005, Best Classic Art award Vanderpoel Gallery, 2006; named Dame Commandeur with Starbust, 1997, with second Starburst, 2003, Sovereign Mil. Order Temple of Jerusalem, 1995 Mem. Presentation Ball Aux.; mem. President's Club, Loyola U., also mem. women's bd. Nat. League Am. Pen Women (v.p. Chgo. br. 1966-68, art chmn. 1978-80, Margaret Dingle Meml. award 1979), Mcpl. Art League Chgo., Nat. Soc. Arts and Letters (art chmn. chgo. chpt. 1982—, apptd. nat. chmn. 1997—), Friends of Austria, Friends of D'Arcy Gallery of Medieval and Renaissance Art., Ill. Cath. Women Club (gov. 1979-), Cuneo Mus. (Vernon Hills, Ill.). Home and Office: 723 W Junior Ter Chicago IL 60613-1512

PALLMEYER, REBECCA RUTH, judge; b. Tokyo, Sept. 13, 1954; arrived in U.S., 1957; d. Paul Henry and Ruth (Schrieber) Pallmeyer; m. Dan P. McAdams, Aug. 20, 1977; 2 children. BA, Valparaiso U., Ind., 1976; JD, U. Ill., Chgo., 1979. Bar: Ill. 1980, U.S. Ct. Appeals (7th cir.) 1980, U.S. Ct. Appeals (11th and 5th cir.) 1982. Judge clk. Minn. Supreme Ct., St. Paul, 1979-80; assoc. Hopkins and Sutter, Chgo., 1980-85; judge, administrv. law Ill. Human Rights Commn., Chgo., 1985-91; magistrate judge U.S. Dist. Ct. (No. Dist.), Chgo., 1991-98, dist. judge, 1998—. Mem. jud. resources com. Jud. Conf. U.S., 1994—2000. Nat. adv. coun. Christ Coll., Valparaiso U., 2001—; bd. dirs. Augustana Ctr., 1990—91. Recipient Profl. Achievement award, Chgo.-Kent Coll. of Law, 2002, Alumni Achievement award, Valparaiso U., 2002, President's Award for Disting. Svc., N.W. Suburban Bar Assn., 2003. Mem.: FBA (bd. mgrs. Chgo. chpt. 1995—2004), Chgo. Bar Assn. (chair devel. law com. 1992—93, bd. mgrs. 2004—06, David C. Hilliard award 1990—91), Fed. Magistrate Judges Assn. (bd. dirs. 1994—97), Womens Bar Assn. Ill. (bd. mgrs. 1995—98), Valparaiso U. Alumni Assn. (bd. dirs. 1992—94). Lutheran. Avocations: choral music, sewing, running. Office: US Dist Ct 219 S Dearborn St Ste 2178 Chicago IL 60604-1877 Office Phone: 312-435-5636.

PALLOZOLA, CHRISTINE, not-for-profit executive; b. St. Louis, Mar. 28, 1952; BS, U. Mo., 1974. Purchasing and sales mgmt. computer industry, Mo., 1984-92; exec. dir. Cahokia Mounds Mus. Soc., Collinsville, Ill., 1993—2001, dir. spl. events, mktg. Arts and Edn. Coun., 2001—04; exec. dir. Am. Acad. Physician and Patient, St. Louis, 2004—. Sec. Businesspersons Between Jobs, St. Louis, 1998—2004. Mem.: Assn. Fundraising Profls. Home: 150 Burtonwood Ballwin MO 63011

PALM, MARY EGDAHL, mycologist; b. Mpls., Jan. 27, 1954; d. Lauren and Mary E.; children: Natalie Elizabeth, Christopher Steven. BA in Biology, St. Olaf Coll., 1976; MSc in Plant Pathology (mycology), U. Minn., 1979, PhD in Plant Pathology (mycology), 1983. Lab. asst. St. Olaf Coll. Biology Dept., Northfield, Minn., 1974, tchg. asst., 1975-76; rsch. asst. U. Minn. plant pathology dept., Mpls., 1976-83, post doctoral rsch. assoc., 1983-84; mycologist (botanist GS12) USDA/APHIS biol. assessment and support staff, Beltsville, Md., 1984-91; mycologist scientific svcs. USDA/Animal and Plant Health Inspection Svc., Beltsville, 1991—, mycologist, dir. morphology, molecular and biochem. diagnostics lab., 2006—. Instr., coord. seminars and tng. sessions for USDA and ednl. sci. group, 1982—; adj. assoc. prof. plant pathology Pa. State U., State College, 1995. Co-author: Deuteromycetes and Selected Ascomycetes That Occur On or In Wood: An Indexed Bibliography, 1979, An Indexed Bibliography and Guide to Taxonomic Literature, 1988, A Literature Guide for the Identification of Plant Pathogenic Fungi, 1987, Fungi on Rhododendron: A World Reference, 1996, Mycology in Sustainable Development: Expanding concepts, Vanishing Borders, 1997, Cultivation and Diseases of Proteaceae: Leucdendron Leucospermum, and Protea, 2004; contbr. articles to profl. jours. Recipient St. Olaf Coll. Hon. Biology scholarship, 1976, Disting. Alumnus Dept. Plant Pathology U. Minn., 1999; grantee U. Minn. Computer Ctr. 1979, 80, 81, 82, V.P Gores Hammer award, 1998. Fellow Mycological Soc. Am.(sec. 1991-94, Am. Inst. Biol. Scis. rep. 1994—, v.p. 1995-96, pres.-elect 1996-97, pres. 1997-98, other coms.); mem. Am. Phytopathol. Soc. (chairperson mycology com. 1988, 89, vice chairperson 1987, mem. 1985, 86, regulatory plant pathology com. 1993—, organizer, moderator colloquim on systematics of plant pathogenic fungi 1987), L.Am. Mycol. Assn. (U.S. liaison), Internat. Assn. Plant Taxonomy (subcom. C of com. on fungi and lichens 1986, 87, 88). Office: USDA Rm 329 B-011A 10300 Baltimore Ave Beltsville MD 20705-2350 Office Phone: 301-504-5327. Business E-Mail: mary.palm@aphis.usda.gov.

PALMA, DOLORES PATRICIA, urban planner, consultant, writer; b. Bklyn. d. Anthony Michael Resse and Eleanor Dorothea (Palma) Graffeo; m. Doyle G. Hyett. BA, CUNY, Bklyn., 1972; M of Urban Planning, U. Mich., 1974. Intern Mich. Mcpl. League, Ann Arbor, 1973-74; park planner Metro Bd. Parks and Recreation, Nashville, 1975; preservation planner Metro. Hist. Commn., Nashville, 1976; sr. cmty. planner Metro Planning Commn., Nashville, 1977-79; exec. dir. Metro Hist. Zoning Commn., Nashville, 1980-82; asst. dir. Mid-Altlantic Regional Office Nat. Trust for Hist. Preservation, Washington, 1983, dir. Office of Neighborhood Conservation, 1984; project dir. urban demonstration program Nat. Main St. Ctr., 1985-87; pres. HyettPalma Inc., 1985—, HyettPalma Publs., 1988—. Author: Salaries, Wages and Fringe Benefits in Michigan Cities and Villages, 1973; Nashville: Conserving a Heritage, 1977, Neighborhood Commercial Buildings: A Survey and Analysis of Metropolitan Nashville, 1983, Business Enhancement Plan for Downtown Poughkeepsie, N.Y., 1987, Future Directions for Seward, Alaska, 1987, Management of Downtown Palmer, Alaska, 1988, Successful Business Recruitment Strategies in the U.S., 1988, Business Plans for Business Districts, 1988, Office Tenant Recruitment for Pittsfield, Mass., 1989, Business Plan for the Heart of Corpus Christi, Tex., 1989, Retail Recruitment Strategies for Reading, Pa., 1989, Seward 2000: Comprehensive Plan, Seward, Alaska, 1990, Business Plan for Downtown Rocky Mount, N.C., 1990, Retail and Restaurant Audit for Rosslyn, Va., 1990, Market Analysis and Enhancement Strategies for Liberal, Kans., 1990, Market Analysis and Enhancement Strategies for Geneva, N.Y., 1990, Building the Vision: Washington Street Corridor, Falls Church, Va., 1990, The Magnetic Mile Vision, Glendale, Ariz., 1990, Downtown Denton (Md.) Devel. Plan, 1991, East Downtown Dearborn (Mich.) Bus. Plan, 1991, Leavenworth/Lansing Market Analysis, 1991; (with Nat. League of Cities), City Commercial Centers Reborn: Building Commercial Distric Dynamism, 1990, Downtown Visions, 1992, Focus Groups for Downtown, 1992, Business Retention and Expansion, 1993, Winning Ways, 1993, Downtown and Utilities, 1994, Downtown Safety: Addressing the Myths and the Realties, 1994, Parking for Downtown Spenders, 1995, Downtown Public Space Maintenance, 1995, How to Revitalize Your Downtown, 1999, America's Downtown Renaissance, 2001. Del. Nat. Assn. Neighborhood Reinvestment Corp., Nashville, 1978; mayoral appointee Neighborhood Housing Svcs., Nashville, 1979-82; dir. Restore the U.S. Capitol Campaign, 1983; publicity dir. Hist. Edgefield, Inc., 1979; Nat. League of Cities Am. Downtown: New Thinking New Life, 1995—, Ind. Downtown, 2001—, Blueprints for Mich. Downtown, 2003—, Blueprints for Pa. Downtown, 2004-; hon. mem. Tenn. State Legislature, 1980; hon. mem. Tenn. State Legislature, 1980. Woodland scholar Nat. Trust for Hist. Preservation, 1976; named one of Outstanding Young Women of Am., 1985, award of excellence Va. Downtown Devel. Assn., 1990, Am. Planning Assn., 1991. Office: HyettPalma Inc 1600 Prince St Apt 110 Alexandria VA 22314-2836

PALMA, KARI MICHELLE, singer, actress, dancer, educator; b. Marion, Ind., July 12, 1968; d. Jerome Frank and Carmen Rochelle Palma. BS in Music Edn., Ind. State U., 1992; BA in Music and Theatre, Marian Coll., 1990. Music educator Honey Creek Mid. Sch., Terre Haute, Ind., 1992—95, Smith and Ctrl. elem. schs., Martinsville, Ind., 1995—; music dir. Nashville Follies Theatre, Ind., 1997—, Brown Co. Live Entertainment, 2005; freelance performer various theatres, Ind., 1988—, Various Theatres, Ohio, 1988—; lead singer Stonehenge Big Band, Terre Haute, Ind., 1990—. Concert liason, bd. dirs. Cmty. Concerts, Martinsville, 1999—2002; chair, fine arts com. MSD of Martinsville Schs., 2001—03. Arranger (music) Various Songs, Medleys, Musicals, 1997—, author, scriptwriter (plays, musicals), 1997—; choreographer (musical) Scrooge, 2000. Children's music dir. Presbyn. Ch., Martinsville, 1998—2000, St. Mary's Episcopalian Ch., 2005; choreographer Indian Creek Cmty. Theatre, Trafalgar, Ind., 2001. Recipient Indpls. 500 Festival Princess, Jr. Miss winner, State Talent Champion, 1st Place State Solo Vocal Competition, Ind. State Music Assn., 1986, Best in Tap Dance, Elite Dance Studio, 2002, Miss Congeniality, Ind. Jr. Miss Pageant, 1986; Liberace Music scholar. Mem.: Ind. State Music Assn., Ind. Orff-Schulwerk Assn. Episcopalian. Avocations: running, marathon runner, choreographer, swimming, gardening. Office: Charles L Smith Elem 1359 E Columbus St Martinsville IN 46151

PALMA, LAURA, lawyer; b. New Haven, Feb. 19, 1958; BA magna cum laude, Dartmouth Coll., 1980; JD, Columbia Univ., 1983. Bar: NY 1985. Ptnr. corp. dept. Simpson Thacher & Bartlett LLP, NYC, 1995—. Harlan Fiske Stone Scholar. Mem.: Assn. Bar City of NY, Phi Beta Kappa. Office: Simpson Thacher & Bartlett 425 Lexington Ave New York NY 10017-3954 Office Fax: 212-455-7143, 212-455-2502.

PALMER, ADA MARGARET, systems analyst, consultant; b. Feb. 8, 1940; d. Mark Lloyd Palmer and Eunice Elizabeth (Thompson) Palmer Schnitzer. AA, Colo. Woman's Coll., 1960; BA, George Washington U., 1962. Programmer, analyst U.S. Navy Dept., Washington, 1962-66, Schroder Trust, N.Y.C., 1967-68; v.p. EDP Learning Systems, N.Y.C., 1968-69; cons. JWI Assoc. Tech. Group, N.Y.C., 1969; adv. sr. programmer Merrill Lynch, N.Y.C., 1969-72; sys. analyst Tchrs. Ins. & Annuity, N.Y.C., 1972-77; sys. specialist N.Y. Times, N.Y.C., 1977-81; computer cons. Applied Sys. Resources, Inc., N.Y.C., 1981-82; asst. sec. Chase Bank, N.Y.C., 1982-94; computer cons. A.Z. Software Shop Inc., Garden City, N.Y., 1994-95; sys. acct. UN, N.Y.C., 1995-99; computer cons. AMP Consulting, Inc., 1999—. Mem. Women's Assn. Wichita Symphony. Recipient George Washington U. Alumni Svc. award, 1992, Am. Overseas Schs. Hist. Soc. Pres. award, 2005. Mem. Colo. Woman's Coll. Alumni Club, George Washington U. Alumni Club of N.Y.C. (past pres.), Am. Overseas Schs. Hist. Soc. (bd. dir. 2002—, archive historian, 2002—, ops. mgr. 2005—, info processing mgr. 2006—). Republican. Presbyterian. Home and Office: Apt 1707 550 W Central Wichita KS 67203-4238 Personal E-mail: ampkansas@aol.com.

PALMER, ANN THERESE DARIN, lawyer; b. Detroit, Apr. 25, 1951; d. Americo and Theresa (Del Favero) Darin; m. Robert Towne Palmer, Nov. 9, 1974; children: Justin Darin, Christian Darin. BA, U. Notre Dame, 1973, MBA, 1975; JD, Loyola U., Chgo., 1978. Bar: Ill. 1978, U.S. Supreme Ct. 1981. Intern Wall Street Jour., Detroit, 1974; freelancer Time Inc. Fin. Publs., Chgo., 1975—77; extern, Midwest regional solicitor U.S. Dept. Labor, 1976—78; tax atty. Esmark Inc., 1978; counsel Chgo. United, 1978—81; ind. contractor Legal Tax Rsch., 1981—89; fin. and legal news contbr. Chgo. Tribune, 1991—, Bus. Week, 1991—, Automotive News, 1993—97, Crain's Chgo. Bus., 1994—2000; contbg. editor Registered Rep, 2002—. Mem.: Chgo. Club. Home: 1570 Christina Ln Lake Forest IL 60045

PALMER, APRIL MARIE, social studies educator; b. Hamilton, Ohio, Feb. 25, 1977; d. Carol Sue Wilson and David Lynn Teague; m. Christopher Chad Palmer, Dec. 20, 1999. BA, U. Fla., Gainesville, 2000, MEd, 2001. Social studies tchr. Williston H.S., Fla., 2002—. Office Phone: 352-528-3542.

PALMER, BEVERLY BLAZEY, psychologist, educator; b. Cleve., Nov. 22, 1945; d. Lawrence E. and Mildred M. Blazey; m. Richard C. Palmer, June 24, 1967; 1 child, Ryan Richard. PhD in Counseling Psychology, Ohio State U., 1972. Lic. clin. psychologist, Calif. Adminstrv. assoc. Ohio State U., Columbus, 1969—70; rsch. psychologist Health Svcs. Rsch. Ctr. UCLA, 1971—77; commr. pub. health L.A. County, 1978—81; pvt. practice Torrance, Calif., 1985—; prof. psychology Calif. State U., Dominguez Hills, 1973—2006. Author: Interpersonal Skills for Helping Professionals Online Course, 2001, 04, reviewer manuscripts for numerous textbook pubs; contbr. articles to profl. jours. Recipient Proclamation, County of L.A., 1972, 1981, Outstanding Prof. award, Calif. State U., 1995; Fulbright Sr. scholar, Malaysia, 2001, Fulbright scholar, Borneo, 2001, Fulbright Sr. scholar, Malaysia, 2004—05, Fulbright scholar, Barbados, 2005. Mem. APA. Office: Calif State U Dominguez Hills Dept Psychology Carson CA 90747-0001 Office Phone: 310-373-6691. Business E-Mail: bpalmer@csudh.edu.

PALMER, CATHERINE E., lawyer; BA, Boston Coll., 1977; JD, Catholic Univ., 1980. Bar: NY 1981. Asst. US atty., chief of criminal divsn. US Attorney's Office, Ea. Dist. NY, 1985—94, spl. assignment asst. US atty., 1996—98; ptnr. Latham & Watkins, NYC, 1994—96, 1998—, and chair, white collar practice and dep. chair, global litig. dept. Office: Latham & Watkins Ste 1000 885 Third Ave New York NY 10022-4834 Business E-Mail: catherine.palmer@lw.com.

PALMER, CHRISTINE (CLELIA ROSE VENDITTI), vocalist, educator, musician; b. Hartford, Conn., Apr. 2, 1919; d. John Marion and Immacolata (Morcaldo) Venditti; m. Raymond Smith, Oct. 5, 1949 (div. June 1950); m. Arthur James Whitlock, Feb. 25, 1953. Student, Mt. Holyoke Coll., 1937-38, New Eng. Conservatory of Music, 1941-42; pvt. studies, Boston, Hartford, N.Y.C., Florence and Naples, Italy; RN with honors, Hartford Hosp. Sch. Nursing, 1941. Artist-in-residence El Centro Coll., Dallas, 1966-71. Pvt. vocal instr.-coach, specializing in vocal technique for opera, mus. comedy, supper club acts, auditions, Dallas, 1962-94; voice adjudicator San Francisco Opera Co., 1969-72, Tex. Music Tchrs. Assn., 1964-75, others; lectr. in field; appearances with S.M. Chartocks' Gilbert and Sullivan Co. Leading operatic soprano N.Y.C. Opera, Chgo., San Francisco, San Carlo, other cities, 1944-62, N.Y. Town Hall Concert, 1951; soloist with symphony orchs. maj. U.S. Cities, 1948-62; soloist Marble Collegiate Ch., Holy Trinity Ch.; coast-to-coast concert tour, 1948; numerous appearances including St. Louis MUNY Opera, Indpls. Starlight Theatre, Lambertville Music Circus; soloist Holiday on Ice, 1949-50; TV performer, including Home Show on NBC, Telephone Hour on NBC, Holiday Hotel; performer various supper clubs, N.Y.C., Atlanta, Bermuda, Catskills, others, including Number One Fifth Avenue, The Embers, The Carriage Club, Viennese Lantern. Hon. mem. women's bd. Dallas Opera Assn.; mem. adv. bd. Tex. Opera News; mem. Tex. Music Tchrs. Cert. Bd., Collegiate Chorale, Don Craig Singers, The Vikings; mem. women's bd., Dallas Bapt. Univ. Oliver Ditson scholar, 1942; recipient Phi Xi Delta prize in Italian, 1937; named Victor Herbert Girl, ASCAP; Spl. Recognition Gold book of Dallas Soc. Mem. Nat. Assn. Tchrs. of Singing (pres. Dallas chpt. 1972-74), Nat. Fedn. Music Clubs, Tex. Fedn. Music Clubs, Dallas Fedn. Music Clubs (pres. 1972-74), Dallas Symphony League, Dallas Music Tchrs. Assn. (pres. 1971-72, Tchr. of Yr. 1974), Thesaurus Book Club (pres. 1990-91, 97-98), Friday Forum (Dallas, bd. dirs.), Dallas Women's C. of C., Eagle Forum, Pub. Affairs Luncheon Club, Dallas Fedn. Music Club, Pro Am., Wednesday Morning Choral Club, Dallas Knife and Fork Club, Prestoncrest Rep. Club. Presbyterian. Home: 6232 Pemberton Dr Dallas TX 75230-4036

PALMER, DENISE E., publishing executive; b. Seymour, Ind., Feb. 12, 1957; m. Gregory G. Palmer. BA, U. Dayton, 1977; MS in Mgmt., Northwestern U., 1984. Sr. auditor Coopers & Lybrand, Dayton, Ohio, 1977—80; corp. auditor Tribune, 1980—86, planning analyst, 1983—86, mgr. planning, 1986—88; dir. fin. WGN Radio, Chgo., 1988—93, sta. mgr., 1993; dir. fin. Chgo. Tribune, Chgo., 1994—95, v.p. fin. & adminstrn., 1996—97, v.p. fin. strategy & fin., 1996—98, v.p. devel., strategy, fin., 1998—2000; pres., CEO CLTV, Oakbrook, Ill., 2000—02; pres., pub., CEO Balt. Sun, 2002—06; pres., pub. Tampa Tribune, 2006—. Bd. mem. Greater Baltimore Com., 2003—. Econ. Alliance of Greater Baltimore, 2003—, Md. Bus. Roundtable for Edn., 2003—; bd. visitors U. Md. Baltimore County, 2003—; mem. adv. bd. U. Dayton; mem. Northwestern U. Coun. of 100 Women. Office: Tampa Tribune 202 Parker St Tampa FL 33606*

PALMER, GRACIOUS ANNE, small business owner; b. NYC, Sept. 28, 1940; d. Frank Carlton Palmer and Grace Ann Travis; m. William Stanley Olsen, June 18, 1988; stepchildren: Stephen Olsen, Archie Olsen, Paul Olsen. AA, City Coll., Long Beach, Calif., 1983; BA, Calif. State U., Chico, 1999. Mgr. Xerox Corp., San Francisco, 1983—89; owner Palmer Enterprises, Shasta Lake, Calif., 2004—; substitute tchr. Shasta County Schs., 2004—. Mem. Citizen's Patrol Shasta County Sheriff's Dept., 2005—; commnr. Planning Commn., Shasta Lake, 2003—05; councelman City Shasta Lake, Calif., 2005—; alternate Regional Transp. Planning Agy., Redding, Calif., 2006—. Mem.: Calif. Elected Women's Assn. (bd. dirs., mem.-at-large 2006—). Democrat. Meth. Avocations: water-skiing, exercise, boating, fishing.

PALMER, IRENE SABELBERG, retired dean, retired nursing educator, genealogist; b. Franklin, N.J., May 28, 1923; d. John Joseph and May (Heiser) Sabelberg. BS, N.J. State Tchrs. Coll., 1945; diploma, Jersey City Med. Center Sch. Nursing, 1945; MA, NYU, 1951, PhD, 1963. Edn. dir. Diploma Schs. Nursing N.J. and Mass, 1948—52; ednl. dir. Glenn Dale (Md.) Hosp. and D.C. Dept. Pub. Health, 1956, dir. nursing svc. and edn., 1956—61; assoc. clin. prof. nursing Georgetown U., Washington, 1960—61; USPHS trainee, 1961—62; assoc. chief nursing svc. for rsch. VA Hosp., San Francisco, 1963—64; rsch. nurse cons. divsn. nursing HEW and USPHS Nursing Rsch. Field Ctr., San Francisco, 1964—66; asst. dean and assoc. prof. nursing U. Colo. Sch. Nursing, Denver, 1966—68; dean and prof. nursing Boston U. Sch. Nursing, 1968—74; prof. Hahn Sch. Nursing U. San Diego, 1974—91, prof. emeritus, 1991—; founding dean Hahn Sch. Nursing, U. San Diego, 1974-87, dean emeritus, 1988—. Lectr. Classical Alliance of the Western States, Uskudar, Turkey, 1994, Italy, 1995. Editor: Nursing Clinics of North America, 1970; Contbr. articles to profl. jours. Served to capt. Nurse Corps U.S. Army, 1953-56. Internat. Nightingale scholar; Nat. Health Svc. fellow; recipient Excellence in Nursing Scholarship award Orgn. Nurse Execs., 1993. Fellow Nat. League Nursing (bd. visitors 1977-87), Am Acad. Nursing; mem. ANA, Am. Assn. History Nursing, Am. Assn. Colls. Nursing (hon.), Boston U. Nursing Archives, German Rsch. Assn. (pres. 1995), Sigma Theta Tau (Leadership award Zeta Mu chpt. 1986, Excellence in Nursing award 1991).

PALMER, JESSICA, diversified financial services company executive; Head of risk mgmt. for corp. and investment banking group Citigroup, NYC, 2003—. Named one of 25 Women to Watch, US Banker mag., 2005. Office: Citigroup 767 5th Ave New York NY 10153*

PALMER, JOCELYN BETH, volunteer; b. Salina, Kans., Dec. 19, 1927; d. Paul Franklin and Josie Murtle (Schultz) Swartz; m. Gerald Keith Palmer, Dec. 28, 1952; children: David, Paula, Brian, April. AA, Christian Coll., Columbia, Mo., 1947; BS with honors, Kans. State U., 1949; MA, U. Iowa, 1951. Grad. asst. psych. U. Iowa, Iowa City, 1949-51; instr. U. Ill., Urbana, 1951-52; co-dir. child devel. ctr. Long Beach (Calif.) City Coll., 1954-56.

Mem. task force Early Childhood Edu., 2000-01. Tchr. trainer, presch. tchr., cons., chmn. nursery com., elder, deacon Presbyn. Ch.; mem. Com. to Develop Stds. for Presch. Handicapped, Salina, 1981-83; pres., bd. dirs. # 305 Salina Sch. Dist., 1975-87; com. chair, bd. dirs. St. Francis Boyd Home, Salina, Ellsworth, 1984-87; bd. dirs. YWCA, 1993-97; bd. dirs. Asburg Hosp. Aux., 1993-96, sec. 1994-96; mem. com. planning early childhood edn. USD 305. Mem. Clippership Mariners (chaplain 1991-93, logkeeper 1994-95, 2000-01, skipper 1997, chaplain, 2002-03), Saline County Med. Alliance (bd. dirs. 1992-96, 98-2000), Twentieth Century Forum (courtesy chmn. 1989-93, 2000—), PEO (pres. 1989-91, 94-95, treas. 1993-95), Salina Downtown Lioness (bd. dirs. 1988-89, 91-93, program chair 1997, pres. 2000-03), Phi Kappa Phi, Omicron Nu. Republican. Avocations: sewing, reading, music, swimming.

PALMER, JUDITH GRACE, university administrator; b. Washington, Ind., Apr. 2, 1948; d. William Thomas and Laura Margaret (Routt) P. BA, Ind. U., 1970; JD cum laude, Ind. U., Indpls., 1973. Bar: Ind. 1974, U.S. Dist. Ct. (so. dist.) Ind. 1974. State budget analyst State of Ind., Indpls., 1969-76, exec. asst. to gov., 1976-81, state budget dir., 1981-85; spl. asst. to pres. Ind. U., 1985-86, v.p. for planning, 1986-91, v.p. for planning and fin. mgmt., 1991-94, v.p., CFO, 1994—. Bd. dirs. Ind. Fiscal Policy Inst., Kelley Exec. Ptnrs.; bd. dirs., treas. Rsch. and Tech. Corp.; bd. dirs. Ind. Farmers Mutual Ins. Bd. dirs., sec.-treas. Columbian Found., 1990-94, 2000—; bd. dirs. Columbia Club, 1989-98, pres. 1995; bd. dirs. Commn. for Downtown, 1984, mem. exec. bd., 1989-92, chmn. cmty. rels. com., 1989-93; mem. State Budget Commn., 1981-85. Named one of Outstanding Young Women in Am., 1978; recipient Sagamore of the Wabash award, 1977, 85, Citation of Merit, Ind. Bar Assn. of Young Lawyers, 1978, Appreciation award, 1980. Mem. ABA, Ind. Bar Assn., Indpls. Bar Assn. Roman Catholic. Office: Ind Univ Bryan Hall Rm 204 Bloomington IN 47405 E-mail: jgpalmer@indiana.edu.

PALMER, LAURA HIGGINS, artist; b. Kans. City, Mar. 16, 1955; d. George Alfred and Isabelle J. Higgins; m. Douglas J. Palmer, Mar. 2, 1975; 1 child, Ada Louise. BFA, Cornell U., 1975; MA, George Washington U., 1978. With exhibits prodn. Smithsonian Instn., Washington, 1975—76; visual libr. Harvard U., Washington, 1976—78; instr. drawing, painting and design MD Hall, Annapolis, Md., 1978—93; designer graphics and computer NASA, Greenbelt, Md., 1994—2000. Artist in residence Md. Hall, Annapolis, 1985—88, Tamarind Inst., Albuquerque, 1991. Numerous one-woman shows including most recently, one-woman shows include Arundel Ctr., Annapolis, Md., 2004, Cultural Arts Found. Anne Arundel County, Md., 2004, Angelfall Studios, Balt., Md., 2004, Via della Scala 67, Rome, Italy, 2004, Paul's Homewood, Annapolis, Md., 2005, Palmer SOL Gallery, Nottingham, England, 2005, Paper Rock Scissors, Balt., Md., 2005, Represented in permanent collections U. Md., U. Coll. Md. Artists Collection, Coll. Pk., Md., Tamarind Inst., U. N.Mex., Albuquerque, N.Mex. Trustee Ballet Theatre Md., Annapolis, 2002—04. Mem.: Coll. Art Assn., Cultural Arts Found. Home and Studio: Palmer Studios 1163 Bay Highlands Dr Annapolis MD 21403

PALMER, LINDA K., psychology educator, writer, editor; b. Chattanooga, Jan. 4, 1954; d. Cornelius N. and Marian Fairchild (Gill) Keeton; m. Jack Andrew Palmer, Feb. 14, 1978; children: Adam Jalal, Nani Faye. MS, U. La., Monroe, 1993; postgrad., La. Tech. U., Ruston, 1995—98. Project mgr. Inst. Behavioral Rsch., U. Ga., Athens, 1985-89; counselor Monroe Alcohol & Drug Abuse Clinic, 1990, N.E. La. Rehab. Hosp., 1996—98; instr. psychology N.E. La. U., Monroe, 1993—95, La. Tech. U., Ruston, 1995—98; mng. editor Edit. Naam Publs., Oreg., 1998—2005. Co-author: Survey Research Methods, 1988, Evolutionary Psychology: The Ultimate Origins; editor-in-chief 10 books, 1998-2006; contbr. articles to profl. jours. Bd. dirs. Montessori Sch., Athens, 1988-89; bd. trustees Know Thyself as Soul Found., 1996-2005. Mem. APA, Southwestern Psychol. Assn., La. Psychol. Assn., Psi Chi (pres. 1992). Achievements include development of wholistic model of well-being with emphasis on moderating role of health habits.

PALMER, LYNNE, writer, astrologer; b. El Centro, Calif., Dec. 14, 1932; d. Clarence Lee and Paquita Mae (Hartley) Hafer; m. Bruno Cazzaniga, Mar. 13, 1964 (div. 1965); m. Sidney Latter, Nov. 29, 1997 (dec. Oct. 2004). Student, Ch. of Light, 1957-62, Calif. Sch. Escrows, L.A., 1960; theatre mgmt. degree, Mus. Arenas Theatres Assn., N.Y.C., 1963. Asst. teller Western Mortgage, L.A., 1957-58; head teller Sutro Mortgage Svc., L.A., 1958-61; freelance astrologer N.Y.C., 1961-92, Las Vegas, Nev., 1962—; owner, operator, tchr. astrology sch. N.Y.C., 1970-72; owner Star Bright Pubs., Las Vegas, 1996—. Spkr. in field; interviewed in N.Y. Post and other major newspapers and mags. including Life and Oggi (Italy), Veja (Brazil), Wall St. Jour., People Mag., Globe, Die Welt am Sonntag (West Germany), New Woman Mag., Forbes. Author: Prosperity, Nixon's Horoscope, Astrological Almanac, Astrological Compatibility (Profl. Astrologers award 1976), Horoscope of Billy Rose, ABC Basic Chart Reading, ABC Major Progressions, ABC Chart Erection, Pluto Ephemeris (1900-2000), Daily Positions, Is Your Name Lucky For You?, Do-It-Yourself Publicity Directory, Your Lucky Days and Numbers, Money Magic, Astro-Guide to Nutrition and Vitamins, Gambling to Win, The Astrological Treasure Map, Dear Sun Signs, Are You Compatible With Your Boss, Partner, Coworkers, Employee, Client?, Bet to Win, Special Report: USA Under Attack, Lucky Days and Winning Numbers; columnist: Self, House Beautiful, Gold; record album: Cast and Read Your Horoscope; TV appearances include The Johnny Carson Tonight Show, What's My Line, 60 Minutes, CBS News Night Watch, Cosmos (BBC), Sci. Series (Italian TV), Fantastico (Brazilian TV), Japan TV, News (Nippon), Do We Really Need It? (ASAHI), The World is Calling (Uranai); contbr. articles to mags. and newspapers. Mem. AFTRA, Am. Fedn. Astrologers (cert.). Avocation: travel. Home: 850 E Desert Inn Rd Apt 912 Las Vegas NV 89169 Office: Lynne Palmer 1155 E Twain Ave Ste 108-248 Las Vegas NV 89169 Office Phone: 800-615-3352. Business E-Mail: lynnepalmer@lynnepalmer.com.

PALMER, MARILYN JOAN, English composition educator; b. Mahoning County, Ohio, Mar. 3, 1933; d. Rudolph George and Marian Eleanor Wynn; m. Richard Palmer, Nov. 10, 1956 (dec. 1987); children: Ricky, Larry, Kevin. Phys. therapy cert., UCLA, 1954, BS, 1955; MA in Philosophy, Ohio State U., 1969; PhD, U. Okla., 1996. Phys. therapist Neil Ave. Sch. for Handicapped, Columbus, Ohio, 1968-69; instr. philosophy Ohio State U., Columbus, 1969; instr. English Youngstown (Ohio) State U., 1970-71; writer, editor The Economy Co., ednl. publs., Oklahoma City, 1977-81; grad. asst. in English U. Okla., Norman, 1981-87, lectr. in English, 1988-90, tech. writing instr. ind. studies, 1988-97. Free-lance editing and cons.; cons. for on-line CD-ROM to accompany a textbook, 2002. Author: Technical Writing for Science, Business and Industry, 1988, An Enthymeme as a Platform for Understanding Audience Values, 1997; editor: Kindergarten Keys Teacher's Guidebook, 1982, author parochial supplement, 1982. Fund-raiser Easter Seal Soc., 1965-68; den mother coord. Boy Scouts Am., 1966, 67. Dept. Energy grantee, 1976. Mem. AAUP, Am. Phys. Therapy Assn., Soc. for Women in Philosophy, Alpha Xi Delta (nat. editor Quill 1984-86). Office Phone: 405-447-6495. Personal E-mail: doclynn@cox.net.

PALMER, MARTHA H., counseling educator, director; b. Chgo., Jan. 10, 1954; d. Thomas Manuel Palmer Sr. and Marie Louise (Cranford-Crawford) Palmer. BA in Psychology, Ea. Ill. U., 1976, MS, 1977; cert. in cmty. law, John Marshall Law Sch., Chgo., 1981; student, U. Ill., Chgo., 1992; postgrad., No. Ill. U., 1995—. Med. asst. health svcs. Ea. Ill. U., Charleston, 1976-77; dir. sch. age and sr. citizen programs YMCA, Chgo., 1978-80; site dir., facilities mgr. Ctr. for New Horizons, Chgo., 1980-85; counselor No. Ill. U., DeKalb, 1985-89; lectr. Malcolm X Coll., Chgo., 1989, recruitment coord., 1989-90; dir. Bethel Self Sufficiency Program, Chgo., 1989-90; asst. prof. counseling Harold Washington Coll. City Coll. Chgo., 1990—2002, acting chair, chmn. dept. counseling, 1999—2001; exec. dir. JEI, 2003—06; lead ednl. cons. Marty Ednl. Svcs., Inc., 1990—. Developer Harold Washington Coll. Sisters Academic Scholarship Program, 1997-2002; coll. bd. coord. Chgo. Youth Ctrs., 2006. Creator of character Marty The Clown, 1978 (U.S. patent, trademark 1998); author poems; contbr. articles to profl. jours. Coord. Afrikan Cultural Pageant, Ea. Ill. U., Charleston and No. Ill. U., DeKalb, 1972-86; mem. Sojourners United Political Action Com.; immediate past pres., pres., mem. Sojourners United Polit. Action Commn., Chgo., 1993-99; founder Harold Washington Coll., Black Women's Caucus, Chgo., 1991-2002; edn. rep. Task Force for Black Polit. Empowerment, Chgo., 1994—; coord. Coll. Support Groups for Self Help, 1991-2002; co-founder Black Maleness Program, 1991-2002; vol. La Rida Hosp., Chgo.; co-convenor Rainbow PUSH Coalition City Coll. Chgo. divsn., 1996-2002; co-founder Sisters in Scholarship Program, Harold Washington Coll., 1997-2002; co-chair 150th Commemoration Women's Rights Nat. Womens Polit. Caucus Greater Chgo. Recipient Sharps and Flats Music Club Adv. award, 1994, BSU award, 1996. Mem. Nat. Assn. Black Psychologists, Ill. Assn. Black Psychologists, Ladies of Peter Claver (Court 129), Delta Sigma Theta. Democrat. New Thought Christian. Avocations: singing, dance, designing, drawing. Personal E-mail: palmerboahene@yahoo.com.

PALMER, NOREEN E., psychotherapist; b. Columbus, Ohio, Nov. 24, 1960; d. Alfred and Lurlena White; m. Charles Edwin Palmer, Apr. 18, 1991; children: Charles Jr., Arianna. BS, Ohio U., 1983; MA, Ohio State U., 1986, MSW, 1988. Lic. ind. social worker. Grad. asst. Ohio State U., Columbus, 1986-88, program coord., 1989—92; social worker Nat. Med. Care, Columbus, 1992-96; profl. liaison Grant/Riverside Hosp., Columbus, 2000—; pvt. practice psychotherapist Pickerington, Ohio, 1995—. Pvt. practice grant writing cons., Columbus, 1990-99; vol. clin. dir. Homeless Families Found., Columbus, 1996-99, v.p., 1997-99; bd. mem. Am. Diabetes Assn.-Heartland Chpt., Columbus. Co-author: Going Off: A Guide for Black Women Who've Just About Had Enough, 2001, Going Off: A Black Woman's Guide for Dealing with Anger and Stress, 2002; guest contbr. Heart and Soul, Black Expressions Mag. Founder Blackboard Literacy Initiative, exec. dir., 1995-97. Recipient Commendation, Canton (Ohio) City Coun., 1988, Appreciation award Pathways Mentors, Columbus, 1989, Vol. award Homeless Families Found., Columbus, 1999, commendation Ohio Ho. of Reps., 2002. Mem. Nat. Coalition of 100 Balck Women (Appreciation award 1997). Avocations: reading, cooking, walking, freelance writing. Office: Grant/Riverside Health Ctr 697B Hill Rd N Pickerington OH 43147-1157 also: 5554 Isaac Rd Canal Winchester OH 43110

PALMER, PAMELA MURRILL, educator; b. Jacksonville, NC, Apr. 21, 1967; d. Roosevelt Dean Lee and Dorsay Ann Mitchell; m. Alan Wade Palmer, Feb. 19, 2000; 1 child, Joshua Alan. BA, Winston-Salem (NC) State U., 1990; MS, NC A&T State U., Greensboro, 1996; cert. in nonprofit mgmt., Duke U. Cmty. and econ. devel. specialist NC A&T State U., 1995—97; prof. High Point U., NC, 1998—. Dir. Nonprofit Leadership Enhancement Program, High Point U., 2005—. Mem., com. leader Love and Faith Christian Fellowship, Greensboro, 2003; sec. United Way of Greater High Point, 2006—; mem. exec. com. Am. Friends Svc. Com.-SERO, Atlanta, 2003; mem. Guilford County Mental Health Bd., Greensboro, 2004. Named Minority Bus. Advocate, High Point C. of C., 2005; recipient Outstanding Faculty award, High Point U. Evening Degree Program, 2004, 2005; grantee Nonprofit Leadership Enhancement Program, Hayden-Harman Found. and High Point U., 2006—. Home: 307 Jackson St Jamestown NC 27282 Office: High Point U 833 Montlieu Ave Campus Box 3471 High Point NC 27262 Office Phone: 336-841-4632. Home Fax: 336-454-9009. E-mail: pmurrill@highpoint.edu.

PALMER, PAMELA S., lawyer; BA, U. Calif., Irvine, 1978; JD, U. So. Calif., 1982. Bar: Calif. 1982. Jud. clk. to Hon. Walter Ely, U.S. Ct. Appeals (9th cir.); with Heller, Ehrman, White & McAuliffe, L.A., ptnr., 1992—96, Latham & Watkins, L.A., 1996—. Office: Latham and Watkins LLP 633 W Fifth St Ste 4000 Los Angeles CA 90071

PALMER, PATRICIA G., writer, retired psychologist; b. Ann Arbor, Mich., Jan. 22, 1928; d. David Hasler and Dorothy (Knapp) G.; m. Charles Franklin Palmer, Dec. 22, 1958 (div.); children: Penelope Anne, Elizabeth Susan. BA English lit., Skidmore Coll., 1953; MA Psychology, U. No. Colo., 1974, EdD, 1977. Lic. psychologist Colo. With Time, Inc., N.Y.C., 1953—56; assoc. dir. vocat. office Smith Coll., Northampton, Mass., 1956—58; pvt. practice psychology Denver, 1975—. Owner, mgr. Assertiveness Tng. Inst., Denver, 1975—85. Author: Liking Myself, 1977, The Mouse, The Monster, and Me, 1977, Teen Esteem, 1989, I Wish I Could Hold Your Hand: A Child's Guide to Grief and Loss, 1994. Home: 101 Kanani Rd Apt 102 Kihei HI 96753-6807 E-mail: pat@drpatpalmer.com.

PALMER, ROSE, humanities educator, writer; b. London, Eng., Feb. 11, 1914; arrived in U.S., 1929; d. Harris Schneider and Rebecca Albeitman; m. Frank Palmer, Apr. 12, 1941 (div. Sept. 1988); children: Diane, Richard, Pamela, Kenneth. Lit. tutor, Chgo., 1985—. Achievements include development of simplified phonics method for tutoring adults and teens. Home: 10 N Summit Ave Apt 200 Park Ridge IL 60068-3310

PALMER, ROSE ANN, television producer, writer, educator; b. Bklyn. BA, St. Joseph's Coll.; MA, Bklyn. Coll.; PhD, N.Y. U., 1997. Lic. H.S. English tchr., H.S. speech tchr., tchr. of deaf, ednl. evaluator, N.Y.C. English tchr. N.Y.C. Bd. Edn., Bklyn., 1957-63; tchr., radio and TV broadcaster WNYE-FM-TV, Bur. Radio and TV, Bklyn., 1963-82; tchr. deaf, lang. coord., edn. edr. N.Y.C. Bd. Edn., 1982-90; producer Telecare TV, Uniondale, N.Y., 1992—; novelist, 1990—. Grad. asst. NYU, 1990; tchr. Bklyn. Coll., 1969, Evelyn Wood Reading Dynamics, 1968. Author: A History of the NY League for the Hard of Hearing in the Context of the Progressive (1900-1918) and Neo-Progressive Eras, 1997. Mem. AAUW, United Fedn. Tchrs., Mystery Writers Am. Avocations: reading, theatre going.

PALMER, ROSLYN WOLFFE, small business co-owner; b. Bainbridge, Ga., May 4, 1952; d. Jake and Bella (Turetzky) Wolffe; m. A. Jackson Palmer, Mar. 27, 1976; 1 child, Mycla Ann. BA in Journalism, U. Ga., 1974. Women's editor The Post Searchlight, Bainbridge, Ga., 1974-78; news editor, dir. WAZA Radio, Bainbridge, Ga., 1978-84; co-owner Jake's Pawn Shop, Bainbridge, Ga., 1984—. Adv. bd. First Port City Bank, Bainbridge, 1992-94; chair Downtown Devel. Authority, Bainbridge, 2001-2005, SW Ga. Regional Libr., Bainbridge, 1989-98. Vol., bd. dirs. Am. Cancer Soc., 1978-90; councilwoman Bainbridge City Coun., 1988—; chmn. Ga. Mcpl. Assn. Cmty. and Human Devel. Policy Com., Atlanta, 1992-94; pres. Jr. Woman's Club, 1977-78, C. of C., Bainbridge, 1993; Leadership Ga. participant, 1992. Recipient Ga. Downtown award Dept. Cmty. Affairs, 1992, Cmty. Involvement award 4-H Club, 1987. Jewish. Avocations: reading, cooking. Home: 2505 Twin Lakes Dr NE Bainbridge GA 39819 Office: PO Box 262 Bainbridge GA 39818

PALMER, SALLY BROADBENT, language educator; b. Ames, Iowa, Oct. 9, 1947; d. Francis Everett Broadbent and Pauline Dayse Winkel; children: David John, Thomas Luther, James Hyrum, Joseph Francis, Matthew Broadbent, Sarah Beth Burford, Jesse Benjamin, Samuel Henry, Elizabeth Irene, Seth William. BA Edn., Brigham Young U., Provo, Utah, 1969; MA English, Brigham Young U., 1993; PhD English, U. Calif., Davis, 1998. Instr. English U. Calif., Davis, 1993—99; instr. Solano C.C., Roseville, Calif., 1998—99; assoc. prof. English S.D. Sch. Mines & Tech., Rapid City, 1999—. Author: (personal essays) David O. McKay Essay Contest (First Pl. 1991 and 1992; Third Pl. 1993); contbr. articles and essays to profl. jours. Pres., sec. Literacy Coun. Black Hills, Rapid City, 2003—06, vol. literacy and ESL tutor, 2001—06; violinist Tempe Symphony, Tempe, 1987—89; tchr. Ch. of Jesus Christ of Latter-day Saints, Tempe, AZ; Davis, CA; Provo, UT; Rapid City, SD; Hillsboro, OR, 1980—2006, organist Rapid City, 2000—06. Recipient Faculty Recognition Award for Excellence in E-Learning, S.D. Bd. Regents, 2004—05. Mem.: Coll. English Assn., 18-19th Century Brit. Women Writers Assn., Jane Austen Soc. N.Am., Proliteracy USA, S.D. Literacy Coun. R-Conservative. Mem. Lds Ch. Home: 4401 Carriage Hills Drive Rapid City SD 57702 Office: South Dakota School of Mines & Technolog 501 E St Joseph Street Rapid City SD 57701 Office Fax: 605-394-5197. Personal E-mail: sbpalmer@hotmail.com. E-mail: sally.palmer@sdsmt.edu.

PALMER, STACY ELLA, periodical editor; b. Middletown, Conn., Oct. 25, 1960; d. Marvin Jerome Palmer and Eileen Sondra (Cohen) Palmer Burke. B in Liberal Arts and Internat. Rels., Brown U., 1982. Asst. editor Chronicle of Higher Edn., Washington, 1982-86, sr. editor, 1986-88; news editor Chronicle of Philanthropy, Washington, 1988-93, mng. editor, 1993-98, editor, 1998—. Bd. dirs. Brown Alumni Monthly, Providence, 1988-91, vice chmn., 1991-93, mem. 1996—, chmn., 2003. Mem.: Brown U. Alumni Assn. (bd. govs. 1997—2001), Brown Club Washington (bd. dirs. 1993—99, pres. 1994—99). Avocations: swimming, bicycling, travel. Home: 3513 30th St Washington DC 20008 Office: Chronicle of Philanthropy 1255 23rd St NW Washington DC 20037-1125

PALMER, STEPHANIE TERESA, elementary school educator; b. NY, June 22, 1949; d. John Ralph and Marie Elvira Tesone; m. Richard Allen Palmer, Dec. 28, 1974; children: Kristen Palmer Bastian, Kimberly, Korinne, Kyra. BA, Fordham U., Bronx, NY, 1971; MA, Manhattan Coll., Riverdale, NY, 1976. Cert. Tchr. N-12 NY Dept. Edn. Tchr. dean of students Eastchester HS, Eastchester, NY, 1972—78; tchr., dir. My Nursery Sch., Armonk, NY, 1989—94; Bedford Bd. elem. tchr. Pleasantville UFSD, Pleasantville, NY, 1994—. Adj. Pace U., Pleasantville, NY, 2003—, L.I. U., Westchester Grad. Ctr., Purchase, NY, 2004—; presenter, workshops in field, 2000—. Cons., reviewer New York Grade 4 BLM, 2003. Pres. PTA, Yonkers, NY, 1985—86; leader Girl Scouts, Westchester, NY, 1986—2005; liaison walk, swim a thon Friends of Karen, Westchester, NY, 1986—2005. Recipient Jerkins award, PTA, 1986. Mem.: Tchrs. Assn. Pleasantville (officer, mem. exec. bd.), NY State United Tchrs., Am. Camping Assn. Avocations: gardening, scrapbooks, travel, reading. Office: Bedrord Rd Elem Sch 289 Bedford Rd Pleasantville NY 10570 E-mail: STPalmer22@optonline.net.

PALMER, VICKI R., food products executive; b. Memphis; m. John E. Palmer; 1 child, Alexandria. B in Econs. and Bus. Adminstrn., Rhodes Coll., 1975; MBA in Fin., U. Memphis, 1980. Corp. loan officer First Tenn. Bank.; head pension investment FedEx, mgr. corp. fin.; mgr. pension investments Coca-Cola Co., 1983—86; asst. treas. Coca-Cola Enterprises Inc., 1986—93, v.p., 1993—99, treas., 1993—, sr. v.p., spl. asst. to CEO, 1999—, bd. dirs., 2001—. Bd. dirs. Spelman Coll., Rhodes Coll., Woodward Acad., First Tenn. Nat. Corp. Named one of 20 Women of Power and Influence in Corp. Am., Black Enterprise Mag., 100 Black Women of Influence, Atlanta Bus. League, 1998; recipient Disting. Alumni award, U. Memphis Alumni Assn. Office: Coca-Cola Enterprises 2500 Windy Ridge Pkwy Atlanta GA 30339

PALMERIO, ELVIRA CASTANO, art gallery director, art historian; b. Cin., July 23, 1929; d. John and Josephine Castano; m. Carlo Palmerio, June 1, 1958 (dec.); 1 child, Marina. B Lit. Interpretation, Emerson Coll., 1950; postgrad., Pius XII Inst., Florence, Italy, 1954—55; student opera with Cesare Sturani. Curator Castano Art Gallery, Boston, 1965-78, dir. Needham, Mass., 1978-98; rschr. for Archivies of Am. Art Smithsonian Instn., Boston, 1988-89; performed voiceover in Italian for Nova PBS TV Series, Nova, Italy, 1997; gov. adv. com., 1997. Vatican translator; interpreter Italian art specializing in Macchiaioli art; Italian interpreter Ritz Carlton Internat. Festival, (Italian) Mayor's Office Sister Cities Internat. Conv.; appointed sec. World Affairs Coun., Boston; tchr. Emmanuel Coll. Boston, 1953. Mem. Rep. Presdl. Task Force, Nat. Rep. Senatorial Com., Presdl. Inner Circle; active Boston chpt. UN; bd. dirs. Needham Hist. Soc., Boston U. Women's Coun.; vol. Sail Boston, 1992; del. Presdl. Trust, 1992; apptd. Gov.'s Com. on Women's Issues; del. to Nat. Fedn. of Rep. Womens Conv., 1999, 2002; vol. WGBH. Cardinal Spellman scholar; recipient Pirandello Lyceum award, I Migliori, 1997, Vol. award Nat. Fedn. Commns. Women, 1999, Nat. Assn. Commissions for Women, 1999. Mem. UN, Boston U. Women's Coun., Boston Browning Soc., Fogg Art Mus. of Harvard U., Friends of Needham Libr., Archives Am. Art Boston, World Boston, World Affairs Coun. Boston (sec.), Nat. Mus. Women in Arts, Needham Hist. Soc. (bd. dirs.), Wellesley Hist. Soc., Nat. Italian Am. Found., French Libr., World Boston. Avocations: current events, international affairs, writing, travel, music. Home: 83 Pickering St Unit B3 Needham MA 02492-0015 Office Phone: 781-449-1050.

PALMIERI, DORA ANN, retired language educator; b. Monmouth, Ill., Dec. 31, 1943; d. Gust John and Ruth Ida Douffas; m. Ronald Ernest Naedele, Feb. 3, 1966 (dec. Sept. 30, 1966); 1 child, Ronnann Naedele-Risha; m. Frank William Palmieri, Jan. 2004. BA in English, Milligan Coll., 1966; MA in English, E. Tenn. State U., 1974. Cert. tchr. Miss., Tenn., N.C., Md., Fla. Editor/asst. editor Courier And Gateway Newspapers, Suitland, Md., 1966—69; English tchr. Long Beach (Miss.) HS, 1969—74, Garinger HS Night Program, Charlotte, NC, 1974—76; curriculum specialist, English instr. Ctrl. Piedmont CC, Charlotte, 1976—81; mgr. tng. and devel. Control Data Corp. and Comml. Credit Corp., Charlotte, Balt., 1980—87; program designer, rschr. Rutledge Coll. Sys., Charlotte, 1987—88; assoc. prof. Daytona Beach (Fla.) CC, 1990—. Lead tchr. adult HS English Daytona Beach CC, 1998—. Co-author: Ecology: The Living World, 1996; author: English All Around Us, vols. 1-4, 1999—2003, Vols. 2, 3, 4. Singles' lay min. South Daytona Christian Ch., 1990—2001. Named Lay Person Of The Yr., Kiwanis Port Orange And South Daytona, 1996. Mem.: Fla. Assn. CCs, Nat. Coun. Tchrs. English. Avocations: photography, theater, writing, crafts, movies. Personal E-mail: hollyhilla@hotmail.com.

PALMISANO, HOLLIE LEAH, personal trainer, athletic trainer; b. Pequannock, NJ, Mar. 22, 1980; d. Gertrude Mary Palmisano. BS in Phys. Edn., William Paterson U., Wayne, NJ, 2004—04. Cert. CPR/AED for profl. rescuer ARC; Nat. Athletic Trainers Assn., tchr. health and phys. edn. NJ. Exercise specialist, personal trainer Plus One, Hopewell, NJ, 2004—; cert. athletic trainer Stuart Country Day Sch. of the Sacred Heart, Princeton, NJ, 2005—. Cert. athletic trainer Olympic Devel. Program for US Field Hockey FUTURES, NJ, 2006—, Sunshine Found. All-Star Football, NJ, 2006—. Named Employee of Month, Plus One, 2005; recipient Academic Excellence award, William Paterson Athletic Dept., 2004, Athletic Tng. Edn. Program Athletic award, William Paterson Exercise and Movement Sci. Dept., 2004. Home: 513 Concord Ave 2d Fl Ewing NJ 08618 Office: Plus One 1750 Merrill Lynch Dr Pennington NJ 08534 Personal E-mail: hpalmisano@plusone.com.

PALMORE, CAROL M., state official; b. Owensboro, Ky., Jan. 13, 1949; d. P.J. and Carrie Alice (Leonard) Pate; m. John Stanley Palmore Jr., Jan. 1, 1982. BS in History and Polit. Sci., Murray State U., 1971; JD, U. Ky., 1977. Social worker Dept. Human Resources, Frankfort, Ky., 1971-74; assoc. Rummage, Kamuf, Yewell & Pace, Owensboro, 1977-81; hearing officer Ky. Bd. Claims, Frankfort, 1980-81; gen. counsel Ky. Labor Cabinet, Frankfort, 1982-83, dep. sec. labor, 1984, 1986-87, sec. labor, 1987-90, 91-94; ptnr. Palmore & Sheffer Attys., Henderson, Ky., 1984-86; dep. sec. Ky. Pers. Cabinet, Frankfort, 1996-98, acting sec., 1998, sec., 1998—. Bd. dirs. Ky. Employer's Mutual Ins., Ky. Retirement Sys., Ky. Pub. Employees Deferred Comp. Authority, Govtl. Svcs. Ctr. Authority, Gov.'s Collective Bargaining Task Force, Gov.'s Minority Mgmt. Trainee Program Task Force, State Parks Commn., Ky. Group Health Ins. Bd.; chmn. Ky. Safety & Health Stds. Bd., Frankfort, 1987-90, 91-94; co-chmn. Ky. Labor Mgmt. Adv. Coun., Frankfort, 1987-90, 91-94; bd. dirs. Ky. Workers' Comp Funding Commn., Frankfort, 1987-90, 91-94, Community Svc. Commn., Frankfort, 1993-94, Ky. Info. Resources Mgmt. Commn., Frankfort, 1994, Sch.-to-Work Partnership Coun., Frankfort, 1994; ex-officio bd. dirs. Pub. Employees Collective Bargaining Task Force, Frankfort, 1994, Ky. Workforce Partnership Coun., Frankfort, 1994. Labor liaison Jones for Gov., Lexington, 1990-91; del. Dem. Nat. Conv., N.Y.C., 1992; mem. inaugural class Ky. Women's Leadership Network, Frankfort, 1993; bd. dirs. Alliant Health Systems Adult Oper. Bd., Louisville, 1992-96, Ky. Commn. Homeless, Frankfort, 1993-94; candidate for Sec. State Commonwealth Ky., 1995; chair Dem. Women's Think Tank, 1995. Mem. Ky. Bar Assn. (del. ho. dels. 1985-86, chair law day/spkr. bur. 1985-86, mem. 1986-90), Ky. Bar Found. (bd. dirs. 1985-92, sec. 1986-89, pres. elect 1989-90, pres. 1990-91), Rotary (program chair Frankfort chpt. 1993-94). Democrat. Episcopalian. Avocations: antiques, reading, vintage jewelry, walking. Home: 2310 Peaks Mill Rd Frankfort KY 40601-9437 Office: Personnel Cabinet 200 Fair Oaks Ln Frankfort KY 40601-1134

PALMQUIST, CAROL ANN, educational association administrator; b. Grand Saline, Tex., Mar. 6, 1943; d. Sam Houston and Erdine (Sellman) Dennington; m. Richard Norman Palmquist, May 23, 1987. BS, U. North Tex., 1965, MEd, 1970. Cert. supr., Tex. Tchr. Midland (Tex.) Ind. Sch. Dist., 1965-69, Port Arthur (Tex.) Ind. Sch. Dist., 1969-85, elem. supr., 1985-89; elem. curriculum coord. Mineral Wells (Tex.) Ind. Sch. Dist., 1990-92, curriculum coord., 1993-96. Bd. dirs., officer Port Arthur Little Theatre, 1970's, Tex. Artist Mus. Soc., 1970's. Recipient Presdl. Svc. award Tex. Artist Mus. Soc. Mem. ASCD, Delta Kappa Gamma, Phi Delta Kappa. Methodist. Avocations: travel, gardening, singing, learning and teaching.

PALOMBO, LISA, artist; b. Providence, Mar. 1, 1965; d. Joseph Christopher Palombo and Catherine Ann Walsh. BFA, R.I. Sch. Design, 1987. Featured artist: (books) The Best of Oil Painting, 1996, Exploring Color, 1998. Recipient honors recognition Artist's Mag., 2003, 2004. Mem.: Oil Painters of Am., N.J. Am. Artists Profl. League. Studio: Lisa Palombo Studios 55 Mountain Ave Caldwell NJ 07006 Office Phone: 973-364-0280. E-mail: art@lisapalombo.com.

PALSER, BARBARA F., retired botanist; b. Worcester, Mass., June 2, 1916; d. G. Norman and Cora A. (Munson) P. AB, Mt. Holyoke Coll., 1938, A.M., 1940, D.Sc. (hon.), 1978; PhD, U. Chgo., 1942. From instr. to prof. botany U. Chgo., 1942-65; from assoc. prof. to prof. botany Rutgers U., New Brunswick, NJ, 1965-83, dir. grad. program in botany, 1973-80; adj. prof. botany U. Mass., Amherst, 1991—. Erskine fellow U. Canterbury, Christchurch, N.Z. 1969; vis. prof. Duke U., Durham, N.C., fall 1962; vis. research fellow U. Melbourne, Parkville, Victoria, Australia, fall 1984-85 Author lab. manual Principles of Botany, 1973, also numerous research papers in bot. jours.; bot. adviser Ency. Brit., Chgo., 1958-59; editor Bot. Gazette, Chgo., 1960-65 Named Outstanding Tchr., Rutgers Coll., 1977 Mem. Bot. Soc. Am. (sec. 1970-74, v.p. 1975, pres. 1976, Merit award 1985), Torrey Bot. Club (pres. 1968), Internat. Soc. Plant Morphologists, N.J. Acad. Scis. (pres. elect 1987-88, pres. 1988-89, Outstanding Svc. award 1985, 90). Avocations: hiking, stamp collecting/philately, photography. Home: Rockridge Retirement Cmty 37 Coles Meadow Rd #303 Northampton MA 01060

PALTROW, GWYNETH, actress; b. L.A., Sept. 28, 1972; d. Bruce Paltrow and Blythe Danner; m. Chris Martin, Dec. 5, 2003; children: Apple Blythe Alison Martin, Moses Martin. Student, U. Calif. Santa Barbara. Grad. Spence Sch., N.Y.C., 1990. Spokesmodel Estee Lauder. Appeared in films: Shout, 1991, Hook, 1991, Malice, 1993, Flesh and Bone, 1993, Mrs. Parker and the Vicious Circle, 1994, Jefferson in Paris, 1995, Moonlight and Valentino, 1995, Seven, 1995, The Pallbearer, 1996, Emma, 1996, Hard Eight, 1996, Sliding Doors, 1998, Out of the Past, 1998 (voice), Great Expectations, 1998, Hush, 1998, A Perfect Murder, 1998, Shakespeare in Love, 1998 (Academy Award for Best Actress, Golden Globe for Best Actress), The Talented Mr. Ripley, 1999, Duets, 1999, The Intern, 2000, Bounce, 2000, The Anniversary Party, 2001, The Royal Tenenbaums, 2001, Shallow Hal, 2001, Possession, 2002, View From the Top, 2003, Sylvia, 2003, Sky Captain and the World of Tomorrow, 2004, Proof, 2005, Infamous, 2006, Love and Other Disasters, 2006, Running with Scissors, 2006; TV films: Cruel Doubt, 1992, Deadly Relations, 1993; Theatre: Picnic, The Adventures of Huck Finn, Sweet Bye and Bye, The Seagull, Proof. Mem. Screen Actors Guild (Outstanding Performance with others). Office: Creative Artists Agy c/o Rick Kurtzman 9830 Wilshire Blvd Beverly Hills CA 90212-1804 also: Screen Actors Guild 5757 Wilshire Blvd Los Angeles CA 90036-3635*

PALULIS, CHRISTINE, biology educator, science educator; d. Greg and Patricia Palulis. BS in Biology, Hofstra U., Hempstead, NY, 1997, MS in Secondary Edn., 1999. Tchr. biology Malverne H.S., NY, 1999—2003; tchr. math. Eagle's Landing Mid. Sch., Boca Raton, Fla., 2003—04; tchr. sci. Don Estridge High Tech. Mid. Sch., 2004—06; tchr. biology Park Vista H.S., Lake Worth, Fla., 2006—. Dir. after sch. program Don Estridge High Tech Mid. Sch., 2004—06, yearbook advisor, 2004—06; advisor class 2004 Malverne H.S., 2000—03, yearbook advisor, 2001—03, asst. dir. marching band, 2002—03, asst. instr. flag core, 2001—02. Participant AIDS Meml. Quilt. Recipient Rho Chi of Yr., Hofstra U. Panhellenic Coun., 1997. Mem.: Nat. Sci. Tchrs. Assn., Nat. Tchrs. Assn., Am. Fedn. Tchrs., Phi Sigma Sigma (life; mem. at large). Democrat. Roman Catholic. Avocations: swimming, reading, travel. Home: 2025 Lavers Circle D-104 Delray Beach FL 33444 Office: Park Vista HS 7900 Jog Rd Lake Worth FL 33467-7909 Office Phone: 561-989-7800. Personal E-mail: cpalulis@hotmail.com. Business E-mail: palulis@palmbeach.k12.fl.us.

PALUMBO, LORRAINE REIKO MINATOISHI, architect, researcher; b. Honolulu, June 3, 1966; d. Merton Chikayuki and Eleanor Machiko (Suda) M.; m. Charles Haigler Palumbo, Feb. 16, 1995; children: Sara Minatoishi, Hana Machiko. BArch, U. Hawaii, 1989; MArch, U. Oreg., 1993; postgrad., Waseda U., Tokyo, 1994-95, PhD in Archtl. History, 1999. Designer, draftsperson DMJM Architects, Engrs. Planners, Honolulu, 1989-91; rsch. intern Mizusawa Constrn. Co., Tokyo, 1992-93; archtl. historian Mason Archs., Inc., 2000—. Seminar leader Waseda U., 1996-97. Editor Hawaii Buddhism Newsletter, 1999—. Grad. tchg. fellow U. Oreg., 1991, Patricia Roberts Harris fellow U.S. Govt., Oreg., 1991-92; recipient Japanese Mombusho scholarship Japanese Govt. Min. of Edn., 1994-98; grantee Toyota Corp. Fellowship, 1997-98. Mem. Archtl. Inst. Japan, Hist. Hawaii Found., U. Oreg. Alumni Assn. Avocations: travel, ocean activities, visiting architectural sites. Office: Mason Archs Inc 119 Merchant St Ste 501 Honolulu HI 96813 E-mail: imp@masonarch.com.

PALUMBO, RUTH ANN, state legislator; b. Lexington, Ky., July 7, 1949; d. James Keith and Dorothy Calvin (Carrier) Baker; m. John Anthony Palumbo II, June 29, 1974; children: John A. III (dec.), Joseph Edward, James Thomas, Stephen Baker. BA in Secondary Edn., U. Ky., 1972. Sales Chez Lissette Boutique, Leysin, Switzerland, 1966; sales, shoes Purcell's Dept. Store, Lexington, Ky., 1966-70; organist Ctrl. Bapt. Ch., Lexington, Ky., 1968; clk. Good Samaritan Hosp., Lexington, Ky., 1968-73; sec. Dr. Joseph Keith, Lexington, Ky., 1971-73; senate clk. aide Ky. Gen. Assembly, Frankfort, Ky., 1974; pub. rels. Palumbo Properties, Lexington, 1974-92; state rep. Ky. Gen. Assembly, 1991—. Mem. LWV, Lexington, 1990-92, Ky. Women's Polit. Caucus, Lexington, 1991-92, NAt. Order Women Legislators, Washington, 1992; sec. Ctrl. Ky. Caucus, Lexington, 1991-92. Mem. Greater Lexington Dem. Women, fin. v.p., 1982; mem. Nat. Order of Women Legislators, Washington, 1992; legis.liaison ACS Breast Cancer Detection Task Force, Ky., 1992; adv. coun. Bryan Sta. Youth Svcs. Ctr., Lexington, 1992; ball chmn. Lexington Philharmonic Women's Guild, 1990; govt. affairs Am. Symphony Orch. League Vol. Coun., Washington, 1992; bd. dirs. Philharmonic Women's Guild, pres., 1986-88; bd. dirs. Am. Cancer Soc., pres., 1988-89; bd. dirs. Lexington Phulharmonic Soc. Recipient Dorothy Moomaw Miles Svc. award Sayre Sch., 1986, Govs. Vol. Activist award Gov. Wallace G. Wilkinson, 1989, named Lexington's Outstanding Young Woman Bluegrass Jr. Woman's Club, 1982, Leadership Lexington, C. of C., 1988, Leadership Am. Found. for Women's Resources, Washington, 1989. Fellow U. Ky. Devel. Coun.; mem. Jr. League LExington (sec. 1989-90), Prof. Women's Forum, Gamma Phi Veta (pres. 1980-82). Baptist. Avocations: playing piano, singing, collecting stamps, music boxes, family. Home: 10 Deepwood Dr Lexington KY 40505-2106 Office: House of Reps State Capitol Annex Rm 370B Frankfort KY 40601*

PANCOAST, BRANDY ELIZABETH, music educator; b. Colville, Wash., Jan. 4, 1976; d. Robert Daniel and Valerie Francis Richartz; m. Tedric Howard Pancoast, July 11, 1999. BM in Piano Performance, Colo. Christian U., Lakewood, 1998, BA in Music, 1998. Cert. nat. profl. piano tchr., profl. piano tchr. Wash., lic. Musikgarten instr. Piano tchr., owner Pancoast Sch. of Music, Kettle Falls, Wash. Presenter in field; coord. Exam Ctr. Royal Am. Conservatory, 2005—. Mem.: Spokane Music Tchrs. (workshop coord. 2001—, Musiclink coord. 2001—, treas. 2005—), Foothills Music Tchrs. (chair Achievement Day 1998—2000, tchr. mentor 1998—2000, v.p. membership 1999—2000, membership survey chmn. 2006—), Wash. State Music Tchrs. Assn., Music Tchrs. Nat. Assn. (v.p. student chpt. 1995—96, pres. student chpt. 1996—98), Am. Coll. Musicians (chair guild adjudication 2001—04). Avocations: gardening, reading, travel, music advocacy. Home: PO Box 809 Kettle Falls WA 99141 Office Phone: 509-738-4913. Business E-Mail: pancoast@theofficenet.com.

PANCRATZ, JEANETTE DIANE, secondary school educator; b. Chgo., Jan. 28, 1953; d. Ernest and Anne Hasser; m. Andrew J. Pancratz, Aug. 5, 1977; children: Mark, Zachary, Jacob, Drewann. BS, DePaul U., Chgo., 1975; MS, George Williams Coll., Downers Grove, Ill., 1982. Cert. tchr. Nat. Bd. Certification, 2003. Tchr., coach Resurrection H.S., Chgo., 1975—89; tchr. Schaumburg H.S., Ill., 1994—. Coach volleyball Schaumburg H.S., 1989—, mem. faculty coun., 2004—, mem. music com., 1999—2004. Recipient award, Ill. Phys. Edn. Profls. Mem.: AAHPERD, PWCA, Ill. AHPERD. Avocation: jogging.

PANDIAN, SHANTHA G., psychiatrist; b. Bklyn., Dec. 19, 1972; d. Dorairaj Sivajothi and Sugirtha Rose Pandian; m. Juan Francisco Rodriguez, Apr. 24, 1998; children: Christopher Rodriguez, Ethan Rodriguez. MBBS, Kasturba Med. Coll., India, 1995. Cert. MD Tenn., Fla., diplomate psychiatry Am. Bd. Psychiatry Neurology. Psychiatry residency E. Tenn. State U., Johnson City, 1997—2001; assoc. chief mental health clin., outpatient psychiatrist James H. Quillen Vets. Admntrn. Med. Ctr., Mt. Home, Tenn., 2001—; asst. prof. psychiatry E. Tenn. State U., 2001—. Chair psychiatry and neurology section Southern Med. Assn., Ala., 2003—. Mem.: Southern Med. Assn. (chair 2003—). Meth. Avocations: reading, exercise, cooking. Office: James H Quillen Vets Adminstrn Med Clinic PO Box 4000 Johnson City TN 37604 Office Phone: 423-926-1171.

PANDOLFI, FRANCES, health facility administrator; b. NYC, Sept. 7, 1944; d. Frank Pandolfi and Rose McGinn; m. Edmund Lewiska Menelik Bobbitt, May 19, 1973. BA, Vassar Coll., 1965; MPA, NYU, 1990. Health planner N.Y.C. Dept. City Planning, 1965-74; planner West Midlands County Coun., Birmingham, Eng., 1974-81, dir. recreation and tourism planning, 1981-85, dir. strategic planning, 1985-86; dep. dir. housing coord. N.Y.C. Mayor's Office, 1987-89; dir. nurses housing N.Y.C. Health & Hosps. Corp., 1989-92, exec. asst. to v.p., 1992-94, asst. v.p., 1994-97; chief of staff N.Y.C. Health and Hosps. Corp., 1998-2001, chief info. officer, 2001—. Dir. Women in Housing and Fin., N.Y.C., 1990-96. Mem.: Am. Soc. Pub. Adminstrn. Office: NYC Health & Hosps Corp 125 Worth St New York NY 10013-4006 Office Phone: 212-788-3437. Business E-Mail: pandolff@nychhc.org.

PANFILE, PATRICIA MCCLOSKEY, psychologist; b. Nanticoke, Pa., May 27, 1952; d. Sylvester John and Albina Patricia (Gorka) McC.; m. Thomas Patrick Panfile, Nov. 25, 1976; children: Joshua McCloskey, Rebecca McCloskey. BA, King's Coll., Wilkes-Barre, Pa., 1974; MS, Pa. State U., 1976. Cert. sch. psychologist, Pa.; lic. psychologist, Pa. Sch. psychologist Berks County Ind. Unit, Reading, Pa., 1976-80; psychologist in pvt. practice Shillington, Pa., 1981-85, Allentown, Pa., 1985—94; psychologist Carbon-Lehigh I.U., 1994—. Psychologist Parkland Sch. Dist., Orefield, Pa., 1989-94, Wt. Mgmt. Ctr., Allentown, Pa., 1989-90, Cedar Park Psychology Assoc., Allentown, Pa., 1988-89, Child Guidance Ctr., Allentown, 1987-89. Contbr. articles to profl. convs. Mem. spl. edn. adv. com. Parkland Sch. Dist., 1989-93; adv. bd. Lehigh Valley shpt. Children with Attention Deficit Disorders), Allentown, 1989; v.p. Oakland Park Homeowners Assn., 1991-92. Mem. Lehigh Valley Psychol. Assn. (v.p. 1990-91, newsletter editor 1990-92, treas. 1994—), Berks Area Psychol. Soc. (pres. 1983-84), Psi Chi, Delta Epsilon Sigma, St. Thomas Aquinas Soc. Roman Catholic. Home: 12 Bastian Ln Allentown PA 18104-9404 Office: 1251 S Cedar Crest Blvd Allentown PA 18103-6205

PANG, JOANNA See ATKINS, JOANNA PANG

PANICH, DANUTA BEMBENISTA, lawyer; b. East Chicago, Ind., Apr. 9, 1954; d. Fred and Ann Stephanie (Grabowski) B.; m. Nikola Panich, July 30, 1977; children: Jennifer Anne, Michael Alexei. AB, Ind. U., 1975, JD, 1978. Bar: Ill. 1978, U.S. Dist. Ct. (no. dist.) Ill. 1978, U.S. Dist. Ct. (ctrl. dist.) Ill. 1987, U.S. Ct. Appeals (7th cir.) 1987, U.S. Dist. Ct. (no. dist.) Ind. 2001, U.S. Dist. Ct. (ea. dist.) Mich. 2003, U.S. Ct. Appeals (6th cir.) 2003, U.S. Dist. Ct. (so. dist.) Ill., 2004. Assoc. Mayer Brown & Platt, Chgo., 1978-86, ptnr., 1986—2001, Mayer Brown Rowe & Maw, LLP, Chgo., 2002—. Bd. dirs. Munster (Ind.) Med. Rsch. Found., 1990—, Pub. Interest Law Initiative, 2003—. Mem. ABA, Fed. Bar Assn., Ill. Bar Assn. Republican. Roman Catholic. Office: Mayer Brown Rowe & Maw LLP 71 S Wacker Dr Chicago IL 60606 Office Phone: 312-701-7198. Business E-Mail: dpanich@mayerbrownrowe.com.

PANKAU, CAROLE, state senator; b. Aug. 13, 1947; m. Anthony John Pankau Jr.; 4 children. BS, U. Ill., 1981. Mem. Ill. House of Rep., 1993—2004, Ill. Senate from 23th dist., 2004—. Mem. DuPage County (Ill.) Bd., 1984-92; committeeman Bloomingdale Twp. Rep. Precinct 70; mem. Keeneyville (Ill.) Sch. Dist. 20; vice chair Bloomingdale Twp. Rep. Orgn. also: One Tiffany Pointe Bloomingdale IL 60108 Office: 105-K State House Springfield IL 62706 E-mail: carole@pankau.org.

PANKEN, SHIRLEY, psychologist; b. N.Y.C, Oct. 11, 1922; d. Harry and Anna; m. Irving Panken, 1946; 1 child, Theodore. MA, NYU, 1947, PhD, 1953. Lic. psychol. assn. N.Y. State. Intern psychologist Bellevue Psychiat. Hosp., N.Y.C, 1946—47; staff psychologist Kings County Psychiat. Hosp., Brooklyn, 1947—53; psychotherapist Bleuer Psychotherapy, Queens, 1953—55; psychoanalyst Pvt. Practice, N.Y.C, 1947—. Editor: Psychoanalytic Review; author: Psychoanalytic Theory and Therapy of Masochism, 1973, The Joy of Suffering, 1983, Virginia Woolf and the Lust of Creation: A Psychoanalytic Exploration, 1987; contbr. articles. Mem.: Nat. Psychol. Assn. Psychoanalysis. Avocations: reading, writing. Home and Office: 505 La Guardia Pl Apt 9A New York NY 10012

PANNKE-SMITH, PEGGY, insurance company executive; b. Chgo., Oct. 26; d. Victor E. and Leona (O'Leary) Stich; m. Craig D. Smith, July 18, 1998; children from previous marriage: Thomas Scott, David Savonne, Heidi Mireille, Peter. V.p. long term care ins. Sales & Seminars, Des Plaines, 1986-90; pres., founder Nat. Consumer Oriented Agy., Des Plaines, 1990—. Cons. on long-term care ins. The Travelers, Tchrs. Inc. & Annuity Assocs., others; spkr. Exec. Enterprises, NYC, 1988—93. Columnist Sr. News, Vital Times, Daily Herald, Sr. Connection, Sr. Marketplace News, Prime Time for Seniors, Pioneer Press, Boulder Daily Camera, Longmont Times-Call, Aurora Sun, Mature Times Lifestyles, 50 Plus Marketplace. Sponsor Ill. Alliance for Aging, Chgo., 1990—, Ill. Assn. Homes for Aging, 1990-91; bd. govs. St. Matthew Luth. Home, Park Ridge, Ill., 1993-95. Recipient Spkrs. awards Health Ins. Assn. Am., Washington, 1990, Ret. Officers Assn., Glenview, Ill., 1991, 93, Nat. Assn. Sr. Living Industries, Denver, 1992, Exec. Enterprises, NYC, 1993, Gov.'s Conf. on Aging, Chgo., 1996, Golden Harvest Long Term Care award Ret. Officers Assn., 2001, Nat. awards UNUM, 2001, AIG 2002, Conseco, 2000, Allianz, 2002, Mut. of Omaha, 2003, Presidents Club, Lincoln Benefit. Mem.: Internat. Soc. for Retirement Planning, Am. Soc. on Aging, Mature Am., Nat. Coun. on Aging (ad hoc com.), Ctr. for Applied Gerontology, Nat. Assn. Long Term Care Profl., Nat. Assn. Sr. Living Industries, Friends of the Colo. Trail, Colo. Mountain Club, Boulder C. of C., Park Ridge C. of C., Kiwanis (bd. dir. Park Ridge 1992—98, pres. 1996—97, Boulder pres. 2006—), Am. Mensa (program dir. in Ill. 1983—85, Colo. chpt. 1999—, pres. Boulder chpt. 2003—). Avocations: showshoeing, travel, sketching wildflowers, hiking, trekking the Colorado Trail. Office: Nat Consumer Oriented Agy 2200 E Devon Ave Ste 303 Des Plaines IL 60018-4505 also: Cherry Creek 300 S Jackson St Denver CO 80209-3176 also: 4450 Arapahoe Ave Boulder CO 80303-9123 also: 250 Parkway Dr 150 Lincolnshire IL 60069 also: 1900 E Golf Rd 950 Schaumburg IL 60173 Office Phone: 800-554-1996. Business E-Mail: NCOAmmp@sbcglobal.net. E-mail: MyBestLTC@sbcglobal.net.

PANTENBURG, MICHEL, health facility administrator, educator, holistic health coordinator; b. Denver, Oct. 6, 1926; d. Arthur Robert and Alice (McKenna) P. Diploma, Providence Nursing Sch., Kansas City, Kans., 1951; BS in Nursing Edn., St. Mary Coll., Leavenworth, Kans., 1958; M. in Nursing, Cath. U. Am., 1960. Joined Sisters of Charity, Roman Catholic Ch., 1945; lic. amateur radio operator. Dir. nursing Providence Hosp., Kansas City, Kans., 1958-62; nursing coordinator Sisters of Charity, Leavenworth, 1962-67; hosp. adminstr. St. Mary Hosp., Grand Junction, Colo., 1967-73, St. Vincent Hosp., Billings, Mont., 1973-84; dir. focus on leadership program Gonzaga U., Spokane, Wash., 1985-92; chaplain pastoral care dept. St. Marys Hosp. and Med. Ctr., Grand Junction, Colo., 1994-99, integrative medicine, 1999—. Dir. Norwest Bank, Billings Co-author, editor: Management of Nursing (CHA award 1969), 1967 Bd. dirs. De Paul Hosp., Cheyenne, Wyo., 1980-85, Ronald McDonald House, Billings, 1982-85, St. Joseph Hosp., Denver, 1994-97. Named Woman of Yr., Bus. and Profl. Women, Billings, 1979 Mem. Cath. Hosp. Assn. (bd. dirs., sec.), Am. Hosp. Assn. (regional del. 1975-80), Am. Coll. Hosp. Adminstrn., Mont. Hosp. Assn. (pres.), Billings C. of C. (v.p. 1977-78). Avocations: hiking, skiing. Office: Pastoral Care Dept St Marys Hosp & Med Ctr Grand Junction CO 81502

PANTZER, MAIREE D., music educator, director; b. Selma, Ala., Jan. 20, 1978; d. Fredrick S. and Sharon Austin Carr; m. David Pantzer, June 18, 2005. MusB in Vocal Performance, Wheaton Coll. Conservatory, Ill., 2000. Music tchr. Chgo. Mennonite Learning Ctr., 2000—04; asst. artistic dir. Children's Chorus Md., Towson, 2004—06, artistic dir., 2006—. Worship pastor Hyde Pk. Vineyard Ch., Chgo., 2002—04; mem. Handel Choir, Balt., 2004—06. Mem.: Am. Choral Dirs. Assn., Orgn. Am. Kodaly Educators. Conservative. Presbyterian. Avocation: running. Office: Childrens Chorus Md 100 East Pennsylvania Ave Suite 202 Towson MD 21286 Office Fax: 410-494-4673. Personal E-mail: maireedee@gmail.com. Business E-Mail: mpantzer@ccmsings.org.

PANZER, MARY CAROLINE, historian, museum curator; b. Flint, Mich., May 29, 1955; d. Milton and Caroline Alice (Weis) P. BA, Yale U.; MA, Columbia U., 1980; PhD, Boston U., 1990. Asst. prof. U. Kans., Lawrence, 1989-91; curator photographs Spencer Mus. Art, Lawrence, 1989-91; asst. dir. SMART Mus. Art U. Chgo., 1991; curator photographs Nat. Portrait Gallery Smithsonian Instn., Washington, 1992-2000; ind. historian N.Y.C., 2000—; adj. faculty NYU, 2002—, Hunter Coll., CUNY, 2003. Author: Philadelphia Naturalistic Photography, 1982, Rudolf Eickemeyer, Jr. and the Art of the Camera, 1986, Mathew Brady and the Image of History, 1997, Halsman: A Retrospective, 1998, Brady 55, 2001, Hine 55, 2002 Separate, But Equal, 2002, Nickolas Muray and Miguel Corarrubias, 2004, Things as They Are: Photojournalism in Context Since 1955, 2005 (winner Infinity award, 2006); contbg. editor Am. Photo, 2002. Mem. Am. Studies Assn., Coll. Art Assn., Oracle, Mid-Atlantic Radical Historians Orgn., Orgn. Am. Historians.

PAOLONI, VIRGINIA ANN, insurance company executive; b. Scranton, Pa., July 26, 1961; d. Edmund James and Virginia (Borick) P. BS in Mktg., King's Coll., 1983; MBA in Mktg., U. Scranton, 1995. CPCU 2004. Underwriter Reliance Ins., Phila., 1983-85; account exec. The Walsh Co., Phila., 1984-87; pres. Paoloni Ins. Agy., Olyphant, Pa., 1987—. Adv. bd. Everett Cash Mut. Ins. co.; mem. pres. coun. King's Coll., mentor. Participant Leadership Lackawanna, Scranton, 1991—; bd. dirs. fin. planning Holy Name of Jesus Ch., Scranton, 1990-94; mem. allocation steering com. United Way, 1992-93; bd. dirs., chair corp. sponsorship Am. Heart Assn.; mem. pub. rels. com. Habitat for Humanity, 1993—. Recipient 1st Agent of Yr. award Utica 1st Ins. Co., 1997. Mem. Greater Scranton Ins. Assn. (bd. dirs., chair edn. com. 1989—, 1st v.p.), Jr. League (chair strategic planning). Republican. Roman Catholic. Avocations: running, gourmet cooking. Office: Paoloni Ins Agy 766 N Valley Ave Olyphant PA 18447-1716 Home: 766 N Valley Ave Olyphant PA 18447-1716

PAOLUCCI, ANNE ATTURA, playwright, poet, literature educator, educational consultant; b. Rome; d. Joseph and Lucy (Guidoni) Attura; m. Henry Paolucci(dec.). BA, Barnard Coll; MA, Columbia U., PhD, 1963; D (hon.), Lehman Coll., CUNY, 1995. Mem. faculty English dept. Brearley Sch., N.Y.C., 1957—59; asst. prof. English and comparative lit. CCNY, 1959—69; univ. rsch. prof. St. John's U., Jamaica, NY, 1969—97, acting head dept. English, 1973—74, chmn. dept. English, 1982—91, dir. doctor of arts degree program in English, 1982—97; ednl. cons.; editl. cons. Bagehot Coun. Fulbright lectr. in Am. drama U. Naples, Italy, 1965-67; spl. lectr. U. Urbino, summers 1965-67, U. Bari, 1967, univs. Bari, Bologna, Catania, Messina, Palermo, Milan, Pisa, 1965-67; disting. adj. vis. prof. Queens Coll., CUNY; bd. dir. World Centre for Shakespeare Studies, Globe project, London; spl. guest Yugoslavia Ministry of Culture, 1972; rep. U.S. at Internat. Poetry Festival, Yugoslavia, 1981; founder, exec. dir. Coun. on Nat. Lits., 1974—; mem. exec. com. Conf. Editors Learned Jour.-MLA, 1975—85; del. to Fgn. Lang. Jours., 1977—85; mem. adv. bd. Commn. on Tech. and Cultural Transformation, UNESCO, 1978—80; vis. fellow Humanities Rsch. Centre, Australian Nat. U., 1979; rep. U.S. woman playwright Inter-Am. Women Writers Congress, Ottawa, Ont., Can., 1978; organizer, chmn. profl. symposia, meetings; TV appearances; hostess Mag. in Focus, Channel 31, N.Y.C., 1971-73; mem. N.Am. Adv. Coun. Shakespeare Globe Theatre Ctr., 1981—; mem. Nat. Grad. Fellows Program Fellowship Bd., 1985—87; mem. Nat. Garibaldi Centennial Com., 1981; trustee Edn. Scholarship, Grants Com. of NIAF, 1990-94; guest spkr. with E. Albee Ohio No. State U., 1990; Apptd. by Pres. Reagan to Nat. Coun. on Humanities, 1986-1993; One of the 10 top Women in Bus. in Queens, 2003. Author (with H. Paolucci) books, including: Hegel On Tragedy, 1962, new edition, 2001, From Tension to Tonic: The Plays of Edward Albee, 1972, new edit., 2000, Pirandello's Theater: The Recovery of the Modern Stage for Dramatic Art, 1974, 2d edit. 2002, Henry Paolucci: Selected Writings on Literature and the Arts; Sci. and Astronomy; Law, Govt., and Pol. Sci., 1999, Dante's Gallery of Rogues, 2001, Do Me a Favor (and other short stories), 2001 (nominated for the Pulitzer Prize), Poems Written for Sbek's Mummies, Marie Menken, and Other Important Persons, Places, and Things, 1977, Eight Short Stories, 1977, Sepia Tones, 1985, 2nd edit., 1986, In Wolf's Clothing, 2004; plays include: Minions of the Race (Medieval and Renaissance Conf. of Western Mich. U. Drama award 1972), video version, 2002, Cipango!, 1985, pub. as book, 1985, 86, videotape excerpts, 1986, revision, 1990; performed NYC and Washington, 1987-88; The Actor in Search of His Mask, 1987, Italian translation and prodn., Genoa, 1987, The Short Season, Naples, 1967, Cubiculo, NY, 1973, German translation, Vienna, 1996, mini-prodn. of Minions of the Race, The Players, 1999, video prodn. 2002, In the Green Room (play), 1999, Three Short Plays, 1995; editor Dino Bigongiari: Background to the Divine Comedy and Readings; editor with introduction: Readings in the Divine Comedy, 2006; poems Riding the Mast Where It Swings, 1980, In the Green Room (orig. play), 1999; Gorbachev in Concert, 1991, Queensboro Bridge (and other Poems), 1995 (Pulitzer prize nominee 1995-96), Terminal Degrees, 1997; contbr. numerous articles, rev. to profl. jour.; editor, author intro. to: Dante's Influence on Am. Writers, 1977; gen. editor tape-cassette series China, 1977, 78; founder Coun. on Nat. Lit.; gen. editor series Rev. Nat. Lit., 1970-2000, CNL/Quar. World Report, 1974-76, semi-ann., 1977-84, ann., 1985-2000; full-length TV tape of play Cipango! and ednl. TV with original music by Henry Paolucci, 1990, grant Queens Pub. TV for 48 Min Videotape of award-winning play, Minions of the Race, 2003, About Thomas More, Thomas Cromwell, and Cardinal Thomas Wolsey, 2003-04; featured in PBS psl. Italian-Americans II: A Beautiful Song, 1998; translations of Selected Poems by Giacomo Leopardi (with Thomas Bergin), 2004 (Italian Ministry Fgn. Affairs prize 2005), The Woman in Dante's "Divine Comedy" and Spenser's "Faerie Quene", 2005; editor: Backgrounds of the "Divine Comedy", 2006. Pres. Reagan appointee Nat. Grad. Fellows Program Fellowship Bd., 1985—86, Nat. Coun. Humanities, 1986—, Ann. award FIERI, 1990; bd. dirs. Am. Soc. Italian Legions of Merit, chmn. cultural com., 1990—; bd. dirs. Italian Heritage and Culture City-wide com., 1986—; pres. Columbus: Countdown 1992 Fedn.; mem. Gov. Cuomo's Heritage Legacy Project for Schs., 1989—; trustee CUNY, 1996—, chairwoman bd. trustees, 1997—99; mem. adv. com. on edn. N.Y. State Senate, 1996—. Decorated cavaliere Italian Republic, commendatore Order of Merit (Italy); named one of 10

Outstanding Italian Ams. in Washington, awarded medal by Amb. Rinaldo Petrignani, 1986; recipient Notable Rating for Mags. in Focus series N.Y. Times, 1972, Woman of Yr. award Dr. Herman Henry Scholarship Found., 1973, Amita award, 1970, award Women's Press Club N.Y., 1974, Gold medal for Quincentenary Can. trustee NIAF, 1990, ann. awards Consortium of Italian-Am. Assns., 1991, Am.-Italian Hist. Assn., 1991, 1st Columbus award Cath. Charities, 1991, Leone di San Marco award Italian Heritage Coun. of Bronx and Westchester Counties, 1992, Children of Columbus award Order of Sons of Italy in Am., 1993, 1st Nat. Elena Cornaro award Order of Sons of Italy, 1993, Golden Lion award, 1997, Can.'s Gold medal Christopher Columbus Can. Commn., 1992, Ann. award Am. Italian Cultural Roundtable, 1997, Am. Italian Tchrs. Lifetime Achievement award, 1997, Italian-Am. Legislator's award, Albany, 1997, N.Y. State Italian-Am. Legis. Lifetime Achievement award, 1997, Columbus Citizens Fedn. Ann. award, 1997, Italian Welfare League award, 1998, Queens Coun. on Arts award, 1998, N.Y. State Conservative Party Bronx com. award, 1998, Woman of Distinction award Kingsborough C.C./CUNY, 1999, Woman of Distinction award N.Y. State Senate, 2000, prize Italian Ministry Fgn. Affairs, 2005; named one of "Ten Top Queens Women in Bus.", 2003; Columbia U. Woodbridge hon. fellow, 1961-62; Am. Coun. Learned Socs. grantee Internat. Pirandello Congress, Agrigento, Italy, 1978; Woodbridge fellow Dept. English and Comparitive Literature, Columbia U., 1961. Mem. Internat. Shakespeare Assn., Shakespeare Assn. Am., Renaissance Soc. Am., Internat. Comparative Lit. Assn., Am. Comparative Lit. Assn., MLA, Am. PEN, Hegel Soc. Am., Dante Soc. Am. (v.p. 1976-77), Am. Found. Italian Arts and Letters (founder, pres.), Pirandello Soc. (pres. 1978-85, 1990-2001), Am. Soc. Italian Legions of Merit (bd. dir. 1990-93). Achievements include pioneering work in multi-comparative literary studies.

PAPA, PHYLLIS MARYANN, performing company executive, dancer, choreographer, educator; b. Trenton, NJ, Jan. 30, 1950; d. Armando Carmen and Mary (Grace) Papa; m. Thomas E. de Ment Jr., Sept. 2, 1979. Student, Royal Ballet Ctr., 1955—62, Am. Ballet Ctr., NYC, 1962—65, Harkness House for Ballet Arts, 1965—68. Dancer Princeton (NJ) Ballet Co., 1963—68, Harkness Youth Co., NYC, 1965—68, Am. Ballet Theatre, NYC, 1968—70, Royal Danish Ballet, Copenhagen, 1970—72; founder, artistic dir. Mercer Ballet (formerly West Jersey Ballet Co.), Mooretown, NJ, 1972—, Ballet Concertante, Mooretown, 1975—; founder Am. Internat. Ballet, Inc., NYC, 1979—, choreographer, prin. dancer S.E. Asia tour, 1980. Artistic dir. Atlantic City Ballet, 1981; founding dir. Atlantic Contemporary Ballet Theatre; tchr. Royal Dance Ctr., Royal Ballet Ctr., Mercer County CC; cons. in field; faculty Richard Stockton Coll. of N.J. Artistic dir., ballet mistress, prin. dancer Stars of Am. Ballet, NYC, prin. dancer Atlanta Ballet Co, 1978, prin. dancer, ballet mistres Ballets Elan, 1980; choreographer over 25 ballets. Recipient Brazilian gold medal of honor, 1998; grantee, NJ State Coun. Arts and NEA, 1975—76, 1982. Office Phone: 609-804-1995. E-mail: ballerina@acbt.org.

PAPAI, BEVERLY DAFFERN, retired library director; b. Amarillo, Tex., Aug. 31, 1949; d. Clarence Wilbur and Dora Mae (Henderson) Daffern; m. Joseph Andrew Papai, Apr. 3, 1976. BS in Polit. Sci., West Tex. State U., Canyon, 1972; MSLS, Wayne State U., 1973. Head extension dept. and Oakland County Subregional Libr. The Farmington Cmty. Libr., Farmington Hills, Mich., 1973-79, coord. adult svcs., br. head, 1980-83, asst. dir., 1983-85, dir., 1985—2005; ret., 2005. Cons. U.S. Office of Edn., 1978, Battelle Meml. Inst., Columbus, Ohio, 1980; presenter in field; libr. cons. 2005-. Contbr. articles to profl. jours. Bd. dirs. Mich. Consortium, 1987-91; bd. dirs. Oakland Literacy Coun., 1998—, vice chair, 2000-01, chair, 2001—; trustee Libr. of Mich., 1989-92, vice chair, 1991, 97-98, chair, 1992; del. White House Conf. on Librs. and Info. Svcs., 1991; founder, treas., fiscal agt. METRO NET Libr. Consortium, 1993—; mem. edn. com. Child Abuse and Neglect Coun. of Oakland County, 1998-2000; mem. Commn. on Children, Youth and Families, 1996—, Multiracial Cmty. Coun., 1995—; chair Edn. and Tng. Com., 2000—04. Recipient Athena award Farmington/Farmington Hills C. of C. and Gen. Motors, 1994, Chairperson's Rainbow award, 2001, Spl. Recognition award Oakland County, 2004; Amarillo Pub. Libr. Friends Group fellow, 1972, Wayne State U. Inst. Gerontology fellow, 1972. Mem. ALA (officer), Mich. Libr. Assn. (chair specialized libr. svcs. roundtable 1975, chair conf. program 1982, chair pub. policy com. 1988-89, chair devel. com. 1994-95, chair ann. conf. and program coms. 1995-96, pres. 1996-97, Loleta D. Fyan award 1975, Libr. of Yr. award 2004), LWV of Mich., Farmington Exch. Club, Coun. on Resource Devel. Democrat. Roman Catholic. Home: 6805 Wing Lake Rd Bloomfield Hills MI 48301-2959 Personal E-mail: papaibev@farmlib.org.

PAPAIOANNOU, EVANGELIA-LILLY, psychologist, researcher; b. Thessaloniki, Greece, Mar. 22, 1963; came to U.S. 1984; d. Nicholas and Ekaterini (Goulias) P. Bus. studies cert. with high honors, Anatolia Coll., Thessaloniki, 1983; BA in Psychology magna cum laude, Smith Coll., 1986; postgrad., Am. U., 1989; PhD in Philos. Psychology, Georgetown U., 2003. Guest researcher NIH, Bethesda, Md., 1986—. Author articles in press and profl. jours. Active in Hellenic Soc. for the Health Scis., Bethesda, 1987—. Recipient: scholarships Smith Coll. and Anatolia Coll. Mem. APA, Jean Piaget Soc., Internat. Platform Assn., Washington Soc. for Jungian Psychology, Washington Soc. for Jungian Psychology, Washington Accueil, Alliance Francaise, Friends of Goethe Internat., Smith Coll. Alumnae Assn., Japan-Am. Soc. Washington, Anatolia Coll. Alumni Assn., Nat. Mus. Women in the Arts, Brazilian-Am. Cultural Inst., Smith Coll. First Group Scholar, Phi Beta Kappa, Psi Chi. Greek Orthodox. Avocations: modern and jazz dance, classical ballet, horseback riding, travel, fencing.

PAPALIA, DIANE ELLEN, humanities educator; b. Englewood, NJ, Apr. 26, 1947; d. Edward Peter and Madeline (Borrin) P.; 1 child, Anna Victoria Finlay. AB, Vassar Coll., 1968; MS, W.Va. U., 1970, PhD, 1971. Asst. prof. child and family studies U. Wis., Madison, 1971-75, assoc. prof., 1975-78, prof., 1978-87, coord. child and family studies, 1977-79. Adj. prof. psychology in pediatrics U. Pa. Sch. Medicine, 1987-89. Author (with Sally W. Olds and Ruth D. Feldman): A Child's World: Infancy Through Adolescence, 1975, Human Development, 1978, with Sally W. Olds and Ruth D. Feldman: 10th edit., 2006;; author: (with Harvey Sterns, Cameron J. Camp & Ruth D. Feldman) Adult Development and Aging, 1996, 3rd edit., 2006; author: (with Dana Gross and Ruth D. Feldman) Child Development: A Topical Approach, 2003; co-author: Psychology, 1985, 2d edit., 1988; contbr. articles to profl. jours. NSF fellow, 1971, Am. Coun. on Edn. fellow, 1979-80; U. Wis. grantee. Fellow: Gerontol. Soc.; mem.: APA, Nat. Coun. Family Rels., Soc. Rsch. in Child Devel., Am. Psychol. Soc., Author's Guild, Psi Chi. Home: Apt 6D 253 W 73d St New York NY 10023 Office Phone: 212-724-4244. Personal E-mail: depapalia@aol.com.

PAPALIAS, TAMARA AHRENS, electrical engineer, educator; b. St. Louis, July 2, 1971; d. Harvey Henry and Florence Irene Ahrens. BSEE, MSEE, Stanford U., Palo Alto, Calif., 1995, PhD in Elec. Engring., 2002. Prin. engr. applications Intersil Corp., Milpitas, Calif., 2005—. Prof. elec. engring. San Jose State U., Calif., 2001—06. Dog trainer Santa Cruz Animal Svcs., Calif., 2002—06. Grantee, Nat. Semiconductor, Agilent Technologies, San Jose State U., 2004—06. Mem.: IEEE (adv. student chpt. 2001—). Office: San Jose State University One Washington Square San Jose CA 95192-0084 Office Fax: 408-924-3925. E-mail: drpapalias@yahoo.com.

PAPANDREOU-SUPPAPPOLA, ANTONIA, electrical engineering educator; b. Famagusta, Cyprus, Oct. 9, 1966; came to U.S., 1985; d. Theodoros and Eleni Papandreou; m. Seth Bowen Suppappola, Aug. 14, 1993; 1 child, Saul. BS, U. R.I., 1989, MS, 1991, PhD, 1995. Rsch. ast. prof. U. R.I., Kingston, 1996-99; asst. prof. elec. engring. Ariz. State U., Tempe, 1999—. Contbr. articles to profl. jours. Grantee Naval Undersea Warfare Ctr., Newport, R.I., 1995, Office of Naval Rsch., Arlington, Va., 1996; Nat. Sci. Found., 2000. Mem. IEEE, IEEE Signal Processing Soc., Comm. Soc., Women in Engring. Soc. Greek Orthodox. Avocations: reading, travel. Office: Ariz State U Tempe AZ 85287

PAPARONE, PAMELA ANN, nurse practitioner; b. Jersey City, N.J., Apr. 16, 1953; d. Thomas Richard and Betty Ann (Richter) Devine; m. Philip William Paparone, Oct 2, 1976; children: Philip, Paige. BSN, Rutgers U., 1974; MSN, Seton Hall U., 1977. RN, N.J.; cert. nurse practitioner; med.-surg. clin. nurse specialist. RN Atlantic City Med. Ctr., 1974-75, surgical inservice nurse Pamona, N.J., 1975-76, clin. nurse specialist, 1978-80; instr. Russell Sage Coll., Troy, N.Y., 1977-78; nurse practitioner, clin. nurse specialist Philip Paparone, D.O., Absecon, 1978—. Lectr. Stockton State Coll., Pomona, 1978-80. Author: The Lyme Disease Coloring Book, 1989; editl. review bd. Jour. Spirochetal and Tick Borne Diseases, 1994-99; contbr. articles to profl. jours. Recipient Nurse Educator of the Year award Am. Assn. Office Nurses, 1989. Mem. Am. Acad. Nurse Practitioners, Sigma Theta Tau. Home: 800 N Harvard Ave Ventnor City NJ 08406-1124 Office: 72 W Jimmie Leeds Rd Absecon NJ 08205-9406

PAPAS, IRENE KALANDROS, English language educator, poet, writer; AA with highest honors, Balt. C.C.; BA magna cum laude, Goucher Coll., 1968; MA in English Lang. and Lit., U. Md., 1974, postgrad., 1980—. Lic. theology profl. Tchr./tutor various schs., Balt., 1965—; tchr. theology U. Md. Free Univ., College Park, 1979—; author/pub. Ledger Publs., Silver Spring, Md., 1982—; TV producer Arts and Humanities Prodns., Silver Spring, 1991—. Lectr. in English, philosophy, Montgomery Coll., Goucher Coll.; instr. English Composition, World Literature, U. Md., College Park, 1968—; adj. faculty various colls.; White House duty, 1997—. Author: Irene's Ledger Songs of Deliverance, 1982, Irene's Ledger Song at Sabbatyon, 1986, Small Meditations, Leaves for Healing, 1996; prodr./dir. tv. progs. Election judge, Montgomery County (Md.) Suprs. Bd. of Elections, 90's; tutor in literacy, 1989, 90. Recipient First Prize Arts and Culture Category Smithsonian Inst., 1991; honored 6th Annual Awards Ceremony Montgomery Community, 1991. Mem. AAUP, Internat. Platform Assn., Nat. Poetry Assn., Phi Beta Kappa. Democrat. Greek Orthodox. Avocations: art/iconography, calligraphy, music, needlepoint. Office: PO Box 10303 Silver Spring MD 20914-0303

PAPATHOMAS, GEORGIA NIKOLAKOPOULOU, technology executive; b. Kato Achaia, Greece, Sept. 11, 1950; d. Andreas and Corina (Fotopoulou) Nikolakopoulos; m. Thomas Vergil Papathomas, Aug. 15, 1976; children: Lia Natassa, Alexander Vergil. BS in Engring. Sci., Columbia U., 1973, MS in Engring. Sci., 1974, PhD in Engring. Sci., 1978; cert. in bus. devel., U. Pa., 1994; cert. in strategic mktg., Harvard U., 1995. Mem. tech. staff Bell Labs., Murray Hill, NJ, 1978-84, supr. Whippany, NJ, 1984-90, program mgr., 1990-93; dir. strategy AT&T, Morristown, NJ, 1993-96, dir. ops. Bedminster, NJ, 1996—2002; v.p. network solutions Lucent Tech., 1998—2002; v.p. info. tech. Pfizer, 2003—. Sloan Found. rsch. fellow, N.Y.C., 1974. Mem. ASCE, Soc. Women Engrs., Sigma Xi. Business E-Mail: georgia.papathomas@pfizer.com.

PAPAYANNOPOULOU, THALIA, hematologist, oncologist, educator; arrived in US, 1964; MD, U. Athens Sch. Medicine, Greece, 1961, DSci, 1965. Resident medicine, dept. clinical therapeutics & Hematology U. Athens, Athens, Greece, 1962—64; postdoctoral trainee cell biology & tissue culture, pathology dept. U. Wash., Seattle, 1965—67, NIH fellow, sr. fellow hematology div., 1968—73, asst. prof. medicine & hematology, 1974—78, assoc. prof. medicine & hematology, 1979—84, full prof. medicine & hematology, 1984—. Mem. Seattle Cancer Care Alliance. Recipient G. J. Stewart award honoring women in Biomedical Sciences, Temple U. Sch. Medicine, 2001. Fellow: Am. Acad. Arts & Sciences; mem.: Am. Soc. Heamatology (W. Dameshek prize 1990). Achievements include research in regulation of hemoglobin production, development of hematopoietic stem cells, and mechanisms of stem cell trafficking. Office: U Wash Hematology Div Box 357710 1959 NE Pacific St HSB K-136 Seattle WA 98195-7710

PAPE, PATRICIA ANN, social worker, consultant; b. Aurora, Ill., Aug. 2, 1940; d. Robert Frank and Helen Louise (Hanks) Grover; children: Scott Allen, Debra Lynn. BA in Sociology, Northwestern U., 1962; MSW, George Williams Coll., 1979. Cert. addictions counselor, Ill.; lic. clin. social worker, sch. social worker, Ill. Pvt. practice family counseling, 1979—; coord. community resources DuPage Probation Dept., Wheaton, Ill., 1977-80; dir. The Abbey Alcoholism Treatment Ctr., Winfield, Ill., 1980-81; prin. Pape & Assocs., Wheaton, 1982—; dir. alcoholism counselor tng. program Coll. of DuPage, Glen Ellyn, Ill., 1982-87. Chgo. affiliate Employee Assistance Program, 1982—; cons. Luth. Soc. Services Ill., 1979-82. Contbr. articles to profl. jours. Mem. alcohol drug task force Ill. Synod Luth. Ch. Am., Chgo., 1985—. Named Woman of Yr., Entrepreneur Women in Mgmt., Oak Brook, Ill, 1986, Social Worker of Yr. Fox Valley Dist., 1998. Mem. Assn. Labor-Mgmt. Adminstrs. Cons. Alcoholism (women's issues com. 1984—), Acad. Cert. Social Workers, Am. Assn. Marriage Family Therapists, Nat. Assn. Soc. Workers, Women in Mgmt. Home: 1330 Shagbark Ln Wheaton IL 60187 Office: Pape & Assocs 618 S West St Wheaton IL 60187-5038

PAPE, REBECCA HOGAN, lawyer; b. Chgo., Feb. 2, 1972; PLDV, U. So. Calif., 1992; JD, U. Mont., 1997. Bar: Mont. Bar Assn. 1997, US Dist. Ct., Dist. Mont. 2002. Law clk. Dist. Ct. Judge McKittrick, 1997—2000; assoc. Sedivy, White and White, P.C., 2000—. Mem.: Mont. Trial Lawyers Assn. (chair new lawyers com. 2002—), State Bar Mont. Office: Sedivy White and White PC 2090 Stadium Dr PO Box 1906 Bozeman MT 59715-1906 Office Phone: 406-586-4311.

PAPPALARDO, FAYE, academic administrator; b. Phila. d. Gregory and Helen (Gregory) P. BS, St. Mary's U., 1968; MS, Johns Hopkins U., 1978; MA, Columbia U., 1991, EdD, 1992. Dept. chair fgn. lang. Cath. Girls High Sch., Balt., 1970-72; dean of coll. Bay Coll. Md., Balt., 1972-76; dir. student life C.C. of Balt., 1978-83, dean student affairs, 1983-88, Carroll C.C., Westminster, Md., 1988-91, exec. v.p., 1991—. Cons. Sci. Rsch. Assn., N.Y.C., 1974-76. Bd. dirs. Multiple Sclerosis Soc., Westminster, 1991-93; mem. Md. Tomorrow, Westminster, 1989-90. Recipient fellowship Franciscan Community, Paris, 1974. Mem. AAUW, Am. Assn. Women in C.C., Am. Assn. Women in Higher Edn. (treas. 1991—, Outstanding Adminstr. award 1994), Md. Assn. Higher Edn. (treas. 1991—), Md. State Deans of Student Affairs (chairperson 1992-93), Johns Hopkins U. Alumni Assn., Columbia U. Alumni Assn. Roman Catholic. Avocation: reading. Office: Carroll CC 1601 Washington Rd Westminster MD 21157-6944

PAPPALARDO, ROSA GLORIA, secondary school educator; b. Bklyn., Mar. 10, 1932; d. Angelo Charles and Rose (Paternostro) Borgia; m. Leonard Thomas Pappalardo, Apr. 16, 1955; children: Marianne, Leonard, Charles, Roseanne. BS, NYU, 1952, MA, 1953; postgrad., Seton Hall U., 1980-81, Rutgers U., 1984. Cert. supr. of art K-12, N.J., N.Y. Art edn. tchr. Islip (N.Y.) Bd. Edn., 1953—54, Herricks (N.Y.) Bd. Edn., 1954-57, 61-62; tchr. spl. edn. Passaic Assn. for Mentally Retarded, Passaic, NJ, 1958—60; supr. art/home edn. Randolph (N.J.) Twp. Schs., 1962—95; adj. prof. Jersey City State Coll., 1971—98, N.J. State U., Trenton, 2002—03; prof. Jersey City State U., 2002—. Art cons.; editor GAINS Leadership Curriculum, Jersey City U.; presenter in field. Co-author art and math. curricula for Randolph Twp. Schs. K-12; contbr. chpt. to books Recipient numerous svc. awards, recognition awards, awards for art edn. and art adminstrn. Fellow: Art Educators N.J. (Disting., pres.); mem.: NABA (pres.), Art Adminstrs. N.J. (pres.), N.J. Art Educators, Arts Coun. of Morris Area (planning com. 2002, Chinese, U.S. and Croatia exhibits), Kiwanis, Delta Zeta (pres.), Phi Delta Kappa. Republican. Roman Catholic. Avocations: swimming, visual arts. Home: 312 Mountain Way Morris Plains NJ 07950-1910 Office: 73 Evans Ln Lake Placid NY 12946-1605

PAPPAS, ALCESTE THETIS, consulting company executive, educator; b. Dix Hills, N.Y., May 5, 1945; d. Costas Ernest and Thetis (Hero) P.; m. Sylvan V. Endich, Sept. 13, 1987. AB, U. Calif.-Berkeley, 1967, PhD, 1978; EdM, Harvard U., 1969. Cert. guidance counselor, Mass., secondary sch. tchr., Mass. Dir. student-young alumni affairs Calif. Alumni Assn., Berkeley, 1969-71; dir. residential programs U. Calif., Berkeley, 1971-73, dir. housing and childcare, 1973-79; sr. cons., mgr. Peat, Marwick, Mitchell & Co., N.Y.C., 1979-80, 80-82, sr. mgr., 1982-84; ptnr. in charge edn., other instns. Peat, Marwick, Main & Co., N.Y.C., 1984-93; pres., CEO Pappas Cons. Group, Inc., Greenwich, Conn., 1993—. Spkr. in field. Author: Reengineering Your Non-Profit Organization: A Guide to Strategic Transformation, 1996; contbr. articles to profl. jours., author monographs. Mem. Merola Opera Bd., San Francisco, 1978-80, Calif. Alumni Council, 1976-79; bd. overseers Regents Coll., 1986-89; bd. dirs., mem. fin. com. Hellenic Coll. and Holy Cross Sch. Theology, Brookline, Mass., 1983-87, Seabury Western Theol. Sem., Evanston, Ill., 1983-89; bd. dirs. N.Y. Chiropractic Coll., 1986-88, Com. on Econ. Devel., 1986-88, Greek Orthodox Archdiocese Council, N.Y.C., 1985-89; bd. dirs., vice chmn. St. Basil Acad., 1983-87; bd. dirs., mem. exec. com. YWCA, N.Y.C., 1985-90, Catalyst, 1988-90; chairperson capital campaign com. U. Calif., Berkeley, exec. v.p. exec. coun. Coll. Letters and Sci.; trustee Clark U., 1993-95, U. Calif. Found., 1993-99; bd. dirs. Nat. Coun. for Rsch. on Women, 1996-98; mem. adv. bd. Grad. Sch. Edn. U. Calif., Berkeley, 2005—. Named mem. Acad. Women Achievers, YWCA, N.Y.C., 1984; recipient award Nat. Mgmt. Assn., 1997. Mem. Mid. States Assn. Schs. and Colls. (bd. dirs., fin. com. 1984-89, planning com. 1988-89), Order of the Ky. Colonels, Mortar Bd., Pi Lambda Theta, Prytanean. Avocations: opera, gourmet cooking, travel, photography. Office: 68 Southfield Ave Stamford CT 06902-7237 Office Phone: 203-357-7058.

PAPPAS, EFFIE VAMIS, language educator, finance educator, writer, poet, artist; b. Cleve., Dec. 26, 1924; d. James Jacob and Helen Joy (Nicholson) Vamis; m. Leonard G. Pappas, Nov. 3, 1945; children: Karen Pappas Morabito, Leonard J., Ellen Pappas Daniels, David James. BBA, Western Res. U., 1948; MA in Edn., Case Western Res. U., 1964, postgrad., 1964—68; MA in English Lit., Cleve. State U., 1986; postgrad., Ind. U. Pa., 1979—86. Cert. elem. and secondary tchr. Ohio. Tchr. elem. schs., Ohio, 1963-70; office mgr. Cleve. State U., 1970-72, adminstr. pub. rels., 1972-73; med. adminstr. Brecksville (Ohio) VA Hosp., 1974-78; lectr. English, econs./bus. mgmt., math., comm., composition Cuyahoga CC, Cleve., 1978-92. Tchg. asst. Case Western Res. U., 1979—80; lectr. bus. comm. Cleve. State U., 1980; participant in sci. and cultural exch. dels. Am. Inst. Chemists, China, 1984, Russia, 89. Feature writer: The Voice, 1970—78, editor, writer: Cleve. State U. newsletter and mag., 1970—73. Cub scout leader Boy Scouts Am., Brecksville, 1960; mem. local coun. PTA, 1965—70; sec. St. Paul's Coun., 1990—91; mem. membership com. St. Paul Ladies Philoptohos, 1990—; active Women's Equity Action League, 1995—2003; mem. Greater Cleve. Learning Project; Sunday sch. tchr., mem. choir Brecksville United Ch. of Christ, 1975—76, mem. bd. missions, 1966—67, mem. membership com., 1993; mem. planning com. edn. Case Western Res. U.; mem. 75th Anniversary steering com. Cleve. Coll. Recipient Editor's Choice award for outstanding achievement in poetry, Nat. Libr. Poetry, 1995, 2000; grantee, Cuyahoga CC, 1982. Mem.: AARP, AAUW (del. meetings, legis. chair 1993—94, co-chair Cleve. br. 1994, 1996—97, legis. chair 1997—98), NAFE, NAE (life named to Nat. Women's Hall Fame), Ohio Edn. Assn. (rep. assembly Columbus 1994, 1999—2001, 2002—03), N.E. Ohio Edn. Assn. (licentiate), Nat. Mus. Women in Arts (hon. roll. mem.). Avocations: travel, art, legal studies, theater, correspondence with national and international friends. Home: 8681 Brecksville Rd Brecksville OH 44141-1912

PAPPAS, EVA, psychologist, psychoanalyst; BA, Pace U., 1962; MA, NYU, 1965, PhD, 1973. Lic. psychologist and psychotherapist, N.Y. Tchr. pub. schs., N.Y.C., 1963-65; counselor P.A.L. Project, N.Y.C., 1965-66; instr. psychology dept. edn. Adelphi U., N.Y.C., 1966-69; tri-lingual psychology intern, 1973—74; sr. staff psychologist Goldwater Meml. Hosp., N.Y.C., 1974—76; fellow Postgrad. Ctr. for Mental Health, N.Y.C., 1976-78, assoc. staff, 1976-80; pvt. practice clin. psychology N.Y.C., 1976—; staff Postgrad. Ctr. for Mental Health, N.Y.C., 1980-83, co-teaching staff, 1982-83, assoc. supervisory staff, 1983-85, psychologist, psychoanalyst, supr. in pvt. practice, 1976—. Cons. Adults Sexually Abused as Children, 1989-93. Author: The Other Son, 2006. Mem. adv. coun. Queens Coll. Ctr. Byzantine and Modern Greek Studies, 1984-88; bd. dirs. Elpides Women's Outreach Program, 1993-97; bd. dirs. Daytop Family Assn., 2003—. Mem. Am. Psychol. Assn., Nat. Registry Health Service Providers in Psychology, N.Y. Soc. Clin. Psychologists (minority groups relations com. 1980-81, employment com. 1981-82), Greek-Am. Behavioral Scis. Inst. (exec. bd., treas. 1983-85). Office: 81 Irving Place Suite 1-B New York NY 10003

PAPPAS, MARGENE, retired music educator; d. Eugene Wallace and Marietta Joan Kirkwood; m. Peter Michael Pappas, Dec. 30, 1973. BS, U. Ill., Champaign-Urbana, 1969, MS, 1973. Tchr. Oswego Dist. 308, Ill., 1969—2006; band dir. Oswego Cmty. Band, 1994—2006; ret., 2006. Guest conductor Ill. All-State Band, 2001. Contbr. articles to NBA Jour. Named to Hall of Fame, Phi Beta Mu, Ill. Chpt., 2003; recipient Studs Terkel Humanitarian award, Village of Oswego, 2002, Sudler Legion of Honor, John Philip Sousa Found., 2003, John P. Paynter Lifetime Achievement award, Quinlan and Fabish Music Co., 2006. Mem.: Bands of Am. (adv. bd. 2001—), Ill. Music Edn. Assn., Am. Sch. Band Dirs. Assn., Nat. Band Assn. (bd. dirs. 2000—06). Achievements include directing the HS Wind Symphony performance at 2004 IMEA All-State; directing Oswego HS Marching Band in the 2005 Tournament of Roses; Margene Pappas Day named in her honor Village of Oswego, May 28, 2006. Avocations: travel, reading, music, hiking, cross stitch. Home: 2469 Lakeside Dr Aurora IL 60504 Office Phone: 630-636-2050. E-mail: tntohsband@aol.com.

PAPPAS, PAMELA A., mathematics educator; BS of Math., Ramapo Coll. of N.J., Mahwah, 1979—83. Sr. software quality engr. Plessey Electronics, Wayne, NJ, 1983—89; v.p. Datatistics Pub. Co., Hawthorne, 1989—93; treas. N. Haledon Nursery Sch., 1994—96; care taker Hawthorne & Wyckoff, 1994—96; math. tchr. Ramapo HS, Franklin Lakes, 1996—. Youth group asst. leader St. Nicholas Greek Orthodox Ch., Wyckoff, 2003—05. Office: Ramapo HS 331 George Street Ave Franklin Lakes NJ 07417 Office Phone: 201-891-1500.

PAPPAS, SANDRA LEE, state senator; b. Hibbing, Minn., June 15, 1949; m. Neal Gosman, 1976; 3 children. BA, Met. State U., 1986; MPA, Harvard U., 1994. Mem. Minn. Ho. of Reps., St. Paul, 1984-90, Minn. Senate, St. Paul, 1990—. Part-time coll. instr. Mem. Dem. Farmer Labor Party. Home: 182 Prospect Blvd Saint Paul MN 55107-2136 Office: Minn State Senate 120 State Capitol 75 Martin Luther King Jr Blvd Saint Paul MN 55155-1601 Office Phone: 651-296-1802.

PAPPAS, SHIRLEY ANN, sales executive; b. Omaha, Nebr., Aug. 18, 1929; d. Ivan Carol Bolen and Irma Elizabeth Sierk; m. George G. Pappas, Feb. 5, 1950; children: Timothy, Kimberley, Tammy. B, U. Nebr., 1950. Sales San Francisco State Coll., 1950—52; baker Roberts Cake Shop, San Francisco, 1952—56; owner Jerry's Donut Shop, San Francisco, 1956—65, Pappas and Son Smokeshop Broadway, San Francisco, 1957—90; sales checker Safeway Market, Daly City, Calif., 1979—92; owner vacation rentals Lavender Ladie Vac Rentals, Daly City, 1995—. Mem. bldg. com. Broadmoor Presbyn., Daly City, 1954—56; den mother Boy Scouts, 1956—58; asst. leader Girl Scouts, 1970—73. Mem.: USA Children's Charities, Cara Charities. Democrat. Protestant. Home: 51 Montgomery Ct Port Ludlow WA 98365 Address: 121 Village Lane Daly City CA 94015

PAPPAS, VIRGINIA M., medical association administrator; m. Bill Pappas; 1 child. BA in Mgmt., George Mason Univ. Various leadership positions to dep. exec. dir. Soc. Nuclear Medicine, Reston, Va., 1978—2002, exec. dir., 2002—. Office: Soc Nuclear Medicine 1850 Samuel Morse Dr Reston VA 20190-5316 Office Phone: 703-708-9000.*

PAPPAS PARKS, KATHERINE LOUIS, artist; b. Detroit, June 1, 1942; d. Louis Epaminonda and Effie (Amolhitou) Pappas; m. William Lee Parks, Oct. 12, 1969; 1 child, Leah Yvonne. BFA, Wayne State U., 1965, cert., 1967, MA, 1972. Cert. secondary tchr., Mich., Wis. Art tchr. Willistead Art Sch., Windsor, Can., 1966-67, Bloomfield Hills (Mich.) Pub. Schs., 1967-69; art instr. Gertrude Herbert Art Inst., Augusta, Ga., 1969-70; art tchr. Solomon

Schector Elem. Sch., Skokie, Ill., 1979-80; art instr. Mayer Kaplan Jewish Community Ctr., Skokie, 1978-81, Evanston (Ill.) Art Ctr., 1990. Presenter art workshop Evanston Twp. H.S., 1988-90; adj. faculty Oakton C.C., Des Plaines, 1980—, Truman Coll., Chgo., 1989-90, 93, 94; curator, exhibitor Suburban Fine Arts Ctr., Highland Park, 1992; curator Figure This, No Exit Gallery, Chgo., 1995. One-woman shows include Kemper Group Gallery, Long Grove, Ill., 1980, Oakton C.C.-Koenline Gallery, 1990, Atrium Gallery, Chgo., 1991, Space 900, Chgo., 1992, Truman Coll., Chgo., 1993, Glen & Viola Walters Cultural Ctr., Hillsboro, Oreg., 2004, IFC Cultural Art Ctr., Portland, 2005; group exhbns. include Palais de Congres, Paris, 1976, Tex. Tech U., 1977, Northwestern U., Evanston, Ill., 1979, 82, 85, West Hubbard Gallery, Chgo., 1980, ARC Gallery, Chgo., 1981, 82, 83, 84, 94, Artemesin Gallery, Chgo., 1984, 87, 89, Chgo. Cultural Ctr., 1984, Name Gallery, Chgo., 1985, 88, Contemporary Art Workshop, Chgo., 1985, Ill. State Mus., Springfield, 1985, Beacon St. Gallery, Chgo., 1987, Paper Press Gallery, Chgo., 1988, Zypher Gallery, Louisville, 1990, Cortesy Gallery, Highland Park, Ill., 1992, 94, Oakton C.C. Art Faculty Visual Arts Ctr., Des Plaines, Ill, 1995, Art Inst. Portland Gallery, 2004, numerous others. Counselor Vista-Home Peace Corp., Chgo., 1974-75. Grantee Ill. Arts Coun. of Chgo., 1981; recipient Purchase award Truman Coll., Ill. Percent for the Arts, 1988, Purchase award Kemper Group, 1979. Mem. NEA, Coalition Artists of Chgo., Space 900 (exhibitor), Artists Residence Chgo. (curator raw space libr. 1981, dir. exhbns. Navy pier, exhibitor). Greek Orthodox. Avocations: tai chi, gardening, cross country skiing, travel. Home: 1626 Washington St Evanston IL 60202-1630 Office: Oakton CC 1600 E Golf Rd Des Plaines IL 60016-1234 Office Phone: 503-690-4505. E-mail: illana.schoinas@is-fine-art.com.

PAPPAS-SPEAIRS, NINA, financial planner, educator; d. Steve E. and Martha (Hicks) Kalfas; m. Harry J. Pappas, 1951 (div.); children: John J., Nicholas S., Vivian E. Pappas Unger, Mark A., Carol A. Pappas Siegel; m. Mitchell F. Speairs, 1992 (dec. 2001). BS, U. Cin., 1950; MA, Northwestern U., 1957; PhD, U. Ill., 1978. Faculty St. Mary's H.S., Chgo., Sch. Dist. 102, LaGrange, Ill., U. Ill., Chgo., 1969-79, U. Tex., Arlington, 1979-82, Tex. Wesleyan Coll., Ft. Worth, 1982-83; realtor Merrill Lynch Realty, Ft. Worth, 1983-84; fin. planner Cigna Corp., Irving, Tex., 1984-90; pvt. practice fin. planning and investments, Ft. Worth, 1990—. Organizer, condr. 1st U.S. Olympic Acad., Chgo., 1977; collaborator Internat. Olympic Acad., Olympia, Greece, 1977, guest lectr., 77, 78; chief of mission to Greece U.S. Olympic Com., 1977; guest lectr. Nat. Olympic Acad. Republic of China, 1982. Author: History and Development of the International Olympic Academy: 1927-1977, 1978; editor: Perspectives of the Olympic Games, 1979; also articles. Vice chair edn. coun. U.S. Olympic Com., 1977—85; sch. bd. Dist. 107, LaGrange, Ill., 1971—74. Recipient Silver Medal Internat. Olympic Acad., Olympia, Greece, 1981. Mem. Lecture Found., Symphony League, Opera Guild (pres. 1982-83), Round Table, Ft. Worth Woman's Club, Women's Wednesday Club (pres. 2003-04), River Crest Country Club, Ft. Worth Boat Club, Ridglea Rejebian Club, Carousel Club. Republican. Greek Orthodox. Avocations: golf, reading, sailing, dance. Home: 7705 Lake Highlands Dr Fort Worth TX 76179-2809

PAPPROTH, JODI RENEE, theater educator; b. Belleville, Ill., Mar. 15, 1971; d. Marcia Janet Rhodes and Robert Eugene Papproth. BFA in Theatre Edn., Drake U., Des Moines, 1993; MA in Theatre Directing, Roosevelt U., Chgo., 2005. Cert. secondary tchr. theatre Colo., 1993. Theatre tchr. Cheyenne Mountain H.S., Colorado Springs, Colo., 1994—. Dir.: (play) Tri Lakes Theatre Group. Mem.: Alliance for Colo. Theatre (pres. 2002—04, Educator of Yr. 2005), Ednl. Theatre Assn. (assoc.). Democrat-Npl. Avocations: hiking, reading, theater. Office: Cheyenne Mountain High School 1200 Cresta Rd Colorado Springs CO 80906 Office Phone: 719-475-6110. Office Fax: 719-475-6116. E-mail: papproth@cmsd.k12.co.us.

PAQET, SHAWNA LEE, museum director; b. Latham, NY, Mar. 26, 1955; BFA, SUNY, Oswego, 1976; MA in Art History Criticism, SUNY, Stony Brook, 1976—79. Edn. curator Mus. Tech., Rochester, NY, 1980—83; collections mgr. Fairbanks Mus., Fairbanks, Alaska, 1983—85; mus. educator Children's Mus., Chgo., 1985—88; asst. prof. sculpture Columbus U., Ga., 1988—97; curator Meriks Gallery, Va. Beach, 1997—. Adj. prof. Tidewater CC, Virginia Beach, 2001—. Art tchr. Beachside Cmty. Ctr., Virginia Beach, 1999—. Mem.: Nat. Coun. Edn. Ceramic Arts, Assn. Art Mus. Curators, Order of Omega, Phi Beta Kappa. Avocations: racquetball, sculpting, crossword puzzles, yoga. Office: Meriks Design 2100 Mediterranean Ave #29 Virginia Beach VA 23451-4153 Personal E-mail: shawnalee326@aol.com. Business E-Mail: paqets@meriksdesign.com.

PAQUIN, ANNA, actress; b. Winnipeg, MB Canada, July 24, 1982; d. Brian and Mary Paquin. Actor: (films) The Piano, 1993 (Academy Award best supporting actress, 1993, Golden Globe nomination best supporting actress, 1993), Jane Eyre, 1995, Fly Away Home, 1996, Amistad, 1997, A Walk on the Moon, 1988, Hurly-burly, 1998, Begin the Beguine, 1998, Sleepless Beauty, 1998, A Walk on the Moon, 1999, She's All That, 1999, X-Men, 2000, Almost Famous, 2000, Finding Forrester, 2000, Buffalo Soldiers, 2001, Darkness, 2002, 25th Hour, 2002, X2: X-Men United, 2003, Steamboy, 2004, The Squid and the Whale, 2005, X-Men: The Last Stand, 2006; (TV films) Member of the Wedding, 1997, Hercules (voice only), 1988, All the Rage, 1999, (voice) Joan of Arc, 2005,: (plays) After Ashley, 2005. Office: Double Happy Talent c/o Gail Cowan PO Box 9585 Wellington New Zealand also: William Morris Agy One William Morris Pl Beverly Hills CA 90212*

PARADIS-KENT, M. ROBIN, music educator; d. Gertrude and Clarence Paradis; m. R. David Kent, Sept. 21, 1985; 1 child, Rachel Kent. BS in English/Polit. Sci., U. Wis., Oshkosh, 1978—83; Post Baccalaureate Cert. in English 6-12, Cardinal Stritch U., Milw., Wis., 1984—85, MEd, 1984—86, Post Baccalaureate Cert. in Music Pre-K-12, 2002—04. Reading Specialist Wis., 1985. English instr. Lakeland Coll., Sheboygan, Wis., 1994—98, Tokyo, 1997—98; english tchr. Dominican HS, Whitefish Bay, Wis., 1989—97; elem. gen. music tchr. Brown Deer Schs., Wis., 2001—. Pvt. piano instr. Stone Ho. Piano Studio, Cedarburg, 1988—2003. Vol., survivor Am. Cancer Soc. - Relay for Life, Cedarburg, 2003—06. Independent. Avocations: travel, reading, music.

PARANTO, SHARON, educator, consultant; BS, No. State U., Aberdeen, SD, 1971; MS, Colo. State U., Ft. Collins, 1986; EdD, U. SD, Vermillion, 1997. Instr. Colo. State U., Fort Collins, 1986—88; prof., dept. coord. No. State U., Aberdeen, SD, 1989—. Mgr. data processing Jewett Drug Co., Aberdeen, SD, 1971—83. Campaign sightfirst ii zone coord. Lions Internat., 2006—; dist. chair campus Lions Dist. 5-SE, SD, 2004—; faculty advisor NSU Lions Club, Aberdeen, 2004—; past pres. Aberdeen Lions Club, 2000—05; past pres. and current sec. Zion Luth. Ch. Coun., 2002—; adv. mem. Noah's Pk. Presch., 2004—; mem., website dir. NSU Luth. Campus Ministries, 2005—; faculty senate pres. No. State U., 2005—06, faculty senate parliamentarian, 2006—. Recipient Lion of Yr., Aberdeen Lions Club, 2000—02, Pres.'s Appreciation award, 2002—03, Cmty. Leadership award, No. State U., 2004, Internat. President's Appreciation award, Lions Internat., 2005—06. Mem.: AAUW, Assn. Info. Tech. Profls., Internat. Assn. Computer Info. Sys., Nat. Assn. Coll. and Employers, Assn. Info. Tech. Profls. Avocations: travel, walking, hiking, reading. Office: Northern State University 1200 South Jay Street Aberdeen SD 57401 Office Phone: 605-626-7726.

PARATORE-ZARZANA, MARY GAY, artist, art educator, lecturer; b. Galveston, Tex., Jan. 10, 1940; d. Owen Albert and Cora Louise (Hunter) Garrigan; m. Philip George Paratore Jr., Aug. 12, 1961 (dec. Feb. 10, 1986); children: Philip G. III, Patrick Owen, Angela Gay, Amber Lynn Marie BA in Art, Sci., Edn., Sam Houston U., 1961; MEd in Art Edn., U. Houston, 1968; student, Art Students' League, 1985, 87, Nat. Acad. Design, 1987. Cert. all level art instr., Tex., Tex. State art cons. Med. illustrator U. Tex., Galveston, 1958, 60; elem. tchr. Stewart Elem., Hitchcock, Tex., 1961-64; art tchr. Ball H.S., Galveston, Tex., 1971-74; art instr. cont. edn. Alvin (Tex.) C.C., 1961-84; head art dept., 1974-75, art instr., 1990-92; sr. adult art instr. Coll. of the Mainland, Tex. City, Tex., 1985-93, art history instr., 1993; art tchr. Manvel Jr. H.S., Tex., 1993—2002; owner Paratore-Zarzana Studio and Gallery, Santa Fe, Galveston, Tex.; pvt. art instr. Hitchcock, Santa Fe, Tex. City, Tex. Demonstrator, lectr. Alvin, Santa Fe, Tex. City, Baytown, Brazosport, Watercolor Art Soc. Houston, Art Leagues, 1961-96; workshop instr. Carrizo Lodge, Ruidoso, N.Mex., 1993; insvc. art cons. Tex. City Ind. Sch. Dist., 1974. One woman exhibns. include Tex. City (Tex.) Assn., 1974, U. Tex., Alvin, 1974, Alvin (Tex.) Pub. Libr., 1978, Tex. Med. Branch, Galveston, 1992, South Shore Harbor, Harbor Club, 2006, Eclectic Home, Houston, 2006, Tremont House and Eibands, Galveston, Tex., 2006; group exhibns. include Nat. Soc. Artists (Best of Show), Art Soc. Houston (First Place), Brazosport Art League, 2005 (First Place), Tex. City Art Festival, 2006, (First Place), Alvin (Tex.) Art League (First Place), ByWater Gallery, Bangor, Maine, Rockport (Tex.) Art Ctr.; featured in Le Review Moderne, 1968; staff artist Cedar Rock Press, 1979-85; designer (cover) poetry book by David C. Yates, 1983. Mem. sch. bd. Our Lady of Lourdes Parochial Sch., Hitchcock, Tex., 1969-73; pres. Santa Fe Friends of the Libr., 1979-81; chmn. spiritual devel. Our Lady of Lourdes Altar and Rosary Soc., 1967; liaison Nat. Soc. Artist and Galveston (Tex.) County Parks and Beach; mem. bd. restoration Alta Loma Cath. Ch., 1988-96. Recipient Dick Blick award, Tex. Art Supply award, Grumbacher award. Mem. Nat. Soc. Artists (founder, Best of Show, pres. 1985-87, 1991-94), Tex. Watercolor Soc. (signature mem.), Art League of the Mainland, Galveston Art Leageu, Tex. Middle Sch. Assn., Assn. Tex. Profl. Educators, Alpha Chi Omega (Delta Kappa chpt.), Delta Kappa Gamma, Beta Sigma Phi (Laureate Eta Psi). Roman Catholic. Avocations: pottery, jewelry making, creative writing, photography, collecting antique glass. Home: 2731-646 N Santa Fe TX 77510 Office Phone: 409-316-1005.

PARCHMENT, ROBYN RENAE, mathematics educator; b. NYC, Aug. 30; d. George and Genevieve Consuela Walker, Norma Jean Walker (Stepmother); m. Ronald Anthony Parchment, Dec. 19, 1998; 1 child, Deborah Genevieve; 1 stepchild, Antonio Julian Small. BS, Pace U., NYC, 1983; MS, CUNY, NYC, 2002. Graphing calculator TI-83 CCNY, 2000, geometer's sketchpad CCNY; cert. math. tchr. NY. Software support rep. Dun & Bradstreet, NYC, 1983—84, programmer Locust Valley, NJ, 1983—84; math. tchr. NYC Dept. Edn. HS, NYC, 1987—; program office asst. Martin Luther King Jr. HS, NYC, 1988—96, grade advisor, 2002—03. Recipient Math Gold medal for excellence in math. for four yrs., Martin Luther King, Jr, HS, 1975—78. Mem.: Alpha Kappa Alpha. Baptist. Avocations: dance, reading, theater, music, travel. Personal E-mail: rparchm@nycboe.net.

PARCHMENT, YVONNE, nursing educator; b. Kingston, Jamaica, July 2, 1943; came to U.S., 1979; d. George Augustus Leslie and Evelyn Maude (Brown) Mitchell; m. Neville McDonald Parchment, Feb. 2, 1963; children: Suzanne Marie, April A. Parchment-Knight, Neville Wade, Everton Jerome. AA, AS, Miami (Fla.) Dade Cmty. Coll., 1982; BSN, U. Miami, 1984, MS in Nursing, 1989; postgrad., Fla. Internat. U., 1996—. RN, Fla. Tchr. elem. sch. Alpha Infant Sch., Kingston, 1974-79; nurse South Miami Hosp., 1979-95; clin. nurse specialist Mt. Sinai Med. Ctr., Miami, 1989-95; clin. asst. prof. Fla. Internat. U., Miami, 1995—. Contbr. articles to profl. jours. Bd. dirs. mental health com. Cmty. Health Ctr., Miami, 1996—. Capt. Army Nurse Corps., USAR, 1989—. Rsch. grantee Fla. League Nursing, 1996. Mem. AACN, Fla. Nurses Assn. (bd. dirs. dist. 5), Jamaica Nurses Assn. of Fla. (past v.p., v.p. 1997—, mem. edn. com., cultural diversity com.), Sigma Theta Tau (mem. by-laws com.). Episcopalian. Avocations: dance, reading, sewing. Office: Fla Internat U North Campus Miami FL 33181

PARDEE, TERESA TANSEY, history educator; b. Dayton, Ohio, Oct. 20, 1954; m. John Woodruff Pardee, May 17, 1980; children: John Woodruff, Christine Marie. BA, Montclair StateU., Upper Montclair, N.J., 1976. Cert. tchr. Nat. Bd. of Profl. Tchg. Standards, 2005. History tchr. Paramus Cath. H.S., NJ, 1979—86; estate adminstr. United Jersey Bank, Hackensack, NJ, 1986—87; tchr. Holy Name Sch., Racine, Wis., 1990—91; tchr. and computer coord. St. Louis King of France Sch., Metairie, La., 1992—99; computer instr. New Horizons Computer Inst., Charlotte, NC, 2000—01; history tchr. Charlotte Mecklenburg Sch. Dist., Charlotte, NC, 2001—. Fellow Yale Nat. Inst., New Haven, 2006—; coord. CMS AP Attack, Charlotte, NC, 2004—05. Named Outstanding Educator, Charlotte Arts and Sci. Coun., 2005; recipient Distinguised Tchg. award, Northwestern State U., 1997, Recognition for Tchg., Ho. of Reps. of La., 1996. Roman Catholic. Avocation: genealogy. Home: 12325 Woodside Falls Rd Pineville NC 28134 Office: East Mecklenburg High School 6800 Monroe Rd Charlotte NC 28212 Personal E-mail: ttpardee@hotmail.com.

PARDIECK, SHERRIE CHAN, education educator; b. Oak Park, Ill., Feb. 27, 1953; d. Oland J. and Yvonne H. (Jensen) Chan; m. David L. Pardieck, May 24, 1975; children: Aaron L., Christina L. AA in Behavioral Sci., Ill. Central Coll., 1973; BA in Elem. Edn., Eureka (Ill.) Coll., 1975; MA in Elem. Edn., Bradley U., Peoria, Ill., 1988, reading specialist endorsement, 1987; EdD, Ill. State U., 2000. Cert. elem. tchr., Ill. Tchr. early childhood edn. at-risk for acad. failure Dist. 323, Dunlap; instr. elem. edn. Bradley U., 1989—. Adv. bd. Bradley Univ. Inst. Gifted and Talented Youth; assoc. prof. tchr. edn. Bradley U. Bd. dirs. BUIGTY; trustee Dunlap Spl. Olympics. Mem. ASCD, NEA, Nat. Assn. for Edn. Young Children, Ill. Assn. for Supervision and Curriculum Devel., Heart of Ill. Assn. for Edn. Young Children, Phi Delta Kappa. Home: PO Box 152 Dunlap IL 61525-0152

PARDINGTON, MARY ELIZABETH, elementary school educator; d. John and Elizabeth Curell; m. David Charles Pardington, July 9, 1993; children: Catherine, Sarah, Veronica, Mary Kate. BS in Elem. Edn., Oakland U., Rochester, Mich., 1987, MA in Curriculum, Instrn., and Leadership, 1991. Continuing tchg. cert. Dept. Edn. Mich., 1991. Elem. tchr. Birmingham (Mich.) Pub. Schs., 1987—. Mem. accreditation team Mich. Accreditation Program, 1990—91; co-head tchr. Beverly Elem. Sch., Beverly Hills, Mich., 1995—, svc. squad leader, 1995—. V.p. Concerned Catholics Shelby Twp., Mich., 1993—, catechism tchr., 1995—; soprano soloist Assumption Grotto Choir, Detroit, 1992—, asst. choir dir., 1994—; dir., prodr. Coffee Ho. Fundraiser, Detroit, 1999—2002. Recipient Workplace Excellence award, Birmingham Pub. Schs., 2002, 2003, award, Friends of Different Learners, 2005; Paul Douglas Tchr. scholar, US Congress, 1986—87, Performance grantee, Birmingham Pub. Schs., 1988. Mem.: NSTA. Republican. Roman Catholic. Avocations: music, old movies, logic puzzles. Office: Beverly Elementary School Beverly Hills MI 48025

PARDUE, MARY-LOU, biology professor; b. Lexington, Ky., Sept. 15, 1933; d. Louis Arthur and Mary Allie (Marshall) P. BS, William and Mary Coll., 1955; MS, U. Tenn., 1959; PhD, Yale U., 1970; D.Sc. (hon.), Bard Coll., 1985. Postdoctoral fellow Inst. Animal Genetics, Edinburgh, Scotland, 1970—72; assoc. prof. biology MIT, Cambridge, 1972—80, prof., 1980—, Boris Magasanik prof. biology, 1995—. Summer course organizer Cold Spring Harbor Lab., NY, 1971—80; mem. rev. com. NIH, 1974—78, 1980—84, nat. adv. gen. med. scis. coun., 1984—86; sci. adv. com. Wistar Inst., Phila., 1976—2004; mem. health and environ. rsch. adv. com. U.S. Dept. Energy, 1987—94; bd. trustees Associated Univs., Inc., 1995—97; mem. Burroughs Wellcome Adv. Com. on Career Awards in Biomed. Scis., 1996—2000, now bd. dirs.; chair Inst. of Medicine Com. on Biol. Basis of Sex and Gender Differences, 1999—2001. Mem. editl. bd.: profl. jours.; contbr. articles to profl. jours. Mem. rev. com. Am. Cancer Soc., 1990-93, Howard Hughes Med. Inst. Adv. Bd., 1993-2000. Recipient Esther Langer award Langer Cancer Rsch. Found., 1977, Lucius Wilbur Cross medal Yale Grad. Sch., 1989; grantee NIH, NSF, Am. Cancer Soc. Fellow AAAS, NAS (chmn. genetics sect. 1991-94, coun. 1995-98), Am. Acad. Arts and Sci. (coun. mem. 1992-96); mem. NRC (bd. on biology 1989-95), Genetics Soc. Am. (pres. 1982-83), Am. Soc. Cell Biology (coun. 1977-80, pres. 1985-86), Phi Beta Kappa, Phi Kappa Phi, Sigma Xi. Office: MIT Dept Biology 68-670 77 Massachusetts Ave Dept 68-670 Cambridge MA 02139-4307 Office Phone: 617-253-6741. E-mail: mlpardue@mit.edu.

PARENT, ANNETTE RICHARDS, free lance writer, artist; b. Elizabeth, N.J., May 5, 1924; d. Edward Carrington Mayo and Elizabeth Veech (Coan) Richards; m. Hiram Lincoln Parent, Mar. 23, 1957; children: Laurence Edward, Anne Mayo Parent Fischer Pasqual. BA, Swarthmore Coll., 1946; postgrad., U. Ariz., Western N.Mex. U. Nat. lit. sec. Woman's Internat. League for Peace and Freedom, Phila., 1946-48; free lance writer various, 1948—. Contbr. poems to ann. anthologies Intermountain Friendly Rev., 1990, 91, 92; contbr. non-fiction articles to numerous publs.; painter, photographer, poet, book reviewer, presenter elderhostel commencement addresses, talks about Quakerism to coll. classes and Presbyn. youth groups; slide talks on Russia; editor: The Troglodyte at Carlsbad Caverns Nat. Park, 1966-80. Mem. search com. for Western N.Mex. U. mus. dir., 1987; co-founder Youth Coun. Against Conscription, Phila., 1946-48; organizer Westtown (Pa.) Sch. peace team, 1940-42; mem. Nat. Coun. Fellowship of Reconciliation, N.Y.C., 1941-46; former mem. safety com. Cralsbad Cacerns Nat. Park; charter mem., officer A Christian Ministry in the Nat. Parks, Carlsbad Caverns Nat. Park, N.Mex., 1970-80, centennial com., 1975; founder, leader of Peace Team, Westtown Sch., 1940-42. Winner N.C. Wyeth 1st in Art award Westtown Sch., 1942, Alumni Assn. 1st in Art award 1942; recipient awards in juried and non-juried art shows Carlsbad Area Art Assn., N.Mex., Grant County Art Guild, Black Range Artists Inc. Mem. AAUW, Nat. League Am. Pen Women (in dual categories of art and letters, v.p., sec., treas., winner non-fiction nat. contest 1955), Soc. Southwestern Authors, Grant County Art Guild, Black Range Artists Inc. (v.p. 1991), Nat. Audubon Soc. (publicity chmn. Southwestern N.Mex. coun. del. 1987-92). Mem. Religious Soc. of Friends. Avocations: hiking, sewing, piano, swimming, reading. Home and Office: PO Box 1319 Silver City NM 88062-1319

PARENT, JILL CARI-STEPANCHAK, elementary school educator; b. Mpls., Nov. 3, 1965; d. John and Alma Jane Stepanchak. BA in Elem. Edn., Coll. St. Catherine, St. Paul, Minn., 1989; MEd in Tchg. and Learning, St. Mary's U., Winona, Minn., 2005; student in Ednl. Adminstrn. and Leadership, U. St. Thomas, St. Paul, Minn., 2005—. Cert. tchr. mid. sch. Minn., 1996. Educator Mpls. (Minn.) Pub. Schs., 1989—, coord. mid. sch., 2004—. Coord. spl. programs Cmty. Edn., Mpls., 1989. Home: 4151 Jefferson Street Ne Columbia Heights MN 55421 Office: Minneapolis Public Schools 2131 12th Ave North Minneapolis MN 55411 Office Phone: 612-668-2800. Personal E-mail: jayce4151@yahoo.com.

PARENT, MARY, film company executive; Past agt. trainee ICM; dir. develop. to v.p. prodn. New Line Cinema, 1994—97; sr. v.p. prodn. Universal Pictures, Universal City, Calif., 1997—2000, exec. v.p. prodn., 2000—01, co-pres. prodn., 2001—03, vice chmn., worldwide prodn., 2003—05, prodr., 2006—. Exec. prodr.: (films) Set It Off, 1996, Trial and Error, 1997, Pleasantville, 1998; prodr.: You, Me and Dupree, 2006; prodn. mgr.: Dangerous Ground, 1997. Named one of 100 Most Powerful Women in Entertainment, Hollywood Reporter, 2004. Office: 100 Universal City Plaza Universal City CA 91608*

PARENT, MIRIAM STARK, psychology educator; b. Phila., June 26, 1950; BA in Psychology, King's Coll., 1971; MA in Counseling, Liberty U., 1985; MA in Clin. Psychology, Biola U., 1987, PhD in Clin. Psychology, 1990. Lic. clin. psychologist, Va., Ill. Registrar, asst. to dean Word of Life Bible Inst., Pottersville, N.Y., 1972-83; adminstr. asst. to dean Liberty U., Lynchburg, Va., 1983-85, assoc. prof. counseling Sch. Religion, 1989-93; therapist Friendly Hills Med. Group, La Habra, Calif., 1985-88; clin. intern univ. psychol. svcs. Kent (Ohio) STate U., 1988-89; assoc. prof. dept. pastoral counseling and psychology Trinity Evang. Div. Sch., Deerfield, Ill., 1993—. Pvt. practice clin. psychology, 1990—. Contbr. articles to profl. jours. Office: Trinity Evang Div Sch 2065 Half Day Rd Deerfield IL 60015-1241 Business E-Mail: mparent@tiu.edu.

PARENT, TANYA H., dance educator, massage therapist; b. Marrero, La., Feb. 4, 1974; d. Kenneth James and Cathie Lee Hill; m. William Harold Parent Jr., May 19, 1996; children: William Harold III, Ava Simone. BFA, U. So. Miss., Hattiesburg, 1996. Cert. Blue Cliff Sch. Massage Therapy. Dancer/performer Dick Feeney Prodns., Biloxi, Miss., 1996—98, Jim Robbins Prodns., Biloxi, 1997—98; owner danceXtreme, Gautier, Miss., 2001—. Prodn. mgr. Gautier Jr. Miss Scholarship Program, Miss., 2005—. Choreographer (jazz/modern dance) Nightmare, 2000 (Best Choreography, by Dance Mag.). Vol. Am. Heart Assn., Gautier, 2003—06. Mem.: Dance Teachers United (assoc.). Conservative. Roman Catholic. Office: danceXtreme PO Box 526 Gautier MS 39553 Office Phone: 228-522-6780. Office Fax: 228-522-1898.

PARENTE, LOUISE, social worker; b. Bklyn., Apr. 11, 1945; d. Frank and Lucy (Coppola) Russo; m. John Parente, Sr., Dec. 23, 1967; children: John Jr., Donald, Steven. B in Social Work summa cum laude, Kean U., Union, N.J., 1984; MSW, NYU, 1985, PhD, 1998. Cert. social worker N.Y., N.J., eating disorder specialist, bd. cert. diplomate. Pvt. practice, S.I., NY, 1989—; staff social worker Very Spl. Pl., Inc., S.I., 1985-86; staff social worker, psychotherapist Children's Cmty. Ctr., S.I. Mental Health Svc., 1986-88; clin. social worker, psychotherapist S.I. Hosp. Outpatient Psychiat. Clinic, 1988-95. Part-time lectr. NYU, N.Y.C., 1995—2000. Chmn. Boy Scouts Am. Mem.: NASW, Internat. Assn. Eating Disorder Profls., Am. Anorexia/Bulimia Assn., Acad. Eating Disorders, Acad. Cert. Social Workers, Soc. Clin. Social Work Psychotherapists (corr. sec.), Kappa Delta Phi, Phi Kappa Phi, Alpha Delta Mu. Office: 312 Bement Ave Staten Island NY 10310 Office Phone: 718-442-1180.

PARETSKY, SARA N., writer; b. Ames, Iowa, June 8, 1947; d. David Paretsky and Mary E. Edwards; m. S. Courtenay Wright, June 19, 1976; children: Kimball Courtenay, Timothy Charles, Philip William. BA, U. Kans., 1967; MBA, PhD, U. Chgo., 1977. Mgr. Urban Rsch Ctr., Chgo., 1971-74, CNA Ins. Co., Chgo., 1977-85; writer, 1985—. Author: (novels) Indemnity Only, 1982, Deadlock, 1984 (Friends of Am. Writers award 1985), Killing Orders, 1985, Bitter Medicine, 1987, Blood Shot, 1988 (Silver Dagger award Crime Writers Assn., 1988), Burn Marks, 1990, Guardian Angel, 1992, Tunnel Vision, 1994, Ghost Country, 1998, Hard Time: A V.I. Warshawski Novel, 1999, Total Recall, 2001, Blacklist, 2003 (Gold Dagger, Brit. Crime Writers Assn.), Fire Sale, 2005 (Publishers Weekly Bestseller hardcover fiction list, 2005), also numerous articles and short stories. Pres. Sisters in Crime, Chgo., 1986-88; dir. Nat. Abortion Rights Action League Ill., 1987—; mentor Chgo. inner-city schs. Named Woman of Yr. Ms mag., NYC, 1987; recipient Mark Twain award for disting. contbns. to Midwestern lit., 1996, Lifetime Achievement award, Private Eye Writers Am., 2005, Cartier Diamond Dagger for Lifetime Achievement, Brit. Crime Writers Assn., 2005. Mem. Crime Writers Assn. (Silver Dagger award 1988), Mystery Writers Am. (v.p. 1989), Authors Guild, Chgo. Network Achievements include being the founder of two scholarships at U. Kans. Office: c/o Dominick Abel Lit Agy #1B 146 West 82nd St New York NY 10024 Business E-Mail: viwarshawski@mindspring.com.*

PARGETER, FREDERICKA MAE (FREDI PARGETER), writer, publisher, insurance salesperson; b. Kirkland, Wash., July 18, 1938; d. Arthur John Bates and Dorothea H. (Workosky) Speed; m. Lincoln R. Perry, May 9, 1965; children: Andrea Lee Gowin, Kenneth R., Pamela E. Perry; m. Denny V. Pargeter, 2002. BA, Wash. State U., 1960. Sales exec. Lincoln R. Perry and Assocs., Bremerton, Wash., 1967—2002; author, pub. Perry Pub., Bremerton, Wash., 1989—2002. Author Kitsap County: A History, 1977, Kitsap County: Year of thy Child, 1979, Kitsap County: A Centennial History, 1979; Port Madison: 1854-1889, 1989, Seabeck: Tide's Out, Table's Set, 1993; co-author: Shelton: The First Century Plus Ten, 1996, Bremerton and PSNY, 2002. Mem. Kitsap County Hist. Soc., Bremerton, Wash., 1972—, Wash. State Hist. Soc., Tacoma, 1976—, Puget Sound Maritime Hist. Assn., Bainbridge Island Hist. Soc., Sanders County Hist. Soc., Mason County Hist. Soc. Mem.: Kitsap County Hist. Soc., Mason County Hist. Soc., Sander County Hist. Soc. (Mont.), Bainbridge Island Hist. So., Puget Sound Maritime Hist. Soc. Avocations: historical research/writing, Pacific Northwestern U.S. Home: PO Box 417 Thompson Falls MT 59873-0417

PARHAM, ELLEN SPEIDEN, nutrition educator; b. Mitchells, Va., July 15, 1938; d. Marion Coote and Rebecca Virginia (McNiel) Speiden; m. Arthur Robert Parham, Jr., Dec. 16, 1961; children: Katharine Alma, Cordelia Alyx. BS in Nutrition, Va. Poly. Inst., 1960; PhD in Nutrition, U. Tenn., 1967; MSEd in Counseling, No. Ill. U., 1994. Registered dietitian; lic. clin. profl. counselor. Asst. prof. to prof. nutrition No. Ill. U., DeKalb, Ill., 1966—2003, coord. programs in dietetics, 1981—86, 1990—2003, coord. grad. faculty sch. family, consumer, nutrition scis., 1985-87, interim chair Sch. Applied Health Professions, 2005—. Cons. on nutrition various hosps., clins. and bus., Ill., 1980-88; founder, dir. Horizons Weight Control Program, DeKalb, 1983-91; founder, leader "Escaping the Tyranny of the Scale" Group, 1994—; co-chair Nutrition Coalition for Ill., 1989-90; ptnr., mgr. Blue Chicory Arts, 1986—; adj. counselor Ctr. for Counsel, Family Svc. Agy. of DeKalb County. Bd. editors Jour. Nutrition Edn., 1985-90, 97—2005, Jour. Am. Dietetic Assn., 1991-97; contbr. articles to profl. jours. Recipient Fisher award, No. Ill. U. Coll. Health and Human Svcs., 2001, Sullivan award, 2002. Mem. Am. Inst. Nutrition, Soc. Nutrition Edn., Am. Dietetic Assn. (named Ill. Outstanding Dietetics Educator 2001, Excellence in Dietetics Edn. award 2001), Soc. Nutrition Edn. (treas. 1991-94, chair divsn. nutrition and weight realities 1995-96, chair jour. com. 2002—05, Weight Realities Cert. of Achievement 1999), N.Am. Assn. Study Obesity. Avocations: painting in watercolor, gardening, reading. Business E-Mail: eparham@niu.edu.

PARHAM, EVELYN LEE, nurse; b. Oxford, N.C., Mar. 17, 1958; d. Mayland and Cora L. Parham. MEd, N.C. State U., 1984; A nursing, Vance Granville C.C., 1992; MSN, U. N.C. Chapel Hill, 2004. RN 1992. Tchr. secondary math. Franklinton H.S., NC, 1980—89; nursing asst. Maria Parham Med. Ctr., Henderson, NC, 1990—92, staff RN, 1992—2005; Cert. Adult Nurse Practitioner Cardiovascular Core N.C., 2005—. Mem.: AACN, ANA, Am. Acad. Nurse Practitioners. Avocations: bicycling, fishing. E-mail: 12halt@msn.com.

PARHAM-HOPSON, DEBORAH, health programs administrator; BSN, U. Cin., 1977; MS in Pub. Health, U. NC, 1979, PhD in Pub. Health, 1990. Rear adm. USPHS Commd. Corps.; dep. assoc. adminstr. Health Resources and Svcs. Adminstrn., HIV/AIDS Bur., HHS, 2000—02, acting assoc. adminstr., 2002, assoc. adminstr., 2002—. Office: US Dept Health and Human Svcs Health Resources Svcs Adminstrn 5600 Fishers Ln Rm 7-05 Rockville MD 20857 Office Phone: 301-443-1993. Business E-Mail: dparham@hrsa.gov.

PARIAG, HAIMWATTIE RAMKISTODAS, information management administrator; b. Golden Fleece, Guyana, Aug. 31, 1967; came to U.S., 1977; d. Ramkisto Das and Surujpati Ramkistodas; m. Moolchand Pariag. BS in Med. Records Adminstrn., C.W. Post Coll., 1988. Registered health info. mgmt. adminstr. Med. records clk. Mary Immaculate Hosp., Jamaica, N.Y., 1986-87; coder Parkway Hosp., Forest Hills, N.Y., 1987, adminstrv. coord., 1987-88, dir. health info. mgmt. svcs., 1988-91; dir. med. records Massapequa Gen. Hosp., Seaford, N.Y., 1991—; dir. health info. svcs./telecom. Brunswick Hosp. Ctr., Amityville, NY, 2000—01; dir. med. records, privacy officer Parker Jewish Inst. Healthcare and Rehab., Hyde Park, NY, 2001—. Mem. Am. Health Info. Mgmt. Assn., N.Y. Health Info. Mgmt. Assn., L.I. Health Info. Mgmt. Assn., Health Info. Mgmt. Assn. N.Y.C. Democrat. Hindu. Avocations: volleyball, raquetball, tennis.

PARIENTE, BARBARA J., state supreme court justice; b. N.Y.C., Dec. 24, 1948; m. Frederick A. Hazouri; 3 children. Grad. with highest honors, Boston U., 1970; JD with highest honors, George Washington U., 1973. Bar: Fla. 1973; cert. civil trial lawyer Fla. Bar; cert. Nat. Bd. Trial Advocacy. Law clk. to hon. Norman C. Roettger, Jr. U.S. Dist. Ct. (so. dist.) Fla., 1973-75; assoc. Cone Wagner and Nugent, 1975—77, ptnr., 1977—83, Pariente & Silber, P.A., 1983; pvt. practice, 1983—2001; judge U.S. Ct. of Appeals (4th dist.), 1993-97; justice Fla. Supreme Ct., Tallahassee, 1997—, chief justice, 2004—06. Participant Twenty-First Century Justice Conf.; mem. Jud. Cir. Grievance Com., 1989-92, chair, 1990-92; mem. nominating com. State Ct. (15th cir.), 1980-84. Bd. dirs. Fla. Bar Found.; mentor Take Stock in Children, 1992-2003; mem. Cities in Schs. mentoring program, 1993, Palm Beach County Commn. on Status of Women; vol. judge Palm Beach County Youth Ct. Program; past chair Supreme Ct. Steering Com. on Families and Children in the Courts Fla. Supreme Ct.; liaison Supreme Ct. Task Force on Treatment-Based Drug Cts., 1999-2004; mem. nat. judges adv. com. Balanced and Restorative Justice Project Dept. Justice. Recipient award for disting. svc. to the arts Palm Beach County Bar Assn., 1987, Civil Litigation Pro Bono award Legal Aid Soc., 1993, Lifetime Achievement award Palm Beach County Jewish Fedn., 1998, Disting. Jud. Svc. award Fla. Coun. on Crime and Delinquency, 2000, Breaking the Glass Ceiling award Jewish Mus. Fla., 2002, Fla. Bar Assn. Family Law Sect. Chair Family Law Visionary award, 2004, William M. Hoevelor Jud. award, 2004, Good Govt. award Palm Beach County LWV, 2005. Mem. ABA (mem. Coalition for Justice 2000-03, Law Day Speech award 1998), Nat. Assn. Women Judges, Am. Inns. of Ct. (founding mem. Palm Beach County chpt.), Acad. Fla. Trial Lawyers (bd. dirs., chair Spkr.'s Bur. program 1984-87, outreach com. 1991-92, co-chair Workhorse Seminar 1991-92), Assn. Trial Lawyers Am. (vice chair profl. rsch. and devel. dept. 1980-82, chair comml. litig. sect. 1984-85, women's trial lawyer caucus 1986-87; mem. ethics com. 1989-90, conv. planning com. 1992-93), Fla. Assn. Women Lawyers (Lifelong Dedication award 2000), Order of Coif. Office: State Supreme Ct of Florida 500 S Duval St Tallahassee FL 32399-1925 Business E-Mail: supremecourt@flcourts.org.

PARILLA, BARBARA V., medicine specialist; b. Queens, NY, May 2, 1960; d. John and Carmela (Cervone) Vassino; m. Frank W. Parilla Jr., Apr. 7, 1990; children: Frank, Michael, Daniel. BS, SUNY, Stony Brook, 1982, MD with distinction in rsch., 1986. Cert. Am. Bd. Ob-Gyn., Am. Bd. Maternal-Fetal Medicine. Resident in ob-gyn., 1986; fellow in maternal-fetal medicine Northwestern U. Sch. Medicine, Chgo., 1990—92; attending physician, dir. fetal assessment team Prentice Women's Hosp., Chgo., 1992—2000; dir. fetal diagnostics Evanston Northwestern Healthcare, Ill., 2000—04; dir. rsch. and scholarly activities Luth. Gen. Hosp., Park Ridge, 2004—. Office: Luth Gen Hosp 1875 Dempster St Ste 325 Park Ridge IL 60068-1127 Office Phone: 847-723-8610. Business E-Mail: barbara.parilla-md@advocatehealth.com.

PARIN-NORRIS, BETH LYNN, art educator, researcher, artist; d. Michael Lynn and Marilyn Jean Parin; m. Ty Curtis Norris, Dec. 7, 2004; children: Isabelle Lynn Norris children: Sage Randall Parin. BFA, St. Mary's Coll., 2000; MFA, Cranbrook Acad. of Arts, Mich., 2002, Govs.' State U., 2006. Online bachelors of fine arts prof. in graphic design Art Inst. Online, Phila.; web designer - summer internship DataNet Techs., Inc., South Bend, Ind., 2001—01; adj. prof.: digital photography and photoshop class Oakland CC, Royal Oak, Mich., 2002—02; tenure track, full photographer & digital design & computer arts Governors State U., University Park, Ill., 2002—; online bachelors of fine arts prof. in graphic design Am. InterContinental U., Hoffman Estates, Ill., 2004—. Vis. digital artist U. Notre Dame, Notre Dame, Ind., 2001; vis. artist, lectr. digital, design seminar Bethel Coll., Mishawaka, Ind., 2002; student art show juror St. Mary's Coll., Notre Dame, 2003—03; art juror Tall Grass Arts Assn., Park Forest, Ill., 2003—03; kaleidoscope class project creator Stanley Clark Sch., South Bend, Ind., 2004—. Photographic based art work, Isolative (Juror's award), 1999, First Pl. award. Ann. St. Mary's Coll. Art Show, Notre Dame, 2000, Best Digital award. Scarab Club, Detroit, MI., Curator's Choice award. Chgo., 2001, Best in Show. Spring Salon Show 2002, Limner Gallery, NYC, NY., 2002), Judz Graham Gallery, Chgo., exhibitions include Agora Gallery, NYC, 2006. Recipient Hon. award for photograph, 2006; scholar Merit award, Cranbrook Acad. of Art, Bloomfield Hills, MI.; scholar., Worldstudio Found., NYC, NY., Nat. Conf. scholar, Soc. Photgraphic Edn., Las Vegas, 2002. Mem.: Agora Gallery, Smithsonian Inst., Nat. Mus. of Women Arts, Blue Sky Gallery, Ceres Gallery, Soc. for Photographic Edn. (life). Avocations: art, theater, music, outdoor activities, photography, travel. Office: Governors State University 1 University Parkway University Park IL 60466-0975 Office Phone: 574-514-3443. E-mail: beth.parin@gmail.com.

PARIS, DEIDRE EILEEN, artificial intelligence researcher, educator; b. Hammond, Ind., Oct. 7, 1968; d. Elizabeth Paris and Dillard Paris Jr. BSEE, So. U., Baton Rouge, 1992; Masters of Sci., Pub. Policy, Ga. Inst. Tech., 1996; MS in Elec. Engring., Ga. Inst. of Tech., 1994; PhD in Civil & Environ. Engring., Ga. Inst. Tech., 2002. Rschr. Constrn. Rsch. Ctr., Ga. Inst. of Tech., Atlanta; fellow GE Med. Sys., Milw., 1991—93, Army Environ. Policy Inst., Atlanta, 1995—97; rschr. Lawrence Livermore Nat. Lab., Livermore, Calif., 1997; asst. prof. Clark Atlanta U., Atlanta, 2002—04; faculty rschr. Oak Ridge Nat. Lab., Tenn., 2003; rsch. participant (NRC) Nuc. Regulatory Commn., Washington, 2004—05; adminstr. fellow NASA Marshall, Ala., 2004—; prof. coll. engring., architectgure & phys. sci. Tuskagee U. Adminstr. fellow Nasa Marshall Space Flight Ctr., Huntsville, Ala., 2002—04; presenter in field. Author, (exbhn.) 17th Internal Symposium on Polymer Analysis and Characterization; contbr. chapters to books. Resident adv. Atlanta Mut. Housing Assn., Atlanta, 2000—03; grad. senator for civil engring. dept. Ga. Inst. Tech. Student Govt. Assn., 1997—99; coord. ReJOYce In Jesus Ministries, LA, 1995—2001; contractor selection com. mem. Hist. Dist. Devel. Corp., 2003—04. Fellow, NASA, ASEE, 2004, GEM, 2003-2006; scholar Ga. Tech Bd. of Regents, Ga. Bd. of Regents, 1999—2001, GM, 1988—91, Motorola Corp., 1992; Adminstv. fellow, NASA, 2004—06, Presdl. Fellow, Ga. Inst. Tech., 1996—2000. Mem.: ASCE (assoc.), Am. Soc. of Civil Engring. (assoc.). Independent. Avocations: dance, reading, exercise. Home: 3672 Hawthorn Ct Auburn AL 36830 Office: Tuskegee U Coll Engring Architecture & Phys Sci 305 Luther Foster Hall Tuskegee Institute AL 36088 Office Phone: 404-429-9469. Home Fax: 256-544-8280; Office Fax: 256-544-8480. Personal E-mail: deidreparis@yahoo.com. E-mail: deidre.e.paris@msfc.nasa.gov.

PARIS, KATHLEEN, secondary school educator; Biology tchr. Bethel High Sch., Spanaway, Wash. Named Wash. State Biology Tchr. of Yr., 1993; recipient Presdl. award in secondary sci., 1997. Office: Bethel High Sch 22215 38th Ave E Spanaway WA 98387-6824

PARIS, NORMA JEAN, psychologist, educator; b. Muskogee, Okla., Jan. 15, 1937; d. Howard Charles and Eleanor Ruth Lewis; m. Barney McKinley Paris, Jr., Feb. 17, 1957; children: Donna Katherine Paris Willis, Cynthia Elizabeth Paris Bickham, Barney McKinley Paris III(dec.). BA summa cum laude, La. State U., 1975, psychologist, 1985, MEd, 1977, PhD, 1997; Edn. Specialist in Counseling, La. Tech. U., 1980. Tchr. Bossier Parish Sch. Bd., Bossier City, La., 1975—84, sch. psychologist, 1984—87, Caddo Parish Sch. Bd., Shreveport, 1987—2001; spl. lectr. Centenary Coll. La., Shreveport, 2001—. Psychol. advisor Compassionate Friends, Shreveport, 1981—92; cons. Children's Advocacy Ctr. Task Force, Shreveport, 1996—98; presenter in field. Bd. mem. Juvenile Justice Bd. Dirs., Shreveport, 1996—2000; exec. bd. mem. Caddo-Bossier Mental Health Assn. Bd. Dirs., Shreveport, 1996—2000. Mem.: La. Sch. Psychologists Assn. (exec. bd. mem. 2001—, La. Sch. Psychologist of Yr. 2001), Assn. Tchr. Educators, Internat. Reading Assn., Mensa. Republican. Baptist. Avocations: bridge, puzzles, water aerobics, travel. Home: 4406 Curtis Loop Bossier City LA 71112

PARIS-DE MONTE, ILEANA M., assistant principal; d. Alfredo Paris Torres and Margarita Badilla Vega; life ptnr. Roland Wyler; children: Adriana M. De Monte, Leonard Alfredo De Monte. BA in Journalism, Calif. State U., Northridge, 1979, Bilingual Tchg. Credential, 1993, M Ednl. Adminstrn., 2005. Cert. adminstr. Calif. Media release officer Bank of Am., LA, 1980; elem. sch. tchr. Serrania Ave. Elem. Sch., LA Unified Sch. Dist., Woodland Hills, Calif., 1988—2002; asst. prin. Napa St. Elem. Sch., Northridge, 2002—. Master tchr. Pepperdine Univ., Nat. U., LA, 1992—2002. Elem. tchr. liaison Taft Complex, LA Unified Sch. Dist., Woodland Hills, Calif., 1997—99. Mem.: ASCD. Office Phone: 818-885-1441. Office Fax: 818-993-4824. Personal E-mail: idemon1@lausd.k12.ca.us.

PARISI, VALERIE MARIE, former dean, medical educator; b. Bklyn., 1952; m. Gary Strong. BS in Biology, Brown U., 1972, MD, 1975; MPH, U. Calif. Sch. Pub. Health, 1980; MBA, U. NC, 2004. Lic. Calif., 1979, Tex., 1984, NY, 1994, NC, 1998, diplomate Nat. Bd. Med. Examiners, 1976, Am. Bd. Ob-gyn., 1981, Am. Bd. Ob-gyn. Divsn. Maternal-Fetal Medicine, 1987. NIH rsch. fellow, Dept. Chemistry and Physics Brown U., Providence, 1970, Noyes Found. rsch. fellow, Dept. Sociology & Divsn. Reproductive Biology and Medicine, 1971; Noyes Found. rsch. fellow, Dept. Ob-gyn. Women and Infants Hosp. RI, Providence, 1972; intern in categorical gen. surgery Brown U. Affiliated Hospitals, RI Hosp., Providence, 1975—76; resident in ob-gyn. Women and Infants Hosp. of RI, Providence, 1976—79; fellow divsn. maternal-fetal medicine, Dept. Ob-gyn. U. Colo. Health Sci. Ctr., Denver, 1982—83, U. Wis. Ctr. for Health Sciences, Madison, 1983—84; instr. Dept. Human Growth and Reproduction Brown U., 1976—79; lectr., divsn. maternal child health U. Calif. Sch. Pub. Health, Berkeley, 1980—81; clin. instr. Dept. Ob-gyn. and Reproductive Sciences, U. Calif., San Francisco, 1980—81, clin. asst. prof., 1981—82; asst. prof. Dept. Ob-gyn. U. Colo. Health Sci. Ctr., Denver, 1982—83, U. Wis. Health Sci. Ctr., Madison, 1983—84; asst. prof. Dept. Ob-gyn. and Reproductive Sciences U. Texas Med. Sch., Houston, 1984—89, assoc. prof. Dept. Ob-gyn. and Reproductive Sciences, 1989—94, dir. divsn. maternal-fetal medicine, 1984—94, asst. prof. Dept. Pediatrics, 1987—89, assoc. prof. Dept. Pediatrics, 1989—94, co-dir. maternal-fetal medicine fellowship program, 1987—94; vis. prof. divsn. neonatology Dept. Pediatrics U. Cin. Med. Ctr., 1991—92; prof. & chair Dept. Ob-gyn. and Reproductive Medicine U. Med. Ctr. at Stony Brook, NY, 1994—97; Robert A. Ross prof. & chair Dept Ob-gyn. U. NC, Chapel Hill, 1997—2004, residency program dir. Dept. Ob-gyn., 1999—2004, rsch. fellow Cecil G. Sheps Ctr. for Health Sciences Rsch., 2003—; dean medicine U. Tex. Med. Branch, Galveston, 2004—06, chief acad. officer, v.p. acad. program adminstrn. and services, 2004—06, adv., 2006—. Attending staff Providence Neighborhood Health Centers, RI, 1977—79; dir. Ob-gyn. Services Bristol County Cmty. Med. Ctr., RI, 1977—79; dir. gynecological services Brown U. Student Health Services, 1978—79; consulting staff Letterman Army Med. Ctr., Presidio of San Francisco, 1979—82; attending staff Kaiser Found. Hosp., Oakland, Calif., 1980, San Francisco, 1980—82; clin. staff Moffitt Hosp. U. Calif. San Francisco Med. Ctr., 1980—82; med. dir. Ambulatory Care Ctr. Dept. Ob-gyn. U. Colo. Health Sci. Ctr., Denver, 1982—83; attending staff Madison Gen. Hosp., Wis., 1983—84, U. Wis. Clin. Sciences Ctr., Madison, 1983—84; consulting staff St. Mary's Med. Ctr., Madison, Wis., 1983—84; attending staff Hermann Hosp., Houston, 1984—94, dir. Maternal-Fetal Spl. Care Unit, 1985—92, obstetrical dir. labor and delivery, 1987—88, Houston, 1992—94, med. dir. Family Ctr., 1992—94; consulting staff St. Joseph's Hosp., Houston, 1987—94, Meml. Southwest Hosp., Houston, 1990—94; active staff Lyndon Baines Johnson Hosp., Houston, 1990—94; ob-gyn. chief U. Hosp., Stony Brook, NY, 1994—97; consulting staff Southampton Hosp., NY, 1995—97, St. Charles Hosp., Port Jefferson, NY, 1996—97; obstetrician-gynecologist-in-chief NC Women's Hosp., Chapel Hill, 1997—2004; attending staff Dept. Ob-gyn REX Hosp., 2002—04. Bd. dirs. Am. Bd. Family Practice, 1999—2004; fin. and investment com., nominating com. Am. Bd. Med. Specialties, 2004; basic examiner Am. Bd. Obstetrics and Gynecology, 1990—, maternal and fetal medicine examiner, 1992—, divsn. maternal and fetal medicine, 1996—2002, bd. dirs. and divsn. chief maternal and fetal medicine, 1998—2002, exec. com., 1999—2002, fin. com., 2004—; mem. Coun. on Residency Edn. in Ob-gyn., 1995—2000; bd. dirs. Planned Parenthood of Suffolk County, 1994—97; exec. bd. Western Perinatal Collaborative Group, 1986—92, chair membership com., 1986—88, vice pres. & pres.-elect, 1988—90, pres., 1990—92. Fellow: Am. Gynecologic and Obstetrical Soc. (nominating com. 1992, fellowship com. 1992—95), Am. Assn. Advancement Sci.; mem.: Tex. Perinatal Assn., Tex. Med. Found., Tex. Med. Assn., Tex. Assn. Obstetricians and Gynecologists, Soc. for Study of Reproduction, Soc. Obstetric Anesthesia and Perinatology (bd. dirs. 1995—99), Soc. for Maternal Fetal Medicine (bd. dirs. 1989—92, scientific program chair 1993, pres.-elect 1993—94, pres. 1994—95), Soc. Gynecological Investigation, Perinatal Rsch. Soc. (exec. coun. 1993—95), NY Obstetrical Soc., Internat. Soc. for Study of Hypertension in Pregnancy, Houston Gynecological and Obstetrical Soc., Harris County Med. Soc., Assn. Reproductive Health Professionals, Assn. Professors of Gynecology and Obstetrics, Am. Med. Women's Assn., AMA, Am. Coll. Obstetricians and Gynecologists (patient edn. com. 1989—91, scientific program com. 1993, edn. commn. 1995—97), Sigma Xi.*

PARISIO, TAMARA LYNN, marketing professional; b. Appleton, Minn., July 4, 1960; d. Merlyn Eugene and Patricia Yvonne (Johnson) Munsterman; m. James Warren Burke, Jr., Mar. 26, 1983 (div. June 1993); 1 child, Madelyn Amanda; m. Douglas Eugene Parisio, Sept. 2, 2000; 1 child, Marco Antonio; stepchildren: Chalynn, BriAnne Lee, Justine. BA, U. Minn., 1982; postgrad., Calif. Luth. U., 1999. Asst. acct. exec. Sheggeby Advt., Mpls., 1982—83, BBDO, Inc., L.A., 1983—84; program mgr. Cable Music Channel, Hollywood, Calif., 1984—85; acct. exec. Ogilvy & Mather, L.A., 1985—88; mgr. mktg. Teleflora, L.A., 1988—93; asst. mgr. mktg. & merchandising Jafra Cosmetics Internat. Inc. (A Gillette Co.), Westlake Village, Calif., 1993—97, mgr. product mktg., 1997—98; mgr. mktg. Jafra Cosmetics Internat. Inc., Westlake Village, 1998—99; mgr. group mktg. Sebastian Internat., Inc., Woodland Hills, Calif., 1999—2001, dir. global mktg., 2001—02; cons. in field, 2002—03; designer, CEO SandDollar Cosmetics, Inc., Woodland Hills, 2004—. Mentor Pepperdine U. Recipient Silver Clio award, 1986, N.Y. Internat. Film and TV Festival bronze award, 1986, Ogilvy & Mather Creative Excellence award, 1986, Disting. Scholar award Calif. Luth. U., 1998, Am. Beauty Assn. award, 2000. Mem. L.A. Mus. Art, L.A. World Affairs Coun., L.A. Conservancy, Rho Lambda, Sigma Beta Delta. Office: SandDollar Cosmetics Inc PO Box 4115 West Hills CA 91308 Office Phone: 818-203-2508. Business E-Mail: tamara@sanddollarcosmetics.com.

PARK, BARBARA, writer; b. Mt. Holly, NJ, Apr. 27, 1947; m. Richard A. Park, 1969; 2 children. Attended, Rider Coll., 1965—67; BS, U. Alabama, 1969. Author: (children's books) Don't Make Me Smile, 1981, Operation: Dump the Chump, 1982 (Tennessee Children's Choice Book award, 1986), Skinnybones, 1982, Beanpole, 1983, Buddies, 1985 (Parents' Choice award, 1985), Kid in the Red Jacket, 1987 (Library of Congress Book of the Yr., 1987), Almost Starring Skinnybones, 1988, Mother Got Married: and Other Disasters, 1989, Rosie Swanson, 1991, Junie B. Jones and the Stupid Smelly Bus, 1992, Junie B. Jones and Her Big Fat Mouth, 1993, Junie B. Jones and a Little Monkey Business, 1993, Junie B. Jones and Some Sneaky Peeky Spying, 1994, Mick Harte Was Here, 1995, Junie B. Jones and the Yucky Blucky Fruitcake, 1995, B. Jones Loves Handsome Warren, 1996, Junie B. Jones and that Meanie Jim's Birthday, 1996, Junie B. Jones Loves Handsome Warren, 1996, Junie B. Jones has a Monster Under Her Bed, 1997, Junie B. Jones is Not a Crook, 1997, Junie B. Jones is a Party Animal, 1997, Junie B. Jones Smells Something Fishy, 1998, Junie B. Jones is a Beauty Shop Guy, 1998, Psst! It's Me.the Bogeyman, 1998, Junie B. Jones is Almost a Flower Girl, 1999, Junie B. Jones and the Mushy Gushy Valentine, 1999, Junie B. Jones has a Peep in her Pocket, 2000, Junie B. Jones is Captain Field Day, 2001, Junie B. Jones is a Graduation Girl, 2001, Junie B. Jones: First Grader, 2001, Junie B. First Grader: Boss of Lunch, 2002, Junie B. First Grader: Toothless Wonder, 2002, Top Secret, Personal Beeswax: A Journal by Junie B., 2003, Junie B. First Grader: Cheater Pants, 2003, Junie B., First Grader: One-Man Band, 2003. Recipient Young Hoosier award, 1985, Milner award, 1986. Office: c/o Random House 1745 Broadway New York NY 10019

PARK, CYNTHIA, sociology educator, consultant; b. Schenectady, N.Y., Feb. 7, 1925; d. Robert Hiram and Miriam Elizabeth Park; m. Robert Wentworth Christy (div.). BA, New Sch. Social Rsch., 1959; MS in Secondary Social Studies, Yeshiva U., 1961; MA in Sociology, Hunter Coll., CUNY, 1969; postgrad., New Sch. U., 1970—75. Permanent lic. secondary social studies N.Y.C. and N.Y. State. Tchr. h.s. sci. and social studies N.Y. Bd. Edn., N.Y.C., 1961, tchr. h.s. social studies Brandeis H.S., 1962—66; tchr. Nassau C.C., L.I., NY, 1970; instr. sociology Bloomfield (N.J.) Coll., 1967—70, Quinnipiac Coll., New Haven, 1971—73, U. New Haven, West Haven, Conn., 1973—75; ind. cons. N.Y.C., 1975—. Cons. Paulo Mesdag Gruppe Rec. Yale U. Archives; owner 98 1/2 McDougal St., N.Y.C., 1951; dir. Coop Gallery, N.Y.C., 1960—65, Westerly Gallery, N.Y.C. Prodr.: (mus. recs.) Music of Finland. Local campaign worker Lexington Dem. Club, N.Y.C., 1963—67. Recipient Fulbright grant to Finland, 1959—60, grants in field. Mem.: Soc. Ethnomusicology, Ind. U., Am. Sociol. Assn., Violoncello Soc., Am. Fedn. Musicians. Democrat. Episcopalian. Avocations: art, violincello, singing. Home: 965 Lexington Ave New York NY 10021

PARK, DOROTHY GOODWIN DENT (MRS. ROY HAMPTON PARK), broadcast executive, publishing executive; b. Raleigh, NC; d. Walter Reed and Mildred (Goodwin) Dent; m. Roy Hampton Park, Oct. 3, 1936; children: Roy Hampton, Adelaide Hinton. Student, Peace Jr. Coll., 1925—33; AB, Meredith Coll., 1936. Sec., dir. RHP, Inc., Ithaca, NY, 1945—, Park Comm., Inc., Ithaca, NY, 1983—95. Pres. Park Found. Inc., Ithaca, 1994—; Bd. visitors Peace Coll., Raleigh, 1968—. Mem.: LWV, DAR (1st vice regent 1955—57), Svc. League Ithaca, Colonial Order of Crown, Sovereign Colonial Soc. Ams. Royal Descent, Daus. Am. Colonists, Nat. Soc. Magna Charta Dames, Descs. Knights of Garter, Ithaca Woman's Club, Garden Club (Ithaca). Presbyterian. Home: 205 Devon Rd Ithaca NY 14850-1409

PARK, GRACE, professional golfer; b. Seoul, South Korea, Mar. 6, 1979; Attended, Ewha Women's U., 2003, Ariz. State U. Winner Kathy Ireland greens.com Championship, 2000, Home Depot Championship, 2001, Cisco Ladies World Matchplay Championship, 2002, Michelob Light Championships, 2003, Kraft Nabisco Championships, 2004. Non-voting mem. LPGA Exec. Com., 2004. Recipient Am. Jr. Golf Assn (AJGA) Player of Yr., 1994, 1996, Rookie of the Yr., LPGA, 2000. Avocation: shopping. Office: c/o LPGA 100 International Golf Dr Daytona Beach FL 32124-1092

PARK, HEE-JUNG (HEE JONG PARK), professional golfer; b. Seoul, Korea, Feb. 27, 1980; Profl. golfer Korean LPGA, 1998—2000, LPGA Tour, 2000—. Winner Australian Jr. Championship, 1996, 97, 98. Achievements include winning several Korean LPGA events including Sports Seoul Ladies Open, 1998, Indonesian Ladies Open, 1999; winner LPGA events including Williams Championship, 2001, Sybase Big Apple Classic, 2002. Avocations: movies, music, video games. Office: LPGA 1000 International Golf Dr Daytona Beach FL 32124-1092*

PARK, LINDA SUE, writer; b. Ill. BS in English, Stanford U. Pub. rels. writer major oil co., 1981—83; writer, 1997—. Author: Seesaw Girl, 1999, The Kite Fighters, 2000, A Single Shard, 2001 (Newbery Medal, 2002), When My Name Was Keoko, 2002, Project Mulberry, 2005. Avocations: cooking, travel, movies, crossword puzzles. Office: Clarion Books 215 Park Ave S New York NY 10003

PARK, MARINA H., lawyer; b. Pasadena, Calif., Nov. 6, 1956; BA with honors, Univ. Calif., Berkeley, 1978; JD, Univ. Mich., 1982. Bar: Calif. 1983. Mng. ptnr. Pillsbury Winthrop LLP, Palo Alto, Calif., 1999—2005; ptnr., Emerging Growth & Tech. practice & mng. ptnr. Pillsbury Winthrop Shaw Pittman, Palo Alto, Calif., 2005—. Office: Pillsbury Winthrop Shaw Pittman 2475 Hanover St Palo Alto CA 94304-1114 Office Phone: 650-233-4770. Office Fax: 650-233-4545. Business E-Mail: marina.park@pillsburylaw.com.

PARK, MARY WOODFILL, information consultant, librarian, writer; b. Nevada, Mo., Nov. 20, 1944; d. John Prossor and Elizabeth (Devine) Woodfill; m. Salil Kumar Banerjee, Dec. 29, 1967 (div. 1983); children: Stephen Kumar, Scott Kumar; m. Lee Crandall Park, Apr. 27, 1985; stepchildren: Thomas Joseph, Jeffrey Rawson. BA, Marywood Coll., 1966; postgrad., Johns Hopkins U., 1983, Goucher Coll., 1986. Asst. to dir. U. Pa. Librs., Phila., 1968-69; investment libr. Del. Funds, Phila., 1969-71; investment officer Investment Counselors Md., Balt., 1980-84, 1st Nat. Bank Md., Balt., 1984-85; founder Info. Consultancy, Balt., 1985—. Lectr. Loyola Coll., Balt., 1991-92, Cath. U., 1993. Author: InfoThink—Practical Strategies for Using Information in Business, 1998; editor, contbr. to profl. publs. Vol. Internat. Visitors' Ctr., Balt., 1979-80, 91; del. White House Conf. on Librs.; v.p. bd. dirs. Friends of Goucher Libr., 1988-90; mem. industry applications com. Info. Tech. Bd., State of Md., 1993-96; mem. info. tech. com. of the

Tech. Coun., Greater Balt. Com., 1993-98. Named One of Md.'s Top 100 Women, Warfield's Bus. Publn., 1996. Mem.: DAR, MD Women's Health Initiative, Huguenot Soc. Md. (1st v.p. 2003—05), Nat. Huguenot Soc., Md. Found. for Psychiatry (bd. dirs. 1998—), Assn. Ind. Info. Profls., Info. Futures Inst., Spl. Librs. Assn. (pres. Md. chpt. 1991—92, v.p. network coord. coun. Sailor project 1993—95, govt. rels. chair 1998—2003, pub. rels. chair 2003—), Daus. of Colonial Wars, Nat. Soc. Daus. Am. Colonists (Md. state 1st vice regent 2003—05, regent Joppa Trail chpt. 2003—05), Nat. Soc. Colonial Dames XVII Century (state rec. sec. 2003—05, 2d v.p. 2005—), Nat. Soc. of the Sons and Daus. of the Pilgrims, Nat. Soc. of U.S. Daus. of 1812 (Md. state rec. sec. 2003—05), Nat. Soc. Dames Ct. Honor, Colonial Dames Am., Nat. Inst. Geneal. Rsch. Alumnae Assn., Soc. of Daughters of Holland Dames, Descendants of Ancient and Honorable Families of New Netherland (coores. sec. 2003—), Friends of New Netherlands, Three Arts Club Homeland, Hamilton St. Club (bd. dirs. 1989—92). Episcopalian. Office: The Information Consultancy 308 Tunbridge Rd Baltimore MD 21212-3803 Business E-Mail: mwpark@informationconsultancy.com.

PARK, NANCY MARIE, art director, illustrator, painter; b. Blackwell, Okla., Nov. 15, 1939; d. Arthur Rue and Nola Marie Steiger; m. Joe Lindley Widows, Jan. 10, 2002; children: Ann Stigers, Drew. Degree, U. Okla., Norman, Okla., 1962. Creative art dir. Lowe Runkle Advertising, Tulsa, Okla., 1970—71; owner Graphic Concepts, Tulsa, Okla., 1971—73; asst. art dir. aircraft Owners & Pilot Assn., Bethesda, Md., 1973—79; artist chief designer Art Display Co., Washington, 1979—80; creative dir. The Drawing Rm., Silver Springs, Md., 1980—84; art editor Am. Vocat. Assn., Arlington, Va., 1984—87; designer, illustrator The Oklahoman, Okla. City, 1987—2002; ret., 2002. Sec. Art Dirs. Okla. City, Okla. City, 1966—70; pres. Okla. Art Guild, Okla. City, 2000—01, dir., 2005—. Mem.: Mensa (local sec. 2000—02), Okla. Art Guild (pres. 2000—01, dir. 2005—). Avocations: singing, reading, travel, painting, puzzles.

PARKE, JANET DIANE, interior designer; b. Winnemucca, Nev., Aug. 20, 1930; d. Willard Virdell and Lois (Carlson) Booth; m. Jack Evan Parke, June 11, 1950; children: Deborah Diane Parke Smith, Cary Evan, James Robert. BA, Brigham Young U., 1950. Interior designer Brunson Homes, Reno, 1972—74, Bakers Interiors, Reno, 1976—81, Tristan Parke Interiors, Reno, 1981—86, Carson Furniture, Reno, 1988—93; designer, mem. sales staff, Thomasville Furniture, 1993—96, Joanies Fashions, 1997—98; sales assoc. Boutique Casablanca, 1998—2005; ret., 2005. Designer showcase homes Designs Ltd., 1987—. Com. mem. Congressman Jim Santini, Reno; bd. dirs. Nev. Jr. Miss Competition, 1969—79; hostess Miss Nev., Reno, 1974—77. Mem.: AIA (assoc.), Nev. Home Builders Assn. (assoc.), Reno Duckettes Ltd. (v.p. 1983—91), Daus. of Nile, Order Ea. Star, Sigma Nu (pres. White Rose chpt. 1952—53). Democrat. Mem. Lds Ch.

PARKE, M(ARGARET) JEAN, retired business owner, editor; b. Akron, Ohio, Aug. 23, 1920; d. Lawrence William and Rosella (Washburn) Beat; m. Harry Morris Parke, July 25, 1942; children: Richard Blake, Catherine Jean. BA magna cum laude, U. Toledo, 1942, MA, 1959. Adminstrv. asst. Dist. Office Price Adminstrn., Toledo, 1943-45; editing cons. Century Press, Inc., Toledo, 1955-72; cons. women's progs. U. Toledo, 1973-75; reports editor Price-Waterhouse & Co., Cleve., 1976-78; fin. officer, ptnr. Parke Supply Co., Avon Lake, Ohio, 1980-86; co-owner, sec. Woodlark Farms, Inc., Georgetown, Ky., 1978-94. Bd. trustees, past pres. Avon Lake Pub. Libr., 1981-90, Friends of the U. Toledo Libr., past pres. 1971-74; founding trustee Friends of Toledo-Lucas county Pub. Libr., 1970-73; trustee Avon Lake Pub. Libr. Found., Inc., 1991-97; organizer, past pres. Parkview Hosp. Evening Guild, Toledo, 1953; incorporator, sec. Ch. Women United of Toledo area, 1963-66; bd. dirs. LWV, Sylvania, Ohio, Avon Lake; mem. Friends of Avon Lak Libr. Jean Parke Conf. Rm. named in her honor Avon Lake Pub. Libr., 1981. Mem. AAUW (past pres., bd. dirs. Toledo br. 1981-90, Ednl. Found. Prog. honoree 1981), Avon on the Lake Garden Club, U. Toledo Alumni Assn. (trustee, officer Blue T award 1981), Chi Omega Alumnae Toledo (officer), Chi Omega Alumnae Ohio (state bd. dirs. 1983-85, Outstanding Ohio Chi Omega Alumna 1982). Republican. Episcopalian. Avocations: travel, great books, theater, college football, needlecrafts. Home: 32821 Tanglewood Ct Avon Lake OH 44012-1540

PARKER, ALICE, composer; b. Boston, Dec. 16, 1925; d. Gordon and Mary (Stuart) P.; widowed; children: David, Timothy, Katharine, Mary, Elizabeth. BA, Smith Coll., Northampton, Mass., 1947; MS, Juilliard Sch., N.Y.C., 1949; MusD (hon.), Hamilton U., 1979, Macalester Coll., St. Paul, 1989, Bluffton Coll., Ohio, 1991, Westminster Choir Coll., Princeton, N.J., 1996. Arranger Robert Shaw Chorale, N.Y.C., 1948-66; artistic dir. Melodious Accord, N.Y.C., 1985—. Tchr., workshop leader Westminster Choir Coll., Princeton, N.J., summers, 1972-98; McDonald chair Emory U., 2003. Composer 4 operas, 41 cantatas, 8 song cycles and numerous anthems and suites. Recipient composer's award ASCAP, 1968—, AGO Disting. Composer of the Yr., 2000, Barlow Endowment, 1992, spl. award Nat. Endowment Arts, 1976, Gottschalk award Pioneer Valley Symphony, 2003, Lifetime Achievement award Choral Arts New Eng., 2004. Fellow Hymn Soc., Hymn Soc. Am. (conf. composer in residence, 2006); mem. Am. Choral Dirs. Assn. (ea. disvn. conf. dedicated in her honor 2006), Am. Condrs. Guild, Chorus Am. (Founders award 1994), Am. Music ctr., Sigma Alpha Iota. Office: Melodious Accord Inc Park West Sta PO Box 20801 New York NY 10025-1523

PARKER, AMY LEE, music educator; b. Owensboro, Ky., May 28, 1980; d. Herbert Franklin Reynolds and Tara Lee (Henderson) Parker; m. Carlos Cristobal Cuenca, June 30, 2003. B.Mus.Edn., U. Louisville, 2002. Cert. tchr. Ky. Clk. Ky. Transp. Cabinet, Frankfort, 1998—2000; singer, section leader, octet mem. 2d Presbyn. Ch., Louisville, 2000—03; music tchr. Myers Middle Sch., Louisville, 2002—04; ch. choir dir. 4th Presbyn. Ch., Louisville, 2003—; music tchr., choir dir. Bullitt Ctrl. H.S., Shepherdsville, Ky., 2004—; cons. Mary Kay Co., Louisville, 2005—. Mem. U. Louisville Cardinal Singers. Vol. Am. Cancer Soc., 2000—; vol. singer various chs., 1996—; vol. Hopeful Hearts, 2004. Named Ky. Col., Gov. and State of Ky., 2000; recipient 3 gold medals, Internat. Choir Olympic Com., Bremen, Germany, 2004. Mem.: Golden Key. Democrat. Avocations: cooking, singing, reading, volleyball, scuba diving.

PARKER, ANN (ANN PARKER NEAL), photographer, graphic artist, writer; b. London, Mar. 6, 1934; d. Russell Johnston and Mildred Grace (Best) P.; m. Avon Neal, Oct. 31, 1964. Student, R.I. Sch. Design, 1952-54; B.F.A., Yale U., 1956. V.p. Thistle Hill Press, North Brookfield, Mass., 1979—; artist-in-residence Altos de Chavon, Dominican Republic, 1983, 84; panel mem. Fulbright Hays Com. for Photography, Film and Video, 1983, 85, 86. Freelance photographer and graphic artist, 1956—; exhbns. include Santa Fe Ctr. Photography, 1982, Focus Gallery, San Francisco, 1983, Altos de Chavon, Dominican Republic, 1984, 86, 87, Nat. Mus. Art, La Paz, Bolivia, 1985, Princeton U. Libr., 1986, Instituto Dominicano de Cultura Hispanica, Santa Domingo, Dominican Republic, 1987, Gallery of Graphic Arts, N.Y.C., 1987, Maxwell Mus. Anthropology, U. N.Mex., Albuquerque, 1988, Gallery Twerenbold, Luzern, Switzerland, 1991, San Antonio Mus. Assns., 1992, Worcester (Mass.) Art Mus., 1993, Gallery of Graphic Arts, N.Y.C., 1994, Lumina Gallery, Taos, N.Mex., 1995, Gallery of Graphic Arts, N.Y.C., 1995, U. Conn., 1996, U. Mass. Med. Ctr., 1996, Ute Stebich Gallery, Lenox (Mass.), 1996, Sony Gallery Am. U. in Cairo, 1997, Casa Chavon, Santo domingo, Dominican Republic, 1999, Tower Hill Botanic Gardens, Mass., 1999, Gallery Graphic Arts, N.Y.C., 2000, Ute Stebich Gallery, Lenox, Mass., 2000, Troyer Gallery, Washington, 2001; work pub. in Smithsonian mag., Am. Heritage Life, Americana, Aperture, Natural History, others; works in permanent collections N.Y. Pub. Libr., George Eastman House, Rochester, N.Y., Met. Mus. Art, N.Y.C., Mus. Modern Art, N.Y.C., Mus. Fine Arts, Boston, Ctr. Creative Photography, Tucson, MIT, Libr. of Congress, Smithsonian Instn., Rosenwald Collection, Mellon Collection, Whitney Mus., others; art books Ephemeral Folk Figures, 1969, Molas Folk Art of the Cuna Indians, 1977, Scarecrows, 1978, Early American Stone Sculpture Found in the Burying Grounds of New England, 1982, Los Ambulantes, 1982, Hajj Paintings: Folk Art of the Great Pilgrimage, 1995, Die Kunst des Hadsh, 1995. Recipient 1st pl. award Mass. Open Photography, 1978, Am. Inst. Graphic Design awards, 1956, 77, 79, Mass. Arts Coun. award, 1988, 96; Ford Found. grantee, 1962-63, 63-64; Fund Four Directions grantee, 1995. Mem. Am. Antiquarian Soc. Address: Thistle Hill Press 126 School St North Brookfield MA 01535-1961

PARKER, ARLENE SANDRA, social worker; b. N.Y.C., June 7, 1948; d. Sam and Sylvia Brotman; m. Franklin Fernandes Parker, Nov. 27, 1983; 1 child, Samantha Joy. BA, SUNY, Albany, 1970; MA, U. Pa., 1971; MSW, Adelphi U., 1977. Diplomate in clin. psychotherapy; ACSW CSW N.Y.; credentialed alcohol and substance abuse counselor N.Y. Asst. social work Cath. Charities, Rockville Centre, NY, 1973—77; sch. social worker Oceanside (N.Y.) Pub. Schs., 1977—. Psychotherapist, Baldwin, NY, 1985—. Scholar Nat. Def. Scholarship, 1969. Mem.: Acad. Cert. Social Workers, NASW, Sisterhood Ctrl. Synagogue. Avocation: travel. Home: 289 Princeton Rd Rockville Centre NY 11570 Office: 865 Merrick Rd Ste 305 Baldwin NY 11510

PARKER, BONITA M., civil rights organization executive; b. Jan. 23, 1968; married; 2 children. Degree in Fin., DePaul U. Several positions with Urban Fin. Services, Am. Bankers Assn.; intern Northern Trust Co., second v.p.; co-owner Skills For Life Tng. Co.; dir., Investments and Econ. Empowerment Salem Bapt. Ch., Chgo.; COO Rainbow/Push Coalition, Chgo. Fin. specialist USAR. Mem.: Nat. Assn. County Officials. Office: RainbowPush Coaltion 930 E 50th St Chicago IL 60615-2702 Office Phone: 773-373-3366. Office Fax: 773-373-3571.*

PARKER, DIANA LYNNE, restaurant manager, special events director; b. Eureka, Calif., June 21, 1957; d. Carol Dean and Lynne Diane (Havemann) P. BA in English, Humboldt U., Arcata, Calif., 1981, postgrad., 1982—84. Lic. real estate agent, Calif. Retail clk. Safeway, Inc., Eureka, 1977-84; caterer, owner TD Catering, Eureka, 1982-84; asst. buyer Macy's Calif., San Francisco, 1984-85; realtor Mason-McDuffie, Alameda, Calif., 1985-87; host, Rotunda Restaurant Neiman Marcus, San Francisco, 1987-89, asst. mgr. Rotunda Restaurant, 1989—96, dir. spl. events, 1989—96, mgr. dining room Rotunda Restaurant, 1996—. Mem.: Nat. Assn. Catering Execs., San Francisco Visitor and Conv. Bur., Women Chefs and Restauranteurs, Mus. Modern Art, Commonwealth Club Calif. Republican. Avocations: gourmet cooking, art, antiques. Office: Rotunda at Neiman Marcus 150 Stockton St San Francisco CA 94108-5807 Office Phone: 415-362-4777.

PARKER, EDNA FAYE, special education educator; b. Laurel, Miss., May 11, 1948; d. William Ray and M. Earlene Allred; m. James Edward Parker, Oct. 18, 1968; children: Nathan Randall, Brent Anthony. BS in Elem. Edn., William Carey Coll., Hattiesburg, Miss., 1981; MS in Elem. Edn., William Carey Coll., 1997, postgrad., 2004. Tchr. Franklin Meth. Ch. Kindergarten, Laurel, 1981—82; tchr. 3d grade Sandersville Elem. Sch., Miss., 1982—83, Title I tchr. grades 1-6, 1983—84; migrant tutorial tchr. Ellisville Elem. Sch., Miss., 1984—88, tchr. 2d grade, 1988—2001, tchr. 3d grade, 2001—02; day treatment tchr. Lillie Burney Elem. Sch., Hattiesburg, Miss., 2002—. Recipient BSU Outstanding Svc. to Children award, Jones County Jr. Coll., 1986. Mem.: Hattiesburg Fedn. Tchrs., Miss. Fedn. Tchrs., Am. Fedn. Tchrs. (Outstanding Svc. award 1987, 2001), Alpha Delta Kappa (chaplain 1988—2005, chpt. pres.-elect 2006—). Baptist. Avocations: gardening, flowers, music. Home: 44 Oloh Church Rd Sumrall MS 39482

PARKER, ELIZABETH RINDSKOPF, dean, law educator; b. Detroit, Dec. 2, 1943; d. Arthur C. and Kathryn G. (Rodgers) Roediger; m. Peter E. Rindskopf, May 25, 1968; 1 child; m. Robert Parker. BA in Philosophy cum laude, U. Mich., 1964, JD, 1968. Bar: Ga. 1968, U.S. Dist. Ct. (no. dist.) Ga. 1969, U.S. Ct. Appeals (5th cir.) 1970, U.S. Supreme Ct. 1971, U.S. Ct. Appeals (6th cir.) 1972, U.S. Ct. Appeals (3rd cir.) 1974, U.S. Ct. Appeals (4th cir.) 1977, U.S. Ct. Appeals (9th cir.) 1978, D.C. 1979. Reginald Heber Smith fellow, mng. atty. Emory Legal Svcs., Atlanta, 1968-71; ptnr. Moore, Alexander & Rindskopf, Atlanta, 1971-74; dir. New Haven Legal Assistance Assn., Inc., 1974-76; dep. dir. Lawyers Com. Civil Rights Under Law, Washington, 1978-78; ptnr. Cohen, Vitt & Annand, Alexandria, Va., 1978-79; acting asst. dir. mergers and joint ventures, dep. asst. dir. health care Bur. of Competition, Fed. Trade Commn., 1979-81; of counsel Surrey & Morse, Washington, 1981-84; gen. counsel Nat. Security Agy., Washington, 1984-89; prin. dep. office of the legal adviser US Dept. State, Washington, 1989-90; gen. counsel CIA, Washington, 1990-95; of counsel Bryan Cave, LLP, 1995—99; gen. counsel U. Wis. Sys., 1999—2002; dean, prof. law U. Pacific Sch. Law, Sacramento, 2003—. Co-operating atty. NAACP Legal Def. and Edn. Fund, Inc., 1971-74; trustee Monterey Inst. Internat. Studies. Contbr. articles to profl. jours. Bd. dirs. Austen Riggs Psychiat. Hosp. Mem. ABA (standing com. law and nat. security, counsel sect. internat. law and politics, adv. bd. Ctr. and Eastern European Law Initiative), Coun. Fgn. Rels. NAS (com. mem. Roundtable on Sci. Comm. and Nat. Security & Commn. on Sci. Comm. and Nat. Security. Office: U of Pacific McGeorge Sch Law 3200 Fifth Ave Sacramento CA 95817 Office Phone: 916-739-7151. E-mail: elizabeth@pacific.edu.

PARKER, ELLEN KOONCE, retired secondary school educator; b. Raeford, N.C., Jan. 1, 1935; d. Lacy Herman Koonce, Sr. and Treva Townsend Koonce; m. Davis Kirkland Parker, Jr. (dec. 2003); children: Davis Kirkland III, Karen Parker Allen. BS in Sci. and Social Studies, Appalachian State U., 1957; M in Guidance and Pers. Svcs., N.C. State U., 1968. Nat. cert. counselor N.C. Clk. Belk Dept. Store, Raeford, 1952—53; measured acerage N.C. Dept. Agr., Hoke County, NC, 1953—56; bus. mgr. coll. newspaper Appalachian, Boone, NC, 1956—57; sci. tchr. Terry Sanford H.S., Fayetteville, NC, 1957—59; math tchr. Dept. of Army, Ft. Bragg, NC, 1959—62; spl. edn. tchr. Seventy First Sch., Fayetteville, 1964—65; dir. guidance Seventy First H.S., Fayetteville, 1965—78, Westover Sr. High, Fayetteville, 1978—92. First pres. Cumberland County Guidance Assn., Fayetteville, 1970, Individual Pupil Svc., NC, 1972; coun. mem., mem. legis. com. N.C. Edn. Assn., 1973; presenter in field. Tchr. N.C. Women's Conf., Banner Elk, NC; v.p. Cumberland County Dem. Party, Fayetteville, NC; organizer Reilly Rd. Presbyn. Ch., Fayetteville, NC. Mem.: Hist. Found. at Montreal, Inc., N.C. Hist. Assn., Alpha Delta Kappa (historian, com. mem. Gamma Sigma), Pi Gamma Mu. Avocations: reading, writing, travel. Home: 9003 Galatia Church Rd Fayetteville NC 28304-6121

PARKER, EMILY, lawyer; b. Winnsboro, Tex., Aug. 17, 1949; d. Roy D. and Helen C. Parker. BA summa cum laude, Stephen F. Austin Coll., 1970; JD cum laude, So. Meth. U., 1973. Bar: U.S. Tax Ct. 1976, U.S. Ct. Appeals (5th cir.) 1977, U.S. Supreme Ct. 1977, U.S. Ct. Claims 1978, U.S. Ct. Appeals (10th and fed. cirs.) 1984; cert. in tax law. Assoc. Thompson & Knight, Dallas, 1973-79, ptnr., 1979—2002; dep. chief counsel IRS, 2002—04, acting chief counsel, 2003—04. Bd. dirs. Child Care Dallas, 1978-83, Easter Seals of Greater Dallas, 1998—. Mem. ABA (natural resources com. chmn. 1991-92, court procedure com. tax sect.), Tex. Bar Assn. (chmn. natural resources com. 1982-84, coun. 1984-87, tax sect.), Dallas Bar Assn. (chmn. coun. tax sect. 1983), Am. Coll. Tax Counsel. Democrat. Avocations: golf, tennis, skiing. Office: Thompson & Knight 1700 Pacific Ave Ste 3300 Dallas TX 75201-4693 Home: Ste 3300 1700 Pacific Ave Dallas TX 75201-4656

PARKER, EVA ANNETTE, librarian; b. North Island, Calif., Nov. 27, 1950; d. R.L. and Eva Mae (Helm) Peters; m. Darrell Dwight Parker, Nov. 9, 1970; children: Geoff, Jenny. BS, Okla. Christian Coll., 1974; MEd, Southwestern Okla. State U., 1984. Cert. libr. media specialist. Tchr. Summer Safari program Oklahoma City Zoo, 1973; libr., tchr. Leedey (Okla.) Pub. Sch., 1983-87; prof. Draughon Tng. Inst., Wichita Falls, Tex., 1988-89; tchr. Region IX Edn. Svc. Ctr., Wichita Falls, 1990; libr. media specialist Vernon (Tex.) Mid. Sch., 1990—2003; libr. Burgess Elem. Sch., Wichita Falls, Tex., 2004—; tchr. art and sci. Vernon Kids Kollege, 1999—. Tutor Vernon Intermediate Sch., 1993—; del. alt. to NEA, Leedey, 1987; storm spotter for City of Grandfield, Okla. Contbg. author: What America's Teachers Wish Parents Knew, 1993; contbr. article to profl. jour. Tchr. Bible sch. Ch. of Christ, Iowa Park, Tex., 1987-93, Grandfield, Okla., 1994—; vol. ARC, Wichita Falls, 1987-93; coach bowling Spl. Olympics, 1992-93; coach track and field Spl. Olympics, Vernon, 1993—; bd. mem. Harvest Playhouse; spl. olympics coach. Libr. improvement grantee Okla. State Dept. Edn., Leedey, 1984, Sch.-to-Work grantee, 1996-2001. Mem. Tex. Libr. Assn., Assn. Tex. Profl. Educators, P.E.O. (pres. Okla. orgn.). Avocations: rock collecting, painting, calligraphy, reading, music. Home: 1303 W 1st St Grandfield OK 73546 Office: Kate Burgess Elem Lang and Prep Acad 3106 Maurine St Wichita Falls TX 76306 Office Phone: 940-716-2850. Personal E-mail: annettep_1@yahoo.com.

PARKER, FAYE C., elementary school educator; b. Madisonville, Ky., Sept. 5, 1954; d. Willis Owen and Mary Agnes (Hill) P. BS, Murray (Ky.) State U., 1976, MEd, 1980, Rank I in elem. edn., 1982. Cert. elem. tchr., Ky. Tchr. Hopkins County Bd. Edn., Madisonville, 1976—94; tchr., extended sch. coord. Jesse Stuart Sch., Madisonville, 1994—. Leader Hopkins County Sch. Sys. Fellow Ky. Edn. Reform Act; named Hopkins County Tchr. of Yr., 1985, 92. Mem. Assn. Childhood Edn. (treas., past local and state pres.), Ky. Reading Assn., Ky. Sci. Tchrs. Assn., Ky. Math. Tchrs. Assn., Hopkins County Edn. Assn., Delta Kappa Gamma. Home: 531 Brown Ln Madisonville KY 42431-1161 Office: Jesse Stuart Sch 1710 Anton Rd Madisonville KY 42431-8514 Office Phone: 270-825-6033. Personal E-mail: parker531@charter.net. E-mail: faye.parker@hopkins.kyschools.us.

PARKER, JACQUELINE KAY, social work educator; b. Yuba City, Calif., June 3, 1934; d. LeRoy George and Veda (Kuster) P. AB, U. Calif., Berkeley, 1959, MSW, 1961, PhD, 1972. Asst. prof. social work Va. Commonwealth U., Richmond, 1973-80, U. Oreg., Eugene, 1983-86; assoc. prof. Cleve. State U., 1986-90; mem. grad. faculty N.Mex. State U., Las Cruces, 1990-94; assoc. prof., MSW program coord. Radford U., Bancroft Libr., U. Calif.-Berkeley, U. Minn. (Social Welfare History Archives), 1994—2000. Cons. Social Rsch. Assocs., Inc., Midlothian, Va., 2000. Author biog. sketches reference books, bibliographic essays, oral histories and articles. Mem. Coun. on Social Work Edn., Friends of the Schlesinger Libr., Cuyahoga (Ohio) County Human Svcs. Adv. Com.; referee Radcliffe Rsch. Scholars Program, Cambridge, Mass.; bd. dirs. Opportunities Industrialization Ctr., Richmond; mem. com. on preparation for ministry Nat. Capitol Presbytery, 2001—; clk. of session Capitol Hill Presbyn. Ch., 2002-04; vol. lawyers project AARP, ESL-Immigrant Ministries, UMC. Mem. NASW (state bd. dirs. Ohio and N.Mex. chpts.). Office: Radford U Sch Social Work PO Box 6958 Radford VA 24142-6958 Personal E-mail: jk3parker@aol.com.

PARKER, JACQUELINE YVONNE, lawyer, educator; b. Urbana, Ill., Jan. 14, 1947; d. Melvin M. and Florence L. (Katz) Pick; m. Bruce Richard Parker, May 30, 1969; children: Kenneth R.L., Michael P., Deborah M. BA, Tufts U., Medford, Mass., 1969; student, U. Calif., Berkeley, 1976—77; JD, New Eng. Sch. Law, 1977; LLM, Harvard U., Cambridge, Mass., 1981. Bar: Mass. 1978, U.S. Ct. Appeals (1st cir.) 1978, U.S. Supreme Ct. 1990. Asst. prof. law New Eng. Sch. Law, Boston, 1978—81, Albany Law Sch., NY, 1981—84; assoc. Parker Coulter Daley & White, Boston, 1984—92; atty. Connelly & Norton P.C., Boston, 1992—2000. Author, co-author (4 vol. treatise) Contemporary Family Law: Principles, Policy & Practice, 1988; contbr. articles to profl. jours. Mem. Children's Adoption & Foster Care Coalition, Boston, 1991—. United Way scholar, 1975, New Eng. Sch. Law Trustee's scholar, 1975-76. Mem. ABA, Nat. Assn. of Counsel for Children (bd. dirs. 1991-2002), Mass. Bar Assn. (family law legis. subcom.), Com. for Pub. Counsel Svcs. (bd. dirs. 1993-2000). Avocations: hiking, jogging, tennis. Office: Law Office of Jacqueline Y Parker Box 590554 Newton Center MA 02459 Office Phone: 617-965-1589. E-mail: jyparker@rcn.com.

PARKER, JENNIFER WARE, chemical engineer, researcher; b. Berkeley, Calif., Apr. 18, 1959; d. Raymond Paul and Maureen Christina (Trehearne) Ware; m. Henrik Davidson Parker, July 30, 1983; children: Katherine Joyce, Nathaniel Henrikson. BSChemE, Princeton U., 1980; MSChemE, UCLA, 1983, PhDChemE, 1986. Devel. engr. Am. Pharmaseal, Glendale, Calif., 1980-81; rsch. engr. Crump Inst. Med. Engring, UCLA, 1986-87; sr. engr. The BOC Group, Murray Hill, NJ, 1987-90, lead engr., 1990-92; sr. rsch. engr. CFM Techs., Inc., West Chester, Pa., 1993-97; v.p. CFMT Inc., Wilmington, Del., 1997-99, pres., 1999—2001, Mattson Tech. IP, 2001—02; founder Adondo Corp., Wayne, Pa., 2002—. Contbr. articles to profl. jours. Mem.: Am. Inst. Chem. Engrs., N.Y. Acad. Scis. Avocations: sports, music, gardening. Home: 201 W Country Club Ln Wallingford PA 19086-6507 Personal E-mail: jhparker@comcast.net.

PARKER, JOAN M., librarian; d. Billy Gene and Mary Jane Parker. BA, Tex. Luth. Coll., Seguin, 1977; MA, Calif. State U., Northridge, 1984; MLS, UCLA, 1986. Libr. Calif. State U., Long Beach, 1986—94, Moss Landing Marine Labs., Calif., 1995—. Chmn. Friends of the Libr., Springville, Calif., 1991—2006. Mem.: Internat. Assn. Aquatic and Marine Sci. Libraries and Info. Ctrs. (pres. 2006—). Democrat. Office: MLML/MBARI Rsch Libr 8272 Moss Landing Rd Moss Landing CA 95039 Office Phone: 831-771-4415.

PARKER, JOEL LOUISE, nursing administrator; d. Hattie Louise and Joe Nmn Williams. BS in nursing, Tex. Christian U., 1975—77; MS in human resources, Golden Gate U., 1988—90; MS in nursing informatics, U. Md., 1997—99, postgrad., 1997—99. CPA; cert. nursing informatic ANCC, 2001. Dept. head, oper. rm. Naval Hosp., Jacksonville, Fla., 1999—2003; dir., ctrl. credentials quality assurance sys. Resources II Program Office, Falls Church, Va., 2003—. Clin. coord., oper. rm. Nat. Naval Med. Ctr., Bethesda, 1994—97; charge nurse pacu/gen. surgery Naval Hosp., Okinawa, Japan, 1991—94; charge nurse ent Naval Hosp. Camp Lejeune, 1988—91; relief charge nurse sicu Veterans Adminstrn. Hosp., Dallas, 1983—87; oper. rm. staff nurse St. Joseph's Hosp., Fort Worth, 1987—88. Pres. ushers bd. First Bapt. Ch. Of Mandarin, Jacksonville, 2000—02. Comdr. USN, 2003—05. Decorated Navy/Marine Corps Achievement medal, Naval Officers Disting. Svc. award, Navy and Marine Corps Overseas Svc. ribbon, Global War on Terrorism Expeditionary medal, Navy Fleet Marine Force ribbon, Joint Meritorious Unit award, Navy Unit Commendation, Meritorious Unit Commendation, Nat. Def. Svc. medal. Mem.: Nat. Naval Officers Assn. (life; pres. 1995—97, Disting. Svc. award 1996), Sigma Theta Tau. Democrat. Bapt. Personal E-mail: texjop@yahoo.com.

PARKER, JUDITH ELAINE, retired language educator; b. Fresno, Calif., July 3, 1938; d. John Harris and Dorothy Henrietta (Nielsen) Oates; m. Brad Hill, Feb. 14, 1959 (div. Feb. 1979); children: Scott, Mark. BA, Fresno State U., 1960, M, 1968. Tchr. lang. arts Fresno Unified Sch. Dist., 1960—2005. Mem. NEA, NOW, Nat. Coun. Tchrs. English, Nat. Mus. Women in Arts, Calif. Assn. Tchrs. English, Fresno Art Mus., Women's Internat. League for Peace and Freedom, Fresno Met. Mus. Democrat. Unitarian Universalist. Avocations: cooking, gardening, travel, reading. Home: 5912 E Hamilton Ave Fresno CA 93727-6225

PARKER, KELLEY D., lawyer; b. Norman, Okla., Apr. 30, 1968; BBA, Univ. Okla., 1990; JD magna cum laude, Georgetown Univ., 1993. Bar: NY 1994. Ptnr., corp. dept., mergers & acquisitions practice Paul Weiss Rifkind Wharton & Garrison, NYC. Office: Paul Weiss Rifkind Wharton & Garrison 1285 Ave of the Americas New York NY 10019-6064 Office Fax: 212-373-3136, 212-492-0136. Business E-Mail: kparker@paulweiss.com.

PARKER, LETITIA, secondary school educator; b. Waukegan, Ill., Jan. 12, 1947; d. Robert Edwin and Lettie M. Parker. AA, Gulf Park Coll., Long Beach, Miss., 1970; BS, Fla. State U., 1972, MS, 1975. Tchr. St. John Elem. Sch., Quincy, Fla., 1972—75, LaFayette Art Ctr., Tallahassee, 1975—76, Henry County Sch., Collinsville, Va., 1976—79, Milton (Wis.) HS, 1979—. Regional chair WAEA Visual Art Classic Competition U. Wis., Whitewater, Wis., 1992—2002. Bd. dirs. Hunziker Endowment Bd., 2000—04. Mem.:

AAUW, Wis. Art Edn. Assn. (bd. dirs. 1979—2005, Pres. award for svc. 1990, 2002), Nat. Art Edn. Assn. Christian Scientist. Avocations: travel, theater. Office: Milton High Sch 114 W High St Milton WI 53563 E-mail: parkerl@mail.milton.k12.wi.us.

PARKER, LINDA BATES, professional development organization administrator; Grad., U. Dayton, U. Cin., Harvard U., 1991. Pres., founder Black Career Women, Cin. Dir. Career Devel. Ctr., mgmt. prof. U. Cin. Author: Career Portfolio; columnist for Nat. Black Collegian Mag.; presenter in field. Office: Black Career Women PO Box 19332 Cincinnati OH 45219-0332

PARKER, LISA E., elementary school educator, gifted and talented educator; b. Decatur, Ga., May 28, 1963; d. Estil Wayne Evans and Ethelene 9Beasley) Allen; m. Donald Wayne Parker, Sept. 29, 1983; childern: Donald Wesley, Matthew Carrson. BS in Edn. cum laude, Tift Coll., 1984; BS in Edn., Ga. So. U., 1984, MEd, 1987, EDS, 1989. Cert. gifted educator; cert. learning disabilities. Tchr. Vidalia (Ga.) City Schs., 1984-86, 1986-88, Treutlen County Bd. Edn., Soperton, Ga., 1988-91, Southeastern Tech. Inst., Vidalia, 1991, instr. devel. studies, 1991—; tchr. 6th grade, math. sci., gifted Montgomery County Mid. Sch., Mt. Vernon, Ga. Instr. devel. studies, 1991—; mem. Devel. Studies Adv. Com. Vidalia, Ga., 1991—; chair S.E. Consortia Devel. Educators, Vidalia, 1993—, vice chair state level; mem. Sex Equity Com., Vidalia, 1991—, Dress Com., Vidalia, 1992, Workroom Orgn., Vidalia, 1992, chairperson state level, 1994-96; commr. faculty forum, 1994-96. Mem. ASCD, Am. Vocat. Assn., Ga. Vocat. Assn., Nat. Assn. Devel. Educators, Coun. Tchrs. Math., Sci. Tchrs. Assn. Republican. Baptist. Avocations: reading, kayaking. Office: Mt Vernon Mid Sch 701 Dobbins St Mount Vernon GA 30445

PARKER, LISA FREDERICK, music educator, Dalcroze specialist; b. N.Y.C., Sept. 17, 1934; d. Karl Telford and Anne (Moore) Frederick; m. Dec. 24, 1966 (div. May, 1979); children: Eden Elizabeth, Wendy Margaret. BA cum laude, Smith Coll., 1956; M of Music in Conducting, New Eng. Conservatory, 1962; Diplôme, Inst. Jacque Dalcroze, Geneva, 1965. Instr. eurythmics, solfége New Eng. Conservatory, Boston, 1959-71; conductor NEC Youth Singers, Boston, 1965-71; dir. Dalcroze Program, Belmont (Mass.) Music Sch, 1970-77; chair Dalcroze dept. Longy Sch. of Music, Cambridge, 1977—. Mem. guest faculty Inst. Jaques Dalcroze, at internat. conf., 1974—; presenter at workshops internationally; tchr., 1999—; founder Boston Ctr. Osteophonie. Author: (children's skit) Curious George Goes to Music School, 1993—; contbr. articles to profl. jours. Active Sane Freeze, Belmont, Mass., 1985-89, All Saints Episc. Ch., Brookline, Mass., 1994—. Recipient George Seamon award Excellence in Tchg., 2003. Mem. Dalcroze Soc. Am. (pres. 1972-75, editor jour. 1975-81), Nat. Music Tchrs. Assn., Dalcroze Soc. Can. Democrat. Avocations: gardening, french language, travel, reading, chamber music. Office: Longy Sch of Music 1 Follen St Cambridge MA 02138-3599

PARKER, LOIS W., retired literature and language professor; b. Corpus Christi, Tex., Sept. 15, 1921; d. Herbert William Barton and Iva Olivia Oatman. MA, So. Ill. U., 1965; PhD in English, U. Ariz., 1970. Assoc. prof. English Southwestern U. Mem.: Austin Harp Soc., Georgetown Music Club, San Gabriel Writers League (co-founder), Wynnewood Music Club. Home: RR 1 Box 277B Oakdale Rd at Atholea Wynnewood OK 73098

PARKER, LYNDA CHRISTINE RYLANDER, secondary school educator; b. Bremerton, Wash., Apr. 21, 1949; d. Richard Algot and Marian Ethelyn (Peterson) Rylander; m. Joseph Hiram Parker, Feb. 7, 1981; 1 child, Joseph Hiram IV. BA in English, Sociology, Pacific Luth. U., 1971, MA in Ednl. Administrn., 1981, prin.'s credential, 1982, postgrad. Tchr. lang. arts Cen. Kitsap Schs., Silverdale, Wash., 1971-74; tchr. English gifted Okanagan Schs., Kelowna, B.C., Can., 1974-78; tchr. lang. arts gifted Federal Way (Wash.) Schs., 1978-86; tchr. lang. arts. remedial reading, humanities gifted Bethel Sch. Dist., Spanaway, Wash., 1986—. Counselor Okanagan Sch. Dist., Kelowna, 1974-78; advisor Ski Club, Cheerleaders, Svc. Club, Pep Club, Kitsap Schs., Silverdale, 1971-74, Cheerleaders, Pep Club, Svc. Club, Ski Club, annual, newspaper, class advisor, Okanagan Sch. Dist., Kelowna, 1974-78, newspaper, Cheerleaders, Bethel Schs., Spanaway, 1986—; multimedia, at-risk program, gifted program, 1996-; presenter of workshops for parents, tchrs., adminstrs., 1988—. Named Christa McAuliffe Outstanding Tchr. of Yr. State of Wash., 1988, Walmart Tchr. of Yr., 2004. Mem. NEA, ASCD, NAFE, Nat. Assn. Secondary Sch. Prins., Wash. Edn. Assn., Wash. Assn. Secondary Sch. Prins., Bethel Educators Assn. Republican. Lutheran. Avocations: piano, skiing, body building. Home: 1721 169th Street Ct S Spanaway WA 98387-9141 Personal E-mail: stefanlay@aol.com.

PARKER, LYNDA MICHELE, psychiatrist; b. Sept. 28, 1947; d. Albert Francis and Dorothy Thomasina (Herriott) P. BA, C. W. Post Coll., 1968; MA, NYU, 1970; MD, Cornell U., 1974; postgrad., N.Y. Psychoanalytic Inst., 1977-82. Diplomate Am. Coll. Forensic Examiners. Intern N.Y. Hosp., N.Y.C., 1975; resident in psychiatry Payne Whitney Clinic, N.Y.C., 1975-78; psychiatrist-in-charge day program Cabrini Med. Ctr., N.Y.C., 1978-79, attending psychiatrist, supr. psychiatry residents, 1978-96, supr. long-term psychotherapy, 1980-82; attending psychiatrist N.Y. Hosp., Cornell Med. Ctr., 1979-96; practice medicine specializing in psychiatry N.Y.C., 1979-96; from instr. psychiatry to asst. prof. Cornell U. Med. Coll., 1979-96; instr. psychiatry N.Y. Med. Coll., 1978-96; assoc. prof., regional chair dept. psychiatry Tex. Tech. U. Health Scis. Ctr., Amarillo, 1996-99, No. region dir. correctional mental health scis., 1999—2002, clin. dir. PAMIO, 1999—2002; pvt. practice, 2002—. Assoc. prof. pharmacy practice in psychiatry Tex. Tech U. Sch. Pharmacy, 1996-99; psychiat. cons. Bldg. Service 32BJ Health Fund, 1983-89, Inwood House, N.Y.C., 1983-86, Time-Life Inc., 1986-96, Ind. Med. Examiners, 1986-96, Epilepsy Inst., 1986-87, asst. med. dir., 1987-88, med. dir., 1988; ind. med. examiner Rep. Health Care Rev. Sys. Mem. adv. bd. St. Bartholomew Community Presch., N.Y.C., 1990-96. Martin Luther King Jr. scholar, NYU, 1968—70. Mem.: AAUW, Tex. Med. Assn., Tex. Soc. for Psychiat. Physicians, Am. Womens Med. Assn., Am. Psychiat. Assn. Episcopalian. Office: 1616 S Kentucky Ste C-200 Amarillo TX 79102 Office Phone: 806-457-9200. Personal E-mail: LyParker@aol.com.

PARKER, MARIETTA, prosecutor; Asst. U.S. atty. Dept. Justice, Kansas City, Mo.; U.S. atty. Dept. Justice, Kansas City, Mo., 1993—.

PARKER, MARY E., educational psychology educator; b. Santa Anna, Tex., Aug. 14, 1945; d. Raymond Martell and Vivian Virginia Eubank; m. Gerald Gray Parker, Aug. 8, 1970; children: James Robert, Jeri Ann, Matthew BS, U. Tex., 1967; MA, West Tex. A&M U., 1969; EdD, Tex. Tech. U., 1994. Cert. secondary tchr. and mid-mgmt. Tchr. Corpus Christi Ind. Sch. Dist., Tex., 1967—68, Hereford Ind. Sch. Dist., Tex., 1974—88; prof. ednl. psychology West Tex. A&M U., Canyon, 1994—. Active Amarillo-West Tex. Partnerships in Edn., 1994-99; presenter in field Contbr. articles to profl. jours Bus. divsn. leader United Way, Hereford, 1980; dir. Mom and Dad's Assn., Canyon, 1994-95; found. chair Divsn. Edn., Canyon, 1996—; key note spkr. Newspaper in Edn., Amarillo, 1999 Sallie Mae grantee, Washington, 1995, Amarillo Nat. Resource Ctr. for Plutonium math./sci. grantee, 1995-2000; C.K. Jefferson scholar Newspaper in Edn., 1997. Mem. U. Women, West Tex. Hist. Assn. (bd. dirs.), West Tex. Alumni Assn. (bd. dirs. 1994-2002, nominee Disting. Alumnus), Delta Kappa Gamma (scholarship com. 1996—), Phi Delta Kappa (found. rep. 1996-2004), Kappa Delta Pi (chpt. counselor 1995—, Ace award 1999, Educator of Yr., Outstanding Found. Prof., Kappan of Yr.) Avocations: reading, writing. Office: West Tex A&M Univ PO Box 60208 Canyon TX 79016-0001 Office Phone: 806-651-3624.

PARKER, MARY-LOUISE, actress; b. Ft. Jackson, S.C., Aug. 2, 1964; 1 child, William Atticus. Attended, Bard Coll. Actress: (theatre) Hay Fever, 1987, The Miser, 1988, The Art of Success, 1989, The Importance of Being Earnest, 1989, Prelude to a Kiss, Broadway, 1990-91 (Theatre World award, Clarence Derwent Award, Tony nomination, 1990), Babylon Gardens, 1991, How I Learned to Drive, 1997 (Lucille Lortel Award for outstanding actress, OBIE Award, 1997), Proof, Broadway (Tony award for best actress in a play, 2001); (films) Signs of Life, 1989, Longtime Companion, 1990, Grand Canyon, 1991, Fried Green Tomatoes, 1991, Mr. Wonderful, 1993, Naked in New York, 1994, The Client, 1994, Bullets Over Broadway, 1994, Boys on the Side, 1995, A Portrait of a Lady, 1996, Reckless, 1995, Murder in Mind, 1997, The Maker, 1997, Let the Devil Wear Black, 1998, Goodbye, Lover, 1998, Five Senses, 1999, Pipe Dream, 2002, Red Dragan, 2002, The Best Thief in the World, 2004, Saved!, 2004, Romance & Cigarettes, 2005, others; (TV movies) Too Young the Hero, 1988, A Place for Annie, 1994, Sugartime, 1995, Legalese, 1998, Saint Maybe, 1998, The Simple Life of Noah Dearborn, 1999, Cupid & Cate, 2000, Master Spy: The Robert Hanssen Story, 2002, Miracle Run, 2004, Vinegar Hill, 2005; (TV miniseries) Angels in America, 2003 (Golden Globe for best supporting actress 2004, Emmy award, Outstanding Supporting Actress in a Miniseries or a Movie, 2004); (TV series) Ryan's Hope, 1975, West Wing, 2001-05,(Emmy nomination, 2002), Weeds, 2005- (Best Performance by an Actress in a TV Series-Musical or Comedy, Hollywood Fgn. Press Assn. (Golden Globe award), 2006. Office: William Morris Agy care Scott Henderson 151 S El Camino Dr Beverly Hills CA 90212-2775*

PARKER, MELISSA BERNICE, advertising executive; d. Marzine Parker, Sr. and Moretha Parker. BS in Agrl. Econs., U. Calif., Davis, 1995; MBA, Calif. State U., Hayward, 2000. Cert. notary pub. Calif., lic. Realtor Calif., property mgmt. Calif. Apt. Assn. Property mgr. M & M Parker & Assocs., Oakland, 1991—; banking officer Citibank F.S.B., San Francisco, 1995—96; sr. claims rep. Farmers Ins. Exch., Pleasanton, Calif., 1996—2000, Richmond, Calif., 1996—2000; applied materials Human Resources Exec. Program, Santa Clara, Calif., 2000; advt. exec. SBC Calif., Oakland, 2001—04, Valley Yellow Pages, Hayward, Calif., 2004—05, Hilltop Learning Corp., 2004—, Jack London Square Realty, Inc., 2005—. Photo journal dvd, Celebrations Article Oakland Tribune Marzine & Moretha Parker Sr. Co-chair Taylor Meml. United Meth. Ch. Ann. Woman's Day; with Marilyn Hickey Ministries; mem. U. Calif.-Davis. Mem.: NAFE, So. Poverty Law Ctr., Pres.'s Cir., Alfred Lepure Soc., Delta Sigma Theta (life). Democrat. United Methodist. Home: 2625 Alcatraz Ave Ste 350 Berkeley CA 94705 Office: 311 Oak St Ste 116 Oakland CA 94607 Office Phone: 510-459-9062. Personal E-mail: parkermel@aol.com. Business E-mail: melissa.parker@jacklondonrealty.com.

PARKER, NANCY KNOWLES (MRS. CORTLANDT PARKER), publishing executive; b. Buffalo, Aug. 30, 1929; d. Ward Emerson and Barbara Louise (Bull) Knowles; m. Cortlandt Parker, Sept. 8, 1951; children: Elizabeth, Cortlandt, Stephen, Nancy Gray. Student, Chevy Chase Jr. Coll., 1949. Copy girl Washington Evening Star, 1947-49; reporter Newark Evening News, 1949-51; asst. pub. rels. dir. Newark Cmty. Chest, 1951-52; writer Suburban Life mag., Summit, NJ, 1952-55; co-founder, assoc. editor, then editor Observer Tribune, Mendham, NJ, 1955-59; cmty. living editor Recorder Pub. Co., Bernardsville, NJ, 1959-84, v.p., 1960—2002; pub. emeritus, 2002—; editor, pub. New Eng., Finger Lakes, L.I. and Va. Wine Gazettes, 1988—. Pres. Greenvale Vineyards, Portsmouth, R.I. Past trustee Somerset Hills Cmty. Chest, North Jersey Tng. Sch., Totowa, Morris-Somerset chpt. UN Assn., Bonnie Brae Ednl. Ctr., Millington, NJ Vis. Homemaker Svc. Somerset County; trustee, bd. dirs. Camp Brett-Endeavor, Clinton, NJ, Morristown (NJ) Meml. Hosp.; mem. Glen Manor House Com., Portsmouth, RI; sec. New Eng. Wine Coun Mem. LWV (chair voters svc. Morris County chpt. 1954-55), Bus. and Profl. Women, Nat. Soc. Arts and Letters, Southeastern New Eng. Grape Growers Assn., Jr. League, Pen and Brush NYC, Friends of Whitehall, Colonial Dames in Am. (past bd. dirs. RI chpt.), Newport (RI) Garden Club (bd. dirs., past pres.), English Speaking Union (bd. dirs. Newport br. 1990-2000), NJ Hist. Soc. (adv. coun. Newark chpt.) Home: 582 Wapping Rd Portsmouth RI 02871-5306 Office: Greenvale Farm & Vineyard 582 Wapping Rd Portsmouth RI 02871-5306 also: 17 Morristown Rd Bernardsville NJ 07924-2312

PARKER, OLIVIA, photographer; b. Boston, June 10, 1941; d. Harvey Perley and Barbara Ellen (Churchill) Hood; m. John Otis Parker, Apr. 4, 1964; children: John Otis, Helen Elizabeth. BA, Wellesley Coll., 1963. Tchr. photog. workshops, 1975—. Photographer, 1969—; author: (monographs) Signs of Life, 1978, Under the Looking Glass, 1983, Weighing the Planets, 1987; portfolios of black and white photographs Ephemera, 1977, Lost Objects, 1980; one-woman shows include Vision Gallery, Boston, 1976, 1977, 1979, 1982, 1983, 1986, 1987, Friends of Photography, Carmel, Calif., 1979, 1981, Marcuse Pfeifer, N.Y.C., 1980, 1983, George Eastman House, Rochester, N.Y., 1981, Art Inst. Chgo., 1982, Photo Gallery Internat., Tokyo, 1983, 1984, 1987, Fotografie Forum Gallery, Frankfurt, Germany, 1985, Lieberman and Saul, N.Y.C., 1988, Mus. Photgraphic Arts, San Diego, 1988, Photographers' Gallery, London, 1990, Brent Sikkema, N.Y.C., 1990, 1991, Parco, Tokyo, 1991, ICAC/Weston, 1992, Vision, San Francisco, 1993, Robert Klein, Boston, 1993, 1996, 1999, 2005, Wooster Gardens, N.Y.C., 1996, (with Jerry Uelsmann) Isabella Stewart Gardner Mus., Boston, 1997, Huntington (W.Va.) Mus. of Art, 2000, Lancaster (Pa.) Mus. of Art, 2000, Toledo (Ohio) Art Mus., 2002, Visual Arts Ctr. Coll. of Santa Fe, 2003, Edelman Gallery, Chgo., 2004, exhibited in group shows at Mus. Fine Arts, Boston, 1978, 1992, 1993, 1996, 1999, Chgo. Art Inst., 1978, Internat. Ctr. Photography, N.Y.C., 1985, 1987, Fogg Art Mus. Harvard U., 1989, Aldrich Mus. Contemporary Art, 2004, Represented in permanent collections Mus. Modern Art, N.Y.C., Art Inst. Chgo., Boston Mus. Fine Arts, Victoria and Albert Mus., London, TV documentary, Africans in America, 1998. Trustee Art Inst. Boston, 1992—; bd. dirs. MacDowell Colony, 1988—. Recipient Wellesley College Alumnae Achievement award, 1996; Artists Found. fellow, 1978. Mem.: Soc. for Photog. Edn., Chilton Club. Office: Robert Klein 4th Fl 38 Newbury St Fl 4 Boston MA 02116-3210 E-mail: glasslight@mac.com.

PARKER, PHYLLIS E., mathematics educator; b. St. Louis, Feb. 24, 1959; d. Donald Eugene and Rosemary Joann Acklin; m. Gary K. Parker, May 19, 1979; children: G. Matthew, Jacob N. BS in Edn., S.E. Mo. State U., Cape Girardeau, 1981; MS in Edn., NW Mo. State U., Maryville, 1995. Elem. math. tchr. West St. Francois County Schs., Leadwood, Mo., 1981—84; 7th-9th grade math. tchr. Fairfax R-3 Schs., Mo., 1984—98, Mount City R-2 Schs., Mo., 1998—. Trustee Mound City Pub. Libr., 2000—; Sunday sch. tchr. St. Patrick's Cath. Ch., Forest City, Mo., 1999—, sec. ch. coun., 2002—. Home: 1704 Sunset Blvd Mound City MO 64470 Office: Mount City R-2 Schs 708 Nebraska Mound City MO 64470

PARKER, PHYLLIS R., secondary school educator; b. Liberty, Tex., Feb. 9, 1947; d. Mark H. and Mary Jane (Stallworth) Richards; m. J. David Parker, Nov. 27, 1970; children: Anson D., J. Nealin, Laura A. BA, Baylor U., Waco, Tex., 1970; M of Pub. Affairs, U. Tex., Austin, 1976. Cert. tchr. Va. Daycare dir. Waco Home and Family Ctr., 1971; tchr., trainer Tex. Dept. Pub. Welfare, Austin, 1972—73, supr. contract devel., 1973; triage Emergency Rm. Group Health Hosp., Seattle, 1980—82; tchr. geography, art Rockbridge County HS, Lexington, Va., 1993—98, tchr. world history, 1998—; intern US Rep. Barbara Jordan, Washington, 1975. Child welfare caseworker Mo. Dept. Pub. Welfare, Jefferson City, 1967—69. Author: Brazil and the Quiet Intervention, 1979. Coord. geography awareness week Va. chpt. Nat. Geographic Soc., 1994; bd. dirs. Rockbridge Assn. for Retarded Citizens, 1986—93. Recipient Excellence in Tchg. award, US State Dept./Am. Coun. for Intermediate Edn., 2000, award, SAR, 2001; fellow, Armonk Found., Germany, 1996, Keizai Koho Ctr., Japan, 1998, Korea Soc., 2002. Mem.: NEA, Va. Geographic Alliance. Avocations: painting, quilting, travel. Home: 22 Hillcrest Ln Lexington VA 24450 Office: Rockbridge County High Sch 143 Greenhouse Rd Lexington VA 24450

PARKER, SARA ANN, librarian, consultant; b. Cassville, Mo., Feb. 19, 1939; d. Howard Franklin and Vera Irene (Thomas) P. BA, Okla. State U., 1961; M.L.S., Emporia State U., Kans., 1968. Adult svcs. librarian Springfield Pub. Libr., Mo., 1972-75, bookmobile dir. Mo., 1975-76; coord. S.W. Mo. Libr. Network, Springfield, 1976-78; libr. developer Colo. State Libr., Denver, 1978-82; state librarian Mont. State Libr., Helena, 1982-88, State Libr. Pa., Harrisburg, 1988-90; Pa. commr. librs., dep. sec. edn. State of Pa., Harrisburg, 1990-95; state libr. State of Mo., Jefferson City, 1995. Cons. and lectr. in field. Author, editor, compiler in field; contbr. articles to profl. jours. Sec., Western Coun. State Librs., Reno, 1984-88, mem. Mont. State Data Adv. Coun., 1983-88, Mont. Telecommunications Coun., 1985-88, WLN Network Coun., 1984-87, Kellogg ICLIS Project Mgmt. Bd., 1986-88; mem. adv. com. Gates Libr. Initiative, 1998—2005; mem. OCLC Strategic Directions and Governance Study Adv. Coun., 2000-01, webjunction adv. coun., 2003—. Recipient Pres.'s award, Nature Conservancy, 1989, Friends award, Pa. Assn. Ednl. Comms. and Techs., 1989, Friend of Sch. Librs. award, Mo. Sch. Librs. Assn., 2000, Bohley Libr. Cooperation award, 2001; fellow Inst. Ednl. Leadership, 1982. Mem. ALA, Chief Officers State Libr. Agys. (pres. 1996-98), Mont. Libr. Assn. (bd. dirs. 1982-88), Mountain Plains Libr. Assn. (sec. chmn. 1980, pres. 1987-88, chair MOREnet adv. coun. 2004—).

PARKER, SARAH ELIZABETH, state supreme court chief justice; b. Charlotte, NC, Aug. 23, 1942; d. Augustus and Zola Elizabeth (Smith) P. AB, U. N.C., 1964, JD, 1969; LHD (hon.), Queens Coll., 1998. Bar: N.C. 1969, U.S. Dist. Ct. (mid., ea. and we. dists.) N.C. Vol. U.S. Peace Corps, Ankara, Turkey, 1964-66; pvt. practice Charlotte, 1969-84; judge N.C. Ct. Appeals, Raleigh, 1985—92; assoc. justice N.C. Supreme Ct., Raleigh, 1993—2005, chief justice, 2006—. Bd. visitors U. N.C., Chapel Hill, 1993—97; pres. Mecklenburg County Dem. Women, Charlotte, 1973; N.C. ct. commr., 1999—; bd. dirs. YWCA, Charlotte, 1982—85. Recipient Disting. Woman of N.C. award, 1997, Woman of Achievement award Nat. Fedn. Women's Clubs, 1997, Humanitarian award N.C. Assn. of Black County Officials, 2003; Named Judge of Yr., N.C. Women Attorneys Assn., 2002. Mem. ABA, Inst. Jud. Adminstrn., N.C. Bar Assn. (v.p. 1987-88), Mecklenburg County Bar (sec.-treas. 1982-84), Wake County Bar Assn., N.C. Internat. Women's Forum, Women Attys. Assn. (Gwyneth David Pub. Svc. award 1986). Episcopalian. Office: NC Supreme Ct PO Box 1841 Raleigh NC 27602-1841

PARKER, SARAH JESSICA, actress; b. Nelsonville, Ohio, Mar. 25, 1965; m. Matthew Broderick May, 1997; 1 child: James. Launched fragrance Lovely perfume, 2005. Actress: (theatre) The Innocents, 1976, The Sound of Music, 1977, Annie, 1978, The War Brides, 1981, The Death of a Miner, 1982, To Gillian on Her 37th Birthday, 1983, 84, Terry Neal's Future, 1986, The Heidi Chronicles, 1989, How to Succeed in Business Without Really Trying, 1996, Once Upon a Mattress, 1996, (films) Rich Kids, 1979, Somewhere Tomorrow, 1983, Firstborn, 1984, Footloose, 1984, Girls Just Want to Have Fun, 1985, Flight of the Navigator, 1986, L.A. Story, 1991, Honeymoon in Vegas, 1992, Hocus Pocus, 1993, Striking Distance, 1993, Ed Wood, 1994, Miami Rhapsody, 1995, If Lucy Fell, 1996, Mars Attacks!, 1996, The First Wives Club, 1996, Extreme Measures, 1996, 'Til There Was You, 1997, The Substance of Fire, 1996, (voice) A Life Apart: Hasidism in America, 1997, Isn't She Great, 1999, Dudley Do-Right, 1999, State and Main, 2000, Life Without Dick, 2001, Strangers with Candy, 2005, The Family Stone, 2005, Failure to Launch, 2006; (TV movies) My Body, My Child, 1982, Going for the Gold: The Bill Johnson Story, 1985, A Year in the Life, 1986, The Room Upstairs, 1987, Dadah Is Death, 1988, The Ryan White Story, 1989, Twist of Fate, 1989, In the Best Interest of the Children, 1992, The Sunshine Boys, 1995, Sex and the Matrix, 2000, (TV series) Square Pegs, 1982-83, A Year in the Life, 1987-88, Equal Justice, 1990-91, Sex and the City, 1998-2004 (Best Supporting Actress Golden Globe award 1999, 2000, 01, 02, 04, Emmy nominee for Outstanding Lead Actress 1999-2002, Outstanding Performance by Female Actor in Comedy Series award 2001, Emmy award Outstanding Lead Actress in a Comedy Series, 2004), (TV pilots) The Alan King Show, 1986; guest appearances The Ben Stiller Show, 1992, The Larry Sanders Show, 1992; co-exec. prodr. Sex and the City. Nat. amb. U.S. Fund for UNICEF. Recipient, Am. Civil Liberties Union award, 1995. Office: Creative Artists Agy care Jane Berliner 9830 Wilshire Blvd Beverly Hills CA 90212-1804*

PARKER, SASHA SMILKA, medical educator, nurse, consultant; b. Neustadt, Holstein, Germany, Nov. 3, 1947; arrived in US, 1952; d. Blagoje Blazo and Sofia Soka Dragic; life ptnr. Richard A. Polemeni; 1 child, Peter Joseph. Student, Ind. U., 1978; AS in Nursing, Broward CC, 1982. Lic. massage therapist Fla., cert. electrologist Fla.; RN Fla.; cert. facial specialist Fla. Asst. surg. adminstr. Am. Med. Inst. Surgery, Ft. Lauderdale, Fla., 1988—89; surg. adminstr. Eye Care & Surgery Ctr., Ft. Lauderdale, 1989—91; clin. supr. Spl. Care Home Health, 1991—97; pres., CEO Gem Homecare Svcs., Inc., Ft. Lauderdale, 1997—2005, Eclectic Skin Inst., LLC, Ft. Lauderdale, 1998—2003; pres., CEO, CFO Esthetic Skin Inst., Inc., 2003—. Cons. Innovative Health Svcs., Inc., Ft. Lauderdale, 1997—; faculty spa mgmt. and hospitality program U. Calif., Irvine, Calif. Vol. Women in Distress, Ft. Lauderdale, Adult Congregate Living Assn., Ft. Lauderdale. Named Ultimate Nurse, Ultimate Nurses, Inc., 2004, Businesswoman of Yr., Nat. Rep. Congrl. Com., Inc., 2004, 2005; recipient Spotlight Entrepreneur award, Nursing Spectrum, 2004. Mem.: Am. Massage Therapy Assn., Nat. Bus. Adv. Coun., Fla. Electrology Assn., Fla. Nurses Assn., Assn. Med. Esthetic Nurses (pres., founder 2004). Avocations: dancing, travel, music, cooking. Office: Esthetic Skin Inst Inc 1120 S Fed Hwy Ste 4 Fort Lauderdale FL 33316 Office Fax: 954-463-4459. Personal E-mail: sashas@bellsouth.net.

PARKER, SUSAN BROOKS, health facility administrator; b. Newport, NH, Nov. 7, 1945; d. Ronald Elliott and Elizabeth Louise (Wiggins) P.; m. Allen D. Avery, 1967 (div. 1978); children: Jeffrey Roberts Avery, Mark Brooks Avery. BS in English and French, U. Vt., 1968; MSW/MSP, Boston Coll., 1978. EMT Vt., 1973-76. Resort hotel mgr., retail buyer Avery Vt. Inns, 1967-75; aftercare psychiat. social worker Orange County Mental Health, Bradford, Vt., 1974-76; exec. dir. Grafton County Planning Coun., Lebanon, NH, 1978-80, N.H. Developmental Disabilities Planning Coun., Concord, NH, 1980-87; commr. Dept. of Mental Health, Augusta, Maine, 1987-89; assoc. commr. U.S. Social Security Adminstrn., Balt., 1989-93; sec. gen. Rehab. Internat., NYC, 1993—98; sr. adv., interim dir. disability program Internat. Labor Office, Geneva, 1998—2002; dir. policy and rsch. Office Disability Employment Policy U.S. Dept. Labor, Washington, 2002—. Cons. Nat. Gov.'s Assn., Washington, 1985-86, Office of Health and Devel. Svcs., Washington, 1987; bd. dirs. Nat. Assn. Devel. Disabilities, Washington, 1983-87, Ctrl. NH Mental Health Ctr., Concord, 1985-87, World Com. Disability, Washington, 1997—, Roeher Inst., Toronto, 1997-2000, Orah.com, Geneva, 2002—, NH Devel. Disabilities Coun., 2002—05; hon. coun. Rehab. Internat., mem. World Assembly, NYC, 1998-. Author: Scheme, 1965, Jamaican Collection, 1973, numerous poems; contbr. articles to newspapers and profl. jours. Pres. Parent Tchr. Orgn., Fairlee, Vt., 1972-73; founder and dir. Fairlee Ford Sayre Ski Program, Dartmouth Coll. Skiway, Fairlee, 1972-76, United Way, Concord, 1983-86; bd. dirs. PTO Rundlett Jr. H.S., Concord, 1982-85; pres. U.S. Coun. for Internat. Rehab., Washington, 1993. Recipient Assn. Retarded Citizens Children's Disability Pub. Policy award, 1992, Kathryn C. Arneson award from People to People, 1992, Commr.'s citation for outstanding efforts in developing policy U.S. Social Security Adminstrn., 1992, Commn.'s citation for outstanding exec. leadership, 1993, Secretary's Performance award U.S Dept. Labor, 2003-2005, Sec.'s Exemplary Achievement award, 2003, 2006; named Outstanding Alumnae Boston Coll., 1991. Avocations: skiing, gardening, canoeing, reading, film and performing arts.

PARKER, SUZANNE MARIE, physical education educator; d. William Reed and Louise Grace Parker. BA, Norfolk State U., Va., 1993; MA, Va. Tech. U., Blacksburg, Va., 1999, PhD, 2002. Lic. tchr. Va., SC, Am. Master Tchr. cert. Tchr. Toano Mid. Sch., Va., 1994—99; grad. asst. Va. Tech. U., 1999—2002; asst. prof. SUNY, Cortland, NY, 2002—05; tchr. Darlington Mid. Sch., SC, 2005—06; asst. prof. Coker Coll., Hartsville, SC, 2006—. Contbr. articles to profl. jours. Mem.: AAHPERD, S.C. Educators Assn., Phi Kappa Phi. Avocations: snowboarding, dirt biking, ATV racing, kayaking.

PARKER, THERESA ANN BOGGS, special education educator, music educator; b. Spencer, W.Va., Jan. 16, 1947; d. Harry Clay and Betty Jean (Richards) Boggs; m. Larry Glen Parker, Apr. 29, 1967; children: Carey Ann, Jill Renee, Timothy Preston, Jeremy David, Leanna Michelle. AA in Secretarial Studies, Glenville State Coll., 1967, BA in Music Edn., 1970; MA in Spl. Edn., Coll. Grad. Studies, 1991; EdS in Ednl. Leadership, W.Va. Grad. Coll., 1996. Cert. tchr. Pvt. practice piano tchr., Spencer, 1967—; sub. tchr. Roane County Schs., Spencer, 1970—71, tchr. spl. edn., 1987—2001, tchr. music K-8, 2001—02, tchr. spl. edn., 2002—06, tchr. music K-8, 2006—, educator team mem.-parent/educator resource ctr., 1989—2002; sub. tchr. Marietta City Schs., Ohio, 1986; adminstr. Sand Hill Day Care Ctr., Reno, Ohio, 1986—87. Spl. edn. rep. W.Va. Dept. Edn., Charleston, 1995-98; dir. Safetytown Roane County, Spencer, 1989-93. Author: (with others) Selected Teaching Models Integrated with West Virginia's Academic Model for Gifted Education, 1991; poet with works appearing in Echoes of Yesteryear, America at the Millennium, 2000, Enlightened Shadows, Miracles of Nature, Best Poems and Poets of 2001, The Road That Never Ends, Internat. Libr. Poetry. Chmn. Cub Scout Pack Boy Scouts Am., Reno, 1983-87, dist. trainer, Parkersburg, W.Va., 1986-87, chmn. Boy Scout Troop, Spencer, 1987-91; Roane County rep. to Clay Ctr. for Arts Charleston, 2005—; organizer First Bapt. Ch. Diabetes Sup. Group, 1995-98. Safetytown grantee W.Va. Dept. Edn., Roane County, 1989, grantee W.Va. Edn. Fund, Roane County, 1992, W.Va. Edn. Fund, Clover Sch., 1992, Diabetes Support Group grantee Benedium Found., Roane and Calhoun/Jackson Counties, 1995, Youth and Edn. grantee Tri-County Partnership, Inc., 1998, W.Va. Humanities Coun., 2000-01, 05, The Edn. Alliance, 2004, 05, Exceptional Tchg. Techniques award RESA V, 2005; named Tchr. of Yr. Spencer Middle Sch., 1999-2000. Mem. MENC, ASCD, W.Va. Profl. Educators, Blue Grass Riding Club, Lions (program chmn., pres. 1997-98, dist. Leo chmn. 1998-00, dist. Flag Day/Peace Poster contest 2000-2001), Roane Arts and Humanities Coun. (charter, pres. 2000—), W.Va. Celtic Soc., Cultural Diversity Soc. Democrat. Baptist. Avocations: reading, sewing, playing piano. Home: 5754 Charleston Rd Walton WV 25286 Office: Roane County Schs 102 Chapman Ave Spencer WV 25276 Office Phone: 304-927-6415. Personal E-mail: partheresa6410@aol.com.

PARKER, TOWANA D., entrepreneur, director; d. John Richard Martin and Bernice Eason; m. Towana D. Parker, Sept. 25, 1976; children: Tanaya S., Yoshaundala S., Edmond II M., Gabriel T. Child Evangelism Metro Child Evangelism, 1985. Entrpreneur Special-T Uniform & Embroidery, Detroit, 1995—; pres. Ladies of Destiny and Purpose Internat., 1997—; exec. dir. Destiny and Purpose Cmty. Outreach, 1999—. Host (television interviewing) Public Report Host, mentor-role model (mentoring (young women 13-18 at risk) Role Model - Mentor (Several from Mayor, State Rep, Youth home & Gov. of State, 2004); contbg. writer. Master puppeteer Kings Kids Puppet Ministry, Detroit, 1986—2004; mem. Detroit Exch. Club, 2004—. Grantee, Detroit Empowerment Zone Devel. Corp., 2002-2004, City of Detroit Neighborhood Opportunity Fund, 2004-2005. Office Phone: 313-533-1931. Home Fax: 313-535-8810; Office Fax: 313-533-1932. Personal E-mail: ladyteedp@aol.com. E-mail: dapco7outreach@aol.com.

PARKES, JACQUELINE, marketing executive; b. 1966; Mktg. dir. Henson Muppets, Major League Baseball, NYC, 1995—2000, sr. dir. mktg., 2000—02, v.p., adv. mktg., 2002—04, sr. v.p., adv. mktg., 2004—. Named one of Forty under 40, Crain's NY Bus., 2004. Office: MLB 75 Ninth Ave 5th Fl New York NY 10011

PARKHURST, BEVERLY SUSLER, lawyer, administrative law judge; b. Decatur, Ill. d. Sewell and Marion Susler; m. Todd S. Parkhurst, Aug. 15, 1976. BA with honors, U. Ill., 1966, JD, 1969. Bar: Ill. 1969, U.S. Dist. Ct. (no. dist.) Ill. 1969, U.S. Ct. Appeals (7th cir.) 1975, U.S. Supreme Ct. 1980. Asst. U.S. atty. U.S. Atty.'s Office U.S. Dist. Ct. (no. dist.) Ill., Chgo., 1974-78, exec. asst. U.S. atty., 1978-81; pvt. practice law Offices of Beverly Susler Parkhurst, Chgo., 1982-86; trial judge Cir. Ct. Cook County, 1996-98; of counsel Witwer, Poltrock & Giampietro, Chgo., 1997—2003, Hedlund & Hanley LLC, 2003—04; appt. fed. adminstr. law judge, 2004—. Faculty Nat. Inst. of Trial Advocacy; bd. dirs. Internat. Forum Travel and Tourism Advs., vice chmn. 2d Internat. Conf., Jerusalem, 1986, regional chmn. 3d Internat. Conf., San Francisco, 1987; chmn. inquiry bd. Ill. Atty. Registration and Disciplinary Commn., 1985-87; guest lectr. legal ethics Washington U., St. Louis, 1986; lectr. on travel law, fed. civic procedures and med. malpractice; adj. prof. John Marshall Law Sch., 1999—; mediator Jud. Disput Resolution. Contbr. articles to profl. jours.; spkr. in field. Mem. Ill. Toll Hwy. Adv. Com., 1985-90; bd. dirs. Ill. Soc. for Prevention of Blindness, Cook County Ct. Watchers, Chgo. State U. Found., 1997—2003. James scholar U. Ill., 1962-66; recipient Spl. Achievement award U.S. Dept. Justice, 1978, Dir.'s award, 1981, Cert. of Profl. Achievement in Mediation, DePaul U. Dispute Resolution Ctr.; U.S. Utility Patent grantee 1984. Mem. ABA (chmn. subcom. alternatives to discovery litigation sect. 1985-87), Ill. Bar Assn. (com. profl. responsibility), Women's Bar Assn., Fed. Bar Assn., Chgo. Bar Assn. (chmn. judiciary commn. 1988-90, bench bar symposium 1988-91, exec. com. Alliance for Women), Nat. Inst. Trial Advocacy (faculty N.E. region), Lincoln Inn of Ct. (v.p.), Legal Club of Chgo. Avocations: scuba diving, swimming, cooking. Office: Fed Adminstr Law Judge Chicago IL 60603

PARKHURST, CAROLYN, writer; b. 1971; BA, Wesleyan U.; MFA in creative writing, Am. U. Author: The Dogs of Babel, 2003 (Best Fiction Book Fort Worth Star-Telegram, 2003, Notable Book New York Times, 2003), (short stories) (included in) North Am. Review, Minn. Review, Hawaii Review, Crescent Review. Office: c/o Douglas Stewart Curtis Brown Ltd 10 Astor Pl New York NY 10003

PARKHURST, VIOLET KINNEY, artist; b. Derby Line, Vt., Apr. 26, 1926; d. Edson Frank and Rosa (Beauchiene) Kinney; student Sch. Practical Arts, Boston, 1941-42, Baylor U., Waco, Tex., 1943, Calif. State U., Los Angeles, 1950-51; m. Donald Winters Parkhurst, Apr. 10, 1948. Fgn. corr. 5 Brazilian mags., 1946-53; tech. illustrator, 1954-55; owner five galleries including Ports of Call, San Pedro, Calif.; artist, specializing in seascapes; work included in permanent collection of Stockholm Mus., many pvt. collections including Presidents Richard M. Nixon, Ford, Reagan, Bush, Gov. Wilson, Mayor of Kobe, Japan, Mayor Yorty of L.A., Rory Calhoun, Barbara Rush, Jim Arness, David Rose, President Hu of China, 2005; one-shows shows at prominent galleries; numerous paintings published. Winner 30 blue ribbons for art. Fellow Am. Inst. Fine Arts. Mem. Ch. of Religious Sci. Author: How to Paint Books, 1966; Parkhurst on Seascapes, 1972. Paintings reproduced on covers South West Art, Arizona Living, Hollywood Bowl Easter Sunrise Service program; ltd. edit. prints published, also ltd. edit. plates. The first artist in the world invited to present a painting to Pres. Jiang Zemin, Beisin, China, 2002; the first western artist to have a painting in China Nat. Mus. of Fine Arts and the Hall of the People. Office: Parkhurst Gallery Ports of Call Village San Pedro CA 90731 E-mail: violet@parkhurstartgalleries.com.

PARKIN, FERN AGNES MARVEL, medical/surgical nurse, nursing educator; b. Pocatello, Idaho, Nov. 22, 1931; d. Clarence J. and May Agnes Cuppett; m. Jesse James Marvel, Apr. 16, 1948 (div. Aug. 28, 1973); children: Alexa Ann Adams, Marco Lewis Marvel, Jill Lynn Osburn; m. William Heber Parkin, Jan. 4, 1991. AA, L.A. Harbor Coll., Wilmington, Calif., 1967; B in Vocat. Edn., Calif. State U., Long Beach, Calif., 1978. RN Calif., Idaho, Ariz., Wyoming, Wash., cert. adult cardiopulmonary resuscitation, Calif., coronary care. Staff nurse, clinic nurse Kaiser Found. Hosp., Harbor City, Calif., 1964—65, 1967—69; charge nurse Bishop Randal Hosp., Lander, Wyo., 1970, Needles Hosp., Calif., 1971, Icelandic Rest Home, Blaine, Wash., 1971—, Shuksans Nursing Home, Bellingham, Wash., 1971—72; nursing instr. LA Unified Sch. Dist., 1973—78; charge nurse Pacific Hosp., Long Beach, Calif., 1972—74; acting head nurse L.A. Harbor Gen. Hosp., Torrance, Calif., 1974—76; LVN nurse instr. YWCA Job Corp, LA, 1976—77; intensive care and coronary care nurse Profl. Nurses Bur., Long Beach, Calif., 1971—77; psychiatric facilitation instr. Atascadero State Hosp., Calif., 1979; dir. staff devel. Paso Robles Convalescent, Calif., 1987—88; welfare missionary Church of Jesus Christ of LDS, Ormoc, Cebu, Bohol, Philippines, 1988—90; charge nurse Twin Cities Convalescent Ctr., Templeton, Calif., 1990—92. Portraits, Pres. Aquina, Pres. Ronald Regan. Counselor relief soc. Ch. Jesus Christ LDS, Wilmington, 1973, mem. choir Pocatello, Idaho, 1969; pres. PTA, Idaho, 1962—63. Mem.: Alpha Gamma Sigma. Democrat. Mem. Lds Ch. Avocations: painting, writing, reading. Home: 200 N PO Box 220667 Centerfield UT 84622

PARKINSON, DIAN, actress; Student, Lee Strasberg Studio, LA. Talk show hostess The Women's Side; appeared on TV shows The Price is Right, The Tonight Show Starring Johnny Carson, Vegas, Bob Hope's Desert Classic, The Bob Hope Christmas Show (Emmy Award Citation); model on cover of Bert Stein, Master of Contemporary Photography, Cosmopolitan mag., commls., posters, billboards, other mags. Named Miss U.S.A.

PARKS, ARVA MOORE, historian; b. Miami, Fla., Jan. 19, 1939; d. Jack and Anne (Parker) Moore; m. Robert Lyle Parks, Aug. 19, 1959 (div. May 1986); children: Jacqueline Carey, Robert Downing, Gregory Moore; m. Robert Howard McCabe, June 20, 1992. Student, Fla. State U., 1956-58; BA, U. Fla., 1960; MA in History, U. Miami, Coral Gables, 1971; LLD (hon.), Barry U., 1996. Tchr. Rolling Crest Jr. H.S., West Hyattsville, Md., 1960-63, Miami Edison Sr. H.S., Fla., 1963-64; grad. asst. U. Miami, Coral Gables, 1964-65; tchr. Everglades Sch. for Girls, Miami, 1965-66; cons., 1966-70; free-lance rsch. historian Miami, 1970-86; adj. prof. U. Miami, Coral Gables, 1986-87; pres. Arva Parks & Co., Miami, 1986—. Cons. thematic and interpretive rsch. and design Harry S. Truman Little White House, Key West, Fla., 1989-91; pres. Centennial Press, 1991—. Author: Miami the Magic City, 1981, rev. edit., 1991, The Forgotten Frontier, 1977 (rev. edit. 2004), Harry Truman and the Little White House in Key West, 1991, Miami: Then and Now, 1992, The Pathway to Greatness, 2001; co-author: (with Gregory M. Bush) Miami: The American Crossroad, 1996, (with Carolyn Klepser) Miami Then & Now, 2002, George Merrich's Coral Gables, 2006; editor Tequesta Jour. Hist. Soc. Fla., 1986-95; writer: (film) Our Miami: The Magic City, 1994. Bd. advs., Nat. Trust for Hist. Preservation, 1984-93, chmn. so. region, 1990-91, Fed. Adv. Coun. Hist. Preservation, 1995-2003; trustee Miami-Dade C.C., 1984-90, U. Miami, 1994—; bd. dirs. Louis Wolfson Media History Ctr., Miami, 1985-90, Orange Bowl Com., 1989—, Bapt. Health Systems of Miami, Inc., 1992—, Dade Found., 1997-2004, Drs. Hosp. Bd., 2004—; cmty. adv. Dade Heritage Trust, Miami, 1988-97, mem. Bi-Racial Tri-Ethnic Adv. Bd., Miami, 1984-99, New World Sch. Arts (exec. com.), Miami, 1986-90, Bok Sanctuary Bd., 2005—, City of Coral Gables Mus. Bd., 2005-; chmn. Vizcaya Trust, 1998-2004, pres. Fla. Forum, 2003-05; chair City of Miami Planning Adv. Bd., 2005—; bd. dirs. Internat. Women's Forum, 2005—. Recipient Historic Preservation award AIA, 1993, Outstanding Women of History award Cuban Am. Women's Club, 1992, Women Helping Women award Soroptimists, 1992, Am. History award DAR, 1987, Pathfinder's award Women's Com. 100, 1985, Outstanding Citizen award Coral Gables C. of C., 1983, Outstanding Preservationist award Dade Heritage Trust, 1983, Good Faith award Black Archives and Rsch. Found., 1981, Mus. of Sci. award, 1981, Cmty. Headliner award Women in Comm., 1980, Humanitarian award Urban League Guild, 1980, award City of Coral Gables Hist. Preservation Bd., 1978, Women of Impact award Cmty. Coalition for Women's History, 1996, Cmty. Star award Family Counseling Svcs. of Greater Miami, 1996, Edward T. Foote Alumnae of Distinction award U. Miami, 2002, Henriette Harris award Dade Heritage Trust, 2004; named to Alumni Hall of Fame Dade County Pub. Schs., 1985, Fla. Women's Hall of Fame, 1986, one of Women Who Made a Difference YWCA, 1988, City Miami Women's Hall Fame, 1996, Woman of Distinction award Soroptimist Internat. of Ams., Woman of Distinction award Girl Scouts Am., 1996, Alumni Women Distinction U. Fla., 1997, Tebeau prize Fla. Hist. Soc. for Am. Crossroad, 1997, Theodore Gibson Unity award, 1999, Vizcayans Cultural Millennium award, 1999, Miami Herald Spirit of Excellence award, 1999, Joseph R. Narot Cmty. Svc. award, 2003, Olympian award Olympia Theater at Gusman Ctr., 2006, Julia Tuttle award Commn. on the Status of Women, City of Miami, 2006. Mem. Internat. Women's Forum, Jr. League. Democrat. Methodist. Avocation: photography. Home and Office: 1601 S Miami Ave Miami FL 33129-1103 Office Phone: 305-854-8087. Personal E-mail: arvamiami@bellsouth.net.

PARKS, CONNIE, elementary school educator; d. Tommy and Mary Rogers; m. Michael Parks, Aug. 11, 1972; children: Charles, Jennifer. BA, Tarleton State U., Stephenville, Tex., 1990. Lic. tchr. Tex. Edn. Agy., 1990. Tchr. Kopperl Ind. Sch. Dist., Tex., 1990—94; asst. mgr. Fossil Co. Store, Hillsboro, Tex., 1995—96; tchr. Hill County Alt. Sch., Hillsboro, 1996—. Home: 2096 Fm 1304 Abbott TX 76621 Office: Hill County Alt Sch 311 S Waco Hillsboro TX 76645 Office Phone: 254-582-0963.

PARKS, GRACE SUSAN, bank executive; b. N.Y.C., Oct. 14, 1948; d. Marco A. and Gloria (Alvino) Vale; m. Louis Parks, Feb. 14, 1988; 1 child, Adam. BS, Pa. State U., 1970; MA, New Sch. for Social Rsch., 1974; cert. in mgmt., Adelphi U., 1979, MBA, 1980; cert. in entrepreneurship, Hofstra U., 1996. Bus. office rep. N.Y. Tel. Co., Rockville Centre, 1971-74; social worker Children's Aid Soc., N.Y.C., 1974-75; EEO officer Edwin Gould Svcs., N.Y.C., 1976-79; v.p. fin. instns. and global markets Bankers Trust Co., N.Y.C., 1979-92; v.p. compensation human resources Chase Manhattan Bank, 1992-96; pres. Loodie Prodns., Inc., 1996; instr. mgmt. Adelphi U. Grad. Sch. Bus. Adminstrn., 1981—; notary pub. State N.Y., 1978—. Mem. Human Resource Planning Soc., Assn. MBA Execs., Am. Compensation Assn., Wall St. Compensation and Benefits Assn. (chmn. 1994-96, pres. 1993-94), N.Y. Compensation Assn., Adelphi U. Businesswomen's Alumni Assn. (pres. 1980-82).

PARKS, JEAN ANNE, retired acute care nurse; b. Grand Rapids, Mich., Aug. 3, 1940; d. Edwin Charles and Ruth Katherine (Skellenger) Paepke; m. Charles Wilbur Parks, Nov. 24, 1961; children: Charles Edwin, Catherine Ann, Michael Allan. Diploma in Nursing with highest honors, Blodgett Meml. Hosp., 1961; BS summa cum laude in Health Studies, Western Mich. U., 1987; MA magna cum laude in Health and Humanities, Mich. State U., 1994. RN. Staff nurse Blodgett Meml. Hosp., Grand Rapids, 1961—62; nurse Ctrl. Mich. Cmty. Hosp., Mt. Pleasant, 1962—64; med.-surg. staff Blodgett Meml. Hosp., 1964—70, part-time staff, 1979—2003; part-time Medicaid evaluator for Kent County, Mich. Dept. Pub. Health, Lansing, 1987—88. Mem. Grand Rapids Symphony Chorus, 1987—2003. Baptist. Avocations: travel, music (toured with chorus to several countries).

PARKS, KATIE MAE, human services manager; b. Hubbard, Tex., Feb. 15, 1922; d. Sylvester and Janice Ruth Toliner; m. James Parks, Feb. 15, 1947 (dec.); children: Joe Keith, Sheryl Janice. Student, Tex. Tech. U. Unit mgr. Meth. Hosp., Lubbock, Tex., 1966—87; outreach specialist Tex. Tech. Wellness Ctr., Lubbock, Tex., 1994—. Bd. mem. Cmty. Health Clinic, Lubbock, Tex., Lubbock (Tex.) Art Commn. Author: (book) Why? - Poetry, 1971, History of African American In Lubbock, 2002. Adv. bd. mem. Martin Luther King, Lubbock, Tex., 1970—; bd. mem. Neighborhood Assn., Lubbock, Tex., 2001—03; pres. Usher Unit #2 Missionary Bapt. Ch., Sunday sch. tchr.; assists Missionary Soc. Nominee Tex. Women Hall of Fame, Gov. Ann Richards, Woman of Yr., Delta Sigma Theta, Clinton's Vol. award. Democrat. Baptist. Avocation: writing. Home: 2402 Cedar Ave Lubbock TX 79404

PARKS, MARGARET LAVERNE, secondary school educator, department chairman; d. Luther L. Parks and Ruth C. Parks-Stowers; adopted children: Nekoda C., Sean M. 1 child, Christopher J. Palmore. B in Sociology, Xavier U., Cin., 1975; MS Criminal Justice, Xavier U., 1977, MEd, 1987. Cert. comprehensive social studies Ohio. Asst. adminstr. Hamilton County Dept. Human Svcs., Cin., 1980—86; social studies dept. chair grades9-12 Cin. Pub. Schs., 1988—. Coll. lectr. U. Cin., Cin., 1975—86. Grantee Nat. Endowment, U. Kans., 1991. Mem.: NAACP, Phi Delta Kappa. Democrat. Avocations: travel, art, music. Office Phone: 513-363-9000.

PARKS, PATRICIA JEAN, lawyer; b. Portland, Oreg., Apr. 2, 1945; d. Robert and Marion (Crosby) Parks; m. David F. Jurca, Oct. 17, 1971 (div. 1976). BA in History, Stanford U., 1967; JD, U. Pa., Phila., 1970. Bar: N.Y. 1971, Wash. 1974. Assoc. Milbank, Tweed, Hadley & McCoy, N.Y.C., 1970-73, Shidler, McBroom, Gates & Lucas, Seattle, 1974-81, ptnr., 1981-90, Preston, Thorgrimson, Shidler, Gates & Ellis, Seattle, 1990-93; pvt. practice Seattle, 1993-99; spl. counsel Karr Tuttle Campbell, Seattle, 1999—. Active Vashon Allied Arts; former bd. dirs. Seattle chpt. Western Pension and Benefits Conf. Mem.: ABA, Pension Roundtable, Seattle-King County Bar Assn., Wash. Women Tax, Wash. State Bar Assn. (past chair gift and estate tax com.), Wash. Native Plant Soc., Wash. Athletic Club. Avocations: kayaking, hiking, contra dancing, birdwatching. Office: 1201 3rd Ave Ste 2900 Seattle WA 98101-3284 Office Phone: 206-224-8094. Business E-Mail: pparks@karrtuttle.com.

PARKS, SUZAN LORI, playwright; b. Fort Knox, KY, 1964; d. Donald and Francis Parks; m. Paul Oscher, 2001. BA, Mount Holyoke Coll., 1985. Guest lecturer Pratt Institute, N.Y.C., 1988, U. Mich., Ann Arbor, Mich., 1990, Yale U., New Haven, 1990—91, NYU, 1990—91; prof. of playwriting Eugene Lang Coll., N.Y.C., 1990; writer-in-residence New School for Social Research (now New School U.), N.Y.C., 1991—92; dir. Theater Projects Calif. Inst. Arts, Valencia, 2000—. Author: (plays) The Sinner's Place, 1985, Betting on the Dust Commander, 1988, Imperceptible Mutabilities in the Third Kingdom, 1990 (Obie award, 1990), Devotees in the Garden of Love, 1992, The Death of the Last Black Man in the Whole Entire World, 1992, The America Play, 1993, Venus, 1996 (Obie award, 1996), In the Blood, 1999, Topdog/Underdog, 2001 (Pulitzer Prize for drama, 2002), (screenplays) Anemone Me, 1990, Girl 6, 1996, (novels) Getting My Mother's Body, 2003. Recipient Rockefeller Foundation grant, 1990, N.Y. Found. for the Arts grant, 1990, Whiting Found. Writers award, 1992, Ford Found. grant, 1995, CalArts/Alpert award, 1996, PEN-Laura Pels award, 2000; fellow MacArthur Found., 2001, Guggenheim Found., 2000; grantee Mary E. Woolley fellowship, 1989, Naomi Kitay fellowship, 1989, Nat. Endowment for the Arts playwrighting fellowship, 1990—91. Office: Calif Inst Arts 24700 McBean Pkwy Valencia CA 91355

PARKS, TAMARA, elementary school educator; b. Berrien Springs, Mich., Nov. 11, 1982; d. Garnet and Jacqualine Spence; m. Brian Parks, May 18, 2003. BS in Elem. Edn., So. Adventist U., 2004. Tchr. East Lake Acad. Fine Arts, Hamilton County Dept. Edn., Chattanooga, 2004—; tutor Newton Learning, Chattanooga, 2006—. Mem.: NEA, Hamilton County Edn. Assn. Seventh-Day Adventist. Personal E-mail: parks_tamara@hcde.org.

PARKS, TRINA, dancer, educator; b. Bklyn., Dec. 26, 1946; d. Charles Heney and Tennel Fern Frazier; m. John Parks (div.); 1 child, Tennel Fern Elder. Student, NY HS Performing Arts, NYC; studied with Katherine Dunham, NYC, 1964. Prin. dancer Katherine Dunham's dance co., NY and France, 1964—66; featured dancer Micael Legrand's TV spl., Paris, 1965; mem. Cleo Quitman Ballet/Modern Dance Co., 1966; lead female dancer Vinnette Carroll's off-Broadway prodn. The Prodigal Son, NY and Europe, 1964—65; prin. dancer Tally Beatty, Rod Rogers & Geoffrey Holder profl. cos., 1966—69; prin. dancer Broadway prodn. Great White Hope, 1968; prin. dancer off-Broadway prodn. House of Flowers, 1968—69; prin. dancer Broadway prodn. Her First Roman, 1969; tchr. Katherine Dunham dance technique LA HS for Arts, 2000—03; tchr. Virgil Jr. HS, LA, 2000. Guest tchr., choreographer Cynthia Kay's Dance Co., Palm Springs, Ark., 2001—02; mem. cast Palm Springs Follies, 2003—; dance tchr. Jane Fonda's Aerobic Dance Sch., Beverly Hills, Calif., 1977—78; aerobics and ballroom dance instr. NYC Coll., 1998—99. Soloist: Swing Low Sweet Chariot, 1965; soloist Dick Shawn TV spl., 1975, featured dancer Dionne Warwick TV spl., 1976, (films) The Blues Brothers, 1980, Sammy Davis TV and live shows, LA and Las Vegas, 1978—79, lead dancer (Broadway prodn.) Snow Queen, 1996—97, spl. guest artist Chester Whitmore's Black Ballet Jazz dance co., 1982—89, Joan Peters and Eugene James dance cos., NY, 1995—98, dancer New Otonie Hotel Club, Tokyo, 1995, choreographer Golden Globe Awards, NBC, 1974, Disco 9000, 1975, Car Wash movie tour, 1979, Carousel, 1980, Tribute to Black Women, Oakland, Calif., 1981, Dr. Martin Luther King, Vigil Concert, NYC, 1997, Bronx Arts Ensemble, The Willy Freeman Story, 1999, (various sch. prodns.). Rec. sec. Kwanza Orgn., LA, 1975—91. Recipient Cert. of Appreciation, Orange County HS of Arts, 2000, Prins.' award, Hosler Mid. Sch. and Roosevelt Elem. Schs., 2000, Best Actress award, NAACP, 1989. Mem.: AFTRA, Actors Equity Assn. Democrat. Avocations: swimming, tennis. Home: PO Box 204 Palm Springs CA 92263 E-mail: teabey@yahoo.com.

PARLE, BERTHA IBARRA, writer; b. El Paso, Tex., Nov. 14, 1947; d. Arnulfo and Bertha (Soto) Ibarra; m. Dennis Jerome Parle, Aug. 16, 1969; children: Joseph, Mónica, Angélica Attended, Loretto Acad., 1965; BA in French, Spanish, U. Tex., El Paso, 1968; MA in Spanish, U. Kans., Lawrence, 1970, H.S. tchg. cert., 1971; postgrad. courses in French, U. Houston, 1990—95. Bilingual tchr. Kans. Remedial Edn. Program, Sharon Springs, 1967, 71, 72; Spanish tchr. Ottawa (Kans.) H.S., 1971-74; ESL instr. North Harris Coll., Houston, 1977-83; modern lang. prof. N. Harris Montgomery C.C. Dist., Houston, 1983-97, head lang. inst., 1997—2002. Cultural cons., sponsor Hispanic students North Harris Coll. and Montgomery Coll., 1983-97, organizer Hispanic cultural events, 1983—, sponsor Cath. Newman Club, 1985-95; lectr., slide show The Nahua Mexica Legacy, 1994-96; participant in field seminars; NEH and Fulbright Ecuador field experience. Author numerous poems; Spanish poetry publ. in Tejidos, Grito al Sol, 1972-94. Hispanic leader St. Leo's Cath. Ch., Houston, 1982-92; del. People to People Am. Program to S. Africa, 2000. Recipient Tchg. Excellence award North Harris Coll., 1997, Excellence award Nat. Inst. for Staff and Orgn. Devel., 1998; Am. Coun. Tchrs. Fgn. Langs. summer scholar U. Montreal, 1999. Mem. AAUW, Am. Coun. Tchrs. Fgn. Langs., Computer Assisted Lang. Instn. Consortium, Am. Assn. C.C. Women, Tex. Fgn. Lang. Assn., Inst. Hispanic Culture., North Harris United Faculty. Avocations: creative writing, study of indigenous language cultures, Hispanic students and Hispanic issues in the community. Office: North Harris Coll 2700 W Thorne Dr Houston TX 77073 Office Phone: 281-618-5546. Business E-Mail: bertha.parle@nhmccd.edu.

PARLEE, MARY BROWN, psychology educator; b. Oak Park, Ill., Feb. 11, 1943; d. Grant Sylvester Brown and Esther (Bonter) de Neufville; 1 child, Elizabeth. BA, Harvard U., 1965; PhD, MIT, 1969. Asst. prof. Wellesley Coll., Mass., 1969-72; fellow Bunting Inst. of Radcliffe Coll., Cambridge, Mass., 1972-74; fellow lab. social psychiatry Harvard U., Boston, 1974-75; assoc. prof. Barnard Coll. of Columbia U., NYC, 1975-78; dir. ctr. for study women and soc. CUNY, 1979-84, prof. psychology grad. ctr., 1984-93; vis. prof. MIT, 1993—99, vis. lectr., 2000—. Contbr. articles to profl. jours. Vol. St. Ignatius, NYC, 1987-88. NIH grantee, 1975-78, 79-82; recipient Publ. award Assn. for Women in Psychology, 1978. Fellow APA (pres. divsn. psychology of women 1983-84); mem. Harvard Club NYC, Radcliffe Club NY (bd. dirs. 1989), Radcliffe Club Boston. Episcopalian. Office: MIT 46-2004 Cambridge MA 02139 E-mail: mbparlee@alum.mit.edu.

PARLIN-MCSHARRY, BARBARA ANN, mathematics educator; b. Evergreen Park, Ill., Nov. 6, 1956; d. James Edward and Margaret Grace Parlin; life ptnr. Glenn W. Bukovsky; 1 child from previous marriage, Thomas McSharry. BS in Math. and Phys. Edn., U. Ill., Chgo., 1978. Cert. tchr. Cook County, 1978. Tchr. phys. edn. grades 1-8 Burbank Sch. Dist. 111, Ill., 1979—89, tchr. math and algebra grade 8, 1989—. Mem.: Ill. Coun. Tchrs. Math. Avocations: water sports, gardening, camping, construction, painting. Home: 205 S Park St Manhattan IL 60442 Office: Liberty Jr HS 5900 W 81st St Burbank IL 60459 Office Phone: 708-952-3255. Business E-Mail: barbaraparlin@burbank.k12.il.us.

PARLOW, CYNTHIA MARIA, professional soccer player; b. Memphis, May 8, 1978; BS in Nutrition, U. N.C., 1998. Profl. soccer player Atlanta Beat, 2001—03. Mem. U.S. Women's Nat. Soccer Team, 1996—, U.S. Under-20 Nat. Team, Nordic Cup championships, Denmark, 1997, U-16 Nat. Team pool. Named All-ACC and ACC Rookie of Yr., 1995, Soccer Am. Freshman of Yr., 1995, Most Valuable Player, 1995 Under-17 U.S. Youth Soccer nat. tournament, World Cup Champion, 1999; recipient Gold medal, Centennial Olympic Games, 1996, Herman Trophy, Mo. Athletic Club Player of Yr. award, 1997, Silver medal, Sydney Olympic Games, 2000. Achievements include helped U. N.C. to NCAA Championship 1996, 97; 1st-Team All-ACC selection in 1997; named to 1997 NCAA All-Tournament Team. Office: US Soccer Fedn 1801-1811 S Prairie Ave Chicago IL 60616

PARMENTER, KELLI DENISE, elementary school educator, small business owner; b. Dallas, Feb. 10, 1963; d. Ted M. and Grace T. Porter; m. Ernest Eugene Parmenter, Jr.; children: Joshua Shane, Clint Martin. MusB in Edn., Baylor U., Waco, Tex., 1986; MEd, Tex. A&M, Commerce, 1994. Tchr. elem. music, mid. sch. choir Mesquite Ind. Sch. Dist., Tex., 1986—; owner Kelli's Angels Animal Sitters, Sunnyvale, Tex., 2002—. Recipient Featured Tchr. award, Mesquite Daily News, 1993. Mem.: Mesquite Edn. Assn. (com. mem. 2006—), Tex. Music Educators Assn. (assoc.). Baptist. Avocations: reading, gardening, travel, horseback riding. Home: 514 E Tripp Rd Sunnyvale TX 75182 Office Phone: 972-288-6411. Personal E-mail: kellisangels@sbcglobal.net.

PARMET, HARRIET ABBEY L., literature educator; b. Phila., July 22, 1928; d. Jacob and Belle Cecil (Popolow) Leibowitz; m. Sidney B. Parmet, June 7, 1950; children: Howard B., Jonathan L. AB, Temple U., 1950, MS, 1960; B in Hebrew Lit., Gratz Coll., 1979; PhD in English, Lehigh U. Cert. secondary edn. tchr., Pa. Tchr. Hebrew Temple U., Phila., 1946-50, Beth Israel, Phila., 1946-51; tchr. English and social studies Gillespie Jr. High Sch., Phila., 1950-55; tchr. Hebrew and Jewish history Temple Beth El, Allentown, Pa., 1964-77; tchr. Hebrew and Israeli lit. Lehigh U., Bethlehem, Pa., 1976—95; prof. emeritus, 1995. Hillel co-advisor, mem. exec. bd. Lehigh U., 1976—. Author: The Terror of Our Days: Four Am. Poets Respond to the Holocaust, 2001; contbr. articles to profl. jours. Vice pres. Temple Beth El Sisterhood, Allentown, 1973-75; mem. exec. bd. Jewish Family Svc., Allentown, 1988—; bd. dirs. Women's Profl. Jewish Fedn., Allentown, 1973-75. Coolodge Colloquim fellow, 1986, Givat Haviva Rsch. fellow, 1987; named Outstanding Alumna Gratz Coll. Centenial Celebration. Mem. Women's Studies Consortium, Lehigh Valley Assn. Ind. Colls., Am. Jewish Congress (pres. Allentown chpt. 1970), Assn. Jewish Studies, Nat. Assn. Hebrew Profs., Temple U. Alumni Assn. (Disting. Alumni award 1995), Gratz Coll. Alumni Assn., Hadassah (life). Home: 1118 N 28th St Allentown PA 18104-2908 Office: Lehigh U Modern Lang Dept Maginnes Hall # 9 Bethlehem PA 18015-3206 Office Phone: 610-758-3090. Business E-Mail: hlpo@lehigh.edu.

PARNAS-SIMPSON, MARIANNA, chorus director, singer; arrived in U.S., 1990, naturalized, 1996; d. Abram and Yeva Parnas; m. Robert Louis Simpson, May 29, 1994; 1 child from previous marriage, Faina Goldstein. BA in in Choral Conducting and Music Edn., Coll. Music Leningrad N.A. Rimsky-Korsakov State Conservatory, St. Petersburg, Russia, 1978; MusM in Choral Conducting and Music Edn., Leningrad N.A. Rimsky-Korsakov State Conservatory, St. Petersburg, Russia, 1983. Dir. children's chorus studio Pioneer Ho. State Ednl. Inst., St. Petersburg, Russia, 1980—89; asst. dir. and vocal instr. Houston Children's Chorus, 1994—99; chorus dir. and music appreciation instr. Parker Elem. Sch., 1999—; chorus dir. Revels Houston. Condr. region 23 treble choir Tex. Music Educators Assn., Houston, 2002; clinician in music appreciation Nat. Suzuki Piano Workshop, Texas City, 2005, 06; clinician and adjudicator Children's Music Festival, Houston, 2006. Performer: Tex. Music Educators Assn. Conv., 2003, 2005. Named Tchr. of Yr., Parker Elem. Sch., 2004—05; recipient First pl., Nat. Children's Chorus Competition, Russia, 1988, Nat. Grammy award, Parker Music Acad., Houston, 2002. Mem.: Am. Choral Dir. Assn., Tex. Choral Dir. Assn., Tex. Music Educators Assn. Avocations: Russian folk songs, travel, reading. Office: Parker Elem Sch 10626 Atwell Dr Houston TX 77076 Office Phone: 713-726-3634. Office Fax: 713-726-3660. Business E-Mail: msimpso1@houstonisd.org.

PARODE, ANN, lawyer; b. LA, Mar. 3, 1947; d. Lowell Carr and Sabine Parode. BA, Pomona Coll., 1968; JD, UCLA, 1971. Bar: Calif. 1972, U.S. Dist. Ct. (so. dist.) Calif. 1972, U.S. Ct. Appeals (9th cir.) 1975, U.S. Supreme Ct. 2000. Assoc. Luce, Forward et al, San Diego, 1971-75; gen. counsel, exec. v.p., sec. San Diego Trust & Savs., 1975-94; with First Interstate Bank, 1994—97; campus counsel U. Calif., San Diego, 1997—. Judge pro tem San Diego Mcpl. Ct., 1978—84; campus counsel U. Calif., San Diego, 1997—. Bd. dirs. San Diego Cmty. Found., 1989-97, chmn., 1994-96; bd. dirs. The Burnham Inst., 1995-2001, Girard Found., 1990-. Mem. Calif. Bar Assn. (corp. law com. 1980-83, client trust fund commn. 1986-90, chmn. 1989-90), San Diego County Bar Found. (founder, bd. dirs. 1979-86, 98-2001, pres. 1980-83), San Diego Bar Assns. (bd. dirs. 1977-81, v.p. 1977-78, 80-81, treas. 1979-80), Law Libr. Justice Found. (pres. 1994). Office Phone: 858-822-1236. Business E-Mail: aparode@ucsd.edu.

PARPIANI, PRIYA, obstetrician, retired gynecologist; b. Karachi, Pakistan, Sept. 24, 1936; arrived in U.S., 1973; d. Deendayal and Vishnadevi Punjabi; m. Vishram Parpiani, Feb. 4. Cert. ob-gyn. Am. Bd. Ob-Gyn. Ob-gyn. resident U. Pa., Phila., Case Western Res. U., Cleve.; asst. clin. prof. ob-gyn. U. Irvine, Orange, Calif., 1999—2002; ret.

PARQUETTE, HEATHER ANN, elementary school educator; b. Toledo, Ohio, Nov. 12, 1968; d. Charles Melford and Lynn Ann Townsend; m. Blake Alexander Parquette, July 24, 1993; children: Tyler Andrew, Alexandra Lynn. BS in Edn., Bowling Green State U., Ohio, 1991; M in Edn., Marygrove Coll., Detroit, 2001. Tchr. Washington Local Sch., Toledo, 1992—. Home: 4925 Tamworth Rd Sylvania OH 43560

PARR, CAROL CUNNINGHAM, academic administrator; b. Chgo., June 3, 1941; d. John W. and Margaret (Boettcher) Cunningham; m. James F. Parr, Jr., Aug. 29, 1964 (div. 1988); children— Lauren Melissa, James Floyd III; m. Ira M. Lechner, Dec. 23, 1989. BA, U. Colo., 1962; MA, La. State U., 1970, PhD, 1972. Tech. translator TVA, Muscle Shoals, Ala., 1962-67; faculty La. State U., Baton Rouge, 1972-75; exec. dir. Women's Equity Action League, Ednl. & Legal Def. Fund, Washington, 1975-80; dir. mgmt. and tng. LWV U.S., Washington, 1981-83; exec. dir. LWV of U.S., 1983-86; assoc. v.p. devel., v.p. Found. U. Md., Adelphi, 1986-88; v.p. Gallaudet U., 1988—. Cons. U.S. Dept. Edn., Washington, Nat. Inst. Edn., Washington, Interam., Washington, others. Author chpts. in books. Edn. Policy fellow, Inst. for Ednl. Leadership, Washington, 1980-81; named one of Outstanding Young Women Am. Mem. Am. Soc. of Assn. Execs., Nat. Soc. Fund Raising Execs., Leadership Washington, Phi Beta Kappa. Office: Gallaudet U 800 Florida Ave NE Washington DC 20002-3660

PARR, SANDRA HARDY, small business owner; b. Atlanta, Dec. 30, 1952; d. Raymond William Hardy and Ruth (Berry) Yancey; m. James Parr Jr., Apr. 14, 1978; 1 child, James Andrew Parr III. Student, Lurleen B. Wallace Jr. Coll., 1972. Sales adminstr. Etec Corp., Hayward, Calif., 1976-77; adminstrv. sec. Cities Svc. Co., Atlanta, 1977-82; sales and planning coord. Intermodal Transp. Co., Norcross, Ga., 1982-83; freelance temp. sec. Atlanta met. area, 1983-86; freelance word processor, cons. Amoco Container Co., Norcross, 1986-88; psychiat. rev. asst. Am. Psychiat. Assn., Atlanta, 1988-89; support svcs. mgr. Parkside Health Mgmt. Corp., Atlanta, 1989-90; med. staff coord. C.P.C. Parkwood Hosp., Atlanta, 1991-98; govt. affairs sr. assoc. Bristol-Meyers Squibb, Atlanta, 1998—; pres. Parr Enterprises, Lawrenceville, Ga., 2002—. Health svcs. asst. Ciba Vision Corp., 1991-93; govt. affairs liaison Philip Morris Govt. Affairs, Alpharetta, Ga., 1993-98. Del. internat. nursing conf., citizen amb. program to People's Republic China, Seattle Washington People to People, Beijing, 1989; part-time exercise instr. Mem. NAFE. Avocations: creative writing, reading, exercising. Address: Bristol Meyers Squibb 950 E Paces Ferry Rd NE Atlanta GA 30326-1180 Home and Office: 1350 Eugenia Ter Lawrenceville GA 30045-7491

PARR, VIRGINIA HELEN, retired librarian; b. Mansfield, Ohio, May 23, 1937; d. Bernard Franklin and Frances Cole (Downes) P.; m. Marvin E. Lickey, June 14, 1959 (div. 1972); children: Sarah Elizabeth, David Andrew, Rachel Alison; m. Laurence E. Steadman, Nov. 27, 1993. AB, Oberlin Coll., 1959; AM, U. Mich., 1961; MLS, U. Oreg., 1973. English and social studies tchr. Whittier Jr. High Sch., Livonia, Mich., 1961-64; libr. U. Oreg. Libr., Eugene, 1973-79, head edn. and psychology, 1979-80, acting asst. univ. libr. for pub. svcs., 1980-82; head reference, rsch. and instrn. svcs. U. Cin., 1982-89, reference libr., bibliographer, 1989—2002, ret., 2002—. Chair, mem. budget com. Eugene Sch., 1976-79. Founding editor: Behavioral and Social Scis. Libr., 1978; contbr. articles to profl. jours. Bd. dirs. Eugene Jr. Symphony Assn., 1979-82; mem. adv. bd. various mental health groups, Eugene, 1971-79. Mem. Assn. Coll. and Rsch. Librs. of ALA (various offices edn. and behavioral sci. sect. 1977-86, numerous coms. reference and adult svcs. divsn. 1981-92), Beta Phi Mu, Pi Lambda Theta. Democrat. Episcopalian. Avocations: reading, classical music, travel. Home: 5532 S Shore Dr 12F Chicago IL 60637-1990 E-mail: v_parr@sbcglobal.net.

PARRA, ELENA BATRIZ-GUADALUPE, psychologist, educator; b. Nogales, Sonora, Mexico, Feb. 1, 1951; d. Francisco Batriz/Parra and Guadalupe Esther (Hoyos) Batriz; m. Fernando Tapia, Dec. 20, 1984 (div. Mar. 2, 1989); m. Ra,pm Castillon; children: Fernando Luis Parra Tapia, Gabriela Guadalupe Tonanzin P Castillon, Tamara Celic parra Castillon. AA, Pima C.C., Tucson, 1972; BA, U. Ariz., 1974, Master, 1975, PhD, 1983, postdoctoral, 1986. Cert. profl. counselor Bd. Behavioral Health Examiners, 2000; lic. psychologist, Ariz., 2001, cert. sch. psychologist Ariz. State Bd. Edn., diplomate Am. Coll. Cert. Forensic Counselors, cert. domestic violence counselor. Assoc. prof. Pima C.C., Tucson, 1975—85; dir. sch. Proyecto de Colores, Tucson, 1976—77; supr. mental health outpatient Santa Cruz Family Guidance Ctr., Nogales, Ariz., 1979—81; sch. psychologist-bilingual diagnostic team Tucson Unified Sch. Dist., 1982—84; supr. clin. psychologist and children's unit San Antonio Mental Health, Bell Gardens, Calif., 1987—89; asst. prof. Calif. State U., Fullerton, 1989—92; clin. dir. Eloy Mental Health Ctr., Ariz., 1992—94; head psychologist Ariz. Dept. of Youth Treatment & Rehab., Tucson, 1992—94; psychologist II Children's Evaluation Ctr., Tucson, 1992—93; clin. dir. Eloy Mental Health Ctr., 1994—95; clin. cons., psychologist La Frontera Clinic, 1995—2000; pres. Multicultural Counseling Ctr., Tucson, 1997—; adj. asst. prof., project coord. U. Ariz., Tucson, 2002—; prof. U. Guadalajara, Jalisco, Mexico. Cons. Chicanos Por La Causa, Tucson, Willcox Eloy, Ariz., 2002—. Author: Daily Life Problems-Recuperation, Adaptation & Adjustment Processes-Spanish, 1993; contbr. articles to profl. jours. Chair Legal Com. for Bilingual Edn., Tucson, 2000—03; dir. Latino Self Help Group, Tucson, 2000—03. Scholar, League Mexican Am. Women and Vocat. Rehab., 1970—74. Mem.: APA, Tucson Assn. for Bilingual Edn., Nat. Assn. Mex. Psychologists and Psychologists in Jalisco (hon.). Roman Catholic. Avocations: poetry, writing, travel, painting, study of Mexican, Mexican-American, Latino-Mexican Indigeneous cultures. Home: 7340 S Camino Bello Tucson AZ 85746 Office Phone: 520-883-3460. Business E-Mail: geparra@u.arizona.edu.

PARRAMORE, BARBARA MITCHELL, education educator; b. Guilford County, N.C., Aug. 29, 1932; d. Samuel Spencer and Nellie Gray (Glosson) Mitchell; m. Lyman Griffis Worthington, Dec. 23, 1956 (div. 1961); m. Thomas Custis Parramore, Jan. 22, 1966 (dec. Jan. 2004); children: Lisa Gray, Lynn Stuart. AB, U. N.C., Greensboro, 1954; MEd, N.C. State U., 1959; EdD, Duke U., 1968. Counselor, thcr. Raleigh City Schs., 1954-59, sch. prin., 1959-65; prof. dept. of curriculum and instrn. N.C. State U., 1970-96, prof. emeritus, 1996—. Acad. specialist Office Internat. Edn., U.S. Info. Svcs., sec. sch. initative program, The Philippines, 1987. Author: The People of North Carolina, 1972, 3rd edit. 1983. Japan Inst. Social and Econ. Affairs fellow, 1980; N.C. AAUW award for juvenile lit., 1973, Holladay medal for excellence N.C. State U., 1994. Mem. ASCD, N.C. ASCD (pres. 1994-96), N.C. Coun. for Social Studies (pres. 1985-87), Assn. Tchr. Educators, Delta Kappa Gamma, Kappa Delta Pi. Home: 5012 Tanglewood Dr Raleigh NC 27612-3135

PARR-CORRETJER, POLLY, singer, music educator; b. Sheffield, Eng., Jan. 9, 1951; arrived in U.S., 1981; d. Stanley and Edith Mary (Charlton) Parr; m. Carlos Ramon Corretjer, Dec. 16, 1978; 1 child, Richard Spencer. Assoc. in Singing and Piano, Royal No. Coll. Music, Manchester, Eng., 1972, Assoc. in Performing, 1973; grad., Royal Schs. Music, 1973; AA in Music and Gen. Studies, Prince Georges C.C., 1991. Featured soloist Cruise Ships, 1973—78; faculty Levine Sch. Music, Washington, 2002—04. Soprano soloist, dir. children's music Universalist Nat. Meml. Ch., Washington, 1989—96; asst. mus. dir., condr. Interact Theatre, Washington, 2001; guest coach for accompanists Washington Bible Coll., Greenbelt, Md.; fine arts vocal judge Grace Christian Sch., Bowie, 1998—2002; pvt. practice vocalist tchr., Bowie, Md., 1978—. Mem.: Music Tchrs. Nat. Assn., Md. State Music Tchrs. Assn. Avocations: sewing, reading, travel. Home: 13201 Idlewild Dr Bowie MD 20715

PARRETT, JANELLE SWILLEY, secondary school educator; b. Meridian, Miss., Nov. 20, 1922; d. Edgar Rowan and Ada Swilley; m. Leslie Loring Parrett (dec. Nov. 2004); children: Ann Loring, John Edward. BS, La. State U., Baton Rouge, 1945; MA, Ohio State U., Columbus, 1949; elem. conversion, Ind. U., South Bend, 1964. Cert. tchr. La., Ohio. Instr. Ohio State U., 1945—49; tchr. elem. Plymouth Cmty. Schs., Ind., 1960—63, tchr. phys. edn. mid. sch., 1963—72, tchr. phys. edn., coach H.S., 1972—75. Mem.: AAHPERD, Ind. Alliance for Health, Phys. Edn. and Recreation (sec. 1963, v.p. 1964—66, chmn. Girls and Women's Sports divsn. 1969), St. Joseph Valley Golf Assn. (v.p. 1999, pres. 2001). Republican. Presbyterian. Avocations: reading, bridge, swimming, golf. Home: 5710 Hampton Woods Blvd Sebring FL 33872

PARRINELLO, DIANE DAVIES, retired pre-school educator; b. West Warwick, RI, Oct. 17, 1939; d. Stanley Duane and Catherine Margaret (Heelan) Davies; m. John Richard Parrinello, Apr. 28, 1962; children: Gregory, Timothy, Bethany, Matthew. BA, U. Rochester, 1961; MS in Edn., Nazareth Coll., 1987. Cert. tchr., N.Y. Biochem. research asst. Syracuse (N.Y.) U., 1962-64; presch. tchr. Jewish Community Ctr., Syracuse, 1964-65; co-owner, mgr. Spl. Creations, Rochester, N.Y., 1979-84; tchr., dir. Winton Rd. Nursery Sch., Rochester, 1983—2005; ret., 2005. Mem. women's council Meml. Art Gallery, Rochester, 1972—; coach Brighton Little League, Rochester, 1975-82; leader Camp Fire Girls, Inc., Rochester, 1975-78; bd. dirs., coach Brighton Soccer League, 1976-85; co-founder Brighton Girls Soccer League, 1976; mem. Arboretum Adv. Bd. Mem. Nat. Assn. for Edn. Young Children (Rochester chpt.). Republican. Roman Catholic. Avocations: reading, golf, paddle tennis. Home: 80 Berkeley St Rochester NY 14607-2209

PARRINELLO, KATHLEEN ANN MULHOLLAND, nursing administrator, educator; b. Syracuse, N.Y., June 26, 1953; d. Bernard Joseph and Mary Catherine (Wicke) Mulholland; m. Richard John Parrinello, June 30, 1973; children: Michael, Jeffrey, Stephen. BS, U. Rochester, 1975, MS, 1983, PhD, 1990. RN, N.Y. Staff nurse U. Rochester (N.Y.)-Strong Meml. Hosp., 1975-78, asst. head nurse, 1976-77, head nurse, 1978-83, assoc. clin. chief, 1983-86, coord. ambulatory care, 1986-88, clin. chief, asst. prof. Sch. Nursing, 1990—; practitioner tchr., asst. prof. Rush Presbyn. St. Luke's Med. Ctr., Chgo., 1988-89. Cons. in nursing U. Wis. Hosps. and Clinics, 1990, 91; prin. investigator State of N.Y. Dept. of Health, 1991. Author pamphlet Arterial Bypass Surgery Patient Booklet, 1981; contbr. articles to profl. publs. Workforce Demonstration grantee N.Y. Dept. Health. Mem. Am. Acad. Ambulatory Nursing Adminstrn. (bd. dirs. 1989-92), Am. Orgn. Nurse Execs., Genesee Valley Nurses Assn., Sigma Theta Tau. Office: Strong Meml Hosp 601 Elmwood Ave Rochester NY 14642-0002

PARRIS, SALLY NYE, real estate agent; b. Evanston, Ill., Apr. 5, 1946; d. Harry Gale Nye Jr. and Bettye (Herb) Sollitt; m. Thomas Baxter Parris, Mar. 25, 1988 (div. Sept. 1985); 1 child, Samantha Ross. AA, Bradford Jr. Coll., 1966; BS in Secondary Edn., Northwestern U., 1968; cert. real estate, Conn. Real Estate Inst., Norwalk, 1985. Lic. real estate agt., Conn. Dir. girls phys. edfn. Latin Sch. of Chgo., 1967-68; dir. Greenwich (Conn.) YWCA, 1972-79; English tchr. Inlingua Sch. Langs., Stamford, Conn., 1981-84; real estate agt. Curtis Assocs., Realtors, Greenwich, Conn., 1985—. Chair profl. divsn. United Way, Greenwich, 1995-98, chair real estate sect. profl. divsn., 1993-94, co-chair campaign kickoff Septemberfest, 1985-99, co-chair Greenwich Pro-Am. Lit. Vol. Benefit, 1995—; v.p., bd. dirs. YMCA, Greenwich, 1993—, chair spl. events com., 1994—, co-chair annual campaign, 1998; bd. dirs., benefit chair Cmty. Answers, Greenwich, 1994—; co-chair 350th Yr. parade Town of Greenwich, 1990; mem. benefits com. Literacy Vols., 1991-93. Recipient Vol. Recognition award Literacy Vols. Am., 1996, Town of Greenwich, 1991, United Way of Greenwich, 1985-97, Thomas Shepard award, 1995, 96. Mem. Conn. Assn. Profl. Women, Greenwich Bd. Realtors (advisor pub. rels. 1985-87, grievance com. 1999), Riverside Yacht Club (winter mem., social register 1960—), Greenwich Country Club (paddle tennis com. co-chmn. 1984-86, quar. editor 1982-86). Republican. Episcopalian. Avocations: swimming, racquet sports, golf, sporting clays, needlepoint. Office: Colwell Banker/Curtis Assocs 278 Sound Beach Ave Old Greenwich CT 06870-1626

PARRISH, CATHY WALDRON, elementary school educator; b. Harrisonburg, Va., July 2, 1944; d. Elmo Preston and Lillian Virginia (Paris) Waldron; m. James Walter Parrish, Aug. 16, 1969; children: James Preston, Cristan Elizabeth. MusB, U. N.C., 1966; MA in Tchg., Winthrop Univ., Rockhill, S.C., 1982; attended 30 hours, Furmar Univ., Greenville, S.C., 1990. Elem. tchr. band and strings Raleigh City Schools, NC, 1967—72; elem. tchr. gen. music Gadsden County Schools, Quincy, Fla., 1972—73, Leon County Schools, Tallahassee, 1973—76, Monroe City Schools, NC, 1977—82; instr. music edn Wingate Univ., NC, 1982—85; elem. tchr. gen music Union County Schs., Monroe, NC, 1985—87, Bethel Elem. Schools, Simpsonville, SC, 1987—. Dir. Bethel Elem. Chorus, Simpsonville, SC, 1987—; children's music dir. Westminster Presbyn. Ch., Greenville, SC, 1994—97, St. Giles Presbyn. Ch., Greenville, SC, 1997—98. Mem. Greenville County Civic Band, Greenville, SC, 1989—, Westminster Presbyn. Ch. Choir, Greenville, SC, 1989—, Westminster Presbyn. Hand Bell Choir, Greenville, SC, 1992—97. Recipient Tchr. of the Yr., Bethel Elem. Sch., 1996—97, Greenville County Fine Arts Ctr., 1996—97, 1999, Tchr. Yr., Mauldin Rotary Club, 2005—06. Mem.: S. C. Foothills Chap. Am. Orff - Schulwerk Assn., Music Educators Nat. Conf., S. C. Music Educators Assn. (v.p. 2003—, pres. elem. divsn. 2001—03). Republican. Presbyterian. Achievements include Bethel Elem. Chorus performing in the Nat. Children's Choir at Carnegie Hall, 1999 and Walt Disney World, Fla., 1997. Avocations: genealogy, reading, cross stitch, furniture refinishing. Home: 8 Dunrobin Ln Simpsonville SC 29681 Office Phone: 864-355-4100.

PARRISH, DEBRA MARIE, lawyer; d. John Charles Pistorino and Kathleen Patricia Moroney; m. Alexander Wells Parrish, Aug. 6, 1988; children: Katherine, Heather, Elizabeth, Laura. BSE, Duke U., Durham, N.C., 1985; JD, Duke U., 1989. Bar: N.C. 1989, D.C. 1990, Pa. 1995, U.S. Patent Office 1994. Assoc. Fulbright & Jawarski, Washington, 1989—92; atty. Office of Gen. Counsel, HHS, Washington, 1992—94; ptnr. Titus & McConomy, LLP, Pitts., 1994—99; pres. Debra M. Parrish, PC, Pitts., 1999—. Dir. Neurolife, Pitts. Contbr. articles to profl. jours. Dir. Nat. In Vitro Diagnostic Ctr., Pitts., 2005—. Mem.: Nat. Assn. Coll. and Univ. Attys., Am. Health Lawyers Assn.

PARRISH, DENISE KAY, regulatory accountant; b. Garden City, Mich., May 20, 1954; d. Lewis William and Carol Ruby (Doederlein) P.; m. Michael Joseph Kraus, Oct. 10, 1986 (div. Apr. 1992); m. Joseph Rickie Walsh, Oct. 2000. BA in Acctg., Mich. State U., 1976. Analyst Mich. Pub. Svc. Commn., Lansing, 1977-81; sr. fin. analyst Colo. Pub. Utilities Commn., Denver, 1981-85; chief rate analyst Ariz. Residential Utilities Consuemr Office, Phoenix, 1985-86, Ariz. Corps. Commn., Phoenix, 1986-91; mgr. rates and pricing Wyo. Pub. Svc. Commn., Cheyenne, 1991—2003, dep. adminstr. office of consumer advocate, 2003—. Faculty mem. Inst. Pub. Utilities Mich. State U.; seminar instr. in field; presenter in field. Mem. ch. coun. local Luth. Ch., 1999—2001, chmn. long range planning com., 2005. Mem. Nat. Assn. Regulatory Utility Commrs. (chair SEC/FASB Task Force 1992-98, vice chmn. 1997-2000, mem. oversight com. on joint telecomm. audits 1991-92, 96-2001, chmn. acctg. subcom. 2000-03, subcom. on internat. rels. 2005—). Lutheran. Avocations: reading, travel, gardening. Office: Wyo Office Consumer Advocate 2515 Warren Ave Ste 304 Cheyenne WY 82001-3113 Office Phone: 307-777-5743. Business E-Mail: dparri@state.wy.us.

PARRISH, JILL NIEDERHAUSER, state supreme court justice; BA, Weber State U., 1982; JD, Yale U., 1985. Bar: Utah 1985, 10th Cir. Ct. Appeals 1987, U.S. Supreme Ct. 2000. Clk. Hon. David K. Winder U.S. Dist. Ct., Utah, 1985; atty. Parr, Wadddoups, Brown, Gee & Loveless, Salt Lake City, 1986—90, shareholder, 1990—95; asst. U.S. atty. Civil Divsn. U.S. Dist. Ct., Utah, 1995—2003; justice Utah Supreme Ct., Salt Lake City, 2003—, mem. tech. com., judicial performance evaluation com., 2003—. Supr. Fin. Litigation Unit U.S. Attys. Office. Mem.: Fed. Bar Assn. (pres.). Office: Utah Supreme Ct PO Box 140210 Salt Lake City UT 84114-0210*

PARRISH, JOANNA FAITH, nursing consultant; (parents Am. citizens); m. Walter E. Parrish. ADN, Hesston Coll., Kans., 1981; BSc in Nursing, Calif. State U., Dominquez Hills, 1998. RN Calif., 1981. QA RN Lanterman Devel. Ctr., Pomona, Calif., 1982—. Contbr. poems to Internat. Libr. Poetry Ann. Anthology (pub. in Internat. Libr. of Poetry Ann. Anthology). Recipient Cert. in Leadership, Summit Inst. at Faith Cmty. Ch., 2005. Conservative. Avocations: travel, singing, dance, painting. Office: Lanterman Devel Ctr 3530 W Pomona Blvd Pomona CA 91769 Office Phone: 909-595-1221.

PARRISH, LORI NANCE, property appraiser; b. Evansville, Ind., July 31, 1948; m. Geoffrey Cohen; children: Gary Brown, Brandi Schmidt. Student, Fin. Inst. Sch., 1968, Fla. Atlantic U., 1969, Clemson U., 1982, Fla. Internat. U., 1988; LHD (hon.), Keiser Coll., 1996; postgrad., U. Ctrl. Fla., 1996—98. Cert. Retail Nurseryman Nova/Davie Cmty. Sch., Fla., 1975, in Credit and Collections Broward CC, Fla., 1980, in Quality Cir. Fla. Atlantic U., 1986, in Target Mgmt. Selection Fla. Internat. U., 1988, County Commrs. Cert. in Fin. Mgmt. Fla. Counties Found., Fla. Assn. Counties, 1997, County Commrs. Cert. in County Govt. Law Fla. Counties Found., Fla. Assn. Counties, 1998, County Commrs. Cert. in Ethics Fla. Counties Found., Fla. Assn. Counties, 1998. Toll operator So. Bell Telephone Co., 1966-68; adminstrv. asst. appraisal and constrn. Loan Dept. Hollywood Fed. Savings & Loan Assn., 1968—72; acct., qualifying agt. Victor Purdo Painting Co., 1972-81; fin. mgr. CRG, Inc., 1982-83; bookkeeper I county and vocat. Sch. Bd. Broward County, South Plantation HS, 1983-84; commr. dist. 5 Broward County, Fla., 1988—2004, vice-chair, 1989—90, 1996—97, chair, 1990—91, 1997—98, 2001—02, property appraiser, 2005—. Citizen's adv. bd. City of Cooper, 1976-77, pers. rev. bd., 1976-77; mem. Property Appraisal Adjustment Bd., 1984-90, 91-94, vice chair, 1987-88, chair 1989-90, 1993-94, 95-96; mem. South Fla. Coordinating Coun., 1985-, Criminal Justice Planning Coun., 1985-90, Nat. Assn. Counties, 1988-2004, Human Svcs. Com., 1988-2004, Broward Econ. Devel. Bd., 1988-89, chair 1991-92; mem. Courthouse Security Com., 1990-93, Pub. Health Trust Com., Environment, Energy Land Use Steering Com., 1991-2004, Health Steering Com. 1989-90, 94-95, Overall Econ. Devel. Planning Com., 1988-90, Met. Planning Orgn., 1988-90, 92-2004, HIV Health Planning Coun., 1992-93, Broward Edn. Planning Initiative Com., Legal, Legis. Subcommittee, 1993, Resource Recovery Bd. 1994-95, 2002-03, vice chair, 1992, chair, 1993, Tourist Devel. Coun. 1997, 2001; mem. select com. water policy, Fla. Assn. Counties', 1995-96, elderly task force mem., 1995; bd. govs. Fort Lauderdale C. of C., 1987-88, 90-91; adv. bd. mem. Water Supply, 1988-94, chair 1991-92; Brady Brigade recruiter, Nat. Orgn. Disability, 1991-93; chair NACO's Subcommittee on Aging, 1993; chair Cooper City Election Reform Com., 1993-94; bd. dirs. Cmty. Health Purchasing Alliance, 1993-96, Fla. Assn. Counties, 1988-2001, South Fla. Regional Transp. Authority, Tri-County Commuter Rail Authority, 1988-2004, vice chair, 1996-97, chair 1997-98; vice chair Broward County Planning Coun., 1991-92, mem. 2002-; spl. projects coord. Davie/Cooper City C. of C.; adminstrv. asst. to bldg. ofcl. City of Cooper City, 1972-81; landscape contractor, owner Earthy Interiors; v.p. Lake Shore Motel and Swap Shop, Inc., 1994-2003, 3290 Sunrise Investments, Inc., 1994-2003, 3291 Sunrise Investments, Inc. (dba Swap Shop), 1994-2003, Fla. Drive-In Theater Mgmt., Inc. 1994-2001, COO Millennium Hollywood's City Pl., 1994-2003; v.p., sec., treas. Swap Shop Mgmt. LLC, 2001-; founder Broward Workshop Criminal Justice Com. Regional Transp. Orgn. Bd. 1996-2003.

Adv. bd. Broward County Libr., 1979-85, Mommas and Poppas of Cooper City High, 1982-90, Broward C.C. Women's Programs Adv. Com., 1981-82; sec. Cooper City Elem. Sch. Adv. Com., 1979-80, chair 1980-82, South Ctrl. Area Adv. Com., 1982-83, sec., 1981-82; legis. chair Broward County Libr. Adv. Bd., 1982-84; active Broward County Sch. Bd., 1984-88, vice-chair, 1986-87, chair, 1987-88; bd. dirs. Pembroke Pines Human Resource Ctr. Adv. Com., 1984-88. Recipient Lifetime Membership award Broward County Phys. Edn. Tchrs., 1988, VIP Female award West Broward Dem. Club, 1988, Lifetime Membership award Young Dems., 1988, Outstanding Svc. award Lauderhill Regular Dem. Club, 1988, Disting. Svc. award Plantation Dem. Club, 1988, Disting. and Dedicated Svc. award Broward County Deputies Assn., 1989, 92, Spl. Achievement award Jefferson-Jackson, 1990, Friend of ARC award Assn. Retarded Citizens of Broward, 1990, Tribute to Success award Pembroke Pines Dem. Club, 1991, Leadership and Dedication award Children's Svcs. Bd., 1991, Desert Storm Family Support award 1991, Disting. Svc. award Women in Distress, 1991-92, Appreciation award Mus. Archaeology, 1992, Ann. Appreciation award N.W. Federated Woman's Club, 1992, Mother's Day award Rainbow Crusaders, 1992, Environ. Appreciation award Sunshine Ranches Homeowners Assn., 1992, Woman Leadership award Assn. Retarded Citizens, 1992, Coconut Creek Disting. Svc. award, 1994, Conservation Legislator of Yr. award Broward County Airboat, Halftrack, Conservation Club, 1994, Honoree Sunrise Regular Dem. Club, 1994, Legislator of Yr. award Broward County Fire Fighters and Paramedics, 1994, Woman of Yr. award Plantation Dem. Club, 1995, Humanitarian of Yr. award Soref Jewish Cmty. Ctr., 1995, Pres.'s award Broward County Fair, 1996, award Manatee Survival Found. 1996, Dream Maker award Jr. League Greater Fort Lauderdale, 1996, Jesse Portis Helms award Dolphin Dem. Club, 1996, Par Excellence award Miramar High Cmty. Sch., 1997, Recognition award North Dade C. of C., 1997, Par Excellence award Miramar High Cmty. Sch., 1997, Criminal Justice Image award Cmty. Reconstruction Inst., 1998, Govtl. Dream Builder award Children's Harbor, 1999, Ray Lisanti Meml. award Gays United to Attack Repression and Discrimination, 1999, Gracias award Hispanic Unity, 1999, Polit. Leader of Yr. award The Vanguard Chronicle, 1999, Environ. Merit award EPA, 2000, Third Ann. Student Life Achievement Corp. Ptnr. of Yr. award Nova Southeastern U., 2002, 2002 Arts Collaboration award 13th Ann. ArtServe Encore awards, Karl Clark Cmty. Involvement award, 2002, Commr. Leadership award Fla. Local Environ. Resource Agencies, 2002, Spirit of Excellence award South Broward Chpt. Am. Bus. Women's Assn., 2002, Edee Greene Good Egg award, 2002, Humanitarian award LWV, 2002, Medallion award Unsung Heroine People with AIDS Coalition Broward County, 2002, Dem. Elected Women Honoree N.W. Dem. Club, 2002, Contbn. to Cmty. award, Pine Island Ridge Civic Orgn. award, 2003, Outstanding Svc. award Engring. Profession Broward Chpt. Fla. Engring. Soc., 2003, Women of Valor Broward County award David Posnack Jewish Cmty. Ctr., 2003, Outstanding Svc. award Washington Pk. Neighborhood Preservation and Enhancement Dist., 2003, South Fla. Commuter Svcs. Transp. Leadership award, 2004, David Posnack Hebrew Day Sch. Lifetime Achievement award, 2004, Outstanding Pub. Ofcl. award Fla. Assn. Mus., 2004-05, Pub. Svc. award Davie Merchants and Indsl. Assn., 2005, Cert. Appreciation Coral Springs C. of C., 2005, Cert. Appreciation Poinsettia Heights Civic Assn., 2005; nominee Feminist of Yr. Fedn. Pub. Employees, 1987; finalist Woman of Yr. Govt., 1987; named Woman of Yr. Sunrise Lakes Phase III Women's Club, 1987, Woman of Yr. City of Hope, 1989, Hon. Conch and Citizen of Fabulous Fla. Keys, 1991, Woman of Yr. Metro Broward Fire Fighters, 1992, Dem. of Yr. Jefferson-Jackson, 1992, 2002, Woman of Yr. Women in Distress, 1993, Environ. Legislator of Yr. Environ. Coalition of Broward County, 1993, Polit. Alliance of Yr. Dolphin Dem. Club, 1999, Humanitarian of Yr. E.A.S.E. Found., 2001, Woman of Yr. South Fla. Mus. Natural History and Pyramid Soc., 2002; named to Broward County Women's Hall of Fame, 1997; Paul Harris fellow Rotary Found. Rotary Internat. Davie Rotary Club, 1997. Mem. ALA, Southeastern Libr. Assn., Davie/Cooper City Friends of Libr. (founder), Ft. Lauderdale Friends of Libr., Broward County Friends of Libr., Amalgamated Transit Union (hon. life, Naval Air Sta., Ft. Lauderdale Hist. Assn. (hon.), Broward County Police Benevolent Assn. (hon.). Office: Broward County Property Appraiser 115 S Andrews Ave Ste 111 Fort Lauderdale FL 33301-1801 Office Phone: 954-357-6904. Business E-Mail: lori@bcpa.net.

PARRISH, NANCY REBECCA, elementary school educator; b. Mulberry, Ark., Jan. 30, 1953; d. Nelson and Lora Duskie Rogers; m. Randy J. Parrish, Aug. 15, 1975; children: Andrew, Lindsay, Cole. BS in Edn., U. Ozarks, Clarksville, Ark., 1975; MEd in Curriculum and Instrn., Union U., Germantown, Tenn., 2002. Tchr. Ft. Smith Pub. Schs., Ark., 1975—76, Van Buren Sch. Dist., 1976—82, Galena Park Ind. Sch. Dist., Tex., 1982—85, Monroe Twp. Sch. Dist., Spotswood, NJ, 1985—87, Amarillo Ind. Sch. Dist., Tex., 1987—90, Dorcester Sch., Woodfliff Lake, NJ, 1990—91, Webster Parish Schs., Springhill, La., 1991—98, Memphis City Schs., 1998—. Mem.: NEA, Tenn. Edn. Assn., Nat. Coun. Social Studies, Kappa Delta Pi. Avocations: reading, piano, quilting, sailing.

PARRISH, PATRICIA ANNE, education educator; b. Bristol, Conn., Dec. 31, 1963; d. Robert L. and Marie J. Chesley; m. David N. Parrish, Apr. 11, 1992; 1 child, Alexandra. Student, Mich. State U., 1981—82; BA, Flagler State Coll., 1985; MA, U. South Fla., 1998, PhD, 2001. Lic. profl. educator Fla., 1985. Tchr. Transfiguration Parrish Sch., St. Petersburg, Fla., 1986—89, Pinellas Assn. Retarded Children, St. Petersburg, 1989—93; tchr. deaf Pinellas County Schs., Largo, Fla., 1993—98; asst. prof. edn. Saint Leo (Fla.) U., 2001—. Mem. adv. bd. San Antonia (Fla.) Elem. Sch., 2003—; mem. sch. adv. coun. Centennial Mid. Sch., Dade City, Fla., 2004—; mem. bd. edn. Reading on the Farm Charter Sch., Dade City, Fla., 2002—04. Co-author: Professional Issues in Special Education, 2001, Bulletproof Vest in Ethic of Care, 2003. Catachist St. Joseph Cath. Ch., Zephychills, Fla., 2003—05. Grantee, Saint Leo U., 2002—03. Roman Cath. Avocations: reading, dance, running. Office: Saint Leo Univ 33701 SR 52 Saint Leo FL 33574

PARRISH, VIRGINIA ELLEN, retired secondary school educator; d. John Richard and Wila Nina (Bonino) Parrish; m. Donald Rogers, June 8, 1969 (div. 1978); children: Jonathan, Hilary; m. William Haes, Dec. 15, 1978 (div. 1987). BA with honors, Rutgers U., 1970. Cert. secondary tchr., N.J. Tchr. French and English West Deptford (N.J.) Twp. Bd. Edn., 1970-71; proofreader Valdosta (Ga.) Daily Times, 1971-72; tchr. French Limestone (Maine) Jr. Sr. High Sch., 1973-74; fin. aid clk. Glassboro (N.J.) State Coll., 1977-78; inside claims adjuster Reliance Ins. Co., Haddonfield, N.J., 1978-79; tchr. English Haddonfield Bd. Edn., 1979-80, Woodstown (N.J.)-Pilesgrove Regional Bd. Edn., 1980-81; tchr. French and English Monroe Twp. Bd. Edn., Williamstown, NJ, 1981—2005. Coord. exch. student program Eurolangues, Internat., N.Y.C., 1981-88. Author: (poem) Note to My Brother, 1986 (3d place award 1986), (short story) The Telescope, (play) Burying Betty, 1995; contbr. poems to anthology. Named Tchr. of Yr., Williamstown Mid.Sch., 2003. Mem. Am. Fedn. Tchrs., NEA. Home: 10 Northridge Dr Mays Landing NJ 08330 Personal E-mail: veparrish@msn.com.

PARR-JOHNSTON, ELIZABETH, economist, consultant; b. NYC, Aug. 15, 1939; d. Ferdinand Van Siclen and Helene H. Parr; m. David E. Bond, Dec. 28, 1962 (div. July 1975); children: Peter V.S., Kristina Aline; m. Archibald F. Johnston, Mar. 6, 1982; children: James, Heather, Alexandra, Margaret. BA, Wellesley Coll., 1961; MA, Yale U., 1962, PhD, 1973; postgrad., Harvard U., 1986; DLitt, U. NB, 2004. Various positions Govt. of Can., Ottawa, Ont., Canada, 1973-76, INCO Ltd., Toronto, 1976-79; chief of staff, sr. policy advisor Ministry of Employment and Immigration, Govt. of Can., 1979-80; various positions Shell Can. Ltd., Calgary, Alta., Canada, 1980-90; pres. Parr-Johnston & Assocs., Calgary, 1990-91; pres., vice-chancellor Mt. St. Vincent U., Halifax, Nova Scotia, N.S., Canada, 1991-96, The U. New Brunswick, Fredericton, Canada, 1996—2002; pres. Parr Johnston Econ. and Policy Cons., Chester Basin, N.S., Canada, 2002—. Instr. U. We. Ont., London, 1964—67, U. B.C., Vancouver, 1967—71; vis. scholar Wesleyan U., Middletown, Conn., 1971—72; acad. rsch. assoc. Carleton U., Ottawa, 1972—73; bd. dirs. Nova Scotia Power, Emera Ltd., Bank of Nova Scotia, Social Rsch. and Demonstration Corp., Can. Found. Sustainable Devel. Tech., Can. Millennium Scholarships Found., Coun. Can. Acads.; spkr. and presenter in field; mem. Fed. Expert Adv. Panel on Equalization, 2005—06; bd. dirs. Coun. Can. Acads. Mem. editl. bd. Can. Econ. Jour., 1980—83; contbr. articles to profl. jours. Planning chmn. John Howard Soc., 1980—84; mem. policy adv. com. C.D. Howe, 1980—85; mem. Ont. Econ. Coun., 1981—84; bd. dirs. Dellcrest Home, 1980—84, Calgary S.W. Fed. Riding Assn., 1985—91, The Learning Ctr., Calgary, 1989—91, Halifax United Way, 1991—92, North/South Inst., 1992—96, Can. Unity Coun., 1993—2005, Vol. Planning N.S., 1992—93, Social Sci. Human Rsch. Coun., 1995—98, FPI Ltd., 1996—2001, Empire Co., 1994—2002, Symphony Nova Scotia, Nat. Theatre Sch. Recipient Canada 125 medal, Queen's Jubilee medal; Hon. Woodrow Wilson fellow, 1962. Mem. Assn. Atlantic Univs. (chair 1994-96), Assn. Univs. and Colls. in Can. (bd. dirs., mem. exec. com. 1994-96), Women in Acad. Adminstrn. (adv. bd. 1991-96), Calgary Coun. Advanced Tech. (exec. 1990-91), Can. Econs. Assn., Inst. Pub. Adminstrn. Can., Sr. Women Acad. Adminstrs. Can., Assn. Commonwealth Univs. (former mem. exec. com.), Phi Beta Kappa. Anglican. Avocations: golf, travel. Home: PO Box 219 Chester Basin NS Canada B0J 1K0 Office Phone: 902-275-3436. Personal E-mail: EPJ@chesterbasin.com.

PARRON, DELORES L., federal agency administrator; b. Red Bank, N.J., Jan. 14, 1944; d. James W. and Ruth Pitts Parron; m. Sherman L. Ragland. BA, Georgian Ct. Coll., 1966; MSW, Cath. U., 1968, PhD, 1977. Psychiat. social worker Hillcrest Children's Ctr., Washington, 1969—71; asst. prof. dept. psychiatry Howard U. Coll. Medicine, Washington, 1971—78; social sci. analyst Pres. Commn. on Mental Health, Washington, 1977—78; sr. program officer Inst. Medicine, NAS, Washington, 1978—83; assoc. dir. Nat. Inst. Mental Health, Rockville, Md., 1983—99; dep. asst. sec. for planning and evaluation U.S. Dept. Health and Human Svcs., Washington, 1999—2001; sci. advisor for capacity devel. NIH, Bethesda, Md., 2001—. Trustee Georgian Ct. Coll., Lakewood, NJ, 1996—2001, Ctr. for the Advancement Health, Washington, 1995—2001. Recipient Disting. Alumnae award, Cath. U. Am., 1993. Fellow: Nat. Acad. Pub. Adminstrn.; mem.: APA (Disting. Leader for Women in Psychology award 1998, Disting. Achievements award minority fellowship program adv. com. 1998). Office: NIH 9000 Rockville Pike Bethesda MD 20892 Office Phone: 301-451-4677. Business E-Mail: parrond@nih.gov.

PARROTT, ANNETTE MICHELE, science educator, consultant; b. NYC, June 25, 1971; d. Janice M. Grey; 1 child, Spencer D. PhD, Ga. State U., 2004. Cert. sci. tchr. Ga. Sci. educator Decatur H.S., Decatur, Ga., 1993—96, Lakeside H.S., Atlanta, 1996—. Team mem. Ga. Aquarium, Atlanta, 2005—. Contbr. to profl. jours., books, websites. Choir dir., tchr. BibleWay Ministries, Atlanta, 1996—2006. Recipient Pres.'s prize for secondary Tchg., Entomol. Soc. Am., award, Ciba Specialty Chems. Edn. Found.; Tandy scholar, RadioShack. Mem.: Nat. Assn. Biology Tchrs. (Hon. mention Outstanding New Biology Tchr.), Southeastern Assn. Educators Sci. (conf. presenter 2000—03), Ga. Sci. Teachers Assn. (adv. bd., secondary rep., author 1994—2006), NSTA (conf. presenter, software reviewer 1993—96), Atlanta Underwater Explorers (presenter 2004—06, Leadership award 2005). Avocations: gardening, music, poetry, photography, scuba diving.

PARROTT, JANICE MORTON, medical/surgical nurse, nursing researcher; b. Atlanta, Apr. 27, 1954; d. James C. and Dorothy Fowler Morton; m. Danny J. Parrott, Feb. 16, 1980; children: Ashley, Olivia. Diploma, Grady Meml. Hosp. Sch. Nursing, Atlanta, 1978; BTh, Christian Life Sch. Theology, 1999, MTh, 2003. Staff nurse Grady Meml. Hosp., 1978-89; rsch. nurse/cardiology Emory U. Sch. Medicine, Atlanta, 1989-91, rschr. preventive medicine, 1991-93, project coord., 1993—99, clin. dir. women's heart rsch., 1999—2003, supr. rsch. nursing, 2003—. Rschr. in field. Assoc. pastor Christian Life Ctr., Covington, Ga. Office: Emory U Sch Medicine 69 Butler St SE Atlanta GA 30303-3073 Home: 326 Hamilton Dr Conyers GA 30094-4130

PARROTT, LOIS ANNE MUYSKENS, humanities educator; b. Willmar, Minn., Aug. 9, 1948; d. Bernard and Janetta Den (Hartog) Muyskens. BA, Dakota Wesleyan U., 1970; MEd, U. North Tex., 1972; PhD, Tex. A&M U., 1982. Tchr. Dallas Ind. Sch. Dist., 1972—75; prof. Richland Coll., Dallas, 1975—. Dir. pub. rels. EBLC, Dallas, 1987—92; multimedia cons. LeCroy Telecomm.-Dallas County C.C. Dist., Dallas, 1991—93; dir. Dist. -wide Computer Users Group, Dallas, 1992—94; spkr. in field; pres. Dallas Ind. Sch. Dist., 2004—05. Contbr. articles to profl. jours. Mem. staff-parish rels. Whiterock United Meth. Ch., youth sponsor, 1999—; vol. Nat. PTA, 1993—94; mem. Dallas County Truancy Task Force; bd. trustees Dallas County Schs., 1994—96; sch. bd. trustee Dallas Ind. Sch. Dist., 1997—, pres. bd. edn., 2004—05. Named Tchr. of Yr., Nat. Inst. Staff and Orgnl. Devel., 1995—96; recipient Cmty. Svc. award, Jane Douglas DAR, 2000; grantee NEH, 1987—89. Avocation: piano. Office Phone: 972-238-6286.

PARRS, MARIANNE M., paper and lumber company executive; b. NYC, 1945; m. Walter Parrs; 3 children. Grad., Brown U. Joined Internat. Paper Co., 1974, sector controller, printing papers Purchase, NY, staff v.p., worldwide responsibility tax planning and compliance, CFO, sr. v.p., 1995—99, exec. v.p. adminstrn., info. tech. and human resources Stamford, Conn., 1999—, CFO, 2005. Bd. dir. Liaison Tech. (formerly Forest Express), CIT Group, 2003—. Bd. dir. Women's Forum. Office: Internat Paper Co 400 Atlantic St Stamford CT 06921 Fax: 914-397-1650. Office Phone: 203-541-8000.*

PARRY, JANET, retired health facility administrator; b. Salt Lake City, Nov. 5, 1943; d. Nathaniel Edmunds Parry and Dortha Nell (Harris) Parry-Miller. BSN, U. Utah, Salt Lake City, 1966. RN Calif. Pres. Med. Mgmt. Cons., Anaheim, Calif., 1970—91; v.p. Parry Devel. Co., Anaheim, 1971—91; property mgr. Parry Profl. Bldg., Anaheim, 1981—95; founding ptnr. Med. Billing Specialist, Anaheim, 1991, PPP Med. Practice Sales, Anaheim, 1995; sales assoc. P & F Investment Property Mgmt., Anaheim, 1994, Boydston Realty, Anaheim, 1994—95; ret. Pres., chmn. bd. dirs. Anaheim Meml. Hosp. Contbr. articles to profl. publs. V.p. Aspen Hollow Homeowners Assn., 2003—05, pres., 2006—; mem. Caritas Chorale of Sun Valley, 2001—, pres., 2005—06, co-chmn. benefit dinner com., 2003—04, bd. dirs., 2003—06, v.p., 2004—05; asst. dir. Promise Christmas Chorale, 2001—02; mem. St. Luke's Hosp. Aux., Sun Valley, 2000—01; bd. dirs. Anaheim Meml. Hosp. Found., 1987—96, v.p., 1991—96, chmn. bd. dirs., 1994; mem. Anaheim Bd. Realtors, 1987—97; mem., bd. dirs., treas. Tustin Main St. Chorus, 1991—94; mem. med. adv. bd. So. Calif. Coll. Med. and Dental Assts., 1972—85; mem. citizen's adv. com. Anaheim Hills Hosp., 1982—84; mem. Anaheim Sister City Com. to Mito, Japan, 1985; exec. prodr. Miss Anaheim Pageant, 1983—84; mem. Anaheim Halloween Festival Com., 1983; treas. Tu Casa Condo. Assn., Carlsbad, Calif., 1976—77; mem. Mormon Tabernacle Choir, Salt Lake City, 1966—68; bd. dirs. U. Utah Coll. Nursing, 2001—03, Am. Heart Assn., 1993—95. Recipient Annie Accolade award, Women's Divsn. Anaheim C. of C., 1984, Women of Achievement award, YWCA, Orange, Calif., 1985. Home: PO Box 3299 Ketchum ID 83340

PARRY, MICHELLE, physics professor; d. Randall Mead and Maureen Parry; m. Cree Santee Hennings, Aug. 3, 1992; 1 child, Nipin Whiporwil Hennings. BS, U. Scranton, 1992; PhD, Purdue U., 1998. Asst. prof. physics Longwood U., Farmville, Va., 1998—2004, 1998—, interim chair, dept. natural scis., 2005—. Recipient Prof. Joseph P. Harper award, U. Scranton, 1992, Lijuan Wang Meml. award, Purdue U., 1997, Akeley-Mandler award, 1998, Edward S. Akeley Meml. award, 1998, Jr. Faculty award, Longwood U., 2001; Spl. Initiative fellowship, Purdue U., 1995-1996. Office: Longwood U 201 High St Farmville VA 23909

PARRY-SOLÁ, CHERYL LEE, critical care nurse; b. Bristol, Pa., Oct. 27, 1960; d. Edmund H. and F. Renee (Platt) P. ADN, Bucks County C.C., 1982. RN NJ, CCRN. Formerly asst. head nurse Deborah Heart and Lung Ctr., Browns Mills, NJ; charge nurse med. ICU Holy Spirit Hosp., Camp Hill, Pa., 1995—2002, tng. ctr. coord., 2001—. Office: Holy Spirit Hosp Edn/Tng/Devel 503 N 21st St Camp Hill PA 17011-2288

PARSHALL, B. LYNNE, science administrator; Ptnr. Cooley Godward LLP; exec. v.p., CFO, dir. Isis Pharm., Inc., Carlsbad, Calif.; also bd. dirs. Bd. vis. Stanford U. Law Sch. Mem.: ABA, San Diego Bar Assn., Calif. Bar Assn., Licensing Execs. Soc. Office: Isis Pharmaceuticals 1896 Rutherford Rd Carlsbad CA 92008-7326

PARSHALL, KAREN VIRGINIA HUNGER, mathematician; b. Virginia Beach, Va., July 7, 1955; d. Maurice Jacques and Jean Kay (Wroton) Hunger; m. Brian J. Parshall, Aug. 6, 1978. BA, U. Va., 1977, MS, 1978; PhD, U. Chgo., 1982. Asst. prof. math. Sweet Briar (Va.) Coll., 1982-87, U. Ill., Urbana, 1987-88; asst. prof. math. and history U. Va., Charlottesville, 1988-93, assoc. prof. math. and history, 1993—99, prof. math. and history, 1999—. Author: (with David Rowe) Emergence of American Mathematics Research Community, 1994; (with others) Experiencing Nature, 1997, James Joseph Sylvester: Life and Work in Letters, 1998, (with others) Mathematics Unbound: The Emergence of an International Mathematical Community, 1800-1945, 2002; Years Ago editor Mathematical Intelligencer, N.Y.C., 1990-93; book rev. editor Historia Mathematica, San Diego, 1990-93, mng. editor, 1994-95, editor, 1996-99; contbr. articles to Archive for History Exact Scis., History of Sci., Jour. of the History of Biology, Archives internationales d'histoire des sciences, Annals of Sci., Historia Mathematica, Notices of the Am. Math. Soc., Am. Math. Mo., Revue d'histoire des mathématiques. Scholars award NSF, 1986-87, 90-93, NSF VPW award, 1996-97; John Simon Guggenheim Found. fellow, 1996. Mem. Am. Math. Soc., History Sci. Soc., Math. Assn. Am., Académie Internationale d'histoire des sciences (corr.), Phi Beta Kappa. Office: U Va Depts Math and History Dept Mathematics P O Box 400137 Charlottesville VA 22904

PARSKY, BARBARA, utilities executive; BA, Rollins Coll. Various mgmt. positions Gen. Electric Co.; ptnr. Porter Novelli, gen. mgr. LA; prin., owner; v.p. corp. comms. Edison Internat., Rosemead, Calif., 2002—. Office: Edison International 2244 Walnut Grove Ave Rosemead CA 91770

PARSONS, ALEXANDRA CLARE, literature and language educator; b. London, Sept. 3, 1975; arrived in U.S., 1976; d. Andrew and Carol Parsons. BA in English cum laude, Wellesley Coll., 1997; MA, Columbia U., Tchrs. Coll., 2001. Permanent tchg. cert. NY, 2001. TV rsch. analyst Katz Media, Seltel, Inc., NYC, 1997—98; broadcast assoc. CBS News Prodns., NYC, 1998—99; media rels. publicity coord. ABC News, NYC, 1999; asst. kindergarten tchr. Marymount Sch., NYC, 1999—2000; English tchr. The Nightingale-Bamford Sch., NYC, 2001—. Scholar, Japan Fulbright Meml. Fund, 2005. Mem.: Nat. Coun. Tchrs. English, Assn. Tchrs. Ind. Sch., Kappa Delta Pi.

PARSONS, ANNE, performing company executive; m. Donald Dietz; 1 child. BA, Smith Coll., 1980. Staff Nat. Symphony Orchestra, Wash., DC, 1981—83; orchestra mgr. Boston Symphony Orchestra, 1983—91; gen. mgr. Hollywood Bowl, LA, 1991—98, NY City Ballet, 1998—2004; exec. dir. Detroit Symphony Orchestra, 2004—. Fellow Am. Symphony Orchestra League, 1980—81. Office: Detroit Symphony Orchestra Max M Fisher Music Ctr 3711 Woodward Ave Detroit MI 48201

PARSONS, CHRISTINA ANNE, writer, photographer, educator; b. Fresno, Calif., Oct. 25, 1979; d. Daniel Charles and Susanne Lee Parsons. Cert. in Mgmt. and Supr., Portland C.C., Oreg., 2001; AS in Adminstrn. and Justice with honors, Fullerton Coll., Calif., 2005. Mktg. strategist and writer Alling Henning Assocs., Vancouver, Wash., 2001—02; mktg. strategist Drake Certivo, Newport Beach, Calif., 2002. Freelance writer; freelance editor; freelance publicist; guest tchr. spl. edn. (autism and severe learning disabilities) Clark County Sch. Dist., Las Vegas, 2005—06. Author: The Metrician's Estuous Phraseology published in Praxis, 2000; contbr. photographs Hawaii-imagazine.com (Photo of the Day multiple times; entire Hawaii photo collection on Hawaii Mag. web site, 2001), articles and photographs to mags. (Editor's Pick (several were awarded this), 2001). Chmn. mktg. com. Clark County Luth. Schs. Assn., Vancouver, Wash., 2001—02. Named Outstanding Transfer Scholar, Fullerton Coll., 2005; recipient Gold Medal award, Academic Decathlon, Calif. H.S., 1995, Silver Medal award, Academic Decathlon, 1996, Soroptimist Club, Whittier, Calif., 1996, Century Club award, Fancy Pubs., 1999; Lena and Faye scholar, Fullerton Coll. Found., 2005. Mem.: Nev. State Educators Assn., NEA, Coun. for Exceptional Children. Conservative. Avocations: travel, walking, reading, writing, photography. Office Phone: 562-682-3514. E-mail: chrisi.parsons@gmail.com.

PARSONS, CINDY MICHELLE, special education educator; b. Shawnee, Okla., Dec. 7, 1967; d. John Walter Loman and Marilyn Sue Ellsworth; m. Ronald D. Parsons, Jr., Dec. 13, 1991; 1 child, Katelyn. BS in edn., U. Cent. Okla., 1991. Tchg. cert. Spl. edn. tchr. Broken Arrow Pub. Sch., Okla., 1994—95, US Dist. #260 Derby Pub. Sch., Kans., 1997—98, Tulsa Pub. Sch., Okla., 1999—2000, Apollo Elem. Sch./Putnam City Pub. Sch., Okla. City, 2000—01, Prairie Vale Elem. Sch./Deer Creek Pub. Sch., Edmond, Okla., 2001—. Mem. Coun. for Exceptional Child, Edmond, 1990, Sight Improvement Com., Edmond, 2003—05; chmn. Soc. Com. Apollo Elem., Putnam City Sch., Okla. City, 2000—01; vol. Autism Summer Camp, Edmond, 1990. Vol. Edmond's Assn. Retarded Citizens, 1991, Fenwick Frog Swim Team, Edmond, 2003; youth Sunday sch. tchr. Named Deer Creek Prairie Vale Tchr. of Yr., 2003—04, Tchr. of Yr., Prairie Vale Elem. Sch., 2004—05; recipient Cert. Achievement for Faculty for No Child Left Behind Blue Ribbon Sch., Sec. Edn., Washington, DC, 2003—04. Mem.: NEA, Okla. Edn. Assn. Baptist. Avocations: reading, antiques, travel. Office: Alice Smith Elem Sch 1070 Beckworth Dr Reno NV 89506

PARSONS, CYNTHIA, writer, consultant; b. Cleve., Jan. 1, 1926; d. Sanford Sherman Clark and Elenore Mann. BA, Principia Coll., Elsah, Ill., 1948; MA, Putney/Antioch Coll., 1956; EdD, Norwich U., Northfield, Vt., 1985. Tchr. various pvt. and pub. schs., 1948-62; edn. editor Christian Sci. Monitor, Boston, 1962-69, 74-82; sr. program office Nat. Inst. for Edn., Washington, 1970-73; founder, dir., coord. SerVermont, Chester, Vt., 1985—2001. Instr. new math Madison Project, Syracuse, N.Y., 1959-61; edn. editor World Bank, Washington, 1969-70; vis. instr. Dartmouth Coll., Hanover, N.H., 1982, 83, 88, U. Vt., Burlington, 1983-88; edn. cons. Robert Coll., Istanbul, Turkey, 1984. Author: Seeds, 1985, Service Learning From A to Z, 1991, George Bird Grinnell, 1992, The Early History of Christian Science in Vermont, 1996, The Discoverer, Mary Baker Eddy, 2000, Yes, I Can Teach a Non-Reader to Read, 2005; co-author: Eleven Awesome Vermont Women, 2004; contbr. newspaper series on edn. Mem. Commn. on Edn. Issues, Boston, 1975-81; bd. mem. Grad. Record Examination, Princeton, N.J., 1978-82, Vt. Coun. on the Humanities, Morristown, 1993-97. Recipient Eleanor Roosevelt medal for pub. svc., Val-kill, N.Y., 1992; grantee Edwin Gould Found. for Children, N.Y. and Vt., 1985-95, MacArthur Found., Chgo. and Vt. Mem. Edn. Writers Assn. (pres. 1970-71). Democrat. Christian Scientist. Avocations: reading, travel, listening to classical music. Home: 4713 N 77th Pl Scottsdale AZ 85251 Personal E-mail: cparsons1@cox.net.

PARSONS, DEBRA LEA, elementary school educator; b. Redding, Calif., May 13, 1960; d. Gary Leon and Leta Barbara Cox. BA in Music Edn., Columbia Christian Coll., 1983; M Music Edn., U. Portland, 1989. Cert. tchr. Calif. Music tchr. David Douglas Sch. Dist., Portland, Oreg., 1984—85, Harold Oliver Sch., Portland, 1987—97, Shasta County Schs., Redding, Calif., 1997—; pvt. music instr. Parsons Music Sch., Shasta Lake City, Calif., 1997—; pvt. tutor math. and lang. arts,computer skills, spanish, and German Parsons Tutoring Svcs., Shasta Lake City, 1997—. Adj. prof. music Columbia Christian Coll., Portland, 1985—91; adj. music instr. Warner Pacific Coll., Portland, 1990—95; adjudicator music competitions Oreg. Music Educators Assn., Portland, 1989—92; grad. tchr. asst. U. Portland, 1986—87. Contbr. poetry to lit. publs. (Editor's Choice award, 98, 99, 00, 01). Vol. Providence Med. Ctr., Portland, 1984—86; asst. sect. leader, libr. Choral Arts Ensemble; asst. dir. Columbia Christian Band. Recipient award for acad. performance, Bank of Am., John Phillips Sousa Band award. Mem.: Music Educators Nat. Conf./Calif. Music Educator's Assn., Delta Kappa Gamma (music chmn.

1996—). Republican. Mem. Ch. Of Christ. Avocations: collecting sea shells, coins, porcelain dolls, sports cards, needlecrafts. Home and Office: 1988 Cabello St Shasta Lake CA 96019 E-mail: debip1@charter.net

PARSONS, ESTELLE, actress, director, theater producer; b. Lynn, Mass., Nov. 20, 1927; d. Eben and Elinor (Mattson) P.; m. Richard Gehman, Dec. 19, 1953 (div. Aug. 1958); children: Martha and Abbie (twins); m. Peter L. Zimroth, Jan. 2, 1983; 1 child, Abraham. BA in Polit. Sci., Conn. Coll. Women, 1949; student, Boston U. Law Sch., 1949-50; DFA (hon.), Conn. Coll., 2005. Stage appearances include Happy Hunting, 1957, Whoop Up, 1958, Beg, Borrow or Steal, 1960, Threepenny Opera, 1960, Mrs. Dally Has a Lover, 1962, Ready When You Are C.B, 1964, Malcolm, 1965, Seven Descents of Myrtle, 1968, And Miss Reardon Drinks a Little, 1971, Mert and Phil, 1974, The Norman Conquests, 1975-76, Ladies of the Alamo, 1977, Miss Margarida's Way, 1977-78, The Pirates of Penzance, 1981, The Shadow Box, 1994; adapted, dir., performer Orgasmo Adulto Escapes from the Zoo, 1983, The Unguided Missile, Baba Goya, 1989, Shimada, 1992, Grace & Glorie, 1996, The Last of the Thorntons, 2000-01, Morning's At Seven, 2002, The Bay at Nice, 2004, Harold & Maude, 2005, Sister Mozart, 2005; film appearances include Bonnie and Clyde, 1966 (Acad. award), Rachel, Rachel, 1967, I Never Sang for My Father, 1969, Dick Tracy, 1990, Boys On The Side, 1995, Looking for Richard, 1996, That Darn Cat, 1997; TV appearances include Roseanne, 1990—. NBC Today, 1951-56; artistic dir. NY Shakespeare Festival Players, 1986, Actors' Studio, 1997-2003; dir. (Broadway play) Salome, the Reading, 2003. Recipient Theatre World award, 1962-63, Obie award, 1964, Motion Picture Acad. Arts and Scis. award, 1967, Medal of Honor, Conn. Coll., 1969; named to Theatre Hall of Fame, 2004. Home: 924 West End Ave Apt T5 New York NY 10025-3543

PARSONS, IRENE ADELAIDE, management consultant; b. North Wilkesboro, N.C. d. Everett T. and Martha (Minton) P. BS in Bus. Edn. and Adminstrn., U. N.C., 1941, LLD (hon.), 1967; MS in Pub. Adminstrn., George Washington U., 1965. Tchr. Roanoake Rapids (N.C.) High Sch., 1941-42; rep. U.S. Civil Svc. Commn., 1942-43; with VA, 1946-74, asst. adminstr. vets. affairs, dir. personnel, dir. equal employment opportunity, 1965-74; mgmt. cons., 1974—. Exec. com. Pres.'s Study Group Careers for Women. Served to lt. USCGR, 1943-46. Recipient Fed. Woman's Outstanding Achievement award, 1966, Silver Helmet award Amvets, 1971, Career Svc. award Nat. Civil Svc. League, 1972, Disting. Alumni Achievement award George Washington U., 1973; named to Brevard Coll. Hall of Fame, 1984 Mem. Assn. Fed. Woman's Award Recipients (chmn. 1972-76) Address: PO Box 2046 North Wilkesboro NC 28659-2046

PARSONS, LINDA L., art dealer; b. Pitts., 1945; B History, U. Colo., 1967; PhD, U. Wis., 1972. Owner Linda L. Parsons Art Sales, Denver, 1971—79, 1984—96, Santa Fe, 1979—84, Cin., 1996—. Contbr. articles to profl. jours. Bd. mem. Santa Fe Animal Shelter. Mem.: Ohio Soc. (bd. mem. 2004—), Am. Art Soc. Cin. (pres. 2004—), Arapahoe Hunt Club, Miami Valley Hunt Club. Avocations: horseback riding, history, travel, walking, conservation. Home and Office: PO Box 1006 Milford OH 45150

PARSONS, LORRAINE LEIGHTON, nurse, pre-school administrator; b. Albany, Maine, Feb. 7, 1939; d. Alfred Elmer Leighton and Arlene Rachael Winslow; m. Jack Arnol Greig (div. July 1982); children: Scotty, Kim; m. Robert Davis Parsons, Dec. 20, 1991. Student, U. Maine. RN, Maine. Office nurse Charles Hannigan, MD, Auburn, Maine, 1961-64; with Stephens Meml. Hosp., Norway, Maine, 1964-69; tchr. spl. edn. W. Paris (Maine) Sch., 1969-73; tchr. reading and math. Buckfield (Maine) Sch., 1974-78; nurse Ledgeview Nursing Home, W. Paris, 1979-80, Central Maine Med. Ctr., Lewiston, 1980-96; child care profl. Marwin Cons. Co., Raymond, Maine, 1996—. Author: Families of the Fox and Geese Quilt, 1997, Homesteads of Hartford, 1997, Quilting is Qumforting, 1999, Town of Hartford, 2000, Military Service, 2000, Marston Homestead, 2000, Crazy Quilt, 2000, Winslow Home, 2001, The Alfred E. Leighton Family, 2001, Rokomeko - Native Americans, 2002, Life - 1870, 1879 & 1881, 2003; co-author: Hartford in Pictures, 1984; author: Rokomeko Indians Native Americans, 2002. Pres., founder Hartford (Maine) Heritage Soc., 1976; program chairwoman Hartford Bicentennial, 1997-98. Recipient Cert. of Honor Bicentennial, State of Maine, 1998, Double-Trouble Nature category Internat. Libr. Photography, 2000; grantee Maine Arts, 1998. Avocations: dolls, stamps, town histories. Home: PO Box 493 Canton ME 04221-0493

PARSONS, MARCIA PHILLIPS, judge; Bankruptcy judge U.S. Bankruptcy Ct. (Tenn. ea. dist.), 6th circuit, Greeneville, 1993—. Office: US Courthouse Ste 321 220 W Depot St Greeneville TN 37743

PARSONS, MARILEE BENORE, science educator; b. Toledo, Nov. 5, 1956; d. Donald Joseph and Mary Kathleen (Poiry) Benore. AA, BA, Thomas More Coll., 1979; PhD, U. Del., 1986. Rsch. tech. Borden Chem., Cin., 1978-80; postdoctoral fellow CIBA-Geigy Pharm., Summit, NJ, 1986-89; mem. faculty U. Mich., Dearborn, 1989—, dir. Will Program, 2006—. Bd. health, Frenchtown, NJ, 1988—89; vol. Girl Scout Sci. Day Camp, Dearborn, 1991—96, 2003—04. Rackham fellow, 1991. Mem.: Am. Soc. Biochemistry and Molecular Biology (Sarah Goddard Power award 2004). Democrat. Roman Catholic. Avocations: biochemistry, women's studies.

PARSONS, MARTHA MCGHEE, rehabilitation nurse; b. Huntington, W.Va., Jan. 24, 1944; d. Orme Winford and Sadie Mae (Dudley) McGhee; children: Laura Beckner, Suzie King; m. Garland Parsons, Oct. 28, 2004. RN, St. Mary's Sch. Nursing, Huntington, W.Va., 1980; student, Marshall U., Huntington, W.Va., 1978-88. Cert. rehab. nurse, cert. case mgr. Surg. head nurse Huntington Hosp. Inc., nursing supr.; quality assurance dir. Am. Hosp. for Rehab., Huntington, 1988-89, DON, 1989-90; rehab. charge nurse Am. Putnam Nursing and Rehab. Ctr., Hurricane, W.Va., 1990—; mgr. health svcs. Mountain State Blue Cross/Blue Shield, Charleston, W.Va., 1995—, mgr. precert., case mgmt. and med. rev., 1995—; owner Sportswear Designs, Hurricane, W.Va. Mem. Assn. for Practitioners in Infection Control. Home: 203 Carper Ln Barboursville WV 25504

PARSONS, MINDY (MINDY ENOS), newsletter editor, publisher, non-profit organization executive; b. Cin., May 18, 1962; d. Max Allen and Margery Ann (White) Enos; m. Judd Lewis Parsons, Sept. 4, 1993; children: Cody Robert and Savannah Anne (twins). AA in Liberal Arts, Brevard Community Coll., 1983; BSBA, Fla. Inst. Tech., 1986; MBA, N.Y. Inst., Boca Raton, Fla., 1992. Mem. adminstrv. support staff IBM, Boca Raton, 1980, 81; dir. mktg. Progressive Pub., Melbourne, Fla., 1986; owner, pub. Echelon Pub. Inc., Melbourne, 1986-87; editor Keuthan Communications Inc., Melbourne, 1987-89; staff writer First Mktg. Corp., Pompano Beach, Fla., 1989-90; assoc. editor Billboard Publs. Inc., Coral Springs, Fla., 1990-92, Caribbean Clipper, Inc., Clearwater, Fla., 1992-93; reporter South Fla. News Network, Coral Springs, 1993-94; owner Creative Communications, Delray Beach, Fla., 1993-96; newsletter editor, pub., founder Breast Cancer Survivor Network Corp., 1997—. Author: How to Save for Your Child's Education, 1990; editor: Soccer for Children, 1988, History of Bahamas, 1990; editor, pub. Breast Cancer Survivor newsletter, 1997—; contbr. articles to profl. publs. Vol. Humane Soc. of Broward County, Coral Springs, 1990-91; founder Breast Cancer Survivor Network; mem. Palm Beach County Breast Cancer Coalition. Mem. NAFE, Newsletter Publishers Assn. Republican. Methodist. Avocations: volleyball, swimming, reading. Home: 1096 SW 26th Ave Boynton Beach FL 33426-7815

PARSONS, SUSAN STEELE, secondary school educator; b. Trenton, NJ, Dec. 7, 1954; d. Elmer Eugene and Barbara Joan Steele; m. Robert Lewis Parsons, Sept. 25, 1982; children: Bret Eugene, Colin Jay. BA in Art Edn., Rowan U., 1976; MA in Edn. and Tech., Georgian Ct. U., 2000, supr. cert., 2001. Instr. Peddie Sch., Hightstown, NJ, 1976—77; tech. assoc. AT&T Bell Labs., Holmdel, NJ, 1977—89; pvt. practice, 1990—95; tech. supr., faculty Millstone Twp. Schs., Millstone, NJ, 1995—2001; tech. instr. Comms. H.S., Wall, NJ, 2001—02, Wall H.S., 2002—. Address: 1914 Shadowbrook Dr Wall NJ 07719-9714

PARSONS, VIRGINIA MAE, psychology educator; b. Milw., Oct. 27, 1942; d. John T. and Mable (Myers) Lakso; m. Ralph F. Parsons, Oct. 5, 1968; children: Ralph F. III, Robert, Jeanne. BA, U. Wis., Milw., 1964; MA, U. Iowa, 1967, PhD, 1970. Asst. prof. U. Wis.-Parkside, Kenosha, Wis., 1970-76; prof. psychology Carroll Coll., Waukesha, Wis., 1976—. Contbr. articles to profl. jours. NSF grantee, 1962-64, 72, 77, Carroll Coll., 1978, 80, 88. Mem. AAAS, Am. Psychol. Soc., N.Y. Acad. Sci., Sigma Xi, Psi Chi. Avocations: photography, swimming, music. Office: Carroll Coll 100 N East Ave Waukesha WI 53186-3103

PARTEN, PRISCILLA M., medical and psychiatric social worker, educator; b. Lowell, Mass., Dec. 7, 1944; d. Ralph Bailey and Margaret Lillian (McDonagh) Newton; m. Samuel L. Parten, June 27, 1965; children: Delora Parten Power, Edward Bailey, Ethan Rogers. BA, Northeastern U., 1968; MSW, Adelphi U., Burlington, Vt., 1987. Lic. ind. clin. social worker, Mass., NH, LCSW, Maine; bd. cert. diplomate NASW. Family support coord. Easter Seal Early Intervention, Derry, NH, 1988-91; med. and psychiat. social worker Salem (NH) Vis. Nurses, 1992-96; home sch. coord. Timberlane Regional Sch. Dist., Plaistow, NH, 1992—; dir. Priscilla M. Parten, MSW, ACSW, BCD, Londonderry, NH, 1992—. Spkr., author, presenter in field, interviewed on Nat. Pub. TV. Bd. dirs. Norwich U. Parents' Assn., 1st v.p., 1999—2001. Recipient commendation Pres.'s Com. on Mental Retardation, 1968. Mem. NASW, Nutfield Exch. Club (bd. dirs. 1994-96). Democrat. Congregationalist. Avocations: skiing, photography, crocheting, gardening, snorkeling. Office: 50 Nashua Rd Ste 214 Londonderry NH 03053-3444 E-mail: senatchie@hotmail.com.

PARTHEMORE, JACQUELINE GAIL, internist, educator, hospital administrator; b. Harrisburg, Pa., Dec. 21, 1940; d. Philip Mark and Emily (Buvit) Parthemore; m. Alan Morton Blank, Jan. 7, 1967; children: Stephen Eliot, Laura Elise. BA, Wellesley Coll., 1962; MD, Cornell U., 1966. Diplomate Am. Bd. Internal Medicine. Resident in internal medicine N.Y. Hosp./Cornell U., 1966-69; fellow in endocrinology Scripps Clinic and Rsch. Found., La Jolla, Calif., 1969-72; rsch. ednl. assoc. VA Hosp., San Diego, 1974-78; staff physician VA San Diego Health Care Sys., 1978-79, asst. chief, med. svc., 1979-83, acting chief, med. svc., 1980-81, chief of staff, 1984—; asst. prof. medicine U. Calif. Sch. Medicine, San Diego, 1974-80, assoc. prof. medicine, 1980-85, prof. medicine, assoc. dean, 1985—. Mem. nat. rsch. resources coun. NIH, Bethesda, Md., 1990—94; mem. VHA Performance Measures Work Group, 2006—. Contbr. chapters to books, articles to profl. jours. Mem. adv. bd. San Diego Opera, 1993—2006; mem. Roundtable and Channel 10 Focus Group, San Diego Millennium Project, 1999; v.p. bd. dirs. San Diego Vets. Med. Rsch. Found., 1989—. Recipient Bullock's 1st Annual Portfolio award, 1985, San Diego Pres.'s Coun. Woman of Yr. award, 1985, YWCA Tribute to Women in Industry award, 1987, San Diego Women Who Mean Bus. award, 1999, Excellence in Leadership award Am. Hosp. Assn., 2002, Local Legend award AMWA/Nat. Libr. Medicine, 2005. Fellow ACP (gov. 2005-, mem. edn. com. 2006-), Am. Assn. Clin. Endocrinologists; mem. Endocrine Soc., Nat. Assn. VA Chiefs Staff/Physician Execs. (pres. 1989-91), Assn. Am. Med. Colls., Wellesley Coll. Alumnae Assn. (1st v.p. 1992-95), San Diego Wellesley Club (pres. 1997-99), San Diego Herb Soc. (co-pres. 2003-04). Avocations: gardening, reading, sailing, cooking, travel. Office: VA San Diego Healthcare Sys 3350 La Jolla Village Dr San Diego CA 92161-0002 Office Phone: 858-552-7419. Business E-Mail: jparthemore@ucsd.edu.

PARTLOW, MADELINE, principal; married; 4 children. Degree in early and mid. childhood edn., Ohio State U.; M in Early and Mid. Childhood, 1995, M in Ednl. Adminstrn., 1997. Tchr. New Albany (Ohio) Mid. Sch., 1979—83, 1985—88; from tchr. to prin. Blacklick Elem., Gahanna, 1992—2000; prin. New Albany (Ohio) Mid. Sch., 2001—. Office: New Albany Mid Sch 6600 E Dublin-Granville Rd New Albany OH 43054-8740

PARTON, DOLLY REBECCA, singer, composer, actress; b. Sevier County, Tenn., Jan. 19, 1946; d. Robert Lee and Avie Lee (Owens) P.; m. Carl Dean, May 30, 1966. Country music singer, rec. artist, composer, actress, radio and TV personality. Entrepreneur, owner entertainment park Dollywood, established 1985. Radio appearances include Grand Ole Opry, WSM Radio, Nashville, Cass Walker program, Knoxville; TV appearances include Porter Wagoner Show, from 1967, Cass Walker program, Bill Anderson Show, Wilburn Bros. Show, Barbara Mandrell Show; rec. artist, Mercury, Monument, RCA, CBS record cos.; albums include Here You Come Again (Grammy award 1978), Real Love, 1985, Just the Way I Am, 1986, Portrait, 1986, Think About Love, 1986, Trio (with Emmylou Harris, Linda Ronstadt) (Grammy award 1988), 1987, Heartbreaker, Great Balls of Fire, Rainbow, 1988, White Limozeen, 1989, Home for Christmas, 1990, Eagle When She Flies, 1991, Slow Dancing with the Moon, 1993 (Grammy nomination, Best Country Vocal Collaboration for Romeo (with Tanya Tucker, Billy Ray Cyrus, Kathy Mattea, Pam Tillis, & Mary-Chapin Carpenter), (with Tammy Wynette and Loretta Lynn) Honky Tonk Angels, 1994, The Essential Dolly Parton, 1995, Just the Way I Am, 1996, Super Hits, 1996, (with others) I Will Always Love You & Other Greatest Hits, 1996, Hungry Again, 1998, Trio II, 1998, Grass is Blue, 1999 (Grammy award for best bluegrass album), Best of the Best-Porter & Doll, 1999, Halos and Horns, 2002, For God and Country, 2003, Makin' Believe, 2003; appears on song "Creepin' In" with Norah Jones, 2004; composer numerous songs including Nine to Five (Grammy award 1981, Acad. award nominee and Golden Globe award nominee 1981); Film appearances include Nine to Five, 1980, The Best Little Whorehouse in Texas, 1982, Rhinestone, 1984, Steel Magnolias, 1989, Straight Talk, 1991; (TV films) A Smoky Mountain Christmas, 1986, Wild Texas Wind, 1991, Unlikely Angel, 1996, Blue Valley Songbird, 1999; (TV series) Heavens to Betsy, 1994, Mindin My Own Business, 1996; Author: Dolly, 1994. Recipient (with Porter Wagoner) Vocal Group of Yr. award, 1968, Vocal Duo of Yr. award All Country Music Assn., 1970, 71, Nashville Metronome award, 1979, Am. Music award for best duo performance (with Kenny Rogers), 1984, Grammy awards for best female country vocalist, 1978, 81, for best country song, 1981, for best country vocal performance with group, 1987, People's Choice award, 1980, 88, Nat. Medal of Arts Nat. Endowment for the Arts, 2005, Kennedy Ctr. Honor, John F. Kennedy Center for Performing Arts, 2006; co-recipient (with Emmylou Harris and Linda Ronstadt) Acad. Country Music award for album of the yr., 1987, (with Brad Paisley) Most Inspiring Video of Yr. for When I Get Where I'm Going, CMT Awards (Country Music TV), 2006, Video of Yr. and Vocal Event of Yr., Acad. Country Music award, 2006; named Female Vocalist of Yr., 1975, 76, Country Star of Yr., Sullivan Prodns., 1977, Entertainer of Yr., Country Music Assn., 1978, Female Vocalist of Yr., Acad. Country Music, 1980; Dolly Parton Day proclaimed, Sevier County, Tenn., designated Oct. 7, 1967, Los Angeles, Sept. 20, 1979; named to Small Town of Am. Hall of Fame, 1988, East Tenn. Hall of Fame, 1988. Address: RCA 6 W 57th St New York NY 10019-3901 Office: Dollywood Co 1020 Dollywood Ln Pigeon Forge TN 37863-4101*

PARTON-STANARD, SUSAN, music educator, voice educator, musician; b. Alton, Ill. d. Raymond Hayes and Dorothy J. (Kaus) Parton; 1 child, Raymond Harris Stanard. MusB in Voice, Opera, Jacksonville U., 1979, MA in Tchg. Music Edn., 1988. Adj. prof. music Jacksonville U., Fla., 1983—95; orch., choral dir. Mayport Jr. HS, Atlantic Beach, Fla., 1985—87; prof. music Fla. CC, Jacksonville, 1999—2002; asst. prof. music Lewis & Clark CC, Godfrey, Ill., 2002—, dept. chair, 2002—. Operatic, concert artist, 1980—; dir. worship, music Isle Faith United Meth. Ch., Jacksonville, 1995—2002; co-dir. choral, vocal edn. Douglas Anderson Sch. Arts, Jacksonville; dir. choral activities, vocal studies, dir. music 12th St. Presbyn. Ch., Alton, Ill., 2004—; organist St. Paul United Meth. Ch., Jacksonville; lectr. in field; vocal coach. Singer, musician: Verdi Requiem, Mozart Requiem, Handel's Messiah; singer: (Operas) Carmen, Cavalleria Rusticana, Tosca, Don Giovanni, Tannhauser. Named Outstanding Artist of Yr., NJ State Opera, 1981, Outstanding Artist N.E. Fla., Cummer Gallery Art, 1982; recipient First Pl. winner, Met. Opera Auditions, Fla. Ea. Regional, 1981—82, Outstanding Tchr. of Yr., Mayport Jr. HS, 1985—86. Fellow: United Meth. Musician in Music Worship Arts; mem.: Am. Guild Organists, Music Tchrs. Nat. Assn., Music Educators Nat. Conf., Am. Choral Dirs. Assn., Nat. Assn. Tchrs. Singing. Avocations: antiques, Depression glass. Home: 4909 Voltaire Dr Godfrey IL 62035 Office: Lewis Clark Cmty Coll Music Dept 5800 Godfrey Rd Godfrey IL 62035 Office Phone: 618-468-4732.

PARULIS, CHERYL, English, drama and speech educator; b. Charlotte, N.C., Apr. 11, 1944; d. Francis August and Evelyn Louise (Scott) Bogacki; m. Albert William Parulis, June 25, 1966 (Apr. 1984); children: Albert William Jr., Christa Suzanne. M in Sports Adminstrn., Mercyhurse Coll., Erie, Pa., 1962-63; student, Indiana U. Pa., 1963-64, U. Que. at Trois Riviers, Can., 1987; BA in English Lit., Clarion U. Pa., 1987, MA in English Lit., 1989; BEd, permanent cert. in English edn., St. Thomas U., Miami, Fla., 1995. Permanet cert. English tchr., Fla. Substitute tchr. Brigantine (N.J.) Pub. Sch. Sys., 1970-72, Dubois (Pa.) Area Sch. Sys., 1982-84, Clarion Intermediate Unit 6, 1984-86; residential aide Pathways, Inc., Clarion, 1987-88; asst. Writing Ctr., Clarion U. Pa., 1987-88, grad. asst., English and computer tutor, 1988-89; tchr. English, St. Jospeh Sch., Miami Beach, Fla., 1991-93, Msgr. Edward Pace H.S., Miami, 1993-98; adj. prof. composition, speech, Am. lit. and drama St. Thomas U., 1994—; adj. prof. English and lit. Internat. Fine Arts Coll., Miami, 1998—. Partitipant Fla. Thespian Festival, 1997, 98; presenter in field; cheerleading coach, Miami, 1995-98. Hospice vol., Miami, 1993-94; vol. Miami Beach Dem. Com., 1994—, Habitat for Humanity, Miami, 1998-99. Recipient Msgr. Edward Pace Golden Apple award of excellence, 1994, 97. Mem. Nat. Coun. Tchrs. English, Dade County Tchrs. Assn., Sigma Tau Delta (life). Roman Catholic. Avocations: theater, film, decorating, stage directing, dance.

PARVIN, RUTHANN, psychological services administrator; b. Ft. Collins, Colo., Sept. 20, 1948; BA, U. Ark., 1966; MA, U. Okla., 1975; JD, U. Nebr., 1977, PhD, 1982. Lic. psychologist, Oreg., Ind., Ill. Therapist Community Mental Health Ctr., Helena, Ark., 1970-71; rsch. asst. FAA, Oklahoma City, 1971-74; therapist Nebr. Childrens Ctr., Lincoln, 1978-79; psychology intern Med. Sch. UCLA, 1979-80; asst. prof. Ind. U., South Bend, 1980-87; dir. psychol. svcs No. Ill. U., DeKalb, 1987-1990; assoc. prof. psychology, dir. clin. tng. Pacific U., Forest Grove, Oreg., 1990-91; dir. counseling Reed Coll., Portland, Oreg., 1991-94; exec. dir. psychol. svcs. A Place to Talk, Portland, 1994—. Legis. asst. U.S. Senate, Washington, 1985-86. Contbr. articles to profl. jours. Congl. Sci. Fellow AAAS and APA, 1985-86 Mem. APA, Feminist Therapy Inst. (steering com. 1989-92, editor Interchange 1991-95), Oreg. Mensa (sec. 2005-06). Avocations: pottery, creative writing. Office: A Place to Talk 2925 SE Taylor St Portland OR 97214-4032

PASCAL, AMY BETH, film company executive; b. LA, Mar. 1958; d. Tony and Barbara Pascal; m. Bernard Weinraub, Aug. 9, 1997; 1 adopted child, Anthony. BA in Internat. Rels., UCLA. With Kestral Films; v.p. prodn. 20th Century Fox, 1986—87, Columbia Pictures, 1987—89, exec. v.p. prodn., 1987—94; pres. prodn. Turner Pictures, 1994—96; pres. Columbia Pictures, Culver City, Calif., 1996-99, chmn., 1999—2002; vice chmn. Sony Pictures Entertainment, Culver City, Calif., 2002—06, co-chmn., 2006—; chmn. Sony Pictures Entertainment Motion Picture Group, Culver City, Calif., 2003—. Bd. trustees Rand Corp. Bd. trustees AFI; mem. UCLA Sch. Theater, Film & Television. Named one of 100 Most Powerful Women in Entertainment, Hollywood Reporter, 2004—05, 100 Most Powerful Women, Forbes mag., 2005—06, 50 Most Powerful People in Hollywood, Premiere mag., 2004—06, 50 Most Powerful Women in Bus., Fortune mag., 2006. Office: Sony Pictures Entertainment 10202 Washington Blvd Culver City CA 90232*

PASCALE, JANE FAY, pathologist; b. New Haven, Conn., May 20, 1932; d. John Adam and Madeline J. (Pompano) P.; m. Joseph H. Kite Jr., Aug. 6, 1970. BA, Mount Holyoke Coll., 1954; MD, U. Chgo., 1959. Cert. anat. and clin. pathology Am. Bd. Pathology; diplomate Nat. Bd. Med. Examiners. Intern, resident in pathology Yale-New Haven Hosp., 1959-63; NIH-NCI spl. fellow dept. microbiology Yale U. Sch. Medicine, 1963-64; NIH-NCI spl. fellow Inst. de Recherches Scientifiques sur le Cancer, Villejuif, France, 1964-66; asst. in pathology Mass. Gen. Hosp. and Harvard Med. Sch., Boston, 1966-68; asst. prof. clin. pathology Yale U. Sch. Medicine, New Haven, 1968-69; attending pathologist Erie County Med. Ctr., Buffalo, 1969-95; clin. asst. prof. pathology SUNY, Buffalo, 1969-90, clin. asst. prof. microbiology, 1991—. Mem. scientific adv. bd. Infectech, Inc., Sharon, Pa., 1995—; scientific del. Citizen Amb. Program People-to-People Internat. Contbr. articles to profl. jours. Recipient Physician's Recognition award AMA, 1981-99. Fellow Am. Soc. Clin. Pathologists, Coll. Am. Pathologists; mem. AMA, N.Y. Acad. Scis., Am. Soc. Cytopathology, Assn. Clin. Scientists. Methodist. Achievements include research in immunopathology of tuberculosis and autoimmune disease.

PASCHAL, BETH CUMMINGS, journalist, editor; b. Lohrville, Iowa, June 26, 1917; d. Harry Ross and Agnes (Baird) Cummings. m. George Washington Paschal Jr., Dec. 20, 1944 (dec. Feb. 1995); children: George Washington III, Laura Huston, Robert Cummings. BS, Iowa State U., 1939. Assoc. editor Farm Jour., Phila., 1939-45. Chmn. 1st N.C. Mus. of Art Beaux Arts Ball, 1973. Editor: A Celebration of Art and Cookery, 1976; columnist Trident Mag., 1940-43; editor State Med. Aux. Newsletter, 1955-63. Arch. selection com. Fine Arts Ctr. Wake Forest U., Winston-Salem, N.C., 1975; chmn. mus. com. Gov. Cultural Adv. Coun., Raleigh, 1980, donor, 1972; hon. chmn. N.C. Mus. Art 50th Anniversary Gala, 1997; pres. N.C. State U. Friends of the Libr., 1979-80; bd. dir. N.C. Mus. Art, 1964—, vice chmn. new bldg. campaign, 1977-78, works art com., 1983-2002, emeritus, docent, 1955-87, emeritus, 1987—, trustee emeritus, 1995—. Named Tarheel of Week, Raleigh News and Observer, 1965; named to YWCA Acad. of Women, 1983, North Caroliniana Soc., 1998; recipient honor, N.C. Mus. Art, Acquisition of Art, 1974, Lifetime Achievement award, N.C. Mus. Art and N.C. Art Soc., 2001, Alumni Merit award, Iowa State U., 1980, Raleigh medal of Arts, 1986, Phi Beta Kappa award, 1995, Thomas Kenan III Leadership Arts award, 2006. Mem. Jr. League Raleigh, Nat. Humanities Ctr. (dir. coun.), Carolina Country Club, Nine O'Clock Cotillion, Mortar Bd., Delta Delta Delta, Theta Sigma Phi. Avocations: reading, tennis, travel, bread baking, sewing. Home: # 301 2701 Glenwood Gardens Ln Raleigh NC 27608

PASCHAL, RHODA JONES, voice educator; b. Savannah, Ga., Apr. 5, 1956; d. Charles Alexander and Rhoda Johnson Jones; m. Robert Sheldon Paschal, June 16, 1979; children: Rhoda Jane, Ann Sheldon. D of musical arts, U. of SC., 1992—95. Certified Teacher of Music Education SC, 2003, International Baccalaureate Music Educator Internat. Baccalaureate Orgn., 2003. Music staff: alto soloist First Presbyn. Ch., Columbia, SC, 1981—; singer, voice tchr. Paschal Acad. of Music, Columbia, SC, 1990—; founder, dir. Palmetto Girls Ensemble, Columbia, SC, 2000—; internat. baccalaureate music educator A. C. Flora High Sch., Richland Sch. Dist. One, Columbia, SC, 2002—. SC dist. chmn. Met. Opera Nat. Coun. Auditions, Columbia, SC, 1990—; artist in residence SC Arts Commn., Columbia, 1990—, cmty. performing tour, 2001—; art affiliate Columbia Music Festival Assn., SC, 2002—; founder Paschal Academy of Music: a comprehensive music program including piano, voice and choral instrn. Singer: performances include operas, recitals, oratorios and musicals; dir.: (plays) including The Sound of Music, Grease, Anything Goes, Music Man. Bible moderator First Prebyterian: Women of the Ch., Columbia, SC, 1980—85; cmty. rsch. Jr. League, Columbia, SC, 1980—85; chmn., jr. garden club Columbia Garden Club, 1980—85. Grad. Assistantship fellowship, Women's Ensemble; SC. Opera Theater: U. of SC, 1988—90, 1992—95. Mem.: Music Educators Nat. Conf. (assoc.), SC. Music Teachers Assn. (assoc.), Nat. Assn. of Teachers of Singing (assoc.), Greater Columbia Opera Guild (assoc.). R-Consevative. Christian/ Presbyterian. Avocations: travel, tennis, bridge. Home: 1713 Roslyn Dr Columbia SC 29206 Office: Paschal Academy of Music 1713 Roslyn Dr Columbia SC 29206 E-mail: paschaliii@msn.com.

PASCOE, CLARA P., public relations executive, property manager; arrived in U.S., 1981; d. Jairo Buritica and Consuelo Antolinez; m. Armon Vakneen, Feb. 14, 2002. Exec. adminstrv. bus. diploma, Inst. Istmo, San Jose, Costa Rica, 1978; secretarial bus. diploma, Alvin C.C., 1983; A in Bus. Adminstrn., West L.A., 1987; BBA, U. Phoenix, Los Angeles, 2002, MBA in Mgmt., 2004. Sec., receptionist Indec Fin. Inc., San Jose, Costa Rica, 1975—81; property mgr., acct. Accurate Records, Inc., L.A., 1987—94; property mgmt. agt. Proactive, L.A., 1994—97; asst. dir. pub. rels. Simon Wiesenthal Ctr., L.A., 1997—. Tax cons. H&R Block, L.A., 1991—95. Avocations: art, dance, writing, reading, sports.

PASCOE, PATRICIA HILL, former state legislator; b. Sparta, Wis., June 1, 1935; d. Fred Kirk and Edith (Kilpatrick) Hill; m. D. Monte Pascoe, Aug. 3, 1957; children: Sarah, Edward, William. BA, U. Colo., 1957; MA, U. Denver, 1968, PhD, 1982. Tchr. Sequoia Union H.S. Dist., Redwood City, Calif. and Hayward (Calif.) Union H.S. Dist., 1957-60; instr. Met. State Coll., Denver, 1969-75, Denver U., 1975-77, 81, rsch. asst. bur. ednl. rsch., 1981-82; tchr. Kent Denver Country Day Sch., Englewood, Colo., 1982-84; freelance writer Denver, 1985—; mem. Colo. Senate, Dist. 32, Denver, 1989—93, Colo. Senate, Dist. 34, Denver, 1995—2003; chair minority caucus Colo. Senate, Denver, 1996-2000, chair policy and planning com., 2001, chair edn. com., 2002. Commr. Edn. Commn. of the States, Denver, 1975-82, 01-05. Contbr. articles to numerous publs. and jours. Bd. dirs. Samaritan House, 1990-94, Cystic Fibrosis Found., 1989-93, chmn. legis. com.; pres. East HS Parent Tchr. and Student Assn., Denver, 1984-85; mem. Moore Budget Adv. Com., Denver, 1966-72; legis. chmn. alumni bd. U. Colo., Boulder, 1987-89; del. Dem. Nat. Conv., San Francisco, 1984, NYC, 1992; mem. Denver Woman's Press Club, 1986—, pres., 2005-06, Colo. Arts Coalition, 1988-97, Conflict Ctr. Bd., 2003-05; bd. dirs. Opera Colo., 1996-02; mem. bd. ACLU Colo. Mem. Soc. Profl. Journalists, Common Cause (bd. dirs. Denver chpt. 1986-88), Lions Club (dir. 2003-05), Phi Beta Kappa. Democrat. Presbyterian.

PASCUAL, MERCEDES, biology professor; PhD in Joint Program, Woods Hole Oceanographic Inst. and MIT, 1995. Asst. prof. dept. ecology and evolutionary biology U. Mich., 2001—. Mem. Ctr. for the Study of Complex Systems U. Mich. Named one of 50 Most Important Women in Sci., Discover mag., 2002; Alexander Hollaender Disting. Postdoctoral Fellow, U.S. Dept. of Energy, Centennial Fellowship, Global and Complex Systems from the James S. McDonnell Found. Office: U Mich Kraus 2045 Ann Arbor MI 48109-1048

PASH, TERESA A., piano teacher, performer; b. Hastings, Mich., May 27, 1963; d. Patrick Joseph Gilmore and Norma Violet Hammond Gilmore Earl; children: Sara, Kyle, Anna. Student, Olivet (Mich.) Coll., 1981-83; BA, U. Puget Sound, Tacoma, 1986. Cert. tchr. Kindermusik, 2004. Tech. writer, desktop pub. H/H Effective Mgmt. Sys., Battle Creek, Mich., 1990-95; pvt. piano tchr. Nashville, Mich. Keyboardist, vocal arranger Holy Smoke Band, Kent, Wash., 1985-88; keyboardist, leader Matthew's House Band, Nashville, Mich., 1996-2002; keyboardist Yesterday's Gospel Band, Hastings, Mich., 1999-2002. Artist/prodr.: (CDs) Classical Alloy & Christmas Memories, 1999, Hymns of the Heart, 2002. Music dir. Cornerstone Cmty. Ch., Kent, 1986-90; band dir. Grace Cmty. Ch., Nashville, 1995-99. Mem.: Battle Creek Area Music Tchrs. Assn. (chair student achievement testing program 1998—2001, pres. 2002—), Mich. Music Tchrs. Assn., Music Tchrs. Nat. Assn. Christian. Avocations: music, songwriting, reading, computers. Home: PO Box 495 Nashville MI 49073-0495 Office Phone: 517-852-9159.

PASHGIAN, MARGARET HELEN, artist; b. Pasadena, Calif., Nov. 7, 1934; d. Aram John and Margaret (Howell) P. BA, Pomona Coll., 1956; student, Columbia U., 1957; MA in Fine Arts, Boston Univ., 1958. Art instr. Harvard-Newton Program Occidental Coll., 1977-78; artist in residence Calif. Inst. Tech., 1970-71. Grants panelist Calif. Arts Coun., Sacramento, 1993. One-woman shows include Rex Evans Gallery, L.A., 1965, 67, Occidental Coll., 1967, Kornblee Gallery, N.Y.C., 1969-72, U. Calif., Irvine, 1975, U. Calif. Santa Barbara, 1976, Stella Polaries Gallery, L.A., 1981-82, Kaufman Galleries, Houston, 1982, Modernism Gallery, San Francisco, 1983, Works Gallery, Long Beach, Costa Mesa, Calif., 1986-92, Malka Gallery, L.A., 1997; exhibited in group shows at Pasadena Art Mus., 1965, Carson Pirie Scott, Chgo., 1965, Calif. Palace of Legion of Honor, San Francisco, 1967, Esther Bear Gallery, Santa Barbara, 1967, 69, Lytton Ctr. of the Visual Arts, L.A., 1968, Salt Lake Art Inst., Salt Lake City, 1968, Mus. Contemporary Crafts, 1969, Second Flint (Mich.) Invitational, 1969, Milw. Art Ctr., 1969, U.S.I.S. Mus., N.Y.C., Mus. Contemporary Art, Chgo., 1970, Studio Merconi, Milan, 1970, Calif. Inst. Tech., Baxter Art Galley, 1971, 1980, Calif. Innovations, Palm Springs Dessert Mus., 1981, Calif. Internat. Arts Found. Mus. Modern Art, Paris, 1982, L.A. Artists in Seoul, Donsangbang Gallery, 1982, An Artistic Conversation, 1931-82, Poland, USA, Ulster Mus., Belfast, Ireland, 1983, Madison (Wis.) Art Ctr., 1994, Calif. State U., Fullerton, 1995, Oakland (Calif.) Mus., 1995, Molly Barnes Gallery, LA, Calif., 2000, Pasadena (Calif.) Mus. Calif. Art, 2002, Patricia Farm Gallery, L.A., 2006, Norton Simon Mus., Pasadena, Calif., 2006; represented in pub. collections at River Forest (Ill.) State Bank, Atlantic Richfield Co., Dallas, Frederic Weisman Collection, L.A., Security Pacific Bank, L.A., Singapore, Andrew Dickson White Mus. Art, Cornell U., Ithaca, N.Y., L.A. County Mus. Art, Santa Barbara Art Mus., Laguna Beach Mus. Art, Portland (Oreg.) Art Mus. Trustee, Pomona Coll, Claremont, Calif., 1987—; parade judge Tournament of Roses Centennial Parade, Pasadena, 1987; bd. dirs. LA Master Chorale, 1992—, Ojai Music Festival, 2004— NEA grantee, 1986. Home: 731 S Grand Ave Pasadena CA 91105-2424

PASIEKA, ANNE W., elementary school educator; b. Chgo., July 20, 1943; d. George Hales and Elizabeth Schultz Wilson; m. Ralph Snodgrass, Jan. 1965 (div. 1977); m. Mark Pasieka, Dec. 17, 1977; children: Helena, Brian, Jeff. BS in edn., Drake U., 1964; MS in adminstrn., Nat. Coll., 1976. Tchr. Quincy (Ill.) Pub. Schs., 1964-67, Univ. City (Mo.) Pub. Schs., 1967-68, Harford County (Md.) Pub. Schs., 1968-70, Comm. Consol. Sch. Dist. 59, Arlington Heights, 1970—. Instructional coun. mem. Byrd Sch., Elk Grove Village. Recipient Tchr. of the Year award Jaycees, Elk Grove Village, Ill., 1974. Mem. AAUW (pres. 1999-2000), NEA, Ill. Edn. Assn., ISTE, ICE, NICE, Delta Zeta, Phi Delta Kappa. Avocation: genealogy. Home: 414 W Hawthorne St Arlington Heights IL 60004-5427

PASINATO, YVONNE LOUISE, science educator; b. L.A. d. William Howard and Elvia Hernandez Catron; m. James Dean Pasinato, Apr. 30, 1983; children: Giovanni James, Ian Lucas. B in Child Devel., Calif. State U., L.A., 1984; M in Sci. Edn., Calif. State U., Fullerton, 1994. Elem. credential Calif., 1985. Elem. tchr. Montebello Unified Sch. Dist., Calif., 1985—89, tchr. sci., 1989—2006. Intervention specialist Montebello Unified Sch. Dist., Calif., 2003—04, staff developer k-12, 2004—. Recipient Hon. Svc. award, Cath. San Gabriel Valley. Office: Montebello Unified Sch Dist 123 S Montebello Blvd Montebello CA 90640

PASKAWICZ, JEANNE FRANCES, pain specialist; b. Phila., Mar. 3, 1954; d. Alex and Lillian (Pyluck) P. BSc, Phila. Coll. Pharmacy; MA, Villanova U., 1973; postgrad., St. Joseph U., 1979; PhD, Kensington U., 1984. Mem. anesthesiology staff Einstein Med. Ctr., Phila., 1990-94, Temple U. Hosp., 1994—; mem. detox./rehab. staff Presbyn. Med. Ctr., Phila., 1984—; house officer Tenet Hosps., Elkins Park, Pa., 1990—; mem. psychiatry staff Hahnemann U. Hosp., Phila., 1984-90; hostage negotiator Office of Mental Health, Phila., 1984-90; mem. surgery/anesthesiology staff Mt. Sinai Hosp., Phila., 1989-91. Bd. dirs. Phila. Coll. Pharmacy, St. Joseph U. Mem. NAFE, Am. Pain Soc., Lambda Kappa Sigma.

PASKMAN, ANDREA, dance specialist; d. Martin Paskman and Jane Sand; m. Anthony Cavoto, Oct. 13, 1973. BS, Temple U., Phila., 1972. Editl. rsch. asst. TV Guide mag., Radnor, Pa., 1972—79; copy editor Panoroma mag., Radnor, Pa., 1980—81; co. mgr. Ballet Klos, Phila., 1983—88; exec. dir. Danserye, King of Prussia, Pa., 1984—; assoc. editor Wyeth-Ayerst Labs., Radnor, Pa., 1993—96; quality liaison ptnr. Astra Pharms., Wayne, Pa., 1996—99; promotional regulatory affairs field assoc. dir. AstraZeneca, Wayne, Pa., 1999—2004, compliance and ethics leader, 2004—. (miniseries-broadcast on cbs) George Washington: The Founding of a Nation, (play) The Cherry Orchard, The Three Sisters, director (dance program) From Minuet to Cakewalk; author (presenter): (series of lectures) Hollywood and Historical Dance; (historical dance) guest choreographer for various organizations including Early Music Department of University of Pennsylvania, teacher (special workshops) for institutions including Swarthmore and Bryn Mawr Colleges, director (programs) covering various historical periods for museums, schs. Achievements include appearance on Jeopardy!; appearance on theme float of nationally broadcast We The People parade to celebrate Bicentennial of Constitution (1987). Business E-Mail: andreapaskman@astrazeneca.com.

PASONICK, KIMBERLY ROSE, elementary school educator; d. Andrew Peter (Francis) and Jeanne Marie Iorio; m. Michael III John Pasonick, Aug. 5, 1995. BS in elem. edn., Edinboro U., Pa., 1989; M in edn. and reading, King's Coll., Pa., 2001. Cert. reading specialist King's Coll., Pa., 2000, reading supr. Marywood U., Pa., 2006. Kindergarten tchr. Kinder-Care Inc., 1990—93, Define Elem., Nanticoke, Pa., 1993—95; pre-kindergarten tchr. Chesterbrooke Acad., Exton, Pa., 1995—96, John Heinz Rehab. Ctr., WIlkes-Barre, Pa., 1996—97; project m.o.m. program Luzerne Intermediate Unit, Kingston, Pa., 1997—2001, remedial math. and reading tchr., 2001—03, reading specialist, 2003—. Coord. family reads program Holy Spirit Acad., Hazelton, Pa., 2002; coord. read across Am. Daniel J. Flood Elem., Wilkes-Barre, Pa., 2005—. Mem. Accredidation for Growth, Wilkes-Barre, Pa., 2006; spkr. Make It Happen Conf., Keystone Reading Assn., Hershey, 2005. Mem.: Instrnl. Support Team, Lucerne County Hist. Soc., Assn. for Supr. and Curriculum Devel. (Exceptional Scholarly Achievement 1999), Internat. Reading Assn., Pa. State Edn. Assn., Alpha Epsilon Lambda. Democrat. Russian Orthodox. Avocations: reading, writing, gardening, travel. Office: Daniel J Flood Elem 565 N Washington St Wilkes Barre PA 18702 Personal E-mail: kpasonick@hotmail.com.

PASS, CHARLOTTE LOUISE, literature educator, consultant; b. Oneonta, Ala., Sept. 2, 1966; d. James Arnold and Betty Jo Pass. Cert. English Edn. Ala., 1998, ESL Ala., 2005. Acad. tutor, supr. U. Ala. Athletic Dept., Tuscaloosa, 1986—93; English/journalism tchr. Tuscaloosa Acad., 1989—91; grad. tchg. asst. U. Ala., Tuscaloosa, 1988—91, grad. instr., 2002—; English/music appreciation tchr. Hillcrest HS, Tuscaloosa, 1998—2001; home sch. tchr. Victory Christian Sch., Tuscaloosa, 2002—04. Literacy cons. Eastwood Mid. Sch., Ala., 2003—; presenter and cons. in field. Mem.: Am. Assn. Applied Linguistics (assoc.), Am. Ednl. Rsch. Assn. (assoc.), Mid-South Ednl. Ednl. Rsch. Assn. (assoc.), Tchrs. of English to Speakers of Other Languages (assoc.), Internat. Reading Assn. (assoc.), Nat. Reading Conf. (assoc.), Nat. Coun. Tchrs. of English (assoc.), Assn. Tchr. Educators (assoc.), ASCD (assoc.), Ala. Reading Assn. (assoc.), Ala. Coun. Tchrs. of English (assoc.), ASPCA, Amnesty Internat., Peta, Nat. Humane Soc., Phi Delta Kappa (assoc.), Phi Kappa Phi (life). Independent. Episcopal. Avocations: reading, piano, singing. Home: 1022 Fairfax Dr Tuscaloosa AL 35406 Office: Univ Ala PO Box 870232 204 Graves Hall Tuscaloosa AL 35487 Office Phone: 205-758-7567.

PASSANANTE, PATRICIA MARIE, middle school educator; b. Bklyn., Apr. 27, 1948; d. Charles and Auriela (Mauro) Casoria; m. Joseph John Passanante, Aug. 8, 1970; children: Laurie Adriana, Kristen Elizabeth. BA, CUNY, 1969; MA in Liberal Studies, SUNY, Stony Brook, 1989. Cert. tchr. Latin 7-12, math. 7-12, N.Y., sch. adminstr., supr. Latin/math. instr. 7-12 Franklin Sch., N.Y.C., 1969-72; Latin/math. instr. 6-8 Harbor Country Day Sch., St. James, N.Y., 1972-76; Latin instr. grades 9-12 Acad. St. Joseph's, Brentwood, N.Y., 1986-89; Latin instr. grades 7-8 Riverhead (N.Y.) Ctrl. Sch., 1989-94, instr. math. grade 8, 1994—, asst. chmn. math., 2003—. 8th grade advisor Riverhead Mid. Sch., 1994-2002, facilitator site-based mgmt. team, 1994-98, conflict mediator, 1993-96; mem. math. grant core team NSF, 2003—. Item writer Latin Proficiency Exam, 1990-95, Tests for Latin Conv., 1989-96. Catechist, Infant Jesus Parish, Port Jefferson, N.Y., 1982-93; jr. leader cons. Girl Scouts U.S., Coram, N.Y., 1983-86, leader, 1982-86. Named to Pres.'s Cir., Girl Scouts U.S., 1986, Tchr. of Yr., Riverhead Ctrl. Faculty Assn., 2000; recipient St. Pius X award Diocese of Rockville Ctr., 1992, Tchr. Yr., Riverhead Ctrl. Faculty Assn., 2000. Mem. Classical Assn. of Empire State (scholar award 1989), N.Y. State Classical League (Co-chair's award 1993), Am. Classical League, Nat. Coun. Math. Tchrs., Suffolk County Classical Soc., Suffolk County Math. Tchrs. Roman Catholic. Office: Riverhead Middle School 600 Harrison Ave Riverhead NY 11901-2786 Office Phone: 631-369-6774. Personal E-mail: mrspassmath@yahoo.com.

PASSLOF, PAT, artist, educator; b. Brunswick, Ga. m. Milton Resnick. Student Queen's Coll., 1946—48; student, Black Mountain Coll., 1948, Willem de Kooning, 1948—50; BFA, Cranbrook Coll., 1951. Prof. art Coll. of Staten Island, CUNY, 1972—. One woman shows at Elizabeth Harris Gallery, 1993, 96, 98, 2000, 02, 05. Fellow John Simon Guggenheim Meml. Found., 1999-2000; recipient award of Merit for painting, Am. Acad. of Arts and Letters, 2000, Purchase award Hassam, Speicher, Betts and Symons Fund of the Am. Acad., 2000, award for achievement in the arts Coun. on Arts and Humanities for S.I., 2001, Edwin P. Palmer award, Nat. Acad. at 181st Ann. Invitational Exhbn., 2006. Address: c/o Elizabeth Harris Gallery 529 W 20th St 6E New York NY 10011

PASSMORE, MARIAN, mathematics educator; d. Henry and Anne Griffin; m. Robert Torres, Aug. 12, 1990; children: Josh, Jessica Torres, Jared Torres. AS in Computer Programming, New Eng. Inst. Tech., Providence, 1984; BS in Computer Oriented Math., Southeastern Mass. U., Dartmouth, 1986; M in Math. Edn., U. Ctrl. Fla., Orlando, 1993. Cert. profl. tchr. Fla. Educator Phillips Coll., Melbourne, Fla., 1987—91, Rockledge (Fla.) HS, 1992—. Mentor FIRST Robotics Team 233, Rockledge, 1999—. Office: Rockledge HS 220 Raider Rd Rockledge FL 32955 Office Phone: 321-636-3711. Office Fax: 321-632-6064. E-mail: passmorem@brevard.k12.fl.us.

PASSUT, CHRISTINE DIANA, special education educator; b. Fairfax, Va., Dec. 9, 1974; d. Robert Charles and Barbara Ann Passut. BA in Psychology, Roanoke Coll., Salem, Va., 1997; M in Spl. Edn., Marymount U., Arlington, Va., 2002. Lic. tchr. learning disabled/emotionally disabled Va. Dept. Edn., 2002. Lead tchr. for four and five yr. olds Child Time Child Care Ctr., Fairfax, 1997—98; pub. health tng. asst. Fairfax County Pub. Schs. - Langley HS, McLean, Va., 1998—99, instrnl. asst. for students with autism, 1999—2000, tchr. for students with autism; tchr. for students with autism and mild mental retardation Fairfax County Pub. Schs. - Annandale HS, Va., 2003—. Support tchr. Tech. Outreach Program, Annandale H.S., 2004, co-sponsor buddies club, 2005—; co-sponsor interlinks club Langley H.S. Mem.: Sierra Club, World Wildlife Fedn., Fairfax Edn. Assn., Endometriosis Assn., Cooking Club Am. (life). Lutheran. Avocations: reading, gardening, cooking, playing with my dogs. Office: Annandale HS 4700 Medford Dr Annandale VA 22003 Office Phone: 703-642-4945. Business E-Mail: cpassut@fcps.edu.

PASSWATER, BARBARA GAYHART, real estate broker; b. Phila., July 10, 1945; d. Clarence Leonard and Margaret Jamison; m. Richard Albert Passwater, June 2, 1964; children: Richard Alan, Michael Eric. AA, Goldey-Beacom Coll., 1963; BA, Salisbury State U., 1981. Notary pub., Md. Sec. DuPont, Wilmington, Del., 1963-65, Nuclear-Chgo., Silver Spring, Md., 1965-67; office mgr. Montgomery County Sch. System, Wheaton, Md., 1977-79; adminstrv. asst. Solgar Nutritional Rsch. Ctr., Berlin, Md., 1979-94, asst. to v.p. R&D, 1995—2001; assoc. broker Prudential-Groff Realty, Berlin, Md., 1983-87, ReMax, Inc., Berlin, Md., 1987-88; broker, mgr,. developers rep. River Run Sales Ctr., Berlin, Md., 1988-96; broker Solgar Realty LLC, Berlin, Md., 1997—98, CAMBR Realty LLC, Berlin, 1998—. Treas. Ocean Pines (Md.) Vol. Fire Dept. Aux., 1981—84, emergency med. tech., 1983—95, life mem., 1996—; sec. Ocean Pines Fire Dept., 1990—95; mem. Citizens Rev. Bd., Snow Hill, Md., 1984—; state bd. del. Child Protection Sys.; bd. dirs. Worcester Gold, 2002—; mem. Worcester County Panel on Child Abuse and Neglect, 2002—; Worcester County organizer Rainbows, 2003—; mem. com. Worcester County YMCA, 2005; Sunday sch. tchr. Cmty. Ch. of Ocean Pines, 1999—2005, co-chair nuture and edn. com., 2001—05. Recipient Woman of the Yr., Worcester County Commn. for Women, 2006. Mem. Coastal Assn. of Realtors of Md., Inc., Worchester County Women's Commn. (Woman Yr., 2006), Beta Sigma Phi, Phi Kappa Phi. Avocations: photography, golf. Office: CAMBR Realty LLC 11017 Manklin Meadows Ln Berlin MD 21811-9340 Office Phone: 410-208-9006. Business E-Mail: cambr@dmv.com.

PASTAN, LINDA OLENIK, poet; b. NYC, May 27, 1932; d. Jacob L. and Bess (Schwartz) Olenik; m. Ira Pastan, 1953; children: Stephen, Peter, Rachel. BA, Radcliffe Coll., 1954; MLS, Simmons Coll., 1955; MA, Brandeis U., 1957. Author: (poetry) A Perfect Circle of Sun, 1971, On the Way to the Zoo, 1975, Aspects of Eve, 1975, The Five Stages of Grief, 1978 (Alice Fay di Castagnola award Poetry Soc. Am. 1978), Setting the Table, 1980, Waiting for My Life, 1981, PM/AM: New and Selected Poems, 1982 (Am. Book award nomination 1982), A Fraction of Darkness: Poems, 1985, The Imperfect Paradise, 1988, Heroes in Disguise, 1991, An Early Afterlife, 1995, Carnival Evening: New and Selected Poems, 1968-98 (nat. Book award nomination 1998), The Last Uncle, 2002, Queen of a Rainy Country, 2006. Recipient Dylan Thomas Poetry award Mademoiselle, 1958, Virginia Faulkner award Prarie Schooner, 1992, Charity Randall citation Internat. Poetry Forum, 1996, Ruth Lilly Poetry prize, 2003; NEA fellow; grantee Md. Arts Coun.; poet laureate of Md., 1991-95. Jewish. Office: 11710 Beall Mountain Rd Potomac MD 20854-1105 Personal E-mail: lpastan@att.net.

PASTEN, LAURA JEAN, veterinarian; b. Tacoma, May 25, 1952; d. Frank Larry and Jean Mary (Slavich) Brajkovich. BA in Physiology with distinction, Stanford U., Davis, 1970; BA in Physiology, U. Calif., Davis, 1970, DVM, 1974; postgrad., Cornell U., Ithaca, N.Y., 1975. Veterinarian Nevada County Vet. Hosp., Grass Valley, Calif., 1975-80; pvt. practice vet. medicine, owner Mother Lode Vet. Hosp., Grass Valley, 1980-96; vet. for Morris the 9-Lives cat (of TV comml. fame), 1985-94; consulting vet. Petlane, 2003—. Lectr. in field; spokesperson Nat. Cat Health Month; guest Today Show on wildlife, raising and tng. mini horses for guide horses for the blind. Author: Malignant, Tarantula Whisperer, Rocky Point Murders; contbg. author: Rocky Point Murders; pub. video How Smart is Your Puppy?, contbr. monthly newspaper column. Bd. dirs. Aguajito Property Owners Assn., Serrano Ranch Property Owners Assn., Sierra Svcs. for the Blind. Mem.: SRPDA (bd. mem.), AOPA, AVMA, ASPCA, Monterey County Vet. Med. Assn. (bd. mem.), Bay Area Vet. Assn. (bd. dirs., Calif. vet. bd. govs.), Monterey Bay Vet Assn. (Carmel wildlife ednl. com., vet. coord. Monterey County Animal Disasters), Carmel Wildlife Edn. Com., Citizens Against Raccoon Extermination, Monterey SPCA, Denver Area Med. Soc., Am. Animal Hosp. Assn. (Mother Lode Hosp. cited for excellence), Mother Lode Vet. Assn., Calif. Vet. Med. Assn. (bd. govs.), Fund Animals Defenders Wildlife, Def. Animals, Inst. Protection Animals, In Def. of Animals, Humane Soc. U.S., Nature Conservancy, Am. Intenrat. Fund Animal Welfare, Internat. Vet. Med. Assn., Sierra Club, Ninety-Nines Pilots Assn., Rep. Womens Found. (bd. dirs.), Nat. Assn. Underwater Instrs., Big Sur Land Trust, Mensa. Republican. Lutheran. Home and Office: 27479 Schulte Rd Carmel CA 93923-9477 Office Phone: 831-626-7227. Personal E-mail: lpasten@aol.com.

PASTERNACKI, LINDA LEA, critical care nurse; b. Green Bay, Wis., May 26, 1947; d. Paul John and Marion M. (Zagzebski) P.; (div.); children: Sam, Dan, Rachel Marie. Nursing diploma, St. Francis Sch. Nursing, Wichita, Kans., 1968; BS, Coll. St. Francis, Joliet, Ill., 1981, MS in Health Adminstrn., 1986. Cert. ACLS, PALS. Med.-surg. nurse geriatrics, psychiatry St. Francis Hosp., Wichita, 1968-70; nurse Critical Care Unit Sunrise Hosp., Las Vegas, Nev., 1970-72; nurse orthopedics Coronary Care Unit Presbyn. Hosp., Albuquerque, 1972-75, nurse cardiac and intensive care, 1986—94; nurse intensive care and coronary care VA Hosp., Albuquerque, 1976-81; nurse emergency rm. Univ. Heights Hosp., Albuquerque, 1981-82; nurse Critical Care Unit Lovelace Med. Ctr., Albuquerque, 1982-86, St. Joseph Med. Ctr., Albuquerque, 1990—94; nurse intensive care Transitional Hosp. Corp., Albuquerque, 1994-97, admissions coord., 1995; nurse HealthSouth, Albuquerque, 1997-98, Bernalillo County Juvenile Detention Ctr., 1997—99, Bernalillo County Detention Ctr., 1999—2000; nurse for Dr. R. Schwend, Chief of Pediatric Orthopedics Carrie Tingly Children's Hosp., U. N.Mex. Hosp., 2000—02; nurse Heart Hosp. of N.Mex., 2002—04; dialysis nurse Fresenius Med. Care, Albuquerque, 2004—05; nurse Maxim Healthcare, Albuquerque, 2005—; clin. nurse cons. LifeMasters Supported Self-Care, Inc., 2005—. Hyperbaric therapy instr. Presbyn. Hosp., Albuquerque, 1975; clin. instr. U. N.Mex. EMT Sch., Albuquerque, 1980. Camp nurse Easter Seals Camps in Calif. and Wash., 2005. Mem. AACN, N.Mex. Nurses Assn. Home: 10605 Central Park Dr NE Albuquerque NM 87123-4844

PASTERNAK, JILL MARGOT, radio producer, musician, educator; b. Newark, Mar. 9, 1934; d. Albert Aaron and Dorothy Vera Bengelsdorf; children from previous marriage: Amy Lydia Pasternak Hendry, William. BS in Harp, Juilliard Sch. Music, NYC, 1955; MA in Pub. Media, Montclair State U., NJ, 1981. Radio broadcasting lic. FCC. Freelance musician, prin. harp Little Orch. Soc. NY, NYC, 1954—56; prin. harp Radio City Music Hall, NYC, 1955—56, 1960—63, 1977—79; prin. harp, soloist Halifax Symphony Orch., NS, Canada, 1956—57, Orlando Symphony Orch., Fla., 1960—63; prin. harp Kenneth Symphony Orch., Kenner Square, Pa., 1991—2001; exec. prodr. WMHT-FM, Schenectady, NY, 1984—87, WFLN-FM, Phila., 1987—97, WRTI-FM, Phila., 1997—. Asst. to pres. Nonesuch Records, NYC, 1977—79; mgr. tng. & devel. Exxon, East Millstone, NJ, 1979—84; coord. MD/PhD program Thomas Jefferson U., Phila., 1987—96; lectr. Arcadia U., Phila., 2003—05, Jewish Cmty. Ctrs., Phila., 2003—; bd. dirs. Strings for Schs., Phila., 1999—2002. Freelance music, prin. harp: albums Broadway shows recs., editl. asst.: Hi-Fi/Stereo Rev. Mag., 1960—62, lit. editl. asst.: New World Records, 1975—77, prodr., host: Crossover, 1998—, Riccardo HWTI, 2005, Thomas Hampson American Songbook, 2006 (Excellence in Broadcasting, 2006). Mem. World Wildlife Fund, 2006, Physicians Ethical Medicine, 2006. Recipient Sarah award, Assn. Women in Comm., 1999, Svc. award, Darlington Arts Ctr., 2004; Fublright scholar, Ecole Normale de Musique, 1956—57. Mem.: Musicians Union, Mu Phi Epsilon. Democrat. Jewish. Avocations: travel, dance. Home: 200 Locust St Apt 18 G Philadelphia PA 19106 Office: WRTI FM Temple Pub Radio 1509 Cecil B Moore Ave Philadelphia PA 19121

PASTINE, MAUREEN DIANE, librarian; b. Hays, Kans., Nov. 21, 1944; d. Gerhard Walter and Ada marie (Hillman) Hillman; m. Jerry Joe Pastine, Feb. 5, 1966. AB in English, Ft. Hays State U., 1967; MLS, Emporia State U., 1970. Reference libr. U. Nebr., Omaha, 1971-77; undergrad. libr. U. Ill., Urbana, 1977-79; univ. libr. San Jose (Calif.) State U., 1980-85; ctrl. univ. libr. So. Meth. U., 1989—97, Temple U., 1997—. Mem. adv. bd. Foothill Coll. Libr., 1983-85; leader ednl. del.librs. to People's Rep. China, 1985, Australia/New Zealand, 1986, Soviet Union, 1988, East & West Germany, Czechoslovakia, Hungary, Austria, 1991, Brazil, 1993. Co-author: Library and Library Related Publicatiosn: A Directory of Publishing Opportunities, 1973; asst. compiler: Women's Work and Women's Stdies, 1973-74,75; compiler prcs. Teaching Bibliographic Science, 1981; editor: Integrating Library Use Skills into the General Education curriculum, 1989,k Collection Development: Present and future in Collection Management, Access to Western European Libraries and Literature, 1992; contbr. articles to profl. publs. Recipient Disting. Alumni Grad. award Emporia State U., 1986, Dudley Bibliog. Instruction Libr. of Yr. award, 1989. Mem. ALA (chmn. World Book-ALA Goal awards jury 1984-85), Assn. Coll. and Rsch. Librs. (editl. adv. bd. BIS Think Tank 1982-85, editl. bd. Choice 1983-85, chmn. Miriam Dudley Bibliographic Instrn. Libr. of Yr. award com. 1984-85, mem. task force on librs. as instrs. 1986-88, chair task force internat. rels. 1987-89, BIS Libr. of Yr. 1989, rep. to AAAS/CAIP 1989—, chair internat. rels. com. 1990-94, ALA pay equity com. 1994—, chmn. rsch. libr. of yr. awards com. 1995-96, acad. status com. 1996—), Libr. Adminstrn. and Mgmtm. Assn. (chmn. stats sect. com. on devel., orgn., planning and programming 1982-83, sec. stats. sect. exec. com. 1982-83, mem. at large 1986-88), ALA Libr. Instrn. round Table (long range planning com. 1986-94), ALA Libr. Rsch. Round

Table, Wash. Libr. Assn., Assn. Libr. Collections & Tech. Svcs. Divsn., Sr. Fellows Inst. (mem. info. resources com. in cause 1996—), Libr. and Info. Tech. Assn., Assn. Specialized and Coop. Libr. Agys. (chair multi-lincs internat. networking discussion group 1990-92), Libr. Rsch. Roundtable, Women's Studies Sect., Eng. and Am. Lit. Studies Discussion Group, Tex. Libr. Assn. (mentor Tall Texans Leadership Inst. 1995-96), Pacific N.W. Libr. Assn., Phi Kappa Phi, Beta Phi Mu. Home: PO Box 4251 Camp Verde AZ 86322-4251

PASTULA, LEAH LYNN, mental health services professional; d. Wendy Jo Haworth and Richard Joseph Pastula. BS, U. Tenn., 1994; MA, Mid. Tenn. State U., 1998; DD (hon.), Universal Life Ch., 1999. Psychol. intern Cmty. Devel. Svcs., Martin, 1994, Tenn. Prison Women, Nashville, 1996—97; crisis response specialist, triage supr., hosp. liaison Centerstone Cmty. Mental Health Centers, Inc., Nashville, 1999—2001; crisis response specialist Vol. Behavioral Health Care Sys., Murfreesboro, Tenn., 2002—. Recipient 1st Pl. 7th Ann. U.S. Open, Tae Kwon Do Championship, 1993, Gold and Silver medal, Tae Kwon Do Championship, U.S., 1994. Mem.: APA, So. Poverty Law Ctr., Psi Chi (sec. U. Tenn. Martin chpt. 1993—94), Phi Kappa Phi, Pinnacle (life). Achievements include research in determining decision making power and relationship satisfaction among heterosexual married, heterosexual cohabiting, and lesbian cohabiting couples. Avocations: guitar, sports, computers, video games.

PATANE, JOYCE A., secondary school educator; d. John and Mary Mayer; children: Lauren, Taylor. AA, Orange County C.C., Middletown, N.Y., 1990; BS, SUNY, Brockport, N.Y., 1995; MS, Nazareth Coll., Rochester, N.Y., 1998. Cert. tchr. gen. earth sci. N.Y., 1995, tchr. elem. edn. N.Y., 1995, spl. edn. educator N.Y., 1998. Tchr. sci. The Norman Howard Sch., Rochester, NY, 1996—, chmn. Dept. Sci., 2002—. Adv. yearbook The Norman Howard Sch., 1999—. Avocations: travel, volleyball, hiking. Office: The Norman Howard School 275 Pinnacle Rd Rochester NY 14623 Business E-Mail: jpatane@normanhoward.org.

PATCH, LISA E., health services director, nurse; b. Macomb, Ill., Jan. 19, 1967; d. Lyle Marlin Swearingen and Mildred Fern Swearingen-Engel; m. Allan Trent Patch, May 25, 1986; children: Breckon Nicole, Brighton Ellen, Brooklyn Leigh. AA in Nursing, N.Mex., 1997; BS, Western Ill. U., 1989. Intern Dona Ana Pub. Health, Las Cruces, N.Mex., 1990—91; pediatric registered nurse Mem. Med. Ctr., Las Cruces, 1997—2000; dir. health svcs. Alamogordo Pub. Schs., Alamogordo, N.Mex., 1999—; registered nurse Dr. Paul's Family Practice, 2000. Adv. bd. N.Mex. State U., Alamogordo, N.Mex., 2002—, preceptor, 2005. Mem. Otero Path, Alamogordo, N.Mex., 2000—03, Otero County Health Coalition, Alamogordo, 2000—, Leadership Alamogordo, 2004; youth leader Wesley United Meth. Ch., Alamogordo, 2004—. Mem.: N.Mex. Sch. Nurse Assn. (exec. bd. mem. 2000—), Am. Sch. Health Assn., Nat. Assn. Sch. Nursing, Sigma Theta Tau. Avocation: travel. Office: Alamogordo Pub Schs 1211 Hawaii Ave Alamogordo NM 88310

PATCHETT, ANN, writer; b. LA, 1963; BA, Sarah Lawrence College. Writer-in-residence Allegheny Coll., 1989—90; vis. asst. prof. Murray State U., 1992. Author: (novels) The Patron Saint of Liars, 1992 (James A. Michener/ Copernicus award for a book in progress, 1990, TV movie, 1997), Taft (also screenplay), 1994 (Janet Heidinger Kafka prize for the best work of fiction, 1994), The Magician's Assistant, 1997 (Nashville Banner Tennessee Writer of the Year Award), Bel Canto, 2001 (PEN/Faulkner prize, 2002), (non-fiction) Truth & Beauty, 2004 (Heartland Prize for Non-Fiction, Chgo. Tribune, Book Sense Honor Book for adult non-fiction, 2005); contbr. articles The New York Times Magazine, Chicago Tribune, Boston Globe, Vogue, GQ, Elle, Gourmet. Fellow Bunting Fellowship, Mary Ingrahm Bunting Institute at Radcliffe College, 1993, Guggenheim, 1994; grantee Residential fellowship, Fine Arts Work Ctr., Provincetown, Mass., 1990. Mailing: c/o HarperCollins Publishers 10 East 53rd Street New York NY 10022

PATCHIN, REBECCA J., anesthesiologist, educator, administrator; b. Detroit, Dec. 8, 1949; d. Robert Ira and Doris J. (Hubert) P.; m. Carl W. Anderson, 1988. ASN, Pacific Union Coll., 1969; BSN, Walla Walla Coll., 1971; MD, Loma Linda U., 1989. Diplomate in anesthesiology and pain mgmt. Am. Bd. Anesthesiology. Resident in internalmedicine Loma Linda U. Med. Ctr., Calif., 1989-90, resident in anesthesiology Calif., 1990-93, fellow in pain mgmt. dept. anesthesiology Calif., 1993-94, asst. prof. anesthesiology, 1994—; assoc. med. dir. Ctr. for Pain Mgmt., Loma Linda, 1995—. Presenter in field. Contbr. abstracts to profl. jours. Mem. AMA (mem. credentials com. 1986—, mem. awards com. bd. trustees 1988-89, del. ho. of dels. 1990—, mem. reference com. 1994—, chair coun. on med. edn. 2002-03, trustee 2003-, Internat. Anesthesiology Rsch. Soc., Internat. Assn. for Study of Pain, Am. Soc. Anesthesiology, Am. Pain Soc., Am. Soc. Regional Anesthesia, Am. Acad. Pain Medicine, Calif. Soc. Anesthesiology (del. resident component 1991-93, mem. com. on young physicians 1994—96, chair com. on young physicians 1996—), Calif. Med. Assn. (mem. reference com. 1988, trustee 1991-93, mem. com. on health professions and licensure 1992—, chair com. on health professions and licensure 1993-96, mem. coun. on legislation 1995-96, chair coun. on legislation 2000—), So. Calif. Cancer Pain Initiative, Riverside County Med. Assn. (sec.-treas 2002, pres. 2004), San Bernardino County Med. Soc. Office Phone: 951-413-0200.*

PATE, JACQUELINE HAIL, retired data processing company executive; b. Amarillo, Tex., Apr. 7, 1930; d. Ewen and Virginia Smith (Crosland) Hail; children: Charles (dec.), John Durst, Virginia Pate Edgecomb, Christopher. Student, Southwestern U., 1947—48; grad., Real Estate Inst., 1998. Exec. sec. We. Gear Corp., Houston, 1974—76; adminstr., treas., dir. Aberrant Behavior Ctr., Personality Profiles, Inc., Corp. Procedures, Inc., Dallas, 1976—79; mgr. regional site svcs. programs Digital Equipment Corp., Dallas, 1979—92; ret., 1992. Realtor Keller Williams Realty, Austin, Tex., 1996—. Active Austin Bd. Realtors, PTA, Dallas, 1958-73. Mem. Daus. Republic Tex. (treas. French Legation state com. 1996). Methodist.

PATE, LISA M., transportation services executive, lawyer; b. 1969; m. Hank Pate; children: Riley, Bealie, Casey. BS, Northwestern U.; JD, Cornell U. Bar: Tenn. 1996. Assoc. Witt, Gaither & Whitaker, PC, Chattanooga, 1996—2002, named shareholder, 2002; now gen. counsel US Xpress Enterprises, Inc., Chattanooga. Office: US Xpress Enterprises Inc 4080 Jenkins Rd Chattanooga TN 37421 Office Phone: 423-510-3000. Office Fax: 423-510-3318.

PATÉ-CORNELL, MARIE-ELISABETH LUCIENNE, finance educator, engineering educator; b. Dakar, Senegal, Aug. 17, 1948; arrived in U.S., 1971; d. Edouard Pierre Lucien and Madeleine (Tournissa) Paté; m. C. Allin Cornell, Jan. 3, 1981; children: Phillip Cornell, Ariane Cornell. Eng. Degree, Inst. Polytechnique de Grenoble, France, 1971; MS in Ops. Rsch., Stanford U., 1972, PhD in Engring.-Econ. Systems, 1978. Asst. prof. in civil engring. MIT, 1978-81; asst. prof. indsl. engring. Stanford (Calif.) U., 1981-84, assoc. prof. indsl. engring., 1984-91, prof. indsl. engring., 1991—, chmn. dept. indsl. engring., 1997-99, chmn. dept. mgmt. sci. and engring., 2000—. Cons. SRI Internat., 1993, Electric Power Rsch. Inst., 1995, Atty. Gen. of N.Mex., 1995, Swiss Re, 2002, Boeing, 2003—; mem. adv. coun. NASA, 1995—98; mem. Marine Bd. NRC, 1995—97; mem. Army Sci. Bd., 1995—97, Air Force Sci. Bd., 1998—2002, Calif. Coun. on Sci. and Tech., 2000—, Pres.'s Adv. Bd. on Fgn. Intelligence, 2001—04; chmn. bd. advisors Naval-Postgrad. Sch., 2004—. Contbr. numerous articles to profl. jours. Numerous rsch. grants. Mem.: Nat. Acad. Engring. (councilor 2001—), Inst. for Mgmt. Scis., Ops. Rsch. Soc. Am., Soc. for Risk Analysis (councilor 1985—86, pres. 1995). Avocations: tennis, swimming, chess, music. Home: 110 Coquito Way Menlo Park CA 94028-7404 Office: Stanford U Dept Mgmt Sci and Engring Stanford CA 94305 E-mail: mep@leland.stanford.edu.

PATENAUDE, PAMELA HUGHES, federal agency administrator; BA, St. Anselm Coll., 1983; MA, So. NH U. Liaison, spl. asst. to dep. asst. sec. for multifamily housing The White House, Washington, exec. asst. to dep. undersec. field coord.; v.p. Manor Homes Builders, Inc., Bedford, NH, 1988—96; mktg. and training dir. NH Small Bus. Ctr.; state dir. and dep. chief of staff Office of U.S. Senator Bob Smith; asst. dep. sec. field policy & mgmt. US Dept. Housing & Urban Devel., Washington, asst. sec. for community planning & devel., 2005—. Former chmn. Bedford Housing Adv. Com.; held leadership positions in various profl. and civic organizations. Office: 451 Seventh St SW Rm 7100 Mall Code D Washington DC 20410 Office Phone: 202-708-2690. Office Fax: 202-708-3336.

PATERAKIS, ANGELA GREGORY, art educator, consultant, writer; b. Oak Park, Ill., June 1, 1932; d. Kostas and Sophia (Spiliotou) Gregory; m. George A. Paterakis, July 31, 1958. B.A.E., Sch. of Art Inst. Chgo., 1954; M.A., U. Ill., 1955; art therapy cert., 1985. Tchr. jr. high sch., Oak Park, Ill., 1955-60; prof. emerita art edn. and art therapy Sch. of Art Inst. Chgo., 1961—; mem. arts advocacy groups, Ill. Author numerous articles, pamphlets on art edn.; pres. Ill. Alliance for Arts Edn.; bd. dirs. Hellenic Mus. and Cultrual Ctr., Chgo., 1990—. mem. Ill. Arts Adv. Com., 1989-91. Recipient Svc. Recognition award Ill. Alliance for Arts Edn., 1985; U. Ill. fellow, 1954-55. Mem. NEA (life), Nat. Art Edn. Assn., Ill. Art Edn. Assn. (named Outstanding Art Educator 1981, Disting. mem., 2000). Office: Sch of the Art Inst Chgo 37 South Wabash Ave Chicago IL 60603-3103

PATERIK, FRANCES SUE, secondary school educator, actress; b. Bloomington, Ill., Feb. 10, 1953; d. Francis LaVerne and Magaline Wilken. Student, Am. Cons. Music, Chgo., 1976—78, N.W. Ind. Opera Co., 1980, Hinsdale Opera Co., Ill., 1981; BA, MA, Western Ill. U., 1984. Tchg. asst. Western Ill. U., Macomb, 1982—84; music tchr. Cardinal Cmty. Schs., Eldon, Iowa, 1985—89, Johnston (Iowa) Cmty. Schs., 1990—94; music/performing arts tchr. Colfax (Iowa)-Mingo Cmty. Sch., 1995—2002, Merrill Middle Sch., Des Moines, 2002—. Dir. handbell choir 1st Christian Ch., Des Moines, 1996—2000; soprano soloist Des Moines Concert Singers, 1989—, Des Moines Choral Soc., 2002—; alto sect. leader St. John's Luth. Ch., 2004—. Actress: (various comedic roles) Ingersoll Dinner Theatre; Playhouse; Drama Workshop; Stage West; actress (various comedic roles) Ankeny Cmty. Theatre, St. John's Luth. Ch. Mem.: Des Moines Choral Soc., Iowa Choral Dirs. Assn., Am. Choral Dirs. Assn., Music Educators Nat. Conf., Nat. Wildlife Fedn., Sierra Club. Democrat. Avocations: gardening, dance. Office: Des Moines Pub Schs Des Moines IA 50312 Business E-Mail: f.paterik@mchsi.com.

PATERNOSTER, KATHLEEN A., secondary school educator; d. John D. Rourke and Anne Heubner; m. Joseph F. Paternoster, Aug. 28, 1983; children: Matthew F., Teresa L. MS in Edn., SUNY, New Paltz, 1993. Cert. biology, chemistry, 7-12 gen. sci., bus., elem. tchr. N.Y., 1993. Tchr. sci. Irvington H.S., NY, 1992—93, Goshen H.S., NY, 1992—93, Hendrick Hudson H.S., Montrose, NY, 1993—. Office: Hendrick Hudson HS 2 Albany Post Rd Montrose NY 10548 Office Phone: 914-737-7500.

PATERSON, EVA, legal association director, educator; b. 1949; BA, Northwestern U.; JD, Boalt Hall Sch. Law, U. Calif., Berkeley. Bar: 1975. Assoc. Legal Aid Soc. Alameda County; staff mem. Lawyers' Com. Civil Rights, 1977—90, exec. dir., 1990—2003; exec. dir., founder Equal Justice Soc., 2003—. Adj. prof. U. San Francisco Sch. Law, Hastings Sch. Law. Co-founder A Safe Place, Oakland, Calif., Calif. Coalition Civil Rights, chair; v.p. ACLU Nat. Bd.; chair Equal Rights Advocates. Named one of Top 25 Lawyers, San Francisco Chronicle, 2002; recipient Fay Stender award, Calif. Women Lawyers, Woman Yr. award, Black Leadership Forum, Earl Warren Civil Liberties award, ACLU No. Calif., Alumni award Merit, Northwestern U. Mem.: San Francisco Bar Assn. (chair). Achievements include first African Am. pres. student govt. at Northwestern U. Office: Equal Justice Soc 220 Sansome St 14th Fl San Francisco CA 94104 Office Phone: 415-288-8700.

PATERSON, HATTIE P., philanthropist; b. Grand Rapids, Mich., Sept. 14, 1944; d. Arthur L. Tyler and Lura B. Henson. BSc, Davenport U. Realtor, 1984; founder, marketer Mich. Utility and Co. Payment Sys., LLC, 1999, Founder Crime, Inc., 1971—. Home: PO Box 1654 Grand Rapids MI 49501

PATERSON, KATHERINE WOMELDORF, writer; b. Huaiyin, China, Oct. 31, 1932; came to U.S., 1940; d. George Raymond and Mary Elizabeth (Goetchius) Womeldorf; m. John Barstow Paterson, July 14, 1962; children: Elizabeth Polin, John Barstow, David Lord, Mary Katherine Nah-he-sah-pe-che-a. AB, King Coll., Bristol, Tenn., 1954; post grad., Kobe Sch. Japanese Lang., 1957-60; MA, Presbyn. Sch. Christian Edn., 1957; MRE, Union Theol. Sem., 1962; LittD. (hon.), King Coll., Bristol, Tenn., 1978; LHD (hon.), Otterbein Coll., 1979; LittD (hon.), St. Mary's of the Woods, 1981; LittD, Washington and Lee U., 1982; LittD (hon.), U. Md., 1982, Shenandoah Coll., 1982; LHD, Washington and Lee U, 1982; LHD (hon.), Norwich U., 1990, Mount St. Vincent U., Halifax, N.S., Can., 1994; LittD, Hope Coll., 1997; DLitt (hon.), Prebyn. Coll., 2002. Tchr. Lovettsville Elem. Sch., Va., 1954-55; missionary Presbyn. Ch., Japan, 1957-61; master sacred studies and English Pennington Sch. for Boys, NJ, 1963-65. Author: The Sign of the Chrysanthemum, 1973, Of Nightingales That Weep, 1974, The Master Puppeteer, 1976, Bridge to Terabithia, 1977, The Great Gilly Hopkins, 1978, Angels and Other Strangers, 1979, Jacob Have I Loved, 1980, Rebels of the Heavenly Kingdom, 1983, Come Sing, Jimmy Jo, 1985, (with John Paterson) Consider the Lilies, 1986, Park's Quest, 1988, The Tale of the Mandarin Ducks, 1990, The Smallest Cow in the World, 1991, Lyddie, 1991, The King's Equal, 1992, Who Am I?, 1992, Flip-Flop Girl, 1994, A Midnight Clear: Stories for the Christmas Season, 1995, A Sense of Wonder, 1995, The Angel and the Donkey, 1996, Jip: His Story, 1996, Marvin's Best Christmas Present Ever, 1997, (with John Paterson) Images of God, 1998, Parzival, 1998, Celia and the Sweet, Sweet Water, 1998, Preacher's Boy, 1999, The Wide-Awake Princess, 2000, The Field of the Dogs, 2001, Marvin One Too Many, 2001, The Invisible Child, 2002, The Same Stuff as Stars, 2002, (with John Paterson) Blueberries for the Queen, 2004, Bread & Roses, Too, 2006; translator: The Crane Wife, 1981, The Tongue-Cut Sparrow, 1987. US nominee for Hans Christian Andersen award, 1979, 89, 97, 98; recipient Nat. Book award, 1977, 79, Newbery medal, 1978, 91, Newbery honor, 1979, New Eng. Book award New Eng. Booksellers Assn., 1982, Union medal Union Theol. Sem., 1992, Scott O'Dell award for hist. fiction, 1997, May Hill Arbuthnot lectr. award, 1997, Lion award NY Pub. Libr., 1998, Literary Light award Boston Pub. Libr., 2000, Living Legend award Libr. of Congress, 2000, Jefferson cup Va. Libr. Assn., 2000, Vt. Gov.'s award for excellence in arts, 2001, Astrid Lindgren Meml. award Swedish Govt., 2006. Mem. Authors Guild, Children's Book Guild Washington. Democrat. Office: Clarion Books 215 Park Ave S New York NY 10003-1603

PATINO-BRANDFON, SYLVIA, retired psychologist; d. Alfonso and Zenobia Moeller Patino; children: Andrea, Thea. AB in English, U. N.Mex., 1956; MS in English, Wis. U., 1958; student, Tavistock Inst., London, 1970—71; MA in Child Study, Tufts U., 1975; PhD in Psychology, Boston Coll., 1980; student in Psychopharmacology, Internat. Coll. Prescribing Psychologist, 1995—97. Lic. psychologist Mass., 1981. Intern psychotherapy Judge Baker Guidance Ctr., Boston, 1972—74; intern McLean Hosp., Belmont, Mass., 1979—80, post doctoral fellow, 1980—81; pvt. practice Quincy and Taunton, Mass., 1982—99; ret., 1999. Spkr. in field. Author: (newsletter) ADHD and Other Behavior Problems, 1994—98. Mem. com. superior cts. Ariz. Supreme Ct., 2004—, mem. jud. performance rev. commn., 2004—, bd. overseeing reporters, 2004. Fellow: APA (life).

PATON, LISA DUPREE, elementary school educator; b. Kingsville, Tex., Dec. 21, 1960; d. Cleve Dupree and Geraldine (Teague) Hawkins; m. Kurt Anthony Paton, Sept. 26, 1987; children: Sarita, Selina. BS in Geology, U. Tex., 1985; alternative cert., Laredo (Tex.) State U., 1989; B in Libr. Sci., Sam Houston State U. Cert. tchr., Tex.; cert ESL and learning resources. Tchr. United Ind Sch. Dist., Laredo, 1989—. Mem. Tex. Libr. Assn. Avocations: scuba, skiing, water-skiing. Office: Finley Elem 2001 Lowry Rd Laredo TX 78045-8552

PATON WALSH, JILL, writer; b. London, Apr. 29, 1937; d. John Llewelyn and Patricia (Dubern) Buss; m. Antony Edmund Paton Walsh, Aug. 5, 1961; Children: Edmund, Margaret, Clare. Author: Hengest's Tale, 1966, The Dolphin Crossing, 1967, Fireweed, 1969, (World Book Festival award 1970), Wordhoard, 1969, Goldengrove 1972, Farewell Great King, 1972, Toolmaker, 1973, The Dawnstone, 1973, The Emporer's Winding Sheet, 1974 (Whitbread prize 1974), The Huffler, 1975, The Island Sunrise: Preshistoric Culture in the British Isles, 1975, Unleaving, 1976 (Boston Globe, Horn Book award 1976), Children of the Fox: Crossing to Salamis, 1977, The Walls of Athens, 1978, Persian Gold, 1978, A Chance Child, 1978, The Green Book, 1981, Babylon, 1982, Parcell of Patterns, 1983 (Universe prize 1984), Lost and Found, 1984, Gaffer Samson's Luck, 1984 (Smarties Grand prix 1984), Lapsing, 1985, A School for Lovers, 1989, Birdy and the Ghosties, 1990, "Grace", 1991, Matthew and the Sea Singers, 1992, When Grandma Came, 1992, The Wydham Case, 1993, Knowledge of Angels, 1994, A Piece of Justice, 1995, Connie Came to Play, 1995, Thomas and the Tinners, 1995, The Serpentine Cave, 1997, When I Was Little Like You, 1997, (with Dorothy L. Sayers) Thrones, Dominations, 1998, A Desert in Bohemia, 2000, (with Dorothy L. Sayers) A Presumption of Death, 2002, Debts of Dinosaur, 2006. Fellow Royal Soc. of Lit. (CBE award 1996). Address: care David Higham Assocs 5-8 Lower John St Golden Sq London W1R 3PE England

PATRICK, CATHY, music educator, administrative assistant; b. Grovehill, Ala., July 7, 1952; d. Charles Edward and Adalena Margarite Patrick. BSc in Music Edn., Auburn U., 1973, MSc in Music Edn., 1975. Band, choral dir. Auburn City Schs., Ala., 1973—78; band dir. Notasulga HS, Ala., 1978—82, Rothschild Mid. Sch., Columbus, Ga., 1982—95, Blackmon Rd. Mid. Sch., Columbus, 1995—2003; adminstrv. asst. to pres. Beacon U., Columbus, 2003—. Assembly Of God. Home: 3624 Sutton Dr Columbus GA 31909 Office: Beacon Univ 6003 Veterans Pky Columbus GA 31909

PATRICK, CONNIE L., federal official; m. John Patrick; 4 children. BA in Criminal Justice, U. Ctrl. Fla.; Grad., FBI Nat. Acad., Fla. Criminal Justice Exec. Inst., Fed. Exec. Inst. Dep. Sheriff's Office Brevard County, 1976—81; various positions including spl. agent, spl. agent supr., asst. spl. agent in charge of Tampa reg. ops. bur., dir. Fla. Criminal Justice Inst. Fla. Dept. Law Enforcement, 1981—95, dir. divsn. human resources & training, 1995—96; dir. gen. training Fed. Law Enforcement Training Ctr., 1996—98, assoc. dir. planning & resources, 1998—2001, assoc. dir. planning & workforce devel., 2001—02, dir., 2002—. Recipient Presdl. Meritorious Rank award, 2001. Office: Fed Law Enforcement Training Ctr 1131 Chapel Crossing Rd Brunswick GA 31524

PATRICK, DANICA SUE, race car driver; b. Beloit, Wis., Mar. 25, 1982; d. T.J. and Bev Patrick; m. Paul Hospenthal, Nov. 19, 2005. With Team Rahal Letterman, 2002—; debut Formula Vauxhall Winter Series, England, 1998, Toronto, Canada, 2002; made her IndyCar Series debut Toyota Indy 300, 2005; signed with Andretti Green Racing, 2006. Co-author (with Laura Morton): Danica: Crossing the Line, 2006. Recipient numerous World Karting Assn. titles including National Points titles in WKA Manufacturs Cup, 1994, 96, five Great Lakes Sprint Series titles and Midwest Spring Series titles, 1996, Grand National championship and Summer National Championship, 1997; Gorsline Scholarship award, 2001 Won 39 of 49 feature karting races, 1996; finished 9th in Formula Vauxhall Championship, Eng., 1991, 2d in Formula Ford Festival (highest finish for an American), 2000, 4th in first appearance in the Indianapolis 500, 2005; became the first female to post a top three result in Atlantic Series, Monterrey, Mex., 2003; first female driver to win pole position in Toyota Atlantic, Portland, 2004.

PATRICK, LAURA DAPHENE LAYMAN, retired physicist; b. Pensacola, Fla., Mar. 29, 1968; d. Richard and Faye Layman; m. Brian C. Patrick, Apr. 3, 1993. BS in Physics, U. Ala., Huntsville, 1993. Analyst Delta Rsch., Inc, Huntsville, Ala., 1993—2001; ret. Home: 112 Blackberry Lane Gurley AL 35748

PATRICK, PAULINE MARGARET, secondary school educator; b. Mpls., Oct. 18, 1949; d. Melvin H. and Margaret P. (Calvelage) Boone; m. Mark H. Patrick, Dec. 18, 1971; children: Lance, Megan. BS, U. Mankato, 1971; MEd, St. Mary's Coll., Winona, Minn., 1993; MA (hon.), Minnetonka U., 1990. Cert. tchr., Minn. Tchr. Edina (Minn.) Sch., 1972-79, Minnetonka (Minn.) Schs., 1986—. Adj. prof. U. St. Thomas, St. Paul, 1989—, mem. T.E.A.C.H., 1991—. Recipient Apple award Ashland Oil Co., 1989. Mem. ASCd, Nat. Coun. Tchrs. English, Nat. Coun. Tchrs. Social Studies. Office Phone: 952-401-5000. E-mail: pelly.patrick@minnetonka.k12.mn.us.

PATRICK, RUTH (MRS. RUTH HODGE VAN DUSEN), botany educator, curator; b. Topeka; d. Frank and Myrtle (Jetmore) Patrick; m. Charles (IV) Hodge, July 10, 1931; 1 child, Charles (V). BS, Coker Coll., 1929; MS, U. Va., 1931, PhD, 1934; LLD (hon.), Coker Coll., 1971; LHD (hon.), Chestnut Hill Coll, 1974; DSc (hon.), Beaver Coll., 1970, PMC Colls., 1971, Phila. Coll. Pharmacy and Sci., 1973, Wilkes Coll., 1974, Cedar Crest Coll., 1974, U. New Haven, 1975, Hood Coll., 1975, Med. Coll. Pa., 1975, Drexel U., 1975, Swarthmore Coll., 1975, Bucknell U., 1976, Rensselaer Poly. Inst., 1976, St. Lawrence U., 1978, U. Mass., 1980, Princeton U., 1980, Lehigh U., 1983, U. Pa., 1984, Temple U., 1985, Emory U., 1986, Wake Forest U., 1986, U. S.C., 1989, Clemson, 1989, Glassboro State Coll., 1992. Assoc. curator microscopy dept. Acad. Natural Scis., Phila., 1939-47; curator Leidy Micros. Soc., 1937-47, curator limnology dept., 1947—, chmn. limnology dept., 1947-73; occupant Francis Boyer Research Chair Acad. Natural Scis., Phila., 1973—, chmn. bd. trustees, 1973-76, hon. chmn. bd. trustees, 1976—; lectr. U. Pa., 1950-70, adj. prof., 1970—; guest Fellow of Saybrook Yale, 1975. Participant Am. Philos Soc. limnology expdn. to Mexico, 1947; leader Catherwood Found. expdn. to Peru and Brazil, 1955; del. gen. assembly Internat. Union Biol. Scis., Bergen, Norway, 1947; bd. dirs. E.I. Du Pont, Pa. Power and Light Co.; chmn. algae com. Smithsonian Oceanographic Sorting Ctr., 1963—68; mem. panel on water bloom Pres. Sci. Adv. Com., 1966; mem. panel on water resources and water pollution Gov.'s Sci. Adv. Com., 1966; mem. nat. tech. adv. com. on water quality requirements for fish and other aquatic life and wildlife Dept. Interior, 1967—68; mem. citizen's adv. coun. Pa. Dept. Environ. Resources, 1971—73; mem. hazardous materials adv. com. EPA, 1971—74, exec. adv. com., 1974—79; chmn. com.'s panel on ecology, 1974—76; mem. Pa. Gov.'s Sci. Adv. Coun., 1972; mem. exec. adv. com. nat. power survey FPC, 1972—75; mem. coun. Smithsonian Instn., 1973—; mem. Phila. Adv. Coun., 1973—76; mem. energy R&D adv. coun. Pres.s Emergy Policy Office, 1973—74; mem. adv. coun. Renewable Nat. Resources Found., 1973—76, Elecric Power Rsch. Found., 1973—77; mem. adv. com. for rsch. NSF, 1973—74; mem. gen. adv. com. ERDA, 1975—77; mem. adv. bd. Sec. Energy, 1975—89; mem. com. on human resources NRC, 1975—76; trustee Biological Abstracts, 1974—76; mem. adv. coun. dept. biology Princeton U., 1975—80; mem. com. on sci. and arts Franklin Inst., 1978—; mem. univ. coun. com. Yale Sch. Forestry and Environ. Studies, 1978—80; mem. sci. adv. coun. World Wildlife Fund-US, 1978—80; trustee Aquarium Soc., Phila., 1951—58, Henry Found.; bd. dirs. Wissahickon Valley Watershed Assn.; bd. govs. Nature Conservancy; bd. mgrs. Wistar Inst. Anatomy and Biology. Author: (series of volumes) Rivers of the United States Vol. 1, 1994, Rivers of the United States Vol. 2, 1997, Chemical and Physical Characteristics Vol. 3, 1995, Rivers of Atlantic and Eastern Gulf Drainage Vol. 4, The Mississipi River and Major Tributaries; co-author (with C.W. Reimer): Diatoms of the United States Vol. 1, 1966, Vol. II, Part 1, 1975; co-author: (with others) (books) Ground Water Contamination in the United States, 1983, 2nd edit.; co-author: (with others) (book) Surface Water Quality: Have the Laws Been Successful?, 1992; mem. editorial bd.with C. W. Reimer: sci. jours. Science, 1974—76, mem. editorial bd.: sci. jours. American Naturalist; contbr. articles over 150 to profl. jours. Recipient Disting. Dau. of Pa. award, 1952, Richard Hopper Day Meml. medal, Acad. Nat. Scis., 1969, Gimbel Phila. award, 1969, Gold medal, YWCA, 1970, Lewis L. Dollinger Pure Environment award, Franklin inst., 1970, Pa. award for excellence in sci. and tech., 1970, Eminent Ecologist award, Ecol Soc. Am., 1972, Phila. award, 1973, Gold medal, Pa. State Fish and Game Protective Assn., 1974, Internat. John and Alice Tyler Ecology award, 1975,

Gold meda;, Phila. Soc. for Promoting Agr., 1975, Pub. Svc. award, U.S. Dept. Interior, 1975, Iben award, Am. Water Resources Assn., 1976, Outstanding Alumna award, Coker Coll., 1977, Francis K. Hutchinson medal, Garden Club of Am., 1977, Golden medal, Royal Zool. Soc., Antwerp, 1978, Green World award, N.Y. Bot. Garden, 1979, Hugo Black award, U. Ala., 1979, Sci award, Gov. Pa., 1988, Founders award, Soc. Environ. Toxicology and Chemistry, 1982, Environ. Regeneration award, Rene DuBois Ctr., 1985, Disting. Citizen award, Pa., 1989, Excellence award, N. Am. Benthological Soc., 1993, Benjamin Franklin medal, Am. Philosophical Soc., 1993, U.S. medal of svc., Pres. Bill Clinton, 1996, Nat. medal for sci., 1997, Nat. Wetlands award, 2000, Sci. Edn. Ctr. named in her honor, U. S.C., 1989. Fellow: AAAS (com. environ. alternatives 1973—74); mem.: Internat. Phycol. Soc., Am. Inst. Biol. Scis., Ecol. Soc. Am., Am. Soc. Naturalists (pres. 1975—76), Am. Soc. Limnology and Oceanography (Lifetime Achievement award 1996), Am. Soc. Plant Taxonomy, Internat. Soc. Plant Taxonomists, Internat. Limnological Soc., Phycol Soc. Am. (pres. 1954), Bot. Soc. Am. (mem. Darbarker prize com. 1956, Merit award 1971), Am. Acad. Arts and Scis., Assn. Metro. Sewage Agys. (Environ. award 1995), Am. Philos. Soc. (Benjamin Franklin Outstanding Sci. Achievement award 1993), Nat. Acad. Engring. (com.environ. engr. study explicit criteria for power plant siting 1973), Nat. Acad. Scis. (chmn. panel com. on pollution 1966, mem.environ. measures panel com. remote sensing earth resources survey 1973—74, mem. nominating com. 1973—75, mem. com. sci. and public policy 1973—77), Water Pollution Control Fedn. (hon.), Soc. Study Evolution, Sigma Xi. Presbyterian. Office: Acad Natural Scis 19th at Benjamin Franklin Pkwy Philadelphia PA 19103 Office Phone: 215-299-1098. Business E-Mail: Patrick@acnatsci.org.

PATRICK, SUSAN D., federal agency administrator; B in English, Colo. Coll.; M in Comm. Mgmt., U. So. Calif. Dir. distance learning campus Old Dominion U.; coord. Digital State Survey 2002 State of Ariz.; dep. dir. Office Edn. Tech. US Dept. Edn., Washington, dir. Office Edn. Tech., 2004—. Office: US Dept Edn Rm FB6-7E208 400 Maryland Ave SW Washington DC 20202 Office Phone: 202-205-4274. E-mail: susan.patrick@ed.gov.

PATRICK, SUSANNE, secondary school educator; d. Marcel and Evelyn De Jonckheere; m. Roy Mark Patrick; 1 child, Colleen Glombowski. MS, Saginaw Valley State U., Mich., 2002. Cert. secondary tchr. Mich. HS math. tchr. East Detroit Pub. Schs., Eastpointe, Mich., 1994—, dept. leader, 2002—. Mem.: Nat. Coun. Tchrs. Math. Avocations: gardening, travel. Office: East Detroit HS 15501 Couzens Eastpointe MI 48044 Office Phone: 586-445-4455.

PATRIE, CHERYL CHRISTINE, elementary school educator; b. Dobbs Ferry, N.Y., June 8, 1947; d. Edward F. and Antoinette C. (Patrie) P. BA in Edn., U. Fla., 1969; MS in Edn., U. Miami, 1979. Cert. assoc. master tchr., Fla. Tchr. Marion County Sch. Bd., Ocala, Fla., 1970, Dade County Sch. Bd., Miami, 1973—. Mem. faculty coun. Lorah Park lem. Sch., Miami, 1979-89, 1991—, career lab. cons., 1983-85, human growth and devel. cons., 1983—, phys. fitness co-chmn., 1984-90, chair dept., 1993—; coord. quality instrn. incentives program, 1984-89; mem. Dade County Elem. Sch. Day Task Force, 1987-88. Mem. United Tchrs. Dade (bldg. union steward 1979-89, mem. crisis in inner city task force 1984-85, mem. sch. adv. com., 1987—, Disting. Svc. award 1984). Office: Lorah Park Elem 5160 NW 31st Ave Miami FL 33142-3439 Home: 555 NE 15th St #28-I Miami FL 33132

PATRON, JUNE EILEEN, former government official; b. N.Y.C., May 15; d. Irving B. and Mollie Patron. BA in Govt. with honors, Clark U., Worcester, Mass., 1965; MA, Am. U., 1967. With U.S. Dept. Labor, 1966-95, dir. Black Lung benefits program, 1976-79, asst. adminstr. pension and welfare benefit programs, 1979-84, assoc. dir. pension and welfare benefit programs, 1984-88, dir. program svcs., 1988-95; ret., 1995. Mem. Sr. Exec. Svc.; ind. contractor, mgmt. cons., 1997-2003. Vol. alumni admissions program Clark U., 1998—. Van Ness Neighborhood Network, 2003—. Recipient various awards Dept. Labor. Mem. Nat. Assn. Ret. Fed. Employees, Sr. Execs. Assn. Home: 3001 Veazey Ter NW Washington DC 20008-5454 E-mail: jpdcny@aol.com.

PATRON, SUSAN HALL, librarian, writer; b. San Gabriel, Calif., Mar. 18, 1948; d. George Thomas and Rubye Denver Hall; m. René Albert Patron, July 27, 1969. BA, Pitzer Coll., 1969; MLS, Immaculate Heart Coll., 1972. Children's libr. LA Pub. Libr., 1972-79, sr. children's libr., 1980—. Reviewer Sch. Libr. Jour., 1980-90, Pubs. Weekly, 1986-91, The Five Owls, 1987-95. Author: (with Christopher Weiman) Marbled Papers, 1979, Burgoo Stew, 1991, Five Bad Boys, Billy Que, and the Dustdobbin, 1992, Maybe Yes, Maybe No, Maybe Maybe, 1993 (ALA Notable Book 1994), Bobbin Dustdobbin, 1993, Dark Cloud Strong Breeze, 1994, The Higher Power of Lucky, 2006. Mem. ALA (Caldecott award com. 1988, Laura Ingalls Wilder award com. 2001), PEN (mem. West Lit. awards jury 1997, 2006), Calif. Libr. Assn. (Patricia Beatty award com. 1987-89, 91-92), Internat. Bd. on Books for Young Children, Soc. Children's Book Writers and Illustrators, So. Calif. Coun. on Lit. for Children and Young People (awards com. 1985), Authors Guild, Friends of Children and Lit. (mem. award com. 1984). Office: LA Pub Libr Childrens Svcs 630 W 5th St Los Angeles CA 90071-2002

PATSICOSTAS, SUSAN JOANNA, mental health services professional, psychotherapist; d. Gordon Howard and Melba Christine Williams; m. Nicholas Patsicostas, May 31, 1970 (div.); children: Thanos Nicholas, William Nicholas, Anthony Nicholas. AA, Ctrl. Fla. C.C., 1989; BA, Stetson U., 1991; MS in Mental Health Counseling, Nova Southeastern U., 1997. Lic. profl. counselor La., mental health counselor Fla., cert. parent trainer Boys and Girls Town, 2001, anger mgmt. and domestic violence counselor 2003. Psychotherapist Lake County Boys Ranch, Ocala, Fla., 1996—2000; clin. dir. Right Choice, LLC, Opelousas, La., 2001—02; owner, dir. New Way Mental Health Resources, LLC, Ville Platte, 2002—. Ct. apptd. adv. for foster children Guardian Ad Litem Program, Ocala, 1993—98. Recipient Above and Beyond award, Guardian Ad Litem Program, 1996. Mem.: Am. Counseling Assn., Assn. Play Therapy (licentiate), Psi Beta, Phi Theta Kappa. Office: New Way Mental Health Resources LLC 1769 West Main St Ville Platte LA 70586 Office Phone: 337-363-3703. Office Fax: 337-363-4008. E-mail: susantexas10@aol.com.

PATTEN, BETSEY LELAND, state legislator; b. Newton, Mass., Apr. 26, 1945; m. Richard C. Patten; 1 child. Student, Kings Coll. With publ. dept. Raytheon Co., 1978—84; rec. sec. Planning and Zoning Bds. of Moultonborough, 1985—91; state rep. N.H. Ho. Reps., chmn. mcpl. and county govt. com. Chmn. Joint Legis. Com. on Adminstrv. Rules, Assessing Standards Bd., Carroll County Rep. Com., 1996—. Home: 46 Patten Hill Rd Moultonborough NH 03254 Office Phone: 603-271-3317. E-mail: rcpatten@worldpath.net.

PATTEN, BRENDA ANNE, secondary school educator; d. Francis Roger and Germaine Josephine Lussier; m. Paul William Patten, May 27, 1978; children: Audrey Anne, Jennifer Lynn. BS and MEd, Bridgewater State Coll., 1982. Lic. tchr. Dept. of Edn., Mass. Tchr. Norton Sch. Dist., Mass., 1975—78, Cathedral Sch., St. Louis, 1978—80, Dighton-Rehoboth Regional Sch. Dist., Mass., 1980—. Curriculum developer (program for scouting weekends) Cadette Sampler (Girl Scout Vol. award, 2003). Leader Girl Scouts of S.E. Mass., Somerset, 1980. Mem.: Mass. Tchr. Assn. (corr.), Boy Scouts of Am. (assoc.; mem. troop leadership team 2002). Office: Dighton Mid Sch 1250R Somerset Ave North Dighton MA 02764 Office Phone: 508-669-4200.

PATTEN, CHRISTINE TAYLOR, artist; b. LA, Oct. 17, 1940; d. Malcolm Clark and Virginia (Strong) Patten; children: Robert Roy Powell Jr., Jonathan Taylor Powell, Matthew Clark Powell, Michael Neal Powell; m. Gendron Jensen, Aug. 15, 1987. Student, Pasadena City Coll., 1958-59, 70-72, U. Oreg., 1959-60; BFA, Otis Art Inst., L.A. County, 1974. Tchr. drawing and painting Pacificulture-Asia Mus., Pasadena Art Mus., 1973-74. Author: O'Keeffe at Abiquiu, 1995, Miss O'Keeffe, 1992; exhibitions include Calif. Mus. Sci. and Industry, L.A., Armory for the Arts, Santa Fe, Mus. N.Mex., Mus. Fine Arts, Santa Fe, Santa Barbara (Calif.) City Coll., Pepperdine U., Malibu, Calif., Harwood Mus., Taos, N.Mex., Ctr. for Contemporary Arts, Santa Fe, Addison-Ripley Gallery, Washington, Albuquerque Mus., Horwitch LewAllen Gallery, Santa Fe, Coll. Santa Fe, Knoedler Gallery, N.Y.C., Exit Art, others, U. Leeds Art Gallery, 2006, Drawing Gallery, London, 2006, Represented in permanent collections L.A. County Mus. Art, Albright-Knox Art Gallery (Mus.), Buffalo, Albuquerque Mus., U. N.Mex., Mus. N.Mex., Mus. Fine Arts, Harwood Mus., The Old Jail Mus., James Kelly Contemporary, Santa Fe, pvt. collections. Santa Fe Arts Coun. grantee, 1985. E-mail: murasaki@laplaza.com.

PATTEN, MAURINE DIANE, psychologist; b. Peoria, Ill., Aug. 30, 1940; d. Maurice H. and Esther Ann (Wilkenson) Foote; m. C. Alfred Patten, Aug. 26, 1961; children: Paul A., Bethany M. BS, Bradley U., 1961; MS, Chgo. State U., 1971; EdD, No. Ill. U., 1977. Lic. psychologist, Ill. Tchr. Elementary Schs., Skokie and Manhattan, Ill., 1961-63; dir. Southwest Coop Presch., Chgo., 1970-74; tchr. spl. edn. Dekalb County (Ill.) Spl. Edn. Assn., 1974-76, asst. dir., 1978-80; resource tchr. Sycamore (Ill.) Sch. Dist., 1976-78; asst. prof. Chgo. State U., 1980-81; pvt. practice as clin. psychologist Sycamore, 1981—2006. Cons. Arthur Andersen & Co., St. Charles, Ill., 1981-88 Fellow APA, Ill. Psychol. Assn. Methodist. Avocations: kayaking, reading. Office: 405 Delnor Glen Dr Saint Charles IL 60174 E-mail: mdpcoach@pattencoaching.com.

PATTEN, ROSE, bank executive; BS, Univ. Toronto. V.p., gen. mgr. Continental Bank of Canada/Lloyds Bank Canada, Toronto, Ontario, 1975—87; sr. v.p. ManuLife Fin., 1987—91; exec. v.p. Nesbitt Burns, Toronto, Ontario, 1992—95; sr. v.p. corp. svcs. BMO Fin. Group, Toronto, Ontario, sr. exec. v.p., human resources. Spkr. in field. Chmn. bus. bd. Univ. Toronto. Named one of 25 Most Powerful Women in Banking. Office: Bank of Montreal 100 King St W 1 First Canadian Pl 21st Fl M5X 1A1 Toronto Canada Office Phone: 416-867-6785. Office Fax: 416-867-6793.

PATTEN STARR, BARBARA SUE BRUMMETT, art educator, textile designer; b. Chillecothe, Ohio, Mar. 3, 1943; d. Charles Ray and Marguerite (Locke) Brummett; m. Lloyd Lee Patten, Nov. 26, 1966 (div.); children: Kimberly Joelle, Kelly Elizabeth; m. Mark Lowell Starr, 1996. AB, Duke U., 1965; MA, Fla. State U., 1966. Dir. fine arts Julius T. Wright Sch., Mobile, ala., 1967-75; asst. dean students Spring Hill Coll., Mobile, 1975-77, dir. fine arts, 1983-88, 94—, assoc. prof. fine arts, 1988—. Art cons. Mobile C. of C., Fine Ares Mus. of South, Mobile Art Assn., Art Patrons League, Mobile Pub. Schs.; represented by Groot & Mislove, Inc., Marilyn Kern, Inc., N.Y.C., The Sagamore Hotel, Bolton Landing, N.Y., 1989. One-woman show Ala. Mobile Coll., 1989; exhibited in group shows at Percy Whting Gallery, Fairhope, Ala., 1985, Little Gallery, Mobile, 1986, Spirit of the Earth, Santa Fe, 1986, Zita, Naples, Fla., 1986, Johnston of Fla., Naples, 1986, In Print, N.Y.C., 1988, Am. Surface Design, 1987, Fine Arts Mus. of South, Mobile, 1982, 84, 89, U. South Ala., Mobile, 1989, others. Pres. Coastal Environ. Alliance Gulf Coast, 1985. Grantee Shell Oil Co., 1981. Mem. Surface Design Assn. (alt. regional del. 1988—), LWV (v.p. Mobile chpt. 1973). Office: Spring Hill Coll 4000 Dauphin St Mobile AL 36608-1780

PATTERSON, AMANDA MARGARET, music educator; b. Luxemburg, Wis., May 15, 1931; d. Alois Milton Arendt and Martha Anastacia Dorner-Arendt; m. Neil A. Patterson (dec.); children: Debra Lee, Patrick Neil, Dean Michael, Jane Marie Mlenar. Student, Milw. State Tchrs. Coll., Wis., 1953. Tchr. music Walworth County, Elkhorn, Wis., 1953—56; tchr. Milw. Music City, 1956—57; tchr. instrumental music City of Milw., 1956—68; tchr. music Greendale, 1968—2006. Musician Anita McKnights All Women Orch., Milw., 1970—81, West Allis Adult Band, Wis., 1972—80. Pres. Wis. State Podiatry Aux. Soc., Milw., 1972—73, Greendale PTA, Wis., 1968—69; chmn. Ballet Co. Friends, Milw., 1973—76; pres. Greendale VFW Aux., Wis., 1980—82, 4th Dist. VFW Aux., Milw., 1992—93; bd. dirs. Milw. Ballet Co., 1973. Mem.: Am. Legion. Roman Catholic. Home: 5342 Lakeview Dr Greendale WI 53129-1928 E-mail: amandamp515@aol.com.

PATTERSON, ANNE WOODS (ANNE BREVARD WOODS PATTERSON), federal agency administrator, former ambassador; b. Ft. Smith, Ark., 1949; m. David R. Patterson; children: Edward, Andrew. BA in Econs., Wellesley Coll.; postgrad., U. N.C. With U.S. Fgn. Svc., 1973—, econ. officer Ecuador, 1974-77, desk officer Nicaragua, analyst for Ctrl. Am., trade specialist Can., econ. counselor Riyadh, Saudi Arabia, 1984-88, polit. counselor U.S. Mission to UN Geneva, dir. Office of Andean Affairs, 1991-93, dep. asst. sec. for Ctrl. Am. and the Caribbean, 1993-95, prin. dep. asst. sec. for inter-Am. affairs, 1995—97, US amb. to El Salvador San Salvador, 1997-2000, US amb. to Colombia Bogota, 2000—03; dep. permanent US rep. UN, NYC, 2004—05, acting permanent US rep., 2005; dep. insp. gen. US Dept. State, Washington, 2003—04, asst. sec., Bur. Internat. Narcotics and Law Enforcement Affairs, 2005—. Recipient Superior Honor award, US Dept. of State, 1981, 88 Meritorious Honor award, 1977, 83, Presdl. award, 1993; Order of the Congress, Congress of Colombia, Order of Boyaca, Govt. Colombia, Order of Jose Matias Delgado, Govt. El Salvador. Office: US Dept State 2201 C St NW Rm 7333 Washington DC 20520 Office Phone: 202-647-8464. Office Fax: 202-736-4885. Business E-Mail: pattersonaw2@state.gov, pattersonz@state.gov.

PATTERSON, BEVERLY ANN GROSS, not-for-profit fundraiser, consultant, social services administrator, writer; b. Pauls Valley, Okla., Aug. 5, 1938; d. Wilburn G. Jack and Mildred E. (Steward) Gross; m. Kenneth Dean Patterson, June 18, 1960 (div. 1976); children: Tracy Dean Patterson, Nancy Ann Patterson-McArthur, Beverly Jeanne Patterson-Wertman; life ptnr. Molly A. Kretz, 1999. AA, Modesto (Calif.) Jr. Coll., 1958; BA in Social Sci., Fresno (Calif.) State U., 1960; M in Community Counseling, Coll. Idaho; postgrad., Stanislaus State Coll., Turlock, Calif., U. Idaho, Boise (Idaho) State U. Cert. secondary tchr., Calif., Idaho, lic. real estate agt., Idaho. Secondary tchr., Ceres and Modesto Calif., Payette and Weiser Idaho, Ontario Oreg., 1960-67; dir. vol. svcs. mental retardation and child devel. State of Idaho, 1967-70, cons. dir. vol. svcs. health and welfare, 1970-72; dir. Ret. Sr. Vol. Program, Boise, 1972-74; exec. dir. Idaho Nurses Assn., Boise, 1974-76; community svcs. adminstr. City of Davis, Calif., 1976-78; dir. devel. and fundraising Mercy Med. Ctr., Nampa, Idaho, 1978-85; exec. dir. St. Alphonsus Med. Ctr. Found., Boise, 1985-87; dir. devel. and gift planning Idaho Youth Ranch, Boise, 1989-94; fund devel. cons. Mercy Housing, Nampa, Idaho, 1994-96, Pratt Ranch Boys Home, Emmett, Idaho, 1994-96, Northwest Childrens Home, Lewiston, Idaho, 1994-96, Idaho Spl. Olympics, Boise, 1994-95, Idaho Found. for Parks and Lands, Boise, 1994-95, St. Vincent de Paul, Inc., Boise, 1995-96, Nampa Shelter Found., Inc., 1994-95, Turning Point Inc., Nampa, 1994-95, Port of Hope Treatment Ctr. Inc., Boise, 1994-97, Idaho Theater for Youth, Inc., Boise, 1995-96, Boise Tennis Coalition, Inc., 1995-2000, El Ada Cmty. Action Ctr., Boise, 1995, Hemophilia Found. Idaho, 1995-96, Boise YWCA, 1996, Marsing (Idaho) Sch. Dist., 1996-98. Founder Fellowship Christian Adult Singles, Boise, 1974; cons., exec. dir. Boise Hotline, 1988-90; co-dir. ACOA workshop leader Child Within Concepts, Inc., Boise, 1987—; cons. coord. Rural Hosp. Edn. Consortium, 1988; cons. hosp. fund devel. and cmty. resources Gritman Meml. Hosp., Moscow, Idaho, 1987-88; cons., conf. coord. State of Idaho, 1987-88; counsel Adult Children of Alcoholics, 1991; pres. Nonprofit Solutions, Inc., Boise, 1995—; co-dir. Child Within Concepts, Inc., Meridian, 1996—; cmty. resource devel. specialist Idaho Dept. Health and Welfare, 1997-2000, United Way Portland, 2000; chmn., pres. Creative Solutions P.A., 2000—; grant writing cons. sch. dist. # 3JT, Oreg., Tillamook Sch. Dist., Oreg., Banks Sch. dist., Oreg., North West Regional Edn. Svcs. Dist., Oreg. Author poetry; contbr. articles to profl. jours. Coord. Idaho Golf Angels Open Pro-Am Tournament, Boise, 1989-91; founding exec. v.p. Coll. Fund for Students Surviving Cancer, 1993-96; bd. dirs. Arthritis Found., Idaho, 1984-86, Idaho Mental Health Assn., 1978-97; founder Ctrl. Vol. Bur., Boise, 1971. Named Idaho Statesman Disting. Citizen, 1985. Mem. Nat. Assn. for Hosp. Devel. (accredited, treas. 1980, accreditation chmn. 1984-86, conf. chmn. 1982, 85), Assn. Healthcare in Philanthrophy (accredited), Nat. Soc. Fund Raising Execs., Idaho Devel. Network, Choices in Giving, Inc. Avocations: golf, woodworking. Address: 9451 N Polk Ave Portland OR 97203-1630

PATTERSON, CARLY, Olympic athlete; b. Baton Rouge, Feb. 4, 1988; d. Ricky and Natalie. Mem. TOPS Nat. Team, 1996, 1997, U.S. Nat. Gymnastics Team, 2000—; gymnast Team USA, Athens Olympic Games, 2004. Achievements include member of US World Championships Gold medal team, 2003; winning silver medal, all-around, World Championships, 2003; won Visa Am. Cup Championship by winning all four events, 2004; winning gold medal, all-around, Athens Olympic games, 2004; member of US Women's Silver medal Gymnastics team, Athens Olympic games, 2004. Office: c/o USOC One Olympic Plz Colorado Springs CO 80909

PATTERSON, CAROLE A., psychologist, educator; d. Clarence L. and Margaret L. Ellison; m. L.A. George Patterson, Oct. 1, 1954; children: Gregory A., Kerry D., Roger L. BA in Psychology, Tex. Tech. U., 1978; MS in Clin. Counseling, Tex. A&M U., 1990. Diplomate Am. Acad. Forensic Counselors, cert. psychologist. Intern Horizon Recovery, Garland, Tex., 1989—90; counselor Counseling Inst. Tex., Garland, 1992—; staff therapist Dallas Life Found., 1996—2005; psychologist Interfaith Housing Coalition, Dallas, 2005—. Therapist Gaston Oaks Bapt. Ch., Dallas, 1991—2001; presenter in field. Family life ministries bd., interdenominational task force Dallas Bapt. Assn., 1995—98. Mem.: Am. Mental Health Counselors Assn., Am. Assn. Counseling and Devel. Methodist. Avocation: travel. Home: 4201 Lomo Alto Dr Apt 305 Dallas TX 75219-1515 Office: Interfaith Housing Coalition PO Box 720206 Dallas TX 75372 Office Phone: 214-827-7220 x103.

PATTERSON, CLAIRE ANN, career technical educator; b. Cin., Dec. 28, 1950; d. Lloyd E. and Ruth T. (Flaherty) Lachtrupp; m. Calvin Stanley Patterson, Jr., July 14, 1973; children: Christopher, Alicia. BS, U. Cin., 1973, MEd, 1980. Cert. elem. tchr., elem. supr., secondary math, secondary prin., asst. supt., Ohio., Va., P.R. Third grade tchr. Acadamia de Aguidilla, P.R., 1973-74; fifth grade tchr. Our Lady of the Rosary, Norfolk, Va., 1974-76; jr. high math and sci. tchr. Yavneh Hebrew Day Sch., Cin., 1976-79; math tchr. Winton Woods City Schs., Cin., 1979-80; math. coord. Great Oaks Inst. of Tech. and Career Devel., Cin., 1980-86, benefits coord./personnel profl., 1986-88, career devel. mgr., 1987-93, asst. dir., 1993-97, dean of instrn., 1998-99, mgr. testing and assessment, 1999—2001, mgr. profl. devel., 2001—03, dir. human resources, 2003—. Ednl. cons. schs. in Ohio, 1988—. Author: Let's Celebrate Math, 1991; contbr. articles to profl. jours. Mem. Ohio Career Devel. Task Frce, 1991-93. Recipient Career Coord. award, State of Ohio, 1993. Mem. Ohio Vocat. Assn. (com. chmn. 1990-93, pres. 1997-2000, Pacesetter award 1991, 92, 93, Trendsetter award 1998, 99), Career Edn. Assn. (pres. 1992-93), Nat. Coun. Local Adminstrs., S.W. Career Coun. (pres. 1991-92), Ohio Vocat. Edn. Leadership Inst. (grad. 1993). Republican. Roman Catholic. Avocations: writing murder-mystery plays, travel, reading. Office: Great Oaks Inst Tech and Career Devel 3254 E Kemper Rd Ste 3 Cincinnati OH 45241-1581 Home: 279 Beechridge Dr Cincinnati OH 45216 Business E-Mail: pattersc@greatoaks.com.

PATTERSON, DEB, women's college basketball coach; Grad., Rockford Coll., 1979. Asst. coach, recruiting coord. No. Ill. U., 1986-91; asst. coach So. Ill. U., 1991-92; top asst. coach, recruiting coord. Vanderbilt U., 1992-96; head coach Kans. State U., 1996—. Asst. coach 1997 World U. Games; women's sr. nat. team asst. coach USA Invitational Tournament of Champions, 1997. Named Women's Coll. Basketball Coach of the Yr. Kans. Basketball Coaches Assn., 1997, Coach of Yr. Ill. H.S. Assn., 1985, Conf. Coach of Yr., 1985, 86. Office: Kansas State U 1800 College Ave Manhattan KS 66502-3308 Fax: 785-532-6093.

PATTERSON, ELIZABETH C., choir director; b. Lakeland, Fla., Mar. 1, 1938; d. Jewell King Patterson and Loreta Marie Woodruff; m. Richard Patterson; children: Richard Pugsley, Wendy Saran. MusM, Milliken U. Dir. Gloriae Dei Cantores, Orleans, Mass., 1988—. CEO Paraclete Press, Brewster, Mass., 1983—90, cons., 1990—. Co-author: (book) The Sound Eternal, 1987. Mem.: NARAS, Am. Choral Dirs. Assn. Avocations: needlepoint, knitting, painting, sewing. Office: Gloriae Dei Cantores PO Box 2831 11 Bayview Dr Orleans MA 02653

PATTERSON, ELIZABETH JOHNSTON, retired congresswoman; b. Columbia, SC, Nov. 18, 1939; d. Olin DeWitt and Gladys (Atkinson) Johnston; m. Dwight Fleming Patterson, Jr., Apr. 15, 1967; children: Dwight Fleming, Olin DeWitt, Catherine Leigh. BA, Columbia Coll., 1961; postgrad. in polit. sci., U. S.C., 1961, 62, 64; LLD (hon.), Columbia Coll., 1987; D Pub. Svc. (hon.), Converse Coll., 1989, M in Liberal Arts, 1999; LLD (hon.), Wofford Coll., 1999. Pub. affairs officer Peace Corps, Washington, 1962-64, VISTA, OEO, Washington, 1965-66; D Pub. Svc. Head Start and VISTA, OEO, Columbia, 1966-67; tri-county dir. Head Start, Piedmont Community Actions, Spartanburg, SC, 1967-68; mem. Spartanburg County Coun., 1975-76, S.C. State Senate, 1979-86, 100th-102nd Congress from 4th S.C. dist., 1987-93; dir. continuing edn., converse II program Converse Coll., 1993—2003; ret. Adj. prof. Spartanburg Meth. Coll., 1993—2001. Trustee Wofford Coll., 1978—90, Columbia Coll., 1991—2003, Spartanburg Meth. Coll., 2004—; pres. Spartanburg Dem. Women, 1968; v.p. Spartanburg County Dem. party, 1968—70, sec., 1970—75, pres., 2004—; bd. dirs. S.C. Ind. Colls. and Univs., 1995—99, Charles Lea Ctr., 1978, Spartanburg Coun. on Aging; chmn., bd. dirs. Bethlehem Cmty. Ctr., 1998—. Mem.: Bus. and Profl. Women's Club, Alpha Kappa Gamma. Democrat. Methodist. E-mail: lizjpatterson@charter.net.

PATTERSON, JAN EVANS, epidemiologist, educator; b. Ft. Worth, May 13, 1956; d. C. Wayne and Zona (Horn) Evans; m. Thomas F. Patterson, June 22, 1985. BA, Hardin-Simmons U., 1978; MD, U. Tex., 1982. Diplomate Am. Bd. Internal Medicine, Am. Bd. Infectious Diseases. Asst. prof. medicine and lab. medicine Yale U. Sch. Medicine, New Haven, 1988-92; assoc. prof. medicine and pathology Health Sci. Ctr. U. Tex., San Antonio, 1993—99, prof. medicine and pathology, assoc. chair medicine, 1999—2005, prof. medicine and pathology, vice chair medicine, 2005—06, prof. medicine and pathology, interim chair medicine, 2006—; chief med. svc. Audie Murphy Vets. Hosp., 2004—06. Hosp. epidemiologist Univ. Health Sys., San Antonio, 1993-2005, Audie Murphy Meml. Vets. Hosp., San Antonio, 1993-95, S. Tex. Vets. Healthcare System, San Antonio and Kerrville, 1995-2005. Contbr. articles to profl. jours. Fellow ACP, Infectious Disease Soc. Am.; mem. Soc. Hosp. Epidemiologists, Am. Soc. Tropical Medicine and Hygiene, Exec. Leadership in Academic Medicine, Alpha Omega Alpha Office: Health Sci Ctr U Tex Divsn Infectious Diseases 7703 Floyd Curl Dr San Antonio TX 78284-6200

PATTERSON, LINDA DARECE, school disciplinarian; b. Casper, Wyo., July 30, 1955; d. James Edward and Decie Mae Patterson; 1 child, Chad Byron Ellingson. MS, Oreg. State U., 1982. Cert. Adminstrv. Tchrs. Practices, Standards. Social studies tchr. Dallas (Oreg.) Sch. Dist., 1977—82; counselor Corvallis (Oreg.) Sch. Dist., 1982—96. Instrnl. vice prin. Gresham (Oreg.) Sch. Dist., 2003—. Dir.: (personalized learning communities) (Appreciation Award, 2002). Recipient Excellent Svc. Spl. Edn. Students, Dallas Sch. Dist., 1982. Mem.: Nat. Assn. Secondary Sch. Prin. (life). Democrat-Npl. Avocations: scuba diving, travel. Office Phone: 503-583-9870. Business E-Mail: lohan007@comcast.net.

PATTERSON, LORIE, literature and language educator; b. Ada, Okla., Oct. 16, 1962; d. Denver Clyde and Wynema Kay Merrell; m. Charles Dennis Patterson, Nov. 8, 1980; children: Christy Denise, Chelsey Danae. BS in Edn., East Ctrl. U., Ada, Okla, 1991. Nominee Nat. Bd. Profl. Tchg. Stds., 2006. Tchr. Pleasant Grove Sch., Seminole, Okla., 1992—94; tchr. spring term Vanoss Pub. Sch., Stratford, 1996, Asher Pub Sch., 1996—. Author: A Dose of Reality, poetry in collections. Named Tchr. of Today, Masonic Lodge

(Macomb, Okla.), 2002, World Champion Roper, Profl. Women's Rodeo Assn., 1992, 1992. Mem.: U.S.Team Roping Championships. Office: Asher Pub Sch PO Box 168 Asher OK 74826-0168 Home: Rt 1 Box 127 Konawa OK 74849

PATTERSON, MADGE LENORE, elementary school educator; b. Vandergrift, Pa., Nov. 9, 1925; d. Paul Warren and Lucy Mae (Lemmon) Schaeffer; m. Stanley Clair Patterson, June 19, 1948 (dec.); 1 child, Stanley Kent. BS in Edn., Ind. State Tchrs. Coll., Pa., 1946, MEd, 1971. Elem. tchr. New Kensington Pub. Schs., Pa., 1946-49, Armstrong Sch. Dist. Schs., Ford City, Pa., 1951-52, kindergarten tchr., 1967-93, Rural Valley Presbyn. Ch., Pa., 1957-67; vol. tutor Adult Lit., Kittanning, Pa., 1993—; co-owner dairy farm. Sunday sch. tchr., choir mem., 1949—; sec. Rural Valley Presbyn. Ch. Women's Assn., 1988-92; vol. tutor Big Bros. and Sisters of Armstrong County, ARIN GED students. Mem. NEA, Pa. Assn. Sch. Retirees, Clara Cockerille Reading Coun. (treas. 1994-98), Pa. State Edn. Assn., Internat. Reading Assn. (Literacy award 2000), Keystone Reading Assn., Assn. Early Childhood Edn., Rural Valley Bus. and Profl. Club, Women's Civic Club (Woman of Yr. 1994), Am. Assn. Ret. Persons, Rural Valley Grange (lectr.). Democrat. Avocations: dancing (line, square, ballroom), reading, camping, music, travel. Home: 204 SR 1028 Dayton PA 16222

PATTERSON, MARIA JEVITZ, microbiology/pediatric infectious disease professor; b. Berwyn, Ill., Oct. 23, 1944; d. Frank Jacob and Edna Frances (Costabile) Jevitz; m. Ronald James Patterson, Aug. 22, 1970; children: Kristin Lara, Kier Nicole. BS in Med. Tech. summa cum laude, Coll. St. Francis, Joliet, Ill., 1966; PhD in Microbiology, Northwestern U., Chgo., 1970; MD, Mich. State U., 1984. Diplomate Am. Bd. Med. Examiners, Am. Bd. Pediatrics Gen. Pediatrics, Am. Bd. Pediatrics Infectious Diseases. Lab. asst., instr. med. microbiology for student nurses Med. Sch. Northwestern U., Chgo., 1966-70; postdoctoral fellow in clin. microbiology affiliated hosps. U. Wash., Seattle, 1971-72; asst. prof. microbiology and pub. health Mich. State U., East Lansing, 1972-77, assoc. prof., 1977-82, assoc. prof. pathology, 1979-82, lectr. dept. microbiology and pub. health, 1982-87, resident in pediatrics affiliated hosps., 1984-85, 86-87, clin. instr. dept. pediatrics and human devel., 1984-87, assoc. prof. microbiology-pub. health-pediatrics-human devel., 1987-90, prof., 1990—. Staff microbiologist dept. pathology Lansing Gen. Hosp., 1972-75; dir. clin. microbiology grad. program. Mich. State U., 1974-81, staff microbiologist, 1978-81; postdoctoral fellow in infectious diseases U. Mass. Med. Ctr., Worcester, 1985-86; asst. dir. pediatrics residency Grad. Med. Edn. Inc., Lansing, 1987-90; med. dir. Pediatrics Health Ctr. St. Lawrence Hosp., Lansing, Mich., 1987-90, Ingham Med. Ctr., 1990-94; cons. clin. microbiology Lansing Gen. Hosp., 1972-75, Mich. State U., 1976-82, Mich. Dept. Pub. Health, 1976—, Ingham County Health Dept., 1988—, Am. Health Cons., 1993, State of Mich. Atty. Gen. Office, 1994-98, Lansing Sch. Dist., 1998—, Mich. Antibiotic Resistance Reduction, 1998—; cons. to editl. bd. Infection and Immunity, 1977; cons. Mich. State U. AIDS Edn. Tng. Ctr, 2001—; presenter seminars. Contbg. author: Microbiology: Principles and Concepts, 1982, 4th edit., 1995, Pediatric Emergency Medicine, 1992, Principles and Practice of Emergency Medicine, 1997, Rudolph's Pediatrics, 2002; item writer certifying bd. examination Bd. Am. Acad. Pediats., 1990—, Am. Bd. Osteopathy, 1997—; contbr. articles to profl. jours. and publs. Mem. hon. com. Lansing AIDS Meml. Quilt, 1993. Recipient award for tchg. excellence Mich. State U. Coll. Osteo. Medicine, 1977, 78, 79, 80, 83, Disting. Faculty award Mich. State U., 1980, Woman Achiever award, 1985, excellence in pediatric residency tchg. award, 1988, 2001, 03, 05, Alumni Profl. Achievement award Coll. of St. Francis, 1991, excellence in diversity award Mich. State U., 2000, Weil Endowed Disting. Pediat. Faculty award, 2001; grantee renal disease divsn. Mich. Dept. Pub. Health 1976-82. Fellow Pediatric Infectious Diseases Soc., Infectious Diseases Soc. Am., Am. Acad. Pediatrics; mem. Am. Coll. Physician Execs., Am. Soc. Microbiology, Am. Soc. Clin. Pathologists (affiliate, bd. registrant), South Ctrl. Assn. Clin. Microbiology, Mich. Infectious Diseases Soc., N.Y. Acad. Scis., Kappa Gamma Pi, Lambda Iota Tau. Roman Catholic. Home: 1520 River Ter East Lansing MI 48823-5314 Office: Mich State Univ Microbiology/Molecular Genetics/Pediat East Lansing MI 48824-4320

PATTERSON, MILDRED LUCAS, retired teaching specialist; b. Winston-Salem, N.C., Jan. 24, 1937; d. James Arthur and Lula Mae (Smith) Lucas; m. James Harrison Patterson Jr., Mar. 31, 1961; children: James Harrison III, Roger Lindsay. BA, Talladega Coll., 1958; MEd, St. Louis U., 1969; postgrad., Webster U., 1970. Classroom tchr. Winston-Salem (N.C.) Pub. Schs., 1959-61, St. Louis Bd. Edn., 1961-72, reading specialist, 1972-88, co-host radio reading show, 1988-91; tchr. specialist Reading to Achieve Motivational Program, St. Louis, 1991-99; ret., 1999—. Bd. dirs. Supt.'s Adv. Com., University City, Mo., 1994—; presenter Chpt. I Regional Conf. Co-author: Wearing Purple, 1996. Bd. dirs. Gateway Homes, St. Louis, 1989-93; mem. com. University City Sch. Bond Issue, 1994; mem. Univ. City Arts and Letters Commn., 1998-99. Recipient Letter of Commendation, Chpt. I. Regional Conf., 1991, Founders' award Gamma Omega chpt. Alpha Kappa Alpha, 1985. Mem. Internat. Reading Assn. (Broadcast Media award for radio 1990, Bldg. Rep. award St. Louis chpt. 1990). Avocations: reading, arts and crafts, storytelling, motivational speaking. E-mail: mildred9@bellsouth.net.

PATTERSON, PATRICIA LYNNE, artist, educator; b. June 13, 1946; BA in Visual Arts, Chatham Coll., 1996; cert. in art edn., Carlow Coll., 1999; MFA, Art Inst. of Boston Lesley U., 2005. Instr. Butler County CC, 1984-88; tchr. Seneca Valley Schs., 1997—2003; represent by La Fond Gallery, Pitts., 2003—. Cons., pub. spkr., Butler, 1978—; resident Va. Ctr. Creative Arts, 2005-06. Exhibited paintings in numerous shows, 1992—; co-author: (play) A Whole New Ballgame, 1994. Stephen min., mem. choir St. Andrews Presbyn. Ch., 1988—; v.p. bd. dirs. Downtown Butler Assn.; bd. dirs. YWCA, Soroptomists, Christian Conciliation Svc., Butler, 1984—92, Grapevine Ctr. (Mental Health Assn. of Butler), 1999—2000, Associated Artists of Butler County, 2003—05. Recipient Disting. Svc. award Butler C. of C., 1986; Heinz fellow, 2005-06; Va. Ctr. for Creative Arts fellow, 2006. Mem.: Associated Artists of Pitts., Pitts. Soc. Artists, Pa. State Tchrs. Assn. Home: 118 Germaine Rd Butler PA 16001-1917 E-mail: patpatt@zoominternet.net.

PATTERSON, PEYTON R., bank executive; b. Weisbaden, Germany; m. Thomas Patterson; 1 child. Degree in Polit. Sci., European Inst. Study, 1977; AB in Polit. Sci., Kenyon Coll., 1978; MBA in Mktg., George Washington U., 1983. From asst. v.p. group product mgr. retail deposit products to v.p. Corestates Fin. Corp., Phila., 1983—85, v.p., 1985—89; from v.p. group product mgr. to sr. v.p. Chemical Banking Corp., NYC, 1989—90, sr. v.p., 1990—95; sr. v.p., dir. nat. fin. svcs. group Chase Manhattan Bank, NYC, 1995—96; exec. v.p., gen. mgr. consumer fin. svcs. Dime Bank Corp., NYC, 1996—2001; chmn., pres., CEO New Haven Savings Bank (now NewAlliance Bancshares, Inc.), 2002—. Co-chmn. Greater N.Y. March of Dimes; mem. Regional Leadership Coun., Arts Coun. Greater New Haven; bd. dirs. United Way. Named One of 25 Most Powerful Women in Banking, US Banker mag., 2003, 2004, 2005; Rockefeller fellow, 2000—01, Henry Crown fellow, Aspen Inst. Office: NewAlliance Bancshares 195 Church St New Haven CT 06510*

PATTERSON, RONNYE WILLIAMS, assistant principal; b. McAllen, Tex., Dec. 19, 1959; d. Charlie and Joy Williams. BS in Edn., SW Tex. State U., San Marcos, 1983; M in Mid Mgmt., U. Houston, Clear Lake, 2006. Dance team dir., dance tchr. Brazosport HS, Brazosport Ind. Sch. Dist., Clute, Tex., 1985—2005, asst. prin., 2005—. Cons. Tex. State Bd. Edn., Austin, 2002—05. Sustaining mem. Jr. Svc. League, Lake Jackson, Tex., 1990—. Named Secondary Tchr. of Yr., Brazosport Ind. Sch. Dist., 2000. Mem.: Tex. Assn. Tchrs. of Dancing (assoc.; treas. 2004—), Tex. Assn. Secondary Sch. Prins. (assoc.), Tex. Dance Educators Assn. (life; past pres., scholarship chair 1988—2006, Dir. of Yr. 2000). Office: Brazoswood HS 302 Brazoswood Dr Clute TX 77531 Office Phone: 979-730-7300 ext 29293.

PATTERSON, SALLY JANE, communications executive, consultant; b. Ontario, Calif., May 28, 1948; d. James Lowell and Barbara Verle (Griffin) Swain; 1 child, Robert Elias Sandoval. BA, Calif. State U., Fullerton, 1970, MA, 1974. Adminstrv. asst. Congressman Jerry Patterson, U.S. House of Reps., Washington, 1978-81; v.p. Pub. Response Assocs., Washington, 1981-87, Hamilton & Staff, Washington, 1987-90; v.p. pub. affairs Planned Parenthood Fedn. of Am., N.Y.C., 1990-93; internat. cons. Mgmt. Sys. Internat., Washington, 1993—; v.p. Wagner & Assocs. Pub. Affairs Cons., Inc., N.Y.C., Washington, 1994-99; pres. Radiant Comms. Inc., 2000—. Cons. Nat. Dem. Inst., Washington, 1994—. Author: Supporting Democracy in The Newly Independent States of The Former Soviet Union, 1994, Women in Government Relations: 20 Years of Vision, Leadership, Education and Networking, 1995, Pursuing a Paradox: Public Attitudes vs. Public Action on Campaign Finance Reform, How does Congress Approach Population and Family Planning Issues?, 1999, Generating Bazz Strategic Communication for Nonprofit Boards, 2005. Trainer Nat. Women's Campaign Fund; bd. dirs Round House Theatre, 2004—. Recipient Gold Key award PR Soc. Am., 1992; named one of 74 Women Shaping Am. Politics, Campaigns and Elections, 1993. Mem. NARAL, Women in Govt. Rels., Inc. (disting. mem., chair leader found. 1985-87, v.p. 1987-88, pres. 1988-89), Coun. Excellence in Govt. (prin.), NARAL Found. (bd. 1993-2005, chair 2001-2004, found. bd. 2001—). Democrat. Episcopalian. Office: Radiant Comms Inc 2121 K St NW Ste 800 Washington DC 20037-1829

PATTERSON, SANDRA MAY, school psychologist; b. Winfield, Kans., Apr. 15, 1937; d. Harold Colonel and Mabel Berniece (Wilson) Riggs; m. Wallace R. Patterson, Nov. 26, 1958; children: Kay Lynn, Carol Ann, Keith Alan. BA in Elem. Edn. cum laude, Wichita State U., 1969, M of Elem. Edn., 1973, M in Student Pers. and Guidance, 1979, cert. sch. psychologist, 1980, ednl. specialist, 1981. Elem. tchr. 4/5 Unified Sch. Dist. 260, Derby, Kans., 1969-79, spl. edn. tchr., 1979-80; sch. psychology intern Unified Sch. Dist., Mulvane, Kans., 1980, sch. psychologist, 1983-92, Unified Sch. Dist. 259, Wichita, Kans., 1981-82, Unified Sch. Dist. 619, Wellington, Kans., 1982-83, Unified Sch. Dist. 353, 1992—98, Unified Sch. Dist. 260, 1998—2002; ret. Practicum lectr. Wichita State U., 1984-85. Author: (children's book) Ben & The Bully, 1999. Mem. NEA (life), Nat. Assn. Sch. Psychologists, Kans. Assn. Sch. Psychologists, Kans. Ednl. Assn. (uniserv rep.). Avocations: farming, ranching. Home: 1369 East 6th St South Oxford KS 67119

PATTERSON, SHIRLEY DRURY, genealogist, editor-in-chief; b. Sterling, Colo., Dec. 30, 1933; d. Carl Walter Drury and Muriel Avis Sheaffer; m. James Riley Patterson, Mar. 28, 1981; m. Donald Eugene Loomiller, May 24, 1953 (div. Jan. 3, 1963); children: Craig Douglas Loomiller, Cynthia Anne Loomiller. BA, U. No. Colo., 1968, N.C. State U., 1984. Pvt. practice profl. genealogist, Loveland, Colo., 1980—; editor in chief Towne Family Assn., Inc., Loveland, 1988—, v.p., 1996—2005, pres., 2005—. V.p. Towne Family Assn., Inc., Auburn, 1996—, genealogist, 1994—97, assoc. genealogist, 1997—. Editor: (journal) About Towne (Cert. of Distinquished Svc., 2001, 1995, Cert. of Disting. Svc., 2002), Atlantic Waves, (newsletter) Columbine Brewgle (Lit. Achievement award, 1998). Mem. of caucus Dem. Party, Ft. Collins, Colo., 1996—2000. Mem.: Boulder County Geneal. Soc. (assoc.), Hardin County Geneal. Soc. (assoc.), South Bend Area Geneal. Soc. (assoc.), The Essex Soc. of Genealogists (assoc.), New Eng. Hist. Geneal. Soc. (assoc.), DAR (life). Democrat. Baptist. Avocations: travel, collector of history books, golf. Home and Office: 4020 Boxelder Dr Loveland CO 80538-2178

PATTERSON, VALERIE, art educator; b. Sidney, N.Y., July 12, 1963; d. Thomas Taylor and Terry Ann (Herter) Patterson BA, Potsdam Coll., N.Y., 1985; MA, Potsdam Coll., 1980. Cert. tchr. art K-12, elem. edn. K-6, N.Y. Tchr. art Brushton-Moira Ctrl. Sch., Brushton, NY, 1985—96, Saranac Lake Ctrl. Sch., NY, 1996—. Mem. edn. adv. bd. Adirondack Park Visitors Ctr. Paul Smiths, N.Y., 1988-92; educator Nat. Spruce-up Am. Program, Paul Smiths, 1992; workshop presenter Exhibited in solo shows Catherine Lorillard Wolfe Art Club, N.Y.C., 1998, 2004, Northeast Watercolor Assn., Conn., 1999, 2000, 01, 02, N.E. Watercolor Soc., Kent, Conn., 1999, 2000-04, Frederic Remington Art Mus., Ogdensburg, N.Y., 2000, Art Assn. Harrisburg, Pa., 2001, Cambridge Art Assn., 2002, Plano (Tex.) Art Assn., 2002, 04, Hudson Valley Art Assn., 2003, Don O'Melveny Gallery, West Hollywood, Calif., 2004, Sarah Jessica Fine Arts Gallery, Provincetown, Mass., 2005, Monkdogz Urban Art Gallery, N.Y.C., 2006; featured in Best of N.Y. Artists Book, 2006; cover illustrations for Manhattan Arts Internat.; featured artist Art Express, PBS-TV, Plattsburgh, N.Y., 2003 Recipient 1st Pl. award for Utiliziing TV in Edn., N.Y. State, 1991, numerous awards for art Mem. N.E. Watercolor Soc Home: 351 County Rt 41 Malone NY 12953 Office Phone: 518-569-5269. Business E-Mail: herter@northnet.org.

PATTON, DEBRA RUTH, elementary school educator; b. Westerly, RI, Feb. 24, 1959; d. Thomas Joseph Patton and Marjorie Roberta DeGrace. BA, Concordia Coll., Bronxville, New York, 1987. Tchr. St. Mark's Luth. Sch., Yonkers, NY, 1987—. Bd. mem. Luth. Schools Assn., Bronxville, NY, 1988—92. Recipient Alpha Chi, Concordia Coll., 1987. Mem.: Nat. Coun. for the Social Studies. Office: St Mark's Luth Sch 7 St Mark's Pl Yonkers NY 10704 Office Phone: 914-237-4944. Office Fax: 914-237-3146. E-mail: stmarklu@optonline.net.

PATTON, JODY, management company executive; With Pacific Northwest Ballet; pres., CEO Vulcan, Inc., Seattle; pres. Vulcan Prodns. Vice-chair First & Goal, Inc.; exec. dir. Experience Music Project, Seattle; co-founder Sci. Fiction Mus. and Hall of Fame, Seattle; bd. dir. Charter Comm. Exec. prodr.: The Blues. Exec. dir. Paul G. Allen Family Found.; bd. dir. U. Wash. Found., Internat. Glass Mus., Oreg. Shakespeare Festival, Theatre Comm. Group. Office: Vulcan Inc 505 Fifth Ave S Ste 900 Seattle WA 98104 Office Phone: 206-342-2000. Office Fax: 206-342-3000.

PATTON, KRISTEN TERESE, music educator; b. Saint Cloud, Minn., Apr. 16, 1981; d. George Timothy and Linda Marie Patton. BA, Coll. of St. Benedict, St. Joseph, Minn., 1999—2003. Nursing asst. St. John's Abbey Retirement Ctr., Collegeville, Minn., 2003—; drama coord. Cathedral HS, Saint Cloud, 2005—; music tchr. Lincoln Elem., Saint Cloud, Minn., 2005—. Pvt. violin & voice tchr., Saint Cloud, 1998—. Musician: (singer/performer) Singers: Minnesota Choral Artists, Kantorie, (violinist) St. Cloud Symphony Orchestra, Amadeus Chamber Orchestra; actor(singer): Dinner Theater. Avocations: softball, travel, exercise. Home: 1237 Whitney Dr Saint Cloud MN 56303 Office: Lincoln Elem 336 5th Ave S Saint Cloud MN 56304 Office Phone: 320-251-6343. Personal E-mail: kristenterese@hotmail.com.

PATTON, MARY RITCHIE, retired pediatric nurse practitioner, consultant; b. Lexington, Ky., Oct. 23, 1942; d. Robert L. Ritchie and Lucille Hisle, John P. Moores (Stepfather); m. John Logan Patton, Aug. 1, 1964; children: Angela Lynn, Stephanie Anne. RN, Ky. Bapt. Hosp. Sch. Nursing, 1964; PNP, Mass. Gen. Hosp. Harvard U., 1972; BSc, St. Joseph Coll., 1986. RN Ky. Bd. Nursing, 1964, lic. PNP, Nat. PNP Assn., 1980. Nurse mgr. James C. Ramsey Med. Care, Frankfort, Ky., 1969—71; PNP Hugh C. Williams Med. Ctr., Carrolton, 1972—74, Wedco Dist. Health Dept., Paris, Ky., 1977—80, maternal and child health nursing dir., 1980—84; nurse cons. Ky. Dept. Health Svcs., Frankfort, 1984—90, perinatal coord., 1990—92; ret., 1992. Adv. com. mem. Ky. Perinatal Assn., Lexington, 1990—92. Adv. com. mem. Ky. Mar. of Dimes, Lexington, 1990—92; vol. disaster svcs. ARC, Lexington, 1992—2005; bd. mem. First Bapt. Ch., Lexington, 1980—94; missionary Ky. Bapt. Assn., Louisville, 1984, 2000; adv. bd. mem. Elkhorn Bapt. Assn., Lexington, 2002—03. Recipient Partnership Evangelism award, Fgn. Mission Bd. of So. Bapt. Conv., 1992, Disaster Svc. award, ARC, 1994, Hours of Svc. award, 1994, 1995. Mem.: Scott County Humane Soc., Georgetown Coll. Women's Assn., Scott County Woman's Club, Rose Rebekka Lodge. Independent-Republican. Christian. Avocations: quilting, travel, reading. Home: 124 E Clinton St Georgetown KY 40324

PATTON, SHARON F., museum director; BA, Roosevelt U., 1966; MA, U. Ill., 1969; PhD in Art History, Northwestern U., 1980. Mem. faculty U. Houston, 1976—79, U. Md., 1979—85; dir. art galleries Montclair State Coll., NJ, 1986—87; chief curator Studio Mus., N.Y.C., 1988—91; assoc. prof. art history U. Mich., Ann Arbor, 1991—98, dir. Ctr. for Arfoamerican and African Studies, 1996—98; dir. Allen Meml. Art Mus. Oberlin Coll., 1998—2003; mem. adv. bd. Nat. Mus. African Art, Washington, 2000—, dir., 2003—. Author: Memory and the Metaphor, the Art of Romare Bearden, 1991, African-American Art, 1998 (Choice Outstanding Book of Yr. award); contbr. articles to publs. in field. Mem. Rapid Transit Pub. Art Commn., Cleve., ArtTable, Cleve.; mem. visual arts jury Cleve. Arts Prize, 2000—02; mem. African Am. adv. coun. and Acquisition adv. com. Cleve. Art Mus. Mem.: ArtTable, Assn. Art Mus. Dirs., Am. Assn. Museums. Office: Nat Mus African Art Smithsonian Instn MRC 708 PO Box 37012 Washington DC 20013-7012

PATTON-NEWELL, JANET LAVELLE, minister; b. Sharon, Pa., Jan. 15, 1965; d. Henry Elbert and Flora Lee Newby; m. Derrick Lamount Newell, June 17, 2000; children: Flora Evette Harris, Kellen Dauntae Newby, Kent Michael Patton, Kaston Moneke Patton, Grace Newell. Diploma in Bible studies, Full Bible Inst. Farrell, Pa., 2002; HHD, diploma in biblical studies, NCI Bible Coll. and Sch. Prophets, 2005; cert., Cambria County Prison Tng. Acad., Pa. Certificate of Congratulations New and Living Way Apostolic Ch. of Jesus Christ, 2003, Certificate of Appreciation ACTS Anointed Call To Singleness, 1999, Wind in the Word Outreach Ministry, 2002, Wind in the Word Outreach Ministry, 2003, Wind in the Word Outreach Ministry, 2004, lic. ordained World Missions Ministerial Assn., minister Ranha Outreach Internat. Orders clk. Mercer County Domestic Rels., (Child Support Bur.), Mercer, Pa., 1996—98; youth and young adult activities coord. Americorp Vista, (Mercer County Housing Authority), Sharon, Pa., 1998—99; evangelist New and Living Way Apostolic Ch. of Jesus Christ, Farrell, Pa., 1998—2000; overseer Paramount Ctr. for Learning, Farrell, Pa.; pastor Rivers Living Water Outreach Ministry, Farrell, Pa., 2000—01, Wind in the Word Outreach Ministry, Farrell, Pa., 2001—. Correction officer Mercer County Prison. Author: (self help) You are a Woman of Excellence, 2001, You are a Man of Excellence, 2001, Our Weapons are not Carnal, 2001; The Three Dimensions of the Prophetic, 2005. Mem. E.R.A.S.E. Anti Drug Coalition, Farrell, 1999, Wheels To Work, (Prince of Peace), Farrell, Pa., 1999; dir. New and Living Way Edn. Dept., Farrell, 1998—2000, Wind in the Word Outreach Ministry Edn. Dept., Farrell, 2001—05; mem. Walking in Black History, Erie, Pa., 1999. E-5 U.S. Army, 1987—2001, Fort Bragg, N. Carolina and Ansbach, Germany. Mem.: Women In Truth Fellowship, Women Speakers, Prophetic Women, Women N Power. Democrat. Apostolic. Avocations: computers, writing. Office: Wind in the Word Outreach Ministry 947 Hamilton Ave Farrell PA 16121 Office Phone: 724-734-1904. Business E-Mail: dr.janetl.newell@windintheword.com.

PAUGH, NANCY ADELE, secondary school educator, school system administrator; BS, N.Y. U., 1975, MA, 1978. Tchr. H.S. math. Woodbridge (N.J.) Schs., 1975-87, supr. secondary math., music and consumer and family sci., 1987—. Contbr. articles to pubs. Mem. Ocean Grove (N.J.) Auditorium Choir, 1984—; organist, choir dir. St. Paul's United Meth. Ch., Tottenville, NY, 1967—71, 1975—. Grantee, NSF, 1995—2001. Mem.: ASCD, Am. Guild Organists, Music Educators Nat. Conf., Am. Math. Soc., Mat. Assn. Am., Nat. Assn. Elem. Sch. Prins., Nat. Assn. Secondary Sch. Prins., Am. Assn. Sch. Adminstrs., Pi Lambda Theta. Office: Woodbridge Schs PO Box 428 Woodbridge NJ 07095-0428 Office Phone: 732-602-8564. E-mail: nancy.paugh@woodbridge.k12.nj.us.

PAUGH, PATRICIA LOU, business consultant; b. Pitts., Oct. 30, 1948; d. Marshall Franklin and Helen Jeanne (Graham) P. BA in English, Columbia U., 1982. Adminstrv. asst. Katz, Robinson, Brog & Seymour, N.Y.C., 1972-75; office mgr. Michael D. Martocci, N.Y.C., 1975-80; adminstrv. mgr. O'Melveny & Myers, N.Y.C., 1982-85, Latham & Watkins, N.Y.C., 1985-88; mgr. Nationwide Legal Svcs., N.Y.C., 1988-89; mgr. legal adminstrn. Aluminum Co. of Am., Pitts., 1990-93; ptnr. Domestic & Overseas Countertrade and Consulting Svcs., Ltd., 1986—; pres. Domestic & Overseas Trading Corp., Pitts., 1993—; mng. dir. Gen. Comml. Svcs., Ltd., 1994—. Mem. Am. Mgmt. Assn., Pitts. C. of C. Republican. Episcopalian. Home: 2403 Charlemagne Cir Pittsburgh PA 15237

PAUL, BESSIE MARGRETTE, retired weather forecaster; b. Absher, Mont., June 24, 1926; d. Fredrick Ernest Bergman and Margrette Marie Daly; m. Theodore Eugene Paul, Dec. 1, 1949 (dec. 1964); 1 child, Barbara Marie. AS, Eastern Montana Coll., 1988; BSBA in bus. adminstrn., Eastern Mont. Coll., 1992. Weather observer, map plotter US Weather Bur., Billings, Mont., 1944—53, map plotter San Francisco, 1955—56; forecaster Nat. Oceanic and Atmospheric Adminstrn., 1956—81; ret., 1981. Mem.: AAUW, Order of Eastern Star, Nat. Assn. Active and Ret. Fed. Employee. Avocations: cooking, baking, gardening, exercise, reading. Home: 2425 Ave B Billings MT 59102

PAUL, CAROL ANN, retired academic administrator, biology educator; b. Brockton, Mass., Dec. 17, 1936; d. Joseph W. and Mary M. (DeMeulenaer) Bjork; m. Robert D. Paul, Dec. 21, 1957; children: Christine, Dana, Stephanie, Robert. BS, U. Mass., 1958; MAT, R.I. Coll., 1968, Brown U., 1970; EdD, Boston U., 1978. Tchr. biology Attleboro (Mass.) High Sch., 1965-68; asst. dean., mem. faculty biology North Shore Community Coll., Beverly, Mass., 1969-78; master planner N.J. Dept. for Higher Edn., Trenton, 1978-80; assoc. v.p. Fairleigh Dickinson U., Rutherford, N.J., 1980-86; v.p. acad. affairs Suffolk Community Coll., Selden, N.Y., 1986-94, prof. biology, 1994-98; ret., 1998. Faculty devel. cons. various colls., 1979-98, title III evaluator, 1985-98. Author: (lab. manual and workbook) Minicourses and Labs for Biological Science, 1972 (rev. edit., 1975); (with others) Strategies and Attitudes, 1986; book reviewer, 1973-77, 94-98. V.p. LWV, Beverly, 1970—74, Cranford, NJ, 1982—83; alumni rep. Brown U., 1972—92; mem. Cape Cod Area LWV, 2001—03; mem. bd. dirs. YMCA of Cape Cod, 2004—, bd. dirs., clk. of bd., 1998—2003. Commonwealth Mass. scholar, 1954-58; recipient Acad. Yr. award NSF, 1968-69, Proclamation for Leadership award Suffolk County Exec., 1989. Mem.: AAUW, AAWCC, AAHE, Nat. Coun. for Staff (nat. exec. bd. 1979—80), Profls. and Orgn. Developers (planning com. 1977—79), Brown Alumni Club of Cape Cod (bd. dirs. 2001—, sec. 2001—04), Pi Lambda Theta, Phi Theta Kappa. Roman Catholic. Avocation: swimming. Address: 26 Martin Circle Winslowe's View at Pine Hills Plymouth MA 02360 Office Phone: artrdpaul@verizon.net.

PAUL, EVE W., retired lawyer; b. NYC, June 16, 1930; d. Leo I. and Tamara (Sogolow) Weinschenker; m. Robert D. Paul, Apr. 9, 1952; children: Jeremy Ralph, Sarah Elizabeth. BA, Cornell U., 1950; JD, Columbia U., 1952. Bar: N.Y. 1952, Conn. 1960, U.S. Ct. Appeals (2nd cir.) 1975, U.S. Supreme Ct. 1977. Assoc. Botein, Hays, Sklar & Herzberg, N.Y.C., 1952-54; pvt. practice Stamford, Conn., 1960-70; staff atty. Legal Aid Soc., N.Y.C., 1970-71; assoc. Greenbaum, Wolff & Ernst, N.Y.C., 1972-78; v.p. legal affairs Planned Parenthood Fedn. Am., N.Y.C., 1979—91, v.p., gen. counsel, 1991—2003; ret., 2003. Bd. dirs. Ctr. Advancement of Women, Inc. Contbr. articles to profl. jours Trustee Cornell U., Ithaca, N.Y., 1979-84; mem. Stamford (Conn.) Planning Bd., 1967-70; bd. dirs. Stamford LWV, 1960-62. Harlan Fiske Stone scholar Columbia Law Sch., 1952. Mem.: ABA, Fairfield County Bar Assn., Assn. Bar of City of N.Y., Conn. Bar Assn., Phi Kappa Phi, Phi Beta Kappa. Personal E-mail: evewpaul@aol.com.

PAUL, JULIA, ancient history researcher; b. Kharkhov, Ukraine, Russia, Dec. 5, 1927; came to U.S., 1937; d. Malham H. and Marazie D. David; m. Joash E. Paul, Feb. 15, 1947; children: Joyce, Joan, Dean, Timothy (dec.), Therese, Bernadette, David. BA, Calif. State U. Stanislaus, Turlock, 1990. Owner Paul's Motel, 15 yrs.; rschr. ancient history and Assyrian history. Host KBSY-TV, Modesto, Calif., 1997—; edn. chair Assyrian Am. Nat. Fedn., 1992-94; entertainment chair Calif. State U. Stanislaus Oratorio Soc. Composer music; handbell player, mem. choir Sacred Heart Ch., Turlock. Founder, organizer Dem. Women's Club of Turlock, 1979, United for Life of Stanislaus County, 1973. Mem. UN Assn. Stanislaus (v.p.). Avocations: golf, bowling, cooking assyrian dishes.

PAUL, MARIANNE, physician assistant; b. Huntington, N.Y., Mar. 21, 1959; d. Coningsby Espin Burdon and Madeline Mary Moisan; m. Christopher Lee Paul, Aug. 11, 1979; 1 child, Justin Matthew. AAS in Radiologic Tech., Nassau C.C., Garden City, N.Y., 1989; BS in Physician Asst., SUNY, Stony Brook, 1995. Cert. physician asst., N.Y., Pa. Radiologic technologist Nassau County Med. Ctr., East Meadow, N.Y., 1989-93; physician asst., clin. mgr. Musculoskeletal Inst., Manhasset, N.Y., 1994-97; physician asst. Dr. Frank P. Cammisa, N.Y.C., 1997—, clin. investigator, rsch. coord., 1997-98; physician asst. Noah S. Finkel, Huntington, N.Y., 1999—. Clin. instr. SUNY, Stony Brook, 1995—; North Shore Univ. Hosp., Plainview, 1996—, Huntington Hosp., 1998—. Author (newsletter) Controlling Back Pain, 1998. Vol. North Shore Univ. Hosp., Manhasset, 1985-87. Mem. Am. Acad. Physician Assts. Republican. Roman Catholic. Avocations: camping, fishing, arts and crafts. Office: 205 E Main St Ste 18 Huntington NY 11743-2923 Fax: 516-427-2134.

PAUL, MELANIE FRANCES, principal; b. Inglewood, Calif., Jan. 8, 1978; d. John Wayne Paul and Mary Alyce Meyer; m. David Leon Block, Mar. 18, 2006. BA in Edn., Ariz. State U., 2000, M Leadership, 2004. Cert. tchr. Ariz. Aims specialist Scottsdale (Ariz.) Unified Sch. Dist., 2001; 3d grade tchr. Litchfield Elem. Sch., Litchfield Park, Ariz., 2001—04; math. tchr. Verrado Mid. Sch., Buckeye, Ariz., 2004—05; instrnl. coach Union Elem. Sch. Dist., Tolleson, Ariz., 1995—96, planning prin., 2006, prin. Sch. # 3, 2006—. Mem.: ASCD. Avocations: hiking, reading. Office: Union Elem Sch Dist 3834 S 91th Ave Peoria AZ 85381

PAUL, NORA MARIE, media studies educator; b. White Plains, N.Y., Mar. 1, 1953; d. Keith and Nancy Miller Doig; m. Robert Lavon Medley, June 1973 (div. Nov. 1974); m. Robert Nathan Paul, Dec. 24, 1982; children: Nathan Augustus, Spencer Bernard. BA, Tex. Women's U., 1975, MLS, 1976. Reference libr. Houston Pub. Libr., 1976-77; cons., co-founder Freelance Rsch. Svc., Houston, 1977-79; editor info. svcs. Miami (Fla.) Herald, 1979-91; faculty Poynter Inst. for Media Studies, St. Petersburg, Fla., 1991—; dir. Inst. for New Media Studies U. Minn. Cons. AP, N.Y.C., 1993-95; vis. faculty European Journalism Ctr., Maastricht, The Netherlands, 1996—. Author: (book) Computer-Assisted Research: A Guide to Tapping Online Information, 4th edit., 1999; co-author: (book) Great Scouts!: Cyber-Guides to Subject Searching on the Web, 1999; contbr. articles to mags. Mem. Spl. Librs. Assn. (Hennebry award news divsn. 1995), Investigative Reporters and Editors. Avocations: writing, tile work. Office: U Minn Inst New Media Studies 111 Murphy Hall 206 Church St SE Minneapolis MN 55455-0488 E-mail: npaul@tc.umn.edu.

PAUL, OUIDA FAY, music educator; b. Deatsville, Ala., Jan. 18, 1911; d. Elza Bland and Martha Eleanor (Hinton) P. AB in Math. and English, Huntingdon Coll., 1930, BS in Music Edn., 1933; MA in Music and Music Edn., Columbia U., 1943, EdD in Music and Music Edn., 1957; postgrad., U. Ill., 1968; studied oil painting, Gloria Foss Sch. of Art, 1978—83. Tchr. math., English and music pub. schs., Ala., 1930—42; tchr. math. Sacred Heart Convent Sch., N.Y.C., 1942-43; tchr. h.s. choral music Kingsport, Tenn., 1943-45; instr., asst. prof. music edn. Greensboro (N.C.) Coll., 1945-49; asst. prof. U. Fla., Gainesville, 1949-61, U. Hawaii, Honolulu, 1961-68; tchr. musicology and voice Leeward C.C., Pearl City, Hawaii, 1968-77; pvt. tchr. voice, Honolulu, 1977-95, Gainesville, 1996—. Choir dir. 1st Presbyn. Ch., Gainesville, 1950-61, Protestant Chapel, USN, Honolulu, 1962-68, Cmty. Ch., Honolulu, 1969-78, Wesley United Meth. Ch., Honolulu, 1978-94; contralto soloist various chs., 1950-94; adjudicator solo and choral auditions and festivals, 1945-94. One-woman art shows include Honolulu Cmty. Theatre, 1980, 84, First United Meth. Ch., 1980; group shows with Honolulu Artists, others; permanent collections René Malmezac, Tahiti; contbr. articles to profl. jours. Cons. to com. on edn. Hawaii Gov.'s Commn. on Status of Women, 1965; English lang. tutor Hawaii Literacy, Inc., Honolulu, 1978-95. Recipient Alumni Achievement award, Huntingdon Coll. Alumnae Assn., 1998. Mem. Music Educators Nat. Conf. (1st v.p. Hawaii 1969-70), Am. Choral Dirs. Assn. (Hawaii chmn. 1963-66), Nat. Assn. Tchrs. Singing, Altrusa (pres. Gainesville 1960-61, past pres. Honolulu), Delta Kappa Gamma (pres. Hawaii Theta chpt. 1963-64, past state music chmn., named one of Makers of Destiny Hawaiian Style 2002.). Methodist. Avocation: painting. Home: 8015 NW 28th Pl Apt B210 Gainesville FL 32606-8607

PAUL, ROCHELLE CAROLE, special education educator; b. East Liverpool, Ohio, July 8, 1951; d. Homer Neil and Dolores Elizabeth (Seiler) P. BS, Clarion State Coll., 1973; MS, Clarion U., 1987; MDiv, Trinity Luth. Sem., Columbus, Ohio, 1992. Cert. tchr., Pa., Ohio. Spl. edn. tchr. Dorchester County Bd. Edn., Cambridge, Md., 1973-78, Forest Area Sch. Dist., Tionesta, Pa., 1979-88; edn. coord. juvenile-probate divsn. Common Pleas Ct. of Licking County, Newark, Ohio, 1993-95; instr. Ctrl. Ohio Tech. Coll., Newark, 1994—; prevention specialist Ctr. Alternative Resources, Newark, 1996-98; program dir. early childhood devel. Ctrl. Ohio Tech. Coll., Newark, 1999-2000; exec. dir. Literacy Network Ctrl. Ohio, 2000—; intervention specialist Treca Digital Acad., 2002—. Rep. Pres.'s adv. bd. Trinity Luth. Sem., 1991-92; active St. Paul's Evang. Luth. Ch., Newark, Ohio; mem. head start cmty. assessment com., LEADS, 1999—, trustee, 2000—, policy coun. chair head start, 2000-2003, chair bd. trustees, 2004—. Mem. ASCD, AAUW, Coun. Exceptional Children (chpt. pres. 1972-73, 98—), Nat. Assn. Edn. of Young Children, Alcohol and Drug Abuse Prevention Assn. Ohio, Ohio Coalition of Assoc. Degree Early Childhood Programs. Avocations: tai chi, reading, writing, vocal and instrumental music, travel. Home: 164 Newton Ave Newark OH 43055-4758 E-mail: rcpaulteacher@netscape.net, rcpaul@alink.com.

PAUL, SALLY JONES, secondary school educator, writer; d. Hugh Parker and Sally George Jones; m. Donald Allan Ferraiuolo, Jan. 4, 2005; children: David Walter children: Clifford Hayden. BA, U. Calif., Davis, 1965. Life tchg. credential Calif., nat. bd. cert. adolescent, early adult visual art. Art dept. chair Winters Mid. Sch., Calif., 1970—89, Winters Joint Unified Sch. Dist., 1989—2005. Author 12 art and design books. Named Educator of Yr., Yolo County Office of Edn., 1998. Mem.: Nat. Art Edn. Assn., Calif. Art Edn. Assn. (statewide sec. 2006—, Outstanding Visual Arts Educator 1996—97). Achievements include design of art to wear garment, Concord Fabrics, Fairfield Batting, international fashion show. Home: 30215 The Horseshoe Winters CA 95694

PAUL, SINDY MICHELLE, preventive medicine physician; b. Phila., Feb. 13, 1957; d. Gerson Stanly and Phyllis (Ostrum) P.; m. Oren Leonard Friedman, Mar. 8, 1986; children: Melissa, Rebecca. AB in Biology with honors, magna cum laude, Bryn Mawr (Pa.) Coll., 1979; MD with honors, Temple U., 1983; MPH, NJ Grad. Program Pub. Health, Piscataway, 1993. Diplomate Am. Bd. Gen. Preventive Medicine and Pub. Health. Med. dir. NJ Dept. Health and Sr. Svcs., Trenton, 1988-96, residency program dir., 1995—, clin. cons. state labs., 1995—, med. dir., 1996—; asst. clin. prof. U. Medicine and Dentistry NJ, Piscataway, 1995—. Mem. exec. com. preventive medicine, pub. health sect. Coll. Physicians of Phila., 1995-2001, exec. com. n.e. regional infection control course N.J. chpts. APIC, 1989—; pres. N.J. Bd. Med. Examiners, 2006. Editor and co-author: (books) Infection Control for Long Term Care Facilities, 1992, HIV/AIDS, 1997; contbr. 200 chpts., abstracts and articles to profl. jours.; mem. editl. adv. bd. (jour.) Infection Control and Hosp. Epidemiology, 1985—, NJ Medicine, Nursing Spectrum, 2000, Jour. Pediat. Infectious Diseases. Divsn. rep. United Way Campaign, Trenton, 1988-89. Grantee Ctrs. for Disease Control and Prevention, Atlanta, 1994-98; recipient Disting. Alumnae award U. Medicine and Dentistry NJ. Mem. Am. Assn. Pub. Health Physicians (exec. com.), Am. Coll. Prevention Medicine (chair joint coun. of residency program dirs., pub. health regent 2006-2008), Assn. for Profls. in Infection Control and Epidemiology, N.J. Pub. Health Assn. (pres.-elect, v.p. 1996-2000, mem. exec. bd., pres. 2001-2003, Ezra Mundy Hunt award, Pres. award for TB, Pres. award for pub. health), Soc. Healthcare Epidemiology Am. (working group 1995—), Ctrs. for Disease Control and Prevention (5 working groups, 1996—), Acad. Medicine NJ (Med. Educator of Yr.). Office: NJ Dept Health and Sr Svcs 50 E State St Ste 4 Trenton NJ 08608-1715 Office Phone: 609-984-6191. Business E-Mail: sindy.paul@doh.state.nj.us.

PAUL, YVONNE C., retired elementary school educator; b. Chgo., July 9, 1934; d. Reuben Douglas Adams and Gladys Winters Bacot; m. William Ralph Paul, Nov. 13, 1962; adopted children: Vanessa, Jonathan. BA, U. Ill., Chgo., 1956; MA in Counseling, San Francisco State U., 1976, MA in Adminstrn., 1983. Classroom tchr. Chgo. Pub. Schs., 1956-59; sch. tchr. Dep. Schs. Europe, Eritrea, East Africa, 1959-60, Stuttgart/Ludwigsburg, Germany, 1960-62; dir. pre-sch. AFB, Killeen, Tex., 1962-63; classroom tchr. Jericho (N.Y.) Sch. Dist., 1964-65; sch. tchr. middle grades Balt. County Schs., Towson, Md., 1965-69; vice prin., tchr. Pittsburg (Calif.) Unified Sch. Dist., 1969-99; ret., 1999. Resource mgr., reading and sci. leadership; classroom tchr., lead math., leader Pittsburg Unified Sch. Dist., 1969-99. Cadet leader Girl Scouts Am., Killeen, 1962; hosp. vol. Killeen Gen. Hosp., 1963; Parent's Booster Club. Technol. Edn. Contra Costa Sch. grantee Alameda/Contra Costa Office Edn., Hayward, Calif., 1985; grant writer awards Technol. Edn. Contra Costa. Mem. No. Calif. Math. Assn., Assn. Calif. Sch. Adminstrs., Artist Guild, Phi Delta Kappa. Roman Catholic. Avocations: writing for publication, reading, gardening, interior design, children's science theater. Home: 488 Lakeview Dr Brentwood CA 94513-5070

PAULEY, BARBARA ANNE, author, educator; b. Nashville, Jan. 12, 1925; d. William Moncrief and Lucile Elizabeth (Dies) Cotton; m. Robert Reinhold Pauley, June 22, 1946; children— Lucinda T., Nicholas Andrew, Robert Reinhold, John Adams. Student Wellesley Coll., 1942. Editorial asst. Ideal Pub. Co., N.Y.C., 1965-70; founder, dir. North Shore Writers' Assn., Wenham, Mass., 1975. Author: (novels) Blook Kin, 1972; Voices Long Hushed, 1976. Pres., Friends of the Library, Wenham, 1979-81. Mem. Mystery Writers Am. Republican. Methodist. Club: Myopia Hunt. Avocation: tennis. Home: 1120 Durham Rd Madison CT 06443

PAULEY, ELSA P., psychologist, educator; b. Memphis, Oct. 28, 1944; d. Arne Eric Pottala and Caroline Arbogast Foust; m. Robert V. Pauley, June 10, 1944 (div. June 1979); children: Matthew V., Tasha; m. Dale A. Johnston, Aug. 14, 1993. Student, U. Calif., Santa Barbara, 1964-65; AB in History, Smith Coll., 1966; MS in Counseling Psychology, U. So. Calif., 1980, PhD in Counseling Psychology, 1983. Lic. psychologist Calif., marriage family therapist Calif. Pvt. practice psychology, L.A., 1981—; ednl. tng. prin. Santa Monica, Calif., 1999—. Worker's compensation intake/report preparation staff Bloch Clinic, L.A., 1981; intern Gateway Hosp., L.A., 1981—83; cons., prin. Pauley, Parks & Brown, L.A., 1983—90; cons., prin. rschr. St. Anne's Maternity Home, L.A., 1984—85; adj. prof. statis. analysis and rsch. design Antioch U., L.A., 1987, U. So. Calif., L.A., 1987—88, U. San Francisco, 1988—90; presenter in field. Deacon Brentwood Presbyn. Ch., 1989—92. Mem.: APA (cert. proficiency in the treatment of alcohol and other psychoactive substance use disorders), Smith Coll. Alumnae Assn., L.A. Smith Coll. Club (pres. 1990, 1966 class sec. 2001—06, 1966 class pres. 2006—). Democrat.

PAULEY, JANE, newscaster, journalist; b. Indpls., Oct. 31, 1950; m. Gary Trudeau; 3 children. BA in Polit. Sci. Ind. U., 1971; D of Journalism (hon.), DePauw U., 1978. Reporter Sta. WISH-TV, Indpls., 1972—75; co-anchor WMAQ-TV News, Chgo., 1975—76, The Today Show, NBC, N.Y.C., 1976—90; from co-anchor to corr. NBC News, N.Y.C., 1976—; prin. writer, reporter NBC Nightly News, 1980—82, substitute anchor, 1990—2003; co-anchor Early Today, NBC, 1982—83; prin. corr. Real Life With Jane Pauley, NBC, 1991; co-anchor Dateline NBC, N.Y.C., 1992—99, prin. anchor, 1999—2003; anchor Time & Again MSNBC, 1999—2003; host The Jane Pauley Show, 2004—05. Author: Skywriting: A Life Out of the Blue, 2004 (Publishers Weekly Bestseller). Mem. adv. bd. Childrens Health Fund, Internat. Coun. Freedom From Hunger; bd. dirs. Pub. Edn. Needs Civic Involvement in Learning. Named Broadcaster of Yr., Internat. Radio and TV Soc., 1986, Best in Bus., Washington Journalism Rev., 1990; named to Broadcasting and Cable Hall of Fame; recipient Emmy award, Edward R. Murrow award, Gabriel award, Nancy Susan Reynolds award, Maggie award, Humanitas award, Commendation award, Am. Women in Radio and TV, Gracie Allen award, Clarion award, Assn. for Women in Comm., Wilbur award, Religious Pub. Rels. Coun., Salute to Excellence award, Nat. Assn. Black Journalists, Leonard Zeidenberg First Amendment award, Radio TV News Dirs. Found., Paul White award, NTNDA. Fellow: Soc. for Profl. Journalists (hon. chair Jane Pauley task force on mass comm. edn.).

PAULEY, SHIRLEY STEWART, religious organization executive; b. Boston, Sept. 13, 1938; d. Charles Norris and Nellie Consuelo (Yorke) Stewart; m. Edward Haven Pauley, May 29, 1964; children: David Stewart, Deborah Jeanne. BA, Gordon Coll., 1960; postgrad., Ariz. State U., 1961, Boston U., 1963. Sec./receptionist Atwell Co., Boston, summer 1956; sec., typist Kelley Girl, Boston, 1956-60; asst. office mgr. Radiator Chem. Corp., Scottsdale, Ariz., 1960-62; sec., clerical worker GM, Westwood, Mass., 1962-64; v.p. Truth Alive Ministries, Dallas, 1995—. Spkr. At Large, Boston, 1956-60; Sunday sch. tchr. Blaney Meml. Bapt. Ch., Boston, 1956-60; choir dir. Sherwood Bapt. Ch., Phoenix, 1961-62, co-youth dir., 1961; co-youth dir. Blaney Meml. Ch., Boston, 1964-66; messenger Bapt. Gen. Conv. Tex., Ft. Worth, 1996; leader bible study Prestonwood Bapt. Ch., Dallas, 2006—; v.p. Truth Alive Ministries, 1996—. Republican. Avocations: photography, reading, music. Office: Truth Alive Ministries PO Box 794945 Dallas TX 75379-4945

PAULIN, AMY RUTH, civic activist, consultant; b. Bklyn., Nov. 29, 1955; d. Ben and Alice Lois (Roth) P.; m. Ira Schuman, May 25, 1980; children: Beth, Sarah, Joseph. BA, SUNY, Albany, 1977, MA, 1978, postgrad., 1979—. Instr. SUNY, Albany, 1978, Queens (N.Y.) House of Detention, 1979; fundraiser United Jewish Appeal Fedn., N.Y.C., 1979-83; dir. devel. Altro Health & Rehab., Bronx, N.Y., 1983-86; fundraising cons. N.Y.C., 1986-88; pres. LWV, Scarsdale, N.Y., 1990-92, Westchester, N.Y., 1992-95; trustee Scarsdale (N.Y.) Village, 1995-99; exec. dir. My Sisters' Place, 1999—. Mem. adv. coun. Family Ct.; co-chair woman Westchester Womens Agenda, Westchester Dept. Social Svcs.; mem. adv. com. Fund for Women & Girls; bd. dirs. Mid. Sch. PTA., 1995-97, Westchester Coalition for Legal Abortion, Scarsdale Open Soc. Assn., 1992-95, United Jewish Appeal Fedn. Scarsdale Women's Campaign; v.p. Westchester Children's Assn.; troop leader Girl Scouts U.S., 1992-96; mem. Town Club Edn. Com., 1983-89; mem. Scarsdale Bowl com., 1992-95, chair, 1994-95; mem. Scarsdale Japanese Festival, 1992-93; mem. Westchester Women's Equality Day, 1987-92; mem. nominating com. Heathcote Neighborhood Assn., 1991-92; bd. advisors Westchester County Found., 1994—; mem. Scarsdale Village Youth Bd., 1992-95; mem. U.S. legislators task force on families at risk Westchester County Bd., 1994—; mem. Updating Voting Equipment Com., 1994; mem. Tobacco Free Westchester, 1993-95, chair 1995—; co-chair Parent Tchr. Coun. Sch. Budget Study, 1991-94; planning chair Kids Base Bd., 1992-95, dir. 1992-94chair parking and traffic subcom. Village Downtown Devel. Com., 1994-95; mem. Westchester Commn. Campaign Fin. Reform, Westchester Commn. Child Abuse, 1996-87; exec. com. Westchester Mcpl. Offcls. Assn., 1996-97; adv. com. Jr. League, 1996-99. Named Westchester County Woman of Yr., 1995, Bridge Fund award, 1998, Women's Health NNetwork Ann. award, 1999. Mem. LWV (bd. dirs. women and children's issues Westchester chpt., dir. social policy N.Y. state), State Communities Aid Assn. (econ. securities com.), N.Y. State Pub. Health Assn. (bd. dirs. Lower Hudson Valley chpt.), N.Y. State Coalition Choice, New Yorkers Against Gun Violence (bd. dirs.). Avocations: swimming, dance. Home: 12 Burgess Rd Scarsdale NY 10583-4410

PAULOSE, RACHEL, prosecutor; Grad., U. Minn. Litigator Dorsey & Whitney; US atty. dist. Minn. US Dept. Justice, 2006—. Bd. mem. Nat. Asian-Am. Bar Assn. Office: US Attys Office 600 US Courthouse 300 S Fourth St Minneapolis MN 55415*

PAULSEN, MARSHA E., counselor; b. Monticello, Ill., Aug. 25, 1951; m. Paul W. Paulsen, July 23, 1977; children: Neil, Derek, Kyle. BS, So. Ill. U., 1973; MA, Murray State U., 1980. Tchr. Hardin County HS, Elizabethtown, Ill., 1973—83; counselor Zion-Benton Twp. HS, Zion, Ill., 1991—. Mem.: ACA, Lake County Counseling Assn., Ill. Counseling Assn. Office: Zion-Benton Twp HS One Z-B Way Zion IL 60099 Business E-Mail: paulsenm@zbths.org.

PAULSEN, RUTH ANN, French and Spanish language educator; b. Cosby, Mo., Dec. 9, 1940; d. Ernest Raymond and Ollie Hasque (Clouse) Thornton; m. Reuben Ray Paulsen, June 15, 1962 (div. 1982); children: Terrill Kent, Jeffrey Alan. AA, St. Joseph (Mo.) Jr. Coll., 1960; BS in Edn., N.W. Mo. State U., 1962; MA, Baker U., 1985; postgrad., U. de Dijon, France, 1982, U. de l'Ouest, 1988, 92. Cert. tchr. French and Spanish 7-12. Tchr. French, Spanish Highland Park High Sch., Topeka, 1962-68, Cen. N. Jr. High Sch., Kansas City, Mo., 1968-70; adult edn. instr. French Johnson County Community Coll., Overland Park, Kans., 1971-73; tchr. French, Spanish Cen. S. Jr. High Sch., Kansas City, 1974-77; tchr. French Ctr. Sr. HS, Kansas City, 1977—95; chair fgn. lang. dept. Ctrl. Sr. HS, Kansas City, 1980—86, 1993—95; tchr. French and Spanish Blue Valley North HS, Overland Park, Kans., 1996—2001. Lectr. French, U. Mo., Kansas City, 1987-95; life mem. Mo. PTA. Author, photographer: (slide and video units with script) France at a Glance, 1989; co-editor: (book) Introduction to Language, 1976. Cub scout den mother Boy Scouts Am., 1969-74; sec. Brookridge Homes Assn., 1980-84. Grantee NDEA, 1964, 65, Rockefeller Found., Angers, France, 1988; Alliance Française scholar, Paris, 1983. Mem. NEA (life), NOW, Am. Coun. Teaching Fgn. Langs., Am. Assn. Tchrs. French, Alliance Française (bd. dirs. 1991—, scholar Paris 1983), Fgn. Lang. Assn. Mo., Kans. Fgn. Lang. Assn. (sec. 1989—), Mo. Edn. Assn., Cen. Edn. Assn. (pres. 1988-89, chief negotiator 1989-90), Planned Parenthood, Phi Theta Kappa, Alpha Delta Kappa. Democrat. Baptist. Avocations: photography, travel. Home: 10932 Rosehill Rd Overland Park KS 66210-1178 E-mail: rpaulsen@aol.com.

PAULSEN, VIVIAN, editor; b. Salt Lake City, May 10, 1942; d. Paul Herman and Martha Oline (Blattmann) P. BA, Brigham Young U., 1964, postgrad., 1965, U. Grenoble, France, 1966. Cert. tchr., Utah. Tchr. French Granite Sch. Dist., Salt Lake City, 1966-67; assoc. editor New Era mag., Salt Lake City, 1970-82; mng. editor Friend mag., Salt Lake City, 1982—. Am. Field Service scholar, 1959; grad. fellow Brigham Young U., 1964-66 Republican. Mem. Ch. of Jesus Christ of Latter-day Saints Office: The Friend 50 E North Temple # F23 Salt Lake City UT 84150-0002

PAULSON, GWEN O. GAMPEL, government relations consultant, life and leadership coach; b. Detroit, Mar. 16, 1945; d. Maurice V. and Lilyan Victor; div.; children: Jill Susan, Mindy Beth; m. Jerome A. Paulson, July 2, 1989. BA, Mich. State U., 1966; MA, Wayne State U., 1974; postgrad., U. Mich., 1981; cert. in Leadership Coaching, Georgetown U., 2005. Lectr. Oakland U., Mich., 1979—80, U. Mich., Ann Arbor, 1981; legis. asst. U.S. Rep. Pete Stark, Washington, 1982—85; mem. profl. staff, ways and means health subcom. U.S. Ho. of Reps., Washington, 1985—89; v.p. for health Capitol Assocs., Washington, 1989—90; pres. Congl. Cons., Washington, 1990—2005, Coaching and Cons. LLC, 2005—. Author: Women and the Structure of Society, 1984. Edward S. Beck fellow U. Mich., Ann Arbor, 1978-79; Rackham Dissertation grant U. Mich., Ann Arbor, 1980. Mem. Coun. for Excellence Govt., Bus. and Profl. Women, Fedn. Am. (co-chair 1999-2001), Internat. Coaching Fedn., Phi Alpha Theta, Tau Sigma Avocations: collecting contemporary glass, travel, history, politics, reading. Office: Coaching and Consulting LLC 1113 N Howard St Alexandria VA 22304-1627 Office Phone: 703-461-7683. Personal E-mail: gwencc@comcast.net.

PAULSON, PATRICIA C., science educator; d. Richard and Dorothy Caldwell; m. Craig Paulson, June 5, 1971; children: Doug, Nels, Peter, David. PhD, Capella U., Mpls., 2005. Cert. tchr. Minn., 1972. Curriculum facilitator Anoka Hennepin Sch. Dist., Coon Rapids, Minn., 1994—99; prof. Bethel U., St. Paul, 1999—. Tchr. Anoka Hennepin Sch. Dist., 1989—99. Grantee Super Saturday Sci. for Wet Cement Kids, 3M, 1999—2003, Nature Trail Devel., Bethel Alumni, 2003. Mem.: ASTE, NARST, ASCD, NSTA. Lutheran. Avocations: reading, golf, fishing. Office: Bethel Univ 3900 Bethel Dr Saint Paul MN 55112 Office Phone: 651-638-6454. Office Fax: 651-638-6001. Business E-Mail: patricia-paulson@bethel.edu.

PAULSON, SONDRA LEE, music educator; b. Jersey City, Mar. 05; d. Robert Luhrs and Edna Agnes Knowsley, Warren Knowsley (Stepfather) and Amanda Troutman (Stepmother); m. Mark Edward Paulson, Aug. 8, 1987; children: Marshall Redford, Elliott Graham, Heidi Joy. BA, Montclair State U., 1988; postgrad., Gratz Coll., 2002—. Cert. music tchr. NJ. Music tchr. Winfield Pub. Sch., Winfield Park, NJ, 1988—92, Grandview Sch., North Caldwell, NJ, 1992—93, Essex Fells (NJ) Sch., 1993—94, Randolph (NJ) Mid. Sch., 1994—98, Darcy Sch., Livingston, NJ, 1998—99, Ridgedale Mid. Sch., Florham Park, NJ, 2000—. Singer Life Christian Ch., West Orange, NJ, 2000—, mem. planning and design team, 2003—04. Innovation grantee, PTA, 2002, 2004, Florham Pk. Bd. Edn., 2004. Mem.: Music Educators Nat. Conf. Independent. Avocations: painting, gardening, cooking, baking, travel. Office: Ridgedale Mid Sch 71 Ridgedale Ave Florham Park NJ 07932 Office Phone: 973-822-3855. Personal E-mail: sondra.paulson@fpks.org.

PAULSON-CRAWFORD, CAROL, conservator, educator; b. Ashland, Ohio, Jan. 15, 1961; d. Donald Howard Paulson and Mary Katherine (Dafoe) Paulson Harris; m. Craig Alan Crawford, May 6, 1995; 1 child, Cole Monroe. BFA, Ohio State U., 1984; MA, U. Wis., 1987, MFA, 1989. Book and paper conservator Wis. Hist. Soc., Madison, 1987-91; conservator Libr. of Congress, Washington, 1992-99; book and paper conservator S.C. Dept. Archives and History, Columbia, 1999-2000; lab. dir., sr. conservator U. S.C., State Park, 2000—02; book and paper conservator Crawford Conservation Inc., 2002—. Author, editor: Boxes for the Protection of Books, 1994; also articles; exhibited at Rockville (Md.) Manson, 1996. Mem. Am. Inst. for Conservation (profl. assoc.), Guild Book Workers, Washington Conservation Guild. Avocations: biking, gardening. Home and Office: 2305 Cardington Dr Columbia SC 29209-3209 E-mail: craigcarolc@aol.com.

PAULSTON, CHRISTINA BRATT, linguistics educator; b. Stockholm, Dec. 30, 1932; arrived in US, 1951; d. Lennart and Elsa Bratt; m. Rolland G. Paulston, July 26, 1963; children: Christopher-Rolland, Ian Rollandsson. BA, Carleton Coll., 1953; MA in English and Comparative Lit., U. Minn., 1955; Ed.D., Columbia U., 1966. Cert. tchr., Minn. Tchr. Clara City and Pine Island High Schs., Minn., 1955-60, Am. Sch. of Tangier, Morocco, 1960-62, Katrineholm Allmanna LarovERk, Katrineholm, Sweden, 1962-63, East Asian Library, Columbia U., N.Y.C., 1963-64; asst. instr. Tchrs. Coll., Columbia U., 1964-66; instr. U. Punjab, Chandigarh, India, summer 1966, Pontificia Universidad Catolica Del Peru, Lima, 1966-67; cons. Instituto Linguistico de Verano, Lima, 1967-68; asst. prof. linguistics U. Pitts., 1969-75, prof., 1975-99, prof. emerita, tchg. pro bono, 1999—, asst. dir. English Lang. Inst., 1969-70, dir. English Lang. Inst., 1970-97, acting dir. Lang. Acquistion Inst., fall 1971, acting chmn. dept. gen. linguistics, 1974-75, chmn., 1975-89. Apptd. internat. advisor in sociolinguistics to Summer Inst. of Linguistics, 1997. Author numerous books and articles on linguistics. Recipient research award Am. Ednl. Research Assn., 1980; Fulbright-Hays grantee, Uruguay, 1985. Mem. Assn. Tchrs. English to Speakers of Other Langs. (2d v.p., conv., chmn. 1972, exec. com. 1972-75, rsch. com. 1973-75, 78-80, chmn. 1973-75, 1st v.p. 1975, pres. 1976), Linguistics Soc. Am. (com. linguistics and pub. interest 1973-77), Internat. Assn. Tchrs. of English as a Fgn. Lang., Am. Coun. on Tchg. of Fgn. Langs., MLA (exec. com. lang. and soc. 1975-76), Ctr.

Applied Linguistics (trustee 1976-81, exec. com. 1980, publs. com. 1981, rsch. com. 1981). Democrat. Episcopalian. Office: U Pitts Linguistics Pittsburgh PA 15260 Office Phone: 412-624-5900.

PAULY, JENNIFER L., director, graphics designer; d. Ronald R. and Clarice M. Pauly. BS in Mass Comm., Advt., St. Cloud State U., 1992; attending, RIT. Chair dept.-comml. art Fla. Met. U., Tampa, 1996—2002; program mgr. design studies S.W. Fla. Coll., Tampa, 2002—06; dept. chair Internat. Acad. Design & Technology, 2006—. Graphic designer, owner JP Creations, Brandon, Fla., 1996—; sch. adv. Ad Illusions. Adj. faculty quarter Fla. Met. U., 1997; catalog designer Lowry Pk. Zoo Ednl. Dept., Tampa, 2002—03; vol. designer Am. Heart Assn., St. Petersburg, Fla., 2003. Scholar, Gen. Mills, 1987-1990. Mem.: Nat. Assn. Photoshop Profls. (assoc.), Am. Advt. Fedn. (assoc.), Tampa Bay Advt. Fedn. (assoc.), Ad 2 Tampa Bay (assoc.), Jr. League Tampa (assoc.), Creative Club Tampa Bay (assoc.; membership chair 1996—2000). Office: International Acad Design & Technology 5104 Eisenbhower Blvd Tampa FL 33634

PAULY, REBECCA MEHL, foreign languages educator; b. Ashland, Ohio, Aug. 30, 1942; d. Robert T. and Blanche Virginia (Scott) Mehl; m. Thomas H. Pauly, July 15, 1967 (div. Sept. 1981); 1 child, Jeffrey Thomas; m. Glenn P. Bentley, Mar. 5, 1985. BA cum laude, Smith Coll., Northampton, Mass., 1963; MA in French, U. Calif., Berkeley, 1966; D Modern Langs., Middlebury Coll., 1984. With dir.'s office St. Francis Hotel, San Francisco, 1963-64; with Dillingham Corp., San Francisco, 1964-65; head French dept. Castilleja Sch., Palo Alto, Calif., 1966-67; with French dept. Anna Head Sch., Oakland, Calif., 1967-70, Tower Hill Sch., Wilmington, Del., 1982; with edn. div. Winterthur (Del.) Mus., 1972-81; instr. French and Italian U. Del., Newark, 1982-84, asst. prof. French and Italian, 1984-87, West Chester (Pa.) U., 1987-92, assoc. prof. French and Italian, 1992—96, prof., 1996—. Mem. editl. bd. Lit./Film Quar. Salisbury, Md., 1990—, Coll. Lit., West Chester, 1990—; author: (videos) La Civilisation Francophone, 2001, L'Italia Alfresco, 2002; (books) The Transparent Illusion, 1993, 2003, Le Berceau et la Bibliothèque, 1989; contbr. articles to profl. jours. Regional coord. Am. Cancer Soc., Chester County, 1975-77. Mem. Am. Assn. Tchrs. French, Am. Assn. Tchrs. Italian, Lit./Film Assn. (nat. v.p. 1989-91, pres. 1995-97), Smith Coll. Club of Del., Am. Soc. Eighteenth-Century Studies. Avocations: sports, photography, design. Office: West Chester U Dept Fgn Lang 109 Main Hl West Chester PA 19383-0001

PAVE, ANGELA, newscaster; b. Columbus, Ohio; B, Capital U., 1977. News dir., reporter Sta. WCLT, Newark, Ohio; reporter Sta. WCMH-TV, Columbus, anchor; cmty. rels. specialist Sta. WBNS-TV, anchor, 1993—. Recipient Outstanding Alumni award, Capital U., Martin Luther King Jr. Humanitarian award, Columbus Edn. Assn., Pi Lamba Educators award, Wink Hess Journalism award, 1983, Golden Rule award, Columbus Sch. Dist., Govs. award Journalism and Cmty. Svc., 1992, Women Acheivement award, WYCA Ctrl. Ohio, 1994. Office: WBNS-TV 770 Twin Rivers Dr Columbus OH 43215

PAVELICH, JUDITH, secondary school educator; b. Bklyn., July 10, 1924; d. Abraham and Anna (Chaikin) Goldstein; m. Martin Pavelich, Dec. 5, 1948; children: Alyce, Susan, Sharon. BA, Moravian Coll., 1954; MA, Lehigh U., 1961; postgrad., Pa. State U., Mainland Inst., Marywood Coll. Tchr. spl. edn., Bethlehem, Pa., 1961—62; counselor Northampton Area Jr. H.S., Pa., 1962—. Coord., sec. Big Bros. and Sisters Northampton Area; mem. cataract support group, treas. Israel Cancer Rsch. Fund; bd. dirs. Lehigh Social Svc. Exch.; vol. Lehigh Valley Ecumenical Soup Kitchen; vol. coord. Reibman for Congress Campaign, Reibman for Judge Campaign; campaign coord. Alan Black for Judge; aide leisure group B'rith Sholom Synagogue; mem. friendship cir. Jewish Cmty. Ctr. With WAVES USNR, 1943—48. Mem.: NEA, Am. Sch. Assn., Pa. Sch. Counselors Assn. (unit rep.), Lehigh Valley Guidance Assn. (sec.), Pa. Educators Assn., Northampton Area Educators Assn., Pa. Pers. and Guidance Assn., Am. Pers. and Guidance Assn. Home: 2235 W Highland St Allentown PA 18104-3631

PAVIET-HARTMANN, PATRICIA, chemist, researcher; b. Cormeilles, France, June 8, 1964; came to U.S., 1997; d. Roland Jean and Josette Juliette (Camus) Paviet; m. Thomas Hartmann, Apr. 27, 1996; 1 child, Josephine Caroline. BS, U. Nice, France, 1986, MS, 1988; PhD Chemistry, U. Paris XI, 1992. Rsch. scientist Commissariat a l'Energie Atomique, Cadarache, France, 1990—92; postdoctoral fellow Lawrence Livermore Nat. Lab., Calif., 1992—93; mem. staff Forschungszentrum, Karlsruhe, Germany, 1993—97, Los Alamos Nat. Lab., 1997—2003, project leader in actinide chemistry, 2000—03; sr. scientist adv. MOX Project, Areva NP, Inc., Aiken, SC, 2003; with Savannah River Site, Aiken, 2006—. Contbr. articles to profl. jours.; patentee in field. Mem. Am. Chem. Soc., Am. Nuclear Soc. Roman Catholic. Avocations: painting, piano, languages (french, english, german, italian, spanish). Home: 134 Steeple Ridge Aiken SC 29803 Office: Savannah River Site PO Box 7097 Bldg 730-2B Aiken SC 29804-7097 Office Phone: 803-502-1889. Business E-Mail: Patricia.PavietHartmann@areva.com.

PAVLAKOS, ELLEN TSATIRI, sculptor; b. Athens, May 25, 1936; d. Andrew and Katherine (Fliskanopoulou) Tsatiri; m. Andrew George Pavlakos, Nov. 2, 1952; children: James, John Andrew. Student, Arsakeion, Athens, 1952, Norton Sch. Art, West Palm Beach, Fla., 1975-79, Nat. Acad. Design, N.Y.C., 1980-81. Solo shows include Brevard Art Mus., 1981, Hess Galleries, Allentown, Pa., 1983, Cultural Ctr. Athens, 1990, 5th Ave. Art Gallery, Melbourne, Fla., 1994, 98; group shows include Le Salon des Nations, Paris, 1984, Nat. Exhbn. of Contemporary Realism in Art, Springfield, Mass., 1984, Springville Mus. Art, Utah, 1985, Capitol Gallery, Fla. Dept. Cultural Affairs, Tallahassee, 1988, Outstanding Am. Women Artists Invitational, Sarasota, 1993, Chamber of fine Arts and Min. of Edn. and Civilization Symposium, Nicosia, Cyprus, 1994, Mus. of Art and Sci., Melbourne, 1996, Appleton Mus. Art, Ocala, Fla., 1997, Sculpture '97, Thessaloniki, Greece, 1997, Dunedin (Fla.) Fine Arts Ctr., 1998, Orlando City Hall Gallery, 1998, 621 Gallary, Tallahassee, Fla., 1999, Lee County Alliance of the Arts, Fort Myers, Fla., 1999, La. State U., Shreveport, 2000, Mt. Dora (Fla.) Art Ctr., 2000, U. Fla. Arts Ctr., Gainesville, 2001, DeLand (Fla.) Mus. Art, 2001, Oceola Art Ctr., Kissimmee, 2002, Visual Arts Ctr. of NW Fla., Panama City, Fla., 2002, Brevard Mus. of Arts and Sci., Melbourne, Fla., 2002, Gadsen Arts Ctr., Lake Wales, Fla., 2004, Atlantic Ctr. for the Arts at Harris, 2004, Seminol Com. Coll., Sanford, Fla., 2004, Lake Wales Art Ctr., Fla., 2004, South Fla. Coll. Mus. Art, Avon Park, 2005, Albany Mus., Ga., 2006, Turner Ctr. Arts, Valdosta, Ga., 2006; bronze sculpture commd. The Harry T. Moore Monument, Titusville Social Svcs. Ctr., 1985, wall relief Knowledge, Brevard Libr., 1993, bronze sculpture Mother Earth, Penakotheke, Athens, 1990, painting Interlude, Penakotheke, Hydrostone sculpture The Flame Keeper, Kennedy Space Ctr., Fla., 1992, Stephen Girard relief Girard Coll., Phila., 1999, Welcoming Christ, bronze sculpture, Holy Name of Jesus CH., Fla., 2004. Recipient best of Show award Brevard Art Mus., 1980; grantee Brevard County Art in Pub. Places, 1990, 93. Mem. Acad. Artists Assn., Medalic Sculpture Assn., Chamber of Visual Arts in Greece, Ten Women in Art. Greek Orthodox. Avocations: art collecting, gardening. Studio: 331 Coral Way W Indialantic FL 32903-4401 Office Phone: 321-773-5046. Personal E-mail: pavlakosstudio@cfl.rr.com.

PAVLEY, FRAN J., state representative; b. LA, Nov. 11, 1948; m. Andy Pavley; children: Jennifer, David. BA, Calif. State U., Fresno, 1970; MA, Calif. State U., 1985. Cert. tchr. Calif. Tchr., 28 yrs.; mem. Calif. Assembly, 2000—. Founder Agoura Hills Disaster Response Team, 1987; mem. adv. com. Santa Monica Mountains Conservancy, 1990—; mem. Coastal Commn., State of Calif., 1995—2000; mem. coun., mayor Agoura Hills, Calif., 1982—97. Democrat. Office: PO Box 942849 Rm 3120 Sacramento CA 95814 Address: 6355 Topanga Canyon Blvd Ste 205 Woodland Hills CA 91367-2108 Office Phone: 916-319-2041.

PAVLICK, PAMELA KAY, nurse, consultant; b. Topeka, Aug. 16, 1944; d. Cy Pavlick and June Lucille Dull. Diploma in nursing, St. Luke's Hosp., Kansas City, Mo., 1966; BA in Psychology magna cum laude, U. North Fla., 1982, MS in Health Adminstrn. summa cum laude, 1987. RN, Mo., Ill., Fla.; cert. ins. rehab. specialist; lic. rehab. providor, Fla., Ga. Clin. instr. St. Luke's Hosp., Kansas City, 1966—70; instr. lic. practical nursing Springfield (Ill.) Sch. Bd., 1970—72; nursing supr. Jacksonville Beach (Fla.) Hosp., 1972—74; pub. health nurse State of Fla., Ocala, 1974—76; dir. nursing Upjohn Health Care, Jacksonville, Fla., 1976—77, mem. adv. com.; med. rep. Travelers Ins. Co., Jacksonville, 1977—84; rehab. cons. Aetna Life & Casualty, Jacksonville, 1985—, rep. nurse cons. adv. coun., 1988—90. Mem. ANA., Am. Assn. Rehab. Nurses, Nat. Assn. Rehab. Providers, Phi Kappa Phi. Republican. Episcopalian. Avocation: boating. Home: 14023 Tontine Rd Jacksonville FL 32225-2025 Office: Aetna Life & Casualty PO Box 2200 Jacksonville FL 32203-2200 E-mail: pampavlick@peoplepc.com.

PAVLISH, CATHERINE ANN, language educator, writer; d. Theodore Joseph and Dorothy Mae Pavlish; m. Gregory A. Carpenter, July 22, 1991; children: Skylar Pavlish Carpenter, Aurora Pavlish Carpenter. BA, Calif. State U., Long Beach, 1985, MA, 1989; PhD, U. North Dakota, Grand Forks, 1998. Cert. secondary tchg. Calif. State U. Long Beach, 1986. Academic advisor, supr. Calif. State U., Long Beach, 1987—92; instr. English Palomar C.C., Vista, Calif., 1999—2001, Mira Costa C.C., Oceanside, Calif., 2000—01, Oreg. Coast C.C., Newport, 2004—. Editor, advisor Waves Literary Program, Newport, 2004—; mem. bd. Writers on the Edge, Newport, 2005—, Internat. Baccalaureate Program, Newport, 2006—. Author: (screenplays) Enough, 2004, Out of the Darkness: An Anthology of Women's Poetry Against Women, 2004, (poetry) A Certain Uncertainty, 2006. Activist anti-poverty programs; advocate human and civil rights, women's rights, consumer rights/protection. Mem.: Am. Fedn. Tchrs., Am. Assn. U. Women, Modern Lang. Assn. Office: Oreg Coast CC 332 SW Coast Hwy Newport OR 97365 Office Phone: 541-574-7129. Business E-Mail: cpavlish@occc.cc.or.us.

PAVONE, JILL RUSSELL, special education educator; b. Jan. 25, 1954; BSEd, SUNY, Geneseo, 1976, MSEd, 1985. Dir. Autism Family Support, Rochester, 1986-91; cons. in pvt. practice, Rochester, 1988—; pvt. instr. Early Intervention, Rochester, 1995—; spl. edn. tchr. Rochester Area Schs., 1977—. Involved in parent and staff tng., 1980—; instr. SUNY Coll. Edn., Geneseo, 1989—. Author: A Sister Named Lily; contbr. articles to profl. jours. Mem. Coun. Exceptional Children, Autism Soc. Am. (pres., v.p.), Rochester Tchrs. Assn. Office: 54 Corwin Rd Rochester NY 14610-1308

PAWEL, NANCY EMMA RAY, oil industry executive, educator, artist; b. Boston, Feb. 14, 1928; d. Carlon Weston and Anna Urban Ray; m. Thomas Ernst Pawel, Sept. 1, 1951 (dec.); children: Margaret Pawel Moore, Elizabeth Thompson, Charlotte Ray Pawel Jonas. BA, Wellesley Coll., Mass., 1949; MA, U. Incarnate Word, San Antonio, Tex., 1989. Lab. asst. Med. Sch. Tufts Coll., Boston, 1949—51; biochemist Sch. Aviation Medicine, Tex., 1952—55; instr. U. The Incarnate Word, 1968—99; pres. Concord Oil Co., San Antonio, 2004—. Adj. faculty S.W. Sch. Art and Craft, San Antonio, 2000—; mem. art adv. com. U. Tex., San Antonio, 1990—95; bd. dirs. San Antonio (Tex.) Art League Mus. Prin. works include Wall Natatorium, U. Incarnate Word, Sleeping Beauty's Castle Garden for Blind, San Antonio (Tex.) Botanic Garden, Towers of San Antonio (Tex.) Children's Mus., Ctrl. Gateway, St. Mary's Hall, San Antonio, exhibitions include Taipei, Taiwan, 1998. Named Outstanding Woman in Art, San Antonio (Tex.) Express News, 1970, Artist of Yr., San Antonio (Tex.) Art League, 1977; recipient Lynn Ford Craftsman award, San Antonio (Tex.) Conservation Soc., 2002. Home: 123 Geneseo Rd San Antonio TX 78209 Office: Concord Oil Co Houston St 1500 Frost Bank Tower San Antonio TX 78205 E-mail: Nerpawel@aol.com.

PAWLING, PATTI J., school system administrator; b. Camden, N.J., Apr. 5, 1957; d. Carl Joseph and Barbara Nancy Niedermayer; m. Charles A. Pawling Jr., July 8, 1955; children: Charles Daniel, Christopher Joseph, David Patrick. BS, Trenton State Coll., Ewing, N.J., 1979. Cert. handicapped tchr. N.J. Dept. Edn., 1979, elem. sch. tchr. N.J. Dept. Edn., 2001, nursery sch. tchr. N.J. Dept. Edn., 1981. V.p. for legislation N.J. Sch. Bds. Assn., Trenton, 1996—2000, pres., 2000—02, 2005—06. Mem. Barrington Bd. of Ed., NJ, 1987—2006, Barrington Fire Co. Ladies Aux., Barrington, 1979—2006; bd. of session First Presbyn. Ch. of Barrington, NJ, 2004—06. Mem.: N.J. Edn. Assn., N.J. Sch. Bds. Assn. Presbyterian. Home: 122 Lawrence Ave Barrington NJ 08007 Personal E-mail: itzpatti2u@comcast.net.

PAWLOWSKI, JANET M., psychologist; b. Erie, Pa., Aug. 21, 1958; d. Charles L. and Mary J. (Seelinger) Dahlkemper; m. Robert S. Pawlowski, Sept. 15, 1984; children: Sara Ann, Krista Mary(dec.). BSN, Villa Maria Coll., 1980; MA in Clin. Psychology, Edinboro U., 1989. Lic. marriage and family therapist, Pa., RN Pa. Nurse St. Vincent Health Ctr., Erie, 1980-89, psychologist, 1989—; pvt. practice Child and Family Guidance Ctr. of Erie, Erie. Mem.: Developmental Delay Resource, Pa. Psychol. Assn., N.W. Pa. Psychol. Assn., Am. Assn. Marriage and Family Therapists. Office: Child and Family Guidance Ctr 9333 Tate Rd 112 Erie PA 16509 Office Phone: 814-824-4515. Personal E-mail: SchoolroomAsso@aol.com.

PAWLUK, ANNETTE MARIE, secondary school educator; b. Sharon, Pa., Nov. 12, 1960; d. Joseph Louis and Helen Katherine (Janosko) A.; m. Paul Pawluk, June 22, 2002. Student, Pa. State U., 1983-85; BE, Edinboro (Pa.) U., 1989; MS in Edn., Youngstown (Ohio) U., 1996. Tchr. math. Farrell Area Sch. Dist., Pa., 1990—2005, tchr. math. secondary sch., 2005—06; ret., 2006. Head math. dept., 1992—. Mem. NEA, Pa. State Edn. Assn. Avocations: walking, weightlifting, aerobics, reading. Office: Farrell Area Sch Dist 1660 Roemer Blvd Farrell PA 16121-1754 Home: 744 N Darby Rd Hermitage PA 16148-9303 Office Phone: 724-509-1230. Business E-Mail: apawluk@fas.k12.pa.us, apawluk@farrellareaschools.com.

PAXTON, JULIA ANN, music educator, director; b. Huntington, W.Va., July 2, 1980; d. George Scott Jackson and Judith Bradley Henson; m. Ethan Franz Paxton, Oct. 4, 2003; 1 child, Aaron Nicholas. BA in Secondary Edn., Marshall U., 2003. Lic. tchr. music edn. K-12 Bd. Edn., W.Va., 2003. Dir. bands Ravenswood (W.Va.) H.S., 2003—. Soprano Sacred Heart Cathedral Choir, Charleston, W.Va., 2006. Mem.: NEA, The Nat. Assn. Music Edn. (Achievment cert. 2002), Tri-M Music Honor Soc. (advisor 2005—06), Kappa Delta Phi (hon.). Democrat. Roman Catholic. Avocations: singing, music, cooking, travel. Home: 102 Hickory hills Place Apt 1 Charleston WV 25314 Office: Jackson County Board of Education PO Box 770 Ripley WV 25271 Office Phone: 304-372-7300.

PAYNE, ANITA HART, reproductive endocrinologist, researcher; b. Karlsruhe, Baden, Germany, Nov. 24, 1926; came to U.S., 1938; d. Frederick Michael and Erna Rose (Hirsch) Hart; widowed; children: Gregory Steven, Teresa Payne-Lyons. BA, U. Calif., Berkeley, 1949, PhD, 1952. From rsch. assoc. to prof. U. Mich., Ann Arbor, 1961-96, prof. emeritus, 1996—; assoc. dir. U. Mich. Ctr. for Study Reproduction, Ann Arbor, 1989-94; sr. rsch. scientist Stanford (Calif.) U. Med. Ctr., 1995—. Vis. scholar Stanford U., 1987-88; mem. reproductive biology study sect. NIH, Bethesda, Md., 1978-79, biochem. endocrinology study sect., 1979-83, population rsch. com. Nat. Inst. Child Health and Human Devel., 1989-93. Assoc. editor Steroids, 1987-93; contbr. book chpts., articles to profl. jours. Recipient award for cancer rsch., Calif. Inst. for Cancer Rsch., 1953, Acad. Women's Caucus award, U. Mich., 1986, Mentor award, Women in Endocrinology, 1999. Mem. Endocrine Soc. (chmn. awards com. 1983-84, mem. nominating com. 1985-87, coun. 1988-91), Am. Soc. Andrology (exec. coun. 1980-83), Soc. for Study of Reproduction (bd. dirs. 1982-85, sec. 1986-89, pres. 1990-91, Carl G. Hartman award 1998, Disting. Svc. award 2004). Office: Stanford U Med Ctr Dept OB GYN Divsn Reproductive Biology Stanford CA 94305-5317

PAYNE, BARBARA ANN, artist, educator; b. Marionville, Mo., Jan. 14, 1938; d. Lewis Michel and Velma Etta Rapp; m. Kenneth L. Payne, Nov. 25, 1956 (dec.); children: Kevin James, Kendra Lynne, Keli Song. AA, Fort Scott Cmty. Jr. Coll., Kans., 1965—67; BS in Edn., Kans. State Coll., Pittsburg, 1967—69. Tchr. Dept. Def. Schs., Yokosuka, Japan, 1969—72, Seoul, Republic of Korea, 1972—74, Spangdahlem, Germany, 1974—75, Bitburg, Germany, 1975—76, West Berlin, 1976—83, Doddea; artist. art instr. Bonn, Königswinter, Germany, 1983—88; artist Würzburg, Germany, 1988—2001, Brussels, Erps Kwerps, 2001—02; ret. Doddea, 2002. Contbr. articles to profl. jours.; one-woman shows include Galerie Fasanenstrasse 71, Berlin, 1983, Am. Embassy Club, Bonn, Germany, 1986, Mobau Wittemann, Aegidienberg, Germany, 1986, Spar-und Darlenhskasse, Aegidienberg, 1987, Stadtbücherei (City Libr.), Bonn-Dottendorf, Germany, 1988, Mehrzweckhalle, Unterpleichfeld, Germany, 1989, 1990, 1991, 1992, 1993, 1994, 1995, 1996, 2001, Kultur Stüble, Höchberg, Germany, 1991, 1992, Hotel Rebstock, Würzburg, Germany, 1993, Firme Volk, Am Markt, 1994, Farewell to Europe exhbn. Erps Kwerps, Brussels, 2002, exhibited in group shows at Berlin Am. Art Guild, West Berlin, Germany and Berlin Am. Cmtys. inside West Berlin, 1977—83, Bildungscentrum des Deutschen Beamtenbundes, Königswinter, Germany, 1986, Akademie Führungskraefte Deutsche Post, Bad Honnef, Germany, 1987, Alte Kirche, Waldbüttelbrunn, Germany, 1990, 1993. Mem. Berlin Am. Art Guild, 1977—83, pres., 1981—82. Mem.: Nat. Mus. Women in the Arts. Avocations: piano, antiques, poetry, art.

PAYNE, DEBORAH ANNE, retired medical company officer; b. Norristown, Pa., Sept. 22, 1952; d. Kenneth Nathan Moser and Joan (Reese) Dewhurst; m. Randall Barry Payne, Mar. 8, 1975 (div.). AA, Northeastern Christian Jr. Coll., 1972; B in Music Edn., Va. Commonwealth U., 1979. Driver, social asst. Children's Aid Soc., Norristown, Pa., 1972—73; mgr. Boddie-Noell Enterprises, Richmond, Va., 1974—79; retail food saleswoman Hardee's Food Systems, Inc., Phila., 1979—81; supr., with tech. tng. and testing depts. Cardiac Datacorp., Phila., 1981—95; tng. supr. Raytel Cardiac Svcs., Forest Hills, NY, 1995—98, supr. tech. support Haddonfield, NJ, 1998—2000; ret., 2000. Mem. NAFE, Delta Omicron (pres. Alpha Xi chpt. 1978-79, pres. Epsilon province 1980-85, chmn. Eastern Pa. alumni 1986-88, Star award 1979), Am. Soc. Profl. and Exec. Women. Democrat. Avocations: music, sports. Home: Park Ter Apts 8040 Rowland Ave Apt A14 Philadelphia PA 19136 Personal E-mail: d.a.payne@att.net.

PAYNE, EMILY MOSLEY, music educator; b. Hopewell, Va., June 17, 1982; d. David Allen and Jeanette Bates Mosley; m. Joseph Barrett Payne, May 29, 2004. BA, Mary Wash. Coll., Fredericksburg, Va., 2000—04. Cert. music tchr. Va., 2004. Music tchr. North/South Elem. Sch., Prince George, Va., 2004—05; sch. chorus music tchr. J.E.J. Moore Mid. Sch., Prince George, 2005—. Piano instr. pvt., Hopewell, 2004—; drama dir. J.E.J. Moore Mid. Sch., 2005—, specialist for gifted music & theater students, 2005—. Dir.: (musical prodn.) A Grand Night for Singing, Once on This Island, Junior. Youth choir dir. First Bapt. Ch., Hopewell, 2004—06, Handbell choir musician, 2004—06, adult choir singer, 2004—06. Mem.: Music Educators Nat. Conf., Mu Phi Epsilon (corr. sec. 2003—04). Baptist. Avocations: acting, baking, piano. Home: 407 Prince George Ave Hopewell VA 23860 Personal E-mail: ermpayne@hotmail.com.

PAYNE, FLORA FERN, real estate broker; b. Carrollton, Mo., Sept. 25, 1932; d. George Earnest and Bernadine Alice (Schaefer) Chrisman; m. H.D. Matticks, Oct. 20, 1950 (div. Oct. 1959); children: Dennis Don, Kathi D.; m. S.L. Freeman, Nov. 25, 1960 (div. Jan. 1973); 1 child, Gary Mark; m. Vernon Ray Payne, Mar. 18, 1988. Student, S.E. C.C., Burlington, Iowa, 1976-77; cert. stenographer, Corr. Sch., Chgo., 1960-61; student, Career Visions Real Estate Sch, 1999. Social svc. designee Mo. League Nursing, 1991. Sec. to v.p. Moore Co., Marceline, Mo., 1973-75; steno to trainmaster A.T. & S.F. Rlwy. Co., Fort Madison, Iowa, 1975-88; with social svc. Brookfield (Mo.) Nursing Ctr., 1990-95; 97-98; candidate for Linn County Pub. Adminstr., 1996; real estate agt. Marceline Realty, Mo., fall 1999; real estate broker Payne Realty, 2000—. Republican. Avocations: poetry, dance, interior decorating. Home: 603 Hickory St Bucklin MO 64631-7282

PAYNE, FRANCES ANNE, literature educator, researcher; b. Harrisonburg, Va., Aug. 28, 1932; d. Charles Franklin and Willie (Tarvin) P. BA, B.Mus., Shorter Coll, 1953; MA, Yale U., 1954, PhD, 1960. adj. fellow St. Anne's Coll., Oxford Eng. Instr. Conn. Coll., New London, 1955-56, U. Buffalo, 1958-60, lectr., 1960, asst. prof., 1960-67; assoc. prof. SUNY, Buffalo, 1967-75, prof. English and medieval lit., 1975—. Adj. fellow St. Anne's Coll., Oxford, Eng., 1966—. Author: King Alfred and Boethius, 1968; Chaucer and Menippean Satire, 1981. Contbr. articles to scholarly publs. AAUW fellow, Oxford, 1966-67; Research Found. grantee SUNY Central, Oxford, 1967, 68, 71, 72; recipient Julian Park award SUNY-Buffalo, 1979. Mem. Medieval Acad. Am., New Chaucer Soc., Internat. Soc. Anglo-Saxonists, Pi Kappa Lambda Office: SUNY-Buffalo 306 Clemens Hall Buffalo NY 14260-4600 Office Phone: 716-645-2575. Business E-Mail: fapayne@buffalo.edu.

PAYNE, GLORIA MARQUETTE, business educator; b. Elkins, W.Va., Dec. 21, 1923; d. Anthony and Roselyn Marquette; m. Carl Wesley Payne, Mar. 6, 1950; 1 child, Mary Debra Payne Moore. BA, Davis and Elkins Coll., MHL (hon.); MA, W.Va. U.; PhD, U. Pitts., 1975; postgrad., NYU Fashion Inst. Tech. Cert. designed appearance cons. Sec. Equitable Ins. Co., Elkins, 1943-44; tchr., dept. head Spencer (W.Va.) H.S., 1944-45; prof. bus. Davis & Elkins Coll., Elkins, 1945-93; image cons. Elkins, 1988-93; bus. cons., 1970-93; mgr. Elkins Wallpaper Shop, 1945-65; owner Merle Norman Cosmetic Studio, Elkins, 1950-56. Dir. tchr. workshops W.Va. U., Marshall U., State Dept. Edn., Charleston, W.Va., summers; dir. machine shorthand workshops for tchrs. throughout the U.S.; dir. designer appearance World Modeling Assn., N.Y.C., 1989—; instr. modeling Davis & Elkins Coll., 1980-93. Author: A Methods Class is Interesting and Challenging, 1970, The Oak or the Pumpkin; mem. editl. bd. Nat. Assn. of Business Teachers Edn. Pub., 1993, 94; contbr. articles to profl. jours. Chair Bi-Centennial, City of Elkins; dir. Elkins Fair, City of Elkins; pres. St. Brendans Parish; judge Mountain State Forest Festival Parades, 1988-2004; rep. Region I at Dallas Nat. Conv., 1994 (one of five nat. finalists); div. chair bus., econs., and tourism. Recipient Outstanding Prof. award Sears-Roebuck Co., Lois Latham award for Excellence in Tchg., Cmty. Svc. award Elkins C. of C., 1992, Outstanding Educator award BPW, 1997, W.Va. Bus. Edn. Assn., W.Va. Vocat. Assn., 1994, 97, Region I award for Outstanding Vocat.Educator, Outstanding Collegiate Tchr. Bus. award, 1997, award of merit Assn. Career and Tech. Edn., 2003-04, Outstanding Prof. of Region award, 2003, 04, 05, Humanitarian award Odd Fellows Lodge, 2004; 1st recipient James S. McDonnell Found. Fully Endowed Acad. Chair in Bus. and Econs.; named Educator of Yr., W.Va. Women's Club, Outstanding Educator AAUW, Randolph County C. of C. Citizen of Yr., 1998, Disting. Citizen, Gov. W.Va., W.Va. Women in Bus. Champion, Small Bus. Assn., 2005. Mem. Am. Bus. Writers Assn., W.Va. Edn. Assn. (past pres., Outstanding Prof., Outstanding Svc. award, Outstanding Bus. Educator award), Tri-State Bus. Edn. Assn. (historian, outstanding svc. award, Tchr.-Educator of the South award 1991), World Modeling Assn. (v.p. 1988-95, modeling award 1989), Designed Appearance U.S. (dir. 1990-98), W.Va. Bus. Edn. Assn. (award 1977, 85, 94, 97), Bus. and Profl. Women's Orgn., W.Va. C. of C., The Fashion Club (advisor), Beta Sigma Phi (advisor), Beta Alpha Beta (advisor), Pi Beta Phi, Phi Beta Lambda (advisor). Democrat. Roman Catholic. Avocations: flower arranging, modeling. Home: 301 Davis St Elkins WV 26241-4030 Office: Davis & Elkins Coll 100 Sycamore St Elkins WV 26241-3996

PAYNE, JAMILA, retail executive, entrepreneur; Grad., Drexel U., 2000. Fashion stylist; founder, pres. Milla by Mail, Phila. Bd. govs. Drexel U. Named one of Phila.'s Most Influential under 40, Phila. Tribune, 2005, 40 Under 40, Phila. Bus. Jour., 2006. Office: Milla by Mail Ground Fl 3225 Arch St Philadelphia PA 19104 Office Fax: 877-645-6245.*

PAYNE, JAN, medical/surgical nurse, educator; b. Berwyn, Ill., Nov. 23, 1942; d. Charles I. and Alice (Nepil) Barberie; m. Neil F. Payne, Jan. 4, 1986; children: Patricia, Sharon, Gail. BSN, U Wis, 1964; MS in Nursing, Loyola U., Chgo., 1970; EdD, No. Ill. U., 1991. Asst. supr. Wesley Meml. Hosp., Chgo.; instr. Loyola U., Chgo.; assoc. prof. Lewis U., Romeoville, Ill.; asst. prof. Elmhurst (Ill.) Coll. Mem. ANA, Assn. for Rehabilitation Nurses, Sigma Theta Tau (eligibility chmn.). Office: Elmhurst Coll 190 Prospect Ave Elmhurst IL 60126-3271 Home: 200 Periwinkle Way Unit 325 Sanibel FL 33957-7422

PAYNE, KERI TOLMAN, dancer, educator; b. Rexburg, Idaho, Apr. 21, 1975; d. Robert William and Teresa Petterborg Tolman; m. Korey Edward Payne, July 25, 1997; children: Kenzie Adjoua, Kassidy Amoin. Assocs. degree, Lewis-Clark State Coll., Lewiston, Idaho, 1995. Dance instr. Danceworks, Dance Unltd., Boise, 1995—2001, Footlight Dance Ctr., Sun Valley, Idaho, 2001—05, Rehle's Dance Studio, Shelley, Idaho, 2005—. Home: 1403 N 1070 E Shelley ID 83274 Personal E-mail: kerithpayne@yahoo.com.

PAYNE, MARY LIBBY, retired judge; b. Gulfport, Miss., Mar. 27, 1932; d. Reece O. and Emily Augusta (Cook) Bickerstaff; m. Bobby R. Payne; children: Reece Allen, Glenn Russell. Student, Miss. U. for Women, 1950-52; BA in Polit. Sci. with distinction, U. Miss., 1954, LLB, 1955. Bar: Miss. 1955. Ptnr. Bickerstaff & Bickerstaff, Gulfport, 1955-56; sec. Guaranty Title Co., Jackson, Miss., 1957; assoc. Henley, Jones, & Henley, Jackson, Miss., 1958-61; freelance rschr. Pearl, Miss., 1961-63; solo practitioner Brandon, Miss., 1963-68; exec. dir. Miss. Judiciary Commn., Jackson, 1968-70; chief drafting & rsch. Miss. Ho. Reps., Jackson, 1970-72; asst. atty. gen. State Atty. Gen. Office, Jackson, 1972-75; founding dean, assoc. prof. Sch. Law Miss. Coll., Jackson, 1975-78, prof., 1978-94, scholar in residence, prof. emerita, 2003—; judge Miss. Ct. Appeals, Jackson, 1995—2001; ret., 2001. Mem. bd. disting. alumnae Miss. U. Women, 1988—2000. Contbr. articles to profl. jours. Founder, bd. dirs. Christian Conciliation Svc., Jackson, 1983-93; bd. dirs. Exchange Club's Child Abuse Prevention Ctr. of Jackson, 1999-2001; counsel Christian Action Com. Rankin Bapt. Assn., Pearl, 1968-92; advisor Covenant Ministerial Fellowship, 1995-2002. Named Miss. Coll. Lawyer of Yr., Miss. Coll. Sch. Law Alumni Assn., 1998, Outstanding Woman Lawyer, Miss. Women Lawyers Assn., 1999, Susie Blue Buchanan award, Women in Profession Com. of Miss. Bar, 2000; recipient Book of Golden Deeds award, Pearl Exch. Club, 1989, Excellence medallion, Miss. U. Women, 1990, Woman of Yr. award, Miss. Assn. Women Higher Edn., 1989, Power of One award, Miss. Govs. Conf., 1996, Disting. Jurist award, Miss. State U., 2004, Lifetime Achievement award, Miss. Bar, 2005. Fellow Am. Bar Found.; mem. Miss. Bar Found., Christian Legal Soc. (nat. bd. dirs. 1992-2001, Skeeter Ellis Svc. to Law Students award 1999, Lifetime Achievement award 2002). Baptist. Avocations: public speaking, travel, needlepoint, sewing, reading.

PAYNE, PAULA MARIE, minister; b. Waukegan, Ill., Jan. 13, 1952; d. Percy Howard and Annie Maude (Canady) P. BA, U. Ill., 1980; MA, U. San Francisco, 1986; MDiv, Wesley Theol. Sem., 1991, postgrad., 1995—; MA in Operational Studies, Air U. USAF, Maxwell AFB, 2005. Ordained to ministry United Meth. Ch., 1990. Chaplain for minority affairs Am. U., Washington, 1988-89; chaplain, intern NIH, Bethesda, Md., 1989-90; pastor Asbury United Meth. Ch., Charles Town, W.Va., 1990—. Supt. ch. sch. United Meth. Ch., Oxon Hill, Md., 1989-90; mem. AIDS task force Wesley Theol. Sem., Washington, 1988-89; mem. retreat. com. Balt. Conf., 1990—; chair scholarship com. Asbury United Meth. Ch., 1990—. Bd. dirs. AIDS Task Force Jefferson County, Charles Town, 1991—, Cmty. Ministries, Charles Town, 1991—; formerly N.H. state v.p. Ch. Women United, now pres.; mem. ethics com. Concord Hosp. Tech. sgt. USAF, 1984-88; chaplain Army N.G., Md., 1994-96, Mass. 2001; chaplain USAFR, 1997. Maj. Air N.G. Recipient Cert. of Recognition, Ill. Ho. of Reps., 1988, 20th Century award of Achievement Internat. Biog. Ctr., Cambridge, Eng., 1993, 1st Five Hundred, Cambridge, 1994, Citizen's citation, City of Balt., 1994, others; Ethnic Minority scholar United Meth. Ch., 1988-89, Brandenburg scholar, 1988-89, Tadlock scholar, 1989-90, Calvary Fellow scholar Calvary United Meth. ch., 1989-90. Mem. AAUW, U. Ill. Alumni Assn. (bd. dirs. 1987-88), Alpha Kappa Alpha (pres. local chpt. 1974-76, v.p. 1973). Republican. Home: 1812 N Gilbert St Danville IL 61832 Personal E-mail: revpmpumc@hotmail.com.

PAYNE, PAULETA POLLY, psychologist; d. Anthony James and Dorothy E. Cerillo; children: Michelle Payne Whitlow, Reubin A., James. BS, Ga. State U., 1981, MS, 1984; PhD, U. Ga., 1989. Lic. clin. psychologist Va., Ga. Clin. psychologist T-Med Svcs., Arlington, Va., Browner Health Svc., Stockbridge, Ga. Home and Office: PO Box 11895 Lynchburg VA 24506

PAYNE, PEGGY, writer; b. Wilmington, N.C. m. Bob Dick. BA in English, Duke U., 1970. Writer sect. and edn. Raleigh (N.C.) Times, 1970-72; freelance writer, 1972—. Scriptwriter, on-camera commentator pub. TV network, N.C., 1975-77; copywriter advt. materials, reports, articles, scripts for orgns., including Office of Gov., State of N.C., IBM, Instrument Soc. Am., N.C. State U.; pub. speaker civic, ednl. and profl. orgns. Author: Revelation, 1988 (selected among editor's weekly choices N.Y. Times), (with Allan Luks) The Healing Power of Doing Good, 1992 (Literary Guild book club selection), Doncaster: A Legacy of Personal Style, 1997; short stories cited in: Best American Short Stories, 1987, New Stories of the South: The Best of 1987; contbr. articles to newspapers, including N.Y. Times, Washington Post, L.A. Times, Chgo. Tribune, others; mags., including Cosmopolitan, Sci. Digest, McCall's, Ms., Family Circle, Food & Wine, others. Indo-Am. fellow, India, 1991; NEH grantee, 1979; award recipient PEN Am. Ctr., 1985; nominee Pushcart prize, 1986. Avocation: travel.

PAYNE, RUBY MAE, secondary school educator; d. L. B. Cloud and Ellen Dyann Brown; m. Bryan Keith Payne, May 21, 1995; children: Dyellen Marie Payne-McKay, Cris Phillip, Bryan Keith Jr., Aarron Lee, Tiffany Anne, Jordan Lynn, Makayla Hope. AA, Taft Coll., 1995; BS, Calif. State U., Bakersfield, 1998, edn. profl. cert., 2000. Cert. online tchr. U. Calif., San Diego, specially designed academic instrn. in English Calif., cCrosscultural lang. acquisition devel. Calif. Instrnl. aide Taft Coll., 1996—98; math. instr. Taft Union HS, 1999—. Cert. Calif. Tech. Assistance Project, Bakersfield, Kern County, Calif., 2000. Vol. Ct. Apptd. Spl. Adv. Kern County, Bakersfield, 2004; pres. Roosevelt Sch. Parent Orgn., Taft, 2004—06; treas. Nat. Health Services, Inc, Shafter, Calif., 1998. Named Mother of Yr., Taft Coll. Children's Ctr., 1994. Mem.: Taft Union HS Tchrs. Assn. (pres. 2005), Calif. Teachers Assn. (assoc.; pres. 2005—05), Alpha Gamma Sigma (life Lifetime Membership 1995). Achievements include design of online courses. Avocations: art, technology, travel, stamps. Office: Taft Union HS 701 7th St Taft CA 93268 Office Phone: 661-763-2300. Office Fax: 661-763-1445. Business E-Mail: rpayne@taft.k12.ca.us.

PAYNE, TABITHA WYNN, psychologist, educator, researcher; b. Balt., Jan. 14, 1970; d. Bruce Gwynn and Wilma Jean Payne; m. Douglas Arthur Hocker. PhD in Exptl. Psychology, Ga. Inst. Tech., Atlanta, 2003. Asst. prof. cognitive psychology dept. psychology and dept. neurosci. Kenyon Coll., Gambier, Ohio, 2002—. Contbg. editor The Psychol. Record. Discrimination counselor SPEAK OUT: Discrimination Adv. Bd., Kenyon Coll. Named Outstanding Grad. Student in Rsch. Psychology, U. Tenn., 1996—97; recipient, 1997—98, Best Presentation award, Psi Chi, 2001; grantee, Wheeler Found., 1996—98, USAF, 1998—2002, Kenyon Alumni, 2005; student tchg. grantee, NSF, 2000—01. Mem.: Assn. Psychol. Sci., Midwestern Psychol. Assn. Achievements include research in individual differences in controlled attention, working memory, perceptual speed, and fluid intelligence; discovery of the ability to control one's attentional focus is critical to making decisions about brief sensory events, such as deciding if two tones are the same in pitch; seasonal affective disorder is similar to major depression, in the sense that both are linked to cognitive failures; design of a laboratory and research to examine eye behavior as an indicator of attention; a specialized computer-interactive course in psychology. Office: Kenyon Coll 118 Samuel Mather Hall Gambier OH 43022 Office Phone: 740-427-5249.

PAYNE, TRACY H., academic director; b. Columbia, SC, May 5, 1970; d. Norman Franklin and Carol Harris Hodges; m. Albert Lee Payne, Sept. 2, 2001; children: Jeremy Lee, Norman Alexander. BS, U. Montevallo, Ala., 1994, MEd, 1998; EdD, U. Ala., Tuscaloosa, 2006. Lead/svc. mem. Ameri-Corps Coll. Bound Program, Washington, 1995—98; Upward Bound student devel. coord. U. Montevallo, 1998—2003, dir. McNair Scholars Program, 2003—. Co-author Ala. Unified State Plan, Gov.'s Office on Nat. and Cmty. Svc., Montgomery, Ala., 1997—98. Named Outstanding Grad. Student for Academic Citizenship, U. Ala. Coll. Edn., 2005; recipient U. Excellence award and scholarship, Chilton County Alumni of U. Montevallo, 1988; fellow, Chi Sigma Iota, 2000; grad. honors scholar, U. Montevallo, 1997. Mem.: Higher Edn. Partnership, Southeas.Assn. Ednl. Opportunity Program Pers., Ala. Assn. Ednl. Opportunity Program Pers. (TRIO Achiever 2006), Kappa Delta Pi, Alpha Epsilon Lambda, Golden Key (hon.). Baptist. Achievements include research in first-generation college students. Avocations: photography, scrapbooks, gardening. Home: 236 County Rd 611 Lawley AL 36793 Office: U Montevallo Sta 6570 Montevallo AL 35115 Office Phone: 205-665-6570. Office Fax: 205-665-6566.

PAYNE, TYANA, psychotherapist; b. Detroit, Jan. 29, 1946; d. Robert David and Virginia Jane (Bubb) P. BSN cum laude, Stanford U., 1969; MPH, Tulane U., 1972, DPH, 1974. Cert. psychiat. and mental health clin. specialist-child and adolescent ANA; lic. psychiat. and mental health nurse practitioner. Crisis stabilization nurse Manattee Mental Health, Bradenton, Fla., 1985-86; project coord. Oreg. Inst. Tech., Klamath Falls, 1979-81; asst. prof. psychiat. and mental health nursing Oreg. Health Sci. U., La Grande, 1987-88; ind. psychotherapist La Grande, 1990—95; pvt. practice pysch/mental health nurse practitioner, 1996—. Contbr. articles to profl. publs. Mem. AAUW, Soc. for Sci. Study of Sex, Population Connection. Office: Crossroads Counseling 409 Pine St Ste 209 Klamath Falls OR 97601 Office Phone: 541-850-9937.

PAYNE, URSULA OCTAVIA, choreographer, educator; b. Charlotte, N.C., Aug. 11, 1969; d. James Oliver and Octavia Clark Payne. BA in Dance, Slippery Rock U., Pa., 1992; MFA in Dance, Ohio State U., 1995. Cert. movement analyst Laban Bartenieff Inst. Movement Studies, N.Y., 1996. Tchr. Slippery Rock (Pa.) U., 1995—. Cons., panelist Dance Advance, Phila., 2003—; faculty Am. Dance Festival, Durham, NC, 2002—. Named one of Top 25 to Watch, Dance Mag.; recipient President's Internat. Initiative award, Slippery Rock (Pa.) U., 2001, Young Alumni award, 2005; fellow, Pa. Coun. of the Arts, 2004, 2006. Mem.: Delta Sigma Theta. Democrat. Avocations: travel, theater. Home: 1707 Highland Ave New Castle PA 16105 Office: Slippery Rock University of Pennsylvania Morrow Field House Slippery Rock PA 16057 Office Phone: 724-738-4509. Office Fax: 724-738-4524. Business E-Mail: ursula.payne@sru.edu.

PAYSEN, BONNIE B., music educator, musician; b. N.Y.C., Mar. 22, 1951; d. Philip and Eilen Merrill Brooks; m. Stephen Patrick Paysen, Aug. 1, 1976; children: Jennifer, Benjamin. BA in Performance, SUNY Albany, 1972; MusM, SUNY Stony Brook, 1977; Edn. certificate, Queens Coll., N.Y., 1986. Profl. French horn player Opera on the Sound, L.I. Brass Guild, Atlantic Winds, N.Y. Metro Area, 1972—2003; pvt. instr. Concert Pops of L.I., Setauket, 1984—86; band dir. Northport, E. Northport Union Free Sch. Dist., 1986—. Mem.: Suffolk County Music Educators Assn., N.Y. State Sch. Music Assn., Music Educators Nat. Conf. Avocations: reading, hiking. Personal E-mail: sbpaysen@optonline.net.

PAYSON, HERTA RUTH, psychotherapist, theater educator, massage therapist; b. Oak Park, Ill., Jan. 31, 1933; d. Joseph Hale and Lily Brush (Bagley) P.; m. Elliott Proctor Joslin, Oct. 12, 1961 (div. Oct., 1984); children: Allen Payson, Rachel Elizabeth, David Elliott. BA, Goddard Coll., 1979; MA, Vt. Coll., 1982; PhD, The Union Inst., 1996. Tchr., dir. Queens (N.Y.) Cmty. Dance Sch., 1954-63; theatrical costumer N.Y.C., 1955-69; costumer Nat. Theatre of the Deaf, Waterford, Conn., 1970-84; asst. prof., theater dept. Conn. Coll., New London, 1970—2004; pvt. practice Groton, Conn., 1980—. Co-owner SYZYGY for little b., N.Y.C., 1964-69; coord. small groups Friends Conf. Religion and Psychology, Haverford, Pa., 1975-79, co-clk., 1978-83. Author: The Dragon's Eye: Envisioning Women's Wisdom, 1998; choreographer for As You Like It, Two Gentlemen of Verona and Romeo & Juliet for N.Y. Shakespeare Festival, Alice in Wonderland for The Little Orch. Soc., others. Mem. ACA, Am. Psychotherapy Assn., Am. CranioSacral Therapy Assn., Conn. Assn. Jungian Psychology, Nat. Guild Hypnotists, Am. Massage Therapy Assn., Fiber Artists on the Cutting Edge. Avocations: gardening, weaving, home improvement. Office: 73 Laurelwood Rd Groton CT 06360-5654 Office Phone: 860-445-8083. E-mail: hpays@conncoll.edu.

PAYTON, CYDNEY, museum director, curator; Owner Cydney Payton Artfolio, 1985—90; co-owner Payton-Rule Gallery, 1990—92; dir. Boulder Mus. Contemporary Art, Colo., 1992—2000; dir., curator Mus. Contemporary Art/Denver, 2001—. Office: Mus Contemporary Art/Denver 1275 19th St Denver CO 80202 Office Phone: 303-298-7554.

PAYTON, SALLYANNE, law educator; b. 1943; BA, Stanford U., 1964, LLB, 1968. Bar: Calif. 1969, DC 1969. Staff asst. to Pres. of U.S. White House Domestic Coun., Washington, 1971-73; chief counsel urban mass transp. adminstrn. U.S. Dept. Transp., Washington, 1973-76; assoc. prof. U. Mich. Law Sch., Ann Arbor, 1976-85, prof., 1985—; William W. Cook Prof. Law. Trustee Stanford U., 1972-82; mem. Adminstrn. Conf. U.S., 1980—; bd. dirs. Roosevelt Ctr. Am. Policy Studies, 1982—. Fellow: Nat. Acad. of Pub. Adminstrn. Office: U Mich Law Sch 336 Hutchins Hall 625 S State St Ann Arbor MI 48109-1215 Office Phone: 734-763-0220. Office Fax: 734-763-9375. E-mail: spayton@umich.edu.

PAYTON, SUE C., civilian military employee; BS, Ea. Ill. U.; MS, U. So. Calif.; grad. exec. program, Goizueta Bus. Sch. Emory U., 1998. Sr. site systems integration mgr. Martin Marietta, 1989—94; v.p. bus. devel. Lockheed Martin Corp., 1994—96; v.p. applied tech. ImageLinks, Inc.; dir. Nat. Ctr. Applied Tech.; acting dir. def. rsch. and engring. US Dept. Def., Washington, dep. under sec. (advanced systems & concepts), 2001—06; asst. sec. acquisition USAF US Dept Def., Washington, 2006—. Office: USAF 1060 Air Force Pentagon Rm 4E964 SAF/AQ Washington DC 20330-1060 Office Phone: 703-697-6446. Office Fax: 703-693-6400. E-mail: sue.payton@osd.mil.*

PAYTON-WRIGHT, PAMELA, actress; b. Pitts., Nov. 1, 1941; d. Gordon Edgar and Eleanor Ruth (McKinley) Payton Wright; m. David Arthur Butler, May 8, 1978 (div. 1989); 1 child, Oliver Dickon Hedley. Grad., St. Mary's Jr. Coll., 1961; BA, Birmingham So. Coll., 1963; postgrad., Royal Acad. Dramatic Arts, London, 1963-65. Actress (Broadway plays) The Show-Off, 1968, Exit the King, 1968, The Cherry Orchard, 1968, Jimmy Shine, 1969, The Crucible, 1972, Mourning Becomes Electra, 1972, All Over Town, 1975, The Glass Menagerie, 1976, Romeo and Juliet, 1977, A Streetcar Named Desire, 1988, Night of the Iguana, 1988, M. Butterfly, 1988—90, Something Unspoken, 1995, Long Day's Journey Into Night, 2003, (off-Broadway) The Effect of Gamma Rays on Man-In-The Wood Marigolds, 1970—71, Jesse and the Bandit Queen, 1975, The Seagull, 1980, Don Juan, 1982, Hamlet, 1982, Mrs. Warren's Profession, 1992, The Replacement, 1995, Richard III, 'Til the Rapture Comes, 1998, What You Get and What You Expect, 2000, Fifth of July, 2003, Duet, 2004, The Day Emily Married, 2004, Indian Blood, 2006, (plays) Skin of Our Teeth, 1972, Aimee, 1973, Othello, Troilus and Cressida, As You Like It, 1976, Lunch Girls, 1977, Summerfolk, 1978, The Greeks, 1982, The Misanthrope, 1982, Tobacco Road, 1984, Passion, 1984—85, Cat on a Hot Tin Roof, 1985, Little Eyolf, 1985, On the Verge, 1986, Our Town, 1987, The Road to Mecca, 1990, Picnic, 1991, The Way of the World, 1991, Quartermaine's Terms, 1993, Misalliance, 1993, Six Degrees of Separation, 1993, Ghosts, 1994, Sea Gull, 1994, The Rivals, 1996, Touch of the Poet, 1996, Glass Menagerie, 1997, Voir Dire, 1997, She Stoops to Conquer, 1997, Blithe Spirits, 1998, Transit of Venus, 1998, Sweet Bird of Youth, 1999, A Fair Country, 2000, Philadelphia Story, 2001, Seascape, 2002, Outward Bound, 2002, Hay Fever, 2005, Equus, 2005, The Learned Ladies of Park Avenue, (films) At the Dark End of the Street, 1980, Going in Style, 1981, Starlight, 1985, My Little Girl, 1985, Ironweed, 1987, The Freshman, 1989, In Dreams, 1999, Saving Face, 2004. Nominee Emmy, 1972, Lucille Lortel, 2003; recipient Fulbright award, 1963, Spl. medal, Edmund Gray prize for high comedy, Herbert Beerbohm Tree citation, Royal Acad. Dramatic Art, 1963—65, Obie award, 1970, 1975, 1976, Clarence Derwent award, Variety Critics' Poll citation, 1970, Drama Desk award, 1972, Best Actress citation, Dallas Theater Critics' Forum, 1994, Balt., 1997, Dean Goodman award, 1999, Joseph Jefferson award, 1996; Fox Grant fellow, 1999. Mem.: Screen Actors Guild, AFTRA, Actors Equity Assn. Episcopalian. Office: Bauman & Assocs 250 W 57th St New York NY 10019-3741

PAZDON, DENISE JOAN, speech pathology/audiology services professional; b. Bklyn., Aug. 28, 1953; d. Robert Edward and Mildred Ella (Volinsky) Strauss; m. John Joseph, Jr. Pazdon, Nov. 3, 1973 (dec.); children: Melissa Joann, John Robert. AS, Coll. Lifelong Learning, Portsmouth, N.H., 1995; BS in Comm. Disorders summa cum laude, Coll. Lifelong Learning, 1997; MS in Comm. Disorders, U. N.H., 2000. Cert. tchr. N.H., lic. speech-lang. pathologist N.H. Speech lang. asst. Garrison Pub. Sch., Dover, NH, 1988—95; speech lang. specialist Kingston-Bakie Sch., Kingston, NH, 1995—98; speech lang. pathologist Pollard Sch., Plaiston, NH, 1998—2001; lang. pathologist, ednl. specialist North Hampton Sch., NH, 2001—03; spl. edn. cons. U. N.H., Durham, 2003—, coop. tchr., supr., 2001—; program designer/instr. Coll. for Lifelong Learning, Portsmouth, 2003—. Contbr. articles to profl. jours. Staff-adult advisor Youth to Youth, Ohio, 1985—87; sch. vol. City of Diver, 1987; bd. dirs. Concerned Citizens for Drug and Alcohol Prevention, Dover, 1980—87. Mem.: Am. Speech Lang. Hearing Assn., N.H. Speech Lang. Hearing Assn., Alpha Sigma Lambda. Avocations: kayaking, travel, skiing, vocalist in band. Home: 41 Ayers Ln Dover NH 03820 Office: North Hampton Sch 201 Atlantic Ave North Hampton NH 03862

PAZNOKAS, LYNDA SYLVIA, elementary school educator; b. Portland, Oreg., Feb. 19, 1950; d. Marley Elmo and Undine Sylvia (Crockard) Sims. BA, Wash. State U., 1972; MS, Portland State U., 1975; EdD, Oreg. State U., 1984. Cert. tchr. Oreg. Tchr. 5th grade, outdoor sch. specialist Clover Park Sch. Dist. 400, Tacoma, 1971-72; tchr. 6th grade, outdoor sch. specialist Hillsboro (Oreg.) elem. Dist. 7, 1972-78, Bend (Oreg.)-La Pine Sch. Dist., 1978-82, elem. curriculum specialist, 1983-85, tchr. 4th grade gifted and talented, 1985-90; grad. teaching asst. Oreg. State U., Corvallis, 1982-84; asst. prof., assoc. prof. No. Ariz. U., 1990-99, chair instnl. leadership, 1997-98; Boeing disting. prof. sci. edn. Wash. State U., Pullman, 1999—. Ednl. cons., tchr. workshops, 1973—; presenter workshop Soviet-Am. Joint Conf., Moscow State U., 1991, Meeting of Children's Culture Promoters, Guadalajara, Mex., 1994, internat. conf. Sci., Tech. and Math. Edn. for Human Devel., UNESCO, Panaji, India, 2001, Nishinomiya Joint Rsch. Conf., Japan, 2001, internat. workshop Promoting Sci. and Tech. Literacy Through Sci. Toys & Out-of-Sch. Sci. Activities, Pattaya, Thailand, 2005, others; faculty Ariz. Journey Schs. for Math. and Sci. Tchg. Improvement; coord. Odyssey of the Mind, Bend, 1985-89, tchr. mentor program for 1st yr. tchrs., Beaverton, Oreg., 1982-83; reviewer Sci. Books and Films AAAS, 1992—; presenter Social Edn. Assn. of Australia, 1997, Nat. State Tchrs. of Yr., Guam, 2005; steering com. Wash. LASER (Leadership and Assistance for Sci. Edn. Reform), 2002—, mem. sci. drafting team sci. curriculum instrnl. frameworks; mem. Nat. Ecol. Obs. Network Design Consortium. Author: Pathways of America: Lewis and Clark, 1993, Pathways of America: The Oregon Trail, 1993, Pathways of America: The California Gold Rush Trail, 1994, Pathways of America: The Santa Fe Trail, 1995, Fifty States, 1997, U.S. Presidents, 1997, U.S. Map Skills, 1997, Human body, 1998, National Parks and Other Park Service Sites, 1999, Our National Parks, 1999, Pathways of America: The California Mission Trail, 2000, Circling the World: Festivals and Celebrations, 2000, Endangered Species, 2001; mem. adv. bd. (jour.) Sci. and Children; contbr. articles to profl. jours.; reviewer Turkish Jour. Sci. Edn. Vol., leader, bd. dirs. Girl Scouts U.S., 1957—; elder First Presbyn. Ch., Bend, 1980—; vol. hist. interpretation High Desert Mus., Bend, 1987-91; docent Mus. No. Ariz.; pres. bd. dirs. The Arboretum at Flagstaff; former sec. and v.p. bd. dirs. Palouse Discovery Sci. Ctr. (pres. bd. dirs.); past pres. Arboretum bd.; mem. Ptnrs. Achieving Leadership in Sci., Wash., D.C., Leadership and Assistance for Sci. Edn. Reform, Wash., D.C. Recipient Excellence in Teaching award Bend Found., 1985-86, 86-87; named Tchr. Yr. Oreg. Dept. Edn., 1982, Higher Edn. Tchr. Yr., Wash. Sci. Tchrs. Assn. (WSTA), 2003; Celebration Teaching grantee Geraldine Rockefeller Dodge Found., 1989, 90, 91, 92, 93, 94, 95, EPA grantee, 1997-99, Eisenhower Math and Sci. Edn. Act grantee, 1997, 99, Grand Canyon Assn. grantee, 1996, 97, 98; commd. Ky. Col., 1993. Mem. NEA, Internat. Coun. Assns. Sci. Edn. (chair pre-secondary and informal sci. edn. of the exec. com. 2004—, editor Stepping Into Sci. Internat. Quar. jour. 2004—, jour/ advisor), Nat. Coun. Tchrs. Math., NSTA (past mem. nat. supervision com., internat. com.), Nat. State Tchrs. of Yr. (nat. pres. 1988-90), Nat. Assn. Rsch. in Sci. Tchg., Oreg. Coun. Tchrs. Math. (bd. dirs. 1981-82), Oreg. Coun. Tchrs. English (bd. dirs. 1981-82), Ariz. Reading Assn. (bd. dirs.), Nat. Coun. for Social Studies, Coun. for Elem. Sci. Internat. (bd. dirs. 1995-98, 99—2003, chair informal edn. com.), Internat. Reading Assn., Oreg.-Calif. Trails Assn., Nat. Sci. Edn. Leadership Assn., Assn. for Sci. Tchr. Edn., Nat. Assn. for Rsch. in Sci. Tchg., Assn. for Sci. Edn., Wash. Sci. Tchrs. Assn. (higher edn. rep. bd. dirs. 2004—), N.W. Oreg.-Calif. Trails Assn., Lewis and Clark Trail Heritage Found., PEO (past corr. sec.), Delta Kappa Gamma (1st v.p.), Phi Delta Kappa (found. rep. 1991-92, v.p. programs 1992-93, historian 1993-94, v.p. membership 1994-95), Golden Key Hon., Pi Lambda Theta, Phi Kappa Phi, Kappa Delta Pi (chpt. counselor, mem. spkrs. bur., nat. Web com., sci. specialist), others. Avocations: cross country skiing, photography, hiking, researching immigrant trails, gardening. Home: 101 Enman-Kincaid Rd Pullman WA 99163

PEABODY, ARLENE L. HOWLAND BAYAR, retired enterostomal therapy nurse; b. Deposit, NY, June 26, 1931; d. Burt and Olive (Oralls) Howland; m. Atilla C. Bayar, Dec. 8, 1956 (div.); m. Norman R. Peabody, Feb. 1, 1975 (dec.); children: Tildy Anne Bayar Sparrow, Carol A. Digilio; m. Robert A. Ehlers, Feb. 15, 2003. Diploma, Ridley's Sec. Sch., Binghamton, N.Y., 1949, Binghamton Sch. Practical Nursing, 1970, Harrisburg Hosp. Sch. Enterostomal Therapy, Pa., 1971; AAS, Empire State Coll., Saratoga Springs, N.Y., 1985; BS in Edn., SUNY, Oneonta, 1990. RN, N.Y.; cert. therapeutic touch practitioner, natural force healing practitioner, enterostomal nurse. Sec. pres.'s office Cornell U., Ithaca, NY, 1949—55; exec. sec. Rudolph Lang, Office Execs. Assn. N.Y. and Prestige Expositions Inc., N.Y.C., 1955—69; enterostomal therapy nurse M.I. Bassett Hosp., Cooperstown, NY, 1972—89; pvt. practice enterostomal therapy nurse Oneonta, NY, 1989—2002. Spkr. in field. Vol. Am. Cancer Soc., 1972-2002, Catskill Area Hospice, 1990-02, Glimmerglass Opera, 1975-2002; bd. dirs. Del. Heritage Inc., 1996-2002; trustee Unitarian Universalist Soc.; active Storytelling Ctr. of Oneonta, Oneonta Concert Assn., Oneonta Contradance. Mem. AARP (bd. dirs. 1986-2002), N.Y. State Hist. Assn., Delaware County Hist. Soc., Wound Ostomy and Continence Nurses Soc., United Ostomy Assn. (N.Y. state field svcs. rep.), Order Ea. Star. Avocations: heirloom quilting, traditional folk music, coutourier clothing, costuming, dance. Home: 13511 Pebblebrook Dr Houston TX 77079-6023

PEACHER, GEORGIANA MELICENT, poet, educator; b. Syracuse, N.Y., Nov. 13, 1919; d. William Catlett and Georgiana (Ruckman) P. BS, Syracuse U., 1941, MS, 1943; PhD, Northwestern U., 1946; MFA, Vt. Coll., 1996. Fellow Northwestern U., 1943-45; dir. speech therapy Neuro-Phys. Rehab. Clinic, Phila., 1946-47; prof. speech pathology and psychology Temple U. Med. Sch., Phila., 1948-67; dir. speech therapy N.Y. Hosp., Cornell U., N.Y.C., 1953-56; ind. rschr. various cities, Russia, Eng., Scotland, 1967-75, C.G. Jung Inst., Zürich, Switzerland, 1975-76; prof. speech and psychology John Jay Coll. CUNY, 1976-90; prof. emerita John Jay Coll. CUNY, 1990—; pres. Pearl Shedding Press, Brunswick, Maine, 1990—. Exhibitor AMA, 1960, Am. Speech and Hearing Assn., 1961. Author: How to Improve Your Speaking Voice, 1966, Folio One: Mesmerists, 1971, Folio Two: Trance Duet, 1972, Folio Three: Thin Wind, 1972, Mary Stuart's Ravishment Descending

Time, 1976, Folio Four: Thunder Wonder, 1983, Speak to Win, 1985, The Skryabin Mysterium, 2004, (plays) Hatshepsut, 1982, (poetry) Elizabeth of Mariana, 1992 (Eva LeFevre French-form award); exhibitions include Pa. Acad. Fine Arts, 1961, Portland Mus. of Art, 2001, Thornton Oaks, 2004, Bowdoin Coll., 2004, U. So. Maine, 2005, Portland Pub. Libr., 2006; contbr. articles to profl. jours. Grantee for performance of Indira India, CUNY, 1988-89, Pharoah Hatshepsut, 1981. Fellow: Am. Speech Hearing Lang. Assn.; mem.: AAAS, APA, Am. Soc. Clin. Hypnosis, Dramatists Guild, Baxter Soc. (sec. 1991—93, pres. 1996—97). Democrat. Avocations: painting, sculpting, book design. Home and Office: 25 Thornton Way Apt 125 Brunswick ME 04011-3282

PEACOCK, FLORENCE F., professional musician, soprano, voice educator; b. Covington, Ga., June 13, 1937; d. Robert Raphael and Louly (Turner) Fowler; m. James Lowe Peacock, Aug. 4, 1962; children: Louly Peacock-Konz, Sara Claire, Natalie F. BA, Hollins Coll., 1959; MMusic, Yale U., 1962. Instrumentalist, singer, dancer Javanese Gamelon, Indonesia, 1963, 64, 96; paticipant, soprano soloist Oberlin Coll.: Baroque Performance Inst., 1978-2001; soprano soloist Franz Schubert Inst., Baden-bei-Wien, Austria, 1995. Presented in recital and concert in Japan, Russia, Indonesia, Eng., Austria, Can. and U.S.; appeared on Nat. Pub. Radio in Performance Today. Bd. dirs. Triangle Opera, Research Triangle Park, N.C.; mem. adv. bd. Chapel Hill-Carrboro Cmty. Chorus; soprano soloist United Meth. Ch. Choir, pres., 1987-88; bd. dirs. nat. devel. coun. U. N.C., Chapel Hill; pres. Preservation Soc., Chapel Hill, 2001; bd. dirs. Chapel Hill Mus., 1999-2001. Recipient citation Chapel Hill Preservation Soc., 1995. Mem. PEO, Nat. Assn. Music Tchrs., Chapel Hill Music Tchrs. Assn. (program chair 1997-98), U. N.C. Woman's Club (pres. 1998-99). Democrat. Methodist. Avocations: swimming, tennis, walking. Home and Office: 306 N Boundary St Chapel Hill NC 27514-7800

PEACOCK, MARILYN CLAIRE, primary school educator; b. Harvey, Ill., Aug. 2, 1952; d. Carmen Anthony and Helen Elaine (Welch) R. AA with high honors, Thornton C.C., 1972; BS in Edn. with high honors, Ill. State U., 1974; MEd, Nat.-Louis U., 1990. Cert. K-9, Ill. Tchr. kindergarten Primary Acad. Ctr., Markham, Ill., 1976-91, tchr. K-3, 1991—. Ill. State scholar, 1969. Mem. Ill. Edn. Assn. (assn. rep. 1976-88), Kappa Delta Pi, Phi Theta Kappa. Republican. Avocations: music, travel. Home: 2447 Clyde St Homewood IL 60430-3103 Office: Acad Ctr 3055 W 163rd St Markham IL 60426-5626 Personal E-mail: mcrpeacock@hotmail.com.

PEACOCK, MARY WILLA, magazine editor, consultant; b. Evanston, Ill., Oct. 23, 1942; d. William Gilbert and Mary Willa (Young) P. BA, Vassar Coll., 1964. Assoc. lit. editor Harper's Bazaar mag., N.Y.C., 1964-69; staff editor Innovation mag., N.Y.C., 1969-70; editor in chief, co-founder Rags mag., N.Y.C., San Francisco, 1970-71; co-founder, features editor Ms. mag., N.Y.C., 1971-77; pub., pres. Rags mag., N.Y.C., 1977-80; sr. editor Village Voice, N.Y.C., 1980-85, style editor, 1985-89; editor-in-chief Model mag., N.Y.C., 1989—, editorial cons., 1991—; fashion dir. Lear's Mag., N.Y.C., 1992-93; dep. editor In Style Mag., 1993-94, Mirabella mag., 1994-95; cons., 1995—2006. Internat. editor InStyle; writer and cons. in field.

PEACOCK, MINDY H., music educator; b. Baton Rouge, La., May 31, 1979; d. Alvin Dermon and Kim Maria (Samson) Hebert. MusB in Edn., La. State U., Baton Rouge, 2001. Asst. band dir. Jackson Mid. Sch., San Antonio, 2001—03; head band dir. Kirby Mid. Sch., San Antonio, 2003—05, Denham Springs Jr. H.S., La., 2005—. Co-instr. La. State U. Leadership Camp, 2000; student tchr. Denham Springs H.S., 2001; organizer Region XII Band, San Antonio, 2002, chmn., 2004—05; camp adminstr. U. Tex. San Antonio Summer Mid. Sch. Band Camp, 2002—05; drum major judge Dist. IV Marching Festival, East Ascension H.S., La., 2003; solo and ensemble judge Spring Branch & NEISD Mid. Schs., San Antonio, 2003—05. Drum major: La. State U. Tiger Marching Band, 1997—2000, performer: San Antonio Mcpl. Band, 2003—04, Sousa Nat. Honors Band, 1997, prin. trumpet: U.S. Collegiate Wind Band European Concert Tour, 1997, drum major: Walker H.S. Band, 1996—97. Recipient Darson award, Kirby Mid. Sch., 2005, Winner Concerto Competition and Music Dir.'s award, La. Youth Orch., 1997, John Philip Sousa award, Walker H.S. Band, 1997, Outstanding Prospective Mem., Sigma Alpha Iota, 1999, Sword of Honor, 2001, James N. Giedman Outstanding Tiger Bandsmen award, La. State U. Tiger Marching Band, 2000. Mem.: Music Educators Nat. Conf., La. Bandmasters Assn., La. Music Educators Assn. Avocations: dance, shopping, organizing. Home: 13580 Landover Dr Denham Springs LA 70726 Office: Denham Springs Jr HS 401 Hatchell Lane Denham Springs LA 70726 Office Phone: 225-665-1681. Business E-Mail: mindy.peacock@lpsb.org.

PEACOCK, MOLLY, poet, educator; b. June 30, 1947; d. Edward Frank and Pauline Ruth (Wright) P. BA magna cum laude, Harpur Coll., Binghamton, N.Y., 1969; MA with hons., Johns Hopkins U., 1977. Adminstr., lectr. in english SUNY, Binghamton, 1970-76; instr. english Friends Sem., N.Y.C., 1981-92; poet-in-residence Bucknell U., 1993-94, Cathedral St. John the Divine, 2000—04; mem. grad. faculty Spalding U., 2001—. Author: And Live Apart, 1980, Raw Heaven, 1984, Take Heart, 1989, Original Love, 1995, Paradise, Piece by Piece, 1998, How To Read A Poem and Start A Poetry Circle, 1999, The Privacy I: Privacy in A Public World, 2001, Cornucopia: New and Selected Poems, 2002, The Shimmering Verge: A One-Woman Show in Poems, 2003; contbg. writer House and Garden mag., 1996-2001; contbr. poems to The New Yorker, The New Republic, The Nation, articles to O, the Oprah Mag., Elle, N.Y. Mag. Named Tennessee Williams Playwright in Residence, Sewanee U., 2006, Elliston poet U. Cin., 2006; Danforth Found. fellow, 1970, Yaddo fellow, 1980, 82, 89, Ingram Merrill Found. fellow 1981, 86, Lila Wallace/Woodrow Wilson fellow 1994, 95, 96, 2001; grantee Creative Artists Pub. Svc. Program, 1977, N.Y. Found. for Arts, 1985, NEA, 1991; Regents scholar U. Calif., Riverside, 1998. Mem. PEN, Poetry Soc. Am. (governing bd. 1988—, pres. emeritus). Home: 109 Front St E #1041 Toronto ON M5A 4P7 Canada Office Phone: 212-677-3535. E-mail: molly@mollypeacock.org.

PEACOCK, PENNE KORTH, ambassador; b. Hattiesburg, Miss., Nov. 3, 1942; m. Fritz-Alan Korth, Dec. 15, 1965 (div. 1997); children: Fritz-Alan Jr., Maria Korth Chieffalo, James Frederick; m. Andrew Peacock, Sept. 21, 2002. Student, U. Tex., 1960—64. Sr. Washington assoc., client liaison and rep. trust and estate div. Sotheby's, 1986-89; amb. to Mauritius, Port Louis, 1989-92; pres. Firestone and Korth Ltd., Washington, 1993-97; commr. US Adv. Commn. Pub. Diplomacy, 1997—. Bd. dir. Chevy Chase Bank, 1993—; rep. Sotheby's Internat., 1997—; adv. com. Sydney (Australia) Cancer Ctr., 2003—. Sr. advisor Ptnrs. in Performance Internat., 2005—; co-chmn. Am. Bicentennial Presdl. Inauguration, Washington, 1988—99; mem. adv. bd. Washington Ballet, 2002—; mem. adv. com. Sydney Cancer Ctr.; bd. dirs. Hillwood Mus. and Gardens; counselor Meridian Internat. Ctr.; bd. dirs. Coun. of Am. Ambs., 1994—. Mem.: Assn. for Diplomatic Studies and Tng. (bd. dir. 1996—2002). Office: 11 Gladswood Gardens Double Bay 2028 NSW Australia

PEACOCK, VIRGINIA C., artist; b. Harrisburg, Pa., June 25, 1958; d. M. Edwin Jr. and Karon Cliffe Green; m. Foulis Munro Peacock, Apr. 20, 1996. BA, Mount Holyoke Coll., 1980. Sec. Mus. Modern Art, N.Y.C., 1982; pub. info. assoc. Nat. Acad. Design, N.Y.C., 1983-87; graphics specialist Fortune Mag., N.Y.C., 1987-95; creative mgr. Bus. Week Mag., N.Y.C., 1995-99. One-woman shows include Ridge Street Gallery, N.Y.C., 1992, 92, 94, Artra Gallery, N.Y.C., 1992, Mercedes-Benz Manhattan, Inc., N.Y.C., 1995, 97, Mercer St. Gallery, N.Y.C., 1999; group exhbns. include The Weisner Gallery, Bklyn., 1987, The New Waterfront Mus., Bklyn., 1987, The Studio Gallery, Bklyn., 1989, B4 ART Gallery, N.Y.c., 1991, The Kentler Internat. Drawing Ctr., Bklyn., 1991, Montserrat Gallery, N.Y.C., 1992, Brookwood Child Care Ctr., Bklyn., 1992, Bklyn. Waterfront Artists Coalition, 1993-96, Time-Warner, N.Y.C., 1993, Krasdale Corp., Bronx, N.Y., 1994, Ridge St. Gallery, N.Y.C., 1994, Fort Hunter Mus., Harrisburg, Pa., 1995, Harbor Cove Cafe, Sag Harbor, N.Y., 1995, St. John's Episcopal Ch., Southampton, N.Y., 1996. Republican. Methodist. Avocations: horse riding, running, gardening, cooking, tennis.

PEAKE, CANDICE K. LOPER, data processing executive; b. Sublette, Kans., Oct. 29, 1953; d. Robert Franklin and Marion Joyce Loper; m. Eugene E. Peake, Aug. 12, 1993. Student, McPherson Coll., Kans., 1971—72; lic. in cosmetology, Crums Beauty Sch., Kans., 1974; student, Garden City Community Coll., Kans., 1975—76, Diablo Valley Coll., 1988—89; BS in Bus./e-Bus., U. Phoenix, 2006; MBA, Colo. Tech. U., 2006—. Cert. data processor ICCP. Owner, operator Candi's For Beautiful Hair, Garden City, 1974-78; systems project librarian Bank of Am., San Francisco, 1980, analyst, 1981, systems analyst, 1981-82, sr. systems analyst, 1982-83, cons., 1983-84, systems cons., team leader, 1984; project mgr. Wells Fargo Bank, Concord, Calif., 1984-86; systems analyst 1st Nationwide Bank, San Francisco, 1986-88; adv. systems engr. Bank Am., Concord, Calif., 1988-89; owner Candi's Visions, Independence, Mo., 1988—; sr. mgr. Computer Scis. Corp., Independence, 1989—. Home: 3419 S Home Ave Independence MO 64052-1239 Office: Computer Scis Corp 3419 S Home Ave Independence MO 64052-1239 Office Phone: 816-506-9614. Business E-Mail: cpeake@csc.com.

PEALE, RUTH STAFFORD (MRS. NORMAN VINCENT PEALE), not-for-profit executive; b. Fonda, Iowa, Sept. 10, 1906; d. Frank Burton and Anna Loretta (Crosby) Stafford; m. Norman Vincent Peale, June 20, 1930; children: Margaret Ann (Mrs. Paul F. Everett), John Stafford, Elizabeth Ruth (Mrs. John M. Allen). AB, Syracuse U., 1928, LLD, 1953; LittD, Hope Coll., 1962; LHD (hon.), Judson Coll., 1988. Tchr. math. Cen. High Sch., Syracuse, NY, 1928—30; nat. pres. women's bd. domestic missions Ref. Ch. Am., 1936-46; sec. Protestant Film Commn., 1946-51; chmn. Am. Mother's Com., 1948-49; pres., editor-in-chief, gen. sec., CEO, chmn. bd. trustees, chmn. emeritus Guideposts Peale Ctr. Christian Living, 1940—; nat. pres. bd. domestic missions Ref. Ch. in Am., 1955-56; mem. bd. N. Am. Missions, 1963-69, pres., 1967-69; mem. gen. program coun. Ref. Ch. in Am., 1968—; mem. com. of 24 for merger Ref. Ch. in Am. and Presbyn. Ch. U.S., 1966-69; v.p. Protestant Council NYC, NYC, 1964-66; co-founder, pub. Guideposts, NYC, 1945—, pres., 1985-92, chmn. bd., 1999—2003, chmn. emeritus, 2003—; pres. Fleming H. Revell, Tarrytown, NY, 1985-92. Appeared on: (nat. TV program) What's Your Trouble, 1952—68; author: I Married a Minister, 1942, The Adventure of Being a Wife, 1971, Secrets of Staying in Love, 1984, A Lifetime of Positive Thinking, 2001; founder, pub. (with Dr. Peale) Guidepost mag., 1945—, co-subject with husband (film) One Man's Way, 1963. Named N.Y. State Mother of Yr., 1963, Disting. Woman of Yr., Nat. Art Assn., Religious Heritage Am. Ch. Woman of Yr., 1969, Woman of Yr., AAUW, 2000; recipient Cum Laude award Syracuse U. Alumni Assn. N.Y., 1965, Honor Iowans award Buena Vista Coll., 1966, Am. Mother's com. award for religion, 1970, Disting. Svc. award Coun. Chs., N.Y.C., 1973, Disting. Citizen award Champlain Coll., 1976, Disting. Svc. to Cmty. and Nation award Gen. Fedn. Women's Clubs, 1977, Horatio Alger award, 1977, Religious Heritage award, 1979, joint medallion with husband Soc. for Family of Man, 1981, Soc. Family of Man award, 1981, Alderson-Broaddus award, 1982, Marriage Achievement award Bride's mag., 1984, Gold Angel award Religion in Media, 1987, Adela Rogers St. John Roundtable award, 1987, Disting. Achievement award Am. Aging, 1987, Paul Harris award N.Y. Rotary, 1989, Leader's award Arthritis Found. Dutchess County, 1992, Dave Thomas Well Done! award, 1994, Norman Vincent Peale award for positive thinking, 1994, Master of Influence award, 1995, The Leadership award Worldwide Leadership Coun., 1998, Cert. for Disting. Svc., N.Y. State Fedn. Women's Clubs, 1999, Light award CANDL Found., 2000, Woman of Distinction awd RCA Women, 2001. Mem. Blanton-Peale Inst. (bd. exec. com.), Am. Bible Soc. (trustee 1948-93, hon. trustee 1993—, bd. dirs.), Nat. Bible Assn. (bd. dirs.), United Bible Soc., Interch. Ctr. (bd. dirs. 1957-92, chmn. 1982-90), Nat. Coun. Chs. (v.p. 1952-54, gen. bd.; treas. gen. dept. United Ch. Women, vice chmn. broadcasting and film commn. 1951-55, program chmn. gen. assembly 1966), N.Y. Fedn. Women's Clubs (chmn. religion 1951-53, 57-58), Home Missions Coun. N.A. (nat. pres. 1942-44, nat. chmn. migrant com. 1948-51), Internat. Platform Orgn. (bd. govs. 1994-2000), Cmty. Action Network (adv. bd. 1998—), Wainwright House (hon. trustee, advisor 2001), PEO, Sorosis (pres. 1953-56, hon. pres.), Alpha Phi (Frances W. Willard award 1976). Republican. Office: Guideposts 66 E Main St Pawling NY 12564-1409 Office Phone: 845-855-5000. Business E-Mail: rpeale@guideposts.org.

PEARCE, BELINDA ALLEN, elementary reading recovery educator; b. Clinton, Ky., May 16, 1951; d. Billie Todd and Ramona (Boswell) Allen; m. Woody D. Pearce, Aug. 23, 1970; children: Kristie Michaela, Jessica Lynne. BS in Elem. Edn., Blue Mountain Bapt. Coll. Women, 1972; MEd in Elem. Edn., U. So. Miss., 1976; postgrad., Jackson State U., 1995. 3d grade tchr. Rienzi (Miss.) Sch., 1972-73; 5th and 6th grade reading tchr. Hancock North Ctrl. Elem. Sch., Pass Christian, Miss., 1973-74, 3d and 4th grade reading tchr., 1974-75, 3d grade tchr., 1975-79, North Bay Elem. Sch., Bay St. Louis, Miss., 1979-86; 2d grade tchr. Waveland Elem. Sch., Bay St. Louis, Miss., 1986-94; Chpt. I reading recovery tchr. North Bay Elem. Sch., 1994-99; tchr. 3d grade Charles B. Murphy Elem. Sch., Pearlington, Miss., 1999—2001; spl. populations coord. Hancock County Vocat. Sch., Kiln, Miss., 2001—. Dept. chmn. Hancock North Ctrl. Elem. Sch., Waveland Elem. Sch. Vol. Bible sch. tchr. First Bapt. Ch., Brazil, summer 1989. Mem. Miss. Profl. Educators, Miss. Edn. Assn. (numerous offices), Delta Kappa Gamma (Alpha Upsilon chpt.). Avocations: swimming (tchr. Red Cross lessons), walking, reading. Home: 916 Victoria St Waveland MS 39576-2635

PEARCE, CAROLE ANN, poet; d. Franklin Richard Markham and Mary Priscilla Jensen; m. Ronald Kent Chirrick, July 12, 1958 (div. 1964); children: Kenneth Scott Chirrick, Ronda Lee Buhler; m. Edwin Garth Pearce, Nov. 26, 1966; 1 child, Edwin Ryan. Degree in bus., Salt Lake Trade Tech. Coll., 1965; AS, Salt Lake C.C., 1998. Lic. real estate assoc. Utah. Real estate assoc. Utah Dept. Bus. Regulation, Salt Lake City, 1976—80. Writer, editor fed. women's coord. U.S. Geol. Survey, Salt Lake City, 1989—94, equal employment opportunities officer, 1993. Contbr. poetry to Great Poems of the Western World, 1990, The Fountain of Peace, 2000, Nature's Gentle Kiss, 2003. Mem.: Dixie Newcomers of St. George (corr.), Acad. Am. Poets, Internat. Soc. Poetry (corr. Poet of Merit 2000, 2002, 2003, 2004). Avocations: swimming, dance, reading. Home and Office: 1831 Lazy River Dr Saint George UT 84790-4420 E-mail: lazypearce@aol.com.

PEARCE, DRUE, federal official, former state legislator; b. Fairfield, Ill., Apr. 2, 1951; d. H. Phil and Julia Detroy (Bannister) P.; m. Michael F.G. Williams; 1 child, Tate Hanna Pearce-Williams. BA in Biol. Scis., Ind. U., 1973; MPA, Harvard U., 1984; cert. exec. program Darden Sch. Bus., U. Va., 1989. Sch. tchr., Clark County, Ind., 1973-74; curator of edn. Louisville Zoo, 1974—76; dir. Summerscene, Louisville, 1976—77; asst. v.p., br. mgr. Alaska Nat. Bank of the North, 1977-82; legis. aide to Rep. John Ringstad Alaska Ho. of Reps., Juneau, 1983, mem., 1984-88, minority whip, 1987—88; mem. Alaska Senate, 1989—2001, chmn. com. oil and gas, mem. exec. com. energy coun., 1989-90, chmn. com. labor and commerce, mem. exec. coms. western state conf., coun. state govts., energy coun., 1991-92, co-chmn. senate fin., chmn. energy coun., vice chmn. com. energy, nat. coun. state govts., 1993-94, mem. select com. legis. ethics and legis. coun., pres. senate, mem. exec. com. energy coun., vice chmn. senate coms. resources and rules, 1995-96, co-chmn. com. senate fin., mem. exec. com. energy coun., vice chmn. com. senate judiciary, 1997—98; sr. adv. to sec. for Alaska affairs US Dept. Interior, 2001—; fed. coord. for Alaskan Natural Gas Transp. Projects Fed. Energy Regulatory Commn., 2006—. Senate pres., 1995-96, 1999-2000, senate rules chmn., 2001; ptnr. Cloverland N., Anchorage, 1993—; resources cons. Arctic Slope Regional Corp., Anchorage, 1987-91, 95-96; sr. adv. Sec. Interior for Alaska Affairs, 2001-. Former bd. dirs. Alaska Women's Aid in Crisis, Anchorage Econ. Devel. Coun., Alaska Aerospace Devel. Corp., Alaska Spl. Olympics, Gov.'s Bd. Mem. DAR, Commonwealth North, Resource Devel. Coun., Alaska Miners Assn., Alaska Fedn. Rep. Women, Aircraft Owners & Pilots Assn., U.S. Trotting Assn. Republican. Office: Office of the Secretary Dept of the Interior 1849 C St NW MS 6020 Washington DC 20240

PEARCE, KAREN LEE, elementary school educator; b. Bethesda, Md., Nov. 4, 1944; d. Norman Donald and Virginia Lee (Copeland) Pearce. AA, San Diego City Coll., 1964; BA in Social Studies, San Diego State U., 1966, postgrad., 1989—91. Cert. learning handicapped tchr. Calif., elem. tchr. Calif., secondary tchr. Calif. 8th grade social studies and English tchr. El Centro Sch. Dist., Calif., 1967—72; 7th-8th grade social studies and English tchr. Dept. Def. Overseas Schs., Heilbronn, Germany, 1972—74, 6th-8th grade social studies tchr. Okinawa, Japan, 1974—77, 5th grade tchr., 1977—80, 1987—89, 5th-6th grade tchr., 1981—84, elem. tchr. learning handicapped, 1984—87; elem. resource specialist San Diego Unified Sch. Dist., 1989—. Girls recreation dir. El Centro Recreation Dept., 1968—70; presenter workshops in field. Co-collaborator: Special Education Handbook for Parents, 1985—86, rev. edit., 1989—90. Vol. Very Spl. Arts Festival for Handicapped Children, Okinawa, 1981—82, Spl. Olympics, Okinawa, 1983—84, sch. liaison, 1985—86. Recipient Cert. of Excellence, El Centro Elem. Tchrs.' Assn., 1971—72, Scroll of Appreciation, US Army Base, Heilbronn, 1972—74. Mem.: Calif. Tchrs.' Assn. (chmn. human rights San Diego Svc. Ctr. 2004—, WHO award 2005), San Diego Educators' Assn. (sch. site rep. 2000—, mem. polit. involvent com. 2001—, mem. Read Across Am. com. 2001—03, mem. cmty. rels. cm. 2000—03), Phi Delta Kappa. Avocations: reading, travel.

PEARCE, SERENA RAY, performing arts educator, music director; b. Charlotte, Nc, Dec. 21, 1950; d. Archie Sereno and Blanche Horton Ray; m. Clyde Thomas Pearce, May 19, 1973; 1 child, Christa Pearce Honeycutt. MusB, U. of NC - Greensboro, Greensboro, NC, 1973; MusM, Meredith Coll., Raleigh, NC, 1987. Lic. tchr. of Music K-12 NC. Chorus and drama dir. Zebulon GT Magnet Mid. Sch., Zebulon, NC, 1973—; adult choir, drama and handbell dir. Bethany Bapt. Ch., Wendell, NC, 1973—. Cultural arts chmn. Zebulon GT Magnet Mid. PTA, Zebulon, NC, 1989—. Mem.: Am. Choral Directors Assn., Music Educators Nat. Conf. Baptist. Avocation: music director for over five groups at a local baptist church.

PEARCE-WORTHINGTON, CAROL, writer, editor; b. Dubuque, Iowa, Dec. 25, 1947; d. Wallace Harry Pearce and Edna Louisa (Williams) Meyer; m. Robert Theodore Worthington, June 23, 1984. BA, Clarke Coll., 1972; MFA, Villanova U., 1974. Sr. editor Show Magazine, N.Y.C., 1975—77; assoc. editor Backstage Newspaper, N.Y.C., 1977—78; sr. editor Weight Watchers Magazine, N.Y.C., 1978—82; writer, editor dept. medicine Meml. Sloan Kettering Cancer Ctr., N.Y.C., 1987—. Featured poetry reader at various readings, N.Y.C., 1995-96. Author: Amelia Earhart, A Biography, 1988, Career Chic, 1990, Harry and Hazel, 2006, the Adventures of Boo in Bubbalooland, Book I-The Wees, 2006; co-author (with J. Francois Eid, M.D.) Making Love Again, 1992; contbr. articles to mags. and pocket books, 1981-91, short stories to Quar. West, Oregon East, Greensboro Rev., Caribbean Writer and other lit. mags.; poetry published in Small Pond, Anemone, Dell Love Poems, Julien's Journal, N.Am. Mentor, Princeton Arts Rev. Recipient Sinipee Nonfiction award Loras Coll., Langston Hughes Poetry award YM-YWCA, N.Y.C., 1982, Annual Poetry award Poetry Soc. Am., 1985, Deer Valley Fiction award U. Utah, 1986; creative writing fellowships to Wesleyan U., Columbia U., Bennington Coll.; poetry and watercolors selected for Cornell Med. Libr. Tri-institutional Art Show, 1994-2003; named artist in residence Millay Colony for the Arts. Mem. AMWA, Princeton Club. E-mail: wordsmiths@excite.com.

PEARCY, SUSAN BETH DUE, artist, printmaker; b. St. Louis, May 6, 1945; d. Waldemar Bernard Henry and Doris Jewel (Hoeger) Due; m. Glen Johnston Pearcy, July 7, 1944; children: Noah Johnston, Rebecca Due. Student, Art Student's League, N.Y.C., 1970; BS in Painting, Graphics and Sculpture, NYU, 1969; student, S.E. Mo. State U., 1963-66. Tchr. various pub. schs., various locations, 1970—, Montgomery County, MD; reviewer The New Art Ctr., Washington, 1987; juror Torpedo Factory Arts Ctr., Alexandria, Va., 1988; pres. Washington Printmakers Gallery, Washington, 1988-90. Tchr. Women's Studio Workshop, N.Y.; bd. dirs. and co-founder Washington Printmakers Gallery; co-chmn. Internat. prints I, Washington, 1989; chmn. Washington Area Printmakers, 1982. Exhibited in group shows include Hudson River Mus., Yonkers, N.Y., 1987, Mus. Modern Art, Buenos Aires, 1987, U. Miss. Mus., 1990, Museu de Arte do Rio Grande do Sul, Brazil, 1989, Visual Arts Ctr., Anchorage, 1989, D.C.&B. Gallery, Brussels, Belgium, 1988, Knoxville Mus. Art, 1988, Nat. Mus. Am. Art, 1988, Silvermine Guild Galleries, New Canaan, Conn., 1988, John Szoke Gallery, N.Y.C., 1988, U. Hawaii at Hilo, 1988, Parkersburg (W.Va.) Art Ctr., 1988, State Tretyakov Gallery, Moscow, 1990, Del. Ctr. for the Contemporary Arts, Wilmington, 1990, Printmaking Coun. of N.J. Nat. Exhibit, 1999, Newman Gallery, Washington, DC, many others; represented in permanent collection at Nat. Mus. Am. Art, Nat. Gallery Art, Pushkin Mus., USSR, Nat. Mus. Women in Arts, 1994, 96, 2002, 03, Corcoran Gallery of Art, 1997, Janner 81 Gallery, N.Y.C., 1998, Nat. Print Biennial and Non-Toxic Prints, Richmond, Va., 1998, FACET, Taos, N.Mex., 1998, others. Co-chair Inclusive Lang. Task Force, Silver Spring, Md., 1989; mem. Stephen's Ministry, 1990. Md. State Arts Coun. grantee, 1989, 1987, Calif. State Arts Coun. grantee, 1977, 79; recipient Equal Merit awards, Art League Gallery, Alexandria, Va., 1987, 86, 85, 84, 83, others. Mem. Md. Printmakers, So. Graphics Coun., Gomez Gallery. Democrat. United Ch. of Christ Avocations: gardening, canoeing. Home: PO Box 63 Barnesville MD 20838-0063

PEARL, HELEN ZALKAN, lawyer; b. Washington, Sept. 12, 1938; d. George and Harriet (Libman) Zalkan; m. Jason E. Pearl, June 27, 1959; children: Gary M., Esther H., Lawrence J. BA with honors, Vassar Coll., Poughkeepsie, N.Y., 1959; JD, U. Conn., Storrs, 1978. Bar: Conn. 1978, U.S. Dist. Ct. Conn. 1978. Mkt. rsch. analyst Landers, Frary & Clark, New Britain, Conn., 1960-61, managerial statistician, 1961-62; real estate salesperson Denuzze Co., New Britain, 1966-70; property mgr. self-employed New Britain, 1970-75; legal asst. Atty. Gen. Office, State of Conn., Hartford, 1978; assoc. Weber & Marshall, New Britain, 1978-83, ptnr., 1983-99, Weber & Carrier, New Britain, 1999—. Hearing officer Commn. on Human Rights and Opportunities, State of Conn., 1980—98; spl. master Conn. Jud. Dept., 1986—. New Britain rep. to Ctrl. Conn. Regional Planning Agy., 1973-75, 84—, chmn., 1990-92; active New Britain Bd. Fin. and Taxation, 1973-77, Conn. State Ethics Commn., 2004-05; co-v.p. Vassar Class, 2004—; vice chair Conn. Citizens Ethics Adv. Bd., 2005; founder, mem. Conn. Permanent Commn. on Status of Women, 1975-82, bd. dirs. Human Resources Agy., 2001—, others. Recipient Book award for torts, Am. Jurisprudence, 1976, Women in Leadership award, YWCA of New Britain, 1988, Vet. Feminists Am. award, 2005. Mem. AAUW (pres. 1970-72), Conn. Bar Assn., New Britain Bar Assn., LWV (Conn. specialist 1987-2004, local pres. 1995-97, co-pres. 2003—), Hartford Vassar Club (sec. 2006—), Phi Beta Kappa. Democrat. Jewish. Avocations: travel, theater, reading, cooking. Home: 206 Hickory Hill Rd New Britain CT 06052-1010 Office: Weber & Carrier 24 Cedar St New Britain CT 06052-1302 Office Phone: 860-225-9463. Personal E-mail: hzpearl@msn.com. Business E-Mail: hpearl@webercarrier.com.

PEARL, MARY CORLISS, wildlife conservationist; b. NYC, July 5, 1950; d. George Carleton and Margaret Lyon (Scheuer) Pearl; m. Don Jay Melnick, Oct. 3, 1981; children: Meredith, Seth. BA, Yale U., 1972, MPhil, 1976, PhD, 1982; DSc (hon.), Marist Coll., 2006. Dir. corp. devel. World Wildlife Fund, NYC, 1983-85, head NY office, 1984-85; adminstr. conservation progs. Wildlife Conservation Soc., NYC, 1985-87, asst. dir., 1988—; exec. dir., pres. Wildlife Trust (formerly Wildlife Preservation Trust Internat.); vis. scholar dept. biol. sci. Stanford U., 1987-88; assoc. dir. Ctr. Environ. Rsch. and Conservation Columbia U. Co-founder Consortium for Conservation Medicine, 1997; adj. rschr. Columbia U., N.Y.C.; cons. UNDP. Editl. adv. Wildlife Conservation mag., 1988; editor: Conservation for the 21st Century, 1989, Conservation Medicine: Ecosystem Health in Practice, 2002; co-editor: Conservation for the 21st Century; columnist Discover Magazine, 2006—;

contbr. articles to profl. jour. Founding mem. Cons. in Higher Edn. Group of the Rainforest Alliance, NYC, 1988; trustee Gomez Found., NYC, 1985—; founder Calvin Hill Daycare Ctr., New Haven, 1970. Recipient David Lapham award, Yale U., 1971. Mem.: AAAS, Am. Soc. Primatologists, Internat. Primatological Soc., AAUW, Ecohealth Soc., Soc. for Conservation Biology (bd. gov. 1990—93), Internat. Union for Conservation of Nature (primate specialist group species survival commn.), Internat. Women's Forum, Cosmos Club. Avocations: squash, birdwatching, reading, history. Office: Wildlife Trust 460 West 34th St 17th Floor New York NY 10001 Office Phone: 212-380-4460. Personal E-mail: pearl@wildlife.com. E-mail: pearl@wildlifetrust.org.

PEARLMAN, ALISON, art educator; b. W. Long Br., N.J., Oct. 7, 1968; d. Daniel Pearlman and Paula Itaya. AB, U. Calif., Berkeley, 1990; MA, U. Chgo., 1991, PhD with departmental honors, 1997. Asst. curator Mus. Contemporary Art, Chgo., 1998—2001; mem. faculty Art Ctr. Coll. Design, Pasadena, Calif., 2001—04; asst. prof. art dept. Calif. State Polytech. U., Pomona, Calif., 2004—. Freelance editor, 2001—04. Fellow Am. Art, Henry Luce Found./Am. Coun. Learned Socs., 1994, Chgo. Humanities Inst. Dissertation fellow, U. Chgo., 1995. Mem.: Assn. Art Editors, Coll. Art Assn. Home: 1750 N Harvard Blvd Hollywood CA 90027

PEARLMAN, AMALIA CECILE, artist, educator; b. Zborov, Czechoslovakia, Oct. 10, 1918; d. Charles David and F. Rachel (Weissman) Rappaport; m. Lester S. Pearlman, June 18, 1939 (dec. 1992); children: Leslie Ellen, Austin Cecil, Lise Ann, Jared Salom, Justin Dana. BA, Bklyn. Coll., 1939; MFA, NYU, 1965, PhD, 1970. Sr. rsch. scientist curriculum devel. for creative arts NYU Sch. Edn.; adj. prof. art De Anza Coll., Calif.; prof. art So. Conn. Coll.; docent in great literature Bridgeport (Conn.) Engring. Inst.; prof. art and art history Western Conn. Coll. Panelist, spkr. in field. One-person shows at Creative Gallery, N.Y., Silvermine Guild Artists, Mystic Art Assn. Gallery, Western Conn. Coll., Mali's Gallery, Rocky Neck Gloucester, San Francisco Open Studios; exhibited in group shows at Collectore of Am. Art, Bloomfield Hills, Ill. (Purchase prize), Hartford (Conn.) Atheneum (Berthe Dion Tucker award), Alameda (Calif.) Fairgrounds (1st Hon. Mention award), Norton Gallery, Palm Beach, Fla. (1st Hon. Mention), Courtyard Mexico City (1st Hon. Mention), Ligoa Duncan Galleries, Paris (Prix de Paris), Silvermine Guild of Artists (Best New Eng. Landscape award), Riverside Mus., N.Y.C., Norwich (Conn.) Art Assn.; represented in archives Nat. Mus. for Women in the Arts, Washington; prodr. audiovisual documentary: Jerusalem, The Living Past, The Emerging Future. Dir. urban evaluation and planning program at Harlem Sch., AIA. Grantee Kress Found., 1975-77, Vinmount Found., 1972, 73. Mem. Rocky Neck Art Assn. (annual demonstrations), Mechanics Inst. Chess Club, Commonwealth Club, Sierra Club. Avocations: reading, gardening, chess, great-grandchildren, theater. Home: Apt 720 2180 Post St San Francisco CA 94115 E-mail: amaliap@pacbell.net.

PEARMAN, GWYNN TAFT, elementary school educator; b. McMinnville, Tenn., Feb. 11, 1955; d. William M. and Laura Edna (Churchwell) Taft; m. Ronald Watson Pearman, Jan. 1, 1986; 1 child, William Michael. BS, Tenn. Tech. U., 1977; MS, U. Tenn., 1981. Tchr. grades 3-4 Norwood Elem., Oliver Springs, Tenn., 1977-80; tchr. grade 5 Claxton Elem., Clinton, Tenn., 1980-85, South Knoxville (Tenn.) Elem., 1985-86; tchr. grade 4 West Hills Elem., Knoxville, 1986—. Mem. SACS com., Clinton, 1994. Author (math program) Geometric Mardi Gras, 1990—. Choir Middlebrook Pike United Meth. Ch., Knoxville, 1986—, tchr., 1990—; mem. Leadership Knoxville (Tenn.) C. of C., 1995. Recipient Knoxville's Best $1,000 award C. of C., Knoxville, 1993, Presdl. award for excellence in sci. and math. tchg., Washington, 1994-95. Mem. Tenn. Sci. Tchrs. Assn., East Tenn. Edn. Assn., Smoky Mountain Math. Educator's Assn., Smoky Mountain Reading Coun., Phi Delta Kappa, Delta Kappa Gamma (nominations com. 1994—). Avocation: skiing. Home: 316 Landoak Ln Knoxville TN 37922-2091

PEARSALL, GLORIA W., retired elementary school educator; d. Fred D. and Pearl M. Williams; m. Freeman Pearsall, Dec. 23, 1958 (dec.); children: Everard F., Corinna D., Heaven-Leigh Rapture. BS, Fayetteville State U., 1954; MEd, Pa. State U., 1958. Tchr. Chinquipin (N.C.) Elem. Sch., 1954—55, P.W. Moore Elem. Sch., Farson, NC, 1955—62, Carver H.S., Mt. Olive, NC, 1964—66, Warsaw (N.C.) Elem. Sch., 1966—93, ret., 1993. Deaconess St. Stephens Amez Ch., Warsaw, 1978; treas. Ministry Kindness, Warsaw, 1963, trustee bd., 1963; compassion worker Bessie Williams Ever Ready Ch., Warsaw, 1970—99. Mem.: NEA, Nat. Assn. Advancement Colored People, N.C. Assn. Edn.

PEARSALL, MARY HELEN, retired counselor; b. Wilmington, N.C., Jan. 22, 1948; d. Stephen Fickett and Lottie Mae (King) P. BA in Religion, Meth. Coll., 1971; MEd in Guidance and Counseling, U. N.C., 1973. Guidance counselor Robinson Sch., Santurce, P.R., 1974-75; rehab. counselor N.C. Rehab. Ctr. for the Blind, Raleigh, 1976—2006; ret. Mem. AACD, Am. Rehab. Counselors Assn., Assn. Educators and Rehabs. In Visual Impairment and Blindness. Democrat. Presbyterian. Avocations: travel, walking, music, church activities. Office: NC Rehab Ctr For the Blind 305 Ashe Ave Raleigh NC 27606-2102

PEARSON, BARBARA LEE, social worker; b. Detroit, July 21, 1951; d. Lee and Muriel (Paddy) Gauchey; m. Arthur Reed Pearson, Oct. 14, 1972 (div. 1987); children: Christopher R., Nicholas A. BS, Oakland U., 1984; MSW, U. Mich., 1986. Cert. social worker. Psychiat. social worker Community Mental Health, Pontiac, Mich., 1986-87, Woodside Hosp., Pontiac, 1987-88, Pontiac Gen. Hosp., 1988-89, Oakland County Sheriff's Dept., 1989-90. Mem. Nat. Assn. Social Workers, Assn. Cert. Social Workers. Lutheran. Avocations: stained glass, playing cello, crewel embroidery, tennis, golf.

PEARSON, CLARA, elementary school educator, music educator; b. Morristown, N.J., Nov. 22, 1956; d. Everett and Lucia Olimpia vander Putten; m. Marshall J. Pearson, July 7, 1995; children: Michaela, Matthew. BA in Music Edn., Kean Coll., 1978. Music tchr. grades K-8 Washington Twp., Robbinsville, NJ, 1978—. Musical dir. Millstone (N.J.) Players, 1979—81; curriculum coord. Washington Twp., Robbinsville, 1999—2003. Children dir. Christmas Show Laurelton Pk. Bapt., Brick, NJ, 1998, 1999. Recipient Gov. Tchr. Yr., 2000, PTA Lifetime award, 2001. Mem.: Music Educators Nat. Conf. Home: 5033 Glenburne Dr Spring Hill FL 34609-0573

PEARSON, DENISE ANNE, music educator; b. Bryn Mawr, Pa., Aug. 16, 1954; d. Albert Hamilton and Helen Pope Anderson; m. James L. Pearson, June 27, 1981; children: James M., Kate E., David A. BS in Music Edn., Indiana U. Pa., 1976. Tchr. Alleghany County Sch. Dist., Covington, Va., 1976—78, Loyalsock Twp. Sch. Dist., Williamsport, Pa., 1978—81, Warren (Pa.) County Sch. Dist., 1996—. Tchr. summer sch. Warren County Summer Music Sch., 1993—. Mem. panel Pa. Ptnrs. in Arts, Erie, 2001—02; chair com. Russell (Pa.) Elem. PTA, 1988—95; dir. choirs First Luth. Ch., Warren, Pa., 1982—; bd. dirs. Warren Concert Assn., 1994—96. Mem.: Philomel (Music Tchr. of Yr. 2001), Delta Kappa Gamma. Republican. Lutheran. Avocations: reading, gardening, cooking, music. Home: 61 S Main St Russell PA 16345 Office: Youngsville Elem Middle Sch 232 Second St Youngsville PA 16371

PEARSON, GAYLE MARLENE, writer; b. Chgo., July 12, 1947; Student, Taylor U., 1965-67; BS in Edn., No. Ill. U., 1970. Asst. news editor Vance Pub., Chgo., 1970-71; child care specialist Ming Quong Children's Ctr., Los Gatos, Calif., 1974-75; area dir. Santa Clara County Info. and Referral, San Jose, Calif., 1977-81; edn. writer, editor free lance San Francisco, 1982-97; author children and young adult lit., 1980—; freelance writer, editor Chgo., 2003—. Author: (books) Fish Friday, 1986 (Best Children's Book 1986 Bay Area), The Coming Home Cafe, 1988, One Potato Tu, 1992, The Fog Doggies and Me, 1993, The Secret Box, 1997, Don't Call it Paradise, 1999. Mem. Soc. Children's Book Writers and Illustrators. Democrat. Avocations: hiking, painting, gardening. Home and Office: 326 S Maple Ave Apt 3F Oak Park IL 60302 Office Phone: 708-848-0371. Personal E-mail: gaylepearson@sbcglobal.net.

PEARSON, GWENDOLYN CURETON, elementary school educator, singer; b. Charlott, NC, Sept. 16, 1952; d. Dan and Hattie Mae Cureton; m. Samar Samuel Pearson; 1 child, Samar II. BS in Sci., Barber Scotia Coll., Concord, NC, 1975; M in Curriculum and Supervision, U. NC, Charlotte, 2003; M in Sch. Adminstrn., Gardner Webb U., Boiling Springs, NC, 2006. Tchr. Charlotte Mecklenburg Schs., 1980—. Directress Crusade Prodns., Charlotte, 1995—97, performer. Actor(directress, singer): (plays) My Grandmother Prayed for Me; A Good Man is Hard to Find (Best Actress award, 1996), Honey, I Got Laid Off, 2006. Fund raiser Diabetic Assn., Charlotte, 2004—05. Nominee Tchr. of Yr., Charlotte Mecklenburg Schs., 2000. Mem.: NTSA (corr.). Democrat. Presbyterian. Avocations: singing, poetry, theater, travel, dance. Home: 5714 Eastbrook Rd Charlotte NC 28215 Office: Quail Hollow Middle School 2901 Smithfield Church Road Charlotte NC 28210 Office Phone: 980-343-3620. Personal E-mail: tassip@aol.com.

PEARSON, HARRIET D., information technology executive; b. N.Y.C. married; 2 children. Degree in engring. with honors, Princeton U.; JD with highest honors, UCLA. Engr. major oil co., La., Tex.; environ. lawyer Washington; dir. pub. affairs, govtl. programs group IBM, 1993, chief privacy officer, 2000—. Active Online Privacy Alliance, BBB's Online Privacy Program; bd. dirs. Internet Edn. Found.; mem. exec. com. Privacy Leadership Initiative; co-chairperson privacy com. Info. Tech. Industry Coun.; keynote spkr. several nat. industry confs. Named Best Thinker, Fast Company mag., 2001; recipient W.E.S.T. award, Working Woman mag., 2001.

PEARSON, LANDON, Canadian senator; b. Toronto, Nov. 16, 1930; 5 children. BA in Philosophy and English, U. Toronto, 1951; MEd in Psychopedagogy, U. Ottawa, 1978, DU, 2002; LLD (hon.), Wilfrid Laurier U., 1995, U. Victoria, 2001, U. Carleton, 2002. Vice-chairperson Can. commn. Internat. Yr. of Child, 1979; pres., chairperson Can. Coun. on Children and Youth, 1984—90; founding mem., chairperson Can. Coalition for Rights of Children, 1990—94; senator The Senate of Can., Ottawa, 1994—2005. Advisor Children's Rights to the Min. of Fgn. Affairs, 1996; personal rep. Prime Min. to the 2002 UN Spl. Session on Children, 1999; adj. prof. Pauline Jewett Inst. Women's Studies, Carleton U., 2006—; assoc. Landon Pearson Resource Ctr. for Study of Childhood and Children's Rights. Author: Children of Glasnost, Letters from Moscow; contbr. articles to profl. jours. Liberal.

PEARSON, LOUISE S., lawyer; b. 1955; BS in Chemistry, U. Wash.; MS in Chemistry, U. Tex.; JD, U. Houston. Bar: 1984. Pvt. practice Kirkland & Ellis, Vinson & Elkins; with Baxter Internat., 1991—2000; v.p., gen. counsel, sec. Dade Behring, Inc., Deerfield, Ill., 2000—. Mem.: ABA. Office: Dade Behring Inc 1717 Deerfield Rd Deerfield IL 60015 Office Phone: 847-267-5300.

PEARSON, LYNDA ANN, music educator; b. Washington, June 1, 1950; d. Frederick Joseph and Nancy Lee Pearson. AA in Music Edn., Luther Rice Coll., Alexandria, Va., 1971, BA in Music Edn., 1973; M in Music Edn., Cath. U. of Am., Washington, 1977. Substitute tchr. Alexandria City Pub. Schs., 1973—77, vocal music tchr., 1977—. Adjudicator Bland Music Competition, Alexandria, 1985. Recipient Good Apple award, Children Together, Alexandria, 2004. Mem.: NEA, Alexandria Edn. Assn., Va. Edn. Assn., Music Educators Nat. Conf., Va. Music Educators Assn. (Dist. 10 rep. 2006—). Baptist. Avocations: counted cross stitch, rubber stamping, collecting bells and Longaberger baskets. Home: 1018 Beverley Dr Alexandria VA 22302-2420 Office: Lyles-Crouch Traditional Acad 530 S Saint Asaph St Alexandria VA 22314 Office Phone: 703-706-4430. Fax: 703-684-0252. E-mail: lpearson@acps.k12.va.us.

PEARSON, REBECCA E., lawyer; b. Balt., Jan. 14, 1964; AB, Duke Univ., 1985; JD, Univ. NC, Chapel Hill, 1989; LLM in Govt. Procurement with highest honors, George Washington Univ., 1996. Bar: Fla. 1989, DC 2000. Assoc. Venable LLP, Washington, ptnr., govt. contract litig., 2004—. Articles editor NC Jour. Internat. Law and Comml. Regulation, 1988—89, student editor-in-chief ABA Public Contract Law Jour., 1995—96; contbr. articles to profl. journals. With USAF, 1989—99. Mem.: ABA. Office: Venable LLP 575 Seventh St NW Washington DC 20004 Office Phone: 202-344-8183. Office Fax: 202-344-8300. Business E-Mail: repearson@venable.com.

PEARSON, SARAH LYNN, elementary school educator; b. Altoona, Pa., June 23, 1982; d. Lynn Robert and Mary Jo Pearson. BA, Indiana U. Pa. 5th grade tchr. Emerald Hill Elem. Sch., Culpeper, Va. Mem.: NEA, Pa. Sci. Edn. Assn., Va. Edn. Assn., Kappa Delta Pi. Roman Cath. Home: 316 Dennison Ct Culpeper VA 22701 Office: Emerald Hill Elementary School 11245 Rixeyville Rd Culpeper VA 22701

PEARSON, SUSAN, elementary school educator; b. Port Arthur, Tex., July 10, 1942; d. Alfred McCallum and Alibel (Elkins) Sherwood; m. Thomas David Pearson, Feb. 1, 1964; children: Kyle, Christopher. BS in Elem. Edn., Lamar U., Beaumont, Tex., 1966. Cert. tchr. of gifted/talented. Tex. Sch. Univ. N. Tex. Tchr. Kirbyville (Tex.) Ind. Sch. Dist., 1964, Gonzales (La.) Elem. Sch., 1964-66, Dixie Elem. Sch., Lexington, Ky., 1966-70, Roanoke (Tex.) Elem. Sch., 1984-85; gifted/talented coord. Denton (Tex.) Ind. Sch. Dist., 1992-96; tchr. Southwood Valley, Coll. Sta., Tex., 1997-2000; tchr. civics and world history 7th and 8th grades Acad. Sci. and Fgn. Langs., Huntsville, Ala., 2003—; tutor Diplomat to Kransnadar Kri., Russia, 2003—05, Diplomat to Uzbekistan, 2005—; dir. project citizen Uzbekistan, 2004—05. Cons. Dixie Elem. Sch., 1968; bd. dirs. City/County Day Sch., Denton, 1994, St. Michael's Acad., Bryan, Tex., 1996-97; long term subsitute, Madison, Ala.; Region 5 North Ala. dir. Project Citizen. Chmn. ball invitations Benefit League, Denton, Tex., 1994—96. Mem.: PEO, AAUW, Denton County Women's Club (pres.-elect 1989—91), Delta Kappa Gamma (treas.), Delta Zeta. Episcopalian. Avocations: gourmet cooking, arts and crafts, reading, travel. Home: 1811 Cross Creek Rd Huntsville AL 35802 Personal E-mail: scp0742@bellsouth.net.

PEASE, ELEANOR JEANNE, humanities educator; b. Phila., Apr. 28, 1935; d. Harold Chandler and Elizabeth (Wright) Hill; m. Richard Bruce Pease, May 26, 1956; children: Richard Bruce Jr., Sharon Pease Andrews. BA in English, Gordon Coll., 1970; MEd in English, Westfield State U., 1973. Educator Gateway Regional Schs., Huntington, Mass., 1970-74; missionary in Japan Christian & Missionary Alliance Hdqrs., Colorado Springs, Colo., 1963-68, 74-93; educator Pasadena Unified Schs., Calif., 1989—95; prof., chair TESOL Nyack Coll., NY, 1995—, chair dept. modern languages and linguistics, dir., instr. summer TESOL inst. Guest lectr. Caransebes Bible Sch., 1996; co-chair Support a Mother project com., 2001--. Contbr. articles to profl. publs. Dir. Womens Ministries, Pasadena Alliance Ch., 1991-95, English Tchrs. Seminar, Hiroshima, 1980-82, 85, 86; coord. homework assistance program Pasadena Schs., 1990-95; vice chmn. Hiroshima (Japan) Internat. Sch. Bd., 1980-83; pres. South Pacific Alliance Women, Pasadena, 1991-93. Mem. TESOL. Avocations: reading, travel. Home: 61 Summit Ave Spring Valley NY 10977-5351 Office: Nyack Coll 1 S Boulevard Nyack NY 10960-3604

PEASE, JENNIFER KELLEY, sports medicine educator; b. Red Bank, N.J., Nov. 12, 1976; d. Richard Edward and Eileen Pease. BS in Movement Sci. with specialization in Athletic Tng., U. Pitts., 2000; MA in Kinesiology, San Jose State U., Calif., 2002. Cert. athletic trainer NATA/PA, 2000, lic. Dept. of State Bur. of Profl. and Occupl. Affairs/Pa., 2004. Athletic trainer - grad. asst. Westmont H.S., Campbell, Calif., 2000—02; fitness specialist Health Fitness Corp., Palo Alto, Calif., 2001—03; athletic trainer Stanford U., Palo Alto, Calif., 2001—03; athletic trainer/clin. instr. U. of Pitts., 2003—. Big sister Big Bros. and Big Sisters Of Greater Pitts., 2005. Mem.: Pa. Athletic Trainers' Assn., Ea. Athletic Trainers' Assn., Nat. Athletic Trainers' Assn., Phi Sigma Pi (alumni and social chairs 1999—2000). Roman Catholic. Avocations: travel, running, reading, hiking, camping. Office: University of Pittsburgh PO Box 7436 Pittsburgh PA 15213 Office Phone: 412-648-7999. Home Fax: 412-648-9177; Office Fax: 412-648-9177. E-mail: jpease@athletics.pitt.edu.

PEASE-PRETTY ON TOP, JANINE B., community college administrator; b. Nespelam, Wash., Sept. 17, 1949; d. Benjamin and Margery Louise (Jordan) Pease; m. Sam Vernon Windy Boy, July 30, 1975 (div. Jan. 1983); children: Rosella L. Windy Boy, Sam Vernon Windy Boy; m. John Joseph Pretty On Top, Sept. 15, 1991. BA in Sociology, Anthropology, Ctrl. Wash. U., 1970; MEd, Mont. State U., 1987, EdD, 1994; HHD (hon.), Hood Coll., 1990; LLD (hon.), Gonzaga U., 1991; DHL (hon.), Teikyo/Marycrest U., 1992; EdD (hon.), Whitman Coll., 1993; HHD (hon.), Rocky Mountain Coll., 1998. Dep. dir. Wash. State Youth Commn., Olympia, 1971; tutor student svcs. Big Bend C.C., Moses Lake, Wash., 1971-72, upward bound dir., 1972-75; women's counselor Navajo C.C., Many Farms, Ariz., 1972; dir. adult & continuing edn. Crow Ctrl. Edn. Commn., Crow Agy., Mont., 1975-79; ednl. cons. Box Elder, Mont., 1979-81; dir. Indian career svc. Ea. Mont. Coll., Billings, 1981-82; pres. Little Big Horn Coll., Crow Agency, 1982—; with Rocky Mountain Coll., Billings, Mont. Exec. com. Am. Indian Higher Ednl. Consortium, Washington, 1983—; bd. dirs. Am. Indian Coll. Fund, N.Y.C., 1988—; sec. Indian Nations at Risk U.S. Dept. Edn., Washington, 1990-91, collaborator task force, 1990-91; 2d vice chmn. Nat. Adv. Coun. Indian Edn., Washington, 1994—. Chmn. Bighorn County Dem. Ctrl. Com., Hardin, Mont., 1983-88; mem. coun. First Crow Indian Bapt. Ch., 1989—; bd. dirs. Ctr. for Rocky Mountain West, 1998—; chmn. Mont. State Reappt. an Distructing Commn., 1999—. MacArthur fellow John D. & Catharine MacArthur Found., 1994. Mem. Nat. Indian Edn. Assn. (Indian educator of yr. 1990), Mont. Assn. Chs. (bd. dirs. 1997—), Crow Tribe Nighthawk Dance Soc.

PEASLEE, MARGARET MAE HERMANEK, zoology educator; b. Chgo., June 15, 1935; d. Emil Frank and Magdalena Bessie (Cechota) Hermanek; m. David Raymond Peaslee, Dec. 6, 1957; 1 dau., Martha Magdelena Peaslee-Levine. AA, Palm Beach Jr. Coll., 1956; BS, Fla. So. Coll., 1959; med. technologist, Northwestern U., 1958, MS, 1964, PhD, 1966. Med. technologist Passavant Hosp., Chgo., 1958-59; med. technologist St. James Hosp., Chicago Heights, Ill., 1960-63; asst. prof. biology Fla. So. Coll., Lakeland, Fla., 1966-68; asst. prof. of biology U. S.D., Vermillion, SD, 1968-71, assoc. prof., 1971-76, prof., 1976, acad. opportunity liaison, 1974-76; prof., head dept. zoology La. Tech. U., Ruston, La., 1976-90, assoc. dean, dir. grad. studies and rsch., prof. biol. scis. Coll. Life Scis., 1990-93; v.p. for acad. affairs U. Pitts. at Titusville, Titusville, Pa., 1993—. Contbr. articles to profl. jours. Fellow AAAS; mem. AAUP, Am. Inst. Biol. Scis., Am. Soc. Zoologists, S.D. Acad. Sci. (sec.-treas. 1972-76), N.Y. Acad. Scis., Pa. Acad. Sci., La. Acad. Sci. (sec. 1979-81, pres. 1983), Czechoslavak Soc. Arts and Scis. (mem. exec. bd. 2004—), Sigma Xi, Phi Theta Kappa, Phi Rho Pi, Phi Sigma, Alpha Epsilon Delta. Office Phone: 814-827-4473. Business E-Mail: peaslee@pitt.edu.

PEATTIE, LISA REDFIELD, retired urban anthropology educator; b. Chgo., Mar. 1, 1924; d. Robert and Margaret (Park) Redfield; m. Roderick Peattie, June 26, 1943 (dec. 1962); children: Christopher, Sara, Miranda, Julia; m. William A. Doebele, 1973 (div.). MA, U. Chgo., 1950, PhD, 1968. Faculty mem. dept. urban studies MIT, Cambridge, 1965—, prof. urban anthropology, 1968-85, now prof. emeritus, sr. lectr. Cons. World Bank, 1975, 76, 81, UN, 1980. Author: The View from the Barrio, 1968, Thinking About Development, 1982, (with W. Ronco) Making Work, 1983, (with Martin Rein) Women's Claims, 1983, Planning: Rethinking Ciudad Guayana, 1987. Recipient Paul Davidoff award, Am. Soc. Collegiate Schs. of Planning, 1989. Mem.: Am. Anthrop. Assn., Soc. Applied Anthropology.

PECHUKAS, DIANA GISOLFI **See GISOLFI, DIANA**

PECINA, KRISTIANNE, secondary school educator; b. Amarillo, Tex., Feb. 27, 1972; d. James Paul and Wanda Kay Stanley; m. Peter Christopher Pecina, Dec. 31, 1994; children: Makenzi, Jake. BS, Stephen F. Austin State U., Nacogdoches, Tex., 1994; M Secondary Edn., Tex. A&M U., Commerce, 2003. Tchr., coach Livingston Ind. Sch. Dist., Tex., 1994—97, Mesquite Ind. Sch. Dist., 1997—. Office: Mesquite HS 300 E Davis St Mesquite TX 75149-4610 Office Phone: 972-882-7833 ext. 2. Business E-Mail: kpecina@mesquiteisd.org.

PECK, CAROLYN, basketball coach; b. Jefferson City, Tenn. BA in Comm., Vanderbilt U., 1988. Mktg. cons., Nashville; salesperson; profl. basketball player Nippondenso Corp., Japan, 1991-93; asst. coach U. Tenn., U. Ky., 1995-96, Purdue U., West Lafayette, Ind., 1996-97, coach, 1997-98; head coach, gen. mgr. Orlando (Fla.) Miracle, 1999—2001; head coach Univ. of Fla., 2002—. Asst. coach USA Jones Cup team, 1997. Named AP Coach of the Yr., 1999, IKON/WBCA Div. I Nat. Coach of the Yr., 1999, Big 10 Coach of the Yr., 1999. Office: U Fla Women's Basketball PO Box 14485 Gainesville FL 32604

PECK, DIANNE KAWECKI, architect; b. Jersey City, June 13, 1945; d. Thaddeus Walter and Harriet Ann (Zlotkowski) Kawecki; m. Gerald Paul Peck, Sept. 1, 1968; children: Samantha Gillian Gildersleeve, Alexis Hilary. BArch, Carnegie-Mellon U., 1968. Architect P.O.D. R&D, 1968, Kohler-Daniels & Assocs., Vienna, Va., 1969-71, Beery-Rio & Assocs., Annandale, Va., 1971-73; ptnr. Peck & Peck Architects, Occoquan, Va., 1973-74, Peck Peck & Williams, Occoquan, Va., 1974-81; corp. officer Peck Peck & Assocs., Inc., Woodbridge, Va., 1981—. CEO interior design group Peck Peck & Assocs., 1988—; mem. archtl. rev. bd. Prince William County, 1998—, chair 2000-2005, mem., 2005—. Work pub. in Am. Architecture, 1985. V.p. Vocat. Edn. Found., 1976; chmn. architects and engrs. United Way, Indsl. Devel. Authority of Prince William, 1976, vice chair, 1977, mem. 1975-79, chmn. Prince William County Arch-Rev. Bd., 2001-04, mem., 2004—; mem. Health Sys. Agy. of No. Va., commendations 1977, Washington Profl. Women's Coop.; developed rsch. project Architecture for Adolescents, 1987-88; mem. inaugural class Leadership Am., 1988, Leadership Greater Washington, D.C. Coun. Metrication, 1992—, D.C. Hist. Preservation League, Rep. Nat. Com. Recipient commendation Prince William Bd. Suprs., 1976, State of Art award for Contel Hdqrs. design, 1985, Best Middle Sch. award Coun. of Ednl. Facilities Planners Internat., 1989, Creativity award Masonry Inst. Md., 1990, First award, 1990, Detailing award, 1990, Govt. Workplace award for renovations of Dept. of Labor Bldg., 1990, Creative Use of Materials award Inst. of Bus. Designers, 1991, 1st award Brick Inst. Md., 1993, award Brick Inst. Va., 1994, Bull Elephant award Prince William County Young Reps., 1995, Detailing & Craftsmanship award Washington Builder's Congress, 1998, Pres.'s citation AIA, Atlanta, 2005; Archtl. Design Competition winner Vis. Pavillion Bur. Engraving and Printing, 2002; named Best Instl. Project Nat. Comml. Builders Coun.; subject of PBS spl.: A Success in Howard Co. Mem. Soc. Am. Mil. Engrs., Prince William C. of C. (bd. dirs.), Soroptimist Club. Roman Catholic. Research on inner-city rehab., adolescents and the ednl. environ. Office: 2050 Old Bridge Rd Woodbridge VA 22192-2447 Office Phone: 703-690-3121. Business E-Mail: dpeck@peckpeck.com.

PECK, MARYLY VANLEER, retired academic administrator, chemical engineer; b. Washington, June 29, 1930; d. Blake Ragsdale and Ella Lillian (Wall) VanLeer; m. Jordan B. Peck, Jr., June 15, 1951; children: Jordan B. III, Blake VanLeer, James Tarleton VanLeer, Virginia Ellaine.; m. 2d, Walter G. Ebert, Sept. 3, 1983 (dec. June 1990); m. 3d Edwin L. Carey, Apr. 13, 1991. Student, Ga. Inst. Tech., 1948, 55-58, Duke U., 1947-48; B.Ch.E., Vanderbilt U., 1951; MSE., U. Fla., 1955, PhD, 1963. Chem. engr. Naval Research Lab., Washington, 1951-52; chem. engr. Med. Field Research Lab., Camp LeJeune, NC, 1952; asso. research and instr. U. Fla., Gainesville, 1953-55; chem. engr., research asso. Ga. Tech. Expt. Sta., Atlanta, 1956-58; lectr. Ga. State Coll., Atlanta, 1957-58; lectr. math. East Carolina Extension, Camp Lejeune, 1959; sr. research engr. Rocketdyne div. N.Am. Aviation Co., 1961-63; self-employed as lectr., 1963; assoc. prof. Campbell Coll., Buie's Creek, NC, 1963-66, prof., 1966; acad. dir. St. John's Episcopal Sch., Upper Tumon, Guam, 1966-68; chmn., prof. phys. scis. U. Guam, Agana, 1968-73, dean Coll. Bus. and Applied Tech., 1973-74, dean Community Career Coll., 1974-77; pres. Cochise Coll., Douglas, Ariz., 1977-78; systems planning analyst Urban Pathfinders, Inc., Balt., 1978-79; dean undergrad. studies U. Md. Univ. Coll., College Park, 1979-82; pres. Polk Community Coll., Winter Haven, Fla., 1982-97, pres. emeritus, 1997—; headmaster All Saints' Acad., 1997-99. Cons. in field. Founder, pres. Guam Acad. Found., 1972-77; bd. dirs. Cochise Coll. Found., 1977-78; charter bd. dirs. Turnaround Inc., 1987-91, chmn. 1990-93; bd. dirs. United Way Ctrl. Fla., 1986-95, vice-chmn., 1992, chair elect, 1993, chmn. 1994; founding mem. Prince George's Ednl. TV Cable Coalition; mem. Prince George's Cable TV Ednl. Adv. Group, 1980-82, Polk County Coun. Econ. Edn., 1982; sec. Polk C.C. Found., 1982-97; mem. Polk County Coord. Coun. Vocat. Edn., 1982-91, PRIDE Adv. Coun.; vice-chmn. Fla. Job Tng. Coord. Coun., 1983-87, Fla. Edn. Fund Bd., 1988-93; active Girls Inc. Bd., 1992—, pres., 2000-2001, hon. mem., 2005; trustee All Sts.'s Acad. 1994-2002; trustee Vanguard Sch., 2001—06, mem. Fdn. Bd., 2001—06; bd. dirs. Theater Winter Haven, 2000—, chair, 2002-03. Named Disting. Alumnus U. Fla., 1992, Woman of Distinction Girls Scouts U.S.A., 1994, Woman of Distinction, 1997; fellow NSF, 1961-63; recipient She Knows Where She's Going award Girls Inc. of Winter Haven, 1995, Cmty. Svc. award Jr. League Winter Haven, 2002, Boy Scout Disting. Citizen award Lake Region Dist. Gulf Ridge Coun. Am., 2005, NDAR Cmty. Svc. award, 2005. Fellow Soc. Women Engrs. (nat. v.p. 1962-63); mem. AAUW, AIChE, DAR (Cmty. Svc. award 2005), Am. Chem. Soc., NSPE, Am. Assn. for Higher Edn., Am. Assn. Cmty. and Jr. Colls., Am. Assn. Univ. Adminstrs., Rotary (sec. 1999-2000, pres.-elect 2003-04, centennial pres. 2004-05), Sigma Xi, Tau Beta Pi, Chi Omicron Gamma, Phi Kappa Phi, Delta Kappa Gamma. Episcopalian. Home: 5390 Woodland Lakes Dr 206 Palm Beach Gardens FL 33418-3959 E-mail: marylypeck@bellsouth.net.

PECK, PHYLLIS HAINLINE, educator; b. Clinton, Iowa, Mar. 14, 1921; d. Russell C. and Julia (Fairchild) Hainline; m. Albert Peck, Jan. 21, 1949; 1 child, Dana Russell. BA, Coll. of St. Catherine, 1942. Adminstrv. analyst Vet. Adminstrn., Washington, 1945—47; instr. in English and bus. Mt. St. Clare Coll., Clinton, 1955-74; instr. in bus. Clinton Community Coll., 1980-93; pvt. practice lectr. Clinton, 1972—90; cons. Ea. Iowa Community Coll. Dist., Davenport, Iowa, 1984—. Cons., lectr. U. Iowa, Iowa City, 1974-85; cons. in humanities Ea. Iowa Community Coll. Dist., 1984—. Author poems (Golden Poet 1989, 90, 91, 92, Poet of Merit, 1989); contbr. articles to bus. jours. Recipient Main St. State award State of Iowa, 1988, Gov.'s Vol. award, 1989. Mem. P.E.O (recording sec. 1986-87, chaplain 1987-91), Profl. Secs. Internat. (hon., life), Alpha Delphian Lit. Soc. (sec. 1986-87, pres. 1987-88). Methodist. Avocations: writing, lecturing, travel. Home: 54 N Church St Apt 21 Fairhope AL 36532-2438

PECTOR, MICHELLE D., lawyer; b. San Antonio, Tex. BA cum laude, U. Tex., Austin, 1997; JD cum laude, U. Houston Law Ctr., 2000. Bar: Tex. 2000, US Dist. Ct. (all dists. Tex.), US Supreme Ct., US Ct. Appeals Fifth Cir. Assoc. Baker Hostetler, Houston. Named a Rising Star, Tex. Super Lawyers mag., 2006. Mem.: Tex. Bar Assn., Assn. Women Attys., Houston Young Lawyers Assn., ABA. Office: Baker Hostetler 1000 Louisiana Ste 2000 Houston TX 77002 Office Phone: 713-646-1326. E-mail: mpector@bakerlaw.com.*

PECZKOWSKI, KRISTIN MARIE, social sciences educator, coach; b. Oak Lawn, Ill., Apr. 8, 1978; d. Barbara Ann Peczkowski; m. Christopher Kuchyt, Dec. 31, 2005. B in Social Sci., Ill. State U., Normal, 2000; paralegal cert., Roosevelt U., 2001; M in Curriculum and Instrn., Concordia U., River Forest, Ill., 2005. Paralegal Earl T. Medansky, Ltd., Chgo., 2001—01; social studies tchr. Oak Lawn (Ill.) Cmty. HS, 2002—. Head swim coach Oak Lawn Cmty. H.S., 2002—. Chaperone Relay for Life, Oak Lawn, 2005. Recipient Outstanding Sportsmanship award, Ill. H.S. Assn., 2004. Mem.: Nat. Coun. Social Studies (life), Pi Beta Phi (life; treas. 1998—99). Office: Oak Lawn Cmty HS 9400 SW Hwy Oak Lawn IL 60453 Office Phone: 708-424-5200. Home Fax: 708-424-5200; Office Fax: 708-424-5278. Personal E-mail: kpeczkowski@olchs.org.

PEDERSEN, ARLENE, web design company executive; b. 1974; Creative dir., owner Pedersen Design Grp. Involved with Tanque Verde Sch. Dist.; mem. Leukemia and Lymphoma Soc. Team in Tng.; mentor Nike Women's Marathon. Named one of 40 Under 40, Tucson Bus. Edge, 2006. Office: Pedersen Design Group 1160 N Craycroft Rd Tucson AZ 85712 Office Phone: 520-270-7863. Office Fax: 520-270-7957.*

PEDERSEN, DARLENE DELCOURT, publishing executive, writer, psychotherapist; b. Westbrook, ME; 1 child, Jorgen David. BSN, U. Conn., 1967; postgrad., U. B.C., 1974-75; MSN, U. Penn., 1996—97. RN bd. cert. clinical specialist, advanced practice registered nurse, bd. cert. in adult psychiatric and mental health nursing, Am. Nurses Credentialing Ctr. Various nursing positions, psychiat. cmty. health, 1967-79; assoc. editor JB Lippincott Co., Phila., 1979-84; sr. acquisition editor WB Saunders Co., Phila., 1984-88, v.p., editor in chief, 1988-91, sr. v.p., editorial dir. books divsn., liaison to London office, 1991-95; domestic and internat. pub. cons. Phila., 1995—; psychotherapist pvt. practice, 1997—. Team leader Northwestern Human Svcs. Delaware County, 1998—99; dir. PsychOptions, 2000—; v.p. content ops. MedCases, Phila., 2000—03; exec. editor Thomson Physicians World, 2003—04; mng. editor FA Davis Co., Phila., 2004—. Author: Canadian Nurse, 1976, PsychNotes, 2005 (Book of Yr. award Am. Jour. Nursing, 2005); contbg. editor: (book) Basic Nursing Skills, 1977; acquisition editor: book Saunders Manual of Medical Practice, Comprehensive Cytopathology. Mem.: ANA, Internat. Soc. Traumatic Stress Studies, U.S. Dressage Fedn., Inc., Am. Orthopsychiat. Assn., Internat. Platform Assn., Assn. Profl. Comm. Cons., Manuscript Soc., Forum Exec. Women, Internat. Soc. Psychiat. Mental Health Nurses, Med. Mktg. Assn., Assn. Am. Pubs., Med. Mktg. Assn., Am. Med. Writers Assn., Am. Med. Pubs. Assn., Am. Psychiat. Nurses Assn., Am. Group Psychotherapy Assn., Emily's List, U. Club Penn., Sigma Theta Tau (Xi chpt.). Avocations: autograph and art collection, travel, music, reading, movies. Office: FA Davis Co 1915 Arch St Philadelphia PA 19103 Office Phone: 215-568-2074. Business E-Mail: ddp@fadavis.com.

PEDERSEN, GLADYS DEL S., volunteer; b. Tilaran, Guanacaste, Costa Rica, Apr. 1, 1932; d. Gilberto Salas and Petronila Masis de Salas; m. Albert R. Pedersen Sr. Assoc. Mgmt., SUNY S.I., 1978; BSBA, St. John's U., S.I., 1984; M Mktg., Wagner Coll., S.I., 1986. Sec. bilingual Bank. Am. Internat., N.Y.C., 1959—67, asst. supr. sec. pool, 1968—72, officer, asst. adminstr., 1972—80, fin. officer, 1980—88. Dir.(play writer): A Family Affair or Monkey Business, 2003, (writer mime Christmas play): The Golden Shoes, 2004. Chair scholarship com. Latin Am. Civic and Cultural Assn., Spring Hill, Fla., 1998—2005; pres., founder Hispanic Scholarships Civic and Cultural Found., Spring Hill, 2005—; tchr. Adult Edn. Literacy Program, 1999—2006; capt. welcome ctr. St. Joan of Arc Roman Cath. Ch., Spring Hill, 1995—. Mem.: Latin Am. Club. Achievements include organizer of annual Spanish heritage festival attended by over 1000 people. Avocations: dance, writing, poetry, classical music. Home: 482 Waterloo Ct Spring Hill FL 34609 Office: Hispanic Scholarship Civic and Cultural Found PO Box 4012 Spring Hill FL 34611 Personal E-mail: gladyspedersen@yahoo.com.

PEDERSEN, KAREN SUE, electrical engineer; b. Indianola, Iowa, Apr. 27, 1942; d. Donald Cecil and Dorothy Darlene (Frazier) Kading; m. Wendell Dean Pedersen, May 6, 1961; children: Debra Ann Pedersen Schwickerath, Michael Dean. AA in Math., Grand View Coll., Des Moines, 1975; BSEE, Iowa State U., 2007; MBA in Econ., Bentley Coll., Waltham, Mass., 1989. Registered profl. engr., Iowa, Mass., Ill. Engr. Iowa Power & Light Co., Des Moines, 1978—80, rate engr., 1980—84; sr. rsch. engr. Boston Edison Co., Boston, 1984—87, sr. engr., 1987—94, prin. rsch. analyst, 1994—98; sr. engr. MidAmerican Energy Co., Davenport, Iowa, 1998—2006; prin. Pedersen Power Solutions, Davenport, 2006—. Ops. chmn. Old South Ch., Boston, 1989-98. Recipient Disting. Svc. award, Iowa Engring. Soc., 2004. Mem. IEEE (chmn. Iowa ctrl. sect. 1983-84, sec. Iowa-Ill. sect. 2003), NSPE (v.p. 1999-2000, v.p. North Ctrl. region 2001-03, Outstanding Svc. award), Mass. Soc. Profl. Engrs. (pres. 1992-93), Eta Kappa Nu. Republican. Congregationalist. Avocations: golf, gardening. Personal E-mail: kspedersen@mchsi.com.

PEDERSON, CELINE, secondary school educator, literature and language educator; b. Rochefort, France, Sept. 21, 1977; BA in French and English Edn., Concordia Coll., Moorhead, Minn., 1999; MEd, St. Mary's U., St. Paul, Minn., 2004. Tchr. French and English Ind. Sch. Dist. 282, St. Anthony, Minn., 2000—.

PEDERSON, LINDA L., music educator; b. Battineau, ND, Apr. 7, 1948; d. Hjalmer and Louise Nordmark; children: Michael, Jeffrey, Sonja. BS in Elem. Edn. and Music Edn., Minot State U., ND, 1970. Music tchr. Valley Sch. Dist., Gilcrest, Colo., 1979—89; mgr. Longmont Country Gen. Store, 1989—93; coord. learning ctr. Loveland H.S., 1993—94; asst. mgr. Ben Franklin, 1994—95; clk. Estes Park 5 & 10, 1995—96, Pizza Hut, 1995—96, Safeway, 1995—97; with Estes Park YMCA, 1995—97; music tchr. Newburg United Sch., ND, 1997—. Pres. Jayceettes, Kenmare, 1973—75; mem. Young Reps., Minot, 1969—70. Named Ourstanding Young Educator, Kenmare Jaycees, ND, 1975—76; recipient Golden Apple award, Newburg Cmty., 1998—99. Mem.: NEA, Band Dirs. Assn., Clin. Dirs. Assn., Sigma Alpha Iota. Avocations: sewing, reading, walking, gardening.

PEDERSON, SALLY, lieutenant governor; b. Muscatine, Iowa, Jan. 13, 1951; d. Gerald and Wineva Pederson; m. James A. Autry, Feb. 6, 1982; children: Rick, Jim Jr., Ronald. Grad., Iowa State U., 1973. With Meredith Corp., 1973-84; sr. food editor Better Homes & Gardens mag.; lt. gov. State of Iowa, Des Moines, 1999—. Pres. Polk County Health Svcs.; bast bd. trustees Nat. Alliance for Autism Rsch.; pres. bd. trustees Autism Soc. Iowa; founding pres. The Homestead Living and Learning Ctr. for Adults with Autism; past cmty. bd. svcs. includes Des Moines Cmty. Playhouse, Very Spl. Arts Iowa, YWCA Aliber Child Care Ctr., YMCA Ctr. Br.; parent rep. Heartland AEA Autism Steering Com.; mem. Iowa State Spl. Edn. Adv. Bd; bd. dirs. Blank Children's Hosp., Mid-Iowa Health Found.; gov.'s appointee State Spl. Edn. Adv. Panel. Democrat. Office: Office of Lt Governor Rm 9 State Capitol Bldg Des Moines IA 50319-0001 Office Phone: 515-281-0225. Office Fax: 515-281-6611.*

PEDESCLEAUX-MUCKLE, GAIL, retired business analyst, writer, artist; b. Cleve., June 20, 1949; d. Alfonso Pedescleaux and Belle Pinkard Pedescleaux; m. Kirk Muckle, Oct. 24, 1997; 1 stepchild, Christopher Corey Muckle. BA in English Lit., Ctrl. Mich. U., 1971. Acct. asst. Travelers Ins. Co., Southfield, Mich., 1972—79, underwriter Garden City, NY, 1979—81, Commerce and Industry, N.Y.C., 1981—83; sr. underwriter Firemans' Fund, N.Y.C., 1983—85; bus. analyst Am. Internat. Group, N.Y.C., 1985—94, sr. quality assurance analyst Livingston, NJ, 1994—2000, sr. bus. analyst Parsippany, NJ, 2000—04; ret., 2004. Cons. in field; patient rep. JFK Family Practice, 2005—. Author: (anthology) America at the Millennium, 2000 (Editor's Choice, 2000), Poetry's Elite: The Best Poets of 2000, 2001 (Editor's Choice, 2001), Throwing Stardust, 2003 (Editor's Choice, 2003), Celebrating Poetry, 2003, Theatre of the Mind, 2003, The Best Poems and Poets of 2003, 2003, Colours of the Heart, 2004, Twilight Musings, 2005 (Editors Choice award, 2005). Mem. DAV: Comdr.'s Club, 1993—, Nat. Multiple Sclerosis Soc., 1994—, Nat. Trust, 1993—, Am. Mus. Natural History, 1996, Nat. Civil Rights Mus., 2002, So. Poverty Law Ctr., 2002, Susan G. Komen Breast Cancer Found., 2003; patient rep. JFK Family Medicine, 2005—; decorating cons. Jazzercise, 2005—. Mem.: Acad. Am. Poets, Edison Arts Soc., N.Y.C. Ballet Guild, Nat. Mus. Women in the Arts, Met. Mus. Art. Avocations: jazzercise, photography, writing, theater, writing children's stories and poetry. Home: 54 Rainford Rd Edison NJ 08820-2903 Personal E-mail: pedymuck@msn.com.

PEDINI, EGLE DAMIJONAITIS, radiologist; b. Kaunas, Lithuania, July 22, 1943; d. Vytautas and Elena Damijonaitis; m. Kenneth Pedini, June 4, 1966; children: David Durand, Julian Adam. BA cum laude, Boston U., 1967, MD, 1967. Diplomate Am. Bd. Radiology. Intern St. Elizabeth's Hosp., Brighton, Mass., 1967—68; resident in radiology Boston City Hosp., 1968—71; radiologist St. John's Hosp., Lowell, Mass., 1972, Chelmsford X-Ray, Mass., 1979—80, Amesbury Hosp./Amesbury Health Ctr., Mass., 1973—98, New Eng. Meml. Hosp./Boston Regional Med. Ctr., Stoneham, Mass., 1973—98, Anna Jacques Hosp., Newburyport, Mass., 1973—98. Ptnr. NE Radiology Assocs., Brockton, Mass., 1980-98; chief radiology Anna Jacques Hosp., Newburyport, Mass., 1984, Amesbury Hosp., 1988, 89, 90. Founder, bd. dirs. Andover Sch. Montessori, Mass., 1974-79; parent ann. fundraising com. Phillips Exeter (N.H.), 1985, 86, 87. Mem. Am. Coll. Radiology, Mass. Radiol. Soc., New Eng. Roentgen Ray Soc., Stonehorse Yacht Club, Chatham Women's Club, Garden Club Harwich.

PEDRETTY, CATHERINE PARTAIN, education educator; b. Birmingham, Ala., May 25, 1928; d. Rufus Johnson and Flora Catherine (McIntyre) Partain; m. William Louis Pedretty, Sept. ll, l949; children: Linda Catherine, Janet Evelyn, Donald William, Mark David. BA, U. Tenn., 1949; MA, U. So. Fla., 1973, PhD, 1987; postgrad., Fla. State U., 1978. Dept. chmn. Pinellas County Bd. Pub. Instrn., Clearwater, Fla., 1971-74, dept. chmn., dir. guidance, 1974—. Adv. Nat. Edn. Assn., Clearwater, 1986-. Mem. Pinellas County Tchrs. Assn., Nat. Edn. Assn., Fla. Assn. Schs., Educators in Industry. Democrat. Home: 1124 Austin Ct Dunedin FL 34698-6100 Office: Dunedin High Sch l65l Pinehurst Rd Dunedin FL 34698

PEDROSA, VERONICA, journalist; b. Manila, Philippines; d. Carmen Navarro Pedrosa; m. Mark Phillips; children: Gabriel, Isabel. Grad., Cambridge U. Television reporter, presenter, prodr. ABS-CBN, Manila; reporter BBC World Television, BBC World Svc. Radio, London; news anchor CNN Internat., Atlanta, news anchor Asia, 2000—05, co-anchor World News Asia; news anchor Al Jazeera Internat., Kuala Lumpar, Malaysia, 2005—. Named Best News Anchor, Asian Television Awards, 2004. Mailing: c/o Al Jazeera International PO Box 23127 Doha Qatar*

PEEBLES, ALLENE KAY, manufactured housing company executive; b. Waukegan, Ill., Feb. 9, 1938; d. Allan Laverne and Kathryn Bernice (McGill) Sedlmayr; m. William Ross Peebles, July 9, 1960; children: Ross William, Robb Allan, Raymond John, Renda Kay (Mrs. Christopher Sivak). BS with high honors, U. Wis., 1960, MS, l967; grad., Realtors Inst., l968. Cert. home economist. Tchr. Horicon (Wis.) High Sch., 1960-61, Oconomowoc (Wis.) High Sch., 1961-67; freelance writer, 1967-70; v.p. Luxury Homes, Inc., Watertown, Wis., 1970-93, Land Devel. Plus Devel. Inc., Watertown, 1970—; co-developer Hidden Meadows Condominium Community, Watertown, 1976-96; gen. ptnr. W and A Elderly Housing Ltd. Partnership, Watertown, 1988—; pres. Housing Am., Inc., Watertown, 1991—2003. Gen. ptnr. Sunrise Housing Ltd., 1990—; builder new and rehab low-income housing, 1983-2003 Active Wis. Gov.'s Conf. on Family, 1980, long range planning team, 1996—2003; dist. membership chmn. Boy Scouts Am., 1984—90; chmn. Ams. Abroad Am. Field Svc., Oconomowoc, 1982—87; del. Wis. Rep. Conv., 1997—; chmn. adminstrv. bd. United Meth. Ch., Oconomowoc, 1974—77, 1996—99, lay leader, 2000—03, pres. United Meth. Women, 2002—06, chmn. family ministry Wis. Conf., del. Wis. conf., 2000—03. Recipient Dist. award of Merit Potawatomi Area coun. Boy Scouts Am., 1986; named Woman of Yr., United Meth. Women, 2003. Mem.: AAUW (pres. Oconomowoc br. 1981—83, pres. Wis. Oconomowoc 1983—85, officer's bd. 1984—93, fin. advisor 1995—2002), NAFE, Wis. Assn. Family and Consumer Scis. (state bd. 1999—, state housing chmn. 2000—02), Met. Builders Assn. Greater Milw., Internat. Fedn. Home Economists (USA internat. del. 1997—), Wis. Manufactured Housing Assn. (bd. dirs. 1979—90, chmn. bd. 1985—88, Mem. of Yr. award 1986), Wis. Builders Assn., Waukesha Bd. Realtors, Wis. Assn. Realtors, Am. Assn. Family and Consumer Scis., Nat. Assn. Realtors, Wis. Home Economists in Bus. (state chmn. 1987—88, internat. rep. 1998—2000, Home Economist in Bus. of Yr. 1987), Internat. Profl. and Bus. Women, Nat. Assn. Home Builders, Nat. Home Economists in Bus. (internat. com. 1985—87, regional U.S. advisor 1990—92), Wis. Home Econs. Assn. (parliamentarian 1988—90), Am. Home Econs. Assn., Phi Lambda Theta, Kappa Omicron Nu, Phi Upsilon Omicron, Phi Kappa Phi. Republican. Avocation: writing. Home: 37788 Mapleton Rd Oconomowoc WI 53066

PEEBLES, BETTY LEA, secondary school educator; b. Schenectady, N.Y., Aug. 3, 1954; d. Allen Jackson and Jean S. (Sasseen) P. BA, Harding U., 1976; MEd, U. S.C., 1992, EdS, 1996; EdD, Ga. So. U., 1999. Tchr. Evans H.S., Ga., 1977—, dept. chmn. Ga., 1985—99. (S.C.) Ch. Christ; tchr. Ga. So. U. 1977-99, dept. chair, 1985-99, asst. prin. 1999—. Mem. NSTA, ASCD, PAGE, Tech. Prep. Avocations: sports, volleyball, gardening, reading. Office: Evans HS 4550 Cox Rd Evans GA 30809-3402

PEEBLES, LUCRETIA NEAL DRANE, education educator; b. Atlanta, Mar. 16, 1950; d. Dudley Drane and Annie Pearl (Neal) Lewis; divorced; 1 child, Julian Timothy. BA, Pitzer Coll., 1971; MA, Claremont Grad. Sch., 1973, PhD, 1985. Special edn. tchr. Marshall Jr. High Sch., Pomona, Calif., 1971-74; high sch. tchr. Pomona High Sch., 1974-84; adminstr. Lorbeer Jr. High Sch., Diamond Bar, Calif., 1984-91; prin. Chapparal Mid. Sch., Moorpark, Calif., 1991-92, South Valley Jr. High Sch., Gilroy, Calif., 1992—95; asst. prof. dept. edn. Spelman Coll., Atlanta, 1995—97; asst. prof. Coll. Edn. U. Denver, 1997—. Co-dir. pre-freshman program, Claremont (Calif.) Coll., 1974; dir. pre-freshman program, Claremont Coll., 1975; cons., Claremont, 1983—. Author: Negative Attendance Behavior: The Role of the School, 1985, Teaching Children Proactive Responses to Media Violence, 1996, Validating Children: A Collaborative Model, 1996, The Challenge of Leadership in Charter Schools, 2000, Charter School Equity Issues: Focus on Minority and At-Risk Students, 2000, Millennial Challenges for Educational Leadership: Revisiting Issues of Diversity, 2000. Active Funds Distbn. Bd.-Food for All, 1987—, Funds Distbn. Task Force-Food for All, 1986; mem. Adolescent Pregnancy Childwatch Task Force. Named Outstanding Young Career Woman Upland Bus. and Profl. Women's Club, 1978-79; Stanford U. Sch. Edn. MESA fellow, 1983, NSF fellow Stanford U., 1981, Calif. Tchrs. Assn. fellow, 1979, Claremont Grad. Sch. fellow, 1977-79, fellow Calif. Edn. Policy Fellowship Program, 1989-90; recipient Woman of Achievement award YWCA of West Edn., 1991. Mem. Assn. Calif. Sch. Adminstrs. (Minigrant award 1988), Assn. for Supervision and Curriculum Devel., Nat. Assn. Secondary Sch. Principals, Pi Lambda Theta. Democrat. Am. Baptist. Home: 39370 Civic Center Dr Apt 531 Fremont CA 94538-6736

PEEBLES, MARY LYNN, nursing home administrator; b. Camden, Tn., Feb. 27, 1943; d. Leonard Nathaniel and Luada Gertrude (Cooper) Peebles; div. 1974; children: Jamie Johnson, Rachel Iversen, Jenny Odle-Madden. AA, Brevard C.C., Cocoa, Fla., 1976; B in Gen. Studies, Rollins Coll., 1978; postgrad. in healthcare adminstrn., U. Tex., Austin, 1983. Administrator Spring Valley ARA, Houston, 1983-84, Rosewood Manor, Memphis, 1984-86, Hillhaven Raleigh, Memphis, 1986-87, Carriage Hill VHA Long Term Care, Fredricksburg, Va., 1988-91; regional v.p. VHA, Memphis, 1991-93; administrator Roper Nursing Ctr., Charleston, S.C., 1993-95; v.p. ops. Diversified Health Svcs., Memphis, 1995-97, regional v.p., 1997-98; pres. Age to Age, 1998-99; regional Cara Vita Sr. Svcs., Roswell, Ga., 1999—. Author: (children's book) The Squirrel's Secret, 1975. V.p. Women's Club. St. James Ch., Memphis, 1985; v.p. Tenn. Health Care Assn., Memphis, 1986; trustee Environ. of God, 1996. Mem. Am. Health Care Assn., S.C. Health Care Assn. (mem. pub. rels. com. 1995), Cruseau. Avocations: writing, photography, reading, hiking.

PEEK, STEPHANIE, artist; b. N.J., Jan. 17, 1940; d. James Desmond and Adeline (Peek) Shevlin; 1 child, Matthew Chase Peek. BA, Wellesley Coll., 1961; MFA, U. Calif., Berkeley, 1996. Artist, San Francisco, 1990—; graphic designer Stephanie Graphic Design, San Francisco, 1971-92. Vis. artist Am. Acad. Rome, Italy, 1997; vis. lectr. U. Calif., Berkeley, 1997; grad. advisor San Francisco Art Inst., 2003-04. Books, Giardini del Sogno, 1997, Time Capsule, 1995, one-woman shows include Triangle Gallery, San Francisco, Friesen Gallery, Seattle & Sun Valley, Represented in permanent collections Harvard, Stanford, Univ. Calif., Berkeley, Santa Cruz, N.Y. Pub. Library. Virginia McPheter Stoltz fellow U. Calif., Berkeley, 1994, J. Ruth Kelsey Travel grantee, 1996, Susan B. Irwin scholarship in visual arts, 1995; recipient Borsa di Studio award Rignano, Italy, 1997, SECA Nominee S.F. Mus. of Modern Art, 2004. Mem. Art Alumni Group (chair 1997-99). Christian Scientist.

PEEL, BARBARA JEAN, science educator; b. Queens, N.Y., Feb. 12, 1953; d. Warren and Jean Helen Schmidt; m. Tony Peel, June 27, 1998. A of Animal Sci., SUNY, Farmingdale, 1971—73; BS in Edn., E. Stroudsburg State Coll., Pa., 1981—83, BA in Biology, 1981—83; MS in Sci. Edn., Queens Coll., N.Y., 1984—86. Cert. Chemistry Tchr. N.Y. Dept. Edn., 1983, Biology Tchr. 1983, Tchr., Gen. Sci. 7-12 1983, Elem. Tchr. 1986, Tchr., Earth Science 1988. Quaity control technician Pfizer, Bklyn., 1973—78; quality control technician Am. Health Found., Valhalla, NY, 1978—81; sci. tchr. Lawrence HS, Cedarhurst, NY, 1983—. Jr. class adv. Lawrence HS, 1985—89, adv. sci. club, 1990—96. Contbr. sch. manuals. Design and create stained glass memorials. Recipient RITIECH award in Sci.; grantee NY State Empire grant, NY State, 1984—86. Mem.: STANYS (life), NY State Edn. Tchrs. (life). Office: Lawrence HS 2 Reilly Rd Cedarhurst NY 11516 Office Phone: 516-295-8007.

PEELE, TAMMY SUE, nurse; b. Cheverly, Md., July 27, 1971; d. Betty Ann Swartz; m. Paul Francis Burkholder, June 3, 1995; 1 child, Caitlin Rose. Nail technician, Wards Corner Beauty Sch., Norfolk, Va., 1990; nurse aide, Madison Career Ctr., Norfolk, Va., 1991; med. office asst., Kees Bus. Coll., Norfolk, Va., 1992. Cert. nurse aide. Nail technician, helper Empress Beauty Salon, Norfolk, 1990—92; nurse aide Sentra Nursing Home, Virginia Beach, Va., 1992—93, Winchester, Va., 1995—2002, Continuing Care, Strasburg, Va., 2002—04; kennel helper GlenEden, Berryville, Va., 2005—; security guard Ctrl. Security Bur., Wincester, 2006—. Kennel helper Carpenter and Pope Vets., Norfolk, 1991—92. Kennel helper Glen Eden, Berryville, Va., 2005—. Republican. Adventist. Avocations: art, reading, writing. E-mail: lordzacharyrascal@yahoo.com.

PEEMOELLER, HELEN CAROLYN, literature educator, department chairman; b. Wilmington, Del., Jan. 24, 1939; d. William Ernest Peemoeller and Helen F. Most; m. Ben Simon, May 16, 1972. AB, Bryn Mawr Coll., Pa., 1960; MA, U. Wis., Madison, 1961. Adj. instr. Rutgers the State U., Camdon, NJ, 1963—65; instr. Moore Coll. Art, Phila., 1966—67, Northampton C.C., Bethlehem, Pa., 1967—70; prof. English, chairperson Reading Area C.C., Pa., 1971—; pres. Berks Real Estate Inst., Reading, 1984—95. Class collector Bryn Mawr Coll. Alumnae Assn., Pa., 1985—95. Fellow, NEH, 1978. Master: Sewing Guild Berks County (pres. 2000—02). Episcopalian. Avocations: sewing, swimming, travel. Home: 4811 Partridge Dr Reading PA 19606-2456 Office: Reading Area Community College 10 S 2d St PO Box 1706 Reading PA 19603 Office Phone: 610-372-4721 5085. Home Fax: 610-779-4810; Office Fax: 610-607-6254. Personal E-mail: hpeemoeller@verizon.net. Business E-Mail: hpeemoeller@racc.edu.

PEEPLES, MARY ANNE BAUMANN, science educator; b. Binghamton, N.Y., July 2, 1941; d. Emmanuel Patrick and Ella Lucille (Woods) Baumann; m. Horace Timothy Peeples, Aug. 21, 1993; children: Charles David Steinkuehler, Ayne Elizabeth Steinkuehler Ray. BS in Edn., Ctrl. Mo. State U., Warrensburg, 1962, MS in Edn., 1969. Cert. Tchr. Mo. Bd. Edn., Kans. Bd. Edn., N.C. Bd. Edn. Sci. tchr., N. Kansas City, Mo., 1962—64, Immaculate HS, Leavenworth, Kans., 1964—72, Easton, Kans., 1972—73, Topeka Pub. Schs., 1973—79, Cumberland County Schs., Fayetteville, NC, 1979—2003; ret., 2003; adj. chemistry tchr. Fayetteville Tech. CC, 1983—. Med. transcriber, radiology Highsmith-Rainey Meml. Hosp., Fayetteville, 1983—97; med. transcriber, orthopedics Cape Fear Orthopaedics, Fayetteville, 1998—2001. With USAR, 1974—80. Recipient NSF award, Tex. A&M, Emporia (Kans.) Coll., 1965, 1972, Citizen Soldier award, 89th ARCOM, USAR, Wichita, Kans., 1977; grantee Merit fellowship-chemistry,

Shell Oil Co., Stanford U., 1966. Mem.: DAR (chpt. regent, state chmn., state officer, state corr. sec. 2005—06), Fayetteville Rep. Women, Woman's Club of Fayetteville (v.p. 2005—06). Republican. Roman Catholic.

PEET, AMANDA, actress; b. NYC, Jan. 11, 1972; d. Charles and Penny Peet; m. David Benioff, Sept. 30, 2006. BA in History, Columbia U., 1994. Actor: (films) Animal Room, 1995, Winterlude, 1996, She's the One, 1996, Virginity, 1996, Grind, 1997, Touch Me, 1997, One Fine Day, 1996, Sax and Violins, 1997, 1999, 1998, Southie, 1998, Playing by Heart, 1998, Origin of the Species, 1998, Simply Irresistible, 1999, Jump, 1999, Two Ninas, 1999, Body Shots, 1999, Isn't She Great?, 2000, The Whole Nine Yards, 2000, Takedown, 2000, Whipped, 2000, Saving Silverman, 2001, High Crimes, 2002, Changing Lanes, 2002, Igby Goes Down, 2002, Whatever We Do, 2003, Identity, 2003, Something's Gotta Give, 2003, The Whole Ten Yards, 2004, Melinda and Melinda, 2004, A Lot Like Love, 2005, Syriana, 2005, Griffin and Phoenix, 2006, The Martian Child, 2005; (TV films) Ellen Foster, 1997, Date Squad, 2001; (TV series) Central Park West, 1995—96, Jack & Jill, 1999—2001, Partners, 1999, Studio 60 on the Sunset Strip, 2006—, (TV appearances) Law & Order, 1995, The Single Guy, 1996, Spin City, 1997, Seinfeld, 1997; (plays) Whale Music, Winter Lies, 27 Sketches: Fear and Misery in the Third Reich, The Country Club, This Is How It Goes, 2005, Escape: 6 Ways to Get Away, 2005, Barefoot in the Park, 2006. Office: The Gersh Agy Ste 201 232 N Canon Dr Beverly Hills CA 90210*

PEET, PHYLLIS IRENE, women's studies educator; b. Winnipeg, Man., Can., Mar. 3, 1943; came to the U.S., 1948; d. Harold Parsons and Gladys Mae (Riley) Harrison; m. Thomas Peter Richman, June 14, 1963 (div. 1969); m. Charles Francis Peet, Sept. 9, 1972. BA in Art, Calif. State U., Northridge, 1972; MA in Art History, U. Calif., L.A., 1976, PhD in Art History, 1987. Sec. L.A. County Supr. Kenneth Hahn, 1960-68; assoc. in art history L.A. County Mus. Art, 1974-75; asst. dir., curator Grunwald Ctr. for the Graphic Arts, U. Calif., L.A., 1975-78; Am. art scholar High Mus. Art, Atlanta, 1984-90; instr. women's studies Monterey (Calif.) Peninsula Coll., 1986—, dir., instr. women's programs/women's studies, 1989—. Dirs.' adv. com. The Art Mus. of Santa Cruz County, 1981-84, 89-94; vis. lectr. Calif. State U., Fresno, 1984; program coord. conf. Inst. for Hist. Study, San Francisco, 1987; lectr. bd. studies in art U. Calif. Santa Cruz, 1991-95; coord. Monterey County Women's Multicultural Conf., 1993-2006. Author, co-curator, editor, compiler: (book and exhbn.) The American Personality: The Artist Illustrator of Life in the United States, 1860-1930, 1976; author, curator: (book and exhbn.) American Women of the Etching Revival, 1988; co-author: American Paintings in the High Museum of Art, 1994; contbr. articles to profl. jours. including Am. Nat. Biography, Fitzroy Dict. of Women Artists, 1997, Dict. Literary Biography, 1998. Vol., activist Dem. Party, L.A., 1960-66, Peace and Freedom Party, L.A., 1967-71; vol. Dem. Party Candidates, Santa Cruz, Calif., 1979-96, Santa Cruz Action Network, 1980-85; mem. nominating com. Girl Scouts of Am., Monterey Bay, 1991-93. Rockefeller Found. fellow UCLA, 1978-80, Dickson grantee U. Calif. LA, 1981-82; recipient Women Helping Women award Soroptimists, Monterey and Carmel, Calif., 1991, 95, Allen Griffin for Excellence in Edn. award Cmty. Found. Monterey County, 1993, Quality of Life award Econ. Devel. Corp., Monterey, 1994, Excellence in Edn. award Monterey Peninsula Coll. Found., 2004, 05, 06; named Tchr. of Yr., Tchrs. of Tomorrow, 2004, Academic Excellence award Monterey Peninsula Coll. Found., 2004, 05, 06. Mem.: NAACP, ACLU, AAUW, NOW, Nat. Mus. Women in the Arts (founding mem.), Coll. Art Assn., UN Assn., Western Assn. Women Historians, Inst. for Hist. Study, Nat. Women's Studies Assn., Planned Parenthood, Monterey Bay Women's Caucus for Art (founder, bd. dirs. 1988—93), Women's Internat. League for Peace and Freedom. Avocations: print collecting, photography. Office: Womens Programs Monterey Peninsula Coll 980 Fremont St Monterey CA 93940-4704 Business E-Mail: ppeet@mpc.edu.

PEETZ, KAREN B., bank executive; married; 2 children. BS, Penn State. U.; MS, Johns Hopkins U. Various client services, sales, credit and risk mgmt. positions JP Morgan Chase (formerly Chase Manhattan Bank and Chemical Bank); sales mgr. global trust services then head global client mgmt. Chase Manhattan Bank, NYC, sr. v.p., bus. mgr. global trust services London; sr. v.p., divsn. head domestic corp. trust bus. Bank of NY, 1998, head global payments services group, haed corp. trust, 2003, sr. exec. v.p., 2006—. Mem. Women's Leadership Initiative Penn State U.; bd. trustees Brooklyn Acad. Music; steering com. Women United in Philanthropy United Way NYC. Mem.: Women's Bond Club. Office: Bank of NY One Wall St 10th Fl New York NY 10286*

PEGS, KAREN ROSAMOND, publishing executive, lawyer; d. Charles Benjamin and Hazel Marie Pegs; 1 child, Desiree Yvette Lee. BA, U. of Calif., Berkeley, 1977, JD, 1980. Bar: Calif. 1980. Atty. Orrick, Herrington & Sutcliffe, San Francisco, 1980—81; project mgr. Safeway, Inc., Pleasanton, Calif., 1987—91. Editor: (lifestyle mag.) Black & Lovely Teen Mag. Vol. Highland Gen. Hosp., Oakland, Calif., 1990—93. With USMC, 1968—70. Scholar, Ford Found., 1973. Mem.: Calif. State Bar (life), Delta Sigma Theta. Democrat-Npl. Baptist. Avocations: writing, singing, acting. Office Phone: 510-825-0528. E-mail: krpe5@aol.com.

PEGUES, JOANN, dietician; BS, Okla. State U.; MPA, U. Colo. Registered dietitian. Program specialist Adminstrn. on Aging U.S. Dept. HHS, Denver. Mem.: Am. Dietetic Assn. (Medallion award 2001). Office: Adminstrn on Aging 1961 Stout St Denver CO 80294

PEICK, ANN LUTZEIER, surgeon; b. St. Louis, 1951; d. Fred Leo and Rose Mary (Steinhoff) L.; divorced; children: Walter Alan, Rebecca Ann. MD, U. Mo., 1981. Resident surgery U. Mo., Columbia, 1981-82, 82-86, fellow pancreas, 1986-87; with Lucy Lee Hosp., Poplar Bluff, Mo.; pvt. practice. Med. dir. S.E. Mo. Area Health Edn. Ctr., Poplar Bluff, 1996-98, Drs. Regional Med. Ctr.; clin. prof. surgery U. Mo., Columbia, 1996-98; with Kirksville Osteo. Surg. Preceptor, Poplar Bluff, 1997-98; dir. trauma St. Anthony's Med. Ctr., St. Louis, 1998. Pres. Mo. Edn. Consortium, 1997; mem. Mid-Mo. Curriculum com., 1997. Mem. ACS, AGA, APA, ASGE, SAGES, AMA, SSAT, Mo. State Med. Assn., Mo. State Surg. Soc. (pres. 1998). Office: Kneibert Clin LLC 686 Lester St Poplar Bluff MO 63901-5025

PEIRCE, CAROL MARSHALL, retired literature educator; b. Columbia, Mo., Feb. 1, 1922; d. Charles Hamilton and Helen Emily (Davault) Williams; m. Brooke Peirce, July 12, 1952. AB, Fla. State U., 1942; MA, U. Va., 1943; PhD, Harvard U., 1951. Head English dept. Fairfax Hall, Waynesboro, Va., 1943-44; instr. English Cedar Crest Coll., Allentown, Pa., 1944-46; instr. Harvard U., 1952-53; asst. dean Radcliffe Coll., Cambridge, 1950-53; head English extension home study U. Va., Charlottesville, 1953-54; asst. dir. admissions Goucher Coll., Towson, Md., 1956-62; prof. English and comm. design U. Balt., 1968—2003, chmn. dept., 1968-94, gen. edn. core coord., 1985-87, Disting. teaching prof. Coll. Liberal Arts, 1981-82, chmn. humanities div., 1972-79; gen. edn. dir., 1995-97; chmn. bd. New Poets Series, 1975—. Vis. scholar Lucy Cavendish Coll., U. Cambridge, Eng., 1977-78; co-coord. On Miracle Ground: The Internat. Lawrence Durrell Conf., 1980, 82, 90, 2000; co-coord. conf. Evermore! Celebrating the 150th Anniversary of Edgar Allan Poe's "Raven," 1995. Author: (with Brooke Peirce) A Study of Literary Types and an Introduction to English Literature from Chaucer to the Eighteenth Century, 1954, A Study of Literary Types and an Introduction to English Literature from the Eighteenth Century to the Present, 1954; editor: (with Lawrence Markert) On Miracle Ground: Second Lawrence Durrell Conference Proceedings, 1984; guest editor: (with Ian S. MacNiven) Lawrence Durrell Issue, Parts I and II, Twentieth Century Literature, Fall, Winter, 1987; contbr. essays to: Poe and Our Times, 1986, Critical Essays on Lawrence Durrell, 1987, Into the Labyrinth: Essays on the Art of Lawrence Durrell, 1989, On Miracle Ground: Essays on the Fiction of Lawrence Durrell, 1990, Dictionary of Literary Biography Yearbook, 1990, St. James Reference Guide to English Literature, 1991, Poe's Pym: Critical Explorations, 1992, Selected Essays on the Humor of Lawrence Durrell, 1993, Lawrence Durrell: Comprehending The Whole, 1994, D.H. Lawrence: The Cosmic Adventure, 1996, Anais Nin: A Book of Mirrors, 1996, others; assoc editor: Deus Loci: The Lawrence Durrell Jour., 1990-92, co-editor, 1993—. McGregor fellow, DuPont fellow U. Va., 1943; Harvard tutor, Anne Radcliffe traveling fellow Harvard U., 1951. Mem. MLA, Edgar Allan Poe Soc. of Balt. (bd. dirs. 1973-89, pres. 1989—), Lawrence Durrell Soc. (bd. dirs. 1983-93, 99—, nat. pres. 1980-82, internat. pres. 1994-98), Md. Assn. Depts. English, Phi Beta Kappa, Chi Delta Phi, Phi Alpha theta, Phi Kappa Phi. Office: Univ Balt Divsn English/ Comm Dsgn Baltimore MD 21201 E-mail: poepeirce@comcast.net.

PEIRCE, GEORGIA WILSON, public relations executive; b. Newton, Mass., Jan. 6, 1960; d. Norris Ridgeway and Anne (McCusker) P. BA, Duke U., 1982. Intern to Speaker of Ho. of Reps., Washington, 1981; prin. PR, etc., Quincy, Mass., 1987-94; dir. media rels. and info. sys. The Mass. Gen. Hosp., Boston, 1994—2004, dir. comm. patient care svcs., 2004—. Cons. Mass. Group Insur. Commn., 1985. Contbr. articles to profl. jours. Mem. cmty. rels. com. Vis. Nurse Assn./Hospice of South Shore; bd. dirs. Ctr. for Nursing Advocacy; mem. com. to elect Mondale-Ferraro, Mass., coord. speakers bur., 1984; mem. charitable trust com. Maj. John F. Regan; com. mem. City of Quincy Recycling Com.; del. Mass. Dem. Conv., 1982, 83; v.p. South Shore Ad Club, 1990-91, mem.-at-large, 1991-92. Recipient 9th Wave awards 1989, 1st pl. in Pub. Rels. award, 1989, merit awards, 1992, Bell Ringer award Cirsis Mgmt.and Print Feature, 2001, Svc. Publicity, 2006, Nat. Patient Safety Leadership fellow, 2004-2005, Golden Lamp award Ctr. for Nursing, 2005, Nat. Patient Safety Leadership fellow, 2005—, Media award Am. Acad. Nursing, 2006. Mem. NAFE, South Shore C. of C., Small Bus. Assn. New Eng., Women's Golf Assn. Mass., Publicity Club New Eng. (v.p. media rels. 1989, Merit Bell Ringer award 2000, 01), Rotary Internat., Eastward Ho! Country Club Chatham (club champion 1977-81, 83, 91, 93, bd. gov. 2003-). Democrat. Roman Catholic. Avocation: golf (many awards including state titles). Office: Mass Gen Hosp Patient Care Svcs Fruit St Bulfinch 230 Boston MA 02114 Office Phone: 617-724-9865. Business E-Mail: gpeirce@partners.org.

PEIRCE, KAREN PATRICIA, education educator; b. Providence, July 12, 1971; d. Raymond Fales and Patricia Kay Peirce. ABH, Rollins Coll., Winter Park, Fla., 1993; MA, Carnegie Mellon U., Pitts., 1997; PhD, U. Ariz., Tucson, 2006. Peer writing cons. Rollins Coll. Writing Ctr., Winter Park, Fla., 1990—93; Fulbright English tchg. asst. Korean Am. Edn. Commn., Ulsan, 1993—94; pub. rels. asst. Embassy of the Republic of Korea, Washington, 1995—96; rsch. asst. Carnegie Mellon U., Pitts., 1996—97; English instr. The Sawyer Sch., Warwick, RI, 1997—98; upper divsn. English tchr. Berkeley Prep. Sch., Tampa, Fla., 1998—2001; grad. assoc. tchg. U. Ariz., Tucson, 2001—06; asst. prof. English U.S. Mil. Acad., West Point, NY, 2006—. Mem.: MLA, Rhetoric Soc. Am., Internat. Writing Ctr. Assn., Conf. on Coll. Composition and Comm., Nat. Coun. Tchrs. English. Home: 281 Hudson St Ste 2 Cornwall On Hudson NY 12520-1039

PEISCH, ALICE HANLON, state legislator; BA, Smith Coll.; JD, Suffolk U. Law Sch. Town clerk Wellesley, 2000—03; state rep. Mass. House, 2003—. Bd. overseers Newton-Wellesley Hosp., 1996—; mem. League of Women Voters of Wellesley, 1986—; bd. mem. Senior Living, Inc., 2001—; mem. Wellesley Svc. League, 1988—; bd. dirs. Wellesley Edn. Found., 1999—2005, adv. bd., 2005—. Democrat. Office: Rm 26 State House Boston MA 02133 Office Phone: 617-722-2080. E-mail: Rep.AlicePeisch@hou.state.ma.us.

PEITSMEYER, NATALIE MARY, science educator; b. Tokyo, Mar. 31, 1965; d. Joseph Michael Rick and Ann Marie Penniston; m. Michael Lloyd Peitsmeyer, Dec. 24, 1985; children: Michael Joshua, Brendan Josiah, Conner Colgate. BA in Biology, U. Colo., Denver, 1989, MA in Curriculum and Instrn., 1997. Lic. profl. tchr. Colo., 1994. Sci. tchr. Cherry Creek Sch. Dist., Centennial, Colo., 1994—. Sci. tech. com. Eaglecrest HS, Centennial, Colo., 2004—, positive behavior support com., 2004—; parent coun. panel Cherry Creek Sch. Dist., Englewood, 2006—. Sci. fair judge Denver Metro Regional, Denver. Recipient Tchr. Yr., Eaglecrest H.S., 2005—06; grantee, Cherry Creek Schs. Found., 2002—03, 2003—04, Biol. Scis. Initiative, 2003—04, 2004—05, Mikkelson Found., 2006. Mem.: Colo. Edn. Assn. (sci. subcom. 2006—), Nat. Assn. Biology Tchrs., Nat. Sci. Tchrs. Assn. Avocations: hiking, travel, reading. Office Phone: 720-886-1104.

PEKELSMA, JUDY ANN, artist, educator; b. Chgo., Apr. 2, 1951; d. Lloyd Michael and Mildred Ruth (Erickson) Pekelsma; m. James Robert Pawlak, June 5, 1982; children: Charlotte Ruth, Simon William. BA, Purdue U., 1974. Sec. Gila Promotions, Silver City, N.Mex., 1997; pres. Yankee Creek Co-op Gallery, Silver City, N.Mex., 1998—2004; sec. Art Co-op, Capitan, N.Mex., 2001. Juror numerous art shows, N.Mex.; GED examiner; participant numerous profl. art and art edn. confs., 1994—; adj. instr. Ea. N.Mex. U., Ruidoso, 1999—; art instr. Eas. N.Mex. U., 2001—; wardrobe mistress Spencer Theater for the Performing Arts, Alto, N.Mex., 2002—; wardrobe and set designer Ruidoso (N.Mex.) Dance Ensemble, 2003—, stage mgr., 2003—, HEAL concert, 2005, 06; presenter, participant Oxford Roundtable on Women's Rights, England, 2006; lead faculty fine arts Ea. N.Mex. U., Ruidoso C.C., 2006—. One-woman shows include Purdue U., 1980—95, Capitan Pub. Libr., 2000, Ruidoso Pub. Libr., N.Mex., 2002, exhibited in group shows at Big Ditch Park, Silver City, 1996—, MacCrae Gallery, Western N.Mex. U., 1997, N.Mex. State Fair, 1998, The Art Loop, Capitan, 2000—01, Spencer Theater Performing Arts, Alto, N.Mex., 2000—, Rio Bonito Valley Artists' Show, Capital Pub. Libr., 2000, Hubbart Mus. Am. West, Ruidoso, 2001, Gov.'s Gallery, Santa Fe, 2001, numerous others, Ea. N.Mex. U., 2003, Represented in permanent collections Unitarian Ch. Las Cruces (N.Mex.), Unitarian Universalist Fellowship Silver City, numerous pvt. collections, painting, N.Mex. State Fair, 2005, various commns., mural, Ruidoso Athletic Club, 2006. Sec., treas. Ballet N.Mex., Inc., Ruidoso, 1998—2000; founder Lafayette (Ind.) Peace Coalition, 1990—96; founder, treas. The New Cmty. Sch., West Lafayette, Ind., 1992—96; flutist Ea. N.Mex. U. Cmty. Orch., 1999—; first flute Musica N.Mex., 2002—03, v.p., 2002—03; founder, flautist High Desert Minstrels, Capitan, N.Mex., 2002—04; stage mgr. Heal Concert, 2005. Mem.: Oxford Round Table Womens Rights, Nat. Mus. Women in the Arts, Women's Art Caucus So. N.Mex., Mimbres Regional Arts Coun. (Silver City, N.Mex.), Southwest Regional Spinners, Art Loop (Capitan), San Vicente Artists, Pecos Valley Potters' Guild. Democrat. Avocations: cross country skiing, fiddling, home education, jogging, knitting. Home: PO Box 37 102 E 2d St Capitan NM 88316 Office Phone: 505-257-2120. Personal E-mail: jpek@zianet.com. Business E-Mail: judy.pekelsma@enmu.edu.

PEKO, LINDA D., elementary school educator; d. Sydney Santo and Kristina Kerchick D'Agata; m. Richard Joseph Peko, Dec. 27, 1975; 1 child, Joy Sydney. AA, Concordia Coll., 1972; BSc, SUNY, Oneonta, 1974. Cert. tchr. N.Y. State Dept. of Edn. Substitute tchr. Mohawk HS, NY, 1975—78, Ilion HS, NY, 1975—78, Herkimer HS, NY, 1975—78; detention supr. Hudson Mid. Sch., NY, 1978—80; tchr. St. Mark's Luth. Sch., Yonkers, NY, 1983—, test coord., 2003—. Coord. bike-a-thon Am. Cancer Soc., Herkimer, 1976. Mem.: Nat. Coun. Tchrs. English. Lutheran. Avocations: reading, singing, gardening, crocheting, birdwatching.

PELAVIN, DIANE CHRISTINE, small business owner; m. Sol H. Pelavin, Aug. 14, 1966. BA, So. Ill. U., 1965; MS, San Jose (Calif.) State U., 1979. Tchr., 1965—68; planning analyst EPRI, Palo Alto, Calif., 1977—78; rsch. analyst NTS Rsch. Corp., Durham, NC, 1978—82; v.p., co-founder Pelavin Assocs., Inc., Washington, 1982—94; pres., co-founder Chesapeake Inst., Washington, 1991—94; sr. v.p. Am. Insts. for Rsch., 1994—. Contbr. articles to profl. jours. U. Chgo. fellow, 1966, NSF fellow, 1968. Mem. Am. Edn. Rsch. Assn. Office: 1000 Thomas Jefferson St NW Washington DC 20007-3835

PELCYGER, ELAINE, school psychologist; b. Jersey City, N.J., Apr. 13, 1939; d. Maurice C. and Bessie (Schneider) Morley; m. Iran Pelcyger, June 4, 1956; children: Stuart Lawrence, Gwynne Ellice, Wayne Farrol. BA magna cum laude, L.I. U., 1983; MS, St. John's U., Flushing, N.Y., 1985. Cert. sch. psychologist N.Y., N.Y.C., nat. cert. sch. psychologist, group psychotherapist, N.Y. Sch. psychologist N.Y.C. Bd. Edn., 1985—2006; trauma and loss sch. specialist; ret., 2006. Mem. Nat. Assn. Sch. Psychologists, Am. Group Psychotherapists, N.Y. Assn. Sch. Psychologists, Psi Chi. Avocations: handicrafts, reading, old time radio.

PELCYGER, GWYNNE ELLICE, school psychologist; b. Bklyn., May 18, 1959; d. Iran and Elaine (Morley) P.; m. Aaron Blum, Dec. 21, 1991 BA, Hofstra U., 1981; MS, St. John's U., 1987. Cert. sch. psychologist, group psychotherapist, cons. Trauma-Loss in Children, Fla. Case mgr. Cath. Charities, N.Y.C., 1986—87; edn. specialist Assn. for Neurologically Impaired Brain Injured Children, N.Y.C., 1987—88; sch. psychologist N.Y.C. Bd. Edn., 1988—92, St. Lucie County Sch. Bd., Fla., 1992—. Program mgr. Profl. Svc. Ctr. Handicapped, N.Y.C.; consulting psychologist Graham Windom, N.Y.C., 1987—89; sch. psychologist Okeechobee County Sch. Bd., Fla., 1994—96; staff psychologist Youth Devel. Ctr. Correctional Svcs. Corp., Pahokee, Fla., 1996—; v.p. juvenile programs Exec. Med. Mgmt. Corp., Port St. Lucie, 1998—. Mem. APA, AACD, Nat. Assn. Sch. Psychologists, N.Y. ACD, Fla. Assn. Sch.Psychologists, Treasure Coast Counselors Assn., Phys-Chi Nat. Honor Soc

PELHAM, ANN, publishing executive, department chairman; BA, Duke Univ., 1974. Reporter The News & Observer, Raleigh, NC, Congl. Quarterly, Washington, Governing Mag.; reporter through exec. editor Legal Times, Washington, 1988—96, assoc. pub., 1996—98, publisher, 1998—; v.p. Duke U. Alumni Assn., 2004—; chmn. Duke Student Pub. Co., 2003—. Editor: The Chronicle (Duke Univ. newspaper). Office: Legal Times Ste 800 1730 M St NW Washington DC 20036 Office Phone: 202-457-0686. Office Fax: 202-457-0718.

PELKOFSKY, JANINE MARIE, special education educator; b. Massapequa, N.Y., Apr. 16, 1971; d. Joseph and Susan (McCloskey) Verdi; m. Ronald Anthony Pelkofsky, July 11, 2002; children: Louis Joseph, Sophia Nicole. AA, Nassau C.C., 1991; Bachelors, Buffalo State U., 1994; Masters, CW Post-Long Island U., 2000. Cert. sch. dist. adminstrn. NY, 2006. Spl. edn. tchr. Sch. for Lang. and Comm. Devel., Glen Cove, NY, 1998—2000; tchr. Hagedorn Little Village Sch., Seaford, NY, 2000—02, coord., 2002—05; autism cons. Massapequa Sch. Dist., Massapequa, 2006—. Mem.: Phi Delta Kappan, CEC, ASCD. Home: 16 Frost Lane Greenlawn NY 11740 Office: Massapequa Sch Dist Merrick Rd Massapequa NY 11758 Office Phone: 516-797-6970.

PELLEGRINO, ROSEANN, science educator; b. Bklyn., Sept. 10, 1964; d. Tony Francis Pellegrino and Laura Marcella Manzo-Pellegrino; m. Franklin David Hoffman (div.); m. Robert Edward Zeblisky, July 12, 1997; children: Timothy Adam Zeblisky, Emily Rose Zeblisky. BA in Philosophy, Stony Brook U., NY, 1987; MEd, Pace U., NYC, 1990. Tchr. sci., substitute Northport High Sch., NY, 1988; tchr. sci. Satellite Acad. High Sch., NYC, 1988—96, Seaford Sch. Dist., Seaford, 1996—. Rsch. lab. tech. Northport Biological, 1985—86. Sea grantee, 1994. Mem.: Nat. Sci. Tchrs. Assn., Phi Delta Kappa. Republican. Methodist. Avocations: softball, hiking, camping. Home: 412 4th Ave East Northport NY 11731 Office: Seaford Union Free Sch Dist 3940 Sunset Ave Seaford NY 11783

PELLET, CAROL, elementary school counselor; b. Newark, N.J., June 1, 1953; d. Michael and Rosemary Shubick; m. Glenn William Pellet, July 20, 1974; children: Heather Marie, Craig Lawrence. Tchr. of Handicapped, Jersey City State, N.J., 1976; MA in Counseling, Montclair U., N.J., 1994. Tchr. of Handicapped N.J. Dept. Edn., LPC N.J. Spl. edn. tchr. Roxbury Bd. Edn., NJ, 1976—94, elem. counselor, 1994—. Parenting instr. Mcpl. Alliance, Roxbury & Mt. Olive, NJ, 1996—. Vol. Crisis Response Team, Mt. Olive, 1997—. Mem.: ACA, N.J. Counseling Assn., Am. Sch. Counseling Assn., Rotary (pres. Mt. Olive 2005—06, adv. for early action 2004—). Avocations: gardening, sewing, yoga. Home: 6 Oakland Rd Budd Lake NJ 07828 Office: Franklin Sch 8 Merker St Succasunna NJ 07876

PELLETIER, MARSHA LYNN, secondary school educator, poet; b. Mt. Pleasant, Mich., July 29, 1950; d. Eugene Russell and Mary Ellen (Edde) Mingle; m. Arthur Joseph Pelletier, May 19, 1973; 1 child, John Frederick. BS in Home Econs. and Edn., Kans. State U., 1971, MS in Edn. Guidance and Counseling, 1972. Lic. real estate broker N.H. Conf. coord., guidance counselor Kans. State U., Manhattan, 1971-73; tchr. home econs. Franklin (Mass.) HS, 1974, Exeter (N.H.) HS, 1974-75, Barrington (N.H.) Mid. Sch., 1975-81, Pentucket Regional Jr. HS, West Newbury, Mass., 1981-82; realtor assoc. Century 21 Ocean and Norword Realty, Portsmouth, NH, 1983-86; tchr. interior design, cons. U. N.H., Durham, 1986-87; tchr. family and consumer sci. Dover (N.H.) Mid. Sch., 1983—2001; tchr. Dover HS, 2001—; mem. legis. adminstrn. com. N.H. Ho. of Reps., Concord, 1992—94, 1996—2002; ind. real estate broker Dover, 1986-2000. Bd. dirs. N.H. State Profl. Bd. Stds., 1999—2004; assessor Nat. Bd. Profl. Tchg. Stds., 2001; tchr. assessor Nat. Tchrs. Bd. Cert., 2002—. Author: (poems) Portsmouth Unabridge: New Poems for an Old City, 2002, Arriving at the Crossroads, 2003, Exeter, New Hampshire: Where the River Meets the Tide, 2005; costume dir. & designer: Guys and Dolls, 2004; actress (hist. dramatization) Factory on Fire. Bd. dirs. Dover Adult Learning Ctr., 1995—98; mem. Health Task Force, Dover, Concord, 1993—94, Cornerstone Dancers, Dover Friends of Pub. Libr., 1996—, bd. supt. adv. com., 2001—06, poetry judge, 2003—, bd. principal's adv. com., 2004—; mem. faculty coun. Dover H.S., 2004—; trustee St. John's Meth. Ch., 1995—97. Named to Nat. Honor Roll for Outstanding Am. Tchrs., 2006; recipient Best Poets award, Internat. Soc. Poetry, 2000, 2001, 2002, 2004. Mem.: NEA (local pres., negotiator, v.p., membership chair, mem. leadership exec. com., bldg. rep. 1979—, N.H. del. to nat. conv.), Seacoast Writers Assn., Nat. Coalition Consumer Econ., Alpha Delta Kappa (v.p., historian, altruistic chmn. 1984—89). Democrat. Avocations: gardening, aerobics, poetry, sewing, cooking. Home: 94 Back River Rd Dover NH 03820-4411

PELLETIER, SHO-MEI, musician, educator; b. Tucson, July 25, 1952; d. Harold W. and Mary Pelletier; m. Dwight E. Shambley, Aug. 12, 1979; children: Aaron Joshua Pelletier-Shambley, Alexis Jessica Pelletier-Shambley. Student, No. Ariz. U., 1965—66, Ariz. State U., 1965—66; MusB in Violin, Ind. U., 1974; student with, Josef Gingold, 1970—75, Ivan Galamian, 1969—75, Sally Thomas, 1969, Sydney Harth, 1967, Angel Reyes, 1968, Dr. Frank Spinosa, 1965—70, Dr. Harold W. Pelletier, 1966. Asst. prin. violinist Dallas Symphony Orch., assoc. prin. violinist, 1975—, solo violinist, 1993, 1995; assoc. prin. violinist Santa Fe Opera, Santa Fe, 1973—98; prin. violinist Dallas Chamber Orch., 1975—92, Dallas Bach Soc., 1975—95. Mem. youth edn. svc. quintet Dallas Symphony Orch., 1978—, charter tchr. Young Strings Minority Scholarship program, 1988; part-time tchr. Booker T. Washington Arts Magnet HS, Dallas, 1982—85. Musician (solo violinist): Sun Valley Music Festival, 1966—67, Interlochen, 1968, Meadowmount, 1969, Walden Ensemble, 1975—, New Arensky Piano Trio, 1975—, Anton A Piano Trio, 1975—, Kodaly Duo, 1975—, Voices Change Ensemble, 1975—, Haydn's Double Concerto for Violin & Harpischord, 1993, The Arensky Violin Concerto in Am. with Dallas Symphony Orchestra as Violin Concerto Soloist, 1995; author: (book) The Simple Dictionary for Classical Musicians, 2000. Charter mem. Nat. Mus. Women Art, Washington; mem. Klanwatch So. Poverty Law Ctr. Named concertmaster, Ariz. All-State Orch., 1968, 1969, Outstanding Young Women of Am., 1982; recipient awards, Plano Art Soc., 1980—, Richardson Art Soc., 1980—. Mem.: Nat. Geog. Soc. Avocations: painting, drawing, photography. Home: 9648 Whitehurst Dr Dallas TX 75243 Office: Dallas Symphony Orch 2301 Flora St Dallas TX 75201-2497 Office Phone: 214-871-4000. Personal E-mail: dwightshambley@sbcglobal.net.

PELLICCIOTTO, NICOLE ALYSSA, special education services professional, consultant; b. Virginia Beach, Va., Feb. 15, 1970; d. Ted and Wanda Pellicciotto; m. Stephen Carl Karcha, Feb. 12, 1994. MEd, George Mason U., 1994, postgrad. in PhD program, 1994—. Cert. Severe and Profound 2-21 Va.,

1995, Early Childhood Spl. Edn. Va., 1995. Pvt. cons. early intervention, Fairfax, Va., 1995—; project mgr. RGB Group, Inc., Fairfax, 2000—. Pvt. cons. DOP; mem. domestic adv. panel Sec. of Def. Contbr. chapters to books. Recipient Tech. award, Va. Assistive Tech. Systems, 1996. Mem.: Coun. for Exceptional Children (assoc.). Personal E-mail: nicpellicc@yahoo.com.

PELLOWSKI, ANNE ROSE, writer, consultant, retired library director; b. Pine Creek, Wis., June 28, 1933; d. Alexander P. and Anna P. (Dorawa) P. BA, Coll. St. Teresa, Winona, Minn., 1955; postgrad., Ludwig Maximilian U., Munich, Fed. Republic Germany, 1955-56, 59; MSLS, Columbia U., 1959; LHD (hon.), U. Colo., Colorado Springs, 1987. Sr. libr. Office Children's Svc., N.Y. Pub. Libr., 1957-66; dir.-libr. Info. Ctr. on Children's Cultures, U.S. Com. for UNICEF, N.Y.C., 1966-82; cons., tchr., libr. storyteller N.Y.C., 1982—. Adj. lectr. Sch. Libr. and Info. Sci., U. Wis., Madison and Milw., 1987—; cons. Biblioteca Nacional, Caracas, Venezuela, 1975-85, HOLP Pubs., Tokyo, 1977—, Children's Libr. Movement, Cairo, 1985-88, Com. on Lit. for Children, Intermadia, Nat. Coun. Chs., N.Y.C., 1987—. Author: World of Children's Literature, 1967, World of Storytelling, 1976, rev. edit., 1990, Made to Measure; Children's Books in Developing Countries, 1979, Story Vine, 1984, Family Storytelling Handbook, 1988; other 5 books; mem. adv. bd. Storytelling jour., 1984-90. Vol. St. Gregory the Gt. Parish, Roman Cath. Ch., N.Y.C., 1968-92, St. Casimir's, Winona, Minn., 1993—. Recipient Constance Lindsay Skinner award Women's Nat. Book Assn., 1980; Fulbright fellow, 1955-56; Libr. Congress scholar Coun. on Libr. Resources, 1965-66. Mem. ALA (mem./chair numerous coms.), Internat. Bd. on Books for Young People (juror Hans Christian Andersen Award 1972-74, 86-90), Nat. Assn. for Preservation. Avocations: reading, making cloth books for children. Office: care H W Wilson Co 950 University Ave Bronx NY 10452-4224

PELOSI, NANCY PATRICIA, congresswoman; b. Balt., Mar. 26, 1940; d. Thomas J. D'Alesandro Jr.; m. Paul Pelosi; children: Nancy Corinne, Christine, Jacqueline, Paul, Alexandra. AB in Polit. Sci., Trinity Coll., 1962. Chair No. Calif. Dem. Party, 1977—81; chmn. Calif. State Dem. Com., 1981—83; committeewoman Dem. Nat. Com., 1976, 1980, 1984; fin. chmn. Dem. Senatorial Campaign Com., 1987; mem. US Congress from 5th Calif. dist., 1987-93, US Congress from 8th Calif. dist., 1993—; minority whip, 2002; minority leader, 2002—; mem. appropriations com., intelligence com.; vice chmn. Dem. Nat. Conv., 1996, co-chmn., 2004. Pub. Svc. award, Fedn. of Am. Societies for Experimental Biology, 1997, Congl. Svc. award, InterAction (Am. Coun. for Voluntary Internat. Action), 1999, Alan Cranston Peace award, Global Security Inst., 2003, Cesar E. Chavez Legacy award, Cesar E. Chavez Found., 2003, Nat. Legis. award, League of United Latin Am. Citizensm 2004, One of 100 Most Powerful Women in World, Forbes Mag., 2005. Democrat. Office: US Ho Reps 2371 Rayburn Ho Office Bldg Washington DC 20515-0508*

PELT, JUDY ANN LOBDILL, artist; b. Grand Island, Nebr., Oct. 21, 1939; d. Oran Russell Lobdill and Sylvia Salome (Dobbs) Acola; m. Thomas Hanna Pelt, Sept. 11, 1960 (div. Feb. 1986); children: Gregory, Paige, Brooke. Student, North Tex. State U., 1957-58, Tex. Christian U., 1958-59, Tex. Tech. U., 1959-60. Tchr. workshops, Longview, Tex., 1987-89; tchr. Imagination Celebration, Ft. Worth, 1990-92, Ft. Worth Womans Club, 1987—. Mem. Pastel Soc. Am. (Master Pastelist 1987), Pastel Soc. Southwest, Knickerbocker Artists U.S.A., Salmagundi Club (assoc.). Avocations: gardening, photography, hiking. Home: 4224 Clayton Rd W Fort Worth TX 76116-8045

PELTO, GRETEL H., nutritional anthropologist, educator; b. Mpls., May 6, 1940; d. Isaac L. and Deana (Harris) Hoffman; m. Pertti J. Pelto, July 27, 1968 (div. Dec. 1995); children: Jonathan, Dunja, Ari; m. Jean-Pierre Habicht, June 13, 1997. Student, Bennington Coll., Vt., 1957—60; BA, U. Minn., Mpls., 1963, MA, 1967, PhD, 1970; DSc (hon.), U. Helsinki, Finland, 1996. Clin. assoc. U. Conn. Sch. Medicine, Farmington, 1970-74; asst. prof. anthropology U. Conn., Storrs, 1974-77, prof. nutritional scis., 1977-92; scientist, child health divsn. WHO, Geneva, 1992-98; prof. nutritional scis. Cornell U., Ithaca, NY, 1998—. Mem. adv. bd. divsn. diarrheal disease control WHO, 1987-92; mem. adv. bd. subcom. on maternal and infant nutrition NAS, Washington, 1980-83; cons. UN U., Washington and Tokyo, 1985, Population Coun., NYC, 1980-82. Co-author: Anthropological Research, 1978, Community Assessment of Natural Food rces of Vitamin A; co-editor: Nutritional Anthropology, 2000; symposium editor: Jour. Nutrition, 2006; mem. editl. bd. Ecology of Food and Nutrition, Maternal and Child Nutrition, Human Orgn. Bd. dirs. Parent-Child Rsch. Ctr. for Eastern Conn., 1974-79; mem. task force Hartford Area Health Edn. Ctr., Conn., 1980-82; mem. adv. com. Travelers Ctr. on Aging, Hartford, 1988-89. Fulbright grantee, 1984; hon. rsch. fellow U. Birmingham, Eng., 1994-97; U.S. AID rsch. grantee, Mex., 1982-87. Fellow Soc. for Applied Anthropology, Am. Soc. for Nutrition (mem. long range planning com. 2001-05, coun. mem. 2004-05, councilor 2004—06, symposium editor 2006); mem. Soc. for Internat. Nutritional Rsch. (bd. dirs. 1989-92), Coun. on Nutritional Anthropology (pres. 1982-84, v.p. 1998-2000), Soc. for Med. Anthropology (bd. dirs. 1980-82). Avocations: photography, cooking. Home: 129 Eastlake Rd Ithaca NY 14850-9700 Office: Cornell U Div Nutritional Sci MVR 3M1 Ithaca NY 14853 Office Phone: 607-255-6277. Business E-Mail: gp32@cornell.edu.

PELTON, MARGARET MARIE MILLER, retired art educator, academic administrator, artist; b. Charlotte, NC, Nov. 5, 1934; d. William Andrew Miller and Helen Cook Miller Margolin; m. Donald Wesley Pelton Jr.; children: Donald W. III, Charles F. BS, U. Miami, 1956; MS, Fla. State U., 1957; EdD in Coll. Adminstrn., Southeastern Nova U., 1979. Art tchr. Miami Dade Pub. Sch., Fla., 1957—70; art instr. Kendall Campus, Miami-Dade Coll., Fla., 1970—79, dept. chair, 1971—79, assoc. dean humanities, Rank prof., 1979—86; founder, vice provost New world Sch. Arts, 1987—96; ret., 1996. Bd. mem. Fla. Very Spl. ART, 1986—96; founder Louis Wolfsou II Fla. Moving Image Archive, Miami, 1986—96, pres., 1986—, v.p., 1996—. Exhibitions include Miami Water Color Soc., Spring Exhbn., 1999, 2001, 2002, 2003 (Outstanding award), Miami Water Color Soc., Fall Exhbn., 2001 (Peoples Choice award), Macon County Fair, Franklin, NC, 2000, Watercolor Soc. NC, Western Regional Show, Asheville, 2001, Watercolor Soc. NC, New Bern, 2003, Macon County Fair, Franklin, NC, 2001, Bet Breira Gallery, 2002 (First award), Fla. Profl. Art Guild, 2003 (Second award), Bascon Louise Gallery, Highlands, NC, 2003, Art League Highlands, 2003, one-woman shows include Kendall Campus Gallery, Miami-Dade Cmty. Coll., 2002, 45 other exhbns. Mem. Dade Commn. Status of Women, Fla., 1983—86; bd. mem. Dade Heritage Trust, Fla., 1995—2001. Recipient Fla. Art Educator of Yr. award, Fla. Art Edn. Assn., 1989. Mem.: DAR, Miami Watercolor Soc. (trustee), Macon County Art Assn., NC Watercolor Soc., Fla. Watercolor Soc., United Daus. Confederacy. Republican. Presbyterian. Home (Winter): 11725 SW 82nd Rd Miami FL 33156-5104

PELTZ, CISSIE JEAN, art gallery director, cartoonist; d. Morton Dunbar Liebshutz and Myrtle Jewel Friedman; m. Richard Walter Peltz, Jan. 1, 1953 (dec. Feb. 21, 1975); 1 child, David Lee. BA, U. Chgo., 1947. Freelance cartoonist Milw. Jour., 1975—77, Chgo. Tribune, 1948—68, Today's Health, Chgo., 1959—71, Cosmopolitan mag., N.Y.C., 1950—85, Look Mag., N.Y.C., 1950—85, N.Y. Times, N.Y.C., 1950—85, Saturday Rev., N.Y.C., 1950—85, Chgo. Mag., 1950—85, Great Books Found., Chgo., 1950—85; owner, dir. Peltz Gallery, Milw., 1989—. Illustrator: book Everyday Speech, 1949, Laugh Your Way to Work, 1977, illustrator: booklets, advt. filmstrips. Named Communicator of Yr., Univ. Chgo., 1963. Mem.: Milw. Art Mus. Contemporary Art Soc., Mil. Art Mus. Print Forum (v.p., pres. 1987—89, bd. dirs. 1989—2002), Milw. Art Dealers Assn. Democrat. Avocations: collecting art, theater, movies. Office: Peltz Gallery 1119 E Knapp St Milwaukee WI 53202 Office Phone: 414-223-4278.

PELTZ, PAULETTE BEATRICE, corporate lawyer; b. Bklyn., May 30, 1954; BA, SUNY, Binghamton, 1976; JD, Am. U., 1979. Bar: D.C. 1980, Va. 1982, Md. 1986. Atty. U.S. EPA, Washington, 1979-83; assoc. Mahn, Franklin & Goldenberg, Washington, 1983-85, Deso, Greenberg & Thomas, P.C., Washington, 1985-87; corp. gen. counsel Western Devel. Corp., Washington, 1987-91; v.p. and corp. gen. counsel Mills Corp., 1992-94; sr. v.p., gen. counsel Charter Oak Ptnrs., 1994—2004; asst. divsn. counsel Charles E. Smith Real Estate divsn. Vornado Realty Trust, Arlington, Va., 2004—. Personal E-mail: ppeltz@vno.com.

PELTZ, RUBY, elementary school educator; b. Youngstown, Ohio, Apr. 22, 1949; d. Peter and Dorothy Raseta Hrelec; m. Kenneth L. Peltz, May 22, 1971; children: Kenneth L. Jr., David A. BS in Edn., Youngstown State U., 1971, MS in Edn., 1975. Educator Campbell (Ohio) City Schs., 1971—. Co-chmn. Bond Issue Com., Campbell, 1999; exec. mem. Campbell Acad. Assn., 1995—, pres. 2002-; memtor Campbell Schs., 1999—. Recipient Outstanding Educator, Indsl. Info. Inst. for Edn., Inc., 2002. Mem. NEA, Ohio Edn. Assn., Ea. Ohio Coun. Tchrs. Math., Campbell City Fest. Com., Campbell Edn. Assn. (blg. rep. 1981-89), Delta Kappa Gamma Democrat. Avocations: reading, kick boxing, skiing, gardening. Home: 71 Creed Cir Campbell OH 44405-1256 Office: Campbell E&M Sch 2002 Community Cir Campbell OH 44405 E-mail: camp_rxp@access.k12.org.

PELUSE, CATHERINE GINA, artist; b. Nova Iguassu, Rio de Janeiro, Nov. 14, 1923; d. Pasquale and Maria Luisa (Battistoni) Lazzari; m. Giuseppe Bertolozzi, July 23, 1949 (dec. Mar. 1970); children: Maria Luisa Blume, Joseph; m. Vincent Peluse, Nov. 7, 1971. Student, Colegio Santo Antonio, Nova Iguassu, Rio de Janeiro. Chairperson "Angolo Artistico" Noi Italiani d'Oggi, Poughkeepsie, N.Y., 1992—. Art coord. 500th Christopher Columbus Italian Ctr., 1991-92. One-woman shows include Ellenville Pub. Lib. and Mus., 1995, Cuneen-Hackett Cultural Ctr., 1995, Civic Ctr. Villa Gori, 1997; exhibitions include RI Watercolor Soc. Gallery, Pawtucket, R.I., 1998, 99, 2000; permanent collections at Mcpl. Bldg. Massarosa-Lucca, Italy, Mt. St. Mary's Coll., Newburgh, N.Y.; appeared in (TV shows) TV Nuovi Orizzonti, Italy, 1997, Media One TV, 1998, TCI, 1998, Dutchess C.C. TV, 2000; contbr. (poem) River of Dreams, Best Poems of the 1990's, Simplicity and Elegance. Past pres. Victory Lodge, Poughkeepsie, 1980, Italian-Am. Cultural Found., 1985; mem. program com. Cuneen-Hacket Cultural Ctr., Poughkeepsie, 1992-96; active Italian Ctr., Ladies Aux., Poughkeepsie, 1996; vol. Frances Lehman Loeb Art Ctr., Vassar Coll., Poughkeepsie, N.Y. Named Editor's Choice, Nat. Libr. of Poetry, 1994, Artist of Yr., Dutchess County, 1996; recipient Merit award Internat. Soc. Poets, 1995, Holiday Exhibit Jeanne Robin Watercolor award Dutchess County, 1996. Mem. Allied Artists of Am., Kent Art Assn. (selection juror 1994), Catskill Art Assn., Dutchess County Art Coun., Dutchess County Art Assn. (panelist 1991-92, pres. 2000). Roman Catholic. Avocations: gardening, cooking, dance, singing, travel. Home: 11 Balding Ave Poughkeepsie NY 12601-2419

PELUSO, MICHELLE, Internet company executive; b. Middletown, NY; B. in Finance and Multinational Mgmt., U. of Pa. Wharton Sch. Bus.; M. in Economics, Phil. and Politics, Pembroke Coll., Oxford U. Mgmt. cons., case leader Boston Consulting Group, NYC, 1995—98; White House Fellow, sr. advisor to sec. of labor, 1998—99; founder, CEO Site59.com (acquired by Travelocity), NYC, 1999—2002; sr. v.p. product strategy and distribution Travelocity, 2002, COO, 2003, pres., CEO, 2003—. Founder A New Generation for Peace. Named Technol. Person of the Year, Travel Agent mag., 2001; named to Fast 50, Fast Co. mag., 2004; recipient Thoroun scholarship, Ernst and Young Entrepreneur of the Year award, 2002. Office: Travelocity 3150 Sabre Dr Southlake TX 76092

PELYPENKO, ELIZABETH, lawyer; b. Chgo., Dec. 17, 1961; d. Mykola and Lydia Pelypenko; m. Arthur Italo, May 31, 1997; 1 child, Valentino Italo. BA Polit. Sci., Northwestern U., Evanston, Ill., 1984; JD, U.Ga., Athens, Ga., 1988. Atty. Pelypenko Law Firm, P.C., Atlanta, 1992—. Lectr. in field. Editor: Calendar Call mag., Verdict mag.; contbr. articles to profl. jours. Named a Ga. Super Lawyer, Atlanta Mag., 2005; named Pre-eminent Lawyer, Martindale-Hubbell Registry, 2005—06. Fellow: Melvin Belli Soc.; mem.: ABA, MENSA, ATLA, So. Trial Lawyers Assn., Roscoe Pound Inst., State Bar of Ga., Ga. Trial Lawyers Assn. (chair CLE com. 2004—), Million Dollar Advocates Forum, Ga. Assn. for Women Lawyers, Athletic Club NE Fencing, Lawyers Club of Atlanta. Independent. Avocation: fencing. Office: Pelypenko Law Firm PC 100 Galleria Pkwy Ste 1320 Atlanta GA 30339 Office Phone: 770-937-0800. Business E-Mail: ep@pelypenkolawfirm.com.

PEMBERTON, BARBARA BUTLER, religious studies educator; d. William Bradley Butler and Elizabeth Ann McGee; m. James Beck Pemberton, Jr., Dec. 7, 1974; children: William Patrick, John David, Michael Beck. BA, U. Miss., Oxford, 1973; MA, Southwestern Bapt. Theol. Sem., Ft. Worth, 1996; PhD, Baylor U., Waco, Tex., 2000. Asst. prof. Christian missions Ouachita Bapt. U., Arkadelphia, Ark., 2001—. Sponsor Chi Rho Phi, Arkadelphia, 2002—, Pruet Sisterhood, Arkadelphia, 2006—; fellow Inst. Ch. and Theology, New Orleans Bapt. Theol. Sem., New Orleans; presenter, spkr. in field. Named Most Inspirational Prof., Ouachita Bapt. U., 2001—02. Fellow: Inst. Ch. and Theology; mem.: Soc. Bibl. Lit., Am. Acad. Religion, Evang. Theol. Soc. Office: Ouachita Bapt U 410 Ouachita street Arkadelphia AR 71998 Office Phone: 870-245-5541. Business E-Mail: pembertonb@obu.edu.

PEÑA, ELIZABETH, actress; b. Elizabeth, NJ, Sept. 23, 1961; d. Mario Peña and Margarita Toirac; married; 2 children. Grad., Sch. Performing Arts. Actor: (plays) Rome and Juliet, Antigone, Blood Wedding, Night of the Assassins, Italian-American Reconciliation, Cinderella, Act One and Only; (films) El Super, 1979, Times Square, 1980, They All Laughed, 1981, Crossover Dreams, 1984, Down and Out in Beverly Hills, 1985, La Bamba, 1986, Batteries Not Included, 1987, Vibes, 1988, Blue Steel, 1989, Jacob's Ladder, 1990, The Waterdance, 1991, Across the Moon, 1992, Free Willy II, 1994, Dead Funny, 1995, Lone Star, 1996 (Independent Spirit award, 1996, Bravo award, 1996), The Pass, 1997, Strangeland, 1997, Rush Hour, 1998, Seven Girlfriends, 1999, Imposter, 2000, Tortilla Soup, 2001 (ALMA award, 2001), Ten Tiny Love Stories, 2001, Zig-Zag, 2001, Keep Your Distance, 2003, Sueño, 2003, How the Garcia Girls Spend Their Summer, 2003, Down in the Valley, 2004, (voice) The Incredibles, 2004, Keep Your Distance, 2005, Transamerica, 2005, Sueño, 2005; (TV films) Fugitive Among Us, 1992, It Came From Outer Space II, Contagious, 1996, Dead Man's Gun, 1997, Aldrich Ames: America Betrayed, 1998, Border Line, 1999, Hollywood Dead Moms Society, 2003, Surburban Madness, 2004; (TV miniseries) Drug War: The Camarena Story, The Invaders; (TV series) Saturday Night Live, Hillstreet Blues, Cagney and Lacey, Dellaventura, I Married Dora, 1987—88, Shannon's Deal, Tough Cookies, Resurrection Blvd., 2000—02, Boston Public, 2003, C.S.I. Miami, 2003, (voice) Maya and Miguel, 2004; dir.: (plays) Celebrando La Diferencia, 1992; (films) The Brothers Garcia, 2002; (TV series) Resurrection Blvd., 2002. Mem.: AFTRA, SAG, Dirs. Guild Am., Actors' Equity Assn. Office: Paradigm care Joel Rudnick 10100 Santa Monica Blvd Fl 25 Los Angeles CA 90067-4003*

PENCE, JEAN VIRGINIA (JEAN PENCE), retired real estate broker; d. William Roscoe and Sophie Cottrell; m. Robert Albert Pence, June 14, 1947; children: Marjorie Pence Tuinstra, Robert J. Grad., Realtors Inst., Ill. Assn. Realtors. Cert. in real estate Central YMCA Coll., 1976. Sales assoc. William Knight Co., Realtors, LaGrange, Ill., 1962—70, sales mgr., 1970—76; pres. Pence & Co., Realtors, LaGrange, 1976—86; freelance writer Sun City Center, Fla., 1999—. Chmn. LaGrange Go-Getters Com. Channel 11 WTTG, Chgo., 1973—74. Author: (genealogy) The Cottrell Adventure With the Wright Connection, (novel) The Apprentice Angel, short stories. Sec. bd. deacons St. Andrew Presbyn. Ch., Sun City Center, 2003—05. Mem.: DAR (vice regent Clearwater chpt. 1984—86), Women's Coun. Realtors (pres. West suburban chpt. 1979—81), DuPage Bd. Realtors, LaGrange Bd. Realtors (sec.-treas. 1973—75, dir. multiple listing service 1978, chmn. profl. standards com. 1985—86), Nat. Assn. Realtors, Coterie (pres. 1982—83), LaGrange Park Woman's (sec. 1967—68), Pierre Chastain Family Assn. (press chmn. 1998—2001).

PENCE, LINDA CAROL, mathematics educator; d. John Princeton and Fern Brown Davis; m. Guy W. Pence, May 27, 1973; children: Colter, Morgan, Sitka. BS in Earth Sci. Edn., Boise State U., 1975. 5th grade tchr. Carson City Sch. Dist., Nev., 1989—96; 7-8th grade math tchr. Meridian Sch. Dist., Idaho, 1996—. Facilitator High Sierra Resource Camp, Carson City, 1992—95. Named Tchr. of Yr., Carson City Sch. Dist., 1993, Environ. Educator of Yr., Nev. Wildlife Fedn., 1994. Mem.: Nat. Coun. Tchrs. of Math. Avocations: skiing, backpacking, travel, snorkeling. Office: Sawtooth Mid Sch 3730 N Linder Rd Meridian ID 83642 Office Phone: 208-855-4200. Office Fax: 208-855-4224. E-mail: pencel@meridianschools.org.

PENCE, LINDA LEE, lawyer; b. Indpls., Dec. 24, 1949; d. Woodrow Wilson and Patsy Mae (Kelley) P. BA in Polit. Sci., Ind. U., 1971, JD, 1974. Bar: Ind. 1974, DC 1982, US Dist. Ct. (no., so. dist. Ind.), US Ct. Appeals (4th, 7th, 9th, 10th, Fed. cir.), US Supreme Ct. Trial atty., chief U.S. Dept. Justice, Washington, 1974-83; assoc. Akin, Gump, Strauss, Hauer & Feld, Washington, 1983-84; ptnr. Spriggs, Bode & Hollingsworth, Washington, 1985-86, Johnson Smith Pence Densborn Wright & Heath, Washington, 1994; dir., ptnr., bus. litig., white collar criminal def. practices Sommer Barnard, Indianapolis. Bd. dir. Indianapolis Symphony Orch.; mem. & past pres. bd. vis. Ind. Univ. Sch. Law; founding mem. & past pres. Ind. Fed. Cmty. Defenders; mem. adv. council Ind. Zoological Soc. Recipient Atty. award Assn. Fed. Investigators, 1982, Atty. Gen. Spl. Commendation award, 1981. Mem. ABA (co-chmn. complex crimes com. 1987-90), Nat. Assn. Criminal Def. Lawyers, D.C. Bar Assn., Ind. State Bar Assn. (chmn. Fed. Judiciary com. 1988-91), Indianapolis Bar Assn. Office: Sommer Barnard Ste 3500 1 Indiana Sq Indianapolis IN 46204 Office Phone: 317-713-3500. Office Fax: 317-713-3699. Business E-Mail: lpence@sommerbarnard.com.

PENCEK, CAROLYN CARLSON, treasurer, finance educator; b. Appleton, Wis., June 13, 1946; d. Arthur Edward and Mary George (Notaras) Carlson; m. Richard David Pencek, July 10, 1971; children: Richard Carlson, Mallory Barbara Rowlinds. BA in Polit. Sci., Western Coll., 1968; Ma in Polit. Sci., Syracuse U., 1975; EdD, Temple U., 1999. Investment analysts asst. Bankers Trust Co., N.Y.C., 1969-71; substitute tchr. Lackawanna Trail Sch. Dist., Factoryville, Pa., 1971-81; instr. polit. sci. Keystone Coll., La Plume, Pa., 1972-73; USGS coding supr. Richard Walsh Assocs., Scranton, Pa., 1975-76; instr. polit. sci. Pa. State U., Dunmore, 1976-77; treas. Creative Planning Ltd., Dunmore, 1988—. Trustee Lourdesmont Sch., Clarks Summit, Pa., 1989—2004, v.p., 2000—04. Bd. dirs. Lackawanna County Child and Youth Svcs., Scranton, 1981—, pres., 1988-90, sec. 2004—; founding mem., sec. Leadership Lackawanna, 1982-84; bd. dirs. N.E. Pa. Regional Tissue and Transplant Bank, Scranton, 1984-88, Vol. Action Ctr., Scranton, 1986-91; founding mem. Women's Resource Ctr. Assn., Scranton, 1986—, pres., 1986-87; v.p. sch. improvement coun. Lackawanna Trail Sch. Dist., 1995-96, sec., 1996-97; mem. adv. bd. Pa. State U., Worthington Scranton, 1998—. Named Vol. of Yr. nominee, Vol. Action Ctr., 1985; Temple U. fellow, Phila., 1991-92. Mem. AAUW (sec. 1973-75, state sel. com. 1979-81), Assn. Jr. Leagues Internat. (area II coun. mem. 1978-79), Jr. League Scranton (v.p. 1980, pres. 1981-83, Margaret L. Richards award 1984), Philharmonic League (v.p. 1976, pres. 1977). Episcopalian. Home: RR 2 Box 2489 Factoryville PA 18419-9649 Office: Creative Planning Ltd 1100 Dunham Dr Dunmore PA 18512-2653 Personal E-mail: spot717@aol.com.

PENCOLA, ANNAMARIA REGINA, elementary school educator; d. Patrick Andrew and Regina Burnette Pencola. BS, Longwood Coll., Farmville, Va., 1977—81, MS, 1988. Sch. leadership team Smithfield Mid. Sch., 2004—05; treas. Isle of Wight Edn. Assn., Va., 2003—. Music director (original musical) A Crack in the Sidewalk; editor: (newsletter) The Real Smithfield Jaycees Newsletter (Best in State- 1st Pl., 1990). Choir dir. Good Shepherd Cath. Ch., Smithfield, 2005—06. Mem.: Women of the Moose, Chi Sigma Iota. Episcopalian/Roman Catholic. Avocations: gardening, animals, music. Office Phone: 757-357-3021. Home Fax: none.

PENDLETON, CYNTHIA M., art educator, artist; b. Detroit, Mich., June 23, 1944; d. James Frederick Murrell and Maculata Florence Damico; m. Robert Brian Pendleton, Feb. 21, 1968 (dec. Mar. 25, 1988); children: James Justin, Katherine Louise Pellerin. BS in art edn., Wayne State U., 1962—66; MLA, Alaska Pacific U., 1981—87. Art Educator State Of Alaska, 1967, Alaska Watercolor Society ALASKA, 1990. Art instr. Madison Heights Sch. Dist., Mich., 1966—67, Anchorage Sch. Dist., 1967—2002. Art cons. Pendleton Productions, Inc., Anchorage, 1969—79. Magazine cover, KRISHNA, collector's pin design, Anchorage Fur Rendezvous, 1989 (First pl., 1989), watercolor, Bridging Cultures (First Nat. Bank Calendar Design Artist, 1995), book illustration, The Needlepoint Book, Chitina Past, commercial film, TAYARU, film, High Road To Alaska (Sunset Film awards, 1972). Liturigical art Holy Family Cathedral, Anchorage, 1975—2005. Finalist Nat. Holiday Greeting Card Design, Am. Diabetes Assn., 2002, Holiday Greeting Card Design, 2003; recipient Nat. Honor Soc., Berkley H.S., 1961—62. Mem.: Alaska Watercolor Soc. (assoc.). Independent. Roman Catholic. Avocations: reading, painting, antiques. Office: Pendleton Fine Arts 3201 Redoubt Ct Anchorage AK 99517-1163 Office Phone: 907-248-4448. Office Fax: 907-248-4448. E-mail: cindy@pendletonfinearts.com.

PENDLETON, FLORENCE HOWARD, shadow senator; b. Columbus, Ga., Jan. 1928; d. John Milton and Elease Brooks Howard; m. Oscar Henry Pendleton, 1943; children: Oscar Henry Jr., Howard Thompson. BS, Howard U., 1949, MS, 1957. Tchr. Columbus Pub. Sch., Ga., 1951—55; instr. Morgan State Coll., Balt., 1957—58; tchr. DC Pub. Sch., Washington, 1958—70, asst. prin., 1970—80, prin., 1980—93; ret., 1993; chmn. Ward Five Dem. Com., Washington, 1979—82; mem. DC Dem. State Party, Washington, 1979—90; DC shadow senator to U.S. Congress, 1995—. Alt. delegate Dem. Nat. Convention, NYC, 1980; commr. Ward Five C07 Advisory Neighborhood Com. Clerk Berean Baptist Ch., 1965—94, clerk emeritus, 1994—. Named Disting. Citizen, Washington, 1980, Outstanding Cmty. Leader Ward Five, Berean Baptist Ch., 1981. Mem.: South St. And Affiliate Streets Block Club (pres. 1975—), Bloomingdale's Civic Assn. (edn. chmn. 1978—80), Ctr. City Cmty. Corp. (mem. chmn. exec. com. 1976—79). Democrat. Office: 441 Fourth St NW Ste 10518 Washington DC 20001 Office Phone: 202-727-8099. Office Fax: 202-483-6301.*

PENDLETON, GAIL RUTH, newspaper editor, writer, educator; b. Franklin, NJ, May 8, 1937; d. Waldo A. and Ruby (Bonnett) Rousset; m. John E. Tyler, Mar. 10, 1956 (div. 1978); children: Gwenneth, Victoria, Christine; m. Jeffrey P. Pendleton, Oct. 1, 1978 (dec. 1992). BA, Montclair State Coll., NJ, 1959; M in Div., Princeton Theol. Sem., NJ, 1973; MA in English, William Paterson Coll., NJ, 1998. Ordained minister Presbyn. Ch., 1974. Tchr. Epiphany Day Sch., Kaimuki, Oahu, Hawaii, 1956-58; editor Women's Sect. Daily Record, Morristown, N.J., 1959-62, reporter, 1963-65; tchr. Hardyston Twp. Sch., Franklin, 1968-69; asst. pastor 1st Presbyn. Ch., Sparta, N.J., 1973-74; reporter N.J. Herald, Newton, 1976-78, editor lifestyle sect., 1978-93, editor Friday entertainment sect., 1993-95, editor spl. sect., 1995-97; pres. Crystal Palace Networking Inc., Newton, 1995—2004. Adj. prof. Ramapo Coll. of N.J., Mahwah, 1998, County Coll. of Morris, Randolph, N.J., 1998, Sussex County C.C., Newton, N.J., 1998—, Centenary Coll., Hackettstown, N.J., 1999—; tchr. Univ. H.S., Newark, 1999-2000. Recipient Ruth Cheney Streeter award Planned Parenthood N.W. N.J., 1985. Mem. N.J. Press Assn. (family sect. layout award 1985, 87, 88, 89, 91, 2nd feature columns award 1986).

PENDLETON, JOAN MARIE, microprocessor designer; b. Cleve., July 7, 1954; d. Alvin Dial and Alta Beatrice (Brown) P. BS in Physics, Elec. Engring., MIT, 1976; MSEE, Stanford U., 1978; PhDEE, U. Calif., Berkeley, 1985. Sr. design engr. Fairchild Semiconductor, Palo Alto, Calif., 1978-82; staff engr. Sun Microsystems, Mountain View, Calif., 1986-87; cons., designer Computer Sci. Dept. U. Calif., Berkeley, 1988-90; dir. engring. Silicon Engring. Inc., Scotts Valley, Calif., 1994-95; CEO Harvest VLSI Design Ctr., Inc., San Jose, Calif., 1988—; dir. ASIC devel. Poseidon Tech., San Jose, 1997-98. Founder Aurora VLSI, Inc., Santa Clara, Calif., 1998—. Contbr. articles to profl. jours.; inventor, patentee serpentine charge transfer device. Recipient 1st, 2d and 3d place awards U.S. Rowing Assn., Fairchild Tech.

Achievement award, 1982, 1st place A award Fed. Internat. Soc Aviron, 1991. 1st and 3d pl. awards World Masters Games in rowing, 2005. Mem. Los Gatos Rowing Club, U.S. Rowing Assn. Avocations: rowing, skiing, backpacking.

PENDLETON, MARY CATHERINE, retired foreign service officer; b. Louisville, June 15, 1940; d. Joseph S. and Katherine R. (Toebbe) Pendleton. BA, Spalding Coll., 1962; MA, Ind. U., 1969; cert., Nat. Def. U., 1990; D (hon.), U. N. Testemitanu, Moldova, 1994. Cert. secondary tchr. Ky. Tchr. Presentation Acad., Louisville, 1962-66; vol. Peace Corps, Tunis, Tunisia, 1966-68; employment counselor Ky. Dept. for Human Resources, Louisville, 1969-75; gen. svcs. Am. Embassy, Khartoum, Sudan, 1975-77, counsular officer Manila, 1978-79, adminstrv. officer Bangui, Central African Republic, 1979-82, Lusaka, Zambia, 1982-84; post mgmt. officer Dept. of State Bur. European and Can. Affairs, Washington, 1984-87; adminstrv. counselor Am. Embassy, Bucharest, Romania, 1987-89; dir. adminstrv. tng. divsn. Fgn. Svc. Inst., Arlington, Va., 1990-92; ambassador Am. Embassy, Chisinau, Moldova, 1992-95, adminstrv. counselor Brussels, 1995-98; consul gen. U.S. Consulate Gen., Montreal, 1998-2001; mgmt. counselor Am. Embassy, Cairo, 2001—04; diplomat in residence U. Memphis, 2004—05; ret., 2005. Bd. dirs. Cairo Am. Coll., 2001—04, Am. Sch. Bucharest, 1987—89. Named to, Hon. Order Ky. Cols., 1988. Democrat. Roman Catholic. Avocation: outdoor activities. Home: 1946 N Cleveland St Arlington VA 22201 Personal E-mail: pendletonmc@gmail.com.

PENGRA, R. RENE, lawyer; b. 1967; BA, U. Wyo., 1988; JD, NYU, 1993. Bar: Ill. 1995, N.Y. 2000. Law clk. to Hon. David B. Sentelle U.S. Ct. Appeals, D.C. Cir., 1993; with Sidley Austin Brown & Wood, Chgo., 1993—, ptnr., 2002—. Office: Sidley Austin Brown and Wood Bank One Plz 10 S Dearborn St Chicago IL 60603

PENHOLLOW, TINA MARIE, health science researcher, educator; b. Dunkirk, N.Y., Sept. 24, 1980; d. Duane Wesley and Christine Ann Penhollow. BS, SUNY Coll. Fredonia, 2001; MS, U. West Fla., Pensacola, 2003; PhD, U. Ark., Fayetteville, 2006. Cert. Health Edn. Specialist Nat. Commn. Health Edn. Credentialing, Inc. Tutor SUNY Coll. at Fredonia, 1999—2001; substitute tchr. Santa Rosa County Sch. Dist., Pensacola, Fla., 2001—02; grad. tchg. and rsch. asst. U. West Fla., 2001—03; health educator women infants and children program Escambia County Health Dept., 2002—03; doctoral acad. fellow and sr. grad. asst. U. Ark., Fayetteville, 2003—06; asst. prof. health promotion Fla. Atlantic U., Davie, 2006—. Presenter in field. Contbr. scientific papers, articles to nat. and internat. periodicals, in profl. jours. Recipient Outstanding Doctoral Student in Health Sci. award, U. Ark., 2005; grantee, U. West Fla., 2001, 2002, 2003; scholar, Western Divsn. Credit Union N.Y., 1997—98; Pace Grad. scholar, U. West Fla., 2001—03, Doctoral fellow, U. Ark., 2003—06. Mem.: AAHPERD, Soc. Sci. Study of Sexuality, Am. Assn. Health Edn. (Horizon Award 2007). Achievements include youngest PhD graduate from the University of Arkansas's program in Health Science. Office: Florida Atlantic Univ ES Building #285 2912 College Ave Davie FL 33314

PENICK, ANGELA LUCAS, elementary school educator; b. Roanoke Rapids, N.C., Sept. 7, 1950; d. George Alexander and Carrie Louise (Hinson) Lucas; m. Charles Inglesby Penick, Jr. (div.); 1 child, Carrie Hayes. AA, Marjorie Hebster Jr. Coll., Washington, 1970; BA in Edn., U. N.C., Chapel Hill, 1972. Cert. tchr. phys. edn., health, presch. handicap. Accounts payable clk. Boddie-Noell Ent., Rocky Mount, NC, 1973—75; tchr. Rocky Mount City Schs., 1975—80; admissions counselor N.C. Wesleyan Coll., 1980—81; dropout counselor Nash C.C., 1981—85; social worker Britthaven Nursing Home, Nags Head, 1988—89; early childhood interventionist Halifax County Mental Health Ctr., Poanoke Rapids, 1989—99, Edgecombe-Nash Mental Health Ctr., Rocky Mount, 1989—99; tchr. Nash-Rocky Mount Schs., 1999—. Chmn. Good Shepherd Day Sch., Rocky Mount, 2000—02; mem. Tar River Orch. & Chorus, Rocky Mount, 2004—05; vol. Episc. Ch. Women, Am. Cancer Soc., March of Dimes; leader Bible Study Fellowship, Rocky Mount, 2004—05; mem. vestry Ch. of the Good Shepherd, Rocky Mount, 1999—2002, mem. search com., 2003—04, mem. youth coun.; bd. dirs., sec. My Sister's House, Rocky Mount, SC, 1995—98. Mem.: Women's Tennis League, U.S. Tennis Assn., Benvenue Country Club. Republican. Episcopalian. Avocations: tennis, gardening, drawing, weight training, jogging. Home: 605 S Taylor St Rocky Mount NC 27803 Office: Nash-Rocky Mount Schools 930 Eastern Ave Nashville NC 27856 Office Phone: 252-937-5622. E-mail: anjo950@aol.com.

PENICK, ANN CLARISSE, minister, counselor; b. Woodstock, Ill., Feb. 17, 1951; d. Preston Edwin and Marjorie Jane Yeoman; m. John William Schoenberger (div.); m. James Lal Penick, Jr., Aug. 9, 1986; stepchildren: Michael Andrew, Katherine Leona. BA in History, No. Ill. U., DeKalb, 1977; MA in History, Loyola U., Chgo., 1987; MA in Counseling, U. Ala., Birmingham, 1995. Cert. minister Diocese Birmingham, Ala., 1993; lic. counselor S.C., 1997, cert. Nat. Bd. Certified Counselors, 1999, lic. mental health counselor Mass., 2006. Substitute tchr. Regina Dominican H.S., Wilmette, Ill., 1987—88; adj. faculty Birmingham (Ala.) So. Coll., 1988—91; tchr. theology John Carroll Cath. H.S., Birmingham, 1993—94; chaplain intern Bon Secours St. Francis Hosp., Charleston, 1996—97; minister Cath. Campus Diocese Charleston, Coll. of Charleston, SC, 1997—2000; pastoral assoc. St. Ann U. Parish, Archdiocese Boston, 2000—02, assoc. cath. chaplain Tufts U., 2002—. Adj. faculty Nat. U., Chgo., 1988; coord. sexual abuse awareness Archdiocese Boston, 2002—, facilitator marriage preparation, 2002—. Contbr. articles to profl. jours. Aid worker Polish Refugee Camp, Vienna, 1982; spokesperson Nat. Night Out, Charleston, 1996; vol. Dem. Nat. Com., Boston, 2004; vol. pastoral counselor Hospice Charleston, 1995—98. Named Advisor of Yr., Emerson Coll., 2001. Mem.: Assn. for Spiritual, Ethical and Religious Values in Counseling, Mass. Mental Health Counselors Assn., Cath. Campus Ministry Assn., Am. Counseling Assn. (bd. dir. 2001—04, Svc. award 2004). Democrat. Roman Cath. Avocations: dance, guitar, singing. Home: 5 Walden Mews Cambridge MA 02140 Office: Tufts Cath Chaplaincy Goddard Chapel 3 on the Green Medford MA 02155 Personal E-mail: annpenick@hotmail.com.

PENICK, CATHERINE TINDAL, literature and language professor; d. Maynard and Ann Tindal; m. Ray Penick, June 10, 1978; children: Macki Smith, Rayce. BS, Miss. U. for Women, Columbus, 1981; MS, Miss. State U., Starkville, 1995. English instr. East Miss. C.C., Scooba, 2004—. Local missions chmn. First United Meth. Ch., Macon, Miss., 2000—06; vol. in prison ministry Whole Man Ministries, Macon, Miss., 2003—06. Mem.: NCTE/TYCA, DAR, Macon Jr. Aux. (life; pres. 1987—88). Avocations: reading, gardening. Home: PO Box 335 Macon MS 39341 Office: East Mississippi CC PO Box 158 Scooba MS 39358 Office Phone: 662-476-5046.

PENICK, PATRICIA AKINS, art educator; b. Waco, Tex., Aug. 27, 1953; d. Frank Earl and Anna Marie (Wernet) Akins; m. Roland Glenn Poertner (div.); 1 child, Joshua Nathan Poertner. Assocs. degree, Kilgore Jr. Coll., Tex., 1972—74; BS, Stephen F. Austin State U., Nacogdoches, Tex., 1976; Masters' degree, So. Ark. U., Magnolia, 1999. Cert. reading, art. Art specialist City of Longview, Tex., 1974—76; reading tchr. Broadway Elem., Gladewater, Tex., 1976—79; homebound tchr. Magnolia Sch. Dist., 1980—85, classroom tchr., 1987—99; 4th grade classroom tchr. Waldo Sch. Dist., Ariz., 1985—87; math. specialist So. Ark. U., Magnolia, 1999—2000; art tchr. Cen. Elem., Magnolia Sch. Dist., 2000—. Faculty sponsor Peer Mediators, East Side Elem., 1998—99; judge regional and state Odyssey of Mind Competition, 2005, 06. Simon Wheat's ABCs, 1998. Mem., dir. Vacation Bible Sch.; dir. prodns. Calvary Bapt. Live Nativity; bd. dirs. Magnolia Arts Coun., 2002—04; counselor Awanas, Calvary Bapt. Ch., 2004—06. Recipient Dr. Guillotine scholarship, Kappa State, 1999, BoBo Shinn Purchase award, Magnolia Arts, 2001; scholar, Longview Tchr.'s Orgn., 1972. Mem.: Magnolia Edn. Assn. (pres., bd. dirs. 2001—03), Delta Kappa Gamma (svc. chair, v.p.). Avocations: painting, sculpting, illustrating children's books, camping, reading. Home: 1401 Shady Ln Magnolia AR 71753

PENMAN, LOREN ANNE, academic administrator; b. Stamford, Conn., Feb. 4, 1953; d. Edgar Douglass and Mary Josephine (Kelly) Lamy; m. Bruce C. Penman, July 13, 1974; 1 child, Brant C. BA, Allegheny Coll., 1974, MEd, 1975; C.A.S., SUNY, Brockport, 1985; postgrad., U. Rochester, 1985—. Cert. secondary, elem. tchr., sch. dist. adminstr. Ohio, N.Y., strategic planner. Tchr. Nordonia High Sch., Macedonia, Ohio, 1974-76, Elba (N.Y.) Central Sch., 1977-79, Batavia (N.Y.) High Sch., 1979-83; dept. chmn. Batavia City Schs., 1983-85; curriculum and staff devel. adminstr. Gates Chili Schs., Rochester, N.Y., 1985-87; instnl. specialist Genesee-Wyoming BOCES, Batavia, 1987-89; asst. supt. Oakfield (N.Y.)-Alabama Schs., 1989-92; prin. Webster Jr. High Sch., NY, 1992—94, Thomas Mid. Sch., 1994—96, Oak Sch., West Indequoit, NY, 1996—2000; dir. learning Byron Bergen Sch., NY, 2000—. Cons. in field. Mem. coun. SUNY-Brockport, 1988—. Recipient Nat. Alumni citation Allegheny Coll., 1983. Mem. N.Y. State Assn. for Supervision and Curriculum Devel., AAUW, N.Y. State Speech Communication Assn. (exec. coun. 1983-85), Nat. Staff Devel. Coun., N.Y. State Staff Devel. Coun. (bd. dirs. 1988-89). Democrat. Office: 6917 West Bergen Rd Bergen NY 14416 Office Phone: 585-494-1220. E-mail: lpenman@bbcs.k1.2ny.us.

PENMAN, ROBBIE MAE, volunteer, political organization worker; b. Memphis, Feb. 25, 1903; d. Robert Rudolph and Emma Jimmie Franklin; m. Edward Thaddeus Penman Sr., June 28, 1923 (dec.); children: Vincent Robert, Edward Thaddeus Jr., Wallace Abraham, Horace Eugene. Student in English and Journalism, Alleghany Coll., Meadville, Pa.; student in Bus. Adminstrn., John Hay Bus. Coll., Cleve.; student in Social Svcs., Case Western Res. U., Cleve.; student in Housing and Cmty. Devel., Cleve. State U. Social svc. outreach worker; dir. day care ctr. Fellowship Bapt. Ch., Cleve. Author: Call Me Russell, 1995. Pres. George Washington Carver Elem. PTA, Cleve., John Borroughs Elem. PTA, Ctrl. Jr. H.S. PTA, East Tech. H.S. PTA; mem. Econ. Opportunity Anti-Poverty Bd., 1962—67; v.p. Model Cities Program, 1972—77, supr. dist. connectors; organizer Cmty. Responsive Dial A Bus; mem. bd. RTA; Am. rep. World Conf. Women, Copenhagen, 1980; asst. to Rev. Donald Jacobs Cleve. Black Ch. Ptnrs. in Ecumenism. Named Outstanding Grandparent of Yr., Ch. LDS, 2005; named to Wall of Tolerance, Montgomery, Ala., 2005; recipient Outstanding Svc. honors, Rep. Louis Stokes. Democrat. Ch. Lds. Achievements include first congressional sr. intern. Avocations: reading, exercise. Home: 6003 Thackeray Ave Cleveland OH 44103

PENN, DAWN TAMARA, entrepreneur; b. Knoxville, Tenn., July 22, 1965; d. Morton Hugh and Virginia Audra (Wilson) P. AS, Bauder Fashion Coll., Atlanta, 1984; postgrad., U. Tenn., 1986; grad., Rasnic Sch. Modeling, Knoxville, 1986. Gen. mgr. Merry-Go-Round, Knoxville, 1984-86; mgr., dancer Lady Adonis Inc. Performing Arts Dance Co., Knoxville, 1987-90; owner, pres. Lady Adonis, Inc. Performing Arts Dance Co., Knoxville, 1990—, also chmn.; owner, pres. Penn Mgmt. and Investment Co. Comml. Real Estate, Knoxville, 1989—; deputized bonded rep. Knox County Sheriff's Dept., Knoxville, 1989-90. Fgn. dance tours include Aruba, Curacao, Caracas, Barbados, Ont., Que., Montreal, Nfld., Labrador, N.S., New Brunswick; cons. The John Reinhardt Agy., Winston-Salem, N.C., 1987—, Gen. Talent Agy., Monroeville, Pa., 1990—, Xanadu, Inc., Myrtle Beach, S.C., 1991—. Author, editor: Lady Adonis Performing Arts promotional mag., 1988; TV and motion picture credits include: Innocent Blood, 1992, The Phil Donahue Show, N.Y.C., 1989, 91. Coord. bridal fair Big. Bros./Big Sisters Knox County, Knoxville, 1985, 86; judge Southeastern Entertainer of Yr. Pageant, Knoxville, 1992—, Miss Knoxville U.S.A. Pageant, Knoxville, 1990—; active Knoxville Conv. and Visitors Bur., 1993-94. Recipient 1st Pl. award for swimsuit TV comml. and runway modeling Internat. Model's Hall of Fame, 1986, 1st pl. award for media presentation Modeling Assn. Am. Internat., 1986; nominee The Pres.'s Commn. on White House Fellowships, U.S. Office Pers. Mgmt., 1994-95. Mem. Internat. Platform Assn., Profl. Assn. Diving Instrs. (cert.). Methodist. Avocations: scuba diving, racquetball, horseback riding, piano, theology. Home: 7320 Old Clinton Pike Apt 9 Knoxville TN 37921-1064 Office: Lady Adonis Inc/Penn Mgmt Ste 9 7320 Old Clinton Hwy Knoxville TN 37921-1064 E-mail: ldyadonis1@aol.com.

PENN, JENNIFER, psychologist, consultant; b. Washington, May 25, 1950; d. William Edward and Constance Payne Jones; m. Donald L. Penn (div.); children: DeNon, Derek, Laura. BS, U. D.C., 1979; MEd, Howard U., Washington, 1982. Lic. profl. counselor; nat. cert. sch. psychologist, cert. Centenco mitigation specialist. Tchr. Nativity Cath. Sch., Washington, 1978—79; grad. asst. Howard U., 1980—82; sch. psychologist D.C. Pub. Schs., 1983—; cons. Penn Hart Cons., 1995—. Nat. del. Nat. Assn. Sch. Psychologists, 1993—95. Sunday sch. tchr. St. John Baptiste de la Salle Cath. Ch., Hyattsville, Md., 1995—2000. Mem.: D.C. Assn. Sch. Psychologists (pres. 1982—). Democrat. Roman Catholic. Avocations: oil painting, watercolor painting. Office: DC Pub Schs 825 N Capitol St NE Washington DC 20005 Office Phone: 202-442-4800.

PENN, LINDA, computer animator; m. Billy Penn; 4 children. B in Home Econs., M in Home Econs., East Tex. State U. From field office staff to East Tex. regional mgr. U.S. Senator Phil Gramm; Head Start Program specialist in adminstrn. for children and families U.S. Dept. Health and Human Svcs., 1992—, Regional Head Start Edn. specialist, regional rep. Region VI Dallas, 2001—. Office: US Dept HHS Ste 1124 1307 Young St Dallas TX 75202

PENN, LYNN SHARON, materials scientist, educator; b. Iowa City, June 18, 1945; m. Arthur Leon Penn, June 24, 1968; 1 child, Ethan. AB, U. Pa., 1966; MA, Bryn Mawr Coll., 1970, PhD, 1974. Chemist Lawrence Livermore Nat. Lab., Livermore, Calif., 1974-78; sr. scientist Textile Rsch. Inst., Princeton, N.J., 1978-80, Ciba-Geigy Corp., Ardsley, N.Y., 1980-83; prin. scientist Midwest Rsch. Inst., Kansas City, Mo., 1983-86; rsch. prof. Polytechnic U., Bklyn., 1987-91; prof. U. Ky., Lexington, 1991—2006; head dept. chemistry Drexel U., Phila., 2006—. Chair Gordon Rsch. Conf. on Sci. of Adhesion, 1992, Gordon Rsch. Conf. on Composites, 2002. N.Am. editor Internat. Jour. Adhesion and Adhesives; contbr. articles to profl. jours. Mem.: Adhesion Soc. (sec. 1982—90, v.p. 2002—04, pres. 2004—06), Fiber Soc., Am. Soc. for Composites, Am. Chem. Soc., Kappa Kappa Gamma. Jewish. Home: 356 S Mill St Lexington KY 40508-2532

PENN, VERNITA LYNN, government agency administrator; d. Welborne L. and Bonita L. Richmond; m. Ray C. Penn, Mar. 21, 1992 (div. Oct. 1994); 1 child, Courtney James. BA, Langston U., 1980; MA, U. Okla., 1992. Lic. tchr. Okla., cert. mediator. Instr. COPE Inc., Oklahoma City, 1998—99; inventory mgmt. specialist Tinker AFB, Midwest City, Okla., 1999—. Bd. dirs. Credit Advisors Am., Midwest City. Mem. Ambs. Concert Choir, Oklahoma City, 1999—, Oklahoma City Beautiful, 2001—. Mem.: Okla. Assocs. Black Journalist, Tinker Mgmt. Assn., Okla. Acad. Mediators and Arbitrators, Nat. Assn. Female Execs., Okla. Bar Assn. (assoc.), Tinker Officers Club, Alpha Kappa Alpha (Silver Soror award 2002). Democrat. Baptist. Avocations: singing, dance, writing, opera, symphony. Home: PO Box 14871 Oklahoma City OK 73113 Office: Tinker AFB 3001 Staff Dr Tinker Afb OK 73145 Office Phone: 405-736-4481. E-mail: vernitavernita@netscape.net.

PENNER, ALICE BRAEKER, clinical social worker; b. Degersheim, St. Gallen, Switzerland, Mar. 1, 1934; came to U.S., 1950; d. Johann and Melanie Olga (Boesch) Braeker; m. Rudolph Gerhard Penner, June 27, 1959; children: Eric Jacob, Brian Gerhard. BA, U. Toronto, 1959; MSW, SUNY, Buffalo, 1963. Diplomate Nat. Bd. Examiners. Case worker Dept. Pub. Welfare, Balt., 1959-61; clin. social worker Hillside Children Ctr., Rochester, N.Y., 1961-62; psychiat. social worker Rochester Mental Health Ctr., 1963-67; ind. contractor Herner Info. Svc., Washington, 1974-77; clin. social worker Chevy Chase Nursing and Convalescence Ctr., Silver Spring, Md., 1978-80; clin. social work cons. Family Svc. of Prince George's County, Lanham, Md., 1980-83, The Fogel Found., Washington, 1983-89, Washington, 1989—; pvt. ind. clin. social work practice, 1989—. Mem. Nat. Assn. Clin. Social Workers, Am. Assn. Marriage and Family Therapy (clin. mem.), Am. Assn. Sex Educators, Counselors and Therapists (clin. mem.). Avocations: abstract painting, crafts, knitting, sewing, embroidery. Home: 3700 Davenport St NW Washington DC 20016-1818 Office: 1090 Vermont Ave NW Ste 800 Washington DC 20005-4961

PENNEY, BETH, language educator, editor, writer; b. Carmel, Calif., Feb. 7, 1955; d. William Carroll Penney and Raylyn Thyrza (Crabbe) Moore. BA in Journalism and English, Calif. State U., Fresno, 1978, MA in English Lit., 1985. Mng. editor Paul Kagan Assoc., Inc., Carmel, Calif., 1980-89; tech. writer Computer Svcs. Corp., Monterey, Calif., 1989-90; publs. mgr. Data Rsch. Assoc., Inc., Monterey, 1990-98; English faculty Monterey (Calif.) Peninsula Coll., 1990—, chmn. English dept., 2005—. Feature writer, reviewer Carmel Pine Cone, 1994—97. Newsletter editor Monterey Peninsula Dickens Fellowship, Pacific Grove, Calif., 1991—. Pres. Pacific Grove (Calif.) Feast of Lanterns, 1995-2000, Friends of the Dickens Project, 1995-2000; founder, hon. sec. Monterey Peninsula Dickens Fellowship, 1991—. Mem. Pacific Grove C. of C. Democrat. Avocations: reading, needlecrafts, collecting depression glass. Home: PO Box 604 Pacific Grove CA 93950-0604 Office Phone: 831-646-4159.

PENNEY, SHERRY HOOD, academic administrator, consultant; b. Marlette, Mich., Sept. 4, 1937; d. Terrance and B. Jean (Stoutenburg) Hood; m. Carl Murray Penney, July 8, 1961 (div. 1978); children: Michael Murray, Jeffrey Hood; m. James Duane Livingston, Mar. 30, 1985. BA, Albion Coll., 1959; MA, U. Mich., 1961; PhD, SUNY, Albany, 1972; LLD (hon.), Albion Coll., 1989; degree (hon.), Quincy Coll., 1999. Vis. asst. prof. Union Coll., Schenectady, NY, 1972-73; assoc. higher edn. NY State Edn. Dept., Albany, 1973-76; assoc. provost Yale U., New Haven, 1976-82; vice chancellor acad. programs, policy and planning SUNY System, Albany, 1982-88; acting pres. SUNY, Plattsburgh, 1986-87; chancellor U. Mass., Boston, 1988-95; pres. U. Mass. Sys., Boston, 1995; chancellor U. Mass. Boston, 1996-2000, endowed prof., 2001—. Chmn., bd. dirs. Nat. Higher Edn. Mgmt. Sys., Boulder, Colo., 1985-87; mem. commn. on higher edn. New Eng. Assn. Schs. and Colls., Boston, 1979-82, Mid. States Assn. Schs. and Colls., Phila., 1986-88; mem. commn. on women Am. Coun. Edn., Washington, 1979-81, commn. on govt. rels., 1990-94; bd. dirs. NSTAR, 1990—, Carnegie Found. for Advancement of Teaching, 1994-2002. Author: Patrician in Politics, 1974; co-author (with James D. Livingston) A Very Dangerous Woman: Martha Wright and Women's Rights, 2004; editor: Women and Management in Higher Education, 1975; contbr. articles to profl. jours. Nat. adv. com. Nat. Initiative for Women in Higher Edn., 2001—05; mem. Internat. Trade Task Force, 1994—96; mem. exec. com. Challenge to Leadership, 1988, chair, 1995—98; bd. dirs. HERS, 1992—, Mary Baker Eddy Libr., Boston, 2001—; trustee Berkeley Div. Sch., Yale U., 1978—82, John F. Kennedy Libr. Found., 1988—2001; bd. dirs. Albany Symphony Orch., 1982—88, U. Mass. Found., 1988—2000, Mcpl. Rsch. Bur., Boston, 1990—2001, New Eng. Coun., 1990—2000, Greater Boston C. of C., 1989—2002, Met. Affairs Coalition, chair, 1999—2001; bd. trustees New Eng. Aquarium, 1990—2004; bd. dirs. Greater Boston One to One Leadership Coun., 1990—2000, NASULGC Commn. Urban Affairs, 1990—2000, The Ednl. Resource Inst., chair, 1996—; bd. dirs. The Environ. Bus. Coun., 1991—97; bd. visitors WEIU, 2002—06. Recipient Disting. Alumna award Albion Coll., 1978, Disting. Citizen award for racial harmony Black/White Boston, 1994, Am. Coun. on Edn./Nat. Identification Program award, Mass., Leadership award, 1995, New Eng. Women's Leadership award, 1996, Pinnacle award for Lifetime Achievement Greater Boston C. of C., 1998, Abigail Adams award, Mass. Women's Polit. Caucus, 2003. Mem. Orgn. Am. Historians, St. Botolph Club, Comml. Club (Boston). Unitarian Universalist. Office: U Mass Boston 100 Morrissey Blvd Boston MA 02125-3300

PENNIMAN, LINDA SIMMONS, retired real estate agent; b. Springfield, Ill., Sept. 26, 1943; d. Robert Leonard Simmons and Frances Jane Day; m. Nicholas Griffith Penniman, IV, Mar. 7, 1938; children: Rebecca, Nicholas G. V. AA, Springfield Jr. Coll., 1963. Sales assoc. Edward L. Bakewell, Inc., St. Louis, 1978—2000, retired, 2000. Chmn., founder Realtors' Housing Assistance Fund, St. Louis, 1996—2000; chair Housing Resources Fund, St. Louis, 1996—2000; chmn. bd. Penniman & Browne, Inc., 2006—. Chair Old Town Assn., Clayton, Mo., 1996—2000, Stop Metrolink Com., Clayton, 1998—99; asst. leader, program chair Greater Naples Leadership, 2003—, bd. dirs., 2003—, vol. com., 2003—, sec., 2005—; founder Women's Com. Forest Park Forever, St. Louis, Butterfly House, St. Louis; pres. Moorings Property Owners Assn.; chair Moorings Property Assn. Recipient Charles H. Evermann Disting. Svc. award, St. Louis Assn. Realtors, 1994. Avocations: golf, reading, politics. Personal E-mail: lindap9043@aol.com.

PENNINGER, FRIEDA ELAINE, retired literature educator; b. Marion, NC, Apr. 11, 1927; d. Fred Hoyle and Lena Frances (Young) Penninger. AB, U. N.C., Greensboro, 1948; MA, Duke U., 1950, PhD, 1961. Copywriter Sta. WSJS, Winston-Salem, NC, 1948-49; asst. prof. English Flora Macdonald Coll., Red Springs, NC, 1950-51; tchr. English Barnwell, SC, 1951-52, Brunswick, Ga., 1952-53; instr. English U. Tenn., Knoxville, 1953-56; instr., asst. prof. Woman's Coll., U. N.C., Greensboro, 1956-58, 60-63; asst. prof., assoc. prof. U. Richmond (Va.), 1963-71; chair. dept. English Westhampton Coll., Richmond, 1971-78; prof. English U. Richmond, 1971-91, Bostwick prof. English, 1987-91, ret., 1991. Author: William Caxton, 1979, Chaucer's "Troilus and Criseyde" and "The Knight's Tale": Fictions Used, 1993, (novel) Look at Them, 1990; compiler, editor: English Drama to 1660, 1976; editor: Festschrift for Prof. Marguerite Roberts, 1976. Fellow Southeastern Inst. of Mediaeval and Renaissance Studies, 1965, 67, 69. Mem.: Friends of The Libr. U. NC Greensboro (bd. dirs. 2005—). Democrat. Presbyterian. Home: 2701 Camden Rd Greensboro NC 27403-1438

PENNINGTON, BEVERLY MELCHER, financial services company executive; b. Vermillion, SD, Feb. 8, 1931; d. Cecil Lloyd and Phyllis Cecelia (Walz) M.; m. Glen D., Sept. 1, 1965 (dec. Aug. 1986); 1 child, Terri Lynn. BS, U. S.D., Vermillion, 1952. Enrolled agt. cert. IRS 1989. Sec. budget dept. Bur. of Indian Affairs, Aberdeen, S.D., 1952-53, pvt. sec., 1953-54, U.S. P.H.S. Indian Health, Aberdeen, 1954-55; adminstr. asst. U.S. Pub. Health Svc., Anchorage, 1955-58, U.S. Pub. Health, Dental Pub. Health, Washington, 1958-61; grant adminstr. Dental Pub. Health, Washington, 1961-65; co-owner Penn Mel Marina, Platte, S.D, 1965-74, Pennington Tax Service, Platte, 1974-86, owner, 1986-93; pres., CEO, White Tiger Fin. Svc., Inc., Platte, 1994—. Contbr. articles to profl. jours. Mem. Platte Women's Club, sec., 1965-68, pres., 1968-70, 89-91; mem. Libr. Bd., Sec., 1982-85, treas., 1995—. Fellow Am. Soc. Tax Profls. (sec. 1989-91, 2d v.p. 1995, 1st v.p. 1996, pres. 1997); mem. NAFE, Platte C. of C. (v.p. 1989, pres. 1990), Lyric Theatre Mus. Soc. (pres. 1988-92, v.p. 2005—), U.S. C. of C., Washington Dakota Cen. Com. Republican. Presbyterian. Avocations: collecting jewelry, reading, dress designing, gourmet cooking. Office: White Tiger Fin Svc Inc 420 Main St Platte SD 57369 Office Phone: 605-337-2603. Business E-Mail: whitetigerfinancial@inbox.com.

PENNINGTON, CLAUDIA, museum director; Dir. Key West Mus. Art & Hist., Fla., 2000—. Office: Key West Mus Art & Hist 281 Front St Key West FL 33040

PENNINGTON, KAREN HARDER, lawyer; b. Amarillo, Tex., June 7, 1956; d. Alvin L. and Rosemary Herskowitz Harder; BS in Biology, W. Tex. State U., 1977; JD, U. Tex., 1986. Bar: Calif. 1986, Tex. 1998, US Patent and Trademark Office 1993, Hopi Tribal Ct. 1993. Assoc. atty. Thelen, Marrin, Johnson & Bridges, L.A., 1986—89, Quinn, Emanuel & Urquhart, L.A., 1989—91, Crosby, Heafey, Roach & May, L.A., 1991—92; atty. Law Office of Karen H. Pennington, Long Beach, Calif., 1993—97, Cath. Charities Immigration Counseling Svcs., Dallas, 1998—2000; immigration atty. Law Office of Karen H. Pennington, Dallas, 2000—. Recipient cover story, Sept. 9 issue, Tex. Lawyer mag., 2002. Mem.: Dallas Bar Assn., LA County Bar Assn., Tex. Bar Assn., Calif. Bar Assn., Am. Immigration Lawyers Assn., North Tex. Coalition Just Peace, United For Peace and Justice, Dallas Peace Ctr. Roman Catholic. Achievements include representation of post-Sept. 11 immigration/national security detainees both before the courts and in FBI interrogations. Office: Law Office of Karen H Pennington Ste 110 701 Commerce St Dallas TX 75202 Office Phone: 214-741-7711. Office Fax: 214-741-7733. Business E-Mail: penningtonlaw@yahoo.com.

PENNINGTON, LISA H., lawyer; b. Wichita Falls, Tex., Oct. 28, 1958; BA magna cum laude, U. Tex., 1981; JD, U. Tex. Law Sch., 1983. Bar: Tex. 1984, US Dist. Ct., Tex. We., Ea., No. & So. Dist. 1984, US Ct. of Appeals, Fifth Circuit 1984, US Supreme Ct. 1992. Coord. labor and employment practice Baker & Hostetler, Houston, 1993—99, mng. ptnr., 1999—, mem. policy com. Named Tex. Super Lawyer, Tex. Monthly, 2004. Mem.: ABA (mem. litigation, employee rights and responsibilities sections), Tex. State Bar Assn., Houston Bar Assn. (bd. dirs., President's award for outstanding com. chair 1995—96). Office: Baker & Hostetler 1000 Louisiana St Ste 2000 Houston TX 77002-5009 Office Phone: 713-646-1303. Office Fax: 713-751-1717. Business E-Mail: lpennington@bakerlaw.com.

PENNINGTON, MELINDA SNIDER, librarian; d. James and Margaret Snider; m. Jodie Ansford Pennington, June 10, 1972; children: Sara Eleanor, Ellen Margaret. BA, Western Ky. U., 1972; MLS, U. Ill., 1974. Head tech. svcs. Tippecanoe County Pub. Libr., Lafayette, Ind., 1983—85, Bowling Green (Ky.) Pub. Libr., 1986—90; humanities reference libr. Western Ky. U., Bowling Green, 1990—93; libr. Winrock Internat., Little Rock, 1996—. Leader 4-H, Bowling Green, 1989—93, Conway, Ark., 1993—99. Mem.: Spl. Libr. Assn. Home: 2034 King Cir Conway AR 72034 Office: Winrock Inter 2201 Riverfront Dr Little Rock AR 72202 Office Phone: 501-280-3066. E-mail: mpennington@winrock.org.

PENNINGTON, VALERIE J., biology professor, dancer; b. Hollywood, Calif. d. John and Barbara Pennington. MS, U. Hawaii, 1996. Prof. biology Southwestern Coll., Chula Vista, Calif., 1996—. Office Phone: 619-421-6700.

PENNISI, LIZ, women's health nurse; b. Bklyn., Nov. 20, 1953; d. Alexander and Marjorie (Soviero) Perillo; children: Stephen, Scott, Greg. Diploma, Beth Israel Sch. Nursing, N.Y.C., 1974. RN, N.Y.; cert. ambulatory women's health nurse. Staff nurse Montefiore Hosp., Bronx, NY, 1974-75; mem. staff Beth Israel Med. Ctr., N.Y.C., 1975-77; office nurse Martin Kurman, M.D., N.Y.C., 1977-80, Adam Romoff, M.D. and Suzanne Yale, M.D., P.C, 1984—. Mem. AWHONN. Avocations: tennis, horseback riding, reading. Office: Drs Romoff and Yale 768 Park Ave New York NY 10021-4153 E-mail: lizpennisi@hotmail.com.

PENNY, LAURA JEAN, librarian; b. Union City, Tenn., June 25, 1956; d. Glen Jones and Harriet Smith (Gould) P. BS in Econs., Lambuth Coll., 1978; MLS, U. Ariz., 1980. Asst. libr. local history and genealogy Pikes Peak Libr. Dist., Colorado Springs, Colo., 1981-84; info. officer Inmos Corp., Colorado Springs, 1984-86; dir. libr. Colo. State Hosp., Pueblo, 1987—. Author: A Tempstuous Voyage, 1987, Abstracts of Strafford County, 1987, Abstracts of Washington County, 1988. Pres. El Paso County Dem. Women's Club, Colorado Springs, 1986-87; chmn. El Paso County Dem. Com., 1987—. Mem. Colo. Coun. Libr. Devel., Pikes Peak Geneal. Soc. (editor 1985-87). Methodist. Avocations: politics, genealogy, writing, skiing.

PENROD, HAZELL. L., music educator; b. Lonepine, La., Dec. 3, 1915; d. John Izac LaFleur and Sally Elizabeth McDonald; widowed Feb. 1994; 1 child, Paula Jean. MusM, Inst. Music, St. Louis, 1957. Piano tchr. Monfrey Music Studio, San Antonio, 1985; pvt. practice piano tchr. San Antonio, 1959. Tchr. ch., San Antonio, Nat. Guild Piano Tchrs., Austin, 1960. Inductee Hall of Fame Piano Guild USA. Mem. Tex. Music Tchrs. Assn., San Antonio Music Tchrs. Assn. Baptist. Home: 503 Wayside Dr San Antonio TX 78213-2842 Office Phone: 210-342-5967.

PENROD, MARIAN PENUEL, personnel consultant, retired school librarian; b. Statesville, Tenn., May 11, 1930; d. Hayden L. Penuel and Zoie L. Cunningham; m. William T. Penrod, Jr., June 8, 1954 (div. Oct. 1979); children: Cheryl Anne Penrod Puryear, Paula Wynn, Laura Lynn Penrod Moseng. BS, Middle Tenn. State Coll., 1952; M of Religious Edn., So. Bapt. Theol. Sem., Louisville, 1955; EdM, U. Miami, 1958. Cert. specialist in pastoral care Pastoral Counseling Ctrs. Tenn., Inc., 2002. Tchr. Parma (Mich.) Elem., 1953—54, Golden Pond (Ky.) Elem., 1955—57, West Jackson (Tenn.) Bapt., 1965—66; tchr., libr. Madison County, Jackson, 1967—69; tchr. Dyer County, Dyersburg, Tenn., 1969—70; sch. libr. Murfreesboro (Tenn.) City Schs., 1972—98; ind. wellness cons. Nikken, Inc., 1998—. Baptist. Avocations: reading, writing, travel, continued education. Office Phone: 615-893-7398.

PENROD, REBECCA LORENE CONNELLY, retired elementary school educator; b. Holland, Mo., July 11, 1921; d. Harry Boyd and Mary Edna (Foster) Connelley; m. Estell Lavon Penrod, Mar. 11, 1944; children: Penelope Childers, Marsha Archer, Samuel (dec.), Stephen, Bruce (dec.), Philip, Stanley. AB, U. Calif., Fresno, 1966; postgrad., SE State Tchrs. Coll., Brigham Young U., U. Calif., Berkeley. Cert. life teaching credential, playwriter, Calif. Prin. Boekerton Sch., Portageville, Mo., 1942—46; tchr. Gideon Dist., Portageville, 1948—50; elem. tchr. Happy Valley Sch., Shasta County, Calif., 1966—67; tchr. kindergarten Alpaugh Sch., Calif., 1967—91, Corcoran Sch., Calif.; ret., 1991. Mem. NEA, Calif. Tchrs. Assn., Alpaugh Tchrs. Assn. (pres., v.p., membership chmn.), Calif. Ret. Tchrs. Assn. Home: 22164 Oak Run Pl Cottonwood CA 96022-7700

PENSABENE, JUDITH K., lawyer; b. 1945; BA, U. Mo., Kansas City; postgrad., U. Houston, 1971; JD, U. Tulsa, 1975. Bar: Okla. 1975, D.C. 1978. Assoc. Holliman Langholz Runnels & Dowart, Tulsa, 1974—78; cons. environ. issues, 1980—89; sr. minority counsel Com. Energy & Natural Resources, U.S. Senate, 1990—95; v.p. & counsel Constellation Energy Group, Washington, 1995—2002; dep. chief counsel Com. Energy & Natural Resources, U.S. Senate, 2002—03, chief counsel, 2003—. Articles editor: U. Tulsa Law Jour. Mem.: Phi Delta Phi, Order of Curule (chair). Office: Committee on Energy and Natural Resources Room 364 Senate Dirksen Office Building Washington DC 20510-6150 Office Phone: 202-224-4971.

PENSACK, SUSAN, elementary school educator; b. Somerville, N.J., Mar. 13, 1956; d. Charles Florence and Eloise Joyce Green; m. Rodney Drew Pensack, June 25, 1977; children: Heather, Ryan. BA in Edn., Rider Coll., 1978; MS in Edn., E. Stroudsburg U., 1991. Cert. elem. tchr. K-8, tchr. handicapped K-12, N.J.; cert. learning disabilities tchr. cons., N.J., 2002. Dir. nursery sch. Surprise House, Belvidere, N.J., 1978-79; head tchr. NORWESCAP, Phillipsburg, N.J., 1979-81; impaired tchr. Washington Nursery, Washington, N.J., 1981-90; tchr. intermediate perceptually Washington Schs., Washington, 1990-91; tutor Masons/Allentown Learning Ctr., Allentown, Pa., 1998—; resource ctr. tchr. Hope Twp. Sch., Hope, NJ, 1991—2001; supr. trainee Masons-Allentown Learning Ctr., Allentown, 1999—; tchr. Lebanon Twp. Valley View Sch., 2001—; resource ctr. tchr. Lebanon Twp. Sch., Califon, NJ, 2001—. Learning disabilities tchr. cons. Lebanon Twp. Sch. Svc. unit dir./leader Girls Scouts Great Valley Coun., Allentown, 1983—; sec. Lower Mt. Bethel Sports. Assn., Martins. Creek., Pa., 1986-94, treas. 1994—. Recipient Outstanding Vol. Leadership award, Girl Scouts, Allentown, 1992, Outstanding Leader, Valley Coun., 1990, Great Valley award, 2000. Mem. NEA, Coun. Exceptional Children, Internat. Dyslexia Assn., N.J. Edn. Assn., Assn. Learning Cons. Democrat. United Meth. United Methodist. Avocations: girl scouts, reading, exercise, walking. Home: 10317 Upper Little Creek Rd Bangor PA 18013-4447 E-mail: pens@epix.net.

PENTON-SMITH, TAMMY L., elementary school educator; b. Picayune, Miss., Apr. 26, 1963; d. Linda and Richard Culpepper; 1 child, Alaina. BS in Bus. Adminstrn., U. So. Miss., Hattiesburg, 2000; alternative rte. elem. tchr., William Carey Coll., Gulfport, Miss., 2001, M of Elem. Edn., 2004. Adminstrv. asst. Tulane U., New Orleans, 1983—96; supr. Kelly Svcs., Gulfport, 2000—01; tchr. 5th grade South Side Upper Elem., Picayune, 2001—05. Coord. sci. fair South Side Sch. Dist., 2002—06; chair grade level South Side Upper Elem., Picayune, 2005—06. Office: South Side Upper Elem 1500 Rosa St Picayune MS 39466

PENTZ, ANNA FAYE, nurse; b. Chambersburg, Pa., Sept. 26, 1944; d. Clarence L. and Betty I. (Armstrong) Weller; children: Ronald, Kimberly, Julie. Diploma, York (Pa.) Hosp. Sch. Nursing, 1965; student, York Coll. Head nurse Meml. Hosp., York, 1968-81, staff nurse operating rm., 1981-84, charge nurse post anesthesia care unit, 1984-89, asst. nurse mgr. perioperative svcs., 1989-94, staff nurse in endoscopy, 1994—. Mem. South Cen. Pa. Ambulatory/Post Anesthesia Nurses.

PENWELL, REBECCA ANN, science educator; b. Dayton, Ohio; d. Harold Russell Penwell, Jr. and Karen Ann Penwell. BS, Allegheny Coll., 1996; MS, Fla. Internat. U., 1999; MEd, U. Fla., 2001, PhD, 2003. Asst. prof. Brenau U., Gainesville, Ga., 2003—. Content specialist Ga. Profl. Stds. Commn., Atlanta, 2003—04. Contbr. articles to profl. jours. Mem.: NSTA, Am. Ednl. Rsch. Assn., Ga. Acad. Sci. Avocations: scuba diving, snorkeling, reading. Office Phone: 770-534-6218. Business E-Mail: rpenwell@brenau.edu.

PENZ, ROXANNE MURRAY, elementary school educator; b. Dallas, July 4, 1966; d. Donald and Ann Murray; m. Daniel Eric Penz, Nov. 11, 2001. BA in Tchg., Sam Houston State U., Huntsville, Tex., 1989. Character Walt Disney World Co., Orlando, Fla., 1990—91; unit supr., performer Busch Entertainment Corp., Tampa, 1991—92; server Colonial Williamsburg Found., Shield's Tavern, Va., 1992—93; receptionist Texakoma Oil & Gas Corp., Dallas, 1993—94; actor Repertory Theatre Am., Corpus Christi, 1994—95; sales support The Met, Arts & Entertainment Newsweekly, Dallas, 1995—96; sales coord. Presidio Media, 1997—98; advt. coord., office mgr. D Mag., 1998—99; talent coach, creative cons., image stylist Media Star, Talk Prodns., Div@ Media, 2000; office mgr. Underground Shopper, 2000; tchr. English, speech, comm. applications Richardson West Jr. High, 2001—04; tchr. theatre Wester Mid. Sch., Frisco, 2004—. Instr., costumer, core co. Scarborough Faire, Renaissance Faire, Waxahachie, Tex., 1998—2006. Scholar, Sam Houston State U., 1984, Alpha Psi Omega. Mem.: NEA, Tex. State Tchrs. Assn. (pres. 2005), Tex. Ednl. Theatre Assn., Frisco Edn. Assn. (pres. 2005). Avocations: acting, travel, cooking, sewing. Office: Wester Middle School 12293 Shepherds Hill Lane Frisco TX 75035 Office Phone: 469-633-4895. Business E-Mail: penzr@friscoisd.org.

PEOPLES, ALICE LEIGH, not-for-profit executive; married; 4 children. Nat. v.p. Jack & Jill of Am., Inc., nat. pres., 2005—. Named one of Most Influential Black Americans, Ebony mag., 2006. Office: Jack & Jill of Am, Inc PO Box 970284 Ypsilanti MI 48197 also: 1930 17th St NW Washington DC 20009 Office Phone: 734-487-7725. Office Fax: 734-487-1596. E-mail: np@jackandjillinc.org.*

PEOPLES, MARIE D., writer; b. Northampton, Mass., Jan. 26, 1950; d. Mary Duress; m. Lamar Peoples, Sept. 16, 1996. BA, Anna Maria Coll., Paxton, Mass., 1974; student in Pre-med, Keuka Coll., Keuka Park, NY, 1968—70; student in History Edn., Assumption Coll., Worcester, Mass., 1975; diploma in Psychology and Social Work with highest honors, Stratford Career Inst., Washington, 2000. Personal care attendant pvt. care, Shelburne Falls, Mass., 2002—; writer Marie Peoples Pub., Bernardston, Mass., 2005. Home: PO Box 224 Bernardston MA 01337 Personal E-mail: mariepeoples@yahoo.com.

PEOT, DEBORAH LYNN, music educator; b. DesMoines, Iowa, May 21, 1972; d. Jerome Keith and Janis Lee Oswald; m. Jason Alan Peot, Aug. 8, 1998; children: Collin Joseph, Chloe Marie. BFA in Violin Performance, DePaul U., 1995, BFA in Music Edn., 1995; M in music edn., U. of Ill., 2000—03. Orch. dir. Sch. Dist. #83, Melrose Pk., Ill., 1995—98, Libertyville Sch. Dist. #70, Libertyville, Ill., 1998—. Mem.: Ill. Music Edn. Assn., Am. String Teachers Assn. Democrat. Cath. Avocations: skiing, bicycling, violin. Home: 3652 N Nora Chicago IL 60634 Office: Highland Mid Sch 310 West Rockland Rd Libertyville IL 60048

PEPER, CHARLOTTE ANN, educational consultant; b. Tucson, Oct. 30, 1949; d. Horace Eric and Marion Monier Bounds; children: Sonya, Jesse, Julie, John, Tina. AA, Pima C.C., Tucson, 1986; BA in Therapeutic Recreation, Prescott Coll., Ariz., 1994, MA in Counseling and Psychology, 2005. Therapeutic recreation provider City of Tucson, 1991—92; tchr. recreation therapy Ariz. Sch. for Deaf, 1992—95; cons. therapeutic recreation Westcenter Rehab. Ctr., 1999—2000; activity dir. Carondelet Holy Family Ctr., 1995—2000; dir. cmty. life Fountains at La Challa, 2000—02; tchr. music San Xavier Mission, 2002—04; exec. dir., cons. The Healing Bow, 1994—. Therapist homeless teens Teens is Transition, 2006—. Recipient Canondelet Mission award, Canondelet Health Network, Tucson, 1998. Mem.: Ariz. Assn. Activity Profls. (co-chair 2002), Am. Counseling Assn. Democrat. Roman Catholic. Personal E-mail: healingbow2@yahoo.com.

PEPIN, FRAN, secondary school educator; b. Pampa, Tex., Sept. 1, 1950; d. William Presley and Lena Faye Tatum; m. Richard Charles (div.); children: Todd Charles, Jill Hansen; m. Richard Pepin, Mar. 11, 2000. BA, Coll. of S.W., Hobbs, N.Mex., 1980; MS, Adams State U., Alamosa, Colo., 1995. Tchr. Lovington Pub. Schs., N.Mex., 1980—83, Farmington Mcpl. Schs., N.Mex., 1984—. Sponsor student coun. Mesa View Mid. Sch., Farmington, 2000—06. Republican. Methodist. Avocations: golf, gardening, camping, fishing. Home: 1301 Gladeview Dr Farmington NM 87401

PEPIN-WAKEFIELD, YVONNE MARY, artist, writer; b. San Francisco, Calif., May 28, 1956; d. Arthur Henry and Mary Alice (Ratté) Pepin; m. Wakefield Tod. BA, Antioch U., 1982; postgrad., Fielding Inst., 1989—, MA in Human Orgn. and Devel., 1991, PhD in Human Orgn. and Devel., 1992. Arts adminstr. Mendocino (Calif.) Art Ctr., 1978-85; founder, dir. Port Townsend (Wash.) Art Edn. Ctr., 1986—94; tchr. Sequim (Wash.) Sch. Dist., 1994—2004; asst. prof. dept. art design Kuwait U. Coll. Women, 2004—. Presenter in field. Author: (book) Cabin Journal, 1984, Three Summers, 1986. Recipient Robert Raushenberg Found. winner, Lab. Sch. Wash.; Fulbright Meml. Fund scholar. Mem.: AAUW, Am. Women's League Kuwait, Nat. Arts Edn. Assn., Am. Ednl. Rsch. Assn. Avocations: painting, teaching, writing. E-mail: wakefieldyvonne@yahoo.com.

PEPPARD, JACQUELINE JEAN, artist; b. Lynwood, Calif., Feb. 12, 1954; children: Nicole Bianca Pedersen, Olivia Christine Pedersen. Student, Colo. U., 1979; AA, Colo. Inst. Art, 1981. Watercolor tchr. Aha Sch. Art, Telluride, Colo., 1994—; cons. for cmty. edn. South Washington Sch. Dist., Cottage Grove, Minn., 1996; represented by Toh-Atin, Durango, Colo., Debra Hudgins Gallery, Santa Fe, N.Mex., Anasazi Gallery, Dallas, Bader-Melnick Gallery, Vail, Colo. Exhibited in group shows at U.S. Open, Taos, N.Mex., 1985 (Hon. mention, 5th Pl. Public's Choice), Brush and Palette Club, Grand Junction, Colo., 1986 (1st Pl. in Watercolor Landscapes), Telluride Watercolor Exhbn., 1986 (Best Regional Artist Purchase award), Riverside (Calif.) Art Mus., 1988, Nat. Arts Club, N.Y.C., 1988, N.Mex. Watercolor Soc., 1989, 90, Collectors Mart, Denver, 1989, Brea (Calif.) Cultural Ctr., 1990, 95, Jackson Hole (Wyo.) Rotary, 1990, El Cajon (Calif.) Performing Arts Ctr., 1990, Denver Mus., 1994, Riverside Mus., Calif., 1995, Nat. Watercolor Society's 75th Annual Exhbn. Brea Cultural Ctr., Calif., 1995; featured in various mags.; posters commd. for Jazz Festival, Telluride, 1987-88, Wine Festival, Telluride, 1988-89, Premier Fly Found., Telluride; represented in permanent collections at Mountain Village Metro Offices, Telluride, DuPont Collection, Telluride, Bank of Telluride, Telluride Arts and Humanities Gallery; contbr. articles to newspapers and mags. Brownie leader Girl Scouts U.S., Telluride, 1995-96. Grantee Telluride Coun. of Arts and Humanities, 1987. Mem. Nat. Watercolor Soc., N.Mex. Watercolor Soc. (2d Pl. award 1990), Watercolor West. Democrat. Avocations: fly fishing, skiing, camping, travel, raising children. Home: PO Box 3075 Bowman CA 95604-3075

PEPPER, BEVERLY, artist, sculptor; b. Bklyn., Dec. 20, 1924; d. Irwin Edward and Beatrice Evadne Stoll; m. Curtis G. Pepper, Oct. 11, 1949; children: Jorie Graham, John Randolph. Studied with, Fernand Leger, Andre L'Hote; student, Pratt Inst., 1939-41, D.F.A. (hon.), 1982; student, Art Students League, N.Y.C., 1944; D.F.A. (hon.), Md. Inst., 1983. Prof. meritus U. Perugia, Italy, 1987. One-woman shows include Marlborough Gallery, N.Y.C., 1969, Mus. Contemporary Art, Chgo., 1969, Galerie Hella Nebelung, Dusseldorf, Ger., 1971, Piazza Margana, Rome, 1971, Parker St. Gallery, Boston, 1971, Qui Arte Contemporanea, Rome, 1972, Marlborough Galleria d'Arte, Rome, 1972, Tyler Sch. of Art, Temple U. Abroad, Rome, 1973, Hammarskjold Plaza Sculpture Garden, N.Y.C., 1975, Met. Mus. Art, Miami, Fla., 1976, San Francisco Mus. Art, 1976, 86, Seattle Mus. Art, 1977, Princeton U., 1978, Indpls. Mus. Art, 1978, Todi Piazza and Sala delle Pietra, 1979, Gimple-Hanover Gallery, Zurich, 1980, Ronald Greenberg Gallery, St. Louis, 1980, Davenport Art Gallery, 1981, Hansen Fuller Goldeen Gallery, San Francisco, 1981, Laumeier Internat. Sculpture Park, St. Louis, 1982, Galleria Il Ponte, Rome, 1982, John Berggrun Gallery, San Francisco, 1983, 1985, Adams-Middleton Gallery, Dallas, 1985, Andre Emmerich Gallery, N.Y.C., 1975, 77, 79, 80, 82, 84, 86, 87, 89, 90, 91, 93, Columbus (Ohio) Mus. Art, 1986, Bklyn. Mus. Art, 1986, Charles Cowles Gallery, N.Y.C., 1987, 90, 94, Albright-Knox Art Gallery 20 yr. traveling survey exhbn., 1986, Visual Arts Ctr. MIT, Cambridge, Mass., 1989, James Corcoran Gallery, Santa Monica, Calif., 1989, 90, Contemporary Sculpture Ctr., Tokyo, 1991, Met. Mus. Art, N.Y.C., 1991, Narni all Rocca, Narna, Italy, 1991; group shows include XXIII Biennale di Venezia, Venice, Italy, 1972, Mus. Phila. Civic Center, 1974, Finch Coll. Mus. Art, N.Y.C., 1974, Marlborough Gallery, N.Y.C., 1974, Janie C. Lee Gallery, Houston, 1975, New Orleans Mus. Art, 1976, Documenta 6, Kassel, Ger., 1977, Quadriennale di Roma, Rome, 1977, Seattle Mus., 1979, Bklyn. Mus. Art, 1987, Bienale de Sculpture, Monte Carlo, 1991, Galleria Comunale d'Arte Moderna, Spoletto, Italy, 1992, Chelsea Harbour Sculpture '93, London, 1993, Queens Mus. Art, Corona Park, N.Y., 1994; represented in numerous permanent collections including Met. Mus. Art, N.Y.C., Fogg Mus., Cambridge, Mass., Albright-Knox Art Gallery, Buffalo, Jacksonville (Fla.) Mus. Modern Art, Galleria d'Arte Moderna, Florence, Italy, Walker Art Center, Mpls., Instituto Italiano di Cultura, Stockholm, Sweden, Power Inst. Fine Arts, Sydney, Australia, Galleria Civica d'Arte Moderna, Turin, Italy, Albertina Mus., Vienna, Hirshhorn Mus. and Sculpture Garden, Washington, Worcester (Mass.) Art Mus., Parkersburg (W.Va.) Art Mus., Smithsonian Inst., Washington, Dartmouth Coll., Hanover, N.H., Atlantic Richfield Co., L.A., Rutgers U., Wright, Runstad & Co., Seattle, Niagara Frontier Transp. Authority, Buffalo, Johns Hopkins Hosp., John Deere Foundry, East Moline, Ill.; commns. include Amphisculpture, AT&T, Bedminster, N.J., 1974-76, Dartmouth Coll., 1976-77, Sol i Onbra Park, 1986-91, City Barcelona, 1986—, Teatre Celle, Villa Celle, Postoia, Italy, 1989-91, Terana Altar II, Smithsonian Inst., Nat. Mus. Am. Art, Washington, 1990-91, Gotanno Community Park, Adachi-ku Machizukuri Corp., Neo-Hodos, Tokyo, 1992, Split Ritual, U.S. Nat. Arboretum, Washington, 1992, Palingenesis, Credit-Suisse, Zurich, 1992-94, The Garden at 26 Fed/ Plz., Gen. Svcs. Adminstrn., N.Y.C., 1992—, Jerusalem Ritual, Jerusalem Found., Israel, 1994. Recipient award Nat. Endowment of Arts, 1976, 79, award GSA, 1975, Honor award Nat. Women's Caucus for Art, 1994.

PEPPER, DOROTHY MAE, nurse; b. Merill, Maine, Oct. 16, 1932; d. Walter Edwin and Alva Lois (Leavitt) Stanley; m. Thomas Edward Pepper, July 1, 1960; 2 children, including Walter Frank. RN, Maine Med. Ctr. Sch. Nursing, Portland, 1954. RN, Calif. Pvt. duty nurse, Lafayette, Calif.; staff nurse Maine Med. Ctr., Portland, 1954-56, Oakland (Calif.) VA Hosp., 1956-58; pvt. duty nurse, dir. RN's Alameda County, Oakland. Mem. Profl. Nurses Bur. Registry, Maine Writers and Pubs. Alliance. Avocation: writing.

PEPPER, DOTTIE, professional golfer; b. Saratoga Springs, N.Y., Aug. 17, 1965; Student, Furman University. Top ranked player LPGA Tour, 1992; ret. as golfer, 2004; commentator NBC, 2005—; lead analyst & commentator The Golf Channel, 2005—. 3 time NCAA All-American; recipient Rolex Player of the Year Award, 1992; recipient Vare Trophy, 1992; leading money winner LPGA, 1992. Achievements include winning tournaments including Mazda Classic, 1989, Crestar Classic, 1990, Nabisco Dinah Shore, 1992, Sega Women's Championship, 1992, Welch's Classic, 1992, Sun-Times Challenge, 1992, LPGA Leading Money Winner, 1992, Wendy's Three-Star Challenge, 1992, PING/Welch's Championship, 1995, JC Penney/LPGA Skins Game, McCall's LPGA Classic, wom four tournaments: Rochester Internat., Shop-Rite LPGA Classic, Friendly's Classic and Safeway LPGA Golf Champ., 1996, 24 tournaments earning $293,652, 1997, tied 2nd at Rochester Internat., tied 3rd at Star Bank LPGA Classic, tied fourth at ShopRite LPGA Classic, 1997, Solheim Cup, 1998, Nabisco Dinah Shore, 1999. Mailing: The Golf Channel 7580 Commerce Center Dr Orlando FL 32819-8947

PEPPER, FLOY CHILDERS, educational consultant; b. Broken Arrow, Okla., Mar. 14, 1917; d. James Alexander and Louise Lena (Barber) Childers; m. James Gilbert Pepper, Mar. 23, 1940; children: James G., Suzanne Pepper Henry. BS, Okla. State U., Stillwater, 1938; MS, Okla. State U., 1939; postgrad., Oreg. U. Home econs. tchr. Bur. Indian Affairs, Ft. Sill, Okla., 1939-40, Chemawa, Oreg., 1940-42, Portland (Oreg.) Pub. Schs., 1945-65; instr. Portland State U., 1967-85; supr. spl. edn. Multnomah Ednl. Svc. Dist., Portland, 1965-83; orientation specialist N.W. Regional Ednl. Lab., Portland, 1983-85; curriculum writer Oreg. State Bd. Edn., Salem, 1987-90; evaluator Native Indian Tchr. Edn. Program U. B.C., Vancouver, 1987-89; cons. Indian edn. Portland Pub. Sch., 1989—. Co-author: Maintaining Sanity in the Classroom, 1971, revised edit., 1982; contbr. articles to profl. jours. Recipient Ed Elliot Human Rights award, Oreg. Edn. Assn., 1996. Mem. Indian Curriculum Com. (alternative chmn. 1990-99), Oreg. Soc. of Individual Psychology, Multicultural Task Force (co-chmn. 1990-99, Dist. Svc. award 1990-91). Republican. Avocations: writing, reading, dance, presenting workshops. Home: 7799 SW Scholls Ferry Rd Apt 138 Beaverton OR 97008

PEPPER, JOLINE ROMANO, psychologist, educator; b. Malden, Mass., Nov. 4, 1971; d. Leo Richard and Geraldine Kathleen Romano; m. Eric Edward Pepper; 1 child, Erica Jade. BA, Merrimack Coll., 1993; MS, U. Mass., 1996. Sch. psychologist North Reading (Mass.) Pub. Schs., 1996—. Adj. faculty mem. Western New Eng. Coll., Mass., 1999—. Recipient Allen J. Ash award, Nat. Honor Soc. in Psychology. Mem.: Nat. Assn. Sch. Psychologists, Psi Chi. Avocation: exercise. Personal E-mail: jpepper@comcast.net.

PEPPER, PAMELA POE, psychologist; b. Erwin, NC, Feb. 21, 1953; d. Thomas Wesley Poe, Jr. and Norma Jean (Ferrell) Poe; m. Eugene Vance Pepper, Jr., May 15, 1976; children: Katherine McIver, Anna Faison. BA in Psychology & English, Salem Coll., 1975; MA in Counseling, U. NC, 1980; PhD in Sch. Psychology, U. NC-Chapell Hill, 1992. Lic. psychologist NC, health svcs. provider, psychologist NC, registered electroencephalography tech. Duke U., cert. provider psychol. svcs. traumatic brain injured students NC Dept. Public Instruction. Postdoctoral fellow in neuropsychology Wake Forest U., Bowman Gray Sch. Med., Winston-Salem, NC, 1993—95; rsch. technologist electroencephalography Epilepsy Rsch. Ctr., Va. Med. Ctr., Durham, NC, 1975—76; clin. assoc. biological psychiatry, program dir. electrophysiological tech. Duke U., Durham, 1978—81; mgr. staff edn. & devel. Durham Regional Med. Ctr., 1981—82; postdoctoral fellow in neurology, divsn. neuropsychology Wake Forest U. Bapt. Med. Ctr., Bowman Gray Sch. Medicine, 1993—95; adj. asst. prof. grad. studies edn. Salem Coll., Winston-Salem, 1994; clin. neuropsychologist Salem Psychiatric Assocs., P.A., Winston-Salem, 1995—97; clin. neuropsychologist, found. ptnr. Tri-Care, P.A., Winston-Salem, 1997—2003; clin. neuropsychologist Pepper Neuropsychol. Consulting., PLLC, Winston-Salem, 2004—. Spkr. in field. Bd. advisors quality assurance Qual Choice Behavioral Health, Winston-Salem, 1996—2001; mem. Jr. League Durham, 1975; pres. Durham/Chapel Hill Salem Coll. Alumnae Assn., 1975—76; bd. dirs. So. Soc. Electroencephalographic Technologists, Atlanta, 1980—81, Mental Health Assn. Forsyth County, Winston-Salem, 2000—02. Recipient Order of Scorpion, Salem Coll., 1973—75. Mem.: APA Clin. Neuropsychology Divsn., APA, Internat.

Neuropsychol. Soc., Brain Injury Assn. NC (spkrs. bureau 1998—). Democrat. Presbyterian. Avocations: reading, writing, gardening, rock collecting, birdwatching. Office Phone: 336-409-4705. Business E-Mail: drpampepper@aol.com.

PERA, RENEE REIJO, biology professor; BS, U. Wis., 1983; PhD, Cornell U., 1993; postdoc., Whitehead Inst. Biomed. Rsch. MIT, 1997. Damon-Runyan fellow Whitehead Inst. Biomed. Rsch. MIT, 1993—97, instr. biology, 1995; asst. prof. in residence U. Calif., San Francisco, 1997—2003, assoc. prof. in residence, 2003—, co-dir. program in human stem cell biology, 2004—, assoc. dir. ctr. reproductive scis., 2004—. Spkr. in field. Contbr. articles to profl. jours. Office: USCF 513 Parnassus Ave Rm HSE 1636 Box 0556 San Francisco CA 94143-0556 Office Phone: 415-476-3178. Office Fax: 415-476-3121.*

PERATONER, HEIDI ESMERALDA, marriage and family therapist intern; b. Boston, June 24, 1962; d. Carlo and Delia Bercerra Peratoner. AA in Spl. Edn., Portland Cmty. Coll., 1985; BA in English, Dominican U., 1994; MS in Clin. Psychology, Argosy U., 2003. Supr. spl. needs student libr. Cedar Mill Libr., Oreg., 1981—82; asst. tchr. spl. edn. Beaverton Sch., Oreg., 1984—85; asst. tchr. Jewish Cmty. Pre-Sch., San Rafael, Calif., 1994—99, 2003—04; marriage family therapist intern, counselor Linda Reed Treatment Svc., San Anselmo, Calif., 2002—05; marriage therapist intern Matrix Family Network and Resource Ctr., Novato, Calif., 2005—. Contbr. poetry. Vol. World Inst. for Ind., Berkeley, Calif., 1986—87; vol., bd. mem. Matrix Resource Ctr. Families of Children with Spl. Needs, Novato, Calif., 1996—2000. Mem.: Calif. Marriage Family Therapist. Avocations: art, crafts, writing, poetry, reading. Personal E-mail: hepenguins@aol.com.

PERCOSKI, KATHRYN JEAN, secondary school educator; b. Memphis, Dec. 12, 1981; d. Tom and Pat Percoski. Bachelor's, Delta State U., Cleve., Miss., 2004. Tchr. and coach Millington Ctrl. H.S., Tenn., 2004—. Coach softball and volleyball Millington Ctrl. H.S., 2004—05. Business E-Mail: kpercoski@scsk12.edu.

PERCY, HELEN SYLVIA, physician; b. Atlanta, May 7, 1923; d. George L. and Sophia (Toulchin) P.; 1 child, Valentina Stewart-Annor. BS, U. San Francisco, 1951; MD, Med. Coll. Pa., 1958. Diplomate Am. Bd. Family Practice. Intern Harbor Gen. Hosp., Torrance, Calif., 1958-59, resident, 1959; physician Maui Med. Group, Lahaina, Hawaii, 1968—; asst. prof. medicine U. Hawaii, Honolulu, 1978—2000. Adv. bd. Maui Community Health Ctr., 1986-89; v.p. Maui AIDS Found., 1986-89. Mem. AMA, Maui County Med. Soc. (councilor 1988—), Hawaii Med. Assn. (Maui councilor). Democrat. Buddhist. Avocation: dance. Office: Maui Med Group 130 Prison St Lahaina HI 96761-1247 Office Phone: 808-661-0051.

PERDIGÓ, LUISA MARINA, foreign language and literature educator; b. Havana, Cuba, Dec. 25, 1947; came to U.S. 1962; d. Mario and Hortensia Dolores (Alvarez) P. AB, CUNY, 1971, MA, 1974, PhD, 1981; MA, Columbia U., 1987. LPN, 2005; cert. translator English/Spanish Am. Translators Assn., ins. and coding specialist. Asst. prof. Spanish, asst. dean St. Thomas Aquinas Coll., Sparkill, NY, 1982-87; asst. prof. Spanish and French CUNY, La Guardia, 1987-88, asst. prof. Spanish, City Coll., 1988-89; asst. prof. Spanish St. Peter's Coll., Jersey City, 1989-91; asst. prof. Spanish and French Clarion U., Pa., 1992-94, Rockland Coll. SUNY, 1995-96, Mercy Coll., 1998—. Author: La Estética de Octavio Paz, 1975, The Origins of Vicente Huidobro's Creacionismo (1911-1916) and its Evolution (1917-47), 1994, The Lyrics of the Troubadour Perdigon, 2002, (poetry) Desde el Hudson/From the Hudson, 1993, Huellas/Footprints, 1997, America at the Millenium, 2000, The Best Poems and Poets of 2002, Theatre of the Mind, 2003; author numerous poems; contbr. articles to profl. jours. Participant seminar in poetry, NEH, U. Kans., 1991; Rsch. fellow Orgn. Am. States, Chile, 1981; grantee CUNY, 1975; scholar Columbia U., 1982-84. Mem. MLA, Clarion Hist. Soc., Circulo de Cultura Panamericano, Sigma Delta Pi, Pi Delta Phi.

PERDIKOU, KIM, information technology executive; BSc. Comp. Sci. and Operational Rsch., Paisley U., Scotland; MA Info. Systems, Pace U. Dir. Network Svcs. Knight Ridder; VP, CIO Women.com Networks, Inc., 1999—2000; CIO Juniper Networks, Inc., Calif., 2000—. Office: Juniper Networks Inc 1194 N Mathilda Ave Sunnyvale CA 94089

PERDUE, BEVERLY EAVES, lieutenant governor, geriatric consultant; b. Grundy, Va., Jan. 14, 1948; d. Alfred P. and Irene E. (Morefield) (dec.) Moore; m. Robert W. Eaves, Jr.; children: Garrett, Emmett. BA, U. Ky., 1969; MEd, U. Fla., 1974, PhD, 1976. Pvt. lectr., writer, cons., 1980-86; pres. The Perdue Co., New Bern, N.C., 1985—; rep. N.C. State Gen. Assembly, Raleigh, 1986-90; senator N.C. Gen. Assembly, Raleigh, 1990-2001; lt. gov. State of N.C., 2001—. Bd. dirs. Nations Bank, New Bern. Bd. dirs. N.C. United Way, Greensboro, 1990-92; exec. mem. N.C. Dem. Party, Raleigh, 1989—; mem. N.C. travel bd. Nat. Conf. State Legislators. Named Outstanding Legislator, N.C. Aging Network, 1989, 92, 100 to Watch, Dem. Leadership Coun. 2003; Toll fellow Nat. Conf. State Legislators, Lexington, Ky., 1992. Mem. Nat. Coun. on Aging, Bus. and Profl. Women, Rotary. Democrat. Episcopalian. Office: Office of Lt Governor 310 N Blount Blvd 20301 Raleigh NC 27699-0401 Office Fax: 919-733-7350, 919-733-6595. E-mail: bperdue@ncmail.net.*

PERDUE, JUDY CLARK, academic administrator; b. N.Y.C. d. Christopher Thompson and Iris Ramona (Turner) C.; m. Tito Perdue, July 27, 1957; 1 child, Melanie. BA, Ind. U., 1967; MA, U. Iowa, 1970; MS, Iowa State U., 1980; PhD, U. Ga., 1987. Cataloger Iowa State U. Libr., Ames, 1970-74, head gifts and exchange, 1974-78; head librarian and asst. prof. biology E. Ga. Coll., Swainsboro, 1988-92; head libr., assoc. prof. biology Floyd Coll., Rome, Ga., 1992-94, chair sci., math. and phys. edn., 1994—. Contbr. articles to profl. jours. Fellow Royal Entomol. Soc. London; mem. Assn. So. Biologists, Ga. Libr. Assn., ALA, Entomol. Soc. Am., Acarological Soc. Am., Delta Kappa Gamma, Delta Phi Alpha. Office: Floyd Coll Libr Hwy 27 Rome GA 30162

PERDUE, THEDA, history professor, writer; b. McRae, Ga., Apr. 2, 1949; d. James Howard and Ouida (Davis) P. AB, Mercer U., 1972; MA, U. Ga., 1974, PhD, 1976. From asst. prof. to assoc. prof. history Western Carolina U., Cullowhee, NC, 1975—83; prof. history Clemson (S.C.) U., 1983—88, U. Ky., Lexington, 1988—98, U. N.C., Chapel Hill, 1998—. Editor Indians of S.E., U. Nebr. Press, Lincoln, 1985—; cons. Smithsonian Instn., Washington, 1989; Fulbright lectr., N.Z., 1988. Author: Slavery and the Evolution of Cherokee Society, 1979, Native Carolinians, 1985, The Cherokee, 1988, Cherokee Women, 1998u, Colulmbia Guide to Indians of the Southeast, 2001, "Mixed Blood" Indians, 2001; editor: Nations Remembered, 1980, Cherokee Editor, 1983, Sifters: American Indian Women's Lives, 2000; co-editor: Southern Women, 1993; mem. editorial bd. Jour. Women's History, 1988—, Ethnohistory, 1992—. Newberry Libr. fellow, 1978, Rockefeller Found. fellow, 1980-8l. Mem. Am. Hist. Assn., Orgn. Am. Historians, Am. Soc. for Ethnohistory, So. Hist. Assn., So. Assn. for Women Historians (pres. 1985-86). Democrat. Office: U Ky Dept History Pot # 1715 Lexington KY 40506-0001

PEREIRA, MELANY, elementary school educator; b. Bombay, Oct. 17, 1945; arrived in U.S., 1976; d. Joseph and Mary Pereira. A in Music, Mt. Aloysius Coll., 1980; degree in elem. edn., St. Francis U., 1983, MEd, 1989. Tchr. elem. edn. St. Ann's Sch., Secunderabad, India, 1969—75, St. Aloysius Sch., Cresson, Pa., 1984—89, All Sts. Cath. Sch., Pa., 1989—. Mission procurator Propagation of Faith, Ebensburg, Pa., 1976—. Named Outstanding Cath., Diocese of Altoona; recipient Educator award, Johnstown, Pa., 1999—2000. Avocations: gardening, sewing, cooking, music, collecting stamps. Office: Mt St Ann Retreat House PO Box 328 Ebensburg PA 15931-0328

PERES, JUDITH MAY, journalist; b. Chgo., June 30, 1946; d. Leonard H. and Eleanor (Seltzer) Zurakov; m. Michael Peres, June 27, 1972; children: Dana, Avital. BA, U. Ill., 1967; M Studies in Law, Yale U., 1997. Acct. exec. Daniel J. Edelman Inc., Chgo., 1967-68; copy editor Jerusalem (Israel) Post, 1968-71, news editor, 1971-75, chief night editor, 1975-80, editor, style book, 1978-80; copy editor Chgo. Tribune, 1980-82, rewriter, 1982-84, assoc. fgn. editor, 1984-90, nat. editor, 1990-95, nat./fgn. editor, 1995-96, specialist writer, 1997—; Yale Law fellow, 1996-97. Recipient Media award, U. Mich., 2000, award, Soc. Women's Health Rsch., 2004. Office: Chicago Tribune 435 N Michigan Ave Chicago IL 60611-4066 Office Phone: 312-222-4330. Business E-Mail: jperes@tribune.com.

PERET, KAREN KRZYMINSKI, health facility administrator; b. Springfield, Mass., Mar. 8, 1950; d. Edward S. and Doris L. (Beaudry) Krzyminski; m. Robert J. Peret, June 19, 1971 (div. Sept. 2003); children: Heather, James, Kaitlin, Matthew. BSN, St. Anselm's, 1972; MS in Nursing Adminstrn., Boston U., 1980; EdD in Orgnl. Devel., U. Mass., 1993. RN, Mass. Staff nurse Boston VA's Hosp., 1972—73; staff nurse pediat. Harrington Meml. Hosp., Southbridge, Mass., 1973—74, instr. edn., 1974—75, relief day asst. dir. nursing, 1975; coord. continuing edn. Ctrl. Maine Med. Ctr., Lewiston, 1975—76; asst. dir. nursing Monson Devel. Ctr., Palmer, Mass., 1977—83, DON, 1983—94; exec. nursing cons. Liberty Healthcare, Waltham, Mass., 1994—98, v.p. ops. Phila., 1998—; ind. mgmt. cons., 1993—. Instr. Quinsigamond Cmty. Coll., Worcester, Mass., 1972-73. Contbr. articles to profl. jours. Mem. ANA, Mass. Nurses' Assn., Am. Assn. on Mental Retardation, Sigma Theta Tau. Home: 79 Sturbridge Rd Holland MA 01521-3123 Office: 401 E City Ave Ste 820 Bala Cynwyd PA 19004-1130 Office Phone: 800-331-7122. Personal E-mail: karenperet@aol.com.

PERETSMAN, NANCY B., investment banker; b. Worcester, Mass., Mar. 27, 1954; d. George Peretsman and Norma (Burofsky) O'Haire; m. Robert Scully, Sept. 17, 1988. AB with hons., Princeton U., 1976; MPPM, Yale, 1979. V.p. Blyth, Eastman, Dillon & Co., NYC, 1979—83; dir., head of media group Salomon Bros., NYC, 1983—95; exec. v.p., mng. dir. Allen & Co., NYC, 1995—. Bd. mem. Charter Comm., Inc. Charter trustee Princeton U., 1976. Named one of 50 Women to Watch, Wall St. Jour., 2005, 50 Most Powerful Women in Bus., Fortune mag., 2006. Office: Allen & Co Inc 711 5th Ave New York NY 10022*

PERETTI, MARILYN GAY WOERNER, human services professional; b. Indpls., July 30, 1935; d. Philip E. and Harriet E. (Meyer) Woerner; children: Thomas A., Christopher P. BS, Purdue U., 1957; postgrad., Coll. DuPage, 1980—2002, U. Wis., 1981—95. Nursery sch. lab. asst. Mary Baldwin Coll., Staunton, Va., 1957-58; tchr. 1st grade, nursery sch. No. Ill. area schs., 1958-61; asst. tchr. of blind Glenbard E. H.S., Lombard, Ill., 1978-80; adminstrv. asst. Elmhurst Coll., 1980-81; dir. vol. svcs. DuPage Convalescent Ctr., Wheaton, 1981-95; dir. cmty. outreach Sr. Home Sharing, Inc., Lombard, Ill., 1996-97; asst. to dir. of Career Vision, graphic designer The Ball Found., 1997-98; adminstrv. asst. Christ Ch. of Oak Brook, 1998-99; asst. for comms. Lombard Mennonite Peace Ctr., 2000—02; owner freelance computer bus., web design Pages by Peretti, 2002—. Prodr. ednl. slide programs on devel. countries, 1988-98; initiator used book collection for libr. project U. Zululand, S. Africa, 1997-98; designer, developer websites for Loretto Ctr., Wheaton, Ill. Maya Ministry, Westchester, Ill., St. Luke Luth. Ch., Glen Ellyn, Ill., DePaul U., 2005, Internat. Crane Found., Baraboo, Wis, 2005. Author, pub. (poetry): Poems of a Woman, 1999, Crack the Rifle in Two, 1999, To Love Cranes, 2000, Let Wings Take You, 2003, Seven Wonders of the Poetry World, 2006, Deep in a Woman, 2006; editor/designer (newsletters) Our Developing World's Voices, 1994-98, The Leaflet, Nature Artists' Guild of the Morton Arboretum, 1997-2000, Ill. State Poetry Soc., 1997-98, LOVE in Action, 2002-2003; exhbns. include The Morton Arboretum, 1992—, Danada Nature Art Show, 2002—, St. Thomas Celebration of the Arts, 2002—, Wheaton Libr., 2003, Glen Ellyn Libr., 2003, Hanging Gardens Gallery, Genoa, Ill., 2004, Downers Grove Libr., 2004, La Spiaza, Wheaton, 2004, DePaul Univ., 2005, DuPage Art League, 2005, Internat. Crane Found., 2005. Bd. dirs. Lombard YMCA, 1977-83, pres., 1980; vol. Chgo. Uptown Ministry, 1979; participant fact finding trips El Salvador, 1988, Honduras, 1989, Nicaragua, 1989, Republic of South Africa, 1991, Guatemala and El Salvador, 1997; mem. Nature Artists Guild of Morton Arboretum, exhibitor, 1992—; mem. DuPage Art League, 2004—, cmty. venue cmdr., 2005—; vol. homeless shelter, 1994-97; initiated sponsorship of ch. missionaries to Gautemala, 2003; assisted local immigrants from Iran, Sudan, 2004. Recipient 1st prize for poetry, Ann Arbor, Mich., 2001, 2d prize for poetry, Nat. Conf. on Aging, 2003. Mem.: Transparent Watercolor Soc. Am. (life), Theosophical Soc. Avocations: swimming, poetry writing, desktop publishing, third world concerns, botanical and animal watercolors.

PERETTI, TERRI L., political science professor, department chairman; d. Jack D. and Lois P. Jennings; m. James R. Zeigler, July 14, 2005; children: Rachel A. Jennings, Michael J. Zeigler. BGS, U. Kans., Lawrence, 1974—78; MA, U. Calif., Berkeley, 1979—80, PhD, 1980—88. Assoc. prof. Santa Clara U., Calif., 1988—, polit. sci. dept. chair, 2002—. Author: (book) In Defense of a Political Court. Mem.: Am. Polit. Sci. Assn. Avocations: hiking, travel.

PEREZ, BARBARA SUE, middle school educator; d. Norman Laverne and Lila Lucilile (Ellis) Svedin; m. Isidro Perez, Mar. 22, 1986; children: Brianna, Marcos, Keila. BA in Elem. Edn., Trinity U., Deerfield, Ill., 1981; MA in Edn., Nova Southea. U., Ft. Lauderdale, Fla., 2002. Tchr. 6th grade math. and sci. Delavan (Wis.)- Darien Sch. Dist., 1986—. Ch. worship leader, treas. Named Tchr. of Yr., Wurbel Assn., Delavan, 1993, 2003. Mem.: ASCD. Avocations: reading, walking. Office Phone: 262-728-2642.

PEREZ, BEATRIZ, marketing executive; V.p. sports and entertainment mktg. N. Am. divsn. The Coca-Cola Co., Atlanta; chmn. bd. dir. Girls Outdoor Adventure for Leadership; bd. trustees Camp Coca-Cola. Named one of Forty Under 40, Sports Bus. Jour., 2001—03; named to Elite Women, Hispanic Bus., 2005. Office: Coca-Cola Co PO Box 1734 Atlanta GA 30301

PEREZ, DORENE MARIE, computer-aided drafting and engineering educator; d. Dario D. and Helen I. Verucchi; m. Robert G. Perez, Aug. 6, 1988; children: Kelli M. Whightsil, Kyle D. Roach, Corri L. Heiden. AS in Engring. Design, Ill. Valley C.C., Oglesby, 1981. Prof. Ill. Valley C.C., Oglesby, 1987—, program coord. for computer aided design, 1995—. Pres. Spring Valley Hist. Soc., Ill., 2000—02. Grantee, NSF, 2005—. Mem.: Am. Soc. Engring. Educators, Soc. Mfg. Engrs. Republican. Evangelical. Avocation: travel. Home: 208 E Cleveland Spring Valley IL 61362 Office: Illinois Valley CC 815 N Orlando Smith Rd Oglesby IL 61348 Office Phone: 815-224-0221. Business E-Mail: dorene_perez@ivcc.edu.

PEREZ, EDITH R., lawyer; BA, U. Calif., Davis, 1976; JD, U. Calif., Berkeley, 1980. Bar: Calif. 1982. Vis. atty. Sergio Augusto Malta Advogados, Rio de Janeiro, Pablo Martinez Cano y Asociados, Mexico City; with Latham & Watkins, L.A., 1984—. Mem. adv. com. on women in svcs. U.S. Dept. Def.; mem. bd. dirs. Hugh O'Brian Youth Leadership Found., Nat. Conf. Christians and Jews, Cmty. Enhancement Corp., Mex.-Am. Legal Def. and Ednl. Fund, ARC, Latino Mus. History, Art and Culture; bd. regents Loyola Marymount U.; mem. adv. coun. on equal opportunity to CEO of So. Calif. Edison; mem. Calif. Gov.'s Task Force on Diversity and Outreach. V.p. L.A. Bd. Recreation and Pks. Commrs., 1994—95; pres. L.A. Bd. Police Commrs., 1997—99; mem. bd. dirs. Nat. Recreation Found., Ctr. for Study of L.A., Loyola Marymount U., Oakwood Sch. Named one of 25 Up-and-Coming Attys. Who Are Making a Difference in Calif., L.A. Daily Jour., 1994, 100 Most Influential Hispanics in U.S., Hispanic Bus. Mag., 1996; recipient Bringing Up Daughters Differently award, NOW Legal Def. and Edn. Fund, 1996, Redesigning Policing award, Nat. Ctr. for Women and Policing, 1997, Cmty. Commitment award, Calif. Latino Civil Rights Network, 1998, Women of Achievement award, Anti-Defamation League, 1998, Legal Svcs. award, Mex.-Am. Legal Def. and Ednl. Fund., 1998, Twice a Citizen award, L.A. Police Res. Found., 1999. Mem.: ABA, Mex. Am. Bar Assn., L.A. County Bar Assn., Calif. State Bar Assn. Office: Latham and Watkins LLP 633 W Fifth St Ste 4000 Los Angeles CA 90071

PEREZ, IRENE, music educator, director; b. San Antonio, Tex., Oct. 29, 1970; d. Tomas Gonzalez and Connie Perez; 1 child, Marina Elaina DeLeon. BA in Music, Tex. Tech U., Lubbock, 1995; MusM, U. New Orleans, La., 1999. Cert. tchr. all-level music pre-K-12 Tex. State Bd. Educator Certification, 2005. Tchr. music Kenedy Elem. Sch., Tex., 2002—; dir. color guard Kenedy H.S. Band, 2004—. Youth music min. Our Lady Queen of Peace Cath. Ch., Kenedy, 2002—. Cpl. USMC, 1995—2000, New Orleans. Decorated Navy Achievement Medal Commdg. Officer Marine Forces Res. Mem.: Tex. Music Educators Assn. Home: 1322 Saint Mary's St Kenedy TX 78119 Office: Kenedy Elem Sch 401 Fm 719 Kenedy TX 78119 Office Phone: 830-583-4100 1331. Business E-Mail: iperez@lion.kenedy.tenet.isd.edu.

PEREZ, JOSEPHINE, psychiatrist, educator; b. Tijuana, Mex., Feb. 10, 1941; came to the U.S., 1960, U.S. citizenship, 1968. BS in Biology, U. Santiago de Compostela, Spain, 1971, MD, 1975. Nuc. medicine technician, EEG technician, supr. Electrographic Labs., Encino, Calif., 1963—69; clerkships in internal medicine, gen. surgery, otorhinolaryngology, dermatology and venereology Gen. Hosp. of Galicia, Spain, 1972-75; resident in gen. psychiatry U. Miami, Jackson Meml. Hosp. and VA Hosp., Miami, Fla., 1976-78; practice medicine specializing in psychiatry, marital and family therapy, individual psychotherapy Miami, 1979—. Emergency room physician Miami Dade Hosp., 1975; attending psychiatrist Jackson Meml. Hosp., 1979—, asst. dir. adolescent psychiat. unit, 1979-83; mem. clin. faculty U. Miami Sch. Medicine, 1979—, clin. instr. psychiatry, 1979—. Mem. AMA (Physicians' Recognition award 1980, 83, 86, 89, 98, 2000, 01, 05), Am. Assn. for Marital and Family Therapy (cert. clin. mem., treas. 1982-84, pres.-elect 1985-87, pres. 1987-89), Am. Psychiat. Assn., Am. Med. Women's Assn., Assn. Women Psychiatrists, Fla. Psychiat. Soc., South Dade Women Physicians Assn. Office: 420 S Dixie Hwy Ste 4A Coral Gables FL 33146-2228 Office Phone: 305-666-7766.

PEREZ, LAURA R., mathematics professor; b. Cleve., Dec. 10, 1952; d. John Sloan Stewart III and Mary Louise Stewart; m. Gilbert Ramirez Perez, Dec. 29, 1996; children: John K. Derby, William S. Derby, Elizabeth L. Borda. Master's, Bowling Green State U., Ohio, 1985. Math. specialist Bowling Green State U., lectr. math., 1991—93; prof. math. Washtenaw C.C., Ann Arbor, Mich., 1993—. Participant DAR, Ypsilanti, Mich., 2004—06. R-Consevative. Catholic. Avocations: volunteer math tutor, swimming, bicycling. Home: 305 S Huron St Ypsilanti MI 48197 Office: Washtenaw Community Coll 4800 E Huron River Dr Ann Arbor MI Office Phone: 734-677-5134. Business E-Mail: lrsperez@wccnet.edu.

PEREZ, LORETTA ANN BRONCHETTI, secondary education educator, small business owner; b. Massena, N.Y., Oct. 8, 1951; d. Joseph Francis and Mary Joanne (Catanzarite) Bronchetti; m. Joel James Perez, Aug. 20, 1977; 1 child, Jennifer Rose. BA, SUNY, Potsdam, 1973, MS in Edn., 1977. Cert. elem. and secondary edn. tchr. Tchr. Massena Ctrl. Sch., 1974—; owner, travel agt. Massena Travel Inc., 1982—. Mem. Nat. Coun. Tchrs. English, Massena Fedn. Tchrs., Massena C. of C., Italian-Am. Assn. (sec. 1990—), Massena Women's Bowling Assn. (pres. 1985-89), Massena Women's Golf Assn. (pres. 1994-96), Massena Women's Coll. Club. Democrat. Roman Catholic. Avocations: golf, travel, reading. Home: 21 Coventry Dr Massena NY 13662-1604 Office: Massena Travel Inc 199 E Orvis St Massena NY 13662-2254 E-mail: mtravel@northnet.org.

PEREZ, LUCILLE C. NORVILLE, medical association administrator, pediatrician; BA, Manhattanville Coll., Bklyn., N.Y., 1974; MD, N.Y. Med. Coll., 1979. Pres. Nat. Med. Assn., Washington, 2001—; assoc. dir. ctr. for substance abuse, prevention, mental health svcs. adminstrn. Dept. Health & Human Svcs., Washington, 2001—. Asst. prof. Mount Sinai Sch. Medicine; assoc. prof. clin. pediat. SUNY Health Sci. Ctr., Bklyn., St. George's Sch. Medicine, Grenada, West Indies; lectr. in field. Recipient Spl. Achievement award, Congl. Black Caucus, Disting. Svc. award, Sec. Health & Human Svcs. Mem.: AMA, Nat. Med. Assn., Medico-Chirurgical Soc. of D.C., Acad. Pediat. Office: Nat Med Assn 1012 Tenth St NW Washington DC 20001

PEREZ, LUZ LILLIAN, psychologist; b. Ponce, P.R., Aug. 7, 1946; d. Emiliano and Maria D. (Torres) P.; children: Vantroi, Maireni. BA, Herbert H. Lehman Coll., 1974; PhD, NYU, 1989. Lic. bilingual (Spanish and English) psychologist, N.Y. Staff psychologist Soundview Throgs Neck Cmty. Mental Health Ctr., Bronx, 1980-88; coord. early childhood program Crotona Park Cmty. Mental Health Ctr., Bronx, 1988-91; cons. psychologist Highbridge Adv. Coun. Preschool Program, Bronx, NY, 1991-93, Coalition for Hispanic Family Svcs., Bklyn., 1991-95, Marathon Child Devel. Ctr., Queens, NY, 1993-94, Bronx Orgn. for Learning Disabled, 1993—, Village Child Devel. Ctr., N.Y.C., 1994-97, Graham-Windham Svcs. to Families and Children, 1994-95, Jackson Child Devel. Ctr., Jackson Heights, NY, 1996-97, Leake & Watts Svcs., Inc., Yonkers, NY, 1996—, Sharon Bapt. Headstart Program, 2005—. Grantee NIMH, 1974-77. Mem. Assn. for Play Therapy, Assn. Early Childhood and Infant Psychology. Avocation: flamenco dancing.

PEREZ, MARITZA E., elementary school educator; b. Bklyn., Nov. 18, 1977; d. Perez A. Jose and Carmen A. Perez (Stepmother), Irma Diaz; m. Steven Brown. Bachelor's, Clayton State U., Morrow, Ga., 2000; Master's, Ctrl. Mich. U., Atlanta, 2003; cert. edml. specialist, postgrad., Argosy U., Atlanta, 2006—. Tchr. Kendrick Mid. Sch., Jonesboro, Ga., 2000—. Coach swimming Kendrick Mid. Sch., Jonesboro, Ga., 2000—, grade level chair, 2002—06, 1:1 wireless tchr., 2005—; profl. devel. facilitator Clayton County Pub. Schs., Jonesboro, 2002—, Ga. Performance Stds. trainer, 2004—. Named Tchr. of Month, Kendrick Mid. Sch., 2000, 2001, 2003, 2004, 2005, 2006; Hope grantee, State of Ga., 1995. Avocations: swimming, reading. Home: 222 Brannan's Walk Mcdonough GA 30253 Office: Kendrick Middle School 7971 Kendrick Rd Jonesboro GA 30238 Office Phone: 770-472-8400. Business E-Mail: mperez@clayton.k12.ga.us.

PEREZ, PATRICIA STREIT, athletic trainer, small business owner; b. Meadowbrook, Pa., Sept. 27, 1975; d. Robert Charles and Nancy M. Streit; m. Wilfredo Perez, July 22, 2000; 1 child, Caleb Streit. BS in Sports Medicine, Barry U., Miami Shores, Fla., 1997; MS in Sports Mgmt., Fla. Internat. U., Miami, 2002. Cert. athletic trainer Nat. Athletic Trainers Assn., 1997, lic. Pa. State Bd. Medicine, 2003, State of Fla., 1997, cert. CPR/AED/first aid/profl. rescuer instr. ARC, 2002. Cert. athletic trainer HealthSouth Doctors Hosp., Coral Gables, Fla., 1997—2000; grad. asst. athletic trainer Fla. Internat. U., Miami, 2000—01; asst. athletic trainer Fla. State U., Tallahassee, 2002—03, Temple U., Philadelphia, 2003—05; founder and CEO One Fit Mama, Oreland, Pa., 2005—. Contbr. articles to periodicals and profl. jours. Recipient Scholarship Key award, Phi Epsilon Kappa, 1997, Pres.'s Cmty. Svc. award, Barry U., 1997; Presdl. scholar, 1993. Mem.: Pa. Athletic Trainers Soc., Nat. Athletic Trainers Assn., Moxie Moms (assoc.), Ea. Montgomery County C. of C., La Leche League Internat. Avocations: health and fitness, family. Office: One Fit Mama 903 Edann Rd Oreland PA 19075 Office Phone: 215-886-2869. E-mail: tricia@onefitmama.com.

PEREZ, ROSIE, actress; b. Bklyn., Sept. 6, 1964; d. Ismael Serrano and Lydia Perez. Actor: (TV) 21 Jump Street, WIOU, Rosie Perez Presents Society's Ride, 1993, Happily Ever After: Fairy Tales for Every Child, 1995, House of Buggin, 1995, One World Jame, 2002, Copshop, 2004, Lackawanna Blues, 2005, Lolo's Cafe, 2006, (films) Do the Right Thing, 1989, White Men Can't Jump, 1992, Night on Earth, 1992, Untamed Heart, 1993, Fearless, 1993 (Acad. award nom. Best Supporting Actress 1994), It Could Happen To You, 1994, Somebody to Love, 1995, A Brother's Kiss, 1997, Perdita Durango, 1997, 24-Hour Woman, 1998, Louis and Frank, 1998, The Road to El Dorado, 2000, King of the Jungle, 2000, Human Nature, 2001, Riding in

Cars with Boys, 2001, Exactly, 2004, Jesus Children of America, 2005, All the Invisible Children, 2005, Just Like the Sun, 2006; exec. prodr.: (TV films) Subway Stories: Tales From The Underground, 1997, I'm Boricua, Just So You Know!, 2006.*

PEREZ, WILMA, microbiologist, researcher; b. Queens, N.Y., June 4, 1961; d. Roberto and Awilda Perez; 1 child, Jadzia Kira Ramos. BS, LI U., NY, 1983. Lab. technologist Bellevue Hosp., N.Y., 1986—91, Columbia Presbyn. Med. Ctr., N.Y., 1991—93; lab. technologist Med. Ctr. NYU, 1993—94; lab. technologist Bklyn (N.Y.) Hosp., 1993—2001; microbiologist N.Y. Eye & Ear Infirmary, 2001—. Contbr. articles to profl. jours. Mem.: Am. Soc. Microbiology, Am. Chem. Soc., N.Y. Acad. Sci. Liberal. Roman Catholic. Avocations: salsa dancing, jogging, weightlifting. Office: New York Eye & Ear Infirmary 310 East 14 Street New York NY 10003 Office Phone: 212-979-4336. Office Fax: 212-674-8604. Personal E-mail: dmwily@yahoo.com. E-mail: wperez@nyee.edu.

PÉREZ-BUSTILLO, MIREYA, language educator, writer, poet, translator; b. Barranquilla, Atlántico, Colombia, Dec. 27, 1942; arrived in U.S., 1947; d. Jaime Enrique Pérez-Moreno and Sylvia Bustillo (Sierra) de Pérez; m. Matthew Hugh Erdelyi (div.); children: Karina Margit, Maya Kristina Julia. BA, Hunter Coll., 1965; student, Yale U., 1965—67; MA, Boston U., 1970; PhD, Rutgers U., 1977; postgrad., One Spirit Interfaith Sem., 2004—. Assoc. prof. Coll. New Rochelle, NY, 1974—; univ. assoc. NYU, 1988—; instr. Latino values and health beliefs Luth. Med. Ctr., Bklyn., 2005; artist-in-residence Byndcliffe Artists Gallery, Woodstock, NY, 2006. Instr. Open Ctr., N.Y.C., 2002; coord. Latino Poets Series Coll. New Rochelle, NY; mem. editl. bd. La Casa del Hada. Author: (poetry collection) Luna Azteca, 2000, Aztec Moon; co-author: The Female Body: Latina Perspectives, 2001, Spanish for Social Workers, 1985. Fulbright fellow, 1993. Fellow: NY U. Faculty Resource Network; mem.: Poet's Ho., One Spirit Learning Alliance, Poet's Cir., Mus. Modern Art, King Juan Carlos Ctr., El Museo del Barrio, Pen Am. Club, Phi Sigma Iota, Sigma Delta Pi. Democrat. Avocations: meditation, yoga, salsa dance, travel, kirtan. Home: 210 Clinton Ave Brooklyn NY 11238 Office: Coll New Rochelle Castle Pl New Rochelle NY 10805 Office Phone: 914-654-5393. Personal E-mail: poema99@aol.com.

PEREZ DE ALONSO, MARCELA, human resources specialist, information technology executive; b. Chile; Grad., Cath. U., Chile. Various sr. level positions in human resources and ops. Citigroup, global consumer head human resources, 1996—99; divsn. head Citigroup North L.Am. Consumer Bank, 1999—2004; exec. v.p. human resources and workforce devel. Hewlett-Packard Co., Palo Alto, Calif., 2004—. Mem. adv. bd. Marshall Bus. Sch. U. So. Calif.; spkr. in field; bd. dirs. Catalyst, NYC, Hewlett-Packard Co. Fin. Svcs. Mem. adv. bd. U. So. Calif. Marshall Bus. Sch.; bd. mem. Next Door Solutions to Domestic Violence. Named Corp. Exec. of Yr., Hispanic-Net, 2005; named one of 50 Most Important Hispanics in Tech. and Bus., Hispanic Engr. & Info. Tech. mag. Office: Hewlett Packard Co 3000 Hanover St Palo Alto CA 94304

PEREZ-OROZCO, JACQUELINE, science educator; b. Oxnard, Calif., Jan. 10, 1975; d. Juan Ramon and Consuelo Perez; m. Gabriel Cesar, July 13, 2002. BA, U. Calif., Santa Barbara, 1997, MEd, 1999; MA, Calif. State U., LA, 2001; EdD, U. So. Calif., 2005. Asst. prin. Hacienda La Puente Ind. Sch. Dist., Industry, Calif., 2001; cons. Action Learning Sys., Inc., Monrovia, Calif., 2001; literacy facilitator Montebello (Calif.) Unified Sch. Dist., 2002, sci. tchr., 2003—.

PERHACS, MARYLOUISE HELEN, musician, educator; b. Teaneck, N.J., June 15, 1944; d. John Andrew and Helen Audrey (Hosage) P.; m. Robert Theodore Sirinek, Jan. 27, 1968 (div. Jan. 1975). Student, Ithaca (N.Y.) Coll., 1962-64; BS, Juilliard Sch., 1967, MS, 1968; postgrad., Hunter Coll., 1976, St. Peter's Coll., Jersey City, N.J., 1977. Cert. music tchr., N.Y., N.J. Instr. Carnegie Hall, N.Y.C., 1966-69; program developer, coord., instr. urban edn. program Newburgh (N.Y.) Pub. Sch. System, 1968-69; adj. prof. dept. edn. St. Peter's Coll., Jersey City, 1976-92; tchr. brass instruments Indian Hills High Sch., Oakland, NJ, 1976; tchr. Jersey City Pub. Schs., 1976-77, N.Y.C. Pub. Sch., Bronx, 1980-84; pvt. tchr. Cliffside Park, NJ, 1976—; vocal music tchr. East Rutherford, NJ, 1990; tchr. music Bergen County Spl. Svcs. Sch. Dist., 1990-91; tchr. gen. music Little Ferry (N.J.) Pub. Schs., 1991-92; tchr. mid. sch. instrumental Paramus (N.J.) Pub. Schs., 1993-94; tchr. vocal music West New York (N.J.) Pub Schs., 1995—. Tchr. music summer enrichment program, West New York, NJ, 1999-2000, tchr. summer instrumental music program Park Ridge (NJ) HS, 1995-96, Waldwick Concert Band, 2003-04; singer, trumpeter Norwegian Caribbean Lines, 1981-82, Jimmy Dorsey Band, Paris and London, 1974; lectr. in field. Singer with Original PDQ Bach Okay Chorale, 1966, Live from Carnegie Hall Recordings, 1970, St. Louis Mcpl. Opera, 1970, Ed Sullivan Show, 1970; singer, dancer, actress (Broadway shows) Promises, Promises, 1969-71, Sugar, 1971-72, Lysistrata, 1972; trumpeter (Broadway shows) Jesus Christ Superstar, 1973, Debbie!, 1976, Sarava!, 1979, Fiddler on the Roof, Lincoln Ctr., 1981, Sophisticated Ladies, 1982; writer, host series on women in music Columbia Cable/United Artists, 1984; recordings: Carnegie Hall Live, Avery Fisher Hall, Lincoln Ctr. Cons. to cadette troop Girl Scouts U.S., Jersey City, 1967-68, Bergen County N.J. Coun., 1995—. Mem. NEA, AFTRA, Actors Equity Assn., Am. Fedn. Musicians (mem. theatre com. local 802 N.Y.C. 1972—, chmn. 1973), Music Educators Nat. Conf., N.J. Music Educators Assn., N.J. Sch. Music Assn., N.J. Edn. Assn., Internat. Women's Brass Conf. (charter mem.), Internat. Trumpet Guild, Mu Phi Epsilon. Democrat. Episcopalian. Avocations: cats, cake decorating, food sculpting, horticulture, sewing. Home and Office: 23 Crescent Ave Cliffside Park NJ 07010-3003

PERI, LINDA CAROL, librarian; b. Johnsville, Pa., Sept. 8, 1943; d. Willard and Ethel F. (Furness) Hinkle. BA, Juniata Coll., 1965; MA, Columbia U., 1967; MLS, Emporia State U., 1995. Sr. lectr. Oslo Inst. Bus. Adminstrn., Norway, 1967-72; Fulbright sr. lectr. Tech. U. Wroclaw, Poland, 1972-75; acad. dir. Inlingua Sch. Langs., Singapore, 1975-82; nat. accts. coord. United Van Lines, Denver, 1982-94; libr. Arapahoe Libr. Dist., Littleton, Colo., 1995-99; libr. Bus. Resource Ctr. Aurora (Colo.) Ctrl. Libr., 1999—. Editor: Mystery in Malacca, 1981. Mem. Am. Libr. Assn., Colo. Libr. Assn., Beta Phi Mu. Avocations: yoga, bridge, book discussion, travel. Personal E-mail: lperi60@yahoo.com.

PERICAK, KRYSANNA, biology educator; b. Evergreen Park, Ill., Jan. 17, 1973; d. Cathy Clare and Steven Frank Trezise; m. David Jason Pericak, Apr. 13, 1996. BA, Trinity Christian Coll., Palos Heights, Ill., 1995; MEd, Saginaw Valley State U., Mich., 1999. Tchr. 8th grade sci. Jeannette Jr. H.S., Sterling Heights, Mich., 1996—2002, tchr. 9th grade biology, 1998—. Chairperson dept. sci. Jeannette Jr. H.S., Sterling Heights, Mich., 2004—. Union rep. Utica Edn. Assn., Sterling Heights, Mich., 2003—06. Home: 11261 Bayberry Dr Romeo MI 48065 Office: Jeannette Jr HS 40400 Gulliver Sterling Heights MI 48310

PERICAK-VANCE, MARGARET A., health facility administrator; b. Buffalo, June 28, 1951; m. Jeff Pericak-Vance; 1 child. PhD in Med. Genetics, Ind. U., 1978. Dir. Ctr. Human Genetics Duke U. Med. Ctr., Durham, NC, James B. Duke prof. medicine, chief, med. genetics sect. Co-recipient McKnight Memory & Brain Disorders award, 2001; named to Century Club: 100 People to Watch as We Move to the Next Millennium, Newsweek Mag., 1997; recipient Louis D. scientific prize, Inst. France Acad. Sci., 2001. Mem.: Inst. Medicine, Am. Coll. Med. Genetics (founding fellow). Office: Duke U Med Ctr Ctr for Human Genetics Box 3445 Durham NC 27710*

PERINGIAN, LYNDA ANN, dietician, writer; d. Mike and Clara A. Peringian. BS in Dietetics, U. Detroit, 1974; MS in Foods and Nutrition, Wayne State U., Detroit, 1976. Registered dietitian, cert. personnel cons. Clin. dietitian North Oakland Gen. Hosp.; chief dietitian Drs. Hosp., Detroit; dir. Healthcare divsn. Roth Young, Detroit, 1977—88; pres. Peringian & Assoc., Dryden, Mich., 1988—. Author: Healthcare Textbook, 1989, THE MIRACLE ROSES - A True Story, 2005. Vol. Birmingham (Mich.) Cmty. House. Avocations: sports, piano, cooking, reading, gardening.

PERINO, DANA MARIE, federal official; m. Peter McMahon. BA in Mass Comm., U. So. Calif., 1994; postgrad., U. Ill. Staff asst. for Rep. Scott McInnis US Congress, Washington, press sec. to Rep. Dan Schaefer; spokesperson US Dept. Justice; dir. comm. White House Coun. on Environ. Quality; spl. asst. to pres., dep. press sec. The White House, dep. asst. to Pres., dep. press sec., 2006—. Office: The White House 1600 Pennsylvania Ave NW Washington DC 20500*

PERKINS, CHERYL A., paper company executive; b. Aug. 1960; m. Mark D. Perkins; 2 children. BS in Chemistry, Ga. Inst. Tech., 1983, M in Polymers, Chemical Engring. Dept., 1989. With Smith-Kline Laboratories, Atlanta; researcher Kimberly-Clark Corp., Roswell, Ga., 1984—87, with nonwovens tech. and product develop. grp., 1987—94, rsch. mgr., absorbent tech. Neenah, Wis., 1994—96, dir., absorbent tech., 1996, dir., feminine care R&D, 1996, v.p., global feminine care R&D, 1999—2000, v.p., sr. tech. officer, 2000—01, chief technical officer, 2001—02, sr. v.p., chief innovation officer Tex., 2002—. Mem. adv. com. Inst. Paper Chemistry Rsch., Atlanta; mem. external adv. bd. for textile and fiber engring. Ga. Inst. Tech.; spkr. in field. Bd. dir. Fox Cities Children's Mus., Appleton, Wis. Named Outstanding Young Engring. Alumni, Ga. Inst. Tech., 2000; named one of 25 Masters of Innovation, BusinessWeek. Achievements include patents in field.*

PERKINS, ELIZABETH ANN, actress; b. Queens, N.Y., Nov. 18, 1960; m. Terry Kinney (div.); m. Julio Macat, June 17, 2000. Grad., Goodman Theatre, Chgo., 1981. Actor (films): About Last Night, 1986, From the Hip, 1987, Sweet Hearts Dance, 1988, Big, 1988, Love at Large, 1990, Enid is Sleeping, 1990, Avalon, 1990, He Said/She Said, 1991, The Doctor, 1991, Indian Summer, 1993, The Flintstones, 1994, Miracle on 34th Street, 1994, Moonlight and Valentino, 1995, Lesser Prophets, 1997, I'm Losing You, 1998, Crazy in Alabama, 1999, 28 Days, 2000, Cats & Dogs, 2001, Try Seventeen, 2002, (voice) Finding Nemo, 2003, Gilded Stones, 2004, Speak, 2004, Jiminy Glick in La La Wood, 2004, The Ring Two, 2005, Fierce People, 2005, The Thing About My Folks, 2005, Must Love Dogs, 2005, Kids in America, 2005; (TV films) For Their Own Good, 1993, Cloned, 1997, Rescuers: Stories of Courage: Two Women, 1997, If These Walls Could Talk 2, 2000, What Girls Learn, 2001, My Sisters Keeper, 2002; (TV miniseries) From the Earth to the Moon, 1998; (TV series) Battery Park, 2000, Weeds, 2005-; theater: Brighton Beach Memoirs, 1984, Playwrights' Horizon, Ensemble Studio Theater, N.Y. Shakespeare Festival, Four Dogs and a Bone, 1995. Office: The Gersh Agy Inc 232 N Canon Dr Beverly Hills CA 90210-5302

PERKINS, ERMA YOUNG, English language educator; b. Greenville, Miss., Feb. 23, 1948; d. Willie and Estella Young; m. Daniel L. Perkins, Aug. 1977. BS, Miss. Valley State U., 1969; MA, Jackson State U., Miss., 1980, postgrad. study in edn., 1981. Cert. tchr., Miss. Proofreader Advocate Print Shop, Greenville, 1965-72; English tchr. Greenville Pub. Schs., 1969-77; asst. sec. Inst. in Community Leadership, Jackson, 1982; Eng. tchr. Jackson Mcpl. Separate Sch. Dist., Jackson, 1977—93. Pres. Le Bonheur Civic Club, Greenville, 1976-77. Mem. NEA, Miss. Assn. Educators, Jackson Assn. Educators. Democrat. Baptist. Avocations: writing, reading.

PERKINS, LOIS ELAINE, retired art educator; b. Asbestos, Que., Can., June 23, 1937; came to U.S., 1940; d. Paul Ernest and Gertrude Anne Bouthillier; m. Harold Lea Perkins, Jan. 19, 1960 (div. Feb. 1962); 1 child, Paul Bouthillier Perkins. Student, Syracuse U., N.Y., 1956—58, Tufts U., Medford, Mass., 1959—60, The Boston Mus. Sch. Fine Arts, 1959—60; BFA, Fla. Atlantic U., 1981. Lic. art therapist, Fla.; cert. nurse asst. Furniture decorator Pilgrim Furniture Co., Merrimack, NH, 1959—60; instr., pottery, painting Broward County (Fla.) Sch. System, 1975-89; instr. painting Broward C.C., Coconut Creek, Fla., 1985-89; freelance artist, 1989—; tchr. painting City of Deerfield Beach, Fla., 1994—2002; ret. Judge local and county art shows, Fla.; instr. youth program Fla. Atlantic U.; store decorator Sears, Pompano, 1987; adj. prof. Brow C.C., 2006. Exhibited in group shows at Boston Globe Show, 1955, Boston Mus. Fine Arts, 1960, Alamance County Festival, N.C., 1960, N.H. League of Arts and Crafts, Concord, 1960-61, D'Onofrio Studio, Serendipity, Miami, Fla., 1964, Beaux Arts, Las Olas Festival, Ft. Lauderdale, Fla., 1963-71, N.Y. Furniture Show, N.Y.C., 1965, Pompano Beach Libr., 1975-98, Broward C.C., Coconut Creek, Fla., 1980, Broward Art Guild, 1980, 82, Am. Savs. Bank, Pompano Beach, 1984, Curzon Gallery, Boca Raton (Fla.) Hotel, Soc. Four Arts, Palm Beach, Fla., 1988, 91, Judge James R. Knott Ctr. for Hist. Preservation, Delray, Fla., Boca Raton Resort and Yacht Club, 2006, others; represented in permanent collections Pompano Beach City Libr., Hebei Province, China; represented in pvt. collections; newspaper columnist Paint Drops, 1996—. Vol. art therapy Salvation Army, Homestead, Fla.; mem. cmty. appearance com., Pompano Beach, Fla., 1980-98. Mem. Fla. Profl. Artists, Inc., Fla. Roster for Fla. Arts in Edn., N.H. League of Arts and Crafts, Sumi-E Soc. Am., Broward Art Guild, Gold Coast Water Color Soc., Norton Artists Guild, Coral Springs Artist Guild, Am. Bus. Women's Assn., Federated Garden Club, Children's Home Soc., Artist Equity Assn., Pi Beta Phi. Methodist. Avocations: art therapy, furniture decorating, travel, gardening, reading. Home: 436 NE 25th Ave Pompano Beach FL 33062-4832

PERKINS, LORENE K., elementary school educator; d. John W. and L. Berneice Turner; m. Edmon L. Perkins; children: Edmon, Rebekah. BS in Edn., East Ctrl. U., Okla., 1974. Tchr. Vanoss Pub. Sch., Ada, Okla., Moss Pub. Sch., Holdenville, Okla., Calvin Pub. Sch., Okla., Byng Pub. Sch., Ada, Okla., Holdenville Pub. Sch., Okla. Home: 4376B N 372 Atwood OK 74827-9738

PERKINS, NANCY ANN, nurse; b. American Fork, Utah, Jan. 31, 1961; d. George Thorvald and Ann Elizabeth (Williamson) Gardner; m. Layne Todd Perkins, Sept. 6, 1986; children: Christian H., Nathaniel B. BSN, Westminster Coll., 1982. RN, BLS, AHA, Utah; designated health care anti-fraud assoc. LPN med./surg. unit staff nurse Holy Cross Hosp., Salt Lake City, 1980-81; RN staff nurse renal St. Marks Hosp., Salt Lake City, 1982-86, RN charge nurse diabetic unit, 1986-87, RN diabetic educator, 1986-87, RN, community educator, 1991—94, RN, charge nurse med. psych. unit, 1987-93; nurse auditor spl. investigation unit Select Health, 2000—04, sr. nurse clin. auditor spl. investigation unit Salt Lake City, 2004, catastrophic care mgr., 1998—2000; RN resource nurse IHC, Salt Lake City, 1993—. Author/educator: (class design syllabus) Adoptive Parenting, 1991. Active Prenatal Boarding Home, Children's Aid Soc., Ogden, Utah, 1992-94; jr. leader Girl Scouts U.S., Salt Lake City, 1984-86; charge first aid clinic Presbyn. USA Gen. Assembly, Salt Lake City, 1990. Mem. Utah Nurses Assn. (Clin. Nurse Practice award 1988). Democrat. Presbyterian. Avocations: hiking, camping, windsurfing, swimming, counted cross stitch. Home: 3682 S 2110 E Salt Lake City UT 84109-4320 Office: Select Health Spl Investigation Unit PO Box 30192 Salt Lake City UT 84130-1472 Office Phone: 801-442-6058. E-mail: nperkins5@aol.com, nancy.perkins@selecthealth.org.

PERKINS, NANCY JANE, industrial designer; b. Phila., Nov. 5, 1949; d. Gordon Osborne and Martha Elizabeth (Keichline) P. Student, Ohio U., 1967—68; BFA, U. Ill., 1972. Indsl. designer Peterson Bednar Assocs., Evanston, Ill., 1972-74, Deschamps Mills Assos., Bartlett, Ill., 1974-75; dir. graphic design Cameo Container Corp., Chgo., 1975-76; indsl. design cons. Sears Roebuck & Co., Chgo., 1977-88; cons. indsl. design, 1988—. Lectr. CUNY, 1995; founder Perkins Design Ltd., Anna Wagner Keichline Gallery, Bellefonte, Pa.; adj. prof. grad. design seminar U. Ill. Chgo., 1982, 88, 91, 93, adj. instr. undergrad. design, 1984, 88, 91, 93; adj. instr. Ill. Inst. Tech., 1987, 91; vis. assoc. prof. Carnegie-Mellon U., 1991; juror annual design rev. Indsl. Design mag., 1986; mem. tech. rev. com. Ben Franklin Partnerships, 1991—; keynote spkr. several major U.S. design groups; spkr. Design in Am. symposium, Nagoya, Japan, 1989. Contbg. author: Design and Feminism, 1999; featured in Bard Grad. Ctrs.' Exhibit, NYC, 2000; contbr. articles to profl. jours.; patents in field. Co-leader Cadette troop DuPage County coun. Girl Scouts US, 1978-79. Recipient Outstanding Alumni award U. Ill. Alumni Jour., 1981, Goldsmith award, 1992; profiled in Indsl. Design mag., 1986, Feminine Ingenuity (by Anne L. Macdonald), 1992, Dun & Bradstreet Reports, 1993; profiled The Phila. Inquirer Mag., 1994; featured in Chgo. Athenaeum "33 plus 20", 1993, Pratt Manhattan Gallery, NYC, 1994. Fellow Indsl. Designers Soc. Am. (treas. Chgo. chpt. 1977-79, vice chmn. 1979-80, chmn. 1981, mem. dist. membership com. 1982, mem. ann. conf. com. 1983, mem. publs. com. 1985-86, dir.-at-large 1987-88, v.p. Midwest dist. 1989-90, nat. sec.-treas. 1991-92, del. Internat. Coun. of the Socs. Indsl. Design 1989, dist. conf. speaker Mideast, 1993, Midwest, 2000, co-founder women's sect. 1992). Office Phone: 888-223-5211. Personal E-mail: njperkins@earthlink.net.

PERKINS, NANCY LEEDS, lawyer; b. Washington, June 19, 1956; d. Roswell Burchard and Joan (Titcomb) P. AB, Harvard U., 1979, M in Pub. Policy, 1987, JD, 1987. Bar: Pa. 1988, D.C. 1989, U.S. Dist. Ct. D.C. 1990. Jud. clk. U.S. Dist. Ct. (ea. dist.) N.Y., Bklyn., 1987—88; counsel Arnold & Porter, Washington, 1988—. Contbr. articles to profl. jours. Recipient Pro Bono svc. award Internat. Human Rights Law Group, 1990. Democrat. Avocation: tennis. Office: Arnold & Porter 555 12th St NW Washington DC 20004-1206 Office Phone: 202-942-5065. Business E-Mail: nancy_perkins@aporter.com.

PERKINS, RITA WADE, historian, educator; b. Burlington, N.J., Aug. 11, 1948; d. Leo Thomas and Anna Dement Wade; m. James Perkins, Dec. 5, 1981; children: David Wesley, Jeffrey Wade, Elise Marie. BA, Rutgers U., Camden, N.J., 1970; MA, Rutgers U., 1979, Villanova U., Pa., 1972. Assoc. prof. Camden County Coll., Blackwood, NJ, 1972—. Lectr./presenter in field, 2003—. Photographer (photography exhibitions with lectures) Bridge of Tears (NJ. Coun. for Humanities Grants, 2003). Fellow, NEH, 1979. Mem.: Am. Conf. of Irish Studies. Achievements include research in Irish Famine Memorials. Office: Camden County College College Dr Box 200 Blackwood NJ 08012 Office Phone: 856-227-7200. E-mail: rperkins@camdencc.edu.

PERKINS- BANAS, MELISSA VERONICA, psychologist; b. New London, Conn., Oct. 28, 1970; d. Roy Dennis and Marian Dana Perkins; m. Joseph Paul Banas, July 3, 1999. BA, U. RI, 1992; MA, U. Hartford, 1995, MS, 1996; PsyD, Yeshiva U., 2004. Cert. Psychologist 1999. Sch. psychologist Norwich Pub. Schools, Norwich, Conn., 1999—2003; psychologist Wheeler Clinic, Plainsville, Conn., 2003—. Post- doctoral neuropsychology fellowship Fielding Inst., NYC, 2004—. Sponsored athlete Adidas Woodbridge Racing Team, Woodbridge, Conn., 2000—02. Recipient Conn. Distance Runner of the Yr., Hi Tek Racing Team, 2001; Cecilia Rothenberg scholarship, Yeshiva U., 2002—03. Mem.: Assn. Advancement of Applied Sport Psychology, Conn. Assn. Sch. Psychologists, NASP, Am. Psychology Assn. (Divsn. 60, clin. neuropsychology), Psi Chi Nat. Honor Soc. Psychology. Roman Catholic. Home: 58 Lake St Norwich CT 06360 Office: Wheeler Clinic 91 Northwest Dr Plainville CT Office Phone: 860-334-0103. Personal E-mail: jpbanas01@snet.net.

PERKINS-MUNN, TIFFANY SABRENA, psychologist, researcher; b. Colorado Springs, Colo., Sept. 12, 1969; d. Gladstone Perkins and Gail Synovia Baldwin; m. Vincent C. Munn, Dec. 28, 1998. BA, Georgetown U., 1991; MA, CUNY, 1998, PhD, 2002. Assoc. rsch. scientist Inst. for Basic Rsch. in Developmental Disabilities, S.I., NY, 1997—2001; dir. rsch. practices Mktg. Metrics, Paramus, NJ, 2001—. Cons. Rockefeller Found., N.Y.C., 2001—. Co-author: (book) Keeping the Struggle Alive, 2002; contbr. articles to profl. jours. Recipient rsch. fellowship, Inst. for Basic Rsch., 1997—2001. Mem.: Am. Statis. Assn., Am. Psychol. Assn. Avocations: writing, racquetball, interior design. Home: 246 6th Ave Roselle NJ 07203-2044 Office: Mktg Metrics 305 Rte 175 Paramus NJ Office Phone: 212-762-2366. Personal E-mail: tiffola@aol.com.

PERKOWSKI, JENNIFER, music educator; BS in Music Edn. magna cum laude, NYU, N.Y.C., 2004. Cert. tchr. music K-12 N.Y. State Dept. of Edn., 2004. Music tchr. Connetquot H.S., Bohemia, NY, 2004—05, Hicksville H.S., NY, 2005—. Music theory/aural comprehension tutor NYU, N.Y.C., 2001—03; spl. edn. tchg. asst. Hicksville Pub. Schs.-Spl. Edn. Summer Program, NY, 2002; vocal dir. for h.s. mus. prodn. Hicksville H.S., 2005—, madrigals select choir advisor, 2005—. Mem.: N.Y. State Sch. Music Assn., Nassau Music Educators Assn., Music Educators Nat. Conf., Kappa Delta Pi, Modern Music Masters (life; sec. 1999—2000).

PERKYNS, JANE ELIZABETH, music educator, composer; b. St. John, New Brunswick, Can., Jan. 17, 1960; arrived in U.S., 1990, naturalized, 2000; d. Joseph Archibald Gormley, Carmelita Anne Gormley; m. John Stephen Perkyns, Aug. 20, 1983; children: Stephen, Nicholas. MusB, Dalhousie U., Halifax, N.S., Can., 1982; MusM, Juilliard Sch., 1983; D in Musical Arts, U. B.C., Vancouver, B.C., Can., 1990. Music adminstr., tchr. Jewish Cmty. Ctr., Houston, 1990—94; adj. music faculty Tex. So. U., Houston, 1990—96, asst. prof. music, 1996—2001, assoc. prof. music, 2001—. Founder, dir. Curtyn Calls Theatre and Pub. Co., Houston, 1995—; co-dir. spl. edn. programs Theatre Under the Stars, Houston, 2000—; dir. Charles P. Rhinehart Piano Festival, 2001—06. Composer: (Musical) The Gift, 1994, Pinnojokio, 1996, Love is a Disability, 1998, Medea's Children, 1999, musician Solo/collaborative recitals. Panelist Cultural Arts Coun. Houston/Harris County, 2000—02. Grantee Mayor's Initiative Grant, Cultural Arts Coun. Houston/Harris County, 2001, Gen. Assistance Grant, Cultural Arts Coun., 2003, Office Civil Rights, 2003. Mem.: Music Educators Nat. Assn., Nat. Assn. for Music Edn., Am. Musicological Soc., Royal Conservatory Music (coord. of exams Houston area 1994—2003), Houston Music Tchrs. Assn. (bd. mem., chair scholarship event 1995—2002), Tex. Music Tchrs. Assn., Music Tchrs. Nat. Assn. (cert.), Coll. Music Soc., Houston Tuesday Musical Club. Avocations: children's arts and crafts, cooking, yoga. Home: 5634 Benning Dr Houston TX 77096 Office: Tex So Univ 3100 Cleburne Houston TX 77004 Office Phone: 713-313-7529. Office Fax: 713-313-1869. Personal E-mail: perkyns_je@tsu.edu. Business E-Mail: perkyns-je@tsu.edu.

PERL, TERI, computer educator; b. N.Y.C., Nov. 19, 1926; d. Nathan and Rose (Gross) Hoch; m. Martin L. Perl, June 24, 1927 (div. 1988); children: Jed, Anne, Matthew, Joseph. BA Econs., Bklyn. Coll., 1947; postgrad., San Jose State U., Calif., 1969; PhD Math Edn., Stanford U., Calif., 1979. Math. cons., resource tchr. Ventura Elem. Sch., Palo Alto, Calif., 1971-79; lectr. San Francisco State U., 1977—79, 1988; project assoc. Stanford U., 1977—79; project assoc., lectr. U. Wis., Madison, 1979—80; dir, co-founder The Learning Co., Fremont, Calif., 1980—87; edn. cons. Teri Perl Assoc., Palo Alto, 1987—. Pres. Expanding Your Horizons Network, Mills Coll., Oakland, Calif Prodr.: (software) MetroGnomes Music, 1992; designer: (software) Gertrude's Secrets, Puzzles, 1982, Math. Rabbit, 1986; author: Math Equals, 1978 (Choice award 1987), Women and Numbers, 1982; co-author: Notable Women in Math., 1998 Mem. Assn. Women Math. (bd. dirs.), Nat. Coun. Tchrs. Math., Internat. Coun. Computers Edn. (contbg. editor SIG Tchr. Edn. Bull. 1988—), Calif. Math. Coun., Women in Math. Edn Avocation: piano. Home and Office: 525 Lincoln Ave Palo Alto CA 94301-3233

PERLESS, ELLEN, advertising executive; b. NYC, Sept. 9, 1941; d. Joseph B. and Bertha (Messinger) Kaplan; m. Robert L. Perless, July 2, 1965. Student, Smith Coll., 1958-59; BA, Bard Coll., 1962. Copywriter Doyle, Dane Bernbach, N.Y.C., 1964-70, Young & Rubicam, N.Y.C., 1970-74, creative supr., 1974-76, v.p., creative supr., 1977, v.p., assoc. creative dir., 1978, sr. v.p., assoc. creative dir., 1979-84; v.p., assoc. creative dir. Leber Katz Ptnrs., 1984-85, sr. v.p., creative dir., 1986-87; sr. v.p., sr. creative dir. Foote Cone & Belding, N.Y.C., 1987-93, sr. v.p., group creative dir., 1994—2002; sr. v.p., sr. creative dir. Euro RSCG Life Becker, N.Y.C., 2003—04; creative cons. pvt. practice Greenwich, Conn., 2004—. Author: numerous poems. Recipient Clio awards, Andy awards, awards Art Dirs. Club N.Y., N.Y. Festivals, One Club. Home: 37 Langhorne Ln Greenwich CT 06831-2611 E-mail: ellen@perless.com.

PERLINGIERI, ILYA SANDRA, art history scholar, writer; b. N.Y.C. d. Nathaniel Gordon and Dr. Naomi Miller Coval-Apel; children: Blake Andrew, Chemynne Alida. BA, U. Mo., 1966; MA, San Diego State U., 1984; PhD, Columbia Pacific U., 1999. Cert. life C.C. credential, Calif. Dir. Ilya Sandra Perlingieri Sewing and Design Sch., San Diego and Miami, Fla., 1973-92; asst. prof., chmn. dept. fashion design Marist Coll., Poughkeepsie, N.Y., 1984-85; mem. faculty Fashion Inst. Design, San Diego, 1986-87, L.A., 1999—2000. Adj. prof. San Diego State U., 1989-92; dir. Textile Arts and Conservation Ctr., San Diego, 1979-83; guest lectr. Met. Mus. Art, N.Y.C., Nat. Gallery, London, Art Inst. Chgo., Los Angeles County Mus. Art, Nat. Gallery, Washington, NYU, Yale U., others; guest PBS-TV, Sta. NPR, NBC-TV, BBC, London. Author: Sofonisba Anguissola: The First Great Woman Artist of the Renaissance, 1992 (transl. into French 1992), The Uterine Crisis, 2003; contbg. editor Threads mag.; contbr. numerous articles on costume and art history to profl. jours. and mags. Dir. edn. Nomad Mus. Tribal Art, Portland, 1999-2001. Recipient award Prague Quadriennale, 1979, Gildred Found., 1980, Samuel H. Kress Found., 1989, 99; French Fgn. Ministry Lecture grantee, 1995, grantee The Thanks to be Grandmother Winifred Found., 2001. Mem. Renaissance Soc. Am., Costume Soc. Am. (charter), Royal Horticultural Soc. (London), Victoria and Albert Mus., Met. Mus. Art, Huntington Libr. and Art Collections, Early Modern Women (charter), Am. Herbalists Guild, Am. Bot. Coun. Avocations: playing classical piano, lyric soprano, organic gardening, needlecrafts, gourmet cooking.

PERLIS, SHARON A., lawyer; b. New Orleans; d. Rogers I. and Dorothy Perlis. BA in French, Principia Coll., 1967; JD, Tulane U., 1970. Officer, dir. Perlis, Inc., New Orleans, 1973—2003; pres. SILREP Internat. Co., Metairie, 1984—; officer, dir. Internat. Adv. Svcs., Inc., New Orleans, 1985-89; prin. Perlis & Assocs., Metairie, 1985—2005; pres. Sharon A. Perlis P.C., 1981—2005. Legal counsel La. Ins. Rating Commn., 1980-84; adminstrv. law judge State of La., 1980-84, mem. Econ. Devel. Adv. Coun., 1982-84; exec. com. small bus. coun. Bd. of Trade, 1987-89, chmn. small bus. coun., 1988, exec. com. East Jefferson coun., 1989-96; dir. World Trade Ctr., 1985-2005, vice chmn. internat. bus. com.; dir. New Orleans br. Fed. Res. Bank of Atlanta, 1982-88, chmn., 1984, 86, 88; dir. Metairie Bank & Trust, 1997-2005; bd. of commr. Port of New Orleans, 1992-96, vice chmn., 1995, chmn. bd., 1996; del. U.S. Def. Dept.'s Joint Civilian Orientation Conf., 1997; adj. prof. A.B. Freeman Sch. Bus., Tulane U.; mem. Coun. for a Better La.; mediator U.S. Postal Svc., Econ. Devel. Commn.; mem. La. Econ. Devel. Commn., Inst. Women in Govt., Nichols State U.; mem. internat. adv. bd. A.J. Butts Sch. Bus., Loyola U. Mem. human rels. commn. City of New Orleans, 1992-93, Commn. To Reorganize City Govt., Leadership La., 2001; mem. exec. bd. La. Coun. Econ. Edn., 1986-89, Pvt. Enterprise Edn. Found., 1986-89; state del. White House Conf. on Small Bus., La. rep. internat. trade issues, 1986; dir. Metro YMCA, 1990-97; exec. com. agy. rels. United Way, 1987-90; mem. exec. com. Jr. Achievement Project Bus., 1987; vice chmn. La. Dist. Export Coun.; bd. dirs. Bur. Govtl. Rsch.; bd. dirs. La. Internat. Trade Commn.; mem. adv. bd. Internat. Program for Non-profit Leadership; mem. Econ. Devel. Commn., State of La.; mem. New Orleans Leadership Inst.; vice chmn. bus.-higher edn. coun. U New Orleans; trustee New Orleans Pub. TV Found.; mem. New Orleans Pub. R.R. Commn.; mem. Jefferson Econ Devel. Commn.; commr. New Orleans Pub. Belt RR. Recipient Achiever's award Woman Bus. owners Assn., 1994, Jefferson Econ. Devel. Commn. award, 1994, Advocacy of Yr. award Small Bus. Adminstrn., 1988, 89, Iberville award New Orleans Pub. Group, 1996, Women of the Yr. award New Orleans Pub. Group, 2000, Patty Strong award Jefferson-25, 2000; named Young Leadership Coun. Role Model, 2001. Fellow Loyla Inst. of Politics, U. New Orleans Govt. Leadership Inst.; mem. ABA, Bankers Assn., Am. Arbitration Assn. (arbitrator/mediator), Jefferson Bar Assn., Orleans Bar Assn., Federal Bar Assn., Adv. Coun. Federalist Soc., La. Estate Planning Coun., La. Bar Assn., Gov.'s Commn. on Internat. Trade Devel., New Orleans Regional C. of C. (bd. dirs. 1990-2001), New Orleans Regional Leadership Inst., New Orleans Area Polit. Action Coun. (pres.), Leadership La., Greater New Orleans Found., New Orleans Estate Planning Coun. Avocations: reading, sailing, tennis. Office: Perlis & Assocs 6069 Magazine St New Orleans LA 70118-6006

PERLMAN, RADIA, communications engineer; BA, MIT, 1973, MS, 1976, PhD, 1988. Sr. disting. engr. Sun Microsystems Labs., Menlo Park, Calif. Mem. exec. team Akaba Inc., Calif., 1999—. Author: Interconnections: Bridges & Routers, 1992; co-author: Network Security: Private Communication in a Public World, 2002. Named Silicon Valley Inventor of Yr., Silicon Valley Intellectual Property Law Assn., 2004; named one of 20 most influential people in info. tech. industry, Data Comm. mag., 1992, 1997; recipient Women of Vision award for Innovation, Anita Borg Inst., 2005. Achievements include invention of Spanning Tree Algorithm; 39 patents. Office: Sun Microsystems Labs umpk16-161 16 Network Cir Menlo Park CA 94025*

PERLMAN, RHEA, actress; b. Bklyn., Mar. 31, 1948; d. Philip Perlman; m. Danny DeVito, Jan. 28, 1982; children: Gracie Fan, Lucy Chet, Jake. Grad. in Drama, Hunter Coll. Co-founder (with Danny DeVito) Colonades Theatre Lab., NYC, Jersey Films. Stage appearances include What! And Leave Bloomingdales?, The Last Night of the Ballyhoo, The Tale of the Allergist's Wife, 2002; TV movies include I Want to Keep My Baby!, 1976, Stalk the Wild Child, 1976, Intimate Strangers, 1977, Having Babies II, 1977, Mary Jane Harper Cried Last Night, 1977, Like Normal People, 1979, Drop Out Father, 1982, The Ratings Game (cable), 1984, Dangerous Affection, 1987, A Family Again, 1987, To Grandmothers House We Go, 1992, A Place To Be Loved, 1993, Houdini, 1998, In the Doghouse, 1999, A Tail of Two Bunnies, 2000, Secret Cutting, 2000; TV series include Cheers, 1982-1993; motion pictures include Love Child, 1982, My Little Pony (voice) 1986, Enid is Sleeping, 1990, Ted and Venus, 1991, Class Act, 1992, There Goes The Neighborhood, 1992, Canadian Bacon, 1995, Sunset Park, 1996, Matilda, 1996, Carpool, 1996, H-E Double Hockey Sticks, 1999; prodr. Pearl, 1996; guest appearances Taxi, 1979, 1980, 1981, 1982, Angie, 1979, St. Elsewhere, 1982, Blossom, 1991, The Simpsons, 1991, Union Square, 1997, Almost Perfect, 1995; author (children's books): Born to Drive, 2006, Canyon Catastrophe, 2006. Recipient Emmy award for Outstanding Supporting Actress in a Comedy Series, 1984, 85, 86, 89, Am. Comedy award for funniest supporting female-TV. Jewish. Office: Creative Artists Agy c/o Jonathan Ruiz 9830 Wilshire Blvd Beverly Hills CA 90212-1804*

PERLMUTTER, BARBARA S., retired advertising executive; b. Hartford, Conn., Oct. 7, 1941; d. Leon and Ethel (Zinman) Sondik; m. Louis Perlmutter, Dec. 11, 1966; children: Kermit, Eric. BA, Smith Coll., 1963; MA in History, Columbia U., 1965; MBA, NYU, 1979. Analyst Celanese Internat. Co., N.Y.C., 1965-69; sr. econ. analyst Nat. Econ. Rsch. Assoc., White Plains, N.Y., 1979-85; dir. pub. affairs Marsh & McLennan Companies, Inc., N.Y.C., 1985-88, v.p. pub. affairs, 1988-99, sr. v.p. pub. affairs, 1999—2006. Avocations: aerobics, reading, tennis.

PERLMUTTER, DIANE F., marketing executive; b. N.Y.C., Aug. 31, 1945; d. Bert H. and Frances (Smith) P. Student, NYU Grad. Sch. of Bus., 1969—70; BA in English, Miami U., Oxford, Ohio, 1967. Writer sales promotion Equitable Life Assurance, N.Y.C., 1967-68; bus. adminstr. de Garmo, Inc., N.Y.C., 1968-69, asst. account exec., 1969-70, account exec., 1970-74, v.p., account supr., 1974-76; mgr. corp. advt. Avon Products, Inc., N.Y.C., 1976-79, dir. comm. Latin Am., Spain, Can., 1979-80, dir. brochures, 1980-81, dir. category merchandising, 1981-82, group dir. motivational comm., 1982-83, group dir. sales promotion, 1983-84, v.p. sales promotion, 1984, v.p. internat. bus. devel., 1984-85, area v.p. Latin Am., 1985, v.p. advt. and campaign mktg., 1985-87, v.p. U.S. operational planning, 1987; cons. N.Y.C., 1987-88; sr. v.p. Burson-Marsteller, N.Y.C., 1988-90, exec. v.p., mng. dir. consumer products, 1991-93, bd. dirs., 1992—98, co-chief oper. officer, 1993-94, chief oper. officer, 1994-96, chmn. mktg. practice/U.S., 1996-98; vice chmn., CEO Cohn & Wolfe, N.Y.C., 1998—2000; CEO Gilda's Club Worldwide, 2001—05, bd. dirs., 2002—; prin. Oxford Hall Assocs., 2005—. Chair ann. meeting Direct Selling Assn., Washington, 1982; v.p. Nat. Home Fashions League, N.Y.C., 1975—76; adj. instr. SUNY/ Fashion Inst. Tech., 1992—; vice chmn. Columbia-Greene Hosp. Found., 2000—; vice chmn., bd. dirs. Olana Partnership, 2000—03; bd. dirs. Double L.P. Industries, Inc. Bd. dirs. Hudson Opera House, 2002—. Named to YWCA Acad. Women Achievers, 1996. Mem.: Women in Comm., Advt. Women of N.Y., Pub. Rels. Soc. Am., Women's Econ. Round Table (bd. dirs. 1998—2000), Miami U. Alumni Assn. (pres., chair 1986), The Women's Forum (bd. dirs. 1998—2000, pres. 2002—04), YMCA of Greater N.Y. (bd. dirs. 1996—2003), Publicity Club N.Y. (bd. dirs. 1994—96). Personal E-mail: dianefperlmutter@yahoo.com.

PERLMUTTER, DONNA, music critic, dance critic; b. Phila. d. Myer and Bessie (Krasno) Stein; m. Jona Perlmutter, Mar. 21, 1964; children: AAron, Matthew. BA, Pa. State U., 1958; MS, Yeshiva U., 1959. Music and dance critic L.A. Herald Examiner, 1975-84; contbr. L.A. Times, 1984—, N.Y. Times, 1994—. Dance critic Dance Mag., NYC, 1980—; music critic Opera News, NYC, 1981-98, Ovation Mag., NYC, 1983-89, Hollywood Reporter, 2001—, L.A. City Beat, 2003—, NY Mag., 1995—, L.A. Mag., 1996—, Daily News, L.A., 1996-97, New Times, L.A., 1997-2002, Performing Arts Mag., 1996-2002; panelist, spkr. in field. Author: Shadowplay: The Life of Antony Tudor, 1991. Recipient Deems Taylor award for excellence in writing on music ASCAP, 1991. Mem. Music Critics Assn. Home: 10507 Le Conte Ave Los Angeles CA 90024-3305 Business E-Mail: jperl@ucla.edu.

PERLOFF, MARJORIE GABRIELLE, literature educator; b. Vienna, Sept. 28, 1931; arrived in U.S., 1998; d. Maximilian and Ilse (Schueller) Mintz; m. Joseph K. Perloff, July 31, 1953; children: Nancy Lynn, Carey Elizabeth. AB, Barnard Coll., 1953; MA, Cath. U., 1956, PhD, 1965. Asst. prof. English and comparative lit. Cath. U., Washington, 1966-68, assoc. prof., 1969-71, U. Md., 1971-73, prof., 1973-76; Florence R. Scott prof. English U. So. Calif., LA, 1976—; prof. English and comparative lit. Stanford (Calif.) U., 1986—, Sadie Dernham prof. humanities, 1990—, prof. emerita, 2000. Vis. prof. U. Utah, 2002; scholar-in-residence U. So. Calif., 2004—. Author: Rhyme and Meaning in the Poetry of Yeats, 1970, The Poetic Art of Robert Lowell, 1973, Frank O'Hara, Poet Among Painters, 1977, 2nd edit., 1998, The Poetics of Indeterminacy: Rimbaud to Cage, 1981, 2d edit., 1999, The Dance of the Intellect: Studies in the Poetry of the Pound Tradition, 1985, 2d edit., 1996, The Futurist Moment: Avant-Garde, Avant-Guerre and the Language of Rupture, 1986, 2d edit., 2003, Poetic License: Essays in Modern and Postmodern Lyric, 1990, Radical Artifice: Writing Poetry in the Age of Media, 1991, Wittgenstein's Ladder: Poetic Language and the Strangeness of the Ordinary, 1996, Frank O'Hara, 2d edit., 1998, Poetry On and Off the Page: Essays for Emergent Occasions, 1998, Twenty-first Century Modernism, 2001, The Vienna Paradox, 2004, Differentials, 2004; editor: Postmodern Genres, 1990; co-editor: John Cage: Composed in America, 1994; contbg. editor: Columbia Literary History of the U.S., 1987; contbr. preface to Contemporary Poets, 1980, A John Cage Reader, 1983. Guggenheim fellow, 1981-82, NEA fellow, 1985; Phi Beta Kappa scholar, 1994-95. Fellow Am. Acad. Arts and Scis.; mem. MLA (exec. coun. 1977-81, Am. lit. sect. 1993—, 1st v.p. 2005, pres. 2006), Comparative Lit. Assn. (pres. 1993-94, mem. adv. bd. Libr. of Am.), Lit. Studies Acad. Home: 1467 Amalfi Dr Pacific Palisades CA 90272-2752 Personal E-mail: mperloff@earthlink.net.

PERLOV, DADIE, management consultant; BA, NYU, 1950; postgrad., Adelphi U., 1963, Vanderbilt U., 1973. Cert. assn. exec., N.Y. Exec. dir. ops. Open City, N.Y.C., 1962-64; field svcs. dir. Nat. Coun. Jewish Women, N.Y.C., 1968-74; exec. dir. N.Y. Libr. Assn., N.Y.C., 1974-81, Nat. Coun. Jewish Women, N.Y.C., 1981-90; founder, prin. Consensus Mgmt. Group, N.Y.C. and Indpls., 1989—. Cons. HEW 1975-76; pres.-elect Internat. Coun. Libr. Assn. Execs., 1979-80; exec. mem. Conf. of Pres., 1981-90; strategic planner, lectr., merger facilitator; bd. devel., structure/governance, ops., audits mgmt. cons. exec. search ABA, Am. Bankers Assn., ALA, Nat. Assn. Home Builders, Am. Coll. Healthcare Execs., Nat. Assn. Ind. Insurers, and more than 500 other maj. trade and profl. assns. Co-author: The Ultimate Association Diet: How to Stay Fit and Trim in the 21st Century; author monthly column Dear Dadie for Assoc. Trends; contbr. articles to profl. jours. Mem. N.Y. Zool. Soc., 1959—, adv. bd. Nat. Inst. Against Prejudice and Violence, 1985-89; bd. visitors Pratt Inst., Bklyn., 1980-84; bd. dirs. Pres. Coun. on Handicapped, 1981—; facilitator Nursing Summit, 1994, 2004. Recipient Recognition award N.Y. Libr. Assn., 1978, BUDDY award NOW Legal Def. and Edn. Found., 1989, cert. N.Y. State Legislature, 1978; named N.Y. State Exec. of Yr., 1980, One of Am.'s 100 Most Important Women, Ladies' Home Jour., 1988. Fellow Am. Soc. Assn. Execs. (cert. 1978, evaluator 1980-91, bd. dirs. 1987-90, bd. found. 1990-92, Excellence award 1983); mem. LWV (chpt. pres. 1960-62), N.Y. Soc. Assn. Execs (pres. 1985, Outstanding Assn. Exec. 1989, Outstanding Svc. award 1991), Global Perspectives in Edn. (bd. dirs.), Nat. Orgn. Continuing Edn. (coun.), Audubon Soc., N.Y. Citizens Coun. on Librs. (bd. dirs. 1981-84), Am. Arbitration Assn. (mem. panel). Avocations: writing, mycology, history, music, art. Fax: 212-874-8068. Office Phone: 212-712-2449.

PERNA, BELINDA A., science educator; b. Connersville, Ind., Nov. 21, 1955; d. Norma J. and Harry M. Smith (Stepfather), Warren Maynard Shenk; m. Roger D. Perna; children: Vincent M., Rebecca D. BS, Ind. State U., Terre Haute, 1977, MA, 1980. Cert. Tchr. Ind., 1988. Med. lab. technologist Terre Haute Med. Lab., Inc., Ind., 1980—85; rsch. asst. Ind. State U., Terre Haute, 1985—88; sci. tchr. Arlington County Pub. Schs., Va., 1988—2001, North Coll. Hill City Schs., Cin., 2001—. Research advisor (exhbn.) Internat. Science and Engineering Fair (2nd Pl. in Environ. Sci., 1995), Westinghouse Science Talent Search; author: (article) Proceeding from the Indiana Acad. of Sci. Choir mem. Terre Haute Choral Soc., Ind., 1984—86; vol. Wolftrap Barns/Filene Fine Arts Ctr., Arlington, Va., 1990—91; youth dir. St. John's Episcopal Ch., Falls Church, Va., 1999—2000; mission outreach work group mem. Wash. United Ch. of Christ, Cin., 2005—06; stewardship com. mem. First United Ch. of Christ, Cin., 2005—06, mission priority com. mem., 2005—06; bd. mem. Opera Americana, Alexandria, Va., 1989—91, Arlington Outdoor Edn. Assn., Arlington, Va., 1990—91; docent Smithsonian Mus. of Natural History, Washington, 1990—92. Fellow, Inst. Advanced Studies in Immunology of Aging Sci. Accelerator; Tchr. Mentor Scholarship, NSF/GWU Young Minority Women in Sci. & Engring., 1992, 1993, Rsch. Fellowship, Coll. of William and Mary, 1993. Avocations: gardening, reading, travel. Home: 1578 Reid Ave Cincinnati OH 45224 Office: North Coll Hill City Schs 1620 W Galbraith Rd Cincinnati OH 45239 Office Phone: 513-728-4783. Personal E-mail: rperna@cinci.rr.com. Business E-Mail: perna.b@nchcityschools.org.

PERNA, JANET, application developer; Various positions including programmer IBM, 1974—81, product development, 1981—91; dir. database tech. IBM Toronto Lab., 1991—96; gen. mgr. info. mgmt. IBM Software Group, 1996—2005; ret., 2006. Mem. IBM World Mgmt. Council; bd. dirs. Deltek Systems, Inc., 2006. Named one of Top 10 Women in IT, Information Week, 50 Smartest People, Sm@rt Partner; named to Hall of Fame, WITI, 2001. Mem.: ARC, IBM World Mgmt. Coun., Habitat for Humanity. Office: IBM 50 Knobloch Ln Stamford CT 06902 Office Phone: 914-299-0268. Business E-Mail: pernaj@optonline.net.

PERNEZNY, LYNN ANNE, music educator; b. Bethlehem, Pa., Nov. 25, 1951; d. Albert and Betty Buralli; m. Kenneth Louis Pernezny, Dec. 28, 1971; children: Benjamin James, Alice Rachel. BA, Moravian Coll., Bethlehem, 1973; MA, Ohio State U., Columbus, 1976; MBA, U. Miami, Coral Gables, Fla., 1978. Credit analyst Barnett Bank, Miami, Fla., 1978—83, Cmty. Bank Homestead, Fla., 1986—88; credit dept. mgr. Suburban Bank, Lake Worth, Fla., 1991—94; credit analyst Prime Bank, Boynton Beach, Fla., 1994—96; music tchr. Glades Day Sch., Belle Glade, Fla., 1996—99, Wellington (Fla.) Landings Cmty. Mid. Sch., 1999—. Children's choir dir. St. Rita Cath. Ch., Wellington, 1989—. Named Regular Educator of Yr., Coun. for Exceptional Children, 2003; recipient T. Edgar Shields Meml. prize in Music, Moravian Coll., 1973; fellow, Ohio State U., 1973—76. Mem.: FMEA, MENC, Fla. Vocal Assn., Pi Kappa Lambda, Phi Alpha Theta. Home: 753 Daffodil Dr Wellington FL 33414 Office: Wellington Landings Middle School 1100 Aero Club Dr Wellington FL 33414 Office Phone: 561-792-8129. Personal E-mail: perneznyk@bellsouth.net. Business E-Mail: perneznl@palmbeach.k12.fl.us.

PERNICIARO, ALISSA A., dancer, educator; b. Manchester, NH, Dec. 29, 1977; d. Richard Henry and Catherine Ann Roberge; m. Giuseppe A. Perniciaro, June 8, 2002; 1 child, Giovanni Antonio. A in Bus. Mgmt., NH Cmty. Tech. Coll., Manchester, 2001; B in Bus. Mgmt., So. NH U., 2006. Instr. Kathy Blake Dance Studios, Amherst, NH, 1997—98; pvt. dance instr. Manchester, 1999—2002; dance educator Rosita Lee Dance Ctr., Derry, NH, 2001—02, Mazza Smith Studio of Performing Arts, Jacksonville, Fla., 2003—05. Adjudicator talent and modeling competitions, NH, 1996—. Vol. Big Bros./Big Sisters; project coord. Americorp, Manchester, 1997—98; spokesperson Cmty. Health and Hospice, Laconia, NH, 2000—01; bd. mem. Miss Greater Manchester Scholarship Program, 2002—04; local titleholder Miss NH Scholarship Program, 1996—2001. Mem.: Delta Mu.

PERO, LOUISE A., elementary school educator; b. Bklyn., Aug. 5, 1952; d. Gene and Beatrice Pero. BA, SI CC, 1975; MA, Richmond Coll., SI, 1985. Tchr. 2d grade St. Joseph Sch., SI, 1979—82, tchr. 3d grade, 1982—92, tchr. 8th grade, 1992—.

PERONTO, JANICE LYNN, principal; d. Richard A. and Bonnie J. Sinkenbring; m. Karl Eric Peronto, June 10, 1995; children: Kolton Richard, Kolby Eric, Konnor Walter. BA in Edn., Purdue U., West Lafayette, Ind., 1991; MEd (hon.), Tarleton State U., Ctrl. Texas, Tex., 2001. Tchr. Cedar Valley Elem., Killeen, Tex., 1992—2002; campus instrnl. specialist Clifton Pk. Elem., 2002—05; asst. prin. Cedar Valley Elem., 2005—. Adv. panel Tex. SBEC, Austin, 1999—; goal III action rsch. coord. Killeen Ind. Sch. Dist., 2002—, mentor coord., 2002—; adv. panel Cedar Valley Elem., 1993—. Mem. Killeen Svc. League, 2003—04. Recipient Excellence Tchg., Killeen Daily Herald, 1997—98, Tchr. of Yr., Walmart Found., 1997—98, Tchr. of Quarter, Exch. Club Killeen, 2001—02. Mem.: Tex. Edn. Assn., Tex. Elem. Prin. Assn. (assoc.), Delta Kappa Gamma (assoc.). Office: Cedar Valley Elementary 4801 Chantz Drive Killeen TX 76542 Office Phone: 254-501-1480. Office Fax: 254-680-6600. E-mail: janice.peronto@killeenisd.org.

PEROTTI, ROSE NORMA, lawyer; b. St. Louis, Aug. 10, 1930; d. Joseph and Dorothy Mary (Roleski) Perotti. BA, Fontbonne Coll., St. Louis, 1952; JD, St. Louis U., 1957. Bar: Mo. 1958. Trademark atty. Sutherland, Polster & Taylor, St. Louis, 1958-63, Sutherland Law Office, 1964-70, Monsanto Co., St. Louis, 1971-85, sr. trademark atty., 1985-91, assoc. trademark counsel, 1991-94, trademark counsel, 1994-96, Polster, Lieder, Woodruff & Lucchesi, 1996—. Honored with dedication of faculty office in her honor, St. Louis U. Sch. Law, 1980. Mem. ABA, Mo. Bar, Bar Assn. Met. St. Louis, Am. Judicature Soc., Friends St. Louis Art Mus., Mo. Bot. Garden. Office: Polster Lieder Woodruff & Lucchesi 12412 Powers Court Dr Ste 200 Saint Louis MO 63131-3615 Office Phone: 314-238-2400. Business E-Mail: rperotti@patpro.com.

PERRAUD, PAMELA BROOKS, human resources professional; m. Jean-Marc Francois Perraud; children: Marc Alexander, Andrea Elizabeth. BA, Conn. Coll., 1970; MA in Urban Studies, Occidental Coll., 1972; MA in Indsl. Rels., U. Minn., 1977. Cert. sr. profl. in human resources, compensation profl., benefits profl., relocation profl., global renumeration profl, global profl. in human resources. Dir. pers. Mpls. Housing and ReDevel. Authority, 1973-75; dir. adminstrn. United Svcs. Orgn., Paris, 1976-78; dir. office svcs. Pechiney Ughine Kuhlmann, Greenwich, Conn., 1979-80; lectr., trainer Monodnock Internat., London, 1981-85; pers. recruiter IBM Europe, Paris, 1989; prof. bus. Am. Bus. Sch., Paris, 1988-92; pres. Women's Inst. for Continuing Edn., Paris, 1992-93; human resource cons. NYC, 1994-97; pres. Global Transitions, 1998—. Chair Women on the Move, Paris, 1990-93; Non-Gov. Orgn. rep. at UN for Fedn. Am. Women's Clubs Overseas, 1998—, co-founder Money Matters for Women Paris, 2005; bd. dirs. METRO Internat., 1998-2002, Assn. Am. Residents Overseas, Families in Global Transition. Co-founder Focus Info., London, 1982; trustee Conn. Coll., New London, 1970-72. Fellow in Pub. Affairs, Coro Found., LA, 1970. Mem. World at Work Assn., Fgn. Policy Assn., Mayflower Soc. of Minn. Avocations: tennis, skiing.

PERRILLES, ANGELA TERESE, physical therapist; b. Peoria, Ill., Apr. 27, 1969; d. William Ernest and Marilyn June Perrilles. BS in Fitness Leadership/Cardiac Rehab., No. Ill. U., DeKalb, 1992; MS in Athletic Tng./Exercise Physiology, Ill. State U., Normal, 1998; AAS, Ill. Ctrl. Coll., East Peoria, 2000. Aide phys. therapy St. Francis Med. Ctr., Peoria, 1988—89; front desk clerk/med. records Health Ctr. No. Ill. U., DeKalb, 1990—95; aide phys. therapy No. Rehab., DeKalb, 1993—95; fitness dir., personal trainer Landmark Health Club, Peoria, 1995—2002; athletic trainer Mustangs Jr. Hockey League, Peoria, 1999—2002; phys. therapist asst. Profl. Therapy Svcs., Peoria, 2000—02; phys. therapist asst./athletic trainer Orthop. Inst./Great Plains, Peoria, 2002—. Coord. cardiac rehab., therapist Jasper County Hosp., Rensselaer, Ind., 1996—97. Contbr.: newsletter Orthop. Inst. Ill., 2004—. Vol. spl. events Peoria Park Dist., 1997—; mem. Peoria Jaycees, 1998—; runner St. Jude Children's Hosp., Peoria, 1999—; chair, organizer Red Kettle campaign Salvation Army, Peoria, 2004—; vol. various charities/events including MS Soc., Arthritis Found., Red Cross, Peoria Humane Soc., others. Recipient Cmty. Svc. award, Peoria Park Dist., 2002. Mem.: Nat. Athletic Trainers Assn. Avocations: running, hot air ballooning, cross stitch, outdoor activities. Home: 617 Rohmann Ct Peoria IL 61604 Office: Orthopedic Inst Ill-Great Plains Rehab 303 N Kumpf Blvd Peoria IL 61605 E-mail: atpatc@insightbb.com.

PERRIN, COURTNEY MASSEY, history educator; b. Gainesville, Ga., Dec. 7, 1977; d. Thomas H. Massey, III and Terry Earnheart; m. Roy Perrin, July 21, 2001; 1 child, Alyson Audress. BA in History, Agnes Scott Coll., Decatur, Ga., 2000. Cert. tchr. Ga., 2000. History tchr. City Schs. of Decatur, Ga., 2000—. Student govt. sponsor City Schs. of Decatur, yearbook sponsor, 2004—.

PERRIN, GAIL, editor; b. Boston, Oct. 14, 1938; d. Hugh and Helen (Baxter) P. BA, Wellesley Coll., 1960. Copy girl Washington Daily News, summers, 1954-57, reporter, 1958, 60-61, acting women's editor, food editor, 1961-62, rewrite reporter, 1963-65; reporter Honolulu Star Bull., 1959; women's editor Boston Globe, 1965-71, asst. met. editor, 1971-74, food editor, 1974-92; food cons., freelance writer, 1992-96; freelance columnist Boston Globe, 1996—2000.

PERRINE, COLLEEN FITZMARTIN, composer, educator; b. Pitts., Aug. 26, 1952; d. Mary Jane and Walter James Fitzmartin; m. Scott Richard Perrine, Sept. 26, 1986; children: Andrew Scott, Gregory Walter. BS in Edn., Ind. U. of Penna, 1974. Tchr. Appleton Schs., Wis.; assoc. music min. Prince of Peace Luth. Ch., Appleton, Wis. Keyboard player, vocalist For A Reason (Contemporary Christian rock band), Appleton, Wis. Composer: (chamber orchestra piece) Y2K Fanfare. Recipient Tchr. of Yr., WalMart Stores, 2004. Avocations: gardening, cooking, writing. Home: 912 W Browning St Appleton WI 54914 Office: Appleton Area Sch Dist 120 E Harris St Appleton WI 54911 Office Phone: 920-832-6161.

PERRINE, VERONICA BEADER, music educator, director; b. Sharon, Pa., Mar. 7, 1955; d. Uros and Vera Pilipovich Beader; m. Robert Alan Perrine, June 12, 1982; 1 child, Natassia Beader. BSc in Music Edn. and Theater, Ind. U., Pa., 1977; MEd in Gifted Spl. Edn., Kent State U., 1980; PhD in Secondary Music Edn., U. Ala., 1989. Cert. Tchr. Pa., 1977, Ohio, 1977, Ala., 1982, NC, 1985, Del., 1989, early adolescent/young adult music Nat. Bd. Profl. Tchg. Stds., 2005. Music tchr., tchr. of gifted Maplewood Elem. Schs., Cortland, Ohio, 1977—82; music tchr. Bessemer City Schs., Ala., 1982—85, Champion Sch. Dist., Ohio, 1988—89, Rehoboth Elem., Jr. HS, Del., 1989—90; choral dir. Lenoir County Schs., Kinston, NC, 1985—88; choral, musical dir. Middletown HS, Del., 1990—, advisor nat.

honor soc., 2002—, advisor tri-m music honor soc., 2002—. Dir. Summer theater children's workshop Everett Theater, Middletown, 1997, 98, 2004. Recipient Tchr. of Yr., Appoquinimink Sch. Dist., 2005, Jessie Ball du Pont Music Educators award, Del. Symphony, 2005. Mem.: Appoquinlink Del. Nat. Edn. Assn., Am. Choral Dirs. Assn. (mem.-at-large 1997—2005), Music Educators Nat. Conf., Del. Music Educator Assn. (all state choir chair 2002—05). Serbian Eastern Orthodox. Avocation: theater. Home: 148 Beech Haven Dr Dover DE 19904 Office Phone: 302-376-4140 x5055.

PERRONE, LISA, mathematics professor; PhD, Emory U., Atlanta, Ga., 2004. Math. instr. Hawaii Pacific U., Honolulu, 1999—2001; asst. prof. math. Tufts U., Medford, Mass., 2004—06. R-Consevative. Avocation: exercise. Office: Tufts Univ 503 Boston Ave Medford MA 02155 Office Fax: 617 627-3966.

PERRONI, CAROL, artist; b. Boston, July 28, 1952; d. Michael John and Mary Agnes (Collett) P.; m. John Richard Mugford, May 23, 1987; 1 child, Jonathan Perroni. Student, Boston Mus. Sch., 1970-71; BA in Art, Bennington Coll., 1976; student, Skowhegan Sch. Painting and Sculpture, 1978; MFA in Art, Hunter Coll., 1983; MEd, The Coll. Santa Fe, 2003. Studio asst. for artist Isaac Witkin, Bennington, Vt., 1973-74; libr. asst. Simmons Coll. Libr., Boston, 1977-78; studio asst. for artist Mel Bochner, N.Y.C., 1979; book-keeper Internat. House, N.Y.C., 1979-80; studio asst. for Lee Krasner, East Hampton, NY, 1980; rsch. asst. Art News Mag., N.Y.C., 1981; intern Greenespace Gallery, N.Y.C., 1982-83; tech. asst. Avery Architectural and Fine Arts Libr. Columbia U., N.Y.C., 1981-83; libr., rechr. Kennedy Galleries, Inc., N.Y.C., 1984-86; program specialist, art tchr. Swinging Sixties Sr. Citizen Ctr., Bklyn., 1986-87; with Arts in Edn. Program, RI, 1993-96. One-woman shows include Boston City Hall, 1978, Hunter Coll. Gallery, N.Y.C., 1983, Ten Worlds Gallery, N.Y.C., 1986, Gallery X, New Bedford, Mass., 1993-94, Hera Gallery, Wakefield, R.I., 1995, 98, AS220, Providence, R.I., 1996, C.C. of R.I., Lincoln, 1996, Boyden Libr., Foxboro, Mass., 1997; group shows include Salem State Coll., Mass., 1978, Fuller Mus. Art, Brockton, Mass., 1989-90, Danforth Mus. Art, Framingham, Mass., 1989, Attleboro Mus., Mass., 1989, Gallery One, Providence, 1992, Gallery X, New Bedford, Mass., 1992-98, Grove St. Gallery, Worcester, Mass., 1993, Bell St. Chapel, Providence, 1994-95, AS220, Providence, 1994, 98, Hera Gallery, Wakefield, R.I., 1993-99, 2000, 01, 04, St. Andrew's Sch., Barrington, R.I., 1994, McKillop Gallery, Salve Regina U., Newport, R.I., 1995, North River Arts Soc., Marshfield Hills Village, Mass., 1995, Providence Art Club, 1995, The Sarah Doyle Gallery, Brown U., Providence, 1995-96, R.I. Watercolor Soc. Slater Meml. Park, Pawtucket, 1995, Fed. Res. Bank, Boston, 1996, Art Adv./Boston, Quincy, Mass., 1996, Rotch-Jones-Duff Mus., New Bedford, Mass., 1997, Dryden Galleries, Providence, 1997, Renaissance Gallery, Fall River, Mass., 1997, 98, Island Arts Gallery, Newport, 1997, Harwood Art Ctr., Albuquerque, 1998, Branigan Cultural Ctr., Las Cruces, N.Mex., 1999, 2000, Atrium Gallery, Providence, 2000, New Haven Pub. Libr., New Haven, 2000, Angelo State U., San Angelo, Tex., 2000, Rockport (Tex.) Ctr. Arts, 2001, Lorain C.C., Elyria, Ohio, 2001, Hiestand Galleries, Miami U., Oxford, Ohio, 2001, South Broadway Cultural Ctr., Albuquerque, 2001, N.Mex. State U. Art Gallery, Las Cruces, 2001, 06, Sedona (Ariz.) Arts Ctr., 2002, Cork Gallery, Avery Fisher Hall, Lincoln Ctr., N.Y., 2002, 03, 04, 05, Keystone Bldg., Santa Fe, 2003, Tishman Hall, Coll. of Santa Fe, 2004, Ctr. Contemporary Arts, Santa Fe, 2004, 05, 06, Roswell (N.Mex.) Mus. and Art Ctr., 2004, 05, Stables Gallery, Taos, N.Mex., 2004, Santa Fe Art Inst., 2004, Headwaters Arts and Conf. Ctr., Dubois, Wyo., 2004, U. N.Mex., Los Alamos, 2005, Peninsula Fine Arts Ctr., Newport News, Va., 2005, Cuyahoga Valley Art Ctr., Cuyahoga Falls, Ohio, 2006, Claremont Forum Gallery, Calif., 2006, Arts Alliance Gallery, Albuquerque, 2006; represented in permanent collection at R.I. Hosp. Art Collection and pvt. collections Bd. dirs. Hera Ednl. Found., 1994—2001. Grantee Artists Space, 1986, Flintridge Found., 1993, fellow Vt. Studio Ctr., Johnson, 1990, Dorland Mountain Arts Colony, 1993, Anderson Ranch Arts Ctr., Snowmass Village, Colo., 2004. Mem.: SOHO 20 Gallery (nat. affiliate mem.), Am. Acad. Women Artists (assoc.). Home and Office: 2089 Plaza Thomas Santa Fe NM 87505-5438 Personal E-mail: carolpi56@msn.com.

PERRY, ANNE MARIE LITCHFIELD, secondary school educator; b. LaJunta, Colo., June 20, 1943; d. Robert Silas and Anne (Kennedy) Hovey, Robert Latta Litchfield (Stepfather); m. Franklin Haile Perry, Dec. 21, 1968; children: Kristina Marie, Tad Kennedy. BE, Drake U., 1966; MA, U. Tex., 1969; PhD, Tex. A&M U., 1977. Grade sch. tchr., San Antonio, 1966—67, Austin, 1967—68; rsch. assoc. R&D Ctr., U. Tex., Austin, 1968; grad. asst., instr. Tex. A&M U., 1969—70; kindergarten tchr., 1970—72; instr. U. St. Thomas, 1973—74; spl. edn. tchr., supr. Cypress, Cypress-Fairbanks Ind. Sch. Dist., Houston, 1974—77, supr. gifted/.talented, bilingual, English lang. devel. programs, 1977—80; mem. adj. grad. faculty U. Houston, 1979—80; lower sch. dir. curriculum and ednl. resources Kinkaid Sch., Houston, 1980—85, dir. young writers workshops, 1985—; tchr., chair lang. arts dept. Klein Intermediate Sch. Dist., Tex., 1986—2001. Vis. asst. prof. Tex. A&M U., 1988—89; cons. in field. Author (photographer): Riders Ready, 1985; author: Teacher Guide and Student Packet for Frindle, 2002, Just Like Always, 2005; editor: Travels in Mexico and California, 1988, Bluebonnet Books-Activities for 1996, Lonestar Books-Activities for 1993-1994 and 1994-1995. Named Tchr. of Yr., Hancock Elem. Sch., 1975. Mem.: NEA, Harley Owners Group-Branzos de Dios, Soc. of Children's Book Writers and Illustrators, Tex. State Tchrs. Assn., Run for the Wall. Methodist. Home: 10965 Clyde Acord Rd Franklin TX 77856-5821 Personal E-mail: aperry@flash.net.

PERRY, ANNETTE OWEN, psychotherapist, educator; b. Dallas, Ga., Apr. 14, 1943; d. Cephus Clyde and Mae Waldrop Owen. BS in Psychology, Ga. State U., 1995; MA in Psychology, State U. of West Ga., Carrollton, 1997; EdS in Guidance/Counseling, State U. of West Ga., 1999. Lic. profl. counselor, nat. cert. counselor. Sec. Atlanta Housing Authority, 1960—69; legal sec. Hansell, Post, Brandon & Dorsey, Atlanta, 1964—67; paralegal Johnson & McCarter, Atlanta, 1967—69; flight attendant TransWorld Airlines, St. Louis, 1969—2000; psychotherapist Focus by the Sea, St. Simons Island, Ga., 2000—. Part-time instr. Coastal Ga. C.C., Brunswick, 2003—. Mem.: Nat. Assn. Addiction Counseling, Lic. Profl. Counselors. Avocations: reading, bicycling. Home: 514 Atlantic Dr Saint Simons Island GA 31522 Office: Focus by the Sea 2927 Demare Rd Saint Simons Island GA 31522 Office Phone: 912-638-1959. Fax: 912-634-9890. E-mail: annetteperry@mindspring.com.

PERRY, BETH ANN, elementary school educator; b. Phila., June 30, 1945; d. Henry Francis and June Elizabeth (Reiff) Perry; m. Michael John Lavish (div.); children: Jennifer Lynn Lavish, Dennis Michael Lavish. BS, Pa. State U., State College, 1967. Cert. tchr. Pa. Tchr. Upper Moreland Sch. Dist., Willow Grove, Pa., 1967—69, 1972—75, LaSalle Coll. H.S., Wyndmoor, Pa., 1969—72; tchr.7th grade life sci. Bristol Twp. Sch. Dist./Benjamin Franklin Mid. Sch., Levittown, Pa., 1999—, coord. sci. dept., 2003—06, coord. Jason Project, 2001—05. Mem. sci. curriculum devel. Bristol Twp. Sch. Dist., mem. strategic planning steering com. Cub scout leader Boy Scouts Am., Carversville, Pa., 1985—89, cubmaster, 1985—89, Weebelos den leader Doylestown, 2005, cubmaster, 2005—06. Mem.: NEA, Bucks County Sci. Tchrs. Assn., Nat. Sci. Tchrs. Assn., Bristol Twp. Edn. Assn., Pa. Edn. Assn. Avocations: reading, photography, skiing. Home: 5927 Stovers Mill Rd Doylestown PA 18901 Office: Bristol Township School District 6401 Mill Creek Rd Levittown PA 19057

PERRY, CYNTHIA, social worker; d. Marvin Olin Smith, Jr. and Alois Elizabeth Smith; children: Ashley Hayden, Robert Craig Jr. BS in Social Work, U. Ala.-Birmingham, 1991. Lic. BSW 1991. Program coord. Bayview Sr. Citizen's Ctr., Pensacola, Fla., 1976—79, nursing home activities dir., 1980—84; work study dept. behavioral sci., psychology dept. U. Ala., Birmingham, 1987—91; positive maturity social work intern United Way Positive Maturity Sr. Companion program, Birmingham, 1991—92; investigator dept. human resources Child Welfare, Mobile, Ala., 1992—93; medical social worker Mercy Medical Hosp., Mobile, 1993—97; case mgr. Ala. Dept. Sr. Svcs., Birmingham, 1999—. Recipient Cert. Appreciation award, Dept. Human Resources, Jefferson County, Ala., 1999. Mem.: Healthcare Social Work Assn., Ala. Gentological Soc., Pensacola Woman's Club. Avocations: travel, cooking, photography, crafts. Personal E-mail: cynthiap27@yahoo.com.

PERRY, DAPHNE, social worker; b. Salt Lake City, June 13, 1926; d. Edwin Samuel and Eunice Naomi (Crosby) Bliss; m. Clarence Kettle, Sept. 6, 1943 (dec. 1947); m. John Calvin Perry, Dec. 20, 1949; children: Don Richard, John David, Scott Edwin, Brian Calvin, Douglas Todd. BA, Calif. State U., Long Beach, 1969; MSW, Portland State U., Oreg., 1985. Caseworker Washington County C.S.D., Hillsboro, Oreg., 1969-80; acting dir. Beaverton (Oreg.) Community Youth Services, 1980; pvt. social work practice Beaverton. Co-owner, sec. Electro-Static Refinishers, Beaverton, 1983-88; vol. cons. Fir Grove Sch., Beaverton, 1980; tchr. Parenting Dynamics classes, Beaverton, 1980-88, 91. Contbr. articles various parenting mags. Founder Beaverton Community Youth Svc. Ctr., 1980, bd. dirs., 1986—; sponsor Parent Anonymous, Beaverton; leader Adult Children of Alcoholics seminars, 1989-91; leader Fairway Village Club, 1998-2005; vol. cons. Mill Plain Sch. Vancover(leadership team 2000-06, vol. of Yr. 2000), 1998-; co-leader teen substance abuse group Evergreen Sch. Dist., 2000-04. Recipient Washington County Super Hero award, 1989. Mem. Nat. Assn. Social Workers, World Beyond War. Independent. Avocations: fishing, art, camping, reading, crafts. Home: 3014 SE 157th Ave Vancouver WA 98683-3756 Personal E-mail: dafpry@aol.com.

PERRY, DIANE SWANEY, mathematics educator; b. Atlanta, Oct. 2, 1969; d. Charles Dale and Juanita Swaney; m. Duke Perry, July 4, 2005. BS in Edn., Ga. State U., Atlanta, 1996, EdM, 1998; Edn. Specialist, Lincoln Meml. U., Harrogate, Tenn., 2000. Cert. tchr. Ga. Profl. Stds. Commn., 1996. 8th grade math tchr. Richard Hull Mid. Sch., Duluth, Ga., 1996—2004, Creekland Mid. Sch., Lawrenceville, Ga., 2004—. Cons. GTAPP, Atlanta, 2005—06. Assoc. UMW Bargain Ho., Greenville, Ga., 2004—06. Named Tchr. of Yr., Richard Hull Mid. Sch., 2002—03; scholar, Joseph Anthony Berne Found., 1995—98. Mem.: Nat. Coun. Tchrs. Math., Ga. Coun. Tchrs. Math. Avocations: tennis, travel. Office Phone: 770-338-4736. Business E-Mail: diane_perry@gwinnett.k12.ga.us.

PERRY, ELISABETH SCHERF, psychologist; b. Kasel-Trier, Germany, Aug. 24, 1952; came to U.S., 1976; d. Willibald and Brigitta (Jakobs) Scherf; m. R. T. Perry. AA in Maths., Columbia Basin Coll., Pasco, Wash., 1978; BS in German Lit., Psychology with honors, U. Wis., 1982; MA in Psychology, Calif. Sch. Prof. Psychology, L.A., 1985, PhD in Clin. Psychology, 1988. Lic. psychologist N.Mex., clin. psychologist N.Mex., cert. Am. Bd. Forensic Examiners. Psychologist Psychol. Health Inc., Albuquerque, 1988-91, Los Lunas Sch. Dist., N.Mex., 1990-91; psychologist, dir., owner S.W. Psychol. Svcs., Santa Fe, 1991—92; clin. and police psychologist pvt. practice, N.Mex., 1988—. Police psychologist Gallup (N.Mex.) Police Dept., 1992-96, McKinley County Sheriff's Dept., Gallup, 1991-96, psychologist, supr. Mesilla Valley, Gallup, 1995-97; sch. psychologist Los Alamos Schs., 1995. V.p. Santa Fe Child abuse Coun., 1991. Mem. APA, N.Mex. Psychol. Assn., Phi Kappa Phi. Avocation: hiking. Office: SW Psychol Svcs 125 E Palace Ave Ste 62 Santa Fe NM 87501-2042 also: 800 Trinity Dr Ste I Los Alamos NM 87544-4105

PERRY, GLENDA LEE, health science librarian; b. Booneville, Ark., Mar. 21, 1940; d. Earnest Asa and Susan Mae (Aaron) P. BS in Elem. Edn., Ark. Tech. U., 1962; MS in Libr. Sci., La. State U., 1972. Elem. sch. tchr. Ark. Pub. Schs., 1962-64, sch. libr., 1965-74; monograph acquisitions libr. U. Tenn. Health Sci. Ctr. Libr., Memphis, 1979-82, serials libr., 1975-78, 82-87; health scis. libr. Met. Nashville Gen. Hosp., 1987—2002; ret. Mem. Med. Libr. Assn. (sr. mem. Acad. of Health Information Profls.), Mid Tenn. Health Sci. Librs. Assn. (sec.-treas. 1992-94), Tenn. Health Sci. Librs. Assn. (union list com. 1988-91). Office: Met Nashville Gen Hosp 72 Hermitage Ave Nashville TN 37210-2110

PERRY, HELEN, medical/surgical nurse, secondary school educator; b. Birmingham, Ala., Mar. 4, 1927; d. Van Mary Ellenol (Thornton) Curry; m. Charlie Pitts, May 1960 (div.); 1 child, Charlenia Pitts; m. George Perry (dec. 1989); children: Hattie Mae(dec.), George Jr., Bishop, Jose Sr. Student, LaSalle Extension U., Chgo., 1968, Georgetown U., 1979; Doctorate/Mayanuis Mosaic Soc., Duke Univ., San Antonio, 1979. Cert. paramedic, of completion Ptnrs. in Health Sheperd Ctr. Am. South Side, 2006; LPN. Tchr. Wenona HS City Bd. Edn., Birmingham, 1977—2005, supply tchr., 2005—. Notary pub., Ala., 1975—; home health nurse U. Ala. Birmingham Hosp., 1988—; math. and reading tutor Princeton Elem. Sch., 2004. Trustee Nat. Crime Watch, 1989; mem. adv. bd. Am. Security Coun., Va., Washington, 1969—91; mem. Coalition for Desert Storm; others; vol. ARC, Birmingham, 1970—; mem. crime watch Am. Police, Washington, 1989; mem. Hall of Fame Pres. Task Force, Washington, 1983—91, Image Devel. Adv. Bd.; nominee Nat. Rep. Com., Washington, 1991, 1992; selected VIP guest del. Rep. Nat. Conv., Houston, 1992; life mem. Rep. Presdl. Task Force, Washington, 1992; mem. Jefferson Com., 2001; mem. adv. bd. Nat. Congl. Com., Washington; mem. fin. com. fundraiser Middleton for Congress Campaign, 1994, Dist. # 59 Bd. Reps.; mem. exec. com. Jefferson County Rep., chairperson legis. dist. 52; chair Harriet Tubman Rep. Com.; del. Commonwealth of Ky. So. Rep. Leadership Conf., 2000; min. Greater Emmanuel Temple Holiness Ch., Birmingham, 1957—, ordained elder, vice champion mother bd.; mem. Nat. Law Enforcement Assn., 1989. Nominee Presdl. Election Registry, Rep. Presdl. Task Force, 1992; named Good Samaritan, Law Envforcement Officers; recipient award, Ala. Sheriff Assn., 1989, Navy League, 1989—91, cert. of appreciation, Pres. Congl. Task Force, 1990, Rep. Nat. Com., 1994, Diamond award, U.S.A. Serve Am., 1992, Rep. Presdl. award, Legion of Merit, 1994, Royal Proclamation, Royal Highness Kevin, Prince Regent of Hutt River Province, 1994, Royal Ceremonial jewel, Svc. award, Ala. Bd. Nursing, Outstanding Sr. Citizen's cert. of recognition. Mem.: Ala. Nurses Assn., Nat. Assn. Unknown Players, Nat. Rep. Women Assn., LaSalle Ext. U. Alumni (life). Avocations: singing, writing, reading, gardening. Home: 2021 10th Ave S Apt 513 Birmingham AL 35205-2716

PERRY, JACQUELIN, orthopedist, surgeon; b. Denver, May 31, 1918; d. John F. and Tirzah (Kuruptkat) P. BE, U. Calif., LA, 1940; MD, U. Calif., San Francisco, 1950; DSc (hon.), U. So. Calif., 1996. Intern Children's Hosp., San Francisco, 1950-57; resident in orthop. surgery U. Calif., San Francisco, 1951-55; orthop. surgeon Rancho Los Amigos Hosp., Downey, Calif., 1955—, chief stroke svc., 1972-75; chief pathokinesiology Rancho Los Amigos Med. Ctr., 1961—; mem. faculty U. Calif. Med. Sch., San Francisco, 1966—, clin. prof., 1973—; mem. faculty U. So. Calif. Med. Sch., 1969—, prof. orthop. surgery, 1972—, dir. polio and gait clinic, 1972—. Disting. lectr. for hosp. for spl. surgery and Cornell U. Med. Coll., NYC, 1977-78; Packard Meml. lectr. U. Colo. Med. Sch., 1970; Osgood lectr. Harvard Med. Sch., 1978; Summer lectr., Portland, 1977; Shands lectr.; cons. USAF; guest spkr. symposia; cons. Biomechanics Lab. Centinela Hosp., 1979—. Served as phys. therapist U.S. Army, 1941-46. Recipient Disting. Svc. award Assn. Rehab. Facilities, 1981, Pres.'s award, 1984, Isabelle and Lenard Goldensen award for tech. United Cerebral Palsy Assn., 1981, Jow Dowling award, 1985, Profl. Achievement award UCLA, 1988, Milton Cohen award Nat. Assn. Rehab., 1993, Tribute Pres. award Ruth Jackson Orthop. Soc., 2004; named Woman of Yr. for Medicine in So. Calif. LA Times, 1959, Alumnus of Yr. U. Calif. Med. Sch., 1980, Physician of Yr. Calif. Employment Devel. Dept., 1994; Jacquelin Perry Neuro Trauma Inst. Rancho Clin. Bldg. named in her honor, 1996. Mem. AMA, Am. Acad. Orthop. Surgeons (Kappa Delta award for rsch. 1977, orthop. rsch. svc., 1976), Am. Orthop. Assn. (Shands lectr. 1988), Western Orthop. Assn., Calif. Med. Soc., LA County Med. Soc., Am. Phys. Therapy Assn. (hon. Golden Pen award 1965), Am. Acad. Orthotists and Prosthetists (hon.), Scoliosis Rsch. Soc., LeRoy Abbott Soc., Am. Acad. Cerebral Palsy, Gait & Clin. Movement Analysis Soc. (mem. emeritus, Lifetime Achievement award 2000), Orthop. Rsch. Soc. (Shands award 1998, 99). Home: 12319 Brock Ave Downey CA 90242-3503 Office: Rancho Los Amigos Med Ctr 7601 Imperial Hwy Downey CA 90242-3456 Office Phone: 562-401-7177. E-mail: pklab@larei.org.

PERRY, JANE A., customer service administrator; b. Anderson, IN, Mar. 14, 1960; d. Richard L. Ward, Shirley A. Ward; m. Will C. Perry, Mar. 14, 1992; 1 child, Devin Ward. A in Bus. Mgr., Acctg. Sci., Indiana Bus. Coll., Anderson, IN, 1990—93. Designee Cardinal Svc. Mgmt. Svcs., New Castle, Ind., 1990—97; caterer Plain J&W Catering, Indianapolis, Ind., 1998—2001; svc. asst. Ind. Ins. Agents Ind., Indianapolis, Ind., 1997—. Planner Ind. Ins. Agents Ind., Indianapolis, 1998—2001. Human rights com. Cardinal Svc. Mgmt. Svcs., New Castle, 1997—2001. Apostilic. Avocations: horseback riding, swimming. Home: 2619 Pearl St Anderson IN 46016-5357 Business E-Mail: perry@bigi.org.

PERRY, JANTINA, retired music educator; b. Bierum, Netherlands, Sept. 14, 1948; d. Koert P. and Itje K. Flikkema; m. David W. Perry, Mar. 24, 1984; m. Paul R. Bassett, Dec. 23, 1969 (div. Sept. 6, 1982); children: Dia E. Bassett, Jonathan K. Bassett. EdD, US Internat. U., San Diego, 2000. Coord. elem. music Nat. Sch. Dist., National City, Calif., 1979—89; tchr. Newport-Mesa Unified Sch. Dist., Costa Mesa, Calif., 1989—2005; ret., 2005. Named Elem. Music Tchr. of Yr., Orange County, Calif., 2002. Protestant. Avocations: singing, travel, gardening, swimming, bicycling. Home: 55 Trinidad Bend Coronado CA 92118 Personal E-mail: jantinap@aol.com.

PERRY, JEAN LOUISE, academic administrator; b. Richland, Wash., May 13, 1950; d. Russell S. and Sue W. Perry. BS, Miami U., Oxford, Ohio, 1972; MS, U. Ill., Urbana, 1973, PhD, 1976. Cons. ednl. placement office U. Ill., 1973-75; adminstrv. intern Coll. Applied Life Studies, 1975-76, asst. dean, 1976-77, assoc. dean, 1978-81, asst. prof. dept. phys. edn., 1976-81; assoc. prof. phys. edn. San Francisco State U., 1981-84, prof., 1984-90, chair, 1981-90; dean Coll. Human and Cmty. Scis. U. Nev., Reno, 1990—2006, spl. asst. to pres. for athletics, academics and compliance, 2006—. Named to Excellent Tchr. List, U. Ill., 1973—79. Mem.: AAHPERD (fellow rsch. consortium, pres. 1988—89), Nat. Assn. Girls and Women in Sports (guide coord., pres.), Nat. Assn. Phys. Edn. in Higher Edn., Am. Ednl. Rsch. Assn., Am. Assn. Higher Edn., Phi Delta Kappa, Delta Psi Kappa. Home: 3713 Ranchview Ct Reno NV 89509-7437 Office: U Nev Legacy Hal/ 232 Reno NV 89557-0001 Office Phone: 775-784-3505.

PERRY, JULIA NICHOLE, psychologist; b. Mpls., July 23, 1972; d. William James and Carolyn Marjorie (Rollins) Perry. BA (magna cum laude with distinction) in Psychology, Hamline U., St. Paul, Minn., 1994; PhlD in Clin. Psychology, U. Minn., 1999. Cons., lic. psychologist Martin-McAllister Consulting Psychologists, Inc., Mpls., 1999—2003; adj. asst. prof. dept. psychology Hamline U., St. Paul, 2002; staff psychologist, team coord. Vets. Affairs Med. Ctr., Mpls., 2003—. Asst. prof. dept. psychiatry U. Minn., 2004—. Author: (book chpt.) Assessment of Treatment Resistance Via Questionnaire, 2002, The BTPI: An Objective Guide to Treatment Planning, 2004. Fellowship for minority students, U. Minn. Grad. Sch., 1994—95. Mem.: Soc. for Personality Assessment, Psi Chi Nat. Psychology Honor Soc., Phi Beta Kappa Nat. Honor Soc. (Zeta chpt.). Dfl. Avocations: travel, photography, reading, writing, research. Office: Vets Affairs Med Ctr One Veterans Dr 116 A Minneapolis MN 55417

PERRY, JUNE CARTER, ambassador; b. Texarkana, Ark., Nov. 13, 1943; d. Bishop W. and Louise (Pendleton) Carter; m. Frederick Majette Perry; children: Chad Douglass, André Frederick. BA cum laude, Loyola U./Mundelein Coll., Chgo., 1965; MA, U. Chgo., 1967. Nat. teaching fellow NC A&T State U., Greensboro, 1967-68; grad./undergrad. lectr. U. Md., College Park, 1969-70; dir. pub. affairs WGMS/RKO Radio, Washington, 1974-77; spl. asst. to dir. pub. affairs Cmty. Svcs. Adminstrn., Washington, 1977-79; dir. pub. affairs ACTION/Peace Corps, Washington, 1979-83; gen. svcs. officer US Embassy, Lusaka, Zambia, 1984-86, polit./labor officer Harare, Zimbabwe, 1986-87; country office for Botswana Bur. African Affairs, Dept. State, Washington, 1987-89; spl. asst. to dep. sec. US Dept. State, Washington, 1989, sr. advisor to asst. sec., 1997—98, amb. to Kingdom of Lesotho, 2004—, dep. amb. to Ctrl. African Rep., 1996—97, dep. amb. to Madagascar, 1998—2000; chief internal polit. affairs and narcotics coord. Embassy Paris, 1990—93; diplomat-in-residence Howard U., 2001—02; dir. Office Social and Humanitarian Affairs Internat. Orgn. Bur., 2002—04; dep. dir. Office of Policy and Plans, Polit. Mil. Affairs Bur. Adv. coun. The Women's Inst., Bethesda, Md., 1983—. Producer, host: Soul of the Classics, WGMS Radio, 1974-77, Heritage Series, RKO Radio, 1974-77, DC Schs. Radio Project, 1973. Bd. dirs. Sign of the Times Art Gallery and Workshop, 1975-77, others in past. Recipient Spl. Achievement award, ACTION, 1981, Mundelein Disting. Alumnae, Mundelein Coll., 1981, Superior Achiever award, RKO Radio, 1977, Superior Honor, Sr. Performance awards State Dept., 1997, 98 2003, 04, 05; Diplomat-in-Residence of Yr. award, US Dept. State, 2002; Woodrow Wilson fellow, 1965, UN Human Rights awardee, 1977, others. Mem. Am. Fgn. Svc. Assn., Cosmos Club, Assn. Black Am. Ambs., Nat. Coun. Delta Sigma Theta (Nat. Coun. Negro Women). Avocations: African art collecting, African-Am. and French history, classical music. Office: US Embassy 2340 Maseru Pl Washington DC 20521-2340 Business E-Mail: perryjc2@state.gov.

PERRY, MARGARET, librarian, writer; b. Cin., Nov. 15, 1933; d. Rufus Patterson and Elizabeth Munford (Anthony) P. AB, Western Mich. U., 1954; Cert. d'etudes Francaises, U. Paris, 1956; MSLS, Cath. U. Am., 1959. Young adult and reference libr. N.Y. Pub. Libr., N.Y.C., 1954-55, 57-58; libr. U.S. Army, France and Germany, 1959-63, 64-67; chief circulation U.S. Mil. Libr., West Point, NY, 1967-70; head edn. libr. U. Rochester, NY, 1970-75, asst. prof. NY, 1973-75, assoc. prof. NY, 1975-82, asst. dir. librs. for reader svcs. NY, 1975-82, acting dir. librs. NY, 1976-77, 80; univ. libr. Valparaiso U., Ind., 1982-93; ret., 1993. Mem. Task Force on Coop. Edn., Rochester, 1972; freelance writer Mich. Land Use Inst., 1995-01. Author: A Bio-bibliography of Countee P. Cullen, 1903-1946, 1971, Silence to the Drums: A Survey of the Literature of the Harlem Renaissance, 1976, The Harlem Renaissance, 1982, The Short Fiction of Rudolph Fisher, 1987; also numerous short stories; contbr. articles to profl. jours. and children's mags. Bd. dirs. Urban League, 1978-80 Recipient 1st prize short story contest Armed Forces Writers League, 1966; 2d prize Frances Steloff Fiction prze, 1968, 1st prize short story Arts Alive, 1990, 2d prize short story Willow Rev., 1990; seminar scholar Schloss Leopoldskron, Salzburg, Austria, 1956, 3d prize short story West Shore C.C., Scottville, Mich., 1995. Mem. ALA. Democrat. Roman Catholic. Avocations: violin and viola, collecting book marks, gardening, reading, travel. Home: 8 Muriel St Ithaca NY 14850 Office Phone: 607-257-3997. Personal E-mail: mperry515@yahoo.com.

PERRY, MISTY J., social studies educator; b. Muncie, Ind., Oct. 12, 1973; d. Robert A. and Danielle Ann Ruddick; m. Brent A. Perry, Jan. 4, 1997; children: McKenna Jo, Mara Ann. Bachelor's degree, Ball State U., Muncie, Ind., 1997. Cert. tchr. Ind., Ohio. Tchr. Muncie Reception and Diagnostic Ctr., 1999—2001; tchr. h.s. social studies Medina County Career Ctr., Ohio, 2001—. Mem.: Nat. Coun. for Social Studies. Democrat. Office Phone: 330-725-8461. Personal E-mail: mjperry@neo.rr.com.

PERRY, NANCY, foundation administrator; m. Ken Perry; 1 child, Brad. BS in Elem. Edn., U. Kans. Kindergarten tchr. Avondale East Elem. Sch.; host local Romper Room TV program; variety/talk show host; pres., CEO United Way of Greater Topeka. Mem. fin. and outreach coms., mem. altar guild Grace Episcopal Cathedral. Mem.: Rotary Club. Office: United Way of Greater Topeka 1315 SW Arrowhead Rd Topeka KS 66604

PERRY, NANCY BLAND, accountant; b. Houston, Miss., Aug. 17, 1955; d. Charles Edward Bland, Minnie Lou Bland; 1 child, Cheryl Elizabeth Crisco; m. Paul D Perry. BS in Edn. with distinction, Miss. Coll., 1975, cert. acctg., 1988. CPA Miss. CPA, acct. various CPA firms, Jackson, Miss., 1983—89; pvt. practice CPA Clinton, Miss., 1989—91; sr. acct. Chem. First Inc.,

Jackson, 1991—2003; asst. v.p. acctg. Denmiss Corp., 2003—. Bd. dirs., various offices Girl Scouts U.S. Mid. Miss., Jackson, 1992—; team mem. Leadership Clinton, 1997—98; bd. dirs., various positions Clinton Pub. Sch. Dist. PTA, 1988—96; bd. dirs., sec. treas. ChemFirst Found., Inc., Jackson, 1996—2002; trustee Clinton Pub. Sch. Dist., 1998—; bd. dirs. Clinton Jr. Miss, 1997—2004; trustee Frances Rushton Meml. Scholarship Trust, 1998—, chair, 2001—. Nominee GIVE, Gov. of Miss., 1995; named Parent of the Yr., Clinton Pub. Sch. Dist., 1995; recipient Metro Jackson's Finest award, Cystic Fibrosis Foundation, 1999, Thanks Badge, Girl Scouts U.S. Mid. Miss., 1995. Mem.: AICPA, Miss. Soc. CPAs, Am. Soc. Women Accts. (bd. dirs., various positions 1996—2001), Jr. Aux. Clinton (bd. dirs., treas. 1996—2000, trustee Francecs Rushton Meml. Scholarship Trust 1999—, chair 2001—), Clinton C. of C. Ch. Of Christ. Business E-Mail: nperry@denkmann-ms.com.

PERRY, NANCY TROTTER, retired telecommunications company executive; b. Cleve., Jan. 1, 1935; d. Charles Hanley and Mable Dora (Lowry) Trotter; m. Robert Anthony Perry, Apr. 27, 1957. Student, Dunbarton Coll., 1952-53; BA, W.Va. U., 1999. Svc. rep. C&P Telephone Co., Balt., 1956-60, adminstrv. asst., 1960-67, staff supr., 1967-69; staff mgr., 1969-79; mgr. consumer affairs C&P Telephone Co., Balt., 1979-91; ret. Bd. dirs., founding dir. Balt. Mus. Industry, Md., Info. and Referral Providers Coun., 1990-2003, sec., 1994-98, v.p. 1999-2002; bd. dirs. Learning Ind. Through Computers, Inc., 1991-99, pres., 1994-96; bd. dirs. Md. Gerontol. Assn., 1991, Md. Consumer Coun., 1991-2000, chair, 1994-96; bd. dirs. Fgn.-Born Info. and Referral Network, 1992-96; bd. dirs. Hearing and Speech Agy., 1989-94, exec. v.p. 1991-94; founding dir. Tele-Consumer Hotline, 1986-92; responding to crisis panel United Way, 1995-2003, vice chmn., 1995-99, 2001-03. Mem. Soc. Consumer Affairs Profls. in Bus., Nat. Fedn. of Blind, Alliance for Pub. Tech., Sons of Italy (v.p. 1997, 2001—, trustee 1999-2005, editor Il Giornale, Fairview writer, photographer, 2003-), Fairhaven Religious Life Com., Fairhaven Residents Assn. (bd. dirs, mem. sec. 2004-06, vice chair, treas., 2006). Avocations: travel, reading. Home: 7200 3rd Ave C150 Sykesville MD 21784-5208 Personal E-mail: ntperry@prodigy.net.

PERRY, SARAH HOLLIS, artist; b. Framingham, Mass., Mar. 24, 1934; d. Hollis Stratton and Mary (Norris) French; m. John Curtis Perry, Sept. 14, 1957; children: Elizabeth, Margaret, Rachel, Lyman, Maria. BA, Smith Coll., Northampton, Mass., 1956; diploma, Sch. Mus. Fine Arts, Boston, 1999, cert., 2000. Syss. svc. rep. IBM, Boston, 1956-57; photog. aide Polaroid, Cambridge, Mass., 1957-74, asst. to chmn., 1974-82; asst. to dir. rsch. Rowland Inst., Cambridge, 1982-92, archivist, 1992-2001, artist in residence, 1992—2002. Mem. teaching faculty Sch. Mus. Fine Arts, Boston, 1999-2000. Recipient Jurors award Hera Gallery, Providence, 1996, 97, Erector Sq. Gallery, New Haven, 1998, Atlanta Paper Mus., 1999-2000; named winner of competition to create sculpture Tufts U. Libr. Lobby, 1997; Travelling scholar Sch. Mus. Fine Arts, 2000, Nancy Graves fellow Millay Colony, 2004 Mem. Phi Beta Kappa (Zeta of Mass. chpt.). Studio: 35 Norwood Heights Gloucester MA 01930-1212 Personal E-mail: shperry@adelphia.net.

PERRY, SUSAN NIGEMANN, education educator, consultant; b. Burlington, Wis., Dec. 3, 1970; d. Karl Nigemann and Regina Niemann; m. Martin Dewitt Perry Jr., Aug. 7, 1991. BS in Elem. Edn., Okla. State U., Stillwater; MEd in Spl. Edn., Loyola Coll., Balt.; degree in Reading Edn., U. Ark., Stillwater, EdD in Higher Edn. Cert. reading recovery tchr. 3d gr. tchr. Anne Arundel Pub. Sch., Annapolic, Md., 1995—95; alt. classroom tchr. Russellville (Ark.) Sch. Dist., 1996—97, spl. edn. resource thcr., 1997—98; spl. edn. resource tchr. Arkaelphia (Ark.) Pub. Sch., 1998—99; grad. asst. U. Ark., Little Rock, 1999—2001, rsch. assoc., 2002—04; asst. to dir. spl. programs Ouachita Bapt. U., Arkdelphia, 2001—02; asst. prof. Hendrix Coll., 2004—. Adj. instr. Ouachita Bapt. U., Arkadelphia, 1999—2000, Arkadelphia, 2001—02; presenter in field. Contbr. articles to profl. jours. Vol. Saline County Humane Soc., 2003—. Grantee, Murphy Found., Conway, Ark., 2003—06, Odyssey Found., Conway, 2003—06. Mem.: ASCD, Reading Recovery Coun. N.Am., Mid-South Ednl. Rsch. Assn., Learning Disabilties Assn., Ark. Reading Assn., Internat. Reading Assn., Children and Adults with Attention Deficit/Hyperactivity Disorder, Nat. Reading Recovery Coun., Coun. for Exceptional Children, Learning Disabilities Assn. Avocations: gardening, walking. Office: Hendrix Coll 1600 Washington Ave Conway AR 72032 Office Fax: 501-450-1446. Business E-Mail: perry@hendrix.edu.

PERRY-CAMP, JANE, music educator, pianist; b. Durham, N.C., Oct. 5, 1936; d. Harold Sanford and Margrid (Hagelberg) Perry; m. John Barton Camp, Aug. 20, 1960 (div. Sept. 1970); m. Harold Anthony Schiffman, June 10, 1978. AB magna cum laude, Duke U., 1958; MusM in Piano Performance, Fla. State U., Tallahassee, 1960, PhD in Music Theory, 1968; studied piano with, Edward Kilenyi, Ernst von Dohnanyi. Asst. prof. music Brevard C.C., Cocoa, Fla., 1968-69; faculty St. Petersburg (Fla.) Coll., 1969-73; asst. prof., assoc. prof. Sweet Briar (Va.) Coll., 1974-80; assoc. prof., prof. Sch. Music, Fla. State U., Tallahassee, 1980-96, prof. emeritus, 1996—, Orpheus chair musicology, 1999. Mem. adv. bd. Fla. State U., Music Theory Soc., Tallahassee, 1982-88; bd. dirs. Fla. State U. Friends of Libr., Tallahassee, 1985-87. Pianist: (CDs) Schiffman: Spectrum, My Ladye Jane's Booke: Eighteen Fugues and Postludes for Piano, 1996, Concerto for Piano and Orchestra, 1999, Chamber Concerto No. 2, 2004, (LPs) Fantasy for Piano, 1986, Chamber Concertino for Piano and Double Wind Quintet, 1987; contbr. articles to profl. jours. and anthologies. Fellow NEH, Paris, London, 1973-74; faculty fellow Sweet Briar Coll., 1979-80; recipient rsch. grants Fla. State U. Found., 1985-86, Internat. Rsch. and Exch. Bd., Krakow, Poland, 1986. Mem. Am. Soc. 18th Century Studies (pres. 1991-92), SE Am. Soc. 18th Century studies (pres. 1987-88), Mozart Soc. Am. (bd. dirs. 1996-2001), Internat. Soc. Study of Time, Am. Musicol. Soc., Coll. Music Soc. Avocations: gardening, hiking, needlework (knitting, crocheting, sewing).

PERSELL, CAROLINE HODGES, sociologist, educator, author, researcher, consultant; b. Ft. Wayne, Ind., Jan. 16, 1941; d. Albert Randolph and Katherine (Rogers) Hodges; m. Charles Bowen Persell III, June 17, 1967; children: Patricia Emily, Stephen David. BA, Swarthmore Coll., 1962; MA, Columbia U., 1967, PhD, 1971. Sr. assoc., then nat. coord. Nat. Scholarship Svc. and Fund for Negro Students, N.Y.C., 1962-66; project dir. Bur. Applied Social Rsch., N.Y.C., 1968-71; asst. prof. NYU, 1971-76, assoc. prof., 1976-86, prof., 1986—, dir. grad. studies dept. sociology, 1984-87, chair dept. sociology, 1987-93, Robin Williams Disting. lectr., 1993-94. Author: Education and Inequality, 1977, Understanding Society, 1984, 3d edit., 1990; author: (with Cookson) Preparing for Power, 1985, Making Sense of Society, 1992; author: (with Maisel) How Sampling Works, 1996; assoc. editor: Tchg. Sociology, 1983—85, Sociology of Edn., 1991—95, Gender & Society, 1992—95; contbr. articles to profl. jours. Carnegie scholar Advancement of Tchg., 2000-01; grantee Fund for Improvement of Postsecondary Edn., 1989-92, NSF Equipment Fund, 1993-96; recipient Faculty Devel. award NSF, 1978-79, Women Educators' Rsch. award, 1978. Mem.: Sociologists for Women in Soc., Ea. Sociol. Soc. (pres. 1995—96), Am. Ednl. Rsch. Assn., Am. Sociol. Assn. (chair sect. 1983—84, chmn. publs. com. 1987—89, chair sect. 1988—89, v.p. 2004—05). Avocations: violin, gardening, opera, sports. Office: NYU Dept Sociology 269 Mercer St New York NY 10003-6633 Office Phone: 212-998-8350. Business E-Mail: chp1@nyu.edu.

PERSKY, KAREN RAE, biologist, educator; b. Joliet, Ill., Dec. 8, 1953; d. Harlan Edward and Diane Elizabeth Asche; m. Bruce Persky, June 3, 1978; children: Jacob, David, Julie, Christina. BA, Drake U., DesMoines, Iowa, 1975; MS, U. N.D., Grand Forks, 1979. Part-time instr. Coll. of DuPage, Glen Ellyn, Ill., 1984—2004, faculty natural sci., 2004—; pres. Complete Microbial Analysis Inc., Oak Brook, Ill., 1995—98; lab instr. Midwestern U., Downers Grove, Ill., 1995—98. Pres. music boosters Dist. 89, Glen Ellyn, 1998—99. Mem.: Am. Soc. Microbiologists, Natural Sci. Tchrs. Assn., Alpha Phi. Roman Catholic. Home: 2160 Stirrup Ln Wheaton IL 60187 Office: College of DuPage 425 Fawell Blvd Glen Ellyn IL 60137

PERSKY, MARLA SUSAN, lawyer; b. Pitts., Feb. 15, 1956; d. Bernard and Elaine (Matus) P.; m. Craig Heberton IV, May 20, 1984. BS, Northwestern U., 1977; JD, Washington U., St. Louis, 1982. Bar: Ill. 1982. Asst. dir. med. records Chgo. Lake Shore Hosp., 1978; sales/mktg. rep. Colgate-Palmolive Co., Chgo., 1978-79; mem. Lurie Sklar & Simon, Chgo., 1982-86; corp. counsel Baxter Healthcare Corp., Deerfield, Ill., 1986-91; lead litigation counsel Baxter Internat. Inc., 1991-94; assoc. gen. counsel Baxter Healthcare Corp., Deerfield, 1994—98, dep. gen. counsel, 1998—2004, acting gen. counsel, corp. sec., 2004—. Dir. Cytyc Corp. Sr. editor Urban Law Ann., 1981-82; contbr. articles to profl. jours. Mem. Chgo. Bar Assn., Ill. Bar Assn. (writing contest award 1983), ABA (vice chmn. medicine and law com. 1984-86), Am. Soc. Law and Medicine, Am. Acad. Hosp. Attys. Democrat. Office: Baxter Internat Inc One Baxter Pkwy Deerfield IL 60015-5281

PERSONETTE, LOUISE METZGER (SISTER MARY ROGER METZGER), mathematics professor; b. Indpls., Dec. 21, 1925; d. Frank Alexander and Frances Lee Ann (Durham) Metzger; m. Marlen William Personette, Dec. 9, 1967 (div. Dec. 1985); 1 stepson: Lyle Scott. BS in Elem. Edn., Athenaeum of Ohio, 1952; MEd, Xavier U., 1964. Nun St. Francis Convent, Oldenburg, Ind., 1942—67; elem. tchr. Cath. Schs., Cin., 1945-56, secondary math tchr. Middletown, Ohio, 1957-63, Evansville, Ind., 1964-65, Hamilton, Ohio, 1966-67; elem. tchr. Kent (Wash.) Schs., 1968-72, math specialist, 1973-82; math cons. greater Seattle Schs., 1983—; GED instr. Muckleshoot Indian Tribe, Auburn, Wash., 1998—2000. Dir. Heatherhill Edn. Ctr., Kent, 1982—, Homework House, Kent, 1987—90; adj. instr. Seattle Pacific U., 1975—95, City U., Seattle, 1975—95; SAT prep. math tutor, 2002—. Co-author: S.O.S. Story Problems, 1980. Mem. Nat. Coun. Tchrs. Math., Math. Assn. Am., Washington State Math Coun., Puget Sound Coun. Tchrs. Math., New Horizons. Home and Office: Heatherhill Education Ctr 564 W Gardner Ct Marion IN 46952 Personal E-mail: louisamath@msn.com.

PERSONS, FERN, actress; b. Chgo., July 27, 1910; d. John William and Alpha Valeska (Solberg) Ball; m. Max I. Persons, Oct. 17, 1935 (dec. Nov. 1971); 1 child, Nancy Janice Persons Rockafellow. BA, Kalamazoo Coll., 1931; BFA, Carnegie-Mellon U., 1933. Faculty mem. speech and drama Ferry Hall, Lake Forest, Ill., 1934-35. V.p. SAG, L.A., 1977-81, nat. bd., 1982-98. Appeared in (films) Prelude to a Kiss, Straight Talk, Curly Sue, Field of Dreams, Hoosiers, Risky Business, Class, Grandview U.S.A., On the Right Track, The Golden Gloves Story, (tv feature films and series) Mario and the Mob, Hard Knox, The Impostor, Under the Biltmore Clock, The Chicago Story, Jack and Mike, Jon Sable, ER, Early Edition, also in regional theatre prodns., 1972-95. Recipient Otto Kahn prize Carnegie-Mellon U., Pitts., 1933; Fern Persons Day named in her honor Mayor Richard M. Daley, Chgo., July 27, 1999. Mem. AFTRA (bd. mem., v.p.), AAUW (scholar 1927), Zeta Phi Eta (v.p. 1971, Disting. Svc. award 1994). Democrat. Methodist. Avocations: travel, reading, walking, gardening, theater. Home: 2700 Woodland Rd Evanston IL 60201-2034

PERSONS, KARI LYNN, physical education educator, basketball coach; b. Seoul, Republic of Korea, Mar. 17, 1975; d. Arthur and Elaine Persons. BA, Cedarville U., Ohio, 1998. Cert. tchr. health and phys. edn. Ohio, tchr. Wis., CPR ARC, SE Wis. Health edn. tchr. Rochester (Minn.) Pub. Schs., 1998—2001; health and phys. edn. tchr. Kenosha (Wis.) Unified Sch. Dist., 2001—. Aquatics dir., unit dir. Salvation Army, Camp Lake, Wis., 1997—2003; athletic dir. Washington Mid. Sch., Kenosha, 2005—, asst. basketball coach, 2005—. Mem.: AAHPERD. Avocations: exercise, fitness, travel, Spanish language, reading. Home: 5612 35th Ave Kenosha WI 53144 Office: Washington Mid Sch 811 Washington Rd Kenosha WI 53140 Office Phone: 262-653-6291. Personal E-mail: lilrunnin@yahoo.com.

PERSONS, MARJORIE ANNABELLE, publishing executive, writer; b. Highmore, S.D., May 27, 1931; d. Orville Manford Kiel and Anna Mabel Shoemaker; m. Clyde Orval Persons, June 15, 1953; children: Larene Kay, Denise Diane, Michelle Lee. BA summa cum laude, Macalester Coll., St. Paul, 1955. Cert. elem. edn. N.J., secondary English edn. N.J., music edn. N.J. Elem. tchr. Rural One-Rm. Sch., Grindstone, SD, 1950—51, Gustin Sch., Flint, Mich., 1964—65; elem. music tchr. Exxon Pvt. Sch., Aruba, Netherlands Antilles, 1965—73, Parochial Sch., Morristown, NJ, 1977—85; tchr. Wycliffe Bible Trans., Oaxaca, Mexico, 1995—97; writer, pub. Classical Magic, Inc., Banner Elk, NC, 1998—. Spkr., clinician numerous state music edn. confs. Author: Themes to Remember, Vols. 1 and 2, 2000, Classical Karaoke for Kids, 2003, Antonin Dvorak, From the New World with Lyrics, 2004. Leader, pres. Girl Scouts Am., Aruba, Phoenix, 1967—73; youth canteen leader Lago Cmty., Aruba, 1970—73; Sunday sch. tchr. various chs. Republican. Presbyterian. Avocations: music, gardening, reading. Home and Office: PO Box 1809 Banner Elk NC 28604 Office Phone: 828-898-7764. Personal E-mail: comapers@skybest.com.

PERTHOU, ALISON CHANDLER, interior designer; b. Bremerton, Wash., July 22, 1945; d. Benson and Elizabeth (Holdsworth) Chandler; m. A. V. Perthou, III, Sept. 9, 1967 (div. Dec. 1977); children: Peter T. R., Stewart A. C. BFA, Cornish Coll. Arts, 1972. Pres. Alison Perthou Interior Design, Seattle, 1972—, Optima Design, Inc., Seattle, 1986-89; treas. Framejoist Corp., Bellevue, Wash., 1973-90; pres. Classics: Interior Design and Constrn., Inc., 1988—, Gemini Holdings LLC, 2004—. Cons. bldg. and interiors com. Children's Hosp., Seattle, 1976—; guest lectr. U. Wash., Seattle, 1980—81. Mem. procurement com. Patrons N.W. Cultural and Charitable Orgn., 1985—, mem. antiques com., 1991—; trustee Cornish Coll. Arts, Seattle, 1973—80, sec. exec. com., 1975—77. Mem.: Am. Soc. Interior Design, Sunset Club, Seattle Tennis Club (mem. house and grounds com. 1974—75). Office: 563 Lake Washington Blvd E Seattle WA 98112-4226 Office Phone: 206-322-7909. Office Fax: 206-322-2335.

PERUGGI, REGINA S., academic administrator; b. NYC; BA in Sociology, Coll. New Rochelle; MBA, NYU; EdD, Columbia U. Drug abuse counselor, N.Y.C.; dir. Community Learning Ctr. York Coll. CUNY, 1974-84, with office of acad. affairs, 1984-86, assoc. dean for adult and continuing edn., 1986-90; pres. Marymount Manhattan Coll., NYC, 1990—2001, Ctrl. Park Conservancy, NYC, 2001—04, Kingsborough Cmty. Coll., CUNY, 2004—. Past chair N.Y. State Adult Leanring Svcs. Adv. Coun.; past pres. Continuing Edn. Assn. N.Y.; active N.Y. State Coun. on Vocat. Edn., N.Y. State Lit. Coun. Office: Kingsborough Cmty Coll 2001 Oriental Blvd Brooklyn NY 11235-2398

PERUO, MARSHA HOPE, artist; b. Mar. 21, 1951; BA, CUNY, Queens Coll., 1971; MFA, Pratt Inst., 1980. Awards chairperson Am. Soc. Contemporary Artists, N.Y.C., 1980—81, corresponding sec., 1981—83, dir., 1983—85, 1st v.p., 1985—87; artist Marsha Peruo, N.Y.C., 1980—. Exhibited nationally Vol. tchr. Cmty. Ch. N.Y., 1989-91 Recipient Dorothy Feigen Meml. award for Graphics, Am. Soc. Contemporary Artists, 1980 Mem. N.Y. Artists Equity Assn Avocations: photography, crafts. Office: Marsha Peruo Artist 55 W 14th St # 9B New York NY 10011-7400

PERUSHEK, DIANE, university librarian; BA, Lake Erie Coll.; MLS, U. Mich.; MA in Asian Studies, Columbia U. Curator Wason Collection, Cornell U., Gest Oriental Libr.; dean collection svcs. U. Tenn.; asst. univ. libr. for collection mgmt. Northwestern U.; univ. libr. U. Hawaii at Manoa Libr., 2001—. Office: U Hawaii at Manoa Libr 2550 McCarthy Mall Honolulu HI 96822 Office Phone: 808-956-7205. Office Fax: 808-956-5968. E-mail: perushek@hawaii.edu.*

PERVALL, STEPHANIE JOY, management consultant; b. San Antonio, Sept. 10, 1963; d. Jessie Elizabeth and Joseph Henry Frank Pervall. Student, Lehigh U., Bethlehem, Pa., 1981—85. Software engr. RCA Missile and Surface Radar, Moorestown, NJ, 1985—88; systems analyst AT&T Chief Fin. Orgn., Piscataway, NJ, systems devel. and support mgr. Basking Ridge, NJ, 1992—96; campus presence mgr. AT&T Chief Fin. Orgn. - Recruiting, 1994—2000; project mgr. AT&T Chief Fin. Orgn., 1996—97; contract writer AT&T Bus. Svcs., Bridgewater, NJ, 1997—2000; ops. mgr. AT&T Bus. Sales, Phila., 2000—01; sr. tech. staff mem. AT&T Consumer Svcs., Somerset, NJ, 2001—02; bus. analyst - contract specialist Chief Process Officer Orgn., Bridgewater, NJ, 2002—. Elder Willingboro Presbyn. Ch., 1999—2004, choir dir., 2003—05. Mem.: Lehigh U. Alumni Assn. (bd. dirs. 2003—05). Presbyterian. Business E-Mail: stephaniejoy@alumni.lehigh.edu.

PERYON, CHARLEEN D., education educator, consultant; b. Milw., Apr. 29, 1931; d. Raymond James Dolphin and Violet Selma Solheim Dolphin Berendes; m. Robert Edward Peryon, Nov. 21, 1953; children: Anne Marie Peryon Noonan, Robert Louis, Lynne Marie Peryon Lang. BA in Biology, Clarke Coll., Dubuque, Iowa, 1953; cert. med. tech., St. Anthony Hosp. Sch. Med. Technology, Rockford, Ill., 1954; MEd in Clin. Reading, U. Guam, 1972; PhD in Spl. Edn., Utah State U., 1979. Cert. tchr. Ill., Iowa, cons. Iowa. Tchr. sci. LaGrange (Ill.) Schs., 1966-68, Washington Sr. High Sch., Mangiloa, Guam, 1968-70; asst. prof. edn. U. Guam, Mangiloa, 1970-71; reading specialist Dept. Edn. Territory of Guam, Agana, 1971-73, state curriculum cons., 1973-75; assoc. prof. reading and spl. edn. U. Guam, Mangiloa, 1975-85; assoc. prof. reading and learning disabilities Clarke Coll., Dubuque, 1985-86; spl. edn. cons. Keystone Area Edn. Agy., Dubuque, 1986-89; prof. spl. edn. U. Dubuque, 1989—. Cons. in field. Author: Distar Teacher Aide's Handbook, 1974; co-auuthor: Reading Specialist's Handbook, 1973; mem. editorial bd. U. Guam Press, Manigloa, 1983-85; contbr. numerous articles to profl. jours. Trustee Cascade Libr.; bd. dirs. Camp Courageous, Monticello, Iowa; vol. Cascade Elem. Sch. Recipient spl. award U.S. Dept. Def. Sch. Dist., Manila, 1976, Internat. Reading Assn. of Newark, 1975. Mem. Internat. Reading Assn. (pres. Guam chpt. 1973-74, chmn. Pacific area 1973-75), Coun. for Exceptional Children (pres. 1992-93), Am. Soc. Clin. Pathologists, Phi Delta Kappa (historian 1977-78, 83-84), Chi Omicron Gamma (pres. 1982-84), Kappa Delta Pi (counselor 1993) Roman Catholic. Avocations: reading, music, cooking, travel. Home: PO Box 127 Cascade IA 52033-0127

PERZ, SALLY, academic administrator, former state legislator; m. Joseph Perz; children: Allison, Julie, Melanie, Andrea, Brian. BA, Siena Heights. Ohio State rep. Dist. 52, 1993; mgmt. cons. Perz, Inc., 1996—; exec. dir. U. Toledo. Active Boy Scouts Am. Recipient Carlson Counyt Mktg. award, 1984-93, Women of Achievement award, 1993. Mem. Toledo Club, Toledo C. of C., Toledo Rotary, Toledo Sisters Cities (exec. bd.). Home: 3245 River Rd Toledo OH 43614-4218 Office: U Toledo 2801 W Bancroft St Toledo OH 43606-3328

PESCH, ELLEN P., lawyer; BA, Barat Coll., 1986; JD, John Marshall Law Sch., 1989; LLM, DePaul U., 1991. Bar: Ill. 1989, U.S. Dist. Ct. (no. dist.) Ill. With Sidley Austin Brown & Wood, Chgo., 1989—, ptnr., 2001—. Mem.: ABA, Internat. Swaps and Derivatives Assn., Stable Value Investment Assn. Office: Sidley Austin Brown and Wood Bank One Plz 10 S Dearborn St Chicago IL 60603

PESCOSOLIDO, PAMELA JANE, graphics designer; b. Chgo., Dec. 28, 1960; d. Carl Albert Jr. and Linda Clark (Austin) P.; m. Larry Carl Vangroningen, Mar. 5, 1994 (div.); 1 child, Harley Austin. BA, Scripps Coll., 1983; JD, Vt. Law Sch., 1990. Bar: Maine 1990. Office mgr., asst. chef The Elegant Picnic, Stockbridge, Mass., 1983; receptionist, sec. Sequoia Orange County, Exeter, Calif., 1983-84; A/R clk. Tropicana Energy Co., Euless, Tex., 1984-85; owner, calligrapher Calligraphic Arts, Great Barrington, Mass., 1986-87; legal intern Pine Tree Legal Assistance, Augusta, Maine, 1989, Office of the Juvenile Defender, Montpelier, Vt., 1990; bookkeeper Badger Farming Co., Exeter, 1991—; owner, legal drafter and researcher Legal Rsch. Svc., Visalia, Calif., 1990—; owner, graphc designer Hourglass Prodns., Visalia, 1995—; owner, mgr. The Angel Within, Artists, Supplies and Gallery, Exeter, Calif. Rsch. editor Vt. Law Rev., Vt. Law Sch., South Royalton, 1989-90. Designer, graphic artist polit. propaganda for Libertarian Party of Calif.; contbr. poetry to Nat. Coll. Poetry Rev. Mem. county cen. com., chair Valley Libertarians, Libertarian Party of Calif., Visalia, 1996—; candidate Libertarian Party Dist. 19, Calif. U.S. Congress, 1996; candidate Libertarian Party Calif. State Contr., 1998. Chase scholar Vt. Law Sch., 1989. Mem. ACLU, AAUW (newsletter editor 1994-96), ABA, Nature Conservancy. Office: The Angel Within LLC 137 North E St Exeter CA 93221-1728

PESICKA, HARLENE NEAVE, mental health services professional; b. Aberdeen, SD, July 27, 1937; d. Harlan Michael and Margaret Marie (Hatzenbeller) Loye; m. William John Pesicka, Dec. 23, 1956; children: William Michael, Sandra Sue, Charlene Marie, Dennis John. BS, No. State U., 1992, MS in Edn. (Counseling and Guidance), 1997. Lic. profl. mental health counselor. Clk. J.J. Newberry, Aberdeen, 1955-56, IRS, Aberdeen, 1957-58; staff asst. Office of Environ. Health Indian Health Svc., Aberdeen, 1958-90; exec. dir. battered women shelter Resource Ctr. for Women, Aberdeen, 1990-92; exec. dir. S.D. Coalition Against Domestic Violence and Sexual Assault, Aberdeen, 1992-95; edn. aide May Overby Sch., Aberdeen, 1996; grad. asst. dept. psychology No. State U., Aberdeen, 1997; therapist, case mgr. Northeastern Mental Health Ctr., Aberdeen, 1997—2004; clinical therapist Luth. Social Svcs., 2005—. Bd. dirs. Resource Ctr. for Women; founding mother Aberdeen Area Rape Task Force, 1976, advocate, spkr., 1977—; bd. dirs. S.D. Peace and Justice, v.p., 1996, pres., 1997, 98; mem. S.D. Advocacy Network for Women, 1984—, pres., 1987; mem. various coms. and bd. dirs., Brown County United Way, chmn. bd., 1980; den mother Boy Scouts Am., also instnl. rep.; mem. S.D. NOW, 1974—, state coord., 1980-90; mgr. Fed. Women's Program Com., nat. EEO counselor, 1975-76; vol. mem. 4-person team on sexism and racism Am. Luth. Ch., N.E. S.D. Dist., 1978-80 Named S.D. Vol. of Yr., 1983, Nat. Vol. of the Yr., Dept. Health and Human Svcs., 1983; recipient award U.S. Dept. Justice, 1992, Athena award Aberdeen C. of C., 1997. Mem.: AAUW, Am. Coll. Cert. Forensic Counselors (diplomate clin. forensic counseling), Pi Gamma Mu, Phi Beta Kappa. Democrat. Home: 13529 386th Ave Aberdeen SD 57401-8754 Office Phone: 605-225-1500.

PESIN, ELLA MICHELE, journalist, public relations executive; b. North Bergen, N.J., Aug. 29, 1956; d. Edward and Helene Sylvia (Rattner) P. BA, Sarah Lawrence Coll., 1978. Press rep. CBS-TV News and Entertainment, N.Y.C., 1978-80; publicist Newsweek Mag., N.Y.C., 1980-81; freelance journalist N.Y.C., 1982-85; publicist Universal Studios MCA Inc., L.A., 1982-83; with publicity and mktg. NBC-TV News, N.Y.C., 1985-86; media exec. Burson Marsteller Pub. Rels., N.Y.C., 1986-87; prin. Pesin Pub. Rels., 1987—. Contbg. editor Cable Age mag., TV Radio Age mag., Advt. Forum, Facts Figures & Film, Advt. Compliance Svc.; syndicated newspaper columnist. Active Israel Bonds/United Jewish Appeal, N.Y.C., Rudolph Giuliani for N.Y.C. Mayor campaign. Mem. Pub. Rels. Soc. Am., Women in Comm., Publicity Club N.Y., Healthcare Pub. Rels. and Mktg. Soc. Avocations: photography, sculpture, modern dance, tennis, skiing. Home and Office: 1483 3rd Ave Apt 22C New York NY 10028 E-mail: eem75p@aol.com.

PESMEN, SANDRA (MRS. HAROLD WILLIAM PESMEN), editor, educator; b. Chgo., Mar. 26, 1931; d. Benjamin S. and Emma (Lipschultz) Zuckerman; m. Harold W. Pesmen, Aug. 16, 1952; children: Bethann, Curtis. BS, U. Ill., 1952. Reporter Radio and Community News Service, Chgo., 1952-53; wire editor Champaign-Urbana (Ill.) Courier, 1953; reporter, feature writer Lerner Chgo. N. Side Newspapers, 1953-55; stringer corr. Wayne (Mich.) Eagle, 1958-61; reporter, feature writer Chgo. Daily News, 1968-78; features editor Crain's Chgo. Business mag., 1978-89; corp. features editor Crain Communications, Inc., 1989-95; tchr. feature writing Northwestern U. Evening Sch., 1972-81. Author: Writing for the Media, 1983, Dr. Job's Complete Career Guide, 1995; editor: Career News Service; author syndicated column Dr. Job, 1985—. Recipient Golden Key award Ill. Mental Health Dept., 1966, 71, award Inst. Psychoanalysis, 1971, Penny Mo. award, 1978, Stick o'Type award Chgo. Newspaper Guild, 1978, award AP, 1975, Peter Lisagor award Soc. Profl. Journalists, 1991; inductee Chgo. Journalism Hall of Fame, 1997. Home: 2811 Fern Ave Northbrook IL 60062-5809

PESNER, CAROLE MANISHIN, art gallery owner; b. Boston, Aug. 5, 1937; m. Robert Pesner (dec. 1983); children: Ben, Jonah; m. Martin Cherkasky, 1995 (dec. 1997). BA, Smith Coll., 1959. Asst. dir. Kraushaar Galleries, Inc., N.Y.C., 1959-86, dir., 1986-90, pres., 1991—. Author, editor publs., catalogues in field. Mem. Art Dealers Assn. Am., Internat. Fine Print Dealers Assn. Office: Kraushaar Galleries Inc 724 5th Ave New York NY 10019-4106 Office Phone: 212-307-5730. Business E-Mail: info@kraushaargalleries.com.

PESTERFIELD, LINDA CAROL, retired principal; b. Pauls Valley, Okla., May 3, 1939; d. D.J. and Geneva Lewis (Sheegog) Butler; m. W.C. Peterfield, Aug. 30, 1958; children: Ginger Carol, Walt James, Jason Kent. Student, East Ctrl. State U., Ada, Okla., 1957, 76, 79; BS, Okla. State U., 1961; postgrad., Ottawa (Kans.) U., 1970, Okla. U., 1979. Tchr. Sumner Elem. Sch., Perry, Okla., 1961-62, Whitebead D-16, Pauls Valley, Okla., 1964-65, Cen. Heights Unified, Ottawa, Kans., 1969-71; prin., tchr. Whitebead D-16, Pauls Valley, 1975-91; adminstrv. asst., curriculum dir. Pauls Valley Sch., P.V., 1991—2003; ret., 2003. Mem. profl. standard bd. State Dept. Edn., Okla., 1988—; presenter in field. Bd. dirs. Positively Pauls Valley, 1987-97, Pauls Valley Gen. Hosp., 2004—; county chmn. Nat. and Okla. 4-H Fund Drive, Garvin County, Okla., 1987-88; mem. orgnl. com. C-CAP-Child Abuse Prevention Orgn., Pauls Valley, 1987—; mem. vision 2000 com. Garvin County Assn. Svcs.; vol. Pauls Valley Main St., 2003-05; mem. women's com. Garvin County Farm Bur., 2005— Named to Gov.'s Honor Roll Recognition and Appreciation for Community Activities, Pauls Valley, Okla., 1985-86; named Pauls Valley Citizen of Yr., 1996; Paul Harris fellow, 1997. Mem. Coop. Coun. Okla. Sch. Adminstrn., Whitebead Ednl. Assn., Okla. Orgn. Dependent Sch., Okla. Assn. Elem. Sch. Prins., AAUW, All Sports Club (v.p. 1984-89, pres. 1985, 90), Okla. Heritage Assn., Pauls Valley Hist. Soc., Pauls Valley C. of C. (pres. 1997, pres. exec. bd. dirs. 1998—), Pauls Valley Alumni (pres. 2005-06), State Found. for Acad. Excellence (forum com.), Rotary (bd. dirs. 1993-96, 1999-2001, 03-06, Paul Harris fellow 1997), Delta Kappa Gamma (past local auditor, parliamentarian, v.p. 2004—, pres. 1979-96, 2005-06), Phi Delta Kappa Democrat. Mem. Ch. of Christ. Home: RR 3 Box 306 Pauls Valley OK 73075-9232 Personal E-mail: wpesterfield@sbcglobal.net.

PETCHIK, MARIAN, mathematics educator; b. Balt., Md., Feb. 26, 1948; d. Ralph and Marian Petchik. BA, Immaculate Coll., 1970; MEd, The Johns Hopkins U., 1975, MS in Adminstrn. & Supervision, 1979. Math. tchr. Balt. County Bd. Edn., 1971—2001. Vol. St. Joseph's Hosp., Balt., 2001—; mem. project attend Dept. of Aging, Balt., 2001—; eucharistic min. St. Ursula Ch., Balt., 1990—, pastoral outreach min., 2001—. Mem.: Catholic Alumni Club (pres. 1980), Delta Kappa Gamma (pres. 2002—04, 2006—). Democrat. Roman Catholic. Avocations: tennis, bicycling. Home: 9603 L Amberleigh Ln Perry Hall MD 21128-9608

PETERA, ANNE PAPPAS, state official; b. Richmond, Va., Feb. 13, 1950; d. Evangel Thomas and Margaret Theresa (McGuire) Pappas; m. Ronald Petera, Sept. 15, 1968; 1 child, Paul Evangel. BS, Va. Commonwealth U., 1980; grad., Realtors Inst. Br. officer Ctrl. Fidelity Bank, Richmond, 1972-79; asst. v.p. Signet Bank, Richmond, 1979-85; sales assoc. Hermitage Realty, Richmond, 1985-92; assoc. broker Napier Old Colony, Richmond, 1992-95, Bowers, Nelms & Fonville & Jefferson-Jones, Richmond, 1995-96; chair Va. Dept. Alcoholic Beverage Control, 1996-97; sec. Commonwealth of Va., 1998—2002; chief of staff to Atty. Gen. of Va., 2002—. Mem. faculty Richmond Assn. Realtors Sch. Real Estate, 1991-96; bd. visitors Va. Commonwealth U., 2001-04, vice rector, 2003-04. Vice-chmn. Hanover (Va.) County Rep. Com., 1990-92, chmn., 1992-94; chmn. 1st Congl. Dist., Rep. Party Va., Richmond, 1994-98, budget dir., 1996-98, treas. 1998-2001; mem. Rep. Nat. Com., 2001—. Named Disting. Achiever, Richmond Assn. Realtors, 1986, 87, 89, 90, 91, 92, 93, 94. Mem. Nat. Alcohol Beverage Control Assn. (dir. 1996-98), Nat. Assn. Realtors, Nat. Assn. Bank Women. Republican. Roman Catholic. Avocations: golf, reading, travel. Office: Office of the Atty Gen 900 E Main St Richmond VA 23219-2725 E-mail: annepetera@aol.com.

PETERMAN, DONNA COLE, communications executive; b. St. Louis, Nov. 9, 1947; d. William H. Cole and Helen A. Morris; m. John A. Peterman, Feb. 7, 1970. BA in Journalism, U. Mo., 1969; MBA, U. Chgo., 1984. Mgr. employee comm. Sears Merchandise Group, Chgo., 1975-80; affairs and mktg. comm. Seraco Real Estate, Chgo., 1980-82; dir. corp. comm. Sears, Roebuck and Co., Chgo., 1982-85; sr. v.p., dir. corp. comm. Dean Witter Fin. Svcs. Group, N.Y., 1985-88; sr. v.p., mng. dir. Hill and Knowlton, Inc., Chgo., 1988-94, exec. v.p. N.Y.C., 1994-96; sr. v.p., dir. corp. comm. Paine Webber Group, Inc., N.Y.C., 1996-2000; mng. dir., regional head comms. and mktg. The Americas, UBS Americas Inc., 2000—03; sr. v.p., dir. corp. comm. PNC Fin. Svcs. Group Inc., 2003—. Media chair DeKalb County Comm., Ga., 1975; media dir., Mo. Atty. Gen., 1971, Rep. Govs. Conf., 1974; copywriter Govt. of Mo., 1971. Chmn. bd. trustees Securities Industry Found. for Investor Edn. Mem. Pub. Rels. Soc. Am., Arthur Page Soc., Pub. Rels. Seminar, Edgewood Country Club, Palmetto Pines Country Club, The Wise Men. Republican. Roman Catholic. Avocations: tennis, golf, sailing, skiing, bridge. Office: The PNC Fin Svcs Group Inc 1 PNC Plaza 249 5th Ave Pittsburgh PA 15222-2707

PETERS, BARBARA WATERMAN, artist, educator; b. Topeka, Nov. 3, 1944; d. L.E. Clifton Bailey and Gertrude Minnie McFarland; m. John Herman Waterman, Dec. 21, 1965 (div. Dec. 1985); m. Larry Dean Peters, May 30, 1986. BFA, Washburn U., 1973; MFA, Kans. State U., 1998. Adj. instr. Washburn U., Topeka, 1985—88, adj. asst. prof., 1989—96, 1999—2001; grad. tchg. asst. Kans. State U., Manhattan, 1997—98, temporary asst. prof., 2004—, asst. prof. painting, 2004—05. Mus. specialist ednl. svcs. Mulvane Art Mus., Topeka, 1987; faculty advisor Washburn Art Students Assn., Topeka, 1994-96; guest curator Water Marks exhbn. Mulvane Art Mus., Topeka, 1995-96; exhbn. juror in field; spkr., reviewer in field. One-woman shows include Bedyk Gallery, Kansas City, Mo., 1983, 88, Collective Art Gallery, Topeka, 1988-90, 96-97, 1999-2000, 2002-2004, 2006, Yost Gallery-Highland (Kans.) C.C., 1989, 95, Art Craft Gallery, Denver, 1994-95, 97, Fourth St. Gallery, Kansas City, 1997, Michael Cross Gallery, Kansas City, 1999-2000, Wichita Ctr. Arts, 2001, Kanas Artist Gallery, Mulvane Art Mus., 2002; group shows include Holman Art Gallery-Trenton State Coll., 1979, N.Mex. Art League, Albuquerque, 1980, Nat. Soc. Painters, N.Y., 1980 (Michael Engle Meml. award), Ball State U. Art Gallery, Muncie, Ind., 1981, Portsmouth (Va.) Cmty. Ctr., 1982, Nelson-Atkins Mus., Kansas City, 1982, Owensboro (Ky.) Mus. Fine Art, 1982 (award), Joslyn Art Mus., Omaha, 1988, others, Women's Conf., Beijing, 1995, Jan Weiner Gallery, Kansas City, 1995, The Columbian Art Gallery, Wamego, Kans., 1997, 2002, Topeka and Shawnee County Pub. Libr., 1997, 2002, 05, Strecker Gallery, Manhattan, Kans., 1999-2000, Cedar Rapids (Iowa) Mus. Art, 1997, Wichita Ctr. for the Arts, 2000, 02, Birger Sandzen Gallery, Lindsborg, Kans., 2001, 2006, U. Kans. Art and Design Gallery, 2002, Strecker-Nelson Gallery, Manhattan, Kans., 2002, 05, 06, Mulvane Art Mus., Topeka, 2003, Emporia Art Ctr., Kans., 2003, Gallery of Framewoods, Topeka, 2004, 05, Kemper Gallery, Kans. State U., 2005, Ctrl. Mo. State U., 2006, Nat. League Am. PEN Women, 2006, Foundry Art Centre, St. Charles, Mo., 2006 (award), Kans./Mo. Artists, Carter Art Ctr., Kansas City, Mo., 2006; visual artist Andrew J. and Georgia Neese Gray Theatre, Washburn U., 1999—; contbr. articles to profl. jours. Vol. art gallery Topeka and Shawnee County Pub. Libr., 1986—; panelist Kans. Arts Commn., Kans. Presswomen, 1990—, N.E. Kans. Music Tchrs. Assn./Topeka Music Tchrs. Assn., 2004; mem. ad hoc com. Kans. Arts Commn., 2002—04, mem. fellowship selection panel, 2004, mem. arts in edn. grants selection panel, 2006; mem. ad hoc com. Topeka Cmty. Found., 2002—03; bd. dirs. Arts Coun. Topeka, 2002—. Recipient Outstanding Achievement award, Am. Inst. Banking, Topeka, 1977, assistantship in lithography, Kans. Arts Commn., 1981, Woman of Distinction in the Arts award, Kaw Valley Girl Scouts, Topeka, 1996, Artist's Residency award, The Raymer Soc., 2001—04, Cert. of Recognition Outstanding Contributions, State Kans., 2003. Mem.: Kemper Mus. Contemporary Art, Am. Arts Action Fund, Nat. League Am. PEN Women, Birger Sandzén Meml. Gallery, Am. Craft Coun., Manhattan Arts Ctr., Assn. Cmty. Arts Agys. of Kans. (bd. dir. 2004—06, sec.-treas. 2006—), Lawrence Art Ctr., The Collective (charter, treas. 1987—89, v.p. 1990—94, 1999—2000, newsletter editor 2000—, pres. 2001—06), Mulvane Art Mus., St. Louis Artists Guild, Kansas City Artists Coalition, Chgo. Artists' Coalition, Nat. Mus. Women in the Arts, Raymer Soc. (bd. dir.), Kans. Authors' Club (conv. workshop presenter 2004, selection com. J. Donald Coffin award 2004—05, v.p. dist. 1 2005—, pres. dist. 1 2006), Kans. Citizens for Arts, Libr. Friends of Art Topeka and Shawnee County Pub. Libr., Friends of Art Bd. Beach Mus. Art (collections com. 1997—), Catharine Lorillard Wolfe Art Club (assoc.). Avocations: reading, writing, travel. Home: 2223 SW Knollwood Dr Topeka KS 66611-1623 E-mail: barbara.r.peters@att.net.

PETERS, BERNADETTE (BERNADETTE LAZZARA), actress; b. Queens, N.Y., Feb. 28, 1948; d. Peter and Marguerite (Maltese) Lazzara; m. Michael Wittenberg, July 20, 1996 (dec. Sept. 26, 2005). Student, Quintano Sch. for Young Profls., N.Y.C. Ind. actress, entertainer, 1957—. Appeared on TV series All's Fair, 1976-77; frequent guest appearances on TV; (films) The Longest Yard, 1974, Silent Movie, 1976, Vigilant Force, 1976, W.C. Fields and Me, 1976, Silent Movie, 1976, The Jerk, 1979, Heartbeeps, 1981, Tulips, 1981, Pennies from Heaven, 1981 (Golden Globe award best actress), Annie, 1982, Slaves of New York, 1989, Pink Cadillac, 1989, Impromptu, 1991, Alice, 1990, Anastasia (voice), 1997, Cinderella, 1997, Snow Days, 1999, Prince Charming, 2001, Bobbie's Girl, 2002, A Few Good Years, 2002, It Runs in the Family, 2003; (TV movies) Cinderella, ABC-TV, 1997, Holiday in Your Heart, 1997; (stage appearances) This is Google, 1957, The Most Happy Fella, 1959, Gypsy, 1961, Curly McDimple, 1967, Johnny No-Trump, 1967, George M!, 1968 (Theatre World award, 1968), Dames at Sea, 1968 (Drama Desk award, 1968), La Strada, 1969, On the Town, 1971, Tartuffe, 1972, Mack and Mabel, 1974, Sally and Marsha, 1982, Sunday in the Park with George, 1983-85 (Tony nom., 1983), Song and Dance, 1985-86 (Drama League award best actress, 1985, Tony award best actress, 1986, Drama Desk award best actress, 1986), Into the Woods, 1987, The Goodbye Girl, 1992-93, Annie Get Your Gun 1998-1999 (Tony award best actress, 1999, Outer Critics Circle award best actress, 1999, Drama Desk award best actress, 1999), Gypsy, 2003; TV mini-series The Odyssey, 1997; rec. artist: (MCA Records) Bernadette Peters, 1980, Now Playing, 1981; CD's include I'll Be Your Baby Tonight, Angel Records, 1996 (Grammy nomination), Sondheim Etc: Bernadette Peters Live at Carnegie Hall, Angel Records, 1997 (Grammy nom.), solo concert Radio City Music Hall, 2002. Founder Ann. Broadway Barks fundraiser. Recipient Hasty Pudding Theatrical award, 1987 Woman of Yr. award, Sara Siddons Actress of Yr. award, 1993-94, Actors Fund medal for artistic achievement, 1999, NYC Parks Citizen award, 2006; named Woman of Yr., Police Athletic League, 1999; named to Theatre Hall of Fame. Office: William Morris Agency c/o Jeff Hunter 1325 Ave of the Americas 15th Fl New York NY 10019*

PETERS, CAROL ANN DUDYCHA, counselor; b. Ripon, Wis., Dec. 23, 1938; d. George John and Martha (Malek) Dudycha; m. Milton Eugene Peters, Aug. 27, 1960 AB, Wittenberg U., 1960, MEd, 1963; leadership devel. cert., Ctr. for Creative Leadership, Greensboro, N.C., 1986; postgrad., U. Toledo, 1973—97, U. Findlay, 1997—99. Lic. profl. counselor, Ohio; nat. cert. counselor, nat. cert. career counselor Nat. Bd. Cert. Counselors, Inc.; cert. basic critical incident stress mgmt. Internat. Critical Incident Stress Found., 1999. Tchr. Springfield City Schs., Ohio, 1960—62, Mad River-Green Local Schs., Springfield, 1962—63; counselor Napoleon Area Schs., Ohio, 1963—70, Findlay City Sch., Ohio, 1970—2000; field counselor Career Relocation Corp. Am., Armonk, 1992—95, 1998—99; sr. lectr. U. Findlay, 1999—2002. Cons., prin. Peters and Peters, Findlay, 1979—; leader Creative Edn. Found., Buffalo, 1980-91, colleague, Hadley, Mass., 1985—; founder ednl. corp. Career Info. Bur. Hancock County, 1974 Pres. Big Bros./Big Sisters Hancock County, 1982-83; bd. dirs. Citizens Opposing Drug Abuse, Findlay, 1982-2005; advisor, leader Hancock Addictions Prevention for Youth, 1985-91; edn. com. Hancock County Cmty. Devel. Found., 1990-93, Findlay/Hancock County Am. 2000 New Sch. Design Team, 1991-92; mem. Hancock County Crisis Response Team, 1991-97, 99—; assets/needs assessment com. United Way, 1997-98; mem. Findlay Juvenile Diversion Task Force, 1997-98; mem. City of Findlay Mayor's Cmty. Issues Visioning Com., 2004-05 Named One of Outstanding Young Women Am., 1967, Outstanding Women in Edn., Bus. and Profl. Women, 1983; recipient Outstanding Citizenship award The Lincoln Ctr., Findlay, 1989, Meritorious Svc. award Big Bros./Big Sisters Hancock County, 1988 Mem. ACA, AAUW, NEA (life), Nat. Career Devel. Assn., Ohio Ret. Tchrs. Assn. (life), Ohio Counseling Assn., Findlay-Hancock County C. of C. (sec. edn. com. 1984-90), Ohio Career Devel. Assn., Black Studies and Libr. Assn. (trustee 2005—, sec. bd. trustees 2006—). Lutheran. Avocations: flower arranging, cooking.

PETERS, CAROL BEATTIE TAYLOR (MRS. FRANK ALBERT PETERS), mathematician; b. Washington, May 10, 1932; d. Edwin Lucius and Lois (Beattie) Taylor; B.S., U. Md., 1954, M.A., 1958; m. Frank Albert Peters, Feb. 26, 1955; children— Thomas, June, Erick, Victor. Group mgr. Tech. Operations, Inc., Arlington, Va., 1957-62, sr. staff scientist, 1964-66; supervisory analyst Datatrol Corp., Silver Spring, Md., 1962; project dir. Computer Concept, Inc., Silver Spring, 1963-64; mem. tech. staff, then mem. sr. staff Informatics Inc., Bethesda, Md., 1966-70, mgr. systems projects, 1970-71, tech. dir., 1971-76; sr. tech. dir. Ocean Data Systems, Inc., Rockville, Md., 1976-83; dir. Informatics Gen. Co., 1983-89; pres. Carol Peters Assocs., 1989—. Home and Office: 12311 Glen Mill Rd Potomac MD 20854-1928 E-mail: carol-peters@comcast.net.

PETERS, ELEANOR WHITE, retired mental health nurse; b. Highland Park, Mich., Aug. 11, 1920; d. Alfred Mortimer and Jane Ann (Evans) White; m. William J. Peters, 1947 (div. 1953); children: Susannah J., William J. (dec.). BA, Jersey City State Coll., 1968; postgrad., U. Del., 1969-70; MS, SUNY, New Paltz, 1983. RN, N.J., N.Y. Staff various hosps., N.J., 1941-58; indsl. nurse Abex, Mahwah, N.J., 1958-68; nurse Liberty (N.Y.) Ctrl. Sch., 1971-76; coord. practical nurse program Hudson County C.C., Jersey City, 1979-80; cmty. mental health nurse Letchworth Village, Thiells, N.Y., 1981-96; ret., 1996. Historian, Bishop House Found., Saddle River, N.J. Mem. AAUW (pres. Liberty-Monticello br. 1988-92), Am. Sch. Health Assn., Alpha Delta Kappa (sec. Mu chpt. 1973-75), Sigma Theta Tau (Kappa Eta chpt.). Republican. Lutheran. Avocations: antiques, history, travel, education of children.

PETERS, ELIZABETH ANN HAMPTON, retired nursing educator; b. Detroit, Sept. 27, 1934; d. Grinsfield Taylor and Ida Victoria (Jones) Hampton; m. James Marvin Peters, Dec. 1, 1956; children: Douglas Taylor, Sara Elizabeth. Diploma, Berea Coll. Hosp. Sch. Nursing, Berea, Ky., 1956; BSN, Wright State U., Dayton, Ohio, 1975; MSN, Ohio State U., Columbus, 1978. Therapist, nurse Eastway, Inc., Dayton, Ohio, 1979-81; therapist, family counseling svc. Good Samaritan-Cmty. Mental Health Ctr., Dayton, Ohio, 1981-83; instr. Wright State U. Sch. Nursing, Dayton, 1983-84; clin. nurse specialist, pain mgmt. program UPSA, Inc., Dayton, 1983-86; staff nurse Hospice of Dayton, Inc., 1985-86, dir. vol. svcs., 1986-89, dir. bereavement svcs., 1986-87; asst. prof. Cmty. Hosp. Sch. Nursing, Springfield, Ohio, 1990-93, prof., 1993-97; ret., 1997; parish nurse Honey Creek Presbyn. Ch., 1998—2003. Co-author (with others): Oncologic Pain, 1987. Mem. Clark County Mental Health Bd., Springfield, 1986-95; mem. New Carlisle (Ohio) Bd. Health, 1990-2003. Mem.: Sigma Theta Tau. Home: 402 Flora Ave New Carlisle OH 45344-1329 E-mail: annjimpeters@sbcglobal.net.

PETERS, ELLEN ASH, retired judge; b. Berlin, Mar. 21, 1930; arrived in U.S., 1939, naturalized, 1947; d. Ernest Edward and Hildegard (Simon) Ash; m. Phillip I. Blumberg; children: David Bryan, James Douglas, Julie Haden Dreisch. BA with honors, Swarthmore Coll., 1951, LLD (hon.), 1983; LLB cum laude, Yale U., 1954, MA (hon.), 1964, LLD (hon.), 1985, U. Hartford, 1983, Georgetown U., 1984, Conn. Coll., 1985, N.Y. Law Sch., 1985; HLD (hon.), St. Joseph Coll., 1986; LLD (hon.), Colgate U., 1986, Trinity Coll., 1987, Bates Coll., 1987, Wesleyan U., 1987, DePaul U., 1988; HLD (hon.), Albertus Magnus Coll., 1990; LLD (hon.), U. Conn., 1992, U. Rochester, 1994, Detroit Mercy Coll. Law, 2001. Bar: Conn. 1957. Law clk. to judge U.S. Circuit Ct., 1954-55; assoc. in law U. Calif., Berkeley, 1955-56; prof. law Yale U., New Haven, 1956-78, adj. prof., 1978-84; assoc. justice Conn. Supreme Ct., Hartford, 1978-84, chief justice, 1984-96; ret., 1996. Judge trial referee Appellate Ct., Hartford, Conn., 2000—. Author: Commercial Transactions: Cases, Texts, and Problems, 1971, Negotiable Instruments Primer, 1974; contbr. articles to profl. jours. Bd. dirs. Nat. Ctr. State Cts., 1992—96, chmn., 1994; bd. mgrs. Swarthmore Coll., 1970—81; trustee Yale-New Haven Hosp., 1981—86, Yale Corp., 1986—92; mem. conf. Chief Justices, 1984—, pres., 1994; hon. chmn. U.S. Constl. Bicentennial Com., 1986—91; mem. Conn. Permanent Commn. on Status of Women, 1973—74, Conn. Bd. Pardons, 1978—80, Conn. Law Revision Commn., 1978—84; bd. dirs. Hartford Found., 1997—2002. Named Laura A. Johnson Woman of the Yr., Hartford Coll., 1996; recipient Ella Grasso award, 1982, Jud. award, Conn. Trial Lawyers Assn., 1982, citation of merit, Yale Law Sch., 1983, Pioneer Woman award, Hartford Coll. Women, 1988, Disting. Svc. award, U. Conn. Law Sch. Alumni Assn., 1993, Raymond E. Baldwin Pub. Svc. award, Quinnipiac Coll. Law Sch., 1995, Disting. Svc. award, Conn. Law Tribune, 1996, Nat. Ctr. State Cts., 1996. Mem.: ABA, Am. Philos. Coun., Am. Acad. Arts and Scis., Am. Law Inst. (coun.), Conn. Bar Assn. (Jud. award 1992, Spl. award 1996). Office: Appellate Ct 75 Elm St Hartford CT 06106-4431 Office Fax: 860-713-2216.

PETERS, JANICE G. SPOTH, elementary school educator; b. Buffalo, July 5, 1941; d. Robert John and Dolores Janice (Vaarwerk) Spoth; m. Carl Jackson Peters, July 25, 1964 (dec.); children: Michelle Ann, Robert Joseph, Charles Martin. BS, SUNY, Buffalo, 1963; postgrad., U. South Fla. Cert. elem. tchr., Fla. Tchr. Paco County Sch. System, Land O'Lakes, Fla.; elem. tchr. Sarasota County Sch. System, Sarasota, Fla., Erie County Sch. System, Tonawanda, N.Y., Centennial Elem. Sch., Pasco County Sch. System, Dade City, Fla. Mem. So. Sch. Accreditation Team; mentor Collegial Coach; thematic unit writer dept. edn. U. South Fla., Pasco County; migrant lead tchr.; team leader, coord. Challengers team; coord. 5 Star Sch. awards; lead Literacy Team, 2005-06. Pub. Centennial newspaper. Dir. religious edn., liturgy leader, lector; den mother. Recipient Best Practices for Lang. Enriched Pupils award, 2000; named Jr. Woman of Yr., Pasco Elem. Sch., 1974, 80, Tchr. of Yr., Centennial Elem. Sch., 1994-95, Walmart Tchr. of Yr., 2006. Mem. Alpha Delta Kappa (pres. Alphi Phi chpt.).

PETERS, JEAN KOH, law educator; AB, Radcliffe Coll., 1979; JD, Harvard U., 1982. Bar: NY 1983, Conn. 1989. Law clk. to Hon. William P. Gray US Dist. Ct., LA, 1982—83; staff atty. Juvenile Rights Div., Legal Aid Soc. NY, 1983—85; asst. clin. prof., assoc. dir. Child Advocacy Clinic, Columbia U., 1986—89; assoc. clin. prof. Yale U., New Haven, 1989—93, clin. prof., 1993—. Contbr. Representing Children in Child Protective Proceedings: Ethical & Practical Dimensions, 2001; contbr. articles to law jours. Office: Yale Law Sch PO Box 208215 New Haven CT 06520 E-mail: jean.peters@yale.edu.

PETERS, JENNIFER R., music educator; b. Pontiac, Mich., Dec. 5, 1968; d. Larry Troy Moehlman and Marjorie Carol Sullivan. B in Music Edn., Mich. State U., 1991; M in Ednl. Adminstrn., Chapman U., Orange, Calif., 1995. Cert. tchr. Mich., Calif., N.D., Colo., Fla. Music tchr. Lompoc (Calif.) Unified Schs., 1992—95, Walhalla (N.D.) Sch. Dist., 1995—97; music store salesperson Colorado Springs (Colo.) Graner Music, 2001—02; music tchr. Brentwood Mid. Sch., Greeley, Colo., 2002—03; band dir. Brevard County Schs., Palm Bay, Fla., 1998—2001, 2003—. Mem. Humane Soc. of U.S., 1992—. Mem.: Colo. Music Educators Assn., Fla. Music Educators Assn., Music Educators Nat. Conf., Fla. Band Assn. Office Phone: 321-952-5800.

PETERS, JOANNA EILENE, music educator; d. Lawrence Edward and Anna Ruth Robinson; m. Gary W. Peters, July 8, 2000. MusB, Shenandoah U., 2000. Lic. tchr. Va. Music tchr. Taunton (Mass.) Pub. Schs., 2000—01, Mullein Hill Christian Acad., Lakeville, Mass., 2001—02; mid. sch. choral dir. Culpeper (Va.) Pub. Schs., 2002—04; h.s. choral dir. Spotsylvania (Va.) Pub. Schs., 2004—. Vol. Potter League Animal Shelter, Newport, RI, 2002; pianist Good Hope Bapt. Ch., Spotsylvania, 2003—05. Named Student Tchr. of Yr., Shenandoah Conservatory, 2000. Mem.: Am. Choral Dirs. Assn., Music Educators Nat. Conf. Office: Spotsylvania HS 6975 Courthouse Rd Spotsylvania VA 22553

PETERS, JUDY GALE, manufacturing executive, educator; b. Dec. 13, 1941; d. Thomas Delbert and Vicie Clarice (Mundy) Hankins; m. Jesse Everitt Lobdell, Jr., Dec. 2, 1963 (div. Jan. 1975); 1 child, Jesse Everett III; m. Kenneth Rae Peters, June 6, 1975 (div. Dec. 1984) 1 stepchild, Kenneth Phillip. BS, Radford Coll., 1964. Tchr. county schs. Licking County, Ohio, 1964-73; buyer Hydrostrut Co., Newark, Ohio, 1974-76, Anchor Coupling Co., Hebron, Ohio, 1976-78; expeditor Diebold Inc., Hebron, 1978-80; buyer, 1980-88; supr. purchasing, 1988-91; strategic procurement mgr. North Canton, Ohio, 1991-97; materials mgr. PSD divsn. Diebold, Inc., Canton, Ohio, 1997—2000, sr. global materials mgr., 2000—. Advisor 4-H Club Band, Licking County, 1965-67. Named Tchr. of Yr., Northridge Local Schs., 1972. Mem. NAFE, Am. Soc. Mfg. Engrs., Soc. Mfg. Engrs., Am. Choral Dirs. Assn. Ops. Mgmt., Newark Women's Bowling Assn. (bd. dirs.), Young Am. Bowling Assn. (bd. dirs. Licking County, Ohio), Am. Soc. Profl. and Exec. Women. Avocations: reading, writing, dance, bowling. Home: 4882 South Blvd NW # 7 Canton OH 44718-1958 Business E-Mail: petersj1@diebold.com.

PETERS, JULIE ANNE, writer; b. Jamestown, N.YU., Jan. 16, 1952; BA, Colo. Women's Coll. Rsch. asst., computer programmer Tracom Corp., Denver, 1975—84; computer sys. designer Electronic Data Sys., 1985—88; ednl. asst. Jefferson County Sch. Dist., Lakewood, Colo., 1990—94; writer, 1994—. Author: The Stinky Sneakers Contest, 1992, Risky Friends, 1993, B.J.'s Billion-Dollar Bet, 1994, How Do You Spell G-E-E-K?, 1996, Revenge of the Snob Squad, 1998, Romance of the Snob Squad, 1999, Love Me, Love My Broccoli, 1999, Define Normal, 2000, A Snitch in the Snob Squad, 2001, Keeping You a Secret, 2003, Luna: A Novel, 2004 (Nat. Book Award finalist, 2004). Recipient Top Hand Award, Colo. Authors' League. Address: 14 Twilight Dr Lakewood CO 80215 E-mail: juliepeters@juno.com.

PETERS, MARGARET ANNETTE, English language educator; BA in English, Tex. A&M U., College Station, 1988; MA in English, Claremont Grad. Sch., Calif., 1993. Asst. prof. English, Santa Fe C.C., 1996—, chair dept. English and speech, 2004—. Adviser Phi Theta Kappa, Santa Fe, 2001—03. Achievements include Gov. of New Mexico declared December 12, 2001, Margaret A. Peters Day throughout the state of New Mexico to commend her work as a teacher. Avocations: book arts, crafts, painting and drawing, journaling. Office: Santa Fe CC 6401 Richards Ave Santa Fe NM 87508 Office Phone: 505-428-1372. Personal E-mail: margpeters@gmail.com. Business E-Mail: mpeters@sfccnm.edu.

PETERS, MARIE T., retired art educator; b. Brockton, Mass., May 27, 1940; d. Louis and Philomena DiMestico; m. Henry Frances Peters, Aug. 8, 1965; children: Michelle, Regina, Angela. BFA, Mass. Coll. Art, Boston, 1962; MA, Rosary Coll., Florence, Italy, 1964; cert. advanced grad. study, Bridgewater State Coll., Mass., 1995. Cert. tchr. Mass. Art tchr. Silver Lake Regional Schs., Kingston, Mass., 1986—2002; ret., 2002. Adj. faculty grad. divsn. Lesley Coll., Cambridge, Mass., 1988—2000, Endicott Coll., Mass., 2001; mem. arts devel. com. Mass. Comprehensive Assessment Sys., 1995—96; mem. visual arts panel Mass. Tchg. Tests, 1998, mem. qualifying score panel visual art, 98. Exhibitions include Nat. Assn. Women Artists, NYC, 1990—, traveling exch. shows, Australia, South Shore Arts Ctr., Cohasset, Mass., 1995—, Monotpye Guild New Eng., 2005, Represented in permanent collections Danforth Mus., Framingham, Mass. Chmn. Mass. Arts

Lottery, Pembroke, 1982—85. Recipient Medal of Honor, 1st prize printmaking, Nat. Assn. Women Artists, NY, 1993, 1994; Smithsonian grantee, Nat. Mus. Am. Art, Washington, 1995. Roman Catholic. Home: PO Box 538 Bryantville MA 02327

PETERS, MARY ANN, ambassador; m. Tim McMahon; 2 children. BA, Santa Clara U.; M Internat. Studies, Johns Hopkins U. With U.S. Fgn. Svc., 1975—, dep. chief of mission Sofia, Bulgaria, econ. counselor Moscow, prin. officer Burma, vice consul Frankfurt, Germany, dep. dir. Office of Pakistan, Afghanistan and Bangladesh Affairs, U.S. State Dept., 1988—90, dep. chief of mission U.S. Embassy Canada, ambassador to Bangladesh Dhaka, 2000—; dir. European and Can. affairs Nat. Security Coun. White House, Washington. Office: DOS Amb 6120 Dhaka Pl Washington DC 20521-6120

PETERS, MARY E., secretary of transportation; b. Phoenix, Dec. 4, 1948; m. Terry Peters; 3 children. BA in Mgmt., U. Phoenix; attended govt. program for state & local govt., Harvard U. Various positions Ariz. Dept. Transp., 1983—98, dir., 1998—2001; adminstr. Fed. Highway Adminstrn., US Dept. Transp., Washington, 2001—05; nat. dir. for transp. policy, cons. HDR, Inc., Phoenix, 2005—06; sec. US Dept. Transp., Washington, 2006—. Past bd. dirs. Project Challenge, Nat. Guard; past chair adv. bd. Hwy. Expansion Loan Program; mem. Gt. Ariz. Develop. Authority; past mem. Growing Smarter Commn. Named Women of Yr., Women's Transp. Seminar, 2004; named one of Most Influential Person in Ariz. Transp., Ariz. Bus. Jour.; recipient George S. Bartlett award, 2005. Mem.: We. Assn. State Hwy. Transp. Officials, Am. Assn. State Hwy. Officials (past chair standing com. on planning, assest mgmt. task force, reauthorization steering com. 2001). Office: US Dept Transp 400 7th St SW Rm 10200 Washington DC 20590*

PETERS, REDEBRA EVYN, music educator; b. Richland Ctr., N.J., July 25, 1972; d. Richard Alan and Pauline Joy Boggs; m. Norman Jules Peters III, Oct. 4, 1997; children: Derek Norman, Caitlyn Joy. MusB in Edn., Lakeland Coll., Sheboygan, Wis., 1994. Tchr. music New Luth. H.S., Green Bay, Wis., 1996—98, Amherst Mid. Sch. and H.S., Wis., 1998—2001; tchr. music, drama Mishicot Mid. Sch. and H.S., Wis., 2001—. Dir. musicals Amherst and Mishicot H.S., Wis., 1999—; adjudicator solo ensemble Wis. State Music, 2000—; founder, coord. Mishicot Cmty. Variety Show Mishicot H.S., 2002—. Singer: Dudley Birder Chorale, 1997—; dir.: Mishicot Cmty. Choir, 2002—, Mishicot Cmty. Musical, 2006. Mem.: Wis. Chorale Dirs. Assn. Avocations: music, cooking, reading. Office: Mishicot Mid Sch and High Sch 660 Washington St Mishicot WI 54228

PETERS, RITA, university administrator; b. Riverhead, N.Y., Sept. 1, 1953; d. Herbert E. and Loni S. Peters. BA, Lycoming Coll., Williamsport, Pa., 1974; MS, U. Calif., Davis, 1990. Cert. fund raising exec.; diplomate nat. cert. sch. psychologist, Sch. Neuropsychology, 2004. Cons. Winning Edge, Stockton, Calif., 1984-92; dir. grants and founds. U. of the Pacific, Stockton, 1992—, dir. corp. and found. rels., 1998. Lilly Endowment Rsch. awardee, 1991; named Paul Harris fellow, 2000. Mem. Nat. Soc. Fund Raising Execs. (cert. fund raising exec.), Rotary. Avocations: travel, computers, swimming, reading, international events. Home: PO Box 218 Hughson CA 95326-0218 Office: Venice HS 18000 Venice Blvd Los Angeles CA 90066

PETERS, ROBERTA, soprano; b. NYC, May 4, 1930; d. Sol and Ruth (Hirsch) Peters; m. Bertram Fields, Apr. 10, 1955; children: Paul, Bruce. Litt.D., Elmira Coll., 1967; Mus. D., Ithaca Coll., 1968, Colby Coll., 1980; L.H.D., Westminster Coll., 1974, Lehigh U., 1977; D.F.A., St. John's U., 1982; LittD, Coll. New Rochelle, 1989; MusD, U. R.I., 1992, Fla. Atlantic U., 1997. Author: Debut at the Met; singer: (Operas) Met. Opera debut as Zerlina in Don Giovanni, 1950, recorded numerous operas, (appeared motion pictures including) Tonight We Sing, 1996, frequent appearances radio and TV, (stage appearances include) The King and I, 1973, Bittersweet, Merry Widow, The Sound of Music, Royal Opera House, Vienna State Opera, Munich Opera, West Berlin Opera, Salzburg Festival, The White House, debuts at festivals in Vienna and Munich, premiered Ani M'amin, Carnegie Hall, 1973, concert tours in U.S., Soviet Union, Scandinavian countries, Israel, China, Japan, Taiwan, South Korea, (debut) Kirov Opera, sang at Bolshoi Opera (1st Am. recipient Bolshoi medal). Trustee, bd. dirs. Carnegie Hall; trustee Ithaca Coll.; dir. Met. Opera Guild; chmn. Nat. Inst. Music Theater, 1991—; apptd. by Pres. Bush to Nat. Coun. Arts, 1991; overseer Colby Coll., Bklyn. Coll. Performing Arts Ctr.; past chair Nat. Cystic Fibrosis Found.; active Israel Bonds, AIDS rsch. Named Woman of Yr., Fedn. Women's Clubs, 1964; recipient honored spl. ceremony on 35th anniversary with Met. Opera Co., 1985, Nat. Medal of Arts, Pres. Clinton, 1998. Avocation: tennis. Office: ICM Artists Ltd 40 W 57th St Fl 16 New York NY 10019-4098

PETERS, SARAH WHITAKER, art historian, writer; b. Kenosha, Wis., Aug. 17, 1924; d. Robert Burbank and Margaret Jebb (Allen) Whitaker; m. Arthur King Peters, Oct. 21, 1943; children: Robert Bruce, Margaret Allen, Michael Whitaker. BA, Sarah Lawrence Coll., 1954; MA, Columbia U., 1966; student, L'Ecole du Louvre, Paris, 1967-68; diplome, Ecole des Trois Gourmandes, Paris, 1968; PhD, CUNY, 1987. Freelance critic Art in Am., N.Y.C. Lectr.-in-residence Garrison Forest Sch., Owings Mills, Md.; adj. asst. prof. art history C.W. Post, U. L.I.; lectr. Bronxville (N.Y.) Adult Sch., Internat. Mus. Photography, 1979, Tufts U., 1979, Madison (Wis.) Art Ctr., 1984, Meml. Art Gallery, Rochester, N.Y., 1988, 91, Caramoor Mus., Katonah, N.Y., 1988, Yale U. Art Gallery, New Haven, Conn., 1989, The Cosmopolitan Club, N.Y.C., 1977, 91, Sarah Lawrence Coll., Bronxville, 1992, The Phillips Collection, Washington, 1993, Mpls. Inst. Arts, 1993, Whitney Mus. Am. Art, Champion, 1994, U. Wis., Parkside, 1994, Nat. Mus. Wildlife Art, Jackson Hole, Wyo., 1995, The Georgia O'Keeffe Mus., Santa Fe, 1997, Bronxville Pub. Libr., 1998, Weatherspoon Art Mus., Greensboro, NC, 2003, Amon Carter Mus, Ft. Worth, 2003, Vassar Coll., 2003, Pa. Acad. Fine Arts, Phila., 2004. Author: Becoming O'Keeffe: The Early Years, 1991, 2d edit., 2001, Pattern of the Past: A Kenosha Memoir, 2001; contbr. essays to Portraits of American Women, 1991, The Dictionary of Art, 1996, Frames of Reference; Works from the Whitney Museum of American Art, 1999, American Art Review, 2003, Georgia O'Keeffe: Color and Conservation, 2006, N.Mex. Hist. Rev., 2006, Seeing American: Painting and Sclupture, 2006; TV appearances include: BBC, London, The Late Show, 1993, A&E Network Biography series on Georgia O'Keeffe, 2004; radio interview: Art Today, Australia Broadcasting Corp., 1999; contbr. articles to profl. jours. Mem. Coll. Art Assn., Bronxville Field Club, The Cosmopolitan Club. Avocations: horseback riding, rock climbing, tennis, cooking. Home: 14 Village Ln Bronxville NY 10708-4806

PETERS, SUSAN, editor; BA, U. Minn., 1974. Reporter The Nat. Culinary Rev., 1996—2004; mng. editor Flavors-The Forum for Atlanta Food Culture and Dining, 03; corr. N.Am. Show Cook website, 2005—; food editor N.Y. Mag., 2006. Adv. bd. Atlanta (Ga.) Sch. Culinary Arts, 1995—99. Mem.: Assn. Food Journalists, Internat. Assn. Culinary Profls., Les Dames D'Escoffier. Office: Sainte Claire Svcs Inc PO Box 46615 Saint Petersburg FL 33741-6615

PETERS, SUSAN P., human resources specialist; married; 1 child. BA, St. Mary's Coll., Univ. Notre Dame, 1975; M Edn., Univ. Va., 1978. Mgmt. positions Gen. Electric, 1979—82; mgr. union rels., profl. rels. mgr. Trane Co., 1982—84; mgr. non-exempt rels. GE Plastics, Pittsfield, Mass., 1984—86, HR mgr. worldwide mktg., prod. mgmt., 1986—89, HR mgr. Europe Bergen op Zoom, Netherlands, 1989—90; mgr. HR staffing & develop. Gen Electric, Fairfield, Conn., 1990—91; mgr. human resources GE Plastics, Pittsfield, Mass., 1991—93; sr. human resources mgr. GE Appliances, Louisville, 1993—2000; exec. v.p. human resources NBC, 2000—01; v.p. exec. develop. Gen. Electric, Fairfield, Conn., 2001—. Office: General Electric 3135 Easton Turnpike Fairfield CT 06828*

PETERSEN, ANNE C. (CHERYL PETERSEN), foundation administrator, educator; b. Little Falls, Minn., Sept. 11, 1944; d. Franklin Hanks and Rhoda Pauline (Sandwick) Studley; m. Douglas Lee Petersen, Dec. 27, 1967; children: Christine Anne, Benjamin Bradfield. BA, U. Chgo., 1966, MS, 1972, PhD, 1973. Asst. prof., rsch. assoc. Dept. Psychiatry U. Chgo., 1972-80, assoc. prof., rsch. assoc., 1980-82; prof. human devel., head Dept. Individual and Family Studies Pa. State U., University Park, 1982-87, dean Coll. Health and Human Devel., 1987-92, prof. health and human devel., 1987-92; dean grad. sch., v.p. for rsch. throughout state U. Minn., Mpls., 1992-94, prof. adolescent devel. and pediatrics, 1992-96; dep. dir., COO NSF, Arlington, Va., 1994-96; sr. v.p. programs W.K. Kellogg Found., 1996—2005; dep. dir. Ctr. Advanced Study Behavioral Scis. Stanford U., 2006—, prof. Dept. Psychology, 2006—. Vis. prof., fellow Coll. Edn., R&D Psychology, Roosevelt U., Chgo., 1973-74; cons. Ctr. for Health Adminstrn. Studies U. Chgo., 1976-78, Ctr. for New Schs., Chgo., 1974-78, Robert Wood Johnson Found. Mathtech, Inc., 1987-89; coord. clin. rsch. tng. program Michael Reese Hosp. and Med. Ctr., Chgo., 1976-80, dir. Lab. for Study of Adolescence, 1975-82; faculty Ill. Sch. for Profl. Psychology, 1978-79; statis. cons. Coll. Nursing U. Ill. Med. Ctr., 1975-83; assoc. dir. health program MacArthur Found., 1980-82, also cons. health program, 1982-88; chair sr. adv. bd. NIMH, 1987-88; nat. adv. mental health coun. NIH, 1997-2003; trustee Nat. Inst. Statis. Scis., 1998-2004. Author: Sex Related Differences in Cognition Functioning: Developmental Issues, 1979, Promoting Adolescent Health: A Diolog on Research and Practice, 1982, Firls at Puberty: Biological and psychosocial Perspectives, 1983, Brain Maturation and Cognitive Development: Comparative and Cross Cultural Perspectives, 1991, Narrowing the Margins: Adolescent Unemployment and the lack of a social role, 1991, Grofit: A Fortran Program for the Estimation of Parameters of a Human Growth Curve, 1972, Girls at Puberty: Biological and Psychosocial Perspectives, 1983, Adolescence and Youth: Psychological Development in a Changing World, 1984, Youth Unemployment and Society, 1994, Transitions Through Adolescence: Interpersonal Domains and Context, 1996; reviewer Jour. Youth and Adolescence, 1975-80, Devel. Psychology, 1979—, Sci., 1979—, Jour. Edn. Psychology, 1979—, Child Devel., 1980—, Jour. Edn. Measurement, 1980, Ednl. Rschr., 1980, Am. Ednl. Rsch. Jour., 1981—, Jour. Mental Imagery, 1982-92, Sex Roles, 1984—; cons. editor Psychology of Women Quar., 1978-82, assoc. editor, 1983-86; adv. editor Contemporary Psychology, 1985-86; mem. editl. bd. various profl. jours.; contbr. chpts. to books and articles to profl. jours. Bd. overseers Lewis Coll., Ill. Inst. Tech., 1980-82; mem. adv. bd. longitudinal data archive project Murray Ctr., Radcliffe Coll., 1985-91, mem. sci. adv. bd., 1983-91 Fellow: APA (chmn. task force on reproductive freedom 1979—81, program chmn. 1981—82, chmn. task force on long range planning 1986—89, pres. divsn. 7 1992—93), AAAS; mem.: NAS (nat. forum on future children and their families 1987—91, chmn. panel on child abuse and neglect 1991—93, mem. forum on adolescence Inst. of Medicine 1997—2000, chair bd. on behavioral, cognitive and sensory scis. 1997—, mem. nat. academics com. sci., engring., and policy 2003—), Global Phys. Therapy Alliance (pres. 2005—), Soc. for Rsch. on Adolescence (pres. 1990—92, past pres. 1992—94, chmn. nominations com. 1992—94, mem. fin. com. 2004—), Acad. Europaea, Psychometric Soc., Behavior Genetics Assn., Assn. Women in Sci. (bd. dirs. 1996—2000), Am. Ednl. Rsch. Assn. (various offices), Internat. Soc. for the Study of Behavioral Devel. (coun. mem. 1995—, pres.-elect 2002—06, pres. 2006—), Inst. for Medicine. Home: 3715 Blackberry Ln Kalamazoo MI 49008-3333 Office Phone: 650-321-2052. E-mail: globalphilliance@yahoo.com.

PETERSEN, CAROLYN ASHCRAFT, psychologist; b. Waxhaw, N.C. d. J. Carl and Carolyn (Ray) Wolfe; m. Thomas L. Ashcraft (div. 1973); children: Anne C., Thomas Wolfe; m. Marvin E. Petersen, Nov. 14, 1982. BS, U. N.C.; MA, Vanderbilt U., PhD, 1963. Lic. psychologist, Pa., Fla. Psychologist Peabody Child Study Ctr., Nashville, 1963-64; rschr. U.S. Dept. Edn.-Peabody, Nashville, 1964-65; assoc. prof. Tenn. State U., Nashville, 1965-66; asst. prof. U. Tenn., Nashville, 1966-69, LaSalle Coll., Phila., 1970-72; adj. instr. U. Pa., Phila., 1970-73; clin. psychologist Overbrook Sch. for Blind, Phila., 1974-76, Fla. Sch. for Deaf and Blind, St. Augustine, 1976-78; asst. prof. psychology U. Tampa, Fla., 1979-82; assoc., adj. prof. S.D. State U., Brookings, 1983-89; ret., 2002. Cons. Tenn. Dept. Edn., Cookeville, 1966-69, Charter Hosp., Tampa, 1979-82; organizer symposia for profl. meetings. Contbr. to profl. publs. Bd. dirs. Brookings Hosp. Aux., 1985-88; v.p. S.D. Art Mus. Guild, 1988-89. Fellow Am. Psychol. Soc., Pa. Psychol. Assn.; mem. APA, Southeastern Psychol. Assn., Nat. Register Psychologists. Republican. Avocations: bridge, travel, art. Home: 103 Silverbell Ct Sun City Center FL 33573-6215

PETERSEN, CATHERINE HOLLAND, lawyer; b. Norman, Okla., Apr. 24, 1951; d. John Hays and Helen Ann (Turner) Holland; m. James Frederick Petersen, June 26, 1973 (div.); children: T. Kyle, Lindsay Diane; m. Lester E.R. Doty, Apr. 17, 2004. BA, Hastings Coll., 1973; JD, Okla. U., 1976. Bar: Okla. 1976, U.S. Dist. Ct. (we. dist.) Okla. 1978. Legal intern, police legal advisor City of Norman, 1974-76; sole practice Norman, 1976-81; ptnr. Williams Petersen & Denny, Norman, 1981-82; pres. Petersen Assocs., Inc., Norman, 1982—2004; ptnr. Petersen, Henson & Meadows, PC, Norman, 2004—. Adj. prof. Oklahoma City U. Coll. Law, 1982, U. Okla. Law Ctr., 1987; instr. continuing legal edn. U. Okla. Law Ctr., Norman, 1977, 79, 81, 83, 84, 86, 89-95; instr. Okla. Bar Assn., ABA, Am. Acad. Matrimonial Lawyers. Bd. dirs. United Way, Norman, 1978-84, pres., 1981; bd. dirs. Women's Resource Ctr., Norman, 1975-77, 82-84; mem. Jr. League, Norman, 1980-83, Norman Hosp. Ayx., 1982-84; trustee 1st Presbyn. Ch., 1986-87. Named among Outstanding Okla. Women of 1980s, Women's Polit. Caucus, 1980, Outstanding Young Women of Am., 1981, 83. Fellow Am. Acad. Matrimonial Lawyers (pres. Okla. chpt. 1990-91, bd. govs. 1991-95); mem. ABA (family law sect., faculty Family Law Inst. 1993—), Cleveland County Bar Assn., Okla. Bar Assn. (chmn. family law sect. 1987-88), Phi Delta Phi. Republican. Home: 4716 Sundance Ct Norman OK 73072-3900 Office: PO Box 1243 314 E Comanche St Norman OK 73069-6009 Office Phone: 405-329-3307.

PETERSEN, DOROTHY VIRGINIA, investment company executive; b. Milw., Sept. 22, 1929; d. Carl Arndt and Loretta Louise Laura (Bremer) Scherer; m. Glenn Charles Petersen, Aug. 27, 1949; children: Dr. Vicki Lynn Abbott, Larry Dean, Dr. Rick Randall. BS magna cum laude, U. Wis.-Parkside, 1975. Repair dept. clk. Eastman Kodak Co., Milw., 1946—47; sec. First Wis. Trust Co., Milw., 1947—49; head sec. art edn. dept. U. Wis., Madison, 1949—50; sec. and asst. Red Star Yeast Co., Milw., 1950—51; exec. sec. Boy Scouts Am., Milw., 1963—65, Applied Power, Pewaukee, Wis., 1965—67; sec., treas. Westshore Muffler Shops, Milw., 1983—2002; asst. sec. and treas. Fastrack, Inc., Mequon, Wis., 2002—. Paintings (Honorable Mention, Wis. Art Show, Twin Lakes, 1976). Head fund drive Town of Greenfield ARC, 1956, helper fund drive, 1955, helper fund, 1957—59; leader Girl Scouts Am., Wauwatosa, Wis., 1960—61; cub pack sec. Boy Scouts Am., Wauwatosa, 1962—63; children's class tchr. Baha'i World Faith, Greenfield, Milw., Burlington, 1959—72, spkr. Milw., Burlington, 1970—99. Mem.: Order Ea. Star (Wauwatosa chpt. #219). Baha'i Avocations: day trading, genealogy, reading, photography, miniature poodles. Home: 7907 W Willowbrook Dr 115N Mequon WI 53097 Personal E-mail: dvpetersen29@hotmail.com.

PETERSEN, JEAN SNYDER, educational association administrator; b. NYC, Oct. 16, 1931; d. Peter Eugene and Helyn Brownell (Parker) Snyder; m. Elton Reed Petersen, Sept. 16, 1954; children— Bruce Brownell, Craig Reed. Student, N.Y. U., 1949-51; degree fgn. banking, Am. Inst. Banking, 1952. Fgn. credit investigator Chase Nat. Bank Hdqrs., N.Y.C., 1952-56; nat. exec. dir. Assn. Children and Adults with Learning Disabilities (name changed to Learning Disabilities Assn. of Am.), Pitts., 1972—. Mem. exec. com., treas. Jr. League, Pitts.; bd. dirs. Found. for Children with Learning Disabilities, N.Y.C., Children's Hosp., Pitts., Music for Mt. Lebanon, Vocat. Rehab. Ctr., Pitts.; bd. dirs., v.p., mem. exec. com. Assn. Retarded Citizens Pa.; ptnr. UN Internat. Yr. of Disabled; ruling elder Presbyn. Ch.Assn. Retarded Citizens Pa.; mem. exec. com. Pat Buckley Moss Nat. Children's Charity Found; chmn. bd. dirs. Masonic Learning Ctrs. for Children. Recipient Sustainers award Jr. League, 1977, Recognition award, 1975, Pres.'s award, 1978. Mem. AAUW, Meeting Planners Internat. (treas.), Am. Soc. Assn. Execs. Republican. Presbyterian. Home: 343 Shadowlawn Ave Pittsburgh PA 15216-1239 Office: 4156 Library Rd Pittsburgh PA 15234-1349 Fax: (412) 5634537.

PETERSEN, JOYCE JEAN, retired elementary school educator; b. Battle Creek, Iowa, Jan. 15, 1931; d. Hugo Jacob Jensen and Adela Charlotte Johannsen; m. William John Petersen, July 15, 1951; children: Timothy Hugh, Joel William, Roxanne Adel. BS in Elem. Edn., Morningside Coll., Sioux City, Iowa, 1965. Tchr. elem. sch. Crawford County Schs., Iowa, 1962—81; ret., 1981. Bd. dirs. Schleswig Pub. Libr., Iowa, 1968—2000, Schleswig Ret. Apt., 1952—. Recipient Outstanding Tchr. award, State of Iowa, 1980, Gov.'s Leadership award, 1980, Friend in Edn. award, 1980. Mem.: VFW Aux. (various offices 1952—), AAUW, Schleswig Golf Club. Avocations: reading, knitting, bridge, gardening, photo albums.

PETERSEN, MAUREEN JEANETTE MILLER, management information technology director, retired nurse; b. Evanston, Ill., Sept. 4, 1956; d. Maurice James and M. Joyce (Mielke) Miller; m. Gregory Eugene Petersen, July 7, 1984; children: Trevor James, Tatyana Brianne. BS in Nursing cum laude, Vanderbilt U., 1978; MS in Biometry and Health Info. Systems, U. Minn., 1984. Nurse U. Iowa Hosps. and Clinics, Iowa City, 1978—82; research asst. Sch. Nursing, U. Minn., Mpls., 1982—83; mgr. Accenture, Mpls., 1984—2001; dir. health info. tech. Park Nicollet, Eden Prairie, Minn., 2003—. Mem.: Project Mgmt. Inst. (proj. mgmt. profl.), Mensa. Methodist. Avocation: travel. Home: 1050 County Rd C2 W Roseville MN 55113-1945 Office: Park Nicollet 7905 Golden Triangle Dr Eden Prairie MN 55344 Office Phone: 952-993-9893. E-mail: peters1050@aol.com, petema@parknicollet.com.

PETERSEN, PATRICIA J., real estate company executive; Pres., CEO Daniel Gale Real Estate. Spkr. in field; adv. bd. several nat. & internat. profl. orgns. including Sotheby's Internat. Realty and Brain Trust. Exec. com., adv. bd. DNA Learning Ctr., Cold Spring Harbor Lab.; bd. dirs. U.S. Broadcasting, Friends for Long Island's Heritage; mem. Nat. Trust for Hist. Preservation. Mem.: Nat. Assn. Realtors, Long Island Bd. Realtors, Women's Real Estate Coun., Internat. Real Estate Fedn., Leading Estates of the World, The Registry. Office: Daniel Gale Real Estate 160 E Main St Huntington NY 11743

PETERSEN, SHANNYN RAE, music educator; b. Cin., Dec. 18, 1981; d. Michael Alan and Robyn Rae Calardo; m. Nicholas Jon Petersen, June 19, 2004. MusB, Grove City Coll., Pa., 2004. Cert. tchr. Pa., Md. Vocal, gen. music tchr. Plum Point Elem. Sch., Huntingtown, Md., 2004—. Pvt. flute tchr., Grove City, 2002—04, Bowie, Md., 2004—; pvt. piano tchr., 2004—. Mem.: Nat. Assn. Music Edn. (chmn. collegiate fundraising 2002—04), Md. State Tchrs. Assn. Avocations: community theater, scrapbooks.

PETERSON, ANN SULLIVAN, physician, consultant; b. Rhinebeck, NY, Oct. 11, 1928; AB, Cornell U., 1950, MD, 1954; MS, MIT, 1980. Diplomate Am. Bd. Internal Medicine. Intern Cornell Med. Divsn.-Bellevue Hosp., NYC, 1954—55, resident, 1955—57; fellow in medicine and physiology Meml.-Sloan Kettering Cancer Ctr., Cornell Med. Coll., NYC, 1957—60; instr. medicine Georgetown U. Sch. Medicine, Washington, 1962—65, asst. prof., 1965—69, asst. dir. clin. rsch. unit, 1962—69; assoc. prof. medicine U. Ill., Chgo., 1969—72, asst. dean, 1969—71, assoc. dean, 1971—72; assoc. prof. medicine, assoc. dean Coll. Physicians and Surgeons, Columbia U., NYC, 1972—80, Cornell U. Med. Coll., NYC, 1980—83; assoc. dir. divsn. med. edn. AMA, Chgo., 1983—86, dir. div. grad. med. edn., 1986—89, v.p. mgmt. cons. corp., 1989—93; ind. cons. Chgo., 1993—2005. Contbr. articles to med. jours. Mem. bd. regents Uniformed Svcs. U. of Health Scis., 1984—90. John and Mary R. Markle scholar, 1965—70, Alfred P. Sloan fellow, MIT, 1979—80. Fellow: ACP; mem.: Mortar Bd., Alpha Omega Alpha, Alpha Epsilon Delta.

PETERSON, ANNE ELIZABETH WALLACE, music educator, composer; b. Aurora, Ill., June 17, 1949; d. Vernon Ammon and Marjorie Lois (Loudon) Wallace; m. Thomas Leonard Peterson (dec. 1990); m. Tim Allen Gasser, Feb. 27, 1993. Attended, Macphail Sch. Music, 1964—67, San Francisco Conservatory Music, 1974—77, U. Edinburgh, 1979, Baroque Performance Inst., 1992; studied with Martha Ivory, 1970, studied with Charlene Brendler, 1978; BA in English and Music, U. Minn., 1971; MA in Music, Lone Mountain Coll., 1978; studied harpsichord, with Laurette Goldberg, 1974—78; studied harpsichord with Peter Williams. Cert. in Tech. Writing De Anza Coll., Cupertino, Calif., 1981. Music tchr. Pillsbury-Waite Cultural Arts Ctr., Mpls., 1971—72, Music Sch., Sunnyvale, Calif., 1991—; tech. writer, editor, rschr. SRI Internat., Menlo Park, Calif., 1973—90. Music tchr. Cmty. Sch. Music and Arts, Mountain View, Calif., 1973—78, Mountain View, 1979—2001; harpsichord performer No. Calif. Renaissance Faire, 1979—85, Minn. Renaissance Festival, 1982; mem. Soc. Tech. Communication, 1979—90, conv. spkr., 1983; keyboard gen. music instr. Boys' and Girls' Club, Redwood City, Calif., 1990—92; pvt. piano and harpsichord tchr., Redwood City, 1980—; musician, Palo Alto, San Francisco, Calif.; conf. workshop presenter in field. Author: (book) Harpsichord Tuning: An Easy Start, 1978, (book, CD) Follow the Rainbow, 2003; musician (harpsichordist): (albums) Then, 1997, Harpsichord at Hampstead, 1999, Starspirations, 2000; musician: Good Company (with Tudor Rose Ensemble), 1997; musician: (harpsichordist) Come and Adore! (Christmas-variety) Starspirations, 1999; musician: (harpsichordist, ensemblist, vocalist) Elizabeth Gambarini, 2000, Cougar Love, 2005. Mem.: Music Tchrs. Assn. (Appreciation award 2000), Music Tchrs. Assn. Calif. (program chair 2000—01), Toastmasters Internat. (Achievement award 1989), Phi Beta (pres. Pi Lambda chpt. 1993—95, program chair 1974—85, 2002—03, Grad. Grant-In Aid award, Marie Logan award 1979, Nat. Historian award 2004). Office Phone: 650-365-5375. Personal E-mail: awpgmusic@yahoo.com.

PETERSON, BARBARA OWECKE, artist, retired nurse, retired real estate agent; b. Winona, Minn., Nov. 25, 1932; d. Adelbert Paul and Hermanda Gilda Bittner; m. Jerome Francis Owecke, Nov. 28, 1953 (div. 1974); children: Paul Richard Owecke, Michael Jerome Owecke, Margaret Francis Owecke (dec.), Stacy Ann Owecke, Wendy Alane Owecke (dec.), James William Owecke, William Harold Owecke; m. Roy Eugene Peterson, May 28, 1983. RN, St. Francis Sch. Nursing, 1953; B Individualized Study, George Mason U., 1994. RN, Va., Wis., Mich., Ill., Ohio, Fla. Staff nurse Commonwealth Hosp., Fairfax, Va., 1973-74; telemetry nurse Fairfax Hosp., 1974-76; med. sales rep. CB Fleet Pharm., Lynchburg, Va., 1976-78; territory mgr. Bristol-Myers Squibb, Northern Va., Washington, 1978-92; realtor Century 21 United, Fairfax, Va., 1974-91; ret., 1992; artist Warrenton, Va., 1992—. Bd. dirs. Fauquier Artists' Alliance, Warrenton, Va., 1993-96, pres., 1994-95. Exhibited in group shows at Fauquier Artists' Alliance, Warrentown, 1994—97, Alexandria Art League, 1994—98, Ctr. for Creative Art, Fredricksburg, Va., 1994—98, George Mason U., Fairfax, Va., 1994, Neighborhood Art Show, The Plains, Va., 1994—97, Japanese Embassy, Washington, 1996, The Campagna Ctr., Alexandria, 1996—97, The Torpedo Factory, Alexandria, Va., 1994—98, Petersburg Area Art League, Va., 1998, Brush Strokes Gallery, Ft. Pierce, Fla., 1998, Treasure Coast Art Assn., Ft. Pierce, 1998—2006, Vero Beach Mus., 1999—2006, Backus Gallery, 1999—2006, Waterways Gallery, 2003—05, Nat. Arts Club, 2006. RN Fauquier Free Clinic, Warrenton, 1993-98; mem. Goldvein Vol. Fire Dept., 1989-94. Mem. Internat. Registry Artists and Artwork, Nat. Mus. Women in the Arts (charter mem.), Archives of Nat. Mus. Women in the Arts, Vero Beach Art Club, Vero Beach Mus., Treasure Coast Art Assn., Art Assocs. of Martin County, Jensen Beach Art League. Roman Catholic. Avocation: tennis. Home: 403 Southstar Dr Ocean Village Fort Pierce FL 34949 Home (Summer): 15 Superior Ln Winona MN 55987 Office Phone: 772-240-4444. Personal E-mail: BaMaBi66@aol.com.

PETERSON, BETTY W., language educator, writer; b. Phil, Ky., Nov. 15, 1944; d. James Delno Withers and Mae Berniece Withers (Luttrell) Emerson, Glen Emerson (Stepfather); m. Danny F. Peterson, Aug. 11, 1962; children:

Angela Yvette Jones, Alisa Yvonne Noritis, Brenton Franklin, Danny Keith. BA English high distinction, U. Ky., Lexington, 1982, MA English, 1986. Instrnl. specialist Somerset C.C., Ky., 1986—89, asst. prof. English, 1989—91, assoc. prof. English with tenure, 1991—2000; prof. English Somerset Cmty. and Tech. Coll., 2000—, tchg. cons., 2006—. Co-editor Ky. writing Somerset C.C., 1989—94, tchg. cons., 2006—. Contbr. articles short stories and poems to profl. jours.;, author plays. Tchr. Gov.'s Scholars Program No. Ky. U., 1996. Named to Who's Who Among Am. Tchrs., 2002, 2005, 2006; recipient Oswald Rsch. and Creativity Award, U. Ky., 1981, Dantzler-Dantzler Acad. Achievement award, 1982, Tchg. Assistantship, U. Ky., 1984—86, Commd. Ky. Col., Hon. Order Ky. Cols., 1996, NISOD Tchg. Excellence Award, Somerset C.C., 2001; scholar, U. Ky. Alumni Assn., 1976—77; Va. Ctr. for Creative Arts Fellow, Ky. Found. for Women, 1993. Mem.: Dramatists Guild Am., Inc. (assoc.), U. Ky. Alumni Assn., Jesse Stuart Found. Independent. Roman Catholic. Avocations: writing, reading, aerobics, theater, guitar.

PETERSON, BRANDI JANELL, elementary school educator; b. Galveston, Tex., Apr. 16, 1982; d. Linda Chyrel Peterson and Raymond Rachal (Stepfather). BA in Sociology, Duke U., Durham, NC, 2004. Cert. math. tchr. Tex. Math tchr. McAdams Jr. HS, Dickinson, Tex., 2004—. Grantee, Kenan Inst. for Ethics, Duke U., 2003; scholar, Tex. N.Mex. Power Co., 2000, Lions Club, 2000; Student-to-Student scholar, Duke U., 2003. Mem.: Alpha Kappa Delta. Democrat.

PETERSON, CANDYCE LEIGH, music educator; b. Kileen, Tex., Mar. 27, 1958; d. Norman Leroy and Marjory Rose Cizek; m. Andrew Allen Peterson, June 4, 1988; children: Courtney Leigh, Kelsey Arline. MusB in Edn., Colo. State U., Ft. Collins, 1980; MEd, Lesley U., Cambridge, Mass., 2001. 7th-12th grade choral tchr. Hugoton Mid. and HS, Kans., 1980—82; orch., elem. music tchr. Arvada West HS, Foster HS, Russell HS, Arvada, Colo., 1982—84; music tchr., band dir. Mesa Elem. Sch., Westminster, Colo., 1984—90; music tchr., handbell and choir dir. Westminster Elem. Sch., Colo., 1991—2005; music tchr. Harris Pk. Elem. Sch., Westminster, 2005—. Sect. leader Arvada Ctr. Chorale, 1984—98. Vol. area schs., Arvada, 2005—06. Named Tchr. of Yr., Westminster Elem. Sch., 1995; Sun Safety grantee, Colo. Dept. Edn., 2003. Mem.: Colo. Music Educators (assoc.). Office: Harris Park Elem Sch Adams # 50 4300 W 75th Ave Westminster CO 80030 Office Phone: 303-428-1721. Business E-Mail: cpeterson@adams50.org.

PETERSON, CLARA MARGARET, elementary school educator; b. Thorp, Wis., June 25, 1930; d. Matthew and Pearl H. Olejniczak; m. Donald Richard Peterson, Dec. 27, 1954; 1 child, Mark Gregory. BS, Wis. State U. Eau Claire, 1964; MS Elem. Edn., U. Wis. LaCrosse, 1975. Tchr. 2d grade pub. sch., Gilman, Wis., 1950—53, tchr. 1st grade Eau Claire, 1953—54, tchr. 2d & 4th grades Trenton, NJ, 1955—56, tchr. 2d grade St. Paul, 1957—58, substitute tchr. La Crosse, 1964—67; tchr. math. 3d & 5th grades La Crosse Pub. Schs., 1967—93. Co-treas. Senate Dance Club, La Crosse; treas. PTA. Mem.: NEA, AAUW, Wis. Ret. Educator's Assn., La Crosse Edn. Assn., We. Wis. Edn. Assn., Wis. Edn. Assn., Delta Kappa Gamma, Kappa Delta Pi. Avocations: piano, swimming, golf, bicycling.

PETERSON, CYNTHIA LYNN, library director, educator; d. Arthur Wayne and D'Alva Rae Peterson. BS in Edn., Baylor U., 1979; MLS, U. North Tex., Denton, 1983; BA, Mars Hill Coll., NC, 1989. Cert. tchr. State of Tex., Texas County libr. Tex. State Libr. Tchr. Richardson Ind. Sch. Dist., Richardson, Tex., 1979—83; libr. Wiley (Tex.) Pub. Libr., 1983—84; libr. instrnl. svcs., coord. music libr. Mars Hill Coll., 1984—89; head of cataloging Henderson State U., Arkadelphia, Ark., 1989—90; head of cataloging libr. U. of Tex. Southwestern Med. Ctr., Dallas, 1990—94, asst. mgr. database devel. and control libr., 1994—96, mgr. database devel. and control libr., 1996—97; dir. libr. svcs. Bluefield (Va.) Coll., 1997—2000, East Tex. Bapt. U., Marshall, 2001—. Mem. work group Tex. Heritage Digitization Initiative, Austin, 2005—; faculty sponsor Delta Pi Theta, East Tex. Bapt. U., Marshall, 2003—. Author: (novels) Background of Eternity; indexer (book) Upper Laurel and Her People. Singer Plano Civic Chorus, 1982—83, Asheville Choral Soc., 1985—88; choir dir. Meml. Bapt. Ch., Bluefield, Va., 1999—2000; dir. children's choir Northway Bapt. Ch., Dallas, 1991—93, editor and author single adult newsletter, 1991—93; mem.choir 1st Bapt. Ch., Longview, Tex., 2006—, mem.ladies ensemble, 2006—; costumer Arkadelphia Little Theatre, 1989—90; reader North Tex. Taping and Radio for the Blind, Dallas, 1993—94; webmaster VikingNet - Alumni Web Page - Valhalla H.S., 1996—2004. Mem.: ALA, Holston Associated Librs. (bd. dirs. 1997—2000), Appalachian Coll. Assn. (mem. task force Appalachian Libr. and Info. Coop. 1998—2000), Tex. Libr. Assn., Assn. of Christian Librns., So. Bapt. Libr. Assn., Assn. Coll. and Rsch. Librs. (mem. leadership com. 2002—04), Beta Phi Mu. Republican. Southern Baptist. Avocations: reading, writing, singing, needlework/sewing, travel. Office: East Texas Bapt Univ 1209 N Grove St Marshall TX 75670 Office Phone: 903-923-2257. Office Fax: 903-935-3447. E-mail: cpeterson@etbu.edu.

PETERSON, DAWN MICHELLE, entrepreneur, writer; b. Rochester, Minn., Oct. 28, 1962; d. Kenneth Eugene and Lois Ann Silker; m. Bud Lamont Peterson, Feb. 14, 1981; children: Jacquline Ann Peterson, Holly Marie Schill, Cassie Jan Wilson. Student, Internet Svcs. Corp. Continuing Bus. Edn., 1985—2005, Legacy Bus. Group Bus. Edn., 2005—. Mgr. of fine dining restaurant and pvt. club Hilton Hotels, Ogden, Utah, 1983—85; pres. B & D Enterprise, Layton, Utah, 1985—; dir. of internat. divsn. Wilson Enterprises, Inc., Ogden, 1991—98; pres. Amma's Daycare, Layton, 2002—, D. S. Peterson Lit. Co., Layton, 2004—. Directorship, Brazilian divsn. Wilson Enterprises, Inc., Ogden, Utah, 1993—95, directorship, Turkish divsn., 1994—96, directorship, Ctrl. Am. divsn., 1994—96, directorship, Polish divsn., 1993—96, directorship, UK divsn., 1993—98, directorship, German divsn., 1993—98, directorship, Mex. divsn., 1993—98, directorship, Australian divsn., 1994—98; US overseer Wilson Enterprises, Inc. and World Wide Dvsn., 1993—98, seminar spkr., 1993—; sr. bus. cons. Victory Devel., Guadalajara, Mexico, 1998—; com. mem. for internet services corp. India launch team Internet Services Corp./Wilson Enterprises, Inc., 1998; organizer and key note spkr. Germany's Women in Bus. Conf., 1996. Author: (novels) Code Breakers; author: (also actor and dir.) (plays) The Tale of the Pigs with the Folders on Their Heads, Barn Yard Animals (Sch. Creativity award, 1970), Laverne and Shirley go into Business; author/speaker (audio presentation) Empowering Women Business Owners, It's an Amazing Trip. Mem. Women In Bus., Ogden, Utah, 1983—85, Ogden C. of C., 1983—85, Rep. Nat. Com., 1987—2005; del. Utah Rep. Party, 1986. Recipient All Around Title, Buckaroo Rodeo, 1974, 1976, Appaloosa Horsemen's Assn., 1980, Endurance Champion, Utah Endurace Racing Assn., 1980, Lake Powell Fesitval of Lights Parade, Lake Powell Festival Com., 2002, 5th in Top 25 Producers, Quixtar Corp., 2002. Mem.: Ind. Bus. Owners Assn. (assoc.). R-Consevative. Christian. Avocations: travel, writing, reading. Office Phone: 801-510-9336. Personal E-mail: bpeterson5673@msn.com.

PETERSON, DONNA RAE, gerontologist; b. Wichita, Kans., Aug. 29, 1948; d. Raymond Houston and Edna Brooks (Waddell) Hobbs; m. William E. Peterson, Nov. 7, 1993; 1 child, Shauna Layne Heath. Student, Wichita State U., 1968—70; BS in Mgmt., N.W. Christian Coll., 1996, MA in Interdisciplinary Studies Gerontology, 2000. Adminstrv. asst. postgrad. edn. Med. Sch. U. Kans., Wichita, 1974—80; activity coord. continuing med. edn. Wesley Med. Ctr., Wichita, 1980—84; mgr. support svcs. 9th dist. Farm Credit Svcs., Wichita, 1984—88; mgr. sales and mktg. Amb. Travel, Eugene, Oreg., 1988—93; dir. mktg. Peterson Design Devel., Eugene, 1993—95; pres. Davinci Designs, Eugene, 1996—2000; owner 2d Half Dynamics, 2000—; dir. Alzheimer's program Sunwest Mgmt., Inc., 2002—04; adult/elder specialist, life coach United Behavioral Health, 2004—. Cons. Jr. League Wichita, 1983, Plancon, Inc., Martinsville, NJ, 1987-88, Changing Creatively, 1997; continuing edn. instr. Lane C.C., 2000—; mem. adv. bd. Lane C.C. Ctr. for Leisure and Learning, 2000—. Mem. Wichita Conv. and Visitors Bur., 1987; mem. events com. Wichita Festivals, Inc., 1987; mem. Eugene Conv. and Visitors Bur., 1988—; mem. Eugene Airport Commn., 1991—, chmn., 1992-93; bd. dirs. Campus Life, chmn., 1993-94; mem. steering com. Eugene Celebration, 1991-94, Oreg. Women Bus. Owners Conf., 1997; bd. pres. Of Coun. for Bus. Edn., 1999-2000. Mem. AAUW, Am. Mktg. Assn. (pres. S.W. chpt. 1991—, pres. 1992-94, bd. dirs.), Soc. Travel Agt. in Govt., Adminstrv. Mgmt. Soc., Forum for Exec. Bus. Women, Gt. Plains Bus. Adminstrn. Group, Assn. Travel Exec., Eugene C. of C. (bus. devel. com. 1990-91), The Gerontol. Soc. Am. (student campus rep. 1999), Alzheimers Assn. (Oreg. chpt., edn. com., 2002—), Eugene High Ground Assn. (chmn.), Delta Gamma Alumni Assn. Republican. Avocations: decorating, writing, skiing, water-skiing, camping. Home: 1460 Olive St Apt 32 Eugene OR 97401-3991 Office Phone: 541-520-2567. Personal E-mail: gerovision@comcast.net.

PETERSON, DOROTHY HAWKINS, artist, educator; b. Albuquerque, Mar. 14, 1932; d. Ernest Lee and Ethel Dawn (Allen) Hawkins; m. John W. Peterson, July 9, 1954; children: John Richard, Dorothy Anne. BS in Edn., U. N.Mex., Albuquerque, 1953; MA, U. Tex., 1979. Freelance artist, 1960—; educator, instr. Carlsbad (N.Mex.) Ind. Elem. Sch. Dist., 1953-54; instr. Charleston (S.C.) County Schs., 1955-56; instr. in painting Midland (Tex.) Coll., 1971-76, Roswell (N.Mex.) Mus. Sch., 1981-83, 91—; instr. in art history Ea. N.Mex. U., Roswell, 1989—2000; instr. painting N.Mex. Mil. Inst., Roswell, 1992—94. Bd. dirs. N.Mex. Arts Commn., Santa Fe; cons. Casa de Amigos Craft Guild, Midland, Tex., 1971-73. One woman shows include Art Inst., Permian Basin, Odessa, Tex., 1994. Tutor Roswell Literacy Coun., 1988-89; bd. dirs. N.Mex. Arts & Crafts Fair, Albuquerque, 1983-85. Named Best of Show, Mus. of the S.W., 1967, 69; recipient Top award, 1973, 75, Juror award N.Mex. Arts & Crafts Fair, 1986, 1st pl. award Profl. Watercolor N.Mex. State Fair, 1988; Talens-d' Arches award, Tex. Watercolor Soc., 1998; Bd. Dirs. award, San Diego Watercolor Soc., 1998, N. Mex. Watercolor Soc., 1998. Mem. Nat. Watercolor Soc. (San Diego Watercolor Soc. award 1988), N.Mex. Watercolor Soc. (2d pl. award 1981, 1st pl. award state fair 1988, Grumbacher award 1993, Wingspread award 1994, 1st pl. award 1995, 1st, 3rd and Graham award 1997, Best of Show 2001, Best of Show 2004, Masterworks award N.Mex. Tricentennial 2005, 3d pl. award 2006, 1st pl. Masterworks, 2006). Office: Dorothy Peterson Studio PO Box 915 Roswell NM 88202-0915 Personal E-mail: dhpeterson@dfn.com.

PETERSON, DOROTHY LULU, artist; b. Venice, Calif., Mar. 10, 1932; d. Marvin Henry and Fay (Brown) Case; m. Leon Albert Peterson, June 21, 1955; 1 child, David. AD, Compton (Calif.) Coll., 1950. Artist Moran Printing Co., Lockport, NY, 1955—; caricature artist West Seneca and Kenmore Creative Artist Socs., 1973-86; commd. artist in pvt. practice, 1986—. Comml. artist Boulevard Mall, Kenmore Arts Soc., NY, 1974—. Works include portraits of Pres. and Mrs. Reagan in Presdl. Libr. Collection, also portraits of Geraldine Ferraro, Pres. Clinton, Pres. Bush, Pres. Nixon, Pres. Ford, Bette Davis, Lucille Ball, Bing Crosby, Elizabeth Taylor, Mickey Mantle; sculpture of Pres. Bush, Princess Diana, John Kennedy Jr., Shirley Temple Black; caricature sculptures of Joan Rivers, Erma Bombeck, Lucille Ball, Shirley Temple Black, Pres. Clinton, Hillary Clinton; author articles, poems. Recipient awards West. Seneca Art Soc., 1975, Kenmore Art Soc., 1982, 86. Recipient Editors award Nat. Poetry Soc., 1997, Editors Choice award Nat. Libr. of Poetry, 1998, Best Poems and Poets of 2001, Internat. Poet of Merit Silver Bowl award, 2002; named to The Best Poems and Poets of the 20th Century, Internat. Libr. of Poets. Democrat. Baptist. Home: 247 Pryor Ave Tonawanda NY 14150-7407

PETERSON, EILEEN M., state agency administrator; b. Trenton, N.J., Sept. 22, 1942; d. Leonard James and Mary (Soganic) Olschewski; m. Lars N. Peterson, Jr., 1970 (div. 1983); children: Leslie, Valerie, Erica. Grad., Internat. Guide Acad., 1998. Cert. Tour dir. Globus, Cosmos, Archers, 1999-2000; lic. realtor, 2002. Adminstrv. sec. State Ins. Fund, Boise, 1983-85; legal asst. Bd. Tax Appeals, Boise, 1985-87, exec. asst., 1987—92, dir., 1992—98; asst. shore excursion mgr. Renaissance Cruises, 2000—01; realtor Keller Williams Realty, 2002—. Ind. distbr. nutritional products USANA Health Scis., Inc., 2005—. Vol. tutor ESL Idaho Refugee Svc., 1997—98; docent Boise Art Mus., 1998—99, 2001—03. Recipient Gov's. Cert. of Recognition for Outstanding Achievement, 1995. Mem. Mensa, Investment Club (pres.), Mountain West Outdoor Club (treas. 1996-98), Idaho Rivers United, Internat. Platform Assn. Avocations: white water rafting, non-fiction reading, teaching esl. Home: 3317 Mountain View Dr Boise ID 83704-4638 Office Phone: 208-869-5842. Business E-Mail: eileen@primetimeproperty.com.

PETERSON, ELIZABETH, retired elementary school educator, advocate; b. Ft. Worth, Tex., July 23, 1920; d. Walter Leonard Peterson and Elizabeth Hudson; m. David Dellinger, Feb. 4, 1942 (dec.); 1 adopted child, Howard children: Patchen, Raymond, Natasha, Daniel, Michele. Student, U. Mich., Ann Arbor, 1938—40, U. Wash., Seattle, 1940—42; BEd, Trenton State Coll., NJ, 1968; MEd in Early Childhood Edn., Antioch U., N.Y., 1974. Cert. tchr. N.J., N.Y., Vt. Tchr. Flemington (N.J.) Elem. Sch., 1960—61, Quakertown (N.J.) Elem. Sch., 1961—67; caseworker Dept. Welfare, Bklyn., 1968—70; tchr. Flatbush Daycare Ctr., Bklyn., 1972—73; caseworker, supr. Talbot Perkins Childrens Svc., Bklyn., 1973—80; tchr. Headstart, Gilman, Vt., 1980—81, Walden (Vt.) Pub. Schs., 1981—82; advocate N.E. Agy. Aging, St. Johnsburg, Vt., 1985—89, 1997—99. Vol. Hospice, St. Johnsburg, 1990—99; mem. peace delegation to release US prisoners of Vietnam war Bratislava, 1967; mem. peace delegration to East and West Berlin England and Germany, 1980; spkr. on peace prevention of nuclear proliferation. Grantee Working for Peace award, Johnson State Coll., 2005. Mem.: Vt. Edn. Assn., Nonviolent Peaceforce, Womens Internat. League Peace, War Resisters League. Avocations: painting, writing poetry. Home: 149 Cronin Rd Schenevus NY 12155

PETERSON, EVONNE STEWART, elementary school educator; d. Richard Allen and Theresa Johnson Stewart; m. Kelvin Osborne Peterson (div.); 1 child, Chelsey Denise. BA in Art Edn., N.C. Ctrl. U., 1979; MA in Art Edn., Winthrop U., 1998; MEd in Reading, Lang., and Literacy, U. N.C., 2001; postgrad., Western Carolina U., 2006—. Cert. K-12 Reading Education Charlotte-Mecklenburg Schools, Charlotte, NC, 2001, K-12 Art Education Charlotte-Mecklenburg Schools, Charlotte, NC, 1991. Adminstrv. svcs. clk. Bachelor Enlisted Quarters, Rota, Spain, 1985—88; tour cons. Am. Airlines, Cary, NC, 1989—90; tchr. afterschool enrichment program Bruns Ave. Elem., Charlotte, 1991—92; tchr. art Lincoln Heights Elem., 1992—2004, tchr. Title I literacy, 2004—, Title I summer sch. site coord., lead tchr., 2005—. Sch. leadership team chair Lincoln Heights Elem., Charlotte, 2002—, tchr. adv. coun. rep., 2001—, mentor, 2000—, literacy/writing com., 2002—, key communicator, 2002—04, diversity facilitator, 2002—04; selected participant Tchg. Fellows Inst., White Oaks, Charlotte, 2005; presenter in field. Recipient Tchr. of Month award, Coca-Cola, 2003; grantee, World Affairs Coun., 1998, IMPACTII, 2000, Charlotte-Mecklenburg Schs., 2001. Mem.: N.C. Educators Assn. (corr.), Internat. Reading Assn. (corr.), Kappa Delta Pi, Phi Kappa Phi. Baptist. Avocations: aerobics/strength training, travel, reading, arts and crafts. Office: Lincoln Heights Elem Sch 1900 Newcastle St Charlotte NC 28216

PETERSON, GINGER, secondary school educator; b. Patrick AFB, Fla., Apr. 18, 1951; m. George E. Peterson Jr., Aug. 12, 1972; children: Jason, Jory, Jake. BS in Math., Religion, Ea. N.Mex. U., 1973, MEd, 1991. Cert. tchr., N.Mex. Jr. high/high sch. math tchr., dept. head math. Floyd (N.Mex.) Schs., 1991-93; math. tchr., head dept. Dora (N.Mex.), 1993—. Adv. bd. mem. Floyd High Sch., 1991-92; interview com. mem. Dora H.S., 1994-99; mem. student assistance team, 2005-. Mem.: Delta Kappa Gamma.

PETERSON, JANE TEMPLE, theater educator; b. Helena, Mont., Mar. 4, 1948; d. George James and Mary Addison Peterson. BA, Tulane U., New Orleans, 1970; MA, Tulane U., New Orleans; PhD, U. Mo., Columbia, 1989. Dramaturg Ind. U., Bloomington, 1985—89; prof. N.J. Inst. Tech., Newark, 1989—94, Montclair State U., 1994—. Judge new play contest Premiere Stages, Union, NJ, 2000—; artist evaluator N.J. Performing Arts Ctr., Newark, 2003—05; adjudicator Samuel French Play Festival, N.Y.C., 2003—05. Co-author: Women Playwrights of Diversity, 1997. Mem.: Am. Theatre and Drama Soc., Am. Soc. Theatre rsch., Assn. Theatre in Higher Edn., Phi Beta Kappa. Avocations: gardening, camping, reading. Office: Dept Theatre and Dance Montclair State Univ Montclair NJ 07043 Office Phone: 973-655-7343. Business E-Mail: petersonj@mail.montclair.edu.

PETERSON, JENNIFER LEIGH, mathematics educator; b. Huron, SD, Dec. 31, 1971; d. Richard Gene and Kandice Kay Boomsma; m. Layne Alan Peterson, Apr. 8, 2006; children: Nate, Alex, Ashley, Jordan, Shanae. BS, Huron (SD) U., 1997; MS, No. State U., Aberdeen, SD, 1999. Spl. edn. tchr. Wolsey Sch., SD, 1997—99; math. tchr., athletic dir., head volleyball coach, head track coach Wolsey-Wessington Sch., SD, 1999—. Office Phone: 605-883-4221.

PETERSON, JILL SUSAN, retired elementary school educator; b. Richland, Wash., July 26, 1946; d. Clarence Edward and Doris Edeline (Ostby) Lange; m. Wallace Peterson Jr., Aug. 10, 1968 (dec. Jan. 1991); 1 child, Dawn Sa Ra. BA, Pacific Luth. U., 1968; MA, U. St. Thomas, 1984; postgrad., Augsburg Coll., U. Minn., U. St. Thomas, U. Calif., Irvine. Tchr. Little Canada Elem. Sch., Minn., 1968—74; tutor title I Red Oak Elem., St. Paul, 1975—79; lead tchr. Sand Creek Elem., Mpls., 1979—88, Andover Elem., Mpls., 1988—2004. Adj. instr. multicultural edn. Hamline U., 1995—99; instr. Seeking Ednl. Equity and Diversity, 1995—. Human rights commr. City Arden Hills, Minn., 1987—90; pres. Children of the World, 1995—99; vol. Ctr. for Victims of Torture, Mpls., 2000—; Women in Soc. del. to Brazil People to People Ambassador Program, 2003; del. Global Peace Initiative to Egypt, People to People Internat., 2005; mem. coun. Roseville Luth. Ch., Minn., 1986—88, 1994—96, 2005—; bd. dirs. Owasso Pointe, 2005—06; mem. Owasso Pointe Bd., 2005—06. Recipient Award of Excellence, Minn. Elem. Sch. Prin. Assn., 1992. Mem.: NEA, Anoka-Hennepin Edn. Minn., Edn. Minn., Alpha Delta Kappa (pres. Alpha Omicron chpt. 1993—94, Regional Scholar of Merit 1994, Tchr. Outstanding Performance 2000). Avocations: reading, swimming, travel, volunteering, investing. Home: 3061 Highpointe Curve Roseville MN 55113

PETERSON, KAMI L., lawyer; BS, Brigham Young U., 1994, JD, 1997. Bar: Utah 1997. Assoc. Scalley & Reading, PC, 1997—2000; gen. counsel Zions Bancorp., Salt Lake City, 2000—. Office: Zions Bancorp 10 E South Temple, 5th Fl Salt Lake City UT 84133 Office Phone: 801-524-4632.

PETERSON, KATHERINE H., federal agency administrator, former ambassador; b. Pasadena, CA; Student, Nat. War Coll.; BA, U. Calif., Santa Cruz. Mem. staff Foreign Svc., 1976, Bureau of African Affairs, Washington; deputy chief of mission Amer. Embassy, Windhoek, Namibia, 1993—96; U.S. ambassador to Lesotho U.S. Dept. State, Washington, 1998—2001; dir. Fgn. Service Inst., Washington, 2001—.

PETERSON, KRISTIN, artist; b. Urbana, Ill., May 17, 1954; d. Theodore Bernard and Helen (Clegg) P. BFA, Kansas City Art Inst., 1978; MFA, U. Calif., 1982. Vis. artist Calif. State U., Humbolt, 1990. Solo exhbn. Diablo Valley Community Coll. Art Gallery, 1981, Meml. Union Art Gallery, 1982, Joseph Chowning Gallery, 87, 89; group exhbns. include Ten Video Artists, 1977, Crosby-Kemper Art Gallery, Kansas City, 1978, The Calif. State Fair Exhibit, 1982, cowtown, Chan-Elliot Gallery, 1983, The Show Box Show, The Art Store Gallery, 1986, Rags, San Francisco Art Commn. Gallery, 1989, Functional Fantasy, The Trans-Am. Pyramid, San Francisco, 1990. Nat. Endowment for the Arts grantee, 1986; Humanities Rsch. grantee, 1981-82. Mem. Emeryville Artists Cooperative.

PETERSON, LINDA H., English language educator; b. Saginaw, Mich., Oct. 11, 1948; BA in Lit. summa cum laude, Wheaton Coll., 1969; MA in English, U. R.I., 1973; PhD in English, Brown U., 1978; DHL, Quinnipiac U., 2004. From lectr. to assoc. prof. Yale U., New Haven, 1977-92, prof., 1992—, dir. undergrad. studies English, 1990-94, chair, 1994-2000, acting chair, 2003, Niel Gray Jr. prof. of English, 2002—, dir. grad. studies, 2005—. Dir. Bass writing program Yale Coll., 1979-89, 90-2004; mem. various departmental and univ. coms. Yale U., 1977-; presenter in field. Author: Victorian Autobiography: The Tradition of Self-Interpretation, 1986, Traditions of Victorian Women's Autobiography: The Poetics and Politics of Life Writing, 1999; co-author: Writing Prose, 1989, A Struggle for Fame: Victorian Women Artists and Authors, 1994; co-editor: Wuthering Heights: A Case Study in Contemporary Criticism, 1992, 2d edit., 2003, The Norton Reader, 11th edit., 2004, Instructor's Guide to the Norton Reader, 2004; mem. editl. bd. Writing Program Adminstrn., 1983-85, Coll. Composition and Comm., 1986-88, Auto/Biography Studies, 1990—; Victorian Poetry, 2002—; contbr. articles to profl. jours. Resident fellow Branford Coll., 1979-87, Mellon fellow Whitney Humanities Ctr., 1984-85, fellow NEH, 1989-90, fellow Harry Ransom Humanities Rsch. Ctr., U. Tex., 1997; life fellow Clare Hall, Cambridge, Eng., 1998—. Mem. MLA (del. assembly 1984-86, mem. program com. 1986-89, mem. non-fiction divsn. com. 1988-92, mem. nominating com. 1993-94, mem. teaching of writing divsn. 1993-98, mem. Victorian lit. divsn. 2004-), Nat. Writing Program Adminstrs. (mem. cons.-evaluator program 1982-95, mem. exec. bd. 1982-84, 89-90, v.p. 1985-86, pres. 1987-88), Nat. Coun. Tchrs. English (mem. CCCC nominating com. 1985, mem. coll. sect. com. 1987-90). Home: 53 Edgehill Rd New Haven CT 06511-1343 Office: Yale U Dept English PO Box 208302 New Haven CT 06520-8302 Office Phone: 203-432-2226. Business E-Mail: linda.peterson@yale.edu.

PETERSON, LINDA LOU, special education educator; b. Bakersfield, Calif., Oct. 17, 1939; d. Wiley Karl and Chrystine Walker Peterson. AA, El Camino Coll., Gardena, Calif., 1959; BS, U. So. Calif., L.A., 1961; postgrad., San Jose State U., 1988—96. Chpt. I tchr. Mt. Pleasant Unified Sch. Dist., Calif., 1986—88; resource specialist in spl. edn. Hayward Unified Sch. Dist., Calif., 1988—. Advisor, dir. Russian Hill Neighbors Bd., San Francisco, 1993—, hospitality and raffle chmn. Named Merit Tchr., San Marino Unified Sch. Dist., 1967. Mem.: NEA (del. to conf. 2004), Hayward Edn. Assn., Vintner's Club. Avocations: reading, exercise, fine dining, travel, jazz. Home: 1001 Pine St #1407 San Francisco CA 94109 Personal E-mail: l_peterson888@hotmail.com.

PETERSON, LINDA S., lawyer; b. Grand Forks, ND, Mar. 15, 1952; BA summa cum laude, U. N.D., 1973; JD, Yale U., 1977. Bar: N.D. 1977, D.C. 1978, U.S. Dist. Ct. D.C. 1979, U.S. Ct. Appeals (D.C. cir.) 1979, U.S. Ct. Appeals (3d cir.) 1982, Calif. 1986, U.S. Ct. Appeals (fed. cir.) 1986. Law clk. Ct. of Appeals for D.C., Washington, 1977-78; ptnr. Sidley & Austin, L.A., 1978—. Dep. counsel Webster Commn., 1992; mem. bd. trustees Southwestern U. Sch. Law, 1995. Recipient Dean Phillips Memorial Award, Vietnam Veterans of America. Mem. State Bar Calif. (rules of ct. com. 1988-91), L.A. County Bar Assn. (conf. dels. 1987-90, trustee 1998-99), Women Lawyers Assn. L.A. (bd. dirs. 1989-99, pres. 1998-99), Phi Beta Kappa. Office: Sidley Austin Brown & Wood LLP 555 W 5th St Ste 4000 Los Angeles CA 90013-3000

PETERSON, M. JEANNE, historian, educator; b. Minn., Nov. 26, 1937; d. Clifford Woodrow and Mildred Amelia (Kukas) P.; divorced. BA, U. Calif., 1966, PhD, 1972. Lectr., asst., assoc. prof. Ind. U., Bloomington, 1971-87, prof. history, 1987—, chairperson dept. history, 1987—93, exec. assoc. dean Coll. Arts and Scis., 1993—99, acting chair gender studies dept., 1999—2000, prof. emerita history, found. prof. emerita gender studies, 2001—. Cons. Jour. Women's History, Bull. Hist. Medicine, U. Mich. Press, Butler U., Indpls., Harvard U. Press, Princeton U. Press, Columbia U. Press, Ind. U. Press, SUNY Press, Food and Foodways, Med. History, ACLS, Am. Hist. Rev., Victorian Studies, NEH, NIH, Can. Coun., U. Nebr., U. Iowa, Adam Matthew Ltd., Johns Hopkins U. Press. Author: The Medical Profession in Mid-Victorian London, 1978, Family, Love, and Work in the Lives of Victorian Gentlewomen, 1989; assoc. editor: Oxford Dictionary of National Biography; co-editor: Lizzie Borden: A Case Book of Family and Crime in the 1890s, 1980; contbr. articles to profl. jours. NEH fellow, 1978-79, Guggenheim Found. fellow, 1984-85, Inst. for Advanced Study fellow Ind. U., 1984-85. Mem. Am. Hist. Assn., Soc. for the Social History Medicine, N.Am. Conf. Brit. Studies, Am. Assn. History Medicine, N.Am. Victorian Studies Assn. Home: 1311 S Rechter Ct Bloomington IN 47401-6173 Office: Ind U Dept Gender Studies 742 Ballantine Rd Bloomington IN 47401-5022 Office Phone: 812-855-0101. E-mail: petersom@indiana.edu.

PETERSON, MARISSA, information technology executive; BS in mech. engrng., Kettering U.; MBA, Harvard U. Mgmt. cons. Booz, Allen and Hamilton; previously held mktg., fin., and engrng. positions Saturn Corp., Gen. Motors; dir. US mfg. Sun Microsystems, Santa Clara, Calif., 1993—95, v.p. worldwide ops., logistics, 1995—98, v.p. worldwide ops., 1998—99, exec. v.p. worldwide ops., 2000—02, exec. v.p. worldwide ops. and chief customer advocate, 2002—. Bd. dirs. Covisint, SuperValu. Bd. trustees Kettering U., Industry Advisory Coun., Alliance for Innovative Mfg., Stanford U.; bd. dirs. Lucille Packard Children's Hosp., Stanford. Named to Top 100 in Bus., SF Bus. Times; recipient Silicon Valley Tribute to Women and Industry, Mgmt. Achievement award, Kettering U. Office: Sun Microsystems Inc 4150 Network Cir Santa Clara CA 95054 Office Phone: 650-960-1300, 800-555-9786. Office Fax: 408-276-3804.

PETERSON, MARTHA, artist; b. Flint, Mich., Sept. 26, 1927; d. Carl J. and Addie Amelia Primm; m. Edward Carlyle Peterson, Sept. 9, 1948; children: Mark, Laura, Michelle. Student, Corcoran Art Sch., Washington, 1966-68, Cath. U., 1966-67, Mich. State U., 1974-76. Art tchr. Forsyth CC, Winston-Salem, NC, 1995-96; pvt. art tchr. Winston-Salem, 1995—. Bd. dirs. Assoc. Arts Winston-Salem, 1995—97; co-founder Quincy Valley Art Students League; mem. Davison County Arts Mus. Mem.: Middletown Art Guild, High Point Arts Coun., Surry County Arts Coun. Unitarian Universalist. Avocations: gardening, reading, travel.

PETERSON, MILLIE M., state senator; b. Merced, Calif., June 11, 1944; BS, U. Utah, 1979, MSW, 1984. Mem. Utah Senate Dist. 12, Salt Lake City, 1991—2002. Susa Young Gates Award, 1998. Mem. NASW. Democrat. Address: 7131 W 3800 S West Valley City UT 84128-3416 Office Phone: 801-566-4423. Personal E-mail: mpeter7131@aol.com.

PETERSON, NANCY, special education educator; AS, Webster State Coll., 1963; BS in Elem. Edn. magna cum laude, Brigham Young U., 1964, MS in Ednl. Psychology, 1966, PhD in Ednl. Psychology, 1969. Instr. in tchr. edn. Brigham Young U., Provo, Utah, 1966-69; asst. prof. edn. dept. spl. edn. U. Kans., Lawrence, 1969-74, dir. spl. edn. classes for handicapped children Clin. Tng. Ctr., 1969-89, project dir. head start tng., 1973-74, coord. edn. univ. affiliated facility Clin. Tng. Ctr., 1969-74, coord. pers. tng. programs in mental retardation, 1973-76, assoc. prof. edn., 1974-88, project dir. pers. tng. programs, 1986-93, prof. edn. dept. spl. edn., 1988—, dept. chair, 1994—. Rsch. sci. Bur. Child Rsch., U. Kans., 1969—; prin. investigator for Kans. U. Kans. Early Childhood Rsch. Inst., 1977-82; Matthew Guglielmo Endowed Chair, Charter Sch. Edn., Calif. State U., LA, 1998-2000; Mary Ann Alia lectureship Charter Sch. Edn. Calif. State U. LA, 1999; prof. spl. edn. U. Kans., 2000—. Recipient J.E. Wallace Wallin award Internat. Coun. Exceptional Children, 1993. Office: U Kans Dept Spl Edn 521 Pearson Hall Lawrence KS 66045-3101

PETERSON, NANCY KAY, poet, editor, writer; b. Madison, Wis., Sept. 18, 1951; d. Roy G. and Margaret J. Peterson; m. Bill C. B. Ng, July 25, 1992. BS Journalism, So. Ill. U.-Carbondale, 1972; MPA, Ind. State U., 1977. Title III coord. St. Francis Coll., Ft. Wayne, 1979—82, asst. to dir. of pub. rels. and dir. devel., 1982—84; asst. dir. devel. St. Mary's U., Winona, Minn., 1984—90; dir. grants and sponsored projects Winona State U., Minn., 1990—, interim sexual harassment officer, 1994—96. Sec./treas. Minn. State U. Assn. Adminstrv. & Svc. Faculty, Winona, 1994—96, local pres., 1998—2000, local grievance officer, 2000—02, v.p., 2002—04. Co-founder/co-editor (literary mag.) Main Channel Voices: A Dam Fine Literary Mag., poet (poem) You'll Catch Your Death of Cold (nominee Pushcart Prize, 2001); author: (short story) For the Love Of (Grand Winner 2001 A Picture is Worth 1000-2000 Words Contest, 2001); poet (poem) North Meets South (quarter finalist New Century Writer's award, 2003), Lost in the Stars (2d pl. FMAM Poetic Mayhem Contest, 2004), Instructions on Chivalry (quarter finalist New Century Writer awards, 2003), Practical Joker (nominee Pushcart Prize, 2002). Elections specialist Mich. Dept. State, Lansing, 1978—79; adult literacy tutor Winona Cmty. Edn., 1987—92; mem. City of Winona Human Rights Commn., 1988—94, co-chair, 1992—94; organizer women's history month ann. poetry reading Winona Arts Ctr., 2002—. Mem.: Nat. Coun. U. Rsch. Adminstrs. Office: Main Channel Voices PO Box 492 Winona MN 55987-0492 Business E-Mail: contact@mainchannelvoices.com.

PETERSON, NORMA JO, retired education educator; b. Knoxville, Tenn., Dec. 26, 1938; d. Henry Beecher and Dorotha (Gross) P. BS, U. Tenn., 1960; MA, E. Tenn. State U., 1976. Cert. Career Ladder Level III elem. tchr. Elem. tchr. Knox County-Halls Elem. Sch., Knoxville, 1960-63; adminstrv. asst. Southeastern Region-Ch. of the Brethren, Bridgewater, Va., 1963-64; dir. Children's Work Nat. Office-Ch. of the Brethren, Elgin, Ill., 1964-69; elem. tchr. Prince George's County-Seabrook Elem. Sch., Seabrook, Md., 1969-70, Kingsport City Schs., Tenn., 1970—98; student tchr. supr. East Tenn. State U., Johnson City, 1998—2005; ret., 2006. Recipient Outstanding Educator award, Kingsport City Schs., Tenn., 1986. Avocations: reading, travel, needlecrafts.

PETERSON, PATRICIA MITCHELL, medical/surgical nurse; b. Danbury, Conn., Feb. 7, 1946; d. James Edward and Dorothy Marie (Brennan) Doyle; children: Eden Ho'onani, Marshall Chance, Paige Alexandra. RN, St. Francis Hosp. Sch. Nursing, Hartford, Conn., 1966; BS, Coll. St. Francis, Joliet, Ill., 1986. RN, Ariz. Pediat. charge nurse Glen Falls (N.Y.) Hosp., 1966; pediat. staff nurse Providence Hosp., Washington, 1966-67; med.-surg. charge nurse Halifax Med. Ctr., Daytona Beach, Fla., 1968-69, Castle Med. Ctr., Kailua, Hawaii, 1988, 89; night supr. Laniolu, Honolulu, 1971-73; pediatric RN Kuakini Hosp., Honolulu, 1973; charge nurse/pediatrics Maui Meml. Hosp., Kahului-Maui, Hawaii, 1973-79; orthopedic RN Humana Hosp., Phoenix, 1981-91, charge nurse night relief renal diabetic unit, 1991-95; Columbia Med. Ctr., Phoenix; high risk ob/pediatric case mgr. Cigna Healthcare Ariz., 1995-98; case mgr. Phoenix Bapt. Hosp., 1998—2001, Med. Mgmt. Health Net Ariz., 2001—04; staff nurse St. Joseph's Hosp., Phoenix, 2004—. Cons. in field. Home: 480 E Ocotillo Rd Phoenix AZ 85012-1021 Office Phone: 602-549-7691. Personal E-mail: pattympeterson@hotmail.com.

PETERSON, PENELOPE LORAINE, dean, education educator; b. Moline, Ill., Nov. 25, 1949; d. Leroy P.; m. W. Patrick Dickson; children: Andrew, Joshua, Elissa. BS, Iowa State U., 1971; MS, PhD, Stanford U., 1976. Asst. prof. dept. ednl. psychology U. Wis., Madison, 1976-80, assoc. prof., 1980-81, prof. ednl. psychology, 1982-85, Sears-Bascom Prof., 1985-87; prof. ednl. psychology & tchr. edn. Mich. State U., East Lansing, 1987—97, co-dir. Inst. Rsch. on Teaching, 1987—97, co- dir. Elem. Subjects Ctr., 1987-92, co-dir. Ednl. Policy Practice Study, 1992—97; dean Northwestern U. Sch. Edn. & Social Policy, Evanston, Ill., 1997—, Eleanor R. Baldwin prof. edn., 1997—. Author chpts. to books; editor: Rev. Ednl. Rsch, 1984-90; contbr. articles to profl. jours. Recipient Palmer O. Johnson award Am. Edn. Rsch. Assn., 1980, Raymond B. Cattell Early Career award Am. Ednl. Rsch. Assn., 1986, Disting. Rsch. award Assn. Tchr. Edn., 1992. Fellow Am. Psychol. Soc. Office: Northwestern U Sch Edn & Social Policy Annenberg Hall Rm 252 2120 Campus Dr Evanston IL 60208 E-mail: p-peterson@northwestern.edu.

PETERSON, REBECCA THORINE, retired voice educator, theater director; b. Durham, N.C., Dec. 23, 1944; d. Thoralf and Polly Ruth Ringdahl; m. John Arven Peterson, May 30, 1964 (dec.); 1 child, Terri Eileen. BS in Edn., Minot State Coll., N.D., 1966; MS in Speech/Theatre, Moorhead State U., Minn., 1979. Cert. tchr. English 1988. Tchr. vocal, instrumental music grades 5-8 New Rockford Pub. Sch., ND, 1966—67; tchr. vocal music grades 1-8 Devils Lake Pub. Sch., ND, 1967—69; tchr. vocal music grades 1-12 Dilworth Glyndon Felton Schs., Minn., 1969—2000; vocal instr. Internat. Cmty. Sch. Abidjan, Ivory Coast, 2000—03; ret., 2003. Cmty. theater dir. various orgns. including Cando Arts Coun. and Ft. Totten Little Theater, ND, 1966—99; pvt. voice, percussion, piano tchr., ND and Minn., 1962—2000; pres. Sun City Concert Band, 2003—. Dir. ch. choir various chs., Minn., 1960—2000. Recipient Tchr. of Yr., Dilworth Pub. Sch., 1975, 1976, Sword of Honor, Fargo-Moorhead Sigma Alpha Iota, Honor award, Minot State Coll. Music Dept., 1966. Mem.: Sigma Alpha Iota Alumni (v.p., pres. 1971—). Avocations: theater, bowling, golf. Home: 11030 W Acacia Dr Sun City AZ 85373

PETERSON, RHONDA LYNN, elementary school educator; b. St. Charles, Ill., Aug. 27, 1956; d. Larkin Edward and Marilyn Ann O'Neal; m. Kevin John Peterson, Sept. 18, 1982; 1 child, Travis Jay; m. Roger Lee Biddle, June 10, 1975 (div. Aug. 0, 1981); 1 child, Thomas Michael Biddle. AS, Waubonsee C.C., Sugar Grove, Ill., 1995; BS in Elem. Edn., No. Ill. U., DeKalb, 1997; M of Edn. in Reading & Literacy, Benedictine U., Lisle, Ill., 2004. Tchr. 1st grade Hinckley/Big Rock Sch. Dist. 429, Ill., 1997—2000, Geneva Cmty. Unit Sch. Dist. 304, Ill., 2000—. Mem. Heartland Elem. Character Edn. Com., Geneva, 2001—, Heartland Elem. Sch. Improvement Team, Geneva, 2002—; chmn. Heartland Elem. Common Vocabulary/Alignment Com., Geneva, 2003—; mem. Geneva Sch. Dist. Math Com., 2004—. Nominee Disney/Hand Tchr. award, 2004, Tchr. of Yr., 2006; recipient Outstanding Pre-Svs. Social Educator award, 1997, Cert. of Commendation for Sallie Mae First Class Tchr. award, 1998. Mem.: NEA, Internat. Reading Assn., Ill. Edn. Assn. Avocations: walking, scrapbooks. Home: 17705 Pleasant St Maple Park IL 60151 Office: Heartland Elem Sch 3300 Heartland Dr Geneva IL 60134 Office Phone: 630-463-3200. Office Fax: 630-463-3209. Business E-Mail: rpeterson@geneva304.org.

PETERSON, ROSETTA HICKS, retired music educator; b. Memphis, Dec. 23, 1932; d. Homer Jackson Hicks and Loretta Jones Hicks Kateo; m. Caleb Theodore Peterson (div.). BA, Spelman Coll., Atlanta, 1954; M in Music Edn., Memphis State U., 1975. Cert. tchr. Ga., Tenn. Music tchr. T.H. Slater Elem. Sch., Atlanta, 1954—60, Porter Jr. HS, Memphis, 1961—71, Vance Jr. HS, Memphis, 1971—94; elem. tchr. Douglas Elem. Sch., Memphis, 1960—61; ret., 1994. Organist Rush Meml. Ch., Atlanta, 1957—60; organist, dir. Mt. Pisgah CME Ch., Memphis, 1966—88, St. John Bapt. Ch., Memphis, 1988—. Singer: (opera chorus) Aida, Memphis Opera, 1969, Porgy and Bess, Lyric Theatre, 1972. Vol. VA Hosp., Memphis, 1964—88, Friends of the Orpheum, Memphis, 1978—82. Named Outstanding Secondary Tchr. Am., Washington, 1974. Mem.: Music Educators Nat. Conf., Zool. Soc., Zeta Phi Beta (life; state dir. 1969—71), Phi Delta Kappa (life; pres. Beta Eta chpt.).

PETERSON, RUTH D., sociologist; BA, Cleve. State Univ., 1969, MA, 1973; PhD, Univ. Wis., Madison, 1993. Asst. prof. Univ. Iowa, 1982—85, Ohio State Univ., 1985—89, assoc. prof., 1989—96, prof., 1996—; dir. Criminal Justice Rsch. Ctr., Ohio State Univ., 1999—. Mem. editl. bd. Race and Society, 1998—2002. Co-editor: Crime and Inequality, 1995; editor (assoc.): Criminology, 1997—2000; contbr. articles to prof. jour. Fellow: Am. Soc. Criminology (v.p. 1999—2000, Herbert Bloch award 1995); mem.: Am. Sociol. Assn. Office: Ohio State University Sociology Department 300 Bricker Hall 190 N Oval Mall Columbus OH 43210

PETERSON, SANDRA KAY, librarian; b. McCook, Nebr., Nov. 21, 1941; d. Walter Rundall and Marjorie Ann (Foster) P. BA, Kearney State Coll., 1963; MLS, U. Pitts., 1967; MS, George Washington U., 1979. Ref. asst. Libr. Congress, Washington, 1965-66; ref. libr. W.Va. State Libr., Charleston, 1967-68, Oberlin Coll., Ohio, 1968-70; documents libr. U. No. Iowa, Cedar Falls, 1970-74, Coll. William and Mary, Williamsburg, Va., 1974-83, Yale U., New Haven, 1984—2003, dir. social svcs. librs. and info. svcs., 2003—. Mem. Depository Libr. Coun. to Pub., Washington, 1983-85, printer. Bd. dirs. Domestic Violence Svcs., New Haven, 1985-91; founder, bd. dirs. Greater Williamsburg Domestic Violence Program, 1978-83. Mem. ALA (coun. mem. 1987-91, chair, sec. Govt. Documents Round Table 1981-83, James Bennett Childs Lifetime Achievement award 1994). Avocations: gardening, basketry, reading, travel. Office: Yale U 38 Mansfield St New Haven CT 06511-3512

PETERSON, SOPHIA, political scientist, educator; b. Astoria, N.Y., Nov. 24, 1929; d. George Loizos and Caroline (Hofstetter) Yimoyines; m. Virgil Allison Peterson, Dec. 28, 1951; children: Mark Jeffrey, Lynn Marie. BA, Wellesley (Mass.) Coll., 1951; MA, UCLA, 1956, PhD, 1969; DHL (hon.), Wheeling Jesuit U., 1997. Instr. Miami U., Oxford, Ohio, 1961-63; with W.Va. U., Morgantown, 1966—, assoc. prof., 1972-79, prof., 1979-97, prof. emerita, 1997—, dir., internat. studies maj., 1980-92. Dir. W.Va. Consortium for Faculty & Course Devel. in Internat. Studies, Morgantown, 1980-97, founding dir., 1997—. Author: monograph Monograph Series in World Affairs, 1979. Recipient gold medal semi-finalist CASE Prof. of Yr. award Coun. for Advancement and Support of Edn., 1987, Outstanding Tchr. award W.Va. U., W.Va. U. Coll. Arts and Scis., 1988, finalist Prof. of Yr. award W.Va. Faculty Merit Found., 1991, Heebink award for disting. state svc. W.Va. U., 1984. Mem. W.Va. Polit. Sci. Assn. (pres. 1984-85). Democrat. Avocations: sailing, travel. Home: 849 Vandalia Rd Morgantown WV 26501-6247 Office: WVa U Dept Polit Sci Morgantown WV 26506 Office Phone: 304-293-7140.

PETERSON, SUSAN, political science professor, dean; d. Phillip (Stepfather) and Janet Chalke, Jack Peterson; life ptnr. Heather Scully; 1 child, Norah. BA, St. Lawrence U., Canton, N.Y., 1983; PhD, Columbia U., N.Y.C., 1992. Vis. asst. prof. govt. Smith Coll., Northampton, Mass., 1991—93; vis. asst. prof. Sch. Internat. Rels. U. So. Calif., L.A., 1993—94; asst. prof. govt. Coll. William and Mary, Williamsburg, Va., 1994—98, assoc. prof. govt., 1998—2004, prof. govt., 2004—, dean ednl. policy arts and scis., 2005—. Exec. editor Security Studies, 2003—05, editor-in-chief, 2005—06. Author: Crisis Bargaining and the State: The Domestic Politics of International Conflict; co-editor: Altered States: International Relations, Domestic Politics, and Institutional Change; contbr. articles to profl. jours. Mem. Peninsula AIDS Found., Newport News, Va., 1997—2000, Our Own Cmty. News, Norfolk, Va., 1997—98; chair Williamsburg AIDS Network, 1998—2000. Recipient Outstanding Internat. Studies Faculty award, Coll. of William and Mary, 2002, 2003; Nat. Security fellow, John M. Olin Inst. Strategic Studies Harvard U., 1989—91, Dwight Eisenhower/ Clifford Roberts fellow, World Affairs Inst., 1990—91. Mem.: Women in Internat. Security, Am. Polit. Sci. Assn., Internat. Studies Assn. Unitarian Universalism. Home: 112 Barrows Mount Williamsburg VA 23185 Office: Coll William and Mary 127 Ewell Hall Williamsburg VA 23187-8795 Office Phone: 757-221-2498. Office Fax: 757-221-2464. Business E-Mail: smpete@wm.edu.

PETERSON, TERESA B., educational consultant; d. Dorothy D. McCraw; children: Lara V, Lynsey R, Andrew T. Doctorate, U. NC, 2006. Cert. Spl. Edn. NC. Compliance facilitator Midwood, TAPS, Morningside, Charlotte, NC, 2004—, exceptional children's specialist, 2004—. Spl. populations coord. Midwood, TAPS, Morningside, 2004—. Co-author: Keys to Successful 21st Century Educational Leadership. Recipient Harris Tchr. of Yr., Sch. Sys., 2002; Para Educator grant, NC Pub. Sch., 1997, Leadership grant, Office Spl. Edn., 2002. Mem.: Coun. Exceptional Children (assoc.). Home: 3518 Campbell Dr Charlotte NC 28205 Office Phone: 980-343-6011.

PETERSON, TERRY NORRIS, lawyer; b. Wichita, Kans. BA, U. Tex., Austin, 1994; JD, South Tex. Coll. Law, 1998. Bar: Tex. 1998. Assoc. Johnson, Spalding, Doyle, West & Trent, L.L.P., Houston. Named a Rising Star, Tex. Super Lawyers mag., 2005; recipient, 2006. Mem.: Greater Houston Soc. Health Risk Mgmt., Garland Walker Inns of Ct., ABA, Houston Bar Assn. Office: Johnson Spalding Doyle West & Trent LLP 919 Milam St Ste 1700 Houston TX 77002 Office Phone: 713-222-2323. E-mail: tpeterson@js-llp.com.*

PETERSON GERSTNER, JANET, English professor; b. Normal, Ill., Nov. 5, 1963; d. Carroll Valleen and Lillian Maxine Peterson; m. Clilnton J. Gerstner, Aug. 1, 1992; children: Isabelle Olivia Gerstner, Alec James Gerstner. BA in English, Colo. State U., Denver, 1991; MA in English, Ariz. State U., Tempe, 1994, PhD in English, 2000. Assoc. prof. English, San Juan Coll., Farmington, N.Mex., 2001—. Recipient Tchg. Excellence award, Nat. Inst. for Staff and Orgnl. Devel., 2003; fellow, Preparing Future Faculty, Fall 1997-Spring 1999. Mem.: MLA, Nat. Coun. of Tchrs. of English, Two-Year Coll. Assn., League for Innovation in the C.C. Office: San Juan Coll 4601 College Blvd Farmington NM 87402 Office Phone: 505-566-3140.

PETIET, CAROLE ANNE, psychologist; b. Newport News, Va., Mar. 1, 1952; d. Gaston Kaleski and Ann (Snyder) Pettit Johnson; m. Lawrence Phillip Bischoff III, Dec. 29, 1973 (div. 1979); m. Robert Jomax Brooks, May 4, 1984 (div. 1989); 1 child, Nicole; stepchildren: Gregory, Randall. BS in Nursing, Baylor U., 1975; MA, Calif. Sch. Profl. Psychology, Berkeley, 1980, PhD, 1982. RN Calif.; lic. psychologist Calif., Colo. Charge nurse Elizabeth Knutsson Hosp., Estes Park, Colo., 1975-76; nurse coordinator, staff nurse Alta Bates Hosp., Berkeley, Calif., 1976-83; pvt. practice psychotherapy, cons., sports psychology Berkeley, Calif., 1982—; tng./clin. cons., rsch. cons. Phoenix Recovery Ctrs., Alameda, Calif., 1980-88; staff psychologist Kaiser Permanente Med. Ctr., Vallejo, Calif., 1982-84. Sports psychology cons. Women's Ski Programs, Aspen, Colo., and B.C., Can., 1986-93; coord. women's studies splty., mem. faculty Rosebridge Grad. Sch., Walnut Creek, Calif., 1986-94; supr., mem. adj. faculty CSPP, Berkeley/Alameda, 1986-89; intern Eden Youth and Family Svcs., Hayward, Calif., 1978-79, No. Calif. State Correctional Med. Facility, Vacaville, 1979-80, Kaiser Vallejo, 1980-81, Kaiser San Francisco, 1981-82; rschr. in field. Contbr. articles, presentations to profl. publs. Scholar Baylor Hosp. Women's Aux., 1974, Soroptimists, 1981; recipient Am. Coll. Scholarship, 1979. Mem. APA, Assn. Women in Psychology, World Fedn. Mental Health, NOW, Amnesty Internat. Democrat. Achievements include research on neuropsychological effects of altitude on women climbers. Office: 2340 Ward St Ste 105 Berkeley CA 94705-1146 Office Phone: 510-843-6760.

PETITO, MARGARET L., foundation president; b. Dallas, Sept. 28, 1950; d. Jacob Charles and Eileen (Shank) Loehr; m. John Haven Petito, 1978 (div. 1984); children: John Christian Robert, David Nelson. BA, So. Meth. U., 1972; MA, Georgetown U., 2006. Mem. Action/Vista Program U.S. Govt., Middlesex, NY, 1972—74; dir., curator Oliver House Mus., Penn Yan, NY, 1975—77; staff asst. Williams & Jensen, P.C., Washington, 1986—89; dir. fed. rels. Chambers Devel. Co., Inc., 1989—92; dir. fed. affairs DSSI-U.S. Biotech., Washington, 1992—94; cons., dir. pub. affairs Embassy Ecuador, Govt. Ecuador, Washington, 1994—96; prin. Petito & Assocs., Washington, 1994—. Dir. external events Internat. Cancer Alliance, Bethesda, Md., 1996—97, Sch. of Bus., Georgetown U., Washington, 1998—99; pres., exec. dir. Friends of Rule of Law in Ecuador, Inc., 2001—. Spl. legis. advisor Drugwatch Internat., Chgo., 1993—; bd. dirs. Nyumbani Orphanage for Kenyan Children with AIDS, Washington, 1989—99; dir. Marshall Ho. Mus., Lambertville, NJ, 1980—82; founder, co-chair Forum for Environ., Washington, 1989—91; pres. Cultural Partnership of the Ams., Washington, 1999—. Mem.: Tex. State Soc. Roman Catholic. Avocations: squash, needlepoint, fishing. Home and Office: Friends of Rule of Law in Ecuador Inc 6008 34th Pl NW Washington DC 20015-1607 Office Phone: 202-537-1327. Business E-Mail: mlp3@starpower.net.

PETKANICS, DONNA M., lawyer; BA, Northwestern U., 1980; JD, U. Calif., Boalt Hall Law Sch., 1985. Staff economist President Carter Adminstrn., Washington; with Wilson Sonsini Goodrich & Rosati, Palo Alto, Calif., 1985—, assoc. mng. ptnr., 1996—97, co-chmn., nominating com., 1997, 1998, mng. dir. - ops., ptnr., mem. exec. mgmt. com. & policy com. Office: Wilson Sonsini Goodrich & Rosati 650 Page Mill Rd Palo Alto CA 94304-1050 Office Phone: 650-493-9300. Office Fax: 650-493-6811. Business E-Mail: dpetkanics@wsgr.com.

PETKE, BEVERLY ANN, music educator; d. Morris Eugene and Geraldine Almina (Snyder) Evans; m. James Robert Petke, July 12, 1975; children: Amy Lavonne (Petke) Greer, Alan Adrian. MusB, Wis. State U., Stevens Point, 1971. Cert. tchr. music Pa. State Dept. Edn., 1989, Wis. State Dept. Pub. Instrn., 1971. Music tchr. Chambersburg Area Sch. Dist., Chambersburg, Pa., 1992—. Office: Chambersburg Area School District 435 Stanley Ave Chambersburg PA Office Phone: 727-263-9281.

PETKO, PATRICIA ANN, music educator; d. Owen M. and Jean A. Bastian; m. Thomas J. Petko, Aug. 29, 1979; 1 child, Thomas Owen Ambler. EdB, West Chester State Coll., Pa.; EdM, West Chester U., Pa., 1973. Music tchr. Coatesville Area Sch. Dist., Pa., 1970—. Musician West Chester Band, 1987—. Recipient Outstanding Svc. award, PTA, 1981, 1984, 1990. Mem.: Music Educators Nat. Conf., Pa. Music Educators Assn. Office: Reeceville Elementary School 248 Reeceville Rd Coatesville PA 19320 Office Phone: 610-383-3785.

PETRAKIS, JULIA WARD, small business owner; b. Englewood, NJ, Apr. 24, 1936; d. William Davis and Elizabeth (Shaw) Ticknor; children by previous marriage: Elizabeth Anne Kinnunen Stam, Allan Conrad III; m. Peter L. Petrakis, Jan. 2, 1988. BA in Biochemistry, Radcliffe Coll., 1958. Ct. reporter Miller Reporting, Washington, 1979-81; sec. Whittaker Corp., Arlington, Va., 1981-82; adminstrv. asst. Entre Computers, Tysons Corner, Va., 1982-84; bus. owner Facts OnLine, Camano Island, Wash., 1984—. U.S. agent MITEK Info. Svcs., Moscow; cons., researcher, book indexer, writer, and instr. in field. Interviewer Harvard-Radcliff Colls., Cambridge, Mass., 1984-85; vol. Cancer Drive, Heart Drive, Annapolis, 1986-89; dir. Cape St. Claire Security Fund, Annapolis, Md., 1988-89; treas. Camano Laguna Vista Community, 1992-94. Avocations: gardening, bird watching, stained glass design. Home: 989 Valerie Dr Camano Island WA 98282 E-mail: factsonline2004@yahoo.com.

PETRAKOS, JOAN, elementary school educator; b. Chgo., Jan. 7, 1965; life ptnr. Matthew Krolak; 1 child, Harper Krolak. BA in Econs., Ill. Benedictine U., Lisle; EdM, DePaul U., Chgo.; M in Ednl. Leadership and Adminstrn., Northeastern U., Chgo. Tchr. Chgo. Pub. Schs., 2000—. Named to Athletic Hall of Fame, Notre Dame H.S., 2005. Home: 5000 N Western Chicago IL 60625 Office: Ames Middle School 1920 N Hamlin Chicago IL 60647 Office Phone: 773-534-4970. Office Fax: 773-534-4975. Personal E-mail: jpetrakos107@hotmail.com.

PETRALLI, MARY JANE, secondary school educator; b. St. Louis, Apr. 3, 1965; d. James Kenneth and Theresa Francis Bax; m. Anthony Louis Petralli, Apr. 6, 1991; children: Emily Nicole, Andrew Louis. BS in Applied Math., U. Mo., St. Louis, 1989, BS in Secondary Edn., 1995, EdM summa cum laude, 2001. Career continuous profl. cert. grades 7-12 math. Info. specialist Internat. Tech., Earth City, Mo., 1989—92; tchr. grades 4-8 St. James the Greater Sch., St. Louis, 1995—98; tchr. grades 9-12 Ritenair Sch. Dist., St. Louis, 1998—. Soccer coach St. William Sch., St. Louis, 1994; volleyball coach Ritenaur H.S., St. Louis, 1998—99, after sch. tutoring lab., 1998—2005. Mem. be. edn. St. William Sch., St. Louis, 1993—94; fundraiser, co-planner, mgr. Kratz Elem. Sch., St. Louis, 2002—04; vol. St. William Holy Trinity Ch., St. Louis, 2000—02. Mem.: Math. Assn. Am., Nat. Coun. for Tchrs. Math. Avocations: reading, hiking, free diving, camping. Home: 9263 Bataan Dr Saint Louis MO 63134 Office Phone: 314-493-6000 ext. 1117. Personal E-mail: TPetralli@sbcglobal.net. Business E-Mail: petrallim@ritenour.k12.mo.us.

PETREE, BETTY CHAPMAN, anesthetist; b. Emmetsburg, Iowa, Sept. 25, 1950; d. David Jr. and Wilma Ruby (Jones) Chapman; m. Howard Gray Petree, Sept. 21, 1974; children: Zachary Gray, Lynsey Taylor. Diploma, Davis Hosp. Sch. Nursing, 1970; cert., N.C. Bapt. Hosp. Sch. Nursing, 1974. RN, N.C. Clin. mgr. pre admit testing N.C. Bapt. Hosp., Winston-Salem, chief nurse anesthetist outpatient surgery, 1990—, asst. dir. nurse anesthesiology, 1997—2005, assoc. dir. nurse anesthesiology, 2005—. Mem. AANA Nat. Re-certification Coun., 1996—2003, v.p., 1997—99, vice chmn., 1998—2002, chmn., 1999—2003. Author: Anesthesia for Kidney Transplantation, Thoracic Aortic Trauma. Recipient Excellence in Teaching award, 1984, 86, 100 Great N.C. Nurses award, 1992. Mem. AANA (Clin. Practitioner award 1988), NCANA (program chmn. 1984-85), NCBH Anesthesia Alumni (sec. 1975-76, pres. 1993-95).

PETRELIS, STELLA MARSHA, writer; b. Tulare, Calif., May 29; d. George Peter and Mersa Soultana Petrelis; m. R.E. Stiles (dissolved). Student, U. Calif., Berkeley, 1962. Freelance writer Fresno Bee, Calif., 1981—93, Visalia Times-Delta, Calif., 1983—91. Recipient Poetry award, Writer's Digest, 1983. Avocations: art, photography, music, horticulture.

PETRI, CHRISTINE ANN, music educator; b. Trenton, NJ; d. Swen Albert Gilberg and Elizabeth Catherine Schutte; m. Joseph Carmen Petri, July 21, 1994. MusB in Music Edn., Westminster Choir Coll., 1971; MA in Music Performance, The Coll. NJ, 1974. Cert. tchr. N.J., 1971. Choral music dir. Hunterdon Ctrl. HS, Flemington, NJ, 1971—84, Hightstown (N.J.) HS, 1984—. Musical dir., prodr. Drama Dept. Hightstown (N.J.) HS, 1984—; pvt. voice and guitar tchr., NJ, 1967—90. Performer: worldwide, 1984—. Mem.: NEA, Ctrl. Jersey Music Educators Assn., Music Educators Nat. Conf., N.J. Edn. Assn. Avocations: antiques, classic cars, cats, guitar, costuming. Home: 1617 Miriam Drive North Brunswick NJ 08902 Office: Hightstown High School 25 Leshin Lane Hightstown NJ 08520

PETRICH, KATHRYN, music educator; b. Parkersburg, W.Va., May 15, 1967; d. Helmut Robert and Johnnie Sue Petrich. MusB Edn., U. Mich., Flint, 1990; MA in Choral Music, Ea. Mich. U., Ypsilanti, 1997. Choral dir. Marshall Pub. Schs., Mich., 1996—. Dir. honors choir activities Mich. Sch. Vocal Music Assn., Big Rapids, 2000—05. Recipient Supts. award for Bldg. Cmty./Sch. Rels., Supt., 1998. Mem.: Marshall Tchrs. Assn. (v.p. 1998—2006). Republican. Presbyterian. Avocation: singing. Home: 42 N McKinley Ave Battle Creek MI 49017-4768 Office: Marshall High School 701 N Marshall Ave Marshall MI 49068 Office Phone: 269-781-1330. Home Fax: 269-781-5304; Office Fax: 269-781-5304. Personal E-mail: mkathrynpetrich@aol.com. Business E-Mail: kpetrich@marshall.k12.mi.us.

PETRIE, LOIS ANN, enterostomy therapy nurse; b. Coraopolis, Pa., Jan. 24, 1941; d. Russell and Helen (McEwen) Hoover; m. Jon Petrie, Dec. 27, 1961. Diploma, Sewickley Valley Hosp., 1961; BS in Health Arts, Coll. St. Francis, 1989, MS in Cmty. Health Administrn., 1996. Staff nurse various hosps., Pitts., 1961-67; head enterostomal therapy West Pa. Hosp., Pitts., 1967-70; cons. pvt. practice, West Palm Beach, Fla., 1970-75; clinician St. Mary's Hosp., West Palm Beach, Fla., 1974-75; cons. Dept. Health, West Palm Beach, Fla., 1974-76; nurse enterostomal therapy St. Joseph's Hosp., Atlanta, 1982-86; cons. North Fulton Med. Ctr., Roswell, Ga., 1984-89; enterostomal therapy coord. St. Joseph's Hosp., 1986-93; enterostomy therapy specialist Northside Hosp., Atlanta, 1993—2001; ret., 2001. Cons., mem. adv. bd. Confortex, Inc., Winona, Minn., 1989-93; faculty preceptor Emory U., Atlanta, 1987— Mem. Nat. Found. Crohn's and Colitis (bd. dirs. Atlanta chpt. 1984-85, bd. dirs. 1998—), Wound Ostomy and Continence Nurses Soc. (regional treas. 1989-93, Outstanding Nurse for S.E. Region award 1992), Am. Cancer Soc. (bd. dirs. 1984-90), Ga. Coun. Nursing Splty. Orgns., United Ostomy Assn.

PETRILLI, MICHELLE LESLIE, lawyer; b. Bridgeport, Conn., Sept. 3, 1953; d. Russell Moreton and Patricia Aldona (Yasonis) Cory; m. Jeffrey S. Welch, May 24, 1978 (div.); 1 child: Stephanie Cory. BA in Biol. sci., U. Del., 1976; JD, Del. Law Sch., Widener U., 1979. Bar: Del. 1979, Pa. 1980. Law clk. Schmittinger & Rodriguez, P.A., Wilmington, Del., 1977—79; jud. clk. Del. Ct. Chancery, Wilmington, 1980—81; assoc. legal counsel Bank of Del. and Bank of Del. Corp., Wilmington, 1981—84, gen. counsel, v.p., 1984—. Mem. exec. com. bd. dirs. Industry Coun. for Tangible Assets, Wash., 1983—86; state rep. Conf. of State Bank Suprs., 1986—. Elected bd. dirs. New Castle County Econ. Devel. Corp., chmn. affordable housing com.; apptd. chair Gov.'s Pub. Safety Coun.; mem. Del. State C. of C., elected dir., 1989. Mem.: Del. Bankers Assn. (govt. affairs com.), Lawyers Forum, Del. Valley Corp. Counsel Assn. (bd. dirs. 1986—89), Fin. Women Internat., Del. Bar Assn., ABA. Republican. Roman Catholic. Home: 2618 Tonbridge Dr Wilmington DE 19810-1217 Office: Bank of Del 222 Delaware Ave Wilmington DE 19801-1621

PETRO, NATALIE ANN, secondary school educator; b. Donora, Pa., Sept. 15, 1979; d. Dimitri Michael and Pauline Petro. Bachelors, U. Pitts., 2002, MA in tchg., 2003. Gymnastics coach B.G.'s Gymnastics Sch., Monessen, 1992—99; dance instr. Shirley Deans Sch. Dance, Belle Vernon, 1997—99; cook Pamela's, Oakland, 2001—03; intern Canon-McMillan HS, Canonsburg, 2002—03, diving coach, 2002—, tchr., 2003—. Mem.: Pi Lamda Theta. Home: 715 Wisteria Ave Apt #3 Pittsburgh PA 15228

PETROFF, LAURA R., lawyer; b. Cleve., July 7, 1955; BA, Denison U., 1977; JD, Vanderbilt U., 1980. Bar: Ill. 1980, U.S. Dist. Ct. Ill. (No. dist.) 1980, Calif. 1986, U.S. Dist. Ct. Calif. (Ctrl. So. and No. dist.) 1986, U.S. Ct. Appeals (9th cir.). Ptnr. Winston & Strawn LLP, L.A., 2000—, mng. ptnr. Chair, ptnr. compensation com. Winston & Strawn LLP, L.A., mem. exec. com., mem. diversity com. Gen. counsel PIHRA Found.; founding mem. Women Rainmakers Roundtable. Mem.: ABA (bd. dirs. pub. counsel law ctr.), State Bar Calif., L.A. County Bar Assn. (co-chair edn. com. 1989—91, mem. exec.com. 1990—92). Office: Winston & Strawn LLP 333 S Grand Ave Los Angeles CA 90071-1543 Office Phone: 213-615-1736. Office Fax: 213-615-1750. E-mail: lpetroff@winston.com.

PETRU, MARIANNE, mathematics educator; b. St. Louis, Nov. 17, 1954; d. Henry August and Lillian Jeanette (Budarek) P. BA, Fontbonne Coll., 1977; MBA, U. Mo., St. Louis, 1983. Cert. tchr., Mo. Math. tchr. St. Joseph's Acad., St. Louis, 1977—. Named Most Influential Tchr., U. Mo., Columbia, 1992. Mem. Nat. Coun. Tchrs. Math., Mo. Coun. Tchrs. Math., Math. Educators Greater St. Louis. Office: St Joseph's Acad 2307 S Lindbergh Blvd Saint Louis MO 63131-3596

PETRUCCI-SAMIJA, MARIA, chemist; PhD in Inorganic Chemistry, McGill U., 1999. Chemist Lumenon Innovative Lightwave Tech., 2000—02; chemist, leader photonics team DuPont Experimental Station, 2002—. Named one of Top 100 Young Innovators, MIT Tech. Review, 2004. Office: DuPont Experimental Station 1007 Market St Wilmington DE 19898

PETRUS, SALLY A., elementary school educator; b. Parma, Ohio, Sept. 20, 1965; d. Salvatore Charles Scherma and Carmie Lizzini-Scherma; m. Ronald M. Petrus, Oct. 13, 1990; children: triplets, Arianne Lee, Brianne Lynn, Carlianne Marie. BFA, Ohio U., Athens, 1987; MEd, Baldwin Wallace Coll., Berea, Ohio, 1991. Tchr. Parma City Sch. Dist., 1989—. Advisor student coun., Parma, 2004—, h.s. cheerleading, 1991—98. Recipient Cleve. Crystal Apple award, Cleve. Plain Dealer, 2001. Mem.: PTA (assoc.). Parma Edn. Assn. (assoc.), Nat. Tchrs. Assn. (assoc.). Home: 14572 Walking Stick Way Strongsville OH 44136 Office: Parma City Sch Dist 5210 Loya Pky Parma OH 44134 Office Phone: 440-885-2418. Personal E-mail: sallypabc@aol.com.

PETRUSKI, JENNIFER ANDREA, speech and language pathologist; b. Kingston, NY, Jan. 28, 1968; d. Andrew Francis and Judith (Cruger) Petruski. BS, SUNY, Buffalo, 1990, MSEd in Speech-Language Pathology, 1992. Cert. tchr. speech-hearing handicapped N.Y., lic. speech-lang. pathology N.Y., cert. of clin. competence. Speech-lang. pathologist Kingston (N.Y.) City Schs., 1992—, student rev. team facilitator, 2002; clin. practicum supr. SUNY, New Paltz, 1996—. Cooperating tchr. SUNY, New Paltz, 1995—2004; ind. contr. speech svcs. Ulster County, 1997; cooperating tchr. Coll. St. Rose, 1997, 2004; summer sch. tchr. New Paltz Sch. Dist., 2002. Mem.: NY State Speech-Lang. and Hearing Assn., Am. Speech and Hearing Assn. (Continuing Edn. award 2004, 2006), Speech and Hearing Assn. Hudson Valley (corr. sec. 1995—2001, newsletter editor 1995—2002, membership com. 1995—2002, treas. 1997, pres. 1999—2000, nominating com. 1999—2000, membership chmn. 2000—02, legis. chmn. 2000—04, website adminstr. 2001—, historian 2001—, continuing edn. adminstr. 2002, program com. 2003, newsletter com. 2003—04), Bd. Regional Assn. Presidents (membership chair 2000—02, pub. info. chair 2003—04, Disting. Svc. award 2005). Home: PO Box 88 Hurley NY 12443 Personal E-mail: jpa1230@verizon.net. E-mail: jpetruski@aol.com.

PETRUZZELLI, JULIE A., lawyer; b. Glen Ridge, NJ, Apr. 18, 1957; BS in Chemistry/Biochemistry, Brown Univ., 1979; JD, Univ. Va., 1982. Bar: NY 1983, DC 1989, US Patent & Trademark Office. Ptnr., head, intellectual property and tech. divsn. Venable LLP, Washington. Mem.: ABA, NY Bar Assn., Women's Bar Assn. DC, NY Patent, Trademark, and Copyright Law Assn., Am. Intellectual Property Law Assn. Office: Venable LLP 575 Seventh St NW Washington DC 20004 Office Phone: 202-344-4010. Office Fax: 202-344-8300. Business E-Mail: japetruzzelli@venable.com.

PETRY, BARBARA LOUISE CROSS, elementary educator; b. Canton, Ohio, Jan. 8, 1954; d. Glenn Griffin and Mary Lucille (Bamberger) Cross; m. Thomas Alan Petry Sr., July 23, 1983; 1 child, Thomas Ala Jr. BA, BS, U. Tampa, 1975; MEd, U. Akron, 1978; cert. tchr. of gifted, Ashland Univ., 1988. Lic. pvt. pilot. Tchr. Our Lady of Peace, Canton, 1975-78; prin. St. Paul Sch., Canton, 1978-82; tchr. Stark County Schs., 1984—2000; tchr. 4th gr. Collier County Publ. Sch., 2000—. Sec., treas. Petry and Assocs. Mem. Aviation Days, Inc., Nat. Alumni Assn. Univ. Tampa, Tampa Alpha Alumni U. Tampa, Omicron Delta Kappa, Alpha Chi Omega, Kappa Delta Pi, Phi Delta Kappa. Republican. Roman Catholic. Home: 150 June Ct Marco Island FL 34145-3533

PETRY, RUTH VIDRINE, retired principal; b. Eunice, La., Jan. 20, 1947; d. Adea and Ruth Alice (Fox) Vidrine; m. Carson Clinton Petry, June 19, 1976. BA, La. Coll., 1971; MEd, McNeese State U., 1984. Cert. Tchr. La. Tchr. jr. h.s. Jefferson Davis Parish, Jennings, La., 1970—72; tchr. h.s. St. Tammany Parish, Mandeville, La., 1972—73, Jefferson Parish, Gretna, La., 1973—81; tchr. jr. h.s. Acadia Parish, Crowley, La., 1981—90; tchr. lang. arts Crowley Jr. H.S., 1981—90; master tchr. assessor La. State Dept. Edn., Lafayette, 1990—91; tchr. Crowley Mid. Sch., 1991—94, instrnl. asst., 1994—95; exec. dir. Assoc. Profl. Educators of La., Baton Rouge, 1995—96; asst. prin. Rayne H.S., La., 1996—2001, prin., 2001—04, ret., 2004. Writing assessment coord. Crowley Jr. H.S., 1984-85, mem. faculty insvc. team, 1986-89, chmn. spelling bee, 1983-90, 92-93, co-chmn. interim self study Crowley Jr. H.S. So. Assn., 1985-86; mem. state selection com. for La. Tech. of Yr., Students of Yr., 1992-93; mem. Tchr. Evaluation Revision Panels, I, III, IV, 1992-93, Prin.'s Evaluation State Com., 1993; adj. prof. edn. La. State U., Eunive, 2002-04; presenter workshops in field. Co-sponsor Nat. Jr. Hon. Soc., 1984-90; mem. La. Gov.-Elect's Edn. Transition Team, 1991-92; mem. La. Goals 2000 steering com. on sch. governance and accountability, 1994-95, mem. sch. fin. commn., 1999-2000. Named Crowley Jr. High Tchr. of Yr., 1985-86. Mem. Assn. Profl. Educators La. (pres. Acadia chpt. 1988-92, dist. VII state exec. bd., 1990-91, state pres.-elect 1991-92, state pres. 1992-94), La. Assn. Prins., La. Assn. for Retarded Citizens, Delta Kappa Gamma (chpt. pres. 1988-90, state leadership scholar 1993). Republican. Baptist. Avocations: music, reading, sewing. Home: 206 Bruce St Lafayette LA 70503-6102 Personal E-mail: ruthpetry@msn.com.

PETTERCHAK, JANICE A., writer; b. Springfield, Ill., Sept. 15, 1942; d. Emil H. and Vera C. (Einhoff) Stukenberg; m. John J. Petterchak, Oct. 5, 1963; children: John A., Julie Gilmour, James. AA, Springfield Coll., 1962; BS, Sangamon State U., 1972, MA, 1982. Supr. hist. markers Ill. State Hist. Soc., Springfield, 1973-74, asst. exec. dir., 1985-87; curator photographs Ill. State Hist. Libr., Springfield, 1974-79, assoc. editor, 1979-83, rep. local history svcs., 1983-85, libr. dir., 1987-95. Author: Mapping a Life's Journey: The Legacy of Andrew McNally III, 1995, Jack Brickhouse: A Voice for All Seasons, 1996, Taming the Upper Mississippi, 2000; To Share: The Heritage, Legend and Legacy of Nathan Cummings, 2000, Out To Sea Again: A Naval Armed Guard in World War II, 2002, Lone Scout: W.D. Boyce and American Boy Scouting, 2003, Where Eagles Soar: A Brief History of Community Banking in Illinois, 2004, Historic Illinois, 2005; editor: Illinois History: An Annotated Bibliography, 1995; assoc. editor Ill. Hist. Jour.; contbr. articles to profl. jours. Grantee NEH, 1987-95 Mem. Ill. State Hist. Soc., Sangamon County Hist. Soc. (bd. dirs. 1991-94, 99-2002, 04—, v.p. 1996-97, pres. 1995-96). Home: 11381 Mallard Dr Rochester IL 62563-8011 E-mail: petterchak@biogwriter.com.

PETTEWAY, DIANE CASHWELL, music educator, musician; b. Laurinburg, N.C., Dec. 21, 1957; d. Berlin Zane Brown and Evelyn Futrell Cashwell; m. Warren Bernard (Bernie) Petteway, July 27, 1996. BA, Meredith Coll., Raleigh, N.C., 1979. Cert. educator academically gifted State of N.C., 1989, educator music State of N.C., 1989, educator K-6 State of N.C., 1989. Music specialist Franklinton City Schs., NC, 1989—93; music integration specialist Duke Sch. Children, Durham, 1993—97, Wake County Pub. Schs., Raleigh, 1997—. Grants panelist United Arts Coun. Wake County, Raleigh, NC, 1999; tchg. artist panelist N.C. State Arts Coun., 2004; tchr. trainer N.C. Ctr. Advancement of Tchg., Cullowhee, 2005—. Director, composer and arranger: A Christmas Carol, 2001 (Best in the Triangle, Spectator Mag., 2001). Dir. M and M Singers ARC Wake County, Raleigh, 2006—. Named Vol. of Yr., ARC Wake County, 2005; grantee, United Arts Wake County, 1998, 1999, Wake Ednl. Partnership, 2003. Fellow: A + Schs. (tchr. trainer 1998—); mem.: ASCD. Methodist. Achievements include design of music curricula that teaches rhythmic and melodic improvisation; development of original band-Contrazz-mixing genres of jazz and New England Contra dance music in live musical settings. Avocations: reading, quilting, journal writing. Home: 2709 Wycliff Rd Raleigh NC 27607 Office: Wake County Pub Schs 2300 Noble Rd Raleigh NC 27608 Office Phone: 919-856-8236. Office Fax: 919-856-7661.

PETTEY, PATRICIA HUGGINS, county official; m. John M. Pettey. Rep. dist. 31 State of Kans., 1993-97; commr. Wyandotte County Unified Govt. Democrat. Home: 3500 Gibbs Rd Kansas City KS 66106-3810

PETTIGREW, L. EUDORA, retired academic administrator; b. Hopkinsville, Ky., Mar. 1, 1928; d. Warren Cicero and Corrye Lee (Newell) Williams; children: Peter W. Woodard, Jonathan R. (dec.). MusB, W.Va. State Coll., 1950; MA, So. Ill. U., 1964, PhD, 1966; PhD honoris causa, U. Pretoria, South Africa, 2002, Holy Family Coll., 2002, Western Conn. State U., 2004. Music/English instr. Swift Meml. Jr. Coll., Rogersville, Tenn., 1950-51; music instr., librarian Western Ky. Vocat. Sch., Paducah, 1951-52; music/English instr. Voorhees Coll., Denmark, SC, 1954-55; dir. music and recreation therapy W.Ky. State Psychiatric Hosp., Hopkinsville, 1956-61; research fellow Rehab. Inst., So. Ill. U., Carbondale, 1961-63, instr., resident counselor, 1963-66, coordinator undergrad. ednl. psychology, 1963-66, acting chmn. ednl. psychology, tchr. corps instr., 1966; asst. prof. to assoc. prof. dept. psychology U. Bridgeport, Conn., 1966-70; prof., chmn. dept. urban and met. studies Coll. Urban Devel. Mich. State U., East Lansing, 1974-80; assoc. provost, prof. U. Del., Newark, 1981-86; pres. SUNY Coll. at Old Westbury, 1986-98. Cons. for rsch. and evaluation Hall Neighborhood House Day Care Tng. Project, Bridgeport, 1966-68, U.S. Ea. Regional Lab., Edn. Devel. Ctr., Newton, Mass., 1967-69; coordinator for edn. devel., 1968-69; cons. Bridgeport Public Schs. lang. devel. project, 1967-68, 70; Lansing Model Cities Agy., Day Care Program, 1971; U. Pitts., 1973, 74, Leadership Program, U. Mich. and Wayne State U., 1975, Wayne County Pub. Health Nurses Assn., 1976, Ill. State Bd. Edn., 1976-77; assoc. prof. U. Bridgeport, 1970, Ctr. for Urban Affairs and Coll. of Edn., Mich. State U., East Lansing, 1970-73; program devel. specialist Lansing Public Schs. Tchr. Corps program, 1971-73; coord. workshop Conflict Resolution The Woman's Role in Our World, 4th Internat. UN Conf. on Women, Beijing, China, 1995; lectr. in field; condr. workshops in field; guest spkr. Internat. Conf. on The New Role of Higher Edn. in the Context of an Ind. Palestinian State, An-Najah Nat. U., Nablus, Palestine, 1996. Tv/radio appearances on: Black Women in Edn, Channel 23, WKAR, East Lansing, 1973, Black Women and Equality, Channel 2, Detroit, 1974, Women and Careers, Channel 7, Detroit, 1974, Black Women and Work: Integration in Schools, WITL Radio, Lansing, 1974, others; editor: Universities and Their Role in World Peace, 2003; contbr. articles to profl. jours. Mem. exec. com. UN Non Govtl. Orgns. Dept. Public Info., 2004; mem. bd. YWCA, New Castle County, 2005-. Recipient Diana award Lansing YWCA, 1977, Outstanding Profl. Achievement award, 1987, award L.I. Ctr. for Bus. and Profl. Women, 1988, Educator of Yr. 100 Black Men of L.I., 1988, Black Women's Agenda award, 1988, Woman of Yr. Nassau/Suffolk Coun. of Adminstrv. Women in Edn., 1989, Disting. Ednl. Leadership award L.I. Women's Coun. for Equal Edn. Tng. and Employment, 1989, L.I. Disting. Leadership award L.I. Bus. News, 1990, Disting. Black Women in Edn. award Nat. Coun. Negro Women, 1991; named Outstanding Black Educator, NAACP, 1968, Oustanding Woman Educator, Mich. Women's Lawyers Assn. and Mich. Trial Lawyers Assn., 1975, Disting. Alumna, Nat. Assn. for Equal Opportunity in Higher Edn., 1990, Woman of Yr., Nassau County League of Women Voters, 1991, Disting. Alumna So. Ill. U., 1997, N.Y. State Senate resolution of commendation, 1998; Elected to Achievers Hall of Fame: Long Island Bus. and Profl. Women's Orgn., 2001 Mem. AAAS, Nat. Assn. Acad. Affairs Adminstrs., Internat. Assn. Univ. Pres. (exec. com., spl. adviser to pres.), Phi Delta Kappa.

PETTINE, LINDA FAYE, physical therapist; b. New London, Conn., Nov. 11, 1958; d. Robert Anderson and Pauline Priscilla (Johnson) Erwin; m. H. Louis Pettine, Jr., Mar. 6, 1982. BS, U. Conn., 1980; post grad., Quinnipiac Coll., Hamden, Conn., 1989-91. Registered phys. therapist Conn. Staff phys. therapist Hahneman Hosp., Worcester, Mass., 1980, Newport Hosp., RI, 1980-82, Middlebury Orthop. Group, Waterbury, Conn., 1982, Easter Seal Rehab. Ctr., Ctrl. Conn., Meriden, Conn., 1982-84; hosp. and rehab. ctr. coord. Easter Seal Rehab. Ctr., Ctrl. Conn., Meriden, Conn., 1984-86; co-founder Pettine and McDiarmid Phys. Therapy, Cheshire and Wallingford, Conn., 1986-88; pres. Keystone Phys. Therapy and Sports Medicine P.C., Cheshire and Wallingford, Conn., 1988-99; facility adminstr. Keystone Phys. Therapy and Sports Medicine, Cheshire and Wallingford, Conn., 1999—2001; facility dir. Conn. Phys. Therapy, LLC, Wallingford, 2001—04, dist. dir., 2002—04; mgr. outpatient rehab. Hosp. St. Raphael, New Haven, 2004—. Lectr. Diabetes Edn. Program, Meriden, Conn., 1985; cons. Waterbury Nursing Ctr., Conn., 1986—87; guest spkr. Conn. chpt. Am. Diabetes Assn., Meriden, 1986, Arthritis Support Group, Meriden, Conn., 1986, Meriden Indsl. Mgr. Assn., Conn., 1986. Mem. adv. bd. Waterbury Continuing Edn. Program, Conn. Katherine Wyckoff and Margaret Wyckoff Moore Endowed Scholar, 1991. Mem.: MD Health Plan (phys. therapist and chiropractor liaison com. 1997). Avocations: reading, needlecrafts, quilting.

PETTIS, PATRICIA AMANDA, secondary school educator, farmer; b. Red Wing, Minn., Jan. 28, 1967; d. Albert A. and Marilyn June (MacAdams) Berg; m. Pettis Steven Mark, Sept. 5, 1992; children: Steven Joseph, Nathan Carl, Allie Amanda, Christopher Mark, Matthew Albert. BS in Edn., St. Cloud State U., Minn., 1990. English instr. LeSueur-Henderson H.S., Minn., 1997—98, Waterville Elysian Morristown Sch. Dist., Waterville, Minn., 1998—. Declamation head coach LeSueur-Henderson H.S., 1997—98; yearbook advisor WEM H.S., Waterville, 1998—2002, lit. mag. advisor, 1998—2003, class advisor, 1998—2006, nat. honor soc. advisor, 2000—. Sunday sch. educator St. Peters Cath. Ch., St. Peter, Minn. Mem.: Minn. Edn. Assn. (assoc.). Avocations: running, gardening, coaching and playing sports. Home: 46364 327th Ave Kasota MN 56050 Office: Waterville-Elysian-Morristown HS 500 East Paquin St Waterville MN 56096

PETTIS-ROBERSON, SHIRLEY MCCUMBER, retired congresswoman; b. Mountain View, Calif. d. Harold Oliver and Dorothy Susan (O'Neil) McCumber; m. John J. McNulty (dec.); m. Jerry L. Pettis (dec. Feb. 1975); children: Peter Dwight Pettis, Deborah Pettis Moyer; m. Ben Roberson, Feb. 6, 1988. Student, Andrews U., Berrien Springs, Mich., 1942—43, student, 1945, U. Calif., Berkeley, 1944—45; PhD (hon.), Loma Linda U., Calif., 2002. Mgr. Audio-Digest Found., LA, Glendale, 1958—61; sec. treas. Pettis, Inc., Hollywood, Calif., 1958-68; mem. U.S. Congress, Calif., 1975—79. Pres. Women's Rsch. Edn. Inst., 1979—80; bd. dirs. Lumbermens Mut. Ins. Co., Kemper Corp., Am. Motors, Am. Mfg. Co. Mem. Former Mems. Congress, 1988—, Pres.'s Commn. Arms Control Disarmament, 1982—85, Commn. Presdl. Scholars, 1990—93; chair bd. Loma Linda U. Children's Hosp. Found.; trustee U. Redlands, Calif., 1980—83, Loma Linda U. Med. Ctr., Calif., 1990—95, bd. mem. Mem.: Morningside Country Club (Rancho Mirage, Calif.).

PETTIT, MELISSA G., special education educator; b. Houston, Nov. 28, 1962; BS in Edn., Miss. State U., 1989, MS in Edn., 1997. Nat. bd. cert. tchr. Spl. edn. tchr., tchr. 9th grade Technology Discovery Vardaman H.S., Miss., 1992—. Office: Vardaman HS Hwy 8E Vardaman MS 38878 E-mail: lpettit@calhoun.k12.ms.us.

PETTUS, MILDRED LOUISE, retired history professor, writer; b. Lancaster County, S.C., Feb. 1, 1926; d. Calvin Hall and Bessie Kathryn (Rodgers) Pettus. BA in History, Winthrop Coll., 1946; MA in History, U. S.C., 1954. Tchr. Kershaw (S.C.) H.S., 1947-48; cotton gin mgr. Pettus Gin Co., Ft. Mill, S.C., 1949-54; tchr. Spartanburg (S.C.) Jr. Coll., 1955-56, Douglas (Ariz.) H.S., 1956-63, Ajo (Ariz.) H.S., 1964-65, Orlando (Fla.) Jr. Coll., 1965-67; asst. prof. Winthrop Coll., Rock Hill, S.C., 1967-89; ret., 1989. Author: Pictorial History of Lancaster County, South Carolina, 1984, The Springs Story, 1986, The Palmetto State, 1989, The Waxhaws, 1993, A Roddery Family, 1998, Leasing of a Nation - The Flawed System of Catawba Indian Land Leases, 2005; columnist: Nearby History, Charlotte Observer, 1985—. Recipient Achievement of Merit award, Am. Assn. Colls. Tchr. Edn., 1973, Outstandign Publ. Editor award, SC Confederation of State and Local History Socs., 1994, Preservation award, Hist. Rock Hill, 2003, York County SC Culture and Heritage Commn. Keeper of the Culture award, 2000, History award, NSDAR, 2000, Alumni Profl. Achievement award, Winthrop U., 2006. Mem.: DAR (Nat. Soc. DAR History award 2001), York County Geneal. and Hist. Soc. (bd. dirs., editor The Quar. 1989—). Democrat. Home: 9227 Whistling Straits Dr Fort Mill SC 29715 Personal E-mail: mlpettus@cetlink.net.

PETTY, M. S. MARTY, publisher; b. St. Louis, Mo., Dec. 17, 1952; married; 2 children. BA in Journalism, Univ. Mo., 1975; MS in Mgmt., Hartford Grad. Ctr. (Rensselaer), 1989. Asst. mng. editor Kansas City Star and Times; mng. editor Hartford (Conn.) Courant, 1983—89, de. exec. editor, assoc. pub., 1989, sr. v.p., gen. mgr.; pub., CEO Hartford (Conn.) Courant, 1997—2000; exec. v.p. St. Petersburg (Fla.) Times, 2000—, pub., 2004—. Trustee Poynter Inst. for Media Studies, Tampa Bay Newspapers Inc.; juror Pulitzer Prize awards; pres. Soc. of Newspaper Design, 1985; bd. dir. Wm. Randolph Hearst Found. journalism bd., 1987—89. Trustee Congressional Quarterly, Governing Mag., Fla. Trend Mag. Named a Woman of Distinction, Girl Scouts of Suncoast Coun., 2004; named Bus. Woman of Yr., Women's Coun., St. Petersburg Area C. of C., 2005. Mem.: Nat. Assn. Minority Media Executives, Newspaper Assn. Am. (diversity bd.), Am. Press Inst. (adv. bd.), Florida Press Assn. (bd. dir.). Office: St Petersburg Times 490 1st Ave S Saint Petersburg FL 33701

PETTY, MARGE D., state senator; b. Ft. Wayne, Ind., Feb. 26, 1946; children: Brandon, Megan. BS, Tex. Christian U., 1968; MEd, Kans. U., 1978; JD, Washburn U. Sch. Law, 1990. Tchr., 1968-69; mgmt. consultant, 1981—94; health educator, 1978-81; mem. City Council of Topeka, 1985-89; dep. mayor Topeka, 1986; mem. Kans. Senate, 1989—2000; dir. pub. affairs and consumer protection Kans. Corp. Commn., 2003—. Mem. Topeka Metro. Ballet, Chamber of Commerce, Mulvane Art Ctr. Episcopalian. Home: PO Box 4262 Topeka KS 66604 Address: 1500 SW Arrowhead Rd Topeka KS 66604-4027

PETTY, RACHEL, academic administrator; BS in Psychology, Howard U., MS; postgrad., George Washington U.; PhD in Human Devel., U. Md. Former mem. faculty dept. edn. Howard U., Washington; instr. dept. psychology Fed. City Coll. (now U. D.C.); from asst. prof. to prof. dept. psychology U. D.C., from asst. dean to dean Coll. Arts and Scis., v.p. acad. affairs, 2001—. Sch. psychologist D.C. Pub. Schs. Title I program, Prince George's County Pub.

Schs.; staff psychologist, cons., clin. program dir. St. Ann's Infant and Maternity Home; consulting psychologist Bd. of Child Care, United Meth. Ch., Balt.-Washington Dist.; cons. child and family svcs. divsn. D.C. Dept. Human Svcs.; cons. Ednl. Testing Svc.; cons., evaluator Everyday Theater Youth Ensemble; cons. D.C. Ednl. Licensure Commn. Contbr. articles to profl. jours. Active Md. State Foster Care Rev. Bd., Conf. on Developing World Class Ednl. Stds. for D.C., Luth. Social Svcs. of Nat. Capital Area, D.C. Child Welfare Consortium. Named one of Outstanding Young Women of the Carolinas; recipient award, Nat. Assn. Equal Opportunity in Higher Edn.; fellow Minority Dissertation, State of Md. Mem.: AAUW, APA, D.C. Psychol. Assn. (bd. dirs.), Am. Psychol. Soc., Psi Chi. Office: U DC 4200 Connecticut Ave NW Washington DC 20008

PETZEL, FLORENCE ELOISE, textiles educator; b. Crosbyton, Tex., Apr. 1, 1911; d. William D. and Eloise Petzel. PhB, U. Chgo., 1931, AM, 1934; PhD, U. Minn., 1954. Instr. Judson Coll., 1936—38; asst. prof. textiles Ohio State U., 1938—48; assoc. prof. U. Ala., 1950—54; prof. Oreg. State U., Corvallis, 1954—61, 1967—75, prof. emeritus, 1975—, dept. head, 1954—61, 1967—75; prof., divsn. head U. Tex., 1961—63; prof. Tex. Tech. U., 1963—67. Vis. instr. Tex. State Coll. for Women, 1937; vis. prof. Wash. State U., 1967 Author: Textiles of Ancient Mesopotamia, Persia and Egypt, 1987; contbr. articles to profl. jours. Effie I. Raitt fellow, 1949—50. Mem. Met. Opera Guild, Sigma Xi, Phi Kappa Phi, Omicron Nu, Iota Sigma Pi, Sigma Delta Epsilon. Home: 150 Downs Blvd Apt A207 Clemson SC 29631

PETZOLD, CAROL STOKER, state legislator; b. St. Louis, July 28; d. Harold William and Mabel Lucille (Wilson) Stoker; m. Walter John Petzold, June 27, 1959; children: Ann, Ruth, David. BS, Valparaiso U., 1959. Tchr. Parkwood Elem. Sch., Kensington, Md., 1960-62; legis. aide Md. Gen. Assembly, Annapolis, 1975-79; legis. asst. Montgomery County Bd. Edn., Rockville, Md., 1980; cmty. sch. coord. Parkland Jr. H.S., Rockville, 1981-87; mem. Md. Ho. of Dels., Annapolis, 1987—, mem. constl. and adminstrv. law com., 1987-93, mem. judiciary com., 1994—2006, chair subcom. on criminal justice, 2003—06, vice chair Montgomery County del., 1995—2006, dep. majority whip, 1999—2002. Chair spl. com. drug and alcohol abuse Md. Ho. Dels., 1999—; mem. transp. planning bd. Nat. Capitol Region, 1989—; vice chmn. assembly on fed. issues Nat. Conf. State Legislatures, 1996-97, chair adv. com. on energy, 1997-99, chair energy and transp. com., 1998-99, pres. women's legis. network, 2004-05, chair transp. com., 2004-05. Editor Child Care Sampler, 1974, Stoker Family Cookbook, 1976. Pres. Montgomery Child Care Assn., 1976-78; mem. Md. State Scholarship Bd., 1978-87, chmn. 1985-87; chmn. Legis. Com. Montgomery County Commn. for Children and Youth, 1979-84; mem., v.p. Luth. Social Services Nat. Capitol Area, Washington, 1980-86; mem. exec. com. coun. Montgomery United Way, 1981-2000. Named Mother of Yr., March of Dimes, 2000; named one of Top 100 Md. Women, Daily Record, 2002, 2004; recipient Statewide award, Gov.'s Adv. Bd. on Homelessness, 1994, recognized for outstanding commitment to children, U.S. Dept. HEW, 1980, Award of Excellence, MADD, 2002, Disting. Legislator award, 2003, Impaired Driving Coalition, 2003, Legis. award, Md. Network Against Domestic Violence, 2003. Mem.: AAUW (honoree Kensington br. 1971, 2002, honoree Md. divsn. 1981), Women Legislators of Md., Md. Women Legislators Caucus (exec. com. 2003—04), Women's Polit. Caucus (chmn. Montgomery County 1981—83). Democrat. Lutheran. Home: 14113 Chadwick Ln Rockville MD 20853-2103 Office Phone: 301-858-3001. Business E-Mail: Carol_Petzold@house.state.md.us.

PEVEAR, ROBERTA CHARLOTTE, retired state legislator; b. Bethel, Maine, July 4, 1930; d. Frank Albert Sr. and Thirza Estella (Hickford) Gibson; m. Edward Gordon Pevear, Aug. 21, 1971. Diploma in Comml. Art, Gould Acad., 1947. Sec. Wilner Wood Products, South Paris, Maine, 1947-50; sec. export dept. Whitaker Cable, North Kansas City, Mo., 1951-56; sec. br. and dist. Anheuser-Busch, Inc., Kansas City, Mo., 1957-59; legal sec. Johnson & Johnson, New Brunswick, NJ, 1960-65, St. John, Ronder & Bell, Kingston, NY, 1966; sec., adminstrv. asst. Sears-Roebuck & Co., Overland Park, Kans., 1967-70, Exeter, NH, 1971-77; salesman Avon Products, Hampton Falls, NH, 1978-86; mem. ho. reps. State of N.H., 1979-88, ret., 1988. Commr. Rockingham Planning Commn., N.H., 1979-88, N.H. Planning Com., 1985-88; clk. Environment and Agrl. Com. N.H. Ho. Reps., 1983-88; del. mem. Rockingham County, 1979-88, exec. bd., 1984-88; chmn. Rockingham County Home, 1987-88. Civil Def. dir., Hampton Falls, NH, 1980—88. Recipient Community Citizen award Hampton Falls Grange, 1982, Seacoast Retired Sr. Service award, 1985. Mem. Nat. Order Women Legislators, N.H. Order of Women Legislators, DAR. Avocations: writing, genealogy, travel.

PEYTON, DIANNA LEAH DAVIS, physical therapist, personal trainer; b. Bowling Green, Ky., Aug. 28, 1968; d. Lorenza Donald and Jeanice Norene Davis; m. Mark Dudley Peyton, Mar. 21, 1998; children: Katherine Danielle, Paul Davis. B of Health Sci., U. Ky., Lexington; M of Health Sci., U. Indpl., Ind., 1999. Lic. phys. therapist, athletic trainer Ky. Phys. therapist/athletic trainer Sports Medicine Group of We. Ky., Madisonville, 1992—. Mem.: Nat. Athletic Trainers Assn., Ky. Athletic Trainers Soc. Avocations: painting, crafts, gardening. Office: Sports Medicine and Rehab Group 900 Hosp Dr Madisonville KY 42431 Office Phone: 270-824-2008. Business E-Mail: dpeyton@trover.org.

PEYTON, ELIZABETH JOY, writer, painter; b. Danbury, Conn., Dec. 20, 1965; d. Paul Leason and Elizabeth Ann (Gordon); m. Rirkrit Tiravanija, July 21, 1991. BA, Sch. Visual Arts, N.Y.C., 1987. Author: Live Forever, 1997, Craig, 1998; exhibitions include Art of Four Decades 1958-1998, San Francisco, Mus. Modern Art, 1998, Examining Pictures, Mus. Contemporary Art, Chgo., 1999, Remix: Contemporary art & pop, Tate Liverpool, 2002, Cher peintre- Peintures figuratives despuis l'ultime Picabia, Centre Pompidou, Paris, 2002, Inaugural Exhbn., Regen Project, LA, 2003, New Paintings, 2003, EDITION SPECIALE, Galerier Suzanner Tarasieve, Paris, 2003, Whitney Biennial, Whitney Mus. Am. Art, 2004. Avocations: swimming, surfing the internet. Office: Regen Projects 633 N Almont Dr West Hollywood CA 90069-5607

PEZESHK, VIOLET, psychologist, educator; d. Mohammad and Gowhar Pezeshk; children: Jhanna Shaghaghi, Natasha Shaghaghi. PhD, Alliant Internat. U., 2000. Cert. hypnotherapist Calif.; DV specialist Minn., 1998. Mem. adj. faculty Dept. Clin. Psychology and MFT Alliant Internat. U., San Diego, 2001—; clin. psychologist Palomar Family Counseling, Escondido, Calif., 2003—04. Program dir. St. Clare's Home, Escondido, 2002—03. Author: (self-help book) Psychological Development of Children from Birth to Adolescence, (children's novel) Ziba, editor weekly clin. article for mag.; exhibitions include Peace on Earth. Mem.: APA (assoc.). Office Phone: 858-635-4754. Personal E-mail: drpezeshk@yahoo.com.

PEZZONI, MERI KATHRYN, music educator; b. Santa Cruz, Calif. d. Antone Victor and Virginia Willa Brenkwitz; m. Delwyn L. Pezzoni, June 29, 1991; 1 child, Caci Benjamin. MusB, U. Calif., Santa Cruz, 1986. Choral dir. Aptos H.S., Calif., 1986—. Mem.: Calif. Music Educators Assn. (state choral rep. 2003—04). Mailing: 402 Vista Del Mar Dr Aptos CA 95003-1832 Office Phone: 831-688-6565.

PEZZULO, JACQUELINE, psychologist, researcher; b. N.Y.C., Aug. 10, 1966; d. John Gerald Johnson and Maria Lopez de Rivera; children: Matthew, John children: Matthew Isaiah Rivera. BS in Psychology, summa cum laude, SUNY, Albany, 1993, MS in Edn. Psychology and Stats., 1996, cert. of Advanced Study, 1996, D in Psychology, 2000. Cert. sch. psychology NY State Dept. of Edn., 1996, psychologist NY State Dept. of Edn., 2003. Cmty. mental health specialist St. Mary's Hosp., Amsterdam, NY, 1998—2000; sch. psychologist Chatham Ctrl. Sch. Dist., Chatham, NY, 2000—01; asst. dir. child and adolescent svcs. rsch. N.Y. State Office Mental Health, Albany, NY, 2001—. Cons. Inst. Cmty. Rsch., Hartford, Conn., 1996—97, VanGuard Comm., 2003—; rsch. cons. SUNY, Buffalo, 1994—96; behavioral health cons. Multiple Sch. Dists. in Urban and Rural Counties, Multiple, NY; presenter in field. Contbr. articles to profl. jours., chapters to books; author: Elminating Barriers for Learning Social and Emotional Factors that Enhance Secondary Education. Adv. and adv. mem. Coalition of Latino Svc. Providers, Amsterdam, NY, 1998—2000; youth mentor Third Ref. Ch. of Am., Albany, NY, 1996—2000; presenter Am. Ednl. Rsch. Assn., San Francisco, 1995; adv. mem. Coordinated Children's Svcs. Intitiative, Amsterdam, NY, 1998—2000. Post-Doctoral Rsch. fellow, Ctr. for Info. Tech. and Evaluation Rsch., 2002—03, State Planning grantee, NIMH, 2003—, Challenge grantee, NY State Divsn. Criminal Justice, 2001—02. Mem.: Nat. Assn. Sch. Psychologists (assoc.), Soc. Rsch. in Child Devel. (assoc.), APA (assoc.), Golden Key, Phi Beta Kappa. Avocations: travel, gardening, dancing and music, theater, reading and writing. Office: NY State Office of Mental Health 44 Holland Ave Floor 6 Albany NY 12229

PFAFF, JUDY, artist; b. London, 1946. Student Wayne State U., 1965-66, So. Ill. U., 1968-69; B.F.A., Washington U.-St. Louis, 1971; postgrad. Yale U., 1970, M.F.A., 1973. Prof. arts, Columbia U., 1992-94, Milton Avery Disting. prof. art, Bard Coll., 1989, 91, 94- One-woman exhbns. include: Webb and Parsons Gallery, New Canaan, Conn., 1974, Artists Space N.Y., 1975, Theatre Gallery, U. So. Fla., Tampa, 1977, Los Angeles Contemporary Exhbn., 1978, Holly Solomon Gallery, N.Y., 1980, Daniel Weinberg Gallery, Los Angeles, 1984, Wacoal, Japan, 1985, Holly Solomon Gallery, 1986, Nat. Mus. Women in the Arts, Washington, 1989, Cleve. Ctr. for Contemporary Art., Cleve., 1990, Fabric Workshop, N.Y., 1991, Rotunda Gallery, N.Y., 1993; group exhbns. include: Whitney Mus. Am. Art, 1975, Hallwalls Gallery, Buffalo, 1976, Art Mus., U. Calif.-Santa Barbara, 1979, Neuberger Mus., SUNY-Purchase, 1979, Contemporary Arts Mus., Houston, 1980, Contemporary Arts Ctr., Cin., 1980, Mus. Modern Art, N.Y.C., 1984, Venice Biennale, 1984, Rotunda Gallery, Bklyn., 1984, Bklyn. Mus., 1985, WHitney Mus. Am. Art., N.Y., 1988, Internat. Art Projects, Asia, 1990, Mis. Modern Art., 1989, Inst. Contemporary Art, Phila., 1991, Cultural Space, N.Y., 1992, Henie-Onstad Art Ctr., Norway, 1992, Whitney Mus. Am. Art at Champion, Stamford, Conn., 1993, Drawing Ctr., N.Y., 1993; commd. work Spokane City Hall, 1984. Nat. Endowment Arts grantee, 1979; Named a Guggenheim fellow, 1983, MacArthur Fellow, 2004; Award of Merit Medal for Sculpture, Am. Acad. of Arts and Letters, 2002. Office: Bard Coll PO Box 5000 Annandale On Hudson NY 12504-5000 E-mail: pfaff@bard.edu.

PFAFF, LAURA KING, auction house executive; b. San Francisco; m. Rick Pfaff. BA in English, U. So. Calif., L.A., 1976. Acct. exec. The Pacific Group, San Francisco, 1986—90; pres. Laura King & Co., San Francisco, 1990—94; sr. v.p., regional dir. Christie's, San Francisco, 1994—2001; chmn. Bonhams & Butterfields, San Francisco, 2001—. Bd. mem. San Francisco Symphony, No. Calif. Cancer Ctr., Calif. Pacific Med. Ctr., Fort Mason Found.; former bd. mem. San Francisco C. of C. Office: Bonhams & Butterfields 220 San Bruno Ave San Francisco CA 94103 Office Phone: 415-861-7500.

PFAFFLIN, SHEILA MURPHY, psychologist; b. Pasadena, Calif., July 31, 1934; d. Leonard Anthony and Honora (Shields) Murphy; m. James Reid Pfafflin, Sept. 7, 1957. BA, Pomona Coll., 1956; MA, Johns Hopkins U., 1958, PhD, 1959. Mem. tech. staff AT&T Bell Labs., Murray Hill, N.J., 1959-75; dist. mgr. AT&T, Morristown, N.J., 1975-98. Chair subcom. on womem Com. on Equal Opportunities in Sci. and Tech., NSF, Washington, 1981-85; mem. adv. coun. Math/Sci. Tchr. Supply and Demand, N.J. Dept. Higher Edn., 1982-83; mem. adv. bd. for Maths., Sci. and Computer Sci. Teaching Improvement Grants, N.J. Dept. Higher Edn., 1984-89. Co-editor: Expanding the Role of Women in the Sciences, 1978, Scientific-Technological Change & the Role of Women in Development, 1981, Psychology & Educational Policy, 1987; contbr. articles to profl. jours. Trustee Ramapo Coll. of N.J., Mahwah, N.J., 1984-96; adv. bd. Project "SMART", Girls Clubs of Am., N.Y.C., 1984-94, Consortium for Ednl. Equity, Rutgers U., New Brunswick, N.Y., 1983-90; pres. Assn. for Women in Sci. Ednl. Found., Washington, 1982-98. Fellow: APA, AAAS, N.Y. Acad. Scis., Assn. for Women in Sci. (pres. 1980—81, Women Scientist award, Met. chpt. 1987); mem.: Phi Beta Kappa, Sigma Xi. Avocation: sailing. Home: 173 Gates Ave Gillette NJ 07933-1719

PFANSTIEL PARR, DOROTHEA ANN, interior designer; b. San Antonio, Nov. 10, 1931; d. Herbert Andraes and Ethel Missouri (Turner) Pfanstiel; m. Thurmond Charles Parr, Jr., Sept. 15, 1951; children: Thurmond Charles, III, Richard Marshall. AA, Coll. San Antonio, 1951. Asst. dean evening divsn. Alamo C.C., San Antonio, 1951; tchr., cons., dir. Humpty Dumpty Early Childhood Devel. Ctr., San Antonio, 1951-58; exec. sec., cons. Thurmond C. Parr, Jr. & Co., San Antonio, 1960-61; founder, pres. Creative Designs, Ltd., San Antonio, 1962—. Liaison, coord. Internat. Students Lang. Sch., Lackland AFB, San Antonio, 1959-65. Adv., cons. Urban Renewal Inner City San Antonio, 1959-61. Named Notable Woman of Tex., Awards and Hons. Soc. Am., 1984-85. Republican. Presbyterian. Avocations: travel, swimming, reading, studying, walking.

PFEFFER, CYNTHIA ROBERTA, psychiatrist, educator; b. Newark, May 22, 1943; d. Edward I. and Ann Pfeffer. BA, Douglas Coll., 1964; MD, NYU, 1968. Assoc. dir. child psychiatry inpatient unit Albert Einstein Coll. Medicine, Bronx, NY, 1973-79; chief child psychiatry inpatient unit N.Y. Hosp. Cornell Med. Ctr., White Plains, NY, 1979-95; assoc. prof. clin. psychiatry Weill Med. Coll. Cornell U., N.Y.C., 1984—. Prof. psychiatry Cornell U. Med. Coll., 1989—; pres. N.Y. Coun. on Child and Adolescent Psychiatry, N.Y.C., 1989—; dir. childhood bereavement program Weill Med. Coll. Cornell U., 1999—. Author: The Suicidal Child, 1986, Difficult Moments in Child Psychotherapy, 1988; editor: Youth Suicide: Perspectives on Risk and Prevention, 1989, Intense Stress and Mental Disturbance in Children, 1996; co-editor: Neurologic Disorders: Developmental and Behavioral Sequelae for Child and Adolescent Psychiatric Clinics of North America, 1999. Recipient Erwin Stengel award Internat. Assn. Suicide Prevention, 1987, Wilford Hulse award N.Y. Coun. on Child & Adolescent Psychiatry, 1989, Sigmund Freud award Am. Soc. Psychoanalytic Physicians, 1994. Fellow Am. Psychiat. Assn., Am. Acad. Child and Adolescent Psychiatry (councillor-at-large 1989—, Norbert Rieger award 1988), Am. Psychopathological Assn.; mem. Am. Assn. Suicidology (pres. 1987, Young Contbrs. award 1981, 82). Office: NY Hosp Westchester Div 21 Bloomingdale Rd White Plains NY 10605-1504 also: 1100 Madison Ave New York NY 10028-0327 Office Phone: 914-997-5849, 212-717-2334. Business E-Mail: cpfeffer@med.cornell.edu.

PFEFFER, JUDITH STADLEN, psychologist, consultant; b. Washington, D.C., Sept. 28, 1942; d. Morris and Marian (Singerman) Stadlen; m. Philip Elliot Pfeffer, Dec. 22, 1962; children: Charles, Ari, Shira. BA, CUNY, 1963; MEd, Rutgers U., 1965; PhD, Temple U., 1981; cert. cognitive therapy, U. Pa., 1985. Cert. sch. psychologist, Pa.; lic. psychologist, Pa. Tchr. Highland Park (N.J.) Sch. Dist., 1963-66; supr., lectr. Hunter Coll. CUNY, 1968-69; cons. learning disabilities Chgo., Phila., N.Y.C., 1968-74; cons. psychologist, rsch. assoc. Montgomery County Intermediate Unit, Norristown, Pa., 1980-82; supr., lectr. Pa. State U., Abington, 1982-83; pvt. practice Warrington, Pa., 1982—. Adj. asst. prof. Temple U., Phila., 1981-82; cons. psychologist Bucks County Intermediate Unit, Doylestown, Pa., 1982—, Bristol Twp. Spl. Edn. Dept., Bristol, Pa., 1987—. Co-author: A Guide to Teaching Children with Learning Disabilities, 1968. Fellow Temple U., 1978. Mem. APA, Pa. Psychol. Assn., Phila. Soc. Clin. Psychologists, Phi Beta Kappa. Home and Office: 812 Lorraine Dr Warrington PA 18976-2218

PFEIFER, LOLA, mathematics educator; M in Curriculum and Instrn., Wichita State U., 2000. Tchr. math. Wichita HS SE, 1992—.

PFEIFER, POLLY LEE, elementary school educator; d. Gerald Edward and Nancy Lee Pfeifer. BA in Edn., Coll. Saint Benedict, St. Joseph, Minn., 1987; MA in Edn., St. Mary's U., Winona, Minn., 1994; student in Libr. Media Scis., Mankato State U., Minn., 2006—. Cert. tchr. Minn., 1987. Tchr. sci. Minnetonka (Minn.) Pub. Schs., 1987—. Mem.: NEA, Minn. Ednl. Media Orgn., Nat. Assn. Sci. Tchrs., Minnetonka (Minn.) Tchrs. Assn. (v.p. 1996). Roman Cath. Avocations: reading, basketball, golf. Office: Minnetonka Mid Sch West 6421 Hazeltina Blvd Excelsior MN 55331

PFEIFER, TRACY M., plastic surgeon; b. Yonkers, NY, Dec. 20, 1960; d. Adrienne K and William A Pfeifer. BA, Rutgers U., 1982—84; MS, Calif. State U., Los Angeles, 1984—85; MD, U. of Medicine and Dentistry of NJ, 1987—91. Bd. cert. Am. Bd. of Plastic Surgery, 2001, Am. Bd. of Surgery, 1999. Plastic surgeon, pvt. practice Pfeifer Plastic Surgery, PLLC, NYC, 1999—. Fellow: Am. Coll. Surgeons; mem.: Am. Soc. Aesthetic Plastic Surgery, Am. Soc. Plastic Surgeons, NY Regional Soc. of Plastic Surgeons (exec. bd. mem. 2000—). Office: Pfeifer Plastic Surgery PLLC 565 Park Ave New York NY 10021 Office Phone: 212-860-0670. Office Fax: 212-593-8823. E-mail: tpfeifer@drpfeifer.com.

PFEIFFER, JANE CAHILL, former broadcasting company executive, consultant; b. Sept. 29, 1932; d. John Joseph and Helen (Reilly) Cahill; m. Ralph A. Pfeiffer, Jr., June 3, 1975. BA, U. Md., 1954; postgrad., Cath. U. Am., 1956—57; LHD (hon.), Pace Coll., 1978, U. Md., 1979; LHD (hon.), Manhattanville Coll., 1979, Amherst U., 1980, Babson Coll., 1981, U. Notre Dame, 1991; LHD (hon.), Bryant Coll., 1995, St. Thomas Aquinas Coll., 2006. With IBM Corp., Armonk, NY, 1955-76, sec. mgmt. rev. com., 1970, dir. comm., 1971, v.p. comm. and govt. rels., 1972-76, bus. cons., 1976-78; chmn. NBC, Inc., N.Y.C., 1978-80; bus. cons., 1980—. Trustee The Conf. Bd., 1991. Pres.'s adv. com. White House Fellows, 1966, Pres.'s Gen. Adv. Commn. on Arms Control and Disarmament, 1977-80, Pres.'s Commn. Mil. Compensation; trustee Rockefeller Found., U. Md., Carnegie Hall, 1981-1986, U. Notre Dame; bd. dirs. Catholic Univ. of Am., 1973-1978, Rockefeller Found., 1973-1985, White House Fellows, 1976-1981, Kettering Found., 1975-1979. Recipient Achievement award Kappa Kappa Gamma, 1974-80, Eleanor Roosevelt Humanitarian award NY League for Hard of Hearing, 1980, Disting. Alumna award U. Md., 1975, Humanitarian award NOW, 1980, Centennial Alumna medallion U. Md., 1988; White House fellow, Washington, 1966, Making Waves award, Greatest 50 Women in Radio and Television-AWRT, 2002. Mem. Coun. Fgn. Rels., Overseas Devel. Coun., Econ. of N.Y. Club. Office: C/O Jonathan L Smith Chesapeake Asset Mgmt LLC 1 Rockefeller Plz Rm 1210 New York NY 10020-2002 Home: Johns Island 1050 Beach Rd Apt 1G Vero Beach FL 32963-3413 Office Phone: 212-218-4044.

PFEIFFER, MARGARET KOLODNY, lawyer; b. Elkin, NC, Oct. 7, 1944; d. Isadore Harold and Mary Elizabeth Kolodny; m. Carl Frederick Pfeiffer II, Sept. 2, 1968. BA, Duke U., 1967; JD, Rutgers U., 1974. Bar: NJ 1974, NY 1976, DC 1981, US Supreme Ct. 1979. Law clk. to Hon. F.L. Van Dusen U.S. Ct. Appeals 3d cir., Phila., 1974-75; assoc. Sullivan & Cromwell, NYC and Washington, 1975-82, ptnr. antitrust, intellectual property, internat. trade and investment practice area, criminal def. and investigations, 1982—. Contbr. articles to profl. jours. Trustee Nat. Law Ctr. on Homelessness and Poverty. Mem. ABA, Internat. Bar Assn., DC Bar Assn., NY State Bar Assn., Assn. of Bar of City of NY, Am. Soc. of Internat. Law. Avocations: gardening, reading, music. Office: Sullivan & Cromwell 1701 Pennsylvania Ave NW Washington DC 20006-5866 Office Phone: 202-956-7540. Business E-Mail: pfeifferm@sullcrom.com.

PFEIFFER, MARY LOUISE, artist, educator; b. Troy, Ohio, Feb. 14, 1944; d. John Edward Dunnick and Helen Elizabeth Johnson-Dunnick; children: William G. II, Scott Edward. AS magna cum laude, Tidewater Coll., Virginia Beach, Va., 1976; BA, Fla. Internat. U., Miami, 1986, MA in Religious Studies, 2004; LLM, St. Thomas U, Miami, 2002. Owner, operator Pfeiffer Originals, Art Glass Designs, Miami, 1976—; adj. prof. dept. religious studies Fla. Internat. U., 2002—, prof. Honors Coll., 2005—. Author: (technical textbook) Basic Radiography. Acting chmn. Navy Relief Soc., Meridian, Miss., 1968—69; pres., sec.-treas. POW-MIA com. NAS Oceana, Virginia Beach, 1970—75; hospitality coord. Performing Arts Cmty. and Edn., Miami, 1982—84; mem. steering com. 5th-7th tribal symposia St. Thomas U. Sch. of Law, 2002—06. Recipient Alumni Assn. Torch award, Fla. Internat. U. Alumni Assn., 2000, Outstanding Svc. award dept. religious studies, Fla. Internat. U., 2000, 2002. Fellow: The Honors Coll.; mem.: Phi Theta Kappa, Theta Alpha Kappa. Avocations: swimming, sailing, golf, travel. Home: 19160 NE 19 Pl North Miami Beach FL 33179-4316 Office: Florida Internat U UP Campus 11200 SW 8th St DM 233 Miami FL 33199 Office Phone: 305-348-4100. Office Fax: 305-348-2118. Business E-Mail: pfeiffer@fiu.edu.

PFEIFFER, MICHELLE, actress; b. Santa Ana, Calif., Apr. 29, 1957; d. Dick and Donna P.; m. Peter Horton, 1981 (div. 1988); 1 adopted child, Claudia Rose; m. David Kelley, Nov. 13, 1993, 1 child. Student, Golden West Coll., Whitley Coll. Actress: (feature films) Falling in Love Again, 1980, Hollywood Knights, 1980, Charlie Chan and the Curse of the Dragon Queen, 1981, Grease II, 1982, Scarface, 1983, Ladyhawke, 1985, Into the Night, 1985, Sweet Liberty, 1986, Amazon Women on the Moon, 1987, Witches of Eastwick, 1987, Married to the Mob, 1988, Tequila Sunrise, 1988, Dangerous Liaisons, 1988 (Acad. award nominee for best supporting actress, 1989, BAFTA award, 1990), The Fabulous Baker Boys, 1989 (L.A. Film Critics Assn. award for best actress, 1989, D.W. Griffith award Nat. Bd. Rev., 1989, N.Y. Film Critics award, 1989, Nat. Soc. Film Critics award for best actress, 1990, Golden Globe award for best actress drama, 1990, Acad. award nominee for best actress, 1990), The Russia House, 1990, Frankie & Johnny, 1991, Love Field, 1992 (Acad. award nominee for best actress, 1993), Batman Returns, 1992, The Age of Innocence, 1993, Wolf, 1994, Dangerous Minds, 1995, Up Close and Personal, 1996, To Gillian on her 37th Birthday, 1996, One Fine Day, 1996, A Thousand Acres, 1997, The Prince of Egypt (voice), 1998, The Story of Us, 1998, A Midsummer Night's Dream, 1999, Deep End of the Ocean, 1999, What Lies Beneath, 2000, I Am Sam, 2001, White Oleander, 2002, Sinbad: Legend of the Seven Seas (voice), 2003; (TV movies) The Solitary Man, 1979, Callie and Son, 1981, The Children Nobody Wanted, 1981, Splendor in the Grass, 1981, One Too Many, 1983, Tales from the Hollywood Hills: Natica Jackson, 1987, Power, Passion and Murder, 1987; (TV series) Delta House, 1979, B.A.D. Cats, 1980; prodr: (films) A Thousand Acres, 1997; exec. prodr.: (films) One Fine Day, 1996. Named Woman of the Yr., Harvard's Hasty Pudding Theater Club, 1995; recipient Crystal award, Women in Film, 1993.

PFEIFFER, PHYLLIS KRAMER, publishing executive; b. NYC, Feb. 11, 1949; d. Jacob N. and Estelle G. Rosenbaum-Pfeiffer; m. Stephen M. Pfeiffer, Dec. 21, 1969; children: Andrew Kramer, Elise Kramer. BS, Cornell U., 1970; postgrad., U. San Diego, 1976-78. Instr. Miss Porter's Sch., Farmington, Conn., 1970; tchr. Dewey Jr. HS NYC Bd. Edn., 1970—73; rschr. Hunter Coll., NYC, 1971—72; account exec. La Jolla (Calif.) Light, 1973—75, advt. dir., 1975—77, gen. mgr., 1977-78, pub., 1978-87; exec. v.p. Harte Hanks So. Calif. Newspapers, 1985—87; gen. mgr. San Diego edit. L.A. Times, 1987—93; pres., pub. Marin Ind. Jour., Novato, Calif., 1993—2000; v.p. advt. and mktg. Contra Costa Times, 2000—04; sr. v.p. advt. San Francisco Chronicle, 2005—. Dir. comm. ctr. San Diego State U., 1980-93. Bd. dirs. La Jolla Cancer Rsch. Found., 1979-82, YMCA, San Diego Ballet, 1980, Dominican Coll., San Rafael, Calif, 1994—, Marin Theater Co., Alvarado Hosp., 1981-88, chmn. fin. com., 1986, sec. bd., 1986; co-chmn. Operation USS La Jolla, USN, 1980—; mem. mktg. com. United Way, 1979-81, chmn., 1983; trustee La Jollan's Inc., 1975-78, Nat. Pk. Trust, 2000-02, Dogs for the Blind, 2001-.; mem. Conv. and Visitors Bur. Blue Ribbon Com. on Future, 1983; mem. resource panel Child Abuse Prevention Found., 1983—; bd. overseers U. Calif., San Diego; mem. violent crimes task force San Diego Police Dept.; dir. Guide Dogs for the Blind, Oakland Mus. Grantee N.Y. Bd. Edn., 1971-72; named Pub. of Yr., Gannet Co., Inc., 1995. Mem. Newspaper Assn. Am., Calif. Newspaper Pubs. Assn. (bd. dirs., exec. com.), Chancellor's Assn. U. Calif.-San Diego, Clairemont Club. Office: 250 The Uplands Berkeley CA 94705 Office Phone: 415-777-7272. E-mail: ppfeiffer@sfchronicle.com.

PFEIFFER, SOPHIA DOUGLASS, retired state legislator, lawyer; b. NYC, Aug. 10, 1918; d. Franklin Chamberlin and Sophie Douglass (White) Wells; m. Timothy Adams Pfeiffer, June 7, 1941; children: Timothy Franklin, Penelope Mesereau Keenan, Sophie Douglass. AB, Vassar Coll., 1939; JD, Northeastern U., 1975. Bar: R.I. 1975, U.S. Ct. Appeals (1st cir.) 1980, U.S. Supreme Ct. 1979. Editl. rschr. Time, Inc., NYC, 1940-41; writer Officer War Info., Washington, 1941-43, NYC, 1943-45; editl. staff Nat. Geog. Mag., Washington, 1958-59, 68-70; editor Turkish Jour. Pediatrics, Ankara, 1961-63; staff atty. R.I. Supreme Ct., Providence, 1975-76, chief staff atty., 1977-86; mem. Maine Ho. Reps., 1990-94; lectr. U. So. Maine, 1995. Bd. dirs. Death and Dying project. Contbr. in field. Chair bioethics study League Women Voters; pres. Karachi (Pakistan) Am. Sch., 1955-56; chair Brunswick Village Rev. Bd., 1986-89; trustee Brunswick Sewer Dist., 2000-05, bd. dirs. Coll. Guild, 2003—, ret., 2005. Home: 15 Franklin St Brunswick ME 04011-2101

PFENNIG, JACQUELINE F., elementary school educator; d. Paul J. and Helen Frisco; m. Dwight R. Pfennig, June 14, 1969; 1 child, Brian. BA, Tusculum Coll., Greenville, Tenn., 1969; MA, Kean U., Union, NJ, 1995; EdD, Nova Southeastern, Ft. Lauderdale, Fla., 2000. 2d grade tchr. Bedford Sch., Middletown, NJ, 1969—75; 2d, 3rd, 6th grade tchr. New Monmouth, Middletown, 1975—86; tchr. Thorne Mid. Sch., Middletown, 1986—. Cons., presenter in field. Fundraiser Fred's Team, NYC, 2000—04, Sherrys House, Worsester, Mass., 2006. Named Tchr. of Yr., Middletown Bd. Edn., 1985; recipient Govs. award, NJ Gov., 1986. Avocations: running, reading. Office: Thorne Mid Sch 70 Murphy Rd Port Monmouth NJ 07758 Personal E-mail: mspfenning@aol.com.

PFENNIGS, KIMBERLY TUCKER, nurse; b. Starkville, Miss., Mar. 31, 1957; d. Robert Anderson and Bobbye Nell Blount Tucker; m. David John Pfennigs, Aug. 16, 1994; children: Andrew Robert Littler, Jacob Guy Littler, Emilyn Grace, Samuel Martin Blount, Jonah David. Certification of Occupl. Proficiency, Eveleth Area Vocat. Tech. Inst., Eveleth, Minn., 1978; BA, Coll. St. Scholastica, Duluth, Minn., 1987; MA, U. No. Colo., Greeley, 1992. RN Minn. Bd. Nursing, 1987. Program mgr. Lighthouse Assessment Ctr., Colorado Springs, 2002—05; civil svc. labor & delivery staff nurse US Fed. Govt., Ft. Carson, Colo., 2005—. Capt. USAF, 1989—94, Operation Desert Shield. Decorated Nat. Def. Svc. Medal USAF; recipient Codman award, JCAHO, 2004. Mem.: MENSA, Sigma Theta Tau. Avocations: gourmet cooking and wines, scrapbooks, creative writing. Home: 4650 Old Farm Circle W Colorado Springs CO 80917-1026 Office Phone: 719-526-7090. Home Fax: 719-591-4534. Personal E-mail: kimberlypfennigs@msn.com.

PFINGSTEN, LYNETTE M., music educator; d. Linda K. Pfingsten. BS in Elem. Edn., So. Nazarene U., Bethany, Okla., 1993; MA in Edn., Baker U., Overland Park, Kans., 2000. Cert. elem. tchr. Kans., 1993. Tchr. 4th grade Mission Trail Elem., Leawood, Kans., 2000—04, tchr. elem. music, 2004—. Tchr. piano, Leawood, Kans., 1998—. Dir.: (directing and choreographing) elem. musicals. Mem.: NEA (life). Avocations: travel, shopping. Home: 15717 S Brookfield St Olathe KS 66062 Office: Mission Trail Elem Sch 13200 Mission Rd Leawood KS 66209 Office Phone: 913-239-6700.

PFISTER, KARSTIN ANN, human services administrator; b. Phila., Apr. 26, 1955; m. William Howard Pfister, July 10, 1979; children: Caitlin Justine, Rebecca Danielle. BA, Cornell Coll., Mount Vernon, Iowa, 1977; MEd, George Mason U., Fairfax, Va., 1983; postgrad., Va. Poly. and State U., 1986, EdD, 1990; grad., Dept. Defense Exec. Leadership Program,Dick Cheney, Sec. of Defense, 1991. lic. profl. counselor, Va.; nat. cert. counselor, lic. marriage and family therapist, cert. clin. mental health counselor, contracting officer's rep. Instr. Nat. Meteorol. Inst., Kabul, Afghanistan, 1977-78; instr. faculty of medicine, faculty of letters Kabul U., 1978-79; program coord. Pepperdine U., Calif., 1979-81; counselor family svc. ctr. Individual Devel. Assoc., Inc., Arlington, Va., 1981-87; acting dir., program coord. family svc. ctr. Hdqrs. Marine Corps., Henderson Hall, 1987-88; dir. family svc. ctr. Hdqrs. Marine Corps., Arlington, Va., 1988—99, dir. marine and family svcs., 1999—. Author: Counseling the Military Family: A Conceptual Framework, Virginia Counselors Journal, 1987; Recognition Memory Processes in Bilingual Students, paper presented at the Iowa Acad. of Sci. ann. meeting, 1979. Recipient Cert. Appreciation U.S. Amb. to Afghanistan, 1979., commendation for Superior Civilian Svc., Commendant of the Marine Corps 1995 and 2002, cert. of recognition from the Sec. of Def., 2002. Mem.: Phi Delta Kappa, Kappa Delta Pi. Office: Marine and Family Svcs HQBN MCNCRC Henderson Ha 1555 Southgate Rd Arlington VA 22214

PFISTER, TERRI, city official; Cert. stenographer, Stenotype Inst. of S.D., 1986. Police pension sec. City of Spokane, Wash., 1991-96, city clk. Wash., 1996—. Office: 808 W Spokane Falls Blvd Spokane WA 99201-3342

PFLAGER, RUTH WOOD, retired communications executive; b. Springfield, Mass., Mar. 3, 1917; d. Walter Guy and Mabel (Munson) Wood; m. Miller S. Pflager, Aug. 31, 1940; children: Sandra P. Wischmeyer, Charlene P. Balistrere, William Wood, Jessie Pflager Avery. BS, U. Mass., 1938; postgrad., Northwestern U., 1939—40. Program chmn., v.p. Radio and TV Coun. Greater Cleve., Inc., 1973—75, pres., 1975—77, exec. dir., 1977—79; ret., 1979. Chmn. Cmty. Mental Health Inst., 1981—82, TV Tune-In, 1988—; Comm. commn. Greater Cleve. Interchurch Coun., 1972—, vice-chmn., 1981—82, chmn., 1983—; comm. coord. Ch. Women United in Cleve., 1974—82, bull. editor, 1974—78; chmn. media concerns Ch. Women United in Ohio, 1979—81; ch. and soc. chair Christ United Meth. Ch., Waynesboro, 1989—; chair Christian social involvement Chambersburg dist. United Meth. Women, 1989—97. Recipient Honor award, Ch. Women United in Cleve., 1980. Mem.: AAUW (life; br. pres. 1977—79, com. on women Ohio divsn. 1979—81, chmn. media concerns task force), Nat. Telemedia Coun. (sec. 1979—80, v.p. 1980—). Home: PO Box 128 Apt 3001 Wesley Dr Quincy PA 17247 Office: 6 W 2nd St Waynesboro PA 17268-2628 Office Phone: 717-762-7042.

PFLUM, BARBARA ANN, retired allergist; b. Cin., Jan. 10, 1943; d. James Frederick and Betty Mae (Doherty) P.; m. Makram I. Gobrail, Oct. 20, 1973; children: Christina, James. BS, Coll. Mt. St. Vincent, 1967; MD, Georgetown U., 1971; MS, Coll. Mt. St. Joseph, 1993. Cons. Children's Med. Ctr., Dayton, Ohio, 1975—2006, dir. allergy clinic, 1983-89; dir. allergy divsn. Hopeland Splty. Clinic, Dayton, 1998-2000; ret., 2006. Fellow Am. Acad. Pediatrics, Am. Acad. Allergy and Immunology, Am. Coll. Allergy and Immunology; mem. Ohio Soc. Allergy and Immunology, Western Ohio Pediatric Soc. (pres. 1985-86) Roman Catholic. Office Phone: 937-293-8263. Personal E-mail: bapflum@hotmail.com.

PHAIR, LIZ, vocalist; b. Cin., Apr. 17, 1967; d. John and Nancy Phair; m. Jim Staskouskas, 1995 (div. 2001) 1 child, James Nicholas Staskouskas Diploma, Oberlin Coll., 1990. Freelance artist, 1990; singer, songwriter, 1992—. Albums include: Exile in Guyville (name Album of Yr. Village Voice), 1993, Whip-Smart, 1994, Whitechocolatespaceegg, 1998, Liz Phair, 2003, Everything to Me, 2005; Actor (films) Cherish, 2002, Seeing Other People, 2004; (TV appearances) America Dreams, 2004 Named Best New Female Vocalist Rolling Stone Critic's Poll. Office: Matador Records 625 Broadway New York NY 10012-2611*

PHALP-RATHBUN, STEPHANIE DAWN, music educator; b. Kansas City, Mo., July 30, 1978; d. Stephen Douglas and Gloria Dean Phalp; m. Robert Eric Rathbun, Sept. 6, 2002. BS, William Jewell Coll., 2000; MusM in Edn., U. Mo., Kansas City, 2005. Dir. orch. Independence Sch. Dist., Mo., 2000—01, Park Hill Sch. Dist., Kansas City, 2001—. V.p. orchs. Kansas City Metro Dist. No. 3, 2002—04, sec./treas., 2004—. Mem.: Mo. Music Educators Assn., Music Educators Nat. Conf., Am. String Tchrs. Assn. (vol. coord. chpt. 2000—04, sec. 2004—, treas. 2004—). Office: Park Hill HS 7701 NW Barry Rd Kansas City MO 64153 Business E-Mail: rathbuns@parkhill.k12.mo.us.

PHAM, LARA BACH-VIEN, small business owner; b. Ba-Xuyen, Vietnam, Jan. 11, 1962; d. Thi Van and Huong Thi Nguyen; m. Thien Van Pham, Apr. 17, 1982; children: Minh-Thu, Sheena, Lisa, Jimmy. Diploma, Brand's Beauty Coll., Charlotte, NC, 1990. Lic. securities NASD, life and health ins., in property and liability, in real estate sales, real estate broker, loan officer, cosmetology tchr. Hair stylist, owner Hair Studio, Charlotte, 1990—; beauty cons. Beauti Control, Charlotte, 1990—93, 2001—; flower arranger Charlotte, 1995—; ptnr. Carolina Choice Realty, Charlotte, 2004—, Charlotte Nails Acad., 2004. Office Phone: 704-566-8966. E-mail: larabvpham@hotmail.com.

PHAN, CHRISTINA, electronic analog design executive; b. Can Tho, Vietnam, Oct. 24, 1961; came to U.S., 1979; d. Thoi Thanh and Loan Kim (Nguyen) Phan; m. Manh Van An, Nvo. 3, 1990; children: Steven An, Jessica An. BSEE, U. Calif., Berkeley, 1983; MSEE, U. Santa Clara, Calif., 1988. Design engr. Nat. Semicondr. Corp., Santa Clara, 1984-97, analog design mgr., 1997—. Patentee in field. Buddhist. Avocation: singing.

PHAN, TÂM THANH, medical educator, psychotherapist, consultant, researcher; b. Hue, Vietnam, June 10, 1949; d. Quê'Dinh and Chánh Thi (Tô) P. BA, Adams State Coll., 1979; MA, Western State Coll., 1980; PhD in Nutrition, Am. Coll. Nutrition, 1983; D of Nutrimedicine, John Kennedy Nutrisci., Gary, Ind., 1986; PhD in Counseling, Columbus Pacific U., 1988; DSc, Lafayette U., 1989. Lic. profl. counselor, marriage and family therapist; cert. nutrimedicine specialist. Counselor Lamar U., Beaumont, Tex., 1980-82; cons. Vietnamese Cmty., Golden Triangle, Tex., 1980—, The Wholistic Clinic, Beaumont, 1980—. Mem. adv. bd. Internat. Homeopathic Clearance, Mo., 1993—. Author: How Western Culture., 1988, Natural Preventive Medicine, The Wholitic Approach, 1992, How to Prevent Mental Illness, 1995, How to Prevent Diabetes, 1996. Fellow Internat. Nutrimedicine Assn., Am. Nutrimedicine Assn.; mem. Interant. Alliance of Nutrimedical Therapists, Internat. Holistic Med. Soc. (bd. dirs. 1996, Cert. of Merit 1996). Avocations: writing, reading, swimming, cooking, knitting. Office: The Wholistic Clinic 1995 Broadway St Beaumont TX 77701-1941

PHANG, MAY, music educator; MusB with honors, McGill U., Montreal, Can., 1992, MusM, 1994; D of Musical Arts, Temple U., 2004. Grad. asst. McGill U., 1992—94; instr. secondary piano Temple U., 1994—97; instr. piano Manayunk Cmty. Ctr. for the Arts, 1997, Settlement Music Sch., 1997; pianist, cello auditions Curtis Inst. Music, 1998; pianist Drexel U., 1999—2000; asst. prof. piano Carroll Coll., Wis., 2000—03; faculty piano Wis. Conservatory Music, Wis., 2001—03; asst. prof. piano DePauw U., Ind., 2003—. Guest artist Montreal Internat. Music Camp, Canada, 2002; faculty New Eng. Music Camp, 2000—01, Adult Chamber Music Workshop, Milw., 2002—03. Singer: DePauw Symphony Orch., MIMC Orch., Wis. Wind Orch., Ambler Symphony Orch., Phila. Orch., Singapore Symphony Orch., Temple U. Chamber Orch., Orch. Symphonique de Trois-Rivières, Banff Festival Chamber Players, Montreal Symphony Orch., McGill Symphony Orch., Temple U. Symphony Orch. Juror Piano Arts Wis. Competition, Wis., 2003; juror, clinician Carroll HS Piano Competition and Masterclass, 2003; juror Waukesha Symphony Concerto Competition, 2001, 2003, Polish Fest Chopin PIano Competition, Milw., 2001—02. Recipient 1st pl., Chopin Young Pianists Competition, Buffalo, 1990, Montreal Classical Music Festival, 1990—91, Concours d'orchestre Symphonique de Montréal, 1991, Can. Music Competition, 1991, Prix du Cercle du cent Associés, 1993, Concours d'orchestre Symphonique de Trois-Rivières, 1994, 2d pl., Pontoise Internat. Young Artists Competition, 1995; Clara Lichtenstein fellow, McGill U., 1992, Maureen Forrester-Montreal Musicians Guild scholar, 1991, Russel Conwell fellow, Temple U., 1994—96, Herbert A. Morse scholar, 1993. Mem.: Coll. Music Soc., Ind. Music Tchrs. Assn. (chair collaborative arts), Music Tchrs. Nat. Assn., Phi Kappa Lambda Soc. Office: Depauw Univ 313 S Locust St Greencastle IN 46135 Office Phone: 765-658-4403. Business E-Mail: mphang@depauw.edu.

PHANTHOURATH, ANOMA T., lawyer; b. Vientiane, Laos, 1972; BA in History, Univ. Tex., Austin, 1994, BA in Journalism, 1994; JD, Univ. Ariz., 1998. Bar: Ariz. 1998, Nev. 2002, US Dist. Ct. Ariz. 1998, US Ct. Appeals (9th cir.) 1999, US Dist. Ct. Nev. 2002. Law clk. Hon. Michael J. Cruikshank; assoc., comml., civil litig. Shughart Thomson & Kilroy PC, Phoenix. Staff mem. Ariz. Law Rev., staff writer The Daily Texan. Bd. dir. Phoenix Tex. Exes Alumni Assn., 2000—, pres., 2005; founder Asian C. of C., Phoenix; fund devel. com. Jr. League, Phoenix; bd. dir., fundraising co-chair Ariz. Fair Housing Ctr.; 2006 Citizens Bond Exec. Com. City of Phoenix, commr., past chair, Pacific Rim Adv. Coun.; adv. com. Maricopa County Colleges Asian Pacific Islander Cmty. Named a Mover and Shaker, AZ Examiner, 2004; named an AZE Emerging Leader, 2004; named one of Best Lawyers Under 40, Nat. Asian Pacific Am. Bar Assn., 2004, Forty Under 40, Phoenix Bus. Jour., 2004, 15 Up and Comers, bizAZ Mag., 2004, five female lawyers affecting change and "Raising the Bar", Ariz. Woman Mag., 2005; recipient Judge Learned Hand Emerging Leadership award, Am. Jewish Com., 2005. Mem.: Clark County Bar Assn. (Nev.), Ariz. Women Lawyers Assn. (steering com. 2002—), Ariz. Asian Am. Bar Assn. (bd. dir. 2003—), Maricopa County Bar Assn. (bd. dir. 2004—). Office: Shughart Thomson & Kilroy PC One Columbus Plz Ste 1200 3636 N Central Ave Phoenix AZ 85012 Office Phone: 602-650-2049. Office Fax: 602-264-7033. Business E-Mail: aphanthourath@stklaw.com.

PHARES, SHARON C., elementary school educator; d. Jack Walter Tompkins and Lillian Howard Creel; 1 child, Kristan Busby Austin. BEd, Southwestern U., Georgetown, Tex., 1963—66. Cert. tchr. Tex. Edn. Agy., 1966. Tchr. Waxahachie ISD, Tex., 1966—71, Leonard ISD, Tex., 1972—73; lead tchr. Irving Ind. Sch. Dist., Tex., 1989—. Tchr. English Inst. China, Beijing, 1990, Zhongshu, 2001. Mem. So. Poverty Law Ctr., Birmingham, Ala., 2004—06; tchr., bd. mem. First United Meth. Ch., Irving, Tex., 1982—2006; mem. Order Ea. Star, Plano, Tex. Recipient Tchr of Yr. award, Union Bower Learning Ctr., Irving ISD, 1992, Stephen F. Austin & Sam Houston award, ATPE, 1999—2005, Teacher of Month award, Irving ISD, 2005, Outstanding Citizen award, STEPS program, Ambassador for Peace award, IIFWP. Mem.: Irving Assn. Tex. Profl. Educators (pres. 2000—01), Revere Pl. Neighborhood Assn. (chair 2004—06), Delta Kappa Gamma (internat. mem.). Independent. United Methodist. Office: Irving Ind Sch Dist 3207 W Pioneer Irving TX 75061 Business E-Mail: sphares@irvingisd.net.

PHARIS, RUTH MCCALISTER, retired bank executive; b. San Diego, Feb. 13, 1934; d. William L. and Mary E. (Beuk) McC.; m. E. Edwin Pharis, Mar. 14, 1953; children: Beth, Tracey, Todd. Grad., Del Mar Coll., Corpus Christi, Tex., 1979. Asst. cashier Parkdale State Bank, Corpus Christi, 1970-72, asst. v.p., 1972-76, v.p., 1976-79, Cullen Center Bank & Trust, Houston, 1979-81, sr. v.p., 1982-93; dir. human resources Scooter Store, Inc., New Braunfels, Tex., 2001—03. Instr. Am. Inst. Banking, 1977—79. Mem. adv. coun. Houston C.C. Mem. Human Resource Mgmt. Assn., Bank Adminstrn. Inst. (v.p. Coastal Bend chpt. 1979), Nat. Assn. Bank Women (ednl. chmn. Coastal Bend group), Am. Inst. Banking (rep.), Tex. Bankers Assn. (coun. 1983-84, instr.), Coastal Bend Personnel Soc. (v.p.), Houston Personnel Assn., New Braunfels (Tex.) Rep. Women (pres. 1999-2002), Corpus Christi C. of C. (mem. women's com. 1976-79), Order Eastern Star. Republican. Baptist. Home: 2779 Morning Star New Braunfels TX 78132-4722 E-mail: rpharis@satx.rr.com.

PHARR, PAIGE ELIZABETH, interior designer, real estate broker; b. New Iberia, La., Sept. 20, 1965; d. Fitzgerald Parker Pharr and Sheila Ferguson Mankin. Student, U. of La. at Lafayette, 1983—86, Am. Intercontinental U., 2001—03. Paralegal Nat. Ctr. for Paralegal Tng., 1990. Paralegal Webb, Carlock, Copeland, Semler & Stair, Atlanta, 1990—92, Resolution Trust Corp., Atlanta, 1992—94; real estate account exec. Koll Real Estate Co., Atlanta, 1994—96, Cushman & Wakefield, Walnut Creek, Calif., 1996—97; v.p. Ackerman & Co., Atlanta, 1997—99; owner Ecclectique, Atlanta, 1999—2003; assoc. dir. Insignia/ESG, Atlanta, 1999—2002; pres. Aria Enterprises, Inc., Atlanta, 2002—. Counsel cancer patients Egleston Children's Hosp., Atlanta, Ga., 1977—83. Mem.: Comml. Real Estate Women. R-Consevative. Episcopal. Avocations: interior design, travel, cooking, photography. Office: Aria Enterprises Inc 3097 Hudson Way Decatur GA 30033 E-mail: paige@ariaenterprises.com.

PHELAN, MARY MICHENFELDER, public relations executive, writer; b. St. Louis, Oct. 6, 1936; d. Albert A. Michenfelder and Ruth Josephine Donahue; m. Gerald Leo Phelan, Aug. 16, 1958; children: Gerald (Grady) Leo, Jr., Joseph (Joe) Leo. BS, St. Louis U., 1958; M in Liberal Arts, Washington U., St. Louis, 1995. PRSA Accreditation Pub. Rels. Soc. of Am., 1987. Counselor, v.p. Fleishman-Hillard, Inc., St. Louis, 1982—94; dir., corp. comm. BJC HealthCare, St. Louis, 1995—2001; exec. v.p. Patrick Davis Ptnrs., St. Louis, 2001—. Author: (children's books) ABCs of Celebration, ABCs of the City of Man. Chair, pub. rels. com. Confluence St. Louis, 1981—85; mem. Citizens for Mo.'s Children, 2004—, Friends of KWMU, Nat. Pub. Radio, St. Louis, 1991—, pres., 1997—99. Recipient One of Top 5 PR Teams in U.S. award, PR WEEK Mg., 2000, Wall of Fame for Achievement in Bus., Nerinx Hall HS, 2001. Mem.: Pub. Rels. Soc. of Am. (life; pres. St. Louis chpt. 1992, Coll. of Fellows 2003).

PHELAN, STEPHANIE ELLEN, artist, graphics designer; b. Montclair/Glen Ridge, N.J., Apr. 25, 1946; d. James Richard and Ellen Irma (McGeehan) P.; m. Richard Kubicz, Jan. 26, 1979 (div. 1983). Student, George Washington U., 1964-65. Asst. buyer, adminstrv. asst. Doyle Dane Bernbach, N.Y.C., 1965-66; asst. art dir. Eye Mag., N.Y.C., 1967-69; assoc. art dir. Nat. Lampoon, N.Y.C., 1969-72; art dir. Grapevine Newspaper, Martha's Vineyard, Mass., 1972-75, Martha's Vineyard C. of C., 1976-78; assoc. art dir. Connoisseur Mag., N.Y.C., 1983-88; dir. print prodn. Calvin Klein Cosmetics, N.Y.C., 1989-90; sr. designer Money Mag., N.Y.C., 1990—2002; creative dir. Mamm Mag., N.Y.C., 2002—05; art dir. Consumer Reports Money Advisor, N.Y.C., 2003—04; freelance designer and dog portraitist N.Y.C., 1991—. Drawing, "Black Dog" logo for the Black Dog Tavern Co., 1976, featured in, NY Mag., County Living Mag., Am. Airlines Mag., Best for Pets Digest. Aux. police officer N.Y.C. Police Dept., 1981—. Recipient commendations N.Y.C. Police Dept., 1983, 86, award of merit, 1989, Dog Art award Westminster Kennel Club, 1993. Roman Catholic. Office Phone: 212-620-0652. E-mail: tucker@phelandogart.com.

PHELPS, ANNETTE FAILLA, realtor; d. Pete Failla and Josephine Priolo; children: Susan, John. Realtor Coldwell Banker, Boca Raton, Fla. Mem. adv. coun. Coldwell Banker, Boca Raton. Pres. Christ Child Soc., Boca Raton. Named to Pres.'s Cir., Coldwell Banker. Mem.: Realtor Assn. Palm Beaches. Home: 2301 Glades Rd Boca Raton FL 33431-7398 Office Phone: 561-362-0045. Personal E-mail: bocarealtor1@aol.com.

PHELPS, CYNTHIA L., medical educator; BA in Biology and Biochemistry, Hope Coll., 1991; PhD in Pharmacology and Toxicology, Mich. State U., 1996. Rsch. asst. dept. pharmacology and toxicology Mich. State U., East Lansing, 1992—95, dissertation rschr., 1995—97; postdoctoral fellow dept. integrative biology U. Tex. Med. Sch., Houston, 1997—2000; rsch. scientist dept. health informatics Sch. Allied Health Scis. U. Tex., 2000—, asst. prof. health informatics, 2000—. Vis. faculty Brandeis U., 1996; lectr. dept. pharmacology and toxicology Mich. State U., 1994—96, tutor dept. osteo. medicine, 1995—96; workshop leader Hands-On Neurosci. Activities Workshop, Soc. for Neurosci., 1998; tchr./trainer Houston Outreach Team "Neural Networks", Am. Physiol. Soc., Houston, 1997—; mentor Project Intercon U. Tex. Med. Sch., Houston, 1997—; creator Brainsurf ednl. web site, 1997—; judge Houston Math and Sci. Fair, 1997—98; distance learning lectr. Sci. in the Classroom, Sch. Pub. Health, U. Tex., 1997—98; lectr. in field. Contbr. articles to profl. jours. Dir. Sci. Theatre, East Lansing, 1995—96; coord. Sci. Day at the Mall/Meridian Mall, 1995—96; mentor GTE Summer Rsch. Program for minority h.s. students, Hope Coll., 1990. Recipient Travel award, Am. Soc. Parasitologists; fellow NRSA postdoctoral fellow award, NIMH; grantee NIMH Edn. grantee, pharmacology/toxicology grad. student tng. grantee, NIH, tng. grantee, NSF/Hope Coll. Mem.: Nat. Biology Tchrs. Assn., Nat. Sci. Tchrs. Assn., Assn. for Women in Sci., Soc. for Neurosci., Tri-Beta. Office: Univ Texas-Houston Health Sci Ctr Dept Health Informatics 7000 Fannin Ste 600 Houston TX 77030

PHELPS, ELAINE L., special education educator; b. Davenport, Iowa, Nov. 4, 1953; d. Emmeft Lawrence Baudendistel and Irene Ann Dinkelman; m. Stanley Floyd Phelps, Mar. 20, 1976; children: Amber Dawn, Alan Richard. BS in Edn., So. Ill. U., Carbondale, 1975, MS in Curriculum Instrn., 1983. Cert. Tchr. K-9, endorsements in reading & lang. arts Ill. Dept. Edn., 1975, Tchr. K-12 Spl. Edn. Ill. Dept. Edn., 1975. Spl. edn. tchr. Akin Grade Sch., Ill., 1975—80, Ewing Grade Sch., 1980—. Bd. mem. Ewing No. Found.; mem. Ewing Focus Com. Congregation leader Thrivant, Mt. Vernon, Ill., 2004—. Mem.: Internat. Reading Assn., Ill. Reading Coun., So. Ill. Reading Coun. (bd. mem. 1980), Ill. Fedn. Tchrs. (pres. local chpt. 1987, co-pres. local chpt. 2006—). Democrat. Lutheran. Avocations: travel, reading, gardening. Home: 4737 N Cherryville Ln Bonnie IL 62816 Office: Ewing No Grade Sch Ewing IL 62836

PHELPS, JAYCIE, gymnast, Olympic athlete; b. Indpls., Sept. 26, 1979; Mem. U.S. Women's World Gymnastics Team, 1994-95, U.S. Olympic Team, Atlanta, 1996. Recipient Sagamore of the Wabash award State of Ind., 1995, Gold medal team competition Olympic Games, Atlanta, 1996; placed 3rd in all around U.S. Olympic Festival, St. Louis, 1994, 2d for team Team World Championships, Dortmund, Germany, 1994, 3rd in all around Coca-Cola Nat. Championships, New Orleans, 1995, 3rd for team World Championships, Sabae, Japan, 1995. Avocations: coaching, swimming, shopping. Office: care USA Gymnastics Pan Am Plz 201 S Capitol Ave Ste 300 Indianapolis IN 46225-1058

PHELPS, MARY ANN BAZEMORE, elementary school educator; b. Cofield, N.C., Sept. 17, 1940; d. Hugh Bazemore and Bertha Elmyra Willoughby; m. Russell Vastie Phelps, Aug. 12, 1967; 1 child, Ann Hope. BS, E. Carolina U., 1962. Cert. elem. tchr. Tchr. Weeksville H.S., Elizabeth City, N.C., 1962-65, Sheep-Harney Sch., Elizabeth City, 1965-67, Colerain (N.C.) Elem. Sch., 1967-92, Windsor (N.C.) Elem. Sch., 1992-93, Ahoskie (N.C.) Christian Sch., 1996-99; tutor Ahoskie, 1996-99. Mem. adv. bd. Bertie County Schs., Windsor, 1985. Mem. Ridgecroft Sch. Bd., Ahoskie, 1993-97; mem. visitor's bd. Chowan Coll., Murfreesboro, N.C., 1994-98; mem. U. N.C. Parents Assn., 1995-99. Mem. NEA, N.C. Assn. Educators (sec. 1963-64). Baptist. Avocations: reading, crossword puzzles, golf, biking. Home: 4407 Willow Moss Way Southport NC 28461-2677

PHELPS, MINDY SHANNON, communications consultant; b. Casper, Wyo., Feb. 5, 1955; d. Greer Pierson Streetman and Patricia Ann Wulff; m. Grant Eaton Phelps, June 20, 1992; children: Patricia Andrea Rosensohn, Elizabeth Susan Lasker Rosensohn. BA, Ea. KY U., Richmond, 1977. Owner Sun Rose Farm, Lawrenceburg, Ky., 1979; evening news anchor WLEX TV, Lexington, Ky., 1983—91; press sec. Gov. of Ky., Frankfort, 1991—92; exec. dir. Ky. Habitat for Humanity, Lexington, 1995—2001; owner Phelps Com, Lexington, 1996—; exec. dir. Ky. Conf. Cmty. & Justice, Lexington, 2005—06. Office Phone: 859-523-2850.

PHELPS, SUSAN WILLIAMS, secondary school educator; d. Glenn Lee and Carole Breese Williams; m. Mark Allan Phelps, June 13, 1980; children: Nathaniel Evan, Joshua Mark, Aaron Michael. BS, SUNY, Binghamton, 1980; MA, SUNY, 1991. Cert. tchr. secondary social studies 7-12 NY. IB/AP Am. history tchr. Binghamton H.S., 2003—. Com. mem. Boy Scout Troop 152, Kattelville, NY, 2000—; lay eucharistic min., vestry St. Mark's Episcopal Ch., Chenango Bridge, NY, 2003—06. Fellow Summer Seminar at Oxford U., Gilder Lehrman Inst. Am. History, 2002; grantee Stony the Rd. Seminar, NEH, 2005, The Lincoln Home, Soc. and Politics in Springfield, Ill., 2005. Mem.: Binghamton Tchrs. Assn. (sec. 2005—). Episcopalian. Avocations: travel, reading, walking. Home: 390 Port Rd Binghamton NY 13901 Office: Binghamton City Sch Dist 98 Oak St Binghamton NY 13905 Office Phone: 607-762-8200. E-mail: phelpss@bcsdgw.stier.org.

PHIBBS, MARY ELLEN, retired secondary school educator; b. Bridgewater, Va., Oct. 25, 1924; d. Minor Cline and Mary Agnes (Shipman) Miller; m. Garnett Ersiel Phibbs, Aug. 18, 1945 (div. June 1972); children: Gerald Edwin, David Miller, Robert Lee. BA, Bridgewater Coll., 1945; MEd, U. Toledo, 1964; postgrad., NYU, 1965, Ariz. State U., 1971, U. Okla., 1972. Tchr. Bassett (Va.) High Sch., 1945-50, Maumee (Ohio) Jr. High Sch., 1964-69, Roosevelt Jr. High Sch., Glendale, Calif., 1969—. Mem. Glendale Sci. Curriculum writing team, 1980-84. Author: How to Teach Students to Listen and Follow Directions, 1991; (audio cassette) Aural Oragami: Lessons in Listening, 1991, When They Hear What Is Said, and Know What To Do, All Students Can Learn Not Just A Few, 1985-1991. Democrat. Methodist. Avocations: gardening, choral singing. Home: 1650 Capistrano Ave Glendale CA 91208-1925 Office: Roosevelt Jr High Sch 1017 S Glendale Ave Glendale CA 91205-2897

PHIFER, EMILY A., elementary school educator; d. Will and Margarette (Jones) Phifer. BS in Early Childhood Edn., Newark State Coll., 1971; BS in Elem. Edn., Kean U., 1971; MS in Edn., Bank St. Coll. Edn., NYC, 1979; EdM, Columbia U., NYC, 1981. Supr. Orange Daycare/Headstart, NJ, 1969—72; tchr. Orange Bd. Edn., 1972—. Cons. in field. Founder, adv. Nat. Jr. Honor Soc., Orange, 2004. Avocations: violin, viola. Home: 115 Polifly Rd Hackensack NJ 07601

PHIFER, RENITA Y., counselor, educator; b. Queens, NY, Jan. 16, 1959; d. Sir Jerry and Velma Lee Phifer; divorced; 1 child, Nygeia Karine Phifer-Dehoyas. AA, Mercy Coll., 1986, degree in Pers. Mgmt., 1988, BSc, 1990, M in English Lit., 2004. Cert. NY State Dept. Edn., in Human behavior NY State Dept. Edn., in Liberal Studies NY State Dept. Edn. Substance abuse counselor Just Caring About People (J-CAP), Queens, NY, 1990—92; mobile crisis counselor Interfaith Hosp., Bklyn., 1992—95; counselor Samaritan Village, Queens, 1995—97, Teen Time, Westchester, NY, 1999—2003; tchr. Even Start, Westchester, 1997—99; academic, vocat. assessment counselor Women's Prison Edn. Partnership, Westchester, 2003—, fundraiser bd. mem., 2004—. Author: (books) The Colors of Life, 2004. Vol. Cath. Charities, 1996—, Rock the Vote, Bklyn., 2004. Recipient Giving Voice to Voiceless award, Puffin Found., Teaneck, NJ, 2003, Blossoms Within Bricks award, 2004, Vale of Tears award, 2005. Mem.: Internat. Libr. Poetry. Democrat. Baptist. Avocations: gardening, paddle ball, bowling, poetry, aerobics.

PHILBIN, ANN, art facility director; b. Boston, Mar. 21, 1952; d. Richard Moore and Ann Theresa (Muller) Philbin BA in art history, BFA in painting, U. NH, 1976; MA in mus. studies/arts adminstrn., NYU, 1982. Rschr. Frick Art Reference Libr., NYC, 1977-79; asst. to dir., program coord. Artists Space, NYC, 1979-80; asst. curatorial coord. The New Mus., NYC, 1980-81; curator Ian Woodner Family Collection, NYC, 1981-83; asst. dir. Grace Borgenicht Gallery, NYC, 1983-85; dir. Curt Marcus Gallery, NYC, 1985-88; account dir., dir. Art Against AIDS Livet Reichard Inc., NYC, 1988-90; dir. The Drawing Ctr., NYC, 1990—99, UCLA Hammer Museum, LA, 1999—. Bd. dirs. Elizabeth Streb, Ringside, NY, 1990, HIV Law Project, N.YC, 1993; founding mem. Women's Action Coalition, NYC, 1991. Recipient Best Monographic Mus. Show Nationally Award for exhibition Lee Bontecou: A Retrospective, Internat. Assn. Art Critics/USA, 2004. Address: UCLA Hammer Museum 10899 Wilshire Blvd at Westwood Blvd Los Angeles CA 90024*

PHILBRICK, MARGARET ELDER, artist; b. Northampton, Mass., July 4, 1914; d. David and Mildred (Pattison) Elder; m. Otis Philbrick, May 23, 1941 (dec. Apr. 1973); 1 child, Otis. Grad., Mass. Sch. Art, Boston, 1937; student, De Cordova Mus., Lincoln, Mass., 1966-67. Juror art shows; exhibited one woman show, Bare Cove Gallery, Hingham, Mass., 1979, Greenwich Garden Ctr., Cos Cob, Conn., 1981; retrospective exhbn. graphics, Ainsworth Gallery, Boston, 1972; exhibited 40 yr. retrospective, Westenhook Gallery, Sheffield, Mass., 1977, 50 yr. retrospective, 1985; group shows, Boston Printmakers, 1948—, USIA tour to Far East, 1958-59, Boston Watercolor Soc., 1956—, Pratt Graphic Art Ctr., N.Y.C., 1966, New Eng. Watercolor Soc., 1982—; represented in permanent collections Nat. Mus. Fine Arts, Hanoi, Library of Congress, Washington, Boston Pub. Library, Nat. Bezalel Mus., Jerusalem, Royal Miniature Soc. 100th Ann. Exhbn., London, 1995; artist, designer: Wedgwood Commemorative Plates, Stoke-on-Trent, Eng., 1944-55, Nat. Mus. of Women in the Arts, Washington, Wiggin Collection Boston Pub. Library, The Margaret Philbrick Collection Westwood (Mass.) Pub. Libr.; illustrator books; exhibited "The Book as Art" Nat. Mus. of Women in the Arts, 1987, "The Book as Art II", 1989. Recipient purchase Libr. of Congress, 1948; recipient 1st graphics Acad. Artist, Springfield, Mass., 1957, Multum in Parvo Pratt-2d Internat. Miniature Print Exhbn., 1966, 1st prize in floral Miniature Art Soc. Fla., 1986, Ralph Fabri award. Mem. NAD (Ralph Fabri 1977), Boston Printmakers Presentation Print (exec. bd. 1951—), Acad. Artists, New Eng. Watercolor Soc., Miniature Painters, Washington Sculptors and Gravers Soc. (Founders award), Miniature Art Soc. N.J., World Fedn. Miniature Artists (charter), Miniature Art Soc. Home and Office: 323 Dover Rd Westwood MA 02090-2439

PHILIP, JOAN MARY, literature and language educator; b. Denton, Tex., Feb. 13, 1960; d. Barron Bevis Collier and Patricia D. Raymond; m. George R. Philip IV, Feb. 14, 1991. BA in English, U. Ark., Fayetteville, 1984. English tchr. Elkins HS, Ark., 1988—. Meals on wheels sponsor Elkins North HS, 1996—. Mem.: US Rose Soc. Democrat. Avocations: golf, gardening, needlework. Office: Elkins HS Highway 16 E Elkins AR 72727 Office Phone: 479-643-3381.

PHILIPP, KARLA ANN, music educator, conductor, musician; b. Milw., Sept. 12, 1955; d. John William and Catherine Ann Philipp. MusB, U. Ariz., 1977; MusM, Memphis State U., 1979. Tchr. itinerant strings Memphis City Schs., 1979—; condr. youth string ensemble and youth sinfonia Memphis Youth Symphony, 1997—. Sect. bass player Tucson Symphony Orch., 1977—78, Memphis Symphony Orch., 1979—89; prin. bass Jackson Symphony Orch., 1989—; note reading tchr., condr. Am. Suzuki Inst., Stevens Point, Wis., 1993—2005; dir. orch. Intermountain Suzuki String Inst., Salt Lake City, 2001—04; notereading tchr., dir. orch. Suzuki Inst. U. Memphis, 2005—, dir. orch. Summer String Camp, 2006—. Mem. Integrity, Memphis, 2003—. Recipient award for tchr. excellence, Rotary Club, Memphis, 1998, Outstanding Tchr. award, Tenn. Gov.'s Sch. for Arts, 1991, 1994, 1995; grantee, Rotary Club, Memphi, 1991, 1997; Haldeman scholar, U. Ariz. Sch. Music, 1974—78. Mem.: Internat. Soc. Bassists, Suzuki Assn. of Ams., West Tenn. Sch. Band and Orch. Assn., Tenn. Music Educators Assn., Music Educators Nat. Conf., Am. String Tchrs. Assn. (west Tenn v.p. 1993—95), Am. Fedn. Musicians Local 71. Episcopalian. Avocations: reading, travel. Office: Ridgeway Mid Sch 6333 Quince Rd Memphis TN 38119 Office Phone: 901-416-1588. E-mail: philippbass@aol.com.

PHILIPPS, JULIE LEIGHANN, elementary school educator; d. Henry Edward and Jean Linda Tobin; m. Mike Philipps; children: Deanna Crystine, Michael Joseph. BA in Edn., Hofstra U., Hempstead, N.Y., 1981—84. Cert. Math. Tchr. Calif. Dept. Edn., 1984, N.Y. Dept. Edn., 1984. Tchr. Bancrof Mid. Sch., San Leandro, Calif., 1989—97, East Ave. Mid. Sch., Livermore, Calif., 1997—2006, Granada H.S., Livermore, Calif., 2006—. Adv. ski clubs various orgns. Coord. Pennies for Patients. Office: Granada HS Wall St Livermore CA 94550 Office Phone: 925-606-4800. Office Fax: 925-606-4763.

PHILIPS, SUZANNE MARGUERITE See CASEY, SUE

PHILLIPS, ALYS SWORDS, surgical nurse; b. Miami, Fla., Apr. 13, 1959; d. Collins Ward and Lea (Turner) Swords; children: Shannon, Carly. AS, Broward Community Coll., Pompano, Fla., 1987. Surg./grad. nurse Holy Cross Hosp., Ft. Lauderdale, Fla., 1988-89; surg./charge nurse Doctor's Hosp. of Hollywood, Fla., 1989-91; surg./orthopedic specialty nurse North Shore Med. Ctr., Miami, Fla., 1991-94, nurse mgr. operating rm., 1994—; nurse mgr. Mt. Sinai Med. Ctr., 2002; staff nurse Meml. Hosp. W., 2002. Contbr. articles to profl. jours. Mem. Assn. Operating Rm. Nurses (pres.-elect Broward chpt.) Republican. Mem. Christian Ch. Avocations: aerobics, fishing, horseback riding. Office Phone: 954-466-7190.

PHILLIPS, ANN Y., art advisor; b. Omaha, July 9, 1955; d. Irvin and Annette Swezey Yaffe; m. Lee Stuart Phillips, Aug. 12, 1984; children: S. Perry, Lucy A. BA, Yale U., 1977; postgrad., Hunter Coll., 1979—81. Adminstr. Pace Gallery, N.Y.C., 1978—79; asst. dir. Rosa Esman Gallery, N.Y.C., 1979—82; dir. Bette Stoler Gallery, N.Y.C., 1982—87; assoc. Hirschl & Adler Galleries, N.Y.C., 1987—93; v.p., art advisor Citibank Art Adv. Svc., N.Y.C., 1993—2000; pvt. art. adv. Ann Yaffe Phillips Fine Art, Inc., 2000—. Mem. art com. Montclair (N.J.) Art mus., 1997—; ptnr. Amiel and Phillips, LLC, 2003— Co-author catalog: Prints of Eugene Delacroix, 1977; co-author, editor catalog: From Architecture to Object--Masterworks from the American Arts and Crafts Movement, 1989; organizer, co-author catalog: Cross Currents: Americans in Paris, 1993. Mem. Am. Assn. Museums, Art Table. Avocations: reading, gardening. Office: Ann Yaffe Phillips Fine Art 329 Park St Montclair NJ 07043-2210 Office Phone: 917-863-9819. Business E-Mail: ann@annphillipsfineart.com

PHILLIPS, BERNICE CECILE GOLDEN, retired vocational education educator; b. Galveston, Tex., June 30, 1920; d. Walter Lee and Minnie (Rothsprack) Golden; m. O. Phillips, Mar. 1950 (dec.); children: Dorian Lee, Loren Francis. BBA cum laude, U. Tex., 1945; MEd, U. Houston, 1968. cert. tchr., tchr. coord., vocat. tchr., Tex. Dir. Delphian Soc., Houston, 1955-60; bus. tchr. various private schs., Houston area, 1960-65; vocat. tchr. coord. office edn. program Pasadena (Tex.) Ind. Sch. Dist., 1965-68, Houston Ind. Sch. Dist., John H. Reagan High Sch., 1968-85, ret., 1985. Bd. dirs. Regency House Condominium Assn., 1991-93. Recipient numerous awards and recognitions for vocat. bus. work at local and state levels. Mem. AAUW (life, 50 yr. mem., Houston Br. v.p. ednl. found. 1987-90, pres. 1992-94, bd. dirs. 1987-96, 50-Yr. mem. cert.), NEA, Nat. Bus. Edn. Assn., Am. Vocat. Assn. (life), Tex. State Tchrs. Assn. (life), Tex. Classroom Tchrs. Assn. (life), Tex. Bus. Edn. Assn. (emeritus, Life Mem. award, numerous other awards), Vocat. Office Edn. Tchrs. Assn. Tex. (past bd. dirs.), Greater Houston Bus. Edn. Assn. (reporter), Houston Assn. Ret. Tchrs., Tex. Assn. Ret. Tchrs., Delta Pi Epsilon (emeritus), Beta Gamma Sigma. Avocations: bridge, reading, arts, crafts, travel. Home: 1824 Glendale Dr Bel Air MD 21015-2544

PHILLIPS, BETTY LOU (ELIZABETH LOUISE PHILLIPS), writer, interior designer; b. Cleve. d. Michael N. and Elizabeth D. (Materna) Suvak; m. John S. Phillips, Jan. 27, 1963 (div. Jan. 1981); children: Bruce, Bryce, Brian; m. John D.C. Roach, Aug. 28, 1982. BS, Syracuse U., 1960; postgrad. in English, Case We. Res. U., 1963—64. Cert. elem. and spl. edn. tchr., N.Y.; cert. interior designer, Calif. Tchr. pub. schs., Shaker Heights, Ohio, 1960—66. Sportswriter Cleve. Press, 1976-77; spl. features editor Pro Quarterback Mag., N.Y.C., 1976-79; bd. dirs. Cast Specialties Inc., Cleve. Author: Chris Evert: First Lady of Tennis, 1977, Picture Story of Dorothy Hamill, 1978 (ALA Booklist selection), American Quarter Horse, 1979, Earl Campbell: Houston Oiler Superstar, 1979, Picture Story of Nancy Lopez, 1980 (ALA Notable book), Go! Fight! Win! The NCA Guide for Cheerleaders, 1981 (ALA Booklist), Something for Nothing, 1981, Brush Up on Your Hair, 1981 (ALA Booklist), Texas.The Lone Star State, 1989, Provençal Interiors-French Country Style in America, 1998, French by Design, 2000, French Influences, 2001, Villa Décor: Decidedly French and Italian Style, 2002 (Foreword Mag. Best Non-Fiction Book, 2003), Unmistakably French, 2003, Emily Goes Wild, 2003 (Tex. Inst. Letters Best Children's Book, 2004), Secrets of French Design, 2004, The French Connection, 2005, Emily Works Out, 2005, Emily's Manners, 2005; contbr. articles popular mags. Mem.: Am. Soc. Interior Designers (profl. mem., cert.), Soc. Children's Book Writers, Delta Delta Delta. Republican. Roman Catholic. Home: 4278 Bordeaux Ave Dallas TX 75205-3718

PHILLIPS, CARLY, writer; b. Mount Vernon, NY, July 7, 1965; d. Leonard Robert and Arlene Weinberg; m. Phillip Drogin, Mar. 23, 1965; children: Jaclyn Lindsay, Jennifer Ashley. BA, Brandeis U., Waltham, MA, 1987; JD, Boston U, 1990. Bar: N.Y. 1991, Conn. 1991. Author: (novels) The Bachelor, 2002 (NY Times Bestseller List, Reading with Ripa Nationally Televised Bookclub, 2002), The Playboy, 2003 (NY Times Bestseller List, 2003), The Heartbreaker, 2004 (NY Times Extended Bestseller List), Summer Lovin', 2005 (NY Times Extended Bestseller List), Hot Number, 2005, Cross My Heart, 2006, Hot Item, 2006 (NY Times Extended Bestseller List). Mem.: Novelists, Inc., Romance Writers of Am. Office: PO Box 483 Purchase NY 10577 E-mail: carlyphillips@optonline.net.

PHILLIPS, CHERYL, reporter; Sports reporter Fort Worth Star-Telegram, Tex.; govt. reporter Great Falls Tribune, Mont.; computer-assisted reporting projects editor Detroit News; computer-assisted reporting editor USA Today; investigative reporter Seattle Times. Bd. dirs. Investigative Reporters & Editors, v.p., 2001—. Office: Seattle Times PO Box 70 Seattle WA 98111 Office Phone: 206-464-2111. Office Fax: 206-464-2261. E-mail: cphillips@seattletimes.com.*

PHILLIPS, CYNTHIA ANN, science educator; b. Plantation, Fla., Nov. 9, 1975; m. Keith A. Phillips, Oct. 7, 1994; children: Macy Ann, Madison Alexis. BS, U. West Ala., Livingston, 1997, MA in Tchg., 1999. Tchr. sci. Thomasville High Sch., Ala., 1999—2000, Demopolis High Sch., 2000—. Sponsor sci. nat. honor soc. Demopolis High Sch., 2000—, chair sci. dept., 2003—. Mem.: Nat. Sci. Tchrs. Assn., Ala. Edn. Assn.

PHILLIPS, DEBORA ROTHMAN, psychotherapist; b. Bklyn. d. Samuel and Iris (Weinstein) Rothman; William Phillips, Jan. 25, 1969 (div. Aug. 1988); children: Ron, Wendy; m. Dennis J. Munjack, Sept. 2, 1989. BA, Barnard Coll., N.Y.; MEd, Chatham Coll., Pa.; ArtsD, Inst. Advanced Study Human Sexuality. Lic. clin. psychologist; cert. sch. psychologist, sex therapist, counselor. Dir. Princeton (N.J.) Ctr. Behavior Therapy, 1970-88; pvt. practice N.Y.C., Beverly Hills, 1988—. Dir. Sexuality Edn. Sconsulting & Health, Princeton, 1973-79; dir. clin. tng. Temple Univ., Phila., 1974-80, asst. clin. prof., 1976-86; cons. Wesley-Westminster Found., Princeton, 1979-81, NBC-TV, 1981, The Doctors, L.A., 1996, Broken Hearts, L.A., 1996;; lectr. child psychiatry Columbia U., N.Y.C., 1980—; asst. clin. prof. U. So. Calif., L.A., 1984-90, 95-96. Author: How to Fall Out of Love, 1978, Sexual Confidence, 1980, How to Give Your Child a Great Self-Image, 1989. Dir. spl. projects Fund End Teen Cruelty, L.A. Recipient Author citation N.J. Inst. Tech., 1981. Fellow Behavior Therapy Rsch. Soc.; mem. Assn. Advancement Behavior Therapy, Soc. Sex Therapy Rsch., Am. Assn. Sex Educators, Am. Assn. Counseling, Cou. Register Health Svc. Providers. Avocations: travel, cinema, theater, french, reading. Office: Beverly Hills Ctr Depression Anxiety 435 N Bedford Dr Ste 216 Beverly Hills CA 90210-4352

PHILLIPS, DONNA ROSE, production artist, writer; b. Cheyenne, Wyo., June 16, 1961; d. Leyson Kirk and Leona Anna (Rasmussen) P.; m. Steven Gary Steinsapir, May 17, 1992; 1 child, Andrew Trevor Steinsapir Student, Mt. San Antonio Coll., Walnut, Calif., 1982—83, Citrus Coll., Azusa, Calif., 1988. Prodn. artist Treasure Chest Advt., Pomona, Calif., 1988—89, Rutland Tool & Supply Co. Inc., Industry, Calif., 1989—92; freelance writer Baldwin Park, Calif., 1992—. Contbg. author: Book of Days, 1989; contbr. articles to mags Recipient award for art Bank Am., Covina, Calif., 1979 Lutheran. Avocations: reading, films, pottery, art, classic cars. Home: 536 S College Ave Claremont CA 91711-5526

PHILLIPS, DOROTHY K., lawyer; BS, U. Pa.; MA, NYU; JD, Villanova Law Sch., 1978. Bar: Pa. 1978, NJ 1978, US Dist. Ct. (ea. dist.) Pa., US Dist. Ct. NJ, US Ct. Appeals (3d cir.), US Supreme Ct. Lectr. Marriage Coun. Phila., U. Pa., Hahnemann Med. Sch., Phila., 1970-75; atty. Adler, Barish, Daniels, Levin & Creskoff, Phila., 1978-79, Astor, Weiss & Newman, Phila., 1979-80; ptnr. Romisher & Phillips. P.C., Phila., 1981-86; prin. Dorothy K. Phillips & Assocs., LLC, 1986—. Judge Reimel Moot Ct. Competition, Villanova Law Sch., 1986; faculty Pa. Bar Inst., CLE Temple U. Sch. Law, 1987-89, Nat. Bus. Inst., lectr. 1998, 2000, 01, 03, 04. Author: The Legal Intelligencer, The Phila. Lawyer, 1998; family law columnist: Pa. Law Weekly, 2005-06; contbr. articles to profl. jours. Named a Super Lawyer Phila. Mag., 2005-06; named one of Top 50 Lawyers Phila. Mag., 2006; featured in Wall St. Jour., Phila. Inquirer, Phila. Bus. Jour., Harper's Bazaar, WPVI-ABC6, KYW-CBS3, WCAU-NBC10, FOX Phila., CN8. Mem.: ATLA, ABA, Lawyers Club, Montgomery County Bar Assn., Phila. Trial Lawyers Assn., Phila. Bar Assn. Custody Rules Drafting Com. (Supreme Ct. Pa., faculty), NJ State Bar Assn., Pa. Bar Assn., Pa. Trial Lawyers Assn. Business E-Mail: dkp@dkphillipslaw.com.

PHILLIPS, DOROTHY REID, retired medical library technician; b. Hingham, Mass., Apr. 21, 1924; d. James Henry and Emma Louise (Davis) Reid; m. Earl Wendell Phillips, Apr. 22, 1944; children: Earl W., Jr., Betty Herrera, Carol Coe. Cert., Durham Vocat. Sch., 1952; B.S. in Comml. Edn., N.C. Central U., 1959; postgrad. U. Colo., 1969; M.Human Relations, Webster Coll., 1979; postgrad. Grad. Sch. Library Sci., U. Denver, 1983. Vocat. nurse Meml. Hosp., U. N.C., Chapel Hill, 1955-59; vol. work, Cairo, Egypt, 1965-67; library technician Base Library, Lowry AFB, Colo., 1960-65, Fitzsimons Med. Library, Aurora, Colo., 1976-93; ret. 1993; mem. Denver Mus. Natural History, Denver Art Mus., Mariners. Mem. AARP, NARFE, AAUW (chpt. community rep. 1982-83, state chmn. edn. found. 1982-84, pres. Denver br. 1984-86), Altrusa Internat. (corr. sec. Denver 1982-83, bd. dirs. 1984-85, pres. Denver chpt. 1988), Friends of Library, Peace Links, Colo. Coordinating Coun. of Womens Orgn., Inc. (pres. coun.), Colo. Library Assn., Council Library Technicians, Federally Employed Women, Delta Sigma Theta (corr. sec. Denver 1964-66), Women's Assn. of Peoples Presbyn. Ch., League of Women Voters, Denver Urban League. Democrat. Presbyterian. Home: 3085 Fairfax St Denver CO 80207-2714

PHILLIPS, GAIL SUSAN, elementary school educator; b. Spokane, Wash., Apr. 17, 1962; d. Vern and Jane Phillips. AA, Spokane Falls CC, Wash., 1982; MB, BE, Ea. Wash. U., 1985, MA, 1992. Tchr. Port Townsend (Wash.) HS, 1986, Gonzaga Prep. HS, Spokane, Wash., 1987—88, Auburn (Wash.) Sch. Dist., 1988—93, Mead (Wash.) Sch. Dist., 1993—94, Totem Jr. High, Federal Way, Wash., 1994—97, Kalles Jr. High, Puyallup, Wash., 1997—. Sec. MENC Student Chpt., Cheney, Wash., 1983—84; v.p. Ea. Wash. MENC Chpt., Spokane, 1987—88; PTA faculty adv. Totem Jr. High, Wash., 1996—97. Office: Kalles Jr High 515 3rd St SE Puyallup WA 98372 Office Phone: 253-841-8729. Business E-Mail: gphillips@nyallup.k12.wa.us.

PHILLIPS, GENEVA FICKER, academic editor; b. Staunton, Ill., Aug. 1, 1920; d. Arthur Edwin and Lillian Agnes (Woods) Ficker; m. James Emerson Phillips, Jr., June 6, 1955 (dec. 1979). BS in Journalism, U. Ill., 1942; MA in English Lit., UCLA, 1953. Copy desk Chgo. Jour. Commerce, 1942-43; editl. asst. patents Radio Rsch. Lab. Harvard U., Cambridge, Mass., 1943-45; asst. editor adminstrv. publs. U. Ill., Urbana, 1946-47; editl. asst. Quar. of Film, Radio and TV UCLA, 1952-53; mng. editor The Works of John Dryden, Dept. English UCLA, 1964—2002. Bd. dirs. Univ. Religious Conf., L.A., 1979. UCLA teaching fellow, 1950-53, grad. fellow 1954-55. Mem. Assn. Acad. Women UCLA, Friends of Huntington Libr., Friends of UCLA Libr., Friends of Ctr. for Medieval and Renaissance Studies, Samuel Johnson Soc. So. Calif., Assocs. U. Calif. Press, Conf. Christianity and Lit., Soc. Mayflower Descendants. Lutheran. Home: 213 First Anita Dr Los Angeles CA 90049-3815 Office: UCLA Dept English 2225 Rolfe Hall Los Angeles CA 90024

PHILLIPS, GLYNDA ANN, editor; b. Riverside, Calif. d. Henry Grady and Patricia (Loflin) P. BA in English, Millsaps Coll., Jackson, Miss., 1977; MS in Comms., Miss. Coll., Clinton, 1996; postgrad., Inst. Children's Lit., West Redding, Conn., 1998—2002. News editor The Magee (Miss.) Courier, 1981-84; editor Miss. Farm Country mag., Jackson, 1984—. Contbr. articles to profl. jours. Recipient first place personal column Nat. Fedn. Press Women, 1984, first place personal column Miss. Press Women's Assn., 1984, 1st Pl. award Miss. Press Women's Assn., 1984, Best Media Campaign award AFBF Info. Contest, 1996, Excellence and Pres.'s award AFBF Pub. Rels. and Info. Program, 2006.

PHILLIPS, GRETCHEN, social worker; b. Erie, Pa., July 14, 1941; life ptnr. Beverly Campbell, June 10, 1989. BA, Mercyhurst Coll., 1966; MSW, Yeshiva U., 1972; postgrad., Advanced Ctr. Psychotherapy, 1972-73, Washington Sq. Inst., 1973-77. Diplomate clin. social work, LCSW NY. Psychiat. social worker, forensic social worker Creedmoor Psychiat. Ctr., Queens Village, NY, 1972-80; med. social worker Bellevue Hosp. Ctr., N.Y.C., 1980-83; intake probation officer N.Y.C. Probation, Family Ct., Bklyn., 1983—. Mem.: NASW. Home: 125 Radford St Apt 3C Yonkers NY 10705-3014 Office: Probation Intake Kings Family Ct 330 Jay St Brooklyn NY 11201-2804 Office Phone: 718-802-2609.

PHILLIPS, GWETHALYN, political organization administrator; Chair Maine Dem. Party, Augusta. Office: Maine Dem Party PO Box 5258 Augusta ME 04332

PHILLIPS, JANET COLLEEN, retired educational association administrator, editor; b. Pittsfield, Ill., Apr. 29, 1933; d. Roy Lynn and Catherine Amelia (Wills) Barker; m. David Lee Phillips, Feb 7, 1954; children— Clay Cullen, Sean Vincent. BS, U. Ill, 1954. Reporter Quincy (Ill.) Herald Whig, 1951, 52, soc. editor, 1953; editorial asst. Pub. Info. Office U. Ill.-Urbana, 1953-54, asst. editor libr., 1954-61; asst. editor Assn. for Libr. and Info. Sci. Edn., State College, Pa., 1960-61, mng. editor, 1961-89, exec. sec., 1970-89; adminstrv. dir. Interlibr. Delivery Svc. of Pa., 1990-99; ret. Mem. Palmer Mus. Arts, State Coll. Cmty. Theatre, Mt. Nittany Med. Ctr. Aux. Mem. Assn. for Libr. and Info. Sci. Edn., Embroiderer's Guild Am., Pa. State Blue Golf Course Club, Univ. Women's Club (Pa. State), Ctr. Hills Country Club, Am. Wine Soc., Cmty. Acad. Lifelong Learning, Delta Zeta. Presbyterian. Avocations: travel, golf, sewing, needlecraft. Address: 471 Park Ln State College PA 16803-3208 E-mail: janph2@aol.com.

PHILLIPS, JEAN BROWN, public relations executive, consultant; b. Phila. d. Harold T. and Elizabeth (Ulrich) Brown; m. John Tudor Phillips (dec.); 1 child, Barbara Jean. BS, Drexel U. Producer, broadcaster Sta. WTVT-TV, Tampa, Fla., 1962—64; pub. rels. exec. Frank Shattuck Co., NYC, 1964—68, Creamer Dickson Basford, NYC, 1968—72; editor Good Food mag., NYC, 1972—75; pres. Phillips Comm., NYC, 1976—. Cons. Displaced Homemaker Program, NYC, 1982—, Midlife Inst. Marymont Manhattan Coll., NYC, 1982—. Prodr.: (TV series) Our Turn, 1982—. Founder, pres. Manhattan Older Women's League, NYC, 1981. Mem.: Pub. Rels. Soc. Am., Am. Home Econs. Assn. (NY State Spotlight award 1982), Am. Women in Radio and TV, Overseas Press Club (NYC).

PHILLIPS, JILL META, writer, critic, astrologer; b. Detroit, Oct. 22, 1952; d. Leyson Kirk and Leona Anna (Rasmussen) P. Student pub. schs., Calif. Lit. counselor Book Builders, Charter Oak, Calif., 1966-77; pres. Moon Dance Astro Graphics, Covina, Calif., 1994—. Author: (with Leona Phillips) A Directory of American Film Scholars, 1975, The Good Morning Cookbook, 1976, G.B. Shaw: A Review of the Literature, 1976, T.E. Lawrence: Portrait of the Artist as Hero, 1977, The Archaeology of the Collective East, 1977, The Occult, 1977, D.H. Lawrence: A Review of the Literature and Biographies, 1978, Film Appreciation: A College Guide Book, 1979, Annus Mirabilis: Europe in the Dark and Middle Centuries, 1979, (with Leona Rasmussen Phillips) The Dark Frame: Occult Cinema, 1979, Misfit: The Films of Montgomery Clift, 1979, Butterflies in the Mind: A Précis of Dreams and Dreamers, 1980; The Rain Maiden: A Novel of History, 1987, Walford's Oak: A Novel, 1990, The Fate Weaver: A Novel in Two Centuries, 1991, Saturn Falls: A Novel of the Apocalypse, 1993, Birthday Secrets, 1998, Your Luck is in the Stars, 2000; columnist Dell Horoscope Mag., Astrology Your Daily

Horoscope Mag., 1998—; contbr. book revs. to New Guard mag., 1974-76; contbr. numerous articles to profl. jours. including Dell Horoscope, Midnight Horoscope, Astrology-Your Daily Horoscope, Am. Astrology. Mem. Young Ams. for Freedom, Am. Conservative Union, Elmer Bernstein's Film Music Collection, Ghost Club London, Count Dracula Soc., Dracula Soc. London, Richard III Soc. Republican. Personal E-mail: queenofwands52@aol.com.

PHILLIPS, JOY LAMBERT, lawyer, banker; b. Ft. Bragg, N.C., Sept. 25, 1955; d. Jurloew Lambert and Mary Carolyn (Gregory) Trivette; m. Frank Warren Phillips, May 10, 1975. AA, N.E. Miss. Jr. Coll., Booneville, 1974; BA, U. Miss., 1976, JD, 1980. Bar: Miss. 1980. Assoc. Daniel, Coker, Horton & Bell, P.A., Jackson, Miss., 1980-85; sr. v.p., asst. gen. counsel Deposit Guaranty Nat. Bank, Jackson, 1985—98; gen. counsel Hancock Bank, Gulfport, Miss., 1999—. Seminar speaker, 1990-91. Treas., Miss. Opera Guild, Jackson, 1990-92; mentor Miss. Coll. Sch. Law, Jackson, 1989-92. Mem. ABA, Miss. Bar Assn. (pres. 2005-06), Hinds County Bar Assn., Harrison County Bar Assn., Miss. Women Lawyers (pres. 1989-90), Jackson Young Lawyers, Kiwanis (dir. 1991-93, pres. 1966). Avocations: reading, walking, dogs, biking. Home: PO Box 819 Gulfport MS 39502-0819 Office: Hancock Bank One Hancock Plz Gulfport MS 39501 Office Phone: 228-563-5755. E-mail: joy_phillips@hancockbank.com.

PHILLIPS, JOYCE MARTHA, human resources executive; b. Bridgeport, Conn., Dec. 18, 1952; d. Stephen and Shirley B. (Howard) Tabory; m. Glenn L. Phillips, July 14, 1974. BA in English, Fairfield (Conn.) U., 1974; MS in Indsl. Rels., U. New Haven, 1982. Tchr. English and Reading Fairfield Woods Jr. High Sch., 1975; asst. to v.p. mktg. Bunker Ramo Corp., Trumbull, Conn., 1975-76; rep. in investor rels. Gen. Electric Co., Fairfield, 1976-77, specialist in manpower rels., 1977-79, specialist in employee benefits Bridgeport, Conn., 1979-80, specialist in employee rels., orgn. and staffing, 1980-84; mgr. hdqrs. personnel and office svcs. Armtek Corp., New Haven, 1984-87, dir. compensation and benefits, 1987-89; v.p. human resources (div. sr. human resources officer) Citibank, N.Y.C., 1989-91, v.p. compensation global fin., 1991-95; sr. v.p. human resources Barclays Bank/BZW, N.Y.C., 1995-96; mng. dir., global head of human resources CIBC World Markets, N.Y.C., 1996-99; evp and mng. dir. global human resources CIBC, N.Y.C, 1999—. Counsel Fairfield U. Alumni Adv. Coun. Avocations: tennis, piano, dance, boating.

PHILLIPS, KAREN, secondary school educator; Physical edn. tchr., adminstr. Walter D. Johnson Jr. H.S., Las Vegas, 1993-97; asst. prin. Lied Mid. Sch., Las Vegas, 1997-99; prin. Clifford J. Lawrence Jr. High Sch., 1999—. Recipient Middle Sch. Physical Edn. Tchr. of the Yr. Nat. Assn. for Sport and Physical Edn., 1993. Office: Clifford J Lawrence Jr High Sch 4410 S Juliano Rd Las Vegas NV 89147-8691

PHILLIPS, KAREN A., urban planner; b. Ocilla, Ga. BA landscape architecture, Sch. Environ. Design U. Ga.; MA landscape architecture, Harvard U. Grad. Sch. Design, 1982. Urban planner, Atlanta, 1975—77; project mgr. econ. devel. dept. N.Y. State Urban Devel. Corp.; co-founder, pres., CEO Abyssinian Devel. Corp., N.Y.C., 1989—2002; mem. N.Y.C. Planning Commn., 2002—. Real estate analyst Port Authority of NY and NJ, 1982—87; adj. prof. Sch. Architecture and Environ. Studies, City Coll, N.Y., 1992; cmty. devel. fellow Milano Grad Sch., New Sch. U., 2002—03. Mem. Parks Coun., Atlanta, 1975—80, Preservation League of NY, Manhattan Coun. Boy Scouts Am.; apptd. design com. Martin Luther King., Jr. Nat. Monument Project; bd. NY Women's Found., 2003—; Mayor's rep. Studio Mus. of Harlem; mem. NY Women's Found. Fellow: Am. Soc. Landscape Arch. Office: NYC Dept City Planning 22 Reade St New York NY 10007-1216 Office Phone: 212-720-3516.

PHILLIPS, KAREN BORLAUG, economist, rail transportation executive; b. Long Beach, Calif., Oct. 1, 1956; d. Paul Vincent and Wilma Borlaug. Student, Cath. U. P.R., 1973-74; BA, BS, U. N.D., 1977; postgrad., George Washington U., 1978-80. Rsch. asst. rsch. and spl. programs adminstrn. U.S. Dept. Transp., Washington, 1977—78, economist, office of sec., 1978—82; profl. staff mem. (majority) Com. Commerce Sci., Transp. U.S. Senate, Washington, 1982—85, tax economist (minority) com. on fin., 1985—87, chief economist (majority) senate com. on fin., 1987—88; commr. Interstate Commerce Commn., Washington, 1988—94; v.p. legis. Assn. Am. Railroads, Washington, 1994—95, sr. v.p. policy, legis. and comm., 1995—98; pres. Policy & Advocacy Assocs., Alexandria, Va., 1998—2000; v.p. N. Am. pub. and govt. affairs Can. Nat. Ry. Co., Washington, 2000—. Contbr. articles to profl. jours. Recipient award for Meritorious Achievement, Sec. Transp., 1980, Spl. Achievement awards, 1978, 80, Outstanding Performance awards, 1978, 80, 81. Mem. Am. Econ. Assn., Women's Transp. Seminar (Woman of Yr. award 1994), Transp. Rsch. Forum, Assn. Transp. Law Profls., Tax Coalition, Can.-Am. Bus. Coun. (bd. dirs.), Blue Key, Phi Beta Kappa, Omicron Delta Epsilon. Republican. Luth. Office: Can Nat Rlwy Co Ste 500 601 Pennsylvania Ave NW Washington DC 20004 Office Phone: 202-347-7816. Personal E-mail: karen.phillips@cn.ca.

PHILLIPS, KATHLEEN GAY, small business owner; b. Clarkston, Wash., Nov. 7, 1952; d. Cecil Martin Phillips and Nellie Florance Robertson; 1 child, John Cecil Dickeson-Phillips. Student, Lewis & Clark State Coll., 1973, Walla Walla C.C., 1990—91, Lewis & Clark State Coll., 1992; grad., H&R Tax Course, 2003. Cert. notary State of Idaho. Accounts clk. Lewis Clark State Coll., Lewiston, Idaho, 1975; co-founder Christina's Creations, Altus, Okla., 1982—, Funmates, Lewiston, 1982; dir. TK Springer, Inc., 1981; asst. mgr. Circle Drive Mobile Home Park, 1982—87. Surveyor Consumer Mail Panel, Palatine, Ill., 2000; restorer Gray Hut Apt. - Hist. Baughman House, Lewiston, 1993—99; rep. Western Modern Jewelry and Jewelry by Kathleen G. Phillips; history cons. Corps. Engrs. at Clarkston. With Medic Alert, 1979—; established Memory Walk & Safe Return, Alzheimer's Assn., 2005; worked with Gov. Kerathoun, Senator Craig, Senator Crapio, House of Rep. Helen Cheenawith, CL Otter. Pvt. U.S. Army, 1991, Gulf War, with USNR. Recipient Oldest Tree award, Pks. & Recreation Bd., 1999. Mem.: Idaho Hist. Soc., Lewiston C. of C., The Planetary Soc., Clan Donald U.S. A., Am. Legion, Order of Ea. Star (life), Pi Beta Lambda. Methodist. Avocations: needlecrafts, painting, archaeology.

PHILLIPS, MARION GRUMMAN, civic volunteer, writer; b. N.Y.C., Feb. 11, 1922; d. Leroy Randle and Rose Marion (Werther) Grumman; m. Ellis Laurimore Phillips, Jr., June 13, 1942; children: Valerie Rose (Mrs. Adrian Parsegian), Elise Marion (Mrs. Edward E. Watts III), Ellis Laurimore III, Kathryn Noel Phillips, Cynthia Louise (Mrs. Charles Prosser). Student, Mt. Holyoke Coll., 1940-42; BA, Adelphi U., 1981. Civic vol. Mary C. Wheeler Sch., 1964-68, Historic Ithaca, Inc., 1972-76, Ellis L. Phillips Found., 1960-91. Bd. dirs. North Shore Jr. League, 1960-61, 64-65, 68-69, Family Svc. Assn. Nassau County, 1963-69, Homemaker Svc. Assn. Nassau County, 1959, 61. Author: (light verse) A Foot in the Door, 1965, The Whale-Going, Going, Gone, 1977, Doctors Make Me Sick (So I Cured Myself of Arthritis), 1979; editor: (with Valerie Phillips Parsegian) Richard and Rhoda, Letters from the Civil War, 1982, Wooden Shoes the story of my Grandfather's Grandfather (F.M. Sisson), 1990, Irish Eyes, family hist. of McTarsneys and Sissons, 1990, The Log Chapel, A History of the Congregational Community Church, Rockwood, Maine, 1999; editor Jr. League Shore Lines, 1960-61, The Werthers in America-Four Generations and their Descendants, 1987; A B-Tour of Britain, 1986; contbr. articles on fund raising to mags. Mem. New Eng. Hist. Geneal. Soc., N.Y. Geneal. Biographical Soc., Hannah Adams Womens Club, PEO Sisterhood, Medfield Garden Club. Congregationalist. Address: 279 North St Medfield MA 02052-1211

PHILLIPS, MARJORIE RUTH, retired elementary school educator; b. N.Y.C., Nov. 9, 1932; d. Leo and Molly (Ringel) Birnbach; m. Bernard S. Phillips, Jan. 30, 1955; children: David Peter, Michael Lee. BS, Cornell U., 1954; MS, Boston U., 1967. Tchr. Beacon Hill Nursery, Boston, 1969-73; coord. early childhood edn. Minuteman Tech High Sch., Lecington, Mass., 1973-82, Middlesex C.C., Bedford, Mass., 1973-93; tchr. sci. Bailey Internat. Sch., Lowell (Mass.) Pub. Schs., 1988—. Democrat. Avocations: rowing, travel.

PHILLIPS, MARY ANN, artist, writer, retired legal assistant; b. Wolfe City, Tex., June 7, 1924; d. Lewis Jennings and Thelma Louise Grace Haywood; m. Delma Phillips, Nov. 3, 1941; children: Anita Sharon, Peggy Ann, James Ralph. Degree, Brantley Draughn Bus. Sch., 1943; studied sculpture with Evaline Sellors, 1962-64; MA in History and Govt., Tex. Woman's U., 1985, MFA, 1988. Legal sec. Zweifel, Floore & Hicks, Ft. Worth, 1943—47; sec. Western Hills Hotel, Ft. Worth, 1957—59; asst. to dist. supr. census dept. Dept. Commerce, Ft. Worth, 1959—60; sec. Rep. Party Tarrant County, Ft. Worth, 1960—65; legal sec. James Morgan Patent Atty., Ft. Worth, 1965, Morgan and Coffey, Ft. Worth, 1965—67. Author: Fletcher Warren Reporting for Duty, Sir, 1995; columnist: Echoes from Yesteryear, 1979—82. Mem.: AAUW, Nat. Assn. Scholars, Tex. Woman's U. Alumni Assn., Delphi Phi Delphi, Phi Alpha Theta. Avocations: travel, theater, reading, writing, poetry. Home: 6208 Abbott Ave Fort Worth TX 76180-6240

PHILLIPS, NANCY CHAMBERS, social worker; b. Danville, Ky., Oct. 11, 1941; d. Alvia Jackson and Virginia Oradell Chambers; m. Eldon Franklin Phillips, Nov. 27, 1968 (div. 1984). BA, Georgetown Coll., 1962; MSW, U. Denver, 1968; postgrad. Tulane U., 1981-85. Tchr., Hazard (Ky.) High Sch., 1962-64; social worker Ky. Dept. Econ. Security, 1964-71; rehab. counselor Ky. Bur. Vocat. Rehab., 1971-72; team leader Cath. Social Services, Bureau, Ky., 1972-74; instr. U. Cin., 1972-77; vis. asst. prof. Fla. Internat. U., 1977-79; asst. prof. social work Idaho State U., Pocatello, 1979-81; rsch. asst. Child Welfare Tng. Ctr. Region VI, Tulane U., New Orleans, 1981-83; village mgr. Countryside Village, Belle Chasse State Sch., New Orleans, 1983-85; asst. supr. case mgmt. svcs. Office Mental Retardation/Developmental Disabilities, Dept. Health and Human Resources, Greater New Orleans Regional Svc. Ctr., 1985-86; social work cons. Depelchin Children's Ctr., Houston, 1986-87; cons. Vis. Nurses Assn. of Brazoria County, Inc., 1987-88; med. social worker Bio-Med. Applications of S.W. Houston, S.W. Houston Dialysis Ctr., 1988-89; social svcs. mgr. vol. and bereavement coord. VNA, Brazoria County, 1988-91; social sorker Brazoaport Meml. Hosp., Lake Jackson, Tex., 1991-2000; dir. social work Angleton Danbury Med. Ctr., 2001-04; cons., 2004—; former mem. profl. adv. bd. Fla. Soc. Autistic Children, South Fla. Soc. Autistic Children, adv. council Ohio State U. Community Edn. Unit. Formerly active children's subcom. Dade and Monroe Counties Mental Health Bd., United Family and Children's Svcs., Family and Child Advocacy in Action Group. Recipient ednl. stipend Ky. Dept. Econ. Security, 1966-68, Nat. Cert. Recognition, South Fla. Soc. Autistic Children, 1979, Disting. Service award, 1979; named Ky. col. Mem. Nat. Assn. Social Workers, Mental Health Profls. Assn. (sec. 1991-92, 93-94, 96-97, v.p. 1995-98, 99-2000), Mental Health Profls. Assn. (pres. 1992—). Home and Office: 1017 San Felipe St Angleton TX 77515-3533 Office Phone: 979-849-2495.

PHILLIPS, NANCY HOPKINS, elementary school educator; b. Richmond, Va., Mar. 4, 1937; d. Garland Evans and Margaret (Lail) Hopkins; m. William Keith Phillips, Aug. 23, 1957; children: William Keith Jr., David R., Susan E., Linda C. BA in Psychology, U. Richmond, d, 1959; MEd in Reading, Va. Commonwealth U., 1975; EdD, U. Mich., 1992—. Cert. K-12 adminstrn., biology and Spanish tchr., Va. Tchr. Trinity Meth. Pre-Sch., Richmond, 1969-72, James River Sch., Richmond, 1972-75, Watkins Elem. Sch., Chesterfield County, Va., 1975-83; asst. prin. Bon Air (Va.) Elem. Sch., 1983-86; instr. Wayne State U. Sch. Edn., Detroit, 1986-89; grad. asst. U. Mich., Ann Arbor, 1988-89; asst. prof. Lynchburg (Va.) Coll. Sch. Edn., 1989—2001, dir. Bickham Early Learning Lab Sch., 1992, prof., 2001; ret. Mem. Va. Assn. Early Childhood Educators (bd. dirs.), Nat. Assn. for Edn. of Young Children, Va. Assn. Tchr. Educators (pres. 1997-99), Assn. Tchr. Educators, Piedmont Assn. Early Childhood Edn. (pres. 1991-1993). Home: 22 Jefferson Grn Waynesboro VA 22980-6595

PHILLIPS, PAMELA B., medical education coordinator; d. Statcher Rogers, Jr. and Frances Elaine (Gooch) Rogers; children: Jasmine Sade Nicole, Stanley Terence Phillips, Jr. BSN, U. SC, Columbia, 1986. RN DC Bd. Nursing, 1986, Ala. Bd. Nursing, 1990, cert. RNC, Am. Nurses Credential Ctr., 1990. Patient care technician coord. Bapt. Health, Montgomery, Ala., 1996—97, continuing edn. and continuing med. edn. coord., 1997—. Mem. Nurse's Guild, Montgomery, 2001. Named Employee of Yr., Bapt. Health, 1999. Mem.: Sigma Gamma Rho (assoc.). Baptist. Avocations: reading, sewing, singing. Office: Baptist Health 2105 East South Blvd Montgomery AL 36111 Office Fax: 334-286-5691. Business E-Mail: pphillips@baptistfirst.org.

PHILLIPS, PAMELA KIM, lawyer; b. San Diego, Feb. 23, 1958; d. John Gerald and Nancy Kimiko (Tabuchi) Phillips; m. R. Richard Zanghetti, Sept. 16, 1989. BA cum laude, The Am. U., 1978; JD, Georgetown U., 1982. Bar: N.Y. 1983, U.S. Dist. Ct. (so. dist.) N.Y. 1983, Fla. 1994, U.S. Dist. Ct. (mid. dist.) Fla. 1994. Assoc. Curtis, Mallet-Prevost, Colt & Mosle, N.Y.C., 1982-84, LeBoeuf, Lamb, Greene & MacRae, N.Y.C., 1984-90, ptnr., 1991—. Mng. editor The Tax Lawyer, Georgetown U. Law Sch., Washington, 1980-81. Mem. coun. The Fresh Air Fund, 1991-94, Youth Leadership Jacksonville, 1999—; bd. dirs. Jacksonville Zoöl. Soc., Inc., 1996—, sec., 1997—; pres. First Coast Venture Capital Group, Inc., 1996-98. Am. Univ. scholar, Washington, 1976-78. Mem. ABA, Bar Assn. City N.Y. (sec. young lawyers com. 1987-89, chmn. 1989-91, second century com. 1990-93, banking law com. 1991-94), Jacksonville Bar Assn., River Club. Democrat. Roman Catholic. Avocations: tennis, travel. Home: 109 Carriage Lamp Way Ponte Vedra Beach FL 32082-1903 Office: LeBoeuf Lamb Greene & MacRae 125 W 55th St New York NY 10019-5369 also: 50 N Laura St Ste 2800 Jacksonville FL 32202-3656 Office Phone: 904-354-8000. E-mail: pamela.phillips@LLgm.com.

PHILLIPS, PAULA L., foundation administrator, artist; b. Tuskegee, Ala., Oct. 3, 1949; d. Paul Jr. and Thelma Lee (McDaniel) Phillips; m. Lloyd Thomas Pate, Apr. 28, 1978 (div. Dec. 1987); children: Chance Edmund, Lloyd Thomas II, Brandy Bianca. BA cum laude, Tex. Wesleyan U., Ft. Worth, 1994; MFA, Md. Inst. Coll. Art, Balt., 1996. Art therapy facilitator Oakgrave Ctr., Ft. Worth, 1990-94; instr. art Friends Sch., Balt., 1996-97, The Md. Inst., Coll. of Art, Balt., 1996-97; instr. comprehensive art Suitland H.S., District Heights., Md., 1997-99; instr. art Anne Arundel C.C., Arnold, Md., 1995—; asst. dir. Cmty. Arts Partnership, Md. Inst. Coll. ARt, Balt., 1998—; dir. Superkids Camp, The Parks and People Found., Balt., 1997—. Exhibited works (mixed media paitings) Smithsonian Anacostia Exhbn., 1999, Govt. House, 1999, Eubie Blake Jazz and Cultural Theater, 1998. Cmty. activist. Named Tchr. of Yr., Suitland H.S., 1997-99. Mem. Creative Alliance Fells Point. Democrat. Avocations: swimming, camping, horseback riding. Home: 1115 Hunter St Baltimore MD 21202-3821 Office: Cmty Arts Partnerships 1300 W Mount Royal Ave Baltimore MD 21217-4134

PHILLIPS, PEGGY V., former biotechnology company executive; b. 1953; MS in Microbiology, U. Idaho. With Immunex Corp., Seattle, 1986—94, sr. v.p. pharm. devel., 1994—99, exec. v.p., COO, 1999—2002; sr. v.p., COO Immunex R & D Corp., 1991—95. Bd. dirs. Immunex Corp., 1996—2002, Dynavax Technologies Corp., 2006—, Portola Pharmaceuticals, 2006—. Bd. dirs. US Naval Acad. Found., 2002—.*

PHILLIPS, RENEÉ, writer; b. Freeport, NY; Student, Art Students League, 1979, Am. Art Sch., 1979, Fashion Inst. Tech., 1980, New Sch. for Social Rsch., 1980. Dir., founder Artopia, not-for-profit art orgn., N.Y.C., 1980-84; pub., editor-in-chief Manhattan Arts Internat., N.Y.C., 1983—2000; editor-in-chief www.Manhattan Arts.com. Juror Excellence in Arts Awards, 1988, N.Y. Lung Assn. Ann. Exhbn., 1990, Manhattan Arts Internat. Ann. Internat. Art Competition, 1992—; juror, co-curator Redefining Visionary Art, Doma Gallery, N.Y.C., 1989; curator Synthesis of Painting and Sculpture exhbn. 1st Women's Bank, N.Y.C., 1984, Salute to Liberty internat. art exhbn., N.Y.C., 1986, HerStory exhbns., 1999-2005, Small Works, 2004-05, The Healing Power of Art, 2002-04; editor-in-chief www.ManhattanArts.com; curator I Love Manhattan, N.Y.C., 2003, The Healing Power of Art, N.Y.C., 2003-05; bd. dirs., v.p. Women's Studio Ctr., L.I., N.Y., 2003—; spkr., lectr. in field Author: The Complete Guide to New York Art Galleries, 1995-2006, Presentation Power Tools for Fine Artists, 1998, 2d edit., 2000, 3d edit., 2002, Success Now! for Artists: A Motivational Guide, 1998, 2d edit., 2003 Recipient award of merit Muscular Dystrophy Assn., 1986, award for outstanding contbns. to arts Mayor of N.Y.C., 1987. Mem. Internat. Assn. Art Critics, N.Y. Artists Equity (former bd. dirs.). Office: Manhattan Arts Internat 200 E 72nd St New York NY 10021-4537 Office Phone: 212-472-1660. Business E-Mail: info@ManhattanArts.com.

PHILLIPS, RUTH AMELIA, retired music educator, artist; b. Gunnison, Colo., Feb. 20, 1922; d. Singleton Harvey and Edna Eloise (Mooseman) Flannery; m. Albert Phillips Jr., Aug. 9, 1942; children: Carl David, Carla Ann. Student, Mesa Satte Coll., Grand Junction, Colo. Cert. music tchr. Colo. Pres., organizer Palisade (Colo.) Art Lovers, 1964—. Pvt. piano and voice tchr. Exhibitions include We. Colo. Ctr. Arts, Grand Junction, Apple Shed Gallery, Cedaredge, Colo., Edge of Cedars Art Gallery, Artist's Hue Art Gallery, Parachute, Colo., Ouray Co. Arts Assn., Ouray, Colo., Glenwood Springs (Colo.) Ctr. Arts, Palisade (Colo.) Meml. Bldg., Delta (Colo.) Fine Arts, Montrose (Colo.) Visual Arts Guild. Music dir. Palisade Christian Ch., 1967—2003. Mem.: Philanthropic Ednl. Org. (pres.). Avocations: singing, painting. Home: 2996 County Rd Grand Junction CO 81504

PHILLIPS, RUTH ANN, retired secondary school educator; b. Greensboro, NC, Nov. 26, 1948; d. Paul Frank and Agnes Elizabeth (Butler) P. AB, Elon Coll., 1971. Cert. health and phys. edn. tchr., N.C. Tchr. health and phys. edn., chmn. dept. Sellars-Gunn Jr. H.S., Burlington, NC, 1972-81, coach tennis, basketball, softball, 1973-81; tchr., coach varsity softball, chmn. health and phys. edn. Walter M. Williams Sr. H.S., Burlington, 1981—2001, ret., 2001. Named Tchr. of Yr., Sellars-Gunn Jr. High Sch., 1975, Secondary Phys. Edn. Tchr. of Yr., N.C., 1998, Eight Who Make A Difference, Homer Thompson Meml., 2001. Mem.: State Employees Assn. NC, N.C. Assn. Educators. Democrat. Methodist. Avocations: racquetball, softball. Home: 2027 S Mebane St Burlington NC 27215-7617

PHILLIPS, RUTHANNE, special education administrator; d. George and Margaret Ann Mitro. BA in Psychology, cum laude, Wittenberg U., Springfield, Ohio, 1979; MS in Spl. Edn., Calif. Luth. U., Thousand Oaks, 1983; MA in Ednl. Leadership, Calif. State U., LA, 2004. Multiple subjects tchg. credential Calif., learning handicapped specialist tchg. credential Calif., severely handicapped specialist tchg. credential Calif., resource specialist cert. of competence Calif., adminstrv. svcs. credential Calif., computers in edn. cert. Calif. Luth. Coll., child mental health specialist Calif. Luth. Coll. and Camarillo State Hosp., specially designed acad. instrn. in English Calif. Grad. student asst. Camarillo (Calif.) State Hosp. and Devel. Ctr., 1979—80, tchg. asst., 1980—81, spl. edn. tchr., 1981—96, Calif. Dept. of Youth Authority at Fred C. Nelles Sch., Whittier, Calif., 1996—97; spl. edn. resource specialist tchr. L.A. County Office of Edn.-Divsn. of Juvenile Cts. and Comty. Schs. at Pacific Lodge Boys Home, Woodland Hills, Calif., 1997—99; spl. edn. tchr. L.A. County Office Edn. Divsn. Spl. Edn. at High Desert Prin.'s Adminstrv. Unit, Palmdale, Calif., 1999—2000; spl. edn. program specialist Antelope Valley Spl. Edn. Local Plan Area, Palmdale, 2000—. Mem. Calif. Sys. of Pers. Devel. Adv. Coun., Sacramento, 2003—05, Calif. Svcs. Tech. Assistance and Tng. Region 11 Coordinating Coun., L.A., 2000—, sec., 2001—02, chairperson, 2002—04; mem. Antelope Valley Family Focus Resource and Empowerment Ctr. Adv. Bd., Palmdale, 2003—05, Chapman U., Antelope Valley Campus Adv. Bd., Palmdale, 2001—03, Pacific Lodge Sch. Site Coun., Woodland Hills, 1997—99. Mem. Friends of the Acton-Agua Dulce Libr., Acton, Calif., 2005—, Friends of Acton Park, Calif., 2005—; liturgy coord. St. Mary's Acton-Agua Dulce Mission, Acton, 2002—, historian, 2000—, lector, 2000—; religious edn. tchr. St. Mary's Acton-Agua Duice Mission, 2001—03; asst. religious edn. coord. St. Mary's Acton-Agua Dulce Mission, Acton, 2004—05; literacy tutor Camarillo, 1992—97, Acton and Palmdale, 2002—. Recipient Wittenberg Alumni scholarship, Wittenberg U., 1975—79. Mem.: ASCD, CEC, Internat. Reading Assn., L.A. County Adminstrs. of Spl. Edn., Assn. Calif. Sch. Adminstrs., Antelope Valley Astronomy Club, Psi Chi, Alpha Xi Delta (Zeta chpt. historian 1978—79). Democrat. Roman Catholic. Avocations: scrapbooking, cardmaking, reading, travel, collecting 1st editions by Stephen King and Dean Koontz. Office: Antelope Valley SELPA 39139 10th Street East Palmdale CA 93550 Office Phone: 661-274-4136.

PHILLIPS, STACI DAVIS, mathematics professor, director; d. Charlie Sanford and Patricia Coldwell Davis; m. Clinton Ray Phillips, Dec. 19, 1998; children: Camon Ray, Isabelle Nicole. BS, Centenary Coll., Shreveport, La., 1997; MS, U. Ark., Fayetteville, 1999. Rsch. asst. agr. dept. U. Ark., Fayetteville, 1997—99; asst. prof. math. Bossier Parish C.C., La., 2000—06, asst. dir. instl. rsch. and assessment La., 2006—. Statis. cons., Shreveport, La., 2003—06. Tchr. Sunday sch. Rose Pk. Bapt. Ch., Shreveport, 2004—. Grantee, Bossier Parish C.C., 2005. Mem.: Bossier Parish C.C. Faculty Senate (corr. sec. 2001—06), SACCR. R-Consevative. Baptist. Avocations: reading, scrapbooks, swimming, travel. Home: 13572 Fm 1998 Waskom TX 75692 Office: Bossier Parish Community Coll 6220 E Texas St Bossier City LA 71111 Office Phone: 318-678-6299.

PHILLIPS, STACY D., lawyer; b. NYC, Sept. 5, 1958; d. Gerald F. and Francine Anne (Kantor) Phillips. AB, Dartmouth Coll., 1980; JD, Columbia U., 1983. Cert.: Family Law Specialist, bar: Calif. 1984, US Dist. Ct. Ctrl. and So. Districts Calif., US Ct. Appeals 9th Cir. Law clk. to Hon. Edward Rafeedie US Dist. Ct., LA, 1983-84; assoc. Wyman, Bautzer, Rothman, Kuchel & Silbert, LA, 1984-85, Jaffe & Clemens, Beverly Hills, Calif., 1986—90; founding ptnr. Mannis & Phillips, LA, 1995—2000, Phillips Lerner, Lauzon & Tamra LLP, LA, 2000—. Guest commentator various TV programs including Good Morning America, Hard Copy, Inside Edition; contbr. Divorce Mag., adv. bd.; bd. dirs. Legal Momentum (previously NOW Legal Def. and Edn. Fund); co-chair Calif. Leadership Coun. Bd. dirs. Vista del Mar Child and Family Services, Levitt & Quinn Family Law Ctr., Bnai Zion Found. Inc.; bd. trustees Alternative Living for the Aging. Named one of 50 Most Powerful Women in LA Law, LA Bus. Jour., 1998, Top 20 Attorneys Under 40 Years Old, LA Daily Jour., 1998, Top 50 Women Litigators in Calif., 2003; recipient Women of Action Award, Israel Cancer Rsch. Fund, 2000, Women of Achievement Award, Bnai Zion Found. Inc., 2001, Women Who Make a Difference Award, LA Bus. Jour., 2001, Patricia McClure Award, Asthma & Allergy Found. Am., 2001, Women of Achievement Award in Family Law and Mediation, Century City C. of C., 2001, 2002; grantee Policy Study Internship, Dartmouth U., 1978—78. Mem.: Beverly Hills Bar Assn. (mem. family law sect., mem. alternative dispute resolutions com.), LA Bar Assn. (mem. family law sect.), State Bar Calif. (mem. child custody and visitation com.), ABA (mem. family law sect.), Chancery Club of LA. Avocations: cooking, tennis. Office: 2029 Century Park E Ste 1200 Los Angeles CA 90067

PHILLIPS, SUSAN MEREDITH, academic administrator, economist; b. Richmond, Va., Dec. 23, 1944; d. William G. and Nancy (Meredith) Phillips. BA in Math., Agnes Scott Coll., 1967; MS in Fin. and Ins., La. State U., 1971, PhD in Fin. and Economics, 1973. Asst. prof. La. State U., 1973—74, U. Iowa, 1974—78; econ. fellow Directorate of Econ. and Policy Rsch., SEC, 1976—78; assoc. prof. fin. dept. U. Iowa, 1978—83, assoc. v.p. fin. & univ. services, 1979—81; commr. Commodity Futures Trading Commn., 1981—83, chmn., 1983—87; prof. fin. dept., v.p. fin. and univ. svcs. U. Iowa, Iowa City, 1987—91; bd. govs. Fed. Res. Sys., Washington, 1991—98; dean Sch. of Bus., prof. fin. dept. George Washington U., Washington, 1998—. Trustee Fin. Acctg. Found., Norwalk, 2006—; bd. dirs. Chgo. Bd. Options Exch., Nat. Futures Assn., Kroger Co., State Farm Mutual Auto. Co. Co-author (with J. Richard Zecher): The SEC and the Public Interest; contbr.

articles to profl. jours. Fellow Brookings Econ. Policy fellow, 1976—77. Office: George Washington U Sch Bus Ste 660 2201 G St NW Washington DC 20052 Business E-Mail: gwsbdean@gwu.edu.

PHILLIPS, TARI, professional basketball player; b. Mar. 6, 1969; Student, U. Ga.; grad., Ctrl. Fla. U., 1991. With Orlando Miracle Women's Basketball Team, Fla., 1999, N.Y. Liberty, N.Y.C., NY, 2000—; player USA Basketball Women's Nat. Team, 2002, 2004. Named Most Improved Player, WNBA, 2000; named to All-WNBA Second Team, 2002; recipient Gold Medal, World Championships, 2002. Office: New York Liberty 2 Penn Plz 14th Fl New York NY 10121

PHILLIPS, VICKI L., school system administrator; b. Marion, Ind., Jan. 15, 1958; d. Denver Phillips and Vivian (Burnette) Fuqua. BS in Edn., Western Ky. U., 1980, MA in Psychology, 1987; doctoral student, U. Ky., 1988—; EdD in instrnl. leadership, U. of Lincoln, Eng., 2002. Dir. devel. tng. dept. Panorama, Bowling Green, Ky., 1978—80; tchr. learning and behavior disorders Simpson County Bd. Edn., 1981—85; exceptional child cons. Ky. Dept. Edn. Office Edn. for Exceptional Children, 1986—90; chief exec. asst. to edn. commr. Ky. Dept. of Edn., 1986—93; dep. dir./chief of staff Nat. Alliance for Restructuring Edn., Wash., DC, 1993—95; dir. Greater Phila. First Partnership for Reform; exec. dir. Children Achieving Challenge, 1995—98; supt. Sch. Dist. of Lancaster, 1998—2003; sec. of edn. Pa. Dept. Edn., Harrisburg, 2003—04; supt. Portland Pub. Schools, Oreg., 2004—. Mem. ASCD, Nat. Coun. for Exceptional Children, Coun. for Behavior Disorders, Nat. Assn. for Sch. Psychologists, Ky. Assn. Sch. Adminstrs., Ky. Assn. for Psychology in the Schs., Ky. Assn. for Family-Based Svcs., Ky. Families for Family-Based Svcs., Ky. Families as Allies. Office: 501 N Dixon St Portland OR 97227-1804

PHILLIPS, WANDA CHARITY, secondary school educator, writer; b. Gettysburg, Pa., Apr. 1, 1947; d. Roy Homer and Frances Marie (White) Kuykendall; m. James E. Phillips; children: Jenny, Peter, Micah. BS in Secondary Edn., Shippensburg U., Pa., 1968; cert. elem. edn., Grand Canyon Coll., 1973; MA in Adminstrn., No. Ariz. U., Flagstaff, 1993. Tchr. Littlestown H.S., Pa., 1969, Phoenix Indian Sch., 1971-72, Peoria Sch. Dist., Ariz., 1973—99; author ISHA Enterprises, Inc., Scottsdale, Ariz., 1985—. Ednl. seminar presenter ISHA Enterprises, Scottsdale, Ariz., 1986—, Assn. Christian Sch. Internat., Calif., 1988—. Author: Easy Grammar, 1986, Daily Grams: Guided Review Aiding Mastery Skills, 1986, Daily Grams: Guided Review Aiding Mastery Skills for Grade 3, 2003, Grade 4, 2003, Grade 5, 2003, Easy Writing, 1991, Daily Grams: Guided Teaching and Review for Grades 2 and 3, 1992, Easy Grammar, Grades 5 and 6, 1994 (children's book) My Mother Doesn't Like to Cook, 1993, Easy Grammar Plus, 1995, Easy Grammar: Grades 4 and 5, 1996, Easy Grammar: Grades 3 and 4, 1998, Daily Grams: Grades 3, 4, 5, 6, and 7, 2002. Raspberry Cottage Tearoom Ministries. Mem.: Nat. Trust for Hist. Preservation, Paradise Valley Women's Club. Office: ISHA Enterprises Inc Easy Grammar Systems PO Box 25970 Scottsdale AZ 85255 Office Phone: 480-502-9454. E-mail: info@easygrammar.com.

PHILLIPS, WINIFRED PATRICIA, radio producer, composer; b. Mobile, Ala., Apr. 13, 1972; d. Winifred Waldron Phillips. BA summa cum laude in Comms., Kean U., 1994. Composer, prodr., actress, writer Nat. Pub. Radio, Washington, 1992—2002; composer, prodr., actress, writer Radio Tales XM Satellite Radio Dramas, Washington, 2002—; owner music and audio prodn. co. Gens. Prodns.; composer Take Two Interactive, NYC, 2005—06. Composer Sony Computer Entertainment Am., Santa Monica, Calif., 2004. Composer, prodr., actress, writer (National Public Radio dramas) Generations Radio Theater Presents: Radio Tales, 1996—2002, (radio dramas) Radio Tales, XM Satellite Radio, 2002—, composer, prodr., actress (radio drama) The Odyssey Trilogy, 2003, Arabian Nights Trilogy, 2003, The Gift of the Magi, 1996, The Yellow Wallpaper, 1996, The Fall of the House of Usher, 1998, Sleepy Hollow, 1998, The Time Machine, 1999, Gulliver's Travels, 1999, The Mummy, 1999, The Island of Doctor Moreau, 2000, Dr. Jekyll and Mr. Hyde, 2000, Journey to the Center of the Earth, 2000, The Pit and the Pendulum, 2000, The Hunchback of Notre-Dame, 2001, Jason and The Argonauts, 2001, War of the Worlds, 2001, Phantom of the Opera, 2001, Beowulf, 2001, Twenty Thousand Leagues Under the Sea, 2001, The Invisible Man, 2001, The Lost World, 2002, composer, actress, author (radio musicals) Celtic Hero, 2000; composer, actress, author: radio musicals Lord of the Celts, 1998; author: (short stories) Breaking Point, 1991, Celtic Beauty for Sword and Sorceress 20 book anthology, 2003, (radio drama script) Light of Truth, 1985; composer: (video games) God of War, 2004, Charlie and the Chocolate Factory, 2005, The Da Vinci Code, 2006. Recipient GRACIE award for best nat./network drama series, Am. Women in Radio and TV, 2001, 2003, 2004, N.Y. Festivals award, Internat. Radio Festivals, 1997, AUDIE Honors award, Audio Pubs. Assn., 1999, GOLDEN REEL Merit award, Nat. Fedn. Cmty. Broadcasters, 2001, GRACIE award for outstanding achievement by an actress, Am. Women in Radio and TV, 1998, N.Y. Festivals award, Internat. Radio Festivals, 2001, N.Y. Festivals World medal, 2004, Outstanding Achievement in Original Music Composition for Videogame, Acad. Interactive Arts Sci., 2005, Best Original Score of Yr. awrd, Game Zone, 2005, Best Original Music award, Game Spot, 2005, Best Original Score award, IGN PS2, 2005, Music of Yr., Game Audio Network Guild, 2005, Best Interactive Score, 2005, Best Cinematic/Cut Scene Audio, 2005, Audio of Yr., 2005; grantee Endowment grantee, Wallace - Reader's Digest Funds, 1996—2002, NEA, 1996—2002, Durkin Hayes Publ., 1998. Mem.: SAG, BMI, NARAS, Game Audio Network Guild, Ind. Game Developers Assn., Am. Fedn. Musicians. Avocations: reading, Web design, computer art, travel. Business E-Mail: phillips@radiotales.com.

PHILLIPS, ZAIGA ALKSNIS, pediatrician; b. Riga, Latvia, Sept. 13, 1934; came to U.S., 1949; d. Adolfs and Alma (Ozols) Alksnis; (div. 1972); children: Albert L., Lisa K., Sintija. BS, U. Wash., 1956, MD, 1959. Fellow Colo. Med. Ctr., Denver, 1961-62; sch. physician Bellevue and Issaquah (Wash.) Sch. Dists., 1970-77; pvt. practice Bellevue, 1977—; staff pediatrician Overlake Med. Ctr., 1977—, Childrens Hosp. and Med. Ctr., Seattle, 1977—, Evergreen Med. Ctr., 1977—. Attending physician Allergy Clinic, Childrens Hosp., Seattle, 1988-2005; cons. and contact to pediatricians in Latvia, 1988—; team mem. to Latvia, Healing the Children Contact with Latvia, 1993-97; bd. mem. Bellevue's Stay in Sch. Program, 1994-97. Mem. Am. Latvian Assn., 1972—, Wash. Latvian Assn., Seattle, 1972—; pres. Latvian Sorority Gundega, Seattle, 1990-93; bd. dirs. Sister Cities Assn., Bellevue, 1992-98, Wash. Asthma Allergy Found. Am., 1992-99. Recipient Recognition award, City of Liepaja, 1995, Latvian Assn. Am., 2003, Recognition cross, Pres. of Latvia, 2005. Fellow Am. Acad. Pediat.; mem. Am. Latvian Physicians Assn. (bd. dirs. 1998—), Wash. State and Puget Sound Pediatric Assn. Office: Pediatric Assn 2700 Northup Way Bellevue WA 98004-1463 Office Phone: 425-827-4600. Business E-Mail: zap@u.washington.edu.

PHILLIPS-JONES, LINDA, consulting psychologist; b. South Bend, Ind. d. Robert Milton and Priscilla Alicia (Tancy) Phillips; m. G. Brian Jones, Feb. 16, 1980; stepchildren: Laurie Darian Jones, Tracy Jones Nino. BS, U. Nev., Reno, 1964; AM, Stanford U., 1965; PhD, UCLA, 1977. Lic. psychologist. Tchrs. trainer Edn. Cons. Ltd. Internat. Tng. Cons., Saigon, Vietnam, 1966-71; rsch. scientist Am. Insts. for Rsch., Palo Alto, Calif., 1979-83; sr. trainer, orgn. devel. cons. SRI Internat., Menlo Park, Calif., 1984-88; psychologist, cons. Coalition of Counseling Ctrs., Grass Valley, Calif., 1980—. Cons. Microsoft, Hewlett-Packard, KPMG, and others, 1980-. Author: Mentors and Proteges, 1982, The New Mentors and Proteges, 1993, Mentoring/Coaching Skills Assessment, 1994; co-author: Men Have Feelings, Too!, 1988, A Fight to the Better End, 1989; contbr. articles to profl. jours. Recipient Civilian Svc. award Govt. of South Vietnam, 1971; grad. fellow UCLA, 1964-65, 72-77; Alumni Profl. Achievement award U. Nev., 2004. Avocations: ranching, horseback riding, gardening, travel. Office: Coalition of Counseling Ctrs The Mentoring Group 13560 Mesa Dr Grass Valley CA 95949-8132 Office Phone: 530-268-1146.

PHILLIPS-LESANE, FAY M., mental health professional; b. Petersburg, Va., Feb. 2, 1956; d. Orlando F. Phillips Sr., Mary E. Phillips. BSW cum laude, Va. State U., 1978; MSW summa cum laude, Howard U., 1981; postgrad., Am. Sch. Profl. Psychology, 1995. LCSW Va., LICSW D.C. Psychiat. social worker Ctrl. State Hosp., Petersburg, Va., 1978—79; mental health specialist Alexandria Cmty. Mental Health, Alexandria, Va., 1979—82; social worker supr., program dir. Luth. Social Svcs., Washington, 1982—88; clin. adminstr. Commn. on Mental Health, Washington, 1988—96; prevention specialist U. D.C., Washington, 1996—2000; pres., CEO Agape Mental Health, Woodbridge, Va., 1998—. Bd. dirs. U. D.C. Dept. Social Work, Christian Hope Child Care, Woodbridge; mem. adv. bd. Nat. Consortium for Am. Children; dir. Inst. Human Devel. Nat. Consortium for African Am. Children. Mem.: Alpha Kappa Alpha. Democrat. Avocations: music, sports, travel, art, bowling. Home: 13400 Forest Glen Rd Woodbridge VA 22191 Office: Agape Mental Health And Consulting Servi PO Box 4986 Woodbridge VA 22194-4986

PHILLIS, MARILYN HUGHEY, artist; b. Kent, Ohio; d. Paul Jones and Helen Margaret (Miller) Hughey; m. Richard Waring Phillis, Mar. 19, 1949; children: Diane E., Hugh R., Randall W Student, Kent State U., 1945; BS, Ohio State U., 1949. Chemist Battelle Meml. Inst., Columbus, Ohio, 1949—53; illustrator periodical We. Res. Hist. Mag., Garrettsville, Ohio, 1974—79; illustrator book AAUW, Piqua, Ohio, 1976; instr. art Edison State C.C., Piqua, 1976; instr. watermedia Springfield Mus. Art, Ohio, 1976—84. Juror art exhbns. state and nat. art groups, 1980—; instr. painting state and nat. orgns., 1980—; lectr. art healing Wheeling Jesuit Coll., W.Va., 1994—96; founder, coord. Nat. Creativity Seminar, Stretching Boundaries for Creative People, 1993, 1995, 1997, 1999, 2002. Author: Watermedia Techniques for Releasing the Creative Spirit, 1992, (chpt.) Bridging Space and Time, 1998; contbr. The Art of Layering: Making Connections, 2004, articles and illustrations to profl. jours.; one-woman shows include Stifel Fine Art Ctr., Wheeling, Springfield Art Mus., Zanesville Art Ctr., Ohio, Ohio U., Lancaster, Ohio U. East St. Clairsville, Cleve. Inst. Music, Columbus Mus. Art, Cheekwood Mus. Art, Bot. Hall, Nashville, Idaho Falls Art Ctr., Monroe C.C., Mich., exhibitions include, N.Y.C., Wheeling, Butler Mus. Am. Art, Youngstown, Ohio, Taiwan Art Edn. Inst., Taipei, 1994, Represented in permanent collections Ohio U., Lancaster and St. Clairsville, Springfield Mus. Art, Heritage Hall mus., Talladega, Ala., Ohio Watercolor Soc., W.Va. Women Artists, U. Charleston, Monroe C.C., Mich., also corp. collections. Co-chmn. Cmty. Health and Humor Program, Wheeling, 1992 Recipient First awards Watercolor West, Riverside, Calif., 1990, Hudson Soc. award Nat. Collage Soc., 1995, Art Masters award Am. Artist Mag., 1996; elected to Hall of Fame, Kent, Ohio, 2000, Hall of Fame, Wheeling, 2000 Mem. Internat. Soc. Study of Subtle Energies and Energy Medicine (art cons. sci. jour. 1992-2006, art and healing workshop 1995), Am. Watercolor Soc. (dir. 1991-93, newsletter editor 1992—,chmn. Jury of Awards, 2003, Osborne award 1975), Soc. Layerists in Multi-Media (nat. v.p. 1988-93), Ohio Watercolor Soc. (sec. 1979-82, v.p. 1982-89, pres. 1990-96, dir. biennial creativity seminars 1993-95, 97, 99, 2002, Gold medal, Best of Show 1993), Nat. Watercolor Soc. (chmn. selection jury 2001), Internat. Noetic Sci., West Ohio Watercolor Soc. (pres. 1979-80, 2d award 1982), Allied Artists N.Y., W.Va. Watercolor Soc. (1st award 1993), Ky. Watercolor Soc., Ga. Watercolor Soc., So. Watercolor Soc. (pres. 1997-98, Silver award 1999) Avocations: hiking, reading, genealogy, music, travel. Home and Office: Phillis Studio 72 Stamm Cir Wheeling WV 26003-5549 E-mail: mhphillis@aol.com.

PHIPARD, NANCY MIDWOOD, retired special education educator, poet; b. Boston, Jan. 31, 1929; d. William Henry and Jean Estelle (Dubbs) McAdams; m. Kenneth E. Brown, June 17, 1949 (div.); children: Christopher M. Brown, Jennifer Progodich, Michael H. Brown, Jeffrey D. Brown; m. Arnold J. Midwood, Jr., July 2, 1980 (dec.); m. Harvey F. Phipard, Jan. 14, 1998 (dec.). Student, Mt. Holyoke Coll., 1946-48; BA, Wellesley Coll., 1973; MEd, Boston Coll., 1975. Dir. confs. and insvc. tng., chmn. bd. Mass. Assn. for Children with Learning Disabilities, Waltham and Framingham, 1969-75; chmn. core edn. teams, cons. to spl. programs, grant writer Needham (Mass.) Pub. Schs., 1974-79; ret., 1979; pres., feature writer S.D. Assocs., Inc., Wellesley, Mass., 1980-81; dir. pub. rels., women's career conf. Babson Coll., Wellesley, 1982. Mem. program evaluation team Mass. Dept. Edn., Quincy, 1978. Author (as Nancy Brown, with Louis Dickstein): Psychological Reports, 1974; author: (poems) Portraits of a Life, 1996, Fields of Gold, 1996, Ever-Flowing Stream, 1997, Best Poems of 1998, 2002, Colors of the Past, 2000, Echoes of Yesteryear, 2000, America at the Millennium, The Best Poems and Poets of the 20th Century, 2000, Memories of Tomorrow, 2000, Journey to Infinity, 2000, Theatre of the Mind, 2003 (The Best Poems and Poets of 2003, 2004, The Best Poems and Poets of 2004, 2005). Bd. dirs., fundraiser Hospice Palm Beach (Fla.) County S., 1993—97; bd. dirs. La Coqueille Villas, Inc., Manalapan, Fla., 1994—98; bd. dirs., chair cmty. rels. Lincoln Child Ctr., Oakland, Calif., 1983—85; docent Calif. Hist. Soc., San Francisco, 1982—87. Recipient Editor's Choice award, Internat. Libr. Poetry, 1996, 1998, 2000, 2003, The Best Poems and Poets of 2003, 2004, 2005. Mem.: Internat. Soc. Poets (disting. mem.), Phi Beta Kappa. Avocations: tennis, travel, duplicate bridge.

PHIPPS, CAROLYN SISK, secondary educator; b. Memphis, July 19, 1946; d. William Edward and Gladys (Hines) Sisk; m. Hardie M. Phipps Jr., Jan. 22, 1968. BS, Memphis State U., 1968, MEd, 1970. Cert. tchr. English, guidance, adminstrn. and supr. Tchr. Memphis City Schs., 1968—. Recipient Tchr. of Excellence award Rotary Club, 1996, Tenn. Tchr. of English Tn. Coun. Tchrs. of English, 1996. Mem. Nat. Coun. of Tchrs. of English (past chair of standing com. on affiliate of tchrs. of English, secondary steering com.), Shelby-Memphis Coun. Tchrs. of English (past pres.), Delta Kappa Gamma. Methodist. Home: 331 Park Manor Ln Collierville TN 38017-7065 Office: St Marys Sch 60 Perkins Ext Memphis TN 38117

PHIPPS, JUDITH A., social worker; b. Youngstown, Ohio, Oct. 19, 1945; d. Sidney and Dorothy Loretta (Zola) Greenberger; m. Bruce E. Phipps. BS, Boston U., 1967; MSS, Bryn Mawr Coll., 1978, M Law & Social Policy, 1984. Lic. Pa., 1990, LCSW Pa., 2001. Staff physical therapist St. Christopher's Hosp. Children, Phila., 1968—69, Magee Meml. Hosp., 1969—72; dir. phys. therapy VNA Abington, 1972—76; staff social worker Doylestown Hosp., 1978—84, VNA No. Chester County, Phoenixville, 1984—89; hospice social worker Wissahickon Hospice, Phila., 1986—89, North Pa. VNA, Lansdale, 1989—90; sr. mgr. The Partnership Group, 1990—93; dir. of. rehab. Manor Care, Pottstown, 1993—99; team supr. Magellan Behavioral Health, King of Prussia, 2000—. Mem.: NASW, Pa. Hospice Network. Avocations: flying, skiing, water-skiing. Home: 1231 Archer Ln Lansdale PA 19446 Office: Magellan Behavioral Health 1100 1st Ave King Of Prussia PA 19406 Office Phone: 610-783-4223. E-mail: j.a.phipps@comcast.net.

PHIPPS, MEG SCOTT, former commissioner; b. Haw River, N.C. d. Bob Scott; m. Robert Phipps, Jr.; children: Margaret, Rob. Grad., Wake Forest U.; M in Agrl. Law, U. Ark. Ptnr. Shoffner, Mosely & Phipps, Graham, NC, 1984—87; asst. atty. gen. N.C. Dept. Justice, 1987—93; assoc. atty. Davis & Humbert, Mebane, NC, 1993—95; adminstrv. law judge Office Adminstrv. Hearings, State of N.C., 1995—2000; commr. agriculture N.C. Dept. Agriculture and Consumer Svcs., Raleigh, 2001—03. Atty. N.C. Dept. Adminstrn., 1984; rsch. asst. Philip Morris, U.S.A., 1983; owner Meville Farms, Haw River. Elder, past Sunday sch. tchr. Hawfields Presbyn. Ch. Office: FPC Alderson Federal Prison Camp Glen Ray Rd Box A Alderson WV 24910

PHIPPS, PATSY DUNCAN, retired auditor; b. New Bern, N.C., July 10, 1934; d. Lawrence C. and Pagie P. Duncan; m. Robert A. Phipps, Sept. 27, 1953 (div. Feb. 2, 1992); children: Kathryn Phipps Sublett, Patricia Phipps Bryant. Cert. in Acctg., U. N.C., Greensboro, 1953; postgrad., U. N.C., 1973; BAI in Auditing, U. Wis., 1986. Regional instr. First Citizens Bank, New Bern, 1976—78; br. mgr. First Citizens Bank & Trust Co., New Bern, 1974—76, supr. account svcs. and ops., 1963—74, v.p., regional audit supr., 1978—97; v.p. auditor So. Bank and Trust Co., Mt. Olive, NC, 1997—99. Cons. Millennia Cmty. Bank, Greenville, NC, 2000—04. Active Broad St.Disciples of Christ Ch. Mem.: Nat. Assn. Bank Women (sec. Ea. N.C. group sec. 1975—76, chmn. 1978—80), Inst. Internal Auditors, New Bern Bus. and Profl. Women's Club (treas. 1973—74, 3d v.p. 1974—75, treas. 1981—82), N.C. Bus. and Profl. Women's Assn. (trustee 1976—82), Nat. Assn. of Bus. and Profl. Women's Club. Home: 1105 Peach Tree Ln New Bern NC 28562-8327 Office: Vespect Consulting Co 1105 Peach Tree Ln New Bern NC 28562-8327 Personal E-mail: patsinfo@cox.net.

PIANALTO, SANDRA, bank executive; b. Valli del Pasubio, Italy, Aug. 4, 1954; B in Economics, U. Akron, 1976; M in Economics, George Washington U., 1985; LHD (hon.), U. Akron, Baldwin-Wallace Coll., Kent State U., Ursuline Coll. Economist bd. govs. Fed. Reserve Sys.; staff mem. budget com. U.S. Ho. of Reps.; economist rsch. dept. Fed. Res. Bank Cleve., 1983—84, asst. v.p. pub. affairs, 1984—88, v.p., sec. bd. dirs., 1988—93, first v.p., COO, 1993—2003, pres., 2003—. Bd. dirs. Cleve. Found., Gr. Cleve. Partnership, U. Hosp. Health Sys., United Way Svcs. Cleve., Rock and Roll Hall of Fame and Mus., N.E. Ohio Coun. Higher Edn., Cath. Diocese Cleve. Found., Ohio Bus. Alliance for Higher Edn. and Economy. Office: Fed Reserve Bank Cleveland PO Box 6387 Cleveland OH 44101-1387*

PIAZZA, MARGUERITE, opera singer, actress, entertainer; b. New Orleans, May 6, 1926; d. Albert William and Michaela (Piazza) Luft; m. William J. Condon, July 15, 1953 (dec. Mar. 1968); children: Gregory, James (dec.), Shirley, William J., Marguerite P., Anna Becky; m. Francis Harrison Berghholdt, Nov. 8, 1970. MusB, Loyola U., New Orleans; MusM, La. State U.; MusD (hon.), Christian Bros. Coll., 1973; LHD (hon.), Loyola U., Chgo., 1975. Singer N.Y.C. Ctr. Opera, 1948, Met. Opera Co., 1950; TV artist, regular singing star Your Show of Shows NBC, 1950-54; entertainer various supper clubs Cotillion Room, Hotel Pierre, N.Y.C., 1954, Las Vegas, Los Angeles, New Orleans, San Francisco, 1956—; ptnr. Sound Express Music Pub. Co., Memphis, 1987—. Bd. dirs. Cemrel, Inc. Appeared as guest performer on numerous mus. TV shows. Nat. crusade chmn. Am. Cancer Soc., 1971; founder, bd. dirs. Marguerite Piazza Gala for the Benefit of St. Jude's Hosp., 1976; bd. dirs. Memphis Opera Co., World Literacy Found., NCCJ; v.p., life bd. dirs. Memphis Symphony Orch.; nat. chmn. Soc. for Cure Epilepsy. Decorated Mil. and Hospittaler Order of St. Lazarus of Jerusalem; recipient svc. award Chgo. Heart Assn., 1956, svc. award Fedn. Jewish Philanthropies of N.Y., 1956, Sesquicentennial medal Carnegie Hall, St. Martin De Porres award So. Dominicans, 1994, Lifetime Achievement award Germantown Arts Alliance, 1998; named Queen of Memphis, Memphis Cotton Carnival, 1973, Person of Yr., La. Coun. for Performing Arts, 1975, Woman of Yr., Nat. Am. Legion, Woman of Yr., Italian-Am. Soc. Mem. Nat. Speakers Assn., Woman's Exchange, Memphis Country Club, Memphis Hunt and Polo Club, New Orleans Country Club, Summit Club, Beta Sigma Omicron, Phi Beta. Roman Catholic. Home: 247 Baronne Pl Memphis TN 38117

PIAZZA, ROSANNA JOY, paralegal; b. Lincoln, Nebr., Sept. 10, 1950; d. Augustine Joseph Piazza and Mary Lou Pease; m. Pennell Spencer, Sept. 20, 1972 (div. Dec. 1979); children: Madeleine, Adrian, Aurora, Angelica, Marissa, Raquel. BA in Psychology, U. Calif., Santa Barbara, 1987, BA in Sociology, 1987, postgrad., 1987-89. Legal asst. Legal Aid, Pacoima, Van Nuys, Calif., 1980-81, Tomas Castelo, Santa Barbara, 1982-84; counselor Battered Women's Network, Santa Barbara, Calif., 1984-89; pres. The Venus Found., Livingston, Mont., 1993; legal asst. Lyman H. Bennett III, Bozeman, 1996—. Poet Mont. Poets, Bozeman, 1989—. Author: (Liberté) (poetry) The Magical Mystical Miracle, 1977, Gods in Exile, Zonderzonde, 1999, The Little Buddha, 1999, The Littlest Page of Lancelot de Lac, 1999. Senate candidate dist. 14 Natural Law Party, Bozeman, 1998; mem. disaster emergency team ARC, Fiver Rivers chpt., 1999—; sec. mission for life Pro Life Orgn., 1998. Mem. AAUW (natual law party), Bus. Women's Assn., Mont. Assn. of Paralegals, Mont. Paralegal Assn., Nat. Assn. of Legal Secs., Mont. State Bar Assn. (paralegal sect.). Avocations: writer, poetry, songwriting, folk guitar and mandolin.

PICARD, LESLIE, publishing executive; With Conde Nast, NYC, 1996—; ad mgr. Vanity Fair, NYC, 1996—98; adv. dir. Conde Nast corp. sales divsn., NYC, 1998—2001, v.p., 2001—04; v.p., pub. Bon Appetit, NYC, 2004—. Office: Bon Appetit Fl 15 4 Times Square New York NY 10036-6522

PICCOLI, SUSAN ELIZABETH, secondary school educator; b. Poughkeepsie, NY, Dec. 2, 1970; BA in History and Art History, Fordham U., Bronx, NY, 1992; MA in History and Edn., SUNY, New Paltz, 1996. Cert. tchr. Vt. Dept. Edn., 2004. History, art history and dance tchr. Oakwood Friends Sch., Poughkeepsie, 1995—99, Woodstock Union HS, Vt., 2000—. Choreographer sch. musicals Oakwood Friends Sch., Poughkeepsie, 1995—99; choreographer for theatrical prodns. Yoh Theatre, Woodstock, 2003—; arts program coord. Woodstock Union HS, 2003—. Class advisor Woodstock Union HS, 2000—04. Recipient award, Nat. Honor Roll for Tchrs., 2005—06, Outstanding Contributions to Arts award, Vt. Arts Edn. Alliance, 2006; grantee Prins. scholarship to Paris, Oxbridge Acad. Programs, 2002, Pearl Harbor, Hawaii scholar, Nat. Endowment for Humanities, East-West Ctr. & Nat. Parks Svc., 2004; Fulbright Meml. Fund Japan scholar, Japanese Govt., 2003, Crow Canyon Archeol. Ctr. Colo. scholar, Nat. Endowment for Humanities, 2003, Fulbright Hays scholar, 2005. Mem.: NEA, Nat. Coun. Social Studies. Avocations: travel, reading, museums. Office: Woodstock Union HS 496-1 Woodstock Rd Woodstock VT 05091

PICCOTTI, CAROLYN M., lawyer; b. 1957; Degree, Dickinson Coll., 1979; JD, Dickinson Sch. Law, 1983. Litig. counsel pvt. litig. firm, 1983—86; law clk. US Dist. Ct., Middle Dist. Pa., Scranton, 1986—88; atty. advisor Bd. Immigration Appeals, Exec. Office Immigration Review, US Dept. Justice, 1988—99; assoc. gen. counsel Office Gen. Council, Exec. Office Immigration Review, US Dept. Justice, 1999—. Sr. policy analyst US Commn. on Immigration Reform, 1995—97. Mem.: Pa. Bar Assn. Office: US Dept Justice Exec Office Immigration Review Office Dir 5107 Leesburg Pike Ste 2600 Falls Church VA 22041

PICK, HEATHER, newscaster; b. Platteville, Wis. m. Joe Pick; 1 child. Reporter, anchor Sta. WREX-TV, Rockford, Ill.; anchor Sta. WBNS-TV, Columbus, Ohio, 2002—. Office: WBNS-TV 770 Twin Rivers Dr Columbus OH 43215

PICK, MARY FRANCES, manufacturing executive; b. Paducah, Tex., Feb. 13, 1929; d. James Claude and Frances Ellen Stewart; m. Sanford Pick, Dec. 27, 1961; 1 child, Cheryl Anne Miller. BA, So. Meth. U., Dallas, 1963; degree, Am. Coll., Dallas, 1992. Real estate broker Paula Stringer Realty, Dallas, 1978—80; mgr. Merrill Lynch Realty, Dallas, 1980—83; owner Mary Pick Realty, Dallas, 1983—84; ins. broker Northwestern Mutual, Dallas, 1988—90; ins. broker, fin. advisor Principal Mutual, Dallas, 1990—96; ind. fin. advisor Dallas, 1990—. Bd. dirs. NDE Quality Inc., Houston, 1991—; owner Millspec, LP, Dallas, 2003—. Bd. dirs. Dallas Theater Ctr., 1964—68, Dallas Ballet, 1965—67. Named Businesswoman of Yr., Nat. Rep. Congl. Com., Jensen Beach, Fla., 2004. Home: 9950 S Ocean Dr Jensen Beach FL 34957 Office: Millspec LP 11695 County Rd 213 Forney TX 75126 Office Fax: 772-229-3080. Personal E-mail: pick3913@aol.com.

PICKARD, KAREN K., parochial school educator; b. Chgo., Aug. 16, 1949; d. Frank J. and Helen T. Kracher; m. Scott S. Pickard, June 20, 1971; children: Christopher, Allison, Katherine. BS in Edn., U. Ill., 1971. Cert. tchr. Ill. Tchr. St. Matthew Sch., Champaign, Ill., 1971—78, 1988—; rsch. interviewer Dept. of Psychology U. Ill., Champaign, 1986—87. Yearbook advisor St. Matthew Sch., 1990—2006, creative dir. musicals, 1993—. Bd. dirs. Jr. League, 1994—96. Named Outstanding Educator, Diocese of Peoria, 1992; named to Outstanding Am. Tchrs., 2006. Mem.: Nat. Cath. Educators Assn., Delta Gamma. Roman Catholic. Avocations: gardening, swimming, reading. Home: 714 S Elm Blvd Champaign IL 61820

PICKART, CAITLIN CAHILL, psychiatrist; d. Gail Patrick Pickart and Geraldine Riley Cahill. BA, Stanford U., 1998; MD, U. Calif., 2003. Lic. Calif., cert. drug enforcement agy. Calif. Resident psychiatrist U. Calif., Irvine Dept. Psychiatry, Human Behavior, Orange, Calif., 2003—. Resident rep. Orange County Psychiat. Soc., Santa Ana, Calif., 2006—. Recipient Outstanding Resident award, U. Calif., Irvine Dept. Psychiatry, Human Behavior, 2004-2005. Mem.: Orange County Psychiat. Soc., Calif. Psychiat. Soc., Am. Psychiat. Assn. Office: U Calif Irvine Med Ctr Dept Psychiatry 101 The City Dr Rt88 Orange CA 92868 Office Phone: 714-456-5770.

PICKEL, DIANE DUNN, education educator; d. Donald and Janice Dunn; m. David E. Pickel, May 30, 1987; 1 child, Emily N. BS in mktg., Pa. State U., 1976—80, MBA, 1985—86. Pub. rels. coord. Huth/PSC Engrs., Lancaster, Pa., 1987—91; mktg. rep. Brinjac, Kambic & Assocs., Harrisburg, Pa., 1991—94; adj. faculty Harrisburg Area C.C., Pa., 1993—2000; prof., bus. adminstrn. Ctrl. Pa. Coll., Summerdale, Pa., 1997—; cons. Entrepreneurial Devel. Ctr., 1998—99, 2004. Vol. Elizabethtown Boys Club Cheerleading Competition, Elizabethtown, Pa., 1997—2003; parent vol. Elizabethtown area sch., 1994—. Sam M. Walton Free Enterprise fellow, 1999—2002. Mem.: Am. Mktg. Assn., Penn State Alumni Assn. Office: Ctrl Pa Coll College Hill and Valley Rd Summerdale PA 17093 Office Phone: 800-759-2727. E-mail: dianepickel@centralpenn.edu.

PICKEL, JOYCE KILEY, psychologist; b. Dec. 20, 1939; m. Edward McDonald, Aug. 24, 1960 (div. Mar. 1977); children: Catherine, Maureen, Edward; m. Mark Pickel, Apr. 6, 1982. BS in Edn., Boston State Coll., 1961; MEd, R.I. Coll., 1968; MA, Mich. State U., 1969; EdD, No. Ill. U., 1990. Tchr., Mass., R.I., 1962-66; guidance counselor Grand Ledge (Mich.) schs., 1966-67; diagnostician Eaton County Intermediate Sch. Dist., Charlotte, Mich., 1968-69; psychometrist Hammond, Ind., 1969-70; coord. programs, sch. psychometrist N.W. Ind. Spl. Edn. Coop., Highland, 1970-72; instr. Ind. U., Gary, 1970-72; program dir. Trade Winds Rehab. Ctr., Gary, 1972-73; supv. sch. psychologist Thornton Fractional Twp. H.S. 215, Calumet City, Ill., 1973—. 1st v.p. Greater Hammond Cmty. Coun., 1974-76; treas. Colonial Club Condominium ASsn., 2003-06, pres., 2006—; regional spkr. teen suicide various confs. Recipient award Hammond Cmty. Coun., 1974, 75, 76, Cmty. Svc. award Greater Hammond Cmty. Coun., 1975; NDEA fellow R.I. Coll., 1967, NDEA fellow Mich. State U., 1967-68. Mem. Nat. Assn. Sch. Psychologists, Coun. Exceptional Children, Am. Fedn. Tchrs., S. Met. Assn. Sch. Psychologists (pres. 1982-83, bd. dirs. 1985-86, v.p. 1994-95), Ill. Sch. Psychol. Assn. (dir. region VIII, mem. governing bd., pres. 1990-91, historian 1995—, Ted Smith Meml. award 1986), Phi Delta Kappa. Office: 1601 Wentworth Ave Calumet City IL 60409-6309 Personal E-mail: pickelj@bellsouth.net.

PICKENS, FRANCES JENKINS, artist, educator; b. Dodd's, Tex., Feb. 26, 1927; d. John Morgan and Mary (Burton) Jenkins; m. Alexander Pickens, Aug. 20, 1955. BA, U. of North Tex., 1947, MA, 1954; MEd, U. Hawaii, 1976. Tchr. art pub. schs., Dallas, 1948-55, Dearborn, Mich., 1955-58, White Plains, N.Y., 1958-59, Athens, Ga., 1960-62; gallery lectr. Honolulu Acad. Arts, 1962—63; tchr. art Punahou Sch., Honolulu, 1963-65, The Kamehameha Schs., Honolulu, 1965-85; jewelry and metal artist Honolulu, 1963—. Instr. jewelry U. Hawaii, Honolulu, 1967, 75, 77. Exhibited works in shows at Mus. of Contemporary Crafts, N.Y., Schmuckmuseum, Germany, Renwick Gallery, Washington, Wichita Nat., Women in Design Internat., Mich. Influence, 1981, Materials Hard and Soft, United States Metal, Hawaii Craftsmen Ann., Artists of Hawaii, 1965— (Disting. Artist 1991), East-West Ctr. Gallery, 2003, retrospective Honolulu Acad. Arts, 2001, KDA Gallery, Honolulu, 2005; represented in permanent collection at Acad. of Arts, The Contemporary Mus., Honolulu, Hawaii State Art Mus., Renwick Gallery, Washington, Wichita Art Assn., Kans.; photographs of work included in Goldsmith's Jour., Jewelry, Contemporary Design and Technique, Jewelry/Metalwork Survey, The Metalsmith's Book of Boxes and Lockets; contbr. articles to Arts and Activities mag., Sch. Arts, Ornament mag. Chmn. state crafts State Fair Tex., Dallas, 1954; Crafts Symposium planning com. Hawaii State Found. Culture and Arts, Honolulu, 1968-69; workshop for instrs. U.S. Army Arts and Crafts, Ft. Shafter, 1975. Named Distinguished Artist of Hawaii, Honolulu Acad. Arts, 1991. Mem. Soc. N.Am. Goldsmiths, Dallas Craft Guild, Hawai Craftsmen (charter, v.p., pres.), Renwick Alliance. Avocations: travel, jewelry, metalwork. Home: 1471 Kalaepohaku St Honolulu HI 96816-1804

PICKERING, ROBERTA ANN, language educator, gifted and talented educator; b. Bloomsburg, Pa., Aug. 26, 1968; d. William Henry and Virginia Lee Rice; m. Robert White Pickering, June 29, 1991. BA English and Theatre Arts, Susquehanna U., Selinsgrove, Pa., 1990; post grad., U. Conn. Cert. Secondary Edn. tchr. Pa. Dept. Edn., 1991. Tchr. AP English and gifted Lewisburg Area H.S., Pa., 1996—. Reader nat. AP English Ednl. Testing Svc., Princeton, NJ, 1999—. Dir.: Ann. Fall Play. Mem.: Pa. Assn. Gifted Edn., Nat. Coun. Tchrs. English, Sigma Tau Delta, Sigma Alpha Iota, Alpha Psi Omega. Home: 518 Maclay Avenue Lewisburg PA 17837 Office: Lewisburg Area High School 815 Market Street Lewisburg PA 17837 Personal E-mail: rwpickr@ptd.net. E-mail: pickering_r@dragon.k12.pa.us.

PICKETT, BETTY HORENSTEIN, psychologist; b. Providence, Feb. 15, 1926; d. Isadore Samuel and Etta Lillian (Morrison) Horenstein; m. James McPherson Pickett, Mar. 10, 1952. AB magna cum laude, Brown U., 1945, ScM, 1947, PhD, 1949. Asst. prof. psychology U. Minn., Duluth, 1949-51; asst. prof. U. Nebr., 1951; lectr. U. Conn., 1952; profl. assoc. psychol. scis. Bio-Scis. Info. Exch., Smithsonian Instn., Washington, 1953-58; exec. sec. behavioral scis. study sect. exptl. psychology study sect. div. research grants NIH, Bethesda, Md., 1958-61; rsch. cons. to mental health unit HEW, Boston, 1962-63; exec. sec. rsch. career program NIMH, 1963-66, chief cognition and learning sect. div. extramural research program, 1966-68, dep. dir., 1968-74, dir. div. spl. mental health programs, 1974-75, acting dir. div. extramural rsch. program, 1975-77; assoc. dir. extramural and collaborative rsch. program Nat. Inst. Aging, 1977-79; dep. dir. Nat. Inst. Child Health and Human Devel., Bethesda, Md., 1979-81, acting dir., 1981-82, dir. Div. Rsch. Resources, 1982-88. Mem. health scientist adminstr. panel CSC Bd. Examiners, 1970—76, 1981—88; mem. coun. on grad. edn. Brown U. Grad. Sch., 1989—91. Contbr. articles to profl. jours. Mem. APA, Am. Psychol Soc., Psychonomic Soc., Assn. Women in Sci., AAAS, Phi Beta Kappa, Sigma Xi. Home: Morgan Bay Rd PO Box 198 Surry ME 04684-0198

PICKETT, CHRISTA LANGFORD, elementary school counselor; b. Hoschton, Ga., Aug. 2, 1943; d. Grady and Ruth Geraldine Langford; children: Mark, Paige Pastor. BA Elem. Edn., Emory and Henry Coll., 1974; MEd Spl. Edn., U. Tenn., Chattanooga, 1981. Cert. sch. counselor (P-12), interrelated spl. edn., elem. edn. Teacher (grades 4/5 &1) Oak Hill Elem., Morganton, NC, 1975—79; tchr. spl. edn. Red Bank Jr. HS, Red Bank, Tenn., 1980—81; teacher (grade 4) Thrasher Elem. Sch., Signal Mountain, Tenn., 1984; tchr. spl. edn. (gifted & handicapped) Lone Oak Elem., Signal Mountain, Tenn., 1985—88; tchr. spl. edn. Berkeley Lake Elem., Duluth, Ga., 1989—99, counselor elem. sch., 1999—. Mem. curriculum and instrn. counsel Berkeley Lake Elem. Sch., Duluth, 1998—, mem. Berkeley Lake team planning com., 1999—, coord. Berkeley Lake Care team, 1999—; facilitator student support team i Berkeley Lake Elem. Sch., Duluth, 1999—, member student support team ii, 2002—. Dir. mediation program Berkeley Lake; mem. Peachtree Presbyn. Ch., Atlanta, 1991—; mem., co-facilitator, facilitator Stephen's Ministry of Peachtree Presbyn. Ch., Atlanta, 1992—; relay for life team mem. of bles Am. Cancer Soc., Duluth, 1999—. Mem.: Am. Sch. Counselor Assn., Am. Counseling Assn., Pi Lambda Theta, Kappa Delta Pi. Protestant. Avocations: painting, reading, exercise. Office: Berkeley Lake Elem 4300 South Berkeley Lake Rd Duluth GA 30096 Business E-Mail: christa_pickett@gwinnett.k12.ga.us.

PICKETT, EUGENIA V., social worker; b. Balt., Mar. 26, 1938; d. Robert Thomas and Eugenia King Valdivia; children: Jennifer Pickett Connoley, Juliana Ewing Harris; 1 stepchild, Jennifer Greenwald. BS, Towson U., 1959; MA, Antioch U., 1975. Diplomate psychotherapy Nat. Bd. Med. Psychotherapy; LCSW MD, cert. group psychotherapy Am. Group Psychotherapy Assn. Educator Balt. City Pub. Schs., 1960—69; staff coord. Greenmount Ave. Medical, Mental Health Clinic, Balt., 1970—76; psychiat. social worker pvt. practice, Balt., 1976—. Educator women's studies, childhood edn. Balt. C.C., Essex, 1978—79; primary trainer Assn. Music, Imagery, Salina, Kans., 1979—2003; cons. Ctr. Living Head Trauma, Balt., 1986—91; primary trainer Creative Therapies Inst., Massapeagua, NY, 1991—2003. Editor: Women: A Journal of Liberation, Journal of the Association for Music and Imagery. Mem. Balt. Def. Com., 1960; mem., pub. spkr. Women's Consciousness Raising Group, Balt., 1965—72; staff counselor, therapist Women's Growth Ctr., Balt., 1970—84; educator, meditation instr. Lotus Garden Buddhist Ctr., Stanley, Va., Balt. Shambhala Ctr., Balt., 1976—2006. Mem.: Md. Soc. Clin. Social Workers (sec. 1999—2002). Democrat-Npl. Buddhist. Office: 500 W U Pkwy 1H Baltimore MD 21210-3236 Office Phone: 410-243-7300. Business E-Mail: epicdharma@aol.com.

PICKETT, SANDRA, information scientist; BS, U. Tex.; MA, U. Houston. Councilwoman City of Liberty, Tex., 1974—98, mayor pro tem, 1976—98; commr., chair Tex. State Libr. and Archives Commn., Austin, 1995—. Past chmn. Liberty County Hist. Commn.; past dir., pres. Preservation Tex.; mem. Nat. Mus. and Libr. Svcs. Bd., Washington, 2004—. Named Citizen of Yr., C. of C., 1981; recipient John Ben Shepperd Leadership award, Tex. Hist. Commn., 1993; Paul Harris fellow, Rotary Internat., 1998. Mem.: Atascosito Hist. Soc. (pres.). Mailing: PO Box 19191 Liberty TX 77575 Office: Tex State Libr and Archives Commn PO Box 12927 Austin TX 78711

PICKETT, SHERRY M., social worker; d. Theo H. and Mable K. McClendon; m. Henry C. Pickett, Mar. 26, 1966; children: Klatra M., Jason A. AS, Oakland C.C., Auburn Hills, Mich., 1992; MSW, U. Mich., 1994. Cert. social worker Mich. Bd. Examiners Social Workers. Social worker State Mich.-Dept. Social Svcs Family Ind. Agy. Children & Family Svcs., Taylor, 1972—97; mgr. Theo & Mable McClendon Found., 1997—. Editor: (newsletter) Bookwomen, 1998—. Pres., founder Theo & Mable McClendon Found., Southfield, Mich., 1994—. Mem.: Bookwomen Reading Club, Lions Club Internat., Detroit Westown Hartford Lions Club (bd. dirs. 2000—05, Achievement award 2002, Pres. Appreciation award 2003). Avocations: travel, reading. Office: Theo & Mable McClendon Found PO Box 2623 Southfield MI 48037 E-mail: pick@umich.edu.

PICKLE, LINDA WILLIAMS, biostatistician; b. Hampton, Va., July 19, 1948; d. Howard Taft and Kathryn Lee (Riggin) Williams; 1 child from previous marriage, Diane Marie; m. James B. Pearson, Jr., Oct. 14, 1984. BA, Johns Hopkins U., 1974, PhD in Biostats., 1977; postgrad., George Washington U., 1986—87. Computer programmer Comml. Credit Computer Corp., Balt., 1966-69; systems analyst, computer programmer Greater Balt. Med. Ctr., Balt., 1969-72; grad. tchg. asst. biostats. Johns Hopkins U., Balt., 1974-77; adj. asst. prof. div. biostats. and epidemiology Georgetown U. Med. Sch., Washington, 1983—88, assoc. prof. div. biostats and epidemiology, 1988-91, dir. biostats. unit, V.T. Lombardi Cancer Rsch. Ctr., 1988-91; biostatistician Nat. Cancer Inst. NIH, Bethesda, Md., 1977-88; math. statistician office rsch. methodology Nat. Ctr. for Health Stats., Hyattsville, Md., 1991-99; sr. math statistician divsn. cancer control/population scis. Nat. Cancer Inst. NIH, Bethesda, Md., 1999—. Author: Atlas of U.S. Cancer Mortality Among Whites: 1950-80, 1987, Atlas of U.S. Cancer Mortality Among Nonwhites: 1950-1980, 1990, Atlas of United States Mortality, 1996, U.S. Predicted Cancer Incidence, 2003; contbr. articles to profl. jours. Recipient Hammer award, US Govt., 2000. Fellow Am. Statis. Assn.; mem. The Biometric Soc., Soc. Epidemiologic Research, Soc. Indsl. and Applied Math., Phi Beta Kappa, Sigma Xi. Achievements include research in statistical methods in epidemiology, mapping health statistics.

PICKOVER, BETTY ABRAVANEL, retired executive legal secretary, civic volunteer; b. N.Y.C., Apr. 20, 1920; d. Albert and Sultana (Rousso) Abravanel; m. Bernard Builder, Apr. 6, 1941 (div. 1962); children: Ronald, Stuart; m. William Pickover, Aug. 23, 1970 (dec. Nov. 1983). Student, Taft Evening Ctr., 1961-70. Sec. U.S. Treasury Dept., Washington, 1942-43; exec. legal sec. various attys., Bronx, N.Y., 1956-70, Yonkers, N.Y., 1971-83, ret., 1983. Chair Uniongram Sisterhood of Temple Emanu-El, Yonkers, N.Y., 1975—, Honor Roll, 1975—, v.p. 1995-97, 98, 99, 2003; sr. citizen cmty. leader Yonkers Officer for Aging, 1984—, Westchester County Sr. Adv. Bd., White Plains, N.Y., 1989-96; v.p. Mayor's Cmty. Rels. Com. of Yonkers, 1985—, historian, photographer, 1988—; mem. Yonkers Flag Day Observance Com., 1998—; mem. adv. coun. Westchester County Office Aging Srs., 1993—; mem. bd. Legislators Task Force for Sr. Citizens Westchester County, 1995-97, 98, 99; Mayor Silver City Coun. Yonkers, 1989; mem. Mayor's Adv. Coun. on Sr. Citizens, 1990. Named to Sr. Citizen Hall of Fame, 1992; recipient Cert. of Appreciation, Westchester County, 1992, Pres. Coun. City of Yonkers, 1992, Merit cert., 1993, Cmty. Svc., City Mayor Yonkers, 1995, 96, 97, 98, 99, 2004, John E. Andrus Meml. Vol., 1995, Cert. of Appreciation, Westchester County Office of County Exec., 1993, 94, Cert. of Disting. Svc., 1997, Merit cert., N.Y. State Senator, 1994, N.Y. State Senator, 1995, 97, 98, 99, 2000, Cert. of Congratulations, N.Y. State Senator, 2001, Merit cert., Proclamation Mayor of Yonkers, 1985, 89, 92, 2 awards, U.S. Ho. of Reps., 1992, Woman of Excellence, Yonkers C. of C., 1993, awards, Mayor of Yonkers, 1985-97, 98, 99, 2000, Cert. of Appreciation, Mayor of City of Yonkers, 2001, awards, N.Y. State Senator and Assemblyman, 1987—97, City of Yonkers, 1993, Cert. of Merit, N.Y. State Assembly, 2001, Cert. of Appreciation, Westchester County Bd. Legislators, 1996, 99, City Coun. Pres., Yonkers, N.Y., 1999, Cert. of Recognition, 2000, Proclamation, Westchester County Bd. Legislators, 2003, 20 Yrs. Vol. Svc. award, Mayor of City of Yonkers, 2004. Democrat. Jewish. Avocations: writing, photography, entertaining at all nursing homes in yonkers, history, public relations. Home: 200 Valentine Ln Apt 5B Yonkers NY 10705-3607

PICKREL, FELICIA RENEE, science educator; d. Linwood Judson and Vivian Oneida Spratley; m. Joseph Scott Pickrel; children: Tia Lynn Scholten, Stacie Leigh Scholten. BS in Biology, Lynchburg Coll., Va., 2001, MEd in Sci. Edn., 2006. Biology and environ. sci. tchr. Appomattox County HS, Va., 2002—. Sgt. USAF. Decorated Basic Tng. Honor Flight medal USAF, Expert Marksman award, NCO Prep Honor Grad., Accomodation medal, Longevity medal. Mem.: Va. Assn. Sci. Tchrs. (life). Home: 133 Bennington Manor Dr Rustburg VA 24588 Office: Appomattox County HS 198 Evergreen Ave Appomattox VA 24522 Office Phone: 434-352-7146. Business E-Mail: frpickrel@appomattox.k12.va.us.

PICOULT, JODI, writer; b. Long Island, NY; m. Tim Van Leer; 3 children. BA, Princeton Univ; MEd, Harvard Univ. Technical writer; textbook editor; English tchr. Author: (novels) Songs of the Humpback Whale, 1992, Harvesting the Heart, 1993, Picture Perfect, 1995, Mercy, 1996, The Pact, 1998, Keeping Faith, 1999, Plain Truth, 1999, Salem Falls, 2001, Perfect Match, 2002, Second Glance, 2003, My Sister's Keeper, 2004 (Publishers Weekly Bestseller, 2005), Vanishing Acts, 2005 (Publishers Weekly Bestseller, 2005), The Tenth Circle, 2006. Avocation: ice hockey. Office: PO Box 508 Etna NH 03750 Business E-Mail: jodi@jodipicoult.com.*

PIECH, MARY LOU ROHLING, medical psychotherapist, consultant; b. Elgin, Ill., Jan. 20, 1927; d. Louis Bernard and Charlotte (Wylie) Rohling; m. Raymond C. Piech, Feb. 12, 1950 (dec. Feb. 1985); 1 child, Christine Piech. BA, U. Ill., 1948, MA, 1953; postgrad., Ill. Inst. Tech., 1966-68, Union Inst., 1991-98. Cert. clin. psychologist, Ill.; diplomate Am. Bd. Med. Psychotherapy. Instr. psychology Elmhurst (Ill.) Coll., 1955-61; asst. prof. psychology North Cen. Coll., Naperville, Ill., 1961-67, Elmhurst (Ill.) Coll., 1968-81; med. psychotherapist Shealy Pain & Health Rehab. Ctr., LaCrosse, Wis., 1977-82, Shealy Inst. Comprehensive Health Care, Springfield, Mo., 1982—. Author, editor: (video series) Mental Health, 1982, (audio tape series) Holistic Mental Health, 1983. Recipient award Lilly Found., Elmhurst Coll., Shealy Inst., 1977. Fellow Am. Bd. Med. Psychotherapy; mem. APA, N.Am. Soc. Adlerian Psychology, Assn. Psychol. Type (life), Phi Beta Kappa, Phi Kappa Phi, Mortar Bd. Office: Shealy Institute Wellness Ctr 5607 S 222nd Rd Fair Grove MO 65648-8192

PIECUCH, DIANE MARIE, music educator; b. Ironwood, Mich., Mar. 25, 1950; d. John H. Meyer and Betty E. Meyer-Lundberg. MusB, Mich. State U., East Lansing, 1972; MusM, George Mason U., Fairfax, Va., 1998. Cert. Orff Schulwerk George Mason U., 1988. Music tchr. Loudoun County Pub. Schs., Sterling, Va., 1972—75, Fairfax County Pub. Schs., Alexandria, Va., 1975—77, 1986—. V.p. PQ Prodns., Alexandria, 1977—96. Composer: (multiple songs) For Corporations And School. Min. of cmty. care St. John's Luth. Ch., Alexandria, 2005—06. Recipient Supts. award, Sch. Bd., 1991—92. Mem.: Fairfax Gen. Music Educators Assn. (assoc.; pres. 1995—97), Am. Orff Schulwerk Assn (assoc.; social chmn. 1989—91). R-Consevative. Lutheran. Avocation: jogging. Home: 6543 Kelsey Point Cir Alexandria VA 22315 Office: Rose Hill Elementary Sch 6301 Rose Hill Dr Alexandria VA 22310 Office Phone: 703-313-4200. Personal E-mail: dpq@cox.net. E-mail: diane.piecuch@fcps.edu.

PIEFFER, PHYLLIS I., music educator; b. Erie, Pa., Apr. 1, 1944; d. Victor Davidson and Margaret Louise Davis; m. Ronald J. Pieffer, June 9, 1966; Liane, Elaine. BMus, Coll. of Wooster, 1966; MA, Eastman Sch. of Music, 1978. Cert. piano, music theory tchr. Music tchr. Gates Chili Sch. Dist., Rochester, N.Y., 1969-70, Ind. Studio, Lakewood, Colo., 1970-98; instr. Colo. Christian U., Lakewood, 1983-90, asst. prof. music, 1990-94, music chair, 1994-98; part-time music faculty Grays Harbor Coll., Aberdeen, Wash., 1998—. Spkr. in field. Vol. Am. Field Svc., 1961, 85-90; mem. Reach to Recovery, Am. Cancer Soc. Mem.: DAR, Wash. State Tchrs. Assn., Music Tchrs. Nat. Assn. (west ctrl. divsn. pres. 1990—92, v.p. for membership 1999—, pres.-elect 2001—03, pres. 2003—05, immediate past pres. 2005—), Pi Kappa Lambda. Presbyterian. Avocations: genealogy, boating, travel. Home: 4852 Wishkah Rd Aberdeen WA 98520-9628 Office: Grays Harbor Coll 1620 Edward P Smith Dr Aberdeen WA 98520-7500 Office Phone: 360-538-4188. E-mail: ppieffer@ghc.edu, pianofil@comcast.net.

PIEHLER, BARBARA F., insurance company executive; BBA in Acctg., U. Wis., Madison. Positions with Arthur Young & Co., Joseph Schlitz Brewing Co., Stroh Brewing Co.; joined contr.'s dept. Northwestern Mutual, 1983, named asst. contr., 1988, asst. to pres., 1990, v.p. corp. svcs., 1991, v.p., asst. to pres., 1994, v.p. policy owner svcs., 1995, v.p. internet, v.p. info. services, 2001, sr. v.p., chief info. officer, 2002. Named one of Premier 100 IT Leaders, Computerworld, 2005. Office: Northwestern Mutual 720 E Wisconsin Ave Milwaukee WI 53202-4797 Office Phone: 414-271-1444.

PIEKNIK, REBECCA ANNE, technologist, educator; b. Detroit, Sept. 30, 1960; AA in Allied Health, Baker Coll., 1998; BS in Health Svc. Adminstrn., Baker Coll. Flint, 2002; MS in Bioethics, Union U., 2005. Cert. surg. technologist, surg. asst. Clin. instr. Baker Coll. Flint, 1999—; cert. surg. technologist Pontiac Osteopathic Hosp., Mich., 2001—02; program dir. surg. tech. Oakland C.C./William Beaumont Hosp., 2002—. Office Phone: 248-898-7685.

PIENE, CHLOE, artist, filmmaker; b. Stamford, Conn., 1972; Exhibitions include Me & More, Kunstmuseum, Luzern, 2003, Whitney Biennial, Whitney Mus. Am. Art, NY, 2004, Spirit, Galerie Nathalie Obadia, Paris, 2004, Videodrome II, Bates Coll. Mus. Art, 2004, Boys Will Be Boys?, Mus. Contemporary Art, Denver, 2005, Getting Emotional, 2005, Mus. Contemporary Art, Denver, 2005, Chloe Piene Galleries Nathalie Obadia, Sandroni Rey Gallery, LA, Klemens Gasser and Tanja Grunert, NYC. Studio: 66 Washington Ave 3rd Fl Brooklyn NY 11205 Personal E-mail: cpstudio@verizon.net.

PIEPER, PATRICIA RITA, artist; b. Paterson, NJ, Jan. 28, 1923; d. Francis William and Barbara Margaret (Ludwig) Farabaugh; m. George F. Pieper, July 1, 1941 (dec. May 3, 1981); 1 child, Patricia Lynn; m. Russell W. Watson, Dec. 9, 1989. Student, Baron von Palm, 1937-39, Deal Conservatory, NJ, 1939, 40, Utah State U., 1950-52; student Baron von Palm, 1937—39, student Deal (N.J.) Conservatory, 1939—40, student Utah State U., 1950—52. One-woman shows include Charles Russell Mus., Great Falls, Mont., 1955, Fisher Gallery, Washington, 1966, Tampa City Libr., 1977-81, 83, 84, Ctr. Pl. Art Ctr., Brandon, Fla., 1985; exhibited in group shows Davidson Art Gallery, Middletown, Conn., 1968, Helena (Mont.) Hist. Mus., 1955, Dept. Commerce Alaska Statehood Show, 1959, Joslyn Mus., Omaha, 1961, Denver Mus. Natural History, 1955, St. Joseph's Hosp. Gallery, 1980, 82, 84-86; represented in pvt. collections. Pres. Bell Lake Assn., 1976-78, 79; mem. Pasco County (Fla.) Water Adv. Coun., 1978—, chmn., 1979-82, 83-84, 86-88, 92—; gov.'s appointee to S.W. Fla. Water Mgmt. Dist., Hillsborough River Basin Bd., 1981-82, 84-87, sec., 1988-91, vice chmn., 1992; active Save Our Rivers program, 1982-84, 85-86, 92—; ad hoc chmn., 1991-92; mem. adv. bd. Fla. Suncoast Expwy., 1988-90; pres. Bell Lake Assn., 1986, 87; mem. adv. bd. Tampa YMCA, 1979-80. Winner photog. competition Gen. Tel. Co. of Fla., 1979; recipient Outstanding Svc. award Bell Lake Assn., 1987, Meml. award Land O'Lake Bd. of Realtors, 1989, Appreciation award Southwest Fla. Water Mgmt. Dist., 1993, finalist, Awds. of Excellence, Photographers winner in top 100 out of 8,000 Nat. Wildlife Fedn. competition, 1986, 1st place photography MacDill AFB, 1991. Mem. VFW (life), Nat. League Am. Pen Women (v.p. Tampa 1976-78, Woman of Yr. award 1977-78), Tampa Art Mus., Ret. Officer's Wives Assn., Land O'Lakes C. of C. (bd. dirs. 1981-82, Outstanding Svc. award 1980), Fla. Geneal. Soc., West State Archaeol. Soc. (distaff mem.), Ret. Officer's Assn., Lutz Club, Land O'Lakes Women's Club, Moose. Home: 3304 E Derry Dr Sebastian FL 32958-8577

PIERANTONI, MARLENE MICHELLE, psychiatrist; b. Arecibo, P.R., Sept. 1, 1978; d. Radames and Myrta Pierantoni. BS in Biology, U. P.R., Mayaguez, 2000; MD, U. P.R., San Juan, 2004. Resident U. S. Fla., Tampa, 2004—. Mem. curriculum com. dept. psychiatry U. South Fla., psychiatry residency recruitment com. mem., educator intern class. Contbr. articles to profl. jours. Grantee, Fla. Psychiat. Soc., 2005; scholar, Am. Psychiat. Assn., 2004. Mem.: AMA, U. P.R. Sch. Medicine Alumni Soc., Fla. Psychiat. Soc. (resident rep.), Am. Psychiat. Assn. Avocations: languages, travel, dance. Office: Univ S Fla 3515 E Fletcher Ave Tampa FL 33613 Office Phone: 813-974-2805. Business E-Mail: mpierant@hsc.usf.edu.

PIERCE, CAROL, success strategist, writer; b. Raceland, La., Dec. 24, 1945; d. Clarence Joseph Pierce and Alice Mae Foret; divorced; children: Monique Ann Gervais Sapia, Nicole Elizabeth Gervais Becnel, Andre Marie Gervais Gros. BA, Nicholls State U., 1966, MEd, 1971. English tchr./libr. Lafourche Parish (La.) Sch. Bd., 1966—94; adj. instr. Nicholls State U., Thibodaux, La., 1994—97; prin., owner Success NOW!, Gonzales, La., 1994—. Master tchr./assessor La. Tchr. Assessment Program, La., 1993-94; side-by-side facilitator Bayou Coun. Alcoholism and Drug Abuse, Thibodaux, La., 1994-95; organizer/chairperson Preparing Students for the World of Work Conf., Thibodaux, 1996, Regional Edn. Com., Bayou Region Parishes, 1996-97; Pre-ACT workshop presenter Nicholls State U., Thibodaux, 1998-99; keynote spkr. Outlook on Health Women's Health Advocates Award Ceremony, Cin., 1999. Author: Jump Now, Look Later: New Ways to Beat YOUR Fears, 1998, Wanna Self-Publish? Here's How, 2000, Thank You, Nicole, 1998, (audio tape) Conquer Procrastination: Jump Now to Accomplish What You REALLY Want, 1999; author: (with others) Sisters Together, 1998, Exceptional Accomplishment, 2000; co-author: (audio tape) Interview with a Survivor: Reclaim Your Life after Abuse, 1998, (audio tape) Abused No More: A Survivor's Story of Courage, 2001. Organizer/facilitator St. Hilary Ch. Divorced/Separated Group, Mathews, La., 1994-95; trustee Leadership Lafourche, Lafourche Parish, La., 1994-97, edn. curriculum com. chair, 1994—2001, mem. alumni, 1994—; mem. Team Cmty. Lafourche, Lafourche Parish, 1995-2002; mem. edn. com. Bayou Vision, Seven Parish Bayou/River Region, La., 1995—; bd. mem. Am. Cancer Soc., Lafourche Parish, 1995-2001, chair Live a Life of Victory Event, 1998—2001, regional v.p., 1999-2001; mem. transitional task force Lafourche Parish Sch. Bd., Thibodaux, La., 1997-98; mem. tech. task force South La. Econ. Coun., Seven Parish Bayou/River Region, 1997-98; v.i.p. Cerebral Palsy Telethon, Lafourche Parish, 1997-98; bd. mem. Chez Hope, Lafourche/St. Mary/Terrebonne/Assumption Parish, 1998-2000; quality assurance steering com. Office Women's Violence, 2006—; developer Cellular Phone Program for Domestic Violence Victims, Lafourche Parish, 1999; steering com., Maria Immacolata Ch., Houma, La., 2002-2004, ch. lector, 2005—; mem. Leadership Lafourche, 1994, Leadership La., 1999, Leadership Terrebonne, 2003; bd. dirs. Bayou Indsl. Group, 2006—. Mem. Nat. Spkrs. Assn. (bd. dirs. New Orleans chpt., chair membership directory 1998-99, Katrina spokesperson found. video 2006), Small Pubs. Assn. N.Am., Ind. Conss. Group, Bayou Indsl. Group, Chamber of Lafourche and the Bayou Region (amb. 1995-2000, edn. com./cmty. devel. com. 1994-2000, Amb. of Yr. 1995), Baton Rouge Area Chamber, Thibodaux C. of C. Roman Catholic. Office: Success NOW! 6033 Courtyard Dr Gonzales LA 70737 Office Phone: 877-586-7669. Business E-Mail: carol@jumpnow.com.

PIERCE, CATHERINE MAYNARD, history educator; b. York County, Va., Oct. 11, 1918; d. Edward Walker Jr. and Cassie Cooke (Sheppard) Maynard; m. Frank Marion Pierce Jr., Oct. 4, 1940 (dec. 1974); children: Frank Marion III, Bruce Maynard. BS in Sec. Edn., Longwood Coll., Farmville, Va., 1939; postgrad., Coll. William and Mary, Williamsburg, 1948, 58, 68. Tchr. York County Pub. Schs., Va., 1939-45; instr. Chesapeake (Va.) pub. schs., 1946-49, 57-74; cons. Vol. Svcs., Williamsburg, Va., 1975—. Author audio-visual hist. narratives for use in pub. schs., 1965-86. Organizer The Chapel at Kingsmill on the James, Williamsburg, 1987—, chmn. governing bd., 1987-97. Mem. DAR (regent Williamsburg chpt. 1980-83). Baptist. Avocations: antiques, genealogy, historic research. Home: 18 Jacobs Mill Ct Elgin SC 29045-8646

PIERCE, DEBORAH MARY, educational administrator; b. Charleston, W. Va. d. Edward Ernest and Elizabeth Anne (Trent) P.; m. Henry M. Armetta, Sept. 1, 1967 (div. 1981); children: Rosse Matthew Armetta, Stacey Elizabeth Pierce. Student, U. Tenn., 1956-59, Broward Jr. Coll., 1968-69; BA, San Francisco State U., 1977. Cert. elem. tchr., Calif. Pub. relations assoc. San Francisco Internat. Film Festival, 1965-66; account exec. Stover & Assocs., San Francisco, 1966-67; tchr. San Francisco Archdiocese Office of Cath. Schs., 1980-87; part-time tchr. The Calif. Study, Inc. (formerly Tchr's. Registry), Tiburon, Calif., 1988—; pvt. practice as paralegal San Francisco, 1989—; tchr. Jefferson Sch. Dist., Daly City, Calif., 1989-91. Author: (with Frances Spatz Leighton) I Prayed Myself Slim, 1960. Pres. Mothers Alone Working, San Francisco, 1966, PTA, San Francisco, 1979, Parent Tchr. Student Assn., San Francisco, 1984; apptd. Calif. State Bd. Welfare Cmty. Rels. Com., 1964-66; block organizer SAFE, 1996; regional dir. South San Francisco Parents TV Coun.; advocate Calif. State Lobby Day, Am. Heart Assn., 2005; neighborhood coord. San Francisco; active feminist movement. Named Model of the Yr. Modeling Assn. Am., 1962. Mem. People Med. Soc., Am. Assn. Univ. Women, Assn. for Rsch. and Enlightenment, A Course in Miracles, Commonwealth Club Calif, Angel Club San Francisco, San Diego Chat Club, Deepak Chopra 7 Spiritual Laws Group, San Francisco Bicycle Coalition. Mem. Unity Christ Ch. Avocation: chess. Address: 1686 34th Ave San Francisco CA 94122-3115 Personal E-mail: deborahkry@juno.com.

PIERCE, DIANNE S., city clerk; b. Hertford, N.C., Nov. 4, 1945; d. Delmar and Mae Curlings Spear; m. William Edward Pierce, June 27, 1964; children: William Mark, Charles David. AAS, Coll. of the Albemarle, 1976. Office mgr. Hertford Frame, Inc., 1973-75; adminstrv. asst. Albemarle Law & Order, Elizabeth City, N.C., 1975-80; adminstrv. sec. City of Elizabeth City, 1980-86, city clk., 1986—; owner, operator Black Gold Express, Inc., Elizabeth City, 1993—. Founding mem. Elizabeth City Teen Svcs. Ctr., 1994-99, dir., 1996-99; active N.C. Transp. Pub. Safety, Raleigh, 1995-97, Mayor's Adv. Bd., Elizabeth City, 1995-97. Mem. Internat. Inst. Mcpl. Clks. (cert. mcpl. clk. 1989, advance acad. edn. 1996, first sustaining edn. 1999, master mcpl. clk., 2003), N.C. Assn. Mcpl. Clks. (dir. 1996-99). Democrat. Baptist. Avocations: reading, travel, tennis, dance. Home: 125 Nancy Dr Elizabeth City NC 27909-9247 Office: City of Elizabeth City 306 E Colonial Ave Elizabeth City NC 27909-4306 also: PO Box 347 Elizabeth City NC 27907-0347

PIERCE, HILDA (HILDA HERTA HARMEL), painter; b. Vienna; arrived in U.S., 1940; m. Herman J. Slutzky; 1 child, Diana Rubin Daly (dec.). Student, Art Inst. Chgo.; studied with Oskar Kokoschka, Salzburg, Austria. Art tchr. Highland Park (Ill.) Art Ctr., Sandburg Village Art Workshop, Chgo., Old Town Art Ctr., Chgo.; owner, operator Hilda Pierce Art Gallery, Laguna Beach, Calif., 1981-85. Guest lectr. maj. art mus. and art tours, Carribean cruises South America, Argentina, Brazil, France, Switzerland, Austria, Italy, Mex., San Diego, China, India, 1998—2002, Russian river cruise and major art mus., St. Petersburg, Moscow, 1994; lectr., Mexico, 1994—2006, U. Calif. Geisel Libr., San Diego, 2003; founder, chmn. Art Encounters, San Diego. One-woman shows include Fairweather Hardin Gallery, Chgo., Sherman Art Gallery, Marshall Field Gallery, exhibited in group shows at Old Orchard Art Festival, Skokie, Ill., Union League Club, Chgo., North Shore Art League, Winnetka, Ill., Art Inst. Chgo., Represented in permanent collections U. Calif. San Diego Art Libr., La Jolla, Carnival Cruise Lines megaliner M.S. Fantasy, megaliner M.S. Imagination, Rebecca and John Moores Cancer Ctr., U. Calif. San Diego, U. Calif. San Diego Geisel Libr.; featured (video) Survivors of the Shoah, Stephen Spielberg Found., 1996; author: A Painting of my Life, 2006; contbr. articles to profl. jours. and newspapers. Recipient Outstanding Achievement in Art award, Chgo. Immigrants Svc. League, 1964. Office Phone: 858-558-7556.

PIERCE, JANIS VAUGHN, insurance executive, consultant; b. Memphis, Dec. 23, 1934; d. Jesse Wynne and Dorothy Arnette (Lloyd) Vaughn; m. Gerald Swetman Pierce, May 27, 1956; children: Ann Elizabeth Swetman, John Willard. BA, U. Miss., 1956, MA, 1964. High sch. tchr., 1957-58; mem. faculty Memphis Univ. Sch., 1965-66, Memphis State U., 1968-75; agent Aetna Life Ins. Co., Memphis, 1977-80, career supr., 1980—, mgr., 1983, supr. prime, career, 1984, chmn. Aetna Women's Task Force, 1980-85; coord. agency tng. specialist Union Ctr. Life Ins. Co., Memphis, 1985-88; agent, v.p., dir., bus. cons. Cons. Sys., Inc., 1975-84, pres., 1984—. Pres. Women's Resource Ctr., Memphis, 1974-77; sec. Tenn. chpt. Women's Polit. Caucus, 1975-76; bd. dirs., treas., mem. exec. com. Memphis YMCA, 1979—; mem. bd. commr. Memphis Area Trans Auth., 1982—; chmn. fin., adminstrn. com., 1983—, chmn. bd. commn., 1990—; pres., bd. dirs. The Support Ctr., Memphis, 1986-87, Supprt Ctrs. Am., 1987—; mem. Tenn. adv. com. U.S. Civil Rights Commn., 1980-85, steering com. Big Break, 1978; mem. adv. bd. Porter Leath Children's Ctr., 1984—, bd. dirs., 1986—; mem. planned giving com. Girl Scouts U.S., 1990—; mem. citizens adv. bd. St. Joseph Hosp., 1991—; mem. Leadership Memphis, 1981. Univ. scholar U. Miss., 1952-56. Mem. AAUW, LWV, United Daus. Confederacy (pres. Albert Sidney Johnson chpt. 1961), Women Leaders Roundtable, Nat. Assn. Life Underwriters, Tenn. Life Underwriters Assn., Am. Pub. Transp. Assn. (bd. dirs. 1991—, gov. bds. com. 1985—, sec. 1987-88, v.p. 1988-90, mem. task force transp. handicapped 1987, pres. 1989, legis. com. 1985—, region III rep. 1991—), Women's Life Underwriters Conf. (bd. dirs., pres. 1985), Memphis Life Underwriters Assn. (bd. dirs. 1982, edn. chmn. 1982, pub. svc. com. 1983, law and legis. chmn. 1984, pres. 1986), Memphis PTA (coun. 1971-72), Memphis Soc. CLUs, Mortar Bd. (regional coord. 1972-78), Memphis CLU Assn., C. of C. (ambassador 1980), Alpha Lambda Delta, Sigma Delta Pi, Le Bonheur Club (bd. dirs.), Memphis State U. Women's Club (pres. 1978). Episcopalian. Republican. Home: 1613 Lyttleton St Camden SC 29020-2906

PIERCE, KACY JONES, assistant principal; b. Birmingham, Ala., Nov. 6, 1954; d. E.A. Casey and Betty Jean Jones; m. George Bradford Pierce, May 6, 1978; children: Elizabeth Ali, Amy Pierce Kirkpatrick, Adam Bradford. BS, U. Ala., Birmingham, 1989, MA, 1998; EdS, Samford U., Birmingham, 2006; BA, Auburn U., 1977. Classroom tchr. Phillips H.S., Birmingham, 1991—98, Louis Pizitz Mid. Sch., Vestavia Hills, Ala., 1998—2003, asst. prin. for curriculum, 2003—. Cons. So. Ctr. for World History, Atlanta, 1993—2000; adj. prof. U. Ala., Birmingham. Office: Louis Pizitz Mid Sch 2020 Pizitz Dr Vestavia Hills AL 35321 Office Phone: 205-402-6356. Office Fax: 205-402-5354. Business E-Mail: piercekj@vestavia.k12.al.us.

PIERCE, LINDA ANN, nurse; b. Middletown, N.Y., Aug. 28, 1958; d. Lenzia R. and Margaret Louise (Waller) Nowlin; divorced; children: Thomas Anthony III, Tiffany Morelle; m. Ron Pierce, May 14, 2005 (dec. May 14, 2005). AAS in Nursing, Sullivan County C.C., 1989. RN, N.Y.; cert. med.-surg. nurse ANCC. Nurse Office of Health Systems Mgmt. Continuing Care Program N.Y. State Dept. Health, 1984—; staff nurse Columbia Presbyn. Med. Ctr., N.Y.C., 1989-91, N.Y. Hosp. Cornell Med. Ctr., Westchester div., White Plains, N.Y., 1991-93, N.Y. State Dept. Health-Office of Health Systems Mgmt., 1994—. V.p. Nurses' Club, Sullivan County C.C., Loch Sheldrake, N.Y., 1987-89. Mem. N.Y. State Nurses' Assn., Phi Theta Kappa. Avocations: reading, writing, poetry, travel. E-mail: 07@health.state.ny.us, Linwil@webtv.net.

PIERCE, LISA MARGARET, telecommunications industry executive, marketing professional, educator; b. Nyack, NY, June 2, 1957; d. William and Elizabeth Pierce. BA with honors, Gordon Coll., Wenham, Mass., 1978; MBA, Atkinson Sch., Salem, Oreg., 1982. Campaign mgr. Carter/Mondale, Manchester, Mass., 1976; investigator Dept. Social Svcs., Nyack, 1977-78; paralegal Beverly, Mass., 1978-79; campaign mgr. Reagan Presdl. Primary, Rockland County, NY, 1980; cons. Sidereal, Portland, Oreg., 1981-82; performance analyst Dept. Social Svcs., Pomona, NY, 1982; market analyst Momentum Techs., Parsippany, NJ, 1983; cons. Booz Allen & Hamilton, Florham Park, NJ, 1984, Deloitte-Touche, Morristown, NJ, 1985; market rschr., forecaster AT&T, Bedminster, NJ, 1985-87, asst. pvt. line product mgr., 1987-89, Integrated Svcs. Digital Network product mgr., 1989-93; dir. Telecom. Rsch. Assocs., St. Marys, Kans., 1994-98; v.p., rsch. fellow Giga Info. Group/Forrester Rsch., Cambridge, Mass., 1998—. Panelist, contbr. TeleCom. Assn., San Diego and Seattle, Internat. Comm. Assn., Atlanta, Ea. Comm. Forum, NY, Nat. Engring. Consortium, Chgo., Super Comm., Soc. Telecom. Consultants, MPLS Forum, Mid Atlantic Venture Assn., GSA Fed. Telecom. Svc. Forums, VoiceCon, EVDO Forum, others; contbr. NY State ISDN/Internat User's Group; feature commentator AP Adio, Nat. Pub. Radio (All Things Considered and MarketWatch), Pub. Broadcasting Svc. Nightly Bus. Report, MSNBC, CNN and CNBC, Radio Wall Street, CBS Evening News Columnist Network World, 2001—02, Bus. Comm. Rev., 2002—. Named one of Top 10 Most Influential IT Analysts, Tech. Mktg. Mag., 2002, 2003; grantee in field. Mem.: IEEE. Personal E-mail: lmpierce@att.net. Business E-Mail: lpierce@forrester.com.

PIERCE, LONNA MCKEON, school librarian; b. Binghamton, N.Y., May 16, 1953; d. Bruno T. and Mary L. Suchowiecki; m. David Paul Pierce, Oct. 17, 1998; children from previous marriage: Anthony McKeon, Finian McKeon, Brendan McKeon, Aria McKeon, Dylan McKeon. BS Edn. summa cum laude, SUNY Oneonta, 1975; postgrad., Hockerill Coll., Bishops Storfford, UK, 1975, SUNY Binghamton, 1981; MLS, Mansfield U., Pa., 2004. Cert. permanent lic. elem. edn. and sch. libr. N.Y. Tchr. elem. Binghamton City Sch. Dist., 1975—77, sch. libr., 2001—, Blessed Sacrament Sch., Johnson City, NY, 1984—90. Profl. storyteller N.Y. State BOCES, Young Artists Rochester, 1990—. Singer (storyteller): A Visit with Laura Ingalls Wilder, 1990—, Baba's Trunk, 1990—, Folktales Around the World, 1990—. Host French visitors La Teste Sister Cities Orgn., Binghamton, 1995—. Mem.: ALA, Sch. Librs. of So. tier (co-pres. 2004—07), N.Y. Sch. Music Assn. (vocal adjudicator 1990—), Am. Assn. Sch. Librs. Episcopalian. Avocations: acting, singing, reading, embroidery. Home: 2 Eland Dr Apalachin NY 13732 Office: MacArthur Elem Sch 1123 Vestal Ave Binghamton NY 13903

PIERCE, MARIAN MARIE, writer, educator; b. Cleve., Mar. 7, 1959; d. William Moses and Thelma Lee Pierce. BA, U. Iowa, 1981, MFA, 1996. Creative writing instr. Marylhurst (Oreg.) U., 1999—, UCLA Ext. Writer's Program, 2000—. Author short stories. Named Frederick Exley Fiction Competition Winner, GQ mag., 1995; Lit. Arts grantee, 2004, Paul Engle fellow, The Iowa Writers' Workshop, 1996—97, MacDowell Colony fellow, 1997. Personal E-mail: marian.pierce@juno.com.

PIERCE, MARY, professional tennis player; b. Montreal, Que., Can., Jan. 15, 1975; d. Jim and Yannick Pierce. Profl. Tennis Player, 1989—. Victories include Comeback Player of the Yr., 1997, Australian Open (singles), 1995, French Open (singles & doubles), 2000, Wimbledon (doubles), 2005; 17 WTA Career Singles Titles, 10 WTA Career Doubles Titles. Office: IMG Ctr 1360 E 9th St Ste 100 Cleveland OH 44114

PIERCE, MARY E., retired elementary school educator, public relations consultant; b. Chgo. d. Henry Harris and Eva Irene (Hanes) P. BE, Chgo. Tchrs. Coll., 1944. One room sch. tchr. Will County, Monee, Ill.; tchr. 5th grade Peotone (Ill.) Sch. Dist.; tchr. elem. and jr. h.s. Steger (Ill.) Sch. Dist., chair lang. arts dept.; ret., 1979; chair sch. improvement plan; pub. rels. cons. Former pres. Steger Edn. Assn.; chmn. bd. dirs. #194 Employee Credit Union, Steger, 1972-95. Village clk. Village of Richton Park, 1992—; pres. Friends of Libr., Richton Park, 1980-2005, v.p.; bd. dirs. So. Suburban Cancer Soc., Tinley Pk., Ill., 1994—, S.E. Chpt. Ill. Credit Union, Calumet City, Ill., 1994-95. Recipient Cmty. Svc. award Cook County Sheriff's Office, Chgo., Merit award S.E. chpt. Ill. Credit Union League. Mem. Delta Kappa Gamma Soc. (Lambda State Beta Beta chpt. treas. 1979-2003). Avocation: golf. Home: 22147 Karlov Ave Richton Park IL 60471-1227

PIERCE, PATRICIA ANN, university administrator; b. Harriman, Tenn., Feb. 13, 1949; d. Fred Ernest and Lela Nora (Jones) P.; m. Jacky Albert Goss, Sept. 21, 1991; children: Wesley Matthew Goss, James Michael Goss. BS, U. Tenn., 1973; cert., Bryn Mawr Coll., 1991. Cert. secondary edn. tchr., Tenn.; cert. diversity trainer. Field rep. Tenn. Human Rights Commn., Nashville, 1973-76, compliance dir., 1976-78; assoc. dir.Opportunity Devel. Ctr. Vanderbilt U., Nashville, 1978-81, dir., 1981—. Cons. Pierce Consulting, Nashville, 1985—; presenter in field. Contbr. articles to profl. jours. Chairperson Mayor's Adv. Com. for People with Disabilities, Nashville, 1988-89; pres. bd. dirs. League for Hearing Impaired, Nashville, 1994-95, Nashville YWCA, 1996-98; spkr. Nat. Intramural Recreation Sports Assn., Nashville, 1994; del. People to People Internat. Learning Disability Del., Beijing, 1995; nongovtl. rep. NGO Forum, 4th World Conf. on Women, Beijing, 1995; People to People Internat. del. to Cuba, 2003; active Gov. Adv. Com. on Equal Employment Opportunity, 1992-96; mem. Leadership Nashville, 2003; commr. Tenn. Human Rights Commn., 2005—; bd. dirs. Internat. Athena, 2004—. Recipient Jean Harris award Rotary 1998, Mary Jane Werthern award Vanderbilt 1997, Nashville ATHENA award, 2003; named to Leadership America 2000; inducted in Acad. of Women of Achievement, 2002. Mem.: Women in Higher Edn. in Tenn. (historian 1999—, pres.), CABLE Profl. Womens Networking Orgn. (pres. 1991—92, historian 2000—, Promote Women award 1993), Am. Coun. Edn. (state facilitator 1994—95, bd. mem. 1994—, mem. Tenn. planning com., Outstandging Contbns. cert. 1995), Internat. Assn. Higher Edn. and Disability (pres. 1988—89, Ronald Blosser Dedicated Svc. award 1989), Women's Polit. Caucus (v.p. 2001—02), Women in Numbers (bd. mem. 2000—, pres. 2003). Avocations: hiking, tennis, photography. Home: 954 Caney Creek Rd Harriman TN 37748 Office: Vanderbilt U VU Station B 351809 Nashville TN 37235-1809 E-mail: patricia.a.pierce@vanderblit.edu.

PIERCE, PONCHITTA ANN, TV host, television producer, journalist, writer, consultant; b. Chgo., Aug. 5, 1942; d. Alfred Leonard and Nora (Vincent) P. Student, Cambridge U., Eng., summer 1962; BA in Journalism cum laude, U. So. Calif., 1964; DHL, Franklin Pierce Coll., 1986. Asst. editor Ebony mag., 1964-65, assoc. editor, 1965-67; editor Ebony mag. (N.Y.C. office), 1967-68; chief N.Y.C. editl. bur. Johnson Pub. Co., 1967-68; corr. news divsn. CBS, N.Y.C., 1968-71; contbg. editor McCall's mag., 1971-77; editl. cons. Philps Stokes Fund, 1971-78; staff writer Reader's Digest, 1976-77, roving editor, 1977-80; co-prodr., host Today in New York, Sta. WNBC-TV, N.Y.C., 1982-87; freelance writer, TV broadcaster, media cons. Co-host Sunday WNBC-TV, 1973—77, The Prime of Your Life, 1977—80; author: Status of American Women Journalists on Magazines, 1968, History of the Phelps Stokes Fund 1911-1972; contbg. editor: Earth Times Monthly, 2002. Del. to WHO Conf., Geneva, 1973; bd. dirs. Morris-Jumel Mansion, Housing Enterprise for the Less Privileged, Third St. Music Sch. Settlement, Inner-City Scholarship Fund, Josephson Inst. Ethics, Marina del Rey, Sta. WNET-TV; active Columbia Presbyn. Health Scis. Adv. Coun.; bd. dirs. U. So. Calif. Ctr. on Pub. Diplomacy, Cuban Artists Fund Recipient Penney-Mo. mag. award excellence women's journalism, 1967; John Russwurm award NYC Urban League, 1968; AMITA Nat. Achievement award in comm., 1974 Mem. NATAS, Women in Comm. (Woman Behind the News award 1969, Nat. Headliner award 1970), Fgn. Policy Assn. (mem. bd. govs., bd. dirs.), Women's Fgn. Policy Group, Coun. on Fgn. Rels., Calif. Scholarship Fedn. (life), Econs. Club N.Y., Lotos Club, Nat. Honor Soc., Mortar Bd.

PIERCE, SHAHEEDA LAURA, nurse midwife, consultant; b. Jersey City, Apr. 13, 1959; d. Lawrence Everett Pierce and Mary Dean Applegate Swing; m. James Shuffield, May 28, 1994; children: Juniper, Rama, Jasmine, Elijah, Jamila, Tara. AAS, Pima Coll., 1984. Cert. paralegal, cmty. meditation svcs., dance leader Dances Universal Peace; cert. profl. midwife. Pvt. practice mediation and paralegal svcs., Tucson, 1991—95, Maui, Hawaii, 1995-96, Tucson, 1996—98, Silver City, N.Mex., 1998-99, Vashon Island, Wash., 1999—. Nat. coord. group Movement For A New Soc., Phila., 1982-83; bd. dirs. Food Conspiracy Cooperative, Tucson, 1993-95; steering com. S.W. Sufi Cmty., Silver City, 1994-95, bd. dirs., 1995-97; mem. faculty adv. bd. Nat. Coll. Midwifery, 2002—; midwife, holistic health cons.; preceptor Birthingway Coll. Midwifery, 2005—. Author: Recipes for the New Children, 1978; contbr. articles to profl. jours.; creator (bd. game) The Healing Game of Life, 1993; composer (musical album on cassette) Full Moon Woman, 1994; co-coord., disc jockey weekly women's radio program KXCI Cmty. Radio, Tucson, 1983. Active Georgians Against Nuc. Energy, Atlanta, 1980-81; organizer Nuc. Free State, Tucson, 1981-82; draft counselor Daring Disarmers, Phila., 1982; vice-chair heavy metals remediation com. Vashon Maury Island Cmty. Coun., 2003, co-chair, 2004. Recipient Ordinary Extraordinary Women's award, 1982. Mem. N.Mex. Midwives Assn., Ariz. Assn. Midwives (co-coord. AHCCCS reimbursement task force 1997-98), Midwives' Alliance Hawaii, Washington Alliance Rural Midwives. Avocations: art, music, dance, nature. Office Phone: 206-463-6246.

PIERCE, SHAYN, biomedical engineer, educator; PhD in Biomedical Engring., U. Va., 2002. Asst. prof. biomedical enging. U. Va. Contbr. articles to profl. jours. Named one of Top 100 Young Innovators, MIT Tech. Review, 2004; recipient Rita Shaffer Young Investigator award, Biomedical Engring. Soc., 2004. Office: U Va Dept Biomedical Engring Box 800759 Health System Rm 2324 Charlottesville VA 22908

PIERCE, SUE, sales executive; b. Shawano, Wis., Oct. 6, 1953; d. Virginia Anne and William Harry Pierce. Student, U. Wis., Superior, 1976—92; grad., Sgt. Maj. Acad., Ft. Bliss, Tex., 1990. Staff sgt. U.S. Army, Ft. McClellan, Ala., 1971—78; sgt. 1st class Ohio Army N.G., Toledo, 1979—83; sales rep. Steam Economies Co., Toledo, 1983—86, Douglas Steam Splty., Menasha, Wis., 1986—90; sales engr. Hercules, Inc., Appleton, Wis., 1990—92; regional sales mgr. Kadant-Johnson Inc., Three Rivers, Mich., 1993—. Budget com. chair U.S. Army Women's Mus. Found., Ft. Lee, Va., 2002—03. Command sgt. maj. USAR, 1971—98. Decorated Legion Of Merit U.S. Army. Mem.: Tech. Assn. of Pulp and Paper Industry (sec. 2002—03). Avocations: travel, water sports, golf. Office: Kadant Johnson Inc 805 Wood St Three Rivers MI 49094 Home: PO Box 1027 Whitehouse TX 75791-1027 Office Phone: 312-961-8169. Personal E-mail: sue.pierce@kadantjohnson.com.

PIERCE, SUSAN RESNECK, academic administrator, literature educator, consultant; b. Janesville, Wis., Feb. 6, 1943; d. Elliott Jack and Dory (Block) Resneck; m. Kenneth H. Pierce; 1 child, Alexandra Siegel. BA, Wellesley Coll., 1965; MA, U. Chgo., 1966; PhD, U. Wis., 1972. Lectr. U. Wis., Rock County, 1970-71; from asst. prof. to prof. English Ithaca (N.Y.) Coll., 1973-82, chmn. dept., 1976-79; program officer Nat. Endowment for Humanities, 1982-83, asst. dir., 1983-84; dean Henry Kendall Coll. Arts and Scis. U. Tulsa, 1984-90; v.p. acad. affairs, prof. English Lewis and Clark Coll., Portland, Oreg., 1990-92; pres. U. Puget Sound, Tacoma, 1992—2003, Boca Raton Comty. Hosp. Found., 2004—05; pvt. practice, 2005—. Vis. assoc. prof. Princeton (N.J.) U., 1979; bd. dirs. Janet Elson Scholarship Fund, 1984-1990, Tulsa Edn. Fund, Phillips Petroleum Scholarship Fund, 1985-90, Okla. Math. & Sci. High Sch., 1984-90, Hillcrest Med. Ctr., 1988-90, Portland Opera, 1990-92, St. Joseph's Hosp., 1992—, Seattle Symphony, 1993—; cons. U. Oreg., 1985, Drury Coll., Springfield, Mo., 1986; mem. Middle States and N. Cen. Accreditation Bds.; mem. adv. com. Fed. Women's Program, NEH, 1982-83; participant Summit Meeting on Higher Edn., Dept. Edn., Washington, 1985; speaker, participant numerous ednl. meetings, sems., commencements; chair Frederick Ness Book Award Com. Assn. Am. Colls., 1986; mem. award selection com. Dana Found., 1986, 87; mem. Acad. Affairs Council, Univ. Senate, dir. tchr. edn., chmn. adv. group for tchr. preparation, ex-officio mem. all Coll. Arts and Scis. coms. and Faculty Council on Internat. Studies, all U. Tulsa; bd. dirs. Am. Conf. Acad. Deans; bd. trustees Hillcrest Med. Ctr.; participant Aspen Inst. Md. 1999, Annapolis Group Media Roundtable, 1996, Harvard Seminar, 1992; former bd. dirs. Assn. Am. Colls. and Univs., 1989-92, Am. Conf. of Academic Deans, 1988-91, Am. Assn. Colls., 1989-92. Author: The Moral of the Story, 1982, also numerous essays, jour. articles, book sects., book revs.; co-editor: Approaches to Teaching "Invisible Man"; reader profl. jours. Bd. dirs. Arts and Humanities Coun., Tulsa, 1984-90, Mizener Pk., 2004-; trustee Hillcrest Hosp., Tulsa, 1986-90; mem. cultural series com., community rels. com. Jewish Fedn., Tulsa, 1986-90; bd. dirs. Tulsa chpt. NCCJ, 1986-90, Kemper Mus. 1996—, Seattle Symphony, 1993-96, St. Joseph Hosp., 1992-93, Portland Opera, 1990-92. Recipient Best Essay award Arix. Quar., 1979, Excellence in Teaching award N.Y. State Edn. Council, 1982, Superior Group Service award NEH, 1984, other teaching awards; Dana scholar, Ithaca Coll., 1980-81; Dana Research fellow, Ithaca Coll., 82-83; grantee Inst. for Ednl. Affairs, 1980, Ford Found., 1987, NEH, 1989. Mem. MLA (adv. com. on job market 1973-74), South Ctrl. MLA, NIH (subcom. on college drinking), Assn. Governing Bds. (coun. of pres.), Nat. Inst. on Alcohol Abuse (presl. advisory group), Soc. for Values in Higher Edn., Assn. Am. Colls. (bd. dirs.), Am. Conf. Acad. Deans (bd. dirs. 1988-91), Coun. of Presidents, Assn. Governing Bds., The Annapolis Group (mem. exec. com.), Phi Beta Kappa, Phi Kappa Phi, Phi Gamma Kappa. Office Phone: 561-212-5103. Business E-Mail: srpconsulting@adelphia.net.

PIERCE, TERRY JO, medical/surgical nurse; b. Winchester, Ind., Dec. 31, 1953; d. Kenneth Eugene and Ilene Marie (Ward) Heltzel; children: Amy Jo, J. Aaron; m. Johnny R. Pierce, Apr. 29, 1995. Cert., Ivy Tech., Richmond, Ind., 1983. LPN, Ind. Nursing asst. Henry County Meml. Hosp., New Castle, Ind., 1982-84; charge nurse Heritage House Convalescent Ctr., New Castle, 1984-89; office nurse, lab. technician McAllister and Meeks Family Practice, New Castle, 1989—2003, Samantha Meeks Family Practice, Inc., New Castle, 2003—. Mem.: Am. Assn. Office Nursing. Home: 2852 E US Highway 40 Lewisville IN 47352-9730 Office: Samantha Meeks Family Practice Inc 3221 S Memorial Dr New Castle IN 47362-1123

PIERCE, THRESIA KORTE (TISH PIERCE), primary school educator; b. Maize, Kans. d. Herman and Marie Adeline (Lubbers) Korte; children: Judith, John, Mark. BS, Friends U., 1955; MS, U. Nev., Las Vegas, 1978. Cert. tchr., Nev., Nev. Life Ins. lic. Office worker Internat. Trust Co., Denver, Colo., 1951, Motor Equipment Co., Wichita, Kans., 1952-53; tchr. Wichita Pub. Schs., 1960-69, Clark County Sch. Dist., Las Vegas, Nev., 1970-2000. Author short stories; contbr. articles to profl. jours. Senator Clark County Edn. Assn., Clark County Classroom Tchrs. Nominee Wichita Women of Yr., 1967. Mem. NEA, Epsilon Sigma Delta (v.p. 1962). bd. dirs. Kansas Newman U., Wichita, 1966-68. Home: Bldg 6 Unit 1106 1600 S Valley View Blvd Las Vegas NV 89102-0547

PIERCE, V. RENEE, music educator; d. Oscar Rudolph and Wylodine Glass; m. D. Thomas Pierce, Aug. 18, 1973; children: Adam, Dustin, Alison. MusB in Edn., U. Montevallo, 1975. Cert. tchr. Tex., Ala. Pvt. piano instr., Oneonta, Ala., 1991—95; elem. music tchr. Pky. Christian Acad., Birmingham, Ala., 1995—98; music assoc. First Bapt. Ch., Boaz, Ala., 1998—; choral dir. Boaz H.S., Boaz, Ala., 2000—. Dir. Young Musician Choir, Boaz, 1998—; pianist First Bapt. Ch., Boaz. Vol. Oneonta City Sch., 1983—98. Mem.: Music Educators Nat. Conf., Ala. Singing Women. Baptist. Avocations: travel, home projects, gardening. Office: Boaz HS 907 Brown St Boaz AL 35957 Office Phone: 256-593-2401. Personal E-mail: tommypierce@bellsouth.net. Business E-Mail: rpierce@boazk12.org.

PIERCY, MARGE, poet, writer; b. Detroit, Mar. 31, 1936; d. Robert Douglas and Bert Bernice (Bunnin) Piercy; m. Ira Wood, 1982. AB, U. Mich., 1957; MA, Northwestern U., 1958; DHL (hon.), Hebrew Union Coll., 2004, Union Coll., 2004, Eastern Conn. State U., 2005. Instr. Gary ext. Ind. U., 1960—62; poet-in-residence U. Kans., 1971; disting. vis. lectr. Thomas Jefferson Coll., Grand Valley State Colls., 1975, 1976, 1978, 1980; vis. faculty Women's Writers Conf., Cazenovia Coll., NY; Elliston poetry fellow U. Cin., 1986. DeRoy Disting. vis. prof. U. Mich., 1992; editor Leapfrog Press, 1997—; poetry editor Lillith, 1999—; fiction editor Seattle Rev., 2003—. Author: Breaking Camp, 1968, Hard Loving, 1969, Going Down Fast, 1969, Dance the Eagle to Sleep, 1970, Small Changes, 1973, To Be of Use, 1973, Living in the Open, 1976, Woman on the Edge of Time, 1976, The High Cost of Living, 1978, Vida, 1980, The Moon is Always Female, 1980, Braided Lives, 1982, Circles on the Water, 1982, Stone, Paper, Knife, 1983, My Mother's Body, 1985, Gone to Soldiers, 1988, Available Light, 1988 (May Sarton award 1991), Summer People, 1989, He, She and It, 1991, Body of Glass, 1991 (Arthur C. Clarke award 1993), Mars and Her Children, 1992, The Longings of Women, 1994, Eight Chambers of the Heart, 1995, City of Darkness, City of Light, 1996, What Are Big Girls Made Of?, 1997 (Notable Book award ALA 1997), Storm Tide, 1998, The Art of Blessing the Day, 1999, Early Grrrl, 1999, Three Women, 1999, Sleeping With Cats, A Memoir, 2002, expanded edit., 2005, Colors Passing Through Us, 2003, Third Child, 2003, Sex Wars: A Novel of the Turbulent Post-Civil War Period, 2005; co-author: (with Ira Wood) So You Want to Write: How to Master the Craft of Writing Fiction and the Personal Narrative, 2001, 2d edit., 2005; (CD) Louder: We Can't Heed You Yet, 2004; author of poetry (16 vols.). Cons. N.Y. State Coun. on Arts, 1971, Mass. Found. for Humanities and Coun. on Arts, 1974; mem. Writer Bd., 1985-86; bd. dirs. Transition House, Mass. Found. Humanities and Pub. Policy, 1978-85, Am. ha-Yam, 1988-98, v.p., 1995-96; gov.'s appointee to Mass. Cultural Coun., 1990-91, Mass. Coun. on Arts and Humanities, 1986-89; artistic adv. bd. ALEPH Alliance for Jewish Renewal, Am. Poetry Ctr., 1988—; lit. adv. panel poetry NEA, 1989; mem. adv. bd. Carrie A. Seaman Animal Shelter. Recipient Borenstone Mountain Poetry award, 1968, 74, Lit. award Gov. Mass. Commn. on Status of Women, 1974, Nat. Endowment of Arts award, 1978, Carolyn Kizer Poetry prize, 1986, 90, Shaeffer-Eaton-PEN New Eng. award, 1989, Golden Rose Poetry prize, 1990, Brit ha-Dorot award The Shalom Ctr., 1992, Notable Book award, 1997, Paterson poetry prize, 2000. Mem.: NOW, PEN, Am. Poetry Soc., Nat. Writers Union, Authors League, Authors Guild, Citizens for the Preservation of Wellfleet, Mass. Audubon Soc., New Eng. Poetry Club. Address: PO Box 1473 Wellfleet MA 02667-1473 Personal E-mail: hagolem@c4.net.

PIERIK, MARILYN ANNE, retired librarian, piano teacher; b. Bellingham, Wash., Nov. 12, 1939; d. Estell Leslie and Anna Margarethe (Onigkeit) Bowers; m. Robert Vincent Pierik, July 25, 1964; children: David Vincent, Donald Lesley. AA, Chaffey Jr. Coll., Ontario, Calif., 1959; BA, Upland (Calif.) Coll., 1962; cert. in teaching, Claremont (Calif.) Coll., 1963; MSLS, U. So. Calif., L.A., 1973. Tchr. elem. Christ Episcopal Day Sch., Ontario, 1959-60; tchr. Bonita High Sch., La Verne, Calif., 1962-63; tchr., libr. Kettle Valley Sch. Dist. 14, Greenwood, Can., 1963-64; libr. asst. Monrovia (Calif.) Pub. Libr., 1964-67; with Mt. Hood C.C., Gresham, Oreg., 1972-98, reference libr., 1983-98, chair faculty scholarship com., 1987-98, campus archivist, 1994-98; ret., 1998; pvt. piano tchr. Gresham, 1998—. Pvt. piano tchr., 1998; mem. site selection com. Multnomah County (Oreg.) Libr., New Gresham br., 1987, adv. com. Multnomah County Libr., Portland, Oreg., 1988-89; bd. dirs. Oreg. Episcopal Conf. of Deaf, 1985-92. Bd. dirs. East County Arts Alliance, Gresham, 1987-91; vestry person, jr. warden St. Luke's Episc. Ch., 1989-92; vestry person St. Aidan's Episcopal. Ch., 2000—; founding pres. Mt. Hood Pops, 1983-88, orch. mgr., 1983-91, 93—, bd. dirs., 1983-88, 91—. Recipient Jeanette Parkhill Meml. award Chaffey Jr. Coll., 1959, Svc. award St. Luke's Episcopal Ch., 1983, 87, Edn. Svc. award Soroptimists, 1989. Mem. AAUW, NEA, Oreg. Edn. Assn., Oreg. Libr. Assn., ALA, Gresham Hist. Soc. Avocations: music, reading. E-mail: pierikm@teleport.com.

PIERRARD-MUTTON, MARY V., artist, educator; b. Steubenville, Ohio, Sept. 22, 1921; d. Frank David and Mary E. (Huffman) Nation; m. Charles Joseph Pierrard, Sept. 5, 1942 (dec. May 1979); children: Karen Marie, Charles Joseph; m. James Mutton, May 27, 1994. Grad., Midway H.S., Pa., 1940. Tchr. China painting home studio, Midway, 1979—; artist Krauses, Washington, Pa., 1980—85; tchr. China painting sr. citizen group, California, Pa., 1993. Demonstrator Pitts. Ctr. of Arts, 1990, Woman's Club, McDonald, Pa., 1992, Garden Club, McDonald, 1992, Fireman's, Midway, 1991, Pitts. Dist. of Chs., Legonier, Pa., 1993. Exhibited in group shows at Washington County Woman's Club, 1981, 90(1st Pl. award), 1990, Pa. Fedn. Woman's Club, 1989, 90 (1st Pl. award), S.W. Dist. Woman's Clubs, 1983 (1st Pl. award); contbr. drawing to book: Years of Duncan, 1980, cover to Internat. Porcelain Artists. Mem. Internat. Porcelain Art Tchrs., Inc., Nat. Mus. Women in Arts, Pitts. Porcelain Artists (treas. 1994-97), Pa. Porcelain Artists (treas. 1985-87), China Painters (pres. Pitts. chpt. 2003-2004), McDonald Woman's Club, Pa. Woman's Club. Home: PO Box 85 Midway PA 15060-0085

PIERRE, MIRELLE, physician, psychotherapist, health facility administrator; b. Port au Prince, Haiti, July 21, 1950; came to U.S., 1970; d. Gustave Pierre and Madeleine Defay; m. Serge Elie, Sept. 30, 1972 (div. Nov. 1982); children: Richard, Lesly Elie. MD, U. Autonoma de Nuevoleon, Monterrey, Mex., 1989; PhD, South Tex. Sch. Nutrition, 1995; postgrad., Clayton Coll. Nat. Health, 1997; CCN, San Antonio Sch. Homeopathy. Physician Guadalpue Psychiat. Ctr., Monterrey, 1990-92; physician, nutritionist Advanced Wellness Clinic, San Antonio, 1993-95; pres., physician, nutritionist Chalumi Health Enterprises, Inc., Bklyn., 1996—. Author: An Ounce of Prevention, 1999, (cassettes) Series of Success Collection, 1999. Mem. Am. Naturopathic Med. Assn., Coalition for Natural Health. Democrat. Pentecostal. Avocations: reading, writing, music. Office: 304 E 35th St Brooklyn NY 11203-3906

PIERREHUMBERT, JANET BRECKENRIDGE, language educator; AB in Linguistics, Harvard Univ., 1975; Rotary Found. grad. fellow, Univ. of Turku, Finland, 1975—76; PhD in Linguistics, MIT, 1980. Cons., dept. linguistics and speech analysis AT&T Bell Labs, 1980—82, technical staff mem., dept. linguistics and artificial intelligence rsch., 1982—89; rsch. assoc., Ctr. for Cognitive Sci. MIT, 1980—82; cons. asst. prof., dept. linguistics Stanford Univ., 1984—85; faculty Linguistic Soc. of Am. Summer Inst., 1986, 1993; visitor, dept. speech transmission and music acoustics Royal Inst. of Tech., Stockholm, 1987—88; assoc prof., dept. linguistics Northwestern Univ., 1989—93, chair, 1993—96, prof., 1993—; faculty, LOT (Dutch post-grad. sch. of linguistics Univ. Nijmegen, 1997; visitor Ecole National Superieure des Telecommunications, Paris, 1996—97; poste rouge Centre Nat. de la Recherche Scientifique, 1997. Assoc. editor Jour. Phonetics, 1989—, adv. editor Oxford Surveys in Generative Phonology, 2000—; co-author (with M. Beckman): (monograph) Japanese Tone Structure, Linguistic Inquiry Monograph, 1988; co-author: (with M. Broe) (books) Papers in Laboratory Phonology V, 2000; contbr. articles to profl. journals, chapters to books. Fellow John Simon Guggenheim Mem. Found., 1996—; grantee NSF Grad. Fellowhip, 1976—79. Fellow: Am. Acad. Arts & Sci. Office: Dept Linguistics Northwestern Univ 2016 Sheridan Rd Evanston IL 60208 Office Phone: 847-467-1570. Office Fax: 847-491-3770. Business E-Mail: jbp@northwestern.edu.

PIERRE-LOUIS, ROSAIRE, elementary school educator, educator; b. North Miami, Fla., U.S., Jan. 10, 1972; d. Brenord and Genevieve (Cantave) Duclona; m. Pierre-Louis, Jan. 28, 1999; children: Brittany, Kasidy. AA, Miami Dade CC; BA, St. Thomas U., Miami; MA, Novasoutheastern Univ. Tchr. Miami Skill Ctr., Fla., substitute tchr. Fla. Home: PO Box 693369 Miami FL 33269-0369 E-mail: Rosaireroro@aol.com.

PIERRI, MARY KATHRYN MADELINE, cardiologist, emergency physician, educator; b. N.Y.C., Aug. 12, 1948; d. Charles Daniel and Margaret Loyola (Pesce) P. BA, Manhattanville Coll., 1969; MD, Med. Coll. Pa., 1974. Diplomate Am. Bd. Cardiology. Med. resident Med. Coll. Pa., Phila., 1974-77; fellow in cardiology N.Y. Hosp., N.Y.C., 1977-79; asst. physician Meml. Hosp., N.Y.C., 1980-89, assoc. physician, 1989-97, chief cardiology svc., 1991—2002, attending physician, 1997—. Assoc. prof. medicine Cornell Med. Coll., 1989—97, prof. clin. medicine, 1997—. Fellow Am. Coll. Cardiology, N.Y. Cardiological Soc.; mem. ACP, Soc. Critical Care Medicine, Alpha Omega Alpha.

PIERROUTSAKOS, SOPHIA L., psychology professor; d. Leonidas Andreas and Margaret Ann Pierroutsakos; m. Garth Silvey; 1 child, Olivia Silvey. BA, Washington U., St. Louis, 1991; MA, U. Ill., 1994, PhD, 1999. Asst. prof. psychology Furman U., Greenville, SC, 1999—2004, St. Louis C.C., Kirkwood, Mo., 2004—. Contbr. articles to sci. jours. Mem.: Internat. Soc. Infant Studies, Cognitive Devel. Soc., Am. Psychol. Soc., Soc. Rsch. in Child Devel. Office: St Louis CC 11333 Big Bend Blvd Kirkwood MO 63122 Office Phone: 314-984-7500.

PIERSON, ANNE BINGHAM, physician; b. N.Y.C., June 9, 1929; d. Woodbridge and Ursula Wolcott (Griswold) Bingham; m. Richard N. Pierson Jr., July 10, 1954 (div. Aug. 1974); children: Richard N. III, Olivia Tiffany Jacobs, Alexandra deForest Griffin, Cordelia Stewart Comfort Smela; m. Richard Taliaferro Wright, Nov. 25, 1978 (div. Sept. 1997); m. Paul H. Altrocchi, May 9, 1998. Student, Katharine Branson Sch., Ross, Calif., 1943-47; BA, Vassar Coll., 1951; MD, Columbia U., 1955, MPH, 1972. Intern Lenox Hill Hosp., N.Y.C., 1955-56; substitute internship AUH, Beruit, Lebanon, 1955; mem. staff 7th Day Adventist Hosp., Taipei, Taiwan, 1957; clinic physician, med. dir. Planned Parenthood of Bergen County, Hackensack, N.J., 1960-74, also bd. dirs., 1966-69; asst. clin. prof. dept. ob-gyn. Columbia U. Coll. Physicians and Surgeons, Internat. Inst. Study of Human Reproduction, 1972-74; med. dir. Memphis Assn. for Planned Parenthood, Inc., 1974-75; staff physician N.Y. Telephone Co., 1976-87; med. dir. Planned Parenthood Assn. Hudson County, 1976-79; physician Sonalysts, Waterford, Conn., 1988—. Mem. nat. med. adv. com. Planned Parenthood-World Population, 1966-69. Pres. Vassar Class 1951, 1986-91; artist mem. Clinton Art Soc., 1989—, East Lyme Art League, 1991—; active Jr. League, 1964-69, sustainer, 1969—. Mem. AMA (Physicians Recognition award 1973—), Nat. Soc. Colonial Dames (life, asst. sec. 1991-94, 2d v.p. 1994-97), Cosmopolitan Club, Lyme Art Assn. (treas. 1998-99, pres. 1999—), Mystic Art Assn., Essex Art Assn. Office: Sonalysts 215 Parkway N Waterford CT 06385-1209

PIERSON, JUANITA (NITA PIERSON), secondary school educator; b. Shreveport, La., Oct. 28, 1921; d. Henry and Rodessa (Scott) Thomas; m. Floyd Allen Pierson, Sept. 18, 1938; children: Annette Marilyn Pieson Poulard, Frederick Allen. Student, U. Md., 1965-66, Centennary Coll., 1967-68, So. U. Coll., 1967-69, Prairie View A&M U., 1969-70, Santa Clara U., 1974; BA, Wiley Coll., 1954; MS, La. Tech., 1975; postgrad., Northwestern U., 1972-74; D (hon.), Shreveport Bible Coll., 1987. Sec. Mooretown Sch., Shreveport, 1957-67; elem. music splst. Caddo Parish Schs., La., 1967-70; secondary edn. tchr., 1970-79. Ptnr. Pierson's Allendale Plz., Shreveport, 1979—; bookkeeper F & F Food Store, Shreveport, 1978—; artistic dir. Performing Arts Studio, 1983—; dir. music Antioch Baptist Ch., 1997—. Instr. Christian Edn., Shreveport, 1970—; organist Shiloh Bapt. Ch., Shreveport, 1975-78; mem. ways and means com. Greenwood Acres Civic Club, 1975-81, mem. econ. devel. and planning com., 1980-81; mem. Ctr. for Families, Shreveport, 1992-99; mem. music and art cultural awareness project, Jackson Heights Housing Cmty., Shreveport, 1998; mem. Shreveport Symphony Guild, Shreveport Little Theatre, Shreveport Opera Guild; min. music Antioch Bapt. Ch., music dir. Jackson Heights Housing Ctr., Avenue B.C. Shreveport. Grantee La. Divsn. Arts, 1995-99, Shreveport Regional Arts Coun., 1995-99; named Educator of Yr. Caddo Parish Sch. Bd., 1978; hon. state senator, La., 1980-81; recipient Cert. of Recognition of Svc. award, Antioch Bapt. Ch., Shreveport, La., 2000; honorarium during African-Am. History Month Celebration, 2002, Movers and Shakers award, Pan Hellinic Coun. of Greek Orgn., 2002, African Am. History Month award Ave. Bapt. Ch., 2004, Mother of Yr. award Ave. Bapt. Ch., 2004, Diamond Svc. award La. Bapt. State Conv., 2004. Mem. NEA, Nat. Coun. Tchrs. English, Shreveport Regional Area Coun., La. Coun. Tchrs. English, Music Tchrs. Nat. Assn., La. State Music Tchrs. Assn., Greater Shreveport Music Tchrs. Assn., Greater Shreveport C. of C. (Woman of the Century award, 2000), Univ. Club, Phi Delta Kappa (Music award Am. History Month 2005), Basileus-Sigma Gamma Rho, Sorority Inc., Eta Psi Sigma Chpt. Baptist. Avocations: music, performing arts. Office: Performing Arts Studio 2332 Jewella Ave Shreveport LA 71109-2412

PIERSON, LINDA KAY, music educator; b. Warsaw, Mo., Mar. 19, 1954; d. Calvin Werby and Helen Roberta Williams; m. Phillip Keith Pierson, July 8, 1978; children: Matthew, Jonathan. B Music Edn., Ctrl. Mo. State U., 1976, M Music Edn., 1982. Instrumental music tchr. Raymore-Peculiar (Mo.) Schs., 1976—. Accompanist H.S. choir and soloists, Peculiar, 1976—. Mem.: NEA, Mo. Music Educators Assn., West Ctrl. Mo. Music Educators (sec.-treas. 1982—90). Methodist. Office: Raymore-Peculiar Schs PO Box 366 211th of School Rd Peculiar MO 64078

PIERSON, NORAH, artist; b. New Haven, June 14, 1940; d. George Wilson and (Mary) Laetitia (Verdery) Pierson; 1 child, (Carl) Ross Palmer. Student, Miss Porter's Sch., Farmington, Conn., 1954—58, Chateau Brillantmont, Lausanne, Switzerland, 1955—56; diploma in graphic design with honors, Sch. Mus. Fine Arts, Boston, 1962. Owner, jeweler Golden Eye, Laguna Beach, Calif., 1971—82, Santa Fe, 1984—. Represented in permanent collections Green & Green, Lambertville, N.J., Squash Blossom, Vale, Colo., Topaz, Atlanta, Spectrum, Willington, N.C.; contbr. articles to publs. Organizer Citizens Nuc. Safety, 1988—. Mem.: Jewelers Bd. Trade, Soc. N.Am. Goldsmiths, Am. Gem Trade Assn. (award 1988). Avocations: painting, gardening, hiking, camping. Office: Golden Eye 115 Don Gaspar Ave Santa Fe NM 87501 Office Phone: 505-984-0040.

PIETRZEN, JULIE LYNN, lawyer; b. Southfield, Mich., Mar. 13, 1974; d. Eugene Victor Pietrzen and Joan Diane Bragg. BA, Albion Coll., Albion, Mich., 1996; JD, Case Western Res. U., Cleve., 2004. LCSW Mich. Patient advocate L&S Assocs., Inc., Haslett, Mich., 1996—97; program coord. YWCA of Western Wayne County, Mich., 1997—2000; atty. Frantz Ward LLP, Cleve., 2004—. Mem.: Cuyahoga County Bar Assn., Cleve. Bar Assn., Ohio State Bar Assn., Phi Delta Phi (province pres. 2004—, Balfour scholar 2003, Grad. of the Yr. 2004). Democrat. Avocations: volleyball, reading, writing, skiing. Office: Frantz Ward LLP 127 Public Sq 2500 Key Center Cleveland OH 44114

PIGG, BRENDA J., music educator; b. St. Louis, June 29, 1959; d. Irvin D. and Wanda J. King; m. Nace M. Pigg, June 27, 1981. BSE, Ark. State U., 1999. Band dir. Doniphan (Mo.) R-1, 1999—. Office: Doniphan R 1 #5 Ballpark Rd Doniphan MO 63935

PIGG, ROBIN CLARK, art educator, interior designer; b. New Orleans, Mar. 25, 1965; d. William Nuschler and Letty Jane Clark; m. Jason Daniel Pigg, Jan. 30, 1988; 1 child, Janiece Marie; 1 child, Davis Clark. B Interior Design, La. State U., 1987. Interior designer VanLandingham Lumber Co., Starkville, Miss., 1998—2003; elem. art tchr. Starkville Acad., Starkville, Miss., 2003—. Dir. interior design dept. Miss. State U., Mississippi State, 2002—03. Chmn. dept. United Way of NE Miss., Starkville, Miss., 1993—94; bd. dirs. Am. Heart Assn., 1990—96; mem. arts and environment com. St. Joseph Cath. Ch., Starkville, 2000—06, sec. pastoral coun., 1990—92. Mem.: Am. Soc. Interior Designers (assoc.), Jr. Aux. Starkville (chmn. safety town update com. 1996—2002). Roman Catholic. Avocations: gardening, travel. Home: 2867 Oktoc Rd Starkville MS 39759-8290

PIGNATELLI, DEBORA BECKER, state official; b. Hoboken, N.J., Oct. 25, 1947; d. Edward and Frances (Fishman) Becker; m. Michael Albert Pignatelli, Aug. 22, 1971; children: Adam Becker, Benjamin Becker. AA, Vt. Coll., 1967; BA, U. Denver, 1969. Exec. dir. Girl's Club Greater Nashua, NH, 1975-77; dir. tenant svcs. Nashua Housing Authority, 1979-80; vocat. counselor Comprehensive Rehab. Assocs., Bedford, NH, 1982-85; specialist job placement Crawford & Co., Bedford, 1985-87; mem. N.H. Ho. of Reps., Concord, 1986—91, mem. appropriations com., 1986-91, asst. minority leader, 1989—91; mem. N.H. Senate, Concord, 1992—2003, v.p. policy, Dem. whip, chair judiciary com., mem. capital budget com., chair enrolled bills com., long range capital budget overview com.; elected mem. N.H. Govs. Exec. Coun., 2005—. Del. Am. Coun. Young Polit. Leaders, Germany, 1987. Asst. coach Little League Baseball, Nashua, 1987—90; del. Dem. Nat. Conv., 1988, Gore del., 2000; mem. steering com. Gephardt for Pres. campaign, NH, 1987—88; bd. dirs. Sky Meadow Condominium Assn. Named one of 10 Most Powerful Women in N.H., N.H. Editions mag., 1995; recipient Meritorious Svc. award, N.H. Women's Lobby, 1997, John F. Kennedy award, Hillsborough County Dems., 2001, Anita and Norman Freedman award, N.H. Dems., 2004, William Paine Domestic Violence award, 2005. Mem.: Women's Lobby, N.H. Children's Lobby. Jewish. Avocations: skiing, swimming, boating. Home: 22 Appletree Grn Nashua NH 03062-2252 Office Phone: 603-271-3632.

PIGOTT, MELISSA ANN, social psychologist; b. Ft. Myers, Fla., Jan. 28, 1958; d. Park Trammell and Leola Ann (Wright) P.; m. David H. Fauss, Jan. 1, 1988. BA in Psychology, Fla. Internat. U., Miami, 1979; MS in Social Psychology, Fla. State U., 1982, PhD in Social Psychology, 1984. Rsch. asst. Fla. Internat. U., 1978-79, Fla. State U., Tallahassee, 1980-84; dir. mktg. rsch. Bapt. Med. Ctr., Jacksonville, Fla., 1984-89; rsch. assoc. Litigation Scis., Inc., Atlanta, 1989-91; sr. litigation psychologist Trial Cons., Inc., Miami, 1991-93; dir. rsch. Magnus Rsch. Cons. Inc., Ft. Lauderdale, 1993—. Adj. prof. psychology U. North Fla., Jacksonville, 1985-89, Nova Southeastern U., Ft. Lauderdale, 1995—. Author: Social Psychology: Study Guide, 1990, Social Psychology: Instructors Manual, 1990; contbr. articles to profl. jours. Mem. ACLU, Am. Psychol. Assn., Am. Psychol. Law Soc., Amnesty Internat., Civitan Internat., Southeastern Psychol. Assn., Soc. for Psychol. Study of Social Issues, Soc. Personality and Social Psychology, Greenpeace, Psi Chi. Democrat. Avocations: concerts, playing piano, going to the beach, bass guitar. Office: Magnus Rsch Cons Inc 1305 NE 23rd Ave Ste 1 Pompano Beach FL 33062-3748

PIGOTT, SUSAN M., religious studies educator; b. Albuquerque, N.Mex., Nov. 22, 1964; d. Ronald E. and Mary Kay Day; m. Kelly D. Pigott, July 28, 1990; children: Nathaniel D., Eliana M. BA, Hardin-Simmons U., Abilene, Tex., 1986; MDiv, Southwestern Bapt. Theol. Sem., Ft. Worth, Tex., 1989; PhD, Southwestern Bapt. Theol. Sem., 1989—95. Instr. of old testament Logsdon Sch. of Theology, Hardin-Simmons U., Abilene, Tex., 1993—95, asst. prof. of old testament, 1995—2000; assoc. prof. of old testament Logsdon Sch. of Theology, Hardin Simmons U., 2000—05; prof. of old testament and hebrew Logsdon Sch. of Theology, Hardin-Simmons U., 2005—. Recipient Disting. Alumni award, Logsdon Sch. of Theology, 1999, President's Merit scholar in Theology, Southwestern Bapt. Theol. Sem., 1989, Logsdon Sch. of Theology award, Logsdon Sch. of Theology, 1986, Broadman Sem. award for outstanding achievement in bibl. studies, Southwestern Bapt. Theol. Sem., 1989, 1995, Albert G. Venting, Jr. Meml. award, 1989, 1995. Mem.: Nat. Assn. of Bapt. Professors of Religion SW Region (pres. 2006—), Nat. Assn. of Bapt. Professors of Religion SW Region (v.p. 2005—06), Soc. of Bibl. Lit., Christian Vegetarian Assn. Bapt. Home: 2309 Shoreline Dr Abilene TX 79602 Office: Hardin-Simmons Univ 2200 Hickory St Abilene TX 79698 Office Phone: 325-670-1296. Business E-Mail: spigott@hsutx.edu.

PIIRMA, IRJA, chemist, educator; b. Tallinn, Estonia, Feb. 4, 1920; came to U.S., 1949; d. Voldemar Juri and Meta Wilhelmine (Lister) Tiits; m. Aleksander Piirma, Mar. 10, 1943; children: Margit Ene, Silvia Ann. Diploma in Chemistry, Tech. U., Darmstadt, Fed. Republic of Germany, 1949; MS, U. Akron, 1957, PhD, 1960. Rsch. chemist U. Akron, Ohio, 1952-67, asst. prof., 1967-76, assoc. prof., 1976-81, prof., 1981-90, prof. emerita, 1990—, dept. head, 1982-85. Author: Polymeric Surfactants, 1992; editor: Emulsion Polymerization, 1982; contbr. articles to profl. jours. Recipient Extra Mural Rsch. award BP Am., Inc., 1989. Mem. Am. Chem. Soc. Avocations: swimming, skiing. Home: 3528 Adaline Dr Cuyahoga Falls OH 44224-3929 Office: U Akron Inst Polymer Sci Akron OH 44325-3909 Personal E-mail: irjapiirma@cs.com, irjapiirma@sbcglobal.net.

PIKE, JUDITH ROBYN, lawyer; b. Newton, July 23, 1959; d. Burton M. and Doris (Weingard) P.; m. Richard A. Miller, July 7, 1990. BA summa cum laude, Tufts U., 1981; JD, U. Pa., 1984. Bar: Mass. 1985, U.S. Dist. Ct. Mass. 1985. Assoc. Rackemann, Sawyer & Brewster, Boston, 1984-86, McDermott & Rizzo, Boston, 1986-90, Kirkpatrick & Lockhart, Boston, 1990—93; founder Law Office Judith R. Pike, Wellesley, Mass., 1993—. Named one of top Boston lawyers, Boston Mag., 2004. Mem.: Wellesley C. of C. (women's bus. network), Mass. Conveyancers Assn., ABA, Mass. Bar Assn., Boston Uncommon (women's accappella quintet) (dir.). Avocations: music, piano. Office: 462 Washington St Wellesley MA 02482 Office Phone: 781-237-2727. Office Fax: 781-237-2737. Business E-Mail: judy@judithpikelaw.com.

PIKE, SHIRLEY, school psychologist; b. Ottumwa, Iowa, Aug. 2, 1949; d. Harold Dewey Pike and Marguerite Cleone Berntsen; m. Michael John Hemmingson, Nov. 9, 1984; children: Marguerite Isajoy, Sara Jean. BA in Psychology, Calif. State U., 1971, MA in Psychol. Svcs., 1975. Nat. cert. sch. psychologist, Md. Sch. psychologist L.A. Unified Schs., 1976-79, S.W. Cook County Edn. Assn., Orland Park, Ill., 1979-81, Grant Wood AEA, Cedar Rapids, Iowa, 1981—. Bd. dirs. Children and Adults with Attention Deficit Disorder, Cedar Rapids, 1989-97; profl. devel. chair East Ctrl. UniServ Unit, Cedar Rapids, 1995-97. Co-author: Assessment and Intervention Children with ADHD, 1994. Pres., past v.p. North Ctrl. region Sri Sathya Sai Baba Orgn., 1995—; precinct capt., steering com. Linn County Dems., Cedar Rapids, 1999; v.p. Inter-Religious Coun. of Linn County, 1998—, past sec., treas.; bd. dirs. Faith in Action, 1997-98. Grantee Iowa Dept. of Pub. Instrn., 1985, 86. Mem. Iowa State Edn. Assn. (exec. bd.), Nat. Orgn. of Sch. Psychologists, Samaritan Counseling Ctr. (bd. dirs.), Phi Beta Kappa, Phi Kappa Phi. Office: Grantwood Area Edn Agy 4401 6th St SW Cedar Rapids IA 52404-4432 Home: 3925 Willowbrook Dr Marion IA 52302-6155

PIKEN, MICHELE RENEÉ (PENN PIKEN), artist, photographer; b. Richmond, Va., Mar. 19, 1946; d. Sam and Dorothy (Klaff) Penn; m. Gerald Piken, Dec. 3, 1967; children: Lara Eden Piken Polner, Charly Brooke Piken. BS, Franklin Sch. Sci. and Arts, 1965; student, Art Inst. Ft. Lauderdale, 1980-81. Photographer, supr. Twin Lakes Travel Park, Ft. Lauderdale, Fla., 1979-81; photographer Miami (Fla.) Jewish fedn., 1988-89; designer Dressed To A Tee Inc., Miami, 1983-85; pres., owner Tickle Pink Inc., Miami, 1985-90; designer, pres. N.V. US Inc., Miami, 1992-95; visual merchandizer Macy's Inc., Aventura, Fla., 1991-92; bookeeper Piken & Assocs. PA, Miami, 1996—. Freelance photographer The Miami Herald, 1998-99. One-woman shows include Eyes of Israel, U. Miami, 1984, Photo Exhibn. of Israel, Yafta Gallery, 1993, Tommy, Houshang Gallery, 1997, Africa & Beyond, Ft. Lauderdale City Hall, 1999. Staff photographer Diabetes Rsch. Found., Miami, 1981-90; vol. Israeli Army, Negev, 1985, Camillus House, Miami, 1988-91, Aventura Regional Hosp., 1994-97. Mem. Dade County Art in Pub. Places, Palm Beach Photographic Ctr. Avocations: painting, sculpting, gardening, candy making, antique restoration. Home: 2466 Eagle Run Way Weston FL 33327-1431

PILAFIAN, AUDREY KALENIAN, music educator; b. Chgo., Sept. 19, 1929; d. Hagop and Adrine Kalenian; m. Harry Pilafian, Sept. 10, 1949; children: Martin, Jack David, Robert John, Mary Katherine. Student, Northwestern U., 1947—49; MusB, U. Miami, 1951, MEd in Supervision and Adminstrn., 1972. Cert. supr./adminstr., gifted edn., music edn., elem. edn. tchr. Fla. Elem. sch. tchr. Miami/Dade Pub. Schs., 1962—76, gifted students tchr., 1976—92; adj. supr. Fla. Internat. U., Miami, 1994—. Musician U. Miami Symphony Orch., Coral Gables, Fla., 1953—56; pvt. cello tchr., Miami, 1970—; cellist Chamber Music Prof. Agy., Miami, 1995—2005. Vol. co-dir. strings ensemble Leewood Elem. Sch., Miami, 1992—2005; state bd. mem. Odyssey of the Mind, Inc., Fla., 1983—98; supt. Sunday Sch. St. Mary Armenian Ch., Hollywood, Fla., 1953—2006. Named Dade County Tchr. of Yr., Fla. Fedn. Woman's Clubs, 1968; recipient Pontifical Blessing Encyclical, His Holiness Karenkin I, Catholicos of all Armenians, 1998. Mem.: Phi Delta Kappa (tchr.), Sigma Alpha Iota (musician/performer, editor, historian), Alpha Delta Kappa (internat. chmn. Fine Arts Grants Bd. 1991—97, internat. music chmn. 2005). Avocations: cello, chamber music, amateur radio, travel, camping. Home and Studio: 9940 SW 60 St Miami FL 33173 Office Phone: 305-271-2512.

PILAT, JEANINE MARIE, medical researcher; d. George and Antoinette Pilat. BA with highest honors, DePaul U., 1999; postgrad., Roosevelt U., 2002—. Intern Inst. Positive Mental Health, Chgo., 1998—99; rsch. asst. religious orders study memory and aging project Rush U. Med. Ctr., Chgo., 1999—2001, asst. coord. religious orders study, 2001—02, rsch. asst. Chgo. health and aging project, 2002—06; rsch. project coord. substrates of emotion study U. Chgo., 2006—. Rsch. participant Sta. WGN-TV, Sta. NBC-TV. Contbr. articles to profl. jours. Grad. scholarship, Roosevelt U., 2003-2005. Mem.: APA (divsn. 40 clin. neuropsychology mem.), Ill. Psychol. Assn., Alpha Lambda Delta, Phi Kappa Phi, Golden Key Nat. Honor Soc. Roman Catholic. Avocations: travel, music, languages. Personal E-mail: jpilat77@yahoo.com.

PILCH, MARGARET L., grant writer, researcher; b. Tacoma, Mar. 6, 1948; d. Bernard Joseph Kern, Jean Katherine Kern; m. Edward Samuel Pilch; 1 child, Christopher Neal Richards. AA, Washburn U., 1979, BA, 1982; MPA, Kans. U., 1987; PhD, Union Inst. and U., 2002. Cert. legal asst. Nat. Assn. Legal Assts., Inc., 1979, grant specialist Nat. Grant Writers Assn., 2003, lic. real estate agt. Va., Kans. Paralegal John Wilkinson, Atty., Topeka, 1978—82, Frank Sabatini, Atty., Topeka, 1982—84; comml. realtor High Plains Realty, Topeka, 1984—85; comml. leasing agent Pembroke Comml. Realty, Virginia Beach, Va., 1985—91; paralegal Goicoechea & DiGrazia, Attys., Elko, Nev., 1992—95, Darlene Reiter, Atty., Sheridan, Wyo., 1995—96, 1997—99; asst. budget dir. Sheridan County Govt., 1996—97; loan processor Sheridan State Bank, 1999—2000; grant reviewer Wyo. Dept. Edn., 2002—04; reader Jacob Javits Scholarship Found. U.S. Dept. Edn., 2004; self-employed grant writer. Cons. in field. Editor: (Handbook) Legal Rights of Women in Wyoming, 2001; author: (Catalog) Catalog for Individuals Seeking Rural Research Grants, 2001, (Dissertation) Workplace Attitudes of Nonfarm Rural Working Women in Sheridan County, Wyoming, 2001; editor: Where to Find Help: People and Places in Wyoming, 2004. Coll. coach Daniels Fund Coll. Prep and Scholarship Program, 2002—03, grad. student supr., 2002—05; mem. legal/legis. com. Wyo. Coun. Women's Issues, 2000—04; judge H.S. Contest Family, Career and Cmty. Leaders of Am., 2004; mem. endowment com. Sheridan Sr. Ctr., 2005, 2006; mem. Spring Creek Assn. Architecture com., 1992—93; com. woman Sheridan County Precinct Rep. Party, 2006; sec., treas. bd. Citco Fed. Credit Union, 2000—; bd. dirs. Wyo. Substance Abuse Treatment and Recovery Ctr., 2003; mem. architecture com. Spring Creek Assn., 1992—93; dist. chmn. Republican Party, Virginia Beach, 1990—91; legis. aide Senator Ben Vidrickson, Topeka, 1984—85; arbitrator Better Bus. Bur., Topeka, 1984—85; rape counselor Citizen's Crime Com., Topeka, 1983—85. Recipient Certificate of Merit, Am. Cancer Soc., 1994, Outstanding Achievement award, 1994—95; grantee, Wyo. Women's Found., 2001. Mem.: AAUW, Inst. Women's Policy Rsch., Am. Assn. Grant Profls., Kans. Legal Assistance Soc. (founder 1977—), Assn. Profl. Rschrs. for Advancement, Rural Sociol. Soc., Women in Rural America Task Force. Avocations: writing, travel, weightlifting, ranching. Home: 875 Lower Prairie Dog Road Sheridan WY 82801

PILCHER, CHRISTIE W., special education educator; b. Jackson, Tenn, Dec. 17, 1944; d. Charles Arthur Sr. and Ruby Mazie (Pope) Walker; m. David Wayne Pilcher, Mar. 20, 1966 (div. 1974); children: David Andrew, Clayton Everett. Student, Mercer U., 1962-63; BA, North Ga. Coll., 1966; MEd, Ga. State U., 1976. Tchr. reading US Army Edn. Ctr., Munich, 1967; tchr. K.G. US Dependent Sch., Munich, 1967-68; tchr. Ga. Acad. for the Blind, Macon, 1974-79; tchr. for visually impaired Bibb County Bd. Edn., Macon, 1979-91, spl. edn. K.G., 1991-94; tchr. visually impaired Troup County Bd. Edn., LaGrange, Ga., 1994—2000, Bartow County Sch. Sys., Cartersville, Ga., 2000—01; tchr. spl. needs kindergarten Bibb County Bd. Edn., Macon, 2001—02, 2005—, tchr. mildly intellectually disabled, 2004—05; ret. Parent advisor Ga. Parent Infant Network for Ednl. Svc., Clarkston, 1985—2004; tchr. summer program Ga. Bapt. Children's Home, Baxley, 1991. Vol. Ga. Radio Reading Svc., 2003—; mem. Mt. Zion Bapt. Ch. Choir, 2005—. Christian Ch. (Disciples of Christ), Deacon, Christian Edn. Com., chair 1991. Avocations: painting, reading, baking, travel, gardening. Home: 939 Clairmont Pl Macon GA 31204-1099 E-mail: christiep@bellsouth.net.

PILEGGI, JENNIFER WENDY, transportation services executive; b. NYC, July 27, 1964; d. Jerome E. Rosenfeld. BA in Art History, cum laude, Yale U., 1986; JD, NYU, 1990. Bar: Calif. 1990. Assoc. Heller, Ehrman, White & McAuliffe, San Francisco, Marron, Reid & Sheehy, San Francisco; joined CNF Inc., Palo Alto, Calif., 1996; corp. counsel Menlo Worldwide Logistics subs., Redwood City, Calif., 1996—99, v.p., corp. counsel, 1999—2003, Menlo Worldwide subs., Redwood City, Calif., 2003—04; sr. v.p., gen. counsel, corp. sec. CNF Inc., 2004—. Mem.: ABA, Calif. State Bar Assn. Office: CNF Inc 2855 Campus Dr Ste 300 San Mateo CA 94403 Office Phone: 650-378-5200. Office Fax: 650-357-9160.

PILEWSKI, JENNIFER MARIE, mathematics educator; d. Walter John and Sandra Kaye Pilewski. BS in Edn., Slippery Rock U., Pa., 1994, MEd with emphasis in Math and Sci., 2000. Cert. math. tchr. Pa., 1994. Math. tchr. Titusville H.S., Pa., 1995—. Student assistance team mem. Titusville HS and Liaisons, Pa., 2001—; part-time math. instr. U. Pitts. at Titusville. Named one of Nat. Honor Roll's Outstanding Am. Teachers, 2005—06. Mem.: NEA, Titusville Edn. Assn., Pa. State Edn. Assn. Democrat. Roman Catholic. Avocation: inline skating. Office: Titusville HS 302 E Walnut St Titusville PA 16354 Office Phone: 814-827-9687. Business E-Mail: jpilewski@gorockets.org.

PILGRAM, SUZANNE, artist, art educator; b. Montclair, NJ, Feb. 25, 1945; d. Hans J. and Florence Ketchum Pilgram; m. Hassan Ghavam, Sept. 3, 1973. BA in Art, Am. U., 1967, MFA in Painting, 1970. Artist, clk. US Com. for UNICEF Children's Culture Ctr., 1970—73; prof. Coll. Translation, Tehran, Iran, 1973—80, Farah Pahlavi U., Tehran, 1977—78, Trenton State Coll., NJ, 1983; assoc. prof. Georgian Court U., Lakewood, NJ, 1981—. Lectr., presenter Ocean County CC, NJ, 1980, NJ, 81, NJ, 82, Pine Shores Art Assn., N.J. State Coun. on Arts, 1998—2006, Columbia U., N.Y.C., 2001. Artwork, Columbia U. Invitational, 2001, painting collage, Trenton Artists Workshop, 2004, paintings, Phoenix Gallery, N.Y.C., 2004—06; printmaking coun. NJ Exhibit "Intolerance", 2006—. Grantee Fulbright-Hayes Group Projects Abroad, U.S. State Dept., Jamaica, 1983, Faculty Rsch. grant, Georgian Ct. U., 2004. Mem.: Trenton Artists Workshop, Women's Studio Workshop, N.J. Project (Grant 1987—). Avocation: gardening. Home: 9 Robin Rd Howell NJ 07731 Office: Georgian Ct Univ 900 Lakewood Ave Lakewood NJ 08701 Office Phone: 732-987-2330. Business E-Mail: pilgrams@georgian.edu.

PILGRIM, DIANNE HAUSERMAN, retired museum director; b. Cleve., July 8, 1941; d. John Martin and Norma Hauserman; divorced. BA, Pa. State U., 1963; MA, Inst. Fine Arts, NYU, 1965; postgrad., CUNY, 1971-74; LHD (hon.), Amherst Coll., 1991, Pratt Inst., 1994. Chester Dale fellow Am. wing. Met. Mus. Art, N.Y.C., 1966-68, rsch. cons. Am. paintings and sculpture, 1971-73; asst. to dirs. Pyramid Galleries, Ltd., Washington, 1969-71, Finch Coll. Mus. Art, Washington, 1971; curator dept. decorative arts Bklyn. Mus., 1973-88, chmn. dept., 1988; dir. Cooper-Hewitt Nat. Design Mus., N.Y.C., 1988-2000, dir. emeritus, 2000—. Mem. adv. com. Gracie Mansion, N.Y.C., 1980; mem. design adv. com. Art Inst. Chgo., 1988; mem. Hist. House Trust N.Y.C., Mayor's Office, 1989-94. Co-author, curator: (book and exhbn. catalogue) Mr. and Mrs. Raymond Horowitz Collection of American Impressionist and Realist Paintings, 1973. The American Renaissance 1876-1917, 1979; (book) The Machine Age in America 1918-1941, 1986 (Charles F. Montgomery prize Decorative Arts Soc.). Bd. dirs. Nat. Multiple Sclerosis Soc., 1989. Recipient Disting. Alumni award Pa. State U., 1991. Mem. Decorative Arts Soc. (pres. 1977-79), Art Deco Soc., Victorian Soc., Art Table.

PILGRIM, JILL, lawyer, consultant; b. London, Nov. 26, 1958; came to U.S., 1969; d. Winslow and Florence L. (Hardy) P. BA, Princeton U., 1980; JD, Columbia U., 1984. Bar: N.Y. 1985. Assoc. Willkie Far & Gallagher, N.Y.C., 1984-86, Cowan Liebowitz & Latman, N.Y.C., 1986-88; of counsel Kurzman Karelsen & Frank, N.Y.C., 1988-89; pvt. practice Pilgrim & Assocs., N.Y.C., 1990—98; gen. counsel, dir. bus. affairs USA Track & Field, Inc., Indpls., 1998—. Examiner in guardianship matters, 1991—; bd. arbitrators Nat. Assn. Securities Delers, Inc.; guest speaker to law students, numerous N.Y. area law schs. Bd. editors The Partnership Handbook, 1986. Mem. Temp. N.Y. State Commn. on Bklyn. Recreation Facilities, 1994—; founder, pres. Ctr. for Protection Athletes' Rights Inc.; bd. dirs., mem. exec. com. Bklyn. Sports Found.; v.p. Friends of Princeton Track; mem. alumni coun. exec. com. Princeton U., 1993-95; bd. dirs. Griffith-Sandiford Family Assistance Fund, Inc.; mem. adv. bd. Bond Street Theater Coalition, Ltd., New Federal Theater. Recipient Essence award Essence Comm., Inc. and Colgate-Palmolive Co., 1990; named Woman of Yr., West Side Residents, 1993. Mem. ABA, Practicing Law Inst., Met. Black Bar Assn., Assn. Bar City N.Y., Assn. Black Women Attys., Sports Lawyers Assn. (bd. mem.), Indpls. Nat. Jr. Tennis Team (bd. mem.), Indpls. Bar Assn. (chairperson sports law sec.), U.S. Olympic Com. (mem. disabled sports com.) Avocations: tennis, field hockey, badminton, volleyball, basketball, track & field. Office: USA Track & Field 1 RCA Dome, Ste 140 Indianapolis IN 46225

PILIBOSIAN, MICHELE MASON, lawyer; b. Metairie, La., Nov. 5, 1970; BA, U. Tex., Austin, 1992; JD cum laude, U. Houston Law Sch., 1998. Bar: Tex. 1998, US Dist. Ct. (ea., no. and so. dists. Tex.) 1999, US Supreme Ct. 2003, US Dist. Ct. (we. dist. Tex.) 2003. Assoc. Baker Hostetler, Houston, 1998—. Candidates editor: Houston Jour. Internat. Law. Named a Rising Star, Tex. Super Lawyers mag., 2006. Mem.: Houston Young Lawyers Assn., Houston Bar Assn., Jr. League Houston. Office: Baker Hostetler 1000 Louisiana St Ste 2000 Houston TX 77002 Office Phone: 713-646-1333. E-mail: mpilibosian@bakerlaw.com.*

PILIGIAN, GEORGETTE A., insurance company executive; BS in bus. computer info. systems, Hofstra U. Positions with E.F. Hutton; joined MetLife Inc., 1987, v.p. e-business applications devel., now chief info. officer corp. systems, 2003—, also sr. v.p. Named one of Premier 100 IT Leaders, Computerworld, 2005. Office: MetLife Inc 200 Park Ave New York NY 10166

PILL, CYNTHIA JOAN, social worker; b. N.Y.C., Mar. 30, 1939; d. Alfred and Edna (Strauss) Fruchtman; m. Robert Pill, July 29, 1961; children: Laura, Daniel, Karen. BS cum laude, Jackson Coll., Tufts U., 1961; MS in Social Work, Simmons Coll., 1963, PhD in Social Work, 1987. Lic. ind. clin. social worker. Clin. social worker Concord (Mass.) Family Sc., 1965-78; coord. family life edn. Family Counseling Svc., Newton, Mass., 1979-83; pvt. practice clin. social work Newton, 1979—; adj. asst. prof., rsch. advisor Smith Coll. Sch. for Social Work, 1988—99. Adj. asst. prof. Simmons Coll. Sch. Social Work, Boston, 1989-93. Contbr. articles to profl. jours. Vol. coord. Hospice at Home, Sudbury, Mass., 1986-88. Mem. NASW, Mass. Soc. Clin. Social Work, Register Clin. Social Workers (bd. cert. diplomate). Address: 435C Dedham St Newton MA 02459 Personal E-mail: docpill123@aol.com.

PILLAERT, E(DNA) ELIZABETH, museum curator; b. Baytown, Tex., Nov. 19, 1931; d. Albert Jacob and Nettie Roseline (Kelley) P. BA, U. St. Thomas, 1953; MA, U. Okla., 1963; postgrad., U. Wis., 1962-67, 70-73. Asst. curator archaeology Stovall Mus., Norman, Okla., 1959-60, ednl. liaison officer, 1960-62; research asst. U. Okla., Norman, Okla., 1962, U. Wis., Madison, 1962-65, cons. archaeol. faunal analysis, 1965—; curator osteology Zool. Mus., Madison, 1965—, chief curator, 1967-92, assoc. dir., 1992—, disting. rschr., 2000—. Bd. dirs. Lysistrata Feminist Coop., Madison, 1977-81, Univ. YMCA, Madison, 1974-77 Mem. Wis. Archaeol. Soc., Okla. Anthrop. Soc., Am. Assn. Mus., NOW, Stoughton Hist. Soc., Am. Ornithological Union, Friends of Stoughton Libr., Friends of Stoughton Auditorium. Home: 216 N Prairie St Stoughton WI 53589-1647 Office: U Wis Zool Mus 434 Noland Bldg 250 N Mills St Madison WI 53706-1708 Business E-Mail: pillaert@facstaff.wisc.edu.

PILLOW-PRICE, KATHY, education educator; b. Paragould, Ark., Dec. 5, 1967; d. Wesley Pillow and Peggy (Mitchell) Wilson; m. Garrick Price, May 13, 2000; children: Kaitlin Pitts, Jake Pitts, Kara Price. BS in Early Childhood/Elem. Edn., Ark. State U., Jonesboro, 1990, MS in Early Childhood Edn., 1997; EdD in Ednl. Leadership, Ark. State U., Jonesboro, Arkansas, 2003. Assoc. prof. edn. Ark. State U., Beebe, 1997—. Cons., trainer Toolbox Tng.; spkr. in field. Pres. Ark. Children's Rights Coun., 2006—. Mem.: NEA, Bus. and Profl. Women, SECA, Ark. Edn. Assn. (mem. state design com.). Office: Ark State U Beebe PO Box 1000 - Iowa St Beebe AR 72012 Office Phone: 501-882-8286. Office Fax: 501-882-8333. Business E-Mail: klpillow@asub.edu.

PILOUS, BETTY SCHEIBEL, medical/surgical nurse; b. Cleve., July 30, 1948; d. Raymond W. and Dorothy E. (Groth) S.; m. Lee Alan Pilous, Sept. 11, 1970; 1 child. Diploma in nursing, Huron Rd. Hosp., Cleve., 1970; BSBA, St. Joseph's Coll., 1989, MHSA, 1996. RN, Ohio; CPHQ. Nurse Huron Rd. Hosp., Cleve., 1970-71, Hillcrest Hosp., Cleve., 1974-77; head nurse, relief supr. Oak Park Hosp., Oakwood, Ohio, 1977-81; head nurse med.-surg. Bedford Hosp., Ohio, 1981-87; dir. inpatient svcs. Meridia Euclid Hosp., Euclid, Ohio, 1987-93. Coord. hosp. info. system for nursing, chair nurse practice com., los com. nursing liaison; DON, Manor Care, Willoughby, Ohio; team leader referral/assessment Hospice Western Res.; dir. clin. svcs. Total Health, 1998, dir. HCQIP, Ohio, 1999, dir. Post Acute Svcs., 2001-; dir. cmty.based svcs. Ohio KePRO, 2005—. Former instr. ARC; chair nurse practice com. Am. Heart Assn.; mem. nursing standards com. Cmty. Hosp. of Bedford; mem. health and safety com. Twinsburg Schs., Ohio, 1984, mem. curriculum com., 1981-83; chairperson standards com. Cmty. Hosp. of Bedford; former counselor jr. high youth 1st Congl. Ch., Twinsburg; past chair adv. bd. chairperson Brecksville Rainbown Assembly for Girls, 1992; mem. Twinsburg Libr. Levy Com., 1991; mem. Gov.'s Task Force on Compassionate Care, 2003-04. Recipient Paradiam award, 1991. Mem. Ohio Citizen League Nursing Nurse Execs. Network (former sec.), Ohio Hosp. Assn., Ohio Orgn. Nurse Execs., Ohio Directors of Nursing Assocs. Long Term Care, Nat. League Nursing, Southeast Cleve. Mid Mgrs. Ohio Orgn. Nurse Exec., Acad. Med.-Surg. Nursing (charter mem.), Networking Group Nurse Mgrs. (initiated), Order Eastern Star, Sigma Theta Tau, Iota Psi. Avocations: hiking, helping children. Office Phone: 216-447-9604. Personal E-mail: bpilous@aol.com.

PINA, MARTHA ELAINE, social worker, marriage and family therapist; b. Guatemala, Jan. 10, 1968; arrived in US, 1970; d. Pedro and Maria Elena Mansilla; m. Robert Pina, Apr. 11, 1987; children: Madeline S., Stephanie C. BA, Calif. State U., Los Angeles, 1995; MA, Antioch U., 2000. Parenting instr. Dept. Children and Family Svcs., L.A., 2000—, domestic violence facilitator, 2001—; lead adult supr. Calif. Youth Correction, L.A., 2001—. Counselor Christian Tabernacle, Santa Ana, Calif., 2004—. Recipient Social Worker of Yr., Foster Parent Assn., 2000. Mem.: Calif. Assn. of Marriage and Family. Democrat. Apostolic. Avocations: camping, water sports, travel. Office: Dept Children and Family Svcs 10355 Slusher Dr Santa Fe Springs CA 90670 Office Phone: 562-903-5163. Business E-Mail: pinama@dcfs.co.la.ca.us.

PINCOMBE, JODI DORIS, health facility administrator; b. Jersey City, Mar. 16, 1954; d. John Joseph and Dorothy Lillian (Wurster) Niemynski; m. JosephAlbert Corvino, Dec. 1, 1973 (div. June 1986); children: Joseph Albert, Jr., Jennifer Lynn, James Michael; m. Raymond Charles Pincombe, July 9, 1988. Student, Saddleback Coll., 1998—. Cert. procedural coder Am. Acad. Procedural Coders, cert. profl. coder hosp. Data adminstr. KeyProcessors, Inc., Cypress, Calif., 1985-88; supr. Ashton-Tate, Torrance, Calif., 1988-90; front office mgr. WillowTree Podiatry, Laguna Hills, Calif., 1990-92; billing mgr. Med. Svcs. Orgn., Laguna Hills, 1990-96; acct. mgr. Argus Med. Mgmt., Long Beach, Calif., 1997—; dir. ops. PFS Tenet Healthcare Sys., Anaheim, Calif., 1997—. Leader seminar Jodi Pincombe, CPC, CPC-H, Mission Viejo, Calif., 1996—. Mem. Am. Acad. Profl. Coders (mem. adv. bd. 1997-2000, Coder of Yr. 1996), Assn. So. Calif. Procedural Coders (pres. 1994-98, pres. elect. Long Beach chpt. 1997-98), Profl. Assn. Healthcare Office Mgrs., Health Care Compliance Assn., 2000. Republican. Home: 26272 Montarez Cir Mission Viejo CA 92691-5302 Office: Tenet 1500 S Douglas Rd Anaheim CA 92806 E-mail: jodi.pincombe@tenethealth.com.

PINCUS, NANCY, architect, web site designer; d. Samuel and Shirley Pincus; 1 child, Ava Leigh Ichikawa. BArch, The Cooper Union for the Advancement of Sci. and Art, 1986. Project arch. Gensler, N.Y.C., 1994—97; archtl. project cons. HLW Internat., N.Y.C., 1997—2001. Designer, developer, webmaster iHaus.com. Vol. Clinton-Gore Campaign, N.Y.C., 1991—92. Mem.: DNC. Achievements include development of iHaus.com and Babybytes.net. Avocations: painting, internet, design, writing, politics. Personal E-mail: npincus@optonline.net.

PINDELL, HOWARDENA DOREEN, artist; b. Phila., Apr. 14, 1943; d. Howard Douglas and Mildred Edith (Lewis) P. BFA, Boston U., 1965; MFA, Yale U., 1967; DFA (hon.), Mass. Coll. Art, 1997, New Sch./Parsons Sch. Design, 1999. Curatorial asst. Mus. Modern Art, N.Y.C., 1969-71, asst. curator, 1971-77, asso. curator dept. prints and illus. books, 1977-79; asso. prof. art SUNY, Stony Brook, 1979-84, prof. art, 1984—. Contbr. articles to profl. jours.; exhbns. include, Mus. Modern Art, Stockholm and 5 European mus., 1973, Fogg Art Mus., Cambridge, Mass., 1973, Indpls. Mus., Taft Mus., Cin., 1974, Gerald Piltzer Gallery, Paris, 1975, Mus. Modern Art, Paris, 1975, Vassar Coll. Art Gallery, 1977; represented in permanent collections, Mus. Modern Art, N.Y.C., Fogg Art Mus., Met. Mus., N.Y.C., Whitney Mus. Am. Art; represented in travelling exhbns. Brandeis U., U. Calif. at Riverside, Cleve. Inst. Arts, SUNY, Potsdam, New Paltz, Wesleyan U., Davison Art Ctr., others. Recipient Artist award Studio Mus. of Harlem, 1994, Joan Mitchell Painting award Joan Mitchell Found., 1994/95, Women's Caucus for Art award for Disting. Contbns. and Achievement in Arts, 1996, Cmty. Svc. award N.Y. State United Tchrs., 1998, Juneteenth award Heckscher Mus., 1999, IAM Pioneer award, 2000; Japan/U.S. Friendship fellow, 1981-82, Guggenheim fellow, 1987-88; Ariana Found. grantee, 1984-85. Mem. Arts Coun. African Studies Assn., Coll. Art Assn. (Best Exhbn./Performance award 1990), Internat. Assn. Art Critics, Internat. House of Japan (acad.). Office: SUNY/Stonybrook Art Dept Stony Brook NY 11794-0001 Office Phone: 631-632-7266. Office Fax: 631-632-7261. Business E-Mail: hpindell@notes.cc.sunysb.edu.

PINE, BESSIE MIRIAM, social worker, columnist; b. Toronto, Jan. 6, 1919; d. Moses and Annie (Rosenberg) Hadler; m. Kurt Pine, Mar 24, 1943 (dec. May 1962); children: Alfred Marc, Annie Laurie Reuveni. BA in Psychology, U. Toronto, 1939; M in Social Work, U. Pitts., 1944. Lic. social worker, N.Y. Br. dir. YM-YWHA, Toronto, 1940-42; case worker Family Svc. of Greater New Haven, Conn., 1944-47, Jewish Family Svc., Phila., 1947-49; divsn. unit supr. Ednl. Alliance, N.Y.C., 1949-51; older adult supr. Kings Bay YM-YWHA, Bklyn., 1955-59; editor pers. reporter Jewish Comty Ctr Program Aids, dir. part time pers. bur., N.Y.C., 1962-67; assoc. dir. pers. svcs. Jewish Comty. Ctrs. Assn., N.Y.C., 1967-93. Editor: (booklet) Viewpoints on Social and Social Work Issues, 1965; author: (rsch. study) Making Retirement Count: Options and Opportunities, 1989; author: (publ.) Looking Back and Looking Forward: A 75 Year Retrospective on the Assn. of Jewish Center Workers, 1993. Recipient Florence G. Heller award Jewish Comty. Ctrs. Assn., N.Y.C., 1994. Mem. Com. to Strengthen Group Work in Jewish Comty. Ctrs. (co-chair 1992-99), Assn. of Jewish Ctr. Profls. (columnist Ask Bessie 1994-2004, Profl. of Yr., Phila. 1990, Tikkun Olam award Balt. 1993), Nat. Assn. Social Workers (cert. social worker). Home: 150 Beaumont St Brooklyn NY 11235-4119

PINEDA, PATRICIA SALAS, lawyer; BA, Mills Coll., 1974; JD, U. Calif., Berkeley, 1977. Bar: Calif. 1977. Dep. pub. defender Calif. State Pub. Defender, 1977-78; assoc. Crosley Heafy Roach & May, 1978-79; sr. counsel Itel Corp., 1980-84; assoc. gen. counsel New United Motor Mfr., Inc., 1984-88, gen. counsel, asst. corp. sec. Fremont, Calif., 1989—2004; group v.p., corp. comm. gen. counsel Toyota Motor North Am. Inc., 2004—. Dir. Levi Strauss & Co.; trustee Rand Corp. Bd. mem. James Irvine Found., 1994—, bd. vice chair, 2006—. Office: Toyota Motor North America Inc Ste 4900 9 W 57th St New York NY 10019-2701 Office Phone: 212-223-0303.*

PINENO, MARIAM DAVIS, retired music educator, poet; b. Nelson, Pa., Feb. 13, 1929; d. Frank Leonard and Rhea J. Chilson Davis; m. Francis Louis Pineno, June 24, 1951; children: Jonathan Phillip, Elizabeth Gayl Pineno Barron, Michael Davis, Martha Louise Pineno Hess. BS in Music Edn., Mansfield State U., 1950; M in Music Edn., Pa. State U., 1953; diploma writing for children & teenagers, Inst. Children's Lit., 1995. Music educator grades 6-8 Olean (N.Y.) Pub. Schs., 1950-51; music educator grades 1-12 Otto Twp., Duke Ctr., Pa., 1951-53; music educator pre K-5 Shikellamy Sch. Dist., Sunbury, Pa., 1967-92. Author of poetry and stories. Choir dir., organist United Meth. Ch., Selinsgrove, 1954-67; pvt. piano instr., Selinsgrove, 1954-67; workshop leader Music Edn. Students, Mansfield, Pa.; vol. hostess Nonprofit Cygnet Studios, Elizabethtown, Pa., 1990-99, poetry reader, 1999. Mem. Pa. Music Educators Assn. (mem. GO com., elem. region IV rep., citation of excellence in elem. music tchg. for dist. 8 1992), Acad. Am. Poets (assoc.), Pa. Assn. Sch. Retirees (Snyder County chpt.), Soc. of Children's Book Writers and Illustrators. Avocations: reading, writing, travel, decorating. Home: 513 N 9th St Selinsgrove PA 17870-1610 E-mail: writemuse@webtv.net.

PINEROS, ELIZABETH, social services administrator, psychotherapist; b. Bogota, Colombia, Mar. 27, 1956; d. Marco Antonio and Ana Lucia (Parra) P.; m. Michael Selvggio, Sept. 18, 1982 (div. July 1988); 1 child, Leonardo. MSW, NYU, N.Y.C., 1982, advaned cert. social work, 1987, PhD, 2000. Diplomate Am. Bd. Clin. Social Work. Case mgr. Mt. Carmel Guild, Union City, N.J., 1982-84; coord. Jersey City Med. Ctr., 1985; clin. supr. La Casa, Newark, 1986-89; clinician II U. Medicine and Dentistry N.J., Newark, 1989-90; clin dir. Proceed, Inc, Elizabeth, N.J., 1990—. Cons. Dover (N.J.) Bd. Edn., 1990-91, Union County Youth Svc., Linden, N.J., 1993-97; mem. Gov.'s Com. on Children's Planning, State of N.J., 1989-91; mem. Profl. Adv. Com. on Alcohol and Drug Abuse, N.J., 1990—; workshop presenter, 1992, 93. Named Person of Spl. Value, Mental Health Assn., Union County, 1999. Mem. Acad. Cert. Social Workers. Roman Catholic. Home: 112 Belgrade Ave Clifton NJ 07013-1004 Office: Proceed Inc 815 Elizabeth Ave Ste 202 Elizabeth NJ 07201-2788

PINES, BEVERLY IRENE, retired clinical psychologist; b. Bklyn., Nov. 11, 1925; d. Solomon and Jeannette (Radin) Grobstein; m. Matthew Pines, Jan. 29, 1949; children: Elyse Pines Rosenstein, Elliot. BA, Bklyn. Coll., 1944, MA, 1948; PhD, NYU, 1957; postgrad., Walden U. Lic. psychologist, N.Y. Student psychologist Kings County (N.Y.) Hosp., 1945-47; med. asst. to physicians, 1942-49; instr., lectr. Bklyn. Coll., 1946-50, group therapist, 1948-50. Pvt. practice psychol. and psychotherapist marriage and divorce counseling, family therapy, geriatric counseling, substance abuse therapy, cmty. health svcs.-health fairs, Bklyn., 1948-2000; pvt. practice psychol. and psychotherapist marriage and divorce counseling, family therapy, geriatric counseling, substance abuse therapy, cmty. health svcs.-health fairs, Bklyn., 1948—; Nat. Register Health Svc. Providers in Psychology, Blue Cross Blue

Shield Wrap Around plus Ins. Plans and Medicaid and Medicare. Mem. APA, N.Y. State Psychol. Assn., Bklyn. Psychol. Assn., Am. Soc. Clin. Hypnosis Edn. and Rsch. Found., Bklyn. Coll. Alumni Assn. Jewish. Address: 637 E 8th St Brooklyn NY 11218-5905

PINES, LORI L., lawyer; b. Aug. 18, 1966; BA in Biology, cum laude, Harvard U., 1988; JD, NYU Sch. Law, 1992; MPAFF, Princeton U., 1992. Bar: NY, NJ, admitted to practice: US Dist. Ct. (So. Dist.) NY, US Dist. Ct. (Ea. Dist.) NY, US Dist. Ct. (NJ). Ptnr. Weil, Gotshal & Manges LLP, NYC. Mem.: Assn. Bar City NY (com. on women in the profession), ABA. Office: Weil Gotshal & Manges LLP 767 Fifth Ave New York NY 10153 Office Phone: 212-310-8692. Office Fax: 212-310-8007. E-mail: lori.pines@weil.com.

PING-ROBBINS, NANCY REGAN, musicologist, educator; b. Nashville, Dec. 19, 1939; d. Charles Augustus and Ruby Phyllis (Perdue) Regan; m. Robert Leroy Ping, June 19, 1959 (div. 1980); children: Robert Alan, Michael Regan, Bryan Edward; m. William Edward Robbins, Jr., Mar. 14, 1981. BMusic, Ind. U., 1964; MA, U. No. Colo., 1972; PhD, U. Colo., 1979. Pvt. instr. piano and flute, 1960—; organist Armed Forces Chapels, Frankfurt, Kaiserslautern, Germany, 1962-66; staff pianist US Armed Forces Spl. Svcs. Theater, Frankfurt, 1963-65; music tchr. Fayetteville Pub. Schs., Ind., 1966-67, Stratton Pub. Schs., Colo., 1967-70; instr. piano, staff piano accompanist U. No. Colo., Greeley, 1970-72; instr. music history U. Colo., Boulder, 1974; instr., asst. prof. music U. NC, Wilmington, 1974-79; assoc. prof. music, coord. music Shaw U., Raleigh, NC, 1979-87; dir. Atlantic CC Com. Arts Sch., 1987-88. Profl. harpsichord accompanist Internat. Inst. in Early Music, 1983; adj. prof. Atlantic Christian Coll. (now Barton Coll.), 1987—88, assoc. prof., 1987—95; mem., pianist Chekker Duo, 1996—2003, 2006—. Recs. include Early Popular Music on Piano/Harpsichord, 1984, En Blanc et Noir, 2001; author: The Piano Trio in the Twentieth Century, 1984, Scott Joplin: A Guide to Research, 1998; editor, compiler: The Music of Gustave Blessner, 1985; music reviewer News and Observer, Raleigh, 1981-96, head music critic, 1989-95; contbr. articles to profl. jours. Sec. Bach Festival Com., Raleigh, 1984; dir. music Bailey United Meth. Ch., N.C., 2000—. John H. Edwards fellow Ind. U., 1961; U. Colo. grad fellow, 1972-74; Mellon Found. grantee, 1982; N.C. Arts Coun. grantee, 1985; NEH summer seminar fellow, 1984. Mem. Am. Musicol. Soc. (sec.-treas. chpt. 1981-83), Soc. for Ethnomusicology (chmn. regional chpt. 1983-84), Wilson Piano Tchrs. Assn. (pres. 1988-90, 95-98), Soc. Am. Music (formerly Sonneck Soc., program com. 1999), Alpha Lambda Delta, Pi Kappa Lambda, Sigma Alpha Iota.

PINHEIRO, GERMANIA ARAUJO, physician, researcher; d. Francisco Arruda and Maria da Conceicao Pinheiro; m. Vinicius Cavalcanti Antao, June 23, 2003; 1 child, Sophie Pinheiro Cavalcanti. MD, Petropolis Sch. of Medicine, Brazil, 1992; MSc, Fluminense Fed. U., Brazil, 1998; PhD, Sao Paulo U., Brazil, 2003. Cert. Pulmonologist Rio de Janeiro State U., 1996, Occupl. Medicine Specialist Gama Filho U., 1998. Assoc. prof. of pulmonology Rio de Janeiro State U., Rio de Janeiro, Rio de Janeiro, 1996—2003; prof. occupl. medicine Gama Filho U., Rio de Janeiro, 1996—2003; pulmonologist Rio de Janeiro State Office for Justice and the Interior, Rio de Janeiro, 1998—2002; mem. State Tech. Commn. of Occupl. Lung Diseases - Rio de Janeiro State Office for Health, Rio de Janeiro, 1998—2003; physician Brazilian Army Ctrl. Hosp., Rio de Janeiro, 1997—99; adj. asst. prof. W.Va. U., Morgantown, W.Va., 2003—; epidemic intelligence svc. officer Nat. Inst. Occupl. Health/Ctrs. for Disease Control & Prevention, Morgantown, 2003—05, sr. svc. fellow, 2005—. Grantee Bronze Sponsorship, European Respiratory Soc., 2002. Mem.: European Respiratory Soc., Am. Thoracic Soc. Home: 132 Bakers Dr Morgantown WV 26505 Office: Nat Inst Occupl Health Ctrs for Disease Control & Prevention 1095 Willodale Rd Morgantown WV 26505 Office Phone: 304-285-6095. Office Fax: 304-285-6111. Personal E-mail: ghp6@cdc.gov.

PINK, (ALECIA B. MOORE), singer; b. Doylestown, Pa., Sept. 8, 1979; m. Carey Hart, Jan. 7, 2006. With Arista Records, 2001—. Singer: (albums) Can't Take Me Home, 2000, M!ssundaztood, 2001, Try This, 2003, I'm Not Dead, 2006, (songs) There U Go, 2000, Most Girls, 2000, (with Mya, Lil' Kim, Christina Aguilera) Lady Marmalade, 2001 (Grammy award Song Yr., 2002, 2 MTV Video Music awards, 2001), You Make Me Sick, 2001, Get the Party Started, 2001 (2 MTV Video Music Awards, 2002), Don't Let Me Get Me, 2002, Just Like a Pill, 2002, Family Portrait, 2002, Feel Good Time, 2003, Trouble, 2003 (Grammy award, Best Female Rock Performance, 2004), God is a DJ, 2003, Stupid Girls, 2006 (MTV Video Music award for Best Pop Video, 2006); actor: (films) Rollerball, 2002, Charlie's Angels: Full Throttle, 2003. Named one of 100 Sexiest Artists, VH1, 2002; recipient World Music award for Best Am. Pop Female Artist, 2003. Office: Box #390 5701 E Circle Dr Cicero NY 13039*

PINKE, JUDITH ANN, state official; b. Ft. Snelling, Minn., Oct. 16, 1944; d. August Henry and Dorothy E. (Bartelt) Hinrichs; m. Kurt G.O. Pinke, June 29, 1974. BA cum laude, St. Olaf Coll., 1966; postgrad., Harvard U., 1980. Supr., tchr. Mpls. Pub. Schs., Mpls., 1966—71; writer, editor U. Minn., Mpls., 1971—72; counselor Secretarial Placement, Edina, Minn., 1972—73; asst. to commr. Minn. Dept. Labor and Industry, St. Paul, 1973—76; mgr. info. resources Minn. Dept. Adminstrn., St. Paul, 1976—77; asst. commr. for fin. and adminstrn. Minn. Dept. Transp., St. Paul, 1977—85; dir. met. sys. dept. Met. Coun. Twin Cities Area, 1985—87; pres. pres. Pinke and Assocs., 1985—; asst. commr. InterTech. Group Minn. Dept. Adminstrn., St. Paul, 1987—. Reader advanced placement exams Ednl. Testing Svc., Princeton, NJ, 1968—71; curriculum planner, faculty Exec. Devel. Inst. Hamline U., 1986—; presenter in field. Active Minn. Info. Policy Coun., 1979—85, chmn., 1982—85; active Twin Cities Metro Futures Task Force, 1988—, chmn., 1988—89; rsch. adv. bd. Kennedy Sch. Govt. Harvard U., 1989. Mem.: LWV, Women Execs. in Govt. (Nat. Leadership Coun., chair spl. membership task force), Women's Transp. Seminar, Minn. Ctr. Women in Govt. (adv. bd., exec. com. 1985—, chmn. long range planning and evaluation com. 1985—86, chmn. alliances com. 1987—), Women in State Employment (co-founder 1976), Loft, Horizon 100. Office: State Minn Dept Adminstrn 50 Sherburne Ave Saint Paul MN 55155-1402

PINKERTON, MARJORIE JEAN, librarian, library science educator; b. Chgo., June 15, 1934; d. Michael Seretto and Evelyn Isabel (Scott) Glass; m. James Ronald Pinkerton, June 29, 1957; children— Steven James, Kathryn Lynn. B.A. in Spanish and History, Carroll Coll., 1956; MA in Spanish, U. Wis., Madison, 1964; MA in Library Sci., U. Mo., 1973. Tchr. high sch., Pardeeville, Wis., 1956-57, Preble, Wis., 1958-59; libr. asst. Meml. Libr., U. Wis., Madison, 1959-64; substitute tchr., librarian Columbia Pub. Schs., Mo., 1965-73; ednl. materials librarian, asst. prof. William Woods Coll., Fulton, Mo., 1973-81, assoc. prof., 1985-93, ret., 1993, dir. Dulany Libr. 1981—93. Co-author: Outdoor Recreation and Leisure, 1969. Contbr. articles to profl. jours. Mem. Bd. Adjustment, City of Columbia, 1971-75, chmn., 1973-74; dir. Nat. Ghost Ranch Found., United Presbyterian Ch., Santa Fe, N.Mex., 1981-84; mem. Columbia Safety Coun., 1967—, pres., 1969-70. Recipient award for cmty. svc. New Democratic Coalition, Columbia, 1976, Outstanding Young Woman award, 1969. Mem. ALA, Mo. Assn. Coll. and Rsch. Libraries (chmn. 1984-85), Mo. Libr. Assn. (com. chmn. 1978-79), Mid-Mo. Associated Colls. and Univs. (chmn. libr. com. 1984-85), Nat. Coun. Tchrs. English, LWV (v.p. 1967-68, 2002—), Nat. Geneal. Soc., Beta Phi Mu (pres. 1974-76, 85-86), Peace Studies Inst., Phi Alpha Theta, Kappa Delta Pi. Presbyterian. Clubs: UN (pres. 1970—), Friends of the Libr. (Columbia, sec.-treas. 1977-78), Gertrude Matthews Soc., Jefferson Club, U. Mo. Libr. Soc. Avocations: genealogy, reading, travel, walking. Home: 1014 Westport Dr Columbia MO 65203-0744 Personal E-mail: mpmidge@aol.com.

PINKETT-SMITH, JADA, actress; b. Balt., Sept. 18, 1971; m. Will Smith, Dec. 31, 1997; 2 children. Actor: (films) Menace II Society, 1993, The Inkwell, 1994, Jason's Lyric, 1994, A Low Down Dirty Shame, 1994, Demon Knight, 1995, The Nutty Professor, 1996, Set It Off, 1996, Blossoms and Veils, 1997 (also exec. prodr.), Scream 2, 1997, Woo, 1998, Return to Paradise, 1998, Bamboozled, 2000, Kingdom Come, 2001, Ali, 2001, The Matrix Reloaded, 2003, The Matrix Revolutions, 2003, Collateral, 2004, (voice) Madagascar, 2005, (TV films) If These Walls Could Talk, 1996, Maniac Magee, 2003, (TV series) A Different World, 1992-93, exec. prodr. All of Us, 2003-; exec. prodr. (films) The Seat Filler, 2004; author (children's book): Girls Hold Up This World, 2004 (NY Times Bestseller list, NAACP Image award for outstanding lit. work-children's 2006).*

PINKHAM, ELEANOR HUMPHREY, retired university librarian; b. Chgo., May 7, 1926; d. Edward Lemuel and Grace Eleanor (Cushing) Humphrey; m. James Hansen Pinkham, July 10, 1948; children: Laurie Sue, Carol Lynn. AB, Kalamazoo Coll., 1948; MS in Libr. Sci., Western Mich. U., 1967. Pub. svcs. libr. Kalamazoo Coll., 1967-68, asst. libr., 1969-70, libr. dir., 1971-93, ret., 1993. Vis. lectr. Western Mich. U. Sch. Librarianship, 1970-84; mem. adv. bd., 1977-81, also adv. bd. Inst. Cistercian Studies Libr., 1975-80. Alice Louise LeFevre scholar, 1967. Mem. ALA, AAUP, ACRL (chmn. coll. libr. sect. 1988-89), Mich. Libr. Assn. (pres. 1983-84, chmn. acad. divsn. 1977-78), Mich. Libr. Consortium (exec. coun. 1974-82, chmn. 1977-78, Mich. Libr. of Yr. 1986), OCLC Users Coun., Beta Phi Mu. Home: #103 4040 Greenleaf Cir Kalamazoo MI 49008-2525

PINKHAM, LISE KUTZMAN, humanities educator; b. Offutt AFB, Nebr., Dec. 12, 1967; d. Nathaniel John and Ellen Joan Kutzman; m. Jeffrey Scott Pinkham, Aug. 8, 1997; children: Benjamin Scott, Lucas Allen John. BA in History and Edn., Mont. State U., Bozeman, 1990. Cert. history, govt., and social studies tchr. Idaho, 1990, social studies tchr. Vt., 2000. History tchr. Eagle Rock Jr. High, Idaho Falls, Idaho, 1990—96, Skyline H.S., Idaho Falls, 1996—99, Northfield Mid./High Sch., Vt., 1999—2000; humanites tchr. Colchester H.S., Vt., 2000—. Personal E-mail: lakpinkham@adelphia.net.

PINKINS, TONYA, actress; b. Chicago, May 30, 1962; m. Ron Brawer, Feb. 12, 1987 (div. 1987); 2 children; 4 children. Attended, Northwestern U., Summer Theater Inst., Chicago, 1978; student, Carnegie Mellon U., 1980—81; BA, Columbia Coll., Chicago, 1996; student, Calif. Western Law Sch., San Diego. Private acting instr. Montclair School of Dance, 1993; visual arts instr., 6th to 8th grades LAUSD, 2000—01; private coach voice, music performance, acting, 2002. Playwriting com. Playwrights' Preview Prodn., 1986—88; instr. cold reading Univ. Calif., San Diego, 2000. Actor: (Broadway plays) Merrily We Roll Along, 1981, Jelly's Last Jam, 1992 (Tony award best featured actress in a musical, 1992, Drama Desk award best featured actress in a musical, 1992, Clarence Derwent award, 1992, Outer Critics Circle award best featured actress in a musical, 1993), Chronicle of a Death Foretold, 1995, Play On!, 1997 (Tony nom. best actress in a musical, 1997), The Wild Party, 2000, Caroline, Or Change, 2004— (Tony nom. best actress in a musical, 2004, Obie award best perf., 2004), (Off Broadway plays) Little Shop of Horrors, 1983, A.My Name Alice, 1985, Just Say No, 1988, Believin'/Psychoneurotic Fantasies, 1990, The Caucasian Chalk Circle, 1990, The Merry Wives of Windsor, 1994, The Vagina Monologues, 2000, The House of Flowers, 2003; (plays) Stealin', Joe Turner's Come and Gone, 1989, The Piano Lesson, 1989, Approximating Mother, 1991, No Niggers, No Jews, No Dogs, 2000, Thoroughly Modern Millie, 2000; (TV series) As the World Turns, 1983—86, University Hospital, 1994, All My Children, 1991—95, 2003—; (TV films) American Dream, 1981, Rage of Angels: The Story Continues, 1986, Strapped, 1993, Against Their Will: Women in Prison, 1994, (TV Guest appearances) Crime Story, 1986, The Cosby Show, 1990, Law & Order, 1990, The Guardian, 2002; (films) Beat Street, 1984, See No Evil, Hear No Evil, 1989, Above the Rim, 1994, Love Hurts, 2002, Romance & Cigarettes, 2005, Premium, 2006; voice (audio books) The Women of Brewster Place, 1992, The Book of Virtues I and II, 1993, The Moral Compass, 1995, Chocolate for a Woman's Soul, 1997, The Silent Cradle, 1998; author: (book) Get Over Yourself: How to Drop the Drama and Claim the Life You Deserve, 2006; singer: (albums) Live @ Joe's Pub. Achievements include co-founder of OPERATION Z: zero tolerance of violence against women and children.*

PINKUS, DEBORAH SUE, special education educator; d. Alvin A. and Nettie Lebowitz; m. Barry Charles Pinkus, July 16, 1978; children: Jason, Joshua, Jonathan, Jared. BA in Elem. Edn., U. Bridgeport, 1975; MA in Spl. Edn., So. Conn. State Coll., 1976. Spl. edn. tchr. Ben Haven Sch., New Haven, 1975—78, Hamden Pub. Schs., 1978—80; para-profl. spl. edn. Highland Elem. Sch., Cheshire, 1990—2000, spl. edn. tchr., 2000—. Ednl. cons. Cheshire Schs., 1988—89, homebound tutor, 1997—2001. Bd. dirs. Playground Without Boundaries, 2004—.

PINKWATER, JULIE, publishing executive; B, Boston U. With Sotheby's Internat. Realty, Network TV Assn; with advertising agency McCaffrey & McCall, Penchina Selkowitz, McCann Erickson; mgr. position Ladies Home Jour.; beauty dir. Allure; advertising dir. More, 1998—2000, pub., 2000—01, Fitness Mag., G&J USA, NY, 2001—04; v.p., pub. Ladies Home Jour., NY, 2004—. Office: Ladies Home Jour 125 Park Ave 20th Floor New York NY 10017-5529 Office Phone: 212-551-7153. Office Fax: 212-455-1313. E-mail: julie.pinkwater@meredith.com.*

PINN, VIVIAN W., federal agency administrator, pathologist; b. Halifax, Va., 1941; BA, Wellesley Coll., 1963; MD, U. Va., 1967. Intern in pathology Mass. Gen. Hosp., Boston, 1967-68, rschr. in pathology, 1968-70; asst. pathologist Tufts U. New England Med. Ctr. Hosp., 1970-77, pathologist, 1977-82; from asst. to assoc. prof. pathology Tufts U., 1971-82, asst. dean student affairs, 1974-82; prof., dept. chair pathology Howard U., 1982-91; first dir. Office Rsch. on Women's Health, NIH, Bethesda, Md., 1991—, assoc. dir. rsch. women's health, 1994—, dir. Office Women's Health Rsch. Pres. Nat. Med. Assn., 1989—90. Office: NIH Office Rsch on Women's Health 9000 Rockville Pike Bldg 1 Rm 201 Bethesda MD 20892 Office Phone: 301-402-1770.

PINNEY, ALESIA L., lawyer; b. Seattle, 1963; m. Jack Brown; children: Keathley, Jon. BA, Seattle U.; MA, U. Denver, 1989; JD, U. Puget Sound, 1991. Acct. Deloitte & Touche, Denver, 1985—89; law clk. Chief Judge Lapsley W. Hamblen Jr. U.S. Tax Ct., 1991—93; employee Bogle & Gaes and Perkins Coie, 1993—98; sr. corp. counsel RealNetworks Inc., 1997; chief privacy officer, v.p., gen. counsel and sec. Drugstore.com, Inc., Bellevue, Wash., 1999—. Office: Drugstore Com 411 108th Ave NE Ste 1400 Bellevue WA 98004-8417

PINSDORF, MARION KATHERYN, diversified financial services company executive, educator, writer; b. Teaneck, N.J., June 22, 1932; d. Charles W. and Katheryn S. (Green) P. BA cum laude, Drew U., 1954; MA, NYU, 1967, PhD, 1976; DSc in Bus. Adminstrn. (hon.), Nichols Coll., 1982. Polit. reporter, editor women's dept. The Record, Hackensack, NJ, 1954—61; assoc. copy editor Good Housekeeping mag., 1962-64; comms. specialist Borden, Inc., 1964-69; v.p. Hill and Knowlton, N.Y.C., 1970-77; v.p. corp. rels. Textron, Inc., Providence, 1977-80; v.p. corp. comms. INA Corp., Phila., 1980-82; ind. mgmt. cons. 1982—. Adj. asst. prof. Brazilian studies Brown U., 1979-89; assoc. prof. grad. sch. bus. Fordham U., 1987-94, sr. fellow in comms., 1994-2003; lectr. in field. Author: Communicating When Your Company Is Under Siege, Surviving Public Crisis, 1987, 3d edit., 1998, German Speaking Entrepreneurs: Builders of Business in Brazil South, 1990, All Crises are Global: Managing to Escape Chaos, 2004; mem. editl. adv. bd. Pub. Rels. Quar.; author book revs.; contbr. articles to profl. jours. Trustee, Drew U., Madison, N.J., 1977-81; pres. Leonia (N.J.) Pub. Libr., 1973-76; bd. dirs. Bergen County Hist. Preservation, 1998—. Home: 114 Leonia Ave Leonia NJ 07605-1916

PINSKY, CHARLOTTE LEE (CHERIE PINSKY), retired academic administrator; b. Hartford, Conn., Aug. 12, 1946; d. David and Charlotte (Abrams) P. BFA, R.I. Sch. Design, 1968. Nutritionist, handicraft developer U.S. Peace Corps., Narino, Colombia, 1971-74; adminstr. dept. radiology U. Calif., San Francisco, 1987—2006; ret., 2006. Mem. de Young Meml. Mus. (docent). Docent Fine Arts Mus., San Francisco. Avocations: 19th century english literature, swimming, skiing. Home: 1925 Leavenworth St Apt 12 San Francisco CA 94133-5303

PINSON, MARGARET ANN, special education educator; b. Whitcha Falls, Tex., Sept. 1, 1951; d. Clyde W. and Annie B. (Musgrove) Buchanan; m. Robert L. Phillips, June 22, 1971 (div. Aug. 29, 1980); children: Chrisopher, Susan; m. E. Thomas Pinson, July 28, 1990. AA, Chipola Jr. Coll., 1971; BA, Fla. State U., 1978; MA, U. West Fla., 1989. Cert. tchr., Fla. Media technician, sec. Chipola Jr. Coll., Marianna, Fla., 1972-74; tchr. aide Calhoun County Sch. Bd., Blountstown, Fla., 1975, compensatory edn. tchr., 1978-81; tchr. Sunland Tng. Ctr., Marianna, 1982-85, 87-88, Grady County Pub. Schs., Cairo, Ga., 1985-87, Boys' Sch., Washington County Sch. Bd., Marianna, 1989; tchr. migrant edn. Washington County Sch. Bd., Quincy, Fla., 1991-92; sr. counselor Camp Discovery, Tallahasse Parks, Tallahassee, Fla., 1991-94; spl. edn. tchr. Gadsden County Sch. Bd., Quincy, 1988—. County coord. Gadsden County Spl. Olympics, Quincy, 1992—; co-county coord. Grady County Spl. Olympics, Cairo, 1985-87; safety com. Sunland Tng. Ctr., Marianna, 1983-85; rep. sch. coun. George Munroe Elem. Sch., Quincy, 1992-95. Rep. to Spl. Olympics Fla. Program Adv. Coun., 1995-96; cmty. hero torch runner 1996 Atlanta Olympic Games. Recipient Marilyn Grisby award, Spl. Olympics, Fla., 2006. Democrat. Methodist. Avocations: storytelling, reading. Office: George W Munroe Elem Sch 1830 W King St Quincy FL 32351-2013 Personal E-mail: mp1001@email.com.

PINTER, ELIZABETH, retired communications educator; b. Weleetka, Okla., Mar. 13, 1924; d. Harry and Nellie (Adamson) Lees; m. Elizabeth Louise Pinter; children: Stephanie Bellows, Claudia Lucke. BS in Journalism & Latin Am. Studies, U. Okla., 1945; MS in Journalism, Columbia U., 1946. Dir. Study Abroad Inc., NYC, 1950—70; prof. Palomar Coll., San Marcos, Calif., 1972—90. Pres. Calif. Assn. Libr. Trustees & Commrs., Sacramento, 1995—96; chair Ctr. for the Arts, Escondido, Calif., 2004—. Mem.: Phi Beta Kappa.

PINTER, SUSANN BARBARA, education educator; Diploma, U. Goettingen, Germany, 1992; Masters in Sci. and Tchg., U. Vt., Burlington, 1995. Tchr. Ridgefield HS, Conn., 1995—96, Marion HS, Ill., 1997—2002; instr. So. Ill. U., Carbondale, 2003—. Author: (jour. articles) Guide for Environmental Sci., 1995, Jour. Geology, 1998, Geological Soc. of Am. Bulletin, 1998, Jour. Geological Edn., 2001. Avocations: fencing, violin. Office: Geology Dept So Ill Univ Carbondale IL 62901 Business E-Mail: spinter@geo.siu.edu.

PINTO, MARIE MALANIA, academic administrator, consultant; b. Tulare, Calif., Aug. 30, 1963; d. Joe Martin and Marie Inez Simoes; m. Joe John Pinto, Dec. 30, 1953; children: Jonathon Joseph, Jameson Jesse, Andrew Clayton, Jordan Michael. B in Bus. Mgmt., U. Phoenix, 2000, MBA, 2002; M in Ednl. Adminstrn., Calif. State U., Fresno, 2003. Cert. vocat. instr. Calif., 1996, adminstrv. svcs. credential 2003. Dept. mgr. Gottschalks, Visalia, Calif., 1984—91, tng. mgr., 1989—91, asst. buyer Fresno, 1991—94, asst. store mgr. Santa Maria, 1994—95; vocat. instr. Tulare Adult Sch., 1996—2002, work experience coord., 1999—2002, adminstrv. intern, 2002—03, asst. dir., 2003—. Staff devel. trainer, cons. Marie Pinto & Associates, Visalia, 1998—. Cons., vol. Visalia C. of C. Recipient School-to-Career Partnership award, Tulare County Office Edn., 2001. Mem.: Calif. Coun. Adult Educators (pres.-elect ctrl. sect.), Tng. and Employment Assn. Tulare County (v.p.), Assn. Calif. Sch. Adminstrs., Calif. Tchrs. Assn., Tulare Soroptimist, Tulare C. of C. Democrat. Roman Catholic. Avocations: aerobics, travel, reading, entertaining, volunteer work. Home: 5548 W Vine Ct Visalia CA 93291 Office: Tulare Adult Sch 575 W Maple Tulare CA 93274 Office Phone: 559-686-0225. Personal E-mail: jjpmmp98@aol.com. Business E-Mail: marie.pinto@tulare.k12.ca.us.

PINTO, MARION, artist; b. NYC, Nov. 7, 1935; d. Stephen Pane Pinto and Anne Mecca. Large scale portraits, NYC, 1968—69, one-woman shows include This Floor, 1970, large scale female nudes, The Venus Triptych, 1972, Junk Site Nude, 1972, Sleeping Church Nude, 1973, American Nude, 1973, large scale male nudes, Man as a Sex Object #1 & #2, 1973, Male Nude with Sculpture, 1974, Double Male Nude, 1974, Male Odalisquie, 1974, one-woman shows include Man as a Sex Object, J. Frederic Lohman Gallery, NYC, 1975, mural, The Ballroom Mural, Ballroom Restaurant, SoHo, NYC, 1976, large scale commd. murals, The Montauk Series, 1978, From the Rainbow Room, 1979, The Jacobs Living Room Mural, 1979, exhibitions include The Egypt Series, 1980—84, Hikawa series, Shimane Festival, NYC, 1991, portrait, The Food Buddha, Ballroom Restaurant, NYC, 1992, exhibitions include Living in the Land of the Gods.and Goddesses (2nd in Hikawa series), NYC, 1996, exhibited in group shows, nat., internat. Democrat. Achievements include studying Japanese art culminating in work more minimal, though realistic, 1986-89. Avocations: swimming, walking, museums, concerts.

PINTOZZI, CHESTALENE, librarian; b. Macomb, Okla., Apr. 4, 1947; d. Otis William and Edith Marie (Jordan) Bowerman; m. Nicola Francis Xavier Pintozzi, Aug. 2, 1967 (div.) Student, U. Okla., 1965-67; BA in English, No. Ill. U., 1969; MLS, U. Tex., 1981. Geology libr. U. Tex., Austin, 1982-84; environ. libr., Ann Marbut Environ. Libr. Sarasota (Fla.) County Pub. Libr. Sys., 1985-87; temporary reference libr. Sci.-Engring. Libr. U. Ariz., Tucson, 1989-90, reference libr. Sci.-Engring. Libr., 1990—. Mem. Geosci. Info. Soc., Soc. for Scholarly Pub., Beta Phi Mu, Phi Kappa Phi. Democrat. Office: U Ariz Bldg 54 Rm 216 Tucson AZ 85720 Office Phone: 602-621-6392. E-mail: pintozzic@u.library.arizona.edu.

PIOU-BREWER, MAGALIE, psychotherapist, educator, small business owner; b. Arthabaska, Que., Can., Apr. 26, 1971; d. Edouard Louis and Jacqueline Dorcal Piou; m. Michael Alexander Brewer, July 21, 2003; 1 child, Anya Lilly Brewer. Student, Cath. U., Leuven, Belgium, 1991—92; BA in Comm., Loyola Coll., Balt., 1993, MS in Pastoral Counseling, 2000; PhD in Clinical Psychology, George Washington U., 2004. Lic. counselor. Assoc. dir. admissions Loyola Coll., Balt., 1994—2001; child psychotherapist Stevenson Psychol. Svcs., Columbia, Md., 2001—03; clin. dir. Bridgeway Counseling Svcs., Columbia, 2004—; exec. dir. MPB Group, Inc., Columbia, 2004—. Adj. asst. prof. Loyola Coll. Grad. Ctr., Columbia, 2005—; spkr. in field. Acad. fellow, George Washington U., 2000—03, Maternal/Child Health grant, Kennedy Kreiger Inst., Balt., 2003. Mem.: APA, Am. Counselors Assn., Am. Mental Health Counselors Assn. Avocations: reading, travel. Office: MPB Group Inc 9650 Santiago Rd Ste 11 Columbia MD 21045 Office Phone: 410-730-2385.

PIPER, ADRIAN MARGARET SMITH, philosopher, artist, educator; b. N.Y.C., Sept. 20, 1948; d. Daniel Robert and Olive Xavier (Smith) P.; m. Jeffrey Ernest Evans, June 27, 1982 (div. 1987). AA, Sch. Visual Arts, 1969; BA in Philosophy, CCNY, 1974; MA, Harvard U., 1977, PhD, 1981; student, U. Heidelberg, Germany, 1977-78; LHD (hon.), Calif. Inst. Arts, 1992, Mass. Coll. Art, 1994. Asst. prof. U. Mich., Ann Arbor, 1979-86; Mellon rsch. fellow Stanford (Calif.) U., 1982-84; assoc. prof. Georgetown U., Washington, 1986-88, U. Calif., San Diego, 1988; prof. philosophy Wellesley (Mass.) Coll., 1990—. Disting. scholar Getty Rsch. Inst., 1998—; speaker, lectr. on both philosophy and art. Artist: one-woman exhbns. include N.Y. Cultural Ctr., N.Y.C., 1971, Montclair (N.J.) State Coll., 1976, Wadsworth Atheneum, Hartford, Conn., 1980, Nexus COntemporary Art Ctr., Atlanta, 1987, The Alternative Mus., N.Y.C., 1987, Goldie Paley Gallery, Phila., 1989, Power Plant Gallery, Toronto, 1990, Lowe Art Mus., Coral Gables, Fla., 1990-91, Santa Monica (Calif.) Mus. Contemporary Art, 1991, John Weber Gallery, N.Y.C., 1989, 90, 91, 92, Whitney Mus. Am. Art, N.Y.C., 1990, Hirschorn Mus., Washington, 1991, Ikon Gallery, Birmingham, Eng., 1991, Cornerhouse, Manchester, Eng., 1992, Cartwright Hall, Bradford, Eng., 1992, Kunstverein, Munich, Germany, 1992, Indpls. Ctr. Contemporary Art, 1992, Manasterio de Santa Clara, Moguer, Spain, 1992, Grey Art Gallery, N.Y.C.,

1992, Paula Cooper Art Galler, 1992, 94; group exhbns. include Paula Cooper Gallery, 1969, Dwan Gallery, N.Y.C., 1969, 70, Seattle Art Mus., 1969, Stadtisches Mus., Leverkusen, Germany, 1969, Kunsthalle Berne, Berne, Switzerland, 1969, N.Y. Cultural Ctr., 1970, Allen Mus., Oberlin, Ohio, 1970, Mus. Modern Art, N.Y.C., 1970, 88, 91, Musee d'Art Moderne, Paris, 1971, 77, 89, Inhibodress Gallery, New South Wales, Australia, 1972, Calif. Inst. Arts, Valencia, 1973, Samuel S. Fleischer Art Meml., Phila., 1974, Mus. Contemporary Art, Chgo., 1975, Newberger Mus., Purchase, N.Y., 1978, Mass. Coll. Art, Boston, 1979, Artemesia Gallery, Chgo., 1979, A.I.R. Gallery, N.Y.C., 1980, Inst. Contemporary Arts, London, 1980, The New Mus., N.Y.C., 1981, 83, 85, Kenkeleba Gallery, N.Y.C., 1983, The Studio Mus. Harlem, N.Y.C., 1985, 89, Mus. Moderner Kunst, Vienna, Austria, 1985, Intar Gallery, N.Y.C., 1988, Whitney Mus. Downtown, N.Y.C., 1988, Art Gallery Ont., Toronto, 1988, Long Beach (Calif.) Art Mus., 1989, Simon Watson Gallery, N.Y.C., 1990, Feigen Gallery, Chgo., 1990, Barbara Krakow Gallery, Boston, 1990, Milw. Art Mus., 1990, Contemporary Arts Ctr., Houston, 1991, John Weber Gallery, 1991, Anne Plumb Gallery, N.Y.C., 1991, Hirschorn Mus., 1991, The Albuquerque Mus. Art, 1991, The Toledo Mus. Art, 1991, Denver Art Mus., Fukui Fine Arts Mus., Fukyui-ken, Japan, 1992-93, N.J. State Mus., Trenton, 1992-93, Philippe Staib Gallery, N.Y.C., 1992, New Loom House, London, 1992, Espace-Lyonnais D'Art Contemporain, Lyon, France, 1993, Am. Acad. Inst. Arts and Letters, N.Y.C., 1993; permanent collections include Met. Mus. Art, Whitney Mus., L.A. Mus. Contemporary Art, San Francisco Mus. Modern Art, The Bklyn. Mus., Denver Art Mus., Kunstmuseum Berne, Musee d'Art Moderne, The Mus. Contemporary Art, Chgo., The Wadsworth Atheneum, Met. Mus. Art; art performances include RISD, 1973, The Whitney Mus. Am. Art, 1975, Kurfurstendamm, Berlin, 1977, Hauptstrasse, Heidelburg, Germany, 1978, Allen Meml. Mus., Oberlin, Ohio, 1980, Contemporary Art Inst. Detroit, 1980, San Francisco Art Inst., 1985, Calif. Inst. Art, 1984, The Studio Mus. Harlem, 1988; performances on video, 1987—; contbr. articles to profl. jours. Recipient N.Y. State Coun. on Arts award, 1989, Visual Arts award, 1990, Skowhegan medal for sculptural installation, 1995, Dance Theatre Workshop award for New Genres, 2000; NEH Travel fellow, 1979, NEA Visual Artists' fellow, 1979, 82, Andrew Mellon Postdoctoral fellow, 1982-84, Woodrow Wilson Internat. Scholars fellow, 1988-89, Guggenheim Meml. fellow, 1989, non-resident fellow N.Y. Inst. for Humanities, NYU, 1996—, Wissenschftskolleg zu Berlin Inst. Adv. Study fellow, 2005-; NEA Artists Forums grantee, 1987; rsch. fellowship NEH, 1998, Getty Rsch. Inst. Disting. scholarship, 1998-99, Internat. Forschungszentrum Kulturwissenschaften fellow Vienna, fellow Wissenschetskolleg zu Berlin Inst. Advanced Study, 2005-. Mem. AAUP, Am. Philos. Assn. (mem. ea. divsn.), Am. Soc. Polit. and Legal Philosophy, N.Am. Kant. Soc. Avocations: Medieval and Renaissance music, fiction, poetry, yoga, German. Office: Adrian Piper Rsch Archives Postfach 54 02 04 D-10042 Berlin Germany Office Phone: 49-30-308-253-18. E-mail: contact@adrianpiper.com, contact@adrianpiper.com.

PIPER, J. K. See GILES, KATHARINE

PIPER, JAMI KATHLEEN, music educator, composer, musician; b. Oakland, California, Dec. 31, 1955; d. Barry Eugene Piper and Margaret Letitia (Weis) Smythe; children: Stephanie June Hauck, Matthew Lewis Hook. MusB, U. Pacific, Stockton, Calif., 1976; MFA, Mills Coll., Oakland, Calif., 1987; postgrad., U. Colo., Boulder. Cert. pre-sch. through 12 tchg. credential in music U. Colo., Boulder, 1997, nat. certified tchr. of music in piano Nat. Music Tchrs. Assn. Piano accompanist, soloist contracted, Calif., 1962—; piano tchr. self employed, Calif., 1976—94, 2004—, Colo., 1996—2002; adj. educator Music Tchr. Assn. Calif., Calif., 1989—, Music Tchr. Nat. Assn., Colo., 1994—2002; vocal, instrumental music tchr. Boulder Valley Sch., Colo., 1995—2002; gen. music, theory, and history tchr. Boulder Arts Acad., Colo., 1995—98; piano accompanist, soloist contracted, Colo., 1995—2002. V.p., treas. Music Tchr. Assn. Calif., Alameda County, 1990—92, pres., 1992—94; v.p. Boulder Area Music Tchr. Assn., Colo., 1994—95; chair of auditions Colo. Music Tchr. Assn., Colo., 1996—98; Am. advisor Kitumusote, Tanzania, 2005. Composer: (hymn) Benediction, 1986, Give Him the Praise, 1986, God Almighty, God of Love, 1987; musician: (solo concert debut U.S.) Oakland, Calif., 1973, (solo concert debut Europe) Mendemblik, Noord-Holland, 1988; arranger: Doulos, 1986. Pres. Daughters of the King, Prince of Peace Chpt., Fair Oaks, Calif., 2006—. Recipient U. Pacific Music Grant, U. Pacific, Stockton, Calif., 1973—76, Calif. State Scholarship, State of Calif., 1973—76, Mary M. Henry Prize, Mills Coll., Oakland, Calif., 1985—87. Mem.: Orgn. Am. Kodaly Educators, Nat. Music Tchr. Assn., Music Tchr. Assn. Calif., Pi Lambda Theta, Kappa Delta Pi. Democrat. Episcopalian. Achievements include arranger, performer, and asst. eng. for the album "Look into the Word" by Dean Ellenwood; world premier performance of "Awaken", by Ken McCaw; artist of the session, Festival Noord Holland. Avocations: sewing, gardening, ballet, figure skating. Home and Office: 5643 Chris Ann Ct Sacramento CA 95841-2800 Personal E-mail: jkpmuses@gmail.com.

PIPER, JOANN LEE ELLIOTT, retired secondary school educator, swim coach; b. Albert Lea, Minn., July 10, 1930; d. Fred Maurice and Anna Frances Lorell (Lee) Elliott; m. Wilmer McMillan Piper, Apr. 19, 1952; children: Brian, Todd, Craig. BS in Speech Edn., U. Wis., 1952; postgrad., Cleve. State U., 1974-75, John Carroll U., Cleve., 1983. Tchr. English, drama and radio Cleve. Schs., 1952-54; instr. swimming West Shore Family YMCA, Westlake, Ohio, 1967-70, Bay Village (Ohio) Recreation, 1968-76, Rocky River (Ohio) Recreation, 1970-73; coach, instr. Lake Erie Cokes Swim Team, Westlake, 1969-75; tchr. TV prodn., broadcast journalism, speech and English Westlake Schs., 1975-93. Mem. TV adv. bds. Cleve. JFK H.S., Parma (Ohio) Normandy H.S., 1988, 90. Prodr., host: (TV series) Gallery, 1980-83; exec. prodr.: TV 4/WHBS News, 1975-93 (Radio TV Coun. award 1977-90). TV prodr. sch. promotions, Westlake, 1975-93, Westlake Arts Coun., 1986, cmty. promotions, 1975-93; author, dir. ch. and sch. celebrations, 1960-74. Recipient Jeannette Wagner TV Tchr. of Yr. award WVIZ (PBS), Cleve., 1982. Mem. NATAS (sec. 1995-2003, historian 2003-, chair workshops, scholarships, Creating Critical Viewers, Emmy statue and plaque 1994), Coll. Club West (trustee 1997-2000, pres. 1999-2000), Gamma Phi Beta (pres. Cleveland West chpt. 1961). Presbyterian. Avocations: theater, travel, reading, swimming, golf. Home: 22870 Laramie Dr Rocky River OH 44116-3067

PIPER, MARGARITA SHERERTZ, retired school system administrator; b. Petersburg, Va., Dec. 20, 1926; d. Guy Lucas and Olga Doan (Akers) Sherertz; m. Glenn Clair Piper, Feb. 3, 1950; children: Mark Stephen, Susan Leslie Piper Weathersbee. BA in Edn., Mary Washington Coll U. Va., Fredericksburg, 1948; MEd, U. Va., 1973, EdS, 1976. Svc. rep. C&P Telephone, Washington, 1948-55, adminstrv. asst., 1955-56, svc. supr., 1956-62; tchr. Culpeper (Va.) County Pub. Schs., 1970-75, reading lab dir., 1975-80; asst. prin. Rappahannock (Va.) County Pub. Schs., 1980-81, prin., 1981-88, dir. pupil pers., spl. programs, 1988-95; ret., 1995. Chair PD 9 regional transition adv. bd. Culpeper, Fauquier, Madison, Orange and Rappahannock Counties, Va., 1991-94; vice chair Family Assessment and Planning Team, Washington, 1992-95. Recipient Va. Gov. Schs. Commendation cert. Commonwealth of Va. Mem. NEA, Va. Edn. Assn., Va. Coun. Adminstrs. Spl. Edn., Va. Assn. Edn. for Gifted, Rappahannock Edn. Assn. Democrat. Methodist. Avocations: creative writing, music, walking, crosstitch, knitting. Personal E-mail: magpi@nc.rr.com.

PIPKIN, MARY MARGARET, artist; b. San Angelo, Tex., Mar. 17, 1951; d. Raymond G. and Lillie Marie (Billie) Pipkin; m. Robert A. Boisture; children: Will, John, Jamie. BFA, MFA, U. Tex.; Max Beckmann Scholar, Bklyn. Mus. Art Sch., 1973—74. One-woman shows include Addison/Ripley Gallery, Washington, Zigler Mus., Jennings, La., 2002, Louisburg Coll., NC, 2003, Art Sta., Stone Mountain, Ga., 2003, Anderson Art Ctr., Ind., 2003, Mus. S.W., Midland, Tex., 2003, US Botanic Garden, Washington, 2003, San Angelo Mus. Fine Art, Tex., 2004, Sci. Mus. We. Va., Roanoke, 2004, Olbrich Botanical Gardens, Madison, Wis., 2004, Mus. Arts & Sci., Daytona Beach, Fla., 2004, Dunedin Fine Arts Ctr., Fla., 2005, Elliot Mus., Stuart, Fla., 2005, Bob Rauschenberg Gallery, Edison Coll., Ft. Meyers, Fla., 2005. Personal E-mail: mmpipkin@aol.com.

PIPPEN, JENNIFER LYNN, therapist, consultant; b. Hinsdale, Ill., Nov. 10, 1975; d. Randy Lynn and Mary Hoekstra Pippen. BA summa cum laude, North Ctrl. Coll., Ill., 1998; M in Counseling Psychology cum laude, Trinity Grad. Sch., Ill., 2002. Lic. profl. counselor Ill., 2002, clin. profl. counselor 2005. Intern therapist Cath. Charities, Waukegan, Ill., 2001—02; therapist Maine Ctr., Park Ridge, Ill., 2002—. Missionary The Navigators, 1998—99; vol. West Suburban Humane Soc., Downers Grove, Ill., 2004. Mem.: ACA, Psi Chi. Avocations: piano, cross stitch. Office: Maine Ctr 819 Busse Hwy Park Ridge IL 60068 Office Phone: 847-696-1570 326.

PIRCH, PAMELA SUE, elementary school educator; b. Lexington, Mo., July 8, 1963; d. Carl David and Kay Lynn (Robinett) Gosoroski; m. Ricky George Pirch, Dec. 31, 1988; 1 child, Nikkole Kaylene. BS in Edn., Ctrl. Mo. State U., 1985, MS, 1994. Cert. tchr., Mo. Tchr. 6th grade Holden R-III Sch. Dist., 1985-87, title I math. tchr., 1987—99, second grade tchr., 1999—. Scholar Holden Tchrs. Assn., 1992. Mem. Mo. State Tchrs. Assn. (pres. local chpt. 1986-87, 92-93, 93-94, sec. local chpt. 1988-89), Delta Kappa Gamma Soc. Internat. Avocations: embroidery, needlecrafts, volleyball, walking, scrapbooks. Home: 1351 NW 565th Rd Holden MO 64040-9499

PIRKLE, MÄNYA HIGDON, artist, craftsman; b. Norris, Tenn., July 3, 1935; d. Samuel Lyle and Mertie Johnson Higdon; m. John Ward Pirkle, Nov. 26, 1967; 1 child, Jonathan Ward; m. William Bullard Monroe, June 18, 1956 (div. 1962); children: Mänette Monroe, Lydia Leigh Monroe Kreips. Illustrator Am. Mus. of Atomic Energy, Oak Ridge, Tenn., 1962, Am. Mus. of Sci. Energy, Oak Ridge, 1974; owner/operator Mänya Art & Graft Gallery, Gatlinburg, Tenn., 1979—81, Oak Ridge, 1981—84; instr. U. Tenn., Knoxville, 1987—88; owner/operator Mänya Collection Art Gallery, Knoxville, Tenn., 1988—92. Exhibitions include clay sculpture, Am. Crafts Coun., 2001, drawings, Knoxville Mus. of Art, 2002. Bd. dirs. Appalacian Ballet. Mem.: Knoxville Art Mkt., Knoxville Art Coun., Knoxville Mus. of Art, So. Highland Handcraft Guild, Foothills Craft Guild (charter mem., standard com.). Avocations: sewing, gardening, crafts, painting, photography. Home: 10201 Thimble Fields Dr Knoxville TN 37922

PIRRO, JEANINE FERRIS, prosecutor; b. Elmira, N.Y., June 2, 1951; d. Leo and Esther Ferris; m. Albert J. Pirro, Aug. 23, 1975; children: Christi, Alexander. BA, U. Buffalo, 1972; JD, Albany Law Sch., 1975. Bar: N.Y. 1975. Legis. aide N.Y. State Senate, Albany, 1973-75; asst. dist. atty. Westchester County Dist. Atty. Office, White Plains, N.Y., 1975-78, chief Victim Witness Unit, 1978-79, chief domestic violence/child abuse bur., 1978-90, dist. atty., 1994—; county judge Westchester County, White Plains, 1990-93. Author, To Punish and Protect, 2003, 2d edit. 2004; contbr. articles to profl. jours. Chair Gov. Pataki's N.Y. State Commn. on Domestic Violence Fatalities Rev. Bd., 1996; bd. dirs. My Sister's Place, 1990—; bd. vis. Pace U. Sch. Law, 1994— Mem. N.Y. State Dist. Attys. Assn. (pres. 1999-2000), Nat. Mus. Women's History (bd. adv.). Republican. Roman Catholic. Office: Westchester County Dist Atty County Courthouse 111 Dr ML King Jr Blvd White Plains NY 10601-2507

PIRRONE, CATHERINE LYNNE, secondary school educator; d. Francis Martin Cole and Catherine Stella Lewandowski; m. John Robert Pirrone, Aug. 19, 1972. BS in math. edn., SUC Buffalo, N.Y., 1973, MS in math. edn., 1976. Math. tchr. Tonawanda Jr. High, NY, 1973—77, Glendale Union HS Dist., Ariz., 1977—82, instrnl. specialist, 1982—87, title I coord., 1987—92, tchr., mentor, 1992—. Recipient Achievement Above All award, 2005.

PIRSCH, CAROL MCBRIDE, retired county official, state senator, community relations manager; b. Omaha, Dec. 27, 1936; d. Lyle Erwin and Hilfrie Louise (Lebeck) McBride; m. Allen I. Pirsch, Mar. 28, 1954 (dec.); children: Pennie Elizabeth, Pamela Elaine, Patrice Eileen, Phyllis Erika, Peter Allen, Perry Andrew. Student, U. Miami, Oxford, Ohio, U. Nebr., Omaha. Former mem. data processing staff Omaha (Nebr.) Pub. Schs.; former mem. wage practices dept. Western Electric Co., Omaha; former legal sec. Omaha; former office mgr. Pirsch Food Brokerage Co., Inc., Omaha; former employment supr., mgr. pub. policy U.S. West Comm., Omaha; mem. Nebr. Senate, 1979-97; commr. Douglas County, 1997—2005, chair, 1999, 2004, vice chair, 2001, 2003. Founder, 1st pres., bd. dirs. Nebr. Coalition for Victims of Crime (Lifetime award 2002); bd. dirs. Centris Fed. Credit Union, 1st v.p., 2003—. Mem. Omaha Douglas County Bldg. Commn., 1997—2003, sec., 2000—03; cmty. cons. Omaha Jr. League, 2002—. Recipient Golden Elephant award, Kuhle award, 1986, Nebr. Coalition for Victims of Crime, Outstanding Legis. Efforts award YWCA, 1989, Breaking the Rule of Thumb award Nebr. Domestic Violence Sexual Assault Coalition, 1989, Cert. of Appreciation award U.S. Dept. Justice, 1988, Partnership award N.E. Credit Union League, 1995, Wings award LWV Greater Omaha, 1995, N.E. VFW Spl. Recognition award for Exceptional Svc., 1995, Victim Rights Week Recognition award, 1995, Victim Adv. Lifetime Achievement award, 2002; Crime Victims Adv. award Nebr. Atty. Gen., 1995. Mem. VASA, Nat. Orgn. Victim Assistance (Outstanding Legis. Leadership award 1981), Freedom Found., Douglas County Hist. Soc., Nebr. Taxpayers Assn., Keystone Citizen Patrol (Comm. Network of Citizen Patrols award, 1995), Audubon Soc., N.W. Cmty. Club, Keystone Task Force (Keystoner of the month, 1987, Queen Keystone, 2002), Benson Rep. Women's Club, Omaha Bus. and Profl. Rep. Women.

PISA, REGINA MARIE, lawyer; b. Cambridge, Mass., Oct. 15, 1955; d. Anthony and Josephine Grace (Talmo) P. AB, Harvard & Radcliffe Cols., 1977; JD, Georgetown U., 1982; MA, Oxford U., Oxford, Eng., 1983. Bar: Mass. 1982, U.S. Dist. Ct. Mass. 1983, U.S. Ct. Appeals (1st cir.) 1983. Assoc. Goodwin, Procter & Hoar, Boston, 1982-89, partner, 1989—2004; chair, managing ptnr. Goodwin Procter LLP (formerly Goodwin Proctor & Hoar)), Boston, 2004—. Past mem. Supreme Judicial Ct. Nominating Com., Mass. Chair bd. dir. Easter Seals Soc., Mass.; mem. bd. dir. & exec. com. Greater Boston C. of C., Franciscan Hosp. Children; bd. dir. Citizens Fin. Group, Jobs for Mass., Mass. Bus. Roundtable; chair & vis. com. Georgetown Univ. Law Ctr.; pres. & bd. dir. Mass. Women's Forum; trustee Simmons Coll., Catholic Charities, Boys & Girls Clubs Am.; pres. & chmn. bd. trustees Somerville Mus., Mass.; mem. bd. vis. Women's Ednl. & Indsl. Union; mem. Dimock Cmty. Health Ctr., Leadership Council, Mass. Mentoring Partnership. Honoree Somerville (Mass.) Pride Night Homefirst Charitable Corp., 1995. Fellow: Boston Bar Found.; mem.: Pro Bono Inst. (mem. adv. com.), ABA, Am. Law Inst., Mass. Assn. Women Lawyers, Internat. Bar Assn., Mass. Bar Assn., Boston Bar Assn., Women's Bar Assn. (Leila J. Robinson award), Women's Fin. Svc. Network, Internat. Women's Forum, Com. of 200, Boston Club, Boston Univ. Club, Chief Exec. Club Boston. Office: Goodwin Procter LLP Exchange Pl 53 State St Boston MA 02109 Office Phone: 617-570-1525. Office Fax: 617-523-1231. E-mail: rpisa@goodwinprocter.com.

PISANESCHI, DENA MARIE, science educator; b. Pitts., Pa., Feb. 25, 1972; d. Steve James and Donna Mae Betarie; m. Brian Albert Pisaneschi, Aug. 6, 1994. B in Psychology, U. Pitts., 1994; MEd, U. South Fla., Tampa, 1997. Nat. bd. cert. tchr. Tchr. 1st grade Lewis Elem., Tampa, 1997—99; tchr. 2d grade Clark Elem., Tampa, 1999—2003, tchr. 4th grade, 2003—05; tchr. 6th grade gifted sci. Liberty Mid. Sch., South Tampa, Fla., 2005—. Team leader Clark, Tampa, 2001—03; mem. dist. adv. coun. Sch. Dist. Hillsborough County, Tampa, 2002—04; chairperson sch. adv. coun. Clark, Tampa, 2002—03, Tampa, 2003—04, Tampa, 2004—05. Contbr. articles to profl. jours. Named Tchr. of Yr., Clark Elem., 2002—03. Mem.: Fla. Assn. for Gifted, Fla. Assn. Sci. Tchrs., Nat. Assn. Gifted Children, Phi Beta Kappa. Avocations: reading, travel, dance. Home: 18904 Wood Sage Dr Tampa FL 33647 Office: Liberty Mid Sch 17400 Commerce Park Blvd Tampa FL 33647

PISANI, MARGARET, elementary school educator; b. Hoboken, NJ, May 13, 1966; d. Nicholas Salvatore and Rose Pisani. BA, Glassboro State Coll., NJ, 1988; MA, NJ City U., Jersey City, 2001; EdM, William Paterson U., Wayne, NJ. Cert. supr. NJ, 2006, adminstr. NJ, 2006, elem. edn. tchr. grades K-8 NJ, 1988, reading specialist NJ, 2001. 7th/8th grade tchr. Epiphany Sch., Cliffside Park, NJ, 1988—90; elem. sch. tchr. North Bergen Bd. Edn., NJ, 1990—99; substitute tchr. Edgewater Bd. Edn., NJ, 2000—01; reading specialist Wayne Bd. Edn., NJ, 2001—. Sch. test coord. Wayne Bd. Edn., 2001—, adminstrv. intern, 2001—. Office Phone: 973-633-3155. Personal E-mail: maggiemay1366@yahoo.com.

PISANO, CARLA ANN, mathematics educator, accountant; d. John and Paula Jahelka; m. Joseph Anthony Pisano, May 16, 1998; children: Paige, Ella. BS in Acctg., Clemson U., SC, 1993; MA in Edn., Va. Inst. Tech., Falls Church, 2000. CPA Va. Staff accountant Am. Systems Corp., Chantilly, Va., 1994—96; supervisory acct. Armed Forces Benefits Assn., Alexandria, Va., 1996—98; math. tchr. Fairfax County Pub. Sch., Falls Church, Va., 1999—. Mem.: Va. Edn. Assn. Office Phone: 571-423-3000.

PISANO, ETTA D., radiologist, educator; AB cum laude, Dartmouth Coll., 1979; MD, Duke U. Cert. Diagnostic Radiology Am. Bd. Radiology, 1988. Radiology resident Beth Israel Hosp., Boston, 1984—88, chief resident, 1986—87, dir. mammography, 1988—89; med. dir. Carolina Screening Mammography, 1989—93; residency program dir. Dept. Radiology U. NC Sch. Medicine, 1992—96, section chief Breast Imaging Sect., 1989—2005, program dir. Post-grad. Continuing Med. Edn. Course in Breast Imaging, 1989—2005, prof. radiology and biomedical engring.; dir. Biomed. Rsch. Imaging Ctr., 2003—. Contbr. articles to profl. jours. Recipient Francis W. Gramlich Philosophy Prize, 1979. Fellow: Soc. Breast Imaging; mem.: Assn. Profl. Women in Medicine and Sci. (mem. Nominating and Salary Equity Com. 1994—), Assn. Univ. Radiologists, Am. Coll. Radiology, Am. Assn. Women's Radiologists, Am. Med. Women's Assn. (Women in Sci. Award 2005), Radiological Soc. North Am., Internat. Digital Mammography Devel. Group (chair 1996—, pres. pro tem 2001—), Am. Roentgen Ray Soc. Office: U NC Sch Medicine 503 Old Infimary Chapel Hill NC 27599 Home: 105 Majestic Ct Chapel Hill NC 27517-8345 Office Phone: 919-966-4397. E-mail: etta_pisano@med.unc.edu.

PISCATELLI, NANCY KELLEY, elementary school educator; b. Boston, Feb. 11, 1953; d. Joseph Murphy and Eleanor Elizabeth (Jeffers) Kelley; m. Thomas George Piscatelli, Apr. 17, 1976; 1 child, Thomas Joseph. BS, Bridgewater State Coll., 1975, MEd, 1979, Boston Coll., 1977; EdD, Northeastern U., 1989. Lead tchr. Boston Pub. Schs., 1975—, dir. exam sch. initiative, 2002—; cons. Boston Plan for Excellence in the Pub. Schs., 1997; dir. summer test preparation program Boston Latin Sch., 2003—. Cons. Tchrs. Corp. Network, 1979-80. Author/editor: (handbook) The Paraprofessional Handbook, 1979; contbr. articles to profl. jours. Campaign worker Dem. Com., Quincy, Mass., 1975—; active sch. vol. pet project of Mrs. George Bush. Mem. Am. Fedn. Tchrs., Boston Tchrs. Union, MassCue. Roman Catholic. Avocations: literature, travel. Home: Pheasant Hill 10 Chickadee Dr Norfolk MA 02056-1741 Office: Boston Pub Schs 26 Court St Boston MA 02108-2505 Office Phone: 617-635-8157. Business E-Mail: npiscatelli@boston.k12.ma.us.

PISCIOTTA, VIVIAN VIRGINIA, retired psychotherapist; b. Chgo., Dec. 7, 1929; d. Vito and Mary Lamia; m. Vincent Diago Pisciotta, Apr. 1, 1951; children: E. Christopher, Vittorio, V. Charles, Mary A. Pisciotta Higley, Thomas Sansone BA Clin. Psychology, Antioch U., 1974; MSW, George Williams Coll., 1984; postgrad., Erickson Inst. No. Ill., 1990. Lic. clin. social worker, Ill.; diplomate in clin. social work. Short-term therapist Woman Line, Dayton, Ohio, 1976—79; psychotherapist Cicero Family Svcs., Ill., 1982—83, Maywood - Proviso Family Svcs., Ill., 1983—84, Maple Ave. Med. Ctr., Brookfield, Ill., 1985—88, Met. Med. Clinic, Naperville, Ill., 1986—88; allied staff Riveredge Psychiat. Hosp., Forest Park, Ill., 1986—97; psychotherapist, pvt. practice Oakbrook, Ill., 1988—96; psychotherapist, co-founder Archer Austin Counseling Ctr., Chgo., 1988—89; founder Archer Counseling Ctr., Chgo., 1989—97; psychotherapist Columbia Hospitals' Columbia Riveredge Hosp., Forest Park, 1997; allied staff Linden Oaks Psychiat. Hosp., Naperville, 1990—97; founder Archer Ctr., Ariz., 1997—99; psychotherapist pvt. practice, 1988—2004; ret., 2004. Substitute tchr. Chgo. Pub. H.S., 1981; instr. Ariz. State U. Livelong Learning Acad., 2002-03; cons. psychotherapy, 2005— Author treatment prog., workshops in field Co-founder Co-op Nursery Sch., Rockford, Ill., 1956; leader Great Books of the Western World series, Piqua, Ohio, 1977, Rockford, 1960-65; leader Girl Scouts U.S., St. Bridget Sch., Rockford, 1968-71 Mem. Assn. Labor-Mgmt. and Cons. on Alcoholism, Soc. Clin. Exptl. Hypnosis, NASW, Acad. Cert. Social Workers, Nat. Social Work Register (cert.), Antioch U. Alumnus Assn., Rockford Coll. Alumnae Orgn. (newsletter contbr. 1972-73), Soc. for Clin. and Exptl. Hypnosis (assoc.), Internat. Soc. for Clin. and Exptl. Hypnosis (assoc.) Republican. Roman Catholic. Avocations: reading, travel, study/research, music, religion. Personal E-mail: arch3456@aol.com.

PISCITELLI, NANCY L., retired special education educator; children: Gina, Joanne, John. BS, Pacific Oaks Coll., 1965, MA, 1978. Coord. tchr. Head Start Pasadena Cmty. Found., Calif., 1965—66; presch. tchr. Villa Esperanza, Pasadena, 1966—67, dir. infant ctr. devel., 1966—80, program dir., 1980—89. Bd. dirs. Villa Esperanza Svcs., Pasadena, 2003—. Chief fin. officer Bone Cancer Internat., Newbury Park, Calif., 1999—2006. Home: 6072 N Shadycreek Dr Agoura Hills CA 91301

PISCOPIO, GERALDINE ANNE, nurse anesthetist; b. Phila., June 24, 1956; d. Daniel Charles and Geraldine Concetta (Salvitti) Mazzafro; children: Christopher, Nicholas. BSN, Holy Family Coll., Phila., 1978; MSN, U. Pa., Phila., 1981. RN, cert. pediatric clin. specialist. Staff nurse anesthetist Lankenau Anesthesia Assocs., Phila., Liberty Anesthesia, Bristol, Pa. Mem. ANA, Am. Assn. Nurse Anesthetists. Home: 6150 Mark Cir Bensalem PA 19020-2472

PISKOR, SUSAN MARIE, secondary school educator; b. Erie, Pa., Apr. 24, 1967; d. Owen Leo and Lucille Ann Hines; m. Daniel Joseph Piskor, July 22, 1989; 1 child, Diana Marie. BS, Edinboro U. Pa., 1989. Cert. tchr. Pa., Va. Biology tchr. Fairfax County Pub. Schs., Lorton, Va., 1989—, chmn. sci. dept., 1998—. Democrat. Roman Catholic. Office: South County Secondary Sch 8501 Silverbrook Rd Lorton VA 22079 Office Phone: 703-446-1600.

PISKOTI, CAROL LEE, art educator; b. Stockton, Calif., Jan. 13, 1949; d. Kyman and Clara Lee; m. James Piskoti, June 16, 1984. BA in Fine Art, Calif. State U. Stanislaus, Turlock, 1971. Tchg. credential Calif. Tchr. Sacramento City Sch. Dist., 1973—. Facilitator, staff Calif. Consortium for Arts Edn., Sacramento, 2002—05. Recipient Hon. Svc. award, PTA-John F. Kennedy H.S., 1989. Mem.: Crocker Art Mus. (tchg. adv. bd. 2002—), Nat. Art Edn. Assn., Calif. Art Edn. Assn. (chair vols. 2001, chair no. area youth art month 2004—06, Award of Merit 2001, Ruth Jansen Outstanding Visual Arts Educator of Yr. award 2004). Avocations: painting, drawing. Office: John F Kennedy HS 6715 Gloria Dr Sacramento CA 95831

PISTERS, KATHERINE M.W., internist, medical educator; b. London, Ont., Canada, July 26, 1962; arrived in US, 1985; d. John Bethune and Rita Margaret Walker; m. Peter W.T. Pisters, June 28, 1984. MD, U. Western Ont., London, 1985. Diplomate Am. Bd. Internal Medicine/Med. Oncology. Intern Cornell Hosps., North Shore U. Hosp. and Meml. Hosp., Manhasset and NYC, 1985—86, resident, 1986—88; med. oncology fellow Meml. Sloan-Kettering Cancer Ctr., NYC, 1988—91, chief resident, 1989—90; instr. Meml.-Sloan Kettering Hosp., NYC, 1991—94; asst. prof. U. Tex. M.D. Anderson Cancer Ctr., Houston, 1994—98, assoc. prof., 1998—2005, prof. medicine dept. thoracic/head and neck med. oncology, 2005—. Instr. thoracic oncology svc. Cornell U. Med. Coll., NYC, 1991—94; spkr., presenter, cons. in field. Contbr. numerous articles to profl. jours., chpts. to books, revs., abstracts in field; sect. editor: Lung Cancer, Current Oncology Reports, 2002—. Named one of Best Cancer Drs., Good Housekeeping, 1999; recipient Career Devel. award, Am. Cancer Soc., 1993—94; grantee, Protocols, 1997—2001; scholar, U. Western Ont., 1980—82; Borden fellow in clin. oncology, 1990—91. Fellow: ACP.

PISTERZI, CANDY, special education educator; b. Moline, Ill., Nov. 15, 1945; d. Homer Noel Jackson and Gladys L. Jackson-Meyer; m. Mike Pisterzi, June 1, 1968; children: Maria Ann, John Anthony, Laura Elaine. BA, Ill. State U., 1967; MA, Columbia U., 1971. Tchr. spl. edn. Homer Sch. Sys., Ill., 1967—68, Poughkeepsie City Sch. Sys., NY, 1968—70, Dutchess County Bd. Coop. Ednl. Svcs., Poughkeepsie, 1971—72, 1989—, Cardinal Hayes Sch., Millbrook, NY, 1986—89. Bd. dirs. Mid-Hudson Tchrs. Ctr., mem. policy bd., 2004—. Grantee, Dutchess County Bd. Of Coop. Ednl. Svcs., 1994, 2003, 2005, Mid-Hudson Tchrs. Ctr., 2005—06. Mem.: Crochet Guild, Delta Kappa Gamma (pres. Alpha Zeta chpt. 2001—04, chmn. state nominations com. 2005—). Avocations: sewing, crocheting, reading, travel. Office: Dutchess County BOCES 5 BOCES Rd Poughkeepsie NY 12601

PISTOR, KATHARINA, law educator; b. Freiburg, Germany, May 23, 1963; m. Carsten G. Bonnemann. JD with honors, U. Freiburgw, 1988; LLM with distinction, U. London, 1989; MPA, Harvard U., 1994; Dr. Jur., U. Munich, 1998. Sr. rsch. fellow Ctrl. European U. Privatization Project, 1993—95; lectr. law Harvard Law Sch., 1994—95; rsch. assoc. Harvard Inst. for Internat. Devel., 1995—98, Max Planck Inst. for Comparative and Internat. Private Law, Hamburg, 1998—99; asst. prof. Kennedy Sch. Govt., Harvard U., 2000—01; assoc. prof. law Columbia U. Law Sch., NYC, 2001—04, prof., 2004—. Vis. prof. Study Ctr. at Gerzensee, Switzerland, 2003, U. Pa. Law Sch., 2004, Inst. for Law and Fin., Frankfurt U., Germany, 2004, Germany, 05. Contbr. articles to law jours. Office: Columbia Law Sch 435 W 116th St, Rm 643 New York NY 10027 Office Phone: 212-854-0068. Office Fax: 212-854-7946. E-mail: kpisto@law.columbia.edu.

PITCOCK, MICHELLE MARIE, science educator; b. Alburquerque, Tex., Oct. 4, 1967; d. Robert Michael and Charlotte Ann George; m. Buck Denton Pitcock, Mar. 13, 2001; children: Allen, Pekkabo. BS, Tex. Tech. U., Lubbock, 1990; MEd, Tex. Tech. U., 2000. Cert. tchg. Tex., GEMS assoc. Lawrence Hall of Sci. Med. rsch. tech. opthalmology Tex. Tech. U. HSC, Lubbock, 1990—2000; tchr. Lubbock Ind. Sch. Dist., 2000—. GEMS assoc. Lubbock Ind. Sch. Dist., 2004—; tchr., presenter Tex. Tech. Sci. It's a Girl Thing, 2005—. Mem.: Nat. Sci. Tchrs. Assn., Tex. State Tchrs. Assn. Avocations: reading, travel, flute, stained glass, clay work. Office: Hardwick Elem Sch 1420 Chgo Ave Lubbock TX 79416 Office Phone: 806-766-0844. Office Fax: 806-766-0842. Personal E-mail: eyemmg@yahoo.com.

PITERNICK, ANNE BREARLEY, librarian, educator; b. Blackburn, Eng., Oct. 13, 1926; arrived in Can., 1956, naturalized, 1965; d. Walter and Ellen (Harris) Clayton; m. Neil Brearley, 1956 (div. 1971); m. George Piternick, May 6, 1971. BA, U. Manchester, Eng., 1948, F.L.A., 1983. Mem. library staff U. B.C., Vancouver, Can., 1956-66, head sci. div., 1960-61, head social scis. div., 1965-66, prof. Sch. Library, Archival and Info. Studies, 1966-91, prof. emerita, 1991—, assoc. dean Faculty of Arts, 1985-90. Mem. Nat. Com. Bibliog. Svcs. Can., 1975-80, chmn. com. on bibliography and info. services for social scis. and humanities, 1981-84; mem. adv. acad. panel Social Scis. and Humanities Research Council, 1981-84; mem. adv. bd. Nat. Libr. Can., 1978-84; mem. Nat. Adv. Com. Culture Stats., 1985-90; organizer Confs. on Can. Bibliography, 1974, 81; pres. Can. Assn. Spl. Librs. Info. Svcs., 1969-70, Can. Libr. Assn., 1976-77. Contbr. articles to profl. jours. Bd. dirs. Vancouver Friends of Chamber Music, 2001—. Recipient Queen's Silver Jubilee medal, 1977, award for Spl. Librarianship Can. Assn. Spl. Librs. and Info. Svcs., 1987, 75th Anniversary medal U.B.C., 1990, Can. 125 medal, 1993; fellow Coun. on Libr. Resources, 1980. Fellow Libr. Assn.; mem. Assn. Profs. Emeriti U. B.C. (pres. 2003-04), Coll. and Univs. Retiree Assns. Can. (bd. dirs. 2005—) Achievements include research in electronic info. svcs. and scholarly comm. Home: 1849 W 63rd Ave Vancouver BC Canada V6P 2H9 Personal E-mail: annebp@interchange.ubc.ca.

PITLUK, ELLEN EIDELBACH, lawyer, mediator; d. Mark Adrian and Baylor Merle Eidelbach; m. Lee Dean Pitluk, Feb. 1, 1985; children: Jessie, Mason. BA in Journalism, Tex. A&M U., College Station, 1981; JD, St. Mary's U., San Antonio, 2002, postgrad. Bar: Tex. 2003, U.S. Dist. Ct. (we. dist.) Tex. 2003. Grad. recruiter Trinity U., Dept. Health Care Adminstrn., San Antonio, 1990—94, 1997—99; rsch. asst. St. Mary's U., Sch. Law, 2000; law clk. Walsh, Anderson, Brown,. Schulze & Aldridge, 2001; law clk. hon. Frank Montalvo 288th Jud. Dist. Ct., Bexar County, 2002; atty., mediator pvt. practice, San Antonio, 2003—. Contbr. articles to profl. jours.;, author of poems. Mem.: ABA, Bexar County Women's Bar Assn., San Antonio Bar Assn., San Antonio Bar Found., Coll. State Bar Tex., State Bar Tex. Office: PO Box 780895 San Antonio TX 78278

PITMAN, URSULA WALL, curator, educator; d. Thomas Joseph and Emily Hruby Wall; m. Lawrence Clymer Pitman, Aug. 19, 1961 (dec. Jan. 1996). BA in History, Northeastern U., 1968, BS in Art History, 1983; MA in History, Boston Coll., 1971, PhD in History, 1978. Cert. history tchr., IBM sys. svc. rep. Computer demonstrator, lectr. IBM, N.Y.C., 1956—59, data processing instr. Boston, 1959—61; art educator Fitchburg (Mass.) Art Mus., 1978—83, curator, 1979—89, dir., instr. docent program, 1982—2000, developer in-mus. and outreach programs, 1982—2000. Advisor on fundraising activities Fitchburg (Mass.) Art Mus., 1978—2000, dir. funded lectr. series, 1980—90, mem. edn. com., 1983—2000; art lectr. Jr. League Boston Sch. Program, Lincoln, Mass., 1976—77; co-dir. Tchrs. Workshop DeCordova Mus., Lincoln, 1980; co-grant writer, implementer Nat. Endowment for the Arts, Washington, 1982—2000. Vol. Harvard U. docent Sachler Mus., Fogg Art Mus., Busch Reisinger Mus., Cambridge, Mass., 1983—93; vol. docent DeCordova Mus., Lincoln, 1976—83; vol. libr. asst. Lahey Clinic, Burlington, Mass., 1996; vol. Nat. Heritage Mus., Lexington, Mass., 1997—. Named Vol. of the Yr., Nat. Heritage Mus., 1999. Avocations: travel, reading, visiting museums, theater. Home: 61 Willard Grant Rd Sudbury MA 01776

PITT, JANE, medical educator; b. Frankfurt, Fed. Republic Germany, Aug. 25, 1938; came to U.S., 1939. d. Ludwig Friederich and Vera (Aberle) Ries; m. Martin Irwin Pitt, Aug. 12, 1962 (dec. 1980); children: Jennifer, Eric Jonathan; m. Robert Harry Socolow, May 25, 1986; stepchildren: David, Seth. BA, Radcliffe Coll., 1960; MD, Harvard U., 1964. Diplomate Am. Bd. Pediatrics, Am. Bd. Pediat. Infectious Diseases. Resident Children's Hosp. Med. Ctr., Boston, 1964-66; fellow Tufts U. Med. Sch., Boston, 1966-67, Harvard U. Med. Sch., Boston, 1967-69; asst. prof. SUNY Downstate Sch. Medicine, N.Y.C., 1970-71; asst. prof. Coll. Physicians and Surgeons Columbia U., N.Y.C., 1971-75, assoc. prof. Coll. Physicians and Surgeons, 1975-2000; prof. Coll. Physicians and Surgeons, 2000—. Mem. instl. rev. bd. Columbia Health Scis. Campus, N.Y.C., 1982—; mem. NIH study sect. Reviewer Jour. of Infectious Diseases, New Eng. Jour. Medicine, 1976—; contbr. articles to profl. jours. NIH grantee, 1974—. Fellow Infectious Disease Soc., Pediat. Infectious Disease Soc., Soc. Pediat. Rsch., Am. Pediatric Soc. Democrat. Jewish. Office: Columbia U Coll Physicians Surgeons 630 W 168th St New York NY 10032-3702 Home: 2620 7TH St Boulder CO 80304-3206 E-mail: jp25@columbia.edu.

PITTA, PATRICIA JOYCE, psychologist; b. N.Y.C., July 3, 1947; d. John Joseph and Mildred (Gioiosa) P.; m. Eric Eugene Kirk; children: Eric Jon, Kevin. BA, Queens Coll., 1968; MS, Hunter Coll., 1972; PhD, Fordham U., 1975. Diplomate Am. Bd. Family Psychology. Recreational therapist Roosevelt Hosp., N.Y.C., 1968-73, psychology intern, 1973-74; staff psychologist NYU Med. Ctr., 1974-78, clin. instr., 1975—; pvt. practice psychology Manhasset, N.Y., 1977—. Chief psychologist St. John's Episc. Hosp., Smithtown, N.Y., 1978-79; cons. North Shore U. Hosp., Manhasset, 1979-84; mem. faculty L.I. family therapy div. Inst. Psychoanalysis; supr. psychologist Clin. Psychology Doctoral Program St. John's U., N.Y.; media psychologist, relationship expert Nat. & Local T.V.; mem. bd. dirs., task force head divsn. pvt. practice APA, 1994—; lectr. in field. Contbr. articles to profl. jours., newspapers. Bd. dirs. Assn. for Retarded Children, 1988-92. Mem. APA (bd. dirs. ind. practice divsn.), Nassau County Psychol. Assn. (pvt. practice com. 1986-88, bd. dirs. 1987—, social issues com. 1988—), Working Woman Manhasset, L.I. Ctr. Bus. and Profl. Women, L.I. Assn. Marriage and Family Therapy (bd. dirs. 1992—, sec. 1993—, pres. 1995—). Avocations: tennis, walking, bicycling, skiing. Office: 35 Bonnie Heights Rd Manhasset NY 11030-1636

PITTARELLI, DIANA, entrepreneur; b. Chgo., Sept. 5, 1951; d. Maurice Seymour Mazel and Harriet Marguerite (Hodgini) Hodges; m. Martin Barry Shapiro, Mar. 4, 1972 (div. June 1989); m. John Pittarelli, Apr. 7, 1990. BA cum laude, Barry U., 1991, MBA, 1993. Lic. real estate sales agt., Fla. Securities broker Herzfeld & Stern, Miami Beach, Fla., 1978-79; NASD broker, dealer IMF Corp., Miami, Fla., 1979-81; outside sales agt. Gold Key Travel, Miami, 1981-84, Maduro Travel/Embassy Travel, Miami, 1981-84; owner, mgr. restaurant/nightclub Biscayne Baby, Coconut Grove, Fla., 1984-89; mgr. Skyline State Bank, Plantation, Fla., 1991-97; pvt. investor. Co-patentee bottle carrying device with pivotable spout; choreographer Miss Fla. USA Pageant, 1988. Mem. Dade County Pub. Rels. Coun., Bob Graham Campaign for Gov., Miami, 1980; capt. cheerleading Miami Dolphins, 1980-85; exec. com. Miami Beach Sr. High Alumni Assn., 1999—, co-chmn. class reunions, 1979, 89, 99. Biscayne Baby named one of Best Night Clubs in U.S. by Playboy mag., 1995. Mem. Am. Bus. Women's Assn., Barry U. Alumni Assn. Avocations: hiking, skiing, theater, travel. Home: Apt 201 201 Van Buren St Hollywood FL 33019-1712

PITTER, TRACY ALANA, athletic trainer; b. Bklyn., Sept. 12, 1980; d. Leonard DeCardova Pitter and Yvonne Elizabeth Taylor-Pitter. BS, Barry U., Miami Shores, Fla., 2001; postgrad., SUNY, Farmingdale, 2004—. Athletic trainer Profl. Phys. Therapy, Queens, NY, 2001—; head athletic trainer St. Mary's HS, Manhassat, NY, 2002—03, Roslyn Mid. Sch., Roslyn, NY, 2004—06. Treas. Best Buddies, Miami, Fla., 2001. Mem.: Nat. Athletic Trainers Assn. Avocations: singing, songwriting, dance, art, fashion design.

PITTMAN, AMANDA NELSON, music educator; d. General Lee and Amanda Hopkins Nelson; m. Marvin Benjamin Pittman, 1964; 1 child, Marvin Benjamin Jr. BMus, U. So. Calif., L.A., 1948, MMus, 1961, DMA, 2003. Gen. tchg. credential in elem. edn. Calif. Tchr. elem. edn. Ft. Worth Schs., 1949—51; tchr. elem. music L.A. City Schs., 1957—64, Montgomery County Schs., Rockville, Md., 1964—66, L.A. City Schs., 1966—75, Beverly Hills Unified Schs., Calif., 1975—90, L.A. City Schs., 1990—91, Clark County Sch. Dist., Las Vegas, Nev., 1992—98, L.A. City Schs., 1999—. Instr. music edn. Pepperdine U., L.A., 1967—70, U. So. Calif., L.A., 1975—77, Calif. State U., L.A., 2002—03. Adminstrv. officer USAFR, March AFB, Calif., 1959—64. Capt. USAF, 1951—56. Mem.: Calif. Music Educators Assn., L.A. City Elem. Schs. Music Assn. (v.p. 2004—06), Internat. Assn. for Jazz Edn., Music Educators Nat. Conf. (presenter 1960—2006), Women in Mil. Svc. for Am. Found. (charter mem.). Home: 8957 Haas Ave Los Angeles CA 90047

PITTMAN, BARBARA N., special education educator; d. Vernon and Bessie L. Pittman. BS in Bus. Edn., U. Wis., Whitewater, 1977; MS in Adult Edn., U. Wis., Milw., 1987. Cert. adminstrv. leadership, spl. edn., alt.edn. Tchr. bus. edn. Sawyer Coll., Milw., 1978—79, Messmer HS, Milw., 1979—83, Stratton Coll. Bus., Milw., 1984—87, Whitefish Bay Schs., Wis., 1987—88; tchr. spl. edn. Milw. Pub. Schs., 1989—. Beauty cons. Mary Kay Cosmetics, Milw., 1989—2000. Leader NBC Canaan Bapt. Ch., Milw., 1996—99, Sunday sch. tchr., 1994—96. Mem.: ASCD, CEC. Avocations: reading, gardening, floral arrangements. Office: Harold S Vincent H S 7501 N Greenville Rd Milwaukee WI 53224-3927

PITTMAN, CONSTANCE SHEN, endocrinologist, educator; b. Nanking, China, Jan. 2, 1929; arrived in US, 1946; d. Leo F.-Z. and Pao Kong (Yang) Shen; m. James Allen Pittman, Jr., Feb. 19, 1955; children: James Clinton, John Merrill. AB in Chemistry, Wellesley Coll., 1951; MD, Harvard U., 1955. Diplomate Am. Bd. Internal Medicine, sub-bd. Endocrinology. Intern Baltimore City Hosp., 1955-56; resident U. Ala., Birmingham, 1956-57; instr. in medicine U. Ala. Med. Ctr., Birmingham, 1957—59, fellow dept. pharmacology, 1957-59, from asst. prof. to assoc. prof., 1959-70, prof., 1970—. Prof. medicine Georgetown U., Washington, 1972—73; mem. diabetes and metabolism tng. com. NIH, Bethesda, Md., 1972—76, mem. nat. arthritis, metabolism and digestive disease coun., 1975—78, mem. gen. clin. rsch. ctrs. com., 1979—83, 1987—90; bd. dirs. Internat. Coun. for Control of Iodine Deficiency Diseases, 1994—; mem. Iodine Deficiency Disorders Elimination Steering Com. Kiwanis Internat., 2002—. Interim editor: ICCIDD Newsletter, 2004—06. Master ACP; mem. Assn. Am. Physicians, Am. Soc. for Clin. Investigation, Endocrine Soc. (coun., 1978-79, pres. women's caucus 1978-79), Am. Thyroid Assn. (pres. 1990-91), Kiwanis (mem. iodine deficiency disorders steering com.). Achievements include research in activation and metabolism of thyroid hormone; kinetics of thyroxine conversion to triiodothyrine in health and disease states; control of iodine deficiency disorders. Emails. Office: UAB Div Endocrinology/Metab Lab Med Ctr Birmingham AL 35294-0001 Office Phone: 205-934-0800. Business E-Mail: cpittman@uab.edu.

PITTMAN, JACQUELYN, retired mental health nurse, nursing educator; b. Pensacola, Fla., Dec. 22, 1932; d. Edward Corry Sr. and Hettie Oean (Wilson) P. BS in Nursing Edn., Fla. State U., 1958; MA, Columbia U., 1959, EdD, 1974. Physician asst. Med. Ctr. Clinic, Pensacola, 1953-55; clin. instr., asst. dir. nursing svc. Sacred Heart Hosp., Pensacola, 1955-56; instr. psychiat. nurse Fla. State Hosp., Chattahoochee, 1958; instr. psychiat. nursing Pensacola Jr. Coll., 1959-60, 62-63; chmn. div. nursing Gulf Coast C.C., Panama City, Fla., 1963-66; asst. prof. U. Tex., Austin, 1970-72, assoc. prof., 1972-80; prof. nursing, coord. curriculum and tchg. grad. program La. State U. Med. Ctr., New Orleans, 1980-99, rep. faculty senate, 1997-99; pres.-elect faculty assembly Sch. Nursing La. State U. Med. Ctr. Sch. Nursing, New Orleans, 1997-98, pres., 1998-99; ret., 1999. Curriculum cons. Nicholls State U., Thibodaux, La., 1982, Our Lady of Lake Sch. Nursing, Baton Rouge, 1983; rsch. liaison So. Bapt. Hosp., New Orleans, 1987-89, Med. Ctr. La., 1992-99; mem. adv. bd. Sister Henrietta Guyot Professorship; mem. planning com. Nichols State U./La. State U. Med. Ctr. Partnership, 1996-99. Mem. ethics com., trustee Hotel Dieu Hosp., New Orleans, 1987—91; judge Internat. Sci. and Engring. Fair Assn., 1990, 1992; del. La. State Nurses' Assn. State Conv., 1992, 1994; assoc. Libr. of Congress, Smithonian Instn.; mem. Dem. Nat. Comm., Presdl. Task Force, 1992, Ctr. for Study of Presidency; tchr. Christian edn. program for mentally retarded St. Ignatius Martyr Ch., 1979—80; tchr. initiation team Rite of Christian Initiation of Adults, Our Lady of the Lake Cath. Ch., Mandeville, La., 1983—86; v.p., bd. dirs. St. Tammany Guidance Ctr., Inc., Mandeville, 1987—91; mem. parish outreach meals-on-wheels program St. Tammany, Covington, La., 2001—02. Mem. ANA, LWV, Am. Assn. Adv. Sci. Directory, N.Y. Acad. Scis., Acad. Polit. Sci., Libr. of Congress Assocs., Nat. Trust for Hist. Preservation, La. Endowment for Humanities, La. Nurses Assn. (archivist 1987-99, state task force com. to preserve hist. documents 1987-99), So. Nursing Rsch. Soc., Nat. League Nursing, Boston U. Nursing Archives, Women's Inner Cir. Achievement N.Am. Cmtys., Internat. Order of Merit, World Found. Successful Women, Wilson Ctr. Assocs., Kappa Delta Pi, Sigma Theta Tau. Democrat. Roman Catholic. Avocations: swimming, golf, travel, reading, louisiana history. Address: 204 Woodridge Blvd Mandeville LA 70471-2604 Personal E-mail: jpit204@aol.com.

PITTMAN, LISA, lawyer; b. Limestone, Maine, Jan. 4, 1959; d. William Franklin and Rowena Paradis (Umphrey) P.; 1 child, Graham Edward Paradis. BA with high honors, U. Fla., 1980, MA, 1981, JD, 1984; LLM with highest honors, George Washington U., 1988. Bar: Fla. 1984, D.C. 1993, U.S Supreme Ct. 1993. Spl. asst. to gen. counsel Nat. Oceanic and Atmospheric Adminstrn., Washington, 1984-85, atty., advisor, 1985-87; minority counsel Com. on Mcht. Marine & Fisheries, Ho. of Reps., Washington, 1987-95; dep. chief counsel Com. on Resources, U.S. Ho. of Reps., Washington, 1995-2001, chief counsel, 2001—02, chief counsel, dep. staff dir., 2002—. Contbr. articles to profl. jour. Home: 7325 Eldorado St Mc Lean VA 22102-2904 Office: US House of Reps 1320 Longworth HOB Washington DC 20515-6201

PITTMAN, MIA N., educational association administrator, entrepreneur; BA, U. Pa.; MBA in Fin., Temple U. With CoreStates Fin. Corp.; with venture capital arm The Reinvestment Fund, Phila.; v.p. comml. lending Progress Fin. Corp.; founder, pres., CEO Start Smart Inc., Upper Darby, Pa. Named one of 40 Under 40, Phila. Bus. Jour., 2006. Office: Start Smart Inc 202 Long Lane - 1st Fl Upper Darby PA 19082 Office Phone: 484-461-3025. Office Fax: 484-461-3562.*

PITTMAN, RACHEL DOBY, science educator; d. Willard James and Evelyn Neal Doby; m. Fred Eli Pittman, June 9, 1978. MEd, U. S.C., Columbia, 1973. Cert. tchr. S.C. Tchr. Clinton Elem. Sch., Lancaster, 1973—78, Ctrl. Elem. Sch., Lancaster, 1978—89, South Mid. Sch., Lancaster, 1989—. Grantee, J. Marion Sims Found., Inc., 2006. Mem.: Palmetto State Tchrs. Orgn. Democrat.

PITTS, AMY KATHLEEN, science educator; b. Portsmouth, Va., Aug. 4, 1977; d. Andrew Joseph and Kathleen Margaret Pitts. BA in Biology, U. NC, Chapel Hill, 1999. Lic. tchr. Va., 2006. Ptnr. exec. Clarke Am., Balt., 2002—04; tchr. sci. Thomas Eaton Mid. Sch., Hampton, Va., 2004—. Yearbook advisor Thomas Eaton Mid. Sch., 2004—; lab. sci. tchr. profl. devel. program participant U.S. Dept. Energy Thomas Jefferson Nat. Accelerator Facility, Newport News, 2005—; participant Chesepeake Bay Acad., Tappahannock, 2004. Vol. Md. Sci. Ctr., Balt., 2003—04. Lt. USN, 1999—2002. Grantee, Dept. of Energy, 2005—06. Office Phone: 757-896-5727. Personal E-mail: akpitts@alumni.unc.edu.

PITTS, BEVERLEY J., academic administrator; m. William Pitts; 2 children. BA in English, Anderson U., 1968; MA in Journalism, Ball State U., 1971, EdD in Higher Edn., 1981. Chair, dept. comm. Anderson U., 1980—85; coord., News Editl. Sequence Ball State U., 1985—88, dir. grad. studies in journalism, 1985—88, dir. gen. studies, 1988—90, dir. academic assessment and general studies, 1990, asst. provost, exec. dir. rsch. and undergraduate curriculum, 1990—92, acting provost, 1994, 2001, acting supr. for information technology, 2000—01, assoc. provost, 1993—2002, provost, v.p. for academic affairs, 2002, acting pres., 2004; pres. U. Indpls., 2005—. Instr. english Anderson U., 1977—80, advisor student publs., 1977—85, asst. prof. comm., 1980—85; assoc. prof. journalism Ball State U., 1985—90, prof. journalism, 1991—. Staff writer, researcher, comm. cons. Nat. Football League Players Assn., Washington, DC (Nat. Football League Players Assn. award of Excellence, 2000); contbr. articles to profl. jours. and newspapers; book review editor College Media Review, 1982—85; design editor College Media Review, 1985—86; reviewer Journalism Educator, 1990—99, grant reviewer Nat. Endowment for the Humanities, 1990, co-publisher (textbook) The Process of Media Writing, 1997, editl. bd. mem. Perspectives, Journal of the Association of General and Liberal Studies, 1997—2001, co-founder Ind. Teachers of Writing, 1981, pres., 1982—83, program chair, fall conf., 1982. Bd. dir. Family Svcs. of Delaware County, 1999—2002, Lyn St. James Found., 2000—02, Cmty. Alliance to Promote Edn., 2001—03, Delaware County CofC, 2003—, Sagamore Inst., 2004—. Ind. Youth Inst., 2000—, chair, 2005; bd. dir. Muncie Rotary Club, 2000—04, sec., 2000—01, pres.-elect, 2001—02, pres., 2002—03; mem. Cmty. Found. Muncie, Ind. Humanities Coun.; bd. dir. pres. Prof. Garfield Found., 2004—; bd. dir. Delaware County Cmty. Found., 2000—, vice-chair, 2003—04, chair-elect, 2005; and several others. Recipient Anderson U. Outstanding Alumni award, 1999, Ball State U. Alumni award, 2000, Woman of Acheivement in Edn. award, Women in Communication; Ottoway Fellowship for Advanced Study, Am. Press Inst., Reston, Va., Ottoway Newspaper Found., 1986, Am. Press Inst. Fellowship for Advanced Study for Journalism Educators, 1987, Fellowship, Think Tank, Coll. of Scis. and Humanities, Ball State U., 1988, Fulbright Scholarship to study in Germany, 1994. Mem.: Assn. for General and Liberal Studies (nat. bd. dir. 1989—94, pres. 1993—94), Assn. for Edn. in Journalism and Mass Comm., Am. Conf. Academic Deans, Am. Assn. U. Adminstrators, Am. Assn. Higher Edn., Nat. Football League Players Assn. (cons. 1984—), Profl. Atheletes Found. (bd. dir. 1990—2004), Sigma Delta Chi. Office: U Indpls 1400 East Hanna Ave Indianapolis IN 46227-3697 Office Phone: 317-788-3211.

PITTS, HOLLY LEA, elementary school educator; d. Thomas Drayton and Barbara Lee Pitts. BS, Sam Houston State U., Huntsville, Tex., 1995. Tchr. 6th grade math, sci. Houser Intermediate Sch., Conroe, Tex., 1995—96; tchr. 7th grade sci. York Jr. H.S., 1996—. Coach cross country York Jr. High, 2005—06, coord. campus sci. fair, 2004—, facilitator student assistance program, 1996—, coord. student mentor program, 2000—05, chair sci. dept., 1999—2005, 1999—2005, coord. sci. fair campus, 2002—. Mem.: Sci. Tchrs. Assn. Tex., Nat. Sci. Tchrs. Am. Office: York Junior High School 27310 Oak Ridge School Road Conroe TX 77385 Office Phone: 832-592-8600. Office Fax: 936-709-7223. Personal E-mail: hpitts@charter.net. E-mail: hpitts@conroeisd.net.

PITTS, JENNIFER LYNN, art educator; b. Houma, La., May 29, 1978; d. Mark Alan and Jane Marie Manes; m. Jason Stephen Pitts, May 27, 2000; 1 child, Luke Warren. BA, U. Ctrl. Ark., Conway, 2000. Cert. tchr. Ark., 2001, Tex., 2001. Tchr. art Town Ctr. Elem., Coppell, Tex., 2001—. Crafts organizer Lakeland Bapt., Lewisville, Tex., 2005—06. Mem.: Tex. Art Educator Assn., Sigma Sigma Sigma (life; pres. 1999—2000). Office: Town Center Elementary 185 North Heartz Road Coppell TX 75019 Office Phone: 214-496-7800.

PITTS, KAREN COLLEEN, art educator; b. Murphy, N.C., Jan. 1, 1957; d. Clyde Edward Lee and Hilda Joan (Pickney) P. AB in Fine Arts, Coll. William and Mary, 1978; MA in Interdisciplinary Art, Va. Commonwealth U., 2002. Cert. tchr., Va. Lectr. art history Patrick Henry C.C., Martinsville, Va., 1980-81; tchr. art Salem Elem. Sch., Fredericksburg, Va., 1981-84, Courtland High Sch., Fredericksburg, 1982-84, Spotsylvania (Va.) High Sch., 1984—. Bd. dirs. Fredericksburg Ctgr. Creative Arts, 1984-86. Mem. NEA, Nat. Art Edn. Assn. Office: Spotsylvania High Sch 6975 Courthouse Rd Spotsylvania VA 22553-3322 Office Phone: 540-582-3882. E-mail: kcpitts@hs.spotsylvania.k12.va.us.

PITTS, SHARON ANN GAMMAGE, nursing administrator; b. Plainview, Tex., Oct. 23, 1956; d. David and Letha Juanita (Howard) Gammage; m. Billy Lee Pitts, May 20, 1978; 1 child, Billy Luke. Diploma, NW Tex. Hosp. Sch. Nursing, Amarillo, 1977. Med. supr. Cen. Plains Regional Hosp., Plainview, Tex., asst. dir. nurses, supr., dir. quality assurance, oper. rm. circulator; adminstr. Covenant Home Health Care, Plainview. Mem. Assn. Oper. Rm. Nurses. Home: 2900 W 17th St Plainview TX 79072-4759

PITTS-CUTLER, MELISSA ANNE, counselor, social worker; b. LA, Aug. 20, 1964; d. William E. and Sadie Lee Pitts; m. Kevin Bernard Cutler, June 7, 1998; children: Allanah Mirelle Cutler, Aniah Drew Cutler. BS, Calif. State U., 1987, MSW, 1993. Cert.: Deliquency Control Inst., U. So. Calif. 2000. Youth counselor Calif. Youth Authority, Norwalk, 1987—91, Whittier, 1991—93, parole agt. LA, 1993—94, asst. supervising parole agt. Westminster, 1994—. Cons. Artshare LA, 2000—05. Author: (fiction) All Men Are.But What About You My Sister, 2005. Donor So. Poverty Law Ctr., 2004. Mem.: Alpha Kappa Alpha. Democrat. Avocations: sports, travel. Office: Calif Youth Authority 8311 Westminster Blvd #260 Westminster CA 92683 Office Phone: 714-890-3381. Office Fax: 562-633-5837. Business E-Mail: kcnmiss@sbcglobal.net.

PITZER, BETTY BRAUN, retired social services administrator; b. Springfield, Ohio, Aug. 7, 1912; d. Frank J. and Alnora (Hagerman) Braun; m. Elwood Gilbert Pitzer, Oct. 2, 1936; children: Philip Elwood, Richard Alan. BA in Bus. Adminstrn. cum laude, Wittenberg U., 1933, LHD (hon.), 2001. Asst. mgr. Baker's Cafeteria, Springfield, 1933—41; fin. sec. Credit Life Ins. Co., Springfield, 1933—41; pres. Ohio Assn. Alpha Delta Pi, Springfield, 1956—58; nat. treas. Alpha Delta Pi Sorority, Atlanta, 1963—79; assoc. dir. United Way Clark County, Springfield, 1965—69; exec. dir. Elderly United Springfield and Clark County, Springfield, 1969—91; ret., 1991. Com. mem. Area Agy. on Aging, Dayton, Ohio, 1979-83, Ohio Gov.'s Conf. on Aging,

Columbus, 1979-81, Home Care Adv. Com., Springfield, 1981-84, Ohio Commn. on Aging State Fair, Columbus, 1979-82; Clark County coord. White House Conf. on Aging, 1971. Pres. Adelphean Found., Atlanta, 1964-71; mem. fiscal rev. com. City of Springfield, 1982; mem. alumni coun. Wittenberg U., Springfield. Recipient Disting. Alumna award Wittenberg U., 1975, gov.'s award State of Ohio, 1982, Svc. to Mankind award Sertoma Club, Springfield, 1984, Meritorious Svc. award Community Hosp. Bd. Trustees, Springfield, 1977-86, Clark County Cmty. Action award, 1986, Hall of Fame award United Way Clark County, 1987, Kiwanis Cmty. Svc. award, 1991, Area Agy. Aging Svc. award, 1991, Springfield Urban League Svc. award, 1991, Clark County ADMH Bd. Svc. award, 1993, Ohio Sr. Citizen Hall of Fame, 1995, Alumni of Distinction award Springfield City Schs., 2006. Mem. Ohio Assn. Sr. Ctrs., Ohio Citizens Coun. (policy bd.), Miami Valley Coun. on Gerontology, Zonta (pres. Springfield 1970-72), Alpha Delta Pi (Alumna of Yr. award 1987). Republican. Lutheran. Home: 111 Englewood Dr Springfield OH 45504

PIVEN, FRANCES FOX, political scientist, educator; b. Calgary, Alta., Can., Oct. 10, 1932; arrived in U.S., 1933, naturalized, 1953; d. Albert and Rachel (Paperny) F.; 1 dau., Sarah. BA, U. Chgo., 1953, MA, 1956, PhD, 1962; L.H.D. (hon.), Adelphi U., 1985. Mem. faculty Columbia, 1966-72; prof. polit. sci. Boston U., 1972-82, Grad. Ctr., CUNY, 1982—. Co-author: Regulating the Poor: The Functions of Public Welfare, 1971, 2d edit., 1993, The Politics of Turmoil: Essays on Poverty, Race and the Urban Crisis, 1974, Poor People's Movements, 1977, New Class War, 1982, The Mean Season, 1987, Why Americans Don't Vote, 1988; editor: Labor Parties in Post Industrial Societies, 1992, The Breaking of the American Social Compact, 1997, Why Americans Still Don't Vote, 2000, Work, Welfare and Politics, 2002, The War at Home, 2004, Challenging Authority, 2006. Recipient C. Wright Mills award Soc. Study Social Problems, 1971, Fulbright Disting. Lectureship award U. Bologna, 1990, President's award APHA, 1993, Annual award Nat. Assn. Sec. of State, 1994, Lifetime Achievement award Pol. Sociology Am. Sociological Assn., 1995, Disting. Career award, 2000, Pub. Understanding of Sociology award, 2003; Guggenheim fellow, 1973-74; Am. Coun. Learned Socs. awardee, 1982. Mem. ACLU, Am. Polit. Sci. Assn. (v.p. 1981-82), Soc. Study Social Problems (pres. 1980-81, Lee founders award 1992), Am. Sociol. Assn. (pres. 2006-). Home: PO Box N Millerton NY 12546-0651 Office: CUNY Grad Sch 365 5th Ave New York NY 10016-4309 Office Phone: 212-817-8674. E-mail: ffox-piven@gc.cuny.edu.

PIZZAMIGLIO, NANCY ALICE, performing company executive; b. Oak Park, Ill., Aug. 22, 1936; d. Howard Joseph and Marian Louise (Henne) Gilman; m. Ernest George Lovas, May 17, 1957 (div. Nov. 1976); children: Lori Dianne, Randall Gilman; m. Albert Theodore Pizzamiglio, Mar. 27, 1978. Student, North Tex. State U., Denton, 1955-56. Stewardess North Cen. Airlines, Chgo., 1956-57; receptionist Leo Burnett Advt. Agy., Chgo., 1957-59; office mgr. Judy Stallons Employment Agy., Oak Brook, Ill., 1973-75; mgr. and escort Prestige Vacations, Inc., Oak Brook, Ill., 1975-76; corp. dir. Al Pierson Big Band U.S.A., Inc., Aubrey, Tex., 1976-2000, Al Pierson, Inc., Aubrey, Tex., 1978—, corp. pres., 1997—, Gilman, Inc. Artists Mgmt., Aubrey, 1982-2000; owner Dancing Horse Ranch, Aubrey, Tex., 1983—; bus. mgr. Guy Lombardo's Royal Canadians, Aubrey, Tex., 1989—. Editor: (newsletter) Property Owners Assn., 1972-73; contbr. articles to profl. jours. Recipient expert award NRA, 1952. Mem. U.S. Lipizzan Registry (bd. dirs. 1986-89, 1996-98, treas. 1996-98), Dallas Dressage Club (bd. dirs. 1988-94), Am. Horse Shows Assn., U.S. Dressage Fedn. (qualified rider 1989, third/all breeds, first level 1989, first/all breeds, fourth level 1991, third Vintage Cup, fourth level 1991, third all-breeds first level 1992, third vintage cup first level 1992), Dallas-Ft. Worth Labrador Retriever Club Inc. (bd. dirs. 2000—, v.p. 2005-06, bd. dirs. 2006-). Republican. Episcopalian. Avocations: showing and training Labrador retrievers, world travel, dog breeding, digital and video photography. Address: Al Pierson Inc 2469 Spring Hill Rd Aubrey TX 76227-3911 Office Phone: 940-365-9491. E-mail: dancehorse@aol.com.

PIZZINGRILLI, KIM, state official; BBA Econ., U. Pitts., Johnstown, 1981; M Govtl. adminstrn., U. Pa., 1988. Auditor, acct., and asst. dir. bur. of audits Pa. Treasury Dept., 1981-87; sr. regulatory analyst Pa. Ind. Regulatory Rev. Commn., 1987-95; spl. asst. to sec. Dept. of State, Harrisburg, Pa., 1995-96, dep. sec. regulatory programs, 1996-98, acting sec., 1998-99, sec. of the commonwealth, 1999—2002; commr. Pa. Pub. Utility Comm., 2002—. Mem. Bd. of Property, Bd. of Fin. and Revenue, State of Pa.; mem. Pa. State Athletic Commn., Pa. State Nav. Commn. for the Delaware River and its Navigable Tributaries, mem. Pa. Mcpl. Retirement Bd.; keeper Great Seal of the Commonwealth. Mem. Nat. Assn. Sec. of State, Women Exec. in State Govt. Republican. Office: Pennsylvania Pub Utility Commn PO Box 3265 Harrisburg PA 17105-3265

PIZZO, PIA, artist, educator; arrived in U.S., 1982, permanent resident, 1985; d. Rosario Pizzo and Rosa Greco; m. Chin Hsiao, Apr. 28, 1962 (div. May 1979); 1 child, Samantha Hsiao (dec.); m. Delbert O. Thompson, June 18, 1985. Diploma, Coll. of Art Orsoline, Milano, Italy, 1956; student, Brera Acad. Art, Milano, Italy, 1957—60; BFA, Ministry Pub. Instrn., Roma, Italy, 1957. Founder, propr. Sama Press, Long Beach, Calif., 1995—. Instr. design and color theory Brooks Coll. Design, Long Beach, Calif., 1998—; instr. art and creativity Dept. Parks, Recreation, Marine, Long Beach, Calif., 1987—; lectr. Dept. Art and Tech. Calif. State U., Long Beach, Calif., 1995—96. Exhibitions include 32 solo exhbns., Europe and USA, 1962—2003, 89 group shows, Europe, USA, Brasil, Taiwan, 1957—; author: The World is Waiting for the Sunrise, 1985 (hon. mention, 1987); co-author (with blind students): 6'x 8' tactile sculptural book-perm. pub. art, 1988; contbr. articles to profl. publs.; author (designer): adult and children books, 1970, 1981. Named Artist of Yr., Disting. Visual Artist, PCA Pub. Corp. for Arts, 1989; recipient Cert. Recognition award, Accademia Tiberina, Roma, Italy, 1957, cert. of Appreciation in Recognition of Outstanding Svc., City of Long Beach, Calif., 2000, permanent pub. art sign project, City of Gardena, Calif., 2001; fellow, Pollock-Krasner Found., NYC, 1984, Calif. Arts Coun., Sacramento, 1987, Pub. Corp. for the Arts, Long Beach, Calif., 2000. Mem.: Long Beach Mus. Art Artist's Coun. (solo exhbn. 1998), The Smithsonian Inst., Internat. Campaign for Tibet, Children Internat., Amnesty Internat. Avocations: classical piano, reading, concerts, museums, languages.

PIZZORNO, LARA ELISE, medical writer, editor; b. N.Y.C., Oct. 5, 1948; d. Daniel A. and Elinor M. (Kugel) Udell; m. John James Leary Jr. (div. 1979); m. Joseph E. Pizzorno; children: Galen Udell. BA magna cum laude, Wheaton Coll., 1970; MAR in Philos. Theology, Yale U., 1973; MA in English Lit., U. Wash., 1986. Lic. massage therapist. Instr. philosophy Edmonds (Wash.) C.C., 1974-78; grants writer Seattle U., 1978-79, asst. dir. devel., 1979-81; devel. cons. Bastyr U., Seattle, 1981-83, copyeditor Textbook of Natural Medicine, 1986-89; instr. English North Seattle C.C., 1986-89; dir. publs. Trillium Health Products, Seattle, 1992-93; owner WordWorks, Seattle, 1993—2000; sr. med. editor Salugenecists, Inc., 2000—. Author: The Complete Book of Bread Machine Baking, 1993; co-author: Natural Medicine Instuctions for Patients, 2001, Ency. of Healing Foods, 2005; contbg. author: Textbook of Functional Medicine, 2006—; editor, contbg. writer: Integrative Medicine: A Clinician's Jour., Choices, Natural Lifestyle and Nutrition mag., Total Wellness, 1996; health and nutrition writer Whole Foods website, 2000—; editor: The World's Healthiest Feeds, Essential Guide, 2006; contbr. numerous articles to popular mags. Mem. Am. Med. Writers Assn., Ctr. Spiritual Living, Phi Beta Kappa. Avocations: healthy cooking, weight training, gardening, bicycling, scuba diving. Home and Office: 4220 NE 135th St Seattle WA 98125-3836 Office Phone: 206-368-5403.

PLACE, JANEY, banking consultant, former bank executive; b. Denver, Jan. 25, 1946; m. Michael Hiles. BA, MA, UCLA, PhD in semiology, 1975, attended Grad. Sch. Mgmt. Info tech. mgr. Hughes Aircraft Co.; corp. mgr. Strategic Tech. Planning Tosco Corp.; sr. v.p. internet strategy, R&D Wells Fargo Bank, 1990—94; exec. v.p. Strategic Tech. Group Bank of Am., 1994—99; pres. Mellon Lab and Online Svcs., N.Y.C., 1999—2003; exec. v.p. Mellon Fin. Corp., N.Y.C., 1999—2003; founder, pres., CEO digitalthinking.com, 1999—. Past lectr. in sys. and comm. theory U. Calif., Santa Cruz, Calif.; bd. dirs. PortBlue; spkr. in field. Contbr. articles to profl. jours.; author: The Western Films of John Ford, 1974, The Non-Western Films of John Ford, 1979. Named One of 25 Women to Watch in Banking, U.S. Banker Mag., 2003.

PLACEWAY, JOELLEN PETERSON, elementary school educator; b. Toledo; d. Jack Douglas and Dolores (Farrell) Peterson; m. Timothy Placeway, May 27, 1978; children: Jared, Jaime Marie, Joshua. MusB, Houghton Coll., NY, 1974; MusM, Mich. State U., East Lansing, 1975. Music instr. Taylor U., Upland, Ind., 1977—80, Marion Coll., Ind., 1977—82; music tchr. prep. dept. Elizabethtown Coll., Pa., 1984—86; music tchr. Elizabethtown Area Schs., 1987—. Asst. prin., section player Ft. Wayne Philharmonic, Ind., 1977—87; music instr. Csehy Summer Sch. Music, Muncy, Pa., 1972—84. Mem.: NEA, Pa. State Educators Assn., Music Educators Assn. Home: 127 Foxbury Dr Elizabethtown PA 17022

PLAINE, LLOYD LEVA, lawyer; b. Washington, Nov. 3, 1947; d. Marx and Shirley P. Leva; m. James W. Hill. BA, U. Pa., 1969; postgrad., Harvard U.; JD, Georgetown U., 1975. Bar: DC 1975. Legis. asst. to US Rep. Sidney Yates, 1971-72; with Sutherland, Asbill & Brennan, Washington, 1975-82, ptnr., 1982—. Fellow Am. Bar Found., Am. Coll. Trust and Estate Counsel (past regent), Am. Coll. Tax Counsel; mem. ABA (past chmn. real property, probate and trust law sect., past coun. sect. of taxation). Office: Sutherland Asbill & Brennan Ste 6 1275 Pennsylvania Ave NW Washington DC 20004-2415 Office Phone: 202-383-0155.

PLAISTED, CAROLE ANNE, elementary school educator; b. Meredith, N.H., Apr. 3, 1939; d. Morris Holman and Christina Martin (Dunn) Plaisted. EdB with honors, Plymouth (N.H.) Tchrs. Coll., 1960; MA, Columbia U., 1966; cert., N.Y. Inst. Photography, 1990. Cert. tchr., N.H. Tchr. Lang St. Sch., Meredith, 1960-61, Mechanic St. Sch., Laconia, N.H., 1961-62, Wheelock Lab. Sch., Keene, N.H., 1963-94; asst. prof. emeritus Keene State Coll. Summer tchr. Cheshire County Headstart, Hinsdale, N.H., 1965; tchr. children's lit. Keene State Coll., 1974, 75; classroom evaluator D.C. Heath Co., Lexington, Mass., 1985-86; dist. trainer for drug edn. supervisory unit, Keene, 1988-94. Author: The Graduates Speak, 1990; co-author curriculum materials; contbr. Kindergarten: A Sourcebook for School and Home, 1984. Trustee Reed Free Libr., Surry, N.H., 1988-2000; program chair Wheelock Sch. PTA, 1964-65. Named Outstanding Elem. Tchr. of Am., 1973. Mem. Cheshire County Ret. Educators Assn., Delta Kappa Gamma (pres. Alpha chpt. 1996-98, 2000-02, corr. sec. Alpha chpt. 1972-76, state scholarship chmn. 1985-2005, Beta Alpha state scholarship 1989, Founders award, 2001). Avocations: reading, gardening, photography.

PLAME, VALERIE ELISE, former intelligence agent; b. Anchorage, Aug. 13, 1963; d. Samuel D. and Diane E. Plame; m. Joseph Charles Wilson IV, Apr. 3, 1998; children: Trevor Rolph, Samantha Finnell Diana. BA in Internat. Rels., Penn. State U., 1985; MA, London Sch. Econs., Coll. Europe, Belgium, 1995. Classified officer CIA, 1985—2003. Became the subject of a wide-spread government controversy when members of the Bush administration were accused of leaking her identity as an undercover CIA agent to members of the media; filed lawsuit against members of the Bush administration in 2006.

PLANDER, SUSAN ELAINE, elementary school educator; d. Harley Meyer and Eileen Margaret Plander (Stepmother), Charlotte Marianne Plander; m. Eugene Francis Hibben, July 27, 1996; 1 child, Marisa Irene. BS in Elem. Edn., Valparaiso U., Ind., 1976, MA in Liberal Studies, 1999. Asst. mgr. Harley's Camarillo Bowl, Calif., 1976—79; loan servicing-customer svc. supr. Guild Mortgage Co., San Diego, 1980—85; elem. sch. tchr. First Luth. Ch. Sch., Camarillo, Calif., 1985—88; gen. mgr. Harley's Camarillo Bowl, Calif., 1988—94; substitute tchr. several No. Ind. sch. dists. Valparaiso, 1995—99; mid. sch. tchr. Carroll County Mid. Sch., Carrollton, Ky., 1999—. Faculty sponsor Panther Pride Publ., Carroll County Mid. Sch., Carrollton, Ky., 2000—06. Editor: (mid. sch. lit. mag.) Panthology. Mem.: NEA, Ky. Coun. for Social Studies, Nat. Mid. Sch. Assn., Sigma Tau Delta. Avocations: quilting, gardening, writing. Office: Carroll County Mid Sch 408 Fifth St Carrollton KY 41008 Office Phone: 502-732-7080.

PLANK, BETSY (MRS. SHERMAN V. ROSENFIELD), public relations counsel; b. Tuscaloosa, Ala., Apr. 3, 1924; d. Richard Jeremiah and Bettye (Hood) P.; m. Sherman V. Rosenfield, Apr. 10, 1954. Student, Bethany Coll., W.Va., 1940-43; AB, U. Ala., 1944. Continuity dir. radio sta. KQV, Pitts., 1944-47; account exec. Mitchell McKeown Orgn., Chgo., 1947-54; pub. rels. counsel Chgo. chpt. A.R.C., 1954-57; dir. pub. rels. Chgo. Coun. on Fgn. Rels., 1957-58; v.p. Ronald Goodman Pub. Rels. Counsel, Chgo., 1958-61; exec. v.p., treas., dir. Daniel J. Edelman, Inc., Chgo., 1961-73; dir. pub. rels. planning AT&T, N.Y.C., 1973-74; dir. external rels. Ill. Bell, Chgo., 1974-90; prin. Betsy Plank Pub. Rels., Chgo., 1990—. Dep. chmn. VII World Congress on Pub. Rels., 1976; co-chmn. nat. commn. on Pub. Rels. Edn., 1984-87; mem. adv. bd. Ill. Issues, 1975—. Bd. dirs. United Way Chgo., 1986-90; chmn. Citizenship Coun. Met. Chgo., 1990-96, Betsy Plank chpt. Pub. Rels. Student Soc. Am., No. Ill. U.; trustee Found. for Pub. Rels. Rsch. and Edn., 1975-80; nat. bd. dirs. Girl Scouts U.S., 1975-85. Recipient Millennium award Coll. Journalism, U. Fla., 2000, Alexander Hamilton award, Inst. Pub. Rels., 2000, Plank Ctr. Pub. Rels. Studies, U. Ala., 2005; named one of World's 40 Leading Pub. Rels. Profls., Pub. Rels. News, 1984, Pub. Rels. Hall of Fame Rowan U., 2005. Fellow Pub. Rels. Soc. Am. (accredited, nat. pres. 1973, Outstanding Profl. award 1977, Outstanding Cmty. Svc. award 1989, Disting. Svc. award 2001, Plank Nat. Scholarships); mem. Ill. Coun. on Econ. Edn. (past chmn., trustee 1974—, Extraordinary Leadership award 2001), Internat. Pub. Rels. Assn., Chgo. Network (chmn. 1980-81), Arthur W. Page Soc. (lifetime achievement award 2000), Union League Club of Chgo., Econ. Club Chgo., Zeta Tau Alpha. Presbyterian.

PLANK, HELENE ELIZABETH, academic administrator; b. Trenton, N.J., Aug. 16, 1957; d. Walter Stephen and Angeline Josephine (Ribavaro) Wasielewski; m. William Stephen Plank Jr., May 31, 1980. AA in Visual Arts, Mercer County Community Coll., 1977; BA in Advt. Design, Trenton State Coll., 1979; MA in Human Svcs. Adminstrn., Rider Coll., 1992. Graphic artist White Eagle Printing Co., Trenton, N.J., 1979-80; arts coun. staff N.J. State Coun. on Arts, Trenton, 1980-84; adminstrv. sec. Mercer County CC, Trenton, 1984-88, coll. researcher, 1988—96, asst. dir. fin. aid, 1996—. Graphic arts cons. in field. Exec. com. mem. Lawrence Arts Coun., 1982-88; adv. bd. mem. Hamilton Twp. Adult/Continuing Edn., Trenton, 1980-81. Recipient Minigrant Mercer County CC Found., 1989, Highest Honors award, 1977, Advisor of the Yr. award, Mercer County CC, 2005, Cmty. Svc. award, 2001 Mem.: NAFE, Mercer County CC Alumni Assn. (exec. coun.), Phi Kappa Phi Nat.Honor Soc. (hon.; staff advisor 2002—). Avocations: drawing, needlecrafts, jewelry design. Office: Mercer County Community Coll PO Box B Trenton NJ 08690-0182 Office Phone: 609-570-3217. E-mail: plankh@mccc.edu.

PLANK, KATRINA JEAN, secondary school educator; b. Lubbock, Tex., May 10, 1949; d. J. W. and Dorthy Jean Hamby; children: Pam Gonzales, Tammye Creek, Machael Chittum, Kindy, Jay William. AS, Lubbock Christian Coll., Tex., 1969; BS in Edn., Abilene Christan Coll., Tex., 1971. Cert. master PAL tchr., PAL svcs. Austin, peer program educator Nat. Peer Helpers Assn., cheer coach level I 1994, cheer coach II 1995. Tchr., coach Ft. Stockton (Tex.) HS, 1971—72; spl. edn. tchr. Tri County Edn. Coop., Stamford, Tex., 1974—77; physical edn. tchr. Anson (Tex.) ISD, 1977—79, spl. edn. tchr., 1990—2005; pvt. preschool Peanuts Club, Anson, Tex., 1980—90; swim tchr. City of Anson, 1980—98; PAL facilitator Anson (Tex.) HS, 1996—2005; swim tchr. M.O.M.S. Pool, 2001—05. Adv. bd. mem. Region XIV Safe & Drug Free Sch., Abilene, Tex., 2000—05, PAL Svcs., Austin, 2002—05; presenter NPHA Nat. Conf., Atlanta, 2003, Austin, 04, Chgo., 05, State Mid. Sch. PAL Conf., Austin, Tex., 2004, Austin, 05, State HS PAL Conf., Austin, Tex., 2005; mem. advocacy com. NAPP, 2005. Tennis coach, 1996—2005; bible class tchr., 1982—. Named one of Leading Educators of World, Internat. Biog. Ctr., 2006. Mem.: Nat. Peer Helpers Assn. Mem. Ch. Of Christ. Avocations: swimming, reading, Bible studies. Home: 1228 14th St Anson TX 79501 Office: Anson HS 1509 Commercial St Anson TX 79501 Office Phone: 325-823-2404. Business E-Mail: kplank@anson.esc14.net.

PLANKENHORN, SHARON A., chaplain; b. Ottawa, Ill., Oct. 8, 1944; d. James O. Plankenhorn and Lista May Johns. BA in Theology, Webster U., St. Louis, 1967; MA in Religious Studies, U. Detroit, Mich., 1973; D in Ministry, Weston Jesuit Sch. Theology, Cambridge, Mass., 1984; MDiv, Eden Theol. Seminary, St. Louis, 2004. Cert. tchr. Mo., 1967. Tchr. religion St. Peter's Parish Sch., Mendota, Minn., 1967—68, Bishop DuBourg H.S., St. Louis, 1968—73; seminar leader Archdiocese St. Louis, 1971—79; chaplain St. Elizabeth Hosp., Belleville, Ill., 1980—81; spiritual dir. Ctr. Religious Devel., Weston Jesuit Sch. Theology, Cambridge, Mass., 1981—84; pastoral assoc. St. Mary's Parish, Brownsville, Tex., 1984—85, Queen of Peace Parish, Harlingen, Tex., 1984—85; programming dir. Maria Stein Retreat, Ohio, 1988—90; chaplain St. Luke's Hosp., Bethlehem, Pa., 1990—92; diversity mgmt. asst. Cochran, Hadden, Royston Assocs., Gloucester, Mass., 1992—93; dir. campus ministry Bentley Coll., Waltham, Mass., 1993—94; co-dir. Vision of Peace Hermitages, Pevely, Mo., 1994—96; religion tchr. John F. Kennedy Cath. H.S., St. Louis, 1996—97; hospice chaplain Pathways Cmty. Hospice, St. Louis, 1998—2002; concierge Brookdale Hallmark, Creve Coeur, Mo., 2003—; hospice chaplain Vis. Nurse Assn., St. Louis, 2003—. Co-author: You Will Receive Power, 1977; editor: The Spirit and The Bride, 1973—78. Charter mem. Profl. Women's Home Offices, St. Louis, 1998—99. Mem.: Spiritual Dirs. Internat. Democrat. Avocations: gardening, hiking, swimming, remodeling. Home: 6702 Michigan Ave Saint Louis MO 63111 Office: Hallmark of Creve Coeur One New Ballas Pl Creve Coeur MO 63146 Office Phone: 314-432-5200. Office Fax: 314-432-5222. Personal E-mail: ssplankenhorn@hotmail.com.

PLASCAK-CRAIG, FAYE DENE, psychology educator, researcher; b. Denver, Jan. 13, 1945; d. Leon Thomas Wolf and Hazel Lucille Schmidt O'Keefe; m. Nicholas D. Plascak, Aug. 20, 1966 (div. Dec. 1988); children: Patricia Plascak, Cynthia Plascak; m. Raymond C. Craig, Dec. 17, 1988. AA, Ind. U., Indpls., 1966; BA, Purdue U., 1981, MS, 1983; PhD, Ind. U., 1988. Dental hygienist in pvt. practice, Indpls., 1966-72; rsch. assoc. Ind.U./Purdue U., Indpls., 1981-83; instr. Marian Coll., Indpls., 1983-84, asst. prof., 1984-89, assoc. prof., 1989-94, prof. psychology, 1994—, chair dept., 1999. Cons. Ivy Tech. St. Coll., Lafayette, Ind., 1996-97. Contbr. chpt. to book. Mem. APA, Midwestern Psychol. Assn., Sigma Phi Alpha, Psi Chi. Avocations: opera, classical music, gardening. Office: Marian Coll 3200 Cold Spring Rd Indianapolis IN 46222-1960

PLATEK, JENNIFER BETHANY, voice educator; b. Wadsworth, Ohio, Aug. 26, 1979; d. Joseph John and Martha Joyce Platek. MusB, Taylor U., Upland, Ind., 1997—2001. Choir dir. N. Royalton City Schs., Ohio, 2002—06. Charity choir organizer N. Royalton HS, 2003—06. Mem.: Ohio Edn. Assn., Music Edn. Nat. Conf., Am. Choral Dirs. Assn. Avocations: reading, running, travel, sports.

PLATIS, MARY LOU, media specialist; b. East Chicago, Ind., Jan. 21, 1946; d. Walter James and Mary Helen (Taus) Campbell; m. James George Platis, Aug. 16, 1974. BS, Ind. State U., 1972, MS, 1974. Tchr. 4th grade Holy Trinity Sch., East Chicago, Ind., 1968-72; tchr. phys. edn. Washington Elem. Sch., East Chicago, Ind., 1972-86; media specialist Ctrl. High Sch. Libr., East Chicago, Ind., 1986—. Recipient 72 Ind. track and field individual state medals, 1983-2001, 72 Ind. state regional individual medals, 1983-2002, 25 All Am. certs., 12 times Masters track and field All Am., 1989-98, 37 Ill. Grand Prix individual titles, 1989-93, 43 Midwest track and field individual titles, 1989-95, 3 times Nat. Masters track and field champion, 7 times Nat. runner-up, Bronze medal Nat. Sr. Games, Pitts., 2005; nat. sr. Olympics qualifier, 1997, 99, 2001, 03, 05; 6th pl. ribbons (2) Nat. Sr. Olympics, 1999; nat. and world ranked masters track and field, 1989-98; individual championship titles in racquetball; named to East Chicago Sports Hall of Fame, 1992. Mem. Nat. Assn. Basketball Coaches. Avocations: racquetball, tennis, working out. Home: 938 Troon Ct Schererville IN 46375 Office: Ctrl High Sch Libr 1100 W Columbus Dr East Chicago IN 46312-2582 Office Phone: 219-391-4046. E-mail: mlplatis@aol.com.

PLATT, JAN KAMINIS, former county official; b. St. Petersburg, Fla., Sept. 27, 1936; d. Peter Clifton and Adele (Diamond) Kaminis; m. William R. Platt, Feb. 8, 1963; 1 child, Kevin Peter. BA, Fla. State U., 1958; postgrad., U. Fla. Law Sch., 1958-59, U. Va., 1962, Vanderbilt U., 1964. Pub. sch. tchr. Hillsborough County, Tampa, Fla., 1959-60; field dir. Girl Scouts Suncoast Coun., Tampa, 1960-62; city councilman Tampa City Coun., 1974-78; county commr. Hillsborough County, 1978—94, country commr., 1996—2004; chmn. Hillsborough County Bd. County Commrs., 1980-81, 83-84, 98-99, ret., 1994, re-elected, 1996, chmn., 1998-99, County Charter Rev. Bd., 2005—06; cp-chair Countrywide Cultural Plan, 2006—. Chmn. Tampa Bay Regional Planning Coun., 1982, West Coast Regional Water Supply Authority, Tampa, 1985, Hillsborough County Coun. Govts., 1976, 79, Agy. Bay Mgmt., Hills Environ. Protection Commn., Sunshine Amendment Drive 7th Congrl. Dist., Tampa, 1976, Cmty. Action Agy., Tampa, 1981, 83-84,chmn. pro tem Tampa Charter Revision Commn., 1975, chmn. Prison Sitting Task Force, Tampa, 1983, Tampa Housing Study Com., 1983, Met. Planning Orgn., Tampa, 1984, Bd. Tax Adjustment, Tampa, 1984, chmn. Hartline, 2002-03, Friendship Trailbridge Oversight Com., 2002-03, Tampa Bay Water, 2003-04; appointee Constn. Revision Commn., Fla., 1977, HRS Dist. IV Adv. Coun., Fla.; mem. Hillsborough County Expy. Authority, Taxicab Commn., Ch. Hills Cmty. Youth Coun.; vice chmn. steering com. Nat. Counties Environ. Task Force; pres. Suncoast Girl Scout Coun., 1973-74, Ch. Head Start Cmty. Found., 2005; chmn. County Charter Rev. Bd., 2005. Bd. dirs. March of Dimes, Tampa, The Fla. Orch., Tampa, Tampa Bay Sierra, Tampa Audubon; trustee Hillsborough County Hosp. Authority, Tampa, 1984-94; pres. Citizens Alert, Tampa, Bay View Garden Club; v.p. Hillsborough County Bar Aux.; mem. adv. bd. Northside Cmty. Mental Health Ctr.: Access House, Tampa; active Arts Coun. Tampa-Hillsborough County, 1983-85, 96-2001, Drug Abuse Coordinating Coun. Orgn., Tampa, Bd. Criminal Justice, Tampa, Fla. Coun. on Aging, Inebriate Task Force, Tampa, Tampa Downtown Devel. Authority Task Force, Tampa Sports Authority, Tampa Area Mental Health Bd., Children's Study Commn., Manahill Area Agy. on Aging, Tampa, Athena Soc., Tampa Area Com. Fgn. Affairs, LWV; pres. Hills Children's Coun., Headstart Found.; bd. dirs. Arts Coun.; exec. com. Tampa Performing Arts Ctr., chmn. charter rev. bd.; mem. Com. of 100. Recipient Athena award, Women in Comm., 1976, Spessard Holland Meml. award, Tampa Bay Com. for Good Govt., 1979, First Lady of Yr. award, Beta Sigma Phi, 1980, First Ann. Humanitarian award, Nat. Orgn. of Prevention of Animal Suffering, 1981, Women Helping Women award, Soroptimist Internat. Tampa, 1983, Good Govt. award, Tampa Jaycees, 1983, LWV, 1983, John Books Meml. award, Fla. Audubon Soc., 1989, Girl Scout Woman of Distinction award, 1996, Girl Scout Thanks award, 1996, Libery Bell award, Hillsborough County Bar Assn., 2000, Black Bear award, Suncoast and Tampa Bay Groups of the Sierra Club, 2001, Eliza Wolff award, Tampa United Meth. Ctrs., Outstanding Leadership in Local Environ. Protection, Fla. Local Environ. Resource Agys., 2002, Lifetime Achievement award for outstanding leadership in local environ. protection, 2004, Communicator of Yr., Tampa Ednl. Cable Consortium, 2005, Disting. Alumna award, Fla. State U., 2005, Tampa Bay Ethics award, Tampa U. Ctr. Ethics, 2005, Dan Hanson Conservationist Yr., Frank Sargenat Fishing Expo, 2006. Mem. Am. Judicature Soc., State Assn. County Commrs. Fla. (at-large dir.), AAUW (bd. dirs.), Mortar Board (Disting. Liftime Mem. award 2006), Garnet Key, Phi Beta Kappa (pres. local alumni), Phi Kappa Phi. Democrat. Episcopalian. Home: 3531 Village Way Tampa FL 33629-8914 Home Fax: 813-805-9522.

PLATT, KATHRYN, special education educator; b. Aurora, Ill., June 20, 1981; d. John R. and Gayl L. Platt. BA, So. Ill. U., 2004. Job coach Batavia (Ill.) HS, 1997—99; tchr.'s aide daycare program So. Ill. U., Carbondale,

2003—04; resource specialist Newark (Calif.) Unified Sch. Dist., 2004—. Mem.: Calif. Tchrs. Assn. (assoc.). Office Phone: 510-818-3400. Personal E-mail: plattinum@gmail.com. Business E-Mail: kplatt@nusd.k12.ca.us.

PLATT, NINA, law librarian; d. Harlan and Ethel (Byron) Thorlacius; m. Vernon Platt, Dec. 21, 1984. BS, U. ND, Grand Forks, 1980; Ms of Libr. and Info. Sci., Dominican U., River Forest, Ill., 1997. Libr. dir. Carnegie Libr., Devils Lake, ND, 1982—85; tech. svcs. mgr. Dorsey & Whitney, Mpls., 1986—95; systems libr. Minn. Office of Atty. Gen., St. Paul, 1995—97; dir. of libr. services Faegre & Benson LLP, Mpls., 1998—. Cons. Nina Platt & Associates, Prior Lake, Minn., 1993—98. Contbr. textbook Knowledge Management for the Information Professional, articles to profl. jours. and web sites. Mem.: Minn. Law Libr. Assn. (Law Librarianship award 2003), Spl. Libraries Assn. (Innovations in Tech. award 2003), Minn. Assn. Law Libraries, Am. Assn. Law Libraries (exec. bd. mem. 2002—), Minn. Libr. Assn. (assoc.), Hekla Club (pres. 1996—97). Achievements include development of Minn. appellate ct. opinions archive. Avocations: motorcycling, gardening. Office: Faegre & Benson LLP 2200 Wells Fargo Ctr 90 S 7th St Minneapolis MN 55402 Business E-Mail: nplatt@faegre.com.

PLATZER, CYNTHIA SIEMEN, lawyer; b. Sarnia, Ont., Can., Aug. 8, 1954; d. Howard John and Gloria Ann (Nugent) Platzer; m. Joel Francis Platzer, May 25, 1979. AA, St. Clair County CC, 1973; BGS, U. Mich., 1975; JD, Detroit Coll. Law, 1981. Bar: Mich. 1982, US Dist. Ct. (ea. dist.)/Mich. 1982. Paralegal/law clk. St. Clair county Prosecutor's Office, Port Huron, Mich., 1979—82; ptnr. Cleland and Platzer, Port Huron, Mich., 1982; commr., parliamentarian Women's Coun. Realtors, Port Huron, Mich., 1982—84; corp. counsel Goodwill Industries, Port Huron, Mich., 1984—; bd. dir., 1983—; 1st v.p., 1986—87; corp. counsel Child and Family Svc., Inc., Port Huron, 1984; Note and comment editor Detroit Coll. Law Rev., 1980—81; 2d v.p. bd dir. Goodwill Industries of St. Clair County, 1983; mem. St. Clair County Met. Planning Commn., 1984, chmn., 1987; magistrate St. Clair County Dist. Ct., 1997—2002; chief judge 72nd Dist. Ct. Mich., Port Huron, 2002—. Named Port Huron Young Career Woman, Nat. Assn. Bus. and Profl. Women, 1985, Young Career Woman Region XII, 1985. Mem.: U. Mich. Alumni Assn., Ea. Mich. Law Enforcement Assn., Mich. Trial Lawyers Assn., Women Lawyers Assn. Mich., St. Clair County Bar Assn., WLAM (pres. St. Clair, sanilac, Mich. 1984—85), Quota (Port Huron).

PLATZNER, LINDA, publisher; Assoc. pub. Modern Bride PRIMEDIA, pub. Seventeen mag. Office: Seventeen 1440 Broadway #21 New York NY 10018-2301

PLAUT, JANE MARGARET, art educator; b. Bklyn., Mar. 31, 1948; d. Charles and Jane Elizabeth (Moore) Rifenberg; m. Harold J. Plaut, Dec. 14, 1968 (div. 1981); 1 child, Harold Jonathan Jr. AAS, N.Y.C. C.C., Bklyn., 1968; BA, Bklyn. Coll., 1978; MA, NYU, 1986. Cert. H.S. art tchr. Staff artist Pastarnack Assn., N.Y.C., 1968, 69; tchr. St. Joseph's Coll., Yokohama, Japan, 1970, St. Maur Internat. Sch., Yokohama, 1970, Good Shepherd Sch., Bklyn., 1978-82, Our Lady Help of Christians, Bklyn., 1978-82, Bishop Kearney H.S., Bklyn., 1982—. Tchr. Saturday humanities enrichment program St. John's U., 2000. One-woman shows include 80 Washington Square East, N.Y.C., 1985, 39 5th Ave., N.Y.C., 1996; works exhibited in group shows at The Paul VI Inst. for Arts, Washington, 1982, 86, Querini Stampali, Venice, Italy, 1983, 84, Bishop Kearney H.S., Bklyn., 1988, 89, Selena Gallery-L.I. U., Bklyn., 1988, St. John's U., Queens, N.Y., 1990, Cathedral Basilica St. James, Bklyn., 2000, others; author, illustrator (children's book): Pierre Le Car, 2001. Recipient commendation for outstanding contbn. to edn. St. Francis Coll., 1991, 92, 94, Gold Photo award Bay Ridge Cmty. Coun., 1999; Fashion Inst. Tech. fellow, 1997, Winning Tchr., Coca Cola Art of Harmony, 2005-06. Mem. Mus. Modern Art, Nat. Art Edn. Assn., Nat. Mus. Women in the Arts (charter) Met. Mus. Art, Bklyn. Mus. Avocations: painting, photography, reading. Office: Bishop Kearney HS 2202 60th St Brooklyn NY 11204-2599 Office Phone: 718-236-6363 ext. 269.

PLAVINSKAYA, ANNA DMITRIEVNA, artist; b. Moscow, Nov. 26, 1960; came to U.S., 1989, naturalized, 1995; d. Dmitri Petrovich and Nina Nicolaevna; m. Gennady Ioffe, Jan 9, 1988 (div. July 1993). Diploma in Costume Design, Theatrical Art Coll., Moscow, 1976-80. Costume designer Evgeny Vahtangov Theater, Moscow, 1980-82; artist freelance Moscow, 1983-89; art restorer pvt. studio, N.Y.C., 1990-93; artist freelance N.Y.C., 1993—. Exhibited in group shows at Gallery Moscow Artists, 1983, Ctrl. Exhbn. Hall, Moscow, 1984, 88, Kuznetzky Most Gallery, Moscow, 1985, Tbilisi Acad. Art, Georgia, 1986, Tallinna Moepaevad '87, Tallinn, Estonia, 1987, Remizovo St. Gallery, Moscow, 1988, Pushkin Sq. Gallery, Moscow, 1988, Textile Art Ctr., Chgo., 1991, Russian Nobility Assn., NYC, 1991, 11th Cleve. Internat. Drawing Biennale, Middlesbrough, Eng., 1993 (2d prize), BWA Gallery, Wroclaw, Poland, 1994, BWA Gallery, Lublin, Poland, 1994, Elblag (Poland) Gallery, 1994, Tatraniska Gallery, Poprad, Tatry, Slovakia, 1994, State Gallery, Ostrova, Czech Republic, 1994, Port Royal Mus. Gallery, Naples, Fla., 1994, Art Addiction Gallery, Stockholm, 1996-98 (cert. merit 1997), Art Addiction Gallery, Venice, Italy, 1998, Internat. Platform Assn., 1998, (1st place, Best of Show), 1999 (1st place award), Le Salon, Paris, 2000, 2002-04 (Bronze medal 2000), Salon Internat. Beziers, 2001-04, 06 (Bronze medal 2001, Prix de La Societe Des Beaux Arts 2002), Salon D'Automne Internat., Luneville, France, 2001, 04, 14e annee Europ'Art Geneve Palexpo, Switzerland, 2005; represented in permanent collections Cleve. Contemporary Art Collection, Middlesbrough, Eng., Zimmerli Art Mus., Norton and Nancy Dodge Collection, NJ. Mem.: Nat. Fedn. French Culture. Russian Orthodox. Avocations: fashion design, antique textile restoration, tennis. Home: 815 W 181st St Apt 3E New York NY 10033-4530 Office Phone: 212-795-4258. Personal E-mail: annaplavinskaya@hotmail.com.

PLAX, KAREN ANN, lawyer; b. St. Louis, June 29, 1946; d. George J. and Evelyn G. Zell; m. Stephen E. Plax, Dec. 19, 1968; 1 child, Jonathan. BA magna cum laude, U. Mo., St. Louis, 1969; JD with distinction, U. Mo., Kansas City, 1976. Bar: Mo. 1976, U.S. Supreme Ct. 1980. Atty. Thayer, Gum & Wickert, Grandview, Mo., 1976-84, Plax & Cochet, Kansas City, Mo., 1984-87; pvt. practice Kansas City, 1987—. Past chair divsn. 3, region IV Mo. Supreme Ct. Com. to review ethical conduct of attys., 1997—98; pres. Collaborative Law Inst. Mo., 2003—06. Author: Missouri Bar Practical Skills, 1998; asst. editor: Racial Integration in the Inner Suburb, 1970; contbr. articles to profl. jours. Recipient Pub. Svc. award U. Mo. Kansas City Law Found., 1998, Woman of Yr. award Assn. Women Lawyers of Greater Kansas City, 1999; named Family Law Practioner of Yr., Mo. Bar, 2005 Fellow: Am. Acad. Matrimonial Lawyers (pres. Mo. chpt. 1999—2001); mem.: ABA (family law sect. 1976—), Mo. Bar Family Law (legis. chair 1997—98, v.p. 1999—2000, Spl. Commendation for Legis. Role in Family Law 1998), Kansas City Met. Bar Assn. Office: Ste 300 1310 Carondelet Dr Kansas City MO 64114-4803 Office Phone: 816-942-1900. Personal E-mail: kaplax@swbell.net.

PLAYER, AUDREY NELL, research scientist; b. Houston, July 17, 1955; d. Tom and Justine Player. BA, N. Tex. State U., 1977; PhD, Wright State U., 1986. Staff scientist Bayer/Triton, Emeryville, Calif., 1990-2000, Nat. Inst. Health, Bethesda, 2000—. Former mem. bd. dirs. Brookdale Cmty. Ctr., Oakland, Calif., former mentor. Mem. Am. Assn. Cancer Rsch. Democrat. Avocations: tennis, hiking.

PLAYER, MICHELLE, performing arts educator, choreographer; b. West Valley City, Utah, Sept. 25, 1970; d. Darville Lynn Anderson and Rebecca Ann Norman; m. Riley Josh Player, Mar. 16, 1991; children: Sawyer Rain, Amelia. BS, U. Utah, Salt Lake City, 1994; MA in Tchg., U. Puget Sound, Tacoma, Wash., 1996. Cert.: U. Utah (criminology) 1994; dance endorsement Utah State Bd. Edn., 2005. Tchr. Becky's Sch. of Dance, Kearns, Utah, 1984—. Suburban Dance Studios, Puyallup, Wash., 1994—96; tchr. / advisor Kearns H.S., Utah, 1996—; tchr. Pk. City Dance Acad., Utah, 2001—. Student advisor Kearns H.S., 1986—; choreographer Kearns H.S., Becky's Sch. of Dance, Pk. City Dance Acad., 1986—; artistic dir. Exhale Dance Studios, Salt Lake City and Magna, 2000—02. Dance choreographer several works created for numerous dance cos. (Best Choreography (Utah Dance Invitational), 1991). Vol. rschr. Utah Rape Crisis Ctr., Salt Lake City, 1994; vol. counselor Salt Lake Juvenile Detention Ctr., 1992, Utah Juvenile Detention Ctr., Salt Lake City. Mem.: Utah Edn. Assn. (assoc.), Utah Dance Edn. Orgn. (assoc.). Achievements include two time nominee for Outstanding American Teachers award; selected as an Ambassador for the People to People Ambassador Program, Western Illinois University. Avocations: travel, guitar, gardening, hiking. Office: Kearns HS 5525 S Cougar Lane Kearns UT 84118 Office Phone: 801-646-5380. Business E-Mail: michelle.player@granite.k12.ut.us.

PLAYER, THELMA B., librarian; b. Owosso, Mich. d. Walter B. and Grace (Willoughby) Player. BA, Western Mich. U., 1954. Reference asst. USAF Aero Chart and Info. Ctr., Washington, 1954-57; reference libr. USN Hydrographic Office, Suitland, Md., 1957-58, asst. libr., 1958-59; tech. libr.br. head USN Spl. Project Office, Washington, 1959-68, Strategic Sys. Project Office, Washington, 1969-76. Mem. ALA, AAUW, English Speaking Union, Spl. Librs. Assn., Nat. Geneal. Socl, Internat. Soc. Brit. Genealogy and Family History, Ohio Geneal. Soc. Royal Oak Found., Daus of Union Vets. of Civil War, David Ackerman Descs. Episcopalian. Home: 730 24th St NW Washington DC 20037-2519

PLAZA, EVA M., lawyer; b. Torreon, Coahuila, Mex., Feb. 13, 1958; d. Sergio and Eva (Torres) P. BA cum laude, Harvard U., 1980; JD, U. Calif., Berkeley, 1984. Trial atty. U.S. Dept. Justice, Washington, 1984-86; assoc. Arent, Fox, Kintner, Plotkin, Washington, 1986-88, Seyfarth, Shaw, Fairweather & Geraldson, Washington, 1988-93; dep. asst. atty. gen. U.S. Dept. Justice, 1993-97; asst. sec. U.S. Dept. Housing and Urban Devel., 1997—2000; chief dep. city solicitor Phila. Mem. ABA, Tex. Bar, Pa. Bar, D.C. Bar, Hispanic Bar Assn. (pres. D.C. chpt.). Democrat. Roman Catholic. E-mail: eva.plaza@phila.gov.

PLEASANTS, GLENNIS JETER, music educator; b. Prince Edward County, Va., July 4, 1961; d. Jarrett Burnett and Ruby Wilson (Maxey) Jeter; children: Brandon, Ben, Chad. MusB, Longwood Coll., Farmville, Va., 1983. Music, computer tchr. Huguenot Acad., Powhatan, Va., 1983—. Pvt. music lessons, Powhatan, 1980—2005. Composer: (music) A Prayer for Americans, 2001. Recipient Tchg. award, Diocese of Richmond, 2004—05. Mem.: Sigma Alpha Iota. Baptist. Avocation: music. Home: 5926 Old Buckingham Rd Powhatan VA 23139

PLEHATY, PHYLLIS JULIETTE, retired curator; b. N.Y.C., Nov. 28, 1920; d. Aaron Neumann and Lillian Caroline Nagel; m. Carl William Plehaty Jr., Oct. 28, 1942 (dec. Jan. 1995); children: Carl. W. III, Phyllis Gretchen- (dec.). Student, Parsons Sch. Design. With design dept. Schumacher-Waverly, N.Y.C., 1940—43; mgr. boutique, antiques The Place, Darien, Conn., 1957—69; archivist, vol. Darien Hist. Soc., 1960—65; photographer, tour guide Swan Ho. Atlanta Hist. Soc., 1969—71; photographer Jamaica Tourism, 1972—74; mgr., buyer Landlords Daughter Vintage '87, Yountville, Calif., 1974—76; curator collections Boulder History Mus., Colo., 1980—99; ret., 1999; antiques art dealer Niwot Antiques, Colo., 2005—. Cons. costume, collection named in hon. Boulder History Mus., 1990—; cons. exhibit Talbots Stores, 2000—; mem. adv. bd. Wise Homestead Mus., Erie, 2000—. Vol. libr. Loraine Davis Children's Libr., Erie, 2003; established Phyllis J. Plehaty Scholarship Univ. Colo.; bd. trustees Boulder Mus. Recipient CU Scholarship, Boulder History Mus. Republican. Lutheran. Avocations: jewelry design, silversmithing, blacksmithing, antiques, painting, crafts.

PLEIN, BEVERLY R., elementary school educator; d. Andrew Michael Reilley and Marilyn Ada Johnson; m. Peter John Plein, July 12, 1980; 1 child, Christopher John. BA, Montclair State U., 1980; MS, LI U., 1998. Cert. K-12 home econs. tchr. NJ. Tchr. home econ. Elmwood Park (NJ) Bd. Edn., 1980—85; tchr. home economics, tech. facilitator Cresskill (NJ) Bd. Edn., 1991—2004; tech. resource tchr. Teaneck (NJ) Bd. Edn., 2004—. Adv. bd. Tech Forum, NYC, 2003—. Co-author: (book) Best Classroom Management Practices for Reaching All Learners What Award Winning Teachers Do. Named Tchr. of Yr., Cresskill Bd. Edn., 1994; recipient Nat. Educator award, Milken Family Found., 2003. Mem.: ASCD, NJ Edn. Assn., Internat. Soc. Tech. in Edn. Home: 191 Boulevard Glen Rock NJ 07452 Personal E-mail: bplein@bellatlantic.net.

PLESHETTE, SUZANNE, actress; b. N.Y.C., Jan. 31; d. Eugene and Geraldine; m. Thomas Joseph Gallagher III, Mar. 16, 1968 (dec. Jan. 2000); m. Tom Poston, May 11, 2001. Student, Sch. Performing Arts, Syracuse U., Finch Coll., Neighborhood Playhouse Sch. of Theatre. Founder, prin. The Bedside Manor (later div. of J.P. Stevens). Theatre debut in Truckline Cafe; star in Broadway prodns. Compulsion, The Cold Wind and the Warm, The Golden Fleecing, The Miracle Worker, Special Occasions; star TV series Bob Newhart Show, 1972-78, Suzanne Pleshette is Maggie Briggs, 1984; starred in TV series Bridges to Cross, 1986-87, Nightingales, 1988-89, The Boys Are Back, 1994-95, The Single Guy, 1996-97; host (CBS spl.) Where Are They Now?, 1997, (TV series spl. appearances) Will & Grace, 2001, 04, 8 Simple Rules, 2004, (TV series) Good Morning Miami, 2002-03; star 30 feature films including The Birds, Forty Pounds of Trouble, If It's Tuesday This Must Be Belgium, Nevada Smith, Support Your Local Gunfighter, hot Stuff, Oh God! Book II, Lion King II Simba's Pride, Spirited Away; TV movies include Flesh and Blood, Starmaker, Fantasies, If Things Were Different, Help-Wanted Male, Dixie Changing Habits, One Cooks, The Other Doesn't, For Love or Money, Kojak, The Belarus File, A Stranger Waits, Alone in the Neon Jungle, Leona Helmsley: The Queen of Mean, 1990, Battling for Baby, 1991-92, A Twist of the Knife, 1993; writer, co-creator, producer two TV series; published author.

PLETCHER, CAROL H., chemicals executive; m. Wayne Pletcher. B in Chemistry, Juniata Coll., Huntingdon, Pa.; M in Phys. Chemistry, U. Mich.; PhD, Coll. Biol. Sciences, U. Minn. Sr. scientist Cargill, Inc., 1983—89, mgr., 1989—92, dir., 1992—93, asst. v.p., 1993—99, v.p., 1999—2001, chief innovation officer, 2001—. Mem. Coll. Biol. Sciences Alumni Soc. Bd. U. Minn., mem.steering com. for Cargill, Inc.; established with husband Pletcher Fellowship, Coll. Biol. Sciences, U. Minn. Named one of 25 Masters of Innovation, BusinessWeek; recipient Outstanding Achievement award, Coll. Biol. Sciences, U. Minn., 2003; Fellowship, Am. Assn. of U. Women. Mem.: Minn. High Tech Assn. (bd. dir. 2006—). Office: Cargill Inc PO Box 9300 Minneapolis MN 55440-9300*

PLETSCH, MARIE ELEANOR, plastic surgeon; b. Walkerton, Ont., Can., May 3, 1938; came to U.S. 1962; d. Ernest John and Olive Wilhemina (Hossfeld) P.; m. Ludwig Philip Breiling, Aug. 25, 1967; children: John, Michael, Anne. MD, U. Toronto, 1962. Diplomate Am. Bd. Plastic Surgery. Intern Cook County Hosp., Chgo., 1962-63, resident, gen. surgery, 1963-64, St. Mary's Hosp., San Francisco, 1964-66; resident in plastic surgery St. Francis Hosp., San Francisco, 1966-69; practice med. specializing in plastic surgery Santa Cruz, Calif., 1969—; Monterey, Calif., 1990—; adminstr. Plasticenter, Inc., Santa Cruz, 1976-88, med. dir., 1987-88. Mem. AMA, Am. Soc. Plastic and Reconstructive Surgeons, Calif. Soc. Plastic Surgeons (mem. coun. 1986-89, sec. 1989-93, v.p. 1994-95, pres. elect 1995-96, pres. 1996-97), Am. Soc. Aesthetic Plastic Surgeons, Calif. Med. Assn., Assn. Calif. Surgery Ctrs. (pres. 1988-92), Santa Cruz County Med. Soc. (bd. govs. 1983-88, 1992-94), Santa Cruz Surgery Ctr. (bd. dirs. 1988-93, 2004—). Roman Catholic. Office: Santa Cruz Can Am Med Group 1669 Dominican Way Santa Cruz CA 95065-1523: 24571 Silver Cloud Ct Monterey CA 93940 Office Phone: 831-462-1000. Personal E-mail: pletsch@pacbell.net.

PLETTE, SANDRA LEE, retired insurance company executive; b. Cambridge, Mass., June 15, 1950; d. Warren M. and K. Towneley Rohsenow; m. André F. Plette, June 23, 1973; children: Nicole Corris, Kristen Towneley. BBA with high distinction, U. Mich., 1972; MBA with high honors, Boston U., 1980. CFA. Investment rsch. assoc. New Eng. Life Ins. Co., Boston, 1972—76; account mgr. ADP Network Svcs., Boston and L.A., 1976—78; various investment positions UNUM Corp., Portland, Maine, 1980—89, v.p. investor rels., 1989—90, v.p. pension underwriting, 1990—93, v.p. fin., 1993—98. Pres. Union Mutual Employees Credit Union, Portland, 1984—88. Fin. com. United Way Greater Portland, 1995—2005; chmn. Tng. Resource Ctr., Portland, 1998—2001, Girl Scouts Kennebec Coun., 1991—; chaplain Maine Med. Ctr., Portland, 2002—; treas. Foreside Cmty. Ch., Falmouth, Maine, 1999—2003, 2005—06; bd. dirs. Coastal Enterprises, Wiscassett, Maine, 1988—91. Mem. United Ch. Of Christ. Avocations: singing, golf, hiking, reading.

PLEVAN, BETTINA B., lawyer; b. Oceanside, N.Y., Nov. 21, 1945; BA, Wellesley Coll., 1967; JD magna cum laude, Boston U., 1970. Bar: N.Y. 1971, US Dist. Ct., (Ea. dist.)NY, US Ct. Appeals, (2nd cir.), 1975, U.S. Supreme Ct. 1977, US Ct. Appeals, (DC cir.), 1977, US Ct. Appeals, (3rd. cir.), 1978, US Dist. Ct. (So. dist.) NY, 1979, US Tax Ct., 1979, US Ct. Appeals, (5th. cir.), 1982, US Ct. Appeals (9th cir.), US Dist. Ct. (No. dist.) NY, 1983, US Ct. Appeals, (4th cir.), 1986, US Dist. Ct. (We. dist.) NY, 1993, US Ct. Appeals, (6th cir.). Editor Boston U. law Review, 1968—70; mem. Proskauer Rose LLP (formerly Proskauer Rose Goetz & Mendelsohn), N.Y.C., 1974—. Pres. Fed. Bar Coun., 1996—98, pres. emeritus, 1998—. Named one of The Best Lawyers in NY, NY mag. Fellow: Am. Acad. Appellate Lawyers, Am. Coll. Trial Lawyers; mem.: ABA (mem. Ho. Delegates 1986—91), NY County Lawyers Assn., NY State Bar Assn., Assn. Bar of the City NY (mem., com. on state courts of superior jurisdiction 1975—78, chair 1978—81, mem. exec. com. 1981—85, chair coun. on jud. adminstrn. 1985—88, mem., long range planning com. 1988—90, chair 1992—95). Office: Proskauer Rose LLP 1585 Broadway Fl 27 New York NY 10036-8299 E-mail: bplevan@proskauer.com.*

PLIMPTON, LESLIE KLOVILLE, lawyer; AB, Washington U.; JD cum laude, Boston Coll.; LLM in Taxation, Boston U. Bar: Mass. 1982. Founder Leslie Kloville Plimpton, atty.-at-law, Boston. Named one of Boston's top lawyers, Boston Mag., 2002. Office: 83 Mt Vernon St Boston MA 02108

PLIMPTON, PEGGY LUCAS, trustee; b. Nov. 3, 1931; d. David Nicholson and Margaret (MacMillan) Lucas; m. Hollis Winslow Plimpton, June 11, 1955; children: Victoria P. Babcock, Priscilla P. Morphy, Hollis Winslow Plimpton III. AB, Duke U., 1954. Trustee Cape Cod Conservatory of Music, 1989—. Bd. trustees Carleton Williard Retirement Home, Bedford, Mass., 1968—, Cape Cod Conservatory Music, 1990—; bd. dirs. Episcopal Ch. Women, 1968-78, Brigham & Women's Hosp., Boston, 1975—; pres. Boston Lying-In Hosp., 1970-72; chmn. Mass. Nat. Cathedral Assn., Boston, 1978-80, 1985-88; pres. bd. trustees Women's Ednl. and Indsl., Boston, 1980-83. Mem. New Eng. Farm and Garden Club (bd. dirs. 1965—, pres. 1995—), Chestnut Hill Garden Club (bd. dirs. 1970-74), Jr. League Garden Club (pres. 1981-83), Colonial Dames (bd. mgrs. 1983-89, v.p. 1993-98, pres. 1998—), Vincent Club, Chilton Club. Republican. Episcopalian. Avocations: gardening, golf, bridge.

PLISKA, STEPHANIE, history educator, special education educator; b. Scranton, Pa., June 6, 1978; d. Thomas Andrew and Helen Myshak Grancey; m. Robert Matthew Pliska, Feb. 15, 1998; children: Miyah, Robert, Alexis, Isabella. BS in Social Sci., Marywood U., Scranton, 2000, MPA/CJ, tchg. cert., Marywood U., Scranton, 2003, postgrad. Cert. tchr. social studies grades 7-12 and spl. edn. grades K-12 Pa. History educator Bishop Hannan H.S., Scranton, 2003—05; history and spl. edn. educator Valley View H.S., Archbald, Pa., 2005—. Adj. prof. Keystone Coll., La Plume, Pa., 2004—; advisor SADD Club, Archbald, 2005; JV cross country coach Valley View HS, JV girls track coach. Leader USA Girl Scouts, Jermyn, Pa., 2004; active Dem. Womens Assn., Scranton, 2002—; pre-sch. tchr. St. Michael's Ch., Jermyn, Pa., 2000—. Mem.: Coun. for Exceptional Children, Elkview Country Club. Russian Orthodox. Avocations: running, yoga, writing, reading.

PLISKIN, BERENICE RITA CHAPLAN, artist; b. NYC, May 21, 1932; d. Bernard Chaplan and Frances Ettinger Chaplan; m. Robert Pliskin, May 11, 1953. BS, CCNY, 1954; MFA, Lehman Coll., 1978. Elem. and art tchr. Bd. Edn., NYC, 1954—90. Author (illustrator): A TrainLoad of Fun, 1981; author: Spanish Word Game Masters, 1987, French Word Game Masters, 1988; co-author: Top 20 ESL Word Game Hits, 1990. Named to Archival File, Nat. Mus. Women in Arts; recipient First prize Nat. Watercolor, Scholastic Arts, 1949, award in oil painting, 1950, Edn./Cmty. award, Westchester Arts Coun., 2002, Digital Delights award, Surface Design Assn., 2003. Mem.: Nat. Mus. Women in the Arts. Avocation: travel.

PLISKOW, VITA SARI, anesthesiologist; b. Tel Aviv, Sept. 13, 1942; arrived in Can., 1951; came to U.S., 1967; d. Henry Norman and Renee (Mushkatel) Stahl; m. Raymond Joel Pliskow, June 30, 1968; children: Tia, Kami. MD, U. B.C., Vancouver, 1967. Diplomate Am. Bd. Anesthesiology. Ptnr. Olympic Anesthesia, Bremerton, Wash., 1971-84, pres., anesthesiologist, 1974-84; co-founder Olympic Ambulatory Surgery Ctr., Bremerton, 1977-83; ptnr., anesthesiologist Allenmore Anesthesia Assocs., Tacoma, 1983—. Staff anesthesiologist Harrison Meml. Hosp., Bremerton, 1971-95, Allenmore Hosp., Tacoma, 1983—. Trustee Tacoma Youth Symphony Assn., 1994—; active Nat. Coun. Jewish Women, 1972—. Fellow Am. Coll. Anesthesiologists, Am. Coll. Chest Physicians; mem. Am. Soc. Anesthesiologists (del. Wash. State 1987—), Wash. State Med. Assn. (del. Pierce County 1993-94), Wash. State Soc. Anesthesiologists (pres. 1985-87), Pierce County Med. Soc. (sec.-treas. 1992). Avocations: classical music, opera, singing (mezzo soprano). Office: PO Box 65274 University Place WA 98464-1274

PLITT, JEANNE GIVEN, librarian; b. Whitehall, NY, Aug. 27, 1927; d. Charles Russell and Anna Marie (Noyes) Given; m. Ferdinand Charles Plitt Jr., Jan. 19, 1952; children: Christine Marie, Charles Randolph. Student, St. Lawrence U., 1945—47; AB, U. Md., 1940; postgrad., Am. U., 1960—61; MLS, Cath. U. Am., 1968. Libr. asst. spl. services divsn. US Army, 1949—51; tchr. secondary various secondary schs., Md. and Va., 1951—67; from reference libr. to asst. dir. Alexandria (Va.) Libr., 1967—70, dir., 1970—. Chmn. librs.' tech. com. Coun. Govts., Washington, 1971—72, Washington, 1980—81. Chmn. No. Va. Libr. Networking Com.; active Little Theatre Group, Alexandria, Alexandria's Ams. with Disabilities Act Com. Recipient Alexandria Pub. Svc. award, 1964, 1974, Recognition award, Am. Assn. Ret. Persons, 1990. Mem.: PTA, ALA, Alexandria Hist. Soc. (bd. dirs. 1974—), Manuscript Soc., Va. Libr. Assn. (legis. com. 1988—), Cath. U. Alumni Assn., Urban League, U. Md. Alumni Assn., Alexandria Assn., Zonta (sec. local chpt. 1972—73, bd. dirs. 1988—), Vernon Country Club. Roman Catholic. Office: Alexandria Libr 5005 Duke St Alexandria VA 22304-2903

PLOECKELMAN, AMY LYNN, athletic trainer; b. Sheboygan, Wis., Feb. 27, 1975; d. Leonard Elmer and Julie Faye Ploeckelman. BS in Kinesiology and Athletic Tng./Sports Medicine, U. Wis., Milw., 2002; postgrad. in traditional Chinese medicine, Acad. Chinese Culture and Health Scis., Oakland, Calif., 2006—. Cert. acupressurist Acupressure Inst. Berkeley, Calif., 2006. Athletic trainer Froedtert Hosp. Sports Medicine Ctr., Milw., 2001—04; head athletic trainer Milw. Profl. Ballet Co., 2002—04; head athletic trainer, performance enhancement dir. Sports and Orthop. Leaders Physical Therapy, 2004—. Athletic trainer, med. staff USA volleyball, Colorado Springs, 2001—05. Lectr., mentor East Bay Scholarship Soc., Oakland, Calif., 2006; vol. Hope through Opportunity. Mem.: Nat. Athletic Trainers Assn. (assoc.). Office Phone: 510-421-1907. Personal E-mail: alp27@sbcglobal.net.

PLONKA, LAVINIA, performing arts educator; b. Chgo., July 15, 1952; d. Leopold Adalbert and Lidia Plonka; m. Ron Morecraft, June 23, 1979. BA, Montclair State U., Upper Montclair, N.J., 1974. Cert. GCFP Feldenkrais Tng. N.Y., 1994. Assoc. dir., performer Claude Kipnis Mime Theatre, N.Y.C., 1977—81; performer Affiliate Artists, N.Y.C., 1981—83; performer, choreographer N.Y.C., 1983—98; dir., tchr. Movement Ctr., Morris Plains, NJ, 1999—2002, Asheville Movement Ctr., NC, 2003—. Assoc. dir., tchr. Youth Theatre N.J., Sparta, 1984—; tchr. Guggenheim Mus., N.Y.C., 1989—98. Editor (Senseability): Feldenkrais Build NA, 1997—; workshop leader Feldenkrais Build NA, 1999—; author: What Are You Afraid Of, 2003. Avocations: Aikido, dance. Office: Asheville Movement Ctr 4 Richmond Ave Asheville NC 28806

PLUMB, PAMELA PELTON, consulting company executive, retired mayor; b. St. Louis, Oct. 26, 1943; d. Frank E. and Dorothey-Lee (Culver) Pelton; m. Peter Scott Plumb, June 11, 1966; children: Jessica Culver, David Scott. BA, Smith Coll., 1965; MA, NYU, 1967. Tchr. Master's Sch., Dobbs Ferry, NY, 1967—69; exec. dir. Greater Portland (Maine) Landmarks, 1969—71; active civic and vol. work, 1971—79; mem. Portland City Coun., 1979—90, mayor, 1981—82; prin. Pamela Plumb & Assocs., 1990—. Vice-chmn. Peoples Heritage Fin. Group. Pres. Nat. League Cities, 1987—88; bd. dirs. Tom's of Maine. Named Portland and Maine Outstanding Young Woman, Jaycees, 1979; recipient Doric Dames's Bullfinch award, 1979, Greater Portland Landmark's Preservation award, 1980, Deborah Morton award, Westbrook Coll., Portland, 1982, Neal W. Allen award, Greater Portland C. of C., 1982, Disting. Svc. award, Kiwanis Club of Portland, 1990. Democrat.

PLUMMER, AMANDA, actress; b. N.Y.C., Mar. 23, 1957; d. Christopher and Tammy (Grimes) Plummer. Student, Middlebury Coll. Has appeared in theatre roles: debut: Artichoke, 1979, A Taste of Honey, 1981(nominee for Tony award, and Drama Desk, recipient Outer Critics Circle and Theatre World awards); A Month in the Country, 1980; The Glass Menagerie, 1983-84; other theatre roles include: Agnes of God (Tony, Drama Desk award, Outer Circle Critics award, Boston Critics award), 1982; A Lie of the Mind, 1985; motion picture debut: Cattle Annie and Little Britches, 1981, The World According to Garp, 1982, Daniel, 1983, Hotel New Hampshire, 1984, Static, 1985, Riders to the Sea, 1987, Courtship, 1987, Made in Heaven, 1987, The Story of the Dancing Frog, 1989, Prisoners of Inertia, 1989, Joe Versus the Volcano, 1990, The Fisher King, 1991, Freejack, 1992, The Lounge People, 1992, So I Married an Axe Murderer, 1993, Needful Things, 1993 (Saturn award, 1994), Pax, 1994, Nostradamus, 1994, Pulp Fiction, 1994, The Final Cut, 1995, The Prophecy, 1995, Search and Destroy, 1995, Butterfly Kiss, 1995, The Vampyre Wars, 1996, Freeway, 1996, Dead Girl, 1996, American Perfekt, 1997, Drunks, 1997, A Simple Wish, 1997, You Can Thank Me Later, 1998, Hysteria, 1998,October 22, 1998, L.A. Without a Map, 1998, Elizabeth Jane, 1998, Great Sex, 1999, Eight and a Half Women, 1999, The Million Dollar Hotel, 2000, Seven Days to Live, 2000, Triggermen, 2002, Ken Park, 2002, Pulp Fiction: The Facts, 2002, My Life Without Me, 2002, The Gray in Between, 2002, The Last Angel, 2002, Satan's Little Helper, 2004, Darkness, 2005; (TV movies) The Unforgivable Secret, 1982, The Dollmaker, 1984, True Blue, 1989, Kojak: None So Blind, 1990, Gryphon, 1990, Miss Rose White, 1992, Sidney Sheldon's The Sands of Time, 1992, Last Light, 1993, Whose Child Is This? The War for Baby Jessica, 1993, Under the Piano, 1995, Don't Look Back, 1996, The Right to Remain Silent, 1996, (voice) Hercules, 1997, The Apartment Complex, 1999, Shadow Realm, 2002, Get a Clue, 2002, Broadway: The Golden Age, by the Legends Who Were There, 2002; (TV series) Stories from My Childhood (voice), 1998; TV appearances include Hallmark Hall of Fame: Miss Rose White (Emmy award supporting actress, 1992), (TV series) Moonlighting, 1987, The Equalizer, 1988, LA Law, 1989, 1990, Tales from the Crypt, 1989, The Outer Limits, 1996, 2000 (Emmy award best guest actress, 1996), Law & Order: Special Victims Unit, 2004 (Creative Arts Primetime Emmy award outstanding guest actress in a drama, 2005), and several other appearances. Recipient Anti-Defamation League award for Women of Achievement, 1988.

PLUMMER, DORIS GOCHNAUER, elementary school educator; b. Lancaster, Pa., Feb. 4, 1956; d. Kenneth Kreider and Wanda Mae Gochnauer; m. Maurice Stephen Plummer, June 18, 1983; children: Jonathan Kenneth, Joshua Olin. BS in Elem. Edn., Millersville U., Pa., 1978. Cert. tchr. N.C. Tchr. North Hills Christian Sch., Salisburg, NC, 1978—, asst. prin., 1990—96, dir. acad. improvement modification program, 2003—. Organist Milford Hills United Meth. Ch., Salisbury, 1996—, dir. children's mus. ministries, 1996—. Recipient Cors Catharine Bitner Music award, Millersville State Coll., 1977, Anne E. Beyer Tchg. award, 1978. Republican. Methodist. Avocations: writing, sewing, music. Home: 2675 W Innes St Salisbury NC 28144 Office: North Hills Christian Sch 2970 W Innes St Mooresboro NC 28114 Office Phone: 704-636-3005. Business E-Mail: splummer4@carolina.rr.com.

PLUMMER, JEANINE D., engineering educator; BS, Cornell U., Ithaca, NY, 1993; MS, U. Mass., Amherst, 1995; PhD, U. Mass., 1999. Assoc. prof. Worcester (Mass.) Poly. Inst., 1999—. Office: Worcester Poly Inst Dept CEE 100 Institute Rd Worcester MA 01609 Office Phone: 508-831-5142. Office Fax: 508-831-5808. E-mail: jplummer@wpi.edu.

PLUMMER, ORA BEATRICE, nursing educator, consultant; b. Mexia, Tex., May 25, 1940; d. Macie Idella (Echols); children: Kimberly, Kevin, Cheryl. BSN, U. N.Mex., 1961; MS in Nursing Edn., UCLA, 1966. Nurse's aide Bataan Meml. Meth. Hosp., Albuquerque, 1958—60, staff nurse, 1961—62, 1967—68; staff nurse, charge nurse, relief supr. Hollywood Cmty. Hosp., Calif., 1962—64; instr. U. N.Mex. Coll. Nursing, Albuquerque, 1968—69; sr. instr. U. Colo. Sch. Nursing, Denver, 1971—74, asst. prof., 1974—76; staff assoc. III We. Interstate Commn. for Higher Edn., Boulder, Colo., 1976—78; DON Garden Manor Nursing Home, Lakewood, Colo., 1978—79, nurse surveyor, cons., 1979—87; ednl. coord. Colo. Dept. Health, Denver, 1987—96. Active in faculty devel. Colo. Cluster of Schs.; bd. dirs. Domestic Violence Initiative. Contbr. articles to profl. jours. Mem. adv. bd. Affiliated Children's and Family Svcs., 1977; mem. Colo. Instnl. Child Abuse and Neglect Adv. Com., 1984-92; trustee Colo. Acad., 1990-96; mem. planning com. State Wide Conf. on Black Health Concerns, 1977; mem. staff devel. com. Western Interstate Commn. for Higher Edn., 1978, mem. minority affairs com., 1978, mem. coordinating com. for baccalaureate program, 1971-76; active in minority affairs, U. Colo. Med. Ctr., 1971-72; mem. ednl. resources com., pub. rels. com., rev. com. for reappointment, promotion and tenure U. Colo. Sch. Nursing, 1971-76, mem. regulatory tng. com., 1989-93; mem. gerontol. adv. com. Met. State Coll., 1989-94; mem. expert panel long term care tng. manual Health Care Financing Adminstrn., Balt., 1989; mem. employee diversity com. Colo. Dept. Health, 1989-96; mem. Nurse Del. to Cuba, 2000. Nominee Nightingale award, Colo., 2003. Avocation: exercise. Office: 4300 Cherry Creek South Dr Denver CO 80246-1523

PLUMMER, PATRICIA LYNNE MOORE, chemist, educator; b. Tyler, Tex., Feb. 26; d. Robert Lee and Jewell Ovelia (Jones) Moore; m. Otho Raymond Plummer, Apr. 10, 1965; children: Patrick William Otho, Christina Elisa Lynne. BA, Tex. Christian U., Ft. Worth, Tex., 1960; postgrad., U. N.C., 1960-61; PhD, U. Tex., Austin, 1964; grad., Bryn Mawr Summer Inst., 1992. Instr., Welch postdoctoral fellow U. Tex., Austin, 1964-66; postdoctoral fellow Dept. Chemistry, U. Ark., Fayetteville, 1966-68; rsch. assoc. Grad. Ctr., Cloud Phys. Rsch., Rolla, Mo., 1968-73; asst. prof. physics U. Mo., Rolla, 1973-77; assoc. dir. Grad. Ctr. Cloud Phys. Rsch., 1977-79, sr. investigator, 1980-85; assoc. prof. physics U. Mo., 1977-85, prof. dept. chemistry and physics Columbia, 1986—. Mem. internat. sci. com. Symposium on Chemistry and Physics of Ice, 1982—, vice chair, 1996—; nat. judge Siemens-Westinghouse Sci. Projects, 1999—. Assoc. editor Jour. of Colloid and Interface Sci., 1980-83; contbr. articles to profl. jours., chpts. to books. Rsch. grantee IBM, 1990-92, Air Force Office Rsch., 1989-91, NSF, 1976-86, NASA, 1973-78; Air Force Office Rsch. summer fellow, 1988, Bryn Mawr Summer Inst., 1992, Faculty fellow Cherry Emerson Ctr. for Sci. Computation, Emory U., 1998-99. Mem. Am. Chem. Soc., Am. Phys. Soc., Am. Geophys. Union, Sigma Xi (past pres., UM-Rolla chptr.). Democrat. Baptist. Avocations: sailing, gardening, tennis, photography. Office: U Mo 201 Physics Bldg Columbia MO 65211-0001 Fax: (573) 882-4195. E-mail: plummerp@missouri.edu.

PLUNKET, DOLORES, art educator, archaeology educator; b. Chgo., Sept. 2, 1916; d. John Nagoda and Evangeline Kompare; m. John T. Plunket, July 15, 1944; children: Lucy Silver, Robert, John T. Jr., Patricia. BS, U. Ill., 1937; MA in Pre-Colombian Art, Nat. U. Mexico, Mexico City, 1975. V.p. Mexican-N.Am. Cultural Inst., Mexico City, 1985-88; dir. lecture series Selby Libr., Sarasota, Fla., 1992-96; lectr. in field. Co-author: (with A.R. L'huillier) Vision del Mundo Maya, 1978; editor Gardening in the Federal District, 1986; contbr. articles to profl. jours. V.p. Friends Selby Libr., 1992-95; pres. Mexico City Garden Club, 1985; bd. dirs. Am. Soc. Mexico, 1986-88. Personal E-mail: jplunket@aol.com.

PLUNKETT, ALEXA, elementary school educator; b. Denison, Tex., Aug. 3, 1980; d. Henry Plunkett and Kathryn Bock Plunkett. BA, Rice U., Houston, 2002; MA in Edn., Wash. U., St. Louis, 2005. Cert. tchr. Mo. Bd. Edn., 2006. English tchr. WorldTeach, San Francisco de Cajon, Perez Zeledon, Costa Rica, 2001, Japan Exch. in Tchg., Niigata City, Niigata Prefecture, Japan, 2002—04; elem. tchr. Fayetteville Montessori, Ark., 2006. Mem.: NEA, Mensa (area rep. 1993). Home: 229 Crosstimber Estates Dr Denison TX 75021

PLUNKETT, MELBA KATHLEEN, manufacturing company executive; b. Marietta, Ill., Mar. 20, 1929; d. Lester George and Florence Marie (Hutchins) Bonnett; m. James P. Plunkett, Aug. 18, 1951; children: Julie Marie Plunkett Hayden, Gregory James. Educated pub. schs. Co-founder, 1961, since sec.-treas., dir. Coils, Inc., Huntley, Ill. Mem. U.S. C. of C., U.S. Mfg. Assn., Ill. C. of C., Ill. Notary Assn. Roman Catholic. Home: 15n170 Sleepy Hollow Rd West Dundee IL 60118-9113

PLYE, KELLY ANN, nurse; b. Pottsville, Pa., July 23, 1969; d. Albert Michael and Barbara Ann (Rakowsky) Wysincavage; m. Edward Charles Plye, May 23, 1992 BS, York Coll., 1991. RN Pa., N.J.; Cert. Post Anesthesia Nurse; nursing lic. Staff nurse med. ICU Hershey Med. Ctr., Pa., 1991—92; staff nurse post anesthesia care unit Kennedy Meml. Hosp., Cherry Hill, NJ, 1992—98; staff Surg. Svc. dept. Kennedy Health Sys., Cherry Hill, 1998—2005; staff South Jersey Surg. Ctr., Mt. Laurel, NJ, 2005—. Avocations: reading, beach. Office: South Jersey Surg Ctr 150 Century Pkwy Ste C Mount Laurel NJ 08054

PNEUMAN, LINDA JACKSON, retired physician; b. Memphis, July 9, 1938; d. John Thomas Jackson, Jr. and Winnie Griffin Jackson; m. Gerald Warnick Pneuman, June 16, 1978 (dec.); m. Terry Robert Cobb, Nov. 8, 1957 (div. 1974); children: Kimberly Winn Kirby, Elizabeth Lankford Fredricksmeyer. BS magna cum laude, U. Memphis, 1961; MD, Meharry Med. Coll., Nashville, 1976. Tchr. chemistry and biology St Mary's Episcopal Sch., Memphis, 1960—62; rsch. asst. Vanderbilt U. Psychopharmacology Rsch. Ctr., Nashville, 1966—67; intern, resident St. Joseph's Hosp., Denver, 1976—77; physician Denver U. Student Health Svc., Denver, 1977—81, US Dept. Def., Bad Aibling, Bavaria, Germany, 1978—79, U. Colo. Student Health Svc., Boulder, 1981—88, Calif. State U., Chico, Calif., 1988—2002; ret. Chair quality assurance U. Colo. Student Health Svc., Boulder, 1985—88; chair human subjects com. U. Colo., Boulder, 1986—88; chair quality assurace Calif. State U., Chico Student Health Svc., 1988—97, acting dir., 2000—01; chief clin. medicine Calif. State U. Chico, 1997—2001. Vol. naturalist City of Boulder Open Space and Mountain Parks, 2005—06; bd. mem. Boulder Valley Women's Clinic, 1986—88; fund raiser Friendship Bridge, Evergreen, Colo., 2005—06. Outstanding Student scholar, Hill Family Found., 1974, 1975. Mem.: Alpha Omega Alpha (life). Democrat. Episcopalian. Home: 205 Devon Pl Boulder CO 80302 Personal E-mail: lpneuman@csuchico.edu.

POAD, FLORA VIRGINIA, retired librarian, retired elementary school educator; b. Roanoke, Va., Oct. 8, 1921; d. Thomas Franklin and Ethlind (Wertz) Huff; m. Stanley Theodore Benton, Dec. 24, 1942 (div. Oct. 1983); children: Peggy, Betty, Mary Jo, Lucy; m. James Joseph Poad, June 6, 1986. Student, Radford Coll., 1939—41, Ohio U., 1956—57; BS in Edn., Ohio No. U., 1960; MA in LS, U. Toledo, 1964; postgrad., Kent State U., 1964—66, postgrad., 1971. Reference asst. Roanoke Pub. Libr., 1939-42; catalog asst. Univ. Libr., Emory U., Atlanta, 1942; sec. ARC, Atlanta, 1943; catalog asst. Pickerington (Ohio) Pub. Libr., 1950-51; tchr. Celina (Ohio) Pub. Schs., 1957-62; tchr., libr. Toledo Pub. Schs., 1962-64; libr. supr. Oregon (Ohio) Pub. Schs., 1964-85; instr. U. Toledo, 1970, reference libr., 1971-86; tchr. Sylvan Learning Ctr., Toledo, 1985-92; ret., 1992. Evaluation team Ohio Dept. Edn., Columbus, 1973; rep. Ohio Gov.'s Conf. on Librs., Columbus, 1974; chmn., adv. bd. libr. sci. dept. Cmty.-Tech. Coll., 1965-69. Editor Ohio Assn. Sch. Librs. Bull., 1968-71. Vol. Am. Cancer Soc., Toledo, 1946—48, 1986—87, Mobile Meals, Toledo, 1986—93, Helping Hands, Toledo, 1994—; vol. libr. Otterbein Portage Valley, 1999—2003. Martha Holden Jennings scholar, 1976—. Mem. Nat. Honor Soc., Delta Kappa Gamma, Pi Lambda Theta, Kappa Delta Pi, Phi Kappa Phi. Avocations: reading, walking, crafts. Home: 3544 Bayberry Pl Oregon OH 43616-2475

POCHMANN, VIRGINIA, retired artist, painter, draftsman; b. Starkville, Miss., Mar. 13, 1938; d. Henry August and Ruth Fouts Pochmann; children: Erica Lynne Weis, Justin Morris Weis. BS, U. Wis., 1959; student, Am. Acad. Art, Chgo., 1966—68, De Burgos Sch. Art, Washington, 1968—70. Exhibitions include Am. Water Color Soc. Ann., N.Y.C., 1982, Rocky Mountain Nat. Watermedia Exhbn., Golden, Colo., 1982, 1984, 1986, Watercolor USA, Springfield (Mo.) Art Mus., 1983, 15th Ann. Watercolor West, Harrison Mus. Art, Logan, Utah, 1983, Watercolor West Ann., Riverside, Calif., 1983, 1985, 1986, West Coast Watercolor Soc., Monterey Peninsula Mus. Art, Calif., 1984, San Diego Watercolor Soc. Internat. Exhbn., 1984, one-woman shows include Fireside Gallery, Carmel, Calif., 1984, 1985, 65th Ann. Nat. Watercolor Soc., Brea, Calif., 1985, Bernard Galleries, Walnut Creek, Calif., 1988, Foliage and Flowers, Sunnyvale, Calif., 1988, Represented in permanent collections City of Sunnyvale Calif.; contbr. articles to painting publs. Recipient Cash award, West Tex. Watercolor Soc., 1985, First award No. Calif. Watercolor Competition, Pacific Art League, 1985. Mem.: West Coast Watercolor Soc. (treas. 1984—85), Artists Equity, Nat. Watercolor Soc. (Purchase award L.A. chpt. 1985). Home: 235 Oak Rd Alamo CA 94507

POCIERNICKI, JANICE LOUISE, artist; b. Rochester, Pa., June 27, 1941; d. Raymond Joseph and Emma Louise Kercovich; m. William Ignatius Pociernicki, June 30, 1966; children: Jennifer Catherine Bitters, William Chad. Sec., Robert Morris U., 1959—60. Art com. mem. Merrick Art Gallery /Mus., New Brighton, Pa., 2002—; pres. Beaver Valley Artists, New Brighton, Pa., 1996—97, historian, 1995—96. Exhibitions include Beaver Valley Artists Annual, West Hills Art League Ann. Show, Pitts. Watercolor Soc. Ann., North Hills Fall Multi Media Show, Pitts. Progressive Artists Show, Pitts. Soc. Artists, one-woman shows include. Mem.: Hoyt Art Assn., Associated Artists of Pitts., Pitts. Soc. of Artists, West Hills Art League (pres. 1995—96), Beaver Valley Artists (pres. 1996—97), Pitts. Prog. Artists, Pitts. Watercolor Soc., Pa. Watercolor Soc. (assoc.). Avocations: travel, knitting, sewing, reading. Home: 270 Southward Drive Moon Township PA 15108-3150 Office Phone: 412-264-2640. E-mail: janpociernicki@verizon.net.

POCKRASS, MARLENE MORGAN, retired literature educator; b. Dales, N.D., Sept. 18, 1936; d. George Michael Morgan and Caroline Erickson; 1 child, Robert Matthew. BS, U. Minn., 1959; MA, Ariz. State U., 1965. Tchr. Brighton H.S., 1959—61, Kamehameha Schs., Honolulu, 1961—64, Mpls. CC, 1965—67, Agtolin Coll., Thesselonika, Greece, 1967—68, Pleege Coll., Athens, Greece, 1968—69, Minn. State U., Manhato, 1969—73, U. Md., 1975—78, U. Minn., Waseen, Md., 1979—94; ret. Fellow, Fulbright Found., 1967—68, 1968—69; grantee, HGU, 1965, USH, 1968. Mem.: NEA. Democrat. Avocations: reading, travel.

POCKWINSE, SHIRWIN M., research scientist, educator; b. Concord, N.H., Nov. 15, 1947; d. Winsor Edmund and Shirley Jane Merrill; m. Richard Carl Pockwinse, Mar. 9, 1974; 1 child, Sarah Winsor-Elizabeth. BA, U. N.H., 1969. Lab. technician U. Mass. Med. Sch., Worcester, 1969—74, profl. technician I, supr. electron microscopy facility, 1974—78, rsch. assoc., adminstr. electron microscopy facility, 1979—2004, faculty, 2004—. From mem. to chmn. adv. bd. U. Mass. Med. Ctr. Child Care Ctr., Worcester, 1975—93. Contbr. articles to profl. jours. Mem.: Baypath Humane Soc. (treas., sec. 1972). Republican. Avocations: skiing, gardening. Home: 2 Peg's Way Hopkinton MA 01748 Office: U Mass Med Sch Cell Biology 55 Lake Ave N Worcester MA 01655

PODANY, AMANDA H., history professor; b. Bromley, Eng. d. Brian and Margaret Hills; m. Jerry Podany; 2 children. PhD, UCLA, 1988. Asst. prof. history Calif State Poly. U., Pomona, 1990—96, assoc. prof. history, 1996—2000, prof. history, 2001—. Exec. dir. Calif. History-Social Sci. Project, LA, 1993—97. Author: (monograph) The Land of Hana: Kings, Chronology, and Scribal Tradition; co-author: The Ancient Near Eastern World; contbr. articles to profl. jours; editor: (series) The World in Ancient Times. Office: Calif State Poly U 3801 W Temple Ave Pomona CA 90020 Office Phone: 909-869-3875.

PODBROS, LINDA ZOE, neuropsychologist, consultant; b. Albany, N.Y., June 25, 1947; d. Robert Selig and Sara (Grodson) P.; m. James Marshall Waters, Sept. 11, 1977; children: David Podbros Waters, Sarah Elizabeth Podbros Waters. BA in Psychology, U. Mass., Boston, 1973; MA in Psychology, SUNY, Stony Brook, 1978, PhD in Neuropsychology, 1981. Lic. psychologist, Mass. Pvt. practice, 1989—; lectr. Mass. Gen. Hosp., 1995; neuropsychology cons. Mass. Statewide Head Injury Program, 1988—; neuropsychologist head trauma unit Spaulding Rehab. Hosp., 1989—; sr. neuropsychologist Rehab. Hosp. Cape and Islands, 1995—. Rsch. asst. U. Mass., Boston, 1973, Boston U., 1974, VA Med. Ctr., Boston, 1973-74; attached sci. worker Nat. Hosp. Nervous Diseases, London, 1976-77; staff neuropsychologist Assn. Help of Retarded Children, Infant's Svcs., 1979-81, Braintree (Mass.) Hosp., 1981-84; chief neuropsychologist New Eng. Med. Ctr., 1984-86; dir. rehab. neuropsychology Tufts-New Eng. Med. Ctr., Boston, 1987-89, spl. and sci. staff, 1984-89; neuropsychology cons. Greenery Skilled Nursing and Rehab. Facility, Brighton, Mass., 1989; faculty mem. clin. neuropsychology externship program Boston Neurobehavioral Inst., 1988-89; asst. prof. dept. neurology Sch. Medicine Tufts U., 1989—, asst. clin. prof. rehab. medicine, 1984—; presenter in field. Contbr. articles to profl. jours. Grantee Sigma Xi, 1978, 80, SUNY, Stony Brook, 1978, New Eng. Med. Ctr. Hosps., 1985-86, Nat. Inst. Disability and Rehab. Rsch., 1986-89; Biomed. rsch. fellow, 1978, 80. Mem. APA, Am. Congress Rehab. Medicine, Mass. Neuropsychol. Soc. (exec. bd. 1991-94, chair pubs. com., mem. sci. com., editor newsletter 1990-95), Mass. Psychol. Assn., Internat. Brain Rsch. Orgn., Internat. Neuropsychol. Assn. (program com. 1992), Nat. Head Injury Found., Soc. Neurosci. Avocations: bicycling, tennis, hiking. Home and Office: 84 Cottage St Sharon MA 02067-2133 Office: 141 Rt 6A/Box 1580 #4 Sandwich MA 02563 Office Phone: 508-833-8893. E-mail: lpodbros@neuropsy.us.

PODD, ANN, newspaper editor; b. Buffalo, Jan. 15, 1954; d. Edward and Florence (Bojan) P.; m. Timothy Murray, 1980; children: Laura, Gregory. AB, Syracuse U., 1976; MBA, SUNY, Buffalo, 1981. Reporter AP, 1977, Buffalo Courier-Express, 1977-80, bus. editor, 1980-82, Bergen (N.J.) Record, 1982-88, N.Y. Daily News, 1988-90, assoc. editor, 1990-92, assoc. editor, dir. human resources, 1992-93; dep. spot news editor Wall St. Jour., N.Y.C., 1994, spot news editor, 1994—2000, nat. TV editor, 2000—03, day editor, 2003—05; Hong Kong mng. editor Wall St. Jour. Asia, Hong Kong, 2005—. Office: Wall Street Journal 25/F Central Plaza 18 Harbour Rd Hong Kong Hong Kong

PODD, MARSHA DIANNE, small business owner, nurse; b. Washington, Apr. 14, 1951; d. John Francis and Gretchen (Green) Podd. BS in Child Devel., U. Calif., Davis, 1973; AA in Nursing, De Anza Coll., 1978. RN, Calif., cert. Lactation Educator. Nurse Palo Alto (Calif.) Med. Clinic, 1973-78, St. Joseph Hosp., Orange, Calif., 1979-80, Diet Ctr., Petaluma, Calif., 1982-89; maternal/child home care nurse specialist, 1991—. Nurse Petaluma Valley Hosp., 1980—86; cons. Diet Ctr., Rexburg, Idaho, 1984—85; co-founder Health in Motion Prodns., 1987—91, maternal/child nurse specialist, 1991—; owner Ctr. for Creative Parenting, 1995—. Nurse Vietnam Refugee Placement, Hamilton AFB, 1980; earthquake relief vol. ARC, San Francisco, 1989-90. Recipient award for one of top ten fastest growing Diet Ctrs. in U.S. and Can., 1987. Mem. Bay Area Diet Ctr. Assn. (pres. 1984, treas. 1987-88), U. Calif. Aggie Alumni Assn. Republican. Avocations: travel, photography, skiing, swimming, bicycling. Home: 1108 Susan Way Novato CA 94947-6919 Office Phone: 415-883-4442. Personal E-mail: marshapodd@aol.com.

PODOLSKY, ANDREA G., lawyer; b. Phila., June 20, 1951; BA summa cum laude, Univ. Pa., 1972; JD, Columbia Univ., 1977. Bar: N.Y. 1978, US Dist. Ct. (ea. & so. dist. NY). Assoc. Cleary Gottlieb Steen & Hamilton LLP, NYC, 1977—88, ptnr., structured fin., intellectual property, 1988—. Editor Columbia Law Rev., 1976-77. Kent scholar. Mem. ABA, N.Y. State Bar Assn., Assn. Bar City of NY, Phi Beta Kappa. Office: Cleary Gottlieb Steen & Hamilton One Liberty Plz New York NY 10006 Office Phone: 212-225-2590. Office Fax: 212-225-3999. Business E-Mail: apodolsky@cgsh.com.

PODUSKA, T. F., artist; b. Cedar Falls, Iowa, Dec. 6, 1925; d. Everett Fleming and Vessie Mitchell; m. Robert D. Poduska, Dec. 27, 1948; children: Ann Poduska McCue, Sue Poduska Niksic. BA, Univ. No. Iowa, 1948. Trustee Denver Art Mus., Denver, 1977—83; bd. mem. Foothills Art Ctr., Golden, Colo. Exhibitions include invitational exhibitions Foothills Art Ctr. 35th Anniversary, 2003, Bus. of Art Ctr., Colo. Springs, Colo., 2003, Gallery of Contemporary Art, U. Colo., 2001, Miriam Perlman Gallery, Chgo., Ill., 1996, Reiss Gallery, Denver, Colo., 1996, exhibitions include Juried Shows Ctr. of The Arts, Tubac, Ariz., 1995, Level to Level, Johnson-Humrikhouse Mus., 1990, Exhibition to India, Bombay, India, 1989, NAWA, 100 Works: 100 Yrs., Nat. Travelling Exhibition, 1989, Nat. Assoc. Women Artists, N.Y.C., 1985, Represented in permanent collections Littleton Hist. Mus., Littleton, Colo., Denver Art Mus., Denver, Colo., Atlantic Richfield Corp., Amoco, Petro-Lewis Corp., Empire Savings, Bill Walters, Exeter, USD West, Mitchell Energy Corp., Piton Found., Ctrl. Bank, Glendale Fed., Laguna Hills, Calif., Marriott Hotels, Syracuse, N.Y., IBM. Recipient Colo. Gov. award, State of Colo., 1977, Cile Bach award, Denver Art Mus., 1991. Mem.: Foothills Art Ctr., Soc. of Layerists in Multimedia, Denver Art Mus. Home: 10233 W Powers Ave Littleton CO 80127 Personal E-mail: tfpoduska@earthlink.net.

PODWALL, KATHRYN STANLEY, biology professor; b. Chgo., Oct. 14; d. Frank and Marie C. Stanley. BS, U. Ill.; MA, NYU. Prof. biology Nassau C.C., Garden City, NY. Developmental reviewer West Ednl. Pub., Amesbury, Mass. and Highland Park, Ill., 1989, 91-92; reviewer AAAS, Washington, 1970—; exec. bd., advisor Women's Faculty Assn., Nassau C.C., 1990—, pres, 2000-2002; lectr. in field. Author: Tested Studies for Laboratory Teaching, vol. 5, 1993; editor: (books and cassettes) Rhyming Simon Books and Cassettes, 1990, Sight Reading Syncopation, 1998, Today's Way To Play the Standards, 2000, Today's Way To Play the Classics, 2000, (book and CD) Cartoons & Car Tunes, 2001, Cartoons & Kid Tunes, 2002, Cartoons and Christmas Tunes, 2003. Recipient L.I. Alzheimer's Found. Svc. award, 2002, Excellence award, Nat. Inst. for Staff and Orgnl. Devel., 2003, Chancellor's award excellence in tchg., SUNY, 2004. Mem. AAUW, Am. Assn. for Women in Cmty. Colls., Nat. Assn. Biology Tchrs. (life), Nat. Sci. Tchrs. Assn. (life), Soc. for Coll. Sci. Tchrs., Met. Assn. Coll. and Univ. Biologists, Nat. Cathedral Assn., N.Y. Acad. of Scis., Friends of Archives (charter), Xerces Soc., Southampton Colonial Soc., LaSalle County Hist. Soc. (life), Garden City Hist. Soc. (life), Soroptimists (bd. dirs. dist. 1 1994-96, club pres. 1992-94, Nassau County Pres. award 2001), U. Ill. Alumni Assn. (life). Avocations: travel, gardening, zoological pursuits. Office: Nassau Community College One Education Dr Garden City NY 11530 Office Phone: 516-572-7575. Business E-Mail: podwalk@ncc.edu.

POE, CHERYL TONI, music educator; b. Denver, Sept. 23, 1943; d. Anthony Joseph Kotwica and Dorothy Jean Rusch; m. Gerald Dean Poe (div. Aug. 1999); children: Lauren, Russell. BA, Western State Coll., 1965; M in Music Edn., U. Portland, 1974. Music tchr. Minot (N.D.) State Coll., 1969—71, Portland (Oreg.) Pub. Schs., 1975—76, Eugene (Oreg.) 4-J Schs., 1976—80, Howard Bishop Mid. Sch., Gainesville, Fla., 1980—82; clk. Sabine Music Ctr., Gainesville, 1983—85; music tchr. Martha Manson Acad., Gainesville, 1985—88, Sch. Bd. Alachua County, Gainesville, 1988—2006; ret. Pres, bd. mem. Alachua County Youth Orch., Fla., 1984—; bd. mem. Found. for Promotion Music, Gainesville, 1998—. Children's ch. choir dir. St. Augustine Cath. Ch., Gainesville, 2000—. Recipient Fla. Music Educator's award, Fla. Music Educator's Assn., 2006. Mem.: Am. Orff Schuwerk Assn., Fla. Elem. Music Educators (pres. 2000—03), Delta Kappa Gamma, Phi Delta Kappa.

POEHLER, AMY, comedienne, actress; b. Burlington, Mass., Sept. 16, 1971; m. Will Arnett, Aug. 29, 2003. Grad., Boston Coll. Cast mem. Second City, Chicago, 1993—96, Upright Citizen's Brigade, 1996—, Saturday Night Live, 2001—. Actor: (films) Saving Manhattan, 1998, Tomorrow Night, 1998, Deuce Bigalow: Male Gigolo, 1999, The Devil and Daniel Webster, 2001, Wet Hot American Summer, 2001, Martin & Orloff, 2002, Mean Girls, 2004, Envy, 2004, Southland Tales, 2006, Man of the Year, 2006; actor, writer, prodr. (films) Wild Girls Gone, 2005, actor, writer (TV series) Upright Citizens Brigade, 1998—2000, appearances include Late Night with Conan O'Brien, 1998—2000, Apt. 2F, 1997, Spin City, 1998, Undeclared, 2002, Arrested Development, 2004. Office: Saturday Night Live NBC Studios 30 Rockefeller Plz New York NY 10112*

POEHLMANN, JOANNA, artist, illustrator, book designer, educator; b. Milw., Sept. 5, 1932; d. Herbert Emil and Lucille (Conover) P. Attended, Layton Sch. Art, 1950-54, K.C. (Mo.) Art Inst., 1954, Marquette U., 1958, U. Wis., 1965, 1985. Assoc. lectr. U. Wis., Milw. Solo exhbns. include (retrospective) Milw. Art Mus., 1966, Bradley Galleries, Milw., 1982, Signature Gallery, John Michael Kohler Art Ctr., Sheboygan, Wis., 1979, 84, Woodland Pattern Book Ctr., Milw., 1988, The Cell Gallery, Rochester, N.Y., 1988, 89, Charles Allis Art Mus., Milw., 1991, Layton Gallery at Cardinal Stritch Coll, Milw., 1993, Univ. Meml. Libr., Madison, Wis., 1993, Wustum Mus. Fine Arts, Racine, Wis., 1994, Villa Terrace Mus., Milw., 1996-97, Grace Chosy Gallery, Madison, 1997, U. Western Mich., Kalamazoo, 1994; two-man shows include Bradley Galleries, 1964, 69, 80, 91, Cardinal Stritch Coll., Milw., 1980; invitational group shows include Cudahy Gallery of Wis. Art, Milw. Art Mus., 1962-85, 92, Bradley Galleries, 1967-79, Lakefront Festival of Art, Milw. Art Mus., 1962-63, 70-72, 76-79, Mount Mary Coll., Milw., 1979, 83, Chosy Gallery, 1980, 81, 86, U. Dallas, 1987, Frick Gallery, Tübingen, Germany, 1991, Spertus Mus. Judaica, Chgo., 1986, World Fin. Ctr., N.Y.C., 1992, Istvan Kiraly Muzeum, Budapest, Hungary, 1992, Artspace, Richmond, Va., 1994, Va. Ctr. For Craft Arts, Richmond, 1994, many others; juried group shows include Milw. Art Mus., 1963, 75, 78, Chgo. Art Inst., 1978, 81, Milw. Fine Arts Gallery, 1980, U. Wis. Fine Arts Gallery, Milw., 1980, The West Pub. Co., St. Paul, 1982, Auburn U., 1983, Zaner Gallery, Rochester, N.Y., 1984, Pratt Graphics Ctr., N.Y.C., 1985, Art 54 Gallery, N.Y.C., 1987, Boston Art Inst., 1987, Bradley U., Peoria, Ill., 1989, Wustum Mus. Fine Arts, 1989, 1992, Trenton State Coll., 1991, numerous others; represented in collections including Victoria & Albert Mus., London, N.Y. Pub. Libr., Mus. Kunsthandwerk, Frankfurt, Germany, Milw. Art Mus., Milw. Pub. Libr., U. Dallas, Orchard Corp. Am., St. Louis, Franklin Furnace Archives - Mus. Modern Art, N.Y., McDonald's Corp., GE Med. Systems Bldgs., Waukesha, Goldhirsh Group, Boston, Marquette U.-Haggerty Mus. Art, others; subject of articles; author: Love Letters, Food for Thought, Cancelling Out. Recipient Merit award Art Dir.'s Club, Milw., 1962, 100 Best award, 1967, 100 Best award Milw. Soc. Communicating Arts, 1973, 76, MGIC award Wis. Painters & Sculptors, 1981, Merit award Illustration Milw. Advt. Club, 1983, 2d award Wustum Mus. Fine Arts, 1983, 4th Purchase Prize award McDonald's Fine Art Collection Competition, 1983, Juror's award Zaner Gallery, 1984, Hopper/Koch award Wustum Mus. Fine Arts, 1985, spl. mention, Purchase award Bradley U., 1985, Purchase award Moravian Coll., 1985, Jack Richeson award Wustum Mus. Fine Arts, 1985, Purchase award U. Del., 1986, Strathmore Paper Co. award Wustum Mus. Fine Arts, 1986, Purchase award U. N.Dak., 1987, Award of Excellence miniature art Metro Internat. Competition, N.Y.C., 1987, 3d award Wustum Mus. Fine Arts, 1987, Purchase award U. Dallas, 1988, Award of Excellence Wustum Mus. Fine Arts, 1992, Individual Art fellowship Milw. County, 1993; Arts Midwest/NEA Regional Visual Artist fellow, 1994—. Roman Catholic. Home: 1231 N Prospect Ave Milwaukee WI 53202-3013

POEKERT, ROSE A(NN), elementary school educator; b. Phila., Jan. 5, 1951; d. Joseph G. and Columbia P. (D'Angelo) Battistelli; m. Anthony F. Poekert, Sept. 2, 1972; children: Sarah M., Amanda J. BS in elem. edn., Chestnut Hill Coll., 1972; postgrad., Villanova U., 1973, U. Nebr., 1975-76, U. Mo., 1979, Notre Dame Coll., Plymouth State U. Cert. elem. tchr. N.H., Mo., N.J. 3rd grade tchr. Walton Elem. Sch., Phila., 1972-73; math. tchr. St. Bridget's Sch., Omaha, 1974-75; tchr. St. Joan of Arc Sch., Omaha, 1975-79, Visitation Sch., Kansas City, Mo., 1979-84; math. tchr. C.D. McIntyre, Whitefield Sch., Whitefield, N.H., 1984-93; tchr. Dalton (N.H.) Elem. Sch., 1993—2003; tchr. 2d grade Lancaster (N.H.) Elem. Sch., 2003—. Mem. NEA-NH Democrat. Roman Catholic. Avocations: travel, gourmet cooking, gardening. Home: 71 Union Rd Dalton NH 03598 Office: Lancaster Elem Sch 51 Bridge St Lancaster NH 03584 E-mail: poekerts@netzero.net.

POEN, KATHRYN LOUISE, music educator, performing arts association administrator; b. Decorah, Iowa, Mar. 4, 1927; d. Arthur Nicolai and Emma Margaret Lomen; m. Roger Dean Walker, Nov. 25, 1949 (div. June 5, 1974); children: Bonnie Jo Walker, Marcia Lee Walker, Randall Craig Walker; m. Monte Mac Poen, May 22, 1982. BA, Iowa State Tchrs. Coll., 1949; MusM, U. Ariz., 1968. Music educator pub. schs., Iowa, 1950—55, Mont., 1960—61, Nogales, Ariz., 1962—76, Flagstaff, Ariz., 1976—90; founder, dir. Flagstaff Light Opera Co., 1995—. Mem. Flagstaff Festival of Arts, 1992—93; dir., mem. Flagstaff chpt.Sweet Adelines, 1990—2000; owner, tchr. pvt. piano practice, 1950—. Composer songs. Mem.: Am. Choral Dirs. Assn., Ariz. Tchrs. of Music Assn., Ariz. Music Educators Assn., Music Educators Nat. Conf. Avocations: travel, collecting. Home: 3703 N Grandview Dr Flagstaff AZ 86004 Office Phone: 928-779-3810. E-mail: pianomewsik@aol.com.

POETHIG, EUNICE BLANCHARD, clergywoman; b. Hempstead, NY, Jan. 16, 1930; d. Werner J. and Juliet (Stroh) Blanchard; m. Richard Paul Poethig, June 7, 1952; children: Richard Scott, Kathryn Aileen, Johanna Klare, Margaret Juliet, Erika Christy. BA, De Pauw U., 1951; MA, Union Theol. Sem., 1952; MDiv, McCormick Theol. Sem., N.Y.C., 1975, STM, 1977; PhD, Union Theol. Sem., 1985. Ordained to ministry Presbyn. Ch., 1979. Missionary United Presbyn. Ch. USA to United Ch. of Christ, The Philippines, 1956-72; mem. faculty Ellinwood Coll. Christian Edn., Manila, 1957-61; mem. faculty, campus ministry Philippine Women's U., Manila, 1962-68. Bd. dirs. Jane Addams Conf., Journey's End Refugee Resettlement Agy., Coun. of Bishops and Execs. of Buffalo Area Met. Ministries; trustee Presbyn. Found., 1991-94, Gen. Bd. Nat. Coun. Chs. Christ, 1995-97; editor New Day Pubs., Manila, 1969-72; curriculum editor Nat. Coun. Chs., Manila, 1962-72; assoc. exec. Presbytery Chgo., 1979-85; exec. Presbytery of Western N.Y., 1986-93; dir. congl. ministries divsn. gen. assembly Gen. Assembly Coun., Presbyn. Ch. (U.S.A.), 1994-98; mem. Coun. Execs., Ill. Coun. Chs., 1980-85. Author: Bible Studies in Concern Response, A.D., 1975, Good News Women, 1987, Sing, Shout and Clap for Joy: Psalms in Worship, 1989, Friendship Press Study on Philippines, 1989, Liturgy 9:1, 1990, Hunger Program Workbook, 1991; editor: (hym book series) Everybody, I Love You, 1971—72, 150 Plus Tomorrow: Churches Plan for the Future, 1982, 2s edit., 1985, Our Living Tradition, 1994, Women of Faith: 1986-1996, 1997, From Slavery to Promised Land, 1999, The Struggle for Equality: Women in Mission, 1999. Active Environ. Def. Fund, Erie County Environ. Mgmt. Coun., NY, 1990—93, NGO Forum UN Fourth World Conf. Women, Beijing, 1995; planning com. Celebrate Adult Curriculum, 1987—93, Transatlantic Dialogue, 2003—04; chmn. governing bd. Stony Point Ctr., 2002—04, PC USA; chmn. PC USA Celebrating the Ordination of Women, 2005—; bd. dirs. Ch. Women United, Chgo., 1974—79, More Light Presbyns., 2000—03; trustee McCormick Theol. Sem., Chgo., 1974—75; bd. dirs., exec. com. Presbyn. Cmty. Ctr., Louisville, 1999—2001; active Women's Ordination Conf. Nat. Presbyn. Ch. Com., Presbyn. Gen. Assembly Challenge to the Ch. Fund., 1989; design team Covenant People Curriculum, 1997; futures com. Highland Presbyn. Ch., chair, 1997—99; organizing bd. Asian Ctr. Theology and Strategy, Chgo., 1974. Recipient Walker Cup, DePauw U., 1951; Nettie F. McCormick fellow in Old Testament Hebrew, McCormick Sem., Chgo., 1975; recipient Disting. Alumni award DePauw U., 2003. Mem. Internat. Platform Assn., Soc. Bibl. Lit., Soc. Ethnomusicology, Assn. Exec. Presbyters (bd. dirs., chairperson 1991-93), Am. Schs. Oriental Rsch., Witherspoon Soc., Nat. Assn. Religious Women, Internat. Assn. Women Mins., Nat. Assn. Presbyn. Clergywomen. Home: 1000 E 53rd St #613 Chicago IL 60615

POETTKER, MARY THERESE, music educator; b. Belleville, Ill., Aug. 29, 1950; d. Delmar Julius and Catherine Rita Thouvenot; m. Robert H. Poettker, Aug. 12, 1972; children: Christina, Scott, Jason, Jennifer. B in Music Edn., So. Ill. U., Edwardsville, 1972, M in Music Edn., 1974. Cert. tchr. vocal and instrument music tchr. K-12 Mo. Vocal music tchr. Ferguson (Mo.)-Florissant Sch. Dist., 1972—79, St. Elizabeth-St. Robert Regional Sch., St. Charles, Mo., 1981—. Dir. music St. Elizabeth Ann Seton Ch., St. Charles, 1983—. Nominee Disney Am. Tchr., Disney Co., 2001. Mem.: Mo. Music Educators Assn. (v.p. jr. high vocal and gen. music St. Louis Metro Dist. 8 1988—2000, 2006—, Merit award St. Louis Metro Dist. 8 2001), Music Educators Nat. Conf., Nat. Pastoral Musicians (chpt. dir. 1998—2004, asst. chpt. dir. 2004—, Outstanding Sch. Music Edn. 1996). Roman Catholic. Avocations: gardening, camping, crafts. Home: 112 Travelers Trail Saint Peters MO 63376-7149

POETZEL, SUSAN MARIE, elementary school educator; b. Mpls., Apr. 9, 1947; d. Carl Gerald and Bernadette Marie (Blakemore) Caspers; m. Roman William Poetzel, Aug. 22, 1970; children: Megan, Adam, Christopher, Karen. BA, Marquette U., 1969; MS, U. Wis., Milw., 1974; MA of Tchg., Nat. Louis U., Evanston, Ill., 1991, Certificate Advanced Studies, 2002. Neighborhood worker Inner City Devel., Milw., 1968-70; rsch. assoc. Greater Milw. Survey, 1971-73; tchr. St. Giles Sch., Oak Park, Ill., 1991—. Author interdisciplinary tchg. unit. Mem., state sec. Nat. Women's Polit. Caucus, Milw., 1975-83; troop leader Girl Scouts U.S., Milw., Downers Grove, Ill., 1980-92; mem. cmty. adv. bd. United Cmty. Svcs., Milw., 1974. HUD urban studies grantee, 1970-71; Keizai Koho Japan fellow, 1994. Mem. ASCD, Nat. Coun. Social Studies, Nat. Middle Sch. Assn., N.C. Soc. Social Studies. Home: 1220 Prairie Ave Downers Grove IL 60515-3554

POFF, SARAH ELLEN, art educator; d. Jack Dalton and Martha Ellen Tucker; m. Alec G. Poff, Dec. 29, 1978; children: John David, Mary Ellen. BS in art edn., S.W. Bapt. Univ, Mo., 1979; M in edn. tech., Lesley U.-Extention, Kansas City, Mo., 2005. Asst. tchr. East Prairie Sch. Dist., Mo., 1978—81; substitute tchr. Cuero Sch. Dist., Tex., 1982—83; mgr. La Posada Apts., Gonzales, Tex., 1983—84; art educator 1st -12th grade Independence Christian Sch., Mo., 1984—85; tchr. Little Angel's Learning Ctr., Blue Springs, Mo., 1986—91; elem. art educator Blue Springs Sch. Dist., Lee's Summit, Mo., 1993—. Watercolor and ink, No Faces, 2001, Face Series (9-11), Overland Park, Kans., 2002, America Wept, We Remember Mag., 2002; author: (children's book) It was a Bright and Sunny Day, 2001; contbr. articles to newspapers. Greeter First Bapt. Ch., Blue Springs, Mo., 2000—06; leader Girl Scouts, Blue Springs, Mo., 1990—92; ch. coun. First Bapt. Ch., Blue Springs, Mo., 1987—91, libr., 1987—92. Recipient PTA Phoebe Appersan Hearst Outstanding Educator, Chapel Lakes Elem. PTA, 1996—97. Mem.: Mo. State Tchr. Assn., Concerned Women of Am. Republican. Baptist. Avocations: digital photography, watercolor, genealogy, writing. Home: 1604 SW 18th Street Ct Blue Springs MO 64015 Office: Poffpaintscom 1604 SW 18th Street Ct Blue Springs MO 64015 Office Phone: 816-225-3824. Personal E-mail: sarah@poffpaints.com. Business E-Mail: spoff@bssd.net.

POGATSHNIK, LEE WOLFRAM, psychologist, educator; b. Camden, NJ, Oct. 12, 1955; d. Harold George and Roseann Monack Wolfram; m. Gerald Joseph Pogatshnik, July 26, 1975; children: Sara, Adam. BA, U. Minn., 1977; PhD, Cornell U., 1983. Lectr. Ea. Conn. State U., Willimantic, Conn., 1983—85; instr. So. Ill. U., Edwardsville, 1989—2005, Ea. Ky. U., 2006—. Mem.: Assn. for Psychol. Sci., Psi Chi. Office: Ea Ky U Dept Psychology 127 Cammack Bldg 521 Lancaster Ave Richmond KY 40475 also: Ea Ky U 127 Cammack Bldg 521 Lancaster Ave Richmond KY 40475 Business E-Mail: lee.pogatshnik@eku.edu.

POGREBIN, LETTY COTTIN, writer, educator; b. NYC, June 9, 1939; d. Jacob and Cyral (Halpern) Cottin; m. Bertrand B. Pogrebin, Dec. 8, 1963; children: Abigail and Robin (twins), David. AB cum laude with spl. distinction in English and Am. Lit, Brandeis U., 1959. V.p. Bernard Geis Assocs. (book pubs.), N.Y.C., 1960-70; columnist The Working Woman column Ladies Home Jour., 1971-81; contbg. editor Tikkun mag., 1988—, Family Circle, 1989—; founding editor Ms mag., N.Y.C., 1971-87, columnist, editor at large, 1987-89, contbg. editor, 1990—; columnist The N.Y. Times, Newsday, Moment Mag., Washington, 1990—, Moment Mag., Washington, 1990—. Cons. Free to Be, You and Me projects, 1972—; lectr. women's issues and family politics, changing roles of men and women, friendship in Am., non-sexist child rearing and edn., Judaism and feminism, Mid-East politics. Author: How to Make It in a Man's World, 1970, Getting Yours: How to Make the System Work for the Working Woman, 1975, Growing Up Free, 1980, Stories for Free Children, 1982, Family Politics, 1983, Among Friends, 1986, Deborah, Golda, and Me: Being Female and Jewish in America, 1991, Getting Over Getting Older: An Intimate Journey, 1996, Three Daughters: A Novel, 2002; mem. editl. bd. Tikkun Mag.; contbr. articles to N.Y. Times, Washington Post, Boston Globe, The Nation, TV Guide, Family Circle, Elle, Travel & Leisure, L.A. Times, N.Y. Daily News, Harpers Bazaar, also other mags., newspapers. Pres. Author's Guild, 1998-2002; pres. Aythors Registry, 2000—; bd. dirs. Ms. Found. for Edn. and Comm., New Israel Fund, Jewish Fund for Justice, PEN Am.; mem. Task Force on Women Fedn. Jewish Philanthropies. Pointer fellow Yale U., 1982, MacDowell Colony fellow, 1979, 89, 94, 2000, Cummington Colony Arts fellow 1985, Edna St. Vincent Millay Colony fellow, 1985; recipient Matrix award Women in Comm., 1981, Gloria Steinem Women of Vision award Ms. Found. for Women, 1990, Abram L. Sachar medal Brandeis U., 1994, Woman of Valor award Jewish Fund for Justice, 1997, Woman of Achievement award N. Shore Child and Family Assn., 1997, Hannah G. Solomon award Nat. Coun. Jewish Women, 1997, Woman of Distinction award Kingsborough Coll., 1998, U.S./Israel Women-to-Women award, 1999, N.Y.C. Contr.'s Jewish Heritage award, 1999, Elle Mag. Readers prize, 2002, Barr Peace award, 2003, Mayor Michael Bloomberg Libr. award, 2003, Lion of Judah Jewish Women's Archive Pioneer award, 2004, Jane Evans Pursuit of Peace award Women of Reform Judaism, 2005; named Woman of Yr. Fifty-Plus Expo, 1997, Outstanding Scholars 21st Century, 2000, Vet. Feminists of Am. Honor Roll, 2002.

POGUE, VELVIE ANNE, nephrologist, educator; d. Henry Robinson and Maggie Mandigo; m. Alfred Robert Ashford; children: Alfred C. Ashford III, Adrienne Ashford. BS, So. U., Baton Rouge, 1970; MD, Harvard U., 1974. Diplomate Am. Bd. Internal Medicine, 1978, nephrology Am. Bd. Internal Medicine, 1980. Intern in internal medicine Harlem Hosp. Ctr., N.Y.C., 1974—75, resident in internal medicine, 1975—77, fellow in clin. nephrology, 1977—79, attending physician, 1979—, chief divsn. nephrology, 1990—; assoc. prof. clin. medicine Coll. Physicians and Surgeons, Columbia U., N.Y.C., 2002—. Rschr. African Am. Study of Kidney Disease and Hypertension, N.Y.C. Named to America's Leading Black Doctors, Black Enterprise Mag., 2001. Mem.: Am. Heart Assn., Nat. Kidney Found., Internat. Soc. Hypertension in Blacks, Nat. Med. Assn., Am. Soc. Nephrology. Achievements include research in complications of hypertension, including hypertensive renal disease in blacks; impact of changes in blood pressure staging on recognized severity of hypertension. Office: Harlem Hospital Center 506 Lenox Ave New York NY 10037 Business E-Mail: vap1@columbia.edu.

POH-FITZPATRICK, MAUREEN B., dermatologist, educator; b. N.Y.C., Feb. 24, 1943; d. Edgar J. and Alice M. (Kennedy) Poh; m. Brian J. Fitzpatrick, Dec. 26, 1970. BS, Siena Coll., 1964; MD, U. Tenn., 1967. Diplomate Am. Bd. Dermatology. Fellow in cardiology Regional Med. Ctr., Memphis, 1968, intern, 1968-69; resident in dermatology Barnes Hosp., St. Louis, 1969-72; asst. Washington U. Sch. Medicine, St. Louis, 1969-72; clin. instr. NYU Sch. Medicine, 1973; from asst. prof. to assoc. prof. dermatology Columbia U. Coll. Physicians & Surgeons, N.Y.C., 1973-86; prof. dermatology and medicine N.Y. Med. Coll., 1987-94; from assoc. prof. to prof. dermatology Columbia U. Coll. Physicians & Surgeons, 1994-98, prof. emeritus, 1998—; clin. prof. medicine U. Tenn. Coll. Medicine, 1998—2002, prof. medicine, 2002—. Grantee Nat. Inst. Arthritis, Musculoskeletal & Skin Diseases, 1976-98. Fellow Am. Acad. Dermatology; mem. Memphis Dermatology Soc., N.Y. Dermatol. Soc., N.Y. Acad. Medicine. Republican. Roman Catholic. Office: 15 Cedar Lane Ter Ossining NY 10562-2919

POHL, KATHLEEN SHARON, editor; b. Sandusky, Mich., Apr. 7, 1951; d. Gerald Arthur and Elizabeth Louise (Neukamm) P.; m. Bruce Mark Allen Reynolds, June 11, 1982. BA in Spanish, Valparaiso U., 1973; MA in English, No. Mich. U., 1975. Producer, dir. fine arts Sta. WNMU-FM, Marquette, Mich., 1981-82; instr. communications Waukesha County (Wis.) Tech. Inst., 1983; editor Ideals mag., Milw., 1983-85; editor, mng. editor Raintree Pubs., Milw., 1985-87; mng. editor, now exec. editor Country Woman mag., Greendale, Wis., 1987—; exec. editor Country Handcrafts mag., Greendale, 1990-93, Taste of Home Mag., Greendale, Wis., 1993—; editor Talk About Pets, Greendale, 1994-95. Author nature book series, 1985-87; sr. editor: Country Woman Christmas Book, 1996—; mng. editor: Irwin the Sock (Chgo. Book Clinic award 1988); exec. editor Taste of Home's Quick Cooking Mag., 1998—. Down the Aisle Countr Style, 2000, Taste of Home's Light & Tasty Mag., 2000—. Mem. Nat. Mus. of Women in Arts, Alpha Lambda Delta (hon.). Home: N54 W26326 Lisbon Rd Sussex WI 53089-4249 Office: Country Woman Mag 5400 S 60th St Greendale WI 53129-1404

POHLMAN, LYNETTE, museum director, curator; BA, Iowa State U., 1972, MA in applied art, 1976. Dir., chief curator Univ. Mus. at Iowa State U. Adj. prof. art & design Iowa State U.; organizer Art in State Bldgs. Prog. Curator Emperors, Shoguns and Kings, 1981, Fiber to Glass, 1987, Land of Fragile Giants: Landscapes, Environments and Peoples of the Loess Hills, 1994—96, The Golden Age of Glass: 1875-1939, 1999. Recipient Christian Petersen Design Award, 2004. Mem.: Assn. Coll. and Univ. Mus. and Galleries (founding mem.). Office: Univ Mus 290 Scheman Bldg Ames IA 50011-1110 Office Phone: 515-294-3342. E-mail: lpohlma@iastate.edu.

POHLMANN, EVELYN GAWLEY, music educator, consultant; b. Pasadena, Calif., May 3, 1942; m. John Ogden Pohlmann, Aug. 8, 1964; children: Alison Pohlmann Espinosa, Victoria Elizabeth. BA, Occidental Coll., 1964. Life tchg. credential Calif. Studio piano tchr., Seal Beach, Calif., 1971—. Tchr. cons. Internat. Piano Tchg. Found., 1976—. Bd. dirs. Long Beach Symphony Assn., 1998—. Recipient Ruby Sword of Honor, Delta Province, Sigma Alpha Iota, 1964. Mem.: Music Tchrs.' Assn. Calif. (pres. 1988—90), Long Beach Symphony Guild (pres. 1994—95).

POHLMANN, MARY MICHAELS, retired medical educator; d. Charles F. and Dorothy M. Michaels; m. John T. Pohlmann, Aug. 24, 1963; children: Joan M., Theresa A. Laurent. BS, Fayetteville State Coll., NC, 1964; MS in Edn., So. Ill. U., Edwardsville, 1972; PhD, So. Ill. U., Carbondale, 1975; MD, So. Ill. U., Springfield, 1983. Cert. tchr. Ill., 1970, Mo., 1966. HS biology tchr. Ferguson/Florissant Sch. Dist., Mo., 1966—70; biology tchr. Centralia HS, Ill., 1970—71; instr., asst prof., rsch. assoc. So. Ill. U., Carbondale, 1974—80; resident in family practice Meml. Hosp. Carbondale, 1983—86; physician Murphysboro Health Ctr., Ill., 1986—87, So. Ill. U. Student Health Programs, Carbondale, 1987—2002, med. chief staff, 1992—96; intern, resident So. Ill. U. Sch. Medicine, Carbondale, 1983—86, clin. asst. prof., 1986; ret. Chmn. Parish Health Cabinet, Carbondale, 2001—06; bd. mem. Jackson County Health Dept., Carbondale, 1988—2006, sec., 1988—2006; bd. mem. Abundant Health Resource Clinic, Carbondale, 2003—06. Recipient Svc. award, Ill. Masters Swimming Assn., 2005. Mem.: AMA, Jackson County Med. Soc., Am. Acad. Family Physicians (life), US Masters Swimming (local masters swimming com. chmn. 2002—05). Avocation: competitive swimming. Home: 405 S Deer Lake Dr E Carbondale IL 62901-5253

POHTO, SUSAN LOUISE, secondary school educator; b. Beverly, Mass., Aug. 16, 1959; d. Ronald Lee Sr. and Eleanor Mae Johnson; m. Larry M. Pohto Jr., July 13, 1986 (div. May 1995); children: Larry M. III, Amberlea S. BS in Chemistry, Westminster Coll., 1981; MEd, John Carroll U., 1997. Rsch. chemist Avery Dennison, Painesville, Ohio, 1981-96; tchr. intern St. Ignatius High Sch., Cleve., 1996-97; tchr. secondary chemistry & math. Mentor (Ohio) Bd. Edn., 1997—. Patentee in field. NSF grantee, 1979. Mem. Am. Chem. Soc. Office Phone: 440-974-5300. E-mail: pohto@mentorschools.org.

POIANI, EILEEN LOUISE, mathematician, academic administrator; b. Newark, Dec. 17, 1943; d. Hugo Francis and Eileen Louise (Crecca) P. BA in Math., Douglass Coll., 1965; MS in Math., Rutgers U., 1967, PhD in Math., 1971. Tchg. asst., grad. preceptor Rutgers U., New Brunswick, N.J., 1966-67; asst. counselor Douglass Coll., New Brunswick, 1967, 69-70; instr. math. St. Peter's Coll., Jersey City, 1967-70, asst. prof., 1970-74, dir. of self-study, 1974-76, assoc. prof., 1974-80, prof., 1980—, asst. to pres., 1976-80, asst. to pres. for planning, 1980-96, exec. asst. to pres., 1996-98, v.p. for student affairs, 1999—. Chair U.S. Commn. on Math. Instrn., NRC of NAS, Washington, 1983-90; founding nat. dir. Women and Math. Lectureship Program, Washington, 1975-81, adv. bd., 1981—; project dir. Consortium for Advancement of Pvt. Higher Edn., Washington, 1986-88; mem. N.J. Math. Coalition, 1991—, Nat. Seminar on Jesuit Higher Edn., 1990-94, strategic planning com. N.J. Assn. Ind. Colls. and Univs., 1990-92; charter trustee Rutgers U., 1992-2004; Nutley panelist Centennial Celebration, 2002; advisor NSF Funded Project of Bank St. Coll. and EDC/Ctr. for Children and Tech., 2003—; mem. learning adv. com. Liberty Sci. Ctr., 2004—. Author: (with others) Mathematics Tomorrow, 1981, Encyclopedia of Mathmatics Education; contbr. articles to profl. jours. Mem. Newark Mus., Nutley (N.J.) Hist. Soc., Friends of Newark Libr.; trustee Nutley Free Pub. Libr., 1974-77, St. Peter's Prep. Sch., Jersey City, 1986-92; active fee arbitration commn. N.J. Supreme Ct., 1983-86, ct. ethics com., 1986-90; U.S. nat. rep. Internat. Congress Math. Edn., Budapest, Hungary, 1988; statewide planning com. NCCJ, 1988-92, youth leadership coun., 1992—; chair evaluation teams Mid. States Assn. Coll. and Schs.; U.S. del. Internat. Congress on Math; trustee The Cath. Advocate, 1993-2003. Recipient George F. Johnson, S.J. Alumni Faculty award, 1976, Douglass Soc. award Douglass Coll., 1982, Outstanding Cmty. Svc. award Christopher Columbus Found., N.J., 1994, Outstanding Svc. award Middle States Assn. Colls. and Schs., 1994, Cert. of Appreciation for outstanding contbns. as nat. dir. women and math. program, 1993, Varsity Letter plaque for leadership and svc. St. Peter's Prep, 1997; named Danforth Assoc., Danforth Found., 1972-86, SPC Legend, Students of St. Peters Coll., 2002, Humanitarian award NCCJ, 2003, N.J. Women of Achievement award N.J. State Fedn. Women's Clubs, 2003, Alumnae Recognition award Douglass Coll., 2003; named to Nutley Hall of Fame, 2003. Mem. AAUP, Math. Assn. Am. (bd. dirs. lectureship program, gov. NJ chpt. 1972-79, chair human resources coun. 1991-96, Outstanding Coll. Tchg. award 1993), Nat. Coun. Tchrs. Math. (spkr. 1974—), Soc. Coll. and Univ. Planning (program com. 1989—, spkr. nat. conf. 1986, 88-90, judge grad. paper competition), Com. on Math. with Disabilities, Com on Devel. of Math., Pi Mu Epsilon (pres. 1987-90, C.C. MacDuffee award for disting. svc. to math. 1995), Phi Beta Kappa, Alpha Sigma Nu, Beta Beta Beta. Roman Catholic. Avocations: gourmet cooking, travel, golf. Office: St Peter's Coll 2641 Kennedy Blvd Jersey City NJ 07306-5997

POINDEXTER, BARBARA GLENNON, secondary school educator; b. Dallas, Oct. 19, 1937; d. Victor and Ruth (Gaskins) Ward; m. Noble Turner Poindexter, Aug. 2, 1994; 1 child, Victoria Angela Russo. BS, Tex. Woman's U., 1958; postgrad., Kans. State U., 1969-70; grad., U. Northern Iowa, 1986. Cert. tchr. S.C., Kans., N.Mex., Tex. Drama and English tchr. Linn (Kans.) H.S., 1968-69; tchr. Mosquero (N.Mex.) H.S., 1973-74, Sumter (S.C.) Sch. Dist., Maywood Sch., 1974-76, Harleyville (S.C.) H.S., 1976-78, Hampton (S.C.) H.S., 1978-79, Centerville Sch., Cottageville, S.C., 1979-80; tchr. English Scurry-Rosser Sch., Scurry, Tex., 1981-82; tchr. French and Spanish Christ the King, Dallas, 1982-83; tchr. French and English, chmn. fgn. lang. dept. Wilmer-Hutchins H.S., Dallas, 1983-94; tchr. French and English Molina H.S., Dallas, 1997—. Mem.: Theta Alpha Phi. Democrat. Methodist. Home: 5315 Maple Springs Blvd Dallas TX 75235-8326 Office: Molina HS 2355 Duncanville Rd Dallas TX 75211-6532 Personal E-mail: edithgassion@yahoo.com.

POINDEXTER, BEVERLY KAY, media and communications professional, real estate broker; b. Noblesville, Ind., Nov. 12, 1949; d. Wayne Francis and Rosalie Christine (Nightenhelser) Hunter; m. Jerry Roger Poindexter, Dec. 7, 1969; children: Nick Ashley, Tracy Lynne, Wendy Dawn, Cory Matthew. Student, Purdue U., Bethany Seminary. Editor Tri Town Topics Newspaper, 1965-69; reporter, photographer Noblesville Daily Ledger, 1969-70; asst. mgr., sales mgr., sports dir. Sta. WHYT Radio, Noblesville, Ind., 1973-79; sales mgr., music dir., DJ, news Sta. WBMP Radio, Elwood, Ind., 1979-88; acct. exec. Stas. WAXT-WHBU Radio, Anderson, Ind., 1988-89; gen. mgr., sales mgr. Sta. WEWZ, Elwood, Ind., 1989-90; now news stringer Sta. WTHR TV-13, Indpls.; real estate broker Booker Realty, Cicero, Ind., 1990-98; real estate broker, owner Poindexter Agy., Noblesville, Ind., 1998—. Area rep. Youth for Understanding, 1993—; pres. bd. dirs. Hamilton Heights Elem. Football, Arcadia, Ind., 1981-83; founder, chmn. Hamilton Heights Elem. Cheerleaders, Arcadia, 1981—; youth leader, counselor Ch. of the Brethren, Arcadia, 1991-94; active Ch. of Brethren Women's Fellowship; active Agape Therapeutic Riding Stables, Cicero. Mem. Nat. Assn. Realtors, Ind. Assn. Realtors, Met. Indpls. Bd. Realtors. Republican. Avocations: horseback riding, canoeing, swimming, singing, dance. Office: 108 Shoreline Ct Apt A Noblesville IN 46062 Office Phone: 765-606-7510. Business E-Mail: thepoindexteragency@yahoo.com.

POITIER, CONSTANCE RENA, music specialist, educator; b. Quincy, Fla., June 1, 1955; d. Leroy Cornelius and Dorothy Louise Parker Harris; m. James Poitier, July 22, 1995; children: Carla Felicia DuPont, Carl Franklin DuPont, Jr. BA, Bethune-Cookman Coll., 1977; ME, Fla. Atlantic U., 1984; ednl. specialist magna cum laude, Nova U., 2004. Nat. bd. cert. tchr. 2004, cert. nat. bd. cert. minority recruiter. Choral dir., gen. music Roosevelt Jr. H.S., West Palm Beach, Fla., 1977-81; drama coach Jupiter (Fla.) H.S., 1985; music specialist Roosevelt Elem., 1981-86, Riverview (Fla.) Elem., 1986-96; min. of music Spring Hill Bapt. Ch., Tampa, Fla., 1994-96; choral dir. Atlantic H.S., Port Orange, Fla., 1996-97; choral dir. Daytona Beach Gospel Choir Daytona Beach Bapt. Ch., Fla., 1996—; music specialist Palm Terrace Elem., Daytona Beach, Fla., 1997—, Bonner Elem., 2004—; asst. to the choral dir. Bethune Cookman Coll., 2003; proprietor Poitier Fin. Svcs. Choral dir. Progress M&E Bapt. State Conv., 1973-76; choral dir., pianist 1st Bapt. Ch. College Hill, Tampa, 1986-96; choir cons., guest dir., clinician for choral workshops; concert and rec. artist; pvt. instr., voice and piano; choral festival judge; gospel music workshop clinician. Author: My Book of Poems, 1996. Fellow NEA, NAACP, Am. Choral Dirs., Westside Bus. and Profls., Fla. Vocal Assn., Fla. Music Educators Assn., Fla. Music Educators Nat. Conf., Zeta Phi Beta. Home: 3801 Birch Mtn Rd Port Orange FL 32129 Office: Bonner Elem Sch George Ingram Blvd Daytona Beach FL 32114-1253 E-mail: connie8082@bellsouth.net.

POKRAS, SHEILA FRANCES, retired judge; b. Newark, Aug. 5, 1935; m. Norman M. Pokras, 1954; children: Allison, Andrea, Larry. Student, Beaver Coll., 1953-54; BS in Edn., Temple U., 1957; JD cum laude, Pepperdine U., 1969. Bar: Calif. 1970, U.S. Dist. Ct. D.C. 1970, U.S. Dist. Ct. Calif. 1970, U.S. Supreme Ct. 1975. Tchr. elem. and secondary schs., Phila. and Newark, 1957-59; pvt. practice law Long Beach, Calif., 1970-78; city councilwoman Lakewood, Calif., 1972-76; judge Long Beach Mcpl. Ct., 1978-80, L.A. Superior Ct., 1980-98; ret., 1998. Supervising judge, 1986; del. Calif. State Dem. Cen. Com., 1975, Calif. State Conv., 1975; mem. Com. on Gender Bias in Calif. Courts, 1986-89 Advisor Jr. League, 1980-85; mem. early childhood adv. bd. Long Beach City Coll.; bd. dirs. Long Beach Alcoholism Coun., 1979-80, Boys and Girls Club Am., 1981-89, Long Beach Symphony, 1985, Jewish Community Fedn., 1982-86, past mem. community rels. com.; active Nat. Women's Polit. Caucus, LWV. Named Woman of Yr., NOW, Long Beach, 1984; recipient Torch of Liberty award, B'nai B'rith Anti-Defamation League, 1974; honoree, Nat. Conf. Christians and Jews, 1986. Mem. ABA, AAUW, Nat. Assn. Women Judges (dist. supr. 1986), Calif. Bar Assn. (judges div.), Calif. Judges Assn. (mem. ann. seminar com. 1981-89), Mcpl. Cts. Judges Assn. (mem. Marshall com. 1979-80), L.A. County Bar Assn. (judges div., mem. arbitration com.), Women Lawyers Assn., L.A. (judges sect.), Women Lawyers Assn. Long Beach, Long Beach Legal Aid Found. (v.p. 1976-78), Long Beach Bar Assn. (active various coms., bd. govs. 1977-78, Judge of Yr. 1987), Long Beach C. of C. (bd. dirs.). Avocations: swimming, golf, jogging, classical music, movies.

POLACCO, PATRICIA, writer, illustrator; Works include: Meteor!, 1987, Rechenka's Eggs, 1988, The Keeping Quilt, 1988, Uncle Vova's Tree, 1989, Boatride with Lillian Two-Blossom, 1989, Thunder Cake, 1990, Just Plain Fancy, 1990, Babushka's Doll, 1990, Some Birthday!, 1991, Appelemando's Dreams, 1991, Picnic at Mudsock Meadow, 1992, Mrs. Katz & Tush, 1992, Chicken Sunday, 1992, The Bee Tree, 1993, Babushka Baba Yaga, 1993, Tikvah Means Hope, 1994, Pink & Say, 1994, My Rotten Readheaded, Older Brother, 1994, Firetalking, 1994, My Ol' Man, 1995, Babushka's Mother Goose, 1995, Aunt Chip and the Great Triple Creek Dam Affair, 1995, I Can Hear the Sun: A Modern Myth, 1996, In Enzo's Splendid Gardens, 1997, Mrs. MacK, 1998, Luba and the Wren, 1999, The Butterfly, 2000, Mommies Say Shhh!, 2005; illustrator: Casey at the Bat, 1992. Office: Penguin Putnam Inc 345 Hudson St Fl 15 New York NY 10014-4502

POLAN, ANNETTE LEWIS, artist, educator; b. Huntington, W.Va., Dec. 8, 1944; d. Lake and Dorothy (Lewis) Polan; m. Arthur Lowell Fox, Jr., Aug. 31, 1969 (div. 1994); children: Courtney Van Winkle Fox, Arthur Lowell Fox III. 1st degree, Inst. des Profs. de Francaise, Paris, 1965; BA, Hollins U., 1967; postgrad., Corcoran Coll. Art and Design, 1968-69. Prof. Corcoran Coll. Art and Design, Washington, 1974—, chmn. painting dept., 1991—. Vis. artist Art Therapy Italia, Vignale, Italy, 1986; dir. summer program La Napoule Art Found., Chateau de la Napoule, France, 1987, Chateau de la Napoule, 88, Chateau de la Napoule, 90; guest lectr., China, 89, China, 96, Japan, 89, Japan, 96. Say What I Am, 1989, Relearning the Dark, 1991, Doers of the Word, 1995, portrait commn., Sandra Day O'Connor, Va. Gov. Gaston Caperton, George Calvert, 1st Lord Baltimore, Edward Villela. Bd. dirs. Washington Project Arts/Corcoran Mus., 1994—2000, v.p., 1995—; bd. dirs. Smith Farm. Mem.: Corcoran Faculty Assn. (pres. 1988—89), Washington Women's Forum, Internat. Women's Forum. Avocations: equitation, skiing. Office: Corcoran Coll Art and Design 1801 35th St NW Washington DC 20007-2211 E-mail: apolan@aol.com.

POLAN, MARY LAKE, obstetrics and gynecology educator; b. Las Vegas, N.Mex., July 17, 1943; Student, Smith Coll., Paris, 1963—64; BA cum laude, Conn. Coll., 1965; PhD in Biophysics and Biochemistry, Yale U., 1970, MD, 1975. Diplomate Am. Bd. Ob-Gyn., Am. Bd. Reproductive Endocrinology, Nat. Bd. Med. Examiners. Postdoctoral fellow dept. biology, NIH postdoctoral fellow Yale U., New Haven, 1970—72, resident dept. ob-gyn. Sch. Medicine, 1975—78, fellow in oncology, then fellow in endocrinology-infertility, 1978—80, asst. instr., then lectr. molecular biophysics-biochemistry, 1970—72, instr., then asst. prof. ob-gyn., 1978—79, 1980—85, assoc. prof., 1985—90; clin. clk. in ob-gyn. and pediat. Radcliffe Infirmary, Oxford (Eng.) U. Med. Sch., 1974; instr. Pahlavi U., Shiraz, Iran, 1978; Katharine Dexter McCormick and Stanley McCormick Meml. prof. Stanford (Calif.) Sch. Medicine, 1990—, chmn. dept. gynecology and obstetrics, 1990—. Vis. prof. Hunan Med. Coll., Changsha, China, 1986; mem. med. bd. Yale-China Assn., 1987—90; liaison com. on ethics in modern world Conn. Coll., New London, 1988—90; mem. med. adv. bd. Ova-Med Corp., Palo Alto, Calif., 1992—95, Vivus, Menlo Park, Calif., 1993—; bd. dirs. Metra Biosys., Mountain View, Quidel, San Diego, Am. Home Products, Madison, NJ, 1994—; mem. reproductive endocrinology study sect. NIH, 1989—90, co-chmn. task force on opportunities for rsch. on woman's health, 1991. Author: Second Seed, 1987; guest editor: Seminars in Reproductive Endocrinology, 1984, Infertility and Reproductive Medicine Clinics of North America: GnRH Analogues, Vol. 4, 1993; editor, with DeCherney: Surgery in Reproductive Endocrinology, 1987;; editor: (with DeCherney, S. Boyers and R. Lee) Decision Making in Infertility; ad hoc reviewer: Jour. Clin. Endocrinology and Metabolism, Fertility and Sterility, Ob-Gyn., others; contbr. chapters to books, articles to med. jours. Fellow, NSRA, 1981—82; grantee, NIRA, 1982—85, HD, 1985—90, NRSA, 1987—88, Johnson & Johnson, 1993—96; scholar, Assn. Acad. Health Ctrs., 1993—96. Fellow: ACOG (PROLOG task force for reproductive endocrinology and infertility 1988—89, rep. to CREOG coun. 1994—97); mem.: Bay Area Reproductive Endocrine Soc., San Francisco Gynecologic Soc., Inst. Medicine (com. on rsch. capabilities of acad. depts. ob-gyn. 1990—91, bd. on health scis. policy 1992—96), Am. Gynecologic and Obstetric Soc., Soc. for Reproductive Endocrinologists, Soc. for Gynecologic Investigation, Am. Fertility Soc., Phi Beta Kappa. Home: 4251 Manuela Ct Palo Alto CA 94306-3731 Office: Stanford U Sch Medicine Dept Gyn OB 300 Pasteur Dr Stanford CA 94305-5317

POLAND, ALISON, artist; Studied, U. Md. Instr. The Corcoran Coll. Art and Design; arch. Bozzuto Homes, Md. Participant 9/11 meml. competition. Featured in The Corcoran Gallery of Art, The Smithsonian, MD Pub. TV, US Army Corps of Engineers. Mem.: US Green Bldg. Coun., Am. Inst. Architects, Urban Land Inst. Office: Bozzuto & Associates 7850 Walker Dr Ste 400 Greenbelt MD 20770 Office Phone: 301-220-0100.*

POLAND, MICHELLE LIND, medical, surgical, and critical care nurse; b. Wheeling, W.Va., Apr. 5, 1956; d. Edwin Ray and Mona Markeeta (Miller) P. Diploma, Belmont Tech. Coll., St. Clairsville, Ohio, 1976, ADN, 1982; BSN, Wheeling Jesuit Coll., 1990, MSN, 1996. Cert. critical care nurse, advanced cardiac life support, pediatric advanced cardiac life support. Staff nurse Peterson Hosp., Wheeling, 1976-81; staff nurse ICU/CCU, instr. nursing edn. Wheeling Hosp., 1982-96, cardiac echo sonographer, 2002—; office nurse Ryncarz Pulmonary Care, Inc., 2002—; cardiac sonographer in cardiac neurovascular unit Wheeling Hosp., 2002—. Adj. nursing instr. Wheeling Jesuit U., 1997—; instr. nursing edn. CPR. Recipient Glorium award. Mem.: AACN, ANA, Sigma Theta Tau (Omicron Mu chpt.), Alpha Sigma Nu. Methodist. Home: 61 Schuberts Ln Wheeling WV 26003-4621

POLASCIK, MARY ANN, ophthalmologist; b. Elkhorn, W.Va., Dec. 28, 1940; d. Michael and Elizabeth (Halko) Polascik; m. Joseph Elie, Oct. 2, 1973; 1 dau., Laura Elizabeth Polascik Jr. BA, Rutgers U., 1967; MD, Pritzker Sch. Medicine, 1971. Jr. pharmacologist Ciba Pharm Co., Summit, NJ, 1961-67; intern Billings Hosp., Chgo., 1971-72; resident in ophthalmology U. Chgo. Hosp., 1972-75; practice medicine specializing in ophthalmology Dixon, Ill., 1975—. Pres. McNichols Clinic, Ltd.; cons. ophthalmology, Jack Mabley Devel. Ctr., 1976-93; mem. staff Katherine Shaw Bethea Hosp. Bd. dirs. Sinnossippi Mental Health Ctr., 1977-82, Dixon Cmty. Trust Mental Health Ctr., 1989—. Mem. Am. Acad. Ophthalmology, Alpha Sigma Lambda, Galena Territory Club. Roman Catholic. Office: 1700 S Galena Ave Dixon IL 61021-9695

POLASKI, ANNE SPENCER, lawyer; b. Pittsfield, Mass., Nov. 13, 1952; d. John Harold and Marjorie Ruth (Hackett) Spencer; m. James Joseph Polaski, Sept. 14, 1985. BA in Psychology, Allegheny Coll., 1974; MSW, U. Pa., 1976; JD, George Washington U., 1979. Bar: D.C. 1979, U.S. Dist. Ct. (D.C. dist.) 1980, U.S. Ct. Appeals (D.C. cir.) 1980, Ill. 1982, U.S. Dist. Ct. (no. dist.) Ill. 1982, U.S. Ct. Appeals (7th cir.) 1982. Law clk. to assoc. judge D.C. Ct., Washington, 1979-80; trial atty. Commodity Futures Trading Commn., Chgo., 1980-84, sr. trial atty., 1984, dep. regional counsel, 1984-88; assoc. Gottlieb and Schwartz, Chgo., 1988-91; staff atty. Chgo. Bd. of Trade, 1991-92, sr. atty., 1992-94, asst. gen. counsel, 1994—. Mem. ABA, Chgo. Bar Assn. Office: Chgo Bd of Trade 141 W Jackson Blvd Chicago IL 60604-2992 E-mail: apolaski@cbot.com.

POLATTY, ROSE JACKSON, civic worker; b. Atlanta, Sept. 17, 1922; d. James Wilmot and Esther Ann (Sweeny) Jackson; m. George Junius Polatty,Nov. 27, 1942; children: George Junius, Robert Wilmot, Rose Crystal, Richard James. AB in Journalism, U. Ga., 1943; postgrad., Oglethorpe U., 1962-63, Ga. State U., 1963. Active U. Ga. Alumni Soc.; pres. Class of 1943 Alumni, 1948-58; bd. mgr., 1966-69; v.p., 1971-73; chmn. seminar, 1971; exec. sec. Atlanta Boy Choir, 1968-69; bd. dirs. Atlanta Arts Coun., 1968-69; adv. com. Kennesaw Coll. on Wheels, 1974-78; bicentennial chmn. City of Roswell (Ga.), 1975-76; sec. hist. preservation commn., 1978-82; chmn., 1983-84. Active Ga. Trust Hist. Preservation, Ga. Conservancy. Mem. adminstrv. bd., chmn. altar guild, Roswell United Meth. Ch., 1977-89. Recipient Recognition award Nat. 4-H Alumni, 1959, Svc. award City of Roswell, 1976, Cmty. Svc. award Roswell Optimist Club, 1977, Roswell Jaycees Leadership award, 1977, Cmty. Svc. award Zion Bapt. Ch., 1977, Vol. award Friends Roswell Libr., 2000. Mem. Roswell Hist. Soc. (charter 1971), Atlanta Symphony Assocs., Colonial Dames XVII Century (charter Nicholas Wallingford chpt. 1979, v.p. 1980-81, pres. 1982-83), U.D.C. (Phillips Legion chpt.), Altanta Audubon Soc., High Mus. Art (charter), PEO (chpt. AA, Ga., charter 1977), DAR (Joseph Habersham chpt.), Roswell Women's (charter 1948, pres. 1966-68), Roswell Garden (charter 1951, pres. 1975-77), N. Fulton Coun. Garden Clubs (charter 1975, pres. 1975-77), Kappa Delta,Delta Omicron, Phi Beta Kappa, Phi Kappa Phi, Kappa Delta Pi. Home: 889 Mimosa Blvd Roswell GA 30075-4436 Personal E-mail: rosejp@aol.com.

POLCE-LYNCH, MARY ELISE, psychologist; b. Geneva, N.Y. d. Anthony Henry and Esther Baumgartner Polce; m. John R. Lynch, Dec. 18, 1987; children: Rachel A., Morgan E. BA in Spl. Edn., Marywood Coll., 1980; MA in Counseling Psychology, James Madison U., 1985, EdS, 1987; PhD in Developmental Psychology, Va. Commonwealth U., 1996. Cert. tchr. spl. edn. Va., 1980, sch. psychologist Va., 1987, lic. profl. counselor Va., 1990. Tchr., coach Frederick County Pub. Schs., Winchester, Va., 1980—85, intern, 1985—87; counselor, clinician Hanover County Cmty. Svcs., Ashland, Va., 1988—2000; asst. dir. counseling Randolph-Macon Coll., Ashland, 2001—. Vis. asst. prof. Randolph-Macon Coll., 1996—, dir. Women's Resource Ctr., 1996, 2000; adv. bd. Black Heritage Soc., Ashland, 1999—2002, Parenting Boys mag., Richmond, Va., 2005—, Journeys mag., 2006; lectr. in field; presenter in field. Author: Boytalk, 2002, Nothing Left Unsaid, 2006; contbr. articles to profl. jours. Vol. Shelter for Abused Women, Winchester, Va., 1983—86; coord. bldg. bridges Cmty. Race Rels. Group, Ashland, 1997—99; coord. children's liturgy St. Ann's Ch., Ashland, 1992—2002; treas. Ashland Swim Team Bd., Ashland, 2004—; women's adv. commn. Richmond Cath. Diocese, Va., 2005—. Recipient John Hill Dissertation award, Va. Commonwealth U., 1996; fellow, James Madison U., 1985—87; Jesse Hibbs Academic scholar, Va. Commonwealth U., 1995. Mem.: APA, Am. Pastoral Counselors, Omicron Delta Kappa (leadership soc. 2006—). Avocations: swimming, running, bicycling, nature. Home: 309 West Francis St Ashland VA 23005 Office: Randolph Macon Coll Ashland VA 23005 Office Phone: 804-752-7270. Business E-Mail: mpolce@rmc.edu.

POLEMITOU, OLGA ANDREA, accountant; b. Nicosia, Cyprus, June 28, 1950; d. Takis and Georgia (Nicolaou) Chrysanthou. BA with honors, U. London, 1971; PhD, Ind. U., Bloomington, 1981. CPA Ind. Asst. productivity officer Internat. Labor Office/Cyprus Productivity Ctr., Nicosia, 1971-74; cons. Arthur Young & Co., N.Y.C., 1981; mgr. Coopers & Lybrand, Newark, 1981-83; dir. Bell Atlantic, Reston, Va., 1983-97; v.p. corp. auditing Columbia Energy Group, Herndon, 1997—2000; pres., CEO Aristion, Inc., Reston, Va., 2000—. Chairperson adv. coun. Extended Day Care Cmty. Edn., West Windsor Plainsboro, NJ, 1987—88. Contbr. articles to profl. jours. Bus. cons. project bus. Jr. Achievement, Indpls., 1984—85. Mem.: AICPAs, NAFE, Princeton Network Profl. Women, Va. Soc. CPAs, N.J. Soc. CPAs (sec. mem. in industry com.), Ind. CPA Soc., Nat. Trust Hist. Preservation. Avocations: water-skiing, tennis. Home: PO Box 2744 Reston VA 20195-0744 Office: 11921 Freedom Dr Ste 550 Reston VA 20190 Business E-Mail: opolemitou@aristion.com.

POLENZ, JOANNA MAGDA, psychiatrist; b. Cracow, Poland, Oct. 20, 1936; came to U.S., 1961; d. Mieczyslaw and Nusia (Goldberger) Uberall; m. Daryl Louis Polenz, July 8, 1962 (div. 1991); children: Teresa Ann, Daryl Philip, Elizabeth Sophia. MD, U. Sydney, Australia, 1960; MPH, Columbia U., 1992. Diplomate Am. Bd. Psychiatry and Neurology. Intern Bklyn. Hosp., 1961-62; resident in psychiatry Mt. Sinai Med. Ctr., N.Y.C., 1962-65, ednl. fellow, 1965-66, rsch. assoc., 1966-67; med. dir. Tappan Zee clin. Phelps Meml. Hosp., Tarrytown, NY, 1968-71, dir. dept. psychiatry, 1972-77; sr. attending psychiatrist Meml. Hosp. Ctr., 1972-93; pvt. practice Briarcliff Manor, NY, 1971-91; physician Joint Commn. Accreditation of Healthcare Orgns., Oakbrook Terrace, Ill., 1993—2004; pres. Sch. of Health.com, N.Y.C., 1998—; assoc. dir. adminstrn. N.Y.C. Health and Hosp. Corp., 2004—. Lectr. in field. Author: In Defense of Marriage, 1981; (with other) Test Your Marriage IQ, 1984, Test Your Success IQ, 1985, The Last Sick Generation, 2000; contbr. articles to profl. jours.; numerous TV appearances including Phil Donahue, 1988, Oprah Winfrey 1984. Grant Found. grantee, 1970. Fellow Am. Psychiat. Assn. (disting. life); mem. AMA, Westchester Psychiat. Assn. (sec. 1982-85, chmn. fellowship com. 1989-98). Avocations: travel, international affairs. Home and Office: SchoolofHealth.com 123 E 75th St Ste 10B New York NY 10021 Office Phone: 212-426-5605. Office Fax: 212-828-2507. Business E-Mail: jpolenz@nyc.rr.com.

POLESHUK, ALICIA L., alcohol/drug abuse services professional; d. William and Nina Poleshuk. BA with honors, Montclair State U., 1995; MSW, Rutgers U., 1998; MS, postgrad., Seton Hall U., 2002—. Lic. social worker N.J. Recreational therapist vol. Bergen Regional Med. Ctr., Paramus, NJ, 1996—97; social work intern Palisades Learning Ctr., Paramus, NJ, 1996—97; student assistance counselor Council on Alcoholism and Drug Abuse of Bergen, Inc., Hackensack, NJ, 1997—; therapist Pascack Mental Health Ctr., Park Ridge, NJ, 1999—. Scholar Hugh McGee scholar, Hackensack U. Med. Ctr., 1995. Mem.: NASW, Marriage and Family Student Assn. (exec. bd. dirs. 2001—), Am. Assn. Marriage and Family Therapy, Am. Psychol. Assn., End DWI. Roman Catholic. Personal E-mail: apoleshuk@aol.com.

POLETO, MARY MARGARET, orthopedic nurse; b. Troy, N.Y., May 4, 1959; d. Vincent P. and Marianne P. BSN, Russell Sage Coll., 1981. Cert. Orthopedic Nurse. Staff nurse Albany (N.Y.) Med. Ctr., 1981-84, asst. nurse mgr., 1984-91, staff nurse, 1991—. Vol. post anesthesia care nurse Albany Plasticare Internat., Dominican Republic. Mem. Nat. Assn. Orthopedic Nurses, Capital Dist. Nurses Assn., Am. Assn. Spinal Cord Injured Nurses, Sigma Theta Tau. Republican. Roman Catholic. Avocations: reading, decorative painting. Office: Albany Med Ctr Hosp New Scotland Ave Albany NY 12208-3491 Home: 54 Patroon Pt Rensselaer NY 12144-8438

POLEVOY, NANCY TALLY, lawyer, social worker, genealogist; b. N.Y.C., May 27, 1944; d. Charles H. and Bernice M. (Gang) Tally; m. Martin D. Polevoy, Mar. 19, 1967; children: Jason Tally, John Gerald. Student, Mt. Holyoke Coll., 1962—64; BA, Barnard Coll., 1966; MSW, Columbia U., 1968, JD, 1986. Bar: N.Y. 1987. Caseworker unmarried mothers' svc. Louise Wise Svcs., N.Y.C., 1967, caseworker adoption dept., 1969-71; caseworker Youth Consultation Svc., N.Y.C., 1968-69; asst. rsch. scientist, psychiat. social worker NYU Med. ctr., N.Y.C., 1973-81; adv. ct. apptd. spl. advs. Manhattan Family Ct., N.Y.C., 1981-82; cons. social work, 1981-86; matrimonial assoc. Ballon, Stoll & Itzler, 1987, Herzfeld & Rubin, P.C., 1987-88; practice NYC. Contbr. articles to profl. jours. Mem. parents' adv. bd. Riverdale Country Sch., 1988—93; mem. outreach bd. Manhattan divsn. United Jewish Appeal Fedn., 1990—94, exec. bd. Manhattan divsn., 1992—94, mem. met. campaign cabinet, 1994—95, mem. task force aging, 2004—; trustee Jewish Assn. Svcs. to Aged, 1996—, v.p., 1999—2003; bd. dirs. Ctr. Jewish History, 1996—; archives com. Ctrl. Synagogue, 1994—2005, chair, 1994—2005; trustee Am. Jewish Hist. Soc., 1992—, asst. treas., 1995—98, v.p., 1998—2003, 2005—. Recipient French Govt. prize, 1963, honor for lifetime cmty. svc., United Jewish Appeal Fedn. N.Y., 2003. Mem.: NASW, Acad. Cert. Social Workers, N.Y. State Bar Assn., Assn. Bar City of N.Y., Barnard Coll. Alumni Assn. (v.p. 1966, class pres. 1966 1996—). Home and Office: 1155 Park Ave New York NY 10128-1209

POLFLIET, SARAH JEAN, physician; b. Austin, Minn., July 4, 1975; d. Richard John and Charlotte Bertha Polfliet. BS in Physiology, U. Calif., Santa Barbara, 1998; MD, U. Va., Charlottesville, 2002; MD in Psychiat., Law, U. Calif., San Francisco, 2006. DEA Certification Med. Bd. of Calif., 2003, lic. MD Med. Bd. of Calif., 2003. Sec. in cmty. rels. U. Calif., 1997—98, asst. instr. of biology lab., 1998, resident physician San Francisco, 2002—; pvt. tutor for nursing student Coll. New Rochelle, Sch. of Nursing, NY, 1998—2001; fin. asst. and sales Isla Vista Bookstore, Isla Vista, Calif., 1994—96; physician Schuman-Liles Cmty. Psychiatry Clinic, Oakland, Calif., 2003—; pvt. practice in psychiat. and psychopharmacology, San Francisco, 2006—; chief resident intensive svcs. Langley Ptnr. Psychiat. Inst., 2006. Rsch. asst. U. Va., Dept. of Psychiatry, Charlottesville, Va., 1999; co-leader for long-term women's depression group U. of Calif., San Francisco, San Francisco, 2004—; psychiatry physician, women's high-risk obstetric clinic San Francisco Gen. Hosp., 2004—05; psychiatry physician, women's mood and hormone clinic U. of Calif., 2004—05, chief of intensive services, langley porter psychiat. inst., 2005—, jr. attending, 2005—; rsch. co-investigator U. of Calif. Dept. of Psychiatry, 2005—. Contbr. numerous articles and presentation to profl. jours. and confs.; author: Where Do Seagulls Go at Night, 2003. Vol. for cmty. outreach program St. Thomas Aquinas Ch., Charlottesville, Va., 1998—2002; vol. Magic Cir. Protective Shelters, Charlottesville, Va., 1999—2002; med. student selection com. U. of Va., Sch. of Medicine, 2001—02; vol. spkr. Med. Youth Soc., San Francisco, 2003—06; vol. St. Elizabeth's Ho. for Battered Women, 2006—. Recipient Julius R. Krevans award for Clin. Excellence, U. Calif., San Francisco, 2003, Dean's List, U. Calif., Santa Barbara, 1993—98, U. Va., Sch. of Medicine, 1998—2002, Pathology Honors, 1999—2000, Edwin Alston award, U. Calif. San Francisco Psychiatric Residency Program, 2006; Bowman's scholarship, U. Va., Sch. of Medicine, 1999—2000, Forensic Fellow, U. Calif. San Francisco, Psychiatry and Law Program, 2006—. Fellow: Am. Psychiat. Assn. (hon.); mem.: Am. Assn. Psychiat. and Law, U. Calif., Santa Barbara, Alumni Assn. (hon.), Alpha Omega Alpha (hon.), Assn. Women Psychiatrists (hon.), No. Calif. Psychiat. Assn. (hon.), U. Va., Sch. of Medicine, Alumni Assn. (hon.). Achievements include research in evaluating training of psychiatry residents about neuroleptic medications; rural suicide outreach programs in Virginia, including composition of suicide outreach survey and meta-analysis of data to further assist tele-psychiatry program. Avocations: jogging, hiking, poetry, writing children's books.

POLHAMUS, BARBARA, nutritionist, educator; d. Helen and Leslie Polhamus. PhD, MPH, U. N.C., Chapel Hill, 1991—97. Registered dietitian Am. Dietetic Assn., 1982. Nutrition dir. Dorchester Ho. Multi-Svc. Ctr., Mass., 1982—84; nutrition dir., maternal and child health Mass. Dept. Pub. Health, Boston, 1984—91; rsch. assoc. U. N.C., Chapel Hill, 1998—2000; nutritionist CDC, Nat. Ctr. for Chronic Disease Prevention and Health Promotion, Divsn. Nutrition and Phys. Activity, Atlanta, 2000—. Tech. cons., Ukraine micronutrient survey CDC, Atlanta, 2002. Contbr. chapters to books, articles to profl. jours., sci. material for web sites. Recipient award of Excellence Pub. Health Tng. and Nutrition Team award, 2005; fellow, Dannon Inst., 1998; grantee, Inst. Nutrition, 1994. Mem.: APHA (elected sect. mem. 2002—04). Liberal. Avocations: yoga, hiking, travel. Office: CDC 4770 Buford Hwy NE MS K-25 Atlanta GA 30341 Personal E-mail: bfp9@cdc.gov.

POLIMENI, REBECCA H., special education educator; b. Albertson, NY, Dec. 13, 1973; d. Vincent and Joan M Polimeni. BA in psychology, Hofstra U., 1995—97; MA in spl. edn., Columbia U., 1999—2001. Tchr. asst. Devel. Disabilities Inst., Young Autism Program, Smithtown, NY, 1997—98; home tutor and parent trainer Pvt. Practice, NY, 1997—; tchr. cons. Autism Help Ctr., Medford, NY, 2000—01; program coord. Devel. Disabilities Inst., Young Autism Program, Ronkonkoma, NY, 2001—03; behavior cons. LI Devel. Cons., Lake Grove, NY, 2003—; behavior consultation Pvt. Practice, NY, 2004—. Staff devel. spkr. LI Devel. Consulting and Pvt. Practice, 2003—. Recipient Adele Leonard Endowed Prize for excellence in Linguistics, Hofstra U., 1997, Provost's Scholar, Hosftra U., 1997, Dean's List, Hofstra U., 1995—97; Academic scholarship, 1995. Mem.: Counsel for Exceptional Children, Psi Chi Nat. Honor Soc., Golden Key Nat. Honor Soc. Independent. Avocations: travel, writing, music, outdoor activities, exercise. Personal E-mail: autad@cs.com.

POLIN, JANE L., foundation official; b. NYC, Sept. 30, 1958; BA, Wesleyan U., Middletown, Conn., 1980; MBA, Columbia U., 1988. Asst. dir. ann. giving Wesleyan U., 1980—82; centennial fund assoc. Met. Opera Assn., N.Y.C., 1982—84; devel. officer Columbia U., N.Y.C., 1984—88; program mgr., comptr. GE Fund, Fairfield, Conn., 1988—99; v.p. cmty. devel. and corp. affairs Sperry & Hutchinson, Inc., 1999—2000, philanthropic advisor, 2001—; bd. dirs. Fred Friendly Seminars, 2005—. Panelist arts-in-edn. Nat. Endowment for Arts, Washington, 1989—90, 1994—95, NEH, 1997; adv. bd. mem. ARC, 1991—99, United Way Am., 1991—99, Inst. for Internat. Econs., 1995—99, Young Audiences, N.Y.C., 1991—2000, mem. Advt. Coun., 1998—2003; judge Frances Hesselbein Cmty. Innovation Fellows Program, 2001—02, Peter F. Drucker Award for Nonprofit Innovation, 1996—2000. Mem.: Alpha Delta Phi. Home and Office: 67 Riverside Dr Apt 7D New York NY 10024-6136 Fax: 212-873-1568. Personal E-mail: janepolin@aol.com.

POLINSKY, JANET NABOICHECK, retired state official, retired state legislator; b. Hartford, Conn., Dec. 6, 1930; d. Louis H. and Lillian S. Naboicheck; m. Hubert N. Polinsky, Sept. 21, 1958 (div.); children: Gerald, David, Beth. BA, U. Conn., 1953; postgrad., Harvard Bus. Sch., 1954. Mem. Waterford 2d Charter Commn. (Conn.), 1967-68, Waterford Conservation Commn., 1968-69; Waterford rep. Town Meeting, 1969-71, S.E. Conn. Regional Planning Agy., 1971-73; mem. Waterford Planning and Zoning Commn., 1970-76, chmn., 1973-76; mem. Waterford Dem. Town Com., 1976-92. Del. State Dem. Conv., 1976, 78, 80, 82, 84, 86, 90, 92; mem. Conn. Ho. of Reps. from 38th Dist., 1977-82, asst. majority leader, 1981-83, chmn. appropriations com., 1983-85, 87-89, ranking mem., 1985-87, minority whip, 1985-86, dep. spkr., 1989-92; dep. commr. dept. adminstrv. svcs. State of Conn., 1993-94, chmn., 1994-95, asst. sec. of state, 1995, commr. utilities ctrl. auth., 1995-97. Trustee Eugene O'Neill Meml. Theatre Ctr., 1973-76, 81-92; corporator Lawrence and Meml. Hosps., 1987-88; mem. New Eng. Bd. Higher Edn., 1981-83; mem. fiscal affairs com. Eastern Conf. Coun. State Govts., 1983-88; mem. Limoge Village Bd., 2000-02; sec. Cascades Master bd., 2000—, sec., 2002—. Named Woman of Yr., Waterford Jr. Women's Club, 1977, Nehantic Women's Bus. and Profl. Club, 1979, Legislator of Yr., Conn. Libr. Assn., 1980. Mem. Order of Women Legislators, Delta Kappa Gamma (hon.). Home: 7141 Haviland Cir Boynton Beach FL 33437-6463 Personal E-mail: naboi1@aol.com.

POLITE, CARLENE HATCHER, writer, educator; b. Detroit; d. John and Lillian Hatcher; m. James S. Patrick, July 21, 2003; children from previous marriage: Glynda Morton, Lila Ashaki. Student, Martha Graham Sch. Dance, N.Y.C., 1952-56; diploma, Acad. Leonardo da Vinci, Rome, 1980. Dancer, student Martha Graham Sch., N.Y.C., 1952-56; dancer Alvin Ailey Dance Co., N.Y.C., 1957-58, Edith Stephen Co., N.Y.C., 1958; dancer, actress Vanguard Playhouse, Detroit, 1960-62; prof. English SUNY, Buffalo, 1971—2000, chair dept. Am. Studies, 1981, prof. emerita, 2000. Tchr. Golden Dragon Kung Fu Acad., 1974-75, Himalayan Inst. Yoga, 1980-82; panelist NEA, Washington, 1981, N.Y. State Coun. Arts, N.Y.C., 1982, N.Y. Found. Arts, 1983, Seattle Arts in Pub. Places, 1989. Author: The Flagellants, 1966, Paris edit., 1967, N.Y. edit., 1968, also other European edits. (Pulitzer prize nominee, 1967, NEA grant, 1967, Rockefeller grant, 1968), Sister X and The Victims of Foul Play, 1975. Coord. Walk to Freedom with Martin Luther King, Detroit, 1963; del., participant UN-Non-Govtl.Orgns. 4th World Conf. on Women, Beijing, 1995. Recipient numerous nat. and internat. awards as artist and educator; invited 1st Ann. Conf. African Presence, Paris, 1991, Internat. Educators and Writers Oxford U., 1997. Avocation: yoga.

POLITE, EVELYN C., retired elementary school educator, evangelist; b. Pineland, SC, Dec. 25, 1937; d. Martin and Mary Brantley Coger; m. Horace Polite, Jan. 1, 1958 (dec. Jan. 1987); children: Horace Lenton, Tracy Polite Floyd. BS, Allen U., 1960; M in Elem. Edn., Armstrong-Savannah (Ga.) State U., 1976; cert. specialist of arts in theology, Zoe U., Jacksonville, Fla., 2000; PhD in Christian Counseling, Zoe U., 2001. Tchr. math. Beaufort County Bd. Edn., Bluffton, SC, 1960—61, Florence County Bd. Edn., Florence, SC, 1961—63, Jasper County Bd. Edn., Ridgeland, SC, 1963—64, 1991—92, Savannah Pub. Schs., 1964—90; math. tutor Dept. Family and Children, Savannah, 1992—94; ret., 1994. Test-item writer Ednl. Testing Svc., Princeton, NJ, 1990; dir. Widows Harvest Ministries, Savannah, Ga.; care and counseling min. Coastal Cathedral Ch. of God. Pres. 42d St Civic Club, Savannah, 2000—03; exec. v.p. Cuyler-Brownsville Neighborhood Orgn., Savannah, 2001—02. Recipient Outstanding Tchr. award, Math.-Sci. Roundtable, Atlanta, 1990. Mem. Ch. Of God. Avocations: world missions, travel, physical fitness, reading Christian literature. Office: Coastal Cathedral Ch of God 2208 E DeRenne Ave Savannah GA 31406 Home: 33 Wild Heron Villas Rd Savannah GA 31419-8981 Office Phone: 912-354-5225. Personal E-mail: evelyn33@bellsouth.net.

POLITE, KAREN E., humanities educator; d. Henry and Rosa Mae Hinton; m. Nelson M. Polite, Jr., Sept. 12, 1998. BA in Social Work, Millersville U., Lancaster, 1995; MSW, U. Pa., Phila., 1997. LCSW Pa. Counselor Eagleville Hosp., Pa., 1995, Wedge Med. Ctr., Phila., 1996; youth worker Philhaven, Mt. Gretna, Pa., 1997—98; counselor Aspen Quality Care, Harrisburg, Pa., 1998—99; program coord. Housing Devel. Corp., Lancaster, 1998; counselor HSA Counseling, Lancaster, 1998—99; assoc. prof. human svcs. Harrisburg Area C.C., Lancaster, 1997—. Adv. bd. Millersville U. Sch. Social Work, Lancaster, 2001—, Family Self-Sufficiency, Lancaster, 2005—. Editor: Sociology: Introduction, 2002. Mem.: Innervisions Inst. for Spiritual Devel. Avocations: exercise, writing. Office: Harrisburg Area Community College 1641 Old Philadelphia Pike Lancaster PA 17602

POLITE, LETTIE WILSON, retired elementary school educator, retired school librarian; b. Asheville, NC, Jan. 5, 1930; d. Lester Vernon and Argatha Foster Wilson; m. Harold Malverse Polite (dec.); children: Harold M. II, Joyce P. Carson. BS in Math. and Social Studies, NC Coll. (now NC Ctrl. U.), Durham, 1951; cert. in libr. sci., Allen U., Columbia, SC, 1955; MEd, NC U., Cullowhee, 1981. Tchr. libr. Asheville (NC) City Schs., 1953—64, tchr. 7th grade. math., 1965—72, tchr. 7th grade math., 8th grade sci., 1972—73, tchr. 6th grade math., 1973—91, tchr. 7th grade math., 1991—92; libr. St. Martin De Porres Sch., New Haven, 1964—65. Tutor, mentor Delta Ho. of Asheville, 1982—; co-chair Uniting for Racial Justice, Women's Internat. League Peace and Freedom, Asheville, 1994—2005; del. Non-Governmental Orgn./World Conf. on Racism, Durban, South Africa, 2001; vol. Reuter Ctr. for Creative Retirement, 1998—; 1st v.p., asst. treas. Asheville Alumnae of Delta Ho., Inc., 1982—; adv. bd. African Am. Affairs Ministry Diocese of Charlotte, NC, 1972—; eucharistic min., mem. choir, pastoral coun., Cath. Daus. of Am. Ct. 412 Basilica of St. Lawrence, Asheville. Recipient cert. of excellence, Leadership Asheville Forum, 2004, NC Black Cath. Recognition award, Diocese of Charlotte, 2004. Mem.: NAACP, Nat. Coun. Negro Women, Links, Delta Sigma Theta. Democrat. Avocations: reading, crafts, travel, singing. Home: 33 Erskine Ave Asheville NC 28801

POLK, EMILY DESPAIN, conservationist, writer; b. Aberdeen, Wash., July 6, 1910; d. John Dove Isaacs and Constance Ashley (DeSpain) Van Norden; m. Benjamin Kauffman Polk, Aug. 23, 1946. Student, U. Oreg., 1928-29, Oreg. State U., 1929-31, Rudolph Shaefer Sch. of Art, San Francisco, 1931-32. Head display & design V.C. Morris, San Francisco, 1931-37; founder, CEO DeSpain Design, L.A. and N.Y.C., 1937-44, 63-64; ornamental & interior design arch. Benjamin Polk Arch., Calcutta and New Delhi, 1952-63; owner Galeria de San Luis, San Luis Obispo, Calif., 1966-68; founder, CEO Small Wilderness Area Preservation, Los Osos, Calif., 1969-79. Author: Poems and Epigrams, 1959 (All India Book award 1959), Delhi Old and New, 1963, A Wild Part of California, 1991, Rockpool Trilogy, 1995, Shadows: A Giant Tree, Vols. I-II, 1995-96, A Pilgrimage through Time, 1996, A Moment in the Mind, 1997, Invisible Thresholds, 1997, Poems for Drums and Woodwinds, 1999, Praises-Hymns Without Music, 2000, From Stress to Serenity, 2001, The Rustle of Leaves-New Poems, 2001; co-author: (with B. Polk) India Notebook, 1987, (with others) Sri Lanka Buddhist Shrines, 1991; editor (poetry): Calcuttan Magazine, 1961-63; contbr. articles to jours.; designer interior and exhibits Internat. Wool Secretariat, World Trade Fair, New Delhi, 1955; hon. interior designer Pres. of India, New Delhi, 1955, Maharanee of Tripura, Calcutta, India, 1962-63, King of Nepal, Kathmandu, 1962-63, Princess Pema Choki, Gantok, Sikkim, 1963; solo exhbns. paintings and montages India, 1963, U.S., 1963, 75, 89, 91, 98, 99, Eng., 1987, jewelry, U.S., 1948, fashion, India, 1955. Mem. coun. Nat. Mus. Women in the Arts, Washington, 1991-93; del., spkr. Pan Asian Cultural Conf., Calcutta, 1963, India House, N.Y., 1963, The Women's Club, 1964, AAUW, 1998. Recipient Kiwanis Citizenship Plaque Inscription, 1928, Golden Bear Conservation award Calif. Pks. and Recreation, Sacramento, 1972, Nat. Conservation award Am. Motors, 1972. Mem. Soc. Women Geographers (Calif. del., spkr. 50th Anniversary Celebrations 1972, Libr. of Congress Oral History Women of Achievement Program 1995), Small Wilderness Area Preservation, Calif. Hist. Soc., Calif. Oaks Found., Am. Women's Club (pres. 1962), Nat. Indian Assn. Women (pres.), English Speaking Union (bd. dirs.), Gyan Chakra Literary Gp. (founder).

POLK, GENE-ANN, retired pediatrician; b. Roselle, NJ, Oct. 3, 1926; d. Charles Carrington and Olive (Bond) Polk; m. Edwin Clay Horne, Aug. 23, 1952; children: Carol Horne Penn, Edwin Christian Horne. BA, Oberlin Coll., 1948; MD, Women's Med. Coll. Pa., 1952; MPH, Columbia U., 1968. Intern Sydenham Hosp., NYC, 1952—53; resident in pediat. Harlem Hosp., NYC, 1953—55; pvt. practice pediat. Englewood, NJ, 1959—68; dir. pediat. ambulatory care Columbia U./Harlem Hosp., NYC, 1968—77, acting dir. pediat., 1977—78, dir. ambulatory care svcs., 1978—88; prof. clin. pediat. Columbia U., NYC, 1988—94, prof. emerita clin. pediat., 1994; ret. Trustee Found. History of Women in Medicine, Phila., 2003—. Fellow: Am. Acad. Pediat.; mem.: AMA, Nat. Medicine Assn. Methodist. Avocations: gardening, travel, history. Home: 374 Miller Ave Englewood NJ 07631

POLK GITLIN, MIMI, film producer; Film prodr. Gitlin Prodns., LA. Prodr.(with Ridley Scott): (films) Thelma & Louise, 1991, The Browning Version, 1994, 1492: Conquest of Paradise, 1992, Monkey Trouble, 1994, White Squall, 1996, Clubland, 1998, Picking Up the Pieces, 1999, Trapped, 2002. Office: 12210 1/2 Nebraska Ave Los Angeles CA 90025-3620

POLLACK, BETTY GILLESPIE, retired health care services executive; b. Oak Park, Ill., Apr. 4, 1940; d. Leon H. and Elta F. Gillespie; m. David Pollack, Dec. 18, 1971; 1 son, Michael Alan. BA, Whittier Coll., 1962; MS, Columbia U., 1964. Cmty. organizer, Boston, 1964-66; faculty mem. Grad. Sch. Social Welfare, U. Calif., Berkeley, 1967-71; exec. dir. Calif. chpt. Nat. Assn. Social Workers, Millbrae, 1971-81; pres., CEO Vis. Nurse Assn., Santa Clara County, Calif., 1981-94; exec. dir. San Francisco Med. Soc., 1994—98, ret., 1998. Mem. exec. com. Assn. United Way Agencies, 1982-85, 91-93; chmn. bylaws commn. of San Mateo County Jr. Hockey Club, 1988-89. Mem. No. Calif. Soc. Assn. Execs. (sec.-treas. 1980-82, pres.-elect 1982-83, pres. 1983-84, program chmn. 1984-85, chmn. nominating com. 1985-86, chmn. publs. com. 1995), Peninsula Profl. Women's Network (sec. 1981-82, chmn. networking conf. 1981, pres. ednl. fund 1981-82), No. Calif. Coalition Vis. Nurse Assns. (v.p. 1983-85, pres. 1985, v.p. reorganized VNA Network No. Calif. 1993-94), Bay Area Profl. Women's Network (mem. newsletter com. 1980-81), Am. Soc. Assn. Execs., Peninsula Forum West, Rotary (San Jose chpt., chmn. program com. 1993-94, youth leadership com., internat. com. 1991-92, chmn. health programs subcom. 1992-94, co-chair Acad. Decathlon San Francisco chpt. 1996, mem. membership com., chmn. program com. 1997-98, bd. dirs. 1998-99), Automate RV Club (pres. 2003-2005), San Carlos Rotary Club. Democrat. Home: 316 Sycamore St San Carlos CA 94070-2020

POLLACK, JESSICA GLASS, lawyer; b. Bridgeport, Conn., June 29, 1964; d. MacEllis Kopel and Judith Wilson Glass; m. Russel Leon Pollack, Apr. 19, 1964; children: Nathaniel Bruce, Jason Henry. BA, Barnard Coll., 1986; JD, U. Chgo., 1990. Assoc. Shearman & Sterling, London, N.Y.C., 1990-94, White & Case, Budapest, N.Y.C., 1994-96; corp. counsel securities and fin. Colgate-Palmolive Co., N.Y.C., 1996—. Office: Colgate-Palmolive Co 300 Park Ave Fl 8 New York NY 10022-7499 Home: 215 E 95th St Apt 30k New York NY 10128-4088

POLLACK, LANA, state senator; b. Ludington, Mich., Oct. 11, 1942; d. Abbie and Genevieve (Siegel) Schoenberger; m. Henry Pollack, 1963; children: Sarah(dec.), John. BA, U. Mich., 1965, MA, 1970; postgrad., Am. U., 1976. Instr. Washtenaw CC, 1975—81; regional coord. gubernatorial campaign, 1981; mem. Mich. State Senate, 1983—. Sr. adminstr. John Howard Compound Sc, Zambia, 1970—71. Trustee Ann Arbor Bd. Edn., 1979—82; chmn. Ann Arbor Dem. Party, Mich., 1975—77; mgr. Campaign for State Senate, 1978, Campaign for 2d Congl. Dist., 1980; candidate for congress, 1988. Democrat. also: Senate House State Capitol Lansing MI 48909

POLLACK, MARSHA, secondary school educator; d. Harry and Rose Grunberg; m. Bertram Pollack, July 14, 1944; 1 child, Meredith Pollack-Richman. BA, Bklyn Coll., 1968, MS, 1973; Specialist Diploma in Adminstrn. and Supervision, Queens Coll., 2003. Cert. tchr. Nat. Bd. Profl. Tchg. Standards, 2001. Tchr. N.Y.C. Dept. of Edn., Bklyn. and Queens, 1968—2002, asst. prin. Queens, 2002—03, tchr./coach/staff devel., 2003—. L.E.A.D. tchr. N.Y.C. Dept. of Edn., 1998—2002, nat. staff devel., 2000; profl. devel. Jericho Mid. Sch., 2003; lesson plan-abstract evaluator Internat. Reading Assn., 2003—05. CAL grantee, Chase Manhattan, 2001. Mem.: Am. Fedn. Tchrs., Nat. Coun. Tchrs. English, Phi Delta Kappa, Internat. Reading Assn., ASCD. Avocations: law, educational research, writing. Office Phone: 718-831-4000. Office Fax: 718-831-4008. Personal E-mail: bjpmhp@aol.com. Business E-Mail: mpollac2@nycboe.net.

POLLACK, PHYLLIS ADDISON, ballerina; b. Victoria, B.C., Can., Aug. 31, 1919; d. Horace Nowell and Claire Melanie (Morris) Addison; m. Robert Seymour Pollack, Sept. 6, 1941 (dec. Jan. 2003); children: Robert Addison, Gwenda Joyce, Victoria Jean, Phyllis Anne. Student, SUNY, 1941—42, San Mateo Tech. Coll., 1958—62, U. Calif., San Francisco, 1962. Owner, dir. Phyllis Addison Dance Studio, Victoria, 1936—38; ballerina Taynton Dancers/Marcus Show Ballet Troupe, 1939—41, Ballet Russe, 1941; x-ray therapy tech. Meml. Hosp., N.Y.C., 1943—45; corr. fgn. telders. dept. N.C.B., N.Y.C., 1945—46; owner, designer Dancing Br. Studio, Sonoma, Calif., 1988—; flower arranger Sonoma Valley Mus. Art, 2000—. Floral designer J. Noblett Gallery, Sonoma, 1988—94, 2002—. Pres. PTA, 1955-56, 62-63; mem. Assistance League San Mateo, Calif., 1960-70. Mem. Metro Club, Bay Area Arrangers Guild, Ikebana Internat., Lifelong Learning Inst. Democrat. Unitarian Universalist. Avocations: dance, choreography, fashion modelling, photography, reading. Home: 384 Ave Barbera Sonoma CA 95476-8069

POLLACK, SONYA A., artist; b. Phila., Nov. 17, 1932; d. Herman and Helene (Spindor) Glick; m. Alfred Pollack; children: Harry, Kenneth, Helena, Daniel. Grad., Pa. Acad. Fine Arts, 1973; BFA, Phila. Coll. Art, 1975. One-woman shows include 3d Street Gallery, Phila., 1982, 84, Woodmere Art Mus., Phila., 1987, Phila. Art Alliance, 1991, 2003, Samuel S. Fleisher Art Meml., Phila., 1999, The X Gallery, 1995; represented in juried and invited group shows at Internat. House, Phila., 1972, Univ. Art League, Phila., 1973, Eastern Coll., Bryn Mawr, Pa., 1973, Vendo Nubes Gallery, Phila., 1973, Woodmere Gallery, Phila., 1975, 76, 79, 81, Civic Center Mus., Phila., 1975, 78, 81, Peale House, Phila., 1981, 84, 85, Allentown (Pa.) Mus., 1982, 84, 86, 94, Glassboro (N.J.) State Coll., 1982, Phila. Art Alliance, 1975, 82, 83, 91, Montgomery County Ct. House, Norristown, Pa., 1982, 83, 84, 3d Street Gallery, 1983, 84, 85, Lancaster (Pa.) Coummunity Gallery, 1984, West Chester (Pa.) State Coll., 1984, Noyes Mus., N.J., 1984, Lehigh (Pa.) U., 1984, Woodmere Art Mus., Phila., 1984, 86, 89, 94, Marion Locks Gallery, Phila., 1984, Pa. Acad. Fine Art Fellowship, Phila., 1984, Cheltenham (Pa.) Ann. Painting Exhbn., 1973, 85, 89, 92, 94, Hopkins House Gallery, N.J., 1987, Pa. Acad. Fine Arts, 1972, 87, Port of History Mus., Phila., 1988, Del. Art Mus., Wilmington, 1989, Muhlenberg Coll., Allentown, 1989, 90, The X Gallery, Nantucket, Mass., 1991, 92, 93, Long Beach Island Found. Arts and Scis., 1991, Berman Mus. Art Ursinus Coll., Collegeville, Pa., 1992, Morris Gallery, Phila., 1994, The X Gallery, Nantucket, Mass., 1999, The American Coll., Bryn Mawr, Pa., 2000, Main Line Art Ctr., N.Y.C., 2002, Satillite Gallery, Phila., Pa., 2003; group shows include: 80 Washington Square East Galleries, N.Y.C., N.Y., 1998, The X Gallery, Nantucket, Mass., 1999, The Am. Coll., Bryn Mawr, pa., 2000, numerous others; contbr. articles to profl. jours. Recipient Hunt award Artist Equity, Drake Press award Pa. Acad. Fine Arts, 1972, Gimble award Pa. Acad. Fine Arts, 1972, Alexander award Cheltenham Ctr. for Arts, 1989, Curator's Choice award Muhlenberg Coll., 1990, Tobeleah Wechsler award Cheltenham Ctr. for Arts, 1994. Mem. Pa. Acad. Fine Arts Fellowship (v.p. 1981-83, chairperson trust fund 1983-88, bd. dirs.). Home: 609 Fairview Rd Narberth PA 19072-1415

POLLACK, SYLVIA BYRNE, retired science educator, researcher, counselor; b. Ithaca, N.Y., Oct. 18, 1940; d. Raymond Tandy and Elsie Frances (Snell) Byrne; children: Seth Benjamin, Ethan David. BA, Syracuse U., 1962; PhD, U. Pa., 1967; MA, Antioch U., 1993. Instr. Women's Med. Coll. Pa., Phila., 1967-68; rsch. assoc. U. Wash., Seattle, 1968-73, rsch. asst. prof., 1973-77, rsch. assoc. prof., 1977-85, rsch. prof., 1985-97, counselor Sch. Nursing, 1993-99; ret., 1999. Asst. mem. Fred Hutchinson Cancer Ctr., Seattle, 1975-79, assoc. mem., 1979-81; mem. study sect. NIH, Washington, 1978-79, 83-85. Contbr. numerous articles to profl. jours.; reviewer for profl. jours. Recipient rsch. grants Am. Cancer Soc., 1969-79, Nat. Health Inst., 1973-97, Chugai Pharm. Co., Japan, 1985-91. Mem. ACA.

POLLAK, CHERYL L., federal judge; b. 1953; AB, Princeton U., 1975; JD, U. Chgo., 1978. Bar: N.Y. Law clk. to Hon. William H. Timbers, U.S. Ct. Appeals for 2d Circuit, 1978-79; assoc. David Polk & Wrdell, N.Y.C., 1979-86; with Office U.S. Atty. for Ea. Dist. N.Y., U.S. Dept. Justice, Bklyn., 1986-91, chief OCDETF unit, 1991-94, dept. chief criminal divsn., 1994-95, internat. and nat. security advisor, 1991-95; magistrate judge for ea. dist. N.Y., U.S. Magistrate Ct., Bklyn., 1995—. Mem.: Assn. Bar City of NY (mem. com. Women in the Legal Profession, litigation com., fed. courts com.), ABA. Office: 225 Cadman Plz E Room 538 Brooklyn NY 11201-1818 Business E-Mail: cheryl_pollak@nyed.uscourts.gov.

POLLAK, JOANNE ELIZABETH, lawyer; b. Cleve., July 16, 1944; m. Mark Pollak, Dec. 26, 1976; children: Elizabeth, Joshua, Rebecca, Benjamin, Jonathan. BA magna cum laude, Dickinson Coll., 1965; JD with honors, U. Md., 1976. Bar: Md. 1976. V.p., gen. counsel The Johns Hopkins Health System Corp./Johns Hopkins Medicine, Balt.; assoc., ptnr. and head of health care practice group Piper & Marbury Law Offices, 1976-93. Instr. bus. of medicine Sch. Medicine, Johns Hopkins U., Internat. Bus. Sch. Bd. dirs. Charlestown Cmty., Inc., 1992—, Mid-Atlantic affiliate Am. Heart Assn., 1991—2004, chair bd. dirs., 2002—03, chair rsch. for life campaign, 1999; mem. bd. advisors U. Md. Law Sch., 2002—. Named One of Md.'s Top Women, Daily Record, 1996, 98, 2000. Office: Johns Hopkins Health Sys Corp Broadway Rsch Bldg 733 North Broadway Ste 102 Baltimore MD 21205 Office Phone: 410-614-3322.

POLLARD, CONSTANCE JO, education educator; b. Belleville, Ill., Dec. 5, 1949; d. Kenneth E. and Mary M. Wyzard; m. Richard Ray Pollard, Jan. 19, 1973; children: Benjamin Jaret, Brittney Maryah. Cert. in bus. edn., U. Mont., 1988; BA in English, U. Wyo., 1972, MA in Edn., 1975; PhD in Adminstrn. Curriculum and Instrn., U. Nebr., 1990. Cert. tchr., Wyo., Alta., Can., B.C., Can., Mont. Tchr. reading clinic U. Wyo., Laramie, summers 1973-76; jr. high sch. tchr. reading Albany County Pub. Schs., Laramie, 1973-75; resource room tchr. Spirit River (Alta.) Sch. Div., 1975-76; elem. tchr. Fernie (B.C.) Pub. Schs., 1976-81; with pub. rels. dept. Overland Exploration Svcs., Denver, 1981-83; broker, owner, mgr. Exec. Realty, Kalispell, Mont., 1983-88; grad. asst. U. Nebr., Lincoln, 1988-89, instr., 1990; asst. prof. edn. U. Idaho, Moscow, 1990—93, prof. edn., 1993—. Reading cons. pub. schs., U.S. and Can., 1972-81; real estate cons. Rocky Bar O Ranch Corp., Northfork, Polebridge, Mont., 1986-88; fin. cons. Kalispell cos., 1986-88. Active conservation activities. Honor scholar U. Wyo., 1967-71. Mem. Nat. Bus. Edn. Assn., Phi Beta Lambda, Pi Omega Pi, Phi Kappa Phi. Avocations: hiking, aerobics, reading, writing. Home: 2895 Harmony St Boise ID 83706-5088

POLLARD, HONORA MAE, elementary school educator; b. Corona, Calif., Aug. 1, 1953; d. Andrew Lawrence and Frances Dorothy (Bowser) Adkins; m. Clyde M. Pollard, Sept. 18, 1992; m. Thomas R. Curry, Mar. 27, 1975 (div. May 4, 1987); 1 child, Darian Leigh Curry. BS in Edn., U. Cumberlands, Williamsburg, Ky., 1986; MEd, Sul Ross State U., Uvalde, Tex., 2005. Cert. tchr. profl. gen. edn. Tex. Edn. Agy., 1988, tchr. ESL Tex. Edn. Agy., 1992, ednl. diagnostician Tex. Edn. Agy., 2005. Tchr. Crystal City (Tex.) Ind. Sch. Dist., 1986—87, La Pryor (Tex.) Ind. Sch. Dist., 1987—89, Carrizo Springs (Tex.) Ind. Sch. Dist., 1989—90, Cotulla Ind. Sch. Dist., Encinal, Tex., 1990—92, Uvalde (Tex.) Consol. Ind. Sch. Dist., 1993—. Author: (non-fiction) Men Begin in Second Grade - Reflections From the Classroom; dir.: Anthon Little Theatre, 2001—. Mem.: Tex. Classroom Tchrs. Assn. Office: Anthon School UCISD PO Box 1909 Uvalde TX 78802 Office Phone: 830-591-2988. Office Fax: 830-591-2993. Business E-Mail: pollardh@ucisd.net.

POLLARD, MARILYN BERGKAMP, retired utility company executive; b. Fowler, Kans., July 7, 1937; d. Frank Henry and Mary Magdalene (Kuhl) Bergkamp; 1 child, Darin. Student, U. Colo., Denver, 1962, U. Denver, 1968, Metro State Coll., Denver, 1969, Colo. Women's Coll., 1977. Ins. underwriter Laurin Jones Agy., Dodge City, Kans., 1955-60; legis. asst. State of Kans., Topeka, 1960-61; various positions Denver, 1961-76; asst. to pres. Pub. Service Co. of Colo., Denver, 1976-86, asst. to chmn. bd., chief exec. officer, pres., 1986-89, asst. to sr. v.p. and gen. counsel, 1989—95, ret., 1995. Bd. dirs. Denver Jr. Achievement, 1979—91, Colo. Found. Dentistry for Handicapped, 1985—91, Am. Humanics, Denver, 1985-91, Artreach, Denver, 1987—91, Denver Civitan Club; incorporator, co-chmn. Colo. for Sensible Energy Policy, Denver, 1982, Denver Salvation Army, 1979—. Recipient Downtown Denver Career Woman award, 1974, Outstanding Achievement in Pub. Relations award, 1972; named Outstanding Vol. Salvation Army, 1999. Mem.: Denver Press (bd. dirs. 1977-78). Avocations: reading, golf, sewing. Office: Pub Svc Co Colo 1225 17th St Ste 300 Denver CO 80202-5506

POLLARD, VERONICA, automotive executive; m. Joel Dreyfuss; 1 child, Justin. Student, U. Wis.; Bachelor's Degree, Boston U.; Master's Degree, Columbia U. First grade tchr., NY; mgr. internat. affairs Cosmo Pub. Rels. Corp., Tokyo; staff writer San Francisco Chronicle; asst. dir. pub. affairs Newsweek Mag.; publicist ABC TV Network, mgr. bus. info.; dir. corp. comm. Capital Cities/ABC, Inc.; v.p. corp. pub. rels. ABC; v.p., external affairs Toyota Motor Corp. Services N.Am., 1998—2002; group v.p. corp. comm. Toyota Motor N.Am., Inc., 2002—. Bd. dirs. Granite Broadcasting Corp.; mem. individual investor adv. com. N.Y. Stock Exch. Former dir. Nat. YMCA of the U.S.A., YMCA Greater N.Y.; trustee Mus. for African Art, NY; active YMCA; hon. bd. mem. West Side YMCA, NY, 1990—98, bd. chair; dir. The Doe Fund, NY. Mem.: Women's Forum. Office: Toyota Motor NAm Ste 4900 Nine West 57th St New York NY 10019

POLLEY-SHELLCROFT, THERESA DIANE, art educator; b. Huntington, W.Va., July 11, 1945; m. John Wesley, II Shellcroft, Jan. 24, 1970; 1 child, Christopher Shellcroft. BS in Art Edn., W.Va. State Coll., Institute, W. Va., 1964—68. Coll. instr. Victor Valley CC, Victorville, Calif., 1980—; h.s. art tchr. Hesperia Unified Sch. Dist., Hesperia, Calif. Painting, quilt art, lecturer, exhibitor, African Inspirations Curator - Exhibit, Road to California, Quilt Show Teacher African American Quilting Trends Agora Gallery, SOHO New York, 2002 (Nat. Endownment for the Humanities, Black Film Studies, 2001; Art Educator of the Yr., 1997; Ca. Visual and Performing Arts Framework Com., 2001). Mem.: Calif. Teachers Assn., NEA, Afro Am. Quilters of LA, San Bernardino Arts Coun., Delta Sigma Theta Sorority. Avocation: travel, reading, swimming,. Office: Studio One Artworks PO Box 2336 Victorville CA 92393 Personal E-mail: tshellcrof@aol.com.

POLLICK, CYNTHIA, lawyer; b. Scranton, Pa., July 17, 1970; d. John and Nancy Ann Pollick. BA, Indiana U. Pa., 1992; JD, U. Pitts., 1999; LLM in Trial Advocacy, Temple U., Phila., 2002. Bar: Pa. 1999, NJ 1999. Ops. res. coord. PEXCO, Waverly, Pa., 1993—96; assoc. Lenahan & Dempsey, Scranton, 1999—2000; owner, civil rights lawyer Employment Law Firm, Pittston, 2000—. Adj. prof. King's Coll., Wilkes Barre, Pa., 1997, Wilkes Barre, 98, Wilkes Barre, 99. Office: Employment Law Firm 126 S Main St Pittston PA 18640-1706

POLLINA, KRISTEN MITTL, child and adolescent psychologist; b. Park Ridge, Ill., Nov. 17, 1973; d. Mary Mittl and Ronald Robert Pollina. BA in Psychology, summa cum laude, New Eng. Coll., Henniker, N.H., 1995; MA in Clin. Psychology, Ill. Sch. Profl. Psychology, Rolling Meadows, 1997, D in Clin. Psychology, 1999. Lic. clin. psychologist State of Ill., 2001. Undergrad. intern in psychology Rape and Domestic Violence Crisis Ctr., Concord, NH, 1993—94, Anna Philbrook Psychiat. Hosp. for Children and Adolescents, Concord, NH, 1994—95; pre-doctoral extern in clin. psychology St. Therese Med. Ctr. Behavioral Medicine Unit, Waukegan, Ill., 1996—97, Family Stress Clinic, Libertyville, Ill., 1997—98; pre-doctoral intern in clin. psychology Depke Juvenile Justice Complex / Hulse Detention Ctr., Vernon Hills, Ill., 1998—99; postdoctoral fellow in clin. psychology Connection's Therapeutic Day Sch., Libertyville, 1999—2000, clin. dir., dir. of clin. tng., 2000—. Instr. Columbia Coll., Park City, Ill., 2000—01. Vol. Connection Crisis Hotline, Libertyville, Ill., 1992—95, A Safe Place, Waukegan, Ill., 1992—95; pres. and mem. Womyn's Network, Henniker, NH, 1991—95; 1st female pres. New Eng. Coll. Greek Coun., Henniker, NH, 1992—95; victim adv. in Jane Doe cases of sexual harassment and assault New Eng. Coll. Jud. Bd., Henniker, NH, 1993—95. Mem.: APA, Assn. for the Advancement of Psychology, Psi Chi, Kappa Phi Sigma (founding pres. 1991—95). Independent. Roman Catholic. Avocations: travel, reading, my pets, yoga. Home: 4582 W Gowin Ln Libertyville IL 60048 Office: Connection's Therapeutic Day Sch 31410 Hwy 45 Libertyville IL 60048 Personal E-mail: dr.kmpollina@comcast.net. Business E-Mail: kpollina@connectionsdayschool.net.

POLLITT, KATHA, writer, educator, poet; b. N.Y.C., Oct. 14, 1949; d. Basil Riddiford and Leanora (Levine) P.; div.; 1 child, Sophie Pollitt-Cohen. BA, Harvard U., 1972; MFA, Columbia U., 1975. Lit. editor The Nation, N.Y.C., 1982-84, contbg. editor, 1986-92, assoc. editor, then columnist, 1992—; jr. fellow council of humanities Princeton (N.J.) U., 1984. Lectr. The New Sch., N.Y.C., 1986-90, Poetry Ctr. 92d St. YMHA and YWHA, N.Y.C., 1986-95. Author: Antarctic Traveller, 1982 (Nat. Book Critics Circle award 1983), Reasonable Creatures: Essays on Women and Feminism, 1994, Subject to Debate: Sense and Dissents on Womes, Politics and Culture, 2001; poetry appeared in The New Yorker, The New Republic, Poetry, and others; contbr. articles to jours. Maggie award, Planned Parenthood Fed Am, 1993; Whiting fellow, 1993, Guggenheim fellow 1987; recipient I.B. Lavan Younger Poet's award Acad. Am. Poets, 1984, Nat. Mag. award 1992; Fulbright grantee, 1985; grantee N.Y. Found. of the Arts, 1987, Nat. Endowment for Arts, 1984. Fellow N.Y. Inst. Humanities. Democrat.

POLLOCK, CONNIE, mathematics educator; b. Pine Bluff, Ark., Dec. 12, 1944; d. Virginia Henry; m. James Henry Pollock, Jan. 8, 1948; children: Karen Diane Harris, Paula Faye Griffith, Jennifer Elaine, Kevin James. Tchr. math grade 7 McCrory Sch. Sys., Ark., 1968, Paragould Sch. Sys., Ark., 1968—69. Mem.: Mo. State Tchrs. Assn., Mo. Coun. Tchrs. Math., Nat. Coun. Tchrs. Math. Baptist. Avocation: music. Home: 335 E Reynolds Ironton MO 63650 Office: Arcadia Valley Mid Sch 550 Park Dr Ironton MO Office Phone: 573- 546-9700. E-mail: cpollock@mail.av.k12.mo.us.

POLLOCK, KAREN ANNE, computer analyst; b. Elmhurst, Ill., Sept. 6, 1961; d. Michael Paul and Dorothy Rosella (Foskett) Pollock. BS, Elmhurst Coll., 1984; MS, North Ctrl. Coll., 1993. Formatter Nat. Data Corp., Lombard, Ill., 1985; computer specialist Dept. VA, Hines, Ill., 1985—. Lutheran. Avocations: cross-stitch, mystery books, bowling, bicycling, softball.

POLLOCK, MARGARET LANDAU PEGGY, elementary school educator; b. Jefferson City, Mo., Oct. 18, 1936; d. William Wold and Grace Elizabeth (Creamer) Anderson; children by previous marriage: Elizabeth, Charles, Christopher, Jeffrey; m. William Whalen Pollock, Jan. 30, 1993. AA, Stephens Coll., 1956; BS in Elem. Edn., U. Mo., Columbia, 1958; MA in Reading Edn., U. Mo., Kansas City, 1987. Cert. elem. tchr., Mo. Kindergarten tchr. Columbia Schs., 1958-59, Moberly (Mo.) Schs., 1960-62; 1st grade tchr. Kansas City Schs., 1962-63; kindergarten tchr. Independence (Mo.) Schs., 1966-75; chpt. I reading specialist Thomas Hart Benton Elem. Sch., Independence, 1975-93; book reviewer Corpus Christi (Tex.) Caller Times, 1994—; children's libr. Corpus Christi Pub. Libr., 1995-97; dir. Johnson City (Tex.) Libr., 1997—. Cons., presenter in field. Bd. dirs. Boys and Girls Club, Independence, 1990-93; coord. Independence Reading Fair, 1989-93; coord. books and tutoring Salvation Army, Kansas City, 1990-92. Mem. AAUW, Internat. Reading Assn. (People to People del. to USSR 1991, local v.p. 1990-91, pres. 1991-92), Internat. Platform Assn., Austin Writer's League, Archeol. Inst. Am., Tex. Libr. Assn., Earthwatch, Nature Conservancy, Sierra Club, Phi Kappa Phi, Pi Lambda Theta (pres. Beta Upsilon chpt. 1992-93). Avocations: native american history, rights and education, archeology, reading, travel, conservation. Home: PO Box 482 Johnson City TX 78636-0482

POLLOCK, SANDRA SUE, retired elementary educator; b. South Lyon, Mich., Mar. 12, 1941; d. Robert Wesley Pollock and Erma Eylene (Westerman) Keating. BS, Ea. Mich. U., 1965. 4th grade tchr. Huron Sch. Dist., New Boston, Mich., 1965-95; ret., 1995. Mem. choir First Congl. United Ch. of Christ, Ypsilanti, Mich., 1985—, Ypsilanti Cmty. Choir, 1995—; vol. patient rels. St. Joseph Mercy Hosp., Ann Arbor, Mich., 1995—; tutor basic lang. skills Washtenaw Literacy, Ann Arbor, 1995—; block capt. Neighborhood Watch, Ypsilanti, 1994—. Recipient Favorite Tchr. award Detroit News, 1968. Mem. AARP, Mich. Assn. Ret. Sch. Personnel. Avocations: writing, singing, baking, canning. Home: 1515 Ridge Rd Lot 311 Ypsilanti MI 48198-3357

POLLOCK, VICKI EILEEN, psychologist; b. Portland, Oreg., Apr. 24, 1956; d. Richard Edward and Margorie Helen (Smith) P. AB summa cum laude, Washington U., St. Louis, 1977; MA, U. So. Calif., 1982, PhD, 1984. Sr. research asst. Mo. Inst. Psychiatry, St. Louis, 1977-79; psychophysiol. lab. chief Psykologisk Inst., Copenhagen, 1979-80; data analyst Ctr. for Longitudinal Rsch., L.A., 1980-83, data coord., 1983-85; psychology intern Neuropsychiatric Inst., L.A., 1984-85; asst. prof. psychiatry (psychology) U. So. Calif., L.A., 1985-91, assoc. prof. psychiatry (psychology), 1991—2000; rsch. dir. EEG Inst., Woodland Hills, Calif., 2002—. Contbr. articles to profl. jours. Fellow Nat. Inst. Alcohol Abuse and Alcoholism, Washington, Grass Found. fellow, 1976. Soc. for Psychophysiol. Research, AAAS, Behavior Genetics Assn., Sigma Xi. Avocations: classical music, swimming. Office: Rsch Dir EEG Inst 22020 Clarendon St ste 305 Woodland Hills CA 91367

POLLOCK-O'BRIEN, LOUISE MARY, public relations executive; b. Tarentum, Pa., Mar. 14, 1948; d. Louis P. and Amelia M. (Ballay) Pollock; m. Vincent Miles O'Brien. BS, Ind. U. of Pa., 1970. Tchr. Archbishop Wood H.S., Warminster, Pa., 1970-75; spokesperson, publicist Calif. Olive Industry, Fresno, 1976-78; account exec. Ketchum Pub. Rels., N.Y.C., 1979-81, account supr., 1982-83, v.p., 1984, v.p., group mgr., 1985-88, sr. v.p., group mgr., 1988-89, assoc. dir., dir. food mktg., sr. v.p., 1990-91; chmn. Aronow & Pollock Comm., Inc., N.Y.C., 1991—2004; pres. Pollock Comm. Inc., N.Y.C., 2004—. Mem. pub. rels. adv. com. Mayor's Vol. Action Com., N.Y.C., 1986; mem. food svc. adv. bd. L.I. City Coll., Bklyn., 1987-88. V.p., fundraiser West 76th St. Block Assn., N.Y.C., 1982. Mem. Internat. Foodservice Editl. Coun. (v.p., bd. dirs. 1984-85). Avocations: watercolor painting, skiing. Office: Pollock Comm Inc 665 Broadway New York NY 10012-4408 Office Phone: 212-941-1414. E-mail: lpollock@pollock-pr.com.

POLOS, IRIS STEPHANIE, artist; b. Oakland, Calif., Feb. 14, 1947; d. Theodore C. and Catherine (Pappas) P.; 1 child Apollo Papafrangou. BFA, Calif. Coll. Arts and Crafts, Oakland, 1968, MFA, 1971. Instr. figure drawing Am. Sch. of Art, Athens, Greece, 1969-71 summers; instr. advanced drawing U. Calif. Extension Open Exchange, San Francisco, 1978-79; artist in residence Chabot Elem. Sch., Oakland, Calif., 1986-92, Mus. of Children's Art, Oakland, 1988—96; art tchr. Arrowsmith Acad., Berkeley, 1991—; instr. Oakland children's hosp. MOCHA, 1995—96. Artist: selected exhibitions include: San Francisco Mus. of Modern Art, 1971, Richmond (Calif.) Art Ctr., 1973, Calif. Coll. of Arts and Crafts, Oakland, 1973, Art for Art Sake Gallery, San Francisco, 1977, Jehu Wong Gallery, San Francisco, 1979, Triangle Gallery, San Francisco, 1981, Bond Gallery, N.Y.C., 1985, 86, Berkeley (Calif.) Art Ctr., 1987, 88, Emanuel Radnitzky, San Francisco, 1990 (2 shows), San Francisco Art Commn. Gallery, 1991, Fine Arts Ctr., Irvine, Calif., 1991, Trojanowska Gallery, San Francisco, 1991, Nelson Morales Gallery, San Francisco, 1992, Morphos Gallery, L.A., 1993, 94, Morphos Gallery, San Francisco, 1994, 95, Hotel Triton Art Fair with Morphos Gallery, San Francisco, 1995, Moreau Galeries, Notre Dame, Ind., 1995, Fort Mason Found., San Francisco, 1995, Magic Theater Lobby, San Francisco, 1995, Chgo.-Artspace, Lima, Ohio, 1997, Catherine Clark Gallery, San Francisco, 1997, 98, 99, Circle Elephant Art Gallery, L.A., 2001, 04, others; permanent collections include the Oakland Mus., Catharine Clark, Gary Noguera, Helen Salz, Daniel Soto, Caroline Zecca, di Rosa Found., Sonoma County, and others; her works also include book illustration and theatre set design; featured artist in Juxtapoz mag., Fall 1998, Chicago Art Fair with C. Clark Gallery, 2001-02, mural projects with Arrowsmith Acad. at Oakland Zoo and at St. Marks Ch., Berkeley. Grantee: Arts in Edn. grant Cultural Arts Divsn., Oakland, 1991-96, Berkeley Repertory Theater, 1995. Democrat. Home: 5801 Broadway Oakland CA 94618-1524 Office: Arrowsmith Acad Art Dept Berkeley CA 94704

POLOWE-ALDERSLEY, STEPHANIE RUTH, English language educator, educational association administrator, legislator; b. Sacramento, July 16, 1945; d. Joseph and Elizabeth Margaret (Nowatka) Polowe; m. Edward S. Downey Jr., Sept. 23, 1967 (div. Jan. 1981); children: Jennifer, Ian; m. Stephen Aldersley, May 30, 1982; 1 child, Jordan. Student, St. Lawrence U., 1963-66; BA in English, Wayne State U., 1967; MA in English, SUNY, Brockport, 1980; EdD in Psycholinguistics, U. Rochester, 1985. Mem. staff United Way of Rochester, N.Y., 1967; tutorial supr. Yonkers (N.Y.) Sch. Bd., 1970-71; reading tchr. Rochester City Schs., 1971-73, substitute tchr., 1973-74; instr. Nat. Tech. Inst. for Deaf at Rochester Inst. of Tech., 1974-82, asst. prof. English, 1982-89, assoc. prof. English, 1989—. Editor newsletter News 'N' Notes, 1987-89, newsletter of Tchrs. of English and Lang. Arts, 1985-87; contbr. articles to profl. publs.; editor Procs. of the Convention of Am. Instrs. of the Deaf, 1991, 93. Sponsor Bluebirds, West Irondequoit, 1977-78; program dir. PTA, West Irondequoit, 1983-84; mem. West Irondequoit Bd. Edn., Rochester, 1986-92, Bd. Coop. Ednl. Svcs., Fairport, N.Y., 1992—; advisor Helmer Nature Ctr., Irondequoit, 1987-88; co-chair Coun. Orgn. Reps. of and for People who are Def or Hard of Hearing, Washington, 1993. Recipient Resolution of Recognition, Conv. Am. Instrs. of the Deaf, 1991; named Hon. Mayor of St. Paul Blvd., Citizens for Preservation of St. Paul Blvd., 1992. Mem. MLA, N.Am. Assn. for Study of Romanticism, Nat. Assn. of Deaf, Coun. on Exceptional Children, Alexander Graham Bell Assn., Nat. Coun. Tchrs. of English, Convention Am. Inst. Deaf (pres.-elect. 1989-91, pres. 1991-93, sec. 1987-89, pres. tchrs. of English and lang. arts 1985-87, resolution of recognition 1989, 91, editor 1991 proceedings 1993), Monroe County Sch. Bds. Assn. (v.p., chair-elect 1992-93, pres. 1993—, co-chair labor rels. 1991-92, steering com. 1991-93). Democrat. Presbyterian. Avocations: collecting, walking, violin, sketching. Office: Nat Tech Inst for Deaf PO Box 9887 Rochester NY 14623-0887

POLSBY, GAIL K., psychotherapist; b. Washington, Jan. 13, 1939; d. Thomas Edward and Elise Wildman (Hammer) Kissling; m. Allen I. Polsby, Aug. 30, 1963; children: Daniel, Abigail. BA, U. Md., Balt., 1960; MSW, Cath. U., Washington, D.C., 1963. Mem. faculty Washington Sch. Psychiatry, 1967—2001, chmn. bd. dirs., 2001—; pvt. practice psychotherapy, Chevy Chase, Md., 1969—; cons. doctoral program Clin. Social Work Inst., Washington, 1999—2003. Sec., bd. dirs. Washington Sch. Psychiatry, 1995—2001, chair faculty coun. Editor quar. newspaper Washington Sch. Psychiatry News, 1997-2005. Mem. Am. Group Psychotherapy Assn., Nat. Fedn. Clin. Social Workers. Avocations: hiking, biking. Home: 5651 Bent Branch Rd Bethesda MD 20816-1049

POLSKY, CYNTHIA HAZEN, artist, art collector, philanthropist; b. NYC, Feb. 16, 1939; m. Leon B. Polsky; 2 children. BA, Marymount Coll., 1978; MBA, Fordham U., 1981. Art collector arts of S.E. Asia and India, 20th century Am. and European paintings, sculpture and 19th and 20th century decorative arts; one-woman shows include U.S. galleries and mus., Represented in permanent collections Corcoran Mus., Washington, DC, Fogg Mus., Cambridge, Mass., Johnson Mus., Cornell U., Ithaca, NY, NY Acad. Scis. and Rockefeller U., NYC. Trustee Met. Mus. Art, NYC, mem. acquisitions com., mem. exec. com., chmn. membership com.; hon. life trustee Asia Soc., Storm King Art Ctr., Mountainville, NY; trustee Pierpont Morgan Libr., NYC; mem. Bryant Park Art Commn.; mem. exec. com. Rockefeller U. Coun.; mem. collector's com. Nat. Gallery Art. Office: 667 Madison Ave New York NY 10021 Office Phone: 212-751-4917.

POMERANTZ, CHARLOTTE, writer; b. Bklyn., July 24, 1930; d. Abraham L. and Phyllis (Cohen) P.; m. Carl Marzani, Nov. 12, 1966; children: Gabrielle Rose, Daniel Avram. BA, Sarah Lawrence Coll., 1953. Children's books include The Bear Who Couldn't Sleep, 1965, The Moon Pony, 1967, Ask the Windy Sea, 1968, Why You Look Like You Whereas I Look Like Me, 1968, The Day They Parachuted Cats on Borneo, 1971 (chosen for Internat. Year of the Child 1977-78), The Princess and the Admiral, 1974 (Jane Addams Children's Book award), The Piggy in the Puddle, 1974 (Featured on Reading Rainbow in Claymation, 1992, NYT Outstanding Picture Book of the Year award 1974), The Ballad of the Long Tailed Rat, 1975, Detective Poufy's First Case, 1976, The Mango Tooth, 1977 (Jr. Literary Guild Selection), The Downtown Fairy Godmother, 1978, The Tamarindo Puppy and Other Poems, 1980 (an ALA Notable Book), Noah's and Namah's Ark, 1980, If I Had a Paka, 1982 (Jane Addams Honor award 1983), Buffy and Albert, 1982, Posy, 1983 (1984 Christopher award), Whiff, Sniff, Nibble and Chew, 1984, Where's the Bear?, 1984, The Half-Birthday Party (Jr. Literary Guild Selection), 1984, All Asleep, 1984, One Duck, Another Duck, 1984, How Many Trucks Can a Tow Truck Tow? (Children's Book of the Year Libr. of Congress 1991) 1987, Timothy Tall Feather, 1987, The Chalk Doll (Top 10 Picture Books of 1989 Boston Globe, Parents Choice award, 1990) 1989, Flap Your Wings and Try, 1989, Serena Katz, 1992, The Outside Dog (One of 100 Books Recommended by the N.Y. Pub. Libr., 1993, ALA Notable) 1993, Halfway to Your House, 1993, Here Comes Henny (based on the wordplay of James Joyce), 1994, Mangaboom, 1997, You're Not My Best Friend Anymore, 1998 (Jr. Libr. Guild Selection 1998), The Birthday Letters, 2000, The Mousery, 2000 (Christopher award), Thunderboom!, 2005; co-author, lyricist play Eureka!, 1997; author radio play Whiff Sniff Nibble and Chew, 1997; contbr. stories to mags.; spl. editorial asst.: Einstein on Peace, 1960; editor: A Quarter Century of Un-Americana, 1963. Address: 260 W 21st St New York NY 10011-3447

POMERANZ, SHARON JANE, lawyer; b. 1962; Degree, San Diego State U., 1986; JD, Southwestern U., 1991. Sr. asst. gen. counsel US Gen. Svc. Adminstrn., Washington, 1991—2003; assoc. gen. counsel Office Gen. Council, Exec. Office Immigration Review, US Dept. Justice, 2003—. Mem.: Calif. Bar Assn. Office: US Dept Justice Exec Office Immigration Review Office Di 5107 Leesburg Pike Ste 2600 Falls Church VA 22041

POMEROY, CLAIRE, dean; m. William Preston Robertson. MD, U. Mich. Coll. Medicine; MBA, U. Ky. Resident in internal medicine and infectious disease U. Minn., fellow internal medicine and infectious diseases, faculty mem., established HIV clinic at Mpls. Veterans' Adminstrn. Med. Ctr.; chief divsn. infectious diseases U. Ky. Coll. Medicine, asst. dean clin. affairs, assoc. dean rsch. informatics, prof.; exec. assoc. dean U. Calif. Davis Sch. Medicine, 2003, prof. infectious diseases and microbiology and immunology, vice chancellor human health sciences, 2005—, dean, 2005—. Faculty senate coun. U. Ky.; reviewer Nat. Institutes of Health, Dept. Veterans' Affairs. Bd. trustee U. Ky. Office: Office of Dean UC Davis Health System 2315 Stockton Blvd Sacramento CA 95817 Office Phone: 916-734-3578. E-mail: cpomeroy@ucdavis.edu.*

POMEROY, ELEANOR LISA BEYEA, psychologist, psychoanalyst; d. Richard Swinney and Eleanor Maude Lorane (Strong) Beyea; children: Deborah Sue, David Randall. BA, U. Tex., Austin, 1965; MPH, U. Tex., Houston, 1970; PhD in Clin. and Devel. Psychology, U. So. Calif., 1975. Accredited psychoanalyst L.A. Inst. and Soc. for Psychoanalytic Studies; lic. psychologist Calif., Va. Chief psychology Westwood Hosp., L.A., 1984—86; clin. dir. Edgemont Hosp., L.A., 1986—88, NU Regional Med. Ctr., L.A.; exec. dir., clin. dir. The Healing Ho., L.A., 1995—2004; pvt. practice. Presenter in field. Contbr. chapters to books, articles to profl. jours. Active Mus. of Tolerance, L.A., Highland Park United Meth. Ch., Trinity Episcopal Ch. Recipient Outstanding Psychologist award, Calif. Assn. Psychology Providers; fellow, Reiss Davis Child Study Ctr., L.A., 1976—78. Mem.: APA (elected member at large psychoanalytic divsn. 2000—03, pres. Psychoanalytic Rsch. Soc. psychoanalytic divsn.), Women Gender and Psychoanalysis (pres.), Group for Advanced Study of Psychotic, Borderline and Narcissistic Disorders, Internat. Psychoanalytical Assn., L.A. Inst. and Soc. for Psychoanalytic Studies, Western States Psychiat. Inst. (v.p.). Republican. Avocations: reading, writing, international relations. Home: 11693 San Vicente Blvd Los Angeles CA 90049 Office: 468 N Camden Dr #200 Beverly Hills CA 90210 Office Phone: 310-860-5177.

POMEROY, HEATHER ALINE, sales executive, marketing executive; b. Laconia, NH, Mar. 4, 1977; d. Robert Dan and Mary Eleanor Pomeroy. BA, Dickinson Coll., Carlisle, Pa., 1999. Asst. to French dieticians Dickinson Coll. en France, Toulouse, 1998; tour cons. EF Edn., Cambridge, Mass., 1999—2001, regional sales mgr. Portland, Oreg., 2001—02; account exec. Internat. Data Collection, Chula Vista, Calif., 2002—03, dir. bus. devel., 2003—04, v.p. sales and mktg., 2004—; dir. bus. devel. Datascension, Brea, Calif., 2005—. Newsletter chair person Market Rsch. Assn., San Diego, 2004—. Editor, writer (newsletter) SoCal MRA Newsletter (Cert. of Appreciation, 2004). Grantee, Dickinson Coll., 1995—99. Mem.: Am. Mktg. Assn. (assoc.), Coun. Am. Survey Rsch. Orgns. (assoc.), Mktg. Rsch. Assn. (assoc.; So. Calif. 2002—05, bd. dirs. 2006—), Tri-Delta Sorority (assoc.). Democrat. Avocations: travel, speaking French, running, yoga, drawing. Office Phone: 619-795-0827. Office Fax: 619-628-2371. Personal E-mail: hpomeroy1@cox.net.

POMERS, TIFFANY LEE, mathematics educator; b. Hackensack, NJ, Nov. 19, 1981; d. Gail and Stanley Pomers. BS, St. Peter's Coll., NJ, 2003. Secondary Edn. NJ. H.s. math tchr. Bayonne H.S., NJ, 2003—, asst. varsity soccer coach, 2003—. Mem.: Math. Assn. of Am.

POMPA, LOUISE ELAINE, secondary school educator; b. Spangler, Pa., Sept. 26, 1958; d. Harry Gregory and Lois Vida Beers; m. David Richard Pompa, Jan. 18, 1985; 1 child, Emilee Louise stepchildren: Angelo, Mary Beth. BS, Pa. State U., 1982; MEd, Ind. U. Pa., 1994. Cert. profl. tchr. Pa. Adult day care provider for mentally handicapped persons Mid-State Intermediate Care Facility for the Mentally Retarded, Altoona, Pa., 1983—84; spl. edn. tchr. Altoona Area Sch. Dist., 1984—86; tchr. Cambria County Children and Youth, Ebensburg, Pa., 1986—87; spl. edn. tchr. Greater Johnstown (Pa.) Vocat.-Tech. Sch., 1987—88, Appalachia Intermediate Unit 8, Ebensburg, 1988—90; spl. edn. tchr., secondary learning support Cambria Heights Sch. Dist., Patton, Pa., 1990—. Author: A Review of the Literature on Motivation and Strategies for Improving Motivation in the Learning Disabled Adolescent: A Comparative Analysis, 1994. Mem.: Kappa Delta Pi, Phi Kappa Phi. Democrat. Roman Catholic. Avocations: health and fitness, gardening, collectibles, quilting. Office: Cambria Heights Sch Dist 426 Glendale Lake Rd Patton PA 16668

POMPEO, ELLEN, actress; b. Everett, Mass., Nov. 10, 1969; Actor: (films) 8 1/2 x 11, 1999, Coming Soon, 1999, Eventual Wife, 2000, In the Weeds, 2000, Moonlight Mile, 2002, Catch Me If You Can, 2002, Daredevil, 2003, Old School, 2003, Undermind, 2003, Nobody's Perfect, 2004, Art Heist, 2004; (TV series) Grey's Anatomy, 2005—, (TV appearances) Strangers with Candy, 1999, Law and Order, 1996, 2000, Get Real, 2000, Strong Medicine, 2001, The Job, 2001. Office: Creative Artists Agy 9830 Wilshire Blvd Beverly Hills CA 90212-1825*

POMPEO, MARIE ANTOINETTE, medical/surgical nurse, nursing educator; b. Jersey City, Feb. 27, 1961; d. Patrick D. and Antoinette (LeFante) Pompeo. Diploma in Nursing, St. Francis Hosp. Sch. Nursing, Jersey City, 1983; BSN, St. Peter's Coll., Jersey City, 1986; MA, Jersey City State Coll., 1990. RN, N.J.; cert. tchr. health edn., sch. nurse, tchr. handicapped. Staff nurse St. Francis Hosp., Jersey City, 1983-86; sch. nurse Jersey City Pub. Schs., 1986—, sch. nurse coord., 1999—. Head cheerleading and dance coach St. Dominic Acad., 1987—, P.S. 8 Bulldog Cheerleaders, 1991-93, St. Peter's Coll., 1991-93, others. Named NFSIA Nat. Spirit Coach of Yr., 1999. Mem. ANA, NEA, N.J. Edn. Assn., N.J. Sch. Nurse Assn., Hudson County Sch. Nurse Assn., N.J. State Nursing Assn., Jersey City Educators Assn., Nat. Fedn. Interscholastic Spirit Assn., Nat. Fedn. Interscholastic Coaches Assn., Am. Assn. Cheer Coaches and Advisors (safety cert.), N.J. Cheerleading Coaches and Assn. Inc. (co-dir. state competition 1993, 94, exec. bd. 1992—, competition dir. 1994-2000, v.p. 2000-04, pres. 2004—, coord. drug awareness resistance edn., cheer competition 1995, nat. cheer dance judging cert.)

POMPLUN, JULIE ANN, secondary school educator; d. Ala and Jill Pomplun. BS, U Wis., La Crosse, 2000; MEd, U. Wis., La Crosse, 2006. Math tchr. Sch. Dist Wauwatosa, Wis., 2001—. Office: Wauwatosa West HS 11400 W Center St Wauwatosa WI 53222

POND, GLORIA DIBBLE, retired educator; b. Merced, Calif., Mar. 10, 1939; d. Frank Burton and Joyce (Rickabaugh) D.; m. J. Lawrence Pond, Nov. 13, 1959; 1 child, Scott Lawrence (dec. 1993). BA, Bennington (Vt.) Coll., 1960; MA, Wesleyan U., Middletown, Conn., 1968; Cert. Adv. Study, Wesleyan U., 1974. Editorial asst. Newsweek mag., N.Y.C., 1956, 58, 59, The Houston Chronicle, 1957; reporter, asst. editor The Rockland Independent, Suffern, N.Y., 1960-62; instr. New Haven U., 1967; from lectr. to prof. Naugatuck Valley Community-Tech. Coll., Waterbury, Conn., 1968-97, prof. emeritus, 1997—. Author: Succeed: Write Now, 1978, Write, Simply Write, 1979; author of poetry; contbr. articles to profl. newspapers, mags. and jours. Founding chmn. Comprehensive Health Planning Coun. Ctrl. Naugatuck Valley, 1968-74; mem. Govs. Clean Air Task Force, Govs. Housing Task Force, 1969-70; founder Wallingford Human Rights Coun.; mem. State Health Coord. Coun., 1974-86, chair State Occupl. Safety Com., 1980-85;

mem. Conn. Siting Coun., 1974-96, chair, 1976-90; mem. Conn. Energy Adv. Bd., Hartford, 1977-91; mem. Adv. Coun. to State Health Commr., 1986—; treas. Regional Mental Health Coun., 1974-86; mem. Woodbury Fair Housing Coun.; mem. Dem. Town Com., 1969-88, State Platform Com., 1974-86, Naugatuck Valley CC Found. Bd., 1998—, Woodbury Scholarship Fund Bd., 1998—, Audubon Stewardship Bd., 2000—. Grantee, Wesleyan U., 1964-70. Mem. Conn. Libr. Assn. (scholar for libr. progs. 1988—), Conn. Humanities Coun. (scholar for community progs.), Western Conn. Bird Club (publicist 1985-90). Democrat. Avocations: sailing, skydiving, skiing. E-mail: gloria_pond@hotmail.com.

POND, PATRICIA BROWN, library and information scientist, educator; b. Mankato, Minn., Jan. 17, 1930; d. Patrick H. and Florence M. (Ruehle) Brown; m. Judson S. Pond, Aug. 24, 1959. BA, Coll. St. Catherine, St. Paul, 1952; MA, U. Minn., 1955; PhD, U. Chgo., 1982. Sch. libr., Minn., N.Y., 1952-62; asst. prof. libr. sci. U. Minn., 1962-63; reference libr. U. Mont., 1963-65; asst. prof. U. Oreg., 1967-72, assoc. prof., 1972-77; prof., dept. chair, assoc. dean Sch. Libr. and Info. Sci. U. Pitts., 1977-85. Mem. ALA (life), Phi Beta Kappa, Beta Phi Mu, Delta Phi Lambda, Kappa Gamma Pi. Home: 15829 SW Village Cir Beaverton OR 97007-3532 Personal E-mail: ppond1@mindspring.com.

POND, PEGGY ANN, librarian; b. Balt., Sept. 27, 1951; d. William Garland and Charlotte Jane (Zepp) Born; m. William Wright Pond, May 13, 1950; children: Stephany Erin, Averil Paij. BA, U. Md., 1973; MLA, We. Md. Coll., 1988. With Carroll County Gen. Hosp., Westminster, Md., 1969-86; tchr. English Carroll County Bd. Edn., Westminster, 1973-76, 86-89; ptnr., mgr. Classic Lady Clothing, Westminster, 1985-89; info. assoc. Carroll County Pub. Libr., Westminster, 1989-90, program asst., 1990-96, libr. assoc., 2000—; dir. youth and family ministry St. Paul's United Ch. of Christ, Westminster, 1996-2000. Tutor Carroll County Bd. Edn., 1979—84; dir. Christian edn. Westminster United Meth. Ch. Fair judge Carroll County 4-H Assn., 1983—; lay dir. Md. Chrysalis, 1993-94; elections judge Carroll County Elections Bd., 1984—. Mem. NEA, Md. Libr. Assn., Puppeteers Am., Order Ea. Star (worthy matron 1982-84). Republican. Methodist. Avocations: reading, needlecrafts, poetry, clowning, quilting.

POND, PHYLLIS JOAN RUBLE, state legislator, educator; b. Warren, Ind., Oct. 25, 1930; d. Clifford E. and Rosa E. (Hunnicutt) Ruble; m. George W. Pond, June 10, 1951; children: William, Douglas, Jean Ann. BS, Ball State U., Muncie, Ind., 1951; MS, Ind. U., 1963. Tchr. home econs., 1951-54; kindergarten tchr., 1961-98; mem. Ind. Ho. of Reps., Inpdls., 1978—, majority asst. caucus chmn., vice chmn. ways and means com., 1995. Active Rep. Precinct Com., 1976—; del. Ind. Rep. Conv., 1976, 80, 84, 86, 88, 90, 92, 96, 2000; alt. del. Rep. Nat. Conv., 1980, del., 1996; alt. del. to Rep. Nat. conv., 2000. Mem. AAUW, Regional Red Cross Bio-Med. Bd., New Haven Am. Legion Aux., New Haven Woman's Club. Lutheran.

PONDER, ANITA J., lawyer; BA, Fisk U.; JD, U. Fla. Bar: Ill. 1985, U.S. Dist. Ct. (No. Dist. Ill.) 1985. Dir. contract compliance Chgo. Dept. Procurement Svcs., 1983—88; ptnr. Holstein, Mack & Klein, Chgo., 1992—94, Altheimer & Gray, 1994—2002, Quarles & Brady LLP, 2002—04, Gardner, Carton & Douglas LLP, 2004—. Spkr. in field. Recipient Cert. of Appreciation, Aurora C. of C., Chgo. N.P. Constrn. Com., Inc., City of Chgo. and Turn Constrn. Co. Constrn. Mgmt. Tng. Program, Mem. of Yr., Cosmopolitan C. of C., Women Bus. Advocate of Yr., U.S. Small Bus. Adminstrn., others. Office: Gardiner Carton & Douglas LLP 191 N Wacker Dr Ste 3700 Chicago IL 60606-1698 Office Phone: 312-569-1153. Office Fax: 312-569-3153. E-mail: aponder@gcd.com.

PONDER, ANNE, academic administrator; b. Asheville, N.C., Apr. 26, 1950; d. Herschel Doyle and Mary Eleanor (Israel) Ponder; m. John Christopher Brookhouse, Mar. 3, 1973; stepchildren: Stephen Christopher, Nathaniel. AB, U. N.C., 1971, MA, 1973, PhD, 1979. Dir. honors Elon Coll., N.C., 1977-85; assoc. acad. dean Guilford Coll., Greensboro, N.C., 1985-89; acad. dean, prof. Kenyon Coll., Gambier, Ohio, 1989—96, v.p. info. tech.; pres. Colby-Sawyer Coll., New London, NH, 1996—2005. Mem. Nat. Collegiate Honors Coun. (pres. 1988-89), N.C. Honors Assn. (pres. 1983), Order of Valkyries. Episcopalian. Office: Colby-Sawyer Coll 541 Main St New London NH 03257

PONDER, CATHERINE, clergywoman; b. Hartsville, S.C., Feb. 14, 1927; d. Roy Charles and Kathleen (Parrish) Cook; 1 child, Richard. Student, Worth Bus. Coll., 1948; BS in Edn., Unity Ministerial Sch., 1956; doctorate (hon.), Unity Sch., 1976. Ordained to ministry Unity Sch. Christianity, 1958. Min. Unity Ch., Birmingham, Ala., 1958-61, founder, min. Austin, Tex., 1961-69, San Antonio, 1969-73, Palm Desert, Calif., 1973—. Author: (books) The Dynamic Laws of Prosperity, 1962, The Prosperity Secret of the Ages, 1964, The Dynamic Laws of Healing, 1966, The Healing Secret of the Ages, 1967, Pray and Grow Rich, 1968, The Millionaires of Genesis, 1976, The Millionaire Moses, 1977, The Millionaire Joshua, 1978, The Millionaire from Nazareth, 1979, The Secret of Unlimited Prosperity, 1981, Open Your Mind To Receive, 1983, Dare To Prosper!: The Prospering Power of Prayer, 1983, The Prospering Power of Love, 1984, Open Your Mind to Prosperity, 1984, The Dynamic Laws of Prayer, 1987, (memoir) Prosperity Love Story, From Rags to Enrichment, 2003. Office: 73-669 US Hwy 111 Palm Desert CA 92260-4033

PONTE, JEAN MOORE, artist, writer, actress; d. Harry Wilbur and Bessie Armina (Daugherty) Moore; m. Joseph Gonsalves Ponte, June 16, 1956; children: Wendy Jean, Joseph Meredith, Malcom Moore. Student, Western Mich. U., Kalamazoo, 1945—47, student, 1949—50; degree in fine arts, Kans. State U., Manhattan, 1994. Actress, bookkeeper Childrens' World Theater, 1947—48; actress Clare Tree Major Players Tour, 1950—51; copywriter Sta. WKZO, Fetzer Broadcasting, Kalamazoo, 1951—52, Aubrey Finley Marley Hodson, Chgo., 1952—54, Jim Mills Prodns., Chgo., 1955—56, Emporium Dept. Store, St. Paul, 1956—57. Author: (novels) Slipping the Fold, 2005; one-woman shows include Manhattan Arts Ctr., 1997, Cube Gallery, Kansas City, Mo., 2001, Unitarian Gallery, 2004. Vol. archeol. digs Mackinaw State Hist. Parks, Mackinaw City, Mich., 1993; vol. Art-of-it-All Gallery, Manhattan, Kans. Recipient cert., North Ctrl. Kans. Guidance, 1980, Mackinaw State Hist. Parks, 1993. Mem.: Columbia Artists, Nat. Mus. Women in the Arts, Manhattan Arts Ctr.

PONTICELLI, CHARLOTTE, federal agency administrator; BA cum laude, Hood Coll.; MA in Spanish Lit., NYU, Madrid, Spain. Dir. Congl. Corr. Office of Legis. Afairs; Congl. liaison officer for Latin Am. and Caribbean US Agency for Internat. Develop.; commr. asst. US. Commn. on Civil Rights; dir. Human Rights and Women's Affairs Bur. Internat. Orgn. Affairs; with Internat. Rep. Inst.; dir. lectures and seminars The Heritage Found.; dep. sr. coord. for Internat. Women's Issues US Dept. State, sr. coord., 2003—. Recipient Veritas Award, Albertus Magnus Coll., 1996. Office: US Dept State 2201 C St NW Washington DC 20520

PONT MARCHESE, MARISARA, former Puerto Rican government official; b. Río Piedras, P.R., Oct. 29, 1941; d. Rafael Pont and Sara Marchese. BA in Humanities cum laude, U. P.R., 1962-63; MS in Libr. Sci., Columbia U., 1971. Asst. to libr. med. scis. campus U. P.R., Río Piedras, 1964-72; spl. aide to Pres. Senate Commonwealth of P.R., San Juan, 1972; dep. aide in mgmt. Office of Gov. of P.R., San Juan, 1973, exec. aide to dir. of communications, 1973-74, dir. communications, 1974-76; pres. Plus Image Devel. and Pub. Rels., San Juan, 1977-86, Comstat/Rowland Pub. Rels., San Juan, 1986—; lectr. U. PR, pres. Commn. of Transition, 2004—05; sec. state Commonwealth of P.R., San Juan, 2005. Mem. Assn. Profl. Pub. Rels. Practitioners of P.R. (pres. 1984-86), Pub. Rels. Soc. Am., Overseas Press Club P.R. (co-chmn. ann. award program 1981-89), P.R. Mfrs. Assn., P.R. C. of C. (pub. rels. award 1985), Bankers Club. Roman Catholic. Business E-Mail: marisarap@comstat-pr.com.

POOL, MARY JANE, writer, editor; d. Earl Lee and Dorothy (Matthews) P. Grad., St. de Chantal Acad., 1942; BA in Art with honors, Drury Coll., 1946; LHD (hon.), Drury U., 2002. Mem. staff Vogue mag., N.Y.C., 1946-68, assoc. merchandising editor, 1948-57, promotion dir., 1958-66, exec. editor, 1966-68; editor House and Garden mag., 1969, editor-in-chief, 1970-80. Cons. Baker Furniture Co., 1981-94, Aves Advt., Inc., 1981-94, bd. dirs.; mem. bd. govs. Decorative Arts Trust; past mem. bd. govs. Fashion Group, Inc., N.Y.C Author: The Gardens of Venice, 1989, The Gardens of Florence, 1992, Gardens in the City-New York in Bloom, 1999; co-author: The Angel Tree, 1984, The Angel Tree—A Christmas Celebration, 1993, The Christmas Story, 2001, editor: 20th Century Decorating, Architecture, Gardens, Billy Baldwin Decorates, 26 Easy Little Gardens. Mem. bus. com. N.Y. Zool. Soc., 1979-86; trustee Drury Univ., 1971—; bd. dirs. Isabel O'Neil Found., 1978—. Recipient award Nat. Soc. Interior Designers, Disting. Alumni award Drury Coll., 1961, Edith Wharton Women of Achievement award, 1999; Pool Art Ctr. at Drury U opened 2004. Address: 1 E 66th St New York NY 10021-5854

POOLE, DOROTHEA VERANETTA, nursing educator; b. Honolulu, Sept. 1, 1964; d. Melvin and Dorothy Jean-Adams Poole. BS in Nursing, Tuskegee (Ala.) U., 1986; MS in Nursing, U. Ala., Birmingham, 1993. RN Ala. Nursing mgr. U. Ala. at Birmingham Hosp., 1986—93, nursing instr., 1993—. Cons. joint commn. accreditation project U. Ala. at Birmingham Hosp., 1993. Mem. health care ministry Faith Chapel Christian Ctr., Birmingham, 2006—. Named Woman of Yr., U. of Ala. at Birmingham Black Student Awareness Com., 2003. Mem.: AACN (Excellenc ein Critical Care Edn., Greater Birmingham chpt. 1998), ANA, Am. Trauma Soc., Am. Burn Assn., Birmingham Black Nurses Assn., Sigma Theta Tau, Alpha Kappa Alpha. Democrat. Avocations: travel, music, classic movies. Office: U Ala at Birmingham 1701 University Blvd Birmingham AL 35294-1210 Office Phone: 205-934-6653. Office Fax: 205-975-6142. E-mail: pooled@uab.edu.

POOLE, EVA DURAINE, librarian; b. Farrell, Pa., Dec. 20, 1952; d. Leonard Milton and Polly Mae (Flint) Harris; m. Tommy Lynn Cole, May 15, 1970 (div. Sept. 1984); 1 child, Tommy Lynn Cole, Jr.; m. Earnest Theodore Poole, Sept. 22, 1990; 1 child, Aleece Remelle Poole. BA in LS, Tex. Woman's U., Denton, 1974, MLS, 1976; postgrad., U. Houston, 1989. Libr. asst. Emily Fowler Pub. Libr., Denton, Tex., 1970-74; children's libr. Houston Pub. Libr., 1974-75, 1st asst. libr., 1976-77; children's libr. Ector County Libr., Odessa, Tex., 1977-80; head pub. svcs. Lee Davis Libr. San Jacinto Coll., Pasadena, Tex., 1980-84; libr. dir. San Jacinto Coll. South, Houston, 1984-90; libr. svcs. mgr. Emily Fowler Pub. Libr., Denton, 1990-93, interim dir., 1993; dir. librs. Denton Pub. Librs., 1993—. Mem. Libr. Svcs. Constrn. Act Adv. Coun., 1994-97, Libr. Svcs. Tech. Act Adv. Coun., 1997-2000; mem. TEXSHARE adv. bd. Tex. State Libr. and Archives Commn., 1999-2005, chmn., 2003-2004; bd. dirs. Denton Area Tchrs. Credit Union, 2003-06; mem. adv. bd. U. North Tex. Sch. Libr. and Info. Sci., 2000—, chair, 2006—; mem. members coun. Online Computer Libr. Ctr., 2004—; mem. presdl. search adv. com. U. North Tex., 2005-06; mem. external constituent bd. Tex. Woman's U. Sch. Libr. and Info. Studies, 2005—. Bd. dirs. Amigos Libr. Svcs., 2000-03, Girl Scouts Cross Timbers Coun., 2002-04, United Way of Denton County, 2002—, exec. com., bd. pres., 2006-, Friends of Librs. U.S.A., 2003—, Named to Outstanding Young Women of Am., 1991. Mem. ALA (chair Loleta Fyan jury com. 1999-2000) Allied Profl. Assn.(chmn. cert. pub. libr. adminstr. program 2005-06, mem. com. orgn., 2005-06), Pub. Libr. Assn. (mem. budget and fin. com. 1999-2002, chair budget and fin. com. 2001-2002, 2004-05, nat. conf. com. 2002-04, chair bylaws and orgn. 2002-03, mem. instnl. scholarships task force 2006), Libr. Adminstrn. and Mgmt. Assn. (program com. 1994-97, mem.-at-large bd. dirs. 2000-02, chair cultural diversity com. 2000-01, com. on orgn. 2002-05, rep. to Freedom to Read Found. 2002-03, strategic planning com. 2005-06), Tex. Libr. Assn. (pub. libr. divsn. sec. 1995-96, chair 1997-98, leadership devel. com. 1995-97, leadership devel. com. chair 1996-97, alumnae 1st class Tex. Accelerated Libr. Leaders 1994, legis. com. 1997-99, Dist. 7 coun. 1996-99, exec. bd. 1998-2000, 2002-05, ad hoc comn. on pub. lib. stds. com. chair 1998-2000, 2002 conf. local arrangements com. 2001-02, chair 2000 conf. program com. 1998-2000, chair awards com. 2001-02, pres.-elect 2002-03, pres. 2003-04, chair Tocker Found. com. 2006—), Pub. Libr. Adminstrs. North Tex. (vice chair 1994-95, chair 1995-96), Tex. Mcpl. Libr. Dirs. Assn. (pres. 1995-96, grantee 1993, Libr. of Yr. 1998), Denton Rotary Club, Tex. Mcpl. League (bd. dirs. 1997-2000). Office: Denton Pub Libr 502 Oakland St Denton TX 76201 Office Phone: 940-349-8750. Business E-mail: eva.poole@cityofdenton.com.

POOLE, KATHERINE, government agency administrator; d. Van B. Poole and Sandee Hawk, Donna Maggert Poole (Stepmother) and Ernie Hawk (Stepfather); m. Brenton Geoffrey Peterson, Apr. 16, 2006. BS in Economics, Fla. State U., Tallahassee, 1991. Asst. to the state economist Office of the Gov., State of Fla., Tallahassee, 1989—92; exec. asst., scheduler, office mgr. U.S. Congressman Charles T. Canady, Washington, 1993—95; chief cabinet aide, sr. cabinet aide Fla. Dept. of Agr. and Consumer Services, Tallahassee, 1995—97; staff dir. Fla. Senate Majority Office, Sr. Legislative Analyst, 1997—2000; press advance rep. Bush Cheney, Washington, 2000; def. fellow and spl. asst. U.S. Dept. of Def., Washington, 2000—01; lead press advance rep. for mrs. bush Presdl. Innaugural Com., Washington, 2000—01; dir. of pub. affairs and bus. rels. U.S. Trade and Devel. Agy., Arlington, Va., 2001—02; spl. asst. to the sec. U.S. Dept. of Labor, Washington, DC, 2002—03; spl. asst. to the under sec. U. S. Dept. of Agr., 2003—. Recipient Outstanding Achievement award, Office of the Sec. of Def., 2001. Avocations: swimming, biking, triathlons.

POOLE, NANCY GEDDES, art gallery curator, writer; b. London, Ont., Can., May 10, 1930; d. John Hardy and Kathleen Edwards (Robinson) G.; m. William Robert Poole, Aug. 15, 1952; 1 child, Andrea Mary. BA, U. Western Ont., 1956, LLD, 1990. Owner, dir. Nancy Poole's Studio, Toronto, Ont., Canada, 1969-78; acting dir. London Regional Art Gallery, Ont., Canada, 1981—, exec. dir. Ont., 1985-89; dir. London Regional Art and Hist. Museums, Ont., Canada, 1989-95. Chair governing coun. Ont. Coll. Art, 1972-73; bd. dirs. Robarts Rsch. Inst., 1995. Author: The Art of London 1939-1980, 1984; editor Jack Chambers, 1978, The Collection, 1990. Bd. govs. U. Western Ont., 1974-85; bd. dirs. Western Area Youth Svcs., 1996; chair Western Area Youth Svcs. Found., 2004, Hazel Cryderman-Wees Found., 2004. Fellow Ont. Coll. Art. Mem.: Order of Can. Office: 420 Fanshawe Park Rd London ON Canada N5X 2S9

POOLER, ROSEMARY S., federal judge; b. 1938; BA, Brooklyn Coll., 1959; MA, Univ. of Conn., 1961; JD, Univ. of Mich. Law Sch., 1965; cert. in Program for Sr. Mgrs. in Govt., Harvard Univ., 1978; degree (hon.), SUNY, Albany, 1986. With Crystal, Manes & Rifken, Syracuse, 1966—69, Michaels and Michaels, Syracuse, 1969—72; asst. corp. counsel Dir. of Consumer Affairs Unit, Syracuse, 1972—73; common counsel City of Syracuse Pub. Interest Rsch. Group, 1974—75; chmn., exec. dir. Consumer Protection Bd., 1975—80; commr. N.Y. State Pub. Services Commn., 1981—86; staff dir. N.Y. State Assembly, Com. on Corps., Authorities and Commns., 1987—94; judge Supreme Ct., 5th Jud. Dist., 1991—94; dist. judge U.S. Dist. Ct. (no. dist.) N.Y., Syracuse, 1994—98; cir. judge U.S. Ct. Appeals, 2nd cir., 1998—. Vis. prof. Syracuse Univ. Coll. of Law, 1987—88; v.p. legal affairs Atlantic States Legal Found., 1989—90. Mem.: Assn. of Supreme Ct. Justices of the State of N.Y. (sec. 1993—94), Women's Bar Assn. of the State of N.Y., N.Y. State Bar Assn., Onondaga County Bar Assn. Office: Federal Bldg 100 S Clinton St Syracuse NY 13261-7395 also: 40 Foley Square New York NY 10007*

POON, CHRISTINE A., pharmaceutical company executive; b. Cin., June 23, 1952; d. James and Virginaia Poon; m. Mike Tweedle. BS in Biology, Northwestern U., 1973; MS in Biology and Biochemistry, St. Louis U., 1973; MBA in Fin., Boston U., 1982. Various mgmt. positions Bristol-Myers Squibb, 1985—2000, v.p., sr. v.p. for Can. and L.Am. pharm. ops., pres., gen. mgr. Squibb Diagnostics' Can. operation, 1994, pres. Med. Devices, 1997—98, pres. internat. medicines, 1998—2000; co. group chmn. pharm. group Johnson & Johnson, New Brunswick, NJ, 2000—01, worldwide chmn. pharms. group, 2001—03, worldwide chmn. medicines and nutritionals, 2003—, vice chmn., mem. exec. com., 2005—. Bd. dirs. Prudential Fin., Inc., 2006—; bd. adv. Healthcare Businesswomen's Assn. Bd. dirs. Fox Chase Cancer Ctr., Phila. Named Woman of Yr., Healthcare Businesswomen's Assn., 2004; named one of 50 Women to Watch, Wall St. Jour., 2005, Most Powerful Women, Forbes mag., 2005, 10 Most Powerful Women in NJ Bus., Star-Ledger, 2006, 50 Most Powerful Women in Bus., Fortune mag., 2006. Office: Johnson & Johnson 1 Johnson and Johnson Plaza New Brunswick NJ 08901*

POOR, SUZANNE DONALDSON, advertising and public relations executive; b. Somers Point, NJ, Oct. 6, 1933; d. James Watt and Roberta (Radford) Donaldson; m. Richard Sumner Poor, Mar. 19, 1955 (div. Sept. 1983); children: Jonathan Scott, Jeffrey Sumner, Sara Suzanne; m. Jasper Raul Gonzalez, Apr. 20, 1996. AB, Mt. Holyoke Coll., 1955; MA, Montclair State Coll., 1975; postgrad., NYU, 1977—83; MPhil, Drew U., 1994, PhD, 1998; photography student, New Sch. Social Rsch., 1979—82. Reporter, copy writer WFLB, WFLB-TV, Fayetteville, N.C., 1955-56; dir. public relations Montclair YMCA, N.J., 1965-69, Girl Scouts Greater Essex County, Montclair, 1969-74; assoc. pub. relations dept. Nat. League Nursing, N.Y.C., 1974; freelance public relations, photography Montclair, 1974-76; dir. communications Insts. Religion and Health, N.Y.C., 1976-78; ptnr., pres. Miller/Poor Assocs., Verona, N.J., 1978—. Freelance writer N.Y. Times, 1988—94; adj. prof. Seton Hall U., 1999—2000, NYU, 2005—. Pres. bd. trustee Doubletree Gallery, Montclair, 1977-79; trustee Friends NJ Network, 1986-93. Mem.: NAFE, Am. Soc. Media Photographers (editor Exposure newsletter 1993—), Exec. Women N.J. (bd. dirs. 1980—83), Am. Woman's Econ. Devel. Corp., Author's Guild, N.J. Ad Club (editor Ad Talk 1982—, bd. dirs. 1983, pres. 2001—03, named to Advt. Hall of Fame NJ 2002). Democrat. Episcopalian. Avocations: bicycling, swimming, tennis, furniture restoration. Home: 30 Plymouth St Montclair NJ 07042-2625 Office: Miller Poor Assocs 261 Bloomfield Ave Verona NJ 07044-2426 Office Phone: 973-857-5161. Personal E-mail: poorsue@aol.com.

POORMAN, CHRISTINE K., television producer; b. Rochester, N.Y., Oct. 19; d. Paul G. and Barbara L. (LiVecchi) Kozlowski; m. Jack Edward Poorman, Sept. 9, 1995. B in Journalism/Fin., U. Ga., 1990. With CNN, Atlanta, 1990, prodn. asst., 1990-94, assoc. prodr., 1995—, producer, 1995-99. Vol. Junior League, 1993—, United Way. Avocations: acting, tennis, travel, food.

POPE, ANNE B., agency head, business executive, lawyer; Degree, Vanderbilt U.; degree Cumberland Sch. of Law, Samford U. Bar: Tenn., DC. Commr. State of Tenn. Dept Commerce and Ins., 1999—2003; fed. co-chair Appalachian Regional Commn., 2003—; assoc. atty. Webster, Chamberlain and Bean, Washington, 1988—92; pres., CEO, v.p., CFO, Parks-Belk Co., 1992—95; pres. Proffitts of the Tri-Cities, 1995—97; exec. dir. Tenn. Film Entertainment, and Music Commn., 1997—99; clk. US Dist. Judge James D. Todd, Jackson, Tenn. Mem. Gov. Sundquist's Coun. of Excellence in Higher Edn., 1997, Gov. Sundquist's Commn. on Practical Govt., 1999. Mem.: Johnson City C. of C. Office: 1666 Connecticut Ave NW Washington DC 20009-1068

POPE, ARLETTE FARRAR, insurance company professional; b. Paterson, NJ, Jan. 30, 1958; d. Arthur James Jr. and Mildred Louise (Johnson) Farrar; m. Leonard Pope, Aug. 12, 1990; children: Tyrell D., Trenace D., Leonard II. BSBA, Fairleigh Dickinson U., 1980. Claim svc. rep. State Farm Ins. Co., Paramus, N.J., 1983-88, claim automation and procedure specialist Parsippany, NJ, 1988—. Trustee The New Beginning Is Now, Paterson, N.J., 1989—; adminstrv. asst. New Christian Tabernacle COGIC, Paterson, 1981—; bd. trustees New Christian Tabernacle Faith in Action Mins., v.p., 1999. Avocations: crossword puzzles, reading, travel. Home: 38 Audrey Ct Stroudsburg PA 18360-8981 E-mail: popepa@earthlink.net.

POPE, ELIZABETH STEPHENS, dance educator; BS in Dance Edn., U. N.C., Greensboro, 1980. Cert. Nat. Cert. Bd. 2003. Dance educator Ligon Magnet Mid. Sch., Raleigh, NC, 1982—2006. Dancer choreographer Ligon Dance Co. Home: 501 Stronwood Ct Garner NC 27529 Office: Ligon Mid Sch 706 E Lenoir St Raleigh NC 27601 Office Phone: 919-856-7929. E-mail: espope@wcpss.net.

POPE, INGRID BLOOMQUIST, sculptor, poet, painter; b. Arvika, Sweden; became U.S. citizen. d. Oscar Emanuel and Gerda (Henningson) Brostrom; m. Howard Richard Bloomquist, Feb. 14, 1941 (dec. Nov. 1982); children: Dennis Howard, Diane Cecile Connelly, Laurel Ann Shields; m. Marvin Hoyle Pope, Mar. 9, 1985 (dec. June 1997). BA cum laude, Manhattanville Coll., 1979, MA in Humanities, 1981; MA in Religion, Yale U., 1984. Exhbns. include Manhattanville Coll., Purchase, N.Y., Yale Div. Sch., Ch. of Sweden in N.Y.C., First Ch. of Round Hill; author: (books) Musings, 1994, Hosannah, Help Please, 1999, Blessings, 2003. Past bd. dirs. N.Y.C. Mission Soc., Greenwich YWCA, Greenwich Chaplaincy, Greenwich Acad. Parents' Assn., past pres; past trustee First Ch. Round Hill, Greenwich; pres. Ch. Women United, Greenwich, 1989-91. Mem. AAUW, Nat. Assn. Pen Women, English Speaking Union, Nat. Wildflower Assn., Yale Club N.Y.C., Lakeview Club (Austin, Tex.), Acad. Am. Poets, Nat. Mus. of Women in Arts, Yale Alumnae Club (Austin and Greenwich, Conn.).

POPE, LENA ELIZABETH, human resources specialist; b. Brookhaven, Miss., Jan. 25, 1935; d. James S. and Elease (Edwards) Smith; m. Roland Van Pope, Dec. 22, 1955 (dec. 1967); children: Nikki D., Ronald V., Ouida. BS, Alcorn A&M Coll., 1955; student, Northwestern U., 1961, DePaul U., 1975-78; MA, Nat. Coll., 1987. Asst. to registrar Alcorn A&M Coll., Lorman, Miss., 1955-57; tchr. Alexander High Sch., Brookhaven, 1957-60, Magnolia High Sch., Moss Point, Miss., 1960-62; asst. student pers. Jackson (Miss.) State Coll., 1962-64; tchr. Chgo. Pub. schs., 1964-65, 78-80; adminstrv. asst. aide U.S. Senator Charles H. Percy, Chgo., 1965-78; tchr. Citywide Colls., Chgo., 1976-79; v.p. human resources Human Resources Devel. Inst., Chgo., 1982—. Cons. Foundatin I, Harvey, Ill., 1989—, Safer Found., Chgo., 1990—, Foster Park Community Orgn., Chgo., 1991—. Office mgr. Percy for Senator, Chgo., 1966, 70, 74, 78; transp. dir. Rep. Nat. Conv., Kansas City, Kans., 1976; vol. Thompson For Gov., Chgo.; sec. Oakdale Covenant Ch., 1985-89. Mem. Alcorn State Alumni (sec., con. 1990—), Eta Phi Beta (Soror of Yr. 1987; pres. Alpha Lambda chpt. 1999—). Republican. Avocations: desk top publishing, travel, reading.

POPE, LILLIE, psychologist, educator, writer, consultant; b. N.Y.C., June 22, 1918; d. Isador and Annie (Chusid) Bellin; m. Martin Pope, June 27, 1947; children: Miriam, Deborah Judith. BA, CCNY, 1937, MS in Edn., 1941; PhD, NYU, 1969. Lic. psychologist, N.Y. Psychologist Bklyn. Jewish Hosp., 1957-64; psychologist day treatment program Infants Home of Bklyn., 1959-64; dir. Bur. Edn. & Tng. Job Orientation Neighborhoods, N.Y.C., 1964-65; founding dir. learning disability clinic Coney Island Hosp., Bklyn., 1965—95, assoc. chief child psychiatry, 1986—95. Adj. prof. Bklyn. Coll., 1972-76; cons., lectr. Head Start and spl. edn. programs, nationwide, 1956—; cons. New Theatre Bklyn., 1983-91; mem. edn. adv. bd. Teaching Exceptional Children, Washington, 1980-86; chair adv. bd. McDowell Ctr. for Learning, Bklyn., 1983-94. Author: Guidelines to Teaching Remedial Reading, 1994. Lectureships U. Anchorage, 1983; bd. dirs. New Theatre Bklyn., 1983-91, Ezra Jack Keats Found., Bklyn., 1987—. NIMH fellow, 1968; United Cerebral Palsy Assn. grantee, 1969, N.Y.C. Bd. Edn. grantee, 1967-98; recipient Mary Hornby award Atlantic Conf. Nova Scotia, 1981. Fellow Am. Acad. Sch. Psychology (Hunter Coll. Hall of Fame, 1997); mem. APA (diplomate), Internat. Reading Assn., Coun. for Exceptional Children (Outstanding Svc. award 1990), Orton Soc., Multidisciplinary Acad. Clin. Edn. (charter), Assn. for Children With Learning Disabilities. Avocations: art, rock hunting, theater.

POPE, MARCIA L., lawyer; b. St. Petersburg, Fla., May 12, 1961; AB, Harvard Univ., 1983; JD, Univ. Va., 1986. Bar: Calif. 1986. Assoc. to ptnr., Employment & Labor practice Pillsbury Winthrop Shaw Pittman, San

Francisco, 1986—, employment counsel. Office: Pillsbury Winthrop Shaw Pittman 50 Fremont St San Francisco CA 94105 Office Phone: 415-983-6487. Office Fax: 415-983-1200. Business E-Mail: marcia.pope@pillsburylaw.com.

POPE, MARY THERESE, retired elementary school educator; b. Erie, Pa., Apr. 4, 1937; d. Joseph Cyril and Rose Isabel (Hoffman) Wittman; divorced; 1 child, Elizabeth Ann. BS in Elem. Edn., Seton Hill Coll., 1959; postgrad., U. Pitts., 1960. Cert. tchr., Pa. Tchr. Erie City Sch. Dist., 1959—65, 1968—99. Leader Blessed Sacrament Cadette troop, 1979-80, Girl Scouts U.S.A., 1983; mem. Blessed Sacrament PTA, Erie, 1972-80, pres. 1973-75; conf. chair Erie Diocese Separated-Divorced Caths., 1974-91; chair Cath. Com. on Scouting, 1986-88, retreat leader, 1990—; parish coun. Blessed Sacrament Ch., 1999—. Recipient St. Anne award Cath. Com. on Scouting, Erie Diocese, 1986. Mem. Seton Hill Coll. Alumna (chair 1971-73). Democrat. Avocations: sewing, reading, needlecrafts.

POPE, MELISSA LOPEZ, law educator; b. Detroit, May 8, 1969; d. Eugene Joe Lopez and Linda Rose Cunningham, Richard Lee Cunningham (Stepfather); m. Morgan Emmor Pope, July 29, 1995; 1 stepchild, Ian Charles. B in Lit., sci. and Arts, U. Mich., Ann Arbor, 1992; JD, Thomas M. Cooley Law Sch., Lansing, Mich., 1999. Bar: Mich. 1999. Acad. adminstrv. intern Office of Academic Multicultural Initiatives, U. Mich., Ann Arbor, 1992—93, multicultural program assoc., 1993—95; receptionist to Spkr. of the House, Mich. Ho. of Reps., Lansing, 1996—97, legal asst. to majority counsel, 1997—98; adj. prof., fed. Indian law Thomas M. Cooley Law Sch., Lansing, Mich., 1999—, asst. dir. and diversity coord. for admissions, 1999—2003, adj. prof., intro. to law, 2000—03, dep. dir., JD program Rochester, Mich., 2003—. Vol. Ann. Ann Arbor Pow Wow, Mich., 1988—; participant Native Am. Critical Issues Conf., Mich., 1993—; law student rep. Am. Indian Law Sect., Lansing, Mich., 1996—99; intern Mich. Commn. on Indian Affairs, Lansing, 1999—99; advisor Native Am. Law Student Assn., Cooley Law Sch., Lansing, Mich., 1999—2003; founder, mem. Thomas M. Cooley Law Sch. MLK Day Planning Com., 1999—; mem. So. Poverty Law Ctr., Montgomery, Ala., 2000—; sec./treas. Am. Indian Law Sect., State Bar of Mich., Lansing, 2000—01; mem. Holocaust Meml. Mus., Washington, 2000—; participant Nat. Conf. on Race and Ethnicity, 2000—; chair-elect Am. Indian Law sect. State Bar Mich., Lansing, 2001—02, chair Am. Indian Law sect., 2002—03; advisor student bar assn. diversity coalition Cooley Law Sch. Oakland U., 2003—, dep. dir. Thomas M. Cooley Law Sch., 2003—, ex-officio Am. Indian Law sect., 2003—. Mem.: Nat. Women's Law Alliance (founding mem., treas. 2002—). D-Liberal. Achievements include Head of Delegation, Four Directions Council, Native American Student Secretariat. Successfully lobbied for inclusion of Indigenous Peoples in the UN Conference on Population & Development document. Office: Thomas M Cooley Law Sch 472 O'Dowd Rochester/Oakland Univ Rochester MI 48309 E-mail: popem@cooley.edu.

POPEJOY, MELANIE ANN, music educator; b. Mexico, Mo., Aug. 13, 1958; d. Joseph Riley and Mildred Fern Monk; m. James Richard Popejoy, Aug. 2, 1980. MusB in Edn., Ctrl. Mo. State U., 1980, MA in Music Edn., 1989. Kodaly certification. Dir. chorus Eldon (Mo.) Schs., 1981—83, Mont. R-I Schs., California, Mont., Iowa City (Iowa) Mid. Sch., 1985—87, Raytown (Mo.) Mid. Sch., 1987—93; specialist elem. music Waco (Tex.) Ind. Sch. Dist., 1993—98; dir. chorus Lewisville (Tex.) Pub. Schs., 1998—2000, Valley Mid. Sch., Grand Forks, ND, 2000—, instr. voice, 2000—. Condr., artistic dir. Waco (Tex.) Girls Choir, 1994—97; founder, artistic dir., condr. Grand Cities Children's Choir, Grand Forks, 2002—. Named Tchr. of Yr., Raytown (Mo.) South Mid. Sch., 1991, N.D. Tchr. of Yr., Sam's Club/Walmart, 2004; recipient Tchr. of Yr., Waco (Tex.) Ind. Sch. Dist., 1996, Delay Mid. Sch., 2000. Mem.: Orgn. Am. Kodaly Educators, Music Educators Nat. Conf., Am. Choral Dirs. Assn. Avocation: singing. Office: Grand Forks Pub Schs Grand Forks ND 58203 Office Phone: 701-746-2360.

POPIAN, LUCIA, artist; b. Bacau, Romania, Sept. 1, 1956; arrived in U.S., 1999; d. Vasile and Maria Bocanet; m. Gabriel Popian, Apr. 11, 1981; 1 child, John. Degree, Nicolae Grigorescu, Bucharest, Romania, 1982; postgrad., Internat. Ctr. Study Presevation and Restoration of Cultural Property, Rome, 1996. Pres. G&L Popian, Pty Ltd., Sydney, Australia, 1993—99, G&L Popian, Inc., N.Y.C., 1999—. Exhibited in group shows at Orizont Art Gallery, Romania, 1985, Juan Miro Competition, Spain, 1986, exhibitions include Fgn. Residents in Italy, 1987. With inf. Romanian Marines, 1982. Recipient Sydney Cove medallion, Gov. NSW, Sydney, 1998. Mem.: Nat. Trust of Am. Republican. Eastern Orthodox. Avocations: pottery, gardening, pet care, tennis, reading. E-mail: archoan@aol.com.

POPLAWSKA, ANNA, artist, educator, art critic; Tchr. in field. Contbr. to monthly art columns in a the following publs.: Footlights Playbill, YogaChicago, Wednesday Jour. of Oak Park.; freelancer Chicago Artist's News. Mem.: Chgo. Art Critics Assn. Address: 1017 S Harlem Forest Park IL 60130 E-mail: poplawska@comcast.net.

POPOFF, EDNA SPIELER, psychologist, consultant; d. Isidor and Rose Spieler; m. William Popoff, June 1, 1946; children: Joshua, Ross, Leslie. BA, Hunter Coll., 1941—45; MA, Columbia U., 1945—47; post grad., Queens Coll., 1958—60; degree, St. John's U., 1960—63. Spl. edn. tchr. NYC Bd. Edn., 1960—65; sch. psychologist Bur. Child Guidance, NYC, 1965—87; guidance cons. Guidance Org. Dist. Office, NYC, 1987—97. Cons. AABB, Queens, NY, 1965—80. Mem.: Am. Psychol. Assn.

POPOVA, NINA, dancer, choreographer, director; b. Novorossisk, USSR, 1922; Student in Paris, studied ballet with Olga Preobrajenska, Lubov Egorova, Anatole Vilzak, Anatole Oboukhov, Igor Schwezoff. Ballet debut with Ballet de la Jeunesse, Paris, London, 1937-39; soloist Original Ballet Russe, 1939-41, Ballet Theatre (now Am. Ballet), 1941-42, Ballet Russe de Monte Carlo, 1943, 47, Ballet Alicia Alonso, Cuba; mem. faculty Sch. Performing Arts, N.Y.C., from 1954; later artistic dir. Houston Ballet, 1975; tchr. Nat. Acad. Arts, Champaign, Ill., also N.Y.C., 1975—, now Eglevsky Ballet Sch., L.I.; tchr. ballet Mexico City, Mex.; asst. choreographer mus. comedy Birmingham So. Coll., Ala., 1960; numerous appearances on Broadway stage, TV; former mem. regular cast Your Show of Shows; currently tchg. N.Y.C. Address: 33 Adams St Sea Cliff NY 11579-1614

POPOVIC, BOZENA (BO POPOVIC), artist; b. Kostajnica, Croatia, Jan. 2, 1957; d. Milorad and Dragica Skvorc; life ptnr. John Richard Tomasello. AA in Mdse., Fashion Inst. of Design & Mdse., San Francisco and L.A., 1977; BFA in Painting, Calif. Coll. Arts & Crafts, 1980; MPA in Pub. Policy Devel., Calif. State U., Hayward, 1997. Adminstr. Claims Tech. Svcs., Oakland, Calif., 1990-93; co-pub., owner Weekender Mag., West Contra Costa Ed., 1993—95; office mgr. Wild Oats Market, San Francisco, 1996-97; cons. fed. funded project Workers to Bus. Owners, Alameda, Calif., 1997; bus. rels. cons. Better Bus. Bur., San Francisco, 1998-99; rschr. Dominican U. of Calif., San Rafael, 1999—2002; devel. assoc. Found. Osteoporosis Rsch. and Edn., Oakland, 2002; devel. coord. Easter Seals No. Calif., Novato, 2002—. Bd. dirs. Women's Refuge, Oakland, 1999; outreach coord. San Pablo Hotel, Oakland, 1995; asst. dir. Voter Registration Project, San Francisco, 1987; active Re-Elect Marge Gibson campaign, Oakland, 1987, Don Perata campaign, Alameda, 1986-87. Mem.: AAUW, San Francisco Bus. Arts Coun., Assn. Fundraising Execs., Calif. Assn. Rschrs. for Advancement, Assn. Profl. Rsch. for Advancement, Soroptimists Internat. (regional del.). Avocations: reading, hiking, sketching. Office: Easter Seals No Calif 20 Pimentel Ct Ste A1 Novato CA 94949 Home: 2001 SE 131st Ave Vancouver WA 98683-6513 E-mail: bpopovic@ca-no.easter-seals.org.

POPP, CHARLOTTE LOUISE, retired health facility administrator; b. Vineland, N.J., July 26, 1946; d. William Henry and Elfriede Marie (Zickler) P. Diploma in Nursing, Luth. Hosp. of Md., Balt., 1967; BA in Health Edn., Rowan U., 1972; MA in Human Devel., Fairleigh-Dickinson U., 1981. Cert. Sch. Nurse, N.J., Health Educator, N.J. Charge nurse Newcomb Hosp., Vineland, N.J., 1967-71; supr. Vineland Rehab. Ctr., 1971-72; charge nurse Bridgeton (N.J.) Hosp., 1972-73; dir. insvc. edn. Millville (N.J.) Hosp., 1973-76; dir. hosp. insvc. edn. Vineland Devel. Ctr. State of N.J., 1976-78, program asst. Vineland Devel. Ctr., 1978-87; dir. habilitation planning services State of N.J., Vineland Devel. Ctr., 1987—2005, lead program coord. Vineland Devel. Ctr., 1981—2001; ret., 2005; adj. prof. practical nursing program Atlantic County Inst. Tech., 2004—; sub. sch. nurse Franklin Twsp., Gloucester County, NJ, 2005—. Exam proctor State of N.J. Bd. Nursing, Newark, 1973—91. Editorial rev. bd. (jour.) Nursing Update, 1973-77. Vol. South Jersey Regional Med. Ctr., 2004—, Am. Red Cross, 2005—; instr. basic life support Am. Heart Assn., bd. dir. Tri-county chpt., 1979—83, bd. dir. South Jersey chpt., 1983—90. Mem. ANA, N.J. State Nurses Assn., South Jersey Insvc. Exch. (life), Smithsonian Assn., Luth. Hosp. of Md. Alumni Assn., Glassboro State Coll./Rowan U. Alumni Assn., Fairleigh-Dickinson U. Alumni Assn. Lutheran. Avocations: reading, travel, collectable plates, animals, horseracing.

POPPE, LAURIE CATHERINE, matrimonial lawyer, social worker, real estate executive; b. Fairfax, Va., Jan. 31, 1964; d. Loren Edward Brunner, Jr. and Elizabeth May Carper, Edward Monroe Peffly, Jr. (Stepfather); m. Christopher Carsten Poppe; 1 child, Sarah Elizabeth. A.Arch., No. Va. C.C., Annandale, 1985; AAS in Restaurant Mgmt., The Restaurant Sch., Phila., 1988; BA in Psychology, Rutgers U., New Brunswick, N.J., 1999; MSW, Rutgers U., 2005; JD, Rutgers U., Newark, 2005. Bar: N.J. 2005; LCSW N.J., 2005. Owner, mem. Dominion Properties, LLC, McLean, Va., 1994—; law clk. to Hon. Ann R. Bartlett, Superior Ct. NJ State Judiciary, Somerville, 2005—; with Norris, McLaughlin & Marcus, P.A., Bridgewater, NJ, 2006—. Scholarship founder for ind. rsch. Douglass Coll., Mabel Smith Honors Program, New Brunswick, 1999—2002. Grantee, Mabel Smith Honor Program, 1998. Mem.: AAUW, NASW, ABA, Somerset County Bar Assn., N.J. State Bar Assn., Psi Chi. Achievements include research in utilization of early intervention programs. Avocations: martial arts, singing, culinary arts, travel. Office Phone: 908-722-0700. Business E-Mail: lcpoppe@nmmlaw.com.

POPPE, PAMELA J., accountant; b. Breckenridge, Minn., Oct. 25, 1948; d. John T. and Anita Ruth (Knudsen) Sanker; m. James Wayne Kelly, May 10, 1969 (div. May 1993); children: Jamison Marc, Brian Lee m. James E. Poppe, Jan. 19, 2000. BA in Music Edn., Concordia Coll., Moorhead, Minn., 1969; BS in Indsl. Adminstrn., Iowa State U., 1980. CPA, Iowa. Band and choir tchr. Danube (Minn.) Ind. Schs., 1969-70; orch. tchr. Raleigh (N.C.) City Schs., 1972-73; French and English tchr. Bethel Acad., Kinston, N.C., 1974; jr. high sch. music tchr. Lenoir County Schs., Kinston, 1974-76; in-charge staff auditor McGladrey Pullen, Des Moines, 1980-82; with internal auditing dept. Am. Fed. Savs. & Loan, Des Moines, 1982-84; v.p. fin. Gentry, Ltd., Des Moines, 1984-89; dir. property mgmt. adminstrn. R&R Investors, Ltd., West Des Moines, Iowa, 1989—96; controller Venter Spooner Inc., Johnston, Iowa, 1997—. Mem. acct. adv. bd. Am. Inst. Bus., Des Moines, 1988-94. Chairperson Holy Trinity Luth. Ch., Ankeny, Iowa, 1991. Recipient Elijah Watts Sells award AICPA, 1980. Mem. Cert. Financial Mgrs. Assn., Iowa Timberline Users Group, Iowa Soc. CPAs, Mensa, Phi Beta Kappa. Avocations: reading, needlecrafts, quilting, dance, bicycling. Home: 909 SE Kensington Rd Ankeny IA 50021-3960 Office: 6500 NW Beaver Dr Johnston IA 50131 Office Phone: 515-331-2800. E-mail: ppoppe@venterspooner.com.

POPPEN, MARCELLA MAY, music educator; b. Aug. 20, 1924; MusM, Eastman Sch. Music, 1952, U. Oreg., 1971; D of Music Edn., Ind. U., 1976. Instr. music Balko Jo Gakuin, Shimonoseki, Japan, 1951-55, Union Free Sch. Dist. #12, Melverne, NY, 1956-68, SUNY, Brockport, 1969-71, North Ctrl. Coll., Mpls., 1984-86; min. of music Evang. Luth. Ch. in Am., Bloomsburg, Pa., Budd Lake, N.J., 1986-93; ind. piano instr. Orange City, Iowa, 1993—. Assoc. in ministry Evang. Luth. Ch. in Am. Ind. U. rsch. grantee, 1976. Mem. Am. Guild of Organists, Music Tchrs. Nat. Assn., Iowa Music Tchrs. Assn., Assn. Luth. Ch. Musicians, Ind. U. Alumni Assn., Mu Phi Epsilon. Personal E-mail: marpo@orangecitycomm.net.

POPPLER, DORIS SWORDS, lawyer; b. Billings, Mont., Nov. 10, 1924; d. Lloyd William and Edna (Mowre) Swords; m. Louis E. Poppler, June 11, 1949; children: Louis William, Kristine, Mark J., Blaine, Claire, Arminda. Student, U. Minn., 1942-44; JD, Mont. State U., 1948. Bar: Mont. 1948, U.S. Dist. Ct. Mont. 1948, U.S. Ct. Appeals (9th cir.) 1990. Pvt. practice law, Billings, 1948-49; sec., treas. Wonderpark Corp., Billings, 1959-62; atty. Yellowstone County Attys. Office, Billings, 1972-75; ptnr. Poppler and Barz, Billings, 1972-79, Davidson, Veeder, Baugh, Broeder and Poppler, Billings, 1979-84, Davidson and Poppler, P.C., Billings, 1984-90; U.S. atty. Dist. of Mont., Billings, 1990-93; field rep. Nat. Indian Gaming Commn., Washington, 1993-2000. Pres. Jr. League, 1964-65; bd. dirs., pres. Yellowstone County Metre Bd., 1982; trustee Rocky Mt. Coll., 1984-90, mem. nat. adv. bd., 1993—; mem. Mont. Human Rights Commn., 1988-90; bd. dirs. Miss Mont. Pageant, 1995—; elected to Billings City Coun., Billings, Mont., 2002; elected dep. mayor coun. woman Ward4, 2002—. Recipient Mont. Salute to Women award, Mont. Woman of Achievent award, 1975, Disting. Svc. award Rocky Mt. Coll., 1990, Disting. Female Alumna award U. Montana Law Sch., 1996, 2004, Status Women award Zonta Club, 2004. Mem. AAUW, Mont. Bar Assn., Nat. Assn. Former U.S. Attys., Nat. Rep. Lawyers Assn., Internat. Women's Forum, Yellowstone County Bar Assn. (pres. 1990, Lifetime Achievement award 2004), Alpha Chi Omega. Republican.

PORAD, FRANCINE JOY, poet, painter; b. Seattle, Sept. 3, 1929; d. Morris H. and Gertrude (Volchok) Harvitz; m. Bernard L. Porad, June 12, 1949 (dec.); children: Laurie, Bruce, Ken, Constance, Marci, Jeffrey. BFA, U. Wash., 1976. Founder, coord. Haiku NW Poets/Readers, Mercer Isle, Wash., 1988—2000; editor Brussels Sprout, Mercer Isle, 1988-95; co-editor Haiku Northwest Anthology, Seattle, 1996, Red Moon Press, Berryville, Va., 1996. Workshop presenter Haiku Can., Toronto and Alymer, Que., Can., 1992, 95, Haiku N.Am., Calif., Toronto, 1993, 95, Haiku N.Am., Oreg., 1997, Haiku Internat., Tokyo, 1997; judge Internat. Haiku Contest New Zealand Poetry Soc., 1995, People's Haiku & Senryu Contest, Canada, 1999, San Francisco Contest for Haiku Poets of North Calif., 1992, Hawaii Edn. Assn., Honolulu, 1995, 99, PEN Women (Seattle) Internat. Poetry Contest, 2000, Fla. State Poetry Assn. Contest, 2003. Author: Connections, 1986, Pen and Inklings, 1986, After Autumn Rain, 1987, Blues on the Run, 1988, Free of Clouds, 1989, Without Haste, 1989 (Cicada Chapbook award 1990), Hundreds of Wishes, 1990, A Mural of Leaves, 1991, Joy is My Middle Name, 1993, The Patchwork Quilt, 1994 (Haiku Soc. Am. Merit Book 1994), Waterways, 1995 (Haiku Can. Sheet Book series 1995), All Eyes, 1995, Ladies and Jellyspoons, 1996, Extended Wings, 1996, Moon, Moon, 1997, Fog Lifting, 1997, All the Games, 1997, Let's Count The Trees, 1998 (Haiku Can. Sheet Selection 1998), (with M. Mountain) Cur*rent, 1998, The Perfect Worry-Stone, 2000, (with K. Kondo and M. Mountain) Other Rens, 2000, Other Rens Book Two and Book Three, 2000, Trio of Wrens, 2000, Second Blooming, 2001, Other Rens Book Five and Book Six, 2001, Other Rens Book Seven, 2001, Other Rens Book Eight, 2002, Other Rens Book Nine, 2002, Other Rens Book Ten, 2003, Probably: 'Real' Renga Sorta, 2002, Probably: 'Real' Renga Sorta 2, 2003, Sunlight Comes and Goes, 2004, (with M. Mountain) Pieces, 2005, Buzzwords, 2005. Recipient 1st prize Internat. Tanka competition Poetry Soc. Japan, Tokyo, 1993, Itoen Tea award Haiku Internat., Tokyo, 1996, 98, Cicada award for Haiku sequences by Amelia, 1999, award Mainichi Internat. Haiku Contest, Tokyo, 1999, Francine Porad's Yearly Haiku award Wash. Poets Assn., 2004, haiku contest award NC Poetry Soc., 2006; named an Hon. Curator Calif. State Libr. Am. Haiku Archive, 2005-06. Mem. Nat. League Am. Penwomen (treas. 1992-94, Owl award 1982, 92, 1st prize state art exhbn. Frye Mus. 1993, 1st pl. Haiku, 1995), Haiku Soc. Am. (pres. 1993-94, Merit book 1994, judge 1997, Brady Senryu Contest H.M. award 1997, Merit book award 2001, San Francisco Internat. Haiku award 2002, Sora award 2004), Heron's Nest award, 2003), N.W. Watercolor Soc. (treas. 1980-85), Women Painters Wash. (v.p. 1987, bd. 1985-93). Avocations: computer fun, travel. Home: 10392 NE 12th I-307 Bellevue WA 98004-4263 E-mail: poradF@aol.com.

PORCH, KATHY M., information technology executive, educator; b. LA, Feb. 17, 1964; d. Donald D. and Joan I. Jones; m. Kerry Porch, Nov. 7, 1987; children: Jason R. Green, John C. MS in Info. Tech. and Info. Security, Capella U., Mpls., 2006. Dir. info. tech. Red Rocks C.C., Lakewood, Colo., 1993—. Office Phone: 303-914-6218.

PORDON, GRACE, writer, poet, artist; life ptnr. Ezequiel Rodriguez Gallegos. Dir. Casa Poema Writer's Retreat, Jalisco, Mexico, 2000—. Dir. Casa Poema Writers' Retreat, Jalisco, Mexico, 2000—. Editor: website. Socialist. Mystic. Office: CasaPoema Writers' Retreat Jalisco Mexico Personal E-mail: casapoema@hotmail.com.

PORGES, AMELIA, lawyer; BA, Cornell U., 1973; MPP, Harvard U., 1980, JD cum laude, 1980. Bar: DC 1980, US Ct. Appeals, Fed. Cir., US Ct. Internat. Trade, cert.: GATT (sr. legal officer). Sr. counsel for dispute settlement, head enforcement US Trade Rep.; counsel Sidley Austin LLP, Washington, DC. Tchr. trade law Sophia U., Tokyo, Johns Hopkins U. Sch. Advanced Internat. Studies; adv. bd. mem. Stanford GATT Digital Archive. Author: Guide to Gatt Law and Practice: Analytical Index; contbr. articles to profl. jours. Mem.: ABA (mem. internat. trade steering group), Am. Soc. Internat. Law. Office: Sidley Austin LLP 1501 K St NW Washington DC 20005 Office Phone: 202-736-8361. Office Fax: 202-736-8711. E-mail: aporges@sidley.com.

PORGES, LUCIE, apparel designer, educator; b. Vienna, Austria, Nov. 23, 1926; arrived in U.S., 1951; d. Eisig and Jetty (Rosner) Eisenstab; m. Paul Peter Porges, June 25, 1951; children: Claudia, Vivette. Attended, Ecole des Arts et Metiers, 1945—48; degree in fashion, Ecole des Arts Geneva. Asst. designer Pauline Trigere, N.Y.C., 1951—94; ret. Tchr. design Drexel U., Phila., 1981—93. Exhibitions include Vienna, 2000. Recipient Chevalier des Arts et Letters, Paris, 1993. Achievements include design of uniforms for United Airlines, 1980. Personal E-mail: styleandhumor@aol.com.

PORIES, MURIEL H., finance company executive; b. Milw., Dec. 19, 1925; d. Jacob and Jean Aronson; m. Walter J. Pories, Aug. 1951 (div. Apr. 1977). BS, U. Wis., Milw., 1951; MA, John Carroll U., 1979; JD, Am. Coll. Law, Brea, Calif., 1984. Cert. prin. Tchr. Irondequoit (N.Y.) Bd. Edn., 1956-59, Shaker Heights (Ohio) Pub. Schs., 1973—77; counselor Lawyers Referral Svc., Santa Ana, Calif., 1983; tchr. Rochester (N.Y.) Bd. Edn., 1984; mng. ptnr. Pories and Klein, Fullerton, Calif., 1984; mktg. analyst Display Techniques Internat., Santa Ana, Calif., 1986; dir. mktg. Peninsula Shipyard, Newport Beach, Calif., 1987-89; pres., owner Mar-Bruc Inc., Laguna Beach, Calif., 2002—. Loan cons. CPM Fin., Ont., 1974; pioneered open edn. Shaker Heights Bd. Edn., 2003; adj. prof. Am. Coll. Law, Anaheim, Calif., 2002—. Author: "That's Because We Love You," 1976, A Program for Dropout Reduction, 1978. Mem. Am. Coll. Law Alumni (pres. 1999). Democrat. Achievements include co-invention of E-Z Cycle Lite. Avocations: swimming, ping pong/table tennis. Home: 227 Cozumel Laguna Beach CA 92651

PORITZ, DEBORAH TOBIAS, retired state supreme court justice, former state attorney general; b. Bklyn., Oct. 26, 1936; m. Alan Poritz; children: Jonathan, Mark. BA, Brooklyn Coll., City U. NY, 1958; JD, U. Penn., 1977. English tchr. Ursinus Coll., Collegeville, Pa., 1967—70; dep. atty. gen. NJ Dept. Law and Pub. Safety, 1977—81, asst. chief environ. protection section, 1981—84, dep. atty. gen. in charge of appeals, chief banking, ins. and pub. securities section, 1984—86, asst. atty. gen., dir. divsn. law, 1986—89; chief counsel to Gov. Thomas Kean State of NJ, Trenton, 1989—90; ptnr. Jamieson, Moore, Peskin & Spicer LLP, Princeton, NJ, 1990—94; atty. gen. State of NJ, Trenton, 1994—96; chief justice NJ Supreme Ct., Trenton, 1996—2006. Recipient Presdl. medal, Bklyn. Coll., 2000.*

PORT, RUTH ELIZABETH, literature and language professor; d. Emory Mahlon and Eunice Funkhouser Kaiser; m. Robert David Port, July 1, 1966; children: Lorinda Elaine Port Williams, Eric Mahlon. BA in English, Hood Coll., 1964; MA in English, U. Md., 1968; PhD in English, No. Ill. U., 1999. Cert. English Secondary Tchr. Md., Pa., Ill. English tchr. Howard County, Md., 1964—65, York County, Dillsburg, Pa., 1967—68, Urbana HS, Ill., 1968—70; English instr., prof. Waubonsee CC, Sugar Grove, Ill., 1982—2000, writing workshop dir., 1990—98, honors com. mem., 1990—2000; edn. field experience supr. Aurora (Ill.) U., 2001—. Author: (poem) Silence, 1994. Host Cmty. Bible Studies, Big Rock, Ill., 1990—. Avocations: gardening, horseback riding, travel, bicycling. Home: 85838 Johns St Big Rock IL 60511

PORTE, BARBARA ANN, writer, librarian; b. NYC, 1943; d. Sol and Dora Porte; m. Floyd Thomas. BS in Agr., Mich. State U., 1965; MS in Libr. Sci., L.I. U. Palmer Sch. Libr. and Info. Sci., 1969. Libr. Freeport Meml. Libr., L.I., NY, Prince Georges County Meml. Libr. Sys., Hyattsville, Md., Nassau Libr. Sys., L.I., NY, 1974—86. Author: Harry's Visit, 1983 (ALA notable book), Jesse's Ghost and Other Stories, 1983, Harry's Dog, 1984 (ALA notable book), Harry's Mom, 1985 (Childrens book of yr. Child Study Assn., 1986), The Kidnapping of Aunt Elizabeth, 1985 (Am. Booksellers Assn. pick of list, 1985), I Only Made Up the Roses, 1987 (Best of the Best for Children award ALA), Harry in Trouble (reprinted as an I Can Read Book, 2002), 1989 (ALA notable book), The Take-Along Dog, 1989, Ruthann and Her Pig, 1989 (Parent's Mag. and Learning best book), Fat Fanny, Beanpole Bertha, and the Boys, 1991, Harry Gets an Uncle (reprinted as an I Can Read Book, 2002), 1991 (Childrens book of yr. Child Study Assn., 1992), Taxicab Tales, 1992, A Turkey Drive and Other Tales, 1993, Leave That Cricket Be, Alan Lee, 1993, When Grandma Almost Fell off the Mountain and Other Stories, 1993, Something Terrible Happened, 1994 (ALA best book young adults), When Aunt Lucy Rode a Mule and Other Stories, 1994, Harry's Birthday (reprinted as an I Can Read Book, 2003), 1994, Chickens! Chickens!, 1995 (Am. Booksellers Assn. pick of list, 1995, Parent's Choice picture book honor, 1995), Black Elephant with a Brown Ear (in Alabama), 1996, Surprise! Surprise! It's Grandfather's Birthday, 1997, Harry's Pony (reprinted as an I Can Read Book, 2004), 1997 (Am. Booksellers Assn. pick of list, 1997), Tale of a Tadpole, 1997 (Am. Booksellers Assn. pick of list, 1997, Sci. Am. best sci. books for children, 1997, NTSA outstanding sci. trade book for children, 1998), Hearsay: Strange Tales from the Middle Kingdom, 1998 (Anne Izard Storyteller's Choice award, 2000), He's Sorry, She's Sorry, They're Sorry Too: Stories, 1998, If You Ever Get Lost: The Adventures of Julia and Evan, 2000 (Parent's Guide to Children's Media award, 2000, Capitol Choices selection, 2000), Ma Jiang and the Orange Ants, 2000 (New Eng. States Touring literary classic selection), Beauty and the Serpent: Thirteen Tales of Unnatural Animals, 2001 (N.Y. Pub. Libr. books for teen age designation, 2003); contbr. short stories and articles to newspapers and popular mags. Mem.: Women's Nat. Book Assn., Children's Book Guild, Author's Guild. Home: PO Box 16627 Arlington VA 22215-1627

PORTEE, CASSANDRA SMITH, elementary school educator, music educator; b. Columbia, SC, Sept. 20, 1960; d. Cheklubia Calvin and Rosa Lee Smith; m. Alvin Portee, Jr., Apr. 4, 1983; 1 child, Allyson Lolita. MusB, Columbia Coll., 1982; Masters Degree, Lesley U., Cambridge, Mass., 2000. Elem. music tchr. Orangeburg Sch. Dist. Six, North, SC, 1982—86, Richland Sch. Dist. Two, Columbia, 1988—. Bd. mem. Ctrl. Midlands Planning Coun., Columbia, 1986—87; philanthropy chair, 3rd v.p. Capital City Rep. Women, Columbia, 2002; hon. bd. mem. Winning Women, Columbia, 2004—. Mem.: SC Music Assn., Eau Claire Music Club, Delta Kappa Gamma. Republican. Baptist. Avocations: travel, reading, crafts. Home: 817 Chester St Columbia SC 29201 Office: Bethel-Hanberry Elementary School 125 Boney Rd Blythewood SC 29016 Office Phone: 803-691-6880. Office Fax: 803-691-6883. Business E-Mail: cportee@bhe.richland2.org.

PORTER, AMY, music educator; d. Richard and Diana Joan Porter; m. Steven Byess, Dec. 27, 1996. MusB, The Juilliard Sch., NYC, 1986, MusM, 1987. Assoc. prof. flute U. Mich. Sch. Music, Ann Arbor, 1999—. Author: (DVD) Karg Elert 30 Caprices: A Study Guide with Amy Porter; arranger: songs Six Songs for Flute and Piano by Benjamine Godard; musician (soloist): (CD) Porter Ambrose King, (Bolcom lyric concerto) Bolcom, Bassett, Daugherty. Named winner, Kobe (Japan) Internat. Flute Competition, 1993, Ville d'Avray Internat. Flute Competition, Paris, 2001; recipient Henry Russel award, U. Mich., 2006. Mem.: Nat. Flute Assn. (bd. mem. 2006—, first prize young artist competition 1990), SE Mich. Flute Assn. (founder, pres. 2002—05, immediate past pres. 2006—). Office: University of Michigan School of Music 1100 Baits Dr Ann Arbor MI 48109 Office Phone: 734-764-7591.

PORTER, CATHERINE (KAY PORTER), therapist, business consultant; b. El Paso, Tex., Jan. 29, 1941; d. Horace Catlin and Lillian (Mier) P. BS, U. Tex., El Paso, 1962; MA, U. Houston, 1966; PhD, U. Oreg., 1972. Systems analyst Univac Corp., Houston, 1963-65; instr. in computers Houston Ind. Sch. Dist., Houston, 1965-67; rsch. assoc. computer ctr. Oreg. State U., Corvallis, 1967-74; asst. prof. U. Oreg., Eugene, 1974-82; pres. Porter Foster Sports & Orgnl. Cons., Eugene, 1983-88, Porter Performance Systems, Eugene, 1988—. Sports psychologist U.S. Olympic Coms., Colorado Springs, Colo., 1987—, U.S.A. Track & Field, Indpls., 1987—, U.S. Tennis Assn., Princeton, N.J., 1987—. Author: The Mental Athlete, 2003, Visual Athletics, 1990; contbr. articles to profl. jours. Coaching walkers to walk Portland Marathon. Mem. Assn. for Advance of Applied Sports Psychology, Profl. Women's Network of Oreg., Oreg. Track Club (bd. dirs. Eugene chpt. 1985-93). Avocations: running, backpacking, hiking, photography, skiing. Office: Porter Performance Systems PO Box 5584 Eugene OR 97405-0584 Office Phone: 541-342-6875. Personal E-mail: kayporter1@aol.com.

PORTER, DONNA JEAN, genealogist; b. Monte Vista, Colo., Aug. 20, 1931; d. George W. and Alma R. (Kile) Bishop; m. Earl Edwin Carmack, Nov. 14, 1949 (div. 1955); m. Paul W. Porter, June 4, 1955; children: LeiLonia Virginia, Paul Benjamin, Rebecca Ann. Registered profl. genealogist. Genealogist, Denver, 1969—; owner Stagecoach Libr. Geneal. Rsch., 1982—2003; staff trainer Lakewood Family History Ctr., 1996—. Instr. and lectr. in field. Co-author: Welding Link, An Introduction to Genealogy, 1968; editor Colo. Genealogist mag., 1970-75; contbr. articles to profl. jours. and mags. Asst. libr. Family History Ctr. Libr., LDS Ch., Denver, 1966-76, mem. acquisition com., instr. spl. geneal. instrn. com.; v.p. Colo. chpt. Palatines to Am., Denver, 1985-86, pres., 1986-87, exhibitor's chair Nat. Conf., 1988. Mem. West Palm Beach Geneal. Soc. (founder, pres. 1964-66), Colo. Geneal. Soc. (corr. sec. 1968-69, pres. 1969-70, 2nd v.p., program chair 1971-73, seminar chair 1974, chair, judge Black Sheep contest 1988), Foothills Geneal. Soc. (pres. 1996-98, genealogist 1983-88, ednl. dir. 1992—, staff genealogist Foothills Inquirere mag. 1983—, Genie of Yr. award 1992), Colo. Coun. Geneal. Socs. (v.p. 1986-87, pres. 1987-90, chair Colo. State Archives Ednl. Gift Fund 1991-03), Nat. Soc. DAR (Peace Pipe chpt. state lineage chair 1970-73, registrar 1971-77), Ind. Hist. Soc., Ind. Geneal. Soc., Nat. Geneal. Soc., Internat. Soc. for Brit. Genealogy and Family History (life: v.p. 2000-03, pres. 2003-05), Ohio Geneal. Soc. (life, Colo. chpt., Champaign County chpt., Madison County chpt., Ross County chpt., Monroe County chpt.), Mo. Geneal. Soc. (life), Md. Geneal. Soc. (life), St. Andrew Soc. (life), Inst. Heraldic and Geneal. Studies, Assn. Profl. Genealogists, Assn. for Gravestone Studies, Palatines of Am. (Colo. chpt.), Lower Delmara Geneal. Soc., Baltimore County Geneal. Soc., Shockey Family Meml. Fellowship (treas. 2005—), Internat. Soc. Brit. Genealogy and Family History (v.p. 1999-2004, pres. 2004-05), Wales Ireland Scotland Eng. Brit. Soc. Colo. (treas. 1994-2002). Home: 1840 S Wolcott Ct Denver CO 80219-4309

PORTER, ELSA ALLGOOD, writer, educator; b. Amoy, China, Dec. 19, 1928; d. Roy and Petra (Johnsen) Allgood; m. Raeford B. Liles, Mar. 19, 1949 (div. 1959); children: Barbara, Janet; m. G. Hinckley Porter, Nov. 22, 1962; children: David, Brian, Wendy. BA, Birmingham-So. Coll., 1949; MA, U. Ala., 1959; M in Pub. Adminstrn., Harvard U., 1971; LHD (hon.), U. Ala., 1986. With HEW, Washington, 1960-73; with U.S. CSC, Washington, 1973-77; asst. sec. Dept. Commerce, Washington, 1977-81; disting. practitioner in residence Washington Pub. Affairs Ctr., U. So. Calif., Washington, 1982-84; v.p. R & D The Maccoby Group, Washington, 1990-96; sr. fellow Meridian Internat. Inst., 1990—. Chair comml. adv. subcom. NASA, 1997—2003. Fellow World Acad. Art & Scis., Nat. Acad. Pub. Adminstrs.; mem. Women's Nat. Dem. Club. Home: 2309 SW 1st Ave Apt 742 Portland OR 97201-5008

PORTER, ETHEL MAE, publishing executive; b. Phila., July 16, 1947; d. Everette Marmon and Ethel Mae Porter. BA in Econs., Mount Holyoke Coll., 1969; MA in Internat. Rels., Yale U., 1971, MPhil in Am. Studies, 1975, PhD in Am. Studies, 1978. Sr. account exec. CTB McGraw-Hill, Monterey, Calif., 2003—04; v.p. Riverside Pub., Itasca, Ill., 2004—. V.p. Harcourt Ednl. Measurement, San Antonio, 1984—2002. Former mem. San Antonio Libr. Found., San Antonio, Tex. Recipient Educator's Hall of Fame, Phi Delta Kappa, Inc.k Gamma Tau Chpt., 1998. Mem.: Nat. Assn. of Black Sch. Educators (life Policy Fellow, Inst. for Edn!. Leadership 1979-1980). Office: Riverside Pub 425 Spring Lake Dr Itasca IL 60143 Office Phone: 630-467-6516. Office Fax: 630-467-7150. Business E-Mail: ethel_porter@hmco.com.

PORTER, JEAN MCRAE, counselor; b. Augusta, Ga., Aug. 1, 1949; d. Hugh Burrell and Ruby Collins McRae; m. Ralph S. Porter, Jr., Aug. 17, 1975; children: Bradford Sloan, Jonathan James. BS, Augusta Coll., Ga., 1970; MEd, Clemson U., S.C., 1973. Cert. secondary adminstrn., guidance, biology, elem., sci. tchg. Tchr. Davenport Jr. H.S., Greer, SC, 1970—71, Greer Middle Sch., 1971—73; counselor Hillcrest Middle Sch., Simpsonville, SC, 1973—75; counselor, tchr. Hughes Middle Sch., Greenville, SC, 1975—84; counselor Wade Hampton H.S., Greenville, 1984—90, Bryson Middle Sch., Simpsonville, 1990—94, Woodmont H.S., Piedmont, SC, 1994—95, Northwood Middle Sch., Taylors, SC, 1995—, 504 accommodations coord., 2002—. Facilitator Christmas Knights, 1995—. Mem.: NEA, Nat. Assn. Mental Illness, Greenville County Edn. Assn., SC Counselors Assn., SC Edn. Assn. Democrat. Avocations: reading, hiking, raising dogs. Home: 111 Brigham Creek Dr Greer SC 29650 Office: Northwood Middle School 710 Ikes Rd Taylors SC 29687 Business E-Mail: jporter@northwd.greenville.k12.sc.us.com.

PORTER, JEANNE SMITH, civic worker; b. Hammond, Ind., Feb. 27, 1930; d. Cyril Augustus and Mary (Mabley) Smith; m. William Harry Porter, Apr. 1, 1953; children: Wendy Alice, David William, Mary Elizabeth, Audrey Jeanne. Student, Hanover Coll., 1948-50; BA in Lit. with honors, Ind. U., 1953. One-woman shows include Art Works Gallery, Holter Mus., Helena, Mont., 2003. Developer, area leader Recovery, Inc., Mont., 1971-82; adv. bd. Mont. House Day Treatment Ctr., Helena, 1980-93; bd. dirs., libr. chmn., Mont. Alliance for Mentally Ill, Helena, 1979—; organizer, planner Columbarium garden, Episcopal Ch., Helena, 1988—; organizer T-House project Mental Health Svcs., 1983-88; developer Social Club-Mentally Ill., 1968—; libr. com. Tucson Episcopal Ch Recipient Disting. Svc. award Jayceens Helena, 1974, Cmty. Svc. award Carroll Coll., 1986, Electrum award Helena Arts Coun., 1988, Long Term Svc. award Mont. Alliance for Mentally Ill., 1989, Vol. of Yr. award Mental Health Assn. Mont., 1989, Dignity award Golden Triangle Mental Health Ctr., 2001. Mem. P.E.O. (philanthropic com. chpt. O 1994—), S.W. Ariz. Watercolor Guild Avocations: painting, drawing, gardening, travel, reading. Home: 4111 E Placita Presilla Tucson AZ 85718-3434

PORTER, JENNIFER MADELEINE, film producer, film director; b. Milw., Oct. 3, 1962; d. John Hamlin and Helen Meak (Smith) P. BA in Comm., Bowling Green State U., 1984. Audio visual supr. Liberty Mutual Ins. Group, Berwyn, Pa., 1985-88; sr. prodr. audio visual Prudential Ins. Co., Mpls., 1988-93; proprietor Shoot The Moon Prodns., Mound, Minn., 1993-96, Shoot the Moon Prodns., Mpls., 1996—. Prodr., dir., writer: (audio visual programs) Phantom Lake.A Lifetime of Memories, 1991 (Best of Show 1991, Script award Assn. for Multi-Image Internat. 1991), Vision.The Gamma Phi Beta Foundation, 1992 (First Place award 1993), prodr., prodn. coord. Stadium Theatre Experience-College Football Hall of Fame (Silver award Assn. for Multi-Image Internat. 1996), the Making of Homo Heights, 1997 (Women in Dirs. Chair Walker Art Ctr.). Mentor U. Minn., Mpls., 1989-96; fundraiser Gamma Phi Beta Found. Philanthropy-Spl. Camping for Girls, Minn., Wis., 1991-99; chairperson 100th Celebration, Phantom Lake YMCA Camp, Mukwonago, Wis., 1994-96. Mem. Assn. for Multi-Image Internat. (exec. bd. local 1986-88), Gamma Phi Beta (internat. officer, pub. rels. speaker/prodr. 1991-99). Avocations: travel, music, sports, camping, canoeing. Home and Office: Shoot The Moon Prodns 5104 26th Ave S Minneapolis MN 55417-1317 E-mail: shootthemoon@usinternet.com.

PORTER, JILL, journalist; b. Phila., Aug. 5, 1946; d. Sidney and Mae (Merion) Chalfin; m. Eric Porter, Mar. 7, 1970 (div. 1975); m. Fred Hamilton, Oct. 28, 1983; 1 child, Zachary. BA, Temple U., 1968. Pub. rels. Manning Smith P.R., Phila., 1968-69; reporter Norristown Times Herald, Norristown, Pa., 1969-72, The Trentonian, Trenton, NJ, 1972-75, The Phila. Daily News, Phila., 1975-79, columnist, 1979—. Instr. Temple U., 1976—80. Contbr. articles to numerous mags. Vol. Phila. Futures, 1994, 95, 96, Phila. Cares, 1997, Career Wardrobe, 2006. Recipient numerous journalism awards. Avocations: dance, biking, reading. Home: 134 Rolling Rd Bala Cynwyd PA 19004-2615 Office: Phila Newspapers Inc Phila Daily News 400 N Broad St Philadelphia PA 19130-4015 Office Phone: 215-854-5850. E-mail: porterj@phillynews.com.

PORTER, JOYCE KLOWDEN, theater educator, director, actress; b. Chgo., Dec. 21, 1949; d. LeRoy and Esther (Siegel) Klowden; m. Paul Wayne Porter, June 8, 1980; 1 child, David Benjamin. BA in Speech Edn., U. Ill., 1971; MA in Theatre, Northwestern U., Evanston, Ill., 1972; postgrad., Northeastern U., Chgo., 1980, Northeastern U., 1989, postgrad., 1998, Ill. State U., Normal, 1985—90. Prof. theatre, play dir. Moraine Valley C.C., Palos Hills, Ill., 1972—2002, emeritus, 2002—, acting theatre coord., 1986-87, theatre coord., 2001—02. Adj. faculty Columbia Coll., 1988—92, Triton Coll., 2004; text reviewer Harcourt Brace Pub., 1997, Simon & Schuster, 1998, Mayfield, 1999, Martins, 2000—, Pearsons Ednl., 2001—03; actress, Chgo., 1972—, LA, 2005—; lectr. Sixth Star Entertainment, 2006—. Author: (textbook) Humanities on the Go, 1992, Experiencing the Arts, 2000. Adv. bd. Oak Park (Ill.) Park Dist., 1983; co-chmn. Moraine chpt. Chgo. Area Faculty for nuclear Freeze, Palos Hills, 1985-87; announcer for blind Chgo. Radio Info. Svc., 1982-83; bd. dirs. Festival Theatre, Oak Park, 1989—, sec. 1996-97, pres., 1997-99, v.p. 2002-2003, pres., 2003—; play selection com. Village Players of Oak Park, 1992; guest dir. Triton C.C., 2000. Mem. Assn. for Theatre in Higher Edn., U.S. Inst. for Theatre Tech., Ill. Theatre Assn., C.C. Humanities Assn (presenter midwest conf. 1993, presenter & planning com. nat. conf. 1999), Ill. Fedn. Tchrs., Nature Conservancy, Zeta Phi Eta. Avocations: acting, singing, travel, antiques. Office: Moraine Valley CC 10900 S 88th Ave Palos Hills IL 60465-2175 Personal E-mail: joyceporter2001@yahoo.com. Business E-Mail: porter@moraine.valley.edu.

PORTER, JUDITH DEBORAH REVITCH, sociologist; b. Phila., Mar. 26, 1940; d. Eugene and Esther (Tulchinsky) Revitch; m. Gerald Joseph Porter, June 26, 1960; children: Daniel, Rebecca, Michael. Student, Vassar Coll., 1958-60; BA, Cornell U., 1962, MA, 1963; PhD, Harvard U., 1967. Lectr. Bryn Mawr (Pa.) Coll., 1966-67, asst. prof., 1967-73, assoc. prof., 1973-79, prof. sociology, 1979—, chair dept. sociology, 1987-93. Author: Black Child, White Child: The Development of Racial Attitudes, 1971; contbr. articles to profl. jours. Committeeperson Haverford Twp. Dem. Party, 1976-96; bd. dirs. Phila. AIDS Fund, 1992-98, Phila. Com. End Homelessness, 1984-, Women Against Abuse, 1995-; vice-chmn. exec. com. drugs and alcohol, Mayor, Phila.; vol. Congreso de Latinos Unidos, Inc., Greater Phila. Coalition Against Hunger. Recipient Shannon award NIMH, 1992-94; Ford Found. fellow, 1973-74; NSF fellow, 1967; NIDA grant Co-PI, 1998-2001. Mem. APHA, Am. Sociol. Assn., Phi Beta Kappa, Phi Kappa Phi. Jewish. Address: 161 Whitemarsh Rd Ardmore PA 19003-1634 Office: Bryn Mawr Coll Dept Sociology Bryn Mawr PA 19010 Business E-Mail: jporter@brynmawr.edu.

PORTER, KATHY LEE, marriage and family therapist, minister; b. St. Louis, Nov. 30, 1953; d. John Elmer and Mabel Elizabeth Porter. BA, Ctrol. Methodist, Fayette, Mo., 1976; MDiv, St. Paul Sch., Kansas City, Mo., 1983; MSW, St. Louis U., 2000. LCSW 2006; ordained min. United Ch. Christ, 1991. Min. United Ch. Christ, Hancock, Minn., 1989—91, Payson Congl. Ch. and Bluff Hall, Ill., 1991—94, Hope United Ch. of Christ, Desoto, Mo., 1994—97; case mgr. BJC Behavioral Health, Farmington, Mo., 2000—02; in-home specialist, therapist Comtrea Mental Health, Festus, Mo., 1998—. Bd. mem. Neighborhood Houses, St. Louis, 1995—2001; mem. nat. Assn. of Soc. Workers, Washington, 2000—. Mem. DeSota Lions Club, DeSota, Mo., 1996—98, Mo. Coalition Against Domestic Violence, Jefferson City, Mo., 2003—; coord. Cmty. Singles, 1997—; mem. St. Luke's United Ch. Christ, Imperial, Mo. Mem.: Nat. Assn. of Soc. Workers (Wash. and Mo. chpts.). United Church Of Christ. Avocations: swimming, horseback riding, reading. Home: 705 Stewart St De Soto MO 63020 Office: Comtrea 21 Municipal Dr Arnold MO 63010 Office Phone: 636-296-6206 ext. 337. E-mail: kleeporter@juno.com.

PORTER, LEAH LEEARLE, food products executive; b. Remington, Va., Sept. 19, 1963; d. James Wallace and Earline Yvonne (Moore) P. BS, U. Md., 1985; MS, Cornell U., 1990, PhD, 1993. Biol. technician USDA, Beltsville, Md., 1981-85; agrl. cons. Md. Dept. Agr., College Park, 1985; grad. rsch. asst. Cornell U., Ithaca, N.Y., 1986-94; mgr. internat. project Glahe Cons. Group, Washington, 1994-95; rsch. mgr. Am. Chemistry Coun., Washington, 1995-97; sci. mgr. ILSI, Washington, 1997-98; exec. dir. CropLife Am., Washington, 1999—2003; v.p. sci. affairs Chocolate Mfgs. Assn., 2004—. Cons., mktg. asst. Le Earle Enterprises, Ithaca, 1988—93. Pres. Cmty. Ministry Prince George's County, 1999—2005, bd. dirs., 1999—2005. Md. State Senate scholar, 1984-85; faculty grad. fellow Cornell U., 1986-87. Fellow N.Y. Acad. Scis.; mem. Am. Phytopathological Soc., Assn. Women in Sci., Alpha Chi Sigma, Zeta Phi Beta. Democrat. Baptist. Avocations: church volunteer, reading, music, weightlifting.

PORTER, LILIANA ALICIA, artist, photographer, painter, printmaker, filmmaker; b. Buenos Aires, Oct. 6, 1941; came to U.S., 1964, naturalized, 1982; d. Julio and Margarita (Galetar) P.; m. Luis Camnitzer, 1965 (div. 1978); m. Alan B. Wiener, May 28, 1980 (div. 1991). Grad., Nat. Sch. Fine Arts, Argentina, 1963. Co-dir., instr. Studio Camnitzer-Porter summer workshops, Lucca, Italy, 1974, 75, 76, 77; prof. art Queens Coll., CUNY, N.Y.C., 1991—. Adj. lectr. SUNY Coll., Old Westbury, N.Y., 1974-76, Purchase br., 1987; co-dir. Studio Porter-Wiener, N.Y.C., 1979-87. One-woman shows of prints/paintings/photographs include Galeria Artemultiple, Buenos Aires, Argentina, 1977, 78, Galleria Arte Comunale, Adro, Brescia, Italy, 1977, Hundred Acres Gallery, N.Y.C., 1977, Mus. Modern Art, Cali, Colombia, 1978, Center for Interamerican Relations, N.Y.C., 1980, Galeria Arte Nuevo, Buenos Aires, 1980, Barbara Toll Fine Arts, N.Y.C., 1979, 81, 82, 84, Galerie Jolliet, Montreal, 1983, Museo de Arte Contemporaneo, Panama City, Panama, 1984, Dolan/Maxwell Gallery, Phila., 1985, U. Alta., Edmonton, 1985, Dolan/Maxwell Gallery, Phila., 1985, Galeria Luigi Marrozzini, San Juan, P.R., 1986, Galería-Taller, Museo de Arte Moderno, Cali, Colombia, 1987, The Space, Boston, 1988, Syracuse U., N.Y., 1990, Steinbaum-Krauss Gallery, N.Y.C., 1993, Galeria Ruth Benzacar, Buenos Aires, 1994, U. Art Gallery, N.Mex. State U., Las Cruces, 1995, Monique Knowlton Gallery, 1996, Ruth Benzacar Gallery, N.Y., 1997, Mus. de Bellas Artes Juan Manuel Blanes, Montevideo, Uruguay, 1997, Espacio Minimo, Murcia, Espana, 1998, 2000, Annina Nosei Gallery, N.Y., 1999, 2000, 02, 04, Artcore Gallery, Toronto, Can., 1999, Ruth Benzacar Gallery, Buenos Aires, 2000, Sicardi Gallery, Houston, 2000, 02, 06, Ctr. Photography, Woodstock, N.Y., 2000, Phoenix Mus., 2000, Galeria Espacio/Mínimo, Madrid, 2000, 03, 04, Brito-Cimino, Sao Paulo, Brazil, 2001, Casas Riegner Gallery, Miami, Fla., 2003, Hosfelt Gallery, San Francisco, 2003, 06, Centro Cultural Recoleta, Buenos Aires, 2003, Palacio Aguirre, Cartagena, Spain, 2004, Eli Marsh Gallery, Amherst Coll., Mass., 2004, Annina Nosei Gallery, N.Y.C., 2004, Galeria Ruth Benzacar, Buenos Aires, 2005, Carrie Secrist Gallery, Chgo., 2005, Sala de Veronicas, Murcia, Spain, 2005, Galeria Petrus, San Juan, P.R., 2005, Galeria Casas Riegner, Bogota, Colombia, 2005, Goya-Girl Contemporary, Balt., 2006; retrospective exhibits 1968-90 Fundacion San Telmo, Buenos Aires, 1990, Museo Nacional de Artes Plasticas, Montevideo, Uruguay, 1991, Centro de Recepciones del Gobierno, San Juan, P.R., 1991, Bronx Mus. Art, N.Y.C., 1992, retrospective exhibit Archer Huntington Art Gallery U. Tex. Austin, 1993, Staller Ctr. for the Art SUNY at Stony Brook, N.Y., 1998, Centro Cultural Recoleta, Sla Cronopios, Buenos Aires, Argentina, 2003; exhibited in numerous group shows including most recently El Mus. del Barrio, N.Y.C., 2000, Casa de America, Madrid, 2000, Contemporary Mus., Balt., 2000, N.Y., others, Mass. Coll. Art, Huntington Gallery, Boston, 2001, ARCO, Madrid, 2001, Centro Cultural Borges, Buenos Aires, 2001, Peter Lewis Theater, Guggenheim Mus., N.Y., 2001, Hosfelt Gallery, San Francisco, 2001, Fundacion Telefonica, Madrid, 2001, Fundacion Joan Miro, Barcelona, 2001, Carrie Secrist Gallery, Chgo., 2001, Contemporary Art Ctr., N.Y., 2001, The Mahady Contemporary Gallery at Marywood U., Scranton, Pa., 2002, Kunst Werke, Berlin, 2003; represented in permanent collections Mus. Phila., Mus. Modern Art, N.Y.C., RCA Corp., N.Y.C., N.Y. Public Libr., N.Y.C., La Biblioteque Nationale, Paris, France, Museo del Grabado, Buenos Aires, Museo Universitario, Mexico City, Mexico, Museo de Art Moderno, Cali, Colombia, Museo de Bellas Artes, Caracas, Venezuela, Met. Mus. Art, N.Y.C. Recipient 1st prize Argentinian Art 78 Mus. Fine Arts, Buenos Aires, 1978, Grand Prix XI, Internat. Print Biennial, Cracow, Poland, 1986, 1st prize VII Latin Am. Print Biennial, San Juan, Puerto Rico, 1986; fellow Guggenheim Found., 1980-81, N.Y. Found. for the Arts, 1985, grantee, 1999. Address: 720 Greenwich St 10G New York NY 10014 Office Phone: 718-997-4800. Personal E-mail: lilianaporter@earthlink.net.

PORTER, LOUISA S., federal judge; Apptd. presiding magistrate judge so. dist. U.S. Dist. Ct. Calif., 1997—2002. Mem.: Fed. Magistrate Judges Assn. (pres. 2003—04). Office: 1140 US Courthouse 940 Front St San Diego CA 92101 Office Phone: 619-557-5383. Office Fax: 619-702-9925.

PORTER, MARGARET EVANS, novelist, lecturer, historian; b. Macon, Ga., Mar. 4, 1959; d. Fred William Jr. and Mariann (Chappell) Evans; m. Christopher John Porter, Oct. 6, 1984 BA Theatre and English, Agnes Scott Coll., 1980; MA Radio, TV and Film, U. Ga., 1983. Instr. writing Colo. Free U., Denver, 1989—93; writer-in-residence Wesleyan Coll., Macon, 1993. Author: (novels) Heiress of Ardara, 1988, Irish Autumn, 1990, Road to Ruin, 1990, Jubilee Year, 1991, Sweet Lavender, 1992, Toast of the Town, 1993, Dangerous Diversions, 1994, The Proposal, 1998, Kissing a Stranger, 1998, The Seducer, 1999, Improper Advances, 2000; also poetry Precinct del. Jefferson City Dem., Colo., 1992; active Episcopal Diocese N.H., columnist Concord Monitor; del. N.H. Dem. Conv., 2002, 06; moderator Diocesan Coun., 2006—; parishioner St. Stephen's Episcopal Ch., Pittsfield, N.H. Recipient Excellence cert. Romantic Times mag., 1991, 94; named Best New Author, Romantic Times mag., 1990 Mem. Authors Guild, Novelists, Inc., N.H. Writers Project, Romance Writers Am., Rocky Mountain Fiction Writers (v.p. 1991-93, Jasmine award 1993), Jane Austen Soc. N.Am Avocations: nature study, theater, music, travel, gardening.

PORTER, MARIE CAROLINE, geriatrics nurse; b. Rochester, N.Y., Sept. 21, 1934; d. Otto Henry and Mildred Magdalena (Christ) Eiffert; children: Stephen, David, Mark, Kevin, Matthew. BSN, Nazareth Coll., 1956. RN, Mass. Staff nurse pediatrics Rochester (N.Y.) Gen. Hosp., 1956-57, nursing arts instr., 1957-58; head nurse pediatrics Syracuse (N.Y.) Meml. Hosp., 1958-59; staff nurse geriatrics Cohasset (Mass.) Knoll Nursing Home, 1978-82; supr. nursing Norwell (Mass.) Knoll Nursing Home, 1982-87, dir. nursing, 1987—. Mem. Nat. Assn. Dir. Nurses Assn. Roman Catholic. Avocations: theater, tennis, reading, travel, music. Office: Norwell Knoll Nursing Home 329 Washington St Norwell MA 02061-1794

PORTER, NANCY LEFGREN, reading recovery educator; b. Council Bluffs, Iowa, Apr. 26, 1945; d. Elvin W. and Verna V. (Hansen) Lefgren; m. Eugene D. Porter, Apr. 3, 1965; children: Theresa McFarland-Porter, M.S., Dr. Tracy K.P. Gregg. BS, U. Iowa, 1976, completed devel. activities program, 1983, MS, 1992. Cert. Reading Recovery trained tchr., reading specialist, 1993. Tchr. Iowa City Sch. Dist., 1976-93, reading recovery Title I tchr., 1993—. Mem. After Sch. Tutoring Program, Iowa City; instr. U. Iowa, 1997. Author (curriculum) Lites and Shadows, 1993, reading curriculum, 1997 (Blue Ribbon award 1997); presenter (cmty. collaboration) NSCI At-Risk, 1994. Precinct chair Dem. Party, Johnson City, Iowa, 1990-96; exec. bd. LWV, 1989-90; WELCA chair Gloria Dei Luth. Ch. Women; mem. corp. bd. Alpha Xi Delta. Grantee K-3 At Risk Grant, 1992, State of Iowa, 1992-97; named Educator of Yr. East Ctrl. Uniserve Unit, 1992. Mem. Iowa State Edn. Assn. (exec. bd. 1993—, Friend of Edn. award 1997, student ISEA), Iowa City Edn. Assn. (pres. 1983-84, 97, govtl. affairs chair 1983—, Educator of Yr. 1992), Delta Kappa Gamma (pres. 1995-96), Pi Delta Kappa (program chair 1994-95). Democrat. Lutheran. Avocations: biking, camping, dance, reading, enjoying grandchildren. Home: 2519 Potomac Dr Iowa City IA 52245-4827

PORTER, ROBERTA ANN, counseling administrator, educator, retired school system administrator; b. Oregon City, Oreg., May 28, 1949; d. Charles Paul and Verle Maxine (Zimmerman) Zacur; m. Vernon Louis Porter, Dec. 27, 1975 (div. Dec. 1998). B in Bus. Edn., So. Oreg. Univ., 1971, M in Bus. Edn., 1977; cert. in counseling, Western Oreg. U., 1986; postgrad., Lewis and Clark Coll., 1995. Cert. in leadership Nat. Seminars. Tchr. Klamath Union H.S., Klamath Falls, Oreg., 1971-73, Mazama Mid./H.S., Klamath Falls, 1973-83; instr. Oreg. Inst. Tech., Klamath Falls, Oreg., 1975-92; counselor Mazama H.S., Klamath Falls, 1983-93; vice prin. Bonanza (Oreg.) Schs., 1993-95; counselor Klamath County Sch. Dist., Oreg., 1995—2004; TAG coordinator Lost River Jr./Sr. H.S., 1995—2002, gender equity team, 1997—. Participant Clinton Cuban-USA Edn. Initiative, Oct. 2000; Blue/Gold Officer USN Acad., 2000—; sch. improvement com. Klamath County Sch. Dist., 2000-04; presenter Oreg. and Nat. Assn. Student Coun., 1989-92, Oreg. Sch. Bds. Assn., Sch. Counselor Assn., 1995, state mini workshops counselors/adminstrs., Western Region Br. leadership tng. ACA, 1999, Klamath Youth Summit, 1999; task force for ednl. reform in Oreg., 1993-94; trainer asst. Leadership Devel. Am. Sch. Counselor Assn.; trainer ACA. Mem. editl. bd. Eldorado Wellness, 1996-99. Trainer U.S. Army and Marines Recruiters, Portland and Medford, Oreg., 1988-89; master trainer Armed Svcs. Vocat. Aptitude Battery/Career Exploration Program, 1992—; candidate Klamath County Sch. Bd., Klamath Falls; interpreter AMTRAK svc. Klamath Dept. Tourism and Nat. Parks, 1998-2005; active Klamath County Crisis Team. Recipient Promising, Innovative Practices award Oreg. Sch. Counselors, 1990. Mem. NEA, ACA (western region parliamentarian 1999-2001), COSA, ASCD, ASCA, Oreg. Sch. Counseling Assn. (presenter, v.p. h.s. 1988-91, com. mem. 1991-93, pres. 1992-95, Pres.'s award), Oreg. Edn. Assn., Oreg. Counseling Assn. (pres. award 1995, parliamentarian 1994-95, area 8 rep. 1995-97, pres.-elect 1997-98, pres. 1998-99, past pres. 1999-2000), Oreg. Assn. Student Couns. (bd. dirs. activity advisors 1989-91), Nat. Assn. Student Couns., Klamath Falls Edn. Assn. (bldg. rep. 1990-93, sec. 1991-92, negotiations team 1992-93), Elks, Delta Kappa Gamma (exec. bd. Alpha chpt. 1985-94, pres. 1990-92, state conv. chmn. 1992, state legis. com. 1991-93, chmn. 1993-95, state expansion com., World Fellowship chair Alpha chpt., scholarship chair 2002-04), Elks (scholarship chair, 2003-05), Ducks Unltd. (Sunset chpt. area chair, Newberg chpt. com. mem.). Avocations: boating, travel, reading, fishing. Home: 13150 SW River Rd Hillsboro OR 97123

PORTER, SALLY LOUISE, artist; b. Madison, Wis., Sept. 22, 1950; d. Donald Edwin and Betty Anne (Selzer) P.; m. Gregory Michael Miller, Oct. 20, 1978; 1 child, Carly Porter Miller. BA, Lewis U.; MEd in Profl. Devel., U. Wis., Whitewater, 1991. Cert. elem. and art tchr., Wis. Substitute art tchr. Wauwatosa (Wis.) Pub. Schs., 1973; math., drama and lang. arts tchr. Kettle Moraine Area Schs., Wales, Wis., 1973, art tchr., 1973—. Ceramics instr. Milw. Art mus., 1980. Ceramics exhibited at various juried shows, 1980—; ceramic works pub. in The Best of Pottery, 1996, Creative Pottery, 1998. Recipient Alexander Purin award Milw. Area Tchrs. of Art, 1980; named Tchr. of Yr. Kettle Moraine Sch. Dist., 2006. Mem. NEA, Wis. Edn. Assn., Nat. Art Art Edn. Assn., Wis. Art Edn. Assn. (3d Place Membership Show award 1991), Nat. Coun. on Edn. to Ceramic Arts, United Lakewood Educators.

Avocations: drawing, ceramics, gardening, reading. Office: Kettle Moraine Mid Sch 301 E Ottawa Ave Dousman WI 53118-9700 Office Phone: 262-965-6500. Business E-Mail: porters@kmsd.edu.

PORTER, SHERI WAGNER, nursing administrator, educator; b. New Orleans, Apr. 9, 1963; d. Donald Whitney and Rita Mae (Remedies) Wagner; m. William Leon Porter, Jan. 23, 1993; 1 child, Meghan Louise. Student, U. New Orleans, 1982-87; AAS in Nursing, N. Harris County Coll., 1991; BSN, Loyola U., 1996. RN, La.; cert. emergency nurse; nat. registered EMT-paramedic; cert. BCLS instr., ACLS instr., pediatric advanced life support instr., Am. Heart Assn.; cert. emergency med. svcs. instr., La.; cert. automatic external defibrillator instr., La.; cert. nonviolent crisis prevention intervention provider, East Jefferson Gen. Hosp.; cert. in interaction mgmt. tactics; cert. selection sys. adminstr. EMT-intermediate New Orleans Health Dept. EMS, 1985-88; paramedic, edn. coord., field supr. Harris County Emergency Corps., Houston, 1988-91; emergency med. svcs. instr. N. Harris County Coll., Houston, 1990, San Jacinto (Tex.) Coll., 1990; nurse, EMS clin. instr. emergency dept. Houston N.W. Med. Ctr., 1990-91; nurse, clin. asst. emergency svcs. Med. Ctr. La. New Orleans, 1991-92; continuing edn. coord. emergency dept. E. Jefferson Gen. Hosp., Metairie, La., 1992-95, edn. coord., instr., cons. comprehensive edn. and early detection program, 1995—. Co-coord. cert. of emergency nurses rev. course E. Jefferson Edn. Dept., Metairie, 1993-95, vice chmn. chest pain evaluation com., emergency dept. continuing edn. com., 1993-95, code-3 com., 1993—, emergency preparedness co-chmn., 1994-95, geriatric edn. task force, 1994—. Mem. coord. coun. adult protective svcs. Edn. and Tng. Performance Group, 1995—. Mem. Emergency Nurses Assn. (cert. emergency nursing pediatric course instr., cert. trauma nursing core curriculum provider, pediatric com. 1994-96, consumer awareness com. 1994-96), New Orleans Area Health and Edn. Tng. Soc., Sigma Theta Tau, Alpha Sigma Nu, Am. Soc. for Training and Devel. Roman Catholic. Avocations: bowling, reading, writing, camping. Office: E Jefferson Gen Hosp Edn Dept 4200 Houma Blvd Metairie LA 70006-2970

PORTER, VERNA LOUISE, lawyer; b. May 31, 1941; BA, Calif. State U., 1963; JD, Southwestern U., 1977. Bar: Calif. 1977, U.S. Dist. Ct. (ctrl. dist.) Calif. 1978, U.S. Ct. Appeals (9th cir.) 1978; cert. Dispute Resolutions Programs Act Mediator, L.A. County Bar Assn., 2005. Ptnr. Eisler & Porter, LA, 1978-79, mng. ptnr., 1979-86; pvt. practice, 1986—. Judge pro-tempore LA Mcpl. Ct., 1983—, LA Superior Ct., 1989—, Beverly HIlls Mcpl. Ct., 1992—; mem. subcom. landlord tenant law, State Calif., panelist conv.; mem. real property law sect. Calif. State Bar, 1983; mem. client rels. panel, vol. LA County Bar Dispute Resolution; ct. appointed arbitrator civil cases, fee arbitrator LA Superior Ct.; mem. BBB Abitrator Automobile Lemon Laws, 2000—. Editl. asst., contbr. Apt. Bus. Outlook, Real Property News, Apt. Age. Mem. adv. coun. Freddie Mac Vendor, 1995—; mem. World Affairs Coun. Mem. ABA, LA County Bar Assn. (client-rels. vol. dispute resolution fee arbitration 1981—; arbitrator lemon law claims), LA Trial Lawyers Assn., Wilshire Bar Assn. Women Lawyers' Assn., Landlord Trial Lawyers Assn. (founding, pres.), Da Camera Soc. Republican. Office: 2500 Wilshire Blvd Ste 1226 Los Angeles CA 90057-4365 Office Phone: 213-385-1568. Business E-Mail: vlporter@vlpesq.com.

PORTERFIELD, AMANDA, religion educator; b. Bronxville, NY, Feb. 6, 1947; d. John Buchanan and Emily Ide (Wheaton) P.; m. Mark D. Kline, Mar. 12, 1979; 1 child, Nicolas. BA magna cum laude, Mt. Holyoke Coll., 1969; MA, Columbia U., 1971; PhD, Stanford U., 1975. Asst. prof. Religion Syracuse (NY) Univ., 1975-82, assoc. prof. Religion, 1982-91, prof. Religion, 1991—94; prof. religious studies Ind. Univ.-Purdue Univ., Indpls., 1994—98, adj. prof. philanthropic studies, 1995—98, adj. prof. Am. studies, 1995—98, dir. women's studies, 1995—98; vis. prof. religious studies Univ. Wyo., 1998—99, prof. religious studies, 1999—2003; Robert A. Spivey prof. religion Fla. State U., Tallahassee, 2003—. Mem. exec. adv. com. Ctr. for Study of Religion and Am. Culture, Indpls.; chair faculty coun. Coll. of Arts and Scis. Syracuse U., Syracuse, 1993—94. Author (books) Feminine Spirituality in America: From Sarah Edwards to Martha Graham, 1981, Female Piety in Puritan New England: The Emergence of Religious Humanism, 1991, The Power of Religion: A Comparative Introduction, 1997, The Transformation of American Religion: The Story of a Late-Twentieth-Century Awakening, 2001, Healing in the History of Christianity, 2005; editor: The People's History of Christianity: Modern Christianity to 1900 (vol. 6), 2005. Sarah Willston scholar, 1966. Mem. Am. Soc. Ch. History (pres. 2001), Am. Acad. Religion, Am. Studies Assn., Am. Hist. Assn., Soc. Sci. Study of Religion, Religious Rsch. Assn., Phi Beta Kappa, Am. Antiquarian Soc. Democrat. Mem. Reformed Ch. of Am. Avocation: tennis. Office: Dept Religion MC 1520 Dodd Hall Fla State Univ Tallahassee FL 32306*

PORTERFIELD-PYATT, CHAUMONDE R., music educator, advocate; b. Visalia, Calif., Oct. 18, 1943; d. Roy E. and Zoisla Saladin; m. Melvin E. Pyatt, June 16, 1984; children: Michelle R. Pyatt children: Brian K. Porterfield, Erik D. Porterfield, Kevin G. Porterfield. AA, Coll. Sequoias, Visalia, Calif., 1963; post grad. with Stanley Glasser, U. London, 1981; BS, U. San Francisco, 1988; degree (hon.), Wessex Theology Coll. Cert. C.C. supr. Calif., 1988, C.C. instr. Calif., 1987, Wellstone Actions Adv. Campaign Mgmt. Sch., 2006. Prof. music Coll. Sequoias, Visalia, Calif., 1981—. Exec. dir. 49th Mozart Festival, 1982; guest soloist Grieg Piano Concerto, No. 1, Opus 16 Kings County Symphony, 1988; state legislative advocate Faculty Assn. Calif. Cmty. Colleges, 1994; conf. presenter Copyright Laws II, Lobbying 101: How to Stalk the Wild Legislator, 2002. Accompanist and singer: Desert Song, 1963, Music Man, 1963; performer (with Maestro Igor Stravinsky): Von Himmel Hoch and Symphony of Psalms, 1965; performer: (with Maestro Aaron Copland) Musica Viva with the San Francisco Symphony, 1966; performer: New J. S. Bach Chorales Premiere, 1988, recitals featuring Composers of Chopin, Rachminoff, Liszt, Debussy, J. S. Bach, and Beethoven, Piano Dedication Concert-Visalia United Methodist Church, 1984; singer: San Francisco Chorale, 1967; contbr. articles to profl. jours. Recipient cert. Appreciation, Fine Arts Divsn. Coll. Sequoias, 2000; Music fellow, Wessex Theol. Coll., Eng., 1989. Mem.: NEA, C.C. Assn. (advocacy chair 1994—, polit. action com. 1994—, lobbying com 1994—, legislation com. 1994—, exec. bd 1998—, advocate 1998—, bd. dir. dist D, W. H. O. award 2004), Coll. Sequoias Tchrs. Assn. (sec. 1989, state rep. 1998—, W. H. O. award 2004), Music Assn. Calif. Cmty. Colleges (legis. advocacy rep. 1984, exec. bd. 1984—), Am. Theatre Organ Soc., Am. Guild Organists (conf. presenter 1984), Calif. State Tchrs. State Coun. (higher edn. rep. 2001), Calif. Teachers Assn. (life; exec. bd. 1989, advocate 1998—, higher edn. dir. at large 2004, com. higher edn. 2004, state dir. 2004—), Calif. Scholastic Fedn. (life), Mu Phi Epsilon (pres. 1967). Achievements include Invited guest to sail on the QE2 from New York to Southampton, England; featuring piano artists Eugene Istomin, Peter Orth, Michael LaGrand, Leonard Pennario and Charles Strauss; Invited guest performer on Steinway pianos once belonging to Vladimir Horowitz, Van Cliburn and Ignace Paderewski. Office: Coll Sequoias 915 S Mooney Blvd Visalia CA 93277 Office Phone: 559-730-3810.

PORTMAN, NATALIE, actress; b. Jerusalem, June 9, 1981; d. Avner and Shelley Hershlag. BS in Psychology, Harvard U., 2003. Appeared in motion pictures including The Professional, 1994, Developing, 1995, Heat, 1995, Beautiful Girls, 1996, Everyone Says I Love You, 1996, Beautiful Girls, 1996, Mars Attacks!, 1996, Star Wars: Episode I-The Phantom Menace, 1999, Anywhere But Here, 1999, Where the Heart Is, 2000, Zoolander, 2001, Star Wars Episode II-Attack of the Clones, 2002, Cold Mountain, 2003, Garden State, 2004, True, 2004, Closer, 2004 (Golden Globe award for best supporting actress, 2005), Domino One, 2005, Star Wars: Episode III-Revenge of the Sith, 2005, Free Zone, 2005, V for Vendetta, 2006; appeared in stage prodns. including Diary of Anne Frank, 1997 (Nominee Tony award), The Seagull, 2001. Office: Creative Artists Agy 9830 Wilshire Blvd Beverly Hills CA 90212*

PORTNOW, MARJORIE, painter; b. NYC, Sept. 30, 1942; d. Julius J. and Bessie M. (Aptaker) P. BA in Art History, Cae-Western Res. U., 1964; MFA in Painting summa cum laude, Bklyn. Coll., 1972; postgrad., Pratt Inst., 1964-65, Skowhegan Sch. Painting, 1965. Mem. faculty Vt. Studio Ctr., 1987—2005, Vt. Studio Sch., Johnson, 1987—95, U. Pa., Phila., 1988—91, Pa. Acad. Fine Arts, Phila., 1988—2003, Snowaggan Sch. Painting and Sculpture, 1989, U. Calif., Santa Cruz, 1991—93, Bklyn. Coll., 1994—96, Phila. Acad. Fine Arts, NY Studio Sch., NYC, 1994—95, Nat. Acad. Design, NYC, 2000—06. One-woman shows include Hollins U., Roanoke, Va., 2000, Peter Rose Gallery, NY, 2003, Oxbow Gallery, North Hampton, Mass., 2005, exhibited in group shows at curated by Graham Nichson, Olana, NY, 2000, fLizan Tops Gallery, East Hampton, NY, 2000, Julie Heller Gallery, Provincetown, Mass., 0201, Lower Manhattan Cultural Coun., NY, 2004, 2005, Sharon Arts Ctr., Peterborough, NH, 2005, exhibitions include Nat. Acad. Design, NY, 2005. Fellow, MacDowell Colony, 1971, 72, 75, Yaddo, 1972, 74, 77; Artists for Environment grantee 1972, Tiffany grantee, 1972-73, 78, Radcliffe Inst. grantee 1973-74, 74-75, 93, Ingram Merrill grantee 1975-76, Nat. Endowment for the Arts grantee, 1980, 94, N.Y. State Creative Artists Pub. Svc. grantee, 1981-82, N.Y. Found. for the Arts grantee, 1986, Radcliffe grantee, 1990, Fullbright grantee, 1993; named juror painting N.Y. Found. for the Arts, 1988. Mem.: Nat. Acad. Design. Office: National Acad Design 5 E 89th St New York NY 10128 Office Phone: 212-925-6321. Office Fax: 212-426-1711.

PORTNOY, LYNN ANN, fashion retailer; b. Detroit, June 13, 1938; d. Morris and Betty (Diamond) P. Student, U. Wis., 1956-57, Harvard U., 1957; BA, U. Mich., 1960. Buyer trainee Joseph Magnin, San Francisco, 1960-65; buyer, pub. rels. Claire Pearone, Troy, Mich., 1968-80; owner, pres. Lynn Portnoy Women's Clothier Inc., Detroit, 1980-97, Southfield, Mich., 1997—. Author: (book) Going Like Lynn, Paris (A Series of Liberating Travel Primers for Women), 1999, Going Like Lynn, New York, 2000, Going Like Lynn, Florence, 2001. Vol. Internat. Vis. Council, South Oakland Shelter, Alzheimers Assn., Mich. Abortion Rights Action League. Mem. Nat. Assn. Women Bus. Owners, Womens Economic Club, U. Mich. Alumni. Avocations: travel, reading, writing, cooking, walking. Office Phone: 248-353-2900. Personal E-mail: info@goinglikelynn.com.

PORTNOY, SARA S., lawyer; b. N.Y.C., Jan. 11, 1926; d. Marcus and Gussie (Raphael) Spiro; m. Alexander Portnoy, Dec. 13, 1959 (dec. 1976); children: William, Lawrence. BA, Radcliffe Coll., 1946; LLB, Columbia U., 1949. Bar: N.Y. 1949, U.S. Dist. Ct. (so. dist.) N.Y. 1952, U.S. Dist. Ct. (ea. dist.) N.Y. 1975, U.S. Ct. Appeals (2d cir.) 1975, U.S. Supreme Ct. 1975. Assoc. Seligsberg, Friedman & Berliner, N.Y.C., 1949-51; atty. AT&T, N.Y.C., 1951-61; vol. atty. Legal Aid Soc. of Westchester, NY, 1966-74; assoc. Proskauer Rose Goetz & Mendelsohn, N.Y.C., 1974-78, ptnr., 1978-94; ret., 1994. Mem. Commn. on Human Rights, White Plains, N.Y., 1973-78; mem. bd. visitors Columbia Law Sch., 1996-02; bd. dirs. Legal Aid Soc. of Westchester County, N.Y., 1975-83, Columbia Law Sch. Assn., 1990-94, Mosholu Montifiore Cmty. Ctr., 1998—; mem. Pres.'s Coun. Yaddo; dir. Muscular Dystrophy Assn., 2000-03. Mem. Assn. Bar City of NY (chair com. legal support staff 1994, mem. Com. on Homeless, Sr. Lawyer's Com. and chair Pub. Svc. Network 2003-06), South Fork Country Club (dir. 1997-2006), The Children's Storefront (dir. 1998—), Legal Momentum (bd. legal advisors 2004—).

PORTO, VICKI A., science educator; b. Pasadena, Calif., Mar. 08; d. Charles F. and Shirley J. Porto. BA, U. Calif., LA, 1976; BS, Calif. Polytechnic U., Pomona, 1982. Cert. tchg. Calif., Wash. Tchr. Alta loma Sch. Dist., Alta loma, Calif., 1982—88, Lake Wash. Sch. Dist., Redmond, Wash., 1991—2005, staff devel. sci., 2005—. Sci. assessment co. Lake Wash. Sch. Dist., 2003—, sci. cirrculum adopt., 2002—03, sci. tchr. leader, 2004—05. Illustrator Tales of the Cucamonga Trail, 1986. Elected area rep. San Bernardino County Ctrl. Com., San Bernardino, 1984—88; v.p. Am. Assn. Univ. Women, Ontorio, 1980—82. Mem.: Nat. Sci. Tchrs. Assn., Assn. for Supr. and Cirrculum Devel., Geol. Assn. Am. Avocations: bicycling, illustrator.

POSER, JOAN RAPPS, artist, writer; b. Plainfield, N.J., Apr. 10, 1940; d. Mandel Max and Marion Davidson Rapps; m. Jay Sanford Poser, Nov. 15, 1964; children: Lester Philip, Toby Anne BA, U. Conn., 1962. Self-employed travel cons., Lancaster, Pa., 1976—79; tchr. McDonogh Sch., Balt., 1982—90; artist's agt. Joan E. Poser Assocs. Agts. in the Arts, Balt., 1978—; co-owner, v.p. Poser's Apparel, Inc., Pa., 1990—95; co-owner Poser's Accessories Sales Reps., 1995—; polit. speech writer, 2005—. Cons. Charmelle, Inc., San Francisco, 2002—. Pres. Lancaster Town Fair, 1974, Temple Beth El Sisterhood, Lancaster, 1973—77, donor chmn., 2000—03; pres. and devel. chmn. Md. Assocs. for Dyslexic Adults and Youth, Inc., 1989—91; campaign chair Bus. and Profl. Women, Assoc. Jewish Charities, Balt., 1985; spl. events chair Cultural Arts Inst. Chizuk Amuno Congregation, 1986—90, trustee, 1986—90; chmn. Lancaster Jewish Cmty. Ctr. 50th Anniversary Gala, 1994, Temple Beth El 50th Anniversary Gala, 1995; bd. dirs. Temple Beth El, 1991—92, Janus Sch., Lancaster, 1991—94, Lancaster Jewish Cmty. Ctr., 1991—93. Mem. Hadassah Democrat. Avocations: opera, sports, architecture, travel, writing. Home: 119 Greenview Dr Lancaster PA 17601-4988 Office Phone: 717-560-7976. Personal E-mail: jerapps@localnet.com.

POSEY, ADA LOUISE, human resources specialist; BA, Carleton Coll. Expense mgmt. and pension operation staff Prudential Ins. Co., 1978—85, internal auditing staff, 1985—89; corp. budgeting staff Minn. Mut., 1989—93; assoc. dir. for gen. svcs. Office Adminstrn., The White House, Washington, 1993-96, dep. dir., 1996-97, dir., 1997-99; spl. advisor Office of Nat. Drug Control Policy, Washington, 1999—; sr. policy advisor Dept. of Energy, Washington, 1999-2001; pres. Posey Cons. Group, 2001—03; dir. diversity and compliance Raytheon Tech. Svcs., Reston, Va., 2003—. Trustee Carleton Coll.; mem. Capital City Links chpt., Washington. Office: Raytheon Tech Svcs 12160 Sunrise Valley Dr Reston VA 21910 Office Phone: 703-295-2259. Personal E-mail: noah0496@aol.com. Business E-Mail: ada_l_posey@raytheon.com.

POSEY, CAROLYN ANN, secondary school educator; b. Hobbs, N.Mex., Jan. 26, 1941; d. Ulman Garrett and Ruby Lee (Worley) Montgomery; m. Lawrence Dare Posey Jr., Dec. 23, 1983; children: James Keith, Carla Ann, Laura Ruth, Paula Lynn. BS, Ea. N.Mex. U., 1962. Apprentice embalmer Wheeler Mortuary, Portales, N.Mex., 1960-62; tchr. Houston Pub. Schs., 1962-63; sec. Baylor Med. Sch., 1963; office mgr. Albuquerque Civ. Light Opera, 1977-78; tchr. Albuquerque Pub. Schs., 1979—97; ret., 1998; owner Deco Designs, 1984—; producer of musicals Carlaw Enterprises, Albuquerque, 1984—; travel agt. Bolack Total Travel, 1987-88. Mem. Wool Warehouse Dinner Theatre, Albuquerque, 1987-88. Producer: George M at the Kimo Theatre, 1986, On The Town, 1987. Office asst. Rep. Party Pete Domenici's, Albuquerque, 1986; alumni bd. Eastern N.Mex. U., Portales, 1988-94; high sch. reunion com., Highland HS., Albuquerque, 1989-1999. Recipient Service award Albuquerque Civic Light Opera, 1985, Crystal Apple award Albuquerque Pub. Schs., 1993, 95, Best in Show Porcelin Dollmaking State Fair, 2005. Mem. Amigos ACLOA (pres. 1975, chmn. edn. com. 1986—). Avocations: painting, tennis, ceramics, writing, travel. Home: 4509 Summer Hill Ln NW Albuquerque NM 87120 E-mail: carlaw49@att.net.

POSEY, GAIL S, music educator; b. Lancaster, Pa., May 11, 1955; d. J. William and Evelyn K. Seitzinger; m. Thomas W. Posey, Sept. 22, 1946; 1 child, Matthew T. BS in Music Edn., Lebanon Valley Coll., Annville, Pa., 1977; MS in Ednl. Adminstrn. & Supervision, Rider U., Lawrenceville, N.J., 1982. Tchr. music Neshaminy Sch. Dist., Langhorne, Pa., 1977—82, 1989—90, Ea. Regional H.S., Voorhees, NJ, 1991—. Rep. Am. Guild English Handbell Ringers, 2002—. Recipient Nat. Exemplary Handbell and Handchime award, Am. Guild English Handbell Ringers, 2001. Mem.: Music Educators Nat. Conf., Suzuki Assn. Am., Am. String Tchrs. Assn., N.J. Music Educators Assn. Home: 16 Trim Rd Levittown PA 19056 Office: Ea Regional HS Laurel Oak Rd PO Box 2500 Voorhees NJ 08043 Office Phone: 856-784-4441 1158. Personal E-mail: gsposey@comcast.net. Business E-Mail: posey_gail@eastern.k12.nj.us.

POSEY, JAN R., music educator; b. Irving, Tex., July 16, 1953; d. John G. and Jeanette Wedeking Reichle; m. Randall C. Posey, May 19, 1973; children: Jennifer M., Kristin R. MusB in Edn., U. Tex., Arlington, 1975. Tchr. elem. music Dobbs Elem. Rockwall ISD, Tex., 1992—93, Shugart Elem. Garland ISD, 1993—. Mem.: Tex. Music Educators Assn. Conservative. Baptist. Avocations: reading, gardening, crafts, travel. Office: Shugart Elementary 4726 Rosehill Rd Garland TX 75043

POSEY, KATYE L., retired school system administrator; b. Talpa, Tex., Oct. 21, 1914; d. Lorenzo Dow Posey and Mary Elizabeth Rodriguez. BA, Northwestern U., Natchitoches, La., 1941; MEd, U. Houston, 1945, D of Edn., 1952. Tchr. elem. Richland Parish Schs., La., Calcasieu Parish Schs., Caddo Parish Schs., elem. prin. La., dir. elem. edn. La.; ret., 1976. Mem.: La. Tchrs. Assn. Baptist. Avocations: reading, gardening, travel, needlepoint. Home: Montclair Assisted Living 9100 E King Hwy Apt 108 Shreveport LA 71115

POSEY, PARKER, actress; b. Balt., Nov. 8, 1968; d. Chris Posey. Student, SUNY, Purchase. Actor (films) Joey Breaker, 1993, Description of a Struggle, 1993, The Wake, 1993, Sleepless in Seattle, 1993, Dazed & Confused, 1993, Coneheads, 1993, Flirt, 1993, Dead Connection, 1994, Opera No. 1, 1994, Iris, 1994, Mixed Nuts, 1994, Amateur, 1994, Sleep With Me, 1994, Drunks, 1995, Frisk, 1995, An Eviction Notice, 1995, Party Girl, 1995, Kicking and Screaming, 1995, The doom Generation, 1995, The Daytrippers, 1996, Basquiat, 1996, Waiting for Guffman, 1996, SubUrbia, 1997, The House of Yes, 1997, Clockwatchers, 1997, Henry Fool, 1997, What Rats Won't Do, 1998, You've Got Mail, 1998, The Misadventures of Margaret, 1998, The Venice Project, 1999, Dinner at Fred's, 1999, Scream 3, 2000, Best in Show, 2000, Josie and the Pussycats, 2001, The Anniversary Party, 2001, Personal Velocity: Three Portraits, 2002, The Sweetest Thing, 2002, The Event, 2003, A Mighty Wind, 2003, Laws of Attraction, 2004, The Sisters of Mercy, 2004, Blade: Trinity, The OH in Ohio, 2006, Superman Returns, 2006; (TV series) As The World Turns, 1991-92; (TV films) First Love, Fatal Love, 1991, Tracey Takes on New York, 1993, Hell on Heels: The Battle of Mary Kay, 2002, Frankenstein, 2004; (TV miniseries) Armistead Maupin's Tales of the City, 1993, More Tales of the City, 1998, Further Tales of the City, 2001; (TV appearances) (voice only) Futurama, 2000, (voice only) The Simpsons, 2000, Will & Grace, 2001, Boston Legal, 2006; (stage) Hurlyburly, 2005, (Lucille Lortel awards, outstanding featured acress, 2005); screenwriter (with Rory Kelly) Dumb in Love, 1995; contributing editor, Open City literary mag. Recipient Spl. Jury prize Sundance Film Festival, 1997; named Queen of Indies by TIME Mag. Office: William Morris Agy 151 S El Camino Dr Beverly Hills CA 90212-2775*

POSEY, SANDRA DALTON, special education educator; b. Phoenix, Az., May 7, 1945; d. Ruth (Privett) Dalton; children: Melinda Ruth, Clay McDowell. BA, Northeast La. U., 1966; MEd, Vanderbilt U., 1981, Trevecca Nazarene Coll., 1989. Tchr. 8th grade Caddo Parish Sch. system, Shreveport, La., 1967; tchr. 7th and 8th grades Monroe (La.) City Sch. System, 1969; tchr. 7th grade Rocky Mt. (N.C.) Sch. System, 1971-73; grad. asst. Peabody Coll. Vanderbilt U., Nashville, 1980-81; resource tchr. Williamson County Sch. System, Franklin, Tenn., 1981-87, gifted coord., 1987—. Asst. dir. Tenn. Acad. for Tchrs. of the Gifted, Nashville, 1989—; mid. Tenn. regional dir. Odyssey of the Mind, 1990, 92; adj. faculty mem. Belmont Coll., Nashville, 1989-93. Mem. Nat. Assn. for the Gifted, Tenn. Assn. for Gifted, Williamson County Assn. for Gifted, Williamson County Assn. for Retarded Citizens, Delta Kappa Gamma, Phi Delta Kappa (v.p. for programs 1991-92, pres. 1992-93). Office: Westwood Elem Sch Springdale AR 72764

POSIN, KATHRYN OLIVE, choreographer; b. Butte, Mont, Mar. 23, 1943; d. Daniel Q. and Frances (Schweitzer) P. BA in Dance, Bennington Coll., 1965; MFA in Interdisciplinary and World Dance, NYU, 1994; studies in composition, 1965-78, studies in ballet, 1965-90, studies in modern dance, 1967-80. Mem. dance co. Am. Dance Theater at Lincoln Ctr., 1965; dancer Anna Sokolow Dance Co., 1965-73; artistic dir. Kathryn Posin Dance Co., NYC, 1972-91; choreographer Eliot Feld Ballet, NYC, 1978, Netherlands Dance Theater, Den Hague, Switzerland, 1980, Alvin Ailey Am. Dance Theater, NYC, 1980; mem. dance faculty U. Wis., Milw., 1984-86, choreographer, 1984-88; tchr., choreographer UCLA, 1988-90, Trinity Coll., Hartford, Conn., 1990-91. Mem. dance faculty, choreographer U. Calif., Santa Barbara, 1986; tchr. dance technique and performance Tchr.'s Coll. Columbia U., spring 1990; tchr. composition and technique Nat. Inst. of Arts, Taiwan, 1991; tchr. world dance Gallatin Sch. NYU; founding chair Joffrey Ballet Sch., New Sch. U. BFA in Dance, 1998. Choreographer (performing cos./orgns.) Cherry Orchard, Lincoln Ctr., NYC, 1978, Alvin Ailey Am. Dance Theater, 1981, Netherlands Dans Theater 84182, Extemporary Dance Co. London, Balletmet, Columbus, Ohio, Milw. Ballet, 1991, 1993, 1995, 1996, Cin. Ballet, 1997, Kansas City Ballet, 2004, Louisville Ballet, 2004, (prin. works) Salvation, Off-Broadway, NYC, 1969, Waves, 1975 (Am. Dance Festival commn.), The Cherry Orchard, NY Shakespeare Festival, 1979, Mary Stuart, Acting Co., 1980, Shady Grove (grantee jt. program of Ohio Arts and Humanities Couns., 1991), The Tempest, Am. Shakespeare Festival, Stratford, Conn., 1982, Midsummer Night's Dream, Arena Stage, Washington, 1982, Boys From Syracuse, Am. Repertory Theater, Harvard U., 1983, The Paper Gramophone, Hartford Stage, 1989, Of Rage and Remembrance, 1990 (Premiere of Yr. in Music and Dance, Milw. Jour.), Stepping Stones, 1993 (co-recipient Meet the Composer/Choreographer award Milw. Ballet, 1993), many others; subject of documentary Kathy's Dance. Grantee Guggenheim Found., 1978, NY State Coun. on Arts, 1977, 79, 80, Jerome Robbins Found., 1972; grantee Nat. Endowment for Arts 1981, 82, 85-87, choreography fellow, 1995-96; Doris Humphrey fellow Am. Dance Festival, New London, Conn., 1968. Office: Kathryn Posin Dance Co 20 Bond St New York NY 10012-2406 Personal E-mail: Pozndance@aol.com.

POSNER, HARRIET S., lawyer; b. Chgo., 1960; BA, Harvard U., 1980; JD, UCLA, 1984. Ptnr. Skadden, Arps, Slate, Meagher & Flom LLP. Bd. dirs. Legal Aid Found., LA, 2002—, NOW Legal Defense, 2004—. Pres., bd. dirs. CityLife, 2000—; bd. trustees Ctr. Early Edn., 2001—. Office: Skadden, Arps, Slate, Meagher & Flom LLP 300 S Grand Ave Ste 3400 Los Angeles CA 90071 Office Phone: 213-687-5237. E-mail: hposner@skadden.com.

POSNER, KATHY ROBIN, retired communications executive; b. Oceanside, N.Y., Nov. 3, 1952; d. Melvyn and Davonne Hope (Hansen) P. BA in Journalism, Econs., Manhattanville Coll., 1974. Corp. liaison Gulf States Mortgage, Atlanta, 1980-82; dir. promotion Gammon's of Chgo., 1982-83; coordinator trade show mktg. Destron, Chgo., 1983-84; pres. Postronics, Chgo., 1984-87; v.p. Martin E. Janis & Co., Inc., Chgo., 1987-90; chmn. Comm 2 Inc., Chgo., 1990—2005, ret., 2005. Editor: How to Maximize Your Profits, 1983; contbg. editor Internat. Backgammon Guide, 1974-84, Backgammon Times, 1981-84, Chgo. Advt. and Media; columnist Food Industry News. Bd. dirs. Chgo. Beautification Com., 1987, Concerned Citizens for Action, Chgo., 1987, Midwest Bd. Shaare Zedek, Med. Ctr. Jerusalem; mem. steering com. Better Boys Found.; campaign mgr. Brown for Alderman, Chgo., 1987; mem. bd. cons. Little City Found.; mem. benefit bd. C.A.U.S.E.S. Mem. NATAS, NOW, Women in Comm., Am. Soc. Profl. and Exec. Women, Women in Film-Chgo. (bd. dirs.), Mensa, Acad. Arts (v.p.), Ill. Restaurant Assn. (mem. adv. bd.), Chgo. Area Pub. Affairs Group, City Club Chgo. (bd. dirs.), Chgo. Legal Clinic (bd. dirs.). Republican. Jewish. Avocations: politics, reading. Home: 100 E Huron # 3505 Chicago IL 60611 Personal E-mail: kathyposner@aol.com.

POSNER, SYLVIE PÉREZ, lawyer; b. Havana, Cuba, Nov. 17, 1954; d. Carlos Miguel Pérez and Emilia Inés Amezaga; m. Michael J. Posner, Aug. 23, 1987; 1 child, Christopher Barrett. BS, Fla. State U., Tallahassee, 1980; JD, U. Miami, Coral Gables, 1988. Bar: Fla. 1989, Fla. So. Dist. 1989, US Ct. Appeals, 11th Cir. 1989. Legislative aide Fla. Senate, Tallahassee, 1981—84; cert. legal intern Dade County Pub. Defender, Miami, 1986—87; rsch. asst. U. Miami Sch. Law, Coral Gables, Fla., 1987—88; law clk. Frumkes and Greene, P.A., Miami, Fla., 1987—88, U.S. Ct. Appeal (4th dist.) Fla., West Palm Beach, 1990—94; asst. atty. gen. Office Atty. Gen., 1994—2000; sr. staff atty. U.S. Ct. Appeals (4th dist.) Fla., West Palm Beach, 2000—05. Mem. Phi Alpha Delta Legal Frat., Coral Gables, Fla., 1985—88, Health and Law Soc., Coral Gables, Fla., 1985—88; participant Trial Advocacy Program, Nat. Inst. of Trial Advocacy, Coral Gables, Fla., 1987; mem. Appellate Law Sect., Fla. Bar, Fla., 1994—, Govt. Law Sect., Fla. Bar, Fla., Broward County Hispanic Bar Assn., Fort Lauderdale, Fla., 1998—2000, Fla. Assn. of Police Attorneys, Fla., 1994—2000; mem. appellate law clk. edn. com. Fla. Supreme Ct., 2002—05. Vol. lawyers program Fla. Bar, Miami, 1989—90; vol. tel. crisis counselor Switchboard of Miami, Inc., Miami, 1981—83; supporting mem. Norton Art Mus., West Palm Beach, Fla., 2003; mem. leadership coun. So. Poverty Law Ctr., 1999—; mem. Emily's List, Washington, DC, 2002; apptd. mem. Dade County Dem. Exec. Com., Miami, 1982—84; exec. v.p. Dade County Young Democrats, Miami, 1988—89; del., fla. dem. conv. Fla. Dem. Party, Orlando, Fla., 1988, del., state dem. conv. Miami, 1984. Nominee Outstanding Young Women of Am., Nat. Fedn. of Dem. Women, 1985, Assoc. Ed., Inter-American Law Review, U. Miami, 1985—88. Mem.: Wellington Country & Golf. Independent. Avocations: swimming, travel, reading, hiking, dancing. Personal E-mail: sylvieposner@yahoo.com.

POSPICHAL, MARCIE W., neuroscientist, psychologist, educator; b. Great Lakes, Ill., Feb. 22, 1959; BS in Psychology, Fla. So. Coll., 1985; MA in Psychology, Neurosci., Vanderbilt U., Nashville, 1990, PhD in Psychology, 1991. Tchg. asst. Vanderbilt U., Nashville, 1988—91, faculty lectr. dept. psychology, 1991—95, rsch. assoc. dept. psychology, 1991—97, editl. asst. Jour. Comparative Neurology, 1992—97, asst. dir. programs Ctr. for Molecular Neurosci., 1996—2001, coord. grad. studies Vanderbilt Brain Inst., 1997—2001, asst. dir. programs in neurosci. edn. Vanderbilt Brain Inst., 1999—2001; adj. instr. dept. psychology Fla. So. Coll., Lakeland, 2001—. Neurosci. cons. Bd. of Nat. Health Mus., 1999; lectr. in field; condr. seminars in field; mem. neurosci. coun. com. Vanderbilt U., Nashville, 1999—2001; Assoc. Vice-Chancellor's planning com. for the 2001 Consortium on Neurogenetics Vanderbilt Med. Ctr., 1999—2001, Vice-Chancellor's Com. on Cmty. Outreach, 1998—2001; mem. neurosci. PhD curriculum com. Vanderbilt U., 1997—2001; adj. mem. Ctr. for Molecular Neurosci. Faculty Recruitment Com., 1997—2001. Contbr. articles and abstracts to profl. jours. Vol. WDCN, Nashville, 1999; mem. Safe and Drug-Free Nashville Metro Schs. Com., 1997; vol. reader for the blind WPLN Listening Libr., Nashville, 1992—93. Co-recipient NSF grantee, 1999; recipient Rsch. Svc. award, Nat., 1995; fellow postdoctoral fellow, Vanderbilt U., 1996, 1993—94, 1991—92, grad. rsch. fellow, 1986—88, 1991; grantee Fight for Sight Postdoctoral Tng. grantee, 1992—93. Mem.: Internat. Brain Rsch. Orgn., Soc. for Neurosci. (com. on neurosci. liberacy 2001—), Assn. of Neurosci. Depts. and Programs. Achievements include research in neurotoxic and electrolytic stereotaxic brain lesioning in rodents; pressure injectin and iontophoretic application of tract tracing substances such as HRP and its conjugates in non-human primates; tract tracing using live slice tissue preparation in non-human primates. Office: thern Coll Dept Psychology Lakeland FL

POSPISIL, JOANN, historian, archivist; b. Schulenburg, Tex., Dec. 10, 1947; d. Edwin James and Jossie Annie (Mica) Krametbauer; m. Gerald Joseph Pospisil, Nov. 19, 1966; 1 child, Ryan Joseph. BA summa cum laude, U. Houston, 1992, MA, 1994. Cert. archivist Acad. Cert. Archivists, 2001. Sec. to v.p. Bohler Bros. of Am., Inc., Houston, 1972-75, asst. corp. sec., 1975-77; archival intern Sul Ross State U. Archives of the Big Bend, Alpine, Tex., 1993; rsch. asst. U. Houston Recovering U.S.-Hispanic Literary Heritage, 1993-94; archival technician Houston Acad. Medicine-Tex. Med. Ctr. Jesse H. Jones Libr., 1995-98; asst. archivist Baylor Coll. Medicine Archive, Houston, 1997—2004, archivist, 2004—. Task force mem., rsch. cons. Houston Urban Coun., 1993; contbg. historian Candelilla Wax Industry, Tex. Archeol. Rsch. Lab., 2004. Contbr. articles to profl. jours. Sec. handbook com. Clay Road Bapt. Parent-Tchr. Orgn., Houston, 1980-81; coord. Houston Police Dept., Houstonians on Watch, 1982-91; sec., membership chair, libr. aide Spring Branch Ind. Sch. Dist. Parent-Tchr. Assn., Houston, 1983-89; presenter geographical and cultural topics to classrooms in Spring Br. Elem. Sch., Northbrook H.S., Houston, 1985-95; interviewer oral history program Alliance Am. Quilts, 1999-; pres., pub. chair, sec. Spring Branch Addition Civic Assn. Inc., pres., 2005—. Recipient Spanish award Houston C.C., 1985, Josephine Del Barto scholar U. Houston, 1989-90, Helen M. Douthitt scholarship in history, 1990-91; named Sadie Iola Daniels scholar Assn. for Study of African Am. Life and History, Washington, 1990. Mem. Ctr. for Big Bend Studies, Soc. Am. Archivists, Tex. Czech Geneal. Soc. (charter), Archvists Houston Area (charter), Soc. Southwest Archivists, Tex. Hist. Assn., West Tex. Hist. Assn. (life, bd. dirs. 2006—), Tex. Oral History Assn. (v.p. 2005-06, pres. 2006—), Phi Kappa Phi, Phi Alpha Theta. Avocations: hiking, genealogy, whitewater rafting, reading non-fiction. Home: 9418 Railton St Houston TX 77080-1431 Office: Baylor Coll Medicine Archives One Baylor Plaza BCMC 177A Houston TX 77030

POST, BARBARA JOAN, elementary school educator; b. Passaic, NJ, June 29, 1930; d. John Ward and Florence Barbara (Barnum) Post; m. Edward Wayne Poppele, Apr. 10, 1954 (dec. Mar. 1978); children: E. Scott Poppele, Sara Elizabeth Poppele, Andrew John Poppele. BSE, William Paterson Coll., 1953; cert. in counseling, Rutgers U., 1981; postgrad., Columbia U., 1983, Northeastern U., 1983. Cert. tchr., N.J. Elem. tchr. Cen. Sch., Glen Ridge, N.J., 1953-55, Middletown (N.J.) Village Sch., 1956, Our Lady of Perpetual Help, Highlands, N.J., 1981-85; reading tchr. Monmouth Reading Ctr., Long Branch, N.J., 1985; tchr. gifted/talented Harmony Sch., Middletown, 1987-88; edn. coord. for Monmouth County Nat. Coun. on Alcoholism, Freehold, N.J., 1988-89; coord. math./sci. consortium Brookdale Community Coll., Lincroft, N.J., 1989-90; tchr., owner Learning Post and Creative Garden of Art for Children, Middletown, 1991—; dir. art Hillel Sch., Ocean, N.J., 1991—. Dir.-owner Learning Post, Middletown, 1986—; art tchr. Art Alliance of Monmouth County, Red Bank, N.J., 1986-88; vol. case mgmt. worker St. Matthews House, Naples, Fla., 1997-98. Author: (poem) The Lift, 1988 (short story) Sarah-Grand, 1984, Hooked on the Classics, 1988; artist (program cover) Country Christmas, 1990, 91. Demonstrator Family Reading Fair, Lincroft, 1989; participant Muscular Dystrophy Telethon, Eatontown, N.J., 1986; tchr. Tower Hill Vacation Bible Sch., Presbyn. ch., Red Bank, N.J., 1998. Mem. AAUW (tchr., mentor for teen women 1989-92, Appreciation award 1989-90), Nat. Soc. DAR (chairperson 1961-62), N.J. Shore Rose Soc. (exhibitor, 2d and 3d prize for roses 1986). Republican. Presbyterian. Avocations: art, swimming, choir, roses, golf. Home: 304 SunBeam Ave Lake Placid FL 33852-5318 E-mail: post@mymailstation.com.

POST, DIANA CONSTANCE, retired librarian; b. Anoka, Minn., Oct. 17, 1929; d. Kenneth Fred and Emma Constance (Fredrickson) Davis; husband dec., June 1996; children: Leslie Post, Paul Post, Tom Post. BS, U. Minn., 1970, MLS, 1976. Cert. libr., media specialist, Minn. Libr., media specialist Lake City (Minn.) H.S., 1970-94. Bd. dirs. Zumbrota (Minn.) Pub. Libr.; mem. SELCO governing bd. regional libr. sys., Rochester, Minn., 1980-86; pres. SELCO exec. com., 1984-86; SELS adv. com., 1990-94. Editor Lake City Sch. Dist. News, 1988-89. Scholar LaVerne Noyes Found., 1947-48, Delta Delta Delta, 1949. Mem. Beta Phi Mu. Avocations: golf, swimming, volunteering. Home: 695 Jefferson Dr Zumbrota MN 55992-1103 E-mail: DPost3@aol.com.

POST, LAURA LEIGH, psychiatrist; b. Manhattan, N.Y., May 8, 1960; d. Robert Donald Polstein and Marna Jane Cohen; m. Judith Elizabeth Avery, Sept. 26, 1988; children: John Andrew Stilwell, Craig Allen. BA in Biology magna cum laude, Harvard U., Cambridge, Mass., 1983; MA in Lit. magna cum laude, U. Paris IV, 1984; MD cum laude, SUNY, Buffalo, 1987; MS, Calif. Coast U., Santa Ana, 1998, PhD, 2002; JD, Novus U., Diamondhead, 2006. Diplomate Am. Bd. Psychiatry and Neurology with added qualifications in addiction psychiatry, Am. Bd. Forensic Medicine, Am. Bd. Sexology. Staff psychiatrist AIDS Independent Direct Support, Calif., 1991—93, Operation Concern of Pacific Med. Ctr., 1991—93, Gladman Day Treatment Ctr. of Telecare Corp., 1992—97, Woodroe Pl. Crisis Residential Program of Alameda County, 1996—97; med. dir. Divsn. Mental Health and Social Svcs., 1997—99, Marianas Psychiat. Svcs., 1999—; psychiatrist Behavioral Health Svcs., Divsn. Corrections, 2000—, Pacific Alcohol/Drug Free Workplace Resources, 2001—02, Health Svcs. Divsn. Corrections, 2002—. Attending physician/cons. Dept. Mental Health and Substance Abuse, Guam, 2001—, STRIDES Assertive Mental Health Outreach, Alameda County, Calif., 1996, Merrithew Meml. Hosp. of Contra Costa County, 1996—97, John George Psychiat. Pavilion of Alameda County, 1996—97, Highland Gen. Hosp. of Alameda County, 1996—97, Mission Crisis Mental Health Outpatient Clinic of San Francisco, 1998—99, Menlo Park VA Med. Ctr., 1988—96; cons. in field; lectr. in field; syndicated columnist Ask Judith & Laura: about sexuality, Muse News: report on women's arts, Saipan Post; condr. and presenter workshops in field; telephone hotline counselor Buffalo AIDS Task Force, 1984—85, Project Pl. of Boston, 1982—83. Contbr. articles to profl. jours.; poet numerous anthologies; author: Backstage Pass: a collection of interviews with women musicians; editor: Marianas Psychiat. Svcs. newsletter, Alliance for Mentally Ill newsletter. Educator Nat. Alliance for Mentally Ill, 2001—; vol. relay for life Am. Cancer Soc., 2002; mem. adv. coun. NMPASI-PAIMI, 2002—04; bd. dirs., sec.-treas. Lao Lao Hts. Devel., 1999—; bd. dirs., sec. Friends of the Arts, 2000—01. Named Best Writer/Journalist, Hot Wire Readers' Choice, 1992, Best Am. Psychiatrist, Consumers Rsch. Coun., 2004—05; recipient, Farney Wurlitzer prize in psychiatry, 1986, Robin Bannerman award for rsch., 1987, 1st prize in essay, Ariz. Authors' Lit. Mag., 1995, Editor's Choice award, Nat. Libr. Poetry, 1995, Gov.'s Arts award for excellence in presrvation of arts and culture, CNMI, 1999—2000; fellow Glenn H. Leak Meml. Oncology Rsch. fellow, Am. Cancer Soc., 1985, Mead-Johnson fellow, Assn. Acad. Psychiatry, 1991; grantee Med. Oncology Rsch. grantee, NIH, 1984; scholar, N.Y. State Regents scholar, 1978—83, Harvard Coll., 1981—82. Fellow: Am. Coll. Forensic Psychiatrists; mem.: Am. Psychiat. Assn., Nat. Writers Union, World Fedn. Mental Health, Am. Acad. Psychiatry and the Law, Acad. Correctional Health Profls., Pacific Basic Med. Assn., Bd. Cert. Correctional Health Profls. Covenant. Episcopalian. Avocations: scuba diving, animal rescue. Office: Marianas Psychiatric Svc PO Box 7920 Saipan MP 96950-7920

POST, ROBIN DEE, psychologist; b. Bronx, N.Y., Feb. 25, 1946; d. Herman D. and Blanche (Simon) P.; m. James Watson Tait, Oct. 3, 1981; 1 child, Victoria Post Tait. BA, Brandeis U., 1966; PhD, Syracuse U., 1973. Lic. psychologist, Colo. Asst. prof. psychology Wash. State U., Pullman, 1973-75, U. Colo. Health Scis. Ctr., Denver, 1975-81, assoc. prof., 1981-89, assoc. clin. prof., 1988—, dir. psychology tng., 1984-89; pvt. practice, Denver, 1988—. Contbr. articles on depression, psychol. assessment and psychology of women in psychology jours. Chmn. enrichment programs com. Belleview Elem. Sch., Englewood, Colo., 1993-96. Fellow APA (coun. reps. 1981-84, chmn. bd. conv. affairs 1987-88); mem. Colo. Psychol. Assn. (presdl. asst. 1984-85, bd. dirs. 1978-85, Ellis Graham award for disting. svc. to psychology 1986), Alliance Profl. Women (bd. dirs. 1991-95, chmn. membership com. 1994-97, spl. recognition award 1995). Avocations: tennis, pets, photography, travel. Office: Robin Dee Post Phd 1777 S Harrison St Ste 840 Denver CO 80210-3933

POST, SHAWN MARIE, elementary school educator; d. Melvin George and Laura Jean VanDenberg; m. Jeff E. Post; children: Stephanie K, Matthew J. Degree in bus. adminstrn. with honors, Webster U., Irvine, Calif., 1997. Registered radiologic technologist; cert. multiple and single subject tchr. Calif. Breast ctr. mgr., technologist Irvine Med. Ctr., 1990—97; breast ctr. mgr. Orange Coast Meml., Fountain Valley, Calif., 1997—98; tchr. Tustin Unified Sch. Dist., Calif., 2000—. Vol. mgr. Susan G. Komen Breast Cancer Found., Costa Mesa, Calif., 1998—99; coach Columbus Tustin Mid. Sch. Nominee Disney Tchr. of Yr., 2001; grantee Replicate This!, 2004. Mem.: Nat. Tchrs. Assn. (assoc.), Am. Alliance for Health (assoc.). Home: 12791 Eveningside Santa Ana CA 92705 Office: Tustin Unified Sch DIst 300 South C St Tustin CA 92780 Office Phone: 714-730-7301. Office Fax: 714-731-5399. Personal E-mail: spost@tustin.k12.ca.us.

POSTELL, CINDY DEBORAH, secondary school educator; b. Savannah, Ga., Aug. 14, 1954; d. George Robert and Sallie Walker Postell. BA in Journalism, U. Ga., 1976; M in Edn., Ga. Southern U., 1980. Sub. tchr. Chatham County Bd. Edn. Choir Cathedral of St. John. Home: 128 W 51stSt Savannah GA 31405

POSTER, MERYL, film company executive; With William Morris Agy.; exec. asst. to co-chmn Harvey Weinstein Miramax Film Corp., 1989—91, dir. devel., 1991—93, v.p. east coast prodn., 1993—94, sr. v.p. prodn., 1994—97, exec. v.p. prodn, 1997—98, co-pres. prodn., 1998—2005. Exec. prodr.: (films) Smoke, 1995, Marvin's Room, 1996, The Pallbearer, 1996, Cop Land, 1997, Wide Awake, 1998, Shakespeare in Love, 1998 (Acad. Award for Best Picture), Cider House Rules, 1999, Chocolat, 2000, Bounce, 2000, The Shipping News, 2001, Kate and Leopold, 2001, Blow Dry, 2001, Chicago, 2002 (Acad. Award for Best Picture), Duplex, 2003; co-prodr.: Music of the Heart, 1999.

POST-GORDEN, JOAN CAROLYN, retired psychology educator; b. Oak Park, Ill., July 3, 1932; d. DeWitt T. and Mary Jane (Lewellen) Post; children: Gregrey Wayne, Jeffrey Scott, Kayle Lynn, Tamara Anne. BS, Manchester (Ind.) Coll., 1964; MS, U. Ga., 1967, PhD, 1970. Lic. psychologist, Colo. Tchr. Clarke County Schs., Athens, Ga., 1964-65; part-time asst. prof. Tex. Tech U., Lubbock, 1968-69; instr. So. Colo. State Coll., Pueblo, 1970-71; asst. prof. U. So. Colo., Pueblo, 1971-76, assoc. prof., 1976-81, prof., 1981—99, chmn. dept., 1991—99, ret., 1999, prof. emeritus, 1999—. Asst. to city mgr., Champaign, Ill., 1980-81; psychologist So. Ctrl. Ill. Devel. Dist., Flora, 1979-80; dir. scholarly and creative activities U. So. Colo., 1988-91 Contbr. chpt. to book and articles to profl. jours. NDEA fellow, 1964-66, Danforth teaching fellow, 1978, faculty fellow Colo. State Div. Mental Health, 1986-87. Mem. APA, Soc. for Rsch. in Child Devel., Rocky Mountain Psychol. Assn., Colo. Psychol. Assn., Psi Chi, Sigma Xi, Alpha Omicron Pi. Avocation: scuba diving. Home: 24 Cactus Dr Key West FL 33040-5632

POSTLETHWAITE, ALEJANDRA, psychiatrist, researcher; b. Mexicali, Mex., Aug. 26, 1975; arrived in U.S., 2001; d. Ernesto and Mayra Topete Postlethwaite; m. Manuel Dario Carrasco, Feb. 26, 2005. MD, U. Autonoma Guadalajara, Jalisco, Mex., 1999. Lic. Calif. Intern Hosp. Gen. Mexicali, Baja California, 1997—98; comty. dr. Secretarai Salud, San Juan Teitipac, Oaxaca, 1998—99; program coord. Sun Valley Behavioral Med. Ctr., El Centro, Calif., 2001—02, rsch. asss.; psychiatry resident Harvard Med. Sch., Bockton, Mass., 2002—05; inpatient chief resident U. Calif., San Diego, 2005—06; edn. and child and adolescent psychiatrist UCLA, 2006—. Psychoanalytic psychotherapy fellow Boston Psychoanalytic Inst., 2004—05. Contbr. articles to profl. jours. Vol. physician Maria Sardina Clinic, San Ysidro, Calif., 2005—. Recipient travel scholarship, U. Autonoma Guadalajara, 1997. Mem.: APA (student mem., minority fellow 2006—), AMA, Am. Psychiat. Assn. Avocations: black and white photography, literature. Home: 3180 Sawtelle Ave Apt 102 Los Angeles CA 90066 Office Phone: 310-825-0138. Business E-Mail: apostlethwaite@mednet.ucla.edu.

POSTON, ANITA OWINGS, lawyer; b. Sylacauga, Ala., Sept. 24, 1949; d. John T. and Margaret Owings; m. Charles E. Poston, June 9, 1973; children: Charles Evans Jr., John W., Margaret Elizabeth. BA, U. Md., 1971; JD, Coll. William & Mary, 1974. Bar: Va. 1974. Atty. Vandeventer Black LLP, Norfolk, Va., 1974—. Substitute judge Norfolk (Va.) Gen. Dist. Cts., 1982-90; mem. Bar Examiners Bd.; mem. bd. visitors Coll. William and Mary. Mem. State Bd. C.C.s, Richmond, 1985-90, chmn. 1988-89; mem. Norfolk Sch. Bd., 1990-2002, chmn. 1998-2002; bd. dirs. WHRO Pub. Broadcasting, chair, 2002-04; bd. dirs. Access Coll. Found., Va. Symphony Orch., Towne Bank, Norfolk. Mem. ABA (law fellows), Va. Bar Assn. (pres. 2000), Norfolk-Portsmouth Bar Assn. (pres. 1998-99), Va. Law Fellows, Am. Inn of Ct. Office: Vandeventer Black LLP 500 World Trade Ctr Norfolk VA 23510-1679 Office Phone: 757-446-8600. Office Fax: 757-446-8670. Business E-Mail: aposton@vanblk.com.

POSTON, ANN GENEVIEVE, psychotherapist, nurse; b. Sioux City, Iowa, July 28, 1936; d. Frank Earl and Ella Marie (Stanton) Gales; m. Gerald Connell Poston, June 27, 1959; children: Gregory, Mary Ann, Susan. BSN, Briar Cliff Coll., 1958; MA, U. Mo., 1978; postgrad., Family Inst. of Kansas City, Inc., 1989-91. RN, Kans., Mo.; lic. counselor, Mo., Kans.; advanced RN practitioner, Kans., Mo. Staff nurse, sr. team leader St. Joseph Mercy Hosp., Sioux City, 1958-59; head nurse St. Anthony's Hosp., Rock Island, Ill., 1960, charge nurse, 1966-69, St. Mary's Hosp., Mpls., 1970-71, North Kansas City (Mo.) Hosp., 1972-73, Tri-County Mental Health Ctr., North Kansas City, 1973-79; psychotherapist VA Med. Ctr., Kansas City, 1979-84, Leavenworth, Kans., 1984-85, The Kans. Inst., Olathe, 1985-95; psychotherapist, marriage and family therapist Psychiatry Assocs., Chartered, Overland Park, Kans., 1994-97; pvt. practice Overland Park, Kans., 1997—. Cons. Synergy House, Parkville, Mo., 1974-75, North Kansas City Hosp., 1978-79, VA Hosps., Kansas City and Leavenworth, 1979-85, Cath. Charities, Kansas City, 1983-87, Olathe Med. Ctr., 1985-95, Humana Med. Ctr. Overland Park, Kans., 1986-95, St. Joseph Med. Ctr., Kansas City, Mo., 1990-95; psychotherapist, marriage & famiy therapist Cath. Charities, Kansas City, Mo., 1996—, Shawnee Mission (Kans.) Med. Ctr., 1996—. Author, presenter (video) Depression & Suicide, 1980. Third officer King's Daus., Moline, Ill., 1960-69; campaign worker Rep. Party, Moline, 1963-68; community asst. New Mark Community Affairs, Kansas City, 1972-76; nursing rep. Combined Fed. Campaign, Kansas City, 1982; coord. mental health program com. Midwest Health Congress, Kansas City, 1981. Mem. ACA, ANA (cert.), Am. Assn. Marriage and Family Therapy (clinical), Nat. Bd. Cert. Counselors, Mo. Assn. Marriage and Family Therapy, Sigma Theta Tau. Roman Catholic. Avocations: theater, travel, bridge.

POSTON, JANICE LYNN, librarian; b. Louisville, Mar. 30, 1965; d. William Kenneth and Loretta Frances (Reece) Ferguson; m. Boyce Day Poston, Jan. 9, 1988. BS in Elem. Edn. with high honors, U. Louisville, 1987; MA in Sch. Media Librarianship, Spalding U., Louisville, Ky., 1992; MLS, U. Ky., Lexington, 2002. Part-time libr. page Louisville Free Pub. Libr., 1981-91; elem. sch. tchr. Jefferson County Pub. Schs., Louisville, 1988-91; cataloging svcs. libr. Spalding U. Libr., Louisville, 1991—2003, reference, instrnl. svcs. libr., 2003—. Active Christian edn. bd. River City Ch. of God. Mem. Ky. Libr. Assn. Republican. Pentecostal. Avocations: teaching sunday school, crafts. Office: Spalding U Libr 853 Library Ln Louisville KY 40203-2170 Office Phone: 502-585-7130. Business E-Mail: jposton@spalding.edu.

POSTON, LINDA, dean, library director; d. Henry and Rosella Derksen; m. Larry A. Poston, May 24, 1975; 1 child, Helena Marie. BS in Christian Edn. and Music, Grace U., 1976; MLS, LI U., NY, 1995. Pub. svcs. asst. Billy Graham Ctr. Libr., Wheaton, Ill., 1995—96; acquisitions libr. Nyack Coll., NY, 1992—95, dir. libr. svcs., 1996—2004, assoc. dean libr. svcs., 2004—. Exec. bd. mem. Westchester Acad. Libr. Dirs. Org., NY, 1997—. Mem.: Assn. Christian Librs. (bd. mem. 2002—04, pres. 2004—). Avocations: gardening, baking, reading. Office: Nyack Coll 1 South Blvd Nyack NY 10960 Office Phone: 845-358-1710 ext. 105.

POSTON, MARTHA ANNE, author, researcher; b. Eden, N.C., Feb. 6, 1936; d. Charlie and Cornelia (Leisure) Hopper. BS in Human Resources, N.C. A&T State U., 1972; AS in Computer Sci., Rutledge Coll., 1985. Monogramist dept. store, Winston-Salem, N.C., 1966-72; ext. officer Peace Corps, Jamaica, 1972-74, vol. Liberia, 1974-78; edn. material specialist Liberian Ministry Agr., 1978-81. Author: In the Service of My God, 1991; editor Human Resource Newsletter, 1979-81. Active Save the Children, Westport, Conn., 1989—; primary tchr. LDS Ch., Atlanta, 1993—. Recipient award Beyond War, Atlanta, 1987. Mem. NAFE, AAUW, Internat. Congress on Arts and Comm. (del. 1994—). Avocations: reading, travel, sports, sightseeing. Home: 479 E Paces Ferry Rd NE Atlanta GA 30305-3311

POSTON, REBEKAH JANE, lawyer; b. Wabash, Ind., Apr. 20, 1948; d. Bob E. and April (Ogle) P. BS, U. Miami, 1970, JD, 1974. Bar: Fla. 1974, Ohio 1977, U.S. Dist. Ct. (so. and mid. dists.) Fla., U.S. Ct. Appeals (11th cir.). Asst. U.S. atty. U.S. Atty.'s Office, Miami, Fla., 1974—76; spl. atty. organized crime and racketeering sect. Strike Force, Cleve., 1976—78; ptnr. Fine, Jacobson, Schwartz, Nash & Block, Miami, 1978—94, Steel Hector & Davis, Miami, 1994—2006, Squire, Sanders & Dempsey LLP, Miami, 2006—. Adj. prof. U. Miami Law Sch., Coral Gables; mem. U.S. sentencing guidelines com. So. Dist. of Fla., Miami. Named one of Best Lawyers in Am., 2003—, Fla.'s Elite Lawyers, Fla. Trend mag., 2004—06; recipient Fla.'s Super Lawyer, Law and Politics, 2006. Mem. Fla. Bar Assn., Nat. Assn. Criminal Def. Attys., Nat. Directory Criminal Lawyers, Am. Immigration Lawyers Assn., Dade County Bar Assn. Democrat. Lutheran. Avocations: power boat racing, swimming. Home: 1541 Brickell Ave Apt 3706 Miami FL 33129-1229 Office: 200 SE 2nd St Miami FL 33131 Office Phone: 305-577-7022. Business E-Mail: rposton@ssd.com.

POSUNKO, LINDA MARY, retired elementary education educator; b. Newark, Dec. 24, 1942; d. Joseph and Mary (Prystauk) P. BA, Newark State Coll., Union, N.J., 1964; MA, Kean U., Union, 1974. Cert. permanent elem. tchr., supr., prin., N.J. Elem. tchr. Roselle (N.J.) Bd. Edn., 1964—65; head tchr. 1st grade Garwood (N.J.) Bd. Edn., 1965—76, 1982—95, head tchr., 1974—76, 1979—82, 1984—86, 1987—88, head tchr. 3d grade, 1976—82, acting prin., 1978, lead tchr. early childhood edn., 1993—95; ret., 1995. Cooperating tchr. to student tchrs.; instr. non-English speaking students and children with learning problems; mem. affirmative action, sch. resource coms.; conductor in-svc. workshops on early childhood devel. practices, 1993. Recipient honor cert. Union County Conf. Tchrs. Assn., 1972-73, The Garwood award N.J. Gov.'s Tchr. Recognition Program, 1983, 88, Outstanding Tchr. award N.J. Gov.'s Tchr. Recognition Program, 1988, Tchr. Recognition award Spanish Nat. Honor Soc., 1999, Most Memorable Tchr. Recognition award Spanish Nat. Honor Soc., 1999; nominee N.J. Gov.'s Tchr. Recognition award, 1993-94. Mem. ASCD, NEA, Internat. Reading Assn. (bd. dirs. suburban coun.), N.J. Edn. Assn., Garwood Tchrs. Assn. (sec., v.p., pres.), High/Scope Ednl. Found. Home: 17 Drake Rd Mendham NJ 07945-1805

POSVAR, MILDRED MILLER, opera singer; b. Cleve. d. William and Elsa (Friedhofer) Mueller; m. Wesley W. Posvar, Apr. 30, 1950; children: Wesley, Margot Marina, Lisa Christina. Degree in Music (hon.), Cleve. Inst. Music, 1946; doctorate (hon.), Cleve. Ins. Music, 1983; diploma, New England Conservatory Music, 1948, doctorate (hon.), 1966; MusD (hon.), Bowling Green State U., 1960; doctorate (hon.), Washington Jefferson U., 1988. Founder Opera Theater of Pitts., 1978—; mem. music faculty Carnegie-Mellon U., 1996—. Operatic debut in Peter Grimes, Tanglewood, 1946; appeared N.E. Opera Theater, Stuttgart State Theater, Germany, 1949-50, Glyndebourne Opera, Edinburgh Festival; debut as Cherubino in Figaro, Met. Opera, 1951; 23 consecutive seasons Met. Opera; radio debut Bell Telephone Hour; TV debut Voice of Firestone, 1952; appeared in films including Merry Wives of Windsor (filmed in Vienna), 1964; Vienna State Opera debut, 1963, appearances with San Francisco, Chgo. Lyric, Cin. Zoo, San Antonio, Berlin, Munich, Frankfurt, Pasadena, Ft. Worth, Kansas City, Pitts., Tulsa and St. Paul operas. Bd. dirs. Gateway to Music. Recipient Frank Huntington Beebe award for study abroad, 1949, 50, Grand Prix du Disque, 1965, Outstanding Achievements in Music award Boston C. of C., 1959, Ohioana Career medal, 1985, Outstanding Achievement in Opera award, Slippery Rock U., 1985, YWCA Ann. Tribute to Women award, 1989, Keystone Salute award Pa. Fedn. Music Clubs, 1994; named one of outstanding women of Pitts., Pitts. Press-Pitts. Post-Gazette, 1968, Person of Yr. in Music, Pitts. Jaycees, 1980. Mem. Nat. Soc. Arts and Letters (pres. 1989-90, Gold medal 1984), Disting. Daus. Pa. (pres. 1991-93), Tuesday Mus. Club, Phi Beta Kappa, Phi Delta Gamma, Sigma Alpha Iota. Office: Opera Theater of Pittsburgh PO Box 110108 Pittsburgh PA 15232-0608

POTASH, JEREMY WARNER, public relations executive; b. Monrovia, Calif., June 30, 1946; d. Fenwick Bryson and Joan Antony (Blair) Warner; m. Stephen Jon Potash; 1 son, Aaron Warner. AA, Citrus Coll., 1965; BA,

Pomona Coll., 1967. With Forbes Mag., NYC, 1967-69, JETRO, San Francisco, 1970-75; v.p., co-founder, pres. Potash & Co. Pub. Rels., Oakland, Calif., 1980—. Founding exec. dir. Calif.-Asia Bus. Coun., Alameda, 1991—; exec. dir. Customs Brokers and editor Cal-Asia Member Alert, 1991—; exec. dir. Customs Brokers and Forwarders Assn., San Francisco, 1990—; adv. bd. Asia Pacific Econ. Rev., 1996—; mem. No. Calif. Dist. Export Coun., 2000—, Pacific Coun. Internat. Policy, 2000—; mem. adv. bd. Ctr. Pacific Rim U. San Francisco, 2005—; mem. adv. bd. China-Am. Bus. and Edn. Ctr., Calif. State U. East Bay, 2005. Editor: Southeast Asia Environmental Directory, 1994, Southeast Asia Infrastructure Directory, 1995-96. Co-founder J.L. Magnes docent program, 1980; pres. NorCal WAORT, 1985—86; bd. dirs. Judah L. Magnes Mus., Berkeley, 1981—94. Named Export Citizen of Yr., U.S. Dept. Commerce, 1998. Mem. Oakland Women's Lit. Soc., Book Club Calif. Office: Potash & Co Pub Rels 1050 Marina Village Pkwy Alameda CA 94501

POTASH, MARLIN SUE, psychologist; b. Paterson, N.J., Oct. 23, 1951; d. Monroe and Perle (Cohen) P.; BS magna cum laude, Tufts U., 1973; MEd, Boston U., 1975, EdD, 1977; m. Thomas P. Ivanyi; children: Laura Potash Fruitman, Hilary Potash Fruitman. Rsch. assoc. Ctr. for Study of Edn., Yale U., 1976; vis. lectr. Tufts U., 1975-76; instr. Emmanuel Coll., 1975-79; dir. clin. svcs., resocialization treatment coord. Columbus Nursing Home, East Boston, 1975-76; asst. prof. behavioral sci., dept. pub. health and community dentistry Boston U. Sch. Grad. Dentistry, 1977-81, asst. clin. prof., 1981-85; pvt. practice psychotherapy, orgnl. cons., 1979—; assoc. Levinson Inst., Cambridge, Mass., 1980-83; instr. Radcliffe Coll. Seminars, 1983-85; psychol. cons. Middlesex Probate Ct., Cambridge, 1980-87; instr. Lesley Coll., 1982-84; supr. grad. internship program in pastoral counseling Danielsen Counseling Ctr., Boston, 1979-80; clin. instr. Mt. Sinai Sch. Medicine, 2006-. Author: Hidden Agendas: What's Really Going On In Your Relationships: In Love, At Work, In Your Family, 1990; co-Author: Cold Feet: Why Men Don't Commit, 1988, (with Laura Potash Fruitman) Am I Wierd or Is This Normal?, 1991; contbr. chpt. to books, articles to profl. jours. Trustee, St. Francis Cill., 1981-82; assoc. commr. Mass. Gov.'s Commn. on Status of Women, 1981-82; commr. Human Relations/Youth Resources Commn. of Brookline (Mass.), 1982-84. Fellow Mass. Psychol. Assn. (bd. profl. affairs 1979-82); mem. APA, Acad. Family Psychology, Am. Assn. Marriage and Family Therapists. Office: Ste 1D 108 E 91 St New York NY 10128-1659 E-mail: mpotash@potashmanagement.com.

POTASH, VELLA ROSENTHAL, lawyer, educator; b. Balt., Oct. 3, 1937; d. Joseph and Rona (Glasner) Rosenthal; m. Michael Donald Potash, June 20, 1957 (div. Aug., 1982); children: James Bennet, John Lawrence. BA in Edn., Goucher Coll., 1959; JD, U. Balt., 1974. Bar: Md. 1975, Pa. 1975, Family Mediation Fla., 1992. Tchr. Balt. Sch. System, 1959-62; pub. rels. dir. Citizens Planning & Housing Assn., Balt., 1968-69; asst. pub. defender Pub. Defender's Office, Balt., 1975-78; lawyer pvt. practice, Balt., 1978-82, Guardian Ad Litem Program Family Law Sect., Broward County, Fla., 1987—2002; family mediator pvt. practice, Broward County, 1992—. Pres., lectr. The Changing Am. Family. Rev. bd. Palm Beach County Foster Care, 1999—2001. Mem. NOW (bd. dirs., chair women's ctr. Boca Raton), Md. Bar, Pa. Bar, Broward County Bar Assn. (assoc.), So. Fla. Goucher Alumnae Assn. (pres.), Broward County Mediation Assn. (bd. dirs.). Avocations: golf, reading. Home: 2900 N Palm Aire Dr Apt 301 Pompano Beach FL 33069-3445

POTE, GRETTA LYNN, music educator; b. Murray, Ky., Dec. 6, 1966; d. Fred W. and Linda W. Shepard; m. Michael Steven Pote; 1 child, Devin Wells. MusB in Edn., Murray State U., Ky., 1990, MusM in Edn., 1994. Band dir. South Marshall Mid. Sch., Benton, Ky., Plainfield Cmty. Mid. Sch., Ind., 1995—98, Ctr. Grove Mid. Sch., Greenwood, 1998—2005, Clay Mid. Sch., Carmel, 2005—. Office: Clay Middle School 5150 East 126th Street Carmel IN 46033 Office Phone: 317-844-7251. Personal E-mail: gpote@ccs.k12.in.us.

POTEAT, PATSY, secondary school educator; b. Danville, Va., Oct. 12, 1952; d. Addison Comer and Anna (Rogers) Moore; m. Paul Trent Poteat, July 16, 1977; children: William Travis, Adam Trent, Alison Moore. BS, Radford (Va.) U., 1975; MS, Va. Poly. Inst. and State U., 1984. Tchr. Pittsylvania County Schs., Chatham, Va., 1975—. Sec. Mt. Hermon PTO, 1991-95, Blairs Mid. PTO, 1997—. Named Tchr. of Yr., Tunstall H.S., 1996-97, Secondary Tchr. of Yr., Pittsylvania County, 2006. Mem. NEA, Va. Edn. Assn., Pittsylvania Edn. Assn., Va. Assn. Tchrs. English, Nat. Coun. Tchrs. English, Journalism Edn. Assn. Baptist. Home: 855 Corn Tassel Rd Danville VA 24540-6019 Office: Tunstall HS 100 Trojan Cir Dry Fork VA 24549-2300

POTEAT, THENA G., psychiatrist; b. Fort Jackson, S.C., Feb. 14, 1967; d. Warren Eugene and Eva Poteat; m. John D. Clemmer, Aug. 19, 1995; m. Nicholas Anthony Szabo, Sept. 19, 1992 (div. May 0, 1994); children: Charles Lewis Clemmer, Jacob Gene Clemmer. AB, Washington U., 1988; JD, Yale U., 1991; MD, Med. U. S.C., 2000. Bar: Mo. 1991, Ill. 1992; diplomate in psychiatry Am. Bd. Psychiatry and Neurology, 2005. Assoc. Thompson & Mitchell, St. Louis, 1991—93; psychiatry resident Yale U., New Haven, 2000—04; psychiatrist Associates in Mental Health, Peoria, Ill., 2004—; asst. prof. U. Ill. Coll. Medicine, Peoria, 2005—. Mem.: Ill. Bar Assn., Mo. Bar Assn., Ill. Psychiat. Soc. (v.p. 2005—06), Am. Psychiat. Assn., Phi Beta Kappa, Alpha Omega Alpha. Office: Associates in Mental Health Ste 580 900 Main St Peoria IL 61602 Office Phone: 309-637-4266. Office Fax: 309-637-9836.

POTEMPA, KATHLEEN M., dean, nursing educator; b. Oct. 3, 1948; Diploma in nursing, Providence Hosp. Sch. Nursing, Southfield, Mich., 1970; BA in Psychology summa cum laude, U. Detroit, 1974; MS in Nursing, Rush U., 1978, D of Nursing Sci., 1986. Charge nurse coronary ICU Holy Cross Hosp., Ft. Lauderdale, Fla., 1970-71; staff nurse, charge nurse cardiovasc. ICU Henry Ford Hosp., Detroit, 1971-74; nurse practitioner Rush-Presbyn.-St. Luke's Med. Ctr., Chgo., 1974-75; nursing edn. coord. dept. nursing Michael Reese Hosp. and Med. Ctr., Chgo., 1975-77, nursing supr., 1977-78; asst. unit leader dept. gerontol. nursing Rush U. Coll. Nursing, Chgo., 1978-79, asst. chmn., 1979-80, assoc. chmn., asst. prof. gerontol. nursing, 1980-85, asst. prof. gerontol. nursing, 1985-86; asst. prof. nursing, dept. internal medicine, practitioner Rush Med. Coll., Rush U., 1987-88; asst. then assoc. prof. dept. med.-surg. nursing Coll. Nursing, U. Ill., Chgo., 1988—96, dir. tng., pre and postdoctoral fellowship instnl. rsch., 1992—94, exec. assoc. dean Coll. Nursing, 1994-95, interim dean Coll. Nursing, 1995-96; prof., dean Sch. Nursing Oreg. Health Scis. U., Portland, 1996—2006, v.p., 2002—06; dean, prof. nursing, Sch. Nursing U. Mich., Ann Arbor, 2006—. Rsch. assoc. Robert Wood Johnson Tchg. Nursing Home Project, VA Edward Hines Jr. Hosp., Hines, Ill., 1985-86, co-dir. Exercise Rsch. Lab., 1985-86; dir. nursing Johnston R. Bowman Health Ctr. for Elderly, Rush Presbyn. St. Luke's Med. Ctr., Chgo., 1980-85. Contbr. articles to profl. jours. Recipient Oreg. Med. Rsch. Found. Mentor award, 2002, Disting. Alumni award, Rush U., 2003. Fellow Am. Acad. Nursing; mem. ANA (coun. nurse rschrs.), Am. Soc. Hypertension, Gerontol. Soc. Am., Midwest Nursing Rsch. Soc., Heart Assn. Met. Chgo., Am. Heart Assn. Oreg., Ill. Coun. Nurse Rschrs., Am. Heart Assn. (coun. cardiovasc. nursing, coun. hypertension, coun. on strokes), Am. Assn. Coll. Nursing Bd. (sec. 2004), Sigma Theta Tau. Office: U Mich Sch Nursing 400 N Ingalls Rm 1320 Ann Arbor MI 48109*

POTOCKY, MIRIAM, social worker, educator, writer; b. Prague, Czech Republic, Feb. 28, 1962; arrived in U.S., 1969; d. Pavel Potocky and Vlastimila Potocka. BA, U. of Colo., 1984; MSW, U. of Kans., 1989, PhD, 1993. Assoc. prof. Fla. Internat. U., Miami, Fla., 1993—. Author: Where Is My Home? A Refugee Journey, 2000, Best Practices for Social Work with Refugees and Immigrants, 2002; author: (under pseudonym Miriam Auerback) Dirty Harriet, 2006; contbr. chapters to books, articles to profl. jours. Office: Fla Internat U Sch Social Work University Park Miami FL 33199 Business E-Mail: potockym@fiu.edu.

POTOK, NANCY ANN FAGENSON, management consultant; b. Detroit, May 20, 1955; d. William and Harriet Fagenson; m. Barry Potok, May 16, 1976; children: Benjamin, Leah. BA, Sonoma State U., 1978; MAS, U. Ala., 1980. Cert. govt. fin. mgr. Presdl. mgmt. intern U.S. Dept. Transp., Washington, 1980-82; budget examiner U.S. Office Mgmt. & Budget, Washington, 1982-89; deputy asst. adminstr. fin. and budget Adminstrv. Office U.S. Cts., Washington, 1989-95; controller U.S. Census Bur., Washington, 1995-97, prin. assoc. dir., CFO, 1997—2002; sr. v.p., sr. assoc. Nat. Opinion Research Ctr., U. Chgo., 2003—05; mng. assoc. McManis & Monsalve Assocs., 2005—. Pres., treas. Women's Transp. Sem., Washington, 1983-84; advisor Presdl. Mgmt. Intern Career Devel. Group, Washington; co-chmn. Census Bur. Labor-Mgmt. Partnership coun., 1997-2002; bd. dirs. The Pub. Mgr Contbr. articles to profl. jours. Chmn. Citizens Adv. Com., Crofton, Md., 1996-98; mem. exec. bd. PTA, Crofton, 1990-95; judge Odyssey of the Mind Creative Problem Solving Competition, Md., 1995; coach Destination Imagination, Creative Problem Solving 1st Pl. Team, 1999. Recipient Arthur S. Flemming award, 1991, Silver medal Sec. Commerce, 1998. Mem. Nat. Acad. Pub. Adminstrn., Am. Asn. Budget & Program Analysts, Am. Soc. Pub. Adminstrn., Am. Statis. Assn., Am. Assn. Pub. Opinion Rsch., Assn. Govt. Accts Avocations: writing, music. Business E-Mail: npotok@mcmanis-monsalve.com.

POTRATZ, WENDY JEAN, athletic trainer, consultant; b. South Saint Paul, Minn., Oct. 25, 1973; d. Ronald Edward and Elizabeth Ann Bruestle; m. Lee Richard Potratz, Sept. 11, 1999; children: Owen Dean, Adeline Grace Elizabeth. BA, Carthage Coll., Kenosha, Wis., 1996; MA, U. Minn., Mpls., 2000. Athletic tng. program dir. Northwestern Coll., Orange City, Iowa, 2000—03; sport psychology cons. Triple Performance Plus, Bemidji, Minn., 2003—. CPR/1st aid instr. ARC, 1997—; cert. examiner Nat. Athletic Trainers Assn. Bd. of Cert., Dallas, 2001—, home study reviewer, 2005—. Author: Agnes Plays Soccer: A Young Cow's Lesson in Sportsmanship. Bd. edn. Trinity Luth. Ch., Bemidji, 2005—. Fellow, U. Minn. Sch. Kinesiology, 1999; grantee, U. Minn. Grad. Sch., 1998. Mem.: Minn. Athletic Trainers Assn. (licentiate), Gt. Lakes Athletic Trainers Assn. (licentiate), Nat. Athletic Trainers Assn. (licentiate; cert. athletic trainer). Avocations: softball, volleyball, gardening, reading, bell choir. Office Phone: 218-368-3189. E-mail: wendy@tripleperformance.com.

POTSIC, AMIE SHARON, photographer, educator, artist; b. Chgo., Dec. 11, 1971; d. William P. and Roberta K. Potsic. BA, Ind. U., 1993; MFA, San Francisco Art Inst., 1999. Cert. Teaching English as a Foreign Language to Adults U. Cambridge, 1996. Adj. faculty, photography instr. San Francisco Art Inst., 1999—; adj. faculty photography instr. U. Calif. Berkeley, 2001—; adj. faculty, photography instr. Ohlone Coll., Fremont, Calif., 2003—. Art/photography cons. Amie Potsic Photography, San Francisco, 2004—. One-woman shows include Seduce Me, Quotidian Gallery, 2000, Thin Skinned Thick, 2002, Doppelganger, The Painted Bride Art Ctr., 2003, 626 Gallery, LA, 2005, publication, exhbn., Ritual and Resilience (Second Pl. Photoessay award, San Francisco Bay Guardian, 1998), publication, Prayer - Jerusalem, Israel (Jerusalem 3000 First pl. award Jewish Exponent, 1996), Casa do Vaticano, Graficos Burti Brazil, exhibited in group shows at Documenta USA, The Mus. of New Art, 2001, Fotosemana, Meseo de Arte Moderno de Bogota, 2002, Piece Process, Athens Inst. Contemporary Art, 2004. Program coord., instr. Shooting Back, Washington, 1993—94. Recipient Award of Excellence, Manhattan Arts Internat. Mag., 1996, Award of Excellence, Coll. Photography Ann., Photographer's Forum, 1999, winner Photo Alliance Slide Competition, San Francisco Art Inst., 2004. Mem.: Coll. Art Assn. Personal E-mail: apotsic@yahoo.com.

POTTEBAUM, SHARON MITCHELL, health educator; b. Champaign, Ill., Jan. 7, 1948; d. Robert D. and Louise M. (Straits) Mitchell; m. Joseph R. Pottebaum; children: Pamela, Nicholas. BS in Secondary Health Edn., Ohio State U., 1969, MA in Health Edn., 1978. Cert. occupl. hearing conservationist 1984, health edn. 7-12 Ohio Dept. Edn., 1969, health edn. K-12 Ohio Dept. Edn., 1978. Health edn. supr. Ctr. Sci. and Industry, Columbus, Ohio, 1970—72; jr. h.s. health tchr., dist. health coord. Scioto-Darby City Bd. Edn., Hilliard, Ohio, 1972—74; Drug, Alcohol, Tobacco & Human Behavior Project coord. Ohio State U., Columbus, 1974—75, instr. health edn., 1975—76; pub. health edn. cons. child health unit Ohio Dept. Health, Columbus, 1978—79; dir. edn. and tng. Family Hosp., Milw., 1980—85; instr. health edn. U. Wis.-Whitewater, 2000—03; mgr. farms, Ill., 2003—. Health edn. cons., tchrs. aide Hillside Elem. Sch., Brookfield, Wis., 1988—97; ind. sales rep. World Book-Childcraft, Brookfield, 1985—88; Head Start tng. tech. assistance project cons. Westinghouse Health Systems, 1979—82; profl. continuing edn. coord. Gtr. Milw. Assn. Hosp. Staff Devel. Dirs. and Wis. Soc. Health Edn. and Tng., 1980—85; adv. mem. geriatric edn. planning com. and indsl. medicine task force coms. Family Hosp., Milw., 1981—84. Co-author (textbook): Teaching Health Science in Middle and Secondary Schools, 1981, Toward A Healthy Lifestyle Through Elementary Health Education, 1980; editor: (monthly newsletter) The Post Graduate, 1990—92 (Wisconsin's "Nellie Bly" First Place Award for Outstanding Branch Newsletter, category of 100+ members, 1992). Recipient cert. of leadership, YWCA Gtr. Milw., 1984. Mem.: AAUW (editor bull. West Suburban-Milw. br. 1990—92, fundraiser 1990—, treas. 1992—94, pres.-elect 1995—96, pres. 1996—97, chair travel group 1997—2000, state historian Wis. chpt. 1998—2000, bd. dirs. Wis. chpt. 1999—2001, historian 1999—2001, chair Women's History Month 1999—2001, co-v.p. program 2006—, scholarship honoree, 5-star br. award 1997), Wis. Assn. Health, Phys. Edn., Recreation and Dance, Upside Investment Club (sec. 2000—01). Avocations: travel, photography, painting, scrapbooks, woodcarving. Home: 2815 Almesbury Ave Brookfield WI 53045 Personal E-mail: s_pottebaum@hotmail.com.

POTTER, ALICE CATHERINE, medical technician; b. Oil City, Pa., June 24, 1928; d. Howard Taylor and Hilda Marian (Lewis) P. BA, U. Findlay, 1949; postgrad., Springfield (Ohio) City Hosp., 1949-50. Registerd med. technologist Am. Soc. Clin. Pathologists; cert. clin. lab. scientist. Med. technologist Mercy Hosp., Springfield, 1950-54, Oil City Hosp., 1954-67; staff med. technologist Thomas Jefferson U. Hosp., Phila., 1968-83, sr. med. technologist, 1983—97, retired, 1997—2002. Vol. Acad. Natural Scis., Phila., 1995-2000 Mem. Am. Soc. Clin. Lab. Scientists, Pa. Soc. Clin. Lab. Scientists (membership chmn. Delaware Valley chpt. 1977-78, chmn. pub. rels. 1982-94, 96-97, bd. dirs. 1989-91, 97-98, 98-99, 99-2004, pres.-elect 1991-92, pres. 1992-93, Scrimshaw award 1992) Republican. Avocations: travel, needlecrafts. Home: 1701 Wallace St Philadelphia PA 19130-3312

POTTER, CORINNE JEAN, retired librarian; b. Edmonton, Alta., Can., Feb. 2, 1930; d. Vernon Harcourt and Beatrice A. (Demaray) MacNeil; m. William B. Potter, Aug. 11, 1951 (div. Jan. 1978); children: Caroline, Melanie, Theodore, William, Ellen. BA, Augustana Coll., 1952; MS, U. Ill., 1976. Br. libr. Rock Island (Ill.) Pub. Libr., 1967-73, children's work supr., 1973-74; dir. St. Ambrose U. Libr., Davenport, Iowa, 1978-97; ret., 1997. Chairperson Quad City Libr. Dir.'s Publicity Com., 1984-88. Chairperson Com. of the Whole for Local Automated Circulation and Online Catalog System, 1989-90. Mem. ALA, Assn. Coll. and Rsch. Librs. (sec., v.p., pres. Iowa chpt. 1979-82), Iowa Libr. Assn. (com. chmn. 1983-84), Iowa Pvt. Acad. Librs. Consortium (sec.-treas. 1986-89), Iowa Online Computer Libr. Ctr. Users Group (v.p.-pres. elect 1988-89, pres. 1989-90), Zonta Club Quad Cities (chair libr. bldg. com. 1993-94, co-pres. 1994-97).

POTTER, CYNTHIA M., art educator, artist; b. Balt., July 15, 1950; d. Percel Celon and Nancy Jane (Williams) Harris; m. Willis M. Potter, Oct. 11, 1975; 1 child, Shomaree. BA, Norfolk State U., 1973, MA, 1983; postgrad., Old Dominion U., 1979, Hampton U., 1984, Va. Commonwealth U. Cert. designated gifted alternative, inservice tng. program for mainstreaming, leadership skills. Summer enrichment art tchr. African Am. art Norfolk (Va.) Pub. Schs., photojournalist tchr., art tchr. Contbr. articles to profl. newsletters. Chair planning com. Ruth Winstead Diggs Scholarship Fund, Inc., 1988—; dir. minority concerns com., 1990—. Recipient Cert. of Recognition, Superior Art Instrn. of Appreciation, 1989; fellow for travel study in West Africa; named Tidewater Elem. Art Tchr. of Yr., for Outstanding Svc., 1988. Mem. Nat. Art Edn. Assn., Nat. Conf. of Artists (exec. sec. 1991-93). Home: 1433 Flintfield Cres Chesapeake VA 23321-2824

POTTER, DEBBY, art educator; b. Boston; BA, Ctrl. Wash. U., Ellensburg, 1976; MA, Portland State U., Oreg., 1982. Tchr. art Raymond H.S., Wash., 1975—78; tchr. art and dept. head Ridgefield H.S., Wash., 1978—. Mem.: Kappa Delta Pi. Office: Ridgefield HS 2630 S Hillhurst Ridgefield WA 98642-9089

POTTER, JUNE ANITA, small business owner; b. La Crosse, Wis., Jan. 22, 1938; d. Christian John and Ethel Marie (Stafslien) Stefferud; m. James Oscar Potter, June 18, 1961; children: Jill Potter Rutlin, Todd. BA in Home Econs., St. Olaf Coll., Northfield, Minn., 1960; postgrad., NY Sch. Interior Design, 1964; MS in Edn., U. Wis., Menomonie, 1977. Sr. high home econs. tchr., FHA advisor Tomah (Wis.) H.S., 1960-64, Black River Falls (Wis.) H.S., 1971-83; freelance interior designer Warrens, Wis., 1964-97; ptnr., mgr. James Potter Cranberry Marsh, Inc., Warrens, 1968—; substitute tchr. Tomah Schs., 2001—. Co-pubr.: Warrens Centennial Book, 1968, Wisconsin Cranberry Centennial Book, 1989. Active various charitable and church orgns.; bd. dirs. Warrens Cranberry Festival, 1984—, chair 25th Anniversary Book, 1997; mem. Warrens Area Bus. Assn., 1990-98; sec. Wis. Cranberry Bd., Inc., 1990—2005; sec. Warren Mills Cemetery Assn., 1993-2000; mem. com. Wis. Alice in Dairyland Finale, 1993 (state Alice award, 2000); mem. Jellystone Campground Ministry, Warrens Wis., 1970-, Millennium Tree Com., Washington, 1999; found. bd. Wis. Exec. Residence, 1994-2003; pres. Gloria Dei Luth. Ch. Women, 1997-2000. Mem.: AAUW (v.p. 1983—2001, Cmty. Leadership award 2006), Wis. State Cranberry Growers Assn. (mem. centennial com. 1988—, pub. rels. com. 1994—2000, State Pres.'s award 2000, Agri-Communicator award 2004), Tomah Pky. Garden Club (corr. sec. 2002—), Beta Sigma Phi (com. mem. 1961—, officer, Nat. Order of Rose 1983, Silver Cir. award 1985, Girl of Yr.). Lutheran. Avocations: flowers, photography, travel, collecting foreign country items. Home and Office: 28353 County Hwy EW Warrens WI 54666-7513 E-mail: jpotter@tomah.com.

POTTER, LORRAINE K., career military officer; m. Robert Saunders. BS, Keuka Coll.; MDiv, Colgate Rochester Div. Sch. Former pastor, N.Y.; clin. pastoral educator Yale-New Haven Med. Ctr.; commd. 2d lt. USAF, 1971, advanced through ranks to maj., 2001; various assignments to command chaplain Hdqtrs. Air Edn./Tng. Command, Randolph AFB, Tex., 1998-99; dep. chief of Chaplain Svc. Hdqtrs. USAF, Bolling AFB, D.C., 1999—. At-large mem. Am. Bapt. Chs. Gen. Bd.; active Ministers Coun. for Chaplains and Pastoral Counselors. Office: Chief Chaplain HQ USAF/Bolling AFB 112 Luke Ave SW Washington DC 20332-5113

POTTER, MYRTLE S., research and development company executive; BA, U. Chgo. Various sales, marketing, and bus. positions Merck and Co., v.p. N.E. Region Bus. Group, 1993—96; v.p. strategy and econ. US Pharmaceuticals Group Bristol-Myers Squibb, 1996—97, group v.p. Worldwide Medicine Group, 1997—98, sr. v.p. sales, US Cardiovascular/Metabolics, 1998, pres. US Cardiovascular/Metabolics, 1998—2000; exec. v.p. Genetech, Inc., South San Francisco, 2000—01, exec. v.p. comml. ops., COO, 2001, president, commercial ops., co-chmn., product portfolio com., cons., 2004—. Bd. dirs. Calif. Healthcare Inst., 2001—, Amazon.com, 2004—. Named Top 50 Most Powerful Women In Business, Fortune, 2003, Most Powerful Black Executives in America, 15 Young Global Business Influentials, Time, Woman of Yr., Healthcare Bus. Women's Assn., 2000; named one of 50 Women to Watch, Wall St. Jour., 2005; recipient National Woman of Distinction Award, Girl Scouts of the USA, 2004. One of the architects of the Astra/Merck joint venture and led the work that set Prilosec on pace to be one of the biggest pharmaceutical products in the world; Won the Merck Chairman's Award for work on the Astra/Merck joint venture. Office: Genetech Inc 1 DNA Way South San Francisco CA 94080*

POTTER, PATRICIA RAE, retired protective services official; d. George Harvey Long and Hazel Marian Hartzell; m. LeRoy Clayton Potter, June 2, 1984; children: Robert Allen Chaffer, René Janine Chaffer Kipp, Suzette Marie Chaffer Brown. Student, Calif. State U., San Jose, 1955—57; BS in Bus. Adminstrn., Coll. Notre Dame, 1982. Cert. advanced police officers and stds. tng. Sec. Pittsburgh-DesMoines Steel, Santa Clara, Calif., 1957—59; sec., computer programmer Monsanto Co., Santa Clara, 1959—63; statis. typist United Tech. Corp., Sunnyvale, Calif., 1963—65; clerk, typist GE, San Jose, 1965—66; statis. typist Boeing Co., Everett, Wash., 1968—69; police officer City of San Jose, 1966—93; ret., 1993. Recipient Best of Show award quilting, Tuolumne County Fair, 2001, 2002, 1st award of excellence, Calif. State Fair, 2001, Distinction award, 2002. Mem.: Internat. Police Assn. (sec. treas. 1998), Calif.-Nev.-Hawaii State Assn. Emblem Clubs (2nd v.p. 2006), Sonora Emblem Club #124 (past pres. 1999—2001). Avocations: travel, quilting, reading, spinning and weaving.

POTTER, POLLY HELENE, elementary school educator; b. San Jose, Calif., Dec. 24, 1941; d. Douglas Roy and Clara Jane (Sterzer) Price; m. Wester Schow Potter, June 6, 1970; children: Elisabeth Potter Boss, Meghan Potter Cannon, Paige Kathleen. BS, U. Utah, 1963; MEd, Utah State U., 1985. Cert. tchr. of gifted 1985. Tchr. Davis County Sch. Dist., Bountiful, Utah, 1963—65, 1969—70, San Francisco Dist., 1967; tchr., facilitator Berkeley Sch. Dist., Calif., 1967—69; tchr. Redwood City Sch. Dist., Calif., 1970—72, Granite Sch. Dist., Salt Lake City, 1978—86, Salt Lake Sch. Dist., Salt Lake City, 1986—2002, 2004—. Student-tchr. supr. U. Utah, Salt Lake City, 2002—03, Salt Lake City, 2005—06; child development instr. U. Phoenix, Salt Lake City, 2003. Recipient Outstanding Sch. Tchr., U. Utah, 2002. Mem.: Nat. Assn. Gifted Children, Utah Assn. Gifted Children (Calvin W. Taylor Outstanding Educator award 2006), Phi Beta Kappa. Mormon. Avocations: reading, needlecrafts, gardening, walking.

POTTER, SUSAN KUNIHOLM, bank executive; BA, Cornell U., 1988; MBA, U. Pa. Sr. mgr. Sotheby's, 1992—94; bus. analyst McKinsey & Co., Cleve., 1994—98, engagement mgr., 1998—2002; exec. v.p. product mgmt. consumer banking group KeyCorp, Cleve., 2002—04, exec. v.p. retail bus. devel., 2004—. Named One of 25 Women to Watch, U.S. Banker Mag., 2003. Office: KeyCorp 127 Public Square Cleveland OH 44114-1306

POTTER, SYLVIA, education educator; b. Buchanan County, Va., Feb. 4, 1942; d. Kelly C. and Virgie E. (Osborn) Runyon; m. Hersel E. Potter, Apr. 23, 1961 (div. 1992); children: Barbara L., Timothy H., Jonathan, Amanda. AS summa cum laude, Southwest Va. Cmty. Coll., 1985; BS summa cum laude, Pikeville Coll., 1987; MA with honors, Va. Tech. Inst., 1994. Lic. reading specialist, early edn. educator, mid. edn. educator, spl. edn., Va. LPN Grundy (Va.) Hosp., 1962-72; tchr. Buch County Schs., Grundy, 1972-76, 89-92, Commonwealth of Va. Dept. of Corrections, Hanover, 1993—. Mem. curriculum com. Dept. Correctional Edn., 1997-99, mem. interview panel for hiring com., 1996-2001. Mem. com. Office on Youth, Grundy, 1991-93; scout leader Boy Scouts Am., 1986-93, com. mem. Matlapanai coun. 1996-99, Order of Arow Brotherhood, Sequoyah coun., 1990-94. Mem. Correctional Edn. Assn., Va. Assn. Correctional Edn., Internat. Reading Assn., VA Assn. for Gifted. Democrat. Mem. Ch. of Christ. Avocations: reading, physical work outs, scouting, camping, travel. Home: 8601 S Fork Ct Fredericksburg VA 22407-8723

POTTER, TERESA PEARL, adult education educator; b. Lakeport, Calif., June 11, 1954; d. William Everett and Irene Evelyn (Hennegar) Heath; m. Gideon Steven James Potter, Mar. 18, 1978 (div. Sept. 1987); 1 child, Abraham Jesse. AA, Portland City Coll., 1976; BA, Pacific Oaks Coll., 1989, MA, 1991. Cert. tchr., Calif. Actress, co-prodr. The Wonder Faire Theater., Portland, Oreg., 1978-81; tchr. Temple Beth Meier Sch., Studio City, Calif., 1982-83; dir. Progress Presch., Santa Monica, Calif., 1983-89, Hill An'Dale Family Learning Ctr., Santa Monica, Calif., 1989-92; tchr. Samata Yoga Studio, L.A., 1989-93, L.A. Unified Sch. Dist., 1992-93; lead tchr. Adult

Edn., Parent Edn. Programs San Juan Unified Sch. Dist., Sacramento, Calif., 1993—. Co-host (cable show) License to Parent, 1997-2000. Pres. Sacramento Parent Edn. Consortium 1997—; chmn. Santa Monica Child Care Task Force, 1997. Mem. Calif. Coun. for Adult Edn., Nat. Assn. for Edn. in Young Children. Democrat. Avocations: golf, reading, swimming, tennis, yoga. Office: San Juan Unified Sch Dist 4640 Orange Grove Ave Sacramento CA 95841-7710

POTTORFF, JO ANN, state legislator; b. Wichita, Kans., Mar. 7, 1936; d. John Edward McCluggage and Helen Elizabeth (Alexander) Ryan; m. Gary Nial Pottorff; children: Michael Lee, Gregory Nial. BA, Kansas State U., 1957; MA, St. Louis U., 1969. Elem. tchr. Pub. Sch., Keats and St. George, 1957-59; cons., elem. specialist Mid Continent Regional Edn. Lab., Kansas City, Mo., 1971-73; cons. Poindexter Assocs., Wichita, 1975; campaign mgr. Garner Shriver Congl. Camp, Wichita, 1976; interim dir. Wichita Area Rape Ctr., 1977; conf. coord. Biomedical Synergistics Inst., Wichita, 1977-79; real estate sales asst. Chester Kappelman Group, Wichita, 1979-98, J.P. Weigard & Sons, Wichita, 1998—; state rep. State of Kans., Topeka, 1985—. Mem. exec. com. Nat. Conf. State Legis. Com. Mem. sch. bd. Wichita Pub. Schs., 1977-85; bd. dirs. Edn. Consol. and Improvement Act Adv. com., Kans. Found. for the Handicapped; mem. Children and Youth Adv. com. (bd. dirs.); active Leadership Kans.; chairperson women's network Nat. Conf., State Legislators; mem. Wichita Children's Home Bd.; vice chmn. Nat. Assessment Governing Bd.; chair edn. com. assembly on state issues Nat. Conf. State legislators. Recipient Disting. Svc. award Kans. Assn. Sch. Bds., 1983, Outstanding Svc. to Sch. Children of Nation award Coun. Urban Bds., 1984, awards Gov.'s Conf. for Prevention of Child Abuse and Neglect, Kans. Assn. Reading. Mem. Leadership Am. Alumnae (bd. dirs., sec) Found. for Agr. in Classroom (bd. dirs.), Jr. League, Vet. Aux. (pres.), Bd. Nat. State Art Agys., Rotary, Ky. Assn. Rehab. Facilities (Ann. award), Nat. Order Women in Legislature (past bd. dirs.), Nat. Conf. State Legislatures (chmn. edn. assembly state issues, exec. com.), Rotary, Chi Omega (pres.). Avocations: politics, travel. Office: Weigard 6530 E 13th St N Wichita KS 67206-1247

POTTS, BARBARA JOYCE, retired historic site director; b. L.A., Feb. 18, 1932; d. Theodore Thomas and Helen Mae (Kelley) Elledge; m. Donald A. Potts, Dec. 27, 1953; children: Tedd, Douglas, Dwight, Laura. AA, Graceland Coll., 1951; grad., Radiol. Tech. Sch., 1953; grad. program for sr. execs. in state and local govt., Harvard U., 1989. Radiol. technician Independence (Mo.) Sanitarium and Hosp., 1953, 58-59, Mercy Hosp., Balt., 1954-55; city coun. mem.-at-large City of Independence, 1978-82, mayor, 1982-90; exec. dir. Jackson County Hist. Soc., 1991-97; ret., 1997. Chmn. Mid-Am. Regional Coun., Kansas City, Mo., 1984-85; bd. dirs. Mo. Mcpl. League, Jefferson City, 1982-90, v.p., 1986-87, pres., 1987, 88; chmn. Mo. Commn. on Local Govt. Cooperation, 1985-90; bd. dirs., Mercantile Bank, 1989-98, chair ind. adv. bd., 1997-99; bd. dirs. Women's Found. of Greater Kansas City, 1997-2003; mem. chancellor's adv. bd. UMKC Women's Ctr., 1996-; mem. adv. bd. Comprehensive Mental Health Svcs., 1997-. Author: Independence, 1985. Mem. Mo. Gov.'s Conf. Edn., 1976, Independence Charter Rev. Bd., 1977; bd. dirs. Hope House Shelter Abused Women, Independence, 1982—, Vis. Nurses Assn., 1990-93, Truman Heartland Cmty. Found., 1990-2003, bd. chmn., 1997-99, Mid-Continent coun. U.S. Girl Scouts, 1991-95, Harry S. Truman Libr. Inst., 1995—, Truman Med. Ctr., 2001—, Coun. on Philanthropy, 2001-03, Leadership 20/20 Vision; adv. bd. Ewing M. Kauffman Fund, 2002-06, Greater Kansas City Cmty. Found., 1999-02, Salvation Army, 1999—; pres. Child Placement Svcs., Independence, 1972-89, Greater Kansas City region NCCJ, 1990-2004; bd. vis. UMKC Sch. Medicine, 2002—; trustee Independence Regional Health Ctr., 1982-90, 94-2001, Park Coll., 1989-99, 2004—, chmn. bd. trustees, 1995-99. Eye Found. Kansas City, 1997-99; mem. Nat. Women's Polit. Caucus, 1978—; mem. adv. bd. Greater Mo. Focus on Leadership, mem. steering com., 1989—. Recipient George Lehr Meml. award for cmty. svc., 1989, Woman of Achievement award Mid-Continent coun. Girl Scouts U.S.A., 1983, 75th Anniversary Women of Achievement award Mid-Continent coun. Girl Scouts, 1987, Jane Adams award Hope House, 1984, Cmty. Leadership award Comprehensive Mental Health Svcs., Inc., 1984, 90, Graceland Coll. Alumni Disting. Svc. award 1991, Disting. Citizen award Independence C. of C., 1993, Outstanding Cmty. Svc. award Jackson County Inter-Agy. Coun., 1994, Outstanding Cmty. Svc. award Cmty. Svcs. League, 1996, Jackson County Humanitarian of Yr. award, 1997, Disting. Citizen award, 1997, Paul Harris award Ind. Rotary Club, 1997, Outstanding Svc. award City of Independence Human Rels. Commn., 1999, Greater Kans. City Coun. Philanthropy Vol. of Yr. award, 2000; named Friend of Edn. Indpendence NEA, 1990. Mem.: LWV (Cmty. Svc. award 1990), Jackson County Hist. Soc., Nat. Trust for Hist. Preservation. Mem. Lds Ch. Home: 18508 E 30th Ter S Independence MO 64057-1904

POTTS, GLENDA RUE, music educator; b. Butler, Ala., Nov. 26; d. Jennings Herschel and Erma Rue (Holdridge) Moseley; m. Billy Wayne Blackwell, June 23, 1963 (div. Aug. 1977); children: William Stephen, Melton Jennings; m. Willis Jones Potts, Jr., July 13, 1985; 1 stepchild, Timothy Brendon. BM in Music, Auburn U., 1963. Organist Beverly Meth. Ch., Birmingham, 1964-65; music tchr. grades 3-8 Birmingham Pub. Schs., 1964-65; music tchr. grades 7-9 Chattanooga Pub. Schs., 1965-66; tchr., owner piano/pipe organ studio Kreative Keyboards, Prattville, Ala., 1967-93, Savannah, 1993-99, Rome, Ga., 1999—. Pipe organist 1st Bapt. Ch., Prattville, 1969-85, 87-93, music asst. dir., 1980-85; pianist, dir. children's choirs, asst. organist Bull St. Bapt. Ch., Savannah, 1995-99; sec., mem. chair Savannah Symphony Women's Guild, 1993-99; soprano Savannah Symphony Chorale, 1993-94; mem. chair Savannah Newcomer's, 1994-95; substitute organist and pianist First Baptist Ch., Rome, Ga., 2000-. Honored as one of Top 400 Women Grads. of Centennial of Admission of Women Students, Auburn U., 1992. Mem. Ga. Music Tchrs. Assn. (pres. Savannah chpt. 1997-99, pres. Rome chpt. 2001-03, treas. 2003—), Music Tchrs. Nat. Assn. (nat. and state cert. tchr. and adjudicator), Nat. Guild of Piano Tchrs. (nat. cert. tchr. and adjudicator, established audition ctrs., chmn. Prattville 1967-93, Rome area fall 2001—, Hall of Fame 1990), Am. Coll. Musicians. Republican. Baptist. Home: 2614 Horseleg Creek Rd SW Rome GA 30165-8583

POTTS, LATONYA G., social studies educator; d. Roosevelt and Barbara Turner; m. Derrick J. Potts, May 8, 2005. BA in History and black studies, Pitzer Coll., Calif., 1997; MA in edn., Claremont Grad. U., Calif., 1999. Cert. social studies tchr. Calif. Tchr. Internat. Polytechnic HS, Pomona, Calif., 1999—2002, Baldwin Park HS, Calif., 2002—.

POTTS, MARTHA LOU, elementary school educator; b. Enid, Okla., May 30, 1939; d. Hugh David and Luaddie (Williamson) P. BA, Northwestern Okla. U., 1961; postgrad., U. Hawaii, 1966, Phillips U., 1967, 75, Citadel, 1980. Tchr. music pub. schs., Vici, Okla., 1961-62, Enid, 1962-67, Tulsa, 1987-88, Garden City, Kans., 1967-70, Dept. Def., Iwakuni, Japan, 1970-76, pub. schs., Charleston, S.C., 1976-86, Hudson, N.H., 1986-87, San Antonio, 1988—. Mem. tribal coun. Tex. Cherokee and assoc. bands. Vol. Cancer Soc., 1977-87, Dem. Party, Charleston, Enid, San Antonio, 1977-97, Neighborhood Watch, San Antonio, 1990-97; mem. tribal coun. Tex. Cherokees Associated Bands, 1998—. Mem. DAR, Am. Assn. Profl. Educators, Music Educators Nat. Conf., Am. String Tchrs. Assn. (People to People award 1997), Tex. Orch. Dirs. Assn., Japanese Am. Cultural Soc., Irish Am. Cultural Soc., Tex. Rangers Assn., Sons and Daus. of Cherokee Strip, Bexar County Geneal. Soc. Civil War Round Table, War of 1812 United Dau. of Confedercy. Roman Catholic. Avocations: travel, genealogy, civil war. Home: 12647 Sandtrap St San Antonio TX 78217-1822 Office: Connell Middle Sch 400 Hot Wells Blvd San Antonio TX 78223-2602

POTVIN, BARBARA DIRKS, librarian; d. Henry Bernhard Dirks and Libbie Marie Travnicek; m. Laurence James Potvin, July 12, 1984; children: Laughlin Ann, James Travnicek, Louis Breckenridge, Curtis Anton. MusB, Ea. N.Mex U., 1980, MusB in Edn., 1980; MLS, U. Ariz., 1988. Cert. Nat. Assn. Music Therapy. Serials libr. asst. Ea. N.Mex U., Portales, 1979—80; elem. music tchr., music therapist Artesia (N.Mex) Pub. Schs., 1981—84; tchr. Pomerene (Ariz.) Elem. Sch., 1984—98; libr. Rim Country Mid. Sch., Payson, Ariz., 1998—. Bd. dirs. Tonto Cmty. Concert Assn., Payson, 1999—2005, Benson (Ariz.) Pub. Libr., 1994—98, sec. Friends of Libr., 1986—98. Named Outstanding mem., Benson chpt., Am. Heart Assn., 1990. Mem.: ALA, Ariz. Libr. Assn. Office: Rim Country Mid Sch PO Box 919 Payson AZ 85547 Office Phone: 928-474-4511. Office Fax: 928-472-2044.

POU, NELLIE, assemblywoman; Degree in mcpl. budget and fin., Rutgers U. Assemblywoman N.J. Gen. Assembly, 1997—; assembly asst. minority leader, 2000—01; dep. spkr., 2002—. Mem. N.J. Dept. Health, Profl. Adv. Com., 1991—92, Passaic County Human Svcs. Adv. Coun., 1991—95, Passaic County-Bergen County HIV Health Svcs. Adv. Coun., 1993—97; chair Mayor's Health Planning Task Force, 1988—97; mem. Passaic County Planning and Policy Partnership Com., 1996—. Commr. Paterson Pub. Libr. Bd. Trustees, 1983—84; mem. N.J. Task Force on Child Abuse and Neglect, 1997—. Democrat. Office: 100 Hamilton Plz Ste 1403-05 Paterson NJ 07505 E-mail: AswPou@njleg.org.

POUILLON, NORA EMANUELA, food service executive, chef; b. Vienna, Oct. 26, 1943; came to U.S., 1965; d. Leopold and Gertraude (Mayr) Aschenbrenner; m. Pierre Pouillon, Dec. 3, 1965 (separated 1978); children: Alexis, Olivier; life ptnr. Steven Damato; children: Nina, Nadia. Baccalaureat, Neuland Schule, Vienna, 1961; Moderne Rechtechnic, Technische Hochschule, Vienna, 1962-63; Bus. Degree, Handelsakademie, Vienna, 1964; drawing cert., Corcoran Sch. Art, 1967; diploma, Internat. Sch. Interior Design, 1968. Tchr. and owner Guerilla Gourmet, Washington, 1973-76; owner Food for Friends, Washington, 1973—75; chef Tabard Inn Hotel, Washington, 1976—78; co-owner, chef Restaurant Nora, Washington, 1979—, City Cafe, Washington, 1986—94, Asia Nora, 1994—. Activist with food safety advocacy groups Green Circle Organics, Walnut Acres, Seaweb's Give North Atlantic Swordfish A Break; founding mem. Chefs Collaborative 2000; charter mem. Seafood Choices Alliance; participant Harvard Sch. Nutrition Roundtable; mem. Internat. Com. Alternative and Complementary Medicine; bd. mem. Foodfit.com, Ctr. Mind-Body Medicine, Women Chefs and Restaurateurs. Bd. mem. Amazon Conservation Team. Restaurant named Top Healthiest Restaurant, Health Mag.; named one of Zagat's Top Ten Restaurants, one of three Power Chefs, Washington Post; Chef of Yr. award of Excellence, IACP; First Book finalist for Cooking with Nora, Julia Child Cookbook award; recipient New Hope Natural Media award for Contbns. Organic Industry; Citizens for Better Health-Nora Pouillon award Sustainable Living, 2003; First Ladies of Cuisine award for Excellence, YMCA, 2004. Mem.: Internat. Assn. Culinary Profls., Les Dames d'Escoffier, Organic Trade Assn. (Spl. Pioneer Leader award 2004). Achievements include having the first certified organic restaurant in the country. Avocations: synergy exercise, yoga, hiking, downhill and cross-country skiing. Office: Restaurant Nora 2132 Florida Ave NW Washington DC 20008-1925 Office Phone: 202-462-5143. Business E-Mail: norap@noras.com.

POULET, ANNE LITLE, museum director, art historian; b. Wash., Pa., Mar. 20, 1942; d. John Francis and Ruth Virginia (Kurtz) Litle; m. Francois Poulet, May 20, 1967. BA cum laude, Sweet Briar Coll., 1964; MA, Inst. Fine Arts, NYU, 1970. Curator Dept. European Decorative Arts and Sculpture Mus. Fine Arts, Boston, 1980—99; curator European Decorative Arts and Sculpture emerita Russell B. & Andrée Beauchamp Stearns, 1999—; dir. Frick Collection, NYC, 2003—. Catalogue, vol. 5, Wrightsman Collection, Met. Mus. Art., NYC, 1967—72, exhibitions include Corot to Braque, Mus. Fine Arts, Boston, 1978—80; author: (exhibit catalogue) Corot to Braque, 1978—80; editor-in-chief Jour. Mus. Fine Arts, Boston, 1989—93; co-author: (catalogue) Clodion (1738-1814), 1992; author, guest curator Jean-Antoine Houdon (1741-1828): Sculptor of the Enlightenment, Nat. Gallery Art, Washington, DC, 2003; contbr. articles to profl. jours. Recipient Iris Fedn. award for decorative arts, 2000; grantee, Ford Found., 1965, Lamb Mellon, 1990, 1998, 2000—01; Kress fellowship, 1976. Fellow: Am. Acad. Arts & Sciences; mem.: Assn. Art Mus. Dir., Am. Fedn. Arts, Am. Assn. Mus., French Heritage Soc. (co-founder, former vice chmn. bd.). Office: The Frick Collection 1 E 70th St New York NY 10021-4967

POULOS, CLARA JEAN, nutritionist; b. L.A., Jan. 1, 1941; d. James P. and Clara Georgie (Creighton) Hill; m. Themis Poulos, Jan. 31, 1960. PhD in Biol., Fla. State Christian U., 1974; PhD in Nutrition, Lafayette U., 1984; D in Nutritional Medicine, Hearts of Jesus and Mary Coll., 1986. Registered nutritionist, cert. hypnotherapist, clin. densitometry technician, in diabetes edn. Dir. rsch. Leapou Lab., Aptos, Calif., 1973—76, Monterey Bay Rsch. Inst., Santa Cruz, Calif., 1976—2001; nutrition specialist Santa Cruz, 1975—2001; dir. nutritional svcs., health enhancement, lifestyle planning, 1983—97; chief tech. and rsch. Osteoporosis Diagnostic Ctr., Santa Cruz, 2000—04; chief tech. rsch. Osteoporosis Care Ctr., San Jose, 2001—. Instr. Stoddard Assocs. Seminars; cons. Biol-Med. Lab., Chgo., Nutra-Med Rsch. Corp., NY, Akorn-Miller Pharmacal, Chgo.; cons. Threshold Lab. Monterey Bay Aquaculture Farms, Calif.; cons. Resurrection Lab., Calif. Author: Alcoholism-Stress-Hypoglycemia, 1976, The Relationship of Stress to Alcoholism and Hypoglycemia, 1979; assoc. editor: Internat. Jour. Bio-Social Research, Health Promotion Features; editor: Nutrition and Dietary Consultant Jour.; columnist: The Connection Newspaper; contbr. articles to profl. jours. Recipient Najulander Internat. Rsch. award, 1971, Wainwright Found. award, 1979, various state and local awards. Fellow: Internat. Acad. Nutritional Consultants, Am. Nutritionist Assn., Internat. Coll. Applied Nutrition; mem.: AAAS, Internat. Fishery Assn. (health assoc.), Calif. Acad. Sci., Am. Public Health Assn., Am. Heart Assn. (pres. Santa Cruz br. 1990—91), Internat. Platform Soc., Am. Diabetes Assn. (profl., pres. Santa Cruz chpt., editor newsletter The Daily Balance Santa Cruz chpt., sec. No. Calif. chpt.), MUSE-Computer Users Group, Am. Women's Bowling Assn., Quota, Toastmistress. E-mail: cjp1918@netscape.net.

POULOS, PAIGE M., public relations executive; b. Woodland, Calif., Apr. 26, 1958; d. Paul William Jr. and Frances Marie (Gibson) Poulos; m. John Stuart Woolley, Jr., Feb. 3, 1990. Student, U. Calif., Davis, 1977-80. Mgr. pub. rels. Somerset Wine Co., N.Y.C. and San Martin, Calif., 1982-88; dir. comm. The Beverage Source, San Francisco, 1988-89, Rutherford (Calif.) Hill Winery, 1989-90; pres. Paige Poulos Comm., Berkeley, Calif., 1990—. Founder, chmn. WINECOM, 1992—; adj. lectr. Culinary Inst. Am./Greystone, 2002, adj. prof. lime comm., 2003 Pub. rels. editor: Practical Winery & Vineyard, 1994; wine, epicurean travel editor Focus Mag. Mem. Pub. Rels. Soc. Am. (accredited 1993, bd. dirs. 1993-95, editor newsletter food and beverage sect. 1993-95, pres. East Bay chpt. 1994-96, sec. 1994, counselors acad. 1994, chmn. food and beverage sect. 1996-97), Women in Comm., Acad. Wine Comm. (program chair 1994, sec. 1998, pres. 2000), Internat. Assn. Bus. Communicators, Am. Inst. Wine and Food, Internat. Assn. Culinary Profls., San Francisco Profl. Food Soc., Sonoma Culinary Guild (bd. dirs. 1998-99). Republican. Episcopalian. Avocations: horseback riding, diving, skiing, wine collecting. Office: Paige Poulos Communications 64 Railroad Ave Richmond CA 94801 E-mail: paige@paigepoulos.com.

POULSEN, DANIALL REI, science educator; b. Kalamazoo, Mich., June 5, 1975; d. Susan Ann and Scott Leroy Davis; m. Andy Dale Poulsen, May 22, 1999; children: Gracie Rei, Easton Andrew. MS Edn., We. Mich. U., Kalamazoo, 2006. Cert. Tchr. Mich., 2000. Tchr. sci. Portage No. H.S., Mich., 2001—. Advisor environ. club Portage No. H.S., 2003—. Mem.: Kalamazoo Astron. Soc. (assoc.). Office: Portage Northern High School 1000 Idaho Portage MI 49024

POULSON, KRISTIE M., secondary school educator; b. Lakeview, Mich., Mar. 30, 1978; d. David J. and Mary L. Poulson. BS, Ferris State U., Big Rapids, Mich., 2001. Tchr. Comstock Pub. Schs., Kalmazoo, Mich., 2003—.

POULTON, LESLEE, language educator; b. Salt Lake City, Oct. 25, 1953; PhD, Ind. U., Bloominton, 1987. Prof. French U. Wis., La Crosse, 1987—. Resident dir. summer study program U. Wis.-La Crosse Summer Study Program, Dubna, Russia, 1990—93. Mem. La Crosse/Epinal (France) Sister City Internat. Orgn., 1994—96; treas. La Crosse Dubna Friendship Assn. Sister Cities Internat., 1993—96. Grantee McGlynn Fund for the Enhancement of Tchg., U. Wis.-La Crosse, 1995; Coll. of Liberal Studies Tchg. grantee, 1994, Faculty Devel. grantee, 1995, Rsch. grantee, 1999, Coll. Liberal Studies Rsch. grantee, 2000, Internat. Faculty Devel. Fund grantee, 2004. Mem.: Am. Assn. Tchrs. French (Wis. chpt., Recognition Tchg. award 1994), Wis. Assn. Fgn. Lang. Tchrs., Midwest MLA. Mem. Lds Ch. Office: Univ Wisconsin-La Crosse 1725 State St La Crosse WI 54601 Office Phone: 608-785-8316. Business E-Mail: poulton.lesl@uwlax.edu.

POULTON, ROBERTA DORIS, nurse, consultant; b. Balt., Oct. 19, 1943; d. Charles Robert and Mary Doris (Guercio) P. Nursing diploma, Md. Gen. Hosp., 1964. Staff nurse Md. Gen. Hosp., 1964-67, Project Hope, Colombia, 1967, Tunisia, 1969-70, St. Agnes Hosp., Balt., 1968-69, team leader, 1972-83, staff nurse-preceptor, 1983-88, nurse mgr. pediatric emergency rm./ambulatory svcs., 1988-93, pediat. hemophilia coord., 1993—2003; cons., 2003—; sch. nurse Mother Secon Acad., Balt., 2004—. Pediat. ambulatory specialty clin. nurse; hemophilia nurse Johns Hopkins Med. Instn., Balt., 1998-2003; cons. Girl Scouts U.S.A., Balt., 1972-2003, Bapt. Conv. Md., 1963-2004. Mem.: ANA, Md. Nurses Assn. Democrat. Baptist. Personal E-mail: rpoulton43@aol.com.

POUNCEY, ALICE GERTRUDE MOORE, psychology and home economics educator; b. Lauderdale County, Miss., July 9, 1939; d. Robert Erby and Julia (Bullard) Moore; m. Kenneth Warren Pouncey, Dec. 20, 1959; children— Alicia Ann, Amy Dawn, Nick Alan. A.A., Jones Jr. Coll., 1959; B.S., U. So. Miss., 1961; M.Ed., Livingston U., 1968; postgrad. Miss. State U., 1970, 82, U. So. Miss., 1969-70, 83. Tchr., Enterprise Jr. High Sch., Miss., 1961-63, Beatrice High Sch., Ala., 1963-65; prof. psychology and home econs. East Central CC, Decatur, Miss., 1969—2001, ret. 2001. Mem. ch. adminstrv. bd., chancel choir Meth. Ch.; mem 4-H Adv. Council. Recipient State 4-H Alumni award. Mem. DAR, Miss. Ret. Edn. Personnel, Miss. Jr. Coll. Faculty Assn., Miss. Profl. Educators, Miss. Assn. Educators, Delta Kappa Gamma, Kappa Kappa Iota. Republican. Methodist. Club: 4-H Vols. (pres. 1963-65), Garden, Woman's, 4-H Honor Club. Avocations: sewing; traveling. Home: PO Box 121 Decatur MS 39327-0121 E-mail: apouncey@hotmail.com.

POUNCEY, ANNIE MOORE, retired secondary school educator; b. Shreveport, La., Mar. 29, 1943; d. Robert Edward and Ora Lee (Boatwright) Moore; (div.); 1 child, Stephanie Andrea Pouncey. BS, Grambling Coll., 1966; MEd, So. U., 1979. Cert. tchr., social sci., speech and adminstrv. Tchr. social studies Webster H.S., Minden, La., 1966-67, Caddo Parish Sch., Shreveport, 1969—, Linear H.S., 1969-70, Linwood Jr. H.S., 1971, Bethune H.S., 1971-73, Huntington High, Shreveport, La., 1973-94; ret., 2001. Presenter in field. Pres. Ingersoll PTA, Shreveport, 1977-81; asst. sec. Delta Lambda Omega, 1990-92; Christian edn. counselor Pleasant Hill Bapt. Ch., Shreveport, 1992—; edn. youth dir. Pleasant Hill Bapt. Ch. Mem. NEA, Caddo Edn. Assn. (faculty rep.), La. Edn. Assn. Democrat. Baptist. Avocations: piano, singing. Office: Huntington High 6801 Rasberry Ln Shreveport LA 71129-2599 Home: PO Box 36964 Shreveport LA 71133-6964

POUNDS, JANICE JONES, elementary school educator; b. Palatka, Fla., May 31, 1953; d. Wallace Linwood and Florence (Warwick) Jones; m. Gary Stephen, Sept. 2, 1973; children: G. Stephen, Kathryn, Jonathan. BEd, U. Fla., Gainesville, 1975; MEd, U. North Fla., Jacksonville, 1987. Tchr. Putnam County Schs., Palatka, 1975-80, curriculum resource tchr., 1980-92, tchr. on spl. assignment, 1993—95; asst. prin. Palatka (Fla.) H.S., 1995—99; prin. Jenkins Middle Sch., Palatka, 1999—2005, Browning Pearce Elem. Sch., San Mateo, Fla., 2005—. Cons. for parenting workshops at local chs., various schs., Palatka, 1989—. Sunday sch. tchr. St. Monica's Cath. Ch., Palatka, 1980-93. Named to Outstanding Young Women of Am., 1987. Democrat. Avocations: water-skiing, bicycling, travel, reading. Home: PO Box 39 Palatka FL 32178-0039 Office: Browning Pearce Elem Sch 100 Bear Blvd San Mateo FL 32187 Office Phone: 386-329-0558. E-mail: jpounds@putnamschools.org.

POUNDS, REGINA DOROTHEA, writer; arrived in U.S., 1980; d. Friedrich and Herta Klein; m. Wayne C. Pounds, June 21, 1968; 1 child, Louis C. Author: Theo's Ghost, 2000, Lord Eaglebeak, 2000, Leonora, 2002, Wild Violets, 2005; contbr. articles to publs. Mem.: Defenders of Wildlife, World Wildlife Fund. Avocations: history, languages, poetry, art. Home: 614 E Grant St Belleville IL 62220 Personal E-mail: oldberliner@yahoo.com.

POUNDSTONE, SALLY HILL, library director; m. Robert Bruce Poundstone; children: Nancy Katrina, Holly Megan, Angus Bruce, Alice Heather. BA, U. Ky., 1954, MA in Libr. Sci., 1955. Asst. head ref. dept. Louisville Free Pub. Libr., 1955-59; libr. Folger Shakespeare Libr., Washington, 1959-60; chief acquisition dept. White Plains (N.Y.) Pub. Libr., 1960-62; libr. Bedford Hills (N.Y.) Pub. Elem. Sch., 1965-66; dir. Mamaroneck (N.Y.) Free Libr. and Emelin Theatre, 1966-87, Westport (Conn.) Pub. Libr., 1987-98; prin. SHP Libr. Consultants, 1998—. Instr. libr. sci. N.Y. U., 1968-69, Coll. of New Rochelle (N.Y.), 1970-71; adv. coun. mem. Pratt Inst. Grad Sch. of Libr. and Info. Sci., 1978-87; adminstrv. svcs. chmn. N.Y. Met. Ref. and Res. Libr. Agy., 1977-79, bd. trustees, 1979-88, 2d v.p. and chair, 1984-85, pres., 1985-88; planning and devel. com. mem. Bibliomation, Inc., 1988-90; chair Conn. State Adv. Coun. for Libr. Planning and Devel., 1988-90. Pres. Garden Club of Mamaroneck, 1969-70, Larchmont-Mamaroneck Film Coun., 1971-72, Mamaroneck Hist. soc., 1976-77, bd. mem., 1976-87; vice chmn. Village of Upper Nyack Planning Bd., 1988-89; leadership com. and task force mem. Westchester 2,000, 1984-87; com. mem. Rotary Club of Westport, 1987—; active Downtown Westport Adv. Com., 1989-90, Rep. Town. Com., Weston, Conn., 1990-93, Westport Bridge & Traffic Com., 1990-97, Honorable Order of Ky. Cols., 1995—, United Way Profl. Adv. Com., 1994-97, Westport Telecomm. Com., 1994-96, and others; v.p., dir. Woodcock Nature Ctr., 1998—, pres., 2001—; mem. Wilton Rep. Town Com., 2000—; mem. Planning and Zoning Bd. Commns., 2000—, sec., 2004-05, vice chair 2005-. Mem. ALA, Conn. Libr. Assn., Fairfield Libr. Adminstrs. Group, Archons of Colophon, Pub. Libr. Dirs. Assn. Westchester County (various offices and chairs), N.Y. Libr. Assn. (sec. treas. adult librs. assn. 1970-72, pres. pub. librs. sect. 1981-82, chair planning com. 1984-85). Home and Office: 48 Sharp Hill Rd Wilton CT 06897-3531 Office Phone: 203-761-0291.

POUR-EL, MARIAN BOYKAN, mathematician, educator; b. NYC; d. Joseph and Mattie (Caspe) Boykan; m. Akiva Pour-El; 1 child. AB, Hunter Coll.; A.M., Harvard U., 1951, PhD, 1958. Prof. math. U. Minn., Mpls., 1968—2000, prof. emeritus, 2000—. Mem. Inst. Advanced Study, Princeton, N.J., 1962-64; mem. coun. Conf. Bd. Math. Scis., 1977-82, lectr. internat. congresses in math. logic and computer sci., Eng., 1971, Hungary, 1967, Czech Republic, 1973, 1998, Germany, 1983, 96-97, Japan, 1985, 88, China, 1987; lectr. Polish Acad. Sci., 1974; lectr. Fed. Republic of Germany, 1980, 1983, 87, 89, 91, 96 Japan, 1985, 87, 90, 93, China, 1987, Sweden, 1983, 94, Finland, 1991, Estonia, 1991, Moscow, 1992, Amsterdam, 1992; mem. Fulbright Com. on Maths., 1986-89; invited spkr. Internat. Congress on Computability and Complexity Theory, Kazan U., Russia, 1997, Workshop on Computability and Complexity in Analysis, held in conjunction with 23rd Internat. Symposium on Math. Founds. of Computer Sci. and Computer Sci. Logic, Brno, Czech Republic, 1998, IEEE Workshop on Real Number Computation, 1998 Author: (with I. Richards) Computability in Analysis and Physics, 1989; contbr. articles to profl. jours. Named to Hunter Coll. Hall of Fame, 1975; NAS grantee, 1966. Fellow AAAS, Japan Soc. for Promotion of Sci.; mem. Am. Math. Soc. (coun. 1980-88, numerous com., spkr., orgn. spl. sessions on math. logic), Assn. Symbolic Logic, Math. Assn. Am. (nat. panel vis. lectr.), Phi Beta Kappa, Sigma Xi, Pi Mu Epsilon (mathematics), Sigma Pi Sigma (physics). Achievements include research in mathematical logic (theoretical computer science) and in computability and noncomputability in physical theory—wave, heat, potential equations, eigenvalues, eigenvectors. Office: U Minn Sch Math Vincent Hall Minneapolis MN 55455-0488 E-mail: pour-el@math.umn.edu.

POURMOTABBED, TAYEBEH, biochemist; b. Kermanshah, Iran, Mar. 25, 1959; d. Ali Akbar Pourmotabbed and Molouk Ghovaalla; m. James Aflaki, Jan. 3, 1998. BA, Coll. of Notre Dame, 1981; PhD, U. Md., 1986. Asst. lectr. gen. chemistry U. Md., Balt., 1985, grad. tchg. asst., 1981-86, supr. undergrad. rsch., 1986-88, postdoctoral rsch. asst. College Park, 1986-88; instr. organic chemistry Howard C.C., Columbia, Md., 1986-87; asst. prof. U. Tenn., Memphis, 1989-92, 1993-98, assoc. prof., 1998—. Vis. prof. Wash. U., Seattle, 1995; invited lectr. in field. Contbr. articles to profl. jours., chpts. to books. Named Disting. Aumnus of Yr., U. Md., 2000. Mem. AAAS, Am. Chem. Soc., Am. Soc. for Biochemistry and Molecular Biology, Am. Coll. Rheumatology, N.Y. Acad. of Scis., Phi Lambda Epsilon. Office: Univ Tenn Molecular Sci Dept 858 Madison Ave Ste G1 Memphis TN 38163-0001 E-mail: tpourmotabbe@utmem.edu.

POVICH, LYNN, journalist, internet executive; b. Washington, June 4, 1943; d. Shirley and Ethyl P.; m. Stephen B. Shepard, Sept. 16, 1979; children: Sarah, Ned. AB, Vassar Coll., 1965. Rschr., reporter, writer, editor, sr. editor Newsweek mag., NYC, 1965—91; editor-in-chief Working Woman mag., NYC, 1991—96; mng. editor, sr. exec. prodr. East coast programming MSNBC Interactive, Secaucus, NJ, 1996—2001. Editor: All Those Mornings at the Post, 2006. Bd. mem. Internat. Women's Media Found., 1998—, co-chair, 2002—05; adv. com. women's rights divsn. Human Rights Watch, 2003—. Recipient Matrix award N.Y. Women in Comms., 1976; named to Acad. of Women Achievers YWCA, 1993.

POVLITZ, JENNIFER, investment company executive; b. 1966; BS, Univ. Ill., 1987. With Merrill Lynch & Co., 1987—, branch dir., private banking and investment Columbia, SC, dir. private banking and investment group NYC, 2004. Named one of Forty Under 40, Crain's Bus. NY, 2004. Office: Merrill Lynch & Co Inc 4 World Financial Ctr 250 Vesey St New York NY 10080

POVSNER, LAURA ELIZABETH, art educator, artist; d. Mitchell Povsner and Marie Mitchell. BFA, Sch. of Art Inst. of Chgo., 1994; MEd, U. Ill., Chgo., 1999. Cert. tchr., art tchr. Ill. Tchr. LA Unified Sch. Dist., Carson, Calif., 2001—02; art tchr. Chgo. Pub. Schs., 2002—, cross country coach, 2004—. Exhibitions include Macy Gallery, Art of Tchg. Exhibit. Grantee, Oppenheimer, 2002—03. Mem.: Nat. Art Educators Assn. (assoc.). Home: 1812 S Dearborn Unit 3 Chicago IL 60616 Office Phone: 773-534-4940. Personal E-mail: lpovsner@yahoo.com.

POWEL, JANE C., educational consultant, elementary school educator; d. John Samuel and Norma Dillemuth Powel; m. Peter John Conigliaro (div.); children: Michael, Andrea, Thomas, Stephen. BS magna cum laude in Elem. Edn., Syracuse U., 1974; MS in Edn., Adelphi U., 1979. Tchr. Garden City Park (N.Y.) Sch., 1974—77; tchr. gifted children New Hyde Park (N.Y.) Sch., 1980; program dir. Roslyn (N.Y.) Pub. Sch., 1982—; pres. Omni Learn Corp., N.Y.C., 2004—. With gate program Point Arena (Calif.) Sch., 1991—2002; dir. edn. Cold Spring Harbor Lab. (N.Y.) DNALC, 1992—97; pres. Cold Spring Harbor Acad. Inc., 1996—2004; dir. advanced learning programs East Woods Sch., Oyster Bay, NY, 1998; spkr. Adelphi U., Garden City, NY, 1998—99. Asst. minister St. Peter's Luth. Ch., Huntington, NY, 2001—03. Mem.: NY Acad. Sci., Assn. Sch. Curriculum and Devel., Kappa Delta Pi. Democrat. Lutheran. Avocations: reading, theater, travel. Home: 303 Greenwich St #3L New York NY 10013 Office Phone: 212-566-3970. Business E-Mail: jane@omnilearncorp.com.

POWELL, ALMA JOHNSON, writer, advocate, foundation administrator; b. Birmingham, Al., Oct. 27, 1937; d. Robert and Mildred Johnson; m. Colin L. Powell, Aug. 1962; children: Michael, Linda, Annemarie. BA, Fisk U., 1957; LHD (hon.), Emerson Coll., 1996. Audiologist Boston Guild Hard of Hearing, 1959—62. Author: (children's books) America's Promise, 2003, My Little Wagon, 2003. Chair nat. coun. Best Friends Found., 1989—2001; chair Alliance for Youth, 2004—. Named one of 100 Most Powerful Women in Wash., Washingtonian mag., 2001.

POWELL, ANNE ELIZABETH, editor-in-chief; b. Cheverly, Md., Nov. 11, 1951; d. Arthur Gorman and Barbara Anne (MacAran) P.; m. John Alan Ebeling Jr., 1972 (div. 1983). BS, U. Md., 1972. Reporter Fayetteville (N.C.) Times, 1973-75; home editor Columbus (Ga.) Ledger-Enquirer, 1976; assoc. editor Builder mag., Washington, 1977-78; architecture editor House Beautiful's Spl. Publs., N.Y.C., 1979-81; editor Traditional Home mag., Des Moines, 1982-87, Mid-Atlantic Country mag., Alexandria, Va., 1987-89; editor in chief publs. Nat. Trust for Hist. Preservation, Washington, 1989-95; editor-in-chief Landscape Architecture Mag., Washington, 1995-98, Civil Engring. Mag., Washington, 1998—. Author: The New England Colonial, 1988. Mem. Nat. Press Club, Am. Soc. Mag. Editors. Home: 1105 Park St NE Washington DC 20002-6317 Office: American Society of Civil Engrs Civil Engring Mag 1801 Alexander Bell Dr Reston VA 20191-4344 Office Phone: 703-295-6213.

POWELL, BETTY CROWDER, artist, educator; b. Madison, N.C., Sept. 13, 1934; d. Roy Pleasant and Virginia (Dean) Crowder; m. George Robert Powell Sr., May 13, 1953; children: George Robert, Stephen Reed, Susan Diane, David Dean. Student, Elon (N.C.) Coll., 1952-53; AA, Wilkes C.C., Wilkesboro, N.C., 1971; BS, Appalachian State U., Boone, N.C., 1973, MA, 1985. Lic. art educator. Asst. gallery dir. Wilkes Art Gallery, North Wilkesboro, N.C., 1973; art tchr. Mulberry Elem. Sch., Traphill Elem. Boomer Ferguson Elem., Millers Creek Primary, 1981-84; art tchr. Wilkes Ctrl. H.S., 1984-85; profl. artist, 1985—. Dir. Wilke County Arts Coun., North Wilkesboro, 1985-86, 90-91. Dir. S.A.F.E., North Wilkesboro, 1996-98. Mem. Northwest Arts League (pres. 1994-95), Nat. Mus. Women in Arts, Blue Ridge Art Clan, Winston Salem Associated Artists, North Wilkesboro Rotary (bd. dirs. 1992-96, Paul Harris fellow 1995, Rotarian of Yr. 2002, Centennial award 2003). Democrat. Presbyterian. Home: 530 Forest Dr Wilkesboro NC 28697-8730

POWELL, CATHY GAIL, secondary school educator; d. Lamar and JoAnn Powell. BS in Comm. Arts magna cum laude, Ga. So. U., Statesboro, 1993, MPA, 1996, MEd, 2003. Cert. Nat. Bd. Profl. Tchg. Stds., 2004. Tchr. H.S. Bulloch County Bd. Edn., Statesboro, Ga., 1999—. Advisor Beta Club Statesboro H.S., Ga., advisor Nat. History Day, chair character edn. com., 2003, mentor, mem. Honors Night com., lead tchr. 9th grade subject area. Participant Habitat Humanity, Statesboro, 2003—04; mem. Parent, Tchr., Student Orgn. Recipient First pl. Presidential Quiz Contest, Statesboro Herald, 2004, top state honors, Ga. Geographic Alliance Geography Awareness Week. Avocations: tennis, reading, singing.

POWELL, DEBORAH ELIZABETH, pathologist, dean; b. Lynn, Mass., Nov. 28, 1939; MD, Tufts U., 1965. Diplomate Am. Bd. Pathology. Intern Georgetown Med. Ctr., Washington, 1965-66; resident in pathology NIH, Bethesda, Md., 1966-69; exec. dean, vice-chancellor clin. affairs U. Kans. Sch. Medicine, Kansas City, 1997—2002; dean, asst. v.p. for clin. scis. U. Minn. Med. Sch., Mpls., 2002—. Past pres. U.S. & Can. Acad. Pathology, Inc.; trustee Am. Bd. Pathology. Mem.: Am. Soc. Investigative Pathologists, Inst. Medicine, Coll. Am. Pathologists. Office: U Minn Med Sch Dean's Office MMC 293 Mayo 8293 420 Delaware St SE Minneapolis MN 55455 Business E-Mail: dpowell@umn.edu.*

POWELL, DIANE MARIE, psychologist; b. Sacramento, Mar. 7, 1941; d. Barrett Robert Powell and Anita Louise Burns; m. Robert Schild Krooth. BA in Psychology, U. Calif., 1962; MA in Psychology, Mich. State U., 1965, PhD in Psychology, 1969; cert. in Psychoanalysis and Human Resources, NYU, 1983. Lic. psychologist N.Y., Conn., advanced profl. cert. in human resources mgmt. NYU, 1986. Asst. prof. U. Pitts., 1970—71, Hofstra U., Hempstead, NY, 1971—76, N.Y. Inst. Tech., N.Y.C., 1976—84; vis. prof. U. New Haven, 1988—89; pvt. practice psychologist Norwich, Conn., 1989—. Pres., founder Heritage Trail Vineyards, Lisbon, Conn., 1996—. Rep. Lisbon Ea. Conn. Tourism Dist., New London, Conn., 1991—2005. Mem.: APA, Conn. Vineyards & Wineries Assn., Nat. Soc. Col. Dames. Avocations: antiques, sailing, gardening. Home: 291 North Burnham Hwy Lisbon CT 06351 Office Phone: 860-887-5361. Personal E-mail: vineyard@snet.net.

POWELL, DINA HABIB, federal agency administrator; b. Cairo, 1973; d. Onsi Habib and Hoda Soliman. BA, U. Tex. Mem. rels. coord. to rep. Dick Army U.S. Ho. of Reps., Washington; dir. congl. affairs, sr. adv. to chmn. of Rep. Nat. Com. Washington, 1999—2001; spl. asst. to pres. for presdl. personnel, Exec. Office of Pres. The White House, Washington, 2001—05; asst. sec. ednl. & cultural affairs US Dept. State, Washington, 2005—. Office: US Dept State 301 Fourth St SW Rm 800 Washington DC 20547 Office Phone: 202-203-5118. Office Fax: 202-203-7469.

POWELL, ELAINE MARIE, writer, educator; b. St. Louis, Nov. 25, 1946; d. Edsel Arthur and Jessie Louise (Whitelaw) Hatfield; m. David Eugene Powell; children: Steven, Bryan. Grad. H.S., Florissant, 1964. Sec. U. Mo., Columbia, 1969—71, Francis Howell Sch. Dist., St. Charles County, Mo., 1985—93; scrapbook instr., cons., 1996—. Author: The Family Heritage Album. Coun. tng. staff Boy Scouts Am., 1980-85, dist. tng. chmn., 1982-85; mem. long range planning coun. Francis Howell Sch. Dist., 1989-93, others. Recipient Dist. award of merit Boy Scouts Am., 1983, Howell of Fame award, 1987, Silver Beaver award Boy Scouts Am., 1991. Mem.: DAR, First Families St. Louis, Ctrl. Fla. Geneal. Soc. (pres. 2003—06). Republican. Presbyterian. Home and Office: 4620 Saddleworth Cir Orlando FL 32826-4126 Personal E-mail: TheHeritageLady@aol.com.

POWELL, ENID LEVINGER, writer, educator; b. Bklyn., Nov. 24, 1931; d. Herbert Roosevelt and Selma Esther (Sherman) Levinger; m. Bert Powell, Nov. 5, 1950; children: Pip Powell Lowe, Jon Lawrence. BA in English, Barat Coll., 1974; MA in English and Creative Writing, U. Ill., Chgo., 1978. Staff writer The Young and the Restless, L.A., 1983-94; tchr. Columbia Coll., Chgo., 1993-95, Newberry Libr., Chgo., 1994—; freelance writer Chgo. Co-author: The Big Steal, 1980, The Divorce Handbook, 1982; contbr. short stories and poetry to popular mags. Nominee for Best Writing award NATAS, 1986, 87, 90-91, 91-92. Mem. ACLU, NOW, Common Cause. Avocations: theater, travel. Home: 1300 N Lake Shore Dr Apt 21B Chicago IL 60610-5152 E-mail: enidbert@awb.us.

POWELL, JILL KIRSTEN, medical educator, obstetrician, gynecologist; b. San Diego, Mar. 31, 1969; d. Robert Dale and Sharon Jean Brouwer; m. Matthew Allen Powell, June 26, 1993; children: Austin Robert, Caroline Elizabeth, Grant Thomas. BS, U. Mich., Ann Arbor, 1991; MD, Mich. State U., East Lansing, 1995. Diplomate Am. Bd. Ob-Gyn., 2001. Resident in ob-gyn. Ohio State U., Columbus, 1995—99; instr. ob-gyn. and women's health St. Louis U., Sch. Medicine, 1999—2002, asst. prof. ob-gyn. and women's health, 2002—, asst. prof. pediat., 2003—. Children's work com. mem. Ladue Chapel Presbyn. Ch., St. Louis, 2002; bd. dirs. Women's Support and Cmty. Svcs., St. Louis, 2006; vol. physician St. Louis U. Health Resource Ctr., Saint Louis, Mo., 2004. Fellow: Am. Coll. Ob-Gyn. (mem. com. on obstetric practice); mem.: Mo. State Med. Assn., St. Louis Gynecol. Soc., N.Am. Soc. Pediat. and Adolescent Gynecology, Assn.Prof. Ob-Gyn., Pi Beta Phi (v.p. St. Louis alumnae chpt. 2006). Office: St Louis Univ Dept Ob/Gyn 6420 Clayton Rd Ste 290 Saint Louis MO 63117 Office Phone: 314-781-1505. Business E-Mail: powelljk@slu.edu.

POWELL, JULIE, writer; b. Austin, Tex. BA, Amherst Coll., Mass. Contbr. articles on food to numerous profl. jours. (James Beard award for food journalism, 2004); author: (novels) Julie and Julia: 365 Days, 524 Recipes, 1 Tiny Apartment Kitchen, 2005 (Quill award for Debut Author Yr., 2006). Office: c/o Author Mall Little Brown and Co 1271 Ave Americas New York NY 10020*

POWELL, KATHRYN A., mathematics educator, athletic trainer; b. Madison, Wis., May 21, 1963; d. Michael F. and Sherrol J. Shea; m. Gregory L. Powell, Mar. 27, 1993; children: Haley, Morgan. BS, Ill. Benedictine Coll., Lisle, 1985; MS, Ill. State U., Normal, 1987. Athletic Trainer Nat. Athletic Trainers' Assn., 1987, Lifeguard, First Aid/CPR/AED Instructor Nat. Pool and Water Parks, 1990; Lifeguard, First Aid, CPR/AED Instructor ARC, 1983, Certified Pool Operator Cert. Pool Operator Assn., 1996. Athletic trainer Waubonsie Valley H.S., Aurora, Ill., 1987—, math tchr., 1987—; instr. athletic tng. student camp No. Ill. U., DeKalb, 2002—. Mgr., lifeguard and diving coach Centennial Beach, Naperville, Ill., 1987—2001; mgr. Oakhurst North Pool, 2003—04. Named Most Influential Tchr., Western Ill. U., 2002. Mem.: Ill. Coun. Tchrs. Math (licentiate), Nat. Coun. Tchrs. Math (licentiate), Nat. Athletic Trainers' Assn. (licentiate), Gt. Lakes Athletic Trainers Assn. (licentiate), Ill. Athletic Trainers Assn. (licentiate; sec. 1989—91). Roman Catholic. Avocations: exercise, golf, travel. Office: Waubonsie Valley HS 2590 Ogden Ave Aurora IL 60504 Office Phone: 630-375-3579.

POWELL, LINDA RAE, educational healthcare consultant; b. Youngstown, Ohio, Sept. 1, 1947; d. Roger Gene and Beverly (Dahlke) P.; m. James Ronald Taylor, Aug. 14, 1985. BSN, Madonna Coll., 1980; MA in Adult Edn., U. Mich., 1988. RN; cert. profl. healthcare quality. Adminstrv. nurse U. Mich., Ann Arbor, 1970-86; coord. exec. spouse program U. Mich. Bus. Sch., Ann Arbor, 1987, 89, exec. dir. Mich. individual entrepreneurial project, 1986-88, bd. dirs. Mich. Individual Entrepreneurial Project, 1991—; ednl. cons. Quality Mgmt. in Healthcare, Ann Arbor, 1988-91; pres., founder Quality Mgmt. Edn. Cons., Ann Arbor, 1991-96; ret., 1996—. Nat. healthcare speaker on quality assessment and improvement. Mag. columnist, 1990-92. Mem. Ronald McDonald House of Ann Arbor, 1988—. Mem. Am. Soc. Healthcare Edn. and Tng., Nat. Assn. Healthcare Quality, Assn. Quality and Participation, Am. Soc. Quality Control, Health Alumni Assn. U. Mich. Avocations: cooking, bicycling, dance. Office: Quality Mgmt Ednl Cons Inc 380 Windycrest Dr Ann Arbor MI 48105-3014

POWELL, LYNNETTE, elementary school educator; b. New Orleans, July 26, 1975; d. James and Linda Knoch; m. Jerry Powell, May 3, 1997; children: Steven, Devin. BA in Elem. Edn., Southeastern La. U., Hammond, 0200. Cert. tchr. La. Tchr. Loranger Mid. Sch., Loranger, La., 2003—, dance team sponsor, 2005—. Office Phone: 985-878-9455.

POWELL, MARGARET ANN SIMMONS, computer engineer; b. Gulfport, Miss., May 26, 1952; d. William Robert and Nancy Rita (Schloegel) Simmons; m. Mark Thomas Powell, Sept. 11, 1983. AS in Math., N.W. Miss. Jr. Coll., 1972; BS in Edn., Memphis State U., 1977; BS in Computer Sci., U. Md., 1988; MS in Computer Sci., Johns Hopkins U., 1991. Tchr. Sacred Heart Sch., Walls, Miss., 1973-80; office mgr. Hyman Builders Supply, Memphis, 1980-84; tech. instr. Bendix Field Engring. Corp., Greenbelt, Md., 1985-87; software engr. Assurance Technology Corp., Alexandria, Va., 1987-89, Naval Rsch. Lab., Washington, 1989-93; computer scientist Naval Info. Systems Mgmt. Ctr., Washington, 1993-97; head software product assurance office Naval Rsch. Lab., Washington, 1997—2004; mgr. software testing Dept. Def., Washington, 2004—. Bd. dirs. Greenbrook Village Homeowners Assn., 1992-96; sec. Greenbelt East Adv. Com., 1994, chair, 1995-96. Recipient Navy Meritorious Civilian Svc. award, 1997, Standardization award Dept. Def., 2001.; named one of Outstanding Young Women Am., 1977, Tech. Leadership award Govt. Exec. Mag., 1996. Mem. IEEE Computer Soc., Assn. for Computing Machinery, Phi Kappa Phi, Kappa Delta Pi, Phi Theta Kappa, Mu Alpha Theta. Episcopalian. Avocation: genealogy. Home: 4652 Kell Ln Alexandria VA 22311-4917 Office: Dept Defense Washington DC 20375-7100

POWELL, MARSHA N., federal program analyst; b. Culver City, Calif., Aug. 31, 1960; d. Raymond Edward Powell and Wynonne Raye Keeling. B Music Edn., S.W. Bapt. U., Bolivar, Mo., 1984; M in Aero. Sci., Embry-Riddle Aero. U., Daytona Beach, Fla., 2006. Cert. K-12 music (vocal) tchr., Mo. Music tchr. Carroll Christian Acad., Westminster, Md., 1984-85; receptionist, PBX operator Criswell Coll., Dallas, 1985-87; critical care asst. Baylor U. Med. Ctr., Dallas, 1987-90; elem. and music tchr. Star of Bethlehem Christian Acad., Triangle, Va., 1990-91; sec. FAA, Washington, 1991-95, program analyst, 1995—. Composer and arranger of music. Music dir. Women's Ministries/Immanuel Bible Ch., Springfield, Va., 1998—, choir mem. and officer, 1991—, dir. Ladies Ensemble, 1999—. Avocations: music, sports, Bible, Dr. Pepper paraphernalia, people. Home: 7908 Inverton Rd Unit 302 Annandale VA 22003-4835 Office: FAA 800 Independence Ave SW Washington DC 20591-0001

POWELL, MICHELE HALL, music educator; b. Norfolk, Va., May 20, 1958; d. Wadsworth and Mable Hall; m. Raymond Powell (div. 1999). BS in pub. sch. music edn., Norfolk State U., 1981, MusM, 1994. Cert. tchr. Va., 1981. Tchr. choral, music Barstow Cogic Christian Sch., Calif., 1982—83, Nuernburg, Germany, 1984—87, Amelia County Mid. and H.S., Va., 1987—88; tchr. asst. Ruffner Mid. Sch., Norfolk, 1988—89; music specialist Windsor Woods Elem. Sch., Va. Beach, Va., 1989—99; tchr. choral, music Brandon Mid. Sch., Va. Beach, 1999—. Mem. Sch. Planning Coun., Va. Beach, 2002—03, PTA Bd., Va. Beach, 2002—03. Named Tchr. of Yr., 2006. Mem.: Music Educator's Nat. Assoc. Home: 1916 Sydenham Trail Virginia Beach VA 23464 Office: Brandon Mid Sch 1700 Pope St Virginia Beach VA 23464 Business E-Mail: Mivhrllr.Poerll@vbschools.com.

POWELL, NANCY JO, federal official, former ambassador; b. Cedar Falls, Iowa; BA, No. Iowa U., 1970. Dep. chief of mission US Embassy, Lome, Togo, 1990—92, consul gen. New Delhi, 1993—95, dep. chief of mission Khaka, Bangladesh, 1995—97; US amb. to Uganda US Dept. State, Kampala, 1997—99, prin. dep. asst. sec. for African affairs, 1999—2001, acting asst. sec. African affairs, 2001, US amb. to Ghana Accra, 2001—02, US amb. to Pakistan Islamabad, Pakistan, 2002—04, prin. dep. asst. sec. & acting asst. sec. for legis. affairs Washington, 2004—05, acting asst. sec. Bur. Internat. Narcotics and Law Enforcement Affairs, 2005, sr. coord. for Avian & Pandemic Influenza, 2005—06; nat. intelligence officer for South Asia, Nat. Intelligence Council Office Nat. Intelligence, Washington, 2006—. Office: Office of Dir Nat Intelligence NEOB 725 17th St Washington DC 20500*

POWELL, PAMELA BAKER, education educator, minister; b. Cin., Ohio, Feb. 22, 1945; d. Earl Milton Baker, Jr. and LaMoine Thompson Baker; m. John Paul Powell, Aug. 20, 1977; children: Stewart Baker Jefferson, Jennifer Powell McNutt, Elliott Hamilton Jefferson. BA, Miami U., Oxford, Ohio, 1967; MDiv, Fuller Theol. Sem., Pasadena, Calif., 1982; DD, Pitts. Theol. Sem., Pitts., Pa., 2000. Ordained Minister Word and Sacrament Presbyn. Ch., 1983. Co-pastor First Presbyn. Ch. of Sherman Oaks, Sherman Oaks, Calif., 1983—88; campus pastor Tex. Tech U., Lubbock, Tex., 1989—91; interim assoc. pastor Westminster Presbyn. Ch., Lubbock, Tex., 1991—92; stated supply pastor Messiah Presbyn. Ch., Lubbock, Tex., 1994—96; pastor First Presbyn. Ch. of Finleyville, Finleyville, 1997—99; assoc. prof. pastoral theology Trinity Episcopal Sch. for Ministry, Ambridge, Pa., 1999—. Pastoral counseling practice Pvt., Lubbock, Tex., 1993—96. Contbr. articles pub. to profl. jour., chapters to books. Judge Young Mothers of Am., L.A., 1984—85; pres. Lubbock Ballet Theatre, Lubbock, Tex., 1995—96; treas. Indpls. Symphony Jr. Group, Indpls., 1975—76; pres. Young Officers' Wives, Eglin AFB, Fla., 1970—71. Nominee Outstanding Young Women of Am., Officers Wives Club -Eglin AFB, 1971; recipient Christian Worker's Award, Fuller Theol. Sem., 1979. Mem.: Nat. Covenant Group, Pitts. Presbytery (com. on ministry 2001—05), Kappa Kappa Gamma (sec. 1966—67). Office: Trinity Episcopal Sch for Ministry 311 Eleventh St Ambridge PA 15243 Home: 2726 Laning Rd San Diego CA 92106-6430 Office Phone: 1-800-874-8754. Office Fax: 724-266-4617. Business E-Mail: pamelapowell@tesm.edu.

POWELL, PATRICIA LYNN, education educator, educator, special education educator, educator; b. Columbus, Jan. 4, 1954; d. Roger Lee and Geraldine (Porter) Triemstra; m. Richard Wayne Powell, Apr. 5, 1980; children: Joshua, Aaron, Kaitlyn. AB in Music and Elem. Edn., Calvin Coll., 1975; EdM in Hearing Impairments, U. Airz., 1976; PhD, U. Ill., Chgo., 2004. Tchr. hearing impaired Ariz. State Sch. for the Deaf and Blind, Tucson, 1976—81; music tchr. disabled students Elim Christian Sch., Palos Heights, Ill., 1986—2001; asst. prof. edn. and spl. edn. Trinity Christian Coll., Palos Heights, 1999—. Mem. com. on disabilities Reformed Ch. in Am., NJ, 2002—03. Recipient Open Hearts award, Pathways Awareness Found., 2001, Ill. Humanities award, Studs Terkel, 2001. Mem.: ASCD, Coun. for Exceptional Children, Am. Ednl. Rsch. Assn. Avocations: flute, quilting, reading, boating, gardening. Home: 12300 Nagle Ave Palos Heights IL 60463 Office: Trinity Christian Coll 6601 W College Dr Palos Heights IL 60463 Personal E-mail: patti_powell@hotmail.com.

POWELL, RUTH AREGOOD, music educator; b. Rising City, Nebr. d. August Walter and Gussie Hobson (Bray) Aregood; m. Jack William Powell, June 27, 1953; children: Stephen Mark, Linda Lou, Timothy Vaughn. BA, Nebr. Wesleyan, Lincoln, 1949; MA, Northwestern U., Evanston, Ill., 1952. Dir. edn. Wauwotosa (Wis.) Meth., 1952-54; self-employed piano tchr. Wis., Hawaii, Ohio, 1955—. Mem. Music Tchrs. Nat. Assn. (pres. East Ctrl. Divsn. 1990-92), Nat. Guild Piano Tchrs., Ohio Music Tchrs. Assn. (pres. 1984-88, pres. ctrl. east dist. 1992-96, named Cert. Tchr. of Yr. 2000-01), Westerville Womens Music Club. Methodist. Avocations: reading, sewing.

POWELL, SHERYL ANN, elementary school educator; 1 child, Kristopher Alan. BS in Interdisplinery Studies, Austin Peay U., Clarksville. Resource math tchr. Richview Mid. Sch., Clarksville, Tenn., 2002—. Recipient Green Apple award, Clarksville Montgomery County Sch. Sys.

POWELL, TRACI E., psychiatrist; BS, U. Ill., Urbana-Champaign, 1994; MD, U. Ill., Chgo., 1999. Diplomate Am. Bd. Psychiatry and Neurology. Consulting psychiatrist Cmty. Mental Health Coun., Inc., Chgo., 2003—; adult psychiatrist Traci E. Powell, MD & Assocs., Chgo., 2005—. Med. student site coord. U. Ill. Coll. Medicine, Chgo., 2004—. 2d v.p. Poe Classical Sch. PTA, Chgo., 2005—06. Mem.: AMA, Nat. Med. Assn., Ill. Psychiat. Soc., Am. Psychiat. Assn., Alpha Kappa Alpha. Office: Traci E Powell MD & Assocs 9415 S Western Ste 201A Chicago IL 60620 Office Phone: 773-779-9700. Office Fax: 773-779-9732.

POWELL, WINONA KAY, music educator; b. Harrisonville, Mo., Feb. 1, 1928; d. Robert James and Naomi Noell Powell; m. Carlos Aguirre, Nov. 14, 1974 (div. Sept. 5, 1975). BA, U. Kansas City, Mo., 1956; MA, Vanderbilt U., Nashville, 1958; MusM, Northwestern U., Evanston, Ill., 1963; MEd, U. Ariz., Tucson, 1977. Tchr. music Kennett H.S., Mo., 1958—59, Kansas City Pub. Sch., 1959—62, Tucson Unified Sch. Dist., 1963—90. Family planning Peace Corps, Barahona, Dominican Republic, 1966—69; airline stewardess TWA, Kansas City, Mo., 1949—55. Vol. Project Hospitality/Salvation Army, Tucson, Neighborhood Watch, Tucson, 1984—86, Tucson Bot. Gardens, 1991—95; trustor U. Ariz. Music Dept. Scholarships; publicity chair Hemlock Soc., 1985—98. R-Consevative. Methodist. Avocations: exercise, reading, swimming, travel. Home: 602 N Avenida Alegre Tucson AZ 85745 Personal E-mail: winonapowell@juno.com.

POWELL GEBHARD, JOY LEE (BOK SIN LEE), small business owner; b. Jan. 29, 1936; arrived in U.S., 1956, naturalized, 1962; d. Yong Joon and Chun Jal Lee; m. Jimmy Wayne Powell, Sept. 24, 1960; children: Chun Jal Lee, Miran Victoria, D. Gebhard; m. Karl Ten Eyck Gebhard, Oct. 15, 1995. Grad., Internat. Speech Acad., Pusan, Korea, 1952, Nat. U. Pusan, 1953—55, McMurry Coll., Abilene, Tex., 1956—58; BA, Wayland Bapt. U., Plainview, Tex., 1966; postgrad., Cen. State U., Okla., 1967—68. Cert. antique appraiser and cons. Nurse Rok Med. Sch., Pusan, 1950—53; news anchor Pusan Radio Sta., 1953; sec., ret. choir organizer chaplain's office U.N. Army divsn. 8069, Pusan, 1954—56, Meth. Mission, Pusan, 1955—56, U.S. A.S.C. Office, Ployada, Tex., 1958, Am. U., Washington, 1958—60; with Washington Post, Ploydada, Tex., 1958, Am. U., Washington, 1958—60; with Washington Post, U.S. Acad. Sci., 1960; with spl. study of prejudice among children grades 1 to 12 Pub. Opinion and Propaganda, 1965—66; tchr. Oklahoma City Sch. Sys., 1968—70; head social studies dept. Dunjee H.S., 1968; tchr. Spanish Carl Albert H.S., 1969; owner Internat. Antiques, Upperville, Va., 1973—; founder, dir. Healing Inc., 1997—. Co-founder, charter mem. lit. mag. Mang

Hiang. Contbr. articles to profl. jours., poetry New Voices in American Poetry, 1978, poems and essays to Korean periodicals. Mem.: World Affairs Coun. Washington, Nat. History Preservation, Smithsonian Assocs. Avocations: music, writing, swimming, collecting, travel. Home and Office: PO Box 221 Upperville VA 20185-0221

POWER, A. KATHRYN, federal agency administrator; m. Brian Power; children: Matthew, Brendan. BA in edn., St. Joseph's Coll., Md.; MEd, Western Md. Coll.; postgrad. Harvard U. Tchr. various pub. schs.; computer systems analyst US Dept. Def.; exec. dir. RI Coun. Cmty. Mental Health Centers, 1985—90; dir. RI Anti Drug Coalition, Gov.'s Drug Program, RI Office Substance Abuse, RI Dept. Mental Health, Retardation and Hospitals, 1993—2003, Ctr. for Mental Health Services, Substance Abuse and Mental Health Adminstrn., HHS, Rockville, Md., 2003—. Pres. Nat. Assn. State Mental Health Program Directors, 1997. Capt. USNR. Recipient Award for Disting. Svc., Sec. US HHS, 2005; fellow Toll fellow, Coun. State Legislators, 1991. Office: Ctr for Mental Health Services 5600 Fishers Ln Rockville MD 20857*

POWER, ELIZABETH HENRY, marketing professional, consultant; b. Hickory, NC, Sept. 28, 1953; d. William Henry Power and Katheryn Otis (Smith) Nelson. Cert. in creative writing, N.C. Sch. Arts, 1971; BA in Sociology, U. N.C., Greensboro, 1977; MEd in Human Resources Devel., Vanderbilt U., 1997. With adoption and foster home recruitment Davidson County Dept. Human Svcs., Nashville, 1980-81; behavioral cons. Nutri-System Weight Loss Ctr., Nashville, N.C., 1982-84; corp. sec., cons. Quantum Leap Cons., Inc., Nashville, 1984-86; owner EPower & Assocs., Granite Falls, N.C., 1980—, MPD/DD Resource & Edn. Ctr., Nashville, 1991-93; dir. instrnl. design Call Ctr. U., 1997-98. Cons. GM/Saturn, 1988-98; dir. instrnl. design Call Ctr. U., 1998; sr. cons. J.D. Power and Assocs., 1998-2005; sr. cons. cars.com, 2000; tng. mgr. Exult, 2001-02. Author: If Change Is All There Is, Choice Is All You've Got, 1990, Managing Our Selves: Building a Community of Caring, 1992; contbg. author: Nonprofit Policies and Procedures, 1992, 98, 2000, 01, More than Survivors: Conversations with Multiple Personality Clients, 1992, 1998; contbr. articles to profl. jours. Vol. West Chester (Pa.) Women's Resource Ctr., 1977; vol. instr. theology Lay Acad. Episc. Diocese Western N.C., Asheville, 1976-77; mem. Burke County Coun. Status Women, Morganton, N.C., 1977-79, sec., 1978; vol. Western N.C. Flood Com., 1977-78; exec. dir. N.C. Rape Crisis Assn., Raleigh, 1979, Foothills Mental Health Ctr., Morganton, 1978-79; mem. task force, writer, convener, facilitator N.C. Gov.'s Conf. Mental Health, 1979; trainer, vol. Rape House Crisis Ctr., Nashville, 1979-81; vol., trainer Rape and Sexual Abuse Ctr., Nashville, 1981-82, bd. dirs., 1981-82; mem. quality circles steering com. Tenn. Dept. Human Svcs., 1980-81; program cons. Women's Resource and Assistance Program, Jackson, Tenn., 1988-92. Recipient award NC Dept. Mental Health/Mental Retardation, 1979, State of NC, 1979, Central Nashville Optimist Club, 1982, Waco YWCA, Waco, Tex., 1985. Mem.: ASTD. Democrat. Home and Office: 1113 Murfreesboro Rd Ste 339 Franklin TN 37064-1307 Office Phone: 615-714-6389. Personal E-mail: epower@epowerinstitute.com.

POWER, MARY SUSAN, political scientist, educator; b. Hazleton, Pa., July 5, 1935; d. Younger L. and Cleo (Brook) Power; 1 child, Catherine Laverne. BA, Wells Coll., 1957; postgrad., Exeter U., Eng., 1955-56, Yale U., 1958-59; MA, Stanford U., 1960; PhD, U. Ill., 1961. Asst. prof. Susquehanna (Pa.) U., 1961-64; assoc. prof. U. Ark., Fayetteville, 1965-68; assoc. prof. polit. sci. Ark. State U., State University, 1968-79, prof., 1979—2000, prof. emeritus, 2000—. Author: (book) Before the Convention, Religion and the Founding Fathers, 1984, Jacques Maritain and the Quest for a New Commonwealth, 1992, Political Philosophy & Cultural Renewal: Collected Essays of Francis Wilson, 2001; columnist (newspaper) The Son, 2005—; contbr., articles to profl. jours. Mem. Fed. Edn. Commn. States, 1982—84; N.E. chair Arkansans for Progress, 1990—96; alt. del. Rep. Nat. Conv., 1972, 1976, 1988, del., 1992; mem. State com. Ark. Rep. Com., 1968—96, sec., 1978—80; mem. Craighead County Election Commn., 1986—88; chmn. Craighead County GOP, 1986—88, vice chmn., 1990—96, N.E. regional chmn., 1988—96; chmn. Craighead County Sheffield for Gov., 1990; mem. exec. com. Ark. Rep. Party, 1990—96, N.E. regional chair, 1988—96; treas. women's soc. Blessed Sacrament Ch., Jonesboro, 1996—2000, chmn. jubilee 2000; chair Silver Caths., 2002—; bd. dirs. Beacons and Bridges, 2005. Relm Found. fellow, 1960, NSF-Am. Polit. Sci. Assn. fellow, 1963, Nat. Def. Seminar fellow, Nat. War Coll., 1973, NEH fellow, 1978, Pres.'s fellow, Ark. State U., 1988—89. Mem.: AAUP (state sec. 1978—80, pres. 1983—90), So. Polit. Sci. Assn., Am. Polit. Sci. Assn., Ark. Polit. Sci. Assn. (bd. dirs., v.p. 1992—93, pres. 1993—94), Phi Kappa Phi (pres. 1991), Phi Gamma Mu (sec.-treas. 1990—2000), Phi Sigma Alpha. Republican. Roman Catholic. Personal E-mail: spower@fastdata.net.

POWER, PEGGY ANN, elementary school educator; b. Chgo., Sept. 17, 1973; d. Edward and Lois Power. BA, U. Ill., Chgo., 1994, MEd, 1996, postgrad., 2004—. Cert. elem. sch. tchr., Ill. Rsch. asst. U. Ill., Chgo., 1991-96; sales asst. Chgo. Bd. Trade, 1991-96; spl. edn. tchr. Gladstone Elem. Sch. Chgo. Bd. Edn., 1995—. Poet: Outstanding Poets of 1994, Best Poems of the 90's, 1992, Distinguished Poets of America, 1993. Active Wis. Dairy Coun., 1996—, Lawry's Menu for Success, Chgo., 1996—, After-Sch. Acad. Ctr., Chgo., 1996—; rep. Chgo. Tchr.'s Union, 1997—, bd. dirs., elem. v.p., 2004—, IFT/AFT del., 2004—. Recipient Gwendolyn Brookes Poet Laureat award, 1990; Baer-Darfler scholar Morgan Park Women's Assn., 1994-96; Marilyn Mucha fellow U. Ill., Chgo., 1995. Mem. ASCD, Coun. Exceptional Children, Nat. Coun. Tchrs. English, U. Ill. Chgo. Alumni Club, Pi Lambda Theta. Democrat. Roman Catholic. Avocations: Karate, poetry, pottery, kayaking. Home: Apt 407 710 Oakton St Evanston IL 60202-2927 Personal E-mail: peggypower@juno.com.

POWER, SAMANTHA J., public policy educator, writer; b. Dungarvan, Ireland, 1970; Grad., Yale U., Harvard U. Law Sch. Reporter covering wars in former Yugoslavia US News & World Report and Economist, 1993—96; polit. analyst Internat. Crisis Group; prof. practice in pub. policy, JFK Sch. Govt Harvard U., founding exec. dir., Carr Ctr. for Human Rights, 1998—2002. Author: A Problem from Hell, America and the Age of Genocide, 2003 (Pulitzer prize, 2003, Nat. Book Critics Cir. award gen. nonfiction, 2003, Artur Ross prize for best book in US fgn. policy, 2003); co-editor (with Graham Allison): Realizing Human Rights, 2000; contbr. articles to pubs. such as The New Yorker, NY Rev. Books, Washington Post, NY Times. Recipient Nat. Mag. award for best reporting, 2005. Office: Carr Ctr Human Rights Policy Harvard Univ - Rubenstein-217 79 John F Kennedy St Cambridge MA 02138 E-mail: samantha_power@harvard.edu.*

POWERS, CECILE LORRAINE, secondary school educator; b. Kansas City, Mo., Dec. 8, 1945; d. Cecil Loran and L. Jean (Howard) Rogers; m. John George Powers, June 8, 1972; 1 child, Nathan John. BA, William Jewell Coll., Liberty, Mo., 1967; postgrad., U. Mo., Kansas City, 1972. Cert. secondary educator, Mo. Tchr., dept. chairperson Consol. Sch. Dist. # 2, Raytown, Mo., 1967—. Bd. dirs. Woman's Missionary Union, 2001—04, pres., 2004—. Named Am. Hist. Tchr. Yr., Little Blue River DAR, Mo., 1988, Tchr. of Yr., Raytown South Middle Sch., 1992-93. Mem. Nat. Coun. Social Studies, Mo. Coun. Social Studies, Mo. State Tchrs. Assn., Raytown Community Tchrs. Assn., Nat. Middle Sch. Assn., Mo. Middle Sch. Assn., Delta Kappa Gamma. Baptist. Avocation: needlework. Home: 815 SW Woods Chapel Rd Blue Springs MO 64015-3333

POWERS, CLAUDIA MCKENNA, state legislator; b. Key West, Fla., May 28, 1950; d. James Edward and Claudia (Antrim) McKenna; children: Gregory, Theodore, Matthew, Thurston. BA in Edn., U. Hawaii, 1972; MA, Columbia U., 1975. Cert. tchr., N.Y. Mem. Greenwich Rep. Town Meeting, Conn., 1979-93, sec. bldg. com., 1982-84, sec. legis. com., 1986—88, 1990—93; mem. Conn. Ho. of Reps., Hartford, 1993—, ranking mem. govt. adminstrn. and elections com., 1995-96, asst. minority leader, 1997-98, vice chmn. Rep. bill rev. com., 1997—2004, house minority whip, 1999—2003, dep. minority leader, 2003—, mem. spl. com. of inquiry into impeachment of the gov., 2004. Mem. editl. bd. Greenwich Mag., 1995-98. Conn. commr. Edn. Commn. of the States, 2000—, also mem. steering com.; campaign chmn. Greenwich Rep. Town Com., 1984, 85, chmn., 1986-90; sec. Rep. Round Table, Greenwich, 1988-90; bd. govts. Riverside Assn., Greenwich, 1987-91, sec., 1991-92; class mother Riverside Sch., Greenwich, 1984-90; mem. altar guild Christ Ch., Greenwich, 1990—, lay eucharistic min., 2004—; adminstrv. coord. Greenwich Teen Ctr., 1990-91; alt. del. Rep. Nat. Conv., New Orleans, 1984—, San Diego, 1996; v.p. LWV of Greenwich, 1990-91; bd. trustees Norwalk Maritime Ctr., 2001—; bd. dirs. Gov.'s Prevention Partnership, 2004—. Episcopalian. Home and Office: 15 Hendrie Ave Riverside CT 06878-1808

POWERS, DEBRA JEAN, medical/surgical nurse; b. Shreveport, La., Mar. 19, 1958; d. Joan Lackey; m. Brian K. Powers, Apr. 18, 1981; children: Joan, Justin. BSN, Northwestern State U., Natchitoches, La., 1980. RN Fla. Staff nurse Schumpert Med. Ctr., Shreveport, 1980, HCA Largo (Fla.) Med. Ctr., 1981—99; charge nurse respiratory med./surg. HCA Largo (Fla.) Med. Ctr. Hosp., house supr. 11-7 shift, 1992—97, emergency rm. nurse, 1997—99, St. Joseph's Hosp., Buckhannan, W.Va., 1999—2003; clinic coord. Gilmer Primary Care, Glenville, 2003—. Mem. Sigma Theta Tau.

POWERS, DORIS HURT, retired engineering company executive; b. Indpls., Jan. 17, 1927; d. James Wallace Hurt Sr. and Mildred (Johnson) Devine; m. Patrick W. Powers, Nov. 12, 1950 (dec. 1989); children: Robert W. Powers, Jaye P., Laura S. Powers. Student, So. Meth. U., 1944-45; BS in Engring., Purdue U., 1949; postgrad., U. Tex., W. Tex., 1952-53, Ecole Normale Du Musique, Paris, 1965-68; grad., Harford County Leadership Acad., 1991. Flight instr. Red Leg Flying Club, El Paso, Lawton, Okla., 1951-57; check pilot Civil Air Patrol, El Paso, Lawton, Okla., 1952-57, ground instr. Washington, Tex., Okla, 1957-61; exec. v.p. T&E Internat., Inc., Bel Air, Md., 1979-88, pres., 1989-91; exec. v.p. T.E.I.S., Inc., Bel Air, 1979-88, pres., 1989-91, Shielding Technologies, Inc., Bel Air, 1987-95; retired, 1995. Mem. Purdue U. Engring. Vis. Com., 1999—2002. Mem. Northeastern Md. Tech. Coun., 1991—; bd. dir. Leadership Acad., 1991-94, Army Alliance, Inc., 1998—; mem. vis. com. dept. engring. Purdue U., 1998-2002; bd. mem. U.S. Mil. Acad. Class 1945, West Point, N.Y., 2004—, Army Alliance, Inc., 2004—. Recipient Svc. award U.S. Army, 1978, Cert. of Appreciation U.S. Army Test and Evaluation Command, 1988, Woman of Distinction award Soroptomist Club, 1996, Outstanding Engr. award Purdue U., 2006; selected as Old Master Purdue U., 1995. Mem. CAP (lt. maj. 1951-58), Soc. of Women Engrs. (sr., v.p. 1977, treas. 1979, sec. rep. 1986-88, 98-00, mentor 1986—, spkr. 1978—, selected to Coll. of Fellows 1993), Engring. Soc. Balt. (spkr. 1980-2005), 99's (pres. 1951-53), Am. Soc. Indsl. Security, Am. Def. Preparedness Assn., Assn. of U.S. Army. Avocations: ice dancing, music. Home: 8535 Olde Mill Cir W Dr Indianapolis IN 46260

POWERS, EILEEN ELIZABETH, lawyer, mediator; b. San Antonio, Mar. 8, 1955; d. Norman Alfred and Ella Mae Powers; m. Charles Frederic Delavan, Apr. 7, 1987; children: Charles Michael Delavan, Elizabeth Leigh Delavan. BA, Cath. U. Am., Washington, 1977, MSW, 1978; JD, George Wash. U., Washington, 1982. Bar: Md. 1982. Assoc. county atty. Prince George's County, Md., Upper Marlboro, Md., 1981—83; asst. countyy atty. Anne Arundel County, Md., Annapolis, 1983—87; assoc. Brassel & Baldwin, P.A., Annapolis, 1987—91; asst. atty. gen. Md. Dept. Natural Resources, Annapolis, 1991—96; of counsel Blumenthal, Delavan & Williams, P.A., Annapolis, Md., 1996—. Pres. Anne Arundel County Ct. Apptd. Spl. Advocates, Annapolis, 1987—2000. Mem.: Md. Bar Assn. Lutheran. Office: Blumenthal Delavan & Williams PA 170 Jennifer Rd Ste 240 Annapolis MD 21401 Office Phone: 410-573-2900. Office Fax: 410-573-2907. E-mail: epowers@bdwlawfirm.com.

POWERS, ELIZABETH WHITMEL, lawyer; b. Charleston, SC, Dec. 16, 1949; d. Francis Persse and Jane Coleman Cotten (Wham) P.; m. John Campbell Henry, June 11, 1994 (dec. Jan. 1997); m. Henry C. B. Lindh, June 16, 2000. AB, Mt. Holyoke Coll., 1971; JD, U. S.C., 1978. Bar: SC 1978, NY 1979. Law clk. to justice S.C. Cir. Ct., Columbia; assoc. Reid & Priest, N.Y.C., 1978—86, ptnr., 1986—97; of counsel LeBoeuf, Lamb, Greene & MacRae, N.Y.C., 1997—2004, ptnr., 2004—. Exec. editor S.C. Law Rev., Columbia, 1977-78. Vol. N.Y. Jr. League, N.Y.C., 1983—; bd. dirs. The Seamen's Ch. Inst., 1996—2006, sec., 1999—2006; trustee Ch. Club, 1991—94, 1997—2001, v.p., 1992—94. Mem.: Nat. Soc. Colonial Dames in State of N.Y. (pres. 1992—95), Nat. Soc. Colonial Dames of Am. (parliamentarian 1994—2000, regent Gunston Hall 2001—02), S.C. Bar Assn., ABA.

POWERS, GAY HAVENS-MONTEAGLE, artist, educator; b. L.A., Mar. 19, 1946; d. Lionel Standar and Jehanne Havens-Monteagle; m. William Pringle, 1969 (div. 1972); m. Joseph Stevens, 1978 (div. 1979). AS in Electronics, Monterey Peninsula Coll., 1972; BA, U. Calif., Davis, 1986; MFA, Mills, 1990. Cert. tchg. multiple subject. Microwave technician Comsat, Carmel Valley, Calif., 1974—79; mgr. univ. art mus. bookstore U. Calif., Berkeley, 1979—80; owner Bonjour Baguette, Davis, Calif., 1981—2000; artist, 2000—; art tchr. Dixon HS, 2003—. One-woman shows include John Natsoulas Gallery, Davis, 1990—2003, exhibitions include Judith Weintraub Gallery, Sacramento, 1989—90, Davis, 1993—, exhibited in group shows at San Francisco Mus. Modern Art Rental Gallery, 1998—2001. Organizer Martin Luther King Freedom Walk, Davis, 1993, Thong Meml. Ann. Awards Dinner, Davis, 1992—93; mem. Human Rels. Commn., Davis, 1993—96. Presdl. grantee, U. Calif. Davis, 1984—86. Mem.: Phi Kappa Phi. Democrat. Home: 1737 E 8th St Davis CA 95616-2408

POWERS, GLORIA DOODY, mathematics educator; b. Houlton, Maine, Sept. 24, 1950; d. Reuben and Edith Grant Doody; children: Angela Powers Folsom, Renee Marie. BS in Edn., U. Maine, Presque Isle, 1972; MS in Edn., U. New Eng., Maine, 2005. Cert. Profl. Educator Dept. of Edn., Maine, 2005. Math tchr. Calais Sch. Dist., Maine, 1973—76, Husson Coll. (off campus location), Calais, Maine, 1978—80, No. Maine CC, Houlton, 1980—85; math tchr. grades 8-12 So. Aroostook Cmty. Sch., Island Falls, Maine, 1984—2000; grade 8-12 math tchr. MSAD#29, Houlton, Maine, 2000—. Subject area coord., dept. head Maine Sch. Adminstrn. Dist. 29, Houlton, 2001—, mentoring, 2002—, mem. dist. leadership team, 2002—; mentoring No. New Eng. CoMentoring Network, Augusta, Maine, 2003—; governor's acad. fellow Maine's Governor's Acad., Augusta, 2003—05. Mem.: Assn. Math. Tchrs. in Maine, Nat. Coun. Tchrs. of Math. Home: 16 Watson Ave Houlton ME 04730 Office: Msad # 29 7 Bird St Houlton ME 04730 Office Phone: 207-532-6551. Business E-Mail: glpowers@houlton.sad29.k12.me.us.

POWERS, JANET F., special education educator; b. Wailuku, Hawaii, Aug. 3, 1948; d. Edward Chokin and Jane Fujiko (Arakaki) Sakugawa; 1 child, Lisa Ann Porter BA, Calif. State U., Long Beach, 1979; MA, Calif. State Poly. U., Pomona, 1988. Cert. tchr., tchr. severely and learning handicapped edn., Calif. Rehab. therapist State of Calif., Costa Mesa, 1979—88, tchr. elem. spl. edn., 1988—. Coach Spl. Olympics; prodr., stage mgr., mem. stage crew La Habra Depot Playhouse, Laguna Playhouse, Cabrillo Playhouse Mem. Niguel Art Assn., Hawaiian Surf Club San Onofre, Golden Key Office: Orange County Dept Edn 200 Kalmus Dr Costa Mesa CA 92628

POWERS, MALA, actress; b. San Francisco, Dec. 20, 1931; d. George Evart and M. Dell (Thelen) P.; 1 child, Toren Michael Vanton. Student, UCLA; studied with Michael Chekhov. V.p. Book Pubs. Enterprises Inc., 1985; internat. lectr. Chekhov Drama Method; entertainer troops USO, Korea, 1951-52; founder, bd. dirs. West Coast Michael Chekhov Drama Group, 1988—; presenter bus. and theater workshops and seminars. Writer, narrator: (sponsored by telephone cos. in various cities) Children's Story, Tele-Story and Dial-A-Story, 1979— (sponsored nationally 1988—); author: Follow the Year, 1985, French edit. 1986; editor: The Secret Seven and the Old Fort Adventure, 1972; rec.: Advent calendar and author book Follow the Star, 1980, Spanish edit., 1981, Italian edit., 1982; films: Cyrano de Bergerac, 1950, Outrage, Edge of Doom, Yellow Mountain, Bengazi, Tammy, Cheyenne, Daddy's Gone A'Hunting, Six Tickets to Hell, 1975;, Hitters, 2003; rec. artist, RCA, records for pre-Christmas, 1977, album Follow the Star; stage prodns. include Absence of a Cello (Broadway), 1964-65; Hogan's Goat, Night of the Iguana, Bus Stop, Far Country, The Rivalry, Mr. Shaw Goes to Hollywood, 2003; also starred in radio and TV prodns. including Medical Story, Ironside, Charlie's Angels; co-star with Anthony Quinn in The Man and the City, 1971-72, Murder She Wrote, 1990. Chmn. So. Calif. Mothers' com. March of Dimes, 1972—; bd. dirs. Layman's Nat. Bible Com., 1981—. Mem. NATAS, Acad. Motion Picture Arts and Scis. (fgn. film com.), ANTA (v.p., exec. com. 1974-75), PEN, Actors Equity Assn.,, Women in Film, Authors Club (London). Mem. Christian Community Ch. Home: 15455-61 Glenoaks Blvd Sylmar CA 91342-2852 Office Phone: 818-367-0022.

POWERS, MARGARET PETTEY, counselor; b. May 27, 1947; BA in Sociology, St. Louis U., 1969; MEd in Secondary Edn. Counseling, U. Mo., 1991. Counselor, coll. advisor St. Thomas Aquinas H.S., St. Louis, 1992-95, Visitation Acad., St. Louis, 1995—2000; pvt. practice St. Louis, 2000—; counselor Birthright Internat., 2005—. Female activist Take Women to Work Day, St. Louis, 1995—. Mem. Am. Counseling Assn., Nat. Career Devel. Assn. Home and Office: 755 Greenview Dr Saint Louis MO 63122-2023

POWERS, MARY ELLEN, lawyer; b. Cleve., 1955; AB, Oberlin Coll., 1977; JD, Univ. Va., 1980. Bar: DC 1980, admitted to practice: US Dist. Ct. for DC 1981, US Ct. of Appeals, DC Cir. 1982, US Ct. of Appeals, Fifth Cir. 1987, US Supreme Ct. 1996. Ptnr.-in-charge DC office Jones Day, Washington. Mem.: Women's Bar Assn. (Star of the Bar 2004), DC Bar Assn. (pro bono com.). Office: Jones Day 51 Louisiana Ave Washington DC 20001-2113 Office Phone: 202-879-3870. Office Fax: 202-626-1700. Business E-Mail: mepowers@jonesday.com.

POWERS, PAULINE SMITH, psychiatrist, educator, researcher; b. Sept. 23, 1941; m. Henry P. Powers; children: Jessica, Samantha. AB in Math., Washington U., 1963; MD, U. Iowa, 1971. Med. intern Emanuel Hosp., Portland, Oreg., 1971-72; psychiatry resident U. Iowa, Iowa City, 1972-74, U. Calif., Santa Barbara, 1974-75; from asst. prof. to assoc. prof. psychiatry Coll. Medicine U. So. Fla., Tampa, 1975-85, prof., 1985—, dir. eating disorder program, 1979—, dir. psychosomatic medicine divsn., 1979—. Author: Obesity: The Regulation of Weight, 1980; editor: The Current Treatment of Anorexia Nervosa and Bulimia, 1984. Fellow: Am. Psychiat. Assn. (Rush Gold Outstanding Exhibit medal 1976, Dorfman Jour. Paper award 1987); mem.: Nat. Eating Disorders Assn. (pres.-elect 2003—05, pres. 2005—, Lifetime Achievement award 2006), Acad. Eating Disorders (founding pres., Women Helping Women award 1995, Profl. Excellence award 1997, Outstanding Clinician award 2000). Office: U So Fla Coll Medicine Dept Psychiatry 3515 E Fletcher Ave Tampa FL 33613-4706 Office Phone: 813-974-2926. Business E-Mail: ppowers@hsc.usf.edu.

POWERS, SHALIA JO, secondary school educator; b. Gate, Okla., Aug. 31, 1950; d. Roy R. and Twila Faye Sutherland; m. Marty Powers, July 1, 1999; children: Cole Sutherland Drake, Dane Roy Drake. Bachelor's degree, Northwestern Okla. State U., Alva, 1972, postgrad., 1972—78. Tchr., coach Southwestern Heights, Plains, Kans., 1972—73; tchr. Fargo Pub. Sch., Okla., 1973—76, Woodward Schs., Okla., 1976—84; tchr., coach Ft. Supply Schs., Okla., 1985—94, Kingfisher Schs., Okla., 1994—2000; sci. tchr. Wynnewood Sch., Okla., 2001—. Co-owner M P Horses, Wynnewood, 1999—; co-owner, mgr. Sutherland Ranch, Gate, 2003—; dir. Wynnewood Sci. Fair, 2002—. Bd. dirs. Kids Inc., Woodward, Okla., 1983; bd. dirs., sec. N.W. O.R. Assn., 1989—93. Named Okla. Jr. High Coach of Yr., 1999, Okla. Asst. Coach of Yr., 2000, Kiwanis Tchr. of Yr., 1988—2001, 2005. Mem.: Alpha Gamma. Democrat. Methodist. Home: PO Box 605 Wynnewood OK 73098

POWERS, SUSAN J., information technology executive; BS in Math., Southern Ill. U.; MBA, Northern Ill. U. V.p. programs Ga. CIO Leadership Assn.; adv. bd. Tech. Assn. Ga., Travel Commerce; v.p. product mktg. Worldspan, 1993, v.p. sales and mktg., sr. v.p. worldwide e-commerce, chief info. officer and sr. v.p. worldwide product solutions. Editl. bd. Bus. Travel News, 2001—. Named Best Product Devel. or Engring. Exec., Am. Bus. Awards, 2003; named one of People of Yr., Travel Agent Mag., 1994, 2000, 100 Most Powerful Women in Travel, 2003; recipient Woman of Yr. Tech. award, (WIT) Women in Tech., 2003. Office: World Headquarters 300 Galleria Parkway Atlanta GA 30339 Office Phone: 770-563-7400.*

POWERS, THERESA MACK, medical/surgical nurse, psychotherapist; b. Thief River Falls, Minn., June 13, 1928; d. Frank John and Alice Genevieve (Denery) Mack; m. Lester Jean Kile, Nov. 18, 1995; stepchildren: Vickie Nussbaumer, Larry Kile, Jeannie Kendall, Cindy Kile; m. Charles James Powers, Sept. 4, 1948 (div. Sept. 11, 1989); children: Maureen, Pam Toffer, Kevin, Peggy Warren, Laurie, Jeff. RN, O.R. Tech., St. Cloud Sch. of Nursing, St. Cloud, Minn., 1948; RN, Columbia Basin Coll., Pasco, Wash., 1963; BA, Tri City Univ. and Eastern Wash. Univ., Cheney, Wash., 1988; MSW, Eastern Wash. Univ., Cheney, Wash., 1990. Lic. Wash.; LCSW Wash. Oper. rm. tech. Our Lady of Lourdes Hosp., Pasco, Wash., 1948—50; oper. rm. tech. (on call) Kennenick Gen., Kennenick, Wash., 1950—63; oper. nurse, office nurse Ray Rose MD Surgeon, Pasco, Wash., 1965—75, Robert Lukson MD Surgeon, Kennenick, Wash., 1965—75; counselor domestic violence A Woman's Pl., Richland, Wash., 1987—89; psychotherapist Cath. Family Svc., Spokane, Wash., 1990—96; dream therapist/analyst pvt. practice, Spokane, Wash., 1996—. RN Red Cross Blood Dr. Am. Nat. Red Cross, Wash., 1960—76; tchr. music, tap dancing, 1960. Performer comedy. Democrat. Roman Cath. Avocations: piano, reading, sewing, walking, ballroom dancing. Home and Office: 5304 N Wash Spokane WA 99205-5144 Office Phone: 509-328-0826. E-mail: t.j.kile@aol.com.

POWROZNIK-TRAEGER, RITA, school counselor; b. Mt. Pleasant, Pa., Apr. 28, 1947; d. John F. and Zita Szczygiel Powroznik; m. Charles F. Traeger, June 25, 1981; children: Sara Danielle Traeger, Karl F. Traeger. BS in Edn., MS in Edn., Duquesne U., Pitts. Cert. in counseling Pa., in secondary edn. Pa. Tchr. McKeesport Area Sch. Dist., Pa., 1968—81, sex equity counselor, 1981—82, sch. counselor spl. edn., 1982—2005. Sec. Pa. Vocat. Spl. Needs Pers., 1985—. Mem.: Allegheny County Counselors Assn., Am. Sch. Counselors, Pa. Sch. Counselors. Republican. Roman Catholic. Avocations: reading, sewing, needlecrafts, music. Home: 3000 Walnut St Mc Keesport PA 15132 Office: McKeesport Area HS 1960 Eden Park Blvd Mc Keesport PA 15132 Office Phone: 412-948-1368, 412-664-3658. Office Fax: 412-664-3621. E-mail: rpowroznik@mckasd.net.

POY, VIVIENNE, Canadian senator, academic administrator, educator; b. May 14, 1941; BA, McGill U.; diploma in Fashion Arts, Seneca Coll.; MA in History, PhD in History, U. Toronto; PhD in Polit. Sci. (hon.), Soongsil U., Seoul, Republic of Korea, 2003. Founder Vivienne Poy Mode, 1981—95; pres. Vivienne Poy Enterprises, 1995—, Calyan Pub.; senator The Senate of Can., Ottawa, 1998—; chancellor U. Toronto; hon. prof. Yanbian U. Sci. and Tech., Yanji, Jilin, China, 2003. Author: A River Named Lee, Building Bridges: The Life and Times of Richard Charles Lee, Hong Kong, 1905-1983, Citizenship and Immigration: The Chinese-Canadian Experience. Chmn. Lee Tak Wai Holdings Ltd.; bd. dirs. Bank East Asia, Canada; gov. McGill U.; hon. patron Chinese Cultural Ctrs. Greater Toronto. Decorated Officer Order St. John; named Kanienkehaka (Mohawk) Ka Tsi Tsa Ken Reh a rare and beautiful flower, T. Brenda Etienne, Bear Clan Kanienkehaka Kanesatake, 2003, Can.'s Most Powerful Women: Top 100, Trailblazer Category, WXN, 2003, Asians in Ontario: Outstanding Asian Can., Can. Multicultural Coun., 2004; recipient Internat. Women's Day award, 1996, Arbor Award outstanding vol. svc., U. Toronto, 1997, Gold medal award excellence race rels., 2002, Queen's Jubilee award, 2002, Seneca Coll. Disting. Alumni award, 2004, Senator Vivienne Poy Youth Cmty. Leadership award, Vancouver Asian Heritage Month Soc. Senator Poy's name. Liberal. Office: 205 Victoria Bldg The Senate of Canada Ottawa ON Canada K1A 0A4

POYNOR, ELIZABETH ANN, surgeon, researcher; b. Nashville, Jan. 9, 1962; d. Paul Clifton and Elizabeth (Gropp) Poynor; m. Richard Shapiro, Feb. 10, 2001; 1 child, Jacob Poynor Shapiro. BS, Princeton U., 1987; MD, Columbia U., 1988; PhD, Cornell U., 2005. Cert. ob-gyn. 1999, gyn.-oncology 2001. Attending surgeon, NYC, 1997—. Avocations: sports, tennis, golf. Home: 444 E 57th St New York NY 10022 Office: 1050 Fifth Ave New York NY 10028 Office Phone: 212-426-2700. Personal E-mail: poynore@hotmail.com.

POZNANSKI, MARGARET MARY, special education educator; b. Bronx, NY, May 6, 1947; d. Joseph Frances and Ruth Ann (Ball) Nelson; m. John A. Poznanski, Mar. 29, 1969; children: Meredith, Melanie, Meghan, Jessica. BA, Notre Dame Coll., Manchester, NH, 1969; MA, Notre Dame Coll., 1987. Cert. elem. edn. tchr. NH, gen. spl. edn. tchr. NH, reading specialist N.H., learning disables specialist N.H. Tchr. Merrimack (NH) Sch. Dist., 1970—71, Pembroke (NH) Sch. Dist., 1981—; presch. tchr. Manchester (NH) Coop. Nursery Sch., 1975—76. Adj. instr. Notre Dame Coll., 1998—2001, So. NH U., Manchester, 2004—. Mem. long range planning com. St. Lawrence Ch., 2002—; eucharistic min. Roman Catholic Ch. Mem.: NEA (del. 1998—), Coun. Exceptional Children, Internat. Dyslexia Assn., Granite State Reading Assn., Internat. Reading Assn., Edn. Assn. Pembroke (pres. 2001—). Office: Pembroke Hill Sch 300 Belanger Dr Pembroke NH 03275

POZNIAKOFF, RITA OPPENHEIM, education software consultant; b. Munich, Nov. 19, 1949; (parents Am. citizens); d. Lester and Pearl Tobia (Waldman) Oppenheim; m. Theodore A. Pozniakoff, Dec. 29, 1985. BS, Cen. Mo. State U., 1973. Dept. mgr. Venture Dept. Stores div. May Co., St. Louis, 1973-75; dist. sales mgr. Seven Up Co., St. Louis, 1975-76; account exec. Christmas Club A Corp., Easton, Pa., 1976-83, Bankers Systems Inc., St. Cloud, Minn., 1983-85; edn. svcs. rep. Control Data Corp., Mpls., 1985-86; edn. specialist Radio Shack bus. products Tandy Corp., Ft. Worth, 1986-87, dist. govt. and edn. mktg. mgr., 1987-88, area edn. mktg. mgr., 1988-89, mgr. govt. accounts Grid Systems Corp. div. Parsippany, N.J., 1989; sr. account rep. N.Y.C. schs. Unisys Corp., White Plains, N.Y., 1989-90; mktg. mgr. N.Y. schs. Jostens Learning Corp., Phoenix, 1990-92, TRO Learning, Inc., Edina, Minn., 1993-96; govt. and edn. sales mgr. CompUSA, Inc., N.Y.C., 1996—. Republican. Home and Office: 7004 Boulevard East 3 1-C Guttenberg NJ 07093-5029

POZUN WATSON, HEATHER DAWN, environmental scientist, educator; b. Lander, Wyo., June 7, 1981; d. Ronald Bruce and Dorothy Lee Pozun. BA in Environ. Sci., M of Tchg., U. of Va., 2004. Cert. elem. tchr. Va. K-2 tchr. Ouzinkie Sch., Alaska, 2004—05; sci. tchr. Nysmith Sch. for Gifted, Herndon, Va., 2005—06; naturalist Reston Assn., Reston, Va., 2006—. Curriculum advisor Explorations Summer Programs, Norwood, Mass., 2004—04. Dir. Va. Pep Band, Charlottesville, Va., 2002—03. Recipient Recognition of Excellence, ETS, 2003; Volvo scholarship, Volvo Corp. and Columbia U., 2000, Linwood-Holton Edn. scholarship, Linwood-Holton Family, 2003. Mem.: NSTA. Avocations: hiking, camping, field studies. Home: 12328 Coleraine Ct Reston VA 20191 Office: Reston Assn 1930 Issaac Newton Sq Reston VA 20190 Business E-Mail: hwatson@reston.org.

POZZ, JENNIFER, art educator; b. Columbus, Ohio, Apr. 12, 1971; d. Jay Edward and Carol Lee Pozz; m. Keith Robert Dotson, July 15, 1995. BA in Art, Hiram Coll., Ohio, 1993. Art tchr. Cleve. Pub. Schs., 1994—95, Bedford City Schs., Ohio, 1995—. Recipient Alice and Patrick McGinty grant, McGinty Ednl. Fund, 1995. Mem.: Nat. Art Edn. Assn. (presenter). Office: Bedford City Schs 481 Northfield Rd Bedford OH 44146

POZZO, MARY LOU, retired librarian, writer; b. L.A., June 18, 1945; d. Clayton Oliver and Violet Elizabeth (Webb) Straub; m. Richard Louis Pozzo, Nov. 10, 1984; stepchildren: Heidi, Peter; m. Richard Lee Horttor, Apr. 15, 1968 (div. 1969). AA, Pasadena C.C., 1965. Asst. legal dept. L.A. City Attys. Office, L.A., 1968—72; sec. fgn. law dept. L.A. County Law Libr., L.A., 1972—78; libr. Musick, Peeler & Garret, L.A., 1979—84, Bronson, Bronson & McKinnon, L.A., 1984—90, Bolton Hall Mus., L.A., 1992—. Pres. Zinnia Press of Tujunga. Author: When Hollywood Came to Sunland-Tujunge-1920-1995, 1997, Founding Sisters: Life Stories of Tujunga's Early Women Pioneers 1886-1926, 2005. Trustee Verdugo Hills Cemetery, Tujunga, Calif., 1992—; regional v.p. Conf. of Calif. Hist. Socs., L.A., 2000—; docent Bolton Hall Mus., Tujunga, 1992—; co-founder Sunland-Tujunga Historic Home & Garden Tour. Recipient Pioneer Women award, LA City Commn. on the Status of Women, 2006, Authorship award, Conf. Calif. Hist. Socs., 2006, Pioneer Woman award, L.A. City Coun. and L.A. City Commn. on Status of Women, 2006. Mem.: Associated Hist. Socs. Los Angeles County (pres. 2004—), Sunland-Tujunga Little Landers Hist. Soc. (pres. 1995—96), The Westerners L.A. Corral, Sunland-Tujunga Women's Club, Bus. & Profl. Womens Club (Cmty. Woman of Yr. award 1998). Avocations: travel, reading, gardening, cooking, animal rescue. Home and Office: 10966 Hillhaven Ave Tujunga CA 91042 Office Phone: 818-353-1718.

PRABHU, VRUNDA P., mathematics professor; b. Bombay, Oct. 10, 1961; d. Sumati Prabhu; m. Shailesh Vengurlekar; 1 child, Sagar; 1 child, Natasha. BSc in Math. and Stats., U. Bombay, 1981, MSc in Math., 1983; PhD, U. Kans., Lawrence, 1993. Assoc. prof. William Woods U., Fulton, Mo., 1993—2002; assoc. prof. Bronx C.C. CUNY, N.Y.C., 2002—. Active cmty. devel. tsunami affected regions, Tamil Nadu, India, 2005—06. Recipient award, War Trauma Found., 2005; grantee, NSF, 2002—06. Mem.: Am. Math. Soc. Achievements include design of FractionsGrid. Office: Bronx CC CUNY W181 University Ave Bronx NY 10453 Office Phone: 267-980-1650.

PRAGER, SUSAN WESTERBERG, academic administrator, law educator; b. Sacramento, Dec. 14, 1942; d. Percy Foster Westerberg and Aileen M. (McKinley) P.; m. James Martin Prager, Dec. 14, 1973; children: McKinley Ann, Case Mahone. AB, Stanford U., 1964, MA, 1967; JD, UCLA, 1971. Bar: N.C. 1971, Calif. 1972. Atty. Powe, Porter & Alphin, Durham, NC, 1971-72; acting prof. law UCLA, 1972-77, prof. Sch. Law, 1977—, Arjay and Frances Fearing Miller prof. law, 1992-99, 2001—06, assoc. dean Sch. Law, 1979-82, dean, 1982-98; provost Dartmouth Coll., Hanover, NH, 1999—2001; pres. Occidental Coll., 2006—. Bd. dirs. Pacific Mut. Life Holding Co., Newport Beach, Calif. Editor-in-chief, UCLA Law Rev., 1970-71. Trustee Stanford U., 1976-80, 87-97. Mem. ABA (council of sect. on legal edn. and admissions to the bar 1983-85), Assn. Am. Law Schs. (pres. 1986), Order of Coif. Office: Occidental Coll / Office of Pres 3rd Fl, Coons Adminstn Bldg 1600 Campus Rd Los Angeles CA 90041-3314 E-mail: prager@law.ucla.edu.*

PRANGER, KATHLEEN, computer science educator; b. Detroit, Dec. 11, 1949; d. Norman Joseph and Mary Ann Pranger. BS, No. Mich. U., Marquette, 1972; MA in Tchg., Oakland U., Rochester, Mich., 1990. Cert. elem. tchr. Mich. Math. tchr. Indpls. Pub. Schs., 1972—74; math. and computer tchr. Houston Ind. Sch. Dist., 1974—87; computer instr. Davenport U., Warren, Mich., 1987—; computer tchr. St. Dennis Elem. Sch., Royal Oak, Mich., 1987—2005, St. Mary's Elem. Sch., Royal Oak, 2004—05. Vice-president Houston Fedn. Tchrs., 1978. Mem.: Indpls. Fedn. Tchrs., Soc. Children's Book Writers and Illustrators. Office: Davenport U Warren MI

PRATHER, DONNA LYNN, psychiatrist; b. Charlotte, N.C., Nov. 4, 1946; d. James Boyd and Ann (Joyner) P. BA, Queens Coll., Charlotte, 1968; MD, U. N.C., 1978. Supr. Meckenburg County Dept. Social Svcs., Charlotte, 1971-74; family practice intern Charlotte Meml. Hosp., 1978-79, resident in family practice, 1979-81; fellow in family medicine U. N.C., Chapel Hill, 1981-82; resident in psychiatry N.C. Meml. Hosp., Chapel Hill, 1982-85; pvt. practice psychiatry Chapel Hill, NC, 1985—. Psychiatrist Person Counceling Ctr., Roxboro, N.C., 1983-92; med. dir. Orange-person-Chatam Mental Health Ctr., Chapel Hill, 1992—; clin. assoc. prof. U. N.C., Chapel Hill, 1985—. Mem. N.C. Psychiat. Assn., N.C. Med. Soc., Am. Psychiat. Assn., N.C. Psychiat. Assn. (chmn., com. for women 1990-91, ethics com. 1997-99). Avocation: music. Office: The Courtyard Ste 27 Chapel Hill NC 27516-2319 Office Phone: 919-929-6519.

PRATHER, LENORE LOVING, former State Supreme Court Chief Justice; b. West Point, Miss., Sept. 17, 1931; d. Byron Herald and Hattie Hearn (Morris) Loving; m. Robert Brooks Prather, May 30, 1957; children: Pamela, Valerie Jo, Malinda Wayne. BS, Miss. Univ. Women, 1953; JD, U. Miss., 1955; D (hon.), Miss. Univ. Women, 2003. Bar: Miss. 1955. Practice with B. H. Loving, West Point, 1955-60; sole practice, 1960-62, 65-71; assoc. practice, 1962-65; mcpl. judge City of West Point, 1965-71; chancery ct. judge 14th dist. State of Miss., Columbus, 1971-82, supreme ct. justice Jackson, 1982-92, presiding justice, 1993-97, chief justice, 1998-2001; interim pres. Miss. U. for Women, Columbus, Miss., 2001—02. V.p. Conf. Local Bar Assn., 1956-58; sec. Clay County Bar Assn., 1956-71 1st woman in Miss. to become chancery judge, 1971, and supreme ct. justice, 1982, and chief justice, 1998-2000; recipient Miss. Bar Found. Professionalism award, 2005; named Outstanding Miss. Woman, Pres.'s Commn. on Status of Women, 1986-87. Mem. Miss. State Bar Assn. (Jud. Excellence award 2000-01), DAR, Rotary, Pilot Club, Jr. Aux. Columbus Club. Episcopalian. Achievements include first female chancellor in Mississippi; first female Supreme Court justice; first female chief justice in Mississippi. Personal E-mail: lenorepr@bellsouth.net.

PRATHER, SOPHIE S., educational administrator; b. Selmer, Tenn., Jan. 23, 1948; d. Argie D. and Doris Prather; 1 child, Kimberly. BEd, Lane Coll., Jackson, Tenn., 1969; MEd, Trevecca U., Nashville, 1987. Cert. ednl. adminstr. K-12, Tenn. Tchr. Milw. Pub. Schs., 1971-72, Juneau Acad., Milw., 1972-76, McNairy County Schs., Selmer, 1977-93; psychiat. tchr. counselor Timber Springs Adolescent Ctr., Bolivar, Tenn., 1993-95, prin., 1995-96, program dir., 1996-98; supr. spl. edn. McNairy County Schs., Selmer, 1998—. Mem. McNairy County Devel. Bd. 1998, McNairy County Health Coun. Adv. Bd., 2001—; mem. bd. trustees Western Mental Health Inst.; mem. adv. coun. S.W. Headstart, McNairy County Family Resource Ctr.; mem. DCS Child Abuse Rev. Team; mem. S.W. Commn. on Children and Youth. Recipient Yoakley award, Tenn. Assn. Adminstrs. Spl. Edn., 2006, Supr. of Yr. award, 2006. Mem. NEA, NAFE, Tenn. Edn. Assn., Phi Delta Kappa, Delta Kappa Gamma. Methodist. Avocations: crafts, embroidery. Office: Spl Edn Ctr 491 High School Rd Selmer TN 38375-3252 Business E-Mail: prathers@k12tn.net.

PRATHER, SUSAN LYNN, public relations executive; b. Melrose Park, Ill. d. Horace Charles and Ruth Anna Paula (Backus) P.; divorced. BS, Ind. U., 1973, MS, 1975. Arts adminstr. Lyric Opera Chgo., 1975; jr. account exec. Morton H. Kaplan Assocs., Chgo., 1976-78, sr. account exec., 1978-81; account supr. Ketchum Pub. Relations, Chgo., 1981-83, v.p., 1983-87, v.p., group mgr., 1985-87; v.p., dir. pub. relations Cramer-Krasselt, Chgo., 1987-95, sr. v.p., dir. pub. rels., 1996—. Cons. Velamints, Foster Wheeler, Kellogg Co., Battle Creek, Mich., 1985—, Village of Rosemont, Ill., PrincCo Personal Comm., Sr. Friendlys, Anti-Cruelty Soc. Chgo., Ill. State Toll Hwy. Authority; founder, prin. pratherpr, 2003-. Singer various recitals; founder, dir. Chgo. Sports Hall of Fame, 1978-81. Mem. archives com. Chgo. Symphony Orch., 1986—, mem. long term planning com., 1987-89; mem. press advance team Papal Visit to Chgo., 1978; mem. White House Press Advance Team, Chgo., 1976-80. Mem. Pub. Rels. Soc. Am. (bd. dirs. Chgo. chpt. 1987—), Internat. Pub. Rels. Assn., Publicity Club (bd. dirs. 1986—, Merit award 1982, Golden Trumpet awards, Silver Trumpet awards), Bus. and Profl. Assn. Lutheran. Avocation: figure skating. Home: 155 N Harbor Dr Apt 2212 Chicago IL 60601-7321

PRATO, ELLEN C., literature educator; b. Denville, N.J., Apr. 4, 1962; d. Charles Patrick and Muriel A. Prato; m. Lyle P. Hough, June 7, 2003; stepchildren: Rachel, Melissa; children: Yolanda Scarpati, Anna Scarpati. BA, Rutgers U., 1984, MA, 1987, PhD in English and American Lit., 1998. Reporter Gloucester County Times, Woodbury, NJ, 1985; tchg. asst. Rutgers U., 1985—96, instr., 1996—2000, Princeton (N.J.) U., 2000—01; prof. Bucks County C.C., Newtown, Pa., 2001—. Home: 79 Morgan Ave Yardley PA 19067

PRATT, ALICE S., music educator; b. Rochester, N.Y., Sept. 28, 1952; d. Nunzio and Elisa Pierleoni Sciscioli; m. Ronald J. Pratt, Aug. 23, 1975; children: Rebecca, Kathryn. BS in Music Edn., Nazareth Coll., 1974. Permanent tchrs. cert. N.Y. Page Rochester Pub. Libr., 1970—73; pvt. piano tchr. Rochester, 1973—; vocal music tchr. Rochester City Schs., 1974—. Presenter in field. Composer: America, America, 2003, Seven Days of Kwanzaa, 2003, various childrens songs for chorus and Orff ensemble. Mentor Rochester City Schs. Recipient Rochester Philharm. Music Educator's award, Rochester Philharm. Orch., 1994. Mem.: N.Y. State Sch. Music Assn. (elem. classroom chair 1996—98), Am. Orff Schulweric Assn. (pres. Greater Rochester chpt. 1985—87, 1994—96, region V rep.), Music Educators Nat. Conf. Avocations: cultural events, camping, travel, gardening, reading. Home: 352 Pine Brook Dr Rochester NY 14616 Office: Rochester City Sch 321 Post Ave Rochester NY 14616 E-mail: barkpratt@aol.com.

PRATT, BONNIE, science educator; b. Durham, NC, Jan. 2, 1961; d. Gerald Jordan and Roselyn Bowen Woolard; m. William A. Pratt, Oct. 2, 1957; children: Cameron Gile, Parker Jordan. BS in Zoology and Microbiology, NC State U., Raleigh, 1983. Tchr. sci. Northview H.S., Duluth, Ga., 2002—. Dir. Project 2011 Northview H.S., Duluth, Ga., 2004—06. Scholar, St. George's U. Med. Sch., 2006. Achievements include developement and implementation of a schoolwide program for incoming freshmen to help them transition into high school. Home: 5620 Timson Lane Alpharetta GA 30022 Office: Northview High School 10695 Parsons Road Duluth GA 30097 Office Phone: 404-783-8895.

PRATT, CARIN, television executive; b. Marshfield, Mass., Aug. 22, 1956; m. John Echeverria; children: Nicholas, Edward. BA, Harvard U., 1978. Staff mem. Nieman Found. Harvard U., Boston, 1977-79; staff mem. Tex. R.R. Commn. Campaign, 1979-80; asst. to Tex. bur. chief Washington Post, Austin, 1981-83, rschr., 1981-83, editor, 1981-83; asst. to assoc. prodr. Face the Nation CBS News, N.Y.C., 1984-87, sr. prodr. Face the Nation, 1987-93, exec. prodr., Face the Nation with Bob Schieffer, 1993—. Office: CBS News 2020 M St NW Washington DC 20036-3369

PRATT, DIANE FORD, science educator; b. Gary, Ind., Oct. 24, 1953; d. Walter Lee Ford and Anna Marie Coates; m. Billy Pratt, Sept. 15, 1979; children: Philip Aaron, Ashley Marie. BS, So. U., Baton Rouge, 1975; MEd, Ind. Wesleyan, 2004. Lic. Biology tchr. Ind. Asst. bacteriologist Lake Co. Health Dept., Crown Point, Ind., 1975—81; rsch. tech. Inland Steel Co., East Chgo., Ind., 1981—91; sci. tchr. Gary (Ind.) Comm. Sch. Corp., 1991—. Troop leader Drifting Dunes Girl Scouts, Gary, Ind.; cheerleader sponsor Bailly Mid. Sch., Gary, Ind. Mem.: Nat. Sci. Tchrs. Assn., Delta Sigma Theta, Inc., Phi Delta Kappa. Mem. Non-Denominational Ch. Avocations: reading, travel. Home: 2432 Jefferson St Gary IN 46407 Office Phone: 219-980-6326.

PRATT, JANICE, hospitality and hotel services educator; b. Bethesda, Md., Aug. 19, 1950; m. Frank Pratt, Dec. 10, 1988. D of Ednl. Leadership, No. Ariz. U., Flagstaff, 2004. Cert. hotel adminstr. Am. Hotel and Lodging Assn. Ednl. Inst. Prof. Ctrl. Ariz. Coll., Coolidge, 1990—, assoc. dean Maricopa Ctr., 2005—06. Mem. Western Pinal County Reps; bd. mem. Internat. Coun. on Hotel, Restaurant and Instl. Edn., Richmond, Va. Recipient John Wiley & Sons award for innovation in tchg., Internat. Coun. on Hotel, Restaurant and Instl. Edn., 2001. Office: Ctrl Ariz Coll 8470 N Ovefield Rd Coolidge AZ 85228 Office Phone: 520-494-5032.

PRATT, KATHERINE MERRICK, environmental consulting company executive; b. Alexandria, Egypt, July 4, 1951; d. Theodore and Bettie (Curland) R.; m. Harry Kenneth Todd (div.); 1 child, Kirsten Todd Pratt. BBA in Mgmt. Systems, U. Iowa, 1980; postgrad., U. Tex., 1985—87. Program data mgr. Rockwell Internat., Dallas, 1981-85; support coord. GTE Govt. Systems, Taunton, Mass., 1987-89, support engr., 1989-93; pres. Enviro-Logistics Inc., Harwood, Md., 1993—; sole propr. Internat. Soc. Logistics. Recipient Rear Admiral Bernard Eccles award, 1997, Cert. Commendation for Superior Performance as Dist. Dir., 1997. Mem. Soc. Logistics Engrs. (officer, mem. standing com. environ. applications, bd. dirs. New Eng. dist. 1996, dir. New Eng. dist., nat. chpt. newsletter judge), U.S. Pony Club (Ctrl. New Eng. championship chmn., nat. recognition for outstanding contbn. 1997). Avocations: sailing, reading, equitation. Office: Enviro-Logistics Inc PO Box 723 West River MD 20778-0723 Office Phone: 410-867-6220. E-mail: envirolog@earthlink.net.

PRATT, LINDA, language educator; b. Mass., May 28, 1948; BA, U. Mass., 1970, MEd, 1975, EdD, 1978. Cert. elem. edn., reading specialist, reading supr. Prof., exec. dir. edn. dept. Elmira (N.Y.) Coll.; prof. Gonzaga U., Spokane, Wash.; insvc. tchr. U. Mass., Amherst; reading specialist Southwick (Mass.) Pub. Sch. System. Author: (with J. Beaty) Transcultural Children's Literature, 1999, Early Literacy in Preschools-Kindergarten, 2003. Mem. IRA, NCTE, Nat. Reading Conf., Kappa Delta Pi, Phi Delta Kappa, Kappa Delta Gamma. Office: Elmira Coll Elmira NY 14901

PRATT, MARY, retired secondary school educator; b. Bridgeport, Conn., Nov. 30, 1918; d. William Young Pratt and Daisy Edna Gore BS, Boston U., 1940; MS, U. Mass. Tchr. Quincy Sch. Dept., Mass., 1941—65, 1968—86, Braintree Sch. Dept., Mass., 1986—88, ret., 1988. Profl. baseball player All Am. Girls Profl. Baseball League, Chgo., 1943-47; supr. recreation Quincy, 1948-68; assoc. prof. Salem State U., Mass., 1965-68; mem., archivist Mass. Assn. Health, Phys. Edn., Recreation and Dance, 1941-88 Named Hon. Aux. Sargent Coll., Boston, 1939, Twiness, 1940; recipient Sports Mus. Legacy award, 2003, Instr. award Planet Fitness Club, 2005, Disting. Svc. award Nat. Athletic Dirs. Assn., 2005, award Mass. Secondary Schs. Athletic Dirs. Assn., 2005 Mem. Mass. Interscholastic Athletic Assn. (game ofcls. com., equity com.), Boston U. Alumni Assn., Sargent Coll. Alumni Assn., Boston U. Hall of Fame (Moose Washburn award 1990), Weymouth Tennis and Fitness Club, Nat. Fedn. H.S. Assn. Hall of Fame Avocations: gardening, tennis. Home: 1428 Quincy Shore Dr Quincy MA 02169-2333 E-mail: prattieko@aol.com.

PRATT, MARY LOUISE, librarian, writer; b. Iowa City, Iowa, May 31, 1953; d. William Winston and Helen Virginia Pratt. BA in Eng., Pa. State U., 1977; MLS, Clarion U. Pa., 1987. Dir. written comm. The Fine Arts Connection, State College, Pa., 1980—81; mgr. Unimarts, Inc., State College, 1981—84; reference libr. Evansville-Vanderburgh County Pub. Libr., Ind., 1987—88; ref. libr. Cabell County Pub. Libr., Huntington, W.Va., 1989—96, adult svcs. coord., 1996—. Cons. br. libr. Cabell County Pub. Libr., Huntington, 1989—, pub. computer instr., 1998—. Actor: (plays) A Christmas Carol, Deathtrap, The Boys Next Door, Ransom of Red Chief; editor: Rural Libraries; columnist: Who Said it?; author: (poem) Mr. Lonely in the City (1st pl. Ctrl. Pa. Festival of Arts Poetry Competition., 1977, 1st pl. Calamity Cafe Poetry Slam, 1999); contbr. articles to profl. jours. Active Cabell-Huntington Coalition for the Homeless, W.Va., 1998—. Mem.: W.Va. Libr. Assn., ALA, Guyandotte Poets, Acad. Am. Poets (assoc.). Democrat. Presbyterian. Avocations: acting, autograph collecting, hiking, travel. Home: 1368 13th St Huntington WV 25701 Office: Cabell County Pub Libr 455 9th St Plaza Huntington WV 25701 Office Phone: 304-528-5700. Personal E-mail: mlpratt007@aol.com. E-mail: mpratt@cabell.lib.wv.us.

PRATT, MINNIE BRUCE, writer, educator; b. Selma, Ala., Sept. 12, 1946; d. William Luther Jr. and Virginia Earl (Brown) P.; m. Marvin Eugene Weaver II, Dec. 19, 1966 (div. Nov. 1976); children: Ransom Jones Weaver, Benjamin Carr Weaver; life ptnr.: Leslie Feinberg, July 31, 1992. BA with honors, U. Ala., 1968; PhD in English Lit., U. N.C., 1979. Lectr. Fayetteville (N.C.) State U., 1975-80; asst. prof. Shaw U., Raleigh, N.C., 1980-82; adj. lectr. Women's Studies Program, George Washington U., Washington, 1984-88; adj. lectr., vis. asst. prof. Women's Studies Program, U. Md., College Park, 1984-93; grad. faculty Union Inst., Cin., 1990—2003; Jane Watson Irwin chair in women's studies Hamilton Coll., 2002—03; prof. writing and women's studies Syracuse U., 2005. Writer-in-residence The Cmty. Writers' Project, Syracuse, N.Y., 1988, The Lit. Festival at St. Mary's Coll., St. Mary's City, Md., 1999, Nat. YMCA Writers Voice Program, N.Y.C., 2000. Author: The Sound of One Fork, 1981, Yours In Struggle: Three Feminist Perspectives on Anti-Semitism and Racism, 1984, We Say We Love Each Other, 1985, Crime Against Nature, 1990 (Lamont Poetry selection of Acad. Am. Poets 1990, ALA Gay and Lesbian Book award for lit. 1991), Rebellion: Essays 1980-1991, 1992 (Outstanding Book award Gustavus Myers Ctr. for Study of Human Rights in US 1992), S/HE, 1995, Walking Back Up Depot Street, 1999 (Best Gay and Lesbian Book of Yr., ForeWord: Mag. of Ind. Bookstores and Booksellers 1999), The Money Machine: Selected Poems, 2003, The Dirt She Ate: Selected and New Poems, 2003 (Lambda Lit. award 2003); mem. editl. bd. Feminary: A Feminist Jour. for the South, Emphasizing Lesbian Visions, 1978-83, Faminist Stuides, 2005—. Fulbright fellow, 1968, Woodrow Wilson fellow, 1968, NDEA fellow, 1968, Creative Writing fellow Nat. Endowment Arts, 1990, NJ State Coun. Arts fellow, 2005; recipient Lillian Hellman-Dashiell Hammett award Fund Free Expression, 1991 Ind. grant lit. DC. Commn. on Arts, 1992, Ind. Artist grant Puffin Found., 1994, Larry Levis award poetry Prairie Schooner mag., 1999, Ind. Artist award Ludwig Vogelstein Found., 2000, Lucille Medwick award Poetry Soc. Am., 2002; named one of Top 31 Alumnae, 1892-1992, XXXI Women's Leadership Hon., U. Ala., 1992. Mem. Poetry Soc. Am. (judge Celia B. Wagner Award 1992), Nat. Writers Union, Southerners on New Ground, Phi Beta Kappa. Office: #227 72 Van Reipen Ave Jersey City NJ 07306 Fax: 201-484-7720. E-mail: mbpratt@earthlink.net.

PRATT, RACHEL C., elementary school educator; d. Craig S. and Dolores J. Pratt. BA, Bethel Coll., Mishawaka, Ind., 2001. Tchr. English Dong Da Sch., Jinci, Shanxi, China, 2001—02; tchr. Discovery Mid. Sch., Granger, Ind., 2002—06, Horizon Elem. Sch., 2006—. Dir drama Discovery Mid. Sch., 2002—06. Primary del. leader People to People Student Amb. Programs, South Bend, Ind., 2005—; women's small group leader Nappanee Missionary Ch., Nappanee, 2005—05. Mem.: Ind. State Tchrs. Assn.

PRATT, REYNA KUSHNER, physics educator; d. Jack and Annetta Horwitz Kushner; m. Laurence Henry Pratt, Sept. 5, 1992; children: Alison Taylor, Harrison Horwitz. BA, Wellesley Coll., 1987; MPhil, The George Wash. U., 1995. Math, physics tchr. Berkshire Sch., Sheffield, Mass., 1987—91; grad. student George Wash. U., Washington, 1991—98; physics tchr. The Madeira Sch., McLean, Va., 1998—. Office: The Madeira Sch 8328 Georgetown Pike Mc Lean VA 22102 Office Phone: 703-556-8341.

PRATT, SANDRA SOWERS, special education educator; b. Worcester, Mass., Oct. 28, 1947; d. Robert Wales Sowers and Phyllis Joyce Nudski; m. David J. Pratt, Apr. 22, 1948; children: Joshua David, Katherine Elizabeth Coutu. BA, Ohio State Un, Columbus, 1973; MEd, Fitchburg State Coll., Mass., 1995, Lesley Coll., Cambridge, Mass., 2000. Cert. spl. edn. tchr. Mass. Tchr. spl. edn. Blackstone Valley Tech, Upton, Mass., 1995—. Adj. prof. Quinsigamond C.C., Worcester, 2004—; presenter in field; adj. prof. U. Mass., Fitchburg State Coll., Boston. Office Phone: 508-529-7771. Personal E-mail: sprattsmilecp@yahoo.com. Business E-Mail: spratt@valleytech.k12.ma.us.

PRATT, SARAH ELLEN, secondary school educator; b. Greensboro, N.C., Sept. 16, 1946; d. Clarence Franklin and Hazel Elleene (Bluster) Moss; m. George Carroll Pratt; 1 child, Todd Franklin. BA, Catawba Coll., 1970, English cert., 1977; MA in Teaching, U. N.C., 1983. Cert. tchr., N.C. Tchr. Salisbury (N.C.) City Schs., 1970-78, Pasadena (Tex.) Ind. Schs., 1978-79, Durham (N.C.) County Schs., 1979-84, McDowell County Schs., Marion, NC, 1984—, personnel dir., 1999—. Cons. N.C. State Dept. Pub. Instrn., 1994—96; bd. dir. Alternative Sch., personnel dir., 2000—. Named N.C. Tchr. of the Yr., N.C. Dept. Pub. Instrn., 1993; named to Nat. Tchr. Hall Fame, 1996. Mem. ASCD, N.C. Assn. Educators (local sec., bldg. rep., conf. del.). Office: McDowell County Schs PO Box 130 Marion NC 28752-9629 Office Phone: 828-652-4535.

PRATT, SUSAN G., architect; b. Kansas City, Mo., Sept. 24, 1951; d. John Bohman and Alice Marguerite (Harris) Grow; m. W. Scott Pratt; children: David, Alice; stepchildren: David, Laura. BArch, Kans. State U., 1973. Registered architect, Mich., Wis. Project arch. Skidmore Owings & Merrill, Chgo., 1973-78, 83-85, Murphy/Jahn, Inc., Chgo., 1978—82, 1986—2004, now v.p.; sr. project arch. Froelich & Marik, L.A., 1982-83, Marshall & Brown, Kansas City, 1985-86; assoc. prin. architect Lohan Caprile, Goettsch, 2004—. Prin. works include New World Ctr., Hong Kong, Group Repertory Theatre, North Hollywood, Calif., Bi State Indsl. Park, Kansas City, Mo., State of Ill. Ctr., Chgo., John Deere Harvester Works Office Facility, Moline, Ill., Two Liberty Pl., Phila., Livingston Pla., Bklyn., North Loop Block 37, Chgo., 1st and Broadway, L.A., Kudamm 119, Berlin, Cologne/Bonn Airport, Cologne, Jeddah Airport, Saudi Arabia, Sony European Hdqrs., Berlin, Munich Airport Ctr., 21st Century Tower, Shanghai, China, South Pointe Condominiums, Miami Beach, Kaufhof Dept. Store, Chemnitz, Germany, Andersen Cons. Hdqrs., Frankfurt, Germany, Deutsche Post Hdqrs., Bonn, Shen Zhen Conv. Ctr., China, Mannheim (Germany) Ins. Co. Hdqrs., Skyline Towers, Munich, Kempinski Hotel, Tokyo Sta., Tokyo, Am. Airlines Terminal, Chgo., Horizon Serono Headquarters, Geneva, Switzerland, Hafen Office Bldg., Dusseldorf, Germany, Nanjing Pl. Retail, China, Convention Ctr. Hotel, Suzhou, China, Greenland Devel. office, hotel, apart., Xi'an, China, Suzhou Hotel, Suzhou, China. Mem. First Presbyn. Ch., Evanston, Ill. Mem. AIA (corp. mem.). Presbyterian. Office: Goettsch Partnership 224 S Michigan Chicago IL 60604 Office Phone: 312-663-1724. Personal E-mail: sspratt@msn.com. Business E-Mail: spratt@gpchicago.com.

PRATTER, GENE E. K., federal judge, lawyer; b. Feb. 25, 1949; d. Eugene Anthony and Laurel Marilyn (Dauer) Kreyche; m. Robert Lawrence Pratter, Oct. 21, 1978; children: Virginia Paige, Matthew Robert. BA, Stanford U., 1971; JD, U. Pa., 1975. Bar: Pa. 1975, U.S. Dist. Ct. (ea. dist.) Pa. 1975, U.S. Ct. Appeals (3d cir.) 1981. Assoc. Duane, Morris & Heckscher, Phila., 1975—83, ptnr., 1983—2004, gen. counsel, 1999—2004; judge U.S. Dist. Ct., (ea. dist.) Pa, 2004—. Judge pro tem Phila. Ct. Common Pleas, 1994—; bd. overseers U. Pa. Law Sch., Phila., 1994—2000; lectr. Ctr. on Professionalism. Contbr. articles to profl. jours. Fund raiser U. Pa. Law Sch. Mem.: ABA (litigation sect. chmn. com. on ethics and professionalism 1995—2000), Phila. Bar Assn., Pa. Bar Assn., Def. Rsch. Inst., Stanford U. Alumni Club (fund raiser, officer 1976—83). Republican. Roman Catholic. Office: 601 Market St Rm 2609 Philadelphia PA 19106-1797

PRAWDZIK, LINDA CONDUSTA, mathematics educator, consultant, director; b. Phila., Aug. 12, 1953; d. Albert D. and Mary B. Condusta; children: Jerome C., Christina Ann, Joseph A. BA in Secondary Edn., King's Coll., Wilkes Barre, Pa., 1975; MS in Secondary Sch. Counseling, Marywood U., Scranton, Pa., 1995. Cert. instrnl. II in secondary math. and secondary sch. counseling Pa. Academic advisor, part time adminstr., adj. faculty math. Corp. Learning Ctr., Wilkes-Barre, Pa., 2001—.

PRAZAK, BESSMARIE LILLIAN, science educator; b. Chgo., June 6, 1941; d. William Felix and Bess Blanch (Kostka) Kolar; m. Charles J. Prazak III, June 15, 1963; 1 child, Robin Marie. BS, Rosary U., 1963; MS, Northwestern U., 1965. Rsch. asst. Argonne Nat. Lab., Lemont, Ill., 1965-68; tchr. Morton Coll., Cicero, Ill., 1968-2000, tchr. emeritus, 2000—. Chair curriculum com. Morton Coll., 1984—2000. Author: Laboratory Manual of Anatomy and Physiology, 1997, Laboratory Manual of Microbiology, 1997, Photo Albums of Anatomy and Physiology Histology, 2002, 2d edit., 2003, Photo Albums of Microbiology, 2004. Mem. AAAS, Nat. Assn. Biology Tchrs., Ill. Assn. C.C. Biologists (sec.-treas. 1978), Human Anatomy and Physiology Soc. Avocations: painting, photography.

PRCHAL, CAROL LOUISE, retired orthopedist; b. Hinsdale, Ill., Oct. 13, 1956; d. Robert and Betty Hooper Prchal. BS, George Williams Coll., Downers Grove, Ill., 1979; MD, U. Ill., Chgo., 1983. Cert. Am. Bd. Orthop. Surgeons, 1992. Orthop. surgeon Burlington Clinic, Wis., 1988—2005. Chairperson dept. surgery Meml. Hosp. Burlington, Wis., 1998—2000. Dir. VIP Svcs., Inc., Elkhorn, Wis., 2006—; vol. coach Spl. Olympics, Walworth County, Wis., 2006—. Recipient Outstanding Scholar award, George Williams Coll., 1979, Disting. Alumni award, Aurora U. (formerly George Williams Coll.), 2004. Mem.: Ice Age Trail Found., Nature Conservancy, Sierra Club, Kappa Delta Pi. Avocations: hiking, gardening, canine agility.

PRECIADO, PAMELA, artist; b. Evanston, Ill., Aug. 30, 1944; d. John James and Lena Day (Stevenson) Wills; m. Harold Prediado, June 1969 (div. July 1984); Student, U. Kans., U. Ill., San Francisco Acad. Fine Art, Am. Acad. Art Chgo., Art Inst. Chg. Comml. portrait artist. Year of the Woman, Dem. and Rep. women of 104th Congress, Black Caucus of 104th Congress, portrait montage Dem. women running for office State of Ill., 1994, exhibitions include Wells Fargo Bank, San Francisco, Godfrey Gallery, Mark Hopkins Hotel, Joseph Alioto Gallery, Macy's Dept. Store, San Francisco, Represented in permanent collections Booth Fisheries of Consol. Foods Corp., DeKalb AgResearch Corp. Mem.: NAFE, LWV, Portrait Soc. Am., Portrait Soc. Am., Chgo. Artists Coalition, Palette and Chisel Acad. Democrat. Avocations: travel, teaching art, tennis. Studio: Fine Art and Portraiture 1838 N Hudson Ave Chicago IL 60614 E-mail: vince188@juno.com.

PREECE, LYNN SYLVIA, lawyer; b. Birmingham, Eng., June 13, 1955; d. Norman and Sylvia Florence (James) Preece. LLB, Leeds (Eng.) U., 1976; postgrad., Washington U., St. Louis, 1978-79; JD, Loyola U., 1981. Bar: Ill., 1981. Assoc. Barnes Richardson, Chgo., 1980-86; from assoc. to ptnr. Burditt & Radzius, Chgo., 1986-88; ptnr. Katten Muchin & Zavis, Chgo., 1988-96, Baker & McKenzie, Chgo., 1996—. Adj. prof. John Marshall Law Sch., 1998—. Contbr. articles to profl. jours. Chair customs com. Chgo. Bar Assn., 1986-87, Am. Bar Sect. Internat. Law, Washington, 1993-95, practitioners workshop bd., 1995-97; sec., dir. Women in Internat. Trade, Chgo., 1986-89, British Am. C. of C., Chgo., 1990; dir. Chgo. Internat. Sch., 1994-96. Recipient Gold medal Duke of Edinurghs award Scheme, London, 1973. Mem.: ABA (program officer, coun. mem., newsletter editor 1996—98), Internat. Bar Assn., Ct. Internat. Trade Bar Assn. Avocation: gardening. Office: Baker & McKenzie Ste 3500 130 E Randolph Dr Chicago IL 60601-6342 Office Phone: 312-861-8022. E-mail: Lynn.S.Preece@Bakernet.com.

PREER, JOAN C., retired assistant principal, retired science educator; d. Clarence Norman and Mary Katherine Casey; m. Andrew Stephen Preer, Sr., May 14, 1965; 1 child, Andrew Stephen Jr. BS in Chemistry, Tenn. A&I State U., Nashville, 1964; M in Adminstrn., Roosevelt U., Chgo., 1980. Ill. tchg. cert. Type 03 Chgo. Pub. Schs., 1969, tchg. cert. grades 3-8 Chgo. Pub. Schs., 1973, gen. sci. endorsement Chgo. Pub. Schs., 1987, sci. tchr. leadership workshop cert. Ill. State Bd. Edn., 1992, adminstrv. cert. Type 75 Ill. State Bd. Edn., 1995. Sci. tchr. Beasley Academic Magnet Ctr., Chgo., 1979—90; sci. coord. Beasley Academic Magnet Sch., Chgo., 1990—96, asst. prin., 1995—2001; ret., 2001. Curriculum writer Bill Kurtis Prodns., Chgo., 1986—2000, Mus. Sci. and Industry, Chgo., 1993—94, Field Mus. Natural History, Chgo., 1995, Brookfield Zoo, Chgo., Argonne Nat. Labs., Chgo., Chgo. Bur. Sci., Chgo., Chgo. Zool. Soc., Chgo.; integrated math., sci. and tech. design team Ill. State U., Normal; middle level childhood sci. stds. com. Nat. Bd. for Profl. Tchg. Stds., 1991—93. Contbg. mem. Nat. Com. to Preserve Social Security and Medicare, 2003—06, Northshore Animal League, Chgo., 2000—06, S.W. Indian Children, 2000—06; active Habitat for Humanity, 2001—06; contbg ptnr. Trinity Broadcasting Network Ministries, Calif., 2001—06. Named Honors Sci. Tchr., Ill. State Bd. Edn.; recipient Golden Apple award, Golden Apple Found., 1988, Cert. Recognition For Excellence In Sci. and Math Tchg., Sigma Xi, 1989, Cert. Recognition For Excellence In Tchg., Ill. Fedn. Tchrs., 1989, Cert. Recognition For Contbns. To Leadership In Sci. Edn., Ill. State Bd. Edn., 1990, Cert. Recognition, Nat. Assn. Precollege Dirs. in Assn. with the AMOCO Corp. Mem.: Chgo. Prins. and Adminstrs. Assn., Ret. Tchrs. Chgo. (life). Achievements include development of a school-level assessment system. Avocations: designing computer programs, travel, designing clothing, designing educational games, writing stories for children.

PREHEIM, KATHY LYNN, elementary school educator; b. Moundridge, Kans., June 30, 1967; d. Jerome Vallee and Bonnie Marie (Schroeder) Kaufman; m. Randall James Preheim, June 4, 1989. BS, Bethel Coll., N. Newton, Kans., 1989; MS, Wichita (Kans.) State U., 2004. Tchr. 5th grade Peabody (Kans.) Elementary Sch., 1989—, dir. dist. curriculum, 2000—. Mem. curriculum com. Peabody Elem. Sch., 2000—; chairperson Quality Performance Accreditation, 1999—. Mem. ASCD. Mennonite Ch. Avocations: skiing, sewing, horseback riding, volleyball, swimming.

PREISS-HARRIS, PATRICIA, music educator, composer, pianist; b. N.Y.C., May 19, 1950; d. Fredric H. and Madeline P.; m. Eric A. Lerner, Nov. 1970 (div. 1975); m. William H. Harris, Aug. 13, 1995. BA, Harvard U., 1973; MFA, Calif. Inst. Arts, 1987. Performer, bassist Carla Bley Band, Willow, NY, 1977—78; instr. piano, composition The Hall Sch., Pittsfield, Mass., 1983—84; instr. music Santa Monica C.C., Calif., 1989; tchr. piano The Hackley Sch., Tarrytown, NY, 1991; tchr. piano and composition Fraioli Sch. of Music, Greenwich, Conn., 1991—2002; accompanist voice dept. SUNY, Purchase, 1991—95; performer, pianist Gary Wofsey Jazz Orch., 1996—, The Jones Factor Big Band, 1999—. Pvt. piano tchr., NY, 1990—2005, Conn., 1990—, Mass., 1980—84; pianist Greenwich Regency Hyatt Hotel, 1995—; solo and ensemble pianist, 1980—; accompanist Blue Notes vocal ensemble, 2000—, Westfair Chamber Singers, 2005—06; attendee Cummington Cmty. Arts, Mass., 1981. Performer Trust in Love, 1981; composer, pianist Jamaica's Album, 1984, When He Calls, 2004, My Brother's song, 2006; composer (piano & flute) Messages, 1980, (women's choir, medieval instruments) Invocations, 1981, (woodwinds) Complete Enlightenment, 1986, (CDs) Harris Bros. Horns, 2003, Aiyb's Song and Dream and co-composer Every Night on Bill Harris' The Extra Mile, 2005; performer, composer (CD) The Nearness of You, 2000 Performance grantee Cambridge (Mass.) Arts Coun., 1977, Artists grantee No. Berkshire Coun. on Arts, 1983. Mem.: Schubert Club. Home: 162 Toms Rd Stamford CT 06906-1031 Office Phone: 203-249-1067. E-mail: patti@pattipreiss.com.

PREJEAN, SISTER HELEN THERESA, human rights advocate, writer, lecturer; b. Baton Rouge, Apr. 21, 1939; d. Louis Sebastian and Gusta Mae (Bourg) P. BA in English, St. Mary's Dominican Coll., 1962; MA in Religious Edn., St. Paul's U., 1973; more than 30, hon. degrees. Joined Congregation of St. Joseph of Medaille, Roman Cath. Ch., 1957. Tchr. St. Frances Cabrini Sch., New Orleans, 1962-66; dir. religious edn. St. Frances Cabrini Parish, New Orleans, 1968-75; dir. novices Sisters St. Joseph Medaille, New Orleans, 1975-81; tchr. Hope House Adult Learning Ctr., New Orleans, 1981-84; chmn. bd. Nat. Coalition to Abolish the Death Penalty, 1993—. Spiritual advisor to death row inmates and murder victims' families, 1982—. Author: Dead Man Walking: An Eyewitness Account of the Death Penalty in the US, 1993 (nominated for Pulitzer Prize). The Death of Innocents, 2004. Recipient Sanctity of Life award So. Christian Leadership Conf., 1990, Abolitionist award Nat. Coalition to Abolish the Death Penalty, 1992, Champion of Liberty award Nat. Assn. Criminal Def. Lawyers, 1994, Ben Smith award, ACLU New Orleans, 1998, Bishop Dingman Peace award Catholic Peace Ministry, Des Moines, Iowa, 2000, Harry F. Fagan Roundtable award, 2001, Ut Diligatis Invicem award Gannon Univ., Erie, Pa., 2002, Cardinal Suenens award John Carroll Univ., 2004, Death Penalty Focus award, 2005; named among America's 20 Most Confident Women, McCalls mag., 1993, dozens of other awards; life and work profiled by N.Y. Times Mag., 1993. Business E-Mail: sisterhelen@deathpenaltydiscourse.org.*

PRELLBERG, JOANNE MARIE, office manager; b. Rockford, Ill., Aug. 27, 1960; d. Frederick Charles II and Dolores Yvonne (Ronk) P.; m. Daniel A. Clay. BS, Boston U., 1983; JD, U. Mo., 1990. Intern Boston (Mass.) Univ. Med. Ctr., 1981-82; pub. rels. specialist Houston (Tex.) NW Med. Ctr., 1982-83; mgr. Bennigans Restaurant, Houston, 1982-84; copy editor HEI Pub., Houston, 1984-85; mgr. Function Junction, Kansas City, Mo., 1985-87; waitress, bartender Houston's Restaurants, Kansas City, 1987-89; law clk. Holbrook, Ellis & Heaven, Merriam, Kans., 1989-91; office mgr. Squaw Peak Animal Hosp., Phoenix, 1991-93; bus. mgr. Coady Enterprises, Inc., 1993-94; office mgr. Tatum Point Animal Hosp., Phoenix, 1994—2003, Grayhawk Animal Hosp., Scottsdale, Ariz., 2003—. V.p. Boston Univ.-Pub. Rels. Student Soc. Am., 1981-83; pres. The Law Coun., Kansas City, 1988-89. Mem. Heartland Bernese Mt. Dog Club (v.p. 1990), Bernese Mt. Dog Club Am. (nat. specialty coord. 1993-97), Grand Canyon State Bernese Mt. Dog Club (pres. 1994), Scottsdale Dog Fanciers Assn. Avocation: breeding and showing purebred dogs. Office: Grayhawk Animal Hosp # 101 20801 N Scottsdale Rd Scottsdale AZ 85262

PREMA, NITYA, marriage and family therapist, artist; b. LA, June 15, 1941; d. James Nicholson and Phyllis Wickersham; children: Fritjof Swenson, Derek Swenson, Krista Mills. AS, Santa Rosa Jr. Coll., Calif., 1977; BA, Sonoma State U., Rohnert Park, Calif., 1980; MA, Profl. Sch. of Psychology, San Francisco, 1983. Lic. marriage and family therapist Bd. of Behavioral Sci., Calif., 1982; psychiat. technician, Bd. of Vocat. Nursing, 1979. Owner, designer and mfr. Nitya Visionary Designs and Gallery, Forestville and Sebastopol, Calif., 1982—92; therapist/social worker O'Connor Hosp. Vista's Program, San Jose, Calif., 1997—99; psychotherapist San Jose Jails/Mental Healtlh, Calif., 1998—2000; pvt. practice family therapist San Andreas and Visalia, Calif., 2000—. Spkr. Internat. Transpersonal Conf., Ireland, 1994; spkr.'s bur. Calif. Assn. of Marriage and Family Therapists, Santa Rosa, 1996. Author: The Spiral Labyrinth Journey: A Pilgrimage into Sacred Space. Activist Rainbow Labyrinth Journey. Mem.: Ebbets Pass Forest Watch, Brewster Kaleidoscope Soc. Achievements include artist and designer of Magic wands and Kaleidoscopes. Office: North Main St San Andreas CA 95249 Office Phone: 209-795-0755. Business E-Mail: artglasscopes@yahoo.com.

PREMACK, ANN J., writer; b. Shanghai, Jan. 5, 1929; interned in Japanese detention ctr., 1943-45; came to the U.S., 1945; d. John Joseph James and Mae Victoria Parker; m. David Premack, Oct. 26, 1951; children: Ben, Lisa, Tim. BS with distinction, U. Minn., 1951. Author: Why Chimps Can Read, 1975; co-author (with D. Premack): The Mind of An Ape, 1983; co-editor: Causal Cognition: A Multidisciplinary Debate, 1995; co-author (with D. Premack): Original Intelligence: Unlocking the Mystery of Who We Are, 2003, French translation, 2003, Japanese translation, 2005; contbr. chapters to books, articles to profl. jours. Avocation: owning and running an avocado grove. Home: 6163 Heatherton Dr Somis CA 93066-9716 Personal E-mail: dpremack@aol.com, dpremack@msn.com.

PRENDERGAST, CAROLE LISAK, musician, educator; b. Chgo., Mar. 15, 1949; d. Chester Matt and Emily Julie (Krupa) Lisak; m. Joseph Thomas Prendergast, Oct. 19, 1974; children: Karin, Colin. MusB, DePaul U., 1971; MA Ch. Music and Liturgy, St. Joseph's Coll., Rensselaer, Ind., 2002. Tchg. cert. K-14, Ill. Music tchr. Chgo. Pub. Schs., 1971-74; music dir. St. Adalbert Ch., 1976-88; freelance musician, 1988—. Piano tchr., Chgo., 1970—; substitute organist St. Adalbert Ch., Chgo., 1965-76; choir accompanist St. Luke Ch., River Forest, Ill., 1993—, music dir., 2000-04; dir. music Queen of Martyrs Ch., Evergreen, Ill., 2004— Chairperson welcome com. Queen of Martyrs Ch., Evergreen Park, 1990— Ill. state scholar, 1968—71, DePaul scholar, 1968. Mem. Am. Guild Organists, Nat. Assn. Pastoral Musicians, Music Tchrs. Nat. Assn., Chgo. Fedn. Musicians, Chgo. Area Suzuki Tchrs., Suzuki Assn. of Ams., Am. Choral Dirs. Assn., Am. Guild English Handbell Ringers Roman Catholic. Avocations: gardening, travel, antiques, cooking. Home: 10417 S Hamlin Ave Chicago IL 60655-3115 Office: Queen of Martyrs Ch 10233 S Central Park Ave Evergreen Park IL 60805 Office Phone: 708-423-8110.

PRESCOTT, BARBARA LODWICH, educational association administrator; b. Chgo., Aug. 15, 1951; d. Edward and Eugenia Lodwich; m. Warren Paul Prescott, Dec. 2, 1979; children: Warren Paul Jr., Ashley Elizabeth. BA, U. Ill., Chgo., 1973, MEd, 1981; MA, U. Wis., 1978; postgrad., Stanford U., 1983-87. Cert. tchr., learning handicapped specialist, cmty. coll. instr., Calif. Grad. rschr. U. Ill., Chgo., 1979-81; learning handicapped specialist St. Paulus Luth. Sch., San Francisco, 1981-83; grad. rsch. asst. Sch. Edn. Stanford (Calif.) U., 1983-87; learning handicapped specialist/lead therapist Gilroy Clinic Speech-Hearing-Learning Ctr., Crippled Children's Soc., Santa Clara, Calif., 1988-89; ednl. dir. Adolescent Intensive Resdl. Svc. Calif. Pacific Med. Ctr., San Francisco, 1989-95; exec. dir. Learning Profiles, South Lake Tahoe, Calif., 1995—. Instr. evening San Jose City Coll., 1988-92. Contbr. articles to profl. jours.; author: Proceedings of Internat. Congress of Linguistics, 1987; editor: Proceedings - Forum for Research on Language Issues, 1986; author videotape: Making a Difference in Language and Learning, 1989. Recipient Frederick Bork Teaching Trainee award San Francisco State U., 1983; Ill. State scholar, 1973. Mem. Calif. Assn. Pvt. Specialized Edn. and Svcs., Phi Delta Kappa (v.p. 1984-86), Pi Lambda Theta (sec. 1982-83), Phi Kappa Phi, Alpha Lambda Theta. Office Phone: 630-924-8052. E-mail: prescott4@netscape.com.

PRESKA, LORETTA A., federal judge; b. 1949; BA, Coll. of St. Rose, 1970; JD, Fordham U., 1973; LLM, NYU, 1978; LHD (hon.), Coll. of St. Rose, 1995. Assoc. Cahill, Gordon & Reindel, NYC, 1973-82; ptnr. Hertzog, Calamari & Gleason, NYC, 1982-92; fed. judge U.S. Dist. Ct. (So. Dist.), NY, 1992—. Mem. N.Y. State Bar Assn., N.Y. County Lawyers Assn., Fed. Bar Coun., Fordham Law Alumni Assn. (v.p.). Office: US Courthouse 500 Pearl St Rm 1320 New York NY 10007-1316

PRESKA, MARGARET LOUISE ROBINSON, historian, educational association administrator; b. Parma, N.Y., Jan. 23, 1938; d. Ralph Craven and Ellen Elvira (Niemi) Robinson; m. Daniel C. Preska, Jan. 24, 1959; children: Robert, William, Ellen Preska Steck. BS summa cum laude, SUNY, 1957; MA, Pa. State U., 1961; PhD, Claremont Grad. Sch., 1969. Instr. LaVerne (Calif.) Coll., 1968-75, asst. prof., asso. prof., acad. dean, 1972-75; instr. Starr King Sch. for Ministry, Berkeley, Calif., summer, 1975; v.p. acad. affairs, equal opportunity officer Minn. State U., Mankato, 1975-79, pres., 1979-92; project dir. Kaliningrad (Russia) Mil. Re-Tng., 1992-96; disting. svc. prof. Minn. State U. Sys., 1993—; pres. Inst. for Effective Tchg. Minn. State U., Winona, 1993—98; owner BuildaBikeInc.com, 2000—. Bd. dirs. XCEL Energy Co., Milkweed Edits.; pres. emerita Minn. State U., Mankato, 1992—; provost, CEO AbuDhabi Campus, Zayed U., United Arab Emirates, 1997-99. Pres. Pomona Valley chpt. UN Assn., 1968-69, Unitarian Soc. Pomona Valley, 1968-69, PTA Lincoln Elem. Sch., Pomona, 1973-74; pres., chmn. bd. Nat. Camp Fire Boys and Girls, 1984-88; mem. Pomona City Charter Revision Commn., 1972; chmn. The Fielding Inst., Santa Barbara, 1983-86; bd. dirs. Elderhostel Internat., 1983-87, Minn. Agrl. Interpretive Ctr. (Farmam.), 1983-92, Am. Assn. State Colls. and Univs., Moscow on the Mississippi - Minn. Meets the Soviet Union; nat. pres. Campfire, Inc., 1985-87; chmn. Gov.'s Coun. on Youth, Minn., 1983-86, Minn. Edn. Forum, 1984; mem. Gov.'s Commn. on Econ. Future of Minn., 1985—, NCAA Pres. Commn., 1986-92, NCAA Cost Cutting Commn., Minn. Brainpower Compact, 1985; commr. Great Lakes Govs.' Econ. Devel. Coun., 1986, Minn Gov.'s Commn. on Forestry. Carnegie Found. grantee Am. Coun. Edn. Deans Inst., 1974; recipient Outstanding Alumni award Pa. State, Outstanding Alumni award Claremont Grad. Sch., YWCA Leader award 1982, Exch. Club Book of Golden Deeds award, 1987; named One of top 100 alumni, SUNY, 1895-1985, 1985, Hall of Heritage award, 1988, Wohelo Camp Fire award, 1989. Fellow Fielding Inst.; mem. AAUW (pres. Mankato 1990-92), LWV, Women's Econ. Roundtable, St. Paul/Mpls. Com. on Fgn. Rels., Am. Assn. Univ. Adminstrs., Rotary, Horizon 100. Unitarian Universalist. Home: 10 Sumner Hls Mankato MN 56001-3931 E-mail: mpreska@hickorytech.net.

PRESLEY, LISA MARIE, singer; b. Memphis, Tenn., Feb. 1, 1968; d. Elvis and Priscilla Presley; m. Danny Keough, Oct. 3, 1988 (div. 1994); children: Danielle Riley Keough, Benjamin Storm Keough; m. Michael Jackson, May 18, 1994 (div. Jan. 18, 1996); m. Nicholas Cage, Aug. 10, 2002 (div. May 16, 2004); m. Michael Lockwood, Jan. 22, 2006. Mgmt. Elvis Presley Trust; owner, chmn. bd. Elvis Presley Enterprises, Inc.; co-owner with mother Priscilla Elvis Presley's Memphis nightclub, operated by Presley Estate, 1997—2003. Singer: (albums) To Whom It May Concern, 2003 (cert. Gold), Lights Out, 2003, Now What, 2005; actor: (music video) You Are Not Alone, Michael Jackson, (car commercial), 1989; appeared on (cover of Vogue mag.), 1996, (cover of Vogue mag. with mother and daughter), 2004, featured in (TV) Elvis by the Presleys, 2005. Internat. spokesperson Citizens Commn. on Human Rights; co-founder (with Isaac Hayes) LEAP (Literacy, Edn., and Ability Program); involved with Fight for Kids. Office: Elvis Presley Enterprises Inc PO Box 16508 3734 Elvis Presley Blvd Memphis TN 38186-0508*

PRESLEY, PAULA LUMPKIN, retired editor; b. Des Arc, Ark., June 8, 1938; d. Herbert Eugene and Clara Erline (Jones) Lumpkin; m. Clifton Jay Presley, Apr. 19, 1958 (div. Mar. 1988); children: Richard Jay, Steven James, Susan Jean. BA in History, Truman State U., Kirksville, Mo., 1985, MA, 1989; MLS, U. Iowa, 1991. Copy and prodn. editor Sixteenth Century Jour., Kirksville, 1982—; asst. editor Thomas Jefferson U. Press, Kirksville, 1986-91, assoc. editor, 1991-98; dir., editor-in-chief Truman State U. Press (formerly Thomas Jefferson U. Press), Kirksville, 1998—2003, ret., 2004; owner Paula Presley Editl. Svcs. Editor (Keywords newsletter): Am. Soc. Indexers, 1997—98; editor: Editing History newsletter, 1996—97; co-editor: Habent sua libelli or, Books Have Their Own Destiny, 1998; editl. com. mem.: Peter Martyr Libr. Series, 1996—; contbr. chpts. to books; contbg. author: What Else Can You Do with a Library Degree: Career Options for the 90s and Beyond, 1997. Mem.: ALA, Conf. Hist. Jours., Calvin Studies Soc., Soc. for Scholarly Pub., Am. Soc. Indexers (newsletter editor 1997—98). Democrat. Presbyterian. Avocations: book indexing, copyediting, research in printing, incunabula, religious history/theology. Home: 820 E Meadow Ln Kirksville MO 63501-2568 Business E-Mail: ppresley@truman.edu.

PRESLEY, PRISCILLA (PRICILLA ANN WAGNER, PRISCILLA BEAULIEU PRESLEY), actress; b. Bklyn., May 24, 1945; m. Elvis Presley, 1967 (div. 1973); 1 child, Lisa Marie; 1 child (with Marco Garibaldi), Navarone. Studied with Milton Katselas; student, Steven Peck Theatre Art Sch., Chuck Norris Karate Sch.; HHD (hon.), Rhodes Coll., Memphis, 1998. Co-owner Bis and Beau Boutique, 1973—76; co-executor, pres. Elvis Presley Enterprise, Inc. (acquired by CKX, Inc.), Memphis, 1979—2005, founder, 1980—2005, exec. cons., 2005—; bd. dir. CKX, Inc., Las Vegas, Nev., 2005—. Launched & developed internat. fragrance line, 1988—, Moments, 1990, Experiences, 1994, Indian Summer, 1996; designer of jewelry line; launched website, 2005—; bd. dir. Metro-Goldwyn-Mayer Inc., 2000—; lectr. SMART TALK. Appearances include (films) The Naked Gun: From the Files of Police Squad!, 1988, The Adventures of Ford Fairlaine, 1990, The Naked Gun 2 1/2, 1991, The Naked Gun 33 1/3: The Final Insult, 1994, (TV series) Those Amazing Animals, 1980-81, Dallas, 1983-88, Melrose Place, 1996, (TV movies) Love Is Forever, 1983, Breakfast With Einstein, 1998 (also exec. prodr.), Hayley Wagner, Star, 1999, After Dallas, 2002; exec. prodr. (TV movie) Elvis and Me, 1988, The Road to Graceland, 1998, Finding Graceland, 1998; co-prodr.(TV mini series) Elvis, 1990; host, Elvis: The Great Performances, 1992; featured in (TV) Elvis 85, 1984, Elvis: Life and Times, 1997, After Dallas, 2002, Elvis by the Presleys, 2005, (TV mini series) Between the Lines, 2004; guest appearances include The Fall Guy, 1983, Tales from the Crypt, 1993, Touched by an Angel, 1997, Spin City, 1999, After They Were Famous, 2002, Oprah Winfrey Show, 2005; author: Elvis and Me, 1987. Amb. Dream Found., 2000—; mem. Citizen's Commn. on Human Rights. Named one of 50 Most Beautiful People in the World, People Mag., 1992. Office: Paul Bloch & Michelle Bega c/o Rogers & Cowan 8687 Melrose Ave 7th Fl West Hollywood CA 90069 Address: Norman Brokaw c/o William Morris Agency 151 El Camino Beverly Hills CA 90212 Office Phone: 310-850-4206, 310-854-8100.

PRESMANES, WILLA SUMMEROUR, behavioral health systems evaluator; b. Baton Rouge, Jan. 12, 1948; d. William Henry and Mildred Katherine (Hazen) Summerour; m. Gregory T. Presmanes, Dec. 26, 1970; 1 child, Alison. BA in Psychology, U. Ga., 1970; MEd in Counseling Psychology, Ga. State U., 1976, MA in Psychology, 1981. Cert. Marriage Enrichment. Psychiat. asst. Northside Hosp. Mental Health Ctr., Atlanta, 1971-74; program evaluator Ga. Mental Health Inst., Atlanta, 1976-79; dir. rsch. and statis.

analyst DeKalb Bd. Health, Decatur, Ga., 1979-93; behavioral health program analyst DeKalb Cmty. Svc. Bd., Decatur, Ga., 1993—. Seminar leader Millinaire DNA (Dollars, Number, Attitude), 2000—, other subjects; radio and TV segments on using your millionaire doce as a magnet to money; nat. cons./lectr. MTM Svcs. Behavioral Healthcare. Author: State of Ga. Comprehensive Service Plans, 1989, Balanced Service System Plans, 1978, Behaviorally Anchored Rating Scales, 1981, Quality Assurance Monitoring, 1977, Georgia Role Functioning Scale, 1982, Outcomes and Accountability Alert: Outcomes Measuring Daily Living Activities, 2000, The Millionaire Code: Unlocking Your Financial Personality and Making More Money, 2003; co-author: Research on Social Work Practice Reliability and Validity of the Daily Living Activities Scale: A Functional Assessment Measure for Serious Mental Disorders, 2000; pub.: Internat. Soc. Quality in Health Care 14th Book of Abstracts, 1997. Mem. Dunwoody United Meth., Atlanta, 1984—, children's cancer cure rsch. vol. Egleston Hosp. Recipient award for publ. Joint Commn. on Accreditation of Healthcare Orgns. Nat. Libr., 1998. Mem. Tri Delta Alumni Soc., Renaissance Inst. Achievements include TV and radio finance and business reports. Avocations: mountain climbing, healthcare, nutrition, exercise.

PRESNELL, JENNY LYNN, librarian; b. Cin., Jan. 24, 1961; d. Joseph Hobart and Carmen Jeanne (Thomas) P. BA in History, Miami U., 1983; MLS, Ind. U., 1984; MA in History, Xavier U., 1992. Libr. Xavier U., Cin., 1984-88, Miami U., Oxford, Ohio, 1988—. Contbr. articles to profl. jours., encys. and books. Mem.: Assn. History and Computing. Methodist. Avocations: knitting, gardening. Office: Miami U King Libr Oxford OH 45056 Office Phone: 513-529-3937. Business E-Mail: presnejl@muohio.edu.

PRESS, AIDA KABATZNICK, retired editor, poet, writer; b. Boston, Nov. 18, 1926; m. Newton Press, June 5, 1947; children: David, Dina Press Weber, Benjamin Presskreischer. BA, Radcliffe Coll., 1948. Reporter Waltham (Mass.) News-Tribune, 1960-63; freelance writer, 1960-63; editl. cons. Mass. Dept. Mental Health, Boston, 1966-72; Waltham/Watertown reporter Boston Herald Traveler, 1963-70; dir. news and publs. Harvard Grad. Sch. Design, Cambridge, Mass., 1972-78; publs. editor Radcliffe Coll., Cambridge, 1978-81, dir., editor of publs., 1981-83, editor Radcliffe Quar., 1971-93, dir. pub. info., 1983-93; cons. editor Regis Coll. Alumnae Mag., Weston, Mass., 1994. Editor emerita Radcliffe Quar., 1993—; contbr. articles to newspapers and mags. Recipient Publs. Distinction award Am. Alumni Coun., 1974, Top 5 coll. Mag., Coun. for Advancement and Support of Edn., 1984, Top 10 Univ Mags., 1991, Gold medal Coll. Mags., 1991, Alumnae Achievement award Radcliffe Coll., 1994, Radcliffe Coll. Presdl. Commendation, 1992. Mem. Phi Beta Kappa. Avocations: hiking, playing recorder.

PRESS, MICHELLE, editor; b. Memphis, Nov. 22, 1940; d. Sam and Rana (Cohen) Appelbaum; m. Roger Koontz, Jan. 2001. BA, New Sch. for Social Research, 1967. Tchr. U.S. Peace Corps, Malawi, Africa, 1962-64; copy editor Japan Quar., Tokyo, 1967-71; asst. editor Am. Scientist, New Haven, 1971-78, mng. editor, 1978-80, editor, 1981-90; mng. editor Scientific American, N.Y.C., 1990—2002, sr editor, 2002—. Mem. Am. Soc. Mag. Editors, Century Assn., Conn. Acad. Arts and Scis. Office: Scientific American 415 Madison Ave Fl 11 New York NY 10017-1179 Office Phone: 212-451-8255. Business E-Mail: mpress@sciam.com.

PRESS, TERRY, marketing executive; children: Gracie, Ethan. Head mktg. DreamWorks SKG. Faculty mem. UCLA Film Sch. Named one of most powerful women in entertainment, Hollywood Reporter, 2005. Office: DreamWorks SKG 100 Universal City Plz # 5121 Universal City CA 91608*

PRESSER, HARRIET BETTY, social studies educator; b. Bklyn., Aug. 29, 1936; d. Phillip Rubinoff and Rose (Gudowitz) Jabish; m. Neil Nathan Presser, Dec. 16, 1956 (div.); 1 child, Sheryl Lynn. BA, George Washington U., 1959; MA, U. N.C., 1962; PhD, U. Calif., Berkeley, 1969. Statistician Bur. Census, Washington, 1959; research assoc. Inst. Life Ins., N.Y.C., 1962-64; lectr. demography U. Sussex, Brighton, England, 1967-68; staff assoc. Population Council, N.Y.C., 1968-69; asst. prof. sociomed. scis. Columbia U., N.Y.C., 1969-73, assoc. prof. sociomed. scis., 1973-76; prof. sociology U. Md., College Park, 1976—99, dir. Ctr. on Population, Gender, and Social Inequality, 1988—2001, disting. faculty rsch. fellow, 1993-94, disting. univ. prof., 1999—; fellow in residence Netherlands Inst. for Advanced Study in Humanities & Social Sci., Wassenaar, The Netherlands, 1994-95. Fellow-in-residence Ctr. for Advanced Study in the Behavioral Scis., Stanford, Calif., 1986-87, 91-92, 2003-04; scholar-in-residence Russell Sage Found., NYC, 1998, 99, 2000; resident scholar Bellagio Study and Conf. Ctr., Rockefeller Found., 2000; acad. visitor Gender Inst. London Sch. Econs and Polit. Scis., 2000. Editl. bd. Time and Soc., 1991-95, Social Forces, 1984-87, Signs, 1975-85, Applied Population and Policy, 2002-, Rose Monograph Series, 2003-05, Jour. of Marriage and the Family, 2003; assoc. editor Jour. Health and Social Behavior, 1975-78; co-editor (with Gita Sen) Women's Empowerment and Demographic Processes: Moving Beyond Cairo, 2000; author: Working in a 24/7 Economy: Challenges for Am. Families, 2003; editor: Population Studies and Demographic Change, Transaction Pubs., 2005-. Nat. Inst. for Child Health and Devel. grantee, 1972-78, 83-88, Population Coun. grantee, 1976-79, NSF grantee, 1982-83, 90-94, 2000-03, Rockefeller Found. grantee, 1983-85, 88-94, William and Flora Hewlett Found. grantee, 1989—, Andrew W. Mellon Found. grantee, 1994-95, W. T. Grant Found., 1996-99, Russell Sage Found., 1976-79, 2003-04; recipient Rosabeth Moss Kanter award for excellence in work-family rsch., 2001, Lawrence R. Klein award, 2003. Fellow AAAS, Sociol. Rsch. Assn.; mem. APHA (coun. mem. population sect. 1976-79), Population Assn. Am. (bd. dirs. 1972-75, 2nd v.p. 1983, 1st v.p. 1985, pres.-elect 1988, pres. 1989), Am. Sociol. Assn. (coun. mem. at large 1990-93, chmn., coun. mem. population sect. 1978-83). Office: U Maryland Dept Sociology College Park MD 20742-0001

PRESSLER, CIARA NICOLE FREY, marketing executive, consultant; b. San Diego, Nov. 1, 1978; d. Timothy Kent and Linda Joyce Pressler, George Thomas Frey. BA in Comm., Seattle Pacific U., 2000. Performing artist, 2000—; performer, artist-in-residence Freestyle Repertory Theatre, N.Y.C., 2002—03; mktg. dir. Capes Coaching Inc., N.Y.C., 2006—. Exec. prodr. 26.2 Prodns., N.Y.C., 2004—. Author: (plays) Marathon, 2004; screenwriter, prin. actor: You Tell Me, 2004; playwright, performer: (plays) Mixed Company, 2002—04. Intern Congresswoman Carolyn B. Maloney, N.Y.C., 2005; vol. various local polit. campaigns N.Y.C., 2005—; prodr. fundraiser to stop domestic violence V-Day Brooklyn, Bklyn., 2006. Mem.: N.Y. Rd. Runners, Am. Mensa. Democrat. Avocation: running.

PRESTAGE, JEWEL LIMAR, political science professor; b. Hutton, La., Aug. 12, 1931; d. Brudis L. and Sallie Bell (Johnson) Limar; m. James J. Prestage, Aug. 12, 1953; children— Terri, James, Eric, Karen, Jay. BA, So. U., Baton Rouge, 1951; MA, U. Iowa, 1952, PhD, 1954; LHD (hon.), U. D.C., 1994, Loyola U., Chgo., 1999; LLD (hon.), Spelman Coll., 1999. Assoc. prof. polit. sci. Prairie View (Tex.) Coll., 1954-55, 56; assoc. prof. polit. sci. So. U., 1956-57, 58-62, prof., 1962—, chairperson dept., 1965-83, dean pub. policy and urban affairs, 1983-89, dist. prof. emeritus, dean emeritus pub. policy, 1989—; prof. polit. sci. Prairie View U., 1989-90; dean Benjamin Banneker Honors College, Prairie View (Tex.) Coll., 1990-98, prof. political sci., 1998—; disting. prof. emeritus polit. sci. Benjamin Banneker Honors Coll., 2000—. Chmn. La. adv. com. to U.S. Commn. on Civil Rights, 1975-85; mem., chmn. nat. adv. coun. on women's ednl. programs U.S. Dept. Edn., 1980-82; dist. vis. prof. U. Iowa, 1987-88. Author: (with M. Githens) A Portrait of Marginality: Political Behavior of the American Woman, 1976; contbr. articles to profl. jours. Rockefeller fellow, 1951-52; NSF fellow, 1964; Ford Found. postdoctoral fellow, 1969-70 Mem. NAACP, Am. Polit. Sci. Assn. (v.p. 1974-75, Frank Goodnow award 1998), So. Polit. Sci. Assn. (pres. 1975-76, Manning Daner award 1998), Nat. Conf. Black Polit. Scientists (pres. 1976-77), Nat. Assn. African Am. Honors Programs (pres. 1993-94), Am. Soc. for Pub. Adminstrn. (pres. La. chpt. 1988-89, nat. exec. coun. 1989-90), Policy Studies Orgn. (exec. coun. 2000), Links Inc., Alpha Kappa Alpha. Home: 11114 Wortham Blvd Houston TX 77065 Office: So Univ PO Box 125 Prairie View TX 77446-0125

PRESTINE, JOAN SINGLETON, writer, educator, editor; b. Salt Lake City, Mar. 11, 1944; d. Herbert William and Frances Bowdidge Singleton; m. Douglas C. Prestine, Apr. 5, 1963; children: Scott, Deb, Jeffrey. BA, U. So. Calif., L.A., 1965. Freelance editor Children's Picture Book, 1989—. Pub. cons., 1987—; lectr. Santa Monica Coll., Pierce Coll., West LA Coll., Ventura Coll., Coll. of Canyons, Moorpark Coll., Oxnard Coll., Learning Tree U., U. Colo., Denver U., 1987—. Author: (picture books My Special Feelings series) I Want This and This and This, 1987, Love Me Anyway, 1987, My Parents Go On a Trip, 1987, Someone Special Died, 1987, Me First, 1987, Sometimes I'm Afraid, 1987, Match Who You Are With What You Do, 1987, How to Write Picture Books for Fun and Profit, 1987, Chipper Chipmunk Cruises, 1989, (picture books Kids Have Feelings Too series) Someone Special Died, 1993, 2003, Sometimes I Feel Awful, 1993, 2003, It's Hard to Share My Teacher, 1994, 2003, Mom and Dad Break Up, 1996, 2003, Moving Is Hard, 1997, 2003, (resource guides) Family Day Care Activities from A to Z, 1989, Earthquake Preparedness, 1990, Helping Children Cope with Death, 1993, Helping Children Understand Their Feelings, 1993, Helping Children Share Their Teacher, 1994, Helping Children Understand Divorce, 1996, Helping Children Cope With Moving, 1997, Easy Activities for Every Kid, 2001. With Jr. League LA, 1976—, St. Joseph Ctr. chair, 1991—, sustainer pres., 2004—; founder Investments Plus, 1983, pres., 1983—86, rec. sec., 1986—; benefactor Huntington Libr.; bd. mem. Parrots Internat., 2005—; mem. Boy Scouts Am., 1972—84, Girl Scouts Am., 1975—80, Peterson Automotive Mus., Nat. Charity League, Checkered Flag 200, 2003—, Pres. Cir. Orthop. Hosp., 2004—; life mem. 11-99 Found., 2002—. Named PTA Parent of Yr., Bellagio Rd. Sch., 1977, Parent of Yr., Parent Tchr. Student Assn., U. HS, 1983; recipient Parenting Shelf, Parents Choice Mag., 1994, 1996, Vol. Cir., St. Joseph Ctr., 1996, Dir.'s award, Early Childhood News, 1997, Carolyn Helman Lichtenberg Crest award, 2002. Mem.: FOCAL, Westside Writer's Guild, Pubs. Mktg. Assn., Soc. Children's Book Writers and Illustrators, So. Calif. Children's Book Writers and Illustrators, Internat. Reading Assn., Childrens Author Network, Book Publicists of So. Calif., Authors Guild, Nat. Assn. Edn. of Young Children (life), Pi Beta Phi (alumni bd., pres. 1996—99, program chair 1993—96). Avocations: car rallies, reading, travel, walking. Office: 2070 South 7th Street, Suite E San Jose CA 95112 Personal E-mail: joanprestine@msn.com.

PRESTO, CATHERINE ANN (KAY PRESTO), media specialist, consultant; b. Erie, Pa., Apr. 26, 1929; d. Frank Peter and Mary Alice Vogel; m. Leon Anthony Presto, Apr. 14, 1951; children: Deborah Ann, Richard Anthony, Lee Ann, Anthony Frank. Student, Chaffey Coll., Calif. State Poly. U., Calif. State U., San Bernardino. Cert. tchr. jr. coll. adult edn. Newcaster, creator, supr. spl. mktg. surveys Sta. KSOM Radio; med. features editor Italics of Health Mag. Riverside Advt. Agy.; pub. info. supr. L.A. County Fair; mgr. pub. rels. dept. Theta Cable TV; media rels. mgr. Ont. Conv. Ctr.; owner Presto Prodns. Talk Show Host WICU-TV; comml. actress; prod. and broadcaster CNN & ESPN Speedweek, Mut. Radio, ABC, NBC, WBBM, KFWB radio networks; spkr. in field. Co-author (non-fiction): Power Basics of Auto Racing, 1986 (2nd place nat., 1987); contbr. articles to books and mags.; co-author: Wake Up.Live the Life You Love - Giving Gratitude, 2005 (No. 6 Barnes & Noble Best Seller List). Promoter House of Ruth Women's Shelter, Claremont, Calif., 1991; condr. drive for supplies Crossroads, Inc., Claremont, Calif., 1998; condr. political campaign Mayor of Ontario, Calif., 1971; bd. dirs. A Spl. Wish Found., Inc. Calif. Divsn., 1998—99; adv. bd. dirs. Inland Valley Daily Bulletin, Ontario, Calif., 1996. Recipient Age of Achievement award, Nordstrom Dept. Stores, 1994, Ava Doner Pioneer award, Women's Referral Svc., Calif., 2001, Outstanding Alumni award, Villa Maria Acad., 2003, Woman of Achievement award, NAFE, 2005, Learning More, Earning More award, CollegeCareerSource.com. Mem.: NAFE, AFTRA (newscaster, sportscaster), Press Club Southern Calif. (former bd. dirs., scholarship chmn.), Am. Writers and Broadcasters Assn. (past western v.p.), World Referral Svc., For You Network, Toastmasters Internat. (v.p. pub. rels. dist. 12, Penny Cole award Dist. 12 2006). Avocations: travel, classical music, reading. Office Phone: 909-985-3041. Business E-Mail: prestoprod@juno.com.

PRESTON, ELIZABETH A., psychologist; b. Missoula, Mont., May 9, 1957; d. Jay William and Elizabeth (Cummings) P.; children, Katherine Jennifer Lee, Jayson Douglas Lee. BA summa cum laude, U. Minn., 1979; PhD, Princeton U., 1984; Postdoctoral Cert., Calif. Sch. Profl. Psychology, 1988. Postdoctoral intern El Dorado County, Placerville, Calif., 1984-85, San Mateo (Calif.) County, 1985-87; adj. faculty Calif. Sch. Profl. Psychology, Berkeley, 1987; postdoctoral intern Kaiser Permanent, Santa Rosa, Calif., 1988-89; therapist Waldenhouse, Inc., San Francisco, 1989; clin. dir. Alinda Youth Svcs., Fairfield, Calif., 1990; therapist Kairos Unltd., Oakland, Calif.; pvt. practice Oakland, Calif., 1994—. Activist No. Calif. War Tax Resistors, Berkeley, 1991. NSF fellow, 1980-83; U. Mont. scholar, 1975-76, 77-78. Mem. Am. Psychol. Assn., Western Psychol. Assn., Phi Beta Kappa, Phi Kappa Phi. Office: 4100-10 Redwood Rd 126 Oakland CA 94619 Office Phone: 510-482-5344.

PRESTON, FRANCES WILLIAMS, music company executive; b. Nashville, Aug. 27, 1934; children: Kirk, David, Donald. Degree (hon.), Lincoln Coll., Ill., Berklee Sch. Music. With BMI (Broadcast Music Inc.), Nashville, 1958—, v.p., 1964-85, sr. v.p. performing rights N.Y.C., 1985, exec. v.p., CEO, 1986, pres., CEO, 1986—2004, pres. emeritus, 2004—. Bd. dirs. Bionovo Inc., 2006—. Mem. Film, Entertainment and Music Commn. Adv. Council State of Tenn.; founding mem. bd. dirs. Leadership Nashville; past pres. bd. dirs. John Work Meml. Found.; chmn. bd. dirs. Country Music Found., Inc., 1983-85, trustee, past pres., chmn. bldg. com.; mem. Commn. on White House Record Library, Carter adminstrn., Pres.'s Panama Canal Study Com., Carter adminstrn.; bd. dirs. Rock & Roll Hall of Fame; mem. adminstrv. council Internat. Confedn. of Socs. of Authors and Composers; v.p. Nat. Music Council; past bd. dirs. Peabody Awards; hon. trustee Nat. Acad. Popular Music; pres. T.J. Martell Fedn. for Leukemia, Cancer and AIDS Rsch.; established Frances Williams Preston Rsch. Labs. for T.J. Martell Fedn., 1993; bd. dirs. R&B Found. Recipient achievement award Women's Equity Action League, spl. citation award NATAS, Golden Baton award Young Musicians Found., Humanitarian award Internat. Achievement in Arts award, 1995, Creative Achievement award Elaine Kaufman Cultural Ctr., 1996, Lester Sill Humanitarian award, 1996, Nat. Trustees award Grammys, 1998; named one of Am.'s 50 Most Powerful Women Ladies' Home Jour.; named to Country Music Hall of Fame. Mem. Country Music Assn. (life mem. bd. dirs., Irving Waugh Award of Excellence), Nashville Symphony Assn. (past sec., bd. dirs.), NARAS Found. (bd. dirs., pres.'s adv. bd.), Nashville Songwriters Assn. (life mem., bd. dirs.), Gospel Music Assn. (life mem. bd., past chmn., past pres.), Am. Women in Radio and TV (past nat. dir.). Clubs: (Friars Found. Applause award). Lodges: Rotary (1st woman mem. Nashville club), Friars. Presbyterian. Office: BMI 320 W 57th St Fl 3 New York NY 10019-3790

PRESTON, JOAN MURIEL, psychology professor, communications educator; b. St. Thomas, Ont., Can., July 28, 1939; d. George Arthur and Vera Victoria (Atkinson) P.; divorced; children: Eric, Stephen. BA with Honors, U. Western Ontario, 1964, MA, 1965, PhD, 1967. Asst. prof. U. Toronto (Can.), 1967-71, Brock U., St. Catharines, Ont., Can., 1971-73, assoc. prof., 1973-78, prof. dept. psychology and comms. studies, 1988—2005; prof. emerita, 2005. Co-founder Comm. Studies Program Brock U., St. Catharines, 1983; head TV Rsch. Unit Brock U., 1987-2005; ptnr. No. Web Design, St. Catharines, 1996-99. Contbr. numerous articles to profl. jours., chpt. to books. Mem. APA, Internat. Comm. Assn., Can. Psychol. Assn. (Sci. Affairs Com., 1995-99). Office: Brock U PO Box 1600 Lewiston NY 14092-5000 Business E-Mail: jpreston@brocku.ca.

PRESTON, KELLY, actress; b. Honolulu, Oct. 13, 1962; m. Kevin Gage, 1986 (div. 1988); 1 child; m. John Travolta, 1991; children: Jett, Ella Bleu. Student, U. So. Calif., UCLA. Represented by Internat. Creative Mgmt., Beverly Hills, Calif. Actor: (films) Mischief, 1985, Space Camp, 1986, 52 Pick-Up, 1986, A Tiger's Tale, 1987, Spellbinder, 1988, Twins, 1988, The Experts, 1989, Run, 1991, Love is a Gun, 1994, Jerry Macguire, 1996, Citizen Ruth, 1997, Addicted to Love, 1997, Nothing to Lose, 1997, The Holy Man, 1998, Jack Frost, 1998, For Love of the Game, 1999, Battlefield Earth, 2000, Daddy and Them, 2001, View from the Top, 2003, What a Girl Wants, 2003, The Cat in the Hat, 2003, Eulogy, 2004, Return to Sender, 2004, Sky High, 2005. Involved with Fight for Kids.

PRESZLER, SHARON MARIE, psychiatric home health nurse; b. LA; d. Rudolph Edward Wirth and Bertha Marie (Thornton) Paddock; m. Alan Preszler, Aug. 31, 1966; children: Brent, Alison. BS in Nursing, Loma Linda (Calif.) U., 1963, MS in Marriage and Family Counseling, 1978. RN, Calif., Idaho; cert. pub. health nurse. Team leader med. fl. Loma Linda U. Hosp., 1963-64; office nurse Dr. Lowell Johnson, Redlands, Calif., 1964-65, Dr. H. Glenn Stevens, Loma Linda, 1965-72; team leader women's oncology Loma Linda U. Hosp., 1974-75; pub. health nurse Riverside County Pub. Health, Hemet, Calif., 1975-78; nurse, staff psychologist Dept. Health and Welfare, Idaho Falls, Idaho, 1989-91, Boise, Idaho, 1991-92; psychiat. nurse Cmty. Home Health, Boise, 1992-94, Mercy Home Health & Hospice, Nampa, Idaho, 1995-99; hospice nurse, home health nurse Mercy Med. Ctr., 1995-99, personal care supr. nurse for medicaid, 1996—; case mgr. Assisted Living of Idaho, 2001, Ada Can, 2001—05; supervising nurse A Full Life, 2005—. Instr. YWCA, Bartlesville, Okla., 1984-88; tchr. Bartlesville Pub. Sch., 1984-88, Heritage Retirement, Boise, 1994. Contbr. to Focus, 1986. Mem. Am. Assn. Marriage and Family Therapy, Sigma Theta Tau. Avocations: reading, tennis.

PRETE, GAYLE COMPTON, advertising and marketing executive; b. Washington, Nov. 28, 1956; d. Walter Dale and Jeanne (Parker) C.; m. Lanny Ross Huff, May 22, 1982 (div. 2002); m. James G. Prete, May 30, 2005. B in Gen. Studies, U. Mich., 1978. Mgr. br. merchandising CBS Records, Chgo., 1978, local promotion, mktg. mgr. Indpls., Boston, N.Y.C., 1978-81; spl. projects supr. Pickwick Internat. Musicland Group, Mpls., 1981-82; account exec. Campbell-Mithun Advt., Mpls., 1982-85; mktg. mgr., communications Universal Foods Corp., Milw., 1985-86; nat. advt. mgr. Thorobred Advt. Agy. (Jockey Internat., Inc.), Wis., 1986-88, dir. consumer and trade advt., 1988-89, v.p. advt., 1990-92; dir. mktg./advt. Allen-Edmonds Shoe Co., Port Washington, Wis., 1993-95; v.p., dir. Fin. Mktg. Plus Direct Mktg. Group, Libertyville, Ill., 1995-97; dir. mktg. & merchandising AR Accessories Group Inc., Milw., 1997-98; v.p. creative svcs. Tucker-Knapp Integrated Mktg. Comms., Schaumburg, Ill., 1998-2000; sr. mgr. creative svcs. Discover Fin. Svcs. (Morgan Stanley Dean Witter), Riverwoods, Ill., 2000—04, dir. mktg. prodn. svcs., 2004—. V.p., sec. Java Masters, Inc., 1992-2005. Mem. Traffic Audit Bur. for Media Measurement (bd. dirs. 1988-93), Assn. Nat. Advertisers (print adv. com., out of home advt. com. 1989-92). Avocations: dance, gymnastics, conga drumming, autocross. Office: Discover Fin Svcs 2500 Lake Cook Rd # 2W Deerfield IL 60015-3851 Personal E-mail: javanuts@aol.com. Business E-Mail: gaylehuff@discoverfinancial.com.

PREUCIL, DORIS BOGEN, music educator; b. Milw., Wis., Dec. 10, 1932; d. Walter Leopold and Adele Anne (Jarvis) Bogen; m. William Warren Preucil, Sept. 4, 1954; children: William, Jr., Walter, Anne, Jeanne. MusB with distinction, Eastman Sch. Music, Rochester, N.Y., 1954; MusM, U. Iowa, 1968; studied with Shinichi Suzuki, Talent Edn. Inst., Japan, 1982. Violinist Rochester Philharm. Orch., 1952—54, Nat. Symphony Orch., Washington, 1954—56; freelance violinist & tchr. Iowa City, 1956—72; asst. prof. Western Ill. U., Macomb, 1972—76; founder, dir., master tchr. Preucil Sch. Music, Iowa City, 1975—97, dir. emerita, tchr., 1997—. Suzuki Professorial chair U. Wis., Stevens Point, 1986; hon. bd. mgrs. Eastman Sch. Music, Rochester, 2005—. Musician (1st violinist): Milw. Symphony, 1948—50, Rochester Philharm., 1952—54, Tri-City Symphony, 1958—72; concertmaster:, 1971—72; musician: Eastman Faculty Quartet, 1951—54, Lydian Trio, 1972—75, Preucil Family Players, 1975—84; author, editor: The Suzuki Viola Sch., 1976—, arranger: The Solo with Orchestra series 2004-. Trustee Nat. Guild Cmty. Schs. Arts, 1988—91; bd. dirs. Amateur Chamber Music Found., 1998—; elder, deacon 1st Presbyn. Ch., Iowa City, 1964—. Named Tchr. of the Yr., Iowa State Music Tchrs. Assn., 2005; recipient Lifetime Achievement award, Eastman Sch. Music, 2004. Mem.: Internat. Suzuki Assn. (founding bd. mem. 1983—95), Suzuki Assn. Am. (cert. tchr., trainer 1980—, pres. 1982—84, Disting. Svc. award 1992), Rotary (mem. music commn. 1989—). Avocations: music, reading, travel. Home: 317 Windsor Dr Iowa City IA 52245 Personal E-mail: wdpreucil@mchsi.com.

PREUDHOMME, MARCIA DENRIQUE, finance company executive, writer; b. San Fernando, Trinidad, West Indies, Nov. 12, 1966; d. Ronald and Sarah Preudhomme. Diploma in gen. draftsmanship, San Fernando Tech. Inst., Trinidad, 1991; cert. in stage mgmt., U. West Indies, Trinidad, 1992; student, Montgomery Coll., 1995. Draftsman San Fernando City Hall, 1994; mgr., team developer Brinker Internat., Inc., Washington, 1997—99; referral coord. Washington Hosp. Ctr., 1999—2001; assoc. BDO Seidman, LLP, Bethesda, Md., 2001—05. Author: Reflections of Realism, 2003, Stranger Than Fiction, 2004 (Urban Spectrum Newspaper award, 2006). Recipient Editor's Choice, Internat. Libr. Poetry, 2003. Avocations: reading, board games, philosophy, exercise. Office Phone: 202-546-1708.

PREUSS, MARY HERGE, Spanish educator; b. Ellwood City, Pa., Aug. 04; d. William J. and Imogene (Lewis) Herge; m. Franklin A. Preuss, Mar. 2l, l964. BA, U. Pitts., l959, MEd, l965, cert. Latin Am. studies, l977, PhD, l98l. Cert. Spanish and English tchr., Pa. Tchr. Spanish Mars (Pa.) Area High Sch., 1959-62, Wilkinsburg High Sch., Pitts., 1962-64, North Hills High Sch., Pitts., 1967-77; lectr. Spanish Chatham Coll., Pitts., 1977, Carlow Coll., Pitts.; prof. Spanish Geneva Coll., Beaver Falls, Pa., 1981-89, chmn. dept. fgn. langs., coord. Latin Am. bus. studies, 1983-89; prof. Pa. State U., McKeesport, 1989—, chair fgn. langs. Author: Gods of the Popol Vuh, 1988, Dioses del Popol Vuh, 1988, Yucatan Maya Stories: From Chen Ja' to the Milpa, 2005; editor Hummingbird Lore and Other Selected Papers from the VI Internat. Symposium on Latin Am. Indian Lits., 1989, LAIL SPEAKS: Selected Papers from the VII Internat. Symposium on Latin Am. Indian Lits., 1989, Past, Present and Future, Selected Papers on Latin Am. Indian Lit., 1991, Stories Yucatec Maya: From Chen Ja' to Milpa, 2005; contbr. numerous articles to profl. jours. Mem. Ross Twp. (Pa.) Rep. Com., l970-79, Ross Twp. Drug Abuse Team, l972-75; bd. dirs. North Hills Youth Ministry, Pitts., l970-75, Friends Hillman Libr., U. Pitts., 1976-80. Am. Philos. Soc. grantee, Geneva Coll. grantee, Pa. State U. grantee. Mem. DAR, Latin Am. Indian Lit. Assn. (founding pres. 1983-87, bd. dirs. 1982—, symposium chmn. 1983-95, editor newsletter 1982-85, editor Latin Am. Indian Lit. Jour. 1985—), MLA, Mid-Atlantic Coun. Latin Am. Studies, Delta Kappa Gamma (scholarship chmn. 1979-80, Laura Braun award 1978, 79). Lutheran. Avocations: travel, reading, gardening, guitar. Home: 145 Timberlane Dr Pittsburgh PA 15229-1058 Office: Pa State U Dept Spanish 6000 University Dr Mc Keesport PA 15132 E-mail: mhpl@psu.edu.

PREVE, ROBERTA JEAN, librarian, researcher; b. Wilmington, Del., Feb. 27, 1954; d. Burton Hugo Sanders and Betsy (Kan) Klein; m. Thomas Alan Preve, Sept. 23, 1978; children: Stephanie Jean, Melanie Marie. BA, U. NH, 1975; MLS, Simmons Coll., 1985. Rschr. U. N.H., Durham, 1974-75; rsch. asst. Eikonix Corp., Burlington, Mass., 1976-79; asst. cashier, credit dept. mgr. Dania (Fla.) Bank, 1980-83; rsch. assoc. Ctr. for Strategy Rsch., Cambridge, Mass., 1984-86; info. svcs. Braxton Assocs., Boston, 1986-87; mktg. adminstr. Summit Tech., Waltham, Mass., 1987-91; mgr. market rsch. AT&T Capital Corp., Framingham, Mass., 1991-95; mgr. Bus. Info. Ctr. Raytheon Co., Lexington, Mass., 1995—. Co-owner T&R Pest Mgmt., Attleboro, Mass., 1988—95. Mem. Spl. Libr. Assn., New England Online (dir., logistics chair 1986-90), Beta Phi Mu. Avocations: hiking, reading, needlecrafts, sports. Office: Raytheon Co 235 Presidential Way Woburn MA 01801 Office Phone: 339-645-8707. Business E-Mail: roberta_j_preve@raytheon.com.

PREWITT, JEAN, not-for-profit organization executive; Degree, Harvard U.; degree in law, Georgetown U. Formerly lawyer Donovan Leisure Newton & Irvine; sr. v.p., gen. counsel United Internat. Pictures, 1982—89; with Nat. Telecomm. and Info. Adminstrn. U.S. Dept. Commerce, 1989—94; prin. Podesta Assocs., Washington, 1994—99; pres. Ind. Film & TV Alliance, L.A., 2000—01, CEO, 2001—; chair Film LA, LA, 2006—. Pres. Casa De Los Amigos, LA, 2003—. Adv. bd. Friends of Cancer Rsch., Washington, 2003—. Office: 10850 Wilshire Blvd 9th Fl Los Angeles CA 90024-4321 Business E-Mail: jprewitt@ifta-online.org.

PREY, BARBARA ERNST, artist; b. N.Y.C., Apr. 17, 1957; d. Herbert Henry and Margaret (Joubert) Ernst; m. Jeffrey Drew Prey, Jan. 11, 1986; children: Austin William Ernst Prey, Emily Elizabeth Prey. BA with honors, Williams Coll., 1979; MDiv, Harvard U., 1986. Sales staff Tiffany and Co., N.Y.C., summer 1977; intern Met. Mus. Art, N.Y.C., summer 1979; pers. asst. Prince Albrecht Castell, Castell, Germany, 1980-81; with modern painting dept. Sotheby's Auction House, N.Y.C., 1981-82; sales asst. Marlborough Gallery, N.Y.C., 1982; tchg. asst. Boston Coll., 1984, Harvard U., Cambridge, Mass., 1984-85; vis. lectr. Tainan (Taiwan) Coll. and Sem., 1986-87; artist Oyster Bay, NY, 1987—. Artist-in-residence Westminster Sch., Simsbury, Conn., 1998; art juror Washington and Jefferson Coll., Washington, 1990; chmn.'s coun. Heckscher Mus.; presenter in field. Illustrator Boys Harbor Cookbook, 1988, A Dream Became You, A City Grows Up, 1991, (cover) Am. Artist Mag., 1994, Barbara Ernst Prey: Watercolors, 1998, Internat. Art Newspaper, 2001, N.Y. Post, 2001, N.Y. Daily News, (PBS) True North, 2001, (PBS) Metro Section, 2001, Arts and Antiques Mag., 2001, 2003, Barbara Ernst Prey: A Trace in the Mind, 2002, NY Times, 2002; illustrator: cover NY Times, 2003; illustrator (cover) NY Times, 2004, 2005, Newsday, 2002, Artwork in the American Embassy Prague, 2002, Artwork in the American Embassy Oslo, 2003, The Robb Report, 2003, LA Times, 2004, White House Christmas Card, 2003, The New Yorker, 2004, Larry King Live CNN, 2004, (PBS) WLIW-NY, 2005, Style Sect., Washington Post, 2005, The New York Times, 2005, NPR, 2005; one-woman shows include Harvard-Yale-Princeton Club, Pitts., 1991, Jensen Fine Arts, NYC, 1999, 2001, exhibited in group shows at Kennedy Space Ctr., Nassau County, N.Y., 1988, Nat. Arts Club, N.Y.C., 1988, Gallery One, Rockland, Maine, 1992, Williams Coll., Williamstown, Mass., 1993, Johnstown (Pa.) Art Mus., 1993, Blair Art Mus., Holidaysburg, Pa., 1993, Phila. Mus. Art Gallery, 1995, Mus. Fine Arts, Westmoreland Mus. Am. Art, Greensburg, Pa., 1996 (Best in Show award), Mus. the Southwest, Midland, Tex., Farnsworth Mus. Art, Rockland, Maine, 1997, Guild Hall Mus., East Hampton, NY, 1998, Portland (Maine) Mus. Art, 1998, U.S. Embassy, Prague, 2002, Heckscher Mus. Art, Huntington, N.Y., 2002, Guild Hall Mus., East Hampton, NY, 2002, 2004, Gilcrease Mus., Tulsa, 2002, NASA Commn.: The Internat. Space Station, 2003, The White House, Collection of Pres. and Mrs. George Bush, 2003, 2004, Kennedy Space Ctr., 2003—06, U.S. Embassy, Oslo, Prague, Liberia, Belarus, 2003, 2004, 2005, U. S. Embassy, Paris, Madrid, 2006, NASA Commn X-43.: Columbia Tribute, 2004, US Embassy, Minsk, 2004, Madrid, 2006, Paris, 2006, NASA Commn: Shuttle Discovery Relaunch, U.S. Embassy, 2005, Kennedy Space Ctr., 2006, Represented in permanent collections Pres. and Mrs. George Bush Farnsworth Mus. Art, NASA, Kennedy Space Ctr., displayed 1997 Holiday Card on 80,000 screens worldwide Bloomberg Bus. Newss; featured on Fox TV News, 1999; contbr. to popular mags., local newspapers. Class agt. Williams Coll., Williamstown, Mass., 1981—91; mem. chmn.'s coun. Heckscher Mus.; lectr. Nat. Gallery Art, Washington, 2005; mem. chmn.'s coun. Heckscher Mus.; active 1st Presby. Ch., Oyster Bay, NY. Fulbright scholar, Germany, 1979-80; grantee Roothbert Fund, Chataugua, N.Y., 1982-84; recipient Ch. History award Gordan-Conwell Sem., S. Hamilton, Mass., 1984, Henry Luce Found., Taiwan, 1986-87, Jean Thoburn award, 1994, Women of Distinction award, N.Y. State Senate, 2004, Women of Distinction award, Distinction Mag., 2005. Mem. Pitts. Watercolor Soc. (Jean Thoburn award 1994), Nat. Mus. Women in the Arts. Avocations: tennis, skiing, birdwatching, reading, squash. Home and Office: 22 Pearl St Oyster Bay NY 11771-2305 E-mail: bprey@optonline.net.

PREY, YVONNE MARY, real estate broker; b. Milw., Mar. 14, 1945; d. Irvin Raymond Reindl and Viola Rose Schneider Maresh; m. John V. Prey, Sept. 2, 1967 (div. Dec. 1984); children: James Carter, Jacquelyn Rue. BS in Sociology, U. Wis., Oshkosh, 1967, postgrad., 1967-69. Lic. real estate broker, Wis.; cert. residential specialist, relocation profl. Social worker Winnebago State Hosp., Oshkosh, 1967-69, Div. Family Svcs., State of Wis., Fond du Lac, 1969-72, Green Bay, 1972-75; real estate broker Action Realty, Inc., Wausau, Wis., 1975-81, Williams Realty, Inc., Wausau, 1982-92, RE/MAX of Wausau, 1992—. Active Habitat for Humanity, Friends of Wausau Hist. Landmarks; sponsor Wis. River Valley Jour. Mem. NAFE, LWV, Wausau Area C. of C. (bd. dirs. Coun. Women Bus. Owners 1990—, Amb. 1975-89, edn. com.), Marathon County Hist. Soc., Wausau Bd. Realtors, Wis. Realtors Assn., Realtors Nat. Mktg. Inst. Roman Catholic. Avocations: reading, gardening, gourmet food preservation. Office: RE/MAX of Wausau 1314 Grand Ave Wausau WI 54403-6672

PREYSZ, SANDRA, music educator; BA, U. Utah, 1973. Cert. tchr. music, profl. piano Music Tchrs. Nat. Assn. Pvt. piano tchr., Salt Lake City, 1977—. Mem. Utah Music Tchrs. Assn. (state bd. dirs., membership chair 1995—), Utah Fedn. Music Club (state bd. dirs., Nat. Festival chmn. 2003—), Nat. Fedn. Music Clubs (bd. dirs. 2003—, nat. festivals chmn., 2003-). Avocations: skiing, sailing, tennis. Personal E-mail: sandrapreysz@msn.com.

PRIBANICH, CHERYL MARIE, music educator; b. Allentown, Pa., Jan. 6, 1955; d. Ronald Earl and Isabel Marie Maurey; m. Mark Michael Pribanich, Aug. 20, 1977; children: Scott Michael, Jenna Marie, Steven Mark. BS Music Edn., Ind. U. of Pa., 1976; M of Music Edn., Temple U., 1982. Music tchr. Parkland Sch. Dist., Orefield, Pa., 1977—78, Allentown (Pa.) Sch. Dist., 1979—. Organist, choir dir. Boulevard E.C. Ch., Allentown, Pa., 1984—92; musician Mcpl., Pioneer, Marine Bands, Allentown, 1970—86. Asst. scout master and troop com. chmn. Boy Scouts of Am., Allentown, 1999—, counselor, 1998—, com. mem., 1997. Mem.: Nat. Edn. Assn., Allentown Edn. Assn., Pa. Music Educators Assn., Pa. State Edn. Assn., Music Educators Nat. Conf., Am. Fed. Musicians. Avocations: singing, needlepoint, reading, performing. Home: 3621 Manchester Rd Allentown PA 18104 Office: Allentown Sch Dist 31 N Penn St Allentown PA 18102 Business E-Mail: pribanichc@allentownsd.org.

PRIBBLE, ELIZABETH J., retired airline administrator; b. Dixon, Ill., Oct. 8, 1929; d. Steve John and Isabel Elizabeth Gall; m. Robert Isom Pribble, Sept. 4, 1954 (dec. Dec. 1970); children: Stephanie Catherine Kerstetter, John Patrick. BS in Edn., No. Ill. U., 1951. Tchr. h.s. Milledgeville (Ill.) Schs., 1951-52; stewardess TACA Internat. Airlines, New Orleans, 1952-54; tool planner Rohr Aircraft Corp., Riverside, Calif., 1954-59; documents libr. U. Calif., Riverside, 1961-66; flight attendant instr. West Coast Airlines, Seattle, 1966-68; flight attendant mgr. Northwest Airlines, Seattle, 1968-94. Campaign mgr. City Coun., Federal Way, Wash., 1995; safety com. advisor Northwest Airlines, Inc., Seattle, 1991-94. Commr., Fire Dept., Federal Way, 1996; mem. Human Svcs. Commn., Federal Way, 1995-98; mem. social justice com. St. Vincent DePaul Ch., 1998—; vol. St. Francis Hosp. Mem. AAUW (bd. dirs. 1995—, v.p. membership), St. Francis Hosp. Vols., Alpha Sigma Alpha (Alumnae Star award 1995). Roman Catholic. Avocations: volunteer work, coin collecting/numismatics, reading, travel. Home: 4301 40th Ave NE Tacoma WA 98422-2492

PRIBBLE, GHADA KHOURY, music educator, singer; b. Amman, Jordan, Feb. 23, 1974; d. Nadeem Wadie Khoury and Nabila Andoni Dabbas; m. Jeffrey Stephen Pribble, Sept. 4, 1996. BS in Music Edn., Pensacola Christian Coll., Fla., 1997, MA in Music Performance, 2000. Mem. voice faculty Pensacola Christian Coll., 2000—03; elem. music tchr. Escambia County Sch. Dist., Pensacola, 2005—. Pres. chorus Pensacola Opera Co., 2006—; counselor Day Camp Sunshine, Liberty Corner, NJ, 2001—02, asst. dir., 2003—04. Singer: (opera and musical theater prodns.) Lucia di Lammermoor, Carmen, Madame Butterfuly, The Elixir of Love, Tosca, Ruddigore, others. Mem.: Music Tchr. Assn. Office Phone: 850-595-6810.

PRICE, ALICE LINDSAY, writer; b. Augusta, Ga., Oct. 21, 1927; d. William Lloyd and Orlana Jerome (Gould) P. BA in Art English Lit., Okla. State U., 1949; MA in English, U. Tulsa, 1970. Mus. asst. Philbrook Art Mus., Tulsa, 1949-51; recreation supr. U.S. Army Europe, 1951-54; neighborhood ctr. dir. City of Monterey (Calif.) Parks and Recreation Dept., 1955-59; art gallery dir., co-owner Gallerie Quais de la Roquette, Arles, France, 1960-62; program dir. City of Tulsa (Okla.) Parks and Recreation Dept., 1963-69; instr. English lit. and creative writing Holland Hall Sch., Tulsa, 1970-86; artist-in residence Okla. State Arts Coun., Oklahoma City, 1986-91; scholar in residence Tulsa City-County Libr. of NEH, Tulsa/Washington, 1988, 90, 91; pub. HCE Publs./ Riverrun Press, Tulsa, 1974—. Acquisitions editor Coun. Oak Books, Tulsa, 1986-89; lectr. Gilcrease Inst., Tulsa, 1984, 86, 90, 94, Trumpeter Swan Soc., Mpls., 1997, Kans. State U., Manhattan, 1997. Author: (poetry) Faces of the Waterworld, 1970, Our Dismembered Shadow, 1981 (Pegasus award 1981); author/illustrator Swans of the World: Nature, Hist., Myth, Art, 1994 (Feldman award 1993), Cranes: The Noblest Flyers in Natural History and Cultural Lore, 2001; editor Tulsa Pub. Artworks, 2006. Mem. Swan Lake Waterfowl Soc., Tulsa, 1986-2000; mem. lit. arts com. Arts and Humanities Coun., 1990—; creative writing workshop dir. Tulsa Ctr. Phys. Ltd., Tulsa, 1990-2000. First pl. Folger scholarship Kans. City Art Inst., 1945; grantee Arts and Humanities Coun., 1990, 92. Mem. Trumpeter Swan Soc., Author's Guild, Internat. Wild Waterfowl Assn., Tulsa Artists Coalition (First Pl. 1997), Living Arts (poetry coord. 1978-85), Phi Beta Kappa. Avocations: travel, listening music, photography. Office: HCE Pubs/Riverrun Arts 3113 S Florence Ave Tulsa OK 74105-2407 Office Phone: 918-748-4411.

PRICE, ALICIA HEMMALIN, retired psychotherapist, alcohol/drug abuse services professional; b. New Bedford, Mass., Nov. 24, 1937; d. William Alton Disbury and Hazel Rogers; m. John Paul Hemmalin, Aug. 11, 1957 (div. 1970); m. John Barrett Price, Nov. 3, 1983 (dec. 1998); children: Karen, Roxanne, Eric. Student, Mass. Coll. Art, 1957—58; BA in Psychology/Art, U. R.I., 1972; MA in Counseling, R.I. Coll., 1978; cert. Jungian/Depth Psychology Counseling, Interfaith Counseling Ctr., Providence, 1990. Cert. chem. dependency profl. Internat. Cert. Reciprocity Consortium for Alcoholism and Other Drug Dependencies. Therapist creative arts Health Care Industry, RI, 1976—87, Mass.; family counselor Family Focus Program, Edgehill Newport, RI, 1987—93; social worker Thundermist Health Assoc., Woonsocket, RI, 1990—91; clinician rsch. team Miriam Hosp., Providence, 1991—2004; ret., 2004. Spkr. in field. Mem.: Jean Baker Miller Tng. Inst. Stone Ctr. Wellesly Coll., East Providence Substance Abuse Prevention Task Force, Nat. Assoc. for Alcoholism and Drug Abuse Counselors, Nat. Mus. Women Artists, Providence Art Club. Independent. Avocations: photography, writing, dance, bicycling. Personal E-mail: adisburyprice@hotmail.com.

PRICE, AMELIA RUTH, not-for-profit foundation president, artist, small business owner; b. Bklyn., Sept. 4, 1942; d. Dr. Alphonse Frederick Pagano and Adele Marie Savarese; 1 child, Ean James. BA, Georgian Ct. Coll., Lakewood, NJ, 1964; MA in Art Hist., Cath. U. of Am., Washington, DC, 1968. Cert. Permanent Certificate, Art State of N.Y. Edn. Dept., 1971. Art tchr. Bd. Coop. Ednl. Svcs., Patchogue, NY, 1967—68; art director Roland Advt. Co., N.Y.C., 1968—69; art dept. chair Bd. Coop. Ednl. Svcs. II, Deer Park, NY, 1969—78; v.p. Delicious Selections Ltd, White Plains, NY, 1991—95; pres., owner Parker Commodities Ltd, Kings Park, NY, 1995—; owner Bubbling Oaks Samoyeds, Commack, NY, 1974—. Co-founder bubbling oaks samoyeds kennels Bubbling Oaks Samoyeds, Commack, NY, 1974—2002. Samoyed Newsletter and other publs.featuring Samoyeds, 1999—; contbr. articles on Samoyeds and their care to various publs., 1999. Pres. Samoyed Club of Am. Edn. and Rsch. Found., Inc., Madison, Wis., 2001—, v.p., 1997—2001. Recipient # 1 Samoyed Bitch, Kennel Rev., 1974, 1975, 1976, 1977, 1978, 1983, 1984, # 3 Samoyed, Dogs in Canada, 1976, Top Winning Team, Orgn. for the Working Samoyed Inc., 1986, 1988. Mem.: Habour Lights Painter, Decorative Artists LI, Soc. Decorative Painters, Nat. Assn. Woman Bus. Owners (pub. affairs com. 2003—), Suffolk County Kennel Club Inc. (chmn. hospitality 1989—99, bd. dirs. 1996—99), Westbury Kennel Association (chmn. of trophies 1985, chmn. judges' transport. 2000), Samoyed Club of America Inc. (pres. 1997—99, Top Winning Bitch 1975, 1976, 1985, Top Winning Team 1985, Top Winning Bitch 1986, Top Winning Team 1987). Home: 128 Cowie Rd Commack NY 11725

PRICE, ARTIS J., retired secondary school educator; b. Hoopeston, Ill., Dec. 10, 1929; d. John William and Marian Elizabeth (Moore) Little; m. Harry Mackey Price, Nov. 28, 1958; 1 child, Kathryn Elizabeth. BS, Purdue U., 1952; postgrad., U. Colo., 1955, Northwestern U., 1958. Cert. tchr. h.s. English, Spanish, speech and phys. edn. Ill. Tchr. English, Spanish and speech Onarga (Ill.) H.S., 1952-53; tchr. English and Spanish Reavis H.S., Oak Lawn, Ill., 1953-58; tchr. phys. edn. Niles Twp. H.S., Skokie, Ill., 1958-59; substitute tchr. Libertyville (Ill.) H.S., 1959-97; tchr. water ski clinics Chgo. Boat Show, 1960-97, Midwest Boat Show, Chgo., 1960-97. Tchr. water ski clinics Boy Scouts, Girl Scouts, Lions Club, Chgo. and suburbs, 1961-98; adv. bd. Lambs Farm Retarded Facility, Libertyville, 1965-68; nutrition cons. Dr. Harry Price, Northbrook, Ill., 1964-98; cons., editor Diamond Video Prodns., Libertyville, 1976-2006. Editor: Water Skiing with Champions, 1969. Vol., Adlai Stevenson Presdl. Campaign, Chgo., 1953-54; founder Ann. Lambs Show Tournament, 1965-99. Recipient 58 Nat. 1st Place Championships, U.S.A. Water Ski, 1957-2006, 4 World 1st Place Championships, 1984, award of distinction U.S.A. Water Ski Hall of Fame, 1998. Mem.: Am. Water Ski Ednl. Found. (award of distinction 1998), U.S.A. Water Ski Assn., Lambs Water Ski Club (hon.; pres. 1965—70), Diamond Lake Water Ski Club (hon.; pres. 1959—64). Home: 1660 Blackwelder Rd De Leon Springs FL 32130-3914

PRICE, BETTY JEANNE, chimes musician; b. Long Beach, Calif., June 12, 1942; d. Grant E. and Miriam A. (Francis) Sickles; m. Harvey H. Price, Aug. 6, 1975; children: Thomas Neil Gering, Timothy Ray(dec.), Pamela Kay(dec.). Degree in Acctg., Northland Pioneer Coll., Show Low, Ariz., 1977. Youth missionary Open Bible Standard Missions, Trinidad, 1958-59; typographer Joel H. Weldon & Assocs., Scottsdale, Ariz., 1980-89; exec. chief acct. Pubs. Devel. Corp., San Diego, 1991-93; coord. music and worship College Ave. Bapt. Ch., San Diego, 1994-95; ChoirChime soloist, 1986—; exec. acct. Advance Reprographics, San Diego, 1996—2003. Chime musician and writer. Author: 101 Ways to Fix Broccoli, 1994, ABC's of Abundant Living, 1995; contbg. author God's Vitamin C for the Spirit, 1995, BounceBook, 1997, You Can Bounce Back Too, 1998, Pathway of Love, One Man's Remarkable Journey, 2002, Breaking Free from Financial Bondage: A Guide to Living Debt Free, 2004; musical arranger: handbell/chime Classical Sounds, 2005, A Musical Tour Around the World, 2005, Music for Special Occasions, 2005, Sounds of Christmas, 2005, A Musical Christmas Story, 2005, Hymns of Faith, 2005; musician: (CD) Classical Chimes, 2005, Chimes of Faith, 2005, Christmas Chimes, 2005. Mem.: ASCAP, Am. Guild English Handbell Ringers. Business E-Mail: chimesoloist@aol.com.

PRICE, BRENDA CHLOÈ, artist, entrepreneur; b. Hockley County, Tex., Mar. 15, 1945; d. Thomas Irby and Mildred Ruth (Bryant) P.; 1 child, Amber Lacy Belcher. Student, West Tex. State U., Canyon, 1963-64; BS in Art Edn., Tex. Tech. U., Lubbock, 1967; postgrad., La. Tech. U., Ruston, 1978-97. Cert. tchr. Tex., N.Mex., Okla. Art tchr. Hurst-Euless-Bedford Sch., 1967—69, Rogers Sch. Okla. City, 1973—74, Okla. Mus. Art, 1979; art tchr., arts coord. Taos (N.Mex.) Valley Sch., 1986—88; artist Gallery Rodeo, Taos, 1991-92, Gallery Touchstone, Taos, 1992—; innkeeper, owner Touchstone, Taos, 1994—. Author: Inside the Wind, 1983; one woman shows include Barnes and Boughton/Gallery 3017, Oklahoma City, 1981, Lutz/Bergerson Gallery, Taos, 1981, Gallery of Fine Art, Oklahoma City, 1982, Ea. Hills Country Club, Albuquerque, 1982, Okla. Art Mus., Oklahoma City, 1983, The Actors' Playhouse, L.A., 1983, Scharf Gallery, Santa Fe, 1983, 84, 85, The Redroom, L.A., 1984, Bent St. Studio, Taos, 1987, Taos Water Gardens, 1988, 25 Yr. Retrospective, Centinel Bank, Taos, 1989, Goettler-Smeltzer Gallery, Albuquerque, 1990, Discover Hollywood Show, Hollywood, Calif, 1991, La Sirena, Taos, 2000, The Gallery, Roswell, N.Mex., 2000; group shows include Okla. Watercolor Assn., 1978, 79, 80, 81, Art Ctr. Mus., Oklahoma CIty, 1981, La. Tech. Univ., 1978, 79, 80, 81, 85, 86, 87, 88, 89, 95, 97, 2001, 02, Taos Today, 1986, 88, 89, Hollywood Arts Coun., 1988, Spring Arts Celebration, Taos, 1989, 90, 91, 92, 93, 94, 95, 96, 97, People's Choice, Taos, 1988, Artists of Taos, 1988, 89, 90, Gallery Rodeo, Taos, 1991 Leda's Pond, Taos, 1994, Taos Gallery, 1996, 97, 98, 99, 2000, Taos 1st NAt. Bank, 1998, and many others. Advisor Med. Arts Found., Taos, 1994—; bd. dirs. for the arts Taos Med. Svcs. Found. Mem. Okla. Watercolor Soc. (past pres.), Nat. Mus. of Women in the Arts. Home and Office: PO Box 1885 0110 Mabel Dodge Ln Taos NM 87571 Office Phone: 505-758-0192. E-mail: brenprice@newmex.com.

PRICE, DEBBIE F., elementary school educator; b. Booneville, Miss., Sept. 9, 1957; d. Grady Lee and Mary Gwen (Berryhill) Nash; m. Joseph Wayne Price, June 1979; children: Dusty Lee, Kayla Nash Price Shipman. BA, Miss. State U., Starkville, 1979, M, 1984. Trained evaluator Miss., Music Tchrs. Assn. Internat. Inc.; cert. tchr. Nat. Bd. Profl. Tchg. Stds. Tchr. grade 3 Biggersville Elem. Sch., Corinth, Miss., 1979—84; tchr. grade 8 East Ctrl. Mid. Sch., Hurley, 1984—86; tchr. grade 4 and social studies grades 5-6 Rienzi Elem. Sch., Rienzi, Miss., 1986—. Sch. rep. Horizon, Inc., Corinth, Miss.; part time retail sales fashion and cosmetics. Rienzi sch. coord. Jump Rope Am. Heart Assn., Miss., 2003—. Nominee Miss. Tchr. of Yr., 2001, Am. Legion Tchr. of Yr., 2006; named Tchr. of Yr, Rienzi Elem. Sch., 1986—87, 1996—97, 1999—2000, 2001—02, Elem.Tchr. of Yr, Alcorn Sch. Dist., 1994—95, 2000—01, Outstanding Am. Tchr., Nat. Honor Roll; grantee, Eisenhower Local Sch. Dist., Horizon, Inc. Mem.: Miss. Profl. Educators. Baptist. Avocation: baking. Office: Rienzi Elem Sch 21 Sch St Rienzi MS 38865 Home: 105 CR 218 Glen MS 38846

PRICE, DONNA J., nurse; b. Edmond, Okla., May 23, 1953; d. Robert Burton and Lois Mae (Cagle) Gaylord; children: Amanda Leigh. Assoc., Okla. State U., Oklahoma City, 1989. Kindergarten tchr. Logos Christian Sch., Oklahoma City, 1980-87; nurse technician St. Anthony Hosp., Oklahoma City, 1988-90, staff nurse, 1990-92; infusion specialist Curaflex Infusion Co., Oklahoma City, 1992-93; managed care nurse Blue Cross/Blue Shield, Oklahoma City, 1993—. Fundraising chmn. Mustang (Okla.) H.S. Band, 1998, sec., 1999; Sunday Sch. tchr. First Bapt. Ch., Mustang, 1998—. Mem. NMA (treas. Oklahoma City chpt. 1996-98, pres. 1999-2000). Republican. Baptist. Avocations: music, reading, cross stitching, car shows, travel. Office: Blue Cross/Blue Shield Okla 3401 NW 63rd St Oklahoma City OK 73116-3716

PRICE, DORIS COLEEN DAVIS, visual artist, printmaker; b. Millsboro, Del., Dec. 1, 1929; d. Robert Henry and Lillie Mae (Johnson) Davis; m. Cyril Hamilton Price, June 9, 1956; children: Alan Curtis, Gary Stuart, Cheryl Lynn. BS in Painting and Writing, SUNY, Old Westbury, 1974. Artist, 1977—. One-woman shows include SUNY, Buffalo, 1977, Am. Internat. Coll., Springfield, Mass., 1980, Jamaica Arts Ctr., Queens, N.Y., 1983, 86, 92, Cellar Gallery, South Nyack, N.Y., 1983, Fordham U. at Lincoln Ctr., N.Y.C., 1984, Spiral Gallery, Bklyn., 1987, Design Masters Art Gallery, N.Y.C., 1988, 90, Delaware State U., Dover, 1994; exhibited in group shows at Salmagundi Club, N.Y.C., 1980, Sarah Lawrence Coll., N.Y., 1980, Automation House, N.Y.C., 1981, Customs Mus. at World Trade Ctr., N.Y.C., 1982, Cork Gallery at Lincoln Ctr., N.Y.C., 1982, Bergen County (N.J.) Mus., 1980, Essex County Coll., Newark, 1983, E. Nelson Galleries, Englewood Cliffs, N.J., 1985, Knickerbocker Artists, N.Y.C., 1986, 90, OPA 3d Internat. Exbn., N.Y.C., Dorsey's Gallery, Bklyn., 1986, Great Neck (N.Y.) Libr., 1986, Queens Coll., N.Y., 1987, 90, Savacou Gallery, N.Y.C., 1990, Medgar Evers Coll., Bklyn., 1990, Design Masters Art Gallery, N.Y.C., 1991, NYNEX Corp., White Plains, N.Y., 1992, Reader's Digest Assn., Pleasantville, N.Y., 1992, Ea. Wash. U., Cheney, 1993 (Purchase award); represented in permanent collections at Apex Mus., Atlanta, Nassau County Mus., L.I., Ea. Wash. U., York Coll., Queens, Medgar Evers Coll., Bklyn., Del. State U., Dover, many pvt. collections. Home: 30692 Mt Joy Rd Millsboro DE 19966

PRICE, ELIZABETH ANNE, lawyer; b. Boston, Aug. 23, 1960; BA, George Washington U., 1983, JD with honors, 1986. Bar: Ga. 1986, U.S. Dist. Ct. (no. dist.) Ga. 1986, U.S. Ct. Appeals (11th cir.) 1986, U.S. Supreme Ct. 1995. Ptnr., litig., trial practice Alston & Bird LLP, Atlanta, 1986—. With U.S. Army, interrogator/Arabic linguist, 1978-81. Mem. State Bar Ga. (access to justice com., ct. futures com.), Atlanta Bar Assn. (bd. dirs. 1996—, pres.). Office: Alston & Bird 1 Atlantic Ctr 1201 W Peachtree St NW Atlanta GA 30309-3400 Office Phone: 404-881-7264. Business E-Mail: lprice@alston.com.

PRICE, FAITH MUNFORD, retired psychiatrist, retired special education educator; d. Robert Sims and Marilu Young Munford; m. Everett Charles Price; children: Paul, Charles, Marilu. AB magna cum laude, Wesleyan Coll., Macon, Ga., 1949; MEd, Emory U., Atlanta, 1951; MD, Emory Sch. Medicine, Atlanta, 1962. Psychiatrist pvt. practice, Houston, 1970—94; tchr. deaf Atlanta Jr. League Speech Sch., 1970—94. Clin. asst. prof. psychiatry Baylor Sch. Medicine, Houston, 1970—94. Elder Meml. Dr. Presbyn. Ch., Houston. Democrat. Episcopalian. Avocations: hiking, writing, reading. Mailing: PO Box 40 Guffey CO 80820

PRICE, GLENDA DELORES, dean, college president; b. York, Pa., Oct. 10, 1939; d. William B. Price and Zelma E. Holmes McGeary. BS, Temple U., 1961, MEd, 1969, PhD, 1979. Clin. lab. specialist. Cytotechnologist Temple U. Hosp., Phila., 1961-67, prof. clin. lab. sci.; faculty Coll. Allied Health Professions, Temple U., Phila., 1967-79, asst. dean allied health, 1979-86; dean allied health Sch. Allied Health Professions, U. Conn., Storrs, 1986—; pres. Marygrove Coll., Detroit, 1998. Pres. Am. Soc. Clin. Lab. Contbr. over 20 articles to profl. jours., chpts. to books. Bd. trustees U. New Eng., Biddeford, Maine, 1989—; bd. dirs. Windham Hosp., Willimantic, Conn., 1989—, E. Hartford VNA, 1989—; allied health adv. Pew Health Prof. Commn., Durham, N.C., 1991—. Recipient Leadership award SUNY-Buffalo, 1982; named Mem. of the Yr., Pa. Soc. Med. Tech., 1979; decorated Legion of Honor, Chapel of Four Chaplains, 1977. Mem. Am. Soc. Allied Health Professions (sec. 1985-87), Am. Soc. Med. Tech. (pres. 1979-80), Alpha Kappa Alpha, Alpha Mu Tau, Alpha Eta, Phi Kappa Phi. Democrat. Baptist. Home and Office: U Conn 358 Mansfield Rd Storrs Mansfield CT 06269-9000

PRICE, HARLENE PAMELA, music educator; d. Harold Hansford and Mabel Lucille Hoffman; m. Calvin Lewis Price, Mar. 29, 1997; 1 child, Joshua Kenneth. MusB, Ohio U., 1985, MusM, 1987. Tchr. Logan-Hocking Sch. Dist., Logan, Ohio, 1989—. Ch. choir dir. Kline Meml. Ch., Logan, Ohio, 1983—; bd. mem. Logan Alumni Band, Inc., 1988—92, v.p., 1992—. Musician soloist with various performing groups. Mem.: NEA, Music Edn. Nat. Assn., Pi Kappa Lambda, Phi Kappa Phi, Sigma Alpha Iota (life). Office: Logan High Sch 50 North St Logan OH 43138 Office Phone: 740-385-2941. Personal E-mail: pprice@loganhocking.k12.oh.us.

PRICE, HELEN BURDON (HELEN LOIS BURDON), artist, retired nursing educator; b. St. Louis, Sept. 23, 1926; d. Kenneth Livingston and Estelle Lois (Pemberton) Burdon; m. John Bryan Price, Jr.; children: Diane Price Baker, Jeannette B., John Bryan III. BS, La. State U., 1946; BS, RN, Johns Hopkins U., 1949; postgrad., Boston U., 1951-52. Head nurse in pediatrics Johns Hopkins Hosp., Balt., 1949-51; instr. nursing sch. Boston Children's Hosp., 1951-52; physician's aide, sec. U.S. Army-Osaka (Japan) Hosp., 1952-54; instr. pediat. nursing Holy Name Hosp., Teaneck, N.J., 1965-67; primary nurse Englewood (N.J.) Hosp., 1974-79; dir.- curator Vineyard Theatre Gallery, N.Y.C., 1980-90; bd. mem., coord. pub. lecture series Ward Nasse Gallery, N.Y.C., 1987-92. Program planner, judge, panel participant, curator Salute to Women in the Arts, Bergen County, N.J.,

1977-95. Fund raiser Women's Aux., Presbyn. Med. Ctr., N.Y. Hosp. Fund, N.Y.C., 1982-90. Mem. Nat. Assn. Women Artists (past sec., v.p., pres., permanent advisor, Akston Found. award 1987, Blake award 1991, Bronze medal 1995, Kreindler Meml. award 1998, Blum Meml. award 1999). Avocations: birdwatching, mycology. Personal E-mail: hbp31@aol.com.

PRICE, HELEN HOGGATT, counseling administrator; b. Lafeyette, La., Aug. 1, 1959; d. Buford James and Barbara Boggan Hoggatt; m. Jahncke Earl Price, Mar. 11, 1978; children: Gretchen Ann, Kayla Ann. BS in Social & Rehab. Svc., U. So. Miss., 1987; M in Counseling & Psychology, Miss. Coll., 1994. Lic. Profl. Counselor Miss., 95, cert. Nat. Cert. Sch. Counselor Nat. Bd. Cert. Counselors, 99, lic. Marriage & Family Therapist Miss., 2000, cert. Psychologist Miss., 2000. Sch. counselor North Pike Elem., Summit, Miss., 1991—95; exec. dir. Crisis Pregnancy Ctr., McComb, Miss., 1995—98; regional dir. S.W. Miss. Mental Health, McComb, 1998—99; sch. counselor McComb Jr. H.S., McComb, 1999—2002, Harrison Ctrl. H.S., Gulfport, Miss., 2002—04, Oak Grove H.S., Hattiesburg, Miss., 2004—. Contbr. Family Counseling in the Schools, 1994, Counselmate, 1994. Scholar Keith Parks scholarship, Miss. Bapt. Conv. Bd., 1993. Mem.: Miss. Marriage & Family Counselors (pres. 1996—98), Miss. Counseling Assn. (pres. 1999—2000, Dr. Charles Scott scholarship 1994, Spl. Recognition award 2001). Republican. So. Baptist. Home: 82 Classic Dr Hattiesburg MS 39402 Office: Oak Grove HS 5198 Old Hwy 11 Hattiesburg MS 39402 Office Phone: 601-264-3623. E-mail: hprice@harrison.k12.ms.us, ttisprice4u@comcast.net.

PRICE, HOLLISTER ANNE CAWEIN, airline project administrator, interior design consultant; b. Memphis, Feb. 11, 1954; d. Madison Albert Cawein and Billie Jeanne (Roberts) Stewart; m. James H. Price, Jr., Oct. 21, 1978 (div. 1985). BA in Communications and Fine Arts, Memphis State U., 1988. Office mgr. Bruce Motor Co., Memphis, 1975-76; br. mgr. Cen. States Agy., Memphis, 1976-78; facility coord. Fed. Express Corp., Memphis, 1978-86, corp. interior designer, project mgr., 1986—; design cons. Smart Shoppes, Inc., Hardy and Trumann, Ark., 1985-86; Fed. Express dept. coord. interior design student interns Memphis State U. Dept. leader Ch. Sch. Edn. Program, Cen. Ch., 1984-85; mem. Arts Svcs. League for Greater Memphis Area, 1986—; active Very Spl. Arts Coun. for Handicapped, Memphis, 1987—. Mem. Nat. Assn. Female Execs., Duration Club (Memphis), Delta Gamma Alumnae. Republican. Episcopalian. Avocations: scuba diving, horseback riding, biking, antique collecting. Office: Fed Express Corp Dept 1870 PO Box 727 Memphis TN 38194-0001

PRICE, ILENE ROSENBERG, lawyer; b. Jersey City, July 2, 1951; d. Irwin Daniel and Mildred (Riesberg) Rosenberg; m. Jeffrey Paul Price, Feb. 18, 1973. AB, U. Mich., 1972; JD, U. Pa., 1977. Bar: Pa. 1977, DC 1978, U.S. Dist. Ct. DC 1979, U.S. Ct. Appeals (D.C. cir.) 1979. Assoc. Haley, Bader & Potts, Washington, 1977-80; staff atty. Mut. Broadcasting System Inc., Arlington, Va., 1980-82, asst. gen. counsel, 1982-85; gen. counsel Multi-Comm Telecommunications Corp., Arlington, 1985-88; east coast counsel Westwood One, Inc., Arlington, 1988-91; gen. counsel Resource Dynamics Corp., Vienna, Va., 1991—2001; legal search cons. The McCormick Group, Arlington, 2001—03; gen. counsel Bluewave Resources, LLC, McLean, Va., 2003—. Mem. Fed. Communications Bar Assn., Wash. Met. Area Corp. Counsel Assn., Women's Bar Assn. D.C. (bd. dirs. 1984-87). Office: Bluewave Resources LLC Ste 310 6830 Elm St Mc Lean VA 22101 Office Phone: 703-448-3400. Business E-Mail: ileneprice@bwres.com.

PRICE, KIM DENISE, counselor; b. Pontiac, Mich., June 29, 1974; d. Priscilla Ann Newell; m. Ethan A. Price, Apr. 20, 1999; children: Destine Zion, Trinitee Davine, Jairahel Zoriah. BS in Orgnl. Comm., Western Mich. U., 1997. Asst. sec. English dept. Western Mich. U., Kalamazoo, 1992—95, orientation leader, 1996; credit adjustor 1st of Am., Kalamazoo, 1997; supr. for abused women Gospel Mission, Kalamazoo, 1998; health mgmt. technician Bronson Meth. Hosp., Kalamazoo, 1999—2000; customer svc. rep. Indy Mac Bank Loan Dept., Kalamazoo, 2000—01; youth treatment provider Lakeside Learning and Treatment Ctr., Kalamazoo, 2001—; psychiatric care specialist Havenwyck Hosp., Auburn Hills, Mich., 2004—06. V.p. of gospel chair Western Mich. U., Kalamazoo, 1996; psychiat. care specialist Havenuryck Hosp., Auburn Hills, Mich., 2004—06. Contbr. poetry International Book of Poetry, 1999—2000, poetry Anthology Book of Poetry. Orgnl. leader divsn. minority affairs Western Mich. U., 1997. Avocations: poetry, creating unique hairstyles, bowling, singing, camping. Home: 7135 Round Hill Dr B Waterford MI 48327

PRICE, LEE ANN, athletic trainer, educator; b. Decatur, Ill., May 3, 1974; d. David L. and Sharon L. Cunningham; m. Kyle W. Price, July 17, 1999; children: Nathan E., Emily E. EdD, Ill. State U., Normal, 2006. Certified Athletic Trainer Nat. Athletic Trainers' Assn. Bd. of Certification, 1996. Athletic trainer Crawford Meml. Hosp., Robinson, Ill., 1997—2002; co-dir. HealthWorks Cmty. Wellness Facility, Robinson, 1997—2002; asst. basketball coach Robinson H.S., 1998—2000; adj. faculty mem. Lincoln Trail C.C., Robinson, 1998—2002; athletic tng. edn. program dir. Ea. Ill. U., Charleston, Ill., 2002—; locum tenens athletic trainer Sarah Bush Lincoln Health Ctr., Charleston, Ill., 2002—; athletic trainer Carle Sportsmedicine, Urbana, Ill., 2003—. Doctoral intern, v.p. academic affairs Millikin U., Decatur, Ill., 2006; athletic tng. edn. panelist Lippincott, Williams and Wilkins, Phila., 2005; presenter in field. Co-author program devel. materials. Vol. coord. athletic svcs. for regional Spl. Olympics, Ea. Ill. U., Charleston, 2005—; vol. athletic trainer state tracks meets. Ill. HS Assn., Charleston, 2002—; vol. athletic trainer Prairie State Games, Edwardsville, Ill., 1995—97; vol. athletic trainer hockey U. Ill., 2006—06. Mem.: Ill. Athletic Trainers' Assn., Gt. Lakes Athletic Trainers' Assn., Nat. Athletic Trainers' Assn. (home study reviewer bd. cert. 2006—, examiner bd. cert.). Avocations: backpacking, camping, travel. Office: Ea Ill U 600 Lincoln Ave Charleston IL 61920 Office Phone: 217-581-7615. Business E-Mail: lprice@eiu.edu.

PRICE, LEONTYNE (MARY VIOLET LEONTYNE PRICE), retired concert and opera singer, soprano; b. Laurel, Miss., Feb. 10, 1927; d. James A. and Kate (Baker) Price; m. William Warfield, Aug. 31, 1952 (div. 1973). BA, Central State Coll., Wilberforce, Ohio, 1949, DMus, 1968; student, Juilliard Sch. Music, 1949-52; pupil, Florence Page Kimball; LHD, Dartmouth Coll., 1962, Fordham U., 1969, Yale U., 1979; MusD, Howard U., 1962; Dr. Humanities, Rust Coll., 1968. Singer: (Operas) (debut) in 4 Saints in 3 Acts, 1952, (appeared) Bess in Porgy and Bess, Vienna, Berlin, Paris, London, under auspices U.S. State Dept., N.Y.C. and U.S. tour, 1952—54; recitalist, soloist (symphonies) U.S., Can., Australia, Europe, 1954—, appeared concerts in India, 1956, 1964, soloist Hollywood Bowl, 1955—59, 1966, Berlin Festival, 1960, role as Mme. Lidoine in Dialogues des Carmelites, San Francisco Opera, 1957; singer: (Operas) NBC-TV, 1955—58, 1960, 1962, 1964, San Francisco Opera Co., 1957—59, 1960—61, 1963, 1965, 1967, 1968, 1971, as Aida at La Scala, 1957;: (Operas) Vienna Staatsoper, 1958, 1959—60, 1961, Berlin Opera, 1964, Rome Opera, 1966, 1968, (recital) Brussels Internat. Fair, auspices State Dept., 1958, Verona Opera Arena, 1958—59, Yugoslavia for, State Dept., 1958; rec. artist RCA-Victor, 1958—, appeared Covent Garden, London, 1958-59, 70, Chgo. Lyric Theatre, 1959, 60, 65, Oakland (Calif.) Symphony, 1980, soloist Salzburg Festival, 1959—63, appeared Tetro alla Scala, Milano, 1960-61, 63, 67, Met. Opera, N.Y.C., 1961-62, 64, 66, 75, 76, since resident mem., until 1985, soloist Salzburg Festival, 1950, 60, debut Teatre Dell'Opera, Rome, 1967, Teatro Colon, Buenos Aires, Argentina, 1969, Hamburg Opera, 1970, recordings A Christmas Offering with Karajani, God Bless America with Charles Gerhardt, Arias from Don Giovanni, Turandot, Aida, Emani, Messa di Requiem, Trovatore, Live at Ordway, The Prima Donna Collection, A Program of Song with D. Garvey, Right as the Rain with André Previn. Co-chmn. Rust Coll. Upward Thrust Campaign; trustee Internat. House.; hon. vice-chmn. U.S. com. UNESCO; Hon. bd. dirs. Campfire Girls. Decorated Order at Ment Italy; named Musician of Year, Mus. Am. mag., 1961; recipient Merit award for role of Tosca in NBC-TV Opera, Mademoiselle mag., 1955, 20 Grammy awards for classical vocal recs. Nat. Acad. Rec. Arts and Scis., citation YWCA, 1961, Spirit of Achievement award Albert Einstein Coll. Medicine, 1962, Presdl. medal of freedom, 1964, Springarn medal NAACP, 1965, Schwann Catalog award, 1968, Nat. Medal of Arts, 1985, Essence award, 1991, others. Fellow: Am. Acad. Arts and Sci.; mem.: AFTRA, Actors Equity Assn., Am. Guild Mus. Artists, Delta Sigma Theta, Sigma Alpha Iota. Inducted into Am. Classical Music Hall of Fame, 1998. Office: Price Enterprises 1133 Broadway Ste 920 New York NY 10010-7901

PRICE, LINDA K., small business owner; b. Dearborn, Mich., Mar. 7, 1952; d. Leroy G. and Mary Anne Hollen; m. Tracy L. Price, Oct. 7, 1989; children from previous marriage: Shannon M. Shepley, Matthew F Gooldy, Krystle E Gooldy. Cert. Ceramic Instr. Mich., 1981. Pres. T.L.C. EnterPrices, Ltd., Canton, Mich., 1991—; co-owner The Handmade Soap Co., Canton, Mich., 2001—. Cath. Achievements include patent for handmade lamp. Avocation: personal improvement. Office: TLC EnterPrices Ltd PO Box 412 Armada MI 48005 Office Phone: 734-454-9028. E-mail: getsometlc@aol.com.

PRICE, LINDA RICE, community development administrator; b. Norman, Okla., Sept. 17, 1948; d. Elroy Leon and Esther May (Wilson) Rice; m. Michael Allen Price, May 17, 1970 (div. June 1998); children: Justin R, Mathew Lyon, David F. BA in Am. History, U. Okla., 1970, M. Regional and City Planning, 1975. Dir. U. Okla. Crisis Ctr., Norman, 1969-70; cardio-pulmonary technician Bethany Med. Ctr., Kansas City, Kans., 1970-72; mgr. congressional campaign Barsotti for Congress, Kansas City, 1972; planning intern City of Seminole (Okla.), 1973-74, City of Tecumseh (Okla.), 1974-75; planner I City of Norman, 1975-76, planner II, 1975-80, community devel. coord., 1980-96, revitalization mgr., 1996—. Adj. prof. U. Okla., Norman, 1986-93; cons. in field, Norman, 1980—; mem. Homeless Here Coalition, Social Svcs. Coordinating Coun.; chair Cleve. County Continuation of Care, 2006. Past pres., mem. LWV Norman, 1979—; chmn. Norman Arts & Humanities Coun., 1983—86; mem. Oakhurst Neighborhood Assn., Norman, Okla., 1991—, v.p., 1991—94; bd. dirs. Women's Resource Ctr., Norman, 1991—92; mem., past pres. bd. Thunderbird Clubhouse, 1992—95; bd. dirs. Ind. Living Svcs. for Youth, pres., 2001—03; gov.'s appt. Rural Housing Incentive Study Task Force, 2000. Named to Leadership Norman, Norman C. of C., 1992, for Exemplary Mgmt. Practice, The Urban Inst., 1989, for Outstanding Performance, HUD, 1988; recipient Citation of Merit, Okla. State Hist. Preservation, 1991, Spl. Recognition, Okla. Hist. Soc., 1991, John J. Gunther Blue Ribbon Practices in Comty. Devel. award, 1997; Best of the Best Practice award HUD, 1999, 2 Best Practice awards, 1999, Okla. Best Practice award, 2000; named to Okla. Mcpl. League Honor Roll of Svc., 2001. Mem. Am. Inst. Cert. Planners (cert.), Am. Planning Assn. (sec. Okla. chpt. 1980-82), Planning and Women (regional coord. 1987-90), Assn. Cen. Okla. Govt. (areawide planning and tech. adv. com. 1979—), Nat. Cmty. Devel. Assn., (bd. dirs. 1998-99, state whip 1988-97, chair nat. membership 1994-96), Rotary. Democrat. Presbyterian. Avocations: softball, travel, music, reading, politics. Office: City of Norman PO Box 370 Norman OK 73070-0370 Office Phone: 405-366-5439. Business E-Mail: linda.price@norman.ok.us.

PRICE, LOIS ANN, elementary school educator; b. North Lawrence, Ohio, Feb. 19, 1936; d. John Henry Rosche and Ruby Dolores Weidner; m. David Louis Price, July 16, 1960; children: Louis David Jr., Geoffrey Christopher. BS in Edn., Bowling Green State U., 1958. 4th grade tchr. Stark County Pub. Sch., Massillon, Ohio, 1956—57, Euclid Pub. Sch., Ohio, 1958—60, Lexinton Pub. Sch., Mass., 1960—62; 1st and 2d grade tchr. Fairfax County Pub. Sch., 1967—93. Edn. assoc. sch. rep., 1976—86. Ch. vol. St. Timothy's Cath. Ch., Chantilly, Va., 1993—; sch. vol. Herndon Elem. Sch., 1993—98; pres. Friends of Chantilly Libr., Va., 2000—01. Recipient Citizen of Yr., Greenbriar Civic Assn., 2004. Mem.: Western Fairfax County Women's Club, Greenbriar Hist. Soc., Greenbriar Garden Club. Avocations: gardening, genealogy, scrapbooks, exercise, reading. Home: 13209Parson Lane Fairfax VA 22033

PRICE, LORI JEAN, humanities educator; b. Loretto, Tenn., May 10, 1968; d. Walter Lee and Peggy Jean Price; m. Michael Houston Scott, July 13, 1996. BS, U. North Ala., 1991; MA, Tenn. Tech. U., 2001. Cert. Teacher Mid. Tenn. State U., 1995. Advtg. coord. The Advocate Newspaper, Lawrencetown, Tenn., 1993—94; case mgr. Giles County Mental Health, Pulaski, Tenn., 1994; english tchr. Clinton H.S., Tenn., 1995—96; humanities tchr. Anderson County H.S., Clinton, Tenn., 1996—. Adult edn. tchr. Old Knoxville High, Tenn., 2003—05. Vol. Shelter, Inc., 1994; rep. Nine Counties, One Vision, 1999. Recipient Tchr. of Yr., Anderson County Schools, 2005—06, Educator of Yr., Knoxville News Sentinel, 2005. Mem.: Anderson County Edn. Assn., Delta Kappa Gamma. Avocations: hiking, swimming, bicycling. Home: 160 Lakeside Loop Norris TN 37828 Office: Anderson County High 130 Mav Circle Clinton TN 37716

PRICE, MARLA, museum director, curator; PhD in art hist. Assoc. curator of 20th-century art Nat. Gallery Art, Washington, DC; chief curator Modern Art Mus. Fort Worth, Tex., 1986—91, dir. Tex., 1991—. Office: Modern Art Mus Fort Worth 3200 Darnell St Fort Worth TX 76107-2872 E-mail: mprice@themodern.org.

PRICE, MARY, elementary school educator; b. Marion, Ohio, Oct. 21, 1963; d. Charles William and Barbara Ann Holcomb; m. Michael Ray Price, July 26, 1986; children: William Joseph, Taylor Ann. BS, The Ohio State U., Columbus, 1986; MA, Marygrove Coll., Detroit, 1999. Cert. elem. tchr., K-8 Ohio Dept. Edn., 1987, reading endorsement Ohio Dept. Edn., 2006. Tchr. kindergarten Fellsmere Elem., Fla., 1987; tchr. 2d grade Elgin South Elem., Prospect, Ohio, 1987—2002, intermediate reading interventionist, 2002—. Mem. literacy com. Elgin Local Sch. Dist., Marion, Ohio, 2002—03; vol. coord. Elgin South Elem., 2002—05, mem. profl. devel. team, 2005—. Vol. coord. Ohio Reads. Grantee, OhioReads-Ohio Dept. Edn., 2002—04, Ohioreads-Ohio Dept. Edn., 2005—. Mem.: Internat. Reading Assn., Ohio Edn. Assn., Elgin Edn. Assn., NEA. Avocations: reading, tutoring, cooking, walking. Office Phone: 740-494-2677.

PRICE, MARY KATHLEEN, law librarian, lawyer; b. Buffalo, Feb. 28, 1942; d. Donn Dale and Mary Elizabeth (Domedion) P. BA, U. Fla., 1963; MS, Fla. State U., 1967; postgrad., Ala. Law Sch., Tuscaloosa, 1967-70; JD, U. Ill., Champaign, 1973. Bar: Ill. 1973, U.S. Dist. Ct. (no. dist.) Ill. 1973. Tchr. Duval and Brevard County Schs., Jacksonville and Titusville, Fla., 1960-63; asst. law librarian U. Ala. Law Sch., Tuscaloosa, 1967-70, U. Ill., Champaign, 1970-73; assoc. firm Ross, Hardies & O'Keefe, Chgo., 1973-75; law librarian, prof. law Duke U. Law Sch., Durham, N.C., 1975-80; dir. law library, prof. law U. Minn., Mpls., 1980-90, acting asst. v.p. acad. affairs, 1985-86; Law Libr. of Congress, 1990—. Mem. acad. adv. bd. Westlaw, St. Paul, 1984-87; vis. prof. law Uppsala U., 1987, 89. Recipient Law Librarianship award Minn. Assn. Law Libraries, 1984, Disting. Alumni award Fla. State U., 1987. Mem. Am. Assn. Law Librs. (pres. 1983-84), Commn. Legal Edn. Exchange with PRC (chmn. libr. subcom. 1984—), Assn. Am. Law Schs. (mem. accreditation com. 1983-87, exec. bd. 1988-90), Order of Coif. Democrat. Roman Catholic. Home: 7901 Takoma Ave Silver Spring MD 20910-5227 Office: Law Libr of Congress Rm 7048 101 Independence Ave SE Stop 3001 Washington DC 20540-3001

PRICE, MARY SUE SWEENEY, museum director; d. William Robert Sweeney; m. Clement A. Price, 1988. BA in English, Allegheny Coll., 1973; D.H.C. (hon.), Caldwell Coll. With textbook pub. co., NYC; supr. pub. rels. Newark Mus., 1975, dep. dir., 1990—93, dir., 1993—. Past pres. ArtTable Inc.; v.p. ArtPrice NJ Inc.; bd. dirs. St. Vincent Acad., Newark Arts Coun. Mem.: Assn. Art Mus. Dirs., Am. Assn. Mus., NJ Assn. Mus. (bd. dirs.). Office: Newark Mus 49 Washington St Newark NJ 07102 Office Phone: 973-596-6550.

PRICE, MYRA B., secondary school educator; d. Marion Elton and Polly J. Barnette; children: Samantha L. Buras, Richard G. IV. BS, U. La., Monroe, 1990. Cert. AMT, Generalist La., 1969, Sci. Edn. La., 1990. Lab. tech. Greater SW Gen. Hosp., Grand Prairie, Tex., 1971—72, Mattie Hersie Hosp., Meredian, Miss., 1972—73, Natchez Charity, Miss., 1971—76, Natchez Med. Ctr., Miss., 1976—78, Dr. Dennis LaRavia, Ferriday, La., 1978—81, Riverland Med. Ctr., Ferriday, La., 1981—2006; educator Hanson Meml. HS, Franklin, La., 1990—93, Ferriday HS, La., 1993—. Mem.: NSTA. Office Phone: 318-757-8626.

PRICE, PAMELA CHAMPION, art educator; b. San Francisco, June 9, 1944; d. John Clyde and Lorraine Clair (Weber) Champion; m. Joel Roderick Price, July 18, 1970. BA in Printmaking, Painting and Drawing, Ga. State U., 1967; MFA in Printmaking, U. Ga., 1970. Teaching asst. Univ. Ga., Athens, 1967-70, instr., 1968-70; adj. instr. Univ. Tex. Permian Basin, Odessa, 1974-75, coord. art, 1975-76, lectr., 1976-77, asst. prof., 1977-83, assoc. prof., 1983-90, prof., 1990—, chmn. art dept., 1992—, Mr. and Mrs. Louis Rochester Prof. of Fine Arts, 1994—. Adv. bd. mem. Women's Ctr., Univ. Tex. Permian Basin, 1986-88; editorial adv. bd. mem. Collegiate Press, Alto Loma, Calif., 1990—. One-woman shows include Art Inst. for Permian Basin, Odessa, 1989, San Angelo (Tex.) Mus. Fine Arts, 1988, Univ. Tex. Permian Basin, 1976, 80, 85, Sul Ross State Univ., Alpine, Tex., 1985, Western Tex. Coll., Snyder, 1981, Coll. of S.W., Hobbs, N.Mex., 1980, Options Gallery Odessa Coll., 1997 (1st Place); represented in permanent collections Equitable Corp., Chgo. Art Inst. for Permian Basin, Ark. Art Ctr., Little Rock, Archtl. Arts, Inc., Dallas, Southwestern Bell Tex. Collection, Redstone Arsenal Bank, Ala., Ga. Commn. on Arts. Exhbn. com. mem. Art Inst. for Permian Basin, 1990—; active 20/20 Foresight, Odessa, 1990—. Recipient Minnie Piper Stevens award Minnie Piper Found., 1992, 2002; named Amoco Outstanding Tchr., Amoco Found., 1985, Statesman of the Arts Odessa Heritage Found., 1998. Mem. Univ. Art Assn. (faculty advisor 1978—), Office: U Tex of Permian Basin 4901 E University Blvd Odessa TX 79762-8122

PRICE, PEGGY REINECKE, writer, researcher; b. Balt., May 19, 1957; d. Norman Raymond and Sheila Marjorie Reinecke; m. Jay Francis Price; children: David Diaz, Alicia Diaz, Christina Diaz, Michael Diaz. BA cum laude, U. Tex., 1997. Bookkeeper Healy Tibbitts Builders, Aiea, Hawaii, 2001—02; writer West Media Group, Latrobe, Pa., 2004—. Co-author and photographer (book) Westmoreland County Resource Guide, 2002. Troop leader Girl Scouts Am., San Antonio, 1992—95; tutor Knowlton Elem. Sch., San Antonio, 1994—95; com. mem. Academics 2000, San Antonio, 1996—97. Staff sgt. USMC, 1979—86. Mem.: Golden Key Nat. Honor Soc. (life), Sigma Tau Delta Internat. English Honor Soc. (life). R-Consevative. Lutheran. Avocations: photography, writing, travel. Office: W Media Group 1305B Clearview Dr Latrobe PA 15650 E-mail: PeebsNJay@yahoo.com.

PRICE, RITA FLEISCHMANN, artist, educator; b. N.Y.C. d. John and Rae (Warschaw) Fleischmann; m. Irving M. Price; children: Allyson Lou, Louis Evan, Jolan Sue. BFA, Sch. of Art Inst. of Chgo., 1982; postgrad., U. Ill., 1984. Asst. dir. admissions Sch. of Art Inst. of Chgo., 1984, asst. dir. non degree, 1985, dir. alumni affairs, 1985-93, mem. faculty, 1990-91, North Shore Art League, Winnetka, Ill., 1983—, Suburban Fine Arts Ctr., Highland Park, Ill., 1995. Bd. trustee Evanston (Ill.) Art Ctr., 1991-97, cons. Sch. of Art Inst. of Chgo., 1992—. Vol. Am. Cancer Soc., Deerfield, Ill., 1985-87, pres. N. Shore Art League, Winnetka, Ill., 1995-97. Recipient award of excellence Mcpl. Art, 1988, Am. Jewish Arts Club, Chgo., 1988-97. Mem. North Shore Art League (pres.), Art Inst. Alumni Assn. Chgo. (bd. dirs.), Evanston Art Ctr., Alumni Assn. Home (Winter): 8204 Casa Del Lago Apt 24C Boca Raton FL 33433-2185 Home: 1665 Dartmouth Ln Deerfield IL 60015

PRICE, RUTHE PAYENSON GEIER, actress, writer, educator; b. New Brunswick, N.J., Dec. 16, 1922; d. Morris Payenson and Anne (Payenson) Dorfman; m. Arnold Geier, July 1, 1951 (div. Nov. 1976); children: Donald Lloyd, Michael Jay; m. Nathaniel Wolfred Price, Oct. 9, 1988 (dec. Nov. 2003). Student, State Tchrs. Coll., Trenton, N.J., 1941-43; BS in Edn., NYU, 1945, MA in Theater, 1946. Dir. Parker Playhouse, Plainfield, N.J., 1947, Newark Acad. Dramatic Art, 1948; asst. dir., theater chair Essex Conservatory, Newark, 1949-51; soc. editor Edison Jour., Miami, Fla., 1954; comptroller Nat. Ins. Cons., Miami, 1974-76; actress Miami, 1977—; mng.editor Starbooks Inc., 1999—. Drama coach, Fla., 1990—; media cons., Fla., 1983—. Appeared in films including Let It Ride, Making Mr. Right, Italian Taxi Driver, The Bellboy, Hardly Working, Last Plane Out, Hot Stuff; TV appearances include Miami Sands, Miami Vice, The Sunset Gang; plays include Save Me a Place at Forest Lawn, Pocket Watch, Ladies in Retirement, Hamlet, You Can't Take it With You, The Male Animal, Blithe Spirit, Lady Precious Stream, As You Like It, Guest in the House, Godperson, Forty Carats, Medea, Skin of Our Teeth, Romeo and Juliet, A Choice to Make; hostess TV talk show Ruthe Geier Presents; hostess radio show Spotlight on Stars; dir. Plays for Living, 1981-86; author: Acting in On-Camera Commercials, 2001; society editor Edison Jour.; contbr. poetry to Harper's mag. Recipient CLIO award, Emmy award, Addy award. Mem. AFTRA (columnist 1985-93, v.p. 1985-93), Screen Actors Guild (bd. dirs. so. dist. 1990-93), Actors Equity Assn. Avocations: stamp collecting/philately, reading, music, theater, travel. Personal E-mail: writegal@bellsouth.net.

PRICE, STACY D., science educator; d. Teresa Tripp and Chandler M. White (Stepfather); m. Stephen M. Price, July 24, 1999 (dec. Mar. 21, 2000). BS in Biology with a minor in Chemistry, Francis Marion U., Florence, SC, 1998. H.s. sci. tchr. South Florence H.S., Florence, SC, 2000—; adult edn. chemistry tchr. Poynor Adult Edn. Ctr., Florence, 2004—. Mem.: Palmetto State Teachers Assn. Office: South Florence HS 3200 S Irby St Florence SC 29505 Office Phone: 843-664-8190. E-mail: sprice@fsd1.org.

PRICE, THEODORA HADZISTELIOU, individual, child and family therapist; b. Athens, Greece, Oct. 1, 1938; arrived in U.S., 1967; d. Ioannis and Evangelia (Emmanuel) Hadzisteliou; m. David C. Long Price, Dec. 26, 1966 (div. 1989); children: Morgan N., Alkes D. L. Diploma in piano tchg., Nat. Conservatory, Athens, 1958; BA in History/Archaeology, U. Athens, 1961; DPhil, U. Oxford, Eng., 1966; MA in Clin. Social Work, U. Chgo., 1988. LCSW, bd. cert. diplomate in clin. social work. Mus. asst., resident tutor U. Sydney, Australia, 1966-67; instr. anthropology Adelphi U., N.Y.C., 1967-68; archaeologist Hebrew Union Coll., Gezer, Israel, 1968; asst. prof. classical archaeology/art U. Chgo., 1968-70; jr. rsch. fellow Harvard Ctr. Hellenic Studies, Washington, 1970-71; clin. social worker Harbor Light Ctr., Salvation Army, Chgo., 1988-89; therapist Inst. Motivational Devel., Lombard, Ill., 1989-90; caseworker Jewish Family & Cmty. Svc., Chgo., 1989-90; staff therapist Family Svc. Ctrs. of South Cook County, Chicago Heights, 1990-91; pvt. practice child, adolescent, family therapy Bolingbrook, Ill., 1991—; dir. counseling svcs., clin. supr., psychotherapist Family Link, Inc., Chgo., 1993; staff therapist Cen. Bapt. Family Svcs., Gracell Rehab., Chgo., 1991, 91-92; casework supr., counselor Epilepsy Found. Greater Chgo., 1992-93; therapist children, adolescents and families dept. foster care Cath. Charities, Chgo., 1993-94; individual and family therapist South Ctrl. Cmty. Svcs. Individual-Family Counseling Svcs., Chgo., 1994-97. Bd. dirs., counselor Naperville Sch. Gifted and Talented, 1982—84; lectr. in field. Author: (monograph) Kourotrophos, Cults and Representations of the Greek Nursing Deities, 1978; contbr. articles to profl. jours. Eleutherios Venizelos scholar, 1962—65, Meyerstein Traveling grantee, Oxford, Eng., 1963, 1964. Mem.: NASW, Am. Bd. Clin. Soc. Workers, Ill. Clin. Social Workers, Nat. Acad. Clin. Social Workers. Avocations: piano, Byzantine chanting, writing. Home and Office: 10 Pebble Ct Bolingbrook IL 60440-1557 Office Phone: 630-378-1187.

PRICE, TINA DENISE, music educator; b. Ceiba, PR, Feb. 8, 1971; d. James Edward and Peggy Dean McFalls; m. David Shane Price (div.); children: Adam, Hilary, Luke, Maria. AA, NE CC, Booneville, Miss., 1991; BS, Blue Mountain Coll., Miss., 1993. Cert. music educator. Tchr. Alcorn Ctrl. HS, Glen, Miss., 1993—94, 2005—. Mem.: Music Educators Nat. Club, Am. Choral Dirs. Assn. Baptist. Avocation: music. Home: 1708 Holley St Corinth MS 38834 Office: Alcorn Ctrl HS BCR 254 Glen MS 38846

PRICE-WARE-KABUTI, THELMA, counselor; d. Abraham Price and Marina Jackson; children: Reon Karsheem Ante' Price-Putnam, Laki David Sullivan Price-Sullivan. Grad. in Secretarial Sci., Ulster County CC, Stone Ridge, NY, 1980. Cert. HIV/AIDS case mgmt. specialist Mass. Dept. Pub. Health, 1993, home health aide Mass. Career Devel. Inst., 1994; alcohol and drug addiction counselor Lloyd Simmon's Sch. Alcohol/Drug Dependency, 1998, New Eng. Sch. Addiction, St. Michael's Coll., 1999. Detox counselor HillCrest Hosp.-McGee Unit, Pittsfield, Mass., 1991—93; case mgr. Tapestry, Springfield, 1993—96; residential counselor Phoenix House of Springfield, Mass., 1995—2000. Cons. Mass. Dept HIV/AIDS Bur. CAB, Boston, 1993—. Coordinator/ chairperson (drop-in center for hiv/aids & families) Family And Friends Come For Support (Appreciation from River Valley Counselling Ctr., 2000), coordinator-chairperson (drop-in center) Family /friends/ and people living with HIV/AIDS (Sidney Borum Award, 1994), leadership & work done on dph-cab (on behalf of people living with hiv/aids) Advocacy, lobbying, and presentations (Mass. Dept. of Pub. Health HIV/AIDS Bur., 2000), leadership & work (advocacy, lobbying, presentations) Establishing HIV/AIDS Services (Sidney Borum Award-Mass. Dept HIV/AID Bur., 1994), work on statewide consumer advisory bd (evaluate and create hiv/aids services) Member of Statewide Consumer Advisory Bd (Appreciation from Mass. DPH-HIV/AIDS Bur., 2000). Bd. mem. Mass. Dept. Pub. Health Statewide Bd., Boston, 1994—2000; presenter AIDS, Medicine & Miracle, Phoenicia, NY; bd. mem. Springfield Mayor's AIDS Coun., Mass., 1999—2001. Recipient 10th Ann. Award of Honour, High World Internat. Orgn., UN Youth XXI, 2000, Excellence in HIV/AIDS award, River Valley Counselling Ctr., 2001; grant, Internat. Aids Conf. Com., 2000. Baptist. Achievements include development of Drop-In Center; instrumental in passing the Stand-by Guardianship law; featured in a book The Right Side of Forty. Avocations: sewing, cooking, travel, crossword puzzles, puzzles. Home: 303 Fernbank Rd #5 Springfield MA 01129 Personal E-mail: thlwar@comcast.net.

PRICHARD, KATHRYN, adult education educator; MEd, Mansfield U., Pa., 1986. Cert. Reading Specialist Mansfield U., 1983, Mid Level Citizenship Edn. grade 7-9 Pa., 2003. Tchr. Athens Area Sch. Dist., Pa., 1988—. V.p. Cherry Grove Cemetery Assn., Nordmont, Pa., 2002—06.

PRICHARD, LONA ANN, retired elementary school educator; b. Mt. Washington, Ky., Jan. 13, 1938; d. Emil Hoke and Ernestine Ray (Hall) Harris; m. Robert Eugene Russell (div.); 1 child, Dora Lynn Russell; m. Richard John Prichard, June 26, 1982; stepchildren: Linda, Rick, Susan, Rita, Pat. Student, U. of the Cumberlands, Williamsburg, Ky., 1956—58; BS in Elem. Edn., Eastern Ky. State U., Richmond, 1961; MS in Elem. Edn., Berry Coll., Rome, Ga., 1974. Cert. tchr. Tchr. 5th and 6th grade Mt. Washington (Ky.) Elem. Sch., 1958-59; thcr. one-rm. sch., grades 1-8 Pulaski County, Somerset, Ky., 1961-62; tchr. 1st grade Osburn Sch., Chickamauga, Ga., 1963-66; tchr. Rock Spring (Ga.) Elem. Sch., 1966-71, North Rossville Elem. Sch., 1971-93; tchr. 1st grade and spl. edn. Rossville Elem. Sch., 1993-2000, ret., 2000. Mem. NEA, Ga. Assn. Educators, Walker County Edn. Assn. Baptist. Avocations: reading, painting, tutoring, conversational English. Home: 1300 Michael Ln Hixson TN 37343-4334 Personal E-mail: rjprichard@msn.com.

PRIDDY, JEAN MARIE, music educator, voice educator; b. Andrews AFB, Md., Apr. 12, 1962; d. Sandra J. and George J. Wanner; m. Greg A Priddy, June 7, 1986. AS, Bluefield Coll., 1986, BA cum laude, 1986; MA in Music Edn., Case Western Res. U., 1990. Profl. Music Edn. Cert. K-12 State of Ohio, 1990. Music tchr. St. Mary's Sch., Collinwood, Ohio, 1990—92, St. Felicitas Sch., Euclid, Ohio, 1990—91; music dir. Lake Cath. H.S., Mentor, Ohio, 1991—2002; voice tchr. Rabbit Run Cmty. Arts Assn., Madison, Ohio, 2002—, Fairport Exempted Village Schs., 2003—, JMPriddy Voice Studios, Mentor, Ohio, 2002—. Sec. Lake County Music Educator's Assn., Mentor, Ohio, 1992—95; pres. Ohio Coll. Music Edn. Assn. CWRU Chpt., 1989—90; mem. play selection com. Rabbit Run Cmty. Arts Assn., Madison, Ohio, 2002; adj. faculty voice Lake Erie Coll., 2006—. Dir.: (musical theater) Once Upon a Mattress, Bye Bye Birdie, Little Shop of Horrors, Starmites, Gold Dust, Anything Goes; singer: Four Spirituals by Needham (World Premier); dir.: Babes In Arms; singer (mother): (opera) Amahl and the Night Visitors; singer: South Pacific at Rabbit Run Theater. Recipient Dennison U. Tchg. Excellence award, Dennison U., 2000, Coll. of Wooster Excellence in Tchg. award, Coll. of Wooster, 2000. Mem.: Lake County Music Educators Assn. (sec. 1992—95, treas. 2003—), Ohio Music Edn. Assn., Music Edn. Nat. Conf., AAUW. Avocations: reading, cooking, jewelry, music, musical theater. Home: 6265 Glenwood Dr Mentor OH 44060 Office Phone: 216-789-0550. Personal E-mail: jmpriddy@multiverse.com.

PRIDE, MIRIAM R., college president; b. Canton, China, June 6, 1948; d. Richard E. and Martha W. Pride; divorced. Grad., Berea College Found. Sch., 1966, Coll. of Wooster, 1970; MBA, U. Ky., 1989. Intern in administrn. in higher edn., head resident Coll. of Wooster, Ohio, 1970-72; accounts payable clk., dir. Boone Tavern Hotel, head resident, dir. student activities Berea Coll., 1972-88; eligibility worker dept. human resources State of Ky., 1975-76; asst. in undergrad. advising Coll. Bus., U. Ky., 1987-89; asst. to pres. for campus life, v.p. for administrn., pres. Blackburn Coll., Carlinville, Ill., 1989—. Chmn. United Way Berea, Carlinville, 1989—92; fin. chmn. Carlinville Hosp., 1995—97; mem. Ill. Commn. on Status of Women; bd. dirs. Land of Lincoln Girl Scouts, 1993—2000, fin. chmn., 1995—2000, mem. nominating com., 2000—; bd. dirs. Carlinville Area Hosp., 1993—97, Assn. Presbyn. Colls. and Univs., Fedn. Ill. Colls. and Univs., 1993—, Federated Ch. Bd., 1998—2001. Mem. Carlinville C. of C. (bd. dirs.), Rotary (bd. dirs. 1996—). Mem. Federated Ch. Avocations: reading, walking, knitting. Office: Blackburn Coll Office of the President Carlinville IL 62626

PRIEBE, SUE, retired secondary school educator, minister; b. Milw., Apr. 29, 1951; d. Russell and Doris Priebe. BS in English Edn., U. Wis., Whitewater, 1973; MEd, Viterbo U., LaCrosse, Wis., 1992. Ordained to minister Faith Bible Ch., 2005. Tchr. Parkview Sch. Dist., Orfordville, Wis., 1974—2006; ret., 2006. Yearbook advisor Parkview HS, Orfordville, 1986—2006; union negotiator Parkview Schs. Edn. Assn., Orfordville, 2004—. Sunday sch. tchr. City of Hope, Janesville, Wis., 1978—2006, music dir., 1980—2005, dir. women's ministry, 2001—06, assoc. pastor, 2005—. Kohl Found. fellow, 2004. Mem.: Am. Assn. Christian Counselors. Avocations: gardening, reading, bicycling, needlecrafts, crocheting. Office Phone: 608-755-0434.

PRIESAND, SALLY JANE, rabbi; b. Cleve., June 27, 1946; d. Irving Theodore and Rosetta Elizabeth (Welch) P. BA in English, U. Cin., 1968; B.Hebrew Letters, Hebrew Union Coll.-Jewish Inst. Religion, 1971, MA in Hebrew Letters, 1972; D.H.L. (hon.), Fla. Internat. U., 1973; DD (hon.), Hebrew Union Coll., 1997. Ordained rabbi 1972. Student rabbi Sinai Temple, Champaign, Ill., 1968, Congregation B'nai Israel, Hattiesburg, Miss., 1969-70, Congregation Shalom, Milw., 1970, Temple Beth Israel, Jackson, Mich., 1970-71; rabbinic intern Isaac M. Wise Temple, Cin., 1971-72; asst. rabbi Stephen Wise Free Synagogue, N.Y.C., 1972-77, assoc. rabbi, 1977-79; rabbi Temple Beth El, Elizabeth, NJ, 1979-81, Monmouth Reform Temple, Tinton Falls, 1981—2006, rabbi emeritus, 2006—; chaplain Lenox Hill Hosp., N.Y.C., 1979-81. Author: Judaism and the New Woman, 1975. Mem. commn. on synagogue rels. Fedn. Jewish Philanthropies N.Y., 1972-79, mem. com. on aged commn. synagogue rels., 1972-75; mem. task force on equality of women in Judaism pub. affairs com. N.Y. Fedn. Reform Synagogues, 1972-75; mem. com. on resolutions Ctrl. Conf. Am. Rabbis, 1975-77, com. on cults, 1976-78, admissions com., 1983-89; chmn. Task Force on Women in Rabbinate, 1977-83, chmn. 1977-79, mem. exec. bd., 1977-79, com. on resolutions, 1989-92, chmn. com. conv. program, 1993-96; mem. joint commn. on Jewish edn. Ctrl. Conf. Am. Rabbis-Union Am. Hebrew Congregations, 1974-77; mem. task force on Jewish singles Commn. Synagogue Rels., 1975-77; mem. N.Y. Bd. Rabbis, 1975—, Shore Area Bd. Rabbis, 1981—; mem. interim steering com. Clergy and Laity Concerned, 1979-81; bd. dirs. NCCJ, N.Y.C., 1980-82, Jewish Fedn. Greater Monmouth County, trustee, 1988-2000, strategic planning commn., 1996—, hon. v.p., 2000—; trustee Planned Parenthood of Monmouth County, 1982-90; v.p. Interfaith Neighbors, 1988-96, pres., 1997—; mem. UAHC-CCAR Joint Commn. on Synagogue Affiliation, 1992-2002; bd. govs. Hebrew Union Coll.-Jewish Inst. Religion, 1993-2005; trustee Union Am. Hebrew Congregations, 1994-98. Cited by B'nai Brith Women, 1971; named Woman of Yr. Temple Israel, Columbus, Ohio, 1972, Woman of Yr. Ladies Aux. N.Y. chpt. Jewish War Vets., 1973, Woman for All Seasons N.L.I. region Women's Am. ORT, 1973, Extraordinary Women of Achievement NCCJ, 1978, Woman of Achievement Monmouth County Adv. Commn. on Status Women, 1988; recipient Quality of Life award Dist. One chpt. B'nai B'rith Women, 1973, Medallion Judaic Heritage Soc., 1978, Eleanor Roosevelt Humanities award Women's div. State of Israel Bonds, 1980, Rabbinical award Coun. Jewish Fedn., 1988, Woman of Leadership award Monmouth Coun. Girl Scouts U.S., 1991, The Woman Who Dares award Nat. Coun. Jewish Women, 1993, Women's Studies Disting. Alumnae award Friends of Women's Studies U. Cin., 1997; named to Alumni Hall of Fame, Fairview Park H.S., 2002. Mem. Hadassah (life), Ctrl. Conf. Am. Rabbis, NOW, Am. Jewish Congress, Am. Jewish Com., Assn. Reform Zionists Am., Jewish Women Internat. (life), Jewish Peace Fellowship, Women's Rabbinic Network, Nat. Breast Cancer Coalition, HUC-JIR Rabbinic Alumni Assn. (sec., treas. 1997-99, v.p. 1999-2001, pres. 2001-03, past pres., 2003-05). Achievements include being the first US women rabbi. Home: 10 Wedgewood Cir Eatontown NJ 07724-1203 Office: 332 Hance Ave Eatontown NJ 07724-2730 Office Phone: 732-747-9365. E-mail: spriesand@monmouth.com.

PRIEST, ALEXIA Z., purchasing agent; b. Waterbury, Conn., Sept. 17, 1954; d. John Joseph and Vera (Mandzik) Zurlis; 1 child, Jason Farrell; m. Alan Priest, Apr. 30, 2004; stepchilden: Brandon, Tyson. BBA, U. Miami, Coral Gables, Fla.; MBA, U. New Haven. Buyer Hewlett Packard, Cupeztino, Calif., 1981-83; purchase mgr. ICI, Redmond, Wash., 1983-84; commodity mgr. No. Telecom, St. Mountain, Ga., 1985-88; mfg. rep. Montgomery Mktg., Norcross, Ga., 1988-90; internat. purchasing agt. Sci. Atlanta, Norcross, Ga., 1990-91; sr. buyer Amphenol, Danbury, Conn., 1992-94; purchasing mgr. Danaher-Gulton Graphic, East Greenwhich, R.I., 1994-96; materials control mgr. Amphenol Corp., Danbury, Conn., 1996-2000; materials mgmt. The Siemon Co., Watertown, Conn., 2000—; purchasing agt. Boehinger-Ingelheim Pharms., Inc., 2001—. Prof. econs., internat. bus., logistics and mgmt. Teikyo Post U. Miami scholar, 1974-75. Mem. Women in Electronics (v.p. sponsors 1989-90, guest speaker 1989), NAFE, Nat. Assn. Purchasing Mgrs. Democrat. Roman Catholic. Avocations: golf, tennis, swimming, reading, jogging. Home: 18 Cynthia St Waterbury CT 06708-2702 Office: Boehringher Ingelheim Purchasing Agt Ridgefield CT 06877 Personal E-mail: aclaryhome@aol.com.

PRIEST, DANA, journalist; married; 2 children. BA, U. Calif., Santa Cruz. Intelligence reporter, Nat. News Desk Washington Post, 1987—. Author: The Mission: Waging War & Keeping Peace with America's Military, 2003 (Pulitzer prize finalist for gen. non-fiction, 2004). Recipient MacArthur Found. Rsch. & Writing grant, 2001, Gerald R. Ford prize for Disting. Reporting on Nat. Def., 2001, Excellence in Journalism award, State Dept., 2001, George Polk award for nat. reporting, 2006, Pulitzer Prize for beat reporting, 2006, Bob Considine award, Overseas Press Club, 2006. Office: Washington Post Nat News Desk 1150 15th St Washington DC 20071-0070 Office Phone: 202-334-4490. Office Fax: 202-496-3883. E-mail: priestd@washpost.com.*

PRIEST, JESSIE SHAW, media specialist; d. Shaw Wesley and Shaw McFadden (Teddie) James; m. David Priest, Dec. 27, 1972; children: David, LaDawndrea Catoria. Cert. edn. tchr. SC State Dept. of Edn., 1967. Reading tchr. Chavis Elem. Sch., Hemmingway, SC, 1967—70; elem. tchr., 1967—73; media specialist Planterville Elem. Sch., Georgetown, SC, 1970—2005.

PRIEST, SHARON DEVLIN, retired state official, not-for-profit developer; b. Montreal, Can. m. Bill Priest; one son Adam. Tax preparer, instr. H & R Block, Little Rock, 1976-78; owner, founder Devlin Co., Ark., 1983-86; account exec. Greater Little Rock C. of C., 1990-94; vice mayor Little Rock, 1989-90, mayor, 1991-92; Sec. of State State of Ark., 1994—2002; exec. dir. The Downtown Partnership, 2002—. Bd. dir. Invesco Inc., New Futures. Bd. dirs., past pres. Metroplan (Environ. Svc. Award 1982), YMCA, Southwest Hosp.; bd. dirs. Fed. Reserve Bank St. Louis; mem. Carter-Baker Commn. Fed. Election Reform Commn., Advt. and Promotion commn., Ark. Internat. Visitors Coun., Pulaski Are Transp. Svc. Policy Com., St. Theresa's Parish Coun., Exec. com. for Ark. Mcpl. League, Nat. League of Cities Trans. and Comm. Steering Com. and Policy Com., adv. bd. M.M. Cohn., Little Rock City Beautiful Commn., 1980-86, Carter Barker Election Reform Commn., 2005, BP Ind. Safety Panel, 2005-06; former bd. dir. Downtown Partnership, S.W. YMCA, 1984, 86, sec.; former mem. Cmty. Housing Resource Bd., 1984-86, Pub. Facilities Bd. S.W. Hosp., 1985-86, S.W. Merchants' Assn., 1985—, 2d v.p., 1985; chmn. Little Rock Arts and Humanities Promotion Commn.; led petition dr. for appropriation for Fourche Creek Plan 7A. Recipient of the Fighting Back Freedom Fighter Award, 1995; Environ. Svc. Award from the Little Rock Metroplan Comm., 1982. Mem. Leadership Inst. Alumni Assn. (4 Bernard de la Harpe Awards), Rotary. Achievements include being selected by Ark. Bus. as one of the Top 100 Women in Ark. Office: Downtown Partnership PO Box 1937 Little Rock AR 72203 Office Phone: 501-375-0121. Business E-Mail: spriest@downtownlr.com.

PRIESZ, CONNIE JOAN, secondary school educator; b. Mpls., Jan. 6, 1956; d. Jerry Jerome and Edna Lenore (Ayer) Lamon; m. Douglas Lee Tietz. BA in Phys. Edn. and Elem. Edn., Augsburg Coll., 1978; MS in Curriculum Instrn., Mankato (Minn.) State U., 1988. Tchr. phys. edn. and health Orono Sch. Dist. 278, Long Lake, Minn., 1978—, coach high sch. gymnastics, 1979—2003; coach high sch. track Orono Sch. Dist. 278, Long Lake, Minn., 1982-88; mid. sch. volleyball coach Orono Sch. Dist. 278, Long Lake, Minn., 1989—93, health curriculum coord., 1996—. Supr. traveling students Sch. Dist. 278 and Isabella Environ. Learning Ctr., Washington, 1983—. Volunteer twin study U. Minn., Mpls., 1973—; coach track and field Spl. Olympics, Mpls., 1985-95; ride mgr. St. Judes Children's Hosp., Loretto, 1986-89; instr. AIDS, ARC, Mpls., 1988—; U.S. cen. team mem. N.Am. Championship Endurance Ride, Carson City, Nev., 1991. Recipient 15-Yr. Svc. Pin Minn. ARC, 1999, Qualified Rider award U.S. Dressage Fedn., 1987, U.S. Nat. Internat. Arabian Horse Assn. Dressage Competition, 1986, Canadian Nat. Internat. Arabian Horse Assn. Dressage Competition, 1990; Top Ten, Internat. Arabian Horse Assn. Nat. Competitive Ride, Endurance Rookie of Yr. award Upper Midwest Endurance and Competitive Riding Assn., 1990, Versitility award AHDRA, 1990, various athletic awards; inducted into Hall of Fame, Minn. Girls' Gymnastics Coaches Assn., 1995, Augsburg Coll., 2002. Mem. NEA, Minn. Edn. Assn., Minn. State High Sch. Coaches Assn. (clinician 1982), Minn. State Girl's Gymnastics Judges Assn. (clinician), Orono Edn. Assn. (membership chmn. 1988—), North Cen. Assn. Colls. and Schs. (validation team Albert Lea, Minn. chpt. 1983), Minn. Mid. Level Educators Assn., Stepfamily Am. Assn. Home: 13401 Marystown Rd Shakopee MN 55379-9131 Office: Orono Sch Dist 278 685 N Old Crystal Bay Rd Long Lake MN 55356-8315

PRIETO, EMILY J., small business owner, consultant; b. Columbus, Ohio, Mar. 6, 1969; d. Paul J. and Dana Navin; m. Thomas Prieto, Aug. 30, 1997. MBA, Franklin U., Columbus, Ohio, 2005. LCSW social worker Ohio, 1995; cert. Activities Dir. Ohio, 1992. Social worker Beverly Health and Rehab, Columbus, 1995—96, MacIntosh Co., Columbus, 1996—97; social worker/program mgr. Heritage Day Health Ctr., Columbus, 1998—2000; owner/operator 2nd Watch Sr. Care, Columbus, 2001—; program mgr. Preservation Ohio, Springfield, 2006—. Vol. guardian Franklin County Vol. Guardian Program, Columbus, 1997—; mem. Ctrl. Ohio Geriatric Social Work Assn., Columbus, 1998—2001. Author (editor): Making the Most of Your Visits, short stories. On air reader for the blind VoiceCorps, Columbus, 2002—06; adv. Columbus Landmarks Found., Columbus, 2002—06; vol. various founds. Recipient Employee of the Yr., Heritage Day Health Ctr., 1999, Nat. Honor Societies: Sociology and Human Svcs., Nat. Assns., 1992, Point of LIght, Pres. Bill Clinton, 1998. Mem.: LWV. Avocations: travel, reading, gardening. Office: 2nd Watch Sr Care LLC Po 6569 Columbus OH 43206 Office Phone: 614-253-0360. Personal E-mail: a2ndwatch@yahoo.com.

PRIETO, MONIQUE N., artist; b. LA, 1962; BFA, UCLA, 1987, Calif. Inst. Arts, 1992, MFA, 1994. One-woman shows include ACME, Santa Monica, Calif., 1994, 1995, 1996, 1997, 1999, 2000, 2001, Bravin Post Lee, N.Y.C., 1996, Anderson Gallery, Va. Commonwealth U., Richmond, 1997, Pat Hearn Gallery, N.Y.C., 1998, Robert Prime, London, 1998, Corvi-Mora, London, Eng., 2000, 2002, Cheim & Read, NY, 2002, 2005, Il Capricorno, Venice, Italy, 2003, Out of the Blue, ACME Gallery, LA, 2004, Scottsdale Mus. Contemporary Art, 2005, exhibited in group shows at Wight Gallery, UCLA, 1987, Bacilla Hernandez Gallery, Long Beach, Calif., 1989, Lockheed Gallery, Valencia, Calif., 1994, Pat Hearn Gallery, N.Y.C., 1996, 1997, Factory Place Gallery, L.A., 1996, Armand Hammer Sales and Rental Gallery, 1997, ACME, Santa Monica, 1997, Orange County Mus. Art, Newport Beach, Calif., 1997, Abstract Painting, Once Removed, Contemporary Arts Mus., Houston, Tex., 1998, Etcetera, Spacex Gallery, Exeter, Eng., 1999, Facts & Fiction II: LA, Arco, Torino, Italy, 1999, Ambient Fiction, Pat Hearn Gallery, NY, 2001, The Figure in the Landscape, Lehmann Maupin Gallery, 2001, The Sensational Line, Mus. Contemporary Art, Denver, 2001, Flatline, Cirrus Gallery, LA, 2002, The Galleries Show, Royal Acad., London, 2002, Before and After Science, Marella Art Contemporanea, Milan, 2003, Drunk vx. Stoned, Gavin Brown's Enterprise, NY, 2005, Extreme Abstraction, Albright-Knox Art Gallery, Buffalo, NY, 2005, Tet a Tete, Greenberg Van Doren, NY, 2005. Herb Alpert scholar, 1992—93, Philip Morris fellow, 1992—94, Skowhegan Sch. Painting and Sculpture fellow, 1994, Louis Comfort Tiffany Found grant, 1998. Mailing: c/o Chem & Read Gallery 547 West 25th St New York NY 10001*

PRIETO, NYCTHIA OPHELIA M., realtor; d. Bernardino R. and Remedios M. Magbanua; m. Daniel Corneja, Jr. Prieto, Sept. 24, 1966; children: Ma-Nerissa, Daniel Bernard III, David John Esquire. BS, U. Philippines, 1957; RN, St. Paul's Sch. Nursing, Philippines, 1961; degree (cum laude), Newark City Hosp. Sch. Nursing, N.J., 1965. Staff nurse New Rochelle Hosp., NY, 1966—67; realtor Long and Foster Nat. Bd. Realtors, McLean, Va., 1983—; ind. stock broker Fairfax, Va., 1992—; ops. R.A. United Airlines, Sterling, Va., 1996—2006; sr. ptnr., agent Alpha Serv Internat. Corp., Fairfax, Va., 2006—. Sponsor, donor Gawad Kalinga, Philippines; mem., vol., contbr. Rep. Party Com., Fairfax County. Mem.: Northern Va. Bd. Realtors, Nat. Bd. Realtors, Philippine Med. Assn. Aux. Republican. Roman Catholic. Office: Alpha Serv Internat Corp Burke VA Personal E-mail: nikiprieto@aol.com.

PRIMACK, ALICE LEFLER, retired librarian; b. Kent, Ohio, Feb. 14, 1939; d. Glenn Q. and Mary S. (Staley) Lefler; m. Robert B. Primack; children: Eric, Mary-Anne, Glenn. BS, Ea. Ill. U., 1961; MLS, U. Wis., 1962. Libr. intern Ohio State U., Columbus, 1962-63, reference, bot. and zool. librarian, 1963-64, head Pharmacy Libr., 1964-66; from asst. to assoc. librarian U. Fla., Gainesville, 1972-92, Univ. librarian, 1992—2005; ret., 2005. Author: How to Find Out in Pharmacy, 1969, Finding Answers in Science and Technology, 1984, Journal Literature of the Physical Sciences, 1992. Mem. adv. bd. 4-H of Alachua County, Fla., 1989—; officer Unitarian-Universalist Fellowship of Gainesville. Mem.: Fla. Free Speech Forum, Spl. Librs. Assn. (pres. Fla. and Caribbean chpt. 1996—98). Democrat. Personal E-mail: theprimacks@bellsouth.net.

PRIMMER, LILLIAN JUANDA, science educator; d. Melvin Palmer and Amanda Severina (Olstad) Bekkum; m. Donald Gale Primmer, June 17, 1967; children: Donald Guy, Jacqueline Juanda Gruber. BS, U. Wis., 1990, MEd, 1993. Tchr. Clintonville Pub. Schs., Wis., 1990—96; part-time tchr. Christa McAulliffe Acad., Appleton, Wis., 2002, 2004. Part-time tchr. Enstein Acad., Green Bay, Wis., 1991; participant/tchr.-facilitator Sci. World, Drummond, Wis., 1994—99; pres. Wis. Elem. & Middle Level Sci. Tchrs., Wis., 1998—99. Merit badge counselor Boy Scouts/Girl Scouts, Clintonville, Wis., 1990—; hunter safety instr. Dept. Nat. Resources, Clintonville, 1994—; fundraiser, participating survivor Relay for Life, Clintonville, Viroqua. Recipient Disting. Tchr. Sci., Wis. Elem. Sci. Tchrs., 1995; grantee Earthwatch grant, Wis. Acad. Scis., Arts & Letters, 1994. Mem.: NSTA, Wis. Soc. Sci. Tchrs. (co-chair forum com., Outstanding Tchr. Sci. 1996). Avocations: hunting, fishing, camping, volleyball, knitting. Home: 69 Ninth St Clintonville WI 54929

PRIMO, JOAN ERWINA, retail and real estate consulting business owner; b. Detroit, Aug. 28, 1959; d. Joseph Carmen and Marie Ann (Nash) P.; m. David James Yared, Sept. 20, 1997; 1 son, Benjamin Primo Yared. BA, Wellesley Coll., 1981; MBA, Harvard U., 1985. Acct. exec. Michigan Bell, Detroit, 1981—82, AT&T Info. Sys., Southfield, Mich., 1983; planning analyst Gen. Motors, Detroit, 1984; v.p. Howard L. Green & Assocs., Troy, Mich., 1985—89; prin., founder Strategic Edge, Inc., Southfield, 1989—. Contbr. articles to profl. jours. Mem. founders soc. Detroit Inst. Arts, 1989—; rsch. advisory task force com. officer Mich. State U; v.p. Detroit County Day Sch., 2005—. Mem.: Internat. Coun. Shopping Ctrs. (faculty, seminar leader 1987—, Mich. state com. officer, rsch. adv. task force), Detroit Country Day Sch.-Lower Sch. Parents Assn. (bd. dirs. 2004—05, v.p. 2005—06, pres. 2006—), Ivy Club Detroit (bd. dirs. 1994—, sec. 1995—99), Harvard Bus. Sch. Club Detroit (bd. dirs. 1994—98, v.p. 1995—96, exec. v.p. 1996—97), Wellesley Club Southeastern Mich. (pres. 1994—98). Republican. Avocations: antiques, travel, theater, gourmet cooking. Home: 224 Woodwind Dr Bloomfield Hills MI 48304-2172 Office: The Strategic Edge 24333 Southfield Rd Ste 211 Southfield MI 48075-2849 Office Phone: 248-557-1664. Business E-Mail: jprimo@thestrategicedge.com.

PRINCE, ANNA LOU, composer, music publisher, construction executive; b. Isabella, Tenn., May 28, 1935; d. Ulysses Gordon and Della Carrie (Hawkins) P.; children: Sandra, Teresa, Vandi. Diploma, Carolina Sch. Broadcasting, 1966; Zion diploma, Israel Bible Sch., Jerusalem, 1970; diploma, S.W. Tech. Coll., 1970; student, United Christian Assn., 1976; MusD, London Inst. Applied Rsch., 1991; diplomatic diploma, Acad. Argentina de Diplomacia, 1993; PhD (hon.), Australian Inst. Coord. Rsch., Victoria, 1993; diploma of honors on internat. affairs, Inst. Des Affaires Internat., Paris, 1994. Lic. Bible tchr. United Christian Acad. Songwriter Hank Locklin Music Co., Nashville, 1963-70; entertainer 1982 World's Fair, Knoxville, Tenn., 1982; ptnr., owner Prince Wholesale Bait Co., Canton, N.C., 1976-82, Grad Builders, Canton, 1982-86, Prince TV Co., Canton, 1986—. Music pub. Broadcast Music, Inc., Nashville, 1982—; mem. prodn. staff, talent coord. (TV series) Down Home, Down Under, 1989-90; host TV show Real Heros of Country Music in Nashville, 1997-2003. Songs recorded on RCA: I Feel a Cry Coming On, 1965 (#1 in Eng.), Best Part of Loving You, (#1 in Eng.), Anna, 1969 (Billboard 1970, recorded in Ireland 1974, hit in Europe and New Zealand); singer, composer I'm In Love With You, 1995; over 20 songs recorded to date; appeared Grand Ole Opry, 1970; exec. prodr., host TV talk show, Real Hereos of Country Music, 1989— (Emmy nomination 1997); author: The Strange Life of Anna Price, 2006. Cand. for county commr. Dem. Party Macon County, N.C., 1984; bd. dirs. Macon County Taxpayers Assn., Inc., 1984, v.p., 1984-86; bd. dirs. Head Start, Topton, N.C., 1969-73; judge Emmy Awards, Am. Registrar Ohio Valley, 2002— Nominated Disting. Women N.C., N.C. Coun. Coun. on Status of Women, 1984, Jefferson award WYFF TV and Am. Inst. for Pub. Svc., Outstanding Bus. Woman Small Bus. Adminstrn., 1984. Mem. BMI, Internat. Parliament Safety and Peace (life, dept. fgn. affairs, dep. mem. assembly), Nashville Songwriters Assn. Internat. (moderator, tchr. 1984-86), Country Music Assn., Reunion Profl. Entertainers, Fraternal Order Police, C. of C., Order of Knight of Templars (dame) Lofsensic Order (dame), Maison Internat. des Intellectuals. Democrat. Personal E-mail: annaprincebook@aol.com.

PRINCE, GINGER LEE, actress, choreographer, educator; b. Stuart, Fla., June 3, 1945; d. Hugh Frederick and Gladys Inez (Davis) P.; children: Jessica Elizabeth McMaster, Jennifer Lee Hall. Student, Stephens Coll. Performing

Arts, 1961. Faculty, bd. dirs. Sande Shurin Acting Studio, N.Y.C., 1981—; adj. prof. Marymount Manhattan Coll., N.Y.C.; guest tchr., dir., chor. Stephens Coll., Columbia, Mo., 1997; lectr. Va. Intermont Coll.; ensemble dir., asst. choreographer Theatre Under the Stars; co-dir., choreographer-in-residence, ballet mistress The Atlanta Ballet; assoc. dir. Southern Ballet of Atlanta; active the Charleston Ballet, Lexington Ballet, Bristol Concer Ballet, Augusta Ballet Co., Louisville Ballet, Tampa Ballet, Southern Ballet Theatre, Orlando, Capital City Ballet, Atlanta, Ruth Mitchell Concert Dance, Atlanta. Choreographer: Tribute to Patti LuPone, Taking My Turn, New Lawrence Welk Show, She Loves Me, Big Band at the Savoy, Company, Lawrence Welk Family Christmas (with the Lennon Sisters), 2000, Carousel, 2001; actress: (Broadway) Gypsy, Ain't Broadway Grand; (off-Broadway) Steel Magnolias (original Broadway cast), After the Dancing in Jericho, The Jericho 7, Tribute to David Merrick; (U.S. nat. tours) La Cage Aux Folles, Pippin, George M!!, Can-Can, Oklahoma, Most Happy Fella; (regional theatre) Pippin, Gilligan's Island, Same Time, Next Year, Vanities, Bus Stop, The Rainmaker, The Odd Couple; (stock) Guys and Dolls, Gypsy, Mame, Peter Pan, Sweet Charity, Pippin, Annie, Something's Afoot, Pal Joey, Goldiggers of 1633, I Do, I Do, Kiss Me Kate, Dames at Sea, Brigadoon, Showboat, Music Man, Oklahoma, Damn Yankees, Driving Miss Daisy, 2000. Appointed mem. by Gov. Jimmy Carter Ga. Coun. for the Arts, 1970-74. Nat. Choreography grantee NEA, 1976, 85. Mem.: SAG, AFTRA, Nat. Assn. Am. Dance Artists, Dance Educators Am., Actor's Equity Assn., Soc. Stage Dirs. Choreographers.

PRINCE, LEAH FANCHON, lab administrator, executive secretary; b. Hartford, Conn., Aug. 12, 1939; d. Meyer and Annie (Forman) Berman; m. Herbert N. Prince, Jan. 30, 1955; children: Daniel L., Richard N., Robert G. Student, U. Conn., 1957—59, Rutgers U., 1962; BFA, Fairleigh Dickinson U., 1970; postgrad., Caldwell Coll. for Women, 1973—75, Parsons Sch. of Design, N.Y.C., 1978. Cert. tchr. art, N.J. Tchr. art Caldwell-West Caldwell Pub. Schs., NJ, 1970—75; pres. Britannia Imports Ltd., Fairfield, NJ, 1979—89; tchr. religious studies Bohrer-Kaufman Hebrew Acad., Randolph, NJ, 1981—82; co-founder, corp. sec. Gibraltar Biol. Labs., Inc., Fairfield, 1970—; dir., co-founder Gibraltar Inst. for Rsch. and Tng., Fairfield, 1984—. Cons. Internat. Antiques and Fine Arts Industries, U.K., 1979-89; cons. in art exhibitry Passaic County Coll., Paterson, N.J., 1989-93; art curator Fairleigh Dickinson U., Rutherford, N.J., 1972-74; curator history of nursing 20th century Bloomfield (N.J.) Coll., 1990-91; lectr. Am. Soc. Microbiology, New Orleans, 1989; spkr. in field. Exhibited in group shows at Bloomfield (N.J.) Coll., 1990, Caldwell Women's Club, N.J., 1991, State Fedn. Women's Clubs Ann. Show, 1992 (1st pl. award 1992), Newark Art Mus., 1992, West (N.J.) Essex Art Assn., 1990, Somerset (N.J.) Art Assn., 1994, Mortimer Gallery, Gladstone, N.J., 1994 (1st pl. award 1998), Tewksbury His. Soc. (1st pl. award 1994, 2004), Tewksbury Hist. Soc., 2001,02, 04, 05, Nat. Meeting Am. Pen Women, Calif., 2002, Washington, 2004 (1st pl. award); one-woman shows include Passaic County Coll., N.J., 1990, Caldwell Coll., 1990; author children's stories. Chair ann. juried art awards Arts Coun. of Essex Bd. Trustees, Montclair, N.J., 1984-90; chair fundraising Arts Coun. Essex County, N.J., 1989. Recipient 1st place award, N.J. Tewksbury Hist. Soc., 1994, 1998, 2004—05, Juried Art award, 2001—02, 2004, 2005. Mem. AAUW, Soc. Childrens Book Writers and Illustrators, Somerset Art Assn., Nat. League Am. Pen Women (pres. N.J. br., Juried Art award 2001, 2004), Barnegat Light Yacht Club. Republican. Avocations: boating, tennis, opera, painting, travel. Home: 5 Standish Dr Mendham Twp Morristown NJ 07960-3224

PRINCE-STOKES, CATHY, neuro-orthopedic nurse administrator; b. McCaysville, Ga., Oct. 6, 1956; d. Joseph H. and Charlene E. (Aaron) Long; m. James Darryl Prince, Aug. 19, 1983; 1 child, Christy Renae McDaniel-Olive; m. Kenneth Stokes, Oct. 27, 1996. Diploma, Dalton Vocat. Sch. Health Occupations, 1979; ASN, North Ga. Coll., 1987. RN, Ga. Nursing asst. Fannin Regional Hosp., Blue Ridge, Ga.; EMT, Gilmer County Emergency Med. System, Ellijay, Ga.; EMT Pickens County Emergency Med. System, Jasper, Ga.; advanced clin. nurse NE Ga. Med. Ctr., Gainesville; DON Mountainside Nursing Home, Jasper, Ga. Home: PO Box 26 East Ellijay GA 30539-0001

PRINCETON, JOY CAROL, retired nursing educator; b. St. Paul, Minn., Dec. 8, 1935; d. Eugene Russell Princeton and Margaret Edna Ehlers Princeton; children: Todd A. Myers, Michael D. Myers, Sarah C. Mooney. BSN, U. Colo., 1969, MSN, 1970, MA in Anthropology, 1975, PhD in Anthropology, 1977. RN Minn., Colo., N.C., Utah. Head nurse, obstetrics Abbott Hosp., Mpls., 1958—65; supr. obstetrics Boulder Meml. Hosp., Colo., 1965—68; asst. prof. U. Co. Sch. Nursing, Denver, 1970—73; assoc. prof. Duke U. Sch. Nursing, Durham, NC, 1978—81; prof. U. Utah Coll. Nursing, Salt Lake City, 1982—95; assoc. dir. U. Hosp., Salt Lake City, 1987—91. Mem. White House Com. on Children & Youth, Colo. Chpt., Denver, 1970—73; expert panel mem. Am. Acad. Nursing, Culturally Competent and Sensitive Health Care, Washington, 1991—93; cons. U. N.C. Med. Sch., Chapel Hill, NC, 1984—85, U. Rochester Sch. of Nursing, NY, 1988, NIH, Nat. Ctr. Nursing Rsch., 1988, U. Capetown Sch. Medicine, South Africa, 1990—91, HHS, PHS Divsn. Nursing, Rockville, Md., 1987—88, 1990—91, St. Louis U. Med. Ctr., 1990—91, Regis Coll. Sch. of Nursing, Denver, 1990—91; adv. Utah State Dept. Health, Salt Lake City, 1991—92; cons. in field, grad. student mentor, 1995—. Author: Maternity Nursing Today, 1973—77 (Am. Nurses Assn. Book of Yr., Parent/Child Nursing, 1973); mem. editl. bd.: Health Care for Women, 1984—94, Medical Anthro Quar., 1984—88, 1993—94, Scholarly Inquiry for Nursing Practice, 1985—90, Jour. Profl. Nursing, 1985—91, 1994—97, Jour. Nursing Edn., 1991—94, Nursing Outlook Jour., 1993—94; contbr. articles to profl. jours.; review panel mem. profl. jours., 1995—2006. Named Nurse of Yr., NC Nurses Assn., 1980; grantee, Dept. Health and Human Svcs., 1982—95; Ednl. grants, Dept. Health, Edn. and Welfare, U. Colo. Programs, 1970—73, grants for master's and doctoral edn., U.S. Pub. Health Svc., 1982—95. Fellow: Soc. Applied Anthropology, Am. Acad. Nursing. Democrat. Avocations: library work, hiking, camping, travel. Home: 2720 14th St Boulder CO 80304 Office Phone: 303-444-8163.

PRINCIPAL, VICTORIA (VICTORIA REE PRINCIPALE), actress, film producer, writer; b. Fukuoka, Japan, Jan. 3, 1946; d. Victor and Ree (Veal) P.; m. Christopher Skinner (div.) m. Harry Glassman, 1985 (separated 2006) Attended, Miami-Dade Community Coll.; studied, Royal Acad. Ballet; studied acting with Max Croft, Al Sacks and Estelle Harman, Jean Scott, Royal Acad. Dramatic Arts. Created product line Principal Secret Skin Care, Color Principal Makeup. Worked as model, including TV commls.; appearences include (film) The Life and Times of Judge Roy Bean, 1972 (Golden Globe Nominee for Most Promising Newcomer), The Naked Ape, 1973, Earthquake, 1974, I Will I Will For Now, 1976, Vigilante Force, 1976, Michael Kael In Katango, 1998; (TV movies) Last Hours Before Morning, 1975, Fantasy Island, 1977, The Night They Took Miss Beautiful, 1977, Pleasure Palace, 1980, Not Just Another Affair, 1982, Mistress, 1987, Naked Lie, 1989 (also exec. prodr.), Blind Witness, 1989 (also co-exec. prodr.), The Burden of Proof, 1990, Sparks: The Price of Passion, 1990, Don't Touch My Daughter, 1991(also exec. prodr.), Just Life, 1992, Seduction: Three Tales from the Inner Sanctum, 1993 (also exec. prodr.), River of Rage: The Taking of Maggie Keene, 1993 (also exec. prodr.), Beyond Obsession, 1994, Dancing in the Dark, 1995, The Abduction, 1996, Love in Another Town, 1997, Time Flies, An Evening of Comic One-Acts; guest host An Evening at the Improv, 1982; exec. prodr. Midnight's Child, 1991; (TV series) Dallas, 1978-87; (theatre) Time Flies, LA Theatre Works, Love Letters, Canon Theatre, LA and Coral Gables Theatre, Fla., Mere Mortals, Second City, Chgo.; (TV miniseries) Greatest Heros of the Bible, 1978; guest appearances Hawaii Five-O, 1979, Fridays, 1982, Home Improvement, 1994, Chicago Hope, 1998, Tracey Takes On, 1999, Just Shoot Me!, 1999, Jack & Jill, 1999, 2001, Titans, 2000, The Practice, 2000, Family Guy (voice), 2000, Providence, 2000, Dallas Reunion: Return to Southfork, 2004; guest lead The Tracy Ullman Show, The Garry Shandling Show; author: The Body Principal, 1983, The Beauty Principal, 1984, The Diet Principal, 1987, Living Principal, 2001 Hon. chairperson, amb. Arthritis Found.; co-chair Victory Over Violence; mem. cmty. adv. coun. LA County Domestic Violence Coun.*

PRINGLE, NORMA JEAN POARCH, translator, educator; b. Kansas City, Mo., May 29, 1934; d. Travis and Frances Gertrude (Millard) Poarch; m. Robert McClelland Pringle, Feb. 17, 1972 (div. May 1983); 1 child, Travis McClelland. BA, Rockford Coll., 1956; MA, U. Mo., Kansas City, 1968; diploma, Agnese Haury Inst. for Ct. Interpreting, U. Ariz., 1985. Accredited translator by exam. Spanish to English Am. Translators Assn. Adj. instr. Spanish Columbia (Mo.) Coll., 1974—. Trainer, ct. interpreters Transimpex, Kansas City, Mo., 1998—; organizer conf. translators, Columbia, Mo., 1982, Columbia, 92. Author: (course outline for study) Judiciary Interpreting, 1998. Grantee Am. Lit., NEH, 1979. Mem.: Mid-Am. Chpt. Am. Translators Assn. (pres., sec., dir.), Nat. Assn. Judiciary Interpreters, Am. Translators Assn. Avocation: flamenco singing and dancing. Office: Columbia Coll 20th and Rogers Columbia MO 65216

PRINGLE, RUTH EVELYN, retired adult education educator; d. Leonard Henry and Edith L. (Henry) Gauger; m. John Philip Pringle, June 13, 1953; children: Lynne Ann Tinsley, Tamra Lea Kerns. Student, Drake U., Des Moines, Iowa, 1949. Draftsman Collins Radio, Cedar Rapids, Iowa, 1951—54; engr. McDonnel Aircraft, St. Louis; sci. and math subsitute tchr. Allen Ind. Sch. Dist., Allen, Tex., 1972—81, adult literacy dir. Adult Right to Read program, 1982—92. Mem. adv. coun. Tex. Ctr. for Adult Literacy and Learning, Tex. A & M U., College Station, Tex. Adult Literacy - Laubach, Austin; spkr. in field. Mem. adv. bd. Allen Pub. Libr., sec., 2001—02; mem. adv. bd. NE Tex. Libr. Sys.; active Allen Cmty. Outreach. Named Founder Allen Pub. Libr., Allen City Coun. and Allen Pub. Libr., 2005; recipient Citizen of Yr., Allen Ind. Sch. District-Community Edn., 1983, Advancement of Adult Literacy award, Collin County Adult Literacy Coun., 1983—84, Celebrate Litercy award, Internat. and NE Tex. Reading Coun., 1991. Mem.: Allen Ret. Educator's Assn. (treas. 2002—04), Friends of Note, Allen Philharm. Orch., Epsilon Sigma Alpha (pres. Beta Pi chpt. 1995—97, Woman of Yr. 1982, Alpha award, Sophia award, Sophrosyne award). Republican. Methodist. Avocations: reading, genealogy, gardening, travel.

PRINS, LAVONNE KAY, programmer analyst; b. Sibley, Iowa, Feb. 28, 1957; d. Henry Simon and Katherine (Schram) Prins. BA, S.W. State U., Marshall, Minn., 1982; postgrad., Mankato (Minn.) State U., 1982-84. Instr. math. Mankato State U., 1982-84; computer operator Sathers, Round Lake, Minn., 1985; law records analyst ITT Consumer Fin. Corp., St. Louis Park, Minn., 1985-86; systems programmer Metaphor, Eden Prairie, Minn., 1987-89; pres. Ablazon Unltd. Inc., Ramsey, Minn., 1990—97; sr. systems programmer Health Risk Mgmt., Edina, Minn., 1989-91; software engr. Dimensional Medicine, Inc., Minnetonka, Minn., 1992-95; programmer analyst DynaMark Inc., Arden Hills, Minn., 1995-98; sr. programmer analyst United Hardware Distbg. Co., Plymouth, Minn., 1998; ind. contractor, 1999—; inspector Boston Sci. Corp., 2000—02; pres. LaVonne's Home Businesses Inc., 2001—; food insp. USDA, 2002—. Sgt. U.S. Army, 1975-79. Republican. Mem. Reformed Ch. in Am. Avocations: sponsoring needy children, studying foreign languages, writing, piano, travel. Address: 1109 7th St S # 109-B Waite Park MN 56387-4626

PRINZ, KRISTIE DAWN, lawyer; b. Columbus, Ga., July 26, 1973; d. Stephen Charles and Helen Ann (Dunlap) P. BA in Spanish and Polit. Sci. summa cum laude, Furman U., 1995; JD, Vanderbilt U., 1998. Bar: Ga. 1998, Calif. 2001. Summer assoc. Rose Immigration Law Firm, Nashville, Tenn., 1996; rsch. asst. Vanderbilt U., Nashville, 1996-97; summer assoc. Bruce, Weathers, Corley, Dughman & Lyle, Nashville, 1997; assoc. Mozley, Finlayson & Loggins, LLP, Atlanta, 1998, Schnader Harrison Segal & Lewis LLP, Atlanta, 1999-2000, Pennie & Edmonds LLP, Palo Alto, Calif., 2000—. Mem. adv. bd. Knoxville Jour., 1990-91. Vol. tchr. English Classes for Refugees, Knoxville, Tenn, 1993; mem. Collegiate Ednl. Svc. Corps. Furman U., Greenville, S.C., 1991-95. Mem.: ABA, Computer Law Assn., Licensing Execs. Soc., Calif. Lawyers for the Arts, Forum for Women Entrepreneurs, Calif. Women Lawyers, Nat. Assn. Women Lawyers, San Francisco Bar Assn., Atlanta Bar Assn. (mem. Therell H.S. Com.), Palo Alto Bar Assn., Churchill Club, Phi Sigma Iota, Sigma Delta Pi, Phi Beta Kappa, Sr. Order Furman U., Kappa Alpha Theta (Elizabeth Staley Leadership award 1995), Phi Sigma Alpha. Avocations: running, playing piano, watching Spanish language movies and programs, tennis.

PRISBELL, KATHLEEN FRANCES, middle education educator, language arts; b. Rahway, N.J., Aug. 9, 1950; d. William Joseph and Helen Frances (Kowaleski) Wolfe; m. Fred Prisbell, Mar. 1, 1973; children: Eric S., Sandra L., Andrew F. BA in English, Kean U., 1972. Cert. secondary educator English N.J., elem. educator N.J., English all grades Nat. Bd. Profl. Tchg. Stds., English and lang. arts all grades Nat. Bd. Profl. Tchg. Stds. Tchr. lang. arts Twp. of Ocean (N.J.) Intermediate Sch., 1972-82, Lakewood (N.J.) Middle Sch., 1986-90, Russell O. Brackman Middle Sch., Barnegat, N.J., 1990—. Site-based mgmt. team Lakewood Middle Sch., 1987-90, com. mem. curriculum devel., 1988; site-based mgmt. core team Russell O. Brackman Middle Sch., Barnegat, 1991—, curriculum coun. chair, 1992—. Writer: (curricula) MAX (Gifted and Talented) Curriculum, 1994, Integrated Music and Social Studies. Tchr. Christian Doctrine St. Mary's Cath. Ch., Barnegat, 1989-93. Recipient Governor's Tchr. Recognition award, 1997. Mem. Nat. Coun. Tchrs. English, N.J. Coun. Tchrs. English, Nat. Arbour Day Found. Democrat. Roman Catholic. Avocations: reading, walking, theater. Home: 6 Maplewood Ct Barnegat NJ 08005-2008 Office Phone: 609-698-5880. E-mail: kprisbell@mail.bts.k12.nj.us.

PRISCO, DOROTHY DESTENO, academic administrator; b. Hoboken, N.J., Jan. 27, 1942; d. Dominick and Martha (Balacco) DeSteno; m. Salvatore Prisco, July 15, 1967; 1 child, Lisa Natalie. BA, Bard Coll., 1964; MA, Jersey City Stat Coll., 1968; MS, U. Ala., Tuscaloosa, 1975; EdD, Rutgers U., 1983. Cert. English tchr., N.J. Tchr. English, Sacred Heart Acad., Hoboken, N.J., 1964-65, North Bergen (N.J.) High Sch., 1965-69, Tuscaloosa Acad., 1969-70; editor, copywriter McCall's Needlework and Crafts mag., N.Y.C., 1974-77; mem. faculty and divsn. chmn. Centenary Coll., Hackettstown, NJ, 1977—84, exec. asst. to pres., 1985—86, v.p. acad. affairs and dean coll., 1986—92, Wesley Coll., Dover, Del., 1992—97, Gwynedd-Mercy Coll., Gwynedd Valley, Pa., 1997—2000; dean sch. grad. and continuing studies, Coll. St. Elizabeth, Morristown, NJ, 2000—. Manuscript cons. Prentice Hall and John Wiley Pub., N.Y.C., 1983-86; mem. evaluation team Mid. States Assn., Phila., 1991—; lectr. series in the humanities funded by N.J. Dept. Higher Edn., 1985-86. Co-author: Fashion Merchandise Information, 1986; contbg. author: (Elizabeth Cartere biography) in Past and Promise: Lives of N.J. Women, 1990; mem. editorial bd. Nat. Assn. Women in Edn., 1991—93. Coord. community svc. Centenary Coll. and United Meth. Ch., Hackettstown, 1989-91. Recipient Disting. Svc. award Rutgers U., 1989; grantee United Meth. Ch., 1989-90, N.J. Dept. Higher Edn., 1989-90, Ronetco Corp., 1990. Mem. Coun. Ind. Colls. (program participant 1991—), Am. Coun. on Edn. (rep. to nat. identification program for advancement women in higher edn. adminstrn. 1985—), Rutgers U. Grad. Sch. Edn. Alumni Assn. (pres. 1991-92). Office: Coll St Elizabeth 2 Convent Rd Morristown NJ 07960

PRISSEL, BARBARA ANN, paralegal, law educator; b. Plum City, Wis., July 7, 1946; d. John Henry and Mary Ann Louise (Dankers) Seipel; m. Stephen Joseph Prissel, Dec. 16, 1967; children: Angela, Benjamin. Grad. with honors, Mpls. Bus. Coll., 1966; at, Moraine Park Tech. Coll., 1983—. Cert. interactive TV, adult edn. instr. Legal sec. Mott, Grose, Von Holtum & Hefferan, Mpls., 1966-67, Whelan, Morey & Morey Attys. at Law, Durand, Wis., 1967-70, Murry Law Office, River Falls, Wis., 1968-70, Potter, Wefel & Nettesheim, Wisconsin Rapids, Wis., 1970-71; paralegal Kilgore Law Office, Ripon, Wis., 1985—2004; sec. to adminstr. Moraine Park Tech. Coll., Fond du Lac, Wis., 1971—72, legal sec. instr., 1995—. Chmn. legal adv. com. Moraine Park Tech. Coll., Fond du Lac, 1996-98, mem. adminstrv. assts. adv. com., 1984-86, mem. legal adv. commn. 1984-. Contbr. poems to newspapers. Ch. rep. Ch. Women United, Ripon, 1984-87; pianist Christian Women's Orgn., Ripon, 1985-95; pianist, organist Our Lady of Lake Ch., Green Lake, Wis., 1987—. Mem.: NAFE, Legal Profls. Assn. (East Ctrl. Wis. pres. 1994—95, sec. 1995—96, chmn. Day-In-Ct. 1999, NALS Fedn. liaison 2000—02, sec. 2001—02, state legal edn. task force 2003—04, v.p. 2003—04, pres. 2003—, v.p. East Ctrl. Wis. chpt. 2004—, chmn. ednl. liaison com., Legal award of Excellence 1995—96), Wis. Assn. Legal Profession (state legal ednl. liaison com. 1997—98, state legal edn. task force 2003—04, ann. meeting com. mem. 2005, mem. nominations and elections com. 2005—06), Nat. Assn. Legal Profession, Nat. Women's History Mus. Roman Catholic. Avocations: teaching and playing piano, creative writing, cooking, swimming, exercising. Home: 129 Wolverton Ave Ripon WI 54971-1144

PRITCHARD, BETTY JEAN, retired art educator; b. Dana, Ind., Nov. 25, 1934; d. Terrence Ellis and Mary Ethel (Wishard) P. BS in Arts and Crafts, Ind. State U., 1957; MA in Art Edn. and Painting, Purdue U., 1972; postgrad., Ball State U., 1958, 66; postgrad. computer graphics works, Ind. U., Bloomington, 1985. Cert. pub. sch. tchr., supt., Ind., Ky., Ill. Art tchr. 1-12 Sheridan (Ind.) H.S., 1957-60; art tchr. 3-12 Danville (Ind.) City Schs., 1961-62; art tchr. 1-12 Brownsburg (Ind.) Comm. Schs., 1962-64; art tchr. 7-12 Blue River Valley S.C., New Castle, Ind., 1964-67; art tchr. 1-8 Twin Lakes Sch. Corp., Monticello, Ind., 1967-69; art tchr. 1-6 Tippecanoe Sch. Corp., Lafayette, Ind., 1972-75; art tchr., children's art Art Ctr. Sch., Albuquerque, 1977-78; tutor supr. Albuquerque Pub. Schs., 1977-78, art lab. asst., 1978-79; art tchr. 7-12 Attica (Ind.) Consolid. Schs., 1979-80; art tchr. 1-8 Southwest Parke C.S., Mecca, Ind., 1983-85; painting instr. Danville Area C.C., Ill., 1987-88; substitute tchr. Albuquerque Pub. Schs., 1989-2000; ret., 2000; night supr. and bookstall clerk Purdue U., 1970—75. One-woman and group shows include Purdue U., Jonson Gallery, U. N.Mex., Union Bldg., U. N.Mex., 1976-78, Arts and Crafts Benefit. Active Neighborhood Watch, Bernalillo, N.Mex., 1995—97, The Nature Conservancy; docent Albuquerque Mus.; vol. greeter Albuquerque Biol. Park; charter mem. WWII Meml. Women's History Mus. Grantee Wabash Valley Projects, Tippecanoe Arts Fedn. and Nat. Endowment of the Arts, Lafayette, 1987. Mem.: Animal Protection Voters, Humane Soc. Legis. Fund, World Soc. Protection of Animals, Nat. Parks Cons. Assn., In Def. of Animals, Humane Soc. of U.S., United Animal Nations, Nat. Park Trust, African Wildlife Fedn., Wild Horse Observors Assn., Voters Union Concerned Scientists, Animal Protection N.Mex., Animal Protection Inst., Animal Legal Def., Internat. Fund for Animal Welfare, Nat. Wildlife Fedn., Doris Day Animal League, Defenders of Wildlife, The Wilderness Soc., Mus. of Albuquerque Found., Nat. Resources Def. Coun. Methodist. Avocations: music, art. Home: 324 E Avenida Bernalillo Bernalillo NM 87004-9018

PRITCHARD, KARRI R., chemistry educator; b. Dallas, Mar. 2, 1978; d. Sherri L. Hejny and Peggy J. Wadsworth, Ralph J. Wadsworth and William Harris Sewell; m. Chris B. Pritchard, June 10, 2000; children: Ashley N., Lanie D. BS in Chemistry, Tex. A & M Commerce, 2001. Tchr. honors chemistry, chemistry, and integraged physics and chemistry Mesquite Ind. Sch. Dist., Tex., 2001—. Republican. Baptist. Avocations: scrapbooks, reading. Office Phone: 972-882-7800.

PRITCHARD, LUCILLE KRAMER, mathematics professor, department chairman; d. Robert Francis Kramer and Immaculate Susan Qualteris; m. Robert Jesse Pritchard, Sept. 28, 1974; children: Robert Jr., Kathryn 1 stepchild, Dawn. BA in English and Math., Turynedd Mercy Coll., Pa., 1970; MA, Villanova U., Pa., 1974. Math. dept. chair Lansdale Cath. HS, Pa., 1970—; assoc. instr. Turynedd Mercy Coll., Turynedd, Pa., 1996—. Middle states steering com. Lansdale HS, Pa.; curriculum com. for secondary math. archdiocese of Thila, 2004—06. Mem.: MAA, NCTM, ATMOPAV. Avocations: golf, reading, hockey.

PRITCHARD, MICHELLE C., lawyer; b. Morganton, N.C., May 6, 1970; d. Cyrus Leon and Olivia Jeanette (Sain) Carswell; m. James Alvin Pritchard, Dec. 6, 1997. BA in Polit. Sci., Davidson Coll., N.C., 1992; JD, Pepperdine U., Malibu, Calif., 1995. Bar: Calif. 1996, N.C. 1999. Assoc. atty. Randolph & Levanas, Santa Monica, Calif., 1996—97, Byrd Byrd Ervin Whisnant & McMahan P.A., Morganton, NC, 1999—. Mem.: N.C. Acad. Trial Lawyers, Nat. Orgn. Social Security Reps. Democrat. Episcopalian. Avocations: triatholons, violin, travel, reading, gourmet food and wine. Home: 115 Staney Ave Morganton NC 28655 Office: Byrd Byrd Ervin Whisnant McMahon 301 E Meeting St Morganton NC 28680 Business E-Mail: mcp@byrdlaw.com.

PRITCHARD, NINA JEAN, communications educator; d. Philip Paris Fields and Mae Ella Jarrett; m. Walter Pritchard, June 28, 1980; 1 child, Davonna Renee. Masters, Nat. Louis U., St Louis, 1990. Cert. tchr. Mo., 1973. Tchr. Mo Bd. Of Edn., St. Louis, 1961—2006. Bd. sec. Transformation Christian Ch., St. Louis. Avocations: reading, editing, crossword puzzles, bowling. Home: 5846 De Giverville Saint Louis MO 63112 Personal E-mail: npritcha5964@stlps.org.

PRITCHARD, SARAH MARGARET, library director; b. Boston, Feb. 8, 1955; d. Wilbur Louis and Kathleen Hunton (Moss) P.; m. Timothy John Brennan, Aug. 20, 1977 (div. 1993); m. Neal Edward Blair, July 15, 2005. BA, U. Md., 1975; MA in French, U. Wis., 1976, MLS, 1977. Intern Libr. Congress, Washington, 1977-78, reference specialist in women's studies, 1978-88, head microform reading rm., 1988-90; sr. program officer Assn. Rsch. Librs., Washington, 1990-91, assoc. exec. dir., 1991-92; acad. libr. mgmt. intern Coun on Libr. Resources Princeton U., NJ, 1988-89; dir. librs. Smith Coll., Northampton, Mass., 1992-99; univ. libr. U. Calif., Santa Barbara, 1999—2006, Northwestern U., Evanston, Ill., 2006—. Editl. advisor Women's Rsch. and Edn. Inst., Washington, 1987-92; bd. dirs. Western Mass. Regional Libr. Sys., 1997-98; bd. dirs. U. Calif. So. Regional Libr. Facility, Gold Coast Libr. Network, Libr. Calif.; mem. steering com. Scholarly Pub. and Academic Resources Coalition, 2006—. Editor: The Women's Annual, 1984; compiler ARL Stats., 1990-92; contbr. articles to profl. jours.; mem. editl. bd. Jour. Acad. Librarianship, 1993-99, Portal: Librs. and the Acad., 2000—; contbg. editor Libr. Issues, 1994-99. Trustee Leroy C. Merritt Humanitarian Fund, 1991-94. Named Wis. Alumni Rsch. Found. fellow, 1975-77, Outstanding Alumna U. Wis. Sch. of Libr. and Info. Studies, 1997. Mem. ALA (chair machine assisted reference sect. 1986-87, chair women's studies sect. 1989-90, coun. 1990-98, 2000-04, chair stds. com. 1998-2002, chair ethics com. 2002-06, Equality award 1997), Nat. Women's Studies Assn., Cosmos Club. Democrat. Office: Northwestern Univ Libr Evanston IL 60208

PRITCHETT, AMY R., aerospace engineer, educator; m. Eric N. Johnson; 1 child. BSc in Aeronautics and Astronautics Avionics Option, MIT, 1992, MSc in Aeronautics and Astronautics, 1994, DSc in Aeronautics and Astronautics, 1996. Joint asst. prof. aerospace engring. Ga. Inst. Tech., Atlanta, 1997—2003, asst. prof. indsl. & systems engring., 1997—2003, joint assoc. prof. aerospace engring., 2003—04, assoc. prof. indsl. & systems engring., 2003—04, joint asst. prof. sch. indsl. and systems engring., 2005—, assoc. prof. aerospace engring., 2005, David S. Lewis Jr. assoc. prof. cognitive engring. Daniel Guggenheim sch. aerospace engring., 2005—. Sr. tech. fellow aerospace engring. Delft U. Tech., Netherlands, 2002; mem. aeronautics and space engring. bd. NRC, 2004—. Contbr. articles to sci. jours.; assoc. editor: AIAA Jour. Aerospace Computation, Info. and Communication, 2003—, mem. editl. adv. bd.: Jour. Cognitive Engring. and Decision Making, 2004—. Recipient Wings Club of Am. Merit award, 1992. Mem.: Am. Soc. Engring. Educators, Soc. Computer Simulation, Human Factors and Ergonomics Soc., AIAA (Lawrence Sperry award 2007), Sigma Gamma Tau (MIT chpt. pres. 1991—92, MIT chpt. treas. 1990—91), Tau Beta Pi. Office: Daniel Guggenheim Sch Aerospace Engring Ga Inst Tech 270 Ferst Dr Atlanta GA 30332-0150 E-mail: amy.pritchett@ae.gatech.edu.*

PRITCHETT, LORI L., real estate broker, secondary school educator; b. Redding, CA, Dec. 21, 1966; d. Lane L. and Linda L. Pritchett. BA, Univ. of the Pacific, Stockton, Calif., 1985—90. Cert. Real Estate Broker Calif., 1993, Tchg. credential Calif., 1989. HS tchr. Red Bluff HS, Red Bluff, Calif., 1989—90; Jr. HS tchr. Anderson Mid. Sch., Anderson, Calif., 1990—91; Jr. HS substitute Evergreen Mid. Sch., Cottonwood, Calif., 1991—; real estate broker Running L Realty, Cottonwood, Calif., 1993—. Mem. Multiple Listing Com., Shasta Assn. of Realtors, Redding, Calif., 1995—, Edn. Com., Shasta

Assn. of Realtors, Redding, Calif., 1995—97, Bus. and Tech. Com., Sahsta Assn. of Realtors, Redding, Calif., 1998—2001, chmn., 1999; chair Multiple Listing Com., Shasta Assn. of Realtors, Redding, Calif., 2003—04. Multiple listing com. chmn. Shasta Assn. of Realtors, Redding, Calif., 2003—03. Mem.: Nat. Assn. of Realtors, Shasta Assn. of Realtors, Calif. Assn. of Realtors. R-Conservative. Avocations: travel, ranching, computer tech., sports. Office: Running L Realty PO Box 616 Cottonwood CA 96022 Home: 15790 Bowman Cottonwood CA 96022 E-mail: lori@runningl.com.

PRITCHETT, RITA JOYCE, educator; b. Pratt, Kans., Feb. 17, 1947; d. Robert Harold and Orvaleen L. BA, Asbury Coll., 1969; MA in Edn., Eastern Ky. U., 1970, specialist in edn., 1971; PhD Candidate, U. Ky. Instr. Asbury Coll., Wilmore, Ky., 1971-74, asst. prof., 1974-78, assoc. prof., 1978—, athletic dir., 1988—98. Pres. Ky. Women's Intercollegiate Conf., 1984-92, Fellowship Christian Athletes, 1989-90; sec. Women's Intercollegiate Athletic Conf., 1985-92. Mem. AAHPERD, Fellowship of Christian Athletes. Republican. Avocations: travel, reading, sports. Office: Asbury College 1 Macklem Dr Wilmore KY 40390-1198

PRITZKER, JEAN, film producer; Formerly with BBC; co-owner Dee Gee Entertainment. Prodr.: (films) The Phantom of the Opera, 1989, Simple Justice, 1990, Hostile Intent, 1997, Ricochet River, 1998, Wedding Planner, 2001, The Wedding Planner, 2001, Mean Creek, 2004, Hooligans, 2005, The Living Hell, 2006. Office: Dee Gee Entertainment Coronet Theater 366 N La Cienega Blvd Los Angeles CA 90048*

PRITZKER, PENNY, investor; b. Chgo., May 2, 1959; d. Donald N. and Sue Ann (Sandel) Pritzker; m. Bryan Traubert, Sept. 10, 1988; children: Donald Pritzker Traubert, Rose Pritzker Traubert. B in Econs., Harvard U., 1981; JD, MBA, Stanford U., 1985. Bar: Ill. 1985. Mgr. Hyatt Devel. Corp., Chgo., 1985-87; pres. Classic Residence by Hyatt, Chgo., 1987—; ptnr. Pritzker & Pritzker, Chgo., 1987—; pres. Pritzker Realty Grp. (formerly Penguin Group, L.P.), Chgo., 1990—; chmn. TransUnion Corp., 2005—. Chmn. exec. com. Encore Sr. Living, Portland, Oreg.; corp. adv. bd. mem. Mayor Daley's Exec. Fellows Prog., Chgo.; mem. Mayor Daley's fin. com.; bd. dirs. William Wrigley, Jr. Co., Chgo., Coast-to-Coast Fin. Corp., NYC, Nat. Investment Conf., Washington. Chair Mus. Contemporary Art, Chgo.; adv. bd. dirs. Chgo. Cares; mem. dean's coun. Harvard U.; mem. Women's Issues Network, Chgo., 1991—, The Chgo. Network, 1992—, Internat. Women's Forum, Chgo., Coun. Fgn. Rels., NY. Named one of 50 Women to Watch, Wall St. Jour., 2005, 100 Most Powerful Women in World, Forbes mag., 2005, 400 Richest Ams., 2006; recipient Brick & Mortar award, Chgo. Equity Fund, 1991, Disting. Svc. award, REIA Kellogg, 1995. Mem. Nat. Assn. Sr. Living Industry Execs. (bd. dirs. 1989-91), Urban Land Inst., Young Pres.'s Orgn. Office: Classic Residence By Hyatt 71 S Wacker Dr Ste 900 Chicago IL 60606-4637*

PRIVAT, RUBY (RUBY THIBODEAUX), elementary school educator; b. Rayne, La., Nov. 4, 1954; d. Cleveland Joseph and Mable (Monceaux) Thibodeaux; m. Pierre A. Privat, Dec. 2, 1972; children: Tiffany, James, George, Jennifer. BS in elem. edn., U. S.W. La., Lafayette, 1987; M in Adminstrn., U. of La. at Lafayette, 2003. Account receivable mgr. Badger Oil Corp., Lafayette, La.; 7th grade reading tchr. Rayne (La.) Cath. Elem. Sch.; 1st grade tchr. Egan (La.) Elem. Sch., 6,7,8 grade tchr., math, social studies. Home: 723 E 2nd St Crowley LA 70526-5217

PRIVATT, KATHY LYNNE, theater educator, theater director, actor; d. Robert Louis and Emma Elizabeth Stewart; m. Jeff Privatt, Dec. 17, 2000. MA, S.W. Mo. State U., 1995; BS magna cum laude in Edn., Ctrl. Mo. State U., 1986; PhD, U. Nebr., 1999. Assoc. prof. theatre arts Lawrence U., Appleton, Wis., 1999—. Presenter in field. Dir.: (plays) Region III Kennedy Ctr.-American Coll. Theatre Festival, 2006. Elder Meml. Presbyn. Ch., Appleton, Wis., 2002—03. Fellow, Fling Fund and Thompson Endowment U. Nebr., Lincoln, 1998—99. Mem.: AAUP (exec. bd. Lawrence chpt. 2004—06), Mid-Am. Theatre Conf., Assn. Theatre in Higher Edn. (comm. coord. theatre as liberal art focus group 2002—06), Phi Kappa Phi. Presbyn. Avocations: sailing, reading, piano. Office: Lawrence University PO Box 599 Appleton WI 54912 Office Phone: 920-832-7248. Business E-Mail: kathy.privatt@lawrence.edu.

PRIVES, CAROL, biologist, educator; PhD, McGill U. Prof. biology Columbia U., N.Y.C., NY, chmn. Dept. Biol. Scis. Mem. Damon Runyon Fellowship Com.; mem. sci. adv. bd. NIH Virology Study Section, N.J. Cancer Commn., Howard Hughes Med. Inst., GeminX. Mem. editl. bd.: Cell, Genes & Devel., Jour. Biology, Chemistry and Cancer Rsch.; editor: Jour. Virology, 1991—99. Fellow: Am. Acad. Arts and Scis.; mem.: Inst. Medicine. Office: Dept Biological Scis Columbia Univ 816 Fairchild Center MC422 1212 Amsterdam Ave New York NY 10027*

PRIVETT, CARYL PENNEY, judge; b. Birmingham, Ala., Jan. 7, 1948; d. William Kinnaird Privett and Katherine Speake (Binford) Ennis. BA, Vanderbilt U., 1970; JD, NYU, 1973. Bar: Ala. 1973, U.S. Dist. Ct. (so. dist.) Ala. 1973, U.S. Dist. Ct. (no. dist.) Ala. 1974, U.S. Ct. Appeals (5th cir.) 1974, U.S. Ct. Appeals (11th cir.) 1981. Assoc. Crawford & Blacksher, Mobile, Ala., 1973—74, Adams, Baker & Clemon, Birmingham, Ala., 1974—76; asst. US atty. no. dist. Ala. US Atty.'s Office, US Dept. Justice, Birmingham, Ala., 1976—94, first asst. US atty., 1992—93, US atty., 1995—97, chief asst., 1997—98; pvt. practice Birmingham, Ala., 1998—2003; city prosecutor City of Mountain Brook, 1998—2003; cir. judge 10th Jud. Cir. of Ala., 2003—. Adj. prof. Cumberland Sch. Law Samford U., 1998—. Active Downtown Dem. Club, Birmingham, Ala.; bd. dir. Legal Aid Soc., Birmingham, Ala., 1986—88, pres., 1988; sec., founder Lawyers for Choice Ala., 1989—92; chair domestic violence com. City of Birmingham, Ala., 1989—91; sustaining mem. Jr. League Birmingham, Ala.; mem. Photography Guild. Named, Outstanding Young Women Am., 1977, 1978; recipient Cert. in Color Photography, U. Ala. Birmingham, 1989, Commr.'s Spl. citation, Food and Drug Adminstrn. Mem.: ABA, Ala. Law Inst., Ala. Acad. Atty. Mediators (pres. 2002), Birmingham Bar Found. (pres. 2001), Birmingham Bar Assn. (exec. com. 1996-98) (Judge Drayton James award 2004), Ala. Bar Assn. (chmn. women in the profession com. 1997-99), Fed. Bar Assn. (pres. Birmingham chpt. 1979), Ala. Solution, Leadership Birmingham, Women's Network, Women's Fund, Altamont Alumni Assn., Summit Club. Presbyterian. Avocation: photography. Home: 30 Norman Dr Birmingham AL 35213-4310 Office: 550 Jefferson County Courthouse 716 Richard Arrington Blvd Birmingham AL 35203 Office Phone: 205-325-5388.

PRIVETTE, JANET BROWN, elementary school educator; b. Raleigh, NC, Mar. 5, 1958; d. Dwight Dale and Peggy Hurt Brown; m. Randy Lee Privette, Dec. 21, 1980; children: Andrew Scott, Todd McLean. BS in Elem. Edn., East Carolina U., Greenville, N.C., 1980; MEd in Elem. Edn., N.C. Ctrl. U., Durham, N.C., 2000. Cert. tchr. Nat. Bd. Edn., 2000. Tchr. kindergarten Franklin County Schs., Louisburg, NC; reading specialist Wake County Pub. Schs., Zebulon, NC. Mem.: Internat. Reading Assn., Internat. Soc. Women Educators, Delta Kappa Gamma. Baptist. Home: 8409 Halifax Rd Youngsville NC 27596 Office: Zebulon Elem Sch 700 Proctor St Zebulon NC 27597

PRIVETTE, LOUISE JUDITH, school psychologist; b. Chgo., May 12; d. Sidney Paul and Mary Goldstein; m. John Joseph Privette, Nov. 18, 2002; 1 stepchild, John Edward. BA in Psychology, Ariz. State U., 1976, M in Counseling, 1978. Nat. cert. sch. psychologist Md., cert. guidance counselor K-12 Ariz., secondary tchr. Ariz., nat. cert. reality therapist Calif. Dir. guidance, tchr. Seton H.S.; sch. psychologist Mesa (Ariz.) Pub. Sch. Dist., 1985—2003, Buckeye (Ariz.) Union H.S. Dist., 2003—. Amb. for edn. Motorola, Ariz., 1996—98; therapist Dobson Bay Psychol. Ctr. Author: (booklet) Watch Me Grow. Luke air force officers' wives club; nat. honor soc. sponsor. Named Sch. Psychologist of Yr., Mesa Assn. Sch. Psychologists, 2000. Mem.: Nat. Assn. Sch. Psychologists (assoc.), Ariz. Assn. Sch. Psychologists (assoc.; regional dir. 1983—84, psychologist of yr. 2001), Pi Lamda Theta, Psi Chi. Office: Buckeye Union H S Dist 902 E Eason Ave Buckeye AZ 85326 Office Phone: 623-327-2415. Office Fax: 623-386-9706. E-mail: louisep@buhsd.org.

PRIVETTE, P(ATRICIA) GAYLE, psychology educator, psychotherapist; b. Zebulon, N.C., Aug. 19, 1935; d. Doris Horton Privette. BA, Wake Forest U., 1956; MEd, U. Fla., 1961, EdD, 1964. Prof. psychology emerita U. West Fla., Pensacola, 1967—2001; psychologist, Pensacola, 1983—; prof. emerita, 2002. Author numerous publs. on human peak performance. Home: 2710 Magnolia Ave Pensacola FL 32503-4947 Office: Counseling Offices 4300 Bayou Blvd Ste 35 Pensacola FL 32503-2671 E-mail: gprivette@cox.net.

PRIZIO, BETTY J., volunteer, retired property manager; b. L.A., Jan. 23, 1928; d. Harry W. and Irene L. (Connell) Campbell; divorced; children: David P., John W., Robert H., James R. AA in Social Sci., L.A. City Coll., 1949. Owner, mgr. indsl. bldgs. and condominiums, mktg. exec., Tustin, Calif., 1976—; ret. Co-chair silent auction Am. Lung Assn., Santa Ana, 1997-2001, co-chair Big Breath Easy charity event; bd. dirs. Founders Chpt. Aux., Providence Speech and Hearing Ctr., 1986-88, aux. pres., 1986-89; vol. Western Med. Ctr. Aux., 1985-89, chmn. gift shop com., 1987-88, 2d v.p., 1992, aux. pres., 1999, jr. vol. adv., bd. dirs. fundraising group, scholarship com., Focus on Women com. 1990—, buyer for gift shop, 1998—, 4th v.p. gift shop, 1993, pres., 1999-2001; adv. coun. Chapman U., Orange, Calif., 1986-87; bd. dirs. Pres. Assocs., 1985-86, Chapman Music Assocs., 1986—, Santa Ana YWCA, 1976-77; adv. coun. Orange County chpt. Freedoms Found. at Valley Forge, 1985—; active United Meth. Ch., Olive Crest Treatment Ctr.; pres. Western Medicine Ctr. Disciplinary, 1999. Named Vol. of Yr., Gift Shop, 1999, Vol. of Nov., hosp. staff and physicians, 2003. Mem.: Tustin Hist. Soc. (bd. dirs. 1988—90), Western Med. Ctr. Aux. (life; pres. 1999, 2000, 2001, Vol of Yr. 1999, 20 Yr. Vol., Regal award). Republican. Avocations: gardening, arts and crafts, travel, photography. Home: 2522 N Tustin Ave Unit D Santa Ana CA 92705

PROBASCO, GAYLA RAE, secondary school educator; b. Geneva, Nebr., Sept. 4, 1949; d. Darien E. and Betty J. (Sluka) Thomsen; m. George W. Probasco, June 5, 1971; children: Todd W., Kari R.(dec.), Ryan K., Erin L. BS in Edn., Kearney State Coll., 1971. Cert. life sci. tchr. Nebr. Sr. high tchr. Holdrege Pub. Sch., Nebr., 1971—72; resource paraeducator Arapahoe Pub. Sch., Nebr., 1983—96, jr.-sr. high sch. tchr., 1996—98; sr. high sch. tchr. Twin Valley Pub. Sch., Bartley, 2001—; middle sch. tchr. SW Pub. Sch., 2004—. Sci. fair judge, Nebr., 1972—. Contbr. small group ministry, teaching, workshops for students and teachers, small group ministry, dedicated service. Cub scout leader Boy Scouts Am., Arapahoe, 1984—87; Brownie leader Girl Scouts USA, Arapahoe, 1984—87; leader Via de Cristo Prison Weekends, York, Nebr., 1996—; dir. Lay Witness Missions, Nebr., 1982—2006; Christian edn. tchr. United Meth. Ch., Arapahoe, 1966—; chmn., dir. Walk to Emmaus, Arapahoe, 1982—; lay pastor small group ministry. Recipient VIP award, First United Meth. Ch. and Arapahoe Pub. Sch., 1992. Mem.: NSTA, Nebr. Tchrs. Sci. Republican. Methodist. Avocations: hiking, gardening, sewing, reading, travel. Home: 1102 Cherry St Arapahoe NE 68922 Office: Southwest Mid Sch 103 West Nebraska Bartley NE Office Phone: 308-692-3223. Personal E-mail: gaylap@atcjet.net. Business E-Mail: gaprobas@esu15.org.

PROCHASKA, ALICE, historian, librarian; m. Franklyn Kimmel Prochaska, June 25, 1971; children: Elizabeth, William. BA in Modern History, Somerville Coll., U. Oxford, 1968; DPhil in Modern History, U. Oxford, 1975. Asst. keeper Pub. Record Office, England, 1975—84; sec. & libr. Inst. Hist. Rsch. U. London, 1984—92; dir. spl. collections Brit. Libr., 1992—2001; univ. libr. Yale U., New Haven, 2001—. Author: History of the General Federation of Trade Unions, 1982, Irish History from 1700: A Guide to Sources in the Public Record Office, 1986; co-editor (with Frank Prochaska): Margaretta Acworth's Georgian Cookery Book, 1987; contbr. numerous articles in scholarly and profl. jours. Named an Hon. Fellow, Royal Holloway U. of London, 2002, Inst. Hist. Rsch. U. London, 2001. Fellow: Royal Hist. Soc. (v.p. 1995—99). Office: Libr Adminstrv Services Sterling Meml Libr Yale U 130 Wall St PO Box 208240 New Haven CT 06520-8240 Office Phone: 203-432-1818. Business E-Mail: alice.prochaska@yale.edu.*

PROCIDANO, MARY ELIZABETH, psychologist, educator; b. New Rochelle, NY, Apr. 1, 1954; d. John D'Arge and Dorothy Diane (Utter) P.; m. Stephen Anthony Buglione, Aug. 9, 1986; children: Daniel Stephen, Katherine Mary, Anne Elizabeth. BS (hon.), Fordham U., 1976; PhD, Ind. U., 1981. Lic. psychologist, N.Y. Assoc. instr. Ind. U., Bloomington, Ind., 1979—80; intern in clin. psychology Inst. of Living, Hartford, Conn., 1980—81; asst. prof. Fordham U., Bronx, NY, 1981—90, asst. chair psychology dept., 1984—87, chair inst. rev. bd. for protection of human subjects, 1986—94, mem. faculty senate, 1992—96, 1998—, mem. coll. coun. and various com., advisor, chair psychology dept., 1996—2002, assoc. prof., 1990—, assoc. chair undergrad. studies, 2005—; pvt. practice, clin. psychology Scarsdale, NY, 1992—96; staff psychologist CHE Sr. Psychol. Assocs., 2005—06. Assoc. dean Fordham U. Grad. Sch. of Art's and Sci., 1996. Cons. editor Jour. of Personality and Social Psychology, 1989-92; contbg. articles and chapters to profl. and scholarly journals and books. Mem. APA, Phi Beta Kappa, Sigma Xi, Psi Chi. Roman Catholic. Avocations: gardening, hiking, cooking. Office: Fordham U Dept Psychology Bronx NY 10458 Office Phone: 718-817-0925. Business E-Mail: procidano@fordham.edu.

PROCKNOW, MARGOT, artist; b. Galesburg, Ill. d. Ross Lincoln and Beulah Ellen (Gillard) Freeman; m. Lloyd L. Henze, Nov. 1953 (div. Dec. 1960; children: Steven Eric, Michael Ross; m. Jene Tremayne Procknow, Sept. 8, 1962; 1 child, Heidi Jene. Student, U. Wis., 1951-53. Artist NASCO, Inc., Ft. Atkinson, Wis., 1960-61; artist/illustrator freelance, Ft. Worth, 1961-77; custom designer fine jewelry Ft. Worth, 1977-89; artist M.E. Procknow Fine Art, Ft. Worth, 1987—. Artist; painting included in Creative Watercolor, 1996, In Watercolor: People, 1996; painting inluded in Nat. Women's Caucus for Art newsletter, 1991. Mem. Nat. League Am. Pen Women, Nat. Mus. Women in the Arts, Soc. Watercolor Artists, Soc. Art of the Imagination, Planetary Soc., Planned Parenthood, NOW, Natural Resources Def. Coun., Audubon Soc., Amon Carter Mus., Nat. Women's History Mus., Kimbell Art Mus. Avocations: reading, rocks, comparative religions, nature studies, science. Home: 1201 Cozby St E Fort Worth TX 76126-3601

PROCOPE, ERNESTA GERTRUDE, insurance company executive; b. Bklyn. d. Clarence and Elvira Forster; m. Albin Bowman (dec. 1952); m. John L. Procope, July 3, 1954. Student, Bklyn. Coll., Coll. Ins., Pohs Inst. Ins.; LLD (hon.), Adelphi U., Marymount Manhattan Coll., 1987, Howard U., 1989; HHD (hon.), Morgan State U., 1978. Founder, pres., CEO E.G. Bowman Co. Inc., NYC, 1953—. Panelist corp. governance and advancement of women US Dept. Labor, 1981. Amb. 10th anniversary independence celebration Republic of Gambia, 1975; trustee NY Zool. Soc., Cornell U., Adelphi U. Named Disting. Black Woman in Corp. Role, Nat. Coun. Negro Women, Inc., 1981, Bus. Person of Yr., Urban Bankers Coalition, 1990; named to African Am. Bus. Hall of Fame & Mus., 2003, Minority Bus. Hall of Fame and Mus., 2006; recipient Achievement award, Thelma T. Johnson Meml. Scholarship Fund, 1972, Interracial Coun. for Bus. Opportunity, 1973, Women of the Yr. award, presented at White House by First Lady Patricia Nixon, 1972, Cmty. Svc. award, F & M Schaefer Brewing Co., 1974, Sojourner Truth award, Negro Bus. and Profl. Women's Club, Inc., 1974, Bus. Achievement award, Nat. Bus. League, 1976, Catalyst award, Women Dirs. of Corps., 1977, Torch of Liberty award, Anti-Defammation League, 1990, Disting. Svc. award, NAACP, 1991, Entrepreneurial Excellence award, Dow Jones/Wall Street Jour., 1992, Whitney M. Young, Jr. award, 1992, Trumpet award, Turner Broadcasting Sys., 2002, Essence Power award, 2004, Women of Power Legacy award, Black Enterprise Mag., 2006. Mem.: Nat. Assn. Ins. Women, Nat. Assn. Ins. Brokers, Cosmopolitan Club, Women's Forum, Alpha Kappa Alpha (hon.). Presbyterian. Office: EG Bowman Co Inc 97 Wall St New York NY 10005-4302 Office Phone: 212-425-8150. Business E-Mail: procope@egbowman.com.

PROCTER, CAROL ANN, retired musician; b. Oklahoma City, June 26, 1941; d. Leland Herrick and Alice (McElroy) Procter. Student, Eastman Sch. Music, 1958—60; MusB, New Eng. Conservatory of Music, 1963, MusM, 1965. Musician (cellist): Springfield (Mass.) Symphony Orch., 1961—65, Cambridge (Mass.) Festival Orch., 1961—65, Boston Symphony Orch. and Boston Pops Orch., 1965—2003, New Eng. Harp Trio, 1971—91; musician: (viola da gambist) Curtisville Consortium, 1972—82; musician: (solo viola da gambist) Boston Symphony Orch., 1976, 1981, 1985; musician: (solo cellist) Boston Pops Orch., 1980, 1987, 2003. Pres. Employees Fed. Credit Union Boston Symphony Orch., 1988—2003; cellist Japan Philharm. Cultural Exch., 1969—70. Recipient Fulbright award, 1965; Fromm fellow, Tanglewood Music Ctr., 1965.

PROCTOR, BARBARA GARDNER, advertising agency executive, writer; b. Ashville, NC; d. William and Bernice (Baxter) Gardner; m. Carl L. Proctor, July 20, 1961 (div. Nov. 1963); 1 son, Morgan Eugene. BA, Talladega Coll., Ala., 1954. Music critic, contbg. editor Down Beat Mag., Chgo., 1958—; internat. dir. Vee Jay Records, Chgo., 1961-64; copy supr. Post-Keyes-Gardner Advt., Inc., Chgo., 1965-68, Gene Taylor Assos., Chgo., 1968-69, North Advt. Agt., Chgo., 1969-70; contbr. to gen. periodicals, 1952—; founder Proctor & Gardner Advt. (divsn. Proctor Comm. Network), Chgo., 1970—, pres., CEO. Pres., CEO Proctor Comm. Network, Chgo.; Mem. Chgo. Urban League, Chgo. Econ. Devel. Corp.; cons. pub. rels. and promotion, record industry; bd. dir. Window to the World Comm., Inc.; bd. trustee 98.7WFMT, WTTW11. Author: (TV documentary) Blues for a Gardenia, 1963. Bd. dirs. People United to Save Humanity, Better Bus. Bur., Window to the World Comm., Inc., Ill. Bell Telephone Co., Northwestern Hosp., Mid-City Nat. Bank, Coun. Chgo. Better Bus. Bur., Louisville Courier-Jour., United Way, Econ. Club; Mem. NARAS, USIA, Chgo. Media Women, Women's Advt. Club, NY Art Dirs. Club, Woman's Day Club, Cosmopolitan C. of C. (dir.); bd. trustee 98.7WFMT, WTTW11; co-chair, State Ill. Gannon-Proctor Commn.; governing coun. mem. Ill. State Bar Assn. Inst. for Pub. Affairs. Recipient Armstrong Creative Writing award, 1954; awards Chgo. Fedn. Advt., Frederick Douglas Humanitarian award, 1975, Headliner award, Assn. for Women in Comm., 1978; named Chgo. Advt. Woman of Yr., 1974; named to Smithsonian Instn. "Black Women Achievements Against the Odds" Hall of Fame and the series' poster-calendar traveling exhbn. Mem. Female Execs. Assn., Internat. Platform Assn., Smithsonian Instn. Assn.

PROCTOR, CARRIE ANN, counseling administrator; d. Charles Nicholas and Barbara Ann Seaman; m. Chad Scott Proctor, June 12, 2004; 1 child, Giuliana Denise. BS, Ohio State U., Columbus, 1992; MEd, S.W. Tex. State U., San Marcos, 1998. Cert. sch. counselor Tex. Spl. edn. tchr. Austin ISD, Tex., 1996—99, sch. counselor, 1999—. Mem.: Capital of Tex. Counseling Assn. (treas., pres. 2001—04, Recognized as Emerging Leader 2004), Tex. Sch. Counseling Assn., Tex. Counseling Assn. (senator 2005—, membership chair 2006—), Ohio State U. Alumni Assn. (past pres.). Episcopalian. Office: Fulmore Middle School 201 E Mary St Austin TX 78704

PROCTOR, GEORGANNE C., investment company executive; b. 1956; m. Robert Proctor. BS in Bus. Mgmt., U. S.D.; MBA in Fin., Calif. State U., Hayward. From fin. analyst Bechtel Financing Svcs. (now part of Bechtel Enterprises), 1982-89; mgr. Bechtel Info. Tech. Group., 1989-91, mgr. project cost controls for Disney MGM Studio project Paris, 1991; dir. fin. & acctg. Buena Vista Home Video Internat., 1991-93; dir. project & divsn. fin. Walt Disney Imagineering, 1993-94; CFO Bechtel Enterprises, 1994-97; sr. v.p., CFO Bechtel Group, Inc., San Francisco, 1997—2002; exec. v.p., CFO Golden West Fin. Corp., 2002—06, Teachers Ins. & Annuity Found. Coll. Retirement Equities Fund (TIAA-CREF), NYC, 2006—. Bd. dirs. The Bechtel Group, 1994—2002. Amb. Calif. State. U., Hayward. Office: TIAA-CREF 730 3rd Ave New York NY 10017*

PROCTOR, JUNE, retired religious organization administrator, writer; b. Lehigh, Okla., June 20, 1936; d. Lowell Lawrence and Martha Fay (Winn) Whitlock; m. Richard Owen Proctor, Nov. 19, 1955; children: Michael Lee, Terrell Glen, Tanya Marie, Richard Lowell, Sheilia Renè, Roger Owen. BA in Psychology, Okla. City U., 1956; MA in Religious Edn. cum laude, Wesley Sch. Theology, 1973; postgrad., U. So. Miss., 1997; MA in History, Tex. A&M U., 2003. Cert. dir. religious edn. US Army Bd. Chaplains, 1984. Dir. religious edn. US Army Post Chapel, Ft. Huachuca, Ariz., 1984—85, Westminster United Meth. Ch., Md., 1981—82, Calvary United Meth. Ch., Paris, Tex., 1995—96; ret., 1996; co-owner Whispering Oaks Ranch, Paris, Tex. Rep. 3d military family symposium US Army War Coll., DC, 1982; curriculum selection com. Bd. US Army Chaplains, Ft. Monroe, Va., 1985; leadership trainer Paris C. of C., 1996. Author: (book) The Night the Angels Cried, 2003 (1st Press Woman Tex., 2004); columnist Stay Tuned with June, 2004— (Nat. Fedn. Press Women, 2d Place, 2005). Pres. Baden-Wurttemberg Dist. Protestant Women of Chapel, Kelley Barracks, Germany, 1980—81; chair youth vols. Am. Red Cross, Ft. Huachuca, 1983—85. Decorated Outstanding Civilian Svc. medal US Dept. Army; recipient Helping Hand Medallion award, VII Corps. Headquarters, Kelley Barracks, 1981, 1st Pl. inspirational books, Press Woman Tex., 2004, 1st Pl. personality profile article, 2005, 1st Pl. personal essay column, 2005, 2d Pl. inspirational books, Nat. Fedn. Press Women, 2004. Mem.: Okla. Writers Fedn., Inc., Nat. Fedn. Press Women, Press Women Tex., US Army War Coll. Assn. (student wife rep. 1982—83), Tex. Archeol. Soc. Field Sch. (registrar 2005—), Valley Caddo Archeol. Soc. (registrar 2003—), Officer's Wives Club, US Army (pres. 1980—81). United Methodist. Avocations: archaeology, writing, public speaking. Home: 18921 FM 1497 Paris TX 75462

PROCTOR, MILLICENT CARLÉ, social worker; b. Chgo., Mar. 9, 1944; d. Harry and Erene (Merriweather) Vinée; m. Donald Proctor (div. 1972); m. James Smith (dec. 1995). BA in Polit. Sci. and History, U. Ill.; MSW, Loyola U.; PhD, 1986. Cert. social worker, Ill.; master addiction counselor. Caseworker, case work supr. Cook County (Ill.) Dept. Pub. Aid; social work supr. dept. children and family svcs. State of Ill.; exec. dir. Adler Adoption Agy., Chgo.; dir. pub. health social svc. Chgo. Dept. Health, coord. mental health info. and edn. Contbr. articles to profl. jours. Active women's bd. Wesley Hosp., materials mgmt. vol. Mem. Am. Pub. Health Assn., Chgo. Child Care Soc., Ill. Child Care Soc., Ill. Psychiat. Assn., Blind Assn. Ill., Acad. Cert. Social Workers, Am. Psychologists Assn., Nat. Assn. Forensic Counselors. Office: Ste 1305 8 S Michigan Ave Chicago IL 60603-3375

PRODOR, LEAH MARIE, secondary school educator; b. Edmonton, Alta., Can., June 27, 1967; d. Leon Brian and Gale Anne (Merrick) P. BA in History, San Diego State U., 1990, MA, 2004. Cert. tchr. Calif. Dept. Edn. Grad. asst., mentor, lectr. San Diego State U., 1987-93; adminstrv. asst. Potomac Sch., McLean, Va., 1993, Winchester Data Corp., San Diego, 1993-94; tchr. San Diego County Office of Edn., 1994—2000, San Diego Union HS Dist., 2000—; adj. prof. San Diego State U., 2005—. Mentor, athletic dept. San Diego State U., 1987-90; head tchr. Polinsky Children's Ctr. Mem. AVID, Juvenile Ct. and Comty. Schs. (chairperson tchr. adv. com. 1998—, communication com. 1998—, equity edn. com., 1998—), San Diego County Office of Edn. (chairperson tchr. adv. com. 1998—, communication com. 1998—, equity edn. com. 1998—), Calif. Tchrs. Assn., Orgn. History Tchrs., Orgn. Am. Historians, Boys and Girls Club of San Diego, San Diego Cross Cultural Educators, Golden Key Honor Soc., Phi Eta Sigma. Avocations: running, horseback riding, dance. Office: San Diego Union HS Dist 675 Encinitas CA 92024 Office Phone: 760-270-4981.

PROENZA, THERESA BUTLER, adult education educator, writer; b. Savannah, Ga., Jan. 18, 1961; d. Lee Bradford Sr. and Theresa Zipperer Butler; m. Luis Mariano Proenza, July 2, 1983. BS in Biology with Spanish minor, U. Ga., 1982; MBA, U. Alaska, 1991. Biology, Spanish and Math. tchr. Jefferson (Ga.) HS, 1982—85; mgr. Gazebo Interiors, Athens, Ga., 1985—86; grant writer, conf. and lectr. corrd. U. Alaska, Fairbanks, 1986—90; rsch. asst. Alaska Dept. Trans. Rsch., Fairbanks, 1990—91; dir. U. Alaska Fairbanks Small Bus. Devel. Ctr., 1991—94; asst. dir. Purdue Ctr. for Internat. Bus. Edn. Rsch., West Lafayette, Ind., 1994—96; adminstrv. dir. Purdue U. Tech. Transfer Initiative, West Lafayette, Ind., 1996—97. Co-chmn. governance com. Summa Health Sys., Akron, 2003; mem. Ohio Supreme Ct. Task Force on Rules of Profl. Conduct, Columbus, 2003—; chair, pers. budget com., lay mem. Ohio Supreme Ct. Bd. Commrs. for Grievances and Discipline; chair-elect Summa Health Sys. Hosps., mem. ethics and fin. com., 2003—04; chair Stan Hywet Hall and Gardens Found. Bd. Dirs., 2003—04. Guest columnist (newspaper bus. column) Fairbanks Daily News-Miner, 1992—94. Recipient Top 100 Women of Summit County, YWCA, 2001. Lutheran. Avocations: cooking, sailing, bicycling, reading, scuba diving.

PROHASKE, DONNA D., social studies educator, department chairman; b. West Islip, NY, June 20, 1969; d. Paul Carl and Diane Marie Prohaske. BA in History, Albright Coll., Reading, Pa., 1991; MA in Liberal Arts, SUNY, Stony Brook, 1995. Cert. sch. dist. adminstr. Tchr., dept. chair West Babylon Schs., NY, 1992—. Curriculum cons. Columbia U., NYC; spkr. Teach Europe Conf. Mem.: ASCD, Nat. Coun. Social Studies. Avocation: travel. Office: West Babylon HS 500 Great East Neck Rd West Babylon NY 11704

PROKOP, SUSAN, disability rights advocate; b. Washington, Aug. 30, 1956; d. Jerome and Lotus (Therkelsen) P.; m. James Shafter Turpin, May 16, 1998. B in Govt., Georgetown U., 1978; MPA, U. Va., 1980. Legis. asst. to Del. James Almand, Richmond, 1980, 81; housing mgmt. specialist Va. Housing Devel. Authority, Richmond, 1981-82; staff asst. Aerospace Industries, Washington, 1982-83; sr. legis. asst. to Congresswoman Marcy Kaptur Washington, 1983-89; dir. health policy Am. Soc. Internal Medicine, Washington, 1989-97; assoc. advocacy dir. Paralyzed Vets. of Am., Washington, 1997—. Mem. Consortium for Citizens with Disabilities, Am. Pub. Health Assoc., Washington, 1997—, Women in Govt. Rels., Washington, 1990—. Bd. dirs. Cmty. Residences, Inc., Arlington, Va., 1995—, Arlington Arts Ctr., 1996-99; del. Dem. Nat. Conv., 1996; mem. Arlington Dem. Comm., 1975—. Democrat. Methodist. Avocations: photography, writing, painting. E-mail: Turkop@worldnet.att.net.

PROM, M. ELAINE, secondary school educator; b. Iowa City, Jan. 28, 1942; d. Kenneth Howard and Elsie Elizabeth (Evans) Fuller; m. James Arthur Prom, June 24, 1967; children: Margot Elaine, Mark Adam. BS, Iowa State U., Ames, 1964; postgrad., Mankato State U.; postgrad., diversified cert., U. Minn.; Masters and Ednl. Specialist studies, Winona State U., Minn. Dept. chairperson John Adams Jr. H.S.; tchr. family life sci. John Marshall H.S., Rochester, Minn. Mem. AAUW, Rochester Bus. and Profl. Women, Rochester Area C. of C., Phi Delta Kappa, Delta Kappa Gamma, Assn. Secondary Curriculum Devel., Am. Home Econ. Assn. Home: 2001 N Normal Ave Tempe AZ 85281-1323

PRONESTI, ROSA C., artist; b. W. Nantmeal Twp., Pa., Aug. 27, 1932; d. Salvatore Maria and Frances (Bavuso-Volpe) P. Student, Hussian Art Sch., Phila., 1954. With Deco Art, Phila., 1950-51; asst. artist Fliesher Art Meml., Phila., 1951-68; mech. artist William F. Bird Studio, Phila., 1952-65, Designers Frank Nofer Inc., Phila., 1968-85. One-woman shows include Cathedral Village Retirement Home, Andora, Pa., 1996, 98, Stone Harbor Miniature 2x3 Art Shows, 1993-2002, Jewish Cmty. Ctr., 2001-04; group shows include Atlantic City (N.J.) Art Ctr., 1997-2003, Long Beach Island Miniature Show, 1985-2001 Surf City, N.J., Yellow Springs Art Show, Chester Springs, Pa., 1997-2001, Ocean City Libr., 2003-04. Mem. Atlantic City Art Ctr. (1st and 2d Pl. awards), Nat. Mus. Women in the Arts, Del. Artist Guild, Woodmere Mus. Art (1st and 2d Pl. awards), Phila. Water Color Soc. Roman Catholic. Home: 28 N Frontenac Ave Margate City NJ 08402-1853

PRONOVOST, AMY LYNNE, dancer, educator; b. Royal Oak, Mich., Aug. 5, 1976; d. Gerald and MaryAnn Pronovost. BA in Dance and English, Western Mich. U., Kalamazoo, 1998. Cert. Stott Pilates, Gyrotonic and pilates for golf. Ballet dir., tchr. Dance Dynamics, Walled Lake, Mich., 2000—. Pilates and gyrotonic instr. Equilibrium, Bloomfield Hills, Mich., 2000—. Home: 7073 Magnolia Ln Waterford MI 48327-4419 Personal E-mail: amypronovosta@sbcglobal.net.

PROPER, KRISTINE SUZANNE, elementary school educator; b. Greenfield, Ind., May 6, 1972; d. William R. and Cinda D. Pearson; m. Michael James Proper; children: Alyson M., Kyle W. BS in Elem. Ed., Ind. U., Indpls., 1994, MA (hon.), 2000. 5th grade sci./lang. tchr. Eden Elem., Greenfield, Ind., 1998—2005; 6th grade sci. tchr. Maxwell (Ind.) Mid. Sch., 2005—. Named Margaret Targett Distinguished Tchr. of Yr.; recipient Golden Apple award, Ind. Power and Light; grantee, Ind. Soil and Conservation, Hancock County Cmty. Found., Vol. Services and Ednl. Support Svcs., Ind. Dept. Environ. Mgmt., 2003. Mem.: Hoosier Assn. Sci. Teachers Inst. (assoc.), Alpha Delta Kappa. Democrat. Avocations: travel, kickboxing, reading. Home: 12 Creek View Dr Greenfield IN 46140 Office: Maxwell Mid Sch 102 N Main St Maxwell IN 46154 Office Phone: 317-326-3121. Office Fax: 317-326-2141. Business E-Mail: kproper@gcsc.k12.in.us.

PROPST, CATHERINE LAMB, biotechnology company executive, pharmaceutical company executive; b. Charlotte, NC, Mar. 10, 1946; d. James Pinckney and Eliza M. Propst. BA magna cum laude, Vanderbilt U., 1967; M of Philosophy, Yale U., 1970, PhD, 1973. Head microbiology div. GTE Labs., Waltham, Mass., 1974-77; various sr. mgmt. positions Abbott Labs., North Chicago, Ill., 1977-80; v.p. rsch. and devel. Ayerst (Wyeth) Labs., Plainview, NY, 1980-83; v.p. rsch. and devel. worldwide Flow Gen. Inc., McLean, Va., 1983-85; pres., CEO Affiliated Sci. Inc., Ingleside, Ill., 1985-97; pres., chmn., CEO Tex. Biotech. Found., Hempstead, Tex., 1997—. Vis. prof. genetics U. Ill., Chgo., 1989—90; founder, exec. dir. Ctr. for Biotech., Northwestern U., 1990—95; pres. Ill. Biotech. Ctr., 1995—97; bd. dirs. several cos.; bd. dirs., mem. sci. adv. bd. Keystone Symposia on Molecular and Cellular Biology, 1997—2002. Author, editor Computer-Aided Drug Design, 1989, Nucleic Acid Targeted Drug Design, 1992; contbr. articles to profl. jours. Named to Outstanding Working Women in the U.S., 1982; recipient many sci. and bus. awards. Fellow: Soc. Indsl. Microbiology (bd. dirs. 1990—93), Nat. Coun. Biotech Ctrs. (bd. dirs. 1995—97); mem.: AAAS, Nat. Wildlife Fedn., Consortium for Plant Biotech. Rsch. (bd. dirs. 1994—99), Phi Beta Kappa, Sigma Xi. Episcopalian. Avocations: horseback riding, skiing, raising Black Angus and Black Brangus cattle. Office: Texas Biotech Found PO Box 17 Hempstead TX 77445-0017 Office Phone: 979-826-3075. Office Fax: 979-826-9710.

PROST, MARY JANE, school nurse; d. George and Mary Anne (Zigon) Klobucher; m. William Andrew Prost, July 17, 1954; children: Willy, Peggy, Beth. Diploma, Canonsburg Gen. Hosp., 1953; BS, California U., Pa., 1973; MA in Psychology, Washington-Jefferson Coll., 1976. Cert. sch. nurse Pa. Mes., surg. nurse Canonsburg Gen. Hosp., Pa., 1953—71; mental health nurse Washington Hosp., 1971—73; sch. nurse Keystone Oaks Sch. Dist., Dorment, 1973—97; ret. Sch. nurse coord. Keystone Oaks Sch. Dist., 1993—97; spkr. in field. Tchr. 1st aid classes ARC, 1975—85, Am. Heart Assn., 1975—90. Named Pa. Sch. Nurse of Yr., Pa. Sch. Nurses Assn., 1995. Mem.: Pa. Western Region Sch. Nurse Assn. (past pres.), Nat. Sch. Nurses Assn., St. Patrick's Women Guild. Home: 419 W McMurray Rd Canonsburg PA 15317

PROST, SHARON, federal judge; b. Newburyport, Mass., May 24, 1951; m. Kenneth F. Greene, June 24, 1984; 1 child, Matthew Prost-Greene. BS, Cornell U., 1973; MBA, George Washington U., 1975, LLM in Taxation, 1984; JD, Am. U., 1979. Bar: D.C. Labor rels. specialist Office of Personnel Mgmt., 1973-76; with Gen. Acctg. Office, 1976-79; trial atty. Fed. Labor Rels. Authority, 1980-83; atty. chief counsel's Office of Dept. of Treasury, 1983-84; assoc. solicitor Nat. Labor Rels. Bd., 1984-89; chief minority labor counsel Senate Com. on Labor and Human Resources, 1989-93; minority chief counsel Senate Com. on the Judiciary, 1993—2001; judge U.S. Court of Appeals, Federal Cir., 2001—. Office: US Court Appeals Fed Cir 717 Madison Pl NW Washington DC 20439*

PROTHO, JESSIE, vocational school educator; d. Duncan and Julia Mae (Edmond) McKenzie; widowed; children: Phyllis Noble, Carl Protho. Diploma, Scientific Beauty Sch., 1947; student, Walker Beauty Coll.; BS in Edn., Indiana U., 1968, MS in Edn., 1971. Lic. vocational dir. Indiana State U., 1979. Cosmetology tchr. Gary (Ind.) Area Career Ctr.; with Johnie's Beauty Shop, 1947-53, Jewelry Tng. Svc., 1948-49, Swartchild and Co., 1949-53; self-employed beauty shop owner, 1953-65; educator Gary (Ind.) Community School Corp., 1965—. Mem. AAUW, NAACP, Ind. U. Alumni Assn., Nat. Cosmetology Assn., Vocat. Indsl. Club, Alpha Phi Omega, Phi Delta Kappa (sec. 1991-92, Tchr. of Yr.). Avocations: bowling, sewing, cooking, creative hair styling. Home: 6710 Adams St Merrillville IN 46410-3407

PROTHROW-STITH, DEBORAH, academic administrator, public health educator; MD, Harvard U., 1979. Resident Boston City Hosp.; state commr. health Pub. Health Commonwealth Mass., 1987; assoc. dean govt. and faculty devel. Sch. Pub. Health Harvard U., Boston, prof. pub. health practice. Author: Peace by Piece: A Guide for Preventing Community Violence, 1995. Co-author: Murder is no Accident: Understanding and Preventing Youth Violence in Am., 2004; Sugar and Spice and No Longer Nice, 2005. Mem. Nat. Commn. Crime Control and Prevention, 1995. Recipient Sec. Health and Human Svc. award, 1989, World Health Day award, 1993. Office: Harvard Sch Pub Health Dept Health Policy & Mgmt 718 E Huntington Ave Boston MA 02115 Business E-Mail: dp-s@hsph.harvard.edu.

PROULX, (EDNA) ANNIE, writer; b. Norwich, Conn., Aug. 22, 1935; d. George Napolean and Lois Nellie (Gill) Proulx; m. James Hamilton Lang, June 22, 1969 (div. 1990); children: Sylvia Marion Bullock Clarkson, Jonathan Edward Lang, Gillis Crowell Lang, Morgan Hamilton Lang. BA cum laude, U. Vt., 1969; MA, Sir George Williams U., Montreal, Can., 1973; DHL (hon.), U. Maine, 1994; LLD, Concordia U., Montreal, 2002; DLitt (hon.), U. Toronto, 2000. Author: Heart Songs and Other Stories, 1988, Postcards, 1991 (PEN/Faulkner award 1993), The Shipping News, 1993 (Chgo. Tribune Heartland award 1993, Irish Times Internat. Fiction award 1993, Nat. Book award for fiction 1994, Pulitzer Prize for fiction 1994), Accordion Crimes, 1996 (Dos Passos prize for lit. 1996), Brokeback Mountain, 1998 (Nat. Mag. award 1998), Brokeback Mountain, 1998 (later adapted into film), Close Range: Wyoming Stories, 1999, That Old Ace in the Hole, 2002, Bad Dirt: Wyoming Stories 2, 2004; contbr. more than 50 articles to mags. and jours.; editor: Best American Short Stories of 1997. Recipient Dos Passos prize for Lit., Longwood Coll., 1997, Ambassador Book award English Speaking Union, 2000, Best Fiction 1999 Book award The New Yorker, 2000, Willa award, 2000, Evil Companions Lit. award, 2001; Kress fellow Harvard U., 1974, fellow Vt. Coun. Arts, 1989, NEA, 1991, Guggenheim Found., 1992; rsch. grantee Inter.-U. Ctr., 1975; resident Ucross Found., 1990, 92. Mem. PEN Am. Ctr., Phi Beta Kappa, Phi Alpha Theta. Avocations: canoeing, reading, fishing.

PROUST, JOYCELYN ANN, retired librarian; d. Merry Aylor and Alice Wilhelmina (Morgan); m. George Edward Proust (dec.); children: Gabrielle Cynara, Bertrand Gerard. BA, U. Denver, 1950, MA, 1955; cert., U. Paris Sorbonne, 1953. Lifetime French tchg. credential Calif. C.C., lifetime libr. credential C.C. Libr. Colo. Sch. Mines, Golden, 1955—62; prof. libr. sci. Long Beach (Calif.) City Coll., 1962—92, prof. emerita, 1992—. Chair Calif. C.C. Libr. Cooperative, 1968—75; exec. dir., pres. Libr./Learning Resources Assn., Calif., 1985—86. Bd. mem. Long Beach Mozart Festival, 1975—95, chair; active 1976 Bicentennial Com., L.A., 1976. Mem.: Alpha Gamma Delta, Phi Sigma Iota, Alpha Lambda Delta. Unitarian. Home: 5249 Village Rd Long Beach CA 90808

PROUT, CAROLYN ANN, controller, personnel administrator; b. Clare, Mich., Jan. 18, 1947; d. Aaron Eugene and Alice Marie (Fall) Prout; m. Stanley George Lyon, July 13, 1968 (dec. May 1971); children: Lori Anne Lyon (dec.), Jamie Lynn Lyon Pier (dec.); m. Dennis Karl Hunt, Jan. 1975 (div. Nov. 1977); 1 child, Julie Marie Baldwin; m. Arthur Roy Przybylowicz, Nov. 3, 1979 (div. Jan. 1998). Cert. acctg., Lansing Bus. U., 1965; BBA summa cum laude, Davenport Coll., 1998. Bank teller Citizens Bank & Trust, Rosebush, Mich., 1965-68; bookkeeper, sec. Doyle & Smith P.C., Lansing, Mich., 1968-74; legal sec. Foster, Swift, Collins & Coey P.C., Lansing, 1974-79; mgr. office ARC, Lansing, 1979-81; controller, personnel adminstr. Mich. Protection & Advocacy Service, Lansing, 1981-88; bus. adminstr. White, Przybylowicz, Schneider & Baird, P.C., Okemos, Mich., 1988-98; faculty sec. Thomas M. Cooley Law Sch., 1998—2002; paralegal Sinas, Dramis, Brake, Boughton & McIntyre, 2002—04; legal asst. Mike Kluck & Assocs., 2005—. Vol. bookkeeper Citizens Alliance to Uphold Spl. Edn., Lansing, 1977-79; coord. bingo IHM Sch., Lansing, 1979-80; mem. St. Casimir Christian Svc., Lansing, 1981-84, chairperson, 1983-84; eucharistic min., 1987-2001; bd. dirs. Immaculate Heart of Mary Sch., Lansing, 1977-80; vol. Ingham County chpt. Am. Cancer Soc., 1989—, Nokomis Learning Ctr., 1990-97; vol. ARC, 1998-2000, WKAR-Radio Talking Book, 1999-2000. Honors scholar Thomas M. Cooley Law Sch., 2001-03. Democrat. Roman Catholic. Avocations: sewing, travel, photography. Office: Mike Kluck & Assocs 4265 Okemos Rd Okemos MI 48864 E-mail: livinlate7@aol.com.

PROVENCHER, JEANNE STANSFIELD, secondary school educator; b. Methuen, Mass., June 30, 1948; d. Ernest Daniel and Rita Marie (Vayo) Stansfield; m. Richard Leonard Provencher, Dec. 15, 1978; children: Matthew, Ryan. BA, Newton Coll. (now Boston Coll.), Chestnut Hill, Mass., 1970; MA, Rivier Coll., Nashua, N.H., 1990. Cert. tchr., Mass.; cert. experienced educator, N.H. Tchr. St. Francis Acad., Nevada, Mo., 1970-71, Salem (NH) H.S., 1971-72, Pelham (NH) Meml. Sch., 1983-87; tchr. English and women's studies Nashua (N.H.) HS South, 1987—. Critical reader Grammar Workshop, 1994; contbg. reader Adventures in Appreciation, 1994; reader/evaluator A.P. Lang. Exams, 2003—06; presenter in field. Lector St. Kathryn Ch., Hudson, N.H., 1988—. Mem. NOW, N.H. NOW, Nat. Coun. Tchrs. English (state judge for student lit. mags. 1994—), New Eng. Coun. Tchrs. English, N.H. Coun. Tchrs. English. Avocations: reading, gardening, bicycling. Office: Nashua HS South 36 RIverside Dr Nashua NH 03062 Office Phone: 603-589-1566. Business E-Mail: provencherj@nashua.edu.

PROVENSEN, ALICE, artist, writer; b. Chgo. d. Jay Horace and Kathryn (Zelanis) Twitchell; m. Martin Provensen, Apr. 17, 1944 (dec.); 1 child, Karen Anna. Student, Art Inst. of Chgo., 1930-31, U. Calif., L.A., 1939, Art Student League, N.Y., 1940-41; D.H.L. (hon.), Marist Coll., 1986. With Walter Lanz Studios, Los Angeles, 1942-43; OSS, 1944-45. Author, illustrator Karen's Opposites, 1963, Karen's Curiosity, 1963, What is a Color?, 1967, author, illustrator (with Martin Provensen) Who's in the Egg?, 1970, author, illustrator The Provensen Book of Fairy Tales, 1971, Play on Words, 1972, My Little Hen, 1973, Roses are Red, 1973, Our Animal Friends, 1974, The Year at Maple Hill Farm, 1978, A Horse and a Hound, A Goat and a Gander, 1979, The Owl and Three Pussycats, 1981, Town and Country, 1984, Shaker Lane, 1987, The Buck Stops Here, 1990, Punch in New York, 1991 (Best Books N.Y. Times, 1991), My Fellow Americans, 1995, Count on Me, 1998 (Book of Yr. Parenting Mag., 1998), The Master Swordsman, 2001, The Magic Doorway, 2001, A Day in the Life of Murphy, 2003 (named One of the Three Best Childrens Books, 2003), Klondike Gold, 2005 (Spur award Western Writers Am., 2006), illustrator (with Martin Provensen) Mother Goose Book, 1976, illustrator Old Mother Hubbard, 1977, A Peaceable Kingdom, 1978, The Golden Serpent, 1980, A Visit to William Blake's Inn, 1981 (Caldecott honor book, 1981), Birds, Beasts and the Third Thing, 1982, The Glorious Flight, 1984 (Caldecott medal, 1984), The Voyage of Ludgate Hill, 1987, also textbooks; exhibitions include with Martin Provensen Balt. Mus., 1954, exhibitions include Am. Inst. Graphic Arts, NYC, 1959, Bolton Group, Boston, 1964, Eric Carle Mus., Amherst, Mass., 2005—06, one-woman shows include Henry Feiwel Gallery, NYC, 1991, Children's Mus., Washington, 1991, Moscarelle Mus. Art, Williamsburg, Va., 1991, Eric Carle Mus. Picture Book Art, Amherst, Mass., 2005—06; books represented Fifty Book of Yr. selections Am. Inst. Graphic Arts, 1947, 1948, 1952 (The Charge of the Light Brigade named Best Illustrated Children's Book of Yr. N.Y. Times, 1964, co-recipient medal Soc. Illustrators, 1960). Named to Soc. Illustrators Hall of Fame, 2000; recipient Empire State award, Youth Svcs. sect. NY Libr. Assn., 2004.

PROVINE, LORRAINE, retired mathematics educator; b. Altus, Okla., Oct. 6, 1944; d. Claud Edward and Emmie Lorraine (Gasper) Allmon; m. Joe A. Provine, Aug. 14, 1966; children: Sharon Kay, John David. BS, U. Okla., 1966; MS, Okla. State U., 1988. Tchr. math. U.S. Grant High Sch., Oklahoma City Schs., 1966-69; tchr. East Jr. High Sch., Ponca City (Okla.) Schs., 1969-70; tchr. Ponca City High Sch., 1978-79, 81-96; lectr. dept. math. Okla. State U., Stillwater, 1996-99. Mem.: Cleve. McClain County Ret. Educators Assn., Ponca City Assn. Classroom Tchrs. (treas. 1983—86, 1991—96), Assn. Women in Math, Okla. Coun. Tchrs. Math, Okla. Edn. Assn., Sch. Sci. and Math Assn., Nat. Coun. Tchrs. Math, Math Assn. Am., Internat. Soc. Tech. in Edn., Coun. for Exceptional Children, Okla. Ret. Educators Assn. (life), Okla. State U. Alumni Assn. (life), U. Okla. Alumni Assn. (life), Okla. Assn. Mothers Club (life; state bd. dirs. 1977—87, pres. 1984—85), Delta Kappa Gamma Soc. Internat. (Delta chpt. treas. 1996—98, chmn. Gamma state essay com. 2005, Eta chpt. treas. 2000—04, Eta chpt. pres. 2004—, chmn. Gamma state essay com. 2005—). Republican. Baptist. Avocations: reading, knitting, sewing, genealogy, quilting. Home: 1019 Greenway Cir Norman OK 73072-6125 Personal E-mail: lorraineprovine@cox.net.

PRUCE, RHODA POSNER, social worker, consultant; b. N.Y.C., Sept. 4, 1944; d. Louis and Anna (Konovitch) Kfare; m. Gary H. Posner, June 27, 1965 (div. Jan. 14, 1989); children: Joseph, Michael; m. Morton S. Pruce, Aug. 22, 1999. BA, Hunter Coll., 1965; MEd, Johns Hopkins U., 1975; MSW, U. Md., 1980. Lic. social worker. Caseworker Family & Children's Svcs., Towson, Md., 1980-86; dir. Gestalt Therapy Ctr., Balt., 1983—; dept. dir. Jewish Family Svcs., Balt., 1991—2000. Bd. dirs. Mid-Atlantic Assn. for Tng. and Consulting, Washington, 1990-96; prof. devel. com. NASW, Balt., 1988-90; local assoc. Nat. Coalition Bldg. Inst. Contbr. articles to profl. jours. Mem. NASW, Nat. Coun. Jewish Women, Nat. Coalition Bldg. Inst. Internat. (local assoc.). Democrat. Jewish. Avocation: dance. Home and Office: 1415 Academy Ln Elkins Park PA 19027 Office Phone: 410-371-0264. E-mail: rpruce@pruceassociates.org.

PRUCHNICKI, JENNIFER ANN, director; m. Nathan Mark Johnson. BA in Journalism, U. Okla., Norman, 2000, JD, 2003. Bar: Okla. 2003. Asst. dir. McNair scholars program Cameron U., Lawton, Okla., 2003—06, dir. student devel., 2006—. Adj. instr. criminal justice Cameron U. Mem.: ABA, Young Lawyers Divsn., Comanche County Bar Assn., Okla. Bar Assn. Office Phone: 580-581-2209.

PRUCINO, DIANE L., lawyer; b. Wilmington, Del., July 15, 1957; d. Lawrence Joseph and Marjorie (Lowe) P. AB summa cum laude, Duke U., 1978; JD, U. Va., 1982. Bar: Ga. 1982, US Dist. Ct. (no. dist.) Ga. 1982, US Ct. Appeals (9th cir.) 1984, US Ct. Appeals (6th cir.) 1985, US Ct. Appeals (DC cir.). Assoc. Kilpatrick & Cody, Atlanta, 1982—97; ptnr., dept. head Labor and Employment and Employee Benefits Practice Group Kilpatrick Stockton LLP, Atlanta, 1997—, mem. exec. com. Mem. editorial bd. Va. Law Review, 1980-82. Bd. dirs. Homes for Children Internat., Inc., Atlanta, 1986—; vol. atty. Atlanta Legal Aid, 1983-84. Mem. ABA, Atlanta Bar Assn. Democrat. Presbyterian. Avocation: travel. Office Fax: 404-541-3350. E-mail: DPrucino@KilpatrickStockton.com.

PRUDHOMME, DONNA POWELL, school counselor; b. Beaumont, Tex., July 12, 1972; d. Donaldson Leo and Wilma Ree Powell; m. Michael Wayne Prudhomme, Apr. 18, 1998; children: Malek Jamal, Mia Brielle. AAS, Lamar U., 1994; BS, Lamar U., Beaumont, Tex., 1994; MA, Prairie View A&M U., Tex., 1996, EdM, 1999; EdD in Ednl. Leadership, Nova Southeastern U., Fort Lauderdale, Fla., 2005. Cert. prin. State Bd. for Educator Certification, 2000, sch. counselor State Bd. for Educator Certification, 2000, classroom tchr. State Bd. for Educator Certification, 2000. Treatment specialist Tex. Dept. Justice, Beaumont, 1994—95, parole officer, 1997—98; drug treatment specialist U.S. Dept. Justice, Beaumont, 1998—99; classroom tchr. Beaumont Ind. Sch. Dist., 1998—2000, elem. counselor, 2001—02, secondary counselor, 2002—. Mem. item rev. com. Bus. Edn. 6-12 Tex. Test. Named Educator of Distinction, Coca Cola Co., 2005. Mem.: ASCD (life), Tex. Alliance Black Sch. Educators (life), Phi Gamma Sigma (life), Alpha Kappa Alpha (life). Office: Beaumont Independent School District 3443 Fannett Beaumont TX 77705 Office Phone: 409-981-7500.

PRUDHOMME, SHIRLEY MAE, small business owner; b. Coleman, Wis., Aug. 14, 1941; d. Harold Joseph and Clara Jean Bolvin; m. Wayne Thomas Prudhomme, Jan. 16, 1960 (dec. 2004); 1 child, Tom Wayne. Grad., Marinette Cath. Ctrl. HS, Wis., 1959. Teletypesetter Marinette Eagle Star, 1959-60; machine operator Stokley Canning Co., Appleton, Wis., 1960; waitress Marc's Big Boy, Appleton, 1960-61; teletypesetter, proofreader Appleton Post Crescent, 1961-69; ptnr., mgr. Shells Restaurant & Bowling, Algoma, Wis., 1969-73; reporter, feature writer, editorial asst. Peshtigo Times, 1974—; co-owner, mgr. Near North Disposal & Salvage, Inc., Crivitz, Wis., 1975—96; author weekly column Country Cousin, 1996—. Supr. Marinette County Bd., 1990—2006. Contbr. poems, essays and short stories to local newspapers, mags. Mem.: Marinette County Tourism Alliance (bd. dirs. 2004—), Crivitz Bus. Assn. (sec., bd. dirs. 1982—91, Citizen of the Yr. 1987), Marinette Assn. Bus. and Industry (bd. dirs. 1992—2006), Crivitz Area Sister Cities (bd. dirs. 2005—). Republican. Roman Catholic. Avocations: reading, history, psychology, cooking, gardening. Home: PO Box 367 N1490 Chickadee Ln Crivitz WI 54114 Office: Peshtigo Times Hwy 41 Peshtigo WI 54157 Personal E-mail: shirleyprudhommechichadee@yahoo.com.

PRUETT, LINDY NEWTON, special education educator; b. Beaver Dam, Ky., Sept. 16, 1940; d. Godfery Eugene Newton and Virginia Irene Cox Levy; m. David Ross Stigler, Sept. 1958 (div. Nov. 1959); 1 child, Charles Michael; m. Wayne Willard Pruett, Aug. 20, 1965; 1 child, Brenda Michelle Baker. BS, Ind. U., 1971, MS, 1974. Cert. in elem. and spl. edn. Tchr. spl. edn. Indpls. Pub. Schs.; faculty mem. online edn. dept. U. Phoenix, 2003—. Mem. NEA, Ind. Edn. Assn., Hoosier Sci. Edn. Assn. Ch. of Christ. Avocations: gardening, knitting, restoring dolls. Home: 1421 N Fenton Ave Indianapolis IN 46219-4105 Office: Arsenal Tech High Sch 1500 E Michigan St Indianapolis IN 46201-3098 E-mail: lwpurett@earthlink.net.

PRUETT-LAWSON, JO ANN, marketing professional, special events coordinator; b. Jacksonville, Fla., Feb. 27, 1961; d. Billy Earl Pruett and Mildred Ann (Reedy) Jewell. AS in Bus. Adminstrn., Fla. C.C., Jacksonville, 1991; BS in Bus. Adminstrn. and Mktg., U. North Fla., Jacksonville, 1993; nail technician lic., Roffler, Jacksonville, Fla., 1994. Cert. image cons., makeup artist, promotional mgr., driving instr. Owner, CEO Black and White Prodns., Jacksonville, 1991—, Depeche Mktg. Group, Inc., Jacksonville, 1996—. Color and makeup cons. Carol Jackson-Color Me Beautiful, Fla., 1990, Fernand Aubrey, Fla., 1990; educator Advanced Edn. for Nail Profls., Jacksonville, 1993—; territory supr. Mktg. Force, Jacksonville, 1993-95; specialty events mgr., Jacksonville, 1993—; sales rep. KMart Corp., Jacksonville, 1995-97; specialty events mgr. Greater Jacksonville Agrl. Fair, 1996. Pres., bd. dirs. Sutton Pl. Homeowners Assn., 1997—; adv. bd. Ronald McDonald Ho., Jacksonville, Fla.; vol. Amelia Island Concour d' Elegance BMW and RM Auction, 2000—. Mem.: First Coast Car Coun. (v.p., show chmn. 14th Ann. Car, Truck, and Motorcycle Show 2001, v.p., show chmn. 2005), Suncoast Jaguar Club, South Fla. Jaguar Club, Jaguar Clubs of N. Am. (mem. BMWCCA First Coast chpt. 1998—, activities dir. 2002—, sanctioned chief judge 2003—, regional v.p. 2006—), Jaguar Car Club North Fla. (pres. 2000—03, founder, chief judge 2000—).

PRUETZ, ADRIAN MARY, lawyer; b. Nov. 13, 1948; Student, U. Wis., 1966—69; BA, Loyola U., Chgo., 1972, postgrad., 1972—73; JD magna cum laude, Marquette U., 1982. Bar: Wis. 1982, Calif. 1985. With Quinn Emanual et al, LA; assoc. Whyte and Hirschboeck, SC, 1982—84, Morrison and Foerster, 1984—88, ptnr., 1988—94, Quinn Emanuel Urquhart Oliver & Hedges, LLP, LA, 1994—, co-chair Intellectual Property Litigation Group. Spkr., lectr. Price Waterhouse Intellectual Property Forum, Licensing Execs. Soc., Am. Soc. Indsl. Security. Named one of One of Calif. Top 50 Litigators, LA Daily Jour., 2001—05, Most Influential Trial Lawyers in Calif., 2002—05, State's Top 25 Intellectual Property Lawyers, 2003—05, Calif.'s Most Successful Lawyers, Calif. Law Bus. Mem.: ABA (past chair com. U.S. lit. affecting internat. patent problems, past chair com. impact 1991 amendments), Los Angeles County Bar, State Bar Calif., Fed. Bar Assn. (spkr., lectr.). Office: 865 S Figueroa St 10th Fl Los Angeles CA 90017 Office Phone: 213-443-3134. Business E-Mail: adrianpruetz@quinnemanuel.com.

PRUITT, ALICE FAY, mathematician, engineer; b. Montgomery, Ala., Dec. 17, 1943; d. Virgil Edwin and Ocie Victoria (Mobley) Maye; m. Mickey Don Pruitt, Nov. 5, 1967; children: Derrell Gene, Christine Marie. BS in Math., U. Ala., Huntsville, 1977; postgrad., Calif. State U., Northridge, 1978—79. Instr. math. Antelope Valley Coll., Quartz Hill, Calif., 1977—78; space shuttle engr. Rockwell Internat., Palmdale, Calif., 1979—81; programmer-analyst Sci. Support Svcs., Inc., Paso Robles, Calif., 1982—85; sr. engring. specialist Loral Vought Sys. Corp., Dallas, 1985—92; dir. concepts and analysis, advanced sys. engring. Nichols Rsch. Corp., Huntsville, Ala., 1992-99; sr. prin. engr. Computer Sci. Corp., Huntsville, 1999—. Mem. DeSoto (Tex.) Coun. Cultural Arts, 1987-89; bd. dirs. Churchill Condominium ASsn., Inc., 2005—. Mem. AAUW (sch. bd. rep. 1982, legal advocacy fund chairperson 1989-91), Toastmasters, Phi Kappa Phi. Republican. Methodist. Avocations: dance, gourmet cooking. Office: PO Box 400002 4090 S Memorial Pky Ste A Huntsville AL 35815-1502 Business E-Mail: apruitt@csc.com.

PRUITT, ANNE LORING, academic administrator, education educator; b. Bainbridge, Ga., Sept. 19, 1929; d. Loring Alphonzo and Anne Lee (Ward) Smith; m. Harold G. Logan; 1 child, Leslie; stepchildren: Dianne, Pamela, Sharon, Ralph Pruitt, Jr., Harold, Minda, Andrew Logan. BS, Howard U., Washington, 1949; MA, Columbia U., N.Y.C., 1950, EdD, 1964; HumD hon., Ctrl. State U., Wilberforce, Ohio, 1982. Counsel for women Howard U., 1950-52; tchr., dir. guidance Hutto H.S., Bainbridge, 1952-55; dean students Albany State Coll., Ga., 1955-59, Fisk U., Nashville, 1959-61; prof. edn. Case Western Res. U., Cleve., 1963-79; prof. ednl. policy and leadership Ohio State U., Columbus, 1979-95, prof. emeritus, 1995—; assoc. dean Ohio State U. Grad. Sch., Columbus, 1979-84; assoc. provost Ohio State U., Columbus, 1984-86, dir. Ctr. for Tchg. Excellence, 1986-94; dean in residence Coun. Grad. Schs., Washington, 1994-96, scholar in residence, 1996—2002. Cons. So. Regional Edn. Bd., Atlanta, 1967-78, So. Edn. Found., Atlanta, 1978-87; co-dir. Preparing Future Faculty program, 1994-2002. Author: New Students and Coordinated Counseling, 1973, Black Employees in Traditionally White Institutions in the Adams States 1975-77, 1981, In Pursuit of Equality in Higher Education, 1987; co-author: (with Paul Isaac) Student Services for the Changing Graduate Student Population, 1995, (with Jerry Gaff and Richard Weibl) Building the Faculty We Need: Colleges and Universities Working Together, 2000, (with Jerry Gaff and Joyce Jentoft) Preparing Future Faculty in the Sciences and Mathematics, 2002, (with Jerry Gaff, Leslie Sims and Daniel Denecke) Preparing Future Faculty in the Humanities and Social Sciences: A Guide for Change, 2003. Trustee Urban League, Cleve., 1965-71, Ctrl. State U., 1973-82, Case Western Res. U., 1987-02, Columbus Area Leadership Program, 1988-91; bd. dirs. ARC, Cleve., 1978-79, Am. West Airlines Found., 1992-95; mem. adv. com. USCG Acad., New London, Conn., 1980-83; Ohio State U. rep. to AAUW, 1989-94; univ. co-chairperson United Way, 1990-91; trustee Marburn Acad., 1991-95; mem. Columbus 1992 Edn. Com., 1988-92; mem. edn. subcom. Columbus Found., 1991-94; mem. exec. com. Renaissance League, 1992-94; mem. vis. panel on rsch., Ednl. Testing Svc., 1996-02; mem. Commn. on Future Clemson U., 1997-98; bd. dirs. Black Women's Agenda, Inc., 1997-, pres. 1998-2002; deacon Peoples Congregational United Ch. of Christ, 1998—; mem. B.E.S.T. Expert Panel, 2002-04; evaluation external expert NSF Grad. Tchg. Fellows in K-12 Edn. Program, 2002-04. Named sr. scholar, Am. Coll. Pers. Assn., 1989, Godmother of Minority Grad. Edn., Black Issues in Higher Edn., 1995, inducted, Ohio State U. Coll. Edn. Hall of Fame, 2004; named one of Am.'s Top 100 Black Bus. and Profl. Women, Dollars & Sense Mag., 1986; recipient Outstanding Alumnus award, Howard U. Alumni Assn., 1975, Disting. Affirmative Action award, Ohio State U., 1988, Disting. Svc. award, 2005, Woman of Achievement award, YMCA, 1993; fellow Am. Coun. on Edn., 1977. Mem. NSF (mem. com. on equal opportunities in sci. and engring. 1989-95), Am. Coll. Pers. Assn. (pres. 1976-77), Coun. Grad. Schs. in U.S. (chairperson com. on minority grad. edn. 1980-84), Am. Ednl. Rsch. Assn., Ohio Assn. Counselor Edn. (pres. 1966-67), Links Inc., Cosmos Club, Alpha Kappa Alpha.

PRUITT, BRENDA SUE BRANSTETTER, secondary school educator; b. Hestand, Ky., Apr. 3, 1953; d. William Edward and Ila Christine (Williams) Branstetter; m. Byron Ross Pruitt, Dec. 27, 1974; children: Ross, Joshua. BS, Western Ky. U., 1975, MA, 1980. Tchr. home econs. Madisonville (Ky.) North Hopkins High Sch., 1976-87, C.O.P.E. Ctr., Madisonville, 1987—, day care dir., 1987—. Bd. dirs. Coalition for Healthy Youth, Madisonville, 1987-93. Leader 4-H Midnight Walkers, Anton, Ky., 1992—; mem. Hopkins County Teenage Pregnancy Coalition, Madisonville, 1987-93. Mem. NEA, Nat. Assn. Family and Consumer Sci. Tchrs. (pres.-elect region 2 1977-78, pres. 1978-79, v.p. 1981-82, treas. 1992-93, sec. 2005-06), Ky. Edn. Assn., Hopkins County Tchrs. Assn. (sec. 1979-80), Hopkins County 4-H Coun. (pres. 2002-04, sec. 2005-06), Phi Upsilon Omicron. Republican. Mem. Ch. of Christ. Avocations: cross stitch, needlepoint, softball. Home: 3390 Tucker Schoolhouse Rd Hanson KY 42413-9641 Office: COPE Ctr 411 Hall St Madisonville KY 42431-2620 Personal E-mail: bpruitt2822@charter.net.

PRUITT, DEBRA MARIE, medical/surgical nurse; b. St. Louis, Aug. 23, 1957; d. Harry F. and Stella (Gibbar) Weber. RN, Luth Med. Ctr., St. Louis, 1978; BSN magna cum laude, Pacific Luth. U., Tacoma, Wash., 1986. Cert. med./surgical nurse. Edn./staff devel. U.S. Peace Corps, Tahoua, Niger, W. Africa, 1978-81; staff nurse St. Anthony's Hosp., St. Louis, 1981-82, Bess Kaiser Hosp., Portland, Oreg., 1982-83; charge nurse Allenmore Hosp., Tacoma, 1983—; mem. patient stds. com. and nursing edn. Instr. Clover Park Vocat./Tech. Nursing Continuing Edn., 1987-90, Pacific Luth. U. Nursing Continuing Edn., 1991—; tri-chair Profl. Nurse Practice Coun., 2003-05. Owner agrl. edn. farm, 1999—. Recipient Nursing Excellence award Allenmore Hosp., 1984, Beyond War Found. award 1987. Mem. Luth. Med. Ctr. Sch. Nursing Alumni Assn., Pacific Luth. U. Sch. Nursing Alumni Assn.

PRUITT, LINDA F., elementary school educator; b. Searcy, Ark., Oct. 10, 1945; d. Hercle Truman and Faye Marie Brandon; m. Bill L. Pruitt, Sept. 27, 1991; children: Robby Boland, Bryce, Tisha Hamilton. BS in Edn., U. Ctrl. Ark., Conway, 1963—67; grad. courses, Harding U., Searcy, Ark., 1967—86, Ark. State U., Jonesboro, 2003. 2d grade tchr. McRae Elem., Searcy; 3rd grade tchr. Chesterfield Heights, Norfolk, Va.; 4th grade tchr. Sidnap Deener Elem., Searcy; 5th grade social studies & sci. tchr. S.W. Mall Sch., Searcy. Kids coll. Harding U., Searcy. Grantee, Searcy Edn. Found., 2004—05, Ark. Sci. & Tech., Little Rock, 2002—05, Walmart, Searcy, 2002—03, 2003—04. Mem.: NASTA. Avocations: gardening, golf. Office: Searcy Pub Sch SW Mid Sch 1000 W Beebe Capps Searcy AR 72143

PRUITT, MARY H., social worker; b. Marianna, Ark., Dec. 12, 1944; d. Florzell and Bonnetta Thelma (Harris) Hawkins; children: Woodie III, Rita Marie. AB, U. Ark., 1967; MSW, Washington U., St. Louis, 1971. Lic. clin. social worker. Case worker Grace Hill Settlement House, St. Louis, 1967-69; social worker Dept. Mental Health, St. Louis, 1972-94; pvt. practice St. Louis, 1990-2000; case mgr. Magellan Behavior Health, St. Louis, 2000—; group leader Liberty Program, St. Louis, 1995—. Bd. dirs. Women in Cmty. Svcs., St. Louis, 1982; mem. Betterment Commn. City of Berkeley, Northside Aides Coun., St. Bartholomew Ch.; supporter numerous charities. Mem. Nat. Assn. Social Workers, Am. Bd. Social Workers, Am. Coun. Social Workers, Assn. Black Social Workers. Home: PO Box 845 Marianna AR 72360-0845

PRUITT, ROSALYN JOLENA, science educator; b. Denville, NJ, Sept. 7, 1977; d. John Henry Jr. and Arlena Cobb Pruitt. BS, U. Memphis, 2001. Lab. technician GTW Analytical Svcs., Memphis, 2000—03; sci. educator Memphis City Schs., 2003. Head softball coach Kirby HS, Memphis, 2005. Profl. Devel. grantee, Exxon/Mobil, 2005. Office: Kirby HS 4080 Kirby Pkwy Memphis TN 38115 Office Phone: 901-416-1960.

PRUITT-STREETMAN, SHIRLEY IRENE, small business owner; b. Atlanta, May 22, 1936; d. Len Harris Strickland, Ellen Jay chadwick-Strickland; m. Charles Carter Pruitt, June 5, 1954 (dec. Sept. 1993); children: Gary C. Pruitt, Patricia L. Pruitt, Dianne S. Pruitt; m. James Dorsey Streetman, Aug. 19, 1999. Student, U. Notre Dame, Ind., 1976, U. Notre Dame, 1978, Degree in Bus. Mgmt., 1980; student in profl. interior design, Sheffield Sch. Interior Design, N.Y.C., 1990. Sec. spl. ins. Hurt & Quin Ins. Co., Atlanta, 1954—56; with Globe Ticket Co., Atlanta, 1956—57, Emmett C. Bennett, CPA, Atlanta, 1958—59; acctg., ptnr. Pruitt's Furniture, TV and Appliances, Alpharetta and Cumming, Ga., 1958—93, owner, pres. Cumming, Ga., 1993—. Contbr. poetry to local papers; co-author: (ch. history) 150 Years of Church History, 1986. Adv. bd. Key Distbrs. of Ga., Clarksville, Ga., 1993—. Recipient Pride award, Dealerscope Mag., 1979, Retailer of the Mo. award, Ga. Retailing Mag., 1976. Mem.: C. of C. Baptist. Avocations: reading, crocheting, embroidery, sketching, genealogy. Office: 3473 Pleasant Grove Rd Cumming GA 30040 also: Pruitts Furniture TV and Appliances 606 Veterans Memorial Blvd Cumming GA 30040

PRUNTY, LEEANN MARSIGLIA, gifted and talented educator; b. Shreveport, La., Dec. 19, 1948; d. Charles P. and Jeannie D. Marsiglia; BA, La. Tech. Univ., Ruston, La., 1980, MA, 1986. Cert. tchr. cons. nat. writing project LSU. Gifted tchr. Bossier Parish Sch. Bd., Benton, La., 1981—2002, Caddo Parish Sch. Bd., Shreveport, La., 2003—. Actor: (plays) Peter Pan Players, 1983—2003; elec. corr. (TV) KTBS. Grad. Leadership Shreveport-Bossier, 1991. Recipient Tchr. of the Yr., Platt Elem. Sch., 2002. Mem.: CADDD Fedn. of Tchrs. Meth. Avocations: travel, writing, sewing, cooking. Home: 608 Linden St Shreveport LA 71104 Office: Fairfield Elem Magnet 6215 Fairfield Ave Shreveport LA 71106 Office Phone: 318-868-9826.

PRUSSING, LAUREL LUNT, mayor, economist; b. NYC, Feb. 21, 1941; d. Richard Valentine and Maria (Rinaldi) Lunt; m. John Edward Prussing, May 29, l965; children: Heidi Elizabeth, Erica Stephanie, Victoria Nicole Johanna. AB, Wellesley Coll., l962; MA, Boston U., l964; postgrad., U. Calif., San Diego, 1968-69, U. Ill., l970-76. Economist Arthur D. Little, Cambridge, Mass., 1963-67, U. Ill., Urbana, 1971-72; mem. county bd. Champaign County, Urbana, 1972-76, county auditor, 1976-92; legis. dir. ERA Ill., 2002—03; founder ERA Yes!, 2003. Mem. local audit adv. bd. Office Ill. Compt., Chgo., 1984-92. Contbr. to Illinois Local Government: A Handbook, 1990. Founding mem. Citizens Forum on Gambling and Campaign Fin. Reform, 1999; downstate program dir. Citizen Action/Ill., 1999; legis. dir. AAUW, Ill., Inc., 2001, lobbyist, 2004; active Champaign-Urbana Mass Transit Dist. Bd., 2004—05; state rep. 103d dist. Ill. Gen. Assembly, 1993—95; Dem. nominee Ill. 15th dist. U.S. Congress, 1996—98; mayor Urbana, 2005—. Named Best Freshman Legislator Ind. Voters Ill., 1994; recipient Friend of Agriculture award Ill. Farm Bur., 1994; named to Legis. Honor Roll Ill. Environ. Coun., 1994. Mem. AAUW, NAACP, LWV, Govt. Fin. Officers Assn., U.S. and Can. (com. on acctg., auditing and fin. reporting 1980-88, Fin. Reporting award 1981-91, Disting. Budget award 1986), Nat. Assn. Local Govt. Auditors (charter), Ill. Assn. County Auditors (pres. 1984-85). Democrat. Home: 2106 Grange Dr Urbana IL 61801-6609 Office Phone: 217-328-2071.

PRUTZMAN, PENELOPE ELIZABETH, elementary school educator; b. Vancouver, Wash., Apr. 25, 1944; d. Delbert Daniel and Jessie May (Lowry) P. BA in Sociology, CUNY, 1975; diploma, Grand Diplôme Cooking Sch. Tchr. Mt. Carmel-Holy Rosary Sch., N.Y.C., 1968—. Active Vol. Svcs. for Children, N.Y.C., 1980—83; vol. St. Mary's Ch., Manhattanville, 2001—. Recipient 10 Yr. Service to Cath. Schs. of Harlem award Office of Supt. Sch. Archdiocese of N.Y., 1979, 20 Yrs. to Cath. Sch. award Archdiocese of N.Y., 1986; named one of Outstanding Elem. Tchrs. of Am., 1974. Mem.: Nat. Cath. Edn. Assn., Fedn. Cath. Tchrs. (sch. del. 1974—94, exec. coun. 1974—95, negotiating com., Cert. of Honor 1982). Democrat. Episcopalian. Avocations: gourmet cooking, travel, collecting cookbooks. Office: Mt Carmel-Holy Rosary Sch 371 Pleasant Ave New York NY 10035-3745 Home: 1915 General Anderson Rd Vancouver WA 98661-6108

PRUZAN, IRENE, musician, educator, public relations executive, art association administrator; b. Watertown, N.Y., Jan. 3, 1949; d. John Edward and Esther (Coahn) P.; m. Charles G. Ullery, Jan. 30, 1972 (div. 1978); m. Charles Robert Freeman, May 20, 1988 (dec. Sept. 2005). Student, U. Ariz., Tucson, 1966-68; MusB, U. So. Calif., 1971; postgrad., San Francisco State U., Calif., 1972-74, U. Minn., 1976-80. Tchr. flute, coach chamber music MacPhail Ctr. for Arts, U. Minn., Mpls., 1976-85, coordinator instrumental music, 1978-81, program dir. instrumental music, 1982-85, div. head of programs, 1985-86; regional dir. Music On The Move, Inc., Valley Cottage, NY, 1986-87; pres. Music On the Move Minn., Inc., St. Paul, 1987—2002; dir. pub. rels. Nat. Flute Assn., 2004—. Founding mem. Crocus Hill Trio, 1976-2004; pub. rels. cons. Sch. of Music, U. Minn., 1991; faculty Nat. Music Camp, Interlochen, Mich., 1983, 84; cons. edn. and festival Ordway Music Theatre, St. Paul, 1985-87; mgr. Sartory String Quartet, Mpls., 1986-93; developer numerous master classes; cons. in field. Writer teaching materials for flute. Bd. directors Twin Cities Friends of Chamber Music, 1982—89; mem. Ariz. Chamber Orch., Tucson, 1967, San Gabriel (Calif.) Symphony, 1968—71; extra player St. Paul Chamber Orch., 1977—91; organizer German jazz residency USIA, Minn. and Wis., 1986; edn. com. Orlando Philharm., 2001—04; cons., program dir. Young Audiences Minn., Mpls., 1986—88. Mem.: AAUW (Orlando br. pub. rels. and web master 2003—), Orlando Musicians Union, Twin Cities Musicians Union, Nat. Flute Assn. (dir. mktg. 1987—90).

PRYCE, DANA A., special education educator; b. Melrose, Mass., Jan. 19, 1977; d. Donald F. and Teresa A. Coholan. BA, Fla. Atlantic U., Boca Raton, 2000. Cert. k-12 exceptional student edn. tchr. Fla. Tchr. for severe autism ARC, Sunrise, Fla., 2001—01; tchr. for profoundly mentally handicapped/medically fragile Broward Children's Ctr., Fort Lauderdale, Fla., 2003—04; tchr. exceptional student edn.- trainable mentally handicapped Sch. Dist. of Palm Beach County, Fla., 2005—. Coord./coach Spl. Olympics, Palm Beach County, Fla., 2005—. Recipient Martin Luther King, Jr. Acad. award, Fla. Atlantic U., 1997-2000, Inspirational Coach award, Spl. Olympics, 2006. Mem.: Mensa. Avocations: art, music. Office Phone: 561-752-1200.

PRYCE, DEBORAH DENINE, congresswoman; b. Warren, Ohio, July 29, 1951; m. Randy Walker (div.); 1 child. BA cum laude, Ohio State U., 1973; JD with honors, Capital U. Law Sch., 1976. Bar: Ohio 1976. Adminstrv. law judge Ohio State Dept. Ins., 1976—78; first asst. city prosecutor, sr. asst. city atty., asst. city mgr. Columbus City Atty.'s Office, Ohio, 1978—85; judge Franklin County Mcpl. Ct., Columbus, 1989, 1990, 1992; mem. US Congress from 15th Ohio dist., 1993—, chair Ho. Rep. Conf., 2003—, mem. fin. svcs. com., chair domestic and internat. monetary policy subcommittee, dep. whip, co-chair cancer caucus. Republican. Presbyterian. Avocation: skiing. Office: US Ho Reps 204 Cannon Ho Office Bldg Washington DC 20515-0001 Office Phone: 202-225-2015.*

PRYCE, MONICA ELIZABETH, music educator; b. Washington, Apr. 7, 1968; d. Frederick Thaddeus Hezikiah and Linett Joyce P. BM, Carleton U., 1995. Cert. tchr. Ch. organist Luth. Ch., Ottawa, Ont., 1985-93, SDA Ch., Ottawa, Ont., 1985-95; piano tchr. Ottawa, 1985-95; ch. pianist United Meth. Ch., Atlanta, 1996—; piano tchr. Atlanta, 1996—; music tchr. DeKalb County Sch. Sys., Atlanta, 1998—. Mem. Music Tchrs.' Nat. Assn. (registered). Avocations: music, sports, reading. Office: Dekalb County Sch Sys 3770 N Decatur Rd Decatur GA 30032-1005 Home: 718 Ivy Chase Ln Norcross GA 30092-4648

PRYOR, CAROL GRAHAM, obstetrician, gynecologist; b. Savannah, Ga. m. Louis O.J. Manganiello, June 11, 1950; children: Carol Helen, Victoria Manganiello Mudano. AB, Ga. Coll., 1943; MD, Med. Coll. Ga., 1947. Rotating intern City Hosps., Balt., 1947-48; asst. resident pathology Baroness Erlanger Hosp., Chattanooga, 1948; intern. obstetrics City Colls., Balt., 1949; coll. physician Ga. State Coll. for Women, Milledgeville, Ga., 1949-50; resident obstetrics City Hosps., Balt., 1950-51; asst. resident gynecology Univ. Hosp., Balt., 1951-52, sr. resident ob-gyn. Augusta, Ga., 1952; pvt. practice ob-gyn. Augusta, 1952—; chmn. ob-gyn. St. Joseph Hosp., Augusta, 1997—. Chair ob-gyn. dept. St. Joseph Hosp., Augusta. Mem., former pres. Iris Garden Club, Augusta; mem. coun. on maternal and infant health State of Ga., Atlanta, 1981-90; mem. edn. found. AAUW, 1961-63, state v.p., state pres., 1963-65. Recipient Cert. of Achievement-Community Leadersip, Ga. div. AAUW, 1982; named Med. Woman of Yr., Ga. br. 51 Am. Med. Women's Assn., 1961; Heritage award Ga. Coll. and State U., 2001, Achievement award, Ga. Coll. U., 1982. Fellow ACS (1st woman mem. Ga. chpt. 1956), ACOG; mem. AMA, Richmond County Med. Soc., So. Med. Assn., So. Surg. Congress, Delta Kappa Gamma. Democrat. Methodist. Office: 2316 Wrightsboro Rd Augusta GA 30904-6220 Office Phone: 706-738-2503. Personal E-mail: cpryor@bellsouth.net.

PRYOR, CAROLYN GALE BARNARD, social work educator; b. Tokyo, Sept. 8, 1940; d. Charles Eugene and Doris Fall (Smith) Barnard; m. David Bruce Pryor, Dec. 24, 1966; children: Aurora Dawn Pryor Beasley, Amanda Zoe Pryor McGuire. BA, Whittier Coll., 1962; MSW, U. Calif., Berkeley, 1964; PhD, U. Mich., 1970. Cert. social worker. Program supr. Lennox Hill Neighborhood Assn., N.Y.C., 1964; psychiat. social worker The Menninger Clinic, Topeka, 1964-66; dir. Green Glacier Cmty. Ctr., Ann Arbor, Mich., 1974-76; sch. social worker Whitmore Lake (Mich.) Schs., 1978-89; assoc. prof. Wayne State U., Detroit, 1989—2000; sch. social worker Northville (Mich.) Public. Schs., 1995—99; environ. educator NC Aquariums, 2002—05; pvt. practice, clin. social work, 2001—. Vis. lectr. U. Mich., Ann Arbor, 1972-74; dir. Parent Alliances for Student Svcs., 1992-94; dir. Priority Sailing Acad., 2006—; presenter in field. Contbr. numerous articles to profl. jours. Pres. People for Peace and Justice, Dexter, Mich., 1988-90, Together for Freedom from Alcohol Abuse, 1990-92; charter sailboat capt., 2002-; commdr. Southport Sail and Power Squadron, 2005. Tng. grant U.S. Dept. Edn., 1992-94; recipient Rsch. award Women of Wayne, 1996. Mem. NASW (del. 1995-97, internat. liaison Mich. chpt. 1993-95), U.S. Power Squadrons. Democrat. United Methodist. Avocations: sailing, gardening, scuba diving, acting. Home: 5900 Dutchman Creek Rd Southport NC 28461-2943 Office: 606 W West St Southport NC 28461 Office Phone: 910-448-1230. Personal E-mail: cbpryor@yahoo.com.

PRYOR, SHANNON PENICK, otolaryngologist; d. Rawley M. Penick and Kathleen R. Ellis; m. Daniel Alexis Pryor, Oct. 8, 1994. BA, Williams Coll., 1989; MD, Tulane U., 1993. Diplomate Am. Bd. Otolaryngology. Intern, resident Johns Hopkins Med. Instns., 1993-98; with NIDCD/NIH, Rockville, Md. Vol., Grillo Health Info. Ctr., Boulder, Colo., 2000. Recipient Leadership award (Young Physicians), AMA Found., 2005. Fellow Am. Acad. Otolaryngology-Head and Neck Surgery; mem. AMA (del., Ho. of Dels., Chgo., 2000—, alternate, 1995-99). Office: NIDCD/NIH 5 Research Ct 2A-37 Rockville MD 20850*

PRYPCHAN, LIDA D., psychiatrist; b. Caracas, DF, Venezuela, July 8, 1960; d. Roman Orestes Prypchan and Edel Sayagues. MD, U. Carabobo, Venezuela, 1986; psychiatrist, U. Ctrl., Venezuela, 1999; postgrad., Mt. Sinai Sch. Medicine, N.Y., 2005. Intern, med. asst. Clinica Residencia Carabobo, Valencia, Venezuela, 1986—89; rsch. assoc. We. Psychiatric Inst. and Clinic U. Pitts. Med. Ctr., 1989—90, sr. rsch. assoc. World Psychiatric Assn., 1990—94; psychiatric resident Hosp. U. Caracas, 1996—99, Elmhurst Hosp. Ctr., NY, 2001—05; fellow Child and Adolescent Psychiatry Elmhurst Hosp. Ctr./Mt. Sinai Sch. Medicine, 2005—. Sr. rsch. assoc. Elmhurst Hosp. Ctr./World Psychiatric Assn., 2003—05. Contbr. articles to profl. jours. Recipient Nat. Sci. Journalism award, Venezuela, 1987, 1988, 1989. Mem.: Acad. Child and Adolescent Psychiatry, Am. Psychiatric Assn. Avocations: movies, theater, travel, walking. Home: 4005 Hampton St #415 Elmhurst NY 11373 Office: Elmhurst Hosp Ctr Dept Psychiatry 7901 Broadway Ave Elmhurst NY 11373 Office Phone: 718-372-6339. Personal E-mail: lidaprypchan@hotmail.com.

PRZYBYLSKI, MERCEDES, retired medical and surgical nurse, health facility administrator; Diploma, Hotel Dieu Sch. Nursing, El Paso; BSN, Madonna Coll., Livonia, Mich.; MS in Adminstrn., Cen. Mich. U. Cert. operating room nurse. Dir. operating room svcs. Pontiac (Mich.) Osteo. Hosp.; dir. operative svcs. Mercy Hosp., Toledo; mgr. ambulatory surgical svcs. St. Vincents Mercy Med. Ctr., Toledo; ret., 1998. Mem. Assn. Oper. Rm. Nurses (pres. Mich. Southeastern chpt. 1991), Mich. Assn. Oper. Rm. Suprs., Am. Acad. Med. Adminstrs.

PSALTIS, HELEN, medical/surgical nurse; b. Rockford, Ill., Nov. 27, 1931; d. Harry and Martha (Triantafelakis) P. Diploma, St. Margaret Hosp., Hammond, Ind., 1953; BSN, DePaul U., 1961; MS in Health Edn., Purdue U., 1971; MSN, Purdue U., Calumet, Ind., 1988. RN, Ind., cert. sch. nurse, Ind. Staff nurse U. Ill. Hosp., Chgo., 1959—61, U. Chgo. Hosp., Billings, Ill., 1962; sch. nurse Pub. Sch. City of East Chicago, Ind.; asst. supr., staff nurse, instr. St. Catherine Hosp., East Chicago, Ind., 1962—63; instr., head nurse, staff nurse St Margaret Hosp., Hammond, 1953—58, 1989—, 1963; staff nurse U. Ill. Rsch. Hosp./Chgo. Hosp., 1959—61; asst. supr., staff nurse, inst. St. Catherine Hosp., East Chicago, 1981—91. Mem. ANA, AACCN, Soc. of Critical Care Nursing, Nat. League for Nursing, Sigma Theta Tau. Home: 4303 Ivy St East Chicago IN 46312-3026

PSARRAS, MARY AUTEN, language educator, tax specialist; b. Bridgeport, Conn., Dec. 26, 1945; d. James Ernest and Mary Dillon Auten; m. Georgios Psarras, Dec. 21, 1974 (dec.); children: Demetrios, Patrick. BA in Modern Spanish and Am. Lit., Brown U., Providence, R.I., 1967; MS in Elem. Edn., U. Bridgeport, Conn., 1973. Cert. tchr. pre-K-8, Spanish grades 7-12, ESL pre-K-12 Conn. Cmty. vol. Peace Corps, Itapuranga, Goias, Brazil, 1967—69; tchr. ESL Bridgeport Bd. Edn., 1970—78, 1984—97, tchr. LAU specialist, bilingual, 1997—. Pres., v.p. and treas. Bridgeport Assn. for Childhood Edn.; pres. and v.p. Conn. Assn. Childhood Edn., 1972—79; mem. steering com. Stratford Tchrs. Applying Whole Lang., 1992—97; mem. election com. Bridgeport Edn. Assn.; del. rep. assy. Conn. Edn. Assn. Grantee, Bridgeport Pub. Edn. Fund, Am. Brands. Mem.: Bridgeport Edn. Assn. (bldg. del. 1997—), Alpha Delta Kappa. Home: 106 Bridgeview Pl Stratford CT 06614 Office: Bridgeport Bd Edn Bilingual Dept 948 Main St Bridgeport CT 06606 Personal E-mail: mpsarras@optonline.net.

PSOMAS, BEVERLY T., music educator, performing arts association administrator; b. Akien, SC, June 23, 1954; d. Alvin Keith and Betty Thurmond Taylor; m. George Achilles Psomas, May 5, 1985; children: Lauren Eaves, Maria, John. BA in Music, U. SC, 1977; MEd in Early Childhood Edn., 83. Tchr., musician Aiken Bapt. Sch., 1976—81; dir. music Main St. Meth. Ch., Greenwood, SC, 1986—93, Westminster Presbyn. Ch., Greenwood, 1994—2005; music tchr. Cambridge Acad., Greenwood, 1995—2004; exec. dir. Greenwood-Lander Performing Arts Lander U., Greenwood, 2005—, mem. music faculty, 2003—. Presenter, spkr. in field. Composer: (ednl. enrichment) Share the Light, 1993—2005, (anthem) Celebrate the Century, 1997. Mem.: Music Educators Nat. Conf., PAM Presbyn. Music. Avocations: walking, travel, theater. Home: 113 Partridge Rd Greenwood SC 29649 Office: Greenwood-Lander Performing Arts 240 Stanley Ave Greenwood SC 29649

PUBANTZ, GLORIA ANNUNZIATA, elementary school educator; d. Joseph Vincent and Mary Velleca Annunziata; m. Jerret James Pubantz, Aug. 29, 1970; children: Joanna Britt, Lisa Nicole, David Jerret, Jeffrey Joseph. BS cum laude in French and Linguistics, Georgetown U., Washington, DC, 1969, MS in French and Linguistics, 1972; MA in Reading Edn., Appalachian State U., Boone, N.C., 2003; student, Appalachian State U., 2005—. Cert. tchr. K-6 elem. edn. N.C., k-12 reading N.C., early-mid. childhood literacy, reading, and lang. arts Nat. Bd. Profl. Tchg. Libr. tech. svcs. Duke U., Durham, NC, 1970—73; tchr. St. Pauls Sch., Spartanburg, SC, 1973—75; tchr., early childhood adminstr. Clemmons Moravian Pre-Sch., NC, 1983—94; lead tchr. Diggs Elem. Sch. Winston-Salem Forsyth County Schs., NC, 1995—. Adj. prof. Appalachian State U., Boone, 2004—. Mem.: Assn. Supr. and Curriculum Devel., N.C. Edn. Assn., Nat. Edn. Assn., Internat. Reading Ass., Phi Beta Kappa. Democrat. Roman Cath. Avocations: gourmet cooking, children's literature, travel. Office: Diggs Elem Visualand Performing Arts Sch 950 Mock St Winston Salem NC 27127 Office Phone: 336-727-2424.

PUCCIO, JANE ANNE, secondary school educator; b. Paterson, N.J., May 6, 1946; d. Roy Rudolf and Thelma Delores (Troll) Muller; m. Frank Sebastian Puccio, Feb. 19, 1977 BA, William Paterson Coll., 1968, MA, 1971. Cert. tchr. social studies and English, N.J. Tchr. social studies Parsippany Bd. Edn., NJ, 1968—. Mem. N.J. Coun. Social Studies, ACLU, Eastham Forum, Phi Delta Kappa Democrat. Avocations: cross country skiing, tennis, bicycling, reading. Home: 30 Alpine Dr Wayne NJ 07470-4202 Office: Parsippany High Sch Vail and Baldwin Rds Parsippany NJ 07054 Office Phone: 973-243-7001 x 7671.

PUCHALLA, MARY KAY, elementary school educator; b. Media, Pa., July 16, 1971; d. Mary Jane Orcutt; m. David Wilson Puchalla, June 25, 1999; children: Kyle David, Korey Wilson. BA, Loyola Coll., Balt., 1993; EdM, Cabrini Coll., Radnor, Pa., 1996. Cert. profl. II Pa., 1993. Math tchr. Marple Newtown Sch. Dist., Newtown Square, Pa., 1996—. Lacrosse coach Paxon Hollow Mid. Sch., Broomall, Pa., 1994—2003, athletic dir., 1999—2001. Home: 1083 Clipper Mill Dr West Chester PA 19382 Office: Paxon Hollow Middle School 815 Paxon Hollow Rd Broomall PA 19008 Office Phone: 610-359-4320. Office Fax: 610-353-4061.

PUCKETT, ELIZABETH ANN, law librarian, educator; b. Evansville, Ind., Nov. 10, 1943; d. Buell Charles and Lula Ruth (Gray) P.; m. Joel E. Hendricks, June 1, 1964 (div. June 1973); 1 child, Andrew Charles; m. Thomas A. Wilson, July 19, 1985. BS in Edn., Eastern Ill. U., 1964; JD, U. Ill., 1977, MS in L.S., 1977. Bar: Kans. 1978, Ill. 1979. Acquisitions/reader services librarian U. Kans. Law Library, Lawrence, 1978-79; asst. reader services librarian So. Ill. U. Law Library, Carbondale, 1979-81, reader services librarian, 1981-83; assoc. dir. Northwestern U. Law Library, Chgo., 1983-86, co-acting dir., 1986-87; dir./assoc. prof. South Tex. Coll. Law Library, Houston, 1987-89; dir./prof. South Tex. Coll. Law Libr., Houston, 1990-94, U. Ga. Law Libr., Athens, 1994—. Co-author: Evaluation of System-Provided Library Services to State Correctional Centers in Illinois, 1983; co-editor Uniform Commercial Code: Confidential Drafts, 1993. Mem. ABA, Am. Assn. Law Librs. (mem. exec. bd. 1993-96). Avocations: reading, antiques. Office: U Georgia Law Libr Athens GA 30602-6018 Office Phone: 706-542-5078. E-mail: apuckett@uga.edu.

PUCKETT, HELEN LOUISE, retired tax consulting company executive; b. Ripley, Ohio, Oct. 29, 1934; d. Joseph and Gladys Muriel (Madden) Haney; m. Marvin R. Puckett, May 26, 1953 (dec.); children: Steven W., Thomas J. Grad., Columbus Bus. U., 1971. Office mgr., sec.-treas. Al-Win Tng., Inc., West Jefferson, Ohio, 1971—, agt., 1977—99; ret., 1999. Notary pub., 1975-88. Sunday sch. tchr. London (Ohio) Ch. of Christ, pres. Women's Fellowship, 1979-81. Mem. London Bus. and Profl. Women (pres.), Coover Soc., Cornerstone Club at Madison County Hosp., Career Women's Cmty. Club, Friends of Libr., Madison County Srs. Office: 485 Glade Run Rd West Jefferson OH 43162-9581 E-mail: hlp@dragonbbs.com.

PUCKETT, KAREN, communications executive; BA, Ind. State Univ., Terre Haute, Ind.; MBA, Bellarmine Coll., Louisville, Ky. Former Chief Tech. Officer CenturyTel, exec. v.p., COO, 2000—; pres., COO, 2002—. Bd. mem. US Telecom. Assn. Mem. bd. dir. St. Francis Med. Ctr.; exec. bd. mem. La. Purchase Coun., Boy Scouts Am. Office: Centurytel 100 Centurytel Dr Monroe LA 71203*

PUCKETT, RUBY PARKER, nutritionist, food service executive, writer; b. Dora, Ala., Nov. 26, 1932; d. John Franklin Parker and Ethel V. (Short) Tuggle; m. Larry Willard Puckett, July 2, 1955; children: Laurel Lynn Puckett Brown, Hollie Kristina Puckett Walker. BS in Food and Nutrition, Auburn U., Ala., 1954; postgrad. in vocat. edn., U. Fla., 1970, 80; MA in Health Sci. Edn., Cen. Mich. U., 1976. Registered dietitian, foodservice adminstr. Dietetic intern Henry Ford Hosp., Detroit, 1955; staff dietitian VA Hosp., Houston, 1955-56; dietitian Matty Hersee Hosp., Meridian, Miss., 1957-58; asst. dir. U. Miss. Med. Ctr., Jackson, 1960-61; dir. dietetics Ft. Sanders Presbyn. Hosp., Knoxville, Tenn., 1961-63, Waterman Meml. Hosp., Eustis, Fla., 1963-68; dir. food and nutrition U. Fla. Shands Hosp., Gainesville, 1968-95; pres. Square One Cons. Service, Gainesville, 1979-85; pres., owner Food Svc. Mgmt. Cons., 1995—. Adv. com. on jr. coll. dietetic programs Fla. Dept. Edn., 1967-69; nominating com. Southeastern Hosp. Conf. for Dietitians, 1969, sec., 1974-75; pres. Field Agy. Nutrition, 1970; instr. U. Fla., 1972-73, 82-85, clin. and cmty. coordinated undergrad. dietetic program adv. bd., 1974-89; instr. Santa Fe Jr. Coll., Gainesville, 1977-81; adv. com. Marquis Libr. Soc., Inc., 1974; health project rev. com. North Ctrl. Fla. Planning Coun., 1974-76; named to White House Conf. on Food and Nutrition, 1976, Senate Select Com. on Food and Nutrition, 1976; com. on animal products NRC Adv. Bd. on Mil. Pers. Supplies, 1978-81; site evaluator dietetic programs in colls and univs., 1998-; mem. Commn. on Accrediation Dietetic Edn., 1997-, program reviewer for dietary mgr. tng., 2003-06; reviewer abstracts, articles Jour. Am. Dietetic Assn.; spkr. in field. Author: Food Service Manual for Health Care Institutions, 1988 (Jim Rose Pub-.award, 2005), 3d edit., 2004, Basic Nutrition and Diet Modification Shands Hospital, 1992, revised edit., 2002, Managing Foodservice Operations, 1992, HACCP The Future Challenge, 4th edit., Nutrition Diet Modification Meal Patterns, 4th edit., Disaster and Emergency Preparedness for Food Service Operations, 2003, Dietary Managers Course by Correspondence, 12th edit., Nutrition for the Elderly, Safety, Sanitation and Security for Food Services Operation, Topics in Practice: Productivity Measures for Food Service Operations, 2005; mem. editl. adv. com.: Stokes Report, 1980—84, editl. advisor: Food Management, 1986—, Topics in Clinical Nutrition, 1988—, Aspen's Focus, 1984—91, Aspen's Hosp. Nutrition and Foodservice Forms; editl. advisor Marketlink, 2006; contbr. articles to profl. jours.; developer nutrition and older adult distance edn.course. V.p. Campus USA Credit Union, 1980—81, pres.-elect, 1981—82; chmn. Shands Hosp. chpt. United Way, 1978, mem. speakers bur., 1985—86; profl. adv. bd. Shands Home Care; vol. Mothers Supporting Daus. with Breast Cancer, 2000—; mem. Sexual Phys. Abuse Bd.; courtesy faculty appt. Divsn Youth, Family and Ext.; election clk., inspector Alachua County (Fla.) Elections, 2000—06; bd. dir. Campus USA Credit Union, 1978—, chmn. bd., 1998—2000; mem. budget and allocations com. United Way, 1983—2005; mem. adv. bd. Harvest Gainesville, 1991—93, Children's Miracle Telethon, 1992—95; adv. bd. Sta. WRUF Pub. Radio, 1992; bd. dir. Fla. 4-H Found., 2000—04, North Fla. Regional Vocat. Sch. Named Alumni of Yr., Auburn U. Sch. Home Econs., 1985, Disting. Woman, Alachua County, Fla., 1992; named to Woodlawn H.S. Hall of Fame, 1982, Fla. Women's Hall of Fame, 1986; recipient Community Leader award, Sta. WRUF-FM, 1972, Ivy award, Restaurateurs of Distinction, 1980, Disting. Pace Setter award, Roundtable for Women in Foodservice, 1984, Award of Distinction, Sch. Human Svc., Auburn U., 1991. Mem.: FCSI (mem. task force needs assessment 2003), Fla. Coun. on Aging (sec. nutrition sect. 1974—76, chmn. 1974—76, adv. bd. 1974—76), Nat. U. Continuing Edn. Assn. (disting. ind. study course 1986, 1989), Nutrition Edn. Soc. (liaison with industry com. 1974, legis. com. 1974, charter), Dietary Mgr. Assn. Found. Fla. (steering com.), Am. Soc. Hosp. Food Service Adminstrs. (edn. com. 1968—71, nomination com. 1978, chmn. publ. com. 1981—82, chmn. legis. com. 1984, adv. bd. Trends 2006, bd. dirs., task force HACCP cert., Jim Rose Pub. award 2005), Gainesville Dietetic Assn. (v.p. 1969, pres. 1970, 1976), Fla. Dietetic Assn. (sec. 1968—70, pres. 1973—74, del. 1980—87, chmn. by-laws com. 1985, numerous other offices), Am. Dietetic Assn. (pres. practice group 41 1982—84, area III coord. 1985—88, chair, Area III ADA Found. 1988—91, area III coord. 1989—, chair practice group mgmt. in food and nutrition svc. 2001, mem. hons. award com. 2005, chmn. stds. of profl. practice, Excellence in Mgmt. Practice award 1994, medal 1996, Marjorie Hulsizer Copher award 2003, Medallion for Profl. Cmty. and Career Achievement), The Athenaeum Soc., Internat. Gold and Silver Plate Soc. (sec. bd. trustees 1983—85), Ivy Soc., Altrusa, Pi Lambda Beta, Kappa Sigma Phi. Democrat. Mem. Lds Ch. Avocations: whitewater rafting, hiking, gardening. Office: 5200 NW 43d St Ste 102-302 Gainesville FL 32606 Office Phone: 352-371-6160. Personal E-mail: puckerp@juno.com.

PUCKETT, SANDY GRAVES, elementary school educator; b. Lebanon, Tenn., July 14, 1961; d. Alice Tomlinson and Oddie Lenning Graves; m. Dwight Edwin Puckett, Apr. 18, 1983; children: Randall Lenning, Corey Jacob. Grad., Lincoln Meml. U., Harrogate, Tenn., 2006. Tchr. Sevier County Bd. Edn., Sevierville, Tenn., 2000—. Master: Nat. Beta Club (sponsor 2003—). Office: Pigeon Forge Mid Sch 300 Wears Valley Dr Pigeon Forge TN 37863 Office Phone: 865-453-2401. Office Fax: 865-453-0799. Business E-Mail: sandypuckett@sevier.org.

PUCKETT, SUSAN, newspaper editor; Exec. food editor features desk Atlanta Jour. and Constn., 1990-97, food editor, 1997—. Author: (cookbooks) A Cook's Tour of Mississippi, 1980, A Cook's Tour of Iowa, 1990, Dips: Great Recipes for Spreads, Salsas, Fondues and Other Party Fare, 1995; co-author: The 5:30 Challenge, 2005. Office: Atlanta Jour and Constn 72 Marietta St NW Atlanta GA 30303-2804 Business E-Mail: spuckett@ajc.com.

PUCKO, DIANE BOWLES, public relations executive; b. Wyndotte, Mich., Aug. 15, 1940; d. Mervin Arthur and Bernice Letitia (Shelly) Bowles; m. Raymond J. Pucko, May 22, 1965; children: Todd Anthony, Gregory Bowles. BA in Sociology, Bucknell U., Lewisburg, Pa., 1962. Accredited in pub. rels. Asst. to pub. rels. dir. Edward C. Michener Assocs., Inc., Harrisburg, Pa., 1962-65; advt./pub. rels. coord. Superior Switchboard & Devices, Canton, Ohio, 1965-66; editorial dir. women's svc. Hutchins Advt. Co., Inc., Rochester, N.Y., 1966-71; pres. Editorial Communications, Rochester and Elyria, Ohio, 1971-77; mgr. advt. and sales promotion Tappan Air Conditioning, Elyria, 1977-80; mgr. pub. affairs Kaiser Permanente Med. Care Program, Cleve., 1980-85; corp. dir. pub. affairs Keystone Health Plans, Inc., Camp Hill, Pa., 1985-86; v.p., dir. client planning Young-Liggett-Stashower, Cleve., 1986; v.p., dir. pub. rels. Marcus Pub. Rels., Cleve., 1987-91; sr. v.p. Proconsul, Cleve., 1991-95, also bd. dirs.; sr. ptnr. pub. rels. Poppe Tyson, Cleve., 1995-96; managing dir. Bozell Pub. Rels., Cleve., 1996-97; sr. counsel Pub. Rels. Ptnrs., Inc., Cleve., 1997—2002. Mgr., role model Women in Mgmt. Field Placement program, Cleve. State U., 1983-92; pub. rels. adv. bd. profl. adviser, Pub. Rels. Student Soc. Am., Kent State U., 1988-2003 Bd. trustees, mem. exec. com., chmn. pub. rels. adv. com. Ronald MacDonald House of Cleve., 1993—2000; bd. dirs., chmn. pub. rels. com. Assn. Retarded Citizens, Cleve., 1987-91; mem. pub. rels.-mktg. com. Beech Brook, 1996—2000; mem. journalism comm. adv. bd. Elon Coll., 1998—2001. Recipient Woman Profl. Excellence award YMCA, 1984, MacEachern award Acad. Hosp. Pub. Rels., 1985, Bell Ringer award Cmty. Rels. Report, 1985, Bronze Quill Excellence award Internat. Assn. Bus. Communicators, 1992, 93, Cleve. Comms. award Women in Comms. Internat., 1993, 95, Tower award Bus./Profl. Advt. Assn., 1993, 95, Creativity in Pub. Rels. award, 1994, Silver Screen award U.S. Internat. Film & Video Festival, 1995, Silver Quill Excellence award Internat. Assn. Bus. Communicators, 1995, 2001, Internat. Assn. Bus. Communicators. Fellow Pub. Rels. Soc. Am. (bd. dirs. 1983-85, 86-94, officer 1991-95, mem. counselors acad. 1986—, Silver Anvil award 1985, Mktg./Consumer Rels. award East Ctrl. dist. 1992, 95, Lighthouse award 1995); mem. Press Club Cleve. (bd. dirs. 1989-96, v.p. 1990-96), Cleve. Advt. Club, Women's City Club Cleve., Nat. Agri-Mktg. Assn. (Nat. Merit award 2000). Republican. Methodist. Avocation: soccer. Home: 656 University Ave Elyria OH 44035-7278

PUDELEK, SHERRY CHARLENE, small business owner; b. Rapid City, S.D., Oct. 4, 1960; d. Clarence Allen Otters and Helen (Ardito) Morreale; m. James Michael Pudelek, Oct. 6, 1979; children: James Walter, Marianne Christine. Student, Triton (Ill.) Jr. Coll., 1978-79. Clk., cashier Jacobs Twin Buick, Chgo., 1979; clk. typist Beardsly & Piper, Chgo., 1979-80; receptionist Gene Wulbert Ford, Oak Park, Ill., 1980; teller Ave. Bank, Oak Park, 1980-81; clk. Wausau Ins., River Forest, Ill., 1981; owner J&M Towing (now J&M Enterprizes), Berwyn, Ill., 1981—85; mgr. Ardito's Amoco, Oak Park, 1985—94; owner J&M Auto Refurnishing, Addison, Ill., 1987-89; asst. svc. mgr. Courtsey Mazda, River Forest, Ill., 1989-90; mgr. Petro Oil Oak Park, Oak Park, Ill., 1990-91; with J & M Auto Ctr., Inc., 1995—2000, Action Transmission, Inc., 2000—. Roman Catholic. Avocations: swimming, boating, cars, cooking, music. Home: 1958 Bristol Ave Westchester IL 60154-4406

PUDLIN, HELEN POMERANTZ, lawyer; b. NYC, June 26, 1949; d. George and Claire Pomerantz; m. David B. Pudlin, Dec. 23, 1973; children: Alexander R., Julia H. BA cum laude, U. Pa., 1970, MS, 1971, JD, 1974. Bar: Pa. 1974. Lectr. U. Pa. Law Sch., 1983-87; asssoc. Ballard, Spahr, Andreas & Ingersoll, Phila., 1974-81, ptnr., 1981-89; gen. counsel Provident Nat. Bank, Phila., 1989-93; sr. v.p., dep. gen. counsel PNC Fin. Corp., Pitts., 1992-93; sr. v.p., mng. gen. counsel PNC Bank Corp., Pitts., 1993; sr. v.p., gen. counsel The PNC Fin. Svc. Group, Pitts., 1993—. Speaker in field. Author: (with others) Review of Antitrust Laws and Procedures, 1983, Criminal Antitrust Litigation Manual, 1983, Pennsylvania Medical Society Handbook, 1989; co-author: Joint Ventures in Healthcare. Former mem. Bd. of Ethics City of Phila.; former mem. bd. dirs. Phila. Facilities Mgmt. Corp.; bd. advisors Pub. Interest Law Ctr. Phila.; former mem. bd. overseers U. Pa.; bd. trustees Wistar Inst. Mem. ABA (antitrust sect., litigation sect., bus. law sect.), Pa. Bar Assn. (former mem. ho. of dels., judiciary com.), Phila. Bar Assn. (bd. govs. 1989-91, fed. cts. com., bus. law sect.), Acad. Natural Scis. (former bd. dirs., trustee), Duquesne Club. Office: The PNC Fin Svc Group 249 5th Ave Pittsburgh PA 15222-2709

PUENTE, MARIA LUZ, bilingual educator; b. Bilbao, Spain, Feb. 8, 1964; came to U.S., 1990; d. Jose L. and Luz (Ordonez) P. BA in History and Arts, U. Complutense, Madrid, 1987; Superior Degree in Classical Piano, Royal Conservatory of Music, Madrid, 1988, Superior Degree in Chamber Music, 1990; MBA, U. Redlands, Calif., 2000. Solfeggio tchr. Royal Conservatory of Music, Madrid, 1988; h.s. tchr. Ministry of Edn., Madrid, 1988-90; bilingual tchr. in elem. sch. Desert Sands Unified Sch. Dist., Indio, Calif., 1990—. Instr. Practising Sch. of Archeology, U. Deusto, Bilbao, 1983. Pianist, performing in concerts, 1974-89; contbr. articles to profl. jours. Mem. La Quinta (Calif.) Hist. Preservatin Commn., 1994—. Roman Catholic. Avocations: photography, piano, collecting, travel, music. Home: 78-620 Forbes Cir La Quinta CA 92253 E-mail: mlpuente@aol.com.

PUERTA, CHRISTY L., construction executive; b. Santa Ana, Calif., May 28, 1966; d. Larry E. and Eileen G. Methvin.; m. Julio E. Puerta, Aug. 28, 1987; children: Nichole, Brittany. BA in Child Devel., Calif. State U., Northridge, 1989. Child care counselor Children's Inst. Internat., L.A., 1985-89; v.p. Larry Methvin Installation Inc., Lodi, Calif., 1984—. Coun. mem. Leadership Prayer Breakfast Coun., 2001—; camp counselor Sch. Bethel Open Bible, Lodi, Calif., 1999—, tchr. Sunday Sch., 2000. Mem. HBANC (assoc.), BIA Superior Calif. (assoc.), Pacific Coast Builders Conf. Republican. Avocations: travel, soccer, family. Office: Larry Methvin Installation Inc 128 N Cluff Ave Lodi CA 95240 Office Fax: 209-367-4938. E-mail: cpuerta@puertafamily.com, lmilodi@aol.com.

PUGACH, MARLEEN CAROL, education educator; b. Englewood, N.J., Apr. 22, 1949; d. Paul Irving and Lillian (Rosenstein) P.; m. William Havens Rickards, June 21, 1978; children: Lev Ian, Anna Yael. BA with distinction, Mt. Holyoke Coll., South Hadley, Mass., 1971; MS in Edn., U. So. Calif., L.A., 1974; PhD, U. Ill., 1983. Vis. asst. prof. U. Ill., Urbana, 1984-85; asst. prof. edn. U. Wis., Milw., 1986-89, assoc. prof., 1989—95, prof., 1996—. Author: (with L. Johnson) Collaborative Practitioners, Collaborative Schools, 1995, 2d edit., 2002, On the Border of Opportunity, 1998, Because Teaching Matters, 2006; editor: (with R. Clift and W. Houston) Encouraging Reflective Practice in Education, 1990, (with H. Barnes and L. Beckum) Changing the Practice of Teacher Education, 1991, (with C. Warger) Curriculum Trends, Special Edition and Reform, 1996, (with L. Blanton, C. Griffin, J. Winn) Teacher Education in Transition, 1997; contbr. articles to profl. jours., chpts. to books. Recipient Margaret Lindsey award Am. Assn. Colls. Tchr. Edn., 1998, Disting. Alumni award Coll. Edn. U. Ill., 2005, Excellence in Tchr. Edn. award Coun. for Exceptional Children, 2005; grantee U.S. Dept. Edn., 1985-88, 99-2002, Carnegie Corp., 2003-; Fulbright grantee U. Alta., 2006. Mem. Am. Ednl. Rsch. Assn., Coun. for Exceptional Children (exec. bd. tchr. edn. div. 1988-91). Office: U Wis PO Box 413 Milwaukee WI 53201-0413 Business E-Mail: mpugach@uwm.edu.

PUGH, ANN BARHAM, writer, educator; b. Ft. Worth, Nov. 19, 1923; d. Edwin Bingham and Ellen Margaret (Bierkamp) Barham; m. Charles Edward Pugh, Feb. 27, 1954; children: Stephen, Michael, Theresa. BA, Tex. Christian U., 1950, MA; postgrad., U. So. Calif. Assoc. prof. speech, drama, and theatre Tex. Christian U., Ft. Worth, 1945-52. Host TV talk show NBC Affilliate, Channel 5, Ft. Worth, 1949-54; speech tchr. Ft. Worth Woman's Club, 1961-62. Author: (children's book) Diggy Armadillo, 1990, Westy the Hare, 1995; playwright: Day They Kidnapped Blanche, 1980 (Am. Theatre Assn. award), (children's musicals) Heidi, 1972, It Happened in Hamelin, 1972, Lilac Connection, 1970; dir., prodr. first Pops Concert, Ft. Worth Symphony, 1963; prodr., musical writer Arts Coun. Greater Ft. Worth, 1963, The Christmas Caffe. Founding pres. Tarrant County Rep. Orgn., 1964-65. Avocations: travel, theater-going.

PUGH, DOROTHY GUNTHER, artistic director; b. Memphis, May 8, 1951; Grad. magna cum laude, Vanderbilt U., 1973; studied with Raymond Clay, studied with Donna Carver, studied with David Howard; student, Royal Acad. Dancing, London. Founder Ballet Memphis, 1985, also artistic dir., 1985—. Named one of city's influential citizens, Memphis Mag.; recipient Woman of Achievement award for Initiative, 1987, Gordon Holl Artistic Adminstr. of Yr. award, State of Tenn., 1999. Office: Ballet Memphis PO Box 3675 Cordova TN 38088-3675 E-mail: info@balletmemphis.com.

PUGH, JOYE JEFFRIES, educational association administrator, consultant, writer; b. Ocilla, Ga., Jan. 23, 1957; d. Claude Bert and Stella Elizabeth (Paulk) Jeffries; m. Melville Eugene Pugh, Sept. 21, 1985. AS in Pre-law, S. Ga. Coll., 1978; BS in Edn., Valdosta State Coll., 1980, MEd in Psychology, Guidance and Counseling, 1981; EdD in Adminstrn., Nova U., Ft. Lauderdale, Fla., 1992. Cert. tchr., adminstr., supr., Ga. Pers. adminstr. TRW, Inc., Douglas, Ga., 1981-83; recreation dir. Ocilla Irwin Recreation Dept., 1983-84; exec. dir. Sunny Dale Tng. Ctr., Inc., Ocilla, 1984-96; employment cons. TPS Staffing and Recruiting, Douglas, 1997-98; mgr. Global Employment Solutions, Inc., 1999—2002; freelance writer, 2002—. Pres. and registered agt. Irwin County Resources, Inc., Ocilla, 1988-97, Camelot Ct., Inc., 1994-97. Author: Colours of Joye, 1975, Antichrist-The Cloned Image of Jesus Christ, 1999, EDEN - The Knowledge of Good and Evil 666, 2006; contbr. articles on handicapped achievements to newspapers, mags. (Ga. Spl. Olympics News Media award, 1987, Assn. for Retarded Citizens News Media award, 1988). Mem. adv. bd. Area 12 Spl. Olympics, Douglas, 1984-88, bd. dirs., 1995-2000; pres. Irwin County Spl. Olympics, 1984-97, mem. adv. task force Spl. Olympics Internat. for 6-7 yr. olds, 1995—97; bd. dirs. Ga. Spl. Olympics, 1995-98, 98-99, mem. comm. and mktg. com., 1995-96, mem. nominations com., 1997-98, outreach and edn. com., 1999-2000; exec. dir., fund raising chmn. Irwin Assn. for Retarded Citizens, Ocilla, 1984-97; arts and crafts chmn. Ga. Sweet Tater Trot 5k/1 Mile Rd. Races, 1993-97; founder, chmn. Joseph Mascolo Celebrity Events, 1985-97; vol. Am. Heart Assn., 2000-02; organist, pianist, soloist, percussionist Satika Bapt. Ch., 2005-. Recipient Spirit of Spl. Olympics award Ga. Spl. Olymics, Atlanta, 1986, Award of Excellence Ga. Spl. Olympic Bd. Dirs., 2000, Cmty. Svc. award Ga. Assn. for Retarded Citizens, Atlanta, 1987, Govs.' Vol. award Ga. Vol. Awards, Atlanta, 1988, Presdl. Sports award AAU, Indpls., 1988, Humanitarian award Sunny Dale Tng. Ctr., Inc., Ocilla, 1988, Golden Poet award New Am. Poetry Anthology, 1988, Outstanding Coach-Athlete Choice award Sunny Dale Spl. Olympics, Ocilla, 1992, Dist. Coach award, 1993, Outstanding Unified Sports Ptnr. of Yr. award, 1995, Coach of Yr. award, 1996; carried Olympic Torch, Ocilla, 1996; Ga. Spl. Olympics State Gold medalist Golf Unified Team, 1996, State Silver medalist Unified Table Tennis Team, 1996, State Bronze medalist Master's Unified Softball Team, 1995. Mem. DAR (Author-Educator-Humanitarian award Nathaniel Abney chpt. 2000), Nat. Soc. Daughters Am. Revolution (mem. Nathaniel Abney chpt.), Mut. Unidentified Flying Object Network (Ga. state sect. dir., asst. state dir., cons. 1994—), Ga. State Assn. for Retarded Citizens, Ctrs. Dirs. Ga., Ocilla Rotary Club (program dir. 1995-97, bd. dirs. 1995-97, sec. 1996-97), Sunny Dale Unified Track Club (founder 1991), Sunny Dale Ensemble (founder 1988), Irwin Assn. Retarded Citizens Inc. (pres., pub. rels. dir. 1984-96). Baptist. Avocations: playing musical instruments, jet skiing, weightlifting, dance, singing. Home and Office: 201 Lakeside Cir Douglas GA 31535-6629 Office Phone: 912-384-9520. Personal E-mail: drjoye@charter.net.

PUGH, MARTHA GREENEWALD, lawyer; b. Washington, Feb. 1, 1913; d. Eugene Ludwig and Mary Martha (Curtis) Greenewald; m. Wallace R. Pugh, Aug. 29, 1935 (div. 1945); children: John Clifford, William Wallace; m. Wallace R. Pugh, Aug. 29, 1975. BA in Physics, U. Colo., 1934; MS in Physics, U. Mich., 1936; JD, Seton Hall U., 1961. Bar: US Patent Office 1947, DC 1964, US Ct. Appeals (DC cir.) 1964, NJ 1965, US Dist. Ct. NJ 1965, US Ct. Customs and Patent Appeals 1966, US Ct. Appeals (3d cir.) 1966, US Supreme Ct. 1977. Instr. physics NYU, NYC, 1941—43; patent staff Bell Telephone Labs., Murray Hill, NJ, 1943—67; patent agt. Gulton Industries, Metuchen, NJ, 1957—58, Summit, NJ, 1958—64; pvt. practice Summit, 1964—81; ptnr. Mathews, Woodbridge, Goebel, Pugh & Collins, Morristown, NJ, 1981—89; of counsel Mathews, Woodbridge and Collins, Parsippany, NJ, 1990—. Active Coalition for Nuclear Freeze, 1983—. Mem.: ABA, Nat. Soc. Inventors (coun. mem.), NJ Patent Law Assn. (2d v.p. 1984, treas. 1985, sec. 1986, 1st v.p. 1987, pres.-elect 1988, pres. 1989), Union County Bar Assn. (trustee 1976—78), NJ Bar Assn. (chmn. patent sect. 1976—77), Women Lawyers of Union County, Nat. Assn. Women Lawyers, Am. Patent Law Assn., Mortar Bd., Green Mountain Club, Pi Beta Phi, Kappa Beta Pi, Sigma Pi Sigma. Democrat. Unitarian.

PUGH, MELANIE SYBIL, elementary school educator; b. Meshoppen, Pa., June 2, 1964; d. Wayne Bevan and Marilyn Joan (Wittmer) P. BS in Elem. Edn., Bloomsburg U., Pa., 1985; MS in edn., Wilkes U., Wilkes-Barre, Pa., 1991. Substitute Tunkhannock Area Sch. Dist., Pa., 1986; kindergarten tchr. Little People Daycare Sch., Scranton, Pa., 1986-87; kindregarten tchr. Tunkhannock Area Sch. Dist., Pa., 1987-89, homebound instr., 1988—, GED instr., 1988-89; kindergarten tchr. Appletree Nursery and Primary Sch., Forty-Fort, Pa., 1989-90; vision therapist Binocular Vision Ctr., Tunkhannock, 1989-91; nursery sch. tchr. Appletree Nursery and Primary Sch., Forty Fort, Pa., 1990—99; tchr. 3rd grade Sesquehanna Prep., 1999—. Deacon Tunkhannock Presbyn. Ch., 1989,, elder, 2003—, sec. deacons, 1991; v.p. PTO Roslund Elem. Sch., Tunkhannock, 1988-89. Republican. Presbyterian. Avocations: sports, reading, travel. Home: 6 Washington St Tunkhannock PA 18657-1215

PUGH, SHANTE CAMILLE, athletic trainer; b. Bklyn., Oct. 17, 1977; d. Hortencia Patricia Owens; m. Esau Pugh III, May 21, 2005. AA, U. South Fla., Tampa, 1997; BS in Health/Sports Medicine, U. North Fla., Jacksonville, 2000. Cert. CPR/AED Am. Heart Assn., 2001; athletic trainer Nat. Athletic Trainers Bd. of Certification, 2001, acad. clin. instr. Athletic Tng. Program-

Sports Medicine/U. Ctrl. Fla., 2006, athletic trainer Fla. Intern athletic trainer Orlando Miracle-WNBA, Fla., 2001. Contract athletic trainer Fla. Hosp., Orlando, 2004—, Disney Wide World of Sports, Orlando, Fla., 2004—05. Contbr. articles to profl. jours. Recipient scholarship, Disney World, 1995, Delta Sigma Theta, 1995. Mem.: S.E. Athletic Trainers Assn., Nat. Athletic Trainers Assn. Avocations: dance, music, teaching, watching horror films, travel.

PUGLIESE LOCKE, RANADA MARIE, nurse; b. Cleve., Sept. 22, 1950; d. Joan Lee Green; m. Thomas L. Locke; 1 child, Kathryn Marie. AA, Los Angeles Valley Coll., 1974; student, Pepperdine U., 1981-82, U. San Francisco, 1985; BA, St. Mary's Coll., 1998; postgrad., Samuel Merrit Coll., 1998-00. Nurse emergency and ICU St. Joseph Hosp., Burbank, Calif., 1968-76; asst. dir. emergency services Brotman Hosp., L.A., 1976-78; clin. instr. Stanford (Calif.) U., 1978-80; dir. emergency services White Meml. Hosp., L.A., 1980-84; coordinator base sta., flight nurse UCLA, 1982-84; flight nurse, dir. med. ops. CALSTAR, 1984-87; coord. base sta. Tahoe Forest Hosp., 1987-98, base sta. coord., staff nurse, house supr. emergency dept.; staff nurse Santa Monica Hosp., 1980-84; firecaptain, EMS coord. North Tahoe Fire Protection Dist., 1990-98. Mem. Emergency Nurses Assn. (pres. local chpt. 1987-78), Flight Nurse Assn., Critical Care Nurses Assn., Calif. State Firefighters Assn. Avocations: backpacking, snow, waterskiing. Home and Office: 68-151 AU St Ph 8 Waialua HI 96791-9456

PUGLISI, MARY JOANNA, psychologist; b. Towson, Md., June 1, 1966; d. Joseph Anthony Butterhoff, Mary Barbara Butterhoff; m. Terrence Anthony Puglisi; children: Meg, Anthony, Cate, Joanna. BA in Psychology, Loyola Coll., 1988, MS in Counseling Psycholgy, 1993. Lic. clin. profl. counselor Md., 2001. Psychologist St. Elizabeth Sch., Balt., 1994—97; PRIDE program coord. St. Anthony of Padua Sch., Balt., 1997—. Cons. (book) Special Needs Resource Directory, 2001. Local coord./team mem. Cath. Engaged Encounter, Balt., 1991. Mem.: Am. Counseling Assn. Home: 8146 Bell Tower Crossing Pasadena MD 21122 Office: St Anthony of Padua Sch 4410 Frankford Ave Baltimore MD 21206

PUIA, MARY BETH, educator; b. Plainfield, NJ, Sept. 28, 1949; d. Elmer Ellsworth Michael and Mary Helen D'Amico; children: Amy Joy, Daniel John, Jenny Marie. BA, Montclair U., NJ, 1972. Tchr. Franklin Bd. Edn., Somerset, NJ, 1993—, Manville Bd. Ed, 1972—. Office Phone: 732-302-2400. Personal E-mail: mepuia@aol.com. E-mail: mpuia@franklinboe.org.

PUJANA, MARIA JOSE, neurologist; MD, Universidad Complutense, Madrid. Former chief resident, neurophysiology dept. Veteran Hosp., Madrid; adj. instructor Ctr. for Global Hlth. and Diseases, Sch. of Med., Case Western Reserve U., 1994—. Pres., designer Marise Jewelry Designs. Former v.p. of council Cleve. Ballet; adv. bd. mem. Cleve. Inst. of Art; trustee Cleve. Found., 2002—; mem. cmty. adv. bd. Rock and Roll Hall of Fame and Museum; bd. mem. Cuyahoga Cmty. Coll. Found., MetroHealth Found., Beck Ctr. for Arts, Cleve. Red Cross. Office: Case Sch of Med 10900 Euclid Ave Cleveland OH 44106*

PULEIO, ANN MARGARET, special education educator; b. Freeport, N.Y., June 28, 1964; d. Raymond Louis and Catherine Grace (Hepburn) Wemssen. BS summa cum laude, L.I. U., 1986; MS magna cum laude, Adelphi U., 1990. Tchr. The Child Study Ctr. N.Y., Bklyn., 1986—90; lead counselor Little Village House, Manhasset, 1989—92; tchr. Sch. Lang. and Communication Devel., North Bellmore, 1990—95, Hagedorn Little Village Sch., Seaford, 1996—. Recipient Acad. Excellence award L.I. U., C.W. Post Coll., Greenvale, N.Y., 1983-86. Mem. Coun. for Exceptional Children. Roman Catholic. Home: 41 Florence Ave Massapequa NY 11758-7841

PULEO, JEAN ANNE, music educator, musician; d. Joseph Alfred and Lucy Stango; m. Joseph Salvatore Puleo, Apr. 6, 1974; children: Jennifer L. Bayley, Lauren J. Grove. B of Music Edn., Temple U., 1970, MusM in Performance, 1973; postgrad., SUNY, Binghamton, 1974—75. Cert. instrnl. II Pa., N.Y. Music tchr. Phila. Bd. Edn., 1970—74, Binghamton (N.Y.) Pub. Schs., 1975—76; violin instr. Suburban Music Sch., Media, Pa., 1990—95; music tchr. Marple Newtown Sch. Dist., Newtown Square, 1995—. Substitute tchr. Substitute Tchr. Svc., Media, 1985—95; profl. violinist Phila. Opera Co., Kennett Symphony of Chester County, Peter Nero and the Philly Pops, Phila. Classical Symphony, Pa. Ballet Orch., Wayne Oratorio Soc., Ocean City (N.J.) Pops. Recipient music scholarship, Phila. Bd. Edn., 1966—70, music grant, Temple U., 1966—70, Ambler music scholarship, 1968—70. Mem.: NEA (mem. tchr.), Music Educators Nat. Conf. (mem. tchr.), Am. Fedn. Musicians Local 77. Avocations: reading, cooking, sports.

PULHAMUS, MARLENE LOUISE, retired elementary school educator; b. Paterson, NJ, Sept. 11, 1937; d. David Weeder and Elfrieda (Ehler) Wemmell; m. Aaron R. Pulhamus, Aug. 20, 1960; children: Steven, Thomas, Nancy. Student, Trenton State U., 1957; BS, William Paterson U., 1959; postgrad., Rutgers U., 1992. Cert. elem. tchr., NJ. Kindergarten tchr. Wayne Bd. Edn., NJ, 1959-63, Paterson Bd. Edn., 1974-75, 2d grade tchr., 1975-81; basic skills instr. Paterson Pub. Schs., 1981—, tchr. accelerated program 1st grade, 1992—; cons. lang. arts, literacy Kendall Hunt Pegasus, Wayne; ret., 1997. Trainer for insvc. groups of learning ctrs. and math. with manipulatives for local pub. schs., trainer for local pub. schs. Contbr. Lessons 4Mat in Action, 3d edit., 4Mat: A Quest for Wholeness, 1977—. Pres. Friends of Eisenhower Libr., Totowa, NJ, 1975-77; coord. ch. sch. Preakness Reformed Ch., Wayne, 1990-93, elder, chair outreach commn.; exec. bd. United Meth. Women Altar GUild, Asbury United Meth. Ch.; sec. VTTC Homeowners Assn., Salisbury, Md. Recipient Gov.'s award for tchg. excellence State of NJ Commn. Edn., 1991, 4Mation program award, 1994. Mem. ASCD, NEA, AAUW, Nat. Coun. Tchrs. Math., Nat. Assn. for Edn. Young Children, NJ Edn. Assn., Passaic County Edn. Assn., Paterson Edn. Assn. (mem. exec. bd., 1985-89, legis. chmn. 1986-89). Personal E-mail: mylilycat@verizon.net.

PULITZER, EMILY RAUH (MRS. JOSEPH PULITZER JR.), art historian, consultant; b. Cin., July 23, 1933; d. Frederick and Harriet (Frank) Rauh; m. Joseph Pulitzer Jr., 1973 (dec. 1993). AB, Bryn Mawr Coll., 1955; student, Ecole du Louvre, Paris, 1955-56; MA, Harvard U., 1963; LHD honoris causa (hon.), U. Mo., 1989; DFA honoris causa (hon.), Aquinas Inst., St. Louis, 2002, St. Louis U., 2003; HHD honoris causa (hon.), Washington U., St. Louis, 2005. Mem. staff Cin. Art Mus., 1956-57; asst. curator drawings Harvard U. Fogg Art Mus., 1957-64, asst. to dir., 1962-63; curator City Art Mus., St. Louis, 1964-73; mem. painting and sculpture com. Mus. Modern Art, 1985—, trustee, 1994—, vice chair paintings and sculpture com., 1996—, mem. drawings com., 2003—; chmn. visual arts com. Mo. Arts Coun., 1976-81; bd. mem. Inst. Mus. Svcs., 1979-84; commr. St. Louis Art Mus., 1981-88, vice chmn., 1988; bd. dir. Pulitzer, Inc., 1993—2005; founder, chmn. Pulitzer Found. for the Arts, 2001—. Bd. dirs. Contemporary Art Mus., St. Louis, 1980-2003, 2004-, pres., 1990-95; bd. dirs. Mark Rothko Found., 1980-89, Grand Ctr., 1993-95,, 99—, arts strategy com. chair, 2003—; bd. trustees St. Louis Symphony Orch., 1994-2004, bd. overseers, 2005—; bd. dirs. arts in transit com. Bi-State Devel. Agy., vice-chmn. and co-founder, 1987-98; mem. Leadership St. Louis, 1990-91; mem. overseers com. to visit Harvard Art Mus., 1990—, chair 2004-; trustee Mus. Modern Art, 1994—; mem. overseer's com. to visit the art mus. Harvard U., 1990—, chair, 2004—, mem. collections com., 1992—, chair, 1992-2004, mem. Fogg Fellows, 1978—, co-chair, 1978-94, bd. overssers, 2006—, pres.'s adv. com. on Allston Initiative, 2005—. Named one of Top 200 Collectors, ARTnews Mag., 2003—06; recipient St. Louis award, Contbn. to Arts Cmty., 2003. Mem. Am. Fedn. Arts (dir. 1976-89), St. Louis Mercantile Libr. Assn. (bd. dirs. 1987-93), Mo. Women's Forum.

PULLEN, PENNY LYNNE, non-profit organization administrator, retired state legislator; b. Buffalo, Mar. 2, 1947; d. John William and Alice Nettie (McConkey) P. BA in Speech, U. Ill., 1969. Tv technician Office Instnl. Resources, U. Ill., 1966-68; cmty. newspaper reporter Des Plaines (Ill.) Pub. Co., 1967-72; legis. asst. to Ill. legislators, 1968-77; mem. Ill. Ho. of Reps., 1977-93, chmn. ho. exec. com., 1981-82, minority whip, 1983-87, asst. minority leader, 1987-93; pres., founder Life Advocacy Resource Project, Arlington Heights, Ill., 1992—. Exec. dir. Ill. Family Inst., 1993-94; dir. Legal Svcs. Corp., 1989-93; mem. Pres.'s Commn. on AIDS Epidemic, 1987-88; mem. Ill. Goodwill Del. to Republic of China, 1987. Summit conf. observer as mem. adhoc Women for SDI, Geneva, 1985; active Nat. Coun. Ednl. Rsch., 1983—88; dir. Eagle Forum of Ill., 1999—2003, pres., 2003—; del. Rep. Nat. Conv., 1984; mem. Rep. Nat. Com., 1984—88; del. Atlantic Alliance Young Polit. Leaders, Brussels, 1977; pres. Maine Twp. Rep. Women's Club, 1997—99, Rep. Women of Park Ridge, Ill., 2001—03, Rep. Women of Wheeling Twp., Ill., 2004—. Recipient George Washington Honor medal Freedoms Found., 1978, Dwight Eisenhower Freedom medal Chgo. Captive Nations Com., 1977, Outstanding Legislator awards Ill. Press Assn., Ill. Podiatry Soc., Ill. Coroners Assn., Ill. County Clks. Assn., Ill. Hosp. Assn., Ill. Health Care Assn.; named Ill. Young Republican, 1968, Outstanding Young Person, Park Ridge Jaycees, 1981, One of 10 Outstanding Young Persons, Ill. Jaycees, 1981. Mem. DAR, Am. Legis. Exch. Coun. (dir. 1977-91, exec. com. 1978-83, 2d vice chmn. 1980-83), Com. on the Status of Women (sec. 1997—).

PULLIAM, GLORIOUS K., elementary school educator; b. Sanford, Fla. d. Godfrey and Harriett Knight; m. Leroy Pulliam, Dec. 19, 1965; children: Leah, Alison, John. BS, Knoxville Coll., Tenn., 1964; MSW, Case We. Res. U., Cleve., 1968; adminstrv. credential, Calif. State U., Hayward, 1994. Child welfare worker Alameda County, Oakland, Calif., 1970—80; sch. adminstr. Hayward Unified Sch. Dist., 1980—99, dir. child devel. program, 1999—. Mem. Citizen's Adv. Commn. City of Hayward, 1999—. Mem.: Child Care Planning Coun., Early Childhood Mentor Tchr. Selection Com., Alpha Kappa Alpha. Methodist. Avocations: walking, dance, travel. Home: 3410 Big Oak Ct Hayward CA 94542 Office: Hayward Unified Sch Dist 24411 Amador St Hayward CA 94540 Office Phone: 510-783-3793.

PULLIN, TANYA, state representative; b. South Shore, Ky, Sept. 15, 1957; d. Norman Keith and Mildred Pauline (Williams) P. JD, Univ. of Ky., 1986; MA, Duke Univ., 1985; BS, Univ. of Ky., 1980. Bar: Ky., 1986, U.S. Ct. Appeals Fed. Cir. 1987. State Rep. House of Rep., Dist. 98, Ky., 2000—; employed Baker & McKenzie, Hong Kong, China, 1995—97, Deacons, Hong Kong, China, 1990—95, Morgan & Finnegan, 1986—90. Bd. dirs., State YMCA of Ky., Frankfort, 1987—. Toll fellow, 2002, Elliott fellow, 2003; recipient Law Day award, 2003. Mem. NY Soc. Ky. Women (treas. 1988—), Kentuckians NY (dinner chmn. 1989—), Rainbow Girls (majority mem.). Democrat. Office: Capitol Capitol Annex Rm 432C Frankfort KY 40601 also: Dist Rural Rt 1 PO Box 486 South Shore KY 41175

PULLIUM, RITA MARIE, educational association administrator, director, psychologist; b. Philippines, Jan. 4, 1947; d. George Lee Huang and Chun Kheng Yu; m. Rush James Pullium; children: Anthea H. Wang, Melissa H. Williams. BA in Psychology, U. Philippines, 1968, MA in Psychology, 1974, PhD in Social Psychology, 1980; postgrad. in Population Psychology, U. NC, 1985. Instr. to asst. prof. psychology Ateneo de Manila U., 1973—84, assoc. prof. psychology, 1981—84, chair psychology dept., 1981—84; postdoctoral fellow, Population Coun. U. NC, Chapel Hill, 1984—85; adj. faculty dept. psychology U. Pitts., 1985—86; faculty dept. psychology Beaver Campus Pa. State U., 1985—86; adj. faculty Rensselaer Polytechnic Inst., NY, 1986—87, vis. asst. prof. NY, 1987—88; asst. prof. psychology Elon U. (formerly Elon Coll.), NC, 1988—93, assoc. prof. psychology NC, 1993—96; v.p., dir. S.E. Asia program United Bd. Christian Higher Edn. in Asia, NYC, 1996—. Cons. Population Ctr. Found., 1978—84; exec. sec. Psychol. Assn. Philippines, 1979—82; area chair Internat. Coun. Psychologists, 1983—84; feedback specialist Ctr. Creative Leadership, Greensboro, NC, 1995—96; presenter in field. Editl. bd. mem.: Philippine Jour. Psychology, 1981—84; contbr. articles to mags., jours. in field. Faculty Devel. grant, Ateneo de Manila U., 1976—80, Faura Rsch. grant, 1977—80, 1983—84, East-West Seminar grant, Honolulu, 1980, Consultancy grant, ASIANetwork, 1994, Asian Studies grant, NEH, 1994, Dept. Edn. Title Y1-A grant, Elon Coll., 1996, Leverhulme fellow, U. Hong Kong, 1979, postdoctoral fellow, Population Coun., 1985—86. Mem.: APA, Asia Soc. Avocation: cross-cultural consultations.

PULOS, VIRGINIA KATE, actress, consultant; b. Dayton, Ohio, Oct. 12, 1947; d. James C. and Mary M. Pulos; m. Georgios S. Georgiou; 1 child, Kate Elizabeth Chiemingo. BFA in Music summa cum laude, U. Cin., 1970. Singer, actor Broadway, Off Broadway, Stock, Film, Regional Theatre, more, 1970-89; founder, pres. Ginny Pulos Comms., Inc., 1989—. Speech, media and tng. cons.; asst. prof comm. NYU Sch. Continuing and Prolf. Studies; speaker confs. in field. Actress: Portrait of Jenny (Eugene O'Neil award, Richard Rodgers award), regular appearances on TV shows: All My Children, As the World Turns, The Doctors, 1982-88; numerous major opera and musical theatre roles, including: (Broadway) A Little Night Music, (Regional) My Fair Lady, others, 1970—; numerous radio and TV commls., 1970-80; guest soloist: Bklyn. Kingsboro Symphony in the Parks, 1984, 85, others. Program chair The Matrix Awards, 1993, 95, 96, others. Named Corbett Found. Internat. Opera fellow, Hamburg, Germany, 1969, N.Y.C., 1970-77. Mem. SAG, Actors Equity Assn., Am. Fedn. TV and Radio Actors, Pub. Rels. Soc. Am. (pres.-elect internat. sect 2005), N.Y. Women in Comm. (bd. dirs. 1992-99). Office: Ginny Pulos Comms Inc 4th Fl 1120 Ave of the Americas New York NY 10036-6700 Office Phone: 212-626-6597. Business E-Mail: info@ginnypulos.com.

PULS, ELAINE ALLISON, retired librarian; b. Grand Junction, Colo., Mar. 14, 1927; d. Ross Edgar and Bertha Margaret (Johns) Allison; m. Gerald Eugene Puls, Sept. 18, 1949; children: Allen Dale, Theodore Joseph. AA, Mesa Jr. Coll., 1947; student, Western State Coll., 1947—48; BLS, U. Denver, 1949. Libr. Denver Pub. Libr., 1949—54; reading guidance libr. Fitzsimmons Army Hosp., Denver, 1954—56; libr. dir. Meeker Grade Sch., Colo., 1958, Rangely Coll. Libr., Colo., 1962—63; acquisitions libr. Colo. Gen. Hosp., Denver, 1963—65; libr. U. Wash., Seattle, 1965—66, VA Hosp. Libr., Seattle, 1965—66; libr. dir. Loveland Pub. Libr., Colo., 1968—89. Chmn. libr. sect. Colo. Mspl. League, 1971—72. Recipient scholarship to Western State Coll., Mesa Jr. Coll., 1947. Mem.: Colo. Libr. Assn. (Lifetime Achievement award 1989). Home: 1634 Weatherby Ln Pueblo CO 81008-1900

PULSIPHER, LYDIA MIHELIC, geographer, educator; d. Joseph L. Mihelic and Lydia Martha Plucker; m. Conrad McCall Goodwin, Aug. 28, 1993; children: Anthony Adlai, Alexander Augustin. BA, Macalester Coll., St. Paul, 1962; MA, Tulane U., New Orleans, 1967; PhD, So. Ill. U., Carbondale, 1977. Prof. U. Tenn., Knoxville, 1980—. Curator (exhibitions) Seeds of Change, Smithsonian Natural Hist. Mus.; author: World Regional Geography: Global Patterns, Local Lifes, 1999. Precinct chmn. Dem. Party, Knoxville, 2003—05. Named Mentor of Yr., Nat. Coun. Geog. Edn., 2005; recipient award for archaeological rsch., Internat. Congress Monuments and Sites and Am. Express, 1992; fellow, NEH, 1990; grantee, Kaypro Computers, 1984, Ctr. Field Rsch., 1981—93, Skaggs Found., 1985—87, Wenner-Gren Found. Anthrop. Rsch., 1987, Ptnrs. of Ams., 1988, Smithsonian Associates, 1990; Fulbright Hays Travel grantee, Fulbright Hays, 1987. Mem.: Assn. Women Faculty U. Tenn. (chmn. bd. dirs. 2002—06), Assoc. Am. Geographers (regional rep. 2003—05), Soc. Slovene Studies, Assn. Am. Geographers (assoc.; honors com., head com. bd. editors, various regional offices 1980—2006), Caribbean Studies Assn. (life), Phi Beta Kappa. Avocations: gardening, cooking, sewing, exercise. Home: 4801 Westover Terr Knoxville TN 37914 Office: U Tenn 309 Burchfiel Geography Bldg Knoxville TN 37996 Office Phone: 865-974-2418. Business E-Mail: lpulsiph@utk.edu.

PUMPHREY, BONNIE JEAN, music educator; b. Urbana, Ill., Jan. 2, 1948; d. Robert Franklin and Edith Mae Harris; m. C. Douglas Pumphrey, Jan. 30, 1971; 1 child, Lara Pumphrey Dueppen. MusB in Edn., U. Ill., Urbana, Ill., 1970; MusM in Choral Music, U. So. Calif., L.A., 1981. Tchr. music Rantoul City Schs., Ill., 1970—74; dir. choral First Presbyn. Ch., Hemet, Calif., 1981—93; office mgr. Imaginart Comms., Idyllwild, Calif., 1985—90; tchr. music Hemet Unified Sch. Dist., Calif., 1993—. Named Tchr. of Yr., Dartmouth Mid. Sch., 1997, Tchr. of Month, Hemet (Calif.) H.S., 2000; recipient Spirit of Festival award, Heritage Music Festival, San Diego, Calif., 1994, Good Apple award, Hemet (Calif.) Unified Sch. Dist., 1995, Spirit of Festival award, Heritage Music Festival, Las Vegas, Nev., 2004. Mem.: Music Educators Nat. Conf., Am. Choral Dirs. Assn., Philantropic Edn. Orgn., So. Calif. Vocal Assn. (adjudicator hon. choir 1994—, v.p. 1993—), Soroptimist Internat. (pres. local chpt. 1986—87). Avocations: travel, home improvement, reading. Home: 27161 Rue De La Shermie Hemet CA 92544 Office: Hemet High School 41701 E Stetson Ave Hemet CA 92544

PUMPHREY, JANET KAY, editor, publishing executive; b. Balt., June 18, 1946; d. John Henry and Elsie May (Keefer) P. AA in Secondary Edn., Anne Arundel C.C., Arnold, Md., 1967, AA in Bus. and Pub. Adminstrn., 1976. Libr. office mgr. Anne Arundel C.C., 1964—2002; mng. editor Am. Polygraph Assn., Severna Park, Md., 1973—98; owner JKP Publ. Svcs., 1990—; dir. Am. Polygraph Assn. Reference Svc., 1995—98; owner Brooke Keefer Ltd.Editions, 1999—. Editor: (with Albert D. Snyder) Ten Years of Polygraph, 1984, (with Norman Ansley) Justice and the Polygraph, 1985, 2d edit., 1998, A House Full of Love, 1990, Mama, There's A Mouse in My House, 1996; pub. Vergennes, Vermont and The War of 1812, 1999; pub.: (with Vickie T. Murphy) An Investigator's Guide to Non-Verbal Communication, 3d edit., 2006. Mem. Rep. Nat. Sustaining Com. Mem. Am. Polygraph Assn. (hon.), Md. Polygraph Assn., Anne Arundel County Hist. Soc., Alumni Assn. Anne Arundel Community Coll. Republican. Methodist. Avocations: travel, poetry, gardening, mystery writer. Home: 3 Kimberly Ct Severna Park MD 21146-3703 Office: JKP Pub Svcs Brooke Keefer Ltd Edits 3 Kimberly Ct Severna Park MD 21146-3703 Personal E-mail: brookekle@worldnet.att.net.

PUNNETT, AUDREY FRANCES, clinical psychologist, educator; b. Bremerton, Wash., Oct. 25, 1947; d. Louis and Marjorie Velma (Gibson) P. AA, Victor Valley Coll., Victorville, Calif., 1967; BS, U. Utah, 1971, MS, 1975; PhD, Calif. Sch. Profl. Psychology, 1981; diploma in Analytical Psychology for Child and Youth, Zurich, Switzerland, 2001. Diplomate Am. Bd. Med. Psychotherapists; cert. play therapist Assn. for Play Therapy. Psychometrist Washington U., St. Louis, Mo., 1974-75; sch. psychologist St. Louis County Sch. Dist., St. Louis, Mo., 1976-78; psychologist Valley Med. Ctr., Fresno, Calif., 1984-85; coord. pediatric rehab. psychology Fresno (Calif.) Community Hosp., 1981-85; pvt. practice, Fresno, 1981—. Clin. psychologist II med. edn. program U. Calif.-San Francisco, Fresno, 1983-84, asst. clin. prof., 1986—; instr. West Hills Coll., Lemoore, Calif., 1983-84; pediat. psychologist Valley Children's Hosp., Fresno, 1985-97; cons. Calif. State U., Fresno, 1988, Exceptional Parents Unlimited, Fresno, 1987-88, Dept. Rehab. Counseling, Fresno, 1988-89. Contrb. articles to profl. jours. Bd. dirs. Ctrl. Calif. Lung Assn., Fresno, 1989—, treas., 1990-91, pres.-elect, 1991, pres., 1992-94. Mem. Fresno Area Psychological Assn. (western regional conf. chair 1988-90), Leadership Fresno (co-chair class project), Assn. For Grad. in Analytical Psychology, Internat. Analytical Assn., Sandplay Therapists of Am., Internat. Soc. Sandplay Therapists, Soc. Pediat. Psychology, Assn. for Play Therapy. Episcopalian.

PUNYON, ELLEN, principal; d. Herbert and Gloria Punyon; m. Rick Saling, Dec. 28, 1980; 1 child, Bryan Marti Saling. BS in edn., Syracuse U., 1973; MEd, U. Wash., 1976. Cert. ednl. adminstr. Office of Supt. Pub. Instrn., 1993. Tchr. Syracuse (NY) Pub. Schs., 1973—75, Issaquah (Wash.) Pub. Schools, 1975—76; spl. edn. tchr. Seattle Pub. Schs., 1984—92, elem. prin., 1992—. V.p. Ptnrs. for Successful Schs., Seattle, 1998—. Mem.: Wash. State Legis. Action Com. (v.p. 2003—05), Assn. Wash. Sch. Prins., Internat. Reading Assn. Avocations: hiking, bicycling, cross country skiing, international travel. Office: Wing Luke Elem Sch 3701 S Kenyon St Seattle WA 98118 Office Phone: 206-252-7630. Personal E-mail: epunyon@yahoo.com.

PURCELL, ANN RUSHING, state legislator, human services manager; b. Reidsville, Ga., May 12, 1945; d. William Robert and Katie (Dasher) Rushing; m. Dent Wiley Purcell, May 26, 1966; children: Edwin Wiley, Mieke Ann, Mikki Marie. BS in Edn., Ga. So. Coll., 1966; degree (hon.), Ga. Future Farmers Am., 1999. Cert. secondary tchr. Tchr. math. Evans (Ga.) High Sch., 1966-68; tchr. math., earth and sci. Beaumont Jr. High Sch., Lexington, Ky., 1969-70; substitute tchr. Tallahassee, 1970's; agt. Noblin Realty, Tallahassee, 1970's; office mgr. Radiation Therapy Assocs., PC, Savannah, Ga., 1979—; state legislator Ho. of Reps. Ga. Gen. Assembly, Atlanta, 1991—2005. Author: Purcells of South Georgia and Other Related Families, 1976. Bd. dirs. Med. Assn. Ga. Polit. Action Com., Atlanta, 1988-89, Girl Scout Coun. Savannah, 1991-93, Effingham YMCA, 1999-, New Ebenezer Retreat Ctr., 2006—; Effingham County fin. chmn. State YMCA, 1991-05, vice chmn. steering com., 1999, bd. dirs., 1999; trustee Ga. So. U. Found., 1992—, Armstrong Atlantic U. Found., 2004-05, sec., 2005—; mem. adv. com. Effingham County Extension Svc., 1992—; chmn. steering com. Effingham YMCA Bd., 2004, 05, 06, chmn. fin. devel., 2005-; mem. adv. com. Treutlin Home, 1999-04; bd. adv. Claxton Youth Detention Ctr. Hon. comdr. 165th Ga. Air Guard Airlift, 1997-04; hon. mem. Civil Air Patrol, 2001-, Ga. State Patrol, 2001; state bd. mem. Ga. Dept. Tech. and Adult Edn., 2005-; mem. adv. bd. Ga. Pacific, 2006—. Decorated WA-PO-HE award Ga. Nat. Air Guard, Minuteman award, Dept. Def. Commendatino medal; named Ga.'s Legislator of Yr., Ga. Sch. Counselors Assn., 1996, Ga. Legislator of Yr., Coastal Conservation Assn. Ga., 1998, Vol. of Yr., Effingham YMCA, 2006; named to Hon. Ga. State Patrol, 2001; recipient Friend of Medicine award, Med. Assn. Ga., 1991, 1993, 1994, 1996, Ga. Vet. award, 2003, Guardian of Small Bus. award, Nat. Fedn. Ind. Bus., 1992, 1994, 1996, Commendation cert., Ga. Emergency Mgmt. Agy., 1995, Vol. of Yr. award, Effingham 4-H, 1998, Nat. Am. hon. degree, Future Farmers Am., 1999, Friend of State 4-H award, 1999, Svc. award, Effingham Recreation Dept., 2000, Cmty. Svc. award, Guyton Masonic Lodge, 2000, Hon. Family Consumer Cmty. Leaders of Ga. award, 2001, Ga. Pub. Health award, 2003, Effingham Jr. Adv. Family Connection award, 2003, 2004, Environ. Leadership award, Ga. Conservation Voters, 2003, 2004, Pub. Rels. award, Ga. Ext. Assn. of Family and Consumer Scis., 2003, Leadership award, Ga. Water Coalition, 2003, 2004, Charles Dick award, U.S. Nat. Guard, 2003, Air Nat. Guardsmen award, Savannah Assn. Flying, 2003, City of Pembroke award, 2004, Bryan County Svc. award, 2004, Friend of Effingham 4-H award, 2005, Friends award, Ga. Med. Soc., 2005. Mem. Aux. to the Med. Assn. Ga. (pres. 1985), Aux. to the Ga. Med. Soc. (pres. 1981-82), Ga. Salzburger Soc. (bd. dirs. 2005, v.p. 2005-), Effingham County Pub. Ofcls. Assn., Rotary Internat. (Paul Harris fellow 2003), Ga. Peace Officers Assn. (hon.), Rincon Noon Lions Club, Exch. Club. Republican. Methodist. Avocations: painting, genealogy, fishing. Home: 410 Willowpeg Way Rincon GA 31326-9157

PURCELL, BONNIE LOU, librarian; b. Tulia, Tex., Sept. 23, 1954; d. Lee Roy and LaVanna Ruth (Schofield) P. BA, Tex. Woman's U., 1977, MLS, 1979. Libr. Winters Ind. Sch., Tex., 1977-81, Rankin Ind. Sch., Tex., 1981-88, libr., tchr., 1989—2004; libr. Pecos Ind. Sch., Tex., 2004—. Cons. libr. Whiteface (Tex.) Ind. Sch., 1981. Tchr., mem. Knitting and Crocheting-Sr. Citizens, Rankin, 1986-89. Named one of Outstanding Young Women of Am., 1983. Mem. Assn. Tex. Profl. Educators, Tex. Libr. Assn., Tex. State Tchrs. Assn. (local pres. 1988-91), Delta Kappa Gamma (historian 1989-91). Avocations: reading, counted cross-stitch, crocheting, knitting, stamp collecting/philately. Home: PO Box 164 Whiteface TX 79379-0164 Office: Pecos Ind Sch 1501 Vets Blvd Pecos TX 79772

PURCELL, CHERYL LINN, music educator; d. Lloyd Howard and Rosaline Elizabeth Goebel; m. Francis Joseph Purcell, Nov. 11, 1977 (dec. May 28, 1980); 1 child, Stephanie Rachel. BS in Edn., U. Mo., 1972, MusM in Edn., 1997. Cert. lifetime tchr. music K-12 Mo., 1972, ch. musician United Meth. Ch. Gen. Bd. Ordained Ministries, 2002. Educator music Gasconade County Schs., Owensville, Mo., 1972—73, Riverview Gardens Sch. Dist., St. Louis, 1973—75, Ft. Zumwalt Sch. Dist., O'Fallon, 1975—78, 1980—2004; ret., 2004; dir. worship arts Faith United Meth. Ch., St. Charles, 1997—. Coord. curriculum performing arts Ft. Zumwalt Sch. Dist., 1999—2004; sec. bd. dirs. St. Charles County Youth Choir, 2005—. Dir.: (performance) Schubert: Mass in G (selected to perform at Carnegie Hall, 2002), Coronation Mass in C, 2005. Mem.: NEA, Fellowship United Meths. Music and Worship

Arts, Ft. Zumwalt Ednl. Assn. (first v.p. 1977—78), Am. Choral Directors Assn., Music Educators Nat. Conf., U. Mo. Alumni Assn. (life), Sigma Alpha Iota (life; v.p. 1971—72). Methodist. Avocations: sewing, gardening, travel. Office: Faith United Meth Ch 2950 Droste Rd Saint Charles MO 63301

PURCELL, DIANE, addiction counselor; b. Salinas, Calif. d. Jared Wightman and Marie Chipman Fox; m. James Edward Purcell children: Jared, Juli, Greg, Heather, Tina. BA, Governor's State U., 1980; MA, Webster U., 1985. Cert. addictions counselor. Addiction counselor Luth. Gen. Hosp., Park Ridge, Ill., 1980-81; mgr. youth program Parkside, Mundelein, Ill., 1981-83, dir., nat. trainer, 1983-89; coord. family program Hinsdale (Ill.) Hosp., 1989-94; pvt. practice addictions counseling Lincolnshire, Ill., 1990—; clin. assoc. Bensinger DuPont & Assocs., Chgo. Author: Sibs, 1986. Avocations: writing, golf. Office: Bensinger DuPont & Assocs 20 N Wacker Dr Ste 920 Chicago IL 60606-2901 E-mail: DJFlog@aol.com.

PURCELL, KAREN BARLAR, naturopathic physician, nutritionist, opera singer, writer; b. Miami, Fla., Dec. 31, 1947; d. Raymond and Elita (Kitzmiller) Barlar; m. John A. Purcell, June 11, 1977 (div. Dec. 1986); 1 child, Carl; m. Roy Gene Autry, Dec. 31, 1987 (dec. Mar. 2003). MusB, U. Cin., 1969; MusM, New Eng. Conservatory Music, Boston, 1971; postgrad., Bastyr U., Seattle, 1997-98; D in Naturopathy, Natural Health Acad. Healing Arts, Tenafly, NJ, 1991. Diplomate Am. Bd. Naturopathic Physicians, 1997, cert. master herbalist, Dallas; ordained to mininstry Progressive Universal Life Ch., 1998. Assoc. prof. U. Miami, 1974-77, Dade County Jr. Coll., Miami, 1974—77; pvt. practice, N.Y.C., 1990—. Assoc. prof. NYU, 1988-92, Strasberg Theater Inst., NYC, 1988-92, UN Internat. Sch., NYC, 1992-96; star mgr. Nature's Sunshine Products; spkr. in field Author: Simplified Nutritional Handbook, 1996, How to Survive a Nuclear Disaster, 2002; opera singer, 1970—. Founder WINS Found. for Moderate to Severe Brain Disorders, 1999—. Mem. Am. Naturopathic Med. Assn., Internat. and Am. Assn. Clin. Nutritionists, Internat. and Am. Assn. Counselors and Therapists, Nat. Spkrs. Assn. Avocations: botany, cooking, travel. Office: 666 West End Ave Ste 15S New York NY 10025-7357 Office Phone: 212-580-3051.

PURCELL, LEE (LEE JEUNE WILLIAMS), actress, film producer; b. Cherry Point, NC, June 15, 1957; m. Alexander Sarenguevo, May 10, 1996 (div.); 1 child, Dylan D. Purcell. Studies with Margot Lister, London; studies with Milton Katselas, Jeff Corey, U.S. Pres., owner Silver Strand Entertainment, L.A., 1995—. Appeared in (films) Adam at 6 A.M., 1970, The Toy Factory, 1971, Dirty Little Billy, 1972, Kid Blue, 1973, Mr. Majestyk, 1974, Almost Summer, Big Wednesday, 1978, Stir Crazy, 1980, Valley Girl, Eddie Macon's Run, 1983, Laura's Dream, 1986, Airplane II, 1989, Trackers, 1990, Money & Murder, 1993, The Joke, 1994, Malaika, 1997, Dizzyland, 1998, The Unknown, 2003, (TV) Hijack, 1973, Stranger in Our House, 1978, Howard, The Amazing Mr. Hughes, 1979, Kenny Rogers as the Gambler, 1980, Killing At Hell's Gate, 1981, My Wicked Wicked Ways: The Legend of Errol Flynn, 1986, Betrayed by Innocence, 1989, Long Road Home (Emmy nominee Lead Actress-Special), 1991, To Heal a Nation, 1992, Dazzle, 1994, Secret Sins of the Father (Emmy nominee Supporting Actress-Special), 1994, Due South (recurring role), 1995-96, Promised Land, 1999, (stage) One Flew Over the Cuckoo's Nest, Richard III, A Streetcar Named Desire, The Taming of the Shrew, A Midsummer's Night Dream. Recipient Bronze Star Halo Career Achievement award So. Calif. Motion Picture Council, 1985, Golden Star Halo award, 1986, Silver Medal award N.Y. Film and TV Festival, 1987. Mem. AFTRA, SAG, Actors' Equity Assn., Acad. Motion Picture Arts and Scis., Acad. TV Arts And Scis. Avocations: writing, collecting antiques and art. Office: PO Box 12581 La Crescenta CA 91224-5581

PURCELL, MARY HAMILTON, speech educator; b. Ft. Worth; d. Josseph Hants and Letha (Gibson) Hamilton; m. William Paxson Purcell, Jr., Dec. 28, 1950; children: William Paxson III, David Hamilton. BA, Mary Hardin-Baylor Coll., 1947, HHD (hon.), 1986; MA, La. State U., 1948; HHD (hon.), U. New Eng., 2000. Instr. dept speech and dramatic arts Temple U., Phila., 1948-53, 60-61; part-time instr. speech Cushing Jr. Coll., Bryn Mawr, Pa., 1966-78. Pres. Pa. Program for Women and Girl Offend, 1968—73, Nether Providence Parent Tchr. Orgn., 1975—76; treas. Virginia Gildersleeve Internat. Fund U. Women, 1975—81, bd. dirs., 1987—93; mem. U.S. del. UN Commn. on Status of Women, 1996; co-chmn. NGO Com. for UNICEF, 1994—2000, mem. global forum, 2001—; mem. Wallingford-Swarthmore Dist. Sch. Bd., 1977—83; bd. dirs. Ministers and Missionaries Fund Am. Bapt. Conv., 1985—94, pres., 1995—2003, Internat. Devel. Conf., 1986—; bd. dirs. Nat. Peace Inst. Found., 1983—86; Big Bros./Big Sisters of Am., 1985—90; bd. dirs. Citizens Crime Commn. of Phila., 1976—, Pa. Women's Campaign Fund, 1985—88, 1993—. Named Outstanding Alumna, Mary Hardin-Baylor Coll., 1972, Disting. Dau. Pa., 1982, v.p., 1994—95, pres., 1995—97, Woman of Yr., DECO Women's Conf., 1998; recipient Eleanor Schnurr award, UNA/USA, 2000. Mem. AAUW (Pa. state pres. 1968-70, v.p. mid. Atlantic region, 1973-77, program v.p. 1979-81, pres. 1981-85, rep. to UN 1985-89), Internat. Fedn. Univ. Women (1st v.p. 1986-89, pres. 1989-92, rep. to UN 1992-2005; pres. UN Dept. Pub. Info. Non Govt. Orgn. ann. conf. 1993), Speech Assn. Am. (Zeta Phi Eta award for excellence in comm. 1983), Pi Kappa Delta, Pi Gamma Mu, Delta Sigma Rho, Alpha Psi Omega, Alpha Chi. Democrat. Baptist. Home: 10 Willowbrook Ave Lansdowne PA 19050 E-mail: mjd1926@aol.com.

PURCELL, MARY LOUISE GERLINGER, retired adult education educator; b. Thief River Falls, Minn., July 17, 1923; d. Charles and Lajla (Dale) Gerlinger; m. Walter A. Kuyawski, June 9, 1950 (dec. July 1954); children: Amelia Allerton, Jon Allerton; m. Dale Purcell, Aug. 26, 1962 (dec. Nov. 2005). Student, Yankton Coll., 1941-45, Yale Div. Sch., 1949-50, NYU, 1949; MA, Columbia U., 1959, EdD, 1963. Teenage program dir. YWCA, New Haven, 1945-52; dir. program in family rels. Earlham Coll., Richmond, Ind., 1959-62, asst. prof. sociology and psychology, 1959-62, conf. coord. undergrad. edn. for women, 1962; chmn. divsn. home and cmty. Stephens Coll., Columbia, Mo., 1962-73, chmn. family and cmty. studies, 1962-78; dir. continuing edn. women Learning Unltd., 1974-78; prof. Auburn (Ala.) U., 1978-88, head dept. family and child devel., 1978-84, chmn. search com. for v.p. acad. affairs, 1984, spl. asst. to v.p. acad. affairs, 1985-86, prof. emerita, 1988—. Developer course, cons. Contemporary Am. Woman, 1962; vis. prof. Ind. U. Summer Sch., 1970; cons. student pers. svcs. Trenton (N.J.) State Coll., 1958—59, 1961. Contbr. articles to coll. bulls., jours. V.p. Falls Villate-Canaan Hist. Soc., 1998—2001, pres., 2002—. Recipient Alumni Achievement award, Yankton Coll., 1975; Alumni fellow, Tchrs. Coll. Columbia U., 1959. Mem.: AAUW, Nat. Coun. Family Rels., Groves Conf. Family (nat. program chmn. 1977, dir., chmn.-elect affiliated couns. 1981—82, chmn. 1982—84, chmn. film awards com., chmn. spl. emphases sect., bd. dirs.), Am. Home Econs. Assn. (bd. dirs. 1967—69, chair 1st subject matter unit 1969, family rels. and child devel. sect. 1986—89), Falls Village Can. Hist. Soc. (v.p. 1998—2001, pres. 2002—), Litchfield County Univ. Club (mem. scholarship com. 2001—, bd. dirs. 2001—), Housatonic Camera Club (co-pres. 1996—2000), Delta Kappa Gamma. Congregationalist. Home: 120 Belden St Falls Village CT 06031-1124 E-mail: mlgp@sbcglobal.net.

PURCHASE-OWENS, FRANCENA, marketing professional, consultant, educator; b. Milw., Nov. 14, 1960; d. Johnny Purchase Sr. and Arlene (Roberts) Pleas Brown. Cert., Mich. Profl. Sch. Modeling, 1980; AA cum laude, Bryant Stratton Coll., 1982; BS in Applied Liberal Studies, Western Mich. U., 1997, M in Ednl. Leadership, cum laude, 2004; MBA, U. Phoenix, Grand Rapids, Mich., 2006. Various office/clerical positions, 1972—84; investment mgmt. sec. M&I Bank, Milw., 1984-85; cons. United Devel. Corp., Milw., 1986-88; paraprofessional Grand Rapids (Mich.) Pub. Schs., 1990-92; temp. helper Dayton Hudson, Grand Rapids, Mich., 1990; customer svc. rep. Kent County Conv. and Visitors Bur., Grand Rapids, 1995; customer svc. rep. children's dept. Meijers, Inc., 1995; mktg. rschr. Wirthlin Worldwide, Grand Rapids, 1996-98; pres. Creative Works, Grand Rapids, 1988—, Francena Purchase Internat. Honor Soc., Grand Rapids, 1999—, Francena Purchase Internat. Applied Studies, 1999—, Francena Purchase Internat. Applied Profl. Studies Soc., 2000—, cons.; pres. Purchase Bus. Inst., Kentwood, 1999—; cons. Urban Bus. X-Change, Grand Rapids, 2005—; adminstrv. asst. to Elizabeth Kubler-Ross Ga. State U., 1980. Sec. Mich. Nat. Bank, Grand Rapids, 1980-81. Volt. Tech. Svcs., Milw, 1980; asst. exec. sec. Manpower Internat. Inc., Milw., 1982-84; cons. NASW; sec., cons. United Devel. Corp; human resource asst., computer programmer, sec., Patricia Stevens Coll., Milw., 1985-86; asst. to pres. Alissia Cosmetics, Miss Black Pageant, 1980; legal sec. to atty. David Clowers, Milw., 1980; student asst. gerontology dept., Ga. State U., Atlanta, 1980; student asst. main office, Ottawa Hills H.S., Grand Rapids, 1976-77; mem. contract divsn. Fed. Govt., Grand Rapids, 1977-78; grad. student adv. bd. Western Mich. U., Kalamazoo, 2000; mem. Nat. Honor Soc. Iroquois Mid. Sch., 1974-75, Grand Rapids, Ottawa Hills Montessori H.S., 1976-79; cons. in field. Co-editor: Smoke Signal, 1975; contbr. articles to profl. jours. Vol. United Way, Grand Rapids, 1990, TV (GVSU-TV) fundraiser, vol. Grand Valley State U.; vol. Cmty. Media Ctr. (GRTV), Cmty. Media Ctr. Scholarships; reading condr. S.E. Neighborhood Assn., Grand Rapids, 1990, Cmty. Media Ctr., GRTV; mem. literacy coun. Kent County Literacy Coun., Grand Rapids, 1991—, task force Dwelling Pl., Grand Rapids, 1999, First Call Help United Way, Grand Rapids, 1992; model Miss J. Fashion bd. Jacobson's Dept. store, East Grand Rapids Mich., 1979; finalist Miss Black Wis. pageant, Milw., 1981; bd. dirs. Program and Quality Com., Pers. Com., Fin. Com., Consumer Adv. bd., Touchstone innoveré mental health, Grand Rapids, 2000—, mem. nominating com, Touchstone Innovative Mental Health, 2000-01, Kent County Cmty. Mental Health, 1999—; mem. Task Force Herkimer Apartment Projects, Weston Apartments Dwelling place of Grand Rapids, 1999; reading program asst. S.E. End Neigborhood Assn., Grand Rapids, 1993, mem. exec. bd. dirs, 2006; rehab. asst. Kent Comty. Hosp. Complex, Grand Rapids, 1991; intake asst. Baxter Comty. Ctr., Grand Rapids, 1989; tutor Kent County Literacy Coun., Grand Rapids, 1988; facilitator trainer Employers Coalition for Healing Racism, Grand Rapids, 1997, Citizens Ctrs. Resource Ctr., Grand Rapids, 1998, Ptnrs. in Pub. Edn., Grand Rapids, 1999, United Way Champions of Diversity, Grand Rapids, 1999; project help tutor Iroquois Mid. Sch., Grand Rapids, 1975; student tutor Washington Elem., Kalamazoo, 1974; fundraiser Spl. Olympics Office Edn. Assn. Ottawa Hills HS, 1978; exec. bd. dirs., asst. sec. First Missionary Bapt. Ch., 2005—; chair cmty. investment coun. United Way, 2006—; pastors asst. First Missionary Bapt. Ch., Grand Rapids, 2005—; vol. Cancer Soc. Recipient Creative Writing award, 1975, Shorthand award Ottawa Hills HS, 1979, Shorthand awards Milw. Stratton Coll., 1981-82, Century award, 1982, Machine Transcription award Milw. Area Tech. Coll., 1981; Phillip Morris scholar Alverno Coll., 1981; Nontraditional Student grantee Western Mich. U., 1994, 00, Thurgood Marshall Profl. Tuition grantee; Thurgood Marshall Assistanship scholar Western Mich. U.1989, 1998; 1st place spkr., 3rd place typist and secretarial job application Office Edn. Assn. Extemporaneous Speaking; 1st Pl. with Letter of Recognition from Senator Berger of Wis. Milw. Area Tech. Coll., 1981; Internat. finalist theatre arts, Milw., 1986; others. Mem.: Parkinson's Assn., Alzheimer's Assn., Western Mich. U. Alumni, Phi Lambda Theta. Avocations: modern dancing, reading, tennis. Address: PO Box 7421 Grand Rapids MI 49510-7421

PURDES, ALICE MARIE, retired adult education educator; b. St. Louis, Jan. 8, 1931; d. Joseph Louis and Angeline Cecilia (Mozier) P. AA, Belleville Area Coll., 1951; BS, Ill. State U., Normal, 1953, MS, 1954; cert., Sorbonne U., Paris, 1964; PhD, Fla. State U., Tallahassee, 1976. Cert. in music edn., elem. edn., secondary edn., adult edn. Tchg. and grad. asst. Ill. State U., 1953-54; music supr. Princeton (Ill.) Pub. Schs., 1954-55; music dir. Venice (Ill.) Pub. Schs., 1955-72, secondary vocal music dir., 1955-72; coord. literacy program Venice-Lincoln Tech. Ctr., 1983-86, chmn. lang. arts dept., 1983-96; ret., 1996. Tchr. in space candidate, 1985. Mem. St. Louis chpt. World Affairs Coun., UN Assn., Nat. Mus. of Women in the Arts, Humane Soc. of Am.; charter mem. St. Louis Sci. Ctr., Harry S. Truman Inst.; contbr. Old Six Mile Mus., 1981, Midland Repertory Players, Alton, Ill., 1991; chair Cystic Fibrosis Spring Bike-A-Thon, Madison, Ill., 1981, Granite City, Ill., 1985. Named to Ill. Sr. Hall of Fame, 2001, Gov's Sr. Hall of Fame, 2001; recipient Gold medal, Nat. Senior Olympics, 1989, 600 others, Sr. World Games, Generations of Success Alumni award, Belleville Area Coll., 1998, several scholarships. Mem.: AAUW, Am. Fedn. Tchrs. (pres. 1957—58), Ill. Adult and Continuing Educators Assn., Am. Choral Dirs. Assn., Ill. Music Educators Assn. (Svc. award 2002), Music Educators Nat. Conf., Ill. State U. Alumni Assn., Slavic and East European Friends (life), Fla. State Alumni Assn., Lovejoy Libr. Friends, Nat. Space Soc., Western Cath. Union, Croation Fraternal Union, St. Louis Numis. Assn., Friends St. Louis Art Mus., Archaeol. Inst. Am., Travelers Abroad (pres. 1966—68, 1989—), Madison Rotary Club (internat. amb., Humanitarian award 1975). Roman Catholic. Avocations: bowling, travel. Home: 1610 4th St Madison IL 62060

PURDUE, PATRICIA, secondary school educator; d. Harold Hansen and Judith Hanssen; m. Purdue Curtis, Nov. 23, 1958; children: Nathan, Ashley, John. BS in Social Sci., U. So. Colo., Pueblo, 2000; M in Behavioral Sci., Cameron U., Lawton, Okla., 2002. Educator Altus Pub. Schs., Okla., 2001—. Mem.: Lions Club (life; advisor 2003—06). Avocations: walking, travel. Office: Altus High School 400 North Park Ln Altus OK 73521 Office Phone: 580-481-2167. Business E-Mail: ppurdue@altusschools.k12.ok.us.

PURDY, JAN RAE, music educator; b. Detroit, Mich., July 11, 1937; d. Fred B. and Irma B. Purdy; m. Norman R. Rapp (div.); children: Lisa Ann Rapp, Lynda Rae Rapp. BA in music, Madonna U., Livonia, Mich., 1992. Tchr. voice and piano Mich. Conservatory, Detroit, Birmingham Conservatory, Mich., Plymouth Music Acad., Mich.; tchr. voice Marion HS, Birmingham, Immaculata HS, Detroit, Ant Ctr. Music Sch., Detroit. Performed with Mt. Clemens Symphony, Dearborn Symphony, Pontiac Symphony, Clarion Symphony Orch., Sarnia, Ont., Cambodia, 2001, Mich. Opera Co., Mich. Opera Theatre Outreach Program, Detroit Lyric Opera, Dearborn Opera Group, Boris Goldovsky Opera Workshop and Performance Co., Verdi Opera Theatre, Oakway Symphony, Warren Symphony, Little Detroit Symphony. Soloist: Mich. Rep. Coun., Pres. Gerald Ford, Sen. Griffin, Detroit Mayor J. Cavanagh, astronaut James A. McDivitt, Detroit Symphony, 1955, 1969, Ctrl. Meth. Ch., Detroit, various area chs. Former mem. Birmingham Musicale; mem. Tuesday Musicale, 2005—. Recipient Belle Isle award, Detroit Symphony, 1955. Mem.: Sigma Alpha IOta. Republican. Avocations: movies, theater, concerts. Home and Office: 23235 Canfield Farmington MI 48336

PURDY, PENNY, music educator; b. Fairmont, W.Va., July 20, 1971; d. Bill and Julie Jones; m. Chris Purdy; children: Tara, Tyler. Masters Degree, Ohio U., Athens, 1995. Music tchr. Vinton County Local Schs., McArthur, Ohio, 1996—98, Athens (Ohio) City Schs., 2001—. Home: 7900 Rolling Hills Dr Athens OH 45701 Office: Athens Middle School 51-55 West State St Athens OH 45701 Office Phone: 740-593-7107. Personal E-mail: ppurdy@athenscity.k12.oh.us.

PURE, PAMELA J., information technology executive; B in Health Adminstrn., U. NC. Various mgmt., product devel. and mktg. positions Shared Med. Sys. (now divsn. Siemens); COO Channel Health Subs. IDX Systems, 1999—2001; grp. pres. product devel. and support McKesson Corp., San Francisco, 2001—02, COO McKesson Info. Solutions, 2002—04, exec. v.p., pres. McKesson Provider Technologies, 2004—. Named Woman of Yr. Tech. (enterprise bus.), (WIT) Women in Tech., 2005. Office: McKesson Corpn 1 Post St San Francisco CA 94104 Office Phone: 415-983-8300. Office Fax: 415-983-9400.*

PURIFOY, SANDRA NABOURS, science educator; b. Alexandria, La., Nov. 30, 1956; d. Joe C. and Marie Riche Nabours; m. William Reese Purifoy, Jan. 25, 1985; 1 child, Lawrence Ashley. BS in Biology, La. Coll., Pineville, 1978; MS in Life Sci., La. Tech. U., Ruston, 1980. Tchr. Rapides Parish Sch. Bd., Alexandria, 1994—95, Allen Parish Sch. Bd., Oberlin, La., 1995—96; instr. biology La. State U., Alexandria, 2002—. Unit commr. Boy Scouts of Am., Alexandria, 2004. Recipient Dist. Award of Merit, Boy Scouts of Am., 2004. Mem.: Human Anatomy Physiology Soc., Nat. Assn. Biology Tchrs., Alpha Epsilon Delta (life). Avocations: gardening, fishing, piano, travel. Home: 1404 Ann Ln Oakdale LA 71463 Office: La State U 8100 Hwy 71 S Alexandria LA 71302

PURKERSON, MABEL LOUISE, physician, educator, physiologist; b. Goldville, SC, Apr. 3, 1931; d. James Clifton and Louise (Smith) P. AB, Erskine Coll., 1951; MD, U. SC, Charleston, 1956. Diplomate Am. Bd. Pediat. Instr. pediat. Washington U. Sch. Medicine, St. Louis, 1961-67, instr. medicine, 1966-67, asst. prof. pediat., 1967-98, asst. prof. medicine, 1967-76, assoc. prof. medicine, 1976-89, prof., 1989-98, prof. emerita, 1998—, assoc. dean curriculum, 1976-94, assoc. dean acad. projects, 1994-98. Cons. in field. Editl. bd. Am. Jour. Kidney Diseases, 1981-87; contbr. articles to profl. jours. Mem. bd. counselors Erskine Coll., 1971—87, trustee, 2000—06; historian St. Louis Symphony Orch., trustee. USPHS spl. fellow, 1971-72. Mem. Am. Heart Assn. Coun. on the Kidney (exec. com. 1973-81), Am. Physiol. Soc., Am. Soc. Nephrology, Internat. Soc. Nephrology, Ctrl. Soc. Clin. Rsch., Am. Soc. Renal Biochemistry and Metabolism, Internat. Assn. History Nephrology, Am. Osler Soc., Explorer's Club (chair St. Louis chpt., 2005-), Sigma Xi (chpt. sec. 1974-76), Alpha Omega Alpha. Home: 20 Haven View Dr Saint Louis MO 63141-7902 Office: Bernard Becker Med Libr Renal Div Dept PO Box 8132 Saint Louis MO 63110-1093 Office Phone: 314-362-4234. Business E-Mail: purkerm@msnotes.wustl.edu.

PURPURA, GRACE, artist, retired art educator; b. N.Y.C., Nov. 3, 1929; d. Michael and Carmela Maligno Purpura; children: Marina, Diana and Valerie Andriola. Student, Cooper Union Sch. Art & Arch., 1946-49, CUNY, 1952, San Jose State U., 1969. Cert. elem., secondary, art tchr., Calif. Art tchr. L.A. City Schs., 1957-62; design instr. L.A. City College, 1960; bilingual tchr. Alum Rock Sch. Dist., San Jose, 1969-91; arts commr. City of San Jose, Calif., 1994-98. Mentor tchr. State of Calif. Dept. Edn., Sacramento, 1984-87; mem. Fulbright Scholar L.Am. project Stanford U., China and Korea/Calif. Dept. Edn., 1987, Calif. Internat. Studies mem., 1985. Exhibited paintings, sculptures and drawings at numerous shows regionally, nat. and internat. including Synopsys, Inc., Mountain View, Calif., Lifescan, Milpitas, Calif., Network Gen. Corp., Menlo Park, Calif., Ohlone Coll., Fremont, Calif., Works Gallery, San Jose, Inst. for Contemporary Art, San Jose, Triton Mus., Santa Clara, Calif., de Saisset Mus., Santa Clara, Denver Art Mus., Raychem Corp., Menlo Park, Forum Art Gallery, N.Y.C.; one-woman shows include San Jose Art League, Casa de la Cultura, Livorno, Italy, Hayward, Calif. City Hall Art Gallery, 2003, Pacific Grove, Calif Art Ctr., 2004, Inst. for Contemporary Art, Calif., 2004, Movimiento Arte y Cultura Latino Americano, Calif., 2004. Bd. dirs. San Jose Art League, 1985-88; arts commr. City of San Jose, 1994-98. Mem. Calif. Art Edn. Assn., Calif. Tchrs. Assn., Paper Gem Printmakers of Silicon Valley (co-founder). Avocations: arts, photography, children's picture books. Home: 2364 Stokes St San Jose CA 95128-4262 Office Phone: 408-971-7588.

PURSCELL, HELEN DUNCAN, sociologist, educator; b. Cottonwood County, Minn., Jan. 8, 1926; d. Arthur Albert Frenzen and Pearl Blanche Pope; m. Boyd Alvah Duncan (dec.); children: Bruce Howard(dec.), Stuart Lachlan(dec.), Scott Boyd; m. Keith William Purscell, June 17, 1994. BA, Mankato State U., 1963, postgrad., 1981—84; MA, U. Iowa, 1967; postgrad., U. Minn., 1969—73. Cert. sex educator Am. Assn. Sex Educators, Counselors and Therapists. Elem. sch. tchr., Redwood County, Minn., 1944—45, Cottonwood County, 1945—46; English tutor Parsons Coll., Fairfield, Iowa, 1964—65; asst. instr. Mankato (Minn.) State U., 1965—66, instr., 1966—68, asst. prof., 1968—90, assoc. prof., 1990—94; ret. Home: PO Box 3639 Mankato MN 56002

PURSLEY, JULIE, newscaster; married. BA in Telecom., Ind. U., 1991. Reporter Sta. WBKO-TV, Bowling Green, Ky.; with Sta. WHAS-TV, Louisville; anchor Sta. WRTV-TV, Indpls., 2001—. Office: WRTV TV 1330 N Meridian St Indianapolis IN 46202

PURTAN, JOANNE, announcer; d. Dick Purtan; m. Eric Purtan; children: Lauren, Adam. B of Telecom., Mich. State U. Morning anchor/reporter WGRB-TV, Albany, NY, 1991—98, co-anchor 5pm, 6pm and 11 pm news, 1994—98; co-anchor Action News This Morning, WXYZ-TV, Detroit, 1998—, reporter Healthy Living, 2002—. Recipient 3 Emmy nominations. Office: WXYZ-TV 20777 W Ten Mile Rd Southfield MI 48037

PURVIS, GAIL, elementary school educator; b. Chgo., June 26, 1945; d. Arthur J. and Elaine (Herron) Hoffman; 1 child, Leo II. BFA, BS in Edn., U. Cinn., 1967; MS in Edn. with honors, U. Miami, 1982; psychology, art edn., fine arts, U. Ill., 1967, DBAE Art Specialist, 1991. Cert. K-12 art tchr., Fla. Instr., art Broward County Schs., Coral Springs, Fla.; tchr., art instr. St. Johns Coll., Nassau, Bahamas; tchr., pottery specialist Queens Coll., Nassau; youth planning specialist Broward Employment Tng. Adminstrn., Ft. Lauderdale, Fla. Adj. prof. Nova SO. U., Ft. Lauderdale, Fla., Barry U., Miami Lakes, Fla. Mem. Nat. Art Edn. Assn., Fla. Art. Edn. Assn., Assn. Supervision Curriculum Devel. E-mail: purvis@nsu.nova.edu.

PURVIS, REBECCA C., transportation executive; d. Russell Andrew and Mary Carol Purvis. BA in Comm., DePauw U., 2001; MA in Tchg. Spl. Edn., We. N.Mex U., 2005. Cert. tchr. level I spl. edn. N.Mex, 2005. Tchr. spl. edn. Gallup McKinley (N.Mex.) County Schs., 2003—05, facilitator, 2005; transp. broker White Diamond Express, LLC, Pitts., 2006—. Coach cheerleading Taft H.S., Chgo., 2001—03. Vol. Pitts. Cares, 2006—, Pitts. Jr. League, 2006—. Fellow, DePauw U., 1997—2001. Mem.: Coun. Exceptional Children. Personal E-mail: purvis_becky@hotmail.com.

PUSCHAK, BETH ANNE, educational consultant; b. Coaldale, Pa, Aug. 1, 1954; d. Frank John and Shirley Mae Horvath; m. John Peter Puschak, July 15, 1978; children: Julie Anne, Kate Lynn, Christine Elise. BS, Pa. State U., State College, 1976; MEd, Kutztown U., Pa., 1984; postgrad., Widener U., Pa., 2000—. Tchg. Cert. K-8, Reading Specialist, Reading Supr. Pa. Dept. Edn. 6th grade tchr. St. Ann Sch., Lansford, Pa., 1977—78; reading specialist Manheim Twp. Sch. Dist., Lancaster, Pa., 1984—99; reading supr. Antietam Sch. Dist., Reading, Pa., 1999—2001; ednl. cons. Leola, Pa., 2001—; tech. asst. Pa. Dept. Edn., Harrisburg, Pa., 2003—. Bd. mem. Lancaster Lebanon (Pa.) Reading Coun. Dir.: (5th grade musical) Neff Sch., 1986—87. Vol. Lancaster Sertoma Club, 1990—. Mem.: Lancaster Lebanon Reading Coun. (bd. mem. 2004—), Keystone State Reading Assn., Internat. Reading Assn. Republican. Roman Catholic. Avocations: cooking, decorating. Home: 41 Magnolia Dr Leola PA 17540 Personal E-mail: bethpuschak@yahoo.com.

PUSKAR, KATHRYN ROSE, nurse, educator; b. Akron, Ohio, Apr. 7, 1946; d. Stanley William and Virginia (Roberts) McKavish; m. George Paul Puskar, Aug. 28, 1969; 1 child, Stacey. Diploma in nursing, Johnstown Mercy Sch. Nursing, 1966; BS, Duquesne U., 1969; MS in Nursing, U. Pittsburgh, 1971, MPH, 1978, DrPH, 1981. Faculty U. Ill., Chgo., 1976-78; cons. Westmoreland Coll., Greensburg, Pa., 1976; clin. specialist McKeesport Hosp., Pa., 1971-73; dir. mental health clinic Frick Hosp., Mt. Pleasant, Pa., 1974-76; prof. U. Pitts., 1980—2006. Cons. Southwood Hosp., 1984-86, VA Med. Ctr., Pitts., 1985—. Contbr. articles to profl. jours.; editor profl. jour. Cons. Newcomers Club, Pitts., 1985-87. NIMH fellowship. Fellow Am. Acad. Nursing, Nat. Acads. Practice; mem. Am. Psychiat. Nurses Assn. (past pres.), Am. Nurses Assn. (cert. psychiat. specialist), Pa. Nurses Assn., Sigma Theta Tau. Republican. Roman Catholic. Avocation: golf. Home: 1795 Robson Dr Pittsburgh PA 15241-2617 Office: U Pitts Sch Nursing 415 Victoria Dr Pittsburgh PA 15261 Office Phone: 412-624-6933.

PUSTER, REBECCA LYNN, music educator, director; d. Edwin Paul Bamber and Evelyn Elaine Gamber; m. David W. Puster, June 18, 1983; children: Matthew, Kristen. BA in Music Edn., U. No. Colo., Greeley, 1982; MA in Sacred Music, Shenandoah U., Winchester, Va., 1999. Choir dir. Illesheim Chapel, US Govt., Germany, 1986; min. music Calvary United Meth. Ch., Frederick, Md., 1983—98; dir. children's choir Chestnut Ave. United Meth. Ch., Newport News, Va., 1988—90; asst. dir. music ministries First Presbyn. Ch., Charlotte, NC, 1999—. Handbell instr. Music and Worship Conf., Montreat, NC, 2000, 2002—03; clinician Handbell Festival, Hickory, NC, 2004—05. Mem.: Am. Choral Dirs. Assn., Am. Guild English Handbell Ringers, Chorister's Guild (chpt. pres. 2004—06).

PUSTILNIK, JEAN TODD, elementary school educator, secondary school educator; b. Ranger, Tex., Dec. 12, 1932; d. Lonnie Elvin and Frances Elvira (Lee) Todd; m. David Daniel Pustilnik, Aug. 15, 1959; children: Palma Elyse, Leslie Royce, Bradley Todd. BA, U. Okla., 1954; MA, St. Joseph Coll., West Hartford, Conn., 1983. Asst. buyer Foley's, Houston, 1954-58; buyer Kerr's, Oklahoma City, 1958-59; mgr. Woodward & Lothrup, Washington, 1959-61; instr. M. Webster Jr. Coll., Washington, 1961-63; tchr. West Hartford (Conn.) Bd. Edn., 1974-92; instr. St. Joseph Coll., 1976-95. Curriculum creator Conn. Home Econs. Dept., Middletown, 1985-88. Dir. Coastal Discovery Mus., 1999-2005. Mem. Am. Home Econs. Assn., Hadassah (pres. 1967-71, 97-2000), Sea Pines Country Club (chair social com. 1997-99). Home: 60 N Sea Pines Dr Hilton Head Island SC 29928-6007

PUTCAMP, LUISE, JR., editor, writer; b. San Diego, Mar. 9, 1924; d. William J. and Luise (Zimmermann) P.; student Phoenix Jr. Coll., 1942-43, So. Meth. U., 1946-47, U. Utah, 1955-56; m. Robert H. Johnson, Feb. 24, 1945; children— Robert H., III, Luise Robin, Jan Leah, Stephanie Neale, Jennifer Anne, Ann Tapia. Reporter, feature writer Anniston (Ala.) Times, 1939-40; Ariz. Republic, Phoenix, 1941-43; asst. news editor Ariz. Network, Phoenix, 1943-44; night news editor Radio Sta WINX, Washington, 1945; telegraph editor Miami Beach Sun-Tropics, 1944, 46; copy editor Dallas News, 1946-51; book page editor Dallas Times Herald, 1951-52; freelance writer, 1953-59; columnist, feature writer Indpls. News, 1961-62; vol. publicist, 1963-66; book page editor Dallas Times Herald, 1968-69; freelance writer, 1973-75; editor, writer The Advocate, Stamford, Conn., 1976-84; freelance writer, Albuquerque, N.Mex., 1984. Recipient Kaleidograph Press award for Sonnets for the Survivors, 1951; Christopher award for short story in Good Housekeeping, 1955. Mem. Nat. Fedn. Press Women (1st pl. award for personal columns 1980) Tex. Inst. Letters, N.Mex. Press Women, S.W. Writers Workshop Internat. Assn. for Near-Death Studies, Inc., Author: Sonnets for the Survivors, 1952; The Christmas Carol Miracle, 1971; The Night of the Child, 1972. Home and Office: 2740 Tramway Cir NE Albuquerque NM 87122-1205 Office Phone: 505-856-5078, 505-856-5078. Personal E-mail: lputcamp@aol.com.

PUTNAM, KERI, film company executive; married; 2 children. Grad., Harvard U. Asst. HBO; with literary dept. Arena Stage, Washington; dir. develop. Devillier Donegan Enterprises, Washington; dir. devel. HBO, 1992—95; v.p. NYC Productions HBO Films, 1995—99, sr. v.p. LA, 1999—2004, exec. v.p., 2004—06; pres. prodn. Miramax Film Unit Walt Disney Co., 2006—. Recipient Excellence in Media award, Women in Film, 2005. Office: Miramax 375 Greenwich St New York NY 10013*

PUTNAM, RUTH ANNA, philosopher, educator; b. Berlin, Sept. 20, 1927; d. Martin and Marie (Kohn) Hall; m. Hilary W. Putnam, Aug. 11, 1962; children: Samuel, Joshua, Maxima. BS in Chemistry, UCLA, 1954, PhD in Philosophy, 1962. Instr. philosophy UCLA, 1957-59; acting asst. prof. U. Oreg., 1959-62; from lectr. to prof. philosophy Wellesley (Mass.) Coll., 1963-98, chmn. dept., 1979-82, 91-93; ret., 1998. Dir. summer seminar NEH, 1986, 89; mem. extramural grad. fellowships Wellesley Coll., faculty benefits com., com. budget, academic review bd., taskforce on affirmative action, bd. of admissions; presenter in field. Editor: Cambridge Companion to William James, 1997; contbr. chpts. to books, articles to profl. jours., and encys. Mem. Am. Philos. Assn. (program com. ea. divsn. 1977). Jewish. Office: Wellesley Coll 106 Central St Wellesley MA 02481-8268 Personal E-mail: raputnam@comcast.net. Business E-Mail: rputnam@wellesley.edu.

PUTNAM, SUSAN K., psychology educator; b. Buffalo; d. Wilford C. Gustavel and Alberta J. Schmitt; m. John S. Putnam, Jr.; children: Alyssa Marie, Nathan John. A in Gen. Studies, Erie CC, Williamsville, NY, 1991—93; BA, Canisius Coll., Buffalo, NY, 1993—95; PhD, SUNY, Buffalo, 1995—2000. Soccer coach Erie CC, Williamsville, NY, 1993—95; rsch. asst. SUNY, 1995—99, postdoctoral fellow in behavioral neuroscience, 1999—2000, vis. asst. prof., 2000—01; assoc. prof. psychology Canisius Coll., 2001—. Mem. autism spectrum disorder rsch. consortium Inter-Institutional, Buffalo, 2004—; mem. Instl. Animal Care and Use Com. of Canisius Coll., 2002—; pres. Penn York Undergraduate Rsch. Assn., Regional, NY, 2003—04; kairos adult leader Canisius Coll., 2005—05; advisor Canisius Coll. Psychology Club, 2005—. Soccer coach Akron Soccer League, NY, 1983—94; mem. Music Ministry Team Surrender; choir dir., organist First Bapt. Ch. Akron, 1983—2006, dir. music ministry, 1985—, youth group leader, 2001—06, mem. pastoral rels. com., 2001—04. Recipient Milton Plezur Excellence in Tchg. award, SUNY, 1999, Chancellor's award for grad. sch. tchg. excellence, 1999, Outstanding Instr. Recognition award, Athletic Dept., SUNY, 1999, Milton Plezur Excellencein Tchg. award, SUNY, 1999, Chancellor's award for grad. sch. tchg. excellence, 1999, Outstanding Instr. Recognition award, Athletic Dept., SUNY, 1999, UPA/Psi Chi Excellence in Tchg. award, SUNY, 2001, Dean's Rsch. grants, Canisius Coll., 2004, 2005, Lay Person of Yr. award, First Bapt. Church Akron, 2003; Dean's Rsch. grants, Canisius Coll., 2002. Mem.: Penn York Undergrrad. Rsch. Assn. (assoc.; pres. 2003—04), Internat. Brain Rsch. Orgn. (assoc.), Am. Neuroendocrine Soc. (assoc.), Soc. Behavioral Neuroendocrinology (assoc.), Alpha Sigma Lambda Hon. Soc. (pres. 1995), Phi Theta Kappa Internat. Honor Soc., Psi Chi Nat. Honor Soc., Alpha Sigma Nu Nat. SJ Honor Soc., Alpha Sigma Nu Hon. Soc. Avocations: sports, animal training, photography, music, camping, canoeing. Office: Canisius Coll 2001 Main St Buffalo NY 14208 Office Phone: 716-888-2895. Office Fax: 716-888-3244. Business E-Mail: putnams@canisius.edu.

PUTO, ANNE-MARIE, reading specialist; b. Windber, Pa., July 20, 1956; d. John Michael and Ann Theresa (Biel) Puto. BS Elem. Edn., U. Pitts., Johnstown, 1978; EdM in Lang. Comms., U. Pitts., 1981; EdM in Ednl. Psychology, Indiana U. Pa., 1989. Reading specialist Conemaugh Valley Sch. Dist., Johnstown, 1978—79, Upward Bound Program, St. Francis U., Loretto, Pa., 1994—2000, Appalachian Youth Svc., Ebensburg, Pa., 1991—2004, Children's Aid Home, Somerset, Pa., 1999—, Appalachia Intermediate Unit 08, Altoona, 1979—. Mem. Cambria Area Reading Coun. Mem.: Keystone State Reading Assn., Pa. Assn. Fed. Program Coords. Avocations: reading, travel, cross country skiing, needlecrafts, theater. Home: 1093 Tener St Johnstown PA 15904

PUTTERMAN, FLORENCE GRACE, artist, printmaker; b. N.Y.C., Apr. 14, 1927; d. Nathan and Jean (Feldman) Hirsch; m. Saul Putterman, Dec. 19, 1947. BS, NYU, 1947; MFA, Pa. State U., 1973. Founder, pres. Arts Unlimited, Selinsgrove, Pa., 1969—; curator Milton Shoe Collection, 1970—; artist in residence Title III Program Cultural Enrichment in Schs. Program, 1969-70; instr. Lycoming Coll., Williamsport, Pa., 1972-74, Susquehanna U., Selinsgrove, PA, 1984—. One-woman shows include Everson Mus., Syracuse, N.Y., 1976, Hagerstown, Md., 1978, Stuhr Mus., Grand Island, N.B., 1979, Muhlenburg Ctr. for the Arts, Pa., 1985, Harmon Gallery, Fla., 1985, The State Mus. of Pa., 1985-86, Segal Gallery, N.Y., 1986, Canton Inst. Fine Arts, Ohio, 1986, Fla. Biennial Polk Mus., Lakeland, Fla., 1987, 89, Artists Choose Artists, Tampa Mus., 1987, Auburn Works on Paper, 1987, Ala., Ruth Volid Gallery, Chgo., 1989, Polk Mus. Art, Lakeland, Fla., 1989, Lowe Gallery, Atlanta, 1990, Mickelson Gallery, Washington, 1990, Palmer Mus., Pa. State U., 1990, Payne Gallery, Moravian Coll., 1991, Everhart Mus., Scranton, Pa., 1991, Lowe Gallery, L.A., 1992, Center Gallery, Bucknell U., Pa., 1993, Lore Degenstein Gallery, Susquehanna U., Selinsgrove, Pa., 1993, Lowe Gallery, Atlanta, 1993, Down Roll Gallery, Sarasota, Fla., Gallery 10, Washington, Donn Roll Contemporary, Sarasota, Fla., 1996, Grand Central Gallery, Tampa Fla., 1997, Walter Wickiser Gallery, N.Y., Hodges-Taylor Gallery, Charlotte N.C., Ziegenfuss Gallery, Sarasota, Burroughs-Chapin Mus., Myrtle Bend, S.C., Lighthouse Gallery, Tequesta, Fla., 1998, Galerie Lumiere, Savannah, Ga., 1999, Walter Wickiser Gallery, N.Y., 1999, Ellen Noel Art Mus., Odessa, Tex., 1999, Spartanburg County Mus. Art, Spartansburg, S.C., 2000, Saginaw (Mich.) Art Mus., 2000, Art Mus., No. Mich. U., Marquette, Lancaster Mus. Art, 2001, Albany (Ga.) Art Mus., 2002, Walter Wickiser Gallery, N.Y.C., 2003, Mira Mar Gallery, Sarasota, Fla., 2003, Waterworks Visual Art Ctr., Salisbury, N.C., 2003, Robeson Gallery, Pa. State U., 2003; 10-yr. retrospective Susquehanna U., 2003, Baisden Gallery, Tampa, Fla., 2004, Pfenninger Gallery, Lancaster, Pa., 2004, Walter Wickisen Gallery, N.Y., N.Y., 2004; exhibited in numerous group shows including: Libr. Congress, Smithsonian Traveling Exhbn., Sarasota (Fla.) Biennial Ringling Mus., 2000, Tampa Mus. Art, 2001, Springfield (Mo.) Art Mus., 2002, Chattahoochee Valley Art Mus., 2002, Butler Inst. Am. Art, 2002, Appalachian Corridors, Charleston, W.Va., 2003, La. State U., Baton Rouge, 2004others. Recipient award Silvermine Guild Conn. Appalachian Corridors, Arena, 1976, Gold medal of honor Audubon Artists ann. competition, Whitehead award Boston Printmakers, 1985, Shellenberg award Artists Equity, 1985, award N.C. Print & Drawing, 1985, award Chautauqua Nat., 1985, Johnson & Johnson award 3rd Ann. Nat. Printmaking Coun. of N.J., 1985, Purchase award N.J. State Mus., 1987, Disting. Alumni award Pa. State U. Sch. Arts & Architecture, 1988, Ethel Klassen Meml. award Fla. Artists Group, 1992, Earl Horter award Phila. Watercolor Club, 1992, award of excellence, 1995, Stella Drabkin Meml. award Colorprint Soc., Award for Excellence Phila. Watercolor Club, 1996, Elizabeth Morse Meml. award Fla. Artists Group, 1996, Daniel Serra Y Navas Meml. award Audubon Artists, N.Y., 1996, Purchase award drawing annual Del Mar (Tex.) Coll., 1997, Purchase award Stockton (Calif.) Arts Commn., 1998, LaGrange Nat. Biennial, 2002; Va. Ctr. for the Creative Arts fellow, 1983-84; Nat. Endowment Arts grantee. Mem. Soc. Am. Graphic Artists (v.p., Daniel Serra Badine award 2004), Nat. Assn. of Women Artists (Nat. Medal of Honor, Elizabeth Blake award).

PUTTMANN, SARA, mathematics educator; b. Iowa, May 18, 1981; BA in Math. Edn. in Math. Edn., U. No. Iowa, Cedar Falls, 1999—2003; MEd in Collaborative Tchg. & Learning, Graceland U., Lamoni, Iowa, 2005—06. Coaching Endorsement Iowa, 2003. HS math. tchr. Mid-Prairie HS, Wellman, Iowa, 2003—, girls basketball coach, 2003—. Office Phone: 319-646-6097.

PUTZEL, CONSTANCE KELLNER, lawyer; b. Balt., Sept. 5, 1922; d. William Stummer and Corinne (Strauss) Kellner; m. William L. Putzel, Aug. 28, 1945; 1 son, Arthur William. AB, Goucher Coll., 1942; LLB, U. Md., 1945, JD, 1969. Bar: Md. 1945. Social worker Balt. Dept. Pub. Welfare, 1945-46; atty. New Amsterdam Casualty Co., Balt., 1947; staff atty. Legal Aid Bur., Balt., 1947-49; mem. Putzel & Putzel, P.A., Balt., 1950-89; pvt. practice Balt., 1989—; instr. U. Balt. Sch. Law, 1975-77, Goucher Coll., 1976-77. Chair character com. Ct. Appeals for 3d Cir., 1976-97. Author: A Practice Guide to Divorce, 1999, Representing the Older Client in Divorce, 1992. Commr. Md. Com. on Status of Women, 1972-76, Com. to Implement ERA, 1973-76; Pres. U. Md. Law Alumni Assn., 1978; bd. dirs. Legal Aid Bur., 1951-52, 71-73. Fellow Am. Acad. Matrimonial Lawyers (chair elder issues com. 1996); mem. ABA (co-chair elder issues com., mem. coun. sr. lawyers divsn. 1996-2000, editl. bd. 1996-99, family law sect.), Md. Bar Assn. (bd. govs. 1972-73, chmn. family law sect. 1978-79, chair sr. lawyers divsn. 2001-03). Home: 7121 Park Heights Ave Unit 401 Baltimore MD 21215-1610 Office: 3835 Naylor s Ln Pikesville MD 21208 Personal E-mail: lawtowson@aol.com.

PYATT, LORI, music educator; d. Lloyd Pyatt and Nadine Rentz. BS in Music Edn., Ctrl. Meth. Coll., Fayette, Mo., 1993. Music tchr. Harrisburg R-8 Schs., Mo., 1993—95; band dir. Gascanade County R-1 Schs., Hermann, Mo., 1997—2001, Marceline Schs., Mo., 2001—02, Dixon R-1 Schs., Mo., 2002—. Mem.: Mo. Women Band Dirs. (sec. 2004—06), Mo. Music Educators Assn., Mo. Bandmasters Assn. Office: Dixon R-1 Schools PO Box A Dixon MO 65459 Office Phone: 573-759-7119.

PYDA, DIANNE SUE, art educator; b. Latrobe, Pa., Mar. 10, 1969; d. Jack G. and Claudia J. Terhorst; m. Joseph E. Pyda, Dec. 13, 1990; children: Patrick A., Andrew J. BS in Edn., Indiana U. Pa., 1992; MEd, California U. of Pa., 1998; cert., Inst. Children's Lit., West Redding, Conn., 2003. Profl. cert. art edn., profl. cert. elem. edn. Tchr. Truxel Pre-sch., Greensburg, Pa., 1990—93; artist, ceramicist Norvelt, Pa., 1993—; tchr. adult art, 1993—; tchr. art Mt. Pleasant (Pa.) Sch. Dist., 1993—. Sponsor Nat. Art Honor Soc., Mt. Pleasant. Exhibitions include (Blue Ribbon award, 1999, 2005, Cert., 1999). With USAR. Mem.: Crafters Assn., Pa. State Edn. Assn., Nat. Art Edn. Assn., Phi Theta Kappa. Avocations: painting, pottery, gardening, writing, reading. Home: Box 232 RD # 1 Mount Pleasant PA 15666 Office: Mt Pleasant Area Sch Dist Box 2222 RD # 4 Mount Pleasant PA 15666

PYDYNKOWSKY, JOAN ANNE, journalist; b. Ft. Riley, Kans., Oct. 2, 1951; d. Fredrick Albert and Mary Elizabeth (O'Connor) Gadwell; m. Michael Stanley Pydynkowsky, Mar. 14, 1981; children: Tricia Lynn Glotfelty, Deborah Findley, Alexandra, Royce M. Pyoynkowsky. BA in Journalism, U. Ctrl. Okla., 1991, MEd in Journalism, 1993. Trust clk. Ill. Nat. Bank, Rockford, 1974-75; engring. aide Barber Colman, Rockford, 1976-77; draftsperson Gen. Web, Rockford, 1979-80, Keeson, Ltd., Rockford, 1981; editor Oklahoma City Marriage Encounter, 1988-89, 94-95; humor columnist UCO Vista, Edmond, Okla., 1990-91; city editor Guthrie (Okla.) Daily Leader, 1991-92; substitute tchr. Edmond (Okla.) Pub. Schs., 1993-94; with N.W. News, Piedmont, Okla., 1994-95, South Oklahoma City Leader, 1995-96; staff writer, columnist, reporter, photographer N.W. News, Piedmont-Surrey Gazette, Okarche Chieftain, Piedmont, 1996—98; city editor Okarche Chieftain, Piedmont, 1996-98, asst. editor, 1998; staff writer, columnist, photographer El Reno (Okla.) Tribune, 1997; horsemanship/hunter/jumper trainer Red Tail Ranch, Piedmont, Okla., 1999-2000. Copywriter, cons., Edmond, 1991—, photographer, 1990—, cartoonist, 1984—, humorist, 1990—; columnist, contbg. writer N.W. News, Piedmont, Okla., 1994-95; reporter and assoc. editor: All About Kids/South Oklahoma City Leader, 1995-96. Artworks include: Turtle (cover), UCO Bus. Rev., winter 2000. Asst. leader Boy Scouts Am., Edmond, 1993-95; league coach Young Am. Bowling Alliance, Edmond, 1993-99; counselor Oklahoma City YWCA Rape Crisis, 1986-88; mem. Tiaras Jr. Women's Honor Soc., 1990-91; mem. selection com. Okla. Journalism Hall of Fame, 1990. Recipient awards State Fair of Okla., 1983-96, 99-2004, Feature Writing award Okla. chpt. Soc. Profl. Journalists, 1992-93, six awards including first place Entertainment, Sports feature, sports column, 1994-95, six awards including first place feature writing, 1995-96, five awards including first place feature writing, 1996-97, eight awards, 1997-98, first place Feature Writing award, State Fair of Okla. Better Newspaper Contest, 1995. Mem. Soc. Profl. Journalists (pres. U. Ctrl. Okla. chpt. 1990, treas. 1989, 91), Internat. Platform Assn., Kappa Tau Alpha. Roman Catholic. Avocations: writing, photography, horsemanship, art. Home: 301 Reynolds Rd Edmond OK 73013-5121 E-mail: asliceofpy@cox.net.

PYLE, CAROL LYNN HORSLEY, small business owner, educational association administrator; b. Dallas, Mar. 29, 1946; d. John Otis and Flora Eileen Horsley; m. Michael R. Pyle (dec. 1995). B Music Edn., East Tex. State U., 1970, MusM, 1973. Cert. music and English tchr., Tex. Choral dir. Dumas (Tex.) Jr. H.S., 1970-72, Haltom H.S., Birdville, Tex., 1981-84, Glen Rose (Tex.) Jr. and Sr. H.S., 1986-88, Springtown (Tex.) H.S., 1988-91, Azle (Tex.) H.S., 1991—; choral dir., vocal coord. Weatherford (Tex.) H.S. and Mid. Schs., 1972-81; English reading tchr. Aledo (Tex.) H.S., 1984-86; tchr. Ft. Worth (Tex.) Ind. Sch. Dist., 1998—99; prin., owner Trebleshooter Svcs., Weatherford, Tex., 1999—. Mem. adv. bd. Tex. Girls' Choir, Ft. Worth; founder, mus. dir. Parker County Choral Soc., Weatherford, 1984-86. Contbr. articles to profl. jours. Founder, bd. dirs., 1st pres. Weatherford Assn. Performing Arts, 1974-77; pres. Weatherford Classroom Tchrs. Assn., Weatherford, 1979-80; soloist, guest condr. various civic, ch. and cmty. choirs, Tex., 1970—; tchr. Azle Ch. of Christ, 1980—; vol. Tarrant County Fine Arts Coun., Parker County Cancer Soc. Named Tchr. of Yr. Weatherford Ind. Sch. Dist./VFW Aux., 1980, Nat. Finalist Tchr. of Yr., Nat. VFW Aux., 1980. Mem. Tex. Music Educators Assn. (chair region VII 1987-88, region V 1991-92), Tex. Choral Dirs. Assn. (state sec. 1980-81), Assn. Tex. Pub. Educators, Assn. Supr. and Curriculum Devel. (mem. nat. staff devel. coun.), Renaissance Consort of Ft. Worth, Schola Cantorum of Tex., Inc. (bd. dirs. 1974-75, 2005-2006, exec. dir. 2006, Mem. of Yr. 1992), Mu Phi Epsilon, Alpha Chi, Alpha Lambda Delta. Office: Trebleshooter Svcs PO Box 443 Weatherford TX 76086 Office Phone: 817-341-7282. Personal E-mail: trebleshooter@hotmail.com.

PYLE, DEBRA LEE, elementary school educator; b. Zeeland, Mich., Sept. 4, 1956; d. Carl Junior and Dorothy Marie Vander Velde; m. James Alan Pyle, June 23, 1978; children: Kelly, Jonathan, Jamie. BA, Hope Coll., Holland, Mich., 1978; MA, Mich. State U., East Lansing, 1984. Elem. tchr. Zeeland Pub. Schs., 1979—. Mem. safe schs. com. Zeeland Pub. Schs., 2000—, mem. gifted-talented com., 2002—. Chair Extreme Mission Team Beaverdam Ref. Ch., Zeeland, 2004—. Grantee, Holland Area Arts Coun., 2005. Mem.: NEA, Zeeland Edn. Assn., Mich. Edn. Assn. Avocations: gardening, travel, reading. Home: 4140 80th Ave Zeeland MI 49464 Office: Zeeland Pub Schs 183 W Roosevelt Zeeland MI 49464

PYLE, ROLANDA, social worker; b. NYC, June 3, 1955; d. Clarence Leroy and Elnora E. (Harris) P. BA, CCNY, 1977; MA, L.I. U., 1984. Notary pub. N.Y., 1994. Sr. counselor Ctrl. Bklyn. Coord. Coun., 1982-85; project coord. Project Teen Aid, Bklyn., 1985; program dir. Family Dynamics, Bklyn., 1985-89; cmty. coord. N.Y.C. Dept. Health, 1989-91; supr. Child Devel., Bklyn., 1992; program dir. Miracle Makers, Inc., Bklyn., 1992-95; dir. Grandparent Resource Ctr., N.Y.C. Dept. Aging, 1995—. Mem. adv. bd. Family Cons. Svcs., Bklyn., 1996-97; mem. Child Welfare Task Force, Bklyn., 1992-95, Interagy. Coun. Aging, Bklyn., 1993-95, Sr. Citizen Task Force, Bklyn., 1992-95. Author (short story) African Voices, 1996; author of poems. Mem. N.Y. Com. Kinship Family Care, co-chiar, 1996-97; mem. N.Y. Kin Care Task Force, Coalition 100 Black women, 1995-97. Fellow Brookdale Ctr. Aging; mem Avocations: travel, reading, writing, art exhibits, music. Home: 1304 Dean St Brooklyn NY 11216-3401 Office: NYC Dept Aging Grandparent Resource Ctr 2 Lafayette St Fl 15 New York NY 10007-1307

PYLES, CAROL DELONG, dean, consultant, educator; b. Oil City, Pa., Apr. 6, 1948; d. William J. and Doris (Gresh) DeLong; 1 child, Whitney Dawn. BS, Alderson-Broaddus Coll., Philippi, W.Va., 1966-70; MS in Nursing, Tex. Woman's U., 1982-85; MA, W. Va. U., 1972-73, EdD, 1974-80. RN, W.Va., Tex., Fla.; cert. health edn. specialist; lic. profl. counselor, Tex., Okla.; nat. cert. counselor. Instr. nursing Fairmont (W.Va.) State Coll., 1971-73, asst. prof. nursing edn., 1973-76, asst. dean Com. Coll., 1976-78, prof. nursing, chmn. divsn. health careers, 1978-81; cons., adj. faculty Salem Coll., Clarksburg, W.Va., 1978-81; officer Allied Health Houston Com. Coll. System, 1981-83, chmn. divsn. sales, mktg. & mgmt., 1983-85; dean Coll. Spl. Arts & Scis., prof. health edn. adminstrn. Cen. State U., Edmond, Okla., 1985-87; dean Coll. of Health, Phys. Edn. & Recreation Ea. Ill. U., Charleston, 1987-91, prof. health studies, 1987-91; dean, prof. med. ctr. campus Miami-Dade (Fla.) C.C., 1991-98; CEO Dr. Carol Pyles & Assocs., Orgn. and Mgmt. Cons., 1998—. Bd. dirs. Dade County Area Health Edn. Ctr., Inc.; treas. bd. dirs. Nat. Network for Health Career Programs in Two Yr. Colls.; pres. cons. seminar devel., P & P Assoc., Inc., Houston; motivational and leadership cons., 1999—, coun. pvt. practice for marriage, life crises, behavior & image problems; vis. prof., dir. Sch. Health, 2000—. Author: articles for Issues in Higher Edn. Mem. South Fla. Health Planning Coun., Indigent Health Care Task Force, Met. Dade County, Fla., Dade County Area Health Edn. Ctr., Inc.; chmn. Indsl. Commn., Charleston (Ill.) Recreation Ctr., 1989; bd. dirs. ARC, East Coles County chpt., Reg. United Way, Coalition Against Domestic Violence, Am. Cancer Soc., Fla. Arthritis Assn., 1998—. Named Personality of Am. 1986, Outstanding Young Leader in Allied Health, 1984, Most Outstanding Young Women of Am., 1983; recipient Svc. award Am. Cancer Soc., 1984. Mem. Am. Coun. Edn., Nat. Identification Program, Am. Cancer Soc., Am. Assn. Coll. for Tchrs. Edn. Inst. Rep., Assn. Schs. Allied Health Professions, Fla. Assn. Community Colls., Alliance of 100 (Fla. Hosp. Assn.), Rotary Internat., Sigma Theta Tau. Avocations: water & snow skiing, bridge, sailing, golf, tennis. Office Phone: 305-348-6992. Business E-Mail: pylescd@fiu.edu.

PYOTT, CAROLINE (PATTY), writer; b. N.Y.C., Nov. 15, 1931; d. Greene Flournoy and Caroline (Lovell) Johnson; divorced; children: Caroline, Richard, Greerson, Laura, Charles. BA, Smith Coll., 1953; MS in Journalism, Columbia U., 1955. Feature writer TV & Entertainment Times, Hong Kong, 1983-86; opinion columnist Hong Kong Standard, 1984-85; spl. asst. to dir. pub. affairs U.S. Office Personnel Mgmt., Washington, 1986-88; v.p. Inst. Ednl. Affairs, Washington, 1990-93, Madison Ctr. Ednl. Affairs, Washington; freelance writer, editor. Author, editor: Common Sense Guide to American Colleges, 1991, 2d edit., 1992. Republican. Episcopalian. Avocations: genealogy, politics. Home: 3020 South Freeman Rd Williamsburg VA 23185 Office Phone: 757-345-6181. E-mail: pyottcj@aol.com.

PYTLEWSKI, LAURA JEAN, chemistry professor; b. Freeport, Ill., Aug. 26, 1959; d. James Franklin and Darlene Ann Donahue; m. James Andrew Pytlewski, Oct. 8, 1983; children: Michael Steven, Matthew John. BS in Biology, St. Xavier U., 1981; MS in Analytical Chemistry, Govs. State U., 1992. Cert. med. technologist Am. Soc. Clin. Pathologists, 1983. Adj. prof. chemistry Moraine Valley C.C., Palos Hills, Ill., 1993—2003; prof. chemistry Triton Coll., River Grove, Ill., 2002—06; adj. prof. chemistry Lewis U., Romeoville, Ill., 2006—; lab. supr. natural sci. dept. U. St. Francis, Joliet, Ill., 2006—. Mem. focus group Benjamin Cummings Publishers, San Francisco, 2004; adj. prof. Govs. State U., Univ. Pk., Ill., 2006—. Author: Biology for Life, 2001; reviewer: Chemistry: A World of Choices, 1998. Mem. com. devel. of new lab. St. Joseph's Sch., Lockport, Ill., 2005—06. Scholar, St. Xavier U., 1980—81. Democrat. Roman Catholic. Achievements include development of a visual factoring method for algebra II. Avocations: painting, reading, rollerblading, swimming, travel. E-mail: pytlewla@lewisu.edu.

PYZEK, TAMERA JEAN, music educator; b. Elmhurst, Ill., Jan. 29, 1981; d. Randolph Edward and Peggy Jean Pyzek. B in Music Edn., U. Ill., 2003. Lead tchr. Prince of Peace Cmty. Early Learning Ctr., St. Joseph, Ill., 2003—04; tchr. Streator Twp. HS, Ill., 2004—06, Milford Pub. Schs., Ill., 2006—. Mem.: MENC, Internat. Tuba-Euphonium Assn., Red and White Booster Club, U. Ill. LaSalle County Alumni Club, U. Ill. Alumni Assn. Home: 100 N Fritz Milford IL 60953 Office: Milford Pub Schs 100 S Chicago St Milford IL 60953 Office Phone: 815-889-4174. Personal E-mail: tamalot03@hotmail.com.

QUACKENBUSH, MARGERY CLOUSER, psychoanalyst, researcher; b. Reading, Pa., Apr. 30, 1938; d. Carl Brumbach and Katherine Elvina (Althouse) Clouser; m. Robert Mead Quackenbush, July 3, 1971; 1 child, Piet Robert. BFA, Pratt Inst., 1960; MA, Calif. Grad. Inst., 1982; PhD in Psychoanalysis, Internat. U. Grad. Studies, N.Y.C., 2001. Cert. in psychoanalysis Ctr. for Modern Psychoanalytic Studies, 1992. Instr. Pratt Inst., Bklyn., 1978-79, Fashion Inst. of Tech., N.Y.C., 1980-81; counselor Wiltwyck, Bronx Ctr., 1981-82; exec. dir. Nat. Assn. for Advancement of Psychoanalysis, N.Y.C., 1982—; pvt. practice in psychoanalysis N.Y.C., 1980—. Adj. prof. Union Inst. Mem. Lenox Hill Dem. Club, N.Y.C., 1993-95; spkr. various cmty. groups, 1991—. Recipient Maison Blanche award, 1959, Miriam Berkman Spotnitz award, 1992, Am. Bd. Accreditation Profl. Svc. award, 2000-04. Mem. Nat. Assn. for Advancement of Psychoanalysis, Nat. Soc. DAR, Alumni Assn. of the Ctr. for Modern Psych. Studies (sec. 1992-94, Alumni Assn. program dir., v.p. 1995-98), Soc. Modern Psychoanalysts. Democrat. Avocations: reading, writing, golf, horseback riding. Home: 460 E 79th St Apt 14E New York NY 10021-1447 Office: Nat Assn Advancement Psychoanalysis 80 8th Ave # 1501 New York NY 10011-5126 Office Phone: 212-741-0515. Personal E-mail: margeryquackenbush@yahoo.com. Business E-Mail: mq@naap.org.

QUADE, VICKI, editor, writer, playwright, theater producer; b. Chgo., Aug. 15, 1953; d. Victor and Virginia (Uryasz) Q.; m. Charles J. White III, Feb. 15, 1986 (div. Aug. 1996); children: Michael, David, Catherine. BS in Journalism, No. Ill. U., 1974. Staff reporter news divsn. The News-Tribune, LaSalle, Ill., 1975-77; staff writer news divsn. The News-Sun, Waukegan, Ill., 1977-81; staff writer ABA Jour., Chgo., 1981-85; mng. editor ABA Press, Chgo., 1985-90, editor, 1990-2000, sr. editor, 1994-2000. Author: (poetry) Rain and Other Poems, 1976, Laughing Eyes, 1979, Two Under the Covers, 1981, (biography) I Remember Bob Collins, 2000; playwright Late Nite Catechism, 1993, Room for Advancement, 1994, Mr. Nanny, 1997, (musical)

Lost in Wonderland, 1998, (musical) Here Come the Famous Brothers, 2001, Put the Nuns in Charge!, 2005; prodr. Late Nite Catechism, Mr. Nanny, Here Come the Famous Brothers, Christopher Carter Messes With Your Mind, Forever Plaid, Cast on a Hot Tin Roof, Verbatim Verboten, Put the Nuns in Charge; U.S. premiere of Drapes, 2005; contbr. to numerous anthologies and publs.; contbd. to: 20th Century Chicago: 100 Years, 100 Voices (contbd. the year 1953), owner/operator Crossroads Theater, Naperville, Ill Recipient numerous awards from Soc. Nat. Assn. Publs., AP, UPI, Spirit of Benedict award Benedictine Sisters Chgo., 2003, Partners in Mission award Sisters of the Living Word, 2005 Mem. Am. Soc. Bus. Press Editors (award), Chgo. Newspaper Guild (award), Am. Soc. Assn. Execs. (Gold Circle award 1989, 90). Avocations: travel, photography.

QUAIFE, MARJORIE CLIFT, retired nursing educator; b. Syracuse, N.Y., Aug. 21; Diploma in Nursing with honors, Auburn Meml. Hosp; BS, Columbia U., 1962, MA, 1978. Cert. orthopaedic nurse; cert. in nursing continuing edn. and staff devel.; BLS instr. Staff instr. Columbia Presbyn. Hosp., N.Y.C., 1968-97, ret., 1997. Content expert for computer assisted instrn. program-ctrl. venous catheters. Contbr. articles to numerous profl. publs. Mem. ANA, N.Y. State Nurses Assn., Nat. Assn. Orthopaedic Nurses, Nat. Assn. Nursing Staff Devel., Nat. Assn. Vascular Access Networks, Intravenous Nurses Soc., Sigma Theta Tau.

QUAM, LOIS, healthcare company executive; m. Matt Entenza; children: Ben, Steve. BA magna cum laude, Macalaster Coll., Minn.; MA in Philos., Politics, Econs., U. Oxford, 1985. Dir. rsch. and eval. United HealthCare, 1989-93, v.p. pub. sector svcs., 1993; sr. adv. White House Task Force Nat. Health Care Reform, 1993-96; CEO AARP/United divsn. United HealthCare, 1996-98; CEO Ovations (formerly Retiree and Sr. Svcs. Co. United HealthCare), Minnetonka, Minn., 1998—. Bd. dirs. George C. Marshall Found., Coun. Fgn. Rels.; adv. com. Am. Democracy Inst. Mem. editl. bd.: British Med. Jour.; contbr. articles to profl. jours. Bd. trustees Macalester Coll. Named one of 50 Most Powerful Women in Bus., Fortune mag., 2006; recipient America-Norway Heritage Fund award, Nordmann-Forbundett Norway-Am. Assn. Office: Ovations UnitedHealth Grp 500 Opus Ctr 9900 Bren Rd E Minnetonka MN 55343-9664*

QUAMINA, JOYCE, management consultant; b. Jan. 4, 1937; d. Da Costa and Beryl Jones; m. Ulric Quamina (dec. May 1985); 1 child, Michelle Quamina Reid. From recording sec. to bus. mgr. WIADCA Inc., Bklyn., 1983—2001. Dir. Caribbean Music Festival, Nassau, Bahamas, 1987—2001; cons. Western Union, NJ, 1994—99; v.p. Westchester Carnival Assn., White Plains, NY, 1989—96. Home: 1150 President St B2 Brooklyn NY 11225

QUANN, JOAN LOUISE, French language educator, real estate broker; b. Phila., Oct. 14, 1935; d. John Joseph and Pauline Cecelia (Karpink) Q. Diploma, U. Paris, 1963; BA in French, U. Pa., 1976; grad., Temple U. Real Estate Inst., 1988; MEd, Temple U, 1994. Lic. real estate broker. Exec. sec. to chief fgn. corr. Newsweek, Inc., Paris, 1964—70, internat. editl. asst. NYC, 1971—73; exec. sec., adminstrv. asst. Richard I. Rubin & Co., Inc., Phila., 1977—91; tchr. French and English to spkrs. of other langs. The Sch. Dist. of Phila., Bd. Edn., 1991—. Judge of elections City of Phila., 1977-81. Mem. AAUW (2d v.p. membership 1985-87, bd. dirs., corr. sec. 1987-91, fin. com. 1993), Alliance Francaise, La Societe Francophone Arts et Loisirs (bd. dirs. 1988—), Am. Coun. on Tchg. of Fgn. Langs., Pa. Acad. Fine Arts (docent 2006—), MLA of Phila. and Vicinity, Phila. Mus. Art (Asian adv. group 2000). Republican. Roman Catholic. Avocations: art history, reading, swimming, travel. Office: Sch Dist of Phila Bd Edn 440 N Broad St Philadelphia PA 19130 Office Phone: 215-537-2519.

QUARTUCCIO, MARYANN, insurance agent, home economist; b. San Jose, Calif., Aug. 26, 1957; d. Anthony Angelo and Catherine Elizabeth (Sunseri) Q. AA, San Jose City Coll., 1979; BS in Home Econs., Calif. Poly. State U., San Luis Obispo, 1984. Lic. ins. agt., Calif. Dept. head Marshall's Dept. Store, San Jose, Calif., 1977-80; food server Servomation Corp., Santa Clara, Calif., 1980-85; sr. customer svc. coord. Prudential Ins., Los Altos, Calif., 1985-90; personal lines account mgr. Alburger Basso Degrosz Ins. Svcs., Belmont, Calif., 1990-95; personal lines mgr. Bandar Covall Ins., San Mateo, Calif., 1995-96, Micheletti & Assocs., San Jose, Calif., 1997-99; personal lines mgr., claims mgr. Dorsey Hazeltine Wynne Ins., Palo Alto, Calif., 1999—2001; ins. agt. Allwest Ins. Brokers, Campbell, Calif., 2001—; acct. mgr. ABD Fin. Svcs. Fin., Redwood, 2005—. Tchg. asst. for the disabled San Jose City Coll., 1978-79. Vol., Second Harvest Food Bank, San Jose, 1999. Mem. Peninsula Ins. Women's Assn. (2d v.p. 1996-97, various coms., Ins. Woman of Yr. 1995), Nat. Assn. Ins. Women, Sons Italy Womens Aux. Republican. Roman Catholic. Avocations: cooking/baking, culinary arts, catering, sports, interior decorating. Home: Apt 71 4951 Cherry Ave San Jose CA 95118-2737 Office: ABD Ins Svcs Fin 305 Walnut St Redwood City CA 94063 Office Phone: 650-839-6291. Personal E-mail: mquartuch@aol.com.

QUAST, PEARL ELIZABETH KOLB, retired elementary school educator; b. Omro, Wis., Nov. 21, 1934; d. Frank Kolb and Lavon Opal Buchanan; m. Arthur Roman Quast; children: Arthur R. Jr., Robert F., John M. BS in Edn., Edgewood Coll., Madison, Wisconsin, 1956; MA in Edn., Cardinal Stritch Coll., Milw., 1971. Cert. tchr. unlimited 0743, K-3 Wis., remedial reading 42 and 27 (K-12), reading specialist 42 and 27 (K-12). Tchr. grade 2 Deerfield (Ill.) Pub. Schs., 1956—58; tchr. grade 3 Whitefish Bay (Wis.) Pub. Schs., 1958—60; tchr. reading Milw. Pub. Schs., 1969—75; reading specialist Germantown (Wis.) Pub. Schs., 1975—91. Seminar presenter Reading Assn., Milw., 1982—86; vol. coord. The Cath. Ctr., Sun City West, 1998—99; coord. lectors Our Lady of Lourdes Ch., Sun City West, 1996—2003, lector, cantor, choir mem., Sun City West and Phoenix, 1995—2005. Bd. trustees Found. for Sr. Living, Phoenix, 1998—2001; group leader founding com. Cath. Ctr. for Srs.' Needs, Sun City and Sun City West, 1995—2001; coord. lectors Our Lady of Lourdes Ch., 1996—2005, mem.; del. Phoenix Diocesan Synod, 2002—03; Bd. trustees Symphony of the West Valley, Sun City West, 1996—2002; mem., bd. dirs. Ariz. Masterwork Chorale, 2003—05. Mem.: AAUW (v.p. membership 1994—96), West Valley Art Mus. (sec. Woman's League 1994—96), Cath. Ctr. (founding officer, v.p. adv. com. 1996—2000, Cert. Appreciation), Found. for Sr. Living, Weavers West Handweaving Guild, Our Lady of Lourdes Church. Roman Catholic. Avocations: handweaving, travel, singing, reading, cultural arts.

QUATTRONE-CARROLL, DIANE ROSE, clinical social worker; b. NYC, July 18, 1949; d. Mario Anthony and Filomena (Serpico) Quattrone; m. Rene Eugene Carroll Jr., June 7, 1980; children: Jenna Cristine, Jonathan Rene. BA cum laude, Bklyn. Coll., 1971; MSW, Rutgers U., 1974. Lic. marriage and family counselor, lic. clin. social worker, N.J.; bd. cert. diplomate in clin. social work. Clin. social worker, field instr. Essex County Guidance Ctr., East Orange, N.J., 1974-82; exec. dir. Psychotherapy Info. and Referral Svc., Madison, N.J., 1982-87; pvt. practice Sparta, N.J., 1982—. Nat. Assn. Social Workers. Avocation: travel. Office Phone: 973-729-2442.

QUAY, JACQUELYN SUE, art educator, consultant; d. Harold Ira and Helen Mary Martin; m. Stanley John Quay, June 12, 1976; children: Patrick William, Kathleen Martin. AB, Wilmington Coll., 1970—73; MEd, Xavier U., 1973—76; EdD, U. of Cin., 1978—87. Music tchr. West Clermont Local Sch. Dist., Batavia, Ohio, 1973—79; adj. prof. U. of Cin., 1988—93; dir., spectra riverside acad. Fitton Ctr. for Creative Arts, Hamilton, Ohio, 1995—. Pres. Ohio Alliance for Arts Edn., 2000—03; co-chair Ohio Arts Edn. Adv. Bd., 2000—02. Co-author: (handbook) Ohio Arts Education Assessment Project Handbook; developed internet graduate courses; contbr. articles. Pres. Sycamore HS Athletic Boosters, Cin., 1995—2000. Nominee Governor's Award for Arts Edn., 2000, 2001, 2002, 2003; recipient Art Adminstr. of the Yr., Ohio Art Edn. Assn., 2003, Arts partnership, Governor's Award, Ohio, 2002, Ohio BEST award, Model Arts Edn. Program, 2002, Model Arts Programming, Ohio Arts Edn. Adv. Com., 2002; Model Arts Demonstration and Dissemination grant, Dept. of Edn., 2000—, 21st Century Learning Cmty. grant, Ohio Dept. of Edn., 2003—, Profl. Devel. Arts Edn. grant, Ohio Arts Coun., Grad. Student scholarship, U. of Cin., 1979—86. Mem.: Ohio Art Edn. Assn. (assoc.), Nat. Assn. of Mid. Schools (assoc.), Americans for the Arts (assoc.), MENC- Ohio Music Edn. Assn. (assoc.), Nat. Art Edn. Assn. (assoc.), ASCD (assoc.), Ohio Alliance for Arts Edn. (assoc.), Phi Delta Kappa (assoc.). Avocations: sewing, golf, softball. Home: 9184 Hopewell Rd Cincinnati OH 45242 Office: Fitton Ctr for Creative Arts 101 South Monument St Hamilton OH 04501-2833 Personal E-mail: jsquay@aol.com. E-mail: jackie@fittoncenter.org.

QUAY, JOYCE CROSBY, writer; b. Dayton, Ohio, Aug. 8, 1928; d. Wilson Hill and Marianne (Mitchell) Crosby; m. John Grier Quay, Nov. 12, 1952; children: Peter Crosby, John Paul, Leslie Quay McMillan. Student, Simmons Coll., 1951, NYU, 1959—60. Ptnr. Quay Assocs., 1961—84. Author: Sam Walton, Founder of Wal-Mart (People to Know), 1994, Early Promise, Late Reward, 1995, (play) Double Destinies, 2000, Portrait of an Era, 2006; contbr. articles to popular publs. Mem. Rep. Nat. Com., 1990, 94-95. Presbyterian.

QUAYLE, MARILYN TUCKER, wife of former United States Vice President, lawyer; b. 1949; d. Warren S. and Mary Alice (Craig) Tucker; m. J. Danforth Quayle, Nov. 18, 1972; children: Tucker Danforth, Benjamin Eugene, Mary Corinne. BA in Polit. Sci., Purdue U., 1971; JD, Ind. U., 1974. Pvt. practice atty., Huntington, Ind., 1974—77; ptnr. Krieg, DeVault, Alexander & Capehart, Indpls., 1993—2001; pres. BTC Inc., Phoenix, 2001—. Author (with Nancy T. Northcott): Embrace the Serpent, 1992; author: The Campaign, 1996. Office: Quayle and Associates Ste 2010 7001 N Scottsdale Rd Scottsdale AZ 85253-3644*

QUEEN, EVELYN E. CRAWFORD, retired judge; b. Albany, N.Y., Apr. 6, 1945; d. Iris (Jackson) Crawford; m. Charles A. Queen, Mar. 6, 1971; children: Angelia, George. BS, Howard U., 1968, JD, 1975. Bar: N.Y. 1976, D.C. 1977, U.S. Ct. Appeals (D.C. cir.) 1977, U.S. Dist. Ct. (D.C. dist.) 1978, U.S. Supreme Ct. 1980. Park ranger Nat. Park Svc., Washington, 1968—69; pers. specialist NIH, Bethesda, Md., 1969—75; staff atty. Met. Life Ins. Co., N.Y.C., 1975—76; atty. advisor Maritime Adminstrn.-U.S., Washington, 1976—78; asst. U.S. atty.-D.C. Justice Dept., Washington, 1978—81; hearing commr. D.C. Superior Ct., Washington, 1981—86, judge, 1986—2001, ret., 2001. Adj. law prof. Howard U., 1988, Dave Clarke Sch. Law, U. D.C., 1993, 94. Contbr. chpt. to book. Recipient spl. achievement awards HEW, 1975, Trefoil award Hudson Valley Coun. Girl Scouts U.S.A., 1988, Spl. Achievement award Dept. Justice, 1981, Sigma Delta Tau Jud. Svc. award, 2001. Mem. Nat. Bar Assn., Washington Bar Assn. Office: DC Superior Ct 500 Indiana Ave NW Washington DC 20001-2191

QUEEN, JOYCE, elementary school educator; b. Cleve., Mar. 17, 1945; d. Wilbur and Mae Closterhouse; m. Robert Graham Queen, Mar. 17, 1973. BA in Biology, Macalester Coll., 1966; MS in Conservation and Natural Resource Mgmt., U. Mich., 1968. Cert. tchr. biol. and earth scis., Ohio. Exhibitor, docent, coord. Grand Rapids (Mich.) Pub. Mus., 1967-68; tchr., naturalist Rose Tree-Media (Pa.) Outdoor Edn., 1967, Willoughby-Eastlake (Ohio) Schs., 1969-70, Independence (Ohio) Schs., 1970-78; sci. tchr. Hathaway Brown Sch., Cleve., 1970—, chmn. dept. primary sci., 1998—. Designer Courtland Woods nature trail, 1986, designer sci. greenhouse, 1990-92; designer sci. classroom Wan Dyke Architects/Hathaway Brown Sch., 1990-92; designer, coord. Dampeer Primary sci. courtyard, 1993, Oliva Herb Garden, 1998, Colini Landscape Design/Hathaway Brown Sch., Shaker Hts., Ohio; ednl. adv. com. William G. Mather Vessel Mus., Cleve., 1992, Holden Arboretum, Kirtland, Ohio, 1992-97, Shaker Lakes Nature Ctr., 2005-06, Squire Valleyvue Farm, 2006; youth divsn. judge Cleve. Botanic Garden Show, 1999, 2000, 02, 05, NOAA Live From Antarctica, 2003; presenter in field. Contbr. articles to profl. jours. Design cons. Cleve. Bot. Garden and Floral Scape, 1998, judge, 1998, 2000, 02, 05; active Belize (Ctrl. Am.) Tchrs. Workshop, 1994; Sagamore Adirondack Great Camps Workshop, 2003; vol. PARI Radio Telescope, 2005; task force, agrl. edn. commn. HB Engring., 2005-06. Catalyst grant Hathaway Brown Sch. Gt. Lks. Curriculum, 1991; recipient Ohio Alliance for Environment, 1986, Presdl. Excellence in Elem. Sci. Tchg. award NSF, 1992, Sheldon Exemplary Equipment and Facilities award, 1992, Garden Club Am. Hull award, 2005; Great Lakes Lighthouse Keepers Assn. scholar, Marine Ecology scholar Marine Resources, Inc., 1989, Internat. Space Sta. Conf. scholar, 2000, Maine Salt Marsh Ecology Curriculum scholar, 2001, Calif. Coastal Wetlands and Desert Study scholar, 2002, Sagamore Inst. Adirondacks scholar, 2003, NASA Mars Mission Scholar, 2006, Hong Kong-Sci./Tech. China scholar, 2006. Mem. NSTA, Cleve. Regional Coun. Sci. Tchrs., Cleve. Natural Hist. Mus., Cleve. Zool. Park, Ind. Sch. Assn. Ctrl. Sts., Internat. Pen Pal Exch. Progam, Great Lakes Sci. Ctr. Holden Arboretum. Presbyterian. Avocations: orchardist, naturalist, horticulturist. Office: Hathaway Brown Sch 19600 N Park Blvd Cleveland OH 44122-1899

QUEENER, DANA BRANDON, elementary school educator; b. Appomatix, Va., Feb. 22, 1975; d. George Preston Smith and Eva Mae Wright-Smith; m. Benjamin Daniel Queener, May 18, 2002; children: Ashton, Brooke, Henry. BS in Elem. Edn., Tenn. Temple U., Chattanooga, 1997; MA, Tenn. Tech. U., Cookeville, 2001, EdS, 2002; postgrad., Capella U., Mpls., 2004—. Tchr. Scott County Bd. Edn., Huntsville, Tenn., 1997—. Coord. sci. fair Robbins Sch., Tenn., 2000—06, coord homecoming, 2000—06; ednl. assoc. Scott County Schs., Huntsbille, 2002—05. Treas. Scott County Schs., 2004—06, negotiator, 2002—05. Named Tchr. of Yr., Robbins, 2005—06. Mem.: Kiwanis, Beta Kappa Gamma. Baptist. Avocations: hiking, basketball, soccer, tennis. Office: Robbins Sch 355 Schoolhouse Rd Robbins TN 37852

QUEENEY, DEBORAH ANN, special education educator; b. Allentown, Pa., Feb. 4, 1949; d. William and Jane Swartz; m. Stephen Francis Queeney, Aug. 5, 1978; children: Nicole Ellen, Jessica Elaine. BSc, Kutztown State Coll., 1972; MEd, U. Pitts., 1975. Tchr. blind, multi-handicapped Lincoln Intermediate Unit 12, York, Pa., 1973—74; tchr. Monmouth Assn. Retarded Children, Shrewsbury, NJ, 1975—78; instrnl. assoc., tutor Amherst Sch. Dist. Regional Svcs. and Edn. Ctr., NH, 1988—91; spl. needs tchr. Milford (N.H.) Sch. Dist., 1991—. Named NH Tchr. of Yr., Assn. Retarded Citizens NH, 1994; recipient Monmouth County Tchr. of Yr., Monmouth Assn. Retarded Citizens, 1977, Excellence in Edn. award, Nat. Ctr. Low Incidence Disabilities, Denver, 2004. Mem.: NH Connections. Avocations: seashell collecting, sketching. Home: 7 Roberts Rd Amherst NH 03031 Office: Milford Mid Sch 33 Osgood Rd Milford NH 03055

QUEEN LATIFAH, (DANA ELAINE OWENS), actress, musician; b. Newark, Mar. 18, 1970; d. Lance and Rita Owens Student, Borough of Manhattan C.C. Co-founder, CEO Flavor Unit Entertainment, 1993—; spokeswoman Revlon. Actress: (films) House Party 2, 1991, Jungle Fever, 1991, Juice, 1992, Who's the Man, 1993, My Life, 1993, Set It Off, 1996, Hoodlum, 1997, The Wizard of Oz, 1998, Living Out Loud, 1998, Sphere, 1998, The Bone Collector, 1999, (voice only) Bringing Out the Dead, 1999, The Country Bears, 2002, Brown Sugar, 2002, (voice only) Pinocchio, 2002, Chicago, 2002 (Acad. Award Nomination for Best Supporting. Actress, 2003), Scary Movie 3, Barbershop 2: Back in Business, 2004, Taxi, 2004, Last Holiday, 2006, (voice only) Ice Age: The Meltdown, 2006, Stranger Than Fiction, 2006; actor, exec. prodr.: (films) Bringing Down the House, 2003; actor, prodr.: (films) The Cookout, 2004, Beauty Shop, 2005; actor: (TV movies) Sister in the Name of Rap, 1992, Mama Flora's Family, 1998, Living with the Dead, 2002, (voice only) Crash Nebula, 2004, The Muppets' Wonderful Wizard of Oz, 2005; (TV appearances) In Living Color, 1991, Fresh Prince of Bel Air, 1991, Living Single, 1993, Mad TV, 1997, Living Single, 1996, 1997, Spin City, 2001, Kung Faux, 2003, The Fairly OdParents, 2004, Eve, 2004; host, exec. prodr.: The Queen Latifah Show, 1999-2001; composer (films) New Jack City, 1991, White Man Can't Jump, 1992, Girls Town, 1996; singer (albums) All Hail the Queen, 1990, The Nature of Sista, 1991, X-tra Naked, 1992, Black Reign, 1994, Order In The Court, 1998, She's the Queen: A Collection of Hits, 2002, The Dana Owens Album, 2004; Author: Ladies First: Revelations of a Strong Woman, 1999, Queen of the Scene, 2006 Recipient Grammy award nomination, 1990, Soul Train Music award, 1995, Sammy Davis Jr. award, 1995, Entertainer of Yr. award, 1995, Grammy award for best rap solo performance, 1995, Arist of the Yr. award, Harvard Found., 2003; named Best New Artist, New Music Seminar, 1990, Best Female Rapper, Rolling Stone Readers' Poll, 1990, Woman of the Yr. Glamour mag., 2006; named one of 50 Most Influential African-Americans, Ebony Magazine 2004, named to Hollywood Walk of Fame, 2005. Achievements include becoming first hip-hop artist honored with star on the Hollywood Walk of Fame. Office: Flavor Unit Entertainment 155 Morgan St Jersey City NJ 07302-2932*

QUELER, EVE, conductor; b. NYC; Student, Mannes Coll. Music, CCNY. Music staff N.Y.C. Opera, 1958-70; assoc. condr. Ft. Wayne (Ind.) Philharm., 1970-71; founder, music dir. Opera Orch., N.Y., 1968; condr. Lake George Opera Festival, Glen Falls, N.Y., 1971-72, Oberlin (Ohio) Music Festival, 1972, Romantic Festival, Indpls., 1972, Mostly Mozart Festival, Lincoln Center, 1972, New Philharmonia, London, 1974, Teatro Liceu, Barcelona, 1974, 77, San Antonio Symphony, 1975; guest condr. Paris Radio Orch., 1972, P.R. Symphony Orch., 1975, 77, Mich. Chamber Orch., 1975, Phila. Orch., 1976, Montreal Symphony, 1977, Cleve. Orch., 1977 (Recipient Martha Baird Rockefeller Fund for Music award 1968, named Musician of Month Mus. Am. Mag. 1972), N.Y.C. Opera, 1978, Opera Las Palmas, 1978, Opera de Nice, 1979, Nat. Theatre of Prague, 1980, Opera Caracas, Venezuela, 1981, San Diego Opera, 1984, Australian Opera, Sydney, 1985, Kirov Opera, St. Petersburg, Russia, 1993, Hamburg Opera, Germany, 1994, Pretoria, South Africa, 1995, Hamilton, Ont., 1995, Hawaii Philharmonic, 1997, Hong Kong Sinfonietta, 1998, Hong Kong Philharmonic, 1999, Orch. dello Stato de Mexico, 1999-2002, Macau Festival, 2000, Festival Euro Mediteranneo, Italy, 2002; Opei Bonn, 1994-96; recording CBS Masterworks, 1974, 76, Hungaroton Records, 1982-85. Decorated Chevalier de l'ordre des Arts et des Lettres; named Woman in Music, N.Y.C., 2002; recipient Butterfly award, Licia Albanese-Puccini Foundation, 1995. Office: Opera Orch 239 W 72nd St Ste 2R New York NY 10023-2734

QUELL, MARGARET ANNE, special education educator; b. Akron, Ohio, Oct. 21, 1942; d. John A and Donna Geraldine (Castello) Quell. BS with hons., Kent (Ohio) State U., 1966; student Inst. des Etrangers, University de Besancon, France, 1962—63; MS in Edn., U. Akron, Ohio, 1976; Grad. studies, U. Aix-Marseille, Aix-en-Provence France, 1968—69; EdD U. Akron, 1982. Cert. Supt. Ariz., Prin. Ariz. Asst. prin., truant officer Wooster (Ohio) City Schs., 1976—80; prin., dir. edn. Apple Creek (Ohio) Devel. Ctr., 1980—81; asst. prin., athletic dir. Mt. Vernon (Ohio) City Schools, 1981—86; cons. child study Columbiana Bd. Edn., Lisbon, Ohio, 1986—87; dir. spl. edn., coord. instrn. Kenston Bd. Edn., Chagrin Falls, Ohio, 1987—90; dir. children's programs Lake County Bd. Mental Retardation/Developmental Disabilities, Mentor, Ohio, 1990—98; dir. spl. edn. Chinle (Ariz.) Unified Sch. Dist., Navajo Nation, 1998—. Mem. adv. bd. Knox County Children's Svcs/, Mt. Vernon, Ohio, 1981—86; exec. dir. Kenston Found., Chagrin Falls, Ohio, 1988—90; mem. exec. coun. Ariz. Sch. for Deaf and Blind, Tucson, 1998—. Author: (Book) Sex Equity in Educational Leadership, 1982; editor: (Book (Hershberger) Amish Life Through a Child's Eyes, 1985. Co-chair silent auction Deepwood Industries, Mentor, Ohio, 1998—98; Lifetime Fellow New Directions Shelter, Mt. Vernon, Ohio, 1984; mem. Proposition 203 Com., Chinle, Ariz., 2000—01. Recipient Innovative Counseling award, John G. Odgers Assn., 1978; fellow Kellogg Fellowship, Kellogg Found. Leadership Program, 1984; grantee Crossage Mentoring, Navajo Workforce Devel., 2000. Mem.: Coun. for Exceptional Children, Nat. Assn. Suprs. Spl. Edn. Programs. Avocations: equine dentistry, music, reading, running, travel. Office: Chinle Unified Sch Dist P O Box 587 Chinle AZ 86503 Business E-Mail: mquell@netscape.net.

QUERY, LOIS A., elementary school educator; b. Ft. Scott, Kans., Sept. 8, 1940; d. Lawrence B. and Ida M. Query. BS in Elem. Edn., Pitts. State U., Kans., 1962, MS in Elem. Edn., 1968. Cert. tchr. Kans. Dept. Edn., 2006. Elem. tchr. Sch. Dist. #1, Hickman Mills, Mo., 1963—65, Ft. Scott Christian Heights, Kans., 1966—73; reading specialist Sch. Dist. R-4, Cabool, Mo., 1974—75; tchr., prin. Tutu Ch. of God Elem. Sch., St. Thomas, Virgin Islands, 1976—81; early childhood tchr. Barton-Dade-Jaspe County Spl. Edn. Coop., Lockwood, Mo., 1989—91; reading specialist U.S.D. #246, Arma, Kans., 1992—2006. Master of ceremonies Title I Parent Meeting, Arma, 2002—06; coord. Young Author's Conf., Arma, 2004, Arma, 06. Treas. Harmony Hill Youth Camp, Fulton, Mo., 1960—68; activities dir. Harmony Hill Girls Camp, Fulton, 1968—75; twp. chmn. Am. Cancer Soc., Ft. Scott, 1974. Nominee Kans. Tchr. of Yr., U.S.D. #246, 2006; Jr. scholar, Pitts. State U., Kans., 1961, Sr. scholar, 1962. Mem.: Phi Kappa Phi, Kappa Delta Pi. Republican. Ch. Of God. Avocations: music, gardening, reading, sewing. Office: USD #246 201 N West Arma KS 66712

QUESADA-EMBID, MARY REGINA CHAMBERLAIN, library media specialist; b. Nov. 25, 1947; BA in English Lit., Cath. U. Am., 1969, MSLS, 1972. Libr. media specialist Charles County Pub. Schs., LaPlata, Md., 1972—, Dr. Thomas L. Higdon Elem. Sch., Newburg, Md., 1972—. Vol. St. Ignatius Cath. Ch., Chapel Point, Port Tobacco, Md., 1996—; mem. Dr. Thomas L. Higdon Elem. Sch. PTA, Newburg, Md., 1988—. Mem. So. Md. Reading Coun., Internat. Reading Assn., El Circulo Cultural Hispánico. Home: PO Box 1 Bel Alton MD 20611-0001

QUEST, KRISTINA KAY, art educator, small business owner; b. Fort Atkinson, Wis., Sept. 22, 1952; d. Duane and Kiwa (Kikuchi) Tessman; m. Michael Charles Quest, July 28, 1973; children: Jennifer, Eric, Sarah. BS Art Edn., U. Wis., 1992; student, U. Wis., Whitewater, 2002—, Madison Area Tech. Coll., Watertown, Wis., 2005—06. Lic. tchr., Wis. Substitute tchr., various cities, 1993—97, 1999—, Lake Mills Sch. Dist., 2003—04, Johnson Creek Pub. Schs., 2005—, St. Peter's Luth. Sch., Helenville, 2005—, tchr. art 7th and 8th grade, 1997; tchr. summer sch. Ft. Atkinson Sch. Dist., 1993—97; tchr. kindergarten, day care 1st Class Presch., before/after sch. day care at Prospect Elem., Lake Mills, Wis., 1997—99; owner Oriental Quest, Oshkosh, Wis., 2000—01, Back Acres Mobile Home Park, Oshkosh, 2000—; tchr. art Wis. Career Acad., Milw., 2002—03; sch. yr. vol. counselor Christian Alpha Life Resource Ctr., 2003—04. Past mem. Jefferson Arts Coun., bd. dirs., 1976-90; workshop fine arts fair judge Lakeside Luth. H.S., Lake Mills, 1991-92; art fair judge for Fort Fest, Fort Atkinson, Crafters, 1993; vol. mentor 7th/8th grades Wis. Career Acad., 2005 Author/illustrator: (book) Tiannamen Square, China's Dark Hours, 1987 (Juried Art Show 1993). Active, donor AIDS Wellness Auction, The Globe, Oshkosh, 1999; mentor future cities competition Milw. Sch. Engring., 2005. Recipient art award Wis. Regional Arts Program/Waukesha Creative Arts League, Madison, 1993, Best Exemplary Model award Wis. Career Acad., 2004-05, Best Mfg. Economy award, 2004-05, Peer award. Mem. Wis. Art Edn. Assn., Nat. Art Edn. Assn., Women in Arts Nat. Mus., Japanese Am. Pub. Mus., U. of Wis.-Whitewater Alumni Assn., Student Tchr.'s Assn. Lutheran. Avocations: watercolor, sketching, painting, Japanese sumi brushstroke painting, block printing. Office: 105 Aztalan St Lot O Johnson Creek WI 53038-9666 Office Phone: 910-699-8533. Personal E-mail: mkquest@tds.net.

QUICK, BARBARA, writer; b. LA, May 28, 1954; d. Harold Chairman and Edith Shepard Tritel; m. John Anthony Quick, Aug. 1, 1988 (separated); 1 child, Julian Anthony. AB in English, U. Calif., Santa Cruz, 1977. Editorial asst. U. Calif., Berkeley, 1978—82, from sr. writer to sr. adminstrv. mgr. Office of Pres., 1982—87; sr. writer, columnist MyPrimeTime.com, San Francisco, 2000. Grant writer, project historian Ctr. for Vulnerable Chilc, Children's Hosp., Oakland, Calif. Author: Northern Edge, 1990 (Discover award), Still Friends, 2000, Under Her Wing, 2000; co-author (with Liz McGrath): (children's bilingual literature) Even More, 2004; co-author: (with Matthew McKay) The Commitment Dialogues, 2005. Recipient Rsch. award, Stuart Found., San Francisco, 1996. Mem.: Authors Guild. Progressive. Avocations: cooking, gardening, foreign languages, travel, Afro-Brazilian dance.

QUICK, ELIZABETH L., lawyer; b. Izmir, Turkey, May 22, 1948; BA, Duke U., 1970; JD with honors, U. NC, 1974. Bar: NC 1974. Mem., trusts & estates Womble Carlyle Sandridge & Rice, Winston-Salem, NC, mem. mgmt.

com. Vis. lectr. U. NC Sch. Law, 1977. Mem. U. NC Law Review, 1973—74, co-author, editor NC Estate Adminstrn. Manual, 1984; contbr. articles to profl. jours. Bd. dir. Cannon Found., Concord, NC, Reynolda House, inc., Winston-Salem, NC; bd. trustee Salem Coll. & Acad., Winston-Salem, NC; mem. Winston-Salem Found. Com. Fellow Am. Coll. Trust and Estate Counsel (past chmn.); mem. ABA, NC Bar Assn. (pres. 1997-98), Forsyth County Bar Assn. (treas.), Order of Coif. Mailing: Womble Carlyle Sandridge & Rice PLLC PO Box 84 Winston Salem NC 27102 Office: Womble Carlyle Sandridge & Rice PLLC One West 4th St Winston Salem NC 27101 Office Phone: 336-721-3638. Office Fax: 336-733-8359. Business E-Mail: equick@wcsr.com.

QUICK, VALERIE ANNE, sonographer; b. Alta., Can., Feb. 14, 1952; came to U.S., 1953; d. Kenneth Conrad and Kathryn (Maller) Bjorge. Grad. high sch., Salinas, Calif. Registered adult and pediatric echocardiographer, abdomen, small parts and ob-gyn sonographer; registered cardiovasc. technician, registered diagnostic cardiac sonographer. Chief EKG technician Natividad Med. Ctr., Salinas, 1978-81, chief ultrasound dept., 1981-94, chief cardiac echo lab., 1995—. Fellow Am. Soc. Echocardiography (elected); mem. Am. Inst. Ultrasound in Medicine, Nat. Soc. for Cardiopulmonary Technicians, Soc. Pediat. ECHO, Soc. Diagnostic Med. Sonographers, Am. Heart Assn., Am. Registry Diagnostic Med. Sonographers. Avocations: reading, photography, travel. Home: 3069 Hermitage Rd Pebble Beach CA 93953-2810

QUIGLEY, DEBORAH HEWITT, adult education educator; d. Merritt Lambert and Gertrude Bush Hewitt; m. Edward James Quigley, III; children: Margaret Sarah, Edward James IV. AA, Coll. Marin, 1972; BA in History with honors, U. Calif., Davis, 1974; multiple subject credential, Dominican Coll., 1975. Clear subject credential with supplementary added math. Calif., 2005, cert. multiple subject tchg. credential with supplementary authorization for math. State of Calif. Commn. on Tchr. Credentialing, 2005. Tchr. Ladybug Presch., Kentfield, Calif., 1975—77; head tchr. Buttons & Bows Nursery Sch., San Rafael, Calif., 1977—78; parent edn. tchr. Nat. City (Calif.) Adult Sch., 1987—, child devel. tchr., 1996—2002, older adult tchr., 2002—. Mem. parent edn. Western Assn. Sch. and Colls. com. Sweetwater Union H.S. Dist., Chula Vista, Calif., 1997—98. Counselor, asst. leader, scout leader Boy Scouts and Girl Scouts, San Diego, 1986—2002; parent assn. mem., newsletter editor Marian Cath. H.S., San Diego, 1998—2002. Lt. j.g. USN, 1978—81. Named Parent Educator of Yr., San Diego Assn. Parenting Educators, 1995, Marian Cath. H.S., 2000, 2002. Mem.: NEA, Calif. Coun. for Adult Edn., Nat. Assn. for the Edn. Young Children. Avocations: reading, sewing, ice skating. Office: Nat City Adult Edn Ctr 517 Miles of Cars Way National City CA 91950 Personal E-mail: quigleydebbie@hotmail.com.

QUIGNEY, THERESA ANN, special education educator; b. East Cleveland, Ohio, June 19, 1952; d. James and Lenora Mary (McDonald) Q.; m. Joseph Carl Lang, July 23, 1983. BA, Notre Dame Coll., 1974; MEd, Cleve. State U., 1980; PhD, Kent State U., 1992. Cert. tchr. handicapped K-12; cert. ednl. adminstrv. specialist edn. of exceptional pupils; cert. ednl. supr.; cert. elem. prin.; cert. h.s. prin. cert. tchr. French K-12, Ohio. Spl. edn. tchr. Newbury (Ohio) Local Schs., 1974—80; county supr., specific learning disabilities and behavior handicaps Geauga County Bd. Edn., Chardon, Ohio, 1980—86, 1987—88; asst. prof. spl. edn. West Chester (Pa.) U., 1992—93; asst. prof. edn. Heidelberg Coll., Tiffin, Ohio, 1993—94; assoc. prof. spl. edn. Cleve. State U., 1994—, coord. spl. edn. program Coll. Edn., 2000—02. Ednl. rschr.; presenter in field. Contbr. articles to profl. jours., chapters to books. Vol. cons. Tchrs. for Action Rsch. South Euclid/Lyndhurst (Ohio) Sch. Dist., 1996—; past participant issues task force Ohio Coun. for Exceptional Children; presenter, participant Oxford Round Table, Oxford U., England; past bd. mem. Camp Sue Osborne, Lake County, Ohio; mem. steering com. State Improvement Grant (Edn.), 2000—02. Grantee Ohio State Supt.'s Task Force on Spl. Edn., 1997, Cleve. State U. Coll. Edn., 1997, Am. Sch. Counselor's Assn.; recipient achievement recognition Assn. for Children and Adults with Learning Disabilities, Ohio, 1980. Mem. CEC, ASCD, Am. Ednl. Rsch. Assn., Learning Disabilities Assn., Mid-We. Ednl. Rsch. Assn., Coun. for Learning Disabilities, Kappa Delta Pi, Phi Delta Kappa, Pi Lambda Theta. Avocations: travel, writing, reading, sketching. Office: Cleveland State Univ Euclid Ave at E 24th St Cleveland OH 44115 Business E-Mail: t.quigney@csuohio.edu.

QUILES, DOLORES, foreign language educator; b. Bronx, N.Y., Aug. 16, 1954; d. Nicolas Ramó Quiles Lopez and Dolores Cortez Quiles; m. David Allan Steres, June 26, 1956; children: Raquel Benedict, Alexander Quiles. AA in Liberal Arts, Columbia (Mo.) Coll., 1975; BA in Spanish, Calif. State U., Chico, 1978; MS in Edn., SUNY, New Paltz, 1991. Fgn. lang. instr. SpeakEasy Ctr., L.A., 1978-81; elem. sch. tchr. L.A. Unified Sch. Dist., 1981-82; health edn. coord. La Union Hispanica, Ctrl. Islip, N.Y., 1982-84; asst. libr. Rosendale (N.Y.) Libr., 1987-91; coll. instr. Ulster County C.C., Stone Ridge, N.Y., 1991—. Libr. trustee Rosendale Libr., 1991—. Scholastic grantee Columbia (Mo.) Coll., 1974. Mem. NOW (Washington pro-choice marcher 1989, 92), LWV, Planned Parenthood, Rondout Literary Soc. Avocation: reading.

QUILES, ESTHER, art educator; b. Bklyn., Nov. 1, 1957; children: John Rivera, Ashley Rivera. BA with honors, Sch. Visual Arts, N.Y.C., 1980; MS, Adelphi U., N.Y.C., 1985. Tchr. art Boys Club N.Y., N.Y.C., 1979—92, West Side H.S., N.Y.C., 1981—2004; tchr. for student tchrs. Sch. Visual Arts, N.Y.C., 1994—97. Vol. tchr. Lehigh U. STAR Acad., Bethlehem, Pa., 2005—06; advisor Aspira N.Y. S.I., 1996—98. Mem. Lation Civic Assn. Inc., S.I., NY, 1995—2006, Calvary Temple Ch., 2002—06; bd. dirs., mem. steering com. Lation Civic Assn. Inc., S.I., NY, 2004—05; art dir. Girls Club N.Y.; mem. sch. bd. Allentown Christian Sch., Pa., 2004—05. Named Outstanding Dedicated Art Tchr., Sch. Art League, Met. Mus. Art, 1997, Tchr. of Yr., N.Y. City Pub. Schs., 1991—93, N.Y.C. Pub. Schs., 1992; recipient Appreciation, Recognition, Contbn., and Cmty. Svc. award, Latino Civic Assn., Inc., Cert. Mem. Congress Recognition Svc. to the Cmty. award, 1998, Proclamation award, City Coun. N.Y., 1998, Recognition of Achievement, N.Y. State Assembly, 1998, Bd. of Edn. award, 8th Ann. Hostos award gala, 1998. Avocations: crafts, interior decorating, singing, horseback riding. Office: West Side HS 140 West 102 St New York NY 10025 Office Phone: 212-678-7300. Office Fax: 212-678-7380.

QUILLEN, TERESA, music educator; b. Haileah, Fla., Sept. 22, 1959; d. Thomas Monroe and Jackie Yvette Dixon; m. David Lawton Quillen; 1 child, Tori Jacquelin. MusB, U. Denver. Cert. tchr. Fla. Head music tchr. ASM Music Sch., Cooper City, Fla., 1982—96; music tchr. Collins Elem. Sch., Dania, Fla., 1996—. Office: Collins Elem Sch 1050 NW 2d St Dania FL 33004-2799

QUILTER, DEBORAH, writer, consultant, educator; b. San Diego, June 24, 1950; d. Edward Sinon and Mary Ann (Murray) Q. BA, San Francisco State U., 1973; postgrad., MIT, 1994. Cert. personal trainer Am. Coun. on Exercise. Consumer reporter, columnist San Francisco Bay Guardian, 1981-82; legal corr. Andrews Litigation Reporter, Westtown, Pa., 1982-85; travel and entertainment editor Better Health and Living, N.Y.C., 1985-87; columnist UDT News, N.Y.C., 1995, Computer Currents mag., N.Y.C., 1997—; contbg. editor Am. Cheerleader, N.Y.C., 1995-96; sr. editor Dance Spirit mag., N.Y.C., 1997—. Cons. and speaker, N.Y.C., 1994—; instr. Marymount Manhattan Coll., N.Y.C., 1996, fitness instr., personal trainer, 1997; faculty mem. Rocky Mt. Inst. Yoga and Agurveda. Co-author: Repetitive Strain Injury: A Computer User's Guide, 1994; contbg. writer: Total Health for Women, 1995; author: The Repetitive Strain Injury Recovery Book, 1998; founding editor in chief Pilates Style mag. Recipient Honorable Mention award for best non-daily newspaper story San Francisco Press Club, 1983. Mem. Authors Guild, Internat. Assn. Yoga Therapists. Avocations: ballet, theater, opera. Home: 140 Riverside Blvd # 1106 New York NY 10069 Office Phone: 212-769-8177.

QUIMBY, JANICE ANN, minister; b. Brunswick, Maine, May 6, 1944; d. Kenneth Blakney Libby and Charlotte Rachel Hill; m. Melvin David Cole (dec.); m. Herbert Leslie Quimby, May 22, 1993. BS in Music Edn., U. So. Maine, 1966. Music tchr. SAD 50, Thomaston, Maine, 1966—67, Bingor Pub. Schs., Okla., 1967—69; exec. program dir. YWCA, Bar Harbor, Maine, 1971—72; music tchr. Woolwich Pub. Schs., 1976—77; accounts receivable clk. L.L. Bean, Freeport, Maine, 1977—88; computer operator Maine Motor Transport, Augusta, 1988—91; pastor Sandy River Chapel, Starks, Maine, 1995—. With USCGR, 1973—87. Republican. Pentecostal Church. Avocations: music, knitting, writing, crocheting. Home and Office: RR1 Box 1401 Starks ME 04917

QUINCE, PEGGY A., judge; b. Norfolk, Va., Jan. 3, 1948; m. Fred L. Buckine; children: Peggy LaVerne, Laura LaVerne. BS in Zoology, Howard U., 1970; JD, Cath. U. of Am., 1975; LLD (hon.), Stetson U., 1999, St. Thomas U., 2004. Hearing officer Rental Accomodations Office, Washington; pvt. practice Norfolk, 1977-78, Bradenton, Fla., 1978-80; asst. atty. gen. criminal divsn. Atty. Gen.'s Office, 1980; apptd. 2d Dist. Ct. of Appeals, 1994-98; justice Fla. Supreme Ct., 1998—. Lectr. in field. Former asst. Sunday sch. tchr., former mem. #3 usher bd. New Hope Missionary Bapt. Ch.; active Jack and Jill of Am., Inc., Urban League, NAACP, Tampa Orgn. for Black Affairs. Recipient award Cath.'s Neighborhood Legal Svcs. Clinic. Mem. Nat. Bar Assn., Fla. Bar, Va. State Bar, George Edgecomb Bar Assn., Fla. Assn. Women Lawyers, Tallahassee Women Lawyers, William H. Stafford Inn. Ct., Alpha Kappa Alpha. Office: Fla Supreme Ct 500 S Duval St Tallahassee FL 32399-1925 Office Phone: 850-922-5624. Business E-Mail: Larryg@flcourts.org.

QUINDLEN, ANNA, journalist, writer; b. Phila., July 8, 1952; d. Robert V. and Prudence Quindlen; m. Gerald Krovatin; children: Quindlen Krovatin, Christopher Krovatin, Maria Krovatin. BA, Barnard Coll., 1974. Reporter New York Post, NYC, 1974-77; gen. assignment, city hall reporter New York Times, NYC, 1977-81, columnist About New York, 1981-83, dep. met. editor, 1983-85, columnist Life in the 30's syndicated, 1986-89, columnist Public and Private, 1990-94; full-time novelist, 1995—; columnist, "Last Word" Newsweek mag. Author: (novels) Object Lessons, 1991, One True Thing, 1994, Black and Blue, 1998, Blessings, 2000, Rise and Shine, 2006, (non-fiction) A Short Guide to a Happy Life, 2000, Being Perfect, 2005 (Publishers Weekly Bestseller non-fiction list, 2005), (children's books) The Tree That Came to Stay, 1992, Happily Ever After, 1997, (compilation) Living Out Loud, 1988, Thinking Out Loud, 1993, Loud and Clear, 2004; wrote text for: coffee table pictorial Naked Babies, 1996, Siblings, 1998. Bd. mem. Nightingale-Bamford Sch., NYC, NARAL Found. Named Woman of Yr., Glamour Mag., 1991; recipient Mike Berger award for disting. reporting, 1983, Pulitzer Prize for commentary, 1992. Mem.: Planned Parenthood Fedn. of Am. (bd. adv.), Author's Guild (coun. mem.), Bd Trustees, Barnard Coll. (chmn. 2003—). Achievements include being first writer to ever appear on fiction, nonfiction & self-help NewYork Times Best Seller lists. Office: c/o ICM 40 W 57th St New York NY 10019-4001*

QUIN-HARKIN, JANET ELIZABETH (RHYS BOWEN), writer; b. Bath, Somerset, Eng., Sept. 24, 1941; d. Frank Newcombe Lee, Margery Lee; m. John Quin-Harkin; children: Clare Broyles, Anne, Jane Hansen, Dominic. BA with honors, U. London, 1963. Author: (children's picture book) Peter Penny's Dance, 1976 (NY Times Best Book of Yr., ALA Book of Internat. Note, 1977), Heartbreak Cafe series novels, Sweet Dreams series, Wanted Date for Saturday Night, 1985 (Reader's Choice award, 1986), Madam Sarah, 1990, Fool's Gold, 1991, Amazing Grace, 1992; author: (as Rhys Bowen) (novels) Evans Above, 1997, Evan Help Us, 1998 (nominated--Barry award, best mystery novel, 1999), Evanly Choirs, 1999, Evan and Elle, 2000, Evan Can Wait, 2001, Murphy's Law, 2001 (Agatha award, 2002, Herodohis award, Reviewer's Choice award, 2002), Death of Riley, 2002 (nominated for Agatha award, nominated for Reviewer's Choice award), For the Love of Mike, 2003 (Anthony award, Bruce Alexander award), Evans Gate, 2004 (Edgar award nominee for best novel, 2005), In Like Flynn: A Molly Murphy Mystery, 2005, Evan Blessed: A Constable Evans Mystery, 2005, Oh Danny Boy, 2006, Evanly Bodies, 2006. Treas. Daughters of the Brit. Empire, San Rafael, 1998—2000. Recipient award for best screenplay, Marin Arts Coun., 1995. Mem.: Soc. Children's Bookwriters, Sisters in Crime, Mystery Writers Am. (regional pres. No. Calif. chpt. 2001). Roman Catholic. Avocations: travel, hiking, singing, tennis. Office: c/o Meg Ruley Jane Rotrosen Agy 318 E 51st St New York NY 10022 Office Phone: 212-593-4330. Personal E-mail: rhys@rhysbowen.com.*

QUINLAN, MARY LOU, former advertising executive, consultant; b. 1953; BA, St. Joseph's U., 1975; MBA, Fordham U., 1982; doctorate (hon.), Alvernia Coll., 1996. Dir. comm. St. Joseph's U., 1975-78; dir. advtg. Avon Products, 1978-89; sr. v.p. Ally & Gargan, 1989-91; exec. v.p., mng. ptnr. DDB Needham N.Y., 1991-94; pres N.W. Ayer & Ptnrs., NYC, 1994-99, CEO, 1995—99; vice chairperson The MacManus Group, NYC, 1999; founder, CEO Just Ask a Woman, NYC, 1999—. Bd. dirs. 1800flowers.com, 2002—; trustee, lectr. St. Joseph's U., 2004—. Author: Just Ask a Woman: Cracking the Code of What Woman Want and How They Buy, 2003, Time Off for Good Behavior: Hardworking Women Can Take a Break and Change Their Lives, 2005. Bd. dirs. St. Joseph's U., Phila. Named Advt. Woman of Yr., Advt. Women of N.Y., 1995. Mem.: N.Y. Women in Comm. (Matrix Award for Advt. 1997). Office: Just Ask a Woman 670 Broadway Ste 301 New York NY 10012

QUINLAN, PATRICIA, retired art educator; b. Coshocton, Ohio, Jan. 1, 1931; d. William J. Quinlan and Margaret E. Hickey. PhB, U. Detroit, 1958; MA, Wayne State U., 1960. Prof. Mercy Coll., Detroit, 1957-62; instr. Soc. Arts & Crafts, Detroit, 1960-65, Wayne State U., Detroit, 1962-65, from asst. prof. to assoc. prof., 1965-76, prof., 1976-94, prof. emeritus, 1994—. Prof. art U. N.C., Chapel Hill, summer 1971; demonstrator Detroit Inst. Arts. Exhbns. include Detroit Artists Market, 1964—, Wayne State U., 1978, 86, Mich. State U., 1976, Oakland U., 1979; group show Starkweather Art Ctr., Romeo, Mich., 2004. Recipient awards Mich. Artists, Detroit Inst. Arts, 1966, Pa. Acad., 1969, Butler Biannual, 1970, 76; grantee Mich. Coun. Art, 1987. Republican. Roman Catholic. Home: 29726 Guy St Southfield MI 48076-1886

QUINLIN, KELLY LEANN, physical education educator; b. St. Joseph, Mo., Feb. 3, 1978; d. Marvin Francis Archer and Sharon Eileen Adwell; m. Joseph Norman Quinlin, June 28, 2002; 1 child, Derek Marvin. BS in Biology, Psychology, N.W. Mo. State U., Maryville, 2000; MS in Athletic Tng., W.Va. U., Morgantown, 2003. Cert. ATC, LAT Mo. Grad. asst. athletic trainer W.Va. U./U. H.S., Morgantown, 2001—03; asst. athletic trainer N.W. Mo. State U., Maryville, 2003—. Examiner Bd. Cert., Omaha, 2002—; home study reviewer Nat. Athletic Trainers BOC, Omaha, 2005—. Lector St. Gregory's Cath. Ch., Maryville, Mo., 2005—. Mem.: Mo. Athletic Trainers Assn., Mid Am. Athletic Trainers' Assn., Nat. Athletic Trainers' Assn. Roman Catholic. Avocations: weightlifting, basketball, golf, running, shopping. Office: NW Mo State Univ 800 University Dr Maryville MO 64468 Office Phone: 660-562-1545. Office Fax: 660-562-1985. Business E-Mail: kellyq@nwmissouri.edu.

QUINN, ALICE FREEMAN, literature educator; BA, Manhattanville Coll., 1970; postgrad., NYU, 1971. Editor Alfred A. Knopf Pub. Firm, 1976—87; fiction editor The New Yorker, 1987—2001, poetry editor, 1987—. Adj. prof. poetry Columbia U., 1994—; lectr. in field. Contbr. articles to Artforum, The New Yorker, The Forward, and Poetry Ireland. Mem. jury Kingsley and Kate Tufts Poetry Awards, 1994—. Mem.: Poetry Soc. Am. (exec. dir. 2001—). Home: 720 Greenwich St #9F New York NY 10014 E-mail: alice_quinn@newyorker.com.

QUINN, CHRISTINE CALLAGHAN, councilwoman; b. Glen Cove, NY, July 25, 1966; d. Mary and Lawrence Quinn; life ptnr. Kim Catullo. BA in Urban Studies and Edn., Trinity Coll., Hartford, Conn., 1988. With Assn. Neighborhood and Housing Develop., 1989—91; chief staff Councilman Thomas K. Duane, 1992—96; exec. dir. NYC Gay and Lesbian Anti-Violence Project, 1996—98; city councilwoman Dist. 3 NYC, 1999—, council speaker, 2006—. Mem. NYC Police/Community Relations Task Force; del. DNC, 2000, mem. platform com., 04. Named one of Fifty Most Powerful Women in NYC, NY Post, Forty Under Forty, Gotham Mag. Avocation: reading. Office: Dist Office Christine Quinn 224 W 30th St Ste 1206 New York NY 10001*

QUINN, HELEN RHODA ARNOLD, physicist; b. Melbourne, Victoria, Australia, May 19, 1943; came to U.S. 1961; d. Ted Adamson and Helen Ruth (Down) Arnold; m. Daniel James Quinn, Oct. 8, 1966; children: Elizabeth Helen, James Arnold. BS in Physics, Stanford U., 1963, MS in Physics, 1964, PhD in Physics, 1967; DSc (hon.), Notre Dame U., 2002, U. Melbourne, 2005. Rsch. assoc. Stanford Linear Accelerator Ctr., 1967—68, 1978—79, mem. permanent sci. staff, 1979—2003, edn. coord., 1988—93, asst. to dir. edn. and pub. outreach, 1998—2003, prof. physics, 2003—; hon. rsch. fellow Harvard U., 1971, rsch. fellow, 1971—72, asst. prof. physics, 1972—76, assoc. prof. physics, 1976—77. Guest scientist (non German postdoctoral rschr.) Deutsches Elektronen Sychrotron, Hamburg, 1968—70; vis. assoc. prof. Stanford U., 1976—78; vis. scientist Stanford Linear Accelerator Ctr., 1977—78. Contbr. articles to profl. jours. Pres. Contemporary Physics Edn. Project, Portola Valley, Calif., 1989-95; vol., chair Town of Portola Valley Trails Com., 1988-98; pres. Am. Phys. Soc., 2004. Decorated Hon. officer Order of Australia, 2005; recipient DIRAC medal Internat. Ctr. Theoretical Physics, Trieste, Italy, 2000; fellow Alfred Sloan Found., 1975-79. Fellow AAAS, Am. Phys. Soc. (pres. 2004); mem. Nat. Acad. Sci. Avocations: hiking, native plants. Business E-Mail: quinn@slac.stanford.edu.

QUINN, HOLLI JO BARDO, social worker, educator, librarian; b. Muncy, Pa., Jan. 7, 1961; d. Emerson David and Beverly Bair Bardo; m. Joel Paul Quinn, Oct. 15, 1983; children: Tara Jo, Austin Paul. BA in Comm., Shippensburg U., 1982; MS in Bible, Phila. Bibl. U., 1997; MA in Religion, Temple U., 1999, postgrad. in Feminist Studies, 2000—01. Mktg. asst. Lower Bucks Cablevision, Levittown, Pa., 1984—87; English composition instr. Temple U., Phila., 1998, Bible instr., 1999; case worker Bucks County Head Start, Bensalem, Pa., 2001—04; prof. humanities Strayer U., Trevose, Pa., 2003—, mgr. Learning Resource Ctr., 2005—06; career svcs. advisor Sunford Brown Inst., Trevose, Pa., 2006—. Impact study rep. Bucks County Head Start, Morrisville, Pa., 2002—04. Author: Sacrifical Offerings, 1989, Fishing, 1995. Vol. A Woman's Place, Doylestown, Pa., 2002; spkr. Women's Ink, Phila., 1989; campaign chair United Way Bucks County Head Start, Bensalem, Pa., 2002, mem. family partnership planning Morrisville, Pa., 2003; active Safety Coun., Bensalem, 2003—04; founding mem. Nat. Campaign for Tolerance, Montgomery, Ala., 2004—06; mem. leadership coun. So. Poverty Law Ctr., Montgomery, 2005—06. Named Wall of Tolerance honoree, So. Poverty Law Ctr., Montgomery, 2005—06; recipient Discovery award in fiction, Bucks County C.C., 1989, Senatorial citation, Pa. Senate, 1992. Republican. Avocations: gardening, landscaping, writing, reading, swimming. Home: 2224 Bent Rd Langhorne PA 19053 Office: Brown Inst 3600 Horison Blvd Ste GL-1 Trevose PA 19053 Office Phone: 215-436-6942.

QUINN, JANE BRYANT, journalist, writer; b. Niagara Falls, NY, Feb. 5, 1939; d. Frank Leonard and Ada (Laurie) Bryant; m. David Conrad Quinn, June 10, 1967; children: Matthew Alexander, Justin Bryant. BA magna cum laude, Middlebury Coll., 1960. Assoc. editor Insiders Newsletter, NYC, 1962-65, co-editor, 1966-67; sr. editor Cowles Book Co., NYC, 1968; editor-in-chief Bus. Week Letter, NYC, 1969-73, gen. mgr., 1973-74; syndicated fin. columnist Wash. Post Writers Group, 1974—2001; contbr. fin. column to Women's Day mag., 1974-95, Good Housekeeping, 1995—; contbr. NBC News and Info. Service, 1976-77; bus. corr. WCBS-TV, NYC, 1979, CBS-TV News, 1980-87, ABC-TV Home Show, 1991-93; contbg. editor Newsweek mag., 1978. Host PBS personal fin. series Take Charge!, 1988; dir. bd. dirs. Bloomberg LP. Author: Everyone's Money Book, 1979, 2d edit., 1980, Making the Most of Your Money, 1991, 2d edit., 1997, A Hole in the Market, 1994, Smart and Simple Financial Strategies for Busy People, 2006; contbr. (software program) Quicken Financial Planner, 1995. Dean's coun. Harvard Sch. Pub. Health; mem. bd. advisors Jerome Levy Econs. Inst. Bard Coll. Named one of 25 Most Influential Women in US, World Almanac; recipient Emmy award for outstanding coverage fin. on TV, Gerald Loeb award for lifetime achievement and disting. bus. and fin. journalism, John Hancock award for excellence in bus. and fin. journalism, Janus award for excellence in TV and bus. reporting, Journalism award for excellence in personal fin. reporting, ICI-Am. U., three-time winner Nat. Press Club award for consumer journalism, two-time winner Nat. Headliner award, honored for outstanding consumer media svc., Consumer Fedn. Am. Mem. Phi Beta Kappa. Office: Newsweek Inc 251 W 57th St New York NY 10019-1802

QUINN, KATHERINE SARAH, psychologist; d. George and Esther Blank; m. Ed Quinn (div. 1994); children: Adam(dec.), Molly Quinn Panepinto. BA in Psychology, U. Nev., 1982, MA in Psychology, 1987; PhD in Psychology (hon.), Calif. Sch. Profl. Psychology, 1999. Intern Children's Behavioral Svcs., Las Vegas, 1980—83, child devel. specialist, 1984—85; rsch. devel. coord. San Diego County Mental Health, 1988—97; intern Southwood Hosp., San Diego, 1991—92; therapist Child Sexual Abuse Treatment Ctr., San Diego, 1992—93; post-doctoral intern Neuropsychological Assessment and Psychotherapy, Solana Beach, Calif., 1999—2002; pvt. practice Solana Beach, 2002—04, Del Mar, Calif., 2004—. Mem.: APA, San Diego Psychol. Assn. Roman Catholic. Avocations: reading, music, opera, theater, hiking. Home: 721 Genter St La Jolla CA 92037 Office: 240 9th St Del Mar CA 92014 Office Phone: 858-720-0682. Business E-Mail: quinnphd@san.rr.com.

QUINN, MAUREEN E., ambassador; b. Spring Lake, N.J. Vice consul, gen. svcs. officer U.S. Consulate Gen., Karachi, Pakistan, 1982—84; econ. officer, comml. attaché Am. Embassy Conakry, Guinea, 1984—86; with Western Hemisphere's Bur. Regional Econ. Affairs, 1986—88, Econ. Bur. Office Internat. Devel. Fin., 1988—90; Pearson fellow U.S. Ho. Reps., Washington, 1990—91; econ. counselor Am. Embassy Dept. of State, Panama, 1991—94, exec. asst., spl. asst. to undersec. for econ., bus. and agrl. affairs, 1994—97, dep. exec. sec., 1997—98, dep. chief of mission Am. Embassy Rabat, Morocco, 1998—2001, U.S. amb. to Qatar, 2001—.

QUINN, PATRICIA K., literary agent; b. Chico, Calif. d. Donald Joseph and Kathleen (Alexander) Q. BA, Bennington Coll.; MFA in Drama, Yale U. Prodr., devel. exec. various Off-Broadway and regional theatres, 1976-84; devel. cons. Sundance Film Inst., Utah, 1983—85; theatrical agt. I.C.M., LA, 1985-90; v.p. comedy devel. Warner Bros. TV, Burbank, Calif., 1990-92; lit. and packaging agt. Met. Talent Agy., LA, 1995—2000. Instr. UCLA Ext., 1995—; spkr., lectr. Nat. Assn. of TV Programming Execs., Fla. Bar, NATAS, Media Xchange (Internat.); mem. TV com. Brit. Acad. Film and TV Arts, 2002-; prof. reps. peer group com. NATAS, 2002-04. Founding mem. N.Y. Theatre Workshop, N.Y.C., 1980—86. Mem.: Women in Film (v.p. 1995—2001, bd. dirs. 2005—). Office: 330 S Spalding Dr #403 Beverly Hills CA 90212 Office Phone: 310-656-5141. E-mail: p_quinn@sbcglobal.net.

QUINN, PEGGY ARMSTRONG, elementary school educator, writer; b. Gorman, Tex., Nov. 12, 1943; d. Lowell Rogers and Alice Humphrey Armstrong; m. Robert Michael Quinn, Aug. 12, 1979; 2 children. BS, Tex. Woman's U., 1965; MEd, San Diego State U., 1976. Cert. elem. tchr. Calif. Dept. Educator, 1975, reading specialist Calif. Dept. Educator, 1975, kindergarten tchr. Calif. Dept. Educator, 1975, elem. tchr. Tex. Dept. Educator, 1981, kindergarten tchr. Tex. Dept. Educator, 1981, ESL tchr. Tex. Dept. Educator, 2001, Learning Resource Specialist Tex. Dept. Educator, 2001. Kindergarten tchr. North Hanover Schs., Wrightstown, N.J., 1966—69; elem. tchr., reading specialist San Diego City Schs., 1970—80; elem. tchr. Garland ISD, Tex., 1986—. Mem. AFT/CIO Educators Group, Dallas, 1987—. Author: (articles) Writer's Digest, 1984 (contest winner), Antique Weekly, 1985. Mem., supporter Weaver PTA, Garland, 1982—; vol. pianist Western Hills Nursing Home, Denton, Tex., 1980—, Comanche, Tex., 2004—05; supporter Dem. Party, Dallas, 2005. Democrat. Baptist. Avocations: music, writing. Home: 8602 Liberty Grove Rd Rowlett TX 75089 Office: Weaver Elem Sch 805 Pleasant Valley Rd Garland TX 75040 Office Phone: 972-494-8311. E-mail: pegqn@yahoo.com.

QUINN, YVONNE SUSAN, lawyer; b. Spring Valley, Ill., May 13, 1951; d. Robert Leslie and Shirley Eilene (Morse) Quinn. BA, U. Ill., 1973; JD, U. Mich., 1976, MA in Econs., 1977. Bar: NY 1978, US Dist. Ct. (ea. and so. dists.) NY 1978,US Ct. Appeals (3d, 5th, 9th, 10th and DC cirs.) 1982, US Ct. Appeals (2d cir.) 1992, US Ct. Appeals (4th cir.) 1994, US Supreme Ct. 1982. Assoc. Cravath, Swaine & Moore, NYC, 1977-80, Sullivan & Cromwell, NYC, 1980-84, ptnr. litig., 1984—, and coord. antitrust practice area. Mem. ABA, Assn. of Bar of City of NY Office: Sullivan & Cromwell 125 Broad St New York NY 10004-2489 Office Phone: 212-558-3736. Office Fax: 212-558-3588. Business E-Mail: quinny@sullcrom.com.

QUIÑONES KEBER, ELOISE, art historian, educator; b. LA; d. Rudy Jr. and Margaret Q. BA, Immaculate Heart Coll., 1966; MA, UCLA, 1967, Columbia U., 1979, PhD, 1984. Lectr. Columbia U., N.Y.C., 1984-86; prof. art history Baruch Coll., The Grad. Ctr., CUNY, 1986—. Author: Codex Telleriano Remensis: Ritual, Divination, and History in a Pictorial Aztec Manuscript, 1995 (Getty Grant Program Publ. Subvention award, 1992); co-author: Art of Aztec Mexico: Treasures of Tenochtitlan, 1983; editor: Chipping Away on Earth: Studies in Prehispanic and Colonial Mexico in Honor of Arthur J.O. Anderson and Charles E. Dibble, 1995, In Chalchihuitl in Quetzalli: Mesoamerican Studies in Honor of Doris Heyden, 2000, Representing Aztec Ritual: Performance, Text, and Image in the Work of Sahaqún, 2002; co-editor: The Work of Bernardino de Sahagun: Pioneed Ethnographer of 16th-Century Aztec Mexico, 1988, Mixteca-Puebla: Discoveries and Research in Mesoamerican Archaeology and Art, 1994; contbr. articles to profl. jours. Mellon postdoctoral fellow Columbia U., 1984-86, fellow Ford Found./NRC, 1986-87, Am. Coun. of Learned Socs. fellow, 1987-88, 93-94, grantee, 1985, 95, NEH fellow, 1993-94, grantee, 1986, 91; grantee Am. Philos. Soc., 1986; fellow Guggenheim Found., 1998; recipient Ralph Waldo Emerson award Phi Beta Kappa Soc., 1996. Mem. Coll. Art Assn., Assn. Latin Am. Art, Am. Soc. for Ethnohistory. Office: CUNY Grad Ctr Art History Program 365 Fifth Ave New York NY 10016 also: CUNY Baruch Coll Dept Fine and Performing Arts 1 Bernard Baruch Way New York NY 10010-1703 Business E-Mail: EQuinones-Keber@gc.cuny.edu. E-mail: equinones@mindspring.com.

QUINT, DAWN DUNAWAY, personnel executive; b. Watertown, NY, Sept. 25, 1955; d. Gordon Paul and Grovene Marie (Champion) Dunaway; 1 child, Gerard Jr. AAS, Jefferson C.C., Watertown, 1975; Bachelor of Gen. Studies, Ea. Conn. State U., 2002. Co-founder, bus. mgr. N.E. Placement Svcs., Eastford, Conn., 1986, exec. dir., 1988—; prin., owner Helping Hands Cleaning Svc., Andover, Conn., 1992—; shelter facilitator United Svcs. Domestic Violence Program, 2003; shelter mgr. Network Against Domestic Abuse of North Central Conn., 2005. Active Lesbian Expressions, U. Conn., Pflag, Coventry, 1987—. Named Continuing Edn. scholar Ea. Conn. State U., 1999, Francisco Martinez Cancer scholar 2000. Mem. Omicron Delta Kappa. Home: 10 Birch Dr Andover CT 06232-1202

QUINTANA-ALLENSON, ANA M., media specialist; b. Chicago, Ill., Oct. 16, 1967; d. Sergio Antonio (Tony) Quintana and Ana Ilia Gonzalez; m. James M. Allenson, May 5, 2006. BA in Comm. cum laude, Loyola U. Chgo., 1989. Cert. Media Rels. Cmty. Media Workshop, 2001, U. of S.C., 2001. Claims rep. Social Security Adminstrn., Chgo., 1993—99, mgmt. support specialist, 2000—01, pub. affairs specialist, 2001—02, acting asst. dist. mgr., 2003, exec. staff asst., 2003—. President-Hispanic task force Gift of Hope Organ and Tissue Donation Network, Elmhurst, Ill., 2002—03. Mem.: Nat. Assn. Hispanic Journalists (mem. Chgo. region Hispanic action com. 1995—, Ill. vice chair 2003—04). D-Liberal. Avocations: photography, reading, drawing, art shows. Office Phone: 312-575-4109. E-mail: ana.quintana-allenson@ssa.gov.

QUIRION, RAMONA SHAW, elementary school educator; b. Skowhegan, Maine, Aug. 9, 1960; d. Patricia Shaw Johnson and Maurice Rueban Shaw; m. Owen Scott Quirion, May 21, 1982. BS in Edn., U. Maine, Farmington, 1982; MS in Edn., SUNY, Binghamton, 1988. Cert. tchr. NY. Tchr. Binghamton City Schs., NY, 1984—2005, Niskayuna Ctrl. Sch. Dist., NY, 2005—. Thanksgiving day dinner coord. Bingnhamton City Schs., NY, 1997—2005. Mem.: ASCD (assoc.). Roman Catholic. Avocations: fitness, wellness, cooking. Office: Niskayuna Ctrl Sch Dist 1620 Balltown Rd Niskayuna NY 12309 Office Phone: 518-862-2511.

QUIRK, KATHLEEN L., mining executive; BS in Acctg., La. State U. With Mobil Oil Corp., Dallas; from mem. staff to treas. Freeport-McMoRan Copper & Gold Inc., New Orleans, 1989—2000, treas., 2000—, sr. v.p., 2003—, CFO, 2003—.

QUIROGA, ALICIA ESPINOSA, physiatrist; b. Manila; d. Eugenio Rillo and Felisa Padiernos (Espinosa) Q. BS, U. Philippines, 1969, MD, 1973. Rotating intern Philippine Gen. Hosp., Manila, 1973-74, resident dept. pediatrics, 1975-77; resident dept. phys. medicine and rehab. U. Md., Balt., 1977-80; fellow in pediatrics & rehab. Children's Hosp. Nat. Med. Ctr., Washington, 1980-81; fellow George Washington U. Hosp., Washington, 1980-81; attending physiatrist, asst. prof. U. Md. Sch. Medicine, Balt., 1981-86; attending physiatrist Sinai Hosp. of Balt., 1986-87; chief rehab. medicine svc. VA Med. Ctr., Augusta, Ga., 1987—. Fellow Am. Acad. Phys. Medicine and Rehab.; mem. Assn. Acad. Physiatrists. also: Macon Rehab Ctr 3330 Northside Dr Macon GA 31210-2559 Home: 11899 Marla Ln Seminole FL 33772-2219

QUISENBERRY, NANCY LOU, academic administrator, educator; b. Washington, Ind., Jan. 29, 1938; d. Joseph Franklin and Maud Helen (Fitch) Forbes; m. James D. Quisenberry, Feb. 6, 1960; 1 child, James Paul. BS in Home Econs., Ind. State Tchrs. Coll., 1960, MS in Home Econs., 1962; EdD, Ind. U., 1971. Cert. tchr. Ind. Home economics tchr. Honey Creek High Sch., Terre Haute, Ind., 1961-62; third grade tchr. Indpls. Pub. Sch., 1962-64; sustitute tchr. Dep. of Def., Baumholder, Fed. Republic Germany, 1964-65; first grade tchr. Wayne Twp. Schs., Indpls., 1966-67; assoc. faculty lang. arts Ind. U.-Purdue U., Indpls., spring 1970; prof. curriculum and instruction So. Ill. U., Carbondale, 1971—98, assoc. dean Coll. of Edn., 1976-96, interim dean, 1996-98; exec. dir. Orpheum Children's Sci. Mus., Champaign, Ill., 2004—. Cons. U. N.C., Durham, 1977, Ministry Edn., Bangkok, 1980, Bangkok, 84, DePaul U., 1990, Ill. State U., 2002, U. Miss., 2001, Loyola U., 2002, Gov.'s State U., 2002; dir. tech. and tng. assistance grant Head Stard-OCD, Carbondale, 1972—74, Cameroon project USAID, Carbondale, 1984—86; mem. Ill. State Tchr. Cert. Bd., 1981—84, 1984—87. Co-author: Early Childhood Education Programs: Developmental Objectives and Their Use, 1975, Play as Development, 1978, Educators Healing Racism, 1999, Racism in the Classroom: Case Studies, 2002. Bd. dirs. Jackson County YMCA, 1988; chair candidacy com. Ctrl. So. Ill. Synod Evang. Luth. Ch. Am., Springfield, 1987—90, sec. multisynodical com. Chgo., 1987—90, synod coun., 1992—95; pres. Epiphany Luth. Ch. Coun., Carbondale, 1984—85, 1989—92, 1994—96. Recipient Dare To Be Great award, Ill. Women Adminstrs. and So. Ill. Region, 1989, Woman of Distinction award, So. Ill. U., 1992; grantee, Bur. Educationally Handicapped, 1979—82, 1990—95. Mem.: World Orgn. for Pre-sch. Edn. (U.S. nat. com., treas. 1997—99, chmn. strategic planning commn. 1999—2002, webmaster 2000—), Assn. Tchr. Educators (chair com. racism from a healing perspective 1995—98), Ill. Assn. Colls. for Tchr. Edn. (pres. 1984—86), Am. Assn. Colls. for Tchr. Edn. (bd. dirs. 1986—88, chair adv. coun. state reps. 1987—88, bd. dirs. 1991—94), Nat. Coun. for Accreditation Tchr. Edn. (bd. examiners 1987—98, new profl. tchr. project elem. edn. stds. drafting com. 1996—98, transition team elem. stds. 1998—2000, chair Rubics devel. com. 2001, exec. bd. 2002—, chair Coun. Profl. Preparation of Educators 2003—), Assn. Childhood Edn. Internat. (chair tchr. edn. com. 1989—93, folio rev. coord. elem. edn. 1989—2001, sec.-treas. 1996—, pres.-elect 1998—2000, pres. 2001—03, past pres. 2003—04, folio rev. coord. elem. edn. 2004—), Internat. Coun. on Edn. for Tchg. (N.Am. v.p. 1992—94, pres.-elect 1997—2000, pres. 2000—02, bd. dirs.), Rotary (pres. Urbana chpt. 2005—). Avocations: gardening, flute, sewing, walking, organ. Home: 1713 E Mumford Dr Urbana IL 61802-8605 Office: So Ill U Coll Edn Carbondale IL 62901-4624 Business E-Mail: nancyq@siu.edu.

QUISGARD, LIZ WHITNEY, artist, sculptor; b. Phila., Oct. 23, 1929; d. Kenneth E. and Elizabeth (Warwick) Whitney; children: Kristin, Berit. Grad. night sch., Md. Inst. Coll. Art, 1947, grad. day sch., 1949; student, Johns Hopkins U., 1952—58; pupil of, Morris Louis, 1958-60; BFA in Painting, Md. Inst., 1966, MFA in Sculpture, 1966. Pvt. tchr. painting, Balt., 1955-65. Tchr. Balt. Hebrew Congregation, 1962-80; mem. faculty Md. Inst. Coll. Art, 1965-76, Goucher Coll., 1966-68, Balt. Jewish Community Ctr., 1974-78, Villa Julie Coll., Stevenson, Md., 1978-80; art critic Balt. Sun, 1969-71, Craft Horizons, 1969-72, The Paper, 1971-72; designer prodns. Center Stage, Goucher Coll., Johns Hopkins U.; lectr. in Md., Va., W.Va., Pa., Ark., Ohio, NY, NJ One-woman exhbns. include Jefferson Place Gallery, Washington, 1960, Emmerich Gallery, NYC, 1962, Goucher Coll., Balt., 1966, U. Md., 1969, Gallery, 707, Los Angeles, 1974, Arts and Sci. Center, Nashua, NH, 1975, Mechanic Gallery, Balt., 1978, Marymount Manhatten Coll., NYC, 1983, Tiffany's windows, NYC, 1984, Starkman Gallery, NYC, 1984, Fordham U., NYC, 1985, Henri Gallery, Washington, 1987, Artemisia Gallery, Chgo., 1987, Savannah Coll. Art and Design, Ga., 1987, Life of Maryland Gallery, Balt., 1988, Franz Bader Gallery, Washington, 1989, Fairleigh Dickinson U., NJ, 1990, Herr-Chambliss Gallery, Hot Springs, Ark., 1990, Huntington Coll., Ind., 1991, Bergdorf Goodman Windows, 1991, Coll. of New Rochelle, NY, 1992, Broadway windows, NYC, 1992, Nexus Found., Phila., 1993, Carnegie Arts Ctr., Leavenworth, Kans., 1994, Asheville Mus., NC, 1995; group exhbns. include, Balt. Mus., 1951-53, 58, Corcoran Gallery Area Show, 1956, 64, Corcoran Biennial Show, 1963, Peale Mus., Balt., 1947, 56, Butler Inst. Am. Art, Youngstown, Ohio, 1957, Provincetown Art Assn., Mass., 1955, Pa. Acad. Am. Art ann., 1964, Chgo. Art Inst., 1965, Gallery 707, 1973, S. Houston St. Gallery, NYC, 1974, Balt. Mus. travelling show, 1978, Mus. of Hudson Highlands, Cornwall, NY, 1983; represented in permanent collections U. Ariz., U. Md., U. Balt., Johns Hopkins U., Lever House, NYC, Center Club, Balt., Libyan Mission to UN, Englewood, NJ, Datalogix Corp., Valhalla, NY, Gt. Northern Nekoosa Corp., Norwalk, Conn., Quality Inns, Newark, Can. Imperial Bank of Commerce, NYC, Rosenberg Diamond Co., NYC, Marsh, Inc., Indpls., Kirkpatrick and Lockhart, Pitts., Fordham U., NYC, Atlantic Realty, Atlanta, Miss. Mus. Art, Jackson, St. Joseph Health Ctr., Hot Springs, Ark., Dermatology Assocs., Pitts., Scudder, Stevens & Clark, Boston, also pvt. collections; executed mural William Fell Elem. Sch., Balt., 1980, Urban Wall, Atlanta, 1990, floor painting Vet.'s Stadium, Phila., 1992, mural Med. Coll. Va., Richmond, 1994. Recipient Best in Show award Loyola Coll. Invitational, Balt., 1966, Florsheim Purchase Grant, 1991; scholar Md. Inst., 1947-49; Rinehart fellow in sculpture, 1964-66. Address: 113 Elizabeth St #B New York NY 10013 Office Phone: 212-571-4283.

QUIST, JEANETTE FITZGERALD, television production educator, choreographer; b. Provo, Utah, July 4, 1948; d. Sherman Kirkham and Bula Janet (Anderson) Fitzgerald; m. G. Steven Quist; children: Ryan, Amy, Michelle, Jeremy. Student, U. Redlands, Calif., 1970; BA, Brigham Young U., 1971; postgrad., Calif. State U., Riverside, 1972, Calif. State U., San Bernardino, 1973. Host, co-producer children's show PBS Sta. KBYU-TV, Provo, 1968-69; buyer ready to wear J.C. Penney & Co., Redlands, 1969-71; tchr. spl. reading program Fontana (Calif.) Elem. Sch. Dist., 1971-73; owner, choreographer Jeanette Quist Creative Dance, Tri Cities, Wash., 1975-79; owner, tchr. Dance Studio, Gridley, Calif., 1979-81; producer, instr. Butte Coll., Oroville, Calif., 1986—2006. Asst. producer Kate Knight Prodn. Co., Chico, Calif., 1987; video producer Gridley Sch. Dist., 1987-88; cmty. svcs. cons. Biggs-Gridley Meml. Hosp., 1999—; presenter in field. Prodr., editor promotional video Police Acad., 1986, commls. for Butte Coll., 1987—; prodr., dir. telecourse Interior Designer, 1988—; prodr., hostess TV talk shows Crossroads, 1988—, NVCA Today, BCTV Forum, 1991—; prodr. (video), Intro to Telecommunications, 1994-98, Butte Environ. Coun., 1995, City of Chico, 1995, Small Bus. Devel. Ctr., 1996, Work Tng. Ctr., 1996, Project Maestros, 1996, Sentencing Video for the Fed. Defs. Office, Ea. Dist. of Calif., 1998; choreographer Kaleidoscope, 1988, South Pacific, 1989, Fantasticks, 1990, Amahl and the Night Visitors, 1990, An Evening of Song and Dance, Butte Coll., 1991, Kiss Me Kate, Butte Coll., 1992, Hello Dolly, Chico Stake, 1992, Tumbleweeds, Butte Theatre, 1994, Joseph and the Amazing Technicolor Dreamcoat, Gridley HS, 1999, Butte Coll. Fine Arts Dept., 2005 State judge Miss. Am. Contest, Provo, 1968; 1st v.p. Friends of Libr., Gridley, 1988; chmn. Regional Fine Arts Festival Tri Cities, 1978; v.p. Gridley High Sch. Parent Club, 1990; chmn. 3D Expo Fine Arts Festival for Oroville, Gridley, and Butte Coll., 1991; cmty. svcs. cons. Biggs-Gridley Meml. Hosp., 1999—, organizer 50th anniversary celebration, 2000. Recipient Acad. Excellence award Butte Coll., 1993-94, What Would We Do Without You award, Butte Coll., 1998; named Assoc. Students Woman of Yr. Instr., Butte Coll., 2004-05; Mask club scholar Brigham Young U., 1967; Project Maestro grantee, 1994, Svc. Learning grantee Butte Coll., 2002. Mem. AAUW (membership v.p. 1989-91, pres. 1997-99, com. for gender equity for Gridley br., Tech Trek chmn. Gridley br. 2001—), Butte County Arts Coun. (spl. com. 1986), Kaleidoscope Arts Coun., Am. Assn. Women in Cmty. Jr. Colls. Republican., Ch. of Jesus Christ Latter-day Saints. Avocations: theater, music, camping, reading.

QUIVERS, ROBIN, radio personality; b. Balt., Aug. 8, 1952; d. Charles and Louise Quivers. Student, U. Md., 1974. Morning anchor W100, Carlisle, Pa., 1980; co-host Howard Stern Show, 1981—; with WWDC, Wash., DC, 1981, WNBC, NYC, 1982—85, WXRK-FM, NYC, 1985—2005, Sirius Satellite Radio, NYC, 2006—. Co-author: Quivers: A Life, 1995; actor: (films) Private Parts, 1997; (TV films) Deadly Web, 1996; co-host (TV series) The Howard Stern Show (WOR-TV), 1990—92, The Howard Stern Show (E!), 1994—2005, Howard Stern On Demand, 2005—; guest appearance: (TV series) The Fresh Prince of Bel-Air, 1993; The Larry Sanders Show, 1993; The Magic Hour, 1998. RN, advanced through ranks to capt. USAF. Office: Sirius Satellite Radio 1221 Ave of the Americas New York NY 10020*

QUNELL, KERRI WYNN, marketing professional; b. Bastrop, Tex., Mar. 16, 1971; d. James Richard Wynn and Lu Ella Johnson; m. Jason Christopher Qunell, Sept. 25, 1999. BA, Tex. State U., 1993. Econ. devel. assoc. Greater Austin (Tex.) C. of C., 1994—97; account exec. Sicola Martin Advt., Austin, 1997—98; mktg. comm. mgr. Dell Computer Corp., Round Rock, Tex., 1998—2001; corp. devel. dir. Sta. KEYE-TV, Austin, 2001—02, cmty. rels. dir., 2002—05; dir. comm. Capital Area Food Bank Tex., Austin, 2005—. Mktg. task force ARC Ctrl. Tex., Austin, 2002—. Bd. mem. Greater Austin Hispanic C. of C., 2002—05. Recipient Vol. of Distinction award, The Dell Found., 2001, Profiles in Power finalist, Austin Bus. Jour. & FOX TV, 2002, Austin Under 40 award, Greater Austin Hispanic C. of C., 2006. Mem.: Women in Comm. Inc., Am. Women in Radio and TV, Am. Mktg. Assn. (bd. mem. 2001—03), Young Women's Alliance Austin (life; pres. 2001—01). Methodist. Avocations: photography, camping, travel, music, interior decorating. Office: Capital Area Food Bank Tex 8201 S Congress Ave Austin TX 78745

QUTUB, EILEEN, state legislator, real estate appraiser; b. York, Nebr., Mar. 2, 1948; m. Abe Qutub. BA in Mgmt. Human Resources, George Fox Coll. Pres., owner Hairtel Internat., Inc., Portland, 1978—83; sales assoc., Realtor Allen Tate Realtors, Charlotte, NC, 1984—87; real estate appraiser City of Charlotte, NC, 1988—91; appraiser III Clark County Assessor's Office, Vancouver, Wash., 1993—94; state rep. Oreg. Dist. 8, Beaverton, Oreg., 1995; state sen. Oregon Dist. 4, Beaverton, Tigard, Oreg., 1997—2001; exec. dir. spl. projects Robert D. & Marcia H. Randall Charitable Trust, Randall Realty Corp., Portland, 2001—03; dir. of sch. advancement Heritage Christian Sch., Hillsboro, Oreg., 2003; non-profit cons. Robert D. & Marcia H. Randall Charitable Trust, Portland, 2003—04; real estate broker Re-Max Equity Group, Beaverton, 2005—. Spkr. and fundraiser in field. Precint Com., alt. del. Oreg. Rep. Orgn.; facilitator engring. dept.-real estate divsn. City of Charlotte, NC; chair, bd. dirs. Pregnancy Resource Ctr. of Greater Portland; bd. dirs. Portland Rescue Mission, Portland, Oregon Right to Life Polit. Action Com., Metro Policy Chaplaincy; advisory bd. dirs. Capital Ministries of Oreg. Republican. Home: 11135 Sw Patridge Loop Beaverton OR 97007 Office: S 210 State Capitol Salem OR 97310 E-mail: qutub.sen@state.or.us.

RAAB, CECILIA MARIE, artist; b. Kansas City, Kans., Apr. 26, 1952; d. Joseph Francis Raab and Eunice Noreen (Nystrom) Hansen. BA in Art Edn., Kans. U., 1974; MA in Studio Art, U. Mo., Kansas City, 1979. Cert. art edn. tchr. K-12, Mo., Kans. Elem. art tchr. Kansas City (Kans.) Pub. Schs., 1974-76; drawing instr. Donnelly Coll., Kansas City, 1977; art instr. Gardner (Kans.) HS, 1979; gallery asst. Hallmark Gallery, Crown Ctr., Kansas City, 1980-81; art techn., sec. Nelson-Atkins Mus. of Art, Kansas City, 1981-82; portrait cons. Photo Corp. of Am.-Midwest Region, 1982-85; English instr. Hengyang Tchrs. Coll., Hunan, Peoples Republic of China, 1990-91; dept. sec. Avila U., Kansas City, 1992—95; desktop publ. Office Max, 1997—2000. Organizer Mirror Image Art Group, Kansas City, 1977-83, Village Printmakers Guild, Shawnee Mission, Kans., 1981-85; instr. Barstow Sch., 2003, adj. prof. humanities, Park U., 2003-04. Exhibited at Kansas City Renaissance Festival, 1981-84, 86-87, 3 art tours to Europe, 1983-84, 89; contbr. articles to profl. jours. ESL instr. Overground RR Orgn., Bapt. Ch., Kansas City, 1985-87; organizer Hyde Park Neighborhood Assn., Kansas City, 1981-84; pres., organizer South Wyandotte/Peaceful Valley Neighborhood Group, 2002-03; vol. Coalition Against Pornography, Kansas City, 1987-88, Historic Kansas City Found. Recipient 1st place printmaking Delta Delta Delta, 1981, 82, City Ctr. Square Art Show, 1978, 1st place drawing, Trinity Religious Art Show, 1999, 1st place printmaking, Trinity Religious Art Show, 2004, Cow Parade, Kans. City, 2001; named one of Outstanding Young Women of Am., 1985. Mem. Christians in Visual Arts, Kansas City Artist's Coalition, People to People Internat., Kans. Alumni Assn., U. Mo. Kansas City Alumni Assn., Aglow Internat. (decorating chair Jo-Wy chpt. 1991-95), Kappa Kappa Iota (pres. Zeta conclave 2002-04). Republican. Avocations: computers, painting, music, travel. Home: 2824 Glenrose Ln Kansas City KS 66106-4554 Personal E-mail: domertist@hotmail.com.

RAAD, VIRGINIA, pianist, educator; b. Salem, W.Va., Aug. 13, 1925; d. Joseph M. and Martha (Joseph) R. BA in Art History, Wellesley Coll., 1947; spl. student, New Eng. Conservatory Music, 1947-48; diplôme, Ecole lôrge Normale de Musique, Paris, 1950; Doctorate with honors (French Govt. grantee 1950-52, 54-55), U. Paris, 1955; student, Alfred Cortot, Jeanne Blancard, Berthe Bert, Jacques Chailley. Artist in residence Salem Coll., W.Va., 1957-70; ind. concert pianist, 1960—; musician in residence at cmty. colls. NC Arts Coun., 1971—. Adjudicator Nat. Guild Piano Tchrs., Nat. Fedn. Music Clubs; panelist, grant reviewer NEH, 1978-84, 92—; mem. com. Nat. Endowment Arts, 1978; Am. rep. Debussy Centennial Colloque, Paris, 1962. Perfomances, concerts, lectrs. master classes at West Ga. Coll., Carrollton, La Grange Coll., Ga., Columbus Coll., Ga., Young Harris Coll., Ga., U. Fla., Gainesville, Norton Gallery, Palm Beach, Fla., Alliance Française de Rollins Coll., Winter Park, Fla., Dixon Gallery and Gardens, Memphis, St. Jude Children's Rsch. Hosp., Memphis, Cleveland State CC, Tenn., Sampson Tech. Inst., Clinton, NC, Wayne CC, Goldsboro, NC, Brevard Coll., NC, Ctrl. Wesleyan Coll., SC, Ky. Wesleyan Coll., Owensboro, Berea Ky., Coll., Alice Lloyd Coll., Pippa Passes, Ky., Coll. of William and Mary, Williamsburg, Va., Eastern Mennonite Coll., Harrisonburg, Va., The Phillips Gallery, Washington, Trinity Coll., Washington, Manhattanville Coll., Purchase, NY, Elmira Coll., NY, Fordham U., NYC, The Piano Tchrs. Congress of NY, Middlebury Coll., Vt., St. Anselm's Coll., Manchester, N.H., Mount St. Mary's Coll., Hooksett, NH, Wellesley Coll., Mass., Curry Coll., Milton, Mass., So. Conn. State U., New Haven, Slippery Rock U., Pa., Seton Hill Coll., Greensboro, Pa., Alliance Française de Pitts. and U. Pitts., Channel 13 WQED (PBS) Pitts., Lincoln U., Oxford, Pa., The Grier Sch., Tyrone, Pa., Mount de Chantal Acad., Wheeling W.Va., Wheeling Jesuit U., among other colls. and univs.; contbg. author: Debussy et l'Evolution de la Musique au XX Siècle, 1965; author: The Piano Sonority of Claude Debussy, 1994; recording artist: EDUCO, 1995—; contbr. articles to profl. jours. Active Amnesty Internat. Urgent Action Network; alumna regional rep. Wellesley Coll.; mem bd. visitors New Eng. Conservatory of Music, 2004—. Named Outstanding W.Va. Woman Educator Delta Kappa Gamma, 1965; presented biography to Schlesinger Library on History of Women in Am. Radcliffe Coll., 1967; grantee Govt. France, Am. Coun. Learned Socs. Mem. Soc. Française de Musicologie, Am. Musicol. Soc. (regional officer 1960-65), Am. Coll. Musicians, Internat. Musicol. Soc., Music Tchrs. Nat. Assn. (adjudicator, musicology program chair 1983-87), W.Va. Music Tchrs. Assn., Audubon Activist, Alpha Delta Kappa (hon.). Republican. Roman Catholic. Avocations: hiking, gardening, birding. Address: 60 Terrace Ave Salem WV 26426-1116 Office Phone: 304-782-2274. Personal E-mail: virginiaraad@aol.com.

RAASH, KATHLEEN FORECKI, artist; b. Milw., Sept. 12, 1950; d. Harry and Marion Matilda (Schwabe) Forecki; m. Gary John Raash, June 13, 1987. BS, U. Wis., Eau Claire, 1972; MFA, U. Wis., Milw., 1978. One-woman and group shows include Sight 225 Gallery, Milw., 1979, 81, Nicolet Coll., Rhinelander, Wis., 1981, 2005, Messing Gallery, St. Louis, 1982, Arts Consortium, Cin., 1982, Ctr. Gallery, Madison, Wis., 1982, Otteson Theatre Gallery, Waukesha, Wis., 1982, Foster Gallery, Eau Claire, 1984, Duluth (Minn.) Art Inst., 1984, West Bend (Wis.) Gallery of Fine Arts, 1987, U. Wis., Waukesha Fine Arts Gallery, 1988, Mount Mary Coll., Milw., 1990, Cardinel Stritch Coll., Milw., 1991, West Bend Art Mus., 1995, 2003, Gwenda Jay Gallery, Chgo., 1995, Wis. Acad., Madison, 1996, Nicolet Coll., Rhinelander, Wis., 1997, 2005, Wausau (Wis.) Ctr. Arts, 1998, Riveredge Galleries, Mishicot, Wis., 2000, Union Theater Gallery, Madison, 2000, Gallery 110, Plymouth, Wis., 2001, Bloomington (Minn.) Art Ctr., 2001, Mt. Seanrio Coll., Ladysmith, Wis., 2001, Regional Art Ctr., Eau Claire, 2002, Ctrl. Wis. Cultural Ctr., Wis. Rapids, 2003; exhibited in group shows at River Edge Galleries, Wis., 1990-91, 94-95, 2000, Peltz Gallery, Milw., 1989-99, 2000-05, Minnetonka Ctr. Arts, Wayzata, Minn., 1996, Paine Art Ctr., Oshkosh, Wis., 1998, 2002, Woodward Gallery, N.Y.C., 2000-01, West Bend Art Mus., 2003, Watrous Gallery, Madison, Wis., 2004; represented in permanent collections United Bank and Trust of Madison, Fine Arts Gallery U. Wis., Miller Brewing Co., Independence Bank Waukesha, Fed. Res. Bank, Mpls., Rhinelander Med. Ctr., Univ. Hosp., Madison, Wis., Porter Boathouse, U. Wis. Recipient Purchase award, Madison Art Ctr., 1978, Hon. Mention, Paine Art Ctr., 2002, Percent Art Direct Purchase award, Wis. Arts Bd., 2001, 2005. E-mail: raashstudio@frontiernet.net.

RABADEAU, MARY FRANCES, protective services official; b. Elizabeth, N.J., July 13, 1948; d. Russell John and Frances (Hanley) R. Student, Union Coll., 1967-69; MEd, Kean Coll., 1976. Officer City of Elizabeth Police Dept., NJ, 1978-82, detective NJ, 1982-83, sgt. NJ, 1983-87, lt. NJ, 1987-91, capt. NJ, 1991-92, dir., 1993-95, dep. chief, 1994; chief N.J. Transit Police Dept., Maplewood, 1995—. Instr. Union County Police Acad. Trustee Blessed Sacrament Ch., Elizabeth, N.J., 1989-99; bd. acad. advisors N.J. state police grad. studies program Seton Hall U.; bd. trustees Benedictine Acad., Elizabeth, N.J. Named one of Outstanding Young Women in Am., 1983, Woman Leader N.J. Assn. Women Bus. Owners, 1997; recipient John H. Stamler Police Acad. Svc. award, 1992, Cert. of Recognition award YWCA, 1992, Disting. Grad. award Nat. Cath. Ednl. Assn., 1995; honoree Union County Commn. on the Status of Women, 1993, Hispanic Law Enforcement Assn. of Union County, 1995, Women Helping Women Recognition award Soroptimist Internat. Ams., 2001. Mem. NAACP, Internat. Assn. Chiefs of Police, N.J. State Chiefs of Police, Essex County Chiefs Assn., N.E. Assn. Women Police (cert., Merit award), Elizabeth Police Patrolman's Benevolent Assn., Elizabeth Police Superior Officers Assn. (treas. 1983-91, v.p. 1991), Am. Soc. Law Enforcement Trainers, Emerald Soc., Union County Urban League, Italian Law Enforcement Officers Assn., Fellas Inc. (hon.), Union County Men's Svc. Orgn., Nat. Assn. of Women Law Enforcement Execs. Democrat. Roman Catholic. Office: NJ Transit Police Dept 180 Boyden Ave Maplewood NJ 07040-2494 Home: 184 Riveredge Dr Chatham NJ 07928-3112

RABB, HARRIET SCHAFFER, academic administrator, lawyer; b. Houston, Sept. 12, 1941; d. Samuel S. and Helen G. Schaffer; m. Bruce Rabb, Jan. 4, 1970; children: Alexander, Katherine. BA in Govt., Barnard Coll., 1963; JD, Columbia U., 1966. Bar: N.Y. 1966, U.S. Supreme Ct. 1969, D.C. 1970. Instr. seminar on constl. litig. Rutgers Law Sch., 1966-67; staff atty. Ctr. for Constl. Rights, 1966-69; spl. counsel to commr. consumer affairs NYC Dept. Consumer Affairs, 1969-70; sr. staff atty. Stern Cmty. Law Firm, Washington, 1970-71; asst. dean urban affairs Law Sch., Columbia U., NYC, 1971-84, prof. law, dir. clin. edn., 1984-99, George M. Jaffen prof. law and social responsibility, 1991-99, vice dean, 1992-93; gen. counsel Dept. Health and Human Svcs., Washington, 1993—2001; v.p., gen. counsel Rockefeller U., NYC, 2001—. Mem. faculty employment and tng. policy Harvard Summer Inst., Cambridge, Mass., 1975-79. Author: (with Agid, Cooper and Rubin) Fair Employment Litigation Manual, 1975, (with Cooper and Rubin) Fair Employment Litigation, 1975. Bd. dirs. Ford Found., 1977-89, NY Civil Liberties Union, 1972-83, Lawyers Com. for Civil Rights Under Law, 1978-86, Legal Def. Fund NAACP, 1978-93, Mex. Am. Legal Def. and Edn. Fund, 1986-90, Legal Aid Soc., 1990-93, The Hastings Ctr., 2004-; mem. exec. com. Human Rights Watch, 1991-93; trustee Trinity Episcopal Sch. Corp., 1991-93; mem. external adv. bd. Columbia U. Ctr. Bioethics, 2002-. Office: Rockefeller U 1230 York Ave New York NY 10021 Office Phone: 212-327-8070. Business E-Mail: hrabb@rockefeller.edu.

RABBITT, LINDA, construction executive; BA, U. Mich., Ann Arbor; MA, George Wash. U. With KPMG (formerly Peat Marwick), 1981—85, dir. mktg., 1982—85; co-founder, co-owner, exec. v.p. Hart Construction Co., Inc.; founder, pres. Rand Contruction, 1989—. Dir. Watson Wyatt & Co., 2002—. Bd. trustees George Wash. U., Federal City Coun. Named Person of Vision, Arlington C. of C., 1995, Bus. Woman Yr., United Cerebral Palsy, 1996, Wash. Woman of Genius, Trinity Coll., 2002, Washingtonian Yr., Washingtonian mag., 2004; named one of 100 Most Powerful Women, 2001; recipient Working Woman 500, 2001. Mem.: Wash. Bd. Trade (past chair), Comml. Real Estate Women (past pres., Annual Achievement award 2003). Office: Rand Construction Corp 2100 Wash Blvd Ste 175 Arlington VA 22204 Office Phone: 703-553-5511. Office Fax: 703-486-3092.

RABE, ELIZABETH ROZINA, hair stylist, horse breeder; b. Granby, Quebec, Canada, Sept. 28, 1953; d. John I. and Christina Maria (De Vaal) Gluck; m. Oct. 21, 1972 (div. 1981); children: Diana Marie Claire, Michelle Diane. Diploma in hairstyling, Art Inst. Film hairstylist Internat. Alliance Theatrical, Stage Employees and Moving Pictures Machine Operators Local 706, L.A., 1977—2004. Recipient Design Patent hock support horse brace U.S. Design Patent Office, Washington, 1994, Emmy award for outstanding achievement for hairstyling in series Carnivale After the Ball, HBO, 2003-04. Mem.: NATAS. Home: 622 Ventura St Altadena CA 91001-4939 Office Phone: 818-385-8269.

RABII, PATRICIA BERG, church administrator; b. Lynn, Mass., Nov. 7, 1942; d. Clarence Oscar and Naomi Ruth (MacHugh) B.; m. S. Rabii, Oct. 26, 1966 (div. 1988); children: Susan M., Elizabeth L. AA, Green Mtn. Coll., Poultney, Vt., 1962; BA cum laude, U. Pa., 1978. Cons. City of Phila., 1981; fin. svcs. officer U. Pa., Phila., 1981-90; asst. to exec. dir. Psi Upsilon Found., Paoli, Pa., 1990-92; parish adminstr. St. David's (Radnor) Episcopal Ch., Wayne, Pa., 1992-98; clergy and parish sec. St. David's Ch., 1998—2006. Co-dir. career planning/pub. rels. Resources for Women, Phila., 1978-81. Counselor direct patient and care ARC, St. Louis, 1967-69; bd. dirs. Upper Merion PTA, 1976-78, Dental Clinic, King of Prussia, 1976-78; leader Girl Scouts U.S.A., King of Prussia, 1976-77, 80-81. Recipient ACT 101 Svc. award, Penn Cap, 1989. Mem. AAUW, U. Pa. Women's Club (bd. dirs. 1975-80, v.p. 1979-80). Avocations: golf, bridge, travel. Home: 5 Drummers Ln Wayne PA 19087-1503 Office Phone: 610-688-7947. E-mail: prabii@stdavidschurch.org, patrabii@comcast.net.

RABINER, SUSAN, editor; b. Bklyn., May 5, 1948; d. Nathan M. and Gloria (Bodinger) R.; m. Alfred G. Fortunato, Mar. 27, 1974; children: Anna, Matthew. BA cum laude, Goucher Coll., 1969. Asst. editor Random House, N.Y.C., 1969-72; editor Oxford U. Press, N.Y.C., 1973-79, sr. editor, 1980-86, St. Martin's Press, N.Y.C., 1986-87, Pantheon Books, N.Y.C., 1987-90, Basic Books, Inc., N.Y.C., 1990-95, editl. dir., 1995—, v.p., 1996-97, pvt. practice literary agt., 1997—. Vis. lectr. Yale U., New Haven, 1983, 84. Co-author (with Alfred Fortunato): Thinking Like Your Editor: How to Write Great Serious Nonfiction and Get It Published, 2002. Office: 240 W 35th St New York NY 10001-2506 Home: 166 Furnace Dock Rd Cortlandt Manor NY 10567 Office Phone: 212-279-0316.

RABINOVICH, RAQUEL, painter, sculptor; b. Buenos Aires, Mar. 30, 1929; arrived in U.S., 1967, naturalized, 1973; d. Enrique Rabinovich and Julia Dinitz; m. Jose Luis Reissig, Feb. 14, 1956 (div. 1981); children: Celia Karen Reissig, Pedro Dario Reissig, Nora Vivian Reissig. Student, U. Córdoba, Argentina, 1950-53, Sorbonne, Paris, 1957, U. Edinburgh, Scotland, 1958-59. Lectr. Whitney Mus., 1983—86, Marymount Manhattan Coll., 1984—90. Exhibitions include Hecksher Mus., Huntington, N.Y., 1974, Susan Caldwell Gallery, N.Y.C., 1975, CUNY Grad. Ctr., 1978, Jewish Mus. Sculpture Ct., N.Y.C., 1979, Ctr. Inter-Am. Rels., 1983, Bronx Mus. Arts, N.Y.C., 1986, Fordham U. Lincoln Ctr., 1985, Ams. Soc., 1990, Erik Stark Gallery, 1991, Montgomery Ctr., 1992, Trans Hudson Gallery, N.Y.C., 1993, 1998, 2000, Noyes Mus., 1994, Nelson Atkins Mus. Art, 1995, Intar Gallery, N.Y.C., 1996, U. Tex. Mus. Art, 1998, Emergences (Hudson River Project), 2001—, Collaborative Concepts, Beacon, N.Y., 2003, Hudson River Mus., Yonkers, N.Y., 2003, Weatherspoon Art Mus., U. N.C., 2004, Yellow Bird Gallery, Newburgh, N.Y., 2005, others, —, Represented in permanent collections World Bank Fine Art Collection, Washington, Univ. Art Mus., Austin, Cin. Art Mus., Walker Art Ctr., others. Fellow, NEA, 1991—92; grantee, N.Y. State Coun. Arts, 1995—96, Pollock-Krasner Found., 2001. Avocations: travel, music. Home: 141 Lamoree Rd Rhinebeck NY 12572-3013 Office Phone: 845-876-7963. E-mail: raquelrabinovich@aol.com.

RABINOWITZ, DOROTHY, television critic; b. N.Y.C. BA, Queens Coll., N.Y.C.; postgrad., NYU, Pratt Inst. Freelance writer, syndicated columnist, commentator Sta. WWOR-TV News, N.Y.C.; editl. page writer and television critic Wall St. Jour., mem. editl. bd. Author: Home Life, 1970, New Lives, 1976, No Crueler Tyrannies: Accusation, False Witness, and Other Terrors of Our Times, 2003; columnist Dorothy Rabinowitz's Media Log. Recipient Pulitzer prize for Disting. Commentary, 2001. Office: Wall St Jour 1155 Ave of the Americas 5th fl New York NY 10036

RABKIN, PEGGY ANN, retired lawyer; b. Buffalo, Apr. 13, 1945; d. Anthony J. and Margaret G. (Catuzzi) Marano; m. Samuel S. Rabkin, June 29, 1969. BA, SUNY, Buffalo, 1967, MEd, 1970, MA, 1972, JD, PhD, 1975. Tchr. Buffalo Pub. Schs., 1967-69; grad. teaching asst. SUNY, Buffalo, 1969-72; case analyst U.S. Equal Employment Opportunity Com., 1974; dir. affirmative action U. Louisville, 1975-78, adj. prof. of law, 1976-77; atty. office for civil rights HEW, N.Y.C., 1978; sr. atty. for labor and employment Am. Home Products Corp., N.Y.C., 1978-86, sr. atty., 1986—. Author: Fathers to Daughters, 1980; editor: Buffalo Law Rev., 1974-75; contbr. articles to profl. jours. Commr. Louisville & Jefferson Co. Human Relations Com., Louisville, 1977-78. Recipient Christopher Baldy fellow, SUNY at Buffalo Law Sch., 1974-75, Regents Coll. Scholarship N.Y. State Bd. of Regents, 1963-67. Mem. ABA, Assn. of Bar of City of N.Y., Am. Corp. Counsel Assn., Soc. of Human Resources Mgmt., U.S. C. of C. (labor com. 1991—). Avocations: skiing, reading, cooking, and nutrition.

RABORN, MARCIA MACARTHUR, primary school educator; b. Birmingham, Ala., Jan. 8, 1945; d. Lee Maurance MacArthur, Jr. and Velma Bosworth Dowling; m. Francis Raborn, Aug. 8, 1970; children: Stephen Francis, Emily Louise. BA, U. Calif., Berkeley, 1968; MA, Oakland U., 1976. Flight attendant World Airways, Oakland, Calif., 1968—70; auditor Nt. Bancorporation, Detroit, 1973—75; dir. religious edn. Christ Ch., Los Altos Hills, Calif., 1989—90, preschool tchr., 1990—93; preschool, kindergarten tchr. Village Green Day Sch., Great Falls, Va., 1998—. Author: Parents and Children Learning Together, 1976. Parenting instr. Cabrini Coll., Wayne, Pa., 1975—76; mem. Assn. Jr. Leagues, 1976—; mem. adv. bd. United Way Phila., 1981—84; cmty. v.p. Jr. League Phila., 1982—88; cmty. leader 4H, Los Altos, 1986—92; various bd. positions U.S. Pony Club, Great Falls, Va., 1994—2002; sustainer bd. Jr. League Washington, 2002—03; bd. mem. PTA, 1980—2002; Sunday sch. tchr. various locations, 1978—94. Mem.: Nat. Mus. Women in the Arts. Episcopalian. Avocations: hiking, travel, reading.

RACCAH, DOMINIQUE MARCELLE, publisher; b. Paris, Aug. 24, 1956; arrived in U.S., 1964; d. Paul Mordechai and Colette Bracha (Madar) Raccah; m. Raymond W. Bennett, Aug. 20, 1980; 3 children. BA, U. Ill., Chgo., 1978; MS, U. Ill., Champaign-Urbana, 1981. Rsch. analyst Leo Burnett Advt., Chgo., 1980-81, rsch. supr., 1981-84, assoc. rsch. dir., 1984-87; pres., pub., owner Sourcebooks, Inc., Naperville, Ill., 1987—; co-CEO Login Pubs. Consortium, Chgo., 1990-99. Author: Financial Sourcebooks' Sources, 1987; editor: Poetry Speaks, 2001, Poetry Speaks to Children, 2005, The Sourcebooks Shakespeare, 2005. Bd. dirs. Com. of 200, Book Industry Study Group. Recipient Blue Chip Enterprise award, 2000, Ernst & Young Entrepreneur of Yr. Ill. and N.W. Ind., 2000; named to Inc. 500 list; inducted into Univ. Ill. Entrepreneurship Hall of Fame, 2001. Mem. Pubs. Mktg. Assn., Am. Booksellers Assn., Am. Assn. Pubs. Office: Sourcebooks Inc 1935 Brookdale Rd # 139 Naperville IL 60563-9245 Office Phone: 630-961-3900. Business E-Mail: dominique.raccah@sourcebooks.com.

RACHLIN RUBIN, JOYCE LINDA, education educator; b. Bklyn., Jan. 25, 1944; d. Nathan and Beatrice (Harris) Rachlin; m. Jerome L. Rubin, June 7, 1964; children: Steven, Shari, Jeffrey. BA in Early Childhood Edn., Bkyn. Coll., 1965, MS in Early Childhood Edn., 1968; D Edn. in Early and Mid. Childhood, Nova U., 1991. Cert. in clin. supervision. Prekindergarten tchr. Project Head Start, Bklyn., 1965; kindergarten tchr. N.Y.C. Bd. Edn., Bklyn., 1965-67; adj. instr. early childhood dept. SUNY, Farmingdale, 1974-77; dir. Giant Step Nursery Sch., 1971-85; instr. dept. early childhood edn. and elem. edn. Fla. Atlantic U., Miami, 1987-88; clin. supr. Tchr. Edn. Ctr., 1991; ednl. cons. Tchr. Edn. Inst., 1988—; adj. instr. Coll. Edn. Fla. Internat. U., 1986-95; asst. prof. early childhood edn. Fla. Atlantic U., 1995-96, Barry U., 1996—. Discussion leader Continuing Edn. Program Baldwin Pub. Schs., PACE, 1977-78; developer, instr. various insvc. courses Early Childhood Edn. Coun. Nassau County, N.Y., 1972-85; developer, presenter workshops Miami-Dade C.C., 1991, 92; ofcl. validator Nat. Assn. Edn. Young Children accreditation system, Washington, 1988—; bd. mem. Nassau County Early Childhood Edn. Coun., 1980-85, Day Care Coun. Nassau County, 1981-85; validator Nat. Acad. Early Childhood Programs, 1987—. Creator videotape Television and the Young Child, Selkirk Cable Systems and B'nai Brith Women, 1987. Mem. Nat. Assn. Edn. Young Children, Assn. Childhood Edn. Internat., Fla. Assn. Children Under Six. Home: 10689 NW 17th Ct Coral Springs FL 33071-4280 Personal E-mail: jlrubin@bellsouth.net.

RACHOW, CINDA LOU, educational association administrator; b. Omaha, Nebr., Mar. 12, 1950; d. Charles A. and Mildred L. Jensen; m. Roger L. Rachow, July 20, 1968 (dec.); children: Christopher M., Kymberli Anne, Ryan Matthew. BA in Psychology, U. Nebr., Omaha, 1973; degree in Elem. Edn., Beuna Vista U., Council Bluffs, Iowa, 1976; MSc in Spl. Edn., U. Nebr., Omaha, 1981. Instr. mobility Ea. Nebr. Office Retardation, Omaha, 1973—74; tchr. emotionally disturbed Ea. Nebr. Office Mental Health, Omaha, 1974—77; tchr. spl. edn. Lewis Ctrl. Cmty. Schs., Coun. Bluffs, Iowa, 1977—91; cons. spl. edn. Loess Hills Area Edn. Agy., Coun. Bluffs, 1991—2003, coord. learning support, 2003—. Mem. steering com. Iowa Dept. Edn., Des Moines, 2002—04; mem. strategic planning team Millard Pub. Sch., Omaha, 2002; rsch. team State of Iowa Assistive Tech., 2002—. Contbr. articles to profl. jours. Mem. rsch. data com. Promise Ptnrs. Iowa, Coun. Bluffs, 2003—06. Recipient Excellence in Svc. award, Griswold Cmty. Schs., 2001. Mem.: ASCD, Phi Delta Kappa. Avocations: piano, violin, reading, gardening. Office: Loess Hills Area Edn Agy 13 29904 Hwy 92 Council Bluffs IA 51503 Office Phone: 712-360-0503.

RACHOW, SHARON DIANNE, realtor; b. St. Joseph, Mo., Apr. 12, 1939; d. Norman DeLos Zancker and Sylvia Lavina (Hawkins) Trouel; m. Thomas Eugene Rachow, Oct. 22, 1968; children: Todd A., Tiffany K. Student, So. Ill. U., 1969-72. Sec. Westab, Inc. (now Mead), St. Joseph, 1957-60, Seitz Packing Co. (now Sara Lee), St. Joseph, 1960-66; exec. asst. to v.p., gen. mgr. Kansas City (Mo.) Chiefs, 1972; co-owner, mgr. Pool 'N Patio Plus, St. Joseph, 1973-84; realtor Coldwell Banker Gen. Realtors, St. Joseph, 1984-93, RE/MAX, 1993—2004, Evans Realty, 2004—. Trustee Nat. Multiple Sclerosis Soc., Mid Am. chpt., Midland M.S. Express Br., 1993-98. Mem.: Real Estate Buyers Agt. Coun. (accredited buyers rep. 1996—), St. Joseph Regional Bd. Realtors (residential specialist 1987—, Multi-List com. 1993—2002, bd. dirs. 1994, forms com. 1994—2002, Top Residential Sales award 1986—, Top 10), Multi Million Dollar Club (quality svc. cert. 2001, quality svc. cert. 2003). Republican. Lutheran. Home: 4211 Country Ln Saint Joseph MO 64506-2454 Office: Evans Realty 606 S Woodbine Rd Saint Joseph MO 64507 Office Phone: 816-390-8000. Business E-Mail: sharonr@stjoelive.com.

RACITI, CHERIE, artist; b. Chgo., June 17, 1942; d. Russell J. and Jacque (Crimmins) R. Student, Memphis Coll. Art, 1963-65; BA in Art, San Francisco State U., 1968; M.F.A., Mills Coll., 1979. Assoc. prof. art San Francisco State U., 1984-89, prof., 1989—. Lectr. Calif. State U., Hayward, 1974, San Francisco Art Inst., 1978; mem. artist com. San Francisco Art Inst., 1974-85, sec., 1980-81. One woman shows include U. Calif., Berkeley, 1972, Nicholas Wilder Gallery, L.A., 1975, San Francisco Art Inst., 1977, Marianne Deson Gallery, Chgo., 1980, Site 375, San Francisco, 1989, Reese Bullen Gallery, Humboldt State U., Arcata, Calif., 1990, Mills Coll. Art Mus., Oakland, Calif., 1998; group shows include Whitney Mus. Art, 1975, San Francisco Sci. Fiction, The Clocktower, N.Y.C., Otis-Parsons Gallery, Los Angeles, 1984-85, San Francisco Art Inst., 1985, Artists Space, N.Y.C., 1988, Angles Gallery, Santa Monica, 1987, Terrain Gallery, San Francisco, 1992, Ctr. for the Arts, San Francisco, 1993, Santa Monica Coll., 1998, 25/25 25th Anniversary Exhbn., So. Exposure Gallery, San Francisco, 1999, Santa Cruz Mus., 2003, Thacher Gallery U. San Francisco, 2004. Bd. dirs. New Langton Arts, 1988-92. Eureka fellow Fleishhacker Found., San Francisco, Va.Ctr. for Creative Arts fellow, Amherst, Va., 2005; recipient Adaline Kent award San Francisco Art Inst., 1976, Djerassi resident, 1994, Tyrone Guthrie Ctr. resident, Ireland, 1995, Millay Colony for Arts resident 1999, Juror's award Artadia San Francisco. Office: San Francisco State U Art Dept 1600 Holloway Ave San Francisco CA 94132-1722 Office Phone: 415-338-6318. Business E-Mail: craciti@sfsu.edu.

RACKE, ANNE MOLLER, winery executive; b. Oberwesel, Germany, Dec. 10, 1961; came to U.S., 1981; d. Werner Jacob and Gerda Johanna Brager; m. Marcus Moller Racke, Aug. 27, 1983 (div. 1993); 1 child, dorothé; m. Saul I. Gropman, May 26, 1995. Grad., Fach Hochschule, Boppard, Germany, 1979. Asst. vineyard mgr. Buena Vista Winery, Sonoma, Calif., 1981-83, vineyard mgr., 1983-90, dir. vineyard ops., 1990-98, v.p., 1998—. Bd. dirs. Carneros Quality Alliance, Napa/Sonoma, Calif. Mem. adv. bd. Sonoma Valley Mus. Art, 1999. Roman Catholic. Office: Buena Vista Winery 27000 Ramal Rd Sonoma CA 95476-9791

RACKIN, PHYLLIS, retired English language educator; b. Newark, N.J., Sept. 15, 1933; d. Milton Philip and Ethel Shulman Finkelstein; m. Donald Rackin, Jan. 1, 1954; children: Rebecca Hoenig, Ethel. BA, N.J. Coll., New Brunswick, 1954; MA, Auburn U., 1957; PhD, U. Ill., 1962. Instr. U. Pa., Phila., 1962—64, from asst. prof. to assoc. prof., 1964—90, prof., 1990—2002, prof. emeritus, 2002—. Author: (book) Stages of History, 1990, Engendering a Nation, 1997, Shakespeare's Tragedies, 1978, Shakespeare and Women, 2005; mem. editl. bd.: Studies in English Literature. Fellow, ACLS, 1988. Mem.: MLA (chair Shakespeare divsn. 1994), Shakespeare Assn. Am. (pres. 1993—94). E-mail: prackin@english.upenn.edu.

RACKLIN, BARBARA COHEN, fundraising consultant; b. N.Y.C., Dec. 3, 1950; d. Harry Cohen and Shari Lillian (Greene) Cohen; m. Arthur Michael Racklin, Aug. 19, 1979 (div.); 1 child, Nicholas Michael. BA in Math., U. Tex., 1972; postgrad., U. LaVerne, 1981-82. Cert. histocompatibility technologist, Am. Bd. Histocompatability and Immunogenetics; cert. fundraising exec. Asst. dir. transplant lab. Med. br. U. Tex., Galveston, 1974-76; transplant immunology specialist Montefiore Hosp., Bronx, N.Y., 1976-77; dir. pediat. immunology lab. Cedar Sinai Hosp., L.A., 1977-79; supr. pathology lab. City of Hope Nat. Med. Ctr., Duarte, Calif., 1979-82, rsch. specialist transplant lab., 1982-85; staff coord. vol. devel. City of Hope Deve. Ctr., L.A., 1986-88; coord. fin. devel. events ARC, Pasadena, Calif., 1995-99; co-owner benefit specialists Fundraising Cons., La Cañada, Calif., 1995-99; chief devel. officer San Gabriel chpt. ARC, 1999—2002; devel. dir. PSW region Anti-Defamation League, 2002—05; assoc. v.p. advancement Music Ctr. L.A. County, 2005—. Tour chmn. City of Hope Ann. Conv., Duarte, 1987, 89, 91. Contbr. or co-contbr. articles to profl. publs. Bd. dirs. City of Hope Med. Ctr., 1986-89, mem. bd. govs., 1991-93; mem. steering com. local parcel tax election, La Cañada, 1992, local sch. bd. election, 1995; mem. sch. bd. La Cañada Unified Sch. Dist., 1997-2001, clk. governing bd., 1999-2000, pres. gov. bd. 2000-01; pres. La Cañada Coun. PTA, 1995-97, City of Hope Aux., 1988-90; bd. dirs. LCF Ednl. Found., past pres., v.p., 1991-97; sec. Children's Hosp. Aux., 1994-97; auditor 1st Dist. PTA, 1997; chairperson youth com. Pasadena Temple, 1996-97; v.p. governing bd. La Canada Unified Sch. Dist., 1998-99; bd. dirs. southwest reg. B'nai B'rith Youth Orgn.; participant Leadership Pasadena, 1999-2000. Recipient Hon. Svc. award La Cañada Coun. PTA, 1996, Svc. award LCF Ednl. Found., 1995, Golden Apple award La Canada Unified Sch. Dist., 1996, Golden Bear award for Fundraising Excellence Am. Red Cross, 2001 Mem.: L.A. World Affairs Coun., Nat. Coun. Planned Giving, Calif. Advancement Rschrs. Assn., Assn. Fundraising Profls. Avocations: skiing, bowling, reading. Office: Music Ctr LA County 135 N Grand Ave Los Angeles CA 90012 Business E-Mail: bracklin@musiccenter.org.

RACO, ELLEN, secondary school educator; b. Queens, NY, June 16, 1959; d. Richard and Carol Wurster; m. Joe Raco, May 24, 1992; 1 child, Christine. BS, Binghamton U., NY, 1981, MS, 1983. Tchr.'s credential CA. Tchr. Tracy Unified Sch. Dist., Calif., 1988—; adj. prof. San Joaquin Delta C.C., Stockton, Calif., 2004—. Cross country coach Tracy HS, 2000—04; vol. track coach West HS, Tracy, 2005—, asst. cross country coach, 2006—. Named Tchr. of Yr., Tracy Unified Sch. Dist., 1995, Woman of Yr., Calif. Interscholastic Fedn., 2000. Office: Tracy HS 315 E 11th St Tracy CA 95376 Office Phone: 209-831-5100. E-mail: eraco@tusd.net.

RADA, RUTH BYERS, retired dean; b. LA, Oct. 3, 1923; d. George and Gerda Marie (Lihm) Byers; children: Kaaren Ruth, Georgene Melanie. AB, U. So. Calif., LA, 1944, MA, 1945; EdD, Nova U., Fla., 1976. Asst. dean instrn. and evening East L.A. Coll., 1964-69, dean instrn., 1969-70; dean student personnel L.A. Harbor Coll., 1970-73, East L.A. Coll., 1973-77, L.A. Mission Coll., 1977-83; prof. biol. sci. East L.A. C.C., 1945-69, ret., 1983. Author: Water Biology, 1950, (with others) Human Body in Health and Disease, 1969, Structure and Function of Human Body, 1970, Laboratory Manual for Introductory Microbiology, 1963. Mem. Calif. Cmty. and Jr. Coll. Assn. (area pres. 1973-74), Calif. Woman Adminstrs. Assn., Los Angeles Coll. Adminstrs. Assn. (sec. 1973-74), Phi Beta Kappa, Phi Kappa Phi, Pi Lambda Theta, Phi Sigma. Republican. Mem. Ch. of Religious Sci.

RADCLIFF, JOYCE B., librarian; d. Robert and Rosanna Bullard; m. Doc Radcliff, June 24, 1968; children: Nicole Lynn, Rasheda Asia. BA, U. South Ala., 1973, MLS, 1996. Tech. asst. U. S. Ala., Mobile, 1974—99; cataloging libr. U. So. Miss., Hattisburg, 1999—2001; serials libr. Tenn. State U., Nashville, 2001—; cons. Libr. of Congress, Washington, 1996; mem. exec. bd. Reading Is Fundamental, Nashville, 2004—. Exec. bd. Libr. Sch. Assn. U. Ala., 1997—2002. Contbr. articles to profl. jours. Advisor ABeneffuo KUO Honor Soc., 1989—99; greeter Frist Mus., Nashville, 2002—; advisor Girl Scouts Am., Mobile, 1982—86. Named Staff of Yr., U. S. Ala., 1999; recipient Award of Appreciation, Libr. Congress, Washington, 1996, Congress award, Congressman Sonny Callahan, 2000. Mem.: ALA, Tenn. Libr. Assn., Delta Sigma Theta. Avocations: walking, reading, travel, computers. Office: Tenn State Univ 330 10th Ave N Nashville TN 37203 Office Phone: 615-963-7383. Personal E-mail: Taylor_Kennedy@hotmail.com.

RADCLIFFE, REDONIA (DONNIE RADCLIFFE), journalist, writer; m. Robert C. Radcliffe; 1 child, M. Donnel Nunes. BA, San Jose State U., Calif., 1951. Reporter, women's editor, county editor The Salinas Californian, 1951-59; free-lance writer Europe, 1959—66; reporter Washington Star, 1967-72; White Ho. reporter, columnist Washington Post, 1972-95. Author: Simply Barbara Bush: A Portrait of America's Candid First Lady, 1989, Hillary Rodham Clinton: A First Lady for Our Time, 1993, reissued as Hillary Rodham Clinton: The Evolution of a First Lady, 1999; contbr.: The Fall of a President, 1974, Guide to Washington, 1989. Trustee Calvert County (Md.) Libr.; bd. dirs. Nat. 1st Ladies' Libr. E-mail: redrad@erols.com.

RADECKI, CATHERINE, psychologist; b. Franklin, N.J., Jan. 23, 1953; s. Alexander Edward and Mary Catherine (Poncharik) R. B.S. in Psychology, U. Md., 1975; M.A. in Psychology, U. Del., Ph.D. in Clin. Psychology, 1982. Lic. psychologist, N.C., N.J., Va. Psychol. examiner West Memphis Mental Health Ctr., West Memphis, Ark., 1978-80; coordinator emergency services N. Ocean Counseling Services, Lakewood, N.J., 1980-83; coordinator adult services Pitt County Mental Health Ctr., Greenville, N.C., 1983-84; dir. Psychol. Services Ctr., Va. Commonwealth U., Richmond, 1984. Contbr. articles to profl. jours. Mem. Com. Task Force Domestic Violence, Richmond, Va., 1985—; mem. United Way of Pitt County, 1984-85. Mem. Am. Psychol. Assn., Psi Chi, Phi Beta Kappa. Office: Ctr for Psychol Svcs VA Commonwealth Psychol 806 W Franklin St Richmond VA 23284-9038

RADEL, EVA, pediatrician, hematologist; b. Vienna, Apr. 10, 1934; came to U.S., 1939; d. Ernest O. and Marian (Feiks) Grossman; m. Stanley Robert Radel, May 31, 1954; children: Carol, Laura. AB, N.Y. U., 1954, MD, 1958. Pediatric intern, resident Bronx Mcpl. Hosp. Ctr., 1958-61; pediatric hematology rsch. fellow Albert Einstein Coll. Medicine, Bronx, 1961-63; pediatrician, head pediatric hematology Morrisania city Hosp., Bronx, 1963-76; assoc. dir. pediatrics North Cen. Bronx Hosp., 1978-82; attending physician pediatric hemetology out patients Montefiore Med. Ctr., Bronx, 1965-79, svc. head pediatric hematology-oncology, 1979—2004; head pediatric hematology North Cen. Bronx Hosp., 1976-97. Responsible investigator Children's Cancer Study Group, 1980-2001; dir. pediatric hematology-oncology Albert Einstein Coll. Medicine, Bronx, 1980-2004; prin. investigator Children's Oncology Group, 2001-05 Fellow Am. Acad Pediatrics; mem. Am. Soc. Hematology, Am. Soc. Pediatric Hematology-Oncology, Soc. for the Study of Blood. Office: Childrens Hosp at Montefiore Sect Pediat Hematology-Oncology 3415 Bainbridge Ave Bronx NY 10467-2401 Office Phone: 718-741-2342. Business E-Mail: eradel@montefiore.org.

RADELL, CAROL K., elementary school educator; b. Rochester, NY, Feb. 22, 1939; d. Harold LaVerne and Ruth Elinor Kruger; m. Eugene Arthur Radell, Apr. 30, 1971 (dec. Jan 18, 1998); children: Terry Jean(dec.), Steven Paul, Marcie Ann. Elem. edn., Long Beach (Calif.) City Coll., 1959; chemistry, Rochester Inst. Tech., 1961; BA, Long Beach (Calif.) City Coll., 1961. Lab. technician Eastman Kodak, Rochester, NY, 1959—63; assoc. tchr. Henrietta Sch. Dist., NY, 1969—71, Fairport Bd. Coop. Edn., NY, 1986—99, Fairport Sch. Dist., 1999—, East Rochester Sch. Dist., NY, 1999—2001, Hemet Unified Sch. Dist., Calif., 1999—2002, Riverside County, Calif., 2000—02. Mem. Safe Celebration Com., Fairport, 1989—90. Mem.: MADD. Avocations: rock climbing, fast walking, reading, volunteer work.

RADEMACHER, BETTY GREEN, retired counselor, consultant; b. Marion, Ill., June 28, 1935; d. Morris Lee and Elva (Davis) Booth; m. Ronald Green, Aug. 21, 1957 (div. 1972); children: Susan Green Berge, Karen Green Townsend; m. David Day Rademacher, June 7, 1975. BS, So. Ill. U., 1957,

MS, 1959. Cert. profl. in human resources. Counselor So. Ill. U., Carbondale, 1958-60, Ill. State U., Normal, 1972-81, staff psychologist, assoc. dir., 1990-99; dir. career edn. Ill. Wesleyan U., Bloomington, 1981-90. Lectr. various profl. confs. Author: (chpt.) New Horizons in Parenthood, 1982; co-author: Williamson County Schools, 1989; contbr. articles to profl. jours. Bd. dirs. United Campus Christian Found., Normal, 1978-98; mem. Womens Div. C. of C., Bloomington, 1989-94; mem., com. chair Bloomington-Normal Human Resource Coun., 1981-99. Mem. Am. Counseling Assn. (Ill. chpt.), Soc. Human Resource Mgmt., Am. Coll. Pers. Assn., Coll. Placement Coun. (midwest chpt.), Ill. Sml. Coll. Placement Assn. (pres. 1988-90), Phi Kappa Phi, Phi Delta Kappa, Pi Lambda Theta. Democrat. Presbyterian. Avocations: skiing, running, antiques, gardening. Home: 702 Broadway St Normal IL 61761-3766

RADER, ANGELA NICHOLE, music educator; b. Buckhannon, W.Va., Dec. 28, 1974; d. Paul Douglass and Leda Linette Koon; m. Brent David Rader, July 5, 1997; 1 child, Jordan McKenzie. B in Music Edn., W.Va. Wesleyan Coll., 1997. Tchr. Waynesboro (Va.) City Schs., 1997—98; tchr., band dir. Lexington (Va.) City Schs., 1998—; girls' basketball coach; dir. choir Trinity Methodist Ch., 2006—. Advisor Waddell Svc. Club, 2004—. Mem. Trinity United Meth. HandBell Choir, 2000—. Mem.: Music Educators Nat. Conf., Va. Music Edn. Assn. Republican. Methodist. Avocations: flute, handbells, coaching girls basketball. Office: Waddell Elem Sch 100 Pendleton Pl Lexington VA 24450

RADER, ELLA JANE See ASHLEY, ELLA JANE

RADFORD, VIRGINIA RODRIGUEZ, retired secondary school educator, librarian; b. Willcox, Ariz., Nov. 17, 1917; d. Domingo Acosta and Maria Ceveriana (Lopez) Rodriguez; m. John Houston Radford, June 5, 1942; children: Mary Jane, Ann Christine, Patricia Mae. BA, BS, U. Kans., 1940, univ. tchrs. diploma, 1940; Librarianship, Benedictine Coll., Atchinson, Kans., 1972-76. Cert. life. tchr. K-12, Kans., master tchr., 1970. Tchr. Spanish, French, English Horton (Kans.) High Schs., 1957-60; 4th and 5th grade tchr. St. Leo's Parochial Sch., Horton, 1961-62; tchr. Spanish, French/librarian Horton High Sch., 1962-82. Translator U.S. War Dept., San Antonio, 1942; past pres. Brown County Ret. Tchrs. Assn., People-to-People (Horton chpt.); silver haired legislator Brown County Northeast Area Agy. on Aging, 2005—; commd. lay min. St. Leo's Ch., 1990; mem. St. Leo's Altar Soc.; pres. bd. dirs. Horton Libr., 1975; bd. dirs. Tri-County Manor, Horton, 2001; adv. bd. mem. Alta Care Corp. Tri County Manor, Horton, Kans. Named Outstanding Secondary Educator of Am., 1975; inducted Kans. Tchrs. Hall of Fame, 1984. Mem.: AAUW, Brown County Assn. Ret. Sch. Pers., Bus. and Profl. Women, Am. Legion Auxiliary, Friends of Libr., Horton Hosp. Aux. (life), Horton Sr. Citizens Club, Inc. (trustee), VFW Aux. Post 3021 (life; v.p.), Delta Kappa Gamma (pres. Alpha Kappa chpt.). Roman Catholic. Avocations: reading, music, travel, photography, collecting letter openers. Home: 439 W 8th St Horton KS 66439-1515 Office Phone: 785-486-3514. Personal E-mail: vradford@carsoncomm.com.

RADICE, ANNE-IMELDA MARINO, museum director, former federal agency administrator; b. Buffalo, Feb. 29, 1948; d. Lawrence and Anne (Marino) R. AB, Wheaton Coll., 1969; MA, Villa SchiFanoia, Florence, Italy, 1971; PhD, U. N.C., 1976; MBA, Am. U., 1984. Asst. curator, staff lectr. Nat. Gallery of Art, Washington, 1972-76; archtl. historian U.S. Capitol, Washington, 1976—81, curator Office of Architect, 1981—85; dir. Nat. Mus. Women in the Arts, 1985-89; chief divsn. of creative arts USIA, 1989-91; sr. dep. chmn. Nat. Endowment for Arts, Washington, 1991-92, acting chmn., 1992-93; exec. v.p. Gray & Co. II, Miami, Fla., 1993; prodr. World Affairs TV Prodn., 1994; assoc. producer Think Tank, 1994; chief spl. projects, confidential adviser Courtney Sale Ross, 1994-96; v.p., COO ICL Internat., 1996; exec. dir. Friends of Dresden Inc., 1998—2001; exec. dir. appeal Conscience Found., NYC, 2001—03; chief staff to sec. US Dept. Edn., Washington, 2003—05; acting asst. chmn. for programs Nat. Endowment Humanities, Washington, 2005—06; dir. The Inst. Mus. & Library Services, Washington, 2006—. Cons. in pub. rels. and TV, 1994—. Contbr. articles to profl. jours. Office: The Inst Mus & Library Services 1800 M St NW 9th Fl Washington DC 20036*

RADIN, AMY JANINE, financial services company executive; b. Mar. 30, 1958; d. Harold I. and Selma M. Friedman; m. Mitchell E. Radin, Nov. 1984; 3 children. BA magna cum laude, Coll. Letters and Spanish, Wesleyan U.; MBA, Wharton Sch., U. Pa. Mktg. develop. mgr. KMG Main Hurdman, NY; various positions in mgmt., customer loyalty, new product develop. and channel mgmt. American Express; exec. v.p., chief mktg. officer Dime Savings Bank of NY; exec. v.p., citi cards e-business Citigroup, Inc., 2000, exec. v.p., customer engagement, 2005, chief innovation officer, global consumer group, 2005—, mem. mgmt. com., mem. global consumer group planning com. Spkr. in field. Trustee The Healthcare Chaplaincy, 2006—; founder, pres. The Small Acts of Kindness Found., Inc. Named one of 25 Masters of Innovation, BusinessWeek. Office: Citigroup Inc 399 Park Ave New York NY 10043*

RADIN, MARGARET JANE, law educator; b. 1941; AB, Stanford U., 1963; MFA in Music, Brandeis U., 1965; doctoral studies in Music History, U. Calif., Berkeley, 1965—68; JD, U. So. Calif. Law Ctr., 1976; LLD (hon.), Ill. Inst. Tech. Chgo.-Kent Sch. Law, 1993. Bar: Calif. 1977. Asst. prof. law U. Oreg. Sch. Law, 1976—78; assoc. prof. U. So. Calif. Law Ctr., 1979—82, prof., 1982—87, Carolyn Craig Franklin prof. law, 1987—89; prof. Stanford Law Sch., 1989—96, William Benjamin Scott & Luna M. Scott prof. law, 1996—, founder & co-dir. Ctr. for E-Commerce, 2002—, co-dir. program in law, science and tech., 1997—2001, dir., 2001—01, dir. LLM program in law, science and tech., 2001—04. Vis. prof. law UCLA Law Sch., 1978—79, Harvard Law Sch., 1984—85, U. So. Calif. Law Ctr., 1989—90, U. Mich. Law Sch., 2004—05. Author: Reinterpreting Property, 1993, Contested Commodities, 1996; co-author: Internet Commerce: The Emerging Legal Framework, 2002. Mem.: Law Professors for the Rule of Law (co-founder), The Copyright Soc. of USA, Computer Law Soc., Am. Intellectual Property Lawyers Assn., Am. Soc. Polit. and Legal Philosophy, Assn. Computing Machinery (law and tech. policy com.). Office: Stanford Law Sch Crown Quadrangle 559 Nathan Abbott Way Stanford CA 94305-8610 Office Phone: 650-725-3803. Business E-Mail: mjradin@stanford.edu.

RADKOWSKY, KAREN, advertising research specialist; b. Washington, Nov. 8, 1957; d. Lawrence and Florence (Kramer) Radkowsky. BA, Columbia U., 1979. Rsch. analyst Cosmair, Inc., N.Y.C., 1979-82, sr. rsch. analyst, 1982-84; asst. rsch. mgr. Am. Express Co., N.Y.C., 1984-85; account rsch. mgr. BBDO, Inc., N.Y.C., 1985-88, v.p., assoc. rsch. dir., 1988-94, sr. v.p., assoc. rsch. dir., 1994-95; sr. v.p., rsch. dir. BBDO N.Y., N.Y.C., 1995-99; sr. ptnr., dir. consumer rsch. Ogilvy & Mather, N.Y.C., 2000—. Bd. dirs. Advt. Rsch. Found., 2001—. E-mail: karen.radkowsky@ogilvy.com.

RADLOFF, MARIE ULREY, music educator; d. Charles Franklin and Patricia Dort Ulrey; m. D. Scott Radloff, July 9, 1996. MusB in Edn., Fla. State U., 1978; MEd, U. of Ctrl. Fla., 1991. Cert. tchr. Fla., 2003. Music specialist Lilburn Elem. Sch., Ga., 1978—87, Bonneville Elem. Sch., Orlando, Fla., 1987—2001, Three Points Elem. Sch., Orlando, 2001—; adj. instr. U. Ctrl. Fla., 2004. Clinician Ctrl. Fla. Orff Chpt., Orlando, Fla., 2002—03; adv. bd. mem., young composers' program Orlando Philharm. Orch., Orlando, Fla., 2003—; chmn. of music assessment writing team Orange County Pub. Schs., Orlando, 2002, clinician on various topics in music edn., 1995—; clinician Fla. Music Educator's Assn., Tampa, Fla., 2002, Arts for a Complete Edn./Fla. Assn. of Arts Educators, Orlando, 2002, U. of Ctrl. Fla., Orlando, 2000, Orange County Pub. Schs. Tchr. Acad., Orlando, 1999; prin. oboist Hollywood Festival Orch., Asian Tour, 2002—03. Author: (book) Making Music Florida Planner. Coun. of ministries mem. First United Meth. Ch., Orlando, 1994—96. Named Tchr. of the Yr., Three Points Elem. Sch., 2002—03; recipient Teacherrific Award for Innovative Tchg. Practices, The Walt Disney Co., 1993, 1994, 2000, Innovative Program/Project award, Fla. Music Educators Assn., 1999; scholar, Orange County Pub. Schs. scholar, 2002. Mem.: Am. Orff Schulwerk Assn., Music Educators Nat. Conf., Fla. Music Educators Assn., Fla. Elem. Music Educators Assn. (dist. chmn. 2003—), Orange County Elem. Music Educators Assn. (dist. chmn. 2000—03), Phi Delta Kappa (chpt. historian 1990—92). Avocations: playing oboe, flute, and handbells, reading, movies. Office: Three Points Elem Sch 4001 S Goldenrod Rd Orlando FL 32822 Personal E-mail: radloffm@earthlink.net. E-mail: radlofm@ocps.net.

RADOMSKI, ROBYN L., marketing executive; b. Pitts., 1956; d. Robert G. and Helen L. Moses; m. A. David Radomski; children: Lauren E., Kristen L. BA in Journalism, Pa. State U., 1975; MBA in Mktg., DePaul U., 1989. Dir. Sedwick-James, Inc., Chgo., 1977-81; v.p. Edelman Worldwide, Chgo., 1981-84, Playboy Enterprises, Inc., Chgo., 1984-91; sr. v.p. Bozell Worldwide, Chgo., 1991-92; v.p. mktg. Fluid Mgmt., L.P., Wheeling, Ill., 1992-96, Wace, The Imaging Network, Chgo., 1998; CMO, v.p. mktg., pub. rels. and physician svcs. Northwestern Meml. Hosp., 1998—99; chief mktg. officer Sonnenschein Nath & Rosenthal, Chgo., 1999—; chmn. worldwide mktg. Lex Mundi, North Am., 2003—. Bd. dirs. Playboy Found., Chgo. Mem. Am. Mktg. Assn., Nat. Investor Rels. Assn., Pub. Rels. Soc. Am., Pub. Rels. Clinic. Internat. Assn. Bus. Communicators (bd. dirs.), Sigma Delta Chi. Avocation: yacht sailing. Office: Sonnenschein Nath & Rosenthal 8000 Sears Tower Chicago IL 60606

RADY, ELSA, artist; b. N.Y.C., July 29, 1943; d. Simon and Lily (Mehlman) R. Attended, Chouinard Art Sch., 1962-66. Designer Interpace, L.A., 1989-94. Designer Swid/Powell, N.Y.C., 1989-94. Exhibited in group shows at Ceramic S102 1974, Oakland Mus., 1974, Drinking Companions, John Michael Kohler Art Ctr., 1977, Women in Crafts, 1977, Am. Ceramics, Phoenix Art Mus., 1980, Am. Porcelain, Renwich Gallery, Smithsonian Inst., 1980, The Am. Hand, Janus Gallery, LA, 1981, Art in Clay 1950's-1980's, Three Decades of So. Calif., Ceramic Art, Evolution, Revolution and Continuation, LA Mcpl. Gallery, 1984, Touring Exhbn., Museo de Ceramica, Barcelona, Spain, 1985, New Acquisitions, Douglas Drake Gallery, Kans., 1986, Am. Potters Today, Victoria and Albert Mus., London, Eng., 1986, Recent Acquisitions in the Decorative Arts, Newark Mus., N.J., 1988, Selections from One Man's Collection: Hubert A. Arnold, The Crocker Mus., Sacramento, Calif., 1989, World War II Holdings, Holly Solomon Gallery, N.Y., 1989, The Vessel: Studies in Form and Media, Craft and Folk Art Mus., 1989, Selections from the Joyce and Jay Cooper Collection of Contemporary Ceramics, Nelson Fine Arts Ctr., Ariz. State U. Art Mus., Building a Permanent Collection: A Perspective on the 1980's, Am. Craft Mus., N.Y., 1990, 28th Ann. Ceramic Exhbn., Everson Mus. of Art, Syacuse, N.Y., 1990, S.E. Bank Collects: A Corp. Views Contemporary Art, Harn Mus. of Art, U. Fla., Here's Looking at Me/A Mes Veaux --Contemporary Self Portraits, Espace Lyonnaise d'Art Contemporain, Lyons, France, 1993, Table Tops: Morandi's Still Lifes to Mappplethorpe's Flower Studies, Calif. Ctr. for the Arts Mus., 1997, Ceramic Still Life: The Common Object, Oliver Arts Ctr. and the Calif. Coll. of Arts and Crafts, 1997, Splendors of Porcelain, LA County Mus. of Art, 1997, Conjunction, Long Beach Mus. of Art, 1999, Color and Fire: Defining Moments in Studio Ceramics, 1950-2000, LA County Mus. of Art, 2000, Chouinard: A Living Legacy, Oceanside Mus. of Art, Calif., 2001; author: Decorative Arts in Modern Interiors, 1971, Clay Work, Form and Idea in Ceramic Design, 1975, Ornaments and Surfaces on Ceramics, Kunst and Handwerk, 1977, Studio Porcelain, 1980, Porcelain: Traditions and New Visions, 1981, Ceramics of the 20th Century, 1982, American Crafts: A Source Book for the Home, 1983, Elsa Rady Porcelain, 1984, American Ceramics 1987 to the Present, 1987, The History of American Ceramics, 1607 to Present, 1988, Modern Design, 1990, The Encyclopedia of Pottery Techniques, 1990, Ceramics of the World From 4000 BC to the Present, 1991, The Craft and the Art of Clay, 1995, The New Ceramic Trends and Traditions, 1996, The Best of Pottery, 1996, Working with Clay, 1998; collections at numerous mus., 1966—98, exhibitions include On and Off the Avenue, The New Yorker, 1981, Janus Gallery, LA, 1981, Mattingly/Baker Gallery, Dallas, 1981, Impressions Gallery, Boston, 1982, Quay Gallery, San Francisco, 1982, Janu Gallery, LA, 1984, Garth Clark Gallery, N.Y., 1985, Jan Turner Gallery, LA, 1987, Holly Solomon Gallery, N.Y., 1987, Jan Turner Gallery, LA, 1988, Holly Solomon Gallery, N.Y., 1990, Ochi Gallery, Idaho, 1990, Isetan Art Mus., Tokyo, Japan, 1991, In Dialogue: The Art of Elsa Rady and Robert Mapplethorpe, Santa Barbara Mus. of Art, 1993, Patricia Faure Gallery, LA, 1995, Holly Solomon Gallery, N.Y., 1995, Ochi Gallery, Idaho, 1995, Long Beach Mus. Art, 2005, Palo Alto Art Ctr., 2005. NEA fellow, Washington, 1981; Calif. Arts Coun. co-grantee, 1983. Home: 12719 Washington Pl Los Angeles CA 90066

RADZINOWICZ, MARY ANN, language educator; b. Champaign, Ill., Apr. 18, 1925; d. Arthur Seymour and Ann (Stacy) Nevins; m. Leon Radzinowicz, June 16, 1958 (div. 1978); children: Ann Stacy Radzinowicz Prior, William Francis Henry. BA, Radcliffe Coll., 1945; MA, Columbia U., 1947, PhD, 1953; MA (hon.), U. Cambridge, Eng., 1960. Prof. Vassar Coll., Poughkeepsie, NY, 1947-50, 52-59, Girton Coll., Cambridge, England, 1960-80, U. Cambridge, 1973-80, Cornell U., Ithaca, NY, 1980-90, Jacob Gould Schurman prof. English emeritus, 1990—. Mem. adv. bd. 2d, 3d, 4th Internat. Milton Symposia, 1985—. Author: Toward Samson Agonistes, 1978 (Hanford prize 1979), Milton's Epics and Psalms, 1989, Milton and the Tragic Women of Genesis, 1995 (Hanford prize); editor American Colonial Prose, 1984, Paradise Lost, Book VIII, 1974; mem. editl. bd. Milton Quar., 1981-2005, Christianity and Lit., 1989—. Mem. MLA, Renaissance Soc. Am., Milton Soc. Am. (honored scholar 1987), John Donne Soc. Home: Ballyconry House Ballyvaughan County Clare Ireland Office: Cornell U Dept English Lit Ithaca NY 14850 Office Phone: 353-65-7077-085. E-mail: manr@eircom.net.

RAE, BARBARA JOYCE, employee placement company executive; b. Prince George, B.C., Can., May 17, 1930; d. Alfred and Lottie Kathleen (Davis) Holmwood; m. George Suart, Feb. 14, 1984; children: James, Glenn, John. MBA, Simon Fraser U., Burnaby, B.C., 1975, LLD (hon.), 1998. Chmn., CEO Adia Can., Ltd., Vancouver, 1953-95; CEO Dekora Staging Inc., Vancouver, B.C., 2003—. Bd. dirs. emeritus Can. Imperial Bank Commerce, Grosvenor Internat. Ltd., Noranda, Inc., Telus, Xerox Can.; dir. VLINX.Com., Can. Inst. Adv. Rsch., 1995-2001, KTCS Pub. Broadcasting; bd. govs. Multiple Sclerosis Soc., 1995—; mem. Fed. Task Force on Future of Can. Fin. Svcs. Sector, 1997-98; past chmn. B.C. Women's Hosp. Found., 1994-97. Chancellor Simon Fraser U., 1987—93; mem. Jud. Appts. Com., B.C., 1988—90; commr. Triennial Commn. Judges Salaries and Benefits; mem. Premier's Econ. Adv. Coun., B.C., 1987—91, Prime Minister's Com. on Sci. and Tech., 1989—94; gen. chmn. United Way Lower Mainland, 1987; chair Salvation Army Red Shield Vancouver Campaign, 1986; bd. dirs. Vancouver Bd. Trade, 1972—76; dir. Royal B.C. Mus.; patron Can. Coun. Christians and Jews; mem. adv. bd. Salvation Army, 1985—2004. Decorated Order of Can., Order of B.C.; recipient Outstanding Alumnae award Simon Fraser U., 1985, Disting. Alumni Svc. award, 1995, Bus. Women of Yr. award Vancouver YWCA, 1986, West Vancouver Achievers award, 1987, B.C. Entrepreneur of Yr. award, 1987, Nat. Vol. award, 1990, Can. Woman Entrepreneur B.C. award, 1992, Queen's Jubilee medal, 2003, Clan Leader award Simon Fraser U., 2004. Home: 3355 Osprey Box 508 Whistler Canada V0N 1B3 Personal E-mail: brae@dekora.com.

RAE, JENEANNE, new product development and innovation development consultant, educator; married; 2 children. BS in Commerce, U. Va.; MBA, Harvard Bus. Sch. Prin., sr. mgmt. team mem. IDEO, Palo Alto, Calif.; co-founder Peer Insight, LLC, Alexandria, Va. Adj. prof. mktg. Georgetown U. McDonough Sch. Bus. Contbr. articles to profl. jours. Named one of Magnificent Seven Gurus of Innovation, BusinessWeek, 2005. Office: Peer Insight LLC 901 King St Ste 400 Alexandria VA 22314 Office Phone: 703-778-5543. Office Fax: 703-535-8176. Business E-Mail: jrae@peerinsight.com.*

RAE, NANCY A., human resources specialist, automotive executive; 1 child. Diploma in Bus. Adminstrn., Ea. Mich. U., M in Indsl. Rels. Interviewer Chrysler Corp., Warren, Mich., 1978; various positions DaimlerChrysler Corp., Auburn Hills, Mich., 1978—92, group personnel exec., procurement and supply and product strategy and regulatory affairs, 1992—94, mgr. workforce diversity and econ. equality, 1994, group personnel mgr., Chrysler Tech. Ctr., 1994—96, group human resources mgr. tech. ops., 1996—98, mgr. health ins. and disability, 1998, v.p. compensation and benefits, 1998—2000, sr. v.p. human resources, 2000—. Office: DaimlerChrysler Corp 1000 Chrysler Dr Auburn Hills MI 48326-2766 Office Phone: 248-576-5741. Office Fax: 248-576-4742.

RAE, SUSANNA-JUDITH, writer, retired marriage and family therapist; b. Cin., July 24, 1946; d. Jess Palfrey Giles and Betty Jane (Zastrow) Kenyon; m. D. David Rogers (div.); children: Robert David Rogers, Michael Dalton Rogers; m. Kenneth Merck. BA, Emory U., 1967; MS, Butler U., 1976, MA, 1986. Lic. marriage and family therapist, clin. social worker, Ind. Tchr. social studies Franklin Ctrl. H.S., Acton, Ind., 1968; cataloger, subs. libr. Carmel (Ind.) Clay Schs., 1975-76; supr. resource ctr. Grad. Sch. Sao Paulo, Brazil, 1977-78; libr., counselor Clark Jr. Coll. Bus., Indpls., 1978-89; pvt. practice Indpls., 1989—98; marriage and family therapist Leap of Faith Counseling Ministry, Indpls., 1998—2004; writer Freelance, Avon, Ind., 2004—. Clin. assoc. Marion County Crisis and Suicide Intervention, Indpls., 1980-82; trainer crisis and suicide intervention Marion county Mental Health Assn., Indpls., 1981-83, mem. spkrs. bur., 1993-96; profl. advisor Rational Recovery Self-Help Network, 1991-95. Contbr. author Rational Recovery Self-Help Network, 1992, 101 Interventions in Family Therapy, 1993; contbr. articles pub. to profl. jours. Dem. party's nominee Hendricks County Coun. Mem., 2002, Hendricks County Commr., 2004; commentator local Nat. Pub. Radio sta, Indpls., 1983—87. Recipient non-fiction and juvenile award Ill. Wesleyan U. Writers Conf., 1979. Mem. Am. Assn. for Marriage and Family Therapy (clin.), Ind. Assn. for Marriage and Family Therapy (clin., sec. 1992-95), Nat. League Am. Pen Women, Mensa (columnist Mind newsletter Indpls. 1984-95), Pi Sigma Alpha, Kappa Delta Epsilon, Kappa Delta Pi. Democrat. United Ch. Of Christ. Avocations: reading, writing, running.

RAEDER, MYRNA SHARON, lawyer, educator; b. NYC, Feb. 4, 1947; d. Samuel and Estelle (Auslander) R.; m. Terry Oliver Kelly, July 13, 1975; children: Thomas Oliver, Michael Lawrence. BA, Hunter Coll., 1968; JD, NYU, 1971; LLM, Georgetown U., 1975. Bar: N.Y. 1972, D.C. 1972, Calif. 1972. Spl. asst. U.S. atty. U.S. Atty's Office, Washington, 1972-73; asst. prof. U. San Fransisco Sch. Law, 1973-75; assoc. O'Melveny & Myers, L.A., 1975-79; assoc. prof. Southwestern U. Sch. Law., L.A., 1979-82, prof., 1983—, Irwin R. Buchalter prof. law, 1990, Paul E. Treusch prof. law, 2002; mem. faculty Nat. Judicial Coll., 1993—. Prettyman fellow Georgetown Law Ctr., Washington, 1971—73. Author: Federal Pretrial Practice, 3d edit., 2000; co-author: Evidence, State and Federal Rules in a Nutshell, 4th edit., 2003, Evidence, Cases, Materials and Problems, 2d edit., 1998. Named to Alumni Hall of Fame, Hunter Coll., 2005. Mem.: ABA (trial evidence com. litigation sect. 1980—, criminal justice sect. 1994—97, adv. to nat. conf. commrs. uniform state laws drafting com. 1996—99, vice-chair planning 1997—98, chair elect 1997—98, chair 1998—99, mem. mag. bd. 2000—, co-chair ad hoc innocence com. 2002—, Commn. Women in the Profession, Margaret Brent Women Lawyers of Achievement award 2002), Youth at Risk Commn., Am. Law Inst., Assn. Am. Law Schs. (chair women in legal edn. sect. 1982, com. on sects. 1984—87, chair elect evidence sect. 1996, chair 1997), Nat. Assn. Women Lawyers (bd. dirs. 1991—98, pres.-elect 1993, pres. 1994—96), Women Lawyers Assn. L.A. (coord. mothers support group 1987—96, bd. dirs., Ernestine Stallhutt award 2003), Am. Bar Found. (life), Order of Coif, Phi Beta Kappa. Office: Southwestern U Sch Law 675 S Westmoreland Ave Los Angeles CA 90005-3905 Business E-Mail: mraeder@swlaw.edu.

RAELIN, ABBY PHYLLIS, school psychologist; b. Bklyn., July 16, 1947; d. Richard and Gertrude P. (Greenberg) Dolin; m. Joseph A. Raelin, Aug. 4, 1974; children: Jonathan, Jeremy. BA in Psychology, Hofstra U., 1969; MEd in Counseling, Boston U., 1970, Counseling and Sch. Pscyhology degree, 1971; PhD in Counseling Psychology, Boston Coll., 1981. Cert. psychologist, sch. psychologist, ednl. psychologist. Counselor Quincy (Mass.) Pub. Schs., 1971-74; psychologist Children's Hosp., Buffalo, 1974-76; counselor Quincy Pub. Schs., 1976-78, dir. Title I presch., 1978-80; sch. psychologist Milton (Mass.) Pub. Schs., 1981—. Mem. APA, Nat. Assn. Sch. Psychologists. Office: Milton Pub Schs Gile Rd Milton MA 02186

RAES, HEATHER REBECCA, special education educator, consultant; b. Newark, N.Y., Oct. 10, 1967; d. William Joseph and Margaret Ruth (Seager) Liddle; m. Mark Edward Raes, May 30, 1987; children: Brianne Rebecca, Brenna Marcail. BS, Nazareth Coll., Rochester, N.Y., 1989, MS, 1992. Cert. bus., elem., spl. edn. tchr., N.Y. Tchr. home econs. Lyons (N.Y.) Jr.-Sr. High Sch., 1989-91, resource room tchr., 1991-92; tchr. spl. edn., cons. Lyons Elem. Sch., 1992—. Mem. Coun. for Exceptional Children, Kappa Delta Pi. Avocations: reading, cross-stitching, cross country skiing, collecting precious moments.

RAESCHILD, SHEILA, writer, humanities educator; b. Pitts., Nov. 4, 1936; d. David Earl Miller and Rae Leoba Seewald; children: Betsy Grawoig Hicks, Susan Grawoig Madison, Paul Grawoig Raedyn, Seth Jurnak. BA, Ga. State U., 1967; MA, PhD, Tulane U., 1971; Cert. Bus. Careers, NYU, 1984. Adj. asst. prof. creative writing U. N.Mex., Albuquerque, 1992—94; part-time instr. English Santa Fe C.C., 1992—94; asst. prof. creative writing U. Cin., 1994—98; adj. asst. prof. humanities Coll. Santa Fe, 1999—; coord. Strengthening Youth City of Santa Fe, 1999. Author: Trolley Song, 1981, The Defiant, 1983, Earthsongs, 1984; contbr. short stories, poetry and non-fiction articles. Fellow, Woodrow Wilson Found., 1967, NDEA, 1967—71, English Speaking Union, 1968, NEH, Johns Hopkins U., 1976. Mem.: Acad. Am. Poets, Poetry Soc. Am., Poets and Writers, Mensa. Office: Coll Santa Fe 1600 Saint Michaels Dr Santa Fe NM 87505-7615 Home: 7 Bajada Place Santa Fe NM 87508 E-mail: sheilaraeschild@peoplepc.com.

RAFFA, JEAN BENEDICT, author, educator; b. Lansing, Mich., Apr. 23, 1943; d. Ernest Raymond and Verna Lois (Borst) Benedict; m. Frederick Anthony Raffa, June 15, 1964; children: Juliette Louise, Matthew Benedict. BS, Fla. State U., 1964, MS, 1968; EdD, U. Fla., 1982. Tchr. Leon County Sch. Sys., Tallahassee, Fla., 1964-69; coord. children's programming WFTV, Orlando, Fla., 1978-80; cons. edn. Tchr. Edn. Ctr. U. Ctrl. Fla., Orlando, 1980-89; writer Orlando, Fla., 1989—; instr. Disney Inst., Orlando, Fla., 1996. Adj. instr. U. Cen. Fla., 1977-85; vis. asst. prof. Stetson U., DeLand, Fla., 1988-89; cons. Lang. Arts Curriculum Com. Orange County Sch. Sys., 1983; inst. The Jung Center, Winter Park, FL, 1997—. Author: Introduction to Television Literacy, 1989, The Bridge to Wholeness: A Feminine Alternative to the Hero Myth, 1992, Dream Theatres of the Soul: Empowering the Feminine Through Jungian Dreamwork, 1994; contbr. articles to profl. jours., articles and meditations to religious jours. Mistress of ceremonies Young Authors' Conf., Orange and Volusia County Sch. Sys., 1984-85; cons. Young Authors' Conf. Orange and Seminole County Sch. Sys., 1985-89; judge Volusia County Pub. Schs. Poetry Contest, 1983, 84, Seminole County Pub. Schs. Lit. Mag., 1985-89; pres. Maitland (Fla.) Jr. H.S. PTA, 1986-87; pres., bd. dirs. Canterbury Retreat and Conf. Ctr. Episcopal Diocese Ctrl. Fla., 1988-90; chair edn. commn. Episcopal Ch. of the Good Shepherd, 1986-89; sr. warden Vestry of Episcopal Ch. of the Good Shepherd, 1988. Mem. Kappa Delta Pi, Phi Delta Kappa. Democrat. Avocations: antiques, horseback riding, travel, reading. Office: 17 S Osceola Ave Ste 200 Orlando FL 32801-2828 Office Phone: 407-648-5141. Personal E-mail: jeanraffa@aol.com.

RAFFERTY, EMILY KERNAN, museum administrator; b. NYC, Mar. 13, 1949; m. John Rafferty; children: Nicholas, Sara. BA cum laude, Boston U., 1971. Arts and philanthropy asst. to David Rockefeller, Jr., Boston, 1971; deputy dir. edn. Inst. Contemporary Art, Boston, 1973—75; adminstr. corp., found. and individual fundraising Met. Mus. of Art, NYC, 1976—81, mgr. devel., 1981—84, v.p. devel. and membership, 1984—96, sr. v.p. devel. and membership, 1996—99, sr. v.p. external affairs, 1999—2005, pres., 2005—. Mem. blue ribbon com Am. Cancer Soc. Found., 1999—2000; lifetime honorary trustee Convent of the Sacred Heart; v.p. bd. Independent Sch.

Chmn. Assn.; pres. Blue Hill Troupe, 1998—99. Mem.: Independent Sector (Met. Mus. rep.), Am. Assn. Museums (devel. com. 1984—94), Women in Financial Devel., Assn. Fundraising Professionals, ArtTable (bd. dirs. 1991—94). Office: Met Museum of Art 1000 Fifth Ave New York NY 10028-1098*

RAFFERTY, GENEVIEVE KENNEDY, social service agency administrator; b. Davenport, Iowa, Jan. 21, 1922; d. Thomas Cyril and Mabel Veronica (Finefield) Kennedy; B.A., St. Ambrose Coll., 1942; postgrad. U. Iowa, 1972; m. Daniel J. Rafferty, Aug. 22, 1942 (dec. 1984); children— Daniel D., Michele M., Genevieve, Thomas K., Eileen M., Margaret M., Sheila M. Real estate saleswoman Manhard Realty, Moline, Ill., 1950-59; substitute tchr., Rock Island, Ill., 1963-67; head start tchr. Rock Island-Scott County Dept. Social Services, 1966; public welfare worker Scott County Dept. Social Services, Davenport, Iowa, 1967-72; exec. dir. Info. and Referral of the Quad-Cities, Rock Island, 1972—92, ret.; mem. Travelers Aid Internat.; chair Rock Island Housing Authority; mem. Quad-City Council on Crime and Delinquency, 1977-80; mem. Rock Island County Council on Alcoholism, 1976-82; chairperson CETA Adv. Bd., 1982-84, bi state regional commn. 1986—; steering com., Quad-City Vision for the Future, 1987; bd. dirs. Quint-City Drug Abuse; chair Just Kids Day Care, 1991—; with United Way Bay Area, 1992-94; Peace Corps vol., Uzbekistan, 1994-96. Named Social Worker of Yr. Quad-City, Nat Assn. Social Workers, 1973, Jefferson award for Cmty. Svc., 2003; Mem. Nat. Assn. Social Workers, Iowa Council Info. and Referral Providers, Nat. Conf. Social Welfare, Ill. Welfare Assn., NOW, Ill. Alliance Info. and Referral Services (dir.). Democrat. Roman Catholic. Office: 2201 25th Ave Rock Island IL 61201-5320

RAFFINI, RENEE KATHLEEN, foreign language professional, educator; b. Racine, Wis., Mar. 10, 1955; d. John Peter and Clara Cecelia (Urli) R.; m. Anthony M. Yezer, Sept. 19, 1984 (div. 1997); children: Claire Eva, Benjamin Anton; m. Mark L. Whipple, June 26, 1999. BA in Econs. and French, U. Wis., 1976; MA in Econs., George Washington U., 1984, MEd, 1996. Cert. secondary edn. tchr. French and social studies, Md. Legis. aide to spkr. Wis. State Assembly, Madison, Wis., 1974—78; credit union advisor/auditor U.S. Peace Corps, Bafoussam, Cameroon, 1978-80; exec. aide George Washington U. Med. Faculty Assn., Washington, 1980-84; fin. economist U.S. Securities and Exch. Com., 1984—89; tchr. of French Bethesda (Md.) - Chevy Chase H.S., 1992-94; history tchr. French Internat. Sch., Bethesda, 1997; tchr. French Walter Johnson H.S., 1994—2005; resource tchr. dept. fgn. lang. Gaithersburg H.S., 2005—. Sponsor Bethesda Comm. Action Team, 1995-2000; student mentor Walter Johnson H.S., 1994—; advisor U.S. Peace Corps Tchg. Forum, Washington, 1997; sponsor French Honor Soc., 1998—. Judge of strokes and turns Montgomery County Swim League, Bethesda, 1997; vestry mem. Grace Episcopal Ch., Silver Spring, Md., 1996-97; active mem. Returned Peace Corps Assns., Washington, 1980—. Grantee Youth Rise, State of Md., Annapolis, 1996-97, Neighborhood Empowerment, Rockville, Md., 1996-97. Mem. Am. Coun. Tchrs. of Fgn. Langs., Am. Econs. Assn., Am. Assn. Tchrs. of French, Les Francomeres (founder 1992—), Les Compagnons de la Parole Française, Friends of Cameroon. Democrat. Avocations: sailing, tennis, photography, camping. Office: Gaithersburg HS 314 S Frederick Ave Gaithersburg MD 20877

RAFFLES, LINDA N., secondary school educator; b. New Britain, Conn., June 14, 1948; d. Peter Anthony and Jacqueline Ann Negrini; m. David Anthony Raffles, Sept. 15, 1978 (div. Oct. 1992); children: Anthony, Sara. BA Math., Ctrl. Conn. State U., 1970, MS Math., 1972. Tchr. math. Gideon Welles Mid. Sch., Glastonbury, Conn., 1970—90, Glastonbury H.S., 1990—2006, East Cath. H.S., Manchester, Conn., 2006—. Prof. MBA U. Conn., Hartford, 1999—; tchr. summer sch., West Hartford, 2000—; cons. Gulf States Project, 2003; pvt. tutor; summer writer Math Connections series Hartford Coll. Women, 1990—95. Author: Stepping Stone Math, 1988. Recipient Presdl. award for excellence in math./sci. tchg., 1987, Glastonbury Tchr. of Yr., 1987. Mem.: Assn. Tchrs. Math. Conn. (publicity chair 1988), Nat. Coun. Tchrs. Math. (publicity chair 1995). Avocations: crafts, travel, reading. Office: East Cath High Sch 115 New State Rd Manchester CT 06040 Business E-Mail: raffesl@glastonburyus.org.

RAFFO, HEATHER, playwright, actress; b. 1970; BA in Literature, U. Mich.; MFA in Acting, USD. Actress (plays) Burn This, Caucasian Chalk Circle, Fathers and Sons, Twelfth Night, Pericles, (off-Broadway) Over the River and Through the Woods, Macbeth, Merry Wives of Windsor, The Rivals, actress/playwright 9 Parts of Desire, 2004—05, actress (films) Road to Nowhere.

RAFFO, SUSAN HENNEY, retired elementary school educator; b. Kendallville, Ind., Feb. 14, 1945; d. Gordon Theron and Sue (Kizer) Henney; m. Lawrence Albert Raffo, Feb. 19, 1977; children: Timothy, Kathleen. BS in Elem. Edn., Ball State U., Muncie, Ind., 1967; M in Spl. Edn., San Francisco State U., 1972. Cert. elem. tchr., Calif. Tchr. East Noble Sch. Corp., Kendallville, Ind., 1967-68, Burlingame Sch. Dist., Calif., 1968-2000, Las Lomitas Sch. Dist., Calif., 2000—06; ret., 2006. Master tchr. San Francisco State U., 1970-95, U. Notre Dame d'Namur, Belmont, Calif., 11996-, instr. grad. edn. dept., supervisor of student tchrs., 2006-. Registrar AYSO, Burlingame, 1987-94; bd. dirs. Burlingame Cmty. Edn. Found., 1989-95, sec., 1992-94. Recipient Svc. award PTA, 1989, J. Russell Kent award for innovative programs San Mateo County Sch. Bds. Assn., 1993; named Tchr. of Yr., Lions Club, 1993. Mem. Calif. Reading Assn., Alpha Delta Kappa, Phi Delta Kappa. Avocations: reading, fabric arts, golf.

RAFTER, TRACY, publishing executive; m. Michael Rafter; 1 child, Haley. With advt. sales mgr., Idaho; gen. mgr. St. Louis; pub. Pa.; group pub. Taunton Daily Gazette and The Herald News, Fall River, Mass.; co-owner Valley Times, Milton-Freewater, Oreg., 1999—2002; sr. v.p. advt. and mktg. L.A. Newspaper Group, 2001—04; pub., CEO L.A. Daily News, 2004—. Office: LA Daily News 21221 Oxnard St POBox 4200 Woodland Hills CA 91365

RAFUSE, NANCY E., lawyer, director; b. Columbia, SC, Dec. 14, 1966; m. Mark Rafuse; 2 children. BBA cum laude, U. Ga., 1988, JD magna cum laude, 1991. Ptnr., chair dept. employment law Paul, Hastings, Janofsky & Walker, Atlanta, 1991—2003; co-founder, mng. ptnr. Ashe, Rafuse & Hill, Atlanta, 2003—. Spkr. in field; mem. bar coun. and disciplinary com. No. Dist. Ga., 2002—05. Contbr. articles to profl. jours. Bd. dirs. Atlanta Urban League, Zoo Atlanta; mem. Atlanta United Way Women's Leadership Coun. Named one of Georgia's Legal Elite, Georgia Trend mag., 2003—04, Top 40 Lawyers Under 40, Nat. Law Jour., 2005. Mem.: ABA (mem. labor and employment law sect.), Atlanta Bar Assn. (mem. labor and employment law sect.), State Bar Ga. (mem. labor and employment law sect.). Office: Ashe Rafuse & Hill LLP 1355 Peachtree St Ste 500 Atlanta GA 30309 Office Phone: 404-253-6002. Office Fax: 404-253-6060. E-mail: nancyrafuse@asherafuse.com.

RAGAN, AMANDA, state senator; b. Mason City, Sept. 1954; m. James Ragan; children: Edith, Charles. AA, N. Iowa Area CC; BA in Human Svcs., cum laude, Buena Vista U. Legis. asst. to Rep. Ed Parker; co-chair Ho. Majority Leader John Groninga, 1987—89; dist. rep. Iowa Dem. State Ctrl. Com., 1992—2002; legis. page Iowa State Senate, 1973, mem. DesMoines, 2002—, asst. leader, co-chair human resources com., mem. agr. com., mem. econ. growth com., mem. rules and adminstrn. com., mem. appropriations com., mem. health & human svcs. com., mem. budget com.; co-chair Senate Human Resources Com. Active Mason City Sesquicentennial Com., Sesquicentennial Com.; mem. Birth Defects Adv. Bd., HAWK-I Bd.; exec. dir. Meals on Wheels, Mason City, Cmty. Kitchen North Iowa, Inc., Mason City; mem. N. Iowa Band Festival Planning Com., Buena Vista Alumni Found., Coun. Social Agencies, Maternal Health Adv. Coun.; active Iowa Dem. Party State Ctrl. Com.; asst. leader Dem. Caucus; mem. Cerro Gordo County Dem. Ctrl. Com.; past chair. Cerro Gordo Re-Elect Clinton-Gore Com.; bd. dirs. Charles City C. of C., Osage C. of C., Francis Lauer Youth Svc. Mem.: N Iowa Fund-Raising Profls. Assn., Mason City C. of C., Mason City Sunrise Rotary (bd. dirs.). Office: State Capitol Bldg East 12th and Grand Des Moines IA 50319 Home: 20 Granite Ct Mason City IA 50401

RAGAN, ANN TALMADGE, media and production consultant, actor; b. Raleigh, NC, July 6, 1951; d. Samuel Talmadge and Marjorie Lois (Usher) R.; m. L. Worth Keeter III, Aug. 22, 1992. Student, U. N.C., 1969-71, Finch Coll., 1972-73, New Sch. Social Rsch., 1973-74, Western Wash. U., 1978. Acct. estimator Benton & Bowles Inc., NYC, 1971-72, media buyer, 1974-77; speechwriter, press aide Senator Robert Morgan, Washington, 1978-79; asst. prodr., casting dir. John F. Murray Inc., NYC, 1979—80; prod., sales dir. Grand St. Films, NYC, 1980-84; ind. prod. for various clients NYC, 1984-86; asst. pub. The Pilot, Inc., Southern Pines, NC, 1986-96, bd. dirs. Prodn. mgr. Anglo Am. Media Workshops, London, 1988—90; dir. SAG Conservatory Am. Film Inst., L.A., 2003—, coach Film Camp, 2005—, cons.; mgr., exec. prodr. films, commercials, audio books Blue Kiss, LLC, 2000—; prodn. mgr., coach Directing Workshop for Women; workshop leader in field. Contbr. articles to newspapers and jours. Life mem. Roanoke Island Hist. Assn.; mem.Moore County Arts Coun., 1986-89. Mem.: SAG (conservatory com., rec. sec. 1997—2006, cons., vice-chair 2003—), AFTRA, Women in Film, Women in Theatre (adminstrv. dir. 1995—97, treas. 1997—99, bd. dirs. 1997—99, pres. 2004—), Actors Equity Assn., Ind. Feature Project West, Kings and Clowns Ednl. Shakespeare Alliance (treas. bd. dirs. 1999—), Pi Beta Phi. Democrat. Methodist. Home and Office: 10542 Bloomfield St Toluca Lake CA 91602-2813 Office Phone: 818-762-6339. E-mail: bluekisslic@aol.com.

RAGAN, CHARLOTTE ANN, music educator; b. Elberton, Ga., May 4, 1929; d. Harry Sanders and Pauline Melissa (Edwards) Bell; m. Gordon Billy Ragan (dec.); children: Gordon Billy Jr., Evelyn Melissa Swanson. BFA, U. Ga., 1950; MA, Columbia U., 1954. Pvt. piano tchr. Dir. hand bells First Bapt. Ch., Milledgeville, Ga., pianist for Merri Maker Choir. Mem.: DAR (state curator 1994—96, state treas. 1996—98, state chorus dir. 2002—), Music Tchrs. Nat. Assn., C. of C., U. Ga. (Sigma Lamda chpt., treas. mortar bd.), Milledgeville Music Club (pres. 1968—70), Alpha Omicron Pi, Sigma Alpha Iota. Baptist. Avocations: dance, bridge, reading. Home: 330 Doles Blvd Milledgeville GA 31061 Office Phone: 478-452-1674.

RAGAN, DEBORAH ANN, music educator; b. Marshalltown, Iowa, May 27, 1951; d. Robert Gerald and Dorothy Lorraine Coughlin; m. Don Edwin Ketelsen (div.); 1 child, Brandon Scott Ketelsen; m. Richard Thomas Ragan, 1990; 1 child, Matthew Robert. AA, Marshalltown C.C., Iowa, 1971; BA, U. No. Iowa, Cedar Falls, 1975. Dir. vocal music Bennett (Iowa) Comty. Schs., 1975—79, Lost Nation (Iowa) Comty. Schs., 1979—81, Bettendorf (Iowa) Comty. Schs., 1981—. Advt. editor sounding bd. Iowa Choral Dirs. Assn.; adjudicator Iowa and Ill. H.S. Music Assns. Vol. John Deere Classic, Coal Valley, Ill. Mem.: NEA, Am. Choral Dirs. Assn. (bd. dirs., hospitality and program chairperson North Cen. Regional Conv.). Avocations: gardening, reading, theater, travel. Home: 1922 W 38th St Davenport IA 52806 Office: Bettendorf H S 3333 18th St Bettendorf IA 52722

RAGANS, ROSALIND DOROTHY, writer, artist, retired educator; b. Bklyn., Feb. 28, 1933; d. Sidney Guy Gordon and Beatrice (Zuckerman) Safier; m. John Franklin Ragans, July 31, 1965; 1 child, John Lee. BFA, CUNY-Hunter Coll., 1955; MEd, Ga. So. Coll., 1967; EdD, U. Ga., 1971. Cert. tchr. art, Ga. Tchr. art Union City (N.J.) Bd. Edn., 1956-62; tchr. 1st grade Chatham Bd. Edn., Savannah, Ga., 1962-64; instr. art Ga. So. U., Statesboro, 1964-69, asst. prof., 1969-76, assoc. prof., 1976-89, prof. emeritus, 1989—. Keynote speaker art edn. confs.; presenter in field. Author: (textbooks) ArtTalk, 1988, 4th edit., 2005, Introducing Art, 1997, 2d edit., 2005, Exploring Art, 1990, 3d edit., 2005, Understanding Art, 1990, 3d edit., 2005; sr. author Art Connections K-5, 1997, 2d edit., 2000, K-6, 3d edit., 2005 Mem. Nat. Assn. Educators (life), Ga. Assn. Educators (life), Nat. Art Edn. Assn. (Southeastern Art Educator of Yr. 1991, Nat. Art Educator of Yr. 1992), Ga. Art Edn. Assn. (Ga. Art Educator of Yr. 1990), Pilot Club Internat. (Ga. dist., Ga. Profl. Handicapped Woman of Yr. 1988). Jewish. Avocation: painting. E-mail: RozRagans@comcast.net.

RAGAVAN, ANPALAKI JEYABALASINKHAM, software developer, researcher; arrived in U.S., 1992; d. George Nagularajah and Thangaranee Veluppillai Jeyabalasingham; m. Ragavan Vinasithamby, July 1, 1993. BS (hon.), U. Sri Lanka, 1985, MPhil (hon.) in Hydrology, 1989; MS in Hydrogeology (hon.), U. Nev., 1996, MS in Civil Engring., 2003, MS in Math., 2004—, MS in Hydrology, 2005, postgrad, 2000—. Cert. BASIC computer programmer, geographic info. sys., Visual Basic programmer, GIS and web design, well drilling with LS 100. Asst. prof. U. Sri Lanka, Kilinochchi, Jaffna, 1989—92; rsch. asst. Ind. State U., Tere Haute, 1992—93; rsch./tchg. asst. U. of Nev., Reno, 1993—96; software developer Bur. Labor Stats., Washington, 1996—99; rsch. asst. U. of Nev., Reno, 1999—. Grad. fellow U. Nev., Reno, 1993—96; presenter in field. Contbr. articles to profl. jours. (Excellence in Abstract Submission award Am. Jour. Pub. Health, 2001); author: (book) Introductory Statistics, Lab-Guide - SAS, 1st edition., 1993, (Nev. health divsn. quar. report) Impact Of Discharge Planning On Adherence to Treatment for Inmates with HIV/AIDS in Nevada, 2001, Surveillance Update: Discharge Planning For Inmates with HIV/AIDS in Nevada, 2002. Named to Great Women of the 21st Century; recipient Excellence in Abstract Submission, APHA, HIV/AIDS Sect., 2001, Cert. Of Appreciation, Nev. State Mental Health and Devel. Services, 2000, Overseas Devel. Adminstrn. scholarship, Govt. Of UK, 1986—89; grantee, State of Nev., 2002; scholar, Asian Inst. Of Tech. in Thailand, 1991, Ind. State U., 1992—93, U. of Nev., Reno, 1993—, Soroptimist Internat. of Reno, Sierra Nev. Region, 2000, Water Resources Assn., 2005, Grad. Student Assn., 2005; Outstanding Grad. Student Rschr. scholar, Grad. Student Assn., U. Nev., Reno, 2006. Mem.: AAAS, Nature Pub. Group, Am. Geophys. Union, Nat. Ground Water Assn., Nev. Water Resources Assn., Am. Math. Soc., Am. Statis. Assn., Geol. Soc. Am., Great Woman of the 21st Century (profl. women's adv. bd.), Alumni Assn. U. Nev. (mem. profl. women's adv. bd.). Mem. Lds Ch. Avocations: dance, music, guitar, swimming, sports. Office: U Nev Dept Internal Med Reno NV 89512 Home: 3952 Clear Acre Ln #276 Reno NV 89512-1202 Office Phone: 775-784-4433. Business E-Mail: ragavan@unr.edu.

RAGGI, REENA, federal judge; b. Jersey City, May 11, 1951; BA, Wellesley Coll., 1973; JD cum laude, Harvard U., 1976. Bar: N.Y. 1977, U.S. Dist. Ct. (ea. dist.) N.Y. 1987, U.S. Ct. Appeals (2d cir.) 2002. Law clerk US Ct. of Appeals, 7th Circuit, 1976—77; assoc. Cahill, Gordon & Reindel, NY, 1977—79; asst. U.S. atty. Dept. Justice, Bklyn., 1979—86; ptnr. Windels, Marx, Davies & Ives, N.Y.C., 1986—87; judge U.S. Dist. Ct. (Ea. dist.) N.Y., 1987—2002, U.S. Ct. Appeals (2nd Cir.), N.Y.C., 2002—. Office: US Courthouse 225 Cadman Plz E Brooklyn NY 11201

RAGGIO, LOUISE BALLERSTEDT, lawyer; b. Austin, Tex., June 15, 1919; d. Louis F. and Hilma (Lindgren) Ballerstedt; m. Grier H. Raggio, Apr. 19, 1941; children: Grier, Thomas, Kenneth. BA, U. Tex., 1939; student, Am. U. Washington, 1939-40; JD, So. Methodist U., 1952. Bar: Tex. 1952, U.S. Dist. Ct. (no. dist.) Tex. 1958. Intern Nat. Inst. Pub. Affairs, Washington, 1939-40; asst. dist. atty. Dallas County, Tex., 1954-56; shareholder Raggio and Raggio, 1956—. Sec. Gov.'s Commn. on Status of Women, 1970-71; trustee Tex. Bar Found., 1982-86, chmn., 1984-85, chmn. fellows, 1993—, Dallas Women's Found., 1993—, Nat. Conf. Bar Founds., 1986-92. Recipient Zonta award, Bus. and Profl. Women's Club award, So. Meth. U. Alumni award, Woman of Yr. award Tex. Fedn. Bus. and Profl. Women's Clubs, 1985, award Internat. Women's Forum, 1990, Disting. Law Alumni award So. Meth. U., 1992, Disting. Trial Lawyer award, 1993, Outstanding Trial Lawyer award Dallas Bar Assn., 1993, Pacemaker award Nat. Bus. Women Owners Assn., 1994, Thomas Jefferson award ACLU, 1994, Courage award Women Journalists North Tex., 1995, Tex. Lawyer award 1999, Entrepreneur award Fortune Sm. Bus. Mag., 2000, Gillian award 2000, Professionalism award Dallas (Tex.) Bar, 2003; named to Tex. Women's Hall of Fame, 1985; named one of Heroes of Sm. Bus., Fortune Sm. Bus. Mag., 2000. Fellow Am. Bar Found.; mem. ABA (chmn. family sect. 1975-76, Best Woman Lawyer award 1995, Lifetime Achievement award 2002), LWV (pres. Austin 1945-46), State Bar Tex. (chmn. family law sect. 1965-67, dir. 1979-82, citation for law reform 1967, Pres.'s award 1987, Sarah T. Hughes award 1993, named one of 100 Tex. Lawyers of Century, 1999, 50 Yr. Lawyer award 2003), Dallas Bar Found. (pres. fellow com. 1991), Am. Acad. Matrimonial Lawyers (gov. 1973-81, trustee found. 1992—), Bus. and Profl. Women's Club (pres. Town North 1958-59), Phi Beta Kappa (pres. Dallas chpt. 1970-71, 90-92). Unitarian Universalist. Home: 3561 Colgate Ave Dallas TX 75225-5010 Office: Raggio and Raggio 3316 Oak Grove Ave Ste 100 Dallas TX 75204-2338 Office Phone: 214-880-7500. E-mail: louise@raggiolaw.com.

RAGINSKY, NINA, artist; d. Bernard Boris and Helen Theresa R.; 1 child, Sofya Katrina. BA, Rutgers U., 1962; studied painting with, Roy Lichtenstein; studied sculpture with, George Segal; studied Art History with Allan Kaprow, Rutgers U. Freelance photographer Nat. Film Bd., Ottawa, Ont., Canada, 1963-81; instr. metaphysics Emily Car Coll. Art, Vancouver, B.C., Canada, 1973-81; painter Salt Spring Island, B.C., 1989—. Sr. artist, jury Can. Coun.; selected Can. rep. in Sweden for Sweden Now Mag., 1979; tchr., lectr. in field, 1973—. One woman shows include Vancouver Art Gallery, Victoria Art Gallery, Edmonton Art Gallery, Art Gallery Ont., San Francisco Mus. Art, Acadia U., Nancy Hoffman Gallery, N.Y.C., Meml. U. Newfoundland Art Gallery; exhibited in group shows at Rutgers U., 1962, Montreal Mus. Fine Arts, 1963, Nat. Film Bd., Ottawa, 1964, 65, 67, 70, 71, 76, 77, Internat. Salon Photography, Bordeaux, France, 1968, Nat. Gallery Ottawa, 1968, Eastman House, Rochester, N.Y., 1969, Vancouver Art Gallery, 1973, 80, Mural for Conf. Ctr. Ottawa, 1973, Field Mus., Chgo., 1976, Edmonton Art Gallery, 1978, 79, Walter Philips Gallery, 1979, Glenbow Mus. Gallery, 1979, Harbour Front Community Gallery, 1980, Hamilton Art Gallery, 1980, Musée Maisil de St. Lambert, 1981, Mendel Art Gallery, 1981, Dunlop Art Gallery, Regina, Can., 1981, Vancouver Art Gallery, 2001; represented in permanent collections Nat. Film Bd. Stills divsn., Ottawa, Ont., Banff (Alta.) Sch. Fine Arts, Nat Gallery Ottawa, Can., George Eastman House, Rochester, NY, Wadsworth Atheneum, Conn., Edmonton Art Gallery, U. Victoria, B.C., various pvt. collections. Bd. dirs. Island Watch, Salt Spring Island, B.C., 1993; founder, coord. Salt Spring Island Ecosys. Stewardship Project, 1993; founder, coord. Salt Spring Island Waterbird Watch Collective, 1994—. Decorated officer Order of Can., 1984; recipient Kees Vermeer award for edn. and conservation Simon Fraser U., 1997, Burns Bog award for environ. excellence, Vancouver, 2005. Mem.: Soc. for Advancement of Slow, Royal Can. Acad. Arts. Avocations: gardening, birding, subject of numerous publs. Home and Office: 272 Beddis Rd Salt Spring Island BC Canada V8K 2J1

RAGLAND, ELLIE, literature and language professor; b. Greensboro, NC, Sept. 16, 1941; d. Lucile Stowe and Terry Porter Ragland; 1 child, Caroline Alexandra Choudhury. BA, Mich. State U., Lansing, 1963; MA, U. Mich., Ann Arbor, 1967, PhD, 1972. Prof. U. Mo., Columbia, 1989—, Frederick A. Middlebush chair English, 1989—. Author: The Logic of Sexuation: From Aristotle to Lacan, 2004 (Outstanding Title, CHOICE Mag., 2004); editor: (Re)-Turn: A Jour. Lacanian Studies, 2003—06. Fellow, NEH, 1980—81. Mem.: MLA (assoc.). D-Liberal. Avocations: travel, cooking, reading. Home: 502 W Rockcreek Dr Columbia MO 65203 Office: Univ Mo English Dept Conley St Tate Hall Columbia MO 65211 Home Fax: 573-882-5785; Office Fax: 573-882-5785. Business E-Mail: raglande@missouri.edu.

RAGLAND, INES COLOM, principal; b. Washington, Mar. 12, 1947; d. Jose Luis Sr. and Frances Yerby (Pannill) Colom; m. Banjamin Michael Ragland, Dec. 17, 1977 (div. May 1991); children: Michelle Elizabeth, Rachael Christine. BA in Secondary Edn., Longwood Coll., 1969, MS in Secondary Adminstrn., 1992. Clk. Va. State Water Control Bd., Richmond, 1969; tchr. Spanish Richmond City Pub. Schs., 1969-74; planning supr. Va. State Water Control Bd., 1974-78; asst. prin., tchr., prin. Grove Ave. Bapt. Christian Sch., Richmond, 1978-83; guidance tchr., asst. prin. Victory Christian Acad., Richmond, 1990—. Cons. in field. Mission participant, El Salvador, 1992. Mem. ASCD. Avocations: Civil War research, church. Office: Victory Christian Acad 8491 Chamberlayne Rd Richmond VA 23227-1550

RAGLAND, TERA DENISE, music educator; b. Louisville, July 18, 1973; d. Robert Noble and Sharron Kay Jones; m. Gordon Ragland, May 29, 1999; 1 child, Anne Elizabeth. B in Music Edn., Georgetown Coll., 1995; M in Music Edn., Murray State U., 1996. Asst. band dir. McLean County Schs., Calhoun, Ky., 1996—2001; music tchr. Russellville (Ky.) Ind. Schs., 2001—. Mem.: NEA, Russellville Edn. Assn., Ky. Edn. Assn., Ky. Music Educators Assn., Music Educators Nat. Conf. Republican. Baptist. Office: Russellville Mid Sch 210 E 7th St Russellville KY 42276 Business E-Mail: tera.ragland@russellvillekyschools.us.

RAGO, ANN D'AMICO, academic administrator, public relations executive; b. Pitts., Aug. 24, 1957; d. Jack and Florence D'Amico; m. John Rago; children: Annie J., Emily J., John Henry. BA, Duquesne U., Pitts., 1979, MA, 1987. From comm. assoc. to dir. pub. rels. Duquesne U., 1979—89, coord. univ. rels., 1989—93, adj. prof. comm., 1990—2000, exec. dir. pub. affairs, 1993—2002; v.p. instnl. rels. Carlow Coll., Pitts., 2002—. Editor University Record, 1989 (silver medal). Bd. dirs. Support, Pitts., 1989-91; sch. dir. Carylnton Sch. Bd., Pitts., 1989-93, pres. sch. bd., 1990. Recipient Gold award for publs./external prospectus 9th Ann. Admissions Advt. Awards, 1994, Gold award for Total Pub. Rels. Campaign, 10th Ann. Admissions Advt. Awards, 1995, Gold award for Total Pub. Rels. Campaign, 11th Ann. Admissions Awards, 1996, 1st Place award in Category 35, Internal Pub. Rels. Campaign, Pitts. chpt. Women in Comm., Inc., 1996, Bronze Cert. for logo and letterhead for Duquesne U.'s Capital Campaign and cert. merit for Duquesne U.'s internal publ. 14th Ann. Admissions Advt. Awards, 1998, Clarion award Assn. for Women in Communications, 2003. Mem. Pub. Rels. Soc. Am. (1st place award 1993), Internat. Assn. Bus. Communicators (award of excellence 1991, award of honor 1993, award of merit 1994), Am. Mgmt. Assn., Assn. for Women in Comm. (Clarion award 2003), Press Club Western Pa., Sigma Delta Chi. Office: Carlow Coll Institutional Relations 3333 Fifth Ave Pittsburgh PA 15213 Office Phone: 412-578-2090. Personal E-mail: adr824@aol.com. Business E-Mail: arago@carlow.edu.

RAGO-MCNAMARA, JULIET MAGGIO, artist; b. Chgo., Mar. 21, 1927; d. Henry Clifford and Grace (Canadeo) Maggio; m. Henry A. Rago, Oct. 7, 1950 (dec. 1969); m. Robert J. McNamara, Aug. 14, 1973 (dec. 1995); children: Christina, Carmela, Anthony, Martha. BFA, Sch. of Art Inst., Chgo., 1950, MFA, 1973; postgrad., Accademia di Belli Arti, Florence, Italy, 1960-61, Vt. Studio Sch., 1988, Putney Painting Intensive, Vt., 1990. Prof. fine arts Loyola U. Chgo., 1969—; art instr. Barat Coll. of Sacred Heart, Lake Forest, Ill., 1970-71. Solo sculpture shows include U. Ill. Med. Ctr., 1978, Loyola U., Chgo., 1979; group sculpture shows include Evanston Art Ctr., 1987, Nina Owen Gallery, Chgo., 1987; solo painting exhbns. include Kerrigan-Hendricks Gallery, Chgo., 1954, Devorah-Sherman Gallery, Chgo., 1963, 65, Rosary Coll., River Forest, Ill., 1970, Wabash Transit Gallery, Sch. Art Inst., Chgo., 1973, Evanston Art Ctr., 1977, Cloud Hands Gallery, Chgo., 1978, Northwestern U., Chgo., 1983, 84, Sykes Gallery, Lancaster, Pa., 1987, Lawrence Perrin Gallery, Chgo., 1989, Space 900, Chgo., 1992, Chgo. Cultural Ctr., 1993, Gallery 1933, 1994, Lincoln Pub. Libr., 1995, Divine Word Gallery, Techny, Ill., 2000, Old Town Sch. Folk Music, 2005, Bemis Hall, Lincoln, Mass., 2005, Cath. Theological Union, Chgo., 2006, many others; group painting shows include Renaissance Soc. Christmas Shows, 1953-69, Old Orchard Art Fair, Skokie, Ill., 1979, Chgo. Bot. Gardens, Glencoe, Ill., 1985, Ill. Arts Coun. Gallery, Chgo., 1986, Assisi, Italy, 1989, Gallery 1933, 1990, 90, Lincoln Pub. Libr., 1994, Fine Arts Gallery, Chgo., Ill., 2002, Lincoln (Mass.) Pub. Libr., 2003, Emerson Umbrella, Concord, Mass., 2003, others; and pvt. collections. Fellow Yaddo Found., 1971, Skowhegan Sch. Painting, 1972, Va. Ctr. Creative Arts, 1986, Vt. Studio Found., 1987, Ragdale Found., 1987, 2006, The Ucross Found., 1988, Byrdcliffe Art Colony, 1991, 92; grantee Ill. Arts Coun., 1979. Mem. Coll. Art Assn. (mem. women's caucus). Avocations: piano, guitar, singing. Home: 1519 Hinman #4-A Evanston IL 60201

RAGSDALE, JANA LYNNE, music educator; b. Oklahoma City, Oct. 18, 1959; d. James and Florence Ward; children: Stephanie, Florence. AA, Oklahoma City C.C., 1989; BS, U. Ctrl. Okla., 1991; MEd in Curriculum and Supervision, U. Okla., 2004. Cert. tchr., prin. Okla. Sec. to pres. Woolsey Brokerage Co., Oklahoma City, 1980—84; exec. asst. Local Fed. Savs., Oklahoma City, 1984—86; music, gifted and talented class tchr. Newcastle (Okla.) Pub. Schs., 1991—. Choir dir. Eastlake Presbyn. Ch. Mem.: Newcastle C. of C., Okla. Edn. Assn., Music Educators Nat. Conf., Phi Kappa Phi. Republican. Avocations: piano, reading, travel. Home: 10900 S Pennsylvania Apt 1824 Oklahoma City OK 73170

RAGSDALE, KATHERINE HANCOCK, Episcopal priest, political activist; d. Ann Hancock and Ambler Coleman Ragsdale. BA, Coll. William and Mary, Williamsburg, Va., 1980; MDiv, Va. Theol. Sem., Alexandria, 1987; Dr. of Ministry, Episcopal Div. Sch., Cambridge, Mass., 1996. Exec. dir. Common Cause, Richmond, Va., 1983—85; dir. IMPACT 88, Washington, 1987—89; pastoral team mem. St. Matthew's Episcopal Ch., Jersey City, 1989—92; program dir. Episcopal Ch. Ctr., NYC, 1989—94; vicar St. David's Episcopal Ch., Pepperell, Mass., 1995—; interim exec. dir. Polit. Rsch. Assocs., Somerville, Mass., 2005—. Co-chair Polit. Rsch. Assocs., 2003—05. Author: (Albany law rev.) The Role of Religious Communities in Domestic Violence, The Role of Religious Institutions in Domestic Violence, (tng. manual) 1001 Ways to Change the World: Advocacy Training; editor: (anthology) Boundary Wars: Intimacy and Distance in Healing Relationships. Bd. dirs. Common Cause, Richmond, Va., 1985—87, NARAL: ProChoice Am., Washington, 2001, mem. exec. com., 2001, mem. transition com., 2001, chair, 2001; mem. Women's Dem. Club; dir. The White House Project, NYC, 1999—; mem. Religious Coalition Reproductive Choice, 1985—2000, treas., 1985—2000, bd. dirs., 1985—2000, chmn. bd., 1992—97; mem. bi-nat. adv. bd. Ctr. Prevention Sexual and Domestic Violence, Seattle, 1991—. Recipient Faith and Freedom award, Mass. Religious Coalition Reproductive Choice, 2000, President's award, Religious Coalition Reproductive Choice Black Ch. Initiative, 2001; grantee, Gloria Steinem/Ms. Found. Women, 2004. Avocation: reading. Office: Polit Rsch Assocs 1310 Broadway Ste 201 Somerville MA 02144 Business E-Mail: k.ragsdale@publiceye.org.

RAGSDALE, MARQUERITA D., ambassador; b. Richmond, Va. BA, Am. U.; MA, PhD, U. Va.; JD, Columbia U. Jr. consular and gen. svcs. officer US Dept. State, Kuwait, 1984, polit. officer US Embassy Mogadishu, Somalia, 1986—88, watch officer Ops. Ctr. Washington, desk officer United Arab Emirates and Oman, 1989—91, polit. econ. officer to dep. chief of mission US Embassy in Doha Qatar, 1992, mgmt. analyst, 1995, dep. dir. Office of Arabian Peninsula Affairs; head polit. sect. Bur. of African Affairs US Embassy in Pretoria, 1999—2002; dep. chief of mission US Embassy in Khartoum; US amb. to Rep. of Djibouti US Dept. State, 2004—. Mem.: Nat. Trust for Hist. Preservation. Avocation: architecture. Office: US Embassy of Rep of Djibouti 2150 Djibouti Pl Washington DC 20521-2150 E-mail: managode@state.gov.

RAGSDALE, SANDRA RUSSELL, special education educator; b. Billings, Mont., Mar. 15, 1957; d. Alexander Emmett and Cleora Jean (Saunders) Russell; children: Naomi Jo, Andrea Renee, James Russell. BS, Mont. State U., 1979, MS in Spl. Edn., 2005, MEd in Reading, 2006. cert. childbirth educator. Spl. edn. and reading tchr. Anchorage Sch. Dist., 2005—06, Matanuska-Susitna Sch. Dist., 2006—. U.S. western dir. Inter Childbirth Edn. Assn., Mpls., 1990-92, pres. elect 1992-94, pres. 1994-95. Contbr. articles to profl. jours. Avocations: skiing, reading, writing, quilting, white-water rafting. Personal E-mail: sandyragsdale1@yahoo.com.

RAGSTER, LAVERNE E., academic administrator; b. St. Thomas, Virgin Islands; BS in Biology and Chemistry, U. Miami, 1973; MS in Biology, San Diego State U., 1975; PhD in Biology, U. Calif., San Diego, 1980. Pres. U. Virgin Islands, St. Thomas, asst. prof. then prof., 1980—90, chair divsn. sci. math., sr. v.p., provost. Trustee U. Virgin Islands, St. Thomas, acting v.p. rsch. land grant affairs, v.p. rsch. pub. svc.; sub-sec. gen. Assn. Caribbean Univs. Rsch. Insts.; coord. Consortium Caribbean Univs. Natural Resource Mgmt. Contbr. articles to profl. jours. Mem.: Caribbean Coun. Sci. Tech. (rep. U.S. Virgin Islands), Nature Conservancy (bd. dirs.), Island Resources Found. (bd. dirs.), Caribbean Conservation Assn. (past v.p.), Caribbean Natural Resources Inst. (bd. dirs., past chair bd. dirs.), Caribbean Studies Assn. (past pres.). Office: Office of Pres U Virgin Islands 2 Hohn Brewers Bay St Thomas VI 00802-9990

RAGUSA, ELYSIA, real estate company executive; V.p. Lincoln Property Co.; pres. S.W. corp. svcs. The Staubach Co., Addison, Tex., pres., COO. Grad. Leadership Dallas; assoc. mem. Dallas Citizens Coun.; bd. dirs. Dallas County C.C. Found., Vis. Nurse Assn.; bd. mem. United Way Met. Dallas, former chmn. ctrl. budget com., former mem. exec. com. Mem.: Internat. Women's Forum, Dallas Breakfast Group. Office: The Staubach Co Ste 400 15601 Dallas Pkwy Addison TX 75001

RAHEJA, KRISHNA KUMARI, retired medical/surgical nurse; b. Muzzaffargarh, India; d. R.R. and Sharda (Devi) Relan; m. B.D. Raheja, Apr. 29, 1956; children: Dalip, Nishtha. Diploma, Lady Hardinge Hosp., New Delhi, India, 1952; BA, Punjab U., 1954; MS in Nursing, Syracuse U., 1967; EdS, No. Ill. U., 1986; EdD, Northern Ill. U., 1988; PhD, Columbia Pacific U., 1987. Cert. transcultural nurse. Staff nurse, head nurse Lady Hardinge Med. Coll. Hosp. New Delhi, New Delhi, India, 1952-54, 54-56, clin. specialist, lectr. India, 1956-66; assoc. head. dept. All India Inst. Med. Scis., New Delhi, India, 1967-70; asst. prof. Alfred (N.Y.) U., 1970-71; asst. prof. Coll. of Nursing U. Ill., Chgo., 1971-80; asst. prof. Ctr. for Nursing Northwestern U., Chgo., 1980-90; assoc. prof. St. Xavier U., Chgo., 1989-2000; ret., 2000. Clin. nursing cons. U. Ill. Hosp. Ambulatory Svcs., Chgo., summer 1971; adj. faculty Northpark U., 1992—. Contbr. articles to profl. jours. Recipient Best Tchr. of the Yr. award, 1984, Internat. Transcultural Excellence award Transcultural Nursing Soc., 1999; named to Sigma Theta Tau Omicron Chpt. Mem. ANA, Ill. Nurses Assn., Transcultural Nursing Soc. (treas.), Transcultural Nursing Assn. Internat. Home: 758 Lilac Way Lombard IL 60148-3641 Office: Saint Xavier Univ 3700 W 103rd St Chicago IL 60655-3105

RAHMAN, YUEH-ERH, biologist; b. Kwangtung, China, June 10, 1928; came to U.S., 1960; d. Khon and Kwei-Phan (Chan) Li; m. Aneesur Rahman, Nov. 3, 1956; 1 dau., Aneesa. BS, U. Paris, 1950; MD magna cum laude, U. Louvain, Belgium, 1956. Clin. and postdoctoral research fellow Louvain U., 1956-60; mem. staff Argonne (Ill.) Nat. Lab., 1960-72, biologist, 1972-81, sr. biologist, 1981-85; prof. pharmaceutics Coll. Pharmacy, U. Minn., Mpls., 1985—2002, prof. emeritus, 2002—, dir. grad. studies, pharmaceutics, 1989-92, head dept. pharmaceutics, 1991-96, 97-98. Vis. scientist State U. Utrecht, Netherlands, 1968-69; adj. prof. No. Ill. U., DeKalb, 1971-85; cons. NIH.; Mem. com. of rev. group, div. research grants NIH, 1979-83 Author; patentee in field. Recipient IR-100 award, 1976; grantee Nat. Cancer Inst., Nat. Inst. Arthritis, Metabolic and Digestive Diseases. Fellow Am. Assn. Pharm. Scientists; mem. AAAS, Am. Soc. Cell Biology, N.Y. Acad. Scis., Radiation Rsch. Soc., Assn. for Women in Sci. (1st pres. Chgo. area chpt. 1978-79). Unitarian Universalist. Home: 939 Coast Blvd Unit 6G La Jolla CA 92037-4115

RAHMING, ETTA LORRAINE, social worker, consultant, psychotherapist, counseling administrator; b. Bronx, Mar. 6, 1957; d. Henry Lewis and Irene (Linen) R. BA in Sociology, CCNY, 1979; MSW, Howard U., 1981. Lic. social worker, N.Y.; lic. counselor, N.Y., alchohol and substance abuse counselor. Investigative probation officer N.Y.C. Dept. Probation, 1981-85; social worker E.N.T.E.R. Alcoholism O.P.D., 1985-86; psychiat. social worker Bronx Lebanon Alcoholism O.P.D., 1986-88; clin. supr. residential treatment program E.N.T.E.R. Inc., 1988-89; supr. Comprehensive Employment Opportunity Support Ctr. Fedn. Employment Guidance Ctr., 1989-92; therapist Our Lady of Mercy Mental Health Clinic, Bronx, 1994—96; sch. psychologist intern Dept, of Svcs. Virgin Islands Dist., 1997—. Dist. mgr. Dept. Human Svc., 1997—. Mem. NASW, Nat. Assn. Black Social Workers, Inc., N.Y. Fedn. Alcoholism Counselors, Nat. Black Alcoholism Coun., N.Y. Women in Criminal Justice. Office Phone: 340-774-0920 4243. Personal E-mail: ettarahming@yahoo.com.

RAHN, SAUNDRA L., councilman; b. Elgin, Ill., Jan. 10, 1936; d. Leonard Herman and Alvina Elizabeth Leetzow; m. Eugene Maurice Rahn, June 25, 1955; children: Connie, Gregory, Pamela. Grad. H.S., Elgin. Councilwoman, Bradenton, Fla., 1970-74, 79-89, 1990-91, 96—. City rep. Nat. Assn. Regional Planning Coun., 1982-84, mem. housing and met. com., 1985-90; city rep. Manatee County Transit Adv. Bd., 1986-90; rep. Ward 5, Bradenton City Coun., 1995-99, met. planning orgn., 1995-97, fire dept. liaison, 1995-97, fin. dept. chmn., 1997-98, pub. works liaison, 1998-99. Pres., lifetime mem. Jr. Woman's Club, Bradenton, 1964; chmn. Tampa Bay Regional Planning Coun., 1973-74, 84, apptd. city rep., 1995-99, legis. chmn., 1999; vice mayor City of Bradenton, 1973, 84; v.p. Sr. Woman's Club, Bradenton, 1989; bd. mem., legis. lobbyist Fla. Regional Planning Coun., 1996-99; rep. City Art League, 1999. Mem. Nat. League Cities (fin., adminstrv. intergovtl. rels. policy com. 1998-99), Fla. League Cities (city rep. intergovtl. rels. com. 1984-90, city rep. fin. and taxation com. 1987-90, intergovtl. rels. com. 1995-97, fin. and taxation com. 1998-99), Woman's Club. Avocations: dance, bowling, gardening. also: PO Box 25015 Bradenton FL 34206-5015

RAI, AISHWARYA, actress; b. Mangalore, Karnataka, India, Nov. 1, 1973; Jury mem. Cannes Internat. Film Festival. Actor: (films) Mamagaru, 1991, Iruvar, 1997,.Aur Pyaar Ho Gaya, 1997, Jeans, 1998, Let's Go Back, 1999, Straight from the Heart, 1999, Taal, 1999, I Have Found it, 2000, Josh, 2000, You Have My Heart, 2000, Dhaai Akshar Prem Ke, 2000, Love Stories, 2000, Albela, 2001, Devdas, 2002, Hum Kisi Se Kum Nahin, 2002, Shakti: The Power, 2002, Heart of Gold, 2003, Choker Bali: A Passion Play, 2003, Don't Say a Word, 2003, The Uniform, 2004, Raincoat, 2004, Kyun.! Ho Gaya Na, 2004, Bride and Prejudice, 2004, Shabd, 2004, (TV commls.) Loreal. Achievements include being crowned Miss World 1994 (also named Miss Photogenic); being first actress and performer from India to appear on cover of Time Mag.(as one of 100 most influential people in world), 2004; being fluent in English, Hindi, Kannada, Tamil and Urdu. Mailing: c/o Wm Morris Agy 1 Wm Morris Pl Beverly Hills CA 90212

RAIFSNIDER, LAURETTA JANE, library administrator and consultant; b. Detroit, Aug. 30, 1947; d. Jack Wilfred and Margaret Pearl (Shannon) Eakin; m. Ronald Dean Raifsnider, June 28, 1968; children— Geoffrey Alan, Kristina Michelle. BA, Ind. U., 1976, MS in Libr. and Info. Sci., 1981. Reference libr. Area 3 Area Libr. Svcs. Authority, Ft. Wayne, Ind., 1980-82, adminstr., 1982. Author: Louis Fortriede Shoes: A Century of Shoemaking in Fort Wayne, 1980; editor Tri-ALSA Newsletter, 1982. Mem. ALA, Assn. Specialized and Coop. Library Agys., Ind. Library Assn. (cons. intellectual freedom com. 1982—), Phi Beta Mu. Home: 1139 Braeview Dr Howell MI 48843-2009 Office: Tri-ALSA PO Box 2270 Fort Wayne IN 46801-2270

RAIL, KATHY LYNN PARISH, accountant; b. Chewelah, Wash., May 21, 1951; d. John Edward and Margaret Irene (Seefeldt) Rail. BBA, Gonzaga U., 1984. CPA, Wash. Legal sec. Redbook Pub. Co., N.Y.C., 1974-75, Howard Michaelson, Esquire, Spokane, Wash., 1975-76; sec. Burns Internat. Security Svcs., Spokane, 1977-79; sec. to contr. Gonzaga U., Spokane, 1979-81, acctg. asst., 1981-82; staff acct. Martin, Holland & Petersen, CPA's, Yakima, Wash., 1984-87; acct., supr. Strader Hallet & Co., P.S., Bellevue, Wash., 1988-91; acct. Miller & Co., P.S., Woodinville, Wash., 1991-93; pres. Parish Rail, CPA, P.S., Redmond, Wash., 1993—. Treas. White Pass Ski Patrol, Nat. Ski Patrol Systems, Wash., 1987-90; chair, chmn. audit com. Mt. Spokane Ski Patrol, 1983-84. Mem. AICPA, Am. Soc. Women Accts. (charter, editor 1987), Wash. Soc. CPA (sec. Sammamish Valley chpt. 1990-92, pres. 1992-93, 93-94), Washington Soc. of Cert. Pub. Accts. (chair adv. coun. 1995-96, tax com., govt. affairs com., dir. 1996-98), Bus. and Profl. Women of Woodinville (treas. 1994-95), Carnation C. of C., Duvall C. of C. Lutheran. Avocations: skiing, piano, golf.

RAILSBACK, SHERRIE LEE, management consultant, educator; b. Phila., Mar. 12, 1942; children: Ricky, Cindy. BBA, U. Ky., 1981. Sales mgr. Marjo Cosmetics, Ft. Wayne, Ind.; asst. dir. patient fin. svcs. Riverside Meth. Hosp., Columbus, Ohio; cons. Railsback and Assocs., Long Beach, Calif.; adoption search/reunion cons., educator Spirited Comm., L.A. Mem.: ASTD, NAFE, Book Publicists So. Calif., Nat. Spkrs. Assn. Office Phone: 310-967-1337.

RAIMAN, ROSEMARY A., advocate; d. Claude and Emma Butch; m. John L. Davidson (div.); children: Jennifer Lynne Davidson, Jacqueline Rose Davidson; m. Irwin Raiman, Aug. 29, 1981. Cert. nat. victims acad. Am. U., 1998, victim assistance specialist Greenville, SC, 2000, trauma svcs. specialist Irmo, SC, 2001, clinically cert. domestic violence counselor Am. Coll. Cert. Forensic Counselors, South Bend, Ind., 2001, credentialed advocate Nat. Advocate Credential, Washington, DC, 2004, cert. roper victim asst. U. Balt., 2004. Program coord. Del. Opportunities Inc., Delhi, NY, 1977—81; dir. Title IIIC Nutrition/Supportive Svcs. for Elderly, Delhi, 1981—85; office coord. Psychol. Svcs. Inc., Annapolis, Md., 1986—91; office mgr. Reliance Comm., Inc., Latham, Md., 1991—94; agy. receptionist Sanders Ins. Agy., LaPiata, Md., 1994—96; cert. victim advocate/admin. asst. Ctr. for Abused Persons, Waldorf, Md., 1996—. Chairperson Charles County Dept. Social Svcs., 1996—2005, bd. mem., 1996—2005; mem. Md. Divsn. Parole and Probation Victim's Adv. Bd., 1998—2001; bd. mem. Md. Assn. Social Svc., 1999—2003; founder Silent Witness Program for Charles County, 1999—, co-coord., 1999—; bd. mem. Md. Network Against Domestic Violence, Bowie, Md., 2000—; crisis respondent Charles County Sheriff's Victim Svc. Unit, LaPlata, 2001—; bd. chair Md. Assn. Social Svc., 2002—03; mem. Family Violence Coord. Coun. Charles County, 2003—, mem. pro bono legal svcs. com., 2003—; co-chairperson Legal Advocates Task Force, Bowie, Md., 2004—; chair Charles County Commn. for Women, 2004—05. Nominee Spirit of Cmty. award, Med. Ctr., Outstanding Cmty. Svc. award, Charles County Comm. for Women, 2006; recipient Silver Tray of Appointment, Del. Opportunities Inc., Outstanding Svc. award, Psychol. Svcs. Inc., Cert. Appreciation, Ctr. for Abused Persons, Charles County Commissioners, Md. Most Beautiful Nominee and 1st Runner-Up, Silent Witness Plaque award, Charles County Co-Coord., Cmty. Svc. award, Commn. for Women, Gov. Victim Assistance award, Crime Control and Prevention Bd. Victims Svc., Bd. Mem. of Yr., Dept. Social Svc., Cmty. Svc. award, Dept. Social Svcs., Appreciation Plaque, Md. State Bd. Mem., Svc. Award Plaque, Ctr. for Abused Persons, Plaque of Appreciation, Charles County Sheriff's Dept., Achievement award, Md. Coalition Against Sexal Assault, 2006. Mem.: Assn. Traumatic Stress Specialist. Republican. Methodist. Office: Ctr for Abused Persons 2670 Crain Hwy Ste 303 Waldorf MD 20601

RAIN, KATHLEEN MARIE, science educator; BS in Edn., Bemidji State U., 1992; MS in Edn., SW State U., 2001. Sci. tchr., chmn. dept. Worthington (Minn.) Mid. Sch., 1992—. Office Phone: 507-376-4174. Business E-Mail: kathy.rain@isd518.net.

RAINE, MELINDA L., academic librarian; b. Boston, Feb. 4, 1951; d. James Agee and Marjorie Elizabeth (Gilstrap) Raine; m. Stephen Richard Brogden, Jan. 1, 1983; 1 child, Nathan Raine Brogden. BA, U. Iowa, 1973, MA, 1974. Info. specialist Pub. Libr. Des Moines, 1974-82, libr. mgr., 1982-90; task force coord. Visio 2020 Project, Conejo Future Found., Thousand Oaks, Calif., 1991-92; mgr. engring. libr. Metters Industries, Camarillo, Calif., 1992-94; govt. publs. libr. Pepperdine U., Malibu, Calif., 1994-98, coord. info. resources, 1998—; assoc. libr. pub. svcs. and programs Pepperdine U. Librs., 2006—. Author: Options for Our Endangered Environment, 1992, Water: Liquid Gold, 1992, The Housing Crisis, 1992, Solid Ideas for Solid Waste, 1992; co-author (with Elizabeth Parang and Trisha Stevenson): Redesigning Freshman Seminar Library Instruction Based on Information Competencies in Research Strategies, 2001. Mem. ALA, AAUW (pub. policy chair 1993-96, v.p. programming 1992-93), Calif. Libr. Assn., Calif. Acad. and Rsch. Librs. Office: Pepperdine U 24255 Pacific Coast Hwy Malibu CA 90263-4786 Business E-Mail: melinda.raine@pepperdine.edu.

RAINES, CHARLOTTE AUSTINE BUTLER, artist; b. Sullivan, Ill., July 1, 1922; d. Donald Malone and Charlotte (Wimp) Butler; m. Irving Isaack Raines, Sept. 26, 1941; children: Robin Raines Collison, Kerry Raines Lydon. BA in Studio Arts magna cum laude, U. Md., 1966. One-woman shows at Castle Theatre, 1988, C.T.V. Awards Hall, Md., 1993, Md. Nat. Capital Park and Planning Commn., 2005; numerous group shows including Corcoran Gallery, 1980, Md.'s Best Exhbn., 1986, Md. State House, 1990, four-artist video documentary, 1992, U. Md. Univ.-Coll. Gallery, 1996; artist publ. cover Writers' Ctr., 1997, Md. State House Print Exhbn., 1999, Washington Women Artists Millenium Show, 2001, Md. State Ho. Complex, 2003; represented in various pvt. collections and permanent collection at U. Md. Univ.-Coll.; selected works in U.S. Dept. State Arts in Embassies Program; contbr. poems to lit. publs. Mem. Artists Equity Assn., Writers' Ctr., Phi Kappa Phi. Avocations: piano, gardening.

RAINES, JUDI BELLE, language educator, historian; b. N.Y.C., July 16, 1955; d. Alfonso Don Raines and Belle Margarite Samuels. BA in Elem. Edn., Adelphi U., 1977, MA in Secondary Edn., 1981; MS in Guidance, St. Johns U., 2000. ESL tchr. Lincoln Farm Camp, Roscoe, NY; project leader Operation Crossroads, Anguilla, B.W.I., 1981; English tchr., sr. activities advisor Andrew Jackson H.S., Jamaica, NY, 1981—83; history and art tchr., step team advisor Magnatech Jr. H.S. 231, Jamaica, NY, 1985—97; English tchr., dorm supr. project Double Discovery Upward Bound, Queens Coll., Columbia Univ. and Queens Coll., 1989—93; English tchr., dean, step team advisor August Martin H.S., Jamaica, NY, 1997—; adj. instr. SAT prep. CUNY, Jamaica, 1999—; guidance counselor Flushing H.S. Step advisor N.Y.C. Bd. End.; adj. instr. Coll. Now, York Coll., 2000—02; dir. book club Martin Van Buren HS, 2004—05. Dir. chorus Ctrl. Bklyn. Model Cities, 1976—77. Recipient Marva Collins Award, cmty. award, 2000, Editors Choice award, 2000—03, Project Prize Educator, Flushing HS, 2002, Gear Up (counselor), 2003. Mem.: ACA, United Fedn. Tchrs., Am. Sch. Counselor Assn., Guilder Lehrman Tchrs. Inst., N.Y. Poetry Forum. Avocations: poetry, chess, swimming, quilt making, computers. Office: Martin Van Buren High Sch 230-17 Hillside Ave Queens Village NY 11427 Personal E-mail: judibelleraines@aol.com.

RAINES, MARTHA ANN, elementary school educator; b. Columbus, Ohio, Jan. 21, 1956; d. Howard Leander and Victoria (Halby) R. BA, Ohio Dominican Coll., 1978; Masters, U. Dayton, 2001. Lic. tchr., Ohio. Tchr. St. Vincent de Paul Sch., Mt. Vernon, Ohio, 1980—2002; prin. St. Rose Sch., New Lexington, Ohio, 2002—. Mem. social studies curriculum com. Diocese of Columbus, Ohio, 1985-86, 90-91. Democrat. Roman Catholic. Office: St Rose School 119 W Water St New Lexington OH 43764 Home: 335 Fort St Bremen OH 43107-1015 Office Phone: 740-342-3043.

RAINES, SHIRLEY CAROL, academic administrator; b. Jackson, Tenn., Apr. 15, 1945; m. Robert J. Canady; 1 stepchild, Brian Scott Smith. BS, U. Tenn., Martin; MS, EdD, U. Tenn., Knoxville; grad. mgmt. program, Harvard Grad. Sch. of Edn. Dept. head Northeastern State U, 1983—87; assoc. prof. edn. George Mason U., Fairfax, Va., 1987—92; prof. and chmn. dept. of childhood/ lang. arts/ reading U. South Fla., 1992—95; prof. U. Ky. Coll. of Edn., 1995—2001, vice chancellor academic svcs. and dean of coll., 1998—2001; pres. U. Memphis, 2001—. Author books; contbr. articles to profl. jours. Recipient Dist. Svc. to Edn., Phi Delta Kappa, Dist. Paper awards, Ednl. Rsch. Assn. Office: U Memphis 341 Adminstrn Bldg Memphis TN 38152

RAINEY, JEAN OSGOOD, public relations executive; b. Lansing, Mich., Apr. 5, 1925; d. Earle Victor and Blanche Mae (Eberly) Osgood; m. John Larimer Rainey, Nov. 29, 1957 (dec. Oct. 1991); children: Cynthia, John Larimer, Ruth. Grad., Lansing Bus. U., 1942. Pub. rels. dir. Nat. Assn. Food Chains, Washington, 1954-59; v.p. pub. rels. Manchester Orgns., Washington, 1959-61; ptnr. Rainey, McEnroe & Manning, Washington, 1962-73; v.p. Manning, Selvage & Lee, Washington, 1973-79, pres. Washington divsn., 1979-84, sr. counsellor, 1985; owner Jean Rainey Assocs., Washington, 1986-87; sr. v.p. Daniel J. Edelman Inc., 1987-96; owner Jean Rainey Assocs., Washington, 1996—. Chmn. bd. Windward Mortgage, 1997—2001. Author: How to Shop for Food, 1972. Pres. Hyde Home and Sch. Assn., Washington, 1969-71; co-chmn. Nat. Adv. Com. for Reelection of the Pres., 1972; chmn. bd. trustees St. John's Presch., 1996-99, vice chair, 2003-04; pres. Sherwood Forest Endowment Fund, 1995-97; adminstr. A Few Good Women-Advancing the Cause of Women in Govt., 1969-74, 97-; bd. dirs. Westchester Corp., 2001-04. Mem. Internat. Women's Forum, Pub. Rels. Soc. Am. (accredited, Hall of Fame 1999), Am. Women in Radio and TV (pres. Washington chpt. 1962-63, mem. nat. bd. 1963-65), Am. News Women's Club (pres. 1973-75), City Tavern Club. Republican. Episcopalian. Home: 4000 Cathedral Ave NW Apt 250B Washington DC 20016-5279 Office: PO Box 251 Main Lobby W 4000 Cathedral Ave NW Washington DC 20016-5249 E-mail: joraineу@aol.com.

RAINEY, PAMELA LEIGH, dance educator; b. Paterson, NJ, Mar. 12, 1975; d. Charles Thomas Rainey and Mary Ann Esposito. BFA in Acting, Marymount Manhattan Coll., 1997. Dance instr. Dance Arts Acad., Lincoln Park, NJ, 2000—05, Miss Patti's Sch. of Dance, Midland Park, NJ, 2004—; voice, acting, dance instr. Hoboken (NJ) Children's Theatre, 2005—; ballet, tap, jazz, hip-hop and ballroom instr. Baird Ctr. of South Orange, NJ, 2003—; ballroom instr. PS 105, Bklyn., 2006—. Actor: (plays) Cats, 2001—02, 42nd St., 1999—2000; singer: Silver Cloud cruise ship, 2000—02. Mem.: Actors Equity Assn. Avocations: piano, aerobics.

RAINIER, ELLEN F., nurse; b. Lafayette, Ind., Apr. 25, 1956; d. Carl Neil and Florence May (Miller) R. BSN, Ball State U., 1978; MS, U. Mich., 1986. Cert. med. surgical nurse 1996, hospice palliative care nurse 2003. Staff nurse Home Hosp., Lafayette, Ind., 1978-81, St. Joseph Mercy Hosp., Ann Arbor, Mich., 1981-87; lectr. U. Mich. Sch. Nursing, Ann Arbor, Mich., 1986-89; staff nurse U. Mich. Med. Ctr., Clinical Rsch. Ctr., Ann Arbor, Mich., 1989-91, St. Vincent Hosp., Indpls., 1991-94. Lectr. Ind. U. Sch. Nursing, Indpls., 1992—, Ivy Tech State Coll., 1994-2004, St. Vincent Hosp, Indpls., 2001-2003. Rsch. grantee Ctr. Rsch. Learning & Teaching U. Mich. Mem. Sigma Theta Tau (rsch. award).

RAINWATER, JOAN LUCILLE MORSE, investment company executive; b. Chattanooga, Mar. 5, 1943; d. Robert Ora and Alma Lucille (Miller) M.; m. Percy Raymond Rainwater (div. 1987); children: Karen Sue, Steven Jay, Robin Rae, Linda Sue. Student, John Robert Powan Sch. Design, 1977-78, Corcoran Sch. Art, 1985-86, Nova U., 1980, 85, 87. Co-owner Rainwater Concrete, Lorton, Va., 1962-87, Undertaking Gallery, Occoquan, 1977-80; cons. in art edn. Occoquan Elem. Sch., Woodbridge, Va., 1969-73; owner Riverside Gallery, Occoquan, 1980-84, Joamen Investments, Occoquan, 1985—. Author: (poems) At Waters Edge, 1995. Founding mem. Hist. Occoquan, 1970, Women's Mus., Washington; pres., v.p. Woodbridge Art Guild, 1980-82. Recipient numerous awards for paintings, various juried shows Washington area, 1977-87. Mem. Unity Ch. Avocations: hiking, reading, esoteric studies.

RAITT, BONNIE LYNN, singer, musician; b. Burbank, Calif., Nov. 8, 1949; Student, Radcliffe Coll. Performer: blues clubs, East Coast, concert tours in Britain, 1976, 1977; albums include Bonnie Raitt, 1971, Give It Up, 1972, Takin' My Time, 1973, Streetlights, 1974, Home Plate, 1975, Sweet Forgiveness, 1977, The Glow, 1979, Green Light, 1982, Nine Lives, 1986, Nick of Time, 1989 (Grammys 1990, Rock-Best Vocal Performance, Female, Pop-Best Vocal Performance, Female, Album of Yr., 1990), I'm in the Mood (with John Lee Hooker) (Grammy 1990, Blues-Best Traditional Record, 1990), The Bonnie Raitt Collection, 1990, Luck of the Draw, 1991 (Grammy, Rock-Best Vocal Performance, Female, Grammy for Best Duet with Delbert McClinton,

1992), Longing In Their Hearts, 1994 (Grammy award Best Pop Album, 1994), Road Tested, 1996, Fundamental, I Can't Make You Love Me, 1998, Silver Lining, 2002, songs include Something to Talk About (Grammy, Best Pop Vocal Performance, Female, 1992), Good Man, Good Woman (with Delbert McClinton) (Grammy, Rock-Best Vocal by a Duo or Group, 1992). Founding mem. Musicians United for Safe Energy, Rhythm and Blues Found.

RAIZEN, SENTA AMON, educational association administrator, researcher; b. Vienna, Oct. 28, 1924; came to U.S., 1940; d. John and Helen (Krys) Amon; m. Abraham A. Raizen, Apr. 18, 1948; children: Helen S., Michael B., Daniel J. BS, Guilford Coll., 1944; MA, Bryn Mawr, 1945; Tchr. Cert., U. Va., 1960. Rsch. chemist Sun Oil Co., Norwood, Pa., 1945-48; rsch. asst. NAS, Washington, 1960-62; assoc. program dir. NSF, Washington, 1962-69, spl. asst., 1969-72; sr. researcher The Rand Corp., Washington, 1972-74; assoc. dir. Nat. Inst. Edn., Washington, 1974-78; ind. cons. Washington, 1978-80; study dir. NAS, Washington, 1980-88; dir. Nat. Ctr. for Improving Sci. Edn., Washington, 1988—. Cons. Nat. Ctr. for Edn. Stats., Washington, 1987—, Ednl. Testing Svc., Princeton, N.J., 1988—, Nat. Goals Panel, Washington, 1990-2000, Third Internat. Math. and Sci. Study, Internat. Assn. Evaluation Ednl. Achievement, The Netherlands, 1990—, SRI Internat., 1998—, Orgns. for Econ. Cooperation and Devel., Paris, 1998—. Contbr. articles to profl. jours., encys., books, reports in field. Pres. Cooperative Nursery Sch., Arlington, Va., 1953-57; leader Brownies, Girl Scouts, U.S. and Cub Scouts, Boy Scouts, Am., Arlington, 1958-64. Recipient Disting. Lifetime award WestEd, 2000; grantee NSF, U.S. Dept. Edn., U.S Dept. Energy, pvt. founds., 1988-2000, fellowship for grad. study NSF, 1944-45, Meritorious Svc. award, 1968, The Network Pres.' award, 1991. Fellow AAAS; mem. Am. Chem. Soc., Am. Ednl. Rsch. Assn. Avocations: dance, swimming, reading, knitting, stitchery. Home: 5513 31st St N Arlington VA 22207-1532 Office: Nat Ctr Improving Sci Edn 1940 Wilson Blvd Ste 400 Arlington VA 22201 Office Phone: 703-875-0496.

RAKAS, PEGGY ANN, music educator; b. Ouizumi, Japan, Dec. 5, 1956; arrived in U.S., 1958; d. Albert Stanley and Margaret Joan Rakas; m. Rick Stuart Krahn, Feb. 29, 1992; 1 child, Leann Rakas Krahn. MusB, Bowling Green State U., Ohio, 1978; MS in Edn., Queens Coll., 1988. Band dir. Norton Schs., Ohio, 1978—81, North Merrick Schs., NY, 1984—. Clinician beginning band techniques U. Dayton and Queens Coll. Co-prodr. Concert for Care Fundraiser for Habitat for Humanity, North Merrick, 2006. Nominee N.Y. State Tchr. of Yr., 1995, Disney Tchr. of Yr., 2005; named Kiwanis Club Tchr. of Yr., 1992, 1995. Mem.: Nassau Music Educators Assn., N.Y. State Sch. Music Assn., L.I. Flute Club. Avocation: gardening. Home: 20 1st St Syosset NY 11791 Office: North Merrick Schs 1057 Merrick Ave North Merrick NY 11566

RAKER, EMILY ELLEN, music educator; b. San Fransisco, Feb. 7, 1960; d. Edward Bernhart and Emilia Marie Schluntz; m. Robert Charles Raker, Aug. 21, 1981; 1 child, Miles Edward. B of Music Edn., Western Wash. U., Bellingham, 1986; MEd, City U., Vancouver, Wash., 2000. Cert. tchr. Wash., 1986, Kodaly Cert. Level I, Oreg., 2002. Tchr. elem. music Syracuse Diocese, NY, 1987—88; tchr. music k-6, band 5-12, Parkrose Sch. Dist., Portland, Oreg., 1989—91; tchr. music k-6, band 5-8, Riverdale Sch. Dist., Portland, Oreg., 1991—92; tchr. music k-5, Evergreen Sch. Dist., Vancouver, Wash., 1992—. Flute Oreg. Symphonic Band, Portland, 1989—2006, Northe Winds, Portland, Oreg., 2004—, S.W. Wash. Wind Symphony, Vancouver, 2006—. Mem.: Greater Portland Area Flute Soc., Nat. Flute Assn. Office: Marrion Elem Evergreen Sch Dist 10119 NE 14th St Vancouver WA 98664 Office Phone: 360-604-6825. E-mail: eraker@egreen.wednet.edu.

RAKER, IRMA S., judge; b. Bklyn. m. Samuel K. Raker. BA, Syracuse U., 1959; cert. of attendance (hon.), Hague (The Netherlands) Acad. Internat. Law, 1959; JD, Am. U., 1972. Bar: Md. 1973, D.C. 1974, U.S. Dist. Ct. Md. 1977, U.S. Ct. Appeals (4th cir.) 1977. Asst. state's atty. State's Atty.'s Office Montgomery County, Md., 1973-79; ptnr. Sachs, Greenebaum & Tayler, Washington, 1979-80; judge Dist. Ct. Md., Rockville, 1980-82, Cir. Ct. for Montgomery County, Md., 1982-94, Md. Ct. of Appeals, 1994—. Adj. prof. Washington Coll. Law, Am. U., 1980—; mem. faculty Md. Jud. Inst., Nat. Criminal Def. Inst., 1980, 81, 82; mem. legis. com. Md. Jud. Conf., mem. exec. com., 1985-89, mem. commn. to study bail bond and surety industry in Md.; mem. spl. com. to revise article 27 on crimes and punishment State of Md., 1991—; mem. inquiry com. atty. Grievance Commn. Md., 1978-81; chair jud. compensation com. Md. Jud. Conf., 1997—. Treas., v.p. West Bradley Citizens Assn., 1964-68; mem. adv. com. to county exec. on child abuse Montgomery County, 1976-77, mem. adv. com. to county exec. on battered spouses, 1977-78, mem. adv. com. on environ. protection, 1980; mem. citizens adv. bd. Montgomery County Crisis Ctr., 1980. Recipient Robert C. Heeney award Md. State Bar Assn., 1993, Dorothy Beatty Meml. award Women's Law Ctr., 1994, Rita Davidson award Women's Bar Md., 1995, Margaret Brent Trailblazers award ABA Commn. on Women in the Profession/Women's Bar Assn. Md., 1995, Elizabeth Dole Woman of Achievement award ARC, 1998, Leadership in Law award The Daily Record, 2001, Nat. Assn. Social Workers' Pub. Citizen of Yr. award, 2001, others; named of Md.'s Top 100 Women Warfield's Bus. Record, 1997, 99, 2001. Fellow Md. Bar Found.; mem. ABA (chair criminal justice stds. com. 1995-96, mem. coun. criminal law sect. 1997—, del. nat. conf. state trial judges, active various coms.), Am. Law Rev., Md. State Bar Assn. (chair coun. criminal law and practice sect., mem. bd. govs. 1981, 82, 85, 86, 90, mem. coun. litigation sect., active coms., chair com. to draft pattern jury instrns. in civil and criminal cases 1980—), Nat. Assn. Women Judges, Internat. Acad. Trial Judges, Am. Law Inst., Montgomery County Bar Assn. (chair criminal law sect. 1978-79, mem. exec. com. 1979-80, active other coms., Outstanding Jurist award 2000), Montgomery County Bar Leaders, Women's Bar Assn. Md., Women's Bar Assn. D.C., Hadassah Women's Orgn. (life), Pioneer Women Na'amat (Celebration of Women award 1985), Pi Sigma Alpha. Office: Ct of Appeals of Md 50 Maryland Ave Rockville MD 20850-2320*

RALEIGH, DAWN KRISTEN, language educator; b. Muncie, Ind., May 31, 1966; d. Gayle Marcus Replogle and Shirley Lee Walker; m. Christopher Alan Raleigh, Mar. 13, 1999; children: Chandler Alan, Andrew Marcus, Abigail LeeAnn. BS, Ball State U., Muncie, 1988, MA, 1991. Lic. tchr. Ind. English tchr., swim coach, acad. coach Delphi (Ind.) Cmty. HS, 1993—97; English tchr. Burris Lab. Sch., Muncie, 1997—2001; English tchr., acad. coach Delta HS, Muncie, 2002—. Actor: (cmty. theatre) A Christmas Carol. Mem.: NEA, Del. Cmty. Classroom Tchrs. Assn., Acad. Coaches Assn. Avocations: swimming, bicycling, sewing, reading. Office: Delta HS 3400 E St Rd 28 Muncie IN 47303 Office Phone: 765-288-5597.

RALEY, BEVERLY SPICKELMIER, systems administrator, educator, writer; b. Lawton, Okla., Aug. 13; d. Ted and Audry Spradlin; m. Richard Raley, Sept. 5, 1981; children: Ray Spickelmier, Lori Spickelmier, Robin Moye, Rolinda Smoak. BS in Curriculum and Instr., Okla. State U., 1970; Master's degree, U. South Fla., 1981. Cert. Bus. Edn. Tchr. Fla., vocat. dir. Tchr. Hillsborough County Pub. Sch., Tampa, 1970—2005, cons., 1975—94. Spkr. Houghton-Mifflin's Spkrs.' Bur., Nation-Wide, 1978—89; adj. prof. U. South Fla., Tampa, 1989—91. Editor: (accounting editor) Business Education Forum, 1984, author articles to profl. jours. Sec. Meadowood Condominium Assn., Tampa, 1985—89, pres., 1985—89. Recipient Outstanding Secondary Bus. Educator, Fla. Bus. Edn. Assn., 1982, Nat. Bus. Edn. Assn., 1983.

RALOFF, JANET, science writer; BS in Journalism, MS in Journalism, Northwestern U. Staff writer, Chemistry mag. Am. Chem. Soc.; mng. editor Energy Rsch. Reports, Boston; writer Sci. News mag., 1977—, online columnist, Food for Thought, 1996—; sci. commentator NPR's Living on Earth show. Author: numerous articles for profl. publications; contbd. to several books. Office: Senior Editor Science News 1719 N St NW Washington DC 20036

RALPH, NANCYJO, retired music educator; d. Alfred M. and Phyllis L. Niles; m. Dwight G. Ralph, Mar. 28, 1970; children: Victoria L. Fortna, Erik C. MusB in Edn., Grove City Coll., Pa., 1969; M in Elem. Edn., Edinboro U. Pa., 1974; postgrad. in Music Edn., Kent State U., Ohio, 1989. Registered music educator. Elem. music tchr. Lakeview Sch. Dist., Sandy Lake, Pa., 1969; h.s. music tchr. Cambridge Springs H.S., Penncrest Sch. Dist., Pa., 1970—2000, elem. music tchr., 2000—05; pvt. piano tchr. Vol. music tchr. Cornerstone Day Care and Penncrest Day Care Ctrs., Penncrest Day Care; with Tool City Bell Ringers, 2005—. Choir mem., pianist, various com. Saegertown (Pa.) United Meth. Ch., 1970—; dir. Justified By Faith, Saegertown, 2002—. Mem.: Pa. Music Educators Assn. (curriculum and instrn. chair dist. 2 1993—2003), Pa. State Edn. Assn. (alt. profl. rights and responsibilities commn. 2001—), Penncrest Area Edn. Assn. (assoc.; v.p. 1982—84, negotiator 1982—86, pres. 1984—86, negotiator 2000—01, v.p. 2001—02, pres. 2001—03), Tool City Ringers. Methodist. Avocations: music, reading, painting. Home: 17768 Grange Center Rd Saegertown PA 16433-4506 Personal E-mail: schoolmarm@zoominternet.net.

RALSTIN, BETTY LOU, religious organization administrator; b. Stanford, Ky., Dec. 29, 1935; d. Eugel Harris Anderson and Elizabeth Ella Campbell; m. John Edward Wasson, Aug. 24, 1954 (div.); 3 children; m. Paul Edward Ralstin, June 23, 1984. Grad. h.s., Manilla, Ind., 1953. Cert. notary Ind., Tenn., Fla. Tax preparation Rafferty & Wood Law Office, Shelbyville, Ind., 1955—61; sec. GE, Shelbyville, 1955—64; acct. William S. Lee CPA, Orlando, 1965—66; office mgr. and tax auditor Milligan & Burke CPAs, Orlando, 1965—66; controller Hallmark Constrn. Co., Orlando, 1966—72; bookkeeper and tax cons. Laurel, Ind., 1972—86; antique and gift shop owner B's Enterprise, Laurel, 1985—89; supr. Book Market, Knoxville, Tenn., 1992—94; portrait cons. United Photographic Industry, Galion, Ohio, 1994—95; 3rd key Foozles, Crossville, Tenn., 1996—97; adminstr. and sec. Lantana Rd. Bapt. Ch., Crossville, 1997—. Named Mrs. Eagle of Yr., FOE 2036, 1985—86. Baptist. Avocations: gardening, travel, going to flea markets, church activities, making baskets. Home: 33 Will Cir Crossville TN 38555 Office: Lantana Rd Baptist Church 3270 Lantana Rd Crossville TN 38572 Office Phone: 931-788-2844. E-mail: paulbetty@frontiernet.net.

RALSTON, BARBARA JO, bank executive; b. Youngstown, Ohio, Apr. 11, 1940; d. Fred Kenneth and Juanita Ruth (Welch) Roof; m. Donald Gene Ralston, Jan. 9, 1960; children: Mark David, Lori Sue. Cert., Pacific Coast Banking Sch. U. Wash., Seattle, 1981; AA in fin., Maricopa County CC. Sec. Bank of Scottsdale, Ariz., 1962-66; adminstrv. asst. Talley Industries, Mesa, Ariz., 1966-73; asst. mgr. Continental Bank, Phoenix, 1973-77; exec. v.p. Continental Bank Service Corp., Phoenix, 1977-85, pres., dir., 1985—86; chmn., pres. to sr. v.p. electronic and convenience banking to exec. v.p. personal banking group Chase Bank of Ariz., exec. v.p., COO; exec. v.p., mgr. northeast Ariz. retail area First Interstate Bank, 1994—95, Phoenix area pres., 1995—96; sr. v.p., mgr. in-store banking Wells Fargo Bank, Ariz., 1996—97; founder, pres., CEO Camelback Cmty. Bank, Phoenix, 1998—. Pres. Ariz. Bus. Leadership. Bd. dirs. Valley Big Bros.-Big Sisters, Phoenix, 1986; mem. Ariz. Acad., Phoenix, 1984; treas. Phoenix Together Town Hall, 1986; chair Am. West Airlines Edn. Found.; immediate past chair, Fresh State Women's Found.; past chair Ariz. Town Hall; past internat. pres. Financial Women Internat. Recipient You Too Can Make A Difference award Valley Christian Ctrs., Phoenix, 1985. Mem. Nat. Assn. Bank Women (state pres. 1981-82), Am. Inst. Banking (state edn. chmn. Ariz. chpt. 1984), Tumbleweed (pres. 1983); Am. Bankers Assn. (state membership chair for Ariz., chair ABA Edn. Found, 2003-), Ariz Bankers Assn. (bd. dirs., 2001-03, pres., 2001-02. Lodges: Soroptimists (pres. 1982, Women Helping Women award 1984). Republican. Methodist. Avocations: reading, travel, sewing. Office: Camelback Cmty Bank 2777 E Camelback Rd Ste 100 Phoenix AZ 85016

RALSTON, JOANNE SMOOT, public relations executive; b. Phoenix, May 13, 1939; d. A. Glen and Viriginia (Lee) Smoot; m. W. Hamilton Weigelt, Aug. 15, 1991 (dec.). BA in Journalism, Ariz. State U., 1960. Reporter The Ariz. Rep., Phoenix, 1960-62; co-owner, pub. rels. dir. The Patton Agy., Phoenix, 1962-71; founder, pres., owner Joanne Ralston & Assocs., Inc., Phoenix, 1971-87, 92—. Pres. Nelson Ralston Robb Comm., Phoenix, 1987—91, Joanne Ralston & Assocs., Inc., Scottsdale, 1991—, Kapaau, Hawaii, 2000—. Contbr. articles to profl. jours. Bd. dirs. Ariz. Parklands Found,. 1984-86, Gov.'s Coun. on Health, Phys. Fitness and Sports, 1984-86; mem. task force Water and Natural Resources Coun., Phoenix, 1984-86; mem. Hawaii Gov.'s Adv. Bd., 2003-05, Hawaii Gov.'s Coun. Advisors, 2005—, others. Recipient Lulu awards (36) L.A. Advt. Women, 1964—, Gold Quill (2) Internat. Assn. Bus. Communicators, Excellence awards Fin. World mag., 1982-93, others; named to Walter Cronkite Sch. Journalism Hall of Fame, Coll. Pub. Programs Ariz. State U., 1987; named one of 25 Most Influential Arizonians, Phoenix Mag., 1991. Mem. Pub. Rels. Soc. Am. (counselor sect.), Internat. Assn. Bus. Communicators, Phoenix Press Club (pres. bd.), Investor Rels. Inst., Phoenix Met. C. of C. (bd. dirs. 1977-84, 85-91), Rotary Internat. Republican. Avocations: horses, dog training. Address: PO Box 808 Kapaau HI 96755-0808 Office Phone: 808-889-6433. Personal E-mail: joanne-ralston@juno.com.

RALSTON, LENORE DALE, academic policy and program analyst; b. Oakland, Calif., Feb. 21, 1949; d. Leonard Earnest and Emily Allison (Hudnut) R. BA in Anthropology, U. Calif., Berkeley, 1971, MPH in Behavioral Sci., 1981; MA in Anthropology, Bryn Mawr Coll., 1973, PhD in Anthropology, 1980. Asst. rschr. anthropology inst. internat. studies U. Calif., Berkeley, 1979-82, rsch. assoc. Latin Am. Study Ctr., 1982-83, acad. asst. to dean Sch. of Optometry, 1990-95, prin. policy analyst, chancellor's office, 1995—; assoc. scientist, rsch. adminstr. Med. Rsch. Inst., San Francisco, 1982-85; cons. health sci. Berkeley, 1986-90. Mem. fin. bd. Med. Rsch. Inst., 1983-84; speaker in field. Co-author: Voluntary Effects in Decentralized Management, 1983; contbr. articles to profl. jours. Commr. Cmty. Health Adv. Com., Berkeley, 1988-90; vice chair, commr. Cmty. Health Commn., Berkeley, 1990-93; mem. bd. safety com. Miles, Inc., Berkeley, 1992-94. Grantee Nat. Rsch. Svc. Award, WHO, NIMH, NSF. Fellow Applied Anthropology Assn.; mem. APHA, Am. Anthropology Assn., Sigma Xi. Home: 1232 Carlotta Ave Berkeley CA 94707-2707 Office Phone: 510-642-5746. Business E-Mail: ralston@berkeley.edu.

RALSTON, MARTHA JANE, retired medical/surgical nurse; b. Chgo., May 23, 1928; d. Joseph D. and Phoebe Josephine (Furguson) Salato; m. Paul R. Ralston, Mar. 10, 1956; children: Craig, Donna, Paula, Barbara. Diploma, Little Company of Mary Hosp., Evergreen Park, Ill., 1950. Cert. in oper. rm. procedures and techniques. Oper. rm. supr. Meml. Hosp., Woodstock, Ill., 1952-62; staff nurse oper. rm. Boulder Community Hosp., 1962-67; staff nurse oper. rm., asst. supr. Boulder (Colo.) Meml. Hosp., 1967-83; ophthalmology recovery rm. staff nurse Rocky Mountain Eye Found. Surgery Ctr., Boulder, 1983-92. Mem. Assn. Oper. Rm. Nurses.

RAM, BONNIE, environmental scientist, consultant; d. Issie Ram and Muriel Model. BA in Geography and Internat. Devel., Clark U., Worcester, Mass., 1979, MA in Environ. Affairs, 1982. Project mgr. Beijer Inst., Swedish Acad. Scis., Harare, Zimbabwe, 1983—85; Bernard Schwartz rsch. felllow Fedn. Am. Scientists, Washington, 1986—87; environ. cons. World Resources Inst., Washington, 1987—88; corp. ops. mgr. Advanced Scis., Inc., Arlington, Va., 1988—94; v.p. environ. programs Energetics Inc., Washington, 1994—. Contbr. articles to profl. jours. Vol. Luther Pl. Shelter, Washington, 1993—2000. Fellow, Jessee Smith Noyes Found., 1983—85, Bernard Schwartz Found., Fedn. Am. Scientists, 1986—87. Mem.: Marine Tech. Soc. (assoc.). Achievements include research in permitting issues associated with ocean renewable technologies; environmental analysis relating to proposed offshore wind power sites. Avocations: scuba diving, world travel. Office: Energetics Inc Ste 100 901 D St SW Washington DC 20024 Office Phone: 202-479-2748.

RAMALEY, JUDITH AITKEN, retired academic administrator, endocrinologist; b. Vincennes, Ind., Jan. 11, 1941; d. Robert Henry and Mary Krebs (McCullough) Aitken; m. Robert Folk Ramaley, Mar. 1966 (div. 1976); children: Alan Aitken, Andrew Folk. BA, Swarthmore Coll., 1963; PhD, UCLA, 1966; postgrad., Ind. U., 1967-69. Rsch. assoc., lectr. Ind. U., Bloomington, 1967-68, asst. prof. dept. anatomy and physiology, 1969-72; asst. prof. dept. physiology and biophysics U. Nebr. Med. Ctr., Omaha, 1972-74, assoc. prof., 1974-78, prof., 1978-82, assoc. dean for rsch. and devel., 1979-81; asst. v.p. for acad. affairs U. Nebr., Lincoln, 1980-82; prof. biol. scis. SUNY, Albany, N.Y., 1982-87, v.p. for acad. affairs, 1982-85, acting pres., 1984, exec. v.p. for acad. affairs, 1985-87; exec. vice chancellor U. Kans., Lawrence, 1987-90; pres. Portland (Oreg.) State U., 1990-97, U. Vt., Burlington, 1997—2001; asst. dir. edn. and human resources NSF, 2001—. Mem. endocrinology study sect. NIH, 1981-84; cons.-evaluator North Cen. Accreditation, 1978-82, 89-90; regulatory panel NSF, 1979-82, bioadv. com., 1994-98; mem. Ill. Commn. Scholars, 1980-90; Vt. tech. coun. Gov.'s Bus. Adv. Coun., Vt. Bus. Roundtable, Com. on Econ. Devel., 1997-2001; presdl. prof. biomed. scis. U. Maine, Orono, 2001—; subcom. on coll. drinking Nat. Inst. Alcohol Abuse & Alcoholism, 1998-01. Co-author: Progesterone Function: Molecular and Biochemical Aspects, 1972; Essentials of Histology, 8th edit., 1979; editor: Covert Discrimination, Women in the Sciences, 1978; contbr. articles to profl. jours. Bd. dirs. Family Svc. of Omaha, 1979-82, Albany Symphony Orch., 1984-87, mem. exec. com., 1986-87, 2d v.p., exec. com., 1986-87, Capital Repertory Co., 1986-89, Assn. Portland Progress, 1990-97, City Club of Portland, 1991-92, Metro Family Svcs., 1993-97, Campbell Inst. for Children, Portland Met. Sports Authority, 1994; vice-chair Ore. Campus Compact, exec. com. 1996-97, nat. adv. coun. Sch.-Work Opportunities, 1996—; bd. dirs. NCAA Pres. Commn., 1991, chair divsn. II subcom., 1994, joint policy bd., 1994; chmn. bd. dirs. Albany Water Fin. Authority, 1987; exec. com. United Way Douglas County, 1989-90; adv. bd. Emily Taylor Women's Resource Ctr., U. Kans., 1988-90; mem. Portland Opera Bd., 1991-92, Portland Leaders Roundtable, 1991-97; bd. devel. com. United Way of Columbia-Willamette, 1991-95; active Ore. Women's Forum, 1991-97, Portland Met. Sports Authority, Greater Burlington Industry Corp., 1998—; progress bd. Portland-Multnomah County, 1993-97; trustee Wilmington Coll. Ohio, 1998—. NSF grantee, 1969-83; fellow Margaret Chase Smith Ctr. for Pub. Policy. Fellow AAAS; mem. Nat. Assn. State Univs. and Land Grant Colls. (exec. com., mem. senate 1986-88, vice-chair commn. urban agenda 1992-94, chair 1995-97), Am. Assn. for Higher Edn. (bd. dirs. 2003—), Assn. Am. Colls. and Univs. (bd. dirs. 1995-98, chair nat. panel on greater expectations 2000-02), ACE (commn. on govt. rels. 1996-2000), Kellogg Commn. on Future of State and Land-Grant Univs., Assn. Governing Bds. Coll. & U. (pres.'s coun. 1998-2000), Endocrine Soc. (chmn. edn. com. 1980-85), Soc. Study Reprodn. (treas. 1983-85), Soc. for Neuroscis., Am. Physiol. Soc., Am. Assn. Schs. and Colls., Am. Coun. on Edn. (chmn. commn. on women in higher edn. 1987-88, commn. on govt. rels., bd. dirs. 1999-2001), Assn. Portland Progress (bd. dirs.), Portland C. of C. (bd. dirs. 1995), Western Assn. of Schs. and Colls. (commr. 1994-97). Office: Edn and Human Resources Directorate Nat Sci Found 4201 Wilson Blvd Arlington VA 22230

RAMALHO-AHRNDT, MARIA GABRIELA, art educator; b. Foz Do Arelho, Portugal, June 14, 1965; arrived in Can., 1967, arrived in U.S., 1991; d. Bernardino Maria and Maria Gabriela (Da Silva) Ramalho; m. Timothy James Ahrndt, Aug. 26, 1995; children: Vincent J. Ahrndt, Alexandra Maria Ahrndt. BA, U. Toronto, Can., 1988; MA in Edn., Mankato State U., 1993. Printing asst. Art Svcs. Agy., Toronto, 1988; gallery asst. Wynick/Tuck Gallery, Toronto, 1988, Odon Wagner Gallery, Toronto, 1989-91, Art Gallery Ont., Toronto, 1990-91; art tchr. Washington Elem. Sch., Mankato, Minn., 1993, Spring Lake Park (Minn.) HS, 1994—. Author, illustrator: Bedtime Stories about Zany Creatures, 2002. Mem.: Am. Arts Crafts Coun., Nat. Art Edn. Assn., Nat. Mus. Women in the Arts. Roman Catholic. Avocations: sculpting, stamp-collecting, art history. Office: Spring Lake Park HS 8001 Able St NE Minneapolis MN 55432-2059

RAMBARAN, SARAH M., music educator; b. Lakeland, Fla., Oct. 17, 1973; d. Stephen L. and Cheryl E. Sorrow; m. Rodney S. Rambaran, Aug. 12, 1995; children: Jared N., Joshua A. BA in Music Edn. K-12, Southeastern U., Lakeland, Fla., 1996. Cert. tchr. Fla., Orff-Schulwerk Levels 1, 2, 3 Am. Orff-Schulwerk Assn., nat. bd. cert. tchr. Music tchr. Wendell Watson Elem., Lakeland, 1996—. Dir. Orff ensemble Polk County Elem. Music Showcase, Lakeland, 1999. Mem. choir Victory Ch., Lakeland, 2005—. Tchr. Incentive grantee, Arts for a Complete Edn.)/FAAE, 2000. Mem.: Polk County Elem. Music Tchrs. Orgn. (pres. 2004—), Fla. Music Educators Assn., Am. Orff-Schulwerk Assn., Music Educators Nat. Conf. Avocations: travel, gardening. Home: 7506 Briarbay Loop Lakeland FL 33810 Office: Wendell Watson Elem 6800 Walt Williams Rd Lakeland FL 33809 Office Phone: 863-853-6060. E-mail: sarah.rambaran@polk-fl.net.

RAMBO, DOMINGO H., elementary school educator; b. Marietta, Tex., Apr. 20, 1924; d. Joseph E. and Elvira (Henderson) Johnson; m. Buford Rambo, Oct. 15, 1951; children: Jennifer Joan, George Alford. BA, Huston Tillotson Coll., Austin, Tex., 1951; postgrad., Calif. State U., L.A., Calif. State U., UCLA, Pepperdine U. Cert. elem. tchr., Calif. Tchr. Greenville (Tex.) Ind. Sch. Dist., L.A. Unified Sch. Dist., profl. expert. Co-founder L.A. Bridge Conservatory Performing and Visual Arts, pres., 1992—. Recipient outstanding and merit award for 35-yrs. svc. L.A. Unified Sch. Dist.; named to Wall of Tolerance, Montgomery, Ala. Mem. NEA, Calif. Tchrs. Assn., UTLA, Phi Delta Kappa.

RAMBO, KELLY CLIFFORD, lawyer; b. Easton, Pa., Apr. 26, 1961; d. Brian D. and Roslyn Clifford; m. William K. Rambo, Apr. 11, 1987; children: William Clifford, Grace Caroline, Luke Evan. BS cum laude, Pa. State U., University Park, 1983; JD with high distinction, Temple U. Sch. Law, Phila., 1986. Bar: Pa. 1986. Assoc. atty. White & Williams, Phila., 1986—87, Cohen & Feeley, Easton, 1987—91; prin. atty. Kelly Clifford Rambo, Atty. at Law, Easton, 1991—95; atty./mng. atty. worker's compensation dept. Post & Schell, Allentown, Pa., 1995—97; ptnr. Cohen & Feeley, Bethlehem, Pa., 1997—. Author: (article) The Legal Field and the Health Care Professional: Weathering Involvement. Fellow Rotary Club, Easton, 2005; mem. Third St. Alliance for Women and Children, Easton, 1994. Mem.: Pa. Trial Lawyers Assn. (assoc.), Pa. Bar Assn. (assoc.), Northampton County Bar Assn. (assoc.). Avocations: travel, reading. Office: Cohen & Feeley 2851 Baglyos Cir Ste 200 Bethlehem PA 18020 Office Phone: 610-332-2718. Office Fax: 610-332-2722. Business E-Mail: krambo@cohenfeeley.com.

RAMBO, SYLVIA H., federal judge; b. Royersford, Pa., Apr. 17, 1936; d. Granville A. and Hilda E. (Leonhardt) R.; m. George F. Douglas, Jr., Aug. 1, 1970. BA, Dickinson Coll., 1958; JD, Dickinson Sch Law, 1962; LLD (hon.), Wilson Coll., 1980, Dickinson Sch. Law, 1993, Dickinson Coll., 1994, Shippensburg U., 1996, Widener U., 1999. Bar: Pa. 1962. Atty. trust dept. Bank of Del., Wilmington, 1962-63; pvt. practice Carlisle, 1963-76; from public defender to chief public defender Cumberland County, Pa., 1974-76; judge Ct. Common Pleas, Cumberland County, 1976-78, U.S. Dist. Ct. (mid. dist.) Pa., Harrisburg, 1979—, chief judge, 1992-99; federal judge U.S. Dist. Ct., Harrisburg, 2000—. Asst. prof., adj. prof. Dickinson Sch. Law, 1974—76; mem. Jud. Conf. Com. on Adminstrn. of Magistrate Judges Sys., 1996—2002. Bd. dirs. Dickinson Sch. Law., Pa. State U., bd. govs., 2000—05, mem. bd. counselors, 2005—. Mem. Pa. Bar Assn. (mem. task force legal svcs. to needy 2000-03, mem. third cir. com. devel. model criminal jury instructions 2004—), Phi Alpha Delta. Democrat. Presbyterian. Office: US Dist Ct Federal Bldg PO Box 868 Harrisburg PA 17108-0868 Office Phone: 717-221-3960.

RAMEY, EUDORA MALOIS, minister; b. Maywood, Ill., Oct. 26, 1923; d. Cleonus and Ora Helen Garner; m. Edward F Ramey, July 27, 1947; children: Jonathan, RoseMary, Paul. Student, Herzl Jr. Coll., Chgo., Peter's Bus. Coll., Master's Sewing Coll., Vennard Bible Coll., Moody Bible Inst. Ordained minister African Episcopal Ch., 1951. Mem. Dist. 9 Bd. Edn., McKinley Sch., Chgo., 1966—75; counselor aide Bd. Edn./Whitney Young Magnet Sch., Chgo., 1975—80; implementor Job Club/Pres.'s Office/Employment Tng., Chgo., 1980—92. Advisor Garfield Pk. Conservatory, Chgo., 1991—, bd. dirs., 1996—. Mem. Chgo. Urban League, 1943—68, PUSH (People United to Serve Humanity), Chgo., 1970—91; ordained local elder/min. St. Stephen AME Ch., Chgo., 1951—; mem. NAACP, Chgo., 1943—68. Recipient Trailblazer for Women in Ministry award, 4th Dist. of the AME Ch., 2001, Cert. of Honor, Internat. Way of Life /City of Chgo., 1999, Chgo. Sr. Citizen's Hall of Fame, 1997. Avocations: Scrabble, Bingo, reading, checkers, crossword puzzles. Personal E-mail: rev.eudora1026@sbc.global.net.

RAMEY, SUSAN DORSEY, elementary school educator; b. Lexington, Ky., Aug. 12, 1949; d. Bernard Ribelin and Martha Eubank Dorsey; m. Charles Kenneth Ramey, Jan. 25, 1980; children: Kristopher Kelly, Amanda Kathryn, Robert Stuart. AA, Ea. Ky U., 1971; BS, Morehead State U., 1991, MS, 1994. Cert. reading specialist Ky. Adult edn. tchr. Fleming County Bd. Edn., Flemingsburg, 1992—93, tchr., 1994—2003, reading first coach, reading specialist, 2003—; reading first master trainer Ramey Livestock Hauling, L.L.C. Exhibitions include J.B. Speed Museum (Images of the Mountain, 1985). Presbyterian. Avocations: horses, Great Danes, painting. Office: Ewing Elem Sch 210 Euclid Ave Ewing KY 41039 Office Phone: 606-267-2601. Business E-Mail: sramey@fleming.k12.ky.us.

RAMIREZ, AINISSA, materials scientist; BSc, Brown U.; MS, PhD, Stanford U. Rschr., scientist Hewlett Packard Lab., Bell Lab., Lucent Tech., sci. curriculum developer pub. sch.; current asst. prof. mech. engring. Yale U. Named one of 100 Top Young Innovators, MIT's Tech. Review, 2003. Office: Yale Univ Mech Engring Dept PO Box 208284 New Haven CT 06520

RAMIREZ, ELISA, mathematics educator; b. Mexicali, Baja California Norte, Mexico, Dec. 5, 1966; d. Jose Luis and Elisa Miranda; m. Julio Cesar Ramirez, Oct. 30, 1993; children: Samantha, Julian, Julio. B, U. Calif., San Diego, 1990. Tchr. math. William Moreno Jr. H.S., Calexico, Calif., 1991—. Chair math. dept. William Moreno Jr. H.S., 2005—06. Recipient Aztec Yr., William Moreno Jr. H.S., 2003, Tchr. Yr., Calexico Unified Sch. Dist., 2004. Office: William Moreno Jr High School 1202 Kloke Rd Calexico CA 92231 Office Phone: 760-768-3960.

RAMIREZ, LEILANI, music educator; b. Frankfurt, Germany, Feb. 8, 1976; d. Sergio and Carla Ramirez. BA, U. Tex., Brownsville, 2000. Disc jockey Sta. 92.7 FM, South Padre Island, Tex., 1995—97; prodn. asst. NBC Studios, Brownsville, Tex., 1997—99; disc jockey Sta. 107.9 KVLY, Weslaco, Tex., 1997—98; elem. music tchr. Resaca Elem., Brownsville, 2001—02, Brownsville Ind. Sch. Dist, Brownsville, 2002—. Cons. San Benito Sch. Dist., Tex., 1999—2005. Musician: S.Tex. Symphony. Mem.: Tex. BandMasters Assn. (assoc.), Tex. Music Educators Assn. (assoc.), Jaycees. R-Liberal. Avocation: travel. Office Phone: 956-831-8728. Personal E-mail: lcramirez@bisd.us.

RAMIREZ, MARI CARMEN, curator; b. San Juan, PR, 1955; m. Hector Olea. M in art history, PhD in art history, U. Chgo. Dir. Mus. Anthropology, History, and Art U. PR, Rio Piedras; curator L.Am. art Jack S. Blanton Mus. Art, U. Tex., Austin, 1989—2001; Worthman Curator L.Am. Art Mus. Fine Arts, Houston, 2001—, dir. Internat. Ctr. for the Arts of the Americas, 2001—. Adj. lectr. art dept. U. Tex., Austin. Editor: (books) El Taller Torres-Garcia: The School of the South and Its Legacy, 1992, Collecting L.Am. Art for the 21st Century, 2002, Questioning the Line: Gego in Context, 2003; co-author (with Hector Olea): Inverted Utopias: Avant-Garde Art in L.Am., 2004; co-curator Re-Aligning Vision: Alternative Currents in South American Drawing, 1997, co-curator (with Hector Olea) (exhibitions) Inverted Utopias: Avant-Garde Art in L.Am., 2004, co-curator (with Beverly Adams) Encounters/Displacements: Alfredo Jaar, Luis Camnitzer, Cildo Meireles, curator Cantos Paralelos: Visual Parody in Contemporary Argentinean Art, Global Conceptualism: Points of Origin (L.Am. sect.). Named one of 25 Most Influential Hispanics, Time Mag., 2005; recipient Peter Norton Family Found. Award for Curatorial Excellence, Ann. award for curatorial excellence, Ctr. for Curatorial Studies, Bard Coll., 2005; Getty Curatorial Residence Fellowship. Office: Mus Fine Arts PO Box 6826 Houston TX 77265-6826

RAMIREZ, MARIA C(ONCEPCIÓN), retired educational association administrator; d. Ines and Carlota (Cruz) Ramirez. BA, U. Incarnate Word, San Antonio, Tex., 1966; MEd, U. Tex., Austin, 1979; postgrad., S.W. Tex. State U., San Marcos, 1980. Cert. elem. tchr., bilingual tchr., supr. Elem. tchr. regular and bilingual Edgewood Ind. Sch. Dist., San Antonio, 1966—69; elem tchr. regular and bilingual Austin Ind. Sch. Dist., Tex., 1969—74, coord. bilingual program, 1974—89, instrnl. coord., 1989—91, asst. prin., 1991—96, bilingual instrnl. coord., 1996—97; ret., 1997. Vol. interpreter Diocesan Law Project Cath. Ch. Ctrl. Tex., Austin, 2002—03; coord. religious edn. Cristo Rey Cath. Ch., Austin, 2002—; dir. Spanish mass choir St. Mary's Cathedral, Austin, 2003—05.

RAMIREZ, MARIA FIORINI, financial consultant; b. Naples, Italy, Jan. 1, 1948; came to U.S., 1961; d. Fernando and Clelia Ambrosio Fiorini; m. George M. Ramirez, 1973. BBA, Pace U., 1972, postgrad., 1974-76. Analyst Meinhard-CIT Comml. Fin., N.Y.C., 1967-68; credit analyst Am. Express Internat. Bank, N.Y.C., 1968-72; credit mgr. Banca Nazionale del Lavoro, N.Y.C., 1972-73; credit mgr., asst. v.p. Merrill Lynch G.S.I., 1973-74, economist, 1974—81, v.p., sr. money market economist Merrill Lynch Econs. Inc., 1981-84; sr. v.p., sr. money market economist Becker Paribas Inc., N.Y.C., 1984; corp. first v.p., money market economist Drexel Burnham Lambert Inc., N.Y.C., 1984-86, mng. dir., chief money market economist, 1986—90; pres. Maria Ramirez Capital Cons. Inc. (subs. Hancock Freedom), N.Y.C., 1990—92; pres., CEO Maria Fiorini Ramirez, Inc., 1992—. Bd. dirs. Statewide Savings Bank, 1989—2000, Arlington Capital, 1991—2000, Security Benefit Life, 1996—98, Independence Community Bank, 2000—06, Schroder Hedge Funds, 2004—, AMF funds, 2005—, Sovereign Bancorp, Inc., 2006—; mem. investment policy com. & product review com. Edward Jones & Co., 1996—. Mem. advisory bd. Pace U. Lunblin Sch. Bus., 1997—; trustee Notre Dame H.S., 2001, Pace U., 2002—. Recipient Lubin Alumni Achievement award, Pace U., 2001, Metro Internat. Fulbright award for Contributing to Internat. Understanding, 2004, Ellis I. Medal of Honor, 2004. Mem.: The Econ. Club NY. Roman Catholic. Office: 675 3rd Ave New York NY 10017*

RAMIREZ, MARY CATHERINE, retired secondary school educator; b. McLeansboro, Ill., Feb. 16, 1921; d. George Washington and Mary Margaret (Lane) Tousley; m. John Ramirez, Oct. 30, 1948 (dec. 1975). BS, Ctrl. U., Edmond, Okla., 1942; MA, U. Okla., 1945. Tchr. Bradley (Okla.) High Sch., 1942-43, McLeansboro (Ill.) High Sch., 1943-46, No. Okla. Jr. Coll., Tonkawa, Okla., 1946-47, Draughon Bus. Coll., Springfield, Mo., 1947-48, VA Hosp., Springfield, Mo., 1948-52, Madison, Wis., 1952-63, Madison pub. sch., 1963-85; tchr. ESL Poland, 1995. Tchr. English (summer), Poland, 1994. Mem. AAUW (publicity chmn. Madison br. 1954-60), NEA, Madison Civics Club. Avocations: travel, photography, coin and stamp collecting, needlecrafts. Home: 971 Wellington Ct Nekoosa WI 54457-9040

RAMIREZ, MONICA E., education educator, consultant; b. New York, NY, Nov. 27, 1952; d. Luis Ramirez de Arellano and Margarete Brendel; m. Neil Allen, Aug. 17, 2002; children: Luis Preiss, Suellen Melzer-Drinnen. BA, MS, U. Munich, 1979; EdS, Novasout Eastern, 1989; PhD, Columbia Pacific U., 1992. Assoc. prof. Fla. Atlantic U., Boca Raton, 1994—97; prof. geology Aims Coll., Greeley, Colo., 1997—2004; assoc. prof. Colo. State U. at Pueblo, 2004—. Stormwater adv. bd. City of Greeley, 2003—; tchr. edn. bd. Colo. State U., 2004—05; geology state chmn. Aims Coll., 2001—04. Contbr. articles to jours.; lang. editor Ctrl. European Sci. Jour., 2002—. Nominee Fla. Governor's award, Fla. Dept. Environ. Edn., 1993; recipient grant, NSF, 2000—04;, Math and Sci. Initiative, Colo. Commn., 2004—05. Avocations: rock climbing, mountain climbing. Office: Colo State U 2200 Bonforte Blvd Pueblo CO 81001 Business E-Mail: monica.ramirez@colostate-pueblo.edu.

RAMIREZ, NOLA MARIE, librarian; b. Painesville, Ohio, July 25, 1953; d. Ruth Alice Young; m. Robert Cisneros Ramirez, Dec. 20, 1983; 1 child, Geoffrey Michael Ross. Attended, West Valley Jr. Coll., San Jose, Calif. Vol. Merced County Libr., Gustine, Calif., 1988—90, libr. asst., 1990—92, branch mgr., 1992—. Co-leader Girl Scouts Am., 1998—. Avocation: reading. Home: 263 Laurel Ave Gustine CA 95322 Office: Merced County Libr Gustine Branch 205 Sixth St Gustine CA 95322 Office Phone: 209-854-3013. Personal E-mail: nolar55@hotmail.com.

RAMIREZ, SARA, actress; b. Mazatlan, Mexico, Aug. 31, 1976; Actress (Broadway plays) The Capeman, 1998, The Gershwins' Fascinating Rhythm, 1999, A Class Act, 2001, Dreamgirls, 2001, Monty Python's Spamalot, 2005 (Tony award, best performance by featured actress in a musical, 2005, Outer Critics Circle award, outstanding featured actress in a musical, 2005), (off-Broadway plays) The Vagina Monologues, (films) You've Got Mail, 1998, actress (voice) UnJammer Lammy, 1999, actress PaRappa the Rapper 2, 2001, Spider-Man, 2002, Washington Heights, 2002, Chicago, 2002, (TV series) Baseball Wives, 2002, (guest appearance) Law & Order SVU, As the World Turns, 2002, NYPD Blue, 2004, Grey's Anatomy, 2006—. Office: Cornerstone Talent Agency 37 W 20th St Ste 1108 New York NY 10011-3713*

RAMIREZ, TINA, artistic director; b. Caracas, Venezuela; d. Gloria Maria Cestero and Jose Ramirez Gaonita. Studied dance with Lola Bravo, Alexandra Danilova, Anna Sokolow. Toured with Federico Rey Dance Co.; founder, artistic dir. Ballet Hispanico, NYC, 1970—. Panelist NEA N.Y. Sate Coun. on Arts; mem. advisory panel N.Y.C. Dept. Cultural Affairs; bd. dirs Dance Theater Workshop. Appearances (Broadway plays) Kismet, Lute Song, (TV series) Man of La Mancha. Bd. mem. The New 42nd Street, Inc. Named one of ten people of yr., AARP Mag., 2004; recipient Arts and Culture Honor award, Mayor of NYC, 1983, Ethnic New Yorker award, NYC, 1986, Gov.'s Arts award, NY State Gov. Mario Cuomo, 1987, honoree Nat. Puerto Rican Forum, Hispanic Inst. for Performing Arts., Hispanic Heritage Award, 1999, Dance Magazine Award, 2002, Nat. Medal of Arts, Nat. Endowment for the Arts, 2005. Office: Ballet Hispanico 167 W 89th St New York NY 10024-1901*

RAMIREZ-CAMPBELL, CHRISTINE M., art council administrator; b. Springfield, Ill., July 1, 1951; d. Philip Joseph Ramirez and Mary Barbara (Dinora); m. R. Michael Patsche, Oct. 1971 (div. 1986); children: Gina Maria Patsche, R. Michael Patsche; m. G. Dennis Campbell, Oct. 1, 1993. AA, Springfield Coll. Ill., 1971; BA, Sangamon State U., 1989. Edn. asst. Ill. State Mus., Springfield, 1989—92; sci. edn. coord. Springfield Children's Mus., 1992—94; dir. cmty. edn. Lincoln Land C.C., Springfield, 1994—2000; exec. dir. Springfield Area Arts Coun., 2000—. Arts trainer, mentor program Ill. Arts Alliance, 2001; v.p. bldg. bd. Springfield Ctr. for the Arts, 2001. Arts chair Springfield Jr. League, 1984; pres. Care Ctr., Springfield, 1984; bd. mem. Brinkenhoff Home Aux., Springfield, 1987. Recipient Paragon award, Assn. Pub. Rels. C.C., 1999, Spl. Recognition Svc. award, Trustees Lincoln Land Cmty. Coll., 2000. Mem.: Downtown Springfield Inc., Springfield C. of C. Office: Springfield Area Arts Council 420 S 6th St Springfield IL 62701-1808

RAMIREZ GARZA, ELIZABETH ANN, biology professor, researcher; d. Joe E. Ramirez Sr. and Diamantina Ramirez; m. Simon Garza, Jr., Sept. 18, 1982; children: Jonathan David Garza, Aaron Zachary Garza, Joshua Joseph Garza, Caleb Daniel Garza. BS in Biology, U. Tex., San Antonio, 1981, MS in Biology, 1986. Cert. radiology Tex. State Bd. Dental Examiners, 1989, dental practice mgmt. asst. Tex., 1990. Rsch. asst. U. Tex. Health Sci. Ctr., San Antonio, 1981—82, 1985—86; student intern genetics lab U. Tex., San Antonio, 1984—85; biology tutor St. Edward's U., Austin, Tex., 1991; lectr. Incarnate Word Coll., San Antonio, 1991—92; adj. faculty biology Austin C.C., 1993—2004, asst. prof. biology, 2004—06; adj. faculty biology Concordia U., Austin, 2002—03. Coll. assistance migrant program mentor St. Edward's U., Austin, 1991—92; biology faculty mentor Dept. Biology, Austin, 1999, biology 1408 com. chmn., 2005. Mem. campus adv. coun. Lyndon Baines Johnson H.S., Austin, 2002—04; active City Charter Commn., Yoakum, Tex., 1987; pres. Bailey Mid. Sch. PTA, Austin, 1999—2000. Nat. Hispanic scholar, Nat. Hispanic Scholarship Com., 1984. Mem.: Tex. C.C. Tchr. Assn. (assoc.). Avocations: hiking, camping, swimming, bicycling. Office: Austin Community College 1212 Rio Grande Austin TX 78701 Office Phone: 512-293-1799 23714. Personal E-mail: lramlgarz@msn.com. Business E-mail: lramirez@austincc.edu.

RAMÍREZ-RUIZ, DORIS M., education educator; b. Aguadilla, PR, Jan. 3, 1956; d. Juan Ramírez and Ramonita Ruiz. BS in Biology, Recinto Univ. Mayagüez, PR, 1978. Lab. instr. Inter Am. U., Aguadilla, PR, 1978; tchr. Bd. Edn., Aguada, PR, 1978—. Advisor student tchrs. Bd. Edn., Aguada, 1997—. Cmty. choir mem. Coro Polifonico de Aguada, Inc., 1995; choir mem. Cath. Ch., Aguada, 1985, cathequist, 1985. Recipient Presdl. Award for Excellence in Math. and Sci. Tchg., NSF, 1998. Mem.: NSTA, Federación de Maestros de PR, Nat. Assn. Biology Tchrs. Roman Catholic. Avocations: singing, travel. Home: PO Box 379 Aguada PR Office Phone: (787)868-2161. Home Fax: (787)252-1024. Personal E-mail: ramirezd@coqui.net.

RAMMINGER, SHELLY LYNN, elementary school educator; b. Binghamton, N.Y., May 1, 1966; d. Thomas Barnard Evans and Phyllis (Chilletti) Savage; m. Thomas Edward Ramminger, Nov. 19, 1988. BS in Edn., SUNY, Geneseo, 1988; postgrad., SUNY, Binghamton, 1989-90; MS in Edn., SUNY, Cortland, 1993. Resource room tchr. Binghamton City Schs., 1988, self-contained tchr., 1988-89; resource rm. tchr. grades 7 through 12 Candor (N.Y.) Cen. Schs., 1989-90, resource rm. tchr. grades 5 through 12, 1990-93; resource rm. tchr. grades kindergarten through 5 Vestal (N.Y.) Cen. Schs., 1993—; self contained tchr. Wyoming Conf. Sch., Hillcrest, N.Y., 1990. Tchr. Nat. Handicapped Sports & Recreation Program, Binghamton, 1989-90, 93; coach Olympics of the Mind, 1989-93; vol. Coty Day Treatment Ctr., 1986-87, Chautauqua Day Ctr., SUNY, Fredonia, N.Y., 1985. Mem. Coun. for Exceptional Children (Cert. of Appreciation 1988), N.Y. State Unified Tchrs. Avocations: skiing, soccer, crafts, reading, music. Home: 9751 Whitewood Trl Charlotte NC 28269-0431 Office: North Meeklenburg HS Statesville Rd Charlotte NC 28269

RAMO, ROBERTA COOPER, lawyer; b. Denver, Aug. 8, 1942; d. David D. and Martha L. (Rosenblum) Cooper; m. Barry W. Ramo, June 17, 1964. BA magna cum laude, U. Colo., 1964; JD, U. Chgo., 1967; LLD (hon.), U. Mo., 1995; LLD, U. Denver, 1995; LHD (hon.), U. Colo., 1995; JD (hon.), Golden Gate U., 1996; LLD (hon.), U. S.C., 2001. Bar: N.Mex. 1967, Tex. 1971. With NC. Fund, Durham, 1967-68; nat. tchg. fellow Shaw U., Raleigh, N.C., 1968-70; mem. Sawtelle, Goode, Davidson & Troilo, San Antonio, 1970-72, Rodey, Dickason, Sloan, Akin & Robb, Albuquerque, 1972-74; sole practice law Albuquerque, 1974-77; dir., shareholder Poole, Kelly & Ramo, Albuquerque, 1977-93; shareholder Modrall, Sperling, Roehl, Harris & Sisk, Albuquerque, 1993—. Lectr. in field., bd. dirs. Merrill Lynch Asset Mgmt., Ednl. Credit Mgmt. Corp. Co-author: New Mexico Estate Administration System, 1980; editor: How to Create a System for the Law Office, 1975; contbg. editor: Tex. Probate Sys., 1974; contbr. articles to profl. jours., chpts. to books. Mem. steering com. World Conf. Domestic Violence, 1996—99; mem. Am. Law Inst. Coun., 1997—, exec. com., 2000—, exec. v.p., 2003—; mem. Martindale-Hubbell Legal Adv. Bd., 1996—2000; bd. dirs., past pres. N.Mex. Symphony Orch., 1977—86; bd. dirs. Albuquerque Cmty. Found., N.Mex. First, 1987—90, Santa Fe Opera, Santa Fe, 2001—; bd. regents U. N.Mex., 1989—94, pres., 1991—93; founding bd. mem. Think N.Mex., 1998—; mem. Civitas Initiative, 1997—; chmn. bd. Cooper's Inc., 1999—. Recipient Disting. Pub. Svc. award Gov. of N.Mex., 1993. Fellow: Am. Bar Found.; mem.: ABA (bd. govs. 1994—97, pres. 1995, Asia Law Initiatives Coun. 1999—2005, chmn. London 2000 com., others), Am. Arbitration Assn. (bd. dirs. 1997—2004, 2004—), Law Inst. Coun., Am. Judicature Soc. (bd. dirs. 1988—91), Am. Bar Retirement Assn. (bd. dirs. 1990—94), N.Mex. Bar Assn. (Outstanding Contbn. award 1981, 1984), Albuquerque Bar Assn. (pres. 1980—81, bd. dirs.), Greater Albuquerque C. of C. (exec. com. 1987—91, bd. dirs.). Address: Modrall Sperling Roehl Harris & Sisk PO Box 2168 Albuquerque NM 87103-2168

RAMO, VIRGINIA M. SMITH, civic worker; b. Yonkers, NY; d. Abraham Harold and Freda (Kasnetz) Smith; m. Simon Ramo; children: James Brian, Alan Martin. BS in Edn., U. So. Calif., DHL (hon.), 1978. Nat. co-chmn., ann. giving U. So. Calif., 1968-70, vice chmn., trustee, 1971—, co-chmn. bd. councilors Sch. Performing Arts, 1975-76, co-chmn. bd. councillors Schs. Med. and Engring. Vice-chmn. bd. overseers Hebrew Union Coll., 1972-75; bd. dirs. The Muses of Calif. Mus. Sci. and Industry, UCLA Affiliates, Estelle Doheny Eye Found., U. So. Calif. Sch. Medicine; mem. adv. coun. L.A. County Heart Assn., chmn. com. to endow Chair in cardiology at U. So. Calif.; vice chmn., bd. dirs. Friends of Libr. U. So. Calif.; bd. dirs., nat. pres. Achievement Rewards for Coll. Scientists Found., 1975-77; bd. dirs. Les Dames L.A., Cmty. TV So. Calif.; bd. dirs., v.p. Founders L.A. Music Ctr.; v.p. L.A. Music Ctr. Opera Assn.; v.p. corp. bd. United Way; v.p. Blue Ribbon-400 Performing Arts Coun.; chmn. com. to endow chair in gerontology U. So. Calif.; vice chmn. campaign Doheny Eye Inst,. 1986; co-chair, bd. overseers Keck Sch. Medicine U. So. Calif., 1999—. Recipient Svc. award Friends of Librs., 1974, Nat. Cmty. Svc. award Alpha Epsilon Phi, 1975, Disting. Svc. award Am. Heart Assn., 1978, Svc. award U. So. Calif., Spl. award U. So. Calif. Music Alumni Assn., 1979, Life Achievement award Mannequins of L.A. Assistance League, 1979, Woman of Yr. award Pan Hellenic Assn., 1981, Disting. Svc. award U. So. Calif. Sch. Medicine, 1981, U. So. Calif. Town and Gown Recognition award, 1986, Asa V. Call Achievement award U. So. Calif., 1986, Phi Kappa Phi scholarship award U. So. Calif., 1986, Vision award Luminaires of Doheny Eye Inst., 1994, Presdl. medallion U. So. Calif., 2002, USC Thornton Sch. of Music Founder's award, 2003. Mem. UCLA Med. Aux., U. So. Calif. Pres.'s Cir., Commerce Assocs. U. So. Calif., Cedars of Lebanon Hosp. Women's Guild (dir. 1967-68), Blue Key, Skull and Dagger.

RAMOS, ALICE M., education educator; b. NYC, June 18, 1948; d. Alejo Ramos and Dominga Mendez de Ramos. BA in French and Spanish, Marymount Manhattan Coll., 1970; MA in French lang. and lit., NYU, 1971, PhD in French Lit., 1979; PhD in Philosophy, U. Navarra, 1985. Spanish instr. Marymount Manhattan Coll., NYC, 1971—72; tchg. asst. in French NYU, 1972—74; instr./asst. prof. in French Coll. of Mt. St. Vincent, Riverdale, NY, 1975—80; lectr. in French U. Navarra, Pamplona, Spain, 1980—85, lectr. in philosophy, 1985—86; asst. prof. philosophy St. John's U., Jamaica, NY, 1987—93, assoc. prof. philosophy, 1993—2002, prof. philosophy, 2002—. Bd. dirs. Murray Hill Inst.; pres. Am. Maritain Assn., 2001—04. Author: (book) Signum: De la Semiótica Universal a la Metafísca del Signo, 1987; editor: Beauty, Art and the Polis, 2000; co-editor: Faith, Scholarship and Culture in the 21st Century, 2002; contbr. articles to profl. jours. Mem.: Philos. Assn., Am. Maritain Assn. (prs. 2001—04). Roman Cath. Avocations: art, music. Office: St John's U Dept Philosophy 8000 Utopia Pkwy Jamaica NY 11439

RAMOS, FLAVIA SALES, education educator, consultant; b. Recife, Pernambuco, Brazil, May 20, 1960; d. Feliciano Sales Ramos and Maria de Fatima Volpini; m. Hedi Mattoussi, June 28, 1996; 1 child, Yasmine Vivian Mattoussi. BA in Art Edn., Universidade Fed. do Rio de Janeiro, Brazil, 1982; MEd in Internat. Edn., U. of Mass., 1989, EdD in Internat. Edn., 1999. Cert. Family and School Bilingual Mediator Ctr. for Human Devel. Springfield, Mass., 1989. Rsch. asst. U. of Mass., Amherst, 1986—96; asst. prof. and dir. of the internat. tng. and edn. program Am. U., Washington, 2002—; vis. asst. prof. of internat. edn. George Wash. U., Washington, 2000—02. Dir. of internat. tng. programs Inst. for Tng. and Devel., Amherst, Mass., 1990—96; rsch. cons. Johns Hopkins U./ USAID, Mogadishu, Somalia; adj. prof. program in intercultural mgmt. Sch. Internat. Tng., Brattleboro, Vt., 1990; outreach network devel. cons. Ptnr. for a Healthier Cmty., Inc, Springfield, Mass., 1996—97; rsch. & edn. cons. Mass. Ctr. for Sudden Infant Death Syndrome, Boston, 1997—; adj. faculty internat. studies U. Conn., Storrs, 2002; ednl. cons. Us Dept. Of Labor, Washington, 2002. Author (illustrator): (children's books) E O Vento Contou Series, (health info. booklets) Read This if You Want to Feel Good and Look Good About Your Baby, Read this if you want your baby to grow happy, safe, and healthy., When a Baby Dies.; contbr. articles to profl. jours. Mem.: Comparative and Internat. Edn. Soc., The Assn. for Women's Rights in Devel., Nat. Assn. of Multicultural Edn. Baha'I. Achievements include development of The FotoDialogo Method. Avocation: travel. Office: American University 4400 Massachusetts Ave NW Washington DC 20016 Office Phone: 202-885-3723. Business E-Mail: framos@american.edu.

RAMOS, MARIA, science educator; d. Joseph Julio and Antoinette Di-Nardo; m. Timothy Ramos; children: Tiffany, Timothy. AAS, Mohawk Valley C.C., Utica, NY, 1981; BS, Syracuse U., Utica, 1983; MS, Rensselaer Poly. Inst., Troy, NY, 1987. Tchr. asst. Rensselaer Poly. Inst., 1984—85; co-op intern IBM, Endicott, NY, 1986; adj. faculty Mohawk Valley C.C., 1987—88, prof., 1988—. Faculty advisor Rome (NY) Returning Adult Student Assn., 1989—; orgnl. cons., Rome and Utica, 1985—; chair academic policy com. Mohawk Valley C.C., 2002—, mem. strategic planning com., 2004—. Vol. Rome Econ. Restructuring, 2004—. Recipient award for excellence in tchg., Mohawk Valley C.C., 1996—97, Chancellor's award for excellence in tchg., SUNY, 1997—98. Mem.: Rotary Internat. Avocations: landscaping, baking. Office: Mohawk Valley CC 1101 Floyd Ave Rome NY 13440 Office Phone: 315-334-7723. E-mail: mramos@mvcc.edu.

RAMOS-CANO, HAZEL BALATERO, caterer, chef, innkeeper, restaurateur, entrepreneur; b. Davao City, Mindanao, Philippines, Sept. 2, 1936; came to U.S., 1960. d. Mauricio C. and Felicidad (Balatero) Ramos; m. William Harold Snyder, Feb. 17, 1964 (div. 1981); children: John Byron, Snyder, Jennifer Ruth; m. Nelson Allen Blue, May 30, 1986 (div. 1990); m. A. Richard Cano, June 25, 1994. BA in Social Work, U. Philippines, Quezon City, 1958; MA in Sociology, Pa. State U., 1963, postgrad., 1966—67. Cert. exec. chef, Am. Culinary Fedn. Faculty, tng. staff Peace Corps Philippine Project, University Park, Pa., 1961-63; sociology instr. Albright Coll., Reading, Pa., 1963-64; rsch. asst. Meth. Ch. U.S.A., State College, Pa., 1965-66; rsch. asst. dept. child devel. & family rels. Pa. State U., University Park, 1966-67; exec. dir. Presbyn. Urban Coun. Raleigh Halifax Ct. Child Care and Family Svc. Ctr., 1973-79; early childhood educator Learning Together, Inc., Raleigh, NC, 1982-83; loan mortgage specialist Raleigh Savs. & Loan, 1983-84; restaurant owner, mgr. Hazel's on Hargett, Raleigh, 1985-86; admissions coord., social worker Brian Corp. Nursing Home, Raleigh, 1986-88, food svc. dir., 1989-90; regional dir. La Petite Acad., Raleigh, 1989-90; asst. food svc. mgr. Granville Towers, Chapel Hill, NC, 1990-92; mgr. trainee Child Nutrition Svcs. Wake County Pub. Sch. Sys., Raleigh, 1993-94; food svc. dir. S.W. Va. 4-H Ednl. Conf. Ctr., Abingdon, 1994-95; caterer, owner The Eclectic Chef's Catering, 1995—; innkeeper, owner Love House Bed and Breakfast, 1996—; pres. Ramos-Cano Inc., 1996—; owner Withers Hardware Restaurant, Abingdon, 2002—; pres. Ramos-Cano Mgmt. Svcs., LLC, 2002—; owner The Frame Shop, Abingdon, 2004—. Cooking instr. Wake Cmty. Tech. Coll., Raleigh, 1986-92; freelance caterer, 1964-95; chair Internat. Cooking Demonstrations Raleigh Internat. Festival, 1990-93. Pres. Wake County Day Care United Coun., 1974-75, NC Assn. Edn. Young Children (Raleigh chpt.), 1975-76; bd. mem. Project Enlightenment Wake County Pub. Schs., 1976-77; various positions Pines of Carolina Girl Scout Council, 1976-85; chmn. Philippine Health and Medical Aid Com., Phil-Am Assn. Raleigh 1985-88 (publicity chmn.); elder Trinity Presbyn. Ch., Raleigh, 1979-81, bd. deacons, 1993-94; elder, session mem. Sinking Spring Presbyn. Ch., 1997—; treas. Abingdon Newcomers Club, 1997—, Presbyn. Women, Sinking Spring Presbyn. Ch., Abingdon, 1999—; master gardener Va. Tech. Master Gardeners Program, 1998—. Rockefeller grant Rockefeller Found., 1958-59; recipient Ramon Magsaysay Presdl. award Philippine Leadership Youth Movement, 1957; Gov.'s Cert. Appreciation State NC, 1990, Raleigh Mayor's award Quality Childcare Svcs., 1990, award for keeping hist. Abington beautiful Abington Kiwanis Club, 1997 Mem. Am. Culinary Fedn., Presby. Women, Raleigh, (historian 1975-76), Penn State Dames (pres. 1968-69). Democrat. Office: Victoria & Albert Inn 224 Oak Hill St Abingdon VA 24210 also: The Love House Bed and Breakfast 210 E Valley St Abingdon VA 24210 also: Withers Hardware Restaurant 260

W Main St Abingdon VA 24210 also: The Frame Shop 115 Charwood Dr Abingdon VA 24210 also: Somethyme Bistro 115 Charwood Dr Abingdon VA 24210 Office Phone: 276-628-1111. E-mail: v&ainn@naxs.com, rcano@naxs.com.

RAMOS-VOIGT, LISETTE D., science educator; b. Ponce, P.R., Mar. 20, 1963; d. Jorge R. Ramos-Lorenzi and Candida R. Cintrón; m. John Gregory Voigt, Nov. 21, 1999; children: John Wren Voigt, Zachary Voigt. BA, Univ. P.R., Mayagvez, P.R., 1985; MA in Sci. Edn., N.Y. Univ., N.Y., 1988; PhD, Capella Univ., Mpls., 2005. Cert. tchg. Mo., P.R. Sci. tchr. San Luis Acad., Lajas, PR, 1987—88; chemistry tchr. Colegio Santiago Apostol, Fajardo, PR, 1988—89; health sci. tech. InterAmerican Univ., Fajardo, PR, 1988—91; biol. earth space sci. tchr. San Juan Consolidated Prep Sch., San Juan, PR, 1991—93; sci. tchr. Westpoint H.S., Kans. City, Mo., 1991—93, Ruskin H.S., Kans. City, Mo., 1993—98; asst. prof. Sanford Brown Coll., Kans. City, Mo., 1996—98; physical sci. Riverview H.S., St. Louis, 1998—99; chemistry tchr. Univ. City H.S., St. Louis, 1999—. Sr. leader trainer Mo. Assessment Program, St. Louis, 2001—; presenter Good Tchr. Conf., Jefferson City, Md., 2000—02; team evaluator Mo. student tchrs. programs Dept. Elem. and Secondary Edn., Mo., writer chemistry curriculum. Contbr. scientific papers. Presenter 4H Kids Group, Rio Grande, PR, 1990; lobbyist Legs. for Edn., Jefferson City, Mo., 1999—2002. Grantee NSF, Univ. Mo., 1992. Mem.: NEA (coord. profl. devel. tchr. conf. 2003), Mo. Nat. Edn. Assn., Sci. Tchrs. Assn., Phi Delta Kappa. Avocations: travel, boating, dance, wine tasting, research. Office: Univ City HS 7401 Balson Ave Saint Louis MO 63130

RAMP, MARJORIE JEAN SUMERWELL, civic worker; b. Kansas City, Mo., July 20, 1924; d. Walter Francis and Helen Louise (Nichols) Sumerwell; m. Floyd Lester Ramp, Sept. 4, 1948; children: David L., Sandra Jean, Paul F., Cheryl Louise. BS Nursing Edn., U. Minn., 1948. RN, Minn. Instr. nursing edn. U. Minn., Mpls., 1948—50; adminstrv. asst. to assn. min. We. Res. Assn. of Ohio Conf. United Ch. Christ, Cleve., 1983—85. Former chmn. hunger task force Ohio Conf. of United Ch. Christ, moderator, 1981-82, moderator We. Res. Assn., 1976-77, mem. nat. exec. coun., 1983-89; mem. United Ch. Bd. for World Ministries, 1971-82; past bd. dirs. We. Res. coun. Girl Scouts U.S.; nat. sec. Campaign for UN Reform, Washington, 1987-2000; pres. Greater Cleve.-Volgograd Oblast Alliance, 1998-99; coord., co-founder Richfield-Wolfach Twin City Program, 1970, bd. dirs., 1970-92; mem. numerous local and nat. peace groups; nongovtl. orgn. rep. Earth Summit, Rio de Janeiro, 1992, del. to UN commn. for sustainable devel.; bd. trustees Kendal at Oberlin Retirement Cmty., 1995-2004. Recipient Golden Trefoil award We. Res. Coun. Girl Scouts U.S., 1972; named Outstanding Woman Ohio Conf., Gen. Synod United Ch. Christ, 1985 Mem. AAUW (pres. Oberlin chpt. 2001-03), LWV, Citizens for Global Solutions (formerly World Federalist Assn. chmn. Ohio 1985—, bd. dirs., nat. exec. com. 1997—, vice-chmn. bd. dirs. 1999-2004, chmn. 2004-06), Delta Kappa Gamma (hon.) Home: 225 Hollywood St Oberlin OH 44074-1011 Personal E-mail: msramp@oberlin.net.

RAMPERSAD, PEGGY A. SNELLINGS, sociologist, consultant; b. Fredericksburg, Va., Jan. 12, 1933; d. George Daniel and Virginia Riley (Bowler) Snellings; m. Oliver Ronald Rampersad, Mar. 19, 1955; 1 child, Gita. BA, Mary Washington Coll., Fredericksburg, 1953; student, Sch. Art Inst. Chgo., 1953—55; MA, U. Chgo., 1965, PhD, 1978. Grad. admissions counselor U. Chgo., 1954—57, adviser fgn. students, 1958, dir. admissions Grad. Sch. Bus., 1958—63, rsch. project specialist, 1970—78, pers. mgr., 1979—80, mgr. orgnl. devel., 1980—82, adminstr. dept. econs., 1983—95; cons. PSR Consulting, Chgo., 1995—. Cons. North Ctrl. Assn. Colls. and Secondary Schs., Chgo., 1964—70, Orchestral Assn. Chgo. Symphony Orch., 1982, Chgo. Ctr. Decision Rsch., 1982, Harvard U., 1993—97. Exhibitions include Va. Mus. Fine Arts, Art Inst. Chgo., others; editor: North Ctrl. Assn. Quar., 1972; contbr. articles to profl. jours. Grad. fellow, U. Chgo., 1963—67. Mem.: AAUW, Am. Acad. Polit. and Social Sci., Am. Econ. Assn., Art Inst. Chgo. (assoc.), Pi Lambda Theta (past pres.). Episcopalian. Avocations: painting, drawing, opera, reading, walking. Home and Office: 28 Seneca Ter Fredericksburg VA 22401-1115

RAMPERSAUD LUNDY, SHERYLL, special education educator; b. Portsmouth, Va., Dec. 30, 1947; d. Rebecca Greene and Freddie Lee Drake; children: Vincent Earle Rampersaud, Sean Derrik Rampersaud, Sharon Antoinette Rampersaud. BS in Acctg., Norfolk State U., 1971—74, Advanced Studies Tchr. Certification, 2000—01. Spl. Educator Emotional Disturbance and Specific Learning Disabilities Va. Bd. Edn., 2002. Fire rates clk. Geico, Friendship Heights, Md., 1968—70; staff acct. Peat, Marwick, Mitchell CPAs, Washington, 1974—76; asst. internal auditor Howard U., Washington, 1976—80; pension acct./ cons. Qualified Pension Consultants/ Compdesign Inc., Bethesda, Md., 1983—98, Thomas F. Barrett, Inc., Bethesda, 1998—99; spl. edn. tchr. The Pines Residential Treatment Ctr., Portsmouth, Va., 2000—. Dir. Sankofa Cultural and Learning Ctr., Inc., Portsmouth, 1999—. Chief officer John F. Kennedy Poling Sta., Portsmouth, 1999—2001. Mem. Christian Ch. Home: 3204 Gwin St Portsmouth VA 23704 Office: The Pines Residential Treatment Center 825 Crawford Pky Portsmouth VA 23070 Office Phone: 757-391-6588. Personal E-mail: srampersaud@cox.net. E-mail: sheryl.rampersaud@absfirst.com.

RAMPHAL, JULIE FRANCES, retired secondary school educator; b. Sioux Falls, SD, Jan. 31, 1944; d. Shelton Russell and Frances Pauline (Hospers) Tilgner; m. Cecil Edward Ramphal, Aug. 29, 1976 (dec. Apr. 2000); stepchildren: Richard Andre, Rani. BA in English, Macalester Coll., 1966; MS in Ednl. Computing, Pepperdine U., 1985. Secondary tchr. Glendora Unified Sch. Dist., Calif., 1966—69, Tustin Unified Sch. Dist., Calif., 1969—2000. Coll. instr. Nat. U., Irvine, Calif., 1987; mentor tchr. Tustin Unified Sch. Dist., Calif., 1995—97; workshop leader Orange County Dept. of Edn., Costa Mesa, Calif., 1998. Workshop presenter Computer Using Educators (CUE) State Confs., Palm Springs, Calif., 1988—95. Recipient Exemplary Achievement in the field of Ednl. Tech., Ednl. Computing Alumni of Pepperdine U., 1992, grant, Women's Action Alliance of NYC, 1991—93, Mentor Tchr. in Tech., Tustin Unified Sch. Dist., 1995—97; grant, Calif. Academic Partnership Program, 1992. Mem.: Am. Assn. of U. Women (v.p. membership 2004—06, legal advocacy fund chair 2006—). Avocations: swimming, singing, gardening, piano, travel. Home: 20141 Crown Reef Lane Huntington Beach CA 92646 Personal E-mail: julieps23@aol.com.

RAMPHELE, MAMPHELA A., international organization administrator, physician, former academic administrator; b. Dec. 28, 1947; Diploma in tropical health and hygiene and pub. health, U. Witwatersrand; B.Com. in Adminstrn., U. South Africa; MD, U. Natal, 1972; PhD in Social Anthropology, U. Cape Town. Sr. rsch. officer U. Cape Town, South Africa, 1986—91, dep. vice chancellor, 1991—95, vice chancellor, 1996—2000; mng. dir. human devel. World Bank, Washington, 2000—. Immediate past chmn. bd. trustees Ind. Devel. Trust; adv. bd. World Bank Econ. Devel. Inst. Contbr. articles to profl. jours.; author: Across Boundaries, A Life, A Bed Called Home, Restoring the Land. Student activist Black Consciousness Movement; trustee Rockefeller Found. Recipient of numerous nat. and internat. awards including 17 hon. doctorates, awards for svc. to cmty., Kilby award, 2003. Mem.: Inst. of Medicine of NAS. Office: The World Bank 1818 H St NW Washington DC 20433*

RAMPONE, CHRISTIE P., professional soccer player; b. Broward County, Fla., June 24, 1975; m. Chris Rampone, Nov. 9, 2001. BS in spl. edn., Monmouth U., N.J., 1997. Mem. N.Y. Power, WUSA, 2001—; soccer player, defender U.S. Women's Nat. Team, 1997, mem. World Cup championship team, 1999. Founding player N.Y. Power, WUSA, 2001. Named First Team All-Mid-Atlantic Region, 1995, 1996, Player of Yr., N.E. Conf., 1995, 1996.

RAMSAY, KARIN KINSEY, publisher, educator; b. Brownwood, Tex., Aug. 10, 1930; d. Kirby Luther and Ina Rebecca (Wood) Kinsey; m. Jack Cummins Ramsay Jr., Aug. 31, 1951; children: Annetta Jean, Robin Andrew. BA, Trinity U., 1951. Cert. assoc. ch. edn., 1980. Youth coord. Covenant Presbyn. Ch., Carrollton, Tex., 1961-76; dir. ch. edn. Northminster Presbyn. Ch., Dallas, 1976-80, Univ. Presbyn. Ch., Chapel Hill, N.C., 1987-90, Oak Grove Presbyn. Ch., Bloomington, Minn., 1990-93; coord. ecum. ministry Flood Relief for Iowa, Des Moines, 1993; program coord. 1st Presbyn. Ch., Green Bay, Wis., 1994—98; owner, sole proprietor Hist. Resources Press, Corinth and Denton, Tex., 1994—. Dir. Godspell tour Covenant Presbyn. Ch., 1972-75; mem. Presbytery Candidates Com., Dallas, 1977-82, Presbytery Exams. Com. Dallas, 1979-81; clk. coun. New Hope Presbytery, Rocky Mount, NC, 1989-90; creator, dir. Thee Holy Fools mime/musical group and This Is Me retreats. Author: Ramsay's Resources, 1983—; co-author: Walking In the Dark, 2006; pub., editor: Patton's Ill-Fated Raid, 2002, Angel Kisses and My Beating Heart, 2004; contbr. articles to profl. jours. Design cons. Brookhaven Hosp. Chapel, Dallas, 1977-78; elder Presbyn. Ch. U.S.A., 1982—; coord. Lifeline Emergency Response, Dallas, 1982-84. Mem. Internat. Platform Assn., Small Publisher's Assn. of N. Am.,Pub. Marketing Assoc., Writer's League of Tex. Office Phone: 940-321-1066.

RAMSDEN, MARY CATHERINE, substance abuse specialist; Diploma, St. Joseph Mercy Hosp., 1966; postgrad., Mason City Jr. Coll., Kirkwood Community Coll. Cert. alcohol and drug counselor; RN Iowa, cert. chem. dependency nurse. Nursing supr. children's unit State Mental Health Inst., Cherokee, Iowa, 1966-69, Iowa Security Med. Facility, Oakdale, 1969; staff nurse psychiatry St. Luke's Meth. Hosp., Cedar Rapids, Iowa, 1969-74, asst. psychiat. nursing instr., 1970-74; mem. staff Sedlacek Treatment Ctr. Mercy Hosp., Cedar Rapids, 1974-85; cons. drug and alcohol CareUnit, Jacksonville Beach, Fla., 1985-86; nursing mgr. adolescent chem. dependency unit Broadlawns Med. Ctr., Des Moines, 1987-88; tng. mgr. Div. Substance Abuse and Heath Promotion Iowa Dept. Pub. Health, 1988-91; clin. program dir. Forest City (Iowa) Treatment Ctr., 1991-92; facilitator Employee & Family Resources Enhancement Women Pr Iowa Correctional Instn. for Women, Mitchellville, 1992-97; cast mgmt. tng. coord. Employee & Family Resources, Des Moines, 1998-99; substance abuse cons., trainer Des Moines, 1999—; sr. counselor Powell Chem. Dependency Ctr. Iowa Luth Hosp., Des Moines, 1999—2003; case mgr., substance abuse counselor drug ct. 5th Jud. Dist., Employee & Family Resources, 2003—. Mem. licensing rev. com. Iowa Bd. of Nursing. Author: (with others) Nurses Quick Reference, 1989. Vol. Project Enduring Families, 2004—. Lt. comdr. Nurse Corps USNR. Named Nurse Expert Coll. Nursing U. Iowa., 1985. Mem.: Iowa Assn. Addiction Profls. (v.p.), Iowa Corrections Assn., Consortium Behavioral Health Nurses and Assoc., Nat. Assn. Alcoholism and Drug Abuse Counselors, Res. Officers Assn. Home: 1519 Idaho St Des Moines IA 50316-2425 Office: 65 Gruber Des Moines IA 50315 Office Phone: 515-242-6982. Personal E-mail: mrrncd@yahoo.com.

RAMSER, WANDA TENE, librarian, educator; b. Atlanta, Ga., June 4, 1951; d. Galen Eugene Ramser and Christine Elizabeth Owen; children: Catherine Nicole Hannabach, David Richmond Hannabach. BA in History, U. Calif., Santa Barbara, 1973; MLS in Libr. and Info. Sci., UCLA, 1976, MLS in L.Am. Studies, 1977. With UCLA L.Am. Ctr., 1973—78; literacy coord. County of L.A. Libr., 1978—83; assoc. faculty South Orange County C.C. Dist., Mission Viejo, 1986, 2002—03, 2005—; with City of Oceanside (Calif.) Libr., 2001—. Chancellors assoc. UCLA, 1993—. Mem.: NOW, ALA (affiliate to Latinos and Spanish spkg., pres. San Diego chpt.), AAUW, Calif. Libr. Assn. (pres. svcs. to Latinos roundtable), UCLA Women Philanthropy, Habitat for Humanity, Mex. Am. Nat. Assn., Palomar Libr. Assn. (pres.). Address: UCLA Alumni Assn PO Box 1484 Beverly Hills CA 90213-1484 Business E-Mail: wanda.ramser@uclalumni.net.

RAMSEY, DORIS THERESA, elementary school educator; b. N.Y.C., Aug. 22, 1933; d. Alfonso Henry and Grace Elizabeth Ramsey. BA in sociology, Lehman Coll., 1973—76; MA in spl. edn., CUNY, City College, 1977—81, MA in reading, 1981—84. Billing clk. Simon & Schuster Publishers, NYC, 1952—65; acctg. clk. Princeton U. Store, NJ, 1965—68; edn. asst. NYC Bd. Edn., 1968—78, tchr., 1978—95; ret. Author: (book) Journey of the Ramsey Moores, 1995; actor: (cmty. theater group) The Hadley Players. Mem. Schemburg Ctr. for Rsch. in Black Culture, Met. Mus. Art. Mem.: Assn. of Black Educators, Alliance of Ret. Americans, Smithsonian Inst., Getty Mus. Avocations: music, travel. Home: 3010 Yates Ave Apt 4H Bronx NY 10469

RAMSEY, EMMA RUTH, secondary school educator; BA in Secondary Edn., Southwestern Okla. State U., Weatherford. Tchr., Viki, Okla.; tchr., drama coach, yearbook advisor Lone Wolf Schs., Okla., 1993—. Contbg. editor Casper Jour.; freelance writer Woodward News, Casper Star Tribune. Actor(cmty. theatre): (plays) Wizard of Oz (Best Actress in Supporting Role, 1998), Sound of Music (Best Actress in Cameo role); dir.(cmty. theatre): Barefoot in the Park. Avocations: genealogy, reading, poetry, drawing, painting.

RAMSEY, GLORIA ROGERS, elementary school educator; b. Memphis, Oct. 6, 1948; d. Reece Jennings and Roberta Mae (Koehler) Rogers; m. Joseph D. Ramsey, Jan. 25, 1969; children: Jessica Jonelle, Sean Michael. BA in Edn., Memphis State U., 1970, MEd. Cert. tchr., curriculum design and tech. Sales clk. Blair House, Memphis, 1968-70; gen. office staff Robert Hall Clothes, Memphis, 1970; tchr. Memphis (Tenn.) City Schs., 1977—. Lead tchr. trainer Memphis (Tenn.) City Schs., 1989-94; tchr. advisory mem. Pink Palace Mus., Memphis, 1993-94; mem. Family Life Adv. Coun., Memphis (Tenn.) City Schs., 1993-95. Recipient Presdl. award for tchg. NSF, 1994. Mem. Nat. Sci. Tchrs. Assn., Tenn. Sci. Tchrs. Assn., Memphis Orgn. Sci. Tchrs. (elem. dir. 1993-95), Phi Delta Kappa. Unitarian Universalist. Office: Memphis City Schs Macon Elem 968 N Mendenhall Rd Memphis TN 38122-1961

RAMSEY, INEZ LINN, librarian, educator; b. Martins Ferry, Ohio, Mar. 25, 1938; d. George and Leona (Smith) Linn; m. Jackson Eugene Ramsey, Apr. 22, 1961; children: John Earl, James Leonard. BA in History, SUNY, Buffalo, 1971, MLS, 1972; EdD in Audiovisual Edn., U. Va., 1980. Libr. Iroquois Ctrl. H.S., Elma, N.Y., 1971-73, Lucy Simms Elem. Sch., Harrisonburg, Va., 1973-75; instr. James Madison U., Harrisonburg, 1975-80, asst. prof., 1980-85, assoc. prof., 1985-91, prof., 1991-98; ret., 1998. Mem. Va. State Library Bd., Richmond, 1975-80; cons. in field. Author: (with Jackson E. Ramsey) Budgeting Basics, Library Planning and Budgeti;g; contbr. to Ency., articles to profl. jours.; project developer Internet Sch. Libr. Media Ctr.; project dir. Oral (tape) History Black Community in Harrisonburg, 1977-78; storyteller, puppeteer. Recipient Pierian Press's Libr. Hi Tech (periodical) award, 1998; rsch. grantee James Madison U., Harrisonburg, 1981, Commonwealth Ctr. State Va., 1989. Mem. ALA, Am. Assn. Sch. Librs., Assn. Edn. Comm. Tech. (exec. bd. DSMS 1989-98, DSMT Meritorious Svc. award 1998), Va. Ednl. Media Assn. (sec. 1981-83, citation 1983, pres. 1985-86, Educator of Yr. award 1984-85, Meritorious Svc. award 1987-88), Phi Beta Kappa (pres. Shenandoah chpt. 1980-81), Beta Phi Mu, Phi Delta Kappa. Home: 3215 S Torrey Pines Dr Las Vegas NV 89146-6529 Personal E-mail: inezramsey@cox.net.

RAMSEY, LUCIE AVRA, small business owner, consultant; b. NY, Mar. 3, 1942; d. Albert and Mazie (Gordon) Miller; m. Charles Allen Ramsey, Feb. 3, 1968; children: Aaron Ramsey (dec.), Jacqueline Hartigan. BS, U. San Francisco, 1986. Cert. mediator, cert. ct. mediator County Riverside Dispute Resolution Ctr. Office mgr. Quicksilver Products Inc., San Francisco, 1962-66; exec. sec. Far West Lab. for Educ. Rsch. and Devel., San Francisco and Berkeley, Calif., 1966-68; office mgr. The Ark Pub. Co., Tiburon, Calif., 1973-75; adminstrv. asst. Nat. Coun. Jewish Women, San Francisco, 1979-80; asst. to the chief Tiburon Fire Protection Dist., 1980; exec. dir. Zionist Orgn. Am., San Francisco, 1980-87; asst. dir. Bay Area Coun. for Soviet Jews, San Francisco, 1987-89; exec. dir. Jewish Community Rels. Coun., Oakland, Calif., 1989-91; pres. Ramsey Cons., Mill Valley, Calif., 1991—. Leader first ever interreligious task force to the USSR. Author: Concerns of the Jewish Community 1930's/1970's. Civic organizer, planner, chairperson Marin County Clergy Group, San Rafael, Calif., 1975-79; asst. area dir. Am. Jewish Com., San Francisco Bay Area chpt., 1994-96. Democratic. Jewish. Avocations: reading, camping, travel.

RAMSEY, MARGIE, librarian; b. Bay City, Tex., Aug. 29, 1921; d. Cyrus Otis Lansford and Myra Lenore Ferrell; m. Joe Bryan Ramsey, July 29, 1945; children: Ronald Lansford, Kevin Bryan. BA in Libr. Sci., Tex. State U., 1942. Cert. tchr., Tex. Libr. Talco (Tex.) Ind. Sch. Dist., 1942-44; sec. Consolidated Aircraft, San Diego, summer 1943; bookkeeper Lockheed Aircraft, Dallas, 1944; libr. Dallas Pub. Libr., 1944-45; sec. Steck Co., Austin, Tex., 1946-48; libr. U. Tex., Austin, 1948-51. Author, poet:. Vol. libr. Hyde Park United Meth., Austin, 1963-2002, Leander (Tex.) Ind. Sch. Dist., 1982-92, Aspen Ridge Lodge, Los Alamos, N.Mex.; mem. The Internat. Libr. of Poetry. Named Outstanding Vol., Nat. Assn. Ptnrs. in Edn., Kraft-Disney, 1989. Fellow AAUW. Democrat. Avocations: teaching, camping, computers, reading, collecting rare books. Home: 1010 Sombrillo Ct # 313 Los Alamos NM 87544 E-mail: laraishere8321@aol.com.

RAMSEY, MARY CATHERINE, mechanical engineer, consultant; b. Dumas, Tex., Sept. 16, 1955; d. E. Edward and Mary V. Roberts; m. Jimmy Paul Ramsey, Aug. 18, 1984. BSME, Tex. Tech U., 1979. Registered profl. engr., Tex. Fatigue and fracture engr. Gen. Dynamics, 1979—80; design engr. Barnard & Burke, Baton Rouge, 1980—81; project engr. Ruston Gas Turbines, Houston, 1981—88, Hawker Siddeley, Houston, 1988—90; project mgr. No. Engring., Houston, 1990—95; project devel. mgr. Air Liquide Am., Houston, 1995—97; cons. Power Project Solutions, Cat Spring, Tex., 1997—. NSF rsch. scholar, 1974; Welch Rsch. Found. grantee, 1974; named Nat. Merit finalist, 1974. Avocations: llama breeding, wildlife rehabilitation, needlecrafts, cooking, piano. Office: 17425 Tranquil Ln Cat Spring TX 78933 Business E-Mail: cramsey@industryinet.com.

RAMSEY, NATALIE D., lawyer; b. Greeneville, Tenn., Dec. 6, 1959; d. William Trent and Nancy Elizabeth (Maupin) Ramsey. BS, U. Del., 1981; JD, Villanova U., 1984. Bar: Pa. 1984, US Dist. Ct. (ea. dist.) Pa., US Ct. Appeals (3d and 11th cirs.), US Supreme Ct. 2004. Assoc. Montgomery, McCracken, Walker & Rhoads, LLP, Phila., 1985-93; ptnr. Montgomery, McCracken, Walker & Rhoads, Phila., 1993—, chair bankruptcy and reorgn. group, 1997—. Dir. Consumer Bankruptcy Advocacy Project, 1998—; chair Ea. Dist. Pa. Bankruptcy Conf., 2005—06. Contbr. articles to profl. jours. Pres. bd. dirs. Delaware County Habitat for Humanity, 1997—2002. Mem.: Turnaround Mgmt. Assn., Comml. Law League. Presbyterian. Avocations: travel, reading. Office: Montgomery McCracken Walker & Rhoads LLP 123 S Broad St Ste 2538 Philadelphia PA 19109-1099

RAMSEY, PRISCILLA R., literature educator; b. Charleston, S.C., Sept. 30, 1940; d. George and Thelma (Lee) Rogers. BA in Psychology, Temple U., 1962; PhD in Literature, The Am. Univ., 1975. Community organizer, 1962-67; secondary sch. educator, 1967-71; asst. prof. English dept. English Dept., Rutgers U., Newark, 1975-79; grad. teaching asst. The Am. U., Washington, 1972-75; assoc. prof. dept. Afro-Am. studies Dept. Afro-Am. Studies, Howard U., Washington, 1979—. Lectr. and presenter in field. Contbr. numerous articles and papers to profl. jours. Recipient Rutgers U. Faculty Rsch. award, 1978-79, The U.S. Dept. Labor award, 1986. Mem. MLA, Coll. Lang. Assn., Middle Atlantic Writers Assn., Critical Theory Study Group. Home: 1121 University Blvd W Apt 118 Silver Spring MD 20902-3317

RAMSEY, SALLY JUDITH WEINE, chemist, research and development company executive; married; 2 children. B in Chemistry, Hiram Coll.; attended grad. study in chemistry, Iowa State U. Co-founder, co-owner, chief chemist Ecology Coatings, Inc., Akron, Ohio, 1990—. Named Best Inventions 2005: Thin Skins, Time Mag.; recipient Silver winner and Materials and other Base Technologies winner, Wall Street Jour. Technology Innovation award, 2005. Achievements include patents-pending coating that waterproofs paper and nanotechnology treatments. Office: Ecology Coating 1238 Brittain Rd Akron OH 44310 Office Phone: 330-633-3500. Office Fax: 330-633-3464.

RAMSEY-GOLDMAN, ROSALIND, physician; b. N.Y.C., Mar. 22, 1954; d. Abraham L. and Miriam (Colen) Goldman; m. Glenn Ramsey, June 29,1 975; children: Ethan Ramsey, Caitlin Ramsey. BA, Case We. Res. U., 1975, MD, 1978; MPH, U. Pitts., 1988, DPH, 1992. Med. resident U. Rochester, NY, 1978—81; chief resident Rochester Gen. Hosp., 1981—82; staff physician U. Health Svc., Rochester, 1982—83; rheumatology fellow U. Pitts., 1983—86, instr. medicine, 1986—87, asst. prof., 1987—91, co-dir. Lupus Treatment and Diagnostic Ctr., 1987—91; asst. prof. medicine Northwestern U., Chgo., 1991—96, assoc. prof. medicine, 1996—2001, prof. medicine, 2001—. Dir. Chgo. Lupus Registry, Northwestern U., Chgo., 1991—, chairperson Systemic Lupus Internat. Collaborating Clinics Group, 2003—; program dir. Gen. Clin. Rsch. Ctr. at NCRR/NIH, 2005— Contbr. rsch. articles to profl. jours. Recipient Finkelstein award Hershey (Pa.) Med. Ctr., 1986. Fellow ACP, Am. Coll. Rheumatology; mem. Soc. for Epidemiologic Rsch., Ctrl. Soc. Clin. Rsch. Office: Northwestern U Feinberg Sch Medicine McGaw Pavilion 240 E Huron Ste M-300 Chicago IL 60611 Office Phone: 312-503-8003. Business E-Mail: rgramsey@northwestern.edu.

RAN, SHULAMIT, composer; b. Tel Aviv, Oct. 21, 1949; U.S. m. Abraham Lotan, 1986. Studied composition with, Paul Ben-Haim, Norman Dello, Joio, Ralph Shapey; student, Mannes Coll. Music, N.Y.C., 1963—67. With dept. music U. Chgo., 1973—, William H. Colvin prof. music; composer-in-residence Chgo. Symphony Orch., 1990—97, Lyric Opera of Chgo., 1994—97. Compositions include 10 Children's Scenes, 1967, Structures, 1968, 7 Japanese Love Poems, 1968, Hatzvi Israel Eulogy, 1969, O the Chimneys, 1969, Concert Piece for piano and orch., 1970, 3 Fantasy Pieces for Cello and Piano, 1972, Ensembles for 17, 1975, Double Vision, 1976, Hyperbolae for Piano, 1976, For an Actor: Monologue for Clarinet, 1978, Apprehensions, 1979, Private Game, 1979, Fantasy-Variations for Cello, 1980, A Prayer, 1982, Verticals for piano, 1982, String Quartet No. 1, 1984, (for woodwind quintet) Concerto da Camera I, 1985, Amichai Songs, 1985, Concerto for Orchestra, 1986, (for clarinet, string quartet and piano) Concerto da Camera II, 1987, East Wind, 1987, String Quartet No. 2, 1988—89, Symphony, 1989—90, Mirage, 1990, Inscriptions for solo violin, 1991, Chicago Skyline for brass and percussion, 1991, Legends for orch., 1992—93, Invocation, 1994, Yearning for violin and string orch., 1995, (opera) Between Two Worlds (The Dybbuk), 1995—97, Soliloquy, 1997, Vessels of Courage and Hope for orch., 1998, (flute concerto) Voices, 2000, Three Scenes for solo clarinet, 2000, Supplications for chorus and orch., 2002, Violin Concerto, 2003, commd. pieces include for Am. Composers Orch., Phila. Orch., Chgo. Symphony, Balt. Symphony, Chamber Soc. of Lincoln Ctr., Mendelssohn String quartet, Da Capo Chamber Players, Sta. WFMT, Lyric Opera Chgo., composer and soloist for 1st performances Capariccio, 1963, Symphonic Poem, 1967, Concert Piece, 1971. Named Guggenheim fellow, 1977, 1990; recipient Acad. Inst. Arts and Letters award, 1989, Pulitzer prize for music, 1991, Friedheim award for orchestral music, Kennedy Ctr., 1992. Office: U Chgo Dept Music 1010 E 59th St Chicago IL 60637-1512

RANADA, ROSE MARIE, retired elementary school educator; b. McClure, Ill., Sept. 21, 1936; d. James F. and Agnes T. (Sullivan) Glaab; m. Anthony Ranada, Oct. 25, 1958; children: James, Thomas. BA, San Jose (Calif.) State U., 1958; MA, U. San Francisco, 1975. Elem. tchr. Alum Rock Sch. Dist., San Jose, Calif., Jefferson Union Sch. Dist., Santa Clara, Calif., Sunnyvale Sch. Dist., Calif. Mentor to student tchrs. Sunnyvale Sch. Dist., Calif., 1963—96. Author: (with J. Rust) Child Care Guidebook for Santa Clara County. Grantee Hewlett Packard Co.

RAND, JOELLA MAE, retired nursing educator, counselor; b. Akron, Ohio, July 9, 1932; d. Harry S. and Elizabeth May (Miller) Halberg; m. Martin Rand (dec.); children: Craig, Debbi Stark. BSN, U. Akron, 1961, MEd in Guidance, 1968; PhD in Higher Edn. Adminstrn., Syracuse U., 1981. Cert. mental health counselor. Staff nurse Akron Gen. Hosp., 1953-54; staff-head nurse-instr. Summit County Receiving, Cuyahoga Falls, Ohio, 1954-56; head nurse psychiat. unit Akron Gen. Hosp., 1956-57; instr. psychiatric nursing Summit County Receiving, Cuyahoga Falls, 1957-61; head nurse, in-service instr.

Willard (N.Y.) State Hosp., 1961-62; asst. prof. Alfred (N.Y.) U., 1962-76, assoc. prof., assoc. dean, 1976-78, acting dean, 1978-79, dean, 1979-90, dean coll. profl. studies, 1990-91, prof. counseling, 1991-2000; ret., 2000. Cons. N.Y. State Regents Program for Non-Collegiate Sponsored Instrn., 1984; cons. collegiate programs N.Y. State Dept. Edn., 1985, Elmira Coll., 1991, U. Rochester, 1992-93; accreditation visitor Nat. League for Nursing, 1984-92; ednl. cons. Willard Psychiat. Hosp., 1992-93; mem. profl. practice exam. subcom. Regents Coll., 1990-95. Vol. Williard Drug Treatment Ctr., 1997—, bd. dirs., Romulus Zoning Bd., 2002—; vol. Red Cross, 2003—, co-capt. disaster team, 2004—05; bd. dirs. Five Point Correctional Facility, Willard Drug Treatment Ctr. Recipient Tchg. Excellence award Alfred U., 1977, Mary E. Gladwin Outstanding Alumni award Akron U. Coll. Nursing, 1983, Alfred Alumni Friends award, 1989, Grand Marshall commencement Alfred U., 1993, Vol. of Yr. award Willard Drug Treatment Ctr., 1999, Cert. Appreciation, Seneca County Cmty. Svcs. Bd., 2005. Mem.: ACA (NAR rep. 2000—04, co-capt. disaster team Red Cross-Finger Lakes chpt. 2003—05, pres. NYCA 2005, Seneca County Med. Reserve Corps. 2005—), Genesee Valley Edn. Com. (chair 1984—86), Western N.Y. League Nursing (bd. dirs. 1991—93), Genesee Regional Consortium (v.p.), N.Y. State Coun. of Deans (treas. 1984—88), N.Y. State Counseling Assn. (v.p.-elect profl. svcs. 1995—96, v.p. profl. svcs. 1996—98, 1999—2000, pres. 2005—06), Sigma Theta Tau (treas. Alfred chpt. 1984—85). Avocations: boating, fishing, public speaking in areas of family and child abuse. E-mail: drand@rochester.rr.com.

RAND, KATHY SUE, public relations executive, consultant; b. Miami Beach, Fla., Feb. 24, 1945; d. William R. and Rose (Lasser) R.; m. Peter C. Ritsos, Feb. 19, 1982. BA, Mich. State U., 1965; MBA, Northwestern U., 1980. Asst. editor Lyons & Carnahan, Chgo., 1967-68; mng. editor Cahners Pub. Co., Chgo., 1968-71; pub. rels. writer Super Market Inst., Chgo., 1972-73; account supr. Pub. Communications Inc., Chgo., 1973-77; divisional mgr. pub. rels. Quaker Oats Co., Chgo., 1977-82; exec. v.p., dep. gen. mgr. Golin/Harris Communications, Chgo., 1982-90; exec. v.p. Lesnik Pub. Rels., Northbrook, Ill., 1990-91; mng. dir. Manning, Selvage & Lee, Chgo., 1991—2002; public rels. cons., 2002—. Dir. midwest region NOW, 1972-74; mem. Kellogg Alumni Adv. Bd.; bd. dirs. Jr. Achievement of Chgo. Mem. Pub. Rels. Soc. Am. (Silver Anvil award 1986, 87), Pub. Club Chgo. (Golden Trumpet awards 1982-87, 90, 94, 95, 97, 98, 99, 00), Vet. Feminists of Am. (bd. dirs., v.p. pub. rels.), Northwestern Club Chgo., Kellogg Alumni Club, Beta Gamma Sigma. Home: 400 Riverwoods Rd Lake Forest IL 60045-2547 Personal E-mail: ksrand@aol.com.

RANDALL, CATHARINE, French educator; b. Lafayette, Ind., Apr. 14, 1957; d. E.V. Jr. and Sally (Shaw) R.; m. W.R. Coats, Nov. 1, 1986 (div. June 1994); 1 child, Sara Shaw Coats. BA in History, Ohio Wesleyan Coll., 1978; MA in French, Boston Coll., 1981; PhD in French, U. Pitts., 1987. Asst. prof. French Montclair (N.J.) State Coll., 1988-89, Rutgers U., New Brunswick, N.J., 1989-91; assoc. prof. French, dir. Intermediate Lang. Program Barnard Coll., N.Y.C., 1991—94; prof. French Fordham U., Bronx, 1994—, chair emerita modern langs. and lit. Presenter papers in field, 1986—; spkr. 16th Century Studies Conf., 1991, 92, 93; organizer, presenter confs.; cons. lang. texts dept. Houghton-Mifflin Pub. Co. Author: Subverting the System: d'Aubigné and Calvinism, 1990, (Em)bodying the Word: Textual Resurrections in the Martyological Narratives of John Foxe, Jean Crespin, Théodore de Bèze, and Agrippa d'Aubigné, 1992; editor (with Daniel Russell) Simon Bouquet's Imitation et traduction des cent dix-huit emblèmes d'Alciat, 1994, Peculiarities of Style: Philibert de L'Orme, 1995, Building Codes: the Calvinist Aesthetics of Early Modern Europe, 1999; contbr. chpts. to books, articles to profl. jours.; reviewer. Princeton Ctr. Theological Inquiry fellow, 1994—, Folger Shakespeare Libr. fellow, 1990-91, Newberry Libr. Rsch. fellow, 1989; grantee Princeton U., 1992, NEH grantee Duke U., 1992. Mem. Phi Beta Kappa, Phi Sigma Iota, Phi Alpha Theta. Episcopalian. E-mail: crandall@fordham.edu.

RANDALL, CLAIRE, retired religious organization administrator; b. Dallas, Oct. 15, 1919; d. Arthur Godfrey and Annie Laua (Fulton) Randall. AA, Schreiner Coll., 1948; BA, Scarritt Coll., 1950; DD (hon.), Berkley Div. Sch., New Haven, Conn., 1974; LHD (hon.), Austin Coll., 1982; LLD (hon.), Notre Dame U., 1984. Assoc. missionary edn. Bd. World Missions Presbyn. Ch., U.S., Nashville, 1949-57, dir. art Gen. Coun. Atlanta, 1957-61; dir. Christian World Mission, program dir., assoc. dir. Ch. Women United, N.Y.C., 1962-73; gen. sec. Nat. Coun. Ch. of Christ U.S.A., NYC, 1974-84; nat. pres. Ch. Women United, NYC, 1988-92; ret., 1992. Mem. Nat. Commn. Internat. Women's Yr., 1975—77, Martin Luther King Jr. Fed. Holiday Commn., 1985. Recipient Woman of Yr. in Religion award, Heritage Soc., 1977, Empire State woman of Yr. in Religion award, State of NY, 1984, medal Order of St. Vladimir, Russian Orthodox Ch., 1984. Democrat. Episcopalian. Avocations: golf, swimming, painting, reading, music. Home: 9965 W Royal Oak Rd # 1214 Sun City AZ 85351-6116

RANDALL, FRANCES, technical writer; b. Frederick, Md., Oct. 6, 1924; d. George Birely and Ruth Carty Delaplaine; m. Myron William Randall, Apr. 10, 1949; children: George Elliott, Myron William Jr., Ruth Ann Randall, Eleanor Jane Randall Luttrell. BA, Hood Coll., 1945; MS, Johns Hopkins U., 1947; DHL (hon.), Hood Coll., 2006. Chemist U.S. Army Lab., Frederick, Md., 1947—49; writer-historian Frederick News-Post, 1965—. Chmn. bd. dirs. The Randall Family LLC, 2001—. Author: Mirror on Frederick, 1998, More Reflections on the History of Frederick, 2005 Bd. dir. Cmty. Found. Frederick County, 1988-96, Braddock Hts. Cmty. Assn., Penn Laurel coun. Girl Scouts U.S. Recipient Cmty. Svc. award, Ch. Transfiguration, Braddock Heights, Md., 1999, Thanks Badge, Penn Laurel Girl Scout Coun., 1988, Alumnae Achievement award Hood Coll., 1998, Woman of Distinction award Penn Laurel coun. Girl Scouts U.S.A., 2000, Families Plus! Cmty. Svc. award, 2004. Mem. DAR (Woman of Yr. in History, 2005), Hood Coll. Alumnae Assn. (pres., sec.), Frederick Woman's Civic Club (publicity chair, pres.), bd. trustees,Hood Coll, 1988-2000, Hist Soc. Frederick County (bd. dir. 2005-) Avocations: swimming, biking, photography, travel, music. Home: 6301 Jefferson Blvd Frederick MD 21703-5809

RANDALL, FRANCES J., psychotherapist; d. George Thomas Randall and Theresa Margaret. BA, Emmanuel Coll., Boston, 1963; MA in Fine Arts, Fla. Atlantic U., Boca Raton, Fla., 1970; postgrad., C.G. Jung Inst., Zurich, 1984, So. Conn. State U., New Haven; MSW, Cath. U., Washington, 1992. Joined Sisters of Notre Dame de Namur. Tchr. Cath. schs., Mass. and Conn., 1954—69; lectr. Tchg. Tng. Coll., Eregi, Kenya, 1969—71, Kenyatta U., Nairobi, Kenya, 1971—84; founder Amani Counseling Ctr., Kenya, 1984—; lectr. US Internat. U., Nairobi, 1985—91; opened 1st counseling ctr. in Africa Nairobi, 1985—91; counselor VNA, Glastonbury, Conn., 1995—2001, Middletown, Conn., 2001—; founder prayer ctr. for recovering addicts Ptnrs. in Prayer; mem. mgmt. com., clin. dir., vice chmn. exec. com. Amani Counseling Ctr., Kenya. Contbr. weekly column to Nation newspaper, Kenya, articles to profl. publs.; numerous book covers, logos, postage stamps. Address: 9 Plano Pl Manchester CT 06040-6520

RANDALL, KAREN, film company executive; BA cum laude, Vassar Coll., 1973; JD, UCLA, 1976. Ptnr. Wyman Bautzer Kuchel & Silbert, 1976; mng. ptnr. Katten Muchin & Zavi, LA; sr. v.p., gen. counsel Universal Studios, 1996—2000; exec. v.p., gen. counsel Vivendi Universal Entertainment, Universal City, Calif., 2000—. Bd. mem. United Internat. Pictures, Hollywood Sign Trust, Hollywood Canteen Found. Named to, YWCA Acad. Women Achievers, The Am. Lawyer's 1995 edit. of "Forty-Five Under 45"; recipient Women of Distinction award, Hollywood C. of C., Pursuit of Justice award, Calif. Women's Law Ctr., Corp. Leadership award, Big Sisters L.A. Mem.: Motion Picture Assn. Am. (Universal's liaison, bd. dirs., mem. spl. policy group), Am. Corp. Counsel Assn. (nat. bd. dirs.). Office: Vivendi Universal Entertainment 100 Universal City Plaza Universal City CA 91608-1002

RANDALL, KAY TEMPLE, accountant, retired real estate agent; b. Chattanooga, Sept. 23, 1952; d. James H. Temple and Hortense N. (Dailey) Goodner; m. Gary F. Goodner, Feb. 9, 1968 (div. July 1972); 1 child, Jeffrey F. Goodner; m. Rodney B. Randall, Oct. 3, 1987. Student, Chattanooga State Coll., 1970-77, 82-83, Am. Inst. Banking, 1977-79. Lic. real estate agt., Tenn., ret.; notary public, Tenn. Ins. rep. Colonial Life Accident and Health, Columbia, SC, 1980-82; real estate appraiser, agt. Chattanooga, 1983-88; acct. Mr. Transmission of Chattanooga, Inc., 1987—; real estate agt. Chattanooga, 1989—. Adminstrv. asst. to legal profession, Chattanooga, 1972-75. Adv. bd. United Meth. Ch., Chattanooga, 1979-82, tchr., 1979-83; fellow cen. br. YMCA, Chattanooga, 1977-97. Fellow Walden's Club. Republican. Episcopalian. Avocation: collecting art. Home: 1858 Rivergate Ter Soddy Daisy TN 37379-5947 Office: Mr Transmission of Chattanooga Inc PO Box 1395 Soddy Daisy TN 37384-1395 E-mail: rodkayj@aol.com.

RANDALL, LILIAN MARIA CHARLOTTE, museum curator; b. Berlin, Feb. 1, 1931; came to U.S., 1938; d. Frederick Henry and Elizabeth Agnes (Ziegler) Cramer; m. Richard Harding Randall, Apr. 11, 1953; children: Christopher, Julia, Katharine. BA cum laude, Mount Holyoke Coll., 1950; MA, Radcliffe Coll., 1951, PhD, 1955; LHD (hon.), Towson State U., 1993; D of Arts (hon.), Mt. Holyoke Coll., 1998. Asst. dir. Md. State Arts Coun., 1972-73; curator manuscripts and rare books Walters Art Gallery, Balt., 1974-85, rsch. curator manuscripts, 1985-95; rsch. cons., 1995-97. Vis. lectr. dept. art history Johns Hopkins U., 1964-68; hon. vis. lectr. U. Mich., Ann Arbor; lectr. in field; bd. dirs. Digital Scriptorium: Electronic Access to Medieval Manuscripts; advisor Union Manuscript Computer Catalogue, 1996—. Author: Images in the Margins of Gothic Manuscripts, 1966; co-editor: Gatherings in Honor of Dorothy Miner, 1974, The Diary of George A. Lucas: An American Art Agent in Paris, 1909-1957, 1979, Illuminated Manuscripts: Masterpieces in Miniature, 1984, Medieval and Renaissance Manuscripts in the Walters Art Gallery, Vol. I, France, 875-1420, 1989, Vol. II, France, 1420-1540, 1992, Vol. III, Belgium, 1250-1530, 1997; contbr. articles to profl. jours. Mem. Williston Libr. com., 1988-89; reviewer, panelist NEH, 1980. Grantee AAUW, 1953-54, ACLS, 1960, 65, Bunting Inst., 1961-63, Ford Found., 1967-69, Am. Philos. Soc., 1971, NEA, 1975, Samuel H. Kress Found., 1979, 81-84, NEH, 1977-84, 89-95; grantee publ. subsidy Md. State Arts Coun., 1972, Mcpl. Art Soc. Balt., 1972, Andrew W. Mellon Found., 1988, Getty Grant program, 1990-92, NEA Mus. program, 1992-93; recipient Festschrift, Walters Art Gallery, ed. Elizabeth Burin, 1996, Sesquicentennial award Mount Holyoke Coll., 1987. Fellow Medieval Acad. Am. (libr. preservation com., various coms. 1985-87, 90-93, 2004—); mem. Internat. Ctr. Medieval Art (bd. dir. 1978-82, 96-99, mem. com. 2004—), Coll. Art Assn. (Arthur Kingsley Porter prize 1957), Balt. Bibliophiles (bd. dir. 1966-80, pres. 1980-83), Pyramid Atlantic (bd. dir. 1985-88), Mus. Fine Arts Boston (vis. com. Art of Europe dept. 2002-2006, adv. bd. Manuscripta 2004—), Grolier Club, Phi Beta Kappa. Home: 370 Adams St Milton MA 02186-4233 Personal E-mail: lmcrand@ix.netcom.com.

RANDALL, LINDA LEA, biochemist, educator; b. Montclair, N.J., Aug. 7, 1946; d. Lowell Neal and Helen (Watts) Randall; m. Gerald Lee Hazelbauer, Aug. 29, 1970. BS, Colo. State U., 1968; PhD, U. Wis., 1971. Postdoctoral fellow Inst. Pasteur, Paris, 1971—73; asst. prof. Uppsala (Sweden) U., 1975—81; assoc. prof. Wash. State U., Pullman, 1981—83, prof. biochemistry, 1983—2000; Wurdock prof. biochemistry U. Mo., Columbia, 2000—. Guest scientist Wallenberg Lab. Uppsala U., 1973—75; mem. study sect. NIH, 1984—88. Contbr. articles to profl. jours.; co-editor: (book) Virus Receptors Part I, 1980; mem. editl. bd.: Jour. Bacteriology, 1982—96. Recipient Eli Lilly award in Microbiology and Immunology, 1984, Faculty Excellence Award in Rsch., Wash. State U., 1988, Parke-Davis award, 1995. Fellow: AAAS, Am. Acad. Arts and Scis., Am. Acad. Microbiology; mem.: NAS, Protein Soc., Am. Soc. Biol. Chemists, Am. Microbiological Soc. Avocation: dance. Office: Univ Mo Dept Biochemistry 117 Schweitzer Hall Columbia MO 65211 Office Phone: 573-884-4160.

RANDALL, LISA, physics professor; BA in Physics, Harvard U., 1983, PhD in Particle Physics, 1987. Rschr. Smithsonian Astrophysical Observatory, 1981, IBM, 1982, Bell Labs, 1983; teaching asst. physics Harvard U., 1984; physics tutor Adams House, 1984—87; president's fellow U. Calif., Berkeley, 1987—87; postdoctoral fellow Lawrence Berkeley Lab., 1989—90; junior fellow Harvard Soc. of Fellows, 1990—91; asst. prof. physics MIT, 1991—95, assoc. prof. physics, 1995—98; prof. physics Princeton U., 1998—2000, MIT, 1998—2001, Harvard U., 2001—; fellow Radcliffe Inst. Fellow, 2002; chair Radcliffe Inst. Cosmology & Theoretical Astrophysics Cluster, 2003. Assoc. editor Nuclear Physics, 1999—; editor Annual Review of Nuclear & Particle Sci., 1997—, Jour. of High Energy Physics, 1997—98, 2000—. Author: Warped Passages: Unraveling the Mysteries of the Univers's Hidden Dimensions, 2005. Recipient Young Investigator award, NSF, 1992, Premio Caterina Tomassoni e Felice Pietro Chisesi award, U. Rome, 2003; grantee Alfred P. Sloan Found. Rsch. Fellowship, 1992, Bell Labs Graduate Rsch. Fellowship for Women. Fellow: AAAS, Am. Acad. Arts & Sciences. Office: Harvard U Physics Dept 17 Oxford St Cambridge MA 02138

RANDALL, LYNN ELLEN, librarian; b. Chgo., Oct. 10, 1951; d. Ward W. and Hazel A. R. BA, King's Coll., 1970; MA, Seton Hall U., 1973; MLS, Rutgers U., 1978. Libr. asst. Newark Coll. Engring, Newark, 1970-75; libr. dir. N.E. Bible Coll., Essex Fells, N.J., 1975-81; reference libr. Seton Hall U., South Orange, N.J., 1983-85; dir. libr. svc. Berkeley Coll., NJ, 1985-89; with Caldwell Coll., NJ, 1989—2006, exec. dir. libr. svcs.; dir. human resources Am.'s Keswick, Whiting, NJ, 2006—. Reference libr., instr. Morris (N.J.) County Coll., 1981-83; panelist/facilitator Middle States Self-Study Inst., 1996, 97, 2004. 05; Evaluator, Middle States, 1994-. Mem. N.J. Libr. Assn. (pres. 1996-97), Am. Libr. Assn. Office: America's Keswick 601 Route 530 Whiting NJ 08759 Business E-Mail: lrandall@americaskeswick.org.

RANDALL, MARILYN KAY, equine studies educator; b. Lewellen, Nebr., Aug. 30, 1947; d. Merlyn Harry and Alvina Anna Thrasher; m. Ray William Randall, Dec. 26, 1970; children: Erin Ann, Matt Thrasher. BS in Health and Phys. Edn., Colo. State U., Fort Collins, 1969; registered phys. therapist, Northwestern U., Evanston, Ill., 1970. Phys. therapist Gen. Rose Hosp., Denver, 1971, U. Minn. Hosp., Mpls., 1971—72; phys. therapist, phys. edn. instr. Bridger (Mont.) Pub. Schs., 1975—82; phys. therapist Yellowstone and Carbon County Pub. Schs., 1982—86; equine profl. Randall Quarter Horses, Bridger, 1982—2005; asst. prof. Equestrian Studies Program N.W. C.C., Powell, Wyo., 1986—92; dir. equine studies Rocky Mountain Coll., Billings, Mont., 1992—98, assoc. prof. Equestrian Program, 1998—2006, asst. program, 1992—2001. Republican. Lutheran. Avocations: showing horses, skiing. Home: 17 Vet Lane Bridger MT 59014 Office: Rocky Mountain College 1511 Poly Dr Billings MT 59102

RANDALL, VICKY, artist, educator, sculptor, small business owner; b. Nashville, Tenn., May 3, 1953; d. R.B. and Mary Helen (Farrell) Randall; m. Carl Jacob Schreiner III, Nov. 22, 1994. BFA, Mid. Tenn. State U., Murfreesboro, 1975; MFA, So. Ill. U., Carbondale, 1979. Asst. prof. art Bethany Coll., Lindsborg, Kans., 1980-85; owner, operator, creator Vicky Randall Studios, Sarasota, Fla., 1989—; in svc. trainer sch. bd. Sarasota Co. Art Tchrs., 1989—2000; children's summer program instr. Sarasota Visual Arts, 1990—95; art. tchr. Ringling Sch. Art and Design, Sarasota, 1996—, studio master, 1998, faculty mem., 2000—; grad. asst. mus. exhibits preparator U. Mus. and Art Galleries So. Ill. U., Carbondale, Ill., 1977—79; tchg. asst., drawing instr. So. Ill. U., 1977—79; asst. prof. art, head sculpture Bethany Coll., Lindsborg, Kans., 1980—85; art. tchr. Emporia State U., Kans., 1982, Penland Sch., NC, 1988. Coord. vis. artist mini-grant ACCK Bethany Coll., 1980, 83; juror over 100 arts and crafts shows, fairs and festivals, 1980—; tech. film advisor studio sets, techniques, artist role devel. Castle Rock Films, 1997; co-chair coordinating docent tng. Sarasota Season of Sculpture, 2006; presenter in field. Exhibited in shows at Dane Hansen Mus., Logan, Ky., 1981, Sandzen Gallery, Lindsborg, Kans., 1983, Trostberger Sculpture Park, Poesch, West Germany, 1985, Penland Sch. Art and Design, 1988, Joan Hodgell Gallery, Sarasota, 1989-91, 92, El Art Festival, St. Petersburg, 1990, 91, 92 (Merit award), Sarasota Arts Assn., 1991, Sarasota Visual Art Ctr. (Artist of Yr. 1993), 1993, (1st Pl. 1994), 94, 97, Ringling Sch. Art and Design, 1996-05, Alyn Gallup Gallery Contemporary Art, Sarasota, 2002, Cognizart Gallery, Osprey, Fla., The Trotzig Gallery, Indian Rocks Beach, Fla., Smokey Hill, Marymount Coll., Salina, Kans., 1982, Salina Arts Ctr., Kans., Ea. Mont. State U., Billings; represented in permanent collections including Home Fed. Bank, Nashville, 1975, Mid. Tenn. State U., 1975, Donaworth, West Germany, 1983-88, Sculpture Garden Sarasota Arts Ctr., 1991, Women's Resource Ctr., Sarasota, 1991, ADP Group, Theater and Arts Dist., 1992, Volker Schlondorff, Pottsdam, Germany, 1997, Rialto Films, LA, 1997, Sarasota Co. Office Complex (2d Pl. Site Specific Competition), 1998, Western Mich. U., 2001-04, Oncology Hematology Ctr., Sarasota, 2003, Krasl Mus., St. Joseph, Mo., 2004-05; represented in over 50 pvt. collections, US and Germany; works include metal sculpture, painted steel wall reliefs, metal furniture; 1st art in Arts and Theater Dist., Sarasota County; internat. sculptor Riverview HS, Sarasota, 2000-04; sculpture and studio featured in Palmetto, 1997; contbr. articles and revs. to profl. jours. Exhbn. com. Arts Coun., Sarasota, 1993—; bd. dirs. Sarasota Visual Arts Ctr., 1990—, tech. advisor, 1996; mem. bd. Pub. Art Com., Sarasota, 2001-04, v.p., 2003; mentor 6th Ann. Selby Scholar Symposium, 2005. Recipient grant to study Henry Moore and Barbara Hepworth in Eng., 1983; named Artist of Yr. Sarasota County, 1993; Bildhauer Symposium grantee, Mertigen, West Germany, 1983; commn. Women's Resource Ctr. for Monumental Garden Sculpture, 1994. Mem. Sculptors Internat. Achievements include first to install Sarasota City's first Art in Public Places piece Clockwork of Convergence, 1992. Home: 727 Hand Ave Sarasota FL 34232-6728 Office: Vicky Randall Studios 1226 Central Ave Sarasota FL 34236-2522 Office Phone: 941-377-5792. Personal E-mail: randall3d@aol.com.

RANDEL, JANE ANN, retail executive; d. Kenneth and Elaine Randel; m. Charles Karel Kliment, June 14, 1998; 3 children. Ed., Wesleyan U. With Hill & Knowlton Public Relations; pub. relations assoc. Liz Claiborne Inc., 1992, v.p. corp. comm., bd. dirs. Bd. dirs., pres. Corp. Alliance to End Partner Violence; bd. dirs. Safe Horizon; adv. bd. infrastructure, safety and environ. RAND Corp.; adv. bd. The Empower Program; nat. adv. bd. Nat. Domestic Violence Hotline; mem. hon. bd. Pa. Coalition Against Rape/Nat. Sexual Violence Resource Ctr.; founding mem. Safe@work Coalition. Named one of 21 Leaders for the 21st Century, Women's eNews, 2005, 40 Under 40, Crain's NY Bus., 2006. Office: Liz Claiborne Inc Church Street Station PO Box 11258 New York NY 10286*

RANDELL, STEPHANIE MCMILLAN, biology professor; d. Robert Hugh and Sieglinde Stephanie McMillan; m. Donald Paul Randell; 1 child, Jacob Nathaniel. BA, U. Houston Clear Lake, 1990; MS, Sul Ross State U., Alpine, Tex., 1996. Lectr. biology Sul Ross State U., Alpine, Tex., 1996—99; instr. biology Angelina Coll., Lufkin, 1999—. Sponsor Angelina Young Democrats, Lufkin, Tex., 2000. Named Outstanding Grad. Student, Sul Ross State U., 1996, Invited Lectr., Tex. Solution '98, 1998; named to Gt. Tchg. Round-up, Angelina Coll. Faculty, 2006; All-American scholar, Sul Ross State U., 1995. Mem.: Tex. C.C. Tchg. Assn. (assoc.). Achievements include research in bird populations and behavior at future windfarm sites in Davis Mountains. Avocations: travel, skiing, snorkeling, reading, hiking. Office: Angelina Coll 3500 S First St Lufkin TX 75901 Office Phone: 936-633-5365. E-mail: srandell@angelina.edu.

RANDER, JOANN CORPACI, musician, educator; b. Waterbury, Conn., June 24, 1954; d. Anthony and Victoria Corpaci; m. David Rander, July 22, 1983. MusB Piano magna cum laude, Hartt Coll. Music, 1976, MusM Piano magna cum laude, 1980; studied classical piano with Paul Rutnam, Juilliard Sch., NYC; studied percussion, with Joe (Skinny) Purcaro, Hollywood, Calif. Musician various org., 1964—; music tchr. Fox Mid. Sch., Hartford, Conn., 1976—77, McDonough Sch., Hartford, 1976—77, Kennelly Sch., Hartford, 1976—77, S. Cath. H.S., Conn., 1977—78, St. Brigid Sch., Elmood, Conn., 1978—80, Wolcott Pub. Sch., Conn., 1980—85; pvt. instr. Zinno Music Studio, Waterbury, Conn., 1985—89. Judge Miss Mattauck Pageant, Conn., 1986, Miss Prospect Pageant, Conn., 1986, Miss Watertown Pageant, Conn., 1986, Miss Cheshire Pageant, Conn., 1987, Music Adjudication Festivals, Hartford, others. Performer: with Buddy Rich Big Band, 1973; performances throughout Fla. including Mar-a-Lago, Gov.'s Club, Four Seasons Hotel, others, conductor, accompanist New Brit. Reperatory Theatre, Miss Conn. and Universe Pageants, 1976—87. Recipient Joseph Summa award; scholar Conn. State scholar, Conn. State Union Barbers Assn. Roman Catholic. Achievements include youngest mem. in musicians union, 1968. Avocations: music performance, piano, percussion, singing, dance.

RANDINELLI, TRACEY ANNE, magazine editor; b. Morristown, N.J., Apr. 6, 1963; d. Andrew R. and Patricia Ann (Brenner) Randinelli. BA in Comm., U. Del., 1985. Copywriter Macy's N.J., Newark, 1985-86; editl. asst. Globe Comms. Corp., N.Y.C., 1986-87; from asst. editor to assoc. editor Scholastic Math and DynaMath Mags. Scholastic, Inc., N.Y.C., 1987-89, editor Scholastic Math Mag., 1989-95; mng. editor Zig Zag Mag. Games Pub. Group, N.Y.C., 1995; sr. editor Contact Kids Mag./ Sesame Workshop, N.Y.C., 1996-2001; freelance writer, 2001—02; sr. editor Pearson Learning Group, 2002—04, supervising editor, 2004—. Mem. Soc. Children's Book Writers, Ednl. Press Assn. Am. (Disting. Achievement award feature articles divsn. 1991, 95, coverdesign 1996, how-to feature divsn. 1998, 99). E-mail: pen4kidz@aol.com.

RANDISI, ELAINE MARIE, accountant, educator, writer; b. Racine, Wis., Dec. 19, 1926; d. John Dewey and Alveta Irene (Raffety) Fehd; m. John Paul Randisi, Oct. 12, 1946 (div. July 1972); children: Jeanine Randisi Manson, Martha Randisi Chaney (dec.), Joseph, Paula, Catherine Randisi Carvalho, George, Anthony (dec.); m. John R. Woodfin, June 18, 1994. AA, Pasadena Jr. Coll., 1946; BS cum laude (Giannini scholar), Golden Gate U., 1978. With Raymond Kaiser Engrs., Inc., Oakland, Calif., 1969-75, 77-86, corp. acct., 1978-79, sr. corp. acct., 1979-82, sr. payroll acct., 1983-86; accts. payable coord. Crosby, Heasfey, Roach & May, Oakland, Calif., 1989—96; acctg. mgr. Lilli Ann Corp., San Francisco, 1986-89; accounts payable coord. Crosby, Heafy, Roach & May, Oakland, 1989—96, ret., 1996. Initiated Minority Vendor Purchasing Program for Kaiser Engrs., Inc., 1975-76; corp. buyer Kaiser Industries Corp., Oakland, 1975-77; lectr. on astrology Theosophical Soc., San Francisco, 1979-99; mem. faculty Am. Fedn. Astrologers Internat. Conv., Chgo., 1982, 84. Mem. Speakers Bur., Calif. Assn. for Neurologically Handicapped Children, 1964-70, v.p., 1969; bd. dirs. Ravenwood Homeowners Assn., 1979-82, v.p., 1979-80, sec., 1980-81, mem. organizing com. Minority Bus. Fair, San Francisco, 1976; pres., bd. dirs. Lakewood Condominium Assn., 1984-87; mem. trustee Ch. of Religious Sci., 1992-95; treas. First Ch. Religious Sci., 1994-98, lic. practitioner, pres., 1990-91, sec., 1989-90. Mem. Am. Fedn. Astrologers, Calif. Scholarship Fedn. (life), Alpha Gamma Sigma (life). Home: # 625 4500 Gilbert St Oakland CA 94611

RANDLE, BARBARA ANN, retired secondary school educator; b. Tupelo, Miss., July 28, 1946; d. William Herman and Gwendola (McMillen) Camp; m. William Clay Ballard, Aug. 12, 1968 (div. Feb. 1977); m. William Fred Randle, May 12, 1979 (dec. 1996); children: Leslie Ann, William Paul Casey. AA, Itawamba Jr. Coll., 1966; BA, U. Miss., 1969, M in Music Edn., 1971, paralegal degree, 2000. Tchr. New Albany Separate Schs., Miss., 1969—70; prin. New Albany Ins. Agy., 1972—76; supr. sales Teleco Mktg. Inc., Memphis, 1976—78; mgr. Brooks McCuller Ins. Agy., Memphis, 1978—79; tchr. speech therapy Itawamba County Sch. Dist., Fulton, Miss., 1979—2003; ret., 2003. Mem. Northeast Miss. Speech and Hearing Assn., Sigma Alpha Iota. Democrat. Methodist. Avocations: piano, singing, cross-stitching. Home: 1905 President Tupelo MS 38801-6218 Office: Wheeler & Franks Law Firm PO Box 681 204 N Spring St Tupelo MS 38802 Office Phone: 662-842-0380.

RANDLE, CANDACE LATRICE, government affairs consultant, political scientist; d. Cynthia F. Randle-Atkins. BA in Polit. Sci., U. Ark., Fayetteville, 2000; MPA, U. Ark., Little Rock, 2005. Leader student affairs orientation U. Ark., Fayetteville, 1997—98, asst. leadership devel., 1998—99, resident asst., 1999—2000; dir. regional briefings Gore-Lieverman Campaign, Nashville, 2000; aide Congl. dist. Office Congressman Vic Snyder, Little Rock, 2001; coord. govt. affairs project Entergy Corp., Little Rock, 2001—05, cons. govt.

affairs project, 2005—. Vol. Walton Arts Ctr., Fayetteville, 2006. Recipient Excellence in Leadership award, U. Ark., 2000, Cy and Betta Carney award, 2005. Mem.: Nat. Assn. Female Execs. Democrat. Bapt. Avocations: painting, reading.

RANDLETT, MARY WILLIS, photographer; b. Seattle, May 5, 1924; d. Cecil Durand and Elizabeth (Bayley) Willis; m. Herbert B. Randlett, Oct. 19, 1950 (div.); children: Robert, Mary Ann, Peter, Susan. BA, Whitman Coll., Walla Walla, Wash., 1947. Freelance photographer, 1949—. One-woman shows include Seattle Sci. Ctr., 1971, Western Wash. State U., 1971, Seattle Art Mus., 1971, Art Gallery Greater Victoria, 1972, Alaska State Mus., 1972, State Capitol Mus., 1983, Whatcom Mus. History and Art, Bellingham, Wash., 1986, Janet Huston Gallery, LaConner, Wash., 1990, Gov.'s Gallery, Office of Gov., Olympia, Wash., 1991, Stonington Gallery, Seattle, 1992, Valley Mus. Art, LaConner, 1992, Grad. Sch. Design Dept. Landscape Arch. Harvard U., Cambridge, Mass., 1996, Mus. N.W. Art, LaConner, 1998, Mary Randlett Portraits in the Arts Cmty., Wright Exhbn. Space, Seattle, 2002—03, Safco Plaza, Seattle and Richmond, Wash., 2003, Seattle's One Percent for Art, 2004, Walla Walla CC, 2004, Wash. State Libr., Olympia, 2005, others, exhibited in group shows at Am. Soc. Mag. Photographers, 1970, Whatcom Mus., Bellingham, Henry Gallery, Seattle, 1971, 1974, Royal Photg. Soc., 1979, Heard Mus., Phoenix, 1979, State Capital Mus., Olympia, Wash., 1983, 1984, 1988, 1989, 1993, Santa Fe Ctr. for Photography, 1987, Tacoma Art Mus., 1989, Helen Day Art Ctr., Stowe, Vt., 1989, Valley Mus. N.W. Art, LaConner, 1991, 1994, 1996—98, Allen Libr. U. Wash., Seattle, 1991, Wing Luke Asian Mus., 1991, Cheney Cowles Mus., Spokane, 1991, 1998, Security Pacific Gallery, Seattle, 1992, Benham Gallery, 1993, Stonington Gallery, 1993, 1998, Rainier Club, Seattle, 1994, Port Angeles (Wash.) Fine Arts Ctr., 1994, Mus. History and Industry, Seattle, 1994, Whatcom Mus., Bellingham, 1994, Pacific N.W. Annual Bellevue Art Mus., Wash., 1995, Skagit Valley Hist. Mus., LaConner, 1995, Seattle Art Mus., 1996—98, Kirkland (Wash.) Arts Ctr., 1997, Bainbridge Arts and Crafts, Bainbridge Island, Wash., 1997, Lucia Douglas Gallery, Bellingham, 1997, Anchorage Mus. History & Art, 1997, Burke Mus. Natural History and Culture, Seattle, 1998, Henderson House, Turnwater, Wash., 1998, Whatcom Arco Exhibit Gallery, Bellingham, 1998, Sea First Gallery, Seattle, 1998, 1999, Citizens Cultural Ctr., Fujinomita, Japan, 1999, Mus. Am. Indian, N.Y.C., 1999, Cheney Cowels Mus., Spokane, 1999, J. Paul Horiuchi Seattle Asian Art Mus., 2000, Mus. NW Art, 2000, Seattle Art Mus., 2002, Whitney Mus. Am. Art, N.Y.C., 2002, High Mus., Atlanta, 2002, Mus. NW Art, 2003, Seattle Art Mus., 2003, Tacoma Art Mus., 2003, Whatcom Mus., 2003, MONA, La Conner, Wash., 2004, Lucia Douglas Gallery, Bellingham, Wash., 2005, U. Wash. Press, Seattle, 2005, U. Portland, Oreg., 2006, and numerous others, Represented in permanent collections Met. Mus., Nat. Collection of Fine Arts, Nat. Portrait Gallery, Washington State Libr., Manuscript divsn. U. Wash., Pacific Northwest Bell, Seattle, Swedish Med. Ctr., Whatcom Mus., Bellingham, Henry Gallery, Seattle, Wash. State Capitol Mus., Olympia, Phillips Collection, Wash.; works appeared in books The Master and His Fish (Roderick Haig-Brown), 1982, Theodore Roethke: The Journey to I and Otherwide (Neal Bowers), 1982, Mountain in the Clouds (Bruce Brown), 1982, Masonry in Architecture (Louis Redstone), 1982, Writings and Reflections from the World of Roderick Haig-Brown, 1982, Pike Place Market (Alice Shorett and Murray Morgan), 1982, The Dancing Blanket, (Cheryl Samuel), 1982, Collected Poems of Theodore Roethke, 1982, Spires of Form (Victor Scheffer), 1983, Assault on Mount Helicon (Mary Barnard), 1983, New as a Wave (Eve Triem), 1983, Sketchbook: A Memoir of the '30's and the Northwest School (William Cumming), 1983, Good Intentions (Jane Adams), 1985, Blackbirds of the Americas (Gordon Orians and Tony Angell), 1985, Historic Preservation in Seattle (Larry Kreisman), 1985, Down Town Seattle Walking Tours (Mary Randlett and Carol Tobin), 1986, Seattle, the Seattle Book, 1986, When Orchids Were Flowers (Kate Knap Johnson), 1986, Jacob Lawrence, American Painter, (Ellen Wheat), 1986, Manic Power: Robert Lowell and His Circle (Jeffrey Meyers), 1987, The Isamu Noguchi Garden Museum (Isamu Noguchi), 1987, Washington's Audacious State Capitol an its Builders (Norman Johnston), 1988, The Bloedel Reserve: Gardens in the Forest (Lawrence Kreisman), 1988, Washingtonians: A Biographical Portrait of the State on the Occasion of its Centennial, 1988, Directory of Literary Biography: Canadian Writers 1920-59, 2d series, 1989, Crafts of America, 1989, The Lone Tree Tragedy (Bruce Brown), 1989, Northwest Coast Handbook of North American Indians, 1990, Dancing on the Rim of the World, 1990, Openings, Original Essays by Contemporary Soviet and American Writers (eds. Robert Atwan, Valeri Vinokurov), 1990, George Tsutakawa (Martha Kingsbury), 1990, Contemporary American Poetry (ed. Al Polin Jr.), 1991, Natural History of Puget Sound Country (Arthur Kruckberg), 1991, Bones (Joyce Thompson), 1991, Cebu (Peter Basho), 1991, Catalogue of Historic Preservation Publications, 1992, Art in Seattle's Public Places (James Rupp), 1992, The Olympic Rainforest (Ruth Kirk with Jerry Franklin), 1992, Steelhead Fly Fishing (Trey Combs), 1992, Illustrated Guidelines for Rehabilitation Historic Buildings, 1993, A History of African American Artists (Bearden and Henderson), 1994, Childrens Literature Review Vol. 1, 1994, Invisible Gardens: The Search for Modernism the American Landscape (Walker and Simo), 1994, Seeing Seattle (Roger Sale), 1994, Reaching Home (Jay and Matson), 1994, Redesigning the American Lawn: A Search for Environmental Harmony (Gordone Geballe, Diana Balmari and F. Herbert Bormann), 1995, Reaching Home: Pacific Salmon, Pacific People (Foves, Jay and Matson), 1995, Carl F. Gould: A Life in Architecture and the Arts (T. William Booth and William H. Wuksib), 1995, Destination Zero (Sam Hamill), 1996, Market Sketchbook, 25th Anniversary Edition, 1996, Spririts of the Ordinary, 1997, Instrument of Change: Jim Schoppert 1947-1992, 1997, Looking for Edulabee Dix (Joann Ridley), 1997, Jack Lenor Larsen: A Memoir, 1998, Museo Nacional Centro de Arte Reina (Mark Tobey), 1998, Fountains Splash, and Spectacle: Water and Design from the Renaissance to Present (ed. Marilyn Symmes), 1998, Ghost Dancing (Anna Linzer), 1998, The Flower in the Skull (Kathleen Alcala), 1998, This Great Unknowing: Last Poems (Denise Levertov), 1999, Building Washington (Paul Dorpat, Genevier McCoy), 1999, The Wright Collection, Seattle Art Museum, 1999, Made to Last: Historic Preservation in Seattle and King County (Larry Kreisman), 1999, Isamu Noguchi: A Study of Space (Ana Maria Torres), 2000, The Tiger Iris (Joan Swift), 2000, The Eighth Lively Art (Wesley Wehr), 2000, All Powers Necessary and Convenient (Mark F. Jenkins), 2000, Ice Breakers: Alaska's Most Innovative Artists (Julie Decker), 2000, Over the Line: The Life and Art of Jacob Lawrence (Peter Nesbett and Michelle Dubois), 2000, Iridescent Light: The Emergence of Northwest Art (Delores Tarzan Ament), 2001, Messages from Frank's Landing, 2000, Leo Kenney: A Retrospective, 2000, Building for Learning: Seattle Public Schools History 1860-2000, 2001, Geology and Plant Life, 2001, and numerous others; works also appeared in newspapers and mags., book, Maritime Seattle, 2002, Picture Bainbridge Island: A Pictorial History, Distant Corner, 2003, Child of the Oemulgee, Passing the Three Gates, 2003, Northwest Mythologies, The Interactions of Mark Tobey, Morris Graves, Kenneth Callahan and Guy Anderson, 2003, The Accidental Collector, Art, Fossils, Friendships, 2004, Isamu Noguchi and Sky Viewing Sculpture, 2004, A San Juan Island's Journal, 2004, Poems From Ish River Country, 2004, American Knees, 2005, Groundswell: Constructing the Contemporary Landscape, 2005. Recipient Wash. State Gov.'s award for spl. commendation for contbns. in field of photography, 1983, Individual Artist award, King County Arts Commn., 1989, Lifetime Achievement award, Artist Trust, 2001, Matrix Table, Seattle Women of Achievement, 1999, Nancy Blankenship Pryor award, 2001, Alumnus of Merit award, Whitman Coll, 2003, History Maker's award, Mus. History and Industry, 2003; grantee, Nat. Endowment for Arts, 1976, Allied Arts Found., 2000. Mem. AIA (hon.), Am. Soc. Mag. Photographers. Home: PO Box 11238 Olympia WA 98508-1238 Office Phone: 360-352-1716.

RANDOLPH, CAROLYN, educational association administrator, educator; BA in Biology, Fisk U., Nashville; MA in Botony, Howard U.; PhD in Sci. Edn., U.S.C. Adj. prof. U. S.C., Coll. Charleston; instr. Fisk U.; sci. tchr., dept. head, dist. sci. coord. Lexington Sch. Dist. Two, West Columbia, SC; v.p. outreach and rsch. SC Gov.'s Sch. Math and Sci. Mem.: Nat. Sci. Teachers Assn. (pres. 2002—03), SC Conservation Edn. and Wildlife Comm. Adv. Bd., SC Sci. Supervisors (past pres.), SC Sci. Coun. (past pres.), Nat. Sci. Found., Nat. Sci. Edn. Leadership Assn. Office: Nat Sci Teachers Assn 1840 Wilson Blvd Arlington VA 22201-3000 Office Phone: 843-383-3900.

RANDOLPH, KATRINA J., literature and language educator; d. Robert N. Randolph and Mary J. Randlph. BS in Edn. K-12 and Spanish, Mo. So. State U., Joplin, 2002. Tchr. English and Spanish Independence Bible Sch., Independence, 2002—. Student liaison faculty adv. bd. Independence C.C., Independence, 1998—99. Named one of NHR's Outstanding Am. Tchrs. Office: Independence Bible Sch 2246 S 10th St Independence KS 67301

RANDOLPH, LYNN MOORE, artist; b. NYC, Dec. 19, 1938; d. Cecil Howard and Dorothy (Didenhover) M.; m. Robert Raymond Randolph, June 5, 1959 (div. June, 1975); children: Robert Cean, Grayson Moore; m. William Simon, July 22, 1986 (dec. June 2000); m. Michael Berryhill, Sept. 14, 2005. BFA, U. Tex., 1961. Pres. Houston chpt. Nat. Women's Caucus for Art, 1979-80. regional v.p., 1982-85, nat. adv. bd. 1986-88, co-chair ann. 1988 ann. conf.; lectr. and conf. participant to art and women's groups, 1980—; set designer, Space, Dance Theater, Houston, 1977, Main St. Theater, 1982; coord. Art Under Duress, El Salvador, Lawndale Art and Performance Ctr., Houston. One-woman shows include Graham Gallery, Houston, 1984, 86, 91, Mary Ingraham Bunting Inst., Cambridge, Mass., 1990, Lynn Goode Gallery, Houston, 1995, U. Tex. Health Sci. Ctr., 1997, Ariz. State U. Mus., 1998, Joan Wich Gallery, Houston, 2003, Joan Wich Gallery, 2006; exhibited in group shows at Contemporary Arts Mus., Houston, 1978-79, 90, 500 Exposition Gallery, Dallas, 1980, Ga. State U. Gallery, 1982, Mus. Fine Arts, Houston, 1986, Aspen (Colo.) Art Mus., 1987, Nat. Mus. Women in Art, Washington, 1988, San Antonio Mus. Art, 1989, Sewell Gallery, Rice U., 1993, Diverse Works, Houston, 1994; works in pub. collections at Ariz. State U., Tempe, The Menil Collection, Houston, San Antonio Mus. of Art, Mary Ingraham Bunting Inst., Cambridge, Houston Mus. Fine Arts, others. Organizer Houston Area Artist's Call Against U.S. Intervention in Ctrl. Am., 1984. Summer fellow Yaddo, Saratoga Springs, NY, 1987, Mary Ingraham Bunting Inst. fellow, Radcliffe Coll., 1989-90. Mem. The Ilusas (women's drum corps), Artists Bd. Lawndale Art and Performance Ctr., Houston. Home: 1803 Banks St Houston TX 77098-5403 Office Phone: 713-528-0909.

RANDOLPH, NANCY ADELE, nutritionist, consultant; b. St. Louis, Sept. 7, 1941; d. Robert Andrew and Mary Jane (Hilliker) R.; m. John Reginald Randolph-Swainson, Sept. 16, 1989. BS, U. Ariz., 1963; MEd, Boston U., 1971; postgrad., Harvard U., 1983. Intern instn. adminstrn. Mills Coll., Oakland, Calif., 1963-64; staff dietitian St. Lukes Hosp., St. Louis, 1964-65; clin. dietitian New England Deaconess Hosp., Boston, 1965-66; dietitian mgr. The Seiler Corp., Waltham, Mass., 1966-67; instr., acting dir. Whidden Hosp. Sch. Nursing, Everett, Mass., 1967-72; instr. nutrition Northeastern U. Coll. Nursing, Boston, 1972; renal/rsch. dietitian Lemuel Shattuck Hosp., Jamaica Plain, Mass., 1979-81; New England regional dietitian coord. Beverly Enterprises, Virginia Beach, Va., 1985-88; state nutritionist, surveyor Mass. Dept. Pub. Health/Health Care Quality, Boston, 1988-89; pub. health nutrition cons., surveyor Agy. for Health Care Adminstrn., State of Fla., Fla., 1995-97; cons. nutritionist Randolph Assocs., Chestnut Hill, Mass., West Palm Beach, Sarasota, Fla., 1972-79, 81-85, 90—. Mem. Am. Dietetic Assn. (cert.), Mass. Dietetic Assn., Nutrition Entrepreneurs, Sports Cardiovascular Wellness Practice Groups, Fla. Dietetic Assn., Mass. Dietetic Assn., Cons. Dietitians in Health Care Facilities.

RANDOLPH, VIRGELLA, retired federal official; d. Russell and Catherine (Smith) Snowden; m. Alphonso L. Randolph, 1960; children: Victor, Pebble, Deborah. At, D.C. C.C., 1976, Georgetown U. Clk. typist census bur. U.S. Dept. Commerce, Suitland, Md., 1955—56; clk. typist to dep. chief fed. acquisition and assistance divsn. Nat. Bur. Stds. (now Nat. Inst. Sci. Tech.) U.S. Dept. Commerce, Gaithersburg, 1956—87; ret. Vol. Providence Hosp., 1987; past mem., pres. We Chick, Inc.; past mem. The Musical Choraleers; past mem., v.p. The Stereophonic Chorale; deaconess Greater First Baptist Ch., Washington, 2004—; mem. Gospel Chorus, Pres., v.p., fin. sec.; mem. Fellowship Choir; co-chair Elevator Ministry. Recipient Bronze medal, U.S. Dept. Commerce, 1974. Mem.: Choir Dirs. and Organists Guils, Hampton U. Annual Minister's Conf. Democrat. Baptist. Achievements include development of in-house procurement training program for Nat. Bur. Stds; subject of Black History Week at Nat. Bur. Stds. for accomplishments. Avocations: flower arranging, singing, writing. Personal E-mail: virgella7@aol.com.

RANDOLPH-BROUGHMAN, MARY ETTA, music educator; b. Staunton, Va., Sept. 11, 1953; d. Morris V. Randolph, Jr. and Claudine (Wimmer) Randolph; children from previous marriage: Katrina Marie Broughman, Sarah Elizabeth Broughman. BA in Music Edn., Bridgewater Coll., 1974; M in Music Edn., James Madison U., 1978; dipoma in music, Mozarteum Hoschschule für Musik und darstellende Kunst, 1980; postgrad., Shenandoah U., 2002—. Tchg. lic. Pvt. piano tchr., Va., 1974—; music tchr. Roanoke (Va.) City Schs., 1974—77, Richmond County Schs., Warsaw, Va., 1978—79, Botetourt County Schs., Fincastle, Va., 1980—81, Montgomery County Schs., Christiansburg, Va., 1981—82, Staunton (Va.) County Schs., 1982—87, Rockridge County Schs., Lexington, Va., 1987—; tchg. asst. piano James Madison U., Harrisonburg, Va., 1977—78. Adjudicator dist. and regional chorus Montgomery and Roanoke Counties, Va.; accompanist, 1974—. Composer, arranger: Come and Worship, Spencer's Mountain. Chmn. Reflections Program, Natural Bridge Dist. PTA, 2004—; vol. 4-H; organist Buena Vista (Va.) Bapt. Ch., 1999—2003; organist, choir dir./accompanist various chs. Fellow, Rotary Internat., Salzburg, Austria, 1979—80. Mem.: Va. Choral Dirs. Assn., Nat. Guild Piano Tchrs., Am. Coll. Musicians, Am. Guild Organists, Va. Music Educators Assn. (25 Yr. Tchg. award 1999), Music Educators Nat. Conf. (25 Yr. Tchg. award 1999). Home: 3017 Forge Rd Glasgow VA 24555 Office: Natural Bridge Elem Sch 42 Natural Bridge School Rd Natural Bridge Station VA 24579 Office Phone: 540-291-2292.

RANEY, CAROLYN E., educational consultant; b. L.A., Aug. 14, 1918; d. Charles Porter Raney and Carrie Elizabeth Schafer; m. Saul Schechtman, July 31, 1952; children: Carol Ruth Kimmel, Julia Schechtman Pabst. MusB, Eastman Sch. Music, 1938; MusM, Case Western U., 1943; PhD in Hist. Music, NYU, 1971; cert. in Bus., Harvard U., 1980. Faculty mem. NYU, N.Y.C., 1968—73, CUNY, S.I., 1968—73, Am. Music and Drama Sch., N.Y.C., 1968—73; dir. grad. dept. Peabody Coll., Johns Hopkins U., Balt., 1973—76; dean arts, v.p. East Stroudsburg (Pa.) State U., 1976—80; faculty Am. creative writing U. Dusseldorf, Germany, 1982—85; dean grad. sch. Schiller Internat. U., Heidelberg, Germany, 1985—90, London, 1985—90, Paris, 1985—90; cons. Mgmt. Inst., Strasbourg, France, 1990—94. Lectr. in field. Author: Francesca Caccini, 1971, (poetry) Portals and Portents, 2005, (poetry volume) Realities and Unrealities, 1993; contbr. articles to publs. Fulbright fellow, NEA, 1963—64. Mem.: Authors Guild, Internat. Musicol. Soc., Acad. Am. Poets (assoc.), Coll. Music Soc. (life; editor 1975—79). Christian Scientist. Avocations: singing, church organist, voice teacher, career advisor. Home: 134 Cathedral Ave Hempstead NY 11550

RANEY, MIRIAM DAY, actress; b. Florence, SC, Sept. 30, 1922; d. Lewis Griffith and Iola Lewis (Edwards) Day; m. Robert William Raney, Mar. 31, 1946 (div. Sept. 1976); children: Robert William Jr., Miriam, Kevin Paige, Megan. BSM in Voice, Music Edn., U. N.C., Greensboro, 1943; student, Julliard Sch. Music, 1942—43; BA in Music History and Lit., U. Ark., Little Rock, 1981; cert., Adam Roarke Film Actors Lab., Irving, Tex., 1989. Singing chorus N.Y.C. Ctr. Opera Co., 1943-44; understudy, singing chorus Oklahoma, Theater Guild, N.Y.C., 1944-45; ingenue lead Connecticut Yankee, Geosan Subway Cir., N.Y.C., 1945; understudy, singing chorus Up In Central Park, Michael Todd, N.Y.C., 1945-46. Beauty cons. Mary Kay Cosmetics, Inc., Dallas, 1993—96. Author: Ark Women in Music, 1982; composer, lyricist: songs The Bend and the Wiillow, 1982, Ballad of Petit Jean, 1983; actor: (plays) Hedda Gabler, 1990, Time of Your Life, 1991, Our Town, 1991, Evening with Women II, 1991; (TV series) Unsolved Mysteries, 1988; (films) Killing Time with Aunt Olene, 1988, commls. and tng. films, 1987—99; reviewer: Ency of Ark. History, 2005—06; print model, Little Rock, Memphis, Ft. Worth, 1988—98. Sec. sr. adult coun. Pulaski Heights United Meth. Ch., 2004—05. Named Illustrious Alumna, U. NC, Greensboro, 1945; recipient Thanks Badge, Girl Scouts USA, Oachita Coun., Little Rock, 1962. Mem.: AAUW (mem. Little Rock br. legis. com., mem. program com. 1973—79, cultural interest rep. 1975—77, 1996—98, state rep. cultural interests 1976—78), Ctrl. Ark. Guild Organists (pres. student chpt. 1977—80), Mus. Coterie. Democrat. Avocations: birdwatching, gardening, reading, movies. Home: 25 Valley Forge Dr Little Rock AR 72212-2613 Personal E-mail: mimraney@comcast.net.

RANK, JANET CAROL, music educator; d. Mark John and Elaine Carol Paider; m. Donald Francis Rank, Aug. 2, 1997; children: Ryan, Rachelle. B of Music Edn., U. Wis., Oshkosh, 1989; MusM, Silver Lake Coll., Manitowoc, Wis., 1999. Dir. h.s. chorus Holmen (Wis.) H.S., 1990; tchr. elem. music Magee & Koening Elem. Schs., Two Rivers, Wis., 1990—. Choir dir. Magee Elem., Two Rivers, 1990—; youth chorale dir. Lake Shore Chorale, Sheboygan, Wis., 1999—2001. Distbr. holy communion St. Francis of Assisi Ch., Manitowoc, 2002—, song leader, 2005—; organist St. Paul's Ch., Manitowoc, 2002—05. Mem.: Assn. Wis. Area Kodaly Educators, Music Educators Nat. Conf., Am. Choral Dirs. Assn. Office: Two Rivers Pub Sch Magee Elem 3502 Glenwood St Two Rivers WI 54241

RANKAITIS, SUSAN, artist; b. Cambridge, Mass., Sept. 10, 1949; d. Alfred Edward and Isabel (Shimkus) Rankaitis; m. Robbert Flick, June 5, 1976. BFA in Painting, U. Ill., 1971; MFA in Visual Arts, U. So. Calif., 1977. Rsch. asst., art dir. Plato Lab., U. Ill., Urbana, 1971-75; art instr. Orange Coast Coll., Costa Mesa, Calif., 1977-83; chair dept. art Chapman Coll., Orange, Calif., 1983-90; Fletcher Jones chair art Scripps Coll., Claremont, Calif., 1990—. Represented by Robert Mann Gallery, N.Y.C.; overview panelist visual arts Nat. Endowment for Arts, 1983, 84; selector Bingham Ednl. Trust, 1997—2002; scholar-in-residence Borchard Found., Missillac, France, 2004; artist-in-residence Europos Parkus, 2005. One-woman shows include LA County Mus. Art, 1983, Internat. Mus. Photography, George Eastman House, 1983, Gallery Min. Tokyo, 1988, Ruth Bloom Gallery, Santa Monica, 1989, 90, 92, Schneider Mus., Portland, Ore., 1990; Ctr. Creative Photography, 1991, Robert Mann Gallery, NYC, 1994, 97, Mus. Contemporary Photography, Chgo., 1994, Mus. Photographic Arts, 2000, Europos Parkas, Vilnius, 2005; represented in permanent collections MOCA, LA, U. N.Mex Art, Ctr. Creative Photography, Mus. Contemporary Photography, Chgo., Santa Barbara Mus. Art, LA County Mus. Art, Mpls. Inst. Arts, St. Louis Art Mus., San Francisco Mus. Modern Art, Art Inst. Chgo., Mus. Modern Art, Lodz, Poland, Princeton U. Art Mus., Stanford U. Art Mus., Contemporary Art Mus., Honolulu, Mus. Contemporary Photography, Art Inst. Chgo., St. Louis Art Mus., others. Active art auction Venice Family Clinic, 1980-2005. Recipient Graves award in Humanities, 1985; fellow NEA, 1980, 88, US, France, 1989, Agnes Bourne fellow Djerassi Found., 1989, Award in the Visual Arts, Flintridge Found., 2004; Durfee Chinese/Am. grantee, 2000-2001, Cultural Affairs grantee City L.A., 2001, grantee Mellon Found., 2005, 06; Borchard Found. scholar-in-residence, France, 2004. Mem. Coll. Art Assn., LA County Mus. Art, Santa Monica Mus. Art, Mus. Contemporary Art. Home: 3117 N Lansbury Ave Claremont CA 91711-4146 Office Phone: 909-607-4439. Business E-Mail: srankait@scrippscollege.edu.

RANKIN, BETTY HILL, retired special education educator; b. Greensboro, N.C., Aug. 28, 1945; d. Wilson Conrad and Elizabeth (Roper) Hill; m. James Whiten Rankin Jr., July 23, 1967; 1 child, John Hunter. BA in History, Winthrop U., 1967; postgrad., U. South Fla., 1971-72, U. Va., 1973-98, George Mason U., 1976-98; MEd, Cambridge Coll., 1999. Tchr. English, history Acad. La Castellana, Caracas, Venezuela, 1967-69; tchr. educable retarded Tampa, Fla., 1970-72; tchr. mentally retarded Loudoun County, Va., 1972—2002; ret., 2002. Lectr. Smithsonian Instn., 1990; presenter N.Am. Conf. Rehab. Internat., Atlanta, 1993; mem. Loudoun County Tech. Steering Com., 1992-93; program dir. Rainbow Ctr. 4-H Therapeutic Equestrian Program, Inc., Manassas, Va., 2001-03; advocate for inclusion and integration of students with mental retardation. Profiled in: (video) The Land of Our Children, Rally Behind the Virginians, Am. Resources Coalition, 1992, (curriculum guide) Reins to Independence, 1999; contbr. articles to mags. Founding mem., treas. N.W. Prince William Citzens Assn., Catharpin, Va., 1986-2002; pres. Save the Battlefield Coalition, Inc., Catharpin, 1988—. Recipient Civic commendation Prince William County Planning Commn., 1987, Peace and Internat. Rels. award Va. Edn. Assn., 1992, Working Women award ABC Ch. 7 News/Washington Toyota Dealers, 2000, Agnes Meyer Outstanding Tchr. award Washington Post, 2001; named Tchr. of Yr., IBM, 1978, Tchr. of Yr., Loudoun County, Va., 2001, Va. Tchr. of the Yr. Region IV, 2002; fellow Internat. Exch. of Experts and Info. in Rehab., U. N.H., 1992; Loudoun Edn. Found. grantee in edn., 1994, 99, 2000; grantee Freddie Mac Found., 2000, 01. Mem. Assn. Retarded Citizens, Coun. for Exceptional Children (nat. presenter 1989, profl. recognized spl. educator 1997), Tchrs. Internat. Exch. (presenter Japan 1992), N.Am. Riding for Handicapped Assn. (registered instr.). Avocations: preservation, equestrian activities, swimming, reading. Home: PO Box 453 Catawba SC 29704

RANKIN, JACQUELINE ANNETTE, communications expert, educator; b. Omaha, May 19, 1925; d. Arthur C. and Virdie (Gillispie) R. BA, Calif. State U., L.A., 1964, MA, 1966; MS in Mgmt., Calif. State U., Fullerton, 1977; EdD, U. LaVerne, Calif., 1981. Tchr. Rowland H.S., La Habra, Calif., 1964-66, Lowell H.S., La Habra, Calif., 1966-69, Pomona (Calif.) H.S., 1969-75; program asst. Pomona Adult Sch., 1975-82; dir. Child Abuse Prevention Program, 1985-86; exec. dir. child abuse prevention Calif. Dept. Pub. Svc., 1985-87; instr. Ind. U., Purdue U., 1993; assoc. prof. speech Ball State U., Muncie, Ind., 1993-94; instr. No. Va. U., 1994—, trainer Loudoun campus, 1996. Faculty evening divsn. Mt. San Antonio C.C., 1966-72; asst. prof. speech Ball State U., Muncie, Ind., 1993; instr. No. Va. U., Alexandria, Annandale, Manassas, Woodbridge, 1995—; assoc. faculty dept. comm. and theatre, Ind. U., Purdue U., Indpls., 1993; trainer internat. convs., sales groups, staffs of hosps., others; spkr., writer, trainer, lectr., cons. in field. Columnist: Jackie's World, Topics Newspapers; author: Body Language in Love and Romance, 1984, Body Language: First Impressions, 1985, Body Language in Negotiations and Sales, 1996, Body Language of the Abused Child, 1999, Using body Language That Kids Trust, Ten Tips for Evaluating Body Language of the Abused Child; contbr. articles to Child Law Practice, ABA and other profl. jours. Mem. Fairfax County Dem. Com.; mem. adv. coun., mem. nat. capital chpt. bd. dirs. ARC. Mem. Internat. Platform Assn., Pi Lambda Theta, Phi Delta Kappa. Home and Office: 9405 General Way Apt 202 Indianapolis IN 46216 Personal E-mail: jackierankin@comcast.net.

RANKIN, JEAN F., lawyer; BA, U. Va.; JD, U. Pa. Clerk for Justice G. Mennen Williams Mich. State Supreme Ct.; assoc. Cravath, Swaine and Moore; with AT&T, AT&T Capital Corp.; counsel Lucent Technologies; sr. v.p., gen. counsel, sec. Agere Sys., Allentown, Pa. Grantee Order of Coif. Office: Agere Sys 1110 American Parkway NE Allentown PA 18109 Office Phone: 610-712-4323.

RANKIN, MARY ANN, dean, biology professor; BS in Biology and Chemistry, La. State Univ., 1966; PhD in Physiology and Behavior of Insects, Univ. Iowa, 1972; postdoctoral study, Harvard Univ., 1972—74. Asst. prof. zoology Univ. Tex., Austin, 1975, chmn., divsn. biol. sci., 1989—94, dean, Coll. Natural Sci., 1994—, prof. zoology, 1996—. Pre-doctoral fellow Imperial Coll. Field Sta., Ascot, England. Office: Coll Natural Sci Univ Tex 1 University Sta G2500 Austin TX 78712 Office Phone: 512-471-3285. Office Fax: 512-471-4998. Business E-Mail: rankin@mail.utexas.edu.

RANKS, ANNE ELIZABETH, retired elementary and secondary education educator; b. Omaha, June 10, 1916; d. Salvatore and Concetta (Turco) Scolla; m. Harold Eugene Ranks, Aug. 20, 1955 (dec.). B in Philosophy, Duchesne Coll., Omaha, 1937; MA, Creighton U., 1947. Tchr. Good Shepherd Parochial H.S., Omaha, 1937-38, St. Benedicts H.S., Omaha, 1938-39, Omaha Pub. Schs., 1939-81. Pres. women's divsn. Dem. Cen. Com., Nebr.; chmn. Gov.'s Profl. Practices Commn. Nebr., 1938-39; vol. Bergan-Mercy Hosp., Omaha, 1980-86, 99—, hosp. mem. aux. bd. dirs., 1985-86; vol. Saddleback Hosp.,

Laguna Hills, Calif., 1989-91; bd. dirs. Sylvia Tischhauser CRTA divsn. Scholarship Found., 1989-94; mem. bd. dirs. Saddleback Valley Ednl. Found., 1990-92; bd. dirs. Orange County Diocesan Coun. Cath. Women, 1989-90, 2d v.p., 1990-94; vol. Bergan Mercy Hosp., 1998-2001. Mem. AAUW (v.p. Laguna Hills br. 1988-91), Nebr. Edn. Assn. (bd. dirs. 1957-60, pres. dist. II 1960-62), Omaha Edn. Assn. (bd. dirs. 1950-55), Womens Club, Cath. Daus. Regent Omaha Ct. (rec. sec. Lake Forest, Calif. Ct. 1988-90), Coll. Club of Leisure World (v.p. 1990-95), Nat. Ret. Tchrs. Assn., Nebr. Ret. Tchrs. Assn., Local Ret. Tchrs. Assn., Cath. Daus. Home: Apt 244 9804 Nicholas St Omaha NE 68114-2180

RANNER, SHANNA, music educator; d. Gare and Shirley Kraemer; m. Christopher Ranner, May 31, 1997; 1 child, Jayson. BA with Instrumental Emphasis, Truman State U., Kirkville, Mo., 1997; MusB in Percussion Performance, Truman State U., Kirksville, Mo, 1997; MusM in Edn., U. Mo.-St. Louis, 2003. Cert. instrumental music edn. K-12 Mo., 2003, vocal music edn. K-12 Mo., 2006. Tchr. music Lincoln County R-III Sch. Dist., Troy, Mo., 2000—04, U. City Sch. Dist., University City, Mo., 2004—. Musician: (mallet keyboard competition) Percussive Arts Soc. Internat. Mallet Keyboard Competition, Music Tchrs. Nat. Assn. Competition-Percussion. Named to Nat. Dean's List, Truman State U., 1995. Mem.: Sigma Alpha Iota, Mo. Music Educators Assn., Music Educators Nat. Conf., Phi Kappa Phi. Lutheran. Avocations: water aerobics, crafts. Home: 12 Fairfield Court Saint Peters MO 63376

RANNEY, HELEN MARGARET, retired internist, hematologist, educator; b. Summer Hill, NY, Apr. 12, 1920; d. Arthur C. and Alesia (Toolan) Ranney. AB, Barnard Coll., 1941; MD, Columbia U., 1947; ScD, U. S.C., 1979, SUNY, Buffalo, 1996. Diplomate Am. Bd. Internal Medicine. Intern Presbyn. Hosp., N.Y.C., 1947—48, resident, 1948—50, asst. physician, 1954—60; practice medicine specializing in internal medicine, hematology N.Y.C., 1954—70; instr. Coll. Phys. and Surg. Columbia, N.Y.C., 1954—60; from assoc. prof. to prof. medicine Albert Einstein Coll. Medicine, N.Y.C., 1960—70; prof. medicine SUNY, Buffalo, 1970—73, U. Calif., San Diego, 1973—90, chmn. dept. medicine, 1973—86, Disting. physician vet. adminstr., 1986—91; cons. Alliance Pharm. Corp., San Diego, 1991—2004; ret., 2004. Master: ACP; fellow: AAAS; mem.: NAS, Am. Acad. Arts and Scis., Am. Assn. Physicians, Harvey Soc., Am. Soc. Hematology, Am. Soc. for Clin. Investigation, Inst. Medicine, Alpha Omega Alpha, Sigma Xi, Phi Beta Kappa. Personal E-mail: hranney@ucsd.edu.

RANNEY, MARY ELIZABETH, small business owner; b. Louisville, Nov. 10, 1928; d. James William and Erna Marie Katerina (Hansen) Connell; m. Glen Royal Ranney, July 26, 1947; children: Darleen Diane Ranney Bowie, Nancy Elizabeth Ranney Pieratt. Student, Monmouth Coll., 1946-47. Cert. profl. sec., nursing asst. Nursing asst. Monmouth (Ill.) Hosp., 1957-63; asst. in fin. Bd. Pub. Instrn. Collier County, Naples, Fla., 1964-68; sec. 1st Nat. Bank, Bonita Springs, Fla., 1969-71; founder, dir. Planned Parenthood, Naples, 1972-76; writer Am. Hibiscus Soc., 1977-82; owner Tree Gallery, Naples and Ft. Myers, 1983—2005. Tchr., seedling judge Am. Hibiscus Soc., 1977-79. Author: (brochure) Abortion, 1976; solo performance Fiddler on the Roof, 1976. Chair Fla. Assn. for Repeal Abortion Laws, Lee and Collier County, 1972; founder Abortion Referral Svc. S.W. Fla., 1972-75; founder, dir. Accordion Band, Naples, 1974-79, Floridian Accordion Band, Ft. Myers, 1989-91; founding officer Naples Concert Band, 1972-79; sponsor Am. hibiscus shows, Naples, 1973-81; founder, codr. City of Ft. Myers String Band, 1998-2005; dir. Bell Choir, 2006. Recipient Prominent Woman of Cmty. award Naples Star, 1977, 78, 79, Mover of 70's award Naples NOW Mag., 1980, Shaker, Mover and Star award Naples NOW Mag., 1983, Life Work Feature award Naples Star, 1981, Great Achiever award Naples Star, 1982. Mem. NOW (charter nat. pres. 1975-77), Am. Hibiscus Soc. (life, founder Ranney chpt. 1973-2003, editor Show Chair Manual 1979, Judges Manual 1980, Pres. Svc. award 1979, Hibiscus of Yr. 1980, 82), Meml. Soc. S.W. Fla. (pres. 1975-77). Democrat. Avocations: musician, seamstress, biker, walker, dancer. Home and Office: 56 Eland Dr North Fort Myers FL 33917

RANNEY-MARINELLI, ALESIA, lawyer; b. Ithaca, NY, 1952; BA, Mich. State U., 1973; JD cum laude, Harvard U., 1977. Bar: Del. 1977, N.Y. 1986. Ptnr. Skadden Arps Slate Flom & Meagher, N.Y.C. Author (and co-editor): Practical Guide to Out-of-Court Restructurings and Prepackaged Plans of Reorganization, 2005. Grantee Am. Coll. Bankruptcy. Office: Skadden Arps Slate Meagher & Flom 4 Times Sq Fl 24 New York NY 10036-6595

RANSIL, DOROTHY MAE, secondary school educator; d. Raymond Augustine and Louise Mary Ransil. BA, Carlow U., 1967; MEd, U. Pitts., 1973. Cert. tchr. Pa. Tchr. St. Anne Elem. Sch., 1950—51, Villa Prep. Sch., 1951—52, St. Martin HS, 1952—53, St. Basil HS, 1953—56, Divine Providence Acad., 1956—58, 1978—84, San Miguel (PR) HS, 1958—61, 1972—73, San Felipe (PR) HS, 1961—65, St. Mary HS, 1965—72, N. Catholic Sch., 1973—78, Serra Cath. HS, McKeesport, Pa., 1984—. With Sisters of Divine Providence, Allison Park, Pa., Sisters Divine Providence, PR, 1972—73. Address: Serra Cath HS 200 Hershey Dr Mc Keesport PA 15132

RANSOM, NANCY ALDERMAN, sociology and women's studies educator, academic administrator; b. New Haven, Feb. 25, 1929; d. Samuel Bennett and Florence (Opper) Alderman; m. Harry Howe Ransom, July 6, 1951; children: Jenny Alderman, Katherine Marie, William Henry Howe. BA, Vassar Coll., 1950; postgrad., Columbia U., 1951, U. Leeds, Eng., 1977-78; MA, Vanderbilt U., 1971, EdD, 1988. Lectr. sociology U. Tenn., Nashville, 1971-76; grant writer Vanderbilt U., Nashville, 1976-77, dir. Women's Ctr., 1978-97, instr. sociology, 1972, 74, lectr. sociology and women's studies, 1983, 90-97. Vol. counselor family planning Planned Parent Assn. of Nashville, 1973—77, mem. adv. coun., 1989—98, v.p., 1981—, pres., 1987—89, Sr. Citizens, Inc., 2001—02, chmn. ann. fund campaign, 2002—03, Sr. Citizens Found., 2004—; mem. planning com. ACE/ACE nat. identification program Women in Higher Edn., 1984—92; spkr. in field. Active Sr. Citizens Found., 2003—. Recipient Women of Achievement award Middle Tenn. State U., 1996, Mary Jane Werthan award Vanderbilt U., 1998; named to Acad. for Women of Achievement, YWCA, 2000, Molly Todd Cup, 2003, Sage award, 2004; Columbia U. residential fellow, 1951; Vanderbilt U. fellow, 1971. Mem.: LWV, NOW, AAUW, Nat. Women's Polit. Caucus, Cable Club, Phi Beta Kappa (v.p. Alpha of Tenn. 1994—95, pres. 1995—97). Business E-Mail: n.a.ransom@vanderbilt.edu.

RANSOM, PEGGY ELAINE, retired education educator; b. Laramie, Wyo., May 12, 1927; d. Edwin Niles and Vera Manila (Cummings) Hitchcock; m. Donald J. Ransom, July 15, 1952. AA, Stephens Coll., 1947; BA, U. Wyo., 1949; MA, Ball State U., 1963, EdD, 1965. Cert. elem. edn. tchr., Wyo., Pa., Ind. Tchr. Laramie Schs., Wyo., 1949-52, Manheim Twp. Schs., Lancaster, Pa., 1952-54, Lancaster Twp. Schs., 1954-59, Marion Schs., Ind., 1959-60; grad. asst. Ball State U., Muncie, 1960-62, instr., 1962-65, doctoral grad. asst., 1963-65, asst. prof., 1965-70, assoc. prof., 1970-75, prof., 1975—96; ret. Cons., speaker in schs. in numerous states, 1965-96. Author: Ten Ideas for Reading Teachers, 1991; co-author (with others) Effective Strategies for Teaching Reading, 1991; contbr. articles to profl. jours. Rsch. com. mem. Ind. Literacy Coun., Indpls. Recipient Sagamore of the Wabash award Ind. State Gov., Indpls., 1984, Contbn. to Edn. in Ind. award Ind. Elem. Prins. Assn., Indpls., 1981. Mem. ASCD, Internat. Reading Assn. (Spl. Svc. award 1990), Am. Reading Forum (v.p. 1986-88), Assn. Tchr. Edn., Ind. State Reading Assn. (pres. 1968-70, contbr. 1981), Ind. State Tchrs. Assn., Delta Kappa Gamma (v.p., pres. 1980-84). Avocations: reading, playing bridge, travel, walking, flying. Home: 1115 Wildwood Ct Marion IN 46952-1222

RANSOM, TASHA ELANA, news production assistant, producer; d. Vincent Allen and Mary Geraldine Ransom. BS, Drake U., Des Moines, 1995; postgrad., Valparaiso U., Ind., 1996—97; MA, Columbia Coll., Chgo., 2002. Law clk. Vickie Pasley & Assocs., Chgo., 1992, 1994; product mgr. Zachs Investment & Rsch., Chgo., 1996; law clk. Hoeppner Wagner & Evans, Valparaiso, Ind., 1997—98; intern Lawyers for the Creative Arts, Chgo., 1999—2000; asst. Linda S. Mensch P.C., Chgo., 1999—2001; intern, prodn. cmty. affairs Fox News Chgo., 2000—01, asst. to news dir., 2001—05, asst. to news dir., prodr., 2005—. Bd. mem. Metro. and Family Svc., 2005—. Recipient Alumni of the Yr., Outstanding Contbn. in the African Am. Cmty., Youth Action Ministry, 2003; Chuck Suber scholarship, Columbia Coll., 2001—02. Mem.: Nat. Assn. Black Journalists, Phi Alpha Delta, Delta Sigma Pi.

RANTA, AMY J., music educator; d. Glenn J and Marnelle H Ranta. MusB in Vocal Performance, U. Conn., Storrs, 1993; MusM in Vocal Performance, U. Conn., 1995. Cert. music tchr. Conn. Dir. of vocal music Putnam H.S., Conn., 1997—2000, Woodstock Acad., Conn., 2000—. Bd. dirs. Theater of Northeastern Conn. at the Bradley Playhouse, Putnam, 2002—04; choral chair Quinnebaug Valley Music Festival, Griswold, Conn., 1998, 2000. Guest conductor (opera chorus concert) Northeastern Conn. Concert Choir, (honors choir-music festival) Quinnebaug Valley Music Festival-Mid. Sch. Divsn.; actor(singer): (musical) Godspell, (play) Steel Magnolias; music dir. (musical) Joseph and the Amazing Technicolor Dream Coat, Cinderella, Godspell, Wizard of Oz, Fiddler on the Roof, Gypsy. Named Tchr. of the Yr., Woodstock Acad., 2005—06; recipient Outstanding Svc. to Sch. Cmty. award, 2001. Mem.: New Eng. Music Festivals Assn., Am. Choral Dirs. Assn., Music Educators Nat. Conf., Conn. Music Educators Assn. (choral chair ea. region 2004, adjudication chair ea. region 2006), Tri-M Music Honor Soc. (hon.), Pi Kappa Lambda, Phi Kappa Phi. Office: Woodstock Academy 57 Academy Rd Woodstock CT 06281 Office Phone: 860-928-6575. Personal E-mail: ajranta@sbcglobal.net. E-mail: aranta@woodstockacademy.org.

RANTS, CAROLYN JEAN, academic administrator, educator; b. Hastings, Nebr., Oct. 3, 1936; d. John Leon and Christine (Helzer) Halloran; m. Marvin L. Rants, June 1, 1957 (div. July 1984); children: Christopher Charles, Douglas John. Student, Hastings Coll., 1954—56; BS, U. Omaha, 1960; EdM, U. Nebr., 1968; EdD, U. S.D., 1982. Elem. sch. tchr. Ogallala (Nebr.) Cmty. Sch., 1956-58, Omaha Pub. Schs., 1958-60, Hastings Pub. Schs., 1960-64, Grosse Pointe (Mich.) Cmty. Schs., 1964-67; asst. prof., instr. Morningside Coll., Sioux City, Iowa, 1974-82, dean for student devel., 1982-84, v.p. for student affairs, 1984-94, interim v.p. for acad. affairs, 1992-94, v.p. enrollment and student svcs., 1994-96, v.p. adminstrn., 1996-99; exec. dir. enrollment svcs. Western Iowa Tech C.C., 1999—, dean of students, 2000—06, interim v.p. instrn. and student svcs. Iowa, 2006—. Pres. New Perspectives, Inc., 1999—2000. New agy. com., chmn. fund distbn. and resource deployment com. United Way, Sioux City, 1987-94, co-chair, United Way Day of Caring, 1996; active Iowa Civil Rights Commn., 1989-97; bd. dirs. Leadership Sioux City, 1988-93, pres., 1992-93; bd. dirs. Siouxland Y, Sioux City, 1985-90, pres., 1988; bd. dirs. Girls, Inc., 1995-2000, Sioux City Symphony, 2001—, Red Cross, 2002—; mem. Vision 2020 Cmty. Planning Task Force, 1990-92; pres. bd. dirs. Siouxland Youth Chorus, 2001—, treas., 2002—; mem. Vision Iowa Bd., 2005—. Mem. Iowa Women in Ednl. Leadership (pres. Sioux City chpt. 1986), Nat. Assn. Student Pers. Adminstrs.(region IV-E adv. bd.), Nat. Assn. for Women Deans, Adminstrs. and Counselors, Iowa Student Pers. Adminstr. (chmn. profl. devel. Iowa chpt. 1988-89, pres. 1991-92, Outstanding Svc. award 1992, Disting. Svc. award 1994), AAUW (corp. rep., coll./univ. rep. 1994-96), P.E.O. (pres. Sioux City chpt., Tri-State Women's Bus. Conf. (treas., planning com. Sioux City chpt. 1987-89), Quota Club (com. chmn. Sioux City 1987-89, v.p. 1992-94, pres. 1994-95, Siouxland Woman of Yr. award 1988), Sertoma (officer, bd. govs., regional dir.), Omicron Delta Kappa (faculty dir. province X 1996-99), Delta Kappa Gamma (state 1st v.p. 1993-95, state pres. 1995-97, internat. com. 1998-2000, 2002-04, N.W. regional dir. 2004-06, 1st v.p. 2006—), Phi Delta Kappa (pres. 1988-89, Excellence in Leadership award 1998, Spl. Commendation Bessie Gabbard award 2001). Republican. Methodist. Avocations: handbells, cross-stitching. Home: 2904 S Cedar St # 4 Sioux City IA 51106-4246 Office: Western Iowa Tech Comm Coll PO Box 5199 4647 Stone Ave Sioux City IA 51102-5199 E-mail: rantsc@witcc.com, cjrants@willinet.net.

RAO-REMY, YVONNE BERNADETTE, special education educator; d. Peter Charles and Noreen Patricia Rao; m. Anthony James Remy, May 1, 2004. MA, Columbia U., NYC, 1997. Cert. tchr. spl. edn. N.Y. Tchr. spl. edn. St. Charles E&T Ctr., Southampton, NY, 1997, Comeswayne Sch. Dist., Pt. Jefferson Station, NY, 2000—01, Miller Place Sch. Dist., NY, 2001—03, Westhampton Sch. Dist., NY, 2003—04, Sag Harbor Sch. Dist., NY, 2004—. Mem.: CEC. Avocations: writing, acting, scuba diving, rock climbing, dance.

RAOUFI, AZADEH, music educator; arrived in U.S., 1998; d. Mohammad Sadogh Raoufi and Fatemeh (Mali) Fakoor-Sevvom. B in Piano and Computer Sci., U. Iowa, 2004, postgrad., 2005—. Tchr. English Shokoh, Mashad, 1995—98; with Info. Tech. Ctr., Iowa City, 2001—02; with internal med. rsch. lab. U. Iowa, Iowa City, 2001—02; piano tchr. West Music, Iowa City, 2002—. Mem.: Iowa City Ind. Piano Tchrs. (v.p.), Iowa Music Tchr. Assn. (pub. rels. person 2004—), Music Tchr. Nat. Assn., Phi Theta Kappa. E-mail: azadeh-raoufi@uiowa.edu.

RAPHAEL, LOUISE ARAKELIAN, mathematician, educator; b. NYC, Oct. 24, 1937; d. Aristakes and Antionette (Sudbeaz) Arakelian; m. Robert Barnett Raphael, June 12, 1966 (div. 1985); children: Therese Denise, Marc Philippe. BS in Math., St. John's U., 1959; MS in Math., Cath. U., Washington, 1962; PhD in Math, Cath. U., 1967. Asst. prof. math. Howard U., Washington, 1966-70, vis. prof., 1981-82, assoc. prof., 1982-86, prof., 1986—; assoc. prof. Clark Coll., Atlanta, 1971-79, prof., 1979-82. Vis. assoc. prof. MIT, Cambridge, 1977-78, vis. prof., 1989-90; vis. mem. Courant Inst. Math. Scis., NYU, 1996-97; vis. scholar Cornell U., 2004. Contbr. over 40 rsch. articles to profl. jours. Program dir. NSF, Washington, 1986—88; acting adminstrv. officer Conf. Bd. Math. Scis., 1985—86. Grantee NSF, 1975-76, 79-81, 89-91, Army Rsch. Office, 1981-89, Air Force Sci. Rsch., 1981-82, 91-95, Nat. Security Agy., 1994-96. Mem.: Soc. Indsl. and Applied Math., Math. Assn. Am. (1st v.p. 1996—98, chmn. minorities in math. task force 1988), Am. Math. Soc. (coun. 2001—04, com. mem.), Sigma Xi. Democrat. Roman Catholic. Office: Howard U Dept Math Washington DC 20059-0001 Office Phone: 202-806-6836.

RAPIN, ISABELLE, physician; b. Lausanne, Switzerland, Dec. 4, 1927; d. Rene and Mary Coe (Reeves) R.; m. Harold Oaklander, Apr. 5, 1959; children: Anne Louise, Christine, Stephen, Peter. Physician's Diploma, Faculte de Medicine, U. Lausanne, 1952, Doctorate in Medicine, 1955. Diplomate Am. Bd. Psychiatry and Neurology. Intern in pediatrics N.Y. U. Bellevue Med. Center, 1953-54; resident in neurology Neurol. Inst. of N.Y., Columbia-Presbyn. Med. Center, 1954-57, fellow in child neurology, 1957-58; mem. faculty Albert Einstein Coll. Medicine, Bronx, NY, 1958—, prof. neurology and pediatrics, 1972—; attending neurologist and child neurologist Einstein Affiliated Hosps., Bronx. Mem. Nat. Adv. Neurol. and Communicative Disorders and Stroke Coun., NIH, 1984-88. Contbr. chpts. to books, articles to med. jours. Recipient award Conf. Ednl. Adminstrs. Serving the Deaf, 1988. Fellow: Am. Acad. Neurology (exec. bd. 1995—99); mem.: AAAS, Assn. for Rsch. in Nervous and Mental Diseases (v.p. 1986), Internat. Neuropsychology Soc., Am. Neurol. Assn. (hon.; v.p. 1982—83), Child Neurology Soc. (Hower award 1987), Internat. Child Neurology Assn. (sec.-gen. 1979—82, v.p. 1982—86, Frank R. Ford lectr. 1990). Office: Albert Einstein Coll Medicine K807 1300 Morris Park Ave Bronx NY 10461-1101

RAPOPORT, JUDITH, psychiatrist; b. NYC, July 12, 1933; d. Louis and Minna (Enteen) Livant; m. Stanley Rapoport, June 25, 1961; children: Stuart, Erik. BA, Swarthmore Coll., 1955; MD, Harvard U., 1959. Lic. psychiatrist. Cons., child psychiatrist NIMH/St. Elizabeth's Hosp., Washington, 1969—72; clin. asst. prof. Georgetown U. Med. Sch., Washington, 1972—82, clin. assoc. prof., 1982—85, clin. prof. psychiat., 1985—; med. officer biol. psychiatry br. NIMH, Bethesda, Md., 1979—82, chief. child psychiatry lab. of clin. scis., 1982—84, chief, child psychiatry div. intramural rsch. programs, 1984—; prof. psychiatry George Washington U. Sch. Med., Washington, 1979—; prof. pediat. Georgetown U., Washington, 1985—. Cons. in field. Author: (non-fiction) The Boy Who Couldn't Stop Washing, 1989 (best seller literary guild selection, 1989), Childhood Obsessive Compulsive Disorder, 1989. Recipient Scolnick award, MIT, 2005. Fellow: Am. Acad. Arts & Sci., Am. Acad. Child Psychiatry, Am. Psychiat. Assn.; mem.: Inst. Medicine, D.C. Psychiat. Assn. Home: 3010 44th Pl NW Washington DC 20016-3557 Office: NIMH Rm 3N202 10 Center Dr Bldg 10 Bethesda MD 20892-0001 Office Phone: 301-496-6081. Business E-Mail: rapoport@helix.nih.gov.

RAPOPORT, NANCY B., law educator; b. Bryan, Tex., June 29, 1960; m. Jeffrey D. Van Niel, Oct. 13, 1996. BA summa cum laude (hon.), Rice U., 1982; JD, Stanford Law Sch., 1985. Bar: Calif. 1987, U.S. Dist. Cts. (no., ea., ctrl., and so. dists.) Calif. 1987, U.S. Ct. Appeals (9th cir.) 1987, Ohio 1993, Nebr. 1999, U.S. Dist. Ct. (no. dist.) Tex. 2003. Jud. clk. Hon. Joseph T. Sneed, U.S. Ct. Appeals (9th cir.), San Francisco, 1985—86; assoc. bus.dept. of bankruptcy and workouts group Morrison & Foerster, San Francisco, 1986—91; asst. prof. Ohio State U. Coll. Law, Columbus, 1991—95, tenured assoc. prof., 1995—98, assoc. dean student affairs, 1996—98, prof., 1998; dean, prof. law U. Nebr. Coll. Law, Lincoln, 1998—2000, U. Houston Law Ctr., 2000—. Invited spkr., panelist, and presenter in field. Co-editor (with Bala G. Dharan): Enron: Corporate Fiascos and Their Implications, 2004. Bd. trustees Law Sch. Admissions Coun., 2001—04; bd. dirs. ADL Southwest Regional Bd., Houston Area Women's Ctr. Named Outstanding Prof. of Yr., Ohio State U. Coll. Law., 1997; recipient Rice U. Dist. Alumna award. Fellow: Am. Coll. Bankruptcy, Am. Bar Found., Houston Bar Found. (selection com. Best Article award 2000—); mem.: ABA (task force atty. discipline 2005—, commn. loan repayment and forgiveness), Assn. Am. Law Sch.'s Profl. Develop. Com., Ohio State Bar Assn. (legal edn. com. 1997—98), Am. Bankruptcy Inst. (law sch. com. 1994—), Bar Assn. San Francisco, Nat. Assn. Coll. and U. Attys., Nebr. State Bar Assn. (Named Legal Pioneer for Women in Law (first women to serve as dean of Nebr. Law Sch. 1999—), Houston Bar Assn., Am. Law Inst. Avocations: ballroom dancing, Latin dancing, black and white photography, blues music. Office: U Houston Law Ctr 100 Law Ctr Houston TX 77204-6060 Office Phone: 713-743-2100. Business E-Mail: nrapoport@uh.edu.

RAPOPORT, SONYA, artist; b. Boston; d. Louis Aaron and Ida Tina (Axelrod) Goldberg; m. Henry Rapoport; children: Hava Rapoport de Fereres, David, Robert. Student, Mass. Coll. Art, 1941-42; BA, NYU, 1945; MA, U. Calif., Berkeley, 1949. Bd. dirs. LEONARDO, Jour. Internat. Soc. Arts, Scis. and Tech.; mem. adv. com. Berkeley Art Mus. U. Calif. One-woman shows include Peabody Mus., Harvard U., 1978, Calif. Palace Legion of Honor, 1963, N.Y.C. Pub. Libr., 1979, New Sch. Social Rsch., N.Y.C., 1981, NYU Grad. Sch. Bus. Adminstrn., 1982, Sarah Lawrence Coll., Bronxville, N.Y., 1984, Kuopio Mus., Finland, 1992, exhibited in group shows at Union Gallery San Jose (Calif.) State U., 1979, Ctr. Visual Arts, Oakland, Calif., 1979, Walker Art Ctr., Mpls., 1981, Nat. Libr., Madrid, 1982, SUNY Libr., Purchase, 1983, Otis Art Inst. Parsons Sch. Design, L.A., 1984, Cleve. Inst. Art, 1984, SIGGRAPH, 1998, N.Y. Digital Salon, 1995, 1996, 1997, 1998, Copenhagen Film Festival, 1996, Scotland Photo Biennial, 1997, Mill Valley Film Festival, 1997, Internat. Symposium Electronic Art, Mpls., 1993, 1995, 1996, 1999, others, Buenos Aires Biennial, 2002, Reina Sofia Mus., Madrid, 2005, Represented in permanent collections Mus. Modern Art, N.Y.C., Stedelijk Mus., Amsterdam, Inpls. Mus. Art, Grey Art Gallery, NYU, San Francisco Mus. Modern Art, San Jose State U. Found.-Union Gallery, Crocker Art Mus., Sacramento, Hall of Justice, Hayward, Calif.; book artist: book Shoe-Field, Chinese Connections, About Me, Objects on My Dresser, interactive book Gateway to Your Ka, Your Fate is in Your Feet, Digital Mudra2; prodr.: A Shoe-In, Biorhythm, Coping with Sexual Jealousy, (computer assisted interactive installations) The Animated Soul, Digital Mudra, 1998, Transgenic Bagel, 1994—95, Redeeming the Gene, Molding the Golem, Folding the Protein, 2001, Make Me a Jewish Man: An Alternative Masculinity, 1999, Arbor Erecta, 1998, Make Me a Man, 1997, Objective Connections, 1996, Brutal Myths, 1996, Smell Your Destiny, 1995; Web books, Redeeming the Gene, Molding the Golem, Folding the Protein, 2001, Rabbalah/Kabul: Sending Emanations to the Aliens, 2004. Home: 6 Hillcrest Ct Berkeley CA 94705-2805 E-mail: sonyarap@lmi.net.

RAPOSO, LAURA I., music educator; b. Johnson City, NY, June 6, 1981; d. Cesar G. and Victoria S. Raposo. MusB, Ithaca Coll., NY, 2003. Tchr. NYASTA String Inst., Ithaca, 2004, NYASTA Viola Fest, Binghamton, 2004, Ithaca City Schs., 2004—, Binghamton City Schs., 2004—. Curriculum leader Binghamton City Schs., 2006; condr. BCMEA, Whitney Point, 2006. Mem.: Broome County Music Educators Assn., Music Educators Nat. Conf., Am. String Tchrs. Assn. Avocations: reading, cooking.

RAPOZA, DONNA LEE, physical education educator; b. Providence, Apr. 15, 1954; d. Henry Joseph and Joan Ann Perry; m. Anthony Joseph Rapoza, June 26, 1992; children: Lauren Marie, Neal Anthony. BS, RI Coll., Providence, 1976; MEd, Providence Coll., 1980. Cert. tchr. RI. Elem. phys. edn. tchr. East Providence (RI) Sch. Dept., 1977—. Mem. PTA. Named RI Phys. Edn. Tchr. of the Yr., RI Coll., 1991; recipient Inspiration award, Nat. Assn. Sport and Phys. Edn., 1991, Alumni Honor Roll award, RI Coll., 1992. Mem.: AAHPERD, RI Alliance Health, Phys. Edn., Recreation and Dance. Home: 478 Enterprize Dr Somerset MA 02725

RAPPAPORT, LINDA ELLEN, lawyer; b. Freeport, NY, Jan. 12, 1952; d. William Jay and Marcia Ann (Weiland) Rappaport; m. Leonard Chazen, June 1, 1980; 1 child, Matthew Ross Chazen. BA, Wesleyan U., Middletown, Conn., 1974; JD, NYU, 1977. Bar: N.Y. 1977. Law clk. Chief Judge James S. Holden U.S. Dist. Ct. Vt., Rutland, 1978; assoc. Shearman & Sterling, NYC, 1979—85, ptnr., 1986—, elected mem. policy com., 1995—, mem. exec. group, 2005—. Bd. dirs. NY Women's Found., NYC, 1995—2001, AIESEC Internat., NYC, 1994—2000; bd. govs. Mannes Coll. Music, 2004—; bd. dirs. Legal Aid Soc. N.Y., 2005—, exec. com., 2005—. Fellow: Am. Coll. Employee Benefits Coun.; mem.: Bar Assn. City of N.Y. (employee benefits com. 1986—, employment law com. 1986—). Office: Shearman & Sterling 599 Lexington Ave Fl 13 New York NY 10022-6069 E-mail: lrappaport@shearman.com.

RAPPAPORT, MARGARET MARY WILLIAMS EWING, psychologist, physician, writer, pilot, consultant; b. Nov. 16, 1947; d. Leo J. and Marie L. (Rischle) Williams; m. Herbert Rappaport (div.); children: Amanda, Alexander. BA, U. Buffalo; MA, SUNY; PhD, MD, U. Colo. Zone Perfect cert. instr. Prof., rschr. U. Dar es Salaam, Tanzania; with Rappaport Assocs., Phila., 1974-94; exec. dir. Inst. for Parent/Child Svcs., Phila., 1978-94; pres., CEO Diabetes Edn. Ctr. Cape Cod, 2002—03. Mem. adj. faculty Temple U., Phila., 1974—94; aviation safety counselor FAA; cons., spkr. in field.; pres. Reach New Heights, Inc., 1994—2005; founder Fit to Fly. Mem. AAUP, Nat. Profl. Spkrs. Assn., Cosmopolitan Club, Orleans Yacht Club. Home: PO Box 1845 Orleans MA 02653-1845 Office Phone: 508-255-9570. Personal E-mail: rappaportmm@yahoo.com.

RAPPAPORT, YVONNE KINDINGER, educator; b. Crestline, Ohio, Feb. 15, 1928; d. Paul Theodore and Florence Iona (Cover) Kindinger; BS summa cum laude, Northwestern U., 1949; MA, Va. Poly. Inst. and State U., 1973, PhD, 1980; m. Norman Lewis Rappaport; children: Michael, Laura, Hilary, Stephen, Jocelyn. Pers. officer, then cons. and mgmt. analyst USAF, 1953-63; cons. mgmt. analysis, pers. and pub. rels., 1963-67; cons. program devel., instr. U. Va., 1967-70, dir. continuing edn. for women, 1970-75, dir. and faculty continuing edn. for adult, 1975-85, dir. for continuing edn., 1986-93, cons. human resources, 1993—, dir., performer theatre, children's theatre, radio and TV, 1953—; bd. dirs. Coalition Adult Edn. Orgns. U.S., 1979—, sec.-treas., 1981-83, v.p., 1983-84, pres.-elect, 1984-85, pres., 1985-87, chair internat. assocs. adult edn., 1987-89; U.S. rep. UNESCO conf., 1983; del. Buenos Aires World Assembly, 1985, Helsinki Peace Conf., 1986, Bangkok World Assembly, 1990; cons. in field. Mem. Va. Legis. Adv. Com. Continuing Edn., 1970-71, No. Va. Adv. Com. Ednl. Telecommunications, 1971—; bd. dirs. Home and Sch. Inst., Washington, 1971—; adv. bd. Svc. League Va., 1976-78. Recipient Meritorious Svc. award USAF, 1959; Career Devel. award ASTD/TOC, 1980, Outstanding Eucator award, Va. Tech, 1998. Mem.

AAUW, PTA, LWV (state dir. 1968-73, nat. pub. rels. com. 1970-75), Nat. Assn. Women Deans, Adminstrs. and Counselors (S.E. regional coord. 1973-76), Adult Edn. Assn. U.S. (nat. leadership award 1973, 74, 76, 78, 79, 82, 83, 86, 88; v.p. 1978-79; chmn. commn. status women in edn. 1972-74, dir. 1973-83, chmn. coun. affiliate orgns. 1974-75, chmn. pub. affairs 1975-78, chair program gen. session 1987), Adult Edn. Assn. Va. (pres. 1971-73; recognition of merit award 1971-73), Pers. and Guidance Assn., Nat. Univ. Extension Assn., Assn. Continuing Higher Edn., World Affairs Coun. (bd. dirs. 1987—), Am. Bus. Women Assn. (award 1960), Fairfax, Va. C. of C. (mem. edn. com. 1987—), Order Ea. Star, Phi Delta Kappa, Phi Delta Theta (v.p. programs, 1994, pres.-elect, 1994). Author handbooks and work books, also radio, TV scripts. Home: 3225 Atlanta St Fairfax VA 22030-2127 Office: Sch Continuing Edn U Va Charlottesville VA 22903

RAPPÉ, TERI WAHL, piano educator; b. Missoula, Mont., Apr. 4, 1945; d. Charley Franklin and Mary Evelyn (Beaver) Wheeler; m. Bruce Dennis Wahl, June 20, 1964 (div. 1982); 1 child, Maradee; m. Gerald Alan Rappé, Sept. 19, 1987; stepchildren: Rick, Susan. BMus with honors, U. Mont., 1971. Cert. secondary tchr. Wash.; nat. cert. music tchr. Piano instr., Missoula, Mont., 1962-72, Wenatchee, Wash., 1972—, Wenatchee Valley Coll., 1976—2004; ch. organist Ctrl. Christian Ch., Wenatchee, 1982-90; ch. pianist First Ch. of God, Wenatchee, 1990—. Accompanist Columbia Chorale, Wenatchee, 1984—98, Appleaires, Wenatchee, 1998—2002, Apollo Club, 2001—; percussionist Wenatchee Valley Symphony. Performer with Wenatchee Valley Symphony, 1992—, Am. Guild of Organists, 1992-99. Mem. Wash. State Music Tchrs. (pres. 1998-2000), Pi Kappa Lambda, Mu Phi Epsilon. Avocations: reading, backpacking, snowshoeing. Home: 227 Grover Ct Wenatchee WA 98801-1811

RAPPLEY, MARSHA D., dean, physician, educator; BS in Nursing, U. Mich., 1980; MD, Mich. State U. Coll. Human Medicine, 1984. Cert. in gen. pediatrics and devel. & behavioral pediatrics Am. Bd. Pediatrics. Resident in pediatrics Mich. State U. Coll. Human Medicine, faculty mem., 1988—, interim assoc. dean acad. affairs, 2002, interim chair Dept. Pediatrics & Human Devel., 2001—03, divsn. dir. gen. pediatrics and dir. gen. pediatric clinics, 1991—2001, assoc. dean acad. affairs, 2003—, prof. Dept. Pediatrics and Human Devel., acting dean, 2005—, divsn. dir. Devel. and Behavioral Pediatrics, dir. Collaborative Devel. Clinic. Office: Office of Dean Univ Mich Coll Human Medicine A118-E Fee Hall East Lansing MI 48824-1316 Office Phone: 517-353-4998. E-mail: rappley@msu.edu.*

RAQUET, MAUREEN GRAHAM, protective services official, educator; b. Seaford, Del., Jan. 28, 1955; d. Robert James and Helen Mary Graham; m. William Jameson Raquet; 1 child, Patrick. BA in Psychology, Lafayette Coll., 1976; MS in Juvenile Justice Adminstrn. and Criminal Justice, Shippensburg U., 1989. Cert. police officer Pa. Police officer Lower Merion Twp. Police Dept., Ardmore, Pa., 1978—80; foster care cons. The Impact Project, Allentown, Pa., 1993—94; juvenile probation officer Montgomery County Juvenile Probation Dept., Norristown, Pa., 1980—92; secure detention coord. Montgomery County Youth Ctr., Norristown, 1992—2000, exec. dir., 2000. Adj. prof. criminal justice West Chester (Pa.) U., 1994—, Montgomery County C.C., Blue Bell, Pa., 1997; mem. adv. bd. Foster Grandparent Program, Norristown, 1998—; bd. dirs. Plays For Living, Norristown, 1995—2000. Recipient Outstanding Scholarship in Juvenile Justice, Pa. Juvenile Ct. Judges' Commn., Ctr. Juvenile Justice Tng. and Rsch., 1989; scholar, Charles A. Dana Found., Lafayette Coll., 1973—76. Mem.: Pa. Assn. Probation, Parole and Corrections, Nat. Coun. Juvenile and Family Ct. Judges, Am. Corrections Assn., Nat. Juvenile Detention Assn., Montgomery County Juvenile Adv. Assn. (v.p. 1991—92), Juvenile Detention Ctrs. Assn. Pa. (mental health adv. bd. 1999—, bd. dirs. tng. commn. 2001—), Alpha Phi Sigma. Office: Montgomery County Youth Ctr 540 Port Indian Rd Norristown PA 19403

RAQUIDEL, DANIELLE COLETTE, language educator, researcher; b. France, 1946; arrived in U.S.A., 1985; 1 child, Sebastien stepchildren: Melissa, Luciano. Degree, U. Lyon, 1968; MA, U. Cinn., 1987, PhD, 1992. Rsch. asst. BBC TV, 1974—76; french prof. French Inst., Caracas, Venezuela, 1976—77, Inst. Univ. Pedagogico, Caracas, Venezuela, 1976—79; prof. Escuela de Artes Plasticas, Barcelona, 1979—81; rsch. asst. U. Cin., 1985—89; French & Spanish prof. U. S.C., Upstate, SC, 1990—. Co-pres. Piedmont Fgn. Lang. Collaborative, SC, 1995—97; mem. exec. coun. Cin. Annual Conf. Romance Lang. & Lit., Cin., 1993—99; region V rep. Am. Assn. Tchrs. French, 2000—06. Contbr. chapters to books Gale's Encyclopedia of World Education, 2001, Gale's Encyclopedia of the Press, 2002; co-author, editor: Ensemble Books 1-2, 1975. Bd. mem. LWV, Spartanburg, SC, 2001. Recipient Disting. Guest award, Nicaragua Govt., 1993, Honduras Govt., 1994. Mem.: Asociacion de Licenciadas y Doctores Españnles en los Estados Unidos, S.C. Fgn. Lang. Tchrs. Assn. Avocations: writing, sculpting, pottery, filmmaking, women's writing in Francophone and Hispanic literature. Office: USC Spartanburg 800 University Way Spartanburg SC 29303 Business E-Mail: draquidel@uscupstate.edu.

RAS, RONDA SUE, secondary school educator; b. Nevada, Iowa, Feb. 2, 1967; d. Ron and Theola Peck; m. Gerard-Jan Martin Ras, June 27, 1992; children: Suzanne Elise, Aaron Christopher, Maria Kathleen. BA in Edn., Wayne State Coll., Nebr., 1990, MA in Edn., 1995. Cert. tchr. Nebr., 1996. Tchr. lang. arts Walthill (Nebr.) H.S., 1990—91; supr. monitor Oak Forest (Ill.) H.S., 1991—93; tchr. lang. arts Winnebago (Nebr.) H.S., 1993—94; tchr. lang. arts and journalism Bancroft-Rosalie (Nebr.) H.S., 1994—. Instr. project challenge Nebr. C.C., Norfolk, Nebr., 1995—; coach varsity speech Bancroft-Rosalie (Nebr.) H.S., 1994—, dir. contest one-act, 1994—; mem. stars cadre Ednl. Svc. Unit 2, Fremont, Nebr., 2004—; mem. Bancroft-Rosalie Preschool Adv. Bd., 2005. Coach youth baseball Bancroft (Nebr.) Ball Assn., 2005—06; mem. governing coun. United Ch. Pender, Nebr., 2000—03. Avocations: piano, softball, travel, reading. Office: Bancroft-Rosalie High School 708 Main Bancroft NE 68004

RASBERRY, DAWN YVETTE, counselor; b. Aug. 1, 1963; BMusic, U. South Ala., Mobile, 1985; MEd, U. Ga., 1990. Acad. advisor U. Ga., Athens, 1987-90; counselor, therapist County Mental Health, Fairhope, Ala., 1991-93, Columbia, S.C., 1993-94; asst. band dir. Mobile County Schs., Mobile, 1994-95, counselor, choral dir., 1995—. Author: Vashti's Star, 1999. Min. of music Highpoint Bapt. Ch., Mobile, 1992-93, 94-97; musician Lily Bapt. Ch., Mobile, 1997—. Mem. Am. Counseling Assn., Nat. Music Tchrs. Assn., Romance Writers Am., Mobile Educators' Union, Omicron Kappa Delta, Sigma Alpha Iota, Abe Neefoo Kuo Honor Soc. (charter). E-mail: rasberry@hotmail.com.

RASCH, ELLEN MYRBERG, cell biology educator; b. Chicago Heights, Ill., Jan. 31, 1927; d. Arthur August and Helen Catherine (Stelle) Myrberg; m. Robert W. E. Rasch, June 17, 1950; 1 son, Martin Karl. PhB with honors, U. Chgo., 1945, BS in Biol. Sci., 1947, MS in Botany, 1948, PhD, 1950. Asst. histologist Am. Meat Inst. Found., Chgo., 1950-51; USPHS postdoctoral fellow U. Chgo., 1951-53, rsch. assoc. dept. zoology, 1954-59; rsch. assoc. Marquette U., Milw., 1962-65, assoc. prof. biology, 1965-68, prof. biology, 1968-75, Wehr disting. prof. biophysics, 1975-78; rsch. prof. biophysics East Tenn. State U., James H. Quillen Coll. Medicine, Johnson City, 1978-94, interim chmn. dept. cellular biophysics, 1986-94, prof. anatomy and cell biology, 1994—2004, prof. emerita, 2004—. Mem. Wis. Bd. Basic Sci. Examiners, 1971-75, sec. bd., 1973-75. Contbr. articles to profl. jours. Recipient Rsch. Career Devel. award, 1967-72, Tchg. Excellence and Disting. award Marquette U., 1975, Kreeger-Wolf vis. disting. prof. in biol. sci. Northwestern U., 1979. Mem. Royal Microscopic Soc., Am. Soc. Cell Biology, Am. Soc. Microscopy, The Histochem. Soc. (Outstanding Svc. award), Phi Beta Kappa, Sigma Xi. Home: 1504 Chickees St Johnson City TN 37604-7103 Office: East Tenn State Univ Dept Anatomy & Cell Biology PO Box 70582 Johnson City TN 37614-0582 Business E-Mail: rasch@etsu.edu.

RASHAD, PHYLICIA, actress, singer, dancer; b. Houston; m. Ahmad Rashad; children: William Bowles, Condola Phylea. Grad. magna cum laude, Howard U., N.Y. Mem. Negro Ensemble Co.; founder Phylicia Rashad and Co., 1990. Actor: (plays) The Cherry Orchard, 1973, Zora, 1981, A Raisin in the Sun, 1984, Gem of the Ocean, 2005, (Off-Broadway) The Duplex, 1972, Zooman and the Sign, 1980—81, Weep Not for Me, 1981, In an Upstate Motel, 1981, Puppetplay, 1983, Sons and Fathers of Sons, 1983; (Broadway plays) Ain't Supposed to Die a Natural Death, 1971, The Wiz, 1975, Dreamgirls, 1981, Into the Woods, 1988, Jelly's Last Jam, 1992—93, A Raisin in the Sun, 2004 (Tony award best actress in a play, 2004, Drama Desk award best actress in a play, 2004), Bernarda Alba, 2006; (films) The Broad Coalition, 1972, The Wiz, 1978, Once Upon a Time When We Were Colored, 1995, Free of Eden, 1999, Loving Jezebel, 1999, The Visit, 2000; (TV films) We're Fighting Back, 1981, Uncle Tom's Cabin, 1987 (Cable ACE award nom. best sup. actress, 1987), False Witness, 1989, Polly, 1989, Polly: Comin Home, 1990, Jailbirds, 1991, Hallelujah, 1993, David's Mother, 1994, The Possession of Michael D., 1995, The Babysitters Seduction, 1996, Free of Eden, 1999, The Old Settler, 2001, Murder, She Wrote: The Last Free Man, 2001; (TV series) One Life to Live, 1983—84, The Cosby Show, 1984—92 (NAACP Image award best actress, 1987, Emmy award nom. best actress, 1985, 1986), Santa Barbara, 1985, Cosby, 1996—2000, (voice) Little Bill, 1999—,; (TV guest appearances) The Love Boat, 1985, A Different World, 1988—90, Blossom, 1991, Touched by an Angel, 1994, 2002, The Cosby Mysteries, 1994, In the House, 1995, Bull, 2001. Recipient Theatre Artist award, Nat. Corp. Theatre Fund, 2006.*

RASKIN, JOY LYNN, art educator, silversmith; b. Manchester, N.H., May 3, 1967; d. Joel Barry and Judith Helena Raskin. BFA, RISD, 1990; MFA, U. Mass., Dartmouth, 1993. Instr. jewelry, silversmithing N.H. Inst. Art, Manchester, 1996—. Juror Am. Craft Coun., Highland, N.Y., 1998—. Exhibns. include Soc. Arts and Crafts, Boston, 1991, League N.H. Craftsmen, Brookfield Crafts Ctr., Conn. Office: PO Box 1422 Concord NH 03302-1422 Office Phone: 603-488-1301. Personal E-mail: spoonladyjr@juno.com.

RASMUSON, LISA MARIE, language educator; b. Fort Dix, NJ, Aug. 1, 1969; d. Christine Mary and John Edward Taintor (Stepfather). BA in Journalism, George Washington U., Washington, 1991, MEd, 1995. Cert. ESL tchr. NJ, 1998, elem. tchr. NJ, 2001. ESL tchr. Prince George's County Pub. Schs., Riverdale, Md., 1995—98, chmn. ESL dept., 1995—97; ESL tchr. Vineland City Pub. Schs., NJ, 1998—2001, Mt. Laurel Bd. Edn., NJ, 2001—. Contbr. articles to newspapers, mags. Founder Thoroughbred Grants in Edn., NJ, Hell's Angel Thoroughbred Rescue Award, NJ, 2003—. Alumni Grant in Edn. grantee, George Washington U., 1994—95, Edn. grantee, Washington Post, 1997. Mem.: NEA (assoc.), US Dressage Fedn., US Equestrian Fedn. Home: 1277 Smithville Rd Bordentown NJ 08505 Home Fax: 609-261-0022. Personal E-mail: lrasmuson@comcast.net.

RASMUSSEN, ALICE CALL, retired nursing educator; b. Grand Rapids, Mich., Dec. 16, 1947; d. Amon Burton and Jessie Pearl (Dann) Call; m. Charles P. Rasmussen, Apr. 16, 1972. BSN, Andrews U., 1971; MSN, Med. Coll. Ga., 1977; postgrad., Ferris State U., 1990. Staff nurse Lockwood-MacDonald Hosp., Petoskey, Mich., 1971—72; instr. Lake Michigan Coll., Benton Harbor, Mich., 1973—87; nursing coord. and health sci. dept. chair Lake Mich. Coll., Benton Harbor, Mich., 1986—2003; ret., 2003. Vice chair Mich. Bd. Nursing, 1998-2000; bd. trustees Watervliet Cmty. Hosp., 2002-Mem. AAUW, NAFE, Mich. League for Nursing, Mich. Coun. Nursing Edn. Adminstrs., Nat. Ordn. ADN, S.W. Mich. Nurse Educator Network, Sigma Theta Tau. Home: 9088 4th St Berrien Springs MI 49103-1637

RASMUSSEN, CAREN NANCY, health facility administrator; b. Ft. Riley, Kans., July 7, 1950; d. Stanley Junior and Katherina Wilhelmina R. AAS, Grand Rapids Jr. Coll., 1970; BS, U. Md., 1977; MS, Johns Hopkins U., 1997. Cert. profl. contracts mgr. Contract specialist Kadena Air Base, Okinawa, 1979-81; med. sec. Walter Reed Army Med. Ctr., Washington, 1970-72, sec. procurement, 1972-76, contract specialist, 1976-79, 81-84, procurement analyst, 1984—, sr. contracting specialist, 1988—2001, Nat. Cancer Inst., 2001—. Fellow NAFE; mem. Nat. Contract Mgmt. Assn. Democrat. Avocations: photography, stamp collecting/philately, gardening, travel. Home: 18632 Clovercrest Cir Olney MD 20832-3057 Office: Nat Cancer Inst Rsch Contracts br Rockville MD 20852 Business E-Mail: cnrasmussen@jhu.edu.

RASMUSSEN, DIANNE, English educator; BA, U. Wis. Eau Claire, 1974; MEd in Profl. Devel., U. Wis. La Crosse, 2001. English instr. Stanley-Boyd H.S., Stanley, Wis., 1974—; adj. prof. U. of Wis. La Crosse, 1999—2005. Cons. Learning Quest Assocs., Inc., Lewiston, Minn., 2000—. Recipient Herb Kohl Ednl. award, 2002, Wal-Mart Tchr. of the Yr. award, Wal-Mart Found., 2004, Gov.'s Svc. award, State of Wis., 2005. Office: Stanley-Boyd High School 507 East 1st Ave Stanley WI 54768 Office Phone: 715-644-5534 147.

RASMUSSEN, JO ANNE DICKENS, speech edueator, theater director; b. Creston, Iowa, Feb. 24, 1928; d. Joseph Harrod and Therese Faye Partello Dickens; m. Richard Jens Rasmussen, June 7, 1953; children: Robin Joel, Lisa Anne. BFA, Drake U., 1945—49. Speech and drama dir. St. Patrick's H.S., Walla Walla, Wash., 1958—60, St. Paul's Sch. For Girls, Walla Walla, 1960—62; speech and acting instr. Whitman Coll., Walla Walla, 1973—84, 1973—84; dir. of traveling theatre for children Walla Walla C.C., 1973—84, speech instr., 1973—84, dir. of drama and speech, 1984—2003. Profl. actress Dartmouth Theatre Co. at Dartmouth Coll., Hanover, NH, 1968. Actor: (plays) Mother Courage by Berthold Brect, Twelth Night by William Shakespeare, Antigone by Annilh; dir.: (outdoor amphitheatre productions) Various Broadway Musicals. Actress, dir. Walla Walla Little Theatre, 1953—83; dir. of living history theatre co. Walla Walla Hist. Soc., 1995—2000. Recipient Allied Arts award, Allied Arts Assn. of Wash., 1986, Exemplary Status, Wash. C.C. Humanities Assn., 1986, Honored for Tchg. Excellence, U. of Tex., 1989, Excellence in Tchg. Cert., Wash. Fedn. of Teachers, 1990, Spl. Recognition for Outstanding Direction, Am. Coll. Theatre Festival, 1992, Excellence in Acting, 1992, Excellence award, Walla Walla C.C. Found., 1994, Cmty. Svc. award, Walla Walla Valley C. of C., 1999, Recognition award, NW Drama Conf., 1998. Mem.: Am. Coll. Theatre Festival (assoc.), Walla Walla Little Theatre (life). Home: 310 Juniper St Walla Walla WA 99362-3331 Personal E-mail: joanne.rasmussen@charter.net.

RASMUSSEN, KATHLEEN MAHER, nutritional sciences educator; b. Dayton, Ohio, Mar. 1, 1948; AB, Brown U., 1970; MSc, Harvard U., 1975, ScD, 1978. Registered dietitian. Tchr. sci. Cape Hatteras Elem. Sch., Buxton, NC, 1971-72; analytical chemist Berkley Machine Works, Foundry Co., Norfolk, Va., 1972-73; rsch. assoc. dept. nutrition Harvard U., Boston, 1978; instr. div. nutritional scis. Cornell U., Ithaca, N.Y., 1981-83, asst. prof., 1983-88, assoc. prof., 1988-96, assoc. dir. grad. affairs, 1992-95, prof., 1996—, assoc. dean, sec. Univ. Faculty, 1997-2000. Com. mem. NAS, Washington, 1988-96; Pew faculty scholar in nutrition Nat. Ctr. Sci. Rsch., Meudon-Bellevue, France, 1989-90. Trustee Cornell U., 2004—. NIH trainee, 1974-80; NIH grantee, 1984-90, 87—, 93—, 2001—, various other grants and awards, 1982-85, 88-89, 89-92, 92-94, 93-96, 97-99, 2001—. Mem.: Internat. Soc. Rsch. in Human Milk and Lactation (pres. 2002—03), Brit. Nutrition Soc., Am. Soc. Clin. Nutrition, Am. Soc. Nutrition Scis. (sec. 1999—2002, pres. 2004—05). Office: Cornell U Div Nutritional Sci 111 Savage Hall Ithaca NY 14853-6301 Office Phone: 607-255-2290. Business E-Mail: kmr5@cornell.edu.

RASMUSSEN, LISA ANNE, art department administrator, art educator, art gallery director; b. Walla Walla, Wash., Mar. 19, 1963; d. Richard Jens and Jo Anne Dickens Rasmussen. AA in Liberal Arts, Walla Walla CC, 1983; BA in Fine Arts, Whitman Coll., 1986; MA in Coll. Instrn. in Art, Ea. Wash. U., 1994. Dir. children's theatre Walla Walla CC, 1980—2002, drawing instr., 1987—99, art dept. chair, fine arts instr., 2000—; tech. asst. Sheehan Gallery, Whitman Coll., Walla Walla, 1986—87; drawing instr. Columbia Basin Coll., Pasco, Wash., 1993; gallery dir. Walla Walla CC Fine Arts Gallery. Sound technician Walla Walla CC Found. Summer Musical Prodns., 1985—98; lighting designer China Pavilion Theatre, Walla Walla CC, 1986—2001. Dir.: (plays) Charlie and the Chocolate Factory. Mem.: Blue Mountain Arts Alliance, Carnegie Art Ctr., Nat. Mus. Women in Arts. Home: 310 Juniper Walla Walla WA 99362 Office: Walla Walla CC 500 Tausick Way Walla Walla WA 99362 Office Phone: 509-527-1873. Personal E-mail: lisa.rasmussen@charter.net. Business E-Mail: lisa.rasmussen@wwcc.edu.

RASMUSSEN, TERESA J., lawyer, insurance company executive; b. Fergus Falls, Minn., Oct. 9, 1956; BS magna cum laude, Moorhead State Univ., 1981; JD, Univ. N. Dak., 1984. CPA 1981; bar: Colo. 1984, Minn. 1986. Trial atty., tax div. US Dept. Justice, Washington, 1984—86; assoc. Oppenheimer Wolff & Donnelly, Mpls., 1986—89; exec. v.p. & gen. counsel Northeast Securities Corp., Mpls., 1989—90; various legal positions up to v.p. & gen. counsel, IDS Life Ins. subsidiary Am. Express Fin. Corp., 1990—2005; sr. v.p., gen. counsel & sec. Thrivent Fin. for Lutherans, Mpls., 2005—. Mem.: ABA, Minn. State Bar Assn., Hennepin County Bar Assn. Office: Thrivent Financial for Lutherans 625 4th Ave S Minneapolis MN 55415-1624

RASOR, DINA LYNN, journalist, private investigator; b. Downey, Calif., Mar. 21, 1956; d. Ned Shaurer and Genevieve Mercia (Eads) R.; m. Thomas Taylor Lawson, Oct. 4, 1980. BA in Polit. Sci., U. Calif., Berkeley, 1978. Editorial asst. ABC News, Washington, 1978-79; researcher Pres.'s Commn. on Coal, Washington, 1979; legis. asst. Nat. Taxpayers Union, Washington, 1979-81; founder, dir. Project on Mil. Procurement, Washington, 1981-89; investigative reporter Lawson-Rasor Assocs., El Cerrito, Calif., 1990-92; pres., CEO, investigator Bauman & Rasor Group, El Cerrito, Calif., 1993—. Author: The Pentagon Underground, 1985; editor: More Bucks, Less Bang, 1983; contbr. articles to profl. jours. Recipient Sigma Delta Chi Outstanding Leadership award Soc. Profl. Journalists, 1986; named to register Esquire Mag., 1986, Nat. Jour., 1986. Mem. United Ch. Christ. Office Phone: 510-235-5021.

RASOR, DORIS LEE, retired secondary school educator; b. Gonzales, Tex., June 25, 1929; d. Leroy and Ora (Power) DuBose; m. Jimmie E. Rasor, Dec. 27, 1947; children: Jimmy Lewis, Roy Lynn. BS summa cum laude, Abilene (Tex.) Christian U., 1949. Part-time sec. Abilene Christian U., 1946-50; sec. Radford Wholesale Grocery, Abilene, 1950-52; tchr. Odessa (Tex.) High Sch., 1967-98. Author play: The Lost Pearl, 1946. Recipient Am. Legion award, 1946. Mem. AAUW, Classroom Tchrs. Assn., Tex. Tchrs. Assn., NEA, Tex. Bus. Educators Assn., "W" Club for Women, Alpha Delta Kappa (pres. 1976-78), Alpha Chi. Mem. Ch. Of Christ. Avocations: reading, cooking, camping, fishing. Home: 3882 Kenwood Dr Odessa TX 79762-7018 Personal E-mail: drjrasor@apex2000.net.

RASSAI, RASSA, electrical engineering educator; b. Tehran, Oct. 15, 1951; d. Farjollah and Farideh (Mofakhami) R. BSEE with high honors, U. Md., 1973, MSEE, 1975, PhD, 1985. Sr. engr. Traycor Electronics Co., Arlington, Va., 1975; project engr. Iran Electronics Industry, Tehran, 1977-79; lectr. U. Md., 1980, 81-91, George Washington U., Washington, 1980-82, George Mason U., Fairfax, Va., 1982; rschr. elec. engring. dept. U. md., 1986-92; prof. No. Va. C.C., Annandale, 1986—, program head engring./elec. engring. tranfer program, 1991. Contbr. articles to profl. jours.; patentee remote telephone links. Mem. NOW Democrat. Avocations: reading, philosophy. Home: 6628 Medinah Ln Alexandria VA 22312-3117

RASTLE, MAXINE SHIFLET COLE, retired elementary school educator; b. Glenville, W.Va., Sept. 6, 1937; d. Walter P. and May (Floyd) Shiflet; m. Charles Cole, Dec. 22, 1960 (dec. 1977); children: C.D., Debra Cole Moss; m. Franklin S. Rastle, June 15, 1979. BA, Glenville State Coll., 1958; MA, W.Va. U., 1961, postgrad., 1992. Cert. elem. tchr., W.Va. Tchr. grade 1 and 3 Lathrop Sch., Painesville, Ohio, 1958-59, 59-60; tchr. Putnam Sch., Marietta, Ohio, 1960-61; phys. edn./health tchr. Weston (W.Va.) Jr. High Sch., 1961-66; tchr. grade 1 and 3 Weston Cen. Sch., 1971—2003, ret., 2003. Active Dem. Women, Glenville, 1992—, Farm Bur., Glenville, PTA/Cen. Sch., 1992; sec. Sunday Sch, substitute tchr. Mem. NEA, W.Va. Edn. Assn., Lewis County Edn. Assn., FFA Alumni Assn. (pres. 1991-93), OES (worthy matron 1966-67). Democrat. Baptist. Avocations: cake decorating, cooking, sewing, crafts. Home: 1760 US Hwy 33W Weston WV 26452 E-mail: mrastle@verizon.net.

RATCHFORD MERCHANT, BETTY JO, retired elementary school educator; b. Huntsville, Ala., Feb. 9, 1937; d. Howard Clyde and Margaret (Kyle) Wikle; m. McClellan Ratchford, 1960 (div.); children: McClellan III, Margaret Lee, Rosalyn Hampton; m. Curtis Merchant, 1992. BS, Auburn U.; MEd, Ala. A&M U., 1998. Cert. tchr. elem. Tchr. elem. Gilbert Sch., Atlanta, Madison County Sch. Sys., Huntsville, Ala., Riverton Elem. Sch., Mt. Carmel Elem. Sch., 2003. Named Tchr. of Yr. for Madison County, 1992. Mem. NEA, AAUW, Ala. Edn. Assn., Environ. Edn. Assn. Ala., Madison County Edn. Assn. Episcopalian. Avocations: poetry, singing, reading, painting, rock climbing. Home: 11033 Everest Cr Huntsville AL 35803

RATHBUN, CHRISTINA SUE, literature and language educator; b. Junction City, Kans., Mar. 14, 1952; d. Alvin Clyde and Jewell Lavon Erichsen; m. Kendall Wade Rathbun, Nov. 24, 1982; children: Nancy Margaret, Emmylou Elizabeth, Sarah Callie. BA, Ft. Hays State Coll., Kans., 1976; MA, Ft. Hays State U., Kans., 1980. Cert. English 7-12 highly qualified Commr. Kans. State Dept. Edn., 2004. English tchr. Ellsworth H.S., Kans., 1976—79, El Dorado H.S., 1980—81, Ellsworth H.S., 1981—. Mem. prof. devel. com. Ellsworth H.S., Kans., 1990—2000. Cm. leader 4-H; Sunday sch. tchr.; Bible sch. tchr. Named Hon. Commr., Nat. Youth Leadership Forum, 2005; recipient 25 Yrs. Svc. award, Unified Sch. Dist. 327 Ellsworth-Kanopolis-Geneseo, 2003, 25 Yr. Appreciation cert., Sch. of Edn. U. Kans., 2003. Presbyterian. Office: Ellsworth HS 11th and Kans Ellsworth KS 67439 Office Phone: 785-472-4471.

RATHER, LUCIA PORCHER JOHNSON, library administrator; b. Durham, N.C., Sept. 12, 1934; d. Cecil Slayton and Lucia Lockwood (Porcher) Johnson; m. John Carson Rather, July 11, 1964; children: Susan Wright, Bruce Carson. Student, Westhampton Coll., 1951-53; AB in History, U. N.C., 1955, MS in Library Sci., 1957; PhD in History, George Washington U., 1994. Cataloger Library of Congress, Washington, 1957-64, bibliographer, 1964-66, systems analyst, 1966-70; group head MARC Devel. Office, 1970-73, asst. chief, 1973-76, acting chief, 1976-77, dir. for cataloging, 1976-91. Chmn. standing com. on cataloguing Internat. Fedn. Library Assns., 1976-81; sec. Working Group on Content Designators, 1972-77; chmn. Working Group on Corp. Headings, 1978-79, Internat. ISBD Rev. Com., 1981-87. Co-author: the MARC II Format, 1968. Recipient Libr. Congress Disting. Svc. award, 1991, Disting. Alumnus award U. N.C. Sch. Libr. and Info. Sci., 1992. Mem. ALA (Margaret Mann award 1985, Melvil Dewey award 1991), Phi Beta Kappa. Democrat. Presbyterian. Home: 438 Heron Point Chestertown MD 21620-1680

RATHKE, BARBARA JOANNE ANDREWS, art educator; b. Carroll, Iowa; d. Wayne Henry and Bernice Marie Andrews; m. Jerome William Rathke, Aug. 31, 1968; children: Benjamin Jerome, Joseph Andrews. BA, North Ctrl. Coll., 1986. Cert. tchr., Ill. Art tchr. Dist. 68, Edgewood Sch., Woodridge, Ill., 1987—. Program chmn. Faithful Circle Quilters, Downers Grove, Ill., 1986; coord. quilt rsch. days Early Am. Mus., Mahomet, Ill., 1988; mem. PTO, Woodridge, 1971—. Recipient Diane Duvigneaud Sr. Art award North Ctrl. Coll., 1986; named to Pres.'s List for Acad. Achievement, North Ctrl. Coll., 1984, 2003. Mem. NEA, Nat. Art Edn. Assn., Am. Quilters Soc., Ill. Edn. Assn., Woodridge Edn. Assn. Avocations: quiltmaking, gardening with hist. roses and native perennials. Office: Edgewood Sch 7900 Woodridge Dr Woodridge IL 60517-3824

RATHKE, SHEILA WELLS, marketing professional, consultant; b. Columbia, S.C., Aug. 9, 1943; d. Walter John and Betty Marie (McLaughlin) Wells; m. David Bray Rathke, Sept. 1966 (dec. 1997); 1 child, Erinn Michele. BA summa cum laude, U. Pitts., 1976, postgrad., 1976-77. Loan coord. Equibank, Pitts., 1961-65; office mgr. U.S. Steel Corp., Pitts., 1966-70; various account and mgmt. positions Burson-Marsteller, Pitts., 1977-87, exec. v.p., gen. mgr., 1987-94, CEO Can. ops. Toronto, Montreal, Ottawa, Vancouver, 1994-95; sr. v.p., dir. corp. devel. Young and Rubicam, Inc., N.Y.C., 1995-99, COO, 1999-2000; asst. provost strategic and program devel. U. Pitts., 2001—. Instr. Slippery Rock Coll., Pitts., 1984-85; adviser Exec. Report Mag., Pitts., 1986-88, A Better Chance, N.Y.C., 1996-2000, N.Y. Philharm., 1997-99. Trustee U. Pitts., 1976-80, mem. alumni bd. dirs., 1990-94; trustee Robert Morris Coll., 1992-95; bd. dirs. Vocat. Rehab. Ctr., 1987-93, Freewheelers, 1989-92, Pitts. Hist. Soc., River City Brass Band, Quantam Theatre, 2003-. Named Disting. Alumnus, U. Pitts., 1992, Legacy Laureate, 2000. Mem. Female Execs. Am., Am. Assn. Advt. Agys. (chair ea. region 1994-95), Pitts. Advt. Club (bd. dirs. 1988-91, pres. 1990), Alpha Sigma Lambda (charter). Avocations: skiing, reading, gardening, travel, photography. Home: 1819 Sarah St Apt 2 Pittsburgh PA 15203 Office: U Pitts Cathedral of Learning Pittsburgh PA 15260- E-mail: sheilarathke@msn.com.

RATHMANN, PEGGY, writer, illustrator; b. St. Paul; BA in Psychology, U. Minn.; student, Am. Acad. Chgo., Atelier Lack, Mpls., Otis Parsons Sch. Design, L.A. Author: Ruby the Copycat (Most Promising New Author Cuffie award Pubs. Weekly 1991), Good Night, Gorilla (ALA Notable Children's Book 1994), Officer Buckle and Gloria (Caldecott medal 1996), Ten Minutes Till Bedtime, 1998 (ALA Notable Children's Book 1998), The Day The Babies Crawled Away, 2003; illustrator: Bootsie Barker Bites, 1992. Office: Penguin Putnam Inc 345 Hudson St Fl 15 New York NY 10014-4502

RATHNAU, HEATHER HEARN, music educator, writer; b. San Antonio, Tex., Mar. 8, 1958; d. Claude Adam Hearn, Jr. and Mildred Ruby Damron; m. Ronald Alan Rathnau, Aug. 1, 1981; children: Alison Renee, Mallory Dawn. MusB magna cum laude, Baylor U., 1980, MusM, 1982. Pvt. music and voice tchr., Houston, 1984—; prin., owner Theory Time, Mo. City, Tex., 1996—. Guest instr. Schmitt Music Expo, 1999, Mpls., 2005; lectr. in field. Author: Theory Time, 1996, 2002. Mem.: Music Tchrs. Nat. Assn., Tex. Music Tchrs. Assn., Forum Music Tchrs. Assn. (pres. 1992—94), Nat. Piano Tchrs. Guild (adjudicator 1990—2005), Houston (Tex.) Music Tchrs. Assn. (v.p. 1989—90), Music Tchrs. Nat. Conf., Houston (Tex.) Fedn. Music Clubs, Mu Phi Epsilon. Republican. Baptist. Avocations: travel, reading, gardening. Home: 6639 Sutters Creek Trail Missouri City TX 77459

RATHORE, UMA PANDEY, utilities executive; b. Mar. 5, 1950; d. O Nath and R Devi Pandey; m. Ram N.S. Rathore, Dec. 18, 1978; children: Dinesh, Rana. BS, Kanpur U., 1967, MS, 1969. Adviser Consul Gen. of Iceland to India, 1976-85; v.p. Nevaid Cons., 1974-82; with North Jersey Utilities, Mount Freedom, N.J., 1983—, pres. Sr. ptnr. Translantic Cons.; founder Maxim Imports, 1994—; ind. mgmt. cons.; bd. dirs. Revel Inc., N.Y. Mem. ethics bd. Randolph Twp., N.J., 1986-91, county and state rep. Shongum Sch. PTA, 1989—, mem. multicultural com., 1993-94; membership chmn. LWV, 1979-81, com. person Dem. dist. 3 Randolph Twp., 1992, 94, mem. ethics com., 1994, mem. com., 1995; mem. drug action com. Randolph Twp., 1994, 95, 96—; mem. Dem. task force N.J. Women's Polit. Caucus, 1994; county and state rep. Randolph Intermediate Sch. PTA, 1993-94, bd. edn. rep., 1996—; mem. PTA coun. Randolph Twp. Schs.; legis. chair Morris County Coun. PTA, 1997—, counselor Region I; mem. Morris Mus., Macculloch Hall, Frelinghuysen Arboretum; mem. Ctr. for Study of Presidency, 1997; mem. DBE, 1999. Mem. Internat. Platform Assn., Dau. Brit. Empire, Acad. Polit. Sci., Kiwanis Club Smithsonian, Libr. of Congress, Fgn. Policy Assn., N.Y. Acad. Scis., Nat. Trust Hist. Preservation, Nat. Wildlife Fedn. Democrat. Avocations: reading, jogging, hiking, mountain climbing. Home and Office: 3 Hickory Pl Randolph NJ 07869-4528

RATICK, RANDIE H., music educator, elementary school educator; b. Ellenville, N.Y., Apr. 14, 1956; d. Saul and Rose Finkelstein; m. Lawrence Richard Ratick, Oct. 1, 1983; 1 child, Benjamin. BFA, SUNY, Buffalo, 1978, MFA, 1979. Cert. tchr. Music tchr. Circleville (N.Y.) Mid. Sch., 1979—85, Hagan Elem. Sch., Poughkeepsie, NY, 1985—. Music coord. k-5 Spackenkill Union Free Sch. Dist. Grantee, Cmty. Found. Dutchess County, 1992—93, Mid-Hudson Tchrs. Ctr., 2001, 2002, Dutchess County Arts Coun., 2001, 2002, 2003, 2004. Mem.: Dutchess County Music Educators Assn. (exec. bd.), Music Educators Nat. Conf., N.Y. State Sch. Music Assn. Avocations: reading, crafts. Home: 454 N Elting Corners Rd Highland NY 12528 Office Phone: 845-463-7840.

RATLIFF, MARGUERITE, special education educator; b. Ft. Walton Beach, Fla., Jan. 6, 1954; d. James Francis and Marguerite (Banister) R. BS, So. Ill. U., 1984; MS in Edn., Western Ill. U., 1994. Cert. tchr., Ill. Tchr. spl. edn. Griggsville (Ill.) Schs., 1984—. Camp cir. Camp Callahan for Handicapped, Quincy, Ill., 2000—; peer ptnr. 4 Rivers Spl. Edn. Dist., 1992—. Writing: plays. Lay ministry assoc. United Meth. Ch., 1997—. Mem. United Meth. Women, Pittsfield Theatre Guild. Avocations: writing, directing plays, collecting St. Nicholas statues, youth activities. Office: Griggsville Schs Stanford and Liberty St Griggsville IL 62340

RATLIFF, MARY JEAN DOUGHERTY, fine arts educator; b. Wichita Falls, Tex., July 25, 1933; d. Robert Byron and Thelma Irene (Dickson) Dougherty; m. Charles Richard Ratliff, Aug. 28, 1953; children: David Charles, Richard Byron, Melany Elaine, James Brett. Student, Tex. Tech. U., 1952-53; AAS, Richland U., 1975; BFA, U. North Tex., 1978. Art instr. Brookhaven Coll., Dallas, 1982-97. Exhibited in Watercolor U.S.A. Show, 1998, 2002. Com. mem. Tex. Bicentennial Com., Farmers Branch, Tex., 1975-76, Imagination Celebration, 1990-91. Named to Notable Women of Tex., 1984-85. Mem.: Internat. Soc. Exptl. Artists (signature mem. status), Nat. Mus. Women in the Arts (charter mem.), Southwestern Watercolor Soc., Tex. Visual Arts Assn. (signature mem. status), Farmers Br. Carrollton Art Assn. (life; founder, twice past pres., v.p., sec., treas.). Republican. Baptist. Avocations: boating, travel, photography, sewing, ping pong/table tennis. Home: 1202 Mackie Dr Carrollton TX 75007-4835

RATNER, ELLEN FAITH, news analyst, news correspondent, writer; b. Cleve., Aug. 28, 1951; d. Harry Ratner and Anne Spott. BA, Goddard Coll., 1974; EdM, Harvard U., 1978. Coord. women's svcs. Homophile Cmty. Health Svc., Boston, 1971-73; co-dir., co-founder Boundaries Therapy Ctr., Acton, Mass., 1973-86; dir. psychiat. day treatment program South Shore Mental Health Ctr., Quincy, Mass., 1974-81; v.p. rsch., devel. and svc., dir. ARC Rsch. Found. Addiction Recovery Corp., Rockville, Mass., 1986-90; health care cons., dir. Found. for Addiction Rsch., 1990-94; White House reporter, bur. chief Talk Radio News Svc., Washington, 1991—, chief polit. corr., news analyst; polit. analyst FOX News Channel, 1997—; Washington bur. chief, polit. editor Talkers Mag., 1996—; CEO Coll. Media News Co. Tchr. Curry Coll., Milton, Mass., 1979-80; cons. program devel. Addiction Recovery Corp., 1984-86; developer, planner The Art's in Mileau Treatment of Phychiatric Outpatients, Quincy, 1980, New Eng.'s first conf. on Chem. Dependency and AIDS, 1988. Author: The Other Side of the Family: A Book for Recovery from Abuse, Incest and Neglect, 1990, 101 Ways to Get Your Progressive Issues on Talk Radio, 1997; mem. adv. bd. The Counselor Mag., 1987-90; appeared on nat. TV and radio shows including C-SPAN, The Oprah Winfrey Show, CNN, Nat. Empowerment TV, others; co-host (radio) Washington Reality Check, Good Day USA, New World Chronicle; polit. corr, Talk Radio Countdown Show; prodr. Talk Daily. Bd. trustees, mem. exec. com., vis. com. presdl. search com. Goddard Col., Plainfield, Vt. 1977-81; bd. trustees Samaritan Coll., L.A., 1988-90; bd. dirs. Nat. Lesbian and Gay Health Found., Washington, 1985-92, pres., exec. com., program com., program chair; v.p. Harry Ratner Human Svcs. Fund, Cleve., 1991—; mem. adv. bd. Women of Washington, Inc., 1992—; bd. dirs. Theater Chamber Players, Kennedy Ctr., Washington, 1988-91, An Uncommon Legacy Found., N.Y.C., 1993—, The Ctr. for Spiritual Enlightment, Falls Church, Va., 1994—. Recipient Cmty. Svc. award Lesbian and Gay Counseling Svc., Boston, 1985, The Addams-Brown award Nat. Lesbian and Gay Health Found., 1993. Mem. Nat. Assn. Radio Talk Show Hosts, Mass. Assn. Day treatment Adminstrs. (chair regulations and standards com. 1979-81), Lily Dale Assembly. Democrat. Jewish. Avocation: writing works on spiritualism. Office: Talk Radio News Svc 2514 Mill Rd NW Washington DC 20007-2950 Address: FOX News Channel 1211 Avenue of the Americas New York NY 10036

RATNER, GAYLE, special education educator; b. Bronx, NY; BS, SUNY, Plattsburgh, 1991, MS in Edn., 1993. Cert. spl. edn. grades K-12 and elem. edn. grades N-6. Spl. edn. tchr. Chazy (N.Y.) Ctrl. Rural Sch., 1991—. Asst. chief reader N.Y. State Tchr. Cert. Examinations, mem. students with disabilities content adv. com.; instr. N.Y. State United Tchrs. Effective Tchg. Program, 1999—, mentor coord.; mem. policy bd. North Country Tchr. Resource Ctr.; new tchr. mentor coord. Chazy Ctrl. Rural Sch. Mem.: N.Y. State United Tchrs., Chazy Tchrs. Assn. (pres. 1995—2005, newsletter editor 2003—), Nat. Bd. Profl. Tchg. Stds. (spl. edn. and elem. edn. com. 2000—, bd. dirs.). Office: Chazy Ctrl Rural Sch 609 Route 191 Chazy NY 12921

RATNER, MARCIA, research scientist; b. Hartford, Conn., June 24, 1960; d. William and Gertrude Chorches Ratner. BA in Psychology, Boston U., 1995, PhD, 2004. Project mgr. dept. neurology Boston U., 1998—2004; rsch. assoc. in neurology Boston U. Sch. Medicine, 1998—, instr. toxicology and forensic toxicology, 2000—, rsch. assoc. pharm., 2004—. CEO, v.p. Chem. Safety Net, Inc., 2002—04; counselor Specialized Housing, Brookline, Mass., 1995—2004. Mem.: N.Y. Acad. Sci., Am. Conf. Govt. Indsl. Hygiene, Soc. Occupl. Environ. Health, Soc. Occupl. Health, Soc. for Neurosci., Mass. Neuropsychol. Soc., Am. Acad. Clin. Toxicology, Internat. Neurotoxicol. Assn., Combined Jewish Philanthropies, Psi Chi, Alpha Phi Omega. Jewish. Avocations: horseback riding, guitar, running, skiing. Office: Boston U Sch Medicine L-603 715 Albany St Boston MA 02118-2526 E-mail: marcia@bu.edu.

RATTNER, KARLENE SUSAN KATHERINE, special education educator; b. Dover, NJ, Jan. 22, 1981; d. Steven Wayne and Jeanne Steffanie Rattner. BA in Edn. and Music, Coll. St. Elizabeth, Morristown, NJ, 2003. Cert. elem. edn. NJ Dept. Edn., 2003, tchr. of the handicapped (pre-k- 12) NJ Dept. Edn., 2003. Resource tchr. Sandshore Elem. Sch., Budd Lake, NJ, 2003—05; spl. edn. tchr. Mt. Olive Mid. Sch., Budd Lake, 2005—. County com. mem., Mt. Olive Township, NJ, 2001; religious edn. tchr. St. Michael's Cath. Ch., Netcong, NJ, youth leader, 2004—. Mem.: EAMO, NEA, N.J. Edn. Assn. Republican. Roman Catholic. Avocations: reading, music, travel, voluteering. Office: Mt Olive Board of Education Route 46 Budd Lake NJ 07828 Office Phone: 973-691-4006. Personal E-mail: kars_song@yahoo.com. Business E-Mail: krattner@mtoliveboe.org.

RATUM, CECILIA BANGLOY, retired psychologist; b. Jones, Isabela, Philippines, Feb. 1, 1935; arrived in U.S., 1968, naturalized, 1974; d. Federico Reyes and Vivina Pastor Bangloy; m. Pablo Agpaoa Ratum, Apr. 21, 1958; children: Nympha, Locelia. Psychology program, U. San Francisco, 1980—81; MA in Elem. Counseling, San Francisco State U., 1975; grad. program, Philippine Normal U., 1963, BS in Elem. Edn., 1955. Cert. tchr. Ilocos Norte Normal Sch., Philippines, 1953, nat. cert. sch. psychologist 1989. Instr. Philippine Wesleyan Coll., Cabanatuan, Philippines, 1955—56; critic tchr. Philippine Women's U., Manila, 1956—57; head tchr., classroom tchr. Philippine Pub. Schs., Jones, 1957—60, dist. guidance coord., 1960—68; filing clk. Pacific Telephone, San Francisco, 1968—69; substitute tchr. San Francisco Unified Sch. Dist., 1969—70, counselor, 1970—78, tchr., 1978—79, counselor, 1979—81, psychologist, 1981—98; ret., 1998—2002; psychologist San Francisco Unified Sch. Dist., 2002—04; ret., 2004. Team leader for sch. pschologist San Francisco Unified Sch. Dist., 1984—86, supr. sch. psychology intern, 1993—96, cadre leader for sch. psychologists, 1997—98. Mem. JCC, San Francisco. Mem.: Calif. Ret. Tchrs. Assn. (San Francisco Divsn.), Sixty Plus San Francisco U. Beta Chpt., Internat. Dyslexia Assn., Calif. Assn. Sch. Psychologists, Nat. Assn. Sch. Psychologists, San Francisco State U. Alumni Assn. (life), San Francisco State U. Osher Learning Inst. (life). Avocations: reading, writing, music, writing. Home: 168 Lowell St San Francisco CA 94112-4307 Personal E-mail: ratum5f@sbcglobal.net.

RATZER, MARY BOYD, librarian, language educator; b. Troy, N.Y., Sept. 6, 1945; d. John Leo and Katherine M. (Van Derpool) Boyd; m. Philip J. Ratzer, July 30, 1972; children: Joseph, David. BA cum laude, Coll. of St. Rose, Albany, N.Y., 1967; MA, SUNY, Albany, 1968, MLS, 1981. Cert. secondary tchr., sch. libr. media specialist, N.Y. Secondary tchr. English, Shenendehowa Cen. Sch., Clifton Park, N.Y., 1968-85; sch. libr. media specialist Shendehowa Cen. Sch., Clifton Park, 1985—2003; internship coord. Sch. Info. Sci. and Policy SUNY, Albany. Coord., mentor tchr. intern program; lectr. SUNY Grad. Sch. Info. Sci. and Policy, Albany; frequent speaker at state-level confs., 1986—; mem. adv. bd. U. Albany Grad. Sch. Info. Sci. and Policy; advocacy cons. Sch. Libr. Sys. Assn.; cons. info. literacy curriculum Regional Bd. Coop. Ednl. Svcs. Sch. Libr. Sys.; mem. adv. coun. sch. libr. media, N.Y. State Edn. Dept.; interim coord. WSW BOCES Sch. Libr. Sys., 2005-06. Contbr.: N.Y. State Teacher Resource Guides for Learning Standards; contbr. articles to profl. jours. Recipient grants. Mem. ALA, Am. Assn. Sch. Librs., N.Y. Libr. Assn., Nat. Coun. Tchrs. English, N.Y. Assn. for Supervision and Curriculum Devel., N.Y. State Acad. for Tchg. and Learning, Libr. User Edn. Roundtable (past pres.). Home: 433 County Route 68 Saratoga Springs NY 12866-6636 Office Phone: 518-442-5110. E-mail: mratzer@wswheboces.org.

RATZLAFF, TERESA, physical education educator; d. Carl and Lula Goines; m. Lowell Ratzlaff, July 26, 1980; children: Kyle D., Kara A. BS, John Brown U., Siloam Springs, Ark., 1975. Nat. cert. tchr. Nat. Bd. for Profl. Tchg. Stds., 2004. Tchr./coach Christian Challenge Schs., Wichita, Kans., 1975—77, Chelsea Pub. Schs., Okla., 1980—83; tchr. Jay Pub. Schs., Okla., 1983—86, Broken Arrow Pub. Schs., Okla., 1986—89, Catoosa Pub. Schs., Okla., 1989—. Assessor Nat. Bd. for Profl. Tchg. Stds., 2001—04, mentor, 2003—; developer Okla. Subject Area Tests, Okla., 2005; presenter in field; mem. phys. edn. profl. tchg. stds., 2001—04, 2006. Coord. Jump Rope for Heart - Am. Heart Assn., Okla., 1980—2006, Kellogg's Statue of Liberty Campaign, Okla., 1983; com. mem. Running for My Sch., Tulsa, 1995—98; sr. v.p. fund-raising Pride of Broken Arrow, 1999—2001; v.p. Parent Faculty Club, Catoosa, 2001—03, parliamentarian, 2003—04; Great Day Svc. vol. Northside Christian Ch., Broken Arrow, 2003—06. Named Elem. Educator of the Month, Broken Arrow Pub. Schs., 1992, Cherokee Elem. Tchr. of Yr., Catoosa Pub. Schs., 2001; recipient Phoebe Apperson Hearst award, Broken Arrow PTA, 1988, 1991, 1999, Cmty. Rels. award, Broken Arrow Pub. Schs., 1995, Innovator award, 1997, Best Practices Award, Catoosa Pub. Schs., 2005; grantee President's Challenge You're It, Get Fit, Burger King Corp., 2004, Cherokee Nation Okla., 2006; Multicultural Enrichment fellow, Fund for Tchrs., Okla. Found. for Excellence, 2006. Mem.: Am. Assn. Health, Phys. Edn., Recreation and Dance (corr.), Okla. Assn. Health, Phys. Edn., Recreation, and Dance (corr. Okla. Elem. Phys. Edn. Tchr. of Yr. 2004, Focus on Excellence award 1989), Nat. Assn. Sports and Phys. Edn. (assoc.), Tex. Assn. Health, Phys. Edn., Recreation and Dance (assoc.). Personal E-mail: gymratz@valornet.com.

RAU, LOUISE BILLIE, interior designer; b. Saginaw, Mich., June 19, 1946; d. Carl and Belinda (Janni) Dolfi; m. Raymond J. Rau, May 2, 1970; children: Allegra L., Katherine M. BS in Edn., Concordia Tchrs. Coll., 1968; MA in Edn., U. Mich., 1970; postgrad., Baker Coll., 1989-91. Cert tchr. Tchr. grade 2 Birch Run (Mich.) Area Schs., 1968-69, Wayne Westland (Mich.) Schs., 1970-72, Clio (Mich.) Area Schs., 1972-74; floor display mgr. Oscar Rau's, Inc., Flint, Mich., 1985-86, direct mktg. coord. Frankenmuth, Mich., 1986-87, interior designer, 1989—; reading tchr. Reese (Mich.) Middle Sch., 1987-89. Docent Art Goes to Sch., Saginaw (Mich.) Art Mus., 1981-84, pres. Mich. Chapt. of Interior Design Soc., 1998—; adj. fac. interior designer, Baker Coll. Flint, 1998. Contbg. designer feature article on Am. style Saginaw News, 1991; designer "Dream Home" Saginaw Parade of Homes, 1991, contbr. articles to profl. jours. Charter pres. AAUW, Frankenmuth, 1976; bd. dirs. Wickson Meml. Libr., Frankenmuth, 1978; ops. com. Frankenmuth (Mich.) Hist. Mus., 1978; mem. sr. mixed choir St. Lorenz Luth. Ch., Frankenmuth, 1980—, mem. liturical arts com., 1991-93. Mem. Interior Design Soc. (profl.), Founders Soc. Detroit Inst. Arts., Eischer Haus Historical Preservation Com., Frankenmuth, MI, 1999—. Avocations: reading, writing, classical music, travel, scuba diving. Home: 725 W Tuscola St Frankenmuth MI 48734-1435 Office: Oscar Rau Furniture Inc 360 S Main St Frankenmuth MI 48734-1635 E-mail: rjrau@concentric.net.

RAU, MARGARET E., writer; b. Shantou, Guangdong, China; (parents Am. citizens); d. George Wright and Mary Victoria (Wolfe) Lewis; m. Neil L. Rau, Jan. 6, 1935 (dec. Nov. 6, 1971); children: Robert, Peter, Mary Margaret Frank, Thomas. Student, U. Chgo., Columbia U.; BA, U. Redlands; student, Riverside Coll. L.S., 1932. Freelance writer. Author: (novels) Band of the Red Hand, 1939; author: (with Neil Rau) (book) My Father Charlie Chaplin, 1960, Act Your Way to Successful Living, 1966, My Dear Ones, Story of the Founding of Recovery, Inc., 1971; author: Dawn from the West, 1964, The Penguin Book, 1965, The Yellow River, The Yangtze River, 1970, Jimmy of Cherry Valley, 1973, Our World: The People's Republic of China, 1974 (notable Children's Trade Book), The People of New China, 1975, Musk Oxen, Bearded Ones of the North, 1976 (Outstanding Sci. Book for Children), The Giant Panda at Home, 1977 (Outstanding Sci. Book for Children), The Gray Kangaroo at Home, 1978, The Snow Monkey at Home, 1979 (Best Non-Fiction Book of the Yr. So. Calif. Coun. Lit. Children), Red Earth Blue Sky, 1981, Minority Peoples of China, 1983, Holding Up the Sky (China's Youth), 1983 (notable Children's Trade Book), Young Women in China, 1989 (Outstanding Book N.Y. Pub. Libr.), The World's Scariest "True" Ghost Stories, 1994, The Ordeal of Olive Oatman, 1997, Wells Fargo's Book of the Gold Rush, 2001, Belle of the West, 2001, The Mail Must Go Through (the story of the Pony Express), 2005. Fellow: So. Calif. Coun. Lit. Children; mem.: Soc. Children's Book Writers and Illustrators, Authors Guild. Avocation: travel. Home: 5700 Via Real # 97 Carpinteria CA 93013

RAU, SHIRLEY A., secondary school educator; b. Morrison, Ill., Dec. 30, 1955; d. Harold A. and Audrey A. (Moore) R. BA, Idaho State U., 1978; MA, Middlebury (Vt.) Coll., 1985; postgrad., Boise (Idaho) State U., 1978—87, Winona (Minn.) State U., 1984—87. Tchr. English, South Jr. High Sch., Nampa, Idaho; instr. freshman composition Boise State U.; tchr. English, Nampa High Sch., cheerleading coach, 1984—. Participant Rockefeller Conf., 1984; workshop presenter. Contbr. articles to profl. jours. Named Nampa Tchr. of Yr., 1981, 89, Idaho State Tchr. of Yr., 1990-91 (finalist Nat. Tchr. of Yr. 1991); Cheerleading Coach of Yr. Internat. Cheerleading Found., 1989; fellow Treasure Valley Writing Project, 1979; Mina Shaughnessy scholar, 1985. Mem. NEA, Nat. Assn. Secondary Sch. Prins. (advisor activities program 1979—), Nat. Coun. Tchrs. English, (women's com.), Idaho Edn. Assn., Nampa Edn. Assn., Idaho Coun. Tchrs. English. Home: 6490 Plantation Ln Boise ID 83703-2642 Office: Nampa High Sch 203 Lake Lowell Ave Nampa ID 83686-6697

RAUCH, CATHERINE KERKES, secondary school educator; b. Ill., Nov. 12, 1951; children: Katie, Elizabeth. BS, Northeastern Ill. U., 1972; MS, U. Ill., Chgo., 1975. Cert. tchr., Ill. Math. tchr. Notre Dame H.S., Chgo., 1973-76, Marillac H.S., Northfield, Ill., 1976-79, Oakton C.C., Des Plaines, Ill., 1979-85; math. tchr., math. team coach Adlai Stevenson H.S., Lincolnshire, Ill., 1985—. Mem. Nat. Coun. Tchrs. Math. (Presdl. Excellence state award 1993, 99, Tandy award for excellence 1998, Edyth Mae Slifte award 2000), Ill. Coun. Tchrs. Math. Office: 1 Stevenson Dr Lincolnshire IL 60069-2824

RAUCH, KATHLEEN, computer executive; b. Franklin Square, N.Y., Oct. 30, 1951; d. William C. and Marian (Shull) R.; B.A., U. Rochester, 1973; M.A. in L.S., U. Mich., 1974; postgrad. N.Y. U., 1981-82. Media specialist Sutton (Mass.) Sch., 1974-76; program cons. Advanced Mgmt. Rsch. Internat., N.Y.C., 1976-79; pub. rels. cons., N.Y.C., 1979; pres. N.Y. chpt. NOW, N.Y.C., 1979-80; computer programmer Blue Cross/Blue Shield of Greater N.Y., N.Y.C., 1981-82; computer programmer analyst Fed. Res. Bank of N.Y., 1983-84; systems officer Citibank, N.A., 1984-85; systems analyst Fed. Res. Bank of N.Y., 1986-89; computer and children's libr. East Meadow (N.Y.) Pub. Libr., 1989-91; pres. Panorama Children's Videos, Inc., 1988-93; microcomputer specialist N.C. State U., 1992-93; prin., v.p. The Computer Lab., Inc., 1993—; prin., v.p., The Computer Lab of Atlanta, Inc., 1994-98. Adv. bd. SafeSkills, Durham, N.C., 1997-98; mem. Coun. on Entrepreneurial Devel., Research Triangle Park, N.C., 1996—. Mem. ALA, NOW (dir. pub. rels. N.Y.C. chpt. 1978, v.p. programs 1978, pres. 1979-80, chmn. bd. 1981, founding mem., sec. Svc. Fund NOW, N.Y.C. chpt. 1981, Raleigh, N.C. chpt.), Assn. for Women in Computing (v.p. membership 1984, exec. v.p. 1985, treas. 1986, mem.-at-large 1987, pres. 1988), Triangle Bus. and Profl. Guild, Friends of the JC Raulston Arboretum. Office: Computer Lab 3737 Glenwood Ave Ste 400 Raleigh NC 27612-5515

RAULERSON, PHOEBE HODGES, school system administrator; b. Cin., Mar. 16, 1939; d. LeRoy Allen and Thelma A. (Stewart) Hodges; m. David Earl Raulerson, Dec. 26, 1959; children: Julie, Lynn, David Earl, Jr., Roy Allen. BA in Edn., U. Fla., Gainesville, 1963, MEd, 1964. Tchr. several schs., Okeechobee, Fla., 1964-79; asst. prin. Okeechobee Jr. H.S., 1979-81, prin., 1983-84; asst. prin. South Elem. Sch., Okeechobee, 1981-82, Okeechobee H.S., 1982-83, prin., 1984-96, asst. supt. for curriculum and instrn., 1996-98, supt., 1998—2004; mem. State Bd. Edn., 2005—. Mem. Dept. Edn. Commr.'s Task Force on H.S. Preparation, 1993-94, chair Task Force Tchr. Preparation and Certification, 1995-96, Edn. Practices Commn., 1998-99, Commr.'s Blue Ribbon Com. on Edn., 1999-2000; mem. shared svcs. network Okeechobee County Exec. Roundtable, 1998-2004; bd. dirs. Small Sch. Dists. Coun. Consortium, 2001-04, Fla. Assn. Dist. Sch. Supts., 1999-2004; mem. Treasure Coast adv. bd. Fla. Atlantic U., 2001, State Bd. Edn., 2005-. Mem. literacy transition team Gov. Jeb Bush, 2002—03; mem. Pres. Frank Brogan's transitional team Fla. Atlantic U., 2003; bd. dirs. Okeechobee County Farm Bur., 1996—2006. Recipient Outstanding Citizen award Okeechobee Rotary Club, 1986, Disting. Citizen award Boy Scouts, 2005; named Fla. H.S. Prin. of Yr., 1990; week named in her honor, Okeechobee County Commrs., 1990. Mem. Am. Bus. Women's Assn., Fla. Assn. Secondary Sch. Prins. (pres. 1993-94, Fla. Prin. of Yr. award 1990), Fla. Assn. Sch. Adminstrs. (bd. dirs. 1992-95), Fla. Assn. Dist. Sch. Supts. (bd. dirs. 2000-2004), Small Sch. Dist. Consortium Com. (exec. com. 2000-2004), Okeechobee Cattlewomen's Assn., Okeechobee C. of C. (bd. dirs. 1995-97), Okeechobee Rotary Club, Okeechobee Exch. Club. Republican. Episcopalian. Home: 3898 NW 144th Dr Okeechobee FL 34972-0930 Business E-Mail: praulerson@okeechobee.com.

RAUSER, CONNIE JEAN, athletic trainer; d. Walter Frank and Anna Winnifred Rauser. BS, Mont. State U., Bozeman, 1983; MS, U. Ariz., Tucson, 1989. Cert. athletic trainer Nat. Athletic Trainers Assn. Athletic trainer Pueblo H.S., Tucson, 1987—89; head athletic trainer Mont. Tech., Butte, 1989—91; asst. athletic trainer U. Idaho, Moscow, 1991—93, Oreg. State U., Coravallis, 1993—96; head athletic trainer Sabino HS, Tucson, 1996—. Office Phone: 520-584-7910. E-mail: connie.rauser@tusd1.org.

RAVA, SUSAN ROUDEBUSH, French language and literature educator, community volunteer; b. St. Louis, June 6, 1939; d. George Shotwell and Dorothy Jean (Coleman) Roudebush; m. John A. Rava, Feb. 20, 1965; children: Ellen D'Arcy, William Cheever, Carol Elisa. BA, Vassar Coll., 1961; MA, Washington U., St. Louis, 1971, PhD, 1977. Mem. staff Am. Field Svc., N.Y.C., 1961-63; tchr. ESL Washington U., 1966-68, lectr. French, 1978-88, sr. lectr. French, 1988—2001, dept. dir. teaching asst. tng., 1990—2001, sr. lectr. emerita, 2001—; tchr. French U. Mo., St. Louis, 1977-78. Author: (short stories) Prairie Schooner, Crescent Rev.; asst. editor Pedagogy French Rev.; contbr. articles to profl. jours., bulls. and revs. Vol. coord. St. Louis Vis. Ctr., 1964-66; bd. dirs., sec. ACLU East Mo., St. Louis, 1967-72; bd. dirs. New City Sch., St. Louis, 1973-75, John Burroughs Sch., St. Louis, 1982-85, Alliance Française Sch., St. Louis, 1991-93; bd. dirs.

Gateway Found., St. Louis, 1992—; mem. bd. deacons Trinity Presbyn. Ch., 1993-96, mem. bd. elders, 1998-2001; bd. dirs. Alliance Francaise St. Louis, 2003—. Recipient Excellence in Teaching award Emerson Electric, 1994. Mem. MLA, Am. Assn. Tchrs. of French. Democrat. Avocations: tennis, writing, travel. Home: 7129 Washington Ave Saint Louis MO 63130-4313

RAVAL, MA FLORENA TENAZAS, retired pathologist; b. Philippines, June 20, 1939; arrived in U.S., 1964; d. Salvador U. Tenazas and Salvacion C. Torrefiel; m. Antonio S. Raval, Nov. 1961; children: Cynthia, Edwin, Jeffrey, Steven. MD, U. Santo Torres, Philippines, 1962. Pathologist Detroit Med. Ctr.; asst. clin. prof. Wayne State U., Detroit. Named one of Am. Top Physicians, Consumers Rsch. Coun. Am., Wash., 2004—05. Fellow: Coll. Am. Pathologists.

RAVDIN, LISA DAWN, neuropsychologist; b. Bklyn., Jan. 29, 1965; d. Richard Lloyd and Susan (Alpert) R.; m. David Neil Deutsch, Oct. 12, 1996; children: Hannah Ravdin Deutsch, Rachel Ravdin Deutsch. BS, Syracuse U., 1987; MD, Chgo. Med. Sch., 1992, PhD, 1994. Lic. psychologist, N.Y. Rsch. asst. North Shore U. Hosp., Manhasset, N.Y., 1987-88; clin. neuropsychology extern Rehab. Inst. Chgo., 1990-91, L.I. Jewish Med. Ctr.-Hillside Hosp., New Hyde Park, N.Y., 1991-93; intern West Haven (Conn.) VA Med. Ctr., 1993-94; neuropsychology fellow in neurology NYU Sch. Medicine/Hosp. for Joint Diseases, N.Y.C., 1994-95; Nat. Rsch. Svc. Award fellow neuropsychology in neurology N.Y. Presbyn. Hosp.-Weill Med. Coll. of Cornell U., N.Y.C., 1995-97, dir. neuropsychology svc., 1997—. Co-dir. Women's Neurologic Health Initiative, N.Y.C., 1998. Contbg. author: Neuropsychology of Aging, 1997; contbr. articles to profl. jours. NIH/NINDS Career awardee, 1998, other grants. Mem. APA, Internat. Neuropsychol. soc., N.Y. Neuropsychology Group (bd. dirs. 1998—, treas. 1999—), Nat. Acad. Neuropsychology. Address: NY Presbyn Hosp Weill Med Coll Cornell U 525 E 68th St New York NY 10021-4870

RAVECHÉ, ELIZABETH SCOTT, immunologist, educator; b. Stuttgart, Federal Republic of Germany, Nov. 21, 1950; (parents Am. citizens); d. Williard Warren and Justine (Dorney) Scott; m. Harold Joseph Ravché, Jan. 26, 1974; children: John, Justin, Bernice, Beth. BS, Seton Hill Coll., 1972; PhD, George Washington U., 1977. Rsch. scientist NIH, Bethesda, Md., 1972-79, sr. investigator, 1980-85; assoc. prof. immunology Albany (N.Y.) Med. Coll., 1985-89; prof. immunology U. of Medicine and Dentistry, Newark, N.J., 1989-96, prof., 1996—. Contbr. 14 chpts. to books, 75 sci. articles to profl. publs.; mem. editl. bd. Oncology Reports, Procs. Soc. Exptl. Biol. Medicine. Sec. PTA, Hoboken, N.J., 1991. Recipient Disting. Alumna Leadership award, Seton Hill Coll., 2002. Fellow Washington Acad. of Sci. (Outstanding Researcher award, 1983); mem. Am. Assn. Immunologists, Am. Assn. Pathologists, Am. Assn. Cancer Rsch. Office: Dept of Pathology U Medicine-Dentistry NJ 185 S Orange Ave Newark NJ 07103-2757 Office Phone: 973-972-5240. E-mail: raveches@umdnj.edu.

RAVEN, ABBE, broadcast executive; b. New York, 1953; 1 child. BA in Theater, U. Buffalo, 1974; MA in Cinema and Theater, Hunter Coll. Prodn. mgr., stage mgr. Manhattan Theater Club, Bklyn. Acad. Music, N.Y.C.; mgr. prodn. Hearst/ABC Video Svcs.; dir. prodn. svcs. A&E TV Networks, 1984-88, sr. v.p. prodn., 1988—95; sr. v.p. programming and prodn. The History Channel and HTV Prodns., 1995-97; sr. v.p. programming The History Channel, 1997—2000, gen. mgr., exec. v.p., 2000—02, A&E Network-USA, pres., 2004—05; pres., CEO A&E Television Networks, 2005—. Instr. various edn1. instns. Active Competition Com. CableACE Awards, chair 12 Ann. Ceremonies; active coms. focusing on violence in TV. Named to Hunter Coll. Hall of Fame; recipient U. Buffalo Alumni award, National History Day Org. Corp. Leadership Award, 2000. Mem. NATAS, Women in Cable, Am. Women in Radio and TV, PROMAX, Nat. Acad. Cable Programming. Office: A&E TV Networks The Hearst Corp 235 E 45th St 9th Fl New York NY 10017-3305*

RAVEN, LINDA F., mechanical engineer; b. Mishawaka, Ind., Oct. 31, 1972; d. Francis Harvey and Therese Strobel Raven. BSME, U. Notre Dame, 1995. Tech. staff Hughes Space & Comm., El Segundo, Calif., 1995—98; cons. engr. Dynatech Engring., Citrus Heights, 1998—99; environ. edn. intern Nat. Parks Svc., Bar Harbor, Maine, 1999; edn. vol. U.S. Peace Corps, Namibia, 1999—2001, HIV-AIDS coord. Windhoek, Namibia, 2002; sales engr. Beacon Power Corp., Wilmington, Mass., 2003—; product mgr. Alternative Energy Store, Worcester, Mass. Asst. scout leader Girl Scouts USA, Roseville, Calif., 1998—99. Avocations: hiking, camping, biking, yoga. Office: 234 Ballardvale St Wilmington MA 01887

RAVEN, PATRICIA ELAINE (PENNY RAVEN), real estate broker, developer, columnist, gas industry executive; b. Oakland, Calif., Apr. 27, 1943; d. Allen James and Patricia Elaine (McClure) Nichelini; m. Larry Joseph Raven, June 15, 1963; children: Laurence Tagge Allen, Corbyn Lance. Student, U. So. Calif., 1961—62, U. Calif., Fresno, 1962—63, Fresno City Coll., 1973. Model, Fresno, Calif., 1960—; owner, operator Del Mar Motel and apts., Fresno, 1963—64; owner R Pantry Markets, 1965—72, v.p., 1968—72; owner Holy Cow Meat Markets, Fresno, 1965—72; real estate salesman, developer, 1973; real estate broker, owner The Raven Co., Fresno, 1974—; v.p. Raven Devel., Inc., 1980—; owner Raven Alcohol Distillery, 1979—89; pres. Am. Gasohol, Inc., 1980—; spl. events cons. Royal Cruise Line, 1986. Columnist: Party Line, Fresno Bee, 1978—87, Central Valley Homes & Lifestyles, 2003—, contbg. editor: Fresno Mag., 2003—; actress: (TV miniseries) Fresno, 1986; co-author: National Handbook on Toll Roads, 1977; actress: (films) Pretty Woman, 1989; Princess Diaries 2, 2004; contbg. editor: Fresno Weekly, 2001—02. Pres. Fresno Cancer League, 1972—73, Jackson Sch. PTA, 1980—82; hon mem. Fresno Zool. Soc.; commr. Fresno County Hist. Landmarks and Records Commn., 2005—; Democratic candidate for lt. gov. Calif., 1978; Fresno County Dem. ctrl. com. alt., 1977; bd. dirs. Women's Symphony League, 1973—74; pres. Huntington Blvd. Homeowners Hist. Assn., 1987—97, officer, 1997—. Named Betty Crocker Homemaker of Tomorrow, 1961; recipient Mayor's award, 1976, Hon. Svc. award, Jackson Sch. PTA, 1982, Appreciation award, United Cerebral Palsy Assn., 1982—86, Fresno Zool. Soc., 1982, Calif. State Senate, 1983, San Joaquin chpt. Assn. Gen. Contractors, 1983, Holland Sch., 1984, Huntington Blvd. Neighbors, 1985, proclamation in her honor, City of Fresno, 1985, others, San Joaquin Valley's Most Fashionable award, 1984, Appreciation award, Huntington Blvd. Neighbors, 1986, hon. mayor, City of Fresno, 1986. Roman Catholic. Home: 3504 E Huntington Blvd Fresno CA 93702-3224

RAVENAL, CAROL BIRD MYERS, artist; b. Bklyn. d. Harry Walter and May (Chalmers) Myers; m. Earl Cedric Ravenal, May 1956; children: Cornelia Jane, John Brodhead, Rebecca Eliza. PhD, Harvard U., 1963. Assoc. prof. R.I. Sch. Design, Providence, 1958—62; asst. prof. R.I. Coll., Providence, 1964-68; assoc. prof. Am. U., Washington, 1969-98; ret., 1998. V.p., pres. Phi Kappa Phi, Washington, 1981-84; chairperson Friends of Art Dept., Washington, 1986-88; v.p. Internat. Psychohistorical Assn., N.Y., 1991-1992; chair Washington Chpt. Internat. Psychohistorical Assn., 1988-90. Contbr. articles to profl. jours.; one-woman exhibits paintings, Harvard, Bkyln. Mus., Providence, Washington, Easton, Md., Germany, Italy. Pres., v.p. Radcliffe Club, 1972-76; bd. mem., chair edn., Acad. of Arts, Easton, Md., 1982-87; bd. mem. Com. Nat. Security, 1984-86; chair Conf. Com. for Nat. Security, 1985; bd. mem. chair, exhbn. com., Art Barn, Washington, 1989-91. Fellow Paul J. Sachs Travelling Harvard U., Sears-Gilbert, Radcliffe Coll.; grantee Am. U., 1979. Mem. Coll. Art Assn., Women's Art Caucus, Internat. Psychohist. Soc., Phi Kappa Phi, Friends of Art Dept. of Am. U., Phi Beta Kappa. Avocations: painting, reading psychobiography, museums, travel, gardening, remodelling historic houses, volunteer teaching. Home: 4439 Cathedral Ave NW Washington DC 20016-3562

RAVENEL, SHANNON, book publishing professional; b. Charlotte, NC, Aug. 13, 1938; d. Elias Prioleau and Harriett Shannon (Steedman) R.; m. Dale Purves, May 25, 1968; children: Sara Blake, Harriett. BA, Hollins Coll., 1960. Mktg. asst., sch. dept. Holt, Rinehart & Winston, Inc., NYC, 1960-61; editl. asst. Houghton Mifflin Co., Boston, 1961-64, editor, 1964—70; editl. cons. pvt. practice, St. Louis, 1973-90; sr. editor, co-founder Algonquin Books of Chapel Hill, NC, 1982-91, editl. dir., 1992-2000; dir. Algonquin imprint Shannon Ravenel Books, 2001—. Series editor: Best American Short Stories, 1978-90; editor: Best American Short Stories of the Eighties, 1990, New Stories From the South, 1986-2005 Recipient Disting. Achievement award Coun. Lit. Mags. & Presses, NYC, 1990, R. Hunt Parker Meml. award for contbns. to the lit. of N.C., 2004. Mem. PEN Am. Ctr. Democrat. Office: Algonquin Books of Chapel Hill PO Box 2225 Chapel Hill NC 27515-2225 Business E-Mail: shannonr@algonquin.com.

RAVITCH, DIANE SILVERS, historian, educator, writer, government official; b. Houston, July 1, 1938; d. Walter Cracker and Ann Celia (Katz) Silvers; m. Richard Ravitch, June 26, 1960 (div. 1986); children: Joseph, Steven (dec.), Michael. BA, Wellesley Coll., 1960; PhD, Columbia U., 1975; LHD (hon.), Williams Coll., 1984, Reed Coll., 1985, Amherst Coll., 1986, SUNY, 1988, Ramapo Coll., 1990, St. Joseph's Coll., N.Y., 1991, Middlebury Coll., 1997, Union Coll., 1998. Adj. asst. prof. Tchrs. Coll., Columbia U., N.Y.C., 1975-78, assoc. prof., 1978-83, adj. prof., 1983-91; asst. sec. office ednl. rsch. and improvement U.S. Dept. Edn., Washington, 1991-93, counselor to the sec. edn., 1991-93. Vis. fellow Brookings Instn., Washington, 1993-94, non-resident sr. fellow, 1994-, editor papers on edn. policy, 1997-05, Brown chair in edn. policy, 1997-05; rsch. prof. NYU, 1994-; mem. Nat. Assessment Governing Bd., 1997-04; com. on edn. policy Nat. Acad. Scis., 2003-05; mem. Koret task force Hoover Instn., 1999-, sr. fellow, 2005-. Author: The Great School Wars, 1974, The Revisionists Revised, 1977, The Troubled Crusade, 1983, The Schools We Deserve, 1985, National Standards in American Education, A Citizens Guide, 1995, Left Back, 2000, The Language Police, 2003; author: (with others) Educating an Urban People, 1981; author: The School and the City, 1983, Against Mediocrity, 1984, Challenges to the Humanities, 1985, What Do Our 17 Year Olds Know?, 1987; editor: The American Reader, 1990; co-editor: The Democracy Reader, 1992, New Schools for a New Century, 1997, City Schools, 2000, Making Good Citizens, 2001, Kid Stuff, 2003, Forgotten Heroes of American Education, 2006, The English Reader, 2006; editor: Learning from the Past, 1995, Debating the Future of American Education, 1995. Chair Ednl. Excellence Network, 1988—91, 1994—96; trustee Nat. Humanities Ctr., 1999—2000, N.Y. Pub. Libr., N.Y.C., 1981—87, hon. life trustee, 1988—; trustee N.Y. Coun. on Humanities, 1996—; mem. Landmarks Preservation Commn., Southold, NY, 2000—02; bd. dirs. Woodrow Wilson Nat. Fellowship Found., 1987—91, Coun. Basic Edn., 1989—91, Thomas B. Fordham Found., 1998—, New Am. Found., 2000—, Albert Shanker Inst., 2002—, Core Knowledge Found., 2003—, Hunt Inst. Ednl. Policy and Leadership, 2002—. Recipient Disting. Svc. award NY Acad. Pub. Edn., 1994, Alumnae Achievement award Wellesley Coll., 1989, Uncommon Book award Hoover Instn., 2004, John Dewey award United Fedn. Tchrs., 2005, Gaudium award Breukelein Inst., 2005, Pub. Svc. award Am. Jewish Hist. Soc., 2006; Guggenheim fellow, 1977-78; Phi Beta Kappa vis. scholar. Mem. Nat. Acad. Edn., Am. Acad. Arts and Scis., Soc. Am. Historians, N.Y. Hist. Soc. (trustee 1995-98), PEN Internat. Office: NYU 82 Wash Sq E New York NY 10003-6644

RAWDON, CHERYL ANN, elementary school educator; b. Dallas, June 13, 1957; d. Billy Wayne and Carol Ann (Murdock) R.; 1 child, Meagan. BS, East Tex. State U., 1979. Cert. kindergarten, elem., jr. high sch. reading and English tchr., Tex. Tchr. reading and spelling Canton (Tex.) Ind. Sch. Dist. Jr. High Sch.; tchr. pre 1st grade Midlothian (Tex.) Ind. Sch. Dist., tchr. kindergarten; tchr. Winnsboro (Tex.) Elem. Sch., 2003—, 2d grade lead tchr., 2005—06. Coord. Angel Tree, 1997-2000; kindergarten rep. to Campus Planning Com., 1999-2000. Mem. First Bapt. Ch., Midlothian, tchr. Sunday sch., mem. choir, mission friends tchr., Awana leader, mem. ch. praise team, 2000; active numerous cmty. orgns.; mem. S.A.M.'s Place, rep., 1998-99; vol. Hope Clinic of Ellis County, 2000; mem. Pine St. Bapt. Ch., Winnsboro, Tex., 2002—, kindergarten tchr., 2004-06, choir 1-6 grade, 2003-05 Recipient Golden Poet award, 1989, 90. Mem. Canton Tchrs. Assn. (pres.), Tex. State Tchrs. Assn., Canton Classroom Tchrs. Assn.

RAWLEY, ANN KEYSER, small business owner, picture framer; b. N.Y.C., July 11, 1923; d. Ernest Wise and Beatrice (Oberndorf) Keyser; m. James Albert Rawley, Apr. 7, 1945; children: John Franklin, James Albert. BA, Smith Coll., 1944. Owner Ann Rawley Custom Framing, Lincoln, Nebr., 1969—. Pres. Friends of Fairview, Lincoln, 1976, Lincoln City Ballet Co., 1983-84; bd. dirs. Lincoln Community Playhouse; mem. adv. bd. Nebr. Repertory Theatre. Mem. Nebr. Art Assn. (sec. 1976-77, life trustee). Republican. Episcopalian. Avocations: travel, tennis, needlework. Home and Office: 2300 Bretigne Dr Lincoln NE 68512-1910

RAWLINGS, ANNETTE, painter; b. Birmingham, Ala., Feb. 23, 1943; d. Henry Buchanan and Doris Naomi (Williams) Rawlings; m. Richard Tucker Sinclair, Mar. 30, 1976; 1 dau., Vanessa. Certificate of Completion, U. Heidleburg, 1961, Escuolade Estraneira, Perugia, Italy, 1967; B.A., U. Miami, 1969. Faculty, Met. Mus. and Art Center, Miami, Fla., 1980-83; cons., lectr. Dade County Pub. and Pvt. Schs., Miami, 1980-83, Coconut Grove Art Assn., 1982-83; one person shows include Yellowplush Gallery, London, 1976, Rogue Gallery Art, Medford, Oreg., 1981, Union St. Gallery, San Francisco, 1981, Virginia Miller Gallery, Miami, 1981; group shows include Met. Mus. of Miami, 1983, Birmingham Mus., 1983, Fla. Internat. U., 1983, Internat. Center Contemporary Art, Paris, 1984, Metropolis Internationale Galerie d'Art, Geneva, 1985, Mandragore Internationale Galerie d'Art, Paris, 1986, Internationale Centre D'Art Contemporain, Paris, 1986, Masters Handmade Paper Exhibit, Met. Mus., Coral Gables, Fla., 1987, 841 Gallery, Miami Beach, Fla., 1987, Met. Mus. Art, Miami, Fla., 1988, 1988 Centre Culturel Paul Du Mail, France (1st place in abstract painting 1988), Ariel Gallery Soho, N.Y.C., 1989, 90, Sorbonne Galerie d'Art, Paris, 1990; represented in permanent collections Raimondos, Corp., Plaza Bank, Miami, Michael Butter, Miami, Brunswick Corp., N.Y.C., Internat. Sch. Art and Design, Miami, Multi-Media Art Ctr. for the Fine Arts, Miami; also pvt. collections; featured in The N.Y. Art Rev., 1990, Am. Artists, 1990. Mem. Met. Mus. and Art Center, Birmingham Mus. Art, Women in Art, Community Art Alliance. Democrat. Episcopalian. Home: 4286 N Douglas Rd Miami FL 33142-4224

RAWLINSON, HELEN ANN, librarian; b. Columbia, S.C., Mar. 30, 1948; d. Alfred Harris and Mary Taylor (Moon) R. BA, U. S.C., 1970; MLS, Emory U., 1972. Asst. children's librarian Greenville (S.C.) County Library, 1972-74, br. supr., 1974-76, asst. head extension div., 1976-78; children's room librarian Richland County Pub. Library, Columbia, 1978-81, sr. adult services librarian, 1981-82, chief adult services, 1982-85, dep. dir., 1985—. Mem. adv. com. S.C. Pre-White House Conf. on Libr. and Info. Svcs., chmn. program com. Recipient Outstanding S.C. Librarian award by S.C. Library Assn., 1998. Mem. ALA, S.E. Libr. Assn., S.C. Libr. Assn. (2d v.p. 1987-89, editl. com. 1993, chmn. pub. libr. sect. 1995), U.S.C. Thomas Cooper Soc. (bd. dirs., v.p., pres.-elect, pres.). Baptist. Home: 1316 Guignard Ave West Columbia SC 29169-6137 Office: Richland County Pub Libr 1431 Assembly St Columbia SC 29201-3101 Office Phone: 803-799-9084. E-mail: harawlin@richland.lib.sc.us.

RAWLINSON, JOHNNIE BLAKENEY, federal judge; b. Concord, N.C., Dec. 16, 1952; BS in Psychology summa cum laude, NC A&T State U., 1974; JD, U. of Pacific, 1979. Private practice, Las Vegas, 1979—80; staff atty. Nevada Legal Services, 1980; from dep. dist. atty. to asst. dist. atty. Clark County Dist. Atty.'s Office, 1980—98; judge U.S. Dist. Ct. Nev., 1998—2000, U.S. Ct. Appeals (9th cir.), 2000—. Office: 333 Las Vegas Blvd S Rm 7072 Las Vegas NV 89101

RAWSKI, EVELYN SAKAKIDA, history professor; b. Honolulu, Feb. 2, 1939; d. Evan T. and Teruko (Watase) Sakakida; m. Thomas G. Rawski, Dec. 16, 1967. BA, Cornell U., 1961; MA, Radcliffe Coll., 1962; PhD, Harvard U., 1968. Asst. prof. history U. Pitts., 1967-72, assoc. prof., 1973-79, prof. history, 1980—; univ. prof., 1996—. Author: Agricultural Change and the Peasant Economy of South China, 1972, Education and Popular Literacy in Ch'ing China, 1979, The Last Emperors: A Social History of Qing Imperial Institutions, 1998; co-author: Chinese Society in the Eighteenth Century, 1987, Worshiping the Ancestors: Chinese Commemorative Portraits, 2001; co-editor: Popular Culture in Late Imperial and Modern China, 1985, Death Ritual in Late Imperial and Modern China, 1988, Harmony and Counterpoint: Chinese Music in Ritual Context, 1996. Grantee Am. Coun. Learned Socs., 1973-74; NEH fellow, 1979-80, Chinese Studies fellow Am. Coun. Learned Socs./Social Sci. Rsch. Coun., 1989, Guggenheim fellow, 1990, Woodrow Wilson Internat. Ctr. fellow 1992-93, NEH fellow, 2006—. Mem.: Assn. Asian Studies (China-Inner Asia coun., bd. dirs. 1976—79, v.p. 1994—95, pres. 1995—96). Home: 5317 Westminster Pl Pittsburgh PA 15232-2120 Office: U Pitts Dept History Pittsburgh PA 15260 Office Phone: 412-648-7458. Business E-Mail: esrx@pitt.edu.

RAWSON, MARJORIE JEAN, lawyer; b. Okolona, Miss., Dec. 5, 1939; d. E.P. and Marjorie J. R. BS, U. Miss., 1961; MS, Ind. U., 1969; JD, John Marshall Law Sch., 1977. Bar: Ind. 1977, U.S. Dist. Ct. (no. dist.) Ind. 1977, U.S. Ct. Appeals (7th cir.) 1983, U.S. Supreme Ct. 1983, Fla. 1988, U.S. Dist. Ct. (mid. dist.) Fla. 1991, U.S. Ct. Mil. Appeals, 1995. Tchr. Munster (Ind.) High Sch., 1966-77; atty. pvt. practice, Munster, 1977-90; deputy prosecutor Lake County Juvenile Ct., Gary, Ind., 1978-90; pvt. practice Naples, Fla., 1991—. Adj. prof. Ind. U., Gary, 1984-87, Purdue U., Hammond, Ind., 1988-90, John Marhsall Law Sch., Chgo., 1984-87, U. South Fla., Ft. Myers, 1992-97; compliance specialist Collier County Pub. Schs., Naples, 1997-99. Author: A Manual of Special Education Law for Educators and Parents, 2000; editor: Handbook for Legal Assistants, 1987. Past pres. Women's Polit. Caucus, Naples, 1995-97, Women's Rep. Club, Naples, 1992-94; mem. adv. bd. Naples Alliance Children, 1997—. Mem. AAUW, LWV, Collier County Bar Assn. (bd. dirs. 1996-99), Naples C. of C. (bd. dirs. 1997—), Zonta Club. Republican. Avocations: jogging, swimming, music. Office: 400 5th Ave S Ste 300 Naples FL 34102-6556

RAWSON, RACHEL L., lawyer; BA magna cum laude, Kenyon Coll., 1987; JD, Columbia U., 1990. Bar: N.Y. 1991, Ohio 1995. With Jones Day, Cleve., 1992—, ptnr., 2003—. Mem.: ABA (bus. law sect.), Cleve. Bar Assn. (banking and bus. law sect.). Office: Jones Day North Point 901 Lakeside Ave Cleveland OH 44114-1190

RAY, AMY, vocalist, guitarist; b. Decatur, Ga., Apr. 12, 1964; BA, Emory U., 1986. Vocalist, guitarist Saliers & Ray, 1980-83, Indigo Girls, 1983—; signed to Epic Records, 1988—2006, Hollywood Records, 2006—. Founder, pres. Daemon Records, Decatur, Ga., 1990—. Musician: (albums) Stag, 2001, Prom, 2005; musician: (with Emily Saliers) Early 45, 1985, Strange Fire, 1987, Indigo Girls, 1989 (Grammy Award for Best Contemporary Folk Album, 1990), Nomads Indians Saints, 1990, Back On the Bus, Y'All, 1991, Rites of Passage, 1992, Swamp Ophelia, 1994, 1200 Curfews, 1995, Shaming of the Sun, 1997, Come On Now Social, 1999, Retrospective, 2000, Become You, 2002, All That We Let In, 2004, Rarities, 2005, Despite Our Differences, 2006, (songs) Closer to Fine, 1989, Hammer and Nail, 1990, Galileo, 1992, Least Complicated, 1994, Shame on You, 1997; appears in (films) Boys on the Side, 1995, Join the Resistance: Fall in Love, 2003, (documentaries) Trudell, 2005, Wordplay, 2006. Nominee Best New Artist, Grammy Awards, 1990; named one of Greatest Women of Rock'n'Roll, VH1. Office: c/o Russell Carter Artist Mgmt Ste 755 315 W Ponce de Leon Ave Decatur GA 30030 Office Phone: 404-377-9900. E-mail: igfan@rcam.com.*

RAY, CAROL RENEÉ, researcher; b. Petersburg, Va. d. Frederick Chester Ray and Brenda Ray-Moore. BSc, Spelman Coll., 1987; MSc, N.C. Agrl. and Tech. State U., 1995; PhD, U. Nebr.-Lincoln, 2003. Tutor coord. U. Nebr., Lincoln, Nebr., 2000, prin. investigator, 1998—2003; instr. chemistry Fayetteville Tech. C.C., 2002; TV tutor comcast U. Md. - Ea. Shore, Princess Anne, 2004, coord. allied health project, 2005; with Johns Hopkins Sch. Medicine, Balt., 2006—. Adj. faculty Sojouriner Douglass Coll., Salisbury, Md., 2004—; cons. Nebr. Divsn. on Aging., 1998. Contbr. articles to profl. jours. Nominee Avon scholarship, 1984; Chemistry Scholarship, Spelman Coll., 1984. Mem.: Phi Upsilon Omicron Nat. Honor Soc. Avocations: flute, reading, tennis, writing. Personal E-mail: carol2004_500@hotmail.com.

RAY, DEBRA ANN, music educator; b. Cleve., Ohio, Nov. 6, 1967; d. Roy Preston and Cleata Ann Ray. AA, Tidewater C.C., Porthsmouth, Va., 1988; BSSE, Old Dominion Univ., Norfolk, Va., 1992, MSEd, 2000. Piano tchr. self employed, Chesapeake, Va., 1986—, Greenbrier Christian Acad., Chesapeake, Va., 1994—98, Currituck County Sch., Curritck, NC, 1998—99; music tchr. Little Creek Elem., Norfolk, Va., 1999—. Mem.: Va. Music Nat. Assn., Music Educator Nat. Conf. (presentor, How Music in the Minor Modes affects Children 2000). Republican. Bapt. Avocations: scrapbooks, reading, bicycling, swimming, gardening.

RAY, DIANE MARIE AYERS, music educator; b. Glens Falls, N.Y., Apr. 28, 1965; d. Robert Edson and Margaret LeClaire Ayers; m. Malcolm Earl Ray, Dec. 24, 1988; children: Zachary Edson, Amanda Doris. BS, Castleton State Coll., 1987. Cert. tchr. music, math. Vt., 1987. Co bus. owner Ray's TV, Poultney, Vt., 1989—99; tchr. music Poultney Elem. Sch., 2002—04; tchr. Beverly, Mass., 2004—; math. and music tchr. Covenant Christian Acad., 2004—. Dir. music United Bapt. Ch., Poultney, 1990—2004. Baptist. Home: 138 Essex St Apt D201 South Hamilton MA 01982-2021

RAY, ELISE, gymnast; b. Tallahassee, Feb. 6, 1982; d. Bill and Ellen Ray. Mem. U.S. Gymnastics Team, 1996-2001, U.S. Olympic Team, 2000. Recipient 1st team Internat. Team Championships, 1997; 1st pl. uneven bars, John Hancock U.S. Gymnastics Championships, 1998; 1st pl. fixed bars, John Hancock U.S. Gymnastics Championships, 1999; 1st pl. All Around uneven bars, John Hancock U.S. Gymastics Championships, 2000; 1st pl. All Around vault, uneven bars, fixed bars, Aussie Haircare Gymnastics Invitational, 2000; 1st team All-Around Champion, Sr. Pacific Alliance Championship, New Zealand, 2000, All-Around Champion, NCAA Championships, 2001, 1st pl. balance beam, NCAA Championships, 2002. Mem. Hill's Angels Club. Avocations: shopping, arts and crafts, movies, family. Address: Womens Gymnastics 1000 S State St Ann Arbor MI 48109

RAY, EVELYN LUCILLE, art association administrator; b. Phila., Oct. 15, 1949; d. William and Erma Lucille (Chadrick) Ray. Sec. City of Phila., 1967, Free Libr. of Phila., 1972-77, Office of City Solicitor, Phila., 1977-81, Water Dept., Phila., 1981-87; program devel. creative cons. Accoutrements for the Arts, Phila., 1989, creative dir., 1993—, meeting planner for small meetings specializing in theme and site selection, 1995—. Comms. support Pa. Acad. of Fine Arts, Phila., 1987-88; creative cons. West Phila. Cultural Alliance, Phila., 1988-89; mem. adv. bd. Internat. Biog. Ctr., Cambridge, Eng., 1995—, Am. Biog. Inst., Raleigh, N.C., 1995—. Republican. Baptist. Avocations: travel, real estate: interior design and preservation, entertaining, classical music.

RAY, JANE ZIMRUDE, retired machine shop executive; b. Strawn, Tex., May 9, 1937; d. M.A. and Susie Matilda (Kitchens) Wooton; m. Earl Vernon Ray, Oct. 19, 1956; children: Marcus Vernon, Martha Ruth Ray O'Grady, Douglas Wayne, Patricia Ann. Grad., Stephenville (Tex.) High Sch., 1955. Bookkeeper Ray's Texaco Svc. Ctr., Ft. Worth, Tex., 1967-74, Ray's Repair & Mfg., Ft. Worth, Tex., 1974-79, pres., 1979-80, Cisco, Tex., 1980-92. Sunday sch. tchr., Cisco, Tex., 1983-92, sub. tchr., 1992—; mem. Civic League of Cisco, 1990—; instr. Community Svc. course Cisco Jr. Coll., 1991.

RAY, JESSICA B., artist, poet, educator; b. Houston, Feb. 10, 1937; d. Raymond Merle Brock and Jessie Lee Evans-Brock; m. Louis A. Williams, Dec. 21, 1969 (div. Dec. 1991); 1 child, Elizabeth Lee Williams. BS, Abilene Christian U., 1959, EdM, 1968. Cert. tchr. Tex. Tchr. English and journalism Ft. Worth/Dallas Ind. Schs., 1959—70; freelance artist/poet Tex., 1970—. Singer Ft. Worth Symphony League, 1995—2001; resident artist Tex. Commn. on the Arts, Austin, 2001—03. One-woman shows include SoHo Gallery, Ft. Worth Tex., 2002—03, Goodrich Gallery, Dallas, 2005, Ft. Worth

Petroleum Club, 2005, exhibitions include One Main Pl., Dallas, 1985, First United Meth. Ch., 2000, 2003, Cook Children's Hosp., Dallas, Tex., 2003, N. Tex. Health Sci. Ctr. Atrium Gallery, 2001, 2002, 2003, 2004, 2005, 2006, Quanah Mus., 2003, Ft. Worth Arts Ctr., 2004—05, Scottish Rite Hosp., Dallas, 2005; author: Mother Earth.Father Sky, 2002, of poems. Recipient Best of Show, Artists, Writers, Composers Am., 2002; Coe Found. fellow, 1961—63. Mem.: Nat. League Am. Pen Women. Methodist. Avocations: gardening, singing. Home: 4407 Bellaire Dr South Fort Worth TX 76109 Office Phone: 817-924-7587.

RAY, JUANITA S., secondary school educator; b. Boone, N.C., Mar. 4, 1962; d. Thomas Willard and Sharon Wheeler Shew; m. Dewayne Lee Ray, Sept. 19, 1987; 1 child, Jacob Thomas. BA in Edn., speech and comm., U. N.C., Chapel Hill, 1984; MEd in theatre arts, U. N.C., Greensboro, 2000. Cert. social studies Randolph Commn., N.C., 2003. Educator Trinity HS, NC, 1985—, N.C. Govs. Sch., Winston-Salem, NC, 2002—, Randolph Early Coll., Asheboro, NC, 2006—. Parent vol. Randolph Co. Spl. Olympics, Asheboro, NC, 2003—. Recipient Diamond Key Coach, Nat. Forensic League, 1993; grantee Belfer Scholar, U.S. Holocaust Mus., 2005, Donors Choose, 2005. Avocations: reading, travel, theater. Home: 6767 Leah Justine Dr Trinity NC 27370 Office: Randolph Early Coll HS 629 Industrial Park Ave Asheboro NC 27205

RAY, LYDIA M., nurse; b. Vineland, N.J., Oct. 18, 1941; d. Charles Elmer and Mary E. (Murphine) Laury; children: Kimberly Morris Farrell, Karen Morris, Robert E. Morris Jr. AS, Cumberland County Coll., Vineland, 1987. Med.-surg. staff nurse Cooper Hosp. Med. Ctr., Camden, NJ; spl. care ICU RN North Ridge Med. Ctr., Ft. Lauderdale, Fla.; clin. nurse Meyerhoff Digestive Disease Ctr.-Endoscopy Johns Hopkins Hosp., Balt., 1994—; clin. II RN Gettysburg Hosp., Pa., 1994—. Recipient Leadership award N.J. League Nursing, 1987. Home: 2881 Pumping Station Rd Fairfield PA 17320-9237

RAY, MARGARET, education educator; d. Ray; children: Kimery Lynch, Kylie Lynch. PhD, Univ of Tenn., 1988. Asst. prof. Tex. Christian U., Ft. Worth, 1989—92, Mary Washington Coll., Fredericksburg, Va., 1992—95, prof., 1995—. Grantee Rsch. grantee, NSF, 1991, 1995, 2006. Office: Univ Mary Washington 1301 College Ave Fredericksburg VA 22401 Office Phone: 540-654-1485.

RAY, MARJORIE, retired financial planner; b. Hemingway, S.C., Mar. 6, 1927; d. James Earl Ray and Maybelle Jordan; divorced; 1 child, Roberta Jill Sharp. AB in English and History, U. Calif., Berkeley, 1962, MLS, 1965; teaching degree, U. Ill., 1966. Lic. real estate agt., Conn. Dir. profl. svcs. Weston (Conn.) Woods Film Studios, 1968-69; asst. dir. Danbury (Conn.) Pub. Libr., 1970-73, Westport (Conn.) Pub. Libr., 1973-74; cons. Conn. State Libr., Hartford, 1974-76, assoc. state libr., 1977-79; broker rep. P&I Equities, White Plains, N.Y., 1980-82, MHA Fin. Corp., Braintree, Mass., 1983-84, Townsley Assocs., Corning, N.Y., 1984-89, v.p. corp. devel., 1985-89; v.p. Planned Mgmt. Co. Savs. Bank Rockville, Conn., 1989-90; sr. v.p. Specialized Investments, 1991-92; investment officer FSC Securities Corp., 1993—97, Conn. regional sales mgr., 1995—; investment officer and asst. treas. Rockville (Conn.) Bank, 1998—2002, ret., 2002. Cons., propr. Colmar, Glastonbury, Conn., 1985—. Mem. Internat. Assn. Fin. Planning (bd. dirs. Hartford 1983-84, Disting. Svc. award 1984), Glastonbury Bus. and Profl. Women. Republican. Congregationalist. Avocations: travel, theater, literature, tennis, golf, ballroom dancing.

RAY, MICHELLE L., physical education educator; b. Alamogordo, N.Mex., Oct. 30, 1971; d. Darwin E. and Sharyn K. Johnson; m. James D. Ray, Aug. 20, 1994; children: Kayla Ann, Courtney Taylor. AA, Johnson County CC, Overland Park, Kans., 1992; BS, Faulkner U., Montgomery, Ala., 1995; MS in Mgmt., Troy U., Montgomery, 2005. Cert. rank 2 tchr. in phys. edn. N-12 Ala. Coord. spl. events Brendle Rentals Inc., Montgomery, 1994—97; tchr. phys. edn., dir. activities Booker T. Washington Magnet H.S., Montgomery, 1997—. Coord., faculty rep. Friends of Arts/Acads. Magnet Edn., Montgomery, 2001—; faculty sponsor jr./sr. prom and grad. Booker T. Washington Magnet H.S., Montgomery, 2001—. Named Tchr. of Month, Booker T. Washington Magnet H.S., 2005—06; grantee, Parent, Tchr., Student Assn., 2005—06. Mem.: AAPHERD, NEA, Ala. Alliance for Health, Phys. Edn., Recreation, and Dance. Avocations: cooking, reading, running. Office: Booker T Washington Magnet H S 632 S Union St Montgomery AL 36104

RAY, NANCY ROBERTA, retired secondary school educator; b. Kansas City, Mo., July 8, 1951; d. Richard Otto and Kathryn Elizabeth (Peden) Helton; m. William D. Ray, June 30, 1972. BS in Social Studies, Cen. Mo. State U., 1973. Tchr. social studies James Bridger Jr. High Sch., Independence, Mo., 1975—2000. Home: 3112 N Miller Dr Independence MO 64058-2262 Office: James Bridger Jr High Sch 18200 E M-78 Hwy Independence MO 64057-1167

RAY, NELDA HOWTON, financial consultant; Grad., U. Montevallo, Ala., 1962. Fin. cons. Merrill Lynch, Tuscaloosa, Ala. Mem.: Rotary Internat. (local and dist. officer). Home: 4704 Oneida Ave Northport AL 35473-1431 Office: Merrill Lynch 302 Merchants Walk Ste 100 Tuscaloosa AL 35406-2214

RAY, RACHAEL, chef, television personality; b. Cape Cod, Mass., Aug. 25, 1968; m. John Cusimano, Sept. 24, 2005. Student, Pace Univ. Mgr. fresh foods dept. Macy's Marketplace, NY; store mgr., buyer Agata & Valentina, NY; mgr., pub and rest. Sagamore Resort, Lake George, NY; food buyer Cowan & Lobel, Albany; editor-in-chief Everyday with Rachael Ray mag., 2005—. Author: 30-Minute Meals, 1999, Veggie Meals, 2001, Comfort Foods, 2001, 30-Minute Meals 2, 2003, Get Togethers: Rachael Ray 30 Minute Meals, 2003, Cooking 'Round the Clock: Rachael Ray's 30-Minute Meals, 2004, Cooking Rocks!: Rachael Ray's 30-Minute Meals for Kids, 2004, 30-Minute Get Real Meals: Eat Healthy Without Going to Extremes, 2005 (Quills award cookbook The Quills Literacy Found., 2005), Comfort Food: Rachael Ray's Top 30 30-Minute Meals, 2005, Rachael Ray 365: No Repeats, 2005 (Quills award cookbook The Quills Literacy Found., 2006), Express Lane Meals, 2006; host 30 Minute Meals, Food Network, 2002—, $40 A Day, 2004—, Inside Dish, 2004—, Rachael Ray's Tasty Travels, 2005—, (syndicated talk show) The Rachel Ray Show, 2006—, guest appearances Pyramid, 2003, The Tony Danza Show, 2004, 2005, Live With Regis and Kelly, 2004, 2005, Sidewalks Entertainment, 2004, Good Day Live, 2004, The View, 2005, Isaac Mizrahi, 2005, Tonight Show with Jay Leno, 2005, Late Show with David Letterman, 2005, Oprah Winfrey Show, 2005, 2006. Named one of 150 Sexiest Women, FHM-US Mag., 2004, 100 Most Influential People, Time Mag., 2006. Office: c/o Everyday with Rachael Ray Fifth Floor 260 Madison Ave New York NY 10016-2402*

RAY, RAEGAN L., science educator; b. Nashville, Mar. 3, 1970; 1 child, Tarra. Degree in Secondary Edn. and Biology, U. Tenn., Martin, 1995. Lic. Va. Dept Edn. Educator Beville Mid. Sch., Woodbridge, Va., 2000—06. Foster parent Prince William County, Manassas, Va., 2004—06. Office Phone: 703-878-2593.

RAY, SUSAN DAVIS, accountant; b. Savannah, Ga., Sept. 28, 1967; d. Shelley Arthur and Ann Swain D.; m. Kevin Christopher Ray, Feb. 7, 1994. BBA in Acctg., U. Ga., 1990, M Acctg. in Taxation, 1991. CPA, 1994. Acct. Robert A. Shuman, CPA, Savannah, Ga., 1991-96; tax mgr. Boswell Davis and Assocs. PC, Savannah, 1996—. Mem. Am. Inst. CPA's, Ga. Soc. CPA's, Savannah Estate Planning Coun., Inst. Mgmt. Accts. Avocations: cooking, reading, needlepoint.

RAY, SUSAN ELAINE, principal; b. Huntington, W.Va. d. Emory Joseph and Frances Fulkerson Ray. BS, Fla. State U., Tallahassee, 1974, MS in Edn., 1976; MS in Edn. Adminstrn., Coll. New Rochelle, N.Y., 2003; post grad., St. Johns U. Cert. tchr. N.Y., Fla., admistr. N.Y., Fla. Tchr. Longwood Ctrl. Schs., Middle Island, NY, 1979—85; instr. Elon Coll., NC, 1986—87; tchr. Riverside H.S., Durham, 1988—2000; instr. edn. Kamuzu Coll., Lilogwe, Malawi, 2000; asst. prin. Lake Grove (N.Y.) Sch., 2001—02, Copiague Mid. Sch., 2003—04; prin. The Broach Sch., St. Petersburg, Fla., 2005—. Staff developer Tchg. Children of Poverty and Tng. New Tchrs., Copiague, NY, 2003—04; dir. The Broach Sch., St. Petersburg, Fla., 2005—. Youth coach U.S. Volleyball Assn., Durham, NC, 1988—99; site dir. Internat. Spl. Olympics, 1999; active Tchrs. Africa Fellowship, 2000—01. Named Durham County Tchr. of Yr., 1998, State Volleyball Coach of Yr., N.C. H.S. Athletic Assn., 1998; recipient Outstanding Achievement in Edn award, Duke U., 1998. Mem.: ASCD, Phi Delta Kappa.

RAY, VIRGINIA H. S., columnist, writer; b. Chgo., Aug. 4, 1931; d. Russell Horton and Cora Virginia Stafford; m. Wilson K. Ray, Nov. 8, 1952 (dec. Oct. 14, 2000); 1 child, Virginia Ray Bouchillon. Writer, reporter South Bend (Ind.) Tribune, 1953—58; freelance writer Lausanne, Switzerland, 1963—68, Tokyo, 1973—79; freelance writer, corr. York County Coast Star, Kennebank, Maine, 1989—2002, Biddeford (Maine) Jour. Tribune, 1990—. Newsletter editor Jr. League Pitts., 1969—70, Tokyo Am. Club, 1974—78; founder libr., Fox Chapel, 1st Internat. Fair, Japan, 1974. Active Pitts. Jr. League, 1958—73; chmn. Three Rivers Art Festival, Pitts., 1962; active Kennebankport Hist. Soc., 1990. Mem.: Portland Jr. League, Brick Store Mus. Republican. Avocations: reading, history, travel, tennis. Home: #15 Pt Arundel PO 1144 Kennebunkport ME 04046-1144 Office Phone: 207-967-4227. Personal E-mail: vsr@gwi.net.

RAY, YVONNE MCCARLEY, elementary school educator; b. Hamilton, Ala., Jan. 15, 1948; d. Emit and Mary Lou McCarley; m. John Murray Ray. BS in Elem. Edn., U. Ala., Tuscaloosa, 1970; MS in Elem. Edn., U. North Ala., Florence, 1976, EdS, 1987. Tchr. 1st grade Phillips Elem. Sch., Bear Creek, Ala., 1970; tchr. 3d grade Hamilton Elem., 1970—80, tchr. 4th grade sci., 1980—. CAP educator, aerospace workshop presenter for tchrs.; presenter astronomy programs; condr. workshops NEWMAST-NASA, 1992, NEWEST-NASA, 1991, U.S. Space Found., 1990, Space Orientation for Profl. Educators, 1988, 89. Named Marion County Elem. Tchr. of Yr., 1987, Outstanding Elem. Tchr. Am., 1972; recipient Am. South Grant for Ednl. Excellence, Am. South Bank, 1992, 1994, First Alt. Christa McAuliffe fellowship, State of Ala., 1991—92. Mem.: NEA, Ala. Edn. Assn., Ala. Sci. Tchrs. Assn., Marion County Edn. Assn., Delta Kappa Gamma, Kappa Delta Pi. Baptist. Avocations: boating, snow skiing, aerobics, reading. Home: PO Box 366 3424 Military St S Hamilton AL 35570 Office: Hamilton Elem Sch 784 10th Ave SW Hamilton AL 35570

RAYBURN, CAROLE ANN (MARY AIDA), psychologist, researcher, writer, consultant; b. Washington, Feb. 14, 1938; d. Carl Frederick and Mary Helen (Milkie) Miller; m. Ronald Allen Rayburn (dec. Apr. 1970). BA in Psychology, Am. U., 1961; MA in Clin. Psychology, George Washington U., 1965; PhD in Ednl. Psychology, Cath. U. Am., 1969; MDiv in Ministry, Andrews U., 1980. Lic. psychologist, Md. Psychometrician Columbian Prep. Sch., Washington, 1963; clin. psychologist Spring Grove State Hosp., Catonsville, Md., 1966—68; pvt. practice, 1969, 1971—; staff clin. psychologist Instl. Care Svcs. Divsn. D.C. Children's Ctr., Laurel, Md., 1970—78; psychologist Md. Dept. Vocat. Rehab., 1973—74; psychometrician Montgomery County Pub. Schs., 1981—85. Lectr. Strayer Coll., Washington, 1969-70; forensic psychology expert witness, 1973—; guest lectr. Andrews U., Berrien Springs, Mich., 1979, Hood Coll, Frederick, Md., 1986-88; instr. Johns Hopkins U., 1986, 88-89; adj. faculty Profl. Sch. Psychology Studies, San Diego, 1987; adj. asst. prof. Loyola Coll., Columbia, Md., 1987; cons. Julia Brown Montessori Schs., 1972, 78, 82—, VA Ctr., 1978, 91-93. Editor: (with M.J. Meadow) A Time to Weep and a Time to Sing, 1985; contbg. author: Montessori: Her Method and the Movement (What You Need to Know), 1973, Drugs, Alcohol and Women: A National Forum Source Book, 1975, The Other Side of the Couch: Faith of the Psychotherapist, 1981, Clinical Handbook of Pastoral Counseling, 1985, An Encyclopedic Dictionary of Pastoral Care and Counseling, 1990, Religion Personality and Mental Health, 1993; co-editor (with Violet Franks) Springer Focus on Women series; author copyrighted inventories Religious Occupational and Stress Questionnaire, 1986, Organizational Relationships Survey, 1987, Attitudes Toward Children Inventory, 1987, State-Trait Morality Inventory, 1987, Body Awareness and Sexual Intimacy Comfort Scale (BASICS), 1993, Inventory in Religiousness, 1996, Inventory on Spirituality, 1997, Sports, Exercise, Leadership and Friendship Questionnaire, 1997, Peacefulness Inventory, Life Choices Inventory, 1998, Inventory on the Supreme and Work, 1999, Children's and Adolescents' Peace Inventory, 2002, Inventory on Well-Being, 2004, TEACH: Traumatic Experiences and Children's and Adolescents' Health, 2005, Creative Personality Inventory, 2005, Intuition Inventory, 2005, Health and Traumatic Experiences in Adults, 2005, Inventory on Religiousness, Children's Version, 2005; cons. editor Profl. Psychology, 1980-83; assoc. editor Jour. Pastoral Counseling, 1985-90, guest editor, 1988; coproposer (with Lee Richmond) The Theory and Field of Theobiology: interfacing of theology and the sciences, 1998; mem. editl. bd. Internat. Jour. Ethics (Nova Sci.), 2004—; contbr. numerous articles to profl. jours. Bd. dirs. Psychologists Ethical Treatment of Animals, 1998-2000. Recipient Svc. award Coun. for Advancement Psychol. Professions and Scis., 1975, cert. D.C. Dept. Human Resources, 1975, 76, cert. recognition D.C. Psychol. Assn., 1976, 1985; AAUW rsch. grantee, 1983. Fellow: APA (editl. bd. Jour. Child Clin. Psychology 1978—82, divsn. psychology women chair task force on women and religion 1980—81, chair equal opportunity affirmative action divsn. clin. psychology 1980—82, clin. psychology women's sect. 1984—86, divsn. psychology issues in grad. edn. and clin. tng. 1988—, program chair 1991—94, pres. divsn. psychology of religion 1995—96, gen. psych. divsn. liaison to commn. internat. rels. 2004—, fellow, divsn. on internat. psychology, divsn. psychology of religion, psychology of women, clin. psychology, cons. psychology, gen. psychology, psychotherapy, state assn. affairs, divsn. media psychology, divsn. family psychology, Mentoring award divsn. clin. psychology, sect. of clin. psychology of women 1997, divsn. psychology of religion 1997, William C. Bier rsch. award divsn. psychology of religion 2000), Md. Psychol. Assn. (editor newsletter 1975—76, chair ins. com. 1981—83, pres. 1984—85, exec. adv. com. 1985—, chpt. recognition 1978), Am. Assn. Applied & Preventive Psychology (sec. 1992—93, chair fellows com. 1992—93), Am. Orthopsychiat. Assn.; mem.: Md. Assn. Counseling and Devel., Md. Asn. Measurement and Evaluation (pres. 2005—), Balt. Assn. Cons. Psychologists (pres. 1991—92), Assn. Practicing Psychologists Montgomery-Prince George's Counties (pres. 1986—88, editor newsletter 1990—, treas. 1996—98), Internat. Soc. Polit. Psychology, Psi Chi (hon.). Achievements include research in stress in religious professionals, women and stress, women and religion, pastoral counseling, state-trait morality inventory, leadership, mentoring, clergy stress, psychotherapy, children, body image; intimacy, peacefulness, spirituality, life choices, religiousness, well-being, work, traumatic experiences and health, creative personality, intuition. Address: 1200 Morningside Dr Silver Spring MD 20904-3149 Personal E-mail: valentinecarole@copper.net.

RAYCE, VALERIE LYNN, secondary school educator; b. Joliet, Ill., May 6, 1968; d. James Ray and Sharon Lynn High; m. Michael Thomas Rayce, Aug. 8, 1992; 1 child, Zachery T. BA, Ind. State U., Terre Haute, 1990; AS, U. Indpls., 1995. Phys. therapy asst., athletic trainer Terre Haute Regional Hosp., 1992—97, Greencastle Phys. Therapy, Ind., 1997—2005; ACT, adminstrv. asst. to athletic dir. South Putnam HS, Greencastle, 2005—; phys. therapy asst. Putnam County Hosp., Greencastle, 2005—. Vol. New Providence Bapt. Food Pantry, Greencastle, 2001—, Ind. Sport Corp., Indpls., 2004—. Mem.: Nat. Athletic Trainers Assn. (cert.), Ind. Athletic Trainers Assn. (All-Star Athletic Trainer 2001, 2006), Ind. HS ATCs. Baptist. Avocations: sports, crafts. Office: South Putham HS 1780 E US Hwy 40 Greencastle IN 46135

RAYMER, JOAN KAY, science educator; b. Chadron, Nebr., June 5, 1952; d. Billie Ray and Juanita Violet Jackson; m. Michael Gene Raymer; children: Craig Jason, Justin Dale children: Jeffrey Allan, Janet Michelle, Ryan Jay. BSc, Chadron State Coll., Nebr., 1996. Teacher State of Nebr., 1996. Sci. tchr. Hay Springs Pub. Sch., Nebr., 1996—. Mem. bd. edn. Hay Springs Pub. Sch., Nebr., 1987—92; sunday sch. tchr. Zion Luth. Ch., Hay Springs, Nebr., 1975—98; leader, instr. LaLeche League, Hay Springs, Nebr., 1978—89. Mem.: NSTA (assoc.), Hay Springs Edn. Assn. (assoc.), Nebr. State Edn. Assn. (assoc.), NEA (assoc.). Office: Hay Springs Pub Sch 407 N Baker St Hay Springs NE 69347 Office Phone: 308-638-4434.

RAYMOND, AMANDA, chemistry educator; b. Ill., 1975; d. Frank and Karen Raymond. BS in Chemistry, U. Ill., 1998; MA, North Ctrl. Coll., Naperville, IL, 2001. Cert. H.S. Teacher Ill. Chemistry tchr. Glenbard West H.S., Glen Ellyn, Ill., 1998—2005, Glenbard South H.S., Glen Ellyn, Ill., 2005. Bilingual/ELL Certification scholarship, Nat. Louis U., 2003—05. Home: 1733 Howe Lane Hanover Park IL 60133 Office: Glenbard South HS 23W200 Butterfield Rd Glen Ellyn IL 60137 Personal E-mail: amy-ray@juno.com.

RAYMOND, DOROTHY GILL, lawyer; b. Greeley, Colo., June 2, 1954; d. Robert Marshall and Roberta (McClure) Gill; m. Peter J. Raymond, June 8, 1974. BA summa cum laude, U. Denver, 1975; JD, U. Colo., 1978. Bar: Conn. 1978, Colo. 1981. Assoc. Dworkin, Minogue & Bucci, Bridgeport, Conn., 1978-80; counsel Tele-Communications, Inc., Englewood, Colo., 1981-88; v.p., gen. counsel WestMarc Communications, Inc., Denver, 1988-91, Cable Television Labs., Inc., Boulder, Colo., 1991-96, sr. v.p., gen. counsel, 1996—. Mem. Am. Corp. Counsel Assn. (pres. 1990-91, Colo. chpt. dir. 1988-94), Colo. Assn. Corp. Counsel (pres. 1987), Sports Car Club Am. (nat. champion ladies stock competition 1981, 85, 86, 88). Avocations: sewing, reading, outdoor activities. Office: Cablelabs 858 Coal Creek Cir Louisville CO 80027-9750

RAYMOND, DOROTHY SARNOFF, communications consultant, former actress, former singer; b. N.Y.C. d. Jacob and Belle (Roossin) S.; m. Milton Harold Raymond, Mar. 15, 1957. BA, Cornell U., 1935. Cons. 5 adminstrns., over 12 years; cons. 5 adminstrns. U.S. Dept. State; founder, chmn. Dorothy Sarnoff Speech Dynamics and Communications Svcs. Inc. subs. Oglivy & Mather, N.Y.C., 1975—2000. Lectr., cons. nat. and internat. orgns., 1975—. Appeared in Broadway plays: Rosalinda, 1942, Magdalena, 1948, The King and I, 1951, My Darling Aida, 1953; debut in opera as Marguerite in Faust, Phila. Opera, 1942; leading roles with N.Y.C., Phila., L.A. and San Francisco Civic Light, New Orleans, St. Louis Mcpl., Salt Lake City operas include La Boheme, Tosca, Tales of Hoffmann, Carmen, Merry Widow, Fleidermaus, Pagliacci, New Moon, Chocolate Soldier, Great Waltz, Vagabond King; soprano soloist with various symphony orchs., soloist and guest on numerous TV programs incl. Ed Sullivan Shows, 1951—; author: Speech Can Change Your Life, 1970, Make the Most of Your Best, 1981, Never Be Nervous Again, 1988, contbr. articles to profl. jours. and mags. Mem. spl. med. adv. bd. N.Y. Cornell Hosp. Recipient Gold Medal of Honor award for disting. svc. to humanity Nat. Inst. Social Scis.; named Woman of Achievement Albert Einstein Med. Coll. Mem. Women's Forum, Women in Communication, Mortar Bd., Tower Club (Cornell U. chpt.), Lotos Club, N.Y. Hosp. Med. Adv. Bd. Home: 150 E 69th St New York NY 10021-5704

RAYMOND, HOLLY CABRINI, secondary school educator; d. William and Linda Graham; m. Thomas C Graham, Apr. 12, 2003. BS in Human Performance, U. So. Miss., Hattiesburg, 1998; MS in Sports Mgmt., U.S. Sports Acad., Daphne, Ala., 2006. Cert. athletic trainer Nat. Athletic Trainer's Assn., 1998; tchr. Fla. Dept. of Edn., 2001. Athletic trainer Healthtrax, Internat. Inc., New Johnsonville, Tenn., 1998—2001; dance tchr. The Dance Ctr., Waverly, Tenn., 1999—2001; tchr. Windermere Prep. Sch., Fla., 2001—03; dance tchr. Olympia H.S., Orlando, Fla., 2003—, athletic trainer, 2003—; mem. Soul Play Modern Dance Fusion, Orlando, Fla., 2005. Mem.: Am. Coll. of Sports Medicine (assoc.), Fla. Alliance for Health, Phys. Edn., Recreation, and Dance (assoc.), Nat. Dance Edn. Orgn. (assoc.), Nat. Athletic Trainer's Assn. (assoc.). Office: Olympia High School 4301 S Apopka-Vineland Rd Orlando FL 32835 Office Phone: 407-905-6400.

RAYMOND, JILLYNNE, literature and language educator; b. Mankato, Minn., Apr. 6, 1961; m. Tom Raymond; children: Josh, Spencer. BA, Macalester Coll., St. Paul, 1981; EdnM, U. Wis., La Crosse, 1998; MA in English, Mankato State U., Minn., 2003. Tchr. Red Wing H.S., Minn., 1993—. Play dir. Red Wing H.S., Minn., 1993—. Dir.: (comty. theatre) Funny Girl. Recipient Grad. Student Achievement award. Mem.: Comm. and Theatre Arts Assn. Minn. (assoc.). Office Phone: 651-385-4600.

RAYMOND, KRISTINA LYNN, special education educator; b. Worcester, Mass., Jan. 23, 1981; d. Roger Marcel Raymond, Jr. and Karen Raymond. BA of Sci. in Edn., Bridgewater State Coll., Mass., 2004. Lic. educator severe disabilities Mass. Bd. Edn. Applied behavior analysis tutor North River Collaborative, Rockland, Mass., 2002—03; substitute Evergreen Ctr., Milford, 2000—03; intense spl. needs tchr. Amesbury Pub. Schs., 2003—04; behavioral mgmt. tchr. Haverhill Pub. Schs., 2004—. Tchr. Discovery Club, Haverhill, 2004—; tutor Haverhill Pub. Schs., 2004—. Mem.: Coun. for Exceptional Children, Psi Chi. Avocations: singing, trumpet, crafts, puzzles.

RAYMOND, LISA, professional tennis player; b. Norristown, Pa., Aug. 10, 1973; d. Ted and Nancy Raymond. Student, U. Fla. Profl. tennis player WTA Tour, 1993—. Mem. U.S. Fed Cup Team, 1997—98, 2000, 2002—03. Recipient 1 Career singles title, 42 Career Doubles Titles, WTA Tour; winner U.S. Open, 1996, 2002, Wimbledon, 1999, Australian Open Grand Slam doubles, 2000, Wimbledon, 2001, U.S. Open Grand Slam doubles, 2001, WTA Doubles Championship, 2001, Mixed Doubles Roland Garros, 2003; named NCAA Singles Champion, 1992, 93. Avocations: shopping, hanging out with friends, watching television, football, volleyball. Office: US Tennis Assn 70 W Red Oak Ln White Plains NY 10604-3602

RAYMOND, SANDRA LYNN, elementary school educator; b. Washington, Mar. 14, 1944; d. Glenn David and Esther Francis (Smith) Thompson; m. Philip John Raymond, Apr. 8, 1967; children: Brian Jon, Bradley Glenn. BS, U. Md., 1966; postgrad., Trinity Coll., Am. U., U. Western Md. Cert. elem. tchr., Md. Spl. edn. tchr. grade 7-8, then tchr. grades 2-3 and coord. Montgomery County Pub. Schs., Rockville, Md., 1985—; tchr. 2nd grade, primary sci. coord. Archdiocese of Washington. Staff devel. educator NCPS; mentor County Kazakhstan. Mem. nursery sch. coun. YMCA; mem. parents coun. Bullis Sch. Greater Washington, 1988-93, bd. dirs., 1988-93, v.p., 1992; elected official mem. State/County Dem Ctrl. Com. Mem. NEA (del. 1992—), Md. State Edn. Assn. (leadership tng. com. 1993—), Montgomery County Edn. Assn., Montgomery County Educators Assn. (officer 1997—, bd. dirs. 1993—, bargaining team mem. 1991-93, bargaining support network 1992—, bargaining support cluster coord. 1992, polit. action seminar mem. 1993, chair mem. benefits 1993—), Md. State Tchrs. Assn. (del. 1990—, Montgomery Women, Delta Kappa Gamma. Office: Darnestown Elementary Sch 15030 Turkey Foot Rd Gaithersburg MD 20878-3907 Address: 1 Meadowcroft Ct Montgomery Village MD 20886-1340

RAYNER, SUZAN L., medical association administrator, physiatrist; BA, Stanford Univ.; MD, Northwestern Univ.; MPH. Cert. Nat. Bd. Medical Examiners, Am. Bd. Physical Medicine & Rehabilitation. Residency Rehabilitation Inst. Chgo. Northwestern Univ.; assoc. prof. medicine UCLA; v.p. ambulatory care VA Greater LA Healthcare Sys.; physiatrist, med. dir., exec. v.p. med. affairs Schwab Rehabilitation Hosp., Chgo.; physiatrist Mount Sinai Hosp., Weiss Meml. Hosp., Univ. Chgo. Hosp., Swedish Covenant Hosp., St. Bernard's Hosp., Loretto Hosp., Bethany Hosp., Lincoln Park Hosp., Kindred Hosp., St. Anthony's Hosp. Bd. dir. RehabCare Corp. Bd. chmn. Sargent Shriver Nat. Ctr. Poverty Law. Mem.: Am. Acad. Physical Medicine & Rehabilitation. Office: Schwab Rehabilitation Hosp 1401 S California Blvd Chicago IL 60608*

RAYNOLDS, ELAINE SPALDING, sales executive, photojournalist; b. Flushing, N.Y., June 26, 1940; d. John Arpad and Thelma Smith Rado; m. Arthur Reginald Raynolds, Nov. 21, 1992; m. Larry Lee Spalding (div.); children: Timothy A. Spalding, Linda Spalding Morrison. Student, Coll. Wooster, Ohio, 1959—60, NYU, N.Y., 1961—62. Administrv. asst. Bus.

Internat., N.Y.C., 1960—64; pub. rels. staff Duke Med. Ctr., Durham, NC, 1967—70; sales exec. Seyforth Labs., Clearwater, 1975—95; adminstrv. aide Pinellas County, Clearwater, Fla., 1980—90; sales exec. Herbalife Internat., Lake Toxaway, NC, 1995—. Photojournalist Mountain Voice, Lake Toxaway, 2004—. Musician: Brevard (N.C.) Cmty. Band, 2003—04; co-author: Art on a Shoestring. Mem. Brevard C. of C., NC. Mem.: Nat. Mus. Women in the Arts, Friends Libr., Transylvania Arts Coun., Transylvania Choral Soc. (treas. 2003—). Avocations: travel, photography, music, nature, wildlife. Home: PO Box 334 Lake Toxaway NC 28747 Personal E-mail: eraynolds@citcom.net.

RAZ, HILDA, editor-in-chief, language educator; b. Rochester, N.Y., May 4, 1938; d. Franklyn Emmanuel and Dolly (Horwich) R.; m. Frederick M. Link, June 9, 1957 (div. 1969); children: John Franklin Link, Aaron Link; m. Dale Nordyke, Oct. 4, 1980. BA, Boston U., 1960. Asst. dir. Planned Parenthood League of Mass., Boston, 1960-62; edit. asst. Prairie Schooner, Lincoln, Nebr., 1970-74, contbg. editor, 1974-77, assoc. editor, 1977-87, acting editor, 1981-83, 85, poetry editor, 1980-87, editor-in-chief, 1987—; prof. dept English U. Nebr., Lincoln, 1990—. Luschei endowed lectr., reader, panelist in field; participant many workshops, symposia, confs.; panelist creativity arts com. NEA, 2000, PEN, 2004; judge Kenyon Rev., 1990, Ill. Art Coun./NEA fellowships, 1987; bd. govs. Ctr. for Great Plains Studies, U. Nebr., 1989-95. Author: The Bone Dish, 1997, What Is Good, 1997, Divine Honors, 1998, Trans, 2001, What Becomes You, 2007; editor: Best of Prairie Schooner: Fiction and Poetry, 2001, Best of Prairie Schooner: Essays, 2000, Living on the Margins, 1999, other books; editor Nebr. Humanist, 1990. Pres. Assoc. Writing Programs, bd. dirs., 1988-89, ex-officio pres., 1989-90, v.p., 1987-88; bd. dirs. Nebr. Libr. Heritage Assn., 1988-91; mem. Mayor's Blue Ribbon Com. on Arts, 1985-88; bd. dirs. Planned Parenthood League Nebr., 1978-83, sec. bd. dirs., 1979-80, chair long-term planning com., 1980-81, 81-82. Recipient Literary Heritage award, Mayor's Art award, Lincoln, 1988, 2002, ORCA award, 2002, May Sartm award, NE Poetry Club, 2004; Bread Loaf scholar editors, 1974, poetry, 1985; Robert Frost fellow, 1988, 89, Mag. Panel fellow, 1993, 94. Avocation: gardening. Home: 960 S Cotner Blvd Lincoln NE 68510-4926 Office: Univ of Nebraska Lincoln Prairie Schooner 201 Andrews Hall Lincoln NE 68588-0334 Office Phone: 402-472-1812. E-mail: HRaz1@unl.edu.

RAZOHARINORO, archivist, historian, researcher; b. Antsirabe, Madagasikara, Republic of Madagascar, Nov. 19, 1936; d. Rakotonjanahary and Razanamanana; m. Eugene Randriamboavonjy; children: Vonimbolanoro, Soalandy, Tianjanahary. Degree in Archives, Ecole Nat. des Chartes, Paris, 1964. Cert. archivist. Archivist Republic of Madagasikar Nat. Archives, Antananarivo, Madagasikara, 1964-69, chief, dir., 1969-2001; instr. history U. Antananarivo, 1973-2001; ret. V.p. Malagascar Acad. Arts, Lit. and Scis. Editor Tantara, 1973-95; author articles and revs. Bd. dirs. Albert Rakoto-Ratsimamanga Mus. Decorated Grand Croix de 2d classe order. Mem.: Madagasikara Acad. Lutheran.

RCHL, BEATRICE CLAIR, editor, art historian; d. William Richard and Alicia Stein Rehl; m. Richard Allan Etlin, July 31, 1995. BA, Princeton U., NJ, 1976; MA, NYU, 1978, PhD, 1984. Editor George Braziller, Inc., NYC, 1983—89; sr. editor humanities Cambridge U. Press, 1989—. Dir. edn. WNET Channel 13, NYC, 1987—89. Editor: Art of the Western World, 1989; translator: Pastels, 1989. Mem.: Am. Inst. Archaeology, Coll. Art Assn. (bd. dirs. 1995—99). Avocations: languages, travel, piano, ballet, theater. Home: 229 E 79 St Apt 15F New York NY 10021 Office: Cambridge U Press 32 Avenue of the Americas New York NY 10013-2473 Office Phone: 212-337-5096.

REA, ANN HADLEY KUEHN, retired social services administrator, marketing professional; b. Arlington, Va, Oct. 14, 1962; d. Alvin Henry Kuehn and Barbara Ann Schanzenbach; m. Burt Richard Rea, June 30, 1990; 3 children. BA in Communications, Va. Poly. Inst. & State U., Blacksburg, 1984; MA in Liberal Studies, Georgetown U., Washington, 1993. Desk asst., prodn. asst. ABC News, Washington, 1986—88; media/info. officer Embassy of Australia, 1988—90; mktg. dir. The Connection for Women & Families, Summit, NJ, 1992—2002, ret., 2002. Mem. LWV. Episcopalian.

REA, ANN W., librarian; b. Jefferson City, Mo., Aug. 3, 1944; d. William H. and Ruby (Fogleman) Webb; m. Glen N. Rea, Sept. 28, 1974; children: Sarah, Rebecca. BA, U. Mo., 1966; MLS, U. So. Calif., 1968. Libr. St. Charles (Mo.) County Libr., 1967-71; libr. adult svcs. Paterson (N.J.) Free Pub. Libr., 1971-74; libr. Beal Coll. Libr., Bangor, Maine, 1983—. Mem ALA, Maine Libr. Assn.(scholarship and loan com.). Office: Beal Coll Libr 99 Farm Rd Bangor ME 04401 Office Phone: 207-947-4591.

REA, ANNE E., lawyer; b. 1959; AB, Brown U., 1981; JD, U. Cgho., 1984. Bar: Ill. 1984. With Sidley Austin Brown & Wood, Chgo., 1984—, ptnr., 1992—. Selected as one of 15 Rising Stars You Won't Want to Oppose in Ct., Ill. Legal Times. Mem.: ABA, Leadership Greater Chgo., Chgo. Bar Assn., Ill. State Bar Assn. Office: Sidley Austin Brown and Wood Bank One Plz 10 S Dearborn St Chicago IL 60603

READ, SISTER JOEL, academic administrator; BS in Edn., Alverno Coll., 1948; MA in History, Fordham U., 1951; degree (hon.), Lakeland Coll., 1972, Wittenburg U., 1976, Marymount Manhattan Coll., 1978, DePaul U., 1985, Northland Coll., 1986, SUNY, 1986, Lawrence U., 1997, Marquette U., 2003. Former prof., dept. chmn. history dept. Alverno Coll., Milw., pres., 1968—2003. Past pres. Am. Assn. for Higher Edn., 1976-77; mem. coun. NEH, 1977-84; bd. dirs. Ednl. Testing Svc., 1987-93, Neylan Commn., 1985-90; past pres. Wis. Assn. Ind. Colls. and Univs.; mem. Commn. on Status of Edn. for Women, 1971-76, Am. Assn. Colls., 1971-77. Bd. dirs. Jr. Achievement, 1991-2003, State of Wis. Coll. Savs. Bd., 2000-03, Greater Milw. Com., Wis. Found. Ind. Colls., 1990-99, Women's Philanthropy Inst., 1997-2000, Wis. Women Higher Edn. Leadership, 1997-2000; bd. dirs. YMCA, 1989-2003, trustee, 2003—; mem. Profl. Dimensions. First recipient Anne Roe award Harvard U. Grad. Sch. Edn., 1980; recipient Morris T. Keaton award, Coun. for Adult and Experiential Learning, 1992; recipient Jean B. Harris award, Rotary; Paul Harris fellow, Rotary. Fellow Am. Acad. Arts and Scis., Wis. Acad. Arts and Scis. Office: Alverno Coll Office of Pres PO Box 343922 Milwaukee WI 53234-3922 E-mail: joel.read@alverno.edu.

READ, SUSAN PHILLIPS, state appeals court judge; b. Gallipolis, Ohio, June 27, 1947; d. Gomer Wesley and Elizabeth Molineaux Phillips; m. Howard John Read. BA summa cum laude, Ohio Wesleyan U., 1969; JD Floyd R. Mechem Prize Scholar, U. Chgo., 1972. Bar: NY 1974. Legal intern US Atomic Energy Commn., 1972—73; asst. counsel SUNY, 1974—77; in-house counsel GE Co., 1977—88, chief environ. counsel, 1980—85; ptnr. Bond, Schoeneck & King, Albany, NY, 1988—94; dep. counsel to Gov. Pataki, 1995—97; judge (confirmed for an unexpired term in 1998 and full term in 1999) NY Ct. of Claims, 1998—2003, presiding judge, 1999; assoc. judge NY State Ct. Appeals, Schenectady, 2003—. Mem.: Phi Beta Kappa. Office: NY State Ct Appeals 20 Eagle St Albany NY 12207-1095*

READE, CLAIRE ELIZABETH, lawyer; b. Waltham, Mass., June 2, 1952; d. Kemp Brownell and Suzanne Helen (Dorntge) R.; m. Earl Phillip Steinberg, Nov. 22, 1980; children: Evan Samuel, Emma Miriam. BA, Conn. Wesleyan U., 1973; JD, Harvard U., 1979; MA in Law and Diplomacy, Tufts U., 1979. Bar: Mass. 1980, D.C. 1983. Sheldon fellow Harvard U., Cambridge, Mass. and, Republic of China, 1979-80; assoc. Ropes & Gray, Boston, 1980-82, Arnold & Porter, Washington, 1982-86, ptnr. internat. law, chmn. Hiring Com., 1987—2006; chief counsel China trade enforcement Office U.S. Trade Rep., Washington, 2006—. Exec. editor: International Trade Policy: The Lawyer's Perspective, 1985; contbr. articles to profl. jours. Mem. ABA (co-chair internat. trade com.), DC Bar Assn., Coun. on Foreign Rels. Office: US Trade Rep 600 17th St NW Washington DC 20508

READE, KATHLEEN MARGARET, paralegal, author, educator; b. Ft. Worth, Tex., Sept. 6, 1947; d. Ralph S. and Margaret Catherine (Stark) R.; 1 child, Kathryn Michelle Carter. BA in English and Polit. Sci., Tex. Christian U., 1978; student, El Centro Coll.; postgrad., Tex. Christian U., Tex. Tech. Asst. land and legal dept. Am. Quasar Petroleum, Ft. Worth, 1971-74; paralegal and office mgr. Law Offices of George Sims, Ft. Worth, 1974-81; asst. Criminal Cts. #2 and #3 Tarrant County Dist. Atty., Ft. Worth, 1981; ind. paralegal Ft. Worth, 1982-84; paralegal Law Offices of Brent Burford, Ft. Worth, 1982-85; sr. paralegal/litigation Law Offices of Windle Turley, Dallas, 1985-90; major case supr. The Dent Law Firm, Ft. Worth, 1990-96, Whitaker, Chalk, Swindle & Sawyer, LLP, Ft. Worth, 1996—. Cons./instr. paralegal program, U. Tex., Arlington, 1996—; active Tex. Christian U. Writer's Continuous Workshop. Author: Plaintiff's Personal Injury Handbook, 1995; contbg. author: Legal Assistant's Letter Book, 1995; editl. com. Tex. Paralegal Jour.; contbr. articles to profl. jours. Recipient scholarship Tex. Christian U., Ft. Worth. Mem. AAUW, Am. Assn. Paralegal Edn., Assn. Trial Lawyers, State Bar of Tex. (Legal Asst. Divsn.), Nat. Assn. Legal Assts., Nat. Paralegal Assn., Ft. Worth Paralegal Assn., Freelance Writers' Network, Austin Writer's League, Okla. Writers' Fedn., Text and Acad. Authors. Home: PO box 101641 Fort Worth TX 76185-1641 E-mail: kmrparal@aol.com.

READIE, COLLEEN BETH, microbiologist; b. Plainfield, NJ, July 8, 1970; d. Henry and Kathleen Elizabeth Readie. BS in Biology, Monmouth Coll., 1992. Microbiologist Thomas J. Lipton Ltd., Englewood Cliffs, NJ, 1993, Integra Life Scis., Plainsboro, NJ, 1994—. Vol. Spl. Olympics, NJ, 2000—. Student Rsch. fellow, Solvay Pharm., 2004. Mem.: PDA. Roman Catholic. Avocations: cycling, triathlons, camping.

READING, MARGERY SCHROCK, psychology professor, artist; b. Pitts., Pa., Oct. 5, 1935; d. Archy Toy and Isabelle Adams Schrock; m. George Paul Reading, Dec. 29, 1984; m. Roger Kenneth Brown (div.); 1 child, Kathryn Lynn. BA cum laude in Art, We. Coll. Women, 1957; MEd in Tchr. Edn., Springfield Coll., Mass., 1961; MA in Clin. and Sch. Psychology, SUNY, Plattsburgh, N.Y., 1972; PhD in Clin. Psychology, SUNY, Albany, N.Y., 1976. Lic. psychologist N.Y., 1977, cert. sch. psychologist Nat. Bd. Certification, 1988, N.Y., 1989. Psychologist Faculty and Counseling Ctr. Siena Coll., Loudonville, NY, 1978—84; from asst. prof. psychology to assoc. prof. emerita Rochester (N.Y.) Inst. Tech., 1985—95, assoc. prof. emerita, 1995—. Vis. prof. Shanghai (China) Inst. Tech., 1990. Exhibitions include U. N.Mex., 1999 (Pres. Choice award, 1999), Taos Open, N.Mex., 1996—2004. Adv. coun. spl. edn. BOCES, Rochester, 1989—92; active Kerry Campaign Dem. Party, Taos, N.Mex., 2004. Scholar, We. Coll. Women, 1953—57. Mem.: Taos (N.Mex.) Soc. Portrait Artists (sec. 2003—05). Democrat. Unitarian. Avocations: archaeology, travel, reading. Home: HCR 74 Box 22624 El Prado NM 87529 Studio: 291 Hondo Seco Rd Arroyo Seco NM 87514

READOUT, ROSALEE JOYCE, retired education educator; b. Urbana, Ohio, Nov. 24, 1936; d. Floyd Emerson and Naomi H. (Hartzler) King; m. R. Morris Stehman July 19, 1953 (div. Nov. 1975); children: Judy Allene, Jerry Allen, Kathy Lynn; m. David Earl Readout, Oct. 29, 1976. AAS, Aims Community Coll., 1977, AA, 1978; B in Edn., Colo. State U., 1979; Masters, Cen. State U., 1986. Cert. educator. Buyer, dept. mgr. Joslins Dept. Store, Greeley, Colo., 1973-77; instr. small bus. mgmt. Larimer County Vocat. Ctr., Ft. Collins, Colo., 1978-79, clk. typist, instr., 1979-82; bus. edn. instr. Ea. Okla. Vocat. Ctr., Choctaw, 1982-86; office mgr. Stalling Ins., Vermilion, Ohio, 1987-88; instr. Bryant Stratton Bus. Inst., Parma, Ohio, 1989—93; payroll, acct. payable San Juan Living Ctr., Montrose, Colo., 1995—97; instr. Pikes Peak CC, Colorado Springs, Colo., 1997—98; sales assoc. Corman's Hallmark, Montrose, Colo., 1998—2002; ret., 2002. Recipient Master Tchr. award Ohio Coun. Pvt. Schs. and Colls., 1992. Mem. Nat. Bus. Edn. Assn. Republican. Avocations: photography, travel, reading, camping. Home: 66340 Largo Ln Montrose CO 81401-7101

REAGAN, BETTYE JEAN, artist; b. Oviedo, Fla., Jan. 27, 1934; d. Andrew and Mary Alice (Powell) Aulin; m. Joel Edwin McGill, Sept. 16, 1952 (dec. July 15, 1956); children: Daniel Lee, Kathleen Ann; m. Donald Thomas Reagan, Mar. 30, 1957; children: Debbie Lynn, Julie Karin, Andrew Scott, Patrick Kelley. Grad., Oviedo (Fla.) High Sch., 1951; student, Arrowmont Arts and Crafts Sch., 1993—96. Co-chmn. 1st St. Gallery, Sanford, Fla., 1986. One-woman shows include G. Sander Fine Art Gallery, Daytona Beach, Fla., 1986, 1987, Artist Hand Gallery, Oviedo, 1983, two-person shows, Ormond Beach (Fla.) Meml. Mus., 1987, 1998, 1st St. Gallery, Sanford, Fla., 1992, exhibited in group shows at Maitland (Fla.) Rotary Art Festival, 1991, St. Johns River Art Festival, 1994, Heathrow Festival of the Arts, 2001, Winter Park Sidewalk Art Festival, 2000, one-woman shows include Ormond Meml. Art Mus., Ormond Beach, 1998, Hope Barton Fine Arts, Clermont, 2001, Steinway Piano Gallery, 2003. Recipient 2nd Place, Maitland Art Festival, 1995, Award of Distinction, Deland (Fla.) Fall Festival of Art, 1995, 1st Place, Beaux Arts 45th Annual Festival Art, 1996, Cert. of Recognition for leadership and role model, Fla. Ho. of Reps., 2001, Poster Artist, Five Fla. Art Festivals, 1991—2002. Mem.: Sanford Seminole C. of C. (chmn. cultural arts com.), Portrait Soc. Am., Pastel Soc. Am. Republican. Baptist. Avocations: tennis, swimming, beach. Home: 2636 Reagan Tr Lake Mary FL 32746 Office: Reagan Studios 2636 Reagan Tr Lake Mary FL 32746 Office Phone: 407-322-8177. E-mail: donbetreagan@aol.com.

REAGAN, JANET THOMPSON, psychologist, educator; b. Sept. 15, 1945; d. Virgil Joe and Carrie (Alexander) Thompson; children: Natalia Alexandria, Robert Barry. BA in Psychology, Berea Coll., 1967; PhD in Psychology, Vanderbilt U., 1972. Mgr. rsch. and eval. Nashville Mental Health Ctr., 1971-72; mgr. eval. Family Health Found., New Orleans, 1973-74; asst. prof. dept. health systems mgmt. Tulane U., New Orleans, 1974-77; dir. eval. Project Heavy West, L.A., 1977-78; asst. prof. health adminstrn. Calif. State U.-Northridge, 1978-83; assoc. prof., dir. health adminstrn., 1983-87; prof., dir. health adminstrn., 1987—. Cons. in field. Contbr. articles to profl. jours., chpts. to books; mem. editl. bd. Jour. Long Term Care Adminstrn., Healthcare Papers. Mem. Am. Pub. Health Assn., Am. Coll. Health Care Adminstrn., Assn. Health Svcs. Rsch., Am. Coll. Health Care Execs. (com. on higher edn. 1987, chmn. 1991), Assn. Univ. Programs in Health Adminstrn. (task force on undergrad. edn. 1985-90, chmn. 1988-90, mem. bd. dirs. 1995, chmn. bd. dirs. 1998-99), Psi Chi, Phi Kappa Phi. Office: Calif State U Dept Health Sci Northridge CA 91330-0001 Office Phone: 818-677-2298. Business E-Mail: janet.reagan@csun.edu.

REAGAN, MELODIE A., communications executive; d. Wyman Reagan and Elaine Edwards; m. Frank Slavick, Aug. 7, 1993; children: Aaron Slavick, Bryce Slavick. BSBA Magna Cum Luade, U. Mo., 1986. Acting dir. Sprint, Kansas City, Mo., 1989—93; sr. mgr. Wiltel, Tulsa, Okla., 1993—94; prin. Telechoice, Montclair, NJ, 1994—97; sr. dir. US West Long Distance, Denver, 1997—99; sr. v.p. Level 3 Comm., Denver, 1999—2001; ceo Auromira Exec. Advantage, Superior, Colo., 2001—. Pres., founder Women Bus. Execs., Superior, Colo., 2001—; founder Colo. Bus. Assn. Coun., Denver, 2002—. Contbr. articles to prof. jours.; presenter in field. Chmn. Women Bus. Executives, Superior, Colo., 2001—03; bd. mem. Wellness for Women, Denver, 2002—03; mktg. chair Denver Shares, Denver, 2003—03; advisor Corybant Iveena, Boulder, Colo., 2002—03. Recipient Nat. Mktg. Hon., Alpha Mu Alpha, 1986, Nat. Bus. Hon., Beta Gamma Sigma, 1986, Women Excellence award, NAFE, 2003. Mem.: Network Denver, Colo. Software Internet Assn., Rocky Women In Tech., Exec. Coun. Avocations: mother, mentor. Office: Auromira Exec Advantage 1825 South Pitkin Ave Superior CO 80027 Business E-Mail: mreagan@auromira.com.

REAGAN, NANCY DAVIS (ANNE FRANCIS ROBBINS), former First Lady of the United States, volunteer; b. NYC, July 6, 1921; d. Kenneth and Edith (Luckett) Robbins, Loyal Davis (Stepfather); m. Ronald Reagan, Mar. 4, 1952 (dec. June 5, 2004); children: Patricia Ann, Ronald Prescott stepchildren: Maureen(dec.), Michael. BA in Theatre, Smith Coll., 1943; LLD (hon.), Pepperdine U., 1983; LHD (hon.), Georgetown U., 1987. Sales clk. Marshall Fields Dept. Store, Chgo.; First Lady of the U.S. Washington, 1981—89. Contract actress, MGM, 1949-56; films include Portrait of Jennie, 1948, East Side, West Side, 1949, Doctor and the Girl, 1949, Shadow on the Wall, 1950, The Next Voice You Hear, 1950, Night into Morning, 1951, It's a Big Country, 1951, Shadow in the Sky, 1952, Talk About a Stranger, 1952, Donovan's Brain, 1953, Hellcats of the Navy, 1957, Crash Landing, 1958, You Can't Hurry Love, 1988, Lunar: Silver Star Story, 1992; TV credits include Schlitz Playhouse of Stars, 1951, Climax, 1954, General Electric Theater, 1953, Zane Grey Theater, 1956, The Tall Man, 1960, 87th Precint, 1961, Wagon Train, 1957, Different Strokes, 1978, Dynasty, 1981; Broadway: Lute Song, 1946; formerly author syndicated column on prisoner-of-war and missing-in-action soldiers and their families; author: Nancy, 1980; (with Jane Wilkie) To Love a Child, 1982, (with William Novak) My Turn: The Memoirs of Nancy Reagan, 1989. Civic worker, visited wounded Viet Nam vets., sr. citizens, hosps. and schs. for physically and emotionally handicapped children, active in furthering foster grandparents for handicapped children program; hon. nat. chmn. Aid to Adoption of Spl. Kids, 1977; spl. interest in fighting alcohol and drug abuse among youth: hosted first ladies from around the world for 2d Internat. Drug Conf., 1985; hon. chmn. Just Say No Found., Nat. Fedn. of Parents for Drug-Free Youth, Nat. Child Watch Campaign, President's Com. on the Arts and Humanities, Wolf Trap Found. bd. of trustees, Nat. Trust for Historic Preservation, Cystic Fibrosis Found., Nat. Republican Women's Club; hon. pres. Girl Scouts of Am. Named one of Ten Most Admired Am. Women, Good Housekeeping mag., ranking #1 in poll, 1984, 85, 86; Woman of Yr. Los Angeles Times, 1977; permanent mem. Hall of Fame of Ten Best Dressed Women in U.S.; recipient humanitarian awards from Am. Camping Assn., Nat. Council on Alcoholism, United Cerebral Palsy Assn., Internat. Ctr. for Disabled; Boys Town Father Flanagan award; 1986 Kiwanis World Service medal; Variety Clubs Internat. Lifeline award; numerous awards for her role in fight against drug abuse. Republican. Presbyterian.*

REAGAN, PENNY A., elementary school educator; b. Thompkinsville, Ky., July 29, 1965; d. Jack T. and Mamie Christine Reagan. BS in Edn., Tenn. Technol. U., Cookeville, 2005. Substitute tchr. Overton County Schs., Livingston, Tenn., 1990—93; youth leader Riverside Assn., Livingston, Tenn., 1990—2006; tchr. Livingston Head Start, Tenn., 1991—; youth dir. Allons Bapt. Ch., Tenn., 2001—06; asst. coach girls basketball Livingston Acad., Tenn., 2005—06. Baptist. Avocations: basketball, volleyball, softball, coaching, referee. Home: 124 Boot Hill Ln Allons TN 38541

REALE, SARA JANE, museum education director; b. Jamestown, N.Y., Jan. 25, 1961; d. Irving Reuben and Frances Goldinger Wolinsky; m. David Anthony Reale, July 28, 1985; children: Michael Joseph, Lauren Rebecca. AS, Jamestown (N.Y.) C.C., 1983; BA, Fredonia (N.Y.) State U., 1985. Mus. tchr. Fenton History Ctr., Jamestown, NY, 1990—95, dir. edn. and pub. programming, 1995—, interim mus. exec. dir., 2003—04; group sales, edn. coord. Lucille Ball/Desi Arnaz Ctr., Jamestown, NY, 2005—. Mem. adv. bd. Roger Tory Peterson Inst., Jamestown, 1997-2001; mem. Chautauqua County Visitors Bur. Motorcoach Com., 1998-; mem. curriculum devel. com. Robert H. Jackson Ctr., Jamestown, 2001-03. Mem. AAUW. Avocations: travel, historical research. Office: 300 N Main Jamestown NY 14701 Office Phone: 716-484-0800 ext. 211. E-mail: sara@lucy-desi.com.

REALS ELLIG, JANICE, marketing professional, human resources specialist; b. NYC, May 14, 1946; d. Otto Peter and Anne (Briganti) Astolfi; m. Paul T. Reals, 1971 (div.); m. Bruce Robert Ellig, July 16, 1994; 1 child, Meredith Evans. BBA, U. Iowa, 1968; MA, Rider Coll., Princeton, N.J., 1978. Dir. Shareholders Mgmt., L.A., 1968—71; v.p. human resources Cooper Med. Ctr., NJ, 1971—80; dir. human resources Pfizer, N.Y.C., 1980—86; v.p. human resources Citibank, 1986—91; sr. v.p. mktg., human resources, adminstrn. Ambac Fin. Group, 1991—2000; prin. Heidrick & Struggles, 2000; pres., owner Gould, McCoy, Chadick, Ellig, 2000—. Chmn. bd. Women's Econ. Roundtable, N.Y.C., 1997—98. Author: What Every Successful Woman Knows, 2001. Bd. dirs. Fountain House, N.Y.C., Nat. Exec. Svc. Corp., N.Y.C., 2000-03, YMCA of N.Y., 2004—; bd. dirs. U. Iowa Found., 2003—, pres. club, 2000—; dir. adv. coun. Bus. Sch., U. Iowa, Iowa City, 1998-2004; bd. dirs. Women in the State and House, Washington, 1998-2006; mem. bus. com. Met. Mus. Art, N.Y.C., 1994—; bd. mem. Women's Forum, N.Y.C., 2004—; mem. adv. coun. Children's Aid Soc., N.Y.C., 1995-97; mem. leadership cir. Women's Campaign Fund, N.Y.C., 1990—2003. Named Woman of Yr., Rhinelander's Children Ctr./Children's Aid Soc., 1999, Woman of Excellence award TV Channel 21, 2002. Mem. Fin. Women's Assn., Econ. Club N.Y.C. Republican. Avocations: writing, gourmet cooking, reading, travel, tennis. Home: Apt 12G 10 Gracie Sq New York NY 10028-7052 Office: Gould McCoy Chadick Ellig 300 Park Ave New York NY 10022 Office Phone: 212-861-5248. Business E-Mail: jrellig@gmcsearch.com.

REAME, NANCY KING, nursing educator; BSN, Mich. State U., 1969; MSN, Wayne State U., Detroit, 1974, PhD in Physiology, 1977. RN. Postdoctoral fellow U. Mich., Ann Arbor, prof. dept. nursing, 1980—; Rhetaugh Graves Dumas Endowed Chair, Nursing Rsch. U. Mich. Health Sys., rsch. scientist, Reproductive Sciences Program, 1990—, dir., Nat. Ctr. for Infertility Rsch., 1990—95. Co-author: Our Bodies, Ourselves; actress The Vagina Monologues, U. Mich., 2002. Bd. dir. N.Am. Menopause Soc. Fellow: AAAS; mem.: Am. Acad. Nursing, Inst. Medicine. Achievements include research in in brain aging and menopause; long-term satisfaction and outcomes after surrogate pregnancy; bioethics of assisted reproduction; gender and health. Office: Univ Mich Sch Nursing 400 N Ingalls Bldg Rm 2238 Ann Arbor MI 48109-0482 Office Phone: 734-647-0134. Office Fax: 734-936-3591. E-mail: nreame@umich.edu.

REAMS, PATRICIA LYNN, retired elementary school educator; b. Fresno, Calif., Dec. 10, 1938; d. Chris H. and Marjorie Lois (nee Maul) Pedersen; m. William Everett Harvey (dec.); m. George William Reams, Nov. 10, 1972; children: Holly, Richard, George, Susan, Kristin. AA, Colo. Women's Coll., 1958; BA, San Jose State U., Calif., 1960. Cert. tchg. life diploma 1966. Tchr. Salinas Sch. Dist., Calif., 1960—61, Cupertino Sch. Dist., Calif., 1961—63, Spreckels Sch. Dist., Salinas, 1963—68, Alisal Sch. Dist., Salinas, 1971—74, Kingsburg Charter Sch., Calif., 1987—2002. BITSA trainer Fresno County Sch., Kingsburg, 1996—98. Pink lady, women's aux. local hosp., Salinas, Calif., 1972—83, Boulder City, Nev., 1984—87; adv. Rainbow Girls, Salinas, 1980—83; sec. PTA, Boulder City, 1984—86; brownie leader, 1985—86; Girl Scout leader, 1986—87; sec. Kingsburg HS Music Boosters, 1992—94; classroom vol. Lincoln Sch., Kingsburg, 2002—06. Recipient Grand Cross of Color award, Rainbow Girls, 1983. Mem.: PEO (pres. 2004—06), Ladies Oriental Shrine. Republican. Avocations: reading, gardening, travel. E-mail: plreams@sbcglobal.net.

REAMY, MICHAELIN, marriage and family therapist, educator, consultant; b. N.Y.C., Feb. 20, 1938; d. Judson Reamy and Eleanor Stevens (McMichael) R.; m. James Donald Cowie, Aug. 29, 1959; children: Jennifer D., James J., David K., Laura S.; m. Richard Ward Stephenson, Aug. 31, 1979. B.S. with Distinction in Human Ecology, Cornell U., 1960; M.S.W., U. Ga., 1979; student of Carolyn Myss and Norm Shealy, cert. program in intuition and energy medicine. Cert. primordial sound meditation instr. with Deepak Chopra, 1996. Tchr. swimming, Conn., E. Africa, Lebanon, 1968-75; social work intern, grad. asst., Atlanta, 1978-79; dir. social services, assoc. dir. and coordinator family therapy adult treatment program Brawner Psychiat. Inst., Atlanta, 1980-82; dir. extramural tng., marriage and family therapist Atlanta Inst. Family Studies, 1982-87; Perspective Ctr. for Psychotherapy, 1988-98; Natural Color & Design, 1988—. Mem. Atlanta Com. Children, 1983-85; instr. Water Safety ARC, 1957—. Recipient DAR Citizen award, 1956; YMCA Service Award, White Plains, N.Y., 1958. Diplomate NASW; mem. Nat. Assn. Social Workers, Am. Assn. Marriage and Family Therapy (com. on supervision), Cornell U. Human Ecology Alumni Assn., Mortar Bd., Omicron Nu, Phi Kappa Phi. Contbr. articles to profl. jours. Kappa Phi. Contbr. articles to profl. jours. Home and Office: Natural Color & Design 11 Garzas Trail Carmel CA 93923 Address: PO Box 190 Apalachicola FL 32329-0190 Office Phone: 831-624-4294.

REARDEN, CAROLE ANN, clinical pathologist, educator; b. Belleville, Ont., Can., June 11, 1946; d. Joseph Brady and Honora Patricia (O'Halloran) R. BSc, McGill U., 1969, MSc, MDCM, 1971. Diplomate Am. Bd. Pathology, Am. Bd. Immunohematology and Blood Banking, Am. Bd. HIstocompatibility and Immunogenetics. Resident and fellow Children's Meml. Hosp., Chgo., 1971-73; resident in pediatrics U. Calif., San Diego, 1974, resident then fellow, 1975-79, asst. prof. pathology, 1979-86, dir. histocompatibility and immunogenetics lab., 1979-94, assoc. prof., 1986-92, prof., 1992—, head divsn. lab. medicine, 1989-94; dir. med. ctr. U. Calif. Thornton Hosp. Clin. Labs., San Diego, 1993—. Prin. investigator devel. monoclonal antibodies to erythroid antigens, recombinant autoantigens; dir. lab. exam. com. Am. Bd. Histocompatibility and Immunogenetics. Contbr. articles to profl. jours.; patentee autoantigen pinch. Mem. Mayor's Task Force on AIDS, San Diego, 1983. Recipient Young Investigator Rsch. award NIH, 1979; grantee U. Calif. Cancer Rsch. Coordinating Com., 1982, NIH, 1983; scholar Nat. Blood Found. Mem. Am. Soc. Investigative Pathology, Am. Soc. Hematology, Am. Assn. Blood Banks (com. organ transplantation and tissue typing 1982-87, tech. com. 13 and 14 edit. tech. manual 1996-2002). Office: U Calif San Diego Dept Pathology 0612 9500 Gilman Dr La Jolla CA 92093-0612 E-mail: arearden@ucsd.edu.

REARDON, NANCY ANNE, food products executive; b. Little Falls, NY, Sept. 19, 1952; d. Warren Joseph and Elizabeth Owen (Tiel) Reardon; m. Steven Jonathan Sayer, Aug. 28, 1976; children: Scott Jason, Kathryn Anne. BS in Psychology, Union Coll., 1974; MS in Social Psychology, Syracuse U., 1978. With GE Co., N.Y.C., 1979-85, Avon Products Inc., N.Y.C., 1985-89, Am. Express, N.Y.C., 1989-91; sr. v.p. human resources Duracell Internat., Inc., Bethel, Conn., 1991-97; sr. v.p. corp. affairs & human resources Borden Inc., Columbus, Ohio, 1997—2004; sr. v.p., chief human resources and comm. officer Campbell Soup Co., Camden, NJ, 2004—. Bd. dir. Warnaco Group Inc. 2006-; adv. bd. mem. Catalyst, 1995. Mem. Human Resource Planning Soc. (bd. dirs. 1991-94, treas. 1992-93), N.Y. Human Resource Planners (bd. dirs., pres. 1989-91), Sr. Pers. Execs. Forum, Nat. Fgn. Trade Coun. (bd. dirs. 1995), Soc. Human Resource Mgmt., Phila. Women's Forum. Avocation: skiing. Office: Campbell Soup Co 1 Campbell Pl Camden NJ 08103-1799

REARICK, ANNE, photographer, educator; BA in English with honors, U. Mass., 1978—82; MFA in Photography with honors, Mass. Coll. Art, 1988—90. Photographer, instr. photography Cambridge Sch. Weston, 1994—. One-woman shows include Dean's Gallery, MIT, Cambridge, 1997, Salle Buscaillet, Bordeaux, France, 2000, Gure Bazterrak, Musée Basque, Bayonne, France, 2005, exhibited in group shows at Erector Sq. Gallery, New Haven, 1997, Conant Gallery, Groton, Mass., 1997, 1999, Photographic Resource Ctr., Boston, 1997, Tufts U., Aidekman Arts Ctr., Medford, Mass., 1997, Whistler Mus., Lowell, Mass., 1999, Galerie Vu, Paris, 1999, Boise (Idaho) Art Mus., 1999, S.E. Mus. Photography, Daytona, Fla., 2001, Soc. Contemporary Photography, Kansas City, Mo., 2001, FNAC, Paris, 2002, Photographic Ctr., Skopelos, Greece, 2002, Recontres Photographiques: Histoires, Chateau de Cadillac, France, 2003, TIME: A Selection from the Permanent Collection, Southeast Mus. Photography, Daytona, Fla., 2003, Human Experience, 2004, Works on Paper, Park Avenue Armory, NYC, 2004, exhibited in group shows, Represented in permanent collections St. Botolph's Club Found. Collection, Boston, S.E. Mus. Photography, Daytona, Rose Art Mus., Brandeis U., Waltham, Mass., Internat. Polaroid Collection, Cambridge, Boise Art Mus., Bibliotheque Nationale, Paris. Recipient Blanche E. Colman award, 1992, Golden Lights award, 1996; fellow, New Eng. Found. for the Arts/Mass. Cultural Coun., 1995; grantee, Polaroid Film, 1990, Somerville Arts Coun., 1990, 1993, 1997, 2003, Janet Wu, 1993, St. Botolph's Club Found., 1995; Fulbright fellow, 1990—91, John Simon Guggenheim Fellowship in Photography, John Simon Guggenheim Meml. Found., 2003—04. Mailing: c/o J Crist Gallery 223 South 17th St Boise ID 83702

REAST, DEBORAH STANEK, small business owner; b. Phila., Feb. 25, 1955; d. Chester Joseph and Thelma Sylvia (Hop) S. AS, Gwynedd Mercy Coll., 1975; Cert. Mgmt., Villanova U., 1987. Cert. med. mgr. Billing clk. Ophthalmic Assocs., Lansdale, Pa., 1971-75, exec. sec., 1975-80, ops. mgr., 1980-99; exec. asst. 24th Sen. Dist., State of Pa., Lansdale, 1999—2002; prin., owner Yours, Mine and Hours-Personal Asst. and Concierge Svcs., Hatfield, Pa., 2003—05, DeborahsVoice.com. Ch. organist Corpus Christi Parish, Gwynedd, 1970-86, Saint Maria Goretti Parish, Hatfield, 1986—, ch. organist, 1986-96. Mem. Internat. Concierge and Errand Assn., Mid-Atlantic Concierge and Errand Assn., Internat. Virtual Assts. Assn., Pa. Assn. Notaries, The Wine Connection, Publicity-St. Maria Goretti Social Com., North Penn C. of C., Hatfield C. of C. Roman Catholic. Avocations: writing, travel, collecting. Office: Yours Mine and Hours PO Box 573 Hatfield PA 19440 Office Phone: 215-778-3704. Office Fax: 215-412-7689. Business E-Mail: deb@yoursmineandhours.com.

REATEGUI, LISA J., lawyer; b. 1966; BA magna cum laude, Princeton U., 1988; MA in Latin Am. Studies, Stanford U., 1990; JD magna cum laude, Northwestern U., 1995. Atty. Sidley Austin Brown & Wood, Chgo., 1995—2003, ptnr., 2003—. Chmn. major gifts fund raising Princeton U.; mem. women's bd. The Field Mus., mem. young profl.'s bd. Mem.: ABA, Chgo. (Ill.) Bar Assn. Office: Sidley Austin Brown & Wood Bank One Plz 10 South Dearborn St Chicago IL 60603

REAVES, LISA GOLDEN, science educator; b. Pell City, Ala., Apr. 27, 1968; d. Bobby Lane and Julia McGuffie Golden; m. Michael Todd Reaves, Nov. 18, 1988; 1 child, Micah. BED in Gen. Sci. Composite, Jacksonville State U., Ala., 1991. Sci. educator Wellborn H.S., Anniston, Ala., 1991—92; sci. educator, coach Ragland (Ala.) H.S., 1992—93, Pell City (Ala.) H.S., 1993—2002, Sylacauga (Ala.) H.S., 2002—. Youth vol. Mignon Bapt. Ch., Sylacauga, 2000—, nursery vol., 2000—, mem. prayer blanket ministry, 2004—. Named St. Clair County Coach of Yr., 1993. Mem.: NEA, Nat. Sci. Tchrs. Assn., Ala. H.S. Athletic Assn., Ala. Edn. Assn. Avocations: swimming, reading. Office Phone: 256-249-0911. Office Fax: 256-245-1026. Business E-Mail: reavesl@mail.sylacauga.k12.al.us.

REAVES, MARILYNN, elementary school educator; d. Carl Ernest and Euphrasia K Dixon; m. Jerry Lynn Reaves, June 2, 1966; children: Robert Lynn, Roger Michael. BA, Harding U., Ark., 1967; MS in Secondary Counseling, Ark. State U., Jonesboro, 1989. Instr. lang. arts Baxter County Schs., Mountain Home, Ark., 1967—69, Malden R-1 Schs., Mo., 1976—. Den mother Cub Scouts Am., Malden, 1977—83. Mem.: Cmty. Tchrs. Assn. (pres. 1986—87, sec. 1987—90, parliamentarian 1990—2004, bldg. rep. 2004—06). Office: Malden R-1 Schs 505 Burkhart Malden MO 63863 Office Phone: 573-276-4546.

REBACK, JOYCE ELLEN, lawyer; b. Phila., July 11, 1948; d. William and Sue (Goldstein) R.; m. Itzhak Brook, Aug. 2, 1981; children: Jonathan Zev, Sara Jennie. BA magna cum laude, Brown U., 1970; JD with honors, George Washington U., 1976. Bar: D.C. 1976, U.S. Dist. Ct. D.C. 1976, U.S. Ct. Appeals (D.C. cir.) 1976, U.S. Ct. Appeals (3d cir.) 1983, U.S. Ct. Appeals (Fed. cir.) 1985. Assoc. Fulbright & Jaworski, Washington, 1976—84, ptnr., 1984—87; legal svcs. cons. IMF, Washington, 1987—. Contbr. articles to profl. jours. Mem. ABA, D.C. Bar Assn., Phi Beta Kappa. Jewish. Office: Internat Monetary Fund 700 19th St NW Washington DC 20431-0001

REBECK, PAMELA JOAN, psychologist; b. Chgo., Sept. 24, 1949; d. Clarence and Jeanette Marion (De Grand) R.; m. James Eugene Clark, Sept. 5, 1981; children: Justin Reid, Colin Taylor. BA in Psychology and Edn., Calif. State U., Northridge, 1971; MS in Psychology, Ill. Inst. Tech., 1973, PhD in Psychology, 1977. Staff psychologist Westside Parents, Chgo., 1973-74; psychosocial team leader Area Svcs. Project, Westchester, Ill., 1974-77; prof. psychology Govs. State U., Park Forest, Ill., 1977-80; assoc. Chgo. Stress Ctr., 1977—; pvt. practice clin. psychology, Naperville, Ill., 1980—. Group leader Anorexia Nervosa and Assoc. Disorders, 1986-91. Vice chmn. Ill. Devel. Disabilities Advocacy Authority, Peoria, 1979-87. Mem. APA, Ill. Psychol. Assn., Nat. Register Health Svc. Providers in Psychology. Avocations: sports, travel, photography. Office: 475 River Bend Rd # 600 Naperville IL 60540-5255 Office Phone: 630-357-9339.

REBEL, AMY LOUISE, elementary school educator; b. Shaker Heights, Ohio, Feb. 26, 1957; d. Paul Vernon Jr. and Louise Alice (Parme) R. BS, No. Ill. U., 1980; postgrad., Nova U., 1992. Cert. tchr., Fla., Ill.; cert. ednl. leadership, Fla.; nat. cert. in water fitness-master level Am. Sport Edn. Program/Nat. Fedn. Interscholastic Coaches Edn. Program instr.; nat. cert. water fitness program coord. Golf coach, mem. support pers. Hinsdale (Ill.) Cen. Twp. High Sch., 1983-85; instructional pers., swimming coach Boca Raton (Fla.) Community Mid. Sch., 1985-86; tchr. phys. edn., swimming coach Boca Raton Community High Sch., 1987; tchr. phys. edn. Whispering Pines Community Elem. Sch., Boca Raton, 1987-88; tchr. phys. and aquatic edn. Sandpiper Shores Cmty. Elem. Sch., Boca Raton, 1989—, ESOL coord., 1991-92; crisis response team Sandpiper Shores Cmty. Elem. Sch., Boca Raton, Fla., 2002—. Personal cons. Water Exercise Programs, Ill. and Fla., 1976—; coach staff swimming Mission Bay Aquatic Tng. Ctr., Boca Raton, 1986-88; co-sponsor Nat. Jr. Beta Honor Soc., 1998-99. Mem. campaign com. Ill. State Rep. 38th dist., 1976; instr. water safety ARC, Fox River Valley, Ill., 1974-90, educator water safety, 1989—. Mem. ASCD, NEA, FTA, Palm Beach County Tchrs. Assn., U.S. Water Fitness Assn. Avocations: commercial acting, aquatics, modeling. Home: PO Box 738 Boca Raton FL 33429 Office: Sandpiper Shores Community Elem Sch 11201 Glades Rd Boca Raton FL 33498-6818 Business E-Mail: rebel@palmbeach.k12.fl.us.

REBELLO, MARLENE MUNSON, speech pathologist; b. San Jose, Calif., Oct. 15, 1948; d. Alfred Vernon and Rose Zita (Pereira) Nunes; m. Steven Del Munson, Mar. 21, 1970 (div. 1982); m. William Wayne Rebello, Dec. 5, 1992. BA, San Jose State U., 1970, MA, 1971; MS in Counseling, U. LaVerne, 1990. Speech pathologist Newark (Calif) Unified Sch. Dist., 1971—; pvt. practice Fremont and Pleasanton, Calif., 1980—; speech pathologist Washington Hosp., Fremont, Calif., 1980-89. Cons. in field. Recipient Bank of Am. award, 1966, Cabrillo scholarship, Nat. Merit scholarship, 1966, Maria Leonard award Outstanding Sr. Grade Point Average, 1970; fellow VA, 1970. Mem. Calif. Speech and Hearing Assn., Pleasanton Sister City Assn. (v.p. 1996-2002, pres. 2003—), Newark Tchrs. Assn. (treas. 1971—), Save Our Sunol Found., Calif. Tchrs. Assn., Arthur & Elena Court Conservation Soc., Pleasanton North Rotary (Paul Harris fellow). Avocations: antiques, decorating, gourmet cooking. Home: 10579 Foothill Rd Sunol CA 94586-9464 E-mail: marspot@aol.com.

REBELSKY, FREDA ETHEL GOULD, psychologist; b. N.Y.C., Mar. 11, 1931; d. William and Sarah (Kaplan) Gould; BA, U. Chgo., 1950, MA, 1954; PhD, Radcliffe Coll., 1961; m. William Rebelsky, Jan. 1, 1956 (dec. 1979); 1 son, Samuel; m. Nicholas Camp, Aug. 14, 1988 (div. Oct. 1993). Counselor, U. Chgo. Orthogenic Sch., 1952-55; rsch. asst. Kenyon & Eckhart, Inc., 1956-58; rsch. asst. lab. human devel. Harvard U., 1959-60, teaching asst. psychology, then instr. edn., 1960-61; rsch. assoc. Speech rsch. lab. Children's Hosp., Boston, 1960-61, M.I.T., 1961-62; mem. faculty Boston U., 1962-96, prof. psychology, 1972-96, dir. doctoral program in devel. psychology, 1969-74, ret., 1996, prof. emerita, 1996; vis. lectr. U. Utrecht (Netherlands), 1965-67; Froman prof. Russell Sage Coll., Troy, N.Y., 1972. Grantee U.S. Office Edn., 1964-65, Boston U. Grad. Sch., 1967-70, OEO, 1967-69. NIMH, 1974-76; Bunting fellow Radcliffe Coll., 1985-86; recipient Disting. Tchr. Psychology award Am. Psychol. Found., 1970; Harbison award excellence teaching Danforth Found., 1971; Metcalf award Boston U., 1978; Disting. Career in Psychology award Mass. Psychol. Assn., 1982; Cmty. Svc. award Boston U. Faculty, 1993. Mem. AAAS, Soc. Rsch. Child Devel. (sec. Boston 1963-65), AAUP (sec. Boston U. 1964-65, pres. 1984-85, 86-88, 91-2002), Am., Eastern, Mass. (chmn. program com. 1962-64) Psychol. Assns., Sigma Xi, Psi Chi. Author: Child Behavior and Development: A Reader, 1969; Child Behavior and Development, 2d edit., 1973: Life: The Continuous Process, 1975; Growing Children, 1976, What's Next? A Guide to Valued Aging and Other High-Wire Adventures, 1996. Address: 1 Billings Park Newton MA 02458-2013 Office Phone: 617-527-9093. E-mail: rebelsky@bu.edu.

REBER, CHERYL ANN, consultant, social worker, trainer; b. Cin., Feb. 7, 1956; d. Randland John and Marcella Catherine (Hollstegge) Reber; m. Michael Zaletel. AA, Xavier U., 1976, BA, 1980. Lic. social worker. Social worker Altercrest, Cin., 1977-79, Hamilton County Dept. Human Svcs., Cin., 1979-85, adoption specialist, social worker, 1985-92, trainer, program developer, 1988-92; social worker, AIDS specialist Hospice of the Miami Valley, 1992-95; ind. trainer Inst. for Human Svcs., Cin., 1996—. Trainer Hamilton County Dept. Human Svcs., Cin., 1988-92; permanency planning cons. Ohio Dept. Human Svcs., 1995-2000, Mem. Cmty. Task Force on Adoption, Cin., 1989-91, 95—. Mem. S.W. Ohio Adoption Resource Exch., Beechmont Players. Democrat. Avocations: whitewater rafting, community theatre, primitive camping and exploration. Personal E-mail: creber4129@aol.com.

REBUEHR, SAGE LEE, secondary school educator; d. Karen Rebuehr. EdM, U. Colo., Boulder, 2003. Lang. arts tchr. Westminster H.S., Colo., 2002—. Office: Westminster High School 4276 W 68th Ave Westminster CO 80221 Office Phone: 303-482-9541.

RECANATI, DINA, artist; b. Cairo, Jan. 15, 1928; Student with Jose de Creft, Art Students League, N.Y.C., 1959—62. Exhibitions include Julie M Gallery, Tel Aviv, Israel, 1981—84, Jewish Mus. Sculpture Garden, NY, 1981—84, Am-Israel Cultural Found., 1984, Hebrew Coll., Boston, 1985, Julie M. Basel Art Fair, 1986, Bklyn. Mus., 1988, Mus. Contemporary Art, Ramat Gan, Israel, 1989, Barbican Art Gallery, London, 1990, Berlin Shafir Gallery, NY, 1990, Tel Aviv Mus. Art, 2001, 2004, Buffalo Arts Studio, 2004, prin. works include Israel Mus. Jerusalem, Tel Aviv Mus., Ben Gurion Airport, Tel Aviv, Tel Aviv U., Jewish Mus., NY, Herzliya Mus., Continental Grain Collection, NY, Israel Embassy, Wash., Hudson Valley, N.Y., NYU, Artomi Fields Sculpture Pk., Hudson Valley, NY, Represented in permanent collections Ministry of Transp., Israel, Am.-Israel Cultural Found., NY, Israel Chancellery, Wash., President's Garden Collection, Jerusalem, Beit Ariella Pub. Libr., Tel Aviv, Weizmann Inst. Sci., Rehovot, Israel; author: Dina Recanati, From the Artists' Notebook, 2001; contbr. chapters to books. Recipient Knickerbocker award, Nat. Arts Club, 1961, Louise Waterman Wise award, Am. Jewish Congress, 1976, King Solomon award, Am.-Israel Cultural Found., 1977. Address: 136 Grand St #6E New York NY 10013-3127

RECH, SUSAN ANITA, obstetrician, gynecologist; b. Summit, N.J., Nov. 5, 1957; d. William F. and Mary Jane (Crooks) R.; m. Marc R. Sarnow; children: Kyle, Nathaniel. BA in Biology, Swarthmore Coll., 1979; MD, U. Medicine Dentistry N.J., Newark, 1984. Diplomate Am. Bd. Ob-Gyn. Resident in ob-gyn. Temple U. Hosp., Phila., 1984-88; pvt. practice, Plattsburgh, N.Y., 1988—; chief dept. ob-gyn CVPH Med. Ctr., Plattsburgh, 1997-2000. Asst. clin. prof. dept. ob-gyn. U. Vt. Sch. Medicine, 1991—; dir. ob-gyn. tchg. program CVPH Med. Ctr., 1998—; bd. dirs. CVPH Med. Ctr., 1999—; mem. med. adv. bd. Planned Parenthood No. N.Y., Plattsburgh, 1989-98, Clinton County Health Dept., Plattsburgh, 1989-96; bd. dirs. Cmty. Providers, Inc., Plattsburgh, 1994-97. Active Newman Ctr., St. Mary's of the Lake Ch., Plattsburgh, 1992-2002; mem. alumni coun. Swarthmore (Pa.) Coll., 1994-96; mem. Seton Cath. H.S. Sch. Bd., Plattsburgh, 1995-98. Rsch. grantee U. Medicine and Dentistry N.J., summer 1980. Fellow ACOG; mem. AMA, Am. Med. Women's Assn. (founding pres. Champlain Valley chpt. 1991), Assn. Women Surgeons, No. N.Y. Ind. Practice Assn. (bd. dirs. 1994-98), Champlain Valley Oratorio Soc. (soloist 1989—), Nat. Honor Soc. Avocations: choral singing, skiing, running, gardening, reading. Home: 15 Point Farm West Grand Isle VT 05458-7021 Office: Assocs in Ob-Gyn PC 25 DeGrandpre Way Plattsburgh NY 12901-2318 Office Phone: 518-563-3260. Business E-Mail: drsrech@obgplb.com.

RECHAK, IVY MARIA, science educator; b. Youngstown, Ohio, Dec. 19, 1967; d. Eduard and Hemma Rechak; children: Kurt Eduard, Sierra Jean Rechak-Lacomba. BS, SUNY Albany, 1995; Masters, Rensselaer Poly. Inst., NY, 2000. Cert. tchr. earth sci. grades 7-12 NY, 2000. Earth sci. tchr. Hudson Falls HS, NY, 1995—96; sci. tchr. Ravena-Coeymans-Selkirk Mid. Sch., NY, 1996—2000; earth sci. tchr. Schuylerville Jr./Sr. HS, NY, 2000—. Roman Catholic. Avocations: swimming, hiking, crafts, scouts. Office: Schuylerville Jr-Sr HS 18 Spring St Schuylerville NY 12871 Office Phone: 518-695-3255. Personal E-mail: rechaki@yahoo.com. Business E-Mail: rechaki@schuylerville.org.

RECK, ELIZABETH TORRE, social worker, educator; b. Winston-Salem, N.C., June 17, 1931; d. Vernon Clark and Mary (Pfohl) Lassiter; m. Mottram Peter Torre, Apr. 13, 1957 (dec.); m. Andrew Joseph Reck, June 17, 1987. Student, Wellesley Coll., Mass., 1948-49; BA, Duke U., 1952; MRE, Union Theol. Sem., 1957; MSW, Tulane U., 1966, PhD, 1972. Cert. social worker, La. Field dir. undergrad. admissions Duke U., Durham, NC, 1952—53; head tchr. primary dept. Riverside Ch., N.Y.C., 1957—60; instr. Sch. Social Work Tulane U., New Orleans, 1966—72, assoc. prof., 1972—2000, coord. Indsl. Social Work Program, 1982—88, mem. faculty senate, 1972—88, prof. emeritus, 2000—. Non-govtl. orgn. rep. UNICEF, World Fedn. Mental Health, 1957—; cons. to v.p. cmty. affairs WETA, Washington, 1979; cons. Office Spl. Symposia and Seminars, Smithsonian Instn., Washington, 1979-86; treas. N.Y. Jr. League, 1961-62, v.p., 1962-63; bd. dirs. Cmty. Vol. Svcs., New Orleans, 1965-68; mem. profl. adv. com. Project Pre-Kindergarten, Orleans Paris Sch. Bd., New Orleans, 1967-69; mem. adv. bd. DePaul Cmty. Mental Health Ctr., New Orleans, 1971-72; mem. citizens adv. com. Orleans Parish Juvenile Ct., New Orleans, 1970-73; mem. Coun. on Social Work Edn. Task Force on Prevention, 1981-87; mem. New Orleans Women's Coalition Task Force on Employers and Working Parents, 1985-90; mem. med. social svcs. subcom. Mayor's Adv. Com. on Domestic Violence, 1995-96; v.p. Torre Realty Bd., 1996—. Grantee NIMH, Summer Inst. grantee Nat. Endowment Humanities, 1982; Newcomb Coll. fellow, 1989-2002. Mem. AAUW (Tulane Corp. rep. 1990-2000), NASW (bd. dir. La. chpt. 1987-89), AAUP (treas. Tulane chpt. 1984-86, 88-91, exec. com. 1991-95, v.p. New Orleans chpt. 1996), Coun. Social Work Edn., Am. Orthopsychiat. Assn. (life), Tulane U. Women's Assn. (v.p. 1996-97, pres. 1997-98, bd. mem. 2006-), Phi Beta Kappa (Tulane chpt. exec. com. 1990-2002, pres. Tulane chpt. 1991, regional sec. 1994—2002). Personal E-mail: ereck@cox.net.

RECKER, STACY, social studies educator; b. Parma, Ohio, Mar. 23, 1975; m. Michael Reiring, Aug. 31, 1996. BA, U. Cin., 1997, MEd, 2005. Lic. tchr. Ohio, 2001. Exec. interviewer The Answer Group, Cin., 1995—99; tchr. social studies Amelia H.S., West Clermont Local Schs., Batavia, Ohio, 2000—. Advisor key club Amelia H.S., 2002—. Medicator Save Animals Found., Cin., 2002, vol. cat com., 2002, fundraiser, 2002. Scholar, U. Cin., 1999—2001, 2004—05. Mem.: Nat. Coun. Social Studies (none). Liberal. Jewish. Avocations: Jewish studies and activities, volunteering with animals. Office Phone: 513-947-7400. Personal E-mail: stacyrecker@fuse.ent. E-mail: recker_s@westcler.org.

RECKERS, MICHELE YVONNE, director, secondary school educator; b. Bloomington, Ill., Oct. 28, 1979; d. Kathryn Evelyn and Scott John Kalina (Stepfather). MusB in Music Edn., Millikin U., Decatur, Ill., 2001. Band dir. Auburn Cmty. Unit Sch. Dist., Ill., 2001—06; 6th grade band dir. Bloomington Jr. H.S., 2006—. Mem.: Ill. Music Educators Assn., Music Educators Nat. Conf., North Am. Brass Band Assn., Sigma Alpha Iota (life; corr. sec. 1999—2000). Republican. Roman Catholic. Avocations: reading, swimming, music. Office Phone: 217-438-6817. E-mail: reckersm@district87.org.

RECTOR, MARY MARGARET, secondary school educator; b. Mpls., Apr. 30, 1946; d. Edmund James and Margaret Ruth (Schaber) Cain; m. William A. Rector, Aug. 4, 1973; children: Meghan, Brian. BS in Home Econs., U. Minn., 1969; MS in Spl. Edn., U. Las Vegas, 1974. Cert. tchr., Minn. Nev. Home econs. tchr. Jim Bridger Jr. H.S., Las Vegas, 1969-71, Rancho H.S., Las Vegas, 1971-73, Chaparral H.S., Las Vegas, 1973—86, Valley H.S., Las Vegas, 1986—2001, 2005—, Foothill H.S., 2002—03. Mem. adv. bd. South Nev. Ext. Nutrition Coun., Las Vegas, 1982-90; spkr. YMCA, Las Vegas, 1983; reader Nutrition Edn. Grants, Las Vegas, 1984; advisor FHA, Las Vegas, 1971—. Contbr. articles to profl. jours. Leader Girl Scouts USA, Las Vegas, 1984-90; voter registrar Clark County Election Dept., Las Vegas, 1976-78; mem. Clark County Dem. Ctrl. Com., Las Vegas, 1976-78; tchr. religious edn. St. Viator, RICA coord., 2004—; participant Nev. Sr. Olympics. Recipient Nev. Family and Consumer Sci. Tchr. of the Yr., 2000; grantee, Clark County Sch. Dist., 1984—85. Mem. Am. Home Econs. Assn. (cert.), So. Nev. Home Econs. Assn. (pres. 1988-90), Clark County Vocat. Assn., Nev. Vocat. Assn. (Outstanding FHA/Hero adviser award 1993, 97), Am. Fedn. Tchrs. (treas. 1974-78), Nev. Assn. Family & Consumer Sci. (pro award 1997). Democrat. Roman Catholic. Avocations: reading, cooking health foods. Office: Valley HS 2839 Burnham Ave Las Vegas NV 89109-1793 Office Phone: 702-799-5450. Personal E-mail: mmrector@aol.com.

RECTOR, SUSAN DARNELL, lawyer; b. Wilmington, Del., Feb. 14, 1959; d. W. Thomas and Barbara Joan (Shafer) Darnell; m. Neil Kenyon Rector, Aug. 7, 1982. BA in Econs., Wake Forest U., Winston-Salem, N.C., 1981; JD, U. N.C., Chapel Hill, 1984. Bar: Ohio 1984. Lawyer Ohio Legislative Svc. Commn., Columbus, Ohio, 1984-87; assoc. Schottenstein, Zox & Dunn, Columbus, Ohio, 1987-93, ptnr., 1993—. Bd. trustees Firstlink, Inc., 1990-95, v.p., 1993, pres., 1994; apt. to Ohio Small Bus. and Entrepreneurship Coun., 1991-95; bd. dirs. The Wilds. Contbr. articles to profl. jours. Mem. allocation com. United Way, Columbus, 1990-96, campaign cabinet, 1991-06, co-chair planning, evaluation and allocation com., 1993-94, bd. trustees, 1996-05, chair health vision coun., 1996-99; trustee Columbus Zool. Park Assn., 2001—, v.p., 2003-04, pres. 2005-06; chmn. devel. com., 2001-03, chmn. zoo fund, 2000; bd. dir., sec., treas. Cmty. Rsch. Ptnrs., 2000-02. Named Harry S. Truman scholar, Truman Scholarship Found., 1979, named one of 10 Outstanding Young Citizens, Columbus Jaycees, 1993, 40 under 40, Bus. (Columbus); grad. Columbus Area Leadership Program; Best Lawyers in Am., 2003, 04, 05. Fellow Am. Bar Found.; mem. Ohio Bar Assn., Columbus Bar Assn. (Cmty. Svc. award 1997), Columbus Bar Found. (trustee 1995—2004, pres. 2003), Women Lawyers of Franklin County, Jr. League of Columbus (bd. trustees, sec. 1989-90, 95-98, pres. 1997-98), Columbus Club, Columbus Met. Club, Columbus Women's Network (Cmty. Leader award), Mortar Bd., Phi Beta Kappa, Omicron Delta Kappa. Home: 67 E Deshler Ave Columbus OH 43206-2655 Office: Schottenstein Zox & Dunn 250 West Street Columbus OH 43215 Office Phone: 614-462-2219. Business E-Mail: srector@szd.com.

RECUPERO, PATRICIA RYAN, hospital president, psychiatrist, lawyer, health facility executive; m. Joseph Recupero. AB, SUNY, 1969; JD, Boston Coll., 1973; MD, Brown U., 1985. Bar: Mass. 1973, RI 1974, Fed. Bar: Dist. of Mass. 1975, Dist. of RI 1975; diplomate Am. Bd. Psychiatry and Neurology, 1990, cert. in Forensic Psychiatry RI, 1994. Assoc. dir. edn./tng. dept. psychiatry and human behavior Brown U., Providence, 1989—94, assoc. dir. edn./tng., 2005—, clin. prof. psychiatry, 1989—91, clin. asst. prof. psychiatry, 1991—2000; asst. prof. medicine Tufts U., 1995—98; vice chair, dept. psychiatry St. Elizabeth's Med. Ctr., Boston, 1995—97, dir. clin. svcs., 1995—97, dir. residency tng. psychiatry, 1996—97; dir. managed care Butler Hosp., Providence, 1990—95, dir. alcohol/drug inpatient svcs., 1991—94, chief forensic psychiatry, 1994—95, med. dir., med. adminstrn., 1997—98, v.p. systems integration/managed care, assoc. med. dir., med. adminstrn., 1998—98, exec. v.p., 1998—98, pres., CEO, 1999—; exec. v.p. behavioral health Care New Eng., Providence, 1999—; clin. assoc. prof. psychiatry Brown U., 2000—05, clin. prof. psychiatry, 2005—. Mem. resource utilization com. Health Advantage, 1993—95; mem. contract for competency to stand trial evaluation program RI Dept. Mental Health Retardation and Hospitals, 1993—95; mem. utilization mgmt. com. Blue Chip RI, 1995—98; forensic evaluations Dept. Disabled Persons Protection Commn., 1995—; ind. med. evaluations Northwestern Ins. Co., 1995—; spl. master RI Supreme Ct., 1996; gender equity/sexual harrassment officer Brown U. Program in Medicine (Office of Women in Medicine), 1997—98; chairperson Butler Hosp. Profl. Lecture Series; mem., ho. delegates RI Bar Assn., 1976—77, mem., confidential assistance com., 1992—95; chair, bylaws revision com. RI Psychiat. Soc., 1989—90, deputy legis. rep., 1989—94, sec./treas., 1991—95, pres. elect., 1995—97, pres., 1997—99, dep. rep. to apa assembly dist. branches, 1999—2003, assembly rep., 2003—, 1997—2000; addiction psychiatry splty. com. Am. Acad. Psychiatry and the Law, 1997—2005, edn. com., 1999—2004, chair, gender issues com., 2000—03, geriatric psychiatry com., 2000, councillor, 1994—; coun. on psychiatry and law corr. mem. Am. Psychiat. Assn., 1994—, mem. com. on quality indicators, 2000—02, chair, workgroup on cyber medicine, 2000—, assembly liaison to coun. psychiatry and law, 2000—02, guttmacher award com. mem., 2003—, task force to rev. guidelines on seclusion/restraint mem., 2003—, coun. on psychiatry and law mem., 2003—; bd. mem. Nat. Assn. Psychiat. Health Systems, 2002—, planning com. mem., 2002—, third v.p., 2003—, membership com., 2003—, exec. com., 2003, pres. elect, 04, pres., 05. Author: (newsletter) e-Health: Enhanced Treatment or Legal Quagmire?, Women in Forensic Psychiatry; contbr. numerous presentations in field, articles to profl. jours., chapters to books. Parole bd. mem. Parole Bd. State of RI, RI, 1993—98; bd. mem. RI Coalition Against Domestic Violence, 1994—95, mem., 1993—98; merit selection panel US Dist. Ct., Dist. of RI, 1998; forensic psychiatry com. on re-cert. Am. Bd.Psychiatry/Neurology, 2000—03; governor's coun. on mental health RI State, 1998—2001; corp. mem. Blue Cross/Blue Shield of RI, 1999—2003; bd. mem. Vis. Nurse Assn./Care New Eng., 1999—2003. Recipient Ann. Exemplary Psychiatrist Award, Nat. Alliance for the Mentally Ill, 2000, Teaching Recognition award, Brown U. Sch. Med., 2001. Fellow: Am. Psychiat. Assn. (disting.); mem.: Internat. Acad. Law and Mental Health, RI Med. Women's Assn., RI Med. Soc., Assn. Women Psychiatrists, Mental Health Assn. of RI, Alliance for the Mentally Ill. Office: Butler Hosp 345 Blackstone Blvd Providence RI 02906

RECUPERO-FAIELLA, ANNA ANTONIETTA, poet; b. Boston, Nov. 22, 1966; d. Vittorio and Anna Maria Recupero; m. Mark Stephan James Faiella, May 30, 1998; 1 child, Dante Vincenzo Faiella. Cert. early edn., Wheelock Coll. Tchr. N. Bennet St. Sch., Boston, 1981-87; clk. Post Office, Boston, 1988—. Art coord. N. Bennett Sch., Boston, 1985-87; acting extra films and commls. Author: A View From the Edge, 1992, Dusting Off Dreams, 1994, Echoes From the Silence, 1995, Treasure the Moment, 1996, Whispers, 1996, Sensations, 1997; co-author: Distinguished Poets of Amercia, 1993, Outstanding Poets of 1994, 1994, Treasured Poems of America, 1995, Treasured Poems of America, 1996, Best Poems of the 90's, 1996, Best Poems of '97, 1997, Ten Years of Excellence, 1998. Co-chair Wall of Tolerance, 2003. Recipient Internat. Writer Yr. award, Internat. Biographical Ctr., 2003, Outstanding Writer award, Internat. Soc. Poetry, 2004, Outstanding Achievement in amateur photography award, Internat. Soc. Photographers, 2004; Mass. State Gen. scholar, 1985. Mem. Internat. Soc. Poets (disting. mem. adv. com. 1994), Nat. Mus. Women Arts, Point of Pines Assn. Democrat. Roman Catholic. Avocations: painting, writing poems, travel, nascar racing, comedy. Home: 40 Bickford Ave Revere MA 02151-1723

RECZEK, CLAIRE E., reading specialist; b. Proctor, Vt., May 7, 1949; d. Charles Edward and Julia (Keavney) White; m. Edward Joseph Reczek, July 1, 1972. BA in English, U. Vt., 1971, MEd, 1976. Cert. reading specialist/coord., elem. edn. tchr., secondary English tchr., reading tchr. Vt. tchr. corps intern Univ. Vt., Winooski, 1974-76; chpt. 1 reading tchr. Rock Point High Sch., Burlington, Vt., 1978-79; tchr., supr. The Learning Ctr., South Burlington, Vt., 1976-79; chpt. 1 reading specialist Bennington Rutland Supervisory Union, Burr-Burton High Sch., 1979-86, Bennington Rutland Supervisory Union, Pawlet Schs., 1986—. Spl. edn. adv. bd. Bennington-Rutland Supervisory Union, Manchester, Vt., 1983—; coll. instr. Coll. of St. Joseph, Rutland, 1991; state tech. com. Nat. Sci. Math Tech., Vt., 1992—. Recipient incentive grants Bennington-Rutland Profl. Devel. Bd., 1988, 89, 90; Woman Distinction award, Delta Kappa Gamma Internat. Soc., 2005, Outstanding Tchr., Bennington Rutland Supervisory Union, 1991. Mem. Delta Kappa Gamma Iota (profl./personal growth chairperson).

REDD, J. DIANE, not-for-profit developer; b. Apr. 10, 1945; d. Robert Fountain and Lillian (Fitts) Redd. BS, W.Va. State Coll., 1967. Instr. bus. subjects Paterson (N.J.) Bus. Edn., 1967—89; with U. Medicine and Dentistry, Newark, 1968—69; adminstrv. asst. rsch. and sponsored programs, 1968—73; asst. dir. health edn., 1973—76; sr. devel. officer, 1976—79; asst. dir. devel., 1979—83; chief devel. and alumni affairs, 1983—89; dir. devel. founds., corps. and major gifts Planned Parenthood Fedn. Am., Inc., N.Y.C., 1989—2002; dir. devel. NAACP-LDF, Inc., N.Y.C., 2002—05; nat. dir. corp. and found. rels. Found. Fighting Blindness, 2005—. Mem. priorities com., devel. com. United Way of Essex and West Hudson, Newark, 1983-85; chmn. human resources com. Cmty. Adv. Bd., U. Medicine and Dentistry N.J., Newark, 1978-82; mem. rsch. bd. advisors Am. Biographical Inst., 1992—. Recipient Recognition of Achievement award Young Women of Am., Inc., Montgomery, Ala., 1979, Black Achiever award YMWCA, 1986. Mem. Assn. of Fund Raising Profls. Inc., Ind. (cert., trustee, v.p., parliamentarian, sec.), Exec. Women N.J. (trustee, chmn. scholarship com.), Women in Fin. Devel. Democrat. Office Phone: 212-965-2205.

REDD, KATHRYN ELIZABETH, education educator, department chairman; b. Hillsbroy, Kans., Dec. 14, 1954; d. Delbert E. and Roberta M. (Johnson) Nikkel; m. Rick L. Redd, Aug. 24, 1974; 1 child, Heidi Renee Redd Simmons. BS, Okla. State U., Goodwell, 1995; MS, Friends U., Wichita, Kans., 1998. Dept. chair, instr. Seward County CC, Liberal, Kans., 1998—. Named Unsung Hero, SW Daily Times, 2005, Outstanding Instr., NISOD, Austin, Tex., 2005, Outstanding Adv., Seward County CC, 2006. Office: Seward County Cmty Coll 1801 N KS Liberal KS 67905

REDDICK, CATHERINE ANNE (CAT REDDICK), Olympic athlete; b. Richmond, Va., Feb. 10, 1982; Majoring in comm., U. N.C., 2000—. Mem. Under-16 Nat. Team, 1998, Under-18 Nat. Team, 1998—99, capt., 2000; mem. Under-21 Nat. Team, 2003; soccer player, defender U.S. Women's Nat. Team, 2000—; mem. U.S. Olympic Soccer Team, Athens, 2004. Co-recipient U-18 Soccer Gold medal, Pan Am. Games, 1999, Nordic Cup, Denmark, 2000, 2001, 2002, 2003; named Defensive MVP, NCAA Final Four, 2000, Freshman All-Am. Team, NSCAA, 2000, Second Team All-Am., 2001, First Team All-Am., 2002; named to First Team All-ACC, 2002. Achievements include being a member of gold medal winning US Women's Soccer Team, Athens Olympic Games, 2004. Office: US Soccer Fedn 1801 S Prairie Ave Chicago IL 60616

REDDICK, JACQUELINE MONIQUE, social worker; b. Newark, July 29, 1972; d. Ethel Lee Reddick; 1 child, Jaleel Tarod. Assoc. of Social Work, Essex County Coll., Newark, NJ, 1997; Bachelor of Social Work, Seton Hall U., South Orange, NJ, 2000; MSW, Kean U., Union, NJ, 2004. Cert. social worker. Med. social worker Irvington Gen. Hosp., NJ, 2000—06; sch. social worker Irvington Bd. Edn., NJ, 2005—. Baptist. Avocations: reading, skating, cooking.

REDDING-LOWDER, CHRISTINE ARNITA, elementary school educator; b. Terrell County, Ga., Mar. 14, 1938; d. Otis Sr. and Fannie Mae (Roseman) Redding; m. Billy Earl Lowder, Feb. 5, 1961; children: Charles DeWayne, Penelope Darcel, Trevor Demetrius. AA, West L.A. Jr. Coll., 1970; BA in Psychology, Calif. State U.-Dominguez Hill, Carson, 1972; MS in Edn., U. So. Calif., 1975; student, Mount St. Mary's Coll., 1998-99. Cert. tchr. K-9, adult edn., Calif., Emergency Response specialist permit. Telephone operator L.A. County Probation Dept., 1964-66; clk. L.A. County Assessor Dept., 1966; clk.-typist Dept. Pub. Social Svcs., L.A., 1966-67; intern L.A. Unified Sch. Dist., 1972-73, tchr., 1973—. Contbr. articles to profl. jours. Pres. Nat. Coun. Negro Women, L.A., 1994; chair polit. subcom. 110th Anniversary 2d Bapt. Ch., L.A., 1995, vice chairperson, chairperson United Teachers L.A. Black Edn. Com., 1978-87; mem. recruiters league, rec. sec. 1992-96; treas., v.p. Marvin Ave. Sch. PTA, L.A., 1967-69. Recipient Negotiation award Pres. United Tchrs. of L.A., 1984, Dedication/Svc. plaque United Tchrs. L.A./Black Educators, 1988, WHO award United Tchrs. L.A./NEA, 1995. Mem. AAUW, NEA (del. rep. assembly 1977—, LWV (v.p., 2005), NEA Black Caucus, Pacific region dir. Black Caucus 1996-98, sec. Black Caucus 1998-2001, treas. Black Caucus 2001-, mem. minority affairs com. 1998-, sec. GAE 2004-), Calif. Tchrs. Assn. (del. state coun. 1977-89, 90-99, vice chair credentials and profl. devel. com. 1983-85, Assn. Better Citizenship com. Dist. J, United Tchrs.-L.A. 1994-2001), Nat. Assn. Univ. Women (regional by-laws chair 1991), Delta Sigma Theta (journalist Century City Alumnae chpt., mem. social action com., Macon Alumnae chpt. 2004-). Democrat. Avocations: travel, reading, theater, stamp collecting/philately, coin collecting/numismatics.

REDDINGTON, MARY JANE, retired secondary school educator; b. New Rochelle, N.Y., July 21, 1923; d. Gordon William and Katharine Regina (Coleman) Kann; m. John Martin Reddington, Oct. 11, 1947; children: Terence, Martha, Robert. BA cum laude, Coll. New Rochelle, 1945; postgrad., Columbia U., 1947—49; MA, Hunter Coll., 1954; PhD (hon.), Iona Coll., 1996. Tchr. St. Gabriel's H.S., New Rochelle, NY, 1945—51, Albert Leonard Jr. H.S., New Rochelle, NY, 1960—81; dir. devel. The Ursuline Sch., New Rochelle, NY, 1981—88; ret., 1988. Active Bd. Edn., New Rochelle, 1983—, v.p., 1985—87, pres., 1987—89, Colburn Meml. Home; active New Rochelle Pub. Libr. Found. Bd., New Rochelle Cmty. Svcs. Bd.; vol. Sound Shore Med. Ctr.; bd. dirs. United Way New Rochelle, 1972—, pres., 1979—82, campaign chair, 1976—82; trustee Coll. New Rochelle, 1967—73; lector Holy Family Ch.; active Holy Family Ch. Ladies Guild. Named to Westchester County Hall of Fame, 2005; recipient Gold Key award, Columbia Scholastic Press Assn., 1976, Ursula Laurus citation, Coll. New Rochelle, 1962, St. Angela Merici medal, 1970, citation, United Way New Rochelle, 1970—82, Spl. Recognition award, 1986, 2001, St. Angela award, The Ursuline Sch., 1977, Nat. Cmty. Svc. award, AARP, 1994, Loyal Svc. and Dedication award, Colburn Home, 1992, Cmty. Salute honoree, New Rochelle Pub. Libr. Found., 1999, Cmty. Svc. award, New Rochelle YMCA, 2001, honoree, Sr. Pers. Placement Bur., 2002, Interreligious Coun. of New Rochelle, 2002, Meals-On-Wheels of New Rochelle, 2003, New Rochelle Fund for Ednl. Excellence, 2004, Marie Vitt award, Sound Share Med. Ctr., 2005. Mem.: Bus. and Profl. Women's Club New Rochelle (past pres., Woman of Yr. 1979), So. Westchester Ret. Tchrs. Assn. (co-pres.), Coll. New Rochelle Alumnae Assn. (past pres.), Ladies of Charity (past pres.), Cath. Women's Club Westchester (founder, past pres.), Woman's Club New Rochelle (pres.), LWV, Alpha Delta Kappa (past pres.). Roman Catholic. Avocations: travel, reading, antiques, writing, cross country skiing. Home: 56 Wykagyl Terr New Rochelle NY 10804

REDEL, VICTORIA, writer, poet, educator; b. NYC, Apr. 9, 1959; d. Irving and Natalie Amalie (Soltanitzky) R.; children: Jonah, Gabriel. BA, Dartmouth Coll., 1980; MFA, Columbia U., 1986. Host/producer Focus on Women, Sta. WNYC-TV, N.Y., 1985-87; mem. faculty Sarah Lawrence Coll., Bronxville, NY, 1996—, Vermont Coll., Montpelier, Vt., 1996—, Columbia U., 2001—. Author: Where The Road Bottoms Out, 1995, Already The World, 1995, Loverboy, 2001, Swoon, 2003; contbr. articles to profl. jours. Recipient Tom and Stan Wick award, Kent State U., 1995, S. Mariella Gable award in fiction, 2001; fellow, Fine Arts Work Ctr., 1986, NEA, 1987. Home: 90 Riverside Dr Apt 12A New York NY 10024-5318 Personal E-mail: vredel@aol.com.

REDFEARN, CHARLOTTE MARIE, nursing administrator; b. Tulsa, Nov. 24, 1949; d. John Edward and Mary Loretta Kirkbride; 1 child, John Patrick. Diploma in nursing, Tulsa Jr. Coll., 1986. Admission nurse Tulsa County Jail, 1992—94; skilled unit mgr. So. Hills Nursing Ctr., Tulsa, 1994—96; asst. dir. nursing Pk. Ter. Nursing Ctr., Tulsa, 1996, Georgian Ct., Tulsa, 1996—97, Manor Care Health Svc., Tulsa, 1997—99; dir. nursing Georgian Cts. Rehab., Tulsa, 1999, Maplewood Care Ctr., Tulsa, 2000—. Roman Catholic. Office: Maplewood Care Ctr 6202 E 61 Tulsa OK 74136

REDFIELD, PAMELA A., state legislator; b. Chgo., Aug. 11, 1948; m. Jerry Redfield; 6 children. BS in Edn., U. Nebr., 1969. Mem. Nebr. Legislature 12th dist., Lincoln, 1998—. Mem. Ralston Bd. Edn. 1992-1998. Coun. State Govt.; Nat. Conf. State Legislatures; Am. Legis. Exch. Conf.; Nat. Coun. Ins. Legislators Mem.: Am. Legis. Exch. conf., Nat. Conf. State Legis., Nat. Coun. Ins. State Legis. Office: State Capitol Dist 12 Rm 1404 PO Box 94604 Lincoln NE 68509-4604

REDGRAVE, LYNN, actress; b. London, Mar. 8, 1943; d. Michael Scudemore and Rachel (Kempson) R.; m. John Clark, Apr. 2, 1967 (div. Dec. 22, 2000); children: Benjamin, Kelly, Annabel. Ed., Queensgate Sch., London, Central Sch. Speech and Drama. Stage debut as Helena in Midsummer Night's Dream, 1962; theatrical appearances include The Tulip Tree, Andorra, Hayfever, Much Ado About Nothing, Mother Courage, Love for Love, Zoo, Zoo, Widdershins Zoo, Edinburgh Festival, 1969, The Two of Us, London, 1970, Slag, London, 1971, A Better Place, Dublin, 1972, Born Yesterday, Greenwich, 1973, Hellzapoppin, N.Y., 1976, California Suite, 1977, Twelfth Night, Stratford Conn. Shakespeare Festival, 1978, The King and I, St. Louis, 1983, Les Liaisons Dangereuses, L.A., 1989, The Cherry Orchard, L.A., 1990, Three Sisters, London, 1990, Notebook of Trigorin, U.S., 1996; Broadway appearances include Black Comedy, 1967, My Fat Friend, 1974, Mrs. Warren's Profession (Tony award nomination), 1975, Knock, Knock, 1976, St. Joan, 1977, Sister Mary Ignatius Explains It All, 1985, Aren't We All?, 1985, Sweet Sue, 1987, A Little Hotel on the Side, 1992, The Masterbuilder, 1992, Shakespeare For My Father (Tony and Drama Desk nominations, Elliot Norton award 1993), 1993, also nat. tour, 1996, West End, 1996, Moon over Buffalo, 1996, The Mandrake Root, 2001, Noises Off, 2001, The Constant Wife, 2005; writer, performer (solo show) Nightingale, 2005; film appearances include Tom Jones, Girl With Green Eyes, Georgy Girl (Recipient N.Y. Film Critics award, Golden Globe award, Oscar nomination for best actress 1967), The Deadly Affair, Smashing Time, The Virgin Soldiers, Last of the Mobile Hotshots, Don't Turn the Other Cheek, Every Little Crook and Nanny, Everything You Always Wanted to Know About Sex, The National Health, The Happy Hooker, The Big Bus, Sunday Lovers, Morgan Stuart's Coming Home, Getting It Right, Shine, 1996, Gods and Monsters, 1998 (Recipient Golden Globe award for best performance by an actress in a supporting role in a motion picture 1998), Strike, 1998, The Annihilation of Fish, 1999, The Simian Line, 2000, The Next Best Thing, 2000, How to Kill Your Neighbor's Dog, 2000, My Kingdom, 2001, Unconditional Love, 2001 (voice) The Wild Thornberrys Movie, 2002, Hansel & Gretel, 2002, Anita and Me, 2002, Charlie's War, 2003, Peter Pan, 2003, Kinsey, 2004, The White Countess, 2005; TV appearances include: The Turn of the Screw, Centennial, 1978, The Muppets, Gauguin the Savage, Beggarman Thief, The Seduction of Miss Leona, Rehearsal for Murder, 1982, Walking On Air, The Faintheartd Feminist (BBC-TV), 1984, My Two Loves, 1986, The Old Reliable, 1988, Jury Duty 1989, Whatever Happened to Baby Jane, 1990, Fighting Back (BBC-TV), 1992, Calling the Shots (Masterpiece Theatre), 1993, Toothless, 1997, Indefensible: The Truth About Edward Brannigan, 1997, Different, 1999, White Lies, 1998, A Season for Miracles, 1999, AFI's 100 Years.100 Stars, 1999, Varian's War, 2000, Lion of Oz and the Badge of Courage (voice), 2000; guest appearances include Carol Burnett Show, Evening at the Improv and Steve Martin's Best show Ever, Circus of the Stars, The Nanny, 1999, Richard & Judy, 2005, The Heaven and Earth Show, 2005; co-host nat. TV syndication Not for Women Only, 1977—79; nat., TV spokesperson Weightwatchers, 1984-92; TV series include House Calls, 1981, Teachers Only, 1982, Chicken Soup, 1989; Rude Awakening, 1998, albums: Make Mine Manhattan, 1978, Cole Porter Revisited, 1979; video: (for children) Meet Your Animal Friends, Off We Go, Off We Go Again: audio book readings include, Pride and Prejudice, The Shell Seekers, The Blue Bedroom, The Anastasia Syndrome, The Women in His Life, Snow In April, Gone With The Wind, 1994, The World of Philosophy, 1996; author: This is Living, 1990, Shakespeare For My Father, 1993; text by: Journal: A Mother and Daughter's Recovery from Breast Cancer. Named Runner-up Actress, All Am. Favorites, Box Office Barometer 1975; recipient Sarah Siddons award as Chgo.'s best stage actress of 1976, 94, Order of Brit. Empire, 2001. Mem. The Players (pres. 1994). Office: Apt 2CB 205 W 57th St New York NY 10019-2198*

REDGRAVE, VANESSA, actress; b. London, Jan. 30, 1937; d. Michael and Rachel (Kempson) Redgrave; m. Tony Richardson, Apr. 29, 1962 (div. 1967); children: Joely Kim, Natasha, Carlo. Student, Central Sch. Speech and Drama, London, 1955-57. First stage appearances include: Reluctant Debutante, Frincton Summer Theater, 1957, Come On Jeeves, Arts Theater, Cambridge, 1957, A Touch of the Sun, Saville Theater, London, 1958, Major Barbara, Royal Court, 1958, Mother Goose, Leatherhead, 1958; Prin. theatrical roles include Helena in Midsummer Night's Dream, 1959, Stella in Tiger and the Horse, 1960, Katerina in The Taming of the Shrew, 1961, Rosalind in As You Like It, 1962, Imogene in Cymbeline, 1962, Nina in The Seagull, 1969, Miss Brodie in The Prime of Miss Jean Brodie, 1966, Cato Street, 1971, Threepenny Opera, 1972, Twelfth Night, 1972, Antony and Cleopatra, 1973, Design for Living, 1973, Macbeth, 1975, Lady from the Sea, 1976, 78, 79, The Aspern Papers, 1984 (Laurence Olivier award for actress of yr. in a revival, 1985), The Seagull, 1969, 85, Chekhov's Women, 1985, The Taming of the Shrew, Ghosts, 1986, Touch of the Poet, 1988, Orpheus Descending, 1989, A Madhouse in Goa, 1989, Chekov's Women, 1989, Three Sisters, 1990, When She Danced, 1991, Heartbreak House, 1991, Maybe, 1993, Brecht in Hollywood, 1994, Vita and Virginia, 1994, Long Days Journey Into Night, 2003 (Tony award for best actress, 2003); films include Behind The Mask, 1958, A Man For All Seasons, 1966, Morgan: A Suitable Case for Treatment, 1966 (Best Actress award, Cannes Film Festival, 1966), Blow-Up, 1966, Red And Blue, 1967, Camelot, 1967, The Sailor from Gibralter, 1967, Isadora, 1968 (Best Actress award, Cannes Film Festival, 1969), The Charge of the Light Brigade, 1968, The Seagull, 1968, A Quiet Place in the Country, 1969, Oh! What a Lovely War, 1969, Daniel Deronda, 1969, Dropout, 1969, The Trojan Women, 1970, The Devils, 1970, The Holiday, 1971, Mary, Queen of Scots, 1971, Murder on the Orient Express, 1974, Winter Rates, 1974, 7 per cent solution, 1975, Julia, 1977 (Academy award for best supporting actress, 1978, Golden Globe award for best supporting actress, 1978), Agatha, 1978, Yanks, 1978, Bear Island, 1979, Playing for Time, 1980, My Body My Child, 1981, Wagner, 1981, The Bostonians, 1983 (Best Actress Nat. Film Critics, Best Actress New Delhi Internat. Film Festival), Wetherby, 1985, Steaming, 1985, Prick Up Your Ears, 1987, Comrades, 1987, Consuming Passions, 1988, Diceria dell'Untore, 1989, The Ballad of the Sad Café, 1990, Young Catherine, 1990, Howard's End, 1992, Crime and Punishment, 1993, The House of the Spirits, 1994, Mother's Boys, 1994, A Month by the Lake, 1995, Little Odessa, 1995, Mission Impossible, 1996, For The Love Of Tyler, 1996, Smilla's Sense of Snow, 1996, Deep Impact, 1998, Celebrity, 1998, Lulu on the Bridge, 1998, Uninvited, 1999, Toscano, 1999, A Rumor of Angels, 1999, Mirka, 1999, An Interesting State, 1999, If These Walls Could Talk 2, 1999, The Cradle Will Rock, 1999, Girl, Interrupted, 1999, A Rumor of Angels, 2000, Crime and Punishment, 2000, The 3 Kings, 2000, The Pledge, 2001, Crime and Punishment, 2002, Good Boy!, 2003, The Fever, 2004, Short Order, 2005, The Keeper: The Legend of Omar Khayyam, 2005, The White Countess, 2005; TV movies and miniseries appearances include Playing for Time, 1980 (Emmy award for outstanding lead actress in a limited series or spl., 1981), Snow White and the Seven Dwarfs, 1985, Three Sovereigns for Sarah, 1985, Peter the Great, 1986, Second Serve, 1986 (Emmy award, Golden Globe award), A Man for All Seasons, 1988, Young Catherine, 1990, Whatever Happened to Baby Jane, 1990, The Three Sisters, 1990, When She Danced, 1991, Playing for Time (Emmy award, TV Times award), The Wall, 1992, Heartbreak House, 1992, Great Moments In Aviation, 1993, Down Came A Blackbird, 1994, The Young Indiana Jones Chronicles, 1992, If These Walls Could Talk 2, 2000 (Emmy award for outstanding supporting actress in a miniseries or movie, 2000, Golden Globe award for best supporting actress in a series, mini-series or motion picture made for TV, 2001, Screen Actors Guild award for best supporting actress in a TV movie or miniseries, 2001) The Gathering Storm, 2002, The Locket, 2002, Byron,2003; Author: Pussies and Tigers, 1964, (autobiography) Vanessa, 1991, Vanessa Redgrave: An Autobiography, 1994. Bd. govs. Central Sch. Speech and Drama, 1963—. Decorated comdr. Order Brit. Empire; recipient 4 times Drama award Evening Standard, 1961-91, Best Actress award, Variety Club, Gt. Brit., 1961, 66, Best Actress award, Brit. Guild TV Producers and Dirs., 1966, Variety Club of Great Britain award, 1992, Laurence Olivier award Actress of the Yr. in a Revival for A Touch of the Poet; fellow Brit. Film Inst., 1988.*

REDICAN, LOIS D., small business owner; b. Portsmouth, Va., Nov. 16, 1944; d. Norman J. and Edna M. Lemay; children: Michelle, Patrick, Ryan. BA, Bridgewater State Coll., 1979. Owner, mgr., diet and nutrition therapist Synergic Weight Loss Ctr., Brockton, Mass. Author: The Smart Dieter's Manual. Mem.: Am. Chem. Soc.

REDINGTON, MARY, music educator; b. St. Louis, Feb. 7, 1940; d. Joseph William Sischka and Jeannette Florence Gorman; m. Eugene Charles Redington (div.); children: Joseph Eugene, Daniel Thomas. BA in Music Edn., Webster U., 1966; postgrad., Ill. State U., Fontbonne Coll., U. Mo., St. Louis, Chapman Coll., Tex. Women's U., Heidelberg Coll., Milliken U., St. Louis C.C. Music tchr. Visitation Acad., St. Louis, 1962-65, Ursuline Acad., St. Louis, 1978-79, Villa Duchesne/Oak Hill, St. Louis, 1981—; pvt. piano and voice tchr., 1968-92. Singer Marty's on Gaslight Sq. Singer, actress, dancer in various prodns. including The King and I; Annie, Bye Bye Birdie, Loretta Hilton Theater Studio J. Prodns.; Tents, Tapers & Tintypes, Encore Prodns; No, No Nannette, The Glennon Players; Jerry's Girls, Villa Duchesne Theater Dept.; vocal backup singer KPLR Channel 11, 1992-93; music dir. numerous theatrical and mus. prodns. Recipient numerous awards for sch. choirs, 1987—. Mem. Nat. Assn. Tchrs. of Singing, Am. Choral Dirs. Assn., Music Educators Nat. Conf., Sigma Alpha Iota. Avocations: swimming, fishing, water sports. Home: 13133 Royal Pines Dr Saint Louis MO 63146-2280 Office Phone: 314-432-2021 360.

REDLINGER, MELINDA, secondary school educator; BA in History, Marquette U., Milw., 1994; MS in Edn., Cardinal Stritch U., Milw., MA in History. Tchr. Greenfield Pub. Schs., Wis., 1994—. Office: Greenfield High School 4800 South 60th St Greenfield WI 53220 Office Phone: 414-281-6200. Business E-Mail: mredlinger@greenfield.k12.wi.us.

REDMAN, BARBARA KLUG, nursing educator; b. Mitchell, SD; d. Harlan Lyle and Darlien Grace (Bock) Klug; m. Robert S. Redman, Sept. 14, 1958; 1 child, Melissa Darlien. BS, S.D. State U., 1958; MEd, U. Minn., 1959, PhD, 1964; LHD (hon.), Georgetown U., 1988; DSc (hon.), U. Colo., 1991; M in Bioethics, U. Pa., 2004, MBE, 2004. RN. Asst. prof. U. Wash., Seattle, 1964-69; assoc. dean U. Minn., Mpls., 1969-75; dean Sch. Nursing U. Colo., Denver, 1975-78; VA scholar VA Cen. Office, Washington, 1978-81; postdoctoral fellow Johns Hopkins U., Balt., 1982-83; exec. dir. Am. Assn. Colls. Nursing, Washington, 1983-89, ANA, Washington, 1989-93; prof. nursing Johns Hopkins U., Balt., 1993-95; dean, prof. Sch. Nursing U. Conn., Storrs, 1995-98; dean Coll. Nursing Wayne State U., Detroit. Vis. fellow Kennedy Inst. Ethics, Georgetown U., 1993-94; fellow in med. ethics Harvard Med. Sch., 1994-95. 2004—; vis. scholar U. Pa. Ctr. for Bioethics, 2004—. Author: Practice of Patient Education, 1968—; contbr. articles to profl. jours. Bd. dirs. Friends of Nat. Libr. of Medicine, Washington, 1987—. Recipient Disting. Alumnus award S.D. State U., 1975, Outstanding Achievement award U. Minn., 1989. Fellow Am. Acad. Nursing. Home: 12425 Bobbink Ct Potomac MD 20854-3005 Office: Wayne State U 5557 Cass Ave Detroit MI 48202-3615

REDMAN, JANIS F., special education educator, department chairman; d. Thomas Edward and Margaret Fletcher (Rush) Fox; m. Timothy Duane Redman, Sept. 5, 1970; children: Megan, Molly, Ashley. BS in Elem. Edn., Ohio State U., Columbus, 1971; MA in Curriculum and Instrn., Ashland U., Ohio, 2002. Cert. spl. edn. Ohio State U., 1972. Tchr. spl. edn. Upper Arlington Schs., Ohio, 1971—74, pvt. tutor home and hosp., 1974—87; dir. edn. St. Patrick's Episcopal Ch., Dublin, 1987—92; tchr. spl. edn. Dublin City Schs., 1992—2003, tchr. spl. edn. intervention, dept. chmn., 2003—. Student coun. advisor Dublin City Schs., 1992—; tutor and cons. math, ACT, SAT tests, 1971—; presenter Sch. Study Coun. Ohio. Stencils, Mt. Carmel Hosp. Oncology Wing, 1977—, Worthington Inn, 1984—, Decorator's Showcase, —. Participant Columbus Marathon, Ohio. Named Wal-Mart Tchr. of Yr.,

Jennings scholar, Ohio State U.; recipient Golden Shamrock award, Excellence in Edn. award. Mem.: ASCD, Kappa Kappa Gamma. Avocations: reading, gardening, walking, scrapbooks. Office: Dublin Coffman HS 6780 Coffman Rd Dublin OH 43017-1027

REDMAN, JOANN A., medical/surgical nurse; b. Owosso, Mich., May 3, 1929; d. Franklin Floyd and Lou Arthur Burkholder; children: Marc William, Amy Laine. A in Nursing, Mid. Mich. CC, Harrison. Nurse Graliot Cmty. Hosp., Alma, Mich., 1982—92; hospice nurse Hospice of Ctrl. Mich., Mt. Pleasant, 1992—. Various positions St. John's Ch., Mt. Pleasant. Democrat. Episcopalian. Home: 708 S University Mount Pleasant MI 48858 Office: Hospice of Ctrl Mich 401 S Main Mount Pleasant MI 48858

REDMOND, ANDREA, executive recruiter; b. Glen Ellyn, Ill., Feb. 21, 1956; m. Bill Ferguson; 1 child, Duke. BS, No. Ill. Univ.; MBA, George Williams Coll. Asst. v.p. First Nat. Bank of Chgo., 1981—86; with Russell Reynolds Assoc., Chgo., 1986—, mng. dir., co-head, CEO/bd. services practice, 1994—. Mutual fund bd. mem. Fischer, Francis, Trees & Watts. Co-author (with Charles A. Tribbett III): Business Evolves, Leadership Endures, 2004. Bd. dir. Y-Me Breast Cancer Orgn., Chgo. Children's Meml. Hosp. Named one of 100 Most Influential Women, Crain's Chgo. Bus., 2004. Mem.: Chgo. Econ. Forum, Chgo. Club, Executives Club. Office: Russell Reynolds Assoc Inc Ste 2900 200 S Wacker Dr Chicago IL 60606-5802 Office Phone: 312-993-0704. Office Fax: 312-876-1919. Business E-Mail: aredmond@russellreynolds.com.

REDMOND, CATHERINE, artist, educator; b. Jamestown, N.Y., 1943; Student, Cornell U., Ithaca, N.Y., 1961-62; AB, Harper Coll., SUNY, Binghamton, 1965; postgrad., Art Students League N.Y., 1969-74. Instr. Art Students League N.Y., 1990—2000; assoc. prof. Pratt Inst., Bklyn., 1999—. Artist-in-residence The Vt. Coun. on the Arts, 1980-82; asst. prof. painting Cleve. Inst. Art, 1985-90; vis. asst. prof. Pratt Inst., Bklyn., N.Y., 1999-2002 Solo shows include Blue Mountain Gallery, N.Y.C., 1985, 88, Bonfoey, Cleve., 1986, 91, The Butler Inst. Am. Art, Youngstown, Ohio, 1987, MB Modern, N.Y., 1996, 98-99, David Findlay Jr., NYC, 2003; exhibited in group shows at Blue Mountain Gallery, N.Y.C., 1991, Mansfield (Ohio) Art Ctr., 1992, Erector Square Gallery, New Haven, Conn., 1992, Babcock Galleries, N.Y., 1993, Gallery Dong Ho, Seoul, Korea, 1995, Gerald Peters Gallery, Santa Fe, 1996, Chuck Levitan Gallery, N.Y.C., 1996, MB Modern, N.Y.C., 1996, 98, Elise Goodheart Fine Art, Sag Harbor, N.Y., 1998, M.D. Modern, Houston, 1998-99, Albright Knox Art Gallery, 1998, Swarthmore (Pa.) Coll., 2003, others; represented in permanent collections Ade Skunta and Co., Cleve., Amerada Hess Corp., N.Y.C., Am. Soc. for Metals, Art Students League N.Y., Butler Inst. Am. Art, Citibank N.Y., Cleve. Indians, Jones, Day, Reavis & Pogue, Cleve., Kemper Group, Luther Coll., Iowa, No. Trust Bank, Chgo., Progressive Ins. Corp., Cleve., Reading Pub. Mus., Pa., 1999, others. Trustee Vt. Alliance for Art in Edn., 1981, Warehouse Dist. Redevel. Corp., Cleve., 1985-87; cons. Vt. Children's Mag., 1981, 92; panel rev. mem. Cleve. Pub. Theater Performance Art Festival, 1989; juror Pen and Brush, N.Y.C., 2002, Fitchberg Mus., Md., 2002. Home: 156 Chambers St New York NY 10007-3505 Office Phone: 212-406-0046. Personal E-mail: catherineredmond@gmail.com. Business E-Mail: credmond@pratt.edu.

REDMOND, GLENIS G., performance poet; b. Sumter, S.C., Aug. 27, 1963; d. Johnny Clifton and Jeanette Vivian Redmond; m. Sherer (div.); children: Vivian Celeste, Maya Amber. BA Psychology, Erskine Coll., Due West, S.C., 1985. Poet in the schs., Greenville, SC, 1994—; educator, performer Kennedy Ctr., Washington; performance poet Lloyd Agy., Asheville, NC. Bd. dirs. Emrys, Greenville, SC, 1998—99, Asheville Area Arts Co., SC, 2003—04, Flat Rock Playhouse, Asheville, 2004—04. Co-author: (book) Backbone, 2000; performer: (Video) Mama's Magic, (audio tape) Coming Forth; contbr. short stories to various literary reviews. Nominee Poet Laureate, Raleigh, N.C., 2002; recipient Carrie McRay Literary award, Spartanburg, S.C., 1995, awards, Johnson Vt. Studio Ctr., 1999, 2002, N.C. Literary award, 2005. Mem.: Nat. Poetry Slam. Democrat. Avocations: reading, exercise, African dance. Home: PO Box 4142 Asheville NC 28805 Office: Loyd Artists PO Box 3048 Asheville NC 28802-3048 Office Phone: 800-476-6240. Office Fax: 828-258-8810. E-mail: poetica11@aol.com.

REDMONT, JOAN, retired language educator; b. Bklyn., Aug. 30, 1918; d. William Rothenberg Sr. and Melanie Tokaji; m. Bernard Sidney Redmont, Mar. 12, 1940; children: Dennis Foster, Jane Carol. BA, Hunter Coll., 1939; diplome de langue Francaise, Alliance Francaise, Paris, 1963; postgrad., Boston U., Goethe Inst., Paris; MA, U. Paris, 1975. Co-founder Coop. Nursery Sch., Mt. Rainer, Md., 1944—45; tchr. Lincoln Bilingual Sch., Buenos Aires, 1948—49; tchr. ESL program Odwin Learning Ctr., Dorchester, Mass., 1983—84, bd. dirs., 1993—98, chmn. bd. dirs., 1995—98; tchr. ESL program Norwood (Mass.) schs., 1996—2000. Editor: Welcome to Moscow, 1978; adaptor, translator: The Herschel Grynspfan Case, 1982. Mem. Jeunes Femmes, Paris, Internat. Women's Group, Paris and Moscow; co-founder Unitarian-Universalist Fellowship, Paris; troop leader Girl Scouts USA, Herkimer, NY; Sunday sch. tchr. Internat. Quaker Ctr.; bd. dirs. Camp Kokosing, Inc., Thetford Center, Vt. Mem.: AAUW, Common Cause. Avocations: gardening, swimming, languages, travel, reading. Home: 220 Del Pond Dr Canton MA 02021

REDSTONE, SHARI E., amusement company executive; 3 children. JD, Boston U., 1978, M in Tax Law, 1980. Lawyer, Boston area, 1978-93; v.p. corp. planning and devel. Nat. Amusements, Dedham, to 1994, exec. v.p., 1994—2000, pres., also bd. dir., 2000—. Mem. exec. com. Boston U. Sch. Law; bd. dir. Midway Home Entertainment, 2004, Viacom, Global Hyatt Corp., LaSalle Bank Corp., The Marmon Group; chmn., CEO Rising Star Media, CineBridge Ventures, Inc.; co-chmn., co-CEO MovieTickets.com; bd. dir., chair governance com. William Wrigley Jr. Co., 1994—2005. Bd. dir. Jewish Philanthropies; bd. overseers Harvard U., 2002—, co-chair com. on Allston; bd. dir., exec. com. Nat. Assn. Theatre Owners; trustee, Dana Farber Cancer Inst. Tufts U.; mem. adv. com. Tufts Hillel. Named one of 50 Women to Watch, Wall St. Jour., 2005. Office: 200 Elm St Dedham MA 02026-4536*

REEBERG, PATRICIA ALDORA, minister, entrepreneur; d. Henrietta Monroe. MDiv., Union Theol. Sem., N.Y.C., 1989. Cert. Cmty. Devel. Leadership Harvard Div. Sch., Mass., 1999, Inst. for Not-for-Profit Mgmt. Columbia U., Grad. Sch. of Bus., NY, 1992. Pres./owner SM&G Corp., Bronx, NY, 1994—; pres./chief exec. officer Concord Cmty. Devel. Corp., Bklyn., 1998—; CEO Coun. of Chs. of the City of NY, 1990—94; asst. pastor St. Paul Bapt. Ch., N.Y., NY, 1985—; chaplain NY State Dept. of Correctional Svcs., N.Y., 1983—89. Cons. Ford Found., N.Y., 2000—01, Rockefeller Found., N.Y., 1997—97, Fedn. of Protestant Welfare Agencies, N.Y., 2002—, NY Work Alliance, N.Y., 2003—. Commr. Civilian Complaint Rev. Bd., N.Y., NY, 1993—95; bd. mem. NY State Regents, N.Y., NY, 1995—2001, Harlem Congregation for Cmty. Improvement, N.Y., NY, 1994—2005. Recipient Good News Maker Award, NY Christian Times, Dedicated Leadership Award, New Voices of Harlem, Outstanding Women Role Model Award, Nat. Assn. of Negro Bus. & Profl. Women's Club, Cert. of Merit, N.Y. Bd. of Rabbis, Elders of Vision Award, Harlem Congregation for Cmty. Devel.; grantee Rsch. Grant, Louisville Inst.; Charles Merrill Fellowship, Harvard Div. Sch. Achievements include the privilege of being the first women elected as of the CEO Coun. of Chs. of the City of N.Y. in its 183 yr. history; first woman appointed Asst. Pastor of St. Paul Baptist Ch. in its 112 year history; also the first chaplain appointed to the N.Y.C. Bd. Edn. Office: SM&G Corp 3403 Cannon Place Bronx NY 10463-4301 Office Phone: 718-548-4386. Home Fax: 718-548-4386; Office Fax: 718-548-4427. Business E-Mail: reebergsmg@aol.com.

REECE, BELYNDA M., minister, consultant, military officer; b. San Diego, May 2, 1956; d. Hubert Jackson and Elizabeth Ann (Seifert) Reece. AS in Environ. Health Tech., Merritt Coll., Oakland, Calif., 1977—83; BS in Liberal Arts, SUNY, Albany, 1994; MDiv in Theology, Colgate Rochester Div. Sch., NY, 1995—97; studied, Capella U., Mpls., 2004—. Gen. duty corpsman Naval Support Activity, New Orleans, 1975—76; gen. duty hosp. corpsman Naval Regional Med. Ctr., New Orleans, 1976—77; preventive medicine tech. Navy Environ. and Preventive Medicine Unit No. 7, Naples, Italy, 1977—80, Navy Environ. and Preventive Medicine Unit No. 5, San Diego, 1980—83; instr. staff Preventive Medicine Tech. Sch., Oakland, Calif., 1983—85; leading chief petty officer, med. dept. Cmdr. Fleet Activities, Chinhae, Republic of Korea, 1985—87; supr., joint coord. preventive medicine svc. Naval Hosp., Camp Pendleton, Calif., 1988—89; leading chief petty officer, med. dept. USS Shenandoah, Norfolk, Va., 1990—92; hosp. corps plan officer Navy Bur. Medicine & Surgery, Washington, 1992—95; chap. Strong Meml. Hosp., Rochester, NY, 1996—97; asst. pastor United Methodist Ch. N. Chili, Rochester, NY, 1996—97, sr. pastor, 2000—04; pastor for spiritual devel. Kenmore United Methodist Ch., NY, 1997—2000; sr. pastor United Meth. Ch., NY, 2002—04; cons. Webb & Assocs. Chap. Cons., Oceanside, Calif., 2004—. Cons. USMC, Camp Pendleton, Calif., 2004—. Decorated Meritorious Svc. Medal, 2 Navy Commendation Medals, Navy Achievement Medal, Good Conduct Medal, Meritorious Unit Commendation, Nat. Def. Medal, S.W. Asia Svc. Medal (with bronze star), Sea Svc. Deployment Medal, 4 Overseas Svc. Ribbons, Kuwait Liberation Medal; finalist Navy Shore Sailor of Yr., 1979, Stephen W. Brown Preventive Medicine Tech. of Yr., HMCM, 1989; recipient Shore Sailor of Yr., Bur. Medicine and Surgery, 1979. Mem.: VFW, Am. Legion, Internat. Critical Incident Stress Found., Am. Assn. Christian Counselors.

REECE, BETH PAULEY, chaplain; b. Warsaw, Ind., June 4, 1945; d. Lester Elden and Genevene (Walter) Pifer; m. Gyle Barry Reece, June 20, 1987. BA, Grace Coll., 1967; interior design degree, Harrington Inst. Design, Chgo., 1995; summer student, Oxford and Cambridge, Eng., 1987, 95, 97; Trinity Coll., Dublin, 1999, U Edinburgh, 2001; grad., Inst. Spiritual Companionship, 2000—02; postgrad., North Park Sem., Chgo., 2005—. Cert. spiritual dir. Grain trader, hedger Ctrl. Soya Inc., Ft. Wayne, Ind., 1973-82; account exec. ACLI Internat. Inc., Chgo., 1982-83; account exec., hedger Ctrl. States Enterprises, Ft. Wayne, 1983-84; account exec. Stotler & Co., Chgo., 1984-89, LaSalle Brokerage Inc., Chgo., 1989—2003; chaplain Rehab. Inst. Chgo., 2004—. Mem. Spiritual Dirs. Internat. Presbyterian. Avocations: reading, sailing, travel. Home: 227 E Delaware Pl Apt 5C Chicago IL 60611-7758 E-mail: bethreece64@msn.com.

REECE, CHERI DODSON, clinical nursing specialist, educator; b. Altoona, Pa., Apr. 17, 1946; d. Paul Francis and Evelyn Pearl (Brown) Dodson; 1 child, Michelle Lynn. Diploma in nursing, Western Pa. Hosp. Sch. Nursing, 1967; BSN, Cedar Crest Coll., 1969; postgrad. nursing, Kent State U., 1979-83; MSN in Perinatal Nursing, Case Western Res. U., 1987. Cert. clinical nurse specialist. Nurse coll. infirmary, 1967-69; staff nurse Western Pa. Hosp., 1968; pvt. duty nurse, 1969, 78, 84-85; staff nurse Nason Hosp., Roaring Spring, Pa., 1969; instr. in-svc. edn. N.D. State Hosp., Jamestown, 1969-71; staff nurse Santa Clara Valley Med. Ctr., San Jose, Calif., 1971-72; instr. nursing San Jose Hosps. and Health Ctr., 1972-74, Kent State U., 1974-75, 78-84, Ohio Valley Hosp., Steubenville, Ohio, 1975-77; staff nurse Ashtabula (Ohio) Medicare Ctr., 1977-78; instr. adult edn. Ashtabula County Joint Vocat. Sch., 1978-79; phys. exam. nurse Phys. Measurements, Inc., Ashtabula, 1978; grad. asst. Case Western Res. U., 1985-86; staff nurse Ashtabula County Home Health, 1986—87; adj. faculty Cleve. State Univ., 1987; perinatal clin. nurse specialist Cape Fear Valley Med. Ctr., 1987—2001; nurse clinician FirstHealth of Carolinas, 2001—04; perinatal clin. nurse specialist Phoebe Putney Meml. Hosp., 2004—; cons. well-baby care and perinatal case revs. Adj. faculty Cleve. State U., 1987; mem. panel of master pool reviewers Nat. Coun. State Bds. Nursing; mem. ednl. adv. group, regional trainer Neonatal Resuscitation Program; preceptor for grad. nursing students. Guest lectr., active in campaign U.S. Rep., Am. Cancer Soc., Am. Heart Fund; patron Straw Hat Theatre; councilmatic aide Ashtabula City Coun., 1981-83; head Ctr. Shop at Ashtabula Arts Ctr., also patron; mem. panel of content experts Nat. Coun. State Bds. of Nursing Licensure Exams.; mem. coms. Fayetteville YMCA, Westminster Presbyn. Ch.; mem. Gov. Commn. on Reduction Infant Mortality, N.C. PTA; cir. moderator Covenant Presbyn. Ch.; active Children's Miracle Network. Mem. AAUW (sec. chpt. 1980-82, treas. 1983-85), AWHONN, Nat. League Nursing, Neonatal Resuscitation Program (regional trainer), Coastal Area Perinatal Assn. (sec.-treas.), Cedar Crest Coll. Alumnae Assn., Alumnae Assn. Greenfield-Kimmel H.S., East Carolina U. Parent's Assn., Douglas Byrd Sr. High Band Booster (pres.), U.S. Masters Swimming, Sigma Theta Tau. Office: Phoebe Putney Meml Hosp 417 Third Ave Albany GA 31702 Office Phone: 229-312-5906.

REECE, JULIA RUTH, systems analyst, entrepreneur; b. Detroit, Oct. 25, 1958; d. William James and Julia Henrietta (Thomas) Coleman; m. Darnell Fuller, Nov. 10, 1984 (div. Dec. 1988); m. Terry Allen Reece, July 2, 2001. BA in Computer Sci., Wayne State U., 1980. Programmer analyst Mich. Bell Telephone Co., Detroit, 1980-82; tech. support analyst Unisys Corp. (formally Burroughs), Detroit, 1982-91; owner JR & Assocs. Computer Svcs., Detroit, 1991—; computer cons. Comprehensive Data Processing, Detroit, 1991-94; sr. programmer, analyst City of Detroit, 1994-00, prin. programmer/analyst, 2000—. Musician Met. Cmty. Tabernacle, Detroit, 1975—84, 1988—2000, Greater Faith New Covenant Assembly, Detroit, 1985—87. Independent. Avocations: reading, travel, music, cooking, computers. E-mail: fullerj@itsd.ci.detroit.mi.us, ladyjr@ameritech.net.

REECE, JULIETTE M. STOLPER, community health and mental health nurse; b. Muskogee, Okla., Oct. 4, 1926; d. Joseph Harry and Marie (Duquesne) Stolper; m. Warren Crane, Apr. 12, 1947; children: Warren Crane, Judith Gayle Crane Cox Fitzpatrick, Janice M. Crane Sharp, Cathy L. Crane Hubble; m. Roy M. Reece Jr., July 16, 1970 (dec.). Diploma, Muskogee Gen. Hosp., 1947; BS in Psychology, Cameron Coll., Lawton, Okla., 1993, postgrad., 1993; student, U. Okla. Cert. pub. health nurse. Indsl. nurse Corning Glass Plant, Mankogee, Okla., 1949; ICU nurse Southwestern Hosp., Lawton, 1976-77; evening charge nurse St. Joseph Hosp., Houston, 1977—78; psychiat. nurse Taliaferro Community Mental Health Ctr., 1977-86; cons. nurse Cedar Crest Manor, Lawton, 1980—85, dir. nursing svc., 1986-87; asst. head nurse Reynolds Family Practice Clinic, Ft. Sill, Okla., 1987-91, head nurse, 1991-95, also diabetes educator, 1991-97; patient/staff edn. coord. dept. family practice Reynolds Army Cmty. Hosp., Ft. Sill, 1996-97; staff nurse Rapid-Temps., 1997-99; nurse cons., owner Jay Mar Assocs., Lawton, Okla., 1998—; sch. nurse Bishop Elem. Sch., Lawton, Okla., 1999—. Vis. mem. Pub. Health Nursing Study Group, USSR, 1979. Vol. for Am. Cancer Soc., Am. Heart Assn., Am. Diabetes Assn., Am. Lung Assn., Am. Assn. Diabetes Educators, Assn. Western Okla. Diabetes Educators, ARC, Easter Seal Programs; tchr. classes for home health care aides, ARC; tchr. med. terminology to hosp. receptionists. Recipient nursing grants. Home: 1601 NW Pollard Ave Lawton OK 73507-2048

REECE, MARLENE WILLIAMS, elementary school educator; b. Marshalltown, Iowa, Dec. 24, 1950; d. Arthur L. and Donna Joan (Parsons) Williams; m. Dennis E. Reece; children: Matthew, Christopher, Allison Lakshmi. Student, William Penn Coll.; BA in Early Childhood Edn., U. No. Iowa, 1973, BA in Elem. Edn., 1981. Cert. early childhood and elem. edn. Tchr., presch. dir. Union (Iowa) Sch.; mid. sch. reading and math. tchr. Eldora (Iowa)-New Providence Schs., tchr. 4th grade and talented and gifted, 1st and 2d multiage classrm. tchr., Title I reading specialist. Mem. NEA, Iowa State Edn. Assn., Iowa Reading Assn., Eldora-New Providence Edn. Assn. (pres., sec.), Hardy Coun. Avocations: music, reading, travel, creative writing. Home: PO Box 73 New Providence IA 50206-0073

REECE-PORTER, SHARON ANN, international human rights educator; b. Cin., Nov. 28, 1953; d. Edward and Claudia (Ownes) Reece; div., 1981; children: Erika Lynn, Melanie Joyce. BS in Textiles and Clothing, Edgecliff Coll., 1975; cert. clerical computer, So. Ohio Coll., 1984; MEd in Gen. Edn., SUNY, Buffalo, 1994; PhD in Internat. Human Rights Devel., Brentwick U., London, 2000; EdD in Global Edn. (hon.), Australian Inst. Coordinated Rsch., Victoria, 1995; postgrad. in photojournalism/profl. photography, NY Inst. Photography, 2002—. Cert. tchr. Ohio. Dept. supr., asst. buyer Mabley & Carew, Cin., 1975—76; claims adjuster Allstate Ins. Co., Cin., 1976—78; sales merchandiser Ekco Houseware, Cin., 1979—80; sales rep. Met. Life Inc., Cin., 1981—83; info. processing specialist GPA/Robert Half/Word Source, Cin., Dallas, 1985—87; tchr. adult edn. Princeton City Schs., Cin., 1984—90; with Rainbow Internat. Non-Profit Adult Ednl. Rsch. Ctr., Honolulu, 1990—98, Norfolk, Va., 1998—; specialist edn. rsch. found. SUNY, Buffalo, 1993; human rights investigator Citizens Commn. on Human Rights Internat., L.A., 2005—. Prof. computer sci. So. Ohio Tech. and Bus. Coll., Cin., 1986-90; computer software tng. cons., 1987-89; part-time tchr. adult GED classes Adult Learning Ctr. Buffalo Bd. Edn., 1994-95; participant Am. Forum for Global Edn., Honolulu; lectr. photography N.Y. Inst. Photography, N.Y.C., N.Y., 2002—. Tutor U.S. divsn. Internat. Laubach Lit., Clermont County, Ohio, 1984; coordinate workshops Dianetics Found., Virginia Beach, Va.; human rights investigator Citizens Commission for Human Rights, Virgina Beach. Fellow Australian Inst. for Coordinated Rsch. (life); mem. NAFE, ASTD, Internat. DOS Users Group, Am. Ednl. Rsch. Assn., Nat. Assn. Women Bus. Owners, UN Assn., World Assn. Women Entrepreneurs, Boston Computer Soc., Cin. Orgn. Data Processing Educators and Trainers, Internat. Platform Assn., Cin. C. of C. (cert. minority supplier devel. coun.), Dianetics Found. (co-coord. workshops). Home: 2941 Chilton Pl Virginia Beach VA 23456 Office: Global Human Rights & Artistic Impressions PO Box 56544 Virginia Beach VA 23456 Personal E-mail: humanrtssharonan@msn.com.

REED, ANGELICA DENISE, sculptor, writer, illustrator; b. Murfreesboro, Tenn., Dec. 16, 1955; d. Keith Kenyon and Lester Faye (Todd) Reed; m. David Earl Myers, Apr. 19, 1975 (dec. Mar. 1978); m. John Gregory Bettis, May 11, 1979. Student, Mid. Tenn. State U., 1973-75, 77-78, UCLA, 1981-82, Venice Sculpture Studio, 1983-85, Brucchion Sch. of Art, Culver City, Calif., 1987-90. Artist-in-residence Reed Studio and Gallery, Venice, Calif., 1990-95, The Jerry Solomon Gallery, L.A., 1997, Belle Art Galleries, Inc. at Bel Age Hotel, West Hollywood, Calif., 2000—. Cons. Sweet Harmony Music, Sunset Beach, Calif., 1978-83, Bettis Paradise Music, Sunset Beach, 1978-85, John Bettis Music, L.A., 1983—, John Bettis Property Mgmt., L.A., 1986—. Fundraiser Children's Hosp./Santa Monica Bay Aux., 1991, Nat. Acad. Songwriters, 1985, SEA Environ. Assn., Bonaventure Hotel, L.A., 1990, 91; mem. L.A. com. P.E.T.A. People for the Ethical Treatment of Animals, 1992; vol. St. John Hosp., 1998. Avocations: gymnastics, scuba diving, travel, ballet. Home and Office: 2251 Mid Tenn Blvd Murfreesboro TN 37130 E-mail: angelicadenise@comcast.net.

REED, ANNE F. THOMSON, management consultant; BA, Goucher Coll., 1973; MPA, Harvard U., 1981. Devel. rschr. Office of Alumni Devel. Vanderbilt U., Nashville, 1973—74; jr. cmty. planner Nashville City Planning Commn., 1974—76; staff asst. to asst. dean for adminstrn. Kennedy Sch. Harvard U., Cambridge, Mass., 1976—77, registrar, admissions officer John F. Kennedy Sch. Govt., 1977—80; presdl. mgmt. intern Dept. Navy, Washington, 1981—83, budget analyst for Naval Sea Sys. Command, 1983—86, numerous mgmt. positions Office Comptroller, 1986—93; dep. asst. sec. agr. for adminstrn. USDA, Washington, 1993—96, chief info. officer, 1997—2000; v.p. govt. global industry group EDS, 2000—02, pres. State and Local Govt., 2002—03; pres. Aquisition Solutions, Inc., 2003—. Office Phone: 703-253-6309.

REED, BERENICE ANNE, cultural organization administrator, educator, artist; b. Memphis; d. Glenn Andrew and Berenice Marie (Kallaher) R. BFA, St. Mary-of-the-Woods Coll., Ind., 1955; MFA in Painting and Art History, Istituto Pio XII, Villa Schifanoia, Florence, Italy, 1964. Cert. art tchr. Tenn. Comml. artist Memphis Pub. Co., 1955—56; arts adminstr., educator pub. and pvt. instns., Washington, Memphis, 1957—70; arts adminstr. Nat. Park Svc., 1970—73; mem. staff U.S. Dept. Energy, Washington, 1973—81, U.S. Dept. Commerce, Washington, 1983—84, Exec. Office of Pres., Office of Mgmt. and Budget, Washington, 1985; with fin. mgmt. svc. U.S. Treasury Dept., Washington, 1985—2004. Ind. art history rschr. Nat. Gallery of Art, Ctr. Advanced Study in Visual Arts, Washington, 1998—; cons. on art and architecture in recreation AIA, 1972-73; artist-in-residence St. Mary-of-the-Woods Coll., Ind., 1965; guest lectr. instr. Nat. Sch. Fine Arts, Tegucigalpa, Honduras, 1968; exec. com. Parks, Arts and Leisure Project, Washington, 1972-73; rschr. art projects, Washington, 1981-83. Developer (video) In Your Interest, 1992; TV interviewer Am. Fin. Skylink satellite programs, 1996-98. Advisor Royal Oak Found.; bd. dirs. Am. Irish Bicentennial Com., 1974—76. Recipient various awards for painting; installed as Dama of Merit, Sacred Mil. Constantinian Order of St. George, Naples, 1997, awarded Star, 2001, installed as Dama, Order of St. Maurice and St. Lazarus, 2000; named one of 150 Women Who Made A Difference in 150 years of St. Agnes Acad., 2001. Mem. Soc. Woman Geographers, Nat. Soc. Arts and Letters, Ctr. Advanced Study in Visual Arts, Art Barn Assn. (bd. dir. 1973-83), Patrons Arts in the Vatican Mus., Irish Georgian Soc. Roman Catholic. Avocations: photography, performing arts. Home: PO Box 34253 Bethesda MD 20827-0253

REED, BRENDA KAY, mathematics educator; b. Greensburg, Ind., Feb. 8, 1966; d. Stanley G and Elizabeth A Reed. BS in Edn., Ball State U., Muncie, Ind., 1989. Cert. tchr. State of Ind., 1989. Math tchr. Decatur County Cmty. Schs., Greensburg, 1990—. Girls jv basketball coach North Decatur Jr/Sr H.S., Greensburg, Ind., 1990—2000, student coun. sponsor, 1990—. Mem.: NEA (life). Office Phone: 812-663-4204.

REED, CATHY LORRAINE, elementary school educator; b. Beckley, W.Va., Sept. 23, 1956; d. Clarence and Beulah mae (Perdue) R. AA, Beckley Coll., 1977; BS in Edn., Concord Coll., Athens, W.Va., 1979; MA, Marshall U., 1989. Cert. tchr. elem. edn. 1-6, reading specialist K-12, W.Va. Tchr. Raleigh County Bd. Edn., Beckley, 1979—. Avocations: sewing, reading, travel. Office: Shady Spring Elem PO Box 2009 Shady Spring WV 25918

REED, CHARLOTTE, education educator, consultant; b. NYC, Apr. 27, 1948; d. Thomas L. and Lillian Marie (Brown) R.; m. Twain M. Peebles, Sept. 12, 1987; 1 child, Mark. BA, Richmond Coll., 1972; MEd, U. Va., 1977, EdD, 1980. Cert. English, speech and drama tchr., N.Y., Va., Ky., secondary prin., Va., Ky., supr., Ky. Tchr. Jr. High Sch. Dist. 13, N.Y.C., 1972-76, Walker Mid. Sch., Charlottesville, Va., 1976-77; project dir. Consultative Resource Ctr. U. Va., Charlottesville, 1977-81; asst. prof. U. Louisville, 1981-87, Alverno Coll., Milw., 1987-89, assoc. prof., 1989-90, Purdue U., Hammond, Ind., 1990-92; program devel. dir. of urban tchr. edn. program Ind. U. N.W., Gary, 1992-93; assoc. prof. edn. Ind. U., 1993—, assoc. dir. program devel. Urban Tchr. Edn. Program, 1993-94; dir. program devel. Urban Tchr. Edn. Program, 1994—. Cons. Hazelwood Sch. Dist., St. Louis, 1985-90, Pvt. Industry Coun. and Louisville Urban League, 1986-87, Cleve. Pub. Schs., 1987-89, Milw. Area Tech. Coll., 1989-90, Coop. Edn. Svc. Agy. Wis., 1990-91; reader Ednl. Testing Svc., 1991—; cons. Mequon-Theinsville (Wis.) Sch. Dist., 1991-92, Hamilton (Wis.) Sch. Dist., 1992, East Chicago (Ind.) Schs., 1992, Gary (Ind.) Community Schs., 1992. Editorial bd. Jour. Invitational Theory and Practice, 1991—. Mem. issues com. Family Svcs. of Milw., 1990—; mem. edn. resource panel Milw. Urban League, 1987-89; bd. dirs. Louisville Youth Commn. Citizens Adv. Bd., 1983-84; chmn. bd. dirs. Cable Bapt. Ch. Day Care Ctr., Louisville, 1985-87. Recipient Svc. award Ky. House Reps., 1984, Gov. Martha Layne Collins, Ky., 1984, Louisville Bd. Alderman, 1984, U. St. Louis Speaker's Bur., 1986-87, St. Louis Pub. Schs., 1989; Nat. Acad. Edn. fellow, 1983; recipient Black Achiever's award Cable Bapt. Ch., 1986, 87. Mem. ASCD, Internat. Alliance for Invitational Edn. (trainer, Svc. award 1983), Am. Edn. Rsch. Assn. (pres. spl. interest group on invitational edn. 1984-85, spl. interest group on rsch. on women and edn., Women Educators Activism award 1993), Am. Assn. Colls. for Tchr. Edn., Nat. Alliance Black Sch. Educators, Assn. Tchr. Educators (spl. interest group on multicultural edn.), Nat. Assn. for Multicultural Edn., Women Educators, John Dewey Soc., Nat. Coun. of Black Studies, Phi Delta Kappa (bd. dirs. N.W. Ind. chpt.). Avocations: singing, acting, volleyball. Office: Ind U NW Urban Tchr Edn Program 217 Sycamore Hall 340 Broadway Gary IN 46408

REED, CYNTHIA KAY, minister; b. Amarillo, Tex., July 10, 1952; d. Carlos Eugene and Marjorie Marie (Daughetee) R B Music Edn., McMurry Coll., Abilene, Tex., 1976; MDiv, Perkins Sch. Theol., Dallas, 1991. Ordained to ministry Meth. Ch., 1989; cert. dir. music. Dir. music and Christian edn. 1st

United Meth. Ch., Childress, Tex., 1976—78, Oakwood United Meth. Ch., Lubbock, Tex., 1978—84, 1st United Meth. Ch., Littlefield, Tex., 1984—86, intern min. Lubbock, 1989—90, assoc. min., 1990—91; min. Meadow and Ropesville United Meth. Chs., 1991—93, Earth United Meth. Ch., Tex., 1993—97, First United Meth. Ch., Colorado City, Tex., 1997—2001, Albany, Tex., 2001—, Moran, Tex., 2001—. Extern chaplain Meth. Hosp., Lubbock, 1989—, Walk to Emmaus Renewal Movement, Lubbock, 1990— Com. mem. Life Gift-Organ Donation, Lubbock, 1991; mem. Arthritis Found., Lubbock, 1991 Georgia Harkness scholar Div. Ordained Ministry, 1989 Mem. Christian Educators & Musicians Fellowship, Am. Guild Organists Office Phone: 325-762-2423.

REED, DAPHNE STEVENSON, artist; b. Hartford, Conn. d. Edward McMurtry and Adele (Vaughan) Stevenson; m: Bruce Penttinen, 2001; children: Bonnie, Laurie, Rory. BA, Am. U.; MFA, U. Mass., 1969. Rschr., author, editor, publisher, artist, Amherst, Mass., 1965—; instr., theatre dir. Mt. Holyoke Coll., South Hadley, Mass., 1970-72; tchr., adminstr., theatre dir. Hampshire Coll. and Amherst Coll., 1972-77; staff asst. Five Colls., Inc., Amherst, 1977-83; adminstr. U. Mass., Amherst, 1977-85; freelance editor, writer, artist, English lang. cons. Amherst, 1986—; writer, pub. Owl Pub., 1993—2006. Broadcaster Radio Reading Svcs. Western New Eng., Springfield, Mass., 1982-88; cons. in field. One woman show Artwork, 1994; author/dir. (plays) I Woman, 1970, This Thing Called Freedom, 1972; author The Secret World of Angels, 1999; editor Owl Angels Jour., 2000—06. Organizer Pioneer Valley (Mass.) chpt. P-FLAG, 1985, leader, 1994—, editor Owl Angels Jour. newsletter, 2001—; founding charter mem. Com. on Race Rels., Amherst, 1970-73. Arts Coun. grantee, Amherst, 1987. Mem. Internat. Women's Writing Guild, Ednl. Theatre Assn., Mothers Against War (organizer 2002). Democrat. Congregationalist. Avocations: theater, literature, writing, painting, metaphysical and political research. Home: 305 Middle St Amherst MA 01002-3016 Office Phone: 413-253-3354. Personal E-mail: owlangels@aol.com.

REED, DIANE MARIE, retired psychologist; b. Joplin, Mo., Jan. 11, 1934; d. William Marion and Olive Francis (Smith) Kinney; m. William J. Shotton; children: Wendy Robison, Douglas Funkhouser. Student, Art Ctr. Col., L.A., 1951-54; BS, U. Oreg., 1976, MS, 1977, PhD, 1981. Lic. psychologist. Illustrator J.L. Hudson Co., Detroit, 1954-56; designer, stylist N.Y.C., 1960-70; designer, owner Decor To You, Inc., Stamford, Conn., 1970-76; founder, exec. dir. Alcohol Counseling and Edn. Svcs., Inc., Eugene, Oreg., 1981-86, clin. supr., 1986, Christian Family Svcs., Eugene, 1986-87; pvt. practice Eugene, 1985-94; co-founder Reed Consulting, Bend, Oreg., 1995—2000; pvt. practice Bend, Oreg., 2000—04; ret., 2005. Evaluator Vocat. Rehab. Div., Eugene, 1982—; alcohol and drug evaluator and commitment examiner Oreg. Mental Health Div., 1981—86. Named Disting. Alumnus, Ctrl. Oreg. region U. Oreg. Coll. Edn., 2003. Mem.: AAUW, APA, Ctr. Ore. Psychological Assn. (pres. elect), Lane County Psychol. Assn. (pres. 1989—90), Oreg. Psychol. Assn., U. Oreg. Nat. Alumni, Ctrl. Oreg. Llama Assn. (pres. 1999—2000), Bend C. of C., Sunriver Area C. of. C. (bd. dirs. 1997—98), Sunriver Women's Club (comm. chair), Toastmasters Internat., Rotary (pres. 1997—98, Rotarian Yr. 1996—97, 1997—98). Avocations: photography, skiing, hiking, backpacking.

REED, DONNA MARIE, editor; b. Dayton, Ohio, Mar. 29, 1950; d. Andrew Levi and Golda Mabel (Branham) Tatman; m. Donald Ray Newsome, May 12, 1973 (div. Sept. 1985); 1 child, Amanda Marie; m. James A. Reed, Sept. 26, 1987. BA, Morehead State U., 1973, MA, 1974. Junior high sch. tchr. English, 1974; part-time corr. Tampa Tribune, Fla., 1974—75, reporter, bur. chief, asst. suburban editor, suburban editor, asst. metro editor, state editor, dep. mng. editor, mng. editor Fla.; dir. comm. Hillsborough County Schs., Tampa, 1990-96. Bd. dirs. Tampa Edn. Channel; com. mem. Hillsborough Edn. Found., Tampa, 1990—. Recipient Sunshine Medallion award Sunshine State Sch. PR Assn., 1991-96, Prin.'s award Armwood H.S., 1994-95. Mem. Fla. Press Assn., Fla. Soc. Newspaper Editors, Hillsborough Assn. Sch. Adminstrs. (Pub. Rels. award 1991, 95), Plant City Little League, Delta Gamma Alumni Assn. Baptist. Avocations: reading, needlecrafts, sports, bike riding. Office: Tampa Tribune 202 S Parker St Tampa FL 33606-2395

REED, FRANCES BOOGHER, writer, actress; b. Marion, Ky., May 29, 1938; d. Charles Boogher and Evelyn Shelby (Roberts) R.; m. José Joaquín Solís, June 1, 1957 (div. Sept. 1964); children: Julie, Michael Charles; m. Arnold Haslund, Jan. 30, 1965 (div. May 1967); 1 child, Elizabeth Evelyn Marie; 1 adopted child, Leni Ellis. BA in English and Spanish, U. Houston, 1960; MPH, U. P.R., 1970. Tchr. English as 2d lang. Author: A Dream With Storms, 1979, Thoughts, Feelings and Dreams, 1985, Black Mexican Necklace, 1990, TOEIC Test Guide, 1997, Miguel's Aztec Calendar, 1997, (with Koji Shimada) From Chocolate Bars to CEO, A MacArthur's Kid, 2000, (with Francisco Diaz Infante M.) Pockets and Jingles: Something for His Pockets, 2000, Love Blooms in Mazatlan, 2004; co-artist (with Francisco Diaz Infante M.) Art Works Gallery, Hilton Head, SC, Museo de Arte, Mazatlan, Mex.; ghostwriter: Life On the Run; actress (television shows) General Hospital, Rescue-911, others, also movies. Mem. Am. Pub. Health Assn., Screen Actors' Guild, Mensa, Phi Kappa Phi. Democrat. Methodist. Avocations: teaching, dance, reading. Home: 239 Beach City Rd Apt 2113 Hilton Head Island SC 29926-4713 Office Phone: 843-689-9258. E-mail: ML888888@aol.com.

REED, GEORGIA MAY, music educator; b. Red Bank, N.J., July 28, 1982; d. Ken and Bonnie Reed. BA, College of N.J., Ewing, 2000—04. Music tchr. Reynolds Mid. Sch., Hamilton, NJ. Swim coach Flanders Valley Swim and Tennis Club, Flanders, NJ, 2000—05. Mem.: NEA, Music Educators Nat. Conf.

REED, HELEN G., poet; b. South Bend, Ind., Nov. 21, 1923; d. Herman F. and Hulda A. (Kinas) Glaser; m. Arthur L. Reed; children: Michael, James. BS magna cum laude, Kalamazoo Coll., 1946; pre-med., U. Chgo., 1944—45. Exec. dir., clinic adminstr. Saint Joseph County Mental Health Assn., South Bend, Ind., 1957—67; program dir. Chgo. Mental Health Assn., 1967—70; exec. dir. Evanston (Ill.) Mental Health Assn., 1970—80. 1st chairwoman United Way Cmty. Coun., South Bend, 1965—66; bd. dirs. National Mental Health Staff Coun., N.Y.C., 1962—67; mem. faculty Nat. Mental Health Staff Coun. In-svc. Tng. Insts., 1967—69; 1st chairwoman Mental Health Consortium, Evanston, 1969—70, Staff Coun. Tng. Inst., Chgo., 1970; cons., supr. Chgo. Vis. Nurses Assn., Chgo. Jr. League, U. Wis. Mgmt. Seminar, U. Chgo. Social Svcs. Students, etc., Evanston and Chgo., 1970—80. Author (poetry): Pulling Up the Dawn, 1992 (Goodman Prize, 1992); contbr. poems to mags. (Edwin Davin Vickers prize, 1993); author (poetry): Riding the Bubbles Down, 1994 (Am. Chapbook prize, 1994, nom. for Pulitzer prize for lit., 1994, Whetstone Poetry prize, 1994, Atlanta Rev. Internat. Merit award, 1996, Willow Rev. Poetry prize, 2002). Mem. vol. Jr. League, South Bend, 1953—67, Chicago, 1967—70, jr. league, Chicago-North Shore, 1970—80; parent rep. Kalamazoo Coll. freshmen, 1964—65. Recipient "Best of the Best" award, Chicago Poets and Patrons, 1990. Mem.: Poetry Ctr. Chgo., Nat. League Am. PEN Women (Librarian, Poetry Contest Chair 2003), Acad. Am. Poets (assoc.). Avocations: birdwatching, gardening, reading, travel, antiques. Home: 345 Cumberland Ln Crystal Lake IL 60014

REED, JANEL M., music educator; d. John R. and Cathy A. Reed. MusB, U. So. Miss., Hattiesburg, 1996—99; M in Music-Performance, U. Mo, Kansas City, 1999—2002, Master in Music-Conducting, 1999—2002; MEd, We. Oreg. U., Monmouth, Oreg., 2003—05. Cert. tchr. Oreg., 2002. Grad. tchg. fellow U. Mo., 2000—02; dir. bands, brass instr. Kans. City Kans. CC, 2001—02; dir. bands McKay HS, Salem, Oreg., 2002—03, Eagle Point HS, Oreg., 2003—05; dir. bands/choirs Eagle Point Mid. Sch., 2003—. Recording reviewer (jour.) Internat. Trumpet Guild Journal. Grantee Grad. Tchg. fellowship, U. Mo., Kansas City Conservatory Music, 2000—02; Oreg. Tchg. & Recruiting/Mentoring grant, Oreg. state, 2004. Mem.: Oreg. Music Educators Assn., Nat. Assn. Music Edn., Phi Eta Sigma (life), Golden Key Nat. Honor Soc. (life), Sigma Alpha Iota (life).

REED, JOAN-MARIE, special education educator; b. St. Paul, Sept. 8, 1960; d. William Martin Reed and Diana-Marie (Miller) Reed Moss. BA, U. Minn., 1982, BS, 1983; MEd, Tex. Woman's U., 1986. Cert. tchr., Tex. Tchr. emotionally disturbed Birdville Ind. Sch. Dist., Ft. Worth, 1984-86, Goose Creek Ind. Sch. Dist., Baytown, Tex., 1986-92, ctr. leader, 1992-93, dept. chairperson, 1987-91; tchr. emotionally disturbed Conroe (Tex.) Ind. Sch. Dist., 1993-94, Willis (Tex.) Ind. Sch. Dist., 1994-95, Jefferson County (Colo.) Pub. Schs., 1995—. Co-editor: New Teacher Handbook, 1986—87, Behavior Improvement Program Handbook, 1987—88, Student Teacher Supervisor, 1997, Intern Supervisor, 2005—. Mem. NEA, Coun. for Exceptional Children. Congregationalist. Avocations: reading, cooking, travel, running. Office: Sobesky Acad Adolescent Day Treatment Program 2001 Hoyt St Lakewood CO 80215 Business E-Mail: jmreed@jeffco.k12.co.us.

REED, JOANN A., corporate financial executive; Dir. fin. planning & analysis, then v.p. controller PAID subsidiary Medco Health Solutions, Franklin Lakes, NJ, 1988—92, sr. v.p. fin., 1992—, CFO, 2002—. Office: Medco Health Solutions 100 Parsons Pond Dr Franklin Lakes NJ 07417*

REED, JULIA CONSTANCE, financial services executive; b. Dunmore, Pa., Nov. 16, 1954; d. James M. and Dorothy C. Reed. BS in Liberal Sci., SUNY, 1994. Enlisted USN, 1973, advanced through grades to chief petty officer, 1989, command master chef Joint Interoperability Test Ctr. Cheltenham, Md., 1991-94, command master chief Naval Med. Ctr. Oakland, Calif., 1994-97, ret., 1997; registered rep. Bayside Fin., Walnut Creek, Calif., 1996-99, registered prin. Middletown, R.I., 1999—; pres. Advantage Tax Svcs., Middletown, R.I., 1997—. Tax cons. R.I. Small Bus. Devel. Ctr., Middletown, 1999—. Bd. dirs. Armed Forces YMCA, Newport, R.I., 1999—, Navy Relief Soc., Newport, 1997—. Recipient Inspirational Leadership award Navy League, 1982. Mem. Fleet Res. Assn., Disabled Am. Vets. Democrat. Roman Catholic. Avocations: reading, golf, chess. Office: Advantage Tax Services Llc 747 Aquidneck Ave Ste 12 Middletown RI 02842-7266

REED, KATHLYN LOUISE, occupational therapist, educator; b. Detroit, June 2, 1940; d. Herbert C. and Jessie R. (Krehbiel) R. BS in Occupl. Therapy, U. Kans., 1964; MA, Western Mich. U., 1966; PhD, U. Wash., 1973; MLIS, U. Okla., 1987. Occupl. therapist in psychiatry Kans. U. Med. Ctr., Kansas City, 1964-65; instr. occupl. therapy U. Wash., Seattle, 1967-70; assoc. prof. dept. occupl. therapy U. Okla. Health Scis. Ctr., Oklahoma City, 1973-77, prof., 1978-85, chmn. dept. occupl. therapy, 1973-85; libr. edn. info. svcs. Houston Acad. Medicine Tex. Med. Ctr. Libr., 1988-97. Cons. Okla. State Dept. Health, 1976-77, Children's Convalescent Ctr., Oklahoma City, 1977-80, Oklahoma City Pub. Schs., 1980-81; vis. scholars program Tex. Woman's U., 1991-94, adj. prof. Sch. Occupl. Therapy, 1992-97, vis. prof., 1997-2006, assoc. prof., 2006—; prof. Houston Ctr. Author: (with Sharon Sanderson) Concepts of Occupational Therapy, 1980, 4th edit., 1999, Models of Practice in Occupational Therapy, 1983, Quick Reference to Occupational Therapy, 1991, 2d edit., 2000, (with Julie Pauls) Quick Reference to Physical Therapy, 1996, 2d edit., 2004; (with S. Cunningham) Internet Guide for Rehabilitation Professionals, 1997; (with Sally Pore) Quick Reference to Speech-Language Pathology, 1999. Vol. crisis counselor Open Door Clinic, Seattle, 1968-72; mem. exec. bd. Seattle Mental Health Inst., 1971-72; Mem. Citizen Participation Liaison Coun., Seattle, 1970-72. Recipient Award of Merit, Can. Assn. Occupl. Therapists, 1988. Fellow: Am. Occupl. Therapy Assn. (Merit award 1983, Slagle lectr. award 1985, Svc. award 1985, 2001); mem.: Soc. for the Study of Occupations, Tex. Occupl. Therapy Found. (pres. 1998—), Neuro-Devel. Treatment Assn., Assn. Advancement Rehab. Tech., Am. Occupl. Therapy Found., Med. Libr. Assn. (Rittenhouse award 1987, Acad. Health Info. Professions), Tex. Occupl. Therapy Assn. (Roster of Merit award 2002, Disting. Svc. award 2004), Okla. Occupl. Therapy Assn. (pres. 1974—76), Coun. Exceptional Children, World Fedn. Occupl. Therapists, N.Am. Riding for Handicapped Assn., Sigma Kappa (Colby award 1994), Pi Theta Epsilon. Democrat. Home: 6699 De Moss Dr Houston TX 77074-5003 Personal E-mail: klreed3@juno.com.

REED, MARY CAROLYN CAMBLIN, retired music educator, retired county official; b. North Platte, Nebr., June 22, 1938; d. Brick and Evelyn Camblin; m. Paul E. Reed, Dec. 20, 1960. BA, U. No. Colo., 1960; MA, Calif. State U., 1964; PhD in Ednl. Adminstrn., U. So. Calif., 1976. Cert. adminstr. Calif., 1970. Music educator Rowland Unified Sch. Dist, Rowland Heights, Calif., 1960—67; tchr and writer instrnl. TV LA (Calif.) County Office Edn.; asst. to supt. and chief dep. supt. LA (Calif.) County Office of Edn., 1976—79; adminstr. Regional Ednl. TV Adv. Coun., LA, 1979—82; ednl. tech. unit adminstr. Calif. State Dept. Edn., Sacramento, 1982—83; dir. media svcs. Sacramento (Calif.) County Office Edn., 1983—94, dir. ednl. media, 1993—94; mng. cons. Northern Calif. Media/Tech. Consortium, 1994—2004, Ctrl. Calif. Ednl. Tech. Consortium, 1994—2004. Cons. music series PBS Sta. WETA, Washington, 1974—76; bd. dirs. LA (Calif.) Music Ctr., AMAN Folk Dance group, LA, 1975—77, PBS Sta. KQED, San Francisco, 1989—95. Musician: Am. Flute Orch., 2001, 2002, Internat. Flute Orch., 2004—, Sacramento (Calif.) Symphonic Band, 1995, 2003, Camellia City Flut Choir, 2000—. Recipient Outstanding Alumnus, U. of No. Colo., 1983. Mem.: Calif. Music Educators Assn. (pres. 1976—78), Cosumnes Cmty. Orch, West Sacramento Orch. (prin. flutist 1990—). Office Phone: 916-928-9332.

REED, MARYANN, nursing administrator; b. Norwood, Mass., May 8, 1964; d. Donald Patrick and Kathleen Emily Curry; children: Mark Myles O'Donnell, Jessica Lynn. BSN, U. Maine, 1986. RN Ill., 1989. Nurse Maine Med. Ctr., Portland, Maine, 1986—93; clin. referral specialist Bayside Neurosehals, Portland, 1991—2003; coord. regional referral Sandy River Health, Portland, 2003; nurse Barron Ctr., Portland, 2003—. Spkr. in field. Ward clk. City South Portland, 2001—03; tchr. Holy Cross Ch., South Portland, Maine, 1993—95. Named Bayside All-Star, Goodwill Industries, 2000; recipient Spot award, 1998. Avocations: gardening, bicycling, walking. Home: 28 Rhode Island Ave South Portland ME 04106 Office: Barron Center 1145 Brighton Ave Portland ME 04102

REED, NANCY BOYD, English language educator, elementary school educator; b. Lodi, Calif., Oct. 10, 1946; d. Leo H. and Anna Gwen (Coombes) Boyd; m. Maurice Allen Reed, Dec. 22, 1966; 1 child, Scot Alastair. AA Recreational Adminstrn. with honors, Delta Coll., 1974; BA Recreational Adminstrn. with honors, Calif. State U., Sacramento, 1976, MA in Edn., English Lang. Devel., 1988; cert. computers in edn., U. Calif., Davis, 1984. Cert. multiple subject, phys. edn., computers in edn. teaching. Tchr. 4th grade Hagginwood Sch., Sacramento, 1980-81; tchr. 4th/5th grade impacted lang. Noralto Sch., Sacramento, 1981-88, bilingual resource tchr., 1988-91, tchr. English lang. devel., 1991-96, English language resource tchr., 1996-98; mentor tchr. North Sacramento Sch. Dist., Sacramento, 1992-95, bilingual resource tchr., 1996-98, English lang. devel. curriculum assoc., 1997-98, ednl. cons., 1998—; English lang. resource tchr. Woodlake Sch., Sacramento, 2001—04; ednl. cons. Reedfusion, 2004—. Fellow, tchr./cons. No. Calif. Math. Project, U. Calif., Davis, 1985—; edn. cons. Reedfusion. Dir. Jasmine Flower Dancers, Sacramento, 1984-96; comty. rep. Am. Host Found., Sacramento, 1976—. Named Outstanding Educator Capitol Svc. Ctr., 1992, Tchr. of Yr., Noralto Sch., North Sacramento Sch., 1996; scholar Fridtjof-Nansen-Akademie, Ingleheim, Germany, 1993, Adenauer Found., Berlin, 1982, 93. Mem. NEA, Nat. Vis. Tchrs. Assn. (bd. dirs. 1994—), Nat. Assn. Bilingual Edn., Nat. Coun. Tchrs. Math., Calif. Tchrs. Assn. (state coun. rep. 1995-96), North Sacramento Edn. Assn. (sec. 1986-88, v.p. 1988-90, pres. 1990-92, outstanding educator 1992). Avocations: travel, photography, camping. Home: 3665 Halter Ct Sacramento CA 95821-3266 Office Phone: 916-201-8038. E-mail: tr6_1971@yahoo.com.

REED, PAMELA, actress; b. Tacoma, Wash., Apr. 2, 1949; d. Vernie Reed; m. Sandy Smolar. BA in Drama, U. Wash. Prin. stage roles include Getting Through the Night, Ensemble Studio Theatre, N.Y.C., 1976, Curse of the Starving Class, N.Y. Shakespeare Festival, Pub. Theatre, 1978, The November People (Broadway debut), Billy Rose Theatre, 1978, All's Well That Ends Well, N.Y. Shakespeare Festival, Delacorte Theatre, 1978, Getting Out, Phoenix Theatre, Marymount Manhattan Theatre, N.Y.C., 1978, Seduced, Am. Place Theatre, N.Y.C., 1979, Sorrows of Stephen, N.Y. Shakespeare Festival, Pub. Theatre, 1979, Fools, Eugene O'Neill Theatre, N.Y.C., 1981, Criminal Minds, Theatre Guinevere, N.Y.C., 1984, Fen, N.Y. Shakespeare Festival, Pub. Theatre, 1984, Aunt Dan and Lemon, N.Y. Shakespeare Festival, Pub. Theatre, 1985, Mrs. Warren's Profession, Roundabout Theatre, N.Y.C., 1985, Haft Theatre, 1986; film appearances include The Long Riders, 1980, Melvin and Howard, 1980, Eyewitness, 1981, Young Doctors in Love, 1982, The Right Stuff, 1983, The Goodbye People, 1984, The Best of Times, 1986, The Clan of the Cave Bear, 1986, Rachel River, 1989, Chattahoochee, 1990, Cadillac Man, 1990, Kindergarten Cop, 1990, Passed Away, 1992, Junior, 1994, Santa Fe, 1997, Bean, 1997, Why Do Fools Fall in Love, 1998, Standing on Fishes, 1999, Proof of Life, 2000; TV series appearances include The Andros Targets, 1977, Tanner, 1988, The Dark Horse (HBO), 1988, Grand, 1990, The Home Court, 1995—; TV films include Inmates: A Love Story, 1981, I Want to Live, 1983, Heart of Steel, 1983, Scandal Sheet, 1985, Born Too Soon, 1993, Mary Hemingway miniseries, 1988, Caroline? (Hallmark Hall of Fame), 1989, Deadly Whispers, 1995, Critical Choices, 1996, Carriers, 1998, Book of Days, 2003, Tanner on Tanner, 2004, Dynasty: The Making of a Guilty Pleasure, 2005, Jane Doe: Now You See It, Now You Don't, 2005.

REED, PAMELA J., lawyer; b. Brockport, NY, 1949; AB, U. Calif., Irvine, 1973, MA, 1974; JD, U. Calif, Berkeley Sch. Law, 1981. Bar: Calif. 1981. Assoc. editor Ecology Law Quarterly, 1979—81; extern to Hon. William H. Orrick U.S. Dist. Ct., No. Dist Calif., 1980; ptnr. Morrison & Foerster LLP, co-mng. ptnr. ops. Mem.: Contra Costa Coun. (past pres.), State Bar Calif., Real Property Sect. (exec. com. 1992—95). Office: Morrison & Foerster LLP 425 Market St San Francisco CA 94105-2482 Office Phone: 925-295-3304. Office Fax: 925-946-9912. Business E-Mail: preed@mofo.com.

REED, ROSEMARY, learning specialist; b. Worcester, Mass., Dec. 11, 1952; d. George Albion and Rose Mae (Duncan) Reed. BS in Speech, Emerson Coll., 1974; MEd, Worcester State Coll., 1976; postgrad., U. Mass., 1980; MBA, Anna Maria Coll., 1986. Cert. tchr. Mass. instr. comm. Suffolk U., Boston, 1976—78, Fitchburg State Coll., Mass., 1978—80; adminstr. edn. Option Program, Haverhill, Mass., 1981—83; dir. edn. Stetson Sch., Barre, Mass., 1983—85; corp. recruiter Positions Inc., Westborough, Mass., 1985; tng. mgr. Future Products, Worcester, 1986—87; tng. cons. A-Z Vacuum Mart, Worcester, 1987—93; libr. Richard Sugden Libr., Spencer, Mass., 1993—2001; dir. edn. Glenhaven Acad., Marlborough, Mass., 2001—03; coord. edn. G. Stanley Hall Sch., Worcester, 2003—05; learning specialist North Ctrl. Charter Essential Sch., Fitchburg, Mass., 2005—. Instr. comm. Suffolk U., 1981—83; tchr. Butler Ctr., Westborough, 1985—91; prin. cons. Jamison Cons. Assocs., Clinton, Mass., 1991—93. Author, editor accreditation programs. Grant writer, treas. Hillside Bapt. Ch., Spencer, 1999—. Named Tchr. of Yr., Bur. Instl. Schs., 1988; Horace Mann Tchg. grant, 1987, 1988. Mem.: NAFE, Lions (Lion of Yr. 1990). Avocations: reading, vegetarian cooking, program devel. rsch. Home: PO Box 408 Spencer MA 01562-2067 Office: One Oak Hill Rd Fitchburg MA 01420

REED, SALLY GARDNER, cultural organization administrator; BA in English, Colo. State U., 1979; MLS, No. Ill. U., 1981. Dir. North Hampton (H.H.) Pub. Libr., 1981-85, Ilsley Pub. Libr., Middlebury, Vt., 1985-93, Ames (Iowa) Pub. Libr., 1993-95; dir. librs. Norfolk (Va.) Pub. Libr., 1995—2001; exec. dir. Friends of Librs. USA, Phila., 2001—. Author: Small Libraries: A Handbook for Successful Management, 1991, 2d edit., 2002, Saving Your Library: A Guide to Getting, Using and Keeping the Power You Need, 1992, Library Volunteers: Worth the Effort!, 1994; editor: Creating the Future: Essays on the Future of Librarianship in an Age of Great Change, 1996, Speaking Out: Voices in Celebration of Intellectual Freedom, 1999, Making the Case for Your Library, 2001, 101+ Great Ideas for Libraries and Friends, 2004, Getting Grants in Your Community, 2005; contbr. articles to profl. jours. Bd. dirs. Sheldon Art History Mus., Middlebury, 1988-93, United Way Story County, Ames, 1994-95; mem. cabinet United Way Norfolk, 1996-97, chair city campaign, 1997. Recipient Recognition award Tidewater Area Minority Libr. Network, 1997, Am. Libr. Assoc. Herb & Virginia White award for Promoting Librarianship, 2000. Mem. ALA (chpt. coun. 1989-93, adv. com. office libr. outreach svcs. 1993-94, nat. libr. week com. 1993-95, presdl. com. pub. awareness 1994-96, councilor at large 1995-99, chair membership com. 1996, resolutions com. 1997, exec. bd. 1997-2001, chair pub. awareness com. 2004-06). Office: Friends Libraries USA 1420 Walnut Ste 450 Philadelphia PA 19102 Office Phone: 215-790-1674. Business E-Mail: sreed@folusa.org.

REED, SUELLEN KINDER, school system administrator; BA in History, Polit. Sci. and Secondary Edn., Hanover Coll., 1967; MA in Elem. Edn. and History, Ball State U., 1970, EdD in Adminstrn. and Supervision, LLD (hon.), 1997; EdD (hon.), Vincennes U., 1996; LittD (hon.), U. Indpls., 1997; LHD (hon.), St. Joseph Coll., 1999, Hanover Coll., 2003; postgrad., Fla. Atlantic U., U. Scranton, Purdue U., Earlham Coll., Ind. U., Ind. State U., U. So. Ind., Butler U., U. Alaska, U. Va. at Edinburgh (Scotland) U., Oxford (Eng.) U. Lic. supt., life lic. in elem. edn., U.S. history, world history, govt., adminstrn. and supervision and endorsement in edn. for gifted and talented K-12, Ind.; lic. adminstr., U.S. history, world history, govt., middle sch. lang. arts, social studies, elem. edn., gifted edn., Fla. Tchr. 5th and 6th grades Rushville (Ind.) Consol. Sch. Corp., 1967-70; tchr. Shelbyville (Ind.) High Sch., 1970-71; tchr. 6th, 7th and 8th grade social studies, curriculum Broward County (Fla.) Sch. Corp., 1971-76; tchr. Rushville Jr. High Sch., 1976-77; asst. prin. Rushville Elem. Sch., 1977-79; prin. Frazee Elem. Sch., Connersville, Ind., 1979-87; asst. supt. Rushville Consolidated Schs., 1987-90, supt., 1991-93; supt. pub. instrn., chairperson bd. edn., CEO dept. edn. State of Indiana, Indpls., 1993—. Pres. N. Ctrl. Regional Edn. Lab., Oak Brook, Ill., 1993—97, Oak Brook, 2002; mem. The Ctr. on Congress Outstanding Tchr. Award Selection Com. Contbr. articles to profl. jours. Bd. trustees Hanover Coll., Commn. Drug-Free Ind., Ind. Commn. Cmty. Svc., Ind. Higher Edn. Telecom. Sys., Ctr. Agrl. Sci. Heritage; hon. bd. mem. Rush County Cmty. Found.; alumni bd. Ball State U. Tchrs. Coll., 1999-; bd. dirs. Nat. Children's Film Festival; trustee, mem. New Salem United Meth. Ch.; bd. dirs. Ind. Historic Landmarks Found., Agy. for Instrnl. Tech., Project Lead the Way, Virtual H.S., 2003—; bd. visitors Ind. U.; hon. bd. mem. Indpls. Zool. Soc. Named Outstanding Sch. Edn. Alumnus, Ball State U., 1994, Govt. Leader Yr., Ind. C. of C., 2001; recipient Pres. award, Ind. Assn. Sch. Prins., 1996, Achievement award, Ind. Network Women Adminstrs., 1996, Alumni award, Hanover Coll., 1997, Legis. award, Ind. Assn. for the Edn. Young Children, 1998, Pres. award, Ind. Middle Level Edn. Assn., 2001, Elizabeth Heywood Wyman award for alumnae, Alpha Omicron Pi, 2001, Friend Youth award, Ind. Sch. Counselors, 2001, Hoosier Heritage Civic Leadership award, 2002, Turn Off the Violence award, Ind. Crime Prevention Coalition, 2002, Ind. Sch. Safety Leadership award, 2002, Citizen's award, Ind. Libr. Fedn., Counselor's award, Assn. for Ind. Media Educators. Mem. ASCD (nat. and Ind. chpts.), Internat. Reading Assn., Nat. Coun. for Accreditation Tchr. Edn. (mem. exec. bd.), Nat. Assn. Elem. and Mid. Sch. Prins. (assoc.), Nat. Assn. Gifted Children (nat. adv. bd.), Internat. Tech. Edn. Assn. (mem. adv. com.), Ind. Assn. Pub. Sch. Supts., Ind. Assn. Elem. and Mid. Sch. Prins. (assoc.), Women's Coun. on Literacy for the Ind. Literacy Found., Rose Hulman Inst. Tech., Network Woman Adminstrs., Indpls. Zoo, Indpls. Art Mus., Indpls. Bd. Assocs., Bus. and Profl. Women of Rushville, Connersville Area Reading Coun., Smithsonian, Rushville Rotary Club, Monday Cir., K-12 Compact Learning and Citizenship (chairwoman), Edn. Commn. States (commr., mem. exec. com. 1994-98, 2002—), Council Chief State Sch. Officers (pres.-elect., 2000-01, pres., 2001-02, v.p., 2002-03), Ind. Hist. Soc., Ind. State Mus., Conner Prairie Farm, Order of Ea. Star (Andersonville chpt.), Delta Kappa Gamma (past pres.), Phi Lambda Theta, Phi Delta Kappa (Conner Prairie). Office: Superintendent Edn Dept 229 State House Indianapolis IN 46204-2798

REED, SUSAN D., prosecutor; m. Robert D. Reed (dec.); 1 child. BA in Econs., U. Tex., JD, 1974. Bar: Tex., U.S. Dist. Ct. (we. dist.) Tex., Fed. Ct., U.S. Supreme Ct., bd. cert. criminal law: Tex. Bd. Legal Specialization. Judge

144th Dist. Ct.; pvt. practice Souls and Reed; chief pros. 144th and 187th Dist. Cts.; adminstrv. judge Dist. Cts. Bexar County, 1996—97; asst. dist. atty. Bexar County, San Antonio, 1974—82, criminal dist. atty., 1998—. Mem. Criminal Justice Policy Coun., Govs. Juvenile Justice Adv. Bd., Bush-Cheney Transition Team for Dept. Justice, Nat. Adv. Coun. on Violence Against Women. Mem. Regional Anti-Terrorism Task Force; co-chair Anti-Crime Commn., 2002. Named to, San Antonio Women's Hall of Fame, 2004; recipient Judge of Yr. award, Tex. Gang Investigators Assn. Mem.: Nat. Dist. Attys. Assn., Tex. Dist. and County Attys. Assn. (pres. 2005—). Office: Bexar County Criminal Dist Atty 5th Fl 300 Dolorosa San Antonio TX 78205-3630 Office Phone: 210-335-2342. E-mail: sreed@bexar.org.

REED, SUSAN J., elementary school educator; d. Eldora L. and James E. Kraby; m. Terry R. Reed, Apr. 15, 1950; children: Jamie R., Daniel C. BS Phys. Edn., N.D. State U., Fargo, 1972; Elem. Edn. Endorsement, Mayville State U., N.D., 1982. Cert. Tchr. Reading N.D. Dept. Pub. Instrn., Title I, 2003, Tchr. Math. N.D. Dept. Pub. Instrn., Title I, 2003. Tchr. h.s. phys. edn. Linton Pub. Sch., ND, 1972—73; office asst. Farmers Home Adminstrn. USDA, Hillsboro, ND, 1974—81; tchr. elem. sch. Hillsboro Pub. Sch., 1984—. Dir. and treas. Hillsboro Scholarship Found., 2002—. Named to Who's Who Among Am. Tchrs., 2006, 2007; recipient Tchr. of Yr., Hillsboro Edn. Assn., 2005. Mem.: Hilsboro Edn. Assn., N.D. Edn. Assn. Avocations: reading, golf.

REED, TERESA F., science educator, elementary school educator; b. Garland, Tex., Apr. 25, 1961; d. L. Roger and Avanelle J. Powell; m. Mike L. Reed, June 18, 1983; 1 child, Bryan M. BS in Edn., Lubbock Christian U., Tex., 1983; MS, Tex. Tech. U., Lubbock, 2003. Tchr. Hunt Elem. Sch., Lubbock, Tex., 1983—88, Honey Elem. Sch., 1988—. Bldg. coord. Regional Sci. Fair, Lubbock, Tex., 1990—. Author: (science curricula) Soil Science, 1998, Change Over Time, 2002. Named Tchr. of Week, KMAC-TV, Spotlight Tchr., Lubbock Ind. Sch. Dist, August Avalanche Jour. Tchr., Lubbock Avalanche-Jour., 2003; recipient Beyond the Call award, Lubbock Christian U., 2002. Mem.: Sci. Tchrs. Assn. Tex. (Sci. and Geography Tchr. of Yr. 2001), Nat. Sci. Tchrs. Assn., Tex. Classroom Tchrs. Assn. Avocations: exercise, church groups, singing. Home: 5402 96th St Lubbock TX 79424-4418 Office: Honey Elem Sch 3615 86th St Lubbock TX 79423 Office Phone: 806-766-0866. Office Fax: 806-766-0864.

REED, VASTINA KATHRYN (TINA REED), child and adolescent psychotherapist; b. Chgo., Mar. 5, 1960; d. Alvin Hillard and Ruth Gwendolyn (Thomas) R.; 1 child, Alvin J. BA in Human Svcs. magna cum laude, Nat.-Louis U., Chgo., 1988; MA, Ill. Sch. Profl. Psychology, 1991; tng. cert., Appelbaum Inst. Child Devel.; cert. family devel. specialist, U. Iowa, 2002; fashion cons. of Evangelist Audey Donson, Good Shepherd Grace Min., 2002—. Notary pub. Ill., lic. profl. counselor Ill., child and adolescent psychotherapist, nat. cert. counselor NBCC. Tchr. early childhood edn. Kendall Coll. Lab. Sch., Evanston, Ill., 1983-85, Rogers Park Children's Learning Ctr., Chgo., 1983-85; child life therapist Mt. Sinai Hosp., Chgo., 1988; child psychotherapist Nicholas Barnes Therapeutic Day Sch., Chgo., 1989-90; presch. instr. YMCA, 1999-2000; crisis line counselor Washington Security Corp., 2000—02; family support specialist Maywood (Ill.) Head Start, 2000—03; health care rep. Care Entrée, 2002—03; mental health svc. coord. Head Start Chgo. Dept. Children & Youth Svcs., 2005—. Den leader Boy Scouts Am., Chgo., 1989-92, scoutmaster, 1992-2000, merit badge counselor, 1999—, troop advisor for Order of the Arrow; vision ptnr., co-labourers Christ Ministry; editor, mem. praise and worship team Christ Outreach Deliverance Ctr. Ministry, 2001—; mem. Ill. Notary Public. Recipient Cub Scouter award Boy Scouts Am., 1990, Scoutmaster award of merit, 1993, 94, Scouters Vet. award, 1994, Scouters Tng. award, 1995, Scoutmasters Key award, 1996, Okpik Cold Weather Camping cert., 1994-95, Outstanding Women of 20th Century medal, 2000, Boy Scout Woodbadge Tng. award, 2001. Mem. APA, Nat. Orgn. for Human Svc. Edn., Order of the Arrow, Charles F. Menninger Soc. (patron), Phi Theta Kappa, Kappa Delta Pi. Democrat. Pentecostal. Avocations: camping, films, singing, music. Home: 1872 S Millard Ave Chicago IL 60623-2542 Office Phone: 773-921-8674. Personal E-mail: treed2010@aol.com.

REED, WARLENE PATRICIA, retired librarian; b. Denmark, Tenn., Aug. 3, 1940; d. Wallace Edward and Louise Greer; m. Jerome Batchelor; children: Angela Batchelor, Edwin Batchelor, Lajuana Batchelor-Counts; m. Billy Matt Reed; 1 child, Byron. BA, Lane Coll., 1962; M in Librarianship, Emporia State U., 1972. Cert. English tchr., libr. Tchr. Crockett County Schools, Alamo, Tenn., 1962—63, Madison County Schs., Jackson, Tenn., 1963—66; tchr., libr. Wichita (Kans.) Pub. Schs., 1966—70; libr. Barnes Hosp. Sch. Nursing, St. Louis, 1971, Francis Howell Sch. Dist., St. Charles, Mo., 1971—2001. Pres. St. Louis Area Libr. Suprs., 1993—95; mem. St. Louis Suburban Libr. Assn., 1983—97. Mem. chancellor's adv. com. U. Mo., St. Louis, 1994—; mem. Charter Rev. Com., St. Charles, 1991—92, Citizens Participation and Adv. Com., St. Charles, 1988—89; bd. dirs. MOsaics Arts Festival Assn., St. Charles, 1996—98; trustee St. Charles City-County Libr. Dist., 1998—. Recipient Alumni award, Lane Coll., 1978, Svc. award, 5th Dist. Lay Orgn.-AME Ch., 1983, Howell of Fame award, Francis Howell Sch. Dist., 1990, Lifetime Disting. Svc. award, St. Charles C. of C., 2002. Mem.: AAUW (pres. 1995—97, gift honoree St. Charles br. 1990), Mo. Assn. Sch. Librs., Howell Found. Bd., St. Charles County Hist. Soc. (black history honoree 2001), Vision-St. Charles County, Sigma Gamma Rho. Mem. Ame Ch. Avocations: reading, travel, youth volunteer. Home: 1135 Olde Saybrook Dr Saint Charles MO 63301

REED, WENDY, management consultant company executive, information technology executive; BS in Computer-Based Mgmt., minor in comm., Clarkson U., 1984. Mem. info. tech. dept. Accenture; with MSA (now Dun & Bradstreet Software), Viasoft, Clarus, Hayes Microcomputer Products. Spkr. in field. Bd. dir. AEA, Revegy, Inc., Milton HS Athletic Assn. Named Woman of Yr. Tech. (small/medium bus.), (WIT) Women in Tech., 2006; named one of 40 Under 40 Georgia's Brightest Stars, Ga. Trend Mag., 2002, Top 50 Entrepreneurs, Catalyst Mag., 2004, 2005; recipient Entrepreneurial Success award, Clarkson U., 2001, Entrepreneur of Yr. award, Ernest & Young, 2006. Office: InfoMentis Inc Ste 160 1750 Founders Parkway Alpharetta GA 30004 Office Phone: 770-667-5352. Office Fax: 770-752-9143.*

REEDE, JOAN YVONNE, academic administrator, medical educator, pediatrician; b. Boston, 1953; 1 child, Loretta Jackson. BS, Brown U., 1977; MD, Mt. Sinai Sch. Med., 1980; MPH, Harvard Sch. Pub. Health, 1990, MS in Health Policy and Mgmt, 1991. Intern Johns Hopkins Hosp., Baltimore, 1980—81, pediat. resident, 1981—83; child psychology fellow Children's Hosp., Boston, 1986—88; med. dir. Cmty. Health Ctr., Boston, Commonwealth of Mass. Dept. Youth Services; dean diversity and cmty. partnership Harvard Med. Sch., 2002—, dir. minority faculty devel. program, faculty dir. cmty. outreach programs, assoc. prof. med.; asst. prof. maternal and child health Harvard Sch. Pub. Health; asst. in health policy Mass. Gen. Hosp. Founder Biomedical Sci. Careers Program, 1991; mem. bd. govs. Warren Grant Magnuson Clin. Ctr.; mem. adv. com. on minority health US Dept. Health and Human Services, 2000—, mem. adv. com. on genetics, health and soc., 2002—; bd. dirs. Mass. Tech. Park. Corp. Named a Ctr. for Disease Control and Prevention/U. Calif. Public Health Leadership Inst. Scholar; recipient Boston NAACP Health award, 1986, Community Service award, Epilepsy Assn. Mass., 1993, Exemplary Models Adminstrv. Leadership award, Am. Assn. U. Adminstrs., 1996. Achievements include being included in the Changing the Face of Medicine exhibit honoring women physicians. Office: Harvard Med Sch 25 Shattuck St Rm 152 Boston MA 02115

REEDER, LINDSAY ERIN, music educator; b. West Chester, Pa., Aug. 28, 1979; d. Robert Allen and Susan Jane Reeder. BS in Music Edn., Penn State U., U. Park, 2002; MusM in Piano Performance, Penn State U., 2002; MusD in Piano Performance, West Chester U., Pa., 2006. Music tchr. Allen HS, Allentown, Pa., 2002—03, Acad. Notre Dame, Villanova, Pa., 2003—. Mem.: Pa. Music Educators Assn., Sigma Alpha Iota (life). Office: Acad Notre Dame 560 Sprout Rd Villanova PA 19085 Office Phone: 610-687-0650. Office Fax: 610-687-1912. Business E-Mail: lreeder@ndapa.org.

REEDY, CATHERINE IRENE, retired elementary school educator; b. Suffolk County, NY, Dec. 27, 1953; d. Edward and Catherine (Spindler) von Grafenstein. AA, Suffolk C.C., Selden, N.Y., 1980; BA in Social Sci. summa cum laude, Dowling Coll., 1983, MS in Edn., 1986. Tchr. coord. sci., tech. regents earth sci. St. Ignatius Sch., Hicksville, NY, 1983—2005, tchr. tech. grades 6-8, 1983—2006; ret., 2006. Contbr. poetry to Beyond the Stars, 1996, Walk Through Paradise, 1995, Best Poems of 1996. Recipient Editor's Choice award Nat. Soc. Poetry, 1996, Nat. Libr. Poetry, 1995. Mem. N.Y. Acad. Scis., N.Y. Sci. Tchrs. Assn., Nat. Poet Soc., Internat. Poets Soc., Alpha Zeta Nu (1st sec.), Phi Theta Kappa, Phi Alpha Sigma, Kappa Delta Pi (pres. Xi Chi chpt. 1985-87). Home: 15 Nikia Dr Islip NY 11751-2630 Office: St Ignatius Sch 30 E Cherry St Hicksville NY 11801-4396 Office Phone: 516-931-0831. E-mail: creedy1@i0.tv.

REEDY, MITSUNO ISHII, artist, painter; b. Furuichi, Osaka, Japan, Jan. 18, 1941; came to U.S., 1961; d. Mitsuyoshi and Teru (Kakehi) I.; m. William Barret Reedy, Apr. 17, 1970 (dec. Apr. 1984); children: Mitsuno Lee, Michele Ann. Student, Laguna Gloria Art Mus. Sch., Austin, Tex., 1976, Elizabeth Ney Mus. Sch., 1977-79, Scottsdale (Ariz.) Art Sch., 1992. Contbr.: The Best of Pastel, 1996, The Best of Oil Painting, 1996, Portrait Inspirations, 1997, Floral Inspirations, 1997, Best of Pastel II, 1998; works include oil portraits in the U. Okla. Sch. of Law, 1984, 1996, Greenwood Cultural Ctr., Tulsa, 1995, Purdue U., 1999, 2003-06, Okla. Fed. Dist. Courthouse, 2001, 02, 06, Heritage Soc., 2005; co-translator: How to Talk so Kids will Listen and Listen so Kids will Talk, Siblings Without Rivalry, How to Be the Paret You Always Wanted to Be. Mem.: Pastel Soc. Am., Pastel Soc. Japan (assoc.). Independent. Methodist. Avocations: power walking, bible study, travel, reading, gardening. Home: 1701 Denison Dr Norman OK 73069-7491 Personal E-mail: mitsuno@flash.net.

REEDY, SUSAN, painter; BFA, Daemen Coll., 1978; MFA, SUNY, Buffalo, 1981. Instr. Niagara County CC, Sanborn, NY, 1983—87, gallery dir., 1984—88; asst. prof. Daemen Coll., Amherst, 1992—. One woman show at Goldman Greenfield Gallery, Amherst, 1985, Castellani Art Mus., Niagara Falls, 1993, Amherst (NY) Mus., 1997; exhibited in 2-person shows at O.K. Harris Gallery, NYC, 1988, Hewitt Gallery of Art, NY, 2002; exhibited in group exhbns. at Butler Inst. Am. Art, Youngstown, Ohio, 1990, 92, Gallery 84, NYC, 1996-97, Albright-Knox Art Gallery, Buffalo, NY, 1993-94, 97, 2004, Meml. Art Gallery, Rochester, NY, 1995-96 (Dirs. Choice award 1995, Dorothy Cripps Salo Meml. award 1996, award for outstanding non-representational painting, 1996), Goldman-Greenfield Gallery, Amherst, NY, 1995; permanent collections include Meml. Art Gallery, Castellani Art Mus., Std. Fed. Bank Hdqrs., Rich Products Corp., Hospice Found. Western NY, Mobil Oil Corp., Roswell Pk. Cancer Inst., Buffalo. Active Roswell Park Alliance Art Com., Roswell Park Cancer Inst., Buffalo, 2004. Recipient Dr. J. Warren Penny award Art Dialogue Gallery, 1995, Mfrs. and Traders Trust Co. award Albright Knox Art Gallery, 1980. Avocation: figure skating.

REEF, GRACE, government official; b. Portland, Maine; m. Don Green, Nov. 9, 1991; children: Megan, Jamie, Ryan. BA, Colby Coll., 1984. Legis. asst. Sen. George Mitchell U.S. Senate, Washington, 1984-94, legis. asst. Sen. Tom Daschle, 1995-97; dir. intergovt. affairs Children's Def. Fund, Washington, 1997-2001; subcom. staff dir. children and families Office of Senator Chris Dodd, Washington, 2001—. Office: Office of Senator Chris Dodd 448 Russell Bldg Washington DC 20510 Business E-Mail: grace_reef@help.senate.gov.

REEL, HEATHER W., educational association administrator; With Sci-Quest, Huntsville, Ala. Mem.: Nat. Sci. Tchrs. Assn., Jr. League, Kappa Delta Alumnae. Office: Sci Quest 102 D Wynn Dr Huntsville AL 35805

REES, MARIAN JANET, librarian; b. Oak Park, Ill., July 3, 1934; d. Ewald and Gertrude Dorothy (Hilbert) Heimert; m. John Robert Rees, Jan. 28, 1956; children: Carol Ellen, John Alton. BA, Ind. U., 1956; MA, Calif. State U.-San Jose, 1973. Mem. acad. staff Inst. Energy Studies, Stanford U., 1974-85, head librarian, dir. info. ctr., 1974-85; head librarian Lifescan, Inc., 1986—88. Cons. in field Author: Energy Modeling: A Selected Bibliography, 1977; editor: Energy Info. Ctr. Selected Acquisitions List, 1975-85. Chmn. fgn. langs. in elem. schs., Wheaton, Md., 1967-69. Mem. Spl. Libraries Assn., AAAS, Internat. Assn. Energy Economists, Western Info. Network Energy (vice chmn. 1980-83), Calif. Library Assn., Energy Librarians Bay Area (chmn. 1979-80) Democrat. Home: 226 West Edith Ave #2 Los Altos CA 94022-2725

REES, NINA SHOKRAII, federal agency administrator; b. Iran; BS in Psychology, Va. Polytech and State U., 1989; MS in Internat. Transactions, George Mason U., 1991. Mem. staff Rep. Porter Goss, Washington, 1990—92; policy analyst Ams. for Tax Reform, Washington, 1992—93; dir. outreach programs Inst. for Justice, Washington, 1993—97; chief edn. analyst The Heritage Found., Washington, 1997—2000; with Bush/Cheney transition team, 2000—01; aide to v.p. U.S. Govt., Washington, 2001—02; asst. deputy sec. Innovation and Improvement US Dept. Edn., 2002—. Contbr. commentaries in newspapers, TV, radio on ednl. issues, 1995. Education adviser to Bush Campaign, Phila., 2000; contbr. to Rep. platform in edn. area Rep. Paty, 2000. Recipient Rita Ricardo Campbell award, Heritage Found., 1999. Office: US Dept Edn 400 Maryland Ave SW Rm 4W317 Washington DC 20202 Office Phone: 202-205-4500. Business E-Mail: nina.rees@ed.gov.

REES, NORMA S., academic administrator; b. NYC, Dec. 27, 1929; d. Benjamin and Lottie (Schwartz) D.; m. Raymond R. Rees, Mar. 19, 1960; children— Evan Lloyd, Raymond Arthur BA, Queens Coll., 1952; Ma, Bklyn. Coll., 1954; PhD, NYU, 1959; D of Arts and Letters honoris causa, John F. Kennedy U., 2001. Cert. speech-language pathology, audiology. Prof. communicative disorders Hunter Coll., NYC, 1967-72; exec. officer, speech and hearing scis. grad. sch. CUNY, NYC, 1972-74, assoc. dean for grad. studies, 1974-76, dean grad. studies, 1976-82; vice chancellor for acad. affairs U. Wis., Milw., 1982-85, from 1986, acting chancellor, 1985-86; vice chancellor for acad. policy and planning Mass. Bd. Regents for Higher Edn., Boston, 1987-90; pres. Calif. State U. East Bay, Hayward, 1990—. Chmn. Commn. Recognition of Postsecondary Accreditation, 1994-96; mem. adv. com. quality and integrity U.S. Dept. Edn., commn. on internat. edn. Coun. on Higher Edn. Accreditation, 2003—. Contbr. articles to profl. jours. Trustee Citizens Govtl. Rsch. Bur., Milw., 1985-87; active Task Force on Wis. World Trade Ctr., 1985-87; bd. dirs. Am. Assn. State Colls. and Univs., 1995-97, Coun. of Postsecondary Accreditation, Washington, 1985-94, Greater Boston YWCA, 1987-90; mem. Calif. Sch. to Career Coun.; bd. dir. Econ. Devel. Alliance for Bus., Alameda County, 1995—; sec. edn. Nat. Adv. Com. Institutional Quality and Integrity, 1998-2002; bd. dirs. Bay Area World Trade Ctr., 2001—. Alameda County Health Care Found., 2002-. Fellow Am. Speech-Lang-Hearing Assn. (honors); mem. Am. Coun. Edn. (com. internat. edn. 1991-93), Am. Assn. Colls. and Univs. (chair task force on quality assessment 1991-92), Nat. Assn. State Univs. and Land Grant Colls. (exec. com. divsn. urban affairs 1985-87, com. accreditation 1987-90), Hayward C. of C. (bd. dirs. 1995-98), Oakland C. of C. (bd. dirs. 1997-2004). Office: Calif State Univ East Bay 25800 Carlos Bee Blvd Hayward CA 94542-3001 Office Phone: 510-885-3877. E-mail: norma.rees@csueastbay.edu.

REES, SARAH LYNN, school psychologist; b. Alhambra, Calif., July 8, 1973; d. Wayne William and Grace Marie Wilke; m. John Corwin Rees, June 16, 2001; 1 child, Drew Corwin. BA, U. Mich., 1995; EdS, Ind. U., 1998. Sch. psychologist Paradise Valley Unified Sch. Dist., Phoenix, 1998—. Mem.: NASP (nat. cert. sch. psychologist). Lutheran. Home: 2719 E Larkspur Dr Phoenix AZ 85032 Office: Cactus View Elementary School 17602 N Central Ave Phoenix AZ 85022 Office Phone: 602-493-6283. Office Fax: 602-548-0137.

REESE, ANNETTE EVELYN, music educator; b. Waynesville, NC, Sept. 23, 1958; d. James F. and Shirley Sharpe Robertson; m. Mark A. Reese, Nov. 22, 1980; children: Caitlan Annette, Sarah Anne. MusB Edn., Mars Hill Coll., 1980; MEd, Belmont Abbey Coll., 1996. Cert. music educator K12. Elem. music specialist Marlboro County Schs., Bennettsville, SC, 1980—81; choral dir. North Gaston H.S., Dallas, NC, 1981—85; dir. of bands East Gaston High/Stanley Mid. Sch., Mt. Holly/Stanley, NC, 1985—95, Belmont Mid. Sch., Belmont, NC, 1995—98, Olympic High/Kennedy Mid. Sch., Charlotte, NC, 1998—. Pres. NC Bandmasters Assn., Charlotte, NC, 2000—, South Ctrl. Dist. Bandmasters, NCBA, Charlotte, NC, 1996—98; sec. NC Bandmasters Assn., Charlotte, NC, 1998—2000; band sect. chair, exec. bd. mem. NC Music Educators Assn., Raleigh, NC, 2000—. Contbr. articles to profl. jours. Troop leader Pioneer Girl Scout Coun., GSUSA, Gastonia, NC, 1996—2002. Mem.: NEA, N.C. Assn. Educators, Music Educators Nat. Conf., N.C. Bandmasters Assn. (pres. 2000—02, Excellence award 1996), N.C. Music Educators Assn. (band sect. chair 2000—02), Delta Omicron Profl. Music Frat. Mem. Evangelical Lutheran Ch. Of America. Avocations: needlework, music, travel. Office: SW Mid Sch 13624 Steele Creek Rd Charlotte NC 28273

REESE, AUDREY MARIA, music educator; b. Atlanta, GA., July 25, 1957; d. Charles and Zola Allen. BA, Columbus U., 1981. Ga. Educator Cert., 1981. Violinist Columbus Symphony Orch., Ga., 1976—81; violinist/violist African Am. Philharmonic Orch., Atlanta, 1988—; violinist Eclectic String Quartet and Just Friends, Atlanta, 1987—, Orch. Atlanta, 1994—96; violinist/violist Music South Corp., Atlanta, 1988—; condr. Still Waters Youth Sinfo-Nia, 2002—04; tchr. orch. Atlanta Bd. Edn., 1981—. Music curriculum writing com. Atlanta Bd. Edn., music adv. team, music textbook adoption com., 2004—. Ga. incentive Atlanta Bd. Edn., 1989; star tchr. achievement Ga. Dept. Edn., 1991. Recipient Tchr. of Yr., Atlanta Pub. Schools, 2002—03. Mem.: Nat. String Orch. Assn., Music Educators Nat. Conf., Ga. Music Assn. (sec. 1995—97). African Meth. Episc. Avocations: reading, dance, music, gardening. Home: 1335 Gates Dr Atlanta GA 30316

REESE, DELLA (DELOREESE PATRICIA EARLY), singer, actress; b. Detroit, July 6, 1931; d. Richard and Nellie Early; m. Vermont Adolphus Bon Taliaferro (div.); m. Leroy Basil Gray (div.); m. Franklin Thomas Lett, Jr. Student, Wayne U. Ordained to ministry Ch. Understanding Principles for Better Living Inc., April, 1987. Choir singer, 1938—, with Mahalia Jackson troupe, 1945-49, Erskine Hawkins, N.Y.C.; solo artist, 1957—; organized gospel group at Wayne U.; appearances include: (radio shows) with Robert Q. Lewis; (TV series) Della, 1969, The Voyage of the Yes, 1972, Twice in a Lifetime, 1974, Cop on the Beat, 1975, Chico and the Man, 1974, 76-78, Nightmare in Badham County, 1976 (Emmy nomination), Roots: The Next Generation, 1979, It Takes Two, 1982, Charlie & Co., 1985, 86, The Kid Who Loved Christmas, 1990, The Royal Family, 1991, You Must Remember This, 1992, Touched By an Angel, 1994-2003, A Match Made in Heaven, 1997, Miracle in the Woods, 1997, Emma's Wish, 1998, The Secret Path, 1999, Having Our Say: The Delany Sisters' First 100 Years, 1999; spl. appearances with Jackie Gleason, Ed Sullivan, McCloud, 1971, Sanford and Son, 1972, Welcome Back, Kotter, 1975, The A-Team, 1983, Night Court, 1984, MacGyver, 1985, Designing Women, 1986, L.A. Law, 1986, Married People, 1990, Dream On, 1990, Picket Fences, 1992, Promised Land, 1996, Anya's Bell, 1999, The Moving of Sophia Myles, 2000; guest host The Tonight Show; actress (films) Let's Rock, 1958, Psychic Killer, 1975, Harlem Nights, 1989, A Thin Line Between Love and Hate, 1996, (voice) Dinosaur, 2000, Beauty Shop, 2005, (plays) Same Time Next Year, Ain't Misbehavin, Blues in the Night, The Last Minstrel Show; recs. for Jubilee, RCA Victor Records, ABC Paramount Records, Jazz Ala Carte, AIR Co. (Grammy nomination 1987); author: Angels Along the Way, 1997, (voice) Dinosaur, 2000. Voted Most Promising Singer of Yr. 1957; recipient Image awards, 1996, 98-2000, Star on Walk of Fame, 1994. Office: William Morris Agy c/o Jeff Kolodny 151 S El Camino Dr Beverly Hills CA 90212-2775

REESE, JACQUELYN L., elementary school educator; b. Bowling Green, Ohio, Sept. 6, 1950; d. Joseph Mark and Gwendolyn Irene (Brim) Gergat; m. Thomas F. Reese, Aug. 11, 1977; children: Laura, Lisa, Mark, David. ADN, Mesa Coll., 1977; BS in Edn., Bowling Green State U., 1974. Clin. RN Colville Indian Health Svc., Nespelem, Wash.; staff RN Coulee Community Hosp., Grand Coulee, Wash.; charge nurse Colville Tribal Convalescent Ctr., Nespelem, Wash.; sch. nurse Nespelem; now elem. tchr. Grand Coulee, Wash. Personal E-mail: tjreese@couleedam.net.

REESE, KATHERINE ROSE, music educator; b. Mannington, W.Va., July 27, 1937; m. Wallace Reese, July 29, 1955; children: Kyla O'Dell, Ann Landers. BA, W.Va. U., 1986. Cert. profl. music tchr. Artist tchr. of piano Fairmont (W.Va.) State Coll., 1986—.

REESE, LINDA MAE, elementary school educator; b. Oelwein, Iowa, Oct. 23, 1955; d. Warren and Eva Byerly; m. Doug Reese, June 25, 1977; children: Dane, Maegan Dunn, Ian. BA in Elem. Edn., U. No. Iowa, Cedar Falls, 1978. Cert. mid. sch. tchr. U. Minn., Mankato. Elem. tchr. Waterloo Pub. Schs., Iowa, 1978—81; preschool tchr. Sunshine Presch., Reedsburg, Wis., 1989—91; ESL tchr. Madison Area Tech. Coll., Reedsburg, 1991—94; mid. sch. tchr. Farmington Pub. Schs., Minn., 1996—. Mem.: NEA, Farmington Edn. Assn. Independent.

REESE, LINDA WILLIAMS, history professor; d. Billie Rae and Edith Dodd Williams; m. John William Reese, June 15, 1968; children: James Conan, Susan Elizabeth, Brian Daniel. BA, U. Okla., Norman, 1968, PhD, 1991; MA, U. Kans., Lawrence, 1971. Asst. prof. N.Mex. Mil. Inst., Roswell, 1974—83; dir. social studies and fgn. lang. Norman Pub. Schs., 1993—94; grad. asst. U. Okla., Norman, 1983—93, vis. asst. prof., 1998—2002, East Ctrl. U., Ada, Okla., 1994—98, assoc. prof., 2002—06. Author: Women of Oklahoma, 1890-1920, 1997; mem. bd. editors: Western Historical Quar., 2002—04; contbr. articles to profl. jours. Bd. mem. Okla. Humanities Coun., Oklahoma City, 2003—06. Named Asa Kyrus Christian Outstanding History Grad. Student, U. Okla., 1985; named to, Outstanding Young Women Am., 1979; recipient Baldwin award for Excellence in Undergraduate Tchg., U. Okla., 1991, Catherine Prelinger award, Coordinating Coun. Women in History, 2003, Tchg. Excellence award, East Ctrl. U., 2006. Mem.: Western History Assn. (assoc.). Avocation: travel. Office: East Central University 1100 E 14th St Ada OK 74820 Office Phone: 580-332-8000. Office Fax: 580-436-3329. Business E-Mail: lreese@ecok.edu.

REESE, SUSAN MARIE, elementary school educator; b. Waseca, Minn., Feb. 21, 1966; d. George Andrew and Donna Frances Cobley; 1 child, David Andrew. BA, U. No. Iowa, Cedar Falls, 1988, MA in Edn., 2006. Cert. Nat. Bd. Profl. Tchg. Stds., 2000. Tchr. Allison-Bristow Cmty. Schs, Allison, Iowa, 1993—2004, North Butler Mid. Sch., Allison, 2004—. Office: North Butler Mid Sch 513 Birch St Allison IA 50602 Office Phone: 319-267-2552. Business E-Mail: sreese@alli-bris.k12.ia.us.

REESE, TRACY, fashion designer; b. Detroit; d. Claude Reese. Degree, Parsons Sch. Design, 1984. Design asst. to Martine Sitbon Arlequin Paris, 1984-87; designer with Marc Jacobs Perry Ellis Portfolio; design dir. Magaschoni, Inc., 1990—95; launched own label Tracy Reese, 1987—89, 1997—, Plenty by Tracy Reese, 1998—, Plenty by Tracy Reese Home. Office: c/o Factory PR 580 Broadway Ste 602 New York NY 10012*

REEVE, AGNESA, writer; b. Waco, Tex., Jan. 1, 1927; d. Philo King and Agnes (McGill) Burney; m. Marshall Perry Reeve, July 16, 1986. BA, So. Meth. U., 1947, MA, 1967; PhD, U. N.Mex., 1983. Instr. El Centro C.C., Dallas, 1967-69, So. Meth. U., Dallas, 1969-74, Santa Fe C.C., 1983-85. Author: From Hacienda to Bungalow, 1988, My Dear Mollie, 1990, Constant Frontier, 1996 (American Association of State and Local History award 1997); co-author: Handful of Ingredients, 1992, Tex Mex New Mex, 1998,

The Small Adobe House, 2001. Pres. bd. dirs. Old Santa Fe Found., 1984-86; bd. dirs. Hist. Soc. N.Mex., Santa Fe, 1991—. Home: 30 Old Arroyo Chamiso Santa Fe NM 87505-6902 E-mail: ajreeve@comcast.net.

REEVES, BARBARA, writer, educator; b. Wellington, Tex., Aug. 29, 1931; d. Edward Decatur Reeves and Ruth Caroline Rich; m. Stanley Kolaski, Jan. 15, 1956 (dec. Feb. 1987); children: Anne Marie, Linda Caroline, John Edward. Writing tchr. San Jacinto Coll. Sys., Houston, 1990—. Curriculum cons. San Jacinto Coll. South, Houston, 1998-2000; cons. and mentor in field. Authro: Georgina's Campaign, 1991, The Dangerous Marquis, 1993, The Much Maligned Lord, 1995, My Buffalo Soldier, 2000, Thunder Moon, 2003. Mem. Romance Writers Am. (founder chpt. 30, chairperson, fundraiser for literacy), Bay Area Writer's League (founder, chairperson). Democrat. Roman Catholic. Avocations: social historian, interior design, family history. E-mail: bk@bkreeves.com.

REEVES, BARBARA ANN, lawyer; b. Buffalo, Mar. 29, 1949; d. Prentice W. and Doris Reeves; m. Richard C. Neal; children: Timothy R. Neal, Stephen S. Neal (dec.), Robert S. Neal, Richard R. Neal. Student, Wellesley Coll., Mass., 1967-68; BA (NSF fellow, Lehman fellow), New Coll., Sarasota, Fla., 1970; JD cum laude, Harvard U., 1973. Bar: Calif. 1973, D.C. 1977. Law clk. U.S. Ct. Appeals, 9th Circuit, Portland, Oreg., 1973—74; assoc. firm Munger, Tolles and Rickershauser, L.A., 1977—78; trial atty. spl. trial sect. Dept. Justice (Antitrust div.), 1974—75; spl. asst. to asst. atty. gen. Antitrust div. Dept. Justice, Washington, 1976—77; chief antitrust div. L.A. field office, 1978—81; ptnr. Morrison & Foerster, L.A., 1981—94, Fried, Frank, Harris, Shriver & Jacobson, L.A., 1995—97, Paul, Hastings, Janofsky & Walker, L.A., 1997—99; assoc. gen. counsel So. Calif. Edison, 1999—2004, v.p. shared svcs., 2004—06; mediator, arbitrator JAMS, 2006—. Mem. exec. com. state bar conf. of dels. L.A. Delegation, 1982-91; del. 9th Cir. Jud. Conf., 1984-88; mem. Fed. Ct. Magistrate Selection Com., 1989; bd. dirs. Pub. Counsel, 1988-92, Western Ctr. Law and Poverty, 1992-98; lectr. in field. Editor: Federal Criminal Litigation, 1994; contbg. author: World Antitrust Law, 1995; contbr. articles to profl. jours. Mem. ABA (litigation sect., antitrust sect.), Fed. Bar Assn. (officer 1998—), Assn. Bus. Trial Lawyers (officer 1997—), Am. Arbitration Assn. (arbitrator, mediator, mem. adv. panel large complex case program), L.A. County Bar Assn. (antitrust sect. officer 1980-81, litigation sect. officer 1988-93 trustee 1990-92, chair alternative dispute resolution sec. 1992-95, L.A. County Ct. ADR com.). Home: 1410 Hillcrest Ave Pasadena CA 91106-4503 Office: 46th Fl 707 Wilshire Blvd Los Angeles CA 90017 Office Phone: 213-620-1133. Business E-Mail: breeves@jamsadr.com.

REEVES, DENISE MOSELEY, dancer, educator; d. Margaret Ann Freeman and Kenneth Stewart Moseley; m. Dennis Dean Reeves, May 15, 1982. BS, U. N.C., Greensboro, 1979; MEd, Frostburg State U., Md., 1984. Cert. tchr. Royal Acad. of Dance, 1988, level 3 master tchr. True Pilates-Romana's Pilates, 2002. Dancer N.C. Sch. of the Arts, Winston-Salem, 1973; tchr. movement edn. sch. King Intermediate Sch., NC, 1978—82; dancer, instr. Hagerstown and W.Va. Youth Ballet Cos., Md., 1982—83; profl. dancer San Jose Dance Theatre, Calif., 1986—88; ballet dir. Pam East Dance, Cupertino, Calif., 1986—92; profl. dancer Santa Clara Ballet, Calif., 1988—92; dance dir., instr. Pebblebrook H.S., Mableton, Ga., 1994—; sch. dir., dancer Ga. Ballet, Marietta, 1992—97; instr., dancer Atlanta Ballet, 1996—98; dance dir. Ga. Gov.'s Honors Program, Atlanta, 1997—97; dir. Pilates Studio of Atlanta, 1999—2002. Coord., instr. Cobb County Schs. Gov.'s Honor Program, Marietta, Ga., 1994—2006. Mem.: Nat. Dance Edn. Orgn., Nat. Dance Assn. (corr.), Ams. for the Arts (corr.), Corps De Ballet Internat. (corr.), Gamma Beta Phi. Achievements include dance ambassador with Santa Clara University to dance in Poland and Soviet Union. Avocations: travel, fitness, musical theatre, dance. Home: 489 Timberlea Lake Dr Marietta GA 30067 Office: Pebblebrook HS 991 Old Alabama Rd Mableton GA 30126 Office Phone: 770-819-2521. Office Fax: 770-819-2524. Personal E-mail: dansin1@hotmail.com. E-mail: denise.reeves@cobbk12.org.

REEVES, DIANNE, singer; b. Detroit, 1956; Student, U. Colo., 1970s. Performed with trumpeteer Clark Terry; recorded sessions with Lenny White, Stanley Turrentine, Alphonso Johnson, 1970s; performer with Night Flight, 1970s, Sergio Mendes tour, 1981, Harry Belafonte, 1983-86; toured as trio with Billy Childs, 1986; rec. artist: (albums) Welcome to My Love, 1982, For Every Heart, 1986, Dianne Reeves, 1987, Never Too Far, 1989, I Remember, 1990, Art and Survival, 1993, Quiet After the Storm, 1994, The Grand Encounter, 1996, That Day., 1997, Bridges, 1999, In the Moment: Live in Concert, 2000, The Calling, 2001, A Little Moonlight, 2003, Christmas Time is Here, 2004, Good Night and Good Luck motion picture soundtrack, 2005; actress (films) Good Night and Good Luck, 2005. Recipient Best Jazz Vocal Album for The Calling, Grammy Awards, 2001, Best Jazz Vocal Album for A Little Moonlight, 2003, Best Jazz Vocal Album for Good Night and Good Luck, 2006. Office: Blue Note Records 150 5th Ave New York NY 10011 Office Phone: 212-786-8600.*

REEVES, HALLIE LAWSON, retired music educator, retired chaplain; d. Andrew William and Gracie Elizabeth (Owens) Lawson; m. William A. Reeves, June 21, 1961 (div.); 1 child, Rona Omega; 1 child, M.C. BA, NC Ctrl. U., 1958; MDiv, Duke U., 1978; PhD in Humane Letters, Nat. Theol. Sem., 1985. Cert. supr. ACPE, 1992. Music tchr. Roxboro Pub. Schs., NC, 1958—59, Oxford Pub. Schs., NC, 1959—60, Durham Pub. Schs., NC, 1960—75; chaplain intern St. Elizabeth's Hosp., DC, 1979—80, chaplain resident, 1980—81, staff chaplain, 1985—2003; dir. chaplain svcs. Provident Hosp., Balt., 1981—85. Owner piano studio, 1958—2003. Mem.: NADCD, Phi Delta Kappa.

REEVES, JOAN HUTCHINS, painter; b. Seattle, June 22, 1932; d. John Marvin and Bess Irene (Sowler) Hutchins; m. George Catherwood Reeves, Sept. 5, 1953; children: David Alan, John Michael. Exhibitions include Whatcom Mus. History and Art. Mem. Art Stall Gallery Coop. (chmn. 1986-89), Nat. Mus. Women in the Arts (charter), N.W. Watercolor Soc. (signature mem., exhbn. chmn. 1986, Purchase award 1988), Women Painters of Wash. (membership chmn. 1986-88, Transparent Watecolor award 1985, 86, 90, Best of Show 1989, 2001, Purchase award, 2004), Mont. Watercolor Soc. (signature mem.), Watercolor West (signature mem.), San Diego Watercolor Soc. (signature mem.) Avocation: travel. Home: 3901 Fremont Ave N Seattle WA 98103-7756

REEVES, KATHLEEN WALKER, English language educator; b. Mt. Pleasant, Mich., Dec. 7, 1950; d. John J. and Gladys M. W.; m. Daniel H. Reeves, Mar. 10, 1972; children: Sheila, Michael. BA, Ctrl. Mich. U., 1973, MA, 1984. English tchr. Shepherd (Mich.) High Sch., 1973-76, Chippewa Hills High Sch., Remus, Mich., 1978-79, Onekama (Mich.) Pub. Sch., 1983-86, Seaholm High Sch., Birmingham, Mich., 1986—. Bd. dirs. Nat. Bd. Profl. Tchg. Stds.

REEVES, LUCY MARY, retired elementary school educator; b. Pewamo, Mich., July 2, 1932; d. Lavaldin Edgar and Marian S. (Lee) Hull; m. Walter Emery Reeves, Jan. 21, 1922. BS, Western Mich. U., Kalamazoo, 1965; postgrad., Western Mich. U., 1965-75. Tchr. Country Sch. One Room, Matherton, Mich., 1956-57, Ionia, Mich., 1957-58, Belding, Mich., 1958-62, Saranac, Mich., Belding, 1965, Belding Area Schs., 1965—89; ret., 1989. Vol. Frederick Meijers Garden, Grand Rapids, Point Man Internat. Ministries, Shiloh Cmty. Ch., United Meml. Health Ctr., Shiloh Cmty. Ch.; vol. United Meml. Health Ctr., Greenville. Mem. NEA, Mich. Edn. Assn., Belding Area Edn., Profl. Businesswomen's Assn. Avocations: computers, reading, travel, sewing.

REEVES, MARY JANE W., interior designer; b. Madison, Wis., Oct. 26, 1949; d. Spencer Hunt and Caroline (Griffith) Watkins; m. Michael Leo Reeves, Nov. 26, 1971 (div.); 1 child, Kristin Ann. BS in Biology, Duke U., 1971; MS in Interior Design, U. N.C., Greensboro, 1975. Interior designer Burdines, Miami, Fla., 1975-78, 81-84; mgr., designer Contract Mktg. Group, Miami, 1981-83; interior designer Burdines, Miami, 1983-84; pres., owner MJR Interiors, Inc., Coral Gables, Fla., 1990—. Mem. bd. govs. Design Ctr. of the Americas, Dania, Fla., 1992-93; bd. dirs. Design Access Adv. Bd., South Fla., 1991-92. Vol. Miami City Ballet, 1991-92. Recipient ASIP Design Excellence Awd. (2), IBD Designer of the Yr., most creative awd., Architectural Digest. Mem. Am. Soc. Interior Designers (profl., bd. dirs. 1989-90, 92—, v.p. 1990-91, pres. 1991-92, pres. IDAF, 1997-99, presdl. citation 1991), Capitol Ctr. Planning Commn. appointment, state of Fla., 1999—, Interior Design Assn. Fla., Nat. Trust Hist. Preservation, Miami Design Preservation League. Office: Mjr Interiors 345 W Palmetto Park Rd Boca Raton FL 33432-3732

REEVES, NANCY RAPP, elementary school educator; BS, Ohio State U., 1991; MA in Tchg., Mary Groves Coll., 2001. Cert. tchr., Ohio. Social studies tchr. East Clinton Mid. Sch., Lees Creek, Ohio, 1991—. Recipient Outstanding Educator award, East Clinton Sch., 2001, 2003, Martha Holden Jennings scholar award, 2005. Mem. Pi Lambda Theta, Phi Kappa Phi, Golden Key Soc. Home: 3816 Bloomingburg New Holland Rd New Holland OH 43145-9611 Office Phone: 937-584-9267.

REEVES, SAMANTHA, professional tennis player; b. Redwood City, Calif., Jan. 17, 1979; d. Jack and Jill. Profl. tennis player, 1995—. Recipient Ranked #1 in U.S. 18-and-under divsn., 1996, WTA Tours Doubles Titles, Quebec City, 2001, 2002, Ranked #76, WTA, Ranked #12 Among U.S. Players, Highest Season Ending Singles Ranking #101, 2002, 2 Women's Circuit Singles Titles, ITF, Rookie of the Yr., 2002, World Team Tennis MVP, 2003. Office: WTA Tour Corporate Headquarters One Progress Plz Ste 1500 Saint Petersburg FL 33701

REFO, PATRICIA LEE, lawyer; b. Alexandria, Va., Dec. 31, 1958; m. Don Bivens; 1 child, Andrew stepchildren: Jody, Lisa. BA with high honors and high distinction, U. Mich., 1980, JD cum laude, 1983. Bar: Ill. 1983, US Dist. Ct. No. Dist. Ill. 1983, US Ct. Appeals 7th cir. 1988, US Ct. Appeals 11th cir. 1989, US Ct. Appeals 5th cir. 1993, Ariz. 1996, US Dist. Ct. Ariz. 1997, US Ct. Appeals 9th cir. 1998, US Tax Ct. Assoc. Jenner & Block, Chgo., 1983—90, ptnr., 1990—96, Snell & Wilmer LLP, Phoenix, 1996—. Mem. faculty Nat. Inst. Trial Advocacy, 1989—; adv. com. on fed. rules of evidence, US Jud. Conf. 2000—; mem. bd. advisors Comml. Lending Liability News, 1989-, Nat. Law Jour., 2005—; lectr. ALI/ABA and Practicing Law Inst. Chancellor Episcopal Parish of St. Barnabas on the Desert, 1999—; bd. dirs. Ariz. Academic Decathlon Assn., 1997—2001, bd. advisors, 2001—; bd. dirs. Ariz. Found. for Women, 1999—2005; dir. Greater Phoenix C. of C., 2005—. Fellow: Ariz. Found. for Legal Services and Edn., Am. Bar Found.; mem.: ABA (sec. sect. litig. 1994—98, exec. com. sect. litig. 1994—, ho. delegates 1998—2001, standing com. on membership 2000—03, chmn. sect. litig. 2003—04, chair Am. Jury Project 2004—05, ho. delegates 2005—). Office: Snell & Wilmer LLP One Arizona Ctr Phoenix AZ 85004-2202

REGALMUTO, NANCY MARIE, small business owner, consultant; b. Bay Shore, N.Y., Aug. 24, 1956; d. Antonio J. Jr. and Agnes C. (Dietz) R. Student, SUNY, Stony Brook. Sales mgr. Fire, Inc., Hempstead, NY, 1976-78; sports handicapper Red Hot Sport, J. Dime Sports, Diamond Sports, Hicksville, NY, 1978—; small bus. owner, pres. Synergy (vitamin/nutritional product mfr. and distributor), Bellport, NY, 1981—. Cons. on medicine, fin., past life, bus. readings, hypnosis, substance abuse, archeology, law enforcement investigations, family, counseling, inter-species comm., animal therapy, psychic surgery, healing, 1989—; lectr. in field, specializing in holistic remedies and therapies, 1989-91. Columnist Daily Racing Form, 1989-91; appeared on numerous TV programs, worldwide radio, mags., newspapers. Lectr., seminar leader, written about in numerous books. Min. Universal Life Ch., 1996, 97, Ch. of Inner Wisdom, 1996, 97. Mem. NAFE, Internat. Platform Assn., Horse Protection Assn., Therapeutic Riding for the Handicapped, World Wildlife Fedn. Office: 18 Woodland Park Rd Bellport NY 11713-2315

REGAN, ELLEN FRANCES (MRS. WALSTON SHEPARD BROWN), ophthalmologist, educator; b. Boston, Feb. 1, 1919; d. Edward Francis and Margaret (Moynihan) R.; m. Walston Shepard Brown, Aug. 13, 1955. AB, Wellesley Coll., 1940; MD, Yale U., 1943. Intern Boston City Hosp., 1944; asst. resident, resident Inst. Ophthalmology, Presbyn. Hosp., NYC, 1944-47, asst. ophthalmologist, 1947-56, asst. attending ophthalmologist, 1956-84; instr. ophthalmology Columbia Coll. Physicians and Surgeons, 1947-55, assoc. ophthalmology, 1955-67, asst. clin. prof., 1967-84; ret., 1984. Mem. AMA, Am. Ophthal. Soc., Am. Acad. Ophthalmology, NY Acad. Medicine, NY State Med. Soc., Mass. Med. Soc., River Club, Tuxedo Club. Home: PO Box 632 Tuxedo Park NY 10987-0632

REGAN, HELEN BROOKS, education educator, educational consultant; b. Wilmington, Del., Jan. 13, 1945; d. Richard Ensign and Helen Townsend (Lewis) Brooks; m. Richard James Regan, Nov. 22, 1980; 1 child, Katherine Helen. BA magna cum laude, Randolph-Macon Woman's Coll., 1966; MA in Teaching, Yale U., 1967; PhD, U. Conn., 1981. Cert. chemistry tchr., intermediate supr., supt., Conn. Tchr. chemistry Glastonbury (Conn.) High Sch., 1967-75; asst. prin. Daniel Hand High Sch., Madison, Conn., 1975-78, 81-83, acting prin., 1979-80; prin. Amity Sr. High Sch., Woodbridge, Conn., 1983-85; assoc. prof. Conn. Coll., New London, 1985—. Cons. Conn. Dept. of Edn., Hartford, 1985—. Co-author: The Staff Development Manager, 1991; contbr. articles to profl. jours. Mem. ASCD, AAUP, Am. Ednl. Rsch. Assn., New Eng. Coalition Ednl. Leaders (pres. 1983-85). Avocations: hiking, cross stitch, bicycling. Home: 165 Gun Point Rd Harpswell ME 04079-3928

REGAN, JUDITH TERRANCE, publishing executive; b. Leominster, Mass., Aug. 17, 1953; d. Leo James and Rita Ann (Imprescia) Regan; children: Patrick, Lara. BA, Vassar Coll., 1975. Reporter Nat. Enquirer; sr. editor, v.p. Simon & Schuster, N.Y.C., 1989—94; pres., pub. Regan Books imprint of HarperCollins, N.Y.C., 1994—. TV prodr. Entertainment Tonight, N.Y.C., Geraldo, N.Y.C.; prodr. 20th Century Fox Films, Fox TV; anchor Full Disclosure, Fox TV; host Judith Regan Tonight, Fox News Channel. Editor, pub. (books) The Way Things Ought to Be (Rush Limbaugh), 1992, Rogue Warrior (Richard Marcinko), 1992, She's Come Undone (Wally Lamb), 1992, Shampoo Planet and Life After God (Douglas Coupland), 1992, Private Parts, Miss America (Howard Stern), 1993, Judge Robert Bork, Slouching Towards Gomorrah, 1993, I Can't Believe I Said That (Kathie Lee Gifford), 1994, Microserfs, 1996, Shabby Chic (Rachel Ashwell), 1996, The Zone (Dr. Barry Sears), 1996, Brain Lock (Dr. Jeffrey Schwartz), 1997, Wicked, 1997, Confessions of an Ugly Stepsister (Gregory Maguire), 1997—2000, Girlfriend in A Coma, 1998, I Know This Much is True, 1998, Marilu Henner's Total health Makeover, 1998, Story (Robert McKee), 1998, Have a Nice Day, Mick Foley (Mankind), 1999, The Rock Says, 2000, and others, —; exec. prodr.: (TV series) Growing Up Gotti, 2004—. Office: Regan Books 10 E 53rd St New York NY 10022-5244

REGAN, MARIE CARBONE, retired language educator; b. Massena, N.Y., July 18, 1936; d. Dominick Carbone, Josephine Trimboli; m. Robert John Regan; children: Shawn, Denise, Gavin, Bridget, Stephanie. BA, SUNY, Albany, 1957; MA, SUNY, Potsdam, 1977. Tchr. English Massena H.S., 1957—60; prof. English SUNY, Canton, 1970—97; ret., 1997. Exec. com. faculty senate SUNY, Albany, 1987—93; evaluator curriculum for two-yr. coll. liberal arts offerings N.Y. State Edn. Dept., Albany, 1990—95. Mem. econ. devel. com. Town of Potsdam, 1994—, dep. town supr., 1994—; com. mem. St. Lawrence County Dem.s, 1994—; edn. alumni bd. SUNY, Potsdam, 2000—; dir. St. Lawrence Valley Tchrs. Ctr., Canton, NY, 1989—90; trustee St. Mary's Ch., Potsdam, 1993—95; vol. Alliance for Mcpl. Power, St. Lawrence County, NY, 1996—. Named Disting. Faculty, SUNY-Canton, 1989; recipient Disting. Svc. Prof., SUNY, 1990. Mem.: AAUW (bd. dirs. St. Lawrence County br., chmn. 1999—2001), Inst. for Learning in Retirement (founding mem., v.p. 2000—01). Democrat. Roman Catholic. Avocations: reading, dance, cooking. Home: 6869 State Hwy 56 Potsdam NY 13676

REGAN, PATRICIA LEE, reading specialist; b. Horton, Kans., May 2, 1950; d. William Herbert and Dorothy Louise (Bower) Moore; m. James Francis Regan, June 7, 1974; 1 child, James Paul. BS, U. Kans., Lawrence, 1972; M in Reading, U. Mo.- Kans. City, 1977. Cert. reading specialist Kans. Bd. Edn., 1977. Reading specialist St. Joseph's Grade Sch., Shawnee, Kans., 1975—77, Wichita Pub. Schs., 1977—78, Shawnee Mission Schs., Kans., 1978—85, Blue Valley Schs., Overland Park, Kans., 1985—. Organizer after sch. reading program DeBois Ednl. Ctr., Kans. City, 2000—01; assisted in establishing living wage More 2, Kans. City, 2005—06; youth sponsor St. Andrew Christian Ch., Olathe, Kans., 2004—06. Nominee Kans. Master Tchr., 1993, 2005; recipient award for Excellence in Edn., Blue Valley Schs., 1993. Mem.: NEA, Kans. Reading Assn., Internat. Reading Assn. Avocations: reading, travel, bicycling, hiking. Office: Cedar Hills Elem Sch 9100 W 165th St Overland Park KS 66210 Office Phone: 913-239-3300.

REGAN, SUSAN WRIGHT, dance educator, small business owner, choreographer; b. Cambridge, Mass., Dec. 12, 1946; d. Stephen Ellis Wright and Angela Louise Domenichello; m. David Joseph Regan, June 29, 1968 (dec.); children: Michele, David, Derek. BS in Edn., Lesley Coll., Cambridge, 1968. Tchr. Chelmsford schs., Mass.; owner, dance tchr., choreographer Susan Wright Sch. Dance, Watertown, Mass., 1964—. Performer NY World's Fair, appearances on numerous TV programs, dance cos. Recipient 2d and 3d pl. medals, NY World's Fair, 1st pl. regionals, Miss Dance New Eng., 5th pl., Miss Dance Am., Charles Burke award outstanding dedication and svc.; Sch. rated Best of the Best, Watertown, 1999—2005. Mem.: Watertown-Belmont C. of C. (Charles Burke award 2005), Dance Masters Am., Dance Tchrs. Club Boston, Sons of Italy. Avocations: travel, gardening, decorating, ballroom dancing, cooking. Office Phone: 617-924-6255. Personal E-mail: swrdance@comcast.net.

REGAN GOSSAGE, MURIEL, librarian; b. NYC, July 15, 1930; d. William and Matilda (Riebel) Blome; m. Robert Regan, 1966 (div. 1976); 1 child, Jeanne Booth; m. Wayne Gossage, 2003. BA, Hunter Coll., N.Y.C., 1950; MLS, Columbia U., 1952; MBA, Pace U., N.Y.C., 1982. Post libr. US Army, Okinawa, 1952-53; researcher P.F. Collier, N.Y.C., 1953-57; asst. libr. to libr. Rockefeller Found., N.Y.C., 1957-67; dep. chief libr. Manhattan Community Coll., N.Y.C., 1967-68; libr. Booz Allen & Hamilton, N.Y.C., 1968-69, Rockefeller Found., N.Y.C., 1969-82; prin. Gossage Regan Assocs., Inc., N.Y.C., 1980-95; pub. svcs. libr. Carlsbad (N.Mex.) Pub. Libr., 1995-2000. Dir. N.Y. Met. Reference and Rsch. Libr. Agy., 1988-95, Coun. Nat. Libr. and Info. Assns., 1991-95; cons. Librs. Info. Ctrs., Gossage Sager Assocs., 2001—. Elder First Presbyn. Ch. of Carlsbad, 1997-99, Stephan min., 2000—, deacon, 2002-03. Mem. Spl. Librs. Assn. pres. 1989-90), Archons of Colophon. Avocations: cats, reading, playing piano, travel. Home: 702 Lakeside Dr Carlsbad NM 88220-5209 Personal E-mail: murielregan@zianet.com.

REGAN-STANTON, CHRISTA MARIA, artist; b. Stuttgart, Germany, Dec. 30, 1930; arrived in U.S., 1952; d. Friedrich Wilhelm and Anna Katharina (Schiller) Hohnhausen; m. James Allen Stanton (dec.); m. James Dale Regan, Apr. 27, 1955 (div. 1983); children: Jessica Ute, Jeffrey William. M Interpretive Dance, Tanzmeister Sch. Vock, Stuttgart, Germany, 1950. Tchr. Christa Studio Dance, Stuttgart, Germany, Athens, Ohio, 1952—54, Miami U., 1955—56; mgr. Treehouse Gallery, Oak Ridge, Tenn., 1983—95; studio potter Oak Ridge, Tenn. Bd. dirs. Upstairs Gallery, Oak Ridge, Tenn.; show dir. Foothills Craft Guild, Oak Ridge, Tenn., 1985. Recipient Honorable Mention award, Oak Ridge Mus. Fine Arts, 1982, First Place award, 1983, Second Place award, 1985. Mem.: Nat Mus. Women in Arts, Southern Highland Crafts Guild, Tenn. Arts and Crafts Assn., Am. Craft Coun., Foothills Craft Guild. Home: 119 Cooper Cir Oak Ridge TN 37830-7156

REGENIE, VICKI, systems engineer; BS in Sys. Engring. Flight sys. engr. NASA Dryden Rsch. Ctr., Edwards, Calif., br. chief flight sys. br., acting program mgr. flight rsch. base R&T program. Avocations: reading, hiking, yard work, camping. Office: NASA Dryden Rsch Ctr PO Box 273 MS 2701 Edwards CA 93523-0273 Business E-Mail: vicki.regenie@mail.dfrc.nasa.gov.

REGENSTEINER, JUDITH GAIL, science educator, research scientist; d. Max Otto and Dorothy Leila Regensteiner; m. Kenneth Schneider, June 8, 1980; 1 child, Alyssa Pauline Schneider. PhD, U. Colo., 1984. Fellow U. Colo. Health Scis. Ctr., Denver, 1984—86, instr. in medicine, 1986—88, asst. prof. medicine, 1988—95, assoc. prof. medicine, 1995—2002, prof. medicine, 2002—. Elizabeth Gee Meml. lectr. U. Colo., 2003; bd. dirs. Ctr. for Womens Health Rsch. Contbr. articles to profl. jours. Recipient Henry Christian award, Am. Fedn. Med. Rsch., 1997. Fellow: Soc. Vascular Medicine and Biology (sec. 1997—). Office: U Colo Health Sci Ctr 4200 E 9th Ave Box B-180 Denver CO 80262

REGES, MARIANNA ALICE, marketing executive; b. Budapest, Hungary, Mar. 23, 1947; arrived in U.S., 1956, naturalized, 1963; d. Otto H. and Alice M. Reges; children: Rebecca, Charles III. AAS with honors, Fashion Inst. Tech., N.Y.C., 1967; BBA magna cum laude, Baruch Coll., 1971, MBA in Stats., 1978. Media rsch. analyst Doyle, Dane, Bernbach Advt., N.Y.C., 1967—70; rsch. supr. Sta. WCBS-TV, N.Y.C., 1970—71; rsch. mgr. Woman's Day mag., N.Y.C., 1971—72; asst. media dir. Benton & Bowles Advt., N.Y.C., 1972—75; mgr. rsch. and sales devel. NBC Radio, N.Y.C., 1975—77; sr. rsch. mgr. Ziff-Davis Pub. Co., N.Y.C., 1977—84; media mgr. Bristol-Myers Squibb Co., 1984—2001, Procter & Gamble Co., 2001—. Mem. Spanish Radio Adv. Coun., N.Y.C., 1986—88, Pan-European TV Audience Rsch. Mgmt. Com., 1988—. Mem. advisor Baruch Coll. Advt. Soc., 1975—; active First Presbyn. Ch., N.Y.C. Mem.: Advt. Rsch. Found., Radio and TV Rsch. Coun., Media Rsch. Dirs. Assn., Am. Advt. Fedn., Am. Mktg. Assn., Anthroposophical Soc., Nature Conservancy, Baruch Alumni Assn., Gilda's Club, Beta Gamma Sigma. Home: 626 E 20th St New York NY 10009-1509 Personal E-mail: marianna10009@hotmail.com.

REGISTER, ANNETTE ROWAN, literature educator; b. Doctors Inlet, Fla., Apr. 5, 1931; d. Ernest Ambors and Frances Perlena (Monroe) R.; Henry Ira Register, Oc. 31, 1954; 1 child, Andrew Henry. RN, Greenville Gen. Hosp. Sch. of Nursing, Greenville, 1948-51; BS, Tex. Woman's U., Denton, 1954; MEd, U. Fla., Gainesville, 1959; SEd, Fla. State U., 1983; student, U. West Fla., Okaloosa Walton C.C. Instrn. dir. nursing edn. Alachua Gen. Hosp., Gainesville, Fla., 1955-57; pub. sch. tchr. Okaloosa County, Ft. Walton Beach, Fla., 1966-93. V.p., Internat. Tng. in Communication Ft. Walton Beach, Fla.; active Inst. Sr. Profls. Okaloosa Walton C.C. Pres. Okaloosa Reading Coun., 1976—80; mem. Okaloosa Walton C.C. Symphony Guild, 1998—; pres. United Meth. Women, Ft. Walton Beach, Fla., 1985—87; dist. v.p. Mem. Fla. C. of C. (amb. 1996—), Phi Delta Kappa (1st v.p.). Methodist. Avocations: crafts, painting, sketching, travel. Office: Okaloosa County Sch Bd 10 Lowery Pl SE Fort Walton Beach FL 32548 Office Phone: 850-243-2250. Personal E-mail: registerannette@yahoo.com.

REGNER, DEBORAH ALLYSON, educator; b. Ann Arbor, Mich., Nov. 9, 1970; d. Stephen Wells Burke and Ruth Ann Webster; m. Robert William Regner, Oct. 30, 1998; 1 child, Ryley Robert. BS in Psychology and Sociology, Ea. Mich. U., Ypsilanti, 1996, MS in Psychology, 1998. Educator health Ea. Mich. U., 1997—2001; dir. campus life Concordia U., Ann Arbor, 2001—04; faculty Washtenaw C.C., Ann Arbor, 2005—06, Schoolcraft Coll., Livonia, 2006—. Grant writer Huron Valley Ambulance, Ann Arbor, 2005—06. Cmty. contact Greater Milan Area Cmty. Found., Milan, Mich., 2006; mem. sexual health com. Milan Area Schs., 2005. Office: Schoolcraft College Psychology Dept 18600 Haggerty Livonia MI 48152 Office Phone: 734-462-4400. E-mail: dregner@schoolcraft.edu.

REGN FRAHER, BONNIE, special education educator; BA, U. Calif., Santa Cruz, 1978; EdS, Rutgers U., 1982, MA, 1983. Cert. tchr. of the handicapped, cert. elem. tchr. Tchr. Search Day Program, Wanamassa, NJ, 1978-87; v.p. Fin-Addict Charters, Wall, NJ, 1987-93; v.p., dir. fin. William

Cook Custom Homes, Wall, 1987-95; v.p. Archtl. Woodworking, 1993-95; tchr. Elmcrest Hosp., 1996—2003; preschool owner Fraher Acad., West Hartford, Conn., 1996—2003; tchr. Palm Beach County Sch. Dist., Fla., 2006—. Mem. Am. Mensa, Autism Soc. Am., Am. Sailing Assn. Avocation: writing.

REGNIER, SOPHIE ANNE MICHELLE, business research consultant; b. NYC, Apr. 13, 1979; MS in Arts Adminstrn., Drexel U., Phila., 2005. Order processing supr. Walnut St. Theatre, Phila., 2000—05; box office mgr. DeSales U. Box Office, Center Valley, Pa., 2005—. Cons. S.A.M. Regnier Cons., Allentown, Pa., 2000—. Fellow, Drexel U., 2003—04. Mem.: Theatre Comm. Group. Office: DeSales University Box Office 2755 Station Ave Center Valley PA 18034 Office Phone: 610-282-3654. E-mail: sophie.regnier@desales.edu.

REGUEIRO-REN, ALICIA, biomedical researcher; b. Madrid, Oct. 31, 1967; came to U.S., Jan. 1995. d. Joaquin Regueiro and Alicia Miguelez; m. Rex. X.-F. Ren, Dec. 27, 1995. BSc, U. La Laguna, Santa Cruz de Tenerife, Spain, 1990, PhD, 1994. Fulbright postdoctoral fellow Columbia U., N.Y.C., 1995-98; rsch. investigator I Bristol Myers Squibb, NJ, 1998—99, rsch. investigator II Conn., 1999—2001, sr. rsch. investigator I, biomed. investigator Conn., 2001—. Contbr. articles to profl. jours.; patentee in field. Mem. AAAS, Am. Chem. Soc., Sigma Xi. Roman Catholic. Avocations: travel, reading. Home: 69 Greenview Ter Middletown CT 06457-8738 Office: Bristol Myers Squibb 5 Research Pkwy Wallingford CT 06492-1951 Fax: 203-677-7202. E-mail: alicia.regueiroren@bms.com.

REHA, ROSE KRIVISKY, retired finance educator; b. N.Y.C., Dec. 17, 1920; d. Boris and Freda (Gerstein) Krivisky; m. Rudolph John Reha, Apr. 11, 1941; children: Irene Gale, Phyllis BS Bus. and Music Edn., Ind. State U., 1965; MA Bus. and Psychology, U. Minn., 1967, PhD Ednl. Psychology and Counseling, 1971. With U.S. and State Civil Svc., 1941—63; tchr. pub. schs., Minn., 1965—66; tchg. assoc., instr. U. Minn., Mpls., 1966—68, 1968—85; prof. coll. bus. St. Cloud State U., Minn., 1968—85, prof. emeritus, 1985—, chmn. bus. edn. & office adminstrn. dept., 1982—83. Advisor Small Bus. Inst., 1972-85, SBA, 1972-85; ct. advocate for women in distress St. Cloud Women's Shelter, 1986-89; adj. prof. profl. and bus. comm. Fla. Atlantic U., Boca Raton, 1989-90; substitute tchr. Broward County, 1990—; tutor (reading) Lauderdale, Fla., 1990-92; moderator, counselor Posnack Jewish Cmty. Ctr., Davie, Fla.; lectr. comm. Soref Jewish Cmty. Ctr. Continuing Edn. for sr. groups, Sunrise, Fla., 1994—; cons., lectr. in field; small bus. cons. Small Bus. Inst. Coll. Bus. St. Cloud State U. Minn.; reviewer bus. comm. and consumer edn. textbooks Contbr. articles to profl. jours Camp dir. Girl Scouts U.S., 1960-62; active various cmty. fund drives; sec., mem. relicensure rev. Com. Minn. Bd. Tchg. Continuing Edn., 1984-85 Recipient Achievement award St. Cloud State U., 1985, St. Cloud State U. Rsch. and Faculty Improvement grantee, 1973, 78, 83 Mem. NEA, ACA (cert.), Am. Vocat. Assn. (cert.), Am. Mental Health Counselors Assn. (cert.), Minn. Econ. Assn., Minn. Women of Higher Edn., Minn. Edn. Assn. (pres. women's caucus 1981-83, award 1983), St. Cloud U. Faculty Assembly (pres. 1975-76), St. Cloud State U. Grad. Coun. (chmn. 1983-85), Fifty-five-plus Sr. Group (moderator 1994-97), Pi Omega Pi, Phi Chi Theta, Delta Pi Epsilon, Delta Kappa Gamma Jewish. Home: 6501 Woodlake Dr Apt 304 Minneapolis MN 55423-1393 Office Phone: 612-866-0544.

REHM, CAROLYN AGNES, pediatrician, educator; b. Queens, NY, Mar. 2, 1952; d. Donald Edward and Agnes Catherine Schanck; m. Steven Thomas Rehm, Oct. 4, 1980; children: Catherine, Tim, Emily. BS, Coll. Mt. St. Vincent, 1974; MD, Columbia U., 1978. Diplomate Am. Bd. Pediats. Intern Johns Hopkins Hosp., Balt., 1978—79, resident, 1979—81; pediatrician Bel Air Clinic, Bowie, Md., 1981—83; pvt. practice pediatrician Huntington, NY, 1983—94; mem. staff pediats. United Cerebral Palsy, Roosevelt, NY, 1994—99; tchr. sci. St. Dominic H.S., Oyster Bay, NY, 1999—2005; prof. Molloy Coll., 2005—. Tchr. sci. Coll. Mt. St. Vincent, Riverdale, NY, 2003—04; dir. Am. Health and Safety Inst., Oyster Bay, NY; moderator student amb. cmty. svc. St. Dominic HS, Oyster Bay, 1999—2005; medical dir. Mill Need Sch. Deaf, NY, 2005—. Author: The Flowerpot Bunnies, 2004. Leader Girl Scouts Am., N.Y., 1986—2005, Boy Scouts Am., N.Y., 1989—94; com. Cath. girl scouts Girl Scouts Am., N.Y., 1999—2004. Recipient Humanitarian award, Columbia Coll. Physicians and Surgeons, 1978, N.Y., 1978, St. Anne award, Girl Scouts, St. Elizabeth award, Outstanding Svc. award, 2000. Fellow: Am. Acad. Pediats.; mem.: Children with Disabilities Am. Roman Catholic. Home: 28 Shamrock Ct Syosset NY 11791

REHM, PATRICE KOCH, radiologist, educator; b. DeSoto, Mo., Nov. 23, 1954; d. James Clarence and Eleanor (Koch) R. BA in Chemistry, U. Mo., 1977; MD, Yale U., 1981. Diplomate Am. Bd. Radiology, Am. Bd. Nuclear Medicine. Intern in medicine Waterbury (Conn.) Hosp., 1981-82; resident in radiology Yale New Haven Hosp., 1982-83, 84-85, fellow in neuroradiology, 1985-86, fellow in nuclear medicine, 1986-87; resident in radiology SUNY Upstate Med. Ctr., Syracuse, 1983-84; clin. assoc. Cleve. Clinic, 1987-88, staff physician, 1988-89, Presbyn. Hosp., Charlotte, N.C., 1989-91, Georgetown U. Med. Ctr., Washington, 1992—; assoc. prof. radiology, dir. nuc. medicine U. Va. Health System, Charlottesville, Va. Fellow Am. Coll. Radiology (dir. nuc. medicine), Radiologic Soc. N.Am., Soc. Nuclear Medicine. Office: U Va Health System PO Box 800170 Charlottesville VA 22908

REHMANI, SHAHIDA, psychiatrist; b. Rawalpindi, Punjab, Pakistan; arrived in U.S., 1990; d. Waheed Abdul and Naima Chowdhry; m. Mohammed Shehbaz Rehmani, Dec. 23, 1985; children: Mustafa, Ahmad, Taaha. MD, Rawalpindi Med. Coll., 1985. Child psychiatrist Strong Meml. Hosp., Rochester, NY, 2000—, Unity Health Sys., 2000—, Life Ho. Program at St. Joseph Villa, 2000—, Livingston County Mental Health, 2003—. Part time faculty Strong Meml. Hosp., Rochester, NY, 2000—; med. dir. Life Ho. Program at St. Joseph Villa, 2000—. Mem.: Am. Acad. Child and Adolescent Psychiatry, Am. Psychiatric Assn., Am. Pakastani Assn. N.Am. Avocations: reading, travel, writing. Home: 43 Park View Dr Pittsford NY 14534-9754 Office: 100 Pinewild Dr Rochester NY Office Phone: 585-368-6703.

REHNKE, MARY ANN, academic administrator; b. Faribault, Minn., Jan. 23, 1945; d. Wesley Arthur and Sarah Frances (Smith) Rehnke; m. Charles Orin Willis, Apr. 18, 1924. BA in English, Cornell Coll., 1967; MA in English, U. Chgo., 1968, PhD in Lit., 1974; MS in Ednl Adminstrn., U. Wis., 1975; Cert. of Completion, Shalem Inst. Spiritual Formation, 2000. Head resident Elizabeth Waters Hall, U. Wis., Madison, 1970-73; asst. prof. English No. Ky. U., Highland Heights, 1973-82, acad. adminstr., 1976-77, dir. summer sessions, 1977-80; dir. conf. planning Am. Assn. Higher Edn., Washington, 1980-82; assoc. dean for faculty relations and acad. programs Coll. St. Catherine, St. Paul, 1982-83; assoc. dean of coll. Daemen Coll., Buffalo, 1983-85; v.p. programs Council of Ind. Colls., Washington, 1986—. Mem. planning com. nat. identification program Am. Council Edn., Washington, 1978-85; mem. program com. Nat. Conf. Women Student Leaders and Women of Distinction, Washington, 1985-88. Author: Women in Higher Education Administration: A Brief Guide for Conference Planners, 1982, Guide to Spiritual Retreats in the Washington, D.C. Area, 1997; editor: Creating Career Programs in a Liberal Arts Context, 1987; editor newsletter N. Ctrl. Regional Women's Studies, 1978-80. Vestry mem Ch. of St. Clement, Alexandria, Va., 1982, vice chair search com., 1986-87. Named one of Outstanding Young Women Am., 1976. Mem.: Nat. Women's Studies Assn., Jane Austen Soc., Soc. Values in Higher Edn., N.Am. Assn. Summer Sessions (rsch. chair 1979—80), Am. Assn. Higher Edn. (coord. nat. conf. roundtable 1982—86), Phi Beta Kappa, Phi Delta Kappa. Democrat. Episcopalian. Office Phone: 202-466-7230.

REHNQUIST, JANET, lawyer, former federal agency administrator; b. Phoenix, May 4, 1957; d. William and Margery (Peck) Rehnquist. BA, U. Va., 1979; JD, U. Va. Law School, 1985. Assoc. counsel to the Pres. The White House, Washington, 1990—93; asst. U.S. atty. (ea. dist.) Va. US Dept. Justice, Washington; insp. gen. US Dept. HHS, Washington, 2001—03; ptnr. Venable LLP, Washington, 2003—, co-chair Wash. Health Care practice. Counsel U.S. Senate Permanent Subcom. on Investigations. Office: Venable LLP 575 7th St NW Washington DC 20004 Office Phone: 202-344-8241. Office Fax: 202-344-8300. E-mail: jrehnquist@venable.com.

REHR, HELEN, social worker; b. NYC, Dec. 16, 1919; d. Philip and Rose (Stern) R. BA, Hunter Coll., 1940; DSc (hon.), CUNY, 1995; MS, Columbia U., N.Y.C., 1943; DSW, Columbia U., 1970. Social worker, asst. dir. Sydenham Hosp., N.Y.C., 1943-45; supr. Grasslands Hosp., Valhalla, N.Y., 1945-47; asst. prof. medicine NYU Bellevue Med. Ctr., N.Y.C., 1947-51; med. soc. cons. Dept. Health, Maternal & Child Health, N.Y.C., 1951-52; assoc. dir. Mt. Sinai Med. Ctr., N.Y.C., 1954—70, dir., 1971—89, Edith J. Baerwald prof. cmty. medicine, 1971—89, prof. cmty. med. emerita, 1998—. Dir. Israel/Australia Leadership Project, 1986—; vis. prof. U. Flinders, U. Melbourne, Australia, 1990, Ben Gurion U., Israel, 1991; Kenneth Pray vis. prof. U. Pa., Phila., 1979-80; cons. Mt. Sinai, 1986—. Author, editor books, jour. and articles in field; mem. editl. bd. Social Work in Health Care, Health and Social Work. Bd. dirs. N.Y. Found., Ctr. for Study of Social Work Practice/Columbia U., Joint Commn. on Accreditation of Hosps.; mem. adv. bd. scholarship and welfare fund Hunter Coll., Jewish Bd. Family Chns Svc. Named Disting. Practitioner, Nat. Acad. Practice; named to hall of fame Hunter Coll., 1978, Columbia U. Sch. Social Work, 1998; recipient Ida M. Cannon award Soc. SW Dir., 1975, Knee-Wittman Lifetime Achievement award NASW, 1990, Columbia I. Alumni medal, 2004. Fellow: Brookdale Ctr. Aging, NY Acad. Medicine, Gerontol. Soc. Avocation: gardening. Home: 27 W 96th St 6C New York NY 10025-6515 Office: Mt Sinai Med Ctr 1 Gustave L Levy Pl New York NY 10029-6500 Office Phone: 212-241-2586.

REHTH, ANN, counselor; b. Pennyan, N.Y., May 28, 1942; d. J. Allen and Jean Eleanor (Stanhope) Henderson; children: Nikki, Douglas, Scott. BA, U. South Fla., 1983; MS, Nova U., 1994. Cert. tchr., ESL tchr. Tchr. Venice H.S., Fla., 1984—94; mental health counselor Meridian Behavioral, Gainsville, Fla., 1994—98, YMCA, Sarasota, Fla., 1998—2001; tchr. Gulf Coast Marine Inst., Venice, 2000—01; tchr. ESOL and reading North Port H.S., Fla., 2001—. Dir. intervention program for children and teens Meridian Behavioral, Gainsville, Fla., 1994—98; cons. to schs. for abuse and crisis intervention YMCA, Venice, Fla., 1999—2001. Mem.: STESOL, Fla. Reading Assn., Sarasota Reading Council. Avocations: reading, volunteering, walking. Personal E-mail: annrehth@comcast.net.

REIBOLD, DOROTHY ANN, accountant, researcher; b. Leigh, Nebr., Feb. 22, 1922; d. Herman Ludwig Marty and Frances Jane Harvey; m. Wayne Henry Reibold, Mar. 27, 1947; children: Lillie Frances, Marty John. BEd, Wayne State Tchrs., 1945. Tchr., prin. Nenzel Sch., Nebr., 1941-42; tchr. Cozad Sch., Nebr., 1942-43; sec. Burroughs Adding Machine, Omaha, 1943-44; tchr. Lyons Pub. Sch., Nebr., 1945-47; office mgr. Yoelin Bros. Wholesale, Denver, 1947-52; freelance bookkeeper Henderson, Colo., 1960-00; bookkeeper Hazeltine Heights Water, Henderson, 1964—; dir. sch. lunch program Zion Luth. Sch., Brighton, Colo., 1969—78; dir. Hazeltine Heights Water, 1982-00. Author: Ecklin Family Story, 1988, Life of Matthias Harvye, 1998. Mem.: DAR. Republican. Lutheran. Avocations: genealogy, travel. Home and Office: 8181 E 104th Ave Henderson CO 80640-9049 Personal E-mail: dotareibold@earthlink.net.

REICH, OLIVE BUERK, artist, educator; b. Bklyn., Mar. 1, 1935; d. Percival G. and Olive Buerk; m. Daniel Oehler Reich, Aug. 4, 1956; children: Peter, Robin, Daniel. BA, Mt. Holyoke Coll., 1956. Tchr. water color technique Olive Reich Studio, Bklyn., 1970—, Aquarelle Studio, Shelter Island, N.Y., 1983-86, Polytech. Preparatory Inst., Bklyn., 1987. Cons. art Union Ch., Bay Ridge, Bklyn., 1984-87, Reich Paper Co., Bklyn, 1986-88, Meta Catering Corp., Bklyn., 1987-88. Illustrator book God's Summer Cottage, 1980, Chronicle of Shelter Island Churches, 1983, Shelter Island Yacht Club, 1986. Pres. Bay Ridge Festival Arts., Bklyn, 1978-80. Mem. Nat. Assn. Women Artists, Artists Equity, Contemporary Artists Guild (corr. sec. 1980-87), Mt. Holyoke Coll. Visual Artists, Artists Alliance of East Hampton, Audubon Artist, Nat. Arts Club (N.Y.C.), Catharine Lorillard Wolfe Art Club (1st v.p. 1982), Bklyn. Watercolor Soc. Avocations: films, ballet, theater, interior decorating. Home: 36 79th St Brooklyn NY 11209-2813 Office: Olive Reich Studio 7518 Third Ave Brooklyn NY 11209 Office Phone: 718-680-3269. E-mail: olive@oliveart.com.

REICH, ROSE MARIE, retired art educator; b. Milw., Dec. 24, 1937; d. Valentine John and Mary Jane (Grochowski) Kosmatka; m. Kenneth Pierce Reich, July 13, 1968. BA, Milw. Downer Coll., 1959; MA, U. Wyo., 1967. Art tchr. Oconomowoc (Wis.) Area Schs., 1959-93, ret., 1993. Mem. Oconomowoc Edn. Assn., NEA (life), Wis. Edn. Assn., AAUW (v.p. membership 1989—), Delta Kappa Gamma (past pres.), Oconomowoc Woman's Club. Roman Catholic. Avocations: newfoundland dogs, needlecrafts, designing stationery, polish paper cutting, restoring old church statues and mannequins. Home: 3717 N Golden Lake Rd Oconomowoc WI 53066-4104

REICH, SUSANNA, children's book author, publicist; b. NYC, Apr. 10, 1954; d. Haskell A. and Nancy B. Reich; m. Gary Golio, May 25, 1980; 1 child, Laurel Alexandra. BFA in Dance, NYU, 1976. Cert. Movement Analyst Laban/Bartenieff Inst. Movement Studies. Dancer Rotante Dance Co., N.Y.C., 1978, Wetzig Dance Co., N.Y.C., 1978-80; mem. faculty Dance Notation Bur., N.Y.C., 1981-85, Laban Inst. Movement Studies, N.Y.C., 1984-85; owner, designer Flowers by Susanna, Briarcliff Manor, N.Y., 1988-98; author children's books Ossining, NY, 1994—; sr. publicist Raab Assocs., Inc., 2000—. Pres. Westchester Dance Coun., Westchester County, N.Y., 1983-85; mem. exec. bd. Ossining Schs. Art Advocates, 1996-99. Author: Clara Schumann: Piano Virtuoso, 1999 (named one of 100 Titles for Reading and Sharing N.Y. Pub. Libr. 1999, NCTE Orbus Pictus Honor Book, ALA Notable Children's Book, ALA Best Book for Young Adults, School Library Journal Best children's Books of 1999), José! Born to Dance: The Story of José Limón, 2005 (named one of 100 Titles Reading and Sharing, N.Y. Pub. Libr., 2005, one of Booklist's Top Ten Arts Books for Youth, Tomas Rivera Mexican Am. Children's Book award, Internat. Latino Book award), Penelope Bailey Takes the Stage, 2006. Named among Outstanding Women Under 40, Women's News, Harrison, N.Y., 1993. Mem.: PEN, Soc. Children's Book Writers and Illustrators (steering com. met. N.Y. chpt.). Home: 5 Belle Ave Ossining NY 10562-3802

REICHBLUM, AUDREY ROSENTHAL, public relations executive, publishing executive; b. Pitts., June 28, 1935; d. Emanuel Nathan and Willa (Handmacher) Rosenthal; m. M. Charles Reichblum, Jan. 25, 1956; children: Robert Nathan, William Mark. Student, Bennington Coll., 1952-53; BS, Carnegie Mellon U., 1956. Founder, creator, chmn. Pitts. Children's Mus., 1970-73; mag. writer Pitts. Mag., 1978; dir. pub. rels. Pitts. Pub. Theater, 1978-79; pres. arPR audrey reichblum PUB. RELS. inc., Pitts., 1980—, arpr, inc., 1996—; pub. "Knowledge in a Nutshell" Series, 1996—99, "The Edible Game A Smart Cookie", 1996—, "Sweet Smarts The Candy With A Brain", 2004. Pub. rels. cons., bd. mem. Pitts. Planned Parenthood, 1980-84, United Jewish Fedn., Bus. and Profl. Women, Pitts., 1980-85, Pitts. City Theater, 1985-94, Pa. Coun. on Aging, 1996-99; chmn. Villa de Marillac Nursing, 1999, Vincencian Collaborative Svcs. Bd.; syndicator The Dr. Knowledge Show. Recipient Gold Cindy award Info. Film Producers Am., 1982, award of excellence Internat. Assn. Bus. Communicators, Pitts., 1986, Matrix award for Three Rivers Arts Festival, Lifetime Achievement award NAWBO-YWCA, Y-Tribute to Women in Comms. award, 1998. Mem. Pub. Rels. Soc. Am. (accredited; award of merit 1983, G. Victor Barkman award for excellence 1984, 1st place award Race For The Cure), Women in Comm. (Matrix-sales promotion award 1987), Nat. Assn. Women Bus. Owners (Life Time Achievement award 1995). Office: 1420 Centre Ave Ste 2213 Pittsburgh PA 15219-3536

REICHELDERFER, BRENDA L., manufacturing executive; b. May 29, 1958; BSEE, Ohio No. Univ. Joined ITT Corp. (predecessor to ITT Industries), 1982; various engring., ops. positions ITT Defense & Electronics, 1982—97; v.p., engring., electrical sys. group, automotive divsn. ITT Industries, 1997—98, pres., fluid specialty group, 1998—2001, pres., motion & flow control group, 2001—03, pres., electronic components group, 2003—05, sr. v.p., chief tech. officer White Plains, NY, 2005—. Bd. dirs. Fed. Signal Corp., 2006—. Office: ITT Industries 4 W Red Oak Ln West Harrison NY 10604 Office Phone: 914-641-2000. Office Fax: 914-696-2950.

REICHERT, KATHLEEN EVELYN, elementary school educator; b. Queens Village, N.Y., Dec. 2, 1945; d. Kenneth Edward and Veronica Rita Merkel; m. Wayne Erwin Reichert, Aug. 1, 1982; 1 child, Wayne Kenneth. BA Elem. Ed, Glassboro State Coll., N.J., 1967; MA Elem. Edn., Rowan U., Glassboro, NJ, 1977. Cert. Tchr. Elem. Edn. K-8 N.J. State Dept. Edn., 1967. Tchr. Paramus Bd. Edn., NJ, 1967—, Hamilton Twp. Bd. Edn., Mays Landing, NJ, 1971—. Coord. basic skills Hamilton Twp. Bd. Edn., Mays Landing, 1989—. Parish mem. St. Martin de Porres Ch., Hammonton, NJ, 1983—. Named Hess Star Tchr. of Yr., 2000; grantee, State Dept. N.J., 1995. Mem.: Phi Delta Kappa. Roman Catholic. Avocation: travel. Home: 200 Lakeview Ave Hammonton NJ 08037 Office: Hamilton Township Bd Education Dennis Foreman Drive Mays Landing NJ 08330

REICHGOTT JUNGE, EMBER DARLENE, retired senator, lawyer, writer, broadcast commentator, radio personality; b. Detroit, Aug. 22, 1953; d. Norbert Arnold and Diane (Pincich) Reichgott; m. Michael Junge. BA summa cum laude, St. Olaf Coll., Minn., 1974; JD, Duke U., 1977; MBA, U. St. Thomas, 1991. Bar: Minn. 1977, D.C. 1978. Assoc. Larkin, Hoffman, Daly & Lindgren, Bloomington, Minn., 1977-84; counsel Control Data Corp., Bloomington, Minn., 1984-86; ptnr. The Gen. Counsel, Ltd., 1987—; mem. Minn. State Senate, 1983-2000, chmn. legis. com. on econ. status of women, 1984-86, vice chmn. senate edn. com., 1987-88, senate majority whip, 1990-94, chmn. property tax divsn. senate tax com., 1991-92, chmn. senate judiciary com., 1993-94, senate asst. majority leader, 1995-2000, chmn. spl. subcom. on ethical conduct. Dem. endorsed candidate Minn. Atty. Gen., 1998; instr. polit. sci. St. Olaf Coll., Northfield, Minn., 1993; bd. dirs. Citizens Ind. Bank, St. Louis Park, Minn. Host cable TV monthly series Legis. Report, 1985-92. State co-chair Clinton/Gore Presdl. Campaign, Minn. Dem. Farmer-Labor Party, 1992, 1996; del. Nat. Dem. Conv., 1984, 1992, 1996; pres. Minn. Women's Polit. Caucus, 2002—04; trustee, bd. dirs. N.W. YMCA, New Hope, Minn., 1983—88, United Way Mpls., 1989—, Greater Mpls. ARC, 1988—2004, chair, 2001—03. Recipient Woman of Yr. award North Hennepin Bus. and Profl. Women, 1983, award for contbn. to human svcs. Minn. Social Svcs. Assn., 1983, Clean Air award Minn. Lung Assn., 1988, Disting. Svc. award Mpls. Jaycees, 1984, Minn. Dept. Human Rights award, 1989, Myra Bradwell award Minn. Women Lawyers, 1993, Disting. Alumnae award Lake Conf. Schs., 1993, Disting. Alumnae award St. Olaf Coll., 1998, awards for leadership Am. Lung Assn., 1999, Am. Heart Assn., 1997, Everyday Hero award Up with People, 1995, Unsung Hero award United Way of Mpls., 1999, 1st recipient of award named in her honor for prevention of sexual assault, 2000; charter inductee Robbinsdale H.S. Hall of Fame, 2000; author of Minn. charter sch. law, winner of "2000 Innovations in Am. Govt. award" Harvard U. and Ford Found., others; named One of ten Outstanding Young Minnesotans, Minn. Jaycees, 1984, Policy Adv. of Yr., NAWBO, 1988, Woman of Achievement, Twin West C. of C., 1989, Marvelous Minn. Woman, 1993; youngest woman ever elected to Minn. Senate, 1983. Mem. Minn. Bar Assn. (bd. govs. 1992-96, Pro Bono Publico Atty. award 1990), Hennepin County Bar Assn., Corp. Counsel Assn. (v.p. 1989-96). Home: 7701 48th Ave N Minneapolis MN 55428-4515 Home Fax: 763-536-1447. Personal E-mail: emberrj@visi.com.

REICHHELD, DEBORAH ANN, retired secondary school educator, language educator; b. Cleve., Feb. 23, 1947; d. John James Pechman Jr. and Ethel M. Pechman; m. Charles A. Reichheld III, Aug. 23, 1969; children: Jennifer Lindsey, Elizabeth Ashley, Deborah Whitney, Chase. BA, Moskingum Coll., 1969; MA Spanish, Kent State U., 1974. Tchr. high sch. Parma City Schs., Ohio, 1969—, dept. chair, 1972—82, 1998—2005, ret., 2005; adj. instr. Spanish Cuyahoga C.C. West, 2005—. Scholar, Muskingum Coll., New Concord, Ohio, 1965—69. Mem.: NEA, Parma Edn. Assn., Ohio Edn. Assn., Phi Sigma Iota. United Ch. Of Christ. Avocations: tennis, aerobics, crafts, baseball. Home: 3313 Hamilton Rd Medina OH 44256 Personal E-mail: deborahreichheld@zoominternet.net.

REICHL, RUTH MOLLY, editor-in-chief; b. NYC, Jan. 16, 1948; d. Ernst and Miriam and (Brudno) R.; m. Douglas Wilder Hollis, Sept. 5, 1970 (div. 1985); m. Michael Singer, 1985; 1 child, Nicholas Singer. BA, U. Mich., 1968, MA in history of art, 1970. Chef, co-owner The Swallow Restaurant, Berkeley, Calif., 1974—77; food writer, editor New West mag., San Francisco, 1977—84; editor restaurant column LA Times, 1984-93, food editor, 1990-93; restaurant critic NY Times, 1993-99; editor-in-chief Gourmet Mag., 1999—. Lectr. in field. Author: Mmmm: A Feastiary, 1972, The Contest Book, 1977, Tender at the Bone: Growing Up at the Table, 1998, Comfort Me with Apples: More Adventures at the Table, 2001; editor: Modern Library Food Series, 2000—, Endless Feasts: Sixty Years of Writing from Gourmet, 2002, Remembrance of Things Paris, 2004, The Gourmet Cookbook, 2004, Garlic and Sapphires, 2005, Tanner Lectures on Human Values, 2005. Recipient James Beard Award for journalism, 1994, James Beard Award for restaurant criticism, 1996, 1998. Office: 4 Times Sq New York NY 10036-6518 Business E-Mail: ruth.reichl@gourmet.com.

REICHMAN, BONNIE S., oncologist; d. Harry and Mildred Reichman. BA, Cornell U., Ithaca, NY, 1976; MD, St. Louis U., 1980. Diplomate Am. Bd. Internal Medicine, Am. Bd. Med. Oncology. Intern Cornell Cooperating Hosps. North Shore U. Hosp./Meml. Sloan-Kettering Cancer Ctr., NYC, 1980—81, resident in internal medicine, 1981—83; fellow med. oncology/immunology Meml. Sloan-Kettering Cancer Ctr., NYC, 1983—84, with rsch. lab. Dr. A. Houghton, 1984—85, clin. rsch. fellow med. oncology, 1985—87, clin. asst. physician, 1987—92; asst. attending physician divsn. hematology/oncology NY Hosp., NYC, 1992—93; assoc. attending physician divsn. hematology/oncology NY Presbyn. Hosp., NYC, 1993—; from clin. assoc. in medicine to clin. assoc. prof. clinical medicine Cornell U. Med. Coll., NYC, 1981—2003; clin. assoc. prof. medicine Well Med. Coll./Cornell U., NYC, 2003—. Assoc. med. dir. Strang Cancer Prevention Ctr., NYC, 1992—97; dir. med. oncology, assoc. dir. Strang-Cornell Breast Ctr., NYC, 1992—97; asst. attending physician divsn. hematology/oncology Beth Israel Med. Ctr., NYC, 1995—2002; med. dir. Comprehensive Cancer Ctr., NYC, 1997—2000; assoc. attending physician St. Vincent's Hosp. and Med. Ctr., NYC, 1997—2000; adv. bd. NYSERNet, Inc., 1994—95. Contbr. articles to profl. jours., chapters to books. Bd. dirs. Nat. Alliance Breast Cancer Orgn., SHARE, 2001—03. Fellow, Am. Cancer Soc., 1984—85. Fellow: ACP; mem.: AMA, Am. Soc. Breast Disease (edn. com. 2004—), Womens Med. Assn. NYC (bd. dirs. 1987—88, fin. assistance com. 1994), NY State Soc. Med. Oncologists and Hematologists (exec. com. 1995—), NY State Soc. Internal Medicine, NY Met. Breast Cancer Group (program com. 1992—95, chair program com. 1993—95, exec. com. 1994—95, sec. 1995—97, v.p. 1997—99, pres. 1999—2001), NY County Soc. Internal Medicine, NY County Med. Soc., NY Acad. Sci., Nat. Coun. on Women in Medicine, Nat. Coun. on Womens Health, Med. Soc. State NY, Internat. Gynecologic Cancer Soc., Am. Soc. Internal Medicine, Am. Soc. Clin. Oncology, Am. Fedn. for Clin. Rsch., Am. Assn. for Cancer Rsch., Meml. Hosp. Alumni Soc. Office: 30 E 60th St New York NY 10022

REICHMANIS, ELSA, chemist; b. Melbourne, Victoria, Australia, Dec. 9, 1953; arrived in U.S., 1962; d. Peteris and Nina (Meiers) R.; m. Francis Joseph Purcell, June 2, 1979; children: Patrick William, Elizabeth Anne, Edward Andrew, Thomas Alexander. BS in Chemistry, Syracuse U., 1972, PhD in Chemistry, 1975. Postdoctoral intern Syracuse (N.Y.) U., 1975-76, Chaim Weizmann rsch. fellow, 1976-78; mem. tech. staff AT&T Bell Labs., Murray Hill, NJ, 1978-84, supr. radiation sensitive materials and applications, 1984-94, head organic and polymer materials, 1994-95; head polymer and organic materials Lucent Techs., Bell Labs., New Providence, NJ, 1996—2000, dir. materials rsch., 2001—. Panel on advanced materials. Japanese Tech. Evaluation Prog., NSF, Washington, 1986, com. to survey materials. rsch. opportunities and needs for electronic industry Nat. Rsch. Coun., 1986, Nat. Materials Adv. Bd., 1993-98, U.S. Nat. Com. for Internat. Union for Pure and Applied Chemistry, 1996-2001. Editor: The Effects of Radiation on High Tech Polymers, 1989, Polymers in Microlithography, 1989, Irradiation of Polymer Materials, 1993, Microelectronics Technology: Polymers for Advanced Imaging and Packaging, 1995, Micro and Nano Patterning Polymers, 1998; patentee in field; assoc. editor Chemistry of Materials, 1996—; contbr. numerous articles to profl. jours. Recipient Soc. Women Engrs. Achievement award, 1993, Engring. Materials award ASM, 1996, Arents Pioneer medal Syracuse U., 2001. Fellow: AAAS; mem.: IEEE, Soc. Women Engrs., Am. Phys. Soc., Soc. for Photo-optical Engrs., Soc. Chem. Industry (Perkin medal 2001), Am. Chem. Soc. (mem.-at-large 1986—90, sec. 1991—92, polymer materials sci. and engring. divsn. 1991—, vice chair 1993, chair-elect 1994, chmn. 1995, pres.-elect 2002, pres. 2003, award in applied polymer sci. 1999), Nat. Acad. Engring. (elected mem.). Avocations: music, reading, needlepoint.

REICHS, KATHY JOAN, forensic anthropologist, educator, writer; BA in Anthropology, Am. U., Washington, DC, 1971; MA in Physical Anthropology, Northwestern U., Evanston, Ill., 1972, PhD in Physical Anthropology, 1975. DABFA Diplomate Am. Bd. Forensic Anthropology, 1986. Asst. prof. Northern Ill. U., 1974—78; instructor Stateville Correctional Facility, Joliet, Ill., 1975—78; asst. prof. Davidson Coll., Davidson, NC, 1981—83; lectr., dept. sociology and anthropology U. NC, Charlotte, 1978—81, 1983—87, asst. prof., dept. sociology and anthropology, 1987—88, assoc. prof., dept. sociology and anthropology, 1988—96, prof., dept. sociology and anthropology, 1996—. Vis. prof., Semester at Sea U. Pitts., 1987; vis. assoc. prof. Concordia U., 1988—89, McGill U., 1988—97; tchr. Symposium for med. and dental students, U. NC Sch. Medicine, Chapel Hill, NC, Symposium for residents in pathology, Laboratorie de Sciences Juciciaires Legales et de medecine legale, Montreal, Canada; instr. Field Course in the Recovery of Human Remains, FBI Acad., Quantico, Va., 1995—; working mem., affiliate Am. Bd. Forensic Anthropology, Inc., Armed Forces Inst. Pathology, Disaster Mortuary Operational Response Team, FBI Lab. Evidence Response, Fed. Emergency Mgmt. Agy., Joint POW/MIA Acctg. Command, RCMP Nat. Police Services Coun.; anthropologue judiciare Govt du Quebec, Ministere de la Securite publique, Laboratoire de Sciences Judiciaries et de Médecine Légale, 1988—; forensic anthropologist cons. Office of the Chief Med. Examiner, State NC, Chapel Hill, NC, 1985—, Mecklenburg County, NC, Medical Examiner's Office, 1985—; cons. osteological analysis Toulouse rsch. project on the skeletal remains of Thomas Acquinas, 1989—90, Remains of Jeam LeBar, Archdiocese Montreal, 1991; cons. Office of Relocation, NC Dept. Transportation, Charlotte, NC; forensic anthropologist Nat. Med. Sys., D-MORT Team, Region 4, 1994—; external cons. in forensic anthropology, casualty, and mortuary affairs ops. ctr. Ctrl. Identification Lab., Hawaii, 1997—99; Commission d'enquete sur les circonstances entourant la disparition et le deces de M. Louis-Georges Dupont (exhumation, analysis), Trois Rivieres/Montreal, 1996; Commission d'enquete Roberge, Govt. du Quebec (exhumation, analysis), Sept Isles/Montreal, 99; frequent expert witness in criminal trials; presenter. lectr. for various profl. associations, conferences, educational institutions, workshops, and literary festivals worldwide. Author: (Temperance Brennan Series) Déjà Dead, 1997 (NY Times Bestseller, Ellis award for Best First Novel, 1997), Death du Jour, 1999, Deadly Decisions, 2000, Fatal Voyage, 2001, Grave Secrets, 2002, Bare Bones, 2004, Monday Mourning, 2004, Cross Bones, 2005; contbr. articles to peer-reviewed publs.; contbr. (TV series) Anatomy of a Murder (CNN), 2005—, guest appearances Leeza, Today Show, Good Morning America, Montell, Investigative Reports, Court TV, Catherine Crier Live, Larry King Live, Discovery Channel, Learning Channel, A&E, WOR-AM-Joan Hamburg, NY Interactive, CBC and BBC (TV and Radio), ABC, TV and Radio programs in South Africa, Australia, New Zealand, Thailand, & Germany. Mem.: Am. Bd. Forensic Anthropology (bd. dir. 1986—93, v.p. 1989—93), Am. Acad. Forensic Sciences (bd. dir. 1996—2002, sec., physical anthropology sect. 1994—95, chair, physical anthropology sect. 1995—96, exec. com., bd. dir. 2000—), Phi Beta Delta. Achievements include traveling to Rwanda to testify at the UN Tribunal on Genocide in 1999; helping identify individuals from mass graves in Guatemala; helping with forensic work at Ground Zero in NYC in 2001; working with the Central Identification Laboratory in Hawaii to identify war dead from WW II; in Southeast Asia, examined the remains from the tomb of the Unknown Soldier.*

REICHS, KERRY E., lawyer; b. Bethesda, Md., Nov. 17, 1970; BA, Oberlin Coll., 1993; MA in Pub. Policy, Duke U., 2000, JD, 2000. Bar: DC, NC. Assoc. Arent Fox Kintner Plotkin & Kahn PLLC, Washington, Sonnenschein Nath & Rosenthal LLP, Washington. Office: Sonnenschein Nath & Rosenthal LLP Ste 600, E Tower 1301 K St NW Washington DC 20005 Office Phone: 202-408-9145. Office Fax: 202-408-6399. Business E-Mail: kreichs@sonnenschein.com.

REICHSLAN, MICHELE B., psychiatrist; b. Phila., Aug. 14, 1952; d. Marvin Leonard and Lettie Bella Bierenbaum; m. Robert Paul Reichslan, Oct. 19, 1977; children: David, Matthew, Jonathon. BA, Conn. Coll., New London, 1974; MD, U. Chgo. Med. Sch., 1978. Cert. Bd. Psychiatry and Neurology, 1990. Pvt. practice psychiatrist, Montclair, NJ, 1990—. Mem.: Am. Acad. Psychoanalysis and Psychotherapy, Am. Psychiatric Assn. Office: 20 Trinity Pl Montclair NJ 07043 Office Phone: 973-741-3887.

REID, DEMETRA ADAMS, insurance company executive; b. Chattanooga, May 13, 1968; d. Willie George Adams, I and Janice Martha Beard; 1 child, Kala Marie. A in pre-Nursing, St. Phillip's Coll., San Antonio, 1993; BSN registered nurse, U. of Tex. Health Sci. Ctr., San Antonio, 1994; MS in Health Adminstrn., Columbia So. U., Orange Beach, Ala., 2001. Cert. case mgr., CCM/TN, 2001. Dir. nursing Quality in Home Health Care, San Antonio, 1996—99; case mgr. NextCare Hosp., San Antonio, 1999—2000; case mgr., sr. health underwriter Blue Cross Blue Shield Tenn., 2000—03; dir. case mgmt. S.E. Bapt. Hosp., San Antonio, 2004—. Cons. Guidance Home Health, San Antonio, 1997—98, Bexar Necessities Home Health, San Antonio, 1997—98; dir., case mgmt. S.E. Bapt. Hosp., San Antonio, 2003—04; mgr. case mgmt. Northside Hosp., Atlanta, 2004—. Author: (novels) Circle With Three Sides, (book of poems) No Rhyme or Reason and No Particular Season. Adopt a family outreach programs mem. Happy Home Bapt. Ch., LaFayette, Ga., 2000—02, choreographer youth dance group. With USAF, 1987—91. Grantee WIN Winners In Nursing grantee, U. of Tex. Health Sci. Ctr., 1993; AMA grantee, 1994. Mem.: Ga. Hosp. Assn., Case Mgmt. Soc. Am., Sigma Theta Tau (life). Christian. Avocations: reading, music, writing. Home: 2186 Mainsail Dr Marietta GA 30062

REID, DOLORES B., retired social services administrator, consultant; b. Pickens, Miss. d. James Edward and Edna (Snow) Scarborough; m. Walter F. Reid; children: Thomas, Amye BS Sociology and Psychology, Loyola U., Chgo., 1954; MSW, Boston U., 1961; postgrad., U. Pa., 1979; PhD Pub. Adminstrn., Union Inst., Cin., 1985. LCSW, Md. Various social work positions, Chgo., St. Paul, N.H., 1954—60; social worker Mass. Soc. for Prevention of Cruelty to Children, Boston, 1961—62; asst. prof. psychiat. social work Hawaii State Hosp./U. Hawaii, Honolulu, 1963—66; psychiat. social worker Mental Health Clinic, Champaign, Ill., 1969—70; dep. dir. regional tng. Ill. Dept. Children and Family Svcs., 1967—71; asst. dir., dir. social svcs. Rock Island Neighborhood Health Ctr., Ill., 1971—73; dep. dir. program support svcs. Ill. Dept. Children and Family Svcs., Springfield, 1973—78; exec. dir. Montgomery County Children Svcs., Dayton, Ohio, 1975—85; various social work positions, 1985—89; chief assessment and monitoring programs Montgomery County, Rockville, Md., 1989—93, chief family preservation svcs., 1993—94; exec. cons. Met. Washington Coun. Govts., 1994—95; chief bur. children svcs. Dept. Human Svcs., Columbus, Ohio, 1995—98, program adminstr. Office Prevention and Protection, 1998—2000, dep. dir. divsn. children and families Phoenix, 2000—05; cons., lectr., trainer social svcs., 2005—06; ret., 2006. Contbr. articles to profl. jours.; presenter in field Mem. Acad. Cert. Social Workers, Child Welfare League Am., Black Adminstrs. in Child Welfare (bd. dirs., v.p., chair kinship care com.), Nat. Network for Social Work Mgrs. (cert. social work mgr.) Office Phone: 623-935-7048. Personal E-mail: dbreid120193@aol.com.

REID, DONNA JOYCE, small business owner; b. Springfield, Tenn., June 25, 1954; d. Leonard Earl Reid and Joyce (Robertson) Kirby; m. Kenneth Bruce Sadler, June 26, 1976 (div. Apr. 1980); m. John Christopher Moulton, Oct. 18, 1987 (div. Dec. 1992); m. Peter Leatherland, Apr. 3, 1993. Student, Austin Peay State U., Clarksville, Tenn., 1972-75. Show writer, producer WTVF-TV (CBS affiliate), Nashville, 1977-83, promotion producer, 1983-85, on-air promotion mgr., 1985-86; gen. mgr. Steadi-Film Corp., Nashville, 1986-90; co-owner Options Internat., Nashville, 1990—2003, Shanti's, Inc., Hermitage, 2003—. Big sister Buddies of Nashville, 1981-87. Named to Honorable Order of Ky. Cols. John Y. Brown, Gov., 1980; recipient Significant Svc. award ARC, 1982, Clara Barton Communications award, 1983. Mem. NAFE, Nat. Assn. TV Arts and Scis., Nat. Film Inst., Nat. Assn. Broadcasters, Internat. Platform Assn., Am. Soc. Prevention of Cruelty to Animals, Humane Soc. U.S. Methodist. Avocations: reading, outdoor sports, travel. Office: Shantis Inc 4715 Andrew Jackson Pkwy Hermitage TN 37076 Office Phone: 615-391-4144. Personal E-mail: donnaoptionspj@aol.com.

REID, FRANCES EVELYN KROLL, freelance/self-employed cinematographer, film director, communications executive; b. Oakland, Calif., Mar. 25, 1944; d. William Farnham and Marion Storm (Teller) Kroll. BA, U. Oreg., 1966. Tchr. secondary sch., Los Angeles, 1968-69; sound recordist Churchill Films, Los Angeles, 1971; freelance sound recordist Los Angeles, 1972-75; freelance dir., prodr., 1975—; freelance cinematographer Berkeley, Calif., 1978—; dir. Iris Films, Berkeley, 1977—; lectr. U. Calif. Grad. Sch. Journalism, 2005. Vol. Peace Corps, Malawi, Africa, 1969-70. Producer/dir. Long Night's Journey Into Day, 2000 (Grand Jury award Sundance 2000, Acad. award nominee 2001); dir. (film) In The Best Interests of the Children, 1977 (Blue Ribbon Am. Film Festival 1978), The Changer: A Record of the Times, 1991, The Faces of AIDS, 1992, Skin Deep, 1995, Talking About Race, 1994, Straight from the Heart, 1994 (Acad. award nominee 1995); cinematographer: (film) The Times of Harvey Milk, 1984 (Oscar 1985), Living with AIDS, 1986 (Student Acad. award 1987), Common Threads: Stories from the Quilt, 1989 (Oscar award 1990), Complaints of a Dutiful Daughter, 1994 (Acad. award nominee 1995). Mem. Film Arts Found., Assn. Ind. Video and Filmmakers, Acad. Motion Picture Arts and Scis. Office: Iris Films 2600 10th St Berkeley CA 94710-2522 Office Phone: 510-845-5414.

REID, GERALDINE WOLD (GERALDINE REID SKJERVOLD), artist; b. Apr. 11, 1944; d. Alden Elroy and Verna (Kocinski) Wold BA in Fine Art, Calif. State U., Sacramento, 1972, MFA, 1975; postgrad., Ind. U. - Purdue U. Instr. dental aux. edn. U. Minn., 1966-70, anthropol. rsch. asst., 1976-78; mng. editor Nat. Arts Guide, Chgo., 1978-80; freelance artist Chgo., 1981-94; pres. Chgo. Art Emerging Inc., 1983-85; graphic artist Reid Design & Illustration, Chgo., 1981-94; dir. show coordination Circle Fine Art, Chgo., 1981. Instr. comm. art and design Alexandria Tech. Coll., Minn., 1994—; seminar lectr., 1977, 86; lectr., art and math. Dept. Math. U. Ill., 1987—88; guest lectr. women's art history AAUW, Alexandria, 1997; lectr. on drawing approaches, 2005. One-woman shows include Artists' Coop. Gallery, Santa Fe, 1976, Artlink, Ft. Wayne, Ind., 1979, 84—, D.E.O. Fine Arts, Inc., Chgo., 1982-83, Union League Gallery, Chgo., 1989, Brodsky Gallery, 1993, Second Floor Gallery, Cen. Square, Glenwood, Minn., 1999, Ann Bickle Heritage House, Glenwood, 2000, Pope County Mus., Glenwood, 2004, Pope Art, Ter. Mill, Minn., 2005; group exhbns. include Crocker Art Mus., Sacramento, 1975, Ft. Wayne Mus. Art, 1978, Artists Guild Chgo., 1982, Charles A. Wustum Mus., Racine, Wis., 1983, Limelight, Chgo., 1986, 87, 88, Neville-Sargent Gallery, 1986, 87, Beacon Street Hull House Gallery, 1988, McDonalds Corp., Chgo., 1988, Prairie Ave. Gallery, Chgo., 1990, Peace Mus., Chgo., 1990, Hyde Park Art Ctr., Chgo., 1990, Lettuce Entertain You Enterprises, Inc., 1990, Olive Tree Gallery, Daley Coll., Chgo., 1991, Crown Ctr. Gallery, Loyola U., Chgo., 1992, Agora Syndicate, Inc., 1992, Kieffer-Nolde/TIC, 1992, Flora '92, 1992, Chgo. Bot. Garden, 1992, Open Spectrum, David Adler Cultural Ctr., 1994, August House Studio, Chgo., 1994—, Upper West Gallery, Alexandria Tech. Coll., Minn., 1995, Plains Art Mus., Fargo, N.D., 1997, Regional Art Exhibit, New York Mills, Minn., 1997, Runestone Mus., Alexandria, 1997-98, Art on the Plains, 3d Ann. Regional Exhbn., Plains Art Mus., Fargo, 31st Ann. Fergus Falls Cmty. Coll. Invitational Art Show, Fergus Falls, Minn., 2002, 03, Pope County Artists Exhibit, Lake Region Arts Coun. Gallery, Fergus Falls, Minn., 2002, Prairie Renaissance Cultural Alliance Gallery, Morris, Minn., 2002-03, Celebration of Lake Region Arts Coun., Fergus Falls, 2002-2003, Fergus Falls C.C. Ann. Invitational, 2003, New York Mills (Minn.) Ann. Regional Exhbn., 2003, Minn. State Cmty. & Tech. Coll., Fergus Falls, 2004, Minn. State Colls. and Univs., 2005-06, Wind and Water exhibit, Lakes Region Arts Coun. Gallery, Fergus Falls, Minn., 2006, Three Havens Art Gallery, Alexandria, Minn., 2006; contbr. artwork to 2 ann. 1994 calendars; artwork selected for inclusion in Alex Tech Coll. greeting card suite, 2005. Mem. New York Mills Cultural Ctr., Mpls. Art Inst., Am. Inst. Graphic Arts, Mpls. Inst. Arts, Glacial Ridge Artists. Business E-Mail: gerrir@alextech.edu.

REID, HELEN VERONICA, dean; b. Reading, Eng., Sept. 25, 1956; d. Alan A. and Teresa H. (Thatcher) Ware; m. Gary B. Reid, May 29, 1976; children: Robert, Jennifer, Kristen. BA in Biology, U. Tex., 1976; BSN, U. Tex., Arlington, 1978; MSN, Tex. Women's U., 1983; EdD, U. North Tex., 2000. CCRN, 1980, cert. CPR instr. Asst. nurse coord., staff nurse, float pool nurse Parkland Meml. Hosp., Dallas, 1979—83, float pool nurse, 1987—93; instr. Trinity Valley C.C., Kaufman, Tex., 1983—86, leader freshman team, 1986—90, dean health occupations, 1990—. Mem.: Tex. Assn. Deans and Dirs. for Profl. Nursing Programs (treas. 2005—), Tex. C.C. Tchrs. Assn., Nat. Orgn. ADN (pub. rels. dir. 1998—2002), Tex. Orgn. for ADN (sec. 1988—92, nominating com. chair 1995—96, pres.-elect 2002—03, pres. 2003—05, past pres. 2005—06), Tex. Assn. Vocat. Nurse Educators, Phi Kappa Phi, Sigma Theta Tau. Office Phone: 972-932-4309. Business E-Mail: reid@tvcc.edu.

REID, INEZ SMITH, lawyer, educator, judge; b. New Orleans, Apr. 7, 1937; d. Sidney Randall Dickerson and Beatrice Virginia (Bundy) Smith. BA, Tufts U., 1959; LLB, Yale U., 1962; MA, UCLA, 1963; PhD, Columbia U., 1968; LLM in Jud. Process, U. Va., 2004. Bar: Calif. 1963, N.Y. 1972, D.C. 1980. Assoc. prof. Barnard Coll. Columbia U., N.Y.C., 1972-76; gen. counsel youth divsn. State of N.Y., 1976-77; dep. gen. counsel HEW, Washington, 1977-79; inspector gen. EPA, Washington, 1979-81; chief legis. and opinions, dep. corp. counsel Office of Corp. Counsel, Washington, 1981-83; corp. counsel D.C., 1983-85; counsel Laxalt, Washington, Perito & Dubuc, Washington, 1986-90, ptnr., 1990-91; counsel Graham & James, 1991-93, Lewis, White & Clay, P.C., 1994-95; assoc. judge D.C. Ct. Appeals, 1995—. William J. Maier, Jr. vis. prof. law W.Va. U. Coll. Law, Morgantown, 1985-86. Contbr. articles to profl. jours. and publs. Trustee emeritus Lancaster Sem., Pa., 2002—; bd. dirs. Homeland Ministries bd. United Ch. of Christ, N.Y.C., 1978—83, vice chmn., 1981—83; chmn. bd. govs. Antioch Law Sch., Washington, 1979—81; chmn. bd. trustees Antioch U., Yellow Springs, Ohio, 1981—82; trustee Tufts U., Medford, Mass., 1988—98, trustee emeritus, 1999—; trustee Lancaster (Pa.) Sem., 1988—2001; bd. govs. D.C. Sch. Law, 1990—96, chmn., 1991—95. Recipient Emily Gregory award Barnard Coll., 1976, Arthur Morgan award Antioch U., 1982, Service award United Ch. of Christ, 1983, Disting. Service (Profl. Life) award Tufts U. Alumni Assn., 1988. Office: DC Ct Appeals 500 Indiana Ave NW Fl 6 Washington DC 20001-2138

REID, IVONNE FIGUEROA, language educator; b. Santiago, Chile, May 25, 1938; d. Hector Francisco Figueroa and Uberlinda Eulojia Cristi; m. Roderic Eugene Reid, June 13, 1963; children: David Alan, Nancy Gail. B in English, U. Chile, 1960; MS in Edn., U. So. Calif., 1963, PhD in Edn., 1972. Rschr. Inst. Statistical Rsch. U. Chile, 1959—63; prof. statistics Family Edn. Inst. Cath. U., Santiago, Chile, 1960—61; rsch. assoc. in evaluation U. S.C. Art in Elem. Edn. Rsch. Project, 1975—80; intermediate sch. tchr. Montebello Unified Sch. Dist., Bell Gardens, 1981—89, h.s. Spanish tchr., 1989—99, literacy facilitator, 1999—2002, cons., 2002—05; vol. cons., 2005—. Presenter Calif. Edn. Rsch. Assn., 1972, 77, 78, Calf. Assn. of Bilingual Edn., 1997—99, 2003. Named High Sch. Tchr. of the Yr., Calif. Bilingual Edn. Assn., Montebello Chapt., 1997; Fulbright scholarship, Dept. State, U. So. Calif., 1961—62. Mem.: Montebello Teachers Assn., Calif. Teachers Assn., Nat. Edn. Assn., Calif. Assn. Bilingual Edn., Am. Ednl. Rsch. Assn. Avocations: travel, music, art, reading. Home: 11102 Orange Dr Whittier CA 90606 Personal E-mail: ivonnereid@earthlink.net.

REID, JACQUELINE, lighting designer; b. Cin., Feb. 13, 1975; d. Gerald and Dorothy Reid. BA, Tufts U., Medford, Mass., 1997; MFA, Northwestern U., Evanston, Ill., 2003. Cert. union lighting designer United Scenic Artists, 2006. Ho. technician Boston Coll., Chestnut Hill, Mass., 1997—2000; tech. dir. Giordano Jazz Dance Chgo., Evanston, Ill., 2003—05; assoc. Luxious Lighting, Inc., L.A., 2004—; tech. dir. Jazz Dance World Congress, Chicago, Ill., 2005—05; lighting designer The Nat. H.S. Inst., Evanston, Ill., 2004—05; adj. lectr. Northwestern U., Evanston, 2003—04. Lighting designer (play) Cradle of Man, The Oresteia, Rembrandt's Gift, Trying, Guinea Pig Solo. Mem.: United Scenic Artists. Office: Luxious Lighting 8117 Manchester Ave #621 Playa Del Rey CA 90293 Office Phone: 773-562-3906. E-mail: jacqueline@jacquelinereid.com.

REID, JOAN EVANGELINE, lawyer, stockbroker; b. Mich., Apr. 22, 1932; d. August W. and Evangeline R. (Brozeau) Rogers; m. Belmont M. Reid. AA in Bus., San Jose State U., 1951; JD, McGeorge Sch. Law, 1989. Bar: Nev.; lic. realtor, life, disability and annuity ins. Officer, dir. Lifetime Fin. Planning Corp., San Jose, Calif., 1967-77, Lifetime Realty Corp., San Jose, 1967-77; co-founder, officer, dir. Belmont Reid & Co., Inc., San Jose, 1960-77; officer, corp. counsel, dir. JOBEL Fin. Inc., Carson City, Nev., 1980—. Past sec., treas. Nev. Fedn. Rep. Women; charter pres. Santa Clara Valley Rep. Women Federated. Paul Harris fellow Rotary. Mem. First Jud. Dist. Bar Assn., State Bar Nev., No. Nev. Women Lawyers Assn., Carson City C. of C., Soroptomist Carson City (past pres., sec.), Carson City Rep. Women's Club (past v.p.).

REID, JODI BELINDA AUSTIN, music educator; m. Michael Sean Reid, Dec. 11, 1999. MusB in Music Edn. cum laude, Va. Commonwealth U., Richmond, 2002. Lic. tchr. isntrumental music K-12 Va. Pvt. instr. violin, Richmond, 2002—; dir. orch. Lloyd C. Bird H.S., Chesterfield, Va., 2003—; dir. orch./guitar Meadowbrook H.S., Richmond, 2003—. Host Ctrl. Regional Orch., Chesterfield, 2006. Recipient scholarship, Guitar Accessories Merchants Assn., 2005; grantee, Domer Family Found., 2005. Mem.: NEA, Internat. Guitar Tchrs. Registry, Va. Band & Orch. Dirs. Assn. (mem. selection com. 2005), Am. String Tchrs. Assn. Achievements include guiding Lloyd C. Bird Orch. to first superior rating in Virginia Band and Orchestra Director's Association District III Festival in nine years. Office: Meadowbrook HS 4901 Cogbill Rd Richmond VA 23234

REID, JUDITH SOLOMON, elementary school educator; b. NYC, Apr. 6, 1951; d. Edwin Lawrence Solomon and Leona Abrams; m. G. Douglas Reid, June 12, 1979; children: Logan, Kelsey. BA with honors, Ohio State U., Columbus, 1973; MEd with honors, Ohio U., Athens, 1977. Tchr. Deer Valley Sch. Dist., Phoenix, 1977—92; reading, literacy specialist Paradise Valley Sch. Dist., Scottsdale, 1992—. Mem. curriculum leadership team Paradise Valley Sch. Dist., 2004—; mem. tchr. tng. team in problem solving, South Africa, 2006. Grantee, Wells Fargo, Phoenix, 2006. Mem.: Creative Problem Solving Inst (coun. mem. 2004—), Paradise Valley Reading Assn., Internat. Reading Assn., Phi Beta Kappa. Democrat. Avocations: hiking, yoga, meditation, gardening, puzzles. Home: 5805 E Grandview Rd Scottsdale AZ 85254 Office Phone: 602-493-6160.

REID, KATHARINE LEE, museum director; d. Sherman E. and Ruth Lee; m. Bryan S. Reid. BA magna cum laude, Vassar Coll.; postgrad., Sorbonne, Paris, 1963, Instiut d'Art et Archaeologie, 1963; MFA, Harvard U., 1966. Mem. curatorial staff Toledo Mus. Art, David and Alfred Smart Mus., U. Chgo., Ackland Art Mus., U. NC, Chapel Hill; asst. dir. Art Inst. Chgo., 1982—86, dep. dir., 1986—91; dir. Va. Mus. Fine Arts, 1991—2000, Cleve. Mus. Art, 2000—05. Bd. dirs. Van Gogh Mus., Amsterdam, Netherlands, Nat. Conf. Cmty. and Justice, Am. Fedn. Arts; chmn. vis. com. Frances Lehman Loeb Art Ctr., Vassar Coll., Poughkeepsie, NY. Fulbright scholar, 1963. Mem.: Am. Assn. Mus. (bd. dirs., former mem. accreditation commn.), Am. Assn. Mus. Dirs. (pres. 2000—01, trustee).

REID, KATHERINE LEE, retired museum director, curator; BA magna cum laude, Vassar Coll; MFA, Harvard U., 1966; studied at, Instiut d'Art et Archaeologie, Sorbonne, Paris. Curator Toledo Mus Art, Ohio, David and Alfred Smart Mus., U. Chgo., Ackland Art Mus., U. NC, Chapel Hill; asst. dir. Art Inst. Chgo., 1982—86, dep. dir., 1986—91; dir. Va. Mus. Fine Arts, 1991—2000, Cleve. Mus. Art, 2000—05. Chair vis. com. Frances Lehman Loeb Art Ctr., Vassar Coll. Bd. mem. Van Gogh Mus., Amsterdam, Nat. Conf. Cmty. and Justice. Mem.: Am. Fedn. of Arts, Am. Assn. Mus., Am. Assn. Mus. Dirs. (pres. 2000—01, past mem. bd. trustees).*

REID, KATHERINE LOUISE, artist, educator, writer; b. Port Arthur, Tex., Mar. 25, 1941; d. Clifton Commodore and Helen Ross (Moore) Reid. BA, Baylor U., 1963; postgrad. in design and illustration, Kans. City Art Inst., 1964; MEd, U. Houston, 1973; cert. supervision, U. Houston-Clear Lake City, 1980; postgrad., San Jacinto Coll., 1982. Litho reprodn. artist Hallmark Cards, Kansas City, Mo., 1963-64; tchr. art high sch. Pasadena (Tex.) Ind. Sch. Dist., 1964-77, supr. art, gifted and talented and photography, 1977-85, supr. art and photography InterAct, 1985-90, instrnl. specialist, 1990-2000, photography and art, 1990-93, instrnl. specialist in art and spl. programs, 1993-96, rsch. planning, data disaggregation, 1996-2000; internet tchr. recruiter, 2001—02; mural artist Old Car Barn, Edna, Tex., 2000—. 4 MAT learning styles trainer DuPont Leadership Devel. Process Trainer, Selective Rsch., Inst., tchr. perceiver specialist, performance quality sys. trainer, coop. learning trainer, outcome based edn. trainer, integrated unit devel. and authentic assessment trainer Greater Gulf Coast Adminstr. Assessment Project, Assessor, 1990-2000; head crafts, asst. dir., dir. summer, winter discovery program-ski camp Cheley Colo. Camps, Denver, Estes Park, 1967-75; awards com. John Austin Cheley Found., 1990-92; staff artist, media workshop Tex. Edn. Agy., Austin, 1961; art enrichment tchr. Port Arthur Ind. Sch. Dist. (Tex.), 1961; head crafts Camp Waluta, Silsbee, Tex., 1960; mem. Tex. Edn. Agy., Art Leadership Inst., 1989-90, Tracking Rsch. Com., 1991, Core Strategic Planning Team, 1992-2000, Outcome Based Edn. Dist. Planning Com., 1991-92, Quality Sys. Improvement Team, 1991-92, Outcome Based Edn. Com. Exit Outcomes, 1991; Region IV data disk trainer, 1998-2000, target teach coord., 1993-2000, multiple intelligence trainer, 1997-2000, data disaggregation trainer, 1997-2000, supt.'s rsch. com., 1999. Author: Through Their Eyes, 1989. Mem. Friends of Fine Arts-Baylor U., Waco, Tex., 1981—, Scholastic Art awards Regional Bd., Houston, 1978-84; bd. dirs. Houston Coun. Student Art Awards, Inc., 1984-90, Pasadena Ind. Sch. Dist. Edn. Found., 2005—; mem. Baylor U. Endowed Scholarship Soc., Baylor U. Old Main Scholarship Soc. Named Outstanding Secondary Educator of Am., 1975, Tex. Art Educator of Yr., 1985, Outstanding Vol., City of Pasadena, 2004. Mem. ASCD, Tex. ASCD, Tex. Art Edn. Assn. (rep. editor newsletter 1982-85, chmn. supervision divsn. 1982-83, v.p. membership 1978-80, chmn. pub. info. com., regional chmn. youth art month 1980-82; regional chmn. membership com. 1976-78, pres. elect 1986, sec. 1991-93, Disting. Fellows award 2004), Tex. Alliance for Arts Edn. (bd. vice chmn. 1984-86, treas. 1988-90), Nat. Art Edn. Assn. (conv. com. 1977, 85), Tex. Assn. Sch. Adminstrs., Houston Art Edn. Assn. (sec. 1969), Tex. Ret. Tchrs. Assn. (Dist. IV historian 2001-03), Pasadena Area Ret. Sch. Employees (parliamentarian 2002-04), Delta Kappa Gamma (2d v.p. 1984-86, pres. 2002-2004, state leadership devel. for chpt. pres. com., 2003-2005, state banner com., 2004, State Leadership Seminar 2005, area III coord. 2005—, Internat. Golden Gift Leadership Seminar 2006). Baptist. Achievements include patents for pet car seat. Home: 106 Ravenhead Dr Houston TX 77034-1520 Personal E-mail: klreid@academicplanet.com.

REID, MARGARET ELIZABETH, elementary school educator, secondary school educator; b. Tampa, Fla., Feb. 8, 1934; d. James Byron and Zella Mae (Thompson) Bruce; m. Arthur M. Reid Jr., Dec. 28, 1955 (div. Dec. 1982); children: Laura Jean, Nancy Ann. BS in Edn., SUNY, Potsdam, 1956; postgrad., SUNY, Stony Brook, 1975—78; MS in Spl. Edn., L.I. U., 1979, postgrad., 1989—. Cert. spl. edn. tchr., N.Y. Tchr. Harborfields Sch. Dist., Greenlawn, NY, 1956—61; tchr. Project Able Three Village Sch. Dist., Stony Brook, 1971—72; substitute tchr. Smithtown Sch. Dist., NY, 1972—75, substitute tchr. spl. edn., 1972—75; substitute tchr. Shoreham Sch. Dist., NY, 1974—76, Mt. Sinai Sch. Dist., NY, 1974—79, Middle Island Sch. Dist, NY, 1974—79; tchr. resource rm. Hempstead Sch. Dist., NY, 1979—96. Tchr. rep. spl. edn. com. Hempstead Sch. Dist., 1985—. Mem. N.Y. Pub. Interest Rsch. Group, N.Y.C. 1987—, Citizens Campaign for the Environment, 1988—, Arthur Murray Sch. Dance (V.I.P. Hon. Student award 2002). NSF grantee Stevens Inst. Tech., 1959. Mem. N.Y. Assn. for Learning Disabled, Hempstead Classroom Tchrs. Assn., Coun. for Exceptional Children, N.Y. Branch Orton Dyslexia Soc., Kappa Delta Pi Republican. Methodist. Avocations: music, art, drama. Home: 64 Walter Ave Hauppauge NY 11788-3425

REID, MARILYN JOANNE, state legislator, lawyer; b. Chgo., Aug. 14, 1941; d. Kermit and Newell Azile (Hahn) N.; m. M. David Reid, Nov. 26, 1966 (div. Mar. 1983); children: David, Nelson. Student, Miami U., Oxford, Ohio, 1959-61; BA, U. Ill, 1963; JD, Ohio No. U., 1966. Bar: Ohio 1966, Ark. 1967, U.S. Dist. Ct. 1967. Trust adminstr. First Nat. Bank, Dayton, Ohio, 1966-67; assoc. Sloan & Ragsdale, Little Rock, 1967-69; ptnr. Reid and Reid, Dayton, 1969-76, Reid & Assocs., Dayton, 1975—; mem. Ohio Ho. of Reps., 1993-98. Mem. health ins. and HMO's com., chmn. ins. com., vets. com., pub. utilities com. Mem. Ohio adv. bd. U.S. Commn. Civil Rights; trustee Friends Libr. Beavercreek, Ohio; bd. dirs. Beavercreek YMCA, 1985—88; pres. Greene County Commn., 2005; chair Miami Valley Regional Planning Commn.; bd. mem. County Commn. of Ohio; chmn., treas. various polit. campaigns, 1975—; chmn. Greene County Rep. Party; active Mt. Zion United Ch. of Christ. Mem. ABA, Ohio Bar Assn., Greene County Bar Assn., Beavercreek C. of C. (pres. 1986-87), Dayton Panhellenic Assn. (pres. 1982), Altrusa (v.p. Greene County 1978-79, pres. 1979-80), Lions (pres. Beavercreek 1975), Greene County Rep. Party (chmn.), Rotary, Kappa Beta Pi, Gamma Phi Beta (v.p. 1974-75). Mem. Ch. Christ. Avocations: tennis, skiing, boating, bridge. Office: Reid & Assocs 3866 Indian Ripple Rd Dayton OH 45440-3448

REID, MARY WALLACE, retired secondary school educator; b. Charlotte, N.C., Oct. 21, 1922; d. Isaac and Mamie Maude (Torrence) Wallace; m. James Samuel Reid, Feb. 13, 1946; 1 child, Virginia Anne. BA, Johnson C. Smith U., 1945; MEd, Temple U., 1970, Secondary Adminstrn. cert., 1982, EdD, 1983. Cert. English, secondary adminstr., French, reading, lang. arts tchr., Pa. Tchr. English, lang, arts, reading Sch. Dist. Phila.; ret., 1988. Title I reading coord., 1976-82; mem. pupil progress com.; past assn. student govt., mem. PFT Bldg. com. Mem. Internat. Reading Assn., Nat. Coun. Tchrs. of English. Home: 1704 Stenton Ave Philadelphia PA 19141-1433

REID, ORIEN, former medical association administrator; b. Oct. 1945; BA, Clark Coll., Atlanta. MSW. Anchor WCAU-TV, Phila., 1979—98; chmn., bd. dirs. Alzheimer's Assn.'s Nat. Bd. Dirs., 1999—2002. Former mem. bd. govs. Nat. Acad. Television Arts and Scis.; former pres. Phila. Consumer Coun. Recipient Best Investigative Reporting, Phila. Press Assn., Excellence in Journalism award, Inst. Food Technologists.

REID, PAMELA JONES, humanities educator; b. Brookhaven, Miss., Jan. 22, 1950; d. Thomas W. and Mary Hutchins Jones; m. Truman Terry Reid, July 22, 1972; children: Emily R. Mulhollen, Carrie R. Jones, Anna. BA, Miss. Coll., Clinton, 1972; MS, U. So. Miss., Hattiesburg, 1976. Instr. Copiah-Lincoln C.C., Wesson, Miss., 1989—. Pres. Jr. Aux. of Brookhaven, 1986. Named Humanities Instr. of the Yr., Miss. Humanities Coun., 1998, Acad. Instr. of Yr., Co-hin Found., 2005. Mem.: Copiah-Lincoln Edn. Assn., Two-Yr. Coll. Assn. of Miss., Delta Kappa Gamma. Presbyterian. Office: Copiah-Lincoln Community College Fine Arts Divsn PO Box 457 Wesson MS 39191-0457

REID, ROSEMARY ANNE, insurance agent; b. Portland, Maine, June 15, 1951; d. Kenneth Bruce and Mary (Hollywood) R.; m. Ronald E. Walls, May 7, 1977 (div. Mar. 1986); children: Rachel A., Tate A. BS in Edn., U. South Maine, Portland, 1973. V.p. ins. Gruntal and Co., Inc., Portland, 1987-91; pvt. practice Portland, 1973—. Mem. Cape Elizabeth Town Coun., 1990, 95-99; mem. Cape Elizabeth Sch. Bd., 1991-94, fin. chair, 1992-93. Recipient 10 Yrs. Nat. Quality, 10 Yrs. Nat. Sale Achievement award, 1979-89, Nat. Assn. of Life Underwriters, 1974—, Am. Hometown Leadership award WalMart, 1998. Mem. Million Dollar Round Table (life and qualifying mem., Top of Table 1984, 86), South Maine Assn. Life Underwriters (bd. dirs. 1985-91, officer 1987-91, pres. 1989-90, regional v.p., pub. svc. chair, others), Life Underwriter Tng. Coun. (chair 1986-87), Maine Assn. Life Underwriters (bd. dirs. 1988-92, v.p. 1991-92, pres. elect 1992). Roman Catholic. Avocations: skiing, swimming, biking. Office: PO Box 927 Portland ME 04104-0927

REID, SHARON LEA, educational facilitator; b. Wheeler, Tex., Apr. 24, 1949; d. George S. and Arvazine (Deering) Robinson; m. Thomas Michael Reid, July 9, 1989. BS, McMurry Coll., 1970; MEd, Tarleton State U., 1979. Cert. tchr., edn. adminstr., supr., Tex. Tchr. Fleming Elem. Sch., San Antonio, 1971-72, Peebles Elem. Sch., Killeen, Tex., 1972-84, Sugar Loaf Elem. Sch., Killeen, 1984-85, facilitator, 1985-98, campus instructional specialist, 1998-99, Duncan Elem. Sch., Fort Hood, Tex., 1999—2004; emotional intelligence trainer Killeen ISD, 1999—2003; ret., 2004. Trainer/dist. Marilyn Burns Problem Solving, Killeen, 1982-85, trainer/campus 4 MAT Lesson Design/Excel, Inc., Killeen, 1994-2000. Mem. Heights Concert Band, Harker Heights, Tex. Recipient music scholarship McMurry Coll., Abilene, Tex., 1968. Mem. ASCD, Nat. Read Across Am. Com., Tex. Elem. Prins. and Suprs. Assn., Tex. State Tchrs. Assn., Internat. Reading Assn., Tex. State Reading Assn., Bell County Reading Assn., Phi Delta Kappa. Avocations: instrumental music, bowling, sewing, cross-stitch. Office: Duncan Elem Sch 52400 Muskogee Dr Fort Hood TX 76544-1099

REID, SUE TITUS, law educator; b. Bryan, Tex., Nov. 13, 1939; d. Andrew Jackson Jr. and Lorraine (Wylie) Titus. BS with honors, Tex. Woman's U., 1960; MA, U. Mo., 1962, PhD, 1965; JD, U. Iowa, 1972. Bar: Iowa 1972, U.S. Ct. Appeals (D.C. Cir.) 1978, U.S. Supreme Ct. 1978. From instr. to assoc. prof. sociology Cornell Coll., Mt. Vernon, Iowa, 1963-72; assoc. prof., chmn. dept. sociology Coe Coll., Cedar Rapids, Iowa, 1972-74; assoc. prof. law. U. Wash., Seattle, 1974-76; exec. assoc. Am. Sociol. Assn., Washington, 1976-77; prof. law U. Tulsa, 1978-88; dean, prof. Sch. Criminology, Fla. State U., Tallahassee, 1988-90; prof. pub. adminstrn. and policy Fla. State U., 1990—. Acting chmn. dept. sociology Cornell Coll., 1965-66; vis. assoc. prof. sociology U. Nebr., Lincoln, 1970; vis. disting. prof. law and sociology U. Tulsa, 1977-78, assoc. dean 1979-81; vis. prof. law U. San Diego, 1981-82; mem. People-to-People Crime Prevention Del. to People's Republic of China, 1982; George Beto Vis. Disting. Prof. criminal justice Sam Houston U., Huntsville, Tex., 1984-85; lecture/study tour of Criminal Justice systems of 10 European countries, 1985; cons. Evaluation Policy Rsch. Assocs., Inc., Milw., 1976-77, Nat. Inst. Corrections, Idaho Dept. Corrections, 1984, Am. Correctional Inst., Price-Waterhouse. Author (with others): Bibliographies on Role Methodology and Propositions Volume D - Studies in the Role of the Public School Teacher, 1962, The Correctional System: An Introduction, 1981, Crime and Criminology, 11th edit., 2006; author: Criminal Law, 6th edit., 2004, Criminal Justice, 7th edit., 2006; editor (with David Lyon): Population Crisis: An Interdisciplinary Perspective, 1972; contbr. articles to profl. jours. Recipient Disting. Alumni award Tex. Woman's U., 1979; named One of Okla. Young Leaders of 80's Oklahoma Monthly, 1980. Mem. ABA, Am. Soc. Criminology, Acad. Criminal Justice Scis., Soc. Criminal Jus. Assn. Avocations: walking, reading, cooking, skiing. Office: Fla State Univ Dept Pub Adminstrn Tallahassee FL 32306 Personal E-mail: suetreid@adelphia.net.

REID, SUSAN G., music educator; b. Balt., Jan. 29, 1969; d. George Palmer and Patricia Ann Callender; m. Scott Reid, Dec. 7, 1996; children: Jordan Scott, Michaela Noel. AA in Music, Harford C.C., Bel Air, Md., 1990; EdB, Millersville U., Pa., 1992; MS in Leadership in Tchg., Coll. of Notre Dame, Balt., 2003. Cert. tchr. Md. Dept. of Edn., 2004. Music tchr. Harford County Pub. Schs., Bel Air, Md., 2000—. Bd. dirs. Constant Friendship Home Owners Assn., Abingdon, Md., 2005—06. Named Tchr. of the Yr., Harford County Boy's and Girl's Club. Mem.: MODA, MCEA. Office: Harford County Public Schools 401 Lewis Ln Havre De Grace MD 21078 Office Phone: 410-939-6608.

REID, SUSAN L., conductor; b. Charlottesville, Va., Apr. 4, 1958; d. L. Leon and Jane S. Reid, Roseann B. Reid. BM, Westminster Choir Coll., 1980; MS, Okla. State U., 1987; MMus, U. Surrey, Guildford, Eng., 1990; DMA, Ariz. State U., 1995; Cert., Royal Coll. of Church Music, Croydon, Eng., 1980. Tchg. asst. U. Surrey, Guildford, England, 1989—90, Ariz. State U., Tempe, 1990—94; dir. of music First United Meth. Ch., Edwardsville, Ill., 1980—83, First Christian Ch., Stillwater, Okla., 1983—89; faculty assoc. in music Ariz. State U., Tempe, 1994—95; dir. of choral activities S.D. Sch. of Mines and Tech., Rapid City, SD, 1995—2000, James Madison U., Harrisonburg, Va., 2000—. Prin., owner Integrated Conducting Inc. Bd. dirs., U.S. corr. Internat. Fedn. Choral Music.

REID, TARA, actress; b. Wyckoff, NJ, Nov. 8, 1975; Owner prodn. co. Hi Happy Films. Actor: (TV series) Child's Play, 1982, Saved by the Bell: The New Class, 1994; (TV films) What We Did That Night, 1999; (films) A Return to Salem's Lot, 1987, The Big Lebowski, 1998, Girl, 1998, I Woke Up Early the Day I Died, 1998, Urban Legend, 1998, Cruel Intentions, 1999, Around the Fire, 1999, American Pie, 1999, Body Shots, 1999, Dr. T and theWomen, 2000, Just Visiting, 2001, Josie and the Pussycats, 2001, American Pie 2, 2001, Van Wilder, 2002, Devil's Pond, 2003, My Boss's Daughter, 2003, Knots, 2004, Alone in the Dark, 2005; TV appearances include: California Dreams, 1996; G vs. E, 2000; Scrubs, 2003—05; host Taradise, E! TV, 2005.

REIDER, SUZIE, Internet company executive, marketing professional; With Ziff-Davis Pub., 1988—2002; sr. v.p. sales and mktg. CNET, 2002—06, gen. mgr. entertainment, 2006; chief mktg. officer YouTube Inc., 2006—. Office: YouTube Inc 71 E Third Ave San Mateo CA 94401*

REID JENKINS, DEBRA L., artist; b. Grand Rapids, Mich., Mar. 24, 1955; d. Russell Eugene and Peggy Ann Reid; m. Garth Edmund Jenkins, Oct. 14, 1978. Student, Kendall Sch. Design, Grand Rapids, 1973-75, Aquinas Coll., 1978-90. Hand decorator Heckman Furniture, Grand Rapids, 1975-80, Widdicomb Furniture, Grand Rapids, 1978-79, LaBarge Mirrors, Holland, Mich., 1980-89; fine artist, illustrator Debra Reid Jenkins Studio, Grand Rapids, 1989-97, Lowell, Mich., 1997—. Illustrator: (books) I Wanted to Know All About God, 1993, I See the Moon, 1997, My Freedom Trip, 1998, Here is Christmas, 2000, Glory, 2001, (mags.) Babybug, 1998, Ladybug, 2001, 2002, 2003. Recipient Emerging Artist award Am. Artist Mag., 1995. Mem. Pastel Soc. Am. (signature mem.), Soc. Gilders, Am. Soc. Portrait Artists, Soc. Children's Book Writers and Illustrators. Avocations: Feldenkrais tai chi, religious philosophy, dog training, kayaking, canoeing. Home and Studio: Debra Reid Jenkins Studio 14200 Thompson Dr Lowell MI 49331 Office Phone: 616-897-7680.

REIDLING, VALERIE ANN, secondary school educator; b. Evansville, Ind., Oct. 24, 1964; d. John Lewis and Rebecca (McAlister) Aulvin; m. David Lowell Reidling, Dec. 21, 1991; children: Coleman, Audrey. BS in Mktg., David Lipscomb U., 1986; MEd in English Edn., Vanderbilt U., 1988. English tchr. Highland Park H.S., Dallas, 1991-98, Highland Park Middle Sch., Dallas, 1998—2002, Plano (Tex.) West Sr. H.S., 2002—. Mem. Nat. Coun. Tchrs. English, PEO Sisterhood. Democrat. Mem. Ch. of Christ. Avocations: aerobics, reading, swimming, tennis. Home: 2005 Ports O'Call Dr Plano TX 75075 Business E-Mail: vreidli@pisd.edu.

REIDY, CAROLYN KROLL, publisher; b. Washington, May 2, 1949; d. Henry August and Mildred Josephine (Mencke) Kroll; m. Stephen Kroll Reidy, Dec. 28, 1974. BA, Middlebury Coll., 1971; MA, Ind. U., 1974, PhD, 1982. Various positions to mgr. subs. rights Random House, Inc., NYC, 1975-83, assoc. pub., 1987-88; dir. subs. rights William Morrow & Co., NYC, 1983-85; v.p., assoc. pub. Vintage Books, NYC, 1985-87, pub., 1987-88, Anchor Books, Doubleday & Co., NYC, 1988; pres., pub. Avon Books, NYC, 1988-92; pres., pub. trade divsn. Simon & Schuster, NYC, 1992—2001, pres. adult publ. divsn., 2001—. Bd. dirs. NAMES Project, 1994—98, Literacy Partners, Inc., 2000—, Nat. Book Found., 2001—. Mem.: NY Women in Comm. (recipient Matrix award 2003), Pubs. Lunch Club. Office: Simon & Schuster 1230 Avenue Of The Americas New York NY 10020-1586 Business E-Mail: carolyn.reidy@simonandschuster.com.

REIDY, FRANCES RYAN, language educator, editor, writer; b. St. Louis, Aug. 5, 1955; d. Edward Joseph and Judith H. Bick. BA in English Lit., Washington U., St. Louis, 1978; cert. in book pub., NYU, 1980; MA in English, U. Mo., 1993, MFA, 2001. Mag. prodn. Antiques World, Art News, N.Y.C., 1980-82; mag. promotion Ziff-Davis Pub., N.Y.C., 1982-83; mag. editor Dun & Bradstreet, N.Y.C., 1983-84; prodn. and proofing Valve Line Survey, 1985—86; prodn., freelance editor Behavior Therapist Mag., N.Y.C., 1985-89; writer, editor Davis Design Co., N.Y.C., 1985-90; freelance editor, writer St. Louis, 1990—; prof. English St. Louis C.C., 1994—. Mem. N.Y. Bus. Press Editors, N.Y.C., 1983-86; bd. dirs. St. Louis Poetry Ctr., 1996—; com. mem. adj. staff devel. St. Louis C.C., 1995-97; adj. prof. Washington U., 2000—. Contbr. poetry to lit. jours., anthologies. Mem. Women Athletes of N.Y., N.Y.C., 1983-88, Prep-Privacy Rights Edn., St. Louis, 1990-93. Recipient winner ann. contests for poetry, St. Louis Poetry Ctr., 1992—98; grantee writer's partial work grantee, Vt. Studio Ctr., 1999—2000; scholar Mo. Women's scholar athlete, State of Mo., 1977—78. Mem. Women in Prodn. (mem. publicity com. 1980-83). Avocations: music, history, philosophy, art, dance, athletics. Home: 3855 Juniata St # 1 Saint Louis MO 63116-4813 E-mail: ReidyFranR@aol.com.

REIDY, GRACE V., retired music educator; b. South Barre, Mass., Dec. 6, 1931; d. John Joseph Valardi and Margaret Tomasello Valardi; m. John James Reidy, July 18, 1953; children: Mary Catherine, Rosemary, Francis, John, Margaret. MusB, New Eng. Conservatory Music, Boston, 1953. Supr. music Ware Pub. Schs., Mass., 1953—56, Hardwick/Hubbard Schs., 1958—60; dir. instrumental music Ware Pub. Schs., 1961—62; supr. music North Brookfield Pub. Schs., 1965, Sterling Pub. Schs., 1965—68; choral dir. Quabbin Regional Sch. Dist., Barre, 1968—72; choral dir., chair dept. Wachusett Regional Sch. Dist., Holden, 1972—94; ret. Condr. Quabbin Singers, 1967—71, Wachusett Singers, 1972—94, Madrigal Dinner, 1981—94. Mem.: NEA (life), Mass. Edn. Assn. (pres. 1990—92), New Eng. Music Festival Assn. (life; pres. 1982—86), Am. Choral Dirs. Assn. (life). Avocations: travel, sports, sewing, knitting. Personal E-mail: grajacriedy@webtv.net.

REIERSON, CAROL ANN, elementary school educator; b. Postville, Iowa, June 4, 1961; d. Dean Orville and Clarian Thelma (Thompson) Gunderson; m. Jeffrey Wade Reierson, May 28, 1983; children: Kristen Marie, Sara Rebecca, Leah Nicole. BA, U. No. Iowa, 1983, MA, 1987. Tchr. spl. edn., multidisability K-6th Postville Comm. Schs., 1983-89; tchr. 5th grade Valley Community Schs., Elgin, Iowa, 1989—. Sci. core curriculum chair Valley Elem. Sch., Elgin, 1992-2001, mentor tchr., 1993-97, peer coaching team organizer, 1992-95; renewed svc. delivery system com. mem. Area Edn. Agy., Dubuque, Iowa, 1991-94; mem. Tchrs Engaged in Advancement Math and Sci., 2001-2004, Literacy Learning Leadership Team, 2005-. Problem solving team supr. Elgin Sch. Dist., 1995-2000. Mem. NEA. Lutheran. Avocations: reading, sewing, fishing, ch. and youth edn., scrapbooking. Office: Valley Elem Sch 23493 Canoe Rd # B Elgin IA 52141-9634 E-mail: reierson_carol@valley.cew.k12.ia.us.

REIF, DEBORAH, manufacturing executive; Grad., Univ. Bridgeport; MBA, Univ. Conn. Fin. positions Gen. Electric, 1973—82; fin. analyst GE Capital, 1982—85; risk mgr. GE Comml. Equipment Fin., 1985—89; chief risk officer GE Vendor Fin. Services, 1990—98; sr. risk officer telecom equipment GE Capital, 1998—99, v.p. global asset mgmt., 2000—01; CEO GE Fin. Guaranty Ins. Co., 2001—03; exec. v.p. fin. restructuring NBC Universal Digital Media, 2004, pres., 2004—05; pres., CEO GE Equipment Services, Fairfield, Conn., 2005—. Office: General Electric 3135 Easton Turnpike Fairfield CT 06828*

REIF COHEN, JESSICA, broadcast executive; m. Bob Cohen; children: AJ, Marisa Rachel. BS in Mktg., NYU, MBA in Fin. and Internat. Bus. Securities analyst, mng. dir. Oppenheimer & Co. Inc.; securities analyst First Boston Corp., Credit Lyonnais, Arnhold & S. Bleichroeder; mng. dir. and sr. media & entertainment analyst Merrill Lynch & Co., 1994, first v.p. rsch., media and global securities. Mem.: Nat. Assn. Television Program Execs., Mus. Television and Radio, Internat. Radio and Television Soc., Media and Entertainment Analysts NY, Beta Gamma Sigma. Office: Merrill Lynch & Co 4 World Financial Ctr New York NY 10080*

REIFF, LAURA FOOTE, lawyer; b. Goldsboro, NC, July 21, 1964; BA in Legal Inst., Econ., Govt., Am. Univ., 1986; JD with honors, George Washington Univ., 1989. Bar: Md. 1989, DC 1990, US Ct. of Internat. Trade. Shareholder, co-chair bus. immigration group Greenberg Traurig LLP, McLean, Va. Co-recipient Outstanding Young Lawyers award, Am. Immigration Law Assn., 1996; recipient Albert Arent Pro Bono award for Cmty. Svc., 1991. Mem.: ABA, Fed. Bar Assn., DC Bar Assn., Md. Bar Assn., Am. Immigration Law Found., Am. Immigration Lawyers Assn. Office: Greenberg Traurig LLP 12th Fl 1750 Tysons Blvd Mc Lean VA 22102-4202 Office Phone: 703-749-1372. Office Fax: 703-714-8372. Business E-Mail: reiffl@gtlaw.com.

REIFF, PATRICIA HOFER, space physicist, educator; b. Oklahoma City, Mar. 14, 1950; d. William Henry and Maxine Ruth (Hoffer) R.; m. Thomas Westfall Hill, July 4, 1976; children: Andrea Hofer Hill, Adam Reiff Hill, Amelia Reiff Hill. Student, Wellesley Coll., 1967-68; BS, Okla. State U., 1971; MS, Rice U., 1974, PhD, 1975. Cert. secondary tchr., Okla., Tex. Resident rsch. assoc. Marshall Space Flight Ctr., Huntsville, Ala., 1975-76; rsch. assoc. space physics and astronomy dept. Rice U., Houston, 1975, asst. prof. space physics and astronomy dept., 1978-81, asst. chmn. space physics and astronomy dept., 1979-85, assoc. rsch. sci., 1981-87, sr. rsch. scientist, 1987-90. Adj. asst. prof. Rice U., 1976-78, disting. faculty fellow, 1990-92, prof. 1992—, chmn. dept. space physics and astronomy, 1996-99, dir. Rice Space Inst., 1999—; mem. sci. team Atmosphere Explorer Mission, Dynamics Explorer Mission; co-investigator Global Geospace Sci. Mission, ESA/Cluster Mission, IMAGE Mission; prin. investigator The Public Connection NASA, Mus. Tchg. Planet Earth Immersive Earth; cons. Houston Mus. Natural Sci., 1986—; adv. com. on atmospheric scis. NSF, Washington, 1988-92; mem. stategic implementation study panel NASA, Washington, 1989-91; mem. space sci. adv. com. NASA, 1993-98, mem. space sta. utilization subcom., 1995-98; mem. adv. com. Los Alamos Non-Proliferation Divsn., 1998-2001; univ. rep. U. Space Rsch. Assn., Washington, 1993—, chair Coun. of Instns., 2001-04; exec. com. George Observatory, Houston, 1989-92, others. Designer Cockrell Sundial/Solar Telescope, 1989; editor EOS (sci. newspaper), 1986-89; contbr. articles to profl. jours. Trustee, Citizens' Environ. Coalition, Houston, 1978-98, pres. 1980-85, adv. com. 1998-2000; mem. air quality com. Houston/Galveston Area Coun., 1980-83, Green Ribbon Com., City of Houston, 1981-83; active coms. Macedonia United Meth. Ch., 1988—. Named rsch. fellow NAS/NRC., 1975, an Outstanding Young Woman Am., 1977, '80, to Houston's Women on the Move, 1990; named Outstanding Aerospace Educator, Women in Aerospace, 1999; NASA grantee 1993, 94, 95, 98, 99; recipient NASA Group Achievement award. Fellow Am. Geophys. Union (fin. com. 1980-82, editor search com. 1992, pub. edn. com.); mem. Cosmos Club, Wellesley Club, Internat. Union of Geodesy and Geophysics (del. 1975, 81, 83, 89, 91, 93, 95, chair working group 2F, 1991-95). Avocations: organic gardening, beef ranching, scouting. Office: Rice U Dept Physics and Astronomy 6100 S Main St Houston TX 77251 Business E-Mail: reiff@rice.edu.

REIFF, RAYCHEL ANN HAUGRUD, language educator; d. Raymond Sanford and Marjorie Colette Haugrud; m. Paul Gerhardt Reiff, Aug. 5, 1973; children: Peder Haugrud, Daniel Paul Haugrud, Marija Elizabeth Haugrud, Rebekah Colette Haugrud. BA, Concordia Coll., Moorhead, Minn., 1967; MA, U. Utah, Salt Lake City, 1969, PhD, 1971. Instr. English Tex. A&I U., 1970—71, asst. prof., 1971—75, U. Wis., River Falls, 1976—77, lectr. Superior, 1990—94, from asst. prof. to assoc. prof., 1994—2003, prof., 2003—. Office Phone: 715-394-8451.

REIG, JUNE WILSON, scriptwriter, television director, television producer; b. Schenectady, N.Y., June 1, 1933; d. Wallace John and Lillian Lucy (Gay) Wilson; m. Robert Maxwell, Nov. 26, 1969. BA summa cum laude, N.Y. State U., 1954; MA in Dramatic Arts, NYU, 1962. Instr. NYU, N.Y.C., 1962—67; prodr., dir. NYU Theater, N.Y.C., 1963—67; dir.-prodr., writer news and pub. affairs NBC TV Network, N.Y.C., 1963—67; dir., writer, prodr. divsn. entertainment NBC-TV Network, N.Y.C., 1967—73; pres. Bunny/Chord Prodns., N.Y.C., 1972—97. Author: (book) Dairy of the Boy King Tut-Ankh-Amen, Charles Scribner's Sons, 1978; writer: (music spl.) The Heart of Christmas with Skitch Henderson, Robert Shaw Chorale and NBC Symphony, 1965; An Afternoon at Tanglewood with Erich Leinsdorf and the Boston Symphony Orch. (Peabody award); writer, dir. (with Johnny Carson) (TV spl.) Stuart Little, 1966 (Peabody award, Prix Jeunesse); writer The Reluctant Dragon, 1968 (Brotherhood award); writer, dir., prodr. (with Burl Ives) Rabbit Hill, 1966 (ALA award); writer, dir., prodr. Bill Cosby As I See It, 1970 (Ohio State award); A Day with Bill Cosby, 1971; Jennifer & Me, 1972; prodr., writer (with Edward Villella and Joanne Woodward) Little Women, the ballet, 1976; prodr., writer (with Orson Welles) Tut, the Boy King, 1978 (Peabody award); writer, dir., prodr.: (TV series) Watch Your Child - The Me Too Show, 1973 (Action for Children's TV Achievement award); films in permanent collections Mus. Broadcasting, N.Y.C. Nominee Emmy award, 1966, 1976; recipient Christopher award. Mem.: NATAS, Dirs. Guild Am., Writers Guild Am., Audubon Soc., NYU Alumni Assn., Internat. Soc. Animal Rights, Friends of Animals, Alan Devoe Bird Club (Old Chatham, N.Y.). Avocations: photography, music, animals. Office: care Howard Comart 450 7th Ave Ste 1701 New York NY 10123-1701

REILLY, ELLEN JANE, elementary school educator; b. Perth Amboy, NJ, Sept. 9, 1945; d. Joseph Charles and Elizabeth Virginia Rafter; m. Robert A. Reilly, Oct. 14, 1967; children: Megan, Sean. AB, Rutgers U., 1967; MA in Edn., Washington U., St. Louis, 1999. Cert. tchr. Ill. Lab. asst. Rutgers U., New Brunswick, NJ, 1964—67; 7th-8th grade sci. tchr. Am. Collegiate Inst., Izmir, Turkey, 1968—69, Air Am. Sch., Udorn, Thailand, 1970—71, St. James Sch., Millstadt, Ill., 1988—92, Whiteside Sch., Belleville, Ill., 1993—; writer, editor Contact mag. Officers' Wives Club, Belleville, 1973—75, 1976—87; tchg. asst. O'Fallon (Ill.) Pub. Schs., 1985—88. Leader Girl Scouts USA, O'Fallon, 1980—91, neighborhood chmn., 1984—86; v.p. Officers' Wives Club, 1981—82; publicity chmn. Cub Scouts, 1981—83; treas. Parent-Tchr. Orgn., 1985—87; mem. River Bluffs Girl Scout Council Gold Award Com., 1990—93. Recipient award of excellence, Regional Office Edn., 1998, Soc. Am. Mil. Engrs., 2003, Sci. Tools award, Armed Forces Comm. and Electronics Assn., 1999, 2003, Nat. Svc. Learning award, US Dept. Edn., 2002, excellence in tchg. award, Emerson Electric, 2003. Mem.: NSTA, Whiteside Fedn. Tchrs. (pes. 2000—02), Ill. Sci. Tchrs. Assn. (Key Leader for Sci. award 2000—). Avocations: reading, bicycling, yoga.

REILLY, KATHLEEN C., director, retired secondary school educator; b. Bridgeport, Conn., Mar. 24, 1937; d. John J. and Lillian (Higgins) Collins; m. Donald Reilly, Aug. 21, 1988; children: Robert L., John, Maura Williams. BS, Boston U., 1958; MA in Teaching, Manhattanville Coll., Purchase, N.Y., 1973; postgrad., Teachers Coll. Columbia U., 1983; CAS, Wesleyan U., 1985. Cert. permanent-English tchr., grades 7-12, N.Y. English tchr. Sch. of Holy

Child, Rye, NY, Edgemont High Sch., Scarsdale, NY; ret., 2000; dir. of tng. Tri-State Consortium. Adj. prof. Hofstra U., Hempstead, N.Y., 1991. Grantee Am. Studies Consortium, NEH, SUNY Tchr. Rsch., 1991, Nat. Coun. Tchrs. English, 1990.; recipient Scarsdale-Westchester Phi Beta Kappa award, N.Y. State Educator of Excellence award, 1996; named Edgemont High Sch. Tchr. Yr.; finalist N.Y. State Tchr. of Yr. Mem. Nat. Coun. Tchrs. of English (tchr. researcher grant). Home: 211 Newtown Tpke Wilton CT 06897-4713

REILLY, NANCY (ANNE CAULFIELD REILLY), painter; b. Bryn Mawr, Pa., Mar. 29, 1927; d. Ralph Caulfield and Claire Helena (Roesch) Goodman; m. Donald Elliott Reilly, May 14, 1949; children: Kevin Caulfield, William Stockbridge, Peter Elliott. Studies with Samuel E. Brown, Westport, Conn., 1955-63; studies with Mimi Jennewein, Larchmont, N.Y., 1964-65. Lectr., demonstrator portrait painting Bridgeport (Conn.) Art League, Milford (Conn.) Art League, Pen and Brush Club, New Haven, Conn. Classic Arts Assn., Allied Artists Am., Kent (Conn.) Art Assn., SCAN, Newtown, Conn. Exhibited in group shows at Nat. Acad. Design, N.Y.C., 1964, 1965, 1969, 1970, Stamford (Conn.) Mus., 1965, Wadsworth Antheum, Hartford, Conn., 1966, 1972, Nat. Acad. Arts and Letters, N.Y.C., 1971, Mus. Sci. and Industry, Bridgeport, 1972, Salmagundi Club, N.Y.C., Nat. Arts Club, Butler Inst. Am. Art, Youngstown, Ohio, 2001, New Britain (Conn.) Mus. Am. Art, 2001, exhibitions include invitational travelling exhbn. Allied Artists Am., 2003—05; included in slide collection Smithsonian Instn., Washington, U. Conn. Health Ctr., Farmington. Vol. artist rehab. unit Norwalk Hosp., 1984—95. Recipient Gold medal for oil painting, Catherine Lorillard Wolfe Art Club, 1965, Silver medal for oil painting, Nat. Arts Club, 1969, George Height award for portrait, 1969, Blanche Farr award, 1991. Fellow: Am. Artists Profl. League (Claude Parsons Meml. award 2003, Leila Gardin Sawyer Meml. award 2005); mem.: Conn. Pastel Soc. (signature, Honors award 2003, 2004, J.D. Altobello Meml. award), Artists' Fellowship N.Y., Kent Art Assn. (Best in Show 1991, Gordon C. Aymar award for oil 1993, Mabel Rowe Aiken award for oil 1995, Frances B. Townley award for portrait 1998, 1999), Hudson Valley Art Assn. (Bronze medal for oil painting 1981, Thora M. Jensen Portrait award 1989, 2005), Pastel Soc. Am. (CPS award 2005), Nat. Arts Club (Silver medal for oil painting 1969, Bruce Stevenson award for portrait 1971, 1988, 1991, First prize 106th Annual Exhibiting Artist Mems. Exbhn. 2005), Allied Artists Am. (bd. dirs. 1991—99, participant in travelling exhibn. 2003—05), New Haven Paint and Clay Club (Merit award 1992, 1997). Home: 9 Marilane Westport CT 06880-1008

REILLY, SHARON, literature educator; b. Milw., Sept. 3, 1951; d. Jerome and Sophie; m. Thomas Reilly; children: Colleen, Michael. BS in Social Work, U. Wis., 1973; BEd, Lakeland Coll., 1989; M in Reading, Cardinal Stretch U., 2003. Cert. literacy coach U. Ark., 2006. Tchr. Oostburg (Wis.) Schs., 1989—96, Sheboygan (Wis.) Schs., 1996—2000, reading specialist, 2000—04, literacy coach, reading specialist, 2004—. Mem.: Internat. Reading Assn., Wis. State Reading Assn. Home: 603 Sch St Kohler WI 53044

REILLY, SUZANNE SWEENEY, art historian, educator; b. Phila., Apr. 14, 1950; d. William Patrick and Vera Sweeney; m. Paul Joseph Reilly, Apr. 26, 1986. BFA, Mass Coll. Art, Boston, 1980; MA, U. Mass., Amherst, 1982. Lectr. Lasell Coll., Newton, Mass., 1986—; tchr. Showa Lang. Inst., Boston, 1995—. Author: A Red Tide in Winter, 2006. Avocations: weaving, travel, art, tour guide, gardening. Home: 11 Corey Terr West Roxbury MA 02132 Office: Lasell Coll 1844 Comm Ave Newton MA 02466 Personal E-mail: spreilly2@verizon.net. Business E-Mail: sreilly@lasell.edu.

REILLY, SUZETTE B., counselor; b. Bethlehem, Pa. AA in Liberal Arts, Northampton Cmty. Coll., Bethlehem, Pa., 1991; BA in Psychology, Cedar Crest Coll., Allentown, Pa., 1995; MA in Counseling Psychology, Immaculata U., Pa., 1998, post grad., 1997—98. Cert. psychologist Profl. Psychology Cert. Bd. N.Am. Assn. Masters in Psychology, 1999, lic. practicing counselor Commonwealth Pa. State Bd. Social Workers, Marriage and Family Therapists and Profl. Counselors, 2002, profl. counselor N.J. Dept. Law and Pub. Safety Divsn. Consumer Affairs Bd. Marriage and Family Therapy, 2003; cert. facilitator groups Ctr. Humanistic Change, Pa., 1991. Instr. Bethesda Day Treatment Ctr., 1991, Warren County C.C., Washington, NJ, 1998—2001, DeSales U., Center Valley, Pa., 1999, St. Luke's Nursing Program Cedar Crest Coll., Bethlehem, 2000; grad. instr. Widener U., Chester, 2000; instr. Alvernia Coll., Reading, 2000, Lehigh Carbon C.C., Schnecksville, Pa., 2001; ombudsman Family Guidance Ctr., Warren County, NJ, 2000—. Presenter to profl. confs. Developer: workshop courses Abnormal Psychology Telecom. Course, 1998, Art Therapy Workshop, 2000, Prosperity: The Creative Connection, 2000; contbr. book reviews to profl. jours. Mem.: ACA, N.Am. Assn. Masters in Psychology, Counseling Assn. Humanistic Edn. and Devel., Pa. Assn. Spiritual, Ethical and Religious Values in Counseling (treas. 2002—, sec. 2003—), Chi Sigma Iota, Beta Mu. Achievements include research in art therapy; hypnosis; ethnicity and multiculturalism; techniques in grief therapy; innovative counseling using empowerment; appropriate ethics for developmental growth. Avocations: flying, sculpting. Mailing: PO Box 5255 Bethlehem PA 18015-2055

REILSONO, LYNDA ANN, elementary school educator; b. Pitts., Sept. 23, 1967; d. Joseph Francis and Grace Angeline (Palombia) Mastandrea; m. Claudio Reilsono, Oct. 24, 1998; 1 child, Ida. BA in Elem. Edn., Point Pk. Coll., Pitts., 1990. Cert. Tchr. K-6 Pa., 1998. Libr. page Mt. Wash. Libr., Pitts., 1984—86; sales clk. Mt. Wash. Thrift Drug, Pitts., 1986—92; tchr. St. Cyril of Alexandria, Pitts., 1991—96, St. James, Sewickly, Pa., 1996—. Clk. Kings Jewelry Store Sales, 1996—2000, Sewickley Pub. Libr., Sewickley, Pa., 1999—2001; teller Bell Fed. Savings and Loan, 1999—2003. South Side Hosp., 1981; fund. raising coord. Edn. Club, 1989; com. woman 19th Ward 8th Dist., Pitts., 1988; eucharistic minister St. Mary of the Mount, Pitts., 1996, lector, 1992. Mem.: Pa. Jr. Acad. Sci. Democrat. Roman Catholic. Avocations: dance, swimming, bowling. Office: St James Sch 201 Broad St Sewickley PA 15143

REIMANN, ARLINE LYNN, artist; b. St. Louis, Nov. 25, 1937; d. Albert Robbins and Bess (Kagan) Miller; m. Hans Reimann, Feb. 24, 1957; 1 child, Robert. BA, Rutgers U., N.J., 1974; MA, Montclair State U., N.J., 1980. Exhibited in group shows at Hunterdon Art Ctr., Clinton, NJ, 1982, 96, Galeria San Jeronimo, San Juan, P.R., 1987, Nat. Arts Club, NYC, 1988, 90—, Interch. Ctr., NYC, Butler Inst. Am. Art, Youngstown, Ohio, 1989, 395 West Broadway Gallery, NYC, 1994, 420 West Broadway Gallery, Soho, NY, 1995, Lever House Gallery, NYC, 1995, Art Ctr. Municipality of Athens, Greece, 1996, West Beth Gallery, Montclair in Manhattan, NYC, 1996, ISE Art Found. NYC, 1996, Soc. Am. Graphic Artists, New Rochelle, NY, 1997, Gallery Art 54, NYC, 1997, Jane Voorhees Zimmerli Art Mus., New Brunswick, NJ, 1998-99, Old Print Shop, NYC, 2004, Art Students League of NY, NYC, 2005, Worldwide Feminist Expo, Balt., 2000, Nat. Assn. Women Artists, UN, 2002, Salmagundi Club, NYC, 2005, Ringling Mus. Sch. Art, Sarasota, Fla., 2006, Goggleworks Ctr. Arts, Reading, Pa., 2006, Venezuelan Consulate, NYC, 2006, Salmagundi Club, NYC, 2006; represented in permanent collections at Jane Voorhees Zimmerli Art Mus., New Brunswick, NJ, Newark Pub. Libr. Fine Print Collection, Newark, Montclair (NJ) State U., Bailey Matthews Mus., Sanibel, Fla., Black Hills Inst., Hill City, SD. Recipient Best in Show award Salute to Women in Arts, Lincoln Ctr., N.Y.C., 1981, Hon. mention award Nat. Juried Exhbn. Small Works Montclair State U., N.J., 1995. Aida Whedon Meml. award Nat. Assn. Women Artists, 1996. Mem. Nat. Assn. Women Artists (bd. dirs., chair traveling print exhbn. 1984-89, printmaking jury 1987-89, 95-97), Audubon Artists (bd. dirs., rec. sec. 1991-97), Soc. Am. Graphic Artists, Phi Beta Kappa. Home: 546 Hillrise Pl Walnut Creek CA 94598-4064

REIMER, JUDY MILLS, pastor, religious executive; m. George G. Reimer, 1964; children: Todd, Troy. BA, Emory and Henry Coll., 1962; MDiv, Bethany Theol. Sem., 1994. Ordained into Set Apart Ministry, Ch. of the Brethren, 1994. Vol. Brethren Vol. Svc. NIH, Bethesda, Md., 1962-64, Hessish Lichtenau, Germany, 1964-65; elem. sch. tchr. Pub. and Private Schs., various cities, 1965-76; deacon Ch. of the Brethren, 1966—; mem Virlina Dist. Bd., 1978-90; chair of nurture com. Ch. of the Brethren Virlina Dist., 1979-82, chair of outdoor ministry, 1983-84, conf. speaker, 1992; founding pastor Ch. of the Brethren, Smith Mountain Lake, Va., 1996-98, gen. bd. exec. dir., 1998—2003; owner, sr. v.p. Harris Office Furniture Co., Roanoke, Va., 1976—. Co-chair and vice-chair of two Virlina Fin. Campaigns, Ch. of the Brethren, 1980s, mem. Gen. Bd., Ch. of Brethren, 1977-90; mem. PTA, United Way Allocation Com., Roanoke Valley Women Owners Assn. (charter mem.); adult advisor Nat. Youth Cabinet. 1991, 92; worship coord. Nat. Youth Conf. 1994 numerous other coms. for Ch. of Brethren; official observer for Nat. Coun. of Chs. at Nicaraguan Election, Feb., 1990; rep. of Ch. of the Brethren, 1989, Atlanta, The Torch of Conscience Campaign to sensitize congregation to the campaign to abolish death penalty; workshop leader across the denomination on leadership devel., pastor/spouse retreats, women's rallies, etc.; ann. conf. moderator elect, 1993-94. Mem. Inst. Indsl. Comml. Chaplains (chmn. bd. dirs. local unit, asst. treas. nat. bd.). Office: Church of the Brethren General Offices 1451 Dundee Ave Elgin IL 60120-1694

REIN, CATHERINE AMELIA, insurance company executive, lawyer; b. Lebanon, Pa., Feb. 7, 1943; d. John and Esther (Scott) Shultz. BA summa cum laude, Pa. State U., 1965; JD magna cum laude, NYU, 1968. Bar: NY 1968, US Supreme Ct. 1971. Assoc. Dewey, Ballantine, Bushby, Palmer & Wood, NYC, 1968-74; with Continental Grp., Stamford, Conn., 1974-85, sec., sr. atty., 1976-77, v.p., gen. counsel, 1980-85; sec., asst. gen. counsel Continental Diversified Ops., 1978-80; v.p. human resources Met. Life Ins. Co., NYC, 1985-88, sr. v.p. human resources, 1988-89, exec. v.p. corp. and profl. svcs. dept., 1989—98, sr. exec., v.p. bus. svcs. grp. and corp. svcs., 1998-99; pres., CEO Met. Life Auto and Home, Warwick, RI, 1999—2004; sr. exec. v.p., chief adminstrv. officer Met. Life Inc., 2004—. Bd. dirs. Bank of NY, First Energy Corpn. Trustee NYU Sch. Law Found. Mem.: ABA, Assn. Bar City of NY. Episcopalian. Avocations: decorating, restoration, cooking. Office: Met Life Inc One Metlife Plz 27 01 Queens Plz North Long Island City NY 11101

REINARD, KATHLEEN ANN, elementary school educator; b. Rock Springs, Wyo., July 19, 1951; d. Louis Edward and Ruth Marie (Nalivka) Gaspar; m. James Henry Reinard, July 28, 1987; 1 child, Richard James. BA, U. Wyo., 1973. Tchr. 4th grade Rocky Boy Sch., Mont., 1973-75; tchr. Thoman Ranch Sch., Green River, Wyo., 1975-78; tchr. 2d grade Washington Sch., Green River, 1978-80, tchr. 3d grade, 1980-93, tchr. 4th grade, 1993—2003, tchr. 3th grade, 2003—. Mem. NEA, Wyo. Edn. Assn., Green River Edn. Assn., Wyo. Wildlife Assn., YWCA, Bus. and Profl. Christian Women's Orgn. (sec. 1983-87). Democrat. Episcopalian. Avocations: gardening, reading, camping, fishing, rock collecting. Home: Star Rt 2 Box 210 Green River WY 82935 Office: Washington Elementary Sch 750 W 5th North St Green River WY 82935-4043

REINARZ, ALICE G., academic administrator; b. Austin, Oct. 25, 1945; d. Earl H. and June Pearl (Knape) Goodwin; m. Ronald B. Reinarz, Aug. 23, 1969 (dec. Aug. 1982); children: David Allen Dean, Lisa Christine. BA, U. Tex., 1967, PhD, 1972. Instr. U. Tex., Austin, 1974-78, lectr., 1978-90, sr. lectr., 1990-97; dir. U. Mich., Ann Arbor, 1997—2003; assoc. dean Tex. A&M U., College Station, 2003—05, asst. provost, prof., 2005—. Cons. U. Tex., Arlington, 1995-2003, Tex. A&M, Galveston, 1996, U. Tex., San Antonio, 2000, Tex. A&M U., College Station, 2001, Bowling Green State U., 2002, U. Tex. Arlington, 2003; adj. prof. U. Mich., 1998-2003. Author: (with others) Encyclopedia of Microbiology, 1998, Academic Advising: A Comprehensive Handbook, 2000; editor: Teaching Through Academic Advising, 1995, Beyond Teaching to Mentoring, 2000. Active Leadership Tex., Austin, 1996, Leadership Am., Washington, 1997. Mem. Am. Soc. Virology, Am. Soc. Microbiology (nat. undergrad. edn. task force 1993-95, Carski Found. Disting. Tchg. award 1990), Nat. Acad. Advising Assn. (chair adminstr.'s commn.), Alpha Epsilon Delta, Phi Eta Sigma, Alpha Lamda Delta. Home: 300 Stone Cove Ct College Station TX 77845 Office: Office of Admissions and Records 217 Koldus College Station TX 77843

REINERT, AGNES FRANCES, chaplain, educator; b. Mott, ND, May 21, 1940; d. Nick Joseph Reinert and Catherine Elenore Frank. BS, U. Mary, Bismarck, ND, 1964; MA, St. Louis U., 1984. RN ND, 1964. Nurse St. Alexius Med. Ctr., Bismarck, 1964—75; supr. ministry students St. Francis Med. Ctr., LaCrosse, Wis., 1992—95; cert. chaplain Cathedral of Holy Spirit, Bismarck, ND, 1997—. Cert. spiritual dir. The Emmaus Program, Bismarck, 2004—. Author: (poetry) The Art of Poetry: A Treasury of Contemporary Verse. Police chaplain Bismarck Law Enforcement, 2002—06; mem. adv. bd. Garrison Meml. Hosp., ND, 2002—06, Spkrs. Bur., Bismarck, 2002—06; mem. sponsorship group Annunciation Monastery, Bismarck, 2005—. Recipient N.D. State Chaplain Rep. for Region VIII, Nat. Assn. of Cath. Chaplains, 1986—89. Mem.: Internat. Conf. Police Chaplains (corr.). Democrat. Roman Catholic. Avocations: cross country skiing, reading, cooking, bicycling. Home: PO Box 5510 Bismarck ND 58506-5510 Personal E-mail: reinertagnes@hotmail.com.

REINERT, JOY ANN, elementary school educator; b. Des Moines, Iowa; d. Willie Earl and Ila Lucille Spoonholtz; m. Wilbert Dean Reinert Jr., May 27, 1961; 1 child, Debra. Student, Cornell Coll., Mount Vernon, Iowa, 1956-57; diploma, Grand View Jr. Coll., Des Moines, Iowa, 1958; BS in Edn., Drake U., Des Moines, 1965. Educator Hubbard Cmty. Sch., Iowa, 1958-66, educator chpt. I Iowa, 1970—88, Hubbard-Radcliffe Sch., Radcliffe, Iowa, 1988-96. Coord. chpt. I Hubbard Sch., 1973-88; coord. talented and gifted Hubbard Sch., 1983-88. Mem. Internat. Reading Assn., Iowa Reading Assn. (v.p. 1988-89, pres.-elect 1989-90, pres. 1990-91), Hardy Reading Coun. (pres. 1983-84, 93-94, 98-2001, asst. chair regional reading conf. 1994-95, co-chair South Plains regional reading conf. 2001-03), Iowa Reading Assn. (state coord. 1997-2000). Missouri Synod Lutheran. Avocations: reading, reading associations, walking, travel. Home: 202 S State St Hubbard IA 50122

REINGLASS, MICHELLE ANNETTE, lawyer; b. LA, Dec. 9, 1954; d. Darwin and Shirley (Steiner) R. Student, U. Calif., Irvine, 1972-75; BSL, Western State U., 1977; JD, Western State U., Coll. Law, 1978. Bar: Calif. 1979, U.S. Dist. Ct. (ctrl. dist.) Calif. 1979, U.S. Ct. Appeals (9th cir.) 1981, U.S. Dist. Ct. (so. dist.) Calif. 1990. Pvt. practice employee litig., Laguna Hills, Calif., 1979—. Instr. Calif. Continuing Edn. of Bar, 1990—, Western State Coll., 1991, Rutter Group, 1994—; chmn. magistrate selection com. U.S. Dist. Ct. (ctrl. dist.) Calif., LA, 1991, 93-95, com. mem., 1997, lawyer rep. to 9th cir. jud. conf.; lectr. in field. Contbr. articles to profl. jours. Pres., bd. dirs. Child or Parental Emergency Svcs., Santa Ana, Calif., 1982-92; bd. dirs. Pub. Law Ctr., Santa Ana, Coalition for Justice, Working Wardrobes; mem. exec. com. and cast CHOC Follies. Recipient Jurisprudence award Anti-Defamation League, 1997; named to Western State U. Hall of Fame, 1993; named one of Top 100 Most Influential Lawyers in Calif., LA Daily Jour., 2001; one of Top 30 Female Litigators in Calif., LA Daily Jour., 2002; one of Top 50 Female Litigators, LA Daily Jour., 2003-04; named to Super Lawyers, LA Mag., 2004, 05. Mem. State Bar Calif., Assn. Bus. Trial Lawyers (bd. dirs.), Orange County Bar Assn. (del. to state conv. 1980-94, bd. dirs. 1983-94, chmn. bus. litigation sect. 1989, sec. 1990, treas. 1991, pres.-elect 1992, pres. 1993), Calif. Employee Lawyers Assn. (com. mem., chair elect)Orange County Trial Lawyers Assn. (bd. dirs. 1987-89, Bus. Trial Lawyer of Yr. award 1995, Employee Trial Lawyer of Yr. award 2004), Orange County Women Lawyers (Lawyer of Yr. award 1996), Vols. in Parole (chmn. adv. com. 1990-91), Peter Elliot Inns Ct. (master), Am. Bd. of Trial Advocates. Avocations: distance running, skiing. Office: 23161 Mill Creek Dr Ste 170 Laguna Hills CA 92653-1650 E-mail: michelle@reinglasslaw.com.

REINHARD, DIANE L., retired university president; B in elem. edn., U. Wis., M in ednl. psychology; PhD ednl. evaluation, Ohio State U. Faculty mem., assoc. dean, acting dean U. of Oreg.; prof., dept. of ednl. psychology W.Va. U., dean, coll. of human resources and edn., acting pres.; pres. Clarion U., 1990—2003; interim pres. Ind. U. of Pa., 2004—05; ret., 2005.

REINHARDT, DEBORAH ANN, music educator; d. James Willard Reinhardt and Wilma Ruth Gibler. MusB in Edn., Baldwin-Wallace Coll., Berea, Ohio, 1973; MusM, Ithaca Coll., NY, 1987; PhD in Music Edn., Case Western Res. U., Cleve., 1990. Music tchr. A.B. Hart Jr. High Cleve. Pub. Schs., 1973—77; music tchr. Kenston Pub. Schs., Chagrin Falls, Ohio, 1977—80, Busby Sch. of No. Cheyenne Tribe, Busby, Mont., 1980—82, Jonesport (Maine) Elem. Sch., 1982—85; asst. prof. music edn. U. Nebr., Lincoln, 1995—2000, Ball State U., Muncie, Ind., 1990—95; assoc. prof. music edn., dir. music edn. Calif. State U., Chico, 2000—. Author: (monograph) A Rich Tapestry: The Music Of Nebraska; contbr. articles to profl. jours. Coord. h.s. honor choir Calif. State U., Chico, 2002—05. Mem.: Calif. Coun. Music Tchr. Educators (chair 2004—), Am. Orff-Schulwerk Assn. (collegiate rep. 2003), Coll. Music Soc., Calif. Assn. Music Edn. (treas. no. sect. 2003—, coord. solo and ensemble festival, coord. large group choral festival 2002). Achievements include research in relationship between creative activities, music learning and curriculum. Avocations: folk dancing, swimming. Home: 5 Delaware Dr Chico CA 95973 Office: Calif State U Chico 103 Performing Arts Ctr Chico CA 95929-0806 Fax: 530-898-4082. Office Phone: 530-898-4639. E-mail: dreinhardt@csuchico.edu.

REINHART, ANNE CHRISTINE, special education educator, consultant; b. Detroit, Mar. 9, 1950; m. Charles Reinhart; children: Kim Meredith, Theodore Justin. BS, Ea. Mich. U., 1972; MA, U. Detroit, 1977. Cert. spl. edn., Mich. Spl. edn. tchr. for emotionally impaired State of Mich. Hosp., Pontiac, Berkley (Mich.) Sch. Dist, 1976—. Co-chair ASSET (support group for gifted and talented students), Birmingham, Mich., 1996-98; com. mem. Mich. Dept. of Edn., Office of Spl. Edn.; particpant Mich Pilot Study grant Quality Assurance Rev., 2000-03. Grantee, Dept. Spl. Edn., Mich., 2000—03. Mem. Kappa Delta Pi. Avocation: writing. Home: 25925 Romany Way Franklin MI 48025-1909

REINHART, KELLEE CONNELY, journalist; b. Kearney, Nebr., Dec. 15, 1951; d. Vaughn Eugene and Mary Jo (Mullen) Connely; m. Stephen Wayne Reinhart, June 15, 1974; children: Keegan Connely, Channing Mullen. BA, U. Ala., 1972, MS, 1974. Advt. copywriter Stas. WTBC-AM, WUOA-FM, 1970-72; asst. mgr. Ala. Press Assn., 1972-74; asst. to the editor Antique Monthly mag., 1974-75, mng. editor, 1975-77; editorial dir. Antique Monthly and Horizons mags., 1977-89; dir. univ. rels. U. Ala. Sys., Tuscaloosa, 1989—2004, vice chancellor for sys. rels., 2004—. Editor: Wild Birds of America: The Art of Basil Ede, 1991, Centennial Memories, Millennial Hopes, 2000, The People's City, 2003. Bd. dirs. Ala. Humanities Found.; bd. dirs. Ala. Writers Forum, pres., 1999—2001. Recipient Druids Arts award, 1995, Betsy Plank Disting. Achievement award U. Ala., 2006. Mem. Soc. Profl. Journalists, Am. Soc. Mag. Editors, Newcomen Soc. U.S., Art Table, XXI/U. Ala. Women's Hon. Soc. Office: 401 Queen City Ave Tuscaloosa AL 35401-1551 Business E-Mail: kreinhar@uasystem.ua.edu.

REINHART, MARY ANN, medical board executive; b. Jackson, Mich., Aug. 14, 1942; d. Herbert Martin and Josephine Marie (Keyes) Conway; m. David Lee Reinhart, Dec. 28, 1963; children: Stephen Paul, Michael David. MA, Mich. State U., 1983, PhD, 1985. Rsch. asst. Mich. State U., East Lansing, 1979-82, 85, teaching asst. dept psychology, 1982-84, asst. prof. Office Med. Edn. R&D, Coll. Human Medicine, 1985-88, chairperson collegewide evaluation com., Coll. Human Medicine, 1985—88, adj. asst. prof. Office Med. Edn. R&D, Coll. Human Medicine, 1988—; assoc. exec. dir. Am. Bd. Emergency Medicine, East Lansing, 1988-95, dep. exec. dir., 1995-2000, exec. dir., 2000—. Reviewer Annals of Emergency Medicine, 1987-95, Acad. Emergency Medicine, 1995-99. Bd. dirs. Neahtawanta Rsch. and Edn. Ctr., Traverse City, Mich., 1991—. Mem. APA (divsn. indsl./orgnl. psychology, health psychology), Phi Kappa Phi. Achievements include application of chart stimulated recall method of assessment in a national medical recertification examination; development and implementation of national longitudinal study of emergency medicine residents and emergency physicians. Office: Am Bd Emergency Medicine 3000 Coolidge Rd East Lansing MI 48823-6319

REINHERZ, HELEN ZARSKY, social worker, researcher; b. Boston, Aug. 4, 1923; d. Zachary and Anna (Cohen) Zarsky; m. Samuel E. Reinherz, Aug. 29, 1943; 1 son, Ellis. AB magna cum laude, Wheaton Coll., 1944; MS, Simmons Coll., 1946; S.M., Harvard U., 1962, Sc.D., 1965. Social worker Newton Family Service, Mass., 1946-49, Mass. Gen. Hosp., Boston, 1949-51; supr. psychiat. social work State Hosp., Waltham, Mass., 1958-61; faculty mem. Simmons Coll., Boston, 1965—, prof. methods rsch., 1972—, dir. research Sch. Social Work, 1968-93, dir. PhD program, 1993-96. Prin. investigator Identifying Children at Risk, 1976—84, Adaption in Adolescence, 1987—93, Adult Rsch. Project, 1998—2001, Early Adulthood Rsch. Project, 1993—97, Simmons Longitudinal Study, 2001—, Study Adolescent Drug Abuse, 1971—73; rsch. cons. Dept. Mental Health, 1970—80; chmn. Gov.'s Adv. Coun. on Mental Health and Retardation, 1972; mem. adv. com. Mental Health Manpower fo Fed. Govt., 1980—82. Author (with H. Wechler, D. Dobbins): Social Work Research in the Human Services, 1976; author: (with M. Heywood, J. Camp) A Community Response to Drug Abuse, 1976; cons., assoc. editor: Jour. Prevention, 1980—91, mem. fed. adv. com.: Rsch. in Prevention Rev., 1984—87, editl. bd.: Jour. Early Adolescence, cons. editor: NASW Jour.; contbr. articles to profl. jours. Recipient Maida H. Solomon award, Simmons Coll. Alumni, 1961, Disting. Career award, Soc. Social Work and Rsch., 2005, Rsch. Achievement award, NASW, 2005; grantee, Grant Found., 1963, Med. Found., 1967—69, NIMH, 1975—84, 1987—; NIH tng. fellow, 1961—65. Fellow Am. Orthopsychiat. Assn.; mem. Acad. Cert. Social Workers, Am. Pub. Health Assn., Coun. Social Work Edn., Harvard Sch. Pub. Health Alumni Assn. (sec.-treas. 1965-68), Phi Beta Kappa, Delta Omega. Home: 17 Corey Rd Malden MA 02148-1116 Office: Simmons Sch Social Work 300 The Fenway Boston MA 02115 Business E-Mail: helen.reinherz@simmons.edu, reinherz@simmons.edu.

REINIKE, IRMA, retired writer, artist, poet, lyricist; b. White Harbor, Long Beach, Miss., Oct. 20, 1927; d. Chester Henry and Edna Claire (Latille) Reinike; children: Harvey Franklin Linn Shows Jr., George David Shows, Thelam Jewell Shows Hoffman. Student, St. Mary's Dominican Coll.; grad., North Light Art Sch., Cin., 1996, 97, 99. Freelance writer, student Famous Writers Sch., Westport, Conn., 1965—69; editor Seabee Courier, writer US Naval Contrn. Battalion Ctr., Gulfport, 1969—71; adminstr. US Army Corps. Engrs.; ret., 1994. Author: Mystery, 1940—41, Long Beach Movie Personality, 1949, My Beach, 1990, Thelma, 1991, (poetry) My Lady of Medjugorje, 1987—88, Irma Reinike Poetry-Book 1, 2002, I Love My Flag, 2000, numerous poems; columnist Round the Town, Long Beach, Miss., 1963—66, The Illustrated Press, Irma Reinike's Personality Parade, New Orleans, 1952; composer: (songs) See You Tomorrow, 1995—96, Days of Love, 1997, The Blue of Your Eyes, 1997, I Am An American, 2006, No Tear Big Enough for Katrina, 2006, others, (stage play) Ethel Chichester, Peg O' My Heart, Kaye Hamilton, Stage Door, 1949, Song, Dance Dixieland Minstrel and Variety Artists, 1950—52, Charity Performer, Le Petit Theatre de Vieux Carre' Sunday Salon, 1996, Destruction by Hurricane Camille, Times Picayune, 1970; Introduction Camille Book-Hurricane, 1969, Ten Acres, 1970—71, Sunrise Lake Ponchartrain, Represented in permanent collections Nat. D-Day Museum, exhibitions include St. Thomas Parish, Long Beach, Miss., Baton Rouge Gallery, Le Petite Theatre, New Orleans, Mandeville, La., City Long Beach, Miss., 2005, many others. Mem. La. Libr. Found. New Orleans Friends Pub. Libr., 1994—96; charter mem. World War II Monument Meml., Washington; mem. Nat. Rep. Senatorial Com., 1994—97, Nat. Rep. Congl. Com., 2000. Named Honored Author, La. Libr. Assn., 1994, 1996, La. State Libr., 1995, Friends Fest New Orleans Pub. Libr., 1994—96, Patron, Le Petit Theatre de Vieux Carre, 1996. Mem.: New Orleans Mus. Art. Republican. Roman Catholic. Avocations: fine arts, songwriting, poetry, lyricist, philosophy.

REININGHAUS, RUTH, retired artist; b. N.Y.C., Oct. 4, 1922; d. Emil William and Pauline Rosa (Lazarik) R.; m. George H. Morales, Feb. 20, 1944; children: George James, Robert Charles; m. Allan Joseph Smith, May 28, 1960. Student, Hunter Coll., NYU, Nat. Acad. Sch. of Design, 1960-61, Frank

Reilly Sch. of Art, 1963, Art Students League, 1964, 68; studied oil painting, with Robert Beverly Hale and Robert Philips, with Morton Roberts and Frank Reilly, Robert Maione, with Rudy Colao. Instr. art Banker's Trust, N.Y.C., 1971-77, 79-99, Kittredge Club for Women, N.Y.C., 1967-77, Bankers Trust Co., 1971-98. Exhibited in group shows at Berkshire Art Mus., 1970s, Hammer Galleries, Inc., N.Y.C., 1974, Far Gallery, N.Y.C., 1974, Mufalli Gallery, N.Y. and Fla., 1983-90, Pen and Brush Club, 1985—, Petrucci Gallery, Saugerties, N.Y., 1988-94, Pastel Soc. Am., 1988—, John Lane Gallery, Rhinebeck, N.Y., 1992-97, Regianni Gallery, N.Y.C., 1994, Catherine Lorillard Wolfe Club, Salmagundi Club, Allied Artists Am., Heidi Newhoff Gallery, N.Y.C., Hudson Valley Art Assn., Knickerbocker Artists, N.Y.C., Pen & Brush Club Inc., Pastel Soc. Am., Heritage Mus.; represented in permanent collections at US Navy Art, US Coast Guard Art Program, Hon. Murtogh D. Guinness, Salmagundi Club; contbr. to popular mags. Active Navy Art Coop. and Liaison, Coast Guard Art Program. Recipient 3d prize in Oils, Murray Hill Art Show, 1959, 69; Washington Sq. Outdoor Art Exhibit scholar Nat. Acad., 1962, Frank Reilly Sch. Art, 1963, NYU, 1963, Talens award, 1963, Robert Lehman award, 1968, Richtone Artists award, 1968, Baker Brush award, 1969, Silver medal Excellence in Pastel Art Spirit Found., 2006; Salmagund scholar, 1969; subject NBC TV show You Are an Artist, 1950s. Fellow: Hudson Valley Art Assn. (Claude Parson's Meml. award 1974), Am. Artists Profl. League (Claude Parsons Meml. award 1974, 2d prize oils 1992, 3d prize pastel 1993, Pres. award 1994, Hon. Mention award 2004); mem.: Navy Art Coop. and Liaison, Knickerbocker Artists (Flora B. Giffuni PSA Pres.' award 1990), Oil Pastel Assn. (Pen and Brush award 1987, Strathmore award 1989, Pen and Brush award 1990, Salmagundi Club award 1991), Allied Artists Am. (assoc.), Washington Sq. Outdoor Art Assn. (bd. dirs. 1983—90), Nat. Arts Club (Reciprocal) Artists Fellowship, Soc. Illustrators (hon. 1983—87), Pastel Soc. Am. (bd. dirs. 1988—90, J. Giffuni purchase award 1988, Pastel Soc. of West Coast award 1997), Coast Guard Art Program, Salmagundi Club N.Y. (pres. 1983—87, curator 1989—97, 2003—04, Philip Isenberg award 1974, Salmagundi Club prize 1985, Franklin B. Williams Fund prize 1987, Tom Picard award 1987, Mortimer E. Freehof award 1988, John N. Lewis award 1988—89, Medal of Honor 1989, Philip Isenberg award 1989—90, Helen S. Coes award 1990, Flora B. Giffuni Pres. award 1990, Thomas Moran award 1990, Samuel T. Shaw award 1990, Alphaeus Cole Meml. award 1991, Salmagundi award 1991, Alice B. McReynolds Meml. award 1991, Philip Isenberg award 1992, 1995, Harry Ballinger Meml. award 2000—01, Philip Isenberg award 2001, Jane Impastato award 2003, 1st prize John N. Lewis award 2004, John N. Lewis award 2004, Best in Show award 2004, Mortimer Freehof award 2005), Pen and Brush Club (Helen Slotman award 1986, OPA Internat. award 1987, Gene Alden Walker award 1988, Pen and Brush Solo award 1992, Margaret Sussman award 1996, 1998, Merit award 2000), Catharine Lorillard Wolfe Art Club (bd. dirs. 1987—97, Anna Hyatt Huntington award 1978, Coun. Am. Artists award 1985, Pastel award 1992, Still Life award 1993, 1st prize 2001), Alpha Delta Pi. Lutheran. Avocations: travel, technical illustration, oil, pastel and watercolor painting, collecting antique music boxes and watches. Home: 222 E 93rd St Apt 26A New York NY 10128-3758 E-mail: reininghaus@netzero.com.

REINISCH, JUNE MACHOVER, psychologist, educator; b. NYC, Feb. 2, 1943; d. Mann Barnett and Lillian (Machover) R. BS cum laude, NYU, 1966; MA, Columbia U., 1970, PhD with distinction, 1976. Asst. prof. psychology Rutgers U., New Brunswick, N.J., 1975-80, assoc. prof. psychology New Brunswick, N.J., 1980-82, adj. assoc. prof. psychiatry, 1981-82; prof. psychology Ind. U., Bloomington, 1982-93, dir. Kinsey Inst. Rsch. in Sex, Gender, and Reprodn., 1982-93; prof. clin. psychology Sch. Medicine, Indpls., 1983-93; dir. emeritus Kinsey Inst., 1993—. Dir., prin. investigator Prenatal Devel. Projects, Copenhagen, 1976—, sr. rsch. fellow, trustee The Kinsey Inst., 1993—; pres. R2 Sci. Comms., Inc., Ind., NY, 1985—; vis. sr. rschr. Inst. of Preventive Medicine, Copenhagen Health Svcs., Kommunehospitalet, Copenhagen, 1994—; cons. SUNY; sr. cons. Mus. of Sex, NYC, 1998, dir. acquisitions and new exhbns., 2003-, v.p. sci. affairs, 2003; exec. dir. Health and Sci. Adv. Bd., 2004-. Author: The Kinsey Institute New Report on Sex, 1990, 94, pub. 8 fgn. edits.; editor, contbr. books Kinsey Inst. series; syndicated newspaper columnist: The Kinsey Report; contbr. rsch. reports, revs., articles to profl. jours.; appeared on TV shows including PBS, BBC, ABC and NBC sci. spls., Discovery, ABC Science Specials, 20/20, Oprah Winfrey, Geraldo Rivera, Charles Grodin, Montel Williams, Sally Jessy Rafael, Good Morning Am., Today Show, CBS This Morning; guest host TV shows including CNBC Real Personal, TalkLive, also fgn. appearances. Founders day scholar NYU, 1966; NIMH trainee, 1971-74; NIMH grantee, 1978-80, Ford Found. grantee, 1973-75, Nat. Inst. Edn. grantee, 1973-74, Erikson Ednl. Found. grantee, 1973-74, grantee Nat. Inst. Child Health and Human Devel., 1981-88, Nat. Inst. on Drug Abuse, 1989-95; recipient Morton Prince award Am. Psychopath. Assn., 1976, medal for 9th Dr. S.T. Huang-Chan Meml. Lectr. in anatomy Hong Kong U., 1988, Dr. Richard J. Cross award Robert Wood Johnson Med. Sch., 1991, Award First Internat. Conf. on Orgasm, New Delhi, 1991, Disting. Alumnae award Tchrs. Coll. Columbia U., 1992, award for su contbn. Profl. al Conocimiento dela Sexualidad Humana, Assn. Mexicana de Sexologia, Mexico City, 1996; named Regents lectr. UCLA, 1999. Fellow AAAS, APA, Am. Psychol. Soc., Soc. for Sci. Study Sex; mem. Internat. Acad. Sex Rsch. (charter), Internat. Women's Forum, Women's Forum. Inc., Internat. Soc. Psychoneuroendocrinology, Internat. Soc. Rsch. Aggression, Internat. Soc. Devel. Psychobiology, Am. Assn. Sex. Educators, Counselors and Therapists, Sigma Xi. Office: SUNY HSCB PBL Box 120 450 Clarkson Ave Brooklyn NY 11203-2056 also: The Kinsey Inst Prenatal Devel Project Ind U Bloomington IN 47405 Business E-Mail: jreinisch@museumofsex.com. E-mail: DrReinisch@aol.com.

REINIUS, MICHELE REED, executive recruiter; b. San Diego, Jan. 17, 1948; d. Wallace Alvin Reed and Dorothy Louise Austin; m. Robin Patric Reinius, Aug. 4, 1990; 1 child, Joselyn Ann Andrews. Supr. Asosa Personnel, Tucson, 1981-83; recruiter TAD Tech., Tucson, 1983-85; co-cowner Migar Personnel, Tucson, 1985-90; mgr. Temps by Encore, Tucson, 1990-2000; pres. Ariz. Recruiting Source, Tucson, 2000—. Democrat. Jewish. Avocations: reading, swimming. Office: Ariz Recruiting Source 7483 E Broadway Tucson AZ 85710 Office Phone: 520-751-0067. Business E-Mail: michelereinius@reinius.com.

REINKE, DORIS MARIE, retired elementary school educator; b. Racine, Wis., Jan. 12, 1922; d. Otto William Reinke and Louise Amelia Goehring. BS, U. Wis., 1943, MS, 1967. Tchr. kindergarten Elkhorn Area Sch. Sys., Wis., 1943—69, prin. bldg., 1968—70, dir. summer sch., 1974—75, tchr. grade 2, 1970—84, chmn. primary dept., 1967—84, administrv. asst., supervising tchr., 1957—83, student tchr., 1984, ret., 1984; tchr. oriented experience Program Area Sch. Sys., Elkhorn, 1966. Pres. Elkhorn Edn. Assn., 1949-50; rep. dist. State Kindergarten Conf., Oshkosh, Wis., 1966; participant early edn. conf. State Early Edn. Conf., Eagle River, Wis., 1968; tchr. Covenant Harbor Elderhostel, 1997, 98; established Doris M. Reinke Resource Ctr., 2002. Author: Doris' Corner newsletter Walworth County Geneal. Soc., 1992—; author: (with Charlotte and William Gates) Guide to Beckwith's History of Walworth County, 2000; author: Images of America-Elkhorn, 2004; contbr. weekly newspaper column Webster Notes, 1989, monthly column in The Week, 1991. Chmn. Sch. Centennial, Elkhorn, 1987; mem. Elkhorn Hist. Preservation Com., 1991—; chmn. Sesquicentennial com., 1997—; dir. Webster House Mus., 1991—; mem. Walworth County Sesquicentennial Com., 1997—98; mem. sesquicentennial com. Walworth County Fair, 1998—; archivist Sugar Creek Luth. Ch., 1992—, mem. ch. coun., 2003, sec., 2005; choir mem. Luth. Ch., 1995—2001; del. dist. constn. conv. Evang. Luth. Ch. Am., Beloit, Wis., 1987; com. mem. Luth. Ch., Elkhorn, 1987, sec., 2005; RSVP Vol. Food Pantry, Elkhorn, 1985—2002, bd. dirs., 1985—88, 1995—. Recipient Wis. Edn. Rsch., West Bend, Wis., 1966, Outstanding Elem. Tchrs., Wash., 1973, Wis. Dept. Edn., Madison, 1980, Local History award State Hist. Soc. Wis., 1993, Outstanding Sr. Citizen award Walworth County Fair, 1999, Cmty. Svc. award Masons, 2000, Disting. Svc. award Rotary, 2004; named one of 50 Who Matter, Janesville Gazette, 2006, Vol. of Yr., Walworth County Area Ret. Educators Assn., 2006. Mem.: Walworth County Ret. Tchrs. Assn. (v.p. 1988, pres. 1991), Nat. Ret. Tchrs. Assn., Walworth County Geneal. Soc. (bd. dirs. 1991—92), Walworth County Hist. Soc. (treas. 1985—89, v.p. 1990—91, pres. 1991—96, v.p. 1999—2000, pres. 2000—05), Elkhorn Women's Club (sec. 1999—2000, v.p. 2003, pres. 2005—), Alpha Delta Kappa (state pres. 1968—70, 1976—78, chpt. pres. 2002—03). Avocations: reading, baseball, bird watching, travel. Home: 516 N Wisconsin St Elkhorn WI 53121-1119 Office Phone: 262-723-4248. Personal E-mail: walcohistory@elknet.net.

REINKE, FRANCES MARYLOU, science educator; b. Gary, Ind., June 10, 1941; d. Theodore George and Helen Stella (Zowal) Kasperek; m. Leonard J. Reinke, June 21, 1969 (dec. 1986). BS, Ind. U., 1963; MA, U. Mich., 1965; postgrad., Mont. State U., 1971; MS, Notre Dame U., 1972; postgrad., Concordia Coll., 1988—. Tchr. Detroit Redford High Sch., 1963-64, Gavit High Sch., Hammond, Ind., 1965-79, Clark High Sch., Hammond, 1980—, chmn. sci. dept., 1987—; instr. sci. Calumet (Ind.) Coll., Ind. U. Tutor Hammond Pub. Schs., 1965—; mem. Air. Force Acad. U.S. Space Found. Mem. Sch. Improvement Program, 1986—, Ind. Book Adoption Com., 1986-87, Hammond Drug and Alcohol Prevention Task Force, Snowflake and Snowball Drug and Alcohol Prevention Jr. and Sr. High Sch. Workshops, Parents Students Tchrs. Assn.; active middle sch. and high sch. sci. fairs; sci. olympiad coach; sponsor, mentor SADD; sponsor Nat. Geography Bee; acad. decathlon coach; active Hoosier Spell Bowl; pentathlon coach Hoosier Super Bowl. Named Tchr. of Yr. Inland Steel, 1986; recipient semi-finalist Presdl. award, 1987, PTSA Life award for Excellence in thcg., 2005; grantee, NSF, Nat. Inst. of Health, 1993, HHMI grant, 2004. Mem. NEA, Am. Fedn. Tchrs., Nat. Sci. Tchrs. Assn., Nat. Assn. Biology Tchrs., Ind. State Tchrs. Assn., Hammond Tchrs. Assn., Hammond Fedn. Tchrs., Calumet Assn. Sci. Tchrs., Nat. Honor Soc. (adv. bd.), Hoosier Assn. Sci. Tchrs. of Ind., Ogden Dunes Women's Club, Sierra Club, Sci. Club (sponsor), Chess Club (sponsor). Roman Catholic. Avocations: travel, painting, skiing, reading, outdoors. Office: Hammond Sch System 1921 Davis St Hammond IN 46327

REINKE, LINDA JEANETTE, retired social worker; b. Harrisburg, Pa., July 18, 1941; d. William M. and Gladys A. Grabill; m. Marvin E. Reinke, June 1963. BS, George Williams Coll., 1963; MSW, Va. Commonwealth U., 1975. Lic. social worker Ill., cert. Acad. Cert. Social Workers, 1977. Social worker, parole agt. Wis. State Parole, Milw., 1965—67; caseworker Calhoun Co. Dept. Pensions and Securities, Anniston, Ala., 1967—68; supr. counseling and evaluation Goodwill Industries, Sioux City, Iowa, 1969—71; social worker Alexandria Social Svcs., Va., 1971—73, 1975—78; social work supr. Fairfax Social Svcs., Va., 1978—88; clin. coord. splty. svcs. Strong Meml. Hosp., Rochester, NY, 1989—90; coord. vol. svcs. Rochester Rehab., 1990—92; adminstr. homemaker program Salvation Army Family Svcs., Chgo., 1993—98. Guest lectr. Va. Commonwealth U., 1978—, George Mason U., 1978—88; field instr. social work Cath. U., Va. Commonwealth U., George Mason U., James Madison U.; chair adv. com. social work program George Mason U. Trainer stroke visitor program Vis. Nurse Svc.; developer stroke support group Strong Meml. Hosp., Rochester; rsch. project, cmty. edn. James City Coun. Social Svcs., Va.; v.p. Sr. Svcs. Coalition Steering Com., Williamsburg, Va., 2005—; coord. home visitor program Williamsburg Social Svcs.; mem. bd., program devel. Williamsburg Area Faith-in-Action, 2001—05; adv. bd. Lakeview Mental Health Ctr., Chgo., 1992—94. Mem.: Va. NASW (nomination and leadership identification com. 1980—84, chair polit. action fundraiser 1985, 1987, coord. continuing edn. and lic. classes Ill. chpt. 1998—99, mem. Va. chpt.), Va. Coun. Social Welfare (conf. co-chair 1979, conf. chair 1980, conf. track coord., bd. mem. no. chpt.). Avocations: reading, travel, history.

REINKING, ANN H., dancer, actress; b. Seattle, Nov. 10, 1949; d. Walter Floyd and Francis Holmes (Harrison) R.; m. Larry Small, 1970; m. Herbert A. Allen; Aug. 25, 1982; (stepchildren): Leslie, Christie, Herbert, Charlie. Student public schs. Guest tchr. NYU, Duke U., Durham, N.C., Rutgers, N.J., Harvard, Cambridge, Mass.; choreographer Pal Joey, Goodman Theater, Chgo., 1988. Broadway appearances include Coco, 1970, Wild and Wonderful, 1972, Pippin, 1973, Over Here, 1974, Goodtime Charlie, 1975, Chicago, 1977, A Chorus Line, 1976, Dancin', 1978, Sweet Charity, 1986-87; TV appearances include Ellery Queen, Doug Henning: Magic on Broadway, 1982, Parade of Stars, 1983, American Treasury, 1985, Salute to Jules Styne, Broadway Salutes Washington, An Introduction to the Dance Gala of the Stars; film appearances include Movie, Movie, 1978, All That Jazz, 1979-80, Annie, 1982, Micki and Maude, 1984; play Ann Reinking.Music Moves Me, 1984; actor, choreographer Broadway shows: Chicago, 1996 (Tony award 1997), Annie Get Your Gun, 1999 (Tony award 1999), Fosse, 2001; choreographer Broadway shows: Annie Get Your Gun, 1999, Look of Love, 2003 Recipient Clarence Derwent award, 1974, Outer Critics Circle award, 1974, Theatre World award, 1974, Dance Educators Am. award, 1979, Harkness Dance award, 1979, two Tony award nominations, Tony award for Choregraphy, 1997; Ford Found. scholar, 1964-66; Robert Joffery scholar, 1967; Harkness scholar; Nat. Dance Educators award. Mem. Actors Equity, AFTRA, Stage Actors Guild. Avocations: horseback riding, skiing, swimming, hiking. also: Steps Contemporary & Classical Dance 2121 Broadway Fl 3 New York NY 10023-1786

REINMANN, CAROL SUE, elementary school educator; married; 2 children. BS in Elem. Edn., MS in Elem. Edn., S.E. Mo. State U. 1st grade May Greene Elem., Charles C. Clippard Elem. Active Hanover Luth. Ch., Sunday sch. tchr., Bible sch. tchr.; mem. Luth. Sch. Bd. Edn.; active Luth. Family and Children's Svcs., Am. Cancer Soc. Reach for Recovery. Recipient Young Educator award Mo. Jaycees, 1974, Elem. Educator of Yr. award Cape Girardeau C. of C., 1994, Eddy award Mo. Pub. Edn., Award of Distinction Vison 2000; named Mo. Tchr. of Yr., 1998. Mem. PEO Sisterhood, Alpha Delta Kappa (Mo. state pres., South Ctrl. regional v.p.). Avocations: collecting antiques, breeding and showing tennessee walking horses. Office: Clippard Elem 2880 Hopper Rd Cape Girardeau MO 63701-3545

REINOLD, CHRISTY DIANE, school counselor, consultant; b. Neodasha, Kans., July 21, 1942; d. Ernest Sherman and Faye Etta (Herbert) Wild; m. William Owen Reinold, Dec. 20, 1964; children: Elizabeth, Rebecca. BA Edn., Calif. State U., Fresno, 1964, MA in Edn. and Psychology, 1964. Cert. counselor, Family Wellness instr.; lic. mental health counselor, Fla. Tchr. Clovis (Calif.) Unified Sch. Dist., 1965-66, Santa Clara (Calif.) Unified Sch. Dist., 1966-67, Inst. Internat. Chateaubriand, Cannes, France, 1968-69; tchr., vice prin. Internat. Sch., Sliema, Malta, 1969-70; elem. sch. counselor Duval City Schs., Jacksonville, Fla., 1977-82, Lodi (Calif.) Unified Sch. Dist., 1982—2004. Cons. Calif. Dept. Edn.; mem. Calif. Commn. on Tchr. Credentialing, Sacramento, 1986—2004, mem. adv. panel, 1998—2004; mem. stds. rev. com. Nat. Bd. Cert. Sch. Counselors, 2002—04. Co-author: The Best for Our Kids; Counseling in the 21st Century; contbr. articles. Chmn. bd. dirs. Oak Crest Child Care Ctr., Jacksonville, 1979-81. Named Anne Upton Sch. Counselor of Yr. for Calif., Calif. Sch. Counselor's Assn., 1995; named to H.B. McDaniel Hall of Fame, Stanford U., 2003; recipient H.B. McDaniel Individual award, 1986, James Saum Legis. award, Calif. Sch. Counselor's Assn., 1991, Donald Hayes Lifetime Achievement award, Assn. Calif. Sch. Counselors, 2002. Mem.: AAUW (3rd v.p. 1974, 1st v.p. 1980, by-laws chmn. 1990, chmn. pub. policy 1991—93, pres. 1993), Lodi Pupil Pers. Assn. (pres. 1986—87), Calif. Alliance Pupil Svcs. Orgns. (bd. dirs. 1988—95), Fla. Sch. Counselors Assn., Calif. Assn. Counseling and Devel., Calif. Sch. Counselor Assn. (legis. chmn. 1985—90, pres. 1991), Am. Sch. Counselor Assn. (govt. rels. specialist 1993—94). Republican. Avocations: history, travel, politics. Home: 1772 Le Bec Ct Lodi CA 95240 Personal E-mail: creinold@earthlink.net.

REINSDORF, JUDITH A., lawyer; b. 1963; BA in Polit. Sci., magna cum laude, U. Rochester; JD, Cornell U. Bar: NY 1990. With Crowell & Morling, Washington; asst. gen. counsel to chief legal counsel Monsanto Co.; v.p., assoc. gen. counsel Pharmacia Corp., 2000—03; v.p., corp. sec. Tyco Internat. Ltd., Princeton, NJ, 2003—04; v.p., gen. counsel, corp. sec. C.R. Bard, Inc., Murray Hill, NJ, 2004—. Mem.: ABA. Office: CR Bard Inc 730 Central Ave New Providence NJ 07974

REINSHAGEN, YOLANDA P., elementary school educator; b. Recife, Brazil, Mar. 18, 1953; came to U.S., 1977; d. Manoel and Irene Ferreira Pessôa; m. Jerald Alfred Reinshagen Sr., Dec. 22, 1977; children: Jerald Jr., Jerlanda, Janice, Joseph, Judith, Jerson. BA in Theology and Edn., Monte Morelos (Mex.) U., 1979; MA in Health Edn., U. West Fla., 1994. Asst. tchr. Educandarion Advents, Belem de Maria, Brazil, 1972-74; chaplain Hosp. La Carlota, Monte Morelos, 1975-77; tchr. Academia Adventista del Oeste, Mayaguez, P.R., 1979, SDA Elem. Sch., Queens, 1980. Office mgr., treas. Family Practice Clinic, Rockport, Ind., 1985-88; ministry dir. Univ. S.D.A.C., Pensacola, Fla., 1992-94 Counselor Pathfinders, 1999; Spanish transl. SDA, 1990. Mem. SMMA (coord. health project 1997, sec. 1997). SDA. Home: 19 North Pt Hattiesburg MS 39402-7708

REIS, JEAN STEVENSON, administrative secretary; b. Wilburton, Okla., Nov. 30, 1914; d. Robert Emory and Ada (Ross) Stevenson; m. George William Reis, June 24, 1939 (dec. 1980). BA, U. Tex., El Paso, 1934; MA, So. Meth. U., 1935; postgrad., U. Chgo., 1937—38, U. Wash., 1948—49. Tchr. El Paso H.S., 1935—39; safety engr., trainer Safety and Security Divsn., Office of Chief Ordnance, Chgo., 1942—45; tchr. Lovenberg Jr. H.S., Galveston, Tex., 1946; parish sec. Trinity Parish Episcopal Ch., Seattle, 1950—65; adminstrv. sec., asst. Office Resident Bishop, United Meth. Ch., Seattle, 1965—94; ret., 1994. Observer Africa U. installation, Mutare, Zimbabwe, 1994; com. on legislation for 1996 gen. conf. Hist. Soc. of United Meth. Ch. Recipient Bishop's award, 1980. Mem. AAUW, Beta Beta Beta. Home: 9310 42nd Ave NE Seattle WA 98115-3814

REIS, LESLIE ANN, law educator, lawyer; b. Plainfield, N.J., Apr. 21, 1958; BS cum laude, Syracuse Univ., 1981; JD, John Marshall Law Sch., Chgo., 1996. Bar: Ill. 1996. Broadcast journalist, 1981—96; legal fellow Reporters Com. for Freedom of the Press, 1996—97; adj. prof. John Marshall Law Sch., 1997—; dir. Ctr. for Info. Tech. & Privacy Law, John Marshall Law Sch., 1997—. Contbr. articles to prof. jour. Mem. Fed. Info. Security & Privacy Adv. Bd. Mem.: Am. Judicature Soc. (past dir., Ctr. for Judicial Independence). Office: Center for Information Technology and Privacy Law John Marshall Law School 315 S Plymouth Ct Chicago IL 60604

REISMAN, ELLEN KELLY, lawyer; b. Oct. 24, 1959; BA summa cum laude, Boston Coll., 1981; JD cum laude, U. Chgo., 1984. Bar: DC 1984, US Dist. Ct., DC 1985, Calif. 1996. Assoc. Arnold & Porter LLP, Washington, 1984, ptnr., 1992—99; gen. counsel, v.p. legal divsn. Wyeth-Ayerst Pharmaceuticals, 1999—2001; ptnr., Product Liability Practice Group Arnold & Porter LLP, LA, 2001—. Named one of Top 50 Women Litigators, The Nat. Law Jour., 2001, The Top 45 Under 45, The Am. Lawyer, 2003. Office: Arnold & Porter 777 S Figueroa St 44th Flr Los Angeles CA 90017-2513 Office Phone: 213-243-4111. Office Fax: 213-243-4199.

REISMAN, FREDRICKA KAUFFMAN, education educator; b. Rochester, N.Y., Sept. 22, 1930; d. Samuel Hopkins and Rosalind (Lessen) Kauffman; 1 dau., Lisa Reisman Halterman. Student, Barnard Coll., 1951; BA, Syracuse U., 1952, MS, 1963, PhD, 1968. Lectr. Syracuse U., 1967-69; adj. assoc. prof. ednl. psychology Maria Regina Coll., Syracuse, N.Y., 1968; asst. prof. elem. edn. U. Ga., Athens, 1969-74, assoc. prof., 1974-79, prof. and chair early childhood middle sch. and elem. edn., prof. math. edn. and spl. edn., 1979-83; vis. prof., dept. human behavior and devel.; coordinator tchr.-scholar program Drexel U., Phila., 1984-85, dir. divsn. instrn. and program, head tchr. preparation, 1991—, prof., dir. tchr. preparation, cert. officer, 1986—. Vis. prof. U. Calif., Riverside, Marianne Frostig Center Ednl. Therapy, Los Angeles; cons. diagnostic teaching math.; mem. program approval com. Pa. State Dept. Edn., 1984—, tchr. cert. com., 1984—; dir. Drexel U. Sch. of Edn. of the Coll. of Arts and Scis., 1997—. Author: Guide to the Diagnostic Teaching of Arithmetic, 1972, 3d edit., 1982, Diagnostic Teaching of Elementary School Mathematics: Methods and Content, 1977, 2d edit., 1981, (with S. H. Kaufman) Teaching Mathematics to Children with Special Needs, 1980, Sequential Assessment in Mathematics, 1985, Elementary Education: A Basic Text, 1987; contbr. articles to profl. jours. Recipient outstanding faculty citizen recognition Am. Assn. Higher Edn., 1994. Mem. Nat. Coun. Tchrs. Math., Am. Psychol. Assn., Internat. Assn. Applied Psychology, Soc. for Rsch. in Child Devel., Sch. Sci. and Math. Assn., ASCD, Assn. for Tchr. Educators, Am. Edn. Rsch. Assn., Sigma Xi, Pi Lambda Theta, Phi Delta Kappa. Office: Drexel U 109 Disque Philadelphia PA 19106

REISMAN, JOAN ANN, executive secretary; b. Brooklyn, NY, Sept. 15, 1936; d. David and Betty Rose Sobel; m. Zane Saul Reisman; children: Mitchell, Eve, Lawrence, Beth. Owner Sno White Cleaners, Bklyn., 1967—70; mgr., owner Hill Park Cleaners, Bklyn., 1970—73; with Handher Murray Law Firm, N.Y.C., 1974—76; mgr., owner Joe Taylor Cleaners, S.I., NY, 1977—78; adminstrv. office mgr. Cobble Hill Health Ctr., Bklyn., 1979—2003. Democrat. Jewish. Home: 21 Gemini Ln Manalapan NJ 07726

REISMAN, JUDITH ANN GELERNTER, media communications executive, educator; b. Hillside, NJ, Apr. 11, 1935; MA in Speech Comm., Case Western Res. U., 1976, PhD in Speech Comm., 1980. Faculty dept. anthropology and sociology Haifa U., Israel, 1981—83; rsch. prof. sch. edn. Am. U., Washington, 1983—85; founder, pres. Inst. Media Edn., 1985—. Cons., reviewer grant proposals audio-visual drug programs for youth Dept. Edn., 1987; rsch. design cons. Alcohol and Tobacco Media Analysis in Mainstream Mags., Dept. HHS, 1987—90; cons., field reviewer Drug Free Youth Sch. Candidates Dept. Edn., 1988; lectr., adj. prof. George Mason U., Va., 1990; expert witness Pres.'s Commn. on Assignment of Women in Armed Forces, 1992, U.S. Atty. Gen. Commn. on Pornography, 1985—86, U.S. Atty. Gen. Task Force on Domestic Violence, Washington, 1985, Mapplethorpe Trial, Cin., 1990, Australian Parliament, 1992, Ga. State Senate, 1992; nominated to panel on sex harassment in the Air Force U.S. Inspector Gen., 2003; sci. advisor Protective Parents Assn.; subcom. junk sci. Am. Legis. Exchange Coun. Edn. Task Force, 1999—2004. Author: Images of Children, Crime and Violence in Playboy, Penthouse and Hustler, 1989, Kinsey, Sex and Fraud, 1990, Softport Plays Hardball, 1991, Kinsey, Crimes and Consequences, 1998, 2003, Kinsey's Attic, 2006; contbr. preme Ct. cases to profl. jours. Co-recipient Scholastic Mag. awards, Dukane award, 1982; recipient Gold Camera award, 1982, Silver Screen award, 1982, Filmstrip of Yr. award, 1981—82, Silver Plaque award, 1982, Family Svc. Assn. Am. 1st pl. award local TV series, 1974, Best of 1965 award, 1965, Scientist of Yr. for Children award, 1993; U.S. Dept. Justice grantee. Mem.: AAAS, Women in Neurosci., Nat. Black Child Devel. Inst., Soc. Sci. Study Sex, N.Y. Acad. Scis., Internat. Comm. Assn., Am. Statis. Assn., Am. Assn. Composers, Authors and Pubs., Nat. Assn. Scholars. E-mail: jareisman@cox.net.

REISMAN, SHARYL A., lawyer; b. NYC, 1967; AB magna cum laude, Dartmouth Coll., 1989; JD cum laude, U. Mich., 1992. Bar: Ill. 1992, NY 1998. Ptnr., environmental law Jones Day (formerly Jones,Day, Reavis & Pogue), NYC. Office: Jones Day 222 E 41st St New York NY 10017-6702 Office Phone: 212-326-3939. Office Fax: 212-755-7306. Business E-Mail: sareisman@jonesday.com.

REISS, DALE ANNE, corporate financial executive; b. Sept. 3, 1947; d. Max and Nan (Hart) R.; m. Jerome L. King, Mar. 5, 1978; children: Matthew Reiss, Mitchell, Stacey. BS, Ill. Inst. Tech., 1967; MBA, U. Chgo., 1970. CPA, Fla., Ill., Mich., Mo. Cost acct. First Nat. Bank, Chgo., 1967; asst. contr. City Colls. of Chgo., 1967-71; dir. fin. Chgo. Dept. Pub. Works, 1971-73; prin. Arthur Young & Co., Chgo., 1973-80; sr. v.p., contr. Urban Investment & Devel. Co., Chgo., 1980-85; mng. ptnr. Ernst & Young LLP, Chgo., 1985-98, Ernst & Young, N.Y.C., 1998-99; global dir. real estate, hospitality and constrn. Ernst & Young LLP, N.Y.C., 1999—. Bd. dirs. Ill. Inst. Tech., Urban Land Inst.; adv. bd. Kellogg Real Estate, Northwestern U., U. Chgo. Grad. Sch. of Bus. Mem. AICPA, Fin. Execs. Inst., Pension Real Estate Assn., Chgo. Network (bd. dirs.), Econ. Chgo. Club, Met. Club, Chgo. Yacht Club, NY Athletic Club. Office: Ernst & Young 5 Times Sq 16th Fl New York NY 10036-6530 E-mail: dale.reiss@ey.com.

REISS, DEBORAH L., elementary school educator; d. M.A. and Lena Doggett; m. Raymond Reiss, Nov. 15, 1975; 1 child, Keleigh. BA magna cum laude, Harding U., Searcy, Ark., 1971; MSW, U. Okla., Norman, 1973; Degree in Tchg., Fla. Atlantic U., Boca Raton, 1993. LCSW Mo. Social worker Meth. Hosps., Memphis, 1986—87; sch. counselor Harding Acad., Memphis, 1987—91; social worker Jackson Meml. Hosp., Miami, Fla., 1991—92; Dds. instr. Mo. So. State Coll., Josplin, 1994—96; dialysis social worker City Health Systems, Springfield, Mo., 1996—99; social worker Smyth County Cmty. Hosp., Marion, Va., 2000—04; tchr. mid. sch. Orange County Pub. Schs., Winterborden, Fla., 2004—. Mem. Smyth County Cmty. Improvement Bd., Marion, Va., 2000—04; adj. instr. univs., Ky., Mo.; presenter women's retreats Va., Tenn. Contbr. articles to profl. jours. Mem.: NASW, Lic. Cert. Social Workers, NCATE, Acad. Cert. Social Workers, Alpha Chi. Avocations: golf, hiking, reading, piano. Home: 207 Twelve League Cir Casselberry FL 32707 E-mail: dlreiss39@aol.com.

REISS, LENORE ANN, language educator, retired secondary school educator; b. Bklyn., Apr. 17, 1936; d. Morris and Alice Shestack; m. Edward Lawrence Reiss, Sept. 13, 1959 (dec. June 5, 2000); children: Stephanie Lynne, Jonathan David. BA cum laude, Boston U., 1957; postgrad., Middlebury Coll., 1956, NYU, 1974—76, U. Miami, 1979. Tchr. Spanish and French Martin Van Buren HS, Queens Village, NY, 1957—59; pvt. tutor N.Y.C., 1960—77; pvt. sch. tchr. Studio on Eleventh St., N.Y.C., 1970—77; tchr. The Livingston Sch., N.Y.C., 1977—78, Chiaravalle Montessori Sch., Evanston, Ill., 1986—87; pvt. tutor Evanston, 1990—95; ret., 1995. Author: White-Robed Recluse: A Study of Emily Dickinson, 1993, Genius of Darkness: A Study of Edgar Allan Poe, 1994, The Good Lady of Nohant: A Study of George Sand, 1995; contbr. poems to jours., articles to profl. jours. Avocations: reading, music, dance, antiques, theater. Home: 2025 Sherman Ave Evanston IL 60201 also: 136 E 76th St New York NY 10021

REISS, SUSAN MARIE, editor, writer; b. Washington, Sept. 14, 1963; m. Paul L. Roney Jr., May 25, 1991. BA in English Lit., U. Va., 1985; MA in English, George Mason U., 1989. Editl. asst. Water Pollution Control Fedn., Alexandria, Va., 1985-87; freelance writer, editor Arlington, Va., 1987-90; staff writer George Mason U., Fairfax, Va., 1988-90, Optical Soc. Am., Washington, 1990-91, news editor, 1991-93, mng. editor, 1993-96; editor On Campus With Women Assn. Am. Colls. and Univs., 1996—2000; freelance writer, editor Arlington, 1996—. Newsletter editor: Arlington County Tennis Assn., 1990-91; contbr. articles to profl. jours. and mags. Mem. Am. Soc. Laser Medicine and Surgery, Nat. Assn. Science Writers, Nat. Press Club, Washington Ind. Writers, D.C. Sci. Writers Assn., Sigma Tau Delta (founding mem. U. Va. chpt.). Avocations: tennis, piano, cross country skiing. Home and Office: 6814 30th Rd N Arlington VA 22213-1602

REISTER, RUTH ALKEMA, lawyer, finance company executive; b. Grand Rapids, Mich., May 30, 1936; d. Henry and Lena (Land) Alkema; m. Raymond A. Reister, Oct. 7, 1967. BA, U. Mich., 1958, JD, 1964; grad. Program in Bus. Adminstrn., Harvard U., 1959, postgrad. Program in Mgmt. Devel., 1976. Bar: Minn., Mich. 1964, U.S. Supreme Ct. 1976. Trust officer Northwestern Nat. Bank, Mpls., 1964-70; asst. counsel, asst. v.p., sec. Fed. Res. Bank, Mpls., 1970-81; asst. sec., bd. govs. Fed. Res. System, 1977; dep. under sec. U.S. Dept. Agr., Washington, 1981-83; pres. First Bank Systems Agrl. Credit Corp., Mpls., 1983-84; pres. Groveland Corp., Mpls., 1986—; dir. Herman Miller, Inc., Zealand, Mich., 1984—. Bd. dirs. United Way, ARC, Jones Harrison Home, Mpls.; bd. dirs., chair Gustavus Adolfus Coll.; chmn. Jones-Harrison Found. Mem. Harvard Bus. Sch. Club Minn., Minn. Women's Econ. Round Table (pres. 1980-81).

REITAN, ANN, psychologist, writer; b. Indpls., Feb. 2, 1964; d. Ralph Meldahl and Ann Reitan. BA in Psychology, U. Wash., Seattle, Wash., 1990; MA in Psychology, Pepperdine U., Irvine, Calif., 1996; PsyD in Psychology, Alliant Internat. U., Fresno, Calif., 2003. Post-doctoral fellow Wash. U., Saint Louis, Mo., 2003—04; clin. psychologist Porterville Devel. Ctr., Porterville, Calif., 2004—05; mem. bd. dir. Greater Fresno Alliance Mental Health. Rsch. asst. Reitan Neuropsychology Lab., Inc., Tucson, 1991—2004. Adv. for mandated dental care for the mentally ill Harborview Hosp., Seattle, 1991—91. Office Phone: 559-485-5336. Personal E-mail: annreitan@sbcglobal.net.

REJENT, MARIAN MAGDALEN, retired pediatrician; b. Toledo, Aug. 12, 1920; d. Casimir Stanley and Magdalen (Szymanowski) R. BS, Mary Manse Coll., 1943; MD, Marquette U., 1946; MPH, U. Mich., 1960. Diplomate Am. Bd. Pediatrics. Intern St. Vincent Med. Ctr., Toledo, 1946-47; resident communicable diseases City Hosp., Cleve., 1947-48; resident pediatrics Childrens Hosp., Akron, Ohio, 1948-50; pvt. practice Toledo, 1950-54; chief div. maternal child health Toledo Bd. Health, 1953-64; dir. pediatrics Maumee Valley Hosp., Toledo, 1964-69; assoc. prof. pediatrics Med. Coll. Ohio, Toledo, 1969-76; med. dir. State Crippled Childrens Program, Columbus, Ohio, 1976-78; attendant pediatrician St. Vincent Med. Ctr., Toledo, 1978-80, 87-99; chief pediatric svcs. Wake County Health Dept., Raleigh, NC, 1980-87; ret. clin. prof. pediatrics Med. Coll. Ohio, 1998; ret., 1999. Exec. com. March of Dimes, 1988-92. Mem. AMA, APHA, Am. Acad. Pediatrics, Am. Med. Women's Assn., Ohio PHA, Ohio State Med. Assn., NW Ohio Pediatric Assn., Acad. Medicine Toledo, Alpha Omega Alpha. Republican. Roman Catholic. Avocations: travel, photography, painting. Home: The Woodlands Apt 401 4030 Indian Rd Toledo OH 43606

REJINO, MONA, music educator, composer; b. Haskell, Tex., Feb. 4, 1959; m. Huey Miller Bledsoe and Patsy Ruth Smith; m. Richard Rejino, Dec. 18, 1982; children: Margaret, Adam. MusB, West Tex. State U., 1981; MusM, North Tex. State U., 1983. Group piano instr. Dallas Ind. Sch. Dist., 1982-84; staff pianist Old San Francisco Steakhouse, Dallas, 1982-92; piano instr. Rejino Piano Studio, Dallas, 1983—. Co-author, composer Hal Leonard Student Piano Libr., 1996—, Hal Leonard Adukt Paino Method Books 1 and 2, 2005; composer, Portraits in Style Intermediate Piano Solos Collection, 2004; co-arranger Popular Piano Solos, Books 3, 4 and 5, 1997-2000, Christmas Piano Solos, Books 1-5, 1997-2000, God Bless America and Other Patriotic Piano Solos, Books 1-5, 2001, More Popular Piano Solos, Books 1-5, 2002, Traditional Hymns, Books 1-5, 2002, Classical Themes, Books 1-5, 2002-03, Christmas Favorites, Book 1, 2005; co-author: Adult Piano Method, Book 1 and 2, 2005; co-arranger: Popular Hits, Books 1-2, 2005-2006, Broadway and Movie Hits, Books 1-5, 2005-06; arranger: Today's Hits, 2006; featured composer in Hal Leonard Showcase Solos Series, 2000-; contbr. to Clavier's Keys Piano Music mag., Keyboard Companion mag., In Touch newsletter. Mem. Music Tchrs. Nat. Assn., Tex. Music Tchrs. Assn., Carrollton Music Tchrs. Assn. (pres. 1989, v.p. 1998—, Tchr. of Yr. 1987-88). Home: 2515 Willowdale Dr Carrollton TX 75006-2032

RELKIN, MICHELE WESTON, artist; b. L.A., Jan. 17, 1946; d. Ruben and Vivian (Demerer) Weston; m. Stephen Relkin, July 18, 1982; 1 child, Gregory Aaron. Student, Santa Monica Coll. Curator, co-founder Gallery 9, Thousand Oaks, Calif., 1994—. Art instr. for children and adults; artist in residence Walnut Canyon Elem. Sch., Moorpark, Calif., Santa Fe Pub. Schs.; visiting artist Santa Fe Pub. and Pvt. Schs. Represented in permanent collections Nat. Archives, Washington, William J. Clinton Presdl. Libr., Ark., The White House, Santa Fe Gallery, Gallera Ortiz, San Antonio, Gabriells Gallery, Santa Fe. Recipient Printmaking award Moorpark Coll., 1992. Mem. Nat. Assn. Women Artists, Thousand Oaks Art Assn. (program dir. 1990—, Art awards), Santa Barbara Printmakers Soc., Santa Fe Book Arts Group. Avocations: walking, pets, nature, teaching children's art. Home: 6 Dandelion Cir Santa Fe NM 87506 Office Phone: 505-986-9517.

RELL, M. JODI, governor; b. Norfolk, Va., June 16, 1946; m. Lou Rell; children: Meredith, Michael. Student, Old Dominion U., Western Conn. State U.; LLD (hon.), Univ. of Hartford, 2001. Mem., dep. minority leader Conn. Ho. Reps., 1984-94; lt. gov. State of Conn., 1995—2004, gov., 2004—. Past vice chmn. Brookfield Rep. Town Com., appt. chair of the Hartford Econ. Devel. Adv. Group, (HEDAG), 1998; trustee YMCA Western Conn; played a key role in raising funds for the Conn. Firefighters Meml.; estab. the Lt. Gov.'s Comm. on State Mandate Reform, Lt. Gov.'s Conn. Treasures award. Named Melvin Jones Fellow, Lions Club Internat. Found., 2003; recipient Leadership award, Nat. Order of Women Legislators (NOWL), Impact award, Conn. Tech. Coun., 2001, First Kids 2001 Policy Leadership award, Conn. Voices for Children, Arnold Markle Public Service award. Mem. Nat. Order Women Legislators (past nat. pres., former v.p., treas., corr. sec.), Women Execs. in State Govt., Brookfield Rep. Women's Club (past pres.), Brookfield Bus. and Profl. Women's Club, Prison and Jail Overcrowding comm., Governor's Law Enforcement Coun., Yale Corp., State Finance Advisory Com. Republican. Office: Office Gov Exec Chambers 210 Capitol Ave Hartford CT 06106 E-mail: Governor.Rell@po.state.ct.us.*

REMER, DEBORAH JANE, elementary school educator; b. Detroit, Dec. 10, 1953; d. Maynard William and Marie Josephine (Wells) Remer. BS, Mich. State U., 1976, MA in Tchg., 1977. Secondary provisional tchg. cert. Mich., secondary continuing tchg. cert. Mich. Sci. tchr. Walled Lake (Mich.) Mid. Sch., 1977-81; substitute tchr. Utica (Mich) Cmty. Schs., 1981-85; sci. tchr. Kingsbury Sch., Oxford, Mich., 1985-86; sci. tchr., sci. dept. chair Walled Lake Consol. Schs., 1986—. Chair 8th grade sci. fair Walled Lake Mid. Sch., 1987, 1989—, coach sci. competition, 1987—94; mem. K-12 sci. com. Walled Lake Consol. Schs., 1990—. Co-author: Environmental Conservation Program Design, 1976; author: The Joachim Ernest Theodore Remer Family in Michigan, 1980, revised, 1995. Archaeology program presenter, pianist Rochester Mills (Mich.) Mus., 1988—, co-dir. archaeology programs, 1989—; tallykeeper Rochester Grangers Vintage Baseball Team. Named winner in conservation, Mich. 4-H Clubs, 1971; recipient Key Club award, 1972, Earl Borden Hist. Preservation award, City of Rochester Hills Hist. Dist. Commn., 1995. Mem.: MADD, NEA, Nat. Trust Hist. Presevation, Oakland County Pioneer and Hist. Soc., Detroit Zool. Soc., Mich. Archeol. Soc., Nat. Wildflower Rsch. Ctr., Archeol. Inst. Am., N.Am. Butterfly Assn., New Eng. Hist. Geneal. Soc., Suffolk County (N.Y.) Hist. and Geneal. Soc., Rochester Avon (Mich.) Hist. Soc. (rec. sec. 1990), Hist. Soc. Mich., Met. Detroit Sci. Tchrs. Assn. (conf. presenter 1993—94), Mich. Sci. Tchrs. Assn. (mem. mid. sch. program com. 1977—81, dir.-at-large 1981, conf. presenter 1993—95), Mich. Earth Sci. Tchrs. Assn., Walled Lake Edn. Assn., Mich. Edn. Assn., Nat. Earth Sci. Tchrs. Assn., Nat. Sci. Tchrs. Assn., Am. Livestock Breeds Conservancy, Mich. Karst Conservancy, Colonial Williamsburg Found., Bat Conservation Internat., Earthwatch, Cranbrook Inst. Sci., Macomb Audubon Soc., Smithsonian Assocs., Founders Soc.-Detroit Inst. Arts, Mich. State U. Alumni Assn., Soc. Preservation Old Mills, Archeol. Conservancy, Alpha Zeta. Republican. Congregationalist. Avocations: archaeology, gardening, reading, music, needlecrafts. Office: Walled Lake Middle Sch 46720 W Pontiac Trl Walled Lake MI 48390-4048 Business E-Mail: remerd@walledlake.k12.mi.us.

REMES, ROBIN EVA, secondary school educator, cartographer; d. Jeremiah and Sarah Remes; m. Fredrick Biddle; 1 child, Patrick Biddle. BS, William Paterson U., 1974; MS, U. South Fla. Cert. tchr. Tex., NJ. World culture studies educator Houston Ind. Sch. Dist., 2004—, reading educator, reading specialist, ESL educator, English educator, chmn. reading dept.; assoc. educator Pinellas County Schools; oil exploration cartographer; computer cartographer Property Appraiser. Elem. sch. tutor, NJ. Author: Cartography Curriculum and H.S. Math Review. Rep. Young Dems., NJ, 1970. State scholar, NJ, 1971—74. Mem.: Houston Fedn. Tchrs. (bldg. steward, Membership Recruiter award 2001). Avocation: travel. Office Phone: 713-943-5700.

REMINGTON, DEBORAH WILLIAMS, artist; b. Haddonfield, N.J., June 25, 1935; d. Malcolm Van Dyke and Hazel Irwin (Stewart) R. BFA, San Francisco Art Inst., 1955. Adj. prof. art Cooper Union, N.Y.C., 1973—97, NYU, 1994—98; tchr. Nat. Acad. Design, N.Y.C., 2003—. One-woman shows include Dilexi Gallery, San Francisco, 1962, 63, 65, San Francisco Mus. Art, 1964, Bykert Gallery, N.Y.C., 1967, 69, 72, 74, Galerie Darthea Speyer, Paris, 1968, 71, 73, 92, Pyramid Gallery, Washington DC, 1973, 76, zola-Leiberman Gallery, Chgo., 1976, Hamilton Gallery, N.Y.C., 1977, Portland (Oreg.) Ctr. for Visual Arts, 1977, Michael Berger Gallery, Pitts., 1979, Mary Ryan Gallery, N.Y.C., 1982, Ramon Osuna Gallery, Washington D.C., 1983, Newport Harbor Art Mus., 1983, Oakland (Calif.) Mus., 1984, Jack Shainman Gallery, N.Y.C., 1987, Shoshana Wayne Gallery, L.A., 1988, Mitchell Algus Gallery, N.Y.C., 2001; group shows include Whitney Mus. Am. Art, N.Y.C., 1965, 67, 72, San Francisco Mus. Art, 1956, 60, 61, 63, 64, 65, Lausanne Mus., Switz., 1966, Fondation Maeght, St. Paul de Vence, France, 1968, Smithsonian Am. Art Mus., Washington, D.C., 1968, Art. Inst., Chgo., 1974, Inst. Contemporary Art, Boston, 1975, Nat. Gallery Modern Art, Lisbon, Portugal, 1981, Toledo Mus. Art, 1975, The 6 Gallery, 1954-57, Natsoulas Gallery, Davis, Calif., 1990, 1st Trienalle des Ameriques Maubeuge, France, 1993, Tamarind Inst. Retrospective, 2000, Worcester (Mass.) Art Mus., 2001, San Jose (Calif.) Mus. Art, 2002, numerous others; represented in permanent collections Whitney Mus. Am. Art, Smithsonian Am. Art Mus., Washington, Art Inst., Chgo., Centre d'Art et de Culture Georges Pompidou, Paris, Carnegie Mus., Pitts. Recipient Hassam and Speicher Purchase award Am. Acad. and Inst. Arts and Letters, 1988; NEA fellow, 1979-80; Tamarind Inst. fellow, 1973; Guggenheim fellow, 1984; Pollock-Krasner Found. grantee, 1999. Mem. NAD (Benjamin Altman prize for painting 178th Ann. Exhbn. 2003). Home: 309 W Broadway New York NY 10013-5325 Office Phone: 212-925-3037. Office Fax: 212-426-1711. E-mail: deborahremington@aol.com.

REMINGTON, KRISTI, lawyer; BA, Denison U., 1992; JD, Am. U., 1995. Counsel to sr. counsel House Govt. Reform Com., U.S. House of Reps., 1996—2001; sr. assoc. Balch & Bingham, Washington, DC, 2001—03; dep. asst. atty. gen. Office Legal Policy, U.S. Dept. Justice, 2003—. Office: Office Legal Policy Rm 4234 Main Justice Bldg 950 Pennsylvania Ave NW Washington DC 20530-0001

REMINGTON, MICHELLE GANIERE, principal; d. John Kenwood and Donna May Ganiere; m. Jesse Ryan Remington, Aug. 1, 1998; children: Blake Allen, Sierra Skye. PhD, U. So. Miss., Hattiesburg, 2002. Cert. sch. administr. and tchr. Mont., Oreg. Elem. tchr. Pub. Sch. Sys., Saipan, Marianas Islands, 1996—98; h.s. English tchr. Colegio Internacional de Caracas, Venezuela, 1998—2001; asst. prin., head K-12 prin. Colegio Internacional Puerto La Cruz, Barcelona, Venezuela, 2001—05; h.s. prin. Am. Cmty. Sch., Abu Dhabi, United Arab Emirates, 2006—. Doctoral mentor Touro Internat. U., Calif., 2005—. Recipient Academic Achievement award, U. So. Miss., 2002; Rogers scholar, Willamette U. and Pvt. Alumni, 1995. Mem.: ASCD, Nat. Assn. Secondary Sch. Prins., Phi Delta Kappa. Avocations: tennis, basketball, volleyball, water-skiing, travel, album collecting. Home: 12897 Sunburst Dr Bigfork MT 59911 Office Phone: 971-2- 681-5115.

REMINI, LEAH, actress; b. Bklyn., June 15, 1970; m. Angelo Pagan, July 19, 2003; 1 child, Sofia Bella. Appearances include (TV series) Living Dolls, 1989, Saved By The Bell, 1991, The Man in the Family, 1991, Getting Up and Going Home, 1992, King of Queens, 1999—, (voice) Gabriel Knight: Sins of the Fathers, 1994, (voice) Phantom 2040: The Ghost Who Walks, 1994, The First Time Out, 1995, Glory Daze, 1996, Fired Up, 1997, Follow Your Heart, 1998, also numerous guest appearances, including Head of the Class, 1988, Who's the Boss?, 1989, Valerie, 1990, Paradise, 1991, Cheers, 1991 & 1993, Blossom, 1992, Evening Shade, 1993, The Commish, 1994, Renegade, 1994, Diagnosis Murder, 1995, Friends, 1995, NYPD Blue, 1996; TV Movies: Legend of the Lost Tribe, 2002 (voice), Hooves of Fire, 1999 (voice); Films: Follow Your Heart, 1998, Old School, 2003. Office: Gold Marchak & Liedtke 3500 W Olive Ave Ste 1400 Burbank CA 91505-5512

REMKUS, CONNIE ELAINE, nutritional consultant; d. Charles Edward and Phyllis Mary Remkus. BSBA in Acctg., San Francisco State U., 1986. Registered nutritional cons. Sch. of Nutritional Sci., San Jose. Flight attendant United Air Lines, Chgo., 1966—2002; self-employed property and investment mgr. Chgo., 1973—2003; tax preparer David Nitz & Assocs., San Mateo, Calif., 1975; nutritional cons., ind. distbr. Diamite Corp., San Carlos, Calif., 1988—95; field v.p. Symmetry Direct, Chgo., 1995—. Mem. South Loop Neighbors, Chgo., 2001—05; vol. SPCA, San Mateo, 1984—87. Mem.: Airline Flight Attendants Union (membership chair grievance com. 1967—70), Bus. Networking Internat. (sec. 2001—03, asst. dir., amb. 2002—03). Avocations: travel, real estate, health and wellness. Office Phone: 312-455-2850.

REMLEY, AUDREY WRIGHT, retired academic administrator, psychologist; b. Dec. 26, 1931; d. Leslie Frank and Irene Lesetta (Graue) Wright; m. Alvin Remley, Mar. 25, 1951 (dec. Mar. 1986); children: Steven Leslie, David Mark. AA, Hannibal-LaGrange Coll., 1951; BS in Edn. cum laude, U. Mo., 1963, MA, 1969, PhD, 1974; LHD (hon.), Westminster Coll., 1996. Lic. psychologist, Mo.; cert. health svc. provider, Mo. From asst. prof. psychology to assoc. prof. to prof. Westminster Coll., Fulton, Mo., 1969-95, prof., assoc. dean faculty, 1989-95, chmn. dept. psychology, 1975-78, dir. counseling svcs., 1975-79, dir. student devel., 1979-80, dir. acad. advising and counseling svcs., 1980-88. Owner It's A Crock Antiques; cons. OVID Bell Press, 1988-89. Mem. adv. bd. Callaway Comty. Hosp., 1988-95, pres., 1992-95; bd. dirs. Serve, Inc., Fulton, 1989-95, pres., 1991-93; mem. adv. bd. social learning program Fulton State Hosp., chair, 1992-94, mng. county govt. task force fin. mgmt. chair; bd. dirs. Cen. Mo. Food Bank, 1995-96, Ft. Worth Symphony League Bd., 1998-2004, pres., 2002-04, v.p. for projects, 2005, exec. advisor, 2005-. Recipient Outstanding Young Woman of Am. award Jaycettes, 1965, Athena award, 1991, Remley Center award (1st recipient) Westminster Coll., 2001; NDEA fellow, 1968; bldg. Remley Women's Resource Ctr. Westminster Coll. named in her honor, 2001 Mem. APA, AACD, Am. Coll. Pers. Assn. (exec. coun. 1982-85, co-editor ACPA Developments 1984-87, v.p. state divns. 1987-89, treas.-elect 1990-91, treas. 1991-93, treas. ednl. found. bd. 1994-96, Outstanding State Divsn. Leader 1982, profl. svc. award 1991, Annuit Coeptis award 1994), Mo. Coll. Pers. Assn. (pres. 1981-82, profl. svc. award 1987), Mo. Psychol. Assn. (lic.), Ft. Worth Newcomers Club (pres. 1998-99), Kiwanis (exec. bd. 1989-92, v.p. 1992, pres.-elect 1992-93, pres. 1993-94, disting. 1995). Presbyterian. Avocations: singing, antiques, knitting.

REMSON, DEBRA S., music educator; b. Buffalo, Sept. 5, 1953; d. Howard and Mildred (Altman) R. Performance cert. in violin, Hochschule für Musik, Graz, Austria, 1973; BA in Music Edn., Fredonia State U., 1975; MA in Urban Edn., U. Buffalo, 1981; MS in Counseling, Canisius Coll., 1995. Tchr. vocal music Buffalo City Sch. Dist., 1977-78; tchr. instrumental music Elmira (N.Y.) City Sch. Dist., 1975-76, Cleveland Hill Sch. Dist., Cheektowaga, N.Y., 1978-79; tchr. vocal music/theater Lockport (N.Y.) City Sch. Dist., 1979-91; tchr. instrumental music Grand Island (N.Y.) Cen. Sch. Dist., 1991—. Guest condr. Niagara County Music Edn. Assn., NCMEA, Niagara County, N.Y., 1985, 90, 1996, 2000, 2004. Campaign asst. Dem. Party, Grand Island, 1997; vol. Ross Perot campaign, 1992. Mem. N.Y. State Music Assn. (adjudicator 1992—, guest spkr. 1991—), Erie County Music Edn. Assn. (guest condr. 1995), N.Y. State Outdoor Edn. Assn. (guest spkr.). Democrat. Avocations: music, fitness training, vocalist with local band. Office: Grand Island Cen Sch Dist 1100 Ransom Rd Grand Island NY 14072-1460

REN, CHRISTINE, surgeon; b. 1966; BS, Holy Cross Coll., Worcester, Mass., 1988; MD, Tufts Univ. Sch. Med., Boston, Mass. Surg. residency NYU Med. Ctr.; founder, dir. prog. surg. weight-loss NY Univ. Sch. Med. Faculty mem. Mt. Sinai Med. Ctr.; asst. prof. surgery NYU Sch. Med. Named one of NY's Premier Female Surgeons, YWCA, 2003; fellow advanced laparoscopic surgery, Mt. Sinai Med. Ctr. Office: New York Univ Sch Med 530 First Ave New York NY 10016

RENARD, MEREDITH ANNE, marketing and advertising professional; b. Newark, Apr. 12, 1952; d. W. Edward and Lois E. (Velthoven) Young; m. Robert W. Renard, Nov. 11, 1995. BA, Caldwell Coll., 1974. Advt., pub. rels. asst. Congoleum Corp., Lawrenceville, NJ, 1974—77; account mgr. Saatchi & Saatchi Compton, N.Y.C., 1977—82; dir. advt., sales promotion Singer Sewing Co., Edison, NJ, 1982—86, dir. product mktg., 1986—88, dir. nat. accounts, 1988—90; sr. mktg. rep. Walt Disney World Co., Lake Buena Vista, Fla., 1990—91; divsn. mktg. rep. Vista Advt., Walt Disney World Co., Lake Buena Vista, Fla., 1991—92; mgr. advt. Walt Disney World Co., Lake Buena Vista, Fla., 1992—94, mgr. Fla. tourist mktg., 1994—97; mgr. spl. events Disney Cruise Vacations, Celebration, Fla., 1997—; mgr. ops. integration Disney Cruise Line, Celebration, Fla., 2000—02, dir. youth activities and ops. integration, 2002—. Contbr. articles to profl. jours. Vol. North Brunswick Dem. Orgn., 1985—87; pub. rels. mgr. Cultural Arts Com., North Brunswick, 1986—87; props chair Adult Drama Group, North Brunswick, 1986—87; mem. mktg. com. Vol. Ctr. Ctrl. Fla., 1993—94. Mem.: Ctrl. Fla. Direct Mktg. Assn. (bd. dirs. 1990—92), Fla. Direct Mktg. Assn. Episcopalian. Avocations: cross stitch, reading. Office: Disney Cruise Line 210 Celebration Pl Ste 400 Celebration FL 34747-4978 Office Phone: 407-566-3651.

RENAUD, BERNADETTE MARIE ELISE, author; b. Ascot Corner, Que., Can., Apr. 18, 1945; d. Albert and Aline (Audet) R. Diploma, Présentation de Marie, Granby, Que., 1962-64. Librarian asst. Schs. of Waterloo, Que., 1964-67, tchr. primary schs. Que., 1967-70; adminstrv. sec. Assn. Medi-Tech-Sci., Montreal, Que., 1972-76. Author: Emilie La Baignoire A Pattes, 1976 (Can. Coun. Children's Lit. prize, 1976, Assn. Advancement of Scis. and Technics of Documentation award, 1976), 2d edit., 2002, Le Chat de l'Oratoire, 1978, Émilie la baignoire à pattes album, 1978, La maison tête de pioche, 1979, La révolte de la courte pointe, 1979, La dépression de l'ordinateur, 1981, Une boîte Magique Très Embêtante, 1981, La grande question de Tomatelle, 1982, Comment on fait un livre?, 1983, The Cat in the Cathedral, 1983, The Computer Revolts, 1984, (book and movie) Bach et Bottine, 1986 (awards for movie, 19 awards across the world, transl. ino 8 langs., subtitled into 18 langs.), Bach and Broccoli, 1986, (short movie) Quand l'accent devient grave, 1989, (novels) Un Homme Comme Tant d'Autres, tome 1, 1992, tome, II, 1993, tome, III, 1994, Prix Germaine Guèvremont, 1995, Gala des Arts du Bas-Richelieu (QC); dir., coord.: Ecrire pour la jeunesse, 1990; author: short stories, adaptations of 8 children's classics, 1977—79, La quête de Kurweena, 1997; dir., coord.: album and CD Le petit violon muet, 1997, Héritiers de l'éternité, 1998, Les Funambules D'un Temps Nouveau, 2001, Les Chemins d'Eve Tome I, 2002, Les Chemins d'Eve Tome II, 2002, Grand Prix du Livre de la Monteregie, 2001, 2002, Émilie, la baignoire à pattes, rééd, 2002, Drôle de nuit pour Miti, 2004, Les gros bisous, 2004, Pas de chouchous, 2004, Les chemins d'Eve Tome III, 2005, Casimir, le maladroit, 2006, Mon chat zoo, 2006, Les chemins d'Eve, tome 4, 2006.

RENCH, ERIN, elementary school educator; d. Diane F. and Leo L. Rench. BA in Art Edn., Western Mich. U., 2004. Technologies tchr. St. Joseph Elem. Sch., Battle Creek, Mich., 2002—03; day care asst. St. Joseph Extended Day, Battle Creek, 2003—05; sub. tchr. St. Joseph Elem. Sch., 2004—05; art tchr. Pendergast Sch. Dist., Phoenix, 2005—06; tchrs. asst. Found. for Blind Children, Phoenix, 2006; art tchr. Dysart Unified Sch. Dist., Surprise, Ariz., 2006—. Profl. mem. Nat. Art Edn. Assn., Ariz., 2004—, Phi Kappa Delta, Mich., 2004—05. Recipient Dean's List, Western Mich. U. Fine Arts Dept., 2004. Mem.: Alpha Gamma Delta (v.p. ops. 2001—02). Liberal. Roman Catholic. Avocations: jewelry design, painting, culinary arts, digital photography. Office Phone: 623-876-7200 ext 1263.

RENDA, LARREE M., retail executive; Exec. v.p. retail ops., human resources, pub. affairs, labor and govtl. rels. Safeway, Inc., Pleasanton, Calif., 1999—, joined, 1974. Office: Safeway Inc 5918 Stoneridge Mall Rd Pleasanton CA 94588

RENDELL, MARJORIE O., federal judge; b. 1947; m. Edward G. Rendell, 1971; 1 child, Jesse. BA, U. Pa., 1969; postgrad., Georgetown U., 1970—71; JD, Villanova U., 1973; LLD (hon.), Phila. Coll. Textile and Sci., 1992. Ptnr. Duane, Morris & Heckscher, Phila., 1972—93; judge U.S. Dist. Ct. (ea. dist.) Pa., 1994—97, U.S. Ct. Appeals (3d cir.), Phila., 1997—. Mem. Am. Jud. Soc., Fed. Judges Assn. Asst. to dir. ann. giving Dept. Devel. U. Pa.,

1973—78; mem. adv. bd. Chestnut Hill Nat. Bank/East Falls Adv. Bd.; mem. alternative dispute resolution com. mediation divsn. Ea. Dist. Pa. Bankruptcy Conf.; active Acad. Vocal Arts, Market St. East Improvement Assn., Pa.'s Campaign for Choice, Phila. Friends Outward Bound; vice chair Ave. of Arts, Inc.; vice chair bd. trustees Vis. Nurse Assn. Greater Phila.; bd. mem. Alumni Trust, U. Penn. Mem.: ABA, Phila. Bar Found. (bd. dirs.), Phila. Bar Assn. (bd. dirs. young lawyers sect. 1973—78), Pa. Bar Assn., Am. Bankruptcy Inst., Internat. Women's Forum, Forum Exec. Women, Phi Beta Kappa. Office: US Courthouse 601 Market St Rm 21613 Philadelphia PA 19106-1715*

RENDER, ARLENE, former ambassador; 2 adopted children. Joined Fgn. Svc., Dept. State, 1970, consular officer Abidjan, Cote D'Ivoire, 1971-73, Tehran, Iran, 1973-76, Genoa, Italy, 1976-78, polit. officer, 1978-79, internat. rels. officer AF/C, 1979-81, dep. chief of mission Brazzaville, Republic of the Congo, 1981-84, consul-gen. Kingston, Jamaica, 1984-86, dep. chief of mission Accra, Ghana, 1986-89, mem. sr. seminar, 1989-90, amb. to The Gambia, 1990-93, dir. Office of Ctrl. African Affairs Washington, 1993—96, amb. to Republic of Zambia, 1996-99, dir. So. African Affairs, 1996—99, U.S. amb. Cote d'Ivoire, 2001—04. Achievements include speaks French and Italian.

RENDICH, ANA, painter, collage artist; arrived in U.S., 1988; d. Ernesto Pedro Rendich and Maria Elena Romero de Rendich; m. Glenn D. Millis, Dec. 31, 1993; children: Sara C. Millis, Amy C. Millis, Sophie A. Millis. Student, Sch. Art U. Salvador, Buenos Aires, 1979—81, Inst. Superior del teatro Colon, 1980—81; master classes with, Victor Callegary, Buenos Aires, 1981, Franco Zeffirelli, N.Y.C., 1996. Chief of characterization Met. Opera House, NYC. Exhibitions include Cork Gallery Lincoln Ctr., NYC, 2003, 2004, 2005, Brush Strokes Art Gallery, Fredericksburg, Va. Mem.: Nat. Coll. Soc. Roman Catholic. Achievements include being the first South American painter to specialize in miniature painting. Avocations: art, opera. Office Phone: 540-368-0560. Personal E-mail: ana_rendich@brushstrokesfredericksburg.com.

RENDL-MARCUS, MILDRED, artist, economist; b. May 30, 1928; d. Julius and Agnes (Hokr) Rendl; m. Edward Marcus, Aug. 10, 1956. BS, NYU, 1948, MBA, 1950; PhD, Radcliffe Coll., 1954. Economist GE, 1953-56, Bigelow-Sanford Carpet Co., Inc., 1956-58; instr. econs. Hunter Coll. CUNY, 1959-60, Columbia U., 1960-61, rschr., 1961-63; sr. economist Nat. Indsl. Conf. Bd., 1963-66; asst. prof. Pace Coll., 1964-66; assoc. prof. Borough of Manhattan C. of C. CUNY, 1966-71, prof., 1972-85. Lectr. econs. CCNY, 1953-58; vis. prof. Fla. Internat. U., 1986; bd. dirs. N.Y.C. Coun. on Econ. Edn.; assoc. mem. Allied Artists Am., Inc., 2004—; cons. in field. Exhibited group shows at in New Canaan Art Show, 1982-85, Am. Soc. Bus. and Behavioral Scis., 1990-96, New Cannan Soc. for Arts Ann., 1983, 85, New Canaan Arts, 1985, Silvermine Galleries, 1986, Stamford Art Assn., 1987, Phoenix Gallery, 1988, N.Y.C., Parkview Point Gallery, 1982-89, Miami Beach, Fla., 1982-89, Art Complex, New Canaan, Miami Beach, 1985—, Lever House, N.Y.C., 1990, Cork Gallery, Lincoln Ctr., N.Y.C., 1990, Women's Caucus for Art, San Antonio, 1990, Artist's Equity, Broome St. Gallery, N.Y.C., 1991, Greater Hartford Architecture Conservancy, 1991, N.H. Arts Ctr., 1997, Just Originals Art Web, Albuquerque, 1999, Ward-Nasse Gallery, N.Y.C., 2000—, Art Complex Gallery, Las Vegas, 2000-, Liliana Fine Art Gallery, Lenox, Mass., 2003—, Artists Gallery, Chelsea, N.Y.C., 2003, Nat. Assn. Women Artists, 2003—, 115-Yr. Anniversary Show, World Trade Ctr., N.Y.C., 2004, Pen and Brush Non-Mem. Show, 2004, Allied Artists Am., N.Y.C., 2005, Nat. Assn. Women Artists, N.Y.C., 2005, Catherine Lorillard Wolfe Art Club, 2005 (Rendl Drawing award 2006), Audubon Artists, N.Y.C., 2005, Real Art Ways Gallery, Hartford, 2006, Karpeles Mus., N.Y., 2006, Port of Call Gallery, Warwick, N.Y., 2006; author (with E. Marcus) Investment and Development of Tropical Africa, 1959, International Trade and Finance, 1965, Monetary and Banking Theory, 1965, Economics, 1969, Economic Progress and the Developing World, 1970, Economics, 1978, Fine Art with Many Equilibrium Prices, 1995; editor Women in the Arts Found. Newsletter, 1986-92; contbr. articles to profl. jours. Founder Rendl Fund for Slavic Art, Mus. of Modern Art, N.Y.C., 1999—, Harvard U. Art Mus. Fund for Slavic Art, Cambridge, 2000—, Harvard Mus. Natural History, Peabody Mus. Archeology and Ethnology, Rendl Fund for the Conservation of Slavic Artifacts, 2000—, Rendl Fund for the Conservation of the Ware Collection of Blaschka Glass Models of Plants, 2001—; mem. mus. coun. Harvard Mus. Natural History, 2001—; founder Rendl Fund for Czech Art, 2006—. Recipient Merit award Manhattan Arts Internat., 1998, Excellence award 1998, Artist Showcase award Manhattan Arts Internat., 1999; Dean Bernice Brown Cronkhite fellow Radcliffe Coll., 1950-51, Anne Radcliffe Econ. Rsch. Sub-Sahara Africa fellow, 1958-59; fellow Gerontol. Assn. Mem. AAUW, Internat. Schumpeter Econs. Soc. (founding), Met. Econ. Assns. (sec. 1954-56), Indsl. Rels. Rsch. Assn., Women's Econ. Roundtable (program planning com.), N.Y.C. Women in Arts, Allied Social Sci. Assn. (artist 1994), Allied Artists Am. Inc. (assoc.), NYU Grad. Sch. Bus. Adminstrn. Alumni (sec. 1956-58), Radcliffe Club, Women's City Club (art and landmarks com.).

RENEE, LISABETH MARY, small business owner, art designer; b. Bklyn., July 28, 1952; d. Lino P. and Elizabeth M. (Dines) Rivano; m. John S. Witanowski, May 15, 1982. Student, U. Puget Sound, 1972-74; BA in Art, SUNY, Buffalo, 1977; MFA, L.I. U., 1982; EdD, U. Ctrl. Fla., 1996. Cert. art tchr., Fla. Adj. faculty L.I. U., Greenvale, N.Y., 1980-82, Rollins Coll., Winter Park, Fla., 1982; art tchr. Phyllis Wheatley Elem. Sch., Apopka, Fla., 1983-85, McCoy Elem. Sch., Orlando, Fla., 1985-86, Lake Howell H.S., Winter Park, Fla., 1986-93; adj. faculty U. Ctrl. Fla., 1994-95, vis. instr., coord. art edn., 1995-96; gallery dir., prof. West Campus Valencia (Fla.) C.C., 1996-98; owner, designer Nartique, 2002—; dir. Renée Studios, Casselberry, Fla. Adj. faculty Valencia C.C., 1995-96; dir. So. Artists Registry, Winter Park, 1984-87; cons. Fla. Dept. Edn., 1989-90, mem. curriculum writing team for arts edn. program; mem. com. Fla. Bd. Edn. Task Force for Subject Area Subtest of Fla. Tech. Cert. Exam.; visual arts dir. Very Spl. Arts Ctr. Fla. Fest, 1996; presenter at profl. confs. Author: The Phenomenological Significance of Aesthetic Communion, 1996, Co-operative Art, 1991; editor: Children and the Arts in Florida, 1990. Visual arts dir. Very Spl. Arts Ctrl. Fla. Festival, 1995; mem. local Sch. Adv. Coun., Winter Park, 1992. Grantee Found. for Advancement of Cmty. Through Schs., 1991, Divsn. Blind Svcs. Invision, 1995, Tangelo Park Project, 1995; ACE scholar Arts Leadership Inst., 1993-96; recipient Tchr. Merit award Walt Disney World Co., 1990. Mem. NEA, ASCD, Nat. Art Edn. Assn., Fla. Art Edn. Assn. (regional rep. 1989-94), Seminole County Art Edn. Assn., Coll. Art Assn., Caucus on Social Theory and Art Edn., Women's Caucus for Art, Phi Kappa Phi, Kappa Delta Pi. Home and Office: Nartique 20 Cobblestone Ct Casselberry FL 32707-5410 Office Phone: 407-921-0257. E-mail: nartiqueinc@yahoo.com.

RENEE (AKA) STEVENS, RITA, actor, theater educator, director; b. Mpls., Sept. 26, 1949; d. Max Rae and Carol Jean Ahrens; children: Zoey Thomas Stevens, Max Norman Stevens, Patrick Dylan Stevens, Michael Lawrence Stevens. Student, U. Minn., Duluth and Mpls., 1967—70; B in Theatre, Calif. State U., Fullerton, 1998, MFA in Theatre, 2001. Profl. art model over 20 instnl. instns. and workshops, LA and Orange County, Calif., 1980—2004; theatre prof., stage dir. Calif. State U., Fullerton, Calif., 2001—; stage and film actor LA area. Bd. dirs., sec. Theatre Neo, Hollywood, Calif., 2004—; theatrical mentor, LA and Fullerton. Actor: (films) Nickey's Birthday Camera, 2004, Forgiven, 2005, Dreammaker, 2005; dir.: (stage play) A Piece of My Heart (best univ. prodn. Orange County Registers, 2003), (stage prodn.) Glimpses of the Divine (meritorious contbn. recognition, 2006); writer (student fiction) The Travels of Father Junipero Serra; actor: (TV) Gen. Hosp., 1984—85, Young and Restless, 1990, Gidean's Crossing, 2001; (plays) Diviners, 1982, Good, 1984, Merchant of Venice, 1980, The Women, 2003, White House Murder Case, 2004. Vol. Sathya Sai Baba Orgn., Glendale and Bangalore, India; sec. Theatre Neo, Hollywood, Calif., 2004—06; hospice vol. LA, 1986—88. Recipient D.R. award for Young Writers, 1958; Mark Cross scholar, South Coast Repertory Theatre, 1980, Front and Ctr. scholar, Calif. State U., 2000. Mem.: SAG, Am. Fedn. TV Assn., Actors Equity. Democrat. Avocations: dancing, singing, sports, travel, gardening. Office: Calif State U 800 N State College Blvd Fullerton CA 92831-3599 Office Phone: 818-404-3726. Personal E-mail: ritasai369@sbcglobal.net.

RENEGAR, JOAN ANN, lawyer; b. Fairfield, Calif., Aug. 7, 1950; d. Alfred Galbert and Frances Lorraine Bissonnette; m. Gregg Randall Renegar, Aug. 17, 1974; children: Eric Christopher, Blake Andrew. JD, Okla. City U., 1979. Bar: Okla. 1979. Atty. U.S. Dept. Treasury, Oklahoma City, 1979—81, Mahaffey & Gore, Oklahoma City, 1982—83, Kornfeld, Franklin, Renegar & Randall, Oklahoma City, 1998—. Adminstr. Robert J. Turner Am. Inn Ct., Oklahoma City, 2005—. Mem.: Assn. of Trial Lawyers of Am. Avocations: travel, cooking, interior design, gardening.

RENEKER, MAXINE HOHMAN, librarian; b. Chgo., Dec. 2, 1942; d. Roy Max and Helen Anna Christina (Anacker) Hohman; m. David Lee Reneker, June 20, 1964 (dec. Dec. 1979); children: Sarah Roeder, Amy Johannah, Benjamin Congdon. BA, Carleton Coll., 1964; MA, U. Chgo., 1970; DLS, Columbia U., 1992. Asst. reference libr. U. Chgo. Libraries, 1965-66; classics libr. U. Chgo. Libr., 1967-70, asst. head acquisitions, 1970-71, personnel libr., 1971-73; personnel/bus. libr. U. Colo. Libr., Boulder, 1978-80; asst. dir. sci. and engring. div. Columbia U., N.Y.C., 1981-85; assoc. dean of univ. librs. for pub. svcs. Ariz. State U. Libr., Tempe, 1985-89; dir. instrnl. and rsch. svcs. Stanford (Calif.) Univ. Librs., 1989-90; assoc. provost for libr. and info. resources Naval Postgrad. Sch., Monterey, Calif., 1993—2005, prof. emerita, 2005—. Acad. libr. mgmt. intern Coun. on Libr. Resources, 1980-81; chmn. univ. librs. sect. Assn. Coll. and Rsch. Librs., 1989-90. Contbr. articles to profl. jours. Trustee Monterey Pub. Libr. Rsch. grantee Coun. on Library Resources, Columbia U., 1970-71, fellow, 1990-92. Mem. ALA, Am. Soc. Info. Sci., Sherlockian Scion Soc., Phi Beta Kappa, Beta Phi Mu. Home: 740 Dry Creek Rd Monterey CA 93940-4208 E-mail: mreneker@pacbell.net.

RENFORTH, DOROTHEA JOYCE, art educator, artist; d. George Glenn and Clara McDonnell (Geisler) Raths; m. Raymond Renforth (div.); children: Rae'Deana Lynn, Reefe Zane, Shawna Leeane, Renetta Dawn; m. Joseph Pritts, Aug. 1988 (dec.). Student, Ctrl. Mich. Coll., 1947—48; tchr. cert., U. Detroit, 1973, continuing cert., 1987. File clk. VA, Detroit, 1946—47; substitute tchr. Chippewa Valley, Royal Oak, Oak Park schs., Mich., 1948—49, Mich., 1955—56; art tchr. Clawson (Mich.) Sch. Dist., 1977—78; tchr. arts and crafts to sr. citizens Van Dyke Schs., Ukranian Village, Warren, Mich., 1987—88. Enumerator U.S. Census, Oakland County, Mich., 1980, Oakland County, 90. Author: (poetry) A Stroll Along Poetry Lane, Run-Away Keno; author, artist: board game License To Play. Mem. Women's Rights Orgn., 1970—85; election worker Hazel Park Election Com. Recipient Golden Poetry award, Eddie How Cole World of Poetry, 1989, Cert. of Achievement, NY Pro-Am. Song Jubilee. Mem.: Ongoing Mich. Artists Program. Democrat. Avocations: poetry, typing, knitting, writing.: 2431 Stockton Blvd Sacramento CA 95817 Home: 99 W Garfield Hazel Park MI 48030-1127

RENFRO, PATRICIA ELISE, library director, academic administrator; b. Nelson, Lancashire, Eng. d. Henry Lawrence and Maud (Thompson) Candlin; m. Charles Gilliland Renfro, June 21, 1969; children: Rebecca Elise, James Lawrence. BA in English and History with honors, U. York, Eng., 1966; acad. postgrad. diploma, U. London, 1968; MA in History, U. Ky., 1981. Libr. asst. Holborn br. London Borough of Camden Pub. Librs., London, 1966-67, sr. asst. libr., 1968-69; dep. acquisitions libr. Folger Shakespeare Libr., Washington, 1969-70; cataloger Libr. Co. of Phila., 1970-72; reference libr. U. Pa. Librs., 1972-73, U. Ky. Librs., 1975-76, head of reference svcs., 1976-78; exec. sec. U. Ky. Libr. Assocs., U. Ky., 1979-80; reference libr. U. Pa., 1982-83, head circulation svcs. Van Pelt Libr., 1983-85, asst. dir. librs. for pub. svcs., 1985-89, assoc. dir. librs., 1989—2000; dep. univ. libr. Columbia U., N.Y.C., 2000—. Mem. programs adv. com. Rsch. Librs. Group, 1991-92; mem. circulation interchange com. NISO 1999-2002; bd. dirs. N.Y. State Higher Edn. Initiative, 2004—. Contbr. articles to profl. jours. Mem. ALA, Assn. Coll. and Rsch. Librs. (rsch. com. 1992-94, ULS program com. 2005). Office Phone: 212-854-2226.

RENFROW, PATRICIA ANNE, secondary school educator; b. Oakland, Calif., Dec. 29, 1951; d. Joseph Montez and Suzanne Leona (Anglada) Galindo; m. Victor E. Renfrow, May 10, 1975; children: Mary Suzanne, Alicia Mariane. BA in Polit. Sci., Calif. State U., Chico, 1973. Spl. edn. instrnl. asst. Vintage H.S., Napa, Calif., 1987-91; instr. ESL Napa Valley Adult Sch., 1992, instr. H.S. diploma program for teen parents, 1992-98, sch. to career liaison, 1994-96, coord. cmty. mentor program, 1996; Cal Works student advisor Napa Valley Coll., 1998—. Teen parent task force Napa Valley Adult Sch., 1992-98, Apple Pie subcom. for pregnancy prevention, 1996—; mem. Calif. Alliance Concerned with Sch. Age Parents, Sacramento, 1992-97. Active Vintage Music Boosters, Vintage H.S., Napa, 1993-97; youth counselor First Unith Meth. Ch., Napa, 1994-96. Named Most Caring Woman, Napa Valley Commn. on the Status of Women, 1995. Mem. AAUW (v.p. membership 1996—). Democrat. Avocations: exercise, reading, collecting disneyania. Office: Napa Valley Coll 2277 Napa Vallejo Hwy Napa CA 94558-6236

RENK, PAMELA JEAN, counselor, psychotherapist, small business owner; b. Pitts., Feb. 23, 1956; d. James Voris and Nancy Marie (Vessels) McClain; m. Randy Allen Renk, June 20, 1976. BA in Social & Behav. Scis. summa cum, Ind. State U., 1982; M in Clin. and Counseling Psychology, Calif. State U., San Bernardino, 1986. Cert. marriage, family and child counselor Bd. Behavioral Sci. Examiners. Intern counselor U. Calif., Riverside, 1984-85, Fontana (Calif.) Med. Group, 1986-87, Harmonium Inc., Mira Mesa, Calif., 1988-89; owner, marriage family child counselor South Bay Counseling, San Clemente, Calif., 1989—. Spkr. in field. Mem. Calif. Assn. Family Therapists. Avocations: skiing, horseback riding, in-line skating, reading, theater. Office: South Bay Counseling 302 N El Camino Real # 210 San Clemente CA 92672-4778 Office Phone: 949-361-7880.

RENNA, CATHY, communications executive, activist; Grad., Adelphi U. Vol. Gay and Lesbian Alliance Against Defamation (GLAAD), NY, 1990, dir. regional media and cmty. rels., 1996—2001, news media dir., 2001—04; media rels. dir. Fenton Comm., NY, 2004—. Office: Fenton Comm 260 Fifth Ave Ninth Fl New York NY 10001 Office Phone: 212-584-5000 319. Office Fax: 212-584-5045. E-mail: crenna@fenton.com.

RENNINGER, MARY KAREN, retired librarian; b. Pitts., Apr. 30, 1945; d. Jack Burnell and Jane (Hammerly) Gunderman; m. Norman Christian Renninger, Sept. 3, 1965 (div. 1980); 1 child, David Christian. BA, U. Md., 1969, MA, 1972, M.L.S., 1975. Tchr. English West Carteret High Sch., Morehead City, NC, 1969-70; instr. in English U. Md., College Park, 1970-72; head network services Nat. Libr. Svc., Libr. of Congress, Washington, 1974-78, asst. for network support, 1978-80; mem. fed. women's program com. Libr. of Congress, Washington, 1978-80; chief libr. divsn. Dept. Vets. Affairs, Washington, 1980-90; chief serial and govt. publs. divsn. Libr. of Congress, Washington, 1991—2006, mem. fed. libr. com., 1980-90, mem. exec. adv. bd., 1985-90; ret., 2006. Mem. USBE pers. subcom., 1982-84; bd. regents Nat. Libr. of Medicine, 1986-90, mem. outreach panel, 1988-89; fed. libr. task force for 1990 White House Conf. on Librs., 1986-90; liaison to The White House Conf. Med. Libr. Assn., 1989-90. Recipient Meritorious Svc. award Libr. of Congress, 1974, Spl. Achievement award, 1976, Performance award VA, ann. 1982-89, Adminstr.'s Commendation, 1985, Spl. Contbn. award, 1986. Mem. ALA (Govt. Documents Roundtable), Libr. Tech. Assn., Med. Libr. Assn. (govt. rels. com. 1985—), DC Libr. Assn., Soc. Applied Learning Tech., Med. Interactive Videodisc Consortium, Govt. Documents Roundtable, Knowledge Utilization Soc., Nat. Multimedia Assn. Am., US Tennis Assn., Phi Beta Kappa, Alpha Lambda Delta, Beta Phi Mu. Home: 840 College Pky Rockville MD 20850-1931 Personal E-mail: KarenRenninger@comcast.net.

RENO, JANET, former United States attorney general; b. Miami, Fla., July 21, 1938; d. Henry and Jane (Wood) R. AB in Chemistry, Cornell U., 1960; LL.B., Harvard U., 1963. Bar: Fla. 1963. Assoc. Brigham & Brigham, 1963-67; ptnr. Lewis & Reno, 1967-71; staff dir. judiciary com. Fla. Ho. of Reps., Tallahassee, 1971-72; cons. Fla. Senate Criminal Justice Com. for Revision Fla.'s Criminal Code, spring 1973; adminstrv. asst. state atty. 11th Jud. Circuit Fla., Miami, 1973-76, state atty., 1978-93; ptnr. Steel Hector and Davis, Miami, 1976-78; US atty. gen. Dept. Justice, Washington, 1993-2001. Mem. jud. nominating commn. 11th Jud. Circuit Fla., 1976-78; chmn. Fla. Gov.'s Council for Prosecution Organized Crime, 1979-80. Recipient Women First award YWCA, 1993. National Women's Hall of Fame, 2000. Mem. ABA (Inst. Jud. Adminstrn. Juvenile Justice Standards Commn. 1973-76), Am. Law Inst., Am. Judicature Soc. (Herbert Harley award 1981), Dade County Bar Assn., Fla. Pros. Atty.'s Assn. (pres. 1984-86). Democrat.

RENO NORTON, TABITHA DAWN, music educator; b. Chattanooga, Tenn., Aug. 25, 1978; d. Tracy Dewayne Reno; m. Justin Darren Norton, July 22, 2000; children: Malachi David Norton, Mary Ruth Dailyn Norton. MusB, Berry Coll., Rome, Ga., 2000. Music specialist Cherokee County Bd. Edn., Canton, Ga., 2000—. Ind. music cons., Ga., 1998; owner and pvt. instr. Cherokee Music Acad., Canton, Ga., 2000. Singer (soloist): The White Ho., 1994; singer: Chattanooga Symphony and Opera, 1996—2000; singer: (soloist) Clock Tower Jazz Ensemble, 1997—98, Carnegie Hall, 1998, Wells Cathedral, 1999, Cherokee Comty. Chorale, 2003; actor: Prospect Theatre Co., 1999. Musical leadership Hopewell Bapt. Ch., Canton, Ga., 2000. Mem.: Ga. Music Educator's Assn., Sigma Alpha Iota (life). Avocations: travel, reading, arts.

RENOUF, ANNE, corporate financial executive, consultant; b. N.Y.C., Apr. 3, 1937; Diploma, Emma Willard Sch., 1954; student, Inst. World Affairs, 1957; AB magna cum laude, honors in Anthropology, Columbia U., 1959; MA, Yale U., 1962, PhD, 1966; JD with honors, Am. U., 1978; postgrad., Duke U. Asst. prof. U. N.C., Chapel Hill, 1966-71; sr. profl. cons. U.S. Govt., Washington, 1972-75; pvt. practice fin. cons. Washington, 1976—; vis. assoc. prof. George Washington U. Sch. Bus. Adminstrn., Washington, 1983-84; gen. ptnr., v.p. Tech. Mgmt. Corp., Montgomeryville, Pa., 1986-88; chmn. Pivot, Inc., 1988—90; founding prin. SaraTech Fin. Inc., 1990-92; pvt. practice fin. cons. Founding dir., chmn. bd., CFO/bd. treas. Initiatives in Industry, Inc., 1996-02; corp. dir.; dir. fin. devel. Ctr. for Space and Advanced Tech., 1990; cons. The Brookings Instn., Washington, 1966, U.S. Dept. State, Washington, 1967, World Bank, 1992—; mem. Pres.'s Commn. Grad. Edn., 1967-68, Nat. Chamber Found. Task Force on Space Commercialization, Washington, 1983-86; vis. scholar Carnegie Endowment for Internat. Peace, N.Y.C., 1968-69; fellow U.S. Dept. State, EUR/RPE, 1967; northeastern dir. Va. Advanced Tech. Assn., 1984-88; fin. and tech. spkr.; mem. Coun. on Competitiveness, 1998—2003, Tech. Coun. Washington, 1998—; mem. Greater Washington Bd. Trade, The Potomac Conf., 1999-2001; mem. The World Bank, The Global Devel. Network, 1998— Contbr. articles on tech. commercialization and fin. to profl. jours. Co-chair, charter mem. U.S./China Capital Cities Coun., Washington, 1985-95; advisor Greater Washington D.C. Bd. Trade, 1985-86, Internat. Red Cross, 1987-90; mem. Mayor's Adv. Coun. on Trade and Investment, 1987-91; mem. adv. coun. Ctr. for Internat. Bus. Edn. U. Alaska, Fairbanks, 1990-91, co-chmn. World Trade Day, 1989; bd. dirs. Nat. Symphony Orch., 1990-99, Greater Washington Met. Boys and Girls Clubs, 1992-2000; dir. Initiatives in Industry, Inc., 1996-02. Recipient citation, Washington D.C. Mayor's Office, 1986; Woodrow Wilson fellow, 1958, Bushnell fellow, Yale U., 1964, Hon. Officer-Faculty fellow, U.S. Dept. State, 1967. Fellow Washington Acad. Scis.; mem. Am. Soc. Internat. Law, Internat. Forum U.S. C. of C., Internat. Energy Seminar-Johns Hopkins Sch. for Advanced Internat. Study, Corcoran Gallery of Art (nat. coun.), Washington Internat. Trade Assn., Assn. for Corp. Growth, Phi Beta Kappa. Office Phone: 202-965-3000, 202-530-5285. Business E-Mail: arenouf@indevone.com.

RENSHAW, JUDITH ANN, special education educator, school system administrator; b. Rome, Ga., June 21, 1960; d. James William and Golda Whiteside LeGrande; m. Robert M. Renshaw, Nov. 2, 1985; children: Lauren Amber, Aimee Shea. MEd, State U. of West Ga., Carrollton, 1985. Lic. Performance Based Tchr.-5 mental retardation (P-12) Ga., Performance Based Tchr.- mid. grades (4-8) Ga., lic. Performance Based Tchr.- interrelated spl. edn. Ga., Performance Based Tchr.- presch. spl. edn. Ga. Spl. edn. tchr. Polk Sch. Dist., Rockmart, Ga., 1982—2005, Pikes Peak Bd. Coop. Svcs., Colorado Springs, 1986—87; spl. edn. coord. Polk Sch. Dist. Bd. Edn., Cedartown, Ga., 2005—. Tchr. support specialist Polk Sch. Dist., Rockmart, 1999—. Mem.: NEA. Baptist. Avocations: travel, dance team coach, sports fan - Atlanta Falcons. Home: 113 Coots Lake Rd Rockmart GA 30153 Office: Polk Sch Dist PO Box 128 Cedartown GA 30125 Office Phone: 770-684-8718. Office Fax: 770-684-3221. Personal E-mail: renshaws@yahoo.com. Business E-Mail: jrenshaw@polk.k12.ga.us.

RENSHLER, ROSEMARY P., retired music educator; d. Charles Allen and Rose Mae Plyley; children: Kevin, Kara, Kristin. MusB in Edn., Capital U., 1961; MA in Music Edn., The Ohio State U., 1979; student, Pa. State U., 1981, Milliken U., 1982, Heidelberg Coll., 1987—88, Otterbein Coll., 1995. Dir. gen. music, choir Clinton Jr. H.S., Columbus, Ohio, 1961—63, Johnson Pk. Jr. H.S., Columbus, 1972—73, Eastmoor Jr. H.S. and Mid. Sch., Columbus, 1973—81; dir. vocal music Northland H.S., Columbus, 1981—; ret., 2004. Dir. choir Oakland Pk. United Meth. Ch., Columbus, 1961—72, Epworth United Meth. Ch., Columbus, 1980—88; dir. music Nat. Rep. Glee Club, Columbus, 1989—2006. Mem. fin. com. Epworth United Meth. Ch., Columbus, mem. com. membership, head usher, mgr. kitchen, cook. Recipient 34 Yr. Svc. award, Columbus (Ohio) Pub. Schs., 2005. Mem.: NEA, Am. Choral Dirs. Assn., Music Educators Nat. Conf., Ohio Educators Assn., Tri-M Internat. Music Hon. Soc. (life; adv. 2002—05). Methodist. Avocations: crafts, dance, gardening, cooking. Home: 1687 Riverbirch Dr Columbus OH 43229

RENSTROM, LISA, environmental organization administrator; married; 2 children. Chair Ctrl. Piedmont Group; exec. dir. Voices and Choices; held leadership positions various orgns. including WTVI Pub. TV, Charlotte, NC, Mus. of Life and the Environment, Raptor Ctr., Riverkeep Found.; bd. dirs. Sierra Club, San Francisco, 2001—, pres., 2005—. Office: Sierra Club Nat Hdqs 85 Second St 2d Fl San Francisco CA 94105 Office Phone: 415-977-5500.

RENT, CLYDA STOKES, academic administrator; b. Jacksonville, Fla., Mar. 1, 1942; d. Clyde Parker Stokes Sr. and Edna Mae (Edwards) Shuemake; m. George Seymour Rent, Aug. 12, 1966; 1 child, Cason Rent Lynley. BA, Fla. State U., 1964, MA, 1966, PhD, 1968; LHD (hon.), Judson Coll., 1993. Asst. prof. Western Carolina U., Cullowhee, NC, 1968-70, Queens Coll., Charlotte, NC, 1972-74, dept. chair, 1974-78, dean Grad. Sch. and New Coll., 1979-84, v.p. for Grad. Sch. and New Coll., 1984-85, v.p. acad. affairs, 1985-87, v.p. cmty. affairs, 1987-89; pres. Miss. U. for Women, Columbus, 1989—2001; disting. prof. sociology Miss. State U. Mem. adv. bd. Nat. Women's Hall of Fame; cons. Coll. Eb. N.Y.C., 1983-89; sci. cons. N.C. Alcohol Rsch. Authority, Chapel Hill, 1976-89; bd. mem. So. Growth Policies Bd., 1992-94; adv. bd. Nat. Women's Hall of Fame, Trustmark Nat. Bank, 1991-97; rotating chair Miss. Instns. Higher Learning Pres. Coun., 1990-91; commn. govtl. rels. Am. Coun. Edn., 1990-93; mem. adv. bd. Entergy/Miss., 1994-97, Freedom Forum 1st Amendment Ctr., 1996-2001; mem. Miss. adv. bd. Trustmark Nat. Bank, 1991-97; mem. Mary Baker Eddy Adv. Group, 2000—; mem. Rhodes Scholar selection com. of Miss., 1996-98; mem. Free Sprit Awards selection com., 1996—; mem. ACE Commn. on Women in Higher Edn., 1999—. Mem. editl. bd. Planning for Higher Education, 1995; contbr. articles to profl. jours.; speeches pub. in Vital Speeches; mem. editl. bds. acad. jours. Trustee N.C. Performing Arts Ctr., Charlotte, 1988-89, Charlotte County Day Sch., 1987-89; bd. visitors Johnson C. Smith U., Charlotte, 1985-89; exec. com. bd. dirs. United Way Allocations and Rev., Charlotte, 1982-88; bd. advisors Charlotte Mecklenburg Hosp. Authority, 1985-89; bd. dirs. Jr. Achievement, Charlotte, 1983-89, Miss. Humanities

Coun., Miss. Inst. Arts and Letters, Miss. Symphony, Miss. Econ. Coun.; chair Leadership Miss. and Collegiate Miss.; chmn. bd. dirs. Charlotte/Mecklenburg Arts and Sci. Coun., 1987-88; Danforth assoc. Danforth Found., St. Louis, 1976-88, Leadership Am., 1989; mem. golden triangle adv. bd. Bapt. Meml. Hosp., 1999—; pres. So. Univs. Conf., 1994-95; mem. commn. govt. rels. Am. Coun. Edn., 1990-93; mem. alumni bd. First United Meth. Ch., 1996—. Recipient Grad. Made Good award Fla. State U., 1990, medal of excellence Miss. U. for Women, 1995, Women Who Make a Difference award IWF, 2000; named Prof. of Yr., Queens Coll., 1979, One of 10 Most Admired Women Mgrs. in Am., Working Women mag., 1993, One of 1000 Women of the 90's, Mirabella mag., 1994; Ford Found. grantee, 1981; Paul Harris fellow, 1992; OWHE fellow, 1999—. Mem. Am. Assn. State Colls. and Univs. (bd. dirs. 1994-96, 99), Sociol. Soc., So. Assn. Colls. and Schs. (mem. commn. on colls. 1996-98), N.C. Assn. Colls. and Univs. (exec. com. 1988-89), N.C. Assn. Acad. Officers (sec.-treas. 1987-88), Soc. Internat. Bus. Fellows, Miss. Assn. Colls. (pres. 1992), Newcomen Soc. U.S., Internat. Women's Forum, Univ. Club, Rotary. Achievements include 1st female pres. of Miss. U. for Women (1st pub. coll. for women in Am.).

RENZI, BETH PAIGE, personal trainer; b. Bridgeton, N.J., Dec. 28, 1980; d. Elwood R and Esther E Renzi. BA in Athletic Tng., Cedarville U., Ohio, 2003; postgrad. in Sports Medicine, Ga. State U., Atlanta, 2005—. Cert. athletic trainer Nat. Athletic Trainers' Assn. Bd. of Certification, 2004, CPR/AED ARC/Ga., 2005. Adminstrv. asst. Cedarville U., 2003—04; head athletic trainer Atlanta Christian Coll., East Point, Ga., 2004—. Named Athletic Tng. Student of the Yr., Cedarville U., 2002—03. Mem.: Nat. Athletic Trainers' Assn. Office: Atlanta Christian Coll 2605 Ben Hill Rd East Point GA 30344 Office Phone: 404-761-8861.

REORDAN, BEVERLY JEAN, artist; d. Albert Wayne Matlaf and Jean Katherine Lang; m. John Robert Suckling, 1951 (div. 1963); children: Leslie Jean Suckling, James Cameron Suckling; m. Robert Geoghegan Reordan, Feb. 1, 1964. Student in Bus., U. So. Calif., 1948—51. Artist, So. Calif., 1965—. Mem. Art A Fair Festival, Laguna Beach, Calif., 1982—, bd. dirs., 1982—87; charter mem. Nat. Mus. Women in Arts, Washington, 1987—; mem. Charter 100 Profl. Women in Orange County, Calif., 1987—89. Original art works pub. by Princess Cruises Fine Arts. Mem. La Quinta (Calif.) Arts Found., 2001—, Palm Springs (Calif.) Desert Mus., 1989—, Artists Coun., Palm Springs, 1990—. Mem.: U. So. Calif. Alumni Assn., Kappa Kappa Gamma. Republican. Avocations: photography, European travel. Home: 60217 Wishbone Ct La Quinta CA 92253

REPINSKI, SARA, library director; d. Stephen Charles and Sharon Ann Gilles; m. Jeffrey Lawrence Repinski, Dec. 10, 1998. BS in History and Art, U. Wis., La Crosse, 1998; MLIS, U. S.C., 2002. Libr. dir. So. Meth. Coll., Orangeburg, SC, 2002—06; catalog libr. Coleman Karesh Law Libr., U. S.C., Columbia, 2006—. Mem. accreditation team Transnat. Assn. Christian Colls. and Schs., Lynchburg, Va., 2002—. Mem.: SC Libr. Assn., Assn. Christian Librs., Civil War Preservation Trust. Avocations: scrapbooks, music, Green Bay Packer football.

REPKA, FRAN ANN, SR., psychologist; b. Toledo, Ohio, Sept. 6, 1942; d. Frank and Helen Marie Repka. BSN, U. Cin., 1970; MA in Clin. Psychology, U. Detroit, 1976; EdD in Counseling Psychology, U. Cin., 1987. Diplomate Am. Assn. Pastoral Counselors; RN; cert. Reiki specialist. Charge nurse, psychiat. nurse St. Charles Hosp., Toledo, 1970—74; dir. Cin. Archdiocesan Consultation Svcs., 1976—89; dir., psychologist Mercy Profl. Svcs., Cin., 1989—94, exec. dir., psychologist, 1994—. Cons., condr. workshops Fedn. of Religious, various locations; psychologist People to People, 1992, Complementary Methods for Self Empowerment and Healing of Mind, 1996—; counselling edn. adv. bd. U. Cin. Contbr. articles to profl. jours. Mental health cons. Sisters of Mercy; mem. pastoral coun. Archdiocese of Cin.; bd. dirs. Mercy Professionals. Recipient Greater Cin. Counseling award, Greater Cin. Counseling Assn., 2003. Mem.: APA, Cin. Assn. of Profl. Psychologists, Cin. Psychoanalytic Psychologists Assn. (pres.), Cin. Psychol. Assn., Ohio Psychol. Assn. (Ohio Psychologist of the Yr. 1999). Roman Catholic. Avocations: dance, reading, travel, swimming. Office: Mercy Professional Services 2330 Victory Pky Cincinnati OH 45206 Office Phone: 513-221-2330.

REPKO, LISA, medical/surgical nurse; b. Boston, Oct. 7, 1954; ADN, Regents Coll., Albany, N.Y., 1980, BSN, 1984; MPH, U. Albany, 1995. RN, N.Y. Staff nurse Albany Med. Ctr. Hosp., 1980—.

REPLOGLE, JEANNE LONNQUIST, artist; b. Evanston, Ill., Apr. 8, 1932; d. William John Lonnquist and Dorothy Muriel Gittere; m. David Robert Replogle, Nov. 6, 1954; children: William, Bruce, Stewart, James, John. Student, Kathyrn Lord's Studio, Evanston, Ill., Studio of Pepino Mangreviti, Wellesley, Mass., Chgo. Art Inst.; BS, Northwestern U. One-woman shows include South Shore Art Ctr., Cohasset, Mass., 1982 (pres. choice, 1982), Artica Gallery, Duxbury, Mass., 2002, exhibitions include Festival Shows, South Shore Art Ctr., Cohasset, 1983—2002 (blue ribbon show, 1994, 2000, 2001, 2002), Annenburg Gallery, Pine Manor Coll., Chestnut Hill, Mass., 1989, Sailor's Valentine Gallery, Nantucket, Mass., 1988, Harvard Univ., Cambridge, Mass., 1993, Mystic (Conn.) Maritime Gallery, 1994, 1995, 1997, 1998, 1999, Small Works Show/Mystic Maritime Gallery, 1995, 1997, The Art of Giving/Mystic Maritime Gallery, 1996, Art of the Sea/Mystic Maritime Gallery, 1997, Fantasy Folk Art, South Shore Art Ctr, Cohasset, Mass., 1999, Folk Art, 1991, Arts Around Boston, 2000, prin. works include numerous to corp. Mem. Nassau Hosp. Aux., Mineola, NY, 1960—76, Mercy League, Rockville Centre, NY, 1960—76, League of Women Voters, Cohasset, Mass., 1976—80. Mem.: Am Soc. of Marine Artists, Stamford Art Assn., Cape Cod Art Assn., Catherine Lorillard Wolfe Art Club, South Shore Art Ctr. Gallery Artists (curator 1991, 1999). Episc. Avocations: golf, tennis.

REPOLE, MARIA, public relations executive; b. NYC, Sept. 9, 1973; m. Peter Leibaron. BA in Sociology, Franklin & Marshall Coll., Lancaster, Pa., 1995. Mktg. asst. Samsung Elecs., Ridgefield Park, NJ, 1995—97; product mgr. Sharp Elecs., Mahwah, 1997—99; dir. pubs. rels. and events Toshiba Am., Wayne, 1999—. Mem.: Pub. Rels. Soc. Am., Consumer Elecs. Assn. (vice chmn. comm. com. 2004—06). Home: 18 Chestnut St Allendale NJ 07401

REPPERT, NANCY LUE, retired municipal official, legal consultant; b. Kansas City, Mo., June 17, 1933; d. James Everett and Iris R. (Moomey) Moore; m. James E. Cassidy, 1952 (div.); children: James E., II, Tracy C. Student, Ctrl. Mo. State U., 1951-52, U. Mo., Kansas City, 1971-75; cert. legal asst., Rockhurst Coll., Kansas City, 1980, cert. risk mgr., 1979. With Kansas City chpt. ARC, 1952-54, N. Ctrl. Region Boy Scouts Am., 1963-66, Clay County Health Dept., Liberty, Mo., 1966-71, city of Liberty, 1971-80; risk mgr. City of Dallas, 1982-83; dir. Dept. Risk Mgmt., Pinellas County, Fla., 1984-94; ind. legal cons. Cedar Rapids, Iowa, 1994—. Mem. faculty William Jewell Coll., Liberty, 1975-80; vis. prof., U. Kans., 1981; adj. prof. dept. polit. sci. masters program, U. South Fla., 1990; seminar leader, cons. in field. Author: Kids are People, Too, 1975, Pearls of Potentiality, 1980; also contbr. articles to publs. Lay min., United Meth. Ch., 1965—; dir. youth devel., Hillside United Meth. Ch., Liberty; co-chmn. youth dir. Collegiate United Meth. Ch. scouting coord. Palm Lake Christian Ch., Exec. Fellow U. South Fla., mem. Coun. Ministries; advancement chmn. Mid-Iowa Coun. Boy Scouts Am., membership chmn. White Rock Dist. Coun., health and safety chmn. West Ctrl. Fla. Coun., 1985—; scouting coord., chmn. youth dept., bd. dirs., pastor's cabinet, diaconate Palm Lake Christian Ch., 1987—; skipper Sea Explorer ship, 1986—; bd. dirs. Neighborly Sr. Svcs., Inc.; vol. sailing master, instr., Boys & Girls Clubs and Hawkeye Coun. Boy Scouts Am., Cedar Rapids. Recipient Order of Merit, Boy Scouts Am., 1979, Living Sculpture award, 1978, 79; Svc. award Rotary Internat., 1979; Internat. awrd of Merit/Leadership Excellence, IBA, 1992; Exec. fellow, U. South Fla., 1988. Mem. NAFE, Am. Mgmt. Assns., Internat. Platform Assn., Risk Mgrs. Soc., Pub. Risk & Ins. Mgmt. Asns., Am. Soc. Profl. & Exec. Women, Am. Film Inst., U.s. Naval Inst., Nat. Inst. Mcpl. Law Officers. Home: PO Box 1590 Laurie MO 65038

REQUARTH, SHERRY LORRAINE, special education services professional; d. Carl D. Olwine and Beatrice R. Ferch, Blaine C. Ferch (Stepfather); m. David R. Rupp, June 2, 1979 (div. Nov. 28, 1988); children: Heather Lindsey Rupp, Joshua Alan Rupp; m. Richard Lee Requarth, Apr. 6, 2002. BS in Elem. Edn. and English, Bowling Green (Ohio) State U., 1970; postgrad., Miami U., Oxford, Ohio, Wright State U., Dayton, Ohio, Xavier U., Antioch U., Wilmington Coll., 1975—95. Cert. Christian Sci. practitioner; notary pub. Ohio, cert. dyslexic reading therapist Ohio. Elem. sch. tchr. Wilmington City Schs., Ohio, 1970—2005, ind. reading tutor, 2005—; demonstrator Tupperware, Dayton, 1980—84; tour guide Airborne Express, Wilmington, 1986—90; jewelry demonstrator Natural Impressions, Painesville, Ohio, 1990—91; dyslexic reading tutor 32 Masonic Learning Ctrs. for Children, Inc., Dayton, 2005—. Gifted and talented summer sch. tchr., Wilmington, 1980—82; tchr., mentor Wilmington City Schs., 1998—99, proficiency testing tutor, 2003—05. Sponsor Compassion Internat., Colorado Springs, 1998—2006; rainbow girl Masonic Lodge, Dayton, 1962—66; fundraiser Heifer Internat., Little Rock, 2004—05; sec. Teenage Reps., Xenia, Ohio, 1964—66; adminstr. The Principle Found., Kansas City, Mo., 2005—06; Sunday sch. tchr. First Ch. of Christ, Scientist, Centerville, Ohio, 1970—2003, grounds maintenance, 2002—06, reader, 2003—06. Recipient Outstanding Young Educator award, Jaycees, 1979, Tchr. of Yr. award, Amerihost Inn, 2004; Martha Holden Jennings scholar, Wilmington City Schs., 1995. Mem.: The Principle Found. (assoc.), Pupils of Frances Fischman, CSB (assoc.), Wilmington Edn. Assn. (assoc.; tchr. rep. 1971—73), Southwestern Ohio Edn. Assn. (assoc.), Ohio Edn. Assn. (assoc.), Phi Kappa Psi (life Sweetheart 1968), Gamma Phi Beta (life; rush asst.). Christian Scientist. Avocations: skiing, swimming, hiking, travel, poetry. Office: PO Box 131 Bellbrook OH 45305 Office Phone: 937-371-2735. Fax: 937-848-9560. E-mail: discernment1@sbcglobal.net.

RESAR, LAURA A., mathematics educator; b. Manitowoc, Wis., Oct. 13, 1979; d. Carol J. and Dean J. Leschke; m. Aaron J. Resar, June 23, 2001; 1 child, James D. BS in Edn., Lakeland Coll., Sheboygan, Wis., 2001. Secondary math tchr. Sioux Falls Pub. Schs., SD, 2002—04, Franklin Pub. Schools, Wis., 2004—. Roman Catholic. Office: Franklin HS 8222 South 51st St Franklin WI 53132-9293 E-mail: resarl@franklin.k12.wi.us.

RESCH, CYNTHIA FORTES, secondary school educator; b. Providence, Dec. 9, 1951; d. Alfred Antone and Mabel (Duarte) F.; m. Joseph Bernard Resch III, June 26, 1982; children: Jeffrey, Jason, Steven, Kayla. BA, R.I. Coll., 1974; postgrad., U. Sorbonne, Paris, 1975, U. Valencia, Spain, 1979, Providence Coll., 1981. Cert. secondary edn. tchr., R.I. Tchr. French and Spanish, North Kingstown (R.I.) H.S., 1977—. Advisor North Kingston HS, Poder, 2004—, Washington D.C. Mission Project, 2004. Mem. North Kingstown Cmty. Chorus, 1996—; advisor North Kingstown H.S. Internat. Club, 1978-2001, La Romana, Dominican Republic Mission Project, 2001, 2006, Washington, DC Mission Project, 2004, 2005. Mem. NEA, Am. Assn. Tchrs. Spanish and Portuguese, R.I. Fgn. Lang. Assn. Avocations: cooking, needlecraft, reading, photography, travel, sewing, aerobics. Office: North Kingstown HS 150 Fairway Dr North Kingstown RI 02852-6202 Office Phone: 401-268-6236. E-mail: cynthia_resch@nksd.net.

RESCH, MARY LOUISE, town agency administrator; b. David City, Nebr., Oct. 26, 1956; d. Ernest John and Mary Jean (Roelandts) Cermak. BS in Psychology, SUNY, Albany, 1984; MS in Counseling and Edn. with high honors, U. Wis., Platteville, 1986. Enlisted U.S. Army, 1974, advance through ranks to sgt., 1982, bomb disposal tech. Ft. Riley, Kans., 1977-79, bomb disposal instr. Indian Head, Md., 1979-80, resigned, 1985; instr., intern family advocacy Army Community Svc., U.S. Army, Ft. Belvoir, 1986; sr. counselor, child therapist Community Crisis and Referral Ctr., Inc., Waldorf, Md., 1986-87; adminstr. Walter Reed Army Med. Ctr. USDA Grad. Sch., Washington, 1987-88, contract mgr. Ft. Jackson, S.C., 1988-91; pres. Athena Cons., Columbia, S.C., 1991-93; dir. spl. programs Newberry (S.C.) Commn. on Alcohol and Drug Abuse, 1993-95; resource devel. coord. Cities in Schs.-SC, Inc., Columbia, 1995-97; exec. dir. S.C. Ctr. for Family Policy, Columbia, 1997—2001; pub. rels. dir. Xpress Group, Inc., 2001—02; resource devel. specialist Town of Lexington, SC, 2002—. Human svcs. cons., Washington, 1986-87; adj. instr. Coker Coll., Ft. Jackson, 1989-95. Active Govs. Juvenile Justice Adv. Coun., Govs. Substance Abuse Prevention Coun.; amb. Greater Lexington C. of C. Mem. S.C. Assn. Prevention Profls. and Advs., State Assn. Crime Prevention Officers, Nat. Contract Mgmt. Assn. (fellow, former pres., mentor). Republican. Lutheran. Avocations: needlepoint, racquetball, reading, bowling, jewelry making. Home: 312 Edgewater Ln West Columbia SC 29169-6957 Office: SC Dept Parks Recreation and Tourism 1205 Pendleton St Ste 517 Columbia SC 29201 Office Phone: 803-734-0078. Personal E-mail: mresch@scprt.com.

RESCH, RITA MARIE, retired music educator; b. Minot, N.D., Dec. 26, 1936; d. Clement Charles and Magdalena Marie (Zeltinger) Resch. BS in Edn., Minot State U., 1957; MM in Music Lit., Eastman Sch. Music, Rochester, N.Y., 1960; MA in English Lit., U. N.D., 1967; MFA in Voice, U. Iowa, 1973, DMA in Piano Chamber Music/Accompanying, 1974. Music tchr. (vocal) Biwabik Sch. Dist., Minn., 1957—58, S. Redford Twp., Detroit, 1958—59; instr. music Fontbonne Coll., St. Louis, 1960—63; asst. prof. music Wis. State U., Stevens Point, 1965—68, Ctrl. Mo. State U., Warrensburg, 1974—79, assoc. prof., 1979—89, prof., 1989—2005, prof. emerita, 2005—. Adjudicator for vocal music Mo. State High Sch. Activities Assn., Columbia, Kans. State High Sch. Activities Assn., Topeka, other orgns., 1976—. Author (with Judith E. Carman, William K. Gaeddert, Gordon Myers): Art Song in the United States: An Annotated Bibliography, 1976, 2001. Assoc. organist Sacred Heart Cath. Ch., Warrensburg, 1980—. Mem.: Mo. Music Tchrs. Assn. (v.p. auditions 1995—98), Music Tchrs. Nat. Assn., Nat. Assn. Tchrs. Singing, Pi Kappa Lambda, Sigma Alpha Iota. E-mail: resch@cmsul.cmsu.edu.

RESNICK, ALICE ROBIE, state supreme court justice; b. Erie, Pa., Aug. 21, 1939; d. Adam Joseph and Alice Suzanne (Spizarny) Robie; m. Melvin L. Resnick, Mar. 20, 1970 PhB, Siena Heights Coll., 1961; JD, U. Detroit, 1964; LLD (hon.), Heidelberg Coll., 1999, U. Akron, 1994. Bar: Ohio 1964, Mich. 1965, U.S. Supreme Ct. 1970. Atty. priv. practice, 1964—75; asst. county prosecutor Lucas County Prosecutor's Office, Toledo, 1964-75, trial atty., 1965-75; judge Toledo Mcpl. Ct., 1976-83, 6th Dist. Ct. Appeals, State of Ohio, Toledo, 1983-88; instr. U. Toledo, 1968-69; justice Ohio Supreme Ct., 1988—. Co-chairperson Ohio State Gender Fairness Task Force. Trustee Siena Heights Coll., Adrian, Mich., 1982—; organizer Crime Stopper Inc., Toledo, 1981—; mem. Mayor's Drug Coun.; bd. dirs. Guest House Inc. Named to Ohio Women's Hall of Fame, 1995; recipient Gertrude W. Donahey award, Ohio Democratic Party, 1999, Woman of Toledo award, St. Vincent Mercy Medical Ctr., 1999. Mem. ABA, Toledo Bar Assn., Lucas County Bar Assn., Ohio State Bar Assn. (Nettie Cronise Lutes award 1995), Nat. Assn. Women Judges (Making A Difference award 1996), Am. Judicature Soc., Toledo Women's Bar Assn., Ohio State Women's Bar Assn. (Alice Robie Resnick Outstanding Lawyer award 1998), Toledo Mus. Art, Internat. Inst. Toledo. Roman Catholic. Office: Ohio Supreme Ct 65 S Front St Columbus OH 43215*

RESNICK, BETH ELENA, special education educator; b. Champaign-Urbana, Ill., Sept. 25, 1974; d. Bruce and Judith Resnick. BS, Utica Coll., NY, 1997; MA in Edn. and Human Devel., George Washington U., Washington, 2000; ednl. specialist, George Washington U., 2005. Cert. generic spl. edn. infant-grade 3 Md. Early childhood spl. educator Montgomery County Infants and Toddlers, Germantown, Md., 2000—. Grantee Low Incidence Disabilities Project, US Dept. Edn., 1998—2000, Ednl. Specialist Leadership Tng. Program, 2003—05. Mem.: Coun. Exceptional Children. E-mail: Beth_Resnick@mcpsmd.org.

RESNICK, ELAINE BETTE, psychotherapist, clinical social worker; b. Orlando, Fla., Apr. 2, 1944; d. Julius Milton and Annette (Chusid) Bernstein; m. Peter Schuyten (div. 1973); m. Richard B. Resnick, May 21, 1975; children: Demian, Jesse, Nora; 1 stepchild, Deborah. Postgrad., NYU, 1992—; MSW, CUNY, 1971; BA (hons.), NYU. Cert. Inst. for Study Psychotherapy, 1979, comprehensive tng. program with chronically and terminally ill patients, 2002; lic. clin. social worker, N.Y.; cert. in hypnosis tng. and supervision Columbia U., 1978; diplomate in clin. social work. Field work supr. NYU, N.Y.C., 1973-82, York Coll., N.Y.C., 1976-77; clin. dir. div. drug abuse N.Y. Med. Coll., N.Y.C., 1977-83, instr., 1978-82, clin. instr., 1982-83; pvt. practice N.Y.C., 1973—; clin. dir. Ctr. Psychiatry & Family Therapy, N.Y.C., 1986—. Field work supr., Wurzweiler Sch. of Social Work, Yeshiva U., 1991—; psychiat. social worker N.Y. State Psychiat. Inst., 1970-71; social worker Intensive Family Counseling Unit N.Y.C. Dept. Social Svcs., 1969-70; psychiat. social worker, St. Vincent's Hosp., 1970; adj. asst. prof. NYU Grad. Sch. Social Work, 1977-82. Contbr. articles to profl. jours.; responsible for numerous presentations in field. Fellow Soc. Clin. Social Work Psychotherapists, Am. Orthopsychiat. Assn.; mem. NASW, Nat. Registry Health Care Providers in Clin. Social Work. Office Phone: 212-678-6949. E-mail: elaine02@mac.com.

RESNICK, RHODA BRODOWSKY, psychotherapist; b. Mar. 22, 1930; d. Isador and Rose (Wasserman) Brodowsky; m. Jack H. Resnick, May 21, 1950; children: Steven E., Caryn B. BS, CCNY, 1951; MS, Queens Coll., 1973; postgrad., Hunter Coll. Tchr. N.Y.C. Bd. Edn., 1960—80, guidance counselor, 1980—; psychotherapist L.I. Cons. Ctr., 1973—77; pvt. practice psychotherapy, 1975—. Fellow, L.I. Inst. Mental Health, 1975. Mem.: PGA, United Fedn. Tchrs., Am. Pers. and Guidance Assn., PGA Hole in One Club, Am. Contract Bridge League (Bronze life). Home: 340 E 64th St New York NY 10021-7503 E-mail: xrojac@hotmail.com.

RESNICK, ROSALIND, multimedia executive; b. N.Y. BA, MA in Italian Renaissance History, Johns Hopkins U., 1981. Bus. reporter The Miami Herald, 1984-89; freelance writer various computer trade mags., 1990-95; founder, pres., CEO NetCreations, Bklyn., 1995—2001; founder, CEO Axxess Bus. Centers, NYC, 2002—, Double R Ventures, NYC. Co-author: The Internet Business Guide, 1995; pub. & editor Interactive Pub. Alert, 1994-97. Bd. mem. Do Something Inc. Mailing: # 15B 39 Fifth Ave New York NY 10003 Office Phone: 917-689-4368.

RESNICK, STEPHANIE, lawyer; b. NYC, Nov. 12, 1959; d. Diane Gross. AB, Kenyon Coll., 1981; JD, Villanova U., 1984. Bar: Pa. 1984, N.J. 1984, U.S. Dist Ct. (ea. dist.) Pa. 1984, U.S. Dist Ct. N.J. 1984, N.Y. 1990, U.S. Ct. Appeals (3d cir.) 1993, U.S. Dist. Ct. (so. dist.) N.Y. 1996, U.S. Dist. Ct. (ea. dist.) N.Y. 2001, U.S. Supreme Ct. 1998. Assoc. Cozen and O'Connor, Phila., 1984-87, Fox, Rothschild LLP, Phila., 1987-92, ptnr., 1992—, mem. exec. com., 2003—. Mem.: ABA, Am. Law Inst., Womens Way (vice-chair 2002, chair 2003—04), N.Y. Bar Assn., N.J. Bar Assn., Phila. Bar Assn. (investigative divsn. Commn. on Jud. Selection and Retention 1988—94, profl. guidance com. 1992—96, profl. responsibility com. 1992—2000, women's rights com., women in the profession com. 1993—, Comm. on Jud. Selection and Retention 1995—2001, chair 1997, fed. cts. com. 2000—, chair 2002—03, bd. govs. 2006—), Pa. Bar Assn. (disciplinary bd. and study com. 1989—91, prof. liability com. 1991—92, commr. on Women in the Profession 1997). Office: Fox Rothschild LLP 2000 Market St Ste 10 Philadelphia PA 19103-3231 Home: 233 S 6th St Apt 2107 Philadelphia PA 19106-3756 Office Phone: 215-299-2082. E-mail: sresnick@foxrothschild.com.

RESNIK, JUDITH, law educator; BA, Bryn Mawr, 1972; JD, NYU, 1975. Orrin B. Evans prof. law U. So. Calif., 1989—97; Arthur Liman prof. law Yale U., New Haven, 1997—. Vis. prof. Harvard U., Yale U., U. Chgo., 1988—90, NYU, 1996—97; founding dir. Arthur Liman Pub. Interest Program and Fund. Co-author: Adjudication and Its Alternatives: An Introduction to Procedure, 2003; author: The Processes of Law: Understanding Courts and Their Alternatives, 2004; contbr. articles to law jours. Recipient Florence K. Murray Service Award, Internat. Assn. Women Judges, 1993, USC Assocs. Award for Creativity in Rsch., 1994. Fellow: Am. Philos. Soc.; mem.: ABA (Margaret Brent Award 1998), Am. Acad. of Arts and Scis., Internat. Assn. of Women Judges (mem. Bd. of Managerial Trustees), Am. Assn. Law Schs. (chair Sect. on Civil Procedure 1991, liaison to ABA Commn. on Women 2000—04, chair Sect. on Civil Procedure 2003). Office: Yale Law Sch PO Box 208215 New Haven CT 06520 E-mail: judith.resnik@yale.edu.

RESNIK, LINDA ILENE, marketing and information executive, writer, publisher, consultant; b. Dallas, Oct. 26, 1950; d. Harold and Reatha (Gordon) R. BJ in Broadcast Journalism, U. Mo., 1971; MA in Journalism, U. North Tex., 1977, MBA in Mktg., 1980. News and documentary producer Sta. KDFW-TV, Dallas, 1971-73; mktg.-info. officer Dallas County C.C. Dist., 1973-79; dir. mktg. The Learning Channel, Washington, 1980-82; dir. Nat. Narrowcast Svc., Pub. Broadcasting Svc., Washington, 1982-85; exec. dir. Am. Soc. Info. Sci., Washington, 1985-89, White House Conf. on Libr. and Info. Svcs., Washington, 1990-91; cons., 1991—; mng. ptnr. FAQs Press, 1998—. Adv. com. ALA Library/Book Fellows Project; fellow Ctr. for Info. and Comm. Scis., Ball State U.; U.S. exec. com. U. of the World; mktg., tng. and telecomm. cons. to ednl. assns., others Author: Food FAQs: Substitutions, Yields & Equivalents, 2000. Youth activities coordinator YMCA, Dallas, 1975-78; spl. event organizer Am. Cancer Soc., Dallas, 1976-77; com. leader Goals for Dallas, 1978-80; co-chair Friends of the Troup (Tex.) Libr., 1996—; mem. com. Tyler Race for the Cure, 1999. Recipient Best TV Feature Story award AP, Tex., 1973. Mem. Am. Soc. Assn. Execs., Am. Soc. Info. Sci. (pub. bull. 1985-89), Women in Cable, Info. Inst., Am. Mktg. Assn. Avocations: travel, racquet sports, reading, theater. Office: PO Box 130115 Tyler TX 75713-0115 E-mail: LIResnik@FAQsPress.com.

RESS, PATRICIA COLLEEN, editor, writer; b. Sioux City, Iowa, Aug. 7, 1945; d. Charles Francis and Alice Joanna (Krofta) Griffin; m. Lawrence Wright Dec. 13, 1969 (dec.); children: Alice Wendy, Cindy Marie; m. Fred Callsen Ress, Sept. 7, 1979; 1 child, Eric Christopher. BS in Edn., U. S.D., 1967; postgrad. studies in Journalism, U. Iowa, 1968, 69; cert. in lab. sci., Gradwohl Sch. Med. Lab. Tech., St. Louis, 1979; environ. lab. sci., S.E. Comty. Coll., Lincoln, Nebr., 1979. Feature writer, columnist Clay County News-Sun, Sutton, Nebr., 1977—; feature writer, photographer Sun Newspapers, Lincoln, Nebr., 1977-78; feature writer -strange and unusual column The Nebr. Voice, Lincoln, Omaha, Kearney, Nebr., 1979-81; reporter, photographer The Walton County Tribune, Monroe, Ga., 1986; feature writer Omaha Met. Update and Midland Bus. Jour., 1990, 91; feature writer, free lance Paragon Publ. Ltd., Bournemouth, England, 1992—; editor The Constitutional Liberator, Omaha, 1995—. Regional story cons. Mike Jarmus radio show; staff feature writer/reporter Lagazette of Broussard, La.; story cons. Doomsday Talk Radio, Media, Pa. Author: Stranger Than Fiction: The True Time-Travel Adventures of Steven L. Gibbs, the Rainman of Time-Travel, 2002, Seven Chilling Things You Should Know About Your Soul, 2002, Travel Tips for Tightwads, 2002, Don't Go To College til' You've Read This Book!, 2002, Time-Travel Odyssey, 2002, Dangerouso Information, 2002, Cures and Treatment You're Not Supposed to Know About - They Actually Work, 2004, Carl's Story, 2004, Invisible Hands of Healing: My Journey Into Trans-Dimensional Medicine, 2004, The Frightenuing Final Piece to the UFO Puzzle, 2004, Conversations With Branton, 2004, Nightsearch RAdio Show of Memphis La Gazette de TVillages, Mind Machines; co-author: Strangers In the Heartland, 1998, Armageddon: The Last Alien Battle, 1998, (plays) Hell Has Windows, 1969; editor: Summary Mag.; pub.; contbr. articles to mags. and newspapers. Mem. Lincoln Civic Symphony and Chorus, Nebr., 1981-82. Recipient scholarship Oelwein (Iowa) Daily Register, 1963, Hon. Mention, Sioux City (Iowa) Jour. Ann. photography contest, 1969, Third Pl. medallion Nat. Libr. of Poetry, Owings Mills, Md., 1995, Editors' Choice award Outstanding Achievement in Poetry, Libr. Poetry, 2004-2005. Mem. Oakcrest Inst. Elkhorn, Nebr. (bd. mem. in charge of pub. rels.) Avocations: playing music, listening to short wave radio, riding horses, cooking, painting. Home and Office: 7016 North 107th Ct Omaha NE 68142

RESSEL, TERESA MULLETT, federal agency administrator; BS in Engrng., MS in Engrng., U. Del.; MBA, Rensselaer Poly. Inst., 1990. V.p., chief compliance officer Kaiser Found. Health Plan, Inc., Kaiser Found. Hosps., Inc.; prin. dep. asst. sec. for mgmt. and budget U.S. Dept. Treasury, Washington, 2001—02, asst. sec. for mgmt. and CFO, 2003—. Recipient Presdl. Citation for Outstanding Alumni Achievement, U. Del., 1996, Disting. Svc. award, Dept. Treasury, 2003. Office: US Dept of the Treasury 1500 Pennsylvania Ave NW Washington DC 20220

RESSLER, ALISON S., lawyer; b. NYC, 1958; AB, Brown U., 1980; JD, Columbia U., 1983. Bar: NY 1984, Calif. 1985. Ptnr., corp. fin. Sullivan & Cromwell, LA, and mem., mgmt. com. Deans coun. Columbia Law Sch.; trustee Brown Univ., Harvard Westlake. Office: Sullivan & Cromwell LLP 1888 Century Park E Los Angeles CA 90067-1725 Office Phone: 310-712-6600. Office Fax: 310-712-8800.

RESSLER, AMY JUNE, theater educator, theater director; b. Dubuque, Iowa, June 9, 1962; d. Elmer John Ressler and Mary Catherine Chapman; m. Marc Steven Muehleip; children: Maxwell, Zoe. BA in Drama, Clarke Coll., Dubuque, Iowa, 1984; MFA in Theater Edn., Ariz. State U., Tempe, Ariz., 1988; MAT in Secondary Edn., Nat. Louis U., Evanston, Ill., 2001. Intern, stage mgr. J.F. Kennedy Ctr., Washington, 1987—89; prof. theater Nat. Louis U., 1990—2002; tchr. English Shullsburg H.S., Shullsburg, Wis., 2003—05; artistic dir. Great Midwestern Edn. Theatre Co., Shullsburg, Wis., 2001—06; prof. theater U. Wis., Platteville, Wis., 2005—. Composer: (Operas) Speading the News, 1998, (nusical theater) Pickle Patch Bathtub, 2005. Children's theatre divsn. Ill. Theater Assn., 1992—94. Recipient Creative Drama award, Ill. Theatre Assn., 2005. Mem.: Am. Alliance fir Theatre & Edn. Achievements include founder Great Midwestern Ednl. Theatre Co. Avocation: camping. Office: U Wisc 180 Doudna Platteville WI 53818

RESTANI, JANE A., federal judge; b. San Francisco, Feb. 27, 1948; d. Roy J. and Emilia C. Restani. BA, U. Calif., Berkeley, 1969; JD, U. Calif., Davis, 1973. Bar: Calif., 1973. Trial atty. U.S. Dept. Justice, Washington, 1973-76, asst. chief comml. litigation sect., 1976-80, dir. comml. litigation sect., 1980-83; judge U.S. Ct. Internat. Trade, N.Y.C., 1983—2003, chief judge, 2003—. Mem. Order of Coif. Office: US Ct Internat Trade 1 Federal Plz New York NY 10278-0001

RETHMEL, CAROL ANN, voice educator, director; b. Takoma Park, Md., Apr. 9, 1953; d. Elmer E. and Donna Elizabeth (Wassum) Parsons; 1 child, Joshua Allan Parsons. MusM, Ea. N.Mex U., Portales, 1988—90. Choral dir. Lea County Pub. Schs., Hobbs, N.Mex., 1996—99, Prince William County Pub. Schs., Woodbridge, Va., 1999—. Mem.: Am. Choral Dirs. Assn. (dist. chmn. 2003—05), Music Educators Nat. Con., Sigmma Alpha Iota. Home: 2849 Chablis Cir Woodbridge VA 22192 Office: Woodbridge Sr HS 3001 Old Bridge Rd Woodbridge VA 22192 Office Fax: 703-497-8172. Personal E-mail: primadiva1@comcast.net.

RETMAN, DEBORAH W., biology educator; b. Xenia, Ohio, Nov. 10, 1961; d. Thomas Elmer and Gail (Nichol) Welsh; m. Mick Retman, Mar. 24, 1990. BA, Ohio U., 1984; MA, Wright State U., 1996. Pharmacy tech. rugs, Xenia, 1977—79; waitress Red Barn, Xenia, 1979—82; sales clk. Tiffany Jewelers, Xenia, 1982—84; biology tchr. Piqua City Schs., Ohio, 1984—. Emt City of Clayton, Ohio, 1990—; coach Piqua City Schs., 1989—. Named Tchr. of the Yr., McDonalds. Mem.: Clayton Fire Assn., Piqua Edn. Assn. (pres. 2003—05). Methodist. Office: Piqua High Sch 1 Indiann Trl Piqua OH 45356-9257

RETSECK, MEGHAN MAERENE, elementary school educator; b. Boynton Beach, Fla., Oct. 3, 1979; d. Cindy Maerene and David Harland Wiest; m. Michael James Retseck, July 13, 2002; 1 child, Mikaela. BA Dance Edn., Meredith Coll., Raleigh, NC, 2002. Cert. tchr. NC. Dance educator East Garner (NC) Magnet Mid. Sch., 2002—; tchr. Step Ahead Dance Studio, Cary, NC, 2003—. Fine arts dept. chair East Garner Magnet Mid. Sch., 2003—. Choreographer Hope Overcoming (Pieces of Gold Showcase award, 2003), Wild Horses (Gold award, 2005), Medea's Vengeance (Gold award, 2006), In the Mood (Garner STARS on Stage Showcase award, 2006). Tchg. Fellows scholar, NC Edn. Found., 1998—2002. Mem.: Nat. Dance Week Orgn. (regional dir. 2006), NDEO, Dance Assn. NC Educators (bd. dirs. 2003), NC AAHPERD. Office: East Garner Magnet Mid Sch 6301 Jones Sausage Rd Garner NC 27529 Office Phone: 919-662-2339. Personal E-mail: mretseck@wcpss.net.

RETZER, MARY ELIZABETH HELM, retired librarian; b. Balt. d. Francis Leslie C. and Edna (Smith) Helm; m. William Raymond Retzer, June 28, 1945; children: Lesley Elizabeth, April Christine. BA, Western Md. Coll., Westminster, 1940; MA, Columbia U., N.Y.C., 1946; postgrad., George Washington U., 1941, Ind. U., 1952, U. Ill., 1958-59, Ill. State U., Normal, 1964-66, Bradley U., Peoria, Ill.; PhD, Western Colo. U., 1972. Faculty Rockville Bd. Edn., Md., 1940-47, elem. supr. Md., 1945-47; staff Peoria Pub. Libr., 1957-63, homebound libr., 1961-63; cons., organizer libr. Bergan High Sch., 1964-67; condr. libr. sci. course in reference Bradley U., 1966-83. Libr. Hines Elem. Sch., 1963-66, Roosevelt Jr. H.S., 1966-69; head media ctr. Manual H.S., Peoria, Ill., 1969-83. Instr. water safety courses ARC, 1938-93; pres. Entre Nous, 1949-51; pres. women's bd. Salvation Army, 1952-54; pres. Peoria Nursery Sch. Assn., 1953-54; mem. legis. action com. Ill. Congress PTA, 1955-56; mem. Crippled Children's Adv. Com., Peoria, 1957-60; active various community drives; women's adv. bd. Peoria Jr. Star, 1970-73; vol. Sarasota Internat. Airport, 1990-98. Mem. AAUW (life), NEA, ALA (life), Ill. Edn. Assn. (life), Peoria Edn. Assn. (life), Ill. Libr. Assn., Ill. Valley Librs. Assn. (pres. 1971-72), Ill. Assn. Media in Edn. (cert. com. 1973-80), Ill. Audiovisual Assn., Internat. Platform Assn., Order Ea. Star (life), Ill. State U. Adminstrs. Club, Willowknolls Country Club, Sarasota Yacht Club, Ladies Oriental Shrine. Republican. Presbyterian. Home: 3240 Lake Pointe Blvd Unit 101 Sarasota FL 34231

RETZLAFF, KAY L., literature educator, writer; d. Robert Stuart and Jean Alice Retzlaff; m. Thomas Ross McCord, Oct. 5, 1985. BA, U. Nebr., Lincoln, 1976, MA, 1981; PhD, U. Maine, Orono, 2004. Cert. tchr. Nebr. Asst. prof. English U. Maine, Augusta, 2003—; paste-up staffer Lincoln (Nebr.) Jour.-Star, 1981; asst. comm. dept. Nat. Assn. Mfrs., Washington, 1981—83; asst. press sec. US Sen. Walter Huddleston Ky., Washington, 1983—85; comm. dir. Nat. Assn. Med. Equipment Suppliers, Alexandria, Va., 1985—86; staff writer FORM Mag., Alexandria, 1987—88; pvt. practice Washington, 1988—. Adj. faculty Ea. Maine Tech. Coll., Bangor, 1994, U. Maine, Augusta, 1994—96, 2000—03, Orono, 1997—; lectr., presenter in field. Author: Ireland: Its Myths and Legends, Women of Mythology; editor: Vietnam Memories: A Cookbook, 2006; contbr. articles to profl. jours. Faculty adv. Celtic Studies Students Assn., 2000—02; vol. Leadership Inst. Waldo County, 1998—99; bd. dirs. Waldo County Coop. Ext., 1997—99, Sta. WERU-FM Cmty. Radio, 1999—2003, Maine Ctr. for Student Journalism, 1994—98. Democrat.

REUBEN, GLORIA, actress, singer; b. Toronto, Ont., June 9, 1964; m. Wayne Isaak, 1999. T.V. and movie actress; backup singer and dancer Tina Turner's World Tour, 2000. Actress (films) Immediate Family, 1989, Wild Orchid II: Two Shades of Blue, 1992, The Waiter, 1993, Time Cop, 1994, Nick of Time, 1995, David and Lola, 1999, Macbeth in Manhattan, 1999, Bad Faith, 2000, Pilgrim, 2000, Happy Here and Now, 2002, Kettle of Fish, 2005, The Sentinel, 2006, (TV films) The Day They Came to Arrest the Book, 1987, Shadowhunter, 1993, Percy & Thunder, 1993, Confessions: Two Faces of Evil, 1994, Dead Air, 1994, Johnny's Girl, 1995, Indiscreet, 1998, Sara, 1999, Deep in My Heart, 1999, Sole Survivor, 2000, The Agency, 2001, Feast of All Saints, 2001, Little John, 2002, Salem Witch Trials, 2002, host (TV series) Polka Dot Door, 1985, actress ER, 1995—99, The Agency, 2001—02, actress, composer, prodr. 1-800-Missing, 2003—04, appearances in Alfred Hitchcock Presents, 1987, 21 Jump Street, 1988, The Flash, 1990—91, Silk Stalkings, 1993, Homicide: Life on the Street, 1995, The District, 2002, Law & Order: Special Victims Unit, 2002, Numb3rs, 2005, actress (plays) Stuff Happens, 2005, A Nervous Smile, 2006; singer: (albums) Just for You, 2004; back-up singer Twenty Four Seven, Tina Turner's World Tour, 2000. Recipient SAG Awards, 1998, 99, Q Award, 1997, 98; named one of 50 Most Beautiful People in World, People mag., 1996. Mailing: c/o Elise Konialian/ Untitled Mgmt Floor 3 23 East 22nd St New York NY 10010 Office Phone: 212-777-1214.*

REUDER, MARY E(ILEEN), retired psychology professor, retired statistician; b. Mpls., Mar. 12, 1923; d. Leo Aloysius and Mary Agnes (McGuire) R.; m. Marvin Alvin Iverson, July 11, 1953 (dec. Dec. 1979); children: Carol Mary, Kent Gery. BA, Coll. St. Catherine, St. Paul, 1944; MA, Brown U., 1945; PhD, U. Pa., 195l. Lic. psychologist, N.Y.; diplomate Am. Bd. Psychol. Specialties. Asst. instr. psychology U. Pa., Phila., 1946-51; work mgmt. specialist U.S. Naval Ammunition Depot, Ft. Mifflin, Pa., 1951-52; rsch. psychologist pers. br. Adj. Gen.'s Office, Dept. Army, Washington, 1952-54; instr. psychology Queens Coll., CUNY, Flushing, 1957-62, asst. prof., 1962-66, assoc. prof., 1966-71, prof., 1971-86, chmn. dept., 1984-85, chmn. acad. senate, 1982-85, prof. emerita, 1986—. Mem. grad. faculty CUNY, 1977-86; mem. adv. bd. Dushkin Press, Guilford, Conn., 1975-84; cons. NATO postdoctoral fellowships NSF, Washington, 1978; cons., manuscript peer reviewer Acad. Psychology Bull., 1980-85, Jour. Profl. Psychology, 1986-88, Am. Psychologist, 1987-88, Psychol. Reports, 1995-96. Contbr. articles to profl. jours. and encys., also monographs, chpt. to book. Cons. com. on rsch. and evaluation Nassau coun. Girl Scouts U.S., 1971-74; bd. dirs. Walker Lake Community Assn., 1993—. Recipient William James award for outstanding contbns. to psychology Acad. Divsn. N.Y. State Psychol. Assn., 1998; grantee NSF, 1964, Sigma Xi, 1962. Fellow APA (pres. divs. 1 and 36 1987-88, exec. com. div. 1 1981-87, div. 36 1979—, coun. reps. div. 36 1980-83, 91-97, 99-2001, 2005—, award for exceptional svc. to divsn. gen. psychology, disting. svc. award by divsn. of psychology of religion, 1996, accreditation site visitor 1996—, Virginia Staudt Sexton Mentoring award divsn. 36 psychology of religion 1996), Am. Psychol. Soc., N.Y. Acad. Scis., Am. Assn. Applied and Preventive Psychology (charter); mem. AAAS (life), Am. Bd. Forensic Examiners, Ea. Psychol. Assn. (adminstrv. coord. 1961-67, 70), Psychometric Soc., Biometric Soc., Am. Statis. Assn., Queens Coll. Faculty Club (past bd. dirs., v.p.), U. Pa. Club L.I. (bd. govs. 1980—, Jack White award), N.Am. Lake Mgmt. Soc., Pa. Lake Mgmt. Soc., Penn Club NY (charter mem.), Sigma Xi (grantee 1962, regional lectr. 1977-86, nat. bd. dirs. 1972-75, 77), Alpha Sigma Lambda, Pi Gamma Mu, Delta Phi Lambda, Kappa Gamma Pi, Alpha Pi Epsilon, Psi Chi. Democrat. Roman Catholic. Avocations: reading, swimming. Home: PO Box C Shohola PA 18458-0080 Office: CUNY Queens Coll Dept Psychology Flushing NY 11367

REUTER, HELEN HYDE, psychologist; b. McGehee, Ark. d. John Lloyd and Sallie Elizabeth (Holcomb) Hyde; m. George S. Reuter Jr.; children: Don N., M. Allan, K.L. BA, Westmar U., 1968; AM, U. S.D., 1969; PhD, Westgate U., 1976; LHD (hon.), Sioux Empire Coll.; LLD (hon.), St. John U., New Orleans; DD (hon.), Temple Bapt. Coll. Ordained So. Bapt. minister. Postmaster U.S. Post Office, College Heights, Ark.; sch. counselor various pub. sch. systems, Mo., Iowa; sch. psychologist Oak Park (Ill.) and River Forest High Sch.; v.p., sec. Internat. Assocs. for Christians, Holden, Mo. Cons. in field. Co-author: One Blood, 1964, 2d edit., 1988, Democracy and Quality Education, 1965, 2d edit., 1986. Named Mother of Yr., City of Monticello, 1960; cited as Psychologist of Yr., Internat. U., Lagos, Nigeria, 1992. Mem. P.E.O. (v.p.), Shakespeare Club (v.p.), Garden Club (v.p.). Democrat. Baptist. Avocations: travel, classical music. Home: 849 Key Largo Ct Auburn GA 30011-2275

REUTER, JOAN COPSON, retired program director; b. London, July 7, 1919; came to US, 1921; d. Denis and Florence (Copson) Soucy; widowed; children: David, Robert N., Joan Ellen Swanson, Alan, Ronald (dec.). AA, Asnuntuck C.C., 1975; BS, N.H. Coll., 1982. Dir. women's ctr. Asnuntuck C.C., Enfield, Conn., 1975—98, ret., 1998. Adj. faculty Asnuntuck C.C., 1984-95, dir. childcare ctr., 1974—; bd. dir. Mentor Program, Town Enfield, After Sch. Program. Bd. dir. Enfield Bd. Edn., 1979-91; justice of peace Town of Enfield, 1980—; sec. Enfield Loan Rev. Com., 1957—. Mem. Women's Club Enfield (sec., bd. dir. 1957—), Asnuntuck Alumni Assn. (v.p., pres.). Republican. Episcopalian. Avocations: reading, walking, gardening. Home: 9 Homestead Dr Enfield CT 06082-4639

REVAK, CLAUDIA ANNE, music educator; d. Claude Adam Pope and Clara Christine Gross; m. Arthur Michael Revak, Oct. 16, 1982; children: Reese Arthur, Christopher Michael. MusB in Edn., Susquehanna U., Selinsgrove, Pa., 1982. Cert. tchr. NJ, Ind., Pa. Dir. of music East Stroudsburg U. Meth. Ch., 1989—2000; musical dir., accompanist Country Gate Playhouse, Belvidere, NJ, 1989—2003; music tchr. LibertyTownship Sch., Great Meadows, NJ, 1990—97; instrumental music tchr. Great Meadows Regional Mid. Sch., 1998—; dir. of music, organist Trinity Episcopal Ch., Mt. Pocono, Pa., 2000—02; organist Zion United Ch. of Christ, Stroudsburg, Pa., 2002—. Festival judge Pa. Fedn. Music Clubs, East Stroudsburg, 1988—2005, festival accompanist, Bethlehem, 1990—; assoc. instr. music edn. Ind. U., Bloomington, 1985—86; prin. chair flute Pa. Intercollegiate Band, 1982. Musician (accompanist): Arts on the Mountain, The French Connection Recital; musician, accompanist The Secret Life of Antonio Vivaldi. Flutist Trinity Cmty. Band, Mt. Pocono, 1991—2002. Recipient Tchr. Recognition Honor, Great Meadows Regional Edn. Found., 2004—06. Mem.: Music Educators Nat. Conf. (assoc.), NJ Music Educators Assn. (assoc.; judge jr. h.s. band-flutes 2002—05, judge and rehearsal acompanist regional chorus 2003—05), NJ Edn. Assn. (assoc.), Music Study Club of Stroudsburg (assoc.; auditor 1990—2006), Sigma Alpha Iota (assoc.; rec. sec., corr. sec. 1979—82, Sword of Honor 1982). United Ch. Of Christ. Achievements include development of NJ arts curriculum framework committee. Avocations: concerts, bicycling, reading. Office Phone: 908-637-4349.

REVELEY, MARY, aeronautical engineer; BS in Aero. Engrng. Accident reconstructionist; expert witness; tchr. h.s. math.; designer fluid sys. NASA, aero. engr. Propulsion Sys. Analysis Office Cleve. Avocation: Avocations: volleyball, soccer, softball, drawing and painting, camping. Office: NASA Glenn Rsch Ctr MS 60-7 Cleveland OH 44135 E-mail: Mary.S.Reveley@grc.nasa.gov.

REVERE, VIRGINIA LEHR, psychologist; b. Long Branch, NJ; d. Joseph and Essie Lehr; m. Robert B. Revere; children: Elspeth, Andrew, Lisa, Robert Jr. PhB, U. Chgo., 1949, MA, 1959, PhD, 1971. Lic. cons. clin. psychologist, Va. Intern, staff psychologist Ea. Mental Health Reception Ctr., Phila., 1959-61; instr. Trenton (N.J.) State Coll., 1962-63; psychologist Trenton State Hosp., 1964-65, Bucks County Psychiat. Ctr., Phila., 1965-67; assoc. prof. Mansfield (Pa.) State U., 1967-77; clin. rsch. psychologist St. Elizabeth Hosp., Washington, 1977-81, tng. psychology coord., 1981-83, psychologist, 1985-91; child psychologist Cmty. Mental Health Ctr., Washington, 1983-85; pvt. practice Alexandria, Va., 1980—. Cons., lectr. in field. Author: Applied Psychology for Criminal Justice Professionals, 1982; contbr. articles to profl. jours. Recipient Group Merit award St. Elizabeth's Hosp., 1983, Community Svc. award D.C. Psychol. Assn., 1978, Outstanding Educator award, 1972; traineeship NIH, USPHS, Chgo., 1963-65; fellow Family Svcs. Assn., 1958-59. Mem. APA, No. Va. Soc. Clin. Psychologists, Va. Acad. Clin. Psychologists. Office Phone: 703-780-4872. E-mail: rrevere923@aol.com.

REVESZ, KINGA, chemist, isotope geochemist, researcher; b. Debreceh, Hungary, Apr. 29, 1943; came to U.S., 1975; d. Bela and Katalin (Harsanyi) Lutter; m. Akos Revesz, Jan. 10, 1975; 1 child, Paul. MS, Eotvos Lorant U., Budapest, Hungary, 1966; PhD, Jozset Attila U., Szeged, Hungary, 1977. Head surface chemistry group Tungsram Rsch. Lab., Budapest, 1971-75; chemist Nat. Bur. Stds., Washington, 1977-78, U.S. Geol. Survey, Water Resources Divsn., Reston, Va., 1983-89, chemist nat. rsch. program, 1989—. Contbr. articles to profl. jours.; patentee in field. Mem. Am. Chem. Soc., Am. Geophys. Union, Geol. Soc. Am., Geol. Soc. Washington. Home: 7910 Park Overlook Dr Bethesda MD 20817-2719 Office: US Geol Survey MS 431 Sunrise Valley Dr Reston VA 20192-0001 Office Phone: 703-648-5865. E-mail: krevesz@usgs.gov.

REVIS-PYKE, ROBIN LYNN, director; b. Orlando, Fla., Feb. 16, 1962; d. Ed Revis and Carol Joan Rogers; m. Scott Douglas Pyke; children: Robert Stevin Revis Pyke, Spencer Douglas Pyke, Barrett Harper Pyke. BS in Comm., Trinity Internat. U., Miami; MS in Higher Edn. Adminstrn., Barry U., Miami, post graduate studies in Edn. Preschool tchr. Miami Shores Baptist Ch., 1996—97, fin. asst., 1997—2000; media comm. coord. Archdiocese of Miami, 2000—01; assoc. dir. admission and fin. aid Miami Country Day Sch., Miami, 2001—06; dean of admission Montverde (Fla.) Acad., 2006—. Assoc. editor The Admission Review. Chair Miami Shores Village Fine Arts Commn., Fla., 1997—2002; mem. Philanthropic Educators Orgn., 1999—2002; exec. bd. mem. Shores Performing Arts Theater, Miami Shores, 2002—04; mem. pres. bd. advisors St. Thomas U.; chair Miami Shores Village Mayors Task Force, Fla., 1998—2001. Mem.: Assn. Ind. Sch. Admission Profls., Secondary Sch. Admission Test Bd., Nat. Coun. Measurement in Edn., Nat. Assn. Independent Schs., Am. Ednl. Rsch. Assn. (grad. student coun. camps liaison 2005—), Am. Assn. U. Women, Phi Delta Kappa, Kappa Delta Pi. Republican. Baptist. Avocations: yoga, cooking, reading, boating, snorkeling. Home: 1800 NE 114 St #2005 Miami FL 33181 Office: Miami Country Day Sch 601 NE 107 St Miami FL 33161 E-mail: robin@revispyke.net.

REXFORD, JENNIFER, communications engineer; BSEE, Princeton U., 1991; MS in Computer Sci. & Engring., U. Mich., 1993, PhD in Computer Sci. & Engring., 1996. Mem. IP network mgmt & performance dept. AT&T Rsch., 1996—. Bd. dirs. Assn. Computing Machinery (ACM) SIGMETRICS, 2003—; mem. tech. adv. bd. Arbor Networks, 2003—; chair Assn. Computing Machinery (ACM) SIGCOMM, 2003—; membership svcs. bd. Assn. Computing Machinery (ACM), 2004—. Contbr. articles to profl. jours. Named one of Top 100 Young Innovators, MIT Tech. Review, 2004. Mem.: IEEE (sr.). Office: AT&T Rsch A139 180 Park Ave Florham Park NJ 07932-0971

REXROAT, VICKI LYNN, occupational child development educator; b. Oklahoma City, Okla., June 12, 1957; d. Troy Bill and Opal Pauline (Flinn) Miller; m. David Edward Rexroat, Sept. 6, 1980; children: Jamie Lynn, Amber Donn, Emily Sue. BS, U. of Sci. and Arts, 1991; MS, U. Ctrl. Okla., 1997. Presch. tchr. Caddo-Kiowa Vocat. Sch., Fort Cobb, Okla., 1981-84, child devel. dir., 1984-89, child devel. instr., 1989—. Rep., advisor Child Devel. Assoc., Washington, 1989—; mem. curriculum team Okla. Dept. of Vocat. Edn., Stillwater, Okla., 1991—; adv. bd. Child Care Careers, Oklahoma City, 1992—. Contbr. articles to profl. jours. Co-chair Reach Out, Inc. Homeless Shelter, Anadarko, Okla., 1995—; founder, vol. Caddo County Welfare Vols., 1989—; friends for life mem. Fort Cobb Sr. Citizens, 1990—; mem. Fort Cobb Booster Club, 1989—. Named Friend of Children Okla. Inst. of Child Advocacy, 1993, New Tchr. of Yr. Okla. Vocat. Assn., 1993. Mem. Friends in the Okla. Early Childhood Assn. (pres. 1989—), So. Early Childhood Assn., Okla. Assn. for the Edn. of Young Children, Nat. Assn. for the Edn. of Young Children, Am. Vocat. Assn. (dist. v.p. 1989—, New Tchr. of Yr. 1994). Democrat. Bapt. Avocations: basketball games, fishing, boating, student organizations. Office: Caddo-Kiowa Vocat Sch North 7th Fort Cobb OK 73038

REYES, CZARINA SUZANNE, mathematics educator; d. Suzanne Paulette Reynolds. BA in Math., So. Meth. U., 1998, MA, 2001; attended in Higher Edn., U. N. Tex. Cert. tchr. Tex., 1999. Math. tchr. Creekview HS, Carrollton, Tex., 1999—2000; faculty math. Dallas County C.C. Dist.-Brookhaven Coll., Farmers Branch, Tex., 2000—. Recipient LENs award Focusin Excellence, Brookhaven Coll., 2006. Mem.: AAUW, Tex. C. C. Tchrs. Assn., Math. Assn. Am., Nat. Scholars, Phi Theta Kappa (Outstanding Student Honor Soc. 2004). Office: Brookhaven Coll 3939 Valley View Ln Farmers Branch TX 75244 Office Phone: 972-860-4338. Office Fax: 972-860-4151. Business E-Mail: creyes@dcccd.edu.

REYES, IRMA V., adult education educator; b. Coamo, P.R., Dec. 10, 1951; d. Nazario Reyes and Gloria E. Miranda; 1 child, Catherine M. Hamade. BA in Edn., U. P.R., Rio Piedras, 1974. Cert. secondary tchr. Spanish and sociology P.R., 1974. Tchr. Ergos Sch., Ponce, PR, 1977—79, intermediate sch. tchr., 1979—84, H.S. tchr., 1984—86, asst. dir. academics and register, 1980—86; part-time H.S. tchr. Cristo Rey Acad., Ponce, 1987—89; intermediate sch. tchr. Pedro Albizu Campos Sch., Ponce, 1986—93; GED Spanish tchr. Perth Amboy (N.J.) Adult Sch., 1994—. Moderator of the student counsel and nat. honor soc. Ergos Sch., Ponce, 1980—86. Mem. Nat. Fedn. Bus. and Profl. Women's Club, Ponce, 1975—77. Mem.: N.J. Assn. Lifelong Learning, Profl. Lit. Am. Tchr., Am. Fedn. Tchrs. Roman Catholic. Avocations: reading, poetry. Home: 541 Hazel Ave Perth Amboy NJ 08861 Office: Perth Amboy Adult Sch 178 Barracks St Perth Amboy NJ 08861 Office Phone: 732-376-6240. E-mail: irmareyes@paps.net.

REYES, JUDY, actress; b. NYC, Nov. 5, 1968; m. Edwin M. Figueroa. Founding mem. Labyrinth Theatre Co., NYC. Actor: (films) Jack & HIs Friends, 1992, Lena's Dreams, 1997, No Exit, 1998, Godzilla, 1998, Bringing Out the Dead, 1999, King of the Jungle, 2000, Home Invaders, 2001, Washington Heights, 2002, King of the Corner, 2004, Dirty, 2005; (TV films) The Prosecutors, 1996, Mind Prey, 1999, WW3, 2001, It's a Very Merry Muppet Christmas Movie, 2002, Our House, 2006; (TV series) Oz, 1999, Scrubs, 2001—; (documentaries) Pieces of Courage: In Search of My Cultural Heroes, 2003; (plays) Some Girls, 2006; exec. prodr.: (films) Moment to Moment, 2003; actor, co-prodr. (films) Taino, 2001, actor, prodr. Glow Ropes: The Rise & Fall of a Bar Mitzvah Emcee, 2005. Recipient Am. Latin Media Arts (ALMA) award for Outstanding Actress in a TV Series, Nat. Coun. La Raza, 2006.*

REYES, SUSANA MARIE, utilities executive, environmentalist; b. Manila, Philippines, Dec. 18, 1954; d. Virgilio T. and Herminia (Fajatin) Reyes; divorced; children: Freya Suzanne Estreller, Sharon Erin Estreller, Jaimee Lauren Estreller, Carissa Mia Estreller. Cert., Fashion Inst. Design and Mdse., L.A., 1983; BA in Comms., St. Paul Coll., Manila, 1976; MA in. Comms., U. Philippines, Manila, 1979. V.p. pub. rels. Apparel Resources Corp., Manila, 1979-81; mdse. specialist Macy's, L.A., 1983-86; mgr. chem. info. ctr. Dept. Water and Power, L.A., 1986-89; mgmt. analyst Dept. Gen. Svcs., L.A., 1990-91; program mgr. city facilities recycling City of L.A., 1991-99; exec. asst. corp. adminstrv. svcs. Dept. Water and Power, L.A., 1999—. Mem. adv. affirmative action com. City of L.A., 1998-99; mem. tech. adv. com. Calif. Resource Recovery Assn., 1992-99. Mem. parent bd. Mayfield Sr. Sch., Pasadena, Calif., 1996; v.p. PTO, Holy Trinity Sch., L.A., 1997. Recipient Good Earthkeeping award City of L.A., 1997. Mem. Sierra Club (mem. polit. com. 1999), All City Employees Benefits Assn. Avocations: reading, writing, event planning, travel. Office: Dept Water and Power 111 N Hope St Rm 1545 Los Angeles CA 90012-2607

REYES-HERNÁNDEZ, MIGDALIA, counselor; b. San Juan, P.R., Oct. 27, 1952; d. José Ramón Reyes and Catalina Hernández; m. Carlos Iván Aponte, Dec. 28, 1974 (div. Feb. 1980); m. Wilfred Román, June 30, 1983; children: Ricardo, Natalia. BA in Edn., U. P.R., Río Piedras, 1973; MA in Counseling, U. Phoenix, Guaynabo, P.R., 1999. Cert. tchr. P.R., guidance counselor. Tchr. Dept. of Edn., PR, 1973—75, Colegio María Auxiliadora, Carolina, PR, 1976—99; counselor Univ. del Este, Carolina, 1999—2000, Colegio María Auxiliadora, Carolina, 1999—2006. Spkr. at conf. Sixth P.R. Congress Investigations in Edn., 2001. Author: (hymns) Himno a María Auxiliadora, 1985, Te cantamos Carolina, 2001. Mem.: Am. Counseling Assn., P.R. Assn. Profl. Counselors (temp. treas. 2000, conf. spkr. 2001). Protestant. Avocations: reading, writing, singing. Home: 1 Fontana Tower Apt 609 Carolina PR 00982 E-mail: migdalia_reyes@hotmail.com.

REYMOND, PATRICIA ANN, social worker; b. Meadville, Pa., Feb. 13, 1935; d. James Thomas and Margaret Alice (Ewing) Bulger; m. Ralph Daniel Reymond, Feb. 4, 1961; 1 child, Eric Daniel. BA, Villa Maria Coll., 1957; MSW, Cath. U., 1960. Caseworker House of Good Shepherd, Balt., 1960-61; sch. social worker Balt. Pub. Schs., 1961-69; social worker Travelers Aid Soc., Balt., summers 1962-69; part-time med. social worker St. Francis Hosp. and Med. Ctr., Topeka, 1988-99. Vol. Shawnee County Med. Soc. Aux., Topeka, 1972—95, Am. Cancer Soc., Topeka, 1978—81, Stormont-Vail Hosp. Aux., Topeka, 1975—95, Capper Found., Topeka, 1989—91, St. Francis Hosp. and Med. Ctr. Aux., Topeka, 1984—88, Meals on Wheels, Topeka, 1993—2003; mem. adv. coun. Kans. Children's Svc. League, Topeka, 1989—92; CASA of Shawnee Co., 1987—2003. Avocations: travel, reading. Home: 2816 SW Macvicar Ave Topeka KS 66611-1705 E-mail: reymunsonwe@aol.com.

REYNARD, MURIEL JOYCE, lawyer; b. Miami Beach, Fla., May 20, 1945; d. Hyman and Faye (Feinstein) Friedkin; m. Brian Patrick Delaney, Nov. 27, 1983; children: Kelly, Charlotte. BA, SUNY, Stony Brook, 1967, MS, 1973; JD cum laude, Yeshiva U., 1983. Bar: N.Y. 1984, U.S. Dist. Ct. (so. and ea. dists.) N.Y. 1984. Health planner Nassau-Suffolk RMP/CHP, Centereach, NY, 1972-74; adminstr. NYC Health and Hosps. Corp., 1974-75; health planner AFSCME Dist. Coun. 37, NYC, 1975-76; adminstr. Inst. Emergency Medicine Albert Einstein Coll. Medicine, NYC, 1977-80; asst. atty. US Atty.'s Office (so. dist.) N.Y., NYC, summer 1982; assoc. Skadden, Arps, Slate, Meagher & Flom, NYC, 1983-85, Paskus, Gordon & Mandel, NYC, 1985-86; v.p., sr. assoc. counsel The Chase Manhattan Bank, N.A., NYC, 1986-96; v.p. assoc. gen. counsel Citicorp Credit Svcs. Inc., NYC, 1997—2002, sr. v.p., assoc. gen. counsel, 2002, sr. v.p., gen. counsel, 2006. Notes and comments editor Cardozo Law Rev.; contbr. numerous articles to law jours. Mem. ABA, N.Y.C. Bar Assn., N.Y. State Bar Assn. Office: Citicorp Credit Services Inc One Court Square New York NY 11120

REYNAUD-ROEPKE, SUZANNE, psychologist; b. Kansas City, Kans., Mar. 26, 1954; d. Raymond Lucien and Donna Jean Reynaud; m. Carl Frank Roepke, Jr., Dec. 22, 1985; children: Peter Hague Roepke II, Lucienne Marie Roepke. BA in Psychology, U. Calif., Santa Barbara, 1976; MEd in Spl. Edn., U. Nev., Reno, 1985; MSEd in Counseling Psychology, U. So. Calif., L.A., 1989, PhD in Psychology, 1995. Cert. clear pupil pers. credential sch. psychology Calif., clear pupil pers. credential Calif., clear specialist credential in learning handicapped Calif., clear multiple subjects credential Calif., sch. psychologist endorsement Nev. Student intern Linda Mar Elem. Sch., Pacifica, Calif., 1978—79; pvt. practice ednl. therapy Gardnerville, Nev., 1984—85; grad. intern Douglas County Sch. Dist., 1984—85; grad. asst. ind. ednl. programs educationally handicapped U. Nev., Reno, 1984—85; psychol. intern Julia Ann Singer Children's Psychiatric Ctr., L.A., 1986—87; outreach L.A. Jewish Orthodox Cmty., 1986—88, Focus on Youth L.A. Unified Sch. Dist., 1988—89; sch. counselor Multnomah St. Magnet Sch., East Los Angeles, 1988—89; psychol. intern Hollywood Counseling Ctr., 1988—89; predoctoral intern Alvarado Parkway Inst., La Mesa, 1991—92; resource specialist North Ter. Elem. Sch., Oceanside, 1994, The Rhoades Sch., Encinitas, 1995; pvt. practice psychology The Dennison Clinic, Carlsbad, 1995—99; NIMH post doctoral rsch. fellow Geriatric Psychiatry Clin. Rsch. Ctr. U. Calif. San Diego Sch. Medicine, 1996—99; sch. psychologist Inyo and Mono Counties Sch. Dists., Calif., 2000—. Doctoral com. mem. LaVerne Coll., Calif.; field work supr. Calif. State U., San Bernardino; spl. edn. cons. region 10 Calif. Preschool Instrnl. Network Spl. Edn. Divsn. Calif. Dept. Edn., 2000—; contract psychologist Cal-Works Dept. Health and Human Svcs., 2000—; presenter to profl. meetings. Co-author (with J. McQuaid, R. Scinta and P. Cutler): Cognitive Behavioral Therapy for Thought Disorder, 1998; co-author: (with J. McQuaid, E. Granholm and F.S. McClure) Group Therapy Manual for Cognitive Behavioral Skills Training (CBSST) for Older Persons with Schizophrenia, 1999; contbr. scientific papers, articles to profl. jours. Task force mem. southwest dist Luth. Ch. (Mo. Synod), Irvine; bd. mem. Bishop (Calif.) Swim Team, 2002—03. Fellow, NIMH, 1996—99; grantee, Am. Assn. Geriatric Psychiatry; Educare scholarship award, U. So. Calif. Sch. Edn., 1985. Mem.: Nat. Assn. Sch. Psychologists, USA Swimming (nat. cert. swim official 1994—), Am. Paint Horse Assn., Phi Delta Kappa (scholarship award 1988). Republican. Lutheran. Avocations: trail riding, photography, cross country skiing, hiking, yoga. Home: 398 Mt Tom Rd Bishop CA 93514-2122 Office: Bernasconi Edn Ctr Big Pine CA 93513 Office Phone: 760-938-2633.

REYNOLDS, BARBARA C., retired mental health educator, dean; b. Syracuse, N.Y. d. Robert J. Clark; m. George L. Reynolds, June 9, 1962 (dec.); children: George L. III, Katherine C.; m. George Barnard, Apr. 17, 2004. BSN, Syracuse U., 1952; MPH, U. Minn., 1968, PhD, 1990. Asst. prof. U. Cin., 1968-75; ind. human resources cons. Cin., 1975-76; asst. prof. sch. pub. health U. Minn., 1976-82; asst. prof. Vanderbilt U., Nashville, 1986-90, N.Y. Med. Ctr. Sch. Nursing, 1964—69, Coll. Mt. St. Joseph, 1973—75; dean sch. nursing Tenn. Tech. U., Cookeville, 1991-98. Contbr. articles to profl. jours. Mem. Leadership Putnam Alumni Assn. (pres. 1995-96), Rotary (Cookeville chpt., bd. dirs.), Sigma Theta Tau, Phi Kappa Phi. Home: 1750 Heathrow Dr Cookeville TN 38506

REYNOLDS, BETTY ANN, retired elementary school educator; b. Plattsburgh, N.Y., Nov. 16, 1942; d. Morton Jay and Thelma Gladys (Baxter) R. BS in Edn., SUNY, Plattsburgh, 1964; MS in Edn., SUNY, Potsdam, 1973. Tchr. 1st grade Ogdensburg (N.Y.) Ctrl. Schs., 1964-65, Massena (N.Y.) Ctrl Schs., 1965-68, 69—; tchr. 2d grade Ft. Richardson (Alaska) On-Base Sch., 1968-69, Ctrl. Schs., Massena, 1969-98—. Mem. N.Y. State Reading Assn. Avocations: reading, cross-county skiing, walking, travel, crafts.

REYNOLDS, CHARLENE JOZINA, music educator, composer; b. Lawrence, Kans., Mar. 13, 1952; d. Charles William and Jozina Irene (Abel) Roberman; m. Nathaniel Dunton Reynolds, Aug. 10, 1974; children: Sarah Jozina, Angela Marie, Amy Ruth. MusB in Edn. summa cum laude, Wichita State U., 1974, M in Music Edn., 2005. Pvt. instr., piano and clarinet, 1968—; elem. music, secondary vocal and instrumental dir. Warner Christian Acad., South Daytona, Fla., 1976—80; elem. music educator Union Hill Sch., Somerville, Ala., 1988—96; pre-K tchr.'s aide Bullfrogs and Butterflies Presch., Andover, 1998—2003; band libr. Wichita State U., 2003—05. Interim min. music First Ch. of God, Huntsville, Ala., 1986—87, 1996; arranger, accompanist Testimony gospel quartet, Huntsville, Ala., 1990—96; composer, arranger Hope Cmty. Ch., Andover, 1997—. Composer: (instrumental music) Prelude and Scherizo: A Duet for English and French Horns with Strings Attached, (pep band composition) Shocker Shout, (praise and worship compositions) To Glorify Your Name, Quiet My Heart, (wedding vow renewal solo) To Have, To Hold. Mem. leadership team Hope Cmty. Ch., Andover, 2001—04. Mem.: Music Educators Nat. Conf., Aux. of Gideons Internat. (chaplain 2002—05), Phi Kappa Phi, Pi Kappa Lambda, Tau Beta Sigma. Home: 912 Maplewood Ct Andover KS 67002 Personal E-mail: cjrjcmusic@yahoo.com.

REYNOLDS, CHARLOTTE N., science educator; d. Nelson R. and Charlotte M. Murray; m. John L. Reynolds, July 14, 1992. BS, U. Wis., Platteville, 1969, MEd, 1984. Phys. edn./sci. tchr. Hazel Green HS, Wis., 1969—76; recreation instr. Chippewa Falls Recreation, 1977—80; sci. tchr. Fennimore HS, 1981—2006. Avocations: horseback riding, camping, needlecrafts, gardening, reading.

REYNOLDS, DEBBIE (MARY FRANCES REYNOLDS), actress; b. El Paso, Tex., Apr. 1, 1932; m. Eddie Fisher, Sept. 26, 1955 (div. 1959); children— Carrie, Todd; m. Harry Karl, Nov., 1960 (div. 1973); m. Richard Hamlett (div. May 1996). Active high sch. plays; screen debut Daughter of Rosie O'Grady; motion pictures include: June Bride, 1948, The Daughter of Rosie O'Grady, 1950, Three Little Words, 1950, Two Weeks With Love, 1950, Mr. Imperium, 1951, Singin' in the Rain, 1952, Skirts Ahoy!, 1952, I Love Melvin, 1953, The Affairs of Dobie Gillis, 1953, Give a Girl a Break, 1953, Susan Slept Here, 1954, Athena, 1954, Hit the Deck, 1955, The Tender Trap, 1955, The Catered Affair, 1956, Bundle of Joy, 1956, Tammy and the Bachelor, 1957, This Happy Feeling, 1958, The Mating Game, 1959, Say One for Me, 1959, It Started With a Kiss, 1959, The Gazebo, 1959, The Rat Race, 1960, Pepe, 1960, The Pleasure of His Company, 1961, The Second Time Around, 1961, How the West Was Won, 1962, My Six Loves, 1963, Mary, Mary, 1963, The Unsinkable Molly Brown, 1964, Goodbye Charlie, 1964, The Singing Nun, 1966, Divorce American Style, 1967, How Sweet It Is!, 1968, What's the Matter with Helen?, 1971, Charlotte's Web, (voice only) 1973, That's Entertainment!, 1974, The Bodyguard, 1992, Heaven and Earth, 1993, (with Albert Brooks) Mother, 1996, That's Entertainment III, 1994, In & Out, 1996, Zack and Reba, 1998; star TV program The Debbie Reynolds Show, 1969; star Broadway show Irene, 1973-74, Annie Get Your Gun, Los Angeles, San Francisco, 1977, Woman of the Year, 1984, The Unsinkable Molly Brown, 1989-90 (nat. tour); author: If I Knew Then, 1963, Debbie-My Life, 1988; creator exercise video Do It Debbie's Way, 1984; recurring role (TV series) Will and Grace; actress (TV movies) Perry Mason, 1989, Battling for Babies, 1991, Halloweentown, 1998, The Christmas Wish, 1998, A Gift of Love, 1999 (Emmy nominee), Virtual Mom, 1999, These Old Broads, 2001, Return to Halloweentown, 2001, Connie and Carla, 2003, Halloweentown High, 2004. Named Miss Burbank, 1948 Office: Debbie Reynolds Studios care Margie Duncan 6514 Lankershim Blvd North Hollywood CA 91606-2409 Office Phone: 818-985-3193.

REYNOLDS, DORIS ELIZABETH, management consultant, poet; b. Nashville, Apr. 16, 1944; children: James Jr., Tony Antonio. BA, Coby Coll., 1990; cert., U. Tenn., Nashville, 2000. Cert. med. terminologist St. Thomas Hosp. Edn. Mgmt. supr. St. Thomas Hosp., Nashville, 1979—90, patient transfer liaison, 1985—90, supr., 1972, 1976. Spkr. in field of people mgmt. Author (under the pseudonym Dynasty): (poetry) Internat. Soc. Poets, 2003 (Cup, 2003). Recipient Cert. of Achievement, Tenn. Hosp. Assn., 1978, George W. Gore honor for outstanding scholarship and acad. excellence, Tenn. State U., 2002. Mem.: Internat. Soc. Poets. Home: 2006 15th Ave N Nashville TN 37208

REYNOLDS, ELIZABETH BURSON, social worker; b. Bronx, N.Y., Mar. 23, 1953; d. John and Rose Marie (Russo) Burson; m. Michael P. Reynolds, May 1, 1983; children: Michael, Christopher. AA, Suffolk C.C., 1973; BSW, Adelphi U., 1975, MSW, 1979. Cert. social worker, sch. social worker. Social worker Indsl. Home for the Blind, Bay Shore, N.Y., 1975-80, S. Oaks Psychiat. Hosp., Amityville, NY, 1980-85, Am. Counseling Found., Smithtown, N.Y., 1985-90, Good Samaritan Long Term Home Health Care Program, Bay Shore, 1988-94, Hope Counseling Ctr., Sayville, N.Y., 1989-94, Just Kids Presch. Learning Ctr., Middle Island, N.Y., 1994—. Part time social worker South Oaks Psychiat. Hosp., 1992, Skills Unlimited Success Day Program, Bohemia, NY, 1993—94. Mem. NASW (diplomate). Roman Catholic.

REYNOLDS, HELEN ELIZABETH, management consultant; b. Minerva, N.Y., Aug. 30, 1925; d. Henry James and Margurite Catherine (Gallagher) McNally; m. Theodore Laurence Reynolds, Feb. 27, 1948; children: Laurence McBride, David Scott, William Herbert. BA, SUNY, Albany, 1967; MA, Union Coll., Schenectady, N.Y., 1971. Cert. realtor Realtors Inst., N.Y. Owner, mgr. Schafer Studio, Schenectady, 1970—73; co-owner, v.p. Reynolds Chalmers Inc., Schenectady, 1971—97; program coord. Schenectady County, 1980—81; adminstr. Wellspring House Albany, NY, 1981—94; pres. HR Mgmt. Cons., Port Charlotte, Fla., 1994—2002; ret. Cons., examiner N.Y. State Civil Svc., Albany, 1971—81; mem. adv. coun. SBA, Washington, 1978—80. Planning bd. Town of Niskayuna, NY, 1977—81, town councilwoman, 1986—94; co-chair Great N.E. Festival Mohawk River, 1989—90; bd. dirs. HAVEN, Schenectady YWCA; mem. N.Y. State Commn. Capital Region, 1994—98, Acad. Women Achievement, Schenectady, 1994; pres. Photo Arts Group Charlotte County, 1998—2003, Buena Vista Property Owners Assn., Port Charlotte, 1998—2003; bd. mem. Charlotte Symphony Orch. Named Woman Vision, 1986—87, Today's Woman, Schenectady YWCA, 1987. Mem.: Assn. Adminstrs. Ind. Housing, Charlotte County Art Guild, Union Coll. Alumni Assn., Charlotte Symphony League (pres.), Antique and Classic Boat Soc. (bd. dirs. 1974—89, Disting. Svc. award 1979), Charlotte Harbor Yacht Club, Zonta (pres. 1981—82). Avocations: photography, reading, golf, skiing, canoeing. Home and Office: 104 Leland St SW Port Charlotte FL 33952-9131

REYNOLDS, JEAN EDWARDS, publishing executive; b. Saginaw, Mich., Dec. 11, 1941; d. F. Perry and Kathrine (Edwards) R.; m. Cary Wellington, Sept. 10, 1975 (div. 1982); children, Bradley, Abigail, Benjamin; m. Jon Haddon, Nov. 8, 1997. BA, Wells Coll., 1963; postgrad., CCNY, 1965-67. Asst. editor, sr. editor trade book div. Prentice-Hall, Englewood Cliffs, NJ, 1963—66, dir. children's books, 1966—69, McCall Pub. Co., N.Y.C., 1969—71; sr. v.p., editorial dir. Franklin Watts Inc., N.Y.C., 1971—75; pres. Pet Projects Inc., Ridgefield, Conn., 1975—81; editor in chief young people's publs. Grolier Inc., Danbury, Conn., 1981—89; founder, pub., exec. v.p. The Millbrook Press, Brookfield, Conn., 1989—2004; assoc. pub. Lerner Publs., Mpls., 2004—06, exec. editor, 2006—. Bd. dirs. Jewish Fedn. Greater Danbury; chair Conn. Ctr. for the Book, 1991-94. Mem. Bd. of Govs. for Higher Edn., State of Conn., 2004—; pres. Jewish Fedn. Greater Danbury, 1991—93, 2003—; bd. dirs. Jewish Home for the Elderly, Fairfield, Conn., 1989—90, 1999, Book Industry Study Group, 1991—98, The Wooster Sch., Danbury, Conn., 1992—, chair headmaster search, 2002—; bd. dirs. Temple Shearith Israel, Ridgefield, Conn., 1994—97, chair Kehila campaign, 2002; bd. dirs. The Children's Book Coun., 1996—2000, vice chair, 1997—98, chair, 1998—99; bd. dirs. Ridgefield Symphony, 2006—. Mem. ALA, Children's Book Coun., Mensa. Jewish. Avocations: skiing, sailing, needlecrafts. Home and Office: 33 Corntassle Rd Danbury CT 06811-3208

REYNOLDS, JUDITH AMY, nutritionist, consultant, animal scientist, educator; d. Jacob Alen and Mary Emeline Lundgren; m. Rodney Roger Reynolds, Aug. 28, 1971; children: Andrea Mary Rickards, James Christopher. AA summa cum laude, Anoka Ramsey CC, 1988; BS summa cum laude, St. Cloud State U., 1990; MS, Tex. A&M U., 1993, PhD, 1997. Cert. Profl. Animal Scientist Am. Registry Profl. Animal Scientists, 1995. Co-owner, mgr. Reynolds Quarter Horses, Palmyra, Mo., 1978—; grad. asst. rschr. Tex. A&M U., College Station, 1990—91, grad. asst. tchr., 1991—95; long term substitute tchr. biology, anatomy physiology, chemistry Princeton and Elk River Pub. Sch. Sys., Minn., 1997—98; divisional equine tech. specialist Archer Daniels Midland Animal Health Nutrition and MoorMan's Inc., Quincy, Ill., 1998—2001; equine nutritionist Archer Daniels Midland Alliance Nutrition Inc., Quincy, 2001—. Asst. prof. William Woods U., Fulton, Mo., 1995—97; assoc. faculty John Woods CC, Quincy, Ill., 2004—; spkr. in field; ofcl. reviewer Nat. Rsch. Coun., Nutrient Requirements of Horses, 2006; mem. Equine Sci. Soc. Nutrition Com., 2006—. Author: (online source) Equine Nutrition in the 21st Century (1st Pl. Online Svc. To Reader, 2003); contbr. articles in to profl. jours. Vol. Princeton Pub. Schools, Princeton, Minn., 1983—90; vol. leader; horse sci., horse bowl, horse advancement, vet. sci. Isanti County 4-H, Minn., 1983—90; vol. leader horse judging, market steers, poultry Bryan HS Future Farmers of Am., Tex., 1992—94; vol. horse judge Brazos County, College Station, Tex., 1991—94, Tex. A&M U., College Station, 1991—95; vol. horse bowl team coach Mo. State 4-H, 1996—97; vol. 4-H horse judge Audrain and Calloway Counties, Fulton, Mo., 1996—97. Recipient High Point All Around Horse, Minn. Quarter Horse Assn., 1980, Two Register of Merit Horses, Am. Quarter Horse Assn., 1980, 1982, Four High-Point and Res. Performance Gelding awards, Five State Champions, Five Res. State Champions, Minn. Quarter Horse Assn., 1980-1983, One Performance Horse Qualified, Outstanding Horses of World, World Equine Rsch. Inst., 1983; Mensa scholarship, Am. Mensa, 1987, Alliss scholarships, Alliss, 1987-1990, Academic scholarships, Anoka Ramsey CC, 1987-1988, St. Cloud State U., 1988-1990. Mem.: Am. Registry Profl. Animal Scientists, Equine Sci. Soc. (nutrition com. 2006—), Am. Quarter Horse Assn., Nat. Reining Horse Assn., Phi Kappa Phi, Psi Chi, Kappa Delta Pi, Phi Theta Kappa, Gamma Sigma Delta. Achievements include development of equine feeds and supplements, SENIORGLO, MOORGLO, PRO-VITA-MIN 20 supplement tubs, FORAGE FIRST horse rewards, MOORGLO Canadian formula, GROSTRONG QuadBLOCK Canadian formula; StaySTRONG metabolic mineral pellets. Avocations: horses, reading, writing, cooking. Office: ADM Alliance Nutrition 1000 N 30th St Quincy IL 62305 Office Fax: 217-222-9060. Business E-Mail: judy_reynolds@admworld.com.

REYNOLDS, JUDITH M., secondary school educator; b. Washington, June 24, 1946; d. Hubert Alberta and Dorothy Jean (Cromer) Massengale; m. Ernest Darden Reynolds Jr., Aug. 21, 1966; children: Judd, Enley. BA, U. Miss., 1968; MEd, Miss. Coll., 1970. Cert. tchr. Miss. Coun. Tchrs. Tchr. Hinds Community Coll., Raymond, Miss., Woodland Hills Bapt. Acad., Jackson, Miss., Jackson Pub. Schs., Clinton (Miss.) Pub. Schs. Mem. Nat. Coun. Tchrs. English, Miss. Coun. Tchrs. English. Home: 1701 Midway Rd Clinton MS 39056

REYNOLDS, KARA STUTSMAN, elementary school educator; b. Detroit, Oct. 30, 1977; d. Albert Chesterfield Stutsman and Cindy Kay Barbieri; m. Ryan Tipton Reynolds, May 18, 2002. B in Comm., U. Mo., Columbia, 2000. Tchr. mid. sch. speech, drama tchr. Berkeley Mid. Sch., Mo., 2003—. Dir. Brentwood Mid. Sch., Mo., 2004. Mem. Speech and Theater Assn. Mo., St. Louis, 2002—06. Mem.: Renissance Com. Home: 835 Albert Ave Glendale MO 63122 Office: Berkeley Middle School 8300 Frost Ave Berkeley MO 63134 Office Phone: 314-524-3883. Personal E-mail: reynoldskara@hotmail.com.

REYNOLDS, KAREN ANN, secondary school educator; b. Poteau, Okla., July 12, 1949; d. Paul Leroy and Ruby Nell (Nummy) Coggins; m. W.D. Reynolds; children: John, Jeffrey. BS, U. Okla., 1975, postgrad., 1987-88; MEd, East Cen. U., 1978. Cert. secondary tchr., Okla. Instr. sci. Ada (Okla.) Sr. High Sch., 1977-81, instr. sci., chmn. sci. dept., 1981—. Spl. cons., ind. study cons. U. Okla., Norman, 1983—; adj. instr. Oklahoma City, Okla. C.C., 1994—. Mem. NEA, Nat. Sci. Tchrs. Assn., Okla. Edn. Assn., Okla. Sci. Tchrs. Assn., Noble Assn. Classroom Tchrs. (v.p. 1982-83), Beta Sigma Phi. Avocations: travel, gardening. Office: Noble Sr High Sch 4601 E Etowah Rd Noble OK 73068

REYNOLDS, KATHLEEN DIANE FOY (KDF REYNOLDS), transportation executive; b. Chgo., Dec. 9, 1946; d. David Chancy Foy and Vivian Anne (Schwartz) R. Student, San Francisco State U., 1964-68. Taxicab medallion permit holder, City and County of San Francisco, 1995—. Studio coord. KTVU-TV, Oakland, Calif., 1968-70; assoc. prodr. KPIX-TV, San Francisco, 1970-72; music publicist Oakland, 1966-78; writer PLEXUS, West Coast Women's Press, Oakland, 1974-82, gen. mgr., 1984-86; screen writer Oakland, 1970—; gen. ptnr. Designated Driver Group, Oakland, 1990-97; assoc. owner DeSoto Cab, San Francisco, 1995-98, ptnr., 1998—; mng. ptnr. Foy Scribes, divsn. The Tallahassee Group, Oakland, Calif., 1997—. Coun. mem. West Coast Women's Press, Oakland, 1975-86; founding assoc. Women's Inst. for Freedom of the Press, Washington, 1977—. Author of periodical news, reviews, features, 1974-82; author of six documentaries for comml. and PBS-TV, 1968-73. Mem. Soc. Mayflower Descendants, Casper, Wyo., 1967—, Chabot Space and Sci. Ctr., Oakland, Calif., Fine Arts Museums San Francisco. Mem. LWV, San Francisco Film Soc. Avocations: archery, reading, film festival attendance. Home: PO Box 2742 Oakland CA 94602-0042 Office Phone: 415-970-1405.

REYNOLDS, LOUISE MAXINE KRUSE, retired school nurse; b. Waynesboro, Va., May 28, 1935; d. Emil Herman and Cora Lee (Hammer) Kruse; m. Elbert B. Reynolds Jr., June 13, 1964; children: David Emil, Jane Marie. Diploma, Rockingham Meml. Hosp., 1956; student, Madison Coll., Tex. Tech U. RN, Tex., Va, cert. sch. nurse. Head nurse orthopedic, opthalmology dept. surgery Duke U., Durham, N.C., 1961-62; head nurse surg. fl. Waynesboro (Va.) Hosp., 1962-64; sch. nurse Lubbock (Tex.) Ind. Sch. Dist., 1974-94, ret., 1994. Pres. Vol. Network Luth. Home, Lubbock, Tex., 1996-2000; sec. Luth. Student Coun., Tex. Tech., Lubbock, 1999-2000. Recipient recognition for contbn. to ch. and cmty., Aid Assn. for Luths. Mem. DAR (sec. Nancy Anderson chpt. 2000-02, chpt. chaplain 2002-04, chpt. treas. 2006—), Va. Nurses Assn. (dist. sec., chair), Tex. Assn. Sch. Nurses (sec., treas. dist. 17, program chair 1989 state conv.). Personal E-mail: lmkreynolds@yahoo.com.

REYNOLDS, LOUISE WEBB, retired volunteer, director; b. Demopolis, Ala., Feb. 22, 1946; d. John Cox Webb, III and Marie Suttle Webb; m. Peter Michael Reynolds; children: Peter Michael Jr., Angie Marie, John Webb. BS, U Ala., 1968. Exec. dir. The Demopolis City Schos. Found., Inc., Demopolis, Ala., 1994—99; tchr. English Demopolis City Schs., Demopolis, Ala., 1968—69; clerk Demopolis Stock Yards, Demopolis, Ala., 1969—72; coord. media West Ala. Mental Health Ctr., Demopolis, Ala., 1974—78; clerk Reynolds Cattle Co., Forkland, Ala., 1986—90. First female chmn. Bd. Edn., Demopolis, 1988—90, Demopolis City Schs. Bd. Edn., 1992—93; active City of Demopolis Cemetery Bd., 2004—06; mem. bd. dirs. Bd. Edn., Demopolis City Schs., Demopolis, 1985—95; vol. counselor "Save-a Life" Crisis Pregnancy Ctr., Demopolis, 1990—94; pres. Demopolis Kappa Delta Alumnae, Demopolis, 1990—93; orgnl. pres., first integrated PTA Demopolis Elem. PTA, Demopolis, 1980—81; reorganizational pres. Marengo County chpt. U. Ala. Alumni Assn., Demopolis, 1977—78; orgnl. pres. Marengo County Assn. Brain Damaged Children, Demopolis, 1971—74; vol. coord. The Achievement Ctr. Spl. Children, Demopolis, 1972—74; orgnl. pres. Marengo County chpt. Nat. Assn. Retarded Children, Demopolis, 1972—74; pres. Demopolis Kappa Delta Alumnae, Demopolis, 1976—77; leader Brownie Scout Tombigee Girl Scout Coun., Demopolis, 1979—83; Cub Scout Den Mother Boy Scouts of Am., Prairie Dist., Black Warrior Coun., Demopolis, 1976—79; orgnl. pres. Pastoral Coun., St. Leo's Cath. Ch., Demopolis, 1993—97; orgnl. coord. "RENEW" St. Leo's Cath. Ch., Demopolis, 1983—88; tchr. Confraternity Christian Doctrine, St. Leo's Cath. Ch., Demopolis, 1973—93; Eucharistic min., lector St. Leo's Cath. Ch., Demopolis. Recipient Disting. Svc. award, Demopolis Jaycees, 1972, Outstanding Chpt. Devel. award, U. Ala., Nat. Alumni Assn., 1979, Paul Harris Fellow, Rotary, 2003. Mem.: The Reading Club (pres. Demopolis chpt. 1982—83, 2003—04). Roman Catholic. Avocations: painting, travel. Home: 303 West Lyon Demopolis AL 36732

REYNOLDS, MARILYN ANN, writer; b. Alhambra, Calif., Sept. 13, 1935; d. Lester Fay Dodson and Esther May Sears; m. Michael Vance Reynolds, Aug. 5, 1967; children: Sharon Lee Reynolds Kyle, Cynthia Lynn Foncannon, Matthew Michael. BA, Calif. State U., L.A., 1967; MS, Pepperdine U., L.A., 1981. Tchr. Alhambra Sch. Dist., Calif., 1972—98; tchr.-in-chg. Elk Grove (Calif.) Unified Sch. Dist., 2000—01. Adj. prof. Am. River Coll., Sacramento, 2001—03. Author: (novel) Telling (Quick Picks for Reluctant Readers, 1996), (non fiction - education) I Won't Read And You Can't Make Me: Reaching Reluctant Teen Readers, (novel) Detour For Emmy (SC. Young Adult Book Award, 1996), Too Soon For Jeff (ALA, Best Books for Young Adults, 1995), (short story collection) Beyond Dreams (ALA, Short Takes, 1996), (novel) But What About Me (NY Pub. Libr., Best Books for the Teen Age, 1997); author: (co-writer) (teleplay) Too Soon for Jeff (Nancy Susan Reynolds Award, 1997); author: (novel) Baby Help (Franklin Award, 1999), If You Loved Me (NY Pub. Libr. Best Books for the Teen Age, 2000), Love Rules (NY Pub. Libr. Best Books for the Teen Age, 2002). Cmty. contbns. com. Unitarian Universalist Soc. of Sacramento, 2000—06. Mem.: Calif. Sch. Libr. Assn., Nat. Coun. of Tchrs. of English. Democrat-Npl. Unitarian Universalist. Home: 2125 Promontory Point Gold River CA 95670 Personal E-mail: mmreynolds@earthlink.net.

REYNOLDS, MARJORIE LAVERS, nutritionist, educator; b. Collingwood, Ont., Can., Jan. 10, 1931; d. Henry James and Laura (Wilson) Lavers; m. John Horace Reynolds, Aug. 17, 1963; children: Steven, Mark. BA, U. Toronto, 1953; MS, U. Minn., 1957; PhD, U. Wis., 1964; AS, State Tech. Inst. Knoxville, 1982. Registered dietitian. Rsch. dietitian Mayo Clinic, Rochester, Minn., 1957-59; rsch. dietitian Cleve. Met. Gen. Hosp., 1959-60; rsch. assoc. U. Tenn., Knoxville, 1963-66; instr. Ft. Sanders Sch. Nursing, Knoxville, 1967-76, State Tech. Inst., Knoxville, 1982-88; substitute secondary sch. tchr. Knox County Schs., Knoxville, 1989-93. Contbr. articles to biochem. and nutrition jours.; newsletter editor Juvenile Diabetes Found., Knoxville, 1985-93. Sec. Midway Rehab. Ctr., Knoxville, 1987—2001. Mem.: LWV, Knoxville Dist. Dietetic Assn. (pres. 1971—72, Outstanding Dietitian 1973—74), Tenn. Dietetic Assn. (pres. 1973—74, Outstanding Dietitian 1973—74), Omicron Nu. Democrat. Presbyterian. Avocations: reading, sports. Home: 7112 Stockton Dr Knoxville TN 37909-2534

REYNOLDS, NANCY REMICK, writer, researcher, editor; b. San Antonio, July 15, 1938; d. Donald Worthington and Edith (Remick) R.; m. Brian Rushton, June 25, 1983; 1 child: Ehren P. Student, Sch. Am. Ballet, N.Y.C., 1951, student, 1953—61, Juilliard Sch. Music, 1957, Martha Graham Sch. Contemporary Dance, 1959, U. Sorbonne, Paris, 1962; BA in Art History, Columbia U., N.Y.C., 1965; postgrad., Goethe Inst., Prien, 1972, U. Chgo., 1974—77, Sarah Lawrence Coll., Bronxville, N.Y., 1974—77. Dancer NYC Ballet, 1956—61; editor Praeger Pubs., NYC, 1965—71; dir. rsch. book Choreography by George Balanchine: A Catalogue of Works, 1979—82; dir. rsch. pub. TV spl. Balanchine, NY, 1983—84; assoc. editor Internat. Ency. of Dance, 1998; dir. rsch. The George Balanchine Found., NYC, 1994—. Co-pub. Twentieth-Century Dance in Slides, 1978-93. Author: Repertory in Review: Forty Years of the New York City Ballet, 1977 (De la Torre Bueno prize 1977), The Dance Catalog: A Complete Guide to Today's World of Dance, 1979, co-author: In Performance, 1980, Dance Classics, 1991 (rec. for teen age NY Pub. Libr.), No Fixed Points: Dance in the Twentieth Century, 2003; editor: Movement and Metaphor: Four Centuries of Ballet (Lincoln Kirstein), 1970, Dance as a Theatre Art: Source Readings in Dance History from 1581 to the Present (Selma Jeanne Cohen), 1974, School of Classical Dance (V. Kostrovitskaya and A. Pisarev), 1978; contbr. (book) Ballet: Bias and Belief, "Three Pamphlets Collected" and Other Dance Writings of Lincoln Kirstein, 1983; contbr. articles to profl. jours Ford Found. Travel and Study grantee, 1974; Mary Duke Biddle Found. grantee, 1990. Mem. Dance Critics Assn. (pres. 1986-87), Soc. Dance History Scholars, Soc. for Dance Rsch., Am. Soc. for Theatre Rsch., European Assn. Dance Historians, Internat. Fedn. for Theatre Rsch. in affiliation with Societe Internat. des Bibliotheques et Musees des Arts du Spectacle, Phi Beta Kappa. Home: 9 Prospect Park W Brooklyn NY 11215-1758 Office Phone: 718-783-4265.

REYNOLDS, PATRICIA JEAN, psychiatric social worker, songwriter; d. Joseph Eustacio D'Angelo and Elizabeth Sophie Jakubczyk; 1 child, Aaron D'Angelo. BA in English, U. Hartford; AS in Mktg., Middlesex Coll., Conn.; MA in Social Work, U. Conn., 1992. Abstract writer Inst. of Living, Hartford; treatment mgr. geriatric and adult units and day program Inst. of Living, Hartford Hosp. Songwriter (CD) New State, New Start, New Man, 2000 (CD of Yr. Conn. Country Music Assn., 2000), Another Country Night, 2005; author: Paradise Park, 2003, various books of poetry. Named Songwriter of Yr., N.Am. Country Music Assn. Internat., 2004. Mem.: Conn. Songwriters Assn. (sec. 2000—, Career Accomplishment award), Nashville Songwriters Assn. Internat., Country Music Assn. Avocations: woodcarving, poetry, novels, sports. Home: PO Box 310762 Newington CT 06131 Office Phone: 860-545-7219. Personal E-mail: patsongs@snet.net.

REYNOLDS, PAULA ROSPUT, energy executive; b. Newport, RI; m. Stephen P. Reynolds, Oct. 2004. BA with highest honors, Wellesley Coll., 1978. Economist consulting firm, Boston; sr. v.p. Pacific Gas Transmission Co.; pres. CEO Duke Energy No. Am., Houston; pres., COO AGL Resources, Atlanta, pres., CEO, 2000—05, chmn., 2002—05; pres., CEO Safeco Corp., Seattle, 2006—. Bd. dir. AGL Resources, Coca Cola Enterprises, Delta Air Lines. Bd. dir. United Way Met. Atlanta, Ga. Rsch. Alliance, Ga. C. of C., Commerce Club, Atlanta. Named one of 100 Most Powerful Women, Forbes Mag., 2006, 50 Most Powerful Women in Business, Fortune mag., 2006; named to Ga. State Univ. Bus. Hall Fame, 2004. Mem.: Am. Gas Assn. (bd. dir.). Office: AGL Resources PO Box 4569 Atlanta GA 30302-4569 Office Phone: 404-584-4000.*

REYNOLDS, PAULINE PHYLLIS, retired primary school educator; b. Detroit, Aug. 21, 1924; d. Paul Wesley and Hazel B. (Rolixman) Baughan; m. Douglas Wilcox Reynolds, June 25, 1950; 1 child: Rene Baughan Reynolds. BS, Ea. Mich. U., 1948; MA, Mich. State U., 1950. 2d grade tchr., Perry, Mich., 1944-46; 1st grade tchr. Ovid, Mich., 1946-47; 2d grade tchr. Owosso, Mich., 1948-93; ret., 1993. Sec. Cemetery Assn., 1952—. Mem. AAUW (hon., life), Delta Kappa Gamma (charter). Home: 600 E Bennington Rd Owosso MI 48867-9794

REYNOLDS, RACHELLE LYNN, elementary school educator; b. Wichita, Nov. 17, 1955; d. Gerald Joe and Karen Yvonne Roberts; m. Myron Leigh Reynolds, Dec. 22, 1992; children: Taylor, Chase, Chance. BS in Edn., Ctr. Mo. State U., Warrensburg. 5th grade tchr. Archie RV, Mo., 3rd grade tchr., title I reading tchr. Sunday sch. tchr. Calvary Bapt. Ch., mem. missionary com. Avocations: flower gardening, reading, bicycling, scrapbooks.

REYNOLDS, REGINA ROMANO, librarian; b. Norristown, Pa., Jan. 31, 1948; d. Michael Anthony and Rose Jeannette (Romano) Romano; m. Gary Kemp Reynolds, May 16, 1970 (div. 1997); 1 child, Elizabeth Alexandra Marie. BA magna cum laude, U. Dayton, 1969; MLS, U. Mich., 1976. Tech. librarian Gen. Atronics Corp., Phila., 1969-70; lib. asst. serials Pa. State U., State Coll., 1970-73; asst. archivist Ins. Co. North Am., Phila., 1973-74; ISDS cataloger Lib. of Congress, Washington, 1976-82, asst. head nat. serials data program U.S. ISSN Ctr., 1982-91, head nat. serials data program, 1992—. Presenter in field. Mem. editl. bd. Serials Review, Greenwich, Conn., 1995—, Jour. of Irreproducible Results, Annals of Improbable Research, 1994—; contbr. articles to profl. jours. Chair CONSER Electronic Resources Task Force, Washington, 1995-96. Mem. ALA (liaison Lib. of Congress com. to study serials cataloging 1992—, digital resources com. 1996—, cons. to com. to study serials stds. 1996—), N. Am. Serials Interest Group, Beta Phi Mu. Avocations: internet communications, watercolor painting, breadmaking, greeting card design. Home: 7603 Marian Ct Falls Church VA 22042-3515 Office: Lib of Congress Nat Serials Data Program Washington DC 20540-0001

REYNOLDS, SALLIE BLACKBURN, artist, volunteer; b. Kansas City, Mo., Feb. 9, 1940; d. Anton and Sallie Churchill (Blackburn) Zajic; m. Jeffrey Calhoun Loker, Mar. 25, 1959 (div. May 1965); children: Toni Lynne Loker, Michael David Loker, Kathryn Lee Loker Simpson; m. Everett Lee Reynolds, Mar. 29, 1969 (dec. Sept. 1992). Student, William Jewell Coll., 1959, BA magna cum laude, 1977; student, U. Mo., Kansas City, 1966-67, Kansas City Art Inst., 1966-70; Cert., Famous Artists Sch., 1965. Cert. tchr., Mo. From clk. to sec. Hdqrs. Strategic Air Command, Offutt AFB, Omaha, 1960-62; sec., wage and hr. law enforcement asst., wage-hr. divsn. U.S. Dept. of Labor, Kansas City, 1963-68, exec. sec. to regional manpower adminstr., 1968-71, spl. asst. to regional exec. com., 1971-72, mgmt. asst. Office of Regional Dir., 1972-73; co-owner Claycomo Skelly Svc. Sta. & Garage, 1970—78; from. clk. to sec. air carrier dist. office FAA, Kansas City, 1978-81; from clk. typist procurement and contracts divsn. to sec. regional pers. officer Bur. of Reclamation, U.S. Dept. of Interior, Boulder City, Nev., 1982—84; editl. asst. divsn. of planning Bur. of Reclamation, Boulder City, 1984-86; substitute tchr.; owner, operator B-Bar-L Wandering Star Ranch (registered angus, polled Herfords and horses, beefalo), Stover, Mo., 1989—; med. support asst. 509 Med. Group, Knob Noster, 2005—06. Editor newsletter Laurie Fine Art, 1989-90; designer historic landmark plaque Clay County, Mo.; designer hist. painting for annual Dogwood Festival pageants Camden County, Mo., 1994. Ofcl. commr., sec., corr. Clay County (Mo.) Bicentennial Commn., 1974-76; mem. Ozark Brush and Palette, Inc., Camdenton, Mo., 1987—, editor newsletter, 1988-89; v.p., sec., life mem. Clay County Hist. Soc., 1972—, active Nat. Wildlife Fedn. (guardian of the wild 2004). Recipient 1st pl. in oil/acrylic painting Nat. Soc. DAR Am. Heritage Contest, 1990, 3d pl., 1991, 1st pl. Gold award, 1992, 1st pl. profl. photography Laurie Fine Art Show, 1991; named one of Top 50 Profl. Artists, Mo. State Fair, 1992. Mem. Nat. Soc. DAR (pub. rels. chmn., rec. sec., archives chmn., corr. sec. Niangua chpt. Camdenton 1987—, Eldon Mo. chpt. 1999—), Nat. Oil and Acrylic Painters Soc., Phi Epsilon of Phi Beta Kappa, Versailles Saddle Club, Mo. Paint Horse Club (sec. 1998). Presbyterian. Avocations: art, history, needlecrafts, music, photography. Home and Office: B-Bar-L Wandering Star Ranch 23688 S 135 Hwy Stover MO 65078

REYNOLDS, SHERI, writer; b. Conway, SC, 1967; BA in English, Davidson Coll., 1989; MFA in creative writing, Va. Commonwealth U., 1992. Assoc. prof., Ruth and Perry Morgan Chair So. Lit. Old Dominion U., Norfolk, Va. Adj. instr. English Va. Commonwealth U., Richmond, 1992. Author: Bitterroot Landing, 1994, The Rapture of Canaan, 1996, A Gracious Plenty, 1997, The Firefly Cloak, 2006, (plays) Orabelle's Wheelbarrow, 2005 (Women Playwrights' Initiative playwriting competition, 2005). Recipient Outstanding Faculty award, State Coun. Higher Education Va., 2003; grantee, Va. Commn. for the Arts in playwriting, 2005. Mailing: Old Dominion U University Village 02 Norfolk VA 23529*

REYNOLDS, VALRAE, museum curator; b. San Francisco, Dec. 18, 1944; d. Ralph Stanley and Valberta May (Eversole) R.; m. Richard Lee Huffman, Sept. 14, 1974; children: Elizabeth Anne, Margaret Lee. BA in Fine Arts with honors, U. Calif., Davis, 1966; MA, NYU, 1969. Asst. curator Asian collections Newark Mus., 1969-70, curator Asian collections, 1970—2002, sr. curator Asian collections, 2003—. Cons. SITES Exhbn., 1988; adj. prof. art history Columbia U., 1996; lectr., presenter in field. Author: From the Sacred Realm, Treasures of Tibetan Art from the Newark Museum, 1999; editor: Newark Mus. Quar., 1976, Tibetan Jour., 1976, Asia Soc., 1977, Arts of Asia, 1989, Explore Tibet, 1992; contbr. over 36 articles and revs. to profl. jours.; prodr. multimedia prodns. in field. Grantee NEA, NEH, 1972-74, 82-83, 85-86, 88-91, 89-92, 99, 2003, J. Paul Getty grantee, 1986, 89-91, Travel grantee Asian Cultural Coun., 1989, NEA grantee, 2003-05, Wallace Found. grantee, 2003-05, Freeman Found. grantee, 2003-05. Office: Newark Mus 49 Washington St Newark NJ 07102

REYNOLDS, VIRGINIA EDITH, sociologist, anthropologist, educator, artist; b. Lafayette, Ind., July 3, 1941; d. Ira Hubert and Harriet G. (Robertson) Reynolds; m. Antonio G. Arroyo, 1961 (div. 1974); children: Mary-Jane R. Arroyo Young, Joanne R. Arroyo Shirley. BS with hons. in Sociology, Columbia U., 1965, MA in Sociology, 1967; postgrad., Pa. State U., 1974—84. Rsch. asst. demographic divsn. Population Coun., N.Y.C., 1968; tchr. CUNY Borough Manhattan C.C., N.Y.C., 1969; asst. prof. sociology and anthropology Lycoming Coll., Williamsport, Pa., 1970—75, Indiana U. Pa., 1975—2001; ret., 2001. Mem. exec. com. Assn. for Asian Studies Mid-Atlantic Region, 1997—99; Tai Chi tchr. Exhibited in group shows at Old Courthouse Office Gallery, 2002 (Hon. Mention award, 2002), 2003 (2d Pl. award, 2003), Centennial of the Union Street Sanctuary, 2004, Presbyn. Ch. of Punxsutawney, 2004. Singer Indiana County Singers and Ch. Choir; mem. Indiana County Dem. Com., Pa., 2001—05. Mem.: AAUW (chair nat. conv. 2005), Touchstone Ctr. for Crafts, Indiana (Pa.) Art Assn., Pitts. Ctr. for the Arts. Episcopalian. Avocations: tai chi, community theatre musicals, international folk dancing, chinese painting. Home and Studio: 1699 Church St Indiana PA 15701 Office Phone: 724-349-4952. E-mail: veren77@hotmail.com.

REYNOLDS, WYNETKA ANN, academic administrator, educator; b. Coffeyville, Kans., Nov. 3, 1937; d. John Ethelbert and Glennie (Beanland) King; m. Thomas H. Kirschbaum; children: Rachel Rebecca, Rex King. BS in Biology-Chemistry, Kans. State Tchrs. Coll., Emporia, 1958; MS in Zoology, U. Iowa, Iowa City, 1960, PhD, 1962; DSc (hon.), Ind. State U., Evansville, 1980; LHD (hon.), McKendree Coll., 1984, U. N.C., Charlotte, 1988, U. Judaism, LA, 1989, U. Nebr., Kearney, 1992; DSc (hon.), Ball State U., 1985, Emporia State U., 1987; PhD (hon.), Fu Jen Cath. U., China, 1987; LHD (hon.), Colgate U., 1993, No. Mich. U., 1995. Asst. prof. biology Ball State U., Muncie, Ind., 1962-65; asst. prof. anatomy U. Ill. Coll. Medicine, Chgo., 1965-68, assoc. prof. anatomy, 1968-73, rsch. prof. ob-gyn, 1973—, prof. anatomy, 1973—, acting assoc. dean acad. affairs Coll. Medicine, 1977, assoc. vice chancellor, dean grad. coll., 1977-79; provost, v.p. for acad. affairs, prof. ob-gyn. and anatomy Ohio State U., Columbus, 1979-82; chancellor Calif. State Univ. system, Long Beach, 1982-90, prof. biology, 1982-90; chancellor CUNY, 1990-97; pres. U. Ala., Birmingham, 1997—2002. Clin. prof. ob-gyn. UCLA, 1985—90; bd. dirs. Abbott Labs., Maytag, Owens-Corning, Humana, Inc., Invitrogen, News-Gazette, Champaign, Ill. Contbr. chapters to books, articles to profl. jours.; assoc. editor: Am. Biology Tchr., 1964—67. Trustee Internat. Life Scis. Inst.-Nutrition Found., 1987—2001, S.W. Mus.; mem. nat. adv. bd. Am. Indian Arts, 1992—97; bd. dirs. Lincoln Ctr. Inst., 1993—. Recipient Disting. Alumni award, Kans. State Tchrs. Coll., 1972, Prize award, Ctrl. Assn. Obstetricians and Gynecologists, 1988, Calif. Gov.'s award for Arts Outstanding Individual Arts in Edn., 1989; NSF Predoctoral fellow, 1958—62, Woodrow Wilson Hon. fellow, 1958. Fellow: ACOG; mem.: Soc. Gynecol. Investigation (sec./treas. 1980—83, pres. 1992—93), Perinatal Rsch. Soc., Sigma Xi.

REYNOLDS COOCH, NANCY D. (MRS. EDWARD W. COOCH JR.), sculptor; b. Greenville, Del., Dec. 28, 1919; d. Eugene Eleuthere and Catherine Dulcinea (Moxham) duPont; m. William Glasgow Reynolds, May 18, 1940 (dec. Jan. 1987); children: Katherine Glasgow Reynolds, William Bradford Reynolds, Mary Parminter Reynolds Savage, Cynthia duPont Reynolds Farris.; m. Edward W. Cooch, Jr., Sept. 6, 2003. Student, Goldey-Beacom Coll., Wilmington, Del., 1938. One-woman shows include Caldwell Inc., 1975, Nat. Museum of Women in Arts, 1998; exhibited in group shows at Corcoran Gallery, Washington, 1943, Soc. Fine Arts, Wilmington, 1937-38, 40-41, 48, 50, 62, 65, Rehoboth (Del.) Art League, 1963, NAD, N.Y.C., 1964, Pa. Mil. Coll., Chester, 1966, Del. Art Ctr., 1967, Del. Art Mus., Wilmington, Wilmington Art Mus., 1976, Met. Mus. Art, N.Y.C., 1977, Lever House, N.Y.C., 1979, Nat. Mus. Women in the Arts, Washington, 1998; represented in permanent collections Wilmington Trust Co., E.I. duPont de Nemours & Co., Children's Home, Inc., Claymont, Del., Children's Bur., Wilmington, Stephenson Sci. Ctr., Vanderbilt U., Nashville, Lutheran Towers Bldg., Travelers Aid and Family Soc. Bldg., Wilmington, bronze fountain head Longwood Gardens, Kennett Square, Pa., bronze statue Brookgreen Gardens, Murrells Inlet, S.C., bronze sculpture "Veiled Lady", Nat. Mus. Women in Arts, Washington, 1998, bronze sculpture U. Del., Newark, 2001, bronze sculpture Biggs Mus., Dover, Del., 2002; contbr. articles to profl. jours. Organizer vol. svc. Del. chpt. ARC, 1938-39; chmn. Com. for Revision Del. Child Adoption Law, 1950-52; pres., bd. dirs. Children Bur. Del.; pres., trustee Children's Home, Inc.; del., past regent Gunston Hall Plantation, Lorton, Va.; mem. adv. com. Longwood Gardens, Kennett Sq., Pa.; garden and grounds com. Winterthur (Del.) Mus.; mem. rsch. staff Henry Francis DuPont Winterthur Mus., 1955-63; mem. archtl. com. U. Del., Newark. Recipient Confrerie des Chevaliers du Tastevin Clos de Vougeot-Bourgogne France, 1960; Hort. award Garden Club Am., 1964, medal of Merit, 1976, Dorothy Platt award Garden Club of Phila., 1980, Alumni medal of merit Westover Sch., Middlebury, Conn., Medal of Distinction, U. Del., 1999. Mem. Pa. Hort. Soc., Wilmington Soc. Fine Arts, Mayflower Descs., Del. Hist. Soc., Colonial Dames, League Am. Pen Women, Nat. Trust Hist. Preservation. Garden Club of Wilmington (past pres.), Garden Club of Am. (past asst. zone 4 chmn.), Vicmead Hunt Club, Greenville Country Club, Chevy Chase Club (Washington), Colony Club (N.Y.C.). Episcopalian. Address: PO Box 3919 Greenville DE 19807-0919

REZ, NANCY BRUBAKER, nurse; b. Ft. Dodge, Iowa, Mar. 27, 1930; d. William Jr. and Anna Pearson Brubaker; m. James Melvin Rez, Sept. 2, 1951; children: David Bradley, Peggy Beth. BA, Occidental Coll., LA, 1951; AA, Pasadena City Coll., Calif., 1976; BS in Nursing, Mt. St. Mary's Coll., LA, 1977; MA, Columbia Pacific U., San Raphael, Calif., 1986. Cert. accupressurist UCLA; RN Calif., 1982; cert. CC instr. Calif., health svcs. Calif. Health clk. Hoover HS, Glendale, Calif., 1970—73; floor nurse Glendale Adventist Med. Ctr., 1977—83; nurse Glendale CC, 1982—85; pvt. practice health cons., accupressurist, Glendale, 1982—. Co-founder free alternative therapies clinic for people with HIV/AIDS, cancer, other diseases Wellness Works, 1989—.

REZNICK, CHARLOTTE, educational psychologist, consultant; b. Bklyn., July 27, 1950; d. Louis and Irene (Sazinsky) R. BA, CUNY, 1971; MS, U. So. Calif., 1974, PhD, 1985. Sch. psychologist L.A. Unifed Sch. Dist., 1979-94; pvt. practice L.A., 1984—; assoc. clin. prof. dept. psychology Grad. Sch. UCLA, 1991—. Cons., creator Imagery for Kids, 1984—, relaxation CDs for kids Discovering Your Spl. Place, 2004, Creating a Magical Garden and Healing Pond, 2005. Contbg. author: Divorce and Family Instability, 1984; contbr. articles to profl. jours. Subccom. mem. alcohol and drug abuse L.A. Task Force on Self-Esteem and Personal and Social Responsibility, 1988-89; mem. Nat. Coun. for Self-Esteem; adv. bd. Wildwoods Found. Mem. L.A. Assn. Sch. Psychologists (Outstanding Psychologist award 1987), Los Angeles County Psychol. Assn., Am. Psychological Assn., Calif. Psychological Assn., Assn. Humanistic Psychology, Assn. Transpersonal Psychology. Avocations: travel, photography, meditation. Office: 11911 San Vicente Blvd Ste 240 Los Angeles CA 90049 Office Phone: 310-889-7859. Business E-Mail: drreznick@imageryforkids.com.

RHA, LIZETTE, social worker; m. Andrew Livingston. BS in Psychology, U. Calif., San Diego, 2000; MSW, San Diego State U., 2002. LCSW. Clin. social worker VA Med. Ctr., LA, 2002—.

RHEA, KAREN HENDRIX, health facility administrator; b. Holladay, Tenn., Dec. 21, 1946; d. John Irvin and Bivian Brown (Hearington) Hendrix; children: Patrick Jeremy, Isaac Brendan, Dylan Garrett. AB, King Coll., 1967; MD, U. N.C., 1973. Diplomate Nat. Bd. Med. Examiners, 1976, Am. Bd. Pediat., 1979, Am. Bd. Psychiatry and Neurology, 1991, Am. Bd. Child and Adolescent Psychiatry, 1992. Resident pediat. Vanderbilt U., Nashville, 1973—76; pediatric practice Franklin, Tenn., 1977—83; child and adolescent psychiatry fellowship Vanderbilt U., Nashville, 1984—86, gen. psychiatry residency, 1987—89, asst. prof. psychiatry, 1989—95; outpatient psychiatrist Columbia HCA, Franklin, 1995—96, Adventist Healthcare Network, Franklin, 1996—2002; v.p. med. svcs. Centerstone, Nashville, 2002—. Mem. med. exec. com. Williamson County Hosp., Franklin, 1979—81. Com. mem. Williamson County Child Abuse Rev. Team, Franklin, 1979—82; bd. mem. Franklin Housing Authority, 1980—85; adv. bd. mem. Bridges to Care / Nashville Consortium, 2004—06. Recipient Am. Med. Women Student award, U. N.C., 1973, Dozier Excellence in Tchg. award in Child and Adolescent Psychiatry, Vanderbilt U.; divsn. Child and Adolescent Psychiatry, 1996. Fellow: Am. Acad. Pediat. (licentiate); mem.: Am. Acad. Child and Adolescent Psychiatry (licentiate), Am. Psychiat. Assn. (licentiate). R-Consevative. Presbyterian. Home: 1015 W Main St Franklin TN 37064 Office: Centerstone 1101 6th Ave N Nashville TN 37208 Office Phone: 615-463-6659. Office Fax: 615-463-6603. Business E-Mail: karen.rhea@centerstone.org.

RHEA, MILDRED LOUISE, writer, poet; b. Cleburne, Tex., Nov. 2, 1911; d. Henry Clay and Bettie (Miller) Bedinger; m. Roy H. Rhea, Nov. 2, 1929 (dec. 1956); children: Allure, Vivian, Marlene, Dale, Howard, Glenda, Karen, Henry. BEd, Humboldt State Coll., Arcata, Calif., 1960. Tchr. Shasta County (Calif.) pub. schs., 1949-53, Mendocino County Pub. Schs., 1953-54, Colusa County (Calif.) pub. schs., 1955-59, Contra Costa County (Calif.) pub. schs., 1959-68, Santa Cruz County (Calif.) pub. schs., 1968—77, ret. Author: Henry and Bettie, A Washington Bedinger Historical Family Story (trilogy), 1990, 91, Homestead on the Prairie, 1990, The War Years, 1993, Papa is Home, 1997, Billie and I and Some Other Guys, 2004, Pomp and Circumstantial Evidence (prose and poetry), 2005; poetry in anthologies: The Barn Loft, The Muse, A Fairy with a Dirty Face, Leo and the Pigs, Glenda, Picking Pie Cherries, Guinea Wink, The New Discovery, Hitch Hikers, Desert Storm Easter. Mem. Am. Assn. Retired Persons. Democrat. Methodist. Avocations: crocheting, painting, poetry, quilting. Home: 1200 Soda Lake Rd Fallon NV 89406

RHEAMS, ANNIE ELIZABETH, education educator; b. Lake Providence, La. d. Curtis Kleinpeter Sr. and Annie Augusta (Webb) Kleinpeter; 1 child, Darryl Jemall Rheams. BA, Grambling (La.) U., 1971; MS, Ala. A&M U., 1975; PhD, U. Wis., Milw., 1989. Cert. tchr. in exceptional edn., adminstrn. Tchr. Ala. A&M U., Normal, 1971-79, adminstr., 1977-79; acad. specialist U. Wis., Milw., 1979-82, Parkside, 1982-84; tchr. diagnostician, adminstr. Milw. Schs., 1984-89; asst. prof. dept. edn. Marquette U., Milw., 1989-96; asst. prin. North Divsn. H.S., Milw., 1996—, Marshall H.S., Milw., 1997—99, tchr. exceptional edn. cognitively disabled, consumer math., 1999—, adminstr., asst. prin., 1999. Career counselor Madison County Career Counseling Svcs., Huntsville, 1975; adj. prof. Oakwood (Ala.) SDA Coll., 1975-78; tchr. Gateway to Engring. Program, Milw., 1984-88; cons. pub. schs./Wee Care Day Care, Milw., 1992-96; condr. workshops in field. Author: P.A.C.E.: A Thematic Approach to Developing Essential Experiences, 1996. Voter registrar/poll watcher NAACP, Lake Providence, 1966; v.p. Work for Wis., Inc., Milw., 1993-94, Messmer H.S. Bd., Milw., 1990-94; com. chmn. Citizen's Rev. Bd., Milw., 1980-82, Met. Milw. Alliance Black Sch. Educators, 1994-95. Assoc. fellow Ctr. for Great Plains Studies, U. Nebr.-Lincoln, 1995; named Outstanding Tchr. Educator, Am. Assn. for Coll. Tchr. Educators Directory, 1995. Mem. Zonta Internat., Alpha Kappa Alpha, Phi Delta Kappa. Avocations: tennis, sewing, ceramics, horseback riding, biking. Home: PO Box 90681 Milwaukee WI 53209-0611 Office Phone: 414-902-8497. Office Fax: 414-902-8315. Business E-Mail: rheams@hotmail.com.

RHENEY, SUSAN O., paper company executive; MBA, Harvard Univ. CPA. Public acctg. auditor Deloitte & Touche; prin. Sterling Group LP (parent co., Mail-Well), 1992—2001; dir. Mail-Well, 1993—97; interim chmn. Cenveo (formerly Mail-Well), 2005—. Bd. dir. Genesis Energy LP, Cenveo, 2003—. Office: Cenveo Ste 400 8310 S Valley Hwy Englewood CO 80112-5806 Office Phone: 303-790-8023. Office Fax: 303-566-7466.

RHIMES, SHONDA, producer, director, writer; b. Chgo., Jan. 13, 1970; 1 adopted child, Harper. BA in English, Dartmouth U., 1991; MFA, U. So. Calif., 1994. Dir., writer: (films) Blossoms and Veils, 1998; writer Crossroads, 2002; The Princess Diaries 2: Royal Engagement, 2004; exec. prodr., writer: (TV series) Grey's Anatomy, 2005—. Office: c/o ABC TV 500 S Buena Vista St Burbank CA 91521-4551*

RHINEHART, ELIZABETH D., psychologist; b. Weymouth, Mass., Jan. 15, 1959; d. George and Joan Rhinehart. AB, Wellesley Coll., 1982; MS, U. Mass., 1987, PhD, 1989. Psychotherapist U. Mass., Psychol. Svcs. Ctr., 1984-86, Hampshire Coll., Amherst, Mass., 1985-86, 87-88, Hampden Dist. Mental Health Clinic, Springfield, Mass., 1986-88, McLean Hosp., Belmont, Mass., 1987-88; psychology intern Inst. Living, Hartford, Conn., 1988-89; psychologist Child & Family Svcs., Hartford, Conn., 1990-92, pvt. practice, West Hartford & Suffield, Conn., 1992—. Contbr. articles to profl. jours. Avocations: skiing, waterskiing, windsurfing, rollerblading. Office: 805 Farmington Ave West Hartford CT 06119 Office Phone: 860-233-0206.

RHINEHART, PETA-GAY CHEN, nurse, consultant; b. Kingston, Jamaica, Nov. 3, 1967; arrived in U.S., 1975; d. Winston Ernest and Margaret Conception Chen; m. James Edmund Rhinehart, Oct. 27, 2000; 1 child, John Stephen Chen Schoettler. AS, Houston CC, 1991, AS in Nursing, 1992; BS in Psychology, U. Houston, 2003, MEd, 2005. RN Tex. Bd. Nurse Examiners, 1992, cert. legal nurse cons., The Am. Legal Nurse Cons. Certification Bd., 2003. RN Meml. City Hosp., Houston, 1999—, Pulse Staffing Agy., Houston, 1999—. Ct. apptd. spl. adv. Child Advocates, Houston, 2004—; mem. com. med. safety Houston Livestock & Rodeo, Houston, 2004—; adj. faculty Meml. Hermann Hosp. Sys., Houston, 1995—; case mgr. Amerigroup Corp., Houston, 1998—2002, cons., 2002—. Mem.: Golden Key Internat., Psi Chi, Phi Theta Kappa, Phi Delta Kappa (v.p. membership 2004—05). Lutheran. Avocation: photography. Home: 9722 Therrell Drive Houston TX 77064 Office: Franklin Cardwell & Jones 1001 McKinney 18th Floor Houston TX 77002 Office Phone: 713-222-6025.

RHINESMITH, HEATHER LYNN, music educator; b. Chilton, NJ, June 22, 1978; d. Kim Brian and Carol Ann Rhinesmith. MusB, Stetson U., Deland, Fla., 2000. Choral dir. Brooksville Christian Ch., Fla., 2001—02. Scholar, Brooksville Music Club, 1996—2000. Mem.: Fla. Vocal Assn. (chair dist. 5 2002—03). Office: Lena Vista Elementary 925 Berkley Rd Auburndale FL 33823 Office Phone: 863-965-5464.

RHO, YANNI, psychiatrist; d. Seung and Yong Rho; m. Matthew Baity, May 29, 2005. BA magna cum laude, U. Tex., 1995; MD, U. Tex. Med. Br., Galveston, 2001; MPH, Harvard U., 2005. Dance tchr. at risk youth project City of Austin, Tex., 1996—97; area coord. Tex. Cancer Coun., Austin, 1996—97; outreach coord. YWCA Encore Plus Women's Health Program, Austin, 1996—97; modern dancer Ballet East, Austin, Tex., 1996—97; internal medicine intern Carney Hosp., Dorchester, Mass., 2001—02; adult psychiatry resident Partners Healthcare, Boston, 2002—05; child and adolescent psychiatry fellow Cambridge (Mass.) Health Alliance, 2005—. Mem. task force Breast Cancer Resource Ctr., Austin, 1996—97; psychiat. cons. City on a Hill H.S., Boston, 2003—04; advising mem. of grad. med. edn. com. Cambridge Heatlh Alliance, Cambridge, Mass., 2005—; lectr. cross-cultural curriculum in psychiatry Mass. Gen. Hosp./McLean Hosp., Boston, 2005—; lectr., presenter in field. Author: (reference guide) Resource Guide for Healthcare: Austin; contbr. articles to profl. jours., appendix to book. Nurse screening asst. Vol. Healthcare Clinic, Austin, 1996—97; tchr. Students Tchg. AIDS to Students, Galveston, Tex., 1997—99; co-founder local chpt. Nat. Alliance on Mental Illness, Galveston, 2000—01; cons. Edn. Devel. Ctr., Inc, Watertown, Mass., 2004—05. Recipient William Todd Midgett, M.D., award, U. Tex. Med. Br., 2000. Mem.: Assn. of Korean Am. Psychiatrists, Mass. Psychiat. Soc., New Eng. Coun. Child and Adolescent Psychiatry, Am. Psychiat. Assn. (mem. com. pub. affairs, fellow substance abuse and mental health svcs. adminstrn. 2004—06), Am. Acad. Child and Adolescent Psychiatry (mem. com. for advocacy), Alpha Omega Alpha. Office: Cambridge Health Alliance 1493 Cambridge St Macht Bldg Cambridge MA 02139 Office Phone: 617-665-3268. Office Fax: 617-665-1973. Business E-Mail: yrho@challiance.org.

RHOADES, EVA YVONNE, retired elementary school educator; b. Henderson, Tex., Sept. 27, 1935; d. Cecil Milton Andrus and Olga Mae Maddox; m. Samuel Jeffery Rhoades (dec. Jan. 1994). BS in Elem. Edn., U. Tex., 1958; ME in Spl. Edn., U. Tex., Tyler, 1982. Tchr. I.W. Popham Elem. Sch., Austin, 1958—62, Kelso Elem. Sch., Houston, 1962—72; tchr. spl. edn. jr. high West Rusk Ind. Sch. Dist., New London, Tex., 1980—94. Mem.: ATPT, Coun. for Exceptional Children, Anna B. Kelso Elem. PTA (life), Rusk County Poetry Soc., Ex-Students U. Tex. (life). Home: 1900 Castlegate Henderson TX 75654

RHOADES, MARYE FRANCES, paralegal; b. Ft. Defiance, Va., Jan. 29, 1937; d. Silas Caswell Sr. and Mary Ann Frances (James) Rhodes; m. Minter James Rowe, May 1964 (div. 1968); children: Margaret Frances Omar, James Robert Rowe; m. Robert Charles Rhoades Jr., July 25, 1980. Student, Mountain State U., 1956-58, 68, U. Charleston, 1962-63, 74, 89, Antioch U., 1972-73; grad., Mike Tyree Sch. Real Estate, 1984, Evans Coll. Legal Studies, 1990. Educator Nicholas County Sch. Sys., Summersville, W.Va., 1958-61; edit. staff, columnist, staff writer, reporter, photographer Beckley Newspapers Corp., 1962-76; educator Raleigh County Bd. Edn., Beckley, W.Va., 1967-68; exec. editor, columnist Local News Jour., Whitesville, W.Va., 1976-77; libr. bookmobile, asst. ref. libr., outreach coord. Raleigh County Pub. Libr., Beckley, 1977-78; agt. Combined Ins. Co., Chgo., 1978-79; legal sec., paralegal W.Va. Legal Svcs. Inc., Beckley, 1979-82; paralegal Appalachian Rsch and Defense Fund Inc., Beckley, 1982-83; exec. dir., owner Rhoades and Rowe, Beckley, 1983—85; paralegal patient advocate Cmty. Health Sys. Inc., Beckley, 1986-96; pvt. practice Beckley, 1996—. Contbr. articles to mags. State bd. dirs., pub. resl. LWV, Beckley; pub. rels., various coms. Raleigh County Dem. Women, Beckley; sec., pub. rels. Orchard Valley Women's Club, Crab Orchard, W.Va.; trustee Fraternal Order Eagles; pub. rels., various coms. Loyal Order Moose, Beckley, Beckley Profl. Bus. Women; com. mem. Nat. Coalition to Save the New River; sales rep. So. U.S. Rep. to U.S. Mil. Acad., West Point, N.Y.; active Am. Legion Aux., Mullens, W.Va. Mem. NEA, Classroom Tchrs. Assn., Nat. Paralegal Assn., Nat. Fedn. Paralegals Assn., Nat. Ind. Paralegals Assn., Nat. Com. Save Soc., Sec. Medicare, Nat. Legal Aid and Def. Assn., Nat. Orgn. Social Security Claimants Reps., State Soc. Sec. Task Force, Nat. Vets. Legal Svcs. Project Inc., W.Va. U. Alumni Assn., Community AIDS Edn. Com., W.Va. Edn. Assn., Am. Disability Repr. Specs. Assn. Democrat. Mem. Ch. of God. Avocations: creative arts and music, walking, nascar, doll collecting, writing. Home: PO Box 2173 Beckley WV 25802 Office: Benefit Services PO Box 7265 Beckley WV 25802 Office Phone: 304-252-8431. Office Fax: 304-252-1098. E-mail: tv65000@charter.net.

RHOADES, PAULA K., dietician, healthcare educator; b. Greenville, Ohio, May 25, 1952; d. Paul and Marcia Rhoades; m. Cleveland Waterman, July 4, 1981; 1 child, Jack Waterman. BS, Miami U., Oxford, Ohio, 1974; MEd, U. Fla., Gainesville, 1977; PhD, U. Calif. Berkeley, 1984. Dietician Shands Tchg. Hosp., Gainesville, Fla., 1974—77; asst. prof. dietetics La. Tech. U., Ruston, 1977—81, 1989—98; supr. child nutrition Caddo Parish Schs., Shreveport, La., 1984—89; renal dietician Dialysis Clinic, Inc., Shreveport and Sacramento, 1998—2004; program dir., dietary mgmt. Bossier Parish C.C., Bossier City, La., 2005—. Mem. dietetics adv. bd. La. Tech. U., 1984—89. Author: (articles) Jour. Am. Dietetic Assn. Coun. pres. Holy Trinity Luth. Ch., Shreveport, 1997. Mem.: La. Dietetic Assn. (pres. 1990—91, Outstanding Dietician 1991), Am. Dietetic Assn. (Outstanding Dietetic Educator 1992). Lutheran. Avocations: golf, walking, reading. Office: Bossier Parish CC 6220 E Texas St Bossier City LA 71111 Business E-Mail: prhoades@bpcc.edu.

RHOADS, GERALDINE EMELINE, editor, consultant; b. Phila., Jan. 29, 1914; d. Lawrence Dry and Alice Fegley (Rice) R. AB, Bryn Mawr Coll., 1935. Publicity asst. Bryn Mawr (Pa.) Coll., 1935-37; asst. Internat. Students House, Phila., 1937-39; mng. editor The Woman mag., N.Y.C., 1939-42; editor Life Story mag., 1942-45, Today's Woman mag., N.Y.C., 1945-52, Today's Family Mag., N.Y.C., 1952-53; lectr. Columbia U., 1954-56; assoc. editor Readers Digest, 1954-55; producer NBC, 1955-56; assoc. editor Ladies Home Jour., 1956-62, mng. editor, 1962-63; exec. editor McCall's mag., 1963-66; editor Woman's Day mag., 1966-82, editorial dir., 1982-84, Woman's Day Resource Center, 1984-89; v.p. Woman's Day mag., 1972—84, CBS Consumer Publs., 1977-84; cons. Woman's Day, N.Y.C., 1989-91. Editorial cons., dir. Nat. Mag. Awards, 1991-94. Author: (with others) Woman's Day Help Book, 1988. Mem. journalism awards com. James Beard Found., 1993-2001. Recipient award for profl. achievement Diet Workshop Internat., 1977; Elizabeth Cutter Morrow award YWCA Salute to Women in Bus., 1977; Recipient Econ. Equity award Women's Equity Action League, 1982; March of Dimes Women Editor's citation, 1982 Mem.: Women's Forum (bd. dirs. 1985—87), Advt. Women in N.Y. (bd. govs. 1983—85, 2d v.p. 1985—87, 1st v.p. 1987—89, bd. dirs. 1989—90, Pres.'s award 1987), N.Y. Women in Comm. (Matrix award 1975), Am. Soc. Mag. Editors (chmn. exec. com. 1971—73), Fashion Group (bd. govs. 1977—79, chmn. bd. govs. 1978—80, bd. dirs. Found. 1980—81, treas. bd. govs. 1983—85, bd. govs. 1987—88), Nat. Press Club (dir.), Bryn Mawr Coll. Alumni Assn. (bd. dirs. 1989—94), Turtle Bay Assn. (bd. dirs. 1989—92), Literacy Vols. of N.Y.C. (bd. dirs. 1986—93), YWCA Acad. Women Achievers, Bryn Mawr Club of N.Y.C. (bd. dirs. 1994—2000), Women's City Club of N.Y. (bd. dirs. 1996—, chair comm. 2001—04, Honoree of Yr. 2004). Home: 185 W End Ave Apt 21A New York NY 10023-5548 Personal E-mail: rhoadsge@aol.com.

RHODA, JANICE TUCKER, writer, educator, musician; b. Lynn, Mass., Mar. 24, 1955; d. Robert Samuel and Cecilia Mary Ann (DiTroia) Tucker; m. David Michael Cleary, Jan. 21, 2001. BMus, New Eng. Conservatory Music, Boston, 1989; Suzuki Tchr. Tng., Ithaca Coll., NY, 1980—81. Pvt. violin tchr., 1975—; violin tchr. Wakefield Pub. Schs., 1979—80, Newton Pub. Schs., 1979—81, All-Newton Music Sch., 1980—84, McGill U., 1982, 1983, Boston Ctr. for Adult Edn., 1992—95, 1997—98, New Eng. Conservatory of Music, Boston, 2000, Cambridge Ctr. for Adult Edn., Mass., 2003—; dir., tchr. Suzuki program Longy Sch. Music, Cambridge, Mass., 1980—87, Brookline Music Sch., Mass., 1992—94; clinician The ABCs of Strings, 1998—, Royal Conservatory Music, Toronto, 2004—05, Vancouver Acad. Music, Canada, 2004—. Author: (book series) The ABCs of Strings; concertmistress North-Eastern Dist. Orch., 1972—73, Mass. All-State Orch., 1972; actor: (DVD) The ABCs of Violin for the Absolute Beginner, 2006. Mem.: Nat. Assn. for Music Edn., Am. String Tchrs. Assn., Suzuki Assn. of Ams., Mu Phi Epsilon. Office: The ABCs of Strings PO Box 400428 Cambridge MA 02140 Office Phone: 888-846-5460. Personal E-mail: abcsofstrings@comcast.net.

RHODE, DEBORAH LYNN, law educator; b. Jan. 29, 1952; BA, Yale U., 1974, JD, 1977. Bar: D.C. 1977, Calif. 1981. Law clk. to judge U.S. Ct. Appeals (2d cir.), N.Y.C., 1977-78; law clk. to Hon. Justice Thurgood Marshall U.S. Supreme Ct., Washington, 1978-79; asst. prof. law Stanford U., Calif., 1979-82, assoc. prof. Calif., 1982-85, prof. Calif., 1985—; dir. Inst. for Rsch. on Women and Gender, 1986-90, Keck Ctr. of Legal Ethics and The Legal Profession, 1994—2003; sr. counsel jud. com. Ho. of Reps., Washington, 1998. Trustee Yale U., 1983-89; pres. Assn. Am. Law Schs., 1998; Ernest W. McFarland prof. Stanford Law Sch., 1997—; sr. counsel com. on the jud. U.S. Ho. of Reps., 1998; dir. Stanford Ctr. on Ethics. Author: Justice and Gender, 1989, (with Geoffrey Hazard) the Legal Profession: Responsibility and Regulation, 3d edit., 1993, (with Annette Lawson) The Politics of Pregnancy: Adolescent Sexuality and Public Policy, 1993, (with David Luban) Legal Ethics, 2005, 4th edit., 2004, Speaking of Sex, 1997, Professional Responsibility: Ethics by the Pervasive Method, 1998, In the Interests of Justice, 2000 (with Geoffrey Hazard, Jr.) Professional Responsibility and Regulation, 2002; editor: Theoretical Perspectives on Sexual Difference, 1990, Ethics in Practice, 2000, The Difference Difference Makes: Women and Leadership, 2002, Access to Justice, 2004, Pro Bono in Principle and in Practice, 2005, (with Katherine Bartlett) Gender and Law, 2005, (with Carol Sanger) Gender and Rights, 2005, Moral Leadership: The Theory and Practice of Power, Judgement and Policy, 2006, In Pursuit of Justice: Scholars, Status, and Academic Culture, 2006; contbr. articles to profl. jours. Mem.: ABA (chmn. commn. on women 2000—02). Office: Stanford U Law Sch Crown Quadrangle Stanford CA 94305

RHODE, KIM, Olympic athlete; b. El Monte, Calif., July 16; Spokewoman for WPRO 7 Guncleaner and Snake Oil. Recipient Bronze medal in women's skeet 1994 USASNC, Bronze medal women's double trap 1995 Seoul World Cup, team Gold medal skeet, team Bronze medal double trap 1995 World Shotgun Championships, Gold medal women's double trap 1995 U.S. Olympic Festival, Gold medal women's double trap Olympic Games, Atlanta, 1996; winner Doubletrap Champion USA Shooting Nat. Championships, 1997. Mem. Safari Club Internat., Women's Sports Shooting Found. Avocations: skiing, hunting.

RHODES, ALICE GRAHAM, lawyer, not-for-profit developer, consultant; b. Phila., June 15, 1941; d. Peter Graham III and Fannie Isadora (Bennett) Graham; m. Charles Milton Rhodes, Oct. 14, 1971 (div. Apr. 21, 1997); children: Helen, Carla, Shauna. BS, East Stroudsburg U. Pa., 1962; MS, U. Pa., 1966, LLB, 1969, JD, 1970, cert. program exec. adminstrn., 2004. Bar: N.Y. 1970, U.S. Dist. Ct. (so. and ea. dists.) N.Y. 1971, U.S. Ct. Appeals (2d cir.) 1971, Ky. 1983, U.S. Dist. Ct. (ea. dist.) Ky. 1985. Staff atty. Harlem Assertion Rights, Mobilization for Youth Office Econ. Opportunity, N.Y.C., 1969-70, coord. Cmty. Action Legal Svcs., 1970-72; assoc. dir. in charge of civil representation HUD Model Cities Cmty. Law Offices, N.Y.C., 1972-73; resource assoc. Commn. on Edn. & Employment of Women, N.C. Dept. Adminstrn., Raleigh, 1975; mgr. policies and procedures Div. for Youth, N.C. Dept. Human Resources, Raleigh, 1976; in-house counsel, petroleum transactional atty. Ashland, Inc. (formerly Ashland Oil, Inc.), 1980-82; corp. atty. core group Ashland, Inc., 1985-87, 88-91; mem. Ashland City Commn. Human Rights, 1993-99; mem. bd. regents Ea. Ky. U., 1994—2000; asst. county atty. Jefferson County, 1999—2000; atty.-advisor EEOC, 2001. Mem. Property Valuation Appeals Commn., Greenup County, 1994, Pub. Members Foreign Svc.; cons. pub. mem. selection and performance stds. review bd. Fgn. Svc., U.S. Dept. State, 1995, Fgn. Agrl. Svc. USDA, 1997; prison program planner, cons. N.Y. City Dept. Corrections, 1971; lectr. N.Y.C. Corrections Acad., Riker's, 1971; lectr. juvenile justice N.C. Law Enforcement Acad., Salemburg, 1976. Driver Meals on Wheels, 1983—91; vol. Am. Heart Assn., 1982—91; mem. adv. com. task force post secondary edn. Gov. of Ky.; mem. Ky. Gov.'s Conf. on Postsecondary Edn., 1999; active Global Interdependence Ctr. U. Pa., 2003—; bd. dirs. exec. com. Boyd County Dem. Women, 1996—2000; mem. missionary soc., scholarship com. St. Matthew AME Ch.; bd. dirs. YWCA Ashland, 1983—84, Ashland Heritage Pk. Commn., 1983—85, Negro Baseball Hall of History; bd. dirs., budget com. United Way, Greenup County, Ky., 1988—92; bd. dirs. Franciscan Sisters of the Poor, Ky. Health Sys. Inc., 1996—99; mem. presdl. search com. Ea. Ky. U., 1997—98. Recipient Cmty. Svc. award Queens Community Corp., N.Y.C., 1972, Ashland C.C., 1986, Cmty. Svc. award NAACP, Ky.; NSF fellow, 1964, 65; faculty friends of Penn scholar U. Pa. Law Sch., 1966-69, Reginald Heber Smith postgrad. law and cmty. econs. devel. fellow, 1969-71; named to Hon. Order of Ky. Cols., 1989. Fellow Ky. Bar Found.; mem. NAFE, AAUW (bd. dirs. Phila. chpt. 1963-65), NAACP (life), N.Y. Bar, Ky. Bar Assn. (mem. edn. law, corp. house counsel, law sects.), Pilot Club (exec. bd. Ashland 1983), Links, Inc., Penn Club (charter mem.), Assn. Gov. Bds. Colls. and Univs., Fgn. Svc. USA (pub. mem.), Global Interdependence Ctr., Pyramid Club of Phila., U. Pa. Edn. Alumni Assn. (bd. dirs.), SC Club. Democrat. Avocations: interior decorating, sports, dance, gourmet cooking, gardening. Address: 658 N 65th St Philadelphia PA 19151

RHODES, BETTY FLEMING, rehabilitation services professional, nurse; b. Franklin, Pa., Nov. 28, 1920; d. John and Twyla Odella (Callen) Fleming; m. Donald Muir Cain, Dec. 31, 1952 (div.); m. Lee Chester Rhodes, June 23, 1962 (dec. Apr. 1997). RN, Allegheny Gen. Hosp., Pitts., 1942. Lic. phys. therapist, Pa. Phys. therapist Office of D.T. Watson, Pitts., 1947, Ky. Soc. for Crippled Children, Louisville, 1947-51, St. Anthony Hosp., Louisville, 1953-78. Nurse U.S. Army, 1943-45; capt. Army Nurse Corps, 1951-52. Decorated Bronze Star. Mem. Am. Phys Therapy Assn. (pres. Ky. chpt.). Roman Catholic. Home: Providence Retirement Home 4915 Charleston Rd Apt 312 New Albany IN 47150

RHODES, DEBORAH J., prosecutor; BA with high honors, Wheaton Coll.; JD with honors, Rutgers U. Law clk. to Hon. J. William Ditter U.S. Dist Ct. (ea. dist.) Pa; mem. Organized Crime & Racketeering sect., Phila. Strike Force U.S. Dept. Justice, Phila., asst. U.S. atty. San Diego, 1990—2004, counselor to asst. atty. gen., criminal divsn. Washington, 2004—05; Us atty. (so. dist.) Ala. US Dept. Justice, Ala., 2005—. Ex-officio commr. U.S. Sentencing Commn., 2003—. Editor (in chief): Rutgers Law Jour. Office: US Attys Office Southern District of Alabama 63 S Royal St Ste 600 Mobile AL 36602*

RHODES, KARREN, public information officer; b. Calif., 1947; 2 children. Diploma in Journalism, U. Utah, 1984. Journalist, Salt Lake City, 1983—85, UPI, Cheyenne, Wyo., 1985—86, Green River (Wyo.) Star, 1986—88; pub. info. officer Nev. Dept. Employment Security, Carson City, 1989—94, Nev. Dept. Employment, Tng. and Rehab., Carson City, 1994—. Trustee Carson Access Found., Carson City, 1996—2001; fundraising chair Mound House Bus. Assn. Recipient Vol. of Yr. award, State of Utah Gov.'s Office, Salt Lake City, 1984, Best of Nat. Collegiate Photography award, 1984. Mem.: Soc. Profl. Journalists. Avocations: photography, graphic design, writing, travel, mentoring.

RHODES, KENDALL WESTBROOK, language arts educator; b. Portsmouth, Va., Jan. 1, 1945; d. William B. and Margaret (Wiersdorf) Westbrook; m. Carl E. Rhodes Jr., Aug. 6, 1966; children: Carl III, William Taylor. BS, Radford Coll., 1966; MS in Edn., Old Dominion U., 1976, postgrad., 1986—91. Cert. tchr., Va. Tchr. Portsmouth Pub. Schs., 1966-67, Tacoma Pub. Schs., 1967-68; tchr., faculty coord. Ct. St. Acad., Portsmouth, 1977—. Pvt. tutor; safety patrol sponsor, yearbook sponsor Ct. St. Acad., Portsmouth. Mem. Portsmouth Svc. League, 1974—; pres. Portsmouth Rep. Women, 1974-; rec. sec. Va. Fedn. Rep. Women, Richmond, 1988-92, pres. 2004-06. Recipient State Tribute, Va. Fedn. Rep. Women, 1984, Most Valuable Mem. award Portsmouth Rep. Women, 1978. Presbyterian. Avocations: travel, cooking, sports. Home: 3412 Churchill Dr Portsmouth VA 23703-3904 Office: Ct St Acad Court And Queen St Portsmouth VA 23704

RHODES, LINDA JANE, psychiatrist; b. San Antonio, May 23, 1950; d. George Vernon and Lucy Agnes (O'Dowd) R. BA, Trinity U., 1972; MD, U. Tex. Med. Br., 1975. Diplomate Am. Bd. Pediat.; bd. certified, Am. Bd. Psychiatry and Neurology. Resident in pediat. U. Tex. Med. Br., Galveston, 1975-78; fellow in ambulatory pediat. U. Tex. Health Sci. Ctr., Houston, 1978-80, asst. prof. psychiatry San Antonio, 1995—, resident in psychiatry, 1990-92, child and adolescent psychiatrist, fellow in biol. psychiatry, 1992-95; pediatrician Kelsey Seybold Clinic, P.A., Houston, 1980-95. Pediat. rep. Tex. Lay Midwifery Bd. Tex. Dept. Health, Austin, 1994-95. Active San Antonio Conservation Soc., San Antonio Herb Soc., Nat. Trust for Hist. Preservation, San Antonio Mus. Assn., Trinity U. Assocs., 1992-95, Witte Mus. Assn.; patron McNay Art Inst.; bd. dirs. Tex. Found. for Psychiatric Edn. & Rsch., 1997—, sec., 1998-99, treas., 1999-2004. Fellow Am. Acad. Pediat.; mem. Am. Psychiat. Assn., Am. Acad. Child and Adolescent Psychiatry (gifts and endowments com.), Ambulatory Pediat. Assn., Tex. Pediat. Soc., Tex. Soc. Psychiat. Physicians, Tex. Acad. Child and Adolescent Psychiatry, Am. Med. Women's Assn., Am. Soc. Clin. Psychopharmacology, Tex. Med. Assn. (com. on child and adolescent health), AMA, Bexar County Psychait. Soc. (sec. 2000-2001, pres. 2002-2003, past pres. 2003-2004).

RHODES, LISA DIANE, minister; b. Bklyn., June 7, 1956; d. Henry Anthony and Rebecca Jane Rhodes. BA, Wheeling Coll., 1978; MSW, U. Md., Balt., 1980; MDiv, Candler Sch. Theology, 1991. Hospice chaplain Grady Hosp. Pastoral Care, Atlanta, 1991—93; coord. for minority health Ctrs. for Disease Control, Atlanta, 1993—96; dir. outreach Interdenominational Theol. Ctr., Atlanta, 1996—98; dir. planning and programs Payne Theol. Seminary, Wilberforce, Ohio, 1998—2001; asst. pastor Ebenezer Bapt. Ch., Atlanta, 1995—2000; dean of the chapel Spelman Coll., Atlanta, 2001—. Mem. Mental Health Assn., Jacksonville, Fla., 1985—87; strategic planning cons. Friendship Bapt. Ch., Gastonia, NC, 1997—99; workshop, retreat facilitator Ptnrs. in Faith, Stone Mountain, Ga., 1998—2001. Editor: Transformative Imperatives, 1998; author: Mediation, 2001. Supporter Children's Def. Fund, Washington, 2001—03. Recipient Theol. Exploration of Vocation award, Lilly Endowment, 2002. Mem.: Am. Assn. Colls. and Univs. Avocations: tennis, reading, swimming. Home: 822 Southland Pass Stone Mountain GA 30087 Office: Spelman Coll 350 Spelman Ln SW Atlanta GA 30314

RHODES, RANDI, radio personality; b. Bklyn. d. Loretta; m. Jim Robertson, 1994 (div. 2004). Jobs at Radio Stations, Seminole, Tex., Mobile, Ala., NY, Dallas, Milw.; former sec., waitress, trucker and US Air Force aircraft mechanic; public relations job then weekend disc jockey WSHE, Coast 97.3 FM, 1987—92; radio talk show host WIOD AM, Miami, Fla., 1992—94, WJNO, West Palm Beach, Fla., 1994—2004, The Randi Rhodes Show, Air Am. Radio, NYC, 2004—. With USAF, 1977. Named Most Outstanding Woman in the Air Force, 1979; recipient Am. Women in Radio and Television award. Mailing: care Carmen Shamwell 4th Fl 641 Sixth Ave New York NY 10019 Office: Air America Radio 641 Avenue Of The Americas Fl 4 New York NY 10011-2038 E-mail: rrhodes@airamericaradio.com.

RHODES, RHONDA COCKRELL, science educator; b. Wilson, N.C., Oct. 27, 1964; d. James Ronald and Shirley Stancil Cockrell; m. Lawrence (Larry) Allen Rhodes, July 28, 1958. BS in Biology, Atlantic Christian Coll., Wilson, N.C., 1988; MEd in Secondary Sci., East Carolina U., Greenville, N.C., 1991. Cert. tchr. NC, 1999. Tchr. sci. So. Wayne H.S., Dudley, NC, 1988—91, Athens Dr. H.S., Raleigh, NC, 1991—2004, Knightdale H.S., NC, 2004—. Chair dept. sci. Knightdale H.S., NC, 2004—. Usher Bible Study Internat., Smithfield, NC, 2005. Environ. Awareness grant, Bright Ideas, 1997?. Mem.: N.C. Sci. Tchrs. Assn., N.C. Assn. of Profl. Educators. Home: 81 Fireweed Pl Clayton NC 27527 Office: Knightdale HS 100 Bryan Chalk Ln Knightdale NC 27545 Office Phone: 919-217-5350. Personal E-mail: rhondarhodes@nc.rr.com. E-mail: rrhodes@wcpss.net.

RHODES, SANDRA LAVERN, elementary school educator; b. Susanville, Calif., June 30, 1944; d. Harold Robert and Verdie Lavern Trussell; m. Oran Wayne Rhodes, Apr. 8, 1966; children: Renee, Kevin, Tracey, Mark. BS in Edn., Abilene Christian U., 1966; MS in Edn., Ctrl. Mo. State U., 1992. Cert. tchr. Tex., Mo. Elem. tchr. Moffat County Ind. Sch. Dist., 1966—67; tchr. Killeen (Tex.) Ind. Sch. Dist., 1985—86, Hickman Mills Consol. Sch. Dist., Kansas City, Mo., 1989—. Tch. advisor Dobbs Elem., Kansas City, 1996—2005, grade level chairperson, 2000—05; curriculum developer Hickman Mills Consol. Sch. Dist., Kansas City, 2002—05. Contbr. articles to profl. jours. Prof. women studies Midwestern Sch. Preaching, Sugar Creek, Mo., 1992—2000; workshop presenter, 1979—99. Nominee Disney Tchr. of Yr., 2000; recipient Appreciation Recognition, Mo. Scholars Acad., 2000. Mem.: Mo. State Tchrs. Assn. (local pres. 1995—97). Republican. Mem. Ch. Of Christ. Avocations: genealogy, travel. Office: Dobbs Elem Sch 9400 Eastern Kansas City MO 64087

RHODES, SUSAN ELIZABETH, secondary school educator; d. Charles Franklin and Nancy McDermott Chick; m. Bruce Gavin Rhodes, Oct. 13, 1977; children: Andrew Gavin, Joshua Lee, Daniel Ray. BS in Elem. Edn., Tenn. State U., Nashville, 1998, MEd, 2006. Cert. tchr. profl. highly qualified status for fed. No Child Left Behind Tenn. Dist. mgr. The Tennessean, Nashville, 1989—99; tchr. 5th grade Wharton Arts Mid. Magnet Sch., Nashville, 1999—. Mem.: NEA, Phi Kappa Phi. Church Of Christ. Avocations: reading, travel, camping. Home: 1202 Riverwood Dr Nashville TN 37216 Office: Wharton Arts Mid Magnet Sch 1625 Dr D B Todd Jr Blvd Nashville TN 37208

RHOE, WILHELMINA ROBINSON, retired science educator; b. Columbia, S.C., Nov. 21, 1936; d. William Howard Taft Robinson, Jessie M. Robinson Howard; m. Reginald Mussolini Rhoe, Nov. 28, 1959; children: Chantaine Rhoe-Bulluck, Reginald M., Jandrette, William O. BS in Biology, Benedict Coll., 1958; MS in Sci. Edn., Clemson U., 1980. Tchr. sci. Ruffin H.S., Ruffin, SC, 1958—59; tchr. biology Sterling H.S., Greenville, SC, 1959—60; tchr. sci. Westside H.S., Anderson, SC, 1961—62; tchr. biology, chemistry, physics, math. New Deal H.S., Starr, SC, 1964—68; chemist, statistician Dow-Badische Co., Anderson, 1968—70; tchr. biology, chemistry, physics, math. McDuffie H.S., Anderson, 1971—92; ret., 1992. Bd. dirs. Anderson Civic Ctr., Anderson, SC, 1992—98; del. Dem. Nat. Conv., Chgo., 1996, L.A., 2000; rules committeeperson S.C. Dem., Columbia, 1994—. Mem.: Anderson County Ret. Tchrs., Order Ea. Star (sec. Thomasena chpt. #206 1984—86). Avocations: reading, sewing, travel. Home: 105 Rhoe Cir Anderson SC 29621

RHONDA, KAROL, dermatologist; b. NYC, Oct. 5, 1962; AB, Harvard U., Cambridge, Mass., 1984; MD, Yale U., New Haven, Conn., 1988. Dermatologist pvt. practice, Forest Hills, NY, 1995—. Fellow: Am. Acad. Dermatology; mem.: L.I. Dermatol. Soc., Phi Beta Kappa. Office: 10848 70th Rd Forest Hills NY 11375

RHONE, ELVIE SUE, educational administrator; b. La., Oct. 06; d. Henry and Clara (McWright) Turner; m. Samuel Rhone, Apr. 24, 1964; children: Debra Lynn, Nedra Lanae. BS, So. U., Baton Rouge, 1962; MEd, Loyola U., Chgo., 1974; MS, Chgo. State U., 1986; EdD, Nova Southeastern U., Ft. Lauderdale, Fla., 1993. Lic. adminstr., supr., guidance, counseling and math. Instr. Cook County Sch. Nursing, Chgo., 1963-65; cons., supr. Cook County Dept. Pub. Aid, Chgo., 1965-66; tchr. Chgo. Pub. Schs., 1966-76, resource tchr., 1976-88, counselor, asst. prin., 1989-94, adminstr. Ctrl. Office Ctr., 1994—. Cons. math. textbook Houghton Mifflin Co., Dallas, 1987. Candidate for alt. del. to nat. conv., Chgo., 1980; bd. dirs. Cmty. Mental Health Coun.,

Inc.; mem. Referral Counselors Real Estate Connection. Recipient Outstanding Svc. award nat. legislation Nat. Cmty. Edn. Assn.; named Outstanding Educator PTA, Chgo., 1987; grantee Ill. State Bd. Edn., Springfield, 1992-94. Mem. ASCD, Nat. Sch. Bd., Assn. for Counselors, Chgo. Area Reading Assn., Phi Delta Kappa (Educator of Yr. 1994). Avocations: writing, gardening, travel, reading. Home: 7027 S Bennett Ave Chicago IL 60649-2007 Office Phone: 773-779-7300. Personal E-mail: phd612@aol.com.

RHONE, SYLVIA MARIE MILLER, recording industry executive; b. Phila., Mar. 11, 1952; BS in Econs. (hon.), U. Pa., 1974; Degree (hon.), Adelphi U., LHD (hon.), 1996. Comml. lending trainee Bankers Trust Co., NYC; sec. Buddha Records, 1974, nat. promotion coord., Bareback Records; regional promotions mgr. ABC Records, 1976—78, Ariola Records, 1978—79; N.E. regional promotions mgr./special markets Elektra Records, 1980—83, dir. mktg./special markets, 1983—85; dir. nat. black music promotion Atlantic Records, NYC, 1985—88, v.p., gen. mgr. black music ops., 1988—88, sr. v.p., gen. mgr. black music ops., 1988—90; CEO, co-pres. EastWest Records America, NYC, 1990—91; chmn., CEO EastWest/Atco Records, NYC, 1991—94; chair/CEO Elektra Entertainment, NYC, 1994—2004; exec. v.p. Universal Records, 2004—06; pres. Motown Records, 2004—06, Universal Motown Records, 2006—. Mem., bd. dirs. Alvin Ailey Am. Dance Theatre, The RIAA, Rock n' Roll Hall of Fame, Jazz at Lincoln Ctr., R&B Found., Studio Mus. of Harlem; bd. dirs. NARAS. Alumni trustee U. Pa., 2001—. Named an Most Influential Black Americans, Ebony mag., 2006; recipient Whitney M. Young Svc. Award, Boy Scouts of Am., 1992, New Music Seminar Joel Webber Prize for Excellence in Music and Bus. award, 1993, Sony Soul of Am. Music Excellence Award, 1993, Legacy Life Mem. award, Nat. Coun. of Negro Women, 1995, Urban Network Exec. Yr. Award, 1995, Herbert H. Wright award, Nat. Assn. Market Developers, 1995, Studio Mus. Corp. award, 1996, Creative Spirit Award, Black Alumni of Pratt Inst., Echo Awards, Trumpet Awards, Turner Broadcasting, 2004. Achievements include became 1st African American and first woman chairman and CEO of a major record company, 1994. Office: Univeral Motown Records 1755 Broadway # 6 New York NY 10019*

RIBBLE, JUDITH GLENN, medical educator; b. Norristown, Pa., Feb. 3, 1938; d. Victor Lewis and Thelma Louise (Coffman) Glenn; m. Darrah Ellsworth Ribble III, June 13, 1959 (dissolved June 1984); children: Darrah, Glenn, Anna; m. Clark Ely Bussey, Aug. 13, 1994; children: Gregory, Will. BA with honors, U. Pa., Phil., 1959; PhD in Social Scis., Med. Coll. Pa., Phil., 1979. Dir. continuing mental health edn. Med. Coll. Pa., Phil., 1979—83, asst. prof. psychiatry, 1979—83; dir. continuing med. edn. Jefferson Med. Coll., Phil., Pa., 1983—84, asst. prof. psychiatry, 1993—95; v.p. profl. edn. Arthritis Found., Atlanta, 1984—87; dir. med. edn. ACP, Phil., 1987—91; dir. continuing med. edn. Lifetime Med. TV, Astoria, NY, 1991—95; v.p. edn. Safeware, Inc., Bellevue, Wash., 1995—96; dir. continuing med. edn. Nat. Ctr. Genome Resources, Sante Fe, 1996—99, Medscape/WebMD, N.Y.C., 2000—06; pres. Nat. Commn. for Cert. Care Profl., 2006—. Adj. asst. prof. family and cmty. medicine U. N.Mex. Sch. Medicine, 2004—. Office Phone: 505-281-1143. Personal E-mail: jribble@sandia.net.

RIBLEY-BORCK, JOAN GRACE, medical/surgical rehabilitation nurse; b. Schenectady, NY, Jan. 5, 1939; d. Harry Jacob and Lillian Josephine (Cheney) Ribley; m. Walter Carl Borck Jr., Oct. 24, 1964; 1 child, Constance Maria. Diploma, Ellis Hosp. Sch. Nursing, Schenectady, 1960; BSN, Russell Sage Coll., Troy, NY, 1981. RN, NY. Staff nurse operating room Columbia Meml. Hosp., Hudson, NY, 1960-63, staff nurse rusk rehab., 1963-64; staff nurse cardiovascular operating room U. Md. Hosp., Balt., 1965-66; staff nurse, evening charge nurse St. Peters Hosp., Albany, NY, 1968-89; substitute staff nurse Wildwood Program, Schenectady, NY, 1989-96, 2001—02, 2002—03; staff nurse Apria Health Care (formerly Homedco Home Care), 1984—; substitute staff, nurse South Colonie Ctrl. Sch., 1996—; staff nurse Gentiva Health Svcs., Schenectady, 2006—. Ind. provider in nursing Medicaid Mgmt. Info. Sys, NY, 2004—. Mem. ANA, NY State Nurses Assn., Albany Coun. Cath. Nurses. Roman Catholic. Home: PO Box 11214 2 Charming Ln Loudonville NY 12211-1818 E-mail: jborck@nycap.rr.com.

RICARD, VIRGINIA BELLE, adult education educator; b. Denver, Nov. 27, 1927; d. Raymond and Loraine Hill; m. W. Kenneth Ricard, Apr. 6, 1953 (dec.); 1 child, Valerie. BS in Chemistry, Marymount Coll. Kans., Salina, 1949; MEd, Colo. State U., Ft. Collins, 1972, MEd in Adult Edn., 1973; PhD, Union Inst. and Univ., Cin., 1978. Med. tech. N.Y. Hosp., N.Y.C., 1950—53; rschr. Colo. State U., Ft. Collins, 1971—73, program coord., 1973—75, program devel. specialist, 1978—80; eval. specialist, cons. Model Edn. Program, DHEW, Denver, 1976—78; pvt. cons. Ft. Collins, Colo., 1980—2002; affiliate faculty mem. Regis U., Denver, 2000—. Author: Developing Intercultural Communication Skills, 1993; contbr. articles to profl. jours. Chair, family selection com. Habitat for Humanity, Ft. Collins, 1988—90; lifetime mem. Girl Scouts USA, first v.p., 1990—93; bd. dirs. Larimer County Food Distbn. Ctr., Ft. Collins, 1995—98, Care, Inc., Ft. Collins, 1996—2002. Recipient Disting. Alumni Award, Marymount Coll. Kans., 1985. Mem.: Colo. Assn. for Continuing and Adult Edn., No. Colo. Weavers Guild, Am. Assn. Adult and Continuing Edn., Phi Kappa Phi. Avocations: art, travel, music, genealogy. Home: 1826 Indian Meadows Ln Fort Collins CO 80525-1421 Office Phone: 970-493-1922.

RICARDO-CAMPBELL, RITA, economist, educator; b. Boston, Mar. 16, 1920; d. David and Elizabeth (Jones) Ricardo; m. Wesley Glenn Campbell, Sept. 15, 1946; children: Barbara Lee, Diane Rita, Nancy Elizabeth. BS, Simmons Coll., 1941; MA, Harvard U., 1945, PhD, 1946. Instr. Harvard U., Cambridge, Mass., 1946—48; asst. prof. Tufts U., Medford, Mass., 1948—51; labor economist U.S. Wage Stabilization Bd., 1951—53; economist Ways and Means Com. U.S. Ho. of Reps., 1954; economist, 1957—60; prof. San Jose (Calif.) State U., 1960—61; sr. fellow Hoover Instn. on War, Revolution, and Peace, Stanford, Calif., 1968—95, sr. fellow emerita, 1995—. Lectr. health Stanford U. Med. Sch., 1973—78; bd. dirs. Watkins-Johnson Co., Palo Alto, Calif., Gillette Co., Boston; mgmt. bd. Samaritan Med. Ctr., San Jose. Author: Voluntary Health Insurance in the U.S., 1960, Economics of Health and Public Policy, 1971, Food Safety Regulation: Use and Limitations of Cost-Benefit Analysis, 1974, Drug Lag: Federal Government Decision Making, 1976, Social Security: Promise and Reality, 1977, The Economics and Politics of Health, 1982, 2d edit., 1985, Resisting Hostile Takerovers: The Case of Gillette, 1997, Chinese transl., 2004; co-editor: Below-Replacement Fertility in Industrial Societies, 1987, Issues in Contemporary Retirement, 1988; contbr. articles to profl. jours. Mem. Western Interstate Commn. for Higher Edn. Calif., 1967-75, chmn., 1970-71; mem. Pres. Nixon's Adv. Coun. on Status of Women, 1969-76; mem. Pres. Ford's Adv. Coun. on Status of Women, 1976-79; mem. task force on taxation Pres.'s Coun. on Environ. Quality, 1970-72; mem. Pres.'s Com. Health Svcs. Industry, 1971-73, FDA Nat. Adv. Drug Com., 1972-75; mem. Pres. Reagan's Econ. Policy Adv. Bd., 1981-90, Pres. Reagan's Nat. Coun. on Humanities, 1982-89, Pres. Reagan's Nat. Medal of Sci. com., 1988-91, Pres. Bush's Nat. Medal of Sci. com., 1991-94; bd. dirs. Ind. Colls. No. Calif., 1971-87; mem. com. assessment of safety, benefits, risks Citizens Commn. Sci., Law and Food, Rockefeller U., 1973-75; mem. adv. com. Ctr. Health Policy Rsch., Am. Enterprise Inst. Pub. Policy Rsch., Washington, 1974-80; mem. adv. coun. on social security Quadrennial Health and Human Svcs., 1974-75; bd. dirs. Simmons Coll. Corp., Boston, 1975-80; mem. adv. coun. bd. assocs. Stanford Libs., 1975-78; mem. coun. SRI Internat., Menlo Park, Calif., 1977-90. Mem. Am. Econ. Assn., Mont Pelerin Soc. (bd. dirs. 1988-92, v.p. 1992-94), Harvard Grad. Soc. (coun. 1991-94), Phi Beta Kappa. Home: Classic Residence Hyatt 620 Sand Hill Rd Apt 308D Palo Alto CA 94304 Office: Stanford U Hoover Instn Stanford CA 94305-6010 Office Phone: 650-723-2074. Personal E-mail: ricardocampbell@sbcglobal.net.

RICCI, CHRISTINA, actress; b. Santa Monica, Calif., Feb. 12, 1980; Appeared in films Mermaids, 1990, The Hard Way, 1991, The Addams Family, 1991, The Cemetery Club, 1993, Addams Family Values, 1993, Casper, 1995, Now and Then, 1995, Gold Diggers: The Secret of Bear Mountain, 1995, Bastard Out of Carolina, 1996, The Last of the High Kings, 1996, That Darn Cat, 1996, Ice Storm, 1997, Little Red Riding Hood, 1997, Souvenir (voice) 1998, Pecker, 1999, I Woke Up Early When I Died, 1998, Fear and Loathing in Las Vegas, 1998, Desert Blue, 1998, Buffalo 66, 1998, The Opposite of Sex, 1998, Small Soldiers (voice only), 1998, Souvenir (voice only), 1998, 200 Cigarettes, 1999, No Vacancy, 1999, Sleepy Hollow, 1999, Bless the Child, 2000, The Man Who Cried, 2000, All Over the Guy, 2001, Prozac Nation (also co-prodr.), 2001, The Laramie Project, 2002, Pumpkin (also prodr.), 2002, Miranda, 2002, The Gathering, 2002, Anything Else, 2003, I Love Your Work, 2003, Monster, 2003, Cursed, 2005; TV appearances include H.E.L.P., 1990, The Simpsons (voice only), 1996, Ally McBeal, 2002, Malcolm in the Middle, 2002, Joey, 2005, Grey's Anatomy, 2006. Office: ICM 8942 Wilshire Blvd Beverly Hills CA 90211-1934*

RICCI, MARGARET THEA, music and piano educator, church organist; b. Maddock, N.D., Sept. 5, 1945; d. Aril Mandor Haugen and Bernetta Dallas (Dyste) Grimes; m. Daniel P. Ricci, Aug. 29, 1970 (dec. July 2001); children: David T., Daniel C. BS in Elem. Edn. and Social Sci., Western Mont. Coll., Dillon, 1967. Cert. in piano and organ instrn., Mont. Music Tchrs. Assn. 2d grade tchr. Jefferson County Sch. Dist., Boulder, Mont., 1965-66, Sch. Dist. 10, Anaconda, Mont., 1968-71, 1st grade tchr., 1971-72; rental property owner/mgr. Anaconda and Butte, Mont., 1986—; organist Hope Luth. Ch., Anaconda, 1979—; piano tchr. Anaconda, 1974—. Entertainer various clubs, Anaconda, 1974—; composer various piano and vocal pieces and ch. svc. setting responses. Weight loss lectr., Weight Watchers, Anaconda, 1974-78; sec. Cmty. Concerts, Anaconda, 1992—; vol. choir dir., Hope Luth. Ch.; sec. trust fund commn., Hope Luth.Ch., 1991-95; entertainment dir. for Good Neighbor Day, Anaconda C. of C., 1984—; pres. Cmty. Concerts, 1999—, Hope Luth. Trust Fund, 1999—. Mem. AFL Musicians Union, Nat. Music Tchrs. Assn., Mont. Music Tchrs. Assn., Butte-Anaconda Music Tchrs. Assn. (sec., v.p., pres. 1975—), Delta Kappa Gamma. Lutheran. Avocations: sewing, the stock market. Home: 1206 W 4th St Anaconda MT 59711-1808

RICCIO, ANGELA, science educator; b. Kankakee, Ill., Dec. 13, 1976; d. Daniel and Patricia Riccio. BS in Elem. Edn., Ill. State U., Normal, 2000; M Sci. Edn., Nat. Louis U., Wheeling, Ill., 2005. Cert. Am. sport edn. program Ill. Sci. tchr. Jefferey C. Still Mid. Sch., Aurora, Ill., 2000—06, Gordan Gregory Mid. Sch., Naperville, Ill., 2006—. Athletic scholar, Ill. State U., 1996—2000. Mem.: NSTA.

RICE, ANNE, writer; b. New Orleans, Oct. 14, 1941; d. Howard and Katherine (Allen) O'Brien; m. Stan Rice, Oct. 14, 1961 (dec. Dec. 9, 2002); children: Michele (dec. Aug. 5, 1972), Christopher. Student, Tex. Woman's U., 1959-60; BA, San Francisco State Coll., 1964, MA, 1971. Author: Interview with the Vampire, 1976, The Feast of all Saints, 1980, Cry to Heaven, 1982, The Vampire Lestat, 1985, The Queen of the Damned, 1988, The Mummy or Ramses the Damned, 1989, The Witching Hour, 1990 (TV series, 2002), Tale of the Body Thief, 1992, Lasher, 1993, Taltos, 1994, Memnoch the Devil, 1995, Servant of the Bones, 1996, Violin, 1998, The Vampire Armand, 1998, Pandora: New Tales of the Vampires, 1998, Vittorio the Vampire, 1999, Merrick, 2000, Blood and Gold, 2001, The Master of Rampling Gate, 2002, Blackwood Farm, 2002, Blood Canticle, 2003, Christ the Lord: Out of Egypt, 2005; (as A.N. Roquelaure) The Claiming of Sleeping Beauty, 1983, Beauty's Punishment, 1984, Beauty's Release: The Continued Erotic Adventures of Sleeping Beauty, 1985 (as Anne Rampling) Exit to Eden, 1985, Belinda, 1986; screenwriter: Interview with a Vampire, 1994.

RICE, BARBARA LYNN, stage manager; b. Hartford, Conn., Nov. 9, 1955; d. Joe Roger and Betty Barbara (Baxter) R. BA in Theatre and French, Ind. U., 1978; MFA in Directing, U. Cin., 1982. Freelance stage mgr., N.Y.C.; dir. The Open Eye: New Stagings, N.Y.C., 1989; prodn. stage mgr. Belmont Italian-Am. Playhouse, N.Y.C., 1994, 95; prodn. assn. Silence, Cunning, Exile, N.Y.C., 1995; asst. stage mgr. The Merry Wives of Windsor, N.Y.C., 1995; stage mgr. The Message of Peace, N.Y.C., 2005. Dir. The Open Eye: New Stagings, N.Y.C., 1989; stage mgr. 20 Years Ago Today, Cin., 1989, Fourscore & 7 Years Ago, Paramus, N.J., 1989-90, Hanging the President, N.Y.C., 1990, Message of Peace (Lotus Music and Dance), N.Y.C., 2004; prodn. asst. Kiss of the Spiderwoman, Purchase, N.Y., 1990, (off-Broadway) Beau Jest, N.Y.C., 1992, Belmont Italian-Am. Playhouse, N.Y.C., 1994, 95, Transformations, 1997; listings editor Back Stage, 1998; contbg. writer The Headset, 2005; stage manager The Message of Peace, Lotus Music and Dance, NYC, 2005. Mem. Actors' Equity Assn., Stage Mgrs. Assn. Presbyterian. Avocations: music, history, art, reading, languages. Home: 412 W 56th St Apt 10 New York NY 10019-3647 E-mail: cincydame@aol.com.

RICE, BRENDA JEAN, operating room nurse, educator; b. Oswego, N.Y., May 12, 1960; d. William Harry Sweeting and Sharon Wildred (Crane) Sagneri; m. David Henry Rice, Aug. 4, 1984. ADN, Cayuga Coll., 1991. RN, N.Y. Staff nurse oper. rm. Oswego Hosp., staff nurse ICU/CCU, staff nurse oper. rm., 1987—. Clin./lab. instr. practical nursing program Oswego Co. BOCES. Firefighter Scriba (N.Y.) Fire Dept., 1988-97, Oswego Town Fire Dept., 1997—; pres. Sears Mdse. Store League, Oswego, 1989-91, Burkes Classic League, Oswego, 1991-93, Scriba Fire Corp., 1993, 94, 97; sec. Lakeview Mixed Cookie League, Fulton, N.Y., 1992-97. Mem. Fulton Womens Bowling Assn. (bd. dirs. 1996—). Republican. Methodist. Avocations: auto racing, fishing, travel, reading, bowling. Home: 124 W Seneca St Oswego NY 13126-1420

RICE, CASSANDREA RAE, music educator; b. Mansfield, Mo., Oct. 20, 1978; d. Andrew and Libby Roth; m. Douglas Rice, June 15, 2002. BS in Music Edn., Mo. State U., Springfield, 2002. Mid. sch. band dir. Mehlville Sch. Dist., St. Louis, 2003—05; asst. band dir. Nixa R-2 Sch. Dist., Mo., 2005—. Mem.: Mo. State Tchrs. Assn., Music Educators Nat. Conf., Pi Kappa Lambda, Kappa Delta Pi. Office Phone: 417-875-5473.

RICE, CLARETHA MAYES, medical/surgical nurse, educator; d. Fred Dossie and Luethisa Mayes; children: William Eugene Mayes, Carisa Denise Brewster. Assoc. in Gen. Studies, C.C. of Phila., 1988. Lic. practical nurse, Pa. Staff nurse Albert Einstein, Phila., 1973—; charge nurse Maplewood Manor, Phila., 1980—84, Stapely Health Care Ctr., Phila., 1984—94; tchr. Sch. Dist. of Phila., 1992—2004. Bereavement counselor Canaan Bapt. Ch., Phila., 1999—. Musician: Canaan Baptist Church Daycare Song (Recommedation from dir. of day care, 1995). Mem. xec. com. Stenton Ave. and Partnership Com., Phila., 1990—2006; tchr. Sunday sch. Disciples of Christ Ch., Phila., 1958—70, Canaan Bapt. Ch., Phila., 1980—2006, deaconess, Bible tchr., 1997—2006, bereavement facilitator and counselor, 1999—2006; coord. women's conf. Canaan Bapt. Ch., Enon Bapt. Ch., Keystone Mercy, 2005. Recipient Cert. of Achievement, Phillippian Bapt. Church-New Hope Ministry, 1999—2006, Cert. of Recognition, Greater Phila. Area Sunday Sch. Assn., Retirement Cert. of Recognition, Am. Fedn. of Tchrs., Cert. of Attendance, Ctr. for Grieving Children, Teens and Families, Cert. of Completion of Mission Study Course, Lott Carey Bapt. Fgn. Mission Conv. of Am.-44Shaw Div. Sch., Name placed on the Wall of Tolerance-So. Poverty Law Ctr., Nat. Campaign for Tolerance, 2005. Democrat. Baptist. Avocations: travel, reading, music, gardening, writing. Personal E-mail: crice63808@aol.com.

RICE, CONDOLEEZZA, secretary of state, former national security advisor; b. Birmingham, Ala., Nov. 14, 1954; d. John Wesley and Angelena Ray Rice. BA cum laude, U. Denver, 1974, PhD, 1981; MA, U. Notre Dame, 1975; PhD (hon.), Morehouse Coll., 1991, U. Ala., 1994, U. Notre Dame, 1995, Nat. Def. U., 2002, Miss. Coll. Sch. of Law, 2003, U. Louisville, 2004, Mich. St. U., 2004; degree (hon.), Boston Coll., 2006. Intern, Bur. of Ednl. & Cultural Affairs US Dept. State, Washington, 1977; intern Rand Corp., Santa Monica, Calif., 1978; polit. sci. cons. Stanford U., 1980—81, asst. prof. polit. sci., 1981—87, assoc. prof., 1987—93, prof., 1993—99; provost Stanford U., 1993-99; spl. asst. to dir. of the Joint Chiefs of Staff US Dept. Def., Washington, 1986; spl. asst. to the Pres. for nat. security affairs NSC, 1989-91, dir. to sr. dir. Soviet & East European Affairs, 1989—91; sr. fellow Hoover Inst., Stanford, Calif., 1991—93; nat. security cons. George W. Bush presdl. campaign, 2000; asst. to the Pres. for nat. security affairs NSC, Washington, 2001—05; sec. US Dept. State, Washington, 2005—. Cons. ABC News, Washington; mem. spl. advisory panel to comdr. and chief strategic air commd.; mem. gov. ind. advisory redistricting the state of Calif.; mem. U.S. Delegation to 2+4 Talks on German Unification; former mem. bd. dirs. Chevron Corp., Charles Schwab Corp., Internat. Advisory Coun. of J.P. Morgan, William & Flora Hewlett Found., U. Notre Dame. Author: Uncertain Allegiance: The Soviet Union and the Czechoslovak Army, 1984; co-author (with Alexander Dallin): The Gorbachev Era, 1986; co-author: (with Philip Zelikow) Germany Unified and Europe Transformed, 1995. Ex officio trustee Nat. Gallery Art. Named one of Most Influential People, Time mag., 2005, 100 Most Influential People, 2006, 100 Most Powerful Women, Forbes mag., 2005—06, The 10 Most Fascinating People of 2005, Barbara Walters Special, Most Influential Black Americans, Ebony mag., 2006; recipient Sch. of Humanities and Scis. Dean's award for Disting. Tchg., Stanford U., 1993, Walter J. Gores award for Excellence in Tchg., 1984, Pres. award, NAACP Image Awards, 2002. Mem. Coun. Fgn. Rels. Republican. Office: US Dept State 2201 C St NW Washington DC 20520 Office Phone: 202-647-4000.*

RICE, CONSTANCE LAMAY, lawyer; b. 1956; BA, Radcliffe Coll.; JD, NYU. Bar: 1984. Law clk. to Honorable Damon Keith, US 6th Circuit Ct. Appeals, 1984—86; atty. to co-dir. LA office NAACP Legal Def. and Edn. Fund; ptnr., civil rights law English, Munger and Rice, LA. Co-dir., co-founder Advancement Project, LA; bd. dirs. Pub. Policy Inst. Calif., Pub. Radio Station KPCC. Named one of State's Top 100 Most Influential Calif. Attys., Calif. Law Bus. Jour., 2000, Am. Top Black Lawyers, Black Enterprise Mag., 2003; recipient Peace prize, Calif. Wellness Found., 2001, John Anson Ford Humanutaruab award, LA County, 2002. Office: English Munger and Rice Ste 800 1545 Wilshire Blvd Los Angeles CA 90001 Office Phone: 213-989-1300.

RICE, DONNA S., educational administrator; b. Tulsa; d. Grady and Mildred Steed; m. Donald Rice, Aug. 3, 1956 (dec. Jan. 1990); children: Michael, Donna E., Nadine. BA in Linguistics, SUNY, Buffalo, 1971, MA in Linguistics, 1973, PhD in Comms., 1985. LPN, N.Y. Asst. dir. English Lang. Inst. SUNY at Buffalo, 1980-85, assoc. dir. edn. opportunity ctr., 1985-86, staff assoc. office of the pres., 1986-87, dir. ednl. opportunity ctr., 1987-90, assoc. vice provost spl. programs, 1990-91, assoc. v.p. spl. programs, 1991-93, assoc. v.p. student affairs, 1993—. Bd. dirs. N.Y.-Pa. region ARC, 1996—; dir.-in-residence English Lang. Inst. SUNY, Beijing, 1981, chair SUNY Com. Promotion of Tolerance and Diversity, Buffalo, 1993—. Contbr. articles to profl. jours. Bd. dirs. King Urban Ctr., 1998—; scholarship com. Humboldt Pkwy. Bapt. Ch., 1985—; mem. policy adv. bd. Bethel Head Start, 1994-98; bd. dirs. Neighborhood Info. Ctr., 1984-97, Leadership Buffalo, 1989—. Recipient Cmty. Svc. award Neighborhood Info. Ctr., 1997, Outstanding Cmty. Svc. award County of Erie, 1990, Leadership award Great Lakes Bapt. Assn., 1989. Mem. Ptnrs. of Am. (life), Am. Assn. Univ. Adminstrs. (bd. dirs. 1987—), Am. Assn. Higher Edn., Nat. Assn. Student Pers. Adminstrs., Delta Sigma Theta. Democrat. Baptist. Avocations: reading, choir, cooking. E-mail: dsrice168@aol.com.

RICE, DOROTHY PECHMAN (MRS. JOHN DONALD RICE), medical economist; b. Bklyn., June 11, 1922; d. Gershon and Lena (Schiff) Pechman; m. John Donald Rice, Apr. 3, 1943; children: Kenneth D., Donald B., Thomas H. Student, Bklyn. Coll., 1938—39; BA, U. Wis., 1941; DSc (hon.), Coll. Medicine and Dentistry N.J., 1979. With hosp., and med. facilities USPHS, Washington, 1960—61; med. econs. studies Social Security Adminstrn., 1962—63; health econs. br. Community Health Svc., USPHS, 1964—65; chief health ins. rsch. br. Social Security Adminstrn., 1966—72, dep. asst. commr. for rsch. and statistics, 1972—75; dir. Nat. Ctr. for Health Stats., Rockville, Md., 1976—82; prof. Inst. Health & Aging U. Calif., San Francisco, 1982—94, prof. emeritus, 1994—. Developer, mgr. nationwide health info. svcs.; expert on aging, health care costs, disability, and cost-of-illness. Contbr. articles to profl. jours. Recipient Social Security Adminstrn. citation, 1968, Disting. Svc. medal, HEW, 1974, Jack C. Massey Found. award, 1978, UCSF medal, 2002. Fellow: Am. Statis. Assn.; mem.: LWV, APHA (domestic award for excellence 1978, Sedgwick Meml. medal 1988), Assn. Health Svc. Rsch. (President's award 1988), Inst. Medicine. Home: 13895 Campus Dr Oakland CA 94605-3831 Office: U Calif Sch Nursing Calif San Francisco CA 94143-0646 Office Phone: 415-476-2771. Business E-Mail: dorothy.rice@ucsf.edu.

RICE, JENNIFER STACY, literature and language educator; b. Sacramento, May 28, 1976; d. Bruce Dean and Jocelyn Karen Reeves; m. Darrin Keith Rice, July 7, 2001; 1 child, Molly Caroline. BA in English, U. Nev., Reno, 1998, MEd in Secondary Edn., 2003. English tchr. Truckee Meadows C.C., Reno, 2000; lang. arts tchr. Dilworth Mid. Sch., Sparks, Nev., 2000—01, Lou Mendive Mid. Sch., Sparks, Nev., 2001—06; English tchr. Billinghurst Mid. Sch., Reno, 2006—. Drama tchr. Mendive Mid. Sch., 2001—, acad. team bus. mgr., 2004—05, acad. intervention tchr., 2001—04. Leader mid. sch. students Reno Christian Fellowship, 2000. Nominee Walt Disney Nat. Tchr., 2006. Mem.: Nat. Coun. Tchrs. of English, Washoe County Tchrs. Assn. D-Conservative. Avocations: pilates, camping, scrapbooks, reading, gardening. Office: Mendive Mid Sch 1900 Whitewood Dr Sparks NV 89434 Office Phone: 775-353-5990. E-mail: jrice@washoe.k12.nv.us.

RICE, JOY KATHARINE, psychologist, education educator; d. Joseph Theodore and Margaret Sophia (Bednarik) Straka; m. David Gordon Rice, Sept. 1, 1962; children: Scott Alan, Andrew David. BFA with high honors, U. Ill., 1960; MS, U. Wis., 1962, MS, 1964, PhD, 1967. Lic. clin. psychologist. USPHS predoctoral fellow dept. psychiatry Med. Sch. U. Wis., Madison, 1964-65, asst. dir. Counseling Ctr., 1966-74, dir. Office Continuing Edn. Svcs., 1972-78, prof. ednl. policy studies and women's studies, 1974-95, clin. prof. psychiatry, 1995—; pvt. practice psychology Psychiat. Svcs., S.C., Madison, 1967—. Mem. State Wis. Ednl. Approval Bd., Madison, 1972—73; mem. Adult Edn. Commn. U.S. Office Career Edn., Washington, 1978; co-chmn. Wis. Lt. Gov.'s Task Force on Women and Depression, 2005—. Author: Living Through Divorce, A Developmental Approach to Divorce Therapy, 1985, 2d edit., 1989; mem. editl. bd. Lifelong Learning, 1979—86; cons. editor: Psychology Women Quar., 1986—88, assoc. editor:, 1989—94, cons. editor: Handbook of Adult and Continuing Education, 1989, Encyclopedia of Women and Gender, 2001, Handbook of Girls' and Women's Psychological Health, 2005; contbr. articles to profl. jours. Pres. Big Bros. Big Sisters Dane County, 2002, bd. dirs.; co-chair Wis. Lt. Gov.'s Task Force on Women and Depression, 2005—06. Recipient Disting. Achievement award, Ednl. Press Assn. Am., 1992, John Fritschler Jr. award for Disting. Achievement, 2004; Knapp fellow, U. Wis., Madison, 1960—62, Tchg. fellow, 1962—63. Fellow: APA (exec. bd. psychology women divsn. 1994—, internat. psychology divsn. 1998—, exec. bd. 1998—, chair internat. com. women 2000—02, chair com. internat. rels. psychology 2005, divsn. pres. 2006, Disting. Leadership award 2000—02); mem.: Am. Assn. Continuing and Adult Edn. (Meritorious Svc. award 1978—80, 1982), Internat. Coun. Psychologists (bd. dir. 1998—2001, sec. 2002—04, bd. dir. 2004—), Nat. Assn. Women Edn. (editl. bd. jour. 1984—88, cons. editor Initiatives 1988—91), TEMPO Internat. (bd. dir., sec. 2000—03, 2006—), Rotary, Phi Delta Kappa. Avocations: interior decorating, painting, gardening, travel. Home: 4230 Waban Hl Madison WI 53711-3711 Office: 2727 Marshall Ct Madison WI 53705-2255 Office Phone: 608-238-9354.

RICE, KAROLYN KAYE, elementary school educator; b. Marinette, Wis., Jan. 16, 1949; d. Rudolph C. and Ruby E. Johnson; m. Roger Ruben Rice, June 15, 1974; 1 child, Melanie Kaye. BA cum laude, U. Wis., 1971. Elem. tchr. Garfield Sch., Marinette, Wis., 1971—74, Jenkins Elem. Sch., Mo., 1978—79; English, music tchr. St. Thomas Aquinas Acad., Marinette, 1979—. Pianist, organist Calvary Temple, 1999—2003, Holy Family Parish, Marinette, 2000—. Recipient Tchr. of Yr., Marinette C. of C., 1984. Bapt. Avocations: travel, reading, knitting. Home: 1640 Stanton ST Marinette WI 54143

RICE, KAY DIANE, elementary school educator, consultant; d. Ray H. and Patricia Quibell; 1 child, Brooke Elise; m. F. Scott Rice. AA in Gen. Edn., Shasta Coll., Redding, 1972; BA in Liberal Studies, Calif. State U., Chico, 1975; EdM in Policy and Govt., U. Wash., 1991. Cert. tchr., Calif., Wash., cert. prin., Wash. Tchr. grade 3 Anderson (Calif.) Schs., 1976-79; tchr. grades 1, 2, and 3 Redding (Calif.) Elem. Schs., 1979-81, tchr. grade 1, 1981-83, tchr. grade 5, 1986-87; tchr. grade 2 Bellevue (Wash.) Pub. Schs., 1987-88; tchr. grade 4 Lake Wash. Sch. Dist., Kirkland, Wash., 1988-89; tchr. grades 3-4 Bellevue (Wash.) Pub. Schs., 1989-90; prin. intern Bellevue (Wash.) and Mercer Island (Wash.) Schs., 1990-91; tchr. grades K-1 Bellevue (Wash.) Pub. Schs., 1991-93, tchr. grades 1-2, 1993—. Mem. early childhood assessment project Bellevue Pub. Schs., 1993-99; presenter in field. Vol. ZEST Sch. Dist. Vol. Program, Bellevue, 1991-93. Recipient Pres.'s Merit award Parent Student Tchr. Assn., 1988, U.S. Presdl. EPA award, 1987; grantee Bellevue Schs. Found., 1987, 95-96, 96-97, 98-2006, Danforth Edn. Leadership grantee Bellevue Pub. Schs., 1990-91, Shunju Club, Japanese Bus. People Wash., 1994, Seattle Chinese Sch., 2004. Mem. ASCD, NEA, AAUW (hospitality com. 1982), PTSA, Wash. Orgn. for Reading Devel., PEO. Avocations: cooking, outdoor sports, reading, writing, religious studies. Home: 6818 205th Ave NE Redmond WA 98053-4721 Office: Somerset Elem Sch 14100 Somerset Blvd SE Bellevue WA 98006-2399

RICE, LEVINA RUTH (SALLY), alderman, retired government agency administrator; b. Deepwater, Mo., June 8, 1932; d. Earl Jackson and Ruth (Hieronymus) Martin; m. William Samuel Rice, Sept. 20, 1949; children: Sandra Ruth, Sheila Marie (dec.), Sonja Leigh, Shelly Jayne, Sherry Lou, Stacy Alyce. Student, Kansas City C.C., 1973-77. Contract specialist, adminstrv. sec. USDA, Kansas City, Mo., 1961-80; co-owner restaurant Sam & Sally's Nu-Way, 1975-85. Chmn. book com., author: The Hieronymus Story, 1997 (Anne Ford Book award 1999). V.p. Hieronymus Family in Am., 1986-94, pres., 1994-96, treas., 1998—; mayor pro-tem Silver Haired City Coun., Kansas City, 1994-96, 2000—, chmn. fin. com., 1998, city ops. com., 1997-98. Mem. Libr. of Congress. Republican. Baptist. Avocations: genealogy, antiques. Home: 200 E 132d St Kansas City MO 64145-1404 E-mail: sallyrrice@msn.com.

RICE, LINDA JOHNSON, publishing executive; b. Chgo., Mar. 22, 1958; d. John J. and Eunice Johnson; m. Andre Rice, 1984, 1 child, Alexa Christine; m. Mel Farr Sr. BA Journalism, Univ. Southern Calif., L.A., 1980; MBA, Northwestern Univ., Evanston, Ill., 1987. With Johnson Pub. Co., 1980—, past v.p. and asst. to pub., COO, 1987—2002; pres. Johnson Pub. Co., Inc., Chgo., 1987—, CEO, 2002—; pres. Fashion Fair Cosmetics, Ill., 1987—. Named one of 100 Most Powerful Women in Chgo., Chgo. Sun-Times, Chicago's 40 Under 40, Crain's Chgo. Bus.; recipient Women of Power award, Nat. Urban League, Trumpet award, Turner Broadcasting, Alumni Merit award, Univ. So. Calif., Alumni of the Year award, Kellogg Grad. Sch. Mgmt.,.stern University. Mem.: Exec. Club Chgo., Econ. Club Chgo., Young Presidents Orgn., Nat. Assn. Black Journalists, Fashion Group Internat., Comml. Club Chgo. Office: Johnson Pub Co Inc 820 S Michigan Ave Chicago IL 60605-2191*

RICE, LINDA LEE, special education educator; b. Milw., Apr. 21, 1954; d. Robert Merrill and Marion Ingrid Rice; m. Larry J. Martin, Nov. 25, 2000; m. David S. Epstein, July 3, 1980 (div. July 17, 1991); children: Andrew Merrill Epstein, Alison Beth Epstein. BS Edn. magna cum laude, U. Mo., Columbia, 1977; MA Edn., Marian Coll., Fond du Lac, Wis., 1997. Cert. Tchr. Emotionally Disabled Wis. and Mo., 1977, Tchr. Cognitive disabled Wis. and Mo., 1977, lic. Prin. Wis., 1997. Tchr. spl. edn. grades 5-6 Walker Sch. West Allis-West Milw. Schs., 1977—81, tchr. spl. edn. grades K-6 Gen. Mitchell Sch., grades 3-4 Irving Sch., 1990—97; tchr. spl. edn. grades 9-12 Nicolet H.S., Glendale, Wis., 1997—2000; tchr. spl. edn. grades K-5 Milw. Acad. Sci., 2000—02; tchr. spl. edn. grades 9-12 Homestead H.S. Mequon Thiensville Sch. Dist., Wis., 2002—. Vol. Schroeder YMCA, Milw., 1989—2000; tchr. rep. task force on delivery edn. svcs. M-T Sch. Dist., Mequon, Wis., 2006—. Mem.: Junior League of Milw. (newsletter editor 1982—84, chairperson edn. com. 1985—86, magazine editor 1985—86), Coun. for Exceptional Children, North Shore Swim Club (bd. mem. 1988—89), Lake Shore Club (bd. mem. 1987—88), Mt. Siani Hosp. Aux. (co-chair annual luncheon 1989), Friends of Children's Hosp. Milw. (com. chair 1985—87, newsletter editor 1987—88), Kappa Delta Pi, Delta Gamma (life). Office: Homestead High School 5000 W Mequon Road Mequon WI 53092 E-mail: lrice@mtsd.k12.wi.us.

RICE, LOIS, mayor; b. Duncan, Okla., May 06; d. William Daniel Wilbourn and Naomi Ruth Lee; m. Karl Gordon Rice, July 18, 1969; 1 child, Phyllis Ann Shepard. Student, Chgo. Inst. Learning. Mgr. Bud's Furniture and Appliance, Plainview, Tex., 1951-69; owner, mgr. Furniture Galleries Canyon, Tex., 1971-96; mayor City of Canyon, 1990—. Governing bd. mem. Better Bus. Bur., Amarillo, Tex., 1996-99; pres. region II, Assn. Mayors, Comm. and Coun., Amarillo, 1996, pres., 1997-99; adv. bd. mem. Atty. Gens. Office, Austin, Tex., 1998. Treas. First United Meth. Ch., 1984—; chmn. bd. Tex. Panhandle Heritage Found., 1988-99; exec. bd. mem. Pvt. Industry Coun., Amarillo, 1988-94; pres. C. of C., Canyon, 1989-90; governing bd. mem. WTAMU Found., 1995—, United Way, 1996—; bd. mem. Tex. Affordable Housing Task Force, Austin, 1998; originator, mentor Boys & Girls Club Canyon, 1999. Recipient Tex. Vocat. Adminstr. and Supr. award Assn. Vocat. Edn., Austin, 1982, Disting. Svc. award Women's Forum, Amarillo, 1991, Regional Svc. award Panhandle Regional Planning Commn., Amarillo, 1997, Career Achievement award Amarillo Womens Network, 1997, Small Town Leadership award Nat. Ctr. for Small Bus., Bentonville, Ark., Washington, 1999; named Citizen of Yr., Canyon C. of C., 1989. Mem. Canyon Rotary Club (past sec. 1997-98, plaque 1998). Republican. Avocations: reading, bridge, travel, card games. Office: 301 16th St Canyon TX 79015-2828

RICE, LOIS DICKSON, retired computer company executive; b. Portland, Maine, Feb. 28, 1933; d. David A. and Mary D. Dickson; m. Alfred B. Fitt, Jan. 7, 1978 (dec. 1992); children: Susan, John Rice. AB magna cum laude, Radcliffe Coll., 1954; postgrad. (Woodrow Wilson fellow), Columbia U., 1954—55; LLD (hon.), Brown U., 1981, Bowdoin Coll., 1984. Dir. counseling services Nat. Scholarship Service and Fund for Negro Students, N.Y.C., 1955-59; with The Coll. Bd., N.Y.C. and Washington, 1959-81, v.p. Washington, 1973-81; sr. v.p. govt. affairs Control Data Corp., 1981-91. Guest scholar The Brookings Inst., Washington, 1991—; bd. dirs. McGraw Hill, Inc., 1987—2003, Internat. Multifoods, 1991—2003, UNUM/Provident Corp., 1992—2003; overseer Tuck Sch. Mgmt. Dartmouth Coll., 1990—94; mem. Pres.'s Fgn. Intelligence Adv. Bd., 1993—2001; trustee George Washington U., 1992—98, trustee Mgmt. Leadership for Tomorrow, 1994—; trustee CNA Corp. Pub. Agenda Found., Harry Frank Guggenheim Found., 1994—. Contbr. articles on edn. to profl. publs.; editor: Student Loans: Problems and Policy Alternatives, 1977. Mem. adv. bd. to dir. NSF, 1981—89, chair, 1986—89; mem. Gov.'s Commn. on Future of Postsecondary Edn. in N.Y. State, 1976—77, Carnegie Coun. on Higher Edn., 1975—80; trustee Radcliffe Coll., 1969—75, Stephens Coll., Mo., 1976—78, Beauvoir Sch., Washington, 1970—76, Children's TV Workshop, 1970—73; bd. dirs. Potomac Inst., 1977—92, German Marshall Fund, 1984—94, Joint Ctr. Polit. and Econ. Studies, 1991—94, Reading is Fundamental, 1991—2004. Recipient Disting. Service award HEW, 1977 Mem. Cosmos Club, Phi Beta Kappa. Episcopalian. Home: 2332 Massachusetts Ave NW Washington DC 20008 Office: The Brookings Instn 1775 Massachusetts Ave NW Washington DC 20036-2103

RICE, LUANNE, writer; b. 1955; B of humane letters, Conn. Coll., 1977, degree (hon.), 2002. Author: Angels All Over Town, 1985, Crazy in Love, 1988, Stone Heart, 1990, Secrets of Paris, 1991, Blue Moon, 1994, Home Fires, 1996, Cloud Nine, 2000, Follow The Stars Home, 2001, Firefly Beach, 2001, Dream Country, 2002, Summer Light, 2002, True Blue, 2002, Safe Harbor, 2003, The Secret Hour, 2003, The Perfect Summer, 2003, Dance With Me, 2004, Summer's Child, 2005. Mailing: c/o Andrea Cirillo Jane Rotrosen Agency 318 E 51st St New York NY 10022

RICE, MARY ESTHER, biologist; b. Washington, Aug. 3, 1926; d. Daniel Gibbons and Florence Catharine (Pyles) R. AB, Drew U., 1947; MA, Oberlin Coll., 1949; PhD, U. Wash., 1966. Instr. biology Drew U., Madison, NJ, 1949-50; rsch. assoc. Columbia U., N.Y.C., 1950-53; rsch. asst. NIH, Bethesda, Md., 1953-61; curator invertebrate zoology and dir. Smithsonian Marine Sta., Smithsonian Instn., Washington, 1966—2002, sr. rsch. scientist emeritus, 2002—. Mem. adv. panel on systematic biology NSF, Washington, 1977-78; mem. com. on marine invertebrates Nat. Acad. Sci., 1976-81; mem. overseers com. on biology Harvard U., Cambridge, Mass., 1982-88. Assoc. editor Jour. Morphology, Ann Arbor, Mich., 1985-91, Invertebrate Biology, 1995—; editor: (with M. Todorovic) Biology of Sipuncula and Echiura, 1975, 2nd vol., 1976, (with F.S. Chia) Settlement and Metamorphosis of Marine Invertebrate Larvae, 1978, (with F.W. Harrison) Microscopic Anatomy of Invertebrates, Vol. 12, 1993; contbr. articles to profl. jours. Recipient Drew U. Alumni Achievement award in sci., 1980. Fellow AAAS; mem. Am. Soc. Zoologists (pres. 1979), Am. Microscopical Soc. (pres. 1999), Phi Beta Kappa. Office: Smithsonian Marine Sta 701 Seaway Dr Fort Pierce FL 34949-3140

RICE, MELISSA ANN, mathematics educator; b. Jerome, Idaho, Dec. 24, 1978; d. Barry Howard and Carolyn Jean Sullivan; m. Todd Douglas Rice, Dec. 31, 2000. BS, BA, Boise State U., Idaho, 2002. H.s. math. tchr. Valley Sch. Dist., Eden, Idaho, 2002—04, Jerome Sch. Dist., 2004—. Tchr., High Schs. That Work site coord. Jerome H.S., 2005—. Mem.: Am. Quarter Horse Assn. Home: 9 Horseshoe Cir Jerome ID 83338 Personal E-mail: ricem@d261.k12.id.us.

RICE, MICHELLE, communications executive; b. 1968; Degree in Journalism, Temple U.; MA in Comm. Mgmt., U. Southern Calif. Mgr., Special Markets and Can. BET, Inc.; dir., Affiliate Sales and Special Markets NBC Cable Networks; northeast regional v.p., Affiliate Rels. and Nat. Accounts iNDemand, 2001—04; v.p., Distbn. Strategy and Ops. TV One, 2004—06, sr. v.p., Nat. Accounts and Affiliate Mktg., 2006—. Named one of 40 Executives Under 40, Multichannel News, 2006. Office: TV One 1010 Wayne Ave Silver Spring MD 20910 Office Phone: 301-755-0400.*

RICE, MONICA ROCHELLE, elementary school educator; b. Peoria, Ill., Oct. 21, 1971; d. Leroy and Helen Hill. AAS, Ill. Ctrl. Coll., East Peoria, Ill., 1991; BS in Elem. Edn., So. Ill. U., Carbondale, 1994; MA in Tchg. and Leadership, St. Xavier, Chgo., Ill., 2006. Tchr. 5th, 6th and 8th grade reading, lit and lang. arts Peoria Pub. Schs., Ill., 1996—99; tchr. 6th-8th computer Matteson Sch. Dist., 1999—2002; tchr. 6th and 7th grade lit. and lang. arts Peoria Pub. Schs., 2002—03, tchr. 6th grade reading and lang. arts, 2003—. Profl. devel. provider Peoria Pub. Schs., 2004—, lead tchr. reading, 2003—. Race for the cure capt. Susan G. Komen Found., Peoria, Ill., 2004—06; sch. cleanup coord. Peoria City Beautiful, 2004—06; ordained min. Ch. Living God, 2004—06, asst. Sunday sch. supt., 2002—06. Democrat. Avocations: travel, reading, Bible study, singing. Home: 4025 N Westport Ct Peoria IL 61615-3905 Office: Chas A Lindbergh Middle School 6327 N Sheridan Rd Peoria IL 61614 Office Phone: 309-693-4427. Personal E-mail: church130@aol.com. E-mail: monica.rice@psd150.org.

RICE, NANCY E., state supreme court justice; b. Denver, June 2, 1950; 1 child. BA cum laude, Tufts U., 1972; JD, U. Utah, 1975. Law clerk U.S. Dist. Ct. of Colo., 1975-76, dep. state pub. defender, appellate divn., 1976-77; asst. U.S. atty. Dist. of Colo., 1977-87; dep. chief civil divn. U.S. Attorney's Office, 1985-88; judge Denver Dist. Ct., 1988-98; justice Colo. Supreme Ct., 1998—. Adjunct prof. law, trial advocacy U. Colo. Sch. of Law, 1987—. Contbr. articles to profl. jours. Mem. Denver Bar Assn. (Judicial Excellence award 1993), Colo. Bar Assn. (bd. govs. 1990-92, exec. coun., 1991-92), Women's Bar Assn., Rhone-Brackett Inn of Ct. (master 1993-97), Women Judges Assn. (co-chair nat. conf. 1990). Office: Colo Supreme Ct Colo State Jud Bldg 2 E 14th Ave Fl 4 Denver CO 80203-2115*

RICE, PAMELA ANN, marriage and family therapist; d. Charles Jefferson Rice, Jr. and Helen Ann (Larsen) Rice. B. of Bibl. Studies, Friends Internat. Christian U., 1983, M. of Bibl. Counseling, 1985, Dr. of Ministry, 1988; MA in Marriage, Family, Child Counseling, Calif. Christian Inst., 1991. Lic. marriage and family therapist Calif., 2000. Program dir. clin. psychiat. unit Van Nuys Cmty. Hosp., Calif., 1991—93; self-employed marriage and family therapist L.A., 2000—. Pastoral staff tng. counselor Vineyard Christian Fellowship, Santa Monica, 1981—86; exec. dir. Homes Of Hope, Hollywood, 1987—89; adminstrv. cons. City of Santa Monica, 1987—89; case mgr. clin. psychiat. unit Buena Pk. Cmty. Hosp., Calif., 1988—91; exec. dir. Mental Health Rehab. Facility, Palmdale, Calif. Recipient Outstanding Achievement award, City of Santa Monica, 1989. Mem.: EMDRIAN (assoc.), Calif. Assn. Marriage and Family Therapists (assoc.). Born-Again Christian. Achievements include receiving a commendation from President Ronald Regan for the development of the Homes of Hope outreach. Avocations: skiing, travel, decorating, poetry. Office: 1460 7th St Se 306 Santa Monica CA 90401 Office Phone: 310-553-2203.

RICE, PATRICIA JANE, journalist; b. St. Louis, Oct. 20, 1942; d. Canice T. and Jane Elizabeth Tobin) R. BA, Maryville Coll., 1964; postgrad., St. Louis U., 1965, 66. Copywriter Wohl Co., St. Louis, 1964-67; free-lance journalist Paris, 1967; copywriter D'Arcy Advt. Co., St. Louis, 1968; feature writer, columnist St. Louis Post, 1969-94, religion editor, 1994—2004, South reporter, 2004—05; freelance writer, 2005—. Moderator Rutgers U./Eagleton Ctr. Women in Politics Conf., 1980, 82, 84; lectr. in field. Author: City House, 1968, The Eclectic Shopper, 1973, A Catholic Funeral, 2005; co-author: In the Running: The New Political Woman, 1981 V.p. The St. Louis Forum, 1997-2002; bd. dirs. Leadership St. Louis, 1985-90. Recipient Quest award Mo. Press Women's, 1998; Knight Ctr. fellow U. Md., College Park, 1996, 2004. Mem. Journalism Found. Met. St. Louis (pres. 1984-91), St. Louis Newspaper Guild (treas. 1977-87), Soc. Profl. Journalists. Avocations: gardening, skiing. Office: Rice Assoc 1221 Locust St Ste 800 Saint Louis MO 63103 Office Phone: 314-241-8000.

RICE, PATRICIA OPPENHEIM LEVIN, special education educator, consultant; b. Detroit, Apr. 5, 1932; d. Royal A. and Elsa (Freeman) Oppenheim; m. Charles L. Levin, Feb. 21, 1956 (div. Dec. 1981); children: Arthur David, Amy Ragen, Fredrick Stuart; m. Howard T. Rice, Dec. 16, 1990 (div. Apr. 1994). AB in History, U. Mich., 1954, PhD, 1981; MEd, Marygrove Coll., 1973. Cert. elem. tchr., Mich. Tchr. reading and learning disabled, cons., Detroit Pub. Schs., 1967-76; assoc. prof., coord. spl. edn., Marygrove Coll., 1976-86; adj. prof. Oakland U., 1987-90, U. Miami, 1989-95; edn. curriculum cons. Lady Elizabeth Sch., Jávea (Alicante) Spain, 1988-91; v.p. Machpelah Non-profit Cemetery Bd., Ferndale, Mich., 1978-87, co-pres., 1987—; adv. bd. Eton Acad., Birmingham, Mich., 1991-93; workshop presenter Dade City Schs., 1992-97; presenter in field. Mem. Mich. regional bd. ORT, 1965-68; mil. affairs and youth svcs. S.E. Mich. chpt. ARC Bd., 1973-79; v.p. exec. bd. Women's Aux. Children's Hosp. Mich., 1968-73; bd. dirs. women's com. United Cmty. Svcs., 1968-73; judge Dade County Schs. for Tchr. Grants, 1996—2004; bd. dirs. Detroit Grand Opera Assn., 1970-75; com. chair morning of music benefits Detroit Symphony Orch.; torch drive area chmn. United Found., 1967-70; benefactor Fla. Grand Opera, 1990-2001, grand benefactor, 2002—, guild exec. bd., 1992-, v.p., 1998-99, co-pres. 2000-02, chair, found. bd. dirs., 2000-01; guild exec. bd. Miami City Ballet, 1996-2000, Choreographers Cir., 1990-; chair Lincoln Rd. Walk, 1996, co-chair All Star Luncheon, 1996, Ball Com., 1992; active Diabetes Rsch. Inst. & Found. Love & Hope Com., Fla. Concert Assn. Cresendo Soc., 1993-97, Villa Maria Angel, 1996—, v.p. angel bd. 1998—2005, found. bd. dirs. 2000—; v.p. Miami Children's Hosp., 2004-05, co-pres., 2005—; panel judge Dade County Cultural Affairs Coun., 2002-04; v.p., amb. Mt. Sinai Hosp. Alzheimer's Bd. Mem. NAACP (life), Navy League, Greater Miami Social Register, Citizens Interested in the Arts (charter, grant chair, exec. bd. 1997—), Williams Island Club, Turnberry Isle Golf Club (signature), Miami Shores Country Club, Surf Club, Phi Delta Kappa, Pi Lambda Theta.

RICE, PATRICIA WEGMANN, counselor; b. New Orleans, Nov. 3, 1943; m. edward Rice, July 31, 1965; children: Ward, Tricia, Lisa, Sean, Kathleen. BA, Loyola U., New Orleans, 1965, MS, 1991. Intern Loyola Counseling and Placement Ctr., 1991; ind. study/child psychiatry Tulane U. Med. Ctr., 1992-94; counselor Acad. of Sacred Heart, 1991—98; counselor pvt. practice Metairie Therapy Ctr., 1998—2006. Vol. Battered Women's Program, New Orleans, 1984-90, Access (Pro Life Group), New Orleans, 1983-90. Fellow Chi Sigma Iota; mem. Alpha Sigma Nu. Home: 308 Homestead Ave Metairie LA 70005-3707 Office Phone: 504-432-6817.

RICE, REBECCA DALE, film producer, writer; b. Albuquerque, May 17, 1953; d. Charles Roy and Marilyn Dale Rice. BS, Tex. Christian U., 1975; MFA, So. Meth. U., 1980. Co-dir. Long on Shorts Film Festival, Dallas, 2001—04. Prodr.: (films) FLMKR, 1999 (Cannes Forum selection, 1999), Stealin' Home, 1995 (Festival awards, 1995); (documentaries) Segregated Sunday, 2000, Join the Food Chain!, 2004 (Emmy nominee, Gracie award). Mem.: Women in Film Dallas. Office: 8575 Stillwater Cir Dallas TX 75243 Personal E-mail: rebdrice@sbcglobal.net.

RICE, REBECCA KYNOCH, writer, consultant, language educator; b. Pittsfield, Mass., June 13, 1954; d. John Hamilton and Nancy Anne (Kynoch) Rice; m. Leonard Charles Feldstein, Oct. 17, 1981 (dec. Dec. 1984); m. Branford Martin Smith, Aug. 14, 1993; 1 child, Oliver Van Santvoord Smith. BA, Sarah Lawrence Coll., 1977; MA, Fairleigh Dickinson U., 1980; MFA, George Mason U., 1996. English tchr. Newark Acad., Livingston, NJ, 1977-79; staff writer, editor Am. Internat. Group, N.Y.C., 1983-85; instr. English George Mason U., Fairfax, Va., 1990-92; mng. editor Green Mountains Rev., Johnson, Vt., 1993-94; freelance writer Johnson, 1994—. Instr. Lone Ridge Writers Group, Redding, Conn., 1998—; grants and publicity mgr. Vt. Studio Ctr., Johnson, 2004—. Author: A Time to Mourn: One Woman's Journey through Widowhood, 1990; contbr. articles to publs. Woodrow Wilson fellow, 1977. Mem.: Authors Guild. Avocation: tennis. Home: 11 Middle St Hadley MA 01060 E-mail: rebeccarice1865@gmain.com.

RICE, REGINA KELLY, marketing executive; b. Yonkers, NY, July 11, 1955; d. Howard Adrian and Lucy Virginia (Butler) Kelly; m. Mark Christopher Rice, Sept. 11, 1981; children: Amanda Kelly, Jaime Brannen. BS in Cmty. Nutrition, Cornell U., 1978. Account exec. J. Walter Thompson Co., N.Y.C., 1978—79; sr. account exec. Ketchum, MacLeod & Grove, N.Y.C., 1979—80; supr. Burson Marstellar, Hong Kong, 1981—83; v.p., dep. dir. food and beverage unit, creative dir. N.Y. office Hill and Knowlton, N.Y.C., 1983—91; mktg. cons. Rice & Rohr, N.Y.C., 1991—93; sr. v.p., dir. consumer mktg. practice Manning, Selvage & Lee, N.Y.C., 1993—97, sr. v.p. global tng. dir., 1999—; chief inspiration officer, dir. corp. devel. Internat. Pub. Rels. Assn., 1999—2001. Writer Fast and Healthy Mag., 1991-2000. Mem. Pub. Rels. Soc. Am. Roman Catholic. Avocation: collecting Provence pottery. Home: 31 Wrangler Ln Bell Canyon CA 91307 Office: Manning Selvage & Lee 6500 Wilshire Blvd Los Angeles CA 90048-4920 Office Phone: 323-866-6023.

RICE, ROSE ANN M., secondary school educator; b. Washington, Mo., Nov. 9, 1948; d. Martin Henry and Mary Ann Kraft; m. Frank William Rice, July 1, 1995. B in Chemistry and Math, Notre Dame Coll., St. Louis, 1971; MS in Edn., Creighton U., 1981. Cert. tchr. Mo. Sci. tchr. St. Gabriel Sch., St. Louis, 1971—75, Hannibal Cath. Sch., Mo., 1975—84, St. Aloysius Sch., St. Louis, 1984—88, Immaculate Conception Sch., Union, Mo., 1991—95, Notre Dame HS, St. Louis, 2001—; sci. and math. tchr. St. Cecilia Sch., St. Louis, 1995—97, St. Dominic Savlo Sch., St. Louis, 1997—2001; prin., sci. and math. tchr. St. Anthony's Sch., Sullivan, Mo., 1988—91. Regional sci. coord. East Ctrl. Coll., Union, 1991—95; tutor Sylvan Learning Ctr., Fenton, Mo., 2002—04, Notre Dame Tutorial Ctr., St. Louis, 2004—05; speech coach, judge in field. Bd. dirs. Phoenix Homeless Shelter, Washington, Mo., 1992—94; mem. ch. coun. Hannibal (Mo.) Cath. Ch., 1980—84, Mary Mother Ch., St. Louis, 2000—01. Recipient ribbons for needlework and crafts, Washington Town & Country Fair; grantee, Litzinger Ctr., Mo. Bot. Gardens, St. Louis, 1998—2001. Mem.: NSTA, Sci. Tchrs. Mo. Roman Catholic. Avocations: needlecrafts, reading, walking, golf, travel. Office: Notre Dame HS 320 E Ripa Ave Saint Louis MO 63125 Business E-Mail: ricer@ndhs.net.

RICE, RUTH ELAINE, music educator; d. Lester Ira and Martha Elizabeth Long; m. Frank Lambert Rice, June 21, 1969; children: Suzanne, Kevin, Lauren. BS in Music Edn., Lebanon Valley Coll., 1968; MS in Edn., Johns Hopkins U., 1980. Tchr. music Lower Dauphin Jr. H.S., Hummelstown, Pa., 1968—69; tchr. music K-6 Northwood Elem. Sch., Balt., 1969—73; tchr. Commonwealth Am. Sch. K-8, Lausanne, Switzerland, 1974—76, Yates Elem. Sch., Schenectnady, NY, 1990—97; tchr. elem. music Elsmere Elem., Bethlehem, NY, 1992—95; tchr. Farnsworth Mid. Sch., Guilderland, NY, 1995—96; tchr. mid. sch. gen. choral Van Antwerp Mid. Sch., Niskayuna, NY, 1996—. Co-author: (music jour.) Teaching Music, 2002. Music dir. Bethlehem Luth. Ch., Delmar, NY, 1982—. Mem.: N.Y. State Sch. Music Assn. (accompanist). Lutheran. Avocations: travel, reading, movies. Home: 5 Darroch Rd Delmar NY 12054 Office: Van Antwerp Middle Sch Storey Ave Schenectady NY 12309 E-mail: singasong123@hotmail.com.

RICE, SUE ANN, retired dean, psychologist; b. Ponca City, Okla., Sept. 17, 1934; d. Alfred and Helen (Revard) R. BS in Edn., U. Okla., 1956; MA, Cath. U., 1979, PhD, 1988. Ensign USN, 1956, advanced through grades to comdr., 1973; ednl. svcs. officer 9th Naval Dist., Great Lakes, Ill., 1956-58; adminstr., asst. staff, comdr. in-chief Pacific Fleet, Honolulu, 1958-61; head edn. div. Naval Air Sta., Lemoore, Calif., 1961-63; instr., acad. dir. Women Officers' Sch., Newport, R.I., 1963-66; head. tng. div. Naval Command Systems Support Activity, Washington, 1966-70; head, ops. support sec. staff, comdr.-in-chief Lant, Norfolk, Va., 1970-74; sr. U.S. rep. NATO, subgroup 5 orgn. JCS, Washington, 1974-77; ret. USN, 1977; head vocation office Archdiocese of Washington, 1977-78; cons. Notre Dame Inst., Arlington, Va., 1989-97, dean of students, 1990-95; ret., 1995. Lectr. Cath. U. Am., Washington, 1983-84; bd. dirs. Villa Cortona Apostolic Ctr., Bethesda, 1984-94. Tech. reviewer Personnel Administration, 1964; editor (newsletter) Vocation News, 1978. Conoco scholarship Continental Oil Co., 1952-56; recipient Meritorious Svc. medal Pres. of U.S., 1977, rsch. grant Cath. U., Sigma Xi, 1986. Mem.: Lay Women's Assn. (internat. v.p.), Cath. War Vets. (nat. membership task force com., nat. youth act com., vets. affairs com., nat. co-chmn. pub. rels. com.), Gamma Phi Beta, Kappa Delta Pi. Roman Catholic. Avocations: travel, music, gardening, woodworking. Home: PO Box 2742 Ponca City OK 74602-2742

RICE, SUSAN A., elementary school educator; d. Terry C. Wells and Dixie L. Rockwell; m. Ralph C. Rice; children: Shelley A. Thompson, Lindsey R. Myers, Mark C. BA in Elem. Edn., Ohio State U., Columbus, 1988. Cert. tchr. Ohio. 3rd grade tchr. Dan Emmett Elem. Sch., Mount Vernon, Ohio, 1989—95; 6th grade tchr. Mt. Vernon Mid. Sch., 1995—2004, 6th grade math tchr., 2004—. Office: Mount Vernon Mid Sch Martinsburg Rd Mount Vernon OH 43050 Office Phone: 740-392-MVMS. Business E-Mail: srice@mt-vernon.k12.oh.us.

RICE, SUSAN ELIZABETH, foreign policy analyst, former federal agency administrator; m. Ian Cameron; children: John D. Rice-Cameron, H. Maris Rice-Cameron. BA in History, Stanford U., 1986; MPhil, Oxford U., 1988, DPhil, 1990. Mgmt. cons. McKinsey and Co., Toronto, Ont., Canada, 1991-93; dir. internat. orgns. and peacekeeping NSC, Washington, 1993-95, spl. asst. to the Pres., sr. dir. African affairs, 1995-97; asst. sec. state African affairs US Dept. State, Washington, 1997—2001; mng. dir., prin. Intellibridge Internat., Washington, 2001—02; sr. fellow fgn. policy The Brookings Instn., Washington, 2002—. Fgn. policy aide Dem. Pres. Campaign, Boston, 1988 Harry S. Truman scholar, 1984, Rhodes scholar, 1986; recipient Walter Frewen Lord prize, Royal Commonwealth Soc., 1990, Assn. prize, Chatham

House-British Internat. Studies, 1992, Samuel Nelson Drew Meml. award, NSC, 2000. Mem. Phi Beta Kappa. Office: The Brookings Instn 1775 Massachusetts Ave NW Washington DC 20036

RICEDORF, AMY ELIZABETH, mental health services professional; b. Williamsport, Md., Sept. 14, 1982; d. Bernard Eugene and Wendy Diane Ricedorf. BS, Towson U., Maryland, 2004; student, Shippensburg U., Pa., 2004—. Resident asst. Towson U. Housing and Residence Life, Md., 2002—04; resident dir. Lebanon Valley Coll. Student Svs., Annville, 2004—; grad. asst. Shippensburg U. Women's Ctr., Pa., 2004—; counselor adv. Domestic Violence Intervention of Lebanon County, Pa., 2005—. Mem.: ACA (student affiliate 2005—06). Independent. Avocations: ballet, art, meditation. Home: 28 Bourbon Red Dr Mechanicsburg PA 17050 Personal E-mail: aerice2000@hotmail.com.

RICE-JONES, ANNIE MAY, retired secondary school educator; b. Nashville, July 28, 1945; d. Gilbert Rice and Carlean (Williams) Frierson; m. Charles Sylvester Alford, June 20, 1970 (div. Feb. 1976); m. Willie R. Jones, July 2, 1983 (dec. June 29, 1997); 1 child, Afiya Shani Alford. BS in Health and Phys. Edn., Tenn. State U., Nashville, 1966; MS in Pub. Health Edn., U. Tenn., Knoxville, 1967; EdD in Curriculum and Instruction with Specializations in Health Edn., U. No. Colo., Greeley, 1983. Lic. missionary Bapt. Ch., 2005, ordained Colo. Christian Fellowship, 2006; cert. tchr. N.C., Conn., Tenn., Colo. Tchr. Hartford (Conn.) HS, 1968-71, Broughton HS, Raleigh, NC, 1971-72, Jefferson County Pub. Schs., Golden, Colo., 1980—. Real estate broker assoc.; instr. health Meharry Med. Coll., Nashville, 1967—68; asst. prof. health edn. Chgo. State U., 1976—78; regional pub. health educator Ill. Dept. Pub. Health, Springfield, 1978—79; survey statistician U.S. Bur. Census, Lakewood, 1979—80. Active cmty. svc.; vol. AIDS educator couns.; vol. chaplain Swedish Med. Ctr., Alliance Clergy Women, Five Points Coalition, Park Hill Residence; mem. St. Joseph's Episcopal Ch. Mem.: NAACP (life), Swedish Med. Ctr. Aux. (life), Phi Delta Kappa, Phi Lambda Theta, Alpha Kappa Alpha. Avocations: reading, travel, interior decorating, water arobics. Personal E-mail: daughterofthunder2000@yahoo.com.

RICH, ADRIENNE, poet; b. Balt., May 16, 1929; d. Arnold Rice and Helen Elizabeth (Jones) R.; m. Alfred H. Conrad (dec. 1970); children: David, Paul, Jacob. AB, Radcliffe Coll., 1951; LittD (hon.), Wheaton Coll., 1967, Smith Coll., 1979, Brandeis U., 1987, Coll. Wooster, Ohio, 1988, CCNY, Harvard U., 1990, Swarthmore Coll., 1992. Tchr. workshop YM-WHA Poetry Ctr., N.Y.C., 1966-67; vis. lectr. Swarthmore Coll., 1967-69; adj. prof. writing divsn. Columbia U., 1967-69; lectr. CCNY, 1968-70, instr., 1970-71, asst. prof. English, 1971-72, 74-75; Fannie Hurst vis. prof. creative lit. Brandeis U., 1972-73; prof. English Douglass Coll., Rutgers U., 1976-79; Clark lectr., disting. vis. prof. Scripps Coll., 1983-84; A.D. White prof.-at-large Cornell U., 1981-87; disting. vis. prof. San Jose State U., 1984-85; prof. English and feminist studies Stanford U., 1986-93. Marjorie Kovler vis. lectr. U. Chgo., 1989. Author: Collected Early Poems, 1950-1970, 1993, Diving into the Wreck, 1973, The Dream of a Common Language, 1978, A Wild Patience Has Taken Me This Far, 1981, Your Native Land, Your Life, 1986, Time's Power, 1989, An Atlas of the Difficult World, 1991, Dark Fields of the Republic, 1995, Midnight Salvage, 1999, Fox, 2001, The Fact of a Doorframe: Selected Poems 1950-2001, 2002, The School Among the Ruins, 2004 (Nat. Book Critics Cir. prize poetry, 2005); (prose) Of Woman Born: Motherhood as Experience and Institution, 1976, 10th anniversary edit., 1986, On Lies, Secrets and Silence, 1979, Blood, Bread and Poetry, 1986, What Is Found There: Notebooks on Poetry and Politics, 1993, 2d edit., 2003, Arts of the Possible: Essays and Conversations, 2001; editor: Muriel Rukeyser, Selected Poems, 2004. Mem. nat. adv. bd. Nat. Writers Union, Rosenberg Fund for Children. Recipient Yale Series of Younger Poets award, 1951, Nat. Inst. Arts and Letters award in poetry, 1961, Eunice Tietjens Meml. prize, 1968, Shelley Meml. award, 1971, Nat. Book award, 1974, Fund for Human Dignity award Nat. Gay Task Force, 1981, Ruth Lilly Poetry prize, 1986, Brandeis U. Creative Arts medal for Poetry, 1987, Nat. Poetry Assn. award, 1989, Elmer Holmes Bobst award arts and letters NYU, 1989, MacArthur fellowship, 1994-99, Dorothea Tanning award Acad. Am. Poets, 1996, others; chancellor Acad. Am. Poets, 1999-2001, Lannan Found. Lifetime Achievement award, 1999, Bollingen prize, 2003, Nat. Found. Jewish Culture award, 2003, Nat. Book Award medal for Disting. Contribution, Nat. Book Found., 2006. Mem. PEN, Nat. Writers Union, A Jewish Voice for Peace. Office: c/o W W Norton Co 500 5th Ave New York NY 10110-0002

RICH, ANDREA LOUISE, museum administrator; BA, UCLA, 1965, MA, 1966, PhD, 1968. Asst. prof. comms. studies UCLA, L.A., 1976, asst. dir. office learning resources, 1976, acting dir. Media Ctr., 1977, dir. office of instructional devel., 1978-80, asst. vice chancellor office of instructional devel., 1980-86, asst. exec. vice chancellor, 1986-87, vice chancellor acad. adminstrn., 1987-91, exec. vice chancellor, 1991-95; pres., CEO L.A. County Mus. of Art, 1995—, pres., Wallis Annenberg dir., 2003—. Office: LA County Mus Art 5905 Wilshire Blvd Los Angeles CA 90036-4597

RICH, CAREN, secondary school educator, hypnotherapist; b. LA, July 2, 1955; d. Jerome Edward and Constance Natalie Finnerman; m. William Rich, July 8, 1995; children: David Lovitch, Zachary Lovitch. BA in Psychology and Sociology, UCLA, 1977; MA in Ednl. Psychology, Calif. State U., Northridge, 1985; PsyD, Ryokan Coll., LA, 1995; MS in Ednl. Adminstrn., Pepperdine U., LA, 2006. Mild/moderate and severe learning disabilities tchg. credentials Calif., cert. hypnotherapist Calif. Tchr. LA Unified Sch. Dist., 1988—; hypnotherapist LA, 1998—. Mem. Sojourn, Santa Monica, Calif., 2005—. Grantee, LA Unified Sch. Dist. Nutrition Network, 1999—. Mem.: Coun. for Exceptional Children (assoc.). Avocations: travel, music. Office: LA Unified Sch Dist 1650 Selby Ave Los Angeles CA 90024 Office Phone: 310-475-8417. Office Fax: 310-474-6517. E-mail: carenrich@earthlink.net.

RICH, DORIS L., writer; b. Saginaw, Mich., Aug. 19, 1920; d. Henry G. Logeman and Mary Alice Corcoran; m. Stanley Rich, June 15, 1948; children: Chris, Lawrence, Deborah. BA, Am. U., Washington, 1972. Reporter Flint (Mich.) Jour., 1941—44; field asst. ARC, Guam, 1944—45; civilian pub. info. officer U.S. Army, Republic of Korea, 1947—48; freelance reporter Hong Kong, Thailand, 1956—70; tchr. Kau Yan Coll., Hong Kong, 1966, Internat. Sch., Accra, Ghana, 1980—82; biographer Smithsonian Instn. Press, Washington, 1989—98. Author: Amelia Earhart: A Biography, 1989, Queen Bess: Daredevil Aviator, 1993, The Magnificent Moisants, 1998. Mem.: Soc. Women Geographers (bd. dirs. 2003—04). Democrat. Roman Catholic. Home: 8100 Conn Ave Apt 403 Chevy Chase MD 20815

RICH, DOROTHY KOVITZ, educational association administrator, writer; BA in Journalism and Psychology, Wayne U.; MA, Columbia U.; EdD, Catholic U. Founder, pres. The Home and Sch. Inst., Inc., Washington, 1964—. Adv. coun. Nat. Health Edn. Consortium; adv. com. Ctr. for Workplace Prep. and Quality Edn., U.S. C. of C.; mem. readiness to learn task force U.S. Dept. Edn., urban edn. team Coun. Gt. City Schs.; legislative nat. initiatives including work on Family/Sch. Partnership Act, 1989, Improving America's Edn. Act, 1994; formulator New Partnerships for Student Achievement program, 1987; creator MegaSkills Edn. Ctr. The Home and Sch. Inst. Inc., 1990; designer MegaSkills Leader Tng. for Parent Workshops, 1988, MegaSkills Essentials for the Classroom, 1991, Learning and Working program for sch.-to-work initiatives, 1996, Career Megaskills, 1999, New MegaSkills Bond Tchr./Parent Partnership, 1994, Career MegaSkills materials and tng., 1998, Adult MegaSkills for Profl. Growth, 1999, MegaSkills Behavior Mgmt. Kit, 2002; developer NEA/MegaSkills nat. mentor tng. initiative, 2000-06, MegaSkills for the Job, 2002, Adult MegaSkills and MegaSkills for Teachers, 2002-06, MegaSkills for Teachers Video Programs, 2003, edn. columns McClatchy Ridder News Svc., 2004-06. Author: MegaSkills in School in Life: The Best Gift You Can Give Your Child, 1988, rev. edit., 1992, What Do We Say? What Do We Do? Vital Solutions for Children's Educationsl Success, 1997, MegaSkills, 3d edit., 1997, 18 tng. books, MegaSkills: Building Children's Achievement for the Information Age, new and expanced edit., 1998, Improving Student Teaching through MegaSkills, All Around the House (early childhood literacy curriculum), 2005, The MegaSkills Way to Reading for Preschool, 2005, New MegaSkills Infancy/Toddler Curriculum, 2006, New Megaskill Respect, 2006; TV appearances include The Learning Channel, NBC Today Show, Good Morning Am.; subject of videos nat. edn. programs in Thailand, Singapore and China: Families and Schools: Teaming for Success, Survival Guide for Today's Parents. Recipient Am. Woman Leader award, Citation U.S. Dept. Edn., Nat. Gov.'s Assn., Alumni Achievement award in edn. Cath. U., 1992, Golden Apple award for MegaSkills Tchrs. Coll., Columbia U., 1996; grantee John D. and Catherine T. MacArthur Found.; named Washingtonian of Yr., ADv. Bd. of McNeil-Lehrer NewsHour, 2004. Mem. Nat. Press Club. Office: MegaSkills Edn Ctr Home and Sch Inst Inc 1500 Massachusetts Ave NW Washington DC 20005-1821 Office Phone: 202-466-3633. Business E-Mail: edstaff@megaskills.org.

RICH, MARY RUTH, music educator; b. Houston, June 20, 1953; d. George Minor and Dolores Tidwell; m. Jerry E. Rich, Jan. 3, 1976; children: Michael Jaye, Jennifer Jane. B.Mus., Baylor U., Waco, Tex., 1975; M.Mus., Baylor U., 1978. Instr. Ind.-Purdue U., Ft. Wayne, Ind., 1987—93; assoc. prof., chair dept. music Lon Morris Coll., Jacksonville, Tex., 1993—, chair divsn. fine arts, 2004—; faculty Baylor U. - Summer Piano Inst., Waco, Tex., 2000—. Adjudicator, Tex., 1993—; pianist, recitals, 1995—; presenter Piano Wellness Seminar, NC, 2001—02, La. State U., 2003—04, U. Tex., Arlington, 2005. Mem.: Music Tchrs. Nat. Assn., Tex. Music Tchrs. Assn. Office: Lon Morris College 800 College Ave Jacksonville TX 75766 Office Phone: 903-589-4127. E-mail: mrich@lonmorris.edu.

RICH, MELODY M., music educator, singer, conductor; d. Kenneth Eugene and Masonia Arquilos; 1 child, Asa Santos. MusB, U. Tex., 1988, MusM, 1994, MusD, 2003. Voice instr. Judson HS, Converse, Tex., 1987—96; adj. instr. U. Incarnate Word, San Antonio, 1995—2000; assoc. minister music Christ Episcopal Ch., San Antonio, 1992—2004; lectr. U. Tex., San Antonio, 2000—; asst. conductor San Antonio Choral Soc., 2004—. Pet partner amb. Delta Soc., San Antonio, 1996—99. Mem.: Tex. Choral Dir. Assn., Am. Choral Dir. Assn., Nat. Assn. Tchrs. of Singing (v.p. 1998—2000, treas. 2001—03). Episcopal. Office: U Tex Dept Music 6900 N Loop 1604 W San Antonio TX 78249 Office Phone: 210-458-5333. Personal E-mail: melodyrich@earthlink.net. Business E-Mail: melody.rich@utsa.edu.

RICH, NANCY JEAN, lawyer; b. Chgo., June 11, 1959; d. John Keith and Phyllis Vallerie (Delaney) R. AB with honors, Loyola U., Chgo., 1981, JD, 1984. Bar: Ill. 1984, U.S. Dist. Ct. (no. dist.) Ill. 1984. Asst. atty. gen. environ. control div. Ill. Atty. Gen.'s Office, Chgo., 1984-87; assoc. Isham, Lincoln & Beale, Chgo., 1987-88, Sidley & Austin, Chgo., 1988-89, Bell, Boyd & Lloyd, Chgo., 1989-91, ptnr., 1992, Katten Muchin Zavis Rosenman, Chgo. Bd. dirs. Pub. Interest Law Initiative. Contbr. to Loyola Consumer Law Reporter, 1991. Adminstrv. asst. Hartigan for Atty. Gen. Campaign, Chgo., 1982; bd. dirs. Suburban Area Agy. on Aging, 1990-2004, pres. bd. dirs., 1999-2001, chmn. resource devel. com., 1991—. Mem. ABA, Ill. Bar Assn., Chgo. Bar Assn. (environ. law com.). Office: Katten Muchin Zavis Rosenman 525 W Monroe St Chicago IL 60661 Office Phone: 312-902-5536. Office Fax: 312-577-8676. Business E-Mail: nancy.rich@kattenlaw.com. E-mail: nancy.rich@kmzr.com.

RICH, S. JUDITH, public relations executive; b. Chgo., Apr. 14; d. Irwin M. and Sarah I. (Sandock) R. BA, U. Ill., 1960. Staff writer, reporter Economist Newspapers, Chgo., 1960—61; asst. dir. pub. rels. and communications Coun. Profit Sharing Industries, Chgo., 1961—62; dir. advt. and pub. rels. Chgo. Indsl. Dist., 1962—63; account exec., account supr., v.p., sr. v.p., exec. v.p. and nat. creative dir. Edelman Pub. Rels. Worldwide, Chgo., 1963—85; exec. v.p., dir. Ketchum Pub. Rels. Worldwide, Chgo., 1985—89, exec. v.p., exec. creative dir. USA, 1990—97, exec. v.p., chief creative officer worldwide, 1998—2001; pres. Rich Rels. A Creativity Consultancy, Chgo., 2002—. Frequent spkr. on creativity and brainstorming; workshop facilitator. Contbr. articles to popular mags. Mem. pub. rels. adv. bd. U. Chgo. Grad Sch. Bus., Roosevelt U., Chgo., DePaul U., Chgo., Gov.'s State U. Recipient Pub. Rels. All-Star award for Creativity, Inside PR mag., 1999. Mem. Pub. Rels. Soc. Am. (Silver Anvil award, judge Silver Anvil awards), Counselors Acad. of Pub. Rels. Soc. Am. (exec. bd.), Chgo. Publicity Club (8 Golden Trumpet awards). Avocations: theater, swimming, bicycling, racquetball. Office: Rich Rels A Creative Consultancy Ste 2603 2500 N Lakeview Ave Chicago IL 60614

RICHARD, CANDACE L., music educator; d. James S. and Nelda M. (Northrup) Terrill; m. Loren D. Richard, July 20, 1974; children: Christopher L., Colby A. MusB in Edn., Emporia State U., 1970; MusM, Kans. State U., 1993. Cert. tchr. Kans. Vocal music tchr. Unified Sch. Dist. 322, Onaga, Kans., 1970—73, Unified Sch. Dist. 457, Garden City, Kans., 1973—76; vocal and instrumental music tchr. Trinity Cath. HS, Hutchinson, Kans., 1982—84; applied vocal music instr. Cloud County CC, Concordia, Kans., 1985—2000; vocal music tchr. Unified Sch. Dist. 333, Concordia, 1990—2000, Unified Sch. Dist. 480, Liberal, Kans., 2000—. Choral clinician, adjudicator, Kans. Bd. dirs. Cmty. Concert Assn., Concordia, 1987—2000, Liberal, 2000—04, Live on Stage II, 2004—. Mem.: NEA, Music Edn. Nat. Conf., Seward County Hist. Soc., DAR, PEO, Delta Kappa Gamma. Lutheran. Avocation: genealogy.

RICHARD, DIANA MARIE, army officer; b. Dallas, Mar. 24, 1958; d. Dee Will and Dorothy Mae (Scott) R. B.S. with honors, Tex. Coll., 1980; student Dallas Bapt. Coll., 1975-76; M.S., Boston U., 1985. Commd. 2d lt., U.S. Army, 1980, advanced through grades to maj., 1983, bn. chem. officer, Stuttgart, Germany, 1983, corps officer, Nellingen, Ger., 1984-86; asst. prof. mil. sci. Prairie View Agrl. and Mech. U., 1987—, bde chem. officer, Hanau, Germany, 1991-95, sr. divsn. chief engr., Ft. Hood, Tex., 1997-99, hr analyst, City of Dallas, 1999—. Mem. Soc. Chem. Officers, NAACP, Delta Sigma Theta. Democrat. Baptist. Lodge: Mem. Order Eastern Star.

RICHARD, ELLEN, theater executive; b. Bridgeport, Conn., Dec. 12, 1957; d. Laurent and Anne (Markham) R. Bus. mgr. Atlas Scenic Studio, Bridgeport, 1977-82; theater mgr. Stamford (Conn.) Ctr. for Arts, 1980-83; bus. mgr. Westport (Conn.) Country Playhouse, 1982-84; gen. mgr. Roundabout Theatre Co. Inc., N.Y.C., 1983—; dir. design and constrn. Am. Airlines Theatre, Studio 54, Harold and Mirium Steinberg Ctr. Theatre, Laurel Pels Theatre, various Broadway Theatres. Dir. design and constrn. Am. Airlines Theatre, Studio 54, Harold and Miriam Steinberg Ctr. for Theatre, Laura Pels Theatre, Broadway theatres. Mng. dir.: (Broadway plays) A View From the Bridge, 1997-98 (Tony award Revival of a Play 1998), Cabaret, 1998-2004 (Tony award Revival of a Musical 1998), The Deep Blue Sea, 1998, Side Man, 1998-99 (Tony award Best Play 1999), Little Me, 1998-1999, Death of a Salesman, 1999, The Lion in Winter, 1999, The Rainmaker, 1999-2000, Uncle Vanya, 2000, The Man Who Came to Dinner, 2000, Betrayal, 2000-01, Design for Living, 2001, Major Barbara, 2001, The Women, 2001-02, An Almost Holy Picture, 2002, The Crucible, 2002, The Man Who Had All the Luck, 2002, An Evening with Mario Cantone, 2002, The Boys from Syracuse, 2002, Tartuffe, 2003, A Day in the Death of Joe Egg, 2003, As Long As We Both Shall Laugh, 2003, Nine, 2003 (Tony award Best Revival of a Musical, 2003), The Look of Love, 2003, "MASTER HAROLD".and the boys, 2003, Big River, 2003, The Caretaker, 2003-04, Twentieth Century, 2004, Assassins, 2004 (Tony award Best Revival of a Musical, 2004); prodr.: Sideman, 1999 (Tony award New Play). Mem. NY Cycling Club. Avocations: bicycling, antiques, art, sailing. Office: 203 Brewster St Bridgeport CT 06605-3112 Personal E-mail: ellrch2@aol.com.

RICHARD, VIRGINIA RYNNE, lawyer; b. Mt. Vernon, N.Y., Aug. 6, 1943; m. Peter L. Richard. BA, Manhattanville Coll., 1965; LLB, NYU, 1969. Bar: N.Y. 1969, Colo. 1973, U.S. Supreme Ct. 1992. Pvt. practice, Denver, 1973-75; assoc. Kane, Dalsimer, Sullivan, N.Y.C., 1970-72, 76-82, ptnr., 1982—99, Winston & Strawn LLP, N.Y.C., 1999—, mem. exec. com., chair IP practice group. Chmn. trademark appeals com. Fed. Cir. Bar Assn., 1991-93; spkr. in field. Mem. editl. bd. Trademark Reporter, 1988-89; contbr. articles to profl. jours. Mem. ABA, Internat. Trademark Assn., U.S. Trademark Assn. (trademark reporter, mem. editorial bd., chmn. subcom. 1982-87), N.Y. Patent, Trademark and Copyright Lawyers Assn., NY Intellectual Property Law Assn. (chair copyright law com. 1994-96). Office: Winston & Strawn LLP 200 Park Ave New York NY 10166-4193 Office Phone: 212-294-4639. Office Fax: 212-294-4700. Business E-Mail: vrichard@winston.com.

RICHARDS, ANITA HENSON, special education educator; b. Houston, July 25, 1956; d. Clyde J. Henson and Jacqueline Morgan Henson Berch BA Tchg. English, Sam Houston State U., 1981; MA Psychology, Houston Bapt. U., 1995. Cert. in secondary English, history, psychology and generic spl. edn., K-12. Tchr. spl. edn. Cypress-Fairbanks Ind. Sch. Dist., Houston, 1982—95. Vol. Gulf Pines Hosp., 1991-93; 4-H leader Waller County, 1990-91, Harris County, 1981-83 Mem. APA, Am. Paint Horse Assn., Pinto Horse Assn., S.E. Tex. Pinto Club (bd. dirs. 1990-91, sec. 1987), Psi Chi (treas. 1993, 94), Alpha Sigma Lambda. Avocations: raising and showing paint and pinto horses, reading. Home: 1415 County Rd 3200 Crockett TX 75835

RICHARDS, ANN ADAIR, psychologist; b. Tulsa, Okla., Jan. 28, 1949; d. William Jenkins and Virginia Ann (Daniels) Richards; 1 child, Desiree Ann Perkins. BS in bus. edn., U. Okla., 1970; BA in theatre arts, U. No. Colo., 1983, MA in agy. counseling, 1985, EdS, 2002. Nationally Certified School Psychologist, lic. Professional Counselor Colo. Regulatory Bd. Workshop coord. Rocky Mtn. Planned Parenthood, Denver, 1977—79; para profl., remedial reading Denver Pub. Schools, 1979—80; generalist clinician Centennial Mental Health Ctr., 1986—95; children and family therapist No. Range Behavior Health, Greely, Colo., 1995—99; pvt. practice Greely, 1999—2000; sch. psychologist intern Northeast Bd. Cooperative Ednl. Svcs., Haxton, Colo., 2000—01; sch. psychologist East Ctrl. Bd. Cooperative Ednl. Svcs., Limon, Colo., 2001—. Mem. crisis response team Colo. Soc. Sch. Psychologists, 2004—; crisis response coord. East Ctrl. Bd. Cooperative Ednl. Svcs., 2001—; chair and vice chair Logan County Sexual Assault Team, Sterling, Colo., 1989—95. Spl. olympics vol. Sterling H.S., 1992—94; bd. mem. Yuma Cmty. Resource Ctr., Yuma, Colo., 1986—88; bdm. mem. Help for Abused Ptnrs., Sterling, Colo., 1989—95, sec., 1989—95; com. mem. Arts Picnic, Greeley, Colo., 1983. Recipient Women of the Yr., Beta Sigma Phi Social Svc. Sorority, 2000, Scholarship, Am. Assn. of U. Women; Circle Key Alumni grant, Kappa Kappa Gamma Found., 1994, 1995, Mildred Guch Scholarship, U. No. Colo., 1984—85. Mem.: Colo. Soc. Sch. Psychologists, Nat. Assn. Sch. Psychologist. Democrat. Luth. Avocations: weightlifting, aerobics, movies, reading, interior decorating. Home: 15400 CR L Box 180 Woodrow CO 80757 Office: East Ctrl Bd Ednl Svcs 820 2d St Limon CO 80828

RICHARDS, CARMELEETE A., computer company executive, network administrator, consultant; b. Springport, Ind., Feb. 8, 1948; d. Gordon K. and Virginia Christine (New) Brown; 1 child, Annasheril. AA in Elem. Edn., No. Okla. Coll., 1969; BS in Edn., Southwestern State Coll., Weatherford, Okla., 1971; postgrad., Ashland (Ohio) Coll., 1981—, U. Phoenix, 1994—; MEd in Instrnl. Design, Am. Intercontinental U., 2004. Cert. tchr. Ohio. 6th grade tchr., Scott City, Kans., 1971; salesperson, customer svc. Jafra Cosmetics, 1979-81; br. asst. mgr. Barclays Am. Fin., Columbus, 1981-84; tng. mgr., ednl. dir. Computer Depot, Columbus, Ohio, 1984-85; corp. trainer, exec. sales Litel Telecommunications, Worthington, Ohio, 1985-87; communications cons. Telemarketing Communications of Columbus, Ohio, 1988-89; corp. computer tng. O/E Learning, Troy, Mich., 1989-98; corp. computer trainer ETOP Cols., Ohio, 1989—; dist. asst. network adminstr. Bexley Sch. Dist., 1998-99; dir. tech., computer instr. MCS, 2001—02; info. tech. specialist, trainer Franklin County Common Pleas Ct., 2002—. Pres. PTA, 1981—82. Recipient Outstanding Participation award Dorothy Carnegie Pub. Speaking; winner Ms. Ohio Beauties of Am. Pageant, 1991. Mem. IEEE, NAFE, Am. Soc. for Tng. and Devel., Columbus Computer Soc., Kappa Delta Pi. Baptist. Avocations: western square dancing, bowling, boating, reading, hiking. Office Phone: 614-462-6792. Personal E-mail: bkar10@yahoo.com.

RICHARDS, CAROL ANN RUBRIGHT, retired editor, retired journalist; b. Buffalo, Sept. 24, 1944; d. Jesse Bailey and Emma Amanda (Fisher) Rubright; m. Clay F. Richards, Aug. 12, 1967; children: Elizabeth Amanda, Rebecca Diana. BA, Syracuse U., 1966. Reporter Rochester (N.Y.) Times-Union, 1966; legis. corr. Gannett News Svc., Albany, NY, 1967-73, White House corr. Washington, 1974-76, regional/nat. editor, 1979-84; founding editor USA Today, Arlington, Va., 1982, mem. editl. bd., 1985-87; dep. editor editl. page Newsday, Melville, NY, 1987—2006; ret., 2006. Adj. prof. journalism Hofstra U., Hempstead, NY, 2006—; freelance editor. Pres. Washington Press Club, 1981-82. Mem.: Women's Press Club N.Y. (named to Hall of Honor 2003), Nat. Press Club. Home: 352 Scudder Ave Northport NY 11768-3021 Office: Newsday 235 Pinelawn Rd Melville NY 11747-4250 Office Phone: 631-896-4571. Business E-Mail: carol.richards@yahoo.com, carol.richards@hofstra.edu.

RICHARDS, CECILE, healthcare network executive; b. 1958; d. Ann Richards; married; 3 children. Grad., Brown U., 1980. Dep. chief of staff to Rep. Nancy Pelosi US Ho. Reps., Washington; founder, pres. America Votes, Washington, 2003—06; pres. Planned Parenthood Fedn. of Am., Inc., NYC, 2006—. Bd. dirs. NARAL Pro-Choice Am., Planned Parenthood Action Fund; founder, bd. dirs. Tex. Freedom Network, 1995. Democrat. Office: Planned Parenthood Fedn Am Inc 434 W 33rd St New York NY 10001-2601 Office Phone: 212-541-7800. Office Fax: 212-245-1845.*

RICHARDS, CHRISTINE P., transportation services executive; b. Amityville, NY, Jan. 8, 1955; BA magna cum laude, Bucknell U., 1976; JD, Duke U., 1979. Bar: Tenn. 1987, NC 1980. Joined FedEx Corp., 1984, corp. v.p. customer and bus. transactions & gen. counsel FedEx Corp. Services, exec. v.p., gen. counsel, sec., 2005—. Office: FedEx Corp 942 S Shady Grove Rd Memphis TN 38120 Office Phone: 901-818-7500. Office Fax: 901-395-2000.

RICHARDS, DENISE, actress; b. Downers Grove, Ill., Feb. 17, 1971; m. Charlie Sheen, June 15, 2002 (separated 2006); children: Sam, Lola. Former model. Actor: (films) Loaded Weapon 1, 1993, Nowhere, 1997, Starship Troopers, 1997, Wild Things, 1998, Lookin' Italian, 1998, Drop Dead Gorgeous, 1999, The World is Not Enough, 1999, Tail Lights Fade Away, 1999, Valentine, 2001, Good Advice, 2001, Empire, 2002, Undercover Brother, 2002, The Third Wheel, 2002, You Stupid Man, 2002, Love Actually, 2003, Scary Movie 3, 2003; (TV films) 919 5th Avenue, 1995, In The Blink of an Eye, 1996, Pier 66, 1996, (guest appearances): (TV series) Spin City, Melrose Place. Office: 722 Elvira Ave #A Redondo Beach CA 90277*

RICHARDS, JACQUELINE, artist, curator; b. Chgo., July 25, 1930; d. Harris Nathan Turner and Henrietta Singer; m. Seymour Richards, Dec. 22, 1949 (div. Dec. 1973); children: Robin, Philip. BS in Cmty. Health, Ga. State U., 1978; postgrad. in art history, U. Chgo., 1949—50; postgrad. in art theory and design, The New Bauhaus, Chgo., 1947—49. Registered dietitian Am. Dietetic Assn., lic. State of Ga. Clin. dietitian Griffin-Spalding Hosp., Griffin, Ga., 1980—86, R.T. Jones Hosp., Canton, Ga., 1986—88; artist, painter Atlanta, 1988—; curator Northside Atlanta Libr., 2004—05. Exhbn. designer Fulton County Librs., Atlanta, 2004—. Illustrated Raymond Lowey Designs an Automobile for Studebaker, 1950; Fanciful Paintings of Porché Motor Car for Automobile Atlanta, 1993, 100 black ink drawings of The Rubaiyat of Omar Khayyam. 1965, one-woman shows include Art Inst. Chgo., 1952—, Northside Atlanta Libr., 2002—03, exhibited in group shows at Am. Fedn. Arts, 1952—59, House of Colors, 2001—. Achievements include development of hypoallergenic skin cream for cancer patients. Avocation: restoration of art objects. Home: 3601 Piedmont Rd Apt 804 Atlanta GA 30305 Office Phone: 404-310-9978.

RICHARDS, KYUNGNYUN KIM, Korean language educator, poet, translator; b. Seoul, Nov. 12, 1940; came to U.S., 1967; d. Johyun and Pongsoon (Ohm) Kim; m. Steffen Francis Richards, June 19, 1971; children: James, Kathleen. BA in French, Ewha Womans U., 1963, MA in French, 1966; MA in Linguistics, U. Calif., Berkeley, 1978. Instr. San Francisco C.C., 1974-80; edn. coord. The Korean Ctr., Inc., San Francisco, 1978-80; lectr. U. Calif., Berkeley, 1980—. Cons. Calif. Dept. of Edn., Sacramento, 1990-91, City Coll. of San Francisco, 1990-91, San Francisco Unified Sch. Dist., 1994-95. Author: College Korean, 1992, Handbook for Teaching Korean-American Students, 1992; contbr. articles and poems to profl. publs.; translator: Dictee, 1997, 2003, Sky, Wind and Stars: Poems by Yun Dong-ju, 2003, I Want To Hijack An Airplane, by Kim Seung-hee, 2004, The Love of Dunhuang, by Yun Humyong, 2005. Bd. dirs. Asian Community Mental Health, Oakland, 1990—. Mem. Internat. Circle of Linguistics, Internat. Assn. of Korean Lang. Educators, Am. Assn. of Tchrs. of Korean (bd. dirs.). Office: U Calif Dept Of East Asian Lang Cutures Berkeley CA 94720-0001

RICHARDS, LACLAIRE LISSETTA JONES (MRS. GEORGE A. RICHARDS), social worker; b. Pine Bluff, Ark. d. Artie William and Geraldine (Adams) Jones; m. George Alvarez Richards, July 26, 1958; children: Leslie Rosario, Lia Mercedes. BA, Nat. Coll. Christian Workers, 1953; MSW, U. Kans., 1956; postgrad, Columbia U., 1960. Diplomate Clin. Social Work, Am. Bd. of Examiners in Clin. Social Work, Nat. Assn. Social Workers; cert. gerontologist. Psychiat., supr., tchg., cmty. orgn., adminstrv., cons. Hastings Regional Ctr., Ingleside, Nebr., 1956-60; supr., cons., adminstrv. VA Hosp., Knoxville, Iowa, 1960-74; field instr. for grad. students U. Mo., 1969-74, 78-90, com. chmn., 1969-70; sr. social worker Mental Health Inst., Cherokee, Iowa, 1974-77; adj. asst. prof. dept. social behavior U. S.D., Cherokee, Iowa, 1974-77, instr. dept. psychiat., 1988-96, Augustina Coll., 1981-86; outpatient social worker VA Med. and Regional Office Ctr., Sioux Falls, SD, 1978-96, med., surg. and intensive care social worker, 1992-96, 1990-92, sur. and intermediate care social worker, 1992-96. EEO counselor. EEO counselor. Mem. Knoxville Juvenile adv. com., 1963-65, 68-70, sec., 1965-66, chmn., 1966-68; sec. Urban Renewal Citizens' adv. com., Knoxville, 1966-68; mem. United Meth. Ch. task force Expt. Styles Ministry and Leadership, 1973-74, adult choir, ch. and society com.; counselor Knoxville Youth Line program; sec. exec. com. Vis. Nurse Assn., 1979-80; canvasser cmty. fund drs., Knoxville; active Cherokee Civil Rights Commn.; bd. dirs., pub. rels., devel. and program devel. cons. YWCA, 1983-85; bd. dirs. Family Svc. Agy., 1989-90, Food Svcs. Ctr., Inc., 1992-96; active SD Symphonic Choir, 1991—, Youth-At-Risk Task Force and Multicultural Ctr. Advocate; deaconess 1st Evang. Free Ch., 1999-2004. Named S.D. Social Worker of Yr., 1983. Mem. NAACP (chmn. edn. com. 1983-85), AAUW (sec. Hastings chpt. 1958-60), Nat. Assn. Social Workers (co-chmn. Nebr. chpt. profl. standards com. 1958-59), Acad. Cert. Social Workers, S.D. Assn. Social Workers (chmn. minority affairs com., v.p. S.E. region 1980, pres. 1980-82, exec. com. 1985-84, mem. social policy and action com.), Nebr. Assn. Social Workers (chmn. 1958-59), Seventh Dist. S.D. Med. Soc. Aux., Coalition on Aging., Nat. Assn. Social Workers (qualified clin. social worker 1991—), Methodist (Sunday Sch. tchr. adult divsn.; mem. commn. on edn.; mem. Core com. for adult edn.; mem. Adult Choir; mem. Social Concerns Work Area). Home: 1701 E Ponderosa Dr Sioux Falls SD 57103-5019

RICHARDS, LYNN, company training executive, consultant; b. Kansas City, Mo., Sept. 2, 1949; d. Robert A. and Betty (Arnold) Nelson. BS in Edn., U. Kans., 1971; MA in Edn., San Diego State U., 1979. Prin. staff ORI, Inc., Silver Spring, Md., 1980-81; sr. corp. trainer Amerada Hess Corp., Woodbridge, N.J., 1981-83; tng. and devel. mgr. Kimberly-Clark Corp., Beech Island, S.C., 1983-85; orgn. devel. mgr. M&M Mars, Hackettstown, N.J., 1985-89; corp. tng. and devel. mgr. Rohr, Inc., Chula Vista, Calif., 1989-93; customer edn. mgr. ComputerVision, Corp., San Diego, 1993-95; leadership devel. cons. Children's Hosp., San Diego, 1995-97; learning tech. cons. Hewlett-Packard Co., San Diego, 1997-98, site learning ctr. mgr., 1998-99; dir. edn. svcs. N.Am. Peregrine Sys., San Diego, 1999—2001. Cons. in field. Contbr. articles to profl. mags. Mem.: Internat. Soc. Productivity Improvement (chmn. awards com. 1988, presdl. citations, achievement awards).

RICHARDS, PATRICIA JONES, artist, poet, musician, composer; b. Pomona, Calif., Nov. 20; d. Earle Feurte Jones and Florence Frable Slawson; m. Addison Whitaker Richards, May 1, 1950 (dec. Mar. 1964). BA, Pomona Coll., 1944; cert. nursery sch. tchr., Scripps Coll., 1944. Acquistions libr. Calif. State Polytechnic U., Pomona, 1979-85. Author: Self-Expression-Poems and Watercolors, 1996, "Old Friends" Through Sun and Showers, 1997, Pensativo-Poems and Watercolors (Golden Leaves award 1996-97, 99-2000), 2000, Afterthoughts - Poems and Watercolors, 2004; pianist Jazz CD, To a Woven Fitness, 2001; co-author, composer A Twist of Hate, a musical, 2004. Personal E-mail: patpj3@yahoo.com.

RICHARDS, PHYLLIS ANDERSON, nurse, health service executive; b. Stuart, Iowa, Sept. 9. 1929; d. John Edward and Verna Mae (Hully) Anderson; m. Herbert Montaque, Mar. 16, 1956; children— Pamela, Herbert, III, Patricia, John. B.S. in Nursing, U. Wash., 1948-53. Surgery nurse Swedish Hosp., Seattle, 1953-54, 1954-56; delivery nurse Kapiolani, Honolulu, 1954; nurse Hawaii Prep. Acad., Kamuela, 1969-90, dir. health services, 1983-90; bd. dirs. Hawaii Island Hosp. Council, 1960-70, Lucy Henriques Med. Center, Kamuela, 1981—96, North Hawaii Cmty. Hosp, 1996—; Bd. dirs., ARC, 1970-83, instr. 1970-88; bd. dirs. Girl Scouts council Pacific Hawaii, 1969. Recipient Alumni award Hawaii Prep. Acad. Alumni, 1983, Thanks award Girls Scouts U.S.A. Mem. Am. Nurses Assn. Club: Hawaiian Republican. Home: Kahua Ranch PO Box 837 Kamuela HI 96743-0837 Office: Hawaii Preparatory Acad Kamuela HI 96743 Office Phone: 808-882-4646.

RICHARDS, PRISCILLA ANN, medical/surgical nurse; b. Providence, Nov. 10, 1949; d. Frank L. Thornton and Dorothy A. Maker; children: Tanya Rene, Jason Edward. Assoc. Degree Nursing, Lincoln Land C.C., Springfield, Ill., 1980. RN Ill., 1980, R.I., 1997. Cert. nursing asst. Meml. Med. Ctr., Springfield, 1971—73, lic. practical nurse, 1973—80, RN, 1980—97, South County Nursing and Subacute Ctr., North Kingstown, RI, 1997—2000, Elmhurst Extended Care, Providence, 2000—05, Maxim Health Care, Providence, 2005—. Sgt. USAF, 1968—71. Baptist. Avocations: reading, swimming, yard work. Home: 71 Wells Ave Warwick RI 02889 Personal E-mail: paramanri@aol.com.

RICHARDS, SUZANNE V., lawyer; b. Columbia, SC, Sept. 7, 1927; d. Raymond E. and Elise C. (Gray) R. AB, George Washington U., 1948, JD with distinction, 1957, LLM, 1959. Bar: D.C. 1958. Sole practice, Washington, 1974—. Lectr. in family and probate law; mem. D.C. Jud. Conf., 1975—2006. Bd. dirs. Coun. for Ct. Excellence. Recipient John Bell Larner award George Washington U., 1958; named Woman Lawyer of Yr., Women's Bar Assn. D.C., 1977. Mem. ABA (ho. of dels. 1988-90), Bar Assn. D.C. (pres. 1989-90, named Lawyer of Yr. 2002), Women's Bar Assn. (pres. 1977-78), Trial Lawyers Assn. of D.C. (bd. govs. 1978-82, 85-2001, treas. 1982-85), D.C. Bar. Home: 530 N St SW Washington DC 20024-4546 Office: PO Box 65466 Washington DC 20035-5466

RICHARDS, VANA JEAN, elementary school educator; b. Cleve, Apr. 14, 1947; d. William Carl and Arlene B. Lau; m. Steven Joseph Richards, June 19, 1971; children: Erica Jean, Aaron Patrick. BA, Humboldt State U., 1969. Cert. elem. tchr. grades K-8 Idaho State Dept. Edn., 1976, life time tchr. grades K-12 Calif. State Dept. Edn., 1969. 4th grade tchr. Healdsburg (Calif.) Elem. Sch., 1969—71; art instr. Inter-Am. U., Ramey AFB, PR, 1972—74; tchr. Horseshoe Bend (Idaho) Elem. Sch., 1977—87, Emmett (Idaho) Sch. Dist., 1998—. Part-time sci. educator Discovery Ctr. Idaho, Boise, 1998—; mem. profl. devel. com. Emmett Sch. Dist., 2001—, new tchr. peer asst., 2001—05; advisor, founder Carberry Schs. Discovery Club, Emmett, 2001—; NASA explorer sch. team lead for Carberrry Elem. Sch. Kenneth J. Carberry Intermediate Sch., Emmett, 2004—, student tchr. mentor, 2005—. Mem. judging panel Toyota Tapestry Grants for Tchrs. NSTA, Emmett, 2006—; sponsor Carberry's Mars Rover Team, Emmett, 2002—06. Finalist Presdl. award for Excellence Sci. Tchg., Idaho State Dept. Edn., 2004; named NASA Airspace Sys. Edn. Cohort, 2006—; recipient Lysol/Nat. Sci. Tchrs. Assn. Sci. Challenge award, Nat. Sci. Tchrs. Assn., 2003, Te@ch award, Best Buy, 2005, Unsung Heroes award, ING, 2005, Governor's Industry award for Notable Tchg. in Sci., Idaho Nat. Lab./Idaho State Dept. Edn., 2006; fellow, Nat. High Magnetic Field Lab., 2003; grantee, Toyota/Nat. Sci. Tchrs. Assn., 2003, Idaho Nat. Lab., 2006; Govs. grantee, Idaho State Dept. Edn., 2000, 2003, 2004, Micron Cmty. grantee, Micron Tech., 2004, Messenger Educator fellow, NASA, 2006—. Mem.: Nat. Mid. Level Sci. Tchrs. Assn. (Vincent J. Marteka Jr. award for creative sci. tchg. 2006), Idaho State Sci. Tchrs. Assn. (region III bd. mem. 2005—), Gem County Tchrs. Assn. (sec., co-pres. 1998—2004, K-6 Tchr. of Yr. Emmett Sch. Dist. 2004), Nat. Tchrs. Assn. (region III bd. mem. 2002—04), Coun. for Elem. Sci. Tchrs. Internat., Idaho Space Grant Consortium (assoc.). Office: Kenneth J Carberry Intermediate School 1950 E 12th St Emmett ID 83617 Office Phone: 208-365-0839.

RICHARDS, WANDA JAMIE, retired education educator; b. Brownwood, Tex., Jan. 11, 1930; d. William Steven and Mary (Effie) Rodgers; m. Kenneth E. Graham, Mar. 29, 1949 (div. Jan. 3, 1963); 1 child, Kenneth Jr.; m. Neill Richards, Mar. 15, 1972 (dec. Dec. 2, 1982). BA, Eastern N.Mex. U., 1962; MA, Colo. State Coll., 1964; EdD, U. No. Colo., 1966. Tchr. spl. edn. Pub. Sch., Roswell, N.Mex., 1961-63; dept. head spl. edn. Eastern N.Mex. U., Portales, 1965-69; curriculum researcher N.Mex. State U., Las Cruces, 1969-71; dir. edn. Inst. of Logopedics, Wichita, Kans., 1971-72; owner W. J. Enterprises, Kans., 1973-89; pres., treas. W.J.G. Enterprise Corp., Sedona, Ariz., 1990—. Pres.'s coun. on spl. edn. Fed. Govt., Washington, 1967-69; planning cons. in field. Contbr. articles to profl. jours. Mem. Citizens for Quality Edn., Sedona, 1991, C. of C., Sedona, 1990-91, Humane Soc., Sedona, 1991. Recipient Fellowship in Spl. Edn., Fed. Govt. Pub. Law 85962, 1963-65; named Faculty Woman of Yr., Eastern New Mex. U., 1967. Republican. Home: 30 Sedona St Sedona AZ 86351-7752 Office Phone: 928-284-0739.

RICHARDS-KORTUM, REBECCA RAE, biomedical engineering educator; b. Grand Island, Nebr., Apr. 14, 1964; d. Larry Alan and Linda Mae (Hohnstein) Richards; m. Philip Ted Kortum, May 12, 1985; children: Alexander Scott, Maxwell James, Zachary Alan. BS, U. Nebr., 1985; MS, MIT, 1987, PhD, 1990. Prof. U. Tex., Austin, 1990—, and Robert M. and Prudie Leibrock Endowed Prof., Engring., and assoc. chair, rsch., biomedical engring. dept. Prof. Howard Hughes Med. Inst., 2002—. Named Presdl. Young Investigator NSF, Washington, 1991; NSF presdl. faculty fellow, Washington, 1992; recipient Career Achievement award Assn. Advancement Med. Instrumentation, 1992, Dow Outstanding Young Faculty awd., Am. Soc. for Engring. Edn., 1992, Y.C. Fung Young Investigator award, Bioengring. Divsn., Am. Soc. of Mechanical Engrs., Howard Hughes Med. Inst. grantee in biomedical engring., 2002. Mem. AAAS, Am. Soc. Engring. Edn. (Outstanding Young Faculty award 1992), Optical Soc. Am., Am. Soc. Photobiology. Achievements include research in photochemistry, photobiology, applied optics and bioengring. Office: Dept Biomed Engring U Texas 1 U Station C0800 Austin TX 78712-0238 Office Phone: 512-471-3604. Business E-Mail: kortum@mail.utexas.edu.

RICHARDSON, ANN BISHOP, foundation executive, lawyer; b. New Rochelle, NY, Dec. 15, 1940; d. Erwin Julius and Mary Frances (Stuart) Heilemann; children: Timothy William, Lynn Patricia, Melanie Elizabeth. BA summa cum laude, Georgetown U., 1977; JD, George Washington U., 1984; cert., Oxford U., Eng., 1986. Bar: Md. 1988, DC 1989. Student counselor Amideast, Beirut, 1967-68, program specialist, 1970-73; adminstrv. asst. UN Devel. Program, Yaounde, Cameroon, 1968-70; adminstrv. mgr. Antioch Sch. Law, Washington, 1977-79; chief adminstrv. officer for internat. ops. Peace Corps, Washington, 1980-84; dir. adminstrn. and fin. African Devel. Found., Washington, 1984-87; atty. Karr and McLain, Washington, 1987-92; v.p., gen. counsel Time Dollar, Inc., Washington, 1992-98; adj. prof. law DC Sch. Law, Washington, 1994-98; prof., acad. dean U. DC David A. Clarke Sch. Law, Washington, 1998—. Bd. dirs. Bur. Rehab., Inc. Active Neighbors, Inc., Washington, 1976—, Time Dollar, Inc. Recipient Spl. Achievement award Peace Corps, 1981, 82, African Devel. Found., 1986. Mem. ABA, ACLU, DC Bar Assn., Am. Women Univ. Grads., Soc. for Internat. Devel., Phi Beta Kappa. Office: David A Clarke Sch Law 4200 Connecticut Ave NW Washington DC 20008-1122

RICHARDSON, BARBARA HULL, state legislator, social worker; b. Danville, Pa., Sept. 30, 1922; d. Robert Alonzo and Clara Lucille (Woodruff) H.; widowed; children: Barbara Follansbee, Lawrence, Christine, Lovel Pratt. BA, Bryn Mawr Coll., 1944; MSW, Smith Coll. School for Social Work, 1973. Social worker child and family svcs. divsn. children and youth svcs. HHS, Keene, N.H., 1969-71, administr. child and family svcs. Concord, N.H., 1975-88, supr. policy writers, 1988-91; mem. N.H. Ho. Reps., Concord, 1992—. Trustee Meeting Sch., 1980—; bd. dirs. Cheshire Housing Trust, 1986-93; adv. bd. Casey Family Svcs. N.H., 1990—; vol. Hospice Monadnock Region, 1991—; mem. community coun. Luth. Social Svcs. New England, 1993—; bd. dirs. Keene Day Care Ctr. Democrat. Home: 101 Morgan Rd Richmond NH 03470-4909 Office: NH Ho of Reps State Capitol Concord NH 03301

RICHARDSON, BETTY H., lawyer, former prosecutor; b. Oct. 3, 1953; BA, U. Idaho, 1976; JD, Hastings Coll. Law, 1982. Staff aide U.S. Senator Frank Church, 1976-77; tchg. asst. Hastings Coll. Law, 1980-82, 1980-82; legal rsch. asst. criminal divsn. San Francisco Superior Ct., 1982-84; jud. law clk. Chamber of Idaho Supreme Ct. Justice Robert C. Huntley Jr., 1984-86; atty. U.S. Dept. Justice, Boise, Idaho, 1993-2001, Richardson & O'Leary, Eagle, Idaho, 2001—; jud. law clk. Chamber of Chief U.S. Dist. Ct. Judge B. Lynn Winmill, Idaho, 2003—. Instr. Boise State U., 1987, 89; mem. U.S. Atty. Gen.'s Adv. Com. subcoms. on environ., civil rights and native Am. issues, others, 1993-2001; mem. hon. adv. bd. for Crime Victims Amendment in Idaho, 1994; mem. Dist. of Idaho Judges and Lawyer Reps. com., gender fairness com., Civil Justice Reform Act com. and criminal adv. com., 1993-2001; Dem. nominee Dist 1 Idaho, U.S. Ho. of Reps., 2003; adj. prof. constnl. law Boise State U., 2004; program planner Idaho State Bar and Law Found., 2004—. Mem. Idaho Indsl. Commn., 1991-93, chmn., 1993; mem. adv. bd. Family and Workplace Consortium, 1995-2001; bd. dirs. Tony Patino Fellowship. Recipient Harold E. Hughes Exceptional Svc. award Nat. Rural Inst. on Alcohol and Drug Abuse, 1999; Tony Patino fellow Hastings Coll. Law, 1982. Mem. FBA, Idaho Bar Assn. (governing coun. govt. and pub. sectors lawyers sect. 1999-01, Pro Bono Svc. award 1988), Idaho State Bar (alt. dispute resolution sect.), Idaho Women Lawyers (Kate Feltham award 2006), Idaho Legal Hist. Soc. Ptnrs. for Justice, Assistance League Boise, YMCA, City Club Boise. Office: Richardson & O'Leary 515 N 27th Boise ID 83702 Office Phone: 208-938-7900.

RICHARDSON, BROWNIE F., accountant; b. Thomaston, Ala., Nov. 29, 1945; d. Cecil G. and Mary G. Foote; divorced; 1 child, Matthew B. BS, U. South Ala., 1997; postgrad., Samford U., Birmingham, Ala., 1998-99. CPA, Ala. Acct. Dudley, Ruland & Chateau, Mobile, Ala., 1990-98, Boohaker, Schillaci & Co., Birmingham, 1998—. Mem. AICPAs, Ala. Soc. CPAs, Ga. Soc. CPAs, Beta Alpha Psi (v.p. 1996). E-mail: brownier@bsccpa.com.

RICHARDSON, DOT (DOROTHY GAY), former Olympic softball player, physician; b. Orlando, Fla., Sept. 22, 1961; m. Bob Pinto. Student, Western Ill. U.; BS in Kinesiology, UCLA; M in Exercise, Adelphi U.; MD, U. Louisville; PhD (hon.), Western Ill. U., 2003, St. Leo Coll., 2004, Adelphi U.; LLD (hon.), Phila. Coll. Osteo. Medicine, 2005. Mem., capt. US Olympic Softball Team, 1996, 2000; resident in orthopedic surg. U. Calif. Med. Ctr.; med. dir. Nat. Tng. Ctr., Clermont, Fla., 2001—. Recipient Gold medal Pan. Am. Games, 1979, 87, 95, 99, ISF Women's World Championship, 1982, 86, 90, 94, 98, South Pacific Classic, 1994, Superball Classic, 1995, Atlanta Olympics, 1996, Sydney Olympics, 2000, Medal of Honor DAR, 2005; ERV Linda Best Defensive Player in Nation award (7 times), Flo Hyman award, 2002; named All-Am. Am. Softball Assn. (16 times), MVP Am. Softball Assn. (3 times), Major Fast Pitch Nat. Championship, Player of Decade for 80s NCAA. Office: Nat Tng Ctr 1099 Citrus Tower Blvd Clermont FL 34711 E-mail: dot.richardson@orhs.org.

RICHARDSON, ELIZABETH WILSON, middle school educator; d. Sally Wilson; m. Bruce Richardson; children: Ross, Lauren. MusB in Edn., U. S.C., Columbia, 1984; MS, Furman U., Greenville, S.C., 1988. Cert. early adolescent English/lang. arts tchr. Nat. Bd., 2003. Lit. tchr. Mid. Sch., Simpsonville, SC, 1985—. Flute tchr., 1980—2006. Dir.: (middle school musicals and dramas) The King and I, Guys and Dolls, Music Man and many others (Who's Who Among America's Teachers, 3X). Grantee Helping the Homeless, S.C. Dept of Edn., 2002. Mem.: S.C. Mid. Sch. Assoc (assoc.), Internat. Reading Assoc (assoc.), Phi Delta Kappa (life), Tau Beta Sigma (life; dist. vice-pres 1983—84). Christian. Avocations: music, reading, football. Office Phone: 864-355-6690.

RICHARDSON, GRACE ELIZABETH, consumer products company executive; b. Salem, Mass., Nov. 22, 1938; d. George and Julia (Sheridan) R.; m. Ralph B. Henderson, Mar. 3, 1979. BS, Simmons Coll., 1960; MS, Cornell U., 1962; MBA, NYU, 1981. Textile technologist Harris Rsch. Lab., Washington, 1962-65; instr. Simmons Coll., Boston, 1965-66; dir. consumer edn. materials J.C. Penney, N.Y.C., 1966-73; dir. residential conservation Con Edison, N.Y.C., 1974-81; dir. consumer affairs Chesebrough-Ponds, Greenwich, Conn., 1981-85; v.p. global consumer affairs Colgate Palmolive, N.Y.C., 1985—2004; chmn. of bd. YMCA of N.Y.C., 2004—. Chair Simmons Coll. Leadership Coun., 1993—97; mem. com. Juilliard Sch., 1996—; bd. dirs. SOCAP, 1996—99, Nat. Coalition Consumer Edn., 1983—93; mem. Cornell U. Coun., chair pub. rels. com., 1988—97; bd. mem. UNIFEM, 2002—. Named Nat. Bus. Home Economist of Yr., Home Economists in Bus., 1979. Mem. Women's Forum, Cornell Club N.Y.C. (bd. dirs. 1989-96). Home: 180 E 79th St New York NY 10021-0437

RICHARDSON, JANE, retired librarian; b. Sept. 16, 1946; d. Robert Clark and Evagene (Davis) Richardson; m. Frank Velasques Martinez Jr., May 28, 1966 (div. July 1970); 1 child, Robert Louis Martinez; m. Dennis Hyduck, Dec. 1, 2001. BA in History, U. Wyo., 1971; MLibr, U. Wash., 1972. Reference and fine arts libr. Clark County Libr., 1973; dept. head Clark County Libr. Dist., 1974-77; br. supr./adminstr. Newport Beach (Calif.) Pub. Libr., 1978-82; on-call libr. Santa Ana and Newport Beach Pub. Librs., Calif. State U., Fullerton, 1984; br. adminstr. Las Vegas-Clark County Libr. Dist., 1985—2003. Mem. Freedom to Read Found. Mem. ALA, Popular Culture Assn., Nev. Libr. Assn., Mountain Plains Libr. Assn., So. Calif. On-Line Users Group, Newport Beach Profl. and Tech. Employees Assn. Office: Las Vegas Clark County Libr 833 Las Vegas Blvd N Las Vegas NV 89101-2059

RICHARDSON, JEAN BROOKS, artist, printmaker; b. Hollis, Okla., Feb. 10, 1940; d. E. Whitson and Mildred E. (Redus) Brooks; m. Ronald A. Richardson, Dec. 29, 1961 (div. 1974); children: Andrea Lynn, Karen Kathleen, Brooks Allen; m. Laurence D. Lucas, Aug. 11, 1977. BFA, Wesleyan Coll., Macon,Ga., 1961. Instr. various mus., Oklahoma City, 1971—. Subject of (books) Plains Myths and Other Tales, Turning Toward Home, The Art of Jean Richardson, 1988; subject of articles to profl. jours.; one-woman shows include Enthios Gallery, Santa Fe, 1984, John Szoke Gallery, N.Y.C., 1985, Cogswell Gallery, Vail, Colo., 1986, Robertson Gallery, Beverly Hills, Calif., 1987, Kirkpatrick Ctr. Mus., Okla. City, 1988, Four Winds Gallery, Sydney, Australia, 1988, Beth O'Donnell Gallery, Aspen, Colo., 1990, Harrington Galleries, Vancouver, B.C., Can., 1990, Merrill Chase Galleries, Washington, 1991, Lucas Gallery, Telluride, Colo., 1995, Kirkpatrick Galleries, Okla. City, Okla., 1997, JR Fine Arts, Scottsdale, Ariz., 1998, Pickard Galleries, Okla. City, 1998, Ventana Gallery, Santa Fe, 2001; represented in permanent collections Okla. State Art Collection, Okla. City, Minn. Mus. Art, Okla. State Capitol. Mem. Okla. State Arts Coun. Democrat. Presbyterian. Avocations: tennis, films. Studio: Jean Richardson Studio PO Box 720225 Oklahoma City OK 73172-0225 Office Phone: 405-728-5557. Business E-Mail: studio@jeanrichardsonstudio.com.

RICHARDSON, JEAN MCGLENN, retired civil engineer; b. Everett, Wash., Nov. 15, 1927; d. Clayton Charles and Marie Elizabeth (Mellish) McGlenn; m. William York Richardson, II, June 11, 1949; children: William York III, Paul Kress II, Clayton McGlenn. BSCE, Oreg. State U., 1949. Registered profl. engr., Ala., Oreg. Engr. Walter Schoel Engring. Co., Birmingham, Ala., 1950-54; office engr. G.C. McKinney Engring. Co., San Jose, Calif., 1972-74; civil design leader Harland Bartholomew & Assocs., Birmingham, 1974-78, Rust Engring. Co., Birmingham, 1978-82; owner, prin. Jean Richardson and Assocs. Inc., 1983-88; cons. engr. Rust Internat. Corp., 1988-90, Fed. Emergency Mgmt. Agy.; sr. engr. City of Portland, Oreg., 1991-94; ret., 1994. Women's engring. del. to China and USSR, 1984; counselor to female students on engring. as a career; state chmn. Mathcounts, Ala., 1986-88, Oreg., 1995—; mem. Girl Scout Coun., Portland, math. vol. pub. schs. Named Woman of Distinction in Engring., 1993; named to, Oreg. State U. Engr. Hall of Fame, 2000. Fellow Soc. Women Engrs.; mem. NSPE, Soc. Women Engrs. (sr. sect. rep. to nat. bd.), Ala. Soc. Profl. Engrs. (pres. Birmingham chpt., state dir., state chmn. Mathcounts, Oreg. 1991-94), Women's Golf Assn. Club, Sunriver Golf Club, Alpha Phi. Republican. Episcopalian.

RICHARDSON, JOELY, actress; b. London, Jan. 9, 1965; d. Tony Richardson and Vanessa Redgrave; m. Tim Bevan, Jan. 1992 (div. July 12, 2001); 1 child, Daisy. Actor: (films) The Hotel New Hampshire, 1984, Wetherby, 1985, Body Contact, 1987, Drowning by Numbers, 1988, King Ralph, 1992, Shining Through, 1992, Rebecca's Daughters, 1992, I'll Do Anything, 1994, Sister My Sister, 1994, Loch Ness, 1994, Hollow Reed, 1996, 101 Dalmatians, 1996, Event Horizon, 1997, Wrestling with Alligators, 1998, Under Heaven, 1998, Toy Boys, 1999, Return to Me, 2000, The Patriot, 2000, The Affair of the Necklace, 2001, Shoreditch, 2003, The Fever, 2004; (TV miniseries) Behaving Badly, 1989; (TV films) Heading Home, 1991, Lady Chatterley, 1993, The Tribe, 1998, The Echo, 1998, Fallen Angel, 2003, Lies My Mother Told Me, 2005; (TV series) Nip/Tuck, 2003—.

RICHARDSON, JUDY MCEWEN, investment banker, consultant, cartoonist; b. Appleton, Wis., June 3, 1947; d. John Mitchell and Isabel Annette (Ruble) McEwen; m. Larry Leroy Richardson, Mar. 19, 1972 (div. Oct. 1983). BA in English, Stanford U., 1968, MA in Edn., 1969; PhD in Higher Edn., U. Wash., 1975. Dir. ednl. rsch. St. Olaf Coll., Northfield, Minn., 1975-79; evaluation specialist Northwest Regional Ednl. Laboratory, Portland, 1980-82; legis. rsch. analyst Ariz. State Sen., Phoenix, 1982-87; dir. sch. fin. Ariz. Dept. Edn., Phoenix, 1987-92, assoc. supt., 1992-94; ednl. cons. Scottsdale, Ariz., 1994-96; exec. dir. Ariz. State Bd. for Sch. Capital Facilities, Phoenix, 1996-98; sch. fin. cons. Peacock, Hislop, Staley & Given, Phoenix, 1998—2002; v.p. Stone & Youngberg, Phoenix, 2002—. Cartoonist for the Ariz. Capitol Times, 1995-96. Office: Stone & Youngberg LLC 2555 E Camelback Rd Ste 280 Phoenix AZ 85016 Office Phone: 602-794-4012. Business E-Mail: jrichardson@syllc.com.

RICHARDSON, LAUREL WALUM, sociology educator; b. Chgo., July 15, 1938; d. Tyrrell Alexander and Rose (Foreman) R.; m. Herb Walum, Dec. 27, 1959 (div. 1972); children: Benjamin, Joshua; m. Ernest Lockridge, Dec. 12, 1981. AB, U. Chgo., 1955, BA, 1956; PhD, U. Colo., 1963. Asst. prof. Calif. State U., Los Angeles, 1962-64; postdoctoral fellow Sch. Medicine Ohio State U., Columbus, 1964-65, asst. prof. sociology, 1970-75, assoc. prof., 1975-79; prof. sociology Sch. Medicine Ohio State U., Columbus, 1979—, prof. cultural studies, edn. policy and leadership; asst. prof. sociology Denison U., Granville, Ohio, 1965-69. Mem. editl. bd. Jour. Contemporary Ethnography, Symbolic Interaction, Gender and Soc., Qualitative Sociology, The Sociol. Quar.; disting. lectr. Acad. Creative Writing, U. Iceland, 2005; Miegunyah disting. fellow U. Melbourne, 2006. Author: Dynamics of Sex and Gender, 1977, 3d edit. 1988, The New Other Woman, 1985, Die Neve Andere, 1987, A Nova Outra Mulher, 1987, Writing Strategies: Reaching Diverse

Audiences, 1990, Gender and University Teaching: A Negotiated Difference, 1995; editor: Feminist Frontiers, 1983, 5th edit., 2000, Fields of Play Constructing an Academic Life, 1997 (Charles H. Cooley award for best sociology book 1998), (with Ernest Lockridge) Travels with Ernest: Crossing the Literary/Sociological Divide, 2004; assoc. editor Symbolic Interaction; author more than 100 rsch. articles and papers. Ford Found. fellow, 1954-56; NSF dissertation fellow, 1960-62; post doctoral fellow Vocat. Rehab., Columbus, 1964; grantee Ohio Dept. Health, 1986-87, Nat. Inst. Edn., 1981-82, NIMH, 1972-74, NSF, 1963-64, NEH, 1992; internat. fellow Copenhagen, 2000, Iceland, 2005, Mienhalow Fellow, Melbourne, 2006; recipient Disting. Affirmative Action award Ohio State U., 1983, Feminist Mentor award, 1998. Mem. Am. Sociol. Assn. (com. on coms. 1980-81, com. on pub. info. 1987—), North Ctrl. Sociol. Assn. (pres. 1986-87), Sociologists for Women in Soc. (coun. mem. 1978-80), Ctrl. Ohio Sociologists for Women in Soc. (past pres.), Women's Poetry Workshop, Soc. for Study of Symbolic Interaction (publs. com.). Avocations: hiking, poetry, book arts. E-mail: richardson.9@osu.edu.

RICHARDSON, LYNN, art educator; b. N.Y.C., June 5, 1950; d. Seymour Harold and Patrie W. Samuels; m. Samuel A. Nogroski (div.); children: Michael D. Nogroski, Ellen Sara Knouse; m. Paul Alton Richardson, Apr. 20, 1984; children: Steve Bennett, Renee Trapane, April Mader. AA, Art Inst., Houston, Tex., 1980; BA, U. Houston, Tex., 1985. Cert. tchr. Tex. Substitute tchr. Dallas Ind. Sch. Dist.; art instr. Bishop's Camp, Tejas Girl Scouts, Samuel Grand Pk. Mem.: NEA. Home: 6924 Wolling Ln Dallas TX 75346 Fax: 214-341-6139. E-mail: lynnrich@sbcglobal.net.

RICHARDSON, M. CATHERINE, lawyer; b. Syracuse, NY, July 14, 1941; d. George Lynch and Margaret (Mansfield) R. BS, State U. Coll., Oswego, N.Y., 1963; MA, U. No. Colo., 1969; JD magna cum laude, Syracuse U., 1977; LLD (hon.), SUNY, 2005. Bar: N.Y. 1978, U.S. Dist. Ct. (no. dist.) N.Y. 1978, U.S. Ct. Appeals (2d cir.) 1982. Math. tchr. Westhill HS, NY, 1963-67, Jamesville-Dewitt (NY) HS, 1969-74; lawyer Bond, Schoeneck & King, PLLC, Syracuse, 1977—. Mem. com. on profession and the cts. and profl. edn. project Chief Judge State N.Y. With St. Camillus Health and Rehab. Ctr.; Frank H. Hiscock Legal Aid Soc. (pres. 1994-96, bd.dir.); mem. Syracuse Rsch. Corp.; mem. State of NY Univ. Hosp. Syracuse Ethics Comm. Recipient Take the Lead award Ctrl. N.Y. Girl Scout Coun., 1988, Athena award Greater Syracuse C. of C. Small Bus. Bur., 1989, Spirit of Am. Women award Girls Inc. of Ctrl. N.Y., 1994, Syracuse Law Rev.'s Alumni Achievement award, 1995; named Outstanding Alumni SUNY Oswego, 1995; Kate Stoneman award, Albany Law Sch., 1996. Fellow ABA (bd. gov. 2003-), Am. Bar Found., N.Y. State Bar Found. (bd. dirs. 1992—, Ruth G. Shapiro award 2002); mem. N.Y. State Bar Assn. (pres. 1996-97), N.Y. State Jud. Inst., Hist. Soc. Cts. State N.Y., Onondaga County Bar Assn. (pres. 1987, Pro Bono award), Onondaga County Bar Found. (bd. dirs.), Am. Law Inst., Nat. Health Lawyers Assn., Am. Acad. Hosp. Attys., N.Y. State Assn. Sch. Attys., Lambda Sigma Tau, Kappa Delta Pi, Delta Kappa Gamma, Phi Kappa Phi, Justinian Hon. Law Soc., Ordr of Coif. Office: Bond Schoeneck & King LLP One Lincoln Ctr Syracuse NY 13202 Office Phone: 315-218-8230. Business E-Mail: crichardson@bsk.com.

RICHARDSON, MARGARET MILNER, retired lawyer; b. Waco, Tex., May 14, 1943; d. James W. and Margaret Wiebusch Milner; m. John L. Richardson, July 22, 1967; 1 child, Margaret Lawrence. AB in Polit. Sci., Vassar Coll., 1965; JD with honors, George Washington U., 1968. Bar: Va. 1968, D.C. 1968, U.S. Dist. Ct. D.C. 1968, U.S. Ct. Appeals (4th, 5th, D.C. and Fed. cirs.) 1968, U.S. Claims Ct. 1969, U.S. Tax Ct. 1970, U.S. Supreme Ct. 1971. Clk. U.S. Ct. Claims, Washington; with Office Chief Counsel IRS, Washington, 1969-77; with Sutherland, Asbill and Brennan, Washington, 1977-80, ptnr., 1980-93; commr. IRS, Washington, 1993-97; ptnr. Ernst & Young, Washington, 1997—2003. Mem. commr.'s adv. group IRS, 1988-90, chair, 1990; bd. advisors George Washington Law Sch.; mem. D.C. Bar Commn. on Multidisciplinary Practice, Presdl. Commn. on Holocaust Assets; bd. dirs. Legg Mason, Inc., JacksonHewitt, Eurasia Found., USA4 UNHCR. Contbr. articles to profl. jours. Assisted Clinton 1992 primary and gen. election campaign; served as team leader Justice Dept./Civil Rights Cluster during Presdl. Transition; mem. bd. Mayor's Transition Team, 1998, Women's Campaign Fund, Nat. Cathedral Sch., Hosp. for Sick Children; trustee Eurasia Found., USA for UNHCR, Woodrow Wilson Coun., U.S.-Russia Bus. Coun., 1999-03; mem. bd. dirs. Nat. Mus. Women in the Arts. Mem. ABA, D.C. Bar Assn. (tax sect.), Va. State Bar, Fed. Bar Assn. (com. taxation), Fin. Women's Assn. N.Y., Washington Women's Forum, Internat. Alliance, U.S. Russia Bus. Coun., Woodrow Wilson Ctr. Avocations: travel, antiques, needlepoint, gardening. Personal E-mail: margaretrichardson@yahoo.com.

RICHARDSON, MARILYN GOFF, small business owner, artist; b. Taunton, Mass., Sept. 9, 1934; d. Laurence Warren and Beatrice Cornelia (Rogers) Goff; m. Winthrop Horton Richardson Jr., July 18, 1959; children: Keith Warren, Kendra Lee. BFA, Boston U., 1956; MS, Ctrl. Conn. U., 1965. Art tchr. New Britain (Conn.) Pub. Schs., 1956-63; elem. tchr. Lakeview Sch. Dist., San Angelo, Tex., 1959-60; prin. Wickettwood Arts & Graphs, Coventry, Conn. and Taunton, Mass., 1980—2006, 2005—. Graphic artist: Bicentennial Cookbook, 1976, Plan of Development, 1978, Recipes from Coventry's First 275 Years, 1987, Exclusively Rhubarb Cookbook, 1988, Exclusively Pumpkin Cookbook, 1992, Exclusively Corn Cookbook, 1995, Exclusively Broccoli Cookbook, 1998, Exclusively Blueberry Cookbook, 2002; works exhibited in galleries in Taos, N.Mex., Women Art, 1985, Springfield, Chicopee and Falmouth, Mass., Hartford, Glastonbury, Willimantic, New Haven, Barnstable, West Hartford, East Hartford, Norwich, New Haven and Manchester, Conn., U. Conn. and N.Y.C.; one woman shows at Casey-Greene Gallery, Willimantic, 1986, The Artery, Ellington, Conn., 1986, Gallery 24, Conn. Pub. TV, Hartford, 1988, U. Maine, Glastonbury Art Guild, Tolland, Conn. Art Ctr., Exposures Ltd. Sec., vice chmn. Coventry Zoning Bd. Appeals, 1969-74; chmn. Coventry Planning Commn., 1974-80; adv. com. supply chmn. Children's Sch. Sci., Woods Hole, Mass., 1976-90; com. mem. Booth and Dimock Meml. Libr., Coventry, 1982-83; mem. Windham Regional Arts Coun., 1986-2004; organizing mem. Coventry Arts Commn., 1986-88, Cape Cod Art Assocs. Mem. AAUW (membership com. Storrs-Willimantic chpt. 1977-79, cultural com. 1985-87), Nat. Mus. Women in the Arts, Falmouth (Mass.) Art Guild, Glastonbury (Mass.) Art Guild, Taunton (Mass.) Art Assn. Avocations: swimming, travel, painting. Home and Office: 130 Fisher St Taunton MA 02780 Personal E-mail: wickettwood@juno.com.

RICHARDSON, MARY L., psychotherapist; b. Topeka, Oct. 4, 1953; d. Darrell and Beverly Nutter; m. Kenneth T. Richardson Jr. children: Shad Martin, Cheralyn Pasbrig, Kenneth T. Richardson III, Russ Richardson. BS in Addictions Counseling, Westbrook U., W.Va. Cert. behavioral health examiner, addictions counselor, Ariz., Hawaii; cert. Nat. Assn. of Alcolism and Drug Abuse Counselors; lic. ind. substance abuse counselor, Ariz. Behavioral Health. Counselor Compcare Alcoholism Ctr. The Meadows Treatment Ctr., Phoenix, 1986-88; co-founder Co-Dependents Anonymous, 1986—; co-dir. Phoenix Cons. & Counseling Assocs., Ariz., 1989—; co-founder Co-Dependents Anonymous, 1986—. Founder, adminstr. The Orion Found., Ariz.; project mem. The Hutoomkhum Cmty. and Support Program, Hopi Reservation, Ariz.; cons. Baywood Hosp., 1988-89; faculty instr. The Recovery Source, 1989-90; chair Nat. Conv. Women, 1992; facilitator Your Healing Journey Workshop, 2002-; co-founder, v.p., treas. The U. of Creative Arts and Scis., 2005-. Author: Women's Acts of Power, 1991-93, Relationship Recover, 1992—, Women's Empowerment, 1992—, Body, Mind & Spirit, 1994—. Mem. Am. Mental Health Counselors, Am. Counseling Assn., Nat. Assn. Alcoholism & Drug Abuse Counselors, Nat. Reciprocity Consortium. Avocations: writing, sculpting, dance, herbology. Home: PO Box 5170 Kailua Kona HI 96745-0519

RICHARDSON, MICHELLE YVETTE, mathematics educator, mathematics professor; b. Plant City, Fla., July 28, 1974; d. Doreatha Lowe and Calvin Earl Mcdonald, Belinda Mcdonald (Stepmother) and adopted d. Henry Lowe; children: Kaidrick Saivon, Kion Rashik. AA, Hillsborough C.C., Plant City, 2000; BS in Math. Edn., U. South Fla., Tampa, 2002; MA in Ednl. Leadership, Argosy U., Tampa, 2003. Math. tchr. McLane Mid. Sch., Brandon, Fla., 2002—, math. subject area leader, 2005—. Adj. math. prof. Hillsborough C.C., Plant City, 2002—. Adult Sunday sch. tchr., praise leader and sec. St. Luke Ind., Plant City, 2005. Named McLane Tchr. of Yr., Hillsborough County Found., 2006—; recipient Ida S. Baker Minorty Tchr. award, 2003—04. Democrat. Avocations: bowling, travel. Home: 506 Lake St Plant City FL 33563 Office: McLane Middle School 306 Knights Ave Brandon FL 33511 Office Phone: 813-744-8100. Office Fax: 813-744-8135. Personal E-mail: michelle.richardson@sdhc.k12.fl.us.

RICHARDSON, NATASHA JANE, actress; b. London, May 11, 1963; d. Tony Richardson and Vanessa Redgrave; m. Robert Fox, 1984 (div. 1993); m. Liam Neeson, July 3, 1994; children: Micheal Richard Antonio, Daniel Jack. Trained, Ctrl. Sch. Speech and Drama. Acting debut on stage at Leeds (Eng.) Playhouse, 1983; appearances include (plays) A Midsummer's Night Dream, Hamlet, 1985, The Seagull, 1985, High Society, 1987, Anna Christie, 1993, (Tony award nominee 1993, Drama Desk award), Cabaret, 1998 (Tony award, Drama Desk award, Outer Critics award), Closer (Broadway, 1999), A Streetcar Named Desire, 2005; (TV) In the Secret State, 1984, Sherlock Holmes, The Copper Beaches, 1984, Ghosts, 1986, Suddenly Last Summer, 1992, Hostages, 1993, Zelda, 1993, (Cable Ace nomination), Haven, 2001; (films) Gothic, 1987, A Month in the Country, 1987, Patty Hearst, 1988, Fat Man and Little Boy, 1989, The Handmaid's Tale, 1990, The Comfort of Strangers, 1991, The Favor, The Watch and the Very Big Fish, 1992, Past Midnight, Widow's Peak, 1994, (Best Actress Karlovy Vary), Nell, 1995, The Parent Trap, 1998, Blowdry, 2001, Wakin Up in Reno, 2001, Maid in Manhattan, 2002, The White Countess, 2005; actor, exec. prodr.: (films) Asylum, 2005. Recipient Most Promising Newcomer award Plays & Players, 1986; named Best Actress by London Theatre Critics, Plays & Players, 1990, Evening Standard Best Actress, 1990; Tony Award, actress in a musical, Cabaret, 1999.*

RICHARDSON, PAMELA F., federal agency administrator; BS in Aeronautical and Astronautical Engring., Ohio State U., MS in Fluid Mechanics. Aerospace engr. NASA Langley Rsch. Ctr., 1975—82, aeronautics engr., 1982—85, with Nat. Aerospace Plane Program, 1985—90; various positions in program mgmt. and program assessment integration NASA Hdqrs. Office: NASA Hdqrs Mail Code Q 300 E St SW Washington DC 20546

RICHARDSON, PATRICIA, actress; b. Bethesda, Md., Feb. 23, 1951; d. Laurence Baxter and Elizabeth (Howard) R.; m. Raymond Baker, June 20, 1982; children: Henry, Roxanne, Joseph. BFA, So. Meth. U., 1972. Appearences include (Broadway) Gypsy, Loose Ends, The Wake of Jamie Foster; (off-Broadway) The Collected Works of Billy the Kid, The Frequency, Vanities, The Coroner's Plot, Hooters, Company, Fables for Friends, The Miss Firecracker Contest, Cruise Control; (regional theatre) King Lear, The Killing of Sister George, Relatively Speaking, The Importance of Being Earnest, Of Mice and Men, The Philadelphia Story, Room Service, Fifth of July, About Face; (nat. tours) Gypsy, Vanities; (films) Gas, 1972, You Better Watch Out, Lost Angels, 1988, In Country, 1988, Ulee's Gold, 1997; (TV) Double Trouble, 1984, Eisenhower & Lutz, 1988, FM, 1989-90, Home Improvement, 1991-99 (Lead Actress in a Comedy Series Emmy award nominee, 1994, Golden Globe award nominee, 1993, 94), Sophie and the Moonhanger, 1995, Undue Influence, 1996, Viva Las Nowhere, 2000. Office: William Morris Agy care Jonathon Howard 151 S El Camino Dr Beverly Hills CA 90212-2775

RICHARDSON, POLLIE, principal; b. Stump City, Ark., Nov. 19, 1949; d. L. C. and Daisy Mae Newman; m. John Wesley Richardson, July 7, 1969 (div.); children: Octavia Ethel, Demetrius Donte', Veritie Potere', Bonita Biaute', Carina Danette. BS in Edn., Harris Stowe State Coll., 1981; EdM, U. Mo., St. Louis, 1995. Cert. administrn. II/secondary prin. Dept. Elem. and Secondary Edn., 1995, elem. edn. Dept. Elem. and Secondary Edn., 1981, learning disabled Dept. Elem. and Secondary Edn., 1981, mentally handicapped Dept. Elem. and Secondary Edn., 1981, behavioral disorder Dept. Elem. and Secondary Edn., 1981, spl. reading Dept. Elem. and Secondary Edn., 1981, math. Dept. Elem. and Secondary Edn., 1995. Asst. prin. Epworth Campus Sch., St. Louis, 1981—96; prin. Mehlville Sch. Dist., St. Louis, 1996—. Instr. Fontbonne U., St. Louis, 1997—98; dir., pioneer alt. sch. Parent to Parent Tng.; spkr. in field. Contbr. articles to profl. jours. Mem.: Leadership Acad., Nat. Assn. Secondary Prins., Coun. Exceptional Children. Baptist. Avocations: sewing, reading, writing, gardening, travel. Office: Mehlville School District 76 Grasso Plaza Saint Louis MO 63123-3108 Home: 2605 Souh Compton Ave Saint Louis MO 63118 Office Phone: 314-631-1047. Personal E-mail: pollier@swbell.net. E-mail: richp@mehlville.k12.mo.us.

RICHARDSON, SALLY KEADLE, academic administrator; b. Mar. 2, 1933; d. Okey P. and Viola Miriam (Graybeal) Keadle; m. Don Rule Richardson, Dec. 15, 1961; children: Miriam Paige, Ruth Evan. AB, Vassar Coll., 1954. Regional pub. info. rep. Columbia Gas Sys., Charleston, W.Va., 1958-62; dir. Children's Mus., Charleston, 1963; coord. space-related sci. project Kanawha County Schs., Charleston, 1967-68; vol. dir. Rockefeller for Gov. Campaign, Charleston, 1972, program dir., 1976, 80; dir. admissions W.Va. Wesleyan Coll., Buckhannon, 1974-75; spl. asst. Office of Gov. State of W.Va., 1977, dep. commr. dept. welfare, 1978-79, dep. dir. dept. health, 1979-83; chmn. W.Va. Health Care Cost Rev. Authority, Charleston, 1983-85. Health care cons., Charleston, 1985-89; dir. W.Va. Pub. Employees Ins. Agy., Charleston, 1989-93; vice-chmn. W.Va. Health Care Planning Task Force, 1992-93; mem. White House Health Care Reform Task Force, Washington, 1993; dir. Medicaid Bur., Health Care Financing Adminstrn., U.S. DHHS, Balt., 1993-96; acting dep. adminstr. HCFA, U.S. DHHS, Washington, 1996-97; dir. HCFA Ctr. for Medicaid and State Ops., 1997-99; mem. U.S. DHHS Governing Coun. on Children and Youth, 1993-97, co-chmn. U.S. DHHS Children's Health Initiative, 1997-99; co-chmn. U.S. DHHS Home and Cmty. Based Svcs. Task Force, 1996-99; mem. U.S. DHHS Pub. Health Coun.'s D.C. Task Force, 1994-99; mem. Nat. Adv. Com. on Rural Health, DHHS, 2000-04; bd. dirs. Molina Healthcare, Inc. W.Va. rep. Task Force on So. Children, So. Growth Policies Bd., 1978-79; co-chmn. exec. com. W.Va. Internat. Yr. of Child, 1979; staff mem. Com. on Human Resources Nat. Gov. Assn., 1983-85; trustee U. Charleston, 1994-; bd. dirs. Children's Home Soc., Charleston, 1999—. Mem. Acad. Health, Nat. Rural Health Assn. Democrat. Office: WVa U Inst Health Policy Rsch 3110 Maccorkle Ave SE Rm 3015 Charleston WV 25304-1210

RICHARDSON, SHIRLEY MAXINE, editor; b. Rising Sun, Ind., May 3, 1931; d. William Fenton and Mary (Phillips) Keith; m. Arthur Lee Richardson, Feb. 11, 1950; children: Mary Jane Hunt, JoDee Mayfield, Steven Lee Richardson. Pers. mgr. Mayhill Pubs., Knightstown, Ind., 1967-87, prodn. mgr., 1975-87, editor, 1967-87; info. staff, assoc. editor Ind. Farm Bur., Inc., 1987-89, dir. info. and pub. rels., 1989-94; genealogy editor AntiqueWeek, 1996-2001; exec. editor Knightstown Banner, 2001—. Avocations: travel, reading, boating, quilting. Home: 366 E Carey St Knightstown IN 46148-1208 Office: 24 N Washington St Knightstown IN 46148-1242 Office Phone: 765-345-2292.

RICHARDSON, SUZANNE MAYS, communication consultant; b. Dayton, Apr. 16, 1944; d. Lewell Newton and Virginia Mays; m. Randolph Wade Richardson, Mar. 20, 1993; children: Rebecca (Nash), William (Nash). BA, Brown U., 1966; MA, Columbia U., 1967, U. Mich., 1970. Spl. asst. to comdg. gen. U.S. Army Materiel Command, Alexandria, Va., 1986-91; strategic initiatives analyst Office Sec. Def., Pentagon, Washington, 1991-93; cons. in field. Chair Colo. Womens Leadership Coalition, 1998-99, sec., 1997; sec. Recording for the Blind and Dyslexic, Denver, 1996-98; bd. dirs. Colo. Women's Hall of Fame, 2000-2004, co-chair, 2002-04, sec.-treas., 2005; bd. dirs. Day of Caring for Breast Cancer Awareness, 2002-05, v.p., 2004. Recipient Woman Leader of Excellence award Colo. Women's Leadership Coalition, 1997. Mem. Assn. Women in Comms. (pres. Denver chpt. 1996-97), Zonta Club of Douglas County (bd. dirs., 2005—, sec., 2005—). Unitarian Universalist. Office: 3864 Castle Butte Dr Castle Rock CO 80109-9638

RICHARDSON, VALERIE, secondary school educator; b. Monticello, Utah, June 6, 1972; d. Billy Joe and Merle Richardson. M in Math. Edn., U. Utah, Salt Lake City, 2006. Tchr. Cyprus H.S., Magna, Utah, 1995—. Adj. tchr. Salt Lake C.C., Salt Lake City, 2005—. Author: (textbook) Lesson Plans On Growth Models. Office: Cyprus High School 8623 W 3100 W Magna UT 84044 Office Phone: 801-646-5300.

RICHARDSON, VETA TERESA, professional society administrator, lawyer; b. Phila., Aug. 4, 1962; d. William Alfred and Teresa Richardson. BS in Bus. Mgmt., U. Md., 1983, JD, 1986. Bar: Pa. 1986, N.Y. 1995, D.C. 1988. Corp. and securities counsel Sunoco, Inc., Phila., 1986-97; v.p. Am. Corp. Counsel Assn., Washington, 1997-2000, exec. dir., CEO, 2001; exec. dir. Minority Corp. Counsel Assn., Washington. Dir. publs. Diversity and the Bar mag., Washington, 2001—; mem. adv. bd. Georgetown Law Sch. Corp. Counsel Inst., Washington, 2000—. Trustee Prince George's Arts Coun., 1997—; mem. steering com. Lawyers for One Am., Washington, 1999-2000. Mem. Nat. Bar Assn., Am. Corp. Counsel Assn., Am. Soc. Assn. Execs., Alpha Kappa Alpha. Avocation: african american art collector.

RICHARDSON, WINIFRED, youth counselor, writer; b. South Gate, Calif., May 7, 1963; d. J.C. and Earline (Evans) R.; 1 child, Joshua AS, Harbor Coll., 1985. Co-editor Southwood Baptist Ch., L.A., 1984-86, word processor, 1987-89; youth counselor State of Calif., 1989—; prin., publisher, 1996—. Author: Balance*Balance*Balance, 1997. Mem. Writers Digest, Reader Digest. Avocations: writing, theater, tennis, piano, reading.

RICHARDSON-BOWMAN, LEQUETTA DEVERA, finance company executive, consultant; d. Edward Richardson and Lonzetta Beatrice Townsend-Richardson; life ptnr. Thomas Michael Sellers; m. Michael Jerome Bowman, Mar. 24, 1987 (div. June 31, 1989); m. Ray Alexander, Dec. 27, 1963 (div. Dec. 13, 1967); children: Malik (Ray) Edward Shakur (Alexander), Briant Leonard Alexander. BA in Psychology magna cum laude, Langston U., 1995; MBA, Okla. City U., 1998. Cost risk analysis course, Dept. of Def. Logistics Mgmt. Coll., sys. acquisition funds mgmt. courses, Dept. of Def. Sys. Mgmt. Coll., Md., contractor performance measurement course, Dept. of Def. Sys. Mgmt. Coll., Md., fed. appropriation law, Grad. Sch. USDA, Okla., federal budget process, Grad. Sch. USDA, Okla., cert. acquisition profl. level I in fin. mgmt., Dept. of Air Force, Ohio, budget estimating techniques, U.S. Office of Pers. Mgmt., Tex., budget formulation, U.S. Office of Pers. Mgmt., Tex., budget execution, U.S. Office of Pers. Mgmt., Tex.; aeronautics Dept. of Transp., FAA, Okla., ISO 9000 implementation and documentation workshop Hartley Group Performance Paradigns, Inc., Okla., ISO 9000 internal quality auditor workshop Hartley Group-Performance Paradigm, Inc., Okla., Outclass the Competition PROTOCOL PLUS through Protocol Sch. of Washington, Profl. Devel. Inst. Symposium Sequoyah chpt. Am. Soc. of Mil. Comptrs., cert. acquisition profl. level I in acquisition logistics Dept. of the Air Force, Ohio, fgn. mil. sales internat. budget workshop Pentagon and Wright-Patterson AFB, appropriations law update in mgmt. field of study Learning Curve Tng. Group, Inc., Okla., cert. acquisition profl. level I in program mgmt. Dept. of the Air Force, Ohio, quality participation for employees USAF, quality leadership for mgrs. USAF. Alterations bookkeeping clk. alterations dept. Al Rosenthal's, Oklahoma City, 1966—67; sec.-receptionist ITT Continental Baking Co., Wonder Bread Regional Sales-Svc. Bus. Office, Oklahoma City, 1967—69; teller Tinker Field Credit Union, Tinker AFB, Okla., 1969; sales-svc. sec. West Coast regional sales svc. office Reynolds Metals Co., L.A., 1969—70; purchasing technician purchasing dept. Memorex Corp., Santa Clara, Calif., 1970—72; pers.-payroll clk. Unit Parts Co.-Borg Warner Corp., Oklahoma City, 1972—73; teller Tinker Field Credit Union, Tinker AFB, Okla., 1972; payroll technician acctg. divsn., C.G. Payroll Br. FAA Mike Monroney Aero. Ctr., Oklahoma City, 1974—81; payroll clk. divsn. WR Grace Petroleum, Bus. Office, payroll sect. TRG Drilling, Oklahoma City, 1981—83; payroll clk. civilian pay Dept. of Def., USAF Acctg. Br., Civilian Payroll Sect., Tinker AFB, 1973—74; mgr., supr. Cmty. Day Care Presch., Bus. Office, Pers. & Payroll, Oklahoma City, 1981; travel clk. FAA, Mike Monroney Aero. Ctr., Acctg. Divsn., Travel Br., Travel Adminstrn. Sect., Oklahoma City, 1983—83; acctg. technician FAA Mike Monroney Ctr., Acctg. Divsn., Accounts Payable Br., Oklahoma City, 1983—85; air traffic control specialist pre-developmental student flight svcs. trainee Dept. of Transp., FAA, Ea. Region, Jamaica, N.Y., Oklahoma City, 1986; mgr.-supr. family bus. Cmty. Day Care PreSch. Bus. Office, Oklahoma City, 1986—87; shipment clk. Def. Logistics Agy., Billing OS & D Sect. (Inbound), Tinker AFB, 1988—90; transp. control clk. Def. Logistics Agy., Freight Terminal Br., Tinker AFB, 1988; customer svc. rep. ATT Sales-Svc. Office, Oklahoma City, 1988; child devel. ctr. supr. HQ 72nd Air Base Wing, 72 Svcs. Divsn., Child Devel. Ctr.-West, Tinker AFB, 1990—91; budget analyst 552 Airborne Computer Squadron, Tinker AFB, 1991—93; budget asst. Okla. City-Air Logistics Ctr., Commodities Mgmt. Directorate, Fin. Mgmt. Br., Tinker AFB, 1991—92; budget analyst Okla. City-Air Logistics Ctr., Tech. and Indsl. Support Directorate, Resource Mgmt. Divsn., Funds Mgmt. Br., Tinker AFB, 1992—97, Okla. City-Air Logistics Ctr., Fin. Mgmt. Directorate Workloading Sect., Tinker AFB, 1998—2001, Okla. City-Air Logistics Ctr., Fin. Mgmt. Directorate, Fin. Analysis Divsn., Tinker AFB, 2001—03. Leader participant League of Black Women, Flossmoor, Ill., 2005; treas. U.S. Green Bldg. Coun., Oklahoma City, 2005; cons. OCU Women As Servant Leaders, Oklahoma City, 2005—06. Named to Vice President's Honor Roll, Rose State Coll., 1991, President's Honor Roll, 1991, 1992; recipient Acad. Achievement award, Langston U., 1994, Spl. Act award, FAA Mike Monroney Aero. Ctr., 1979, Svc. award, 1983, Performance award, Okla. City-Air Logistics Ctr., Tech. and Indsl. Directorate, Resource Mgmt. Divsn., Funds Mgmt. Sect., 1996, Okla. Scholar-Leadership Enrichment Program' Elizabeth George Seminar fellowship, Okla. State Regents for Higher Edn. through the U. of Okla., 1995. Mem.: Friends Earth, Nat. Wildlife Fedn., Price Tower Arts Ctr., League Black Women, Sustainable OKC, T&L Golf Club. Episc. Avocations: cooking, gardening, hiking, yoga, reading. Office Phone: 405-235-2905.

RICHARDSON-LOWRY, MARY, lawyer; b. June 26, 1957; BA, U. San Francisco State, 1981; JD, Tex. So. U., 1984. Bar: U.S. Dist. Ct. (No. Dist. Ill.) 1986, Ill. Supreme Ct. 1986. Asst. corp. counsel Dept. Law City of Chgo., 1987—92, sr. supervising atty., 1992—94; asst. to Mayor Richard M. Daley City of Chgo., 1994—98, commr. dept. bldgs., 1998—2002; ptnr. Mayer, Brown, Rowe & Maw LLP, Chgo., 2002—. Chmn. Cmty. Devel. Commn. City of Chgo., 2004—. Office: Mayer Brown Rowe Maw Llp 230 S La Salle St Ste 400 Chicago IL 60604-1407 Office Phone: 312-701-8442. Office Fax: 312-706-8427. E-mail: mbrl@mayerbrown.com.

RICHARDSON-MELECH, JOYCE SUZANNE, music educator, singer; b. Perth Amboy, N.J., Nov. 15, 1957; d. Herbert Nathaniel and Fannie Elaine (Franklin) Richardson; m. Gerald Melech, July 28, 1990. MusB, Westminster Choir Coll., 1979, MusM, 1981; postgrad., Rutgers U., 1999—. Cert. music tchr. N.J., supr. N.J. Musical play dir. Perth Amboy H.S., 1989-92, asst. band dir., 1984-94; music tchr. Perth Amboy Bd. Edn., 1981—, gifted and talented music tchr., 1992-96; vocal soloist N.Y.C. Vocal soloist N.Y. Philharm. and Westminster Symphonic Choir, 1977, United Moravian Ch., N.Y.C., 1980-81, Ctrl. Jersey Concert Orch., Perth Amboy, 1994-96; mezzo-soprano soloist in The Messiah, John Hus Moravian Ch., Bklyn., 1998; master tchrs. collaborative with N.J. Symphony Orch., 2000-01, 2003, 2005 Contbg. author: Teacher's Resource Book, 2000, 2001, 2003, 2005, illustrator: The Peacock of Half-Way Tree: A Caribbean Fable, 2004; actor: Perth Amboy Adult Cmty. Theatre, 1983. Participant Perth Amboy Adult Cmty. Theatre, 1983. Recipient award for excellence in tchg., NJ Symphony Orch., 2000, 2001, 2003, 2005, Lois Bailey Glenn award for tchg. excellence, Nat. Music Found., 2004; grantee, Am. Music Edn. Initiative for Programmatic Ragtime, 2004. Mem. NAACP, Internat. Platform Assn., Am. Mus. Natural History (assoc.), Am. Fedn. Tchrs., Am. Fedn. Musicians (local 204-373), Music Educators Nat. Conf., Orgn. Am. Kodaly Educators, Alliance for Arts Edn. N.J., Ctrl. Jersey Music Educators, N.J. Music Educators Assn., Alpha Phi Omega. Democrat. Episcopalian. Avocations: travel, Art Deco antiques, needlecrafts, knitting, crocheting. Home: 148 Carson Ct Somerset NJ 08873-4790 Office: Samuel Shull Sch 380 Hall Ave Perth Amboy NJ 08861-3205 Office Phone: 732-376-6060 26662. Business E-Mail: joycrichardson@paps.net.

RICHARDSON-TOUSON, F. MICHELLE, director; d. Richard B. and Hazel O. Richardson; m. Philip W. Touson, June 24, 2000. AA, City Coll. San Francisco, 1996; BS, Howard U., Washington, DC, 2000; MS, Fla. State U., Tallahassee, 2001. Intern NIKE Inc., Beaverton, Oreg., 1997—98; tutorial coord. U. Calif., Berkeley, 2002—03; grad. asst. U. N.Mex - Office of African Am. Student Svcs., Albuquerque, 2005—. Com. mem. U. N.Mex - Huey P. Newton Birthday Celebration, 2005—06, U. N.Mex - Black Panther Party 40th Anniversary, 2005—06. Regents Fellowship, U. N.Mex, 2006. Mem.: Nat. Assn. Athletic Academic Advisors, North Am. Soc. for the Sport of Sociology, North Am. Soc. Sport Mgmt., Am. Alliance Health, Phys. Edn., Recreation and Dance, Nat. Assn. Collgiate Women Athletic Adminstrs. Office Phone: 505-277-5645. Office Fax: 505-277-4095. Business E-Mail: mtouson@unm.edu.

RICHARDSON-WENINEGAR, LORETTA LYNNE, biologist, educator; b. Ft. Riley, Kans., Sept. 19, 1954; d. Woodrow and Florence Myrtle Denton; children: Jennifer Lynne Weninegar-Canady, Jessica Leigh Weninegar, James Christopher Weninegar. BS in Biology and Secondary Edn./Minor Psychology, U. Mobile, 1976, MSEd in secondary edn./biology, 1993; MS in biology, Jacksonville State U., 2002. Cert. Tchr. #252735, Type B Ala., 1976, Tchr. #252735, Type A Ala., 1993. Sci. tchr. Arnold Sch. of Ala., Mobile, 1976, Berney Points Sch., Birmingham, Ala., 1977—79, Hueytown H.S., Ala., 1995—98, Jacksonville H.S., Ala., 1990—91; grad. tchg. asst., biology Jacksonville State U., Ala., 1993, adj. instr. biology, 1993—98; asst. project dir. Ala. Sci. in Motion Ala. A&M U., Huntsville, 1998—; tchr. of sci. Columbia H.S., 2006—. Field technician, botanist Natural Resource Conservation Svc., Ala., 1996; chmn., pers. com. Berney Points Sch., Birmingham, 1979—81; asst. dir. Chattooga river environ. edn. and water quality project Jacksonville State U., Ala., 1994—95, facilitator environ. edn. From Awareness to Action, 1993, staff, Little River Field Sch., 1993—97; trainer Ala. Water Watch Ala. A&M U., Huntsville, 1998—; adj. instr. Biology Calhoun C.C., Decatur/Huntsville, Ala., 2004—. Spkr. bur., hike leader The Land Trust of Huntsville and North Ala.; mem. strategic planning com. Columbia H.S., Huntsville, 2005—; outdoor amb. Ala. Bur. Tourism and Travel, 2006, amb. yr. outdoor Ala., 2006; spkr. Ala. Wildflower Soc., Huntsville. Mem.: NEA, Nat. Sci. Tchr. Assn., Nat. Assn. Biology Tchrs., Ala. Edn. Assn., The LandTrust of Huntsville and North Ala. (speaker's bur., hike leader), Beta Beta Beta, Delta Kappa Gamma (membership chmn. 2002—04). Achievements include research in water quality analysis of Cane Creek in Calhoun County, Ala; lysozyme crystal experiment; Vascular Flora of Choccolocco Creek, Calhoun, Cleburne, and Talladega Counties, Ala. Avocations: hiking, camping, gardening, birdwatching, dance. Home: 9507 Hemlock Dr SE Huntsville AL 35803-1161 Personal E-mail: bcdh@aol.com.

RICHARDS-VITAL, CLAUDIA, small business owner, recreational facility executive; b. Banes, Oriente, Cuba, May 18, 1935; arrived in U.S., 1951; d. Vasper Zacharia Richards and Ana Louisa Coombs - Vital; m. Eugene Blackman, July 22, 1956 (div. Apr. 20, 1965); children: Emery, John, Veronica. AA in Bus. Adminstrn./English, Havana Bus. Acad., 1951; diploma in Early Childhood Devel., Miami Dade C.C., 1972. Pvt. practice nanny, Miami Beach, Fla., 1951—56; seamstress Playboy Club, Miami, Fla., 1961—65; prodn. supr. So. Bakery, 1965—69; care mother James E. Scott Cmty. Agy., 1970—75; nurse asst. North Shore Hosp., 1970—75; home health aide Total Care Home Health Agy., 1975—85; site dir. YMCA, 1985—95; sole propr. Veronica's Boutique, 1982—89, Claudia's Formal Wear, 1989—. Pres. Local #249 Am. Bakery and Confectionery Workers Internat. AFL-CIO, Fla., 1966—69. Named Parent of Yr., Metro Dade County, 1993; recipient Diamond Pendant, Queen Elizabeth II, 1965, cert. of Appreciation, YMCA of Miami, Fla., 1990. Mem.: NAFE, NAACP. Democrat. Roman Catholic. Avocations: sewing, decorating, gardening, babysitting, animals. Home: 1915 NW 49 St Miami FL 33142 Office Phone: 305-637-2090. Personal E-mail: claudia@claudiaformalweareleganza.com.

RICHE, WENDY, television producer; b. N.Y.C., Jan. 8, 1945; d. Elliot and Janice (Fantel) Fields; m. Alan Riche, Dec. 4, 1966; children: Tim, Peter. Student, Syracuse U. Sec. ABC, 1973, program coord. Late Night Programs, 1974, assoc. prodr. In Concert series and specials, 1974; developer, prodr. Levenback/Riche and Wittman/Riche Prodn. Co., 1975-78; prodr. Universal TV, 1978-86; exec. prodr. ABC Entertainment, 1986-89; sr. v.p. prodr. Fox Broadcast Co., 1989-91; exec. prodr. Gen. Hosp. ABC-TV, 1992-99, exec. prodr. Port Charles, 1997-00; exec. prodr. WR Prodns., 2000—04; co-exec. prodr. Laguna Beach: The Real Orange County MTV, 2004—. Prodr. (movies of the week) Who Will Love My Children? (8 Emmy award nominations), Madame X, I Saw What You Did, Friendships, Secrets, and Lies, Deadly Care; exec. prodr. (ABC pilot) Never Again, (movies for TV, dir. programming ABC Entertainment) God Bless the Child, David (Emmy award nomination), My Name is Bill W (Emmy award winner), Women of Brewster Place, Unspeakable Acts, Our Sons, Fight for Life, (exec. producer daytime drama) General Hosp. (Emmy award for outstanding drama series 1994/95, 95/96, 96/97, 97/98, 98/99, 99/2000), (after school spl.) Positive: A Journey Into Aids (3 Emmy award nominations). Recipient Soap Opera Update Editors award, 1993, Pub. Svc. award Nat. Kidney Found., 1994, Soap Opera Hall of Fame, 1994, 96, Nancy Susan Reynolds award, 1994, 95, 96, Chair's award Am. Cancer Soc., 1994/95, 15th Media Access award, 1995, Imagen award, 1996, Komen award, 1996, Ryan White Youth Svc. award, 1996, Daytime TV Mag. Readers Poll award for best show, 1996/97, Soap Opera Digest award for Gen. Hosp. favorite show, 1997, 98, 99, 2000, Media Access Michael Landon award, 1997. Mem. Writes Guild Am., Producers Guild Am.

RICHERSON, KRISTINA MARIE, social studies educator; b. Gainesville, Fla., Dec. 27, 1972; d. Charles Joseph Kuhr and Patricia Darlene Reynolds; m. Edward Lee Richerson, Jan. 21, 1974; children: Christopher, Shelby Lyn Kuhr, Phillip Carl. BA in Social Sci. Edn., U. North Fla., 2003. Cert. Social Sci. Edn. 6-12 Fla., 2003. Food svc. worker crew chief Subway, Belle Chasse, La., 1996—2000; seventh grade social studies tchr. Baker County Mid. Sch., Macclenny, Fla., 2003—. Pre-k tchr. (summer) Westside Nursery/Preschool, Glen Saint Mary, Fla., 2006—. Conservative. Avocations: flute, reading, crocheting, cross stitch. Home: 10774 Westside Loop Glen Saint Mary FL 32040

RICHES, WENDY, magazine publishing executive; Dir. pub. rels. Save the Children Fund, dir. mktg. and fundraising U.K., 1985-90; exec. creative dir. Ogilvy & Mather Direct, London, 1990-92; mng. dir. Ogilvy & Mather Direct (now Ogilvy One), London, 1995-98; chmn., CEO OgilvyOne N. Am.; pres., global mktg. & e-commerce Hasbro Inc., 1998—2000; former pres. D'Arcy Mktg. Comm. Group; exec. v.p., integrated mktg. Meredith Pub. Group, NYC, now exec. v.p., 2006—. Mem., bd. dirs. Columbia House Co., Direct Marketing Association, 2000—. Office: Meredith Publishing 125 Park Ave New York NY 10017 Office Phone: 212-557-6600.*

RICHESON, JENNIFER ANNE, psychology professor, researcher; b. Sept. 1972; ScB, Brown U., 1994; PhD in Social Psychology, Harvard U., 2000. Asst. prof. psychol. and brain scis. Dartmouth Coll., Hanover, NH, 2000—05; assoc. prof. Dept. Psychology Northwestern U., Evanston, 2005—, faculty fellow Inst. for Policy Rsch., 2005—. Vis. fellow Rsch. Inst. for Comparative Studies in Race and Ethnicity, Stanford U., 2004—05. Contbr. articles to profl. jours. Grantee Ford Found. Odyssey Grant, 1993, NIMH Individual Rsch. Svc. Award, 1999—2000, Walter and Constance Burke Rsch. Initiation Award, 2000—06, NIMH B/START Grant, 2002—04, NSF, 2002—05; MacArthur Fellow, John D. and Catherine T. MacArthur Found., 2006. Mem.: Soc. for Psychol. Study of Social Issues, Soc. for Personality and Social Psychology, Am. Psychol. Soc., Am. Psychol. Assn. Office: Dept Psychology Northwestern U 2029 Sheridan Rd Evanston IL 60208-2710 Office Phone: 847-467-1331. E-mail: jriches@northwestern.edu.*

RICHEY, ELLEN, credit card company executive; BA summa cum laude, Harvard U.; JD, Stanford U. Law clk. Hon. Lewis F. Powell, Jr. U.S. Supreme Ct.; law clk. Hon. Charles B. Renfrew U.S. Dist. Ct. (no. dist.); ptnr. Farella, Braun & Martel, San Francisco, 1980—94; from gen. counsel, sec. Providian Fin. Corp., San Francisco, 1995—, exec. v.p., 1997—99, vice chmn. Enterprise Risk Mgmt., 1999—. Office: Providian Financial Corp 201 Mission Street Lobby San Francisco CA 94105 Office Phone: 415-278-4634. Business E-Mail: ellen_richey@providian.com.

RICHEY, MARY ELLEN, lawyer; b. Boston, Mar. 16, 1949; BA summa cum laude, Radcliffe Coll., 1970; JD, Stanford U., 1977. Bar: Calif. 1978. Law clk. to Hon. Charles B. Renfrew U.S. Dist. Ct. (no. dist.) Calif., 1977-78; law clk. to Hon. Lewis F. Powell, Jr., assoc. justice U.S. Supreme Ct., 1979-80; with Farella, Braun & Martel, San Francisco; assoc. Providian Fin. Corp., San Francisco, 1980—85, ptnr., v.p., sec., 1985—93, gen. counsel, 1985—, vice chmn., 2001—. Symposium editor Stanford Law Rev., 1976-77. Mem. ABA (bus. law sect., real property probate and trust law sect.), State Bar Calif. (bus. law sect., real property law sect.), Bar Assn. San Francisco, Phi Beta Kappa, Order of Coif. Office: Providian Fin Corp 201 Mission St San Francisco CA 94105-1831 Office Phone: 415-543-0404. Office Fax: 415-278-6028.

RICHEZZA, AMANDA, athletic trainer; b. Waterbury, Conn., July 11, 1976; d. Richard John Richezza and Phyllis Pepe. BPE, Ctrl. Conn. State U, 2000. Intern The Taft Sch., Watertown, Conn., 1999—2000; intern for exhbn. game WNBA vs. USA Olympic Team, Bridgeport, Conn., 1999; camp athletic trainer NY Giants, East Stroudsburg, Pa., 2003; athletic trainer Jamestown H.S., Williamsburg, Va., 2001—. Mem.: Va. Athletic Trainers Assn., Nat. Athletic Trainers Assn. Avocations: coin collecting/numismatics, reading, exercise, running. Office: Jamestown HS 3751 John Tyler Hwy Williamsburg VA 23185

RICHIE, MARGARET BYE, architectural historian; PhD, U. Pa., 1987. Author: Victorian Sketch Book, 1980, Stone Houses, Homes of Traditional Pennsylvania's Bucks County and Brandywine Valley, 2005. Mem. Bucks County Archtl. Rev. Bd. Fellow: Sigma Pi Kappa. Avocations: architecture, history, politics, sociology, languages. Address: Woodland Crossing T04 300 Linden Ponds Way Hingham MA 02043

RICHIE, NICOLE, television personality; b. Berkeley, Calif., Sept. 21, 1981; d. Lionel and Brenda Harvey Richie. Co-star: (TV series) The Simple Life, 2003; The Simple Life 2: Road Trip, 2004; The Simple Life 3: Interns, 2005; The Simple Life 4: 'Til Death Do Us Part, 2006; guest appearance Punk'd, 2003; Mad TV, 2004; Rock Me Baby, 2004; Six Feet Under, 2004; actor: (films) Kids in America, 2005; author: The Truth About Diamonds, 2005 (Publishers Weekly hardcover fiction bestseller list). Office: Creative Artists Agy 9830 Wilshire Blvd Beverly Hills CA 90212*

RICHLER, ZENIA H., naturopath educator, health facility administrator; B in Bio-Energetics, Acad. Bio-Energetics, 1997, M in Bio-Energetics, 1999, D in Bio-Energetics, 2001; D of Naturopathic Medicine, So. Coll. Naturopathic Medicine, 2001. Dir. Health Alternatives, Atlanta, 1986—98, dir., nmd Humansville, 1998—; pres., CEO, chief instr. Acad. BioEnergetics, Humansville, Mo., 1999—. Assoc. dir. new bus. devel. Transformation Group, Inc., Houston, 2006—; acad. cons. EMR Techs., Inc., Las Vegas, Nev., 2006—; instr. Neurotherapy BioFeedback Certification Bd., 2006—; cert. instr. SounderSleep, 2006—. Fellow: AAIM, Am. Assn. Integrated Medicine; mem.: Am. Assn. Drugless Practitioners, Noetic Scis., Natural Resources Def. Coun., Coalation for Natural Health, Nat. Health Fedn., Am. Holistic Health Assn., Am. Alternative Med. Assn. Avocations: swimming, reading, yoga. Office: Acad BioEnergetics 18820 E Hwy N Humansville MO 65674 Office Phone: 417-754-8469. Business E-Mail: academybe@tri-lakes.net.

RICHMAN, ARLEEN, professional society administrator; b. N.Y.C., Jan. 1, 1941; d. Abraham Friedel and Judith Anne Hecht; m. Sheldon B. Richman, May 26, 1970. AAS, Hofstra Coll., 1960; BBA in Acctg. summa cum laude, Adelphi U., 1969, postgrad., 1969-71. Women's page editor AP, N.Y.C., 1960-69; adminstrv. positions various assns., Washington, 1976-80; mng. editor Trips Travels, Washington, 1980-83; comm. mgr. Appropriate Tech. Internat., Washington, 1984-90; grants adminstr. Coun. for Internat. Devel., Washington, 1990-93; dir. comm. and spl. projects U.S. Parachute Assn., Alexandria, Va., 1993-97; mgr. spl. projects Nat. Soc. Accts., Alexandria, 1997—2001, comm. mgr., 2001—; editor Nat. Pub. Acct., 2001—. Cons. various UN Devel. Program and AID projects, 1986-93; cons., editor, writer Com. on Internat. Liaison for Agr., Puebla, Mexico, 1988-90. Author: Opening the Marketplace to Small Enterprise, 1990; editor: High Impact Case Studies, 1989, (jour.) The Profl., 1995-97; contbr. numerous articles to newspapers and jours. Com. mem. local homeowners assn., Alexandria, 1984—; vol. friend Mental Health Assn., Alexandria, 1992—; vol. mentor Alexandria Jail, 1998—. Recipient Keep Am. Beautiful award Keep Am. Beautiful Fedn., Washington, 1966, Point of Light award Compeer, Alexandria, 1998, 2000. Mem. Am. Soc. Assn. Execs. Jewish. Avocations: tennis, birdwatching. Home: 2741 Carter Farm Ct Alexandria VA 22306-3242 Office: Nat Soc Accts 1010 N Fairfax St Alexandria VA 22314-1504 E-mail: arichman@nsacct.org.

RICHMAN, JOAN M., lawyer; b. Chgo., Dec. 15, 1965; Diploma in Internat. Bus., The Netherlands Sch. Bus., 1989; B of Commerce with distinction, McGill U., 1988; JD, Georgetown U., 1992. Bar: Ill. 1992. Summer assoc. Baker & McKenzie, Chgo., 1991, assoc., 1992—99, ptnr., 1999—. Office: Baker and McKenzie One Prudential Plz 130 E Randolph Dr Chicago IL 60601

RICHMAN, RACHEL L., food scientist, microbiologist, educator; b. Valley City, N.D., Jan. 23, 1975; d. Mary E. Cockerill; m. George M. Richman, May 26, 1973; 1 child, Iris G. MS in Food Sci., U. Minn., 2002. Instr. Minn. State U., Moorhead, 2002—03; lectr. N.D. State U., Fargo, 2003—. Office: ND State Univ Veterinary/Microbiolo Sci Dept 1523 Centennial Blvd Fargo ND 58105 Office Phone: 701-231-7184. Business E-Mail: rachel.l.richman@ndsu.edu.

RICHMAN, SOPHIA, psychologist; b. Lwow, Poland, Jan. 28, 1941; arrived in US, 1951; d. Leon and Dorothy Weiss Richman; m. Spyros D. Orfanos, Nov. 25, 1976; 1 child, Lina Joanna Orfanos. BA in Psychology, CCNY, 1962, MS in Psychol. Svcs., 1965; PhD in Psychology, NYU, 1970, cert. in psychoanalysis, 1975. Lic. psychologist N.Y., 1972, N.J., 1993, diplomate in psychoanalysis Am. Bd. Profl. Psychology. Testing asst. Hunter Coll., N.Y.C., 1965—68; rsch. assoc. Harvard U., Boston, 1967—68; counselor to students NYU, N.Y.C., 1968—72; clin. psychologist SS Rockaway (N.Y.) Mental Health, 1972—74, Student Ctr. Roosevelt Hosp., N.Y.C., 1974—75; cons. psychologist Diocese of Bklyn., 1974—80; pvt. practice psychotherapy and psychoanalysis NY, 1972—, NJ, 1991—93. Adj. prof. Fordham U., Baruch Coll., N.Y.C., 1986, N.Y.C., 87; supervising analyst ICP, CCAPS, NY, 1986—, NJ, 1995—; supr. postdoctoral program NYU, NY, 2003—. One-woman shows include Cornelia St. Café, 2005; author: A Wolf in the Attic: The Legacy of a Hidden Child of the Holocaust, 2002; contbr. articles to profl. jours., chapters to books. Holocaust testimony Fortunoff Video Archive, Yale U., Conn., 1990, Survivors of the Shoah Visual History Found., L.A., 1998; pub. edn. spkr. on the holocaust various elem. and middle schs. NJ, 1994—95. Recipient scholarship, Jewish Women's Caucus of Assn. Women in Psychology, 2003; Fellowship grant, Meml. Found. for Jewish Culture, 2000—01. Fellow: Acad. Psychoanalysis; mem.: APA (divsn. 39 sect. 3 and 5 treas.), The Pen and Brush Club. Avocations: painting, writing, music. Office: Ste 5 303 Second Ave New York NY 10003 Office Phone: 212-533-3383. Personal E-mail: sophiarichman@aol.com.

RICHMOND, ALICE ELENOR, lawyer; b. NYC; d. Louis A. and Estelle (Muraskin) R.; m. David L. Rosenbloom, July 26, 1981; 1 child, Elizabeth Lara. BA magna cum laude, Cornell U., 1968; JD, Harvard U., 1972; grad. Owners and Pres.'s Mgmt. Program, Harvard U., Harvard Bus. Sch., 2001; DLH (hon.), North Adams State U., 1987. Bar: Mass. 1973, U.S. Dist. Ct. Mass. 1975, U.S. Ct. Appeals (1st cir.) 1982, U.S. Supreme Ct. 1985. Law clk. to justices Superior Ct., Boston, 1972-73; asst. dist. atty. Office of Dist. Atty., Boston, 1973-76; spl. asst. atty. gen. Office of Atty. Gen., Boston, 1975-77; asst. prof. New Eng. Sch. of Law, Boston, 1976-78; assoc. Lappin, Rosen, Boston, 1978-81; ptnr. Hemenway & Barnes, Boston, 1982-92, Deutsch, Williams, Boston, 1993-95, Richmond, Pauly & Ault, Boston, 1996—2003; prin. Richmond & Assocs., Boston, 2003—. Asst. team leader, faculty Trial Advocacy Course, 1978—82; examiner Mass. Bd. Bar Examiners, Boston, 1983—; trustee Mass. Continuing Legal Edn., Inc., Boston, 1985—96, Boston, 1998—2004; treas. Nat. Conf. Bar Examiners, 1995—2005, chmn., 2003—04; analyst CBS TV WBZ, 1991—; v.p., bd. dirs. Am. Bar Ins., Inc., 1995—; bd. dirs. Valora Tech., Inc. Conbr. chpts. to book; contbr. articles to profl. jours. Mem. Pres. Adv. Com on the Arts, 1995—99; bd. overseers Handel & Haydn Soc., 1985—94, bd. govs., 1994—, v.p., 1996—2002; mem. Boston 2000 Millennium Commn., 1997—98; sec., dir. Boston 2000, Inc., 1998—2001; mem., pres. Coun. of Cornell Women, Cornell U. Coun.; trustee Red Auerbach Youth Found., Fund for Justice and Edn., 1997—2002; mem. adv. bd. Ctrl. and Ea. European Law Initiative, 1998—2002; mem. Angell Meml. Hosp. Coun. of Fellows, 2001—. Named one of Outstanding Young Leaders, Boston Jaycees, 1982; Sloan Found. Urban fellow, N.Y.C., 1969. Fellow: Am. Coll. Trial Lawyers; mem.: NOW, Legal Def. and Edn. Fund (trustee 1995—2002, sec. 1998—2002), ABA (ho. of dels. 1980—, vice chmn. com. on rules and calendar 1986—88, bd. govs. 2002—05, task force on gats 2003—, standing com. on audit 2005—), Latin Am. Legal Initiatives Coun., Mass. Bar Found. (pres. 1988—91), Mass. Bar Assn. (pres. 1986—87), Am. Law Inst., Bostonian Soc. (dir.), Boston Club, Harvard Club. Office: Richmond & Assocs 39 Brimmer St Boston MA 02108 Office Phone: 617-523-8187. Business E-Mail: arichmond@rpalaw.com.

RICHMOND, DAPHNE KAY, science educator; d. James Buell and Nettie Mae Willis; m. Arthur Dale Richmond, Nov. 27, 1970; children: Scott Darren, Kenneth Dale, Robin Denise Douglas, Sammi Dale Coney, Meredith Dyan Burnett. BSE, U. Ark., Fayetteville, 1984. Tchr. 7th & 8th grade sci. Mountainburg Mid. Sch., Ark., 1991—. Mem.: NSTA (assoc.). Office: Mountainburg Middle School 129 Highway 71 SW Mountainburg AR 72946 Office Phone: 479-369-4506.

RICHMOND, DINA RAE, retired secondary school educator; b. Shawnee, Okla., Apr. 29, 1929; d. Jack H. Williams and Bertha B. (Megehee) Williams McNair; children: Gregory, Mark, Stephanie. BA in Edn., U. Cen. Okla., 1952; MA in Edn., S.W. Tex. State U., San Marcos, 1977. Tchr. Cotton County Ind. Sch. Dist., Randlett, Okla., 1952-53, Terrell County Ind. Sch. Dist., Sanderson, Tex., 1967-71, Luling (Tex.) Ind. Sch. Dist., 1971-87, Lexington (Tex.) Ind. Sch. Dist., 1987-90, Brenham Ind. Sch. Dist., 1990—91; ret., 1991. Mem. NEA, Tex. State Tchrs. Assn., Delta Kappa Gamma. Democrat. Baptist. Home: 1613 Luza Ln Bryan TX 77802-1517 E-mail: drichmond2929@cox.net.

RICHMOND, DONNA, speech-language pathologist; b. Huntington, W.Va., Aug. 19, 1961; d. Joseph Roy and Marie (Cunningham) Wright; m. David Lawrence Richmond, Nov. 3,1990; children: Jonathan Andrew, Lydia Brooke. BA in Speech-Lang. Pathology, Marshall U., 1983, MA in Comm. Disorders, 1992; postgrad., U. Ky., 1996-98. Lic. in speech pathology, N.C., Ky.; cert. clin. competence, 1994. Speech therapist, itinerant Greenup County Bd. Edn., Greenup, Ky., 1983-84; speech pathologist Lawrence County Bd. Edn., Louisa, Ky., 1984-94; speech pathologist, floater NOVA, Gallipolis, Ohio, 1993-94; speech pathologist Boyd County Bd. Edn., Ashland, Ky., 1994-98; co-lead speech pathologist Orange County Bd. Edn., Hillsborough, N.C., 1998—. Univ. practicum supr. U. N.C., Chapel Hill. Mem. N.C. Speech-Lang. Assn., Ky. Speech-Lang. Assn., Am. Speech-Lang.-Hearing Assn., Coun. for Exceptional Children (profl.). Avocations: reading, crafts. Home: 7 Chartwell Ct Durham NC 27703-3739 Office: CW Stanford Mid Sch 308 Orange High School Rd Hillsborough NC 27278 Business E-Mail: donna.richmond@orange.k12.nc.us.

RICHMOND, GAIL LEVIN, law educator; b. Gary, Ind., Jan. 9, 1946; d. Herbert Irving and Sylvia Esther (Given) Levin; children: Henry, Amy. AB, U. Mich., 1966, MBA, 1967; JD, Duke U., 1971. Bar: Ohio 1971, U.S. Claims Ct. 1986, U.S. Ct. Mil. Appeals, 1994; CPA, Ill. Acct. Arthur Andersen & Co., Chgo., 1967-68; assoc. Jones, Day, Cleve., 1971-72; asst. prof. Capital U. Law Sch., Columbus, Ohio, 1972-73, U. N.C. Law Sch., Chapel Hill, 1973-78; vis. asst. prof. U. Tex. Law Sch., Austin, 1977-78, Nova U. Law Ctr., Ft. Lauderdale, Fla., 1979-80, assoc. prof., 1980-81, assoc. prof., assoc. dean, 1981-85, prof., assoc. dean., 1985-93, 95—, prof., acting dean, 1993-95. Author: Federal Tax Research, 6th edit., 2002; co-author: Tax Planning for Lifetime and Testamentary Dispositions, 1997, A Complete Introduction to Corporate Taxation, 2006; contbr. articles to profl. jours. Pres. Greater Ft. Lauderdale Tax Coun., 1987-88; trustee Law Sch. Admission Coun., 1994-99, chair audit com., 1991-93, chair svcs. and programs com., 1997-99. Mem. ABA (chair commn. on individual income, tax sect. 2001-03, supervising editor News Quar. 2006—, chair AMT task force 2003-2004, chair adj. com., legal edn. sect. 2002-05), Am. Assn. Atty.-CPAs (dir. Fla. chpt. 1992-98), Assn. Am. Law Schs. (audit com. 1992, chair sect. adminstrn. of law schs. 1996, pres. S.E. chpt. 1993-94, sec. S.E. chpt. 1995-2002), S.E. Assn. Law Schs. (pres. 2002-03, sec. 2004—). Democrat. Jewish. Avocation: reading. Office: Nova Southeastern U Shepard Broad Law Ctr 3305 College Ave Fort Lauderdale FL 33314-7721

RICHMOND, GERALDINE LEE, chemist, educator; BS in Chemistry magna cum laude, Kansas State U., 1975; PhD in Phys. Chemistry, U. Calif., Berkeley, 1980. Rsch. and teaching asst. Kans. State U., 1973-76, U. Calif., Berkeley, 1976-80; asst. prof. chemistry Bryn Mawr Coll., 1980-85; assoc. prof. chemistry U. Oreg., Eugene, 1985-91, dir. rsch. experience for undergrad. program, 1987—2004, dir. chem. phys. inst., 1991-95, prof. chemistry, 1991—, Knight prof. liberal arts and sci., 1998—2001, Richard M. and Patricia H. Noyes prof. chemistry, 2001—. Mem. adv. bd. Chemistry, NSF, 1986-89, Materials Sci., 1989-92; mem. adv. bd. Accounts of Chem. Rsch., 1991-94, Analytical Chemistry, 1992-95; chair, founder Com. Advancement Women Chemists (COACh), 1998-2005; mem. governor's sci. adv. bd., State of Oreg., 1986-89; mem., Basic Energy Sci. Adv. Com. Dept. Energy, 1995-2003, chair, 1998-2003; regent Oregon State Bd. Higher Edn. (Gov. Kitzhabor appointee), 1999-2003, system strategic planning com., 1999-2000, Budget and Fin. Com., 2000-03, regent, v.p. (Gov. Kulongoski appointee), 2002-, mem. exec. com., 2003-05, v.p. and interim pres., 2004, chair, chancellor's office reorganization com., 2004-05; mem. Coun. on Chem. Sciences, Dept. Energy 1996-2001; mem. bd. chem. sci. and tech. matter, NAS/NRC, 1989-92, mem.bd. on solid state sciences, 1991-94, mem. chem. sci. roundtable 2003-;chair, NAS Frontiers in Sci. Symposium, 1993-94, Women Faculty Resource Network, U. Oreg., 1992-2004;lectr. in field. Mem. editl. bd. Critical Reviews and Surface Anatomy, 1991-95, Analytical Chemistry, 1992-95, Accounts of Chemical Research, 1991-94, Vibrational Spectroscopy, 1990-94, Jour. Physical Chemistry, 1989-1994, Applied Spectroscopy, 1993-96, Langmuir, 2001-03; adv. bd. mem. Chemical and Engineering News, 2002-04; assoc. editor, Annual Review of Physical Chemistry, 2005-; contbr. articles to profl. jours. King Meml. scholar, 1973-75; Alfred P. Sloan rsch. fellow, 1985-89; recipient Rosalyn Schwartz award, 1982, NSF Presdl. Young Investigator award, 1985-90, Camile and Henry Dreyfus Tchr. award, 1986-90, Chemistry Dept. Alumni award, Kansas State U., 1986, Women Scientists and Engrs. Faculty award, NSF, 1991-96, Rsch. Creativity award, NSF, 1991, Agnes Faye Morgan Rsch. award, 1993, Coll. Arts & Sciences Alumni award, Kansas State U., 1997, Presdl. award Excellence Sci. and Engring. Mentoring White House, 1997, Women Helping Women award Soroptomist Internat., 1998, Rsch. Creativity award, NSF, 2000, Advance Leadership award, NSF, 2001, Oregon Outstanding Sci. award Oregon Acad. Sci., 2001, Spiers medal, Royal Soc. Chemistry (UK) Faraday divsn., 2004 Fellow AAAS, Am. Phys. Soc.(mem. adv. com. laser sci. topical group, 1990-95), Am. Acad. Arts & Sciences; mem. Am. Chem. Soc. (Analytical Chemistry award 1973, Francis P. Garvan medal, 1996, Women

Chemist Com. Regional award Diversity, 2002, Spectrochemical Analysis award, 2002, award for Encouraging Women into Careers in Chem. Sci. 2005), Assn. Women in Sci., Coblentz Spectroscopy Soc. (mem. exec. com., 1988-91, award 1989), Electrochem. Soc., Soc. Applied Spectroscopy, Western Spectroscopy Assn. (exec. bd. mem. 1986-1989) Office: Dept Chemistry 1274 Univ Oregon Eugene OR 97403 Office Phone: 541-346-4635. Office Fax: 541-346-5859. Business E-Mail: richmond@uoregon.edu.*

RICHMOND, LEE JOYCE, psychologist, educator; b. Balt., May 31, 1934; d. Alexander J. and Anne (Morganstern) Blank; m. Aug. 9, 1953 (div. 1983); children: Ruth, Stephen, Sharon, Jessica. BS, Loyola Coll., 1961; MEd, Johns Hopkins U., 1968; PhD, U. Md., 1972. Licensed psychologist. Prof. psychology Dundalk Community Coll., Balt., 1971-75; prof. edn. Johns Hopkins U., Balt., 1975-86, Loyola Coll., Balt., 1986—; pvt. practice Balt., 1974—. Author of numerous articles and books; co-author: Soulwork: Finding the Work You Love-Loving the Work You Have, 1998, What Brings You to Life?, 2001, To Promote Good Will; co-editor: Connections Between Spirit and Work, 1997. Recipient Outstanding Contbn. to Psychology award Md. Psychol. Assn., 1986, Disting. Svc. award Nat. Vocat. Guidance Assn., 1984, Eminent Career award Nat. Career Devel. Assn., 2002. Mem. Coun. for the Accreditation of Coun. and Ednl. Related Programs (bd. dirs. 1999-2000), ACA (gov.'s coun. 1988-90, pres. 1992, mem. ins. trust 1994-99, chair 1998-99, Appreciation cert. 1990), Nat. Career Devel. Assn. (pres. 1988-89, Past Pres. award 1990, chmn. profl. stds. com. 2003-), Balt. Psychol. Assn. (pres. 1998-99), MD Assn. Coun. and Devel. (pres. 2003-); fellow Nat. Career Devel. Assn., Am. Counseling Assn. Home: 8907 Greylock Rd Baltimore MD 21208-1004 Office: Loyola Coll Grad Ctr 2034 Greenspring Ave Lutherville Timonium MD 21093

RICHMOND, MARILYN SUSAN, lawyer; b. Bethesda, Md., Oct. 19, 1949; d. Carl Hutchins Jr. and Elizabeth Adeline (Saeger) R. BA with honors, U. Fla., 1971; JD, Georgetown U., 1974. Bar: Md. 1974, D.C. 1975. Atty. Office of Gen. Counsel, FTC, Washington, 1974-77, antitrust atty. Bur. of Competition, 1977-81; counsel, consumer subcom. of com. on commerce, sci. and transp. U.S. Senate, Washington, 1981-85; assoc. Heron, Burchette, Ruckert & Rothwell, Washington, 1985-87, ptnr., 1987-90; dep. asst. sec. for govtl. affairs U.S. Dept. Transp., Washington, 1990-91, acting asst. sec. for govtl. affairs, 1991-92; cons. Raffaelli, Spees, Springer & Smith, Washington, 1993-94; asst. exec. dir. govt. rels. APA Practice Orgn., 1995—. Lectr. Brookings Instn. Ctr. for Pub. Policy Edn., Washington, 1985-88. Active Lawyers for Bush-Quayle, Washington, 1988. Mem. ABA (antitrust, adminstrv. law sect., vice chair transp. industry com. antitrust sect. 1992-99). Republican. Methodist. Avocations: horseback riding, tennis. Home: Apt 601 2725 Connecticut Ave NW Washington DC 20008-5305 Office Phone: 202-336-5889.

RICHMOND, ROCSAN, television executive producer, small business owner; b. Chgo., Jan. 30; d. Alphonso and Annie Lou (Combest) Richmond; 1 child from previous marriage, Tina S. Student, Wilson Jr. Coll., 1963, 2d City Theatre, Chgo., 1969, Alice Liddel Theatre, 1970; cert. fingerprint classifier, LA City Coll., 1996. Lic. 3d class radio/tel. operator FCC. Vegetarian editor Aware mag., Chgo., 1977—78; investigative reporter, film critic Chgo. Metro News, 1975—81; prodr., talk show host Sta. WSSD, Chgo., 1980—81; dir. pub. rels. IRMCO Corp., Chgo., 1981—82; dir. pub. rels., newsletter editor Hollywood (Calif.) Reporter, 1985—86; exec. prodr. Donald Descendent's Prodns., Hollywood, 1983—, Future News, TV show, 1983—86; pres. Richmond Estates; tchr. TV prodn. Profl. Bus. Acad., Hollywood, 1998—2000; founder, pres. Richmond Acad. Fine Manners, 2000—; v.p. adminstrv. svcs. S.G. Mgmt. Co., Manhattan Beach, Calif., 2006—. Invention invisible drapery tieback. Jehovah'S Witness. Achievements include invention of invisible drapery tieback. Office: PO Box 665 Los Angeles CA 90078-0665 E-mail: aaaaatoner@aol.com.

RICHSTONE, BEVERLY JUNE, psychologist, writer; b. N.Y.C., June 8, 1952; d. Max and Rosalyn Richstone. BA summa cum laude, Queens Coll., 1975; MEd, U. Miami, 1978; PsyD, Nova U., 1982. Lic. clin. psychologist. Clin. fellow Harvard Med. Sch., 1982-83; staff psychologist Met. State Hosp., Waltham, Mass., 1983-85; asst. attending psychologist McLean Hosp., Belmont, Mass., 1983-84; asst. psychologist Cambridge Hosp./N. Charles Mental Health Rsch./Tng. Found., Cambridge, Mass., 1984-85; assoc. dir. Coastal Geriatric Svcs., Hingham, Mass., 1985-86, Alpha Geriatric Svcs., Hingham, 1986-87; freelance writer Tucson, 1987—. Instr. psychology Harvard Med. Sch., Boston, 1983-84; consulting psychologist Coastal Geriatric Svcs., Hingham, 1985. Author: From Harvard to Humility, 2000; contbg. author: The New Our Bodies, Ourselves, 1992, Our Bodies, Ourselves For The New Century, 1998. Mem. APA, Phi Beta Kappa.

RICHTER, DORIS LOUISE, retired elementary school educator; b. Martin, S.D., Apr. 18, 1935; d. Edgar W. and Rhoda E. (Jackson) Gardner; m. Wendelyn Richter, June 3, 1960 (div. Jan. 1977); children: Michael J., Pamela J., Suzanne L. BS in Edn., Black Hills State Coll., 1969. Tchr. fourth grade Erskine Elem., Sturgis, SD, 1969—95; ret. Mem. S.D. Edn. Assn., Nat. Edn. Assn. Republican. Lutheran. Avocations: bowling, reading, gardening.

RICHTER, ELIZABETH LEE, artist; b. Mount Vernon, N.Y., Feb. 1, 1927; d. Frank George and Edna Marguerite (Heese) Lee; m. Edwin Walter Richter, Apr. 10, 1948; children: Marilyn E. Tuma, Barbara J. Walker. BA summa cum laude, U. Bridgeport, 1986. Freelance needlework designer, tchr., 1973-87; freelance artist, 1987—. Restoration asst. New Canaan (Conn.) Hist. Soc. Costume Mus., 1976-81. Mem. Rowayton Arts Ctr., Inc. (bd. dirs. 1992-95), Silvermine Guild Artists, Phi Kappa Phi, Alpha Sigma Lambda. Avocations: films, theater, dance, classical music. Home: 15 Winthrop Woods Rd Huntington CT 06484-5025

RICHTER, JUDITH ANNE, pharmacologist, educator; b. Wilmington, Del., Mar. 4, 1942; d. Henry John and Dorothy Madelyn (Schroeder) R. BA, U. Colo., 1964; PhD, Stanford U., 1969. Postdoctoral fellow Cambridge (Eng.) U., 1969-70, U. London, 1970-71; asst. prof. pharmacology Sch. Medicine Ind. U., Indpls., 1971-78, assoc. prof. pharmacology and neurobiology, 1978-84, prof., 1984—. Vis. assoc. prof. U. Ariz. Health Sci. Ctr., Tucson, 1983; mem. biomed. rsch. rev. com. Nat. Inst. on Drug Abuse, 1983-87. Mem. editl. bd. Jour. Neurochemistry, 1982-87; contbr. numerous articles to sci. jours. Fellow, Wellcome Trust, 1969—71; scholar, Boettcher Found., 1960—64. Mem. AAAS, Am. Soc. for Pharmacology and Exptl. Therapeutics (exec. com. neuropharmacology div. 1989-91), Am. Soc. for Neurochemistry, Internat. Soc. for Neurochemistry, Soc. for Neurosci., Women in Neurosci., Assn. Women in Sci., Phi Beta Kappa, Sigma Xi. Achievements include research in neuropharmacology, especially barbiturates, neurobiology of mutant mice and dopaminergic systems, and regulation of sensory neuron glutamate release. Office: Ind U Sch Medicine 635 Barnhill Dr Indianapolis IN 46202-5126 Office Phone: 317-274-7593. Business E-Mail: jrichter@iupui.edu.

RICHTERMEYER, BEVERLY SUMMERS, special education consultant; b. Hardin, Mo., Mar. 29, 1932; d. Llroy B. and Elna Aurel (Ficke) Summers; m. Herbert Henry Richtermeyer, Dec. 17, 1950; children: Lisa Ann, Lita Kay. BS Edn., Mo. Valley Coll., 1967; MEd, U. Mo., 1975, postgrad., 1989—98; edn. specialist, Ctrl. Mo. U., 1985. Cert. tchr., Mo. Tchr. Carrollton Pub. Schs., Mo., 1967—75; cons. learning disabilities, sch. psychology examiner Marshall Pub. Schs., Mo., 1975—. Adult lit. cons. Saline County, Marshall, 1988—; mem. edn. com. Marshall C. of C., 1987—; spl. edn. cons. South Australia Pub. Schs., 1989; grant writer Saline County and Pub. Schs., 1980— Active Saline/Johnson County Water Dist., 1992—, City Coun., Grand Pass, Mo., 1989—; advisor Saline County 4-H; organizer Santa Fe Trail Wagon Train, 1992, 93; mayor Grand Pass, 2004—; adv. com. Mo. Dept. Transp., 2004—; dir. Saline County Mental Health Bd. Mem. DAR, Order Ea. Star, Dau. of 1812-1983, United Dau. Confederacy, Delta Kappa Gamma (hon. internat. tchr.) Mem. United Ch. of Christ. Avocations: horseback riding, reading, travel. Home: RR 2 Box 10-25 Malta Bend MO 65339-9633 Office Phone: 660-493-2560.

RICHWINE, HEATHER, technology support manager; d. David and Gayle Richwine. BA, U. N.C., 1991. Legis. asst. Office of Congressman Ike Skelton, Washington, 1991-96; spl. asst. Lightspan Partnership, Washington, 1996-97; tech. support mgr. Deloitte Cons. LLC, Washington, 1997—2003. Vol. Folger Shakespeare Libr., 1997-99. Mem. Jr. League of Washington. Avocations: hiking, reading, languages. Home: 6705B Washington Blvd Arlington VA 22213-1038 Office: Deloitte Cons 555 12th St NW Ste 450 Washington DC 20004-1200

RICK, ROSELEEN P., lawyer; b. NYC, 1941; BA, Va. Commonwealth Univ., 1976; JD, Univ. Richmond, 1980. Bar: Va. 1980. Ptnr., practice group leader, multi-family housing Troutman Sanders LLP, Richmond, Va. Mem.: ABA, Nat. Assn. Women Bus. Owners, Va. Bar Assn., Richmond Bar Assn. Office: Troutman Sanders LLP Bank Am Ctr 1111 E Main St Richmond VA 23219 Office Phone: 804-697-1462. Office Fax: 804-698-6007. Business E-Mail: roseleen.rick@troutmansanders.com.

RICKABAUGH, VICKI, horse farm owner, mayor; b. Phila., June 22, 1951; d. William C. and Marilyn Kirschner; m. Charles David Rickabaugh Jr., Sept. 15, 1973; children: Gloria, George, Peggy, Marc. AA, Brookdale C.C., 1981; BS in Edn., Monmouth U., 1972. RN, N.J., state cert. EMT, N.J.; cert. elem. tchr., N.J. Owner, instr. Blue Spruce Horse Farm Dressage Ctr., Jackson, N.J., 1972—; dep. mayor Jackson Twp. (N.J.) Com., 1996, 99, mayor, 1997-98; owner, instr. Blue Spruce Farm Dressage Ctr. Founder, dressage advisor East Coast Regional Dressage Assn., Medford, N.J., 1993—; lectr. in field. Author: (book) Horse Riding for Beginners, 1985; author: (lecture series) Trace and Equine Circle of Needs, 1982—; contbr. articles on dressage and horses to East Coast Regional Dressage Assn. newsletter, 1994—. Bd. dirs. Jackson Twp. Bd. of Edn., 1991-94, v.p., 1992; Rep. committeewoman Ocean County (N.J.) Rep. Orgn., 1995—; committeewoman Jackson Twp. Com., 1996; founder, mem. Jackson Coun. for Arts, 1998—, Tourism and Bus. Coun., Jackson, 1997-99; EMT Jackson Twp. 1st Aid Squad, 1989-95; mem. Jackson Twp. Mcpl. Alliance for Prevention of Alcohol and Drug Abuse, 1995-99. Recipient Proclamation to Mayor Rickabaugh, N.J. Gov. Christine Todd Whitman, N.J. Exec. Dept., Trenton, 1997, Senate and Gen. Assembly Joint Legis. Resolution for disting. svc. State of N.J., 1997, Svc. award Jackson Coun. for Arts, 1998. Mem. Am. Horse Show Assn. (life), U.S. Dressage Fedn. (L judge), Ea. States Dressage and Combined Tng. Assn. (life), Pathfinders (founder). Republican. Avocations: horses, tennis, sailing. Home: 5 Stanley Pl Jackson NJ 08527-4454 Fax: 732-833-0255. E-mail: v.rickabaugh@usa.net.

RICKARD, ANNE COLTON, art educator, artist; b. Cleve., Aug. 28, 1960; d. Theodore Joseph and Nancy Braun Colton; m. John David Rickard, June 27, 1987; 1 child, Georgianna. BA, Ohio No. U., 1982; MA in Liberal Studies, SUNY, Plattsburgh, 1988. Cert. art tchr. grades K-12 N.Y. State Edn. Dept., 1982, elem. edn. grades N-6 N.Y. State Edn. Dept., 1982. Hosp. pharmacy technician Albany (N.Y.) Med. Ctr. Hosp., 1982—84; art tchr., dept. chairperson Lake Placid (N.Y.) Mid./H.S., 1984—. Yearbook advisor Lake Placid Mid./H.S., 1988—91, coord. Winter Carnival, 1995—2000. Authored art exposure project for H.S. students Adirondack Pk. Vis. Interpretive Ctr.; vol., fundraiser Skating Club of Lake Placid, 2000—03. Recipient Tchr. Inst. of Contemporary Art, Sch. Art Inst. Chgo., Nat. Endowment of the Arts, 2001; Art Educator's fellow, Maine Coll. Art, 2003. Mem.: Nat. Art Edn. Assn. (assoc.), N.Y. State Art Tchrs. Assn. (assoc.). Home: 21 Holly Hill Rd Lake Placid NY 12946 Office: Lake Placid Middle/High School 250 Main St Lake Placid NY 12946 Personal E-mail: jrickard@adelphia.net.

RICKARD, LISA ANN, lawyer; b. Englewood, N.J., Oct. 22, 1955; d. Joseph Mitchell and Ann Marie (Samen) Moore; m. J. Scott Rickard, June 18, 1977; children: Jack Taylor, Justin Moore. BA in Govt. and French, Lafayette Coll., 1977; JD, Am. U., 1982. Legis. asst. Bank of Am., Washington, 1977-78; spl. asst. and press asst. to Sen. Richard Stone, Washington, 1978-80; legis. asst. to Sen. Frank Murkowski, Washington, 1981; assoc. and ptnr. Akin, Gump, Strauss, Hauer & Feld, Washington, 1982-93; v.p. federal affairs Ryder System, Inc., Washington, 1993-97, sr. v.p. govt. affairs, 1997; v.p. fed. & state govt. affairs Dow Chemical Co.; pres. U.S. C. of C. Inst. for Legal Reform, Washington. Bd. dirs., mem. corp. adv. coun. Women's Rsch. and Edn. Inst., Washington, 1991—. Diplome D'Etudes Francaises Cours Moyen, Deuxieme Degres, U. Strasbourg, France, 1976. Mem. ABA, D.C. Bar Assn. Episcopalian. Avocation: travel. Office: Institute for Legal Reform 1615 H St NW Washington DC 20062-2000 Office Phone: 202-463-3107. E-mail: lrickard@uschamber.com.

RICKARD, MARGARET LYNN, library director, consultant; b. Detroit, July 31, 1944; d. Frank Mathias and Betty Louise (Lee) Sieger; m. Cyriac Thannikary, Nov. 13, 1965 (div. Feb. 1973); 1 child, Luke Anthony Thannikary; m. Marcos T. Perez, Mar. 1973 (dec. Oct. 1973); m. Lui Gotti, Dec. 23, 1984 (dec. Aug. 1997); m. William A. Rickard, Aug. 22, 1998 (dec. Aug. 21, 2005). AB, U. Detroit, Mich., 1968; MLS, Pratt Inst., Bklyn., 1969; postgrad., NYU, 1976—77. Cert. libr. N.Y. Sr. libr. Queens Pub. Libr., Jamaica, NY, 1969-77; libr. dir. El Centro (Calif.) Pub. Libr., 1977-99; ret., 1999. Vice chmn., chmn. Serra Coop. Libr. Sys., San Diego, 1980—82, libr. cons., 1998—; county libr./cons. Imperial County Free Libr., 1993—99. Pres. Hist. Site Found., El Centro, 1988—99, 1992, sec., 1989, trustee, 1989—99, v.p., 1991—92; mem. Downton El Centro Assn., mem. arches bus. improvement dist.; mem. comm. and arts task force Imperial County Arts Coun.; coord. arts and culture com. City of El Centro Strategic Plan; fin. sec. St. Elizabeth Luth. Ch., El Centro, 1988. Recipient Disting. Svc. award, El Dorado County ACSA, 2004, El Dorado County Disting. Employee Svc. award, ACSA, 2004; Title IIB fellow, Pratt Inst., 1968—69. Mem.: AAUW (v.p. El Centro 1988), ALA, Calif. County Librs. Assn., Calif. Libr. Assn., Toastmasters, El Centro C. of C., Women of Moose (sr. regent El Centro 1988—89, ednl. advancment chmn. 1999—2000), Soroptomists (life; v.p. El Centro 1978, corr. sec. 1990—91, 1st v.p. 1991—92, pres. 1992—93, 2d v.p. 1995—96, 1998—99, rec. sec. 1997—98). Democrat. Lutheran. Home and Office: 6169 Terrace Dr PO Box 232 Pollock Pines CA 95726 E-mail: rickmeg@worldnet.att.net.

RICKARD, RUTH DAVID, retired history professor, retired political science professor; b. Fed. Republic Germany, Feb. 20, 1926; came to U.S., 1940; d. Carl and Alice (Koch) David; m. Robert M. Yaffe, Oct. 1949 (dec. 1959); children: David, Steven; m. Norman G. Rickard, June 1968 (dec. 1988); 1 stepson, Douglas. BS cum laude, Northwestern U., 1947, MA, 1948. Law editor Commerce Clearing House, Chgo., 1948; instr. history U. Ill., Chgo., 1949-51, instr. extension program Waukegan, 1960-67; instr. history Waukegan Schs., 1960-69; original faculty, prof. western civilization, polit. sci. Coll. of Lake County, Grayslake, Ill., 1969-92. Mem. Inter-Univ. Seminar on Armed Forces and Soc.; mem. Hospitality Info. Svc. for Diplomatic Residents and Families affiliate Meridian Internat. Ctr.; spkr. in field. Author: History of College of Lake County, 1987 (honored by city of Waukegan 1987), (poem) I Lost My Wings, 1989, Au Revoir from Emeritusdom, 1993, Where are the Safety Zones, 1994; contbg. author: History of National Press Club: Reliable Sources, 1997; contbr. articles to profl. jours. Mem. Econ. Devel. Com., Waukegan, 1992-93; working with homeless through Samaritans of Greater Washington area, 2000—. Scholar Freedoms Found. Am. Legion, Valley Forge, Pa., 1967. Mem. AAUW (pres. Waukegan chpt. 1955-57, scholarship named for her 1985, program co-chair McLean chpt. 1997-2000), LWV (charter, v.p. Waukegan chpt.), Nat. Press Club D.C., Northwestern U. Alumni Washington (bd. dirs.). Avocations: writing, travel, lecturing, reading, theater.

RICKEL, ANNETTE URSO, psychology and psychiatry researcher, educator; b. Phila. d. Ralph Francis and Marguerite (Calcaterra) Urso; 1 child, John Ralph Rickel. BA, Mich. State U., 1969; PhD, MD, U. Mich., 1972. Lic. psychologist, Mich. Faculty early childhood edn. Merrill-Palmer Inst., Detroit, 1967-69; adj. faculty U. Mich., Ann Arbor, 1969-75; asst. dir. N.E. Guidance Ctr., Detroit, 1972-75; asst. prof. psychology Wayne State U., Detroit, 1975-81; vis. assoc. prof. Columbia U., N.Y.C., 1982-83; assoc. prof. psychology Wayne State U., 1981-87, asst. provost, 1989-91, prof. psychology, 1987-95; Am. Coun. on Edn. fellow Princeton and Rutgers Univs., 1990-91; clin. prof. dept. psychiatry Georgetown U., Washington, 1995—2000; program officer Rockefeller Found., 2000—03; pres. Annette Urso Rickel Found., 2003—; prof. Weill Cornell Med. Sch., 2005—. AAAS and APA Congl. Sci. fellow on Senate Fin. Subcom. on Health and Pres.'s Nat. Health Care Reform Task Force, 1992—93; prof. Weill Cornell Med. Sch., 2005. Cons. editor Jour. of Cmty. Psychology, Jour. Primary Prevention; co-author: Social and Psychological Problems of Women, 1984, Preventing Maladjustment., 1987; author: Teenage Pregnancy and Parenting, 1989, Keeping Children From Harm's Way, 1997, High Risk Sexual Behavior, 1998, Understanding Managed Care, 2000, Attention Deficit Hyperactivity Disorder in Children and Adults, 2006; contbr. articles to profl. jours Mem. Pres.'s Task Force on Nat. Health Care Reform, 1993; bd. dirs. Children's Ctr. of Wayne County, Mich., 1989—, The Epilepsy Ctr. of Mich., 1984-92, Nat. Symphony Orch., 1997—, Reading is Fundamental, 2000—, Chamber Music Soc. of Lincoln Ctr., 2002—, Soc. Meml. Sloan Kettering Cancer Ctr., 2002—, The Kellogg Found., 1996-97, The John D. and Catherine T. MacArthur Found., 1998-99. Grantee NIMH, 1976-86, Eloise and Richard Webber Found., 1977-80, McGregor Fund, 1977-78, 82, David M. Whitney Fund, 1982, Katherine Tuck Fund, 1985-90, NIH, 2000; recipient Career Devel. Chair award, 1985-86. Fellow APA (div. pres. 1984-85); mem. Internat. Women's Forum, Soc. for Rsch. in Child Devel., Soc. for Rsch. in Child and Adolescent Psychopathology, Internat. Assn. of Applied Psychologists, Sigma Xi, Psi Chi. Roman Catholic. Office Phone: 212-659-7760. Personal E-mail: rickelau@aol.com.

RICKERT, JEANNE MARTIN M., lawyer; b. Cambridge, Mass., May 13, 1953; d. Robert Torrence and Margaret (Mutchler) Martin; m. Scott Edwin Rickert, Aug. 19, 1978. BA, Cornell U., 1975; JD, Case Western U., 1978. Bar: Ohio 1980, admitted to practice: US Dist. Ct. (No. Dist.) Ohio 1980. Law clk. to Judge Leroy J. Contie Jr. U.S. Dist. Ct. Ohio, Akron, 1978-80; assoc. Jones, Day, Reavis & Pogue, Cleve., 1980-86; ptnr. Jones & Day, Cleve., 1987—. Author: The Limited Liability Company in Ohio: 1994 Senate Bill 74, with Commentary and Practice Pointers, 1994; co-author (with John Currivan): Ohio Limited Liability Companies, 1999. Mem.: ABA, Ohio State Bar Assn. (corp. law com. 1985—), Cleve. Bar Assn., Order of the Coif. Office: Jones Day Reavis & Pogue N Point 901 Lakeside Ave E Cleveland OH 44114-1190 Office Phone: 216-586-7220. Office Fax: 216-579-0212. Business E-Mail: jmrickert@jonesday.com.

RICKETSON, MARY ALICE, psychotherapist; b. Centralia, Wash., Mar. 11, 1948; d. Luke Alonzo and Marian Elizabeth (Callahan) Peavey; m. Emory Lee Ricketson, Oct. 10, 1970 (div. Jan. 2003); 1 child, Lee Forrest; m. William D. Killen, Sept. 17, 2005. BA, Our Lady of the Lake Coll., 1969; MA, Western Carolina U., 1979; postgrad., Gestalt Ctr. South. Nat. cert. counselor; cert. cln. mental health counselor; lic. profl. counselor. Pub. welfare worker State Dept. Pub. Welfare, San Antonio, 1970, Bexar County Child Welfare, San Antonio, 1971-72, Tarrant County Child Welfare, Ft. Worth, 1972-74; instr. Tri County Tech. Inst., Murphy, N.C., 1974-77; vocat. adjustment coord. Indsl. Opportunities, Inc., Marble, N.C., 1975-78; clin. social worker Smoky Mountain Area Mental Health, Marble, 1978-87; med. social worker Good Shepherd Home Health Agy., Hayesville, N.C., 1987-91; counselor White Oak Counseling Clinic, Brasstown, N.C., 1987-89; pvt. practice Murphy, NC, 1989—; practicioner Neurofeedback, 1999—; Reike practitioner, 2001—; practicioner Internat. Inst. Visualization Rsch., 2002—. Cons., counselor, co-founder Rape Edn. and Awareness, Caring and Help, Inc., Murphy, 1982—, spkr., 1982, bd. dirs., vol. advocate, 1978—98; coord. Women's Resource Ctr., 1992—94; program coord. REACH, Inc., 1993—94; presenter SE Mental Health Symposium, Myrtle Beach, SC, 1985. Columnist women's columns The Cherokee Scout, Carolina newspapers. Bd. dirs. Cherokee County Sharing Ctr. for Needy, 1988; adv. com. Assn. for Retarded Citizens, Cherokee and Clay Citizens, 1991; primary emotional energy recovery facilitator, 1992—. Recipient Person of the Decade award REACH, Inc., Murphy, 1987. Mem. Am. Counseling Assn., Assn. Retarded Citizens, N.C. Counseling Assn., N.C. Coalition Domestic Violence. Avocations: gardening, hiking, photography, reading, sewing. Office: 225 Valley River Ave PO Box 742 Murphy NC 28906-0742 Home: 447 Pet Ln Rd Murphy NC 28906 Office Phone: 704-837-4107. Personal E-mail: maryricketson11@hotmail.com.

RICKETSON, MARY E., dean, lawyer, educator; m. Nathan Ben Coats. JD, U. Denver, 1978. Asst. atty gen., Colo.; dep. dist. atty. Colo.; private practice specializing in employment dispute mediation; exec. dir. Colo. Lawyer's Com.; dean, univ. prof. U. Denver Sturm Coll. Law, 2000. Affiliated Judicial Arbitrators and Mediators. Trustee Dian Fossey Found. Internat.; co-chair Mayor Wellington Webb's 2025 Commn., 2002. Recipient Women of Distinction award, Mill High Girl Scouts, 2004, Edwin Wolf award, Lawyers Com. Civil Rights Under Law, 2004, Mile High Coun. Girl Scouts award, 2004. Mem.: Colo. Hispanic Bar Assn. (Cmty. Svc. award 2003, award 2003), Colo. Profl. Soc. on Abuse of Children (former pres.), Colo. Women's Bar Found. (former pres.), Colo. Women's Bar Assn. (Mary Lathrop Award 2003).

RICKETTS, AMY RENE, elementary school educator, writer; b. Adrian, Mich., July 21, 1975; d. John and Cheri Ricketts. AB in Edn., U. Mich., Ann Arbor, 1997; MS in Edn., U. So. Calif., LA, 2004. Cert. tchr. Mich., 1997, profl. clear tchg. credential Calif. Commn. Tchr. Credentialing, 1997, cert. cross-cultural lang. and devel. Calif., 1997. Tchr. 1st grade Golden View Elem. Sch., Huntington Beach, Calif., 1997—2000, tchr. 5th grade, 2000—01; tchr. phys. sci. 8th grade John Muir Mid. Sch., Burbank, Calif., 2001—. Curriculum writer Skirball Cultural Ctr., L.A., 2004. Author: (curriculum manual) Einstein: A Teacher's Guide. Recipient Tchr. of Yr., Burbank Unified Sch. Dist., 2005. Mem.: Calif. Sci. Tchrs. Assn., NSTA. Office: John Muir Mid Sch 1111 N Kenneth Rd Burbank CA 91504 Office Phone: 818-558-5320. Personal E-mail: missamyricketts@yahoo.com.

RICKETTS, VIRGINIA LEE, historian, researcher; b. Jamestown, Kans., Jan. 12, 1925; d. Roy Earl Eastman and Alma Anna Hunter; m. Clair Keith Ricketts, June 3, 1944; children: Keith Alan, Dennis Lee, Donald Gene. Grad. H.S., Filer, Idaho. Clk. dist. ct., auditor, recorder Jerome County, Idaho, 1972—79; pvt. practice historian, rschr. Jerome, 1979—. Mem. Idaho State Hist. Records Adv. Bd., Boise, 1976-2002; pres. Idaho Assn. Recorders and Clks., 1977-78; cons. Idaho State Supreme Ct., Boise, 1979-81; tour dir., instr. Coll. So. Idaho, Twin Falls, 1984-97; mem. Bur. Land Mgmt. Adv. Bd., Shoshone, Idaho, 1989-95, Upper Snake River Ecosystem Adv. Bd., Idaho, 1995-98; Internat. Toastmistress communicator, 1988; lectr. in field Author: The History of the North Side-The First 75 Years, 1982, Greater Twin Falls Historical Guide, 1988, A History of the Middle Snake River, 1996, Then and Now in Southern Idaho, 1998, Shoshone Falls the Magnificent Spectacle, 2005 Organizer Friends St. Stricker Ranch, Inc., Twin Falls, 1984 Recipient Cert. of Commendation, Am. Assn. for State and Local History, 1984, Cert. of Resolution of Appreciation, Idaho State Bd. Edn., 1998, Esto Perpetua award Idaho State Hist. Soc., 2004; named Idaho Disting. Citizen, Idaho Statesmen, 1988, Centennial Citizen, Citizens of Jerome County Idaho, 1990 Mem. Idaho State Hist. Soc. (trustee 1987-99, chair bd. trustees 1991-98), Oreg. Calif. Trails Assn. (organizer Idaho chpt. 1984, treas. 1985-99), Jerome County Hist. Soc., Inc. (co-organizer 1984, former pres., curator 1985-2004), Idaho Assn. Mus. (Outstanding Svc. award 1998), Soroptimist Internat. Am. (Woman of Distinction 1999), PEO (historian Ea. Idaho chpt. 1987-98) Republican. Presbyterian. Avocations: needlecrafts, gardening, sports, family activities. Home: 516 E 300 S Jerome ID 83338-6747

RICKEY, BETTY L., nursing educator; d. Albert H. and Elinor E. Lyons; m. Micheal P. Rickey, Apr. 16, 1971. MS in Nursing, Wayne State U., Detroit, 1991. Lic. practical nurse. Cert. nurse asst. Lakeview Hosp., Battle Creek, Mich., 1969—70; nurse several hosps. and offices Mich., 1970—82; ADN 3 hosps. Mich., 1982—85; nursing instr. to prof. of nursing Delta Coll., University Center, Mich., 1985—. Nursing program coord. Delta Coll., University Center, 2001—05. Recipient Don Laughner for Creative Change and League for Innovation award, Delta Coll., 1996, Delta Coll. Svc. award, 1997. Mem.: ANA, Mich. Nurse's Assn. (pres. charter in area region), Mich. League for Nursing (bd. mem. 2001—06), Nat. League of Nursing, Sigma Theta Chi. Office: Delta Coll 1961 Delta Rd University Center MI 48710 Office Phone: 989-686-9278. Office Fax: 989-667-2230. Business E-Mail: bettyrickey@delta.edu.

RICKS, DALLIS DERRICK BIEHL, pianist; b. Columbia, S.C., June 8, 1938; d. Bennie Carlisle and Pearl (Bradshaw) Derrick; m. Robert W. Burgess, Feb. 15, 1958 (div. 1978); children: Donna Ann Burgess Hegeman, Robert Russell; m. Albert George Biehl Jr., Aug. 19, 1978 (dec. 1989); m. Griffith M. Ricks, Oct. 30, 1991 (dec. 1999); 1 stepchild, Stephen M. Pvt. studies with, Dr. Parker, 1955-56; student, Am. Savs. and Loan Inst., 1970-71; Cert. in Piano, Major Conservator of Music, 1955. With S.C. Nat. Bank, Columbia, 1956-59, First Nat. Bank, Columbia, 1959—65, Standard Savs. & Loan, Columbia, 1970-72, State of S.C., Columbia, 1978-82, State of Fla., Palm Beach, 1988—. Boca Raton (Fla.) Welcome Wagon Club, 1984—. Mem. Nottingham Garden Club, Beta Sigma Phi (v.p. Columbia chpt. 1962-69). Republican. Lutheran. Home: 74 Vista Del Rio Boynton Beach FL 33426-8829

RICKSON, MARY JANE, counseling administrator; m. Matthew Rickson, Feb. 28, 1992; 3 children. BA, We. New Eng. Coll., Springfield, Mass., 1990. Cert. tchr. social studies Mass., 1990. Peer mediation coord. Roger L. Putnam Vocat. Tech. H.S., Springfield, 1990—; sch. committe mem. Quaboag Regional Sch. Dist., Warren, Mass., 2003—. Coach t-ball, soccer Warren Youth Sports, Mass. Recipient Tchr. of Yr., Wal-Mart Corp., Springfield, 2002. Mem.: Mass. Assn. of Sch. Coms. (corr.). Independent. Office Phone: 413-787-7811.

RICKS-STANFORD, HOPE YVETTE, elementary school educator; b. Jacksonville, Fla., July 3, 1976; d. Norman Lawrence and Ruth Willie Ricks; m. Donald Devon Stanford, June 11, 1996; children: Brent Déjon Stanford, Chico Devon Stanford, Dymond Dajane Stanford. BA in Child Devel., Calif. State U., L.A., 2003; student, Calif. State U., Carson, Calif., 2003—. Tchr. Inglewood (Calif.) Unified Sch. Dist., 2003—. Gate facilitator Inglewood (Calif.) Unified Sch. Dist., 2004—. Mem.: Real Estate Investors Club. Avocations: tennis, travel.

RICO, STEPHANIE ALLCOCK, art educator; b. Washington, Oct. 25, 1955; d. Harry M. and Ann Orlosky Allcock; m. Vincent F. Rico, Sept. 17, 1983; children: Cara Ann, Gianna Ann. BA, U. Md., 1979. Freelance muralist Stephanie Rico Fine Art, Silver Spring, Md., 1978—; visual art educator Studio in the Glen, Montgomery County, Md., 1979—, Montgomery County (Md.) Schs., 1994—. Pres., founder Art Horizons, Brookeville, Md., 1993—; art cons. Miles and Stockbridge, Wash., DC, 1994—2000; advisor, cons. Montgomery County (Md.) Schs., 2000—; bd. dirs. Huntingridge, Brookeville, Md., 2001. Author: (book) Art Horizons American Art, 1997. Mem. Worth Ea. Montgomery County (Md.) Polit. Action Com., 2000—. Mem.: Nat. Assn. Cath. Tchrs., Nat. Mus. for Women in the Arts, Phi Kappa Phi. Avocations: painting, sculpting, photography, gardening. Office: Art Horizons Studio in the Glen 21309 Ridgecroft Dr Brookeville MD 20833 Personal E-mail: arthorizons@comcast.net.

RICORD, KATHY, diversified financial services company executive; Grad., Denison U.; degree in City and Regional Planning and Bus. Adminstrn., Ohio State U. With Nationwide Mutual Ins. Co., 1986—, asst. to CEO, 1997—99, sr. v.p. mktg. and strategy, 2002—03, exec. v.p., chief mktg. officer, 2003—. Office: Nationwide Mutual Ins Co One Nationwide Plaza Columbus OH 43215-2220

RIDDELL, TINA MARIE, secondary school educator; EdM, Grand Canyon U., Ariz., 2005. Cert. tchr. Mass., 1994. Phys. edn. tchr. John F. Kennedy Mid. Sch., Northampton, Mass., 1996—2001, Ralph C. Mahar Regional H.S., Orange, 2001—. With U.S. Army, 1991—99. Office: Ralph C Mahar Regional HS 507 S Main St Orange MA 01364 Office Phone: 978-544-2542.

RIDDIFORD, LYNN MOORHEAD, biologist, educator; b. Knoxville, Tenn., Oct. 18, 1936; d. James Eli and Virginia Amalia (Berry) Moorhead; m. Alan W. Riddiford, June 20, 1959 (div. Jan. 1966); m. James William Truman, July 28, 1970. AB magna cum laude, Radcliffe Coll., 1958; PhD, Cornell U., 1961. Rsch. fellow in biology Harvard U., Cambridge, Mass., 1961-63, 65-66, asst. prof. biology, 1966—71, assoc. prof., 1971—73; instr. biology Wellesley (Mass.) Coll., 1963—65; from assoc. prof. to prof. zoology U. Wash., Seattle, 1973—2003, prof. biology, 2003—, Virginia and Prentice Bloedel prof., 2000—05, assoc. chmn., 2003—04. Mem. study sect. tropical medicine and parasitology NIH, Bethesda, Md., 1974—78, 1997; mem. Competitive Grants panel USDA, 1979, 89, 95; mem. regulatory biology panel NSF, 1984—88, 2001, 05; mem. governing coun. Internat. Ctr. for Insect Physiology and Ecology, 1985—91, chmn. program com., 1989—91; chmn. adv. com. SeriBiotech, Bangalore, India, 1989; mem. biol. adv. com. NSF, 1992—95; mem. coun. Internat. Cong. Entomology, 1988—, pres., 2000—04; mem. coun. Internat. Fedn. Comparative Endocrine Socs., 1996—, pres., 2001—05. Mem. editl. bd. profl. jours.; contbr. articles to profl. jours. Bd. dirs. Entomol. Found., 1998—2001, chmn., 2001; bd. dirs. Whitney Lab., 2000—04, chmn., 2004. Recipient Gregor J. Mendel award, Czech Republic Acad. Scis., 1998; fellow, NSF, 1958—60, 1961—63, NIH, 1960—61, 1986—87, John S. Guggenheim Found., 1979—80, NIH, 1986—87; grantee, NSF, 1964—65, 1967—, Rockefeller Found., 1970—79, USDA, 1978—82, 1989—, NIH, 1975—. Fellow: AAAS, Entomol. Soc. Am. (Recognition award in insect physiology, biochemistry and toxicology), Royal Entomol. Soc., Am. Acad. Arts and Sci.; mem.: Soc. Exptl. Biology, Soc. Devel. Biology, Am. Soc. Biochem. and Molecular Biology, Soc. Integrative and Comparative Biology. Methodist. Home: 16324 51st Ave SE Bothell WA 98012-6138 Office: U Wash Dept Biology PO Box 351800 Seattle WA 98195-1800 Business E-Mail: lmr@u.washington.edu.

RIDDLE, ANNA LEE, retired elementary school educator, retired music educator; b. Washington, Pa., Jan. 19, 1933; d. Don Elliott and Carrie Mae Porter; m. Richard Dean Riddle, Dec. 28, 1954; children: Richard Dean Riddle II, Robert Eliott, Lee Ann Riddle-Fink. MusB, W.Va. U., 1954. Cert. advanced profl. music Md. Dept. Edn. Music tchr. Monongalia County Schs., Morgantown, W.Va., 1954—55; choir dir. First Presbyn. Ch., Elyria, Ohio, 1958—67, Presbyn. Ch. Atonement, Silver Springs, Md., 1968—82; music tchr. Montgomery County Pub. Schs., Rockville, Md., 1970—95; choir dir. First Presbyn. Ch., Weston, W.Va., 1998—. Chmn., founder Montgomery County Elem. Honors Chorus, Rockville, 1984—95. Sec. Garden Club, Weston, 1998—2001; pres. AAUW, Weston, 1999—2001, Federated Club, Weston, 2000—01; vol. Hosp. Aux., 1998—. Named Md. Music Tchr. of Yr., Md. Music Educators Nat. Conf., 1992. Mem.: DAR, Order Ea. Star. Republican. Presbyterian. Avocations: sewing, ceramics, swimming. Home: 324 E 7th St Weston WV 26452

RIDDLE, ELSIE KATHLEEN, elementary school educator, school librarian; b. Phila., Apr. 11, 1939; d. Pervie Olivet and Marian Grasso Riddle. AA, San Jose City Coll., 1961; BA in Edn., San Jose State U., 1966, MLS, 1974; postgrad., Santa Clara U., 1970—97. Cert. elem. tchr. Calif., secondary tchr. Calif., libr. San Jose State U., 1966. Libr. grades K-6 Sunnyvale Elem. Sch. Dist., Calif., 1966—72, tchr. elem., 1972—98. Tchr. remedial reading Cherry Chase Elem. Sch., Sunnyvale, 1999—2002. Active Triton Mus. Art, Cupertino Sr. Ctr., Santa Clara Sr. Ctr., Nat. Mus. Women in the Arts, Sunnyvale Hist. Assn., Orchard Gardens; mem. vocal music choir Golden Tones, Santa Clara County Reading Coun., Saratoga Hist. Mus. Mem.: AAUW, PTA, NEA (life; life), Assn. of Am. Ret. Persons, Sunnyvale Edn. Assn., Calif. Tchr. Assn., Calif. Libr. Assn., Calif. Ret. Tchrs. Assn. (life), San Jose State U. Alumni Assn., Santa Clara Caroliers, Lions Club, Elks, Alpha Delta Kappa. Democrat. Avocations: gardening, reading, travel, hiking, all fine arts.

RIDDLE, MELANIE TIMMS, secondary school educator; b. Anderson, S.C., Feb. 17, 1958; d. Delbert Silas and Norma Hincher Timms; m. Thomas David Riddle, July 8, 1978; children: Timothy David, Carrie Morgan. AA, Anderson Coll., S.C., 1977; BA, Erskine Coll., Due West, S.C., 1980; MEd, Clemson U., S.C., 1984; D of Ministry, So. Bapt. Sch. Bibl. Studies, Jacksonville, Fla., 2005. Profl. tchg. cert. S.C. Dept. Edn., 1980. Tchr. Crescent H.S., Iva, SC, 1980—; dir. Shekinah Bible Inst., Greer, SC, 2003—. Bd. dirs. Internat. Cathedral of Prayer, Greer, 2002—06. Mem.: NEA (assoc.). Pentecostal. Avocation: reading. Office: Crescent HS 9104 Hwy 81 South Iva SC 29655 Office Phone: 864-352-6175. Business E-Mail: riddlem@anderson3.k12.sc.us.

RIDE, SALLY KRISTEN, physics professor, research scientist, retired astronaut; b. LA, May 26, 1951; d. Dale Burdell and Carol Joyce (Anderson) R.; m. Steven Alan Hawley, July 26, 1982 (div.). BA in English, Stanford U., 1973, BS in Physics, 1973, PhD in Physics, 1978. Tchg. asst. Stanford U., Palo Alto, Calif., rschr. Dept. Physics; astronaut candidate, trainee NASA, 1978-79, astronaut, 1979-87, on-orbit capsule communicator STS-2 mission Johnson Space Ctr. Houston, on-orbit capsule communicator STS-3 mission, mission specialist STS-7, 1983, mission specialist STS-41G, 1984; sci. fellow Stanford (Calif.) U., 1987-89; dir. Calif. Space Inst. U. Calif. San Diego, La Jolla, 1989—96, pres. space com., 1999-2000; prof. dept. physics9 U. Calif. San Diego, 1989—96; pres., CEO Imaginary Lines, Inc., 2001—. Mem. Presdl. Commn. on Space Shuttle Challenger Accident, 1986, World Resources Inst. Global Coun., 1993—, Presdl. Com. of Advisors on Sci. and Tech., 1994—, Univ. Calif. Oversight Com. for the Nat. Labs, Pacific Coun. on Internat. Policy; pres., CEO Space.com, 1999—2000; intiated NASA EarthKAM project; bd. dir. Nat. Rsch. Coun. Space Studies, Congressional Office of Tech. Assessment, Carnegie Instn. Washington; past bd. dir. NCAA Found.; bd. trustee Caltech; lectr. in field. Author: (with Susan Okie) To Space and Back, 1986, (with T.O'Shaughnessy) Voyager: An Adventure to the Edge of the Solar System, 1992, The Third Planet: Exploring the Earth From Space, 1994, (revised 2004), The Mystery of Mars, 1999, Exploring Our Solar System, 2003. Named to The Nat. Women Hall of Fame, 1988, Astronaut Hall of Fame, Kennedy Space Center, 2003; recipient Jefferson award for Pub. Svc., Nat. Spaceflight medal (twice), Von Braun award, Lindbergh Eagle award, Silver Anniversary award, NCAA, 1998, Theodore Roosevelt award, 2005. Fellow: Am. Physical Soc. Achievements include becoming the first American woman to orbit Earth when she flew aboard Space Shuttle Challenger, June 18 1983. Avocations: tennis, running, volleyball, softball, stamp collecting. Office: U Calif San Diego Dept Physics 0426 La Jolla CA 92093-0426 Address: Sally Ride Science 9191 Towne Centre Dr San Diego CA 92122

RIDENHOUR, MARILYN HOUSEL, retired accountant; b. Madison, Nebr., July 12, 1931; d. Kenneth Virgil Housel and Edna Christina Reese Housel; m. Henry Clifton Ridenhour, Apr. 25, 1954 (dec.); children: Keith James, Susan Marie Ridenhour Redelfs, Jill Housel Ridenhour Cortese. Student, Nebr. Wesleyan U., 1949—50; BS in Bus. Adminstrn. with distinction, U. Nebr., 1953. CPA Mo., 1957. CPA Price Waterhouse & Co., St. Louis, 1953—54, Adolph Kahn, St. Louis, 1954—57; ptnr., CPA Adolph Kahn & Co., St. Louis, 1957—61, Kahn, Ridenhour & Co., St. Louis, 1961—65, Ridenhour Hylton & Co., St. Louis, 1965—91; cons. Baird Kurtz & Dobson, St. Louis, 1991—92, ret., 1992. Citizen leader Chesterfield, Mo. 2d Congl. Dist., 2005. Mem.: Rep. Leadership Found. (founding mem.), Am. Women's Soc. CPA, Am. Soc. Women Accts. (charter pres. 1959), Dawn Hope Soc., Soaring Eagle, Nat. Law Enforcement (founding mem. 2005), Century Soc., U. Nebr. Alumni Assn., St. Labre Indian Sch. Ednl. Assn., Chancellors Club U. Nebr., Beta Gamma Sigma, Phi Chi Theta, Alpha Lambda Delta, Delta Delta Delta. Republican. Methodist. Personal E-mail: hermhr@wchtv.net.

RIDENOUR, AMY MORITZ, research center administrator; b. Pitts., Nov. 9, 1959; d. Karl Berkoben and Carol Lee (Riley) M. B or Econs., U. Md., 1981. Exec. dir. Nat. Ctr. for Pub. Policy Rsch., Washington, 1982-88, trustee, 1986—; pres. The Nat. Ctr. for Pub. Policy Research, Washington, 1988—; formerly host Scoop!, Nat. Empowerment Television, Washington; nationally sundicated columnist UPI and Knight-Ridder Tribune, 1998—. Chmn. Liberty Inst., Washngton. Assoc. pub. Cath. Study Coun. Bull.; editor Nat. Policy Watch Jour., Liberation Bull.; exec. editor Liberty Letter; contbr. articles to Policy Rev. and other profl. jours. Regional coord. Reagan-Bush Nat. Campaign, Washington, 1980; bd. dirs., v.p. Internat. Youth Yr. Commn. for U.S., 1985; chmn. Md. Fedn. Coll. Rep. Clubs, 1978-80. Mem. Accuracy in Academia (adv. bd.). Lutheran. Avocations: skiing, books, history. Office: Nat Ctr for Pub Policy Rsch 501 Capitol Court Washington DC 20002

RIDENOUR, DEBORAH HUGHES, elementary school educator; b. Balt., Sept. 26, 1945; d. George Wilson and Goldie Holton Hughes; m. Kenneth Henry Ridenour, June 27, 1970. BS in Elem. Edn., Frostburg State U., 1967; MLA, Johns Hopkins U., 1981. Tchr. Balt. County Pub. Sch., 1967—. Named Tchr. of Yr., Essex-Middle C. of C., 2002; recipient Excellence in Edn. award, Balt. County C. of C., 1990. Mem.: NEA, Tchrs. Assn. Balt. County, Md. State Tchrs. Assn. Methodist. Avocations: aerobics, travel, reading, golf, motorcycling. Office: Middleborough Elem Sch 313 West Rd Baltimore MD 21221

RIDENOUR, JOEY, medical association administrator, operations research specialist; BSc in Nursing, Ariz. State U.; MN, U. Phoenix. RN Ariz. COO Maricopa Health Sys., Phoenix, 1975—95; exec. dir. Ariz. State Bd. Nursing, 1995—98; pres. Nat. Coun. State Bds. of Nursing, Chgo., 1998; exec dir Ariz State bd of nursing. Pres. Ariz. State Bd. Nursing, Phoenix, 1986—89, 1994—95; adj. faculty Ariz. State U. Recipient Disting. Achievement award, Am. Soc. Pub. Adminstrn., Ariz. State U. Coll. Nursing, U. Phoenix; fellow, Wharton. Office: Boards of Nursing Natl Coun of State 111 E Wacker Dr Ste 2900 Chicago IL 60601-4277

RIDER, FAE B., freelance writer; b. Summit Point, Utah, Mar. 1, 1932; d. Lee Collingwood and Jessie (Hammond) Blackett; m. David N. Rider, Jan. 26, 1952; children: David Lee, Lawrence Eugene. BS, No. Ariz. U., 1971, MA, 1974; postgrad., U. Nev., Las Vegas, 1985-88. Lic. tchr. in elem., reading, spl. edn. Learning specialist, Las Vegas, summers 1974-76; tchr. kindergarten Indian Springs (Nev.) Pub. Schs., 1971-76; reading tchr. Las Vegas Pub. Schs., 1976-80; curriculum coord. Indian Springs Pub. Schs., 1980-91; tchr. 1st grade Las Vegas Pub. Schs., 1991-92, reading specialist, 1992-93; pvt. edn./reading cons. Las Vegas, 1993—. Author booklet: Door to Learning - A Non-Graded Approach, 1978. Bd. dirs. Jade Park, Las Vegas, 1988. Recipient Excellence in Edn. award, 1988, Outstanding Sch.and Cmty. Svc. award, 1990. Mem. Internat. Reading Assn., Ret. Tchrs. Assn., Am. Legion Aux., A.R.E study group, Delta Kappa Gamma (pres., Rose of Recognition), Kappa Delta Phi. Avocations: reading, writing, travel.

RIDER, RUTH WHEELER, elementary school educator; b. Jacksonville, Fla., Dec. 2, 1944; d. Ralph Stanley and Ruth Bernice Wheeler; m. Sydney Bertram Alexander (div.); children: Amy Elizabeth, Stephen Shane, Jeremy Scott, Allison Ruth. BA in Christian Edn., Asbury Coll., 1966. Certification for Exceptional Student Education U. North Fla., 1990. Tchr. Duval County Sch. Bd., Jacksonville, Fla., 1989—2005; reading tchr. Jefferson Davis Mid. Sch., 2005—06, stds. coach, 2006—. Leadership team for Jefferson Davis, Jacksonville, 2004—. Author: (book) Spotlight on Teachers, 2005, Nerd-Face Tag Along, 2006. Missionary to Indonesia World Gospel Mission, 1969—73; mem., asst. music dir. Real Life Christian Fellowship, 1997—; mem. PTA. Recipient Region III Tchr. of Yr., 2002—03, Jefferson Davis Tchr. of Yr., 2000—01, 2002—03, Editor's Choice award for outstanding achievement in poetry, 2005. Mem.: Internat. Soc. Poets, Duval Teachers United. Republican. Protestant. Avocations: writing, baking, singing. Home: 2349 Hugh Edwards Dr Jacksonville FL 32210 Office: Jefferson Davis Mid Sch 7050 Melvin Rd Jacksonville FL 32210 Office Phone: 904-573-1060. Personal E-mail: ruthrider1@netzero.net.

RIDGE, LINDA KISER, secondary school educator; b. Arlington, Va., Mar. 4, 1955; d. Patricia H. Rosensteel; m. Timothy S. Ridge, June 12, 1981; children: Jennifer A., William S. BS, Radford U., Va., 1977; MA in Natural Scis., U. S.C., Columbia, S.C., 1990. Lic. tchr. Va., S.C., Tenn. Tchr. Orange (Va.) County Schs., 1977—81, Orangeburg County Schs., Cordova, SC, 1981—84, Bamberg (S.C.) County Schs., 1984—96, Morgan County Schs., Oakdale, Tenn., 1996—99, Cumberland County Schs., Crossville, Tenn., 1999—. Cons. earth sci. U. S.C., Columbia, 1991—96; cons. Vol. Emergency Preparedness Team, Crossville, Tenn.; vol. homecoming Nat. Guard-278th, Crossville; vol. Red Cross, Crossville. Recipient Multiple Yr. Recipient, Who's Who Among America's Teachers, 1994, 1998, 2000, 2002, 2004 (2X's); grantee Classroom Rsch./Activities, Savannah River Nuc. Plant, Classroom Rsch. for Seeds in Space Project, NASA. Mem.: Delta Kappa Gamma. Office: Cumberland County High School 660 Stanley St Crossville TN 38555 Office Phone: 931-484-6194.

RIDGEWAY, TERESA DRIVDAHL, weaver, educator; b. Big Timber, Mont., May 10, 1936; d. Emil L. and Margaret Lamach Drivdahl; m. Hallas H. Ridgeway, Sept. 15, 1963; children: Lesley, Benton, Kristoffer. BA in English, U. Mont., 1958. Tchr. English Flathead County H.S., Kalispell, Mont., 1958—60; tchr. English and French Fife (Wash.) H.S., 1960—61; tchr. English as fgn. lang. Ecole des Arts et Metiers, Phnom Penh, Cambodia, 1961—63; tchr. English and French Coventry (Conn.) H.S., 1964—65. Tchr., lectr. Que. Weavers' Conf., 1994; weaving tchr. New Eng. Weavers Conf., Mass., 2005; spkr. in field. Contbr. articles to mags.; rugs, tapestries, Represented in permanent collections U. Conn. Libr., U. Montana, Aetna Ins. Tng. Ctr., Mass., numerous pvt. homes in the US and Europe. Named Weaver of Distinction, New Eng. Weavers' Conf.; recipient Smith-Mundt tchg. grant to Cambodia, 1961—63. Mem.: Handweavers' Guild of Conn. (life; weaving tchr. 1980—, Master Weaver). Democrat. Congregational. Avocation: knitting. Home: 318 Phoenixville Rd Chaplin CT 06235 Office: Handweavers Guild of Conn 127 Carriage Dr Glastonbury CT 06033 Office Phone: 860-455-9392.

RIDGWAY, DELISSA ANNE, federal judge; b. Kirksville, Mo., June 28, 1955; d. Kenneth Driggs and Margaret Anne (Warner) R. BA with honors, U. Mo., 1975, postgrad., 1976; JD, Northeastern U., 1979. Bar: DC Ct. Appeals 1979, US Dist. Ct. DC 1980, US Ct. Appeals (DC cir.) 1980, US Supreme Ct. 1983, US Ct. Appeals (1st cir.) 1988. Law clk. to presiding justice U.S. Dist. Ct. D.C., Washington, 1979; assoc. Shaw, Pittman, Potts & Trowbridge, Washington, 1979-88, counsel, internat. practice group, 1988—94; chair, US Fgn. Claims Settlement Commn. US Dept. Justice, Washington, 1994—98; judge US Ct. Internat. Trade, NYC, 1998—. Lectr. nuclear and environ. law to various orgns. Mem. Women's Legal Def. Fund. Recipient: Hardin-Craig fellow U. Mo., Columbia, 1974, Frederick B. Abramson award, DC Bar Assn., 1996, Earl W. Kintner award, Fed. Bar Assn., 2000, Woman Lawyer of The Year, Washington, 2001. Mem. ABA, Women's Bar Assn. (sec. 1989-90), Fed. Bar Assn. (chair adminstrv. law sect. com. agy. adjudication 1985-89, chair adminstrv. law sect. com. regulatory reform 1984-85), Am. Law Inst., Fellow, Am. Bar Found. Roman Catholic. Office: US Ct Internat Trade One Federal Plz New York NY 10278-0001

RIDGWAY, MARCELLA DAVIES, veterinarian; b. Sewickley, Pa., Dec. 24, 1957; d. Willis Eugene and Martha Ann (Davies) R. BS, Pa. State U., 1979; VMD, U. Pa., 1983; MS, U. Ill., 1997. Diplomate Am. Coll. Vet. Internal Medicine. Intern U. Ill., Urbana, 1983-84, resident in small animal internal medicine, 1984-87; small animal vet. Vet. Cons. Svcs., Savoy, Ill., 1987-97; clin. asst. prof. small animal vet. medicine U. Ill., Urbana, 1997—. Contbr. articles to profl. jours. Mem. Am. Vet. Med. Assn., Acad. Vet. Clinicians, Ea. Ill. Vet. Med. Assn. (pres. 2000-2001), Savoy Prairie Soc. (pres. 1989—), Grand Prairie Friends (bd. dirs. 1993-96), Sangamon Valley Conservancy (bd. dirs. 1995-2005 Avocations: prairie conservation activities, hiking, canine collectibles, running, dog obedience training. Office: U Ill Vet Med Teaching Hosp 1008 W Hazelwood Dr Urbana IL 61802-4714 Home: 808 Indigo Savoy IL 61874

RIDGWAY, ROZANNE LEJEANNE, corporate director, retired ambassador; b. St. Paul, Aug. 22, 1935; d. H. Clay and Ethel Rozanne (Cote) R.; m. Theodore E. Deming. BA, Hamline U., 1957, LLD (hon.), 1978, George Washington U., 1986, Elizabethtown Coll., 1990, U. Helsinki, 1992; LLD in Pub. Svc. (hon.), Coll. of William and Mary, 1994; DHL (hon.), Hood Coll., 1994; LLD (hon.), Albright Coll.; DHL in Pub. Adminstrn. (hon.), The Citadel, 2003; DHL (hon.), Ill. Coll., 2003. Career diplomat U.S. Fgn. Svc., 1957-89, amb. at large for oceans and fisheries, 1975-77, US amb. to Finland Helsinki, 1977—80; counselor State Dept., 1980—81, spl. asst. to sec., 1981, amb. to German Dem. Republic, 1982-85, asst. sec. Europe and Can., 1985-89; pres. Atlantic Coun. US, 1989-92, co-chmn., 1993-96; chmn. Baltic-Am. Enterprise Fund, Washington, 1994—. Bd. dirs. 3M Corp., Emerson Electric Co., Boeing Co., Sara Lee Corp., Manpower, Inc., New Perspective Fund, Europacific Fund, New World Fund. Life trustee Hamline U.; trustee Nat. Geog. Soc., Ctr. Naval Analyses. Decorated Grand Cross Order of the Lion (Finland); recipient Profl. awards Dept. State, Presdl. Disting. Performance awards, Joseph C. Wilson Internat. Rels. Achievement award, 1982, Sharansky award Union Couns. Soviet Jewry, 1989, U.S. Presdl. Citizens medal, 1989; named Person of Yr. Nat. Fisheries Inst., 1977, Knight Comdr., Order of Merit, Germany; inducted into Nat. Women's Hall of Fame, 1998. Fellow Nat. Acad. Pub. Adminstrn.; mem. Am. Acad. Diplomacy, Army-Navy Country Club.

RIDINGS, DOROTHY SATTES, former association executive; b. Charleston, W.Va., Sept. 26, 1939; d. Frederick L. and Katharine E. (Backus) Sattes; m. Donald Jerome Ridings, Sept. 8, 1962 (dec. June 1997); children: Donald Jerome Jr., Matthew Lyle. Student, Randolph-Macon Woman's Coll., 1957-59; BSJ, Northwestern U., 1961; MA, U. N.C., 1968; D.Pub. Svc. (hon.), U. Louisville, 1985; LHD (hon.), Spalding U., 1986; LLD (hon.), U. Charleston, 1999. Reporter Charlotte Observer, NC, 1961-66; instr. U. N.C. Sch. Journalism, 1966-68; freelance writer Louisville, 1968-77; news editor Ky. Bus. Ledger, Louisville, 1977-80, editor, 1980-83; communications cons., editor, 1983-86; mgmt. assoc. Knight-Ridder Inc., Charlotte, NC, 1986-88; pres., pub. Bradenton Herald, Fla., 1988-96; pres., CEO Coun. on Founds., Washington, 1996—2005. Adj. prof. U. Louisville, 1982-83; v.p. Nat. Mcpl. League, 1985-86; bd. dirs. com. on Constl. Sys., Nat. Com. Against Discrimination in Housing, 1982-87, Com. for Study of Am. Electorate, 1982—; bd. dirs. Ind. Sector, 1983-88, 92-97; mem. exec. com. Leadership Conf. Civil Rights, 1982-86; mem. Accrediting Coun. on Edn. in Journalism and Mass Comm., 2000-06. Pres. LWV U.S., 1982-86, 1st v.p., 1980-82, human resources dir., 1976-80, chair edn. fund, 1982-86, 1st vice chair, 1980-82, trustee, 1976-80, pres. Louisville/Jefferson County, 1974-76, bd. dirs., 1969-76; chmn., bd. dirs. Nat. Civic League, 2000-04; trustee Louisville Presbyn. Theol. Sem., 1992—, chmn., 2000—; trustee Ford Found., 1989-96, Manatee C.C., 1992-96; bd. dirs. Benton Found., 1989-96, Fla. Press Assn., 1994-96, Leadership Ky., 1984-87, Leadership Louisville, 1983-86, Louisville YWCA, 1978-80, Jr. League Louisville, 1972-74; mem. ABA Accreditation Com., 1987-93, ABA coun. legal edn. and admissions to bar, 1997-03, Gov.'s Coun. Ednl. Reform, 1984-85; chair Prichard Com. Acad. Excellence, 1985-86; mem. Gov.'s Commn. Full Equality, 1982-83; mem. state adv. coun. U.S. Commn. Civil Rights, 1975-79; mem. steering com. Task Force for Peaceful Desegregation, 1974-75; elder 2d Presbyn. Ch., 1972-75, 78-81; mem. adv. coun. on ch. and soc. United Presbyn. Ch. in USA, 1978-84; mem. bd. visitors U. N.C., 1993-96; mem. Nat. Commn. on Presdl. Debates, 1997—; mem. Urban Librs. Coun. Exec. Bd., 2005—; bd. dirs. Editl. Projects in Edn., 2004—. Recipient Northwestern U. award of merit, 1994, Disting. Alumna award U. N.C., 1995, Leadership award Nat. Assn. Cmty. Leadership

Orgns., 1986, Alumnae Achievement award Randolph-Macon Woman's Coll., 1985, Disting. Citizen award Nat. Mcpl. League, 1983; inducted into Northwestern U. Medill Sch. Journalism Hall of Fame, 1996, U. N.C. Journalism Hall of Fame, 1997.

RIDLEN, JUDITH ELAINE, minister; b. Champaign, Ill., Nov. 10, 1948; d. Samuel Franklin and Helen Louise (Camp) R. BS in Home Econs., Ill. State U., 1970; M. Religious Edn., Lexington Theol. Sem., 1974; D. Ministry, McCormick Theol. Sem., 1984. Ordained to ministry Christian Ch. (Disciples of Christ). Assoc. regional minister Christian Ch. in Ill.-Wis., Bloomington, Ill., 1974-84; sr. minister Northside Christian Ch., Knoxville, Tenn., 1984—92. 1st vice-moderator Christian Ch. in Tenn., Nashville, 1988-1992; bd. dirs. Christmount Christian Assembly, Black Mountain, N.C., 1986-1992, Div. Homeland Ministries, Indpls., 1975-81; sec. Assn. Christian Ch. Educators, Indpls., 1983-84. Mem. Ch. Women United (officer Knox County unit 1986-1992).

RIDLEY, BETTY ANN, theology studies educator; b. St. Louis, Oct. 19, 1926; d. Rupert Alexis and Virginia Regina (Weikel) Steber; m. Fred A. Ridley, Jr., Sept. 8, 1948; children: Drue Alexis, Clay Kent. BA, Scripps Coll., Claremont, Calif., 1948. Christian Sci. practitioner, Oklahoma City, 1973—. Tchr. Christian Sci., 1983—; mem. Christian Sci. Bd. Lectureship, 1980-85. Trustee Daystar Found., 1990-; mem. First Ch. of Christ Scientist, Boston, 1956-2005, Fifth Ch. of Christ Scientist, Oklahoma City. Mem. Jr. League Am. Home: 2933 Lansdowne Ln Oklahoma City OK 73120-4343 Office: Suite 100-G 3000 United Founders Blvd Oklahoma City OK 73112 Office Phone: 405-848-7565. Personal E-mail: baridley@aol.com.

RIDLEY, JULIE A., biologist, educator; b. Summerville, SC, Feb. 17, 1966; d. Floyd and Julie Franklin; m. Brad Ridley, Jan. 23, 1988; children: Justin, Ben. BS, Berry Coll., Rome, Ga., 1986. Cert. Tchr. 4-12 Ga., 1993. Tchr. 9th grade biology Murray County Bd. Edn., Chatsworth, Ga., 2002—. Mem.: NSTA. Office Phone: 706-695-1414.

RIDOLFI, DOROTHY PORTER BOULDEN, nurse, real estate broker; b. SI, NY, Jan. 24, 1937; d. David Porter and Helen Marie (McCloskey) Boulden; m. Edward Benjamin Ridolfi, Aug. 16, 1958; children: Edward Brian, Judyann Nixon, Jacqueline Ryan. RN, St. Francis Hosp., 1957; student, Seton Hall U., 1958, Mercer CC, 1974, student, 1984, Thomas Edison Coll., 1979—84. Cert. coronary and critical care nurse; real estate cert. South Jersey Sch. Profl. Bus., 1976, lic. real estate instr. NJ, broker NJ, sales person NJ, cert. residential broker, residential specialist. Owner Stay 'N Play Day Camp, 1963—65; nurse Princeton (NJ) Med. Ctr., 1972—73; pres., broker Ridolfi Realty Inc., Trenton, NJ, 1977—91; nurse Hamilton (NJ) Hosp., 1982—85; instr. real estate Mercer County CC and Career Devel. Sch. Trustee NJ Assn. Realtors Edn. Found., No. Regional Adv. Bd. Bank Mid Jersey. Corr. sec. Hist. Soc., Hightstown, NJ, 1971—72; bd. dirs. Campfire Girls and Boys, 1984; committeewoman Burlington County Dem. Com., Willingboro, NJ, 1966—67, Mercer County Dem. Com., East Windsor, NJ, 1969—72. Mem.: TREND, Mercer County Multiple Listing, Nat. Assn. Realtors, Nat. Fedn. Ind. Bus. (RPAC chmn. 1989), NJ Assn. Realtors (bd. dirs., v.p. 5th dist. 1989, Make Am. Better award 1982), Mercer County Bd. Realtors (bd. dirs. 1981—83, treas., v.p., pres. 1988—, 1997), Soroptomist Internat. of Am. and NJ, Mercer County C. of C. Roman Catholic. Avocations: genealogy, travel, reading. Office: Gloria Nilson Realtors GMAC Real Estate 1970 Rt 33 Hamilton Square NJ 08690 Personal E-mail: dotridolfi@aol.com.

RIECHMANN, DEB, reporter; Grad., U. Kansas William Allen White Sch. Journalism & Mass Communication, 1980. Writer AP, Washington. Recipient Merriman Smith award for excellence on deadline, White House Corrs. Assn., 2006. Office: AP Washington Bur 6th Fl 2021 K St NW Washington DC 20006-1082 also: AP Headquarters 450 W 33rd St New York NY 10001 Office Phone: 212-621-1500.*

RIEDEL, JUANITA MAXINE, writing educator; b. Overbrook, Kans., Nov. 17, 1918; d. Albert Ernest and Gladys Jennie (Hadsell) Smith; m. Richard Joseph Riedel, May 16, 1943 (dec. Aug. 1988); children: Nancy Riedel Basford, Linda Riedel Haynes. BE, U. Kans., 1944. Instr. creative writing Jackson (Mich.) C.C., 1979-86; instr. Creative Writers Workshop, Jackson, 1982—. Author: Words--Power and the Pattern, 1981, Church on Main Street, Jackson, MI, 1984, Wahroonga, 1994, Sidewalks, 1995; editor numerous books. Mem. AAUW (pres. 1976-78, grantee 1980), Beta Sigma Phi (various offices 1949 Republican. Home: 3149 Halstead Blvd Jackson MI 49203-2553

RIEDMAN, MARY SUZANNE, lawyer; b. June 1951; JD, Yale U. Bar: Wash. 1980, DC 1983, Calif. 1988. Various positions Beverly Enterprises Inc., Forth Smith, Ark.; counsel Vencor Inc., Louisville, 1995—96, assoc. gen. counsel, 1996—97, v.p., assoc. gen. counsel, 1997—98; (In 1998 Vencor Inc. split into Vencor Inc. and Ventas Inc.); v.p., assoc. gen. counsel Vencor Inc. (renamed Kindred Healthcare Inc. in 2001), Louisville, 1998—99, sr. v.p., gen. counsel, 1999—. Office: Kindred Healthcare Inc 680 S 4th St Louisville KY 40202-2412

RIEFF, HARRIET LILLIAN, librarian; b. Bklyn., Feb. 15, 1923; d. Samuel and Eva (Raphael) Rosenbaum; m. Edward Rieff, Sept. 19, 1948; children: Samuel Evan, Raymond. BA, NYU, 1951, MA, 1959. English tchr. Great Neck (N.Y.) H.S., 1962-84; creator lasting literary Great Neck Libr., 1985—. Great books leader Great Neck Libr., 1985—; performer classical lit. librs., 1985—; ednl. TV & curriculum advisor Great Neck Sch. Dist., 1970-84; advisor to dir. Tilles Cultural Ctr., Greenvale, N.Y., 1992-94. With USN, 1943—48, WAVES. Mem. Am. Fedn. Tchrs., Great Books Assn., Nat. Coun. Arts, N.Y. State Tchrs. Assn., Vet. Adminstrn., Great Neck Tchrs. Assn., Actor's Guild. Avocations: theater, music, travel. Home: 18 Baker Hill Rd Great Neck NY 11023-1436

RIEGER, BIN HONG, secondary school educator, elementary school educator; b. Kota Bharu, Kelantan, Malaysia, Oct. 6, 1948; came to U.S., 1974; d. Kee Teong and Leng Yean (Tan) Teo; m. Paul Leonhard Rieger, Aug. 1, 1979; 1 child, Natasha Irina. BA, Ambassador Coll., 1978; MA, Calif. State U., L.A., 1982. Cert. tchr., Calif.; cert. lang. devel. specialist. Temporary tchr. Zainab Secondary Sch., Kota Bharu, 1971, Islah Nat. Primary Sch., Kota Bharu, 1972-74; contract tchr. L.A. Unified Sch. Dist., 1979—, presenter dance workshop, 1988. Presenter workshop fair L.A. Ednl. Partnership, 1987-89, presenter emergency immigrant edn. assistance program, 1989-90, 92-2001; participant Korean Bilingual Staff Devel. Project, Seoul, 1992, English Edn. Curriculum Internat. Explore Korea Program, 2001, 02; numerous presentations in field. Presenter folk dance 14th Ann. Citywide Elem. Tchrs. Staff Devel., 1987, LA City Elem. Schs. Music Assn., Inc. Staff Devel., 2001, 8th Annual Title VII Conf. for LA Unified Sch. Dist., 2002, LAUSD Dual-Lang. Inst., 2004, 05; Fun Day coord. Pacific Asia Mus., Pasadena, Calif., 1988. Nominee 17th Annual BRAVO award, Music Ctr. Edn., LA, 1999; recipient Outstanding Tchr. of Yr. award, Wilshire Rotary Club of LA, 1996; Grant, LA Ednl. Partnership, 1986, 1989, Fulbright Meml. Fund Tchr. program, Japan, 2005. Avocations: folk dancing, swimming, travel. Home: 4906 Viro Rd La Canada Flintridge CA 91011-3746 Office Phone: 213-386-6303. Personal E-mail: plrieger@sbcglobal.net.

RIEGNER, ELIZABETH JANE, counselor, educator, mental health nurse; b. West Reading, Pa., Mar. 9, 1944; d. George Connard and Elizabeth Jane (Livingood) R.; children: Philip Donald (dec.), Joel Wesley, Matthew Eric. RN, Meth. Hosp., Phila., 1966; BS in Edn., Millersville State U., 1968; MS, West Chester State U., 1977; postgrad., Fla. State U. Lic. clin. mental health counselor, nat. cert. counselor, clin. supr., RN, registered play therapist-supr. Instr. Reading Hosp. Sch. Nursing, West Reading, 1967-68; charge nurse Ephrata (Pa.) Community Hosp., 1970-74; nurse, counselor Wilmington (Del.) Med. Ctr., 1976-79; mental health counselor Seneca Nation of Indians, Steamburg, N.Y., 1980-81; pediatric nurse Dr. Richard Lisciandro, Jamestown, N.Y., 1981-83; counselor Pastoral Counseling Svc., Jamestown, 1983—90; nurse Big Bend Hospice, Tallahassee, 1991—92; child therapist, nurse cons. Carondelet Psychiat. Care Ctr., Richland, Wash., 1992-93; pvt. practice Pt. Orange, Fla., 1993—. Cons. Seneca Nation of Indians, Steamburg, 1980-85; mental health counselor pvt. practice, Jamestown, 1983-90; instr. Fla. State U., Tallahassee, 1991-92; co-therapist Domestic Violence Offenders Program, Tallahassee, 1991. Co-founder The Compassionate Friends, Jamestown, 1983; performer/soloist The Chautauqua Chamber Singers, Jamestown, 1983-90; musician Bach Festival Choir, 2004—. Mem. Am. Mental Health Counselors Assn., Am. Assn. Marriage and Family Therapists, Assn. for Play Therapy. Avocations: music, travel, photography. Home: 6018 Hickory Grove Ln Port Orange FL 32128-7096 Office: 3959 S Nova Rd Ste 28 Port Orange FL 32127-9229

RIEHECKY, JANET ELLEN, writer; b. Waukegan, Ill., Mar. 5, 1953; d. Roland Wayne and Patricia Helen (Anderson) Polsgrove; m. John Jay Riehecky, Aug. 2, 1975; 1 child, Patrick William. BA summa cum laude, Ill. Wesleyan U., 1975; MA in Comm., Ill. State U., 1978; MA in English, Northwestern U., 1983. Tchr. English Blue Mound (Ill.) H.S., 1977-80, West Chicago (Ill.) H.S., 1984-86; editor Child's World Pub. Co., Elgin, Ill., 1987-90; freelance writer Elgin, 1990—. Author: Dinosaur series, 24 vols., 1988, UFOs, 1989, Saving the Forests, 1990, Irish Americans, 1995, The Mystery of the Missing Money, 1996, The Mystery of the UFO, 1996, Stegosaurus, 1998, Triceratops, 1998, Tyrannosaurus, 1998, Velociroptor, 1998, A Ticket to China, 1999, Greece, Sweden, 2000, George Lucas, 2001, The Emancipation Proclamation, 2002, The Osage Nation, 2002, The Cree Nation, 2002, Indonesia, 2002, The Plymouth Colony, 2002, The Settling of Jamestown, 2002, The Settling of St. Augustine, 2002, The Siege of the Alamo, 2002, Benjamin Franklin, 2003, Daniel Boone, 2003, The Wampanoag, 2003, Ulysses S. Grant, 2004, William McKinley, 2005, Respect, 2005, Citizenship, 2005, Cooperation, 2005, Iguanodon, 2006, Dipladoens, 2006, Pteranodon, 2006, Megalodon, 2006. Nat. dir. Kids Love a Mystery, 1999-2004. Recipient Summit award for best children's nonfiction Soc. Midland Authors, 1988. Mem. Soc. Am. Magicians, Soc. Children's Book Writers and Illustrators (network rep. 2006), Mystery Writers Am. (midwest bd. dirs. 2000-04), Sisters in Crime, Phi Kappa Phi. Democrat. Baptist. Avocations: reading, hiking, dinosaur hunting. Office Phone: 847-695-9781. Personal E-mail: jr@janetriehecky.com.

RIEHL, JANE ELLEN, education educator; b. New Albany, Ind., Oct. 17, 1942; d. Henry Gabbart Jr. and Mary Elizabeth Willham; m. Richard Emil Riehl, June 15, 1968; 1 child, Mary Ellen. BA in Elem. Edn., U. Evansville, 1964; MS, Ind. U., Bloomington, 1966; postgrad., Spalding U., 1979, Ind. U. S.E., New Albany, 1991—2002. Cert. 1-8 and kindergarten tchr., Ind.; lic. profl. elem adminstrn., reading minor kindergarten tchr., Ind. Elem. tchr. Clarksville (Ind.) Cmty. Sch., 1964-68, 70-75, 81-82, tchr. kindergarten, 1975-81; elem. tchr. Chapelwood Sch. Wayne Twp., Indpls., 1968-70; lectr. edn. Ind. U. S.E., 1988-97, dir. tchg. and rsch. project, 1990-91, 92-93, dir. field and career placement, cert./lic. grad advisor New Albany, 1998, coord. elem./spl. edn. field and career placement, license and grad. advisor, 1998—. Cons. Riehl Assocs., Jeffersonville, Ind., 1995—. Co-author: An Integrated Language Arts Teacher Education Program, 1990, The Reading Professor, 1992, Multimedia: HyperStudio and Language Education, 1996, Technology: Hypermedia and Communications, 1997, others; author procs. Parent vol. Girl Scouts U.S.A., Jeffersonville, 1988-95; mem. adminstrtv. bd. Wall Street United Meth. Ch., Jeffersonville, 1993-95; mem. women's health adv. coun. Clark Meml. Hosp., Jeffersonville, 1995—; bd. dirs. Clark Meml. Hosp. Found., vice chair, 1999, chair 2000, sec. 2002-03; team mem. People to People Citizen Amb. Program, 1993, 95, 96; chair internat. bylaws Altrusa Internat., Inc., 2001—. Named Young Career Woman of Yr. Bus. and Profl. Women New Albany and Dist. 13 Ind., 1966; tchg. and rsch. grantee Ind. U. S.E., 1990, 94, 95, 96, 97, 2000; recipient Disting. Tchg. award Ind. U. S.E., 1997, Tchg. Excellence Recognition award, 1997. Mem. Nat. Coun. Tchrs. English, Profs. Reading Tchr. Edn., Ind. State Med. Assn. Alliance (v.p. so. area 1999-2000), Clark County Med. Soc. Alliance (pres.-elect 1997-98, pres. 1998-99), Altrusa Internat. Inc. (internat. bd. 1993-95, dist. gov. 1993-95, svc. award 1995), Phi Delta Kappa (v.p. 1991-92, pres. 1997—, svc. award 1991), Kappa Kappa Kappa (pres. Jeffersonville 1975-76, 90-91, Outstanding Mem. award 1987). Avocations: travel, reading, crafts, decorating. Home: 1610 Fox Run Trl Jeffersonville IN 47130-8204 Office: Ind U SE 4201 Grant Line Rd New Albany IN 47150-2158

RIEHL, LORI JO, art educator; d. Dale D. Ziemann and Bonnita Joann Jochim-Ziemann; m. Russell W. Riehl, Dec. 28, 1990; children: Riley J., Hannah J. BA in Art Edn. and Theatre Comm., Dickenson State U., N.D., 1991; EdM, Coll. St. Catherine, St. Paul, 2004. Lic. profl. educator ND Dept. Pub. Instrn. Visual art instr. Mo. Hills Consortium, Garrison, ND, 1991—94; edn. svcs. coord. ND Divsn. Emergency Mgmt., Bismarck, 1994—97; artist and edn. svcs. coord. ND Coun. on the Arts, Bismarck, 1997—2000; visual art instr. Bismarck Pub. Sch., 2000—. Drama club dir. Simle Mid. Sch., Bismarck, 2001—03, Horizon Mid. Sch., Bismarck, 2004—; art club advisor Horizon Middle Sch., Bismarck, 2004—. Mem. environ. com. St. Anne Ch., Bismarck, 2004—06. Recipient Svc. to the Profession award, ND Speech and Theatre Assn., 2003. Mem.: ND Speech and Theatre Assn., Nat. Art Edn. Assn.

RIELY, CAROLINE ARMISTEAD, gastroenterologist, educator; b. Washington, Feb. 1, 1944; d. John William and Jean Roy (Jones) Riely. AB, Mt. Holyoke Coll., 1966; MD, Columbia U., 1970. Diplomate Am. Bd. Internal Medicine. Med. intern Presbyn. Hosp., N.Y.C., 1970-71, resident in medicine, 1971-73; fellow in liver disease Yale U., New Haven, 1973-75, asst. prof., 1975-80, assoc. prof., 1980-88; prof. medicine U. Tenn., Memphis, 1988—. Fellow ACP, Am. Coll. Gastroenterology; mem. Am. Assn. Study Liver Disease, Internat. Assn. Study Liver, N.Am. Soc. for Pediatric Gastroenterology and Nutrition. Home: 1756 Central Ave Memphis TN 38104-5116 Office: U Tenn 951 Court Ave Rm 555D Memphis TN 38103-2813

RIENZI, BETH ANN MENEES, psychologist, educator, director; b. Grand Rapids, Mich., Jan. 31, 1944; d. Thomas Orville and Sylvia Anna (Graham) Menees; m. William David Sanders (dec. 1972); children: Michael Remington, Genevieve Demontremare, Jeannette Sanders, James William Sanders AA, Porterville Coll., Calif., 1972; BA, Calif. State U., Bakersfield, 1974, MA, 1978; PhD, Calif. Sch. Profl. Psychology, Fresno, 1983. Lic. psychologist, Calif. Pvt. practice, Visalia, Calif., 1975—80; clin. psychologist Kings View Mental health, Visalia, Calif., 1980—85, Tulare County Mental Health, Visalia, 1985—88; prof. psychology Calif. State U., Bakersfield, 1988—, coord. faculty mentor program. Deafness specialsit Kings View, 1980-85; sr. rsch. scientist Applied Rsch. Ctr., 1989—; cons. Head Start-Home Base, Tulare County, 1984-88; coord. faculty mentor program, Calif. State U., Bakersfield, assessment dir., 2000-205, assoc. dean Humanities and Social Scis., 2005—, dir. Osher Lifelong Learning Inst., 2005— Contbr. articles to profl. jours Recipient Alumnus of Yr. award Calif. State U., Bakersfield, 1996; Kern County Mental Health grantee, 1991-95 Mem. APA, Am. Bd. Forensic Examiners (diplomate), Am. Psychology Soc. (charter), We. Psychology Assn., Assn. Women in Psychology, Coun. Tchrs. Undergrad. Psychology, Alliance Against Family Violence (vol. sexual assault response team 1993-97), Psi Chi (nat. coun., we. v.p. 1995-97, life) Avocations: travel, exercise, sign language, spanish. Office: Calif State U Humanities and Social Scis 9001 Stockdale Hwy 12DDH Bakersfield CA 93311-1022

RIES, MARCIE BERMAN, ambassador; b. Boston; m. Charles Parker Ries; 2 children. BA, Oberlin Coll., 1972; MA, Johns Hopkins Sch. of Advanced Internat. Studies, 1974. Mgr., internat. investment policy Motor Vehicle Manufacturers Assn., 1975—78; consular/polit. officer US Embassy Santa Domingo, 1978—80; internat. relations officer Office of Strategic Nuclear Policy, Bureau of Politico — Military, 1981—83; polit. officer US Embassy Ankara, Turkey, 1984—86; desk officer, Malta and the Vatican Office of Western European Affairs, 1986—88; dep. head, polit. section Office of European Regional Polit. Military Affairs, 1988—90; officer in charge, French desk Office of Western European Affairs, 1990—91; Pearson fellow House Internat. Relations Com., 1991—92; dep. polit. counselor US Mission to European Union, Brussels, 1992—96; polit. counselor US Embassy London, 1996—2000; dir., Office of UN Polit. Affairs US Dept. State, 2001—03; chief of mission US Office Pristina, Kosovo, 2003—04; US amb. to Albania US Dept. State, Tirana, 2004—. Recipient Superior Honor awards, US State Dept. Office: US Dept State 9510 Tirana Place Washington DC 20521-9510

RIESELMAN, DEBORAH SUE, editor; b. Cin., Jan. 15, 1953; d. Robert Henry and Gail Dixon (Cato) R.; div. Apr. 1995; 1 child, Charles R. Hamilton. Student, U. Ky., U. Aberdeen, Scotland, U. Cin. News editor Dixie News, Florence, Ky., 1974-79; mng. editor Recorder Newspapers, Burlington, Ky., 1979-84, Christian Music Place, Close to Home Website, 1996-97; editor, asst. dir. U. Cin., 1984—. Writing instr. U. Cin., 1999—; editl. judge Internat. Assn. Bus. Communicators, 1992-99, Cath. Press Assn., 2001, 05, Cin. (Ohio) Overature Awards, 2005. Editor, author (mag.) Horizons, 1988— (49 awards Cin. Editors Assn. 1988-2000, 33 awards Internat. Assn. Bus. Communicators 1992-2005, IABC Gold Quill medal Coun. Advancement and Support of Edn. 1998, Regional CASE award 2004); contbg. author: Mentors, Models and Mothers, 1997. Pub. chmn. 2 state senatorial races, Ky., 1980s; site coord., pub. rels. dir. NAMES Project AIDS Meml. Quilt, Cin., Covington, Ky., Lexington, Ky., Washington, 1989-98; interpreter and storyteller Cin. Hist. Soc., 1996-2001; bd. dirs. Women of Evang. Luth. Ch., Ind.-Ky. Synod, 1999-2002. Named Outstanding Citizen of Erlanger, Erlanger (Ky.) City Coun., 1982, one of Outstanding Young Women of Am., 1985. Mem. Internat. Assn. Bus. Communicators (Bronze Quill judge 1995—), Cin. Editors Assn. (various membership coms. 1988-00), U. Cin. Assn. Women Adminstrs. (former bd. dirs.), Kappa Kappa Kappa. Lutheran. Avocations: teaching clogging, mountain dulcimer performer. Fax: 513-556-3237. Office Phone: 513-556-5225. E-mail: Deb.Rieselman@UC.edu.

RIFE, ELIZABETH, musician, educator; b. Zebulon, Ga., Feb. 23, 1938; d. Jack and Ouida Dorothy (Walker) Bridges; m. Robert M. Hill, June 25, 1959 (div.); 1 child, Dorothy Hill Bremer; m. C. David Rife, Feb. 15, 1986. BS in Music Edn., Ga. State Coll. and U., 1959; postgrad., Ga. State U., 1976-81, Vanderbilt U., 1977-79. Music tchr., Marietta, Ga., 1959—; choir master, organist Holy Trinity Luth. Ch., Marietta, 1966-79. Pres., chmn. bd. Assist, Inc., Marietta, 1982-84. Guest columnist Marietta Daily Jour., 1980-84, Horizons mag., 1997. Dir. WSB-TV Call for Action, Atlanta, 1980—82; spkr. Foster Children Program, Marietta, 1980—83, United Way, 1982—83; sec. bd. dirs. Help for Hispanics, 2002; conducted seminars, workshops on hunger ch. and civic groups, Atlanta, 1981—; concert coord. Musica Sacra Atlanta, 2003—; mem. steering com. Presbyn. Answer to Hunger, 1991—; vol. Must Ministries, 2002—. Mem. Music Tchrs. Nat. Assn., Music Educators Nat. Assn., Ga. Music Educators Conf. (adjudicator piano competition 1967—), Cobb County Music Tchrs. Assn., Guild Music Sacra of Atlanta, Sigma Alpha Iota. Presbyterian. Avocations: running, reading, travel, fashion consulting, tutoring. Home: 1296 Poplar Pointe SE Smyrna GA 30082-2213

RIFFEL, LAURA ANN, director, special education educator; d. Melvin Ell and Deloris Ann Warford; m. Thomas Edward Riffel, Dec. 23, 1978; children: Jessica Regan, Brandon Daniel. BS in elem. edn., Kans. State U., Manhattan, 1979, MS in Spl. Edn., 1986; PhD in Spl. Edn. U. Kans., Lawrence, 2002. Tchr. LD grades 1 and 3 Geary County Schs., Junction City, Kans., 1979—87; tchr. EMH grade 4 Cabarrus County Schs., Concord, NC, 1987—89; tchr. LD kindergarten, grade 6 and SMH grades 3 and 4 Olathe (Kans.) Dist. Schs., 1989—2000; tchr. asst. U. Kans., Lawrence, 2000—02; dir. Behavioral Intervention Program, Forest Park, Ga., 2002—; webmaster Office of Spl. Edn. Programs Tech. Assistance Ctr. Positive Behavior Support, Eugene, Oreg., 2000—; rschr. Abt Corp., Balt., 2001—02. Adj. prof. applied behavior analysis Ga. State U.; presenter parent mentor programs State of Ga., 2000—; mem. steering com. Effective Behavioral and Instl. Supports, Ga., 2001—; agy. trainer functional behavior assessment and mgmt. Contbr. articles to profl. jours. Finalist Kans. Tchr. of Yr., 1997. Mem.: TASH, Assn. Behavior Analysis, Assn. Positive Behavior Support (web cons. 2002—), Coun. Exceptional Children, Phi Kappa Phi, Delta Kappa Gamma, Pi Lamda Theta. Methodist. Avocations: decorating, knitting, children's drama. Home: 345 Winthrop Ln Mcdonough GA 30253 Office Phone: 404-362-2025.

RIFFKIND, RANDI JAN, psychologist; d. Raymond and Gladys Riffkind; 1 child, Kimberly Christensen. BA in Sociology, Calif. State U., 1966; M in Psychology, Loyola Marymount, LA, 1974; PhD in Psychology, Internat. Coll., LA, 1984. Cert. psychologist Calif., 1985, bd. behavioral sci. marriage, family, child mgmt. Calif., 1975. Lic. psychologist Dept. Social Svcs., Disability Evaluation Divsn., LA, 1992—; commr. Dept. Consumer Affairs, Bd. Psychology, Calif., 1996, Calif., 1997, Calif., 1999, Calif., 2000; lic. psychologist pvt. practice, LA, 1984—; co-founder Advanced Psychological Svcs., 1996—; expert witness Social Security Adminstrn., Office of Hearings and Appeals, 1998—. Bd. dirs. LA Psychological Assn., 1986—2000; exec. v.p. So. Calif. Clinical Analysis Soc., LA, 2004, LA, 05. Author: (book) Sucessfully Single, 2000. Recipient Women of Achievement award, Mayor of LA, 1990. Office: Randi Riffkind Psychological Corp 10801 Nat Blvd Ste 240 Los Angeles CA 90064 Office Phone: 310-470-2626. E-mail: drriffkind@adelphia.net.

RIFKA, JUDY, artist, educator; b. Bklyn., Sept. 25, 1945; d. Irving David Tenenbaum and Pearl Fessler; children: John Reed, Matthew Lenski. BA, SUNY, Old Westbury, 1993; MA, Adelphi U., 1994. Asst. prof. SUNY, Rochester, NY, 1974; artist-in-residence Princeton U., NJ, 1976, Tamarind Inst., N.Mex., 1983, Columbia U., NY, 1994, Md. Inst. Mt. Royal, Balt., 1985, Skowkegan Sch., Maine, 1989, Tandem Press, Madison, Wis., 1991. Grants juror NY State Coun. Arts, NYC, 1983, Mass. Coun. Arts, Boston, 1984, Nat. Found. Arts, 1988. One-woman shows include numerous others, 1974—2001, Brooke Alexander Gallery, 1982—85, Galerie de France, Paris, 1984, Anna Friebe Gallery, Cologne, Germany, 1985—86, Brooke Alexander Gallery, 1987—88, Tobias Hirschmann, Frankfurt, Germany, 1988, Pyramide Arte Contemporeane, Florance, 1989, Brooke Alexander Gallery, 1991, Hofstra U., 1996, prin. works include murals Madison Sq. Garden, 1989, Union Sq. Cafe, NY, 2004; author: Opera of Worms, 1984; Exhibited in group shows at Brooke Alexander Editions, 2004, N.Y. Studio Sch., 2005, Austin Mus., Tex., 2006, Andy Warhol Mus., 2006, Berkely Art Mus., Calif., 2006, Grey Gallery NYU, 2006. Jewish. Home: 53 Market St New York NY 10002 Office Phone: 212-285-1532. Personal E-mail: jrifka@nyc.rr.com.

RIFKIND, ARLEEN B., pharmacologist, researcher, educator; b. NYC, June 29, 1938; d. Michael C. and Regina (Gottlieb) Brenner; m. Robert S. Rifkind, Dec. 24, 1961; children: Amy, Nina. BA, Bryn Mawr Coll., 1960; MD, NYU, 1964. Resident Bellevue Hosp., N.Y.C., 1965; clin. assoc. Endocrine br. Nat. Cancer Inst., 1965—68; rsch. assoc., asst. resident physician Rockefeller U., 1968—71; from asst. prof. to assoc. prof. Weill Med. Coll. Cornell U., N.Y.C., 1971—83, prof. pharmacology Weill Med. Coll., 1983—, chmn. Gen. Faculty Coun. Weill Med. Coll., 1984—86. Mem. Nat. Inst. Environ. Health Scis. Rev. Com., 1981-85, chmn., 1985-86; mem. toxicology study sect. NIH, 1989-91, chmn., 1991-93; bd. sci. counselors USPHS Agy. for Toxic Substances and Disease Registry, 1991-95; adv. com. FDA, Spl. Studies Relating to the Possible Long-Term Health Effects of Phenoxy Herbicides and Contaminents, 1995-99; external adv. bd. Environ. Health Scis. Ctr., Wayne State U., 1999—. Assoc. editor Drug Metabolism and Disposition, 1997-2005; mem. editl. bd. Toxicology and Applied Pharmacology, 1996-2002, Biochem. Pharmacology, 1996—2003; contbr. articles to profl. jours. Chair Friends of Libr., Jewish Theol. Sem. Am., 1984-86; trustee Dalton Sch., 1986-92; bd. govs. Am. Jewish Com., 1999—; bd. dirs. N.Y. chpt. Am. Jewish Com. Recipient Andrew W. Mellon Tchr.-Scientist award, 1976-78, Tchg. Excellence award Weill Med. Coll. Cornell U., 2004 Mem. AAAS, Internat. Soc. Study Xenobiotics, Am. Soc. Clin. Investigation, Am. Soc. Pharmacology and Exptl. Therapeutics, Endocrine Soc., Soc. Toxicology. Office: Cornell U Med Coll Dept Pharmacology 1300 York Ave New York NY 10021-4805 Business E-mail: arifkind@med.cornell.edu.

RIFKIND, IRENE GLASSMAN, legal secretary; b. Houston, June 27, 1921; d. Benjamin Wolf and Celia Pesses Glassman; m. Sydney E. Rifkind, Feb. 8, 1942 (div.); children: Jeffrey Allen, Stephen Paul. Sec. Mo. Dept.

Edn., St. Louis, 1967—69, Metal Goods Corp., St. Louis, 1969—71; legal sec. LaBarge Inc., St. Louis, 1971—75; sr. legal sec. Maritz Inc., St. Louis, 1975—91; ret., 1991. Recipient Hon. Svc. cert., Office Civil Def., St. Louis, 1945, Meritorious Svc. cert., ARC, St. Louis, 1946. Mem.: Exec. Women Internat. (pres. 1985—86), The Miriam Found. (vol. 1948—, pres. 1958—59). Jewish. Avocations: sewing, reading, needlecrafts. Home: 633 Broadmoor Dr Apt C Chesterfield MO 63017

RIFMAN, EILEEN, music educator; b. Bklyn., June 10, 1944; m. Samuel Sholom Rifman, Aug. 12, 1972; children: Edward, Aimee. MusB, Manhattan Sch. Music, 1966, M Music Edn., 1967; MusM, Ind. U., 1970; cert., Fontainebleau, France, 1967. Music specialist N.Y.C. Pub. Sch. System, 1966-67; instr. Long Beach (Calif.) City Coll., 1970-72, Immaculate Heart Coll., Hollywood, Calif., 1971-74, U. Judaism, Hollywood, 1973-74; co-coord. Community Sch. Performing Arts, L.A., 1974-82, instr., 1973-83; pvt. piano tchr. Manhattan Beach, Calif., 1963—; tchr. gifted and talented edn. program GATE, Manhattan Beach, Calif., 1990-91. Tchr. Etz Jacob Hebrew Acad., L.A., 1991-95, Ohr Eliyahu Acad., Culver City, 1995-96; peer counselor Beach Cities Health Dist., 1997-2005. Performer Pratt Inst., Clinton Hill Symphony, N.Y.C., 1962, Sta. WNYC-FM, 1964. Chair Cultural Arts Com., Manhattan Beach, 1985-86; bd. dirs. Hermosa Beach (Calif.) Community Ctr., 1990-91. Mem. Nat. Fedn. Music Clubs (adjudicator 1970). E-mail: eileenrifman@hotmail.com.

RIGDON, NANCY KENWAY, music educator; d. Edward Northwood and Rita Johnson Kenway; m. Kevin William Rigdon; children: Matthew Alexander, Suzanne Virginia. MusB, U. Hartford, 1983; MusM, Eastern Conn. State U., 1992. Cert. profl. educator. Music tchr. Coventry Pub. Schs., Conn., 1983—84, Norwich Pub. Schs., Conn., 1984—99, East Lyme Pub. Schs., Conn., 1999—. Creator, dir. East Lyme Mid. Sch. Drama Club; creator Seashore Praise and Worship Contemporary Worship Team/Svc. Recipient Eugene O'Neill award, Eugene O'Neill Meml. Theatre Ctr., New London, 2001—02. Mem.: Nat. Assn. for Music Edn., Conn. Music Educators Assn. (choral chair 2001—02), Am. Choral Dirs. Assn., World Wildlife Fund, Nat. Wildlife Fedn., Nat. Gardening Club. Avocations: musical theatre, kayaking, quilting, gardening. Office: East Lyme Mid Sch 31 Society Rd Niantic CT 06357 Personal E-mail: rigda@hotmail.com.

RIGELWOOD, DIANE COLLEEN, insurance adjuster, administrator; b. Savannah, Ga., Apr. 24, 1950; d. William Howell III and Ruth Colleen (Treanor) Bridges; 1 child, Stephanie Michelle Rigelwood Eichstead. Student, Savannah Tech., 1968-69. Ins. adjuster GAB Bus. Svcs., Inc., Savannah, 1974-86, Cramer Johnson White & Assocs., Savannah, 1986-89, Gay & Taylor, Savannah, 1989-94; service location supr. GAB Robins N.A., Inc., Savannah, 1994—. Pres. Isle of Hope PTA, Savannah, 1978; mem. Rep. Nat. Com., Ga. Rep. Party, Savannah Area Rep. Women. Mem. NAFE, Nat. Assn. Ins. Women Internat. (mem. nat. conv. adv. panel 2001), Savannah Claims Assn. (past pres.), Atlanta Claims Assn., Ga. Coun. Nat. Assn. Ins. Women (internat., state dir., immediate past state dir., nat. conv. adv. panel 2001), Ins. Profls. of Savannah (past pres.). Republican. Avocations: walking reading, fishing. Office: GAB Robins N Am Inc PO Box 16955 Savannah GA 31416 E-mail: d.rigelwood@worldnet.att.net.

RIGERMAN, RUTH UNDERHILL, mathematics professor; b. Batavia, N.Y., Feb. 1, 1944; d. George E. and Caroline E. (Cooper) Underhill; m. David Rigerman, Nov. 17, 1967; children: Cliff, Eileen, Matthew, Glenn, Ardeen. BS, SUNY, Brockport, 1965, MS, 1967. Instr. math. Genesee C.C., Batavia, 1982—; tech. specialist Genesee Advanced Studios, Batavia, 1990—; instr. SUNY, Brockport, 1990—. Named Master Tchr., U. Tex., 1992, 96. Mem. Math. Assn. Am. Home: 4749 Batavia Elba Townline Rd Batavia NY 14020-1035 Office: Genesee C C 1 College Rd Batavia NY 14020-9703

RIGG, DAME DIANA, actress; b. Doncaster, Yorkshire, Eng., July 20, 1938; d. Louis and Beryl (Helliwell) R.; m. Menahem Gueffen, July 6, 1973 (div. Sept. 1976); m. Archibald Hugh Stirling, Mar. 25, 1981 (div. Apr. 1993); 1 child, Rachael Atlanta. Grad., Fulneck Girls' Sch., Pudsey, Yorkshire; student, Royal Acad. Dramatic Art, London; D (hon.), Stirling U., Eng., 1988, Leeds U., 1992, Southbank U., 1996. Prof. of theater studies Oxford U., 1998—. Stage debut as Natella Abashwilli in The Caucasian Chalk Circle, Theatre Royal, York, Eng., 1957; joined Royal Shakespeare Co., Stratford-on-Avon, 1959, debut as Andromache in Troilus and Cressida, 1960; London debut as Philippe Trincant in The Devils, London, 1961; numerous repertory appearances; joined Nat. Theatre, 1972; appeared in Jumpers, Macbeth, 1972, The Misanthrope, 1973, Pygmalion, 1974, Phaedra Britannica, 1975, Night and Day, 1978, Colette, 1982, Heartbreak House, 1983, Little Eyolf, 1985, Antony and Cleopatra, 1985, Wildlife, 1986, Follies, 1987, Love Letters, 1990, All for Love, 1991, Putting It Together, 1992, Berlin Bertie, 1992, Medea, 1992 (Tony award, Broadway prod., 1994, Eve. Standard award, Variety Club award), Mother Courage and Her Children, 1995, Who's Afraid of Virginia Wolf, 1996, Humble Boy, 2001, Honour, 2006; film appearances include A Midsummer Night's Dream, 1968, The Assassination Bureau, 1969, On Her Majesty's Secret Service, 1969, Julius Caesar, 1970, The Hospital, 1971, Theatre of Blood, 1973, A Little Night Music, 1977, The Great Muppet Caper, 1981, Evil Under the Sun, 1982, A Good Man in Africa, 1994, Parting Shots, 1998, Heidi, 2005; co-starred as Emma Peel in Brit. TV miniseries: Charles II: The Power and the Passion, 2003. TV series The Avengers, 1965-67; star TV series Diana, 1973-74; numerous TV movies including This House of Brede, 1975, Hedda Gabler, 1981, Little Eyolf, 1982, Witness for the Prosecution, 1982, King Lear, 1983, Bleak House, 1984, A Hazard of Hearts, 1987, Worst Witch, 1987, Unexplained Laughter, 1989, Mother Love (Broadcasting Guild Award, BAFTA), 1989, Genghis Cohn, 1994, Zoya, 1995, The Haunting of Helen Walker, 1995, Moll Flanders, 1996, Samson and Delilah, 1996, Rebecca, 1997 (Emmy award, 1997); host PBS series Mystery, 1989—, Mrs. Bradley Mysteries, 1999—, In the Beginning, 2000, The American, 2000, Victoria & Albert, 2001; author: No Turn Unstoned, 1982, U.S. edit., 1983, So To The Land, 1994. Decorated comdr. Brit. Empire; created dame, 1994; recipient Tony award nomination as best actress in Abelard and Heloise and The Misanthrope; Plays and Players award for Phaedra Britannica and Night and Day; Variety Club Gt. Britain award for best actress for Evil Under the Sun; Brit. Acad. Film and TV Arts award for best TV actress in Mother Love, 1989, Award for Women in TV & Film, 2001. Mem. United Brit. Artists (co-founder, dir. 1982—). Address: c/o Lionel Larner Ltd 119 W 57th St New York NY 10019-2303*

RIGGIO, KERRY KERSTIN, elementary school worker, researcher; d. Patrick Peter and Giedre Grazina (Lisauskas) Riggio. BA in Econs., Pa. State U., University Park, 1993. Cert. United Animal Nations Emergency Rescue Svc., EMT NJ. Patient care rep. Hunterdon Med. Ctr., Flemington, NJ, 1998—2000; statis. analyst A.M. Best, Oldwick, NJ, 2000; aftercare asst. Immaculate Conception Sch., Annandale, NJ, 2003—. Author: Calls of the Tame: Dog Sounds Explainec, 1999. Pet therapy vol. St. Hubert's Geralda, Madison, NJ, 1994; CCD aide Immaculate Conception Ch., 2004. Recipient award for slogan, Mellon Bank, 1992; Garden State scholar. Mem.: Am. Mensa Ltd., Lithuanian-Am. Club No. NJ. Roman Catholic. Avocations: collecting Sleeping Beauty memorabilia, ceramics. E-mail: savekoala@aol.com.

RIGGLE, PATRICIA CAROL, special education educator; b. Gallipolis, Ohio, May 28, 1965; d. Pat and Freadith Fay Price; m. Richard Allan Riggle; children: Alana, Emily. BS, U. Rio Grande, 1989. Sub. tchr. Gallia County Local Schs., Gallipolis, Ohio, 1989—92, Gallipolis City Schs., Gallipolis, Ohio, 1989—92; tchr. Wellston City Sch., Wellston, Ohio, 1992—; child care provider Rio Grande Child Devel. Ctr., Rio Grande, Ohio, 1992—93. Vol. asst. dir. drama club Wellston HS, Wellston, Ohio, 1998—; career assessment adv. com. Gallia-Jackson-Vinton Joint Vocats. Sch. Dist., Rio Grande, Ohio, 2001—03. Youth Sunday sch. tchr. Okey Chapel, Scottown, Ohio, 1985—2000. Mem.: NEA, Ohio Farm Bur., Wellston Tchrs. Assn., Ohio Edn. Assn. Avocations: camping, travel, crafts. Home: 4767 Hannan Trace Rd Patriot OH 45658 Personal E-mail: star1@aceinter.net.

RIGGS, BARBARA, federal agency administrator; b. Albany, NY; B in Internat. Studies, Cornell U., 1974. With U.S. Secret Svc., 1975—, assigned to field office LA, NY, with presdl. protective divsn. Washington, asst. dir. office protective rsch., head tech. security divsn, head Nat. Threat Assessment Ctr., 1998, chief of staff, dep. dir., 2004—. Mem. White House Security Rev., 1995. Recipient Meritorious Exec. Presdl. Rank award, 2002. Achievements include first female supervisory agent assigned to presdl. protective divsn.; first female to serve as dep. dir. Office: US Secret Svc US Dept Homeland Security 245 Murray Dr Bldg 410 Washington DC 20223*

RIGGS, KRISTA DYONIS, music educator, librarian; b. Aurora, Colo., June 17, 1977; d. Donald Eugene and Jane (Vasbinder) Riggs. MusB summa cum laude, Ariz. State U., 1999; MusM, Ind. U., 2000, MLS, 2004, MusD with high distinction, 2004. Libr. Woodward Park Regional Libr., Fresno, Calif., 2004—; tchr. oboe and music theory Calif. State U., Fresno, 2006—. Invited spkr. World Conf. Internat. Soc. Music Edn., Internat. Symposium on Philosophy of Music Edn., Nat. Conf. Coll. Music Soc.; invited peformer recital Internat. Double Reed Soc. Author: (articles) Double Reed Jour., Philosophy of Music Edn. Rev. Recipient Nina Neal merit scholarship, Ind. U., 2000—04. Mem.: Internat. Double Reed Soc., Coll. Music Soc., Internat. Soc. Philosophy of Music Edn. Office: Calif State Univ Music Dept 2380 Keats Ave M/S 77 Fresno CA 93740 Business E-Mail: kdriggs@csu.fresno.edu.

RIGGS, RORY B., pharmaceutical executive; b. Orange, N.J., May 5, 1953; d. Thomas Jeffries and Virginia (Griggs) R. BA, Middlebury Coll.; MBA, Columbia U. Mng. dir. PaineWebber, Inc.; CEO RF&P Corp.; mng. dir. Pharma Ptnrs. LLC; pres. Biomatrix Inc., Ridgefield, N.J., 1995—. Bd. dirs. Biomatrix, Inc. 1990—; bd. mem. Fibrogen Corp., Spartan Corp., Pharma Ptnrs, LLC. Mem. Young Pres. Orgn. Office: Biomatrix Inc 65 Railroad Ave Ste 3 Ridgefield NJ 07657-2176

RIGGS, WILLIAM W., social sciences educator; b. Decatur, Ill., Apr. 26, 1945; d. William and Doris Mae Riggs; m. Karen Sue Henderson, May 19, 1998 (div.); children: William, Christopher. BA, The Citadel, 1967; MS, U. So. Miss., 1989; PhD, U. New Orleans, 1999. Commd. 2d lt. USMC, 1967, advanced through grades to maj., ret., 1987; tchr. Coast Episcopal High Sch., Pess Christian, Miss., 1987—89; asst. prof. polit. sci. Tex. A&M Internat. U., Larado, 2001—04, chair dept. social scis., 2004—. Vis. prof. U. West Ala., Livingston, 1989—90; external reviewer N.W. State U., Nachitoles, La., 2004; presenter in field. Contbr. chapters to books. Chair Logistics Cmty. Anchorage Sch. Dist., 2000—01; bd. dirs. Anchorage Mus., 1998—2001. Fellow, TAMU. Mem.: NEH, Am. Soc. Pub. Adminstrn. (v.p. 2004—). Avocations: golf, bridge, travel. Office: Tex A&M Internat U 5201 Univ Blvd Laredo TX 78041

RIGGSBY, DUTCHIE SELLERS, education educator; b. Montgomery, Ala., Oct. 26, 1940; d. Malcolm Sellers and Marcelia Sellers Dickman; m. Ernest Duward Riggsby, Aug. 25, 1962; 1 child, Lyn. BS, Troy State Coll., 1962, MS, 1965; postgrad., George Peabody Coll., 1963; EdD, Auburn U., 1972. Cert. tchr., Ala., Ga.; cert. libr., Ga. Tchr. Montgomery Pub. Schs., 1962—63, Troy City Schs., 1963—67; instr. Auburn U., Ala., 1968—69, dir. media svcs., 1972—77; asst. prof. Columbus Coll., Ga., 1972—77, assoc. prof., 1978—83, prof., 1983—. Vis. prof. U. P.R., Rio Piedras, 1972—73; leader various workshops, 1989, 1993—; sorfware reviewer NSTA; chmn. publicity Ga. Ednl. Tech. Conf., 1997—, bd. dirs.; bridal cons. Hist. Moments, Inc., 1998—2001, v.p., 1998—2001; chair scholarship com. Ga. Ednl. Consortium, 1999—; coord. instrnl. Tech. Sch. Edn., 1996—97; coord. program Ednl. Founds., 2001—04. Contbr. more than 90 articles on state, regional, nat., and internat. programs to profl. jours., 1968—. Active Internal Aerospace Edn. CAP, Maxwell AFB, 1980-90; dir. Air and Space Camp for Kids, 1990-98; apptd. selection com. Coll. Edn. Columbus State U. Hall of Fame, 2005— Recipient STAR Tchr. award NSTA, 1968; named to Lee H.S. Hall of Fame, Montgomery, 1997. Mem.: Ga. Assn. Instrnl. Tech. (bd. dirs. 1982—84), World Aerospace Edn. Orgn. (v.p. for Ams. 1996—98, pres. for Ams. 1998—, pres. 1999—), Nat. Congress on Aviation and Space Edn. (dir. spl. promotions 1986—90), Assn. for Ednl. Commn. and Tech. (awards com. 1994—96, non-periodical publs. com. 1994—99, chair meml. awards com. 1996—99), Phi Delta Kappa (pres. Chattahoochee Valley chpt. 1986—87, membership v.p. 2005—06, pres. Chattahoochee Valley chpt. 2006—, Svc. award 1989, Svc. Key award 1993). Baptist. Avocations: photography, mining for gemstones. Office: Columbus State U Coll Edn 4225 University Ave Columbus GA 31907-5679 Office Phone: 706-565-7802.

RIGHINI, MARILOU MAUSTELLER, editor, consultant; b. Savannah, Ga., June 17, 1937; d. John Ellis and Ethel Mae Mausteller; m. Massimo A. Righini, May 5, 1962; children: Giovanna, John Paolo. BA in Polit. Sci. magna cum laude, Mich. State U., East Lansing, 1958; attended, Johns Hopkins U., Bologna, Italy, 1958—60; MA in Internat. Rels., Johns Hopkins U., Washington, DC, 1963. Editor Internat. Legal Materials Am. Soc. Internat. Law, Washington, 1968—97, dir. pubs., 1992—97; editor, mem. editl. bd. Transnational Pubs., Inc., Ardsley, NY, 1998—, aquisitions editor, cons., 1998—2001. Translator IBM, Milan, 1960—61; tchr. polit. sci., internat. law, am. lit. Istituto Ugo Foscolo, Bologna, Italy, 1961—62; rschr., editl. asst. Washington Ctr. Fgn. Policy Rsch., 1963—68; program chmn. Internat. Devel. Conf., Washington, 1977; program coord. Washington Fgn. Law Soc., 1980—81, bd. govs., 1980—82; chmn. Coun. Washington Reps. UN, 1983—85; tchr. internat. law and orgn. Trinity Coll., Washington, 1985; elected com. rep. DC Dem. State Com., Ward 1, 1988—92; chmn., nominating com. Worldwise 2000, 1989, bd. dirs., 1989—91; ann. mtg. roundtable chair Am. Soc. Internat. Law, 1991, ann. mtg. panel chair, 92; program developer Am. Assn. Law Librs., 1999, 2000. Mem.: Mich. State U. DC Study Devel. Coun., Am. Soc. Internat. Law, UN Assn. U.S.A., Meridian Internat. Ctr., Delta Gamma.

RIGSBY, LINDA FLORY, lawyer; b. Topeka, Kans., Dec. 16, 1946; d. Alden E. and Lolita M. Flory; m. Michael L. Rigsby, Aug. 14, 1963; children: Michael L. Jr., Elisabeth A. MusB, Va. Commonwealth U., 1969; JD, U. Richmond, 1981. Bar: Va. 1981, D.C. 1988. Assoc. McGuire, Woods, Battle & Boothe, Richmond, Va., 1981-85; dep. gen. counsel and corp. sec. Crestar Fin. Corp., Richmond, 1985-99, gen. counsel, 1999-2000; mng. atty. Sun Trust Banks Inc., 2000—, deputy gen. coun., 2006. Mem. audit com. Bon Secours Health Systems, Richmond, 1999—. Bd. dirs. Commonwealth Cath. Charities, 2004-. Recipient Disting. Svc. award U. Richmond, 1987; named Vol. of Yr. U. Richmond, 1986, Woman of Achievement, Met. Richmond Women's Bar, 1995. Mem. Va. Bar Assn. (exec. com. 1993-96), Richmond Bar Assn. (bd. dirs. 1992-95), Va. Bankers Assn. (chair legal affairs 1992-95), U. Richmond Estate Planning Coun. (chmn. 1990-92). Roman Catholic. Avocations: music, gardening. Home: 163 W Square Pl Richmond VA 23233-6157 Office: SunTrust Bank 919 E Main St Richmond VA 23219-4625 Office Phone: 804-782-7738. E-mail: linda.rigsby@suntrust.com.

RIGSBY, MARY SUE, retired elementary school educator, adult education educator; b. Big Stone Gap, Va., June 22, 1936; d. Sherman Coomer and Jenelle Kilbourne; m. Hobert Herchel McElyea (div. 1978); children: Gary A. McElyea, Tammy Sue McElyea, Jeffrey Earl McElyea; m. Elmer Virgil Rigsby Jr., June 1, 1985 (dec. July 12, 2000). BS, East Tenn. State U., Johnson City, 1979, MEd, 1989. Cert. postgrad. profl. Va., early edn., mid. edn., learning disabilities tchr., reading specialist Va. Tchr. aide Lee County Schs., Pennington Gap, Va., 1971—74; tchr. Tazewell County Pub. Schs., Tazewell, Va., 1979—86, Rogersville City Schs., Tenn., 1988—89, Scott County Pub. Schs., Gate City, Va., 1989—2004, part-time tchr. adult edn. Weber City, Va., 2004—. Home: 101 Milton Ct Kingsport TN 37664-3570

RIGSBY, SHEILA GOREE, accounting firm executive; b. Macon, Ga., June 13, 1955; d. David Wendell and Carolyn (Canington) Goree; children: Jason, Ryan. Student, Macon Coll., 1979. cert. tax preparer. Tax preparer Better Income Tax Svc., Macon; acct. Bass Tool and Indsl. Supply, Macon, Padgett Bus. Svc., Macon; owner Ind. Acctg. Svcs., Macon. Mem. NAFE, Nat. Fedn. Ind. Businessmen, Nat. Soc. Tax Profls., Nat. Assn. Tax Preparers, Nat. Assn. Tax Practitioners, Ga. Assn. Pub. Accts. Office: 4000 Mercer University Dr Macon GA 31204-5702

RIHA, JANET M., elementary school educator; d. John and Vivian A. Mizia; children: Jason M., Krystin M. BS in Math., Western Ill. U., Macomb, 1976; MEd in Math., National-Louis U., Evanston, Ill., 1992. Cert. tchr. Ill., 1976. Tchr. Plainfield Sch. Dist. 202, Ill., 1976—. Mem.: Nat. Coun. Tchrs. Math. (assoc.). Office Phone: 815-436-6128. Business E-Mail: jriha@learningcommunity202.org.

RIHANNA, (ROBYN RIHANNA FENTY), singer, actress; b. St. Michael, Barbados, Feb. 20, 1988; d. Ronald and Monica Fenty. Singer: (albums) Music of the Sun, 2005, A Girl Like Me, 2006, (songs) Pon de Replay, 2005, SOS, 2006 (Best New Video Artist, MTV Video Music Awards Japan, 2006), Unfaithful, 2006; actor: (films) Bring It On: All or Nothing, 2006. Recipient Best Internat. Artist award, MuchMusic Video Awards, 2006, Female Breakout Artist award, Teen Choice Awards, 2006, Choice R&B Artist award, 2006, Best R&B award, MTV Europe Music Awards, 2006. Office: Def Jam Entertainment Cambridge MD 21613*

RIIHIMAKI, CATHERINE ANNE, geologist; b. Hartford, Conn., Jan. 7, 1976; d. Arthur Alexander and Barbara Diane Riihimaki; life ptnr. Kira Trillium Lawrence. BA, Williams Coll., Williamstown, Mass., 1998; PhD, U. Calif., Santa Cruz, 2003. Vis. asst. prof. geology Colby Coll., Waterville, Maine, 2003—04; Keck post-doctoral fellow dept. geology Bryn Mawr Coll., Pa., 2004—. Deacon Westminster Presbybn. Ch., West Hartford, Conn., 1992—94. Nat. Merit Scholar, 1994, Grad. Student fellow, NSF, 1999—2002, Summer Rsch. fellow, Coun. Undergraduate Rsch., 1997, Regents fellow, U. Calif., 1998—99, Student fellow, Nat. Assn.Geosciences Tchrs., 1998, post-doctoral fellow, Keck Found., 2004—, Lewis and Clark Fund grantee, Am. Philos. Soc., 2005, rsch. grantee, NSF, 2005—. Mem.: Coun. Undergraduate Rsch., Assn. Women Geoscientists, Geol. Soc. Am., Am. Geophys. Union, Phi Beta Kappa, Sigma Xi. Democrat. Avocations: soccer, trumpet, photography, hiking. Office: Bryn Mawr College 101 North Merion Ave Bryn Mawr PA 19010 Office Phone: 610-526-7971.

RIIKONEN, CHARLENE BOOTHE, international health administrator; b. Washington, June 10, 1942; d. John Edward and Frances Elizabeth (Jett) Boothe; m. Esko Riikonen, 1989; children: Cynthia Lee, Anthony John, Jennifer Elizabeth. AA with high honors, Howard C.C., 1977; BA magna cum laude, U. Md., 1979. Asst. dir. univ. rels., alumni dir. U. Md., Catonsville, 1977-81, assoc. dir. univ. rels. and devel. College Park, 1982-83; sr. devel. officer Internat. Ctr. Diarrhoeal Disease Rsch., Dhaka, Bangladesh, 1984-86; exec. v.p. Child Health Found. (formerly Internat. Child Health Found.), Columbia, Md., 1985-97; pres. Cera Products, LL., Jessup, Md., 1997—, mng. dir., CEO. Cons. to organize symposium oral rehydration therapy Nat. Coun. Internat. Health, Washington, 1987; organizer internat. symposium on food-based oral rehydration therapy Aga Khan U., Pakistan, 1989; organizer consensus conf. cereal-based oral rehydration therapy, Columbia, Md., 1993. Author: (tng. manual) Prevention and Treatment of Childhood Diarrhea with Oral Rehydration Therapy, Nutrition and Breastfeeding, 1992; editor procs. Oral Rehydration Therapy Symposia, 1987, 89, 93, 94; editor Child Health News, 1993—; contbr. articles to profl. jours. Pub. affairs chmn. United Way, Washington Capital Area, Prince Georges County, 1981-83; v.p. Waterfowl Assn.; pres. Windstream Assn., 1988-89; v.p. Waterfowl Terrace Assn., 1994—; mem. pub. rels. com. Md., Del. Cable TV Assn., Balt., 1981-83. Mem. APHA (internat. maternal-child health com.), AAUW, Nat. Coun. Internat. Health Assn., U. Md. Balt. County Alumni Assn. (bd. dirs. 1979-83), Women's Internat. Pub. Health Network. Clubs: Columbia Assn. Athletic (Md.) (capt. women's traveling racquetball team 1979-83). Democrat. Avocations: racquetball, windsurfing, skiing, painting. Office Phone: 410-309-1000. Business E-Mail: sales@ceraproducts.us.

RIKE, SUSAN, public relations executive; b. N.Y.C., Aug. 29, 1952; d. George Carson and Mildred Eleanor (Geehr) R. BA cum laude, Bklyn. Coll., 1975. Editl. asst. Artforum Mag., N.Y.C., 1975-77; co-owner Say Cheese, Bklyn., 1977-80; editl. asst. The Star, N.Y.C., 1980-82; acct. sec. Robert Marston and Assocs., N.Y.C., 1983-84; asst. acct. exec. Marketshare, N.Y.C., 1984; acct. exec. Doremus Pub. Rels. BBDO Internat., N.Y.C., 1984-86; pres. Susan Rike Pub. Rels., Bklyn., 1986—. Democrat. Avocations: travel, music festivals and concerts, literature. Office: Susan Rike Pub Rels 335 State St Ste 3C Brooklyn NY 11217-1719

RIKHOFF, JEAN, writer; b. Chgo. children: Allison Branson, Jeffrey Branson. BA, Mt. Holyoke Coll.; MA, Wesleyan U. Divsn. chair Adirondack Cmty. Coll., Queensbury, N.Y. Author: (novels) Dear Ones All, 1961, Voyage In, Voyage Out, 1963, Rites of Passage, 1966, Buttes Landing, 1973 (Book of Month Club alternate), One of the Raymonds, 1974 (Book of the Month Club alternate), The Sweetwater, 1976, Where Were You in '76?, 1978, (juvenile) Writing About the Frontier: Mark Twain, 1963, Robert E. Lee: Solider of the South, 1968 (anthologies) The Quixote Anthology, 1968, North Country Anthology, 1986 (chapbook) David Smith, I Remember, 1984; founder, editor Quixote, The Glens Falls Rev.; contbr. numerous articles to profl. publs. Eugene Saxton fellowship, 1958, Nat. Endowment for the Humanities fellowship, 1972, SUNY Creative Writing fellowship, 1973, 79. Democrat. Avocation: painting. Home: 42 Sherman Ave Glens Falls NY 12801-2753 E-mail: jrikhoff@iopener.net.

RILEY, BETSY LEA, music educator; b. Loudon, Tenn., May 22, 1971; d. Jack Douglas and Etta Lee Hawke; m. Craig Eugene Riley, Aug. 1993; children: Paytyn Lea, Ella Jane, Sydney Elizabeth. Bachelors, Tenn. Wesleyan Coll., Athens, 1994. Cert. Music Edn. Tenn., 1994. Music tchr. Monroe County Schs. Vonore Elem. Sch., Tenn., 1994—. Baptist. Office: Vonore Elem Sch Hwy 411 Vonore TN 37885 Office Phone: 423-884-6485.

RILEY, BETTY ANNE, psychologist, educator; d. James Andrew Riley and Elizabeth Riley Deurloo; m. Ronald Robert Teed, June 14, 1997. BA in Music, Wheaton Coll., 1969, MA in Christian Edn. with highest honors, 1971, MA in Counseling Psychology, 1985; PsyD in Clin. Psychology, Ill. Sch. Profl. Psychology, 1992. Lic. clin. psychologist Ill., 1993. Dir. of Christian edn. Naperville Bible Ch. (now called Grace Pointe), Ill., 1971—78; vis. instr. Wheaton Coll., Wheaton, Ill., 1980—81; writer and editor Scripture Press Pubs. Inc., Wheaton, Ill., 1971—76; pre-primary dept. mgr. Scripture Press Pubs., Inc., Wheaton, 1976—83; clin. psychologist Psychotherapy & Consultation Svcs., Wheaton, 1985—97; founder and dir., clin. psychologist Bethel Ctr. for Psychotherapy, Wheaton, 1997—. Vol. cons. Solomon Klein Orphanage, Cochabamba, Bolivia, 1988; provide respite for refugee ctr. workers The Alpenland Life Ctr., Crikvenica, Croatia, 1995—95; lectr. in field. Author: (leader's guide) Leader's Guide for Building Stronger Families; co-author (with Mary Lebar): You Can Teach 4s and 5s; editor, composer (song book) Let's Sing! for 4s and 5s; prodr.: (cassettes) Motions 'N Music 1; Motions 'N Music 2; Let's Sing! for 4s and 5s; contbr. chapters to books. Youth ministries bd. Evangel Bapt. Ch., Wheaton, Ill., 2002—03; co-founder (with husband) and co-pastor Village Ch. of Wheaton, Wheaton, Ill., 2003—. Recipient Rech award in Psychol. Studies, Wheaton Coll., 1985. Mem.: Christian Assn. for Psychol. Studies, Am. Assn. for Marriage and Family Therapy, APA, Christians for Bibl. Equality. Christian Evangelical. Avocations: attending concerts, cooking, golf. Office: Bethel Center for Psychotherapy 213 W Wesley St Ste 204 Wheaton IL 60187 Office Phone: 630-681-1900.

RILEY, CAROLE A., music educator, religious institute director; b. Pitts. d. Francis King and M. Gertrude Daube; m. Walter Joseph Meserve, June 18, 1981. Student, Carlow Coll., 1959-61, Royal Conservatory, Montreal, Ont., Can., 1966-67; BS in Music Edn., Duquesne U., 1968, MusM, 1972, MA in Formative Leadership, 1978, PhD in Formative Spirituality, 1983; cert. in pastoral counseling, Pitts. Pastoral Inst., 1972-74; studies with Gregory Sebok, Adirondack Inst., 1972; postgrad., U. Pitts., 1978, Slippery Rock U.,

1984. Joined Congregation Divine Providence, Roman Cath. Ch., 1959; cert. tchr., Pa. Staff, spiritual dir. Cenacle Retreat House, Pitts. and Charleston (W.Va.), 1972—2000; prof. Duquesne U., Pitts., 1972—, prof. piano, 1982—; asst. dean Duquesne U. Sch. Music, Pitts., 1982-85; exec. dir. Inst. Formative Spirituality Duquesne U., Pitts.; wxec. dir. W.Va. Inst. Spirituality, 2000—. Adj. prof. U. Charleston, Parkersburg, W.Va., 1983-88, St. Mary Coll., Moraga, Calif., 1983, U. San Diego, 1984, 86; lectr. in Thailand, Korea, Germany, Australia, Brazil, 8 countries in Africa. Fellow Am. Assn. Pastoral Counselors; mem. Coll. Theology Soc., Coll. Music Soc., Music Tchrs. Nat. Assn., Pa. Music Tchrs. Assn., Pitts. Piano Tchrs., Soc. for Sci. Study of Religion, Religious Rsch. Assn. Avocations: sewing, walking, cooking. Home: 700 Forbes Ave Ste 214 Pittsburgh PA 15219-4722 Office: Duquesne U 600 Forbes Ave Pittsburgh PA 15219-3002 E-mail: rileyc@duq.edu.

RILEY, CHERYL, artist, educator; b. Houston, Tex., Dec. 1, 1952; d. Bennie Riley and Gladys Mae DuBois. AA in Fashion Fine Art, Columbia Coll., 1973. Advt. exec. Levi Strauss & Saatchi Saatchi, San Francisco, 1979—84; instr. mixed media Penland (N.C.) Sch. Crafts, 2004; instr. wood decorative surfaces Haystack Mountain Sch. Crafts, Deer Isle, Maine, 2003; instr. mixed media Arrowmont Sch. Arts and Crafts, Gatlinburg, Tenn., 2001; instr. visual concepts N.Y. Sch. Interior Design, N.Y.C., 2001—05; artist, furniture designer Right Angle Designs, San Francisco, 1986—99; artist, designer N.Y.C., 2000—. Designer, cons. selected site art and graphics San Francisco Redevel. Agy., 1992; designer, think tank cons. Design Revival, Rock Hill (S.C.) Art Coun., 1999, 2000; conceptualist, think tank cons. Alternative Design for Walt Disney Industries, Jersey City and Orlando, Fla., 1998; keynote spkr. ann. conf. Furniture Soc. Am., Purchase, NY, 1997; artist, comty. facilitator Mosaic Mural on Exterior of 911 Emergency Ctr., San Francisco, 1994—98; artist, civic artist Lifetime Cultural Achievement from San Francisco Bus. and Profl. Women, Inc., 1997. Included in book and panel, Women Designers in the USA, 1900-2000, 2000. Bd. dirs., chair membership com. Mus. Arts and Design, N.Y.C., 2000—; bd. dirs., chair SECA aux. San Francisco Mus. Modern Art, 1996—99; bd. dirs., exec. bd. sec. Am. Craft Coun., N.Y.C., 1992—97; bd. dirs., exec. bd. dirs., chair Capp St. Project, San Francisco, 1990—97; fundraiser Ndebele tribe-inspired wall panels for Carver Acad. Elem. Sch. and Bayview Police Sta.'s Cmty. Conf. Rm., San Francisco. Recipient visual art grant, Fleishacker Found. and Tamarack Found., 1997, design arts individual grant, NEA, 1994. Mem.: Bead Soc., Orgn. of Black Designers (panel discussion participant 1997), Furniture Soc. Avocations: reading, swimming, walking, fine dining, opera, gallery and museum visits. Office: 22 Copeces Ln East Hampton NY 11937 E-mail: mail@cherylriley.com.

RILEY, CHERYL M., prosthodontist, military officer; b. Biloxi, Miss., Aug. 4, 1963; d. William Richard and Gloria Lucille Morgan; m. Kevin Gerard Riley; 1 stepchild, Jared Nolan. BS in Chemistry magna cum laude with high honors, Millsaps Coll., 1985; RDH, U. Ala., 1987, DMD, 1989; MS in Oral Scis., SUNY, Buffalo, 1993. Diplomate Am. Bd. Prosthodontics. Dental specialist Miss. Army N.G., 1983—85; dental hygienist Ala. Army N.G., 1985—87; NBC officer, phys. tng. officer, retention officer La. Army N.G., 1987—89; dental officer, NBC officer N.Y. Army N.G., 1989—90; resident in prosthodontics SUNY, Buffalo, 1990—93; NBC officer USAFR, NY, 1990—93; tng. officer, divsn. officer, chmn. children's dental health care month USN, Quantico, 1993—96, head prosthodontic dept., weapons officer Palms, 1996—97; chief prosthodontics, PROFIS officer U.S. Army, Ft. Bragg, NC, 1997—2003, chief prosthodontic mentor, 2004—05; comdr. 257th Med. Detachment. Part-time instr. SUNY, Buffalo, 1991—93. Decorated Bronze Star, Army Commendation medal, Navy Commendation medal, NATO medal Bosnia Theater, others; Merit scholar, Millsaps Coll., 1981—82, Acad. scholar, 1982—83, 1983—84, 1984—85, Ruth Cushman scholar, 1984—85, Emma Lou Ohsburg scholar, U. Ala., 1986—87, Dorothy Perkins Campbell scholar, SUNY, Buffalo, 1991—92. Fellow: Am. Coll. Prosthodontics (diplomat); mem.: Aircraft Owners and Pilots Assn., U.S. Parachute Assn., Tri Chi, Beta Beta, Omicron Delta Kappa, Phi Eta Sigma, Eta Sigma, Alpha Epsilon Delta (pres.), Theta Nu Sigma (v.p.), Phi Mu. Personal E-mail: aeropros@aol.com. Business E-Mail: cheryl.riley@us.army.mil.

RILEY, DAWN C., educational philosopher, researcher; b. Rochester, NY, Mar. 18, 1954; d. John Joseph Jr. and June Carol (Cleveland) R. BA in Edn., Polit. Sci., SUNY, 1976; MEd, in Special Edn., summa cum laude, U. Ariz., 1980; PhD, Univ. Calif., Berkeley, 1994. Cert. multiple subject credential (K-Coll.), specialist credential (K-12), Calif., coun. of educators for deaf; elem. permanent credential, N.Y. Elem. sch. tchr., 4th grade Escola Americana do Rio de Janeiro, Brazil, 1975; pvt. practice, comml. artist Rochester, 1972-80; elem. tchr. Rochester City Sch. Dist., 1976-78; rsch. asst., summer vestibule program The Nat. Tech. Inst. for Deaf, 1976-79; tchr. English, 7th-12th grades The Calif. Sch. for Deaf, 1980-94; rsch. asst. to Dr. Richard J. Morris The Univ. Ariz., 1978-80; rsch. asst., Calif. new tchr. support project The Far West Lab. for Ednl. R & D., San Francisco, 1989; chair high sch. English dept. The Calif. Sch. for Deaf, 1990-96; prin. Calif. Sch. for the Deaf, Fremont, 1996-97; asst. prof. edn. founds. So. Ill. U., 1998—2003; with ednl. founds. Skidmore Coll., 2003—, dir. student tchg. Coord. & devel. Practical Lang. in Applied Settings Program, 1981-82; chair Computer Curriculum Com., 1982-84, Critical and Creative Thinking Skills Com., 1983-84; coord. Gifted and Talented Program, 1983— Recipient Kate Navin O'Neill Grad. scholar Univ. of Calif., Berkeley, 1989; University fellow, 1978-80, Evelyn Lois Corey fellow, 1990; Recipient Sustained Superior Accomplishment award Calif. Dept. Edn., 1991. Mem. AAUW, Nat. Coun. Tchrs. English, Far Western Philosophy of Edn. Soc., Am. Ednl. Rsch. Assn., Am. Assn. Colls. for Tchr. Edn., Philosophy of Edn. Soc., John Dewey Soc., Soc. Profs. Edn. (bd. dirs. 2001-03)m Phi Beta Kappa (Berkeley chpt.). Office: Skidmore Coll Edn Studies Dir Student Tchg Saratoga Springs NY 12866 Office Phone: 518-580-5149. Business E-Mail: driley@skidmore.edu.

RILEY, DYANNE SCHROCK, music professor; b. San Diego, Feb. 16, 1944; d. Ralph Ellis Schrock and Coral Jean Clark; m. Michael Arthur Riley; children: Michael Timothy, AnnaMarie, David Patrick, Keri Jo, Suzanne. BA with distinction in music, San Diego State U.; MusM, Brigham Young U. Tchr. Mt. Miguel High Sch.; grad. asst. Brigham Young U., Provo; asst. prof., dir. choral activities Utah Valley State Coll. Vocal specialist Tng. Sch. of Mormon Tabernacle Choir, 2003—; condr. Utah Valley Choral Soc.-Wasatch Chorale, 2005—. Singer: Mormon Tabernacle Choir, 1995—2004. Recipient Adj. faculty of Yr., Utah Valley State Col., 1998—99, 2002—03. Mem.: Soc. Music Theory, Am. Choral Dirs. Assn., Nat. Assn. Tchrs. Singing. Avocations: harp, quilting, outdoor activities. Home: 4323 N Imperial Way Provo UT 84604 Office: Utah Valley State Coll 800 W Univ Pky Orem UT 84058 Office Phone: 801-863-7432. Business E-Mail: rileydy@uvsc.edu.

RILEY, FAITH LYNCH, retired historian, writer; b. Lockesburg, Ark., Sept. 16, 1940; d. Lester Doss and Nina Pettigrew-Doss Shuffield; m. Bryan Riley, Mar. 12, 1962; children: Reed Lynch, Costa Lynch, Alex Lynch. BS of Edn., Henderson State Tchrs. Coll., Arkadelphia, Ark., 1962. Tchg. Ark. Dept. of Edn., 1962. Dir. SW Ark. Regional Archives, Washington, Ark., 2002—; flight attendant Delta Airlines, Dallas, 1963—64; tchr. Crawfordsville H.S., Ark., 1962—63; columnist Mena Star Newspaper, Mena, Ark., 1980—92; writer, owner Riley Publications, Wickes, Ark., 1994—, ret. Author (publisher): (oral history) Legacy of Arkanas, Somewhere The Sun Is Shining: Eyewitness Accounts of the Great Depression, To Do Or Die: Ouachita Mountain Men Remember World War II; editor: (non-fiction) 25 Years at Southwest Archives: True Stories From the Collections of Southwest Arkansas Regional Archives, Washington, Arkansas. Chmn. Rich Mountain CC, Mena, Ark., 1988—89, mem., 1983—2000. Baptist. Achievements include research in History of Schools Since 1836 in Twelve SW Arkansas Counties. Avocations: working on the ranch, fishing/hunting, piano playing, nature photography, four wheeling in the back woods and trails near the Cossatot River. Home: 740 Hwy 278 Wickes AR 71973 Personal E-mail: faithriley@alltel.net.

RILEY, FRANCENA, nurse, retired non-commissioned officer; b. New Smyrna Beach, Fla., May 5, 1957; d. Willard Harrell and Jacqueline Delores (Griffen) R. 1 child, Daniel Albert Cross (dec.). AA, U. Md., Heidelberg, Fed. Republic Germany, 1987; BS, Upper Iowa U., 1994; MA in Edn., Ctrl. Mich. U., 2001. Enlisted U.S. Army, 1980, advanced through grades to sgt. 1st class, 1991, expert field med. badge, parachustist; practical nurse emergency room Keller Army Hosp., West Point, N.Y., 1981; bn. tng. noncommd. officer 34th Med. Bn., Ft. Benning, Ga., 1988-89, practical nurse 2d Mobile Army Surg. Hosp., 1989-91; wardmaster intensive care unit #1 2d MASH, 1990-91; practical nurse pediatric ward Walter Reed Army Med. Ctr., Washington, 1982-84; practical nurse, then nursing supr. 913th Med. Detachment, Kaiserslautern, Fed. Republic Germany, 1984-86; wardmaster surgery clinic Army Regional Med. Ctr., Landstuhl, Fed. Republic Germany, 1987; with 2D MASH 44th med. brigade operation desert shield U.S. Army, Saudi Arabia, 1990-91; ops. non-commd. officer 2d MASH, 1991-92; wardmaster newborn nursery USA MEDDAC, Ft. Polk, La., 1992-94; wardmaster med. surg. unit USAMEDDAC, Ft. Polk, 1994-95; ret., 1995; distbn. clk. USPS, Atlanta, 1995-2000; anesthesia nurse Northside Hosp., Atlanta, 2002—04; jr. planner Eagle Group Internat. Inc., Atlanta, 2004—. Maintenance support clk. USPS, Atlanta; adj. instr. Ga. Perimeter Coll., Clarkston, Ga., 2001—. Mem. handbell choir, sr. usher bd. hist. com. Ebenezer Bapt. Ch., Atlanta. Recipient med. badge U.S. Army, 1991. Baptist. Avocations: bicycling, plate collecting, visiting zoos and nature parks. Home: 8773 Valley Lakes Ct Union City GA 30291-6011 Personal E-mail: alberta959@aol.com.

RILEY, JOCELYN CAROL, writer, television producer; b. Mpls., Mar. 6, 1949; d. G.D. Riley and D.J. (Berg) Riley-Jacobson; m. Jeffrey Allen Steele, Sept. 4, 1971; children: Doran Riley, Brendan Riley. BA in English, Carleton Coll., Northfield, Minn., 1971. Mng. editor Carleton Miscellany, Northfield, Minn., 1971; mkgt. asst. Beacon Press, Boston, 1971-73; freelance writer, editor, prodr., 1973—. Author: (books) Only My Mouth is Smiling, 1982, Crazy Quilt, 1984; prodr.: (TV series) Her Own Words, 1986, Belle: The Life and Writings of Belle Case La Follette, 1987, Gold Medal Internat. Film and TV Festival, 1988, Zona Gale, 1874-1938, 1988, Patchwork, 1989, Prairie Cabin, 1991, Winnebago Women Songs & Stories, 1992, Ethel Kvalheim, Rosemaler, 1992, Her Mother Before Her, 1992, Women in Construction, 1993, America Fever, 1994, Women in Policing, 1994, Sisters & Friends, 1994, Big Sister, Little Sister, 1995, Audrey Handler, Glass Artist, 1995, Women in Dentistry, 1996, Sewing Together, 1996, Women in Nontraditional Careers, 1996, Women in Firefighting, 1996, Women in Machining, 1997, Women in Welding, 1997, Prairie Child, 1997, Math at Work, 1998, Writing on the Lakes, 1998, Women in Engineering, 2000, Work Talk, 2000, Women in Highway Construction, 2001, Women in Building Construction, 2002, The Art of Ethel Kvalheim, 2002, Writing at Work, 2003, Shifting Gears: Changing Careers, 2004, Women Entrepreneurs, 2005, Women in the Automotive Industry, 2005, Women in Electronics, 2006; columnist: Wis. State Jour., 1986—91; contbr. articles to profl. jours. Active United Way of Dane County, 1984-90, On-Site Rev. Com., Madison Area Tech. Coll., 1993, Boy Scouts Am., 1996—. Hon. fellow Women's Studies Rsch. Ctr., U. Wis., Madison, 1986-91; Film in the Cities Regional Film/Video grantee; Dane County Cultural Affairs Comm. grantee, 1986-94, 96-97, 2002, 04; Wis. Arts Bd. grantee, 1986, 88-93; Wis. Humanities Coun. grantee, 1997; Wis. Sesquicentennial grantee, 1997, Madison CitiArts grantee, 1986-87, 89-90, 92-93, 96-97, 2002; Bronze Apple award Nat. Ednl. Film & Video Festival, 1988; cert. of commendation Am. Assn. State and Local History, 1988, Gold medal Internat. Film & TV Festival, 1988, cert. of recognition Wis. Dept. Pub. Instrn. Am. Indian History & Culture Program, 1991, Write Women Back into History award Nat. Women's History Project, 1995, ALA award, 1996, Barb Landers Meml. award Assn. for Gender Equity Leadership in Edn., 2004. Mem. Women in Comm. (pres. Madison chpt. 1984-85, nat. del. 1983, Writer's Cup 1985), Coun. for Wis. Writers (1st pl. for nonfiction article 1986), Authors Guild, Madison Assn. for Multi-Image (pres. 1986-87, nat. del. 1986), Downtown Madison Rotary Club. Address: PO Box 5264 Madison WI 53705-0264

RILEY, LYNNE F., lawyer; b. Boston, Oct. 31, 1959; BA cum laude, U. Mass., 1981; JD cum laude, Suffolk U. Law Sch., 1992. Bar: Mass. 1992, U.S. Dist. Ct. Mass. 1993, U.S. Ct. Appeals First Ct. 1993. Ins. agent Fidelity Nat. Title Ins. Co., Lawyers Title Ins. Co. Title examiner Mass. Land Ct., 1994—. Author: Recent First Cir. Devel. & Persisting Problems Regarding Avoidance of Impairing Liens, 1999. Named an top Boston lawyers, Boston Mag., 2004. Mem.: U.S. Panel Bankruptcy Trustees Dist. Mass. (mem. 1995), Mass. Conveyancer's Assn., Internat. Women's Insolvency & Restructuring Confederation (network chairperson), Am. Bankruptcy Inst., Women's Bar Assn. Mass., Boston Bar Assn. (bankruptcy sect.). Office: Riley & Esher LLP 69 Thorndike St Cambridge MA 02141 Office Phone: 617-876-3755. Office Fax: 617-876-3155.

RILEY, MARGARET FOSTER (MIMI RILEY), law educator; b. NYC, 1959; AB in History and Polit. Sci., magna cum laude, Duke U., 1981; JD, Columbia U., 1985. Bar: NY 1986, Pa. 1988. Assoc. Rogers & Wells, NYC, 1985—88, Pepper, Hamilton & Scheetz, Phila., 1988—92; asst. prof. U. Va. Sch. Law, 1992—98, named assoc. prof., 1998, now prof., co-dir. Legal Rsch. and Writing Program, 1992—. Office: U Va Sch Law 580 Massie Rd Charlottesville VA 22903-1789 Office Phone: 434-924-4671. E-mail: mf9c@virginia.edu.

RILEY, MARY JANE STEWART, secondary school educator; d. Norman Stewart and Martha Veronica Venzuch; m. Richard Michael Riley, Jan. 11, 1980 (div. Mar. 23, 1987); children: Megan Stewart, Erin Courtney Stewart. BS, We. Mich. U., Kalamazoo, 1967—71; MA in Tchg., Oakland U., Rochester, Mich., 1971—77. Cert. tchr. Mich. Guest tchr. Birmingham Pub. Schs., Mich., 1993—95; HS tchr. Ferndale Pub. Schs., Ferndale, Mich., 1995—96; HS tchr. in adult edn. Royal Oak Pub. Schs., Mich., 1995—97; mid. sch. tchr. Sch. Dist. Pontiac, Mich., 1996—. Exec. bd. mem. Mich. Coun. Social Studies (MCSS), Ann Arbor, Mich., 1996—98, state conf. chmn., 1999—2005; state contest judge Mich. Social Studies Olympiad (MSSO), Shelby Twp., Mich., 1996—; tech. writer social studies curriculum Pontiac Public Schs., 1996—; ednl. cons. Mich. Dept. Edn.; mem. tchr. del. to Kusatsu, Japan. Chmn. Marine Safety Edn. Commn., Lansing, Mich., 1989—90; mem. ho. dels. Nat. Coun. Social Studies (NCSS). Recipient Top Fellow award, Goethe Inst., 2002. Mem.: Pontiac Edn. Assn. (dir. 2006—). Independent Thinkers. Achievements include writing a senate bill in 1989 for boating safety that passed the Michigan state legislature, and signed into law by former Governor James Blanchard, causing boating regulations in other states. Avocations: golf, travel, reading, photography, karaoke. Office: Madison Mid Sch 1275 N Perry St Pontiac MI 48341 Office Phone: 248-451-8010.

RILEY, NANCY C., state legislator; b. Tulsa, Okla., June 20, 1958; m. Jerry A. Riley; children: Dan, Robin, Patrick stepchildren: Steve, Phil. Student, Okla. Christian U., 1976-79; BSE, UCT Langston, 1985. Tchr. Tulsa Pub. Schs., 1986—; mem. Okla. Senate from 37th dist., Oklahoma City, 2001—. Active PTA, Berryhill Hoover, S.W. Tulsa Chamber, Sand Springs Chamber, Bixby Chamber, Green Country Campfire Adv. Coun., Interagency Coun. Early Childhood Intervention, Okla. Fedn. Rep. Women, Okla. First Ladies, Tulsa Rep. Men's Club, After Five Rep. Women's Club, Tchr. Recruitment Com. for Minorities. Mem. Tulsa Classroom Tchrs. Assn. (del. 1986-2000), Rolling Oaks Homeowners Assn. (past pres. 1999-2000), Delta Kappa Gamma (sec. 1994-97). Republican. Mailing: State Capitol Bldg Rm 528A 2300 N Lincoln Blvd Oklahoma City OK 73105 E-mail: Rileyn@lsb.state.ok.us.

RILEY, NANCY J., real estate broker; b. Pitts., Pa., Sept. 25, 1947; d. Albert William and Frances Louise (Abaray) Torchia; m. J Thomas Riley, Dec. 31, 1976; children: Jennifer Torchia Davis-Wells, Alison Kathleen Davis-Bearnarth. Cert. Residential Specialist Nat. Assn. Realtors, 1992, Internat. Property Specialist Nat. Assn. Realtors, 2002, in Leadership Tng. Women's Coun. of Realtors, 1996. Developer sales Pinellas & Dade County, Fla., 1973—83; broker, owner Country Club Properties, Inc., Clearwater, Fla., 1983—91; broker, assoc. Century 21 Gateway Properties, Inc., St. Petersburg, Fla., 1992—95; residential real estate broker Coldwell Banker Residential Real Estate Co., St. Petersburg, Fla., 1995—. State com. woman Fla. Rep. Party, Pinellas County, 2000—; bd. dirs. Rep. Party Of Fla., 2001—. Recipient Realtor Of The Yr., Clearwater Assn. Of Realtors, 2000. Mem.: Nat. Assn. Realtors (bd. dirs. 1995—2006), Fla. Assn. Realtors (dist. v.p. 2000—01, treas. 2004—05, sec. 2003—04), Clearwater Assn Realtors (pres. 1999—2000, Realtor of Yr. 2000). Republican. Office: Coldwell Banker Residential Real Estate Co 3401 Fourth St No Saint Petersburg FL 33704

RILEY, PAMELA JANERICO, artist; b. Winchester, Mass., Aug. 27, 1970; children: Samuel Adrian Jenkins, James Mark Jenkins. Student, So. Maine Tech. Coll. Ordained to ministry Universal Life Ch., Calif. Data entry clk. Orlando Pub. Libr., 1999. Vol. Caring Unltd., Sanford, Biddeford, Maine, 1999; parent St. Louis Childcare Devel. Svcs., 1999; crime watcher Forest Green Apt. Complex, York County, 1999.

RILEY, REBECCA MICHELLE, music educator; b. Carthage, Mo., June 23, 1974; d. Russell and Ruby Richmond; m. Ben Lee Riley; children: Raecancia Ann, Matthew Lee. M, William Woods U., Fulton, Mo., 2003. Cert. tchr. Mo. Elem. music tchr. Diamond (Mo.) Elem. Sch., 1997—2000; music tchr. Jasper (Mo.) HS, 2000—02, Noel (Mo.) Sch., 2002—. Mem.: Mo. State Tchrs. Assn. (assoc.), Music Educators Nat. Conf. (assoc.), Mo. Music Educators Assn. (assoc.).

RILEY, SALLY JEAN, science educator; b. Pasadena, Calif., Feb. 24, 1941; d. Richard Dunlap Hopping and Nelle Bernice Webb-Hopping; m. Robert William Riley, Sept. 27, 1977; children: Stacie Lynn Scripter, Derrick Wayne, Stefanie Lyn Campbell. BA, Calif. State U., L.A., 1963; Tchg. Credential, U. Calif., Irvine, Calif., 1982. Social worker County of LA, Covina, Calif., 1967—71, County of Orange, Santa Ana, Calif., 1974—76; sci. tchr. Irvine Unified Sch. Dist., Irvine, Calif., 1982—. Mem. Sch. Site Coun., Irvine, Calif., 1995—. Vol. Pacific Wildlife Orgn., Laguna Niguel, Calif., 2000—04. Mem.: NEA, Calif. Tchrs. Assn., Irvine Tchrs. Assn. R-Liberal. Christian Scientist. Achievements include Dean's List - Univ. Calif., Irvine. Avocations: genealogy, gardening, reading, travel. Office: Venado Mid Sch 4 Deerfield Irvine CA 92604 Office Phone: 949-936-6856. Business E-Mail: sriley@iusd.org.

RILEY, SHARON LYNN, elementary school educator; b. Anchorage, Aug. 24, 1957; d. Harvey Clayton and Beverly Ann (Laurence) Dzomba; 1 child, Erin Michelle. BEd, U. Toledo, 1978; MEd, John Carroll U., 1992. Tchr. Northwood (Ohio) Local Schs., 1978-82, Cleveland Heights/University Heights (Ohio) Bd. Edn., 1985—. Mem. ASCD, Phi Delta Kappa. Office: Coventry Elem Sch 2843 Washington Blvd Cleveland Heights OH 44118-2009 Office Phone: 216-371-7110.

RILEY, THERESA MARIE, elementary school educator; b. Clayton, Mo., Oct. 11, 1949; d. Theodore John and Agnes Josephine Hake; m. James Whitcomb Riley Jr., June 12, 1981; children: James William, Kelly Elizabeth. BS in Elem. Edn., Spalding U., Louisville, 1971. Tchr. St. Lucy Sch., St. Louis, 1971—73, All Souls Sch., 1973—2002, St. Cletus Sch., St. Charles, 2002—. Mem. Parish Tchr. Com., St. Louis, 2004—. Roman Catholic. Avocations: reading, cross stitch, travel. Home: 644 Village Sq Hazelwood MO 63042-3312 Office: St Cletus Sch 2721 Zumbehl Rd Saint Charles MO 63301 Office Phone: 636-946-7756. E-mail: triley492002@yahoo.com.

RILEY-DAVIS, SHIRLEY MERLE, advertising agency executive, marketing consultant, writer; b. Feb. 4, 1935; d. William Riley and Beatrice Estelle (Whittaker) Byrd; m. Louis Davis; 1 child, Terri Judith. Student, U. Pitts., 1952. Copywriter Pitts. Mercantile Co., 1954-60; exec. sec. U. Mich., Ann Arbor, 1962-67; copy supr. N.W. Ayer, N.Y.C., 1968-76, assoc. creative dir. Chgo., 1977-81; copy supr. Leo Burnett, Chgo., 1981-86; freelance advt. and mktg. cons., 1986—. Advt. and mktg. dir. Child and Family Svc., Ypsilanti, Mich., 1992-96; advt. mktg. dir. Jude Entertainment, 1998; vis. prof. Urban League Black Exec. Exch. Program; print, radio, and TV commls. Mem. adv. Cmty. Diabetes, past bd. dirs. People's Hope for Housing, Ypsilanti; adv. bd., founding mem. African Am. Alzheimer's Support Group, Ypsilanti, 1995—; bd. dirs. housing bur. for Srs. U. Mich. Med. Ctr., 1995-96; vol. Washtenaw County Foster Grandparent Program. Recipient Grand and 1st prize N.Y. Film Festival, 1973, Gold and Silver medal Atlanta Film Festival, 1973, Gold medal V.I. Film Festival, 1974, 50 Best Creatives award Am. Inst. Graphic Arts, 1972, Clio award, 1973, 74, 75, Andy award of Merit, 1981, Silver medal Internat. Film Festival, 1982, Corp. Mgmt. Assistance Program award, 1986, Good Sam award, 1981, Svc. Advt. Creativity of Distinction cert., 1981; Senatorial scholar. Mem. Women in Film, Facets Multimedia Film Theatre Orgn. (founding bd. dirs.), Greater Chgo. Coun. for Prevention of Child Abuse, Internat. Platform Assn., Epilepsy Found. Chgo. (past bd. dirs.), Silver Club (mem. adv. bd.), Washtenaw County Sr. Leaders. Democrat. Roman Catholic. Avocations: dance, poetry, design, writing, volunteering. Personal E-mail: shirleyrileydavis@yahoo.com.

RILL, VICKI LYNN, healthcare educator, physical education educator; b. Westminister, Md., June 7, 1964; d. Sterling and Martha Rill. BS, Frostburg State U., Md., 1986; M, Frostburg U., 1988. Tchr. Bethesda Chevy Chase H.S., Md.; resource tchr. Kennedy H.S., Silver Springs, Md. Chmn. U. of Tex.Libr Friends, 2002—05. Mem.: ABA, Sevier County Bar Assn., Tenn. Bar Assn. (mem. bd. governors 2003—05). Office: Ogle, Coass & Richardson PC 103 Bruce St Sevierville TN 37862

RIMA, INGRID HAHNE, economics professor; b. Fed. Republic of Germany; d. Max F. and Hertha G. (Grunsfeld) Hahne; m. Philip W. Rima; children: David, Eric. BA with honors, CUNY, 1945; MA, U. Pa., 1946, PhD, 1951. Prof. econs. Temple U., Phila., 1967—. Author: Development of Economic Analysis, 1967, 6th edit., 2000, Labor Markets Wages and Employment, 1981, The Joan Robinson Legacy, 1991, The Political Economy of Global Restructuring, Vol. I, Production and Organization, Vol. II, Trade and Finance, 1993, Measurement, Quantification and Economic Analysis, 1994, Labor Markets in a Global Economy, 1996. Fulbright Disting. Lectr., Lingnan U., China, 2000. Fellow Ea. Econ. Assn.; mem. Am. Econ. Assn., History of Econs. Soc. (pres. 1993-4), Phi Beta Kappa (pres. chpt. 2006). Office: Temple U Broad & Montgomery Ave Philadelphia PA 19122 Personal E-mail: irima@aol.com.

RIMBACH, EVANGELINE LOIS, retired music educator; b. Portland, Oreg., June 28, 1932; d. Raymond Walter and Viola Clara (Gaebler) Rimbach. BA, Valparaiso (Ind.) U., 1954; MMus, Eastman Sch. Music, Rochester, N.Y., 1956; PhD, Eastman Sch. Music, 1967; student, Pacific Luth. U., Parkland, Wash., 1950—52. Vocal music instr. Goodwin Jr. High Sch., Redwood City, Calif., 1956-57; music instr. Calif. Concordia Coll., Oakland, Calif., 1957-62; prof. music Concordia U., River Forest, Ill., 1964-97, chmn. dept., 1989-97; ret., 1997. Contbg. editor: Church Music, 1965—80; editor: (book) Johann Kuhnau: Magnificat, 1980, (cantata) Johann Kuhnau: Lobe den Herrn, 1993; contbr. (essays) Hymnal Supplement '98 Handbook, Keywords in Church Music, 2004; contbr. articles to profl. jours. Bd. dirs. Civic Symphony of Oak Park-River Forest, 1974-80, concert com. chmn., 1976-78, prog. annotator, 1976-80; mem. choir Grace Luth. Ch., River Forest, 1964-97. AAUW postdoctoral fellow, 1969-70; DAAD grantee, Munich, 1980; recipient Rose of Honor award, Sigma Alpha Iota, 1987. Mem. Am. Musicol. Soc., Assn. Luth. Ch. Musicians (editor newsletter 1998—), Sigma Alpha Iota (Rose of Dedication award 1997). Republican. Lutheran. Avocations: travel, cooking, needlecrafts. Home: Apt L-206 12121 Admiralty Way Everett WA 98204-7507 Home Fax: 425-265-0837. Personal E-mail: rimbachtwo@earthlink.net.

RIMEL, REBECCA WEBSTER, foundation administrator; BS, U. Va., 1973; MBA, James Madison U., 1983. Head nurse, emergency dept. U. Va. Hosp., Charlottesville, 1973-74, coord. med. out-patient dept., 1974-75, nurse practitioner dept. neurosurgery, 1975-77, instr. in neurosurgery, 1975-80, asst. prof., 1981-83; program mgr. health Pew Charitable Trusts, Phila., 1983-84; asst. v.p. Glenmede Trust Co., Pew Charitable Trusts, Phila., 1984-85; v.p. for programs Pew Charitable Trusts, Phila., 1985-88, exec. dir., 1988-94, pres., 1994—. Mem. Coun. on Founds., Washington; prin. investigator dept. neurosurgery U. Va., 1981—83; adv. com. Boxing U.S. Olympics, 1983—86; adv. coun. Nat. Inst. of Neurol. Disorders and Strokes, 1988—91, bd. dirs., Thomas Jefferson Meml. Found., Deutsche Banc Flag Investors Fund. Contbr. chpts. in books, articles and abstracts to profl. jours. Recipient Disting. Nursing Alumni award, U. Va., 1988; fellow Kellogg Nat. fellow, 1992. Mem.: APHA, ANA, Va. State Nurses Assn. (membership and credentials com. 1982—86), Emergency Dept. Nurses Assn., Am. Assn. Neurosurg. Nurses, Am. Acad. Nursing.

RIMER, BETH A., director; d. Thomas G. and Yvonne J. Hutchins; m. Scott A. Rimer, Jan. 29, 1994; children: Meghan, Jill. B in English Edn., Bowling Green State U., Ohio, 1992; M in Curriculum and Tchr. Leadership, Miami U., Oxford, Ohio, 1999. Tchr. NW Local Schs., Cin., 1993—96, Sycamore Cmty. Schs., Blue Ash, Ohio, 1996—2002; asst. dir. Ohio Writing Project - Miami U., Oxford, 2002—. Office Phone: 513-529-5245.

RIMERMAN, JANET MALAINE, art educator, artist; d. Jack Ellis and Mollyann Rimerman. BA, Willamette U., Salem, Oreg., 1978; postgrad., U. Wash., Seattle, 1979, Portland State U., 1980—82. Art tchr. Shelton H.S., Wash., 1978—81, Milwaukie Jr. H.S., Oreg., 1981—91, Hazelbrook Middle Sch., Tualatin, Oreg., 1991—96, Tigard H.S., Oreg., 1996—. Curator Lake Oswego Festival of Arts, Oreg., 1992—; juror various local art competitions; workshop presenter. Recipient Educator award, Balinki and DuPrey Gallery, 2002, Human Rights award, Tigard H.S., 2003. Mem.: Watercolor Soc. Oreg., Colored Pencil Soc. Am. (dist. chpt. pres. 1994—96, nat. publicity dir. 1997—99). Avocations: photography, travel, antique glass. Home: PO Box 1350 Lake Oswego OR 97035

RIMES, LEANN, country music singer; b. Jackson, Miss., Aug. 28, 1982; m. Dean Sheremet, Feb. 23, 2002. Singer: (albums) Blue, 1996, Unchained Melody: The Early Years, 1997, You Light Up My Life: Inspirational Songs, 1997 (Contemporary Christian Album of Yr., 1998), Sittin' on Top of the World, 1998, LeAnn Rimes, 1999, I Need You, 2001, God Bless America, 2001, Twisted Angel, 2002, Greatest Hits, 2003, What a Wonderful World, 2004, This Woman, 2005; co-writer: (TV films) Holiday in Your Heart, 1997; guest appearance (TV films) Holiday in Your Heart, 1997, (TV series) American Dreams, 2003, (TV) Days of Our Lives, 1998, Moesha, 1999, MadTV, 2000, Tinseltown TV, 2003, and several others, (films) Coyote Ugly, 2000, host Nashville Star, 2003—; performer: (TV) LeAnn Rimes Live, 2003, LeAnn Rimes: Custom Concert, 2004; author: (children's books) Jag, 2003, Jag's New Friend, 2004; singer: (soundtrack) Can't Fight The Moonlight for Coyote Ugly (Favorite Song, Blockbuster award, 2001), Looking Through Your Eyes for Quest for Camelot, (soundtrack-TV miniseries) I Need You for Jesus, 2000. Internat. spokesperson Children's Miracle Network; established LeAnn Rimes Adventure Gym (Vanderbilt Children's Hosp.), Nashville. Nominated Best Country Singer award, Country Music Assn., 1996; recipient Best New Artist,(youngest person to win a top award) & Best Female Country Vocal Performance, Grammy award, 1997, Song of Yr. & Single Record of Yr., Blue, Top New Female Vocalist, Acad. of Country Music, 1997, Horizon award, Country Music Assn., 1997, Favorite Female Artist, Blockbuster award, 1998; named Female Rising Video Star of Yr., Country Music Television (CMT), 1997, New Country Act of Yr., Internat. Touring Talent Pub., Internat. Rising Star, British Country Music Awards, Artist of Yr., North Tex. Music Festival, Country Single Sale Artist of Yr., Female Country Artist of Yr., Contemporary Christian Artist of Yr., Billboard, 1998 and others. Office: care Curb Records 3907 W Alameda Ave 2d Fl Burbank CA 91505-4332

RIMLAND, LISA PHILLIP, writer, composer, lyricist; b. Stamford, Conn., Mar. 27, 1954; d. Maurice Louis and Eva (Kreiz) R. BA, U. Conn., 1978. Owner Ph Rimland Press, Storrs, Conn., 1991—. Composer numerous songs, including Your Heart or Mine, 1990, Drive Me Crazy, 1991, Send Me an Angel, 1992, Geography of Heaven, 1990, 2002, The Winds of Time (The Cloning Song), 2003; author: The Candida Manual: Candida Overgrowth and the Quest for Human Wellness, 1999, Voices From the Farm, 1999, Machronomarker Observations Conducted During the First Three Months of the Life of a Cloned Heifer Dairy Calf, 2000, An Evaluation of Machronomarker Observations, 2001, Amy and Aspen: Behavioral Observations of a Cloned Holstein Cow and Her Genetic Donor Living Together In Pasture, 2003, Betty and Cathy With Aspen In Summer, 2004, Behavioral Observations of Two Cloned Holstein Cows and Their Genetic Donor Living Together in Pasture, 2006; contbr. articles, poems, essays to profl. jours. Vol. dairy barn U. Conn., 1992—, vol. photographer Morgan horse facility, 1982-91. Recipient DAR award, 1969, Soc. Women Engrs. award, 1971, Editor's Choice award Nat. Libr. Poetry, 1995, 96; Nat. Merit scholar, 1972. Mem. ASCAP. Avocations: film and drama, art, poetry, athletics, morgan horses. Home: PO Box 408 Storrs Mansfield CT 06268-0408

RIMLER, ANITA A., former state official; b. 1944; m. George W. Rimler. Campaign aide, legis. asst. former Del. Rob James, 1975; asst. to atty. gen. Mary Sue Terrry State of Va., Richmond, 1985—91; dir. fin. ops. Terry for Gov. campaign, 1993, Robb for Senate campaign, 1994, Warner's U.S. Senate campaign, 1996; sr. advisor, dir. fin. ops. Warner for Gov. campaign; sec. of state State of Va., Richmond, 2002—06. Democrat.*

RIMM, SYLVIA BARKAN, psychologist, media personality educator; b. Perth Amboy, N.J., Apr. 16, 1935; d. Harry and Reva (Cisser) Barkan; m. Alfred A. Rimm, Jan. 27, 1957; children: Ilonna Rimm Madsen, David, Eric, Sara Rimm-Kaufman. BA, Rutgers U., 1957; MS, U. Wis., 1971, PhD, 1976. Lic. psychologist, Wis. Elem. classroom tchr., Hamburg, Franklin, Sussex, N.J., 1957-58, Wilson, N.Y., 1965-67, Watertown (Wis.) Unified Sch. Dist., 1968; lectr. Mount Mary Coll., Milw., 1977-80, asst. prof., 1980-82; dir. Family Achievement Clinic, Oconomowoc, Wis., 1981-93; psychologist dir. Family Achievement Clinic Metro Health Med. Ctr., Cleve., 1993—; clin. prof. of psychiatry and pediatrics Case Western Reserve U., Cleve., 1993—. Gubernatorial apptd., v.p. Wis. Psychology Examining Bd., Madison, 1986-93; host. nat. pub. radio show Family Talk with Sylvia Rimm; contbr. monthly series NBC's Today Show. Author: (with Gary A. Davis) Education of the Gifted and Talented, 1985, 89, 94, 98, 2003, Underachievement Syndrome: Causes and Cures, 1986, Guidebook: Underachievement Syndrome, 1989, How to Parent So Children Will Learn, 1990, Learning Leads Q-Cards, Teacher Tips, Parent Pointers, Student Stepping Stones, 1990, Gifted Kids Have Feelings Too, 1990, Exploring Feelings: Discussion Book for Gifted Kids Have Feelings Too, 1990, Parenting for Achievement, 1994, Keys to Parenting the Gifted Child, 1994, Why Bright Kids Get Poor Grades, 1995, Dr. Sylvia Rimm's Smart Parenting, 1996, Raising Preschoolers, 1997, See Jane Win: The Rimm Report on How 1000 Girls Became Successful Women, 1999 (N.Y. Times bestseller), How Jane Won: 55 Successful Women Share How They Grew From Ordinary Girls to Extraordinary Women, 2001, See Jane Win for Girls, 2003, Rescuing the Emotional Lives of Overweight Children, 2004, Growing Up Too Fast, 2005; syndicated columnist Sylvia Rimm on Raising Kids. Mem. bd. edn. Watertown (Wis.) Unified Sch. Dist., 1969-81; bd. dirs. Watertown (Wis.) Community Child Care Ctr., 1974-77, Watertown Coun. for Creative Edn.; bd. trustees Univ. Lake Sch., 1985-88. Mem. APA, Am. Ednl. Rsch. Assn., Nat. Assn. for Gifted Children (bd. dirs. 1987—), Wis. Psychol. Assn., Wis. Sch. Psychologist Assn., Counsel for Exceptional Children, Wis. Assn. of Educators for Gifted/Talented (past pres., Meritorious Svc. award 1987), Wis. Coun. for Gifted and Talented (treas., charter founding mem.), Ohio Psychol. Assn., Pi Lambda Theta. Avocations: swimming, bicycling, writing, sailing. Home: 3901 E Lake Rd Sheffield Lake OH 44054-1009 Office: Family Achievement Clinic Ste 410 26777 Lorain Rd North Olmsted OH 44070 Office Phone: 800-795-7466. E-mail: srimm@sylviarimm.com.

RINALDI, JACQULEINE BLANCHE, education educator, director; b. Mt. Vernon, NY, Feb. 5, 1935; d. Emile Joseph Tellier; m. Nicholas Miichael Rinaldi, Aug. 29, 1959; children: Christina Marie Banas, Paul Francis, Stephen Emile, David Nicholas. PhD, U. Conn., Storrs, 1999. Adj. prof. English Fairfield U., Conn., 1972—, Sacred Heart U., Fairfield, 1979—, dir. learning ctr., 1991—. Home: 595 Gilman St Bridgeport CT 06605 Office: Sacred Heart U 5151 Park Ave Fairfield CT 06825 Office Phone: 203-371-7823. Home Fax: 203-396-8049; Office Fax: 203-396-8049. Business E-Mail: rinaldij@sacredheart.edu.

RINALDI, RENEE ZAIRA, physician; b. NYC, Dec. 10, 1949; d. John James and Concetta Rinaldi; m. Kenneth Robert Ballard, June 16, 1977; children: Claudia Michele, Celeste Noelle, Christopher Charles. BA, Barnard Coll., Columbia U., 1971; EdM, Harvard U., 1973; MD, N.Y. Med. Coll., 1976. Diplomate Am. Bd. Internal Medicine and Rheumatology. Intern Met. Hosp., N.Y.C., 1976—77; resident in medicine San Fernando program UCLA, Sepulveda Campus, 1977—79; staff internist Olive View Hosp., Van Nuys, Calif., 1979—80; fellow rheumatology UCLA, 1980—82; practice medicine specializing in rheumatology L.A., 1983—; asst. clin. prof. medicine ULCA, 1983—; clin. chief rheumatology Cedars Sinai Med. Ctr., L.A., 1996—2000. Jane Wyman Clin. fellow, 1981. Mem. So. Calif. Rheumatology Soc., L.A. County Women's Med. Assn., Am. Coll. Rheumatology Office: 150 N Robertson Blvd Ste 224 Beverly Hills CA 90211 Office Phone: 310-659-5905.

RINALDO, SHARON ANN, special education educator; b. Hartford, Conn., May 13, 1952; d. Jerry and Mary (Sullivan R.). BS, So. Conn. State U., New Haven, 1974, M in Counseling, 1979, postgrad., 1983. Co-dir. summer youth work experience program T.E.A.M., Derby, Conn., 1977-82; asst. dir. group home Derby, 1978-79; therapist Cath. Family Svcs., Ansonia, Conn., 1980-81; pvt. therapist, 1980-85; spl. edn. tchr. Derby Bd. Edn., 1974—. Chair bd. dirs. Ansonia Battered Women's Project, 1982-84; cons. Irving After Sch. Program, Derby, 1997-98; counselor DART Program Derby H.S., 1992-95; co-pres. Derby Edn. Assn. Tchrs. Union, 1982-83. Mem. NEA, Coun. Exceptional Children, Conn. Edn. Assn., Derby Edn. Assn. Avocations: travel, reading, woodworking, arts and crafts, exercise. Office: Derby HS 8 Nutmeg Ave Derby CT 06418-1126

RINDLISBAKER, CANDACE MAY, elementary school educator; b. Soda Springs, Idaho, May 13, 1947; d. Richard Earl and Vernona Mendenhall Garbett; m. Leon G. Rindlisbaker, May 31, 1968; children: Richelle Gollaher, Shad Larin. BA, Idaho State U., Pocatello, 1970. Cert. tchr. Idaho State Bd. Edn. Tchr. Grace Sch. Dist. 148, Idaho, 1967—68, 1970—72, 1982—83, Pocatello Sch. Dist. 91, Idaho, 1968—69, North Gem Sch. Dist. 149, Bancroft, Idaho, 1983—. Head tchr. N. Gem. Elem. Sch., Bancroft, Idaho, 1990—95, N. Gem. Mid. Sch., Bancroft, Idaho, 1997—99; site coord., Learning for the 21st Century N. Gem Sch., Bancroft, Idaho, 1999—2000, h.s. drama dir., 2000—. Recipient Christa McAuliffe Tchr. Recognition, N. Gem Sch. Dist., 1991—92, Tchr. of Yr., 1997—98. Home: 1752 Lund Rd Bancroft ID 83217 Office: North Gem Sch 360 S Main Bancroft ID 83217

RINE, PATTY DAVIS, music educator; d. Jackie and Peggy Blackwell Davis; m. C. Michael Rine, July 15, 1978; 1 child, Carolyn G. MusB in Edn., Sam Houston State U., Huntsville, Tex., 1978; M in Elem. Edn., Steven F. Austin, Nacogdoches, Tex., 1980; Kodaly Cert., Sam Houston State U., Huntville, Tex., 1986. Tchr. grade 1 Hemphill Ind. Sch. Dist., Tex., 1978—79, tchr. grade 4, 1979—80; tchr. music grades 4-5 Jackson Elem. Sch. Lamar Consolidated Ind. Sch. Dist., Roseneber, 1980—85, Meyer Elem. Sch. Lamar Consolidated Ind. Sch. Dist., Richmond, 1985—93; tchr. music grades k-5 Jane Long Elem. Sch. Lamar Consolidated Ind. Sch. Dist., 1993—. Solo & ensemble accompanist Lamar H.S. Lamar Consolidated Ind. Sch. Dist., Rosenberg, Tex., 1994—2002, Briscoe Jr. H.S. Lamar Consolidated Ind. Sch. Dist., Richmond, 2002—; asst. drir. Select Choir Lamar Consolidated Ind. Sch. Dist., Rosenberg, 2005—. Mem. pub. rels. com. Foster Band Boosters, Richmond, Tex., 2005—; tchr. vacation bible sch. South Pk. Bapt. Ch., Alvin, 1969—76; dir. children's choir First Bapt. Ch. Hemphill, 1978—80, First Bapt. Ch. Rosenberg, 1984—, tchr. vacation bible sch., 1985—, dir. children's choir chimes, 1994—, choir mem., 1994—, camp sponsor, 1995—; founding mem. Singing Women South East Tex., Houston, 1994—. Mem.: Tex. State Tchrs. Assn. (assoc.), Kodaly Assn. (assoc.), Tex. Music Educator Assn. (assoc.). Baptist. Avocation: travel. Home: 5002 Whitewing Dr Richmond TX 77469 Office: Jane Long Elem Sch 907 Main St Richmond TX 77469 Office Phone: 832-223-1900. Business E-Mail: prine@lcisd.org.

RINER, DEBORAH LILLIAN, mental health services professional; b. Brunswick, Ga., Mar. 20, 1960; d. Lee Calvin and Lillian Rosebell Jacobs. A in Allied Health, Calif. Coll. Health Sci., 2005. Cert. medical hypnotherapist, difficult & complex issues Omni Hypnosis Tng. Ctr., 2002, notary pub. Ga. Exec. sec. Greater Jax Christian Sch., Jacksonville, 1984—87; med. transcription coord. St. Vincent's Med. Ctr., Jacksonville, 1987—89; claims processor Allen Med. Claims Adminstrs., Ft. Valley, Ga., 1990—91; registration technician Houston Health Care Complex, Perry, Ga., 1991—92; med. asst. Peace Sun Med. Clinic, Khamis Mushayt, Saudi Arabia, 1993—95; owner and hypnotherapist Coastal Hypnosis Ctr., Brunswick, 2002—. Pres. HealthGlynn.com. Mem. Chronic Disease Coalition, Brunswick; coord. Glynn County Blood Pressure Monitoring Program; amb. Am. Cancer Soc., 2006—. Mem.: Nat. Guild Hypnotists, Nat. Guild Hypnotists, Brunswick Golden Isles C. of C., Order Ea. Star. Mem. Ch. Of Christ. Avocations: genealogy, travel, antiques, Reiki. Office: Coastal Hypnosis Ctr 40 Carteret Ct Brunswick GA 31525 Office Phone: 912-261-8906. Business E-Mail: coastalhypnosis@aol.com.

RING, ALICE RUTH BISHOP, retired preventive medicine physician; b. Ft. Collins, Oct. 11, 1931; d. Ernest Otto and Mary Frances Bishop; m. Wallace Harold Ring, July 26, 1956 (div. 1969); children: Rebecca, Eric, Mark; m. Robert Charles Diefenbach, Sept. 10, 1977. BS, Colo. State U., 1953; MD, U. Colo., 1956; MPH, U. Calif., Berkeley, 1971. Diplomate Am. Bd. Preventive Medicine. Physician cons. Utah State Divsn. Health, Salt Lake City, 1960—65; med. dir., project head start Salt Lake City Cmty. Action Program, 1965—70; resident Utah State Divsn. Health, 1969—71; asst. assoc. regional health dir. USPHS, San Francisco, 1971—75, med. cons. Atlanta, 1975—77, dir. primary care, 1977—84; dir. divsn. diabetes control Ctrs. Disease Control, Atlanta, 1984—88; dir. WHO Collabor Ctr., Atlanta, 1986—91; dir. preventive medicine residency Ctrs. Disease Control, Atlanta, 1988—93; exec. dir. Am. Bd. Preventive Medicine, 1993—98. Trustee Am. Bd. Preventive Medicine, 1990—92; lectr. Emory U. Sch. Pub. Health, 1988—94; bd. dirs. Redwood Coast Med. Svcs., v.p., 1994—2004; mem. adv. com. Shamli Hospice, Gualala, Calif.; mem. adv. coun. Sonoma County Area Agy. on Aging, Santa Rosa, Calif., 2001—, sec., 2004—06, v.p., 2006—; bd. dirs. Alliance Rural Cmty. Health, Calif., 2002—04. Co-author: Clinical Diabetes, 1991; author: History of the American Board of Preventive Medicine, 2002. Bd. dirs. Diabetes Assn. Atlanta, 1985—90. Recipient Disting. Svc. award, Am. Bd. Med. Splties, 2004. Fellow: Am. Coll. Preventive Medicine (bd. dirs. 1990—94, Spl. Recognition award 1998); mem.: AMA (grad. med. edn. adv. com. 1993—97), Steering Com. Environ. Commons, Am. Bd. Med. Specialists (Disting. Svc. award 2004), Am. Acad. Pediat., Assn. Tchrs. Preventive Medicine. Office: PO Box 364 Gualala CA 95445-0364 Business E-Mail: ard@mcn.org.

RING, KRISTEN M., physical education educator; d. Roger (Stepfather) and Nicke Flynn. BS, U. Tenn., Knoxville, 1994; MS, U. Ark., Fayetteville, 1996. Lic. athletic trainer Tex. Dept. Health, 2000, cert. Nat. Athletic Trainers Assn., 1994. Asst. athletic trainer U. Ark., Fayetteville, 1994—99; head athletic trainer/lectr. Tex. Woman's U., Denton, 1999—. Staff rep. Tex. Woman's U. Student-Athlete Adv. Com., 1999—; mem. Tex. Woman's U. P.E.A.C.E. Team, 1999—. Mem.: Nat. Athletic Trainers Assn. Office: Tex Woman's Univ PO Box 425349 Denton TX 76204 Office Phone: 940-898-2593. Office Fax: 940-898-2372. Business E-Mail: kring@twu.edu.

RING, LUCILE WILEY, lawyer; b. Kearney, Nebr., Jan. 2, 1920; d. Myrtie Mercer and Alice (Cowell) W.; m. John Robert Ring, Mar. 28, 1948; children: John Raymond, James Wiley, Thomas Eric. AB, U. Nebr., Kearney, 1944; JD, Washington U., 1946. Bar: Mo. 1946, U.S. Dist. Ct. (ea. dist.) Mo. 1947, U.S. Ct. Appeals (8th cir.) 1972. Atty.-adviser, chief legal group adjudications br. Army Fin. Ctr., St. Louis, 1946-52; exec. dir. lawyer referral svcs. St. Louis Bar, 1960-70; pvt. practice St. Louis, 1960-2000; staff law clk. U.S. Ct. Appeals (8th cir.), St. Louis, 1970-72; exec. dir. St. Louis Com. on Cts., 1972-85. Legal advisor Mo. State Anat. Bd., 1965-95; adj. prof. adminstrv. law Webster Coll., Webster Groves, Mo., 1977-78; mem. Mo. Profl. Liability Rev. Bd., State of Mo., 1977-79. Author, editor: Guide to Community Services - Who Do I Talk To, 1974, 75, 76-79, St. Louis Court Directories, 1972, 73, 74, 75, Felony Procedures in St. Louis Courts, 1975; author: Breaking Barriers: The St. Louis Legacy of Women in Law 1869-1969, 1996; author (series): Women Lawyers in St. Louis History, 1996, Women Breaking Barriers, 1998; contbr. articles to profl. jours. Mem. Mo. Mental Health Authority, 1964-65; bd. dirs., v.p. Drug and Substance Abuse Coun., met. St. Louis, 1976-83; mem. adv. coun. St. Louis Agy. on Tng. and Employment, 1976-83; mem. Mayor's Jud. Reform Subcom., St. Louis, 1974-76. Recipient letter of commendation Office of Chief of Fin., U.S. Army, 1952, Outstanding Alumni award, U. Nebr., Kearney, 1994, Disting. Alumni award, 2005; scholarship, Washington U. Sch. Law, 1944—46, 1st Mo. woman nominated for Mo. Ct. Appeals, St. Louis Dist., Mo. Appellate Commn., 1972, 1st woman nominated judgeship Mo. Non-Partisan Ct. Plan, 1972. Mem. Bar Assn. Met. St. Louis (v.p. 1975-76), Legal Svcs. Ea. Mo., Inc. (v.p. 1978-79, dir.), Legal Aid Soc. St. Louis City and County (bd. dirs. 1977-78), HUD Women and Housing Commn. (commr. 1975), Women's Bar Assn. (treas. St. Louis chpt. 1949-50), Mo. Assn. Women Lawyers (treas. 1959-60, pres. 1960-61), Washington U. Dental Faculty Wives (pres. 1972-74), Mortar Board, Pi Kappa Delta, Sigma Tau Delta. Methodist. Home and Office: 2041 Reservoir Loop Rd Selah WA 98942-9616 Office Phone: 509-697-7740.

RING, RENEE ETHELINE, lawyer; b. Frankfurt, Germany, May 29, 1950; arrived in U.S., 1950; d. Vincent Martin and Etheline Bergetta (Schoolmeesters) Ring; m. Paul J. Zofnass, June 24, 1982; children: Jessica Renee, Rebecca Anne. BA magna cum laude, Catholic U. Am., 1972; JD, U. Va., 1976. Bar: NY 1977. Assoc. Whitman & Ransom, NYC, 1976-83, Carro, Spanbock, Fass, Geller, Kaster & Cuiffo, NYC, 1983-86, ptnr., 1986, Finley Kumble Wagner et. al., NYC, 1987; of counsel Kaye, Scholer, Fierman, Hays & Handler, NYC, 1988; ptnr. Kaye, Scholer, Fierman, Hays & Handler, LLP, NYC, 1989-97, Hunton & Williams, NYC, 1997—2002, McKee Nelson LLP, NYC, 2006—. Trustee The Spence Sch., 2001—02; advisor WestWind Found., 2001—; mem. exec. com. Lawyers for Clinton, Washington, 1991—92; team capt. Clinton Transition Team, Washington, 1992—93; mem. Nat. Lawyers Coun. Dem. Nat. Com., 1993—98; trustee The Clinton Legal Expense Trust, 1998—2002, Pound Ridge Land Conservancy, 2003—; v.p. Queens Bot. Garden Soc., 2005—, mem. exec. com., 2005—, mem. alumni coun. U. Va. Sch. of Law, 1997—2005, 2d v.p., 2000—01, 1st v.p., 2001—03, pres., 2003—05. Mem.: ABA. Democrat. Roman Catholic. Office Phone: 917-777-4527.

RING, YVONNE ANN, special education educator; b. Miami, Fla., Dec. 2, 1960; d. Thomas Charles and Diane Esther Fisher (Stepmother); m. John Michael Ring, Oct. 19, 1991; children: James William Jobbitt, II, Stephanie Ann Jobbitt. BS in Spl. Edn., Piedmont Coll., Demorest, Ga., 1996, Ednl. Specialist, 2002—03; MS in Interrelated Spl. Edn., North Ga. Coll. and State U., Dahlonega, 2001. Cert. tchr. interrelated spl. edn. Ga., 2001, tchr. mental retardation spl. edn. Ga., 1996, tchr. middle grades, math., social sci., reading, interrelated spl. edn. 2006, Wilson reading tchr. 2006. Interrelated spl. edn. tchr. Rabun County Mid. Sch., Tiger, Ga., 2000—, North Habersham Mid. Sch., Clarkesville, Ga., 1996—2000. Practicum Clayton Elem., Clayton, Ga., 1994—94. Recipient Spl. Recognition, Coun. For Exceptional Children, 2000—, Recognition of Participation, Hand-in-Hand Mentor Program, 2001—; Tony Molinaro Scholarship, Ga. Coun. of Aminstrs. of Spl. Edn., 2003. Mem.: Nat. Assn. Spl. Educators, Internat. Reading Assn., Profl. Assn. of Ga. Educators (assoc.), Coun. for Exceptional Children (assoc.), Internat. Dyslexia Found. (assoc.). Avocations: tutoring, travel, continuing education, professional conferences, museums. Home: PO Box 242 Clayton GA 30525-0007 Office: Rabun County Mid Sch 108 Wildcat Hill Drive Tiger GA 30576 E-mail: yring@rabun.k12.ga.us.

RINGGOLD, FAITH, artist; b. NYC, Oct. 8, 1930; BS, CCNY, 1955, MA, 1959; DFA (hon.), Moore Coll. Art, Phila., 1986, Coll. Wooster, Ohio, 1987, Mass. Coll. Art, Boston, 1991, CCNY of CUNY, 1991, RI Sch. Design, 1994, Russell Sage Coll., NY, 1996, Parsons Sch. Design, 1996, Marymount Coll., 1999, Mary Grove Coll., 2000, William Patterson U., 2001, Chgo. Art Inst., 2001, Bloomfield Coll., 2005; DSc (hon.), Brockport State U., NY, 1992, Calif. Coll. Arts and Crafts, Oakland, 1993; DHL (hon.), Malloy Coll., 1997, Bank St. Coll., 1999, William Patterson U., 2001, St. Joseph Coll., 2004; DEd (hon.), Wheelock Coll., 1997. Art tchr. N.Y. Pub. Schs., 1955-73; lectr. Bank St. Coll. Grad. Sch., N.Y.C., 1970-80; prof. art U. Calif., San Diego, 1984—2002, prof. emeritus, 2002—, ret., 2002. Solo exhbns. include Bernice Steinbaum Gallery, 1991, ACA, 2000, Spectrum Gallery, N.Y.C., 1967, 70 10 year retrospective, Studio Mus. in Harlem, N.Y.C., 1984, Bernice Steinbaum Gallerym N.Y.C., 1987-88, Balt. Mus., Deland (Fla.) Mus., Faith Ringgold 25 Yr. Survey Fine Arts Mus. L.I., Hempstead, 1990-93, Textile Mus., Washington, 1993, Children's Mus. of Manhattan, N.Y.C., 1993-95, Hewlett-Woodmere Pub. Libr., Hewlett, N.Y., 1993-94, St. Louis Art Mus., 1994, Athenaeum, La Jolla, Calif., 1995, A.C.A. Gallery, N.Y.C., 1995, 98, Ind. U. of Pa., 1995, Bowling Green State U., Ind., 1996, New Mus. Contemporary Art, N.Y.C., 1998; exhibited in group shows at Harlem Cultural Coun., N.Y.C., 1966, Meml. Exhibit for MLK, Mus. Modern Art N.Y.C., 1968, Chase Manhattan Bank Collection, Martha Jackson Gallery, N.Y.C., 1970, Am. Women Artists, Gedok, Kunstalle, Hamburg, Ger., 1972, Jubliee, Boston Mus. Fine Arts, 1975, Major Contemporary Women Artists, Suzanne Gross Gallery, Phila., 1984, Committed to Print Mus. Modern Art, N.Y.C., 1988, The Art of Black Am. in Japan, Terada Warehouse, Tokyo, Made in the USA, Art in the 50s and 60s U. Calif. Berkeley Art Mus., Craft Today Poetry of the Physical, Am. Craft Mus., N.Y.C., Portraits and Homage to Mothers Hecksher Mus. Huntington, 1987, N.J. State Mus., Trenton, 1992-94, Fukui Fine Art Mus., Fuki, Japan, 1992, Takushima Modern Art Mus., Japan, 1993, Otani Meml. Art Mus., Japan, 1993, Salina Art Art., Kans., 1993, Bruce Watkins Ctr. Kansas City, Mo., 1993, Barton County C.C., Great Bend, Kans., 1993, Del. State Coll. Arts Ctr. Gallery, Dover, 1993-94, Roswell Mus. and Art Ctr., N.Mex., 1994, Aknaton Gallery, Cairo, Alexandria, Egypt, Exit Art, N.Y.C., 1994, New Mus. Contemporary Art, N.Y.C., 1996, Spellman Coll. Mus., Atlanta, 1996, Whitney Mus., N.Y.C., 1996, Centre Georges Pompidou, Paris, 1997, Mus. Art, Ft. Lauderdale, Fla., 1997, N.J. Ctr. Arts, Summit, N.J., 1997, Trout Gallery Dickenson Coll., Carlisle, Pa., numerous others; represented in collections at Chase Manhattan Bank, N.Y.C., Philip Morris Collection, N.Y.C., Children's Mus., Bklyn., Newark Mus., The Women's House of Detention, Rikers Island, N.Y., The Studio Mus., N.Y.C., High Mus., Atlanta, Guggenheim Mus., Met. Mus. Art, Boston Mus. Fine Arts, MOMA, AARP, Washington, Am. Craft Mus., N.Y.C., Clark Mus., Williamstown, Mass., ARCO Chem., Phila., Coca-Cola, Atlanta, Ft. Wayne Mus. Fine Art, Ind., Harold Washington Libr. Ctr., Chgo., Lang Comm. Corp., Coll., Phila. Mus. Art, Pub. Art Pub. Schs., P.S. 22, Bklyn., Spenser Mus. Lawr., Kans., St. Louis Mus. Art, Balt. Mus., Nat. Mus., Washington, Woman's Mus., Washington, Eugenio Maria de Hostos C.C., N.Y.C., MTA 125th St. IRT subway sta. installation, N.Y.C., numerous others; author: Tar Beach, 1991, Aunt Harriet's Underground Railroad in the Sky, 1992 (Picture Book award 1993, Best Children's Book of Yr. 1993), Dinner at Aunt Connie's House, 1993 (Reading Magic award 1993), We Flew Over the Bridge: Memoirs of Faith Ringgold, 1995, Talking to Faith Ringgold, 1995, Bonjour Lonnie, 1996, My Dream of Martin Luther King, Jr., 1996, The Invisible Princess, 1999, If a Bus Could Talk: The Story of Rosa Parks, 1999, Counting to Tar Beach, 1999, Cassie's Colorful Day with Daddy, 1999, Cassie's Word Quilt, 2000, O Holy Night, 2004, Three Witches, 2006; author: (video prodn.) Goodnight Moon: and Other Sleepy Time Tales, Tar Beach, 2000; contbr. articles to profl. jours. Recipient AAUW travel award to Africa, 1976; John Simon Guggenheim Meml. Found. Fellowship (painting), 1987, N.Y. Found. for Arts award (painting), 1988, Nat. Endowment Arts award (sculpture), 1978, (painting) 1989, La Napoule Found. award (painting in So. of France), 1990, Video and Software award Calif. children's book, 1991, Parent's

Choice Gold award, 1991, Artist award Studio Mus., Harlem, 1991, Artist of Yr. award Sch. Art League N.Y., 1991, Coretta Scott King award for illustration, 1992, Dist. Artist award Nat. Coun. Art Adminstrs., 1992, award, 1993, Arts Internat. award (travel to Morocco), 1992, Honors award for outstanding achievement in the visual arts Woman's Caucus Arts, N.Y., 1994, Towsend Harris medal City Coll. Alumni Assn., 1995, N.J. Artist of Yr. award N.J. Ctr. Visual Arts, 1997, 31st NAACP Image award, 1999, Visionary Woman award, Moore Coll. Art & Design, 2005. Home: PO Box 429 Englewood NJ 07631-0429 Office: ACA Galleries 529 W 20th St Fl 5 New York NY 10011-2800 Office Phone: 858-576-0397. Personal E-mail: ringgoldfaith@aol.com.

RINGHOFFER, WINNIFRED MIRIAM, music educator, consultant; b. Seattle, July 21, 1928; d. Boy Norfleet and Almyra Damron Collier; m. Stephen M. Ringhoffer, Aug. 8, 1953 (div. July 1975); children: Myra Jean Hoane, Mary Ellen Haltiner, Margaret Helena Billingsley. BA in Music, Whitman Coll., 1950; AM in Musicology, Boston U., 1952. Music tchr. Baker (Oreg.) Pub. Sch., 1952—53; adj. lectr. voice Whitman Coll., Walla Walla, Wash., 1953—58, 1974—94; ret., 1994; music tchr. Walla Pub. Sch., 1953—54. Pvt. music tchr., Walla Walla, 1994—; adjudicator Dist. Met. Opera Auditions, Spokane, Wash., Seattle. Past pres. Jr. Club of Walla Walla; instr., Quest program Walla Walla C.C., 2000—06; past bd. dirs. Walla Walla Cmty. Concert, Walla Walla Symphony. Mem.: PEO (chpt. pres. 2000—02), Music Tchrs. Nat. Assn. (permanent profl. cert. tchr. music in voice), Wash. State Music Tchrs. Assn. (adjudicator), Nat. Assn. Tchrs. of Singing (past pres. Inland Empire chpt., past gov. Intermountain Region), MLB Book Club, Profl. Ski Instrs. Assn. (level I cert.), Rainbow, Ea. Star. Avocations: sewing, reading, travel, skiing, biking. Home and Studio: 119 Leonard St Walla Walla WA 99362

RINGLESBACH, DOROTHY LOUISE, retired nurse, writer; b. Ft. Wayne, Ind., Aug. 14, 1925; d. Paul Frederich and Elizabeth Barbara Sauerteig; m. Robt J. Salisbury, 1946 (div.); children: David, Claudia Ann, Evelyn, Claude, Jane; m. John C. Ringlesbach, July 5, 1980. RN, Wishard Meml. Hosp., 1947. RN Ind., Ky., Va. RN staff Mary Chiles Hosp., Mt. Sterling, Ky., 1958—60; interperter Colonial Williamsburg, Williamsburg, Va., 1968—73; house supr. Williamsburg Cmty. Hosp., Williamsburg, Va., 1973—80, 1985—93; ret. Author: OSS Stories that can Now Be Told, 2005; contbr. articles pub. to profl. jour. Mem. US Cadet Nurse Corps., 1944—47; state pres. Aux. to Kymedical Assn., Louisville, 1965—66, rec. sec., 1962—65. Cadet nurse corps, 1944—47. Mem.: OSS Com. Vets, OSS Soc. Luth. Avocations: reading, raise orchids, travel, writing. Home: 303 Farmville Ln Williamsburg VA 23188 Office Phone: 757-564-8299. Personal E-mail: esp22693@widomaker.com.

RINGLEY, KATHLEEN J., director; b. Massillon, Ohio, Mar. 02; d. Paul Charles Ringley and Rita Estelle Bachtel. B of Music Edn., Mt. Union Coll., Alliance, Ohio, 1981; MusM, U. Akron, Ohio, 1992. Cert. tchr. K-12 music Ohio. Dir. choir, asst. band dir. Tuslaw Local Schs., Massillon, Ohio, 1982—89; grad. tchg. asst. U. Akron, 1990—92; music tchr. Massillon City Schs., 1992—94; dir. vocal music and drama Cen. Cath. H.S., Canton, Ohio, 1995—. Music dir. Players Guild of Canton. Composer summer prodn. workshops songs. Named Outstanding Sr. Music Maj., Mt. Union Coll., 1981, Outstanding Grad. Student in Music, U. Akron, 1992; recipient Sterling Achievement award, Mu Phi Epsilon, 1981. Mem.: Nat. Assn. Cath. Sch. Tchrs., Ohio Music Edn. Assn., Music Educators Nat. Conf. Avocations: travel, attending Broadway musicals, operas, concerts, collecting Woodstock and Peanuts memorabilia. Home: 822 Stratford Ave NE Massillon OH 44646 Office: Cen Cath H S 4824 Tuscarawas St W Canton OH 44708

RINGPFEIL, FRANZISKA, dermatologist; b. Sept. 13, 1967; MD, 1992. Diplomate Am. Bd. Dermatology. Pvt. practice dermatology, Phila.; asst. prof. Jefferson Med. Coll. Thomas Jefferson U., 2000—. Contbr. articles to profl. jours. Mem.: Society Pediatric Dermatology, Soc. Investigative Dermatology, Phila. Dermatologic Soc., Nat. Assn. Pseudoxanthoma Elasticum, Dermatology Found., Am. Acad. Dermatology (Young Investigators award 2001). Office: Thomas Jefferson Univ Jefferson Med Coll 233 S 10th St Rm 409 Philadelphia PA 19107 Office Phone: 215-503-8259. Office Fax: 215-503-5788. E-mail: franziska.ringfeil@jefferson.edu.*

RINGSTEAD, DEE ANN, principal; b. Ames, Iowa, July 1, 1949; d. Virgil Melvin and Marleen Theresa Davis. BS, U. Iowa, Iowa City, 1972; MS, Calif. State U., Fullerton, 1979. Tchr. Santa Ana Unified Sch. Dist., Calif., 1974—93, adminstr., 1993—2000; prin. Santa Maria Joint H.S. Dist., 2000—. Adj. instr. Calif. State U., Fullerton, Calif., 1990—2000. Bd. mem. Ethel Pope Auditorium Found., Santa Maria, 2000—, Coastal Voices, Calif., 2001—, Santa Maria Youth and Family, 2002—. Named Orange County Tchr. of Yr., 1999—2000. Mem.: ASCD, Delta Kappa Gamma. Avocations: travel, cooking, reading.

RINGWALD, MOLLY, actress; b. Sacramento, Feb. 18, 1968; d. Bob and Adele Ringwald; m. Valery Lameignère, July 28, 1999 (div. Nov. 2002); life ptnr. Panio Gianopoulos; 1 child, Mathilda Ereni. Grad. high sch., Los Angeles. Actress: (stage prodns.) The Glass Harp, 1973, Annie, 1977, Cabaret, 2001, Enchanted April, 2004, When Harry Met Sally, 2004, Sweet Charity, 2006;(feature films) Tempest, 1982, Spacehunter: Adventures in the Forbidden Zone, 1983, Sixteen Candles, 1984, The Breakfast Club, 1985, Pretty in Pink, 1986, The Pick-Up Artist, 1987, For Keeps, 1988, Betsy's Wedding, 1990, Seven Sunday, 1994, Office Killer, 1996, Kimberly, 1999, Requiem For Murder, 1999, Teaching Mrs. Tingle, 1999, Cut, 2000, In the Weeds, 2000, Ring of Fire, 2000, Not Another Teen Movie, 2001, The Tulse Luper Suitcases: The Moab Story, 2003; (TV movies) Packin' It In, 1983, P.K. and the Kid, Something to Live For: The Alison Gertz Story, 1992, Twice Upon a Time, 1998, Since You've Been Gone, 1998, The Big Time, 2002; (TV mini-series) The Stand, 1994; regular (TV series) The Facts of Life, 1979-80, Townies, 1996; guest-star: (TV shows) Diff'rent Strokes, The Merv Griffin Show; (Album) Molly Sings, 1974. Office: William Morris Agy 151 S El Camino Dr Beverly Hills CA 90212-2775*

RINO, BARBARA ELIZABETH, music educator, musician; b. Lincoln, Nebr., Jan. 14, 1945; d. Howard Gillette and Elizabeth Lucille Cook; m. Louis Stanislaus Rino, Dec. 22, 1974 (dec. Aug. 31, 2004); 1 child, John Gaspare. MusB (with distinction), Nebr. Wesleyan U., Lincoln, 1966; violin study, Harold Wippler, Denver, Colo., 1974—77. Lic. tchr. Colo., 1967. Violinist Lincoln Symphony Orch., Lincoln, Nebr., 1962—66; music educator Denver Pub. Sch., Denver, 1966—68; orch. dir. Adams County Sch. Dist. 50, Westminster, Colo., 1969—78, Adams County Sch. Dist. 12 Five Star Schs., Thornton, Colo., 1988—2001; pvt. studio tchr. self employed, Westminster, Colo., 1971—; concertmaster Brico Symphony Orch., Denver, 1972—74; dir. orch. Denver Youth Musicians Inc., 1973—77, 1984—89; free lance violinist Denver Musicians Assn., Denver, 1973—95; orch. clinician, adj. Solo and Group Competitions Youth Orch. Chair Auditions, Colo., 1973—; concertmaster Rocky Mountain Chamber Orch., 1985—87. Conductor: Colo. Music Educators State Conf., 1972, 1975; musician: Disneyland and Universal Studios, Kennedy Arts Ctr., 1976, Expo '86; author (curriculum): Dist. Orch. grades 6-12, 1990. Music activities Westminster United Meth. Ch., Colo., 1980—. Recipient Outstanding Alumni award, Nebr. Wesleyan U. Dept. Music, 2006. Mem.: Music Tchrs'. Nat. Assn., Am. String Tchrs. Assn. (Colo. Outstanding Tchr. of the Yr. 2003), Music Educators Nat. Conf., Phi Kappa Phi, Kappa Delta Pi. Meth. Achievements include with pvt. violin and viola students consistently chosen to participate in Colo. All State HS Orch., Western States Honor Orch., Denver Young Artist Orch., MTNA divsn., Nat. solo competitions.

RINSCH, MARYANN ELIZABETH, occupational therapist; b. L.A., Aug. 8, 1939; d. Harry William and Thora Analine (Langlie) Hitchcock; m. Charles Emil Rinsch, June 18, 1964; children: Christopher, Daniel, Carl. BS, U. Minn., 1961. Registered occupational therapist Calif., lic. Calif., 2003. Staff occupational therapist Hastings (Minn.) State Hosp., 1961-62, Neuropsychiat. Inst., L.A., 1962-64; staff and sr. occupational therapist Calif. Children's Svcs., L.A., 1964-66, head occupational therapist, 1966-68; researcher A. Jean Ayres, U. So. Calif., L.A., 1968-69; pvt. practice neurodevel. and sensory integraton Tarzana, Calif., 1969-74; pediat. occupational therapist neurodevel. & sensory integration St. Johns Hosp., Santa Monica, Calif., 1991-95; pvt. practice, cons. Santa Monica-Malibu Unified Sch. Dist., 1994-2001; pvt. practice, 2001—. Mem. alliance bd. Natural History Mus., L.A. County, 1983—, pres., 1998-99; cub scouts den mother Boy Souts Am., Sherman Oaks, Calif., 1986-88, advancement chair Boy Scout Troop 474, 1989-92; mem. Vol. League San Fernando Valley, Van Nuys, Calif., 1985-93; trustee Viewpoint Sch., Calabasas, Calif., 1987-90; bd. dirs. Valley Women's Ctr., 1990-91. Mem. Am. Occupational Therapy Assn., Calif. Occupational Therapy Assn. Home: 19849 Greenbriar Dr Tarzana CA 91356-5428 Personal E-mail: merinsch@sbcglobal.net.

RINTA, CHRISTINE EVELYN, nurse, air force officer; b. Geneva, Ohio, Oct. 4, 1952; d. Arvi Alexander and Catharina Maria (Steenbergen) R. BSN, Kent State U., 1974; MSN, Case Western Res. U., 1979. CNOR. Staff nurse oper. room Euclid (Ohio) Gen. Hosp., 1974-76, oper. room charge nurse, 1977-79; commd. 1st lt. USAF, 1979, advanced through grades to lt. col.; staff nurse oper. room Air Force Regional Hosp., Sheppard AFB, Tex., 1979-82; staff nurse oper. room, asst. oper. room supr. Regional Med. Ctr. Clark, Clark Air Base, Philippines, 1982-83; chief, nurse recruiting br. 3513th Air Force Recruiting Squadron, North Syracuse, N.Y., 1983-87; nurse supr. surg. svcs. 432d Med. Group, Misawa Air Base, Japan, 1987-89; course supr., instr. oper. room nursing courses 3793d Nursing Tng. Squadron, Keesler Med. Ctr., Keesler AFB, Miss., 1989-92; asst. dir., then dir. oper. room and ctrl. sterile supply Keesler Med. Ctr., Keesler AFB, Miss., 1992-93; comdr., enlisted clin. courses flight 383d Tng. Squadron, Sheppard AFB, Tex., 1993-94; comdr., officer clin. courses flight 383rd Tng. Squadron, Sheppard AFB, Tex., 1994-95; comdr. enlisted courses flight 383rd Tng. Squadron, Sheppard AFB, Tex., 1995-96; ops. officer, oper. room svcs. 74th Med. Ops. Squdron, Wright-Patterson AFB, Ohio, 1996-2000; ret., 2000. Decorated Air Force Commendation medal, Air Force Achievement medal, Meritorious Svc. medal. Mem. Ohio Nurses Assn., Assn. Operating Rm. Nurses, Air Force Assn., Sigma Theta Tau. Home: 3110 Cymar Dr Beavercreek OH 45434-6355 Personal E-mail: maxine1988@aol.com.

RIOS, ELENA, health association administrator; BA, Stanford U., 1977; M in Health Policy and Planning Analysis, UCLA, 1980, MD, 1987. With State of Calif. Office of Statewide Health Planning and Devel.; mem. Nat. Health Care Reform Task Force; coord. outreach groups for White House; advisor regional and minority women's health U.S. Dept. Health and Human Svcs., 1994—98; pres., CEO Nat. Hispanic Med. Assn. Primary care health svcs. rsch. fellow UCLA, 1990; CEO Hispanic-Serving Health Professions Schools, Inc.; bd. dirs. Nat. Hispanic Leadership Agenda, Women's Policy Inc., Partnerships for Prevention; co-chair Hispanic Health Coalition; mem. advisory panel Medicare Edn.; lectr. in field. Named one of Top 10 Latinos in Healthcare, LatinoLeaders mag., 2004. Office: Nat Hispanic Med Assn 1411 K St NW Ste 1100 Washington DC 20005*

RIOS, EVELYN DEERWESTER, columnist, musician, artist, writer; b. Payne, Ohio, June 25, 1916; d. Jay Russell and Flossie Edith (Fell) Deerwester; m. Edwin Tietjen Rios, Sept. 19, 1942 (dec. Feb. 1987); children: Jane Evelyn, Linda Sue Rios Stahlman. BA with honors, San Jose State U., 1964, MA, 1968. Cert. elem., secondary tchr. Calif. Lectr. in music San Jose (Calif.) State U., 1969-75; from bilingual cons. to assoc. editor Ednl. Factors, Inc., San Jose, 1969-76, mgr. field rsch., 1977-78; writer, editor Calif. MediCorps Program, 1978-85; contbg. editor, illustrator Cmty. Family Mag., Wimberly, Tex., 1983-85; columnist The Springer, Dripping Springs, Tex., 1985-90. Author, illustrator, health instr. textbooks elem. schs., 1980—82. Author: The Best of It Seems To Me, 2002. Chmn. Dripping Springs Planning and Zoning Commn., 1991—93; music dir. Cambrian Park (Calif.) Meth. Ch., 1961—64; choir dir. Bethel Luth. Ch., Cupertino, Calif., 1965—66, 1968—83; dir. music St. Aban's Ch., Bogota, Colombia; organist Holy Spirit Episcopal Ch., Dripping Springs, 1987—94. Mem.: Am. Guild Organists (dean 1963—64), Phi Kappa Phi (pres. San Jose chpt. 1973—74). Avocations: weaving, stitching, painting. Home: PO Box 3175 Atascadero CA 93423-3175

RIPLEY, CHARLENE A., lawyer; BA, U. Alberta; JD, Dalhousie U., Nova Scotia. Counsel Amoco Can. Petroleum Co. Limited, 1990—97; sr. counsel Norcen Energy Resources Limited (predecessor to Anadarko Can. Corp.), 1997—98, v.p., gen. counsel, corp. sec., 1998—2003; v.p., gen. counsel Anadarko Petroleum Corp., 2003—, corp. sec., 2004—. Mem.: Alberta Arbitration & Mediation Soc., Tex. State Bar, API Gen. Com. on Law, Tex. Gen. Counsel Group, Assn. Corp. Counsel, Law Soc. Alberta, Can. Bar Assn. Office: Anadarko Petroleum Corp 1201 Lake Robbins Dr The Woodlands TX 77380-1046 Office Fax: 832-636-8220, 832-636-1000.

RIPMA, MARY, librarian; b. St. Johns, Mich., Aug. 7, 1952; d. Charles William and Vera Elizabeth Austin; m. Mark Gale Ripma, Apr. 29, 1978; children: Lee, Tye, Clay. BA, Mich. State U., 1974; MLS, San Jose State U., Calif., 1977; cert. in bus. mgmt., Cañada Coll., Redwood City, Calif., 2000. Dir. editl. Info. Access Corp., Redwood City, 1977—83; info. advisor Mothers with Babies, Menlo Park, Calif., 1983—88; reference libr. Menlo Park Pub. Libr., 1988—92; bus. specialist Dialog Inc., Mountain View, Calif., 1992—98; mgr. Menlo Park Rsch. Inc., 1998—2001; mgr., owner www.y-ourgetawayhouse.com, Santa Cruz, Calif., 2001—. Vol. libr. Kristin Sch., Albany, New Zealand, 2004—; music program organizer, rm. mother PTA, Menlo Park, 1987—2004. Seeburg scholar, San Jose State U., 1977. Mem.: AAUW, Forest & Bird, Warkworth Quilting Club, Collie Club of Am. Democrat. Unitarian. Avocations: quilting, swimming. Home: 217 Goatley Rd Warkworth 1241 New Zealand Mailing: 849 Almar Ave Ste C 190 Santa Cruz CA 95060 E-mail: ripma@hotmail.com.

RIPPLE, PAULA G., literature and language educator; d. Robert F. and Jan Cooper Gantz; m. David E. Ripple; children: Shelley Ripple Rodriguez, Jacob Paul. BA, Kans. State U., Manhattan, 1972; MA, Kans. State U., Ft. Hays, 1996. Cert. tchg. St. Mary of the Plains, 1991. Sec. Ctrl. Elem. Sch., Dodge City, Kans., 1982—91; tchr. English Dodge City H.S., 1991—. Adj. instr. English Dodge City C.C., Kans., 1998—2000. Mailing: 1901 La Mesa Dr Dodge City KS 67801-6420

RIPSTEIN, JACQUELINE, artist; b. Mexico City, Apr. 18, 1952; came to U.S., 1996; d. Maximiliano and Josephine Ripstein; widow; children: Stephanie, Arlette. Grad. high sch., Mexico City. Participant more than 160 expositions and tours, U.S., Mex., Europe. Developer, patentee Invisible Art & Light Technique; group shows include: Libr. Mus. Show, Cuernavaca, Morelos, Mex., 1978, C.V.M. Art. Co., N.Y., 1979, MGM Grand Gallery, Las Vegas, 1980, Govt./Inst. del Petroleo, Mex., 1982, Lanai Gallery, Mex., 1982, Praxis Gallery, 1988, Dyansen Gallery, Beverley Hills, Calif., 1988, CFE Tech. Mus., Mex., 1991, San Carmen Mus., Mex., 1991, Jewish Cmty. Ctr., Houston, 1992, Sefarad, Posada de la Hermandad Art and Cultural Ctr., 1992, 94, Art Expo Phillips-Samuels Gallery, Miami, 1993, Salon d'Automne, Grand Prix de Sud Ouest, 1995, Biennale d'Aquitain (prize 1994): Mus. d'Art Moderne d'Unet, France, 1995 (recognition prize Fort Lauderdale Philarmonic Soc. 1994), Grand Prix de Paris d'Art Plastique: Found. Napoleon, Unet, 1995, Biennale Diploma Honneur/D'EncouragementPub. Paris, Wirtz Gallery, South Beach, Fla., 1996, Kolel Art Show, Caracas, Venezuela, 1996, The World Spritual U., JR's Art, Heart Sanctuaries, 1998, Art Frenzie, 1998, Vibrations through Music and Art, Steven Halpern and JR's Art, 1999, Vibrations through Music, UN Philarmonica, JR's Art, 1999; spl. events include: Day of Awakenings, Miami Arena, U. Wisdom Found., 1998; commd. Our Lady of the Universe: God's Gift to the World, Thy Will Be Done, Holy Family Inst., Calif., Boston, N.C., Phila., Chgo., New Orleans, Palm Beach, Fla., Naples, Fla., 1997; appeared in publs. Hola Mag., 1994, Fine Art Index N.Am., 1994, Voces Esteticas de Ignacio Flores Antunez, Quinientos Anos Editores, Artistas Plasticos, 1981, Directorio Artistico, 1986, Art Expressions Mag., Sedona Mag., others. Recipient Proclamation, City of Toledo, 1994, Nat. Competition award, Mex., 1994, Laureat prize '95, 1994, Certificate of appreciation, Aspira of Fla., United Way Edn. Program, South Beach Alternative Sch., 1995. Mem. Aventura Mktg. Coun.

RISEN-WHITE, ANGELA LORRI, systems analyst; b. Bloomington, Ind., Nov. 2, 1970; d. Thomas Gary and Margie Bea (Gilbert) Risen; m. Jerry Leslie White, Oct. 19, 1996. BS in Acctg., Ind. U., 1994. CPA, CMA. Bookkeeper Hoosier Hills Food Bank, Bloomington, Ind., 1993-94; fin. devel. program assoc. Baxter Healthcare, Deerfield, Ill., 1995, Baxter Healthcare Can., Mississauga, Ont., 1995-96; with inventory acctg. Allegiance Healthcare, Waukegan, Ill., 1996-97, sr. fin. analyst V. Mueller divsn., 1997-98, sr. fin. ops. analyst V. Mueller divsn., 1998-99, bus. sys. analyst V. Mueller divsn., 1999—. Foster home coord. Guardian Angel Basset Rescue, Ill. Mem. Ill. CPA Soc., Inst. Mgmt. Accts., Jr. Achievement (vol. tutor). Office: Allegiance Healthcare 1430 Waukegan Rd # Kb-b2 Mc Gaw Park IL 60085-6787

RISHER, MARY LOU BISHOP, artist; b. Tulsa, Jan. 6, 1929; d. George W. and Frances Pearl (Hendrix) Nesmith; m. Thomas Ray Bishop, Sept. 1, 1951 (div. 1996); children: Thomas R. Bishop II, Frances Joann Bishop Faber; m. Jack Risher, May 26, 1998. Student, Columbia U., 1948; BA, U. Houston, 1949, MEd, 1951; student, U. Wash., 1954; postgrad., U. Houston, 1983-84; pvt. studies with, James Jennings, Opal Walls, Ruth Pershing Uhler, Lowell Collins. Cert. tchr., Tex., Wash. Fine artist, painter specializing in portraits, 1951—; freelance artist, 1975—; pvt. tchr. pastels and oils. Condr. portrait seminars Tidwell Art Ctr., Houston. Exhibited in one-woman shows in Washington, Ala., Tex.; group shows at Bellevue Arts Fair, Washington; represented in permanent collections at 1st Bapt. Ch., Houston, Unitarian Ch., Huntsville, Ala., also corp. and pvt. collections in U.S. and Europe; executed murals for Unitarian Ch., Huntsville; portraits represented at Mary Doerr's images of Austin and the Southwest, Austin. Recipient scholarship Houston Mus. Fine Art, 1939-50, numerous awards for art. Mem. AAUW, Houston Soc. Illustrators, Profl. Picture Framer's Assn., Phi Kappa Phi, Phi Theta Kappa, Kappa Delta Pi. Unitarian Universalist. Avocations: portrait work, piano, gardening, landscape painting, travel. Home: 16 Cypress Meadow Loop Slidell LA 70460-5214

RISIMINI, BARBARA LYNN, secondary school educator; b. Vineland, N.J., Sept. 26, 1975; d. Peter Daniel Dell'Aringa and Joy Wanette Tullar; m. Kevin Joseph Risimini, July 21, 2000. BS, Cumberland County Coll., Vineland, 1995; degree, Rowan U., Glassboro, N.J., 1998. Office: Oakcrest HS 1824 Dr Dennis Foreman Dr Mays Landing NJ 08330-2640

RISING, CATHARINE CLARKE, author; b. Berkeley, Calif., Jan. 7, 1929; d. Philip Seymour and Helen Katharine (Davis) Clarke; m. Boardman Rising, Sept. 16, 1950. BS, U. Calif., Berkeley, 1950, PhD, 1987; MA, San Francisco State U., 1979. Cert. cmty. coll. instr., Calif. Author: Darkness at Heart: Fathers and Sons in Conrad, 1990, Outside the Arch: Kohut and Five Modern Writers, 1999; contbr. articles to profl. jours. Mem. MLA, Phi Beta Kappa.

RISKIN, VICTORIA, former trade association administrator; d. Robert Riskin and Fay Wray; m. David Rintels. Pres. Writers Guild Am., West, 2001—04. Author: (TV films) My Antonia, 1995; prodr.: (TV films) The Last Best Year, 1990, A Town Torn Apart, 1992, World War II: When Lions Roared, 1994, The Member of the Wedding, 1997.

RISKO, VICTORIA J., language educator; BS, U. Pitts., 1966; MS, W.Va. U., 1969, EdD, 1971; postgrad., U. London, 1975. Fellow Learning Disabilities Inst. W.Va. U., 1969—70; tchr. Johnstown (Pa.) Pub. Sch. Sys., 1967—68; tchr. remedial reading Johnstown (Pa.) Pub. Sch. Dist., 1967; instr. home econs. W.Va. U., 1968—69, instr., supr. reading clinic, 1969; rschr.-tchr. Robert F. Kennedy Youth Ctr., Morgantown, W.Va., 1969—70; tchr.-cons. inservice edn. of tchrs. Belair-Manchester Schs. of Mandeville, Jamaica, 1974—75; instr., asst. prof., assoc. prof., dir. reading clinic programs, mem. grad. faculty SUNY, Fredonia, 1970—75; rsch. scientist Learning Tech. Ctr., mem. faculty interdisciplinary team Child Study Ctr., Kennedy Ctr. Peabody Coll., Vanderbilt U., Nashville, 1978—89, assoc. prof., 1975—94, prof. lang. and learning, 1994—. Vis. prof. reading W.Va. U., 1971. Recipient Disting. Svc. and Leadership award, Coll. Reading Assn., 1995, Disting. Rsch. in Tchr.'s Edn. award, Assn. Tchr. Educators Conf., 1992. Office: Vanderbilt U Peabody Coll 367 Wyatt Ctr Box 330 Nashville TN 37203

RISSER, HILARY S., mathematician, educator; m. Scott D. Risser, June 3, 2000; 1 child, Ellie. BS, BA, So. Meth. U., 2000, MS, 2001; PhD, Sothern Methodist U., 2005. Tchg. asst. So. Meth. U., Dallas, 1998—2002; math. tchr. Plano (Tex.) Ind. Sch. Dist., 2002—06; asst. prof. math. Tex. Women's U., Plano, Tex., 2006—. Recipient Betty McKnight Spears Award, So. Meth. U. Math dept., 2001; Nat. Merit Scholar, 1996. Mem.: Am. Math. Soc., SIAM, Tau Beta Pi, Gamma Phi Beta (rec. sec., area reference chair, Dallas alumnae webdesigner 1997—2003). Avocations: Tae Kwon Do, quilting, needlepoint.

RISSMAN, BARBARA SUSAN ZIMMER, psychotherapist; b. Copiague, N.Y., May 14, 1951; d. Samuel and Hilda (Krebs) Zimmer; m. Randall S. Rissman, June 20, 1976; children: Jesse, Dahlia. BS, Boston U., 1973; MSW, Rutgers U., 1980. Diplomate Am. Bd. Examiners. Family therapist The Children's Annex, Woodstock, N.Y., 1980-83, Catskill Family Inst., Kingston, N.Y., 1980-86; family therapist dir. Maverick Family Counseling, Woodstock, 1984—. Cons. Compuserve-Human Sexuality Svc., Woodstock, 1987—. Mem. NASW. Office: Maverick Family Counseling 404 Zena Rd Woodstock NY 12498-2620 Office Phone: 914-679-8650. Personal E-mail: bzrissman@gmail.com.

RISSMILLER, CAROLE, school system administrator; d. John and Alice Geary. MS, East Stroudsburg U., 1999; postgrad., Widener U., 2003—. Cert. supt. Pa., secondary math. tchr. Pa., elem. and secondary prin. Pa. Math tchr. Pleasant Valley Sch. Dist., Brodheadsville, Pa., 1985—97, chmn. math dept. Pleasant Valley HS, 1996—97, HS asst. prin., 1997—99, elem. prin., math supr., 2001—03, asst. supt., 2003—; HS prin. Stroudsburg (Pa.) Sch. Dist., 1999—2001. V.p. Quiet Valley Living Hist. Farm, Stroudsburg, 2005—. Bd. dirs. Pocono Area Transitional Housing, Stroudsburg, 2003. Mem.: Pa. Assn. Sch. Administrators, Kiwanis. Office: Pleasant Valley Sch Dist #1 School Lane-Route 115 Brodheadsville PA 18322 Office Phone: 570-402-1000. Office Fax: 570-992-1902. Business E-Mail: rissmiller.carole@pvbears.org.

RISTOW, GAIL ROSS, art educator, paralegal, children's rights advocate; b. Carmel, Calif., Oct. 18, 1949; d. Kenneth E. and Lula Mae (Craft) Ross; m. Steven Craig Ristow, Sept. 15, 1971. BS in Biochemistry, Calif. Polytech State U., San Luis Obispo, 1972; MEd, Ariz. State U., 1980. Cert. tchr., Calif. Asst. instr. Calif. State Polytech U., Pomona, 1972; grad. asst. Calif. Polytech State U., Pomona, 1973-74; tchr. Mt. Carmel High Sch., L.A., 1974-76, Cartwright Sch. Dist., Phoenix, 1976-80; pres., owner Handmade With Love, Bay City, Tex., 1984-88; tchr. art Aiken, S.C., 1989-96. Tchr. Community Edn., Bay City, 1986-88, Palacios, Tex., 1987. Sec. Chukker Creek Homeowners, Aiken, S.C., 1989-96; mem. S.C. Foster Care Rev. Bd., 1991-96; vol. tchr. elem. schs., Korea. Mem. AAUW, Am. Chem. Soc., Nat. Soc. Tole and Decorative Painters, Aiken Newcomer's Club (sec. 1989-91), Aiken Lioness Club (pres. 1991-94), Aiken Lions Club, Kennawick Newcomer's Club (sec. 2005—), Richland Newcomers Club, Bechtel Wives Group, Alpha Delta Kappa (v.p. 1986-87). Avocations: painting, woodworking, sewing, reading, children's rights advocacy. Home: 396 Lombardy Ln Richland WA 99352

RISTOW, THELMA FRANCES, retired elementary school educator; b. Plymouth, Wis., Sept. 9, 1938; d. Ambrose J. and Marie A. (Lauby) Enders; m. William A. Ristow, Nov. 7, 1964; children: James, Lora, Kim Marie, Robert, Donald. BS, U. Wis., Oshkosh, 1960, MS in Edn., 1995. Cert. elem. tchr. Peer coach Oshkosh Area Sch. Dist., 2000—, ret., 2003. Contbr. chapters to books; co-author (with Dr. Ava McCall): Teaching State History: A Guide to Developing a Multicultural Curriculum. Mem. Internat. Reading Assn. (state coord.), Wis. State Reading Assn., Ctrl. Wis. Reading Coun., Mid-East

Reading Coun., Wolf River Reading Coun., Fox Valley Reading Coun., Headwaters Reading Coun., Phi Delta Kappa, Kappa Delta Pi. Home: 1600 Northpoint St Oshkosh WI 54901-3119 Office: Oshkosh Area Sch Dist Adminstrn 215 S Eagle St Oshkosh WI 54903 Personal E-mail: tfristow@sbcglobal.net.

RISTUCCIA, LAVERN K. COLE, psychologist, consultant; b. Balt., Mar. 14, 1952; d. Vernon Geyer and Viola Cecilia (Riley) Cole; m. Bruce Michael Ristuccia, Oct. 26, 1990; 2 children. BA, U. Md., Balt., 1974; MA in Clin. Psychology, Antioch Coll., 1982; PhD in Psychology, Nova Southeastern, Ft. Lauderdale, Fla., 1993. Lic. psychologist, N.Y. Practica Nova Southeastern Mental Health Clinic, Ft. Lauderdale, 1987-89; intern psychologist U. Rochester (N.Y.) Med. Ctr., 1989-90; psychologist Monroe Devel. Ctr., Rochester, 1990-92, Lifetime Assistance, Rochester, 1992-94, Park Ridge Hosp., Rochester, 1994-97; psychologist in pvt. practice Rochester, 1997—. Cons. Arbor Hill Living Ctr., Rochester, 1996-97, Indsl. Medicine, Inc., Rochester, 1996-97; adivsor to bd. dirs. Canandaigua (N.Y.) Montessori Sch., 1998-2000. Mem. APA, N.Y. State Psychologists Assn., Genesee Valley Psychol. Assn. Democrat. Methodist. Avocations: travel, antiques. Office: 3180 West St Canandaigua NY 14424-1722

RITCH, KATHLEEN, diversified financial services company executive; b. Harbor Beach, Mich., Jan. 23, 1943; d. Eunice (Spry) R. BA, Mich. State U., 1965; student, Katharine Gibbs Sch., 1965—66. Exec. sec., adminstrv. asst. to pres. Katy Industries, Inc., N.Y.C., 1969-70; exec. sec., adminstrv. asst. to chmn. Kobrand Corp., N.Y.C., 1970-72; adminstrv. asst. to chmn. and pres. Ogden Corp., N.Y.C., 1972-74, asst. sec., adminstr. office svcs., and asst. to chmn., 1974-81, corp. sec., adminsr. office svcs., 1981-84, v.p., corp. sec., adminstr. office svcs., 1984-92, v.p. corp. sec., 1992-2000; freelance executive NYC, 2000—. Co-owner Unell Mfg. Co., Port Hope, Mich., 1966-87. Bd. dir. Young Concert Artists, Inc. Home: 500 E 77th St New York NY 10162-0025

RITCHEY, LAURETTA MARIE, secondary school educator; b. Chgo., Oct. 17, 1947; d. Thomas Joseph and Marien LaFond Fay; m. Richard Wayne Ritchey, July 17, 1971; children: Richard Thomas, Christopher Milo, Timothy James. BA, Dominican U., River Forest, Ill., 1969; MA in Tchg. in Biology, Northeastern U., Chgo., 1975; CAS Early Childhood, Nat. Lewis U., Evanston, Ill., 1982. Cert. secondary tchr. Ill. Sci. tchr. Proviso West HS, Hillside, Ill., 1969—78, ValleyView Sch. Dist., Romeoville and Bolingbrook, Ill., 1986—91, Carl Sandburg HS, Ill., 1991—. Tchr. rep. Pk. Dist., Orland Park, 2005—06. Recipient Connections award (2), State of Ill. Mem.: NIABT. Home: 15W770 82nd St Burr Ridge IL 60527 Office: Carl Sandburg HS 131st and LaGrange Road Orland Park IL 60462 Office Phone: 708067103100. Business E-Mail: lritchey@d230.org.

RITCHIE, ANNA SPEARS, music educator; b. Concord, NC; d. Carl Lindley Spears Jr. and Zelma Grantham Spears; m. Marshall Wainwright Ritchie, July 13, 1985; children: Mary Frances, Marshall Wainwright Jr. MusB, Meredith Coll., Raleigh, NC, 1985. Cert. K-12 music educator NC. Elem. music tchr. W.M. Irvin Elem. Sch., Concord, 1985—. Facilitor for integrated studies, nat. presenter brain injury assn. Cabarrus County Schs., Concord. Fundraiser ARC, Cabarrus County, Concord, 2006—. Named Tchr. of Yr., R. Brown McAllister Elem., W.M. Irvin Elem.; recipient Impact on Education award. Presbyterian. Avocations: travel, cooking, reading, walking, weight training. Office Phone: 704-782-8864. E-mail: aritchie@cabarrus.k12.nc.us.

RITCHIE, BETH BRADLEY, elementary school educator; b. Lynchburg, Va., Feb. 23, 1970; d. Parmer Harding Bradley and Lois Dull (Bradley) Ocheltree; m. Robert John Ritchie, Oct. 9, 1993; children: Elsie Alexander, Caroline Wallace, Virginia Grace. BS in Early Childhood Edn., Longwood Coll., 1992. Learning disabled resource tchr. Thomas Dixon Elem., Staunton, Va., 1992—93, long-term substitute tchr. 6th grade, 1993—94; tchr. sci./health reading 6th grade Bessie Weller Elem., Staunton, 1994—95; tchr. K-4 Sea Island Presbyn. Ch., Beaufort, SC, 1999—2002; K4 tchr. Advent Day Sch., 2005—. Bn. key vol. coord. 3d Bn. / 11th Marines, 29 Palms, Calif., 1996—98; soccer coord. Advent Episcopal Day Sch., 2002—05. Recipient Molly Pitcher award, 3d Bn. / 11th Marines, 1998. Mem.: Officer's Wives Club (club officer 1997—98). Republican. Episcopalian. Avocations: running, being with children, gardening. Home: 3414 Stoneleigh Dr Birmingham AL 35223-2218 Office Phone: 205-252-2535. E-mail: britchie@advent.pvt.k12.al.us.

RITCHIE, DORIS LEE, executive secretary; b. Oak Park, Ill., May 18, 1926; d. Joseph Bulicek and Janette Louise Whitmire; m. H. R. Ritchie, Nov. 7, 1947 (dec.); children: H. Russell III, Jane Lee, Dara Kim. AA, Harper Coll., Palatine, Ill., 1972; BA, Elmhurst Coll., Ill., 1975; MS, Northern Ill. U., 1979; EdD, No. Ill. U., 1987. Exec. sec. Motorola, Chgo., 1943—45, Englander Bedding, Chgo., 1945—48, Pioneer Press, Oak Park, Ill., 1949—50, ABC, Chgo., 1948—49; tchr. Rolling Meadows Ill. Sch. Dist., 1979—81; vol. cons. Palatine, Ill., 1980—83. Spkr. in field. Sr. commr. City of Carlsbad, 1986—91, housing commr., 2000—06. Recipient Woman of Distinction, Soroptimist Club, 1990, DAR, 2000, Rookie of Yr., Hi Noon Rotary Club, 1989. Mem.: Hospice of North Coast, Belleek Collector's Soc., Country Friends (life), Widows and Widowers Club. Avocations: antiques, reading, bridge. Home: 3379 Garibaldi Pl Carlsbad CA 92010 Personal E-mail: dl-ritchie@sbcglobal.net.

RITCHIE, INGRID MARIA, environmental scientist, educator; b. Munich, May 26, 1949; arrived in US, 1952; d. Curtis Huey and Johanna Leokadia (Kroll) Ritchie. AS, Murray State Coll., 1969; BS summa cum laude, Southwestern State U., 1971; MS, U. Minn., 1973, PhD, 1980. Rsch. scientist Air Quality Minn. Pollution Control Agy., Mpls., 1974—76, Regional Copper-Nickel Study, Mpls., 1976—79; health risk assessment Minn. Dept. Health, Mpls., 1979—82; assoc. prof. Ind. U. Sch. Pub. and Environ. Affairs, Indpls., 1982—. Vice-chmn. Sci. and Tech. Resource Adv. Coun. to Minn. Joint Legis. Com. on Sci. and Tech.; mem. Indpls. Air Pollution Control Bd.; task force on kerosene heaters Underwriters Labs., Inc. Fellow, USPHS, 1980. Mem.: APHA, Nat. Environ. Health Assn., Nat. Air Pollution Control Assn. Office: Ind U BS-SPEA Room 4083 801 W Michigan St Indianapolis IN 46202-5199

RITCHIE, KELLIE WINGATE, lawyer; b. Lincoln, Nebr., June 21, 1962; d. John and Lynn Wingate; children: Matthew, Jennifer, Kaitlyn. BA in Psychology, Stephens Coll., Columbia, Md., 1984; JD, U. Mo., 1988. Bar: Mo. Rsch. atty. Mo. Adminstrv. Hearing Commn., Jefferson City, Mo., 1988—89; asst. pub. defender Buchanan County Pub. Defender, St. Joseph, Mo., 1989—90; asst. pros. atty. Buchanan County Prosecutor's Office, St. Joseph, 1990—96, Clinton County Prosecutor's Office, Plattsburg, Mo., 1999—2005; atty. Langdon & Emison, Lexington, Mo., 2005—06; pvt. practice, 2006—. Bd. mem. Prevent Child Abuse Mo., Jefferson City, 1995—97, St. Joseph Preservation Inc., 1990—92; pres., mem. Jr. League, St. Joseph, 1991—2006; fundraising Allied Arts Coun., St. Joseph, 1995—97; bd. mem. NW Mo. Children's Advocacy Ctr., St. Joseph, Mo., 2000—03; jud. candidate Fifth Jud. Circuit, St. Joseph, 1994; bd. mem. YWCA Women's Shelter, St. Joseph, Mo., 1995—97; pres. Ho. of Hope, Lexington, Mo., 2006. Recipient Outstanding Victim Advocacy award, CASA, 1993, Outstanding Woman Leader award, YWCA St. Joseph, 1994, Hist. Preservation award, St. Joseph Landmark Commn., 1996. Mem.: ATLA, Lafayette County Bar Assn. (pres. 2005—06), Mo. Assn. Trial Atty., Assn. Women Lawyers, Kans. City Met. Bar Assn. Home: 27 Ussery Dr Lexington MO 64067 Office: Kellie Wingate Ritchie Atty at Law 1021 Franklin Lexington MO 64067 Office Phone: 660-259-6110. Personal E-mail: kritchie@sbcglobal.net. Business E-Mail: mail@kelliewingateritchielaw.com.

RITMAN, BARBARA ELLEN, counselor; b. L.A., Oct. 19, 1946; d. Jack and June Harriett (Marcus) R. AA, Long Beach City Coll., 1969; BA (magna cum laude), Calif. State U., Long Beach, 1974; MA, Chapman Coll., 1976. Lic. marriage, family and child counselor. Instr. Mt. San Antonio Coll., Walnut, Calif., 1976-78; mental health worker Orange County (Calif.) Mental Health, 1978-80; therapist Family Svc., Long Beach, Calif., 1980-82; clin. dir. Neighborhood Youth Assn., Wilmington, Calif., 1981-88; head psychology svcs. Bellflower (Calif.) Med. Group, 1988-89; chem. dependency counselor Kaiser Permanent, Orange, Calif., 1990—. Cons. Child Abuse Info. Ctr., L.A., 1976-78, Action Seminars for Progress, Santa Monica, Calif., 1976-82. Vista vol., Salt Lake City, Houston, 1967—68. Fellow mem. Calif. Assn. Marriage & Family Therapists. Avocations: film, music, theater. Office: Kaiser Permanente Chem Dependency Recovery Program 4201 W Chapman Ave Orange CA 92868-1505

RITTENHOUSE, NANCY CAROL, elementary school educator; b. Humeston, Iowa, May 26, 1941; d. Myrl Matthews and Opal L. (McCartney) Hixson; m. J. Kent Rittenhouse, Dec. 18, 1960 (div. Mar. 1984); children: Brenda L. Carroll, J. Aaron, Timothy K. Grad., Kirksville State Tchrs. Coll., 1960; student, St. Mary of the Plains Coll., 1984-87; degree in elem. edn., Ft. Hays State Coll., 1989. Cert. tchr., Kans. Reading instr. Sacred Heart Sch., Dodge City, Kans., 1984; elem. tchr. Miller Sch., Dodge City, Kans., 1985-86, Washington Sch., Hays, 1987; city-county recreation dir. Sherman County, Goodland, 1988; elem. tchr. Northside Sch., Larned, 1989-90; with Great Bend (Kans.) Tribune. Artist numerous paintings; author poetry. Mem. Menninger Found., Topeka, 1984—; hon. mem. Boy Scouts Am., 1978; camp instr. Spl. Olympics Blind Found., Junction City, Kans., 1985-90, Dodge City, 1984; leader Girl Scouts USA, 1975-77. Recipient Hon. award Spl. Olympics, 1984, 1st pl. poetry award, 1990, watercolor award, 1990, oils award, 1988, pen and ink award, 1984. Mem. AAAS, Nat. Trust for Hist. Preservation, Nat. Geog. Soc., Planetary Soc., Smithsonian Assn., MIT. Republican. Avocations: painting, drawing, walking, swimming, writing prose. Home: PO Box 1872 Great Bend KS 67530-1872 Office: Great Bend Tribune 2012 Forest Ave Great Bend KS 67530-4014

RITTER, ANN L., lawyer; b. N.Y.C., May 20, 1933; d. Joseph and Grace (Goodman) R. BA, Hunter Coll., 1954; JD, N.Y. Law Sch., 1970; postgrad. Law Sch., NYU, 1971-72. Bar: N.Y. 1971, U.S. Ct. Appeals (2d cir.) 1975, U.S. Supreme Ct. 1975. Writer, 1954-70; editor, 1955-66; tchr., 1966-70; atty. Am. Soc. Composers, Authors and Pubs., N.Y.C., 1971-72, Greater N.Y. Ins. Co., N.Y.C., 1973-74; sr. ptnr. Brenhouse & Ritter, N.Y.C., 1974-78; sole practice N.Y.C., 1978—. Editor N.Y. Immigration News, 1975-76. Mem. ABA, Am. Immigration Lawyers Assn. (treas. 1983-84, sec. 1984-85, vice-chair 1985-86, chair 1986-87, chair program com. 1989-90, chair spkrs. bur. 1989-90, chair media liaison 1989-90), N.Y. State Bar Assn., N.Y. County Lawyers Assn., Assn. Trial Lawyers Am., N.Y. State Trial Lawyers Assn., N.Y.C. Bar Assn., Watergate East Assn. (v.p., asst. treas. 1990—). Democrat. Jewish. Home: 47 E 87th St New York NY 10128-1005 Office: 420 Madison Ave Rm 1200 New York NY 10017-1171 Personal E-mail: annlritter@aol.com.

RITTER, HEATHER DAWN, language educator; b. Bedford, Ind., Sept. 18, 1980; d. Gary Dean and Anita Catherine Ritter. BS in Elem. Edn., Ind. U., Indpls., 2004. Tchr. English as 2d lang. Stout Field Elem. Sch., Indpls., 2004—. Avocations: reading, gardening.

RITTER, JODI GOTTESFELD, lawyer; b. Bklyn., May 1966; BA cum laude, SUNY, Albany, 1988; JD, NY Law Sch., 1992. Bar: NY 1993, Conn. 1993, US Dist. Ct. So. Dist. NY, US Dist. Ct. Ea. Dist. NY, US Supreme Ct. Asst. dist. atty. Kings County Dist. Atty.'s Office, NY, Spl. Narcotics Prosecutor's Office; ptnr. Wilson, Elser, Moskowitz, Edelman & Dicker LLP, NYC. Mem.: NY State Bar Assn. Office: Wilson Elser Moskowitz Edelman & Dicker LLP 23rd Fl 150 E 42nd St New York NY 10017-5639 Office Phone: 212-490-3000 ext. 2245. Office Fax: 212-490-3038. Business E-Mail: ritterj@wemed.com.

RITTER, LAURA LINGERFELT, music educator; b. Morristown, Tenn., June 6, 1968; d. Harold Kenneth and Peggy Kenley Lingerfelt; m. Greg Edward Ritter, Jan. 8, 1994; 1 child, Cameron Kenley. MusB, Furman U., Greenville, SC, 1990; MusM, U. Ill., Urbana-Champaign, 1991. Assoc. prof. music Walters State C.C., Morristown, Tenn., 1994—; dir. music Buffalo Trail Bapt. Ch., Morristown, 1996—99. Named Disting. Alumni, All Saints Episcopal Sch., 2006. Mem.: PEO (pres. 1997—2006), Am. Choral Dirs. Assn. (repertoire and stds. chmn. 2001—04), Gen. Federated Women's Club (treas. 1995—2006). Christian. Avocation: singing. Office: Walters State CC 500 South Davy Crockett Parkway Morristown TN 37814 Office Phone: 423-585-6969. Personal E-mail: glritter@charter.net. Business E-Mail: laura.ritter@ws.edu.

RITTER, NADINE M., research scientist; AS, San Jacinto Coll., Pasadena, Tex., 1976—78; BS, U. Houston, Clear Lake, Tex., 1980—84; MS, PhD, Rice U., Houston, 1984—88. Principle cons. NMRBiotech Cons. Svcs., Germantown, Md., 2001—; sr. cmc cons. Biologics Cons. Group, Alexandria, Va., 2005—. Home: 13613 Anndyke Pl Germantown MD 20874 Office: Biologics Cons Group 13613 Anndyke Pl Germantown MD 20874 Office Phone: 240-372-4898. Personal E-mail: nmrbiotech@ritterward.com. E-mail: nritter@bcg-usa.com.

RITTER, RENÉE, artist, educator; b. Bronx, N.Y. d. Marvin and Helen Gaylinn; m. Seymour David Ritter; children: Edward, Steven, Jennifer. BA, Queens Coll.; MFA, L.I. U. Adj. prof. art CW Post Coll., L.I. U., Greenvale, N.Y., 1982—. Juror scholastic art and writing awards Alliance for Young Artists and Writers, Inc., 1999—2000; adj. prof. art history Nassau C.C., 2000—. One-woman shows include Elaine Benson Gallery, Bridgehampton, N.Y., 1988, 91, 97, Islip (N.Y.) Mus., 1992, 2004, Viridian Gallery, N.Y.C., 1981, 82, 84, 86, 91, 92, Nassau County Mus. of Art, Roslyn, N.Y., 1988, Smithtown Arts Coun., Mills Pond House, Smithtown, N.Y., 1988, Danville Mus. of Art, 1987, others.; group exhibits include Guild Hall, East Hampton, N.Y., 1998, Heckscher Mus., Huntington, N.Y., 1990, 92, 94, 96, Silvermine Guild, New Canaan, Conn., 1992, 94, Bergen County Mus. of Art, Paramus, N.J., 1983, 91, Ft. Hays Kansas State U., 1991, Lubbock Fine Arts Ctr., Tex., 1992, Reece Gallery, N.Y.C., 1995, Francine Ellman Gallery, L.A., 1991, NAWA Traveling Centenary Exhibit, 1987, Parrish Art Mus., Southampton, 1984, Muscarelle Mus., Va., 1994, 96, Smithtown Twp. Arts Coun.-Mills Pond House, St. James, N.Y., 1994, Md. Fedn. Art, 1994, 95, 96, Valdosta (Ga.) State U., 1996, Eleftherias Park Art Ctr., Athens, Greece, 1996, others; represented in permanent collections Muscarelle Mus. of Art-Coll. of William and Mary, Williamsburg, Va., Jane Voorhis Zimmerli Mus. Art-Rutgers U., New Brunswick, N.J., Hillwood Mus.-L.I. U., Greenvale, Islip Mus. Art, FAMLI Mus., Hempstead, N.Y., Danville (Va.) Mus. Arts Docent Nassau County Mus. Art, Roslyn, N.Y., 1979-92. Recipient awards Nassau County Mus. Art, Roslyn, 1986, Islip (N.Y.) Mus. Art, 1987, Heckscher Mus. Art, Huntington, N.Y., 1996, Muscarelel Mus. Art, Williamsburg, 1996. Mem. Nat. Assn. Women Artists, Nat. Drawing Assn. (exec. bd. 1991-98). E-mail: renee@vitter.net.

RITTERHOUSE, KATHY LEE, librarian; b. Hutchinson, Kans., May 24, 1952; d. Fayne Lee and Elizabeth Rose (Tener) R.; m. Michael Raymond Demmitt, July 8, 1972 (div. Apr. 1990). BA in English, Kans. State U., 1974; MLS, U. Okla., 1979. Circulation libr. Grand Prairie (Tex.) Meml. Libr., 1979-80, libr. dir., 1980—. Bd. dirs. Grand Prairie Arts Coun., 1980-2000, pres., 1989. Recipient Women in History award, 1999; named Pub. Svc. Employee of Yr. Grand Prairie C. of C., 1989. Mem.: ALA (intellectual freedom com. 1998—2001), Tex. Libr. Assn. (Tex./SIRS Intellectual Freedom award 1993), Metro Rotary Club (bd. dirs. 1992—99, pres. 2003—04, dist. new generations chair 2001—04), Beta Phi MU. Office: Grand Prairie Meml Libr 901 Conover Dr Grand Prairie TX 75051-1521 E-mail: kritterh@gptx.org.

RITTI, ALYCE RAE, artist; b. Moline, Ill., Jan. 18, 1934; d. Raymond Russell and Alice Linnea Matilda (Arvidson) Keagle; m. Raymond Richard Ritti, Jan. 26, 1957; children: Lesley, Jocelyn, Matthew, Susanna. BA with departmental honors, Grinnell Coll., 1956; MS, Purdue U., 1957; PhD, Columbia U., 1973; postrad., Pa. State U., 1985-90. Advanced cert. Am. Speech, Lang., and Hearing Assn. Speech therapist Rockford (Ill.) Coll. Summer Speech Ctr., summer 1956; instr. speech Cornell U., Ithaca, N.Y., 1957-59; exec. sec. Art Alliance of Cen. Pa., Lemont, 1978-80; test manual coord. NEA, Washington, 1980-82; rsch. assoc. E.P. Sys. Group, State College, Pa., 1980-82; visual artist Pt. Matilda, Pa., 1984—. Com. mem., ad hoc projects Cen. Pa. Festival of Arts, State College, 1988—, artist in action, 1989-91, 93-94, instr. accessible arts collages, 1994-95; artist World's Women Online, 1995-2002; instr. art Cmty. Acad. Lifelong Learning Ctr., State College, 1997-2002, writer Active Life, 1998-2001; artist-in-residence Pa. Coun. on Arts, 2001—04; panelist Art Alliance SCORE Workshops, 1999, 2001; judge Gen. Fedn. Women's Clubs Pa. Arts Festival, 2001, judge Clare Dahlia Snetsinger art award 2006. Artist numerous solo shows including Studio Z Gallery, Pitts., 2002, The Stage Gallery, Merrick, NY, 2002, Woskob Gallery, Pa. State Downtown Theatre, Ctr., State Coll., Pa., 2003, Paul Robeson Cultural Ctr. Univ. Pk., Pa., 2005; exhibited in internat., nat. and regional shows and galleries, 1990—, including So. Alleghenies Mus. Art Triennial VI, Salon d'Automne, Paris, 2002, 03, Assoc. Artists Pitts. Warhol Mus., 2002, Triennial VII (Mus. Purchase award), Biennials I and II, Art of the State, State Mus. Pa., Harrisburg, 2003, Great Plains Nat., Hays, Kans., 2004, Alliance Women Artists, City Hall, Oslo, Norway, 2004, Alliance of Women Artists, Galleria Tondinelli, Rome, 2005, Art of the State, State Mus. Pa., Harrisburg, 2005, Hopper Ho. Gallery, Nyack, 2005, Winter Salon, Spruce Creek, Pa., 2006, Gallery at Gamble Mill Bellefonte, Pa., 2006, Art Alliance Open Juried Show, Lemont, Pa., 2006, show Altoona, Pa., 2006; contbr. articles to numerous publs. Bd. dirs., officer sch. dist. PTAs, PTOs, couns., Stamford, Conn., 1963-70, State College, 1971-87. Office of Edn. fellow Columbia U. Tchrs. Coll., 1969, 70; Unified Art Event grantee (2) Cen. Pa. Arts Coun., 1984, 86. Mem. Nat. Mus. Women in the Arts, Art Alliance of Ctrl. Pa. (life, bd. dirs. 1981-86, v.p. 1982), Alliance of Women Artists, Associated Artists Pitts., Art in Common, Phi Beta Kappa. Avocations: bicycling, theater, walking, reading, romping with dog. Home: 170 Cherrywood Way Port Matilda PA 16870-8904 Personal E-mail: rrr@psu.edu.

RITTINGER, PATRICIA ANN, secondary school educator, mathematician; b. Rockaway Beach, N.Y., Dec. 13, 1944; d. Philip J. and Margaret Mary Foran; m. John Patrick Rittinger, July 13, 1966; children: Barbara Rittinger Rigo, Michael Patrick. BS, St. Bonaventure U., Alleghany, N.Y., 1966; MA, U. Notre Dame, Notre Dame, Ind., 1968. Cert. tchr. math grades 7 - 12 Bd. Regents, N.Y., 1970. Tchr. math. South Bend (Ind.) Ctrl. Schs., 1966—69, Herricks Pub. Schs., New Hyde Park, NY, 1970; substitute tchr. Vestal (N.Y.) Ctrl. Schs., 1972—77; tchr. math. Union-Endicott (N.Y.) Ctrl. Schs., 1977—. Advisor mathletes Union Endicott (N.Y.) H.S., 1985—; pres. Broome County Mathletes, NY, 1990—. Mem. parish coun. St. Vincent's Ch., Vestal, 1990—94. Named Mathletes Coach 2006, N.Y. State Math League, 2006. Mem.: Assn. Math. Tchrs. N.Y., So. Tier Math. Tchrs. Assn., Delta Kappa Gamma (treas. 1994—96). Reform. Roman Catholic. Avocations: bridge, reading, sudokus. Home: 601 Queensbury Court Vestal NY 13850 Office: Union-Endicott High School 1200 East Main Street Endicott NY 13760 Office Phone: 607-757-2181. Personal E-mail: prittinger@cs.com. Business E-Mail: prittinger@uegw.stier.org.

RITVO, EVA CAROLINE, psychiatrist, educator; b. KA, Nov. 22, 1961; d. Edward Ross Ritvo and Jean Anita Krag; m. Mark Steven Nestor, Jan. 10, 1988; children: Marissa Joy Nestor, Jillian Nestor. BS, Harvard U, 1983; MD, UCLA, 1987. Diplomate Am. Bd. Psychiatry and Neurology. Asst. prof. U. Miami, Miller Sch. Medicine, Miami Beach, Fla., 1991—99, assoc. prof. psychiatry, 1999—; chmn. dept. psychiatry Mt. Sinai Med. Ctr., Miami Beach, 2000—. Co-editor: book Concise Guide to Marital and Family Therapy. Bd. dirs. United Cerebral Palsy, Miami, Fla., 2005—06. Mem.: Am. Psychiat. Assn., Am. Coll. Psychiatrists. Avocations: tennis, golf. Office: Miller Sch Medicine 4300 Alton Road Miami Beach FL 33134 Office Phone: 305-674-2194. Home Fax: 305-535-7321; Office Fax: 305-532-5241. Personal E-mail: ritvomd@earthlink.net.

RITVO, HARRIET, historian; b. Cambridge, Mass., Sept. 19, 1946; d. Martin and Zelma R. AB, Harvard U., 1968, PhD, 1975; attended, U. Cambridge, Eng., 1968-69. Staff assoc. AAAS, Boston, 1976-79; from asst. to full prof. MIT, Cambridge, 1979—, assoc. dean humanities & social scis., 1992-95, Arthur J. Conner prof. of history, 1995—, head history faculty, 1999—2006. Author: The Animal Estate, 1987, The Platypus and the Mermaid, 1997; co-editor: Macropolitics of 19th Century Literature, 1991. Rsch. fellow Stanford Humanities Ctr., 1985-86, fellow NEH, 1989, Guggenheim fellow, 1990, sr. fellow Nat. Humanities Ctr., 1990, 2002-03; recipient Whiting Writer's award Whiting Found., 1990. Fellow: Am. Acad. Arts and Scis. Office: MIT E51-285 Cambridge MA 02139 Office Phone: 617-253-6960. Business E-Mail: ritvo@mit.edu.

RIVAUX, LOIS ELAINE, music educator; b. Galveston, Tex., Aug. 4, 1947; d. Jake Richard and Lois Catherine Dodson; children: Tania R., Rich, Benjamin R., Jorge Ariel Nevarez-Rivaux. BS in Elem. Edn., Southwestern Adventist U., Keene, Tex., 2003. Cert. tchr. Tex. Exec. dir. YMCA, Galveston, 1988—94; paraprofl. Groesbeck (Tex.) Ind. Sch. Dist., 1995—2002; tchr. elem. music Galveston Ind. Sch. Dist., Galveston, 2002—. Children's min. First United Meth. Ch., Groesbeck, Tex., 1999—2002. Named Citizen of Yr., Groesbeck C. of C., 2000; recipient Disting. Honor award, 1988. Democrat. Lutheran. Home: 6922 Youpon Galveston TX 77551 Office: L A Morgan Elem 1410 37th Galveston TX 77550 Office Phone: 409-763-1333. Personal E-mail: ler4@hotmail.com.

RIVELLI, SUSAN VERONICA, nurse; b. Des Moines, Aug. 28, 1954; d. Thomas James Dobberthein and Naomi M. (Edwards) Dutch; 1 child, Carly Vanessa; m. Prospero Rivelli, Jr., Aug. 20, 1989. Diploma in practical nursing, Des Moines Area CC, 1976; ASN, St. Petersburg Jr. Coll., 1983, AA, 2001. RN, Fla.; cert. risk mgr., Fla., quality assurance profl.; cert. hospice and palliative nurse. Dir. quality assurance and med. records Horizon Hosp., Clearwater, Fla., 1980-89; DON Palm Gardens of Clearwater, 1989-90; quality assurance/risk mgr. liaison, cons. The Manors, Tarpon Springs, Fla., 1990-94; instr. Ultimate Learning Ctr., Clearwater, Fla., 1994—; shift adminstr. The Manors, Tarpon Springs, Fla., 1994-97; staff nurse Hospice of Fla. Suncoast, Largo, Fla., 1997—2001; sr. staff nurse Hospice of the Fla. Suncast, Largo, 2002—03; admissions nurse Hospice of the Fla. Suncoast, Largo, 2003—04, admissions clin. coord., 2005—. Cons. in field. Pres. Knollwood Civic Assn., Largo, Fla., 1985, editor, pub. newsletter, 1984. Scholar Tampa Bay Orgn. Nurse Exec., 2001. Mem. Am. Health Info. Mgmt. Assn., Nat. Assn. of Quality Assurance Profls., Bay Area Healthcare Risk Mgrs, Nat. Hospice/Pallrative Care Orgn., West Coast Fla. Hospice and Palliative Nurse Assn. (sec.), Phi Theta Kappa. Roman Catholic. Avocations: writing, reading, alpine skiing. Home: 3149 Harvest Moon Dr Palm Harbor FL 34683-2124

RIVERA, BAVI EDNA (NEDI RIVERA), bishop; b. 1946; d. Bishop Victor Manuel Rivera; m. Rev. Bob Moore, 1979. AB in Physics, Wheaton Coll., Norton, Mass., 1968; MDiv, Ch. Div. Sch. of the Pacific, Berkeley, Calif., 1976; cert. in Parish Revitalization, Vancouver Sch. Theology. Ordained priest, 1979; served at churches in Diocese of Calif., Diocese of El Camino Real; rector St. George's Episcopal Ch., Salinas, Calif., 1984—93, St. Aidan's Episcopal Ch., San Francisco, 1994—2005; ordained & consecrated bishop suffragen Diocese of Olympia, 2005—. Achievements include Ordained as first Hispanic woman bishop, Meydenbauer Ctr., Bellevue, Wash., Jan. 22, 2005. Office: Diocese of Olympia PO Box 12126 1551 10th Ave E Seattle WA 98102 Office Phone: 206-325-4200 ext. 312. Business E-Mail: nrivera@ecww.org.

RIVERA, CAROLINE CLARK, biologist, educator; b. Milw., Apr. 3, 1972; d. Marshall Charles and Delores Brennan Clark; m. Mark Daniel Rivera, June 7, 1998; 1 child, Kiernan Clark. BA, Fla. Atlantic U., Boca Raton, Fla., 1997; MA in Anthropology, N.Mex. State U., Las Cruces, 1999; postgrad., Old Dominion U., Norfolk, Va., 2001—. Asst. prof. biology Tidewater C.C.,

Norfolk, 2002—. Mem.: Va. C.C. Soc., Am. Assn. Phys. Anthropologists, Human Anatomy and Physiology Soc., Phi Kappa Phi. Avocation: yoga. Office: Tidewater Community College 300 Granby St Norfolk VA 23510

RIVERA, CHITA (CONCHITA DEL RIVERO), actress, singer, dancer; b. Wash., Jan. 23, 1933; d. Pedro Julio Figuerva del Rivero; m. Anthony Mordente. Student, Am. Sch. Ballet, N.Y.C. Broadway debut: Call Me Madam, 1952; appeared on stage in: Guys and Dolls, Can-Can, Seventh Heaven, Mister Wonderful, West Side Story, Father's Day, Bye Bye Birdie, Three Penny Opera, Flower Drum Song, Zorba, Sweet Charity, Born Yesterday, Jacques Brel is Alive and Well and Living in Paris, Sondheim-A Musical Tribute, Kiss Me Kate, Ivanhoe, Chicago, Bring Back Birdie, Merlin, Jerry's Girls, 1985, The Rink, 1984 (Tony award 1984), Can-Can, 1988, Kiss of the Spider Woman (Tony award, Best Actress in a musical), 1993, The Dancer's Life, 2005; performs in cabarets and nightclubs around world; starred in: film Sweet Charity, 1969; numerous TV appearances include Kojak and the Marcus Nelson Murders, 1973, The New Dick Van Dyke Show, 1973-74, Kennedy Ctr. Tonight-Broadway to Washington!, Pippin, 1982, The Mayflower Madam, 1987, Sammy Davis Jr.'s 60th Birthday Celebration, 1990, Ira Gershwin at 100: A Celebration at Carnegie Hall, 1997, Venecia, 2001, Anything Goes, 2000, The Visit, 2001. Recipient Best Actress, Outer Critics Circle award, 1993, Drama League award, Spider Woman, 1993, Best Leading Actress in a Musical, Tony award, Ellis Island Medal of Honor, 2000, Kennedy Center Honor, 2002—02, Rolex Dance award, Career Transition for Dancers, 2006. Mem. AFTRA, SAG, Actors Equity Assn. Office: William Morris Agy c/o Samuel Liff 1325 Ave of the Ams New York NY 10019*

RIVERA, GEORGINA PEREIRA, mathematician, educator; b. Hartford, Conn., Dec. 7, 1973; d. Fernando Duarte and Idalina C. Pereira; m. Arnaldo Rivera, July 19, 2003. M in Math Edn., Ctrl. Conn. State U., New Britain, 2004. Cert. tchr. Conn., 1997. Math coord. Chippens Hill Mid. Sch., Bristol, Conn., 2004—. Vol. Crossroads Cmty. Cathedral, East Hartford, Conn., 2000. Mem.: NCTM.

RIVERA, JENNY, law educator; b. NYC, Dec. 8, 1960; d. Manuel and Belia (Thomas) R. AB, Princeton U., 1982; JD, NYU, 1985; LLM, Columbia U., 1993. Bar: NY, U.S. Dist. Ct. (so. and ea. dists.) NY, US Ct. Appeals (3rd cir.), US Supreme Ct. Pro se law clk. 2nd Cir. Ct. Appeals, NYC, 1985-87; staff atty. Legal Aid Soc., NYC, 1987-88; assoc. counsel Puerto Rican Legal Def. and Edn. Fund, NYC, 1988-92; law clk. to Hon. Sotomayor U.S. Dist. Ct. (so. dist.) NY, NYC, 1993-94; asst. prof. Law Sch. Suffolk U., Boston, 1994-97; assoc. prof. Law Sch. CUNY, 1997—2002, prof., 2002—. Contbr. articles to profl. jours. Participant Spanish Domestic Violence Hotline Adv. Com., Middletown, NY, 1995-97; co-chairperson Latina Rights Initiative Adv. Com., NYC, 1995-2000; bd. dirs. Latina Roundtable on Health, NYC, 1995-98; mem. NYC Commn. on Human Rights. Honoree for women's rights work Pres. of Manhattan Borough, NYC, 1992; recipient Felipe Torres award Puerto Rican Bar Assn., 1995-96, Flor de Maga award, 2005; named one of Hispanic Bus. Elite Women, 2005. Mem.: NYC Commn. on Human Rights. Avocations: travel, movies, running, hiking, swimming. Office: 6521 Main St Flushing NY 11367-1358

RIVERA, JOSIE, elementary school educator; b. Victoria, Tex., Apr. 29, 1947; d. Jose Jr. and Emilia (Ramirez) Lopez; m. Mike Rivera, Jan. 10, 1964; children: Diana Lynn, Mike Jr., Michele Yvonne. AA, Victoria Coll., 1983; BS in Edn., U. Houston, 1984, MEd, 1985, 1995, EdD, 1997. Tchr., aide Bloomington Ind. Sch. Dist., Tex.; vis. prin. Bloomington ISD Supt.; tchr. Victoria Ind. Sch. Dist., asst. prin.; adj. prof. Victoria Coll.; spl. projects U. Houston-Victoria. Mem. spl. projects com. U. Houston-Victoria, 2004—, pres.'s adv. cun. Mem. Vision Victoria, U. Houston PAC; pres., bd. dirs. Affectionate Arms; v.p. bd. dirs. Hope Chest; v.p. Latina Forum; bd. dirs. DeTar Healthcare Sys.; co-chair FOU Fundraising foe U. Houston-Victoria. Named one of South Tex. Women, 2000. Mem. Tex. Elem. Prins. and Suprs. Assn. (Nat. Disting. Prin. 1999), Tex. Assn. Biligual Educators, Alpha Delta Kappa, Phi Delta Kappa. Home: PO Box 129 Placedo TX 77977-0129 Office Phone: 361-570-4187. E-mail: Jo1947@hotmail.com.

RIVERA, MAIRA, elementary school educator; b. Bronx, Nov. 6, 1969; d. William and Edith Soto; m. Ismael Rivera, July 23, 1988; children: Jose Enrique, Christina Marie, Daniel Luis. BA, Herbert H. Lehman Coll., Bronx, 2000, MS in Edn., 2003. Ednl. asst. Bd. Edn., NYC, 1993—2000, tchr. spl. edn., 2000—04; early intervention ind. contractor G & Y Kids Power, Yonkers, 2003; tchr. Orange County Pub. Schs., Orlando, Fla., 2004—. Named Michael McCoy'sTchr. Yr., Orange County Pub. Schs., 2006; recipient Lehman Urban Tchr. Edn. award, 2006. Mem.: Kappa Delta Pi (Kappa Delta Pi 2003). Home: 12504 Hyanis Ct Orlando FL 32828

RIVERA, MIRIAM, information technology executive, lawyer; AB, Stanford U., AM in Spanish, JD, MBA, Stanford U. Assoc. bus. and tech. Brobeck, Phleger & Harrison; strategy cons. Andersen Consulting (now Accenture); co-founder On Your Mind; in-house counsel Ariba Inc., Sunnyvale, Calif.; v.p., dep. gen. counsel Google Inc., Mountain View, Calif. Bd. sec. Google Found. Vol. A Better Chance, La Casa de las Madres, First Congregational Ch. of Palo Alto. Office: Google Inc 1600 Amphitheatre Pky Mountain View CA 94043 Office Phone: 650-253-0000. Office Fax: 650-253-0001.*

RIVERA, YELISSA MARIE, science educator, coach; d. Ramon Rivera and Yolanda Rodriguez; 1 child, Evandro Emmanuel Melton Rivera. BS in Gen. Sci., U. PR, Rio Piedras, 2000; MA in Math. Edn., Interamerican U. PR, Metro Campus, 2002. Cert. tchr. Fla., 2005. Tchr. St. John's Sch., Santurce, PR, 2000—02, Roosevelt Roads Mid./H.S., Ceiba, PR, 2002—04, St. Elizabeth Seton Elem. Sch., Naples, Fla., 2004—05, Golden Gate H.S., Naples, 2005—. Office Phone: 239-377-1600.

RIVERA-MARTINEZ, SOCORRO, retired elementary school educator, assistant principal; b. Mayagüez, P.R., Apr. 19, 1942; d. Sotero R. and Rafaela Martinez; m. Carmelo Torres, Dec. 26, 1965; 1 child, Yolivette. AEd, Catholic U., 1963, BA in Elem. Edn., 1980. Cert. tchr., mentor tchr. Tchr. 1-6 grades P.R. Dept. Edn., Mayagüez, 1962-93; auxilliary administr. Colegio San Agustin, Cabo Rojo, P.R., 1993-94, asst. principal, 1994-98. Tchr. in charge Rio Hondo Sch. Mayagüez, 1964-70, 73-93, gifted children club, 1990-91, dir.'s resource for tng., 1985-93; math and sci. counselor Rio Hondo, Sch., Castillo Sch., 1971-93. Co-leader troop 384 Girl Scouts Am., Rio Hondo Sch., Mayagüez, P.R., 1975-79; vol. leader Catholic Ch. Summer camp, Cabo Rojo, P.R., 1990-92. Recipient Presidential award Excellence in Sci. and Math. Tchg. The White House, 1993, State award Excellence in Math. Nat. Coun. Math. Tchrs., 1993, Excellence in Math. award Dept. Edn., 1993; named Tchr. of the Year Dept. Edn., 1975, 82. Mem. Educadores Puertorriqueños en Acción, Coun. Elem. Sci. Internat., Coun. Presidential Awardees. Roman Catholic. Avocations: reading, poetry, writing, wire craft, gardening. Home: L22 Calle 3 Borinquen Cabo Rojo PR 00623-3324 Office: Colegio San Agustin Cabo Rojo PR 00623

RIVERA MATOS, CARMEN LOURDES, lawyer; b. San Juan, PR, June 17, 1952; d. Luciano Rivera and Margarita Santiago; m. Jorge Omar Matos, July 1, 1977; children: Emily, Paula, Sarah. BA, Douglas Coll., New Brunswick, NJ, 1974; MA, Rutgers U., New Brunswick, 1977; JD, Temple U., Phila., 1980. Bar: Pa. 1980. Atty. advisor Dept. Housing and Urban Devel., Phila., 1980—81; trial atty. U.S. EEOC, Phila., 1981—86, supervisory trial atty., 1986—95, assoc. regional counsel, 1991—95; assoc. Stewart, Wood & Branca, Norristown, Pa., 1995—2001; pvt. practice Law Offices of C. Matos, Doylestown, Pa., 0012—2006; ptnr. Stewart, Wood & Matos, Norristown, Pa., 2006—. Bd. trustees Richard Stockton Coll., 1999—2005. Mem.: ABA, Montgomery County Bar Assn., Nat. Employment Lawyer's Assn., Hispanic Bar Assn. Office: Stewart Wood & Matos 411 Cherry St Norristown PA 19401 Office Phone: 610-277-2520. Personal E-mail: crm617@aol.com.

RIVERA-SINCLAIR, ELSA, psychologist, consultant, researcher; b. Lima, Peru, Dec. 2, 1927; came to U.S. 1954; d. Jorge Maximo Rivera Bodero and Hortencia Resurreccion Vega Alvarado; m. Walter Ward Sinclair, Oct. 30, 1957; children: Harold Anthony, Thomas Edgar (dec.), Ian Paul. AA in Gen. Edn., Montgomery Coll., Takoma Park, Md., 1976; BA in Psychology, U. Md., College Park, 1979; MA in Clin. Psychoolgy, U. Md., Baltimore County, 1982; PhD in Counseling Psychology, U. Md., College Park, 1988. Diplomate in clin. psychology Am. Bd. Psychol. Spltys., 1998. Psychology intern Spring Grove Hosp., Catonsville, Md., 1980-81, Veterans Administrn. Med. Ctr., Washington, 1985-86; clin. psychologist PHS evaluation facility/inpatient care St. Elizabeths Hosp. Immigration/Naturalization, Washington, 1989; clin. psychologist acute care St. Elizabeths Hosp., Washington, 1989; clin. psychologist DC Dept. Mental Health, Washington, 1996—2003. Bd. mem. Mayor of D.C. Multicultural Task Force, 1992-94, CMHS, Dept. Human Svcs. Recipient Vol. award Andromeda Transcultural Hispano Mental Health Ctr., 1998; APA fellowship, Am. Psychological Assn. Mem. APA (fellowship 1982), DC Psychol. Assn., Md. Psychol. Assn., Phi Kappa Phi. Avocations: travel, painting, reading, poetry, classic music. Home: 116 Fleetwood Ter Silver Spring MD 20910 E-mail: universe@erols.com.

RIVERA-VELAZQUEZ, MARIA, marketing professional; BA in Econs. cum laude, U. P.R., San Juan, 1993; MA in Econs., U. Wis., Milw., 1995. Statistician Blue Shield P.R., San Juan, 1996—97; rsch. analyst Info. Resources, Inc., Chgo., 1998—2001; sr. rsch. analyst Northwestern Mut., Milw., 2001—04, mgr. corp. and market rsch., 2004—. Spkr. Wis. SAS Users Group Conf., Milw., 2003. Vol. Vecinos Unidos Pro Macun, Toa Baja, PR, 1996—97; vol. United Way campaign Northwestern Mut. Friends, Milw., 2001—; pres. Young Dems. Macun, Toa Baja, PR, 1990—94. Scholar, NEA-P.R. chpt., 1994—95. Mem.: Am. Mktg. Assn. Office: Northwestern Mutual 720 E Wisconsin Ave Milwaukee WI 53202

RIVERO, ANDRIA, education educator; b. Alacranes, Matanzas, Cuba, Feb. 04; came to the U.S., 1956; d. Javier and Juana Maria Rivero; m. Hermann E. Diehl (div. Dec. 1983); children: Hermann J., Karina J. BS, Fla. Internat. U., 1974; MS, Nova U., 1981. Elem. tchr. St. Patrick Cath. Sch., Miami Beach, Fla., 1979-81; instr., dean instrn. Ft. Lauderdale Coll., Miami, Fla., 1981-84; prof., disability svcs. advisor St. Thomas U., Miami, 1984-99. Edn. specialist Accrediting Commn. for Colls. and Tech. Career Schs., 1993—; adv. bd. Tech. Career Inst., Miami, 1997-2000; adj. prof. MDC, 2000—, Fla. Internat. U., 2000—; lic. cmty. assn. mgr., Dore County, Fla., 2000. Mem. safety com. City of Miami Beach, 1995-97. Roman Catholic. E-mail: arivero@bellsouth.net.

RIVERO, MARILYN ELAINE KEITH, state legislator; b. Burlington, Vt., Aug. 22, 1942; d. Kenneth Charles and Irene (Haskell) Keith; m. Victor Paul Rivero, Sr., 1966; children: Lina, Mita, Victor Jr., Amy, Nicholas. BS, U. Vt., 1964, MS, 1988; postgrad., Middlebury Coll., 1973, St. Michaels Coll., 1986. Vol. Peace Corps., 1964-66; mem. Vt. Ho. of Reps., 1991—; mem. health and welfare com., 1991—. Recipient Beyond War award. Mem. ANA, Vt. Nurses Assn., Returned Peace Corps. Vol., Am. Assn. Retired People. Roman Catholic. Home: PO Box 37 Milton VT 05468-0037 E-mail: m149rivero@aol.com.

RIVERS, ALMA FAYE, secondary school educator; b. Marion, N.C., Oct. 13, 1949; d. Arthur Henry and Lena (Deyton) Letterman; m. Charles Edwin Rivers, June 29, 1980. BA, Mars Hill Coll., 1971; MEd, W. Ga. Coll., 1978. Tchr., choral dir. W. Fannin H.S., Blue Ridge, Ga., 1971-76, W. Fannin Jr. H.S., Blue Ridge, 1976-80; tchr. Truett-McConnell Coll., Young Harris, Ga., 1975-76, 78-80, Sprayberry H.S., Marietta, Ga., 1980—. Student tchr. supr. State of Ga., 1988—, tchr. mentoring program, 1990—; tchr., cons. Kennesaw (Ga.) State U., 1995—; presenter workshops, confs., and confs. on 19th century women's lit. and multiculture lit. Mem. Standing Peachtree NA, Atlanta, 1994—; vol. PGA Tournament. NEH fellow, 1995. Mem. Nat. Coun. Tchrs. English, Ga. Coun. Tchrs. English, Thomas Wolfe Soc., Cooking Club of Am., Alpha Delta Kappa. Methodist. Avocations: golf, piano, literature, travel, book collecting. Office: Sprayberry High Sch 2525 Sandy Plains Rd Marietta GA 30066-5799

RIVERS, BEVERLY D., former district secretary; b. 1965; JD U. Ala. Sch. Law; BS in bus. mgmt., Oakwood Coll., Huntsville, Ala. Sec. D.C.; spl. asst. CFO; chief legis. asst. State Senator Henry L. Marsh, Richmond, Va.; atty. Hill Tucker Firm, Marsh Firm; acting sec. of dist. D.C. Govt., 1999, sec. of dist., 1999—2003. Mem.: Nat. Forum Black Pub. Adminstr., Wash. Bar Assn., Ala. Bar Assn., D.C. Bar Assn.

RIVERS, LYNN N., former congresswoman; b. Augres, Mich., Dec. 19, 1956; 2 children. BA, U. Mich., 1987; JD, Wayne State U., 1992. Mem. sch. bd. City of Ann Arbor, Mich., 1984-92; mem. Mich. House of Reps., 1992-94, U.S. Congress from 13th Mich. dist., 1994—2002; mem. edn. and workforce com., sci. com., 1994. Mem.: Nat. Adv. Bd., Univ. Mich. Depression Center, 2003-. Democrat.

RIVERS, SHERRY DIANE, educational administrator, consultant; b. Conway, Ark., Nov. 22, 1948; d. Edward Lee and Lorene Ann (Fleming) Shock; m. Pat Lee Mansfield, Feb. 6, 1970 (div. Sept. 1979); children: Jonathan Scott, Amy Christen; m. Douglas B. Rivers, Dec. 17, 1983. BSE, U. Cen. Ark., 1971, MSE, 1972; EdD, U. Ark., 1986. Classroom tchr. Ark. Schs., Hot Springs, Ark., 1971-78; edn. examiner Hot Springs Schs., 1979-80; instr. U. Cen. Ark., Conway, Ark., 1980-81; dir. spl. edn. Faulkner County Day Sch., Conway, 1979-83, Springdale (Ark.) Pub. Schs., 1983-84; asst. prof. Western Ill. U., Macomb, Ill., 1984-85; dir. spl. edn. Bi-Co. Spl. Edn. Coop., Morrison, Ill., 1984-86; dir. spl. edn., asst. curriculum dir. Clinton (Iowa) Community Schs., 1986-87; coord. mid. schs. Birmingham (Ala.) Pub. Schs., Birmingham, 1989—; curriculum coord. Vestavia Hills City Schs., Birmingham, Ala., 1987—; coord. mid. schs. Birmingham Pub. Schs., 1989—; ednl. and tech. cons. IBM/USA, 1990—. Adj. asst. prof. U. Ala., Birmingham, 1987-90; mem. adv. bd., pres. Community Providers Assn., Little Rock. Co-author: Christian Ladies in the Eighties: And Other Balancing Acts, 1986; author: Quest for Educational Quality, 1991. Community advisor B'hon Jr. League of B'hon; pres. Rep. Women's Club, Clinton, 1987-88; alt. del. Nat. Fedn. Rep. Women Conv.; mem. Rep. Cen. com., Clinton, 1987. Devel. Disabilities Svcs. grantee, 1982-83, Found. Exceptional Children grantee, 1985-86, South Cen. Bell Mini grantee, 1989, grantee, team leader MDC, 1992. Mem. ASCD, AAUW, Am. Assn. Sch. Adminstrs., Coun. for Exceptional Children, Rotary Internat. (chair, sec.), Phi Delta Kappa, Delta Kappa Gamma, Kappa Kappa Kappa. Baptist. Avocations: reading, tennis, public speaking, travel. Office: 200 Narrows Pky Ste A Birmingham AL 35242

RIVERS, WILGA MARIE, language educator; b. Melbourne, Australia, Apr. 13, 1919; arrived in U.S., 1970; d. Harry and Nina Diamond (Burston) Rivers. BA, U. Melbourne, 1939, diploma in Edn., 1940, MA, 1948; Licence es L., U. Montpellier, France, 1952; PhD, U. Ill., 1962; MA (hon.), Harvard U., 1974; PhD of Langs. (hon.), Middlebury Coll., 1989. H.S. tchr., Victoria, Australia, 1940-48; asst. in English lang. France, 1949-52; tchr. prep. schs., 1953-58; asst. prof. French No. Ill. U., DeKalb, 1963-64; assoc. prof. Monash U., Australia, 1964-69; vis. prof. Columbia U., 1970-71; prof. French U. Ill., Urbana-Champaign, 1971-74; prof. Romance langs. and lit., coord. lang. instrn. Harvard U., 1974-89, prof. emerita, 1989—. Cons. NEH, Ford Found., Rockefeller Found., others; lectr 44 countries and throughout U.S.; mem. adv. bd. Modern Lang. Ctr., Ont. Inst. for Studies in Edn., Nat. Fgn. Lang. Ctr., Lang. Acquire Rsch. Ctr., San Diego. Author: The Psychologist and the Foreign-Language Teacher, 1964, Teaching Foreign-Language Skills, 1968, 2d edit., 1981, Speaking in Many Tongues, 1972, 3d edit., 1983, A Practical Guide to the Teaching of French, 1975, 2d edit., 1988, 3d edit. (on Web), 2001, Opportunities for Careers in Foreign Languages, 1993; co-author: A Practical Guide to the Teaching of German, 1975, 2d edit., 1988, A Practical Guide to the Teaching of Spanish, 1976, 2d edit., 1988, A Practical Guide to the Teaching of English as a Second or Foreign Language, 1978, Communicating Naturally in a Second Language, 1983, Teaching Hebrew: A Practical Guide, 1989, others; editor, contbr. Interactive Language Teaching, 1978, Teaching Languages in College: Curriculum and Content, 1992, Down Under/Up Top: Creating a Life, 2004; writing translated into 11 langs.; editl. bd. Studies in Second Language Acquisition, Applied Linguistics, Language Learning, Mosaic, System; adv. com. Can. Modern Lang. Rev.; contbr. articles to profl. jours. Decorated chevalier des Palmes Académiques; recipient Disting. Fgn. Lang. Leadership award N.Y. State Assn. Fgn. Lang. Tchrs., 1974, Disting. Alumni award U. Ill., 1999, Dean's Disting. Svc. award Harvard Continuing Edn., 2004. Mem. MLA, Am. Assn. Applied Linguistics (charter pres.), Am. Coun. on Tchg. Fgn. Langs. (Florence Steiner award 1977, Anthony Papalia award 1988), Mass. Fgn. Lang. Assn. (Disting. Svc. award 1983), Tchrs. of English to Spkrs. of other Langs., Am. Assn. Tchrs. French, Linguistic Soc. Am., Am. Assn. Univ. Suprs. and Coords. Fgn. Lang. Programs Northeast Conf. (Nelson Brooks award 1983), Internat. Assn. Applied Psycholinguistics (v.p. 1983-89), Japan Assn. Coll. English Tchrs. (hon.), Am. Assn. Tchrs. German (hon.), Internat. Assn. Lang. Labs. (hon.). Episcopalian. Home and Office: 84 Garfield St Watertown MA 02472-4916 Personal E-mail: wmrivers@comcast.net.

RIVET, JEANNINE M., insurance company executive; BS in Nursing, Boston Coll.; MPH, Boston U. Sch. Public Health. V.p. grp. ops. Prudential Ins. Co. Am.; v.p. health svc. ops. to CEO United HealthCare, Minnetonka, Minn., 1990-98, CEO, 1998—2000, Ingenix; exec. v.p. UnitedHealth Grp., 2000—. Office: UnitedHealth Group 9900 Bren Rd E Minnetonka MN 55343-9664

RIVLIN, ALICE MITCHELL, economics professor, former federal official; b. Phila., Mar. 4, 1931; d. Allan C. G. and Georgianna (Fales) Mitchell; m. Lewis Allen Rivlin, 1955 (div. 1977); children: Catherine Amy, Allan Mitchell, Douglas Gray; m. Sidney Graham Winter, 1989. AB, Bryn Mawr Coll., 1952; MA, Radcliffe Coll., 1955, PhD, 1958; LLD (hon.), U. Mich., 1975, U. Md., 1975; DSc (hon.), U. Ind., 1976; LLD (hon.), Yale U., 1984; DSc (hon.), N.J. Inst. Tech., 1998; LLD (hon.), U. Dist. of Columbia, 1999, Harvard U., 2001. Mem. staff Brookings Instn., Washington, 1957-66, 69-75, 83-93; dir. econ. studies Brookings Inst., 1983-87; dir. Congl. Budget Office, 1975-83; prof. pub. policy George Mason U., 1992—93; dep. dir. Office Mgmt. and Budget Exec. Office of the Pres., Washington, 1993-94, dir., 1994-96; vice chmn. Fed. Res. Sys., Washington, 1996-99; chair Fin. Assistance and Mgmt. Authority, 1998—2001; sr. fellow, econ. studies program Brookings Instn., Washington, 1999—; Henry J. Cohen prof. New Sch. U., 2001—; co-dir. Greater Wash. Rsch. Program, Brookings Instn., 2001—. Dep. asst. sec. program coordination HEW, Washington, 1966-68, asst. sec. planning and evaluation, 1968-69; mem. Staff Adv. Commn. on Intergovtl. Rels., 1961-62; bd. dirs. NY Stock Exch., 2005-06, NYSE Group, Inc., 2006-, BearingPoint, Inc., Washington Post Co. Author: The Role of the Federal Governemnt in Financing Higher Education, 1961, (with others) Microanalysis of Socioeconomic Systems, 1961, Systematic Thinking for Social Action, 1971, (with others) Economic Choices 1987, 1986, (with others The Swedish Economy, 1987, (with others) Caring for the Disabled Elderly: Who Will Pay?, 1988, Reviving the American Dream, 1992, The Economic Payoff from the Internet Revolution (co-edited with Robert E. Litan), 2001, Beyond the Dot.Coms: The Economic Promise of the Internet (with Robert E. Litan), 2001. MacArthur fellow, 1983-87, Elliot J. Richardson prize for excellence in pub. svc., 2002, Barnard medal of distinction, Barnard Coll., 2002. Mem. Am. Econ. Assn. (nat. pres. 1986), Nat. Acad. Pub. Administrn., Nat. Acad. of Social Insurance, Coun. on Fgn. Rels., Women's Econ. Roundtable Office: Brookings Instn 1755 Massachusetts Ave Washington DC 20036 also: NYSE Group Inc 11 Wall St New York NY 10005

RIVLIN, RACHEL, lawyer; b. Bangor, Maine, Sept. 1, 1945; d. Lawrence and A. Sara (Rich) Lait. BA, U. Maine, 1965; MA, U. Louisville, 1968; JD, Boston Coll., 1977. Bar: Mass. 1977, U.S. Dist. Ct. Mass. 1978, U.S. Ct. Appeals (1st cir.) 1983, U.S. Supreme Ct. 1985. Audiologist Boston City Hosp., 1969-72; dir. audiology Beth Israel Hosp., Boston, 1972-74; atty. Legal Sys. Devel., Boston, 1977-78, Liberty Mut. Ins., Boston, 1978-82; counsel, sec. Lexington Ins. Co., Boston, 1982-85, v.p., assoc. gen. counsel, sec., 1985—. Mem. task force fin. literacy students U.S. Bankruptcy Ct. and Boston Bar Assn., 2004—05. Mem. civil rights com. Anti-Defamation League, Boston, 1982—2005; bd. dirs. Dance Art, Inc., Boston, 1985—92. Mem.: ABA (mem. ins. regulation sect. 1980, vice chair internat. ins. law com. 1983—84, chair internat. ins. law com. 1985—86, sr. vice chair nat. inst. insurer insolvency 1987—88, sr. vice chair pub. regulation of ins. 1987—90, nat. inst. reins. collections and insolvency 1988, chair excess surplus lines and resins. com. 1988—89, nat. inst. insurer insolvency 1989, vice chair internat. ins. law com. 1997—2005, task force ins. and corp. counsel interests and involvement 1999—2003, vice chair corp. counsel com. 2003—05), Boston Bar Assn. (mem. coun. 1983—86, chmn. corp. counsel 1987, steering com. corp. bus. law and fin. sect. 1987—89, chmn. ins. law. com. 1987—90, nominating com. 1988, edn. com. 1989, 1990—91, chmn. ins. com. 1990—93, ethics com. 1993—2005, edn. com. 1994, multi-disciplinary practice task force 2000—02, comprehensive revision Mass. corp. law 2000—02, mem. coun. 2002—05, edn. com. 2003, mem. task force fin. literacy students 2004—05), Boston Coll. Law Sch. Alumni Assn. (ann. fund com. 1981—89, chmn. telethon com. 1989—94, nominating com. 1990, search com. for dean 1993, search com. for law sch. fund dir. 1993, leadership gifts exec. com. 1994—98, search com. for dir. instl. advancement 1995, reunion com. 2002, Father James Malley award 1996). Office Phone: 941-870-3326. Business E-Mail: rachelrivlin@aol.com.

RIVO, SHIRLEY WINTHROPE, artist; arrived in U.S., 1953, naturalized, 1960; m. Julian David Rivo, Mar. 22, 1953; children: Morissa, Sandra, Philip. BA, Kean U., 1977, MA, 1980. Cert. arts tchr. K-12. Window display designer Belgium Stores, Toronto, 1945-53; needlepoint design Creative Kits, Inc., N.J., N.Y., 1965-72. Chair person exhbn. We Love New York, Lever House, N.Y., 1996; guest spkr. Old Guard of Summit, 2004; spkr. in field. One-woman shows include New Hampshire House, Summit, N.J., 1970, Chemical Bank, N.Y.C., 1977, St. Barnabas Med. Ctr., Livingston, N.J., 1978, N.J. Ctr. for Visual Arts, Summit, 1979, 85, Ciba-Geigy, Summit, 1979, AT&T, Basking Ridge, N.J., 1982, Exxon, Warren, N.J., 1985, Chubb Corp. World HQ, Warren, N.J., 1985, B'nai Jeshurun, Short Hills, N.J., 1987, John Trapp Gallery, Summit, 1988, Johnson & Johnson, New Brunswick, N.J., 1994, 2004, Schering-Plough, Kenilworth, N.J., 1994, photography, Johnson & Johnson Health Care Systems, Piscataway, N.J., 2004, Summit Free Pub. Libr. Gallery, N.J., 2006; two-person exhbn. Overlook HOsp., Summit, N.J., 2003; group shows include N.J. Ctr. for Visual Arts, N.Y.C., 1970, 72, 76, 81, Kean Coll., Union, N.J., 1972, 80, 87, 88, 89., Visual Arts, Merck & Co., 1990, Papermill Playhouse, N.J., 1972-2000, Somerset Art Assn., 1973, 74, 77, Drew U., Madison, N.J., 1978, Allied Arts of Am., Nat. Arts Club, 1982, Morris County Cultural Ctr., 1983, Morris Mus., Morristown, N.J., 1984, Hunterdon Art Ctr., 1987, Visual Spectrum, Schering-Plough, 1993, 2000, numerous others; permanent collections include Morris Mus., Morristown, Johnson & Johnson, New Brunswick, Nabisco Hdqs., Hanover, N.J., Deloitte and Touche LLP, Parsippany N.J., Nat. Baseball Hall of Fame, Cooperstown, N.Y., Yankee Stadium, Bronx, N.Y., Bklyn. Bot. Garden, Statue of Liberty, N.J., N.Y. Bot. Garden, Bronx. Recipient Best in Show, Millburn Short Hills Art Ctr. 1985, other awards, 1972, 74, 86, 88, 89, 90, 91, 1st prize Papermill Playhouse and in 1995, award of excellence, Pauline Wick award Am. Artists Profl. League Mems. Show, 1990, award for photography Pepermill Playhouse, 2003, Outstanding Achievement Amateur Photography award Internat. Soc. Photographers, 2004, numerous others. Mem. N.J. Ctr. Visual Arts (program chair 1979-84, chair spl. events, 1982-84, chair classes 1990-98), Millburn Shorthills Arts Ctr. (trustee, 1990-2006, chmn. pub. rels. 1986-92, chmn. corp. exhibits, 1986-96, 1st v.p. 2006). Avocation: writing. Home: 32 Summit Rd New Providence NJ 07974-2750

RIYAZ, NAJMUN, psychiatrist; b. Springar, India, Mar. 17, 1971; arrived in U.S., 1997; d. Assadullah and Hamida Sham; m. Riyaz Bashir, May 24, 1996; children: Medina, Haroun. MBBS, Govt. Med. Coll., Toledo, Ohio, 1996; MD, Med. U., 2003. Resident psychiatry St. Elizabeth's Med. Ctr.,

Boston, 1999—2002, Med. U., 2002—03; psychiatrist Fulton County Health Ctr., Waseon, Ohio, 2003—. Pres. Najmun Riyaz Inc., Toledo, 2003—. Mem.: APA, Nat. Alliance Mentally Ill, Ohio Psychiatrist Assn. Avocations: interior decorating, cooking, travel, painting.

RIZER, MAGGIE, model; b. Watertown, NY, Jan. 9, 1978; Model Elite Modeling Agy.; appeared in ads for Calvin Klein, Versace, the Gap. Actor(guest appearances): (TV series) Sex and the City, The Victoria's Secret Fashion Show, 2001, America's Top Model, 2003. Office: Elite Premier 111 E 22nd St New York NY 10010

RIZZI, MARGUERITE CLAIRE, music educator; b. New York, NY, Aug. 4, 1955; d. Joan Henderson, Norman Henderson (Stepfather), John N. Rizzi; life ptnr. Brenda June Mottram. BA, Clark U., 1976; MusM, New Eng. Conservatory, 1991; EdD, Boston U., 2000. Cert. std. tchr. cert. music, spl. edn. tchr. Coord. guitar program Boston U., Boston, 1993—99; tchr. Beacon H.S., Brookline, Mass., 1993—2001. Musician (recording): Sympatico, 1999 (listed for grammy nomination, 1999). Capt. sailing vessels. Mem.: Boston Women's Jazz Coalition, Am. Profl. Capt.'s Assn., Internat. Assn. Jazz Edn., Music Educators Nat. Conf. Democrat. Avocations: sailing, bicycling, reading. Office: 74 Green St Brookline MA 02446-3305 Personal E-mail: mottriz@attbi.com.

RNIX, REGINA LEIGH, performing arts educator, small business owner; d. William Eugene and Dorothy Ann Lednicky; m. Mark Alan Nix, Sept. 18, 1999. AA, McLennan CC, Waco, Tex., 1991; BS in Dance and Bus. cum laude, Tex. Woman's U., Denton, 1993. Owner, dir. All That Jazz Acad Dance, Hewitt, Tex., 1993—; pre-kindergarten, asst. dir. Lorena United Meth. Childcare Ctr., Tex., 2000—. Choreographer Grease, Tin Bldg. Theatre, Clifton, Tex., 2005 (Best Choreography OMAR, 05). Recipient Best Costume, Co. Dance, Dallas, 2005, Best Choreography, Creation Dance Championships, 2006. Mem.: Dance Educators Am. Republican. Roman Catholic. Avocations: fishing, sewing. Office: All That Jazz Acad Dance 235 N Hewitt Dr Ste 3 Hewitt TX 76643 Office Phone: 254-666-0118.

ROACH, CAROLE HYDE, music educator; d. Clyde Eugene Hyde and Mary Evelyn Springer; m. Samuel Frederick Roach, Nov. 14, 1970. BMus, Ga. State U., 1962; MusM, Fla. State U., 1963; postgrad., U. Ga., 1974. Nat. cert. voice and piano Tchrs. Nat. Assn., 1974, cert. piano & voice Music Tchrs. Nat. Assn., 1985. Voice & piano tchr. Mary Hardin-Baylor Coll., Belton, Tex., 1964—65, Kennesaw State U., Ga., 1967—70, Perimeter Coll., Decatur, Ga., 1970—71; choral dir. Jerusalem Ave. Jr. HS, North Bellmore, NY, 1965—67; choir dir. Ch. of Ascension, Cartersville, Ga., 1993—96, St. Teresa's Episcopal Ch., Acworth, Ga., 2000—; mezzo-soprano soloist Peachtree Presbyterian, Atlanta, 1967—84, Peachtree Meth., Atlanta, 1984—86. Soloist Fletcher Wolfe Chorale, Atlanta, 1968—71, state vocal auditions chmn., 2003, Atlanta, 04; soloist Atlanta Chamber Opera, 1968—71; musical dir. Canton Theatre, Canton, Ga., 2004. Actress: Gooch (Best Supporting Actress, 1991); Bloody Mary (Best Supporting Actress, 1995); dir.: Fantasticks (Best Dir., 1998), Lend Me a Tenor (Best Dir., 1999), I Hate Hamlet (Best Dir., 2000). Pres., treas. Pumphouse Players, Cartersville, Ga., 1990—2003. Mem.: Music Tchrs. Nat. Assn., Ga. Music Tchrs. Assn., Greater Marietta Music Tchrs. Assn. (pres. 2003—), Cobb County Music Tchrs. Assn. (pres. 1975—76, state chair for vocal auditions). Democrat. Episcopal. Avocations: theater, travel, dog breeding, dog showing, dog rescue. Office: Music Acad So Keyboards 1898-B Leland Dr Marietta GA 30067 Home: 22 Glory Ln Cartersville GA 30120 Personal E-mail: roachs@msn.com.

ROACH, HILDRED ELIZABETH, education educator; BA, Fisk U., 1957; MusM, Yale U., 1962. Instr. Tuskegee Inst., 1957-58, 59-60, Fayetteville State Coll., 1962-66; piano tchr. Howard U., 1966-67, history of African-Am. Music tchr., spring 1992, 93; asst. prof. Va. State U., 1967-68; assoc. prof. to prof. Federal City Coll. (U. D.C.), 1968—. Lectr. Cath. U., 1972, MENC Conf. in Boston and Milw., 1973, DCMEA Meeting, Kennedy Ctr., 1973, Fisk U., 1973, Montgomery County Region of Md. Assn. of Student Coun., 1973, Wilmington (Del.) Music Tchrs. Assn., 1973, Martin Luther King Libr., Black Studies Div., 1974, Music Tchrs. Assn., 1975, Music Educators Conf., Phila., 1975, Hood Coll., 1980, Talladega U., Howard U. Ethnic Music Conf., 1973, Peoples Congrl. Ch., 1980, others; vol. D.C. Piano Competition Steering Com., 1985. Author: Black American Music: Past and Present, Boston, 1973, Vol. 1 and 2, 2d edit. 1992; solo concerts Livingston Coll., 1956, Fisk U., Sr. Recital, 1957, Tuskegee Inst., Faculty Concert, 1958, 59, Yale U. Master Recital, 1962, Fayetteville State Coll., Faculty REcital, 1962-66, Howard U., Faculty Recital, 1967, Va. State Coll., Faculty Recital, 1968, Eastern Mennonite Coll., Vis. Faculty, 1972, Fed. City Coll., Faculty Recital, 1973, Peoples Congrl. Ch., 1981, others. Recipient Ford Found. Early Entrant Scholarship to Fisk, 1953-57, Sarah McKim Maloney award, Fisk U., 1954, Rieser Alumni Scholarship to Juilliard, 1958, John Hay Whitney Scholarship to Yale, 1960, State of Ala. Scholarship to Yale, 1960-62, Lockwood Competition Scholarship award, 1961-62; grantee Am. Forum, 1969, Ctr. of Applied Rsch., 1989. Mem. Afro-Am. Creative Assn., Am. Music Tchr., Black Music Caucus, Nat. Assn. Negro Musicians, Nat. Assn. for Advancement of Colored People. Nat. Assn. Negro Musicians, NEA, Alpha Kappa Alpha, Phi Beta Kappa. Office: U DC 4200 Connecticut Ave NW # 46 Washington DC 20008-1122

ROACH, KATHLEEN LYNN, lawyer; b. Santa Monica, Calif., Nov. 6, 1962; d. William Russell and Margaret Rose (Balogh) R. AB, U. Calif., Berkeley, 1982; JD, U. Chgo., 1985. Bar: Ill. 1985, Calif. 1988, U.S. Dist. Ct. (no. dist.) Ill. 1985, U.S Dist Ct. (ea. dist.) Calif. 1988, U.S. Ct. Appeals (7th cir.) 1985. Assoc. Sidley & Austin, Chgo., 1985-93, ptnr., 1993—. Bd. dirs. AIDS Legal Coun., Chgo., 1990—; bd. govs. Chgo. Coun. of Lawyers, 1992—. Office: Sidley & Austin 1 S First National Plz Chicago IL 60603-2000

ROACH, MARGARET, editor-in-chief; Editor., mgr. NY Times; garden columnist Newsday Newspapers; creative developer Martha Stewart Living Omnimedia, 1995; gardening editor Martha Stewart Living; mgr. devel. and exec. editor marthastewart.com; editor-in-chief Martha Stewart Living, NYC, 2001—. Author: A Way to Garden, 1998 (Garden Writers Assn. Am. Best Book, 1998). Mailing: Martha Stewart Living 11 West 42nd St 25th Floor New York NY 10036*

ROACH, MARGOT RUTH, retired biophysicist, educator; d. Robert Dickson and Katherine Roach; m. Franklyn St. Aubyn House, Dec. 20, 1994 (wid. Feb. 2000). B.Sc. in Math. and Physics with honors, U. N.B., Fredericton, Can., 1955; MD, C.M. cum laude, McGill U., Montreal, Can., 1959; PhD in Biophysics, U. Western Ont., Can., 1963; D.Sc. (hon.), U. N.B., St. John, Can., 1981. Jr. intern Victoria Hosp., London, Ont., Can., 1959-60, fellow in cardiology, 1962-63, asst. resident in medicine, 1963-64, Toronto Gen. Hosp., 1964-65; mem. faculty, dept. biophysics U. Western Ont., London, 1965—98, head dept. biophysics, 1970-78, prof., 1971-98, asst. prof. medicine, 1965-72, assoc. prof., 1972-78, prof., 1978-98, prof. emeritus Biophysics & Med., 1998. Mem. staff dept. medicine Victoria Hosp., 1967-72, U. Hosp., London, 1972-98; Commonwealth vis. sci., dept. applied math. theoretical physics Cambridge U., 1975; vis. sci. Bioengring. Inst., Chonqing U., People's Republic of China, 1991; mem. bioengring. grants com. Med. Rsch. Coun. Can., 1993-96; cons. and lectr. in field. Mem. editl. bd.: Imprints, 2003—06. Active civic orgns. and coms. including Univ. Rsch. Coun., 1976-79; mem. interview bd. London Conf. of United Ch., 1967-90; steward United Ch. of Can., 1967-73, elder, 1973-82, mem. com. on ministry vocations, 2004-06, chair unified bd. Tatamagouche Pastoral Charge, 2001-; chmn. stewardship devel. com. Colborne St. United Ch., 1990-93. Recipient A. Wilmer Duff prize in physics U. N.B., 1955, Cushing prize in pediatrics, 1959, Ciba Found. award for research in aging, 1959, Teaching award Faculty of Medicine U. Western Ont., 1990, Dean's award, 1997, Women of Distinction award YWCA, 1997; Med. Research Council fellow U. Western Ont., 1960-62, Arthur Guyton award Internat. Soc. Cardiovascular Medicine and Sci., 1997; numerous other fellowships and grants in medicine. Fellow Royal Coll. Physicians (Can.), Am. Coll. Cardiology (Young Investigator's award 1963); mem. Can. Physiol. Soc., Can. Cardiovascular Soc. (of council), Can. Clin. Investigation Soc. (council 1980-84), Can. Soc. Internal Medicine. Address: RR #1 104 Sea Shore Dr Tatamagouche NS Canada B0K 1V0 Personal E-mail: mroach@pchg.net.

ROACH, MARTHA S., art educator; b. Lawrence, Kans., Aug. 9, 1961; d. Harold John and Marie Elizabeth Brohammer; m. John B. Roach, Apr. 2, 1994; children: Jason, Rose, Amanda. B of Art Edn., U. Kans., Lawrence, 1984. Tchr. Richland R-4 Schs., Mo., 1985—88, Cheney Unified Sch. Dist. #268, Kans., 1988—2000, Hillsboro Unified Sch. Dist. #410, 2000—02, Haysville Unified Sch. Dist. #261, 2002—06. Office: Campus High Sch 2100 W 55th S Wichita KS 67217 Office Phone: 316-554-2236. E-mail: mroach@usd261.com.

ROACH, PAM, state legislator; m. Jim Roach; 5 children. BA in History, Brigham Young U., 1970. Mem. Wash. Legislature, Olympia, 1991—, mem. govtl. ops. and election com., mem. internat. trade and econ. devel. com., mem. ways and means com., mem. sentencing guidelines commn. Past mem. Gov.'s Juvenile Issues Task Force; mem. local coun. Boy Scouts Am.; past mem. adv. com.; founder, dir. Escuela de Esperenza; mem. Joint Com. Vets. and Mil. Affairs; mem. Sentencing Guidelines Commn. Mem. Wash. Policy Coun., Rotary. Republican. Office: 202 Irving Newhouse Bldg Olympia WA 98504-0001 also: PO Box 40431 Olympia WA 98504 Office Phone: 360-786-7660. Business E-Mail: roach-pam@leg.wa.gov.

ROACHÉ, SYLVIA, social worker; b. Sept. 21, 1923; d. James E. and Iris E. Lawrence; m. Leonard E. Roaché, Oct. 12, 1950; children: Patrick, Grace Roaché Greenidge, Daniel. Diploma, Jamaica Sch. Theology, Wis., 1950; LPN, Practical Nursing Sch., Toledo, 1958; BA in Social Work, U. Pitts., 1977, MSW, 1979. Assoc. pastor 1st Ch. of God, Toledo, Sav-la-mar, Jamaica; nurse Toledo Hosp., Shadyside Hosp., Pitts.; social worker Vintage, Pitts.; co-pastor Lincoln Ave. Ch. of God, Pitts. Author: Reflections, 1976, Life's Unforgettable Moments, 2001, Ruth and Naomi Find Joy After Tragedy, 2004; contbr. articles to mags. Mem.: Nat. Assn. Ch. of God (founder min.'s wives assn.), Am. Assn. Christian Counselors (charter mem.). Avocations: sewing, writing. Home: 3268 Winter Wood Ct Marietta GA 30062-7001

ROARK, BARBARA ANN, librarian; b. Evanston, Ill., July 24, 1958; d. Edward B. and Ann H. Rowe; m. Paul E. Roark, Sept. 18, 1982; children: Sarah, John. BA in History, U. Ky., 1981, MLS, 1982. Dir. Hopkins County Madisonville (Ky.) Pub. Libr., 1983-85; ops. mgr. Wurzburg Inc., Nashville, 1985-91; dir. Spies Pub. Libr., Menominee, Mich., 1991-98, Franklin (Wis.) Pub. Libr., 1998—. V.p. adv. coun. Mid-Peninsula Libr. Coop., Mich., 1993-95, sec. adv. coun., 1991-93; chair tech. adv. com. Milwaukee County Federated Libr. Sys., 2001—. Grant writer Title II, 1994, Title I, 1995. Treas. Franklin Area Jr. Woman's Club. Recipient Cert. of Excellence Libr. of Mich., 1995, Cert. of Appreciation Menominee Area C. of C., 1998. Mem. ALA, Wis. Libr. Assn. (pers. and profl. concerns com. 1999—, Muriel Fuller award 2002), Spies Pub. Libr. Found., PEO, Order Ea. Star, U. Ky. Alumni Assn., Franklin Area Jr. Women's Club (treas. 1999—), Kiwanis (pres. Milw. suburban S.W. chpt. 2002—), Zeta Tau Alpha. Methodist. Avocations: golf, reading, cross stitching, travel. Office Phone: 414-425-8214. E-mail: barbara.roark@mcfls.org.

ROARK, MARY LOU, educator, counselor; b. Greene, Iowa, Oct. 25, 1938; d. Alfred H. and Anna M. (Voigts) Heuer; m. Eldridge W. Roark, Jr., June 20, 1964; children Lisa K., Michael E. BA, Wartburg Coll., 1961; MA, Syracuse U., 1964; EdD, Va. Poytech. Inst. & State U., 1978. Nat, cert, counselor. (Nat. Bd. for Cert. Counselors). Tchr. Madison (Wis.) City Schs., 1961-62, Iowa City (Iowa) Schs., 1964-65, Syracuse (N.Y.) City Schs., 1965-67; coop. edn. coord. Va. Polytech. and State U., Blacksburg, Va., 1977-78; from assoc. prof. to prof. edn. dept. SUNY, Plattsburgh, 1980-93, counseling programs coord., 1989-95, prof., 1993-98, acting dean profl. studies, 1998, ret., 1998, prof. emeritus, 1998—. Bd. dirs. Campus Violence Prevention Ctr., Towson, Md., 1989—; cons., counselor, pvt. practice, Plattsburgh, 1980—. Author: (handbook) Guide to Preventing Campus Violence, 1988; contbr. articles to profl. jours., chpts. to books. Pres. LWV, Plattsburgh, 1983-85; chair Community Svcs. Bd., Plattsburgh, 1985-89; moderator Dist. Atty.'s Child Sex Abuse Coun., Plattsburgh, 1991-92; v.p. N.Y. Bd. for Cert. Profl. Counselors, Inc., 1996-98. Mem. Northeastern N.Y. Counselors Assn. (pres. 1992-93), Am. Coll. Pers. Assn. (chair task force 1985-90), Phi Kappa Phi (pres. 1992-94), Omicron Delta Kappa, Phi Delta Kappa.

ROBAK, KIM M., lawyer; b. Columbus, Nebr., Oct. 4, 1955; m. William J. Mueller; children: Katherine, Claire. BS with distinction, U. Nebr., 1977, JD with highest distinction, 1985. Tchr. Lincoln Pub. Schs., Nebr., 1978—82; clerk Cline Williams Wright Johnson & Oldfather, 1983; summer assoc. Cooley Godward Castro Huddleson & Tatum, San Francisco, 1984, Steptoe & Johnson, Washington, 1985; ptnr. Rembolt Ludtke Parker & Berger, Lincoln, 1985—91; legal counsel Gov. E. Benjamin Nelson/State of Nebr., 1991—92, chief of staff, 1992—93; lt. gov. State of Nebr., 1993—98; v.p. external affairs, corp. sec. U. Nebr., 1999—2004; with Ruth Mueller Robak, LLC, Lincoln, Nebr., 2004—. Chair Prairie Fire Internat. Symposium on Edn., 1986; bd. dirs. Fiserv, Inc., First Ameritas Life Ins. Corp. NY, Union Bank & Trust Co. Program com. Leadership Lincoln, 1987—90; chair program com. Leadership Lincoln Alumni Assn., 1987, selection com., 1990; mem. Toll Fellowship Program, 1995; chair Nat. Conf. Lt. Govs., 1996; hon. chair Daffodil Day Campaign An, Cancer Soc.; hon chair Walktoberfest Am. Diabetes Assn.; hon. chair Prevent Blindness Campaign, Nebr.; hon. mem. Red Ribbon Campaign Mothers Against Drunk Driving, 1994—95; active Groundwater Found., 1997, Medicaid Managed Care Commn., 1993—98; bd. dirs. Nebr. Health Sys., 1997—2004, Nat. Found. Women Legislators Found., 1997—98; chair Nebr. Info. Tech. Commn., 1997—98; hon. Christmas chair Salvation Army, 1997; cert. program chair Nat. Order Women Legislators, 1997; mem. Martin Luther Home Soc., 1999—2001, Dem. Gen. Counsel, Nebr., 1985—92; bd. dirs. women's ministries First Congl. Ch., 1988—91, trustee, 1991—99, asst. moderator, 1999—; trustee Plymouth Congl. Ch., 1998—; bd. dirs. Doane Coll., 1997—, Lincoln Pub. Sch. Found., 1998—2004, Lincoln Partnership for Econ. Devel. Bd., 2000—, Nebr. Found. for the Humanities, 2003—, Lincoln Cmty. Found., 2004—, United Way of Lincoln and Lancaster County, 2000—, Strategic Air and Space Mus., 2006—, Exec. Women's Golf Assn., 2005—. Named Notable Woman, First Plymouth Congl. Ch.'s Bd. Women's Ministries, 1996; fellow, Leadership Lincoln, 1986—87. Mem.: ABA (steering com. 1997—), Lincoln Bar Assn., Nebr. State Bar Assn. (ethics com. 1987—92, chair com. yellow pages advt. 1988, vice chair com. pub. rels. 1988—92, ho. of dels. 1988—95), Nat. Inst. Trial Advocaty, Alzheimers Assn. (hon. chair Lincoln-Greater Nebr. chpt. 1996—98), Updowntowners, Exec. Women's Golf Assn. (trustee 2005—), Order of Coif, U. Nebr. Coll. Alumni Assn. (bd. dirs. 1986—89). Office: Ruth Mueller Robak LLC 530 S 13th St Ste 110 Lincoln NE 68508 Business E-Mail: robak@ruthmueller.com.

ROBB, BABETTE, retired elementary school educator; b. St. Paul, Minn., Jan. 25, 1923; d. Roy F and Eda Johnson; m. David L Robb, July 23, 1945; children: Deborah G. Jankura, Pamela W. BA, So. Meth. U., Dallas, 1945; Elem. Educator, U. Wis., River Falls, 1948. Asst. to county auditor Washington County, Stillwater, Minn., 1945—46, county sch. tchr. Stillwater, 1947—53; elem. sch. tchr. Stillwater (Minn.) Dist. 834, 1953—81. Author: (elem.sch. text) St. Croix Valley Story, 1970; contbr. articles Childrens Mags., 1979. Chmn. Washington County Young Reps., Stillwater, 1946—50; mem. bd. dirs. Family Svc., Stillwater, Minn.; Grand Marshall of 4th of July Parade Afton (Minn.) Hist. Soc., 1973. Recipient Drama award, Minn. Regional Speech Contest, 1940; chosen to christen SS Ernie Pyle, U.S. Maritime Commn. Mem.: AAUW (life; Founder local chpt. 1946), St. Croix Valley Ret. Tchrs. Assn. (bd. dir.), Minn. Ednl. Assn. (sec. local br. 1953—), Delta Kappa Gamma (Sec. 1972—). Methodist. Achievements include first to introduce Spanish to Elementary Students in 1958. Avocations: modeling, photography, swimming, writing, water biking. Home (Summer): 2803 S St Croix Tr Afton MN 55001 Home (Winter): Apt 407-408 3500 S Ocean Blvd Palm Beach FL 33480

ROBB, JANET, secondary school educator; b. McKeesport, Pa. d. Nicholas Robb and Pauline Elizabeth Sowa. BA, Slippery Rock U., Pa.; M, U. Pa., Pitts. Tchr., pub speaking McKeesport Area Sch. Dist. Play dir. McKeesport Area HS, forensic coach. Lector St. Mark's Ch., Port Vue, 1985—. Named 5th Diamond Coach, Nat. Forensic League, 2004; named to Hall of Fame, Pa. HS Speech League, 1994.

ROBB, KATHY MCCLESKEY, lawyer; b. Bklyn., Nov. 14, 1954; BA cum laude, spl. honors, Plan II, Univ. Tex., 1976; JD, Univ. Va., 1980. Bar: Va. 1982, NY 1989, US Dist. Ct. (ea. and so. dists.) NY, US Supreme Ct. Law clk. to Hon. Glen M. Williams US Dist. Ct. (we. dist.) Va., 1980—81; ptnr. resources, regulatory and environ. law Hunton & Williams LLP, NYC, 1988—. Adv. bd. BNA's Environ. Due Diligence Guide. Fellow: ABA; mem.: Assn. of City Bar of NY. Office: Hunton & Williams LLP 200 Park Ave New York NY 10166 Office Phone: 202-995-1128, 212-309-1128. Office Fax: 202-309-1100. Business E-Mail: krobb@hunton.com.

ROBB, LYNDA JOHNSON, writer; b. Washington, Mar. 19, 1944; d. Lyndon Baines and Claudia Alta (Taylor) Johnson; m. Charles Spittal Robb, Dec. 9, 1967; children: Lucinda Desha, Catherine Lewis, Jennifer Wickliffe. BA with honors, U. Tex., 1966. Writer McCall's Mag., 1966-68; contbg. editor Ladies Home Jour., 1968-80; lectr., bd. dirs. Reading Is Fundamental, 1968—, Lyndon B. Johnson Family Found., 1969-95. Past mem. Va. State Coun. on Infant Mortality, Va. Maternal & Child Health Coun.; mem. Nat. Commn. to Prevent Infant Mortality, 1987-93; chmn. Pres.'s Adv. Com. for Women, 1979-81; pres. bd. dirs. Nat. Home Libr. Found.; chmn. Va. Women's Cultural History Project, 1982-85; chmn. Reading is Fundamental, 1996-2001. Mem.: Zeta Tau Alpha. Office: Reading is Fundamental Ste 400 1825 Connecticut Ave NW Washington DC 20009-5708

ROBBEN, TRICIA ELIZABETH, protective services official; d. Joseph William and Margaret Kelly Robben. BS, John Carroll U., 1993—97; MPA, Fla. Atlantic U., 2002—. Cert. Victim Advocate Office of the Atty. Gen./FL. Rsch. coord. U. Hospitals of Cleve. and Case Western Res. U., 1997—99; sales assoc. First Union Securities, Boca Raton, 1999—2000; elder crime specialist Boca Raton Police Services Dept., Fla. Hospice ethics com. mem. Hospice by the Sea, Boca Raton, Fla. Recipient Civilian of the Month, Dec. 2002 and June 2003, Cmty. Policing award, Internat. Assoc. of Chiefs of Police, 2003, Civilian of Yr. 2003, Chiefs Achievement award, Boca Raton Police Dept., 2003; Stanley scholar, Stanley Found., 1997. Avocation: swimming. Office: Boca Raton Police Services Department 100 NW Boca Raton Blvd Boca Raton FL 33432 Office Phone: 443-285-3135. Personal E-mail: troben@verizon.net. Business E-Mail: trobben@ci.boca-raton.fl.us.

ROBBINS, ANDREA M., science educator; d. Nicholas and Stephanie Ann Glucki; m. Donald A. Robbins, May 12, 1984; children: Christine M., Donald A. BS in Chemistry, Villa Maria Coll., Erie, Pa., 1982; MS in Chemistry, SUNY, Fredonia, 1998. Asst. instr. chemistry U. Pitts., Bradford, Pa., 1982—99, instr. chemistry, 1999—. Contbr. articles to profl. jours. Mem.: Am. Chem. Soc. (alt.councilor 1988—99, councilor 2000—). Home: Box 164 Rixford PA 16745 Office: U Pitts Bradford 300 Campus Dr Bradford PA 16701

ROBBINS, ANNE FRANCIS See REAGAN, NANCY

ROBBINS, AUDREY, county official; b. Chgo., Mar. 1, 1932; d. Philip I. and Manya Lehr; children: Dana Merfeld, Cindy Buss. BA, DePaul U., Chgo., 1993. Mfrs. rep. Museum Reprodns. - Marwall Industries, N.Y.C., 1969—79; asst. to chief counsel Arthur Andersen & Co., Chgo., 1979—98; mem. staff Office of Chief Judge, Cook County Cir. Ct., Chgo., 1999—. Author: Goldblatt's Galloping Gourmets, 1974 (Tribune award, 74). Vol. intensive care infants Northwestern Meml. Hosp., Chgo., 1979—80; vol. Art Inst. Chgo., 1984—86; touring docent Terra Mus. Am. Art, Chgo., 1999—2004, Clarke/Glessner House, 2005—, Loyola U. Mus. Art, 2005—; bd. dirs., sec., pres. Nathan & Francis Goldblatt Soc. for Cancer Rsch., 1955—83. Mem.: Golden Key (life). Avocations: art history, watercolors, cooking. Home: 910 N Lake Shore Dr # 718 Chicago IL 60611 Office: Cir Ct Cook County 50 W Washington Chicago IL 60602

ROBBINS, CARRIE FISHBEIN, costume designer, educator; d. Sidney W. and Bettye A. (Berman) Fishbein; m. Richard D. Robbins. BS, BA, Pa. State U., 1964; MFA, Yale Drama Sch., 1967. Costume designer including over 30 Broadway shows, NYC, Death in Venice, Glimmerglass Opera and NYC Opera, 2005, City Center Encores! series A Tree Grows in Brooklyn, 2005, Irving Berlin's White Christmas (the new musical from the film), 2004, 2005, San Francisco, LA, Boston, 2006, St. Paul, Detroit, Seattle, Thetre Royal, Eng., A Class Act at the Ambassador Theatre, 2001—, Grease (Tony nomination best costumes), Over Here (Tony nomination best costumes), Secret Affairs of Mildred Wilde, Yentl, Cyrano, Iceman Cometh, Octette Bridge Club, Look to the Lillies, Sweet Bird of Youth, Agnes of God, Boys of Winter, The First, Frankenstein, Shadow Box, Samson et Dalila, San Francisco Opera, 1980, LA Opera, 1999, Houston Grand Opera, 2002, Rigoletto, Russlan et Ludmilla, Taverner, Bernstein's Mass, Opera Co. Boston, 1975-76, 1986, 1989, Hamburg State Opera (W.Ger.), 1979, Washington Opera Soc., 2005, 06, designed for NY Shakespeare Festival, Jules Irving's Lincoln Ctr. Repertory Theatre, Tyrone Guthrie Theatre, Mpls. (including Hamlet, Julius Caesar and Three Penny Opera), Mark Taper Forum, LA (including The Tempest with Anthony Hopkins, Fashion Inst. Tech. Surface Design award, Flea in Her Ear (Dramalogue Critics award), The Wedding Banquet, Seattle and Taiway, 2003, Williamstown, Chelsea Theatre Ctr., Bklyn., John Houseman's City Ctr. Acting Co., Juilliard Sch., NYC, WNET and cable TV, off-broadway theatres, NYC including Promenade Theatre, It's Only a Play, Big Potato, Women's Project's Exact Center of the Universe, Two-Headed, Westport Country Playhouse's Bench in the Sun, Arclite Theatre Tennessee Williams Remembered, Paper Mill Playhouse Rags, (TV) Saturday Night Live-NBC, 1985-86, The Rita Show; (film) In the Spirit, 1987; designer sets and costumes Tallulah Hallelujah; tchr. Henry Le Tang Profl. Sch. Tap Dance, 1989-91; vis. guest lectr. costume design U. Ill., UCLA, Oberlin Coll., Pa. State U., others; master tchr. costume design NYU; designer apparel Rainbow Room, Rockefeller Ctr., 1987-97, Aurora Grill, 1988, Empress Ct., Caesar's Palace, Las Vegas, 1988, Windows on the World Restaurant Complex, 1996 (Image of Yr. award Nat. Assn. Uniform Mfrs. and Distbrs. 1997); regional theatres including Berkshire Theatre, Mass., Toys in the Attic, Fla. Stage It's Only a Play, M. Butterfly for Arena State, DC, 2004, On the Verge, 2006; one-woman show Cen. Falls Gallery, NYC, 1980; exhibited in group shows at Cooper Hewitt Mus., Pa. State U., Wright-Hepburn Gallery, NYC, Scottsdale, Ariz., Salmagundi Club, 1983, 1984; illustrations and calligraphy pub. ann. calendar Soc. of Scribes competition, Ms. mag.; original costume work photographed in books; Costume Design, 1983, Fabric Painting and Dying for the Theatre, 1982; original drawing reproduced Time-Life Series: The Ency. of Collectibles; profiled in Costume Design-Techniques of Modern Masters, 1996, Contemporary Designers, 1990, 1997; designer loft conversions, comml. lobby space, studios, others; contbr. articles Stage Directions Mag.; illustrator: Who Was Wolfgang Amadeus Mozart?, 2003; contbr. to profl. jours. Named Disting. Alumna, Pa. State U., 1979; recipient Antoinette Perry nominations for Best Costumes for a Broadway Show, 1971-72, 73-74, Drama Desk award, Am. Theatre Wing, N.Y.C., 1971, 72, Maharam award for design, Joseph Maharam Found., N.Y.C., 1975, nomination, 1984, Juror's Choice award for surface design, Fashion Inst. of Tech., 1980, Dramalogue Critics' award for Outstanding Achievement in Theatre Costume Design, L.A., 1982, Silver Medal, 6th Triennial of Theatre Design, Novisad, Yugoslavia, 1981, Diplome L'Honneur, 1990, Audelco nomination, 1990, Henry Hewes nomination, 1999, League N.Y. Theatres, N.Y.C., 1971-72, 73-74. Mem. League Profl. Theatre Tng.

Programs (steering com.), League Profl. Theatre Women (bd. dirs. 2001—, Designing Woman of Yr. 2004), Graphic Artists Guild, Soc. Scribes, Am. Soc. Interior Designers, United Scenic Artists Local 829; adv. com. The Costume Collection of Theatre Devel. Fund. Home and Office: 11 W 30th St 15th Fl New York NY 10001 E-mail: crobb10001@aol.com.

ROBBINS, DOROTHY ANN, foreign language educator; b. Little Rock, Mar. 17, 1947; d. W. E. and Ina (Spencer) Robbins. BA in Sociology, U. Ark., 1971; cert., U. Heidelberg, Germany, 1975; PhD, U. Frankfurt, Germany, 1981. Cert. state translator, Germany. Prof. Ctrl. Mo. State U., Warrensburg, 1999—. Author: (introduction) Collected Works of L. S. Vygotsky, 1999, Vygotsky's Psychology-Philosophy: A Metaphor for Language Theory and Learning, 2001, Voices within Vygotskian Non-Classical Psychology: Past, Present and Future, 2002, L.S. Vygotsky's and A.A. Leontiev's Russian Educational Semiotics and Psycholinguistics: Applications for Second Language Theory, 2003; editor: A.R. Luria and Contemporary Psychology, 2005; guest editor Jour. Russian and East European Psychology; contbr. articles to profl. jours. Fulbright-Hays Travel fellow to Russia, 1994, sr. level Fulbright fellow to Moscow, 1999. Mem. Internat. Vygotsky Soc. (exec. bd.), Luria Gesellschaft, Phi Beta Delta (campus pres. 1994-95). Avocations: travel to russia, russian language and literature, writing prose, trips to the sea, candlelight meals. Office: Ctrl Mo State U Martin 236 Warrensburg MO 64093 Business E-Mail: drobbins@cmsu1.cmsu.edu.

ROBBINS, ELLEN SUE, lawyer; b. Chgo., Mar. 15, 1967; d. Sheldon Neal and Barbara Lynn (Corenman) R. BS in Bus. Adminstrn. summa cum laude, U. Ill., 1988; JD magna cum laude, Harvard U., 1991. Bar: Ill. 1991. Jud. clk. to Judge Charles P. Kocoras U.S. Dist. Ct., Chgo., 1991-92; ptnr. Sidley & Austin, Chgo., 1999—. Adj. prof. law DePaul Coll. Law, Chgo. Mem. ABA, Chgo. Bar Assn. Avocations: jogging, golf, sports. Office: Sidley & Austin One South Dearborn Chicago IL 60603 Office Phone: 312-853-2931. E-mail: erobbins@sidley.com.*

ROBBINS, HULDA DORNBLATT, artist, printmaker; b. Atlanta, Oct. 19, 1910; d. Adolph Benno and Lina (Rosenthal) Domblatt. Student, Phila. Mus's. Sch. Indsl. Art, 1928-29, Prussian Acad., Berlin, 1929-31, Barnes Found., Merion, Pa., 1939. Poster designer and maker ITE Circuit Breaker Co. Inc., Phila., 1944; instr. serigraphy Nat. Serigraph Soc. Sch., N.Y.C., 1953-60; instr. creative painting Atlantic County Jewish Cmty. Ctrs., Margate, Atlantic City, NJ, 1960-67. Represented by William P. Carl, Fine Prints, Boston, Picture Store, Boston. One-woman shows include Lehigh U. Art Galleries, 1933, ACA Galleries, Phila., 1939, 8th St. Gallery, N.Y.C., 1941, Serigraph Gallery, 1947, Atlantic City Art Ctr., 1961, 1971, exhibited in group shows at 2d Nat. Print Ann. Bklyn. Mus., Carnegie Inst., Libr. of Congress, LaNapoule Art Found., Am. Graphic Contemporary Art, Represented in permanent collections Met. Mus. Art, N.Y.C., Mus. Modern Art, Biblioteque Nationale, Smithsonian Instn., Art Mus. Ont., Can., Victoria and Albert Mus., London, U.S. embassies abroad, Lehigh U., Princeton Print Club, 6 prints, Phila. Mus. Art. Recipient Purchase prize, Prints for Children, Mus. Modern Art, N.Y.C., 1941, prize, 2d Portrait Am. Competition, 1945, 2d prize, Paintings by Printmakers, 1948. Mem.: Serigraph Soc. (mem. founding group, charter sec., Ninth Ann. prize 1948, 1949), Graphics Soc., Print Club, Am. Color Print Soc. Home and Office: 16 S Buffalo Ave Ventnor City NJ 08406-2635 Office Phone: 609-823-7314.

ROBBINS, JANE BORSCH, library and information science professor; b. Chgo., Sept. 13, 1939; d. Reuben August and Pearl Irene (Houk) Borsch; married; 1 child, Molly Warren. BA, Wells Coll., 1961; MLS, Western Mich. U., 1966; PhD, U. Md., 1972. Asst. prof. library and info. sci. U. Pitts., 1972-73; assoc. prof. Emory U., Atlanta, 1973-74; cons. to bd. Wyo. State Libr., 1974-77; assoc. prof. La. State U., Baton Rouge, 1977-79; dean La. State U. Sch. Library and Info. Sci., 1979-81; prof., dir. Sch. Library and Info. Studies U. Wis., Madison, 1981-94; dean, prof. Fla. State U. Sch. Info. Studies, Tallahassee, 1994—. Author: Public Library Policy and Citizen Participation, 1975, Public Librarianship: A Reader, 1982, Are We There Yet?, 1988, Libraries: Partners in Adult Literacy, 1990, Keeping the Books: Public Library Financial Practices, 1992, Balancing the Books: Financing American Public Library Services, 1993, Evaluating Library Programs and Services: A Manual and Sourcebook, 1994, Tell It! The Complete Manual of Library Evaluation, 1996; editor Libr. and Info. Sci. Rsch., 1982-92; contbr. articles to profl. jours. Bd. dirs. Freedom to Read Found., 1997-99. Mem.: ALA (councilor 1976—80, 1991—95), Fla. Libr. Assn. (bd. dirs. 1997—99), Wis. Libr. Assn. (pres. 1986), Assn. for Libr. and Info. Sci. Edn. (dir. 1979—81, pres. 1984), Am. Soc. Info. Sci., Beta Phi Mu (exec. dir. 2000—04). Democrat. Episcopalian.

ROBBINS, JANE LEWIS, retired elementary school educator; b. New Iberia, La., Dec. 14, 1942; d. William Lewis and Maurine (James) Robbins. BS, U. Okla., 1965; ME, So. Meth. U., 1972; postgrad., Tex. Women's U., 1981, 83, 85; cert. in edn. adminstrn., Tex A&M U. Commerce, 1991. Tchr. Lone Grove Ind. Sch. Dist., Okla., 1964-65, Concord-Carlisle (Mass.) Regional Sch. Dist., 1966-67, Newton (Mass.) Pub. Schs., 1967-68, Highland Park Ind. Sch. Dist., Dallas, 1968—2000, instrnl. specialist, dist. appraiser, coord. dist. gifted and talented, coord. student tchrs., mentor new tchrs., coord. instrnl. leadership program, interim elem. prin., 1990-93; asst. prin. McCulloch Intermediate Sch., Dallas. Instr. reading clinic So. Meth. U., 1972-75, Sch. Edn., summer 1978, adj. prof. Div. Ednl. Studies; chmn. English dept. McCulloch Middle Sch.; regional coordinator Tex. Acad. Pentathlon, 1985-89. Hosting com. Goddard Ctr. Visual and Performing Arts; planning com. CSARA Found.; bd. dirs. Main St. Auth.; chair Gloria Ainsworth Day Care Ctr., 2006—; bd. trustees YWCA; bd. dirs. Greater S.W. Hist. Mus.; mem. bd. Oak Hill Episc. Sch. Mem. ASCD, Tex. Assn. Improvement Reading, Tex. Assn. Gifted and Talented, Assn. Children with Learning Disabilities, Internat. Reading Assn. (North Tex. Coun.), Tex. Elem. Prins. and Suprs. Assn. (Acad. III), Nat. Coun. Tchrs. of English, Tex. Mid. Sch. Assn., Mid. Sch. Consortium, Tex. Assn. Secondary Sch. Prins., Friends Chickasaw Regional Libr., Ardmore Holly Garden Club, Pi Beta Phi (v.p.), Delta Kappa Gamma, Tex. Ret. Tchrs. Assn. Republican. Episcopalian.

ROBBINS, JANET LINDA, language educator; b. LaJunta, Colo., Jan. 16, 1947; d. Richard Carl and Ruth Janet Robbins. B in Music Edn., Drake U., Des Moines, Iowa, 1969; BA, U. Minn., Mpls., 1974. Cert. life office mgmt. ins. cos., Iowa, 1970, tchg. music K-12, psychology 9-12 Iowa, 1969. Acctg. clerk Ctrl. Life Assurance Co., Des Moines, 1970; reader, tutor, intern Minn. State Svcs. for the Blind, St. Paul, 1973—74, 1975; tng. asst. psychology Mankato State U., Minn., 1974—75; intern mentally retarded St. Peter State Hosp., Minn., 1975; tchr. bi-lingual (Spanish and English) So. Minn., 1976; substitute tchr. pvt. students St. Louis Park Pub. Schs., Minn., 1977—81; care of aged and child care Okaloosa, Iowa, 1981—; instr. ESL Indian Hills C.C., Okaloosa, 1987—. Intern pvt. co., Washington, 1987; tchr. Sunday Sch. Presbyn. Friends, Meth. Chs.; owner Janet L. Robbins Bookkeeping and Ednl. Svcs., 1987—. Author: numerous newspaper articles and poetry. Vol. some Dem. Party campaigns; youth asst. 1st Bapt. Ch., Okaloosa, 1987—88. Recipient Vol. award, Gov. Iowa, 1993, 2000, Ten County Literacy Tutor award, IHCC, 2001. Mem.: Iowa Life Long Learning Assn., U. Minn. Alumni Assn., Drake U. Alumni Assn. Democrat. Methodist. Avocations: piano, writing, tutoring. Mailing: PO Box 576 Oskaloosa IA 52577

ROBBINS, LILLIAN CUKIER, psychology educator; b. Nancy, France, Sept. 6, 1933; came to U.S., 1943; BA, CCNY, 1954; MA, U. Ill., 1956; PhD, NYU, 1961. Cert. psychologist, N.Y. Research psychologist NYU Med. Ctr., 1962-67; asst. prof. Hunter Coll., N.Y.C., 1967-70, CCNY, 1970-71; assoc. prof. Rutgers U., Newark, 1971-76, prof., 1976—. Prin. investigator Citizen's Com. for Children, N.Y.C., 1973-75; dir. coll. honors program Rutgers U., Newark, 1980-97. Contbr. articles to profl. jours. Chair women's issues Am. Jewish Com., N.Y.C., 1984-86. Mem. AAAS (life), AAUP (exec. coun. 1980-2005), Am. Psychol. Assn., Phi Beta Kappa. Democrat. Jewish. Avocations: skiing, tennis, gardening, knitting, reading. Home: 49 E 96th St New York NY 10128-0782 Office Phone: 973-353-5440 x225.

ROBBINS, M. JOAN, mental health services professional, sexual addictions therapist; b. Phila., Oct. 2, 1935; d. James Blair and Elsie May Hickle; m. Harry D. Robbins, Oct. 6, 2000; children: Patricia McPhillips, Joseph Maguire. BA in Social Psychology, Fla. Atlantic U., 1995, MEd in Mental Health Counseling, 1998. Cert. counselor Nat. Bd. Cert. Counselors, 2000, juvenile sexual offender counselor Kent Sch. Social Work, Ky., sexual addiction therapist, corrective thinking practitioner. Youth worker Cathedrale St. Esprit, Istanbul, Turkey, 1990—91; crisis intervention Covenant Ho., NYC, 1991—92; counselor Corrections Corp. Am. Youth Tng. Ctr., Okeechobee, Fla., 1998—2000; therapist Vision Quest, Okeechobee, 2001—02; mental health counselor pvt. practice, Okeechobee, 2002—. Vol. AA Recovery Program Amerikan-Bristol Hosp., Instanbul, 1990—91; leader Girl Scouts Greater Phila., 1967—72; vol. ARC, Okeechobee, 2003—, Medical Res. Corps., Lee County, Fla., 2003—. Fellow: Nat. Soc. Advancement Sexual Health, Am. Mental Health Counseling Assn.; mem.: Nat. Assn. Addictions Profls. Avocation: amateur radio. Office Phone: 863-610-1396.

ROBBINS, MARY, concert pianist; b. Shelby, N.C., Feb. 14, 1950; d. Clyde Hugh and Hazel Marguerite (Lovett) Robbins; m. Carl Brockman, Jan. 16, 1983. Student, Converse Coll., Spartanburg, S.C., 1968-71; BMusic, U. Tex., 1973, MMusic, 1975, D Musical Arts, 1992. Concert coord. Austin (Tex.) Virtuosi, 1980-82; piano clinician Alfred Music Pub., Van Nuys, Cailf., 1991-94; pianist various chamber org., Austin, 1976-91; pvt. piano instr. for adults and children Austin, 1971—; tchg. asst., instr. piano U. Tex., Austin, 1971-75; founder, prin. pianist A. Mozart Fest, Austin, 1991—, artistic dir., 1991—; founder, prin. pianist A. Mozart Fest Kidskonzerts, Austin. Accompanist U. Tex., Austin, 1971-84; invited lectr. Mozart Internat. Bicentennial Congress, Salzburg, Austria, 1991. Composer music and cadenzas following Mozart's style for his piano concertos, 1989—; composer, performer CD, A. Mozart Fest, 1998, CD with Austrian pianist Paul Badura-Skoda, 2002, CD with pianist Anton Nel, 2005. Presenter, Music Tchr. Nat. Assoc. Conf., 2003. (Presenter of session on stylistic issues of interpretation in Mozart). Vol. music class tchr. First English Luth. Ch., Austin, 1992; founder combined groups Classical Music Consortium, Austin, 1997. Grantee Tex. Commn. on Arts, 1991, 93, City of Austin, 1992—. Mem. Austin Dist. Music Tchrs. Assn. (v.p. 1997-98, chair adult programs 1997—, chair festivals 1997-98, Pre-Coll. Tchr. of Yr. 1998), Mu Phi Epsilon. Lutheran. Avocations: cooking, entertaining, dance, outdoor sports, visual arts. Home: 2600 La Ronde St Austin TX 78731-5924

ROBBINS, NANCY SLINKER, volunteer; b. New Kensington, Pa., Jan. 28, 1923; d. Charles Morris and Nancy Grace (Moore) Slinker; m. James Bingham Murray, Aug. 1, 1946 (div. 1959); m. Daniel Harvey Robbins, Nov. 21, 1964; children: Nancy Caroline, Christina Chapman. BA, Westminster Coll., 1945; grad., U. Pitts., 1946. Cert. tchr., Pa. Tchr. Lower Burrell Sch., New Kensington, 1945-48; asst. buyer Gimbel's, Pitts., 1951-53, buyer, 1953-57, La Salle's, Toledo, 1957-61, Sibley's, Rochester, N.Y., 1961-66. Editor: Fan Fare, 1980-81. Pres. bd. Woman's Edn. and Indsl. Union, Rochester, 1973-76, Women's Coalition for Downtown, Rochester, 1982-84; pres. bd. Ronald McDonald House, Rochester, 1986-90, adminstr. grants program, 1996—2004; chmn. Pub. TV Auction, Rochester, 1980. Recipient Jefferson award Am. Inst. Pub. Svc., 1988, Forman Flair award for outstanding volunteerism, 1990, DeWitt Clinton award for pub. svc. Masons, 1989, Miracle Maker award Golisano Children's Hosp., 2005. Avocations: antiques, travel, cooking. Home: 35 Schoolhouse Ln Rochester NY 14618-3231 E-mail: nandan0035@aol.com.

ROBBINS, SUSAN PAULA, social work educator; b. Bklyn., Aug. 15, 1948; d. Harold Jess and Rose (Bernstein) R. AA, Manhattan C.C., 1972; BA summa cum laude, Hamline U., 1974; MSW, U. Minn., 1976; PhD, Tulane U., 1979. Adj. instr. dept. sociology and social work Augsburg Coll., Mpls., 1975-76; part-time instr. women's studies program U. Minn., Mpls., 1976; rsch. and grant cons. Seminole Tribe of Fla., Hollywood, 1978-79, child and adolescent caseworker, program planning cons., 1979-80; coord. criminal justice/corrections program St. Mary's Dominican Coll., New Orleans, 1979-80; asst. prof. social work New Orleans Consortium, 1978-80, U. Houston, 1980-86, assoc. prof., 1986—, assoc. dean acad. affairs, 1998-2000. Cons. ABA Multi Door Program, Houston, Cmty. Svc. Option Program, Houston; mediator Dispute Resolution Ctrs., Houston, 1982—; trainer Tex. Dept. Protective Svcs. Tng. Inst., 1995—. Author (with others): Encyclopedia of Social Work, Social Workers' Desk Reference; contbr. articles and book chpts. to profl. jours. Women's Club of Mpls. fellow, 1975, Nat. Inst. of Mental Health fellow, 1976-78; recipient Nat. Faculty Excellence award Univ. Continuing Edn. Assn., 1998. Mem. NASW, Coun. on Social Work Edn., Social Welfare Action Alliance, Assn. for Cmty. Orgn. and Social Adminstrn., So. Sociol. Soc., Phi Kappa Phi (sec. Houston chpt. 1984—). Democrat. Jewish. Office: Univ Houston 4800 Calhoun Rd Houston TX 77204-4013 Office Phone: 713-743-8103. Business E-Mail: srobbins@uh.edu.

ROBBINS-O'CONNELL, MINDY, special education educator, consultant; b. Uniontown, Pa., Apr. 24, 1978; d. Richard and Barbara Robbins; life ptnr. Carrie O'Connell, Aug. 5, 2005. BS, Ind. U. Pa., 2000; MBA, Averett U., Danville, Va., 2006. Cert. tchr. Va. Tchr. of deaf Norfolk Pub. Schs., Va., 2001—, tchr. of Va. students of learning after sch. program, 2001—04; ednl. cons. Conn. State Ednl. Resource Ctr., 2005—. Cons. diversity and leadership, Norfolk, 2005—; in-house diversity specialist Norfolk Pub. Schs., 2005—. Mem. Youth Crisis Network, Norfolk, Va., 2006—06. Avocations: music, travel.

ROBBINS-WILF, MARCIA, educational consultant; b. Newark, Mar. 22, 1949; d. Saul and Ruth (Fern) Robbins; 1 child, Orin. Student, Emerson Coll., 1967-69, Seton Hall U., 1969, Fairleigh Dickinson U., 1970; BA, George Washington U., 1971; MA, NYU, 1975; postgrad., St. Peter's Coll., Jersey City, 1979, Fordham U., 1980; MS, Yeshiva U., 1981, EdD, 1986; postgrad., Monmouth Coll., 1986. Cert. elem. tchr., N.Y., N.J., reading specialist, N.J., prin., supr., N.J., adminstr., supr., N.Y. Tchr. Sleepy Hollow Elem. Sch., Falls Church, Va., 1971-72, Yeshiva Konvitz, N.Y.C., 1972-73; intern Wee Folk Nursery Sch., Short Hills, NJ, 1978-81, dir. day camp, 1980-81, tchr., dir., owner, 1980-81; adj. prof. reading Seton Hall U., South Orange, NJ, 1987, Middlesex County Coll., Edison, NJ, 1987-88; asst. adj. prof. L.I. U., Bklyn., 1988, Pace U., N.Y.C., 1988—. Ednl. cons. Cranford High Sch., 1988; presenter numerous workshops; founding bd. dirs. Stern Coll. Women Yeshiva U., N.Y.C., 1987; adj. vis. lectr. Rutgers U., New Brunswick, N.J., 1988. Chairperson Jewish Book Festival, YM-YWHA, West Orange, N.J., 1986-87, mem. early childhood com., 1986—, bd. dirs., 1986—; vice chairperson dinner com. Nat. Leadership Conf. Christians and Jews, 1986; mem. Hadassah, Valerie Children's Fund, Women's League Conservative Judaism, City of Hope; assoc. bd. bus. and women's profl. divsn. United Jewish Appeal, 1979; vol. reader Goddard Riverside Day Care Ctr., N.Y.C., 1973; friend N.Y.C. Pub. Libr., 1980—; life friend Millburn (N.J.) Pub. Libr.; pres. Seton-Essex Reading Coun., 1991-94. Co-recipient Am. Heritage award, Essex County, 1985; recipient Award Appreciation City of Hope, 1984, Profl. Improvement awards Seton-Essex Reading Council, 1984-86, Cert. Attendance award Seton-Essex Reading Counci, 1987. Mem. N.Y. Acad. Scis. (life), N.J. Council Tchrs. English, Nat. Council Tchrs. English, Am. Ednl. Research Assn., Coll. Reading Assn. (life), Assn. Supervision and Curriculum Devel., N.Y. State Reading Assn. (council Manhattan), N.J. Reading Assn. (council Seton-Essex), Internat. Reading Assn., Nat. Assn. for Edn. of Young Children (life N.J. chpt., Kenyon group), Nat. Council Jewish Women (vice chairperson membership com. evening br. N.Y. sect. 1974-75), George Washington U. Alumni Club, Emerson Coll. Alumni Club, NYU Alumni Club, Phi Delta Kappa (life), Kappa Gamma Chi (historian). Clubs: Greenbrook Country (Caldwell, N.J.); George Washington Univ. Avocations: reading, theater. Home: 242 Hartshorn Dr Short Hills NJ 07078-1914 E-mail: dr.mrw349@aol.com.

ROBEK, MARY FRANCES, business education educator; b. Superior, Wis., Jan. 30, 1927; d. Stephen and Mary (Hervert) R. BE, U. Wis., 1948; MA, Northwestern U., 1951; MBA, U. Mich., 1962, PhD, 1967. Tchr. Bergland (Mich.) High Sch., 1948, Tony (Wis.) High Sch., 1948-50, Sch. Vocat. and Adult Edn., Superior, 1950-58; prof. bus. edn. and office tech. Ea. Mich. U., Ypsilanti, 1958-93; instr. Jazyckova Gymnasium, Banská, Stiavnica, Slovakia, 1994. Author: Information and Records Management, 1995. Assn. of Records Mgrs. and Adminstrs. fellow, 1992. Mem. Assn. Records Mgrs. and Adminstrs. (life), Inst. Cert. Mgrs. (pres. 1980-81, Emmett Leahy award 2000), Cath. Daus. Am., Delta Pi Epsilon, Delta Kappa Gamma, Pi Lambda Theta. Republican. Roman Catholic. Home: 515 Clough Ave Superior WI 54880 Personal E-mail: RobekMary@aol.com.

ROBEL, LAUREN, dean, law educator; b. Dec. 1953; BA, Auburn U., 1978; JD, Ind. U., 1983, postgrad., 1985. Bar: US Supreme Ct., Ind., Ill. Law clk. to Hon. Jesse Eschbach, U.S. Ct. Appeals (7th cir.), 1983—85; dean, Val Nolan prof. law Ind. U. Sch. Law, Bloomington. Vis. faculty U. Panthenon-Assas, Paris; reporter rules com. U.S. Dist. Ct. (so. dist.) Ind.; mem. rules com. Ind. Supreme Ct. Author: Les États des Noirs: Federalisme et question raciale aux États-unis, 2000, Federal Courts: Cases and Materials on Judicial Federalism and The Lawyering Process, 2005; contbr. articles to profl. jours. Mem.: Ind. State Bar Women (Law Recognition award), Ind. Bar Found. (Pro Bono Publico award), Order of Coif. Office: Ind Univ Sch Law 211 S Indiana Ave Bloomington IN 47405 Office Phone: 812-855-8885. Business E-Mail: lrobel@indiana.edu.

ROBELOT, JANE, anchor; b. Greenville, S.C., Oct. 9, 1960; married; 1 child. BA in Econs., Clemson U. News and sports dir., reporter WCCP-AM Radio, Clemson, SC; anchor, reporter WSPA-TV, CBS affiliate, Spartanburg, SC, 1983—90; gen. assignment reporter WCAU-TV, Phila., 1990—92, co-anchor 6:00 PM news, 1991—92, co-anchor 11:00 PM news, 1992—95; co-anchor CBS Morning News, N.Y.C., 1995; news reader This Morning CBS News, N.Y.C., 1995—96, co-anchor This Morning, 1996—99, co-anchor CBS Atlanta News, 1999—. Office: WGCL TV 46 Meredith Corp 425 14th St NW Atlanta GA 30318-7965

ROBERSON, DEBORAH LYNN, special education educator; b. Sharon, Pa., Sept. 24, 1954; d. James and Helen Kathryn Adair; m. Bobby Ray Roberson, Mar. 3, 1979; children: Manuel, Edward Lee, Bobby Ray, Michael Eugene. BSc in edn., Slippery Rock U., 1990; AA, Pa. State U., 1987; M in edn., Slippery Rock U., 1999. Spl. edn. tchr. Georgetown County Schools, SC, 1990—91; title I aide Sharon City Sch. Dist., Pa., 1991—92; headstart tchr., case mgr. Mercer County, Farrell, Pa., 1992—93; learning support tchr. Farrell Area Sch. Dist., Pa., 1993—99, elem. tchr., 1999—2000, learning support tchr., 2000—, 2001—. Mem. prin. adv. Farrell Sr. H.S., 2003—; mem. superintendent's adv. Farrell Sch. Dist., 2002—; spl. edn. contact Midwestern Intermed. Unit, 2002—. Bd. mem. Shenango Valley Cmty. Health Bd., Sharon, Pa., 2004—. Mem.: Pa. State Educators Assn., Farrell Educators Assn. Avocations: crafts, gardening, travel. Office: Farrell Area Sch Dist 1600 Roemer Blvd Farrell PA 16121

ROBERSON, DORIS JEAN HEROLD, retired social worker; b. N.Y.C., Oct. 15, 1924; d. Albert and Rosalind (Lowenstein) Herold; m. Lloyd Willis Roberson, Aug. 31, 1949; children: Lynn, Patricia, Katherine, Irene. BA cum laude, Mount Holyoke Coll., 1945; MSW, Fordham U., 1947. lic. master social worker, N.Y. Social worker Children's Aid Soc., N.Y.C., 1947-52, Yonkers (N.Y.) Pub. Schs., 1966-89; ret., 1989. Mem. NASW, Acad. Cert. Social Workers, N.Y. State Sch. Social Workers Assn., Phi Beta Kappa. Home: 145 Hoover Rd Yonkers NY 10710-3408

ROBERSON, JANET L., manufacturing executive; b. Rochester, N.Y., Oct. 4, 1955; d. Joseph Rollin and Patricia Jean Nightingale; m. Joe Frank Briseno, June 24, 1977 (div. Dec. 1979); 1 child, Bradley Christian; m. Kenneth Mark Roberson, Aug. 9, 1997; stepchildren: Brandon, Ashley. BS in Bus., LeTourneau U., Longview, Tex., 1993. Tech. writer Gen. Dynamics, Ft. Worth, 1979-82, tech. editor, 1982-84, sr. tech. editor, 1984-86; chief tech. data Lockheed Martin, Ft. Worth, 1986—. With USAF, 1976-78. Mem. Inst. Cert. Profl. Mgrs. (cert.), Nat. Mgmt. Assn. Republican. Roman Catholic. Avocations: painting, working out, reading. E-mail: jan.l.roberson@lmco.com.

ROBERSON, LINDA, lawyer; b. Omaha, July 15, 1947; d. Harlan Oliver and Elizabeth Aileen (Good) R.; m. Gary M. Young, Aug. 20, 1970; children: Elizabeth, Katherine, Christopher. BA, Oberlin Coll., 1969; MS, U. Wis., 1970, JD, 1974. Bar: Wis. 1974, U.S. Dist. Ct. (we. dist.) Wis. 1974. Legis. atty. Wis. Legis. Reference Bur., Madison, 1974-76, sr. legis. atty., 1976-78; assoc. Rikkers, Koritzinsky & Rikkers, Madison, 1978-79; ptnr. Koritzinsky, Neider, Langer & Roberson, Madison, 1979-85, Stolper, Koritzinsky, Brewster & Neider, Madison, 1985-93, Balisle & Roberson, Madison, 1993—. Adj. faculty U. Wis. Law Sch., Madison, 1977-2004. Co-author: Real Women, Real Lives, 1981, Wisconsin's Marital Property Reform Act, 1984, Understanding Wisconsin's Marital Property Law, 1985, A Guide to Property Classification Under Wisconsin's Marital Property Act, 1986, Workbook for Wisconsin Estate Planners, 2d edit., 1993, 5th edit., 2003, Look Before You Leap, 1996, Family Estate Planning in Wis., 1992, rev. edit. 2003, The Marital Property Classification Handbook, 1999. Chmn. elect Divorce Coop. Inst., 2004. Fellow: Am. Bar Found., Am. Acad. Matrimonial Lawyers (pres. Wis. chpt. 2001); mem.: ABA, Internat. Soc. Family Law, Nat. Assn. Elder Law Attys., Legal Assn. Women, Dane County Bar Assn., Wis. Bar Assn., Family Law Coun. of Cmty. Property States (del. 1996—, chair 2004). Office Phone: 608-259-8702. Business E-Mail: lr@b-rlaw.com.

ROBERSON, SUZANNE, librarian, researcher; d. Donald Charles and Joanne Roberson; m. James Richard Hobin, Sept. 21, 1986. BA, SUNY, Albany, 1977, MLS, 1985. Asst. libr. Albany Inst. History & Art, 1978-84; researcher U. Albany Librs., 1984-85; asst. libr. Capital Newspapers, Albany, 1985-87; dir. rsch. & records Emma Willard Sch., Troy, N.Y., 1988-94; cons. sr. rsch. analyst, 1994—. Researcher for William Kennedy N.Y. State Writers Inst., U. Albany, 1986—. Mem. Assn. Profl. Rschrs., N.Eng. Prospect Rsch. Assn. Home: 149 Manning Blvd Albany NY 12203-1739

ROBERSON-BROWN, LINDA MARIE, social studies educator; d. James Edward and Ethel Vera Roberson; m. Earl Belmont Brown, Oct. 10, 1918. BA in Child Devel., Spelman Coll., Atlanta, Ga., 1978. Cert. tchr. Ga., 1978. Tchr. Cobb County Sch. Sys., Marietta, Ga., 1980—. Presenter Kennesaw State U., Ga., 2003—. Events planner Mt. Pilgrim Dist. Congress of Christian Edn., Birmingham, Ala., 2004—06. Mem.: Cobb County Assn. of Educators (v.p. 1998—2004, com. chairperson 2005—06). Democrat. Baptist. Avocations: travel, reading, walking. Home: 875 Amber Pl NW Atlanta GA 30331 Office: Tapp Mid Sch 3900 Macedonia Rd Powder Springs GA 30127 Office Phone: 770-222-3758. E-mail: linda.robersonbrown@cobbk12.org.

ROBERT, ELLEN, university administrator; b. Jackson, Mich., May 24, 1944; d. Paul Jules and Beryl Ruth R.; m. Michael F. Winter, Sept. 6, 1970; children: Christopher Robert-Winter, Laurel Robert-Winter. BA, Western Mich. U., 1966, PhD, 1973. Faculty in sociology Kalamazoo (Mich.) Coll., 1969-70, U. Minn., Morris, 1973-80, faculty in women's studies Mpls., 1980-84; dir. advising San Francisco State U., 1984-91; dir. student learning ctr. U. Calif., Berkeley, 1991-94, dir. McNair scholars program, lectr. sociology Davis, 1995—. Bd. dirs. Davis Cmty. Meals, 1996-98. Mem. Sigma Zi. Democrat. Episcopal. Office: U Calif Davis Grad Studies One Shields Ave Davis CA 95616 E-mail: errobert@ucdavis.edu.

ROBERTS, ANGELA CHRISTINE, audiologist; b. Okinowa, Japan, June 27, 1977; d. John Alan Roberts and Teresa Ann Spagnoli; m. Faraz Khandwala, May 7, 2004; children: Alexandra Khandwala, Madeline Khandwala, Mason Khandwala, Laylah Khandwala, Kasim Feroz Khandwala. AA in Sign Lang., Am. River Coll., Sacramento, 2001; BS in Speech Pathology and Audiology, Calif. State U., Sacramento, 2003, MS in Audiology, 2005. Lic. profl. Speech-Language Pathology and Audiology Bd., 2006, cert. occupl. hearing conservationist Coun. Accreditation in Occupl. Hearing Conservation, 2005. Schools/indsl. program mgr. Agy. Hearing, Sacramento, 2001—06; audiologist Kaiser Permanente, Roseville, Calif., 2006—. Mgr., coord. health fair Agy. Hearing, Sacramento, 2001—06. Mem.: Am. Speech-

Lang.-Hearing Assn. Avocations: photography, art. Office: Kaiser Permanente 1600 Eureka Rd Roseville CA 95661 Personal E-mail: audiodoc14@netscape.net. Business E-Mail: angela.c.roberts@kp.org.

ROBERTS, ANNE MARGARET, secondary school educator; b. Auburn, Ind., Sept. 5, 1972; d. James Alfred and Rachel Sherwood Roberts. BA, Hanover Coll., 1995; MA in Fgn. Lang. and Lit., Purdue U., 2004. Cert. tchr. Ind., 1995, lic. real estate agt. Ind., 1998. U.S. history and French tchr. Sci. Acad., Mercedes, Tex., 1995—97; real estate agt., realtor Coldwell Banker Roth Wherly Graber, Auburn, Ind., 1998—99; French tchr. Eastside Jr./Sr. H.S., Butler, Ind., 2000—02; edn. specialist Ind. U., Purdue U., Fort Wayne, Ind., 2004—. Grantee Hanover Coll., 1994. Mem.: Am. Assn. Tchrs. French, Phi Mu (life; Alumnae Chair 1994—95). Avocations: travel, tennis, piano. Personal E-mail: anne_m_roberts@alumni.purdue.edu.

ROBERTS, BETTY JO, retired librarian, speech therapist; b. Ft. Worth, Tex., Nov. 11, 1927; d. Harry Pulliam and Mamie Josephine (Parker) Easton; m. Robert Lester Roberts, Jr.; children: Jo Lu, Lee Ann. Student, Tex. State Coll. Women, Denton, 1945-47, Tex. Wesleyan Coll.; BS, SW Tex. State U., 1952. Tchr. Milton H. Barry Sch. for Physical Rehab., Houston, United Cerebral Palsy Ctr., Ft. Worth, Tex., San Marcos Pub. Schs., Tex., 1952-53; supr. practice tchrs. S.W. Tex. State, 1952-53; tchr. Waco (Tex.) Ind. Schs., 1953-54; speech therapist Providence Crippled Children's Hosp., Waco; tchr. phonics, creative art Latin Am. Ctr., Waco, 1961-69; ch. librarian Trinity United Methodist Ch., Waco, 1979-88; ch. lib. Cen. United Methodist Ch., Waco, Tex., 1988-91. Compilor, Editor: Swedishes and More 1984. Democrat. Methodist. Address: 3248 Village Park Dr Waco TX 76708-1582

ROBERTS, CAROLYN JUNE, real estate broker; b. Reading, Mass., June 10, 1938; d. Frank Hiram and Blanche Laura (Robertson) Gifford; m. Roy Dale Roberts, Apr. 4, 1956; children: Kathleen, Charles, Cindy. BS in Microbiology, San Diego State U., 1973, MBA, 1982. Lic. med. tech.; real estate broker, Calif. Microbiologist Kaiser Permanent, San Diego, 1973-74; mgr. anesthesiology U. Calif., San Diego, 1975-81; dir. ambulatory care Merced (Calif.) Community Med. Ctr., 1983-84; mgr. medicine U. Calif., San Francisco, 1984-89, mgr. surgery San Diego, 1989-94. Pres. Acad. Bus. Officers San Francisco (Calif.) Gen. Hosp., 1986-87; chief adminstrv. Dept. Med. Univ. Utah, Salt Lake City. Co-author: (novels) The Forgotten Middle. Mem. Am. Assn. Med. Colls. on Bus. Affairs (program com. 1991-92), Soc. Rsch. Adminstrn. (western sect. pres. elect 1993-94), Sigma Iota Epsilon. Avocations: scuba diving, sailing, travel. Home: 3174 Central Ave Spring Valley CA 91977-2512

ROBERTS, CELIA ANN, librarian; b. Bangor, Maine, Feb. 6, 1935; d. William Lewis and Ruey Pearl (Logan) Roberts. AA, U. Hartford, 1957, BA, 1961; postgrad., So. Conn. State Coll., 1963—. With catalog, acquisition and circulation depts. U. Hartford Libr., 1956-65; libr. Simsbury Free Libr., Simsbury, Conn., 1965-69; reference libr. Simsbury Pub. Libr., 1969—. Tchr. ballet, 1965—66; tchr. genealogy, 1977—; ballet mistress Ballet Soc. Conn., Inc., 1968—70; with corps de ballet Conn. Opera Assn., 1963—64; active in prodns. Simsbury Light Opera Assn., 1964—69. Contbr. articles to profl. jours. Vol. Family History Ctr., 1970—. Mem.: DAR (Abigail Phelps chpt.), AAUW (past pres. Greater Hartford br.), ALA, Simsbury Hist. Soc., Conn. Libr. Assn., Denison Soc., Inc., Daus. of Scotia, Simsbury Geneal. and Hist. Rsch. Libr., Chateauguay Valley Hist. Soc., New Brunswick Geneal. Soc., Conn. Hist. Soc., Dance Masters Am. (Conn. Dance Tchrs. Club chpt.), Soc. Mayflower Descs. Conn., Conn. Soc. Genealogists (registrar Hartford 1983), Pro Dance, New Eng. Historic Geneal. Soc., Ont. Geneal. Soc. Unitarian Universalist. Office: Simsbury Public Libr 725 Hopmeadow St Simsbury CT 06070-2243 Business E-Mail: croberts@simsburylibrary.info.

ROBERTS, COKIE (CORINNE BOGGS ROBERTS), newscaster; b. New Orleans, Dec. 27, 1943; d. Thomas Hale and Corinne Morrison (Claiborne) Boggs; m. Steven V. Roberts, Sept. 10, 1966; children: Lee Harriss, Rebecca Boggs. BA in Polit. Sci., Wellesley Coll., 1964; degree (hon.), Amherst Coll., Columbia Coll., Loyola U. of the South, Manhattanville Coll., Gonzaga U., Boston Coll., Hood Coll., Chestnut Hill Coll., Miss. Women's U., Notre Dame U., Duke U. Assoc. prodr., host Altman Prodns., Washington, 1964—66, prodr. L.A., 1969—72; reporter, editor Cowles Comm., N.Y.C., 1967; prodr. Sta. WNEW-TV, N.Y.C., 1968, Sta. KNBC-TV, L.A., 1972—74; reporter CBS News, Athens, Greece, 1974—77; sr. news analyst. Nat. Pub. Radio, Washington, 1977—; corr. MacNeil/Lehrer Newshour, Washington, 1984—88; spl. Washington corr. ABC News, Washington, 1988—92; interviewer, commentator This Week With David Brinkley, Washington, 1992—96; co-anchor This Week with Sam Donaldson & Cokie Roberts, 1996—2002; chief congrl. analyst ABC News, 1998—; polit. commentator, analyst ABC News, World News Tonight and other ABC News broadcasts. Lectr. in field. Co-host weekly pub. TV program on Congress The Lawmakers, 1981—84, prodr., host pub. affairs program Sta. WRC-TV, Washington; prodr.: Sta. KNBC-TV Serendipity (award for excellence in local programming, Emmy nomination for children's programming); author: We Are Our Mother's Daughters, 1998, Founding Mothers: The Women Who Raised Our Nation, 2004; contbr. articles to newspapers, mags.; writer of a weekly column along with husband for newspapers around the country by United Media; contbg. editor (with husband): USA Magazine; co-author: From this Day Forward. Bd. dir. Presidential Commn. on Service and Civic Participation, Dirksen Ctr., Pekin, Ill., 1988—95, Fgn. Students Svc. Ctr., Washington, 1990—, Manhattanville Coll., Purchase, NY, 1991—99, Children's Inn at NIH, Bethesda, Md., 1992—. Named one of 50 Greatest Women in the History of Broadcasting, Am. Women in Radio and Television; named to Broadcasting Hall of Fame, Cable Hall of Fame; recipient Broadcast award, Nat. Orgn. Working Women, 1984, Distinguished Alumnae Achievement awards, Wellesley Coll., 1985, Everett McKinley Dirksen disting. reporting of Congress, 1987, Weintal award, Georgetown U., 1987, Corp. Pub. Broadcasting award, 1988, Edward R. Murrow award, Corp. Pub. Broadcasting, 1990, Broadcast award, Nat. Women's Polit. Caucus, 1990, David Brinkley Comm. award, 1991, Mother of Yr. award, Nat. Mother's Day Com., 1992, Emmy award news and documentary, 1991. Mem.: Radio-TV Corrs. Assn. (pres. 1981—82, bd. dirs. 1980—94), U.S. Capitol Hist. Soc. Roman Catholic. Mailing: 1717 DeSales St NW Washington DC 20036

ROBERTS, CRISTINA ABEJA, volunteer; BSLS, Escuela Nat. Bibliotec-conomia Archivonomia, Mexico, 1979; student, U. Americas, Mexico City, 1979—83. Head librarian ENEP/UNAM, 1982—88; office adminstr. Needle-point by D, 1993—94; office mgr. Lieberman Advt. Agy., 1994—96; librarian Perris HS, 1997—2000; libr. asst. El Centro Pub. Libr., Calif., 2000—02; freelance translator El Centro, 2002—. Paraeducator bilingual II Temescal Canyon HS, 1998—2000; presenter in field. Contbr. articles to profl. jours. Vol. Culver City Sr. Ctr., 1989—96, Culver City Friends of the Libr., 1994—, Culver City Sister City Com., Gio's Mobil Home Estates, 2005, AARP, 2001—; bd. dirs. Perris Valley Hispanic C. of C., 1997—2000. Named on Wall of Tolerance, Ala., 2001. Home: 1850 W Lincoln Ave Spc 120 El Centro CA 92243-1245

ROBERTS, DELLA, artist; b. Norfolk, Va., Feb. 13, 1929; d. Lee Clifford and Elsie Leone (Kothmann) Watkins; m. Edgar Parsons Roberts, Feb. 17, 1951; children: Edgar Parsons Jr., Clifford Kent, Glenn Adele. BA, Randolph Macon Womans Coll., 1950. Tchr. Sawtooth Ctr. Visual Design, Winston-Salem, N.C., 1952, 53, 76, 79, bd. dir.; conducted workshops Art Gallery Originals, Winston-Salem, 1980, 81, Guild of Charlotte Artists, 1980, Danville Mus. Fine Arts and History, Danville, Va., 1981. Artist: one woman shows including Randolph-Macon Women's Coll., Lynchburg, Va., 1977, Hammer Galleries, N.Y.C., 1978, Danville Mus. Fine Arts and History, 1980, Wilkes Gallery, 1981, Conacher Galleries, San Francisco, 1983, 85, 87, 89, 91, Sawtooth Ctr. Visual Design, Winston-Salem, 1987; featured artist (mags.) Pace mag., 1978, Charlotte mag., 1978, "G" mag., 1980, Southern World mag., 1981, Am. Artist mag., 1981, US Art mag., 1988, Southern Accents mag., 1981, (book) Southern Seasons, 1983, Women Artist, 1990. Recipient Pica award The Printing Industry of The Carolinas, Inc., 1984; named Artist of Yr. City Winston-Salem and Sawtooth Ctr. for Visual Design, 1986-87. Mem. Winston-Salem Associated Artists (bd. dir. 1972-74), Winston-Salem Arts Coun. (bd. dir., sec. 1967, 68), Art Gallery Originals (bd. dir. 1969—), Sawtooth Ctr. for Visual Design (bd. dir. 1988-2006). Avocations: gardening, tennis.

ROBERTS, DORIS, actress; b. St. Louis, Nov. 4, 1930; d. Larry and Ann (Meltzer) R.; m. Michael E. Cannata, June 21, 1950; 1 child, Michael R.; m. William Goyen, Nov. 10, 1963 (dec.). Student, NYU, 1950-51; studies with Sanford Meisner, Neighborhood Playhouse, N.Y.C., 1952-53, Lee Strasberg, Actors' Studio, 1956. Ind. stage, screen and TV actress, 1953—. Profl. stage debut, Ann Arbor, Mich., 1953; appeared in summer stock Chatham, Mass., 1955; Broadway debut in The Time of Your Life, 1955; other Broadway and off-Broadway appearances include The Desk Set, 1955, The American Dream, 1961, The Death of Bessie Smith, 1961, The Office, 1965, The Color of Darkness, 1963, Marathon 33, 1963, Secret Affair of Mildred Wilde, 1972, Last of the Red Hot Lovers, 1969-71, Bad Habits, 1973 (Outer Circle Critics award 1974), Cheaters, 1976, Fairie Tale Theatre, 1985, The Fig Tree, 1987, It's Only a Play, 1992, Bye Bye Birdie, 2004; movie debut Something Wild, 1961, film appearances include: Barefoot in the Park, 1968, No Way to Treat a Lady, 1973, A Lovely Way to Die, 1969, Honeymoon Killers, 1969, A New Leaf, 1970, Such Good Friends, 1971, Little Murders, 1971, Heartbreak Kid, 1972, Hester Street, 1975, The Taking of Pelham, One, Two, Three, 1974, The Rose, 1979, Good Luck, Miss Wyckoff, 1979, Rabbit Test, 1979, Ordinary Hero, 1986, #1 with a Bullet, 1987, For Better or for Worse-Street Law, 1988, National Lampoon's Xmas Vacation, 1989, Used People, 1992, The Night We Never Met, Momma Mia, 1994, Walking to Waldheim, 1995, The Grass Harp, 1995, A Fish in the Bathtub, 1997, My Giant, 1998, All Over the Guy, 2001, Dickie Roberts-Child Star, 2003, Lucky 13, I Can See You.Com, Grandma's Boy, 2005; TV debut on Studio One, 1958, Mary Hartman, Mary Hartman, 1975, Mary Tyler Moore Hour, 1976, Soap, 1978-79, Angie, 1979-80, Remington Steele, 1984-88, Lily Tomlin Comedy Hour, Barney Miller, Alice, Full House, Perfect Strangers, Sunday Dinner, A Family Man, The Fig Tree (PBS), 1987, (TV films) The Story Teller, 1979, Ruby and Oswald, 1978, It Happened One Christmas, 1978, Jennifer: A Woman's Story, 1979, The Diary of Anne Frank, 1982, A Letter to Three Wives, Blind Faith, 1989, A Mom For Christmas, 1990, The Sunset Gang, 1990, Crossroads, 1993, Dream On, 1993, The Boys, 1993, A Time To Heal, 1994, A Thousand Men and a Baby, 1997, One True Love, 2000, Sons of Miseltoe, 2001, A Time to Remember (Hallmark channel) 2003, Raising Waylon, (CBS) 2003, Lucky 13, 2004, (Hallmark channel) Our House, 2005, Grandma's Boy, 2005, Keeping Up With The Sterns, 2006; (TV series) include St. Elsewhere, 1982 (Emmy award best sup. actress drama) Murder She Wrote, 1990, Step By Step, 1994, Burk's Law, 1994, Walker Texas Ranger, 1995, High Society, 1996, Everybody Loves Raymond, 1996-05 (Amer. Comedy award, 1999, Emmy award outstanding supporting actress in a comedy series, 2001, 02, 03, 2005, Gracie Allen award, 2004). Recipient People's Choice award, 2006. Mem. SAG (Ensemble award 2002), AFTRA, Actors Equity Assn., Dirs. Guild Am.

ROBERTS, DOROTHY E., law educator; BA magna cum laude, Yale U., 1977; JD, Harvard U., 1980. Bar: NY 1981. Law clk. to Hon. Constance Baker Motley US Dist. Ct. (so. dist.) NY, 1980—81; assoc. Paul, Weiss, Rifkind, Wharton & Garrison, NYC, 1981—88; assoc. prof. Rutgers U. Sch. Law, Newark, 1988—94, prof., 1994—98; vis. prof. Northwestern U. Sch. Law, Chgo., 1997, prof., 1998—2001, Kirkland and Ellis prof., 2001—, faculty fellow Inst. for Policy Rsch., faculty affiliate Joint Ctr. for Poverty Rsch., 1998—. Vis. assoc. prof. U. Pa. Law Sch., 1994; fellow Program in Ethics and the Professions Harvard U., 1994—95; vis. prof. Stanford Law Sch., 1998; fulbright fellow Ctr. for Gender and Devel. Studies U. West Indies, Trinidad and Tobago, 2002—03. Author: A First Amendment Anthology, 1994, Constitutional Law Anthology, 1996, Killing the Black Body: Race, Reproduction, and the Meaning of Liberty, 1997, Shattered Bonds: The Color of Child Welfare, 2002; co-author: Frug's Women and The Law, 1998, Constitutional Law: Cases, History and Dialogues, 2000, First Amendment Law: Cases, Comparative Perspectives, and Dialogues, 2003; contbr. articles to profl. jours. Office: Northwestern U Sch Law 357 E Chicago Ave Chicago IL 60611 Office Phone: 312-503-0397. E-mail: d-roberts@law.northwestern.edu.

ROBERTS, ELIZABETH ANNE STEPHENS, educational consultant; b. Bklyn., Oct. 23, 1942; d. Edward Joseph and Mary Agnes (Donlon) Stephens; m. James Patrick Roberts, July 31, 1976; children: Sean Michael, Kerri Elizabeth Stephens. BA in Latin, Seat of Wisdom Coll., Litchfield, Conn., 1967; MA in English, CUNY, 1972; PhD in Adminstrn. and Supervision, L.I. U., 1976. Cert. tchr. Latin N.Y., tchr. English N.Y., sch. adminstrn. and supervision N.Y., sch. dist. adminstrn. N.Y. Tchr. Christ the King HS, Middle Village, NY, 1964—73, asst. prin., 1973—74; asst. prin., tchr. English Elwood (N.Y.) Sch. Dist., 1974—78; ednl. cons. Huntington, NY, 1978—87, 2002—; instr. English, adminstr. Touro Coll, Huntington, 1987—91; tchr. Latin South Huntington (N.Y.) Sch. Dist., 1990—2002, chairperson world langs. dept. grades 6-12, 1997—2002. Coord. student internat. travels South Huntington Schs., 1990—2002. Coord. parish-wide renew program Our Lady Queen Martyrs Ch., Centerport, 1987—90. Mem.: Fgn. Lang. Assn. Chairpersons and Suprs. (pres. 1997—2002), Classical Assn. N.Y. State, N.Y. State Assn. Fgn. Lang. Tchrs., Am. Classical League, Phi Delta Kappa (treas. 1990—). Avocations: travel, reading, crossword puzzles. Home: 24 Platt Pl Huntington NY 11743-3528 Personal E-mail: JSEKR@aol.com.

ROBERTS, ESTHER LOIS, lawyer, music educator, composer, writer; b. Rockwood, Tenn. d. Reva Gretchen (Crowder) H. BA in Biology, U. Tenn., Knoxville, BA in Botany, BM in Piano Lit./Pedagogy, MM in Piano Lit./Pedagogy, U. Tenn., Knoxville; JD, U. Tenn. Knoxville, 2001. Bar: Okla. 2000, Tenn. 2001. Patent atty. Dept. of Energy, Oak Ridge, Tenn., 2001—. Author: (children's book series) Sam the Horse, Sam Gets Ready for School, others, 1996; contbr. to Tenn. Law Review. Mem. ABA, Okla. Bar Assn., Tenn. Bar Assn., Am. Musicians Coll., Am. Indian Horse Registry, Nat. Soc. DAR, Scottish Clan Donnachaidh. Christian Scientist. Home and Office: 8216 Strawberry Plains Pike Knoxville TN 37924 E-mail: starlight.farm@worldnet.alt.net.

ROBERTS, EVELYN SMITH, elementary school educator; b. Lawrence, Kans., Dec. 3, 1948; d. Jerome Oak Jr. and Almeda Smith; children: David, Emily, Christopher. BS, U. Tulsa, 1972, MA, 1974, PhD candidate, 1993. Cert. tchr., supt., psychometrist, elem. educator, jr. high lang. arts educator, reading specialist, Okla. Asst. libr. German-Am. Jr.-Sr. High Sch., Nurnberg, Germany, 1972-73; clinician, diagnostician Mabee Reading Clinic, U. Tulsa, 1972-80; test adminstr. Stillwater Pub. Schs., Okla., 1976; reading, English, social studies tchr. Union Middle Sch., Tulsa, 1975-76, 77; reading specialist Roy Clark Elem. Sch., Tulsa, 1977-88; reading specialist, spl. svc. coord. Christa McAuliffe Elem. Sch., Tulsa, 1988—99; enrichment specialist Ct tchr. Moore Elem. Sch., 1996—. Nursery sec. Boston Ave. Meth. Ch., Tulsa, 1984—; accompianist for musical programs Clark & McAuliffe Elem. Schs., Tulsa, 1977-99. Finalist Okla. Tchr. of Yr., 1992-93; named Dist. Tchr. of Yr., 1991-92, Tchr. of Yr., 1991-92, 85-86, Dist. Tchr. of the Month, Union Pub. Schs., 1985. Mem. NEA, ASCD, Tulsa County Reading Coun. (exec bd., sec., v.p. 1980-86), Okla. Reading Coun., Internat. Reading Assn., Union Classroom Tchrs. Assn., Okla. Edn. Assn., Kappa Delta Pi, Phi Kappa Phi. Methodist. Avocations: reading, piano, travel. Office: Union Pub Schs 6515 S Garnett Rd Broken Arrow OK 74012-8529

ROBERTS, GLORIA JEAN, writer; b. Bklyn., Aug. 4, 1959; d. Albert Brown and Alma Julia Ruth Brooks; m. Floyd D. Roberts, Apr. 23, 1982; stepson: Charles Richard Roberts. Student, Ohio Art Inst, 1977-81. Author: The Stienhardt Memoirs, 1998, vol. 2, 2000, Maxx Mann Series, 1998; one-woman shows include C.W. Post Coll., Brookville, N.Y., 1997, exhibited in group shows at Harborsfield Gallery, Greenlawn, N.Y., 1999—2000, Ward-Nasse Gallery, N.Y.C., 2001—; composer: Love 'Em and Leave Em Behind, 2000, Thoughts of a X-Mas Long Ago, 2001; performer: (plays) Inspector Calls, 2004—05, A Christmas Carol, 2004—05. Mem. Minstrel Players of Northport; Sunday sch. tchr., vestry mem., lay reader, former choir mem. Trinity Ch. Democrat. Avocations: collecting teddy bears, photography, poetry, yoga, tennis. Home: 205 Duncan Elder Dr Greenlawn NY 11740-2429 Office Phone: 631-398-0302. Personal E-mail: gloria631TS@aol.com.

ROBERTS, HOLLY LYNN, artist; b. Boulder, Colo., Dec. 22, 1951; d. Harold Albert Roberts and Emma Jane (Holmes) Evangelos; m. Robert H. Wilson, Dec. 1, 1989; children: Ramey Wilson, Teal Wilson. Student, Bellas Artes de Mex., San Miguel de Allende, Mex., 1971, U. N.Mex., Quito, Ecuador, 1971-72; BA with spl. distinction, U. N.Mex., 1973; MFA, Ariz. State U., 1981. One woman shows include Roth Art Series, Hobbs, N.Mex., 1980, Harry Wood Gallery, Ariz. State U., Tempe, 1981, Etherton Gallery, Tucson, 1983, 85, 87, Linda Durham Contemporary Art Gallery, Santa Fe, 1986, 87, 89, 91, 95, Jayne H. Baum Gallery, N.Y.C., 1989, 91, Baker Gallery, Kansas City, 1990, Friends of Photography, San Francisco, 1990, Etherton-Stern Gallery, N.Y.C., 1991, 95, Benteler-Morgan Gallery, Houston, 1991, Gallery 210, U. Mo., St. Louis, 1992, Ehlers/Caudill Gallery, Chgo., 1992, 95, Ctr. Photographic Art, Carmel, Calif., 1993, Robert Koch Gallery, San Francisco, 1994, others; group exhbns. include Hunterdon Art Ctr., Clinton, N.J., 1978, U. N.Mex. Art Mus., Albuquerque, 1979, 83, Am. Consulate Gen., Hermosillo, Mex., 1982, Phoenix Art Mus., 1982, 83, 84, Houston Ctr. for Photography, 1983, Robert Freidus Gallery, N.Y.C., 1984, Santa Fe Ctr. for Photography, 1984, John Michael Kohler Arts Ctr., Sheboygan, Wis., 1984, 89, Laurence Miller Gallery, N.Y.C., 1984, Ctr. for Contemporary Arts, Santa Fe, 1985, Mus. Fine Arts, Santa Fe, 1985, 86, 94, Robert Koch Gallery, San Francisco, 1986, Mus. Photographic Art, San Diego, 1987, Mus. Contemporary Photography, Chgo., 1988, Blue Sky Gallery, Portland, Oreg., 1989, Graham Modern, N.Y.C., 1990, Palm Springs (Calif.) Desert Mus., 1990, Pratt-Manhattan Gallery, N.Y.C., 1991, Art Inst. Chgo., 1991. L.A. County Art Mus., 1992, The Light Factory, Charlotte, N.C., 1993, Spectrum Gallery, Rochester, N.Y., 1995, U. Galleries, Coll. Fine Arts, U. Fla., Gainesville, 1996, Atrium Gallery, Sch. Fine Arts, U. Conn., Storrs, 1996, Soros Ctr. Contemporary Art, Kyiv, Ukraine, 1996; represented in permanent collections Mus. Photographic Art, San Diego, Phoenix Mus. Art, Prudential Ins., Ctr. for Creative Photography, Tuscon, San Francisco Mus. Modern Art, Mus. Fine Arts, Santa Fe, Mus. Fine Arts, Houston, Albuquerque Mus. Art, Monterey (Calif.) Peninsula Mus. Art, Calif. Mus. Photography, Riverside, L.A. Mus. Contemporary Art, Art Inst. Chgo., Green Libr. Stanford U., others. Ferguson grantee Friends of Photography, 1986, grantee Nat. Endowment for Arts, 1986, 88.

ROBERTS, JANET LYNN LEKOWSKI, science educator; b. El Paso, Tex., Apr. 17, 1958; d. Joseph Charles and Doris (Stahlhut Lekowski; m. David Carroll Roberts, Dec. 23, 1988. BA in Journalism, U. Tex., El Paso, 1980, MEd in Sci. Edn., 1984. Cert. elem. Biology tchr., Life-Earth Sci. tchr., Tex.; cert. ESL, Tex. Edn. Agy., 1999. Elem. tchr. Ysleta Ind. Sch. Dist., El Paso, 1983-88, mid. sch. tchr., 1988-89; ESL tchr., 1999—2006, Arizona Fleming Elem. Sch., Houston, 2006—. Faculty rep. PTA, El Paso, 1987-88. Recipient Rudy Telles scholarship U. Tex. Sch. Journalism, 1979, grant Advt. Fed., 1980, named Outstanding Grad. Student, 1985. Mem. Assn. Tex. Profl. Educators (sec. 1988-89, del. 1988, faculty rep. 1984-88)Eastwood Knolls (campus communication com. 1988-89), Tierra del Sol (campus communication com. 1986-87). Republican. Avocations: photography, aerobics, physical fitness. Office: Arizona Fleming Elem Sch 14850 Bissonnet Houston TX 77083

ROBERTS, JEANNE ADDISON, retired literature educator; b. Washington; d. John West and Sue Fisher (Nichols) Addison; m. Markley Roberts, Feb. 19, 1966; children: Addison Cary Steed Masengill, Ellen Carraway Masengill Coster. AB, Agnes Scott Coll., 1946; MA, U. Pa., 1947; PhD, U. Va., 1964. Instr. Mary Washington Coll., 1947-48; instr., chmn. English Fairfax Hall Jr. Coll., 1950-51; tchr. Am. U. Assn. Lang. Center, Bangkok, Thailand, 1952-56; instr. Beirut (Lebanon) Coll. for Women, 1956-57, asst. prof., 1957-60, chmn. English dept., 1957-60; instr. lit. Am. U., Washington, 1960-62, asst. prof., 1962-65, asso. prof., 1965-68, prof., 1968-93. Dean faculties Am. U., 1974; lectr. Howard U., 1971-72; seminar prof. Folger Shakespeare Libr. Inst. for Renaissance and 18th Century Studies, 1974; dir. NEH Summer Inst. for HS Tchrs. on Teaching Shakespeare, Folger Shakespeare Libr., 1984-86; dir. NEH summer inst. Va. Commonwealth U. 1995-96 Writings By and About Women in The English Renaissance; study group leader Inst. Learning in Retirement, Am. U., 1999-, mem. study groups. Author: Shakespeare's English Comedy: The Merry Wives of Windsor in Context, 1979, The Shakespearean Wild: Geography, Genus and Gender, 1991; editor: (with James G. McManaway) A Selective Bibliography of Shakespeare: Editions, Textual Studies, Commentary, 1975; (with Peggy O'Brien) Shakespeare Set Free, vol. 1, 1993, vol. 2, 1994, vol. 3, 1995, (with Georgianna Ziegler) Shakespeare's Unruly Women, 1997; contbr. articles to profl. jours. and scholarly collections. Danforth Tchr. grantee, 1962—63, Folger Sr. fellow, 1969—70, 1988. Mem. MLA (chmn. Shakespeare div. 1981-82), Renaissance Soc. Am., Milton Soc., Shakespeare Assn. Am. (trustee 1978-81, 87-89, pres. 1986-87), AAUP (pres. Am. U. chpt. 1966-67), Southeastern Renaissance Conf. (pres. 1981-82), English Speaking Union (bd. dirs. 2005-06), Phi Beta Kappa, Mortar Board, Phi Kappa Phi. Episcopalian. Home: 4931 Albemarle St NW Washington DC 20016-4359 Personal E-mail: jeannerobe@aol.com.

ROBERTS, JO ANN WOODEN, school system administrator; b. Chgo., June 24, 1948; d. Tilmon and Annie Mae (Wardlaw) Wooden; m. Edward Allen Roberts Sr. (div.); children: Edward Allen Jr., Hillary Ann. BS, Wayne State U., 1970, MS, 1971; PhD, Northwestern U., 1977. Speech, lang. pathologist Chgo. Bd. Edn., 1971—78, adminstr., 1987—88; project dir. Ednl. Testing Svc., Evanston, Ill., 1976—77; instr. Chgo City C.C., 1976—77; exec. dir. Nat. Speech Lang. and Hearing Assn., Chgo., 1984—86; dir. spl. svcs. Rock Island (Ill.) Pub. Schs., 1988—90; supt. Muskegon Hts. (Mich.) Pub. Schs., 1990—93; dep. supr. Chgo. Pub. Schs., 1993—96; supt. of schs. Hazel Crest (Ill.) Sch. Dist. #152 1/2, 1996—98; cons. Chgo. Pub. Schs., 1998—2000, dep. accountability svcs., 1999—, InterVention officer, 2000—01, chief troubleshooter, 2001—. Hon. guest lectr. Gov.'s State U., U. Pk., Ill., 1983—86; cons. in field. Author: Learning to Talk, 1974. Trustee Muskegon County Libr. Bd., 1990, Mercy Hosp. Bd., Muskegon, 1990, St. Mark's Sch. Bd. Dirs., Southborough, Mass., 1989, United Way Bd., Muskegon, 1990; mem. Mich. State Bd. Edn. Systematic Initiative in Math and Sci., 1991, Gov. John Engler Mich. 2000 Task Force, 1991, Chpt. II Adv. Commn., 1991. Recipient Leadership award Boy Scouts Am., 1990; named finalist Outstanding Young Working Women, Glamour Mag., 1984, Outstanding Educator, Blacks in Govt., 1990. Mem. Am. Assn. Sch. Adminstrs., Nat. Alliance Black Sch. Educators, Mich. Assn. Sch. Adminstrs., Assn. Supervision & Curriculum Devel., Phi Delta Kappa. Avocations: creative writing, peotry, modern dance, theater, drawing. Address: Chgo Pub Schs 125 S Clark St Chicago IL 60603-5200

ROBERTS, JOAN ILA, psychologist, educator; b. Salt Lake City, June 26, 1935; d. Wallace Bryan and Ila Nelson Roberts. BS, U. Utah, Salt Lake City, 1957; MA, Columbia U., N.Y.C., 1960, EdD, 1970. Cert. tchr. Utah, 1957. Asst. prof. Dept. Ednl. Policy Studies U. Wis., Madison, Wis., 1968—75; from assoc. prof. in social scis. to prof. emerita SUNY, Syracuse, NY, 1976—94, prof. emerita, 1994—. Coord. Wis. Coordinating Coun. of Women in Higher Edn., 1971—78; project dir. Model Caregivers Tng. Project N.Y. State Dept. Social Svcs., 1981; vis. prof. Women's Studies Program U. Utah, Salt Lake City, 1988; v.p. Ctr. for a Human Future, Syracuse, 1977—, bd. dirs.; spkr. in field. Co-author (with S. Akinsanya): Schooling in the Cultural Context: Anthropological Studies of Education, Vol. II, 1975, Educational Patterns and Cultural Configurations: The Anthropology of Education, Vol. I, 1976; co-author: (with T. Group) Feminism and Nursing: An Historical Perspective on Power, Status, and Political Activism in the Nursing Profession, 1994, Nursing, Physician Control, and the Medical Monopoly: Historical Perspective on Gendered Inequality in Roles, Relationships, Rights, and Range of Practice, 2001; contbr. articles to profl. jours. Co-pres. Seneca Falls (Utah) Nat. Women's Ctr. and Ednl. Inst., 1983—; mem. com. on family violence and incest Nat. Women's Health Network, 1981—83; mem. com. on bibliographic rsch. Coun. on Anthropology and Edn., 1975—78. Mem.:

AAUW, NOW (mem. task force on edn. 1973—75, del. White House Conf. 1980, mem. search com. N.Y. chpt. 1980, bd. dirs. N.Y. chpt. 1980, Woman of Courage award 1978), Nat. Women's Studies Assn. (mem. nat. task force def. of women tchg. women's studies courses 1981—82), Am. Psychol. Assn., Am. Anthrop. Assn., U. Women's Club, London. Home: 7307 E Rose Lane Scottsdale AZ 85250

ROBERTS, JUDITH MARIE, librarian, educator; b. Bluefield, W.Va., Aug. 5, 1939; d. Charles Bowen Lowder and Frances Marie (Bourne) Lowder Alberts; m. Craig Currence Johnson, July 1, 1957 (div. 1962); 1 child, Craig Jr.; m. Milton Rinehart Roberts, Aug. 13, 1966 (div. 1987). BS, Concord State Tchrs. Coll., 1965. Libr. Cape Henlopen Sch. Dist., Lewes, Del., 1965—91; with Lily's Gift Shop, St. Petersburg, Fla., 1991—. Pres. Friends of Lewes Pub. Libr., 1986—90; chmn. exhibits Govs. Conf. Librs. and Info. Svcs., Dover, Del., 1978; mem. Gov.'s State Libr. Adv. Coun., 1987—91. Mem.: NEA, ALA, Del. Learning Resources Assn. (pres. 1976—77), Del. Library Assn. (pres. 1982—83), Sussex Help Orgn. for Resources Exch. (pres. 1984—85), Del. State Edn. Assn. Methodist. Office Phone: 727-867-7974. Business E-Mail: judyoffice2003@yahoo.com.

ROBERTS, JULIA FIONA, actress; b. Smyrna, Ga., Oct. 28, 1967; d. Betty and Walter Roberts; m. Lyle Lovett, Jun. 25, 1993 (div. March 22, 1995); m. Daniel Moder, July 4, 2002; children Hazel Patricia, Phinnaeus Walter. Actress (films) Blood Red, 1986, Satisfaction, 1987, Mystic Pizza, 1988, Steel Magnolias, 1989 (Acad. Award nominee, Golden Globe award), Pretty Woman, 1990 (Acad. Award nominee, Golden Globe Award), Flatliners, 1990, Sleeping With the Enemy, 1991, Hook, 1991, Dying Young, 1991, The Player, 1992, The Pelican Brief, 1993, I Love Trouble, 1994, Ready to Wear (Prêt-à-Porter), 1994, Something To Talk About, 1995, Mary Reilly, 1996, Everybody Says I Love You, 1996, Michael Collins, 1996, My Best Friend's Wedding, 1997, Conspiracy Theory, 1997, Stepmom, 1998 (also exec. prodr.), Notting Hill, 1999, Runaway Bride, 1999, Erin Brockovich, 2000 (Acad. award for Best Actress, Golden Globe for Best Performance by an Actress), The Mexican, 2001, America's Sweethearts, 2001, Ocean's Eleven, 2001, Full Frontal, 2002, Confessions of a Dangerous Mind, 2002, Mona Lisa Smile, 2003, Closer, 2004, Ocean's Twelve, 2004, (voice) The Ant Bully, 2006; (TV movies) Baja Oklahoma, 1988, Before Your Eyes: Angelie's Secret (voice only), 1995; (TV appearances) Crime Story, 1987, Miami Vice, 1988, Friends, 1996, Murphy Brown, 1998, Sesame Street, 1998, AFI's 100 Years.100 Movies, 1998, In the Wild, 1998, Law & Order, 1999; Broadway plays include Three Days of Rain, 2006. Involved with UNICEF; lent celebrity name to help raise money for research to develop a cure for Rett Syndrome. Named Female Star of the Yr., Nat. Assn. Theatre Owners, 1991; recipient People's Choice awards Favorite Motion Picture Actress, 1991, 98, Favorite Comedy/Dramatic Motion Picture Actress, 1992, Favorite Dramatic Motion Picture Actres, 1994; recipient Woman of Yr. award Hasty Pudding Theatricals, 1997, Spl. award Internat. Star of Yr., ShoWest Conv., 1998; named one of '50 Most Beautiful People in the World, People Mag., 1990, 1991, '50 Most Beautiful List', People Mag.(USA), 2000, 2002, '25 Most Intriguing People, People Mag., 2001, Top Entertainers, E!, 2001.; named one of 50 Most Powerful People in Hollywood Premiere mag., 2002-06. One of the most popular and sought-after talents in Hollywood; highest paid actress in film history. Office: c/o Kevin Huvane Creative Artists Agency 9830 Wilshire Blvd Beverly Hills CA 90212-1825*

ROBERTS, KARLENE ANN, education educator; b. San Francisco, June 12, 1937; d. Carl Joachim and Doris Elizabeth (Hosman) Hahn; m. Sept. 7, 1963 (div. June 1981); 1 child, Donald Brett. BA, Stanford U., 1959; PhD, U. Calif., Berkeley, 1967. Rsch. assoc. Stanford (Calif.) U., 1967-69; lectr. U. Calif., Berkeley, 1967-70, asst. prof., 1970-73, assoc. prof., 1973-78, prof., 1978—. Cons. in field; reviewer in field. Mem. editorial bd. Acad. Mgmt. Jour., 1976-81, Jour. of Applied Psychology, 1977-87, Jour. of Vocat. Behavior, 1974-76, Orgnl. Behavior and Human Decision Processes, 1978-87, Calif. Mgmt. Rev., 1981-88, Acad. Mgmt. Exec., 1987; author: Comparative Studies in Organizational Behavior, 1972, Communication in Organizations, 1977, Toward an Interdisciplinary Science of Organizations, 1978, New Directions in Methodology: Aggregation Issues in Organizational Science, 1980, Organizational Behavior, 1991, New Challenges to Understanding Orgns., 1993.

ROBERTS, KATHARINE ADAIR, retired bookkeeper; b. Columbus, Ga., June 4, 1930; d. William Lynn and Ella Miller (Adair) R. BA, U. Redlands, 1955; postgrad., San Bernardino Valley Coll., 1971—74, Calif. State U., San Bernardino, 1975—78. Bookkeeper Rettig Machine Shop, Inc., Redlands, Calif., 1970-97, ret., 1997. Pres. Dem. Study Club, San Bernardino, 1967-68, Redlands Dem. Club, 1976, Wilsonian Club, San Bernardino, 1986; chair Redlands/San Bernardino chpt. Citizens for Global Solutions, 1987—, San Bernardino leader ptnrs. for global change program; active San Bernardino County Dem. Ctrl. Com., treas. 1977-80. Named one of 63 Women of Distinction, 63rd Assembly Dist., Calif., Assemblyman Bill Emmerson, 2005; recipient Citizen Achievement award, LWV, 1989. Mem. Dem. Luncheon Club (George E. Brown Amb. of Peace award 2000), Humane Soc. of San Bernardino Valley, Redlands Humane Soc., Redlands Dem. Club (treas.), LWV, Inland Empire Debating Soc. (treas.). Democrat. Home: 798 W 18th St San Bernardino CA 92405-4235

ROBERTS, KATHLEEN ANNE, lawyer, former federal judge; b. LA, Oct. 2, 1945; BA in English summa cum laude, U. Mass., Boston, 1971; PhD program in English Lit., Yale U., 1971-72, JD, 1977. Bar: N.Y. 1979, U.S. Dist. Ct. (so. and ea. dists.) N.Y. 1979, U.S. Ct. Appeals (2d cir.). Rsch. dir. Conn. Citizen Rsch. Group, 1972-73; investigator, monitor, evaluator grants, cons. Fund for City of N.Y., 1973-77; law clk. U.S. Dist. Ct. (so. dist.) N.Y., 1977-79; asst. U.S. atty. criminal div. So. Dist. N.Y., N.Y.C., 1979-83, asst. U.S. atty. civil div., 1983-85, U.S. magistrate, 1985-95; ADR neutral and dir. profl. svcs. JAMS/Endispute, N.Y.C., 1995—. Law clk. San Francisco Neighborhood Legal Assistance Found., summer 1975, U.S. Attys. Office, So. Dist. N.Y., criminal div., summer 1976; adj. prof. law, trial advocacy instr. Bklyn. Law Sch., 1983—. Mem.: NY County Lawyers' Assn.

ROBERTS, KATHLEEN JOY DOTY, secondary school educator; b. Jamaica, NY, Apr. 19, 1951; d. Alfred Arthur and Helen Caroline (Sohl) Doty; m. Robert Louis Roberts, Nov. 24, 1974; children: Robert Louis, Michael Sean, Kathleen Meagan. BA in Edn., CUNY, 1972, MS in Spl. Edn., 1974; cert. advanced study in ednl. adminstrn., Hofstra U., 1982; Ednl. Specialist, Nova Southeastern U., 2003, PhD Computing Tech. in Edn., 2004. Cert. sch. adminstrn., tchr. math., N.Y.; cert. N.Y. Dept. Mental Hygiene; lic. spl. edn. supr., ednl. adminstr., N.Y. Tchr. health conservation Woodside (N.Y.) Jr. H.S., 1973-77; coord. spl. edn. dept. Ridgewood (N.Y.) Jr. H.S., 1977-81; adminstrv. asst., health, compliance and mainstream coord., grant writer Grover Cleveland H.S., Ridgewood, 1981—2004, also coord. transition linkage, resource tchr. mentor, 1981—2004; tech. staff developer Region 4, N.Y.C. Dept. Edn., 2004—06; collaborative team tchr. Queens H.S. for Tchg., 2006—. Instr. Grad. Sch. U. Phoenix. Author: Closed Circuit TV and Other Devices for the Partially Sighted, 1971, Nat. Soc. Colonial Daughters of the Seventeenth Century Lineage Book (Centennial Remembrance edit.), 1999; contbr. articles to profl. jours. Legis. chmn. Fairfield Jr. and Sr. H.S. PTA and Massapequa coun., 1987-92. Mem.: ACM, DAR, NEA, Internat. Soc. Tech. in Edn., N.Y. State Tchrs. Assn., Colonial Dames of the XVII Century, Colonial Daus. of the XVII Century (pres. 1985—91, nat. chmn. hist. activities com. 1988—91, registrar, historian Founders chpt. 1991—94, nat. councillor, publicity chmn. 1991—94, centennial com. 1994—96, registrar gen. nat. soc. 1997—2000, pres. 2000—), Pilgrim Edward Doty Soc. Republican. Home: 52 Hicksville Rd Massapequa NY 11758-5843 Office: NYC Dept Edn Region 4 Queens Plaza N Long Island City NY 11101 Business E-Mail: drkathyroberts@yahoo.com.

ROBERTS, KATHLEEN MARY, retired school system administrator; b. Syracuse, NY, Apr. 15, 1947; d. Casimer and Lorrayne Arletta (Molloy) Piegdon; m. James C. Roberts, June 29, 1968 (div. Sept. 1988). BA, Cen. State U., Edmond, Okla., 1968, MEd, 1971; PhD, U. Okla., 1977. Cert. tchr., prin., supt., Okla.; cert. supt., N.Y. Tchr. Putnam City Schs., Oklahoma City, 1960-72; reading specialist Moore (Okla.) Pub. Schs., 1973-74, Crooked Oak Pub. Schs., Oklahoma City, 1974-77, 1990-95; rsch. assoc. Oklahoma City Pub. Schs., 1977-80; supt. Okla. Dept. Corrections, Oklahoma City, 1980-86, Healdton (Okla.) Pub. Schs., 1986-90; supr. Crooked Oak Schs., Oklahoma City, 1990—95; supt. Piedmont (Okla.) Pub. Schs., 1995-98, ret., 1998; registered fin. advisor McDonald & Assocs., 1998—. Contbr. articles to profl. publs. Bd. dirs. United Meth. Prism Ministry, Oklahoma City, 1986—, Children's Shelter, Ardmore, Okla., 1989-90; mem. State Vocat. Edn. Coun., Oklahoma City, 1980-85. Recipient citation Okla. State Senate, 1986. Mem. ASCD, Internat. Reading Assn., Am. Assn. Sch. Adminstrs., Okla. Assn. Sch. Adminstrs., Piedmont C. of C. (v.p. 1997—), Phi Delta Kappa, Alpha Chi, Kappa Delta Phi. Democrat. Roman Catholic. Avocations: furniture refinishing, reading, gardening.

ROBERTS, KATHY DESMOND, executive director educational facility; b. Washington, Mar. 24, 1953; d. James Michael and Jean Langrish Desmond; m. John D. Roberts, Aug. 5, 1989; children: John, Kyle, Jenny; stepchildren: Jason, Jesse, Tatum. BA, Coll. New Rochelle, 1981; student, Tchrs. Coll. Columbia. Rsch. asst., 1982-83; founder, pres. Am. Inst. Neuro-Integrative Devel., Fairfield, Conn., 1982—; founder, exec. dir. Giant Steps Sch., Fairfield, Conn., 1992—. Bd. dirs. Autism Soc. Conn.; tissue resource com. Autism Rsch. Found., Boston, 1996—; adv. bd. Autism Soc. Am. Found., 1997—; founder Fairfield County Autism Soc., Conn., 1989. E-mail: SASCO54@aol.com.

ROBERTS, LIA, investor, political organization worker; b. Bucharest, Romania, 1949; arrived in U.S., 1979, naturalized, 1982; married; 1 child. Degree in Geology and Geotechnical Engring., U. Bucharest. Prin., owner, Las Vegas, 1979—93; pvt. investor, 1993—; chmn. Nev. Rep. Party, Las Vegas, 2003—. Mailing: Nevada Republicatn Party Chmn 8625 W Sahara Ave Las Vegas NV 89117

ROBERTS, LISA DAWN, elementary school educator; d. Jamie D. and Mary D. Roberts. BS in Early Childhood and Elem. Edn., Auburn U., Montgomery, Ala., 1996. 4th grade tchr. Millbrook Mid./Jr. H.S., Ala., 1996—. Office: Millbrook Mid/Jr High Sch 4228 Chapman Rd Millbrook AL 36092 Office Phone: 334-285-2100.

ROBERTS, LOUISE NISBET, philosopher, educator; b. Lexington, Ky., Apr. 21, 1919; d. Benjamin and Helen L. Nisbet; m. Warren Roberts, June 14, 1952 (dec.); children: Helen Ward Roberts Hill, Valeria Lamar Roberts Emmett. AB, U. Ky., 1942, MA, 1944; PhD, Columbia U., 1952. Instr. philosophy Fairfax Hall, Waynesboro, Va., 1943—44, Fairmount Casements, Ormond Beach, Fla., 1944—45; mem. faculty Newcomb Coll., Tulane U., 1948—, prof. philosophy, 1969—85, dept. head, prof. emeritus, 1985—. Contbr. articles to profl. jours. Univ. scholar, 1945-46. Mem. AAUW (fellow 1947-48, pres. New Orleans chpt. 1986-88), DAR (vice regent New Orleans chpt. 1987-90, 2002-03), So. Soc. Philosophy and Psychology, Phi Beta Kappa (chpt. pres. 1956-57), Delta Delta Delta (fellow 1946-47). Democrat. Episcopalian. Office: Tulane U Dept Philosophy New Orleans LA 70118

ROBERTS, LYNNE JEANINE, physician; b. St. Louis, Apr. 19, 1952; d. H. Clarke and Dorothy June (Cockrum) R.; m. Richard Allen Beadle Jr., July 18, 1981; 2 children. BA with distinction, Ind. U., Bloomington, 1974; MD, Ind. U., 1978. Diplomate Am. Bd. Dermatology, Am. Bd. Pediatrics, Am. Bd. Laser Surgery. Intern in pediats. Children's Med. Ctr., Dallas, 1978-79, resident in pediats., 1979-80; resident in dermatology U. Tex. Southwestern Med. Ctr., Dallas, 1980-83, chief resident in dermatology, 1982-83, asst. instr. dermatology and pediatrics, 1983-84, asst. prof., 1984-90, assoc. prof., 1990-99; prof., 1999—; physician Cons. Dermatol. Specialists, Dallas, 1990-93; pres. Lynne J. Roberts, MD, PA, Dallas, 1993—. Dir. dermatology Children's Med. Ctr., Dallas, 1986-2000; dermatology sect. chief Med. City Dallas Hosp., 1994-95, 95-97. Contbr. articles to profl. jours., chpts. to books. Recipient Scholastic Achievement Citation Am. Med. Women's Assn., 1978. Fellow Am. Acad. Dermatology, Am. Soc. Laser Medicine and Surgery (bd. dirs. 1994-97); mem. Soc. Pediatric Dermatology, Am. Soc. Dermatologic Surgery, Tex. Med. Assn., Kappa Alpha Theta, Alpha Omega Alpha. Avocations: horseback riding, reading, fishing, swimming, camping. Office: Ste 330 7502 Greenville Ave Dallas TX 75231 Office Phone: 469-232-9300.

ROBERTS, MARGARET HAROLD, editor, publisher; b. Aug. 18, 1928; AB, U. Chattanooga, Tenn., 1950. Editor, pub. series Award Winning Art, 1960-70, New Woman mag., Palm Beach, Fla., 1971-84; editor, pub. BONKERS mag., 1992—2001. Author: juvenile book series Daddy is a Doctor, 1965.

ROBERTS, MARGARET REYNOLDS, art educator; b. Nashville, Oct. 10, 1914; d. Elijah and Margaret (Sanders) Brugh; m. Morgan Boaz Reynolds, June 3, 1937 (dec. Mar. 1976); children: Margaret, Susanne, Morgan, Brugh, Liza, Elaine; m. William Clyde Roberts, Apr. 23, 1977 (dec. Aug. 2004). Student, Ward-Belmont Jr. Coll., Nashville, 1934; BA, Vanderbilt U., 1936; postgrad., William and Mary Coll., 1937-38, U. Wis. Tchr. decorating Watkins Inst., Nashville, 1965-70; tchr. Cheekwood, Nashville, 1973-74; tchr. period furniture Belle Meade Club, Nashville, 1994, 1994. One-woman exhibits include Vanderbilt U., 1986, 88, 94, 2001, Belmont U., 1989, Barnes & Noble, The French Shoppe, Belle Meade Plantation, 2002, 06, Bookstar, 2003, The Corner Market, 2003, Partheun Mus., 2005. Mem. Tenn. Art League, Le Petit Salon Literary Club (pres. 1979-80), Marsh Creek County Club, Centennial Club, Belle Meade Club, Kappa Alpha Theta. Roman Catholic. Avocations: tennis, golf, painter. Home and Office: 5100 Boxcroft Pl Nashville TN 37205-3702

ROBERTS, MARGOT MARKELS, art association administrator; b. Springfield, Mass., Jan. 20, 1945; d. Reuben and Marion (Markels) R.; children: Lauren B. Phillips, Debrah C. Herman. BA, Boston U. Interior designer Louis Legum Furniture Co., Norfolk, Va., 1965-70; buyer, mgr. Danker Furniture, Rockville, Md., 1970-72; buyer W & J Sloane, Washington, 1972-74; pres. Bus. & Fin. Cons., Palm Beach, Fla., 1976-80, Margot M. Roberts & Assocs., Inc., Palm Beach, 1976—. Dealer 20th century Am. art and wholesale antiques Margot M. Roberts, Inc., Palm Beach, 1989—; v.p., dir. So. Textile Svcs. Inc., Palm Beach. Pres. Brittany Condominium Assn., Palm. Beach, 1983-87; v.p. South Palm Beach Civic Assn., 1983-88; South Palm Beach Pres.'s Assn., 1984-88; vice chmn. South Palm Beach Planning Bd., 1983-88, 90-91; chair Palm Beach County Beach and Shores Coun., 1998-2000; town commr. Town South Palm Beach, Fla., 1991-92, vice mayor, 1992-93, mayor, 1993-2000, chair Palm Beach Countywide Beaches and Shores Bd., 1998-2000; mem. Commn. on Status of Women of Palm Beach County, 1992-95; voting mem. Palm Beach Country Mcpl. League, 1991-2000; mem. Palm Beach County Intergovtl. Planning and Rev. exec. com., 1999; vice chair Commn. Status of Women of Palm Beach County, 1994-95; bd. dirs. Palm Beach County Juvenile Justice Bd., 1998-99. Mem. Nat. Assn. Women in Bus., Palm Beach C. of C. Republican.

ROBERTS, MARIE DYER, retired computer systems specialist; b. Statesboro, Ga., Feb. 19, 1943; d. Byron and Martha (Evans) Dyer; m. Hugh V. Roberts, Jr., Oct. 6, 1973 (dec. 2001). BS, U. Ga., 1966; student, Am. U., 1972. Cert. sys. profl.; cert. in data processing. Mathematician, computer specialist U.S. Naval Oceanographic Office, Washington, 1966-73; sys. analyst, programmer Sperry Microwave Electronics, Clearwater, Fla., 1973-75; data processing mgr., asst. bus. mgr. Trenam, Simmons, Kemker et al, Tampa, Fla., 1975-77; mathematician, computer specialist U.S. Army C.E., Savannah, Ga., 1977-81, 83-85, Frankfurt, West Germany, 1981-83; ops. rsch. analyst U.S. Army Constrn. Rsch. Lab., Champaign, Ill., 1985-87; data base adminstr., computer sys. programmer South Pacific divsn. U.S. Army C.E., San Francisco, 1987-93; computer specialist, IDEF repository coord. Functional Process Improvement Expertise/Def. Info. Sys. Agy, Arlington, Va., 1993-95; computer specialist Ctrl. Integration Def. Info. Sys. Agy., MacDill AFB, Fla., 1995—, ret., 2001. Instr. computer scis. City Coll. of Chgo. in Frankfurt, 1982-83. Author: Harris Computer Users Manual, 1983. Recipient Sustained Superior Performance award Dept. Army, 1983, 2 Nat. Peformance Rev. Hammer awards V.P. Al Gore, 1996, DISA Dirs.'s award for Project of Yr., 1999. Mem. Assn. Info. Tech. Profls., U. Ga. Alumni Assn., Sigma Kappa. Personal E-mail: hurob@juno.com.

ROBERTS, MARY LOIS, music educator; b. Kalamazoo, Mich., Feb. 12, 1934; d. Gerben Zichterman and Anna G. Booden; children: Kathleen, Kerry. BA, Grand Canyon U., 1963. Cert. tchr. Ariz., Ill. 4th grade tchr. Bible Chapel Christian Sch., Phoenix, 1963, 2d and 3d grade tchr., 1963—64; 1st grade tchr. Maple Sch. Elem. Sch., Des Plaines, Ill., 1965, 2d grade tchr., 1965—66; substitute tchr. Goshen (Ind.) Pub. Schs., 1980—82; music tchr. Roberts Studio, 1982—. Accompanist H.S. choir Goshen H.S., 1983—89; organist 8th St. Mennonite Ch., 1991—92, St. James Episcopal Ch., Goshen, 1992—. With USAF, 1953—55. Mem.: Music Tchrs. Nat. Assn., Goshen/Elkhart Music Tchrs. Assn. (pres. 2001—03). Avocations: swimming, travel. Home: 215 E Douglas Goshen IN 46526

ROBERTS, MICHELE A., lawyer; b. NYC, Sept. 14, 1956; BA, Wesleyan U., 1977; JD, Boalt Hall Sch. Law, U. Calif., Berkeley, 1980. Bar: Wash. DC 1980. Atty. Pub. Defender Svc., Washington, 1986—92; ptnr. Rochon & Roberts, 1992—2001, Shea & Gardner, 2001—04; ptnr., civil/white collar litig. Akin Gump Strauss Hauer & Feld LLP, Washington, 2004—. Former mem. adj. faculty George Wash. U. Sch. Law; former lectr. Pub. Defender Svc. Tng. Program; past instr. Nat. Inst. Trial Advocacy; mem. adj. faculty Harvard Law Sch.; serves on DC Adv. Commn. on Sentencing. Named First Among Washington's Top 75 Lawyers, Washingtonian mag. survey, 2002; named one of 75 Best Lawyers in Washington, 2004, Am. Top Black Lawyers, Black Enterprise Mag., 2003. Fellow: Am. Coll. Trial Lawyers; mem.: Nat. Assn. Criminal Def. Lawyers, Nat. Bar Assn., ABA, DC Bar. Office: Akin Gump Strauss Hauer & Feld LLP Robert S Strauss Bldg 1333 New Hampshire Ave NW Washington DC 20036-1564 Office Phone: 202-887-4306. Business E-Mail: mroberts@akingump.com.

ROBERTS, NANCY, computer scientist, educator; b. Boston, Jan. 25, 1938; d. Harold and Annette (Zion) Rosenthal; m. Edward B. Roberts, June 14, 1959; children: Valerie Friedman, Mitchell, Andrea. AB, Boston U., 1959, MEd, 1961, EdD, 1975. Elem. tchr. Sharon (Mass.) Pub. Schs., 1959-63; asst. prof. Lesley U., Cambridge, Mass., 1975-79, assoc. prof., 1980-83, prof., 1983—, dir. grad. programs in tech. in edn., 1980—99, dir. Project Bridge, 1987-92, dir. divsn. tchg., learning and leadership, 2001—04; dir. Ctr. for Math., Sci. and Tech. in Edn., Cambridge, Mass., 1990-91. Rsch. assoc. MIT, Cambridge, 1976-79;mem. nat. steering com. Nat. Edn. Computing Conf., Eugene, Oreg., 1979-96, co-chmn. nat. conf., 1989, vice chmn. steering com., 1991-95. Author: Dynamics of Human Service Delivery, 1976, Practical Guide to Computers in Education, 1982, Computers in Teaching Mathematics, 1983, Introduction to Computer Simulation, 1983 (J.W. Forrester award 1983), Integrating Computers into the Elementary and Middle School, 1987, Computers and the Social Studies, 1988, Integrating Telecommunications into Education, 1990, Computer Modeling and Simulation in Science and Mathematics Education, 1999; mem. editl. bd. Jour. Ednl. Computing, 1983—, Jour. Rsch. in Sci. Teaching; editor Computers in Edn. book series, 1984-89. Mem. Computer Policy Com., Boston, 1982-84, mem. adv. bd. Electronic Learning, 1989-91; bd. dirs. Computers for Kids, Cambridge, 1983-85; mem. State Ednl. Tech. Adv. Coun., 1990-93; bd. dirs. Boston Ctr. Adult Edn., 2000—, Citizens Charter Schs., 1997-05; pres. bd. Littleton Mus. Fine Arts, 2003—. Grantee, NSF, 1985—96, DOE, 1994—2003. Mem. System Dynamics Soc. (bd. dirs. policy com. 1987-89). Republican. Jewish. Home: 300 Boylston St Apt 1102 Boston MA 02116-3940 Office: Lesley Coll 29 Everett St Cambridge MA 02138-2702 Office Phone: 617-349-8419. Business E-Mail: nroberts@lesley.edu.

ROBERTS, NANCY CAROLYN, retired counselor, elementary educator; b. Lenoir, N.C., Mar. 18, 1935; m. John C. Long, Sept. 4, 1954 (div. Sept. 1976); children: Jennifer Long Petresky, Donald Long; m. Jesse Porter Roberts, Aug. 5, 1977 (dec. 1995). Student, Heidelberg Coll., 1953-55; BS, U. Akron, 1957, student, 1972-73, Ohio State U., 1974-75; MEd, U. Cen. Fla., 1981. Cert. guidance counselor, elem. tchr., Fla. Classroom tchr. Akron (Ohio) Pub. Schs., 1976-77, Seminole County Sch. Dist., Winter Park, Fla., 1977-85, elem. guidance counselor, 1985—97; ret., 1997. Leader parenting workshop Wright State U., Dayton, Ohio, 1988, Seminole Community Coll., Sanford, Fla., 1989—. Author theme curriculum for guidance, 1988. Named Fla. Elem. Counselor of Yr., 1994. Mem. AACD, ACA, Seminole Counseling Assn. (pres.-elect 1991—), Fla. Counseling Assn. (v.p. elem.), Phi Delta Kappa, Delta Kappa Gamma. Republican. Avocation: golf. Home: 603 Shorewood Dr Unit F401 Cape Canaveral FL 32920-5053

ROBERTS, NANCY COHEN, art dealer, marketing professional; b. Washington, Oct. 12; d. Norman G. and Roberta B. Cohen; m. Marc R. Roberts, Aug. 22, 1985; 2 children. BA, U. Pa., Phila., 1976; MBA, NYU, 1982. Actress, 1976—80; exec. tng. program Bloomingdales, 1980—82; advt. salesperson Hearst Corp., N.Y.C., 1982—84; dir. pub. rels./mktg. Karastan, N.Y.C., 1984—2005. Bd. dirs. Manhattan Theatre Club, N.Y.C., Children's Mus. Manhattan, N.Y.C., Auction Live, Washington. Active ann. fundraiser Chapin Sch., N.Y.C.; active capital campaign Riverdale Country Sch., N.Y.C., 1995—2001; grade rep. Edward R. and Rosalind Roberts Found., N.Y.C. Mem.: NY Athletic Club, Breakers Country Club, Club Colette, Army Navy Club, Vassar Club.

ROBERTS, NORA, writer; b. Silver Spring, Md., Oct. 10, 1950; m. Ronald Aufdem-Brinke, 1970 (div. 1983); children: Dan, Jason; m. Bruce Wilder, 1985. Former legal secy. Author: Promise Me Tomorrow, 1984, Hot Ice, 1987, Sacred Sins, 1987, Brazen Virtue, 1988, Sweet Revenge, 1989, Public Secrets, 1990, Genuine Lies, 1991, Carnal Innocence, 1992, Divine Evil, 1992, Honest Illusions, 1992, reprint, 1993, Private Scandals, 1993, Hidden Riches, 1994, Born in Fire, 1994, Born in Ice, 1995, True Betrayals, 1995, reprint, 1996, Born in Shame, 1996, Daring to Dream, 1996, Montana Sky, 1996, reprint, 1997, Holding the Dream, 1997, Finding the Dream, 1997, Sanctuary, 1997, Rising Tides, 1998, Once Upon a Castle, 1998, Homeport, 1998, Sea Swept, 1998, The Reef, 1998, Inner Harbor, 1999, Jewels of the Sun, 1999, River's End, 1999, Heart of the Sea, 2000, Tears of the Moon, 2000, Carolina Moon, 2001, Heaven and Earth, 2001, The Villa, 2002, Three Fates, 2002, Chesapeake Blue, 2002, Key of Knowledge, 2003, Key of Light, 2003, Once Upon a Midnight, 2003, Birthright, 2003, Blue Dahlia, 2004, Once Upon a Moon, 2004, Northern Lights, 2004, A Little Fate, 2004, Key of Valor, 2004, Black Rose, 2005, Blue Smoke, 2005 (Quill award romance The Quills Literacy Found., 2006); (under pseudonym J.D. Robb) Naked in Death, 1995, Glory in Death, 1995, Immortal in Death, 1996, Rapture in Death, 1996, Ceremony in Death, 1997, Vengeance in Death, 1997, Holiday in Death, 1998, Loyalty in Death, 1999, Conspiracy in Death, 1999, Judgment in Death, 2000, Witness in Death, 2000, Betrayal in Death, 2001, Seduction in Death, 2001, Interlude in Death, 2001, Purity in Death, 2002, Reunion in Death, 2002, Imitation in Death, 2003, Portrait in Death, 2003, Visions in Death, 2004, Survivor in Death, 2005, Origin in Death, 2005, Memory in Death, 2006; author numerous category romances for Silhouette. Recipient Lifetime Achievement award Waldenbooks. Mem. Romance Writers Am. (charter, mem. Washington chpt., inductee Hall of Fame, Centennial award, Lifetime Achievement award 1997), Mystery Writers Am., Sisters in Crime, The Crime League of Am., Novelists, Inc. Office: GP Putnams Sons 375 Hudson St New York NY 10014-3658*

ROBERTS, PAMELA RANGER, secondary school educator; b. Royal Oak, Mich., May 19, 1960; d. Richard Lee and Carol Bruce (Roland) Ranger; m. John Jack Roberts, Sept. 23, 1989. BA Anthropology, U. Colo., 1983. Retail sales book buyer Neptune Mountaineering, Boulder, Colo., 1985—92; tchr., coach, advisor Phillips Acad., Andover, Mass., 1989; tchr. Spanish Broomfield (Colo.) H.S., 1992—97; retail sales, floor mgr. Neptune Mountaineering, 1997—99; tchr. Spanish Broomfield H.S., 1999—. Dept. chair world lang. Broomfield High Sch., 2001—, mem. emergency first response team, 1999—.

Mem.: Am. Assn. Tchrs. Spanish and Portguese, Sigma Delta Pi. Avocations: rock climbing, skiing, surfing, swimming, travel. Home: 130 S 33d St Boulder CO 80305 E-mail: pam.roberts@bvsd.org.

ROBERTS, ROBYN RENAY, elementary school educator, coach; b. Utica, NY, May 13, 1976; d. Wayne Arnold and Linda Irene Roberts. BS in Psychology, SUNY, Brockport, 1999, BS in Phys. Edn., 1999, MA in Liberal Studies, 2003. Cert. tchr. N.Y. Fitness instr. and party coord. Midtown Athletic Club, Rochester, NY, 1998—; phys. edn. tchr. Rochester City Sch. Dist., 1999—; owner and instr. Athletics Unlimited, 2005—. Dir. sch. fundraisers Sch. No. 1, Rochester, NY, 1999—; organizer Jump Rope Heart, 1999—, Sch. Walks Diabetes, 1999—, Hoops for Heart; founder after-sch. program Go Girls Go - Sch. No. 1, 2003—; HS girls softball umpire Ctrl. West NY Bd., 2004—; boys and girls varsity tennis coach Sch. Arts, 2005—. Lobbyist Am. Heart Assn., Albany, NY, 2003. Named to Women's Empire State Softball Team, 1998, 1999; grantee, Rochester Ednl. Assn., 2002, Women's Sports Found., 2004, 2005, Spiritus Christi, 2005, 2006; scholar, SUNY, Brockport; Ruth A. Garis Tennis scholar, 1997. Mem.: PTA (mem. coord. 2002—), AAHPERD, N.Y. State AHPERD. Democrat. Avocations: violin, tennis, golf, skiing, kayaking. Office: Martin B Anderson Sch 1 85 Hillside Ave Rochester NY 14610-2406 Office Phone: 585-473-1533. Fax: 585-256-8993. E-mail: affinity13@msn.com.

ROBERTS, RUTH W., retired elementary school educator; b. Reading, Pa., Jan. 24, 1936; d. Jason W. and Margaret J. (Smith) White; m. James B. Steffy, Dec. 23, 1956 (div. Aug. 1974); m. George R. Roberts, Sept. 8, 1995; children: James M., John W., Susan E. BS in Elem. Edn., West Chester (Pa.) U., 1956; MA, Commonwealth of Pa., 1985. Tchr. Selinsgrove (Pa.) Area Schs., 1965-66, Lewisburg (Pa.) Area Sch. Dist., 1966—99. Curriculum cluster leader Lewisburg Area Sch. Dist., 1984—. Mem. NEA, Pa. Edn. Assn., MENSA, PASR (Union County chpt. v.p.). Avocations: cross stitch, reading, travel. Home: 156 Redtail Ln Lewisburg PA 17837-9615

ROBERTS, SHERRIE LYNN, special education educator, secondary school educator; b. Albia, Iowa, Dec. 1, 1958; d. Glenn D. and Evelyn M. Klyn; m. Ronald D. Roberts, June 1, 1980; children: David, Daniel, Dana. BS in Edn., Northeast Mo. State U., 1980; degree in Spl. Edn., Morningside Coll., 2004. Various secretarial positions, 1980—2001; pvt. piano instr., 1995—2000; tchr. spl. education Albia (Iowa) H.S., 2001—03; tchr. Evans Mid. Sch., Ottumwa, Iowa, 2003—. Part-time instr. adult basic edn. Indian Hills CC, Ottumwa, Iowa. Mem.: Beta Sigma Phi (v.p. 1986—). Lutheran. Avocations: travel, reading, scrapbooks. Home: 18780 Copperhead Rd Ottumwa IA 52501 Office: Resource Tchr Evans Middle Sch 812 Chester Ave Ottumwa IA 52501-4150

ROBERTS, SUZANNE CATHERINE, artist; b. San Antonio, Oct. 27, 1953; d. Thomas Simons and Marceline Margaret (Conrady) Garrett; m. Ted Blake Roberts, May 22, 1976; 1 child, Elizabeth. BS Radio-TV-Film, U. Tex., 1975, B Journalism, 1977; MA Interdisciplinary Studies, Corpus Christi State U., Tex., 1982; MS Gen. Counseling, Corpus Christi State U., 1989; MA Polit. Sci., S.W. Tex. State U., 1995. News announcer Sta. KIXL Radio, Austin, Tex., 1976, Sta. KSIX Radio, Corpus Christi, 1977—78; news anchor Sta. KZTV-TV, Corpus Christi, 1979, news reporter, 1977—80; news announcer, reporter Sta. KRYS-AM-FM, Corpus Christi, 1983—87; freelance reporter UPI, Austin, 1989—94, Tex. State Network, Austin, 1995—97, Des Moines, 1997—2000; artist, 1998—.

ROBERTS, THOMASENE BLOUNT, entrepreneur; b. Americus, Ga., Sept. 5, 1943; d. Thomas Watson and Mary Elizabeth (Smith) Blount; m. Henry Lee Roberts, Apr. 24, 1970 (div. 1991); 1 child, Asha Maia. Student, Fisk U., 1960-63; BA, Morris Brown Coll., 1965; MA, Atlanta U., 1970, postgrad., 1979-82, Clark Atlanta U. Social worker Gate City Day Nursery Assn., Atlanta, 1965-66; ticket agt. Delta Air Lines, Inc., Atlanta, 1966-68; clk. accounts payable Kraft Foods, Inc., Decatur, Ga., 1968; cons. family svcs. Atlanta Housing Authority, 1970-72, supr. family svcs., 1972-73, mgr. family relocation, 1974-79; grad. rsch. asst. Sch. Edn. Atlanta U., 1979-82; city coun. asst. City of Atlanta, 1984-88, rsch. asst. Dept. Pub. Safety, 1988; dir. govtl. rels. Morris Brown Coll., Atlanta, 1988-93; owner TBR Ent., Atlanta, 1993—2002; adminstrv. analyst human svcs. City of Atlanta, 1995-97, adminstrv. analyst, prin. dept. adminstrv. svcs., 1997; owner Dream Catcher Events, Inc., 1997—; psychol. svcs. specialist City of Atlanta, 1998—2002. Researcher/intern Project Focus Teen Mother Program, Atlanta, 1981-82; moderator Nat. Black Women's Health Project, Atlanta, 1985; workshop leader Assn. Human Resources Mgrs., Atlanta, 1989; pres.'s rep. U. Ctr. Devel. Corp., Inc., 1989-93; cons. entrepreneur devel. workshop Morris Brown Coll. Chairperson Ida Prather YWCA Cmty. Bd., Atlanta, 1985-90; bd. dirs. YWCA Met. Atlanta, 1986-90, Met. Atlanta Coalition 100 Black Women, 1988-90, 92-2001, sec., mem. bd. dirs., 1994-96, 1st v.p., 1997-2000; trustee Hammonds House Mus., 1995-2001; active fund dr. com. Jomandi Prodn., 1988-89; v.p. maj. gifts com. Camp Best Friends, City of Atlanta, 1989; mem. Multi-Cultural Leadership Group, Gov.'s Coun. on Developmental Disabilities, 1990; bd. dirs. Atlanta Black/Jewish Coalition, 1997-2000; apptd. mem. Atlanta Sister Cities Commn.; presenter, cons. Youth Motivation Task Force, 1998-2001; co-chmn. Atlanta AIDS Partnership Fund, 2000-04. Mem. Atlanta-Trinidad/Tobago Exch. (sec., treas. 1983-89, Pt. of Spain cert. 1986), Nat. Polit. Congress Black Women (corr. sec. 1989-90), Nat. Assn. for Equal Opportunity Higher Edn. (coll. liaison 1988-93), Coun. for Advancement-Support of Edn., Info. Forum, Atlanta Urban League, Inc., Nat. Assn. for Equal Opportunity in Higher Edn. (Disting. Alumni award 1991), Nat. Soc. Fund-Raising Execs. (cert. 1992), Nat. Soc. Fund-Raising Execs. Leadership Inst., Friends of Morehouse Sch. Medicine, Assn. Bridal Cons., Internat. Spl. Events Soc. (v.p. programs 2001-02), Atlanta Bus. League, Delta Sigma Theta (pub. rels. asst. 1986-89). Avocations: theater, music, films, art, fine dining. Home and Office: 1817 King Charles Rd SW Atlanta GA 30331-4909 Office Phone: 404-344-5052. Home Fax: 404-344-0378. E-mail: dreamcatcherevents2000@yahoo.com.

ROBERTS, TIFFANY MARIE, former soccer player; b. Petaluma, Calif., May 5, 1977; BA in Comm. Studies, U. N.C., 1998. Mem. U.S. Women's Nat. Soccer Team, 1994—; including CONCACAF Qualifying Championship Montreal, 1994; 3d place FIFA Women's World Cup Sweden, 1995; gold medal U.S. Olympic Team, 1996; mem. Under-20 Nat. Team 1997 Nordic Cup, Denmark; mem. Tri Valley Team, San Ramon, Calif.; profl. soccer player Carolina Courage, 2001—03. Named 1994 Calif. H.S. Player of Yr., Most Valuable Player, Far Western Regional, 1993, World Cup Champion, 1999. Achievements include member U. N.C. NCAA national championship teams, 1996, 97. Office: US Soccer Fedn 1801-1811 S Prairie Ave Chicago IL 60616

ROBERTS, TONI, small business owner, jewelry designer; b. Dec. 20, 1948; d. William James and Blanche Alexandria (Michael) Guyhto; children: Danielle Ahmed, Marc Roberts. BA in Spanish Edn., CCNY, N.Y.C., 1960; MEd, Herbert H. Lehman Coll., N.Y.C., 1973. Dist. reading coord., sch. reading specialist, tchr. N.Y.C. Bd. Edn., 1961-75; asst. to dir. of devel. Malcolm King Coll., N.Y.C., 1978-79; sales promotion and mktg. copywriter, audio visual prodr. Avon Products, Inc., N.Y.C., 1980-83; sales promotion and advt. mgr. Gralla Publs., Inc., N.Y.C., 1988-89; program developer, coord. Bronx Writers Corps, Bronx Coun. on Arts, N.Y.C., 1994-95; counselor Adult Learning Ctr., Lehman Coll., N.Y.C., 1996; craftswoman, direct to pub. marketer Bold of Spirit Jewelry Line, 1994—. Facilitator Women's Creative Self-Discovery Workshops, 1997—; founder, facilitator Womanwrite, 1992-94; tchr. mentor, trainer, educator, motivator, program and workshop developer, facilitator Bronx Mus. Arts, 1995—, Am. Craft Mus., Bronx C.C., Bronx Creative Arts for Youth, Learning Alliance, N.Y. Pub. Libr., Arts Connection Young Talent Program, Sponsors for Ednl. Opportunity; mem. panels RAPP, Bronx Coun. Arts, N.Y. Found. for Arts and Bronx Coun. on Arts, The African Experience, Schomburg Ctr. for Rsch. in Black Culture, Crystal Quilt and the Found. for African Am. Women, after sch. program developer, coord. Arts Connection, N.Y.C., 1989-94, life coach, spirit mentor pvt. practice, cons. domestic violence facilities, 1998—. Author: God and Modern Woman, 1977, Reading with Love, 1978; interpreter: The Greatest in the Kingdom, 1979; reader N.Y. Pub. Libr., The Crystal Quilt at Ctrl. Park Conservatory; narrator, scriptwriter Retumba Con Pie at Lincoln Ctr.; MC CBGB Gallery, The Nuyorican Cafe; interviewee Cityscape WFUV-FM radio, Joy's Jour., WBAI-FM radio, Numbers Are You, The God of My Father, WBLS-AM radio, Aurora Borealis, Channels D & 17, N.Y. Cable TV. Mem. N.Y.C. Commn. on Status of Women, 1979-81. Recipient Fiction fellowship N.Y. Found. for Arts, 1989, Fiction award Bronx Coun. Arts, 1991. Avocations: african drumming, photography, computers. Personal E-mail: orisha2003@aol.com.

ROBERTS, VERNA DEAN, music educator; b. Sherman, Tex., Apr. 11, 1925; d. Vern Holbrook and Sarah Aileen Wells (Shoffner) Smith; m. James Bruce Roberts, Jan. 22, 1947; children: Gregory Bruce, Debra Deane, Pamela Anne. B in Music Edn., Phillips U., 1947; MS in Elem. Edn., Okla. State U., 1950; postgrad., U. Ill., 1960—, William Rainey Harper Coll., 1960—. Pvt. tchr. piano, 1940—; pvt. tchr. voice, 1945—; music instr. pub. schs. Durant, Stillwater, Southard, Okla., 1947-51, Sacred Heart of Mary High Sch., Rolling Meadows, Ill., Elk Grove Village (Ill.) High Sch.; dir. children's choirs, adult choirs Okla., Ill.; singer with choruses & show choirs; music adjudicator Okla., Ill. Faculty mem. Am. Coll. Musicians Piano Guild. Charter mem., elder emeritus, deacon, Sunday Sch. tchr., dir. adult and children's choirs, dir. stewardship drive, pres., treas. Disciple Women, mem. handbell choir Christian Ch. (Disciples of Christ), Arlington Heights, Ill.; del. Nat. Issues Conv., We the People, Phila., 2003. Named to Hall of Fame, Am. Coll. Musicians Piano Guild, 1973. Mem. Nat. Music Tchrs. Assn., Ill. State Music Tchrs. Assn. (state membership chmn.), Northwest Suburban Music Tchrs. Assn. (charter mem., 1st v.p., 2nd v.p., chmn. numerous coms.), Assn. Disciples Musicians, Ill. Music Assn., Arts Coun. Co-op. Republican. Avocations: music performance, reading, poetry, swimming, cooking. Office: Roberts Sch Music 623 Sycamore Dr Elk Grove Village IL 60007-4624 Office Phone: 847-437-2067.

ROBERTS, VICTORIA LYNN P., antique expert; b. N.Y.C., Sept. 15, 1953; d. Edgar Alan Parmer and Nina Joyce (Ash) Gross; m. George E. Roberts, Dec. 1, 1978 (div. 1985); 1 child, Joshua Henry. BA in Polit. Sci., Am. govt., const. law, Yale U., 1998; MBA, Fairfield U., 1999. Lic. real estate broker N.C., 2005, Conn., 2005. Pres. High Gear Creative Svcs., Savannah, Ga., 1979-81; v.p. Rossignol Modeling Agy., N.Y.C., 1981-82; mgr., dir. Parc Monceau Antiques, Westport, Conn., 1982-85; pres., owner, CEO Victoria & Cie LLC, Custom Furniture Mfg., Norwalk, Conn., 1985—; pres., owner L.L.C. Custon Furniture Mfg.; with Prudential Conn. Real Estate, 2005. Antiques tchr. Sacred Heart U., Fairfield, Conn., 1988, 89, Norwalk Community Coll., 1989; antique lectr. various hist. socs., Conn., 1989-90; speaker in antiques field; antique expert seminars to interior designers, Norwalk, 1989; creator, sole contbr. spls. on antiques CNBC TV, 1989, 90. Antiques editor Brooks Community Newspaper, Westport, 1989-91; contbr. Antiques Mag., 1991—. Mem. Appraisers Assn. Am. (sr.), Coll. Arts Assn., Norwalk Rotary, Yale Club (N.Y.C. admissions com. mem.), Alpha Sigma Lambda. Avocations: scenic photography, bicycling, history, rose gardening. E-mail: victoria@victoriacie.com.

ROBERTS-MAMONE, LISA A., lawyer; BA magna cum laude, Grove City Coll., 1985; JD magna cum laude, Case Wester Res. U., 1988. Bar: Ohio 1988. With Jones Day, Cleve., 1988—, ptnr., 2000—. Mem. Estate Planning Coun. of Cleve.; trustee The Laub Found.; mem. Estate Planning Discussion Group, Cleve.; mem. diamond adv. group U. Hosps. Cleve.; mem. Case Western Reserve U. Estate Planning Adv. Coun., Hathaway Brown Sch. Profl. Advisors Com. Mem.: Cleve. Bar Assn. (estate planning, probate and trust law sect.), Ohio State Bar Assn. (estate planning, trust and probate sect.). Office: Jones Day North Point 901 Lakeside Ave Cleveland OH 44114-1190 Office Phone: 216-586-7172.

ROBERTSON, ANNE FERRATT, language educator, researcher; b. Dallas, Mar. 19, 1946; d. Thomas Littelle and Elisabeth (Fentress) Ferratt; m. Edwin David Robertson, Sept. 7, 1968; 1 child, Thomas Therit. BA, Hollins Coll., 1968; MA, NYU, 1990, PhD, 1994. Web pub. Ancient Near Eastern Marking, N.Y.C.; profl. cons., 1994—. Author articles. Mem. Am. Oriental Soc., Egyptological Seminar of N.Y. (treas.). Avocation: soprano. Home and Office: 315 E 72nd St Apt 6H New York NY 10021-4627 E-mail: arobe@nyc.rr.com.

ROBERTSON, BRENDA, senator; b. Sussex, NB, Can., May 23, 1929; m. Wilmont W. Robertson (dec.); children: Doug, Leslie, Tracy. BS, Mount Allison U.; DHL (hon.), Mount St. Vincent U., 1973; DSc (hon.), U. Moncton, 1983. Legislator NB Legislature, 1967—83; senator The Senate of Can., Ottawa, 1984—2004. Progressive. Address: Ste 207 50 Assomption Blvd Moncton NB Canada E1C 0C5

ROBERTSON, CAROL A., science educator; d. Andrew A. and Elizabeth A. Jumper; m. Bruce A. Robertson; children: Sam, Jeff. BS in Edn., U. Mo., Columbia, 1978—82. Lifetime cert. tchr. in biology (7-12) Mo. Bd. Edn., 1982, cert. NCATE in Chemistry Mo. Bd. Edn. Sci. tchr. Hallsville HS, Mo., 1982—83, Fulton HS, Mo., 1984—88, 1992—. Master tchr. U. Mo. Summer Genetics Inst., Columbia, 2003; software tester, cons. Concord Connection - Molecular Logic, Concord, Mass., 2004—06; adv. bd. Fulton Pub. Schs. Found., Mo., 2004—; adv. Nat. Honor Soc., Fulton Chpt., Fulton HS, 2004—. Contbr., tchr. ideas: book by Evan Adkins How to Survive & Thrive on the First Three Weeks of School, 2006. Sponsor Fellowship of Christian Athletes, Fulton HS, 2002—05. Recipient Outstanding Svc. in Edn. award, Fulton Pub. Schs., 2003, Tchr. of Yr., 2005; grantee fellowship, Partnership for Rsch. & Edn. in Plants, U. Mo., Columbia, 2005—06. Mem.: NSTA, Mo. State Tchrs. Assn., Sci. Tchrs. Mo., Delta Kappa Gamma. Republican. Baptist. Avocations: photography, sports, hunting, fishing. Office: #1 Hornet Dr Fulton MO 65251

ROBERTSON, CONNIE LYNN, elementary school educator; b. Pearisburg, Va., Dec. 27, 1952; d. James E. and Louise (Ferguson) Boothe; m. Steven L. Robertson, Oct. 4, 1975; children: Gary L., James L., Jason W. BS in Elem. Edn., Concord Coll., 1974. Tchr. 1st grade Peterstown (W. Va.) Elem. Sch., 1974-75, tchr. 1st, 2nd grades, 1988—; tchr. 1st, 2nd, 3rd, 5th grades Ballard (W.Va.) Elem. Sch., 1975-88. Treas. Monroe County Reading Coun., Peterstown, 1980—. Tchr. Peterstown Bapt. Ch., 1974—. Home: RR 1 Box 120 Peterstown WV 24963-9707

ROBERTSON, DAWN H., retail executive; b. Birmingham, Ala. m. Tom Robertson; 2 children. BA in Fashion Merchandising, Auburn U., 1976. Buyer, exec. trainee Davidson's (divsn. R.H. Macy & Co.), Atlanta, 1977; various positions The May Co., 1983—96; pres., CEO McRae's, (divsn. Sak's Inc.), Jackson, Miss., 1997—98; exec. v.p. for men's/children's/home Fed. Merchandising Group, 1998—2000; pres., chief merchandising officer Federated Stores Direct, NYC, 2000—02; mng. dir. Coles Meyer, Australia, 2002—06; pres. Old Navy Gap Inc., San Francisco, 2006—. Named one of 50 Most Powerful Women, Fortune Mag., 2005. Office: Gap Inc Two Folsom St San Francisco CA 94105*

ROBERTSON, DONNA VIRGINIA, architect, educator, dean; b. Richmond, Va., Feb. 26, 1952; d. Charles Henry and Florence (Givens) R.; m. Robert M. McAnulty, May 24, 1986; 1 child, Robertson. Cert. theater arts studies, Webster Coll., St. Louis, 1972; BA, Stanford U., 1974; MArch, U. Va., 1978. Registered arch., N.Y. Asst. prof. Harvard U., Cambridge, Mass., 1983-84; asst. prof. Barnard Coll. Columbia U., N.Y.C., 1984-92; dean Sch. Arch. Tulane U., New Orleans, 1992-96; dean Coll. Arch. Ill. Inst. Tech., Chgo., 1996—; ptnr. Robertson McAnulty Archs., Chgo., 1986—; owner Donna V. Robertson Archs., N.Y.C., 1982-86; sr. designer Kohn Pedersen Fox Archs., N.Y.C., 1980-82, Mitchell Giurgola Archs., N.Y.C., 1979-80. Adj. asst. prof. Barnard Coll., Columbia U., N.Y., 1982-83, dir. arch. program, fall 1985-92; vis. critic in design Harvard U., Cambridge, fall 1990, U. Va., Charlottesville, fall 1991; organizer, panelist Arch. and Lit. Symposium, N.Y.C., 1985; jury chair Am. Collegiate Schs. Arch., Boston, 1996; mem. bd. dirs. Nat. Archtl. Accrediting Bd., 2000-03; profl. advisor Ford Calumet Environ. Ctr. Competition, City of Chgo., 2004. Prin. arch. Fishback residence, New Orleans, Sunkel residence, New Orleans, Pisar residence, N.Y.C., Dachs residence, N.Y.C.; pres. Nat. Archtl. Accrediting Bd., 2002-03; profiled in Archtl. Record May 2004. Juror invitational competition Seoul Performing Arts Ctr., Republic of Korea, 2006. Named one of Most Influential Women in Chgo., Crain's Chgo. Bus., 2004; recipient Honor award, Chgo. Landmarks Commn., 2005. Mem. AIA (juror annual design hons. awards 1996, Educators and Practitioners Network, co-chair tchrs. seminar 2006, mem. Chgo. bd.), Coll. Fellows of AIA, Am. Coll. Student Assn. (co-chair 2006), Chgo. Network-Internat. Women's Forum, Raven Soc. (U. Va.), Arts Club (Chgo.), Phi Beta Kappa. Office: Ill Inst Tech Coll Architecture 3360 S State St Chicago IL 60616 Office Phone: 312-567-3263. E-mail: robertson@iit.edu.

ROBERTSON, HEATHER ANDERSON, musician, educator; b. Danville, Va., Apr. 28, 1977; d. S. Wayne and Susan Blair Anderson; m. Jerry Wayne Robertson, July 27, 2002. BA, Averett U., 1999. Music tchr. K-12 Commonwealth of Va., 2001. Info. specialist City of Danville, Va., 2000—01; tchr. music Pittsylvania County Schs., Chatham, 2001—. Ch. musician Chatham Bapt. Ch., 1998—2004; dir. music Watson Meml. United Meth. Ch., 2004—. Author of poems. Mem. The United Friends and Family, Danville, 1999—2001; vol., hon. mem. 4-H, Chatham, 1986—2003; bd. mem. Ext. Leadership Coun., 1993—96. Named 4-H All-Star, Pittsylvania County Coop. Ext., 4-H, 1994. Mem.: Va. Choral Directors' Assn. (assoc.), Am. Criminal Justice Assn. (assoc.), Va. Music Educators Assn. (assoc.), Mensa, Climax Ruritan Club (hon.). Church Of Christ. Avocations: reading, piano pedagogy, writing, horseback riding, travel. Office: Pittsylvania County Schs 100 Trojan Cir Dry Fork VA 24549 Personal E-mail: heather.robertson@pcs.kas.va.us.

ROBERTSON, JANE RYDING, marketing executive; b. Dallas, Apr. 11, 1953; d. Ronald and Olive Stacey (Hodgkinson) Pearce; m. James Randall Robertson, May 25, 1974; children: James Andrew, Jessica Ryding. Assoc. degree, Tyler Jr. Coll., 1972; BS, Tex. Tech U., 1974. Store mgr. trainee Montgomery Ward, Dallas, Lubbock, Tex., 1974-75; dist. sales rep. Max Factor & Co., Dallas, 1975-78; sr. asst. buyer cosmetics Sanger Harris, Dallas, 1978-88, also cosmetic mktg.-divisional mktg. account exec., 1978-88; v.p. mktg. Dallas Market Ctr., 1988-90; dir. mktg.-pub. rels. Galleria/Hines Dallas, 1990—2002; sr. v.p. mktg. Dallas Market Ctr., 2003—. Pub. rels. bd. Easter Seals, 1996—2000; mem. corp. adv. bd. So. Meth. U., 2000—05; mem. nat. bd. dir. Susan G. Komen Found. for Breast Cancer, Dallas, 1990—95; bd. dir. Ctr. for Profl. Selling, Baylor U., Waco, Tex., 1989—95. Mem. Internat. Coun. Shopping Ctr. (sr. cert. mktg. dir.), Fashion Group Internat. (bd. dir. 2005—), Univ. Club (bd. dir. profl. women's com. 1990-92). Methodist. Avocations: reading, youth activities, interior decorating. Office: Dallas Market Ctr 2100 Stemmons Freeway MS 405 Dallas TX 75207 Office Phone: 214-655-6173. E-mail: jrobertson@dmcmail.com.

ROBERTSON, JEAN ELIZABETH, sociology educator; b. Galashiels, Scotland, Sept. 20, 1956; arrived in U.S., 1998; d. Frank Robertson and Jean Isabella Connochie; m. Mohan Narayanasamy; children: Sonja Jean Lowit, Simon David Lowit, Nicholas Ian Lowit. MA, U. Aberdeen, Scotland, 1995. ESOL tchr. Spanish Cath. Ctr., Gaithersburg, Md., 1999—2001; adjuct faculty mem. Strayer U. Online, Newington, Va., 2002—, cons. course development, 2006—. Vol. Montgomery County Dept. Health and Human Svcs., Rockville, Md. Home: 19105 Plummer Dr Germantown MD 20876 Office: Strayer U Online Newington VA Office Phone: 301-515-1337. Home Fax: 301-515-1337. Personal E-mail: jerliz56@yahoo.com.

ROBERTSON, KARI DAWN, athletic trainer; b. Othello, Wash., Sept. 15, 1976; d. Gregory Lawrence and Sandra Lee Robertson. BS in Kinesiology, Wash. State U., Pullman, 1999; MS in Kinesiology, Calif. State U., Northridge, 2006. Cert. athletic trainer Nat. Bd. Athletic Trainers Assoc. Bd. Certification, 1999. Head cert. athletic trainer and athletic dir. Saint Monica Cath. HS, Santa Monica, Calif., 1999—2000; cons. Data Select Sys., Inc., Westlake Village, Calif., 2000—06; head cert. athletic trainer Calabasas HS, Calabasas, Calif., 2001—03. Athletic trainer U.S. Field Hockey Assn., Moorpark, Calif., 2003—06; site dir. US Field Hockey Assoc. Futures Program, Moorpark, 2006—06. Young adult ministries Malibu Presbyn. Ch., Calif., 1999—2004. Mem.: Nat. Athletic Trainers' Assn. (assoc.). Presbyterian. Avocations: travel, athletics, music, outdoor activities. Personal E-mail: karidrobertson@yahoo.com.

ROBERTSON, LAURA ELIZABETH, science educator; d. Roy Lee and Judith Ann Robertson. BS in Biology, U. Tenn., Knoxville, 2000, MS in Edn., 2001. Cert. elem. edn. 1-8, secondary sci. biology 7-12. Tchr. mid. sch. sci. East Tenn. State U., Johnson City, 2001—. Named Employee for Outstanding Svc., East Tenn. State U., 2004. Mem.: Tenn. Sci. Tchr. Assn., Nat. Sci. Tchr. Assn. Office: East Tenn State U PO Box 70632 Johnson City TN 37614

ROBERTSON, LAVERNE, minister; MS, Nova Southeastern U., 1995; D Divinigy, Miracle Theol. Coll. Pastor Mansion Ave. Triumphant Bapt. Ch., Richmond, Va., 2001—04; founder, dir. Va. Triumphant Coll. and Seminary, 2006. Singer: (songs) Freedom Day Has Come. Gospel music writer and performer, Richmond, 1980—99. Named 3rd runner up, Miss Black Richmond Pageant. Office: Mansion Ave Triumphant Baptist Ch PO Box 24245 1801 Mansion Ave Richmond VA 23224 Office Phone: 804-232-6046. Personal E-mail: laverroberts@aol.com.

ROBERTSON, LINDA F., educational administrator; b. Powell, Wyo., July 15, 1946; d. Lee and Dorothy W. (Schweighart) Brunk; m. Darrell G. Robertson II, July 2, 1965; 1 child, Michelle. BA in elem. edn., U. Wyo., 1968; MA in edn. adminstrn., U. Akron, 1978; PhD in higher edn. adminstrn., Kent State U., 2005. Cert. supt., elem. prin., secondary prin., Ohio. Elem. prin. Aurora (Ohio) City Schs., asst. supt., high sch. prin.; dir. Ctr. for Internat. and Intercultural Edn., Kent State U. Named Ohio Prin. of Yr., 1992. Mem.: Kappa Delta Pi, Phi Delta Kappa. Home: 8220 Timber Trl Chagrin Falls OH 44023-5071 Business E-Mail: lfrobert@kent.edu.

ROBERTSON, LISA RAE, music educator; b. Cedar Falls, Iowa, May 2, 1960; d. Robert Dale and Betty Jane Frey; m. Norman Mark Robertson, Feb. 9, 1980. BA in Fine Arts and Humanities, U. Wyo., 1988. Art gallery asst. Sheridan (Wyo.) Inn, 1981—83; music divsn. mgr. Gospel Gardens, Sheridan, 1984; piano tchr. Sheridan, 1980—; art instr. Three Peaks Christian Sch., Sheridan, 1996—; vocal music accompanist Sch. Dist. No. 2, Sheridan, 1984—. Republican. Baptist. Avocations: reading, fitness walking, church involvement. Home: 8 Taxi Dr Sheridan WY 82801 Office: Sch Dist No 2 PO Box 919 Sheridan WY 82801

ROBERTSON, LOUISE WILKES, pediatrician, cardiologist; b. Berryville, Va., Oct. 9, 1933; d. Archibald Francis Robertson and Louise Miller Wilkes; m. Willys Moore Monroe, Oct. 6, 1990; children: Alexander Gaylord Monroe, Susan Monroe, Randolph. BS, Mary Washington U., Fredericksburg, Va., 1956; MD, Va. Commonwealth U., Richmond, 1960. Intern Va. Commonwealth U., 1960—61, resident, 1961—63, instr., 1965—67, asst. prof., 1967—74, assoc. prof., 1974—. Cons. in field. Fellow, Va. Commonwealth U., 1963—65. Fellow: Am. Acad. Pediatrics, Am. Coll. Cardiology; mem.: Alpha Omega Alpha. Democrat. Episcopalian. Avocations: singing, piano, reading. Home: 806 College St Bedford VA 24523-1934 Office: Va Commonwealth U Box 980223 Richmond VA 23298-0223 Office Phone: 804-828-9610. Personal E-mail: drlwrobertson@msn.com.

ROBERTSON, MARGARET MOORE, information technology educator; b. Greenville, Sc, Feb. 13, 1953; d. Michael Judson Moore and Mary Lou Shaffer; children: Suzanne Michelle, Mary Kristin. MA in Libr. Sci., Hollins U., Va., 1999. Assoc. prof. info. systems tech. Patrick Henry CC, Martinsville, Va., 1998—. Home: 1312 Chatham Rd Martinsville VA 24112 Office: Patrick Henry CC PO Box 5311 Martinsville VA 24115 Office Phone: 276-656-0251. Business E-Mail: mrobertson@ph.vccs.edu.

ROBERTSON, MARIAN ELLA (MARIAN ELLA HALL), small business owner, handwriting analyst; b. Edmonton, Alta., Can., Mar. 3, 1920; d. Orville Arthur and Lucy Hon (Osborn) Hall; m. Howard Chester Robertson, Feb. 7, 1942; children: Elaine, Richard. Student, Willamette U., 1937-39; BS, Western Oreg. State U., 1955. Cert. elem., jr. high. tchr., supt. (life) Oreg.; cert. graphoanalyst. Tchr. pub. schs., Mill City, Albany, Scio and Hillsboro, Oreg., 1940-72; cons. Zaner-Bloser Inc., Columbus, Ohio, 1972-85, assoc. cons., 1985-89; pres. Write-Keys, Scio, 1980-90; owner Lifelines, Jefferson, Oreg., 1991-94. Tchr. Internat. Graphoanalysis Soc., Chgo., 1979; instr. Linn-Benton C.C., 1985-89; del. Oreg. Water Resources Congress at Seaside, 2002; mem. Ptnrs. of the Ams., Costa Rica, 2003. Master gardener vol. Marion County, Oreg. State U. Extension Svc., 1992; floriculture judge Marion County Fair, 1992; master gardener clinic Oreg. State Fair, 1992; sr. intern 5th Congl. Dist. Oreg., Washington1984, mem. sr. adv. coun.; mem. precinct com. Rep. Ctrl. Com., Linn County, 1986, alt. vice chair, 1986, parliamentarian, 1988—; candidate Oreg. State Legislature, Salem, 1986; del. N.W. Friends Yearly Meeting, Newberg, Oreg., 1990—92; clk. Marion Friends Monthly Meeting, 1992—93. Mem.: Ptnrs. of Ams.-Costa Rica., Port Orford Heritage Soc. (hon.). Republican. Mem. Soc. Of Friends. Avocations: piano, organ, violin, gardening, writing. Home: 2757 Pheasant Ave SE Salem OR 97302-3170 Office Phone: 503-371-5940.

ROBERTSON, MARY AMOS, mathematics educator; b. Fairmont, W.Va., Apr. 10, 1963; d. Robert Newton and Martha Evelyn Amos; m. W Scott Robertson, July 6, 1989. B in Math Edn., Fairmont State U., Fairmont, W.Va., 1984; M in Ednl. Leadership, Nova Southeastern U., Ft. Lauderdale, Fla., 1993. Cert. profl. tchg. Fla., 1986. Tchr. Mononghalia County Sch., Morgantown, W.Va., 1985—86, Sch. Dist. Lee County, Ft. Myers, Fla., 1986—. Mem. Matlacha (Fla.) Hookers, 1998—2006. Named Math Tchr. of Yr., Lee County Sch., 2004—05. Mem.: Lee County Math Coun. (pres. 1996—97), Floridia Coun. Tchrs. Math. (regional dir. 1998—99), Nat. Coun. Tchrs. Math. Methodist. Office: Ft Myers High Sch 2635 Cortez Blvd Fort Myers FL 33901 Office Phone: 239-334-2167. Office Fax: 239-334-3095. E-mail: maryar@leeschools.net.

ROBERTSON, MARY LOUISE, archivist, historian; b. LA, May 19, 1945; d. Snell and Dorothy (Tregoning) R. BA, UCLA, 1966, MA, 1968, PhD, 1975. Teaching asst. dept. history UCLA, 1967-70; acting instr. UCLA Extension, 1973-74; acting instr. dept. history Pepperdine U., L.A., 1970, Calif. State U., Northridge, 1972-73; asst. curator manuscripts Huntington Libr., San Marino, Calif., 1975, assoc. curator, 1977, chief curator, 1979—. Adj. prof. English Claremont Grad. Sch., 1994. Author: Guide to British Historical Manuscripts in the Huntington Library, 1982; co-author, editor: Guide to American Historical Manuscripts in the Huntington Library, 1979; co-editor: State, Sovereigns & Society in Early Modern England, 1998; contbr. articles on Tudor history to profl. jours. Mabel Wilson Richards dissertation fellow, 1970-72. Mem. Am. Hist. Assn., Soc. Calif. Archivists, N.Am. Conf. on Brit. Studies, Pacific Coast Conf. on Brit. Studies (treas. 1986-88, pres. 1988-90), Phi Beta Kappa. Office: Huntington Libr 1151 Oxford Rd San Marino CA 91108-1299

ROBERTSON, MERLE GREENE, art historian, academic administrator; b. Miles City, Mont., Aug. 30, 1913; d. Darrel Irving and Ada Emma (Foote) McCann; m. Wallace McNeill Greene, Dec. 2, 1936 (div. Sept. 1950); children: Barbara Merle Greene Metzler, David Wallace Greene; m. Lawrence William Robertson, Dec. 19, 1966 (dec. May 1981). Student, U. Washington, 1933-35; BA, U. San Francisco, 1952; MFA, U. Guana Guato, Mex., 1963; LHD, Tulane U., 1987. Cert. tchr., Calif. Camp dir. Camp Tapawingo, Sequim, Wash., 1951-53; tchr. San Rafael Mil. Acad., 1952-64; camp dir. Marin County Camp Fire Girls, San Rafael, Calif., 1954-56; expedition dir. Tulane U., New Orleans, 1962—; tchr. Monterey (Calif.) Penninsula Coll., 1974-76, Robert Louis Stevenson Sch., Pebble Beach, Calif., 1967-76; exec. dir. Pre-Columbian Art Rsch. Inst., San Francisco, 1971—. Adj. curator H.M. de Young Meml. Art Mus., San Francisco, 1991—, com. mem. pre-Columbian art, 1990—; rsch. assoc. Middle Am. Rsch. Inst./Tulane U., New Orleans, 1976—, U. Calif. Archaeol. Rsch. Facility, Berkeley, 1982—, Calif. Acad. Scis., San Francisco, 1985—; dir. Archaeol. Recording Maya Art in Mex., Gualemala, Belize, Honduras, 1962—. Author: Sculpture of Palenque, 4 vols., 1983-91, Ancient Maya Relief Sculpture, 1967 (Best Design 1967), (CD-ROMS) Merle Greene Robertson's Rubbings of Maya Sculpture; editor: Palenque Round Table, 10 vols., 1973-95; prin. works include over 4500 rubbings of Maya Sculpture, Merle Greene Robertson Rare Manuscript Archives, Tulane U.; exhbns. including rubbings in most major mus. in US and Europe. Merle Greene Robertson Sch. named in her honor, Chiapas, Mex., 1981; recipient Order of the Aztec Eagle award Mexican Govt., 1994, Orden del Pop award, Guatemala, 2004, Reconocimento Especial "TOH", Merida, Yue, 2004. Fellow AAAS, The Explorers Club, Soc. for Am. Archaeology; mem. 47th Internat. Cong. Americanists (hon. v.p. 1992), Am. Anthropol. Assn., Assn. de Artistes Mougins. Avocations: travel to exotic countries, painting, hiking. Home and Office: 1100 Sacramento St Apt 1004 San Francisco CA 94108-1918 Personal E-mail: pari-merle@mindspring.com.

ROBERTSON, ROBIN ALAYNE, headmaster, anthropologist; b. Tex. B, U. Penn.; M in Anthropology, PhD in Anthropology, Harvard U. Former asst. prof. So. Methodist U., former assoc. dean for gen. ed., 1984—90; head of sch. Emma Willard Sch., Troy, NY, 1990—99, Milton Acad., Milton, Mass., 1999—. Trustee-at-large CASE; bd. v.p. Nat. Coalition of Girls' Schools, 1994—; mem. pres. council Sage Colleges, Troy, NY. Mem. Troy Redevelopment Found., 1994—, pres., 1995—96. Office: Milton Acad 170 Centre St Milton MA 02186

ROBERTSON, ROSE MARIE, cardiologist, educator; b. Detroit, May 15, 1945; d. Joseph Michael and Rose Marie (Pink) Stevens; m. David Robertson, Oct. 31, 1978; 1 child, Rose Marie. BA, Manhattanville Coll., 1966; MD, Harvard Med. Sch., 1970. Diplomate Nat. Bd. Medicine, 1971, Am. Bd. Internal Medicine, 1974, Cardiovascular Medicine, 1975. Intern in medicine Mass. Gen. Hosp., Boston, 1970-71, resident in medicine, 1970-72; fellow in cardiovasc. medicine Johns Hopkins Med. Sch., Balt., 1973-75, asst. prof. medicine, 1976—77, Vanderbilt U. Med. Ctr., Nashville, 1975-82, assoc. prof. medicine, 1982-89, dir. cardiovasc. tng. program, 1990—2000, assoc. dir. cardiology, 1987—2000, prof. medicine, 1989—. Mem. adv. bd. Robert Wood Johnson Found., 1990-, chair, 2003-; mem. adv. bd. Assn. for Patient-Oriented Rsch.; mem. cardiovasc. study sect. NIH, Bethesda, Md., 1993-97; invited spkr., lectr. Contbr. articles to profl. jours., chpts. to books. Fellow Am. Coll. Cardiology, Am. Heart Assn. (pres. 2000-01, chief sci. officer 2003-), European Soc. Cardiology; mem. Am. Autonomic Soc., Am. Fedn. for Clin. Rsch., Am. Soc. Clin. Investigation, Am. Clin. and Climatol. Assn., Assn. Univ. Cardiologists. Home: 4003 Newman Pl Nashville TN 37204-4308 Office: 7272 Greenville Ave Dallas TX 75240 Office Phone: 214-706-1295. E-mail: rosemarie.robertson@heart.org.

ROBERTSON, SARA STEWART, private investigator, entrepreneur; b. NYC, Feb. 4, 1940; d. John Elliott and Mary Terry (Schlamp) Stewart; m. James Young Robertson, Nov. 29, 1975 (dec. Mar. 1988). BA, Conn. Coll., 1961; MBA, Am. U., 1969. From trainee to officer First Nat. Bank/First Chgo. Corp., 1969-75, v.p., 1975-92; prin. Royall Enterprises, Chgo., 1992—; prin., dir. Zeppelin Press, Inc., Miami, Fla., 1995—. Chair individuals fundraising, exec. com. Youth Guidance, Chgo., 1993-95. Bd. dirs. Harbor House Condominium Assn. Chgo., 1990-92; trustee Sherwood Conservatory Music, 1993-2005, chair bd. devel., 1993-95, 97-99; mem. allocations com. and family priority grants com. United Way-Chgo., 1992-95; co-founder, v.p., sec.-treas. Animal Support Kindness and Kinship, Inc., 1999-2005, v.p., sec., 2001-05. Mem.: Club 13 Palm Beach (pres. 1996—98, v.p. 2003—05, pres. 2005—). Personal E-mail: saisairob@aol.com.

ROBERTSON, TINA BARBARA, dancer, educator; b. Plainfield, NJ, Jan. 24, 1973; d. Walter Baker and Barbara Rose Stiglitz; 1 child, Derek Brandon. Dance instr. Sch. Contemporary Dance and Theatre, South Plainfield, NJ, 1990—92; dance instr., choreographer Fran's World of Dance, Piscataway, NJ, 1992—2000, Ms. Kim's Sch. of Dance, North Plainfield, NJ, 2000—01, Happy Feet Dance Studio, Englishtown, NJ, 2003—04, Bound Brook H.S. Drama Club, Boundbrook, NJ, 2004—05, Broadway Bound Dance Ctr., Lebanon, NJ, 2003—. Mem.: Nat. Dance Assn., Am. Alliance for Health and Dance, Dance Tchr. Mag. Avocations: singing, writing. Home: 346 Walnut St Dunellen NJ 08812 Office: Broadway Dance Ctr 1386 US Hwy 22 Lebanon NJ 08836

ROBERTSON, VIRGINIA MARIE, small business owner, publisher; b. Doyle, Kans., Jan. 19, 1946; d. Lloyd G. and Cleda A. (Frost) Cox; m. J. Lynn Robertson, July 26, 1974; 1 child, Dina M. BFA, Washburn U., 1973; MFA, Idaho State U., 1975. Art instr. Washburn U., Topeka, 1965, Topeka Recreation Dept. Cultural Arts, 1965-68; fabric dept. mgr. Montgomery Ward, Tokepa, 1968, display dept. mgr. Pocatello, Idaho, 1968-73; art prof. continuing edn. Idaho State U., Pocatello, 1975-76; art instr. continuing edn. Peninsula Coll., Port Angeles, Wash., 1976-77; quilting instr. Washburn U., 1978-81; owner, publisher Osage Co. Quilt Factory, Overbrook, Kans., 1978—2005, Robertson's Quilt Shop, Cortez, Colo., 2005—. Owner Osage County Quilt Shop, Overbrook, 1982-89. Pub. and designer quilt and craft books and patterns, 1978-89; numerous one-woman shows, Kans., Idaho, Wash., 1966-89. City coun. City of Overbrook, 1986, 87. Recipient Best Oil of Show award Mid-Am. Show, Topeka, 1966. Republican. Office: Robertson's Quilt Shop 15 E Main Dolores CO 81323 Address: Robertsons' Enterprises PO Box 357 Dolores CO 81323-0357

ROBEY, SHERIE GAY SOUTHALL GORDON, secondary school educator, consultant; b. Washington, July 7, 1954; m. Robert Jean Claude Robey; children: Michael Gordon, Robert Robey, Jamie Robey. BS, U. Md., 1976; MA in Edn. and Human Devel., George Washington U., 1988. Tchr. Esperanza Mid. Sch., Hollywood, Md., 1980-84, Chopticon High Sch., Morganza, Md., 1984—. Coach Odyssey of the Mind, 1985-95; sponsor Future Tchrs. Am., Morganza, 1990-2002, S.H.O.P/S.A.D.D., Morganza, 1990-2002; cons. Ednl. Cosn., Waldorf, 1980—; pres. BNA Swim Team, 1990-2002; driver edn. classroom and lab instr. 1996-2005. Parish com. Good Shepherd United Meth. Church, 1999, 2004—. Named Inclusion Tchr. of Yr., St. Mary's County, 2004; recipient Tchr. of Yr., Nammec, 2002, Inclusion Tchr. of Yr., St. Mary's County, 2005; Tchr. Scholarship, Target, 2001—02. Mem. Ednl. Rep. Assn. St. Mary's County, Lighthouse Hist. Soc. Methodist. Avocations: swimming, writing, visiting lighthouses, collection miniature lighthouses, photography. Home and Office: 11181 Carroll Dr Waldorf MD 20601-2656 Office Phone: 301-475-0215. E-mail: lightbeacon2@yahoo.com.

ROBFOGEL, SUSAN SALITAN, lawyer; b. Rochester, NY, Apr. 4, 1943; d. Victor and Janet (Rosenthal) Salitan; m. Nathan Joshua Robfogel, July 12, 1965; children: Jacob Morris, Samuel Salitan. BA cum laude, Smith Coll., 1964; JD, Cornell U., 1967. Bar: N.Y.1967, U.S. Dist. Ct. (we. dist.) 1968, U.S. Ct. Appeals (2d cir.) 1971, U.S. Supreme Ct. 1971, U.S. Dist. Ct. (no. dist.) 1974, D.C. 1982. From asst. corp. counsel to sr. asst. corp. counsel City of Rochester, NY, 1967-70; assoc. Harris, Beach & Wilcox, Rochester, 1970-75; ptnr. Harris, Beach, Wilcox, Rubin & Levey, Rochester, 1975-85, Nixon, Peabody, LLP, Rochester and N.Y.C., 1985—; chair bd. Office of Compliance, Washington, 1999—. Panel mem., Fed. Svc. Impasses Panel, Washington, 1983-94; mem., past chair Data Protection Rev. Bd., Albany, N.Y., 1984—. Recipient Brockport Coll. Found. Community award, 1989. Fellow Am. Bar Found., N.Y. State Bar Found., Coll. Labor and Employment Lawyers; mem. ABA, N.Y. State Bar Assn., Washington D.C. Bar Assn., Monroe County Bar Assn. (Rodenbeck award 1988). also: 437 Madison Ave New York NY 10022-7001 Home: 9182 Luckenbach Hill Rd Springwater NY 14560 Office Phone: 212-940-3116. Business E-Mail: srobfogel@nixonpeabody.com.

ROBICHAUD, DONNA LYNN, career planning administrator; b. Chgo., Apr. 12, 1958; d. Kenneth Lamar and Sheila Wolf; m. Terry Lionel Robichaud, May 27, 1978 (dec. Dec. 9, 1990); 1 child, Jenafer Elisa. AA, Siena Heights U., 1999, BFA cum laude, 1999, MA in Cmty. Counseling, 2006. Cert. Vol. Hospice Lenawee, MI. Case mgr. Cmty. Action Agy., So. Ctrl. Mich. Works, Adrian, Mich., 2001—03, work first career mgr. Jackson, Mich., 2003—04; career mgr. Human Resource Devel. Inc., SCMW, Hillsdale, Mich., 2004—. Exhibitions include Memories, Quintuplets, Love and Loss; author: (poetry) Morning Tea (Poet of Yr., 1992); contbr. Vol. Hospice Lenawee, Adrian, Mich., 1992. Recipient Lambda Iota Tau, Siena Heights U., 1995, Alpha Sigma Lambda, 1996. Mem.: ACA, Assn. Death Edn., Counseling, Am. Acad. Bereavement. Avocations: travel, computers, reading. Home: 579 Stockford Dr Adrian MI 49221 Office: S Ctrl Mich Works HRDI 21 Care Dr Hillsdale MI Office Phone: 517-437-3381.

ROBIN, CLARA NELL (CLAIRE ROBIN), English language educator; b. Harrisonburg, Va., Feb. 19, 1945; d. Robert Franklin and Marguerite Ausherman (Long) Wampler; m. Phil Camden Branner, June 10, 1967 (div. May 1984); m. John Charles Robin, Nov. 22, 1984 (div. Dec. 1990) BA English, Mary Washington Coll., 1967; MA English, James Madison U., 1974; postgrad., Jesus Coll., Cambridge, Eng., 1982, Princeton U., 1985—86, Auburn U., 1988, U. No. Tex., 1990—91. Cert. tchr. English, French, master cert., Tex. Tchr. 7th grade John C. Myers Intermediate Sch., Broadway, Va., 1967—68; tchr. 10th grade Waynesville H.S., Mo., 1968—70; tchr. 6th, 7th, 8th grades Mary Mount Jr. H.S., Santa Barbara, Calif., 1970—72; tchr. 9th grade Forest Meadow Jr. H.S. Richardson Ind. Sch. Dist., Tex., 1972—78, tchr. 10th grade Lake Highlands H.S., 1972—84; tchr. 11th, 12th grades Burleson H.S. Burleson Ind. Sch. Dist., Tex., 1986—2003; tchr. 9th and 10th grade English Ft. Worth Country Day Sch., 2003—. Instr. composition Hill Coll., 1989-90 Contbg. author: (book revs.) English Jour., 1989-94, (lit. criticism) Eric, 1993 Vol. Dallas Theater Cir., 1990—96; active Kimbell Art Mus., Ft. Worth, 1990—, Modern Art Mus., Ft. Worth, 1992—, KERA Pub. TV, Dallas, 1990—, Amon Carter Mus., Ft. Worth, 2001—. Fellow NEH, 1988, 89, 92, 95, Fulbright-Hays Summer Seminar Abroad, 1991; ind. study grantee Coun. Basic Edn., 1990; recipient Chpt. Achievement award Epsilon Nu Delta Kappa Gamma, 1993, Hon. Mention Tex. Outstanding Tchg. of Humanities award, 1995, Burleson Ind. Sch. Dist., Campus Ednl. Improvement Com., 1997-2000, Dist. Ednl. Improvement Com., 1998-2001 Mem.: Tex. State Reading Assn., Nat. Coun. Tchrs. English (spring conf. presenter 2000, 2002), Epsilon Nu of Delta Kappa Gamma (1st v.p. 1988—94, v.p. 1992—94, profl. affairs com. 1996—98, comms. chair 1998—). Avocations: bicycling, travel, reading, writing, landscaping. Home: 4009 W 6th St Fort Worth TX 76107-1619 Office: Ft Worth County Day Sch 4200 Country Day Ln Fort Worth TX 76109-4299 Office Phone: 817-302-3203 ext. 102. Personal E-mail: crbkrd@aol.com. Business E-Mail: crobin@fwcds.org.

ROBINOWITZ, CAROLYN BAUER, psychiatrist, educator, director; b. Bklyn., July 15, 1938; d. Milton Leonard and Marcia (Wexler) Bauer; m. Max Robinowitz, June 10, 1962; children: Mark, David AB, Wellesley Coll., 1959; MD, Washington U., 1964. Diplomate Am. Bd. Psychiatry and Neurology. Chief physician tng. NIMH, Bethesda, Md., 1968-70; dir. pediatric liaison U. Miami Sch. Medicine, Fla., 1970-72, dir. child psychiatry tng., 1971-72; dir. edn. George Washington U. Sch. Medicine, Washington, 1972-74; project dir. Psychiatrist as Tchr., Washington, 1973-75; dep. med. dir. Am. Psychiat. Assn., Washington, 1976-86, dir. Office Edn., 1976-87, sr. dep. med. dir., 1986-94, COO, 1986-94, treas., 2004—05, sec.-treas., 2005—06, pres.-elect, 2006—. Assoc. dean Georgetown U. Sch. Medicine, 1995—98, dean, 1998—2000, lectr., 1976—82, professorial lectr., 1982—94, prof., 1995—2000, clin. prof., 2000—; dir. Am. Bd. Psychiatry and Neurology, Evanston, Ill., 1979—86, sec., 1984, v.p., 85, pres., 86; clin. prof. psychiatry and behavioral scis., child health and devel. George Washington U., 1984—98, 2001—; professorial lectr. Uniformed Svcs. U. of Health Scis., 1986—. Editor: Women in Context, 1976; contbr. articles to jours., chpts. to books Admissions com. Wellesley Coll. Club, Washington, 1983-84. Served with USPHS, 1966-69. Recipient NIMH Mental Health Career Devel. award, 1966-70, NIMH grantee, 1974-94. Fellow Am. Psychiat. Assn. (Disting. Svc. award 1991, Vestermark award 1995, Adminstrv. Psychiatry award 1999), Am. Coll. Psychiatrists (bd. dirs. 1993-96, 1st v.p. 1996-97, pres. 1999-00, past pres. 2000-04, sec. gen. 2005—, Bowis award 1994, Disting. Svc. award 2001); mem. AMA (coun. psychiatry sect. 2000-, coun. on sci. affairs 2001-05, coun. on sci. and pub. health 2005—), Assn. for Acad. Psychiatry (disting. life., pres. 1994-95, dir. 1992-96, 03-, Lifetime Achievement award 2003), Group for Advancement of Psychiatry (dir. 1982-84, pres. 1989-91), Coun. Med. Splty. Socs. (dir. 1977-82, pres. 1981-82). Office: #514 5225 Connecticut Ave NW Washington DC 20015 Office Phone: 202-237-1466. E-mail: cbrobinowitzmd@usa.net.

ROBINS, CYNTHIA LOU, journalist, jewelry designer; b. Mansfield, Ohio, July 30, 1939; d. Jack I. and Rhoda M. Shore; children: Harlan Wayne, Daniel Shore. BA in English, Ohio State U., 1961, MA in Theatre, 1969. TV critic Columbus Dispatch, Columbus, Ohio, 1973—77; reporter, columnist San Francisco Examiner, Calif., 1977—2001; beauty editor Chronicle, San Francisco, 2001—02; designer, owner CynCity Design, Las Vegas. Freelance writer, 1977—2006.

ROBINS, FAYE E., principal, elementary school educator; b. Bklyn., Jan. 11, 1951; d. Leo and Sarah Zusman; children: Jeffrey Scott, Rebecca Ann. BSc, Bklyn. Coll., 1979, MSc, 1987; cert. in Advanced Study, NYU, 1991. Cert. tchr. N.Y., 1985. Tchr. N.Y.C. Bd. Edn., Bklyn., South Country Ctrl. Sch. Dist., Bellport, NY, chm.; asst. prin. Longwood Ctrl. Sch. Dist., Mid. Island, NY, dir.; prin. South Huntington (N.Y.) Unified Sch. Dist. Mem.: ASCD, NMSA. Office: Stimson Mid Sch 401 Oakwood Rd Huntington Station NY 11746

ROBINS, JUDY BESS, sculptor; b. Chgo., Oct. 24, 1942; d. Hubert W. and Zelpha Doris Plain; children: Philip, Tamara Robins Jensen. AA in Fine Arts, William Rainey Harper Coll., 1982; studied with Sem Ghelardini, Pietrasanta, Italy, 1991. Exhibitions include Sedgwick Studio, Chgo., 2005, prin. works include Che-ca-guo/Wild Onion limestone sculptures, Chgo. Navy Pier, 1999, Art Walk, William A. Koehnline Gallery, Oakton C.C., Des Plaines, Ill., Gwyneth outdoor sculpture. Mem.: Internat. Sculpture Assn., Chgo. Sculpture Internat., Chgo. Artists Coalition (past co-chmn. for com. artists rights, past chmn. bd.). Avocations: bicycling, swimming. Studio: 1804 S Kilbourn Chicago IL 60623 Personal E-mail: judy.robins@comcast.net.

ROBINS, JUDY ROSELYN, interior designer; b. Cleve., Sept. 2, 1948; d. Stanley and Esther (Resnick) Waxman; m. Kenneth Michael Robins, Sept. 26, 1971. AAS, Fashion Inst. Tech.; BS, NYU, 1970, MA, 1972. Fabric coord. Celanese Corp., N.Y.C., 1970—71; merchandiser Bayly Corp., Denver, 1973—74; instr. Metro State Coll., Denver, 1977—81; self-employed interior designer Denver, 1975—. Bd. dirs. Waxman Industries. Mem. steering com. Denver Art Mus., trustee, 1986—96, collections com., devel. com.; founding mem. Young Women's Leadership Cabinet United Jewish Appeal, 1977—82, Nat. Jewish Ctr. Bd., 1984—87, Nat. Women's Bd., 1984—; v.p. Mizel Mus. Judaica; bd. dirs. Nat. Found. for Jewish Culture; bd. govs. Nat. Jewish Ctr. for Immunology and Respiratory Medicine; mem. steering com. Alliance Contemporary Art; women's bd. Nat. Jewish Hosp., 1978—80, bd. dirs., 1984—88; bd. dirs. congregation Jewish Family and Children's Svc. Colo., 1975—83, Anti-Defamation League, 1987—90; bd. dirs., v.p. leadership Allied Jewish Fedn., assoc. campaign chmn., 1985, gen. chmn., 1987—88. Recipient Young Leadership award, Allied Jewish Fedn., 1977, Afkey award, Denver Art Mus., 1995, Kipness-Friedland Lion of Judah award, United Jewish Communities, 2004. Mem.: United Jewish Appeal (nat. women's divsn. exec. com. 1985—98, nat.-vice chair 1990—98). Address: 2165 E Alameda Ave Denver CO 80209-2710 Office Phone: 303-777-8485. E-mail: kennyrobin@aol.com.

ROBINS, LEE NELKEN, medical educator; b. New Orleans, Aug. 29, 1922; d. Abe and Leona (Reiman) Nelken; m. Eli Robins, Feb. 22, 1946 (dec. Dec. 1994); children: Paul, James, Thomas, Nicholas; m. Hugh Chaplin, Aug. 5, 1998. Student, Newcomb Coll., 1938-40; BA, Radcliffe Coll., 1942, MA, 1943; PhD, Harvard U., 1951. Mem. faculty Washington U., St. Louis, 1954—, prof. sociology in psychiatry, 1968-91, prof. sociology, 1969-91, prof. social sci. and social sci. in psychiatry, 1991-2000, prof. emeritus, 2001—. Past mem. Nat. Adv. Coun. on Drug Abuse; past mem. task panels Pres.'s Commn. on Mental Health; mem. expert adv. panel on mental health WHO; Salmon lectr. NY Acad. Medicine, 1983; Cutter lectr. Harvard U., 1997. Author: Deviant Children Grown Up, 1966; editor 11 books; mem. editl. bd. Psychol. Medicine, Jour. Studies on Alcohol, Social Psychiatry and Psychiatric Epidemiology, Epidemiol. e Psichiat. Sociale; contbr. articles to profl. jours. Recipient Rsch. Scientist award USPHS, 1970-90, Pacesetter Rsch. award Nat. Inst. Drug Abuse, 1978, Radcliffe Coll. Grad. Soc. medal, 1979, Sutherland award Am. Soc. Criminology, 1991, Nathan B. Eddy award Com. on Problems of Drug Dependence, 1993, Spl. Presdl. Commendation Am. Psychiat. Assn., 1999, Am. Acad. Arts and Scis., 1999, Commendation and Appreciation award Harvard Inst. Psychiat. Epidemiology and Genetics, 2000, Disting. Sci. Devel. award Soc. Rsch. in Child Devel., 2003, Peter Raven Lifetime award Acad. Sci. St. Louis, 2006; rsch. grantee NIMH, Nat. Inst. on Drug Abuse, Nat. Inst. on Alcohol Abuse and Alcoholism. Fellow Am. Coll. Epidemiology, Royal Coll. Psychiatrists (hon.), Am. Soc. Psychiatrists (hon.), Soc. Study of Addiction (hon.); mem. APHA (Rema Lapouse award 1979, Lifetime Achievement award sect. on alcohol and drug abuse 1994), Internat. Fedn. Psychiat. Epidemiology (com.1992-2002), World Psychiat. Assn. (sect. com. on epidemiology and cmty. psychiatry, 1985-2002, co-chmn. sect. on rsch. instruments in psychiatry), Soc. Life History Rsch. in Psychopathology, Am. Coll. Neuropsychopharmacology, Inst. Medicine, Am. Psychopath. Assn. (pres. 1987-88, Paul Hoch award 1978), World Innovation Found. (hon. mem. 2004). Office: Washington U Med Sch Dept Psychiatry Saint Louis MO 63110 Business E-Mail: robinsl@psychiatry.wustl.edu.

ROBINS, NATALIE, poet, writer; b. Bound Brook, N.J., June 20, 1938; d. Louis Robins and Mildred (Levy) Robins-Vogel; m. Christopher C.H. Lehmann-Haupt, Oct. 3, 1965; children: Rachel Louise, Noah Christopher. BA, Mary Washington Coll., Fredericksburg, Va., 1960. Author: (poetry) Wild Lace, 1960, (poetry) My Father Spoke of His Riches, 1966, (poetry) The Peas Belong on the Eye Level, 1971, (poetry) Eclipse, 1981, (non-fiction) Savage Grace, 1985 (Edgar award Mystery Writers of Am., 1985), (non-fiction) Alien Ink, 1992 (Hefner Found. 1st Amendment award, 1992), (non-fiction) The Girl Who Died Twice, 1995, Living in the Lightning: A Cancer Journal, 1999, Copeland's Cure, 2005. Personal E-mail: nrobins@speakeasy.net.

ROBINSON, ALICE HELENE, language educator, administrative assistant; b. Cleve., Oct. 16, 1946; d. Alford B. and Willie Helena (Knuckles) R. BA, Cleve. State U., 1968, MA, 1992; postgrad., John Carroll U. Cert. tchr. English, Ohio. English language educator Cleve. Bd. Edn., Ohio. Presenter 1st Celtic Conf. Cleve. State U., 1993. Contbr. poetry to anthologies. Cleve. Edn. Fund scholar, 1991. Mem.: Cleve. Mus. Art. Episcopalian. Avocations: stamp collecting/philately, artifacts, puzzles, logic problems. Home: 3344 E 142nd St Cleveland OH 44120-4009 Office: Cleve Bd Edn 1380 E 6th St Cleveland OH 44114-1606 Personal E-mail: twitcentral@hotmail.com.

ROBINSON, ALICE JEAN MCDONNELL, retired drama and speech educator; b. St. Joseph, Mo., Nov. 17, 1922; d. John Francis and Della M. (Mavity) McDonnell; m. James Eugene Robinson, Apr. 21, 1956 (dec. 1983). BA, U. Kans., 1944, MA, 1947; PhD, Stanford U., 1965. Tchr. Garden City (Kans.) High Sch., 1944-46; asst. prof. Emporia (Kans.) State U., 1947-52; dir. live programs Sta. KTVH-TV, Hutchinson-Wichita, Kans., 1953-55; assoc. prof. drama and speech U. Md. Baltimore County, Balt., 1966-99, rsch. theatre history. Author: The American Theatre: A History in Slides, 1992, Betty Comden and Adolph Green: A Bio-Bibliography, 1993; co-editor: Notable Women in the American Theatre, 1989; appeared in plays, including Landscape, 1983, Tartuffe, 1985, Rockaby, 1990. Mem. Am. Soc. Theatre Rsch., Assn. Theatre Higher Edn., Phi Beta Kappa. Republican. Avocations: travel, reading, acting, directing. Home: 111 N Main St Caldwell KS 67022-1535

ROBINSON, AMINAH BRENDA LYNN, artist, illustrator; b. Columbus, Ohio, Feb. 18, 1940; d. Leroy Edward William and Helen Elizabeth (Zimmerman) R.; m. Clarence Adrian Robinson (div. 1981); 1 child, Sydney Edward (dec. July 17, 1994). Student, Columbus Coll. of Art & Design, 1956-60, Ohio State U., 1960-61, Franklin U., 1961-62, Bliss Coll., 1963. Asst. libr., illustrator, artist Ohio Pub. Libr., Columbus, 1958-64; draftsman Mountain State Telephone Co., Boise, Idaho, 1964-66; illustrator TV Oper. Br. TV, Miss., 1966-67; sr. illustrator N.Am. Rockwell Corp., Columbus, 1971; with City Recreation and Pks. Dept., Columbus, 1972—. Lectr. to numerous orgns., 1971—; spkr. numerous workshops, 1970—. One woman shows include Otterbein Coll., Worthington, Ohio, 1982, 89, 91, Columbus Mus. Art, 1983, 90, 2003, Esther Saks Gallery, Chgo., 1984, Akron Art Mus., 1987, 88, So. Ohio Mus., Portsmouth, 1990, U. Wis., Greenbay, 1990, Museo Nacional de Bellas Artes, Santiago, 2004; exhibited in group shows at Wexner Art Ctr., Columbus, 1992, Nat. Mus. Women in the Arts, Washington, 1990, 91, Memphis Brooks Mus. Art, 1991; represented in permanent collections Cin. Art Mus., Newark Art Mus., Otterbein Coll., Nat. Underground R.R. Freedom Ctr.; numerous others; seried artist: Pages in History, 1981-, Afrikan Pilgrimage: the Extended Family, Sapelo Series, New York Stories, People of the Book, Chilean Suite; author: A Street Called Home; illustrator: Elijah's Angel, 1992, Sophie, 1994, A School for Pompey Walker, 1995, To Be A Drum, 1998. Ohio Arts Coun. fellow 1979-80, 86-87, 88-89, 991-92, Travel-Study fellow Am. Forum for Internat. Study, 1979, PSI Residency fellow, 1989; resident Israel, 1998, Santiago, Chile, 2004; recipient Gov.'s award for the visual arts in Ohio, 1984, Columbus Star of 1980 Achievement award, 1980; named Outstanding Citizen in the Community, Nat. Epicureans, 1974, named a MacArthur Fellow, 2004.

ROBINSON, AMORIE ALEXIA, psychologist, educator; b. Detroit, Oct. 19, 1956; d. David Everett Robinson, II and Jane Marian Robinson; m. Hattie Corine Francis, Oct. 17, 2001. BA in Psychology, Oberlin Coll., Ohio, 1978; MA in Ednl. Psychology, U. Mich., 1979, PhD in Clin. Psychology, 1996. Dir. counseling svcs. Lewis Coll. Bus., Detroit, 1981—84; admissions counselor U. Detroit, 1984—89; forensic psychologist Recorders Ct. Psychiat. Clinic, Detroit, 1996—2002; psychotherapist Counseling Assocs., Farmington Hills, Mich., 1996—; guest lectr. U. Mich., Ann Arbor, 2002—. Adv. bd. Gay Lesbian Straight Edn. Network, Detroit, 2004—; co-founder Com. for Study of Culture, Class and Mental Health, U. Mich., 1990—96; condr. workshops in field; lectr. in field; designer Kofi Kards. Illustrator, cartoonist children's coloring books, 1975—2004; author: There's A Stranger in This House: African American Lesbians and Domestic Violence in Battered Black and Blue: Violence in the Lives of Black Women, 2000, Misunderstood, Misled, & Misfit: The Marginalization Experiences of African American Lesbian Youth, 2000. Co-founder, v.p. bd. dirs. Ruth Ellis Ctr., Detroit, 1999—; co-founder, pres., bd. dirs. Karibu House, Inc., Detroit, 1997—; co-founder, bd. dirs. African-Am. Lesbians Organized to Renew Dignity and Empowerment, Detroit, 1994—, Unity Fellowship Ch., Detroit, 1989—. Recipient Catalyst Activist award, Triangle Found., Detroit, 2001, Lorraine Hansberry award, Affirmations Gay and Lesbian Cmty. Ctr., 1997, Coretta Scott-King Black Achievement award, Alpha Phi Alpha, 1989; fellow half-term fellow, U. Mich., 1994—95, Rackham Minority Merit fellow, 1989—95. Mem.: APA (Sci. Directorate award 1993), Detroit Metro Assn. Black Psychologists (sec. 1997—, Outstanding Svc. award 2002), Assn. for Women in Psychology (suite coord. 1993—95). Avocations: violin, tennis, African drumming. Office: Counseling Associates 33045 Hamilton Ct #W-300 Farmington Hills MI 48334 Business E-Mail: kofi@umich.edu.

ROBINSON, ANDREA J., lawyer; b. 1960; AB magna cum laude, Harvard Univ., 1981; JD, Univ. Va., 1984. Bar: NY 1985, DC 1988, Mass. 1990. Atty. Debevoise & Plimpton, NYC, Washington; ptnr., Litigation dept. Wilmer Cutler Pickering Hale & Dorr, Boston, 1990—, co-vice chmn., Securities dept. Spl. asst. dist. atty. Middlesex County, Mass., 1994. Named a Mass. Super Lawyer, Boston Mag., 2004, Top 50 Female Mass. Super Lawyer, 2004. Mem.: ABA, Boston Bar Assn., Phi Beta Kappa, Order of the Coif. Office: Wilmer Cutler Pickering Hale & Dorr 60 State St Boston MA 02109 Office Phone: 617-526-6360. Office Fax: 617-526-5000. Business E-Mail: andrea.robinson@wilmerhale.com.

ROBINSON, ANGELA REGINA, secondary school educator; d. Alvin Samuel and Deloris Ann (Howell) White; m. Donnie Joe Robinson, Aug. 13, 1988; children: Amber, Donni. BA, U. S.C., 1983; MS, SUNY, New Paltz, 1991; postgrad., The Citadel, 2003—. Cert. tchr. Tchr., coach Richland County Sch., Columbia, SC, 1983—86; tchr. Berkeley County Schs., Moncks Corner, SC, 1986—88, 1992—, Newburgh (N.Y.) Schs., 1988—92; English dept. chairperson Timberland H.S., Moncks Corner, 2004—. Sec. Visions for the Family, Moncks Corner, 1992—; vol. tchr., tutor Friendly Aid Soc., Moncks Corner, 1998—; advisor Delta Teens, Moncks Corner, 2002—. Named Tchr. of Yr., 2005—06; Sojourner Truth fellow. Mem.: Nat. Coun. Tchrs. English, Berkeley County Tchr. Forum, Delta Sigma Theta. Avocations: promoting reading, travel, writing. Office: Berkeley County Schs Main St Moncks Corner SC 29461

ROBINSON, ANGELA TOMEI, clinical laboratory technologist, manager; b. Bklyn., June 5, 1957; d. Leo James and Nina Angela T.; m. John C. Robinson, Sept. 27, 1987. BS, St. John's U., 1979, MS, 1985. Cert. lab. technologist. Exec. sec. Stead-fast Temporaries, Inc., NYC, 1975—79; chief med. technologist Winthrop-U. Hosp., Mineola, NY, 1979—98, adminstrv. lab. coord., edn. coord., lab. info. mgr., 1998—; coord., founder Nat. Med. Lab. Week, Mineola, 1981—; tech. supr., lab. mgr., cons. Hilton Med. Group, Hempstead, NY, 1993—96; lab. technologist Cardiovasc. Group, Garden City, NY, 1996—2000, lab. mgr., 2000—03. Lab. cons. Gastroenterology Group, Mineola, 1998—2000; staff contbr. newsletter, in pub. rels. Winthrop-U. Hosp., Mineola, 1981—, com. mem., clin. instr. for retng. pers. in lab., chmn. com. to petition salary increases, 1987—90, Vision 2000 redesign team, 1997—98; adj. prof. seminar C.W. Post Coll., Westbury, NY, 1992—, edn. coord., 1998—2002; adj. prof. SUNY, Farmingdale, 1999—, advisor, 1999—, com. advisor, Stony Brook, 1995—, Jr. Achievement, 2003; rep. Nassau Suffolk Health Manpower Plan, 1991; team mem. vision 2000 NIH, 1997—98; com. rep. St. John's U. Ann. Clin. Lab Seminar, 1998—; jr. vol. cons., 2002; advisor Nassau C.C., 1999—; cons. Mentorship of L.I., 2003—; lectr. in field; mem. com. clin. lab bd. Dept. Edn. Office of Profl. Author: (poetry) Our World's Best Loved Poems, 1984 (2d place merit cert. 1983) contbr. articles to profl. jours. Singer Blessed Sacrament Ch. Choir, Bklyn., 1971-73, coord., singer ch. folk group, 1971-79; mem. MADD, 1985-87, Nat. Rep. Congl. Com., 1984-86, Am. Health Found., 1986-87, DAV, 1984-87, Noise Pollution Clearinghouse, 2003—; fundraiser Statue of Liberty/Ellis Island Found., 1985-86, 95-96, Hands Across Am., 1986, U.S. Olympic Team Spirit, 1992—, U.S. English First, Nat. Mus. Am. Indians; mentoring ptnr. L.I. Mentor, 2003—, jr. vol. mem., 2003—; mem. Noise Pollution Clearinghouse, 2003—; mem. com. World War II Meml., 2000—; mem. com. clin. lab. bd. N.Y. State Dept. Edn. Bd. Regents, 2005—. Recipient cert. of merit NY State Senate, 1985, citation Gov. NY State Pres. Soc., 1975; award St. John's U. Med. Tech. Alumni, 1992 Mem. Am. Soc. Clin. Lab. Sci., Profl. Stds. Coalition Clin. Lab. Pers., Am. Soc. Clin. Pathologists (registered), Made in the U.S. Found., NY State Soc. Clin. Lab. Sci. (chmn. govt. liason com., state bd. dirs. 1988—, Outstanding Med. Tech. Student award 1979, Mem. of Yr. award 1995, founding officer Nassau-Suffolk chpt. 1985-86, bd. dirs., seminar moderator 1985-87, pres.-elect 1986-87, 90-91, pres. 1991—, membership com. 1991, state chairperson 1993—), Profl. Stds. Coalition (pub. rels. chair 1993—, co-chair 1997—, contbg. editor Lab Medicine 2005), Theta Phi Alpha (alumni chmn. 1976-77, alumni-collegiate rep. 1986-87). Avocations: piano, guitar, gardening, singing, tennis.

ROBINSON, ANNETTMARIE, entrepreneur; b. Fayetteville, Ark., Jan. 31, 1940; d. Christopher Jacy and Lorena (Johnson) Simmons; m. Roy Robinson, June 17, 1966; children: Steven, Sammy, Doug, Pamela, Olen. BA, Edison Tech. U., 1958; BA in Bus., Seattle C.C., 1959. Dir. pers. Country Kitchen Restaurants, Inc., Anchorage, 1966—71; investor Anchorage, 1971—. Cons. Pioneer Investments, Anchorage, 1983—, M'RAL, Inc. Retail Dry Goods, Anchorage, 1985; owner Cons. Co., Reno, 1998—. Mem. Rep. Presdl. Task Force, Washington, 1984—, Reps. of Alaska, Anchorage, 1987; mem. chmn. round table YMCA, Anchorage, 1986—; active Sta. KWN2, KQLO, Reno, Nev.; active in child abuse issues and prosecution; dir., sec. Hunter Lake Townhouse Assn., Reno, Sta. KSRU and KHOG-Radio, KIHM Cath. Radio, Reno, 1996—, KOZZ Radio, 2000—; mem. Cmty. Assn. Inst. Condo/Coop./Townhouse Law, 1999—. Named Woman of Yr. Lions, Anchorage, 1989, marksman first class Nat. Rifle Assn., 1953. Mem. Porsche Club of Am. (racing team 1998—). Avocations: egyptology, theology, archaeology, shooting, fishing.

ROBINSON, BARBARA JON, librarian; b. Beatrice, Nebr., Feb. 28, 1944; d. Beryl William and Beulah Rose (Burgess) Potter; m. J. Cordell Robinson, Aug. 12, 1967 (div. 1987); children: Lisa Maria, Hilton Clifton. BA, Smith Coll., 1966; MA, Ind. U., 1967, MLS, 1969. Libr. Universidad de Los Andes, Bogotá, Colombia, 1969-70, Ind. U., Bloomington, 1970-71, U. Calif., Riverside, 1974-85, U. So. Calif., L.A., 1985—. Author: The Mexican American: A Critical Guide to Research Aids, 1980; editor: Artistic Representation of Latin American Diversity: Sources and Collections, 1993. Fellow Gulbenkian Found., 1966, Ford Found., 1967, Fgn. Area fellow, 1968-69. Mem. Seminar Acquisition Latin Am. Libr. Materials (pres. 1988-89), Phi Beta Delta. Methodist. Avocations: travel, skiing, reading, violin. Office: U So Calif Doheny Meml Libr Univ Pk Los Angeles CA 90007

ROBINSON, BARBARA PAUL, lawyer; b. Oct. 19, 1941; d. Leo and Pauline G. Paul; m. Charles Raskob Robinson, June 11, 1965; children: Charles Paul, Torrance Webster. AB magna cum laude, Bryn Mawr Coll., 1962; LLB, Yale U., 1965, Order of the Coif. Bar: N.Y. 1966, U.S. Dist. Ct. (so. and ea. dists.) N.Y. 1975, U.S. Tax Ct. 1972, U.S. Ct. Appeals (2d cir.) 1974. Assoc. Debevoise & Plimpton LLP, NYC, 1966-75, ptnr., 1976—, with Trusts and Estates Dept.; commr. Mayor's Commn. on Women's Issues, 2002—. Mem. adv. bd. Practicing Law Inst.; bd. dirs. Am. Arbitration Assn., 1997—2003. Mem. bd. editors: Chase Jour., 1997—2001; contbr. articles to profl. jours. Mem. adv. coun., bd. vis. CUNY Law Sch., Queens, 1984—90; active Coun. on Fgn. Rels.; trustee Trinity Sch., 1982—88, pres., 1986—88; bd. dirs. Found. for Child Devel., 1988—2000, 2001—, chmn., 1991—2000; bd. dirs. Catalyst, 1993—, treas., 1993—; bd. dirs. Fund for Modern Cts., 1994—2003, Wave Hill, 1994—. Garden Conservancy, 1996—2002, Lawyers Com. for Civil Rights Under Law, 1997—2003, William Nelson Cromwell Found., 1993—, Irish Legal Rsch. Found. Inc., 1996—, Citizens Union Found. Inc., 1996—2004, Am. Friends Brit. Mus., 2003—, The Ocean Conservancy, 2004—, Teagle Found., 2005—. The Grumwall Found., 2006—, The John A. Found., 2006—; trustee Bryn Mawr Coll., 2000—. Recipient Laura Parsons Pratt award, 1996. Fellow Am. Coll. Trust and Estate Counsel, Am. Bar Found., N.Y. Bar Found.; mem. ABA (commn. on women in profession 1999-2002), N.Y. State Bar Assn. (vice chmn. com. on trust adminstrn., trusts and estates law sect. 1977-81, ho. of dels. 1984-87, 90-92, com. ann. award 1993-94), Assn. of Bar of City of N.Y. (chmn. com. on trusts, estates and surrogates cts. 1981-84, judiciary com. 1981-84, coun. on jud. adminstrn. 1982-84, chair nominating com. 1984-85, 99-2000, exec. com. 1986-91, chair 1989-90, v.p. 1990-91, chair com. on honors 1993-94, com. on long-range planning 1991-94, co-chair coun. on childen 1997-98, pres. 1994-96), Assn. of Bar of City of N.Y. Fund Inc. (bd. dirs. 2000-03, pres. 1994-96), Women's Forum, Yale Coun., Yale Law Sch. Assn. N.Y. (devel. bd., exec. com. 1981-85, 93—, pres. 1988-93), The Century Assn., Yale Club, Washington Club. Office: Debevoise & Plimpton LLP 919 Third Ave New York NY 10022 Office Phone: 212-909-6325. Business E-Mail: bprobinson@debevoise.com.

ROBINSON, BERNICE JOYCE, secondary school educator; d. Edwin Samuel and Ruth Selena Mckinley; m. Padmore Agbemabiese, May 2, 2003; children: Marc, Sherri, Sena Agbemabiese, Elikplim Agbemabiese. MA, Hunter Coll., N.Y.C., 1958. Music tchr. N.Y. Bd. Of Edn., N.Y.C., 1958—63, Columbus Bd. of Edn., Ohio, 1965—. Min. of music St. Philip Episc.l Ch., Columbus, 1983—. Dir.(performer): (classical jazz keyboardist). Music condr. Mass Ecumenical Choirs, Columbus, 1975—2003. Recipient Cmty. Svc. award, Omega Psi Phi, 2003. Mem.: Delta Omicron (corr.). Episcopalian. Avocation: drama. Home: 7669 Swindon St Blacklick OH 43004 Office Phone: 614-365-5465.

ROBINSON, BRENDA KAY, editor, public relations executive; b. Flint, Mich., May 15, 1946; d. Albert Coleburn and Kathryn Mary (Salay) Moore; m. Richard F. Robinson, Feb. 6, 1970; 1 child, Kelly Dawn. AS in Fashion, Garland Jr. Coll., 1967. Actress Actor's Workshop and Repertory Co., West Palm Beach, Fla., 1980-82, 2002—03; asst. store mgr. Pavo Real Sculpture Gallery, Boca Raton, Fla., 1987-88; freelance artist, illustrator, coloring book designer Troy, Mich., 1972—; freelance editor, writer Delray Beach, Fla., 1995—; v.p., editor Dick Robinson Co., Delray Beach, 1979—; editor, writer Legacy Scribe LLC, 2003—; pub. rels. dir. Unity of Delray Beach Ch., 1996-99, 2004—; sales office profl. mem's dept. and designer salon Saks Fifth Ave., Troy, Mich., 1968-72. Cons. Mary Kay Cosmetics, 1983-84. Author, illustrator (coloring book with text) Boca Raton Animal Shelter Coloring Book, 1993. Puppeteer Kids on the Block shows Assn. for Retarded Citizens, West Palm Beach, Fla., 1981-85; bd. treas. Windemere House Condominium Assn., Delray Beach, 1993, bd. sec., 1994, 2003. Mem.: Bill Gove Golden Gavel Toastmaster Club, Quail Ridge Country Club. Republican. Avocations: Web surfing, walking, bichon frise dogs, improvisational comedy acting. Home and Office: 3677 Quail Ridge Dr N Boynton Beach FL 33436-5331 E-mail: brendarobinson@legacyscribe.com.

ROBINSON, CARRIE, pastor; b. Balt., Jan. 11, 1945; d. Charles Dingle and Anna Lemmon; m. Bill Robinson, Nov. 26, 1977 (dec. June 2, 2003); children: Michael Stukes, Maurice Johnson, Monica Johnson. Doctorate, Interdenominational Coll.; degree in Christian edn., Theol. Sem. and Coll. Notary pub. With Verizon Tel. Co., 1968—; pastor Prayer and Faith Ministries Bapt. Ch., Balt., 1987—. Sec. United Bapt. Conf., Balt., 1990—, v.p., 2000—. Mem.: Internat. Women Ministerial Alliance (v.p. 2000—), Order of Ea. Star (Helen Benton House # 34). Avocations: singing, reading, computers, drumming. Office: Prayer and Faith Ministries Bapt Ch Inc 1865 N Gay St Baltimore MD 21213 Home: 2705 Hamilton Ave Baltimore MD 21214-1912 Office Phone: 410-675-0047. E-mail: bishopcrobinson3@aol.com.

ROBINSON, CHARLOTTE HILL, artist; b. San Antonio, Nov. 28, 1924; d. Lucius Davis and Charlotte (Moore) Hill; m. Floyd I. Robinson, Mar. 1943; children: Floyd I. Jr., Lawrence H., Elizabeth H. Student, Incarnate Word Coll., 1942—45, NYU, 1947-48, Corcoran Sch. Art, 1951-52. Painting instr. Art League No. Va., Alexandria, 1967-75. Condr. Art World Seminar Washington Women's Art Ctr., 1975-80, drawing workshop Smithsonian Instn. Resident Assocs. Program, Washington, 1977; program dir. Nat. Women's Caucus for Art, 1979; project coord., exhbn. curator The Artist and the Quilt, nat. mus. traveling exhbn., 1983-86; vis. artist S.W. Craft Ctr., San Antonio, 1983-85; lectr. WFUV 90 FM, Fordham U., NYC, 1990, San Antonio Art Inst., 1991, Nat. Mus. for Women in Arts, Washington, 1991, Iowa State U., Ames, 1991; panelist Nat. Mus. Women in Arts, 1997, Woman and the Arts, Douglass Coll./ Rutgers U., 1998, Washington Women's Caucus for Art at the Millenium Art Ctr., 2001. Editor: The Artist & The Quilt, 1983; one-person shows include Thames Sic. Ctr., New London, Conn., 1991, Brunner Gallery & Mus., Iowa State U., 1991, 92, San Antonio Art. Inst., 1991, Fordham U., 1991, de Andino Fine Arts, Washington, 1992, Masur Mus. Art, Monroe, La., 1993, 96, 2001, Lee Hansley Art Gallery, Raleigh, NC, 1993, 97, 2001, Sol Del Rio, San Antonio, 1995, 97-98, 1812 Artic Gallery, Virginia Beach, Va., 1995, Savannah Coll. Art and Design, 1997, Duke U. Sch. Law, 1998, No. Va. CC, 1999, McLean Project for the Arts, 2002, Southwest Sch. Art & Craft, San Antonio, 2003; exhibited in group shows at Franklin Square and Watkins Gallery, Washington, 1992, Rutgers U., New Brunswick, NJ, 1992, 96, 98, Brody's Gallery, Washington, 1992, Lee Hansley Art Gallery, Raleigh, 1993, 96, 98-2001, 02, 03, 05, 06, Emerson Gallery, McLean, 1993, 95, 99, No. Va. CC, 1994, 99, Harvard U., 1996, Ceres Gallery, NYC, 1999-2000, Millennium Art Ctr., Washington, 2001, Am. Ctr. Physics, 2003. Trustee Bronx Mus., NY, 1977; bd. dirs. Washington Women's Art Ctr., 1977, New Art Examiner, 1985-86; nat. bd. dirs. Women's Caucus for Art, 1983-84. Recipient Concourse award Corcoran Sch. Art, 1952; Telfair Acad. Art scholar, Savannah, Ga., 1959; Nat. Endowment for Arts grantee, 1977-81; fellow Va. Ctr. for Creative Arts, Sweet Briar, Va., 1985. Address: Lee Hansley Gallery 225 Glenwood Ave Raleigh NC 27603 Office Phone: 703-941-3865. E-mail: bjohnb@mchs1.com, chardyrob@cox.net.

ROBINSON, CHERYL JEAN, human services specialist, advocate; b. Bklyn., June 26, 1947; d. George Harry and Maude DeCota Williams; life ptnr. Sybil Virginia Jones, Dec. 1, 1979; children: Zuleika Marie Nathaniel, Karima Melody. AS, San Diego Mesa Coll., 1982. Cert. cmty. econ. devel. San Diego State U., 1997, meeting and event planning San Diego State U., 2002. Asst. storefront dir. Ctr. for Women's Studies and Svcs., San Diego, 1979—84; circulation mgr. The Longest Revolution, San Diego, 1980—84; bookkeeper Potts by Patt, San Diego, 1984—88; human svc. specialist County of San Diego - Health and Human Svc. Agy., 1988—. Treas. U.S.S. Dixion Legal Def. Fund, San Diego, 1980—82, San Diego Gay Ctr., 1981—82; bd. mem. San Diego Lesbians, Gay, Bisexual and Transgender Pride, 1991—2001; student project advisor cmty. econ. devel. cert. program San Diego State U., 1999—; cmty. activist San Diego City Police LGBT Adv. Bd., 2001—; comm. chair Ebony Pride, San Diego, 2002—. Area 1 del. Internat. Assn. of Lesbian, Gay, Bisexual and Transgender Pride Coords., 1993—94; mem. Lesbians of Color, San Diego, 1978—80; facilitator Lesbian Solidarity, San Diego, 1980—83; publicity chair Spectrum, San Diego, 1986—88; promotional chair North Pk. Main St., San Diego, 1996, spring festival chair, 1996—2002; cmty. mem. San Diego Police Lesbian, Gay, Bisexual, Transgender Adv. Bd., San Diego, 2001—03; mem. San Diego Dem. Club, 2002; pers. chair San Diego Lesbian, Gay, Bisexual, Transgender Pride, 1991—2000; mem. San Diego Electric Streetcar, Inc, 2002. Recipient Spl. Commendation, City Coun. San Diego, 1994, City San Diego - Dist. Three, 1997, Cert. of Appreciation, San Diego Lesbian and Gay Pride, 1999, Presidents Award for Com. Mem. of the Yr., North Pk. Main St., 2001. Liberal. Achievements include development of California Main Street Certification. Home: 3251 College Pl Apt 49 Lemon Grove CA 91945-1452 Personal E-mail: cj.robins@cox.net.

ROBINSON, CHERYL JEFFREYS, special education educator; d. William Charles and Dorothy Crawford Jeffreys; m. Norman Norris Robinson, June 21, 1975; children: Nicole Lorraine, Natalie Lavonne. BS summa cum laude, DC Tchrs. Coll., 1976; MA, George Washington U., 1977; EdD, Nova Southeastern U., 2003. Advanced profl. cert. Md. State Dept. Edn., adminstrv. and supervisory cert. Md. State Dept. Edn., 2005. Diagnostic-prescriptive tchr. Prince George's County Md. Pub. Schs., 1977—83, spl. edn. resource tchr., 1984—90, regional spel. edn. specialist, 1990—2005, spl. edn. area office mgr., 2001—02; spl. edn. supr. Montgomery County Pub. Schs., 2005—. Mem. adv. com. rep. Summer Inst. Nova Southeastern U., Ft. Lauderdale, Fla., 1997; planned and facilitated tchr. ADHD tng., 1998—2001; facilitator sch. staff/parent program ADHD students, 2000—01; mem. sch. CEO's faculty support team, 2003—. Mem.: AAUW (Career Devel. grantee 1997—98), Montgomery County Assn. Adminstrv. and Supervisory Personnel, Nat. Educators Assn., Coun. Exceptional Children, Nat. Coun. Negro Women, Kappa Delta Pi, Alpha Kappa Alpha. Democrat. Baptist. Avocations: art, crafts, antiques, theater. Office: Montgomery County Public Schools Carver Ednl Svcs Ctr 850 Hungerford Dr Rm 230 Rockville MD 20855 Office Phone: 301-279-3837. Personal E-mail: robinson@radix.net.

ROBINSON, CLEO PARKER, artistic director; Degree in Dance Edn. Psychology, Denver U., DFA (hon.), 1991. Founder, exec. artistic dir., choreographer Cleo Parker Robinson Dance, Denver. Mem. dance, expansion arts and inter-arts panels NEA; bd. dirs. Denver Ctr. Performing Arts; tchr. in workshops. Co-creator (documentary) African-Americans at Festae, Run Sister Run, (film) Black Women in the Arts, (music video) Borderline. Apptd. Nat. Coun. on Arts, 1999. Recipient Thelma Hill Ctr. for the Performing Arts award, 1986; Choreography fellow NEA; named one of Colo. 100, 1992, Colo. Governor's award for Excellence in the Arts; named to Blacks in Colo. Hall of Fame, 1994. Mem. Internat. Assn. Blacks in Dance (2nd v.p.). Office: 119 Park Ave W Denver CO 80205 Office Phone: 303-295-1759. Business E-Mail: cleodance@aol.com.

ROBINSON, CRYSTAL, professional basketball player; b. Atoka, Okla., Jan. 22, 1974; d. Billy and Nancy Robinson. Grad., S.E. Okla. State, 1996. Forward, WNBA New York Liberty, N.Y.C., 1999—. Named MVP, U.S. Sports Festival, 1993; named to Nat. Assoc. of Intercollegiate Athletics Hall of Fame, 2003; recipient ABL Rookie of the Yr. award, 1996—97.

ROBINSON, DEBORAH J., counselor, educator, consultant; b. Buffalo; d. Daniel L. and Barbara A. Robinson. BA, Canisius Coll., Buffalo, 1974; MS in Student Pers. Adminstrn., Buffalo State Coll., 1981. Notary pub., N.Y. Counselor U. Buffalo-Buffalo Ednl. Talent Search, 1982; residential mgr. Women's Residential Resource Ctr., Buffalo, 1986-88; GED coord. aide and tutor JUSENDO, Buffalo, 1988-89; counselor, coord. Trott ACCESS Ctr. Niagara County C.C., Sanborn, N.Y., 1989-91, coord. women in tech. program, 1992, CEOSC counselor, 1992-93, placement counselor, 1993-95, counselor, 1995—. Cons. Cmty. Action Orgn., Edn. Task Force, Buffalo; mem. Ellicott Dist. Concerned Taxpayers, Buffalo; evaluator commn. on higher edn. Middle States Assn. Colls., 1998—. Mentor Buffalo Youth for Golf, Inc., 2002. Recipinet Niagara County Black Achievers, Inc. award, 1998. Mem. AAUW, Career Devel. Orgn., Di GAmma. Avocations: collecting elephants, reading, stock market. Office: Niagara County CC 3111 Saunders Settlement Rd Sanborn NY 14132-9487

ROBINSON, DEBRA JOANN, science educator; b. Monroe, Miss., Mar. 24, 1959; d. John Robert and Violet Ruth Rothenberger; 1 child, Shardae Cheree. BS in Criminial Justice, U. Tex., Arlington, 1981; M in Edn., U. Phoenix, 2006. Teaching Certification La Tournea U., 2004. ICU, cardiac catheter lab. HCA Hosp., Arlington, Tex., 1984—94; exec. dir. Alterrra Assisted Living, Cedar Hill, Tex., 1994—99; h.s. sci. tchr. Faith Family Acad., Dallas, 1999—. Sponsor Faith Family Acad., Dallas, 2003—. Avocations: reading, painting, crafts. Home: 1404 Legget Arlington TX 76018 Office: Faith Family Acad 300 W Kiest Dallas TX 75224

ROBINSON, DEVETTE LORRAINE, music educator; d. Horace Edward and Cassie Jones; m. Claude Jones, Oct. 10, 1992; 1 child, Clarisa. MusB, MA, Prairie View A&M U., Tex., 1981. All-level music cert. Tex. Edn. Agy. Choir dir., Houston, 1994—96; band and percussion dir., 1996—2000; choir dir., 2000—03; choir dir., aux. dir., 2000—03; choir dir., 2003—04, Sheldon Ind. Sch. Dist., Houston, 2004—. Singer: (jazz ensemble) Salute to Martin Luther King and Mahalia Jackson. Named Tchr. of Yr., Sch. Campus and Adminstrv. Office, 2000—01. Mem.: Tex. Music Educators Assn., Iota Phi Lambda (assoc.), Delta Sigma Theta (assoc.). Democrat. Baptist. Avocations: travel, walking, Karate.

ROBINSON, DIXIE FAYE, elementary and secondary school educator; b. Lexington, Ky., Feb. 7, 1944; d. John David and Betty Lou (Taylor) Moore; m. Jim Darrell Robinson, June 25, 1978. BA, Georgetown (Ky.) Coll., 1966; MA in Edn., Ball State U., 1972; postgrad., Miami U., Oxford, Ohio, 1989—, Ind. U., 1990-92. Cert. tchr., Ind. Tchr. Richmond (Ind.) Community Schs., 1966-91, adminstr., 1991-97, alt. sch. tchr., 1997—. Team leader Richmond Community schs., 1983-90, mentor tchr., 1989-91, 2004—, coop. learning staff devel. mem., 1989-91, coord. ptnrship in edn., 1990-91, site-base convenor, 1990-91; v.p. Richmond Area Reading Coun., 1984. Pres. Historic Richmond, Inc., 1982; tour guide Richmond-Wayne County Tourism Bur., 1986-87; vice-chmn. Richmond Area Rose Festival, 1988-89; adv. bd. Palladium Item, Richmond, 1990. Recipient Hoosier Meritorious award Ind. Sec. of State, 1986, Nat. Energy Edn. Devel. award, Washington, 1991, Exemplary Program award for alternative schs. State of Ind., 2001 Cmtys. in Schs. Wayne County Tchr. of Yr., 2005; grantee Newspapers in Edn., 1986. Mem. NEA, NAFE, ASCD, Nat. Mid. Sch. Assn., Assn. Tchr. Educators, Nat.

Assn. Secondary Sch. Prins., Nat. Coun. Tchrs. English (Ctr. of Excellence award 1988-91), Ind. Coun. Tchrs. of English (Hoosier Tchr. English 1991), Ind. Middle Level Inst., Richmond Area Reading Coun., Kappa Delta Gamma, Phi Delta Kappa. Avocations: historic preservation, antiques, community affairs, reading, travel. Home: 100 NW 8th St Richmond IN 47374-4055

ROBINSON, DOROTHY K., lawyer; b. New Haven, Feb. 18, 1951; children: Julia Robinson Bouwsma, Alexandra Toby Bouwsma. BA in Econs. with honors, Swarthmore Coll., 1972; JD, U. Calif., Berkeley, 1975; MA (hon.), Yale U., 1987. Bar: Calif. 1975, N.Y. 1976, Conn. 1981, U.S. Ct. Appeals (2d cir.) 1975, U.S. Dist. Ct. (so. dist.) N.Y. 1981. Assoc. Hughes Hubbard & Reed, N.Y.C., 1975-78; asst. gen. counsel Yale U., New Haven, 1978-79, assoc. gen. counsel, 1979-84, dep. gen. counsel, 1984-86, gen. counsel, 1986—95, dir. fed. rels., 1986-88, acting sec., 1993, v.p., gen. counsel, 1995—. Mem. Calif. Law Rev., 1973-75. Trustee Hopkins Grammar Day Prospect Hill Sch., New Haven, 1983-88, sec., 1986-88; trustee Wenner-Gren Found. Anthrop. Rsch., 1991-2003; bd. dirs. Cold Spring Sch., New Haven, 1990-95; mem. adv. bd. Conn. Mental Health Ctr., New Haven, 1979-89; bd. dirs. Nat. Assn. Ind. Coll. and Univs., 1995-98; mem. alumni coun. Swarthmore Coll., 1999-2002. Fellow Ezra Stiles Coll. Yale U., Am. Bar Found.; mem. ABA, Nat. Assn. Coll. and Univ. Attys. (bd. dirs. 1987-90), Conn. Bar Assn., Calif. Bar Assn., Assn. Bar City N.Y., Phi Beta Kappa. Office: Yale U Office of VP and Gen Counsel PO Box 208255 New Haven CT 06520-8255 Office Phone: 203-432-4949.

ROBINSON, ELIZABETH LEIGH, special education educator; b. Nashville, Apr. 12; BS in Spl. Edn./English magna cum laude, Vanderbilt U., 1982. Spl. edn. tchr., grades 9-10 Hickman County High Sch., Centerville, Tenn., 1982—, dept. chmn. Mem.: ACTE.

ROBINSON, ELLA GARRETT, editor, writer; b. Decatur, Ala., Apr. 12, 1954; d. Calvis Clemon and Jewell Helms Garrett; m. Daniel Robinson, May 7, 1976. BA, Samford U., Birmingham, AL, 1972—76. Editl. asst. Woman's Missionary Union, Birmingham, Ala., 1976—94; copy editor/writer freelance, Pleasant Grove, Ala., 1994—. Author: (book) A Guide to Literary Sites of the South, 1998. Mem.: Ala. Media Profls. Home: 735 Seventh Pl Pleasant Grove AL 35127 Personal E-mail: ERobnson@aol.com.

ROBINSON, EMILY SUE, music educator; b. Henryetta, Okla., Mar. 1, 1952; d. William Gilbert and Frances (Meyer) Campbell; m. Robert Thomas Robinson, Apr. 16, 1972; children: Juliette Renae Kidd, Tamara Kaye Clemence, Samuel Thomas. MusB, Oklahoma City U., 1974; MusM, U. Okla., 1990. Piano instr., Midwest City, Okla., 1976—; accompanist Rose State Coll., Midwest City, 1986—, adj. prof., 1988—2000, prof., 2000—; accompanist Midwest Choral Soc., Midwest City, 1992—2000. Organist Midwest Blvd. Christian Ch., Midwest City, 1971-74; accompanist Chouteau Acad. Ballet, Oklahoma City, 1972-75, music dir. Eastminster United Presbyn. Ch., Del City, 1975—. Mem. Okla. Music Tchrs. Assn. (adjudicator 1994—), Ctrl. Oklahoma Music Tchrs. Assn. (historian 1996-98). Home: 332 W Campbell Dr Midwest City OK 73110-3318 Office: Rose State Coll 6420 SE 15th St Midwest City OK 73110-2704

ROBINSON, EVELYN EDNA, secondary school educator; b. St. John, Maine, Feb. 23, 1911; d. Registe Jalbert and Olive Michaud; m. Carl Robinson, July 19, 1939; children: Robert, James. BA in Math., U. Maine, 1934; MS, U. N.H., 1963; MEd, Hillyer Coll. U., 1960. Tchr. English and math. Ft. Kent (Maine) H.S., 1934; tchr. English and math., coach girls basketball Madewaska (Maine) H.S., 1935-55; tchr. math. Stamford (Conn.) H.S., 1955-56; tchr. math and English, Bristol (Conn.) H.S., 1956-63; prof. math. Worcester (Mass.) State Coll., 1963-77, chmn. dept., 1970-77. Coord. cmty. bus. Worcester State Coll., 1970-77, class advisor, 1968-72, salary equity bd., 1971-73. Vol. libr. Madawaska Pub. Libr., 1936-55; lector Christ the King, Worcester, 1974-2000. Mem. Delta Kappa Gamma. Republican. Roman Catholic. Avocations: decorating, flower arrangements, ceramics, tailoring. Home: 167 N Spencer Rd Spencer MA 01562-1232

ROBINSON, EVELYN ETTA, principal; b. Pocatello, Idaho, Nov. 5, 1946; d. Luther Nelson Robinson and Marian Rose Smith. Tchr. diploma, Bapt. Bible Coll., 1968; BA, U. Ill., Springfield, 1978, MA, 1979; edn. specialist, Idaho State U., Boise, 1988. Cert. elementary tchr., sch. prin., superintendent. 1st grade tchr. Villa Christian Sch., Broadview, Ill., 1968—74, North Jacksonville Elem., Jacksonville, Ill., 1978—79, Bonneville Elem., Pocatello, Idaho, 1979—88; edn. supr. Grace Acad., Springfield, Ill., 1977—78; prin. Westfair Acad., Jacksonville, 1977—84, Lewis & Clark Elem., Pocatello, Idaho, 1988—. Instr. Idaho Sate U. Coll. Edn., Pocatello, 1987—, District #25 Tech. Portfolio, 1997—; curriculum instr. Integration of Tech. into Idaho history, 1999—; inservice instr. District #25, Pocatello, 1988—; mentor District #25 Tech. Mentor Program, 1996—; mem. District #25 Curriculum Com., 1996—2000, Leadership for the 21st Century Com., 1997—, Home Page Devel. Com., 1999—, Tchr. Evaluation Com., 2000—01, Sch. Improvement Criteria Com., 2000—01, Enhancement Learning Project Com., 2000—; commr. Idaho State Bd. Edn. Accountability Commn., 2003—; presenter in field. Author: Lewis & Clark School Improvement Profile, 1988—2005. Tchr. children's program Idaho State Mus. Natural History, Pocatello, 1984; mem. Salvation Army Canned Food Drive Com., Pocatello, 1994—, Neighborhood Watch Program, Pocatello, 1994—, Neighborhood Support Group for the Elderly, Pocatello, 1996—, Ross Park Zoological Soc., Pocatello, 2003—; tchr. Sunday Sch. Workshop Nazarene Ch., Pocatello, 1985—; bd. dirs. Pocatello Zoo, 2003—. Nominee Idaho Tchr. of Yr., 1982—83, Outstanding Adminstr., Pocatello Edn. Assn., 1994; named Tchr. of Yr., Bonneville Elem. Parent-Tchr. Assn., 1982—83, Bonneville Elem., 1988—89; recipient Outstanding Svc. award, Messiah Baptist Ch., 1972, Outstanding Leadership award, Am. Assn. Sunday Schools, 1977, Sunday Sch. Leadership award, Westfair Baptist Ch., 1979, Dedication to Youth award, Ctr. for Leadership, Edn., and Devel., 1989, 8 Who Make a Difference award, Idaho Channel 8, Pocatello, 1997, Woman of Achievement award, ZONTA Internat., 2005, Excellence in Edn. award, Northwest Regional, 2006, Idaho's Excellence in Edn. award, Alpha Delta Kappa, 2006. Mem.: SE Idaho Reading Assn. (bldg. rep. 1983—88, chair newspaper in edn. week 1984—88), Internat. Reading Assn. (chair newspaper in edn. 1986—87, chair Idaho Honors coun. 1987—88), Assn. Supervision and Curriculum Devel., District #25 Assn. Elem. Sch. Principals (v.p. 1989—90, pres. 1990—91), Region V Assn. Elem. Sch. Principals, Idaho Assn. Sch. Administrators, Idaho Assn. Elem. Sch. Principals (Idaho Gem award 1990—91, Idaho's Nat. Disting. Prin. award 2005), Nat. Assn. Elem. Sch. Principals, Internat. and Portneuf Valley Audubon Assn., Phi Delta Kappa (chair program com. 1987—88, v.p. program com. 1988—89, v.p. membership 1989—90, pres. 1990—91), Alpha Delta Kappa (sgt. at arms 1982—84, chair altruistic com. 1986—88, chair courtesy com. 1990—92, historian 1992—94, Idahos Excellence in Edn. award 2006). Avocations: gardening, hunting, fishing, birdwatching, hiking. Office: Lewis & Clark Elem 800 Grace Dr Pocatello ID 83201 Business E-Mail: robinsev@d25.k12.id.us.

ROBINSON, FLORINE SAMANTHA, marketing executive; b. Massies Mill, Va., Feb. 4, 1935; d. John Daniel and Fannie Belle (Smith) Jackson; m. Frederick Robinson (div. 1973); children: Katherine, Theresa, Freda. BS, Morgan State U., 1976; postgrad., U. Balt., 1977-81, Liberty U., 1987. Writer, reporter Phila. Independent News, 1961-63; freelance writer, editor Balt., 1963-71; asst. mng. editor Williams & Wilkins Pubs. Inc., Balt, 1971-76; mktg. rep., then mktg. mgr. NCR Corp., Balt., 1977-93; assoc. minister, trustee Christian Unity Temple, Balt., 1976—; pres. ABCOM, Inc., Balt., 1993—. Bd. dirs. Armstrong & Bratcher, Inc., Balt. Editor: Stedman's Medical Dictionary, 1972; contbr. articles to profl. jours. Active PTA, Balt., 1963-65; bd. dirs. Howard Pk. Civic Assn., Balt., 1967—, pres. 1991—; leader, cons. Girl Scouts USA, 1970-73. Recipient Excellence in Rsch. award Psi Chi, 1976, Citizen citation Mayor of Balt. Mem. NAFE, Mid-Atlantic Food Dealers Assn., Am. Soc. Notaries, Internat. Platform Assn., Edelweiss Club, Order of Eastern Star. Democrat. Avocation: piano. Home: 3126 Howard Park Ave Baltimore MD 21207-6715

ROBINSON, GAIL PATRICIA, retired mental health counselor; b. Medford, Oreg., Dec. 31, 1936; d. Ivan T. and Evelyn H. (Hamilton) Skyrman; m. Douglas L. Smith; children: Shauna J., James D. BS in Edn., Oreg. State U., 1958, PhD in Counseling, 1978; MS in Counseling, Western Oreg. State Coll., 1974. Tchr. Monterey (Calif.) Pub. Schs., 1958-59, Corvallis (Oreg.) Pub. Schs., 1959-62, 69-75, counselor, 1977-81; pvt. practice Corvallis, 1977-95. Vol. therapist Children's Svcs. divsn., Linn and Benton Counties, 1982-83; asst. prof. Western Oreg. State coll., 1977, counselor, 1982-83; mem. grad. faculty Oreg. State U., Corvallis, 1978-95; presenter workshops, lectr. in field. Contbr. articles to profl. jours. Mem. Benton County Mental Helath Citizens Adv. Bd., 1979-85, chair, 1982-83; trustee WCTU Children's Farm Home, 1978-84, chair child welfare com., 1982-83, pres., 1984; mem. Old Mill Sch. Adv. Bd., 1979-85, chair, 1979-81; bd. dirs. Cmty. Outreach, 1979-83; mem. Benton Com. for Prevention of Child Abuse, 1979-85, v.p., 1982; mem. Oreg. Bd. Lic. Profl. Counselors and Therapists, 1989-95, chair, 1989-90, Aurora Colony Historical Soc., vol., 2000-, bd. mem. 2005-. Mem. ACA (govt. rels. com. 1988-91, professionalization com. 1988-92, pres. 1996-97), Am. Mental Health Counselors Assn. (chair consumer and pub. rels. com. 1988-91, bd. dirs. Western region 1989-91, chair strategic planning com. 1994-95, pres. 1992-93), Oreg. Counseling Assn. (chair licensure liaison com. 1985-91, exec. bd. 1985-88, steering com. 1986-87, register editorial com. 1985-86, Disting. Svc. award 1985, 87, Leona Tyler award 1989), Oreg. Mental Health Counselors Assn. Personal E-mail: robinsgp@comcast.net.

ROBINSON, GEORGIA MAY, retired education educator; b. Detroit, Sept. 6, 1926; d. George J. and Lena C. (Behrendt) Levin; m. Ralph M. Robinson, Apr. 15, 1956; children: Aron David, Stephen Mark. BS, Elmhurst (Ill.) Coll., 1950; MAT, Nat. Coll. of Edn., Evanston, 1978. Tchr. Am. Echod Congregation, Waukegan, Ill., 1966-74, AAUW Nursery Sch., Waukegan, 1965-76, Nat. Coll. Edn., Evanston, 1977-87; instr. childhood edn. Nat. Louis U., Evanston, 1977-96. Cons. Am. Sch. of Lima, Peru, 1979, Ill. State Bd. of Edn., Springfield, 1986-91; scrip cons. Coronet Ednl. Films, Chgo., 1981-82; adv. coun. Mus. of Sci. and Industry, Chgo., 1980-81; chmn. for Ferguson lecture series Nat. Coll. Edn., 1984-85; presenter in field. Mem. cmty. adv. coun. Waukegan Sch. Dist. 60, 1977—78; mem. scholarship selection com. Altrusa, Waukegan, 1984—90; chmn. sch. bd. Am Echod Congregation, 1994—96; bd. dirs. Waukegan Sch. Found., 1991—98. Mem. Nat. Assn. for Edn. of Young Children (validator for accredidation process 1987-96), Ill. Assn. for the Edn. of Young Children, Chgo. Assn. for the Edn. of Young Children, Midwest Assn. for the Edn. of Young Children, Ill. Soc. Early Childhood Profls. (membership chair 1992-96), Assn. for the Advancement of Therapeutic Edn. (founder, co-pres. 1987-92). Avocations: mixed media painting, sewing, golf. Home: 705 Colville Pl Waukegan IL 60087-5026

ROBINSON, GLENDA CAROLE, pharmacist; b. Johnson City, Tenn. d. Harry and Jackie Evelyn Bowers; m. Richard Haynes Robinson, 1967 (div. 1985); children: Rachel Corianne, Fredrick David. BS in Pharmacy, U. Tenn., 1967. Pharmacist supr. Sommers Drug Stores, San Antonio, 1968-69; staff pharmacist Crawford Long Hosp., Atlanta, 1971-72, Rich's Pharmacy, Atlanta, 1973-74; relief staff pharmacist Atchley Drug Ctr., Greeneville, Tenn., 1977-86; staff pharmacist Takoma Hosp. Pharmacy, Greeneville, 1983-86, Greene Valley Developmental Ctr., Greeneville, 1987-91, dir. pharmacy, 1991—. Mem. First Dist. Pharmacy Assn. East Tenn., Greeneville Jr. Women's Club (sec., internat. affairs chair), Greeneville Morning Rotary Club (pres., Polio Plus chair, Outstanding Rotarian 1996-97, Found. Dist. Svc. award 1998-99).

ROBINSON, GWENDOLYN NEINA, elementary school educator; d. John Henry and Beatrice Robinson; m. Ronald E. Peterson; children: Wadiya K. Peterson, Zakia N. Peterson, Neimah G. Peterson. BA, Coll. New Rochelle, NY, 1985; MA, CUNY, NYC, 2000; postgrad., Touro Coll., NYC, 2006—. Tchr. Gates Acad., Bronx, 1988—89, Cmty. elem. Sch. 114X, 1989—90, Macombs Hr. H.S. 82X, 1990—95, CES 64X, 1995—99, Sisulu Children's Acad., NYC, 1999—2000, Kasholu Montefiore Daycare, Bronx, 2000—01, CES124X, 2001—. Tchr., co-chair Sch. Leadership Team, Bronx, 2005—; advisor Bronx Arts Ensemble, 2005—06. Mem.: NAACP, Alumni Assn. City Colls. Baptist. Office: Bd Edn 175 W 166th St Bronx NY 10452

ROBINSON, HELENE M., retired music educator; b. Eugene, Oreg., May 30, 1912; d. Kirkman K. and Emily A. Robinson. BA in Music, U. Oreg., 1935; MusM, Northwestern U., Evanston, Ill., 1945. Piano tchr. No. Ariz. U., Flagstaff, 1952—60, Calif. State U., Fullerton, 1960—61, U. Calif., Santa Barbara, 1961—62, Ariz. State U., Tempe, 1963—77. Author: Basic Piano for Adults, vol. I and II, 1964, Intermediate Piano for Adults, vols. I and II, 1970; author: (with others) Teaching Piano in Classroom and Studio; contbr. articles to profl. jours. Mem.: Music Tchrs. Nat. Assn. (spkr. convs. 1974—76), Phi Beta. Avocation: piano. Home: 1300 NE 16th Ave Ste c/o Hcc Portland OR 97232-4421

ROBINSON, HELENE SUSAN, pharmacist; b. Cleve., July 10, 1956; d. Martin Stanley and Elaine (Steinhardt) Grumbach; children: Marie, Michelle, Michael. BS in Pharm. Scis., U. Cin., 1979; cert. Women in Mgmt., Ursuline Coll., Pepper Pike, Ohio, 1983. Asst. mgr. Cunningham Drugs, Cleve., 1979-80; staff pharmacist St. Luke's Hosp., Cleve., 1980-84, oncology pharmacist, 1984-85; dir. of pharmacy Care Plus-Cleve., Beachwood, Ohio, 1985-87; staff pharmacist Kaiser Permanent, 1987-88; pharmacist HMSS, Cleve., 1988-94, Coram, Cleve., 1995-97; asst. dir. pharmacy Mt. Sinai Med. Ctr., Richmond Heights, Ohio, 1998; dir. pharmacy Mt. Sinai East Med. Ctr., 1999-2000; pharmacist Marc's Pharmacy, Solon, Ohio, 2000—. Vol. Music and Drama Depts. Solon (Ohio) HS, 2002—. Participant strategic planning com. Solon Schs., 2001—02. Mem. Cleve. Soc. Hosp. Pharmacists (chmn. oncology 1984-85), Ohio Soc. Hosp. Pharmacists, Am. Soc. Hosp. Pharmacists, Kappa Epsilon. Avocations: needlepoint, reading, sewing. Office: Marc's Pharmacy 6239 Som Center Rd Solon OH 44139

ROBINSON, JANET L., publishing executive; BA in English cum laude, Salve Regina Coll., Newport, R.I., 1972; diploma in Exec. Edn., Dartmouth U., 1996; DBA (hon.), Salve Regina U., Newport, R.I., 1998. Tchr., reading specialist, 1972—83; account exec., Tennis Mag. The N.Y. Times Co., 1983—85, nat. resort and travel mgr., Golf Digest/Tennis, 1985—87, advt. dir., Tennis Mag., 1987—90, v.p. advt. sales and mktg., The Women's Mag. Group, 1990—92, group sr. v.p., advt. sales and mktg., The Women's Mag. Group, 1992—93, v.p., dir. advt., 1994, sr. v.p. advt., 1995, pres., gen. mgr., N.Y. Times newspaper, 1996—, sr. v.p. newspaper ops., 2001—04, exec. v.p., COO, 2004—, dir., 2004—, pres., CEO, 2005—. Cons. Dept. Edn., Mass., 1977—83; chair. Advertising Council, 2004—. Mem. Literacy Vols. N.Y.; mem. adv. bd. Salve Regina Coll.; trustee Carnegie Corp., 2004—. Named Outstanding Newspaper Exec., Frohlinger's Mktg. Report, 1994; named one of 100 Most Powerful Women in World, Forbes Mag., 2005—06. Mem.: Women in Comm., Advt. Women N.Y., Advt. Club N.Y. Office: NY Times 229 W 43rd St New York NY 10036-3959*

ROBINSON, JENNIFER JEAN, lawyer; b. Chgo., Aug. 23, 1975; d. Ivan M. and Roberta E. Rittenberg; m. Richard A. Robinson. BA in Anthropology with honors, U. Iowa, Iowa City, 1997, JD with highest distinction, 2003. Assoc. Rittenberg, Buffen & Gulbrandsen, Ltd., Chgo., 2003—. Office: Rittenberg Buffen & Gulbrandsen LTd 309 W Washington St Ste 900 Chicago IL 60606-3209

ROBINSON, JEWELL, arts and education administrator, actor; d. Maxie Cleveland and Doris Jones Robinson; m. James Douglass Shepperd (div.); children: Randall Jeffrey Shepperd, Scott Douglass Shepperd. BA, George Washington U., Wash., DC, 1959; LHD (hon.), Goucher Coll., Towson, Md., 2003. Exec. asst. to dir. Wash. Urban League; staff assoc. to pres. Nat. Coun. Negro Women, Washington; divsn. mgr. United Givers Fund (United Way), Washington; v.p. TransCentury Corp., Washington; dep. dir. Nat. Bd. YMCAs, Washington, NOAA Office of Congl. Affairs, Washington, 1978—79; exec. dir. Ellington Fund (Ellington Sch. of the Arts), Washington, 1978—82. Mem. bd. Wash. Ballet, 1979—81, Wash. Stage Guild, 1990—. Author: (script) Mother Lange: The French Soul, 1998, Unforgettable: Nat King Cole, the Man and His Music, 2000, The Whole World in His Hands: the Life and Music of Paul Robeson, 2004, Rita Hayworth: Latin Love Goddess, 2001, What Made Sammy Run? The Life and Music of Sammy Davis, Jr., 1999, Black Mary, 1998, Alice, 1998, Miss Anderson's Music: The Life and Music of Marian Anderson, 2002, Blond Ambitianss: Marlene Dietrich, Mae West & Tallulah Bankhead, 2002; co-author: Thomas Jefferson and His Slave, Betty Hemings, 1993; actor: numerous theatre and TV roles. Mem. bd. Whitman Walker AIDS Clinic, Washington, 1992—2000; vol. AIDSWalk, Washington. Recipient Mary Goldwater award, Theatre Lobby, 1992, award, Audelco, 2001, Helen Hayes award, 2001. Mem.: Am. Fedn. TV and Radio Artists, Screen Actors Guild, Actors Equity Assn. Democrat. Protestant. Avocations: reading, writing, sewing, art. Office: Smithsonian Nat Portrait Gallery Washington DC 20015 Business E-Mail: robinsonj@si.edu.

ROBINSON, JOANNE ADELE, retired secondary school educator, volunteer; b. Alameda, Calif., May 9, 1936; d. Herbert William and Jeanne Adele (Stoddard) Justin; m. William Grant Robinson, Aug. 26, 1961; children: Deann Adele, Scott William, Paul Justin. BS in Physical Edn./Bio. Sci., San Francisco State U., 1958. Cert. secondary tchr. Calif., 1959. Phys. edn. tchr. San Mateo Union High Dist., Menlo Park, Calif., 1959—64, Alameda Unified Sch. Dist., 1964—66; program dir. Girls Club Am., Alameda, 1975—80, Camp Fire Boys & Girls, Inc., Oakland, Calif., 1980—85; phys. edn. tchr. Alameda Adult Sch., 1990—2004; ret., 2004. 1st aid/CPR instr. Am. Red Cross, Alameda, 1960—2006, team leadership coord., 1978—2006. Pres., fundraiser bd. mem. Alameda Girls Club, 1967—89; mem. UNA E. Bay Chpt., Alameda, 1968—2006; summer faire chairman Alameda Welfare Council, 1981—2006; area rep. Youth For Understanding Internat. Exchange, Alameda, 1986—91; vol. coord. food distribution to low-income families SHARE No. Calif., 1988—98; v.p., program coord. Ch. Women United, Alameda, 1985—2006. Recipient Gulick award, Camp FIre Boys & Girls, Inc., 1982, Woman of Yr. award, City of Alameda, 1996. Mem.: PEO, Womans Nat. Sports Assn. (nat. acquatics judge 1959—67), Calif. Assn. Health, Phys. Edn., Recreation & Dance (life), Delta Kappa Gamma Internat. Avocations: hiking, bicycling, kayaking, drawing. Home: 2857 Lincoln Ave Alameda CA 94501

ROBINSON, JOYCE ELAINE, science educator; d. Eugene Carl and Daisy Belle Anderson; m. Gary Leonard Robinson, Oct. 27, 1979; children: Gary Leonard II, Jaron D'Andre. AA, Butler County C.C., El Dorado, Kans., 1977; BS, Emporia State U., Kans., 1978; MS, Our Lady of The Lake U., San Antonio, 2002. Cert. sci. composite tchr. Tex., life-earth sci. tchr. Tex. Subsitute tchr. Wichita (Kans.) Pub. Sch. Dist., 1991—93; sci. tchr. NE Ind. Sch. Dist., San Antonio, 1994—. Mentor tchr. Rural South Tex. Regional Collaborative, San Antonio, 2002—. Named one of Outstanding Young Women of Am., 1978; grantee NSF, 2000—02; NASA Space/Geoscis. Project grantee, 2000—02, Comet grantee, 2000—02. Mem.: Delta Sigma Theta (life; founder's day com. chmn. 1989—91, asst. fin. sec.). Baptist. Avocations: racquetball, travel, shopping, modeling. Office: 4538 Vance Jackson San Antonio TX 78230 Office Phone: 210-442-0550.

ROBINSON, JUDITH ADELL, elementary school educator; b. Youngstown, Ohio, Jan. 13, 1940; d. Nicholas Hamilton and Virginia Lee (Cross) Hayden; m. William Albert Kata (dec.); 1 child, Tiffany Kata stepchildren: Terie Kata, William Tyson Kata, J. Todd Kata; m. Bruce Alan Robinson, Feb. 25, 2003; stepchildren: Curtis, Randall. BS in edn., Youngstown State U., 1966; MS in edn., Kent State U., 1969. Tchr. Austintown Kindergarden Assn., Austintown, Ohio, 1963—66, Yongstown City Sch., Youngstown, Ohio, 1966—2001. Bd. mem. Youngstown City Sch., Credit Union, Youngstown, Ohio, 1978—94, v.p., 1994—2004, pres., 2004—. Mem. The Jr. League of Youngstown, Youngstown, Ohio, 2001—, Youngstown Area Federation of Women's Clubs, Youngstown, 1959—, Fortnighly IV, Youngstown, 1959—. Mem.: Ohio Edn. Assn., Mahoning County Ret. Tchrs., Mahoning Valley Lit. Assn., Thursday Nine Golf Club, Saxon Club Couples Bocce League, Duffers Couples Golf Club, Order Eastern Star, Delta Kappa Gamma. Republican. Presbyterian. Avocations: travel, reading, golf, bridge, gambling. Home: 1330 Millicent Ave Youngstown OH 44505 Home (Winter): 3430 Auburndale Ave The Villages FL 32162 E-mail: jkata13@aol.com.

ROBINSON, JULIE ANN, judge; b. 1957; BS, U. Kans., 1978, JD, 1981. Bar: Kans. 1981. Asst. U.S. atty. for dist. Kans. U.S. Dept. Justice, Kansas City, Kans., 1983—94, sr. litigation counsel, 1991—94; law clk. to hon. Benjamin E. Franklin, U.S. Bankruptcy Ct. for Dist. Kans., Kansas City, Kans., 1981—83, bankruptcy judge, 1994—2001; judge bankruptcy appellate panel U.S. Ct. Appeals (10th cir.), Topeka, 1996—2001; U.S. dist. judge State of Kans., 2001—. Instr. trial practice U. Kans. Sch. Law, 1989—90. Fellow: Am. Bar Found.; mem.: ABA, Kans. Bar Assn. Office: US Dist Ct 405 US Courthouse 444 SE Quincy Topeka KS 66683

ROBINSON, JUNE KERSWELL, dermatologist, educator; b. Phila., Jan. 26, 1950; d. George and Helen S. (Kerswell) R.; m. William T. Barker, Jan. 31, 1981. BA cum laude, U. Pa., 1970; MD, U. Md., 1974. Diplomate Am. Bd. Dermatology, Nat. Bd. Med. Examiners, Am. Bd. Mohs Micrographic Surgery and Cutaneous Oncology. Intern Greater Balt. Med. Ctr., Hanover, NH, 1974, resident in medicine, 1974—75; resident in dermatology Dartmouth-Hitchcock Med. Ctr., Hanover, 1975—78, chief resident, clin. instr., 1977—78, instr. in dermatology, 1978; fellow Mohs; chemosurgery and dermatologic surgery NYU Skin and Cancer Clinic, N.Y.C., 1978—79; instr. in dermatology NYU, N.Y.C., 1979; asst. prof. dermatology Northwestern U. Med. Sch., Chgo., 1979, asst. prof. surgery, 1980—85, assoc. prof. dermatology and surgery, 1985—91, prof. dermatology and surgery, 1991—98; prof. medicine and pathology, dir. divsn. dermatology Cardinal Bernardin Cancer Ctr., Loyola U. Med. Ctr., 1998—2004, program leader skin cancer clin. program, 1998—2004; prof. medicine Med. Sch. Dartmouth U., 2004—05, chief Dermatology Sect. Hitchcock Med. Ctr., 2004—05; prof. clin. dermatology Feinberg Sch. Medicine, Northwestern U., Chgo., 2006—. Mem. consensus devel. conf. NIH, 1992; mem. panel on use of sunscreens Internat. Agy. for Rsch. on Cancer, WHO, 2000; lectr. in field. Author: Fundamentals of Skin Biopsy, 1985, also audiovisual materials; editor: (textbooks) Atlas of Cutaneous Surgery, 1996, Cutaneous Medicine and Surgery: An Integrated Program in Dermatology, 1996, Surgery of the Skin, 2005; mem. editl. bd. Archives of Dermatology, 1988-97; sect. editor The Cutting Edge: Challenges in Med. and Surg. Therapeutics, 1989-97, editor, 2004—; contbg. editor Jour. Dermatol. Surgery and Oncology, 1985-88; mem. editl. com. 18th World Congress of Dermatology, 1982; contbr. numerous articles, abstracts to profl. publs., chpts. to books. Bd. dirs. Northwestern Med. Faculty Found., 1982-84, chmn. com. on benefits and leaves, 1984, nominating com. 1988. Grantee Nat. Cancer Inst., 1985-91, 2004—, Am. Cancer Soc., 1986-89, Skin Cancer Found., 1984-85, Dermatology Found., 1981-83, Northwestern U. Biomed. Rsch., 1981, Syntex, 1984. Fellow: Am. Coll. Chemosurgery (chmn. sci. program ann. meeting 1983, chmn. publs. com. 1986—87, chmn. task force on ednl. needs 1989—90, co-editor bull. 1984—87); mem.: Chgo. Dermatol. Soc., Women's Dermatol. Soc. (pres. 1990—92, Wilma Bergeld, MD Visionary and Leadership award 2002), Soc. Investigative Dermatology, Am. Soc. Dermatol. Surgery (pres. 1994—95), Dermatology Found. (trustee 1995—98), Am. Acad. Dermatology (asst. sec.-treas. 1995—98, sec.-treas. 1998—2001, bd. dirs. 1993—95, Stephen Rothman Lectr. award 1992, Presdl. citation 1992, 2000), Am. Dermatol. Assn., Am. Cancer Soc. (pres. Ill. divsn. 1996—98, St. George Disting. Svc. medal 2004). Office: Northwestern U Feinberg Sch Med Dept Dermatology 132 E Delaware Pl #5806 Chicago IL 60611

ROBINSON, KAREN ANN, marketing executive; b. Roswell, N.Mex., Nov. 15, 1957; d. Conard Roe and Shirley Maxine (Donahey) Shelnut; m. Raymond Lee Robinson Jr., Dec. 5, 1987. BA in Economics and Polit. Sci., U. Redlands, Calif., 1980. Exec. trainee, dept. mgr. May Co., L.A., 1980, div. sales mgr., 1981; mgr. phone ctr. Pacific Bell/AT&T, L.A., 1982-83; regional sales mgr. AT&T, L.A., 1983-85, mgr. strategic planning Basking Ridge, N.J., 1985-86, nat. applications mgr. Atlanta, 1986-87; v.p. strategic planning Ernest Telecom, Atlanta, 1988; v.p. sales and mktg. Nat. Data Corp., Atlanta,

1989—91, Amnex, 1991—93; CEO Electronic Power Tech. Inc., Enrev Corp.; pres., CEO Prime Point Media, Ga., 2001. Former pres. Tech. Exec. Round Table; spkr. in field. Contbr. articles to profl. jours. Named one of Top 20 Women in Wireless Industry, Wireless Weekly, 2000; recipient Women of Yr. Tech. award, (WIT) Women in Tech., 2000. Mem. Sales and Mktg. Execs. of Atlanta, NAFE, Committee 200. Presbyterian. Avocation: scuba diving. Office: Prime Point Media Ste 170 680 Engineering Dr Norcross GA 30092 Office Phone: 637-966-0100 ext. 303. E-mail: krobinson@primepointmedia.com.*

ROBINSON, KAREN L., music educator; 1 child. BA in Music Edn., Ohio State U., Chico, 1991; M in Conducting, U. Oreg., Eugene, 1994. Cert. tchr. Calif. Tchr. K-8 music Sunriver Prep Sch., Oreg., 1994—95; choral dir. Acalanes H.S., Lafayette, Calif., 1995—99, Carlmont H.S., Belmont, Calif., 2000—03; artistic dir. Peninsula Womens Chorus, Palo Alto, Calif., 2001—03; interim condr. Cantabile Youth Choir, Los Altos, Calif., 2005—. Composer: works for treble choir, solo voice and piano. Recipient Max Risinger award, U. Oreg., 1991. Mem.: Music Edn. Nat. Conf., Am. Choral Dir.'s Orgn. Avocations: singing, skiing, hiking, bicycling. E-mail: Karen@ksings.com.

ROBINSON, KAREN VAJDA, dietician; BS in Home Econs., Montclair State Coll., 1980; MS in Health Scis./Dietetics, James Madison U., 1992. Cert. food svc. sanitation mgr., N.J. 1984. Dietician Roosevelt Hosp., Edison, NJ, 1980-85; asst. mgr. UVA (U. Va.) Dining Svcs., Charlottesville, 1985-86; temp. sales sec., mem. banquet prep. staff Boar's Head Inn, Charlottesville, 1986-88; head diet counselor Diet Ctr., Charlottesville, 1986-90; dietetic intern VA Med. Ctr., Hampton, Va., 1991; pub. health nutritionist Cen. Shenandoah Health Dist., Waynesboro (Va.) Health Dept., 1993-97. Grad. dietetic intern mentor, 1993—97; cons. dietitian Hebrew Hosp. Home, Bronx, NY, 1998; food svc. mgr. Sodexho Marriott Svcs., Morningside House Nursing Home, Bronx, 1998—99; clin. dietitian Yonkers (NY) Gen. Hosp., 1999—2001; cmty. svcs. instr. Westchester C.C., Valhalla, NY, 2001; inpatient/out patient dietitian Park Care Pavilion (formerly Yonkers Gen. Hosp.), 2001—; clin. dietitian St. John's Riverside Hosp., Yonkers, 2002—; outpatient dietitian St. John's Riverside, Valentine Lane Family Practice, Yonkers, 2005. Contbr. articles to local newspapers. Mem. Charlottesville Health Promotion Coalition, 1993-97. Mem.: Westchester Rockland Dietetic Assn. (health fairs chair 1998—2001, scholarship com. 2000—06, pub. rels. co-chair 2000—01, sec. 2001—07, chmn. nominating com. 2003—04, health fairs com. 2005—06, grantee 2000), Va. Dietetic Assn. (exec. bd. 1996—97), Blue Ridge Dietetics Assn. (nat. nutrition month coord. 1993—95, editor newsletter 1993—96, mem. exec. bd. 1993—97, pres.-elect 1995—96, scholarship com. 1996, pres. 1996—97), Va. Public Health Assn. (sec. 1995, awards chair 1996—97), Dietitians in Nutrition Support, Gerontol. Nutritionists Practice Group, Cons. Dietitians in Health Care Facilities, Am. Dietetic Assn. (registered). Home: 10-02 Hunter Ln Ossining NY 10562 Office Phone: 914-964-4216. Personal E-mail: kvrobinson@aol.com.

ROBINSON, KRISTINA PARKER, secondary school educator; b. Macon, Ga., Jan. 27, 1977; d. Terry and Lynn Parker; m. John Christopher Robinson, June 28, 2003. MEd, Ga. Coll. & State U., 2003. Cert. tchr. sci. and gifted edn. Ga. Sci. tchr. Tift County Bd. Edn., Ga., 2003—, Houston County Bd. Edn., Warner Robinson, Ga., 1999—2003. Girls basketball coach Tift County HS, 2003—. Mem.: Ga. Sci. Tchrs. Assn. Baptist. Home: 608 46th St Tifton GA 31794 Personal E-mail: jcrkpr@friendlycity.net.

ROBINSON, LAURA ANN, music educator; d. Larry and Sharon Robinson. B of Music Edn., Western Mich. U., Kalamazoo, 1991; M of Music Edn., Northwestern U., Evanston, Ill., 1996. Dir. bands Escanaba Mid. Sch., Mich., 1991—; prin. oboe Marquette Symphony, Mich., 1996—. Oboist, English horn Superior Festival Orch., Upper Mich., 1997—; guest condr. U. Wis., Green Bay, 1997—; oboist, English horn Sault St. Marie Symphony, Ont., Canada, 2004—. Vol. Players de Noc Theater, Escanaba, 1991—, Bonifas Fine Arts Ctr., Escanaba, 1991—; instr. Escanaba Colorguard, 1991—. Recipient award, Japan Fulbright Fund, 2004, Regional Tchr. of Yr. award, Wal-Mart, Escanaba, 2005, Spotlight on Excellence award, Mich. Edn. Assn. Mem.: AAUW, Music Educator Nat. Conf., Mich. Sch. Band Orch. Assn. (Dist. Tchr. of Yr. and state finalist 2006). Avocations: performing, travel, cooking, gardening, sports. Office: Escanaba Mid Sch 1500 Ludington St Escanaba MI 49829 Office Phone: 906-786-7462 ext. 133. Office Fax: 906-786-5958. E-mail: lars1@chartermi.net.

ROBINSON, LINDA GOSDEN, communications executive; b. LA, Jan. 10, 1953; d. Freeman Fisher and Jane Elizabeth (Stoneham) Gosden; m. Stephen M. Dart (div. June 1977); m. James Dixon Robinson III, July 1984. Student, UCLA, 1970-72; BA summa cum laude in Psychology, U. So. Calif., 1978. Dep. press sec. Reagan Presdl. Campaign, LA, 1979; press sec., dir. pub. relations Rep. Nat. Com., Washington, 1979-80; dir. pub. affairs US Dept. Transp., Washington, 1981-83; sr. v.p. corp. affairs Warner Amex Cable Communications, NYC, 1983-86; chmn. Robinson Lerer & Montgomery, LLC, NYC, 1986—, CEO, 1986—2002. Bd. dirs. Revlon, Inc., NYC; dir. BlackRock, Inc., NYC. Del. Rep. Nat. Conv., 1985; trustee NYU Sch. Medicine Found. Bd., vice chair; trustee NYU Hosp. Ctr.; bd. dirs. Lustgarten Found. Pancreatic Rsch. Mem.: Phi Beta Kappa. Avocations: tennis, horseback riding.

ROBINSON, LINDA SCHULTZ, artist, educator; b. Oakland, Calif., Mar. 15, 1949; d. James Richie Schultz and Dorothy Louise Koster-Schultz; m. Steven R. Robinson, Aug. 10, 1980; children: Laura Anne, Chelsea Marie, Emily Louise. AA in Art, Mauna Olu Coll., 1970; BA in Criminal Justice, Calif. State U., Sacramento, 1979. Cert.: Calif. (paralegal). Legal typist U.S. Govt., Concord, Calif., 1975—79; paralegal Alternative Legal Choices, Pleasant Hill, Calif., 1985—87; spl. edn. para-profl. Acad. Sch. Dist., Colorado Springs, Colo., 1995—96; pvt. art instr. to spl. needs individuals Colorado Springs, 1999—. Art therapist Meml. Hosp., Colorado Springs, 2001—. Exhibitions include Colorado Springs Art Guild, 2001. Bd. dirs. Interfaith Hospitality Network, Colorado Springs, 1995—99; vol. art tchr. Acad. Dist. 20 Schs., Colorado Springs, 2001—. Avocations: guitar, reading, crafts.

ROBINSON, LYNDA HICKOX, artist; b. Bakersfield, Calif., June 26, 1932; d. George Philip and Naida (Hathaway) Hickox; m. Arthur C. Robinson; children: Jill, Scott. BA, U. Calif., Berkeley, 1953; MA, Mills Coll., 1957. 1st v.p. San Francisco Women Artists, 1985-86, pres., 1986-87; chair gen. meeting East Bay Women Artists, Montclair, Calif., 1994—2006. Invited artist Glasgow Scotland City of Culture Exhbn., 1990; dance tchr. Exhbns. include San Francisco Women Artists Gallery, 1992-94, Kaiser Cmty. Gallery, 1992-03, Alta Bates Cmty. Gallery, 1994-02, Valley Art Ctr. Gallery, 1992-02, Royal Ground Gallery, 1994-2006, Lindsay Dinkx Brown Gallery, 2003, Wente Winery, 2006; represented in permanent collections Fuji Vending, Dr. Louise Annand MacFarquar, Prof. and Mrs. Fred Casmir; contbr. artworks to jours. and mags. Recipient Tchg. fellowship Mills Coll., 1954, Francis Coen cash award, 1993. Mem. Phi Beta Kappa.

ROBINSON, MARGUERITE STERN, anthropologist, educator, consultant; b. NYC, Oct. 11, 1935; d. Philip Van Doren and Lillian (Diamond) Stern; m. Allan Richard Robinson, June 12, 1955; children: Sarah Penelope, Perrine, Laura Ondine. BA, Radcliffe Coll., 1956; PhD, Harvard U., 1965. Assoc. scholar Radcliffe Inst. for Advanced Studies, Cambridge, Mass., 1964-65; asst. prof. anthology Brandeis U., 1965-72, assoc. prof., 1972-78, prof., 1978-85, dean Coll. Arts and Scis., 1973-75; assoc. fellow Inst. Internat. Devel. Harvard U., Cambridge, 1978-80, fellow Inst. Internat. Devel., 1980-85, inst. fellow Inst. Internat. Devel., 1985-2000, inst. fellow emeritus Inst. Internat. Devel., 2000—; dir. Cultural Survival Inc., 1981-99, Am. Inst. Indian Studies, Chgo., 1977—, chmn., 1983-84; faculty mem. Microfinance Tng. Program, Boulder, Colo. and Turin, Italy, 1995—2006. Cons. in field. Author: Political Structure in a Changing Sinhalese Village, 1975, Local Politics: The Law of the Fishes, 1988, Pembiayaan Pertanian Pedesaan, 1993, The Microfinance Revolution, Vol. 1: Sustainable Finance for the Poor, 2001, Vol. 2: Lessons from Indonesia, 2002, Mobilizing Savings from the Public: Basic Principles and Practices, 2005, The Future of the Commercial Microfinance Industry in Asia, 2005, Commercial Microfinance and Employment in Developing Countries, 2005; contbg. author: Cambridge Papers in Social Anthropology 3, 1962, Cambridge Papers in Social Anthropology 5, 1968, Enterprises for the Recycling and Composting of Municipal Solid Waste, 1993, The New World of Microenterprise Finance, 1994, New Perspectives on Financing Small Business in Developing Countries, 1995, Assisting Development in a Changing World, 1997, New World of Microfinance, 1997, Agricultural Development in the Third World, 1998, Strategic Issues in Microfinance, 1998, Microfinance: Conversations with the Experts, 1999, Microbanking: Creating Opportunities for the Poor Through Innovation, 2005; contbr. articles to profl. jours. Mem. internat. coun. advisors Calmeadow Found., 1996-2000; pres. The Greatest Gift Corp. Fellow NIH, 1964-65; grantee NSF, 1966-70, Ford Found., 1972-74, 79, Calmeadow Found., 1994; fellow Indo-Am. Fellowship Program-Indo-U.S. Subcommn. on Edn. and Culture, 1976-77, Am. Inst. Indian Studies, 1976-77; grantee Calmeadow Found., 1994. Fellow Am. Anthrop. Assn., Soc. Bunting Inst. Fellows; mem. Assn. Asian Studies, India Internat. Centre. Personal E-mail: MRobinso1@aol.com.

ROBINSON, MARILYNNE, writer; b. Sandpoint, Idaho, Nov. 26, 1943; d. John J. and Ellen (Harris) Summers; children: James, Joseph. BA, Brown U., 1966; PhD in English lit., U. Wash., 1977. Mem. faculty Writer's Workshop U. Iowa, 1991—. Spkr. in field. Author: (novels) Housekeeping, 1981 (PEN/Hemingway Award, 1981, Richard and Hinda Rosenthal Award, AAAL), Gilead, 2004 (Nat. Book Critics Cir. prize for fiction, 2004, Pulitzer Prize for fiction, 2005, Publishers Weekly Hardcover Bestseller list, 2005), (non-fiction) Mother Country: Britain, the Welfare State and Nuclear Pollution, 1989, (essay collection) The Death of Adam: Essays on Modern Thought, 1998; Has contbd. to Harper's, Paris Rev., The NY Times Book Rev., others. Recipient Mildred and Howard Strauss Living Award, AAAL, 1998; Lila Acheson Wallace Reader's Digest Grant, 1991. Office: Farrar Straus & Giroux 19 Union Sq W New York NY 10003*

ROBINSON, MARLA HOLBROOK, community care nurse; b. Grass Valley, Calif., Sept. 15, 1934; d. Hilmer Harrison and Mable Lucille (Kline) Holbrook; m. Donald Wilson Robinson Jr., June 25, 1961; children: Jeffrey Brian, Jennifer Lee. BSN, PHN, U. Calif. Chico, 1956. RN; cert. audiometer. Nurse U. Calif. San Francisco Hosp., 1956-59; supr. clinic St. Luke's Hosp., San Francisco, 1959-60; sch. nurse, pub. health nurse San Francisco City and County, 1960-62; sch. nurse All Saints Sch., Carmel, Calif., 1969-79; cmty. care nurse, founder Care & Choice Home Health Care, 1994. Mem. Carmel Found., 2003. Mem. AAUW, Quata Internat. Monterey Peninsula (pres. 1993), Jacettes (pres. 1967), Long Term Dir. of Nursing Salinas, Calif., Ea. Star Monterey (50 Yr. mem.). Episcopalian. Avocations: growing orchids, crafts, reading, travel. Office: Community Care 80 Garden Ct Ste 105 Monterey CA 93940 Office Phone: 831-657-1994, 831-657-1998. Personal E-mail: marlarob@yahoo.com.

ROBINSON, MARLENE THERESA, special education educator; b. Rochdale, Mass., Jan. 4, 1938; d. Mark Raymond and Juliet T. (Moffitt) Mullin; m. Harry Matthew Robinson, Aug. 28, 1968; children: Julie Anne, Mary Mullin. BA, Our Lady of the Elms, Chicopee, Mass., 1959; MEd, Worcester State Coll., 1961; postgrad., Assumption Coll., 1965-68, R.I. Coll., 1968-78. Cert. tchr. and spl. edn., R.I., Mass. Elem. tchr. grade 1 Chaffee Elem. Sch., Oxford, Mass., 1959-62; spl. edn. primary tchr. Julia Bancroft Sch., Auburn, Mass., 1962-68; spl. edn. secondary tchr. N.A. Ferri Mid. Sch., Johnston, R.I., 1968—. Writer, dir. video prodn. Say No to Drugs, 1986. CYO advisor St. Gregory the Great, Warwick, 1988-91; sec. Cedar Hill PTA, Warwick, 1983-86; block capt., pres. Love Lane Assn., Warwick, 1990-92; hostess Warwick City Coun., 1985; candidate Constl. Conv., Warwick, 1986; com. worker Dem. party, Warwick, 1985-88; tchr., sec. liaision Parent's Group for Learning Disabled, 1978-82; religious edn. tchr. confirmation class St. Gregory's Ch., 1971-92. Mem. Coun. Exceptional Children, Warwick Figure Skaters (sec., test chmn. 1979-89, Outstanding Dedication award 1979-89). Democrat. Roman Catholic. Home: 224 S Cobble Hill Rd Warwick RI 02886-9333 Office: NA Ferri Mid Sch 10 Memorial Ave Johnston RI 02919-3222

ROBINSON, MARY CATHERINE, artist; b. Oshkosh, Wis., Aug. 18, 1934; d. Edward Charles Leupold and Nora Alice O'Laughlin; m. Charles Benjamin Robinson, Sept. 10, 1960; children: Charles Edward, Jeanne Marie, David James. Student, U. Wis., Milw., 1953—54, Ringling Art Sch., Sarasota, Fla., 1954—56, Layton Art Sch., Milw., 1957—58. Owner Tree Top Studio, Nokomis, Fla. Represented by, Karchelles Gallery, Sarasota, Artemsia Gallery, Venice, Fla., exhibitions include Puerto Del Sol/Costa Del Sol, Torremolinos, Spain, 2002, Ampalius/Vilamoura, Portugal, 2003, Selby Gallery, Sarasota, Maggior Consiglio, Treviso, Italy, 2004, Womens Resource Ctr., Sarasota, 2005, Roscamp Ctr., 2006, Represented in permanent collections Selby Bot. Garden. Recipient First prize painting, Fla. State Fair, 1959. Mem.: Portrait Soc. Am., U.S. Tennis Assn. Avocations: painting, sculpting, tennis, photography, fishing. Home: 1609 Hammock Dr Nokomis FL 34275 Office Phone: 941-488-6444. E-mail: robinsonmary@webtv.net.

ROBINSON, MARY ELIZABETH GOFF, retired historian, researcher; b. East Providence, R.I., Jan. 3, 1925; d. Newell Darius and Eva Agnes (Crane) Goff; m. Charles Albert Robinson, July 30, 1954; 1 child, Thomas Goff (dec.). BA, Wheaton Coll., Norton, Mass., 1947. Cataloger, fine arts Chester County Hist. Soc., Pa., 1973-80, trustee Pa., 1974-80. Cataloger artifacts Chadds Ford (Pa.) Hist. Soc., 1992-95. Co-author: (monograph) Ada Clendenin Williamson, 1983, (history) The Ingalls and the Hoyts, The Crane Sawmill, The Ingalls-Crane House, 1995; author: (monograph) The Life of a Young Entrepreneur at the Turn of the Twentieth Century, 1992; editor: A Quiet Man from West Chester, 1974. Mem. Jr. League, Providence, 1957-62, Providence Athenaeum, 1955-63, Providence Preservation Soc., 1959-63, Brandywine Conservancy, Del. Symphony Orch., Winterthur Mus.; donor Newell D. Goff Fund Chester County Cmty. Found.; founder Chester County Artists Register, Chester County Art Assn., acting libr., 1994-2000. Donor T. Morris Longstreth Libr. endowment West Chester U., Quest Lewes (DE) Found., Friends of Lewes Pub. Libr. Mem. AAUW, R.I. Hist. Soc. (trustee 1994-99, founder Newell D. Goff Edn. Ctr.), Danville (Vt.) Hist. Soc., Hershey's Mill Country Club, Hope Club (Providence), Chester County Cmty. Fdn. Avocations: writing, reading, hiking, travel.

ROBINSON, MARY JO, pathologist; b. Spokane, Wash., May 26, 1954; d. Jerry Lee and Ann (Brodie) R. BS in Biology, Gonzaga U., 1976; DO, Des Moines U., 1987. Diplomate Nat. Bd. Osteo. Med. Examiners, Am. Osteo. Bd. Pathology; cert. anatomic pathology, lab. medicine and dermatopathology. Med. technologist Whitman Cmty. Hosp., Colfax, Wash., 1977—81, Madigan Army Med. Ctr., Ft. Lewis, Wash., 1981—83; intern Des Moines Gen. Hosp., 1987—88; resident in pathology Kennedy Meml. Hosp., Stratford, NJ, 1988—92; asst. prof. pathology Sch. Medicine U. Medicine and Dentistry of N.J., Stratford, 1995—; staff pathologist Kennedy Meml. Hosp., Cherry Hill, NJ, 1995—; fellow in dermatopathology Jefferson Med. Coll., Phila., 1994. Fellow Coll. Am. Pathologists; mem. AMA, Am. Osteo. Assn., Am. Soc. Clin. Pathologists, Am. Osteo. Coll. Pathologists (pres. 2003-04, 1st prize resident paper 1992), N.J. Assn. Osteo. Physicians and Surgeons, Am. Osteo. Bd. Pathologists (chmn. 2003-06). Avocations: astronomy, antiques, science fiction. Office: Pathology UDP 3600 42 E Laurel Rd Stratford NJ 08084 Office Phone: 856-488-6561. Business E-Mail: robinsmj@umdnj.edu. E-mail: m.robinson@kennedyhealth.org.

ROBINSON, MARY LOU, federal judge; b. Dodge City, Kans., Aug. 25, 1926; d. Gerald J. and Frances Strueber; m. A.J. Robinson, Aug. 28, 1949; 3 children. BA, U. Tex., 1948, LL.B., 1950. Bar: Tex. 1949. Ptnr. Robinson & Robinson, Amarillo, 1950-55; judge County Ct. at Law, Potter County, Tex., 1955-59, (108th Dist. Ct.), Amarillo, 1961-73; assoc. justice Ct. of Civil Appeals for 7th Supreme Jud. Dist. of Tex., Amarillo, 1973-77, chief justice, 1977-79; U.S. dist. judge No. Dist. Tex., Amarillo, 1979—. Named Woman of Year Tex. Fedn. Bus. and Profl. Women, 1973; recipient Sandra Day O'Connor award profl. excellence, 2005. Mem. Nat. Assn. Women Lawyers, ABA, Tex. Bar Assn. (Outstanding 50-Yr. Lawyer award 2002), Tex. Bar Found. (Samuel Pessara Outstanding Judge award), Amarillo Bar Assn., Delta Kappa Gamma. Presbyterian. Office: US Dist Ct Rm 226 205 E 5th Ave # F13248 Amarillo TX 79101-1559 Office Phone: 806-468-3822.

ROBINSON, MARY LU, retired accountant, artist; b. Bloomington, Ind., Nov. 11, 1919; d. Louis Cleveland and Ruby Olive (King) Welch; m. Robert Newlin Robinson, Sept. 27, 1948; children: Richard Louis, Rebecca Jane. Student, Ind. U., Bloomington, 1937-40, Ind. U., South Bend, 1954-55, Tex. Christian U., Ft. Worth, 1989, 90, 99. Ptnr. Robert N. Robinson, CPA, South Bend, 1950-82. Exhibited in group shows at Composers, Authors, Artists Am., N.Y.C., 1990, Soc. Watercolor Artists, Ft. Worth, 1989—, Internat. Soc. Exptl. Artists, 1992, Womans Club, Ft. Worth, 1989—, Women of Worth, Ft. Worth, Tex., 2005. Den mother Boy Scouts Am., South Bend, 1956-59; bd. dirs. Neoclassic group Nelson-Atkins Mus. Art, Kansas City, Mo. Mem. DAR, Nat. Assn. Pen Women, Inc. (chpt. pres. 1999—), Colonial Dames XVIIC (chpt. pres. 1995-97), Daus. Colonial Wars (state pres. 1992-95), Magna Charta Soc., Colonial Order of the Crown, Daus. Am. Colonists, Daus. of 1812, Washington Family Descs., Nat. Trust Historic Preservation, Order Eastern star (assoc. matron 1969-70), Johnson County Master Gardner Assn. Avocations: genealogy, travel, history, bridge, gardening. Home: 1401 Hyde Park Ln Arlington TX 76015-2236 E-mail: marylrobinson@sbcglobal.com.

ROBINSON, MAUREEN LORETTA, retired secondary school educator; b. NYC, May 17, 1945; d. Arthur Vincent and Paula (Dillon) R.; m. Derish Michael Wolff, Feb. 13, 1992. BA in English, Wagner Coll., 1967; MS, CUNY, 1970; LHD (hon.), Wagner Coll., 2003. Cert. tchr. secondary sch. English, K-12 reading, N.Y. Tchr. English Curtis H.S., S.I., NY, 1968-95, coord. student activities, 1985-94. Vis. lectr. Coll. of S.I., 1982; guest lectr. NYU, 1991, Pace U., N.Y.C., 1993; dir. Soc. de Management de Projets Internat., Paris, 1996—. Class agt. Wagner Coll., 1995—; mem. nat. alumni bd.; trustee Wagner Coll., 1998—, vice chair bd. trustees, 2001—03; pub chair Bernardsville Garden Club, 1995—97, pres., 1997—99, sec., 1999—2001, pub chair, 2001—03, nominations chair, 2004—, bd. dirs., yearbook chair, 2005—; trustee Somerset Hills Edn. Found., 1996—97; pub. chair Friends of the Bernardsville Libr., 1996—2002, bd. dirs., nominations chair, 2004—; elected mem. Somerset Hills Bd. Edn., Bernardsville, NJ, 1997—2003; v.p. Somerset County Ednl. Svcs. Commn., Raritan, 2000—02, pres., 2002—03; bd. dirs. Clarence Dillon Pub. Libr., 2002—03; sec. Friends for a Greener Bernardsville Inc., 2003—04, pres., 2005, co-pres., 2006—. Staff sgt. USAR, 1979—85. Recipient Human Rels. award Greater N.Y. Region of NCCJ, 1994, Army Achievement medal Dept. of Army, 1983, Bernardsville Vol. of Yr. award, 2003, Outstanding Comty. vol. award Borough Coun. and Mayor Bernardsville, 2003. Mem. AAUW, Wagner Coll. Nat. Alumni Assn. (1st v.p. 1999-2001), Friends of the Shelter. Avocations: reading, gardening, skiing, cooking, travel. Home: 160 Jockey Hollow Rd Bernardsville NJ 07924-1312

ROBINSON, MILDRED WIGFALL, law educator; b. Charleston, SC, Dec. 1, 1944; d. Switzon Samuel and Mildred Gwendolyn (Mance) Wigfall; m. William Hudson Ravenell, Aug. 29, 1969 (div. Apr. 1986); children: William Samuel, Teressa Emlynne; m. Armstead Louis Robinson, June 27, 1987; 1 child, Allison Louise Wigfall. BA, Fisk U., 1965; JD, Howard U., 1968; LLM, Harvard U., 1971. Bar: Mass. 1971. Dir. admissions, asst. dean Boston U., 1971-72; asst. prof. law Fla. State U., Tallahassee, 1972-76, assoc. prof., 1976-84, assoc. dean, 1983-84; vis. assoc. prof. U. Va., Charlottesville, 1984-85, assoc. prof., 1985-88, prof., 1988—, currently Henry L. & Grace Doherty Charitable Found. prof. law. Currently trustee Martha Jefferson Hosp.; bd. dir. Law Access, Inc., 1993—96; mem. exec. com. Assoc. Am. Law Sch., 2000—03; commr. Nat. Conf. of Commn. on Uniform State Laws, 1990—94; bd. visitors J. Reuben Clark Law Sch. Brigham Young U., Provo, Utah, 1993—96. Mem.: ALI, Phi Beta Kappa. Democrat. Episcopalian. Avocations: aerobics, needlecrafts, reading. Office: U Va Sch Law 580 Massie Rd Charlottesville VA 22901 E-mail: mwr@virginia.edu.

ROBINSON, MOLLY JAHNIGE, statistician, educator; b. Cleve., July 8, 1936; d. John White and Mary Tayler (Sullivan) McCaslin; m. Thomas Paul Jahnige (dec.); m. Donald Leonard Robinson, Jan. 1, 1983; children: Katherine Jahnige Mathews, John Samuel, David Wynn, Paul John Jahnige. Student, Swarthmore Coll., Pa., 1954—56; BA, Pomona Coll., Claremont, Calif., 1958; MA, Claremont U., 1962. Tchr. 4th, 7th, and 8th grades Claremont Sch. Dist., 1958—63; instr. stats. Smith Coll., Northampton, Mass., 1973—2004. Leader Girl Scouts USA, 1957—; vol. Cmty. Found. We. Mass., 2000—05, Ashfield Youth Commn., 1995—2005; Sunday sch. dir., youth leader St. John's Episcopal Ch., Northampton, 1973—75, 2002—04; coord. Episcopal Relief and Devel. We. Mass., 2005—; mem. sch. bd. Mohawk Region, Ashfield, Mass., 2003—06; edn. chair Wells Trust Fund, Greenfield, Mass., 1996—; chair Town Common Com., Ashfield, 2003—. Recipient World Friendship medal, Girl Scouts USA. Democrat. Avocations: writing, working with children.

ROBINSON, MURIEL COX, psychiatrist; d. Henry Willard and Veola Garry Cox; m. Julius Ceasar Robinson (div.); children: Julius W., Rosalyn P. Student, Ohio State U., 1948; MD, Meharry Med. Coll., 1952. Psychiatry resident Homer Phillips Hosp./Washington U., St. Louis, 1953—56; staff psychiatrist St. Louis Child Guidance Ctr., St. Louis, 1956—57, Napa (Calif.) St. Hosp., 1958, Cmty. Mental Health Centers, Richmond, Calif., 1958—75; pvt. practice psychiatry Calif., 1960—79; staff psychiatrist East Oakland Mental Health Ctr., Calif., 1976—79, Calif. Youth Authority, Sacramento, 1979—92; with Locum Tenens Physicians Group, 1992—94. Mem. mental health adv. bd. Contra Costa County, Martinez, Calif., 1960—64. Bd. dirs. North Richmond Neighborhood Ho., Calif., 1961—63. Mem.: AAAS, AMA, NAACP, Am. Psychiat. Assn. (life). Avocations: block flute, keyboards. Home: PO Box 292148 Sacramento CA 95829-2148 Office Phone: 916-427-8070.

ROBINSON, NANCY A., writer; b. Dewey, Okla., June 19, 1939; d. Joseph K. and Velma D. Green; m. McDonald Robinson, June 11, 1961; children: Ehren, Shannon, Adam. BA Letters and Sci., U. Calif., Berkeley, 1961; MA, Drew U., 1993. Tchr. gifted and talented, Lexington, Mass., 1962—66; writer AT&T, Morristown, NJ, 1982—85, Santa Barbara Mus. Natural History, Calif., 1989—92; founder, pub. Green River Press, Santa Barbara, 1999—. Author: Touched by Adoption, 1999, On Becoming, 2004. Founder Bill Downey Writers Scholarship, Santa Barbara, 1996—2003; clk. Santa Barbara Friends Meeting, 2000—03; v.p. Ednl. Found. AAUW, Santa Barbara, 1990—91. Quaker. Office: Green River Press 5880 Hidden Ln Goleta CA 93117 Office Phone: 805-964-4475. Business E-Mail: narob@cox.net.

ROBINSON, NANCY MAYER, psychology educator; b. Houston, Aug. 30, 1930; d. Sidney L. and Bertha-Louise (Heyman) Mayer; m. Halbert B. Robinson, June 24, 1951 (dec. Mar. 1981); children: Christine Halberstadt, Laura Nicholson, David Robinson, Elizabeth Robinson. BA, Stanford (Calif.) U., 1951, MA, 1953, PhD, 1958. Lic. psychologist, Wash. Asst. prof. edn. U. N.C., Chapel Hill, 1966-69; sr. rsch. assoc. U. Wash., Seattle, 1969-74, assoc. prof. psychiatry and behavioral scis., 1974-82, prof. psychiatry and behavioral scis., 1982—, chief psychologist Child Devel. and Mental Retardation Ctr., 1974-88, dir. Ctr. for Study of Capable Youth, 1981—2000, prof. emeritus, 2000—. Cons. U.S. State Dept. Office Overseas Schs., Washington, 1986—; mem. nat. adv. bd. Nat. Inst. Child Health and Human Devel., Bethesda, Md., 1979-83; trustee Am. Psychol. Found. Author: (with H.B. Robinson) Mentally Retarded Child, 1965, 76; editor Am. Jour. Mental Deficiency, 1979-86. Recipient Edn. award Am. Assn. Mental Deficiency, 1982, Presidential award, 1986. Fellow APA, Am. Psychol. Soc.; mem. Acad. Mental Retardation (sec. 1983-86), Soc. Rsch. in Child Devel., Nat. Assn. Gifted Children. Home: 5005 NE 45th St Seattle WA 98105-3805 Office: Halbert and Nancy Robinson Ctr Young Scholars U Wash PO Box 351630 Seattle WA 98195-1630

ROBINSON, NANCY NOWAKOWSKI, academic administrator; b. Pitts., Nov. 2, 1945; d. Theodore Joseph Nowakowski and Martha Radick; 1 child, David A. BA cum laude, U. Pitts., 1983, MA, 2000. Founding mem. bd. dirs., treas. Extrasolar Planetary Found., Pitts., 1980—97; mem. adv. com. Nazareth Housing Svcs., 1995—; assoc. Sisters of the Holy Family of Nazareth, Pitts., 1998—; pres. City of God Found., Pitts., 2000—02, bd. dir., 2000—, treas., 2004—. Author: Institutional Anti-Judaism: Pope Pius VI and the Edict Concerning the Jews, 2004; editor: Pittsburgh Lubber's Line, 2003—05. Chaplain and diversity advisor divsn. 7, 8th eastern region U.S. Coast Guard Aux., 2003—, publs. officer, 2003—05; treas. City of God Found. Recipient Sister Noel Kernan award, Seton Hill Coll., 1999, Weiner Israel Heritage Nationality Rms. award, U. Pitts., 1999; Dorot Found. grantee for study in Israel, 1999, Pax Christi grantee, Pax Christi, 1999. Mem.: Soc. Bibl. Lit., Am. Acad. Religion, Golden Key. Roman Catholic. Avocations: Jewish/Catholic relations, history, music, travel, outdoors. E-mail: nancy1@pitt.edu.

ROBINSON, NELL BRYANT, nutrition educator; b. Kopperl, Tex., Oct. 15, 1925; d. Basil Howell and Lelia Abiah (Duke) Bryant; m. Frank Edward Robinson, July 14, 1945 (dec.); 1 child, John Howell. BS, North Tex. State U., 1945; MS, Tex. Woman's U., 1958, PhD, 1967. Registered dietitian, Tex. Tchr. Comanche H.S., Tex., 1945-46, Kopperl H.S., 1946-48; county extensin agt. Agrl. Extension Svc., Tex., 1948-56; prof. nutrition Tex. Christian U., Ft. Worth, 1957—92, chmn. dept. nutrition and dietetics, 1985-91; ret., 1992. Contbr. chpt. to book. Pres., bd. dirs. Sr. Citizens Svcs. Greater Tarrant County, 1990-91. Named Top Prof., Tex. Christian U. Mortar Bd., 1978. Mem. Am. Dietetic Assn. (del. 1983-88, ethics com. 1985-88, coun. edn. 1988-90, chmn. coun. on edn. divsn. edn. accreditation and approval 1989-90, Medallion award 1990), Am. Assn. Family and Consumer Scis., Tex. Dietetic Assn. (pres. 1972-73, Disting. Dietitian awafd 1981), Tex. Assn. Family and Consumer Scis. (pres. 1978-80, Home Economist of Yr. award 1975), Ft. Worth Women's Club, Order Ea. Star. Home: 4459 Kirkland Dr Fort Worth TX 76109-4952

ROBINSON, OLA MAE, accountant; b. Worsham Ranch, Tex., Nov. 17, 1903; d. Franklin Earle and Jennie Rachael (Gay) R. B of Acctg., Draughons Bus. Coll., 1935. Tchr. rural schs., Tex., 1924-34; bookkeeper Ins. Cos., Wichita Falls, Tex., 1935-40; acct., bookkeeper U.S. War Dept., Washington, 1941-50; acct. Air Force Acctg. & Fin. Ctr., Denver, 1951-65; bookkeeper 1stMeth. Ch., Denver, 1966-70. Author, editor: Robinson Family, 1995. Recipient Pres. award Denver Rose Soc., 1980. Mem. Nat. Assn. Retired Persons, Nat. Genealogical Soc., Am. Rose Soc. (pres.), Clay County Hist. Soc. Republican. Methodist. Avocations: travel, photography, reading, writing, gardening. Home: 400 W 14th Ave #213B Amarillo TX 79101-4140

ROBINSON, PAULA LEKATZ, artist; b. Thermopolis, Wyo., Jan. 26, 1953; m. Thomas Tucker Donovan (dec.); 1 child, Bonnie Lynn Larsen; m. Everett Lawson Robinson, Oct. 3, 1998 (dec.); 1 child, Equezance Fawn Marie. BA in History & Sociology, U. Minn., 1976; BA in English, St. CLoud State U.; MA in Tchg., Webster U., 1983; MA in English, St. Cloud State U., 1994. Painter U. Minn., Morris, 1973; intern Mille Lass Co., Milacg, 1974; adminstrv. asst. St. Cloud State U., 1983—94; owner, printer Ostby Printing, Duluth, 1981—89, Crosby Printing, Crosby, 1981—89; owner, quilter Waboos Enterprises, Ironton, 1989—2005. Author: Arapaho Tribal Culture, 1985, (plays) Feather, 1993. Vol. Hellett Meml. Libr., Crosby. Mem.: Am. Legion Aux. (mem. Ironton aux. 2005). Democrat. Roman Catholic. Office Phone: 218-545-2180. E-mail: waboos1985@yahoo.com, waboos1985@emily.net.

ROBINSON, REBECCA LYNNE, medical researcher; b. Evansville, Ind., Dec. 9, 1967; d. Sherman Joseph and Joyce Jeane Black; m. Robert Wayne Robinson, Aug. 8, 1992; children: Calder Luke, Mary Helen Ellie. BA, U. So. Ind., 1990; MS, Purdue U., 1995. Tchg. asst. Ind. U.-Purdue U., 1990—92; rsch. asst. Osgood Lab. for Cross-Cultural Rsch., Indpls., 1990—93; rsch. analyst Regenstrief Inst./Bowen Rsch. at Ind. U. Sch. Medicine, Indpls., 1993—98; rsch. scientist St. Vincent Hosp., Indpls., 1996—98; health outcomes rsch. cons. U.S. Med. Divsn., Eli Lilly and Co., Indpls., 1998—. Cons. Osgood Lab. for Cross-Cultural Rsch., 1993—98, Ind. Hand Ctr., Indpls., 1996—98, Ind. State Dept. Health, Indpls., 1996—98; presenter in field. Contbr. articles to profl. jours. Facilitator, team leader, participant Ministry of Moms, Nativity Ch., Indpls., 2001—05. Recipient Outstanding Grad. Student award, Purdue U., 1992, Best Author Presentation award, 17th World Congress on Psychosomatic Medicine, 2003, Marketscan Rsch. award, 2005; grantee Agy. for Health Care Policy and Rsch., 1990—95. Office: Eli Lilly and Co Lilly Corp Ctr Indianapolis IN 46285 Office Phone: 317-433-1323. Office Fax: 317-277-7444. E-mail: rlrobinson@lilly.com.

ROBINSON, ROBIN, newscaster; b. Chgo. m. Terrence Brantley, 1986 (div. 1989). B, San Diego State U., 1980. Reporter KGTV, San Diego, 1979—81; consumer reporter CBS affiliate, Denver, 1981—84; reporter WBBM-TV, Chgo., 1984—87; co-anchor Fox News at 9 WFLD-TV, Chgo., 1987—. Co-recipient Emmy awards. Office: WFLD-TV 205 N Mich Ave Chicago IL 60601

ROBINSON, ROBIN WICKS, lawyer; b. Roanoke Rapids, NC, June 5, 1961; d. Wallace Wayne and Rozelle Royall Wicks; m. James Hendry Robinson, Jr., Nov. 7, 1992; children: James Hendry Robinson III, Wallace Katherine McLean Robinson. BA in Politics (hon.), Converse Coll., Spartanburg, S.C., 1982; JD, U. N.C., Chapel Hill, 1985. Bar: N.C. 1986; 5th Jud. Dist. 1986, U.S. Dist. Ct. (ea. dist.) 1987; U.S. Dist. Ct. (we. dist.) 1997, 5th Jud. Dist. Arbitrator 1993, Superior Ct. Cert. Mediator, family fin. mediator, specialist in family law, NC. Assoc. atty. Ryals, Jackson & Mills, Wilmington, NC, 1986-90; ptnr. Pennington & Wicks, Wilmington, NC, 1990-93; pres, profl. corp. Ryals, Robinson & Saffo P.C., Wilmington, NC, 1993—. Ethics com. N.C. State Bar, Raleigh, N.C., 1990-93; exec. com. New Hanover County Bar Assn., Wilmington, 1994-97. Bd. mem. Cape Fear Mus. Assocs., Inc., Wilmington, N.C., 1991-2000, v.p. 1994-97, pres. 1997-2000; bd. mem., counsel Wilmington Symphony Orchestra, Inc., Wilmington, N.C., 1991-99; commn. mem. USS N.C. Battleship Commn., Wilmington, N.C., 1989-93; mem. Bd. Deacons First Presbyn. Ch., Wilmington, N.C., 1996-99, Chancel Choir, 1988—. Recipient Women of Achievement New Hanover Commn. for Women, Wilmington, N.C., 1997, Trustee Merit Scholarship Converse Coll., Spartanburg, S.C., 1978-82; named Mortar Bd. Converse Coll., Spartanburg, S.C., 1981—, Crescent Converse Coll., Spartanburg, S.C., 1979-80, Pro bono publico award Legal Svcs. of the Lower Cape Fear, 1997, 2002. Mem. Am. Bar Assn., N.C. Bar Assn., N.C. Acad. Trial Lawyers, New Hanover County Bar Assn., Phi Delta Phi, Phi Sigma Iota, Pi Gamma Mu. Republican. Presbyterian. Avocations: travel, piano, choral, swimming, tennis, sailing. Home: 1940 Hawthorne Rd Wilmington NC 28403-5329 Office: Ryals Robinson & Saffo PC 701 Market St Wilmington NC 28401-4646 E-mail: rrspc@bellsouth.net.

ROBINSON, ROXANA BARRY, writer, art historian; b. Pine Mountain, Ky., Nov. 30, 1946; Student, Bennington Coll., 1964—66; BA, U. Mich., 1969. Art cataloguer Sotheby's, N.Y.C., 1970-74; exhbn. dir. Terry Dintenfass Gallery, N.Y.C., 1974-76; freelance writer, 1976—. Author: (novels) Summer Light, 1988 (Washington Irving award Westchester Libr. Assn.), This is My Daughter, 1998 (Notable Book of the Yr. award N.Y. Times, 1998, Washington Irving award Westchester Libr. Assn.), Sweetwater, 2003 (named Notable Book, N.Y. Times), (biography) Georgia O'Keeffe: A Life, 1989 (Notable Book of the Yr. award N.Y. Times, 1989, Washington Irving award Westchester Libr. Assn.), (short stories) A Glimpse of Scarlet, 1991 (Notable Book of the Yr. award N.Y. Times, 1991), Asking for Love, 1995 (Washington Irving award Westchester Libr. Assn., Notable Book of the Yr. Nat. Libr. Assn.), A Perfect Stranger, 2005. Trustee Eugene Lang Coll., NY, Nat. Humanities Ctr., NC, 1995—, PEN Am. Ctr., NY, 1998—. Recipient Lit. Lion award, N.Y. Pub. Libr., 1991; fellow, Nat. Endowment Arts, 1987, MacDowell Colony, 1999; John S. Guggenheim Found. fellow, 2000. Office: c/o Lynn Nesbit Janklow-Nesbit 445 Park Ave New York NY 10022

ROBINSON, RUTH CARLESON, retired secondary school educator; b. Salem, Oreg., Aug. 27, 1937; d. Richard Victor and Opal Charlotte Carleson; m. Kenneth Oliver Robinson, Aug. 2, 1959; children: Grant Kenneth, Victoria Ruth BS, Oreg. State U., 1959. H.S. tchr. Hillsboro Sch. Dist., Oreg., 1959—60, Gresham-Barlow Sch. Dist., Oreg., 1976—2002. Site coun. Sam Barlow H.S., Gresham, 1994—2002, chair site coun., 1998—2002. Contbr. Portland Opera Assn., 1982—; mem. Portland Classical Chinese Garden, Portland Art Mus., Met. Mus. Art, N.Y.C., Asian Art Mus., San Francisco, Asia Art Coun., Portland. Mem. AAII, AAUW, NEA, Oreg. Edn. Assn., Gresham-Barlow Edn. Assn. (v.p. 1994-95, pres. 1995-96), Multnomah County UniServ (sec. 1989-92, pres. 1993-95) Avocations: opera, travel, collecting. Home: 2934 NE 38th Ave Portland OR 97212-2854

ROBINSON, SALLY SHOEMAKER, lay associate; b. NYC, Dec. 31, 1931; d. Samuel M. and Helen Dominick Smith S.; m. James Courtland Robinson, Dec. 31, 1931; children: Samuel Shoemaker, W. Courtland, A. Alexander, Ellen Whitridge Robinson Mihalski. BA cum laude, Bryn Mawr Coll., 1953; postgrad. studies, Yonsei U. Lang. Inst., Korea, 1960-62, Children's Theatre Assn., 1964; MA, Towson State U., 1974. Ordained elder Brown Meml. Presbyn. Ch., 1985. Commd. missionary to Korea United Presbyn. Ch., Republic of Korea, 1959-71; dir. Brown Meml. Tutorial Program, 1974-84; exec. dir. Episcopal Social Ministries Diocese of Md., Balt., 1984-97; canon for social ministry Episcopal Diocese of Md., Balt., 1985-96; chair, global bd. United Bible Societies, 2001. Trustee Am. Bible Society. Met. chmn. 10th Decade Campaign Bryn Mawr Coll.,, 1974-76, nat. chmn. Centennial Campaign. 1980-85, trustee, 1985—; trustee Am. Bible Soc., 1988—, v.p., 1993—, chmn. bd., 1996-2001; chmn. global bd. United Bible Socs., 2001—; trustee United Bd. for Christian Higher Edn. in Asia, 1990-95; trustee emeritus Bryn Mawr Coll., 1997—. Home: 10522 Burnside Farm Rd Stevenson MD 21153-2024 Office: Brown Meml Ch 1316 Park Ave Baltimore MD 21217-4185

ROBINSON, SALLY WINSTON, artist; b. Detroit, Nov. 2, 1924; d. Harry Lewis and Lydia (Kahn) Winston; m. Eliot F. Robinson, June 28, 1949; children: Peter Eliot, Lydia Winston, Sarah Mitchell, Suzanne Finley. BA, Bennington Coll., 1947; postgrad., Cranbrook Acad. Art, 1949; grad., Sch. Social Work, Wayne U., 1948, MA, 1972; MFA, Wayne State U., 1973. Psychol. tester Detroit Bd. Edn., 1944; psychol. counselor and tester YMCA, N.Y.C., 1946; social caseworker Family Svc., Pontiac, Mich., 1947; instr. printmaking Wayne State U., Detroit, 1973—. Tchr. children's art Detroit Inst. Art, 1949-50, now artistic advisor, bd. dirs. drawing and pring orgn. One-woman shows include, U. Mich., 1973, Wayne State U., 1974, Klein-Vogel Gallery, 1974, Rina Gallery, 1976, Park McCullough House, Vt., 1976, Williams Coll., 1976, Arnold Klein Gallery, 1977, exhibited in group shows, Bennington Coll., Cranbrook Mus., Detroit Inst. Art, Detroit Artists Market, Soc. Women Painters, Soc. Arts and Crafts, Bloomfield Art Assn., Flint Left Bank Gallery, Balough Gallery, Detroit Soc. Woman Painters, U. Mich., U. Ind., U. Wis., U. Pitts., Toledo Mus., Krannert Mus., Represented in permanent collections. Bd. dirs. Planned Parenthood, 1951—, mem. exec. bd., 1963—; bd. dirs. PTA, 1956-60, Roeper City and Country Sch., U. Mich. Mus. Art, 1978; trustee Putnam Hosp. Med. Rsch. Inst., 1978; mem. Gov.'s Commn. Art in State Bldgs., 1978-79; mem. art and devel. coms. So. Vt. Art Ctr., 1987-88; mem. vol. com. Marie Selby Gardens; patron Graphic Art Studio, U. So. Fla., Tampa; patron, benefactor Clark Mus., Williamstown, Mass. Fellow: Williams Coll. Mus. Art (mem. visiting com.); mem.: Bloomfield Art Assn. (program co-chmn. 1956), Birmingham Soc. Women Painters (pres. 1974—76), Detroit Soc. Women Painters, Detroit Artists Market (dir. 1956—, hon. bd. mem.), Founders Soc. Detroit Inst. Art, Bennington Coll. Alumnae Assn. (regional co-chmn. 1954), Cosmopolitan Club (N.Y.C.), Founders Garden Club (Sarasota, Fla.), Garden Club Am. (bd. dirs.), Oaks Club (Fla.), Women's City Club (coord. art shows Detroit 1950), Village Women's Club (Birmingham, Mich.). Unitarian Universalist. Home: 209 Hills Point Rd Charlotte VT 05445-9698 also: 639 Eagle Watch Ln Osprey FL 34229 Personal E-mail: sallyrobinsonflorida@msn.com.

ROBINSON, SANDRA DARLENE, nursing educator; b. Burbank, Calif. d. Darwin Grant and Louise Hall Moe. Diploma, Blessing Hosp. Sch. Nursing, Quincy, Ill.; BA in Health Sci., Quincy U.; MS in Healthcare Adminstrn., LaVerne U., Pomona, Calif.; BSN, Calif. State U., Bakersfield. RN, cert. CCRN, BLS, ACLS. Nurse dir. Antelope Valley Hosp., Lancaster, Calif., Lancaster Cmty. Hosp., St. Mary's Med. Ctr., Apple Valley, Calif.; nursing instr. Antelope Valley Coll., Lancaster. Cons. Fresno Cmty. Hosp., Fresno, Calif., 1989. Vol. Am. Cancer Soc., Lancaster, 2003—. Sgt. USAF, 1968—70. Mem.: AACN. Republican. Roman Catholic.

ROBINSON, SARA CURTIS, arts administrator; b. Amarillo, Tex., Jan. 6, 1967; d. Don Teel Curtis and Suzanne (Stokes) Brent; m. Benjamin Rowland Robinson, Oct. 5, 1991; children: Rowland Wyatt, Tristan Rodman, Spalding Rhys. BA, Pine Manor Coll., 1989. Asst. dir. Sorota Fine Arts, Boston, 1989; asst. to curator Asiatic art Mus. Fine Arts, Boston, 1990-91; from devel. officer to dir. devel. Bank of Boston Celebrity Series, 1992—96. Mem. Women in Devel., Boston, 1993-96, Boston Arts Mktg. Group, 1992-94. Mem. Jr. League Boston, 1990-95, com. chair, 1993; mem. Mass. Advocates for the Arts, Boston, 1993-96, Cultural Diversity Com. for the Arts, Boston, 1993-96; com. Newbury St. League Auction, Boston, 1989. Mem. Internat. Soc. Performing Arts Adminstrs., Nat. Soc. Fundraising Execs. Episcopalian.

ROBINSON, SARAH BONHAM, artist, educator, mental health services professional; b. Mar. 16, 1939; d. Robert and Eleanor Bonham; m. Bruce Robinson, Aug. 28, 1961 (div. 1975); children: Christopher, David Brooke, Megan, Andrew. BA, Wilson Coll., 1961; MFA, U. Pa., 1962; art edn. cert., Kean Coll., 1979. Asst. art instr. Wilson Coll., Chambersburg, Pa., 1960-61; educator art Newark Acad., Livingston, NJ, 1966-68; therapist arts J. E. Runnells, Berkeley Heights, NJ, 1974; therapist creative arts Dept. Psychiatry, asst. dir. psychiat. rehab. Elizabeth (N.J.) Gen. Med. Ctr., 1974—95, dir. activity therapy, 1976—95, clin. chief partial hosp., 1978-85, chmn. quality assurance psychiatry, 1980-83, asst. dir. rehab. svcs., 1983—95; exec. dir. Am. Day Treatment Ctr., Cranford, NJ, 1995—97; sr. dir. programs Mental Health Assoc. Essex County, 1997—2005; semi-ret., 2005; ind. behavioral health cons., 2005—. Adj. instr. Rutgers U., New Brunswick, N.J., 1967; cons. Children's Specialized Hosp., Mountainside, N.J., 1976-91; bd. dirs. Mental Health Assoc. Monmouth County. Paintings exhibited in eastern U.S., 1960—; prodr., editor: Changes, 1974; illustrator: Miller-Cory Colonial Cooking, 1975. Artist, mem. Sane, Union County, N.J., 1969-90; bd. dirs. Bridgeway Inc., 2005—; mem. emergency response team Ocean County, N.J. Woodrow Wilson fellow, 1961; N.J. Coun. Arts grantee Women for Women Union County Art Workshop, 1992. Mem. Am. Assn. Partial Hosps., N.J. Assn. Partial Hosps. (regional chmn. 1983-87, co-founder). Home: 261 Beach Front Manasquan NJ 08736-3937 Personal E-mail: sbrstudio@optonline.net.

ROBINSON, SHARON BETH, health science association administrator; b. Balt., Sept. 28, 1959; BS, Towson State U., 1981; MS, Johns Hopkins U., 1986. Exec. asst. Congress of Neurol. Surgeons, Balt., 1983-86; office adminstr. Md. Inst. Emergency Med. Svcs., Balt., 1986-87; coord. spl. projects U. Md. Med. Systems, Balt., 1986-88; adminstr. Am. Bd. Med. Genetics, Bethesda, Md., 1988—, Am. Coll. Med. Genetics, Bethesda, 1992-98, Am. Bd. Genetic Counseling, Bethesda, 1993—. Mem. Catonsville Community Coll. Alumni Assn. (bd. dirs. 1984-89, sec. 1986, v.p. 1987, pres. 1988). Office: ABMG/ABGC 9650 Rockville Pike Bethesda MD 20814-3998 E-mail: srobinson@genetics.faseb.org.

ROBINSON, SHEILA FRANCES, special education educator; b. Terre Haute, Ind., Mar. 18, 1955; d. Dean V. and Frances Murphy; m. Jack L. Robinson, Dec. 27, 1980 (div. Feb. 1984); 1 child, Aaron. BS in Retail, So. Ill. U., 1977. Cert. tchr. Ind., 1997, tchr. Type 10 Ill., 1997. Various advt. and retail positions, Terre Haute, Dayton, Ohio; resource tchr. learning disabilities Martinsville Jr. and Sr. H.S., Ill., 1997—. Mem.: Alpha Sigma Lambda, Phi Kappa Phi, Kappa Delta Pi. Avocations: gardening, reading, poetry. Office: Martinsville Jr Sr HS PO Box K Martinsville IL 62442

ROBINSON, SHIRLEY S., coach, educator; b. Miami, Fla., Mar. 10, 1946; d. Henry Early and Catherine Lampley Snell; m. Grover G. Robinson, Mar. 2, 1970 (div. May 1982); 1 child, Wayne Anthony. BA, Bethune Cookman U., 1969; postgrad., U. Miami, 1973-74, Nova U., 1988-89. Staff organizer North Dade Newspaper, Opa Locka, Fla., 1963-64; coach Spl. Olympics, Miami, 1989—, Sports Disabled Program, Miami, 1989—, Shake A Leg, Miami, 1997—. Advisor Miami Edison Sr. H.S., 1989—, Tech. Student Assn., Miami, 1990-92; tchr. ministry Antioch Bapt. Ch., Miami, 1999—; founder Phys. Challenge Club of Miami Edison Sr. High. Mem. 1st delegation Assocs. on Higher Edn. and Disability Profls., Republic of Vietnam, 1993; advocate for people with disabilities; mem. feeding ministry Antioch Bapt. Ch., 1999. Dade County Sch. Bd. grantee for higher edn., 1973-74. Mem. NAACP, Coun. for Exceptional Children (trophy 1982), United Tchrs. of Dade, Bethune Cookman Coll. Alumni Assn. (sec., scholarships com., trophy 1997), Nat. Coun. Negro Women, Sigma Gamma Rho. Home: 15831 NW 37th Ct Opa Locka FL 33054-6333

ROBINSON, STEPHANIE NICOLE, education educator; b. Chgo., July 8, 1974; d. Thomas Earl and Lola Jean Robinson; m. Melvin Douglas Burch. BA, U. Ill., Champaign, 1996, MA, 2000, PhD, 2002. Rsch. asst. U. Ill., 1997—2000, tchg. asst., 2000—02; substitute tchr. Champaign Pub. Schs., 1998—2002; asst. prof. Ball State U., Muncie, Ind., 2002—04; substitute tng. instr. Dept. Def., Camp Lejeune, NC, 2005; faculty mentor Western Govs. U., Salt Lake City, 2005—. Contbr. to book: Greenwood Dictionary of Education, 2003; author: History of Immigrant Female Students, 2004. Vol. ARC, NC, 2005; mem. com. Martin Luther King Sch., 2005. Mem.: Nat. Assn. Multicultural Edn., Officers Wives Club. Roman Catholic. Avocations: tennis, golf, crafts.

ROBINSON, SUE L(EWIS), federal judge; b. 1952; BA with highest honors, U. Del., 1974; JD, U. Pa., 1978. Assoc. Potter, Anderson & Corron, Wilmington, Del., 1978-83; asst. U.S. atty. U.S. Attys. Office, 1983-88; U.S. magistrate judge U.S. Dist. Ct. (Del. dist.), 1988-91, dist. judge, 1991—, chief judge. Named to U. Del. Wall of Fame, 1994. Mem.: Del. State Bar Assn. (sec. 1986—87). Office: US Dist Ct J Caleb Boggs Fed Bldg 844 N King St Lockbox 31 Wilmington DE 19801-3519

ROBINSON, VERNA COTTEN, retired librarian, real estate manager; b. Enfield, N.C., Oct. 6, 1927; d. Ernest and Ida (Faulcon) Cotten; m. Elbert Crutcher Robinson, Aug. 14, 1953 (dec. Feb. 1992); children: Angela, Elbert Cotten. BS, N.C. Cen. U., 1948; MS in Libr. Sci., Carnegie Mellon U., 1950. Br. libr. Blyden br. Norfolk (Va.) Pub. Libr., 1950-51; serials libr. Howard U., Washington, 1951-52; sch. libr. Spingarn H.S., Washington, 1952-53, Cardozo H.S., Washington, 1955-60, Roosevelt H.S., Washington, 1960-67, 70-85; ret. D.C. Pub. Schs., 1985. Pres. Robinson Property Mgmt. Inc., Washington, 1993—; bd. dirs. New Birth Corp., Miami. V.p. D.C. Assn. Sch. Librs., Washington, 1972-74; vice-chair Diaconate Lincoln Congrl. Temple/United Ch. of Christ, 1999—, chair, 2000-02. Recipient Elder Wise Woman award, Ctrl. Atlantic Conf. of United Ch. of Christ, 2002, Pioneer's Achiever's award United Ch. Christ, 1995; Daisy Scarborough scholar N.C. Cen. U., 1946-48, Carnegie Libr. Alumni scholar Carnegie Libr. Sch. Alumni Assn., 1948-50. Mem. African Am. Women's Assn. (internat. com. 1992-95), Delta Sigma Theta (tuition scholar Grand chpt. 1948-50), Delta Sigma Theta Alumnae Assn. (Wash. D.C. Chpt., 1970-). Avocations: reading, walking. Office Phone: 202-882-1737.

ROBINSON, VIRGINIA LYNN, elementary school educator; b. Paintsville, Ky., Aug. 19, 1950; d. John Cromwell Conley and Dolores Jean (Wilcox) McFaddin; m. Charles Robert Turner, Mar. 11, 1971 (div. 1987); children: Bethany Leigh, Ashley Lauren; m. Ronald Lee Robinson, Sept. 19, 1989. MusB, Morehead State U., 1972, elem. endorsement, 1979. Cert. tchr., Ky. Music tchr. Marion County Schs., Lebanon, Ky., 1975-76, Johnson County Schs., Paintsville, 1976-81, lang. arts/fine arts tchr., 1983—2006; ret., 2006. Active, officer PTA, Oil Springs, Ky., 1984—; judge Jenny Wiley Festival, Prestonsburg, Ky., Ky. Apple Festival, Paintsville; music dir. United Meth. Ch., Oil Springs, 1990—. Named Golden Apple Achiever Ashland Oil, 1990. Mem. Ky. Edn. Assn., Ky. Coun. Tchrs. English/Lang. Arts, Morehead State Alumni Assn., Ky. Poets Soc., Ky. Acad. Assn. (ofcl. 1990—), Delta Kappa Gamma. Democrat. Avocations: creative writing, singing, reading, dance, theater production. Home: 8772 Kentucky Route 580 Oil Springs KY 41238-9124

ROBINSON, WENDY Y., school system administrator; Under grad., DePauw U., Ind. U.-Purdue U., Ball State U. Tchr. Ward Elem., 1973—86; asst. prin. Meml. Pk. Mid. Sch., 1986—87, Weisser Pk. Elem., 1987—89; prin. Price Elem., 1989—91; area admin., asst. supt. Wayne HS, 1991—95; dep. supt. Fort Wayne Comm. Schs., 1995—2003, supt. Fort Wayne, Ind., 2003—. Office: Fort Wayne Comm Sch 1200 S Clinton St Fort Wayne IN 46802

ROBINSON PEETE, HOLLY, actress, writer; b. Phila., Sept. 18, 1964; d. Matthew T. and Dolores Robinson; m. Rodney Peete, June 10, 1995; children: Rodney Jackson, Ryan Elizabeth, Robinson James, Roman. BA in French and Psychology, Sarah Lawrence Coll., 1986. Cofounder (with Rodney Peete) HollyRod Found., 1997—. Actress (TV films) Dummy, 1979, Howard the Duck, 1986, Killers in the House, 1998, After All, 1999, Earthquake, 2004, (TV miniseries) The Jacksons: Am American Dream, 1992, (TV series) 21 Jump Street, 1991, Hangin' With Mr. Cooper, 1996, For Your Love, 1998, Like Family, 2003, Love, Inc., 2005, appeared on Sesame Street, 1969, ABC TGIF, 1990, Booker PI, 1990, Gabriel's Fire, 1991, Pacific Blue, 1997, Touch By An Angel, 1997, Strong Medicine, 2001, One on One, 2001—02, Pepsi Smash Superbowl Bash, 2006; author: Get Your Own Damn Beer, I'm Watching the Game!: A Woman's Guide to Loving Pro Football, 2005 (Quills award sport The Quills Literacy Found., 2006). Recipient Women of Conscience award, 1999, Am. Mentor award, Buddy award, Nat. Orgn. Women Legal Def. and Edn. Fund, Cmty. Svc. award, So. Calif. Broadcasters Assn., Gerald R. Ford People Helping People award, 2004, Healthy Babies, Healthy Futures award, March of Dimes, 2004, Woman of Distinction award, U. So. Calif., 2004, Anheuser Busch John E. Jacob Cmty. Svc. award, Disting. Achievement award, Huntington Disease Soc., Mentor award, Girls, Inc., 2004. Avocations: hiking, travel, pilates, football. Mailing: c/o HollyRod Foundation Ste LL15 9250 Wilshire Blvd Beverly Hills CA 90212*

ROBISON, EMILY BURNS, musician; b. Pittsfield, Mass., Aug. 16, 1972; d. Paul and Barbara Burns; m. Charlie Robison, May 1, 1999; children: Charles Augustus, Julianna Tex, Henry Benjamin. Performer Blue Night Express, 1984—89; banjo player, guitarist, vocalist Dixie Chicks, 1989—. Musician: (albums) Thank Heavens for Dale Evans, 1990, LIttle Ol' Cowgirl, 1992, Shouldn't a Told You That, 1993, Wide Open Spaces, 1998 (Maximum Vision Clip of Yr., Billboard, 1998, Best New Country Artist Clip of Yr., Billboard, 1998, Best Country Album, Grammy Awards, 1998, Album of Yr., Acad. Country Music, 1998, Best Selling Album, Can. Country Music Awards, 1999, Song of Yr., WB Radio Music Award, 1999, Album of Yr., ACM, 1999), Fly, 1999 (Best Country Album, Grammy Awards, 1999, Best Selling Album, Can. Country Musc Awards, 2000, Internat. Album, British Country Music Award, 2000, Country Album of Yr., Billboard Awards, 2000, Album of Yr., ACM, 2000, Album of Yr., CMA, 2000), Home, 2002 (Favorite Country Album, Am. Music Awards, 2002, Best Recording Package, Grammy Awards, 2002, Best Country Album, Grammy Awards, 2002), Top of the World Tour: Live, 2003 (Grammy award for Best Country Group Vocal Performance, 2005), Taking the Long Way, 2006; performer: (documentary) Dixie Chicks: Shut Up and Sing, 2006. Named Most Significant New Country Act, Country Monitor, 1998, Top New Country Artist, Billboard, 1998, Top Vocal Group, Acad. Country Music, 1998, Country Artist of Yr., Rolling Stone, 1999, Top Country Artist, Billboard, 1999, Internat. Rising Star, British Country Music Awards, 1999, Artist of Yr. (Country), WB Radio Music Award, 1999, Favorite New Artist (Country), AMA, 1999, Vocal Group of Yr., CMA, 1999, Country Artist of Yr., Billboard, 1999, 2000, Entertainer of Yr., CMA, 2000, ACM, 2000, Vocal Group of Yr., 2001, Entertainer of Yr., 2001, Favorite Musical Group or Band, People's Choice Award, 2002, Vocal

Group of Yr., Country Music Assn., 2002, others; named one of 100 Most Influential People, Time Mag., 2006; recipient Horizon award, CMA, 1998. Office: Monument Sony Nashville 34 Music Sq East Nashville TN 37203*

ROBISON, JUNE LEANNE, music educator; d. Charles and Hisako Henderson; m. Kenneth Dale Robison; children: Steven Dale, Andrew Lee. MusB cum laude, U. North Tex., Denton, 1983. Music and chorus tchr. Mexia Mid. Sch., Tex., 1983—85, St. Stephen's Elem. Sch., Conover, Tex., 1998—, mem. bldg. leadership team, 2000—03, mem. character edn. com., 2004—. Composer: (children's mus.) Paws and Tales, 2001, The Five Feuding Tribes, 2003, Katie's Bully, 2005. Chmn. edn. com. Humane Soc. Catawba County, Hickory, NC, 2002. Named Vol. of Yr., Humane Soc. Catawba County, 2002, NC Character Educator of Yr., Kenan Inst., 2002, KIND Tchr. of Yr., Nat. Assn. Humane and Environ. Edn., 2003; recipient Promising Practice award, Character Edn. Partnership, 2003, 2005; grantee, Catawba Valley Found., 2002, Hickory Cmty. Rels. Coun., Hickory City Coun., 2006; Wachovia/Ben Craig Elem. Educator of Yr. in Catawba County, 2002. Mem.: NC Music Edn. Nat. Assn., Music Edn. Nat. Assn. Avocation: scrapbooks.

ROBISON, PAULA JUDITH, flutist; b. Nashville, June 8, 1941; d. David Victor and Naomi Florence R.; m. Scott Nickrenz; Dec. 29, 1971; 1 child, Elizabeth Hadley Amadea Nickrenz. Student, U. So. Calif., 1958-60; BS, Juilliard Sch. Music, 1963. Founding artist, player Chamber Music Soc., N.Y.C., 1970-90, NY ChôroBand, 1994; co-dir. chamber music Spoleto Festival, Charleston, SC, 1978-88; Filene artist-in-residence Skidmore Coll., Saratoga Springs, NY, 1988-89; mem. faculty New Eng. Conservatory Music, 1991—, mem. faculty, Donna Heiken flut chair 1st occupant, 2005—; co-dir. Gardner Chamber Orch., Boston, 1995—; artist-in-residence Gardner Mus., 2005. Faculty Juilliard Sch., N.Y.C., 1978-82; annual concert series, Met. Mus. Art, N.Y., 1990—, With Art series, P.S. 1 Art Gallery, N.Y., 2000, Mass. Mus. Contemporary Art, 2001; dir. Vivaldi in the Courtyard, Gardner Mus., Boston, 2002—, faculty NE Conservatory, 2005—; founder, Pergola Recordings, 2006; collaboration with Sol LeWitt, Variations on a Theme, Gardner Mus., 2005. Soloist with various major orchs., including N.Y. Philharm., London Symphony Orch.; player, presenter Concerti di Mezzogiorno, Spoleto (Italy) Festival, 1970-2003; commd. flute concertos by Leon Kirchner, Toru Takemitsu, Oliver Knussen, Robert Beaser, Kenneth Frazelle; premiered works by Pierre Boulez, Elliott Carter, William Schuman, Thea Musgrave, Carla Bley, John Tavener, Michael Tilson Thomas; premiered Rio Days Rio Nights, Music Theatre Group prodn. in N.Y.C., 1998; participant Marlboro Music Festival, 1999-05; founder Pergola Recs., 2005; author: The Paula Robison Flute Warmups Book, 1989, The Andersen Collection, 1994, Paula Robison Masterclass: Paul Hindemith, 1995, The Sidney Lanier Collection, 1997, Frank Martin: Ballade, 2002, To a Wild Rose, 2003, MasterClass Series, Diller-Quaile Sch. of Music, 2004-; co-author: Places of the Spirit, 2003; recs. on CBS Masterworks, Music Masters, Vanguard Classics, New World Records, Omega, Arabesque, Sony Classical, King Recs., Mode Recs., Artemis Recs.; two person show Gardner Mus., Boston, 2005; featured in PBS documentary and book: Juilliard. Recipient First prize Geneva Internat. Competition, 1966, Adelaide Ristori prize, 1987, Lifetime Achievement award Nat. Flute Assn., 2004; named Musician of Month, Musical Am., 1979, House Musician for Isamu Noguchi Garden Mus., N.Y.C., 1988; Martha Baird Rockefeller grantee, 1966; Nat. Endowment for Arts grantee, 1978, 86; Fromm Found. grantee, 1980; Housewright Eminent scholar Fla. State U., 1990-91. Recipient Disting. Svc. award, Music Tchrs. Nat. Assn., 1989, Laurence Lesser Presdl. award, 1999, Lifetime Achievement award, Usdan Ctr. for Creative and Perfomring Arts, 2000, Hon. Citizen for Life award, City of Charleston, S.C., 2002, Lifetime Achievement award, Nat. Flute Assn., 2004. Mem. Sigma Alpha Iota (hon.). Office: Kirshbaum Demler & Assoc 711 W End Ave #5KN New York NY 10025

ROBISON, SUSAN MILLER, psychologist, speaker, consultant; b. Chgo., Nov. 15, 1945; d. William Louis and Constance Mary (Maloney) Miller; m. Philip Dean Robison, Dec. 27, 1969; 1 child, Christine Gray. BS, Loyola U., Chgo., 1967; MS, Ohio U., 1969, PhD, 1971. Lic. psychologist, Md. Asst. prof. psychology Ohio U., Lancaster, 1970-72; prof. psychology Coll. Notre Dame, Balt., 1972—; pvt. practice Ellicott City, Md., 1982—. Leadership cons. Nat. Coun. Cath. Women, Washington, 1987—99; co-owner BossWoman (leadership seminars and coaching). Author: Sharing Our Gifts, 1987, 2d edit., 1992, Discovering Our Gifts, 1989, 2d edit., 1993, Thinking and Writing in College, 1991. Mem. APA, Assn. for the Advancement Behavior Therapy, Am. Assn. Sex Educators, Counselors and Therapists, Nat. Spkrs. Assn. Avocations: writing, skiing, dance, jogging, quilting. Home: 3725 Font Hill Dr Ellicott City MD 21042-4932

ROBISON, SYLVIA POTTER, retired academic administrator; b. Little Rock, Ark. m. Olin Robison; 3 children. BA, Baylor U. summa cum laude, 1959; postgrad., Wesleyan U., 1968-70; LLD (hon.), Middlebury Coll., 2000. Tchr., Ft. Worth, Tex., 1959-60, Dept. Def. Sch. RAF, Greenham Common, Eng., 1961, tchr., prin. jr. high Brize Norton, Eng., 1961-63. Speaker Burlington Vt. YWCA Women's Day, 1978; lectr. Inst. USA and Can. Studies, Acad. Scis. of USSR, 1977, Bowdoin Coll. sr. seminar, 1973. Mem. nat. adv. bd. Reading Is Fundamental, Washington, 1976-91, Vt. Humanities Coun., 2002—; chmn. Vt. State Bd. Librs., 1987-89; bd. trustees Vt. Symphony Orch., 1984—, v.p., 1987-89, pres. bd. trustees, 1989-90, Vt. Folk Life Ctr., 1987-92, Am. Symphony Orch. League, 1989-92; mem. adv. bd. Sheldon Mus., 1982-95; trustee Frog Hollow State Craft Ctr., 1983-87; vol. Portland Symphony Orch., Pejepscot Hist. Soc., Walker Art Mus.; bd. dirs. Porter Hosp. Aux., Middlebury, 1975-85; bd. Vt. Folklife Ctr., 1985-90, Joint Urban Ministry Project, 1999-2003; bd. mem. Vt. Stage Co., 1998-2004. Mem.: AAUW (pres. Vt. 2000—05).

ROBLE, CAROLE MARCIA, accountant; b. Bklyn., Aug. 22, 1938; d. Carl and Edith (Brown) Dusowitz; m. Richard F. Roble, Nov. 30, 1969. MBA with distinction, N.Y. Inst. Tech., 1984. CPA, Calif., N.Y. Compt. various orgns. various orgns., 1956-66; staff acct. ZTBG CPA'S, L.A., 1966-67; sr. acct. J.H. Cohn & Co., Newark, 1967-71; prin. Carole M. Roble, CPA, South Hempstead, NY, 1971-90; ptnr. Roble & Libman, CPAs, Baldwin, NY, 1990-93; prin. Carole M. Roble, CPA, Baldwin, NY, 1993—. Speaker, moderator Found. for Acctg. Edn., N.Y., 1971—; lectr. acctg. various schs. including New Sch., Queens Coll., Empire State Coll., Touro Coll., N.Y. Inst. Tech., N.Y.C., Parsons Sch., 1971—. Guest various N.Y. radio and TV stas., 2 noted various newspapers. Treas. Builders Devel. Corp. of L.I., Westbury, N.Y., 1985; dir. Women Econ. Devels. of L.I., 1985-87. Recipient Sisterhood citation Nat. Orgn. Women, 1984, 85, cert. of Appreciation Women Life Underwriters, 1988, Women in Sales, 1982, 84; named top Tax Practitioner Money Mag., 1987, one of Top 100 Most Influential People, Acctg. Today, 1999. Mem. AICPA (mem. small firm advocacy com. 1996—), Am. Acct. Assn. (auditing sect.), Am. Soc. Women Accts. (pres. N.Y. chpt. 1980-81), Am. Woman's Soc. CPAs, Nat. Conf. CPA Practitioners (trustee L.I. chpt. 1981-82, sec. 1982-83, treas. 1983-84, v.p. 1984-85, 1st v.p. 1985-86, pres. 1986-87, nat. nominating com. 1983-84, 88-89, nat. continuing profl. edn. chmn. 1988-90, nat. treas. 1991-94, nat. v.p. 1994-96, exec. v.p. 1996-98, first woman nat. pres. 1998-99), Calif. Soc. CPAs, N.Y. State Soc. CPAs (bd. dirs. Nassau chpt. 1981-86, 91-93, bd. dirs. profl. devel., 1982-86, sec., mem. fin. acctg. standards com. 1990-95), Kiwanis (program chmn. County Seat chpt. 1989-90, sec. 1990-91, pres. 1991-92), Baldwin C. of C. (treas. 1990-93). Avocations: golf, gourmet cuisine, water-skiing, music. Home: 626 Willis St Hempstead NY 11550-8000

ROBLES, DIANA M, administrative assistant; d. Matt and Laura Robles. AAS in Liberal Arts, Eastfield Coll., Mesquite, Tex., 1999; BFA in Tech. Theatre, Sam Houston State U., Huntsville, Tex., 2003. Dept. asst. Eastfield Coll. Admissions, Mesquite, 1997—99; hostess ops.: attractions/spl. events Walt Disney World Resort, Orlando, Fla., 2002, vacation planner, 2002; resident charge scenic artist Sam Houston State U., Huntsville, 2002—03, scenic artist, 2000—03, tchg. asst.: scene painting, 2003; divsn. asst. Eastfield Coll., Mesquite, 2004—05, divsn. sec., 2005; asst. to v.p. of instrn. Mountain View Coll., Dallas, 2005—. Theatre technician, Tex., 1999—. Mem.: Sam Houston State U. Alumni Assn., US Inst. Tech. Theatre, Tex. Assn. Chicanos in Higher Edn. (hon.). Catholic. Avocations: painting, photography, cake decorating, sewing. Office: Mountain View Coll 4849 W Illinois Ave Dallas TX 75211

ROBLES, MARICELA, architect; b. 1975; Sr. designer D.R. Horton Homes. Mem. Tucson Xicano Mexicano Com. for Self-determination, Access Tucson Cmty. TV, National Chicano Moratorium Com.; co-founder Radio Chicana. Named one of 40 Under 40, Tucson Bus. Edge, 2006. Mem.: Am. Diabetes Assn., La Raza Unida Club (co-founder). Avocations: kickboxing, bikram yoga, mariachi music. Office: D R Horton Homes 5255 E Williams Circle Tucson AZ 85711*

ROBLES, ROSALIE MIRANDA, elementary school educator; b. L.A., Oct. 30, 1942; d. Richard and Carmen (Garcia) Miranda; m. Ralph Rex Robles, July 12, 1986; children: Gregory, Eric, Karen Cassandra. BA, Calif. State Coll., L.A., 1964; postgrad., Northridge State Coll. Playground supr. L.A. City Schs., 1961-64; elem. tchr. Montebello Unified Schs., Calif., 1964—; sch. site rep., faculty club chair, PTA La Merced Elem., 2006—. Rep. Montebello Credit Union, 1973-75, Bilingual Com., 1983-88; mem. Sch. Site Coun., 1989-92, chmn. 1980-83; union rep. Montebello Unified Schs. Chmn. Monterey Park Christmas Food Baskets, 1973-91; boys coord. Am. Youth Soccer, 1993-94, girls coord.; chmn. Boy Scouts Am., 1980-85; exec. bd. PTA, 1978, 80, 85, 87, 92—, pres. 1990-92; sec. St. Paul Parent Group, 1992-93, Palimentarian, 1993—; rep. Cost Containment Com., 1994-96; Eucharistic minister Roman Cath. Ch.; team mother Boys and Girls Club, 2005-06. Recipient Hon. Svc. award PTA, 1979, Hon. Svc. Continuing award, 1982, Golden Oak award, 1995. Mem. AAUW (pres. 2001-2003, v.p. program 2003—, cultural chair), Montebello Tchrs. Assn. (facuLyt club chair), Delta Kappa Gamma (sec., recording sec., pres., 2004—). Roman Catholic.

ROBOTHAM, SATTANYA A., private school educator; b. Kingston, Jamaica, Aug. 2, 1974; d. Vincent and Virginia Robinson. B Spanish, Queens Coll., Flushing, NY, 1997. Asst. tchr. Pkwy. Sch., Bklyn., 1997—2000; 4th grade tchr. St. Stephen Luth. Sch., Bklyn., 2000—01; electives tchr. Covenant Christian Ministries Acad., Marietta, Ga., 2001—. Office: Covenant Christian Ministries Acad PO Box 4065 Marietta GA 30061-4065

ROBSON, BARBARA S., elementary school educator; b. Phila., July 4, 1938; d. Robert John and Gladys Blodwyn (Williams) Smith; m. William John Robson, Oct. 1, 1960; children: William Charles, Robin Lynne, Robert Bruce. BS, West Chester U., 1960; postgrad., Pa. State U., Millersville U., Fla. State U. Cert. elem. edn. Tchr. Lansdowne (Pa.) Aldan Sch. Dist., No. Lebanon Sch. Dist., Fredericksburg, Pa., Ea. Lebanon County Sch. Dist., Myerstown, Pa. Cooperating tchr., mentor Lebanon Valley Coll., curriculum coord. grade K-1. Delta Kappa Gamma scholar. Mem. NEA, Internat. Reading Assn., Assn. Supervision and Curriculum Devel., Pa. Edn. Assn., Ea. Lebanon County Edn. Assn., Lebanon County Ednl. Honor Soc., Delta Kappa Gamma. Home: 205 Phillip Dr Myerstown PA 17067 Address: 1007 Alden Way Lebanon PA 17042

ROBSON, CAROL ANN SHAFFNER, retired secondary school educator; b. Jacksonville, Ill, July 19, 1936; d. Carl Merle and Patricia Beatrice (Brown) Shaffner; children: David, Glen, Anne, Patricia, Susan. BA, Ill. Coll., 1958; MS, So. Conn. State U., 1978, diploma in Advanced Studies, 1991. Cert. tchr., Ill., Conn., Mass. Tchr. New Berlin Bd. Edn., Ill., 1958-59, Arenzville Bd. Edn., Ill., 1960, Weston Bd. Edn., Mass., 1960-63, Hamden Bd. Edn., Conn., 1975-79, Elkhart Grade Sch., Ill., 1979-80, Hartford Bd. Edn., Conn., 1984—2002, ret., 2002. Tchr. Hamden Adult Edn., 1984—. Mem. Hamden Orgn. Women Educators, Hartford Fedn. Tchr., Conn. Coun. Adult Educators, Weston Tchrs. Assn. (pres. 1962-63), New Haven County Ret. Tchrs. Assn., Conn. Coun. English Tchr., Alpha Delta Kappa, Phi Delta Kappa, Delta Kappa Gamma. Republican. Avocation: cooking. Home: 331 Broadway Hamden CT 06518-2617

ROBSON-MCCOY, JEANIE ANN, secondary school educator; b. Idaho Falls, Idaho, July 28, 1954; d. Thomas D. and Glenny Robson; m. James Paul McCoy, Jan. 2, 1988; children: Randi Moore, Joshua McCoy. BS, Utah State U., Logan, 1976. Tchr. Gallup-McKinley Pub. Schs., Tohatchi, N.Mex., 1976—80, Echo (Oreg.) Sch. Dist., 1980—84, Blackfoot (Idaho) Sch. Dist., 1984—85, Idaho Falls Sch. Dist. 91, 1985—. Author: numerous poems. Named Speech Arts Tchr. of Yr., Speech Arts Tchrs. Idaho, 1992. Mem.: NEA, Nat. Coun. Tchrs. English. Democrat. Home: 725 11th St Idaho Falls ID 83404 Office: Idaho Falls High Sch 601 S Holmes Idaho Falls ID 83401 Home Fax: 208-522-6352. Personal E-mail: jeanie@srv.net.

ROBY, PAMELA ANN, sociologist, educator; b. Milw., Nov. 17, 1942; d. Clark Dearborn and Marianna (Gillman) Roby; m. James Peter Mulherin, July 15, 1977 (div. 1987). BA, U. Denver, 1963; MA, Syracuse U., N.Y., 1966; PhD, NYU, 1971. Instr. ednl. sociology NYU, N.Y.C., 1966; asst. prof. George Washington U., Washington, 1970—71; asst. prof. sociology and social welfare Brandeis U., Waltham, Mass., 1971—73; assoc. prof. U. Calif., Santa Cruz, 1973—77, prof. sociology and women's studies, 1977—, chair cmty. studies bd., 1974-76, 79, dir. sociology doctoral program, 1988—91, 2006—, chair sociology dept., 1998—2001. Mem. social sci. rsch. rev. com. NIMH, Washington, 1976—80; vice chair Nat. Commn. Working Women, Washington, 1977—80; cons. James Irvine Found., San Francisco, 1986; mem. sociology program rev. com. Northeastern U., Boston, 1990; mem. anthropology, linguistics and sociology panel NSF, Washington, 1993; assessor Social Scis. and Humanities Rsch. Coun. Can., Toronto, 1993; mem. U. Calif San Francisco Sociology Grad. Dept. External Review Panel, 2005, Ford Found. Post-Doctoral and Dissertation Fellowship Evaluation Panel, 2005, 06. Co-author: The Future of Inequality, 1970; editor: Child Care: Who Cares? Foreign and Domestic Infant and Early Childhood Development Policies, 1973—75, The Poverty Establishment, 1974; author: Women in the Workplace, 1981; adv. editor: Social Quar., 1990—93, Gender and Society, 1986—89. Vis. scholar, Indian Coun. Social Sci. Rsch., 1979, U. Wash., Seattle, 1991—92; Andrew W. Mellon Sr. scholar, Wellesley Coll., 1978—79. Mem.: Alpha Kappa Delta, Re-Evaluation Counseling (coll. and univ. faculty reference person 1980—), Eastern Sociol. Assn. (exec. coun. mem.-at-large 1973—74), Pacific Sociol. Assn. (v.p. 1996—97), Internat. Sociol. Assn. (rsch. coun. mem.-at-large 1978—82), Am. Sociol. Assn. (chair sect. sex and gender 1974—78, exec. coun. mem.-at-large 1975—78), Sociologists Women in Soc. (pres. 1978—80), Soc. Study Social Problems (pres. 1996—97), Phi Beta Kappa. Avocations: camping, hiking, painting, swimming, pen and ink drawing. Office: U Calif Dept Sociology C8 Santa Cruz CA 95064

ROCA DE TORRES, IRMA ENEIDA, retired psychology professor; b. Arecibo, P.R., Sept. 30, 1942; d. Fernando and Angelina (Saavedra) Roca; m. Francisco A. Torres-Santos, Dec. 26, 1966; children: Javier, Irmarylis (dec.), Leilani, Ilianai. BA in Psychology, U. P.R., 1962; MA in Clin. Psychology, U. Minn., 1964; PhD in Sch. Psychology, Temple U., 1987. Lic. psychologist, sch. psychologist, P.R. Social scis. educator U. P.R., Río Piedras, 1964-66, psychology educator, 1966—2000, assoc. dean, 1990—98; psychologist Head Star, San Juan, P.R., 1966-68. Contbr. articles to profl. jours. Bd. dirs. ballet sch., San Juan, 1978-91; actress, asst. dir. Children's Theater Group, San Juan, 1960-2000; advocate for children with handicaps. Recipient Certificate of Honor for Disting. Alumni Temple U., 1995, Lifetime Career award P.R. Psych. Assn., 2005; grantee U. P.R., Río Piedras, 1984-87, 1989-91. Mem. APA (grantee 1989), Am. Assn. Mental Retardation, Interam. Soc. of Psychology (nat. rep. 1993-95), P.R. Psychol. Assn. (sec. 1969-70, v.p. 1975-76, pres. 2003), Nat. Assn. Sch. Psychologists (pres. P.R. mental health planning, adv. coun., 2003-06). Roman Catholic. Avocations: theater, ballet, reading. Home: 6 Calle 1 La Campina San Juan PR 00926

ROCCA, CHRISTINA B., ambassador, former federal agency administrator; b. Washington, 1957; m. Gordon L. Rocca; 2 children. BA in History, King's Coll., London, 1980. Staff ops. officer, Directorate of Ops. CIA, Washington, 1982—97; fgn. affairs advisor to Senator Sam Brownback US Senate, Washington; asst. sec for South Asian Affairs US Dept. State, Washington, 2001—06; US perm. rep. & amb. UN Conf. on Disarmament, Geneva, 2006—.*

ROCCHI, ROBIN HENNING, financial executive, automotive company executive; BA, Dartmouth Coll., 1983; MBA, Northwestern U., 1988. Lending officer Manufacturers Hanover, N.Y.C., 1983-86; fin. analyst, treas. office GM, N.Y.C., 1988-91, mgr., 1991-94, dir., 1994-2000; dir. internat. strategy GM Asset Mgmt., N.Y.C., 2000—01, dir. global equity strategy, 2001—04, gen. dir., 2004—05, v.p. investment programs, 2005—. Office: GM Asset Mgmt 767 5th Ave Fl 16 New York NY 10153-0023

ROCCHIO, GLORIA D., cultural organization administrator; Pres. Ward Melville Heritage Orgn., Stony Brook, NY; founder, pres. North Shore Promotion Alliance. Pres. Eagle Realty Holdings, Inc. Sec. N.Y. State, Long Island, North Shore Heritage AreaPlanning Commn.; treas. bd. dirs. Long Island Conv. and Visitors Bur.; mem. Industry's Small Bus. Coun. Mem.: Three Village C. of C. (bd. dirs.), Long Island Assn. Commerce. Office: Ward Melville Heritage Orgn 111 Main St Stony Brook NY 11790

ROCCO, NIKKI, film company executive; m. Joseph Rocco. Sales dept. Universal Pictures, 1967, asst. to gen. sales mgr., 1981—84, v.p. distbn., 1984—90, sr. v.p. distbn. and mktg., 1990—95, exec. v.p., distbn., 1995—96, pres., distbn., 1996—. Bd. dirs. Will Rogers Motion Picture Pioneers Found. Named one of 100 Most Powerful Women in Entertainment, Hollywood Reporter, 2004, 2005; recipient Crystal award, Women in Film, 2000. Office: Universal Pictures 100 Universal City Plaza Universal City CA 91608*

ROCHA, CYNTHIA J., social sciences educator, consultant; b. Alton, Ill., Aug. 16, 1960; d. Ernest Leroy and Joyce Marilyn Gasperson; m. Bill Hnath; 1 child, Clarissa. B. U. Tex., Austin, 1987, MSW, 1991; PhD, Washington U., St. Louis, Mo., 1994. Dir., counseling svcs. Ladies Ctr., Austin, Tex., 1989—91; asst. prof. U. Tenn., 1994—2000; assoc. prof. Coll. of Social Work, U. Tenn, Knoxville, 2000—06. Bd. mem. Laurel HS, Knoxville, Cmty. Partnership Ctr., Knoxville, 1996—2002; program evaluator, cons. in field, St. Louis; adv. Corp. Bd. Dir., Knoxville, 2000—05; program evaluator, cons. in field, Knoxville, 1993—; presenter in field. Contbr. articles to profl. jours. and pubs. Recipient Nat. State Policy Plus One award, Nat. Commn. for Educating Students to Influence Policy & Legis., 1998, Chancellor award, U. Tenn., 2001. Mem.: NASW, Coun. Social Work Edn. Avocations: camping, singing, travel, dance. Home: 1053 Brantley Dr Knoxville TN 37923

ROCHA, OSBELIA MARIA JUAREZ, librarian, principal; b. Odessa, Tex., Aug. 3, 1950; d. Tomas R. and Maria Socorro (Garcia) Juarez; m. Ricardo Rocha, July 8, 1972; children: Nidia Selina, René Ricardo. AA, Odessa Coll., 1970; BA, Sul Ross State U., 1972; MA, Tex. A&I U., 1977; MLS, Tex. Woman's U., 1991; mid-mgmt. cert., U. Tex., Permian Basin, 1999. Cert. life provisional reading specialist, learning res. tchr., secondary English, math. Tex., mid-mgmt. adminstr. Math. tchr. Del Rio (Tex.) Jr. HS, 1972-78, Ector HS, Odessa, 1979-81, Permian HS, Odessa, 1981-88; reading tchr. Del Rio HS, 1978-79; libr. Blackshear Elem. Magnet Sch., Odessa, 1988-93, Bowie Jr. HS, Odessa, 1993-95, Ector Jr. HS, Odessa, 1995-96, Permian HS, Odessa, 1996-2000; asst. prin. Big Spring HS, Tex., 2000—02; prin., curriculum dir. Weimar HS Ind. Sch. Dist., 2002—. Reviewer children's and adolescent's books MultiCultural Rev.; contbr. articles to profl. jours. Mem.: ASCD, Tex. Coun. Women Sch. Execs., Tex. Elem. Prins. and Suprs. Assn., Tex. Libr. Assn., Tex. Reading Assn., Tex. Assn. Bilingual Edn., Tex. Assn. Secondary Sch. Prins., Delta Kappa Gamma, Beta Phi Mu. Roman Catholic. Avocations: reading, needlecrafts, collecting realia from various cultures. Office: Cavaos Elem 9301 W 16th St Odessa TX 79763 Home: 1717 W 24th St Odessa TX 79763-2309 Personal E-mail: osbeliar@yahoo.com. Business E-Mail: rochaosm@ector-county.k12.tx.us.

ROCHA, PATRICIA KENNEDY, lawyer; b. Providence, Oct. 16, 1957; d. Gilbert Thomas and Joan Kennedy Rocha; m. James Hilton Lerner, June 30, 1982; children: John Lerner, Christopher Lerner, Matthew Lerner. BA with honors, Brown U., Providence, R.I., 1979; JD, Boston Coll., Newton, Mass., 1982. Bar: R.I. 1982, Mass. 1983, U.S. Dist. Ct. R.I. 1983, U.S. Dist. Ct. Mass. 1983. Atty. Adler Pollock & Sheehan, Providence, 1982—. Mem. faculty RI Fed. Bd. Bar Examiners for US Dist. Ct. Pres. Boston Coll. Law Sch. Alumni Chpt. Recipient 75th Anniversary Alumni award, Boston Coll. Law Sch., 2005. Mem.: R.I. Character and Fitness Com., R.I. Bar Found. (dir.), R.I. Def. Counsel (dir. 2005—06). Office: Adler Pollock and Sheehan PC One Citizens Plz 8th Fl Providence RI 02903 Office Phone: 401-274-7200. Office Fax: 401-351-4607. E-mail: procha@apslaw.com.

ROCHBERG, FRANCESCA, historian; d. George and Gene Rochberg; children: Jacob Rochberg-Halton, Gemma Rochberg-Halton. BA, U. Pa., Phila., Pa., 1975; PhD, U. Chgo., Chgo., Ill., 1980. Assyrian dictionary project U. Chgo., Oriental Inst., 1980—82; prof. history U. Notre Dame, Ind., 1982—93, U. Calif., Riverside, Calif., 1994—. Recipient John Frederick Lewis award, Am. Philos. Soc., 1999; fellow, John D. and Catherine T. MacArthur Found., 1982—87, John Simon Guggenheim Found., 1993—94. Mem.: Internat. Assn. Assyriology, The Oriental Inst. U. Chgo., Archaeological Inst. Am., Am. Schs. Oriental Rsch., History Sci. Soc., Am. Oriental Soc. Achievements include research in ancient Near East, assyriology, history of science. Office Phone: 951-827-5401.

ROCHE, BARBARA ANNE, retired minister, editor; b. Long Beach, Calif., Aug. 28, 1934; d. Claire Peter and Agnes Louise (Elford) Roche. BA, Stanford U., 1956; cert., United Theol. Coll., Bangalore, India, 1961; MDiv, Princeton Theol. Sem., 1960; DMin, San Francisco Theol. Sem., 1984. Ordained min. Presbyterian Ch., 74. Clk. typist Smithsonian Instn., Washington, 1956—57; dir. religious edn. Emmanuel Presbyn. Ch., Spokane, 1962—66; area rep. Commn. on Ecumenical Mission and Rels., Chgo., 1966—73; dir. student svcs. Pacific Sch. of Religion, Berkeley, Calif., 1973—76, dean of students, 1976—84; editor Concern Mag. and Newsfold, N.Y.C., 1985—88, Horizons Mag. and Bible Study, Louisville, 1988—97, ret., 1998. Assoc. Consultation on Ch. Union, Princeton, NJ, 1973—80; parish assoc. St. John's Presbyn. Ch., Berkeley, 1981—84; judge H.S. jours. Assoc. Ch. Press, 1998—99. Editor: (jours.) Living the Word, 1999—2000, (mag.) Stewardship Part 2, 1998, (book) Dear House, Mission Becomes You, 2000; contbr.: book Celebrating Our Call, Ordination Stories of Presbyterian Women, 2006. Named Woman of Decade, Grad. Theol. Union Women's Ctr., 1975. Mem.: NOW, Assn. Presbyn. Women Clergy, Presbyn. Writers' Guild, Presbyn. Women (life), Amnesty Internat. Democrat. Presbyterian.

ROCHE, GAIL CONNOR, editor; b. Phila., Aug. 14, 1953; d. Donald Russell Connor; m. Richard Roche, Nov. 21, 1981; children: Alex James, Clare Evelyn. AB cum laude, Franklin & Marshall Coll., Lancaster, Pa., 1975; MA with distinction, Rider U., 1988. Cert. tchr., Pa. Tchr. Pennsbury Schs., Fallsington, Pa., 1975-76, Cen. Bucks Sch., Doylestown, Pa., 1977-79; reporter Trenton Times, NJ, 1979-82; editor Dow Jones & Co., Princeton, NJ, 1982-95; mem. adv. bd. Dow Jones Women's Network, Princeton, 1990-95; tech. editor Bloomberg News, Princeton, 1995-2000; sr. editor, letters editor Bloomberg Markets, 2000—. Contbr. articles to mags. Mem. Phi Beta Kappa. Home: 23 Jericho Run Washington Crossing PA 18977-1027 Office Phone: 609-394-0738. Personal E-mail: groche@bloomberg.net.

ROCHE, PAULINE JENNIFER, artist; b. London, Sept. 22, 1961; arrived in U.S., 1995; d. Walter Daniel and Doreen Molly Roche; m. Hany Massarany, Feb. 27, 1986; children: Thomas Daniel, Natalie Jane. BS, Monash U., Melbourne, Australia, 1982. Rsch. physiology dept. physiology Monash U., Melbourne, 1983—86; rsch., policy and planning officer Victorian State Govt. Dept. Edn./Pub. Svc. Bd., Melbourne, 1986—92; artist, 1989—. Exhibitions include Sherbrooke Art Award exhbns., 1991—97, Victorian Artists Soc. Ann. Exhbns., 1992—2001, Alice Bale Ann. Nat. Exhbns., 1993—98, Camberwell Rotary Ann. Juried Art Exhbn., 1992—98,

1993, 2000, Kew Gallery Invitational Exhbn., 1994, Victorian Artists Soc. Artist of Yr. Invitational Exhbn., 1997, Salmagundi Club 20st Ann. Open Exhbn., Salmagundi Club, 1997—98, Catherine Lorillard Wolfe Art Club Exhbn., 1997, 2004, Am. Artists Profl. League 69th Grand Nat. Exhbn., 1997, Newbury Fine Arts, Boston, 1998—2006, Newbury Fine Arts Figurative Art Group Exhbn., 2000, Celebrate! Exhbn., Tucson, 2002, Catherine Lorillard Wolfe Art Club 109st Art Exhbn., 2004, El Presidio Gallery, Tucson, 2005—06, one-woman shows include Cato Gallery, Victorian Artists Soc. Galleries, Melbourne, 1994, Ventana Med. Sys. Nat. Hdqs., Tucson, 2003. Recipient Gold Medal of Honor, Audubon Artists 55th Ann. Exhn., 1997, Hans Heysen award, Sherbrooke Art Soc., 1992, Award for Oil Painting, Alice Bale Nat. Art Awards, 1994, Mavis Hill Acquisitive Award, Sherbrooke Spring Exhbn., 1995, Gordon Moffat award, Victorian Artists Soc., 1997, Highly Commended, Victorian Artists Soc. Dep. Lord Mayor's Exhbn., 1999, N.J. Chpt. award for artistic excellence, Am. Artists Profl. League, 1997, Pres. award, Salmagundi Club, 1997, Artist Showcase award, Manhattan Arts Internat., 1997, 1998, Leonard J. Meiselman Meml. award, Catherine Lorillard Wolfe Art Club, 1997, Sharon and Danielle Ortlip Meml. award, Salmagundi Club, 1998, Highly Commended award, Australian Guild Realist Artists, 2006. Mem.: Australian Guild Realist Artists, Portrait Soc. Am., Victorian Artists Soc. (signatory mem., Gordon Moffat award 1997). Office Phone: 520-219-2902. E-mail: paulineroche@comcast.net.

ROCHELLE, DOROTHY, educational consultant; b. Danville, Va., Nov. 8, 1922; d. Morton Dean and Eunice Pearl Edwards; m. James Edward Rochelle, Feb. 17, 1946; children: Michael, Deborah, Stephen, Patricia. Diploma in Nursing, St. Phillips Sch. Nursing, Richmond, Va., 1945. RN, Va., Calif. Charge nurse L.A. Gen. Hosp., 1948, Calif. Luth. Hosp., L.A., 1949, White Meml. Hosp., L.A., 1950-52, St. Francis Hosp., Lynwood, Calif., 1952; cmty. liaison L.A. Unified Sch. Dist., 1977—. Title I parent U.S. Congress, Washington, 1973. Mem. Urban League, L.A., 1999—, Black Women's Forum, L.A., 1999—; chairperson 1st Calif. State-wide Parent Conf. on Title I, Marin County, Calif., 1973; mem. L.A. Mayor's Adv. Com. on Edn.; cons. U.S. Dept. Edn. on New Regulations for Title I Funds, 1972-78; founder Advocates for Black Children, L.A., 1999—; life mem. PTA, L.A., 1999—. Recipient Mayor's Human Rels. award, L.A., 1970; hon. by Nat. Assn. Sch. Adminstrs. Mem. NAACP, NOW, Nat. Coalition of ESEA Title I Parents (founding and emeritus). Democrat.

ROCHELLE, LUGENIA, academic administrator; b. Maple Hill, N.C., July 14, 1943; d. John Edward and Ruby Lee (Holmes) R. BA, St. Augustine's Coll., 1965; MS, N.C. A & T State U., 1969; D of Pedagogy, Barbar-Scotia Coll., 1993. Cert. tchr., N.C. Tchr. French, English Butler High Sch., Barnwell, SC, 1965-67; instr. English N.C. A & T State U., Greensboro, 1970-77, St. Augustine's Coll., Raleigh, NC, 1977-86, dir. freshman studies program, 1986-91, dean lower coll., 1991-95, asst. to v.p. acad. affairs, 1991-92; dir. gen. studies, asst. prof. English Voorhees Coll., Denmark, SC, 1996-98, spl. asst. to pres. external affairs, 1999—2002, dir. Hons. Coll., 1999—, dean, Coll. of General Studies, 2002—. Dir. Mellon program St. Augustine's Coll., Raleigh, 1980-83; adv. bd. cooperating Raleigh Colls., 1986—, Off to Coll., Montgomery, Ala., 1993—; mem. profl. practices commn. N.C. Dept. Pub. Instrn., 1994-96; coord. Title III, 1999-00, coord. Bd. Trustees Rels., 1999-02; dir. Ctr. Excellence in Humanities, Vorhees Coll., April 2000-02; Hostess for Radio Talk Show, Views and News from Voorhees Coll., Sept. 2001-03. Author: English Manual of Writing, 1980, (with others) Off to College, 1997, 98, reprinted, 1999, 2000, 01; editor: Can't Nobody Do You Like Jesus, 1998. Judge oratorical contests, Optimist Club, Raleigh, 1985-93; chair pro tem Raleigh Bicentennial Hist. Com., Raleigh, 1991-92; initiated, effected chartering of Phi Eta Sigma St. Augustine's Coll., 1995; bd. dirs. Garner Rd. YMCA, Raleigh, 1994-1996; coord. Honda Campus All-Star Challenge, 1996—; lay min., sec. vestry St. Philip's Episcopal Ch., 1997—; instnl. rep. S.C. Women in Higher Edn., Voorhees Coll., 1998—. Nat. teaching fellow N.C. A & T State U., Greensboro, 1968-70. NCTE Fellow Nat. Coun. Tchrs. English; mem. ASCD (assoc.), Am. Assn. U. Women (pres. Denmark Br.), Cardinal Club. Avocations: reading, collecting antique birds, travel. E-mail: rochelle@voorhees.edu.

ROCHLIN, JOYCE TRETICK, researcher; b. Balt., Apr. 13, 1941; d. Louis Tretick and Rose Schwartz Tretick Rosenbloom; m. Jerry S. Sopher, June 25, 1961 (div.); children: Keith A. Sopher, Maura Sopher; m. Paul R. Rochlin, July 12, 1973; children: Greg, Jennifer. BA, U. Md., 1983; MA, Towson State U., 1986; EdD, Nova Southeastern U., 1991. Adj. asst. prof. psychology; rsch. for AIDS Adminstrn. of Md., Balt., 1990-91. Contbr. articles to profl. jours. Avocations: golf, travel, computer programming.

ROCK, BETH MARIE, voice educator, director; d. Babe and Lowene Darnell; m. Steven Joseph Rock, May 11, 1991; children: Jason Steven, Emily Lauren, Jenna Elizabeth. MusB, Ea. Ill. U., Charleston, 1988. Choral dir. Palisades Mid. Sch., Burr Ridge, Ill., 1988—90, Woodland Sch. Dist., Streator, Ill., 1990—92, Midland Sch. Dist., Varna, Ill., 1994—; asst. music dir. Peoria Area Civic Chorale, Ill., 1998—. Recipient Talented Student award, Ea. Ill. U., 1985—88, Dvorak Meml. award, 1987, Choral Conducting award, 1988, award, Sigma Alpha Iota, 1986, Outstanding Am. Tchr., Nat. Honor Roll, 2006. Mem.: Music Educator's Nat. Conf. Avocations: reading, bicycling, travel. Office: Midland HS 1830 State Rt 17 Varna IL 61375 Office Phone: 309-463-2095.

ROCK, CARO, publisher; b. Kansas City, Mo., Aug. 4, 1953; d. Paul Jr. and Barbara Uhlmann; m. Robert Henry Rock, Dec. 20, 1975; children: William, Thomas. Student, Wheaton Coll., 1971-72; BA, Tulane U., 1975; postgrad., Temple U. Asst. editor Ames Pub. Co., Phila., 1975-76; lending officer Provident Nat. Bank, Phila., 1976-78; asst. v.p. Fidelity Bank, Phila., 1978-83; spl. sections Montgomery Newspapers, Ft. Washington, Pa., 1987-95; assoc. pub. Main Line Life, Ardmore, Pa., 1995—. Bd. mem. Free Libr. Phila.; chmn. bd. Rock Sch. Ballet; adv. bd. Main Line Art Ctr.; fin. com. Haverford Sch.; assocs. bd. Phila. Art Mus. Named to Pa. Best 50 Women in Bus., 1997. Mem. Main Line C. of C. (bd. mem.).

ROCK, JENNIFER ELIZABETH, elementary school educator; b. Melbourne, Fla., June 30, 1977; d. Robert Dale Rock and Joanne Leslie Cox, Steven Robert Cox (Stepfather). BA in Music Edn., Southeastern U., Lakeland, Fla., 2001. Tchr. chorus Stone Mid. Sch., Melbourne, Fla., 2001—. Leader youth Calvary Chapel, 2005—06, singer worship team, 2002—06. Scholar, Brevard C.C., 1996—98, State of Fla., 1996—2001. Mem.: Fla. Vocal Assn. (assoc.; dist. sec. 2006—), Music Educators Nat. Conf. (assoc.). Republican. Avocation: travel.

ROCK, MARY ANN, artist, educator; b. St. Louis, Mar. 2, 1931; d. Clobert Bernard and Mary Henrietta (Jones) Broussard; m. William Ralph Rock, Mar. 18, 1960 (div. Sept. 1967); 1 child, John Henry C. BS, Bennett Coll., 1952; postgrad., Chgo. Art Inst., 1953—54, So. Ill. U., Carbondale, 1955. Instr. arts and crafts Presidio Hill Sch., San Francisco, 1966; dir. gallery Cannery House Gallery, Friday Harbor, Wash., 1974—76; co-founder Island Artisans, Friday Harbor, 1980—85; gallery asst. Waterworks Gallery, Friday Harbor, 1986—95; with European study tour, 1996; patron sponsored painting sabbatical, 2001—03; prin., owner Dream Keeper Art Card Co., 2002—. Guest instr. Spring St. Sch., Friday Harbor, 2001, Friday Harbor, 02; presenter art workshops Friday Harbor Elem. Sch., 1976, 87, Portland CC, 1989, 90. Author, illustrator: DreamKeeper, 1995; brochures, one-woman shows include Trofes Gallery, Seattle, 2006, exhibitions include 13th Saloon Internat. del Alpha, Lyon, France, Waterworks Gallery, Friday Harbor, 1986—, 7th Whatcomb County Mus., Bellingham, 1988, Portland CC, 1990, Chetwynn Stapleton Gallery, Portland, 1989—98. Curator African art exhibit NAACP, San Francisco, 1961. Vt. Studio Ctr. fellow, Johnson, 1999. Democrat. Avocations: collecting ethnic artifacts, skiing, rock climbing, travel, reading.

ROCKABOVE, MAGDALENE M., special education educator; d. Walter M. Stewart Sr. and Meto M. Stewart; married; 3 children. AA, Mont. State U., 1996, BS in Elem. Edn., 1997, M in Spl. Edn., 2001; student, Mont. State U., Bozeman, 2006—. Clk. Indian Health Sci., Billings, Mont., 1999—2000, stats. asst., 2000—01; spl. edn. tchr. Lodge Grass (Mont.) H.S., 2001—05. Mentor Mont. Youth Leadership, Dillon, 2004—; mem. World Vision, 2000—. Recipient Partnerships for Diversity award, U. Mont., 2004—05. Mem.: Civil Rights Movement. Democrat. Avocations: jogging, reading, singing. Home: PO Box 176 Pryor MT 59066 Office: Lodge Grass High Sch PO Box 810 Lodge Grass MT 59050

ROCKAS, ANASTASIA T., lawyer; b. Rochester, N.Y., 1963; BA, Smith-Coll., 1985; JD with hons., U. Conn., 1990. Bar: Conn. 1990, N.Y. 1993. Atty. Skadden, Arps, Slate, Meagher & Flom LLP, N.Y., 1992, ptnr. Office: Skadden Arps Slate Meagher & Flom LLP Four Times Sq New York NY 10036

ROCKBURNE, DOROTHEA GRACE, artist; b. Montreal; naturalized; Student, Black Mountain Coll.; PhD (hon.), Coll. of Creative Studies, Detroit, 2002. Milton and Sally Avery Disting. prof. Bard Coll., 1986. Trustee Ind. Curators Inc., N.Y., Art in Gen.; artist in residence Am. Acad. in Rome, 1991; vis. artist Skowhegan Sch. Painting and Sculpture, 1984; Rockefeller Found. resident Bellagio (Italy) Conf. and Study Ctr., 1997. One-woman shows at Sonnabend Gallery, Paris, 1971, New Gallery, Cleve., 1972, Bykert Gallery, NYC, 1970, 72-73, Galleria Toselli, Milan, Italy, 1972-74, Galleria D'Arte, Bari, Italy, 1972, Lisson Gallery, London, 1973, Daniel Weinberg Gallery, San Francisco, 1973, Galerie Charles Kriwin, Brussels, 1975, Galleria Schema, Florence, Italy, 1973, 75, 92, John Weber Gallery, NYC, 1976, 78, Galleria la Polena, Geona, Italy, 1977, Tex. Gallery, Houston, 1979-81, Xavier Fourcade Gallery, NYC, 1981-83, 85-86, David Bellman, Toronto, 1980-81, Margo Leavin, Calif., 1982, Arts Club Chgo., 1987, André Emmerich Gallery, NYC, 1988-89, 91-92, 94-95, Rose Art Mus., 1989, P. Fong & Spratt Galleries, San Jose, Calif., 1991, Sony Music Hdqs., NYC, 1993, Frederick Spratt Gallery, San Jose, 1994, Guild Hall Mus., Easthampton, N.Y., 1995, Portland Mus. Art, Maine, 1996, Ingrid Raab Gall., Berlin, 1997, Art in Gen., NY, 1999, Greenberg, Van Doren, NYC, 2000, Dieu Donné Papermill, NYC, 2003, Jan Abrams Fine Art, NY, 2003; group exhbns. at Leo Castelli Gallery, NYC, 1966, Whitney Mus. Am. Art, 1970, 73, 77, 79, 82, 05, Mus. Modern Art, NYC, 71, 73, 81, 84, 86, 91, 93-94, 05, Buenos Aires, 1971, Kolner Kunst Market, Cologne, Germany, 1971, Stedelijk Mus., Holland, 1971, Spoleto (Italy) Festival, 1972, Palazzo Taverna, Rome, 1973, Nat. Gallery Victoria, Melbourne, Australia, 1973, Art Gallery NSW, Sydney, 1973, Auckland (New Zealand) City Art Gallery, 1973, Inst. Contemporary Art, London, 1974, Mus. d'Arte de la Ville, Paris, 1975, Galerie Aronowitsch, Stockholm, 1975, Stadtiches Mus., Manchengladbach, Germany, 1975, Galleria D'Arte Moderna, Bologna, Italy, 1975, Art Gallery Ont., Toronto, Can., 1975, Mus. Fine Art, Houston, 1975, Contemporary Arts Ctr., Cin., 1973, 75, 81, Mus. Contemporary Art, Chgo., 1971, 77, 86, Corcoran Gallery of Art, Washington, 1975, 87, Städtisches Mus., Leverkusen, Germany, 1975, Cannaviella Studio d'Arte Rome, 1976, Phila. Coll. Art, 1976, 83, New Mus., NYC, 1977, 80, 84, 83, Renaissance Soc. of U. Chgo., 1976, Lowe Art Mus., U. Miami, Fla., 1976, Inst. Contemporary Art, Boston, 1976, Seibu Mus. Art, Tokyo, 1976, NY State Mus., Albany, 1977, Drawing Ctr., 1977, Kansas City (Mo.) Art Inst., 1977, Smithsonian Inst., Washington, 1977, Kassel, Fed. Republic Germany, 1972, 77, Ackland Art Ctr., Chapel Hill, NC, 1979, 84, Milw. Art Ctr., 1978, 81, Biblioteca Nacional, Madrid, 1980, Gulbenkian Mus., Lisbon, Portugal, 1980, Bklyn. Mus., 1981, 89, Guggenheim Mus., 1982, 88-89, 2004, Albright Knox Art Gallery, Buffalo, 1979-80, 88-89, Kuustforeningen Mus., Copenhagen, 1980, Venice Biennale, 1980, Cranbrook (Mich.) Acad. Art, 1981, Mus. Fine Arts, Boston, 1983, Contemporary Arts Mus., Houston, 1983, Norman Mackenzie Art Gallery, U. Regina, Sask., Can., 1983, Galleriet, Sweden, 1983-84, Seattle Art Mus., 1979-84, Nat. Mus. Art., Osaka, Japan, 1984, Fogg Art Mus., Cambridge, Mass., 1984, Am. Acad. and Inst. Arts and Letters, NYC, 1984, 87, LA County Mus. Art, 1984, 86, Wadsworth Atheneum, Hartford, Conn., 1981, 84, Evehart Mus., Pa., 1984, Grey Art Gallery, NYU, 1977, 84, 87, Avery Ctr. Arts, Bard Coll., N.Y., 1985, 87-88, Stamford (Conn.) Mus., 1985, Aldrich Mus., Conn., 1979, 82, 95, Bronx Mus. Arts, N.Y.C., 1985, High Mus., Atlanta, 1975, 81, Phila. Mus. Art, 1986, Nat. Gallery Art, Washington, 1984, 94, 97, Mus. Art, Ft. Lauderdale, Fla., 1986, Nat. Mus. Women in Art, Washington, 1987, Xavier Fourcade Gallery, 1982, 83, 86-87, LA County Mus. Modern Art, 1986-87, The Hague, The Netherlands, 1986, Carnegie-Mellon Art Gallery, Pitts., 1979, 87, Balt. Mus. Art, 1975-76, 88, Ctr. for Fine Arts, Miami, 1989, Milw. Art Mus., 1989, Cin. Art Mus., 1989, New Orleans Mus., 1989, Denver Art Mus., 1989, Parrish Art Mus., South Hampton, NY, 1990-91, 99, Margo Leavin Gallery, LA, 1991, Guild Hall Mus., East Hampton, NY, 1991, Am. Acad., Rome, 1991, Mus. Contemporary Art, LA, 1991, 99, Hunter Coll., NY, 1991, CentroCultural/Arte Contemporanea, MexicoCity, 1991, Hilton, San Jose, Calif.,1992, Hillwood Art Mus., L.I., NY, 1992, Am. Acad. and Inst. Arts and Letters, 1992, Neuberger Mus., 1992, 00, Kohn-Abrams Gallerie, LA, 1993, Gallery at Bristol Myers Squibb, NJ, 1993-94, Friends of Art and Preservation in Embassies, NYC, 1993, Andre Emmerich Gallery, NYC, 1993, Fred Spratt Gallery, San Jose, Calif., 1994, Raab Galarie, Berlin, 1994, NY Studio Sch., NYC, 1995, 02, Rose Art Mus., Brandeis U., 1996, Addison Gallery Am. Art, Andover, Mass., 1997, 04, Fine Arts Mus. San Francisco, 1997, Wexner Ctr., Columbus, 1997, Dieu Donne Papermill, Inc., NYC, 1998, Pub. Sch. 1, Long Island City, NYC, 1999, Gemini G.E.L., 1998, Am. Acad. Arts and Letters, 1999, 01, Parsons Sch. Design, NYC, 1999, David Dorsky Gallery, NY, 2000, Greenberg Van Doren Fine Art, NYC, 2000, 02, 04, 05, 06, NAD, NYC, 2002, Armory Show, NYC, 2002, Nat. Gallery of Art, 2001, Krannert Art Mus., 2002, Selby Gallery, Fla., 2002, Geffen Contemporary, LA, 2002, Marcus Ritter, NYC, 2002, Bowdoin Coll. Mus. Art, 2002, Reina Sophia Mus., Madrid, 2003, Cleve. Mus. Art, 2003, New Britain (Conn.) Mus. Am. Art, 2003, Mus. New Zealand, 2003, Guggenheim Mus., NYC, 2004, ACA Galleries, NYC, 2004, Bruce Mus., Greenwich, Conn., 2004, MOCA at Calif. Plz., L.A., 2004, Boca Raton Mus. Art, 2005, Betty Cunningham Gallery, 2005, Spanierman Gallery, East Hampton, NY, 2005, Black Mtn. Coll. Mus., Asheville, NC, 2005, Mus. Modern Art, NYC, 2006, Nat. Acad. Design, NYC, 2006, Yellow Bird Gallery, Newburgh, NY, 2005, Pa. Acad. Fine Arts, Phila., 2006, Cleve. Mus. Art, 2006, Weatherspoon Mus., Greensboro, NC, 2006, Morgan Libr., 2006, others; print exhbns. at Nat. Gallery, Washington, 1994, 97, 2001, Kate Ganz, Ltd., NYC, 2000, David Adamson Gallery, Washington, 2000, Fine Arts Mus. San Francisco, 1997, Bklyn. Mus., 1989, Mt. Holyoke Coll. Art Mus., 1987, Harcus Gallery, Boston, 1985, Xavier Fourcade Gallery, NYC, 1982, Mus. Modern Art, NYC, 1981, 91, Yale U. Art Gallery, New Haven, 1981, New Gallery Contemporary Art, Cleve., 1978, Art Gallery Ont., Toronto, 1978, Stadtiches Mus., Monchengladbach, Germany, 1971, Mus. New Zealand Te Papa Tongarewa, Wellington, 2003, Ralls Collection, Washington, 2004, Addison Gallery Am. Art, Mass., 2004, Mus. Fine Arts, Boston, 2003, 04, 05; represented in permanent collections Milw. Art Ctr., Mus. Modern Art NYC, Fogg Mus., Cambridge, Mass., Phila. Mus. Art, High Mus. Art, Atlanta, Houston Mus. Fine Arts, Corcoran Gallery, Washington, Mpls. Art Inst., Mpls. Art Mus., Met. Mus. Art, NYC, Guggenheim Mus., NYC, Nat. Acad. Design, NYC, J. Paul Getty Trust, LA, Ludwig Mus., Aachen, Fed. Republic Germany, Holladay, Washington, Saatchi, London, Bard, Albright-Knox Art Gallery, Buffalo, Whitney Mus. Am. Art, NYC, U. Mich., Ann Arbor, Ohio State U., Columbus, Gilman Paper Co., NY, Auckland (New Zealand) City Art Mus., Portland (Oreg.) Art Mus., Aaken Art Mus., Oberlin, Ohio, Highhold Internat., South Africa, U. Ohio Art Gallery, Columbus, HHK Charitable Found., Milw., Art Gallery Ont., Nat. Mus. Women in Art, Washington, Chase Manhattan Bank, NYC; installations: Hilton Hotel, San Jose, Calif., Sony Music Hdqrs., Aldridge Mus., Conn., Edward T. Gignoux Courthouse, Portland, Maine. Recipient Witowsky prize, Art Inst., Chgo., 1976, Creative Arts award, Brandeis U., 1985, Bard Coll., 1986, Alliance for Young Artists and Writers Inc. award, 1997, Jimmy Ernst Lifetime Achievement award in art, Am. Acad. Arts and Letters, 1999, Pike award, Nat. Acad. of Art and Design, 2002, Adolph and Clara Obrig prize, Nat. Acad. Design, 2002, Pollock Krasner award, 2002, 2004, Omi Internat. Francis J. Greenberger award, 2003; fellow, Guggenheim fellow, 1972; grantee, Nat. Endowment Arts, 1974, Am. Acad. Rome, 1991. Mem.: AAAL. Personal E-mail: drockburne@gmail.com.

ROCKEFELLER, ALLISON HALL W., conservationist; b. Manhattan, N.Y., Nov. 20, 1958; d. George Carroll and JoeAnn (Feeley) Whipple; m. Peter Clark Rockefeller, Dec. 19, 1987; 2 children. BA, Hamilton Coll., Clinton, N.Y., 1980. Asst. dir. pub. rels. Sotheby's Internat. Realty, N.Y.C., 1980-83; dir. pub. rels. and corp. comms. Douglas L. Elliman & Co., N.Y.C., 1983-88; founder residential sales divsn. Elliman East; residential sales assoc. Brown Harris Stevens, N.Y.C., 1988-90; founder Henry Hudson Soc. of Historic Hudson Valley, Inc., 1988—; trustee, devel. com. mem. Mus. of City of N.Y., 1993—; trustee, chmn. devel. com. Student Conservation Assn., Charlestown, N.H., 1987-95, chmn. bd., 1995—. Mem. Pres.'s coun. Mission Soc., N.Y.C., 1994—. Mem. Nat. Soc. Fund Raising Execs., Delta Psi. Presbyterian. Avocations: horticulture, historic houses, american history, writing, landscape architecture. Office: 30 Rockefeller Plz Rm 5600 New York NY 10112-0002

ROCKEFELLER, SHARON PERCY, broadcast executive; b. Oakland, Calif., Dec. 10, 1944; d. Charles H. and Jeanne (Dickerson) Percy; m. John D. (Jay) Rockefeller IV; children: John, Valerie, Charles, Justin. BA cum laude, Stanford U.; LLD (hon.), U. Charleston, 1977, Beloit Coll., 1978; LHD (hon.), West Liberty State Coll., 1980, Hamilton Coll., 1982, Wheeling Coll., 1984. Founder, chmn. Mountain Artisans, 1968—78; teacher's asst., Head Start Head Start program, Coal Branch Heights, W.Va.; chmn. Corp. Pub. Broadcasting, Washington, 1981—84; bd. dirs. Stas. WETA-TV-FM, Washington, 1987—89, pres., CEO, 1989—. Bd. dirs. Pub. Broadcasting Svc., W.Va. Edn. Broadcasting Authority, PepsiCo, Smithsonian Instn., Nat. Gallery of Art, Nat. Cathedral, Stanford Univ., Chgo. Univ., George Washington Univ., Phillips Collection, Colonial Williamsburg Found.; trustees coun. Nat. Gallery of Art. Mem.-at-large Dem. Nat. Conv., del., 1976, 1980, 1984; trustee Fed. City Coun.; bd. dirs. Rockefeller Bros. Fund; former mem. bd. dir. Sunrise Mus., W.Va.; bd. mem. Sotheby's, NYC, Mus. Modern Art, NYC, Colonial Williamsburg Found; former chmn. Va. Assn. Pub. TV Stas. Named Washingtonian of Yr., Washingtonian Mag., 1994; named one of Top 200 Collectors, ARTnews Mag., 2004, 2005, 2006; recipient Charles Frankel Prize, Nat. Endowment for the Humanities, 1994, Distinguished Broadcaster Award, 1994, Woman of Vision Award, Women in Film & Video, CINE Lifetime Achievement Award. Fellow: Am. Acad. Arts & Sciences, Smithsonian Am. Art Commn. (bd. mem.); mem.: Stanford-in-Washignton Coun. (former chmn.). Avocation: collecting 19th-century Am. art and Am. impressionism. Office: Sta WETA-FM 2775 S Quincy St Arlington VA 22206-2236*

ROCKEFELLER, SHIRLEY E., court clerk; b. Sayre, Pa., May 24, 1938; d. Clayton A. and Eva M. Baldwin Wilbur; m. Richard L. Rockefeller, Sept. 27, 1937; 1 child, Randy L. Student, Ridley's Sec. Sch., 1956-57. Legal sec. A.S. Moscrip, Esq., Towanda, Pa., 1961-64; clk. Register and Recorder's Office Bradford County, Towanda, 1965-75; register, recorder and clk. of orphan's ct. Bradford County Courthouse, Towanda, 1976—. Hospitality chmn. Rep. Women, Towanda, 1996-99, scrapbook chmn., 1998—. Mem. DAR (regent), Order of Ea. Star (sec. 1965-99), Tuscarora Hist. Soc., Pa. Register of Wills Assn. (exec. bd. 1998-99). Republican. Mem. United Ch. of Christ. Avocations: crocheting, cooking, travel, fishing. Home: RR 2 Box 425 Rome PA 18837-9568 Office: Bradford County Courthouse 301 Main St Towanda PA 18848-1824

ROCKENSIES, EILEEN REGINA, retired nursing educator; b. Bklyn., Jan. 14, 1942; d. Theodore Charles and Susan Rita Dros; m. Kenneth J. Rockensies, June 6, 1970 (dec.); children: Kevin John, Patricia Ann, Regina Marie. BSN, Coll. Misericordia, Dallas, Pa., 1964; MSN, Russell Sage Coll., Troy, N.Y., 1968. RN N.Y. Gen. nurse St. Clares Hosp., N.Y.C., 1964—65; prof. med. surg. nursing St. Clares Hosp. Sch., N.Y.C., 1965—66; asst. prof. nursing CUNY, Bklyn., 1966—71; ret. Vol. pub. rels. Our Lady of Fatima Rehab. of Liberia, Liberia. Mem.: ANA, Nat. League Nursing, Nat. Sci. Tchrs. Adminstrn. Home: 47 Harford Ave Shavertown PA 18708

ROCKHILL, MARSHA, special education educator; AA, Gulf Coast CC, Panama City, Fla., 1976; BA in Music Edn. - Choral, Fla. State U., Tallahassee, 1978; M in Social Sci. Edn., Fla. State U., Panama City, 2002; student, Fla. State U., Tallahassee, 2003—. Cert. art tchr. Fla. Dept. Edn., Tallahassee, 2000. Spl. edn. tchr. Rosenwald Mid. Sch., Panama City, 1988; music/art tchr. St. Andrew Sch. Ctr. for Exceptional Students, Panama City, 1989—; music tchr., physically handicapped Margaret K. Lewis, Panama City, 1993—98. Founder, coord. Very Spl. Art Festival, Bay County, 1990—; charter mem. Fla. League Arts Tchrs., Tallahassee, 1999—; bd. mem. Svc. Learning Coun., Bay County, 2002—; artist in residency Fla. Dept. Very Spl. Arts, Tampa, 2004—; historian St. Andrew Waterfront Project, 1989—; oral history project coord. St. Andrew Sch., 2005—; presenter in field. Recipient Tchr. of Yr. award, St. Andrew Sch., Panama City, 1995, 2006, Golden Spike award, Bay Arts Alliance, Panama City, 2001; grantee scholarship, Bay Edn. Found., 2004, 2005, John David Jones ABCD scholarship, 2005. Mem.: Garnet and Gold Honor Soc., Pi Lambda Theta. Avocations: singing, writing plays. Office: St Andrew Sch 3001 W 15th St Panama City FL 32401

ROCKLEN, KATHY HELLENBRAND, lawyer; b. NYC, June 30, 1951; BA, Barnard Coll., N.Y.C., 1973; JD magna cum laude, New England Sch. Law, 1977. Bar: NY 1978, US Dist. Ct. (so. and ea. dists.) NY 1982, US Dist. Ct. (no. dist.) Calif. 1985. Interpretive counsel NY Stock Exchange, NYC; 1st v.p. E.F. Hutton & Co. Inc., NYC; v.p., gen. counsel, sec. S.G Warburg (USA) Inc., NYC; mem. Proskauer Rose LLP, NYC. Adj. prof. Fordham Sch. Law. Vice-chair, mem. exec. com. NY lawyers Pub. Interest; mem. exec. com. lawyers divsn. Am. Friends Hebrew U.; mem. lawyers' divsn. exec. com. ADL; mem. adv. bd. NY Women's Bar Found. Mem. NY State Bar Assn., NY Women's Bar Assn., Assn. Bar City NY (v.p., chmn. exec. com., chmn. drugs law com., chmn. fed. legis. com., chmn. libr. com., securities law com., sec. 2d century com., sex law com., young lawyers' com., corp. law com.). Office: Proskauer Rose LLP 1585 Broadway New York NY 10036 Office Phone: 212-969-3755. E-mail: krocklen@proskauer.com.

ROCKWELL, ELIZABETH DENNIS, retirement specialist, financial planner; b. Houston, Tex., 1921; d. Robert Richard and Nezzell Alderton (Christie) Dennis. Student, Rice U., 1939—40, U. Houston, 1938—39, student, 1940—42, D (hon.), 1999. Purchasing agt. Standard Oil Co., Houston, 1942—66; v.p. mktg. Heights Savs. Assn., Houston, 1967—82; exec. dir. investments CIBC Oppenheimer Corp., Houston, 1982—2001; exec. prof. U. Houston Coll. Bus., 1992—. Contbr.: articles on retirement planning, tax planning and tax options, monthly article 50 Plus sect. for Houston Chronicle newspaper. V.p. Desk and Derrick Club Am., 1960—61; bd. dirs. ARC, 1985—91, Houston Heights Assn., 1973—77; sr. v.p. Oppenheimer, 1986—; mem. found. bd. Coll. Bus. U., Houston, 1990, mem. million dollar roundtable, 1991—, mem. ct. of the table, 1991—, Top of Table, 1996—; mem. U. Houston Sys. Planned Giving Coun., U. Houston Found., 2000—; mem. coll. bus. adv. bd. U. Houston Coll. Bus., 1992—, mem. alumni bd., 1987—95; apptd. trustee U. Houston Sys. Found., Inc.l, 1992; bd. govs. Houston Forum; active Tex. Leader's Round Table, 1994; pres. U. Houston Coll. Bus. Adminstrn. Found., 1986—2000; mem. Houston C.C. Adv. Bd. for Ednl. TV. Named Disting. Alumnae, Coll. Bus. Alum. Assn., U. Houston, 1992, YWCA Outstanding Woman of Yr., 1978; recipient Disting. Alumna, U. Houston Alumni Orgn., 1996, award, Freedoms Found., 2004, Jesse H. Jones award for philanthropy, ARC, 2004, Roger Eichhorn Leadership Svc. award, U. Houston Coll. Engring., 2004. Mem.: Houston Heights Assn. (charter, dir. 1973—77), U.S. Savs. and Loan League (com. on deposit acquisitions and adminstrn.), Soc. Savs. Instns., Fin. Mgrs., Inst. Fin. Edn., Savs. Inst. Mktg. Soc. Am. (Key Person award 1974), Am. Savs. and Loan League (chpt. pres. 1971—72, pres. 1972—73, state dir. 1973—76, Leaders award 1972), Greater Houston Women's Found. (charter), U. Houston Alumni Orgn. (life), U. Houston Bus. Women's Assn. (pres. 1985), Rice U. Bus. and Profl. Women, Harris County Heritage Soc., Friends of Bayou Bend, Forum Club, River Oaks Bus. Women's Exch. Club.

ROCKWELL, ELIZABETH GOODE, dance company director, consultant, educator; b. Portland, Oreg., Sept. 10, 1920; d. Henry Walton and Elizabeth (Harmon) Goode; m. William Hearne Rockwell, Feb. 3, 1948;

children: Enid, Karen, William. BA, Mills Coll., 1941; MA, NYU, 1946. Instr. dance Monticello Jr. Coll., Alton, Ill., 1941-42; dir. masters program in dance Smith Coll., Northampton, Mass., 1946-48; 1st dir. dance dept. High Sch. of Performing Arts, N.Y.C., 1948-51, 53-54; dir. Elizabeth Rockwell Sch. Dance, Bedford, N.Y., 1956-86, Rondo Dance Theater Internat. Dance Touring Co., Bedford, 1971-93; tchr. continuing dance classes CCAE, 1994—; with Martha Graham, 1944-46; with Hanya Holm, 1946-48; with José Limon, 1949-52. Mem. adv. ednl. com. Calif. Ctr. for Arts, Escondido, Calif., 1993-95, dir. dance classes, 1994—; tchr. master class, choreographer Waitukubuli Dance Theater, Dominica, 1999; dir. prime dance performance Artists Coming of Age, U. San Diego, 1999. Choreographer (suite of dances) Jazz Suite, 1966, (50-minute dances) Catch the Wind, 1969, Genesis, 1972, (narrative modern ballet) The Executioner, 1974, Decathalon, 1982; dir. (subscription series) Dance-Art-Poetry-Jazz, 1978-79, (dance/music 1600-1900) Stages in Ages, 1981, (Am. dance revivals) Masterpieces of American Dance, 1982-84, Dances of the Decades, 1985-90, (revival & new choreography) Dances of Our Times, 1991; dir. dance workshops for Calif. Ctr. Arts, 1994, 95, 96; creator, founder performing group of older dancers Golden Connections Dance Ensemble of Women, CCAE, (touring San Diego area), 1996—. Bd. dirs. Coun. for Arts in Westchester, White Plains, N.Y., 1978-79, affiliate, 1978— Recipient Medal for Performance, Israeli Army, 1966, Award for Excellence in Arts Edn. Alumnae of High Sch. of Performing Arts, 1990, Tommy Dance award of distinction San Diego Area Dance Alliance, 1999; various grants N.Y. State Coun. on Arts, 1971-93, Coun. Arts in Westchester, 1973-92, dance touring program grant Nat. Endowment for Arts, 1975-79. Mem. Am. Dance Guild, Westchester Dance Coun. (program dir. 1965-69), Assn. Am. Dance Cos., San Diego Area Dance Alliance (bd. dirs. 1995—). Avocations: writing, swimming, touring, reading. Home: 205 Tampico Gln Escondido CA 92025-7359

ROCKWOOD, MARCIA, magazine editor; Exec. editor Reader's Digest, Pleasantville, N.Y. Office: Reader's Digest Reader's Digest Rd Pleasantville NY 10570-7000

RODAK, SHARON LORRAINE, elementary school educator, researcher; b. San Francisco, July 20, 1962; d. James Langdon Rodak and Florence Nerona Hunt; 1 child, Samuel Joseph Oakes. AA, MiraCosta C.C., Oceanside, Calif., 1984; BA, San Diego State U., 1988; postgrad., Ind. U., 2002. Tchg. credential Calif., 1990, Ind., 1994, cert. ESL instr. Calif. Cmty. Colleges, MiraCosta C.C., 1989. ESL educator Mira Costa C.C., Oceanside, 1989—92; elem. educator Murrieta (Calif.) Valley Unified Sch. Dist., 1990—93, mid. sch. educator, 1993—95, Carlsbad (Calif.) Unified Sch. Dist., 1991—; ESL educator Vista (Calif.) Unified Sch. Dist., 1993—94; gifted and talented educator Met. Sch. Dist. Martinsville, Ind., 1997—99; tchr. educator assoc. instr. Ind. U. Sch. Edn., Bloomington, 1999—2001. Gifted and talented site coord. E. Hale Curran Elem. Sch., Murrieta, 1991—92; doctoral dissertation participant Ind. U. Sch. Edn., Bloomington, 2000—01; site coun. mem. Aviara Oaks Mid. Sch., Carlsbad, Calif., 2001—; presenter in field. MiraCosta Spartan scholar, MiraCosta C.C., 1980, Mildred R. Lowel scholar, Ind. U. Sch. Edn., 1999, 2000, 2001. Mem.: NEA, Calif. Tchrs.' Union, Nat. Art Edn. Assn., Am. Ednl. Rsch. Assn., Pi Lambda Theta. Democrat. Roman Catholic. Achievements include development of Vocational English As A Second Language Curriculum and Instruction; research in arts integration curriculum and instruction. Avocations: reading, exercise, art. Home: 1351 Enchante Way Oceanside CA 92056 Office: Carlsbad Unified Sch Dist 6225 El Camino Real Carlsbad CA 92008

RODAMAKER, MARTI TOMSON, bank executive; m. Bill Rodamaker; children: Mackenzie, Meeghan. BA in Econs., U. No. Iowa; MBA in Fin., U. St. Thomas. Credit analyst Marquette Bank, Mpls., 1984—87; field examiner Norwest Bank, 1987—93; from mem. staff to pres. First Citizens Nat. Bank, Mason City, Iowa, 1993—2000, pres., 2000—. Mem. adv. coun. Fed. Res. Iowa. Chmn. Hosp. Found.; treas. campaign YMCA; bd. regents Luther Coll., 2003—. Named One of 25 Women to Watch, U.S. Banker Mag., 2003. Mem.: Iowa Ind. Bankers Assn. (pres. 2001), Mason City C. of C. (bd. dir.). Office: First Citizens National Bank 2601 Fourth St SW Mason City IA 50401-1708

RODE, DEBORAH LYNN, accountant; b. Guymon, Okla., Mar. 17, 1962; d. Darrel G. and Virginia E. (Bressler) Rhind. BA Acctg. and English, North Ctrl. Coll., Naperville, IL, 1984; M Acctg., DePaul U., Chgo., 1999. CPA, Ill., 1996, cert. Internal Auditor, Ill., 1997. Mgr. customer fin. svcs. Quaker Oats, Chgo., 1988—91; sr. cons. Software divsn. Dun & Bradstreet, Schaumburg, Ill., 1991—97; mgr. corp. acctg. and fin. assurance SBC/Ameritech, Hoffman Estates, Ill., 1997—2001; asst. contr. DePaul U., Chgo., 2001—05; contr. Global Water, Phoenix, 2005—06; acct. Phoenix, 2006—. Recipient Grad. With Highest Honors Distinction, DePaul U., 1999; Presdl. Leadership Scholarship, North Ctrl. Coll., 1980—84. Mem.: AICPA, Inst. Internal Auditors, Mensa (life).

RODEN, CAROL LOONEY, retired language educator; b. Boston, Jan. 10, 1939; d. William Vincent and Margaret Carey Delaney; m. Vincent James Looney, Feb. 11, 1961 (div. Nov. 1995); children: Vincent J. III Looney, Kara A. Putnam, Douglas B. Looney, John W. Looney; m. Thomas Edward Roden, July 7, 1997. BA, Emmanuel Coll., 1960; postgrad., SUNY, Albany, 1974. Spanish tchr. Hingham (Mass.) H.S., 1960—61, Kennedy H.S., Utica, NY, 1974—80, Waterville (N.Y.) Cen. Sch., 1983—94, Archbishop Carroll H.S., Wayne, Pa., 1995—96; ret., 1996. Author (numerous poems); photographer. Pres. PTA, Whitesboro, NY, 1971; v.p. Newcomers Group, Utica, NY, 1970; vol. Puerto Rican Cmty. House, Boston, 1959. Fellow, U. Kans., 1960; scholar Gov. Furcolo scholar, State of Mass., 1956. Mem.: AAUW (v.p. membership 1995—99, Gift honoree 1999, Outstanding Woman of Yr. 2000), Alpha Mu Gamma. Democrat. Roman Catholic. Home: 119 Sawgrass Dr Blue Bell PA 19422

RODEN, MARY JANE, mathematician, educator; d. Jerome James and Joan Katherine Kittok; m. Terry Evan Roden, June 28, 1986; children: Nicholas, Noelle, Netanya, Nathan. B of Liberal Arts, U. Minn., Morris, 1986; Cert. in Secondary Edn., U. St. Thomas, St. Paul, Minn., 1994; M in Curriculum, St. Cloud State U., Minn., 1996. Cert. elem. edn., math. tchr. Minn. Tchr. 5th grade St. Charles Brromeo Cath. Sch., Mpls., 1986—90, tchr. 6th-8th grade math., 1990—94; tchr. 7th grade math. Centennial Ind. Sch. Dist. 12, Circle Pines, Minn., 1994—2004, math. curriculum facilitator, dist. assessment coord., 2004—. Collaboration trainer Minn. Dept. Edn., Mpls., 1996—2003, assessment cons., 2003—. Author: (7th grade curriculum) Image of God, 1993. Mem. com. Pack and Troop 711, Boy Scouts of Am., Mpls., 2000—01; treas. St. Charles Borromeo Coun. Cath. Women, Mpls., 2004—06. Recipient Centennial Tchr. of Yr. award, Centennial Ind. Sch. Dist. 12, 1997. Mem.: Minn. Coun. Math. Tchrs., Nat. Coun. Math. Tchrs. Avocations: cooking, reading, watching children participate in activities. Home: 3884 Stockdale Dr Vadnais Heights MN 55127 Office: Centennial Ind Sch Dist 12 4707 North Rd Circle Pines MN 55014 Office Phone: 763-792-6186. Office Fax: 763-792-6180. E-mail: mroden@isd12.org.

RODENBAUGH, MARCIA LOUISE, retired elementary school educator; b. Pitts., Nov. 11, 1942; d. E. Thomas and Lucy Indiana (Fry) Wimer; m. John Anthony Lee, Mar. 21, 1964 (div. Nov. 1971); m. Richard Alan Rodenbaugh, Aug. 3, 1975 (div. Dec. 1989); stepchildren: Ken, Tiffany, Tricia. BA in Edn., Westminster Coll., New Wilmington, Pa., 1964, MEd in Remedial Reading, 1966. Tchr. North Hills Sch. Dist., Pitts., 1964-69, Ctrl. Bucks Schs., Doylestown, Pa., 1969—2001. Fellow Pa. Writing Project, West Chester U., 1990; presenter in field. Author children's books: Marci Books (set of 6), 1983-99. Pres. Maple Leaf Day Care Ctr. Bd., Warminster, Pa., 1971; pres. Wesley Coll. Parents Assn., Dover, Del., 1985-86; vol. Meals on Wheels, Phila. inner-city schs.; bd. dirs. Friends of the Libr., Doylestown br. Bucks County Libr., 2002—, sec. 2003—; local judge History Day, Ursinus Coll.; home tutor; bd. pres. Chestnut Grove Condo Assn., 2004-05, bd. dirs., 2005—. Mem. NEA, Pa. Edn. Assn., Ctrl. Bucks Edn. Assn. Republican. Presbyterian. Avocations: reading, sailing, writing, piano, church choir. Home: 7-16 Aspen Way Doylestown PA 18901-2756 Office: Ctrl Bucks Sch Dist 315 Weldon Dr Doylestown PA 18901-3525 Personal E-mail: wimerml@aol.com.

RODENBERG, JOHANNA KRISTINE, education educator, consultant; d. Edward Ellis and Francess Irene Rodenberg; m. Andrew Thomas Myers, Sept. 3, 1994; children: Justin Grant, Jeffrey Richard Myers, Jakob Edward Myers. AA in Fine Art, Mesa C.C., 1980; BA in Linguistics, San Diego State U., 1982; MA in Ednl. Psychology, U.S. Internat. U., San Diego, 1987; postgrad., U. San Diego/San Diego State U., 2000—. Cert. Nat. Bd. Profl. Tchg. Stds. English lang. tchr. EF Internat. Sch., San Diego, 1983—90; reading specialist San Diego Unified Sch. Dist., 1996—99, peer coach/staff developer, 1999—2002, peer assistance and support consulting tchr., 2002—. Ednl. cons. Nat. Ctr. on Edn. and the Economy, Washington, 1998—2002; ind. ednl. cons., faculty devel., 2003—; faculty San Diego State U., 2000—; spkr., presenter in field. Rm. mom Holmes Elem. Sch., San Diego, 2003. Mem.: ASCD, Internat. TESOL, Nat. Coun. Tchrs. of English, Internat. Reading Assn. Avocations: cooking, reading, gardening. Office: San Diego Unified Schs/SDSU San Diego CA Office Phone: 858-496-1883. Personal E-mail: jkr1007@earthlink.net.

RODEWALD, NANCY BEAL, history educator; d. Charles Archibald and Marjorie Hyatt Beal; m. Jeffrey Paul Rodewald, Aug. 27, 1977; children: Matthew, Katherine. BS in edn., Ball State U., Ind., 1977; MA in edn., Olivet Nazerene U., Ill., 2002. Young adult program tchr. Muskogee Pub. Schs., Okla., 1978—79, 8th grade civics tchr., 1979—80; 8th grade Am. History tchr. Elgin Dist. U-46, Ill., 1990—. 8th grade basketball coach Kimball Mid. Sch., Elgin, Ill., 2000—03, 7th grade girls basketball coach, 2001—03, 7th grade girls volleyball coach, 2003. Mem.: Nat. Philanthropy Coun. Ball State U., Geneva Hist. Soc., Geneva Acad. Found., Kappa Alpha Theta. Roman Catholic.

RODGER, MARION MCGEE, medical/surgical nurse, administrator; b. Waterville, Maine, Feb. 21, 1949; d. Audrey Renee (Kilgore) McGee. Diploma, Albany Med. Ctr., 1970; student, U. Calif., San Diego, 1994. RN, Calif.; cert. in psychiat.-mental health nursing. Clin. nurse med.-surg. Albany Med. Ctr., 1970-84, mgr. vascular/trauma unit, 1970-78; ICU nurse Sharp Meml. Hosp., San Diego, 1984, divsn. mgr. orth., neuro-pulm., surg., med., 1985-91; br. dir. Nat. Staffing Agy., 1992; health facilities evaluator nurse State of Calif., 1994-99; supr. licensing and cert. div., supr. San Diego dist. office Dept. Health Svcs., State of Calif., 1999—. Home: 731 Avocado Pl Del Mar CA 92014-3943 E-mail: mrodger@ca.gov.

RODGERS, BETTY JO, mathematics educator; b. Pamlico, N.C., Aug. 6, 1946; m. Roy L. Rodgers, May 7, 1965; children: Kevin Wade, Joannis Louise. BS, East Carolina U., 1971; MA, Appalachian State U., 1980. Cert. tchr., N.C. Math. tchr. Iredell County Schs., Statesville, NC, 1976—79, West Henderson (N.C.) H.S., 1979—80, Aurora (N.C.) H.S., 1981—86, Gates County H.S., Gatesville, 1986—89, Asheville (N.C.) Christian Acad., 1989—92; coll. algebra tchr. We. Piedmont C.C., Morgantown, 1991—95, We. Youth Inst., Morgantown, 1995—96; math tchr. Pender H.S., Burgaw, 1996, Bladen H.S., Elizabethtown, 1997—99, Goldboro H.S., 1999—2001, Dept. Pub. Instrn., Raleigh, 2001—03, Pamlico County H.S., Bayboro, 2004—06; ret. Tchr. Pamlico Tech. Inst., Grantsboro, N.C., 1980-82; coll. algebra tchr. Mitchell C.C., Statesville, 1978-79, A-B Tech., Inst., Asheville, 1989-90; presenter, cons. in field. Mem. Nat. Coun. Tchrs. Math., N.C. Coun. Tchrs. of Math. Avocations: mission trips, bible study, computers, singing. E-mail: bjrodgers77@earthlink.net.

RODGERS, CHERYL L., elementary school educator, small business owner; d. William Thanal and Earl Lee Mitchell; m. Rick W. Rodgers, Dec. 20, 1991; 1 child, Richie W. II. BSAS, Sam Houston State U., Huntsville, Tex., 1992; MS, U. Houston, 2006. Cert. tchr. Tex., prin. Tex. Reading tchr. Aldine Middle Sch., Houston, 1992—99; reading, lang. arts and social studies tchr. Drew Intermediate Sch., Crosby, Tex., 1999—. Mem.: Tex. Fedn. Tchrs., Phi Delta Kappa. Baptist.

RODGERS, DIANA LYNN, elementary school educator; b. Mt. Clemens, Mich., Sept. 25, 1971; d. Alice Jane and James Bruce Carter; m. James Edward Rodgers, Oct. 19, 1996; children: Colin James, Jacob Carter. BMus, Wayne State U., Detroit, 1994, M in Elem. Edn., 2002. Asst. band dir. L'Anse Creuse H.S., Harrison Twp., Mich., 1994—95; elem. music tchr. Gt. Oaks Elem., Chesterfield Township, Mich., 1995—. Pvt. music instrn., Macomb Twp., 1990—; flute soloist, Mich., 1990—. Flute soloist St. Lawrence Cath. Ch., Utica, Mich., 1993—2000. Home: 21128 Glenview Ct Macomb MI 48044 Office: Great Oaks Elem 32900 24 Mile Rd Chesterfield MI 48047 Office Phone: 586-725-2038. Personal E-mail: jimdirodgers@aol.com. E-mail: drodgers@abs.misd.net.

RODGERS, KATHY, lawyer; Attended, Smith Coll., Columbia U. Atty. Poletti, Freidin, Prashker, Feldman and Gartner; gen. counsel, v.p. Barnard Coll., acting pres., 1993—94; pres. Legal Momentum (formerly NOW Legal Def. and Edn. Fund). Bd. mem. Lawyers Alliance, Nat. Coun. Rsch. on Women, Fair Labor Assn., Nat. Council Women's Orgns. Mem.: Bar Assn. City of NY. Office: Legal Momentum 395 Hudson St New York NY 10014

RODGERS, LANA LORETTA LUSCH, retired elementary school educator; b. Lehighton, Pa., Jan. 26, 1943; d. Charles Norman and Loretta Margaret (Gaumer) Lusch; m. Harold Eugene Rodgers, Aug. 15, 1964; children: Jacqui Rodgers Kirchner, Travis Dustin. BS in Elem. Edn., Kutztown U., Pa., 1964, BS in Blind and Partially Sighted Edn., 1967; M Elem. Edn., Kutztown U., 1968, specialist in reading, 1983. Tchr. Honey Brook Elem. Sch., Twin Valley Sch. Dist., Elverson, Pa., 1964—67, 1986—2000, Berkshire Bldg., Wilson Sch. Dist., Reading, Pa., 1967—68; substitute tchr. Robeson Elem. Sch., Twin Valley Sch. Dist., 1981—83, reading tchr., 1985; ret. Portrait artist; English tchr. Reading Area CC. Sec. Twin Valley Sch. Dist. Tchr.'s Orgn., Elverson, 1966; leader Girl Scouts USA, Wyomissing, Pa., 1966—68; vol. Ct. Apptd. Spl. Advocates, Reading Ct., 2000—; mem. Literacy Coun., 1977—79; Stephen min. West Lawn United Meth. Ch. Recipient CASA Cert. Recognition, Pa. Sen. Michael O'Pake, 2001—05, Cert. Recognition, West Lawn United Meth. Ch., 1998, Tutor award, Reading Area CC, 2004. Mem.: AAUW. Republican. Avocations: piano, painting, surfing, motorcycling, ice skating. Home: 106 Halsey Ave Reading PA 19609-2110

RODGERS, LOIS EVE, secondary school educator; BA, U. So. Miss.; MEd, William Carey Coll.; student, Bread Loaf Sch. English. Tchr. Hattiesburg (Miss.) High Sch. Named Miss. State English Tchr. of Yr., 1993.

RODGERS, MARY COLUMBRO, literature educator, writer, academic administrator; b. Aurora, Ohio, Apr. 17, 1925; d. Nicola and Nancy (DeNicola) Columbro; m. Daniel Richard Rodgers, July 24, 1965; children: Robert, Patricia, Kristine. AB, Notre Dame Coll., 1957; MA, Western Res. U., 1962; PhD, Ohio State U., 1964; postgrad., U. Rome, 1964-65; EdD, Calif. Nat. Open U., 1975, DLitt, 1978. Tchr. English Cleve. elem. schs., 1945-52, Cleve. secondary schs., 1952-62; supr. English student tchrs. Ohio State U., 1962-64; asst. prof. English U. Md., 1965-66; assoc. prof. Trinity Coll., 1967-68; prof. English D.C. Tchrs. Coll. U. D.C., 1968—2000; pres. Md. Nat. U., 1972—2006; founder, chancellor Open U. Am., 1965—; dean Am. Open U. Acad.; ret., 2000; ind. rschr., writer, 2000—. Author: A Short Course in English Composition, 1976, Chapbook of Children's Literature, 1977, Comprehensive Catalogue: The Open University of America System, 1978-80, Open University of America System Source Book, V, VII, VII, 1978, Essays and Poems on Life and Literature, 1979, Modes and Models: Four Lessons for Young Writers, 1981, Open University Structures and Adult Learning, 1982, Papers in Applied English Linguistics, 1982, Twelve Lectures on the American Open University, 1982, English Pedagogy in the American Open University, 1983, Design for Personalized English Graduate Degrees in the Urban University, 1984, Open University English Teaching, 1945-85: Conceptual History and Rationale, 1985, Claims and Counterclaims Regarding Instruction Given in Personalized Degree Residency Programs Completed by Graduates of California National Open University, 1986, The American Open University, 1965 to 1985: History and Sourcebook, 1986, New Design II: English Pedagogy in the American Open University, 1987, The American Open University, 1965 to 1985: A Research Report, 1987, The American Open University and Other Open Universities: A Comparative Study Report, 1988, Poet and Pedagogue in Moscow and Leningrad: A Travel Report, 1989, Foundations of English Scholarship in the American Open University, 1989, Twelve Lectures in Literary Analysis, 1990, Ten Lectures in Literary Production, 1990, Analyzing Fact and Fiction, 1991, Analyzing Poetry and Drama, 1991, Some Successful Literary Research Papers: An Inventory of Titles and Theses, 1991, Catalogue for the Mary Columbro Rodgers Literary Trust, 1992, A Chapbook of Poetry and Drama Analysis, 1992, Convent Poems, 1943-1961, 1992, Catholic Marriage Poems 1962, 1979, 1993, Catholic Widow with Children Poems 1979-1993, 1994, First Access List to the Mary Columbro Rodgers Trust by Year, 1994, Nicola Columbro: A Brief Biography, 3d edit., 1994, Biographical Sourcebook I: Mary Columbro Rodgers 1969-1995, 1995, Catholic Teacher Poems, 1945-1995, 1995, Fables and Farm Stories for Fiction Analysis, 1995, Second Access List to the Mary Columbro Rodgers Literary Trust by Alphabet, 1995, Third Access List to the Mary Columbro Rodgers Literary Trust by Subject, 1996, Fourth Access List to the Mary Columbro Rodgers Literary Trust for K-PhD Open Learning-Open University Methods with Data Batches Delineated, 2002, Journals: Reflections and Resolves 1992-2002, 03, 04, 16 vols., 2002, Fifth and Final Access List to the Mary Columbro Rodgers Literary Trust with Annotations, 2004, Journals: Reflections and Resolves, 2005, Catholic Open University of America System Poems, 1962-2005, 2005; contbr. articles to profl. jours. Fulbright scholar U. Rome, 1964-65. Fellow Cath. Scholars; mem. U.S. Distance Learning Assn., Poetry Soc. Am., Nat. Coun. Tchrs. English, Am. Ednl. Rsch. Assn., Am. Acad. Poets, Pi Lambda Theta. Home and Office: Coll Heights Estates 3916 Commander Dr Hyattsville MD 20782-1027 Office Phone: 301-779-0220. Personal E-mail: openuniv@aol.com.

RODGERS, SUZANNE HOOKER, physiologist, consultant; b. Rochester, N.Y., Dec. 26, 1939; d. John Ashmead and Priscilla May (Bodman) Rodgers AB, Vassar Coll., 1961; PhD, U. Rochester Med. Ctr., 1967. Postdoctoral fellow USPHS Middlesex Hosp., London, 1966—68; ergonomist Eastman Kodak Co., Rochester, 1968—82; cons. Rochester, 1982—. Author: Working With Backache, 1985; tech. editor, prin. author Ergonomic Design for People at Work, 1983, 86, co-editor, contr. Kodak's Ergonomic Design for People at Work 2d edit., 2003 Bd. dirs., chmn. com., v.p. Rochester Philharm. Orch. Inc., 1969-75; bd. dirs. Opera Theatre Rochester, 1969-75; bd. dirs., chmn. com., pres. Monroe County Bd. Health, Rochester, 1979-88 Mem. Human Factors and Ergonomics Soc., (pres. We. N.Y. chpt. 1971-72), Am. Coll. Sports Medicine Avocations: photography, gardening, reading, silent films. Home and Office: 169 Huntington Hls Rochester NY 14622-1121 Office Phone: 585-544-3587. Personal E-mail: shrodgers@aol.com.

RODGERS SMITH, KIMBERLY JEANNE, lawyer; b. Des Moines, May 11, 1978; d. Larry Richard and Leona Ruth Rodgers; m. Shane Eugene Smith, Apr. 22, 2006. JD, Drake U., Des Moines, 2003. Bar: Iowa 2004. Assoc. Roehrick Law Firm, P.C., Des Moines, 2003—. Com. mem. Iowa Bar Assn. Mock Trial Com., Des Moines, 2004—. Mem. St. Boniface Young Adults Group, Waukee, Iowa, 2003—06. Mem.: ABA, Am. Trial Lawyer Assn., Iowa Bar Assn. Conservative. Roman Catholic. Avocations: travel, bicycling, reading, sports. Office: Roehrick Law Firm PC 505 5th Avenue Suite 535 Des Moines IA 50309-2320 Office Phone: 515-243-1403. Personal E-mail: krsmithjd@aol.com.

RODI, KATHRYN KELLY, elementary school educator; b. Miami, Fla., Sept. 17, 1969; d. Robert Scott and Linda Dawn Johnson; m. Mark Jeffrey Rodie, Sept. 30, 1988; children: Zachary Thorton Rodie, Joshua Sterling Rodie. Bachelor's, Auburn U., Montgomery, Ala., 1999. Cert. early childhood edn. Ala., 1999. Tchr. grade 2 Eclectic Elem., Ala., 2000—. Home: 1940 Pleasant Hill Rd Wetumpka AL 36092 Office: Eclectic Elementary 35 Harden St Eclectic AL 36024 Office Phone: 334-541-2291. Personal E-mail: miamijets8@yahoo.com.

RODIN, JUDITH SEITZ, foundation administrator, former academic administrator, psychologist, educator; b. Phila., Sept. 9, 1944; d. Morris and Sally R. (Winson) Seitz. m. Paul Verkuil. AB, U. Pa., 1966; PhD, U. Columbia, 1970. Asst. prof. psychology NYU, 1970—72; assoc. prof. Yale U., 1975—79, prof., dir. grad. studies, 1982—89, Philip R. Allen prof. psychology, medicine and psychiatry, 1984—94, chmn. dept. psychology, 1989—91, dean Grad. Sch., 1991—92, provost, 1992—94; pres. U. Pa., Phila., 1994—2004, prof. psychology, medicine and psychiatry, 1994—2004; pres. Rockefeller Found., NYC, 2005—. Chmn. John D. and Catherine T. MacArthur Found. Rsch. Network on Determinants and Consequences of Health-Promoting and Health-Damaging Behavior, 1983-93; vice chair coun. press. U. Rsch. Assn., 1994-95, chair, 1995-96; mem. Ind. Panel to Review Safety Procedures at The White House, 1994-95; chair adv. com. Robert Wood Johnson Found., 1994—; mem. Pres. Clinton's Com. Advisors Sci. and Tech., 1994—; mem. Coun. Competitiveness, 1997—; mem. nominating com. N.Y. Stock Exch., 1998—; bd. dirs. Aetna, Electronic Data Sys., AMR, Citigroup Inc., 2004- . Author: (with S. Schachter) Obese Humans and Rats, 1978, Exploding the Weight Myths, 1982, Body Traps, 1992; chief editor Appetite Jour., 1979-92; contbr. articles to profl. jours. Mem. Pa. Task Force on Higher Edn. Funding, 1994; bd. dirs. Catalyst, N.Y.C., 1994—; trustee Brookings Inst., 1995—; pres. steering com. Am. Reads, 1997—. Recipient Phila. award, 2004, William Penn award; grantee NSF, 1973—82, NIH, 1981—. Fellow AAAS, APA (bd. sci. affairs 1979-82, pres. divsn. 38 health psychology 1982-83, Outstanding Contbn. award 1980, Disting. Sci. award 1977, Lifetime Achievement award 2005), Am. Acad. Arts and Scis., Soc. Behavioral Medicine; mem. AAU (mem. exec. com. 1996—), Am. Philosophical Soc., Inst. Medicine of NAS, Acad. Behavioral Medicine Rsch., Ea. Psychol. Assn. (exec. bd. 1980-82), Phi Beta Kappa, Sigma Xi (pres. Yale chpt. 1986-87). Office: Rockefeller Found 420 Fifth Ave New York NY 10018 Business E-Mail: president@rockfound.org.

RODIN, RITA ANGELA, lawyer; b. NYC, 1968; BS magna cum laude, Boston Coll., 1990; JD, St. John's U., 1990. Bar: N.J. 1994, N.Y. 1994. Law clk. Hon. Thomas C. Platt U.S. Dist. Ct. (ea. dist.) NY, 1993—94; atty. Skadden, Arps, Slate, Meagher & Flom LLP, NYC, 1994—2001, ptnr. Intellectual Property and Tech. Group, 2001—. Office: Skadden Arps Slate Meagher & Flom LLP Four Times Sq New York NY 10036 Office Phone: 212-735-3774. Business E-Mail: rrodin@skadden.com.

RODITTI, ESTHER C(LAIRE), lawyer, writer; b. LA, Feb. 7, 1933; d. David and Lucy Roditti; m. Oscar H. Schachter, Aug. 8, 1957 (div. Oct. 1992); children: Charles David, Susan Dayana. BA, UCLA, 1954; JD, Harvard U., 1957. Bar: N.Y. 1959. Assoc. Stickles, Hayden and Kennedy, N.Y.C., 1957-62; asst. dir. Legis. Drafting Fund Columbia U., N.Y.C., 1962-65, cons., 1965-67, N.Y.C. Air Pollution Control Dept., 1965-67; instr. and cons. New Sch. for Social Rsch., N.Y.C., 1968-70; cons. Internat. League for Rights of Man, N.Y.C., 1969, Rand Inst., N.Y.C., 1969, U.S. Soviet Environ. Studies Program, UN Assn., N.Y.C., 1969; sr. rsch. assoc. Ctr. for Policy Rsch. Columbia U., 1970-73; sr. program officer Ford Found., N.Y.C., 1972-78; pres. Esther Roditti Schachter, P.C., N.Y.C., 1978-83; ptnr. Schachter & Froling, N.Y.C., 1983-85, Schachter, Courter, Purcell & Kobert, N.Y.C., 1985-92; pres. Esther C. Roditti, P.C., 1992—. Spkr., lectr., panelist profl. assn. confs., forums, workshops, U.S., Can., Tokyo, London. Author: N.Y.C. Air Pollution Control Code Annotated, 1965, Enforcing Air Pollution Controls, 1979, Financial Support of Women's Programs in the 1970's, 1979, Computer Contracts Reference Directory, 1979-83, Hiring and Firing Knowledge Workers, 1995, Tax and Business Handbook for Consultants and Clients, 1998; co-author: Charities and Charitable Foundations, 1974; author, co-author articles in field; legal editor: Computer Economics, 1983-89; editor Computer Law & Tax Report, 1984-86, pub., editor, 1986-2000; author, editor Computer Contracts-Negotiating Drafting Treatise, 1992—. Nat. governing bd. Common Cause, 1979-82, mem. state governing bd., N.Y., 1982-84; mem. com. on urban environ. Citizens Union, N.Y.C., 1969-73; mem. West Side Dem. Club, 1958-63. Recipeint Outstanding Svc. award Brandeis U., Nat. Women's Com., 1973; grantee Ford Found., 1970, NSF, 1971. Mem. ABA (lectr. 1987), Assn. Bar City NY (founder, chmn. com. on computer law 1980—), NY State Bar Assn., Computer Law Assn. (lectr. 1985, bulletin editor 1998-, bd. dirs. 2000-), Am. Arbitration Assn. (chair com. for computer disputes 1985-), Phi Beta Kappa. Office Phone: 212-879-3322.

RODKEY, FRANCES THERESA, elementary school educator; b. Germantown, Pa., Sept. 3, 1952; d. Joseph Milton and Elizabeth Jane Parsons; m. Glenn Leroy Rodkey, May 1, 1976; children: Jennifer, Rachel. Student, Immaculata Coll., 1970—72; BS in Elem. Edn., Bloomsburg U., 1975; MA, Marygrove Coll., Mich., 2006. Cert. emergency edn. Pa., 1986. Substitute tchr. Coatesville Sch. Dist., Pa., 1984—89, tchr. 6th grade, 1989—2003, head dept. social studies, 2000; head dept. social studies Scott Mid. Sch., 2003—. Mem.: NEA, Pa. State Edn. Assn. Republican. Roman Catholic. Avocations: reading, camping, hiking. Home: 1111 Oak St Coatesville PA 19320 Office: Coatesville Area School District 545 E Lincoln Hwy Coatesville PA 19320-5404 Office Phone: 610-383-6946. Business E-Mail: rodkeyf@coatesville.k12.pa.us.

RODKIN, LOREE, jewelry artist; Studied film making, art history, design, N.Y.C. Hollywood actors mgr., interior designer; jewelry maker Loree Rodkin Gothic Jewelry, Beverly Hills, Calif. Designer of In Memory Ring to honor friend, lover, or family mem. proceeds donated to Elton John AIDS Found. Office: Loree Rodkin Gothic Jewelry 453 Rodeo Dr Beverly Hills CA 90209 Fax: 310-276-8104. E-mail: lrodkin@instanet.com.

RODLEY, CAROL A., federal agency administrator; b. Mass. married; 3 children. Grad., Smith Coll. Dep. chief of mission Am. Embassy, Phnom Pehn, Cambodia, 1997—2000; dep. exec. sec. US Dept. State, Washington, 2001—03, prin. dep. asst. sec. Bur. Internat. Orgn. Affairs, 2003—, acting asst. sec. Bur. Intelligence and Rsch., 2005—. Recipient Christian A. Herter award, Am. Fgn. Svc. Assn., 2000, Sr. Performance award, US Dept. State, Human Rights & Democracy award, James Clement Dunn award for Leadership, Dir. Ctrl. Intelligence Exceptional Humint Collector award, Intelligence Community Seal Medalion. Office: Bur Intelligence and Rsch US Dept State 2201 C St NW Washington DC 20520

RODMAN, SARAH, music critic; b. 1969; Popular music critic, staff columnist Boston Herald, 2000—06; popular music critic Boston Globe, 2006—. Office: Boston Globe 135 Morrissey Blvd Boston MA 02125 Mailing: Boston Globe PO Box 55819 Boston MA 02205-5819*

RODMAN, SUE A., wholesale company executive, artist, writer; b. Ft. Collins, Colo., Oct. 1, 1951; d. Marvin F. Lawson and Barbara I. (Miller) Lawson Shue; m. Alpine C. Rodman, Dec. 13, 1970; 1 child, Connie L. Rodman; m. Graham L. Jackson. Student, Woodbury Bus./Arts Coll., Calif., 1969, Colo. State U., 1970—73. Silversmith Pinel Silver Shop, Loveland, Colo., 1970-71; asst. mgr. Traveling Traders, Phoenix, 1974-75; co-owner, co-mgr. Native Am. arts and crafts company Deer Track Traders, Loveland, 1975-85; v.p. Deer Track Traders, Ltd., Loveland, 1985—. Author: The Book of Contemporary Indian Arts and Crafts, 1985, short stories; contbr. articles to popular mags. Mem. U.S. Senatorial Club, 1982-87, Rep. Presdl. Task Force, 1984-90; mem. Civil Air Patrol, 1969-73, 87-90, pers. officer, 1988-90. Mem.: Indian Arts and Crafts Assn., Western and English Sales Assn., Crazy Horse Grass Roots Club. Mem. Am. Baptist Ch. Avocations: museums, piano, recreation research, fashion design. Office: Deer Track Traders Ltd PO Box 448 Loveland CO 80539-0448

RODRIGUEZ, ANNABELLE, judge, former attorney general; b. Santurce, PR; m. Francisco de Jesus-Schuck; children: Ricardo Enrique Candle, Fernando Manuel Vela. BA in history magna cum laude, U. PR, JD, 1985. From asst. solicitor gen. to solicitor gen. PR Dept. Justice, 1986—93; ptnr. Martino, Odell & Calabria, Hato Rey, PR, 1993—96; judge US Dist Ct. (PR dist.), 1996; sec. justice PR, 2001—04; assoc. judge PR Supreme Ct., 2004—. Democrat. Office: Tribunal Supremo de PR PO Box 2392 San Juan PR 00902*

RODRIGUEZ, CAROLYN, lawyer; b. N.Y.C., Sept. 26, 1961; d. Emilio and Emma (Vasquez) R.; m. Warren Dondero, Jan. 4, 1991; children: Michelle Alicia, Nikki Taylor, Alexis Nicole. BA, Fordham U., 1982; JD, Pace U., 1987. Bar: Conn. 1987, N.Y. 1988, U.S. Dist. Ct. (so. and ea. dists.) N.Y. 1990. Asst. corp. counsel N.Y.C. Law Dept., 1987-89; assoc. David M. Lee, Esquire, N.Y.C., 1989-95; pvt. practice Suffolk, N.Y., 1995—. Mem. N.Y. State Trial Lawyers Assn., P.R. Bar Assn., Assn. Trial Lawyers of Am., N.Y. State Bar Assn.

RODRIGUEZ, DENISE RIOS, lawyer; b. Detroit, Apr. 5, 1951; AA, Henry Ford Cmty. Coll., 1971; BA with distinction, Wayne State U., 1975; JD cum laude, U. Mich., 1979. Bar: Mich. 1979, Calif. 1988, U.S. Dist. Ct., Ctrl. Dist. Calif. 1988. Gen. counsel to Health Care Fin. Admin. U.S. Dept. Health & Human Svc.; ptnr. Foley & Lardner LLP, L.A., chairperson health payments/compliance practice group. Mem.: ABA (health law sect.), Am. Health Lawyers Assn., Healthcare Fin. Mgmt. Assn., Mex.-Am. Bar Assn., Hispanic Nat. Bar Assn. Fluent in spanish. Office: Foley & Lardner LLP 2029 Century Park E Ste 3500 Los Angeles CA 90067 Office Phone: 310-277-2223. Office Fax: 310-557-8475. Business E-Mail: drodriguez@foley.com.

RODRIGUEZ, DORIS JONES, retired science educator; d. Joseph Jones Jr. and Rebecca Monroe Jones; m. Felix A. Rodriguez, Dec. 28, 1965; 1 child, Andrea Dionna Marie. BS, S.C. State U.; MS, L.I. U., 1975; postgrad., NYU, 1971—75, Adelphi U., 1995. Tchr. elem. sch. North Augusta Pub. Schs., SC, 1963—69; tchr. biology, health edn. Oquinas High Sch, Bronx, 1969—72; tchr. biology, health edn., gen. sci. Roosevelt High Sch., 1972—2000; ret., 2000. Vol. Am. Literacy Assn.; tutor students regents Biology and Sci. test N.Y. State; advocate for tolerance justice and fair needs. Grantee, NSF, 1972—72. Mem.: NSF, So. Poverty Law Ctr., United Fed. Tchrs. Found., Roosevelt Ret. Tchrs. Orgn., N.Y. State United Tchrs. Assn. Baptist. Avocations: piano, singing, walking, travel. Home: 197 Mill Run North Augusta SC 29891 also: 50 Virginia Ave Freeport NY E-mail: aerlnaandrea@hotmail.com.

RODRIGUEZ, ELAINE FLUD, lawyer; BA, Loyola U., 1978; JD, Tulane U., 1982. Bar: La. 1982, Tex. 1983. Assoc. Akin, Gump, Strauss, Hauer & Feld, Atlas & Hall; gen. counsel, sec. Zoecon Corp., 1991—93; v.p., gen. counsel, sec. CellStar Corp., Carrollton, Tex., 1993—2000, sr. v.p., gen. counsel, sec., 2000—. Office: CellStar Corp 1730 Briercroft Ct Carrollton TX 75006 Office Phone: 972-466-5021. E-mail: erodriguez@cellstar.com.

RODRIGUEZ, GAIL LEE, music educator; b. Akron, Ohio, July 18, 1955; d. Norman Ralph Cox and Esther Hannah Starman; m. Dario Rosendo Rodriguez, Apr. 9, 1983; children: Dario Norman, Elena Diane. Student, Baldwin Wallace Coll., 1973—75; MusB, Ohio U., 1977, MusM, 1978. String specialist Cabbell County Pub. Schs., Huntington, W.Va., 1978—80; 4th grade tchr., music tchr. St. Joseph's Parish Day Sch., Queens Village, NY, 1980—84; music tchr. Our Lady of Blessed Sacrament Sch., Bayside, NY, 1990—, St. Kevin Sch., Flushing, NY, 1994—2000. Workshop presenter Diocese of Bklyn. Cath. Schs., 2003—06. Co-dir. youth choir Our Lady of the Blessed Sacrament Ch., music min. Bayside, NY, 1987—. Mem.: Music Educators Nat. Assn. Roman Catholic. Avocation: sewing.

RODRIGUEZ, GERMAINE, radiologist; b. San German, PR, Oct. 29, 1968; d. Raul Rodriguez and Asela Ferrer. BS magna cum laude, Interam. U. P.R., 1989; MD cum laude, U. Ctrl. Caribe, 1993. Diplomate Am. Bd. Diagnostic Radiology. Resident in diagnostic radiology Mt. Sinai Med. Ctr., Miami Beach, 1989-93; fellow in abdominal imaging Brigham & Women's Hosp., Boston, 1997-98; staff radiologist Gables Imaging, Miami, 1998-99, Specialist Diagnostic Imaging, Sunrise, Fla., 1999—. Recipient Janet M. Glasgow achievement award Am. Women's Med. Assn., 1993. Mem. Am. Coll. Radiology, Radiol. Soc. N.Am., Am. Inst. Ultrasound Medicine, South Fla. Radiol. Soc., Am. Cancer Soc., Alpha Omega Alpha. Avocations: reading, rollerblading. Office: 13798 NW 4th St Ste 305 Sunrise FL 33325-6227

RODRIGUEZ, GLORIA E., science educator; d. Heriberto Rivera and Ketty Román; m. Benigno V. Rodriguez, Apr. 11; children: Winston, Daina, Arayoán, González. AS, BS, InterAmerican U., P.R.; MS, Phoenix U., P.R., 1990; ABD, State U. Buffalo, 1994. Cert. tchr. N.Y., Fla., P.R. Elem. edn. tchr. Carvin Sch., Carolina, PR, 1976—78; sci. resource tchr. P.R. Bd. of Edn., San Juan, PR, 1978—80; sci. tchr. Edison Sch., Miami, 1980, C.E. Acad., Miami, 1980—85, Our Lady of Mercy, Hato Key, PR, 1985, Buffalo Bd. of Edn., 1993—. Office: PS 76 Herman Badillo Bil Acad 300 S Elmwood Acad Buffalo NY 14201-2361

RODRIGUEZ, IRMINA BESTARD, science educator; b. Havana, Cuba, Apr. 29, 1945; came to U.S., 1961; d. Gaspar and Ester Antonia (Bas) Bestard; m. Luis Felipe Rodriguez, June 8, 1968; children: Damien Brandon, Leslie Christina. BA in Chemistry, Coll. of New Rochelle, 1967; postgrad., U. Bridgeport, 1969-71, Barry U., Fla. Internat. U. Cert. tchr. Fla. Rsch. technician in pharmacology N.Y. Med. Coll., N.Y.C., 1967-70; rsch. chemist Clairol, Inc., Stamford, Conn., 1970-74; pre-sch. instr. Happi-tymes, Miami, 1981-84; educator St. John Neumann Sch., Miami, 1984-92; sci. educator Carrollton Sch., Miami, 1992—. Coord. sci. dept. Carrollton Sch., 2004—. Contbr. articles to profl. jours. Mem. ways/means chmn. Stamford Women's Rep. Club, 1975-79, v.p. 1979. Mem. AAUW, Nat. Sci. Tchrs. Assn., Fla. Sci. Tchrs. Assn., Dade County Sci. Tchrs. Assn. Republican. Roman Catholic. Avocations: swimming, biking, reading, art collecting, ecology club advisor. Office: Carrollton Sch of the Sacred Heart 3747 Main Hwy Miami FL 33133-5907 Office Phone: 305-446-5673. Business E-Mail: irodriguez@carrollton.org.

RODRIGUEZ, JOANNE H., literature and language educator, department chairman; b. St. Petersburg, Fla., Nov. 15, 1946; d. Jesse Ray and Joanne Mary Hansell; m. Ronald Lee Rodriguez, June 23, 1973; 1 child, Erica Gabrielle. AA, St. Petersburg Jr. Coll., Fla., 1965; BA, U. South Fla., Tampa, 1966, MA, 1969; post grad., Fla. Internat. U., Fla. Atlantic U. Cert. tchr. Fla. Instr. English St. Petersburg H.S., Fla., 1967—78; adj. instr. St. Petersburg Jr. Coll., 1980—87, assoc. prof. English, 1987—96; chairperson dept. English Monsinor Edward Pace H.S., Miami, 1996—. Yearbook sponsor St. Petersburg H.S., Fla., 1967—76; mentor Women on the Way St. Petersburg Jr. Coll., 1990—96; forensics sponsor Monsignor Edward Pace H.S., Miami, 1998—2003, cand. coord. Silver Knights, 1998—; adj. instr. St. Thomas U., 1998—99, 2002, Fla. Internat. U., 1999—; reviewer comm. textbooks; presenter to profl. confs. Contbr. articles to jours. and periodicals. Music lady Shorecrest Prep., St. Petersburg, Fla., 1984—96; mem. Neighborhood Crime Watch, St. Petersburg, 1990—96; participant Miami AIDS Walk, 2006. Named Tchr. of Yr., Deaver Found., 2004; scholarship for AP Workshop, Coll. Bd., 1998. Mem.: Nat. Cath. Educators Am., Nat. Coun. Tchrs. English. Roman Catholic. Avocations: arts and crafts, writing, reading, gardening, antiques. Office: Monsignor Edward Pace HS 15600 NW 32d Ave Miami FL 33054-2273

RODRIGUEZ, JOSEFA NIEVES, special education educator, language educator; b. Mantanzaz, Cuba, Nov. 7, 1942; d. Basilio Gonzalez Santana and Edelmira Margarita Escalona; m. Manuel B. Rodriguez, June 17, 1972; children: Josie, Aimee, Manuel Jr. B in Secretarial Sci., Barry U., Miami Shores, Fla., 1965, BS, 1980, MS, 1992. Profl. educator's cert. Fla., cert. ESOL, Spanish, specific learning disabilities, mentally handicapped. Sales agt. Eastern Airlines, Inc., Miami, Fla., 1965—90; pre-sch. tchr. Archdiocese Miami, 1994—96; ESOL tchr. adult edn. Dade County Pub. Schs., Miami, 1996—, spl. edn. tchr., 2000—, tchr. of students with phys. impairments, 2005—06. Substitute tchr. Dade County Pub. Schs., Miami, 1992—2000; adj. prof. Miami Dade CC, Miami, 1997, ESOL instr., 2000; facilitator U. Miami Reading Inst.; ESOL tutor adult edn. Dade County Pub. Schs., Miami, 2005—06. Mem.: AFT, NEA, Dade Art Educators Assn., Coun. for Exceptional Student Edn., Fla. Edn. Assn., United Tchrs. Dade, Barry U. Alumnae Assn. Republican. Roman Catholic. Avocations: opera, piano, painting, tennis, languages. Office: Dade County Pub Schs 1500 Biscayne Blvd Miami FL 33132 Office Phone: 305-995-1000.

RODRÍGUEZ, LILIANA CRISTINA, mathematics educator; b. Valencia, Carabobo, Venezuela, May 19, 1975; d. Rodolfo Rodríguez and Ana Rosa Sanabria de Rodriguez; m. Harold Enrique Torrence, Dec. 22, 1999; children: Jonathan Enrique Torrence, Susana Andreina Torrence. BS in Math and Learning Disabilities (hon.), U. of Carabobo/Nat. Open U., Valencia, 1999. Cert. 7-12 Mathematics tchr. Minn. Dept. of Edn., 2002. Bilingual Spanish-English tchr. Aurora Charter Sch., Mpls., 2000—03; secondary math tchr. Hazel Pk. Acad. (St. Paul Pub. Sch.), St. Paul, 2003—. Music tchr. Aurora Charter Sch., Mpls., 2000—03. Musician (singer): (music writer) Mensaje de Hermandad. Chorus dir. Holy Rosary Ch., Mpls., 2000—06. Scholar Cum laude scholar, U. of Carabobo -Venezuela, 1999—2003. Mem.: Nat. Coun. of Tchrs. of Math. (assoc.). Achievements include development of Spanish curriculum for children. Avocations: swimming, music, travel, drawing, painting. Home: 6145 Courtly Alcove Unit C Woodbury MN 55125 Office: Saint Paul Public School 360 Colborne St Saint Paul MN 55102 Office Phone: 651-767-8100. Personal E-mail: lilianac75@hotmail.com. E-mail: liliana.rodriguez@spps.org.

RODRÍGUEZ, MARIA, social worker, counselor; b. Mayaquez, P.R., Jan. 2, 1953; d. Pablo Velez and Genara Valle; m. Carlos A. Rodriguez (div. 1990); children: Carlos A. Jr., Leslie A. Student, Passaic C.C., Patterson, N.J. Cert. HIV specialist. Case mgr. Mayaquez (P.R.) Med. Ctr., 1970-71, Hispanic Multi-Purpose Ctr., Patterson, N.J., 1989-90, Cure AIDS Now, Miami, Fla., 1991-93; adminstrv. asst. Carles Imports & Exports, Patterson, 1975-80; tchg. asst. St. John's Sch., Patterson, 1981-87; counselor Passaic (N.J.) City Hall, 1987-89; hot line counselor Health Crisis Network, Miami, 1990-91; job placement coord. Alternatives Svcs., Hialeah, Fla., 1993-94; social worker Beckham Hall for Homeless, Miami, 1994, Metro Dade Human Resouces, Miami, 1994—. Dep. registrar Metro Dade Elections Dept., Miami, 1991; chairperson L.Am. Com., North Miami Beach, Fla., 1993; advocate people with disabilities Archdiocese of Miami, 1994; active Voters Coun. North Miami Beach, 1993; active LWV of Dade County, Policemen's Benevolent Assn. Recipient Appreciation cert. Coalition of Homeless, 1993, City Hall of North Miami Beach for svcs. in cmty., 1993, State of Fla., 1993. Mem. NAFE. Democrat. Roman Catholic. Avocations: reading, writing, social events. Home: 1301 NE 181st St North Miami Beach FL 33162-1327

RODRIGUEZ, MARTHA JEANNE, biology educator; b. Lawrence, Kans., May 26, 1977; d. Rich Phillip and Debbie Jean Rodriguez. BA in Liberal Studies, Calif. State U. Monterey Bay, Seaside, 2000. Biology tchr. Caruthers (Calif.) Unified Sch. Dist., 2001—.

RODRIGUEZ, MICHELLE (MAYTE MICHELLE RODRIGUEZ), actress; b. Bexar County, Tx, July 12, 1978; Actor: (films) Girlfight, 2000, 3 A.M., 2001, The Fast and the Furious, 2001, Resident Evil, 2002, Blue Crush, 2003, S.W.A.T., 2003, Control, 2004, Sian Ka'an (voice), 2005, BloodRayne, 2005; (TV series) Lost, 2005— (Outstanding Performance by an Ensemble in a Drama Series, Screen Actors Guild award, 2006, Outstanding Supporting Actress in a TV Series, Nat. Coun. La Raza ALMA award (Am. Latin Media Arts), 2006); voice over: (video game) True Crime: Streets of L.A., 2003; Driv3r, 2004; Halo 2, 2004.

RODRIGUEZ, NORA HILDA, social worker; b. Brownsville, Tex., Dec. 26, 1964; d. Raul and Julia Rodriguez; 1 child, Carlos. AS, Tex. Southmost Coll., 1986; BS, Tex. A&M U., 1987, B.A.A.S.; AA in Social Work, Tex. Southmost Coll., 1997; BA in Sociology, U. Tex., Brownsville, 1997; MSSW, U. Tex., 2003. Med. billings Valley Counseling and Wellness, Brownsville; tchr. asst. spl. ed. Garden Pk. Elem. Sch., Brownsville, Tex., 1998; case mgr. Valley AIDS Coun., McAllen, Tex.; case worker Cath. Social Svcs., Brownsville, Tex., 2002—. Scholar, Cath. Daughters Am., 1985; Hispanic scholar, L & F Distributors, Ltd., 1998—99. Fellow: Internat. Fedn. Social Workers (assoc.); mem.: Am. Trauma Soc., Social Work Grad. Alumni Assn. (assoc.), NASW (assoc.), Phi Theta Kappa. D-Conservative. Roman Catholic. Avocations: teaching, travel, hiking, scuba diving, reading. Home: 9401 US Military Hwy 281 Brownsville TX 78520 Office: Catholic Social Svcs 47 W Elizabeth Brownsville TX 78520 Personal E-mail: icbluestars@hotmail.com. E-mail: nrodriguez@cdob.org.

RODRIGUEZ, RITA MARIA, economist; b. La Havana, Cuba, Sept. 6, 1944; came to U.S., 1960; Tomas and Adela (Mederos) R.; m. E. Eugene Carter, Jan. 7, 1972; 1 child, Adela-Marie R. Carter. BBA, U. PR, 1964; MBA, NYU, 1968, PhD, 1969. Bus. adminstrn. asst. prof., then assoc. prof. Harvard Bus. Sch., Cambridge, Mass., 1969-74, 74-78; fin. prof. U. Ill., Chgo., 1978-82; dir. Export-Import Bank of U.S., Washington, 1982-99. Cons. Polaroid Corp. and Indsl. Devel. Bank in Ecuador (Corporacion Financiera Nacional), 1978-82, U.S. IRS, 1982; bd. dirs. Acad. Ednl. Devel., Washington, 1989-93, 2000—; bd. advisors Pew Econ. Freedom Fellows, Washington, 1991-94, World Bank, MIGA, Washington, 2000; bd. dirs. Affiliated Mgrs. Group, Boston, 2000-, Pvt. Export Funding Corp., N.Y., 2001—; sr. fellow Woodstock Theol. Ctr., Georgetown U., Washington, 2002—; bd. dirs. ENSCO, Dallas, 2003—. Author: (with E. Eugene Carter) International Financial Management, 1976, 2d edit., 1979, 3rd edit., 1984, (with Heinz Riehl) Foreign Exchange Markets: A Guide to Foreign Currency Operations, 1977, Foreign Exchange Management in U.S. Multinationals, 1980 (with Heinz Riehl) Foreign Exchange and Money Markets, 1983, Japanese, Spanish, Portuguese translations, The Export-Import Bank at Fifty, 1987; co-editor (with G.C. Hufbauer) Ex-Im Bank: Overview, Challenges, and Policy Options in the Ex-Im Bank in the 21st Century, 2001; editor (with Gary Hufbauer) The Ex-Im Bank in the 21st Century; contbr. numerous fin. articles to profl. publs. Bd. dirs. Am. Friends of Turkey, 2001. Recipient Outstanding Achievement award Nat. Coun. of Hispanic Women, 1986; Outstanding Hispanic Achievement award Hispanic Corp. Achievers, 1988; Nat. Leadership award Government The Nat. Network of Hispanic Women, 1989. Mem.: Coun. Fgn. Rels. Roman Catholic. Avocations: gardening, music. Office: 3075 Ordway St NW Washington DC 20008-3255

RODRIGUEZ-VELEZ, ROSA, prosecutor; Bar: PR 1977. US Atty., PR US Dept. Justice, 2006—. Office: US Attys Office Torre Chardon Ste 1201 350 Carlos Chardon Ave San Juan PR 00918*

RODRIGUEZ-WALLING, MATILDE BARCELO, special education educator; b. Santiago, Cuba, Aug. 15, 1950; d. Humberto Jacinto and Matilde Amelia (Cuervo) Barcelo; m. Luis Alfredo Rodriguez-Walling, June 29, 1973; 1 child, Alfredo Luis. BA, U. Miami, Fla., 1972; MS in Diagnostic Tchg., Fla. Internat. U., 1981; EdS, Barry U., 1988. Cert. ednl. specialist computer edn., Fla. Tchr., chair fgn. lang. dept. Notre Dame Acad., Miami, Fla., 1972-80; tchr., coord. English as 2d lang. adult edn. program Dade County Pub. Schs., Miami, elem. sch. tchr., tchr. middle sch. spl. edn. Homestead, Fla., elem. spl. edn. tchr. Miami, 1986—, behavior mgmt. specialist, exceptional edn. dept. chair; tchr. on spl. assignment Fla. Dept. of Edn., 1994—. Mem. spkrs. bur. Nat. Clearinghouse for Professions in Spl. Edn.; sch. adv. chairperson Blueprint 2000; presenter and spkr. at state and nat. profl. confs.; coord. Fla. Spkrs. Bur.; mem. Fla. Edn. Stds. Commn. Commr. Fla. Edn. Stds. Commn.; mem. State Adv. Com.; mem. Commrs. Blue Ribbon Panel Edn. Governance; co-chair Nat Commn. Improve Spl. Edn. Teaching & Learning. Recipient Gran Orden Martiana, Cuban Lyceum, Miami, 1976. Mem. Coun. Exceptional Children (sec. 1989, v.p. 1990, pres. 1991-92, multicultural chair 1992-93, Mainstreaming Tchr. of Yr. 1983, region finalist Dade County Tchr. of Yr. 1991, Fla. Tchr. of Yr.), Fla. Fedn. Coun. for Exceptional Children (pres. 1997-98, past pres. 1998-99), Coun. Children with Behavior Disorders, Nat. Bd. for Profl. Tchg. Stds. (exceptional needs com.), Internat. Coun. for Exceptional Children (Tchr. of Yr. 1994), Delta Kappa Gamma (Epsilon chpt.). Roman Catholic. Avocations: travel, guitar. Office: Miami-Dade County Pub Schs 1500 Biscayne Blvd Ste 409G Miami FL 33132-1400 Home: 12501 SW 78th St Miami FL 33183-3516 E-mail: mrodriguez-walling@dadeschools.net.

RODRIQUEZ, EMILY KAY, elementary school educator; b. Ft. Wayne, Ind., June 8, 1981; d. Ronald D. Rodriquez and Carol R. Wencel, Michael Wencel (Stepfather) and Jessica L. Rodriquez (Stepmother). BS in Secondary Edn., U. Nev., Las Vegas, Nev., 2003; MA in Ednl. Administrn. and Supervision, U. Phoenix, Las Vegas, Nev., 2006. Server Applebee's Inc., Las Vegas, 2000—; tchr. history Sedway Mid. Sch., Las Vegas, 2003—. Adv. student coun. Sedway Mid. Sch., 2003—. Youth vol. Warm Springs Bapt. Ch., Las Vegas, 1996—2003. Independent. Avocations: music, travel, current events, fashion, movies. Office Phone: 702-799-3880.

ROE, CHARLOTTE E., diplomat; d. Edward Gaynor Roe and Eloise Tarbell; m. Hector Gabriel Bravo, Feb. 25, 1989. BA, U. Colo., Boulder, 1964; MA, Ohio State U., Columbus, 1982. Bus. mgr. New Am., NYC, 1964—65; youth affairs fellow NY Friends Group, NYC, 1965—67; exec. dir. Frontlash, NYC, 1967—74; legis. rep. Internat. Ladies Garment Workers Union, Washington, 1975—76; nat. field rep. AFL-CIO, Columbus, Ohio, 1976—83; fgn. svc. officer Dept. State, Washington, 1983—. Commr. Mint US-Hungry Sci. and Tech. Fund, Budapest, Hungary, 1997—99. Adv. com. US Ctrl. and Ea. Europe Environ. Found., Arlington, Va., 2000—03; exec. bd. NOW, NYC, 1968—70; elections officer Bd. Elections, Arlington County, 2004—. Recipient Meritorious Honor award, US Embassy, Santiago, Chile, 1988, Superior Honor award, Dept. State, 2004. Mem.: Nat. Resources Def. Coun., Diplomatic Assn. for Edn. and Tng., Hist. Harp Soc. Avocations: tai chi, horseback riding, harp. Office: Dept State WHA/PPC 20th and C St NW Washington DC 20520

ROE, KATHRYN JANE, elementary school educator; b. Indpls., July 25, 1958; d. Max Richard and Marthana Jane Kidwell; m. Patrick Allen Dawson, June 14, 1980 (div. Jan. 15, 1996); 1 child, Gregory Scott Dawson; m. William R. Roe, Jr., July 24, 2006. BS, Ball State U., 1987, MA in Edn., 1992. Cert. tchr. NC, Ind. Aide Blue River Valley Schs., Mt. Summit, Ind., 1987—88; grad. asst. Ball State U., Muncie, Ind., 1988—92, adj. faculty, 1992—97; tchr. Muncie Cmty. Schools, 1997, Cumberland County Schs., Fayetteville, NC, 2005—. Article reviewer Ind. Reading Quar., Muncie, 1994—97; presenter in field. Author: (textbook) Academic Survival Skills: Batteries Not Included. Active lit. walk-a-thon Cumberland County Schs., Fayetteville, NC, 2005; active Habitat for Humanity, Ball State U., Muncie, 1994—96; mem. walk-a-thon Longfellow Student Coun., Muncie, 2002—03; mem. neighborhood clean-up Whitely Assn., Muncie, 2004. Named Longfellow Tchr. of Yr., Muncie Cmty. Schools, 2003, Tchr. Vol. of Yr., Longfellow PTA, 2003, Student Body Tchr. of Yr., Longfellow Student Coun., 2003; grantee, Florence Rogers Charitable Trust, 2005, Armed Services Sci. Tchg. award, 2005, Buddy Project, 2003—04; Buddy grantee, Buddy Writing Project, 1999—2005. Mem.: Internat. Reading Assn. (assoc.). Independent. Pentecostal. Avocations: travel, reading, writing, choral singing. Office: Cumberland County Schs 3876 Sunnyside School Rd Fayetteville NC Home: 7141 Canary Dr Fayetteville NC 28314 Office Phone: 910.483.4319. Office Fax: 910.483.5711. Personal E-mail: kjdawson58@peoplepc.com. Business E-Mail: kathrynroe@ccs.k12.nc.us. E-mail: kidiewell@yahoo.com.

ROE, LESA B., federal agency administrator; b. 1963; m. Ralph Roe. B. in elec. engring., U. Fla., Gainesville; M. in elec. engring., U. Ctrl. Fla., Orlando. Satellite comm. analyst Hughes Space & Comm., El Segundo, Calif.; with NASA, 1987—, comm. engr. Space Shuttle Engring. Directorate Kennedy Space Ctr., Fla., 1987, payloads office mgr. Internat. Space Sta. (ISS) Program Office, Johnson Space Ctr. Houston; assoc. dir. bus. mgmt. Langley Rsch. Ctr., NASA, Hampton, Va., 2003—04, dep. dir., 2004—05, dir., 2005—. Office: Bldg 1219 Rm 213 Mail Stop 106 Hampton VA 23681-2199 also: Langley Rsch Ctr 100 NASA Rd Hampton VA 23681 Office Phone: 757-864-4111. E-mail: lesa.b.roe@nasa.gov.*

ROE, WANDA JERALDEAN, artist, retired educator, lecturer; b. Batesville, Ark., Nov. 9, 1920; d. William Melvin and Luna Eva (Cockrum) Finley; m. Roy A. Roe, Dec. 25, 1940; children: Ramona Jeraldean, Roy A. II. BS in Edn., U. Cen. Ark., Conway, 1954; MS in Edn., Ark. State U., 1965; diploma Exec. Devel. Ctr., U. Ill., 1984; postgrad., U. Ark., 1981. Cert. educator, Ark.; lic. profl. counselor, Ark. Counselor Fountain Lake H.S., Hot Springs, Ark., 1965-68; instr. art and home econs. Foreman (Ark.) H.S., 1968-72; profl. counselor Pea Ridge (Ark.) H.S., 1972-83; instr. art No. Ark. C.C., Rogers, 1980-90; profl. artist Rogers (Ark.) Art Guild Gallery, 1983-94, Big Spring Gallery, Neosho, Mo., 1989-98, Ark. Artists Registry, Little Rock, 1983—; instr. art Wishing Springs Gallery, Bella Vista, Ark. Art display coord., dir. workshops State Dept. Edn., Little Rock, 1965-83; supr. for practice tchrs. and counselor interns. Ark. Colls. and Univs., 1968-83; art instr. War Eagle Seminar, 1996; presenter in field. Exhibited in one-person show at Walton Art Ctr., 1996; group show at Philbrook Mus., Tulsa, 2004; author numerous poems; mem. editl. bd. Cmty. Pubs. Inc., 1994-97; art work pub. Internat. Bu. Delta Kappa Gamma Soc., 2001; editor, publ. Arkansas Diamonds, 2005. Mem. State Adv. Coun. for Gifted/Talented Edn., Little Rock, 1989-96; mem. Ark. Leadership Acad., 1996, G/T Coalition, 1996-97; juror for art contests; guide for County Constn. Day, Benton County, 1987; pres. United Meth. Women, Pea Ridge, 1973-75; cmty. vol.; sec. Benton County Dem. Ctrl. Com., 1996-2005; White House vol., 1996; rsch. bd. advisors Internat. Directory of Disting. Leadership, 1992—; keynote spkr. Dem. County Conv., AAUW State Conv Travel Study grantee Delta Kappa Gamma, 1987; named Art Educator of Yr., N.W. Art Educators Assn., 1983; recipient numerous art awards. Mem.: AAUW (state pres. 1985—87, state exec. bd.), Rogers Art Guild (pres. 1991—92), Ozark Pastel Soc. (pres. 1990—93, Signature mem.), Internat. Assn. Pastel Socs. (Outstanding Vol. award 1997), Spiva Art Ctr., Ark. Art Educators Assn. (Svc. award for contbn. to art profession 1997), Nat. Art Educators Assn., Dem. Women's Club (v.p. 1996—98), Village Art Club (pres. 1998—2001, bd. dirs. 2002—03, chmn. bd. dirs. 2004—05, Gallery Tour coord. 2005, mem. gallery bd. 2005—06, wishing spring gallery bd. 2006), Delta Kappa Gamma (stete pres. 1983—85, internat. nominations com. 1998—2002, cover artist internat. sem. 2002—06, state exec. bd.). Democrat. Methodist. Avocations: music, lecturing, directing workshops.

ROEBUCK, JUDITH LYNN, retired secondary school educator; b. Huntington, W.Va., Jan. 1, 1946; d. Russell Vance and Janice Lee (Adams) Dickey; m. William Benjamine Roebuck Jr., Mar. 28, 1970; children: Lisa, Paul. AB, Marshall U., 1968; MA, W.Va. U., 1973; postgrad., Marshall U., 1973—, W.Va. U., 1973—. Cert. tchr., adminstr., W.Va. Tchr. art, English Vinson High Sch., Huntington, 1967-68; tchr. art Wayne (W.Va.) and Crockett Elem. Sch., 1968-69; tchr. art, speech Ona (W.Va.) Jr. High/Mid. Sch., 1969-91; tchr. speech, debate Huntington H.S., 1991-92; tchr. art Barboursville (W.Va.) H.S., 1992-94, Cabell Midland H.S., Ona, W.Va., 1994—96, ret., 1996; chair related arts team Ona Mid. Sch., 1988-91, sch. improvement team, 1990-91; ret., 1996. Adv. bd. Teen Inst., Huntington, 1990—, W.Va. Teen Inst., 1995, leader, 1990—; mem. drama and debate program, Huntington, 1991-92, Invitationalism Coun., Huntington, 1990—, Cabell County Curriculum Coun., Huntington, 1991-92, Cabell County Reading Coun., 1991-92, Cabell County Tchrs. Acad., Tchr. Expectancy Student Achievement, W.Va. Health Schs. Program, 1998; mediator, trainer Helping Improve Peace, 1994; mentor, tchr. Impact. Contbr. articles to profl. jours. Counselor, Coll. Scouts Program, 1994—; vol. nat. disaster ARC, 1996—, human rels. liaison officer, 1996—; mem. citizen's emergency response team Homeland Security, 2004-, skywatch team Nat. Weather Bur., 2004; mem. Nat. Critical Incident Stresss Mgmt. Team., 2000—. Mem. NEA, DAR (sec. 1988—), Nat. Art Edn. Assn. (curriculum coun., art chair 1993-96, county del. 1994), W.Va. Edn. Assn., Cabell Edn. Assn. (membership chair 1989-91), Horizons, Phi Delta Kappa (pres. 1998—). Avocations: crafts, sewing, reading, diet and health, walking.

ROEDER, GLORIA JEAN, civil rights specialist, retired private investigator; b. Des Moines, Dec. 4, 1945; d. Gerald Arthur and Dorothy Jean (Pardekooper) R. BA, Simpson Coll., Indianola, Iowa, 1970; postgrad., Iowa State U., Ames, 1991. Examiner disability determination divsn. Disability Determination Divsn. State of Iowa, Des Moines, 1970-75; owner, pres. Aaron Investigations, Des Moines, 1975-98; pvt. investigator Des Moines; ret., 2001. Cons. All Area Detective Agy., Des Moines, 1965-78. Civil rights specialist Iowa Civil Rights Commn., Des Moines, 1978—2002, local liaison; vol. Luth. Social Svcs., 1988—, eucharistic min., 1996—98. Mem. Nat. Assn. Human Rights Workers, Nat. Assn. Prevention Child Abuse (bd. dirs. 1988-91), Iowa Assn. Pvt. Investigators (chair constn. com. 1994-95, sec. bd. dirs. 1996). Avocations: poetry, drawing, painting, swimming, reading.

ROEDER, PHOEBE ELIZABETH, science educator; b. Portland, Oreg., Nov. 30, 1946; d. Sumner J. and Gretchen Barber; m. Stephen B.W. Roeder, June 28, 1969; children: Adrienne H.K., Roland C.W. BA in Chemistry, U. Oreg., 1969; PhD in Chemistry, U. Calif. San Diego, LaJolla, 1974. Liberal studies program coord. San Diego State U., 1992—, instr. sci. Office: San Diego State U 5500 Campanile Dr San Diego CA 92182-1623 Home: 6789 Alamo Way La Mesa CA 91941 Office Phone: 619-594-4812.

ROEDER, REBECCA EMILY, software engineer; b. Findlay, Ohio, Nov. 2, 1959; d. Brian Eldon and Barbara Lee (Melton) R.; m. Stephen William Bigley, May 28, 1983. BS in Edn. and Computer Sci., Bowling Green State U., 1983, MS in Computer Sci., 1993. Sys. analyst NCR Corp., Dayton, Ohio, 1983-84; sr. sys. analyst Unisys (Burroughs) Corp., Detroit, 1984-88; asst. dir. St. Vincent Med. Ctr., Toledo, 1988-95; sr. cons. Advanced Programming Resources, Inc., Columbus, Ohio, 1996; sr. software engr. Qwest Comm., Dublin, Ohio, 1996—2002; sys. analyst Ohio Bur. of Worker's Compensation, Columbus, 2002—03; supr. info. tech. Ohio Dept. Edn., 2003—. Active Sta. WGTE/WGLE Pub. Radio, Toledo, 1984—96, Sta. WOSU Pub. Radio, Columbus, 1996—, Toledo Mus. Art, 1988—96, Toledo Zoo, 1993—96, Dawes Arboretum, 1996—, Stratford Festival Friend, 1997—, Columbus Zoo, 1997—2004, Columbus Symphony Orch. Concerto Club, 1998—2005; presenter Women in Sci. Career Day, Lourdes Coll., 1992; active Sta. WCBE Radio, Columbus, 1996—98, 2001—06, Franklin Pk. Conservatory, 2004—. Marathon scholar Marathon Oil Co., Findlay, 1978, Hancock scholar Findlay Area C. of C., 1978. Mem.: Assn. for Computing Machinery. Unitarian Universalist. Avocations: instrumental and choral music, drum and bugle corps, reading. Office: Ohio Dept Edn 25 S Front St Columbus OH 43215 Home: 3165 Leeds Rd Columbus OH 43221

ROEDER VAUGHAN, MIMI, small business owner; b. Balt., Nov. 21, 1948; m. Arky Vaughan; children: Gina Pizza, Kelly Vaughan, Ryan Vaughan. BA, U. Tenn., 1970; postgrad., U. Hawaii, 1972. Founder, CEO Roeder Travel, 1973—, Kailua Property, 1973—, Md. Sch. Travel, 1976—, Roland Park Travel, 1984—92, Falls Road Travel, 1990—. Mem. bd. Augusta Bank, 1990—91. Dir., sec. Civic Works, 1998—2000; pres., founder Baskets and Books, 1995—2000; co-founder Kingston Orphanage Group, 2000. Named One of Md.'s Top 100 Women, Daily Record, 1995, 1999, 2001; recipient Sabre Star award, Am. Airlines, 1999, 2000, Gold Spike award, Amtrak, 1998. Mem.: GBC Leadership (bd. dirs. 2000, class rep. 1995 1995—2000), Network 2000 (co-chair mentoring 1999—2000, membership com. 1998—2000). Office: 9805 York Rd Cockeysville Hunt Valley MD 21030

ROEDIGER, JANICE ANNE, artist, educator; b. Trenton, N.J. d. John and Anne Balint; m. Paul Margerum Roediger; children: Pamela Anne, Matthew Paul, Joan Margaret. Student, Beaver Coll., 1975-78; grad. cert., Pa. Acad. Fine Arts, 1988. Instr. multi-media Jane Law Long Beach Island Gallery, Surf City, N.J., 1992-95; instr. drawing Long Beach Island Found., Loveladies, NJ, 1994—2006. Docent Mus. Am. Art, Pa. Acad. Fine Arts, Phila., 1992—. Exhibited in group shows at Rittenhouse Galleries, Phila., 1988-94, Phila. Mus. Art, ASR Gallery, 1992—, Schaff Gallery, Cin., 1995-96, Lambertville (N.J.) Gallery of Fine Arts, 1997—. Mem. vestry, rector's warden St. Anne's Episcopal Ch., Abington, Pa., 1970-73; chair med. staff aux. Abington Meml. Hosp., 1973-7, chair scholarship com., 1974; coord. student com. Pa. Acad. Fine Arts, Phila., 1986-88; active Phila. Mus. Art, 1972—. Recipient Rohm & Haas Outstanding Achievement award Pa. Acad. Fine Arts, 1987, Pearl Van Sciver award Woodmere Mus., 1991, Blumenthal award Cheltenham Ctr. for Arts, 1991, Pres. award, 2001, Lance Lauffler award for visionary painting Pa. Acad. Fine Arts, 1988, Award of Merit Long Beach Island Found., 1994, 96, Woodmere Mus. Memorial Endowment award, 1999, Outstanding Achievement award Long Beach Island Found., 2002. Mem. Nat. Mus. Women in Arts, Phila. Art Alliance, Artists Cultural Exch. (bd. dirs. 1989—). Episcopalian. Avocations: writing, collecting, golf, walking, travel. Home: 1250 Greenwood Ave Jenkintown PA 19046 Studio: 1913 Guernsey Ave Abington PA Personal E-mail: imjanroe@aol.com.

ROEHL, KATHLEEN ANN, financial executive; b. Chgo., June 1, 1948; d. Walter Steven and Catherine (Puss) Kalchbrenner; m. Eric C. Roehl, June 28, 1969; children: Aaron C., Marc E. BA with honors, U. Ill., 1969. Registered investment advisor; cert. fin. mgr.; CFP. Tchr. Ft. Huachuca (Ariz.) Accomodation Schs., 1969-70; interior designer Key Kitchens, Dearborn Heights, Mich., 1979-80; stockbroker, fin. cons. Merrill Lynch, Dearborn, Mich., 1980-81, v.p., registered investment advisor, fin. mgr. Northbrook, Ill., 1982—2004, v.p., wealth mgmt. advisor Crystal Lake, Ill., 2004—. Bd. dirs. ATA Info. Systems. Mem. Ill. Govt. Fin. Officers Assn., Internat. Assn. for Fin. Planning (bd. dirs. 1987-88), Fin. Planning Assn., Northbrook C. of C. (bd. dirs. 1991-93), Northbrook Early Risers Rotary (charter mem.). Avocations: horticulture, architecture, photography. Office: Merrill Lynch 360 Memorial Dr Ste 210 Crystal Lake IL 60014 Office Phone: 815-788-2440. Business E-Mail: kathleeen_roehl@ml.com.

ROEHL, NANCY LEARY, marketing professional, educator; b. Natick, Mass., Mar. 25, 1952; d. Norman Leslie and Dorothy (Holmquist) Pidgeon; m. Patrick J. Leary, Sept. 17, 1977 (div. May 1984); m. Patrick F. Roehl, July 2, 1995. AA, Mass. Bay Coll., Wellesley, 1979; BS, Lesley Coll., Cambridge, Mass., 1988; MA Edn. Arts and Scis., U. South Fla., 1992. Cert. tchr., Fla. Sec. GTE Corp., Needham, Mass., 1973—78; coord. edn. Cullinet Software Inc., Westwood, Mass., 1983—84, adminstrv. asst., 1984—85, mgr. adminstrn., 1985—86; specialist product mktg. Cullinet Co., Westwood, 1986—88; v.p. mktg. and adminstrn. Jonathan's Landscaping, Bradenton Beach, Fla., 1988—89; tech. support staff A Plus Tax Product Group, Arthur Andersen, Inc., Sarasota, Fla., 1989—90; cons. Palmetto, Fla., 1990—; tchr. Manatee County, 1992—; editor Objex, Inc., 2000—. Mem.: AAUW, Nat. Trust for Hist. Preservation, Phi Kappa Phi. Office: Objex Inc PO Box 38 Terra Ceia FL 34250 Business E-Mail: nancy@roehl-consulting.com.

ROEHLIG, NICOLE, elementary school educator; d. Reinhard and Dorothy Roehlig. BS, Winona State U., Minn., 1998, U. Wis., Oshkosh, 2003. Paralegal, Milw., 1998—2000; tchr. Bonduel (Wis.) Mid. Sch., 2003—. Office Phone: 715-758-4840.

ROEMER, CAROL KALUGA, art educator; b. Cleve., Sept. 24, 1941; d. Joseph and Helen (Belavich) Kaluga; m. William Daniel Roemer, Dec. 21, 1974 (dec. Mar. 1998). BA, Calif. State U., Long Beach, 1970, MA, 1972; PhD, Claremont (Calif.) Grad. Sch., 1992. Cert. c.c. tchr., Calif. Classroom tchr. Holy Spirit Sch., L.A., 1966-67; adj. instr. Cerritos C.C., Norwalk, Calif., 1972-81, Calif. State U., Long Beach, 1973-79, Golden West Coll., Huntington Beach, Calif., 1980-81; replacement instr. (full-time) Pasadena City Coll., 1977-80; prof. art Long Beach City Coll., 1981—2004, prof. emeritus, 2004—. Author: The Bread of Angels: Charles Eliot Norton's Art History, 1992; multi-media author/developer: Looking at Art, 1997-98. Recipient Tchg. Excellence award Nat. Inst. for Staff and Organizational Devel., U. Tex., 1995. Mem. Coll. Art Assn., Mus. Latin Am. Art, Long Beach Mus. Art (guest lectr. 1990-93), L.A. County Mus. Art (guest lectr. 1997), Cairn Terrier Club of So. Calif. (bd. dirs., newsletter editor). Avocations: cairn terrier exhibitor, breeder.

ROEMER, ELIZABETH, retired astronomer, educator; b. Calif., Sept. 4, 1929; d. Richard Quirin and Elsie Roemer. BA with honors, U. Calif., Berkeley, 1950, PhD (Lick Obs. fellow), 1955. Tchr. adult class Oakland pub. schs., 1950-52; lab technician U. Calif. at Mt. Hamilton, 1954-55; grad. research astronomer U. Calif. at Berkeley, 1955-56; research asso. Yerkes Obs. U. Chgo., 1956; astronomer U.S. Naval Obs., Flagstaff, Ariz., 1957-66; asso. prof. dept. astronomy, also in lunar and planetary lab. U. Ariz., Tucson, 1966-69, prof., 1969-97; prof. emerita, 1997—; astronomer Steward Obs., 1980-97, astronomer emerita, 1997—. Chmn. working group on orbits and ephemerides of comets commn. 20 Internat. Astron. Union, 1964-79, 85-88, v.p. comm. 20, 1979-82, pres., 1982-85, v.p. commn. 6, 1973-76, 85-88, pres., 1976-79, 88-91; mem. adv. panels Office Naval Research, Nat. Acad. Scis.-NRC, NASA; researcher and author numerous publs. on astrometry and astrophysics of comets and minor planets including 79 recoveries of returning periodic comets, visual and spectroscopic binary stars, computation of orbits of comets and minor planets. Recipient Dorothea Klumpke Roberts prize U. Calif. at Berkeley, 1950, Mademoiselle Merit award, 1959; asteroid (1657) named Roemera, 1965; Benjamin Apthorp Gould prize Nat. Acad. Scis., 1971; NASA Spl. award, 1986. Fellow AAAS (council 1966-69, 72-73), Royal Astron. Soc. (London); mem. Am. Astron. Soc. (program vis. profs. astronomy 1960-75, council 1967-70, chmn. div. dynamical astronomy 1974), Astron. Soc. Pacific (publs. com. 1962-73, Comet medal com. 1968-74, Donohoe lectr. 1962), Internat. Astron. Union, Am. Geophys. Union, Brit. Astron. Assn., Phi Beta Kappa, Sigma Xi. Office: U Ariz PO Box 210092 Lunar & Planetary Lab Tucson AZ 85721-0092

ROEMMICH, DALONNES KAY, music educator; b. Bismarck, N.D., Sept. 14, 1951; d. Edmund and Verna Roemmich. MusB in Music Composition, Dickinson State U., N.D., 1972; MusM, U. N.D., 1987. Nat. registered music tchr., nat. cert. music tchr. 1st-12th grade vocal/instrumental music tchr. Sykeston (N.D.) Pub. Sch., 1972—77; 5th-12th grade instrumental music tchr. Hazen (N.D.) Pub. Schs., 1977—80; K-6th grade gen. music tchr. Carrington (N.D.) Pub. Sch., 1980—99; 5th-12th grade vocal music tchr. Bottineau (N.D.) Pub. Schs., 1999—. Dir. N.D. Gov.'s Choir, 2004—05. Author: (jour. article) N.D. Music Educators Jour., 1998. Piano accompanist Women's Cmty. Choir, 2001—05; clarinet player N.D. Centennial Band, 1989; piano accompanist Grace Lutheran Bretheran Ch., 2001—05, Bethel Chapel Ch., Carrington, ND, 1972—99. Recipient Golden Apple award, 2004—05. Mem.: NEA, Soc. Gen. Music (N.D. chmn. 1985), Am. Choral Dirs. Assn., Bottineau (N.D.) Edn. Assn., Music Educators Nat. Conf., Music Educator Assn., N.D. Music Educator Assn. (15 Yr. Career Achievement, 25 Yr. Career Achievement), N.D. Music Edn. Assn. (N.E. bd. mem. 1990—98). Home: 319 Sinclair St Bottineau ND 58318 Office: Bottineau Pub Schs 301 Brandon St Bottineau ND 58318 Office Phone: 701-228-2629.

ROENICKE, NORMA JEAN, music educator, pianist, organist, small business owner; b. Saginaw, Mich., Oct. 28, 1942; d. Walter William and Evelyn Hulda (Riethmeier) Moderow; m. W. Ruppal (div. 1966); m. Walter Allen Roenicke, Oct. 25, 1967; children: Scott Walter, Charisse Leigh Roenicke Taylor. Student, Delta Coll., U. Mich. Music tchr., performer Grinnell Bros., Saginaw, Mich., 1960-69; organist, choir accompanist Resurrection Luth Ch., Saginaw, Mich., 1974-97; organist, choir dir. Messiah Luth. Ch., Bay City, Mich., 1998—; accompanist Germania Club, Saginaw, Mich., 1997—; sub. organist St. Lorenz Luth. Ch., Frankenmuth, Mich., 1975—. Bd. dirs. Saginaw Symphony, 1985-94. Mem. Am. Guild Organists, Mich. Music Tchrs. Assn., Nat. Music Tchrs. Assn., PEO (pres. 1995-97, 2004-), Rotary (internat. svc. dir. Frankenmuth chpt. 1997-99, Paul Harris fellow). Republican. Lutheran. Avocations: travel, reading, skiing, walking. Office Phone: 989-777-7000. E-mail: njrpiano@hotmail.com.

ROER, RICKI E., lawyer; b. NYC, May 22, 1956; BA, U. Pa., 1978; JD, Am. U., 1981; LLM in internat. law, Oxford U., 1982. Bar: NY 1982, US Dist. Ct. Ea. Dist. NY, US Dist. Ct. So. Dist. NY, US Ct. Appeals 2nd Cir. Ptnr. Wilson, Elser, Moskowitz, Edelman & Dicker LLP, NYC, head nat. employment litig. team. Mem.: ABA, NY State Women's Bar Assn., Assn. of the Bar of the City of NY. Office: Wilson Elser Moskowitz Edelman & Dicker LLP 23rd Fl 150 E 42nd St New York NY 10017-5639 Office Phone: 212-490-3000 ext. 2375. Office Fax: 212-490-3038. Business E-Mail: roerr@wemed.com.

ROERDEN, CHRIS (CLAIRE ROERDEN), editor, business owner, publishing consultant; b. NYC, Aug. 28, 1935; d. Marion Smolin; m. Harold H. Roerden (div. 1985); children: Ken, Doug. BA in English summa cum laude, U. Maine, 1969, MA in English, 1971. Mem. pub. rels. staff Shell Oil Co., N.Y.C., 1952-55; asst. to pub. rels. dir. Interchem. Corp., N.Y.C., 1956-59; staff editor Newkirk Assocs., Albany, N.Y., 1960-62; instr. in English U. Maine, Portland, 1969-71; mentor Empire State Coll., SUNY, Rochester and Syracuse, 1973-74; mng. editor CPA Digest, Brookfield, Wis., 1983; owner Edit It, Brookfield, 1984—99, Market Savvy Book Editing, Greensboro, NC, 1999—. Lectr. U. Wis., Milw., 1991—98, 2006, Telesis Inst., Alverno Coll., 1995—97; presenter Pub.'s Mktg. Assn. Pub. U., 1996—, S.E. Mystery Writers of Am., 1998—2006, Harriette Austin Writers Conf., 2000—, Of Dark and Stormy Nights, 2001; moderator Malice Domestic, 2006, Bouchercon, 2006; keynote spkr. in field. Author: Collections from Cape Elizabeth, 1965, Oops 'n Options Game, 1982, Open Gate: Teaching in a Foreign Country, 1990, What Two Can Do: Sam & Mandy Stellman's Crusade for Social Justice, 2000, Don't Murder Your Mystery, 2006; editor: Life Skills Parenting Series, 1994-96, Mrs. Wheeler Goes to Washington (Elizabeth Wheeler Colman), 1989, Give This Man a Hand (Earl Harrell), 1990, Genetic Connections: A Guide to Documenting Your Individual and Family Health History, 1995 (Benjamin Franklin award and 6 others), The Safety Minute (R.L. Siciliano), 1995, The Cassidy McCabe Mystery Series (Alex Matthews, Love is Murder Reader's Choice award Best Series Continuing Character 1999): Secret's Shadow, 1995, Satan's Silence, 1997, Vendetta's Victim, 1998, Wanton's Web, 1999, Cat's Claw, 2000, Death's Domain, 2001, Wedding's Widow, 2003; The Body in the Transept (Jeanne Dams), 1995 (Agatha award), Down But Not Out (Jeanne Sexson), 1996, The Battering Syndrome (Michael Groetsch), 1996, Nonviolent Crisis Intervention (Crisis Prevention Inst.) 1996, He Promised He'd Stop (Michael Groetsch), 1997, Failure is Not an Option (Donna Jordan), 1998, New Millennium Guide to Managing Money (John T. McCarthy), 1998, Should I Stay or Go? (Lee Raffel), 1998, The M-Files (Jay Rath), 1998, Walking Tours of Wisconsin, 1998, Citizen Power (Robin Epstein), 1999, Divorcing the Corporation (Rosalyn Reeder), 1999, When the Dead Speak (Sandra Tooley), 1998, The Good Die Twice (Lee Driver), 1999, Nothing Else Matters (S.D. Tooley), 2000, Path to the Soul (Ashok Bedi, M.D.), 2000, Zachronyms (David Zach), 1998, ShapeWalking (Marilyn Bach), 1999, The Herbal Drugstore (Rodale), 2000, Breast Cancer Survivors' Club (Lillie Shockney), 1999, The Susan Chase Mystery Series (Steve Brown), Stripped to Kill, 2000, Dead Kids Tell No Tales, 2000, When Dead is Not Enough, 2001, Radio Secrets, 2000, Fallen Stars, 2001, Hurricane Party, 2002, River of Diamonds, 2002, Rescue, 2002, The Boy Who Invented Television (Paul Schatzkin), 2002, Sanctuary of Evil (Steve Brown), 2003, The Unseen (Lee Driver), 2004, Mad Cow Nightmare (Nancy Means Wright), 2005, Murder Passes the Buck (Deb Baker), 2006, Dolled Up for Murder (Deb Baker), 2006. Pres. Brookfield Civic Chorus, 1986-88; v.p. Brookfield Civic Music Assn., 1989-91. Recipient cert. of honor Korean Nat. Commn. for UNESCO, 1989, Kate Mooney Vol. Svc. award Counseling Ctr. Milw., 1991, Disting. Tech. Commn. awards (2) STC, 1995, award of achievement STC, 1995, Merit award, 1996, 1st pl. tech. editing award MAPA Book awards, 1995, 96, 2d pl. interior design award MAPA Book awards, 1995, 97. Mem.: NOW (Wis. pres. 1978—81, Positive Action award for Leadership 1977), Feminist Bus. and Profl. Women's Forum (coord. 1990—99), Wis. Women's Network (founding), Wis. Bus. Women's Coalition (bd. dirs. 1988), Pubs. Mktg. Assn. (coord. Wis. chpt. 1997—99), Mystery Writers Am. (bd. dirs. S.E. chpt. 2001—06), Women in Comm. S.E. Wis. (bd. dirs. 1988), Soc. for Tech. Comm. (Wis. bd. dirs. 1991—95), Mid-Am. Pubs. Assn. (pres. 1995—97), Mensa Internat., Phi Kappa Phi. Address: 3683 Waterwheel Ct Greensboro NC 27409-8103 Office Phone: 336-323-1032. Business E-Mail: CRoerden@aol.com.

ROERDINK, LISA MARIE, elementary school educator; b. Valrico, Fla., Feb. 16, 1979; d. Fredrick Joseph and Susan Lizette Franceschini; m. Jeffrey John Roerdink. BA in Elem. Edn., Covenant Coll., Lookout Mountain, Ga., 2002. Cert. tchr. Ga. Tchr. LaFayette Mid. Sch., Ga., 2002—. Chair Highlands Presbyn. Missions Com., LaFayette, 2004—06. Mem.: Ga. Educator's Assn. (assoc.). Republican. Presbyterian. Home: 1206 W 50th St Chattanooga TN 37409 Office: La Fayette Acad 301 N Cherokee St La Fayette GA 30728 Office Phone: 706-638-6440. Business E-Mail: lisaroerdink@walkerschools.org.

ROESSER, JEAN WOLBERG, state official; b. Washington, May 8, 1930; d. Solomon Harry Wolberg and Mary Frances Brown; m. Eugene Francis Roesser, Aug. 3, 1957 (dec.); children: Eugene Francis, Jr., Mary Roesser Calderon, Anne. BA, Trinity Coll., Washington, 1951; postgrad. in econs., Cath. U. of Am., 1951-53. Congl. relations asst. U.S. Info. Agy., Washington, 1954-58; news reporter for Montgomery County Coun., Suburban Record, 1983-86; mem. Md. Ho. of Dels., Annapolis, 1986-94, Md. Senate, Annapolis, 1994—2002; mem. fin. com., ethics com. State Senate, Md. Gen. Assembly, Annapolis, 1994—2002, joint com. welfare reform, 1996, joint com. healthcare delivery & financing, 1996—2002, joint budget & audit com., 1997—2002, chair joint com. on welfare reform, 2002; sec. Md. Dept. Aging, 2003—. Former mem. Md. Gov.'s Task Force on Energy; former pres. Montgomery County Fedn. Rep. Women, Potomac Women's Rep. Club; former 3d v.p. Md. Fedn. Rep. Women; founding mem. Montgomery County Arts Coun.; alt. del. Rep. Nat. Conv., 1992, del., 1996. Named one of Md.'s Top 100 Women, Daily Record, 2002; recipient Cmty. Achievement award, Washington Psychiat. Soc., 1994, 1998, Trinity Coll. Leadership award, 1994, Common Cause Md. award, 1993, Md. Underage Drinking Preventio Coalition award, 1994, Legislator of the Yr. award, Montgomery County Med. Soc., 1996, 2000, Best in Class award, Md. C. of C., 1997, Cmty. Svc. award, Washington Psychiatric Soc., 1998, Legislator of Yr. award, Md. State's Atty.'s Assn., 2000. Republican. Roman Catholic. Home: 10830 Fox Hunt Ln Potomac MD 20854-1553 E-mail: jeanroesser@aol.com.

ROESSLER, CAROL ANN, state legislator; b. Madison, Wis., Jan. 16, 1948; m. Paul Roessler. BS, U. Wis., Oshkosh, 1972. Dir. nutrition program for older adults County of Winnebago, Wis., 1973-82; elected to assembly, 1982—86; mem. Wis. Assembly, Madison, 1983-87; elected to senate in spl. election, 1987; mem. Wis. Senate from 18th dist., Madison, 1987—. Instr. pre-retirement planning Fox Valley Tech. Inst., 1978-81. Home: 1506 Jackson St Oshkosh WI 54901-2942 Office: PO Box 7882 Madison WI 53707-7882 E-mail: Sen.Roessler@legis.state.wi.us.

ROETHLIN, MARY JANE, science educator; d. Joseph Patrick and Mildred Costello Corcoran; m. Siegfried Martin Roethlin, Oct. 22, 1966; children: Douglas Martin, Christine Roethlin Najjar, Mark Edward, Michael Corcoran. BA, Coll. of Notre Dame of Md., Balt., 1964; MA in Tchg., Montclair State U., N.J., 1991. Cert. sci. tchr. N.J., 1991, supr. edn. N.J., 2005. Rsch. biologist Chas. Pfizer & Co., Maywood, NJ, 1964—67; tchr. sci., dept. head Paramus Cath. Girls H.S., NJ, 1977—92; tchr. biology/sci. program leader Glen Ridge H.S., NJ, 1992—. Home: 77 Old Orchard Dr Hawthorne NJ 07506 Office: Glen Ridge HS 200 Ridgewood Ave Glen Ridge NJ 07028 Office Phone: 973-429-8300 2330. E-mail: mroethlin@glenridge.org.

ROFFÉ, SARINA, public relations executive; b. Bklyn., Feb. 16, 1955; d. Abe J. and Reneé (Salem) Missry; m. David Roffé, June 4, 1974; children: Simon, Harriet, Abraham. BA in Journalism, U. Md., 1992; MA in Jewish Studies, Touro Coll., 2005. Reporter Gazette Newspaper, Gaithersburg, Md., 1991—93; news editor Richner Publs., Lawrence, NY, 1993—94; mng. editor Queens Tribune, 1994; interpreter of deaf Montgomery County Pub. Schs., Rockville, Md., 1980—93; writer, editor freelance Bklyn.; dir. pub. affairs NYC Dept. Juvenile Justice, 1996—2002; founder, exec. dir. NY Cued Speech Ctr., Inc., 1995—2004; nat. dir. comms. Jewish Nat. Fund, 2002—05, Am. ORT, 2005—. Contbg. author: Choices in Deafness-A Parent's Guide,

1987, Cued Speech Resource Guide for Parents, 1993, Jewish Cooking in America, 1994; contbr. articles to profl. jours. Pres. Montgomery County Assn. Hearing Impaired Children, Silver Spring, 1981—83; fundraising v.p., treas. B'nai B'rith Women, Gaithersburg, 1975—93; dir. Magen David Sephardic Congregation Bd., Rockville, 1989—93. Named Best in the Bus., Am. Correctional Assn., 1999; recipient 1st Pl. award, Am. Sephardic Fedn., 1991. Mem.: Sephardic Cmty. Fedn., Am. Sephardi Fedn. (bd. dirs. 2002—), Nat. Cued Speech Assn. (v.p. 1999—2002, pres. 2002—), Acad. Women Achievers of the YWCA, Jewish Women Internat., Hadassah, Sephardic Voters League (v.p. 1999—2003, bd. dirs. 2003—05), Deadline Club. Democrat. Jewish. Avocations: Mid East cooking, Jewish genealogy. Personal E-mail: sarinaroffe@aol.com. Business E-Mail: sroffe@waort.org.

ROG, DOROTHY ANN, elementary school educator; b. Chgo., July 15, 1942; d. John Stanley and Wanda Leona Stopka; children: Linda Rochelle Westerberg, Michelle Lynn Flatley. Bachelors Degree, St. Xavier U., Chgo., 1964; EdM, Nat. Louis U., Wheaton, Ill., 1991. Cert. elem. edn. Ill., 1964. Lower elem. tchr. Dist. #111, Burbank, Ill., 1964—68; fifth grade tchr. Maercker Sch., Westmont, Ill., 1978—. Mem.: Maercker Edn. Assn. (sec.). Avocations: travel, viewing the arts, reading. Office Phone: 630-968-6165.

ROGACHEFSKY, ARLENE SANDRA, dermatologist; b. Rochester, NY, June 29, 1970; d. Hymen Rogachefsky and Deanna Rogachefsky Luntz; m. David Black, Oct. 27, 2001; children: Mitchell Harris Black, Ellie Rachel Black. BA with honors, Brown U., Providence, 1992; MD magna cum laude, SUNY, Buffalo, 1996. Diplomate Am. Bd. Dermatology, cert. Am. Coll. Mohs Micrographic Surgery and Cutaneous Oncology. Intern in internal medicine Cleve. Clinic Found., 1996—97, resident in dermatology, 1997—2000; fellow Mohs and cosmetic laser surgery Office of Dr. David Goldberg, Westwood, NJ, 2000—01; assoc. Skin Laser and Surgery Specialists NY and NJ, Hackensack and Westwood, NJ, 2001—03, Affiliated Dermatologists and Dermatol. Surgeons, Morristown, NJ, 2005—. Contbr. articles to profl. jours. Home: 160 Myrtle Ave Millburn NJ 07041 Office: Affiliated Dermatologists and Dermatologic Surgeons 182 S St Ste 1 Morristown NJ 07960 Office Phone: 973-267-0300. E-mail: arogachefsky@hotmail.com.

ROGACZEWSKI, SHERRIE REECE, small business owner, singer; b. Greenwood, S.C., Nov. 23, 1966; d. George Washington and Hazel Irene Reece; m. Wayne Robert Rogaczewski, Nov. 29, 1986; 1 child, Brett. Grad. high sch., Greenwood, S.C. Singer, songwriter Sherreece, New Orleans, 1990—; co-owner World Gym, 2001—. Singer, songwriter: recs. Wild Life, 1997, New Age Dawning, 2000, Holy of Holies, 2004. Mem.: Gospel Music Assn. Avocations: history, archaeology. Office Phone: 504-813-8486. E-mail: sherreece@hotmail.com.

ROGALSKI, CAROL JEAN, clinical psychologist, educator; b. Chgo., Sept. 25, 1937; d. Casimir Joseph and Lillian Valentine Rogalski. BS, Loyola U., Chgo., 1961; PhD, NYU, 1968; cert. in psychoanalysis, Postgrad. Ctr. Mental Health, 1973. Lic. clin. psychologist, N.Y., Ill. Rsch. assoc. William Alanson White Inst., N.Y.C., 1961-66; rsch. asst., intern Hillside Hosp., Glen Oaks, N.Y., 1966-68; cons. Mt. Sinai Hosp., N.Y.C., 1968-73; staff psychologist Jesse Brown VA Hosp., Chgo., 1974—; clin. asst. prof. psychiatry Med. Sch. U. Ill., 1996—. Instr. technique and history of illuminated manuscripts Morton Arboretum, Lisle, Ill. Mem. editorial bd. Internat. Jour. Addictions, 1994-98; contbr. articles to profl. publs. Mem.: Guild of Natural Sci. Illustrators, Nature Artists' Guild, Chgo. Soc. for Psychotherapy Rsch. (chair 1988—91), Communal Studies Assn. Avocations: watercolors, illuminated manuscripts. Office: Jesse Brown VA Hosp 820 S Damen Ave Chicago IL 60612-3728 Office Phone: 312-569-7490. E-mail: carol.rogalski@med.va.gov.

ROGALSKI, LOIS ANN, speech and language pathologist; b. Bklyn. d. Louis J. and Filomena Evelyn (Maro) Giordano; m. Stephen James Rogalski, Jun e 27, 1970; children: Keri Anne, Stefan Louis, Christopher James, Rebecca Blair, Gregory Alexander. BA, Bklyn. Coll., 1968; MA, U. Mass., 1969; PhD., NYU, 1975. Lic. speech and lang. pathologist, N.Y.; cert. Nat. Acad. Sports Medicine; cert Powerhouse Pilates; cert. for yoga. Speech, lang. and voice pathologist Rehab. Ctr. of So. Fairfield County, Stamford, Conn., 1969, Sch. Health Program-P.A. 481, Stamford, 1969-72, pvt. practice speech, lang. and voice pathology Scarsdale, NY, 1972—. Cons. Bd. Coop. Ednl. Svcs., 1976-79, Handicapped Program for Preschoolers for Alcott Montessori Sch., Ardsley, N.Y., 1978—; rsch. methodologist Burke Rehab. Ctr., 1977. Mem. profl. adv. bd. Found. for Children with Learning Disabilities, 1978—; bd. dirs. United Way of Scarsdale-Edgemont, 1988-89; instr. religious instr. CCD Immaculate Heart of Mary Ch., Scarsdale, 1991—; bd. dirs. Scarsdale Teen Ctr., Inc., 1998—. Fellow Rehab. Svcs. Adminstrn., 1968-69; N.Y. Med. Coll., 1972-75. Mem. N.Y. Speech & Hearing Assn., Westchester Speech & Hearing Assn., Am. Speech, Hearing & Lang. Assn. (cert. clin. competence), Coun. for Exceptional Children, Assn. on Mental Deficiency, Am. Acad. Pvt. Practice in Speech Pathology & Audiology (bd. dirs., treas. 1983-87, pres. 1987-89), Internat. Assn. Logopedics & Phoniatrics, Sigma Alpha Eta. Avocations: yoga, pilates.

ROGAN, ELEANOR GROENIGER, oncologist, educator; b. Nov. 25, 1942; d. Louis Martin and Esther (Levinson) G.; m. William John Robert Rogan, June 12, 1965 (div. 1970); 1 child, Elizabeth Rebecca. AB, Mt. Holyoke Coll., 1963; PhD, Johns Hopkins U., 1968. Lectr. Goucher Coll., Towson, Md., 1968-69; rsch. assoc. U. Tenn., Knoxville, 1969-73, U. Nebr. Med. Ctr., Omaha, 1973-76, asst. prof., 1976-80; assoc. prof. Eppley Inst., dept. pharm. scis. U. Nebr., Omaha, 1980-90, prof. dept. pharm. scis. and dept. biochem. & molecular biol, 1990—. Contbr. articles to profl. jours. Predoctoral fellow USPHS, Johns Hopkins U., 1965-68; recipient Linus Pauling Functional Medicine award, 2006. Mem. AAAS, Am. Assn. Cancer Rsch., Soc. Toxicology. Democrat. Roman Catholic. Home: 8210 Bowie Dr Omaha NE 68114-1526 Office: U Nebr Med Ctr Eppley Inst 986805 Nebr Med Ctr Omaha NE 68198-6805 Office Phone: 402-559-4095. Business E-Mail: egrogan@unmc.edu.

ROGENESS, MARY SPEER, state legislator; b. Kansas City, Kans., May 18, 1941; d. Frederic A. and Jeannette (Hybskmann) Speer; m. Dean Rogeness, Aug. 31, 1964; children: Emily, James, Paul. BA, Carleton Coll., 1963. Computer analyst Dept. Def., Ft. Meade, Md., 1963-66; freelance writer, editor Longmeadow, Mass., 1982-91; mem. Mass. Ho. of Reps., Boston, 1991—, asst. minority leader, 2003—. Editor: Reflections of Longmeadow, 1983. Mem. Longmeadow Rep. Town Com., 1983—; bd. dirs. Goodwill Industries Hartford-Springfield, 1996—2004; mem. Longmeadow Sch. Com., 1982-88. Mem. Am. Legis. Exch. Coun., World Affairs Coun. of Western Mass. Office: Mass House of Reps State House Rm 124 Boston MA 02133 Office Phone: 617-722-2100.

ROGER, JANICE LOWENSTEIN, cantor; b. Chgo., July 6, 1951; d. Herbert and Gertrude Tauf Lowenstein; m. Brandon Anthony Roger, Nov. 30, 1980; children: Edwin Sidney, Miles Lawrence. B of sacred music, Hebrew Union Coll.Jewish Inst. of Religion, 1975—79; MusB, Roosevelt U., 1969—73; MusD (hon.), Hebrew Union Coll.-Jewish Inst. of Religion, 2004—04. Cantor Am. Conf. of Cantors, 1979. Cantor Indpls. Hebrew Congregation, 1979—. Cantorial chmn., nat. commn. on cantorial/congl. rels. Union for Reform Judaism, NY, 1995—; chmn., conv. adminstrn. com. Am. Conf. of Cantors, NY, 2004—, v.p., 1991—95, conv. co-chairman 1987, 1993; mem., artist evaluation com. Young Audiences, Indpls., 1991—92; bd. mem. Indpls. Chamber Orch., 1997—99; com. mem. Ind. Arts Coun., 2002. Singer: (concert) Hymns and Anthems, Ronen Chamber Ensemble; collaborating producer (dance performance) Avodah Dance Ensemble. Allocations com. United Way, 1990—91. Creative Renewal, Arts Coun. of Indpls., 1999. Mem.: Coalition on Advancements in Jewish Edn., Music Educators' Nat. Conf., Am. Conf. of Cantors. Avocations: reading, knitting, playing scrabble. Office: Indpls Hebrew Congregation 6501 North Meridian St Indianapolis IN 46260 Office Phone: 317-255-6647. Personal E-mail: janicer@ihcindy.org.

ROGERS, ALISON M., special education educator; b. Hackensack, NJ, Sept. 7, 1979; d. Thomas and Kathleen Mary Rogers. B in Tchg. of Handicapped, Kean U., 2001, M in Spl. Edn., 2004. Resource ctr. tchr. Elmwood Park (NJ) Sch. Dist., 2001—02, Bogota (NJ) Sch. Dist., 2002—; reading and math summer clinic Kean U., 2002—. Pvt. tutor, 2001—. Mem.: Coun. for Exceptional Children, Bogota Ednl. Assn., Kappa Delta Pi. Office: Lillian M Steen Sch W Main St Bogota NJ 07603 E-mail: alison785@aol.com.

ROGERS, AUDREY PATRICIA, social studies educator, consultant; d. William Green, Jr. and Ann Green; m. David Merrill Rogers, Aug. 12, 1989; children: Benjamin, Meryl. BA, Tufts U., Medford, Mass., 1988; MEd, U. Mass., Lowell, 1989; MA, U. N.H., Durham, 1997. Social Studies Tchr., 5-12 N.H. Bd. Edn., 1989. Ednl. cons. Rogers Enterprises, Merrimack, NH, 2001—; social studies tchr. Nashua HS, NH, 1989—2001. Pres. N.H. Coun. for Social Studies, Concord, 2004—. Author: (book) Cooperative Learning Basics, 1995, Trail of Tears, 2005, Rosa Parks and Montgomery Bus Boycott, 2004, Chinese Exclusion Act, 2004. Recipient Social Studies Tchr. of Yr.

ROGERS, CAROL ROSENSTEIN, social worker, educator; b. N.Y.C., Apr. 25, 1947; d. Herman R. and Shirley Rosenstein; m. Martin M. Rogers, Aug. 10, 1969; children: Eric J., Beth S. BA cum laude, SUNY, Albany, 1969; EdM, Boston U., 1970, MSW, 1995. LCSW Mass.; permanent cert. tchr. secondary French N.Y., cert. tchr. secondary French and Spanish Mass. Tchr. French and Spanish grades 7-12 Town of Chelmsford (Mass.) Pub. Schs., 1970—81; educator, counselor for infertility and adoption Resolve Inc., Somerville, 1982—86; adoption educator Bedford, 1982—; adoption social worker Concord Family and Adolescent Svcs., Acton, 1997—2000; sch. social worker City of Newton (Mass.) Pub. Schs., 1997—2000; pvt. practice clin. social worker Burlington, 2002—. Mem. Archway interdisciplinary adoption study group; developer, implementor adoption tng. Mass. Gen. Hosp., Boston, Harvard U., Mass. pub. schs.; presenter confs. Com. mem. Bedford Parent-Tchr. Assn., Bedford, Mass., 1987—91; pub. spkr. LWV, Bedford, 1999; bd. dir. Temple Isaiah Sisterhood, Lexington, 1990—92, Open Door Soc./Adoption Cmty. of New Eng., Holliston, Mass., 2000—01. Mem.: NASW, Pi Delta Phi. Avocations: women's causes, travel, cooking, reading, gardening. Home: 47 Glenridge Dr Bedford MA 01730 Office: 1 Garfield Cir Burlington MA 01803 Office Phone: 617-529-4495. Personal E-mail: carol_rogers@comcast.net.

ROGERS, CATHERINE ALICE, obstetrician, gynecologist; b. Highland Falls, NY, Feb. 17, 1967; d. Gordon Byram Rogers and Nenette ter Bush Finley; m. David Scott Fuhrmann, Oct. 8, 2000; 1 child, Stuart Finley Fuhrmann. BA in Internat. Rels., Stanford U., 1989; MD, U. N.Mex., 1995. Diplomate Am. Bd. Ob-Gyn. Resident in ob-gyn. U. N.Mex. Health Svcs. Ctr., Albuquerque, 1996—99; physician, owner Sound Women's Care, Edmonds, Wash., 1999—. Mem.: ACOG, Wash. State Obstet. Assn., Wash. State Med. Assn., Seattle Gyn. Soc. Office: Sound Women's Care 21616 7th Ave W Ste 205 Edmonds WA 98026 Office Phone: 425-640-4810.

ROGERS, CHERYL ANN, speech pathology services professional; b. Schenectady, N.Y., July 8, 1948; d. George Michael Rogers and Viola Mary Santore. BS Speech and Language Pathology, State Univ. N.Y., Buffalo, N.Y., 1970; MA Speech and Language Pathology, Univ. Buffalo, Buffalo, N.Y., 1972. Lic. CCC/Sp N.Y., cert. tchr. of speech/hearing handicapped. Speech lang. pathologist Aspire, Buffalo, 1971—. Clin. adj. lectr. Univ. Buffalo, 1975—; lectr. Medaille Coll., 1975—; instr. BOCES Region #1, 1980—85. Prof. adv. bd. Hospice, Buffalo, 1980; vol. Luth. Ch. Home; eucharistic min.; pres. union UCPEU Local 3721, Buffalo, 1991—96; co-founder Dignity Buffalo, 1986. Mem.: Amnesty Internat. Human Rights Campaign, Am. Speech Hearing Lang. Assn., Kappa Delta Pi. Democrat. Roman Cath. Avocations: Reiki Level II hypnotherapy, painting, writing. Home: 44 Manchester Pl Buffalo NY 14213 Office: Aspire of NY 4632 Union Rd Cheektowaga NY 14225

ROGERS, COLETTE, counseling administrator; d. Sherzol and Dorothy Heater; m. Quint Rogers, Sept. 24, 2005; children: Michael Todd Johnson, Brittany Beth Johnson, Ryan Ty Johnson. BS, Tex.A&M U., 1978; MS, Tex. A&I U., 1985. Cert. guidance & counseling Tex. Edn. Agy., 1985. Health and phys. edn. instr. Freer ISD, Tex., 1978—79, counselor/tchr., 1981—90; health and phys. edn. instr. Aransas Pass HS, Tex., 1979—80; elem. PE tchr. Klein ISD, Houston, 1980—81; guidance dir. St.Joseph Acad., Brownsville, Tex., 1990—93; counselor/dept. chair counseling So. Tex HS for Health Professions, Mercedes, 1993—. Spkr. in field. Avocations: reading, decorating, writing. Office: S Tex HS for Health Professions 700 Med High Dr Mercedes TX 78570 Office Phone: 956-565-2454. Office Fax: 956-565-4039. Business E-Mail: colette.johnson@stisd.net.

ROGERS, ELAINE P., art educator; d. Henry Moore Rogers Jr. and Carolyn Kavanaugh Rogers; m. Brendan Timothy Hayes, Sept. 29, 1984; children: Austin Rogers Hayes, Stephen Pearce Hayes. BA, U. Richmond, 1980; BFA, Va. Commonwealth U., 1982; MA, U. Wis., 1983, MFA, 1984. Asst. coord. Art Gallery-Artist Run, Richmond, Va., 1986—87; instr. art St. Catherine's Sch., 1986, Henrico County Pub. Schs., 1988; faculty Upper Sch. Art Collegiate Sch., 1989—98; adj. asst. prof. art and art history U. Richmond, 2001—. Vis. asst. prof. U. Va., Charlottesville, 1987; adj. faculty art J. Sgt. Reynolds C.C., Richmond, 1985—88, Va. Commonwealth U., 1988—89, Va. Mus. Fine Arts, 1988—93; artist mem., emeritus 1708 East Main Gallery, 1985—. One-woman shows include Marsh Gallery, Richmond, 1985, Ea. Va. Med. Sch., Norfolk, 1985, 1708 East Main Gallery, 1986, Mentor Gallery, Charlottesville, 1990, Clark Pollock Gallery, 1991, Artspace, Richmond, 1995, Main Art Gallery, 1995, Collegiate Sch., 1999, Artspace at Plant Zero, 2004, exhibited in group shows at Marsh Gallery, 1983, Ctr. Gallery, Madison, Wis., 1984, Allen Priebe Gallery, Oshkosh, Wis., 1984, Madison Art Ctr., 1984, Sweet Briar Coll., Va., 1988, Anton Gallery, Washington, 1986, Fayerweather Gallery, Charlottesville, 1987, Richmond Internat. Airport, 1988, Peninsula Fine Arts Ctr., Newport News, Va., 1990, MCV Hosps. Galleries, Richmond, 1991, Va. Mus. Fine Art, 1992, Art at Powerhouse Gallery, Cleve., 1994, 1708 Gallery, Richmond, 1995, 1708 Underground Gallery, 1996, Coinicidence Gallery, 1997, Les Yeux du Monde, Charlottesville, 2000, 1708 Gallery, 2001, 2002, 2003, 2005, The Cultural Arts Ctr., Glen Allen, Va., 2004, Faculty Exhbn., U. Richmond, 2005, 2006, Art Space, 2005, numerous others. Fellow, U. Wis., Madison, 1983—84, Va. Mus. Fine Arts, 1988—89; grantee, U. Richmond, 1980. Avocations: walking, reading, bicycling, swimming. Personal E-mail: erogers@richmond.edu.

ROGERS, ELIZABETH (BETTY) CARLISLE, education educator, consultant; d. Charles Bunyan and Maggie Era (Little) Carlisle; children: Kellie Elizabeth, Sean Lewis. BS, U. Miss., 1972, MS, 1974; PhD, U. Ga., 1997. Chair divsn. sci. and math. Truett-McConnell Coll., Cleveland, Ga., 1974—84; chair dept. math. Lakeview Acad., Gainesville, Ga., 1984—89; prof. math. and edn. Piedmont Coll., Demorest, Ga., 1989—; prin. R&H Analytics, 2004—. Pres. BCR Inc., Gainesville, Ga., 1990—; ptnr. The Ednl. Solutions Task Force, Washington, 2000—. Author: (profl. book) A Study of Curriculum and Pedagogy, 1997; editor (contbg. author): Cooperative Learning In Undergraduate Mathematics, 2001; author: (textbook) Mathematics for Agriculture, 2000. Chair, ceremonies and events Spl. Olympics of Ga., 2001—04. Grantee Faculty Devel. in Ga., State of Ga., 1992—95; scholar Carrier Scholarship, Carrier Found.; Tchg. Fellow, U. of Miss., 1971—73. Mem.: Women in Math., Math. Assn. of Am., Alpha Delta Pi (Dorothy Shaw Leadership award), Alpha Lambda Delta (pres.), Kappa Delta Phi (pres.), Phi Kappa Phi. Achievements include research in advantages of coop. learning for undergraduate math. students; history of math. in Ctrl. and South Am. Home: 4733 Highland Rd Gainesville GA 30506 Office: Piedmont Coll Ctrl Ave Demorest GA 30535 Office Phone: 770-287-4634. Personal E-mail: b.rogers@prodigy.net. E-mail: brogers@piedmont.edu.

ROGERS, ELIZABETH LONDON, retired geriatrics services professional; MD, Jefferson Med. Sch., 1971. Lic. internal medicine, gastroenterology, and geriatrics Am. Bd. of Internal Medicine. Chief of staff Balt. VA Med. Ctr., 1982—93; prof. dept. of medicine U. of Md. Med. Sch., Baltimore, 1990—93; assoc. dean for clin. medicine Duke U. Med. Sch., Durham, NC, 1993—96; acting chief of staff VA Healthcare Sys., New Haven, 1996—2002; ret., 2002. Pres. Bradmer Biotech, Miami, 2002—05; dir. Cardiome Pharma, Vancouver, B.C., Canada, 2003—04. Recipient Geriat. scholarship, Hartford Found., 1984—85. Fellow: ACP.

ROGERS, EVA MARIE VANLEUVEN, artist, poet; b. Poughkeepsie, NY, May 27, 1958; d. Clyde Benjamin Van Leuven and Gloria Alice (Stanton) Myers and Wilton E. Myers; m. Bruce L. Rogers. Exhbns. include one-woman shows, Adorondack Ctr. for the Arts, Blue Mt. Lake, N.Y., Tinker Street Cafe; group shows include Woodstock Artists Assn., 1994, 95, Springfield Art League 75th Ann. Nat. Exhibit, Small Works '94/Catskill Art Soc., The Tonawanda Ann. Nat. Juried Show/Carnegie Art Ctr., N.Y., Art WYO'94/West Wind Gallery, Casper, Wyo., Baystreet Galleria Nat. Open, Balboa Island, Calif., Nat. Soc. of Artists, '95, Santa Fe, others; prodr. Woodstock pub. access TV. Recipient Fire and Rose award Artspirit Internat., Marlbourgoh, Mass., 1996, Spl. Recognition award Baystreet, Balboa Island, Calif., 1994, awards profl. divsn. Nat. Soc. of Artists, Santa Fe, Tex., numerous others. Mem. Woodstock Artists Assn., Catskill Art Soc. Personal E-mail: vision375@aol.com.

ROGERS, GAIL ELIZABETH, library director; b. Charlotte, N.C., May 6, 1947; d. James Yates and Marian Elizabeth (Church) Rogers. BA, Salem Coll., 1969; MLS, U. N.C., 1971. Cert. libr., Ga. Br. libr. Atlanta Pub. Libr., 1970-77; br. coord. Dekalb Libr. System, Decatur, Ga., 1977-82; asst. dir. West Ga. Regional Libr., Carrollton, 1982-83, Cobb County Pub. Libr., Marietta, Ga., 1983-90, dir., 1991—. Mem. Leadership Cobb, Cobb County, 1985-86. Mem. ALA, Ga. Libr. Assn. (2d v.p. 1987-89), Southeastern Libr. Assn. (v.p.-pres. elect. 1990-92, pres. 1992-94), Urban Librs. Coun., Kiwanis Club Marietta (bd. dirs. 1991-92, sec. 1992-93, sec.-treas. 1993-94, pres. 1995-96). Office: Cobb County Public Lib 266 Roswell St SE Marietta GA 30060-2005

ROGERS, GLENDA NELSON, writer, photographer; b. Greenville, N.C., Mar. 6, 1962; d. Luther Sullivan and Thelma Olivia (Joyner) Nelson; m. Theodore Courtney Jr. Rogers, July 30, 1983. BA in Psychology cum laude, So. Meth. U., 1984. Loaned exec., campaign coord. United Way, Fort Worth, Tex., 1985; human resources dept. MCorp, Fort Worth, 1985; investment counselor S.W. Savs., Dallas, 1985-88; br. mgr. S.W. Fed. Savs. Assoc., Dallas, 1988-90; pres. The Daily Grind, Inc., Plano, Tex., 1990-95; missionary, dir. receipting Global Missions Fellowship, Dallas, 1995-97; v.p. WISE Ministries, 1998—. Annuities cons. S.W. Savs., 1987-90; spkr. various fellowship groups. Active cmty. svc. East Dallas Asian Outreach, 1987-88. Mem. Soc. for Children's Book Writers and Illustrators, Kappa Delta Pi, Psi Chi. Evangelical. Avocations: dogs, travel, nature and wildlife studies, cultural studies. Office: WISE Ministries 1130 Tumbleweed Trail Kennesaw GA 30152 Home: 1130 Tumbleweed Trl Kennesaw GA 30152-5445

ROGERS, JEAN CLARK, writer; b. Wendell, Idaho, Oct. 1, 1919; d. John Harvey and Josie Maud (Powers) Clark; m. George William Rogers, Nov. 27, 1942; children: Shelley, Geoffrey, Sidney, Gavin (dec.), Sabrina, Garth. Teaching cert., Albion State Normal Sch., 1939; BA, U. Calif., Berkeley, 1943; LHD (hon.), U. Alaska, 2002. Author: (juvenile fiction) Good Bye My Island, 1983, King Island's Christmas, 1985, The Secret Moose, 1985 (Best Book of 1985, Children's Reading Coun.), Dinosaurs are 568, 1988 (Parent's Choice award 1990), Runaway Mittens, 1988, Raymond's Best Summer, 1990, Leftfield Bear, 1996. Mem., chmn. Alaska State Pub. Offices Commn., Juneau, 1982-87; mem., v.p. Alaska State Broadcasting Commn., Juneau, 1987-92; hon. lifetime mem. Bartlett Meml. Hosp. Guild, 1994—; mem. Friends of Libr., Juneau Hist. Soc., Friends of Mus., Juneau. Recipient Honored Author Citation, Alaska State Reading Assn., 1982, Golden Apple award for svc. to edn.,awarded Outstanding Ednl. Profl. Outside the Dist., 2004—. Delta Kappa Gamma, 1990. Mem. ALA, Alaska State Libr. Assn. (hon. lifetime mem. 1994), Soc. Children's Bookwriters and Illustrators. Avocations: reading, cooking, singing. Home: 1790 Evergreen Ave Juneau AK 99801-1422

ROGERS, JOANN VEDDER, library and information science educator; b. Pitts., July 28, 1940; d. Sanford Elihu and Helen (Gottbraith) Vedder; m. John C. Rogers, 1970 (div. 1974). B.A., Conn. Coll., 1962; M.L.S., Columbia U., 1967; Ph.D., U. Pitts., 1977. Cert. library media specialist, N.Y., secondary tchr., N.Y., Va. Prof. Coll. Library Info. Sci., U. Ky., Lexington, 1974. Author, editor: Libraries and Young Adults, 1979; author: Nonprint Cataloguing for Multimedia Collections, 1982, 2d edit., 1987. Contbr. articles to profl. jours. Ctr. for Devel. Change fellow, Lexington, 1978. Mem. ALA (council 1984-87), Assn. Library Info. Sci. Edn., AAUP (chpt. pres. 1987-88, 89-90), Beta Phi Mu. Home: 620 Seattle Dr Lexington KY 40503-2125

ROGERS, JUDITH ANN WILSON, federal judge; b. NYC, 1939; AB cum laude, Radcliffe Coll., 1961; LLB, Harvard U., 1964; LLM, U. Va., 1988; LLD (hon.), D.C. Sch. Law, 1992. Bar: D.C. 1965. Law clk. Juvenile Ct. D.C., 1964-65; asst. U.S. atty. D.C., 1965-68; trial atty. San Francisco Neighborhood Legal Assistance Found., 1968-69; atty. assoc. atty. gen.'s office U.S. Dept. Justice, 1969-71, atty. criminal divsn., 1969-71; gen. counsel Congl. Commn. on Organization of D.C. Govt., 1971-72; coordinator legis. program Office of Dep. Mayor D.C., 1972-74, spl. asst. to mayor for legis., 1974-79, corp. counsel, 1979-83; assoc. judge D.C. Ct. Appeals, 1983-88, chief judge, 1988-94; judge U.S. Ct. Appeals (D.C. cir.), 1994—. Mem. D.C. Law Revision Commn., 1979-83; mem. grievance com. U.S. Dist. Ct. D.C., 1982-83; mem. exec. com. Conf. Chief Justices, 1993-94. Bd. dirs. Wider Opportunities for Women, 1972-74; mem. vis. com. Harvard U. Sch. Law, 1984-90; trustee Radcliffe Coll., 1982-88. Recipient citation for work on D.C. Self-Govt. Act, 1973, Disting. Pub. Svc. award D.C. Govt., 1983, award Nat. Bar Assn., 1989; named Woman Lawyer of Yr., Women's Bar Assn. D.C., 1990. Fellow ABA; mem. D.C. Bar, Nat. Assn. Women Judges, Conf. Chief Justices (bd. dirs. 1988-94), Am. Law Inst., Phi Beta Kappa. Office: US Ct Appeals Fed Cir 717 Madison Pl NW Washington DC 20001-2866 also: US Courthouse 333 Constitution Ave NW STE 5800 Washington DC 20001*

ROGERS, KAAREN LEA, music educator; b. Estherville, Iowa, Oct. 12, 1963; d. Lawrence Michael Slifka and Mary Jeanette Mittag; 1 child, Jillian Faye Carstensen. BA, Buena Vista U., Storm Lake, Iowa, 1999. 6-12 grade vocal music dir., musical theater dir. Acta Cmty. Sch., Iowa, 1999—2006; vocal music dir. Gilbert HS, Iowa, 2006—. Dir. children's theater workshops NW Iowa; dir. Iowa All State Choir, All State Speech Festival. Mem.: Iowa Choral Dirs. Assn., Am. Choral Dirs. Assn. Avocations: musical theater, quilting.

ROGERS, KAREN BECKSTEAD, gifted studies educator, researcher, consultant; b. L.A., Nov. 28, 1943; d. Maurice Webster and Helen Dorothy (Nalty) Beckstead; m. William Geoffrey Rogers, Sept. 11, 1965; children: Jeanne Elizabeth Rogers Armstrong, Jennifer Lynn Rogers Hasbrouck, William Carey. BA in Humanities, U. Calif., Berkeley, 1965; MA in Spl. Edn., San Diego State U., 1969; MA in Ednl. Psychology, U. Minn., 1983, PhD in Curriculum and Instrn. Sys., 1991. Cert. elem. tchr., Calif. Coord. Pace project West Jr. Paul Schs., 1975—77; dir. Omnibus project Jr. League of Mpls., 1978—83; instr. U. Minn., Mpls., 1985—95; instr. gifted studies U. St. Thomas, Mpls., 1984—87, from asst. prof. gifted studies to prof., 1987—2004; prof. edn., rsch. dir. gerric U. NSW, Sydney, Australia, 2004—, dir. rsch. gerric, 2005—. Cons., Burnsville, Minn., 1978—. Author: Ability Grouping and Gifted Learners, 1991 (Early Scholar award, 1991), Talent Development in Context, 1998, Re-Forming Gifted Education, 2002; contbg. editor Roeper Rev., 1994—, contbg. reviewer Jour. Secondary Gifted Edn., 1994—, Jour. for the Edn. of the Gifted, 1994—, Gifted Edn. Internat., 1998—, Gifted Child Quarterly, 1997—; contbr. chapters to books, articles to profl. jours. Docent Mpls. Inst. Arts, 1975—. Recipient Lifetime Achievement award Minn. Coun. for Gifted and Talented, 1989. Mem. Coun. for Exceptional Children (pres. The Assn. for the Gifted 1994-96), Nat. Assn. for Gifted Children, Am. Ednl. Rsch. Assn. Democrat. Avocations: art collecting, art history, music appreciation, writing, reading. Home: 22 Las Fieras Rancho Santa Margarita CA 92688 Office: Univ New South Wales 2/23 Birriga Rd Sydney -2025 2052 Australia Office Phone: 61-2-9385-1944. Business E-Mail: k.rogers@unsw.edu.au.

ROGERS, KATHARINE MUNZER, retired English language educator, writer; b. NYC, June 6, 1932; d. Martin and Jean (Thompson) Munzer; B.A. summa cum laude, Barnard Coll., 1952; Fulbright scholar, Newnham Coll., Cambridge U., 1952-53; Ph.D., Columbia U., 1957; m. Kenneth C. Rogers, Aug. 4, 1956; children: Margaret, Christopher, Thomas. Instr. English, Skidmore Coll., Saratoga Springs, N.Y., 1954-55, Cornell U., 1955-57; lectr. to prof. English, Bklyn. Coll., 1958-88; mem. doctoral faculty CUNY, 1972-88. Author: The Troublesome Helpmate: A History of Misogyny in Literature, 1966; William Wycherley, 1972; Feminism in Eighteenth Century England, 1982; Frances Burney: The World of "Female Difficulties", 1990, The Cat and the Human Imagination, 1998, L. Frank Baum: Creator of Oz: A Biography, 2002, First Friend: A History of Dogs and Humans, 2005. Editor anthologies: The Signet Classic Book of 18th and 19th Century British Drama; Selected Writings of Samuel Johnson, 1981, The Meridian Anthology of Early American Women Writers, 1991, The Meridian Anthology of Restoration & Eighteenth Century Plays by Women, 1994; co-editor: (with William McCarthy) The Meridian Anthology of Early Women Writers: British Literary Women from Aphra Behn to Maria Edgeworth, 1987. Contbr. articles to profl. jours.

ROGERS, KATHIE ANNE, accountant; b. Patchogue, N.Y., Aug. 20, 1951; d. William Arthur and Rosemary Anne (Falvey) Rogers; m. James M. Castiglione, Sept. 27, 1969 (div.); children: James W. Castiglione, John S. Castiglione; m. Timothy L. Buckley, July 21, 2002. AAS, Suffolk C.C., Riverhead, N.Y., 1982; BBA, Dowling Coll., 1984; MST, L.I. U., 1990; DBA, Nova Southeastern U., 2000. CPA NY. Acct. Center Moriches Libr., 1983—; adj. asst. prof. Suffolk C.C., Riverhead, 1987-94; instr., lectr. L.I.U.-C.W. Post Campus, Brookville, NY, 1992-94; asst. prof., chair dept. St. Francis Coll., Brooklyn Heights, NY, 1994-2000; assoc. prof. Suffolk C.C., Riverhead, NY, 2000—. Mem.: AICPA, Am. Acctg. Assn. Avocation: fitness enthusiast. Office Phone: 631-548-3535. Business E-Mail: rogersk@sunysuffolk.edu.

ROGERS, LISA ANN, music educator; b. Easton, Pa., Aug. 19, 1961; d. Mortimer Fred and Shirley Marie Kuebler Rogers; life ptnr. Maureen R. Monczewski. BA in Music, Elizabethtown Coll., Pa., 1983; MS in Edn., Wilkes U., Wilkes Barre, Pa., 2004. Pa. Instrnl. II tchr. cert. State Pa. Dept. Edn., 1990. Orch. dir., strings tchr. Stroudsburg (Pa.) H.S., 1997—; music tchr. Franklin Twp. Elem. Sch., Quakertown, NJ, Wilson Area Mid. Sch., Easton, Holland Twp. Elem. Sch., Milford, NJ, Washington (N.J.) Borough Sch. Dist., Our Lady of Mt. Carmel Elem. Sch., Doylestown, Pa. String instr. Nazareth (Pa.) Music Ctr., 1995—; folk group dir. St. Joseph Roman Cath. Ch., Easton, 1984—2001. Mem.: NEA (assoc.), Pa. Music Educators Assn., Stroudsburg Area Edn. Assn. (assoc.), Pa. Edn. Assn. (assoc.), Music Educators Nat. Conf. (assoc.). Office: Stroudsburg High School 1100 West Main St Stroudsburg PA 18610 Office Phone: 570-421-1991. Office Fax: 570-424-1383. Business E-Mail: larogers@stroudsburg.k12.pa.us.

ROGERS, LORENE LANE, university president emeritus; b. Prosper, Tex., Apr. 3, 1914; d. Mort M. and Jessie L. (Luster) Lane; m. Burl Gordon Rogers, Aug. 23, 1935 (dec. June 14, 1941). BA, N. Tex. State Coll., 1934; MA (Parke, Davis fellow), U. Tex., 1946, PhD, 1948; DSc (hon.), Oakland U., 1972; LLD, Austin Coll., 1977. Prof. chemistry Sam Houston State Coll., Huntsville, Tex., 1947-49; research scientist Clayton Found. Biochem. Inst. U. Tex., Austin, 1950-64, asst. dir., 1957-64, prof. nutrition, 1962-80, assoc. dean Grad. Sch., 1964-71, v.p. univ., 1971-74, pres., 1974-79, mem. exec. com. African grad. fellowship program, 1966-71; research cons. Clayton Found. for Research, Houston, 1979-81. Vis. scientist, lectr., cons. NSF, 1959-62; cons. S.W. Research Inst., San Antonio, 1959-62; mem. Grad. Record Exams Bd., 1972-76, chmn., 1974-75; adv. com. ITT Internat. Fellowship, 1973-83; dir. Texaco, Inc., Gulf States Utilities, Republic Bank, Austin. Bd. dirs. Tex. Opera Theatre, Austin Lyric Opera; chmn. bd. trustees Texaco Philanthropic Found.; chmn. council of presidents Nat. Assn. State Univs. and Land-Grant Colls., 1976-77, mem. exec. com., 1976-79; mem. com. on identification of profl. women Am. Council on Edn., 1975-79, mem. com. on govt. relations, 1978-79; mem. target 2000 project com. Tex. A&M U. System; mem. ednl. adv. bd. John E. Gray Inst., Lamar U., Beaumont, Tex. Eli Lilly fellow, 1949-50; Recipient U. Tex. Students Assn. Teaching Excellence award, 1963; Disting. Alumnus award N. Tex. State U., 1972; Outstanding Woman of Austin award, 1950, 60, 71, 80; Disting. Alumnus award U. Tex., 1976; Honor Scroll award Tex. Inst. Chemists, 1980 Fellow Am. Inst. Chemists; mem. AAAS, Am. Chem. Soc. (sec. 1954-56), Am. Inst. Nutrition, Am. Soc. Human Genetics, Nat. Soc. Arts and Letters, Assn. Grad. Schs. (internat. edn. com. 1967-71), Sigma Xi, Phi Kappa Phi, Iota Sigma Pi, Omicron Delta Kappa. Achievements include research in hydantoin synthesis, intermediary metabolism, biochem. nutritional aspects of alcoholism, mental retardation, congenital malformations. Home: 4409 Gaines Ranch Loop Apt 211 Austin TX 78735-6523

ROGERS, LYNNE CARY, artist, painter; b. Hampton, Va., Jan. 2, 1953; d. John Grayson and Virginia Sledd Rogers. At, Longwood Coll., Farmville, Va., 1971—72; BFA in Sculpture, Va. Commonwealth U., Richmond, 1976. Owner Lynne Cary Creations, Cape Charles, 1985—90; restoration artist and designer Sommerset Hunterdon Stream Navigation, Inc., East Millstone, NJ, 1990—92; owner Zane Carrot Prodns., Wachapreague, Va., 1992—. Extended substitute tchr. art Northampton Mid. Sch., Machipongo, Va., 1988; theatre mgr. asst. Odd Duck Studio, Seattle, 1999—2000; video prodn. asst. Imago, Seattle, 2000. Exhibitions include Town Tavern, Port Townsend, Wash., 1977, 1980, Town Café, 1978, Towards a New Mythology, 1980, Stanley Gallery, Norfolk, Va., 1986, Palmer-Rae Gallery, Va. Beach, 1986, Va. Mus. Fine Arts, Richmond, 1987, Chrysler Mus., Norfolk, Va., 1987, Peninsula Fine Arts Ctr., Newport News, 1988, Riverrun Gallery, Lambertville, N.J., 1993, Trilogy Gallery, Salisbury, Md., 1995, ESO Art Ctr., Belle Haven, Va., 1997—98, Fountain Café, Port Townsend, Wash., 2000, Café Rosso, Norfolk, Va., 2002—, featured in, An Illustrated Survey of American Artist Leading Contemporaries by Les Krantz, 1990, My Place in the Sun BBC travel series, 2004; flutist and vocalist: music groups The Myrtles, Urban Folk. Mem. and advocate Richmond Living Wage Coalition, 2001; chair art com. Ea. Shore Tourism Commn., Melfa, Va., 2006—. Democrat. Avocations: yoga, foreign films. Home: PO Box 11 Wachapreague VA 23480 Studio: 31176 Bunting Port Rd Wachapreague VA 23480 Office Phone: 757-787-3243. Business E-Mail: zanecarrot@yahoo.com.

ROGERS, MARGARET ELLEN JONSSON, civic worker; b. Dallas, Aug. 7, 1938; d. John Erik and Margaret Elizabeth (Fonde) Jonsson; m. Robert D. Rogers; children: Emily, Erik, Laura. Student, Skidmore Coll., 1956—57, So. Meth. U., 1957—60. Civic worker, Dallas. Dir. Sta. KRLD radio, Dallas, 1970-74; dir. 1st Nat. Bank, Dallas, 1976-85, vice-chmn. dirs. trust com.; trustee Meth. Hosps., 1972-82, mem. exec. com., 1977-82, corp. bd. mem., 1990-94, mem. fin. com., 1990-93; bd. dirs. Lamplighter Sch., 1967—; past mem. vis. com. dept. psychology MIT; mem. vis. com. Stanford U. Librs., 1984-90; bd. dirs. Callier Ctr. Communication Disorders, 1967-90, Winston Sch., 1973-85; bd. dirs., mem. exec. com. Episc. Sch., 1976-83; chmn. Crystal Charity Ball; co-chmn. nat. major gifts com. Stanford Centennial Campaign; bd. dirs. Children's Med. Ctr., Hope Cottage Childrens' Bur., Baylor Dental Sch., Dallas Health and Sci. Mus., Dallas YWCA, Day Nursery Assn.; mem. devel. bd. U. Tex., Dallas, 1988-90; bd. govs. The Dallas Found., 1988-95, chmn. investment com. 1991-92; trustee So. Meth. U., mem. investment com., 1988—, chmn. investment com., 1992-99; mem. vis. com. Dedman Coll., 1989-90; life trustee Dallas Mus. Art, mem. investment com.; mem. collectors com. Nat. Gallery Art; bd. dirs. Dallas Arboretum, 1991-92; trustee, mem. fin. com. Monterey Bay Aquarium, 1995—, chair devel. com., 1995-2000, mem. fin. com., 2000—. Mem. internat. coun. Mus. Modern Art; pres. MJR Fund, Jonsson Found. Margaret Jonsson Charlton Hosp. of Dallas named in her honor, 1973. Mem.: The Lamplighter Sch. (life).

ROGERS, MEGAN ELIZABETH, mental health therapist; b. Bradford, Pa. d. James Russell and Martha Ann (Spencer) R.; m. Thomas J. Sarac, Oct. 17, 1992; children: Issac W. Sarac, Rhianna A. Sarac. BA in Psychology with deptl. honors., Coll. of Wooster, 1985; MA in Psychology, U. Chgo., 1991; D in Clin. Psychology, Minn. Sch. Profl. Psychology, 2001. Social worker Selfhelp Cmty. Svcs., N.Y.C., 1985-87; tchg. asst. U. Chgo., 1988-89; rsch. asst. U. Chgo. Hosp., 1988-90; mental health therapist Counseling and Personal Devel., Phillips, Wis., 1991-94; intern in clin. psychology Battle Creek VA Med. Ctr., 1998-99; prof. psychology Inver Hills C.C., Minn., 2001—02, Centery C. C., Minn., 2002—. Contbr. articles to profl. jours. Coord. soup and bread program, Wooster, 1982-85. U. Chgo. fellow, 1989. Mem. APA, Phi Beta Kappa. Democrat. Presbyterian. Home: 3401 Glen Oaks Ave White Bear Lake MN 55110 E-mail: megan.rogers@century.edu.

ROGERS, MIMI, actress; b. Coral Gables, Fla., Jan. 27, 1956; m. Jim Rogers, 1977 (div. 1980); m. Tom Cruise, May 9, 1987 (div. 1990); m. Chris Ciaffa, Mar. 20, 2003; children: Lucy Julia, Charlie. Appeared in films Blue Skies Again, 1983, Gung Ho, 1985, Someone to Watch over Me, 1987, Street Smart, 1987, Hider in the House, 1989, The Mighty Quinn, 1989, Desperate Hours, 1990, The Palermo Connections, 1990, The Doors, 1991, The Rapture, 1991, Dark Horse, 1992, The Player, 1992, Monkey Trouble, 1994, Far From Home: The Adventures of Yellow Dog, 1995, Lost in Space, 1998, Austin Powers: International Man of Mystery, 1997, Seven Girlfriends, 1999, Ginger Snaps, 2000, The Upgrade, 2000, Dumb and Dumberer: When Harry Met Lloyd, 2003, Seeing Other People, 2004, The Gunman, 2004, The Door in the Floor, 2004, Dancing in Twilight, 2005, others; appeared on TV series The Rousters, 1983-84, Paper Dolls, 1984, The Geena Davis Show, 2000, The Loop, 2006-; appeared on TV spls. and pilots; TV movies include Divorce Wars, 1982, Deadlock, 1991, Fourth Story, 1991, Ladykiller, 1992, A Kiss to Die For, 1993, Tricks, 1997, The Christmas List, 1997, Weapons of Mass Distraction, 1997, Virtual Obsession, 1998, Host, 1998, Devil's Arithmetic, 1999, Manchester Prep, 1999, Common Ground, 2000, My Horrible Year!, 2001, Reel Comedy: Austin Powers in Goldmember, 2002, Charms for the Easy Life, 2002, Cave In, 2003, Stone Cold, 2005, Selling Innocence, 2005. Office: Creative Artists Agy c/o Jane Berliner 9830 Wilshire Blvd Beverly Hills CA 90212-1825*

ROGERS, NANCY HARDIN, dean, law educator; b. Lansing, Mich., Sept. 18, 1948; d. Clifford Morris and Martha (Wood) Hardin; m. Douglas Langston Rogers, Jan. 30, 1970; children: Lynne, Jill, Kim. BA with highest distinction, U. Kans., 1969; JD, Yale U., 1972. Bar: D.C. 1975, Ohio 1972, U.S. Ct. Appeals (6th cir.) 1973, U.S. Dist. Ct. (no. dist.) Ohio 1974, U.S. Dist. Ct. (so. dist.) Ohio 1975. Law clk. U.S. Dist. Judge Thomas D. Lambros, Cleve., 1972-74; staff atty. Cleve. Legal Aid Soc., 1974-75; vis. asst. prof. Coll. of Law Ohio State U., Columbus, 1975-76, asst. prof., 1976-78, 83-89, assoc. prof., 1989-92, prof., assoc. dean acad. affairs, 1992-97, prof., 1992—, Joseph S. Platt, Porter, Wright, Morris & Arthur prof. law Columbus, 1995—2001, vice provost acad. adminstrn., 1999—2001, dean, Michael E. Moritz chair in alternative dispute resolution Michael E. Moritz Coll. Law, 2001—. Adj. prof. Ohio State Coll., 1981-83; vis. prof. law Harvard Law Sch., 2000. Author (with Frank E.A. Sander, Sarah R. Cole, Stephen B. Goldberg): (Book) Dispute Resolution: Negotiation, Mediation and Other Processes), 2003; author: (book with Craig A. McEwen and Sarah R. Cole) Mediation: Law, Policy, Practice, 2nd edit., 1994; mem. (adv. bd.) World Arbitration and Mediation Report, 1991—, Alternatives, 1992—, co-chair (editl. bd. with Frank E.A. Sander) Dispute Resolution mag., 1994—2002; contbr. chapters to books, articles to profl. jours. Bd. dirs. Assn. for Developmentally Disabled, Columbus, 1980-85; Legal Svcs. Corp. 1995-2003. Named Outstanding Prof., Ohio State U. Coll. Law Alumni Assn., 1996; recipient Book prize, Ctr. Pub. Resources for A Student's Guide to Mediation and the Law, 1987, Ctr. Pub. Resources for Mediation: Law, Policy, Practice, 1989, Peacemaker of Yr. award, Cmty. Mediation Svcs. Ctrl. Ohio, 1990, Disting. Svc. Recognition, Soc. Profls. in Dispute Resolution, 1990, Whitney North Seymour sr. medal, Am. Arbitration Assn., 1990, Svc. Recognition award, Legal Aid Soc. Columbus, 1996, Ritter award, Ohio State Bar Found for outstanding contbns. to adminstrn. of justice, 1998; grantee Exxon Edn. Found., 1986, William and Flora Hewlett Found., 1990, Ohio State U. Interdisciplinary Seed, 1990, Ohio State U. Symposium, 1992, William and Flora Hewlett Found., 1992—96, Nat. Sci. Found., 1993—95, State Justice Instn., 1994, Fund for Improvement Post-Secondary Edn., U. Mo., 1996—97, William and Flora Hewlett Found., 1997—2003. Mem. ABA (chair, standing com. dispute resolution 1988-91, D'Alemberte-Raven award sect. on dispute resolution 2002), Assn. Am. Law Schs. (pres.-elect 2006—), Phi Beta Kappa. Office: Ohio State U Coll Law 55 W 12th Ave Columbus OH 43210-1306 Office Phone: 614-292-0574. Business E-Mail: rogers.23@osu.edu.

ROGERS, NATALIE, psychologist; b. Rochester, N.Y., Oct. 9, 1928; d. Carl Ransom and Helen (Elliott) R.; m. Lawrence Howard Fuchs, June 5, 1950 (div. Oct. 1970); children: Janet Pearl, Frances Sarah, Naomi Ruth. AA, Stephens Coll., Columbia, Mo., 1946; BA, DePauw U., Greencastle, Ind., 1948; MA, Brandeis U., Waltham, Mass., 1960. Lic. psychologist, Mass. Psychologist Counseling Ctr., U. Hawaii, Honolulu, 1965-66, Cambridge (Mass.) Guidance Ctr., 1964-65, Children's Hosp., Boston, 1967-68, North Shore Family Therapy Inst., Boston, 1970-71, Coll. Mental Health Ctr., Brookline, Mass., 1970-71; pvt. practice, Santa Rosa, Calif., 1974—. Workshop facilitator, Europe, Latin Am., Japan, USSR, 1975—; founder, dir. The Person Centered Expressive Therapy Inst., Santa Rosa, 1984—. Author: Emerging Woman: A Decade of Midlife Transitions, 1980; contbr. articles to profl. jours. Bd. dirs. Resources for Creativity and Consciousness, Santa Rosa. Radcliffe scholar Bunting Inst., Cambridge, 1966-67. Mem. APA, Assn. Humanistic Psychology (bd. dirs.), Assn. Transpersonal Psychology. Democrat. Avocations: sculpting, painting, dance, gardening, photography. Home and Office: 171 Nelson Way Santa Rosa CA 95404

ROGERS, OLIVIA JOHNSON, elementary school counselor; b. Hays, Kans., Nov. 23, 1947; d. Norman Bruce and La Rene (Miller) Johnson; m. John E. Rogers, Mar. 23, 1991. BS in Edn., Emporia State U., 1971; MS in Edn., Kans. State U., 1976; EdS in Counseling, Wichita State U., 1990. Lic. profl. counselor; nat. cert. counselor. Elem. sch. tchr. Topeka Pub. Schs., 1972-82; spl. edn. tchr. Wichita Pub. Schs., 1982-87, elem. sch. counselor, 1987-91; counselor Diabetes Ctr. at St. Joseph-Via Christi Med. Ctr., Wichita, 1987-91; counselor, clinician CPC Gt. Plains Hosp., Wichita, 1987-91; elem. sch. counselor Salina (Kans.) Pub. Schs., 1991—. Counselor, Child Abuse Prevention Svcs., Salina, 1997—, Rogers Counseling Svcs., Salina, 1997—. Ednl. cons. Topeka Girls Club, 1980-81. Mem. Am. Counseling Assn., Am. Sch. Counselor Assn., Kans. Sch. Counselor Assn., Kans. Mental Health Assn.

ROGERS, PATRICIA LOUISE, education educator, consultant; b. St. Paul, 1956; life ptnr. W. S. Larson. BS, U. Minn., Twin Cities, 1979, MA, 1982, PhD, 1997. Lic. tchr. art and theatre Minn., 1979. Tchr. St. Paul Schs., 1979—82; cancer rschr. U. Minn. Sch. Pub. Health, Mpls., 1984—95; prof. Bemidji State U., Minn., 1996—2006; dean Sch. Edn. and Grad. Studies Valley City State U., ND, 2006—. Cons. and trainer for online tchg. Minn. State Colls. and Univs., Twin Cities, cons., 1998—; spkr. in field. Editor: (book) Designing Instruction for Technology-Enhanced Learning, Ency. of Distance Learning, Teaching, Technologies and Applications; contbr. articles to profl. jours. Vice chair Minn. Online Coun., 2003—04, chair, 2004—. Grantee, Minn. State Colls. and Univs. under a FIPSE Grant, 2001—02; scholar, Fulbright, Coun. for Internat. Exch. Scholars, 2000—01; Dissertation fellow, Getty Ctr. for Arts in Edn., 1996. Mem.: Nat. Art Edn. Assn., Assn. for Ednl. Comm. and Tech., Rotary Internat. (assoc.). Dfl. Office: Valley City State Univ Sch Edn and Grad Studies 101 College St SW Valley City ND 58072 Office Phone: 701-845-7300. Business E-Mail: patricia.rogers@vcsu.edu.

ROGERS, PJ, artist; b. Rochester, NY, June 13, 1935; d. Frederick John Pfluke and Louise Elizabeth Goldsmith; children: Sarah Jeanne, Susan Rogers-Swaney. BA, Wells Coll., Aurora, NY, 1947. Art preparator Buffalo Mus. Sci., NY, instr. painting NY; SP instr. U. Akron, Akron, Ohio. One-woman shows include Harris-Stanton Gallery, Ohio, 2001, 2004, exhibitions include over 100 intenat. and nat., Represented in permanent collections. Mem. Hosp. Bd., Buffalo. Mem.: Soc. Am. Graphic Artists, Boston Print Makers. Avocations: tennis, reading, exercise. Business E-Mail: proger2@neo.rr.com.

ROGERS, RITA RUTH, psychiatrist, political scientist; b. Radauti, Romania, July 30, 1925; arrived in U.S., 1953; d. Schaje and Helen Stenzler; m. G. Allen Rogers (dec.); children: David, Judith, Sheila. Candidate in medicine, Charles U., Prague, 1948; MD, U. Vienna, 1953; M of Polit. Sci., UCLA, 1970. Lic. Calif. State Bd. Med. Examiners, 1960, Mich. State Bd. Med. Examiners, 1960, diplomate Am. Bd. Psychiatry and Neurology, Am. Bd. Child Psychiatry. Founder, chief divsn. child and adolescent psychiatry Harbor-UCLA Med. Sch., Torrance, 1962—85. Lectr. in field; disting. clin. prof. dept. psychiatry UCLA, 2005. Contbr. numerous articles to profl. jours.; co-author: (autobiography) The Alchemy of Survival, 1988. Recipient Gold medal, World Assn. Dynamic Psychiatry, 1990; grantee NIMH, L.A. County Harbor-UCLA Med. Ctr. Fellow: Am. Acad. Child Psychiatry, Am. Coll. Psychiatrists (life), Am. Psychiat. Assn. (life; trustee-at-large 1979—82, disting.); mem.: World Assn. Med. Law (founding), South Bay Psychiat. Soc., So. Calif. Psychiat. Soc. (pres. 1994—97). Address: 2316 Via Pinale Palos Verdes Estates CA 90274 Office Phone: 310-376-5801.

ROGERS, RUTH FRANCES, retired microbiologist; b. Chgo., Nov. 5, 1925; d. Frank Joseph and Ruth Elizabeth (Abbott) Kucera; m. James Alvin Rogers, June 17, 1950; children: Kenneth James, David Wayne. BS, U. Ill., 1948. Microbiologist No. Rsch. Ctr., Nat. Ctr. for Agrl. Utilization Rsch., Peoria, Ill., 1963—85; ret., 1985. Contbr. articles to profl. jours. Recipient Sustained Superior Performance award USDA, 1984. Methodist.

ROGERS, SHARON, art educator; b. Detroit, May 6, 1950; d. William Farland and Helen Jane Lowe; m. Bruce M. Rogers, June 6, 1972; 1 child, Katherine Marie. BA, N. Tex. State U., 1972; MA, So. Meth. U., 1982. Art tchr. Slaughter Jr. High, McKinney, Tex., 1975-76; advance placement art history and portfolio art instr. Lakeview Centennial H.S., Garland, Tex., 1977-78, head fine arts dept., 1978—2001; advance placement portfolio art instr. Naaman Forest H.S., Garland, 2002—. Asst. girls' soccer coach Lakeview Centennial H.S., 1999—2001. Adult Sunday Sch. tchr. St. Philip's United Meth. Ch., Garland, 1980—, vol. family ministries, 1990-99 Mem. Assn. Tchrs. Profl. Edn., Nat. Art Edn. Assn., Garland Tchr.'s Orgn. Avocations: drawing, painting. Office: Naaman Forest HS 4834 Naaman Forest Blvd Garland TX 75040 Home: 1609 Fairway Cir Garland TX 75043-1122

ROGERS, SHARON J., education consultant; b. Grantsburg, Wis., Sept. 24, 1941; d. Clifford M and Dorothy L (Beckman) Dickau; m. Evan D Rogers, June 15, 1962 (div. Dec. 1980); m. Joseph Y. Ruth, Dec. 22, 2003. BA summa cum laude, Bethel Coll., St. Paul, 1963; MA in Libr. Sci., U. Minn., 1967; PhD in Sociology, Wash. State U., Pullman, 1976. Lectr., instr. Alfred (N.Y.) U., 1972-76; assoc. prof. U. Toledo, 1977-80; assoc. dean Bowling Green (Ohio) State U. Librs., 1980-84; univ. libr. George Washington U., Washington, 1984-92, asst. v.p. acad. affairs, 1989-92, assoc. v.p. acad. affairs, 1992-97, co-dir. Univ. Teaching Ctr., 1990-97; cons. in higher edn. and librs., 1997—. Mem Online Computer Library Ctr Users Coun, 1985—92; pres. Online Computer Library Ctr Users Coun., 1989—90, rsch. advt. com., 1990—92; trustee Online Computer Library Ctr., 1992—2002; exec dir Assn Libr. and Info. Sci. Edn., 1997—2000. Contbr. articles to profl jours. Bd dirs CapAccess, 1993—97, treas, 1993—95; bd dirs ACLU, Toledo, 1978—84. Fellow Jackson, Univ Minn, 1964—65; grantee NSF, Wash State Univ, 1969—72. Mem.: ALA (exec coun 1987—91, pub comt 1989—93, chair 1990—93), Universal Serials and Book Exchange (bd dirs, treas 1987), Washington Research Library Consortium (bd dirs 1987—90), Am Sociological Asn, Asn Col and Research Libraries (pres 1984—85). Home: 2922 24th St N Arlington VA 22207 E-mail: sjdrr@verizon.net.

ROGERS, SHERRY ANNE, physician; b. Syracuse, NY, Apr. 15, 1943; d. Rodney Wellington and Jayne Hammond; m. Robert Hamilton Rogers, June 30, 1970. BA, Syracuse U., 1969; MD, SUNY, 1969-70. Diplomate Am. Bd. Family Practice, 1973, Am. Bd. Environ. Medicine, 1985. Intern Health Scis. Ctr. Syracuse, 1969-70; pvt. practice pediat., Auburn, NY, 1970-71; emergency physician Cmty. Gen. Hosp., Syracuse, NY, 1971-72; pvt. practice family medicine, Syracuse, 1972-85; pvt. practice environ. medicine, 1978—. Lectr. in field. Author: (books) Total Health, 1989, Tired or Toxic?, 1990, Wellness Against All Odds, 1994, Chemical Sensitivity, 1995, You Are What You Ate, The E.I. Syndrome, 1997, Depression Cured At Last, 1997, Alternative and Complementary Veterinary Medicine, 1998, No More Heartburn, 2000, The Cure is in the Kitchen, The Scientific Basis of Environmental Medicine Techniques, 2000, Pain Free in 6 Weeks, 2001, Detoxify or Die, 2003, The High Blood Pressure Hoax, 2005, Total Wellness, 2006; editor: Internal Medical World Report, 1992—93; contbr. articles to profl. jours., chapters to books Molds & Mycotoxins, Arch. Environ. Health, others. Fellow: Am. Coll. Nutrition, Am. Coll. Asthma, Allergy and Immunology. Office: Northeast Center Environmental Medicine PO Box 2716 Syracuse NY 13220-2716 Office Phone: 800-846-6687, 315-488-2856.

ROGERS, SUZANNE C., actress; d. Grant Christian Crumpler and Edna Mary Allen. Diploma, Christine Parks Sch. Dance, Petersburg, Va., 1957, Marion Mease Sch. Dance, Richmond, 1961, Stella Adler Drama Sch., N.Y.C., 1963. Rockette Radio City Music Hall, 1961—63. Performer: (Broadway plays) CoCo, Music Man, 110 In The Shade, Funny Girl, Halleliah Baby & Follies; actor: (TV series) Days Of Our Lives, 1973—. Recipient Best Actress, Daytime TV Mag. Annual Readers Poll, 1977, Best Supporting Actress Emmy, Days of Our Lives, 1979, Women in Film Living Legacy Humanitarian award, 2002. Home: 11266 Canton Dr Studio City CA 91604-4154

ROGERS, THOMASINA VENESE, federal commissioner; Student, Northwestern U.; JD, Columbia U. Chmn. Adminstrv. Conf. U.S., Washington, 1994-95; presdl. pers. staff The White House, Washington; dep. legal counsel, then legal counsel EEOC, Washington; mem. Occupl. Safety and Health Rev. Commn., Washington, 1998—, chmn., 1999—2002. Bd. dirs. Children's Nat. Med. Ctr. Mem. Am. Arbitration Assn. (bd. dirs.) Office: Occupl Safety and Health Review Commn One Lafayette Ctr 1120 20th St NW Washington DC 20036-3457

ROGERS, VIRGINIA MARIE BUXTON, industrial psychologist; b. Phila., May 18, 1952; d. Robert Stevens and Dorothy Louise (Miller) Buxton. BS, Pa. State U., 1974; MA, U. Md., 1977, PhD, 1979. 0pers. rsch. specialist BP Am., Cleve., 1979-81; rsch. cons. Pers. Decisions Rsch. Inst., Washington, 1978-79; staff tng. assoc. BP Am., Cleve., 1981-83, mgr. exec. assessment and devel., 1983-88, mgr. exec. tng. and devel., 1988-90, v.p. group tng., 1990-97; v.p. human resources Downstream Oil, 1997-99, Global Retail Mktg., 1999—2003; v.p. Weston Hemisphere HR Svcs., 2003—. Home: 1631 Treasure Oaks Dr Katy TX 77450-5088 Office: Weston Hemisphere HR Svcs 501 Westlake Park Blvd Houston TX 77079

ROGERS, WANDA FAYE, vocalist; b. Oct. 24, 1929; d. John Riley and Bessie Louise Narmore; m. Weldon Nelson Rogers Sr., Feb. 27, 1959 (div. 1967); 1 child, Weldon Nelson. Student, Modesto Jr. Coll. Lic. radio broadcast. Author: (song book) Wanda Faye Song Book, 2004; singer: (CD) UFO, recorded with Jewel Records, 1958-64, Germanys Bear Import Records, 1998, Columbia Records, 1965, The Sunset Westerners, Sta. KGFL, 1946—53, Sta. WBAP, Ft. Worth, Tex., 1954—57. Named to, Cowgirl Mus. Hall of Fame, 2002, Hall of Fame, Western Swing Soc., Sacramento, 2003. Avocations: music, writing songs. Office: PO Box 583372 Modesto CA 95350

ROGGE, RENA WOLCOTT, librarian; b. Bklyn., Nov. 3, 1920; d. Ralph Stratton and Mona Florence (Shannon) Wolcott; m. Carl Frederick Rogge Jr., Aug. 4, 1942; 1 son, Carl Frederick Rogge. B.A., Elmira Coll., 1941; M.L.S., Rutgers U., New Brunswick, N.J., 1966; M.A.L.S., New Sch. Social Research, N.Y.C., 1972, D. Info. Services, Nova Univ., 1987. Sec. Sch. Dist. South Orange, Maplewood, N.J., 1958-65; head reference librarian Cranford (N.J.) Pub. Library, 1966-68; readers' advisor Jersey City, 1968-69; reference librarian Newark State Coll., Union, N.J., 1969—; reference coordinator, asst. dir. for info. services Kean Coll. Library, sec. faculty senate, 1978-79, archivist faculty senate, 1979—, chmn. constn. revision, 1982—, grad. research com. 1983. Recipient Outstanding Pub. Employee award, State of N.J., 1972, merit Award, 1983; online research grantee, Kean Coll. N.J., 1979. Mem. N.J. Library Assn., Am. Soc. Indexers, N.J. State Coll. Librarians' Assn., Kean Coll. Fedn. Tchrs. (exec. com.). Club: Elmira Coll. Home: 27 Bodwell Ter Millburn NJ 07041-1201 Office: Kean Coll Nancy Thompson Library Morris Ave Union NJ 07083-7117

ROGGENSACK, PATIENCE DRAKE, state supreme court justice; b. Joliet, Ill., 1941; BA, Drake U., 1962; JD, U. Wis. Law Sch., 1980. Atty. Dewitt Ross and Stevens, 1980—96; judge Wis. Ct. of Appeals, 1996—2003; justice Wis. Supreme Ct., 2003—. Mem.: ABA, Wis. Bar Assn. Office: Wis Supreme Ct PO Box 1688 Madison WI 53701-1688

ROGILLIO, KATHY JUNE, musician, director, small business owner, educator; b. Baton Rouge, La., Nov. 4, 1950; d. David Hunter and Thelma Ruth (Tucker) R. MusB, La. State U., 1972, MusM, 1974. Organist Plains Presbyn. Ch., Zachary, La., 1963-73; teacher's aid Gifted/Talented East Baton Rouge Parish, Baton Rouge, La., 1974-75; staff accompanist La. State U., Baton Rouge, 1975-76; music enrichment tchr. Episcopal H.S., Baton Rouge, 1976-77; organist, choirmaster Grace Episcopal Ch., St. Francisville, La., 1977-82; piano-technician So. U., Baton Rouge, La., 1977-84; apprentice in piano rebuilding and concert tuning, 1978-81; music tchr., organist, choirmaster St. Patrick's Episcopal Day Sch. and Ch., Zachary, La., 1985-86; vis. organist, dir. Numerous Chs., La. and Miss., 1982—; piano rebuilder pvt. practice, Zachary, La., 1986—. Ind. contract work Santi Falcone, Falcone Piano Co., Haverhill, Mass., 1987-88, part time organist/choirmaster St. Patrick's Episcopal Ch., Zachary, La., 1999-2000; pvt. piano tchr. La. Sch. for Visually Impaired, 2000-04; recitalist, vis. organist.; music dir., organist Faith Presbyn. Ch., Baton Rouge, La., 2002-, aff. mem., 2004; guest organist First Bapt. Ch., Baker, La., 2003. Arranger: Piano-Trio Arrangement Brahms Intermezzo Opus 118, #2, 1986 (2d pl. Composer's Guild Farmington, Utah, 1986). Treas. Beulah Plains Cemetery Assn., Zachary, La., 1987; mem. Landowners for Equitable Flood Control, Zachary, La., 1994—; Dem. candidate for U.S. Ho. of Reps. from 6th Dist. La., 2000. Mem. Am. Guild Organists, Baton Rouge Musicians' Assn. (exec bd. 1990-92, v.p. 1992-94, pres. 1994-96), La. Endowment for the Humanities, La. Pub. Broadcasting, Order Ea. Star, Pi Kappa Lambda (profl. mus. hons. frat.). Democrat. Episcopalian. Avocations: needlework, cooking. Home and Office: Artist Pianos 18153 Barnett Rd Zachary LA 70791-8114 Office Phone: 225-654-8555. E-mail: k.rogillio@worldnet.att.net.

ROGOSKI, PATRICIA DIANA, corporate financial executive; b. Chgo., Dec. 29, 1939; d. Raymond Michael and Bernice Rose (Konkol) R. BS in Acctg. and Econs., Marquette U., 1961, postgrad., 1965-66, NYU, 1966-68, St. John's U., N.Y.C., 1975-76; cert. mgmt. acct., 1979. Sr. fin. analyst Blackhawk Mfg. Co., Milw., 1961-66; mgr., sr. analyst Shell Oil Co., N.Y.C., 1966-71; mgr. data processing Bradford Nat./Penn Bradford, Pitts., 1971-75; asst. mgr. fin. controls ITT, N.Y.C., 1975-79; v.p., comptr. ITT Consumer Fin. Corp., Mpls., 1979-80; sr. v.p. fin. ITT Fin. Corp., St. Louis, 1980-84; v.p., exec. asst., group exec. ITT Coins, Secaucus, NJ, 1984-85; pres. Patron S., Ltd., Wilmington, Del., 1986—; CFO, sr. v.p. Guardsmark, Inc., Memphis, 1989-94; sr. v.p. Peoplemark, Inc., Memphis, 1989-94. Bd. dirs. St. Louis Repertory Theater, 1983-84. Named to Acad. Women Achievers, YWCA, N.Y.C., 1980. Mem. Fin. Execs. Internat., Inst. Mgmt. Acctg., Econ. Club, Memphis Symphony Chorus. Avocation: duplicate bridge. Office: Patron S Ltd 2711 Centerville Rd Ste 400 Wilmington DE 19808-

ROGOWSKI, CHERYL, farmer; AS, Orange County CC, 1981; BS, Mount St. Mary Coll., 1984. Farm mgr., 1977—. Founder Warwick Valley Farmer's Market, 1993; mentor New Farmer Devel. Project. Named MacArthur fellow, John D. and Catherine T. MacArthur Found., 2004. Achievements include establishment of the first low-income Cmty. Supported Agrl. program (CSA) in NY; creation of literary programs for migrant farm workers. Mailing: 327-329 Glenwood Rd Pine Island NY 10969 Office Phone: 845-258-4574.

ROHLFING, DORLEE CLARK, school system administrator, educator; b. Bristol, Conn., June 21, 1936; d. Morgan William and Doris Nelson Clark; m. David Christian Rohlfing, June 14; children: Mark Christian Morgan(dec.), Alison Leslie Marie. AA, Hartford Coll. for Women, Conn., 1958; BS summa cum laude, U. Wis., Milw., 1972, MS, 1975. Presch. tchr. Newark Pre-Sch. Coun., 1965—66; tchr. Milw. Pub. Schs., 1986—96, student svcs. specialist, 1986—96; supr., lectr. U. Wis., Milw., 1997—.

ROHLIN, DIANE ELIZABETH, financial relations executive; b. N.Y.C., June 18, 1958; d. Edward F. and Elaine (Wittenstein) R. BA, Mich. State U., 1979. Account exec. Prudential Bache, Chgo., 1980, A.G. Becker, Chgo., 1981-82; sr. ptnr., assoc. dir. market intelligence Fin. Rels. Bd., Chgo., 1983-99, now assoc. mng. ptnr., 1999—2001. Republican. Avocations: reading, golf, horseback riding.

ROHNE, EMILY HOGAN, medical nurse; b. Shreveport, La., Dec. 6, 1959; d. Joseph A. and Emily E. (Jamison) Hogan; m. Ronald E. Rohne, July 31, 1981; children: Kelly, Eric, Scott. Diploma, Deaconess Hosp. Sch. Nursing, St. Louis, 1983; student, U. Mo., Columbia, 1978-79, U. Mo., St. Louis, 1979-80. RN, Ga.; cert. oncology nurse. Staff nurse Northside Hosp., Atlanta, asst. unit mgr., charge preceptor, 1984-89; hosp. nurse Dr. Pradeep Jolly, Atlanta, 1989-90; staff nurse Riverview Hosp., Noblesville, Ind., 1992-93; office nurse Dr. William Terpstra Family Practice, Noblesville, Ind., 1993-95; staff nurse Denton Regional Hosp., Denton, Tex., 2002—05, Baylor Grapevine Hosp., Grapevine, Tex., 2004—.

ROHNER, BONNIE-JEAN, small business owner, computer scientist, consultant; b. Waltham, Mass., Aug. 2, 1946; d. Gerrit John and Marjorie Lorraine (Hollis) Rohner; children: David Harrison Sackett, Amanda Marjorie Sackett. BFA in Fashion, Pratt Inst., Bklyn., 1967; BA in Biology, Adelphi U., 1983; MS, CIS, U. New Haven, 1993. Freelance fashion designer, Garden City, NY, 1971-76; owner, mgr. Printing Workshop, Massapequa, NY, 1976-78; personnel mgr. Doron Ltd., Norwich, Conn., 1978-79; computer related trainer Gen. Dynamics, Groton, Conn., 1979-89; acad. computing coord. Three Rivers Com./Tech. Coll., Norwich, 1989-94; owner, mgr. bytestream, Norwichtown, Conn., 1993—. Tech. advisor Countywide Network Com., 1989—90; computer cons. U. New Haven, Groton, 1990—92; sec. Connbug, Rocky Hill, Conn., 1992—93; tech. cons. Am. Online, 1996—. Mem.: ACM, AAUP, AAUW, NAFE, Women's Network S.E. Conn. Avocations: creative writing, Web surfing. Office Phone: 860-886-7977. Business E-Mail: bonnie-jean@bytestream.org.

ROHR, CAROL ANN, composer, music educator; d. Herbert Samuel and Cecil Leotta Neale; m. Stephen P. Rohr, May 30, 1968. MusM, U. S.D., 1967—71. Composer: (piano composition) Dorian Grey for Piano (Cedar Rapids, Iowa Beethoven Club, 2004), (piano, violin and cello composition) Stream of Consciousness (Iowa Composer's Concert, 1994), (piano composition) Sonata and Postlude (Iowa Composers Forum Ann. Concert at Coe Coll., Cedar Rapids, Iowa, 1980). Chair, orgn. support Cedar Rapids City Music Contest, 1975—2004. Scholar Swensrud scholarship award, Northwood Pub. Sch., 1955—58. Mem.: Nat. Music Tchrs. Assn. (assoc.), Iowa Music Tchrs. Assn. (assoc.; student performance auditions and festivals 1980—), Iowa Composers Forum (assoc.), Beethoven Club of Cedar Rapids, Iowa (assoc.; libr./historian 1995—2005). Home: 4008 Glen Elm Drive NE Cedar Rapids IA 52402-2667 Office: Carol A Rohr Private Piano Instruction 4008 Glen Elm Dr NE Cedar Rapids IA 52402-2667

ROHRBACH, HEIDI A., lawyer; b. Buffalo, Jan. 25, 1953; d. William R. and A.T. R.; m. Leonard Lance, Aug. 9, 1996; 1 child, Peter R. Frank. BA, Northwestern U., 1974; JD, Vanderbilt U., 1977. Bar: NY, 1978. V.p., asst. gen. counsel J.P. Morgan Chase & Co., NYC, 1985—2004.

ROHRBOUGH, ELSA CLAIRE HARTMAN, artist; b. Shreveport, La., Sept. 26, 1915; d. Adolph Emil and Camille Claire (Francis) Hartman; m. Leonard M. Rohrbough, June 19, 1937 (dec. Jan. 1977); children: Stephen, Frank, Leonard. One-woman shows include Le Petit Theatre du Vieux Carre, New Orleans World Trade Ctr.'s Internat. House, Singing River Art Assn., Pascagoula, Miss., La. Font Inn, Pascagoula, Mandeville (La.) City Hall, St. Tammany Art Assn., Covington, La., others; exhibited in groups shows at 1st Guaranty Bank, Hammond, La., St. Tammany Art Assn., Ft. Isabel Gallery, Covington, S.E. La. State U., La. State Archives, Massur Mus. Art, Monroe, La., Mobile (Ala.) Art Gallery, Gulf Coast Juried Exhibit, Mobile, Juried Arts Nat., Tyler, Tex., Greater New Orleans Nat., La. Watercolor Soc. Internat., Ky. Watermedia Nat., So. Watercolor Ann., La. Women Artist; represented in permanent collection at St. Tammany Parish Ct. House, Mandeville City Hall, Bellingrath Gardens, Theodore, Ala. Mem.: St. Tammany Art Assn. (instr. 1977—78, bd. dirs. 1985—86, classes chmn. 1986—88, bd. dirs. 1987), La. State Assn. (pres. 1998—2000), Nat. League Am. Pen Women (v.p. S.E. La. br. 1986—87, pres. 1987—92, 1994—98, v.p. S.E. La. br. 2002—04). Republican. Roman Catholic. Avocations: flower arranging, gardening, ethnic cooking, american antiques. Home: 100 Christwood Blvd Apt 106 Covington LA 70433-4601

ROHREN, BRENDA MARIE ANDERSON, therapist, educator; b. Kansas City, Mo., Apr. 18, 1959; d. Wilbur Dean and Katheryn Elizabeth (Albright) Anderson; m. Lathan Edward Rohren, May 10, 1985; 1 child, Amanda Jessica. BS in Psychology, Colo. State U., 1983; MA in Psychology, Cath. U. Am., 1986. Lic. mental health practitioner, alcohol/drug counselor. Mental health therapist, sr. case mgr. Rappahannock Area Community Svcs. Bd., Fredericksburg, Va., 1986-88, mental health therapist, case mgmt. supr., 1988; rsch. assoc. Inst. Medicine, NAS, Washington, 1988-89; supr. adult psychiat. program Lincoln (Nebr.) Gen. Hosp., 1989, program supr. mental health svcs., 1989-91; adj. instr. S.E. Community Coll., Lincoln, 1990—; assessment and referral specialist Rivendell Psychiat. Ctr., Seward, Nebr., 1993-95; therapist Lincoln Day Treatment Ctr., Lincoln, Nebr., 1993-95; mental health and substance abuse therapist Cmty. Mental Health Ctr., Lincoln, 2004—. Adj. instr. Coll. of St. Mary, 1994—2001; therapist Rape/Spouse Abuse Crisis Ctr., Lincoln, 1996—2002; substance abuse counselor Independence Ctr., Lincoln, 2002—; computer cons. Syscon Corp., Washington, 1983—84; mental health clinician Cmty. Mental Health Ctr., 2004—; domestic abuse therapist Bryan LGH Med. Ctr., Lincoln, Nebr., 2004—; asst. coord. Lancaster County Behavioral Health Coalition, 2005—. Author: (report) Bottom Line Benefits: Building Economic Success Through Stronger Families; editor: (newsletter) Alliance for Mentally Ill, Lincoln, 1993-2002. Active Nat. Alliance for the Mentally Ill-Lincoln, Nebr. Domestic Violence/Sexual Assault Coalition; asst. coord. Lancaster County Behavioral Health Coalition, 2005— Mem. APA (assoc.), ACA, Nat. Assn. Alcohol and Drug Abuse Counselors, Nebr. Psychol. Assn. (assoc.), Nebr. Counseling Assn Democrat. Roman Catholic. Avocations: interior decorating, reading, landscaping, camping. Home: 3821 S 33rd St Lincoln NE 68506-3806 Office: Independence Ctr 1650 Lake St Lincoln NE 68502 Office Phone: 402-481-5390. Personal E-mail: brenda@neb.rr.com.

ROHRER, SUSAN EARLEY, film producer, film director, scriptwriter; b. Richmond, Va., Mar. 24; d. Charles Marion Jr. and Gloria Jean (Ripley) Earley; m. Mark Brooks Rohrer. BA in Art cum laude, James Madison U. Prodr., dir., co-story writer (tv shows) Never Say Goodbye, 1988 (Emmy award, Humanitas Prize finalist), Terrible Things My Mother Told Me, 1988 (Emmy nomination, Gold award Nat. Ednl. Film Festival); prodr., dir. (TV movies) For Jenny With Love (TV Movie award), Mother's Day, 1989 (3 Image award nominations), prodr., dir., writer (TV show) The Emancipation of Lizzie Stern, 1991 (Angel award, Bronze award Nat. Ednl. Film Festival, Emmy nomination, Monitor award finalist, TV Movie award), If I Die Before I Wake, 1993 (Emmy nomination, Humanitas Prize finalist, Cine Golden Eagle, TV Movie award); dir. (TV show) Sweet Valley High, 1996; dir. TV pilot Dojo Kids, 1996; prodr., dir., co-writer About Sarah, TV movie, 1998 (award of excellence Film Adv. Bd., Best of Festival award Breckenridge Film Festival, The Christopher award, Angel award, N.Y. Festivals finalist); writer (TV movies) Another Pretty Face, 2002, Book of Days, 2003. Recipient Resolution of Recognition Virginia Beach City Coun., 1988. Mem. ATAS, SAG, Writers Guild Am., Dirs. Guild Am. Office: Josh Schechter IPG 9200 Sunset Blvd Ste 820 Los Angeles CA 90069

ROHR-KIRCHGRABER, THERESA M.B., adolescent medicine; BA, Cornell U., 1984, MD, 1988. Cert. Internal Medicine, Adolescent Medicine. Intern U. Hosp. Cleveland, 1988—89, resident, 1989—91; hosp. appointment Meridia Huron Hosp., Cleve., 1991—94, Crouse-Irving Meml. Hosp., Syracuse, 1994—2003, Grady Hosp., Atlanta, 2004, SUNY Health Sci. Ctr., Syracuse, 1994—2003, academic appointment, 1994—2003, Case Western U., Cleve., 1991—94, Morehouse Sch. Medicine, Atlanta, 2004; asst. prof. Emory U. Sch. Medicine, Atlanta, 2005—. Fellow: Am. Coll. Physicians-Am. Soc. Internal Medicine; mem.: Soc. for Adolescent Medicine. Office: Emory U Sch Medicine 1440 Clifton Rd NE Atlanta GA 30322*

ROIN, JULIE, law educator; b. 1955; BA in Social Studies, magna cum laude, Radcliffe Coll., 1977; JD, Yale U., 1980. Bar: DC 1981. Law clk. to Hon. Patricia M. Wald US Ct. Appeals DC Cir., 1980—81; assoc. Caplin & Drysdale, Chartered, Washington, 1981—84; asst. prof. law U. Va. Sch. Law, 1985—90, prof., 1990—98, Class of 1963 rsch. prof. law, 1992—95, Henry L. and Grace Doherty Charitable Found. prof. law, 1996—98; prof. law U. Chgo. Law Sch., 1998—, Seymour Logan prof. law, 2002—. Vis. asst. prof. law Yale Law Sch., 1986—87, U. Va. Sch. Law, 1984—85; vis. prof. law Harvard Law Sch., 1990—91, U. Chgo. Law Sch., 1993, U. Mich. Law Sch., 1997; Jack N. Pritzker disting. vis. prof. law Northwestern U. Law Sch., 1998. Co-author (with P. Stephan & D. Wallace): International Business and Economics: Law and Policy, 1993. Office: U Chgo Law Sch 1111 E 60th St Chicago IL 60637 Office Phone: 773-702-5314. E-mail: julie_roin@law.uchicago.edu.

ROITMAN, JUDITH, mathematician, educator; b. N.Y.C., Nov. 12, 1945; d. Leo and Ethel (Gottesman) R.; m. Stanley Lombardo, Sept. 26, 1978; 1 child, Ben Lombardo. BA in English, Sarah Lawrence Coll., 1966; MA in Math., U. Calif., Berkeley, 1971, PhD in Math., 1974. Asst. prof. math. Wellesley (Mass.) Coll., 1974-77; from asst. prof. to prof. math. U. Kans., Lawrence, 1977—. Author: Introduction to Modern Set Theory, 1990; contbr. articles to profl. jours. Grantee, NSF, 1975—87, 1992—95. Mem. Assn. Symbolic Logic, Am. Math. Soc., Assn. Women in Math. (pres. 1979-81, Louise Hay award 1996), Kans. Assn. Tchrs. Math., Nat. Assn. Tchrs. Math. Avocation: poetry. Business E-Mail: roitman@math.ku.edu.

ROLAND, ANNE, registrar Supreme Court of Canada; m. Alphonse Morissette; 1 child, Julien BA Philosophy, Caen, France, 1965; diploma, Inst. Supérieur d'interprétation et de traduction, 1969; lic. in law, Paris, 1969; LLB, U. Ottawa, 1979. Bar: Quebec 1980. Legal trans., revisor, Can., 1971-75; chief trans. svcs. customs and excise Sec. of State, Can., 1975-76; spl. asst. to chief justice Can., 1976-81; chief law editor Supreme Ct. Can., 1981-88, dep. registrar, 1988-90, registrar, 1990. Mem. Can. Bar Assn., Assn. Can. Ct. Adminstrs., Assn. Francophone Jurists, Can. Inst. Adminstrn. Justice, Assn. Reporters Jud. Decisions. Office: Supreme Ct Can Office Reg 301 Wellington St Ottawa ON Canada K1A 0J1 Office Phone: 613-996-9277. E-mail: rolanda@scc-csc.gc.ca.

ROLAND, MEG, literature educator; PhD, U. Wash., Seattle, 2002. Asst. prof., chair English dept. Marylhurst U., Oreg., 2003—. Mem.: Medieval Acad. of Am., Internat. Arthurian Soc., MLA, Soc. for Textual Scholarship (sec. 2006). Office: Marylhurst University 17600 Pacific Hwy Marylhurst OR 97036 Office Phone: 503-636-8141. E-mail: mroland@marylhurst.edu.

ROLAND, REGINA E., elementary school educator, educational consultant; b. Evanston, Ill., Aug. 1, 1949; d. Melvin J. and Rosemary G. (Malone) Ahrens; m. James I. Roland, Feb. 14, 1970. BA, No. Ill. U., 1971; MEd, Nat. Louis U., 1985. Educator St. John the Bapt. Sch., Winfield, Ill., 1972—74; Spanish/ESL/bilingual tchr. Des Plaines (Ill.) Cmty. Consol. Sch. Dist., 1974—2004; ednl. cons. and mentor, 2004—. Presenter workshops in field. Co-author: A Hat for All Seasons, Hats on the Go; contbr. articles to mags. Scholar, Ill. State67. Mem.: NEA, Assisi Animal Found. Roman Catholic. Avocations: reading, walking, jewelry-making, writing, volunteer work. Home: 61 Dundee Ln Barrington IL 60010 Personal E-mail: Jasroland@sbcglobal.net.

ROLAND, SALLY, music educator; b. Omaha, Apr. 22, 1957; d. Chester Henry Sr. and Marie Elaine (Hysom) Dreesen; m. Ronald L. Roland, June 26, 1977 (div.); children: Alexander Jacob, Melissa Christine. BAE, Wayne (Nebr.) State Coll., 1979, MSE, 1998. Cert. in K-12 adminstrn., specific learning disabilities and elem. edn., Nebr.; endorsement in mild/moderate spl. edn. 7-12. K-6 classrm. tchr. Cuming County Dist. 33, Oakland, Nebr., 1979-80; substitute tchr. local sch. dists., 1980-89; itinerant resource tchr. Ednl. Svc. Unit 2, Fremont, Nebr., 1989-93; secondary resource tchr. West Point (Nebr.) H.S., 1993-2000; secondary spl. edn. tchr. Omaha (Nebr.) Pub. Schs., 2000—. Adj. faculty in edn. Wayne State Coll., 1996; pres. Sch. Age Child Care Coalition, West Point, 1990; mem. West Point Cmty. Edn. Bd., 1993-95. Leader, Youth for Christ, West Point, 1992-97; leader 4-H Club, West Point, 1990-96, foods judge at area county fairs, 1997—. Mem. ASCD, NEA, Learning Disabilities Assn., Coun. for Exceptional Children, Nebr. State Edn. Assn., Kappa Delta Pi. Democrat. Lutheran. Avocations: computers, surfing the net, reading, writing, cooking. Home: 5255 S 157th Ct # 165 Omaha NE 68135-6466

ROLE, LORNA W., medical educator; Prof. anatomy and cell biology Columbia U., N.Y.C. Contbr. articles to profl. jours. Mem.: Soc. for Neurosci. Achievements include research in on the mechanisms underlying the maturation and maintenance of synapses between neurons. Office: Columbia Univ Dept Anatomy and Cell Biology 630 W 168th St New York NY 10032-3702

ROLENC, SISTER ANITA, parochial school educator, archivist; d. Joseph Ernest Rolenc and Agnes Marie Polak. BS, Coll. St. Mary, Omaha, 1964; MA, U. Lincoln, Omaha, 1975. Tchr. St. Ludmila Sch., Cedar Rapids, 1954—58, Assumption Sch., Dwight, Nebr., 1958—60, St. Michael Sch., Harlan, Iowa, 1960—63, St. Wenceslaus Sch., Spillville, Iowa, 1963—64, Our Lady Lourdes, Porcupine, SD, 1967—68, St. Adalbert Sch., Omaha, 1964—67, St. John Nepomucene Sch., Weston, Nebr., 1968—70, Notre Dame Acad., Omaha, 1970—74, Neumann HS, Wahoo, Nebr., 1975—81, St. Wenceslaus Sch., Dodge, Nebr., 1981—82, Assumption Sch., Omaha, 1982—85; parish minister St. Patrick Parish, O'Neill, 1985—86; tchr. St. Mary's Sch., O'Neill, Nebr., 1986—. Archivist Notre Dame Sisters, Omaha, 1989—2006. Roman Catholic. Avocations: embroidery, reading, music, walking. Office: Saint Marys HS 300 N 4th St Oneill NE 68763 Business E-Mail: arolenc@esu8.org.

ROLER, JO ANNE CARUSO, education educator, consultant; b. Chgo., Apr. 13, 1951; d. Charles James and Dorothy Serra Caruso; children: Bryan Matthew, Scott Andrew. BA, Purdue U., West Lafayette, 1973; MA, Nat. Louis U., Ill., 1996. Nat. Bd. Cert. Tchr. Nat. Bd. for Profl. Tchg. Stds., 1999. Tchr. Sch. Dist. 159, Matteson, Ill., 1974—81, Sch. Dist. 103, Lincolnshire, Ill., 1991—; profl. devel. provider State of Ill., Waukegan, 2000; adj. prof. DePaul U., Lake Forest, 2004, So. Ill. U., Carbondale, 2004—. Cons. Coll. Bd., Evanston, Ill., 1999—; presenter Chgo. Pub. Sch. AP Vertical Teams Workshop, 2000, AP Vertical Teams Conf., Tulsa, 2000; cons., educator Truman State U., Kirksville, Mo., 2001; presenter Coll. Bd. Midwestern Regional Meeting, Chgo., 2001, Ill. Sch. Districts 96, 102, 103, and 125 Common Inst., Lincolnshire, 2001; cons., instr. Augsberg Coll., Mpls., 2001; cons., educator U. Ark., Little Rock, 2002—; cons., instr. Tex. Christian U., Ft. Worth, 2002—05; cons. State of N.Mex, Albuquerque, 2004; cons., educator U. Okla., Norman, 2005; cons. Sch. Dist. 109, Deerfield, Ill., 2006—. Co-author: (manual) AP Social Studies Vertical Team Guide, 2001. Avocations: travel, reading, violin. Office: Sch Dist 103 1370 Riverwoods Rd Lincolnshire IL 60069 Office Phone: 847-295-1560. Business E-Mail: jroler@comcasst.net.

ROLES-WALTER, JENNIE RUTH, art educator, artist; b. Winchester, Tenn., Aug. 17, 1980; d. Ernest Gordon and Brenda Williams Roles; m. Cameron Arthur Walter, Oct. 4, 2004. AS, Motlow CC, Tullahoma, Tenn; B in Art Edn., Tenn. Tech. U., Cookeville; M in Art Edn., Ala. A&M U., Normal. Art tchr. Huntland HS, Tenn., Franklin County HS, Winchester. Mural lead artist Franklin County Internat. Dogwood Festival, 2005. Exhibitions include Appalachian Ctr. for Crafts Gallery, Smithville, Tenn., Gallery 111, Dalton, Ga., Tenn. Tech. U. Student Show, 2002, Dalton, Ga. Art Guild, 2003, Fayetteville, Tenn. Art League, 2003, Ala. A&M U. Gallery, 2004, KP Arts Gallery, Fayetteville, Tenn., 2004, one-woman shows include North Windows Gallery, Appalachian Ctr. for Crafts, Smithville, Tenn., 2003. Recipient Lincoln Davis 4th Congl. Outstanding Art Tchr. award, 2005, Secondary New Tchr. of Yr. Award, Franklin County HS, 2005; grantee PENN scholarship, Winchester, Tenn., 2005. Mem.: NAEA. Avocations: sports, travel, music, entertainment.

ROLL, MARILYN RITA BROWNLIE, social worker; b. Bay City, Mich., Dec. 7, 1946; d. John P. and Rita (Himpele) Brownlie; m. Charles S. Roll Jr., Dec. 28, 1968; 1 child, Brian. BS, Cornell U., 1969; MSW, Rutgers U., 1986. Diplomate Am. Bd. Clin. Social Work; Lic. clin. social worker, NJ; cert. practitioner in psychodrama, cert. in EMDR, cert. in Imago relationship therapy for couples and singles, cert. in clin. hypnosis, cert. family life educator, cert. secondary sch. tchr., cert. sch. social worker, NJ, cert. parent effectiveness instr., cert. stepfamily counselor, ACSW. Home econs. tchr. Scotch Plains Fanwood (NJ) H.S., 1970, 1973—78; dir., co-founder, program developer Family Life Resources, Fanwood, 1982—; sch. social worker Somerset Elem. Sch., North Plainfield, NJ, 1984-85; psychotherapist, intervention counselor Resolve Cmty. Counseling Ctr., Scotch Plains, 1985-87; pvt. practice psychotherapist Westfield, NJ, 1987—. Evaluative cons. Bank St. Coll. Internat. Work and Family Life Study, NYC, 1986; program developer, parent educator Mothers Ctr., Scotch Plains, 1977-83. Mem. Sch. Dist. Substance Abuse com., Scotch Plains, 1987-88. Mem. NASW, Nat. Coun. on Family Rels., Am. Soc. Group Psychotherapy and Psychodrama, Stepfamily Found., Family Resource Coalition, Alumni Assn. Sch. of Social Work Rutgers U., Alumni Assn. Cornell Univ. Sch. Human Ecology, Phi Lambda Theta. Home: 184 Burns Way Fanwood NJ 07023-1604 Office: 128 S Euclid Ave Westfield NJ 07090-5103 Office Phone: 908-789-3335.

ROLL, RENÉE F., retired psychologist, publishing executive; d. Leo and Helen Feldman; children: Stewart Daniel, Jeri Ann. BA, U. Calif., 1965, MS, 1967. Lic. psychologist Bd. Med. Examiners, Calif., 1973, marriage and family therapist Bd. Behavioral Scis. Calif., 1968, cert. diplomate psychologist Am. Psychotherapy Assn., 1998, therapist Nat. Bd. Cognitive Behavioral Therapists, 1999. Tchr. Manesquan Sch. Dist., NJ, 1959—60, Montebello Unified Sch. Dist., Calif., 1961—70, psychologist, 1961—70; pvt. practice counselor Glendale, Calif., 1970—73; pvt. practice psychologist Chico, Calif., 1974; ret., 1974; cons. Dr. J.P. Haddock, Chico, 1975—82. Author: The Seeds of Growth, A History for the Future, 2002 (appears in the Libr. of Congress, DC), A Crooked Christmas Tree, 2004, A Tale of Two Boys and Wolf Pups, 2006. Vol. fireman Calif. Dept. Forestry, Butte Meadows, Calif., 1983. Recipient Outstanding Achievement award, Internat. Soc. Poets, 2003, Poet of Merit award, 2003, Outstanding Achievement in Poetry award, 2006.

Mem.: AAUW, Nat. Assn. Female Execs., Natural Wildlife Assn., Writing Group Stockton, Purse Club. Avocations: piano, poetry, flowers, writing. Home: 4089 Five Mile Dr Stockton CA 95219 Office Phone: 209-481-0273. Personal E-mail: reneeroll@comcast.net.

ROLLAND, CLARA, pianist, educator; b. Budapest, Hungary, Apr. 20, 1916; arrived in U.S., 1939; d. Alexander and Katalin (Stein) Szekely; m. Paul Rolland, Dec. 24, 1940 (dec. Nov. 9, 1978); children: Peter Thomas, John Paul. Grad., Royal Franz Liszt Acad. Music, 1939, Cleve. Inst. Music, 1941; diploma (hon.), Franz Liszt Acad. Music, 1990. Founder, instr. prep. dept. piano, theory and ear tng. Simpson Coll., Indianola, Iowa, 1941—45; pvt. studio Urbana, Ill., 1946—73; founder, tchr. fun with music class Fine Arts Ctr., Clinton, Ill., 1966—70; co-dir. Music Divsn. Nat. Acad. Arts, 1973—79. Judge Three Rivers Piano Competition, St. Louis, 1978; lectr. in field. Performer, WILL-FM, 1950—55. Mem.: Music Tchr. Nat. Assn. (Baldwin Jr. Achievement award 1972, 1973, 1974, 1975, 1977, Mason & Hamlin Tchr. Achievement award 1974, H.S. Auditions winner 1974), Am. String Tchr. Assn. (life), Mu Phi Epsilon (pres. Mu Alpha chpt. 1961).

ROLLAND, KATHY ANN, elementary school educator; b. Pottsville, Pa., May 10, 1963; d. Kenneth Warren Rolland, Sr. and Lilla Catherine Telepchak. BS in Early Childhood Edn., Pa. State U., 1985; MEd in Sch. Leadership and Instrn., Wilmington Coll., 1998. Cert. generalist, early childhood Nat. Bd. Profl. Tchg. Stds. Tchr. Colonial Sch. Dist., New Castle, Del., 1990—. Mem. Investigations Math. Adv. Bd., New Castle, 2002—, Bridges Learning Sys. Dist., New Castle, 2002—. Vol. Freedom Outreach, Wilmington, 1999—. Excellence in Edn. grantee, MBNA Found., 2002. Mem.: NEA, Del. Coun. Tchrs. Math., Del. State Edn. Assn., Phi Lambda Theta. Avocations: travel, guitar, volunteering. Office: So Elem Sch 795 Cox Neck Rd New Castle DE 19720 Office Phone: 302-323-2828.

ROLLÉ, JANET LYDIA, Internet company executive; b. Mt. Vernon, N.Y., Dec. 25, 1961; d. William Arthur and Barbara Monica (Goldson) Rollé; m. Mark Damon Keye, Apr. 14, 1995; 1 child. BFA in Dance, SUNY, Purchase, 1984; MBA in Mktg. and Film, Columbia U., 1991. Profl. dancer, London, 1984-88; spl. asst. to chmn. Home Box Office, NYC, 1991-92, mgr. multiplex mktg., 1992-93; dir. mktg. HBO Home Video, 1993-96, dir. mktg. and sales promotion, 1996—2001; v.p. Programming Enterprises & Bus. Devel. for VH1 and CMT MTV Networks, 2001—05; v.p., gen. mgr. AOL Black Voices, 2005—. Mentor Harlem YMCA Mentoring Program, NYC, 1993—; sponsor Black Filmmaker Found. Recipient Black Achievers in Industry award Harlem YMCA, 1993. Mem. Am. Film Inst. (3d decade coun.), NY Women in Film and TV, USTA (mem. Multicultural Participation Com.) Avocations: tennis, golf. Office: AOL 22000 AOL Way Dulles VA 20166*

ROLLE, MYRA MOSS See MOSS, MYRA

ROLLER, JEANNE KEENEY, education educator; b. Geneseo, Ill., July 3, 1948; d. Marvin C. and Irma A. (Hopkey) Keeney; m. Larry Richard Roller, Dec. 27, 1969; 1 child, Derek C. BA, St. Ambrose U., 1973; MST, U. Wis., Eau Claire, 1979; EdD, Nova Southeastern U., Ft. Lauderdale, 1996. Cert. tchr., Iowa; cert. reading specialist, Iowa. Tchr. Mahomet (Ill.)-Seymour Sch. Dist. 3, 1973-76; pre-sch. dir. Mt. St. Clare Coll., Clinton, Iowa, 1980-87, reading instr., 1979-82, edn. instr., 1980-85, prof., chair dept. edn., 1985-92, dir. Flavian Ctr., 1989-92; part-time instr. off-campus program St. Ambrose U., Davenport, 1988—92, instr., 1988—92, asst. prof. edn., 1992—96, chair dept. edn., 1995—98, assoc. prof., 1996—2001, prof., 2001—, assessment coord., 2003—06. Mem. Internat. Reading Assn., Nat. Assn. for the Edn. Young Children, Assn. Childhood Edn. Internat., Kappa Delta Pi. Roman Catholic. Avocations: genealogy, children's literature, walking.

ROLLER, MARION, sculptor; b. Boston; Student, Vesper George Sch. Art, Art Students League; BA in Art, Queens Coll., 1980. Sculptor in residence, 1999-2000. Instr. Fashion Inst. Tech., N.Y.C., Sculpture Ctr.; head design dept. Traphagen Sch. of Fashion. Exhbns. include The Newark Mus., 1995-96, Nat. Acad. Design, N.Y., 1994, Nat. Sculpture Soc., N.Y., 1996-97, Scottsdale, Ariz., Serravezza, Italy, 1994, Transco Mus., Phila., U.S. Mint, San Francisco, Denver, Albany, NY, Inst. History and Art, Pittsfield, Mass., Mus., Fedn. Internat. de la Medaille, Helsinki, Finland, Budapest, Hungary, 1993, Price Waterhouse Galleries, NYC, 1997, Janus Gallery, Santa Fe, Chesterwood, Stockbridge, Mass., 1997, Hillsdale, Mich., Coll., 1997, Nat. Sculpture Soc., 2000, 2001, UN, NYC, 1995, Cannon House Rotunda, Washington, Butler Inst. of Am. Art, 2001, Nat. Acad. Annual, 2001, others; first sculptor in residence, designer Plantation Life medal, The Wall, Brookgreen Gardens; commns. include Nassau Ctr. for Emotionally Disturbed Children, St. Mary's Children and Families Found., Traphagen Sch. Fashion, Rosemary Harris Meml., Brookgreen Gardens, medal Nat. Acad. Design, Butler Mus., others; contbr. articles, book reviews to Sculpture Review. Recipient Helen Gapen Oehler Meml. award Allied Artists, 1991, Samuel Cashwan Meml. award Audubon Artists, 1992, Audubon Artists award, 1994, Pen & Brush award for Watercolor, 1997, Nat. Sulpture Soc. Annual Exhibit award, 1998, Lou Magnani award Salmagundi Club, 1998, Gold medal of Honor 56th Annual Audubon Artists Exhibit, 1998, medal Internat. Exhibit of Medallic Art Museium Beelden ann Vee, 1998, award for Medallic Sculpture Pen & Brush, 1999, medal of Ethel Traphagen Medallic Art Co., 2001. Fellow Nat. Sculpture Soc. (sec., Kalos Kagathos Found. prize, C. Percival Dietsch Sculpture prize, Tallix Foundry prize, Edith H. & Richman Proskauer prize, Joel Meisner Foundry award); mem. Nat. Acad. Design (academician), Audubon Artists (treas., past pres., Gold medal of honor, Art Students League award, 1999), The Pen & Brush (chmn. sculpture sect., Pen and Brush award for watercolor, 1997, Bronze medal for sculpture, Chaim Gross Found. award, 1996, Samuel Cashwan meml. award, 1992, Margaret Sussman award 2000, Charlotte Dunwiddie award for medallic art 2000), Allied Artists Am. (past pres., Silver medal honor, Sybil and Bob Porton award, Helen Gapen Oehler Meml. award, 1991), Am. Medallic Sculpture Assn., Fine Arts Fedn. (bd. mem.).

ROLLER, PAMELA JO, elementary school educator; b. Logansport, Ind., Mar. 22, 1952; d. Glen B. Roller and Clara Evelyn Sizemore. BS, Ind. U., Kokomo, 1974; MS, Ind. U./Purdue U. Indpls., 1976. Cert. CFG Coach for Nat. Sch. Reform Faculty 2006. Tchr. 5th and 6th grade Southeastern Sch. Corp., Logansport, 1974—76, tchr. 1st grade, 1976—79, tchr. 2d grade, 1979—82, tchr. 1st grade, 1982—88, readiness tchr. 1st grade, 1988—94, tchr. 2d grade, 1994—2006. Founder/coord., mentoring program K-12 Tender Loving Care, 1989—; coord. Young Astronauts, 1988—; founder/coord. Sch. on Sat., Galveston, Ind., 1994—2006; third grade tchr., Bolivia, 2004. Flight dir. Mission Possible, Galveston, 1996—; dist. lay spkr. United Meth., Logansport, Ind., 1992—. Recipient Disney's Am. Tchr. Awards Honoree, Calif., 2003, Make a Difference award, USA Weekend Mag., 2006; scholar, Japan Fulbright Meml. Fund, 2005. Mem.: NSTA, Profl. Assn. in Edn., Hoosier Assn. Sci. Tchrs., Ind. State Tchrs. Assn., Pi Lambda Theta. Democrat. Methodist. Achievements include classroom business called chocolate lollipops, Inc. has earned over 5,000 dollars, and given to numerous charities. Office Phone: 574-699-6687. Personal E-mail: proller1@msn.com.

ROLLE-RISSETTO, SILVIA, foreign languages educator, writer, artist; b. Rosario, Argentina, Apr. 19, 1967; d. Dante and Gladys Rolle. BA in Spanish, Calif. State U., Long Beach, 1987, BA in French and Italian, 1987, MA in Spanish, 1990; PhD in Spanish, U. Calif., Riverside, 1996. Assoc. prof. Spanish, grad. coord. and fgn. lang. assessor of Spanish and Italian, dept. world langs. and lit. Calif. State U., San Marcos, 1996—, chair, world lang. & hispanic lit., 2000—. Participant numerous confs. Author: La Obra de Ana Maria Fagundo: Una Poetica Fememino-Feminista, 1997, Plazas: un lugar de encuentro para la hispanidad (lab manual); contbr. articles to profl. jours.; translator. Recipient Patrons of Italian scholarship U. degli Studi di Siena, 1987. Mem. MLA, Nat. Hispanic Soc., Asociacion de Literatura Femenina Hispanica, Hispanic Assn. of the Humanties, Letra Femeninas, Mairena, Assn. Internat. Hispanistas. Democrat. Office: Calif State U San Marcos World Langs & Hispanic Lit 333 S Twin Oaks Valley Rd San Marcos CA 92096-0001 Business E-Mail: srolle@csusm.edu.

ROLLIN, BETTY, writer, television journalist; b. NYC, Jan. 3, 1936; d. Leon and Ida R.; m. Harold M. Edwards, Jan. 21, 1979. BA, Sarah Lawrence Coll., 1957. Assoc. features editor Vogue mag., 1964; sr. editor Look mag., 1965-71; network corr. NBC News, N.Y.C., 1971-80, contbg. corr., 1985—2003; network corr. ABC News Nightline, 1982-84. Contbr. corr. Religion and Ethics Newsweekly PBS; lectr. in field. Profl. actress: on stage and TV, 1958—64; author: I Thee Wed, 1962, Mothers Are Funnier Than Children, 1964, The Non-Drinkers' Drink Book, 1966, First, You Cry, 1976, reissue, 2000, Am I Getting Paid for This?, 1982, Last Wish, 1985, reissue, 1998; columnist: Hers, N.Y. Times; contbr. articles to popular mags. Bd. mem. Death With Dignity Nat. Ctr., 1997—. Office: Care NS Bienstock Inc 1740 Broadway New York NY 10019-4315 Office Phone: 212-664-7171.

ROLLINGER, MARY ELIZABETH, school counselor; b. Jamestown, N.Y., May 12, 1950; d. Ernest Robert and June Armina (Carlson) Furlow. BS, Edinboro U., 1974; MEd, St. Bonaventure U., 1994. Cert. secondary edn. and elem. edn., N.Y., adv. cert. in counseling, 1996; advanced tng. in critical incident stress debriefing, 1996. English tchr. Bemus Point (N.Y.) Ctrl. Sch., 1974—2000; part-time clothing buyer Good Morning Farm, Stow, N.Y., 1976-84; part-time GED instr. Erie 2 BOCES, Fredonia, N.Y., 1979-84; sch. counselor Bemus Point Ctrl. Sch. Dist., 2000—06; ret. Creative writing tchr. Chautauqua County Sch. Bd., Fredonia, 1986—; adj. prof. SUNY, Fredonia, 1994-96; turnkey trainer for N.Y. State syllabus N.Y. State Dept. Edn., Albany, 1985. Vol. Reg Lenna Civic Ctr., Jamestown, 1992; tchr. rep. Parent/Tchr./Student Assn., Bemus Point, 1980-94; bd. dirs. Amicae-Hotline for Rape/Battering/Abuse, Jamestown, 1986-88, Mutuus Mime Theater, Jamestown, 1982-86. Mem. Am. Counseling Assn., Am. Sch. Guidance Counselors Assn., Chautauqua County Counselors Assn., NY State Sch. Counselors Assn., Delta Kappa Gamma (publicity chair 1985-90). Avocations: photography, reading, travel, walking, soaring. Home: PO Box 551 Bemus Point NY 14712-0551 Personal E-mail: mer@cecomet.net.

ROLLINS, CAROLE ANN, writer, artist; b. Stockton, Calif., Feb. 3, 1948; d. Jack Elmer and Gladys Ester (Bartholomew) Rollins. BS in Conservation of Natural Resources, U. Calif., Berkeley, 1971, AB in Arch., 1971, MA, 1974, postgrad., 1975; postgrad. in environ. studies, U. Nev., Las Vegas, 2000—. Coord., initiator IDS 120 course U. Calif., Berkeley, 1970-74; ptnr., initiator Ca Song Records, N.Y.C., 1976-86; trustee, founder Environ. Celebration Found., Las Vegas, 1994—. Co-owner Nature Tech. Internat., 2004—. Author, illustrator: Me and My Friends, 1992, The Ecology Book, 1996; co-author: Adding Biology, 2006; singer writer Nostalgia Goes Country, 1986; author of essays, poetry. Nat. Wildlife Fedn. fellow, 1973-74; NEA grantee, 1974-75. Avocations: singing, dance, poetry, plants. Office Phone: 415-898-5895.

ROLLINS, DIANN ELIZABETH, occupational health nurse, primary school educator; b. Newark, Dec. 13, 1943; d. Lewis Paul and Letitia Lavinia Rollins. RN, Meth. Hosp. Sch. Nursing, Phila., 1964; postgrad., Howard U., 1966, Milton Coll., 1969—72, West Chester State Coll., 1972—79; cert. bldg. maintenance, John F. Kennedy Vocat. Tech., 1992; BSN, Thomas Jefferson U., 2000. RN Pa., N.J.; lic. religious sci. practioner United Ch. Religious Sci., 2003. Nurse Meth. Hosp., Phila., 1964—66, 1967—69, Mercy Hosp., Janesville, Wis., 1969—72, Chester County Hosp., West Chester, Pa., 1972—74, Cheyney U., Pa., 1974—75, Embreeville State Hosp., coatesville, 1976—78; agy. nurse Norristown, Phila., 1978—86, Medox, Olsten, Kimberly, Phila., 1985-86; RN supr. New Ralston House, Phila., 1986-87, 88-89; agy. nurse Kimberly, Quality Care, Olsten, Medox, others, Phila., 1987-89; info. and referral specialist Nat. Mental Health Consumer Self Help Clearing House, Phila., 1992-93; intern ACT NOW Southeastern Mental Health Program, Phila., 1993-94; nursery sch. tchr. Bambino Gesu Child Devel. Ctr., Phila., 1994-99; primary instr. nursing assts. ARC, 2000—01, Clin. Pathways Educators Ins., 2001—02; supplemental staff nurse Breslin Learning Ctr., 2002—, LPN instr., 2003—; staff nurse Bayada Nurses, 2002—; postal nurse (occupl. health nurse) U.S. Post Office, 2003—. Spkr. in field. Vol. instr. program Franklin Inst., Phila., 1973-74; vol. multimedia first aide instr. ARC, Wilmington, Del., 1975-83; vol. plan II nurse blood mobiles ARC, S.E. Pa., 1982-85. Recipient Stella M. Mummert maternal/child care award, Meth. Hosp., 1964. Mem. Alumnae Meth. Hosp. Sch. Nursing, Four Chaplains Legion of Honor. Avocations: reading, writing, walking, singing. Office Phone: 215-829-1609. Personal E-mail: dynamyte19107@yahoo.com.

ROLLINS, DORIS CALLELA, music educator, pianist, performing accompanist; arrived in U.S., 1925; d. Samuel Ezekiel and Ismay Henrietta Jones; m. Valdemar W. Rollins, Sept. 9, 1951; 1 child, Gabrielle Valerie. MusB, Oberlin Conservatory, Ohio, 1945; M in Music Lit., Eastman Sch. Music, 1950; postgrad., NYU, Columbia U., N.Y.C., Manhattan Sch. Music, Julliard Sch. Music. Cert. music tchr. N.Y. Music tchr.-piano Fisk U., Nashville, 1945—52; music tchr.-gen. Yorkville H.S., N.Y.C., 1952—53; tchr. music-choral and gen., choral music dir. James Monroe H.S., Bronx, NY, 1955—65; tchr. music choral-gen., choral music dir. Isaac E. Young Jr. H.S., Bronx, 1970—86; tchr. music history Coll. New Rochelle, 1990—93. Choir dir. St. Lukes Episcopal Ch., St. Catherine AME Zion Ch., New Rochelle; piano music tchr. Rye Country Day Sch., NY; piano music tchr., accompanist Greenwich Acad., Conn. Pres. Womens Aux. to Nat. Med. Assn.; pres., v.p., treas. The Group. Mem.: Southwestern Ret. Tchrs. Assn. (v.p.), NY State Music Tchrs. Assn., Music Educators Nat. Conf., Alpha Kappa Alpha (choral dir.). Democrat. Episcopalian.

ROLLINS, MARGARET ANN, communications and theater educator; d. Frank N and Margaret Elizabeth Whitson; m. William Stephen Rollins, Aug. 6, 2001; 1 child, Kelli Elizabeth Stuart. B, Sam Houston State U., Huntsville, 1975. Tchr. Woodville H.S., Tex., 1979—2001, Athens Mid. Sch., Tex., 2001—. Sunday sch. tchr. First United Meth. Ch., Woodville, Tex., 1985—2001. Named Tchr. of Yr., 1989, 1996, Wal Mart Tchr. of Yr., 1999, Tchr. of Month, Athens Mid. Sch., 2005; recipient Tchr. of Yr., Tyler County Rotary Club, 1999, Mirabeau B. Lamar award, Masonic Lodge, 1999. Avocations: reading, gardening, knitting, exercise. Office Phone: 903-677-3030.

ROLLMAN, CHARLOTTE, artist, educator; b. Harrisburgh, Ill., Oct. 15, 1947; d. Joseph and Beulah (Overton) R.; m. Edward H. Shay, 1971 (div. 1982); m. William B. Holland, 1987; 1 child, Danielle Suzanne Holland. BFA, Murray State U., 1969; MFA, U. Ill., 1971. Instr. art Ball State U., Muncie, Ind., 1971-75; supr. hand-painted silk garments Nicole, Ltd., Chgo., 1980-84; textile designer, stylist Thybony Wallcovering, Chgo., 1983-88; prof. art No. Ill. U., DeKalb, 1987—. Exhibitions include New Harmony (Ind.) Gallery Art, Charlotte Brauer, Munster, Ind., Jan Cicero, Chgo., Roy Boyd, Chgo, Locus, St. Louis, Suzanne Brown, Scottsdale, Ariz, Nestle's Corp., DeKalb, Capitol State Bank, St. Louis, others; illustrator New Internat. Dictionary Music, 1991; AV coord. Women's Caucus Art, Beijing, 1995. Grad. Sch. Rsch. grantee No. Ill. U., 1993, Faculty Enhancement grantee, 1995, Undergrad. Improvement grantee No. Ill. U., 1996. Mem. AAUW, Women's Caucus Art, Nat. Mus. Women Arts, Chgo. Area Women's Studies, DeKalb Area Women's Ctr. Office: No Ill U Sch Art Dekalb IL 60115

ROMA, AIDA CLARA, artist; b. Phila., July 17, 1924; d. Carlo and Giustina S. R.; widowed; 4 children. Student, Camden County Coll., 1990-99. Dental Dr. Martin Apother, Runnemede, N.J., 1956-66; owner Rogers Auto Sales, Runnemede, N.J., 1966-90; tchr. St. Joseph's Sch., Camden, N.J., 1955-56. Author of poems, Jealousy, 1999, My 2 Best Friends, 2001, "Pal" My Pal, 2004. Art tutor, Haddenfield, N.J.; v.p. Girl Scouts Am., Runnemede, 1964; sec. Boy Scouts Am., 1960; mem. St. Teresa's Choir, 1993—, Atlantic City Choirs. Recipient Internat. Poet award, Artistic Artistry award, England, 2004. Mem. Sons of Italy. Republican. Achievements include invention of Rack on the Back auto addition. Avocation: singing. Home: PO Box 2076 Laurel Springs NJ 08021

ROMAN, JANE SEDGEWICK, nurse; b. Valleyvield, Que., Can., Jan. 27, 1946; d. William Middleton R. and Patricia Mitchell Tuttle; m. Allen J. Latham, June 21, 1982 (div. Jan. 1992). Diploma in nursing, Genesee Hosp., 1966; BA in Nursing and Biology, Goddard Coll., 1975; MEd, Cambridge Coll., 1991. RN, Mass.; cert. oper. rm. nurse, nursing adminstr. Coord. surg. tech. program Dimock Cmty. Health Ctr., Boston, 1974-77; terr. mgr. Cilco Corp., Huntington, W.Va., 1979-84; clin. instr. surg. svcs. Boston U. Med. Ctr., 1988-93; dir. surg. svcs. Frisbie Meml. Hosp., Rochester, N.H., 1993-94; clin. instr. surg. tech. Bunker Hill C.C., Boston, 1995, dir. surg. tech., 1998—; oper. rm. nurse Beth Israel Deaconess Med. Ctr., Boston, 1996—; dir. surg. tech. program Bunker Hill C.C., 1998—. Team mem., instr. partnership program Boston U., Erevan, Armenia, 1993. Capt. USAR, 1976-81. N.Y. Bd. Regents scholar, 1963-66. Mem. Am. Urol. Assn. Allied (v.p. 1991-92, pres. 1992-94), Genesee Hosp. Alumni Assn., Goddard Coll. Alumni Assn. (sec. 1975-77), Greater Lynn Photographic Assn. Democrat. Unitarian Universalist. Avocations: photography, sailing, skiing. Home: 49 Jackson Rd Medford MA 02155-2160 Office: Bunker Hill CC Chelsea Campus 175 Hawthorne St Chelsea MA 02150-3243 E-mail: jroman@bhcc.state.ma.us.

ROMAN, MARY, city official; b. Great Barrington, Mass., Sept. 30, 1939; d. Arthur Roger and Beatrice Louise (Cable) Barboza; m. Granville Smith Roman, Apr. 3, 1954; children: Warren David, Kenneth Roger, Michael Stuart, Craig Garfield, Gerald Spencer. Student, Springfield Coll., 1954, Am. Inst. Banking, Stamford, Conn., 1965-69. Teller, loan officer, v.p. Merchants Bank, Norwalk, Conn., 1965-89; br. mgr. Gateway Bank, Norwalk, Conn., 1989-99, Shawmut Bank, Norwalk, Conn., 1989-99, Fleet Bank, Norwalk, Conn., 1989-99; city clk. City of Norwalk, 1999—. Bd. dirs. Soc. to Aid Retarded, Norwalk, Conn., 1992—, Family and Children's Agy., Norwalk, 1997—; mem. Oak Hills Golf Authority, Norwalk, 1998—; mem., past grand marshall Conn. Sr. Olympics; mem. Am. Legion Aux., U.S.A. Track and Field. Recipient awards Celebrate Women, Inc., 1995, Norwalk Old Times, Inc,. 1995. Mem. Oak Hills Women's Golf Assn. (past pres.). Avocations: horseback riding, golf, masters and senior olympics track and field. Home: 1 Birchside Dr Norwalk CT 06850-1513 Office: City of Norwalk 125 East Ave Norwalk CT 06851-5702

ROMAN, NANCY GRACE, astronomer, consultant; b. Nashville, May 16, 1925; d. Irwin and Georgia Frances (Smith) R. BA (Joshua Lippincott Meml. fellow), Swarthmore Coll., 1946; PhD, U. Chgo., 1949; D.Sc., Russell Sage Coll., 1966, Hood Coll., 1969, Bates Coll., 1971, Swarthmore Coll., 1976. Asst. Sproul Obs., Swarthmore Coll., 1943-46; asst. Yerkes Obs., U. Chgo., at Williams Bay, Wis., 1946-48, research asso., 1949-52, instr. stellar astronomy, 1952-55, asst. prof., 1955; research asso. Warner and Swasey Obs., Case Inst. Tech., Cleve., summer 1949; physicist radio astronomy br. U.S. Naval Research Lab., Washington, 1955-56, astronomer, head microwave spectroscopy sect., 1956-58, astronomer cons., 1958-59; head observational astronomy program Office Space Flight Devel., NASA, Washington, 1959-60, chief astronomy and solar physics, geophysics and astronomy programs, 1960—79, chief astronomy and relativity programs, 1965—80, program scientist for space telescope, 1979-80; astronomy cons., 1980-89; prin. scientist Astronomical Data Ctr., NASA, 1981—97. With McDonnell Douglas Space Systems, 1988-94. Contbr. articles to sci. periodicals. Trustee Russell Sage Coll., 1973-78; bd. mgrs. Swarthmore Coll., 1979-83. Recipient Fed. Woman's award., 1962; citation for pub. service Colo. Woman's Coll., 1966; 90th Anniversary award Women's Ednl. and Indsl. Union, 1967; NASA Exceptional Sci. Achievement award, 1969; NASA Outstanding Leadership medal, 1978 Fellow AAAS, Am. Astronautical Soc. (William Randolf Lovelace II award 1980); mem. AAUW, Am. Astron. Soc., Internat. Astron. Union (editor symposia 1956-58), Astron. Soc. Pacific. Acheivements include rsch. on stellar clusters, high velocity stars, radio astronomy; 1st noted correlation of metallic lines in stars with their space velocity; asteroid named Roman, 1989. Personal E-mail: nancy.roman6@verizon.net.

ROMAN, ROBIN, anesthesiologist; b. Newark, N.J., July 7, 1956; d. Lee and Estelle (Kukolnik) R.; m. Gregory August Stork, Oct. 12, 1991; 1 child, Heather. BS, Georgetown U., 1978; MD, U. Med. & Dentistry N.J., 1982. Diplomate Am. Bd. Anesthesiology with added qualifications in pain mgmt. Resident Hartford (Conn.) Hosp., 1985; fellow dept. anesthesiology NYU, 1986; anesthesiologist Hartford Anesthesia Assocs., 1986—; med. dir. Health-South, Hartford, Conn. Mem. AMA, Am. Soc. Regional Anesthesia, Am. Soc. Anesthesiologists, Internat. Anesthesia Rsch. Soc., Soc. for Cardiovascular Anesthesiology, Soc. for Pediat. Anesthesia, Conn. State Med. Soc., Hartford County Med. Soc. Roman Catholic. Avocations: piano, tennis, swimming, ice skating, Karate. Home: 14 Talcott Mountain Rd Simsbury CT 06070-2515 Personal E-mail: 3storks@sbcglobal.net.

ROMANA, KATHLEEN, writer; b. Boston, Oct. 30, 1957; Student, Mus. Sch. Art, Boston, 1973-75; diploma, Butera Sch. Art, Boston, 1979; AA, Back Bay C.C., Boston, 1981. Freelance illustrator various advt. agys., Boston, 1981-92, freelance copywriter, 1990-92; poet/writer Austin, Tex., 1993—; owner Odyssey Vintage Clothing Store, 2000—. Author, poet, illustrator: Dreamscapes and Other Wanderings, 1998; author, editor, illustrator: Thy Kingdom Come, 1998; author of poetry included in anthologies: Outstanding Poets of 1998, The Isle of View, 1998, Daydreams, 2000, Tides of Memory, 2000, Treasured Poems of America, 2000, Internat. Libr. Poetry, 2000, Ovations, 2001, Best Poems and Poets of 2001 (anthologies) Homecomings, The Silence Within, Acclamations; published Austin Daze Newspaper, Sept. 2003; Austin Poets for Peace, 2003; Illustrator Austin Poets for Peace, 2003; performer, Forest Fest Poetry Festival, 2003; Expressions, Austin 2003 Recipient Editors Choice award and Poet of Merit award Internat. Libr. Poets, Pres.'s award for Lit. Excellence, Iliad Press, 2001, The Pres. award Literary Excellence, 2002; others. Mem. Internat. Soc. Poets (disting.), Nat. Libr. Poetry. Avocations: samurai saber, tai chi, fan form.

ROMANELLO, MARGUERITE MARIE, retired librarian; b. San Francisco, Feb. 14, 1939; d. Antonio Joseph and Josephine Remilda (Magliano) R. BA cum laude, Lone Mountain Coll., 1960, MA, 1961. Cert. secondary tchr. and librarian, Calif. Instr. Portola Jr. High Sch., San Francisco, 1961-74, Abraham Lincoln High Sch., San Francisco, 1978-81; libr. Francisco Jr. High Sch., San Francisco, 1974-75, instr., 1975-78; libr., media specialist Raoul Wallenberg Traditional High Sch., San Francisco, 1981—; test reader math and English San Francisco Sch. Dist. Assessment Office, 1981—2000; ret., 1998. Judge U.S. Acad. Decathalon, San Francisco, 1988, 89. Author: MOSAIC, 1975, (play) Scenes from Sense and Sensibility, 1986; editor San Francisco Guitar Soc. Newsletter, 1975-76; exhibitor Festival of Needlework, San Francisco, 1979. Founder, curator Raoul Wallenberg Mus., San Francisco, 1981—; active in Community Adv. Coun., San Francisco, 1968-70, KRON Community Adv. Com., San Francisco, 1985-94, Adopt-A-Sch. Program, San Francisco, 1988—, San Francisco Opera Guild; vol. Humanities West, 1993-96. Grantee Office of Supt., San Francisco, 1972, Calif. State Assembly, Sacramento, 1988; hist. Dickens Fellowship of San Francisco, 1992. Mem. Jane Austen Soc. North Am. (chmn. mem. 1986-89, mem. ann. grand meeting planning com. 1996—), Assoc. Alumni of Sacred Heart, Alpha Psi (treas. Alpha Delta Kappa chpt. 1978-80, corr. sec. 1976-78, 92-94, recording sec. 1994-96, chaplain 2004-06, sunshine com. chair 2000-06, sixty plus gamma mem. co-chair 2002-04, corr. sec. 2004-06), Catholic Profl. Women's Club (recording sec. 2005-). Roman Catholic. Avocations: reading, piano, guitar, writing, walking. Home: 15 Red Rock Way Apt 301N San Francisco CA 94131-1715 Office: Wallenberg High Sch 40 Vega St San Francisco CA 94115-3826

ROMANO, CLARE, artist; b. Palisade, NJ, 1922; m. John Ross; 2 children. BFA, Cooper Union, NY; student, Inst. d'Arte, Florence, Ecole des Beaux Arts, Fontainebleau. Faculty New Sch., NYC, Univ. Wash., Seattle, Vt. Studio Sch., Okla. Arts Inst., Pratt Inst., NYC, 1964—; prof. emeritus Pace Univ.

Co-author (with John Ross): Complete Printmaker, 1972, (rev. ed. with Tim Ross), 1990, John Ross and Clare Romano: Artists and the Book, 2001; one-woman shows include AAA Gallery, NYC, Galleria Segno Grafica, Venice, Jane Haslem Gallery, Washington, NJ State Mus., Represented in permanent collections MoMA, Whitney Mus., Met. Mus. Art, Bklyn. Mus., Tokyo Art Ctr., Queensland Mus., Moderna Gallorija, Ljubljana, Slovenia, British Mus. Grantee Fulbright Fellow, Louis Comfort Tiffany Grant, NJ States Coun. Arts grant, five fellowships to MacDowell Colony. Mem.: NAD (Academician 1979—). Mailing: PO Box 1122 New York NY 10159-1122

ROMANO, MENA N., artist, educator; b. Bronx, N.Y., Oct. 16, 1943; d. Gerardo and Paulina (Sciurba) DeSanctis; m. Nicholas Romano, Nov. 23, 1963; children: Dina Marie Girola, Nicholas Carmine, Jr.(dec.). AS in Fine Arts, Suffolk County CC, Selden, N.Y., 1983; BFA summa cum laude, Long Is. U., 1986, MFA, 1988. Coord. art internships Nassau CC, Garden City, NY, prof. art, 1996—; adj. asst. prof. art Suffolk County C C, Selden, NY, 1988—. Vis. artist B.O.C.E.S. Art in Edn. program, 1992-; curator art, exhbns. Chess Collectors Internat., 1990; lectr. in field. Exhbns. include Islip Art Mus., S.W. Tex. State U. Gallery, Fine Art Mus. Long Island, The Pen and Brush Club N.Y.; permanent installations Meditation Garden, Garden City, 13th St. Garden Portals, Chgo., Adelphi U. Campus, Garden City, NY. Grantee Artist Space, N.Y., 1990, others. Mem. Nat. Drawing Assn. (chair membership 1990-91), Long Island Craft Guild (pres. 1994-95), Phi Theta, Pi Alpha Sigma. Avocations: travel, gardening.

ROMANO, SHEILA JUNE, telecommunications industry professional, writer, artist; b. Elko, Nev., June 11, 1951; d. John Lewis and June Florene (Lani) C. BA, U. Nev., 1974. Various svc. positions Citizens Comm. (formerly Alltel-Nevada Inc.), Elko, 1974-78, svc. rep., 1978-84, bus. office supr., 1984-87, bus. supr. Nev. office, 1987-94, bus. supr., state pub. rels. coord., 1994-97, results coord., project mgmt. support person Elk Grove, Calif., 1997, supr. customer ops. escalations and exec. complaints, 1998-2000, specialist state gov. affairs, 2001—02; sr. regulatory analyst Frontier Comm., 2002—. Active Citizens Amb. program People to People Internat., 1995—98; writer, artist, 1974—. Contbg. author: Fence Post to Fiber, 1998. Officer, organizer Freedom Com., Elko, 1984; mem., treas. Elk Grove Cmty. Action Team, 1997-98. Mem. NOW, AAUW (editor newsletter Elko 1980-82, v.p. programs 1991-93, sec. 1995-96), Soroptimists Internat. (treas. 1992-93, sec. 1993-94, v.p. 1995-96, pres. 1996-97). Office: Frontier PO Box 340 Elk Grove CA 95759-0340

ROMANOFF, MARJORIE REINWALD, retired education educator; b. Chgo., Sept. 29, 1923; d. David Edward and Gertrude (Rosenfield) Reinwald; m. Milford M. Romanoff, Nov. 6, 1945; children: Bennett Sanford, Lawrence Michael, Janet Beth (dec.). Student, Northwestern U., 1941-42, 43-45, Chgo. Coll. Jewish Studies, 1942-43; BEd, U. Toledo, 1947, MEd, 1968, EdD, 1976. Tchr. Old Orchard Elem. Sch., Toledo, 1946-47, McKinley Sch., Toledo, 1964-65; substitute tchr. Toledo, 1964-68; instr. Mary Manse Coll., Toledo, 1974; instr. children's lit. Sylvania (Ohio) Bd. Edn., 1977; supr. student tchrs. U. Toledo, 1968—73, 1985—2001, instr. advanced comms., 1977, rschr., 1973-74; instr. Am. Lang. Inst., 1978—2002. Asst. prof. elem. edn. Bowling Green (Ohio) State U., 1978—88; chair rsch. com. Am. Lang. Inst., U. Toledo, 1985—94, asst. prof. elem. edn. in lang. arts, 1985—87, asst. prof. elem. edn., ESL specialist, 1978—2002; condr. workshop Internat. Conf./Teaching Langs., U. Cin., 1996; presenter in field. Author: Language and Study Skills: For Learners of English, Prentice Hall Regents, 1991. Trustee Children's Svcs. Bd., 1974-76; pres. bd. Cummings Treatment Ctr. for Adolescents, 1978-80; mem. Crosby Gardens Adv. Bd., 1976-82, Cmty. Planning Coun., 1980-84, Citizens Rev. Bd. of Juv. Ct., 1979—; allocations com. Mental Health and Retardation Bd., 1980-81; active Bd. Jewish Edn., 1976—, pres., 1982-84; active Jewish Family Svc., 1978-85, v.p., 1980-85; allocations com. Jewish Welfare Fedn., 1980, 89-91; bd. dirs. Family Life Edn. Coun., 1984-90, sec., 1988-90; budget and allocations com. Jewish Fedn., 1989-93; bd. dirs. Friends Toledo-Lucas County Librs., 1991—, bd. pres., 1991-93; program chair U. Toledo Women's Commn., 1991-93; bd. dirs. Ohio Friends of Pub. Librs., 1992-94. Named One of Ten Women of Yr., St. Vincent's Hosp., Guild, 1984, Outstanding Instructional Staff Woman, U. Toledo, 1990, Excellence award Citizen's Rev. Bd., 2003. Mem. Tchrs. English to Speakers Other Langs., Toledo Libr. Legacy Found., Orgn. Rehab. and Tng. (named Outstanding Woman in Cmty. Svc. 1987), Hadassah (chpt. pres. regional bd. 1961-64), Northwestern U. Alumni Assn., Phi Kappa Phi, Phi Delta Kappa, Kappa Delta Pi (pres., faculty adv. 1971-75, Point of Excellence award 1992), Pi Lambda Theta (chpt. pres. 1978-80, nat. com. 1979-84). Home: Stratford in the Hills 4343 W Bancroft St Apt 4B Toledo OH 43615

ROMANO-MAGNER, PATRICIA R., English studies educator, researcher; b. NYC, Mar. 22, 1928; d. Al and Nicole (Siriani) Romano; m. Ralph M. Magner, Dec. 24, 1954. AA, BA, L.A. City Coll.; MA, Calif. State U., L.A.; D (hon.), Stanford U., Cambridge (Eng.) U., Queens Coll. Master tchr. Burbank (Calif.) Unified Sch. Dist., L.A. City Schs., Stanford (Calif.) U. Sch. for the Gifted; prof. Calif. State U., L.A., curriculum lab. asst. LA. Mem. AAUW, AAUP (award 2000), Am. Legion Aux., Sierra Club, Natural Resources Def. Coun., The Friends of the William J. Clinton Presdl. Libr. (founding mem.), Scholarship Soc. of Calif. State U. L.A. Republican. Avocation: horseback riding. Home: 5975 N Odell Ave Chicago IL 60631-2358 Address: Box 31195 Chicago IL 60631-0195

ROMANOVICH, PATRICIA M., parochial school educator; b. Akron, Ohio, Dec. 11, 1937; d. Joseph and Mary (Dorosz) Siwik; m. Paul Romanovich, Sept. 13, 1958; children: Paula Marie, Gregory Joseph, Jeffrey John, Martin Paul. BS in Edn., St. John Coll., Cleve., 1971; M.Curriculum and Instrn., Cleve. State U., 1988. Tchr. St. Josaphat Sch., Parma, Ohio, 1964—87, tchr., tech. coord., 1998—2004, tech. advisor, 2004—; tchr. St. Columbkille Sch., Parma, 1987—90; tchr., computer coord. St. Anthony Sch., Parma, 1990—93, Greenbriar Jr. H.S., Parma Heights, Ohio, 1993—98. Tech. adv. bd. chair St. Josaphat Sch., 1998—2004, curriculum chair, 1998—2004, drama club dir., 1998—; creator, rschr. flip chart Sch. Crisis Mgmt. Plan, 1999—2003. Named one of Outstanding Elem. Tchrs. of Am., 1974; recipient Excellence in Tchg. award, Diocese of Cleve., 2001; grantee Tech. grantee, Sch. Net, Columbus, 2001. Mem.: Korean War Vets. Assn. Ukrainian Catholic. Avocations: reading, travel, country walks. Home: 5400 Sandy Hook Dr Parma OH 44134 Office Phone: 440-884-1812. Personal E-mail: sandyvalley@sbcglobal.net.

ROMANOWSKI, SARAH REBECCA, secondary school educator; b. St. Louis, Sept. 11, 1976; d. Roy Arthur and Barbara Ann Zoller; m. Louis Frank Romanowski, Nov. 27, 2004. B, St. Ambrose U., Davenport, Iowa, 1998. Tchr. Potosi Sch. Dist., Mo., 1999—2001, Webster Groves H.S., St. Louis, 2001—. Dir. Webster Groves H.S., 2001—. Dir.: (high school theater) Seussical the Musical. Office: Webster Groves HS 100 Selma Saint Louis MO 63126 Office Phone: (314) 918-4153.

ROMANSKI, JOYCE MARIE, secondary school educator, small business owner; b. Bklyn., July 15, 1936; d. Harold Joseph and Mildred Helen Grace (Mills) Culkin; m. Andrew Henry Romanski, Sept. 17, 1966 (dec. Nov. 1996). AA, Ctrl. Fla. C.C., 1976; BA in Psychology, U. Fla., 1979, M of English Edn., 1982, EdS in Curriculum and Instrn., 1985. Clk. Manhattan Savs. Bank, N.Y.C., 1956-58, sec. ins. divsn., 1959-61, exec. sec. real estate, 1961-64, asst. sec. securities, 1966-70, dep. sec., asst. to pres., 1970-71, dep. sec., asst. to CEO, 1971-74; tutor North Marion Mid. Sch., Citra, Fla., 1979-80, tchr., 1980—. Cons. Abacuss Tng., Citra, FCAT Tng., Crown Region, Fla., Tech. for Educators, Citra, Connections Dept. of Edn., Tallahassee, 1999—, Grants for Great Ideas, Public Education Foundation, 2002-2003; panalist Nat. Bd. for Profl. Tchg. Stds., 1993; mem. Marion County Writing Prompt Com. for FCAT Student Preparation, 2003; mem. Marion county Final Lang. Arts Exam Devel. Com., 2004— Mem. posse Marion County Sheriff's Dept., Ocala, 1986—89, lt. posse, 1989—92, capt. mounted posse, 1992—97; coord. US/USSR Exch. program, 1988—89, US/Latvia Student Exch. program, 1989—90; elected Marion County Exec. Com. Precinct Woman, 2004—; reps. exec. com. precinct woman Merion County, 2004—; candidate Marion County Sch. Bd., 2006—. Butcher scholar Ctrl. Fla. C.C., 1976; Marion County Sch. Sys., Tchrs. mini-grantee, 1988; grantee Dept. of Edn. Tech., 1999, Grants for Great Ideas, 2002. Mem. Fla. Assn. Compputers in Edn., Image Tech. Team, Ocala Ladies Golf Assn., Stride Dressage Club, Arredondo Dressage Soc. Republican. Lutheran. Avocations: horseback riding, dressage training and showing, golf, swimming, bowling. Home: Pegasus Farm PO Box 1059 Fairfield FL 32634-1059 Office: Pegasus Enterprises 15895 NW 115th Ct Reddick FL 32686 Office Phone: 352-816-1379. Personal E-mail: diamondpegasus_586@yahoo.com. Business E-Mail: diamondpegasus58@aol.com.

ROMANUCCI-ROSS, LOLA, anthropologist, educator; b. Hershey, Pa., June 13, 1928; d. Ignazio and Josephine (Giovannozzi) R.; m. John Ross Jr., Aug. 26, 1972; children: Deborah Lee, Adan Anthony. BA, Ohio U., 1948; MA, U. Minn., 1953; postgrad., Ecole des Hautes Etudes, Paris, 1961-63; PhD in Anthropology, Ind. U., 1963. Rsch. assoc. Am. Mus. Natural History, N.Y.C., 1963-67; assoc. prof. U. Hawaii, Honolulu, 1967-68; from asst. prof. to prof. family and preventive medicine and anthropology Sch. Medicine U. Calif., San Diego, 1969—. Mem. study sect. HEW Maternal and Child Health, Bethesda, Md., 1973-75; cons. NSF, 1988—. Author: Conflict, Violence and Morality in a Mexican Village, 1973, 2d edit., 1986, Mead's Other Manus: Phenomenology of the Encounter, 1985, One Hundred Towers; an Italian Odyssey of Cultural Survival, 1991; editor: Ethnic Identity, 1975, 4th edit., 2006, The Anthropology of Medicine, 1982, 3d edit., 1997, When Law and Medicine Meet: A Cultural View, 2004; mem. editl. bd.: Anthropology and Humanism Quarterly, Interdisciplinary Jour. Study of Health, Illness and Medicine, 1997—, contbr. articles to profl. jours., book chpts. Grantee Wenner-Gren Found. for Anthropol. Rsch., 1974-75. Fellow Am. Anthropol. Soc.; mem. Soc. Med. Anthropology, Soc. Psychol. Anthropology, Soc. Anthropology of Europe, Soc. Cultural Anthropology, Soc. Health and Human Values. Achievements include research in New Guinea, South Pacific, Italy and Mexico. Avocations: music, hiking, literature, writing.

ROMEO, JOANNE JOSEFA MARINO, mathematics educator; b. Youngstown, Ohio, Nov. 21, 1943; d. Joseph James and Ann Marie (Bonamase) Marino; m. John Homer Romeo, Aug. 14, 1965; children: Christopher, Chrisanne, Jonathan; m. Harwood D. Schaffer, Apr. 25, 2003. BS, Ohio State U., 1965; postgrad., Youngstown State U., 1969-70; MS, Purdue U., 1974; postgrad. in computer sci., U. Tenn., Knoxville, 1982-91. Substitute tchr., Columbus, Ohio, 1964-65; tchr. geometry, math. and French Hamilton Sch. Dist., Columbus, Ohio, 1965-66; tchr. gifted children Bluegrass Elem. Sch., Knoxville, Tenn., 1976-77; tchr. math. and sci. Webb Sch., Knoxville, 1977-85, also developer computer sci. program, 1977-85; headmistress Greenbrier Acad., Sevierville, Tenn., 1985-86; instr. math. Pellissippi State Tech. Community Coll., Knoxville, Tenn., 1986—; dir. religious edn. Sacred Heart Parish, Knoxville, Tenn., 1987—2001; tchr. advanced math. Knox County Sch., Knoxville, Tenn., 2000—02; math. dept. chair, Washburn H.S. Grainger County Schs., Washburn, Tenn., 2004—. Delegate to go to Russia and Lithuania Ministries of Edn., NCEA. Vol dir. religious edn. Sacred Heart Parish, Knoxville, 1979-87, lay pastoral minister, 1988-2004. Mem. Nat. Council Tchrs. Math., Nat. Cath. Edn. Assn., Nat. Council Parish and Religious Coordinators and Dirs., Nat. Sci. Tchrs. Assn., Nat. Assn. Exec. Females, Ohio State U. Alumni Assn., Tenn. Assn. Dirs. Religious Edn., Purdue U. Alumni Assn., Alpha Gamma Delta. Independent. Home: 1708 Capistrano Dr Knoxville TN 37922-6302 Personal E-mail: joannejmr@yahoo.com.

ROMER, ANN ELIZABETH, school psychologist; b. Jamestown, N.Y., June 21, 1940; d. Andrew Martin and Ellen Jean (Chiverton) Gunnarson; m. Paul A. Romer, July 14, 1962; children: Kirsten, Daniel, Erika. BA, Alfred U., 1962; MEd, Kent State U., 1979, Ednl. Specialist, 1980. Lic. sch. psychologist, Ohio, N.Mex.; assoc. psychologist, Tex. Sch. psychologist Astabual County Bd. Edn., Jefferson, Ohio, 1980-85, Trumbull County Bd. Edn., Warren, Ohio, 1985-90; ednl. diagnostician Gadsden Ind. Sch. Dist., Anthony, N.Mex., 1992-93, level I sch. psychologist, 1993-94, level II sch. psychologist, 1994—2000; sch. psychologist Vacaville Unified Sch. Dist., Calif., 2001—04, part-time contract work, 2004—06; ret., 2006. Cons. sch. psychologist. Listener Trumbull Contact, Warren, 1972-74; co-leader Girl Scouts U.S., 1971-74. Mem. Nat. Assn. Sch. Psychologists, N.Mex. Assn. Sch. Psychologists (So. state rep. 1993-95, pres.-elect 1995-96, pres. 1996-97). Mem. Christian Ch. Avocations: reading, gardening, bowling, needlecrafts, stamp collecting/philately.

ROMER, CAROLE JOYCE, volunteer; d. Thomas Sydney and Lola Lillian (Spiegel) Cohen; m. William Romer, July 7, 1957 (dec.); children: Lisa Melanie, Kevin Douglas. Student, U. Miami, 1951—52, Miami Dade Coll., 1960—70. Chairmanships B'nai B'rith Women, Fla., 1969—90, internat. pres., 1990—95; pres. Fla. Hillel Bd., B'nai B'rith Youth Orgn. State Assn.; chmn. So. Fla. Women's Courses, Hero's Help, Fla., City Adv. Commn. Dade County. V.p. Highland Oaks PTA, Fla.; vol. Heart Fund Assn., Cancer Soc.; chmn. Jewish Women's Polit. Courses, Fla.; com. mem. Jewish Cmty. Ctr., Fla.; founding bd. mem. Mathew Forbes Romer Found., 1995. Named Honoree, Hillel Bd. Found., 1987, B'nai B'rith Youth Orgn., 1988. Avocations: bridge, tennis, reading.

ROMER, DENISE PATRICE, lawyer; b. Tulsa, Jan. 11, 1975; d. Franz Karl and Trudy Maria Romer. BS in Sociology, Okla. State U., 1997; M in Alternative Dispute Resolution, Pepperdine U., 2000, JD, 2000. Bar: Calif. 2001, Wis. 2002, Okla. 2004. Clk. Tulsa Early Settlement - Divsn. Tulsa County Ct. Sys., 1999—99, Tulsa County Office Dist. Atty., 1998—98; asst. to counsel Nat. Assn. Securities Dealers, L.A., 1999—99; legal clk. Calif. Lawyers for Arts, Santa Monica, 2000—00; assoc. atty. Korenberg, Abramowitz & Feldun, Sherman Oaks, Calif., 2001—02; criminal def. atty. Boyle, Boyle & Paulus, S.C., Milw., 2002—03; litig. and employment support GE Med. Sys., Waukesha, Wis., 2003—; assoc. atty. Gibbs, Armstrong, Borochoff, Hillican & Hart, 2003—. Apprentice KFAQ Talk Radio, Tulsa, Okla., 2004. Author poetry. Rep. internet team leader Rep. Nat. Com., Tulsa, Okla., 2003—; supporter/ mem. So. Poverty Law Ctr.- Nat. Campaign for Tolerance, L.A., 2001—. Mem.: ABA (assoc.), State Bar Okla. (assoc.), State Bar Calif. (assoc.), State Bar Wis. (assoc.), L.A. County Bar Assn. (assoc.), The Smithsonian Instn. (assoc.), Pepperdine U. Alumni Assn. (life). Conservative. Roman Catholic. Avocations: writing, yoga, travel. Home: 6904 White Walnut Way Braselton GA 30517 Personal E-mail: romer33@hotmail.com.

ROMERO, ANNETTE LOUISE, multi-media specialist, educator; d. Walter Joseph and Emma Louise Romero. BS Edn., U. Tex., Austin, 1978; M Edn., Sam Houston State U., Huntsville, Tex., 1980. Tchr. phys. edn. Conroe Ind. Sch. Dist., The Woodlands, Tex., 1978—79, Spring Branch Ind. Sch. Dist., Houston, 1980—90; coord. tech. Meml. H.S., Houston, 1995—2005, tchr. tech. applications, 1999—. V.p. Tex. Assn. Golf Coaches, 2004—; coach volleyball and track Conroe Ind. Sch. Dist., The Woodlands, 1978—79; coach varsity volleyball Spring Branch Ind. Sch. Dist., Houston, 1980—95, coach varsity boys golf, 2000—; coach varsity girls golf Meml. H.S., Houston, 1990—, sch. webmaster, 1999—. Office: Memorial High School 6316 Crab Orchard Houston TX 77024 Office Fax: 713-365-5138. E-mail: annette.romero@springbranchisd.com.

ROMERO, CHRISTIANE, German language educator; married; 2 children. Matura mit auszeichnung, Realgymnasium, Vienna, 1959; lehramtsprüfung in German and English, PhD, U Vienna, 1963; diploma in French, La Sorbonne, Paris, 1964; MPhil in Comparative Lit., Yale U., 1967. Lectr. in German Yale U., 1964-67; asst prof. Emmanuel Coll., Boston, 1970-73, Tufts U., Medford, Mass., 1973-78, assoc. prof., 1978-85, prof., 1985—, acting chair dept. German and Russian, 1983, chair dept. German, Russian, and Asian Langs. and Lits., 1988—. Lectr. women's studies, social justice and peace program, intro. to inetrnat. rels. Tufts U., past mem. student honors com., undergraduate admissions and fin aid com., ednl. policy com., grad. sch. policy com., faculty personnel com., grievance panel com., univ. planning and budget proirities com., tenure and promotion com., mem. internat. rels. exec. com., women's program adv. bd. com., comm. cluster exec. com, com. on coms., 1991—, faculty rep. to trustee com. on acad. affairs, 1985-86, faculty rep. to trustee com. on devel., 1991—; vis. asst. prof. German Duke U., 1967-70; coord. sect. Internat. Symposium on GDR, Conway, N.H., 1978—; panelist on German films Goethe Inst. workshop Middlebury (Vt.) Coll., 1979; mem. selection com. U.S. Congress-German Bundestags Exch. Program, 1983-88; panelist Fourth New England Workshop on German Affairs, Boston, 1983, Ctr. for European Studies, Harvard U., 1984; mem. exec. com. Grad. Consortium in Women's Studies, Radcliffe Coll., 1991—; lectr. Bryn Mawr Coll., 1977, Fletcher Sch. Law and Diplomacy, 1981, Cornell U., 1981, Smith Coll, 1982, Simmons Coll., 1984, U. Mass., Amherst, 1989, MIT, 1989, Timburlane Regional High Sch., N.H., 1989, Mich. Symposium, Ann Arbor, 1990, ctr. for internat. studies U. Pitts., 1991. Author: Simone de Beuvoir, 1978, 12th rev. edit., 1994, Anna Seghers, 1993; editor: Kritische Intelligenz, 1982; contbr. articles to profl. jours.; presenter papers in field. Fellow Yale U., 1964-67; Summer Rsch. fellow Tufts U., 1975, 84, 95; grantee Am. Philos. Soc., 1981; summer grantee NEH, 1981; rsch. grantee Am. Coun. Learned Socs., 1981-82; grantee Dept. Edn. (FIPSE), 1989. Mem. MLA (chair seminars 1975, 1988 (two), mem. exec. com. divsn. 20th century German lit. 1986-90), AAUP (exec. com., past chair com. W, v.p., pres. Tufts chpt.), Am. Assn. Tchrs. German (pres. Mass. chpt. 1983-84, past. sec., v.p., pres.-elect), Northeast MLA (chair 19th century German lit. 1977, 81, v.p. 1988-89, pres. 1989-90), Women in German. Office: Tufts U Dept German Russian & Asian Langs & Lits Medford MA 02155

ROMERO, JANE PATRICIA, nursing administrator; b. NYC, Oct. 9, 1949; d. Edmund Aloysius and Catherine Clara Marano; m. Gary Eugene Romero, June 19, 1976; 1 child, Miranda; 1 child, Carina. BS, Chapman U., Orange, Calif., 1979; BSN, George Mason U., Fairfax, Va., 1996; chef cert., Cambridge Sch. Culinary Arts. RN Calif., 1972; CLC Kaplan U., 1998. Clin. rsch. nurse NIH, Bethesda, Md., 1988—96, adminstrv. coord., 2004—; home health infusion specialist Olsteen/Quantum, Marlboro, Mass., 1996—2000; rsch. nurse Clinica Medica, Waltham, Mass., 2000—02; supr. nursing Mass. Eye and Ear Infirmary, Boston, 2000—03; supr. IV pharmacy Kaiser Permanente, San Francisco, 2003—04. Coach Spl. Olympics, Landstuhz, Germany, 1985—86; spkr., founder advocacy group for parents of handicapped children Germany, 1986; pres. Lynbrook Elem. PTA, Fairfax County, Va., 1990—92; sec. Higashi PTA, Randolph, Mass., 1997—99. Capt. USAF, 1975—78. Mem.: Nat. Guild Hypnotists (cert. hypnotist). Office: NIH 9000 Rockville Pike Bethesda MD 20814

ROMERO, TRACI BAUDOIN, science educator; b. Lafayette, La., Oct. 12, 1977; d. Larry James and Deanna Gaspard Baudoin; m. Dalton Joseph Romero, Mar. 20, 1998; children: Andrew Jospeh, Alli Elizabeth. BA in Elem. Edn., U. La., Lafayette, 2001. Cert. tchr. La. Dept. Edn., 2001. Tchr. 7th grade life sci. Anderson Mid. Sch., New Iberia, La., 2002—. Leader AMS 4H Club, New Iberia, La., 2003—. Religion tchr. OLPS Chouch, New Iberia, 2005—06. Democrat. Roman Catholic. Home: 5905 Coteau Road New Iberia LA 70560 Office: Anderson Middle School 1059 Anderson Street New Iberia LA 70560 Office Phone: 337-365-3932. Office Fax: 337-367-8285. Business E-Mail: trromero@iberia.k12.la.us.

ROMERO-RAINEY, REBECA, bank executive; d. Martin and Cheryl Romero; m. John Rainey. Degree, Wellesley Coll. Pres., CEO Centinal Bank Taos, N.Mex., 1999—, bd. dir., 1999—. Bd. admissions Wellesley Coll. V.p. Taos Chpt. Habitat for Humanity; sec., treas. Bridges Project Edn. Taos; mem. Leadership N.Mex.; treas. N.Mex. Cmty. Found.; bd. dir. Taos (N.Mex.) Feeds Taos; treas. bd. dirs. Rocky Mountain Youth Corps. Named One of 25 Women to Watch, U.S. Banker Mag., 2003. Mem.: Ind. Cmty. Bankers Assn. N.Mex. (bd. dir. 2003—).

ROMETTY, GINNY (VIRGINIA M. ROMETTY), information technology executive; b. 1957; BS in Computer Sci., Elec. Engring. with high hon., Northwestern U. Applications, sys. devel. GM Corp.; bus., IT cons. IBM, 1985—91, supr. ops. ins. rsch., gen. mgr. strategy mktg., sales ops., gen. mgr. global services Am., mng. ptnr. bus. cons. services, 2002—05, sr. v.p., global bus. services, 2005—. Mem. bd. IBM Worldwide Mgmt. Coun., Sr. Leadership Team; bd. dirs. Am. Internat. Group (AIG), 2006—. Named a Global Bus. Influential, Time Mag., 2002; named one of 50 Most Powerful Women in Bus., Fortune mag., 2006. Office: IBM Corp 1133 Westchester Ave White Plains NY 10604*

ROMIJN, REBECCA, actress, model; b. Berkeley, Calif., Nov. 6, 1972; m. John Stamos, Sept. 19, 1998 (div. Mar. 1, 2005); children: Jaap Romihn Stamos, Elizabeth Kuizenga Stamos. Attended, U. Calif., Santa Cruz. Model Sports Illustrated, Christian Dior, Victoria's Secret, Biotherm, Clarins, Dillards, Escada, Furla, Got Milk?, J.Crew, La Senza, Liz Claiborne, Matrix Essentials, Maybelline, Pantene Pro V, Tommy Hilfiger, various others. Actor: (films) Dirty Work, 1998, X-Men, 2000, Rollerball, 2002, Femme Fatale, 2002, X2, 2003, The Punisher, 2004, Godsend, 2004, The Alibi, 2006, Man About Town, 2006, X-Men: The Last Stand, 2006; (TV films) Hefner: Unauthorized, 1999; (TV series) Just Shoot Me, 1999—2000, Pepper Dennis, 2006—, (TV appearances) Friends, 1997, Jack & Jill, 2000. Office: Bragman Nyman Cafarelli 8687 Melrose Ave West Hollywood CA 90069-5701*

ROMNEY, PATRICIA ANN, psychologist, educator; b. N.Y., June 14, 1944; d. Hubert Forbes and Bernetta J (Taylor) R.; m. Joaquin Rosa, Aug. 25,1973 (div. 1980); children: Joaquin Maceo, Imani Romney; m. Paul Henry Wiley, June 2, 1984; 1 child, Maya Pacem. BA, Good Counsel Coll., White Plains, N.Y., 1966; PhD, CUNY, 1980. Lic. Clin. Psychologist. Coll. psychologist Mt. Holyoke Coll., South Hadley, Mass., 1981-86, vis. assoc. prof. psychology, 2001—; assoc. prof. psychology Hampshire Coll., Amherst, Mass., 1986—96; pres. Romney Assocs., Amherst, 1996—; pvt. practice Amherst, 1996—. Cons. Brown U., Phillips Acad., Smith Coll., U. Maine at Orono, 1988—. Contbr. articles to profl. jours. Mem. APA, Am. Family Therapy Acad. Avocations: reading, travel. Office: Romney Assocs 64 Carriage Ln Amherst MA 01002-3303 Office Phone: 413-253-5630. Business E-Mail: promney@romneyassociates.com.

ROMNEY-MANOOKIN, ELAINE CLIVE, retired music educator, composer; b. Salt Lake City, July 11, 1922; d. Joseph Campbell Clive and Katie Winifred Gilroy; m. Eldon Brigham Romney, May 5, 1941 (dec. May 1998); children: Ruth Romney Powell, Frederic Clive Romney, Clive Jay Romney, Stanley Clive Romney, Eldon Clive Romney, Roslyn Kay Romney Reynolds, Rae Lynne Romney Johnson, Vincent Clive Romney; m. Stuart Midgley Manookin. Studied piano, violin and cello, Clive Music Studios, Salt Lake City, 1938; cert., U. Utah, 1941; studied organ, U. S.C., 1954; studied piano with Frederic Dixon, McCune Sch., 1938—42; studied paino with Alton O'Steen, Juilliard, 1936. Musician: Assembly Hall with McCune Symphony, 1941, author organ book for beginning organists; composer: (sch. song) South H.S., 1939, Skyline H.S., 1962, Wasatch Jr. H.S., 1964; organist Grandview Second Ward, 2001—; organist: Columbia (S.C.) Stake Ctr., 1953—54, East Millcreek Stake, 1956—, Monument Pk. Stake, 1955—56. Bd. dirs. Utah Hemophlia Found., Salt Lake City, 1965—99; vol. specialist Welfare Employment; vice chmn. dist. Rep. Party, Salt Lake City, 1970—90. Recipient Dedicated Svc. award, Hemophilia Found., 1991. Mem.: Alpha Dorian Fine Arts Soc. (past pres.), AXO Luncheon Club (pres.), Agalia Mu (past pres.). Avocations: travel, writing, volunteering. Address: 2987 Hartford St Salt Lake City UT 84106-3468

RONALD, PAMELA C., plant pathologist, educator; Diploma in French Lang. Studies, U. Strasbourg, France, 1981; BA in Biology, Reed Coll., Portland, Oreg., 1982; MA in Biology, Stanford U., Calif., 1984; MS in Plant Physiology, U. Uppsala, Sweden, 1985; PhD in Molecular and Physiol. Plant Biology, U. Calif., Berkeley, 1990. Rsch. asst. dept. biology Stanford U., Calif., 1983—84; Fulbright fellow Inst. Botany U. Uppsala, Sweden, 1984—85; postdoctoral fellow dept. plant breeding Cornell U., 1990—92; asst. prof. dept. plant pathology U. Calif., Davis, 1992—97, assoc. prof.,

1997—2002, prof., 2002—. Founder, CEO Tellus Genetics, Davis, Calif., 1998—2000; Guggenheim fellow Lab. Molecular Biology of Plant-Microorganism Interactions Nat. Ctr. Sci. Rsch., Nat. Inst. Agronomic Rsch., Castanet-Tolosan, France, 2000; hon. scientist Nat. Inst. Agrl. Biotechnology, Republic of Korea, 2002—; chair plant genomics prog. U. Calif., Davis, 2004—05; external adv. Zhejiang U. Agrl. Inst., 2005—. Contbr. articles to sci. jours.; mem. editl. bd.: Planta, 1997—2002, Molecular Plant Pathology, 2002—, assoc. editor: Transgenic Rsch., 2003—, sr. editor: Molecular Plant Microbe Interactions, 2003—. Mem.: AAAS, Internat. Soc. Molecular Plant-Microbe Interactions, Am. Soc. Plant Biologists, Am. Phytopathological Soc. Office: Genome and Biomedical Scis Facility U Calif Davis 451 E Health Scis Dr Davis CA 95616-8816 E-mail: pcronald@ucdavis.edu.*

RONDEAU, DORIS JEAN, entrepreneur, consultant; b. Winston-Salem, N.C., Nov. 25, 1941; d. John Delbert and Eldora Virginia (Klutz) Robinson; m. Robert Breen Corrente, Sept. 4, 1965 (div. 1970); m. Wilfrid Dolor Rondeau, June 3, 1972. Student Syracuse U., 1959-62, Fullerton Jr. Coll., 1974-75; BA in Philosophy, Calif. State U.-Fullerton, 1976, postgrad., 1976-80. Ordained to ministry The Spirit of Divine Love, 1974. Trust real estate clk. Security First Nat. Bank, Riverside, Calif., 1965-68; entertainer Talent, Inc., Hollywood, Calif., 1969-72; co-founder, dir. Spirit of Divine Love, Huntington Beach, Calif., 1974—; pub., co-founder Passing Through, Inc., Huntington Beach, 1983—; instr. Learning Activity, Anaheim, Calif., 1984—; chmn. bd., prin. D.J. Rondeau, Entrepreneur, Inc., Huntington Beach, 1984—; co-founder, dir. Spiritual Positive Attitude, Inc., Moon In Pisces, Inc., Vibrations By Rondeau, Inc., Divine Consciousness, Expressed, Inc., Huntington Beach, Doris Wilfrid Rondeau, Inc., Huntington Beach, Calif. Author, editor: A Short Introduction To The Spirit of Divine Love, 1984; writer, producer, dir. performer spiritual vignettes for NBS Radio Network, KWVE-FM, 1982-84; author: Spiritual Meditations to Uplift the Soul, 1988. Served with USAF, 1963-65. Recipient Pop Vocalist First Place award USAF Talent Show, 1964, Sigma chpt. Epsilon Delta Chi, 1985, others. Mem. Hamel Bus. Grads., Smithsonian Assocs., Am. Mgmt. Assn., Nat. Assn. Female Execs. Fax: (714) 841-3286. Avocations: long-distance running, body fitness, arts and crafts, snorkeling, musical composition.

RONE, MONIKA HIEDI, mental health services professional, consultant; b. Hindsdale, Ill., Oct. 7, 1971; d. Donald Jacob and Agneta Elisabeth Sibrava; m. Jason Lee Rone (div.); 1 child, Jordin Elisabeth. BA, U. Ctrl. Ark., Conway, 1994; M Rehab. Counseling, Ark. State U., Jonesboro, 1997. Lic. profl. counselor Ark. Mental health therapist Mid South Health Sys., Pocahontas, Ark., 1997—2001, Ark. Counseling Assoc., Pocahontas, 2001—02, Families, Inc., Pocahontas, 2002—03, Life Strategies Counseling, Inc., Pocahontas, 2003—. Owner Monika Rone's Pvt. Counseling, Pocahontas, 2003—; presenter in field. Contbr. articles to profl. jours. Active Action on Smoking and Health, Pocahontas, 2004—. Recipient Honor of Appreciation award, Mid South Health Sys., 1998. Mem.: Ark. Counseling Assn. Democrat. Avocations: gardening, exercise, writing, travel. Office: Monika Rones Pvt Counseling Ctr 202 W Broadway Pocahontas AR 72455

RONEY, ALICE LORRAINE MANN, poet; b. Hartford, Mich., Dec. 6, 1926; d. Paul Douglass and Margaret Alice (Widener) Mann; m. Robert Kenneth Roney, Oct. 6, 1951; children: Stephen Paul, Karen Margaret. AA, Santa Monica Coll., 1946; BA, UCLA, 1950. Tech. writer Hughes Aircraft Co., Culver City, Calif., 1949—52; chmn. Ebell Jr. Blind Recording, LA, 1959—63; librarian St. Augustine-by-the-Sea Episcopal Day Sch. Santa Monica, Calif., 1961—68. Author: Those Treasured Moments, 1972, The Seeds of Love, 1975, Psalms for My Lord, 1975; co-author: Singing for Joy, 1989, numerous poems. Sch. bd. Episcopalian Ch., 1964—67, asst. directress altar guild, 1967—69, directress altar guild, 1969—71; treas. Diocese of LA Churchwomen, 1970—73. Recipient Ebell Jr. Svc. award, 1959, 2d pl. for poetry creative writing divsn. marina dist., Calif. Fedn. Women's Clubs Fine Arts Festival, 1979, 3d pl. for inspirational poetry, 1979, 2d and 3d pl., 1981, 1st and 2d pl., 1982, 1st pl., 1985, 2d pl., 1986, 3d pl. for light verse, 1980, 1st pl. for children's stories, 1983, 1985. Fellow: World Lit. Acad.; mem.: PEO (pres. chpt. QB 1969—71, 1976—78, 1986—88), Nat. Fedn. State Poetry Socs., Ky. State Poetry Soc., World Poetry Soc. (life), Calif. State Poetry Soc., Internat. Poetry Soc., Santa Monica Bay Woman's Club (1st v.p. 1980—82, pres. 1982—84, 2d v.p. 1984—86, pres. 1986—93, 1997—2005). Episcopalian. Home and Office: 1105 Georgina Ave Santa Monica CA 90402-2027

RONEY, CARLEY, wedding company executive, writer; m. David Liu; 2 children. BFA, NYU Tisch Sch. Arts, Inst. Film & TV; MA Cultural Studies, NYU. Creative dir., editor Nat. Mus. Am. History, McGraw-Hill Co., Simon & Schuster, 1988—94; cofounder RunTime Inc., 1994, pres., 1994—96; cofounder The Knot, 1996, v.p. creative devel., 1996—99, editor in chief, 1996—; syndicated columnist Scripps Howard News Svc., 2003—. Author: The Knot's Complete Guide to Weddings, 1998, The Knot Ultimate Wedding Planner, 1999, The Knot Book of Wedding Vows & Traditions, 2000, The Knot Book of Wedding Gowns, 2001, The Knot Book of Wedding Flowers, 2002, The Knot Complete Guide to Weddings in the Real World, 2003, The Knot Guide for the Groom, 2005, The Knot Guide for the Mother of the Bride, 2005; author: (foreword) Forever & a Day, 1999; author: (syndicated column) Ask Carley, 2003—; contbr.: NY Times, Wall St. Jour., USA Today, Glamour, Vogue, Elle, Self, Naples Daily News; appearances on Oprah, The View, ABC, Today Show, NBC, The Early Show, CBS. Achievements include The Knot named Best Wedding Hub 4 years in a row by Yahoo! Internet Life. Office: The Knot 6th Fl 462 Broadway New York NY 10013 Office Phone: 212-219-0724. Office Fax: 212-219-1929.*

RONEY, SARAH DAVIS, elementary school educator; b. Burlington, N.C., Nov. 22, 1977; d. Jerry Donald and Nancy Jackson Davis; m. Bryan Michael Roney, July 13, 2002; children: Elizabeth Grace, Andrew Davis. BS in Elem. Edn. and English cum laude, U. N.C., Greensboro, 2000, M in Sch. Adminstrn., 2002. Lic. tchr. N.C. Kindergarten tchr. Orange County Schs., Hillsborough, NC, 2000—03, 2d grade tchr., 2003—. Co-chair sch. governance com. Ctrl. Elem. Sch., Hillsborough, 2002—03; mem. adv. bd. U. N.C. Sch. Edn., Greensboro, 2001—03. Named Most Outstanding 1st Yr. Tchr., Orange County Schs., 2000—01. Mem.: ASCD, N.C. Assn. Educators, Kappa Delta Pi. Baptist. Avocations: exercise, aerobics. Office: Ctrl Elem Sch 154 Hayes St Hillsborough NC 27278

RONEY, SARAH GORDON, dancer, educator; d. Michael and Suzanne Gordon; m. James Matthew Roney, June 18, 2005. BS in Dance, Performance and Choreography, Goucher Coll., Balt., 2001. Dance tchr. Cecil Dancenter, North East, Md., 1998—2000, dance tchr., choreographer, 2006—; choreographer Providential Prodns., Rising Sun, Md., 1998, 2000; dancer, tchr. Ballet New Eng., Portsmouth, NH, 2001—06, outreach coord., choreographer, 2004—06. Guest tchr. Ballet Regent, Saratoga Springs, NY, 2004, Saratoga Springs, 05, Phillips Exeter Acad., NH, 2006; creator artist-in-residence North Hampton Sch., NH, 2006. Mem.: Phi Beta Kappa. Avocation: knitting. Office: Cecil Dancenter 25 Flint Dr North East MD 21901

RONGO, LUCILLE LYNN, medical center executive; b. N.Y.C., Sept. 15, 1958; d. Vincent Frank and Lucy Ann (Guilano) R. BS, Mercy Coll., Dobbs Ferry, N.Y., 1984. Asst. supr. accounts receivable Montefiore Med. Ctr., Bronx, 1978-81, asst. mgr. accounts payable, 1981-83, payroll mgr., 1983-87, spl. funds mgr., 1987-97, asst. contr. spl. funds/payroll, 1997-99, bus. info. system ops. cons., 1997-99, dir. bus. info. sys./logistics, 1999—. Mem. NAFE, Am. Mgmt. Assn., Am. Payroll Assn., Healthcare Fin. Mgmt. Assn. Avocations: collecting miniatures; art; dance, skiing, tennis. Home: 2 Fountain Ln Scarsdale NY 10583-4625 Office: Montefiore Med Ctr 111 E 210th St Bronx NY 10467-2401 Business E-Mail: LRongo@montefiore.org.

RONIS, GWENDLYN, musician, educator; b. Bklyn., Sept. 5, 1926; d. Morris W. Haber and Sarah Danzig; m. Charles Murray Ronis (dec. Apr. 1974); children: Linda Kass, David. BA, Bklyn. Coll., 1947; MA, NYU, 1950. HS music tchr. N.Y.C. Bd. Edn., 1950—55; pvt. piano instr., 1940—2006; student advisor adjudicator Five Towns Coll., Merrick, NY, 1979—87, adj. assoc. prof. theory, sightsinging and piano, 1979—87; adj. assoc. prof. theory, sightinging and piano Molloy Coll., Rockville Centre, 1999—2006. Pianist 2 solo recitals at Carnegie Chamber Hall, guest soloist (with Little Orch. Soc.) Town Hall, N.Y.C. Creator of after-school piano program N.Y. Bd. Edn., N.Y.C., 1965—67. Mem.: Assn. of Piano Tchrs. of L.I. (pres. 1991—93, treas. 1995—2003), Friday/Woodmere Music Club (pres. 1995—97). Avocations: painting, museums, theater. Home: 819 Broadway Woodmere NY 11598

RONSON, BONNIE WHALEY, literature educator; b. Tampa, Fla. d. Terrell Allen and Audie Lou Whaley; 1 child, Tyler Beeby. BA, Mercer U., 1975; MEd, U. Tampa, 1980; DPA, Nova U., 1989. Prof. English, Hillsborough C.C., Tampa, 1988—. Author: (books) Lessons All Around You, 1998, More Lessons All Around You, 1999. Office: Hillsborough C C Ybor City Campus Tampa FL 33610 Office Phone: 813-253-7000. E-mail: drronson@gte.net.

RONSTADT, LINDA MARIE, singer; b. Tucson, July 15, 1946; d. Gilbert and Ruthmary (Copeman) R. Rec. artist numerous albums including Evergreen 1967, Evergreen Vol. 2, 1967, Linda Ronstadt, The Stone Poneys and Friends, Vol. 3, 1968, Hand Sown, Home Grown, 1969, Silk Purse, 1970, Linda Ronstadt, 1972, Don't Cry Now, 1973, Heart Like a Wheel, 1974, Different Drum, 1974, Prisoner In Disguise, 1975, Hasten Down the Wind, 1976, Greatest Hits, 1976, Simple Dreams, Blue Bayou, 1977, Living in the U.S.A., 1978, Mad Love, Greatest Hits Vol. II, 1980, Get Closer, 1982, What's New, 1983, Lush Life, 1984, For Sentimental Reasons, 1986, Trio (with Dolly Parton, Emmylou Harris), 1986, 'Round Midnight, 1987, Canciones de Mi Padre, 1987, Cry Like a Rainstorm-Howl Like the Wind, 1989, Mas Canciones, 1991, Frenesi, 1992, Winter Light, 1993, Feels Like Home, 1995, Dedicated to the One I Love, 1996, We Ran, 1998, Trio 2, 1999 (with Emmylou Harris & Dolly Parton), Western Wall: The Tucson Sessions (with Emmylou Harris), A Merry Little Christmas, 2000, Hummin' to Myself, 2004, Adieu False Heart, 2006; starred in Broadway prodn. of Pirates of Penzance, 1981, also in film, 1983, off Broadway as Mimi in La Boheme, 1984. Recipient Am. Music awards, 1978, 1979, Grammy awards, 1975, 1976, 1987 (with Emmylou Harris and Dolly Parton), 1988, 1989 (with Aaron Neville), 1990, 1991, (with Aaron Neville), 1992 (2), 1996, 2000, Acad. Country Music award, 1987, 1988; named one of 100 Greatest Women of Rock 'n' Roll, VH1, 1999. Office: Electra Records 75 Rockefeller Plz New York NY 10019-6908

ROOD, CYNTHIA HOOPER, landscape architect, consultant; b. Columbus, Miss., Jan. 22, 1944; d. James Fullerton and Virginia Fite Hooper; children: Virginia Rood Pates, Amelia Gordon. BS in Landscape Architecture, U. Ga., Athens, 1966. Registered landscape arch. Miss., 1974, landscape designer, horticultural supr. Ala., 2005. Landscape arch., assoc. Olmsted Assocs., Landscape Archs., Brookline, Mass., 1966—67; budget and design US Naval Air Systems Command, Adak, Alaska, 1968—69; landscape arch. C. H. Rood, Landscape Arch., Columbus, Miss., 1969—. Pres. AMD, Inc., Columbus, 1990—; pres. Miss. chpt. Am. Soc. Landscape Archs., Jackson, 1991—92, dep. chmn. residential design com., Washington, 2002—03. Author: (articles) Miss. Dental Assn. Jour. Bd. dirs. Nat. Assn. Jr. Auxiliaries, Greenville, Miss., 1983—86, pres., 1984—85; mem. Nat. Assn. Colonial Dames Am., Washington, 1970—, Golden Triangle Regional Med. Ctr., Found., Columbus, 1986—90. Finalist, Nat. Merit Scholarship Found., 1962; recipient E. C. Martin scholarship, U. Ga., 1962—66, Award of Excellence, Nat. Coun. Tchrs. English, 1962, Alpha Zeta Scholarship Award, Alpha Zeta Chpt., U. of Ga., 1963, Queen of Pilgrimage Ball, Nat. Assn. Jr. Auxiliaries Columbus chpt., 1966, Award of Merit, Am. Soc. Landscape Archs. Miss. chpt., 1989, Merit award, Associated Builders and Contractors, 1994, Award of Merit, Main St. Columbus, Inc., 1996. Mem.: Magowah Country Club (life), Chi Omega Frat. (life; state pres. 1985—86, Outstanding Chi Omega in Miss. 1985). Office: C H Rood Landscape Architect 80 Eighth St N Columbus MS 39701 Office Phone: 662-327-6498. E-mail: abraco@aol.com, chr@amddesign.com.

ROOF, CYNTHIA WHITE, special education educator; d. William Eugene and Ivylin Howell White. BS in Edn., Augusta Coll., Ga., 1975, EdM, 1979. Cert. tchr. S.C. Spl. edn. tchr. Richmond County, Augusta, 1975—85, Anderson Dist. Fire, SC, 1985—. Named Tchr. of Yr., South Fant Elem., 2001—02, South Fant Early Childhood and Edn. Ctr., 2005—06. Mem.: S.C. Edn. Assn., Coun. for Exceptional Children. Presbyterian. Avocations: scrapbooks, crocheting, reading. Office: South Fant Early Childhood and Edn Ctr 1700 S Fant St Anderson SC 29624

ROOF, SALLY JEAN-MARIE, library and information scientist, educator; b. Cleve., Dec. 29, 1947; d. James William and Marie Monreal Roof; m. Christian John Hoffmann III, Sept. 22, 1973; children: Christian Graham Hoffmann, Joscelyn Nicole Hoffmann, Gavin Leigh Hoffmann. BA in English Lit., Dunbarton Coll. of Holy Cross, Washington, D. C., 1969; MS in Libr. and Info. Sci., Cath. U. of Am., 1972; degree in Profl. Mgmt. (hon.), Miami U., 1976; MA in Elem. Edn., No. Ariz. U., 2001. Cert. tchr. in libr. media ctr. adminstrn. Nat. Bd. of Cert. Tchrs., 2004. Asst. libr. U.S. Postal Svc. Libr., Washington, 1971—72; head of acquisitions George Wash. U. Libr., Washington, 1972—74; libr. adminstr. and mgr. Calgon Corp. Libr. Merck Inc., Pitts., 1974—77; libr. info. specialist U. of Phoenix, 1979—81; reference libr. Grand Canyon U., Phoenix, 1990—91; reference libr. West Campus Libr. Ariz. State U., Phoenix, 1994—95; libr. tchr. info. specialist Madison Meadows Sch., Phoenix, 1998—. Libr. cons. U. of Phoenix, 1981—82; presenter Ariz. Libr. Assn., Scottsdale, 2003; mem., presenter People to People Amb. Program Children's Lit. Del., Spokane, Wash., 2004; participant rep., 04; cons. in field. Editor: Serial Titles in the Washington, D. C. University Consortium Libraries, No School Left Behind at Your Library. Librarians Meet Arizona Legislators, 2004; author: (pamphlet) Madison Meadows Library Media Center; designer (school website) Madison Meadows Sch. website. Chmn. grade level patroness Nat. Charity League, Phoenix, 1994—99; pres. Phoenix (Ariz.) Mus. of History, 1991—94. Mem.: ALA (assoc.), Ariz. Libr. Assn. (assoc.), Phi Kappa Phi, Beta Phi Mu, Jr. League of Phoenix. Democrat-Npl. Roman Catholic. Avocations: yoga, fast walking, reading, bicycling. Office: Madison Meadows School 225 W Ocotillo Rd Phoenix AZ 85013 Office Phone: 602-664-7640. Personal E-mail: sroofhoff@cox.net. E-mail: sroof@msd38.org.

ROOK, VICKI LYNN, safety specialist; b. Denton, Tex., Oct. 14, 1954; d. Lonzo Lester and Myrtle Jodelle Roberts; m. Rickey Hugh Rook, Jan. 27, 1979; children: Brandon Nicholas, Katy Lynn Student, Richland Jr. Coll., Dallas, 1974-75. Safety supr. United Parcel Svc., Dallas, 1975-81; pers., safety adminstr. Boeing Airport Equipment, Carrollton, Tex., 1981-83; safety rep. Loral Vought Sys. Corp., Grand Prairie, Tex., 1983-95; sr. safety specialist Fed. Express Corp., Dallas, 1995—. Mem. workers comp claims mgmt. various cos., Dallas, 1975—; mgr. union contract negotiation Boeing Airport Equipment, Dallas, 1983; com. mem. mgmt. safety program tng. Fed. Express, Memphis, 1997-2001 Tchr. Sunday sch. Walnut Ridge Bapt. Ch., Mansfield, Tex., 1997-2001, 1st Bapt. Ch., Grand Prairie, 1980-82, counselor ch. camp, 1980-82; vol. ednl. TV Loral Vought Sys., Dallas, 1993. Named Safety Specialist of Yr. Fed. Express, 1997. Mem. Am. Soc. Safety Engineers, Nat. Safety Coun. Republican. Office Phone: 469-524-4623. Business E-Mail: vlrook@fedex.com.

ROOKE, MICHELE A., lawyer; b. Springfield, Mass., July 22, 1963; d. Richard E. and Margaret M. Oumet; m. Timothy J. Rooke; 2 children. BS, Sprinfield Coll., Springfield, Mass., 1981; MEd, Springfield Coll., 1992; JD, Western New Eng. Law Sch., 1999. Bar: Mass. 1999, (U.S. dist. ct.) 2001. Victim witness advocate Hampton City Dist. Atty. Office, Springfield, 1990—99, asst. dist. atty., 1999—2002; atty. Doherty Wallace Pilliburgh & Murphy, 2002—. Youth soccer and softball coach. Office: Doherty Wallace Pillsburg and Murphy One Monarch Pl Springfield MA 01144 Office Phone: 413-733-3111.

ROOK-NYKRIN, MARY CAROL, special education educator; d. Edward Earl and Marie Therese (Riley) Rook; m. Edward J. Nykrin, Dec. 21, 2002; children: Sarah Riley, Sean Riley, Brendan Riley. BS in Edn., Ill. State U., 1970; MS in Edn., Chgo. State U., 2000; MA in Edn. Adminstrn., Gov.'s State U., 2002. Cert. learning behavior specialist. Educator Blue Island (Ill.) Pub. Sch., 1970—80; spl. edn. educator AERO Spl. Edn. Coop., Burbank, Ill., 1998—. Office Phone: 708-458-1152 ext. 217.

ROOKS, JUDITH PENCE, nurse midwife, consultant; b. Spokane, Wash., Aug. 18, 1941; d. Lawrence Cyrus and Christine Atrice (Snow) Pence; m. Peter Geoffrey Bourne, Mar. 1972 (div.); m. Charles Stanley Rooks, Sept. 21, 1975; 1 child, Christopher Robert. BS, U. Wash., 1963; MS, Cath. U. Am., 1967; MPH, Johns Hopkins U., 1974. Cert. edpidemiology, nursing, nurse-midwifery, mediation. Staff nurse King County Harborview Hosp., Seattle, 1963—64, The Clin. Ctr., NIH, Bethesda, Md., 1965; asst. prof. nursing dept. San Jose (Calif.) State Coll., 1967-69; epidemiologist Ctrs. for Disease Control, Atlanta, 1970-78; asst. prof. dept. ob-gyn. Oreg. Health Sci. U., Portland, 1978-79; expert Office of the Surgeon Gen., Dept. HHS, Washington, 1979-80; project officer U.S. AID, Washington, 1980-82; prin. investigator Sch. Pub. Health Columbia U., N.Y.C., 1988-89, assoc. Pacific Inst. for Women's Health, 1993-2001; cons. Portland, 1982—. Mem. tech. adv. com. Family Health Internat., Research Triangle Park, N.C., 1986-97; mem. midwifery adv. com. Frontier Nursing Svc., Hyden, Ky., 1997-2002; mem. com. Inst. of Medicine NAS, Washington, 1983-85; academic faculty cmty.-based nurse-midwifery edn. program Frontier Sch. Midwifery and Family Nursing, Hyden, Ky., 1993-95; dir. N.Y. Acad. Medicine/Maternity Ctr. Assn. evidence-based symposium on The Nature and Management of Labor Pain, 1999-01. Author: Midwifery and Childbirth in America, 1997; co-author: Nurse-Midwifery in America, 1986, Reproductive Risk in Maternity Care and Family Planning Services, 1992; mem. editl. bd. Birth, 1996—; editl. cons. Jour. Nurse Midwifery, 1992-2000, Jour. Midwifery and Women's Health, 2002--; contbr. articles to profl. jours. Mem bd. advisors World Affairs Coun. Oreg., Portland, 1987-90; bd. dirs. Planned Parenthood of the Columbia/Willamette, Portland, 1987-90; chm. Ga. Citizens for Hosp. Abortion, Atlanta, 1969-70; assoc. Pacific Coun. on Internat. Policy, 1995-97. Recipient nat. award Nat. Perintal Assn., 1999. Mem. APHA (chair com. on women's rights 1982-83, mem. governing coun. 1976-77, 79-82, Martha May Eliot award for svc. to mothers and children 1993, Hattie Hemschemeyer award for cont. outstanding contbns. to nurse-midwifery and maternal and child health care 1998), Am. Coll. Nurse-Midwives (life, pres. 1983-85). Avocations: gardening, walking, reading, travel, cooking. Home and Office: 2706 SW English Ct Portland OR 97201-1622 Office Phone: 503-243-2253. E-mail: jprooks1@comcast.net.

ROOKS, LINDA, writer; d. Harold John and Marianna Wieck; m. Marvin Edward Rooks, Dec. 19, 1967; children: Juliana Wolf, Laura Katherine Voorhees. BA, San Francisco State U., 1965. Tchr. Seminole Jr. H.S., Fla., 1970—72; pro-life liaison for Paula Hawkins senatorial campaign Nat. Right to Life, Winter Park, Fla., 1986; asst. editor Ctr. Stage Mag., Maitland, Fla., 1987—89; office coord., newsletter editor Adoption by Shepherd Care, Orlando, Fla., 1994—2000; freelance writer Maitland, 2000—. Author: Broken Heart on Hold, 2006, (devotional) Tapestry; scriptwriter: radio and tv Testimony of An Unborn Child (Cammeo Award for Best of Show, 1987); contbr. articles to profl. jours. Pres. Ctrl. Fla. Right to Life, 1984—85, 1990—96; staff position state coord. for families Bob Dole Presdl. Campaign, Fla., 1995—96; pub. rels. co-chmn. Nat. Right to Life Conv., Orlando, 1983. Mem.: Word Weavers Writers Group (sec. steering com. 2002—). Republican. Avocation: travel. Office: PO Box 241 Winter Park FL 32790-0241 Personal E-mail: linda@brokenheartonhold.com.

ROOMBERG, LILA GOLDSTEIN, lawyer; b. Bklyn., Oct. 21, 1929; d. William H. and Mary (Abramowitz) Goldstein; m. Lawrence A. Simon (div. 1965); 1 child, Virginia Simon Feil; m. Gerald Arnon Roomberg (dec. 1995). BA, NYU, 1949, JD, 1951. Bar: N.Y. 1952, Pa. 1963. Assoc. Ballard, Spahr, Andrews & Ingersoll, Phila., 1959-71, ptnr., 1971-91, of counsel, 1992—. Mem. Pa. Bar Assn., Phila. Bar Assn., Phila. Bar Found. (sec. 1984-87, trustee 1981-87). Home: 120 Spruce St Philadelphia PA 19106-4315 Office: Ballard Spahr Andrews & Ingersoll 1735 Market St Ste 5100 Philadelphia PA 19103-7599 E-mail: roomberg@ballardspahr.com.

ROOME, KRISTINE ANN, college administrator; b. Pequannock, N.J., Sept. 3, 1967; d. Michael Wesley and Joan Ann (Dooley) Roome. BS, Montclair State U., 1990; postgrad. in anthropology, Columbia U., 1993—. Fin. acct. JP Morgan Co., N.Y.C., 1990-93; sr. acct. Tchr.'s Coll. Columbia U., N.Y.C., 1993, asst. dir. office of instnl. studies, 1993—. Assoc. dir. Wright Gallery, N.Y.C., 1994—, curator several exhbns., 1995. Alumni scholar, Student Govt. Assn. scholar Montclair State U., 1989, 90, Columbia U. Tchr.'s Coll. scholar, 1995, travel grantee, 1995, Field Lang./Area Studies fellowship Inst. for African Studies Columbia U., N.Y.C., 1996—. Mem. NAFE, Assn. Inst. Rschrs. Avocations: art, tennis, reading.

ROONEY, CAROL BRUNS, dietician; b. Milw., Dec. 20, 1940; d. Edward G. and Elizabeth C. (Lemke) Bruns; m. George Eugene Rooney Jr., July 1, 1967; children: Steven, Sean. BS, U. Wis., 1962; MS, U. Iowa, 1965. Registered dietitian; cert. nutrition specialist; disting. health care food svc. adminstr.; cert. dietitian, Wis. Intern VA Med. Ctr., Hines, Ill., 1962-63, resident in nutrition and food svc. Iowa City, 1963-65, dietitian nutrition clinic Hines, 1965-67, 69-70, chief clin. dietetics, 1970-71, chief adminstrv. dietetics, 1971-73, clin. dietitian Memphis, 1967-68; asst. chief nutrition and food svc. Zablocki VA Med. Ctr., Milw., 1974-85, chief nutrition and food svc., 1985-96, divsn. mgr. cons. care, 1996-98, cons. nutrition and food svc. mgmt., 1995—, bus. enterprise mgr., 1998-2000. Adj. lectr. Loyola U. Coll. Dentistry, Maywood, Ill., 1969-72; investigator nutrition VA/Med. Coll. Wis., Milw., 1975-2000, co-dir. ann. clin. nutrition symposium, Milw., 1979-94; chmn. task force on ration allowance VA, Washington, 1977-84, nutrition and food svc. spl. interest users group, 1983-85, chmn. tech. adv. group region IV, 1986; mem. Dept. Vets. Affairs Mktg. Ctr. Subsistence Task Force, 1991-95, dietetic internship adv. bd. St. Luke's Hosp., Milw., 1983-87; mem. Dept. Vets. Affairs Nat. Cost Containment Ctr. Nutrition & Food Svc. Benchmarking Tech. Adv., 1995-96; nutrition and food svc. policy manual rev. task force, chiefs, food and nutrition svc. mentor group, 1992-96; lectr. in field Author: (videocassette) VA Ration Allowance as a Management Tool 1976; editor: Nutrition Principles and Dietary Guidelines for Patients Receiving Chemotherapy and Radiation Therapy, 1980; contbr. articles to profl. jours., 1978—. Profl. edn. com. Milw. South unit Am. Cancer Soc., 1976-86, bd. dirs. Milw. South unit, 1984-86, Milw. divsn., 1986-87, Wis. divsn., 1987-91, media spokesperson, 1983-91, del. to Milw. divsn., 1984-85, mem. orgnl. and expansion com. Milw. divsn., 1986-87, profl. edn. com. Milw. divsn., 1986-87, Wis. divsn., 1987-91, taking control Wis. divsn., 1987-91, chmn. nutrition Wis. divsn., 1989-91; med. adv. com. YMCA Met. Milw., 1985-2000; mem. Marquette U. HS Mothers Guild, 1990-94. Named Dept. Vets. Affairs Dietitian of Yr., 1994; recipient Disting. Svc. award, Am. Cancer Soc. Milw. South unit, 1980, Women of Achievement award, Girl Scouts USA Milw. area, 1987, Leadership award, VA, 1989, Dept. Vets. Affairs Fed. Women's Program cert. merit for outstanding profl. leadership, 1994, commendation, Dept. Vet. Affairs, 2000, rsch. grantee, Paralyzed Vets. Am., 1981—83. Fellow Am. Dietetic Assn. (registered, practice groups in mgmt. responsibilities in health care delivery, gerontology nutrition 1980-2000, dietetics in phys. medicine and rehab. 1983-97, clin. nutrition mgmt. 1987-2001, amb. nat. media spokesperson 1983-89, Resource Amb. 1991—, Outstanding Svc. award 1983-89), FADA; mem. AAUW, Am. Soc. Health Care Food Svc. Adminstrs. (dir.-at-large Wis. chpt. 1993-95, pres.-elect Wis. chpt. 1995-96, pres. 1996-97, immediate past pres. 1997-98, Disting. Health Care Food Svc. Adminstr. 1995—), Wis. Dietetic Assn. (co-chmn. divsn. mgmt. practice 1976-77, chmn. 1977-78, bd. dirs. 1981-83, coord. cabinet 1984-91, pres. 1988-89, chmn. nominating com. 1989-90, chmn. long-range planning com. 1989-90, legis. com. 1988—, Wis. Medallion award 1986), Milw. Dietetic Assn. (cmty. nutrition and clin. dietetics and rsch. coms. 1975-76, chair ad hoc com. for nutrition and oncology patients 1976-79, clin. dietetics and rsch. study group 1981-90, chair 1983-85, pres. 1982-83, by-laws com. 1983-84, chair policies and procedures com. 1983-87, pub. rels. com. 1983-87, chair nominating com. 1984-85), Am. Cancer Soc., Fed. Execs. Assn., Coll. Endowment Assn., Leadership Vets. Affairs Alumni Assn. (charter, life), Phi Upsilon Omicron, Kappa Delta, Kappa Delta Alumnae Assn., Milw. Kappa Delta Alumnae Assn. (rep. Milw. Panhellenic coun. 1998-99, treas. 1999-2004). Avocations: tennis, golf. Home: 18230 Le Chateau Dr Brookfield WI 53045-4922

ROONEY, GAIL SCHIELDS, academic administrator; b. Feb. 15, 1947; BA, U. Colo., 1969; MS, George Williams Coll., 1974; PhD, U. Ill., 1982. Asst. dir. Spl. Svcs. Program Cleve. State U., 1970-71; admissions counselor George Williams Coll., Downers Grove, Ill., 1972-73; coord. of career exploration ctr. Women's Programs Cuyahoga Community Coll., Cleve., 1973-76; vis. asst. prof. Sch. Clin. Medicine U. Ill., Champaign, 1981-82; counselor, instr. Cuyahoga Community Coll., Cleve., 1982-84, dir. counseling, career and psychol. svcs., 1984-85; dir. career, counseling and health svcs. Briar Cliff Coll., Sioux City, Iowa, 1985-88, v.p. for student devel., 1988-95; adj. faculty, psychology dept. Mesa (Ariz.) C.C., 1995; asst. prof. counselor edn. Wayne (Nebr.) State Coll., 1997-99; dir. career and employment svcs. U. Kans., Lawrence, 1999—2003; dir. Career Ctr. U. Ill., Urbana, 2003—. Cons. on team devel., continuous improvement, and orgnl. effectiveness, 1996-99; program presenter Myers Briggs Type Indicator, 1986—. Bd. dirs. St. Luke's Gordon Recovery Ctr., Sioux City, 1988-95. Mem. Midwest Assn. Colls. and Employers, Nat. Assn. Colls. and Employers, Am. Coll. Pers. Assn., Nat. Assn. Student Pers. Adminstrs. Home: 1626 Cobblefield Rd Champaign IL 61822 Office Phone: 217-244-1497. E-mail: grooney@uiuc.edu.

ROONEY, MICHELE LYNN, music educator; b. Albany, N.Y., Dec. 13, 1959; d. Walter William Wieczerzak; m. Arthur Patrick Rooney, Sept. 21, 1991; children: Timothy Ryan, Colleen Lyra. BS in Music Edn., Coll. St. Rose, Albany, N.Y., 1984, M in Learning Disabilities, 1986. Cert. tchr. N.Y. State, 1986. Gen. music tchr. Hackett Mid. Sch., Albany, 1984—2005, chorus instr., 1984—2005; gen. music tchr. Myers Mid. Sch., Albany, 2005—, chorus instr., 2005—. Pvt. piano tchr., Albany, 1983—. Contbr. Americans for the Arts, L.A., 2003—06. Mem.: NYSSMA/MENC (corr.). Roman Catholic. Avocations: travel, geocacheing, embroidery, golf, cooking. Home: 331 S Main Ave Albany NY 12209 Office: Myers Mid Sch 100 Elbel Ct Albany NY 12209 Office Phone: 518-475-6425. Office Fax: 518-475-6427. Personal E-mail: hootyhoo331@hotmail.com.

ROOS, SYBIL FRIEDENTHAL, retired elementary school educator; b. LA, Jan. 29, 1924; d. Charles G. and Besse (Weixel) Friedenthal; m. Henry Kahn Roos, May 8, 1949 (dec. Dec. 1989); children: Catherine Alane Cook, Elizabeth Anne Garlinger, Virginia Ann Bertrand. BA in Music, Centenary Coll., 1948; MEd, Northwestern State U., 1973. Cert. elem. edn. tchr., spl. edn. tchr. Tchr. Caddo Parish Schs., Shreveport, 1968-75, Spring Branch Ind. Schs., Houston, 1975-85; vol. Houston Grand Opera/Guild, 1979—, Houston Mus. of Fine Arts/Guild, 1990—, Houston Symphony Soc./Guild, 1997—. Pres. Nat. Coun. Jewish Women, Shreveport, 1958; life mem. Mus. Fine Arts; area coord. Spl. Olympics, Shreveport, 1974-75; bd. dirs. U. Houston Moore Sch. Music. With USN, 1944-46. Mem. AAUW (pres. Spring Valley Houston chpt. 1985-87), Houston Grand Opera Guild (pres. 1989-91), Houston Symphony League, Houston Ballet Guild, Am. Needlepoint Guild, Delta Kappa Gamma (bd. dirs., treas. 1987-89), Phi Mu. Republican. Avocations: music, tennis, needlepoint, volunteering. Home: 10220 Memorial Dr Apt 78 Houston TX 77024-3227 Personal E-mail: s.roos@worldnet.att.net.

ROOST, ALISA, theater educator; b. San Francisco, Nov. 9, 1971; d. Eric Robert-Tissiot Roost and Anna Lyons-Roost. BA, U. Calif., Santa Cruz, 1992; MA, U. Ill., Urbana, 1995; MPh, CUNY Grad. Ctr., 1998, PhD, 2001. Grad. tchg. fellow CUNY, 1997—98, writing fellow, 1999—2000; vis. artist acting and directing Winthrop U., 2001—02; asst. prof. theatre Monmouth (Ill.) Coll., 2002—. Dir.: (staged reading) The Choice, 1997, (musical) Flahooley, 1998; (plays) Bloomer Girl, 2000; contbr. articles to profl. jours. Mem.: Middle Eastern Studies Assn., Am. Soc. Theatre Rsch., Assn. for Theater in Higher Edn. (conf. coord. 1999—2001, talent coord 2005). Democrat. Episcopalian. Avocation: ice skating. Personal E-mail: flahooley@hotmail.com. E-mail: flahooty@earthlink.net.

ROOT, JANET GREENBERG, private school educator; b. Atlantic City, N.J., May 16, 1936; d. Louis and Edith (Shapiro) Greenberg; m. Allen W. Root, June 15, 1958; children: Jonathan, Jennifer, Michael. BS, U. Md., 1958. Tchr. Bd. Edn., Brighton, N.Y., 1958-60; dir. music/art parent program, chmn. dept. arts-humanities Shorecrest Prep. Sch., St. Petersburg, Fla., 1989—. Trustee Shorecrest Prep. Sch., 1980—86, 1990—96, 1998—, dir. cultural enrichment program, 1978—; mem. ednl. bd. Bayfront Ctr., 1993—2000; mem. exhbns. and collections com. Tampa Bay Holocaust Mus., mem. edn. com., 2003—; trustee Salvador Dali Mus., 1998—, chmn. edn. com., mem. long range bldg. com., mem. exec. com., 2001—04; trustee Order of Salvador, 1999—. Named Honoree, Nat. Philanthropy Day.

ROOT, NINA J., librarian, writer; b. 1934; d. Jacob J. and Fannie (Slivinsky) R. BA, Hunter Coll.; MSLS, Pratt Inst.; postgrad., USDA Grad. Sch., 1964-65, CUNY, 1970-75. Reference and serials libr. Albert Einstein Coll. Medicine Libr., Bronx, NY, 1958-59; asst. chief libr. Am. Cancer Soc., N.Y.C., 1959-62; chief libr. Am. Inst. Aeros. and Astronautics, N.Y.C., 1962-64; head ref. and libr. svcs. sci. and tech. divsn. Libr. Congress, Washington, 1964-66; mgmt. cons. Nelson Assocs., Inc., N.Y.C., 1966-70; dir. libr. svcs. Am. Mus. Natural History, N.Y.C., 1970-97; freelance mgmt. cons. and libr. planning, 1970-99. Trustee Barnard Found., 1984-91; mem. libr. adv. coun. N.Y. State Bd. Regents, 1984-89, trustee Metro, 1987-92; bd. dirs. Hampden/Booth Libr. Players, 1990-97, Sutton Area Cmty., 1997-2001; trustee Mercantile Libr. N.Y., 1993-95; dir. emerita Libr. AMNH, 1998—. Recipient Meritorious Svc. award Libr. of Congress, 1965, Founders medal SHNH, 1997. Mem. ALA (preservation com. 1977-79, chmn. libr./binders com. 1978-80, chmn. preservation sect. 1980-81, mem. coun. 1983-86), Spl. Librs. Assn. (sec. documentation group N.Y. chpt. 1972-73, 2d v.p. N.Y. 1975-76, treas. sci. and tech. group N.Y. 1975-76, mus. arts and humanities divsn. program planning chairperson-conf. 1977), Archons of Colophon (convener 1978-79), Soc. for Hist. of Natural History (N.Am. rep. 1977-85), N.Y. Acad. Scis. (mem. publs. com. 1975-80, 89-91, archives com. 1976-78, search. com. 1976), Explorers Club. Home: 400 E 59th St New York NY 10022-2342

ROOT, PHYLLIS IDALENE, writer; b. Ft. Wayne, Ind., Feb. 14, 1949; d. John Howard and Margaret Esther (Trout) R.; children: Amelia, Ellen. BA, Valparaiso U., 1971. Tchr. complete scholar program U Minn., 1997—; tchr. MFA writing for children Vt. Coll., 1998—2006, Hamline U., 2006—. Author: Moon Tiger, 1985, Soup for Supper, 1986, The Listening Silence, 1992, The Old Red Rocking Chair, 1992, Coyote and the Magic Words, 1993, Sam Who Was Swallowed By a Shark, 1994, Rosie's Fiddle, 1997, One Windy Wednesday, 1996, Contrary Bear, 1996, Mrs. Potter's Pig, 1996, Aunt Nancy and Old Man Trouble, 1996, The Hungry Monster, 1996, What Baby Wants, 1998, One Duck Stuck, 1998, Aunt Nancy and Cousin Lazybones, 1998, Turnover Tuesday, 1998, Grandmother Winter, 1999, Here Comes Tabby Cat, 2000, Hey Tabby Cat, 2000, Meow Monday, 2000, Foggy Friday, 2000, Kiss the Cow, 2000, All for the Newborn Baby, 2000, Rattletrap Car, 2001, Soggy Saturday, 2001, Mouse Goes Out, 2002, Mouse All Year Round, 2002, Oliver Finds His Way, 2002, Big Momma Makes the World, 2002, 2003 (Boston Globe Horn Book award for picture books 2003), What's That Noise? (with M. Edwards), 2002, If You Want to See A Caribou, 2004, Ten Sleepy Sheep, 2004, Quack, 2005, Hop!, 2005, The House That Jill Built, 2005, Looking for a Moose, 2006, Lucia and the Light, 2006. Mem. Authors Guild, Soc. Children's Book Writers and Illustrators. Avocations: gardening, sailing, canoeing.

ROOTH, SIGNE ALICE, editor, consultant; b. NYC, Aug. 14, 1924; d. Gerhard Teodor and Florence Elizabeth (Miner) Rooth. BA summa cum laude, U. Miami, 1944; MA, U. So. Calif., 1945; PhD, U. Chgo., 1953. Translator IMF, Washington, 1954—56, UN Secretariat, NYC, 1956—58, editor Official Records Editing sect., 1958—69; translator/interpreter UN Mission to Congo, Leopoldville, 1962—63; editor/sr. editor divsn. Gen. Assembly Affairs UN Secretariat, NYC, 1969—84, cons. editor UN Devel. Programme, 1985—92, cons. editor trusteeship dept., dept. pub. info., dept. gen. assembly and conf. mgmt., 1993—2006. Editor Econ. and Social Commn. for Asia and the Pacific, Bangkok, 1999; bd. mem. Assn. Culturelle Francophone, UN Secretariat. Author: Seeress of the Northland: Fredrika Bremer's American Journey, 1849-1851, 1955; editor: Procs. of UN Congress on Pub. Internat. Law: International Law as a Language for International Relations, 1995; contbr. articles and essays to jours. Recipient Am. Swedish Woman of Yr., Woman's Auxiliary of Am. Swedish Hist. Mus., Phila., 1984. Mem.: French Inst./Alliance Francaise, Swedish Women's Ednl. Assn., Am. Scandinavian Soc., Am.-Scandinavian Found., Am. Swedish Hist. Found. (life), Southampton Hist. Mus., Rogers Meml. Libr., Parrish Art Mus., Paris Am. Club. Avocations: reading, travel, art, music, collecting F. Bremer autographs.

ROPERS-HUILMAN, BECKY LYNN, education and humanities educator; b. Boscobel, Wis., Sept. 30, 1970; d. Raymond Gale and Rosa Marie (Pleviak) Ropers; m. Brian David Ropers-Huilman, Aug. 21, 1992. BA, U. Wis., Eau Claire, 1991; MS, U. Wis., Madison, 1993, PhD, 1996. Assoc. prof. La. State U., Baton Rouge, 1996—. Author: Feminist Teaching in Theory and Practice, 1998. Mem. Am. Ednl. Rsch. Assn., Assn. for Study of Higher Edn., Nat. Women's Studies Assn. Avocations: reading, singing, health and fitness activities. Home: 2313 Ebony Ave Baton Rouge LA 70808-2152 Office: La State U 121C Peabody Hl Baton Rouge LA 70803-0001 Office Phone: 225-578-2892. Business E-Mail: broper1@lsu.edu.

ROPPLE, LISA M., lawyer; b. June 25, 1962; BA summa cum laude, Holy Cross Coll., 1984; JD magna cum laude, Boston Coll., 1989. Bar: Mass. 1989, US Ct. Appeals (1st cir.). Ptnr., co-chair litigation dept. Ropes & Gray, Boston, 1989—. Editor (articles): Boston Coll. Law Rev. Office: Ropes & Gray 1 International Pl Boston MA 02110-2624 Office Phone: 617-951-7554. Office Fax: 617-951-7050. Business E-Mail: lisa.ropple@ropesgray.com.

RORIE, KATHY MARIE, artist; b. Monroe, N.C., Aug. 23, 1949; d. Paul E. Price and Verna Lee Melton; m. Marion Buxton Rorie, Oct. 28, 1969; 1 child, Megan Marie. Instr. painting Anson Stanly C.C., Monroe, NC, 1991—92, Union County Schs., 1992—. Tchg. artist Blumenthol Performing Arts Ctr., Charlotte, NC, 2006—06. Exhibitions include Art Prospect '97, La Jolla, Calif., numerous others, Represented in permanent collections Loll Assocs., Lake Wylie, S.C., Allen Tate Realtors, Charlotte, Nation's Bank, numerous others. Named Emerging Artist, N.C. Arts & Sci., Charlotte, 1993. Mem.: Union County Art League (pres. 1999), Charlotte Art League (bd. dirs. 1991—97), Nat. Coll. Soc., Nat. Mus. Women in Arts. Methodist. Home: 1865 Tanglebriar Ct Matthews NC 28104 Personal E-mail: kathyrorie@aol.com.

RORIE, NANCY CATHERINE, retired secondary school educator; b. Union County, N.C., May 31, 1940; d. Carl Evander and Mary Mildred (Pressley) Rorie. BA, Woman's Coll. U. N.C., 1962; MEd, U. N.C., 1967; EdD, Duke U., 1977. Cert. curriculum and instrnl. specialist, social studies tchr. for middle and secondary levels, English tchr., N.C. Tchr. social studies and English Guilford County Schs., Greensboro, NC, 1962—67; instr. social studies Lees-McRae Coll., Banner Elk, NC, 1967—76; tchr. social studies and English Monroe City Schs., NC, 1977—93, Union County Schs., Monroe, 1993—2002; ret., 2002. Bd. mem. Wingate Univ. Friends of the Arts, NC, 2006—. Mem.: Monroe Aquatics And Fitness Ctr. Home: 2401 Old Pageland Monroe Rd Monroe NC 28112-8163

RORKE-ADAMS, LUCY BALIAN, pathologist, educator; b. St. Paul, June 22, 1929; d. Aram Haji and Karzouhy (Ousdigian) Balian; m. Robert Radcliffe Rorke, June 4, 1960 (dec. Mar. 31, 2002); m. Boyce M. Adams, Apr. 16, 2004 (dec. June 21, 2006). AB, U. Minn., 1951, MA, 1952, BS, 1955, MD, 1957. Diplomate Am. Bd. Pathology. Intern Phila. Gen. Hosp., 1957-58, resident anat. pathology and neuropathology, 1958-62, asst. neuropathologist, 1963-67, chief pediat. pathologist, 1967-68, chief neuropathologist, 1968-69, chmn. dept. anat. pathology and chief neuropathologist, 1969-73, chmn. dept. pathology, 1973-77, pres. med. staff, 1973-75; neuropathologist Children's Hosp., Phila., 1965—, pres. med. staff, 1986-88, acting pathologist-in-chief, 1995-2000. Cons. neuropathologist Wyeth Rsch. Labs., Radnor, Pa., 1961—87, Wistar Inst. Anatomy and Biology, Phila., 1967—93; assoc. prof. pathology U. Pa. Sch. Medicine, Phila., 1970—, prof. pathology, 1973—, clin. prof. neurology, 1979—, clin. prof. pediat., 1997—; forensic neuropathologist Office Med. Examiner, Phila., 1977—2004. Author: Myelinization of the Brain in the Newborn, 1969, Pathology of Perinatal Brain Injury, 1982; mem. editl. bd. Jours. Neuropathology Exptl. Neurology, 1980—85, 1993—98, Pediat. Neurosurgery, 1984—2002, Child's Nervous Sys., 1984—88, Brain Pathology, 1990—95; contbr. articles to profl. jours. NIH fellow, 1961—62, NIH grantee, 1963—68. Fellow: Coll. Am. Pathologists; mem.: AMA, Phila. Coll. Physicians (trustee 2002—04, treas. 2004—), Burlington County Med. Soc., Am. Neurol. Soc., Am. Soc. Neuroradiology (hon.), Am. Assn. Neuropathologists (exec. coun. 1976—85, v.p. 1979—80, pres. 1981—82, Meritorious Svc. award 1999), Phila. Neurol. Soc. (v.p. 1971—72, editor transactions 1973, pres. 1975—76). Office: Childrens Hosp Phila 324 S 34th St Philadelphia PA 19104-4399 Home: into 126 E Maple Ave Moorestown NJ 08057-2014 Business E-Mail: Rorke@email.chop.edu.

RORSCHACH, KIMBERLY, museum director; m. John Hart; 2 children. BA, Brandeis U.; PhD in art hist., Yale U. Curator Phila. Mus. Art, Rosenbach Mus. & Libr., Phila.; Dana Feitler dir. Smart Mus. Art, U. Chgo., 1994—2004; dir. Nasher Mus. Art, Duke U. (scheduled to open Oct. 2005), Durham, NC, 2004—. Mem.: Assn. Art Mus. Dirs. (trustee). Office: Nasher Mus Art PO Box 90732 Durham NC 27708 Office Phone: 919-684-8420.

RORTY, AMELIE, philosopher, educator; b. Antwerp, Belgium; 1 child, Jay Adam. PhD, Yale U., New Haven, Conn. Vis. prof. Harvard U., Cambridge, Mass., 2003—. Mem.: Am. Philosophic Assn. Office: Harvard University Hilles Library 56 Shephard Street Cambridge MA 02138

ROSA, MARGARITA, agency executive director, lawyer; b. Bklyn., Jan. 5, 1953; d. Jose and Julia (Mojica) R.; 1 child, Marisol Kimberly Rosa-Shapiro. BA in History cum laude, Princeton U., 1974; JD, Harvard U., 1977. Bar: N.Y. Assoc. Rosenman & Colin, N.Y.C., 1977-79, Rabinowitz & Boudin, N.Y.C., 1981-84; staff atty. Puerto Rican Legal Def. Edn. Fund, N.Y.C., 1979-81; teaching fellow Urban Legal Studies program CUNY, 1984-85; gen. counsel N.Y. State Div. Human Rights, N.Y.C., 1985-88, exec. dep. commr., 1988-90, commr., 1990-95; exec. dir. Grand St. Settlement, 1995—. Vice chmn. N.Y. State Task force on ADA Implementation, 1991-95; mem. N.Y. Gov.'s Task Force on Sexual Harassment, 1992; mem. Mayor's Commn. on the Judiciary, 2002-04, mem. Mayor's commn. on women's issues, 2002—; adj. prof. law Fordham Law Sch., 1995; adj. prof. pub. policy Wagner Grad. Sch. NYU, 1995—, Baruch Coll. Exec. MPA program, 1998; bd. dirs. Martin Luther King Jr. Commn. N.Y. State, 1990-95, Feminist Press CUNY, 1990-95; mem. adv. bd. N.Y.C. Ind. Budget Office, 1996-2001, vice chair, 2000-01. Bd. dirs. United Neighborhood Houses, 1995-97, Legal Svcs. for Children, 1999-2003, Non-Profit Coordinating Com., vice chair, 2001—, Found. for Child Devel., 2004-, sec. 2005-, Nat. Philanthropic Trust, 2001-. Recipient Hispanic Women Achievers award N.Y. State Gov.'s Office Hispanic Affairs, 1990, Woman of Excellence award CUNY, 1992, Oscar García Rivera award P.R. Bar Assn., 1996, N.Y. State Atty. Gen.'s award for disting. pub. svc. in the legal profession, 2002; Lombard Assn. fellow Office of U.S. Atty., So. Dist. N.Y., 1975; Revson Teaching fellow Charles Revson Found., 1984-85. Mem. N.Y. State Bar Assn. (com. on minorities in the profession 1997), Assn. Bar City N.Y. (commn. future of CUNY 1999-2000). Office: Grand St Settlement 80 Pitt St New York NY 10002-3516 Office Phone: 212-674-1740 ext. 212. Business E-Mail: mrosa@grandstreet.org.

ROSA-BRAY, MARILYN, physician; b. Arecibo, PR, Feb. 17, 1970; d. Tomas Rosa and Maria Mercedes Lopez; m. Franklin A. Bray, Mar. 21, 2001; 1 child, Allen M. Bray. BS in Biology, U. P.R., Rio Piedras, 1988—92; MD, U. P.R., San Juan, 1992—97. Diplomate Am. Bd. Internal Medicine. Instr. KAPLAN, San Juan, PR, 1996—97; intern in neurology San Juan V.A. Hosp., PR, 1997—98; intern McLaren Regional Med. Ctr., Flint, Mich., 1998—99; sr. rsch. fellow U. Wash., Dept. Neurology, Tacoma, 1999—2000; in-patient geriatric physician Western State Hosp., Seattle, 1999—2000; med. and lab. dir. Biomat USA, Seattle, 1999—; anatomy and physiology prof. Shoreline C.C., Wash., 1999—2001, Seattle Pacific U., 2000; physician Va. Mason Med. Ctr., Seattle, 2001—03, Carolyn Downs Family Medicine Ctr., Seattle, 2002—03, Valley Med. Ctr., Newcastle, Wash., 2003—; clin. preceptor Seattle U. Coll. Nursing, 2005. Mortality and morbidity external reviewer Western State Hosp., Tacoma, 2000—. Spkr., cmty. edn. Golden Care Sr. Group, Renton, Wash., 2003; cmty. educator Va. Mason Med. Ctr., Seattle, 2003. Named Outstanding Citizen of PR, 2005; recipient Outstanding Woman of Hatillo, P.R., Rotary Club, 1992. Mem.: ACP, AMA (assoc.), Wash. State Med. Assn., Med. Assn. P.R. (assoc.), Genesse County Med. Soc. (assoc.), Am. Student Med. Assn. (pres. 1991—92), Biology Honor Soc. (v.p. 1990—92). Avocations: sailing, walking. Office: Valley Med Ctr Int Med 7203 129th Ave SE Ste 200 Newcastle WA 98056-1412 Personal E-mail: marilynrosa@hotmail.com. E-mail: marilyn_rosabray@valleymed.org.

ROSALES, JENNIFER, professional golfer; b. Manila, Philippines, Sept. 17, 1978; Attened, U. So. Calif. Winner Philippine Ladies Amateur Open, 1994—98, Chick Fil-A Charity Championship, 2004. NCCC individual champion, 1998; winner Golf World Invitational, 1998. Achievements include being tied for lead after three rounds of the 2004 US Open. Avocations: shopping, movies, pets. Office: c/o LPGA 100 International Golf Dr Daytona Beach FL 32124-1092*

ROSALES, SUZANNE MARIE, hospital coordinator; b. Merced, Calif., July 23, 1946; d. Walter Marshall and Ellen Marie (Earl) Potter; children: Anita Carol, Michelle Suzanne. AA, City Coll., San Francisco, 1966. Diplomate Am. Coll. Utilization Review Physicians. Utilization review coord. San Francisco Gen. Hosp., 1967-74; mgr. utilization review/discharge planning UCLA Hosp. and Clinics, 1974-79; nurse III Hawaii State Hosp., Kaneohe, 1979-80; review coord. Pacific Profl. Std. Review Orgn., Honolulu, 1980-81; coord. admission and utilization reviewq The Rehab. Hosp. of the Pacific, Honolulu, 1981-85; coord. Pacific Med. Referral Project, Honolulu, 1985-87; dir. profl. svcs. The Queen's Healthcare Plan, Honolulu, 1987-88; utilization mgmt. coord. Vista Psychiat. Physician Assocs., San Diego, 1989; admission coord. utilization review San Francisco Gen. Hosp., 1989-91, quality improvement coordinator, 1991—. Cons. Am. Med. Records Assn. Contbr. articles to profl. jours. Mem. Nat. Assn. Utilization Review Profls. Home: 138 Alta Vista Way Daly City CA 94014-1402 Office: San Francisco Gen Hosp 1001 Potrero Ave San Francisco CA 94110-3594

ROSALES-SAID, MARTA MILAGROS, elementary school educator; b. Bilbao, Bizkaia, Spain, Aug. 5, 1959; d. Elias and Milagros (Franco) Rosales; m. Haroon Said, Sept. 8, 1984; 1 child, Iskander. BEd, Escuela de Magisterio, Spain, 1980; Spanish Final Diploma, London Inst. Linguistics, 1986. Spl. edn. tchr. Colegio INTXA Verondo, Durango, Spain, 1981-83; tchr. Pasadena (Calif.) Unified Sch. Dist., 1988—, mentor tchr., 1991—. Prodr., editor, dir.: Bilingual Education (video), 1991. Pasadena Ednl. Found. grantee, 1989-90; recipient Tchr. Excellence, Pasadena Rotar Club, 1995. Mem. London Inst. Linguists, Nature Conservancy. Avocations: drama, reading, story telling, translator children's books.

ROSANDER, LYNDA SUE, elementary school educator; b. Wamego, Kans., Sept. 11, 1941; d. Russell Lynn and Genevieve Augusta (Lelievre) Grutzmacher; m. James Edwin Rosander, June 27, 1965; children: Jennifer Lynn, Julian, April Lee Flagor. BA and B of Edn., Washburn U., 1964. Tchr. Jefferson County Pub. Schs., Denver, 1964-65, Topeka Pub. Schs., 1965-67, Clinton County R-III Schs., Plattsburg, Mo., 1984—93, Ind. Sch. Dist., 1993—2002. Co-dir. Northwest Mo. Sci. Olympiad, 1987-92; coach Nat. Ranking Sci. Olympiad Team, 1989-93; northwest Mo. coun. Mo. Energy Resources Program, 1988-90. Co-developer Nature Study Area, Plattsburg, 1989, Community Recycling Campaign, Plattsburg, 1989. Mo. Incentives grantee, 1986, Mo. Energy Resources Program grantee, 1989; recipient Citizen of Yr. award Plattsburg C. of C., 1991, Mo. State TIE award, 1993; nominee Tchr. of Yr. Mo., 1992. Mem. Nat. Sci. Tchrs. Assn., Mo. State Tchrs. Assn., Sci. Tchrs. Mo., Plattsburg Community Tchrs. Assn., Plattsburg PTA, Delta Kappa Gamma. Republican. Lutheran. Avocations: walking, reading, bridge, gardening.

ROSATO, JENNIFER L., dean, law educator; BS, Cornell U., 1983; JD, U. Pa., 1987. Law clk. to Hon. Thomas N. O'Neill, Jr. Fed. Dist. Ct., Ea. Dist. Pa.; assoc. Hangley Connolly Epstein Chicco Foxman and Ewing, Phila.; prof. Villanova Law Sch.; assoc. dean student affairs, co-dir. Ctr. for Health, Sci. and Pub. Policy Brooklyn Law Sch.; assoc. dean students, sr. prof. Coll. Law, Drexel U., Phila., 2006—, acting dean, 2006—. Vis. prof. U. Pa. Law Sch. Contbr. articles to profl. jours. Office: Drexel U Coll Law 3141 Chestnut St Philadelphia PA 19104 E-mail: jennifer.l.rosato@drexel.edu.*

ROSCKOWFF, CAROL MARTHA, pediatrician; b. Menomonie, Wis., Apr. 19, 1944; d. Cyril Hamlin and Jenny Wilhelmina Christina (Fjelstad) Evenson; m. Miekelawf W. Rosckowff (div.); children: Jenny Maria Roberts, Sven Evenson, Kari Ingrid; m. David Stanhope, June 22. BA, Augustana Coll., Sioux Falls, S.D., 1966; MD, U. Wis., Madison, 1970. Bd. cert. pediatrician Am. Bd. Pediats. Part-time pediatrician Midelfort Clinic, Eau Claire, Wis., 1974—75; pediat. educator family practice residency program U. Wis., Eau Claire, 1975—76; pediat. coord. Wyoming Valley Family Practice Residency Program, Kingston, Pa., 1977—86; part-time pediatrician Runet Health, Wilkes-Barre, Pa., 1980—88; pvt. practice Franciscan Skemp Healthcare, Mayo Health Sys., LaCrosse, Wis., 1988—2005; part-time pediatrician Good Night Pediats., Phoenix, 2005—. Mem. Women's Mental Health Task Force, Pa., 1985—86. Fellow: Am. Acad. Pediats. Avocations: reading, bicycling, water aerobics, writing. Home: # 31 2310 S Farnsworth Dr Mesa AZ 85209 Office: Good Night Pediats 325 E Baseline Rd Phoenix AZ 85042

ROSE, BEATRICE SCHROEDER (MRS. WILLIAM H. ROSE), harpist, educator; b. Ridgewood, NJ, Nov. 15, 1922; d. Henry William and Ida (LeHovey) Schroeder; m. William Harrison Rose, Apr. 10, 1954; 1 child, Daniel. Student, Inst. Musical Art, 1940—41, Mannes Coll. Music, 1942—44; studies with, Lucile Lawrence and Carlos Salzedo. Concert and radio debut NY World's Fair, NYC, 1939; soloist Damrosch Music Appreciation Hour broadcast, 1940, Duke of Windsor's Save the Children Fund, Nassau, The Bahamas, 1941; assoc. harpist Radio City Music Hall Orch., NYC, 1944-50; various radio and solo performances NY area, 1944-51; concert artist Italy, US and Can., 1952; prin. harpist Houston Symphony, 1953-84; prof. harp Moores Sch. Music, U. Houston, 1953—98. Soloist Contemporary Music Soc., 1959, 60, Houston Chamber Orch., 1969; dir. Christmas Festival of Harps, Houston Harp Ensemble, PBS, 1978, Harps of Gold, 1983; staff harpist Heritage Club, 1987-95, High Tea Ritz Carlton, 1996-97, St. Regis, 1998-2003. Author: The Harp in the Orchestra: A Reference Book for Harpists, Teachers, Composers and Conductors, 2003; composer works include Enchanted Harp, rev. edit., 1995; recs. for Houston Symphony, Stokowski, Everest, Capitol, Comissiona, Vanguard Records. Recipient 1st prize Federated Music Clubs Contest, 1936; NY Hour of Music award, 1945. Mem. Am. Harp Soc., Tex. Music Educators Assn. (adjudicator All-State competitions), Nat. Fedn. Music Clubs (harp adviser 1991), Phi Beta. Home: 1315 Friarcreek Ln Houston TX 77055-6714 Office: U Houston Sch Music Houston TX 77004

ROSE, CAROL ANN, retired air transportation executive; b. Toledo, Ohio; d. Donald Lucien and Dorothy Josephine (Maus) Edmunds; m. Saul Rose, Feb. 3, 1971 (div. 1976). BA, Kent State U., 1963. Entertainer, restaurant supr. S.S. Aquarama Cruiseship, Cleve., 1961-63; airline reservation agt. United Airlines, Cleve., 1963-68, internat. passenger svc. rep. Miami, Fla., 1969-70, V.I.P. customer svc. receptionist-expediter Phila., 1971-79, account exec., 1980-84, spl. events mgr. Chgo., 1984-87, red carpet club coord., 1987-88, corp. meeting planner, 1988-90, comml. aircraft weight and balance planner Seattle, 1991-96, comms. coord., 1996-98, mktg. and promotion coord., 1998-99, coord. workers compensation-comm./return to work Chgo., 1999—2001; ret., 2001; vol. editor Spiceline cmty. newsletter. Speaker Am. Mktg. Assn., Chgo., 1989. Author: Red Carpet Club Procedure Manual-O'Hare, 1987, Corporate Meeting Planners Manual, 1989, United Airlines Foundation Community Connection Report; Editor: Sky Lines Seattle Station Newsletter, 1992, United Airlines Workers' Compensation Newsletter, 1999 Vol. Relay for Life Am. Cancer Soc. Recipient Oustanding Svc. award Airline Passengers Assn., Phila., 1981, Outstanding Contbn. award Muscular Dystrophy Assn.-Jerry Lewis Telethon, Las Vegas, 1985, 86, 89, Leadership award United Way Campaign, Chgo., 1988. Mem. Meeting Planners Assn., Mgmt. Club (v.p. 1983, pres. 1984), Women United (exec. bd. 1982-83), Spicer Estates Homeowners Assn. (pres.), Delta Zeta. Avocations: reading, walking, writing, dance. Home: 468 Woodruff Trl Mullica Hill NJ 08062-2026

ROSE, CAROL LEE, artist, educator; b. Balt., Nov. 20, 1955; d. George Edward and Mary Theresa (Rinehart) Hubbard; m. David Bair, Aug. 2, 1975 (div. Aug. 1985); 1 child, David Michael Bair; m. David William Rose, Aug. 18, 1990. A in Fine Arts, Anne Arundel C.C., Arnold, Md., 1985; BS in Interdisciplinary Studies, Midwestern State U., 1995; MA in Art History, Tex. Woman's U., Denton, 2006. Cert. tchr., Tex.; cert. secondary art. Ednl. aide Sam Houston Elem., Wichita Falls, Tex., 1990-95, ednl. tutor, 1995-96; art tchr. Washington Jackson Math Sci Ctr, Wichita Falls, 1996—. Art club supr. Washington Jackson Math Sci Ctr., Wichita Falls, 1996-. Exhibited in juried show Breckenridge Fine Arts Ctr., 1993 (Hon. Mention award 1993); created sculpture Whirligig, 1995 (merit award in sculpture 1995). Active Washington Jackson PTA, Wichita Falls, 1996—. Mem. Tex. State Tchrs. Assn., Wichita Falls Art Assn. Republican. Roman Catholic. Avocations: painting, sculpture, nascar winston cup car racing. Home: 3034 Pool St Wichita Falls TX 76308-3539 Office: WFISD Washington Jackson Sci Ctr 1300 Harding St Wichita Falls TX 76301-7328 Office Phone: 940-720-3145. E-mail: crose@wfisd.net.

ROSE, CAROL MARGUERITE, law educator; b. Washington, Apr. 12, 1940; d. J. Hugh and Marie (Meenehan) R. BA, Antioch Coll., 1962; MA, U. Chgo., 1963, JD, 1977; PhD, Cornell U., 1970. Bar: Ill. 1977, Calif. 1978, D.C. 1978. Instr. history Ohio St. U., Columbus, 1969-73; assoc. dir. So. Govtl. Monitor Project, Atlanta, 1975-76; law clk. to judge U.S. Ct. Appeals (5th cir.), Austin, Tex., 1977-78; asst. prof. law Stanford U., 1978-80; acting prof. law U. Calif., Berkeley, 1980-82; prof. law Northwestern U., Chgo., 1982-88, Yale U., 1989—90, Fred A. Johnston prof. New Haven, 1990—94, Gordon Bradford Tweedy prof. of law and orgn., 1994—2005; emerita, 2005—. Bd. editors Found. Press, Mineola, N.Y., 1986—. Mem. Am. Assn. Law Schs., Am. Acad. Arts and Scis., Order of Coif. Office: U Ariz Coll of Law PO Box 210176 Tucson AZ 85721-0176 E-mail: carol.rose@yale.edu.

ROSE, DARLENE JOYCE, speech pathology/audiology services professional; b. St. Paul, Oct. 10, 1942; d. Earl Ambrose and Marie Helen (Rivard) Martin; m. Frederick Conrad Rose, Aug. 6, 1966; 1 child, David. BA cum laude, Briar Cliff Coll., 1964; MS magna cum laude, Marquette U., 1966. Supr. dept. speech Curative Adult Rehab. Ctr., Milw., 1966—71; student supr. Marquette U., Milw., 1969—71; speech/lang. pathologist Phys. Therapy Svcs., Inc., Milw., 1973—82, Rehab. Assocs., Inc., Mequon, Wis., 1982—91; rehab. facility coord. Nova Care Inc., Milw., 1991—93; sr. speech pathologist, clin. student supr. Covenant Health Care, Brookfield, Wis., 1993—. Lectr. phys. medicine Mt. Mary Coll., Wauwatosa, 1987—89; TV spokesperson Covenant Health Care, Milw., 1994—2000; cons., video course presenter Waukesha County Tech. Coll., Pewaukee, 2004. Pres. PTA, Wauwatosa, Wis., 1976, Brookfield (Wis.) Libr. Bd., 1991—94; vol. Repertory Theater, Milw., 1993—2001; mem. beautification com. Village of Elm Grove, 1993—. Named Mrs. Wis., 1977; recipient degree of distinction, Nat. Forensic League, 1958, 2d pl., Worldwide Miracle-Gro Garden Contest; grantee, Vocat. Rehab. Assn., 1964. Mem.: Am. Speech and Hearing Assn. Republican. Cath. Avocations: gardening, travel, reading, modeling, baking. Home: 13535 Wrayburn Rd Elm Grove WI 53122

ROSE, DEBRA FIELDS See FIELDS, DEBBI

ROSE, DEEDIE POTTER, arts patron; BA in French, Tex. Christian U. Mem. Nat. Coun. on Arts Nat. Endowment for Arts, 2002—; past pres. bd., bd. trustee Dallas Mus. Art; bd. dir. Dallas Ctr. for Performing Arts, Dallas Theater Ctr., Dallas Inst. for Humanities and Culture, Dallas Architectural Forum, Pub. Radio Internat., Channel 13/KERA 90.1, Tex. Internat. Theatrical Arts Soc., Dallas Found., Tex. Christian U.; adv. bd. U. Tex. Sch. Architecture; coun. mem. Dallas Women's Found. Recipient Neiman Marcus Silver Cup award, TACA, 1997. Mailing: Nat Endowment for Arts 1100 Pennsylvania Ave NW Washington DC 20505*

ROSE, DORI, real estate agent; b. Bklyn., Aug. 20, 1939; d. Murray Lewis and Frances Rose Fenig; m. Joel A. Rose, Apr. 12, 1964; children: Susan, Terri Rose Angstreich. BS cum laude, Bklyn. Coll., 1961; MS, Bklyn. Coll., 1964. Tchr. N.Y.C. Pub. Schs., 1961—66; real estate salesperson Weichert Realtors, Cherry Hill, NJ, 1982—93, Remax of Cherry Hill, 1993—. Named to Million Dollar Club, 1984—2004, Disting. Sales Club, 2000. Mem.: Silver Million Dollar Club, Remax Hall of Fame, Remax 100% Club. Avocations: antiques, travel. Office: Remax of Cherry Hill 1736 Rt 70 E Cherry Hill NJ 08003

ROSE, DORIS ANN, elementary school educator; b. MIddletown, Ohio, Apr. 10, 1947; d. Roy Patton and Anita Theresa Craft. AA, Temple Coll., Tex., 1971; BA, U. Mary Hardin Baylor, Belton, Tex., 1974. Cert. tchr. Tex. Social studies tchr. Galveston Ind. Sch. Dist., Tex., 1975—76; history and English tchr. Killeen Ind. Sch. Dist., Tex., 1978—. Grader Tex. Edn. Agy., Austin, 2006. Editor: (newspaper) Ea. Hills Times, 2005—06. Mem. Tex. Watch, Austin, 2006. Named Tchr. of Month, Killeen Ind. Sch. Dist., 1995; recipient Cert. of Merit, Nat. League Jr. Cotillions, 2005. Mem.: Am. Fedn. Tchrs. (rep. 1994—95), Killeen Fedn. Tchrs. (sec. 1994—95). Democrat. Avocations: gardening, reading, writing, sewing, cooking. Home: PO Box 385 Eddy TX 76524 Office: Ea Hills Mid Sch 300 Indian Tr Harker Heights TX 76548

ROSE, EDITH SPRUNG, retired lawyer; b. N.Y.C., Jan. 7, 1924; d. David L. and Anna (Storch) Sprung; m. David J. Rose, Feb. 15, 1948; children: Elizabeth Rose Stanton, Lawrence, Michael. BA, Barnard Coll., 1944; LLB, Columbia U., 1946. Bar: N.Y. 1947, N.J. 1973. Adminstr. Practising Law Inst., N.Y.C., 1947-48; ptnr. Smith, Lambert, Hicks & Miller, Princeton, N.J., 1974-88; counsel to Drinker, Biddle & Reath, Princeton, 1988-91; ret., 1991. Mem. ABA, N.Y. Bar Assn., N.J. Bar Assn., Princeton Bar Assn., Womens Law Caucus of Mercer County, Princeton Club (N.Y.C.). Home: 201 Lambert Dr Princeton NJ 08540-2308

ROSE, JANE A., financial planner; b. Phila., Sept. 30, 1940; d. Maurice and Miriam (Blank) Auritt; divorced; children: Lynne C., Wendy J., Debora J. Rose-Stewart. Student, Pa. State U., 1958; BA, Rutgers U., 1975; MBA, Temple U., 1978, postgrad., 1978-80. CPA, N.J.; CFP; cert. mgmt. acct., personal fin. specialist. Asst. v.p. Data Control Ctr., Cherry Hill, N.J., 1966-70; statistician, sr. staff asst. I.U. Internat. Corp., Phila., 1970-72; ops. mgr. Bus. Data Ctr., Cherry Hill, N.J., 1972-75; instr. acctg. and mgmt. Rutgers U., Camden, N.J., 1975-80; cost acctg. supr., acctg. mgr. Phila. Nat. Bank, 1980-82; asst. dir. fiscal planning N.J. Dept. Higher Edn., Trenton, 1982-85; contr., CFO Essex County Coll., Newark, 1985-87; v.p. fin. Horizon House, Inc., Phila., 1987-89; v.p. RTD Fin. Advisors Inc., Phila., 1989—. Instr., advisor Cen. Mich. U., McGuire AFB, N.J., 1978-80; instr. MBA Program, Widener U., Chester, Pa., 1980-82; rsch. asst. Temple U. Sch. Bus., Phila., 1975-76. Trustee Contact Cmty. Helpline, Cherry Hill, N.J., 1987-97, v.p., 1988-89, pres., 1989-94, mem. fin. com., 1995—; chair planned giving com. Women's Way, 2001—. Fellow Temple U. Sch. Bus., Phila., 1976-78. Fellow N.J. Soc. CPAs (chair subcom. 1985-89); mem. AICPA (grader CPA exam. 1987), Am. Woman's Soc. CPAs, Inst. Mgmt. Accts. (sec. South Jersey chpt. 1971-73, v.p. 1982-84, bd. dirs. 1971-75, 84-85, 91-93; grader, cons. CMA exam. 1986-99), Fin. Planning Assn., Am. Soc. Women Accts. (sec. Phila. chpt. 1972-74, bd. dirs. 1970-75), Choral Arts Soc. Phila. (singer, 2003—). Office: RTD Fin Advisors Inc 30 S 17th St Ste 1720 Philadelphia PA 19103-1752 Office Phone: 215-557-3800. E-mail: jrose@rtdfinancial.com.

ROSE, JOANNA SEMEL, volunteer; b. Orange, NJ, Nov. 22, 1930; d. Philip Ephraim and Lillian (Mindlin) Semel; m. Daniel Rose, Sept. 16, 1956; children: David S., Joseph B., Emily, Gideon G. Cert., Shakespeare Inst., U.K., 1951; BA summa cum laude, Bryn Mawr Coll., 1952; postgrad., St. Hilda's Coll., Oxford U., 1953; grad., CUNY Ctr. for Humanities. Mem. exec. com. Am. Friends St. Hilda's Coll., former chmn.; bd. dir., former pres. Paper Bag Players, N.Y.C.; former bd. dir., current mem. adv. coun. Poets and Writers, Inc., N.Y.C.; former chmn. adv. bd. Partisan Rev., N.Y.C.; mem. adv. coun. Nat. Dance Inst., N.Y.C.; bd. mem. NY Coun. for Humanities. Bd. dir. Bay St. Theatre, Sag Harbor; former bd. dir. Am. Friends Jewish Mus. Greece; assoc. fellow Berkeley Coll. Yale U.; mem. N.Y. Inst. for Humanities; bd. dirs. N.Y. Gate Coun. for Humanities; bd. dirs. Ctr. Humanities CUNY. Former bd. dirs. Eldridge St. Project, N.Y.C. Named an Hon. fellow, St. Hilda's Coll. Oxford. Mem. Cosmopolitan Club, Bryn Mawr Club of NY, LVIS East Hampton. Home: 895 Park Ave New York NY 10021-0327 also: 1 Lily Pond Ln East Hampton NY 11937

ROSE, JOANNE W., rating service executive; BA in Polit. Sci. and History magna cum laude, U. Rochester; JD, Columbia U. Assoc. White & Case, NYC; sr. mng. dir., gen. counsel Standard & Poor's Rating Svcs. divsn. McGraw Hill, NYC, 1989—99, chair rating policy bd.; exec. mng. dir., structured fin. ratings Standard & Poor's, NYC, 1999—. Office: Standard & Poors 55 Water St New York NY 10041-0003

ROSE, JODI, artistic director, film producer; b. Phila., Nov. 27, 1952; d. Hubert Michael and Rita Gervase (Schubert) Rosenberger; m. Edward A. Caycedo; children: Gervase-Teresa, Thomas Schubert, Tanya-Katrina, Edward-Michael. Student, Vienna (Austria) Hochshule, 1973; BS in Edn. and Music, Chestnut Hill Coll., Phila., 1974; postgrad. in performing arts, NYU, 1976-77. Leading roles in 35 musicals or operas throughout country, U.S. and Europe, 1974-87; founder, artistic dir. Opera on the Go, Ltd., 1988—. Prodr., dir., choreographer: Goldilocks, Little Red Riding Hood, The Tortoise and the Hare, The Pirate Captains, Telephone, Sweet Betsy from Pike, The Medium, La Pizza Con Funghi, others Founder, dir. musical theater workshops for youth, Queens Theater, N.Y., 1993—2002 Grantee NY State Coun. on Arts, NYC Dept. Youth Svcs.; guest performer at Lincoln Ctr., NYC Republican. Roman Catholic. Avocations: ballroom dancing, scuba diving, water-skiing, swimming, horseback riding. Office: 603 N Delavan Ave Margate City NJ 08402-1915 E-mail: jodimrose@comcast.net.

ROSE, JOLENE RENEE, music educator; b. Ravenna, Ohio, Jan. 29, 1960; m. Dennis Ray Rose, July 26, 1986; children: Becca Rae, Hayes Ray. MusB in Edn., Kent State U., Ohio, 1982. Instr. music Arthur County H.S., Nebr., 1982—. Mem.: NEA, Nebr. Edn. Assn., Music Educators Nat. Conf., Zeta Mu (pres. 2004—05). Independent. Avocations: music, swimming, reading, jet skiing, scrapbooks.

ROSE, KATHLEEN DIANE, elementary school educator; b. Torrington, Wyo., Oct. 10, 1951; d. Henry and Rachael Korell; m. Robert Clifford Rose; children: Justin Levi, James Henry, Joshua Robert. MusB, U. Wyo., Laramie, Wyo., 1988, MA, 2005. Cert. tchr. Dept. Edn., Wyo., 2000. Elem. music specialist Brownsville Ind. Sch. Dist., Tex., 1990—95; tchr. music Hilltop Bapt. Acad., Cedar Park, Tex., 1996—98; elem. music specialist Carbon County Sch. Dist. One, Rawlins, Wyo., 2000—. Supervising tchr. Carbon Sch. Dist. One, 2004—05. Musician: Wyo. Student Baroque Ensemble. Com. woman Carbon County Rep. Com., Rawlins, 2006; pianist, tchr. Sinclair Cmty. Ch., Wyo., 2002—06. Named Tchr. of Yr., Wyo. Dept. Edn., 2006; recipient Kuehn award, U. Wyo., 1987; scholar, Ea. Wyo. Coll., 1970, U. Wyo., 1986—88. Mem.: Music Educators Nat. Conf., Am. Orff Schulwerk Assn. Republican. Evang. Avocations: bible reading, running, needlecrafts. Home: PO Box 53 Sinclair WY 82334 Office: Highland Hills Elementary 1525 Darnley Rd Rawlins WY 82301 Office Phone: 307-328-9299.

ROSE, LEATRICE, artist, educator; b. NYC, June 22, 1924; d. Louis Rose and Edna Ades; m. Sol Greenberg (div.); children: Damon, Ethan; m. Joseph Stefanelli, Oct. 10, 1975. Student, Cooper Union, 1941-45, Arts Students League, 1946, Hans Hoffman Sch., 1947. Faculty Phila. Coll. Art, Sch. Visual Arts, SUNY, Bklyn. Coll. Solo exhbns. include Hansa Gallery, N.Y.C., 1954, Zabriskie Gallery, N.Y.C., 1965, Landmark Gallery, N.Y.C., 1974, Tibor de Nagy Gallery, N.Y.C., 1975, 78, 81, 82, Elaine Benson Gallery, Bridgehampton, N.Y., 1980, Armstrong Gallery, N.Y.C., 1985, Benton Gallery, Southampton, N.Y., 1987, Cyrus Gallery, N.Y.C., 1989; group exhbns. include Sam Kootz Gallery, N.Y.C., 1950, Peridot Gallery, N.Y.C., 1952, Poindexter Gallery, N.Y.C., 1959, Tanager Gallery, N.Y.C., 1960, 62, Riverside Mus., N.Y.C., 1964, Frumkin Gallery, N.Y.C., 1964, Pa. Acad. Fine Arts, Phila., 1966, N.Y. Cultural Ctr., 1973, The Queens (N.Y.) Mus., 1974, 83, Nat. Acad. Design, N.Y.C., 1974, 75, 76, 92, 93, Weatherspoon Art Gallery, Greensboro, N.C., 78, 81, Whitney Mus. Am. Art, N.Y.C., 1978, Albright-Knox Gallery, Buffalo, 1978, 81, Met. Mus. Art, 1979, Vanderwoude Tananbaum Gallery, N.Y.C., 1982, Benton Gallery, 1986, 87.; public collections include Albrect Gallery, St. Joseph, Mo., Guild Hall Mus., East Hampton, N.Y., Tibor de Nagy, Met. Mus. Art. Grantee N.Y. State Coun. Arts, 1974, The Ingram Merrill Found., 1974, AAUW, 1975, NEA, 1977, Esther and Aldolph Gottlieb Found., 1980, 88; recipient Altman prize NAD, 1974, Phillips prize NAD, 1992, award AAAL, 1992, Am. Inst. Art award. Mem. NAD, 1992- (Academician, 1994-). Avocations: reading, walking. Office: 463 West St Apt A924 New York NY 10014-2038

ROSE, MARY MCNALLY, federal official; b. Apr. 10, 1946; d. Hugh B. and Margaret (Brady) McNally; m. Philip David Rose, Sept. 12, 1970; children: Sarina Josephine, Aimee Elizabeth, Michael Roddy, Maureen Erin. RN, Bon Secours Sch. Nursing, 1967. Spl. asst. to dir. Fed. Exec. Inst., Washington; asst. dir. office exec. personnel The White House, Washington, 1983-85, asst. office personnel mgmt., 1985, dir. personnel, 1985-86; dep. under sec. for mgmt. U.S. Dept. Edn., Washington; vice chmn. Fed. Salary Coun.; mem. US Merit Systems Protection Bd, Washington, 2005—. Office: US Merit Systems Protection Bd 1615 M St NW Rm 680 Washington DC 20419*

ROSE, MARYA MERNITZ, lawyer; b. Sept. 1962; m. Anthony J Rose. BA, Williams College, Williamstown, Mass.; JD, Ind. U. Corp. counsel Cummins Inc, 1997—98, corp. counsel & dir. public relations, 1998—99, corp. counsel & dir. public relations & comm. strategy, 1999—2000, v.p., gen. counsel, 2001—. Office: Cummins Inc 500 Jackson St Columbus IN 47202

ROSE, NANCY JOY, social worker; b. Phila., Apr. 4, 1954; d. William Humphrey and Elizabeth Charlotte (Young) R.; m. Trevor B. Jones, Aug. 18, 1984; 1 child, Tracy Lynn. B.A., Temple U., 1975; cert. program for elem. edn. Glassboro State Coll., 1984-85. Cert. paralegal, 1989. Park ranger Independence Hist. Park, Phila., 1978; researcher Colonial Penn Ins. Co., Phila., 1978-79; customer service rep. Del. Mgmt. Co., Phila., 1979; case worker Dept. Pub. Welfare, Phila., 1979-84; health and safety com. mem. Pa. Social Services Union, Phila., 1980-83; health and safety rep. Snyder Dist. Welfare Office, Phila., 1980-84. Chairperson human needs com. First Councilmatic Dist., Phila, 1982-83; English in Action vol. English Speaking Union, Phila., 1983-87; legal med. clerk Ear Nose and Throat Profl. Assocs., Millville, NJ., 1990-1995. Mem. Am. Archeol. Soc., Mus. Natural History, Smithsonian Instn., Bibl. Archeology Soc., N.J. Archaeology Assn., N.J. Archeol. Soc. Office Phone: 856-694-5280.

ROSE, NORMA LOUISE, retired human services manager; d. Elzie Mars and Hattie Mae Rose. MBA, Chapman U., Orange County, Calif., 1979. With Hewlett-Packard Co., Pasadena, Calif., 1959—98, prodn. worker, 1959—78, order processing clk., prodn. supr., pers. rep., coll. recruiting mgr., human resources mgr.; ret., 1998. Home: 24218 Via Llano Murrieta CA 92562-5581 Personal E-mail: normar@murrieta.net.

ROSE, PEGGY JANE, artist, educator, gifted education advocate; b. Plainfield, NJ, Oct. 4, 1947; d. Kenneth Earl and Mary Elizabeth (Taylor) R.; m. Byram Soli Daruwala, July 30, 1988; 1 child, Mathew Byram Daruwala. BA magna cum laude, U. Tex., Austin, 1971; BFA with distinction, Acad. of Art Coll., San Francisco, 1980; student of, Burton Silverman. With curriculum devel. com. Calif. Coll. Arts and Crafts, Oakland, 1985-86; with Walnut Creek (Calif.) Civic Arts, 1985-95; with faculty exec. com. Acad. of Art Coll., 1983-97; featured artist Sausalito (Calif.) Art Festival, 1986. Art exhbn. juror, No. Calif., 1994-97; instr. painting, drawing. One-woman shows include Dragon Gallery, Mill Valley, Calif., 1987, Brenda Hall Gallery, San Francisco, 1993, exhibited in group shows at US Art, 1994, Marin Arts Coun., San Rafael, Calif., 1996, exhibitions include Acad. Art Faculty Exhibits, Carmel Gallery, 1990, City of Walnut Creek, 1994—97, Mercer County Ann. Exhibit, 2003 (Juror's Choice award, West Windsor Arts Coun. award, 2003); author: Whistler's Pastels in Venice; editor: Resource Notebook for Teaching Gifted Children. Founder advocacy group Raising Exceptionally Able Children; co-chmn. G&T Resource Com., West Windsor-Plainsboro Regional Sch. Dist.; advocate gifted edn. Recipient Parent of Yr. award, NJ Assn. Gifted Children, 2002, Nat. Assn. Gifted Children. Mem.: Alamo Danville Artists Soc. (Best of Show Gold Medallion 1984), San Francisco Women Artists Gallery (Merit award 1987), N.Y. Soc. Illustrators (Lila Atcheson Wallace award), San Francisco Acad. Art Coll., Marin Soc. Artists (Grumbacher Gold Medallion awards), Arts Coun. Princeton, master Pastelist, Internat. Assn. Pastel Socs., Pastel Soc. Am. (Sauter-Margulies award 1998, Bd. Dirs. award 2003), Pastel Soc. West Coast (signature mem., Best of Show 1996, Handell award 1996, Ferrari Color award 1997, award 2004), Arts Coun. Princeton (Juror's Choice awards 2001, 2002), Audubon Artists, Allied Artists Am. (signature mem., Gold Medal of Honor 2002), Portrait Soc. Am., Calif. Art Club, Catherine Lorillard Wolf Art Club (Gold Medal of Honor 2002). Avocations: music, gifted education advocacy. Studio: 12 Perry Dr Princeton Junction NJ 08550-2803 Office Phone: 609-275-1633. Business E-Mail: prose47@comcast.net.

ROSE, ROSLYN, artist; b. Irvington, N.J., May 28, 1929; d. Mark and Anne Sarah (Green) R.; m. Franklin Blou, Nov. 26, 1950; 1 child, Mark Gordon Blue (dec.). Student, Rutgers U., Newark, NJ, 1949—51, Pratt Ctr. for Contemporary, 1969; BS, Skidmore Coll., Saratoga Springs, N.Y., 1976. One-woman shows include Midday Gallery, Caldwell, N.J., 1972, Caldwell Coll., 1972, Kean Coll., Union, N.J., 1973, Art Corner Gallery, Millburn, N.J., 1974, Brandeis U., Mass., 1974, Newark Mus., 1974, George Frederick Gallery, Rochester, N.Y., 1981, Robbins Gallery, Washington, 1981, Arnot Art Mus., Elmira, N.Y., 1982, Douglas Coll. Rutgers U., New Brunswick, 1987, Nathans Gallery, West Paterson, N.J., 1984, 86, 89, 97, 99, The Pen and Brush, N.Y.C., 1998, New Century Artists Gallery, N.Y.C., 2003, Symposia, Hoboken, N.J., 2005, Hoboken Hist. Mus., 2006; exhibited in group shows at Seattle Art Mus., Portland (Oreg.) Mus., NYU U., Montclair Art Mus., N.J., Women in the Arts, Florence and Naples, Italy, Art Ctr. Athens, Greece, Middlesex County Mus., Piscataway, N.J., New Century Artists, N.Y.C., Noyes Mus., Oceanville, N.J., Grounds for Sculpture, Hamilton, N.J., Mountain Art Show, Bernardsville, NJ, 2002 (Best in Show award), Manhattan Arts Internat., N.Y.C. (Artist Showcase award) 2004, J.W. Starks Galleries, Tex A&M U., 2004, Stevens Inst., Hoboken, 2005, Hoboken Hist. Mus., 2006, others; represented in permanent collections including N.J. State Mus., Trenton, Citibank of N.Y., Moscow, N.J. State Libr., Trenton, Roddenbery Meml. Libr., Cairo, Ga., Rosenberg Libr., Galveston, Tex., Newark Mus., Newark Pub. Libr., AT&T, BASF Wyandotte Corp., First Fed. Bank, Rochester, Gulf & Western Industries, Irving Trust Co., N.Y., McAllen Internat. Mus., Tex., Nabisco Brands Corp., East Hanover, N.J., Readers Digest Collection, Voorhees-Zimmerli Mus., Rutgers U., New Brunswick, N.J., The Noyes Mus., Ceres Gallery, NYC (study collection), Oceanville, N.J., Stevens Inst., Hoboken, others; featured artist New Century Artists Gallery, N.Y.C., 1998-2001, 2003, 2004, Internat. Soc. Exptl. Artists, 1999-2005, Period Gallery, Omaha (Dirs. award 2001), Cambridge Art Assn., 2002, Studio Seto, Boston, 2004, Somerville Art Mus., 2005, Fort Worth Art Ctr., 2005, Ceres Gallery, N.Y.C.; creator UNCIF cards, 1979-80; founding mem. Hob'art Cooperative Gallery, Hoboken, N.J. Recipient graphic award Westchester (N.Y.) Art Soc., 1973, Best-in-Show award Livingston (N.J.) Art Assn., 1971, Best-in-Show award N.J. Ctr. for Visual Arts, Summit, 1969, Mixed Media Merit award Salmagundi Club, N.Y.C., 1995, Exptl. Art award Western Colo. Art Ctr., 2000, Period Gallery Alternative Photography award, 2000, 2001, Mountain Art Show; numerous others. Mem.: Internat. Soc. Exptl. Artists, Nat. Assn. Women Artists (v.p. 1997—2001, exec. bd. 2001—03), Innovative Painting award 1990, Hazel Witte Mem. Computer Art award 2003), Pen and Brush Club N.Y.C. (Mixed Media award 1996, 1997, 1998, Photography award 2000, 2001, Best-in-Show award Mountain Art Show 2002). Office: Roslyn Rose Studios 321 Newark St Hoboken NJ 07030-2434 Business E-Mail: bluerose@roslynrose.com.

ROSE, SARA MARGARET, English as a second language educator; b. Johnstown, Pa., Sept. 22, 1950; d. William S. and Mary Margaret (Leberknight) R.; m. Akbar Ahamadian (common law, separated); 1 child, Meryem Rose. Student, U. Copenhagen, Denmark, 1971-73; MEd, Blagard Tchrs. Seminarium, Copenhagen, 1981. Cert. tchr., Denmark. Lang. tchr. and cons. Adult Edn., Hillerød, Denmark, 1981-90; cons. on immigrant and refugee issues Danish Dept. Welfare, Hillerød, 1983-88; ESL instr. Balt. City C.C., 1991-94, Catonsville C.C., Balt., 1992-96, Balt. Hebrew U., 1993-95, Balt. County Adult Edn., 1990-96, ESL facilitator, adminstr., 1994-96; dir. English Lang. Inst. Coll. Notre Dame of Md., Balt., 1996-99; ESL instr. U. Md., Baltimore County, 2000—03; ES instr. Towson U., 2003—. Cmty. coord. Au Pair Care, Balt., 1991-98. Lectr. on Immigrant and Refugee Issues, AOF Hillerød, 1983-90; founder, adminstr. Fgn. Women's Social Club, Hillerød, 1985-87; mem. People's Movement Against Racial Hatred and Discrimination, Denmark, 1983-90. Recipient Study Tour to Turkey, Danish Ministry of Edn., 1986, Cert. of Appreciation Balt. City C.C., 1993. Mem. TESOL, Md. TESOL (pres. 1999-2000, past pres. 2000—), Amnesty Internat., Greenpeace. Methodist. Avocations: reading, travel, music, theater, time with daughter. Home: 3905 Darleigh Rd Apt 2H Baltimore MD 21236-5808

ROSE, SHIRLEY KELLY, retired language educator; b. Marianna, Fla., Jan. 22, 1939; d. James Williams and Alice Elizabeth (White) Kelly; children: William Timothy Livingston, Kelly Livingston Carlton. BA, Fla. State U., Tallahassee, 1960; MS in Adult Edn., Troy State U., Montgomery, Ala., 1979, MS in English, 1990. English tchr. Bay County HS, Panama City, Fla., 1960—62, St. James HS, Montgomery, 1972—73, Patterson State Tech Coll., Montgomery, 1973—2000, chmn. gen. edn., 1990—2000; ret., 2000. Tech. coll. rep. State Policy Adv. Comm., Montgomery, 1986—99, Postsecondary Exec. Com., Montgomery, 1985—99. Coord. edn. divsn. United Way, Montgomery; organizer, pres. Jr. Woman's Club, Mobile, Ala., 1965—67; co-chmn. mother's march March of Dimes, Montgomery and Mobile, 1965—68; bd. dirs. Cystic Fibrosis, Montgomery. Named Disting. Young Woman, Montgomery Jaycettes, 1969, Outstanding Clubwoman, Montgomery Jr. Woman's Club, 1969, Outstanding Tech Coll. Faculty Mem., Ala. Coll. Sys., 1992; recipient Davenport Meml. award, Nat. Coun. Higher Edn., 1996. Mem.: Ala. Edn. Assn. (pres. postsecondary divsn. 1986—87, Outstanding Postsecondary Mem. 1995). Methodist. Avocations: travel, reading, bridge, exercise. Home: 8620 Lillian Pl Montgomery AL 36117

ROSE, SUSAN PORTER, management and governmental affairs consultant; b. Cin., Sept. 20, 1941; d. Elmer Johnson and Dorothy (Wurst) Porter; m. Jonathan Chapman Rose, Jan. 26, 1980; 1 child, Benjamin Chapman. BA, Earlham Coll., 1963; MS, Ind. State U., 1970; HDL (hon.), Rose-Hulman Inst. Tech., 2002. Staff asst. Congressman Richard L. Roudebush, Washington, 1963-64; asst. dean George Sch., Bucks County, Pa., 1964-66; asst. dir. admissions Mt. Holyoke Coll., South Hadley, Mass., 1966-71; asst. dir. correspondence First Lady Pat Nixon The White House, 1971-72, dir. of scheduling to First Lady Pat Nixon, 1972-74, to First Lady Betty Ford, 1974-77; spl. asst. to asst. atty. gen. Office Improvements in Adminstrn. Justice, Washington, 1977-79; spl. asst. to dep. asst. atty. gen. Justice Mgmt. divsn. U.S. Dept. Justice, Washington, 1978-81; chief of staff to Barbara Bush, asst. to U.S. v.p. Washington, 1981—89; chief of staff to First Lady Barbara Bush, dept. asst. pres. of U.S. The White House, 1989—93; commr. U.S. Commn. Fine Arts, 1993-98. Bd. dirs. Barbara Bush Found. for Family Literacy, 1993—2002; trustee Bush Presdl. Libr.; mem. alumni coun. Earlham Coll., 1977—78, pres. alumni assn., 1978—81. Recipient Disting. Alumni award, Earlham Coll., 1992, Ind. State U., 1991. Mem.: Ind. Acad. Home: 5955 Ranleigh Manor Dr Mc Lean VA 22101-2428

ROSE, TERRY DENISE, secondary school educator; b. Knoxville, Tenn., Mar. 14, 1958; d. William Ray and Barbara Diane (Moore) R. BS, U. Tenn., Knoxville, 1981, MS, 1987, EdD, 1991. Cert. tchr., Tenn. Instr. in math. Walter State Community Coll., 1990-92; asst. prof. dept. elem. edn. We. Carolina U., 1992—. Mem. Smoky Mountain Math. Educators Assn. (past chair), Tenn. Math. Tchrs. Assn. (past v.p.), Spring Hill Mid. Sch. Math. (tchr., chair 1981-88), Nat. Coun. Tchrs. Math., Phi Delta Kappa, Phi Eta Sigma. Home: 10744 Mercury Dr Knoxville TN 37932-2447

ROSE, TESSIE E., special education educator, consultant; b. Galveston, Tex., Aug. 13, 1974; d. Carolyn and Kenneth Rose; m. Tom Nay, July 7, 2001. BS in Outdoor Recreation for Spl. Populations, Ferrum Coll., Va., 1993—96; MS in Therapeutic Recreation, U. Utah, Salt Lake City, 1996—98, PhD in Spl. Edn., 2001—05; Post Doctorate - Spl. Edn., Lehigh U., Bethlehem, Pa., 2005—06. Lic. Spl. Edn. Severe Disabilities Endorsement Utah Bd. Edn., 2002, cert. Spl. Edn. Mild/Moderate Utah Bd. Edn., 2004, AIMSweb Trainer Edformation, Inc., 2005. Spl. edn. tchr. Murray Sch. Dist., Utah, 2002—05; adj. faculty, dept. spl. edn. U. Utah, Salt Lake City, 2003—05; rsch. assoc. Ctr. for Promoting Rsch. to Practice, Bethlehem, Pa., 2005—. Trainer AIMSweb- Edformation, Inc., Minn., 2005—; project coord., mp3 model demo grant Lehigh U., 2005—, project coord., tchr. study group, 2005—; mgr., transition and assessment Lehigh U. & Pocono Mountain Sch. Dist., Pocono, Pa., 2005—; edn. cons., Salt Lake City, 1999—. Author: (rsch. and presentation) Effectiveness of Personalized Level Systems (Outstanding Profl. Performance award, CCBD, 2005); contbr. chapters to books, articles to profl. jours. Trip coord. YouthLINC, Holliday, Utah, 2003—05; fund raising com. Nat. Ability Ctr., Park City, Utah, 1998—2003; scholarship com. Lehigh Women's Group, Bethlehem, 2005—06. Recipient Tchr. of Yr. Nomination, Key Bank, Utah, 2004, The Rose award, Grant Elem., 2005; grantee Leadership grant, U. Utah, 2001—04. Mem.: AAHPERD, Coun. for Exceptional Children. Avocations: rock and ice climbing, travel. Office Phone: 610-758-6932. Personal E-mail: queentessie@yahoo.com.

ROSE, TRACEY ANNE, education educator; d. Richard William Mitchell and Patricia Carolyn Mitchell-Iversen; m. James L. Rose, May 1984; children: Grae Savannah, Keegan Indiana. BA in Elem. Edn., Ark. State U., State University, 1986; MA, So. Nazarene U., Bethany, Okla., 1991; AA in Am. Sign Language, Okla. State U., Oklahoma City, 2001; PhD in Indsnl. Leadership and Academic Curriculum, U. Okla., Norman, 2006. Cert. elem. prin., deaf/hard of hearing, spl. edn., early childhood edn., elem. tchr. Elem. tchr. Blytheville Pub. Schs., Ark., 1986—87, Oklahoma City Schs., 1987—93, Putnam City Schs., Oklahoma City, 2000—06; instr. Oklahoma City CC, 1995—2000, U. Okla., Norman, 2002—05; prof. Okla. State U., Stillwater, 2006—. Mem.: Gamma Beta Phi, Delta Kappa Gamma. Avocation: marathon running.

ROSE, VIRGINIA SHOTTENHAMER, secondary school educator; b. San Jose, Calif., Feb. 3, 1924; d. Leo E. and Mae E. (Slavich) Shottenhamer; m. Paul V. Rose, June 21, 1947; children: Paul V. Jr., David P., Alan P. AB, W. Calif., San Jose, 1945, MA, 1972. Tchr. grades 5-6 Evergreen Sch. Dist., San Jose, 1945-47; 6th grade tchr. Washington Sch., San Jose, 1947-57; elem. tchr. San Jose Unified Sch. Dist., 1967-82, reading specialist, tchr. grades 6-8, 1982-92; ret., 1992. Cons. in field; mem. project literacy San Jose Unified Schs., 1987-91; mem. instrnl. materials evaluation panel Calif. State Edpt. Edn., Sacramento, 1988; master tchr. U. Calif., San Jose, 1991. Co-author: Handbook for Teachers' Aides, 1967. Active Alexian Bros. Hosp. League, San Jose, 1965, bd. dirs., chair libr. cart, 1966-76; vol. San Jose Hist. Mus., 1992—. Mem. AAUW (com. chair 1978-81), Internat. Reading Assn., Calif. Reading Assn. (Margaret Lynch award for Outstanding Contbn. to Reading 1999), Santa Clara County Reading Coun. (pres. 1986-87, Asilomar conf. chair 1991, IRA honor coun. pres. club 1987, bd. dirs.), Santa Clara U. Calala Club (bd. dirs. 1994-96), Soroptimist Internat. (sec. 1993-94), Pi Epsilon Tau (pres. 1944-45), Kappa Delta Pi (pres. 1943-45), Pi Lambda Theta (pres. San Jose chpt. 1987-89, auditor 1980, sec. 1985-86, Biennium award 1987). Avocations: reading, hiking, biking, gardening, cooking. Office: Willow Glen Ed Park S 2001 Cottle Ave San Jose CA 95125-3502

ROSE, WENDY MICHELLE, science educator; b. Dyersburg, Tenn., Sept. 10, 1971; AS, Dyersburg State C.C., Tenn., 1991; BS, Austin Peay State U., Clarksville, Tenn., 1993; MS, U. Memphis, 2006. Instr. sci. Dyersburg State C.C., Tenn., 1994—. Conservative. Roman Catholic. Achievements include research in protein chemistry. Avocations: travel, reading, hiking. Home: PO Box 237 Dyersburg TN 38025 Office: Dyersburg State Community College 1510 Lake Road Dyersburg TN 38024 Office Phone: 731-286-3293. Business E-Mail: rose@dscc.edu.

ROSE-ACKERMAN, SUSAN, law and political economy educator; b. Mineola, NY, Apr. 23, 1942; d. R. William and Rosalie Rose; m. Bruce A. Ackerman, May 29, 1967; children: Sybil, John. BA, Wellesley Coll., 1964; PhD, Yale U., 1970. Asst. prof. U. Pa., Phila, 1970-74; lectr. Yale U., New Haven, 1974-75, asst. prof., 1975-78, assoc. prof., 1978-82; prof. law and polit. economy Columbia U., N.Y.C., 1982-87; Ely prof. of law and polit. econ. Yale U., New Haven, 1987-92, co-dir. Ctr. Law, Econ. and Pub. Policy, 1988—, Henry R. Luce prof. jurisprudence law and polit. sci., 1992—. Vis. rsch. fellow World Bank, 1995-96. Author: (with Ackerman, Sawyer and Henderson) Uncertain Search for Environmental Quality, 1974 (Henderson prize 1982); Corruption: A Study in Political Economy, 1978, (with E. James) The Nonprofit Enterprise in Market Economies, 1986; editor: The Economics of Nonprofit Institutions, 1986, (with J. Coffee and L. Lowenstein) Knights, Raiders, and Targets: The Impact of the Hostile Takeover, 1988, Rethinking the Progressive Agenda: The Reform of the American Regulatory State, 1992, Controlling Environmental Policy: The Limits of Public Law in Germany and the United States, 1995, Corruption and Government: Causes, Consequences and Reform, 1999 (Levine Prize 2000), (with Janós Kornai) Building a Trustworthy State in Post-Socialist Transition, 2004, (with Kornai and B. Rothstein) Creating Social Trust in Post-Socialist Transition, 2004, From Elections to Democracy: Building Accountable Government in Hungary and Poland, 2005, International Handbook on the Economics of Corruption, 2006+; contbr. articles to profl. jours.; mem. editl. bd. Jour. Law, Econs. and Orgn., 1984—, Internat. Rev. Law and Econs., 1986—, Polit. Sci. Quar., 1988—. Guggenheim fellow 1991-92, Fulbright fellow, Free U. Berlin, 1991-92; fellow Ctr. for Advanced Study in the Behavioral Scis., Stanford, Calif., 2002, Collegium Budapest, 2002. Mem. Am. Law and Econs. Assn. (bd. dirs. 1993-96, 2002-04), Am. Econ. Assn. (mem. exec. com. 1990-93), Am. Polit. Sci. Assn., Assn. Am. Law Schs., Assn. Pub. Policy and Mgmt. (policy coun. 1984-88, treas. 1998-2000). Democrat. Office: Yale U Law Sch PO Box 208215 New Haven CT 06520-8215 Office Phone: 203-432-4891. Business E-Mail: susan.rose-ackerman@yale.edu.

ROSEBOROUGH, TERESA WYNN, lawyer; b. Iowa City, Nov. 28, 1958; d. Robert Larry Wynn Jr. and Ethel (Crawford) Wynn; m. Joseph Anthony Roseborough, May 24, 1980. BA, U. Va., 1980; MEd, Boston U., 1983; JD with high honors, U. N.C., 1986. Bar: Ga. 1987, U.S. Ct. Appeals (4th cir.) 1987, U.S. Dist. Ct. (no. dist.) Ga. 1989, U.S. Ct. Appeals (11th cir.) 1989, U.S. Ct Appeals (5th, 6th and 7th cir.), U.S. Supreme Ct. Counselor U.S. Dept. of Army, Giebelstadt, Fed. Republic of Germany, 1980-83; law clk. to hon. Judge J. Dickson Phillips U.S. Ct. Appeals (4th cir.), 1986-87; law clk. to hon. Justice John Paul Stevens U.S. Supreme Ct., Washington, 1987-88; assoc. Sutherland, Asbill & Brennan, Atlanta, 1988-93; dep. asst. atty. gen. office legal counsel U.S. Dept. Justice, Washington, 1994—96; ptnr. Sutherland Asbill & Brennan LLP, Atlanta. Adj. prof. litig. Emory U. Sch. Law, 1996—98. Editor in chief U. N.C. Law Rev., 1985-86. Bd. dirs. Howard Schs., Atlanta, 1990—, Neighborhood Justice Ctr., 1993—, Nat. Assn. for Pub. Interest Law, The Children's Sch.; chair pro bono com. Atlanta Coun. Younger Lawyers, 1990-92, bd. dirs., 1990-93. Named to Am.'s Top Black Lawyers, Black Enterprise mag., 2003. Mem. ABA (vice chair young lawyers sect. pro bono com. 1990-92, vice chair water quality com. sect. on natural resources energy and environment 1992—), Am. Constn. Soc. (chair, 2004-), State Bar Ga., Gate City Bar Assn., Ga. Assn. Black Women Attys., Order of Coif. Avocations: skiing, golf. Office: Sutherland Asbill & Brennan LLP 999 Peachtree St NE Atlanta GA 30309-3996 Office Phone: 404-853-8100. E-mail: teresa.roseborough@sablaw.com.

ROSEBROUGH, CAROL BELVILLE, cable television company executive; b. Ironton, Ohio, June 5, 1940; d. Lindsey and Bessie (Reed) Belville; m. John R. Rosebrough, Mar. 4, 1960 (dec. Nov. 1974); children: G. Suzanne, John R., Rebecca J. Student, Columbia (Mo.) Coll., 1958-59; BSBA, Franklin U., 1985. Cons. CBR and Assocs., Columbus, 1978-82; dir. adminstrn. United Cerebral Palsy Columbus and Franklin County, 1972-82; bus. mgr. Times Mirror, Newark, Ohio, 1982-83, ops. mgr., 1983-85, gen. mgr. Logan/Waverly/Greenfield, Ohio, 1985-86, Times Mirror doing bus. as Dimension Cable Svcs., Marion, Ohio, 1986-88; v.p., gen. mgr. Cable TV div. Comcast of S.E. Pa. (formerly Susquehanna Comms., Times Mirror and Cox Comms.), Williamsport, Pa., 1988—. Bd. dirs United Way, Marion County, 1987-88, Lycoming County, 1989-2000, 2001-, Williamsport/Lycoming C. of C.; personal and bus. coach Coach U., 2002. Named one of Pa.'s Best 50 Women in Bus., 1997, One of Top 100 Bus. Persons in the State of Pa., 1997-99; fellow Betsy Magness Leadership Inst. 1999-2000, Pa. Economy League 2003—. Mem. Ohio Cable TV Assn. (bd. dirs. 1986-88), Pa. Cable TV Assn. (bd. dirs. 1990-96), Pa. Edn. Comms. Sys. (bd. dirs.), Pa. Rural Devel. Coun. (exec. com. telecomms. task force 1992-95), Mid-Ohio Regional Planning Commn. (transp. com. 1980-82), Internat. Women's Writers Guild, Internat. Assn. Counselors and Therapists. Avocations: writing, reading, music, arts/therapies. Office: Susquehanna Comms 330 Basin St Williamsport PA 17701-5216 Personal E-mail: carolrosebrough@suscom.net. Business E-Mail: carol_rosebrough@cable.comcast.com.

ROSEBROUGH, CATHERINE MARIE, special education educator, consultant; b. Marion, Ohio, Feb. 1, 1972; d. George Edward and Cheryl Sue Rosebrough. BS in Spl. Edn., U. Akron, Ohio, 1994; MS in Ednl. Adminstrn., U. Dayton, Ohio, 1998. Permanent tchg. cert. in spl. edn. Ohio, adminstrv. lic. Ohio. K-6 resource spl. edn. educator Lancaster (Ohio) City Schs., 1994—99; 3-6 inclusion/resource spl. edn. educator London (Ohio) City Schs., 1999—. Intervention coord. St. Patrick Sch., London, 2001—; cons. Edn. Made Easy, London, 2002—; intervention coord. Madison-Clark Christian Acad., London, 2004—; coord. Positive Behavior Support Team, 2004—. Mem. com. Habitat for Humanity, London, 1999—2006; bd. dirs. Domestic Violence Shelter, London, 1999—2004; mem. Signs of Christmas, Columbus, Ohio, 2005. Recipient Ashland (Ohio) Tchr. Golden Apple award, 1998; Presdl. scholar, U. Akron, 1990—94. Mem.: NEA, Kappa Delta Pi (nat. convocation del. 1990—94). Republican. Roman Catholic. Avocations: reading, walking. Office: London Elem Sch 380 Elm St London OH 43140 Office Phone: 740-845-3272. Office Fax: 740-845-3282. E-mail: catherine.rosebrough@london.k12.oh.us.

ROSELL, SHARON LYNN, physics and chemistry professor; b. Wichita, Kans., Jan. 6, 1948; d. John E. and Mildred C. (Binder) Rosell. BA, Loretto Heights Coll., 1970; postgrad., Marshall U., 1973; MS in Edn., Ind. U., 1977; MS, U. Wash., 1988. Cert. profl. educator, Wash. Assoc. instr. Ind. U., Bloomington, 1973-74; instr. Pierce Coll. (name formerly Ft. Steilacoom (Wash.) Community Coll.), 1976-79, 82, Olympic Coll., Bremerton, Wash., 1977-78; instr. physics, math. and chemistry Tacoma (Wash.) Community Coll., 1979-89; instr. physics and chemistry Green River Community Coll., Auburn, Wash., 1983-86; researcher Nuclear Physics Lab., U. Wash., Seattle, 1986-88; asst. prof. physics Cen. Wash. U., Ellensburg, 1989—. Faculty senate Ctrl. Washington U., 1992-98. Lector and dir. Rite of Christian Initiation of Adults, St. Andrew's Ch., Ellensburg, Wash., 1993—, mem. parish coun., 1995-2000. Mem.: Soc. Physics Students (councilor zone 17 1998—2004, com. judging Nat. Outreach and Rsch. awards 2000—01, 2003—05, nat. nominating com. 2005—), Pacific NW Assn. Coll. Physics (bd. dirs. 1997—99, 2001—, treas. 2002—), Internat. Union Pure and Applied Chemistry (affiliate), Am. Chem. Soc., Am. Assn. Physics Tchrs. (rep. com. on physics for 2-yr. colls. Wash. chpt. 1986—87, v.p. 1987—88, pres. 1988—89, v.p. 1994—95, pres. 1995—96, past pres. 1996—97), Am. Phys. Soc. Democrat. Roman Catholic. Avocations: leading scripture discussion groups, reading, poetry, needlecrafts. Home: 1100 N B St Apt 2 Ellensburg WA 98926-2570 Office: Ctrl Wash U Physics Dept Ellensburg WA 98926 Office Phone: 509-963-2757. Business E-Mail: rosells@cwu.edu.

ROSEMAN, KIM, gallery director; b. 1970; BFA, Monmouth U., NJ. Owner Karin Newby Gallery and Sculpture Garden. Tubac chpt. founder Hearts and Hooves; mem. Tubac Mus. of Arts, Tubac Ctr. for Arts, Tucson Plein Air Painters Soc. Named one of 40 Under 40, Tucson Bus. Edge, 2006. Office: Karin Newby Gallery 19 Tubac Rd Tubac AZ 85646 Office Phone: 520-398-9662. Office Fax: 520-398-2861.*

ROSEN, ADELE R., interior designer; b. Utica, NY, Feb. 2, 1933; d. Nat and Faye Marsh; children: Liz Payson, Barbara Dollar. BA, SUNY, Utica. Interior designer Self-Employed, Santa Barbara, Calif.; dir. Beyond Tolerance Ctr., Santa Barbara. Pres. S.B.Jewish Fedn. Homons Bd.; bd. mem. Child Abuse Listening Mediation; dir. Anne Frank exhibit, Santa Barbara, 1998—; bd. mem. S.B. Art Mus. Named Person of Yr. Disting. Cmty. Svc.award, Anti Deformation League, 1996. Home: 827 Via Granada Santa Barbara CA 93103

ROSEN, ADRIENNE, artist, educator; b. St. Louis, Dec. 18, 1940; d. Charles and Rena Gallop; m. Alex Paul Tucker, June 21, 1961 (dec. June 1965); m. Martin M. Rosen, Dec. 1967; 4 children. BFA, Washington U., St. Louis, 1972. Illustrator, designer Internat. Shoe Co., St. Louis, 1961; owner, illustrator, graphic designer A.R. Art Studio, St. Louis, 1961—; painter portraits of people and pets St. Louis, 1995—. Art tchr. St. Louis Artist Guild; art tchr. Coll. for Kids program Meramec C.C.; pvt. instr. Adrienne's Acad. Art; juried mem. The Best of Mo. Hands, 2005—06. Designer, illustrator (dolls) Bethany Farms Inc., 1990—. Vol. artist Leukemia Soc. Am., St. Louis, 1999, Animal Aid, St. Louis, 1975, Am. Med. Ctr., St. Louis, Cystic Fibrosis Found.; vol. St. Louis Showstoppers for Breast Cancer Rsch. Named Artist of Month, Ballwin, Mo., 2004; recipient 2d pl. award, Jewish Cmty. Ctrs. Assn., St. Louis, 1997, University City Art Assn., St. Louis, 1999, award of mention, South County Art Assn., St. Louis, 1998, Recognition award, Art Happening, 2001—02, 1st pl. award profl. watercolor, Jewish Cmty. Ctrs. Assn., 2002, 2003, Hon. Mention Award, Mo. Art Tchrs. Exhibit, William Woods Coll., Fulton, 2005, Hon. Mention award, Jewish Cmty. Ctr., 2005, 2006, 1st place profl. watercolor, St. Olympics Art Show, 2006. Mem.: Artists Boutique (publicity chair 2005—06), Greater St. Louis Art Assn. (publicity dir. 1994—99, sec. 1995—98, v.p. 1998—2000, pres. 2000—02, exhibits chair 2002—03, publicity chair 2004—05, pres. 2006), St. Louis Watercolor Soc. (signature mem.), St. Louis Artist Guild (bd. dirs. 1993—94), Art World Art Assn. Avocations: dance, photography, marathon race running. Office: AR Art Studio 1717 Seven Pines Dr Saint Louis MO 63146-3713 Office Phone: 314-576-7137. Personal E-mail: Arosen3125@aol.com.

ROSEN, ANA BEATRIZ, electronics executive; b. Guayaquil, Ecuador, May 16, 1950; came to U.S., 1962; d. Luis A. and Luz Aurora (Rodriguez) Moreira; m. Manuel Jose Farina, Dec. 15, 1979 (dec. Apr. 1990); children: Kevin, Mark; m. Michael G. Rosen, June 6, 1992 (dec. Oct. 2001). AA, Latin-Am. Inst., 1971. Adminstr. asst. M&T Chem. Inc., N.Y.C., 1971-75; mgr. sales Singer Products Co., N.Y.C., 1975-78; v.p. Argil Internat. Ltd., N.Y.C., 1978-83; pres. KMA Enterprises Inc., Bklyn., 1983-94, KMA Industries Inc., Palm Beach Gardens, Fla., 1994—. Mem. U.S Trade Adv. Bd.; v.p. Miro Sales, Inc. Bd. dirs. Palm Beach County chpt. ARC. Mem. ARC, World Trade Coun. (Palm Beach County), Gold Coast Bus. and Profl. Women of the Palm Beaches, County Bus. & Profl. Coun. Roman Catholic. Office Phone: 561-627-5090.

ROSEN, CAROL MENDES, artist; b. N.Y.C., Jan. 15, 1933; d. Bram de Sola and Mildred (Bertuch) Mendes; m. Elliot A. Rosen, June 30, 1957. BA, Hunter Coll., 1954; MA, CUNY, 1962. Tchr. art West Orange (N.J.) Pub. Schs., 1959—85. Co-curator exhibit Printmaking Coun. N.J., Somerville, 1981; exhibit curator 14 Sculptors Gallery, N.Y.C., 1988; collection: Nat. Collection of Fine Arts, Smithsonian Instn., Newark Mus., N.J. State Mus., Bristol-Myers Squibb, AT&T, Noyes Mus., N.Y. Pub. Libr., Zimmerli Art Mus., Mus. of Modern Art, Whitney Mus., Libr. Collection Bklyn. Mus., Victoria & Albert Mus., Nat. Art Gallery, London, Mus. of Tolerance, L.A., Hunterdon Mus. Art, Nat. Mus. Women in Arts, Tel Aviv U. and The Jewish Nat. & U. Libr., Jerusalem, Houghton Libr., Harvard U., Yale U., Clark Art Inst., Skidmore, Williams Coll. Mus. Art, Oberlin Coll., William Paterson U., Stanford U., Smith Coll., Wellesley Coll., Tate Britain, Kreitman Rsch. Ctr. Contbr. articles to arts mags. Recipient Hudson River Mus. award, Yonkers, 1983; fellow, N.J. State Coun. Arts, 1980, 1983. Jewish. Avocations: gardening, reading. Home: 10 Beavers Rd Califon NJ 07830-3433 Personal E-mail: earosen@earthlink.net.

ROSEN, RHODA, obstetrician, gynecologist; b. Trenton, N.J., Jan. 17, 1933; d. Max and Gussie (Thierman) R.; m. Seymour Kanter, Aug. 19, 1956; children: Cynthia, Gregg, Larry, Brad. BA, U. Pa., 1954, MD, 1958. Diplomate Am. Bd. Obstetrics and Gynecology. Intern Albert Einstein Phila. Med. Ctr., 1958-59, resident, 1959-62, assoc. staff gynecology exec. com.; clin. prof. ob-gyn. Temple U. Med. Sch., Phila.; attending physician Rolling Hill Hosp., Elkins Park, Pa.; pvt. practice ob-gyn. Phila., 1962—. Chmn. gynpathology com. Albert Einstein Med. Ctr., Phila.; arbitrator N.Y. Stock Exch. Bd. dirs. Joseph J. Peters Inst.; docent Barnes Found., Merion, Pa. Fellow ACOG, ACS; mem. AMA, Nat. Assn. for Arbitrators for N.Y. Stock Exchange, Pa. Med. Soc., Phila. Colposcopy Soc. (past pres.), Ex-Residents Assn. (past pres. Albert Einstein Med. Ctr.), Philadelphia County Med. Soc. (com.), Phila. Bar Assn. (com.). Jewish. Avocations: bicycling, art, swimming, music. Home: 1420 Locust St Apt 35K Philadelphia PA 19102

ROSEN, ROBERTA, philosophy educator; b. Madawaska, Maine, Aug. 9, 1935; d. Bernard and Dolores (Bourgoin) Dionee; m. Frank Rosen, June 8, 1963; children: Ruth, Rachael, David, Sarah. BA, Gov. State U., University Park, Ill., 1975, MA, 1976; PhD, Walden U., 1977; postdoctoral, K.A.M.I.I. Temple. Free-lance writer, Chgo.; dir. religious edn. ASFU, Chgo.; minister All Souls 1st Universalist Soc., Chgo., 1975—95; prof. philosophy Prairie State Coll., Chicago Heights, Ill., 1976—89. Leader seminars on prevention of child abuse, 1976-1999. Author: (novel) Call Her Dolores, (children's) Johnny Linny's Nightmare; contbr. articles to religious jours. Bd. trustees Gov. State U., Unitarian-Universalist Women's Fedn. Recipient Humanitarian award, Humane Soc. award; named Best Tchr. Mem. Unitarian-Universalist Women's Assn. (life).

ROSEN, SARAH PEREL, social worker; b. Russia, Sept. 19, 1946; arrived in U.S., 1961; married, Apr. 8, 1970; children: Esther, Bayla, Yehoshua, Yakov, Levi, Nechoma, Menachem, Chana, Rochel. BA, Hunter Coll., N.Y., 1969; MA, Columbia U., N.Y., 1974; MSW, Hunter Coll., N.Y., 1997. LCSW, lic. Acad. Cert. Social Workers, cert. group therapist Ctr. Advancement Group Studies. Social worker Maimondes Hosp., Bklyn., 1995—97, North Shore Children and Family Svcs., Roslyn, NY, 1997—, supr., 1997—; pvt. practice psychotherapist Bklyn., 2002—. Provider Luth. Elem. Sch., Bklyn., 2005—. Grantee, United Jewish Appeal, 1996; scholar, Jewish Found. Edn. Women, 1995. Mem.: NASW, Nat. Assn. Advancement Psychoanalysis, Am. Group Psychoanalytic Assn., Acad. Clin. Social Workers. Jewish. Avocations: exercise, literature, dance. Home: 423 Kingston Ave Brooklyn NY 11225 Office: North Shore Child and Family 480 Old Westbury Roslyn NY 11577

ROSEN, WENDY WORKMAN, advertising executive; b. Miami, Sept. 17, 1954; d. Robert L. and Mildred E. (Duck) Workman; m. Steven David Rosen, June 22, 1972, children: Rebecca, Jeffrey. AS, Santa Fe Coll., 1974; BS, U. Fla., 1976. Cert. exhbn. mgr. Advt. exec. Balt. News Am., 1978-80, Balt. Mag, 1980-82; pres. The Rosen Group, Inc., Balt., 1982—. Cons. Times Pub. Group, Balt., 1982; gen. ptnr. Mill Ctr. Artists Studios, Balt.; pres. Am. Craft Showroom; founder The Buyers Markets of American Crafts, founder Craft Bus. Inst. Author: Crafting as a Business, Cash For Your Crafts; pub.: Niche mag., Am. Style mag., Market Insider. Bd. mem. Craft Emergency Relief Fund. Mem. Natl. Assn. Exposition Mgrs., Glass Art Soc. Democrat. Jewish. Avocation: gardening. Office: The Rosen Agy 3000 Chestnut Ave Ste 300 Baltimore MD 21211-2769

ROSENBAUM, BELLE SARA, religious studies educator, religious organization administrator; b. N.Y.C., Apr. 1, 1922; d. Harry and Hinda (Sits) Heimowitz; m. Jacob H. Rosenbaum, Mar. 12, 1939; children: Linda Zelinger, Simmi Brodie, Martin, Arlene Levene. Cert., N.Y. Sch. Interior Design, 1945; MA in Judaic Art, U. B.C., 1997, PhD, 1997. Sr. mem. Am. Soc. Appraisers, Washington, 1979—; tchr. Judaica Yeshiva U., 1984—; dir. Mus. Contemporary Judaica; pres. Jarvis Designs, Inc., Union City, NJ, 1955-75, Design Assocs., BLS, Monsey, NY, 1970-78; v.p. Lord & Lady Inc., Union City, 1955-70, Cardio-Bionic Scanning, Inc., Spring Valley, NY, 1975-78; v.p., treas. Rapitech Sys., Inc., 1985; exec. bd. State of Israel Bonds Orgn., 1992—. Author short stories, 1947-48, Chronicle of Jewish Traditions, 1992, Upon Thy Doorposts, 1996; contbr. articles on interior design to profl. jours. Chmn. bd. artifacts Rockland Holocaust Ctr., 1991—; trustee Rockland Ctr. Holocaust Studies, 1994; pres. Ednl. Ctr. Jewish Values Jerusalem Gt. Synagogue, Israel, 1998—; co-chair Nat. Jewish Art Week, 2000; curator arts Holocaust Mus. Rockland County, 2000; Bd. dirs. Midgal Ohr Schs., 1971—, Shaare Zedek Hosp., Jerusalem, 1998—, Jewish Fedn. Rockland County, 1999—, Riverdale (N.Y.) Jewish Mus., 1999—, Am. Guild Judaic Art, 1999—, Judaica Mus. Riverdale, 2001—.

ROSENBAUM, JOAN HANNAH, museum director; b. Hartford, Conn. d. Charles Leon and Lillian (Sharasheff) Grossman; m. Peter S. Rosenbaum, July 1962 (div. 1970). AA, Hartford Coll. for Women, 1962; BA, Boston U., 1964; student, Hunter Coll. Grad Sch., 1970-73; cert., Columbia U. Bus. Sch. Inst. Non Profit Mgmt., 1978; DHL (hon.), Jewish Theol. Sem., 1993. Curatorial asst. Mus. Modern Art, N.Y.C., 1966-72; dir. mus. program N.Y. Council on Arts, N.Y.C., 1972-79; cons. Michal Washburn & Assocs., N.Y.C., 1979-80; dir. Jewish Mus., N.Y.C., 1980—. Mem. adv. bd. Pub. Ctr., N.Y.C.; bd. dirs. Creative Time. Bd. dirs. Artists Space, 1980-93; mem. coun. Am. Jewish Mus., 1981-90; mem. policy panel Nat. Endowment Arts, 1982-83. Created knight (Denmark); recipient Disting. Alumni award Boston U. Coll. Libera Arts, 1994, Woman of Distinction award Hadassah, 1997, diploma Chevalier of Order of Arts and Letters (France), 1999; European travel grantee Internat. Coun. Mus., 1972. Mem. Am. Assn. Mus. (cons. 1979—), Assn. Art Mus. Dirs. (com. chair), N.Y. State Assn. Mus. (mem. coun. 1981-90), Art Table. Office: Jewish Mus 1109 5th Ave New York NY 10128-0118

ROSENBAUM, LINDA JEAN, elementary school educator; b. Peoria, Ill., June 2, 1952; d. James Leo and Phyllis Jean (Sosamon) R BS Elem. Edn., Ill. State U., 1974, MS Elem. Edn., 1984. Cert. tchr., Ill. Tchr. Dwight Elem. Sch., Ill., 1974—. Presenter workshops on coop. edn., 1986— Contbr. articles to edn. publs Unit Leader, counselor-in-tng., asst. dir., dir. Kickapoo coun. Girl

Scouts U.S.A., 1975-82, leader, neighborhood chmn., mem. program com., bd. dirs., camp dir. Centrillio coun., 1975—; bd. dirs. Dwight Crafts Guild, 1990. Mem. NEA, Ill. Edn. Assn., Dwight Edn. Assn. (pres., 1976-77, 82-83, 86-87, 2002-03) Republican. Avocations: hiking, camping, bicycling, hand crafts, reading. Office: Dwight Elem Sch 801 S Columbia St Dwight IL 60420-1347

ROSENBAUM, LOIS OMENN, lawyer; b. Newark, Apr. 10, 1950; d. Edward and Ruth (Peretz) Omenn; m. Richard B. Rosenbaum, Apr. 4, 1971; children: Steven, Laura. AB, Wellesley Coll., 1971; JD, Stanford U., 1974. Bar: Calif. 1974, Oreg. 1977, D.C. 1974, U.S. Supreme Ct. 1990, Wash. 2001. Assoc. Fried, Frank, Harris, Shriver & Kampelman, Washington, 1974-75, Orrick, Herrington, Rowley & Sutcliffe, San Francisco, 1975-77, Stoel Rives LLP (formerly Stoel, Rives, Boley, Jones & Grey), Portland, Oreg., 1977-81, ptnr., 1981—. Lawyer rep. 9th Cir. Jud. Conf.; mem. U.S. Dist. Ct. Mediation Panel. Bd. dirs. Providence Med. Found., 1990-95, Robison Jewish Home, 1994-97, Jewish Family & Child Svc., 1997-2000, Am. Jewish Commn., 2000-04; past mem. Nat. Legal Com. Am. Jewish Com. Wellesley Coll. scholar, 1971. Mem. ABA, Multnomah County Bar Assn. (arbitration panel), Wellesley Club (pres. 1987-88). Office: Stoel Rives LLP 900 SW 5th Ave Ste 2600 Portland OR 97204-1268 Office Phone: 503-294-9293. Business E-Mail: lorosenbaum@stoel.com.

ROSENBAUM, MARY HELÉNE POTTKER, writer, editor; b. Highland Park, Ill., Mar. 13, 1944; d. Ralph Eugene and Olga Norma (Somenzi) Pottker; m. Stanley Ned Rosenbaum, Sept. 2, 1963; children: Sarah Catherine, William David, Ephraim Samuel. Student, Bard Coll., 1962-63; BA magna cum laude, Dickinson Coll., 1975. Writing dir. Black Bear Prodns., Inc., Carlisle, Pa., Boston, Ky., 1989—; co-advisor Dickinson Coll. Hillel, Carlisle, 1991-92; exec. dir. Congregation Beth Tikvah, 1990-92. Coord. Interfaith Family Resources, 1995-97; exec. dir. Dovetail Inst. Interfaith Family Resources, 1997—. Co-author: Celebrating Our Differences: Living Two Faiths in One Marriage, 1994; columnist Interfaith Newsletter, 1995; mem. pubs. com. Cumberland County Hist. Soc.; editl. cons. Writers Cramp Inc., 1989—; assoc. editor Dovetail: A Jour. by and for Jewish/ Christian Families, 1996-98, editor, 1998-2003; editor/adminstr. Shalom newspaper of Ctrl. Ky. Jewish Fedn., 2005—; contbr. articles to profl. jours. Mem. Cable Commn., Carlisle, 1991-92. Recipient Jean Gray Allen Non-fiction award Harrisburg Manuscript Club, 1978, Founder's Fiction award, 1978. Mem. League Women Voters Carlisle Area (pubs. coord. 1990-92, pres. 1988-90). Democrat. Roman Catholic. Avocations: dramatic reading, walking, cooking, folk singing. Home: 815 Simon Greenwell Rd Boston KY 40107-8524 Office: Dovetail Inst Interfaith Family Resources 775 Simon Greenwell Ln Boston KY 40107 Office Phone: 800-530-1596. E-mail: di-ifr@bardstown.com.

ROSENBERG, ALISON P., public policy officer; b. Miami, Fla., Sept. 5, 1945; d. Mortimer I. and Gail (Sklar) Podell; m. Jeffrey Alan Rosenberg, May 4, 1969; 1 child, Robert Aaron. BS in Econs., Smith Coll., 1967. Mng. officer Citibank, N.Y.C., 1967-69; legis. aide Senator Charles Percy, Washington, 1969-80; profl. staff mem. Senate Fgn. Rels. Com., Washington, 1981-85; assoc. asst. adminstr. Agy. for Internat. Devel., Washington, 1985-87; dir. African affairs Nat. Security Coun., Washington, 1987-88; dep. asst. sec. for Africa State Dept., Washington, 1988-92; asst. admnstr. for Africa Agy. for Internat. Devel., Washington, 1992-93; lead partnerships specialist (Africa) The World Bank, Washington, 1993—. E-mail: arosenberg@worldbank.org.

ROSENBERG, AURIA ELEANOR, secondary school educator; b. Detroit, Mar. 27, 1935; d. Paulino and Emelia (Phillip) Aromin; m. Jonah Rosenberg, Jan. 23, 1967 (div. June 1974); children: Pamela Reynée, Jonathan David, Deena Robyn. BA in French, Univ. Wash., 1961; MA in edn., Nat.-Louis Univ., 1992. Cert. tchr. Ill., Wash. Tchr. Tyee Jr H.S., Bellevue, Wash., 1961-62, Bais-Yaakov Parochial Sch., Chgo., 1979-84, Audy Home Cook County Detention Ctr., Chgo., 1984-89, Pleasant Ridge Elem. Sch., Glenview, Ill., 1988-90, Lyon Elem. Sch., Glenview, Ill., 1989-91; chair world lang. dept. Phillips Acad., Chgo., 1991—. Rep. committeewoman of 49th ward, Chgo., 1970-82, mem. Cook County Rep. Committeewomens Orgn. Chgo., 1970-82, sec., 1970-74. Recipient Merit award Excellence for Outstanding Tchr. of Yr., Ill. State Bd. Edn. Mem. Alumni Assn. Univ. Wash., Nat. Coun. Tchg. Fgn. Lang., Ill. Coun. Tchg. Fgn. Lang. (adv. coun., ctrl. states), Ctr. States Coun. Tchrs. Fgn. Langs. (mem. adv. coun.), Internat. Reading Assn., Ill. Reading Assn., Pi Lambda Theta (v.p. 1996-98, sec. 1992), Delta Kappa Gamma (historian 1994—), Phi Delta Kappa. Republican. Avocations: watercoloring, illustration. Home: One Ct of Harborside Northbrook IL 60062 Office Phone: 312-773-1503. Personal E-mail: laprof61@yahoo.com.

ROSENBERG, BETSY, radio personality, environmentalist; Reporter, anchor KCBS, San Francisco, host Trash Talk, 1997; host EcoTalk, Air Am. Radio, 2004—; nat. anchor CBS Radio, NYC. Recipient awards, EPA, Nat. Recycling Assn., Calif. Resource Recovery Assn., Peninsula Cmty. Conservation Fund, Keep Calif. Beautiful. Office: KCBS 865 Battery St San Francisco CA 94111

ROSENBERG, DEBORAH A., special education educator; d. Samuel and Ethelle Wells Luque; married, June 6, 1970; children: Aimee, Corey. BSc in Bus. Adminstrn. Pers. Mgmt., SUNY, Albany, 1971; MSc in Spl. Edn., LI U., 1987; profl. diploma in Adminstrn. and Supervision, St. Johns U., 2003. Cert. Sch. Dist. Adminstr. U. of State of NY Edn. Dept., Provisional Cert. in Sch. Adminstrn. and Supervision. Prodn., sales office mgr. Electronic Essentials, Inc., Woodside, NY, 1974—85; reading, English tchr. NYC Bd. Edn., Bushwich, NY, 1985—88, tchr. Rikers Island, NY, 1988—89, spl. edn. tchr. Jamaica, NY, 1989—92, edn. evaluator Hollis, NY, 1992—2003; spl. edn. math. tchr. NYC Dept. Edn., Flushing, NY, 2003—. Pvt. tutor, NYC, 1985—; adult edn. tchr. Phoenix House, LI, NY, 1987—93; reading tchr. Jamaica Learning Ctr., NYC, 1993—2002. Mem.: Assn. of Tchrs. of Math. NYC, Phi Delta Kappa (UFT chpt. leader JHS189 2006—). Democrat. Avocations: reading, crossword puzzles, role playing games. Office: JHS189Q Dist 25 Region 3 144 80 Barclay Ave Flushing NY 11355 Office Phone: 718-359-6676. Personal E-mail: debrose49@aol.com.

ROSENBERG, ELLEN Y., religious association administrator; married; 2 children. Student, Goucher Coll.; BS in Edn., Mills Coll.; postgrad., Columbia U. Assoc. dean for acad. affairs Marymount Manhattan Coll., N.Y.C.; exec. dir. Women of Reform Judaism/Fed. Temple Sisterhoods, 1992—. Bd. dirs. Mazon, World Union for Progressive Judaism, Jewish Braille Inst. Am., Union Am. Hebrew Congregations. Jewish. Office: WRJ 633 3rd Ave New York NY 10017-6706

ROSENBERG, EMILY, psychiatrist; b. N.Y.C., Aug. 29, 1953; d. Irving and Dorothy Rosenberg; m. Thomas A. Miller, Feb. 17, 1996; children: Alice, Scott. BS, City Coll. N.Y., N.Y.C., 1974; MS, Rensselaer Poly. Inst., Troy, N.Y., 1977; PhD, U. Okla., Oklahoma City, 1982, MD, 1984. Diplomate Am. Bd. Psychiatry & Neurology, 1993. Pvt. practice, Oklahoma City, 1988—92; med. dir., post traumatic stress disorder program VA Med. Ctr., Oklahoma City, 1992—. Fellow: Am. Psychiatric Assn.; mem.: AMA. Avocation: marathon running. Office: VA Med Ctr - 183-A 921 NE 13th St Oklahoma City OK 73104

ROSENBERG, JANE, author, illustrator; b. N.Y.C., Dec. 7, 1949; d. Abner Emmanuel and Lily (Quittman) R.; m. Robert F. Porter, May 30, 1982; children: Melo Ann Porter, Ava Hermine Porter, Eloise Pearl Porter. BFA, Beaver Coll., 1971; MA in Painting, NYU, 1973. Painter, freelance illustrator, N.Y.C., 1974-82; art tchr. Ethical Culture Sch., N.Y.C., 1974-75; art dir. N.Y. News for Kids, N.Y.C., 1979-80; children's book author, illustrator N.Y.C., L.A., 1982—. Author, illustrator: Dance Me a Story: Twelve Tales from the Classic Ballets, 1985, Sing Me a Story: The Metropolitan Opera's Book of Opera Stories, 1989, Play Me a Story: A Child's Introduction to Classical Music through Stories and Poems, 1994; one-woman shows include Every Picture Tells a Story Gallery, L.A., 1991, Summerlin Libr. and Performing Arts Ctr., Las Vegas, Nev., 1995. Mem. Authors' Guild, Soc. Children's Book Writers and Illustrators.

ROSENBERG, JILL, realtor, civic leader; b. Shreveport, La., Feb. 17, 1940; d. Morris H. and Sallye (Abramson) Schuster; m. Lewis Rosenberg, Dec. 23, 1962; children: Craig, Paige. BA in Philosophy, Tulane U., 1961, MSW, 1965; grad., Realtor Inst., 1994. Cert. residential specialist Residential Sales Coun. Social worker La. Dept. Pub. Welfare, 1961-62, 63-64; genetics counselor Sinai Hosp., Balt., 1967-69; ptnr. Parties Extraordinaire, Cons., 1973-77; realtor assoc. Robert Weil Assocs., Long Beach, Calif., 1982—. Pres. we. region Long Beach Edn. Found., 1972—73; pres. Long Beach Cancer League, 1987—88, exec. bd. dirs., 1984—96; pres. Long Beach Jewish Cmty. Sr. Housing Corp., 1989—91; v.p. fundraising S.E. unit Long Beach Harbor chpt. Am. Cancer Soc., 1989—90; trustee St. Mary Med. Ctr. Found., 1991—; pres. nat. conf. NCCJ, 1994—96, bd. dirs., 1989—, Leadership Long Beach, 1992—2000, pres., 1994—95, hon. bd. govs., 2000—; dean's adv. bd. Sch. Bus. Adminstrn. Calif. State U., Long Beach, 2000—04; assoc. coun. Long Beach Edn. Found., 2003—05; v.p. Jewish Cmty. Fedn. Long Beach and West Orange County, 1983—86, bd. dirs., 1982—86, Long Beach Symphony Assn., 1984—85, Westerly Sch. Assoc., 1991—2000, Phoenix Long Beach Mus. Art, 1992—98, Am. Diabetes Assn., Long Beach., Calif., 1997—99, Stramski Children's Devel. Ctr., Long Beach Meml. Med. Ctr., 1998—, Arts Coun. for Long Beach, 2002—, Long Beach Day Nursery, 2000—02; leadership devel. chair Pub. Corp. for Arts, 2003—. Recipient Young Leadership award Jewish Cmty. Fedn. Long Beach and West Orange County, 1981, Jerusalem award State of Israel, 1989, Hannah G. Solomon award Nat. Coun. Jewish Women, 1992, Alumnus of Yr. award Leadership Long Beach, 1995, Humanitarian award The Nat. Conf., 1997, Disting. Leadership award Calif. Assn. Leadership Programs, 2000; named Rick Racker Woman of Yr., 1999; scholar La. Dept. Pub. Welfare, 1962, NIMH, 1964. Mem. Arts Coun. Long Beach (v.p. 2003-05), Rotary Club (bd. dirs. 2000-01, 05—, v.p. 2005—06). Office: Robert Weil Assocs 5220 E Los Altos Plz Long Beach CA 90815-4251 Office Phone: 562-494-7000. Personal E-mail: jillsold@yahoo.com.

ROSENBERG, JILL L., lawyer; b. New Hyde Park, NY, 1961; AB cum laude, Princeton U., 1983; JD, U. Chgo., 1986. Bar: N.Y. 1987, U.S. Dist. Ct., So. Dist. N.Y. 1988, U.S. Dist. Ct., Ea. Dist. N.Y. 1988, U.S. Ct. Appeals, second cir. 1992, U.S. Supreme Ct. 1992. Assoc. Baer Marks & Upham, N.Y.C., 1986—91; ptnr. Orrick Herrington & Sutcliffe LLP, N.Y.C., 1991—, ptnr. in charge pro bono program. Recipient James H. Fogelson Young Leadership Award, Lawyers Division UJA Fedn. N.Y. Mem.: N.Y. Legal Assistance Group (bd. dir.), ABA (labor & employment law sect., litig. sect.), N.Y. State Bar Assn. (labor & employment law sect.), Assn. Bar City N.Y. Office: Orrick Herrington & Sutcliffe LLP 666 Fifth Ave New York NY 10103 Office Fax: 212-506-5151, 212-506-5215. Business E-Mail: jrose@orrick.com.

ROSENBERG, MARILYN ROSENTHAL, artist, poet; b. Phila., Oct. 11, 1934; m. Robert Rosenberg, June 12, 1955; 2 children. B in Profl. Studies in Studio Arts, SUNY, Empire State Coll., 1978; MA in Liberal Studies, NYU, 1993. Represented in permanent collections Avant Writing Collection, The Ohio State U. Librs., Whitney Mus. Libr., N.Y.C., Tate Gallery Libr., London, Mus. Modern Art Libr., NYC, Bklyn. Mus. Lib., Bibliotheque Nat., Paris, Fogg Arts Lib., Harvard U., one-woman shows include Westchester CC, Valhalla, N.Y., 2002, exhibited in group shows at Fla. Atlantic U., Boca Raton, Fla., 2000, U. Ctrl. Ark., Conway, 2000, Ocean Grove Libr., Victoria, Australia, 2000, City Gallery, Székesfehervár, Hungary, 2000, 2006, The Temple Judea, Elkins Park, Pa., 2001, Art Acad. Cin., 2002, Ohio State U. Librs., Columbus, 2002, Cuesta Coll. Art Gallery, San Luis Obispo, Calif., 2002, Pensacola (Fla.) Mus. Art, 2002, U. Indpls. (Ind.) Gallery, 2002, Lowenstein Gallery, Miami, Fla., 2003, Starr Gallery, Newton Ctr., Mass., 2003, Wexford (Ireland) Arts Centre, 2003, The Buddy Holly Ctr., Lubbock, Tex., 2003, Peck Arts Ctr. Gallery, Ctrl. Wyo. Coll., Riverton, 2003, Purdue U. Galleries, Lafayette, Ind., 2003, Ellipse Art Ctr., Arlington, Va., 2003, The Ctr. for Book Arts, NYC, 2003, 2005, Durango Art Ctr., Colo., 2004, Neopolis Gallery, Cleve., 2004, Ceres Gallery, NYC, 2004, 2005, dfsdfsdf, 2006, Westchester Gallery/Westchester Art Workshop, 2004, 2006, Futernic Gallery, Alper Jewish Cmty. Ctr., Miami, Fla., 2005, Art Ctr. Hasselt Belgium, 2005, Gallery Durban Segnini, Miami, Fla., 2005, Rutgers U., Camden, N.J., 2005, Gallery 308, Mpls., 2005, Pelham (N.Y.) Art Ctr., 2006, works in exhib. catalogs, reviews, ref. books, anthologies and websites. Home: 67 Lakeview Ave W Cortlandt Manor NY 10567-6415

ROSENBERG, PAMELA, opera director, conductor; b. LA, 1945; m. Wolf Rosenberg (dec. 1996); 2 children. Diploma, London Opera Ctr.; B, U. Calif. at Berkely, 1966; M in Russian hist., Ohio State U. Various positions Frankfurt Opera, 1974—87; dir. of ops. Deutscher Schauspielhaus, Hamburg, Germany, 1987—88; mgr., artistic affairs Netherlands Opera, 1988—90; co-gen. dir. Stuggart Opera, 1990—2000; gen. dir. San Francisco Opera, 2001—06, exec. adv., 2006. Office: San Francisco Opera 301 VanNess Ave San Francisco CA 94102*

ROSENBERG, SARAH ZACHER, retired cultural organization administrator; b. Kelem, Lithuania, Jan. 10, 1931; came to U.S., 1938; d. David Meir Zacher and Rachel Korbman; m. Norman J. Rosenberg, Dec. 30, 1950; children: Daniel, Alyssa. BA in History, U. Nebr., 1970, MA in Am. History, 1973. Rsch. historian U. Mid-Am., Lincoln, Nebr., 1974-78, program developer dept. humanities, 1978-79, asst. dir. div. acad. planning, 1980-81, dir. program devel., 1981-82; exec. dir. Nebr. Humanities Coun., Lincoln, 1982-87, Nebr. Found. for Humanities, Lincoln, 1984-87, Am. Inst. for Conservation Hist. and Artistic Works, Washington, 1987-97, exec. dir. found., 1991-97; program officer, spl. cons. mus. div. NEH, Washington, 1987, external reviewer, 1981, 89; pvt. practice Potomac, Md., 1997—2004; ret., 2004. Lay participant long-range planning conf. Nebr. Bar Assn., Hastings, 1986. Co-editor: The Great Plains Experience: Readings in the History of a Region, 1978; contbr. articles to profl. jours. Action mem. Hadassah, Lincoln, 1961—87, Tifereth Israel Synagogue, Lincoln, 1961—87, Beth El Congregation, Besthesda, Md., 1988—2001, Kol Shalom Congregation, 2001—; bd. dirs. Sta. KUCV, affiliate Nat. Pub. Radio, Lincoln, 1986—87, Lincoln Cmty. Playhouse, Lincoln, 1986—87. NEH grantee, 1981, 86, merit awards, 1983, 87; Humanities Resource Ctr. grantee, Peter Kiewit Found., 1984. Mem. Am. Hist. Assn., Western Hist. Assn., Alpha Theta. Democrat. Home: 8102 Appalachian Ter Potomac MD 20854-4050 Personal E-mail: srosenb435@aol.com.

ROSENBERG, SHELI Z., investment company executive; Degree, Tufts U., Northwestern U. Atty. Cotton, Watt, Jones & King, 1966—70; mng. ptnr. Schiff Hardin & Waite, 1976—80; from gen. coun. to vice-chmn. Equity Group Investments, LLC, Chgo., 1980—2000, vice-chmn., 2000—. Bd. dirs. CVS Corp., Capital Trust, Cendant Corp., Manufactured Home Communities, Inc., Equity Residential Properties Trust, Equity Office Properties Trust, Ventas, Inc.; adv. bd. J.L. Kellogg Grad. Sch. Bus. N.W. Univ. Trustee Rush Presbyn. St. Luke's Med. Ctr., exec. com.; co-founder, pres. Ctr. for Exec. Women, J.L. Kellogg Grad. Sch. Bus., 2001—. Office: Equity Group Investments LLC 737 North Michigan Ave Ste 1405 Chicago IL 60611 E-mail: szr312@aol.com.

ROSENBERG, TINA, reporter; b. Bklyn., 1958; BS, Northwestern U., 1981, MS, 1982. Fgn. policy editl. writer The New York Times, freelance writer New York Times mag., 1983-96, fgn. policy editl. writer, 1996—, mem. editl. bd.; adj. prof. internat. rels. Columbia U., N.Y.C. Vis. fellow Nat. Security Archive; former sr. fellow World Policy Inst., New Sch. U. Author: Children of Cain: Violence and the Violent in Latin America, The Haunted Land: Facing Europe's Ghosts After Communism (Pulitzer prize for general nonfiction, Nat. Book award, 1996); contbr. articles to publs. Recipient MacArthur Fellowship "genius" award. Office: NY Times Editl Bd 229 W 43rd St New York NY 10036

ROSENBERG-CORTES, STEFANIE DEANNE, secondary school educator; d. Dennis Wayne Rosenberg and Kathleen Anne Huitt; m. Mario Ernesto Cortes, May 28, 2005. BS in Edn., Drake U., Des Moines, 2005. Cert. in social studies. Tchr., coord. Thomas Jefferson Bilingual Sch., Mexico City, 2000—01, I Have a Dream Found., Des Moines, 2003—04; tchr. Des Moines Pub. Sch., 2005—. Treas. bd. dirs. Iowa Literacy Coun., Des Moines, 2002—; ct. apptd. spl. adv. abused-neglected children Des Moines, 2002—. Recipient award, Nat. Coun. Youth Leadership, 2000, Presdl. Vol. Svc. award, Pres.-Exec. Br., 2002. Mem.: Iowa State Edn. Assn. (vice chair exec. bd. student program), Mortar Bd., Kappa Delta Pi, Alpha Lambda Delta, Phi Alpha Theta. Avocations: scrapbooks, travel, reading.

ROSENBERGER, JANET THUMA, retired elementary school educator; b. Marietta, Pa., Feb. 9, 1939; d. Benjamin E. and Mary Ellen (Engle) Thuma; m. Lyle L. Rosenberger, June 6, 1959; children: Kathie, Karen, Kyna Rosenberger. BS in Edn., Gwynedd Mercy, Gwynedd Valley, Pa., 1977; MS in Edn., Beaver Coll., Glenside, Pa., 1980. Cert. elem. educator, reading specialist. Tchr. 1st grade Souderton (Pa.) Area Sch. Dist., 1977—2003; ret., 2003. Avocations: hiking, gardening, theater, piano, reading. Office: Souderton Area Sch Dist 760 Lower Rd Souderton PA 18964-2094

ROSENBERGER, MARGARET ADALINE, retired elementary school educator, writer; b. Micanopy, Fla., Oct. 30; d. Eugene David and Lillian Adeline (Bauknight) Rosenberger. Student, Stetson U., 1946—48; BA in Edn., U. Fla., 1949, MEd, 1952. Drama sec. Nat. Youth Adminstrn., Gainesville, Fla., 1939—40; civil svc. clk. U.S. Army, Camp Blanding, Fla., 1940—46; tchr. J.J. Finley, Gainesville, 1949—52; prin., tchr. Micanopy Jr. H.S., 1952—55; gen. supr. Alachua County Schs., Gainesville, 1955—57, elem. supr., 1958—59; tchr. U.S. Army Dependents' Sch., Heidelberg, Germany, 1957—58; prin. Littlewood Elem. Sch., Gainesville, 1959—73, Prairie View Elem. Sch., Gainesville, 1973—82, ret., 1982; owner Rose Hill Publs. Mem. sch. adv. com. Prairie View Elem. Sch., 1975—82. Author: My God of Love, Mercy, Miracles and Angels, 1996, Secrets and Songs of Payne's Prairie, 1998, vol. 2, 2004—, A Teacher's Odyssey, 2001, My Pets and I, 1999, Poems for Children, 2001, My Angels and I, 2001, Spiritual Interpretations of God's Truths, 2002, The Birth and Growth of the Village, 2003, The Other Sides Where Love Knows No Color, 2005, numerous poems; co-author: Reflections of Light, 1995; co-author: (with Frances B. Head) A Lifetime of Humor, 2005; author, composer: St. Augustine Song; contbr. articles to local newspapers. Pres. Govs. Children's Commn., Gainesville, 1956—57; dir. The Village Chorus, Gainesville, 1987—; mem. Gainesville Schs. PTA, 1959—82, PTA Micanopy, 1952—55; Dem. candidate Fla. House Rep., 1974; pianist, organist Village Vespers on Sunday Evenings, 1990—; bd. dir. Foster Grandparents, Gainesville, 1974—76; v.p. bd. dir. No. Fla. Retirement Village, Inc., 1981, chmn. bd. dir., 1982—86, rep. bd. dirs., 1986—, chmn. bd. dir., historian, 1988—. Named Woman of Distinction for Alachua and Bradford Counties, 2005; recipient Disting. Alumna award, U. Fla., P.K. Yange Devel. Rsch. Sch., 2006. Mem.: Internat. Soc. Poets, Am. Soc. Composers, Authors & Pub., Micanopy Hist. Soc., Altrusa Internat. Club Gainesville (chmn. internat. com., chmn. newsletter, spkr. for programs), Order of Eastern Star, Delta Kappa Gamma (internat. soc. 1959—). Democrat. Baptist. Avocations: stamp collecting/philately, coin collecting/numismatics, book collecting, post card collecting, creative writing. Home: 410 SW Wacahoota Rd Micanopy FL 32667 Mailing: 8015 NW 28th Pl B 110 Gainesville FL 32606

ROSENBLAD, HELEN VIOLA, social services administrator; b. Hutchinson, Kans., Dec. 14, 1923; d. Raymond Grant Streeter and Edith May Hunter; m. Ralph Alexander Rosenblad, June 8, 1946; children: Signe Elizabeth, Eric Lee, Kirstin Patricia, Lars Jon. BA in Sociology, Baker U., 1945. Dir. girls work Kingdom House, St. Louis, 1945—46; youth worker Morgan Meml. Youth and Children's Ctr., Boston, 1946—50; pricer Goodwill Industries, Springfield, Mass., 1950—52; EMT Downs (Kans.) Ambulance Svc., 1985—87; coord. Mother-To-Mother Ministry, Hutchinson, Kans., 1987—91. Transp. cons. S.W. Kans. Area Agy. on Aging, Dodge City, 1970—79. Author: The Flitting of Rose Leaves, 1983, 1997, Streeters in Europe and America, 2004. Leader Girl Scouts, Boston, Springfield, Lowell, Andover, Mass., 1946—60; clothing and foods leader 4H, Winfield, Bushton, Stafford, Kans., 1960—75; founder Downs Hist. Soc., 1983—87, Downs Sr. Citizens, Inc, 1983—87; dir. Fed. Commodity Distbn., Osborne County, Kans., 1984—87; founder, bd. dirs. Interfaith Housing Svcs., Hutchinson, 1990—2006; adv. bd. Youthbuild, Inc., Hutchinson, 1993—96; active Hutchinson Cmty. Improvement Commn., 1995—2001, 2006—, Hutchinson Housing Commn., 1995—2005, Hutchinson Housing Authority Bd., 1998—, Mayor's Task Force for Cmty. Diversity, 2004—; founder, bd. dirs. Stepping-Stones for Youth, Inc., Hutchinson, 1997—2004; delivery person Meals on Wheels, Hutchinson, 1997—; missions com. United Meth. Ch., 1960—; bd. dirs. Area Agys. on Aging, Kans., 1970—87, Hutchinson Ams. with Disabilities Act, 2004—. Named Vol. of the Cmty., Hutchinson News, 2002; grantee to establish Sr. Ctr., S.W. Kans. Area Agy. on Aging, Minneola, Kans., 1976, N.W. Kans. Area Agy. on Aging, Downs, 1984. Mem.: United Meth. Women. Avocation: genealogy. Home: 814 E 30th Apt 301 Hutchinson KS 67502

ROSENBLATT, ALICE F., healthcare insurance company executive; With The New Eng., William M. Mercer, Inc., Mut. of NY; chief actuary, sr. v.p. HMO and grp. svcs. Blue Cross of Calif., 1987—89; sr. v.p., chief actuary Blue Cross/Blue Shield Mass., 1989—93; prin. health and welfare grp. Coopers & Lybrand, Boston; chief actuary, exec. v.p. integration planning and implementation Wellpoint Health Networks, Inc., 1996—2004; exec. v.p. integration planning/implementation, chief actuary WellPoint, Inc. Commr. Medicare Payment Adv. Commn. Fellow: Soc. Actuaries (bd. dirs.); mem.: Am. Acad. Actuaries (bd. dirs.). Office: WellPoint Inc 120 Monument Cir Indianapolis IN 46204

ROSENBLATT, JOAN RAUP, mathematical statistician; b. N.Y.C., Apr. 15, 1926; d. Robert Bruce and Clara (Eliot) Raup; m. David Rosenblatt, June 10, 1950. AB, Barnard Coll., 1946; PhD, U. N.C., 1956. Intern Nat. Inst. Pub. Affairs, Washington, 1946-47; statis. analyst U.S. Bur. of Budget, 1947-48; rsch. asst. U. N.C., 1953-54; mathematician Nat. Inst. Standards and Tech. (formerly Nat. Bur. Standards), Washington, 1955—, asst. chief statis. engring., 1963-68, chief statis. engring. lab., 1969-78, dep. dir. Ctr. for Applied Math., 1978-88; dir. Computing and Applied Math. Lab., Gaithersburg, 1988-93, dir., 1993-95, guest rschr. Statis. Engring. Divsn., 1996—. Mem. com. on indsl. rels. Dept. Stats. Ohio State U., 1981-90; mem. adv. com. in math. and stats. USDA Grad. Sch., 1971—; mem. Com. Applied and Theoretical Stats., Nat. Rsch. Coun., 1985-88. Mem. editorial bd. Communications in Stats., 1971-79, Jour. Soc. for Indsl. and Applied Math., 1965-75, Nat. Inst. Stds. and Tech. Jour. Rsch., 1991-93; contbr. articles to profl. jours. Chmn. Com. on Women in Sci., Joint Bd. on Sci. Edn., 1963—64. Rice fellow, 1946, Gen. Edn. Bd. fellow, 1948-50; recipient Fed. Woman's award, 1971, Gold medal Dept. Commerce, 1976, Presdl. Meritorious Exec. Rank award, 1982. Fellow AAAS (chmn. stats. sect. 1982, sec. 1987-91), Inst. Math. Stats. (coun. 1975-77), Am. Statis. Assn. (v.p. 1981-83, dir. 1979-80, Founders award 1991), Washington Acad. Scis. (achievement award math. 1965); mem. AAUW, Royal Statis. Soc. London, Philos. Soc. Washington, Internat. Statis. Inst., Caucus Women Stats. (pres. 1976), Assn. Women Math., Exec. Women Govt., Phi Beta Kappa, Sigma Xi (treas. Nat. Bur. Standards chpt. 1982-84). Home: 2939 Van Ness St NW Apt 702 Washington DC 20008-4628 Office: Nat Inst Stds and Tech 100 Bureau Dr Stop 8980 Gaithersburg MD 20899-8980 Business E-Mail: jrr@nist.gov.

ROSENBLUM, ELLEN F., judge; b. 1951; m. Richard Meeker. BS, Sociol., U. Oreg., 1971, JD, 1975. Bar: Oreg. 1975. Atty. priv. practice, Eugene, Oreg., 1975—80; asst. U.S. atty. Eugene, Oreg., 1981—89; circuit ct. judge Multnomah County Ct., Portland, Oreg., 1989—. Trustee Nat. Jud. Coll.; past chmn., Jud. Conduct Comm. Oreg. Jud. Conf.; chmn. Gov. Adv. Comm. Corrections, Oreg. Citizens Just. Conf., 2000. Chmn. Oreg. Citizen's Justice Conf. Recipient Pres. Public Svc. award, Oreg. State Bar, Andrea Swanner Redding Mentoring award, Lewis & Clark Law Sch., Honorary Alumna award, Merit. Svc. award, Univ. Oreg. Law Sch.; Alumni Fellow, Univ. Oreg.

Coll. Arts & Sci., 1990. Fellow: Am. Bar Found. (life); mem.: U.S. Dist. Ct. Oreg. Hist. Soc. (past pres.), Owen M. Panner Am. Inn of Ct. (past pres.), Oreg. Women Lawyers (founding bd. mem. 1989, Justice Betty Roberts award 2000), ABA (bd. govs., sec. 2002—, mem. Comm. Racial & Ethnic Diversity). Office: Multnomah County Courthouse Rm 512 1021 SW 4th Ave Portland OR 97204

ROSENBLUM, JUDITH A., law educator; b. Chgo., June 12, 1951; BA, U. Rochester, 1973; JD, University Mich., Ann Arbor, 1976. Atty. Gordon, Elden, Schlack, Glickson & Gordon, 1976—77; staff atty. Ctr. Judicial Conduct Organs. American Judicature Soc., Chgo., 1977—83, staff atty. Ednl. Programs, 1977—80, sr. staff atty., 1980—83; legal writing instr. Northwestern U. Sch. Law, Chgo., 1984—98, acting dir. legal writing, 1992, 1995, asst. dir. legal writing, 1998—2000, academic support coord., 1996—, dir. comm. and legal reasoning. Contbr. articles to profl. jours. Mem.: Chgo. Bar Assn. Office: Northwestern U Sch Law 357 E Chicago Ave Chicago IL 60611 Office Phone: 312-503-8943. E-mail: j-rosenbaum2@law.northwestern.edu.

ROSENBLUM, MINDY FLEISCHER, pediatrician; b. Bronxville, NY, June 5, 1951; d. Herman and Muriel (Gold) Fleischer; m. Jay S. Rosenblum, June 22, 1971; children: Meira, Tamar, Rafi, Rachel. BA, Yeshiva U., 1972; MD, Albert Einstein Coll., 1976. Diplomate Am. Bd. Pediat., Am. Bd. Pediatric Endocrinology. Intern in pediat. Bronx Mcpl. Hosp. Ctr., 1976-77, residency in pediat., 1977-79; fellow in pediatric endocrinology Children's Hosp. of Phila., 1981; asst. prof. U. Pa., Phila., 1981—95; attending physician Bryn Mawr (Pa.) Hosp., 1981—, Lankenau Hosp., Wynnewood, Pa., 1983—; clin. assoc. Children's Hosp. of Phila., 1995—. Fellow Am. Acad. Pediat.; mem. Phila. Pediat. Soc. (bd. dirs. 1988-92), Am. Diabetes Assn., Lawson Wilkins Pediatric Endocrine Soc. Office Phone: 610-642-9200. Personal E-mail: jmr101@comcast.net.

ROSENBLUM, NANCY LIPTON, political science professor; BA with high honors, Radcliffe Coll., 1969; PhD, Harvard Univ., 1973; LHD (hon.), Kalamazoo Coll., 1993. Asst. prof. Harvard Univ., 1973—77, assoc. prof., 1977—80; prof. Brown Univ., 1980—97; vis. prof. Harvard Univ., 1985; chair, Polit. Sci. dept. Brown Univ., 1989—95, Henry Merritt Wriston prof., 1997—2001, founder & dir., Stephen Robert Inst. for Study of Values, 1998—2000; Sen. Joseph Clark prof. of ethics in politics & govt. Harvard Univ., 2001—. Mem. exec. com. Conf. for Study of Polit. Thought, 1988—; rev. editor Political Theory, 1989—93, mem. editl. bd., 1993—97; council mem. Am. Polit. Sci. Assn., 1991—93, Tocqueville Soc., 2001—; mem. vis. com. dept. Polit. Sci. Brandeis Univ., 1986, Univ. Mich., Ann Arbor, 1993, Queens Coll., 1993, Stanford Univ., 1994, Univ. Alta., Canada, 1995; mem. vis. com. Dept. Polit., Princeton Univ., 2002. Author: Membership & Morals: The Personal Uses of Pluralism in America, 1998, Another Liberalism: Romanticism and the Reconstruction of Liberal Thought, 1987, Bentham's Theory of the Modern State, 1978; editor: Obligations of Citizenship and Demands of Faith, 2000, Liberalism and the Moral Life, 1993; co-editor: Breaking the Cycles of Hatred, 2002, Civil Society and Government, 2002; contbr. articles to profl. jour., chapters to books. Bd. dir. Civil Liberties Union Mass., Fine Arts Work Ctr., Provincetown, Mass. Recipient David Easton award, APSA, 2002; Bunting Inst. Fellow, Radcliffe Coll., 1988—89. Fellow: Am. Acad. Arts & Sci. Office: Harvard University Littauer 318 Cambridge MA 02138 Office Phone: 617-384-5851. Business E-Mail: nrosenblum@latte.harvard.edu.

ROSENBLUM, ZINA MICHELLE ZARIN, psychology professor, marketing professional, researcher; b. N.Y.C., Mar. 4, 1949; d. Harry and Miriam (Bachrach) Zarin; m. Martin Jerome Rosenblum, May 31, 1975; children: Steven David, Richard James. BA magna cum laude, Queens Coll., 1971; MEd, Columbia U., 1973, MEd Counseling Psychology, 1973. Prof. psychology Marymount Manhattan Coll., N.Y.C., 1971—73; addictions counselor Manhattan Vets. Hosp., N.Y.C., 1971—73; project dir. BBD&O Advt., N.Y.C., 1973—74, Grey Advt., N.Y.C., 1974—75; supr. market rsch. Doyle Dane & Bernbach, N.Y.C., 1975—77, SSC& B, N.Y.C., 1977—78; dir. rsch. Hershey Co., Pa., 1978—79; adminstr. Suncoast Eye Clinic, St. Petersburg, Fla., 1979—97; prof. psychology St. Petersburg Coll., Seminole, Fla., 1997—. Sec. Nat. Coun. Jewish Women, Fla., 1980—81; docent Fla. Holocaust Mus., 2005—. Scholar, Columbia U., 1971; Nat. Merit acholar, Coll. Bd., 1970. Mem.: APA, Phi Beta Kappa. Office: Suncoast Eye Clinic Martin Rosenblum 2200 16th St North Saint Petersburg FL 33704 Office Phone: 727-822-4729. Personal E-mail: zcurl@aol.com.

ROSENFELD, IRENE B., food products company executive; b. Bklyn., 1953; BA in Psychology, Cornell U, 1975, MS in Bus., 1977, PhD in Mktg. & Statistics, 1980. With Dancer, Fitzgerald Sample Advertising (now Saatchi and Saatchi), 1979—81, Kraft Foods Inc., 1981—2004, exec. v.p., gen. mgr., beverages divsn., 1991—94, exec. v.p., gen. mgr. desserts & snacks divsn., 1994—96; pres. Kraft Foods Canada, 1996—2004; group v.p. Kraft Foods Inc., 2000—04; pres. Kraft Food N. Am., 2003—04; chmn., CEO Frito-Lay Inc. (divsn. of PepsiCo Inc.), Plano, Tex., 2004—06; CEO Kraft Foods Inc., 2006—. Bd. dirs. AutoNation, Inc. Mem. YWCA Acad. Women Achievers; bd. trustees Cornell U. Named one of Most Powerful Women, Forbes Mag., 2006, 50 Most Powerful Women in Bus., Fortune mag., 2006; recipient The Masters in Excellence award, Jewish Student Cmty. at Cornell Univ., 2005. Office: Kraft Foods Inc 3 Lakes Dr Northfield IL 60093*

ROSENFELD, RHODA LYNN, reading specialist; b. Weehawken, NJ, Nov. 16, 1939; d. Martin and Gladys Auerbach; m. Howard Rosenfeld (dec.); m. Alan Arnold Simon (div.); children: Stephanie Distasio, Jill Simon. BS in Elem. Edn., Fairleigh Dickinson U., 1961; ME in Reading Specialist, William Paterson Coll., 1976. Cert. Elementary Teacher 1964, NJ Supervisor's Certificate Montclair State Coll., 1980. Pvt. reading tutor The Galloway, Atlanta, 2006; adj. prof. Palomar Coll., San Marcos, Calif., 1997; adj. prof. in reading Lake Sumter Cmty. Coll., Leesburg, Fla., 1995—96. Reading specialist Parsippany Troy Hills Bd. Edn., 1975—94; pre-sch. tchr. Troy Hills Sch., Parsippany; elem. sch. tchr. Teaneck Bd. Edn. Mem.: Atlanta Botanical Garden, NJ Retired Edn. Assn. Avocations: reading, yoga, piano, exercise. Home: 2865 Lenox Rd NE Atlanta GA 30324

ROSENFELD, SARENA MARGARET, artist; b. Elmira, NY, Oct. 17, 1940; d. Thomas Edward and Rosalie Ereny (Fedor) Rooney; m. Robert Steven Bach, June 1958 (div. 1963); children: Robert Steven, Daniel Thomas; m. Samson Rosenfeld III, June 5, 1976. Student, Otis/Parson Art Inst., L.A., 1994-98, Idyllwild Sch. Music and Arts, 1994-98. One-woman shows include Robert Dana Gallery, San Francisco, Gordon Gallery, Santa Monica, Calif., Hespe Gallery, San Francisco, Art Expressions, San Diego, L.A., La Jolla, Calif., Aspen, Colo., New Orleans, Honolulu, La Sierra U., Riverside, Calif., U. Enklinik, Bochum, Germany, Ruhr U., Germany, U. Benjamin Franklin, Berlin, 2002, Gallery 444, San Francisco, exhibited in group shows at Ergane Gallery, NYC, Orlando Gallery, Sherman Oaks, Calif., Bradford Gallery Blue Sq., Newport Beach, Calif., 2001, LA, Soho, NYC, Santa Barbara, Calif., Tanglewood, Mass., Johannesburg, South Africa, Coda Gallery, Palm Desert, Calif., Johnson Art Collection, LA, Convergence Gallery, Santa Fe. Mem., vol., animal handler Wildlife Waysta., Angeles Nat. Forest, Calif.; vol. animal keeper L.A. Zoo. Recipient Best of Show award Glendale Regional Arts Coun., 1984-85, 1st pl. awards Santa Monica Art Festival, 1982, 83, 84, 85, 86, Sweepstakes award and 1st pl., 1986, Purchase prize awards L.A. West C. of C., 1986-87, Tapestry in Talent Invitational San Jose Arts Coun., 1986, 1st pl. awards Studio City and Century City Arts Couns., 1976-84, 1st award Pacific Palisades Art Affair XII, 1997, Sherman Oaks Fall Arts Festival, 1997. Mem. Nat. Mus. of Women in the Arts. Republican. Home: 6570 Kelvin Ave Canoga Park CA 91306-4021

ROSENHEIM, MARGARET KEENEY, social welfare policy educator; b. Grand Rapids, Mich., Sept. 5, 1926; d. Morton and Nancy (Billings) Keeney; m. Edward W. Rosenheim, June 20, 1947; children: Daniel, James, Andrew. Student, Wellesley Coll., 1943-45; JD, U. Chgo., 1949. Bar: Ill. 1949. Mem. faculty Sch. Social Service Adminstrn., U. Chgo., 1950—, assoc. prof., 1961-66, prof., 1966—, Helen Ross prof. social welfare policy, 1975-96, dean, 1978-83; lectr. in law U. Chgo., 1980-97. Vis. prof. U. Wash., 1965, Duke U., 1984; Helen Ross prof. emerita U. Chgo., 1996—; acad. visitor London Sch. Econs., 1973; cons. Pres.'s Commn. Law Enforcement and Adminstrn. Justice, 1966-67, Nat. Adv. Commn. Criminal Justice Stds. and Goals, 1972; mem. Juvenile Justice Stds. Commn., 1973-78; trustee Carnegie Corp. N.Y., 1979-87; trustee Children's Home and Aid Soc. of Ill., 1981—, chair, 1996-98; chair CHASI Sys. Inc., 1998-2001; dir. Nat. Inst. Dispute Resolution, 1981-89, Nuveen Bond Funds, 1982-97; mem. Chgo. Network, 1983—. Editor: Justice for the Child, 1962; contbr. 2d edit., 1977; editor: Pursuing Justice for the Child, 1976; editor: (with F.E. Zimring, D.S. Tanenhaus, B. Dohrn) A Century of Juvenile Justice, 2002; editor: (with Mark Testa) Early Parenthood and Coming of Age in the 1990s, 1992; contbr. articles to profl. jours. Office: 969 E 60th St Chicago IL 60637-2677 Home: Apt 303 1 Thomas Moore Way San Francisco CA 94130-2942 E-mail: mrosenhe@midway.uchicago.edu.

ROSENKRANTZ, BARBARA GUTMANN, science and medicine historian; b. NYC, Jan. 11, 1923; d. James and Jeanette (Mack) G.; m. David P. Bennett, Sept. 5, 1942 (div.); 1 child, Louise; m. Paul Rosenkrantz, Apr. 19, 1950 (dec. 1986); children: Judith, Deborah; m. J. Nathaniel Marshall, 1988. AB, Radcliffe Coll., 1944; PhD, Clark U., 1970. Rsch. assoc. Harvard U., Cambridge, Mass., 1970-71, lectr., 1971-73, assoc. prof. history of sci., 1973-75, prof., 1975-93, prof. emeritus, 1993—, chmn. history of sci. dept., 1984-89, master Currier House, 1974-79, faculty adminstr. Author: Public Health and the State, 1972, (with William A. Koelsch) American Habitat, 1973; editor for history Am. Jour. Pub. Health, 1985-89. NIH research grantee, 1970-72; Rockefeller Found. fellow, 1979-80; Ctr. for Advanced Study in Behavioral Scis. fellow Stanford U., 1984, Inst. Medicine fellow; Sherman Fairchild Disting. Scholar, Calif. Inst. Tech., 1989. Fellow: Am. Acad. Arts and Scis., Mass. Hist. Soc.; mem.: Am. Hist. Assn., History of Sci. Soc., Am. Assn. for History of Medicine. Jewish. Office: Harvard U Dept History Sci Ctr 371 Cambridge MA 02138 Office Phone: 617-496-2239. Fax: 617-495-3344.

ROSENSAFT, JEAN BLOCH, university administrator; b. N.Y.C., Jan. 6, 1952; d. Sam E. and Lilly Bloch; m. Menachem Rosensaft, Jan. 13, 1974; 1 child, Joana Deborah. BA in Art History, Barnard Coll., 1973; postgrad., NYU, 1978. Gallery lectr. in spl. exhbns. Mus. of Modern Art, N.Y.C., 1977-80; NEA lectr. on collections Modern Art Edn. Dept., 1979-80, spl. asst. for ind. sch. program, 1980-83, spl. asst. for publs., 1983-84; coord. pub. programs The Jewish Mus., N.Y.C., 1984-86, asst. dir. of edn., 1986-89; sr. nat. dir. for pub. affairs and institutional planning Hebrew Union Coll.-Jewish Inst. of Religion, N.Y.C., 1989—, exhbns. dir., 1994—2000, mus. dir., 2000—. Author: Chagall and the Bible, 1987; editor: Ann Sperry: 30 Pieces/30 Years, 2003, The Art of Aging, 2003, Archie Rand: The Nineteen Diaspora Paintings, 2004, Aliza Olmert: Tikkun, Jan Aronson: A Reverence for Nature, 2005, Carol Hamoy: Psalm Song, 2005, Mary Grünberg: Selected Works 1966-2006, 2006, Tamar Hirschl: Cultural Alarm, 2006, The Eye of the Collector: The Jewish Vision of Sigmund R. Balka, 2006. Mem. collections and acquisitions com. U.S. Holocaust Meml. Mus., Washington, 1980—; mem. steering com. Coun. of Am. Jewish Mus., N.Y.C., 1995—; chair task force on the arts UJA/Fedn. Women's Task Force, N.Y.C., 1995—; v.p. Internat. Network of Children of Jewish Holocaust Survivors, N.Y.C., 1987—; chair Park Ave Synagogue H.S. Parents Assn., N.Y.C., 1993-96, sch. bd., 1993—, adv. bd. 1996—. George Welwood Murray fellow Barnard Coll., 1973. Home: 179 E 70th St New York NY 10021-5109 Office: Hebrew Union Coll-Jewish Inst Religion 1 W 4th St New York NY 10012-1105 Office Phone: 212-824-2209. Business E-Mail: jrosensaft@huc.edu.

ROSENSTEIN, ELYSE S., secondary school educator; b. Bklyn., Jan. 23, 1951; d. Matthew and Beverly Irene (Grobstein) Pines; 1 child, Michael Howard. BS, Adelphi U., Garden City, NY, 1987, MS, 1994. Cert. tchr. physics and gen sci. NY. Tchr. sci. NYC bd. dirs., 1988—96, Brentwood UFSO, Brentwood, NY, 1996—97; adj. instr. Bklyn. Coll. CUNY, Bklyn., 1997—2000; sci. tchr. Hempstead H.S., Hempstead, NY, 1997—2000, Malverne H.S., Malverne, NY, 2000—. Mem.: NY Acad. Scis., LI Physics Tchrs. Assn. Avocations: reading, cooking, guitar. Home: 1910 Henry St Bellmore NY 11710 E-mail: physicsteacher@earthlink.net.

ROSENSTOCK, LINDA, dean, medical educator; b. NYC, Dec. 20, 1950; m. Lee Bailey; children: Adam Lee, Matthew Lynn. AB in Psychology, Brandeis U., 1971; student, U. B.C., Vancouver, Can., 1971-72; MD, MPH, Johns Hopkins U., 1977. Diplomate Am. Bd. Internal Medicine, Am. Bd. Preventive Medicine; lic. physician and surgeon, Wash. Med. resident then chief resident U. Wash., Seattle, 1977-80, resident in preventive medicine, instr. medicine, 1980-82, asst. prof., 1982-83, 83-87, lectr. environ. health, 1982-83, adj. asst. prof., 1983-86, mem. grad. sch. faculty, 1985—, assoc. prof., 1987-93, prof. medicine and environ. health, 1993—94, also dir. programs, 1994; dir. Nat. Inst. Occupational Safety and Health, Washington, 1994—2000; dean UCLA Sch. of Pub. Health, 2000—, prof. environ. health sciences, 2000—; prof. medicine UCLA Sch. Medicine, 2000—. Dir. Harborview Med. Ctr., Seattle, 1981-87, acting sect. head, 1992-94; dir. Nat. Inst. Occupational Safety and Health, Washington, 1994—. Assoc. editor Internat. Jour. Occupational Medicine and Toxicology, 1991—; mem. editorial bd. Am. Jour. Indsl. Medicine, 1985-94, Jour. Gen. Internal Medicine, 1987-90, Environ. Rsch., 1987—, Western Jour. Medicine, 1990—; contbr. numerous articles to profl. jours. Mem. exec. bd. Physicians for Human Rights, 1990—; mem. occupl. health adv. bd. United Auto Workers GM, 1990-94, chair, 1993-94; mem. task force on pneumoconioses Am. Coll. Radiology, 1991-94; mem. external adv. panel Agrl. Health and Safety Ctr., 1992-93; mem. adv. com. Ctrs. for Disease Control, 1992-94; mem. com. to survey health effects of mustard gas and lewisite Inst. Medicine, 1992, mem. bd. health promotion and disease prevention, 1993-94; mem. bd. sci. counselors HHS, 1993-94, mem. exec. com. nat. toxicology program, 1994—; mem. med. adv. bd. Teamsters Internat., 1993-94. Recipient Upjohn Achievement award Harborview Med. Ctr., 1978, Jean Spencer Felton MD award Western Occupational Med. Assn., 1988, Environ. and Occupational Medicine award Nat. Inst. Environ. Health Scis., 1991-94; Robert Wood Johnson scholar, 1980-82, Henry J. Kaiser scholar, 1984-89. Fellow ACP (health promotion subcom. 1989-90, clin. practice subcom. 1990-91), Collegium Ramazzini; mem. APHA (chair membership com. 1983-85, chairperson occupational helath and safety sect. 1985-86, gov. coun. 1986-88), Am. Coll. Occupational Medicine (mem. jud. com. 1989-94), Am. Thoracic Soc. (com. health care policy and clin. practice 1990-93), Internat. Commn. Occupational Health (sci. com. epidemiology in occupational health 1989—), Soc. Gen. Internal Medicine (program planning com. 1987, Glaser award com. 1993-94), Western Assn. Physicians, Pacific Interurban Clin. Club. Office: UCLA Sch Pub Health 16-035 Ctr for Health Sciences Box 951772 Los Angeles CA 90095*

ROSENSTOCK, SUSAN LYNN, orchestra administrator; b. Bklyn., Nov. 2, 1947; BS, SUNY, Cortland, 1969; MBA, So. Meth. U., 1977, MFA, 1978. Asst. mgr. Columbus (Ohio) Symphony Orch., 1978-82; grants program dir., info. officer Greater Columbus Arts Coun., 1982-83, asst. dir. grants and adminstrn., 1983-84; dir. ann. giving and spl. events Columbus Symphony Orch., 1984-86, dir. devel., 1986-90, orch. mgr., 1990-98, gen. mgr., 1998—. Panelist Ohio Arts Coun. Music Panel, 1986, 87, NEA, 2002, Challenge Grants Panel, 1991, J.C. Penney Gold Rule Award Judges Panel, 1993, 94. Mem. Am. Symphony Orch. League (devel. dirs. steering com. nat. conf. 1987, 88), Nat. Soc. Fund Raising Execs. (program com. Ctrl. Ohio chpt. 1988-94, chmn. program com. 1993, 94, bd. dirs. 1993-95, treas. 1995). Office: Columbus Symphony Orch 55 E State St Columbus OH 43215-4203 E-mail: susanr@columbussymphony.com.

ROSEN-SUPNICK, ELAINE RENEE, physical therapist; b. N.Y.C., May 7, 1951; d. Oscar Arthur and Sydell (Zimmerman) R.;m. Jed Supnick, Apr. 21, 1985. BS, CUNY, 1973; MS, L.I. U., Bklyn., 1977; D of Health Sci., U. St. Augustine, 1998. Cert. orthop. specialist/Am. Bd. Phys. Therapy Specialists. Phys. therapy cons. Lenox Hill Hosp. Home Care, N.Y.C., 1977-83, Group Health Ins., Queens, N.Y., 1977-83, Vis. Nurse Assn., Bklyn., 1977-83; sr. phys. therapist Bird S. Coler Hosp., Roosevelt Island, N.Y., 1973-77; assoc. prof. CUNY-Hunter Coll., 1977—; ptnr. Queens Phys. Therapy Assocs., Forest Hills, N.Y., 1982—. Fellow Am. Acad. of Orthop. Manual Phys. Therapists; mem. Am. Phys. Therapy Assn. (bd. cert. orthop. specialist, cert. phys. ther Democrat. Jewish. Office: Queens Phys Therapy Assocs 6940 108th St Flushing NY 11375-3851 E-mail: elaine.rosen@hunter.cuny.edu.

ROSENTHAL, DONNA MYRA, social worker; b. Rochester, NY, Feb. 23, 1944; d. Harry Lionel and Leila Estelle (Eber) Rosenthal; m. Thomas Robert Kolar, Aug. 5, 1979. BA, George Washington U., 1965; MS, Columbia U., 1967. Cert. social worker. Cmty. organizer Health & Welfare Coun. Nassau County, Uniondale, NY, 1967-68; field rep. NY State Office Aging, NYC, 1968-73; asst. dir. United Neighborhood Houses, NYC, 1973-84; exec. dir. Nat. Down Syndrome Soc., NYC, 1984-94; exec. vice chmn. CLAL-The Nat. Jewish Ctr. for Learning and Leadership, NYC, 1994—. Pres. Exec. Women in Human Svcs., NYC, 1985—89. Pres. Congregation Beth Elohim, Bklyn., 1991-94; pres. Columbia U. Social Work Alumni, NYC, 1989-91; 3rd vice-chmn. adv. coun. Columbia U. Sch. Social Work, 1991-2000, co-chair centennial com., 1995-98, chmn. adv. coun. 2000-06; treas. Alumni Fedn. Columbia U., 1995-97, sec., 1997-99, v.p., 1999-2001, pres. 2001-03. Recipient Alumni medal Columbia U., 1991; NIMH fellow Columbia U., 1966-67; Regents scholar, 1961. Mem.: Columbia Alumni Assn. (bd. dirs. 2005—), Columbia Club (bd. dirs. 2004—, v.p. 2005—). Avocation: music. Office: CLAL 440 Park Ave S New York NY 10016-8012 Office Phone: 212-779-3300.

ROSENTHAL, ELIZABETH ANNE, writer, entrepreneur; b. San Rafael, Calif., Mar. 3, 1963; d. Mason P. and Lynne G. Rosenthal. BA, U. Mich., Ann Arbor, 1985; MBA, U. Chgo., 1993, PhD, 1996; MPH, U. Calif., Berkeley, 1989; Cert. of Completion, Ecole Centrale, HEC, Institut d'Etudes Politiques, Paris, 1991. Sec. edn. dept. Healthcare Forum, San Francisco, 1986—87; cons. Pub. Health Divsn., State of Mich., Ypsilanti, 1990; project asst. planning and bus. devel. ArcVentures, Inc., Chgo., 1991—92; quality auditor W.A. Golomski & Associates, Chgo., 1992—93; subject matter expert Unext, Deerfield, Ill., 2000—04; mem. faculty Cardean U., Deerfield, 2003—04; founder and pres. Loving Living Life, Inc., Chgo., 1997—, life coach, 1999—2003; founder, exec. dir. Healing Centers United, Inc., Chgo., 2005—. Author: Where to Go When You're Hurting: A Healing Resource Guide, 1998; contbr. articles to profl. publs. Named Vol. of Yr., Christopher Ho., 2002; rsch. fellow, Am. Soc. Quality Control, 1994. Home and Office: PO Box 14684 Chicago IL 60614 Personal E-mail: drbeth@lovinglivinglife.com.

ROSENTHAL, ELIZABETH ROBBINS, physician; b. Bklyn., Feb. 10, 1943; d. Marc and Ruth Jackson (Oginz) Robbins; m. Samuel Leonard Rosenthal; children: Thomas, Benjamin, Marc. AB, Smith Coll., 1963; MD, NYU, 1967. Diplomate Am. Bd. of Dermatology. Intern in pediatrics Upstate Med. Ctr., Syracuse, NY, 1967-68; resident in dermatology Henry Ford Hosp., Detroit, 1968-69, Roosevelt Hosp., N.Y.C., 1969-70, Boston U. Med. Ctr., 1972-74; pvt. practice Mamaroneck, NY, 1976—; attending United Hosp., Pt. Chester, NY, 1994—2004. Asst. clin. prof. Albert Einstein Coll. Medicine, Bronx, 1978—. Bd. dirs. Community Counseling Ctr., Mamaroneck, N.Y., 1982—. Fellow Am. Acad. Dermatology; mem. N.Y. State Med. Soc., NOW, Westchester County Med. Soc., Am. Med. Women's Assn. Office: 1600 Harrison Ave Mamaroneck NY 10543-3145 Office Phone: 914-698-2190. E-mail: drelizrose@verizon.net.

ROSENTHAL, HELEN NAGELBERG, county official, advocate; b. NYC, June 6, 1926; d. Alfred and Esther (Teichholz) Nagelberg; m. Albert S. Rosenthal, Apr. 10, 1949 (dec.); children: Lisa Rosenthal Michaels, Apryl Meredith Rosenthal Stuppler. BS, CUNY, 1948; MA, NYU, 1950; postgrad., Adelphia U., LI U., Lehman Coll., 1975. Cert. early childhood and gifted edn. tchr., NY, NJ, elem. and secondary tchr., Fla. Tchr. gifted students NY Bd Edn., Bklyn., 1949-77, 79-87, Baldwin Pub. Schs., NY, 1977-79; rep. community affairs County of Dade, Fla., 1988-92; ret., 1992; condo dir. Pembroke Pines, 1999—. Author: Criteria for Selection and Curriculum for the Gifted, 1977, Science Experiments for Young Children, 1982, Music in the Air.and in Our Minds. Dir. Condominium, 1989-91. Recipient Departmental award, 1948. Mem. Concerned Citizens for Educating Gifted and Talented (officer NYC chpt.), Assn. Gifted and Talented Edn. (NY chpt.), Am. Inst. Cancer Rsch., Bklyn. Coll. Alumni Assn. (pres. Broward-Dade chpt. 1995-96, v.p. membership 1996—).

ROSENTHAL, JANE, film company executive; b. Providence, 1957; d. Martin and Ina; m. Craig Hatkoff; children: Juliana, Isabella. Student, Brown U.; BA, NYU, 1977. Rsch. staff CBS Sports, NY; editor program practices CBS Entertainment, 1977, program exec. miniseries L.A., 1978, assoc. dir. motion pictures for TV, 1979; v.p. feature prodn. Universal Studios, 1984—85; v.p. in charge of motion pictures and TV Walt Disney, 1985—87; v.p. in charge of movies and miniseries Warner Bros. TV, 1987—88; co-founder (with Robert DeNiro), ptnr. Tribeca Film Ctr., N.Y.C., 1989—; co-founder Tribeca Film Festival, N.Y.C., 2002. Prodr.: (films) Thunderheart, 1992, Night and the City, 1992, A Bronx Tale, 1993, Faithful, 1996, Marvin's Room, 1996, Wag the Dog, 1997, Analyze This, 1999, Entropy, 1999, Meet the Flawless, 1999, The Adventures of Rocky & Bullwinkle, 2000, Meet the Parents, 2000, Prison Song, 2001, Showtime, 2002, About a Boy, 2002, Analyze That, 2002, House of D, 2004, Stage Beauty, 2004, Meet the Fockers, 2004, Rent, 2005; (TV series) Tribeca, 1993; exec. prodr.: (films) Nine, 1996, The Repair Shop, 1998; (TV films) Witness to the Mob, 1998, Holiday Heart, 2000. Office: Tribeca Prodns 6th Fl 375 Greenwich St New York NY 10013*

ROSENTHAL, LUCY GABRIELLE, writer, editor, educator; b. N.Y.C. d. Henry Moses and Rachel (Tchernowitz) Rosenthal. AB, U. Mich., 1954; MS in Journalism, Columbia U., 1955; MFA, Yale Sch. Drama, 1961; postgrad. Writers Workshop, U. Iowa, 1965—68. Asst. editor Radiology mag., Detroit, 1955—57; free-lance editl. cons. various pub. houses, lit. agts. NYC, 1957—73; mem. admissions staff Writers Workshop U. Iowa, Iowa City, 1965—68; editor Book-of-the-Month Club, NYC, 1973—74, mem. editl. bd. judges, 1974—79, sr. editl. advisor, 1979—87. Mem. biography jury Pulitzer Prize, 1980; mem. bd. Am. Book Awards, 1981-82; adj. prof. English, NYU, 1986—; mem. guest faculty in writing Sarah Lawrence Coll., 1988-96, regular faculty writing, 1996—; lectr., adj. asst. prof. writing program Columbia U., 1990-96, Humanities faculty, 92nd St. YM/YWCA, 1987; fiction workshop The Writer's Voice, West Side YMCA, summer 1991; adj. prof. NYU Sch. Continuing Edn., 1988; mem. faculty Sarah Lawrence Ctr. for Continuing Edn., 1989, 90; instr. fiction writing course Art Workshop Internat., Assisi, Italy, summer 1993. Plays produced at Eugene O'Neill Meml. Theater Ctr., 1966, 1967; author: The Ticket Out, 1983; editor: Great American Love Stories, 1988, The World Treasury of Love Stories, 1995, The Eloquent Short Story: Varieties of Narration, 2004; contbr. to Global City Rev., 1995, articles and revs. to mags. and periodicals. Pulitzer fellow critical writing, 1968. Mem. Authors Guild, Authors League, Nat. Book Critics Circle, Women's Media Group (bd. mem. 1979-81), PEN, Phi Beta Kappa, Phi Kappa Phi. Office: Sarah Lawrence Coll Bronxville NY 10708 E-mail: lrosenth@slc.edu.

ROSENTHAL, LYOVA HASKELL See GRANT, LEE

ROSENTHAL, MARILYN, school librarian, educator; b. Cambridge, Mass., Oct. 8, 1941; d. Edward and Helen Ruth Goldman; m. Stephen Alan Rosenthal, Apr. 11, 1964; children: Diane Wood, David. AB, Vassar Coll., 1963; MA in French, NYU, 1965; MS in Libr. Sci., Palmer Sch. Libr. and Info. Sci., 1979. Reference trainee Post Ctr. for Bus. Rsch., Brookville, NY, 1978—79; adj. reference libr. North Bellmore (N.Y.) Pub. Libr., 1979—83; adj. libr. Nassau C.C. Libr., Garden City, NY, 1983—88, instr., 1988—93, asst. prof., 1993—98, assoc. prof., reference libr., 1998—2003, prof., 2004—. Mem. interlibr. loan com. L.I. Libr. Coun., 1988—, chmn., 1989—95; presenter in field.; mem. adv. panel on info. literacy Mid. States Commn. on Higher Edn., 2002—; v.chmn. academic senate Nassau C.C., 1997—2001.

Contbr. chapters to books, articles, revs. to profl. publs. Del. SUNY Librs. Assn. Coun., 1990—2001. Recipient Chancellor's award for Excellence in Librarianship, SUNY, 1996. Mem.: Assn. Coll. Rsch. Librs. (symposium planning com.), Assn. Coll. and Rsch. Librs. (vice chmn. L.I. sect. 1992, membership sec. 1994—2000, v.p. 2000, mem. chpts. coun. 2000—02, pres. 2001, past pres. 2002, L.I. sec. 2003), Women's Faculty Assn. Nassau C.C. (membership sec. 1993—96, pres. 1996—2000, past pres. 2000—02, recording sec. 2003—). Home: 17097 Huntington Park Way Boca Raton FL 33496-2921

ROSENTHAL, NAN, curator, educator, author; b. N.Y.C., Aug. 27, 1937; d. Alan Herman and Lenore (Fry) R.; m. Otto Piene (div.); m. Henry Benning Cortesi, Sept. 5, 1990. BA, Sarah Lawrence Coll., 1959; MA, Harvard U., 1970, PhD, 1976. Asst. prof. art history U. Calif., Santa Cruz, 1971-77, assoc. prof., 1977-84, prof., 1985-86, chair dept. art history, 1976-80; curator 20th-century art Nat. Gallery Art, Washington, 1985-92; sr. cons. dept. modern art Met. Mus. of Art, N.Y.C., 1993—; Lila Acheson Wallace vis. prof. fine arts NYU Inst. Fine Arts, N.Y.C., 1996, 2000. Vis. prof. art history Fordham U., Lincoln Ctr., 1981, 85; vis. scholar N.Y. Inst. for Humanities, NYU, 1982—83; vis. lectr. visual arts Princeton U., 1985, 88, 92; adj. prof. art history Columbia U., 2002. Author: George Rickey, 1977; also exhbn. catalogues, catalogue essays and articles; art editor Show, 1963-64; assoc. editor, then editor at large and contbg. editor Art in Am., 1964-70. Radcliffe Inst. fellow, 1968-69, scholar, 1970-71; travelling fellow Harvard U., 1973-74, rsch. fellow U. Calif., 1978, Ailsa Mellon Bruce curatorial fellow Nat. Gallery of Art, 1988-89; rsch. and travel grantee U. Calif., Santa Cruz, 1974, 77-80, 82-85. Office: Met Mus of Art Dept Modern Art 1000 Fifth Ave New York NY 10028-0113 E-mail: nan.rosenthal@metmuseum.org.

ROSENTHAL, SHIRLEY LORD, cosmetics magazine executive, novelist; b. London, Aug. 28; came to U.S., 1971; d. Francis J. and Mabel Florence (Williamson) Stringer; m. James Hussey; m. Cyril Lord; m. David Anderson; m. A. M. Rosenthal, June 10, 1987; children: Mark, Richard. Student, S.W. Essex Coll., London, 1948—50. Reporter London Daily Mirror; fiction editor Woman's Own, 1950-53; features editor Good Taste mag., 1953-56; features, fiction editor Woman and Beauty, 1956-59; women's editor Star Evening newspaper, 1959-60, London Evening Standard, 1960-63, London Evening News, 1963-68; beauty editor Harper's Bazaar, London, 1963-71, N.Y.C., 1971-73; beauty, health editor Vogue mag., Condé Nast Publs., N.Y.C., 1973-75; v.p. corp. rels. Colgate, Helena Rubinstein, N.Y.C., 1975-80; beauty dir. Vogue mag., 1980—95, contbg. editor, 1995—. Chairwoman media coun. The Am. Acad. Dermatology, 1995—; corp. v.p. content iBeauty.com, 1999—2002; enrichment advisor Silverson Cruises, 2004—. Syndicated Field columnist on beauty, health; author 3 beauty books; also novels: Golden Hill, 1982; One of My Very Best Friends, (Lit. Guild Selection), 1985; Faces, 1989; My Sister's Keeper, 1993, The Crasher, 1998. City commr. Craigavon City, No. Ireland, 1963-68. Address: 131 E 66th St New York NY 10021-6129 E-mail: Shirlord3@aol.com.

ROSENTHAL, SUSAN LESLIE, psychologist; b. Washington, Sept. 27, 1956; d. Alan Sayre and Helen (Miller) R. BA, Wellesley Coll., Mass., 1978; PhD, U. N.C., Chapel Hill, 1986; grad., Hedwig van Ameringen Exec. Leadership in Acad. Medicine Program for Women, 2006. Diplomate child and adolescent psychology 2005. Postdoctoral fellow Yale Child Study Ctr., New Haven, 1986-88; asst. prof. pediatrics U. Cin., 1988-93, assoc. prof. pediatrics, 1993-2000, prof. pediatrics, 2000-01, dir. psychology divsn. adolescent medicine, 1988-01, dir. post-doctoral tng., divsn. psychology, 2000-01; dir. Divsn. Adolscent and Behavioral Health, sr. scientist Sealy Ctr. Vaccine Devel. U. Tex. Med. Br., 2001—. Mem. study sect. NIH, MCHB; mem. numerous adv. coms. Merck, FHI, others; mem. Coun. Soc. Devel. and Behavioral Pediat. Contbr. articles to profl. jours.; spl. reviewer in field. NIH grantee, 1994—, Merck & Co., Inc. grantee, 1995, Wyeth-Ayerst Labs. grantee, 1995—2000, SmithKlineBeecham Biols. grantee, 1997—98, Glaxo-SmithKline grantee, 2001—. Fellow APA (program chair divsn. 37 1992, sec. 1996-98); mem. N.Am. Soc. Pediatric & Adolscent Gyn. (mem. at-large, bd. dirs., 2005—), Soc. Pediatric Rsch., Soc. Devel. and Behavioral Pediatrics (coun. mem.). Office: Univ Tex Med Br Divsn Adolescent and Behavioral Health 301 University Blvd Galveston TX 77555-0319 Business E-Mail: slrosent@utmb.edu.

ROSHONG, DEE ANN DANIELS, dean, educator; b. Kansas City, Mo., Nov. 22, 1936; adopted d. Vernon Edmund and Doradell (Kellogg) Daniels, d. Ken Garner and Lucille Cronin Davidson; m. Richard Lee Roshong, Aug. 27, 1960 (div.). BMusEd., U. Kans., Lawrence, 1958; MA in Counseling and Guidance, Stanford U., Calif., 1960; postgrad., Fresno State U., U. Calif., Berkeley; EdD, U. San Francisco, 1980. Counselor, psychometrist Fresno City Coll., 1961-65; counselor, instr. psychology Chabot Coll., Hayward, Calif., 1965-75, coord. counseling svcs. Livermore, Calif., 1975-81, asst. dir. student pers. svcs., 1981-89, Las Positas Coll., Livermore, Calif., 1989-91, assoc. dean student svcs., 1991-94, dean student svcs., 1991—2003, life coach, 2000—; counselor Experience Unltd., Pleasant Hill, Calif., 2004—; symposium organizer Calif. State U., East Bay, 2004—. Writer, coord. I, A Woman Symposium, 1974, Feeling Free to Be You and Me symposium, 1975, All for the Family Symposium, 1976, I Celebrate Myself Symposium, 1978, Person to Person in Love and Work Symposium, 1978, The Healthy Person in Mind and Spirit Symposium, 1980, Change Symposium, 1981, Sources of Strength Symposium, 1982, Love and Friendship Symposium, 1983, Self Esteem Symposium, 1984, Trust Symposium, 1985, Prime Time: Making the Most of This Time in Your Life Symposium, 1986, Symposium in Healing, 1987, How to Live in the World and Still Be Happy Symposium, 1988, Student Success is a Team Effort, Sound Mind, Sound Body Symposium, 1989, Creating Life's Best Symposium, 1990, Choices Symposium, 1991, Minding the Body, Mending the Mind Symposium, 1992, Healing through Love and Laughter Symposium, 1993, Healing Ourselves Changing the World Symposium, 1994, Finding Your Path Symposium, 1995, Build the Life You Want Symposium, 1996, Making Peace With Yourself and Your Relationships Symposium, 1997, Everyday Sacred Symposium, 1998, Wisdom of the Heart Symposium, 1999, Inner Wisdom Symposium, 2000, Second Half of Life Symposium, 2001, A Celebration of Life Symposium, 2003, Viewing Mental Health and Mental Illness From a Multi-Cultural Perspective Symposium, 2004, Promoting Mental Health in Multi-Cultural Settings Symposium, 2005, Building Bridges to Hope and Recovery: Healing Ourselves, Transforming the System Symposium, 2006; mem. cast TV prodns. Eve and Co., Best of Our Times, Cowboy; chmn. Falling Awake Symposium, 2002, Calif. C.C. Chancellor's Task Force on Counseling, Statewide Regional Counseling Facilitators, 1993-95, Statewide Conf. Emotionally Disturbed Students in Calif. C.C.s, 1982—, Conf. on the Under Represented Student in Calif. C.C.s, 1986, Conf. on High Risk Students, 1989. Author: Counseling Needs of Comunity College Students, 1980. Bd. dirs. Teleios Sinetar Ctr., Ctr. for Cmty. Dispute Resolution, 1998—, Pleasanton Youth Collaborative Bd., 1997-2002, Pleasanton Youth Master Plan Bd., 1998—; choir dir., 1996-99; pres. bd. Tri-Valley Unity Ch., 1998-2005, v.p. 2005, lay minister 2005, Tri-Valley Haven bd., 2000—, Calif. State U. East Bay Inst. Mental Illness and Wellness Edn. bd., 2000—. Ellis Life Coach Tng., 1999—, Interspiritual Mentor Tng. Program, 2005; title III activity dir. Las Positas Coll., 1995-99, dir. pace program, 1999-2003, dir. quest program, 2000-03. Mem.: Calif C.C. Counselors Assn. (svc. award 1986—87, award for Outstanding and Disting. Svc. 1986—87, Pleasanton Mayor's award 2000—01, 2002), Calif. Assn. C. C. (chmn. commn. on students svcs. 1979—84), Assn. Counseling and Devel., Nat. Assn. Women Deans and Counselors, Western Psychol. Assn., Assn. Humanistic Psychologists. Home and Office: 1856 Harvest Rd Pleasanton CA 94566-5456 Personal E-mail: deeroshong@comcast.net.

ROSIAK, FRANCES RUTH, elementary school educator; b. Erie, Pa., Dec. 28, 1949; d. Adam Anthony and Ann Theresa (Staszewski) R. BA, Mercyhurst Coll., Erie, 1971; MEd, Edinboro U. Pa., 1976. Cert. tchr., Pa. Tchr. St. Titus Elem. Sch., Titusville, Pa., 1969-70, St. Michael Sch., Greenville, Pa., 1970-71, Our Lady of Mt. Carmel Sch., Erie, 1971-89, Chestnut Hill Elem. Sch., Millcreek, Pa., 1989-90, Belle Valley Elem. Sch., Millcreek, 1990—. Presenter in field. Dir. folk group Our Lady of Mt. Carmel Parish, 1975-88. Recipient State award Presdl. Awards for Excellence in Sci. and Math. Tchg., 1993; grantee Presque Isle Rotary Club, 1990, 91, 94, EdCore, 1990, GE, 1991, Kearsarge Rotary Club, 1995, Presdl. award for excellence in sci. tchg. PSTA Bd. of Dirs. (NWA Pa. Region VII Rep.), 2006. Mem. NSTA, Pa. Edn. Assn., Pa. Sci. Tchrs. Assn. (presenter 1989, 90, 91, 92, presenter, keynote speaker educator's symposium of Am. horticultural soc. and Montessori found. 1993, 94), Internat. Reading Assn. Democrat. Avocations: reading, nature study, hiking, camping, gardening. Office: Belle Valley Elem Sch 5300 Henderson Rd Erie PA 16509-4094 Business E-Mail: frosiak@mtsd.org.

ROSICKI, MARIA TRZETRZEWINSKA-TRETT, clinical psychologist; b. Warsaw, Dec. 13, 1925; d. Walter and Irena (Cywinska) T.; m. Tadeusz Rosicki, Nov. 26, 1960. BA summa cum laude, CUNY, 1956; MA, Fordham U., 1959, PhD in Clin. Psychology, 1969. Cert. psychologist, psychoanalyst, N.Y. Vocat. guidance counselor Archdiocese of N.Y., N.Y.C., 1958-61; staff psychologist, supr. Cath. Guardian Soc., Bklyn., 1963-92; psychotherapist, supr. Advanced Inst. for Analytic Psychotherapy, Queens, N.Y., 1970-78; pvt. practice psychotherapy, psychoanalysis Glen Cove, N.Y., 1978—. Mem. Sigma Xi, Phi Beta Kappa. Roman Catholic.

ROSITA, ALMA See DAVIES, ALMA

ROSKAM, CATHERINE S., bishop; b. May 30, 1943; m. Philip K. Roskam, Sept. 3, 1966; 1 child, Gemma. BA in theatre, Middlebury Coll., 1965; MDiv, Gen. Theol. Sem., NYC, 1984. Worked in theatre as an actress and prodr., NYC; ordained deacon, 1984, priest, 1984; asst. rector Holy Apostles Ch., NYC; priest-in-charge Holy Innocents' mission congregation, San Francisco; interim rector Ch. of Our Savior, Mill Valley, Calif.; diocesan missioner Episcopal Diocese of Calif., 1991—95; consecrated bishop, 1996; suffragen bishop Episcopal Diocese of NY, 1996—. Mem. exec. coun. Episcopal Ch. in the USA, 2000—; mem. Anglican Consultative Coun., 2001—; mem. bd. trustees Gen. Theol. Sem., NYC, vice chair, 2001—02. Office: Episcopal Diocese of NY 1047 Amsterdam Ave New York NY 10025 Office Phone: 212-316-7400. Office Fax: 212-316-7405.

ROSKEY, CAROL BOYD, social studies educator, dean, director; b. Columbus, Ohio, Mar. 9, 1946; d. Clarence Eugene and Clara Johanna (Schwartz) B.; m. Joseph Meeks, Aug. 17, 1968 (div. 1981) m. William A. Roskey, Nov. 16, 2003; children: Catherine Rachael, Tiffany Johannah. BS, Ohio State U., Mex., 1968; MS, Ohio State U., 1969, PhD, 1972. Rsch. asst., assoc. Ohio State U., Columbus, 1968-71; internship Columbus Area C. of C., Ohio, 1970; lectr. Ohio State U., Columbus, 1970, 72; asst. prof. U. Mass., Amherst, 1972-74, Cornell U., Ithaca, N.Y., 1974-78, assoc. prof., 1978-80; legis. fellow Senate Com. Banking, 1984; supr. economist, head housing section USDA, Washington, 1980-85; assoc. prof. housing and consumer econs. U. Ga., Athens, 1985-90, prof., 1990-97, head housing and consumer econs., 1992-97; dean Coll. Family and Consumer Scis. Iowa State U., Ames, 1997—2003, dir. Family Policy Ctr., 2003—. Rsch. fellow Nat. Inst. for Consumer Rsch., Oslo, Norway, 1992; cons. Yale U., 1976-77, HUD, Cambridge, Mass., 1978, MIT Ctr. for Real Estate Devel. Ford Found. Project on Housing Policy; del. N.E. Ctr. for Rural Devel. Housing Policy Conf. Reviewer Home Econ. Rsch. Jour., 1987—01, ACCI conf., 1987—; contbr. articles to profl. mags. Mem. panel town of Amherst Landlord Tenant Bd.; bd. dirs. Am. Coun. Consumer Interests; mem. adv. coun. HUD Nat. Mfg. Housing, 1978-80, 91-93; chair Housing Mfg. Inst. Consensus Commn. on Fed. Standards. Recipient Leader award AAFCS, 1996, Disting. Alumni award Ohio State U., 1999; named one of Outstanding Young Women of Am., 1979; Columbus Womens Chpt. Nat. Assn. Real Estate Bds. scholar, Gen. Foods fellow, 1971-72, HEW grantee, 1978, travel grantee NSF bldg. rsch. bd., AID grantee, USDA Challenge grant, 1995-98. Mem. Am. Assn. Housing Educators (pres. 1983-84), Nat. Inst. Bldg. Sci. (bd. sec. 1984, 85, 89-92, bd. dirs. 1981-83, 85, 87-93), Internat. Assn. Housing Sci., Com. on Status on Women in Econs., Nat. Assn. Home Builders (Smart House contract 1989, treas. bd. human sci. 2001-03), Epsilon Sigma Phi, Phi Upsilon Omicron, Gamma Sigma Delta, Phi Beta Delta, Kappa Omicron Nu (v.p. of programs 1995-96), Phi Kappa Phi, others. Office: Iowa State U 2354 Palmer Ames IA 50011-0001 Office Phone: 515-294-3028. Business E-Mail: cbroskey@iastate.edu.

ROSKO, MARYANN A., nurse; b. McKeesport, Pa., Sept. 22, 1930; d. George Rosko and Anna Makar. Grad. in Nursing, Homestead Hosp., Pa., 1951; postgrad. in Nursing, Chgo. Lying In, Ill., 1952—53. RN Pa. RN staff Homestead Hosp., Pa., 1951—55; RN supr. McKeesport Hosp., Pa., 1959—62, RN staff devel., 1963—68; RN insvc. edn. Magee Women's, Pitts., 1968—85. 1st lt. U.S. Army Nurse Corp, 1955—58. Home: 2605 Sunset Dr West Mifflin PA 15122-3564

ROS-LEHTINEN, ILEANA CARMEN, congresswoman; b. Havana, Cuba, July 15, 1952; arrived in US, 1959; d. Enrique Emilio and Amanda (Adato) Ros; m. Dexter Lehtinen; 2 children, 2 stepchildren. AA, Miami-Dade Community Coll., Fla., 1972; BA, Fla. Internat. U., 1975, MS, 1987. Prin. Ea. Acad., from 1978; mem. Fla. Ho. of Reps., Tallahassee, 1983—86, Fla. Senate, 1986—89, U.S. Congress from 18th Fla. dist., 1989—; mem. govt. reform com., internat. rels. com. Recipient Nat. Legis. award LULACH, 1999, Official of the Year, Youth Crime watch of Am., 2001. Republican. Episcopalian. Office: US Ho of Reps 2160 Rayburn Ho Office Bldg Washington DC 20515-0918 also: Dist Office Ste 100 9210 Sunset Dr Miami FL 33173

ROSMAN, PAULA, anthropologist, educator; AB, Hunter Coll., NYC, 1953; PhD, Columbia U., NYC, 1963. Part-time instr. grad. dept. ednl. sociology and anthropology NYU Sch. Edn., NYC, 1964; rsch. assoc. anthropology Columbia U., 1964—65; lectr. in anthropology Barnard Coll., Columbia U., 1965—66, asst. prof., 1966—70, assoc. prof., 1970—74, prof., 1974—98, prof. emerita, 1998—; lectr. anthropology Hunter Coll., 1963—64; rsch. assoc. dept. anthropology Am. Mus. Natural History, 1995—. Author: Feasting with Mine Enemy: Rank and Exchange Among Northwest Coast Societies, 1986; contbr. articles to profl. publs.; author: The Tapestry of Culture, 1980, 2d edit., 1985, Your Own Pigs You May Not Eat: A Comparative Study of New Guiea Societies, 1978. Grantee, NIMH, 1960—63, 1964—65, NEH, 1986—87; faculty rsch. grantee, SSRC, 1968, rsch. grantee, NSF, 1969—72, 1974—75, 1986—87, Barnard Coll., 1972—73, 1978—81, 1989, 1991—92, Guggenheim fellow, 1986—87. Home: 560 Riverside Dr Apt 18P New York NY 10027-3238

ROSMUS, ANNA ELISABETH, writer; b. Passau, Germany, Mar. 29, 1960; d. Georg Rudolf and Anna Johanna (Friedberger) R.; divorced; children: Dolores Nadine, Beatrice Salome Kassandra M Sociology, German Lit. and Fine Arts, U. Passau, 1994; PhD (hon.), U. S.C., 2000. Spkr. and organizer in field. Author: Resistance and Persecution, 1983 (Geschwister Scholl prize, 1984), Exodus in the Shadow of Mercy, 1988, Robert Klein A German Jew Looks Back, 1991, Wintergreen Suppressed Murders, 1993 (Conscience in Media award, 1994), Pocking End and Renewal, 1995, What I Think, 1995, Out of Passau, 1999, Against the Stream, 2002, Leaving a City Hitler Called Home, 2004; guest talk shows, including documentaries and features in Germany, Austria, Gt. Britain, Denmark, Holland, France, Italy, Sweden, Poland, Can., U.S., S.Am., Australia, 1983-. Fundraiser Anne Frank Found., Jewish Cmty. Ctrs., Holocaust Ctrs., others, 1992—. Recipient Immigrant Achievement award Am. Immigration Lawyers Assn., 1998; named Best German Writer, European essay Competition, 1980; Sarnat award Anti Defamation League, 1994; Anna Rosmus Day, City of Santa Cruz, 1994. Mem. PEN Internat. Avocations: environment protection, multicultural projects, minority programs. Personal E-mail: passau11@yahoo.com.

ROSNER, ANN See SEAMAN, BARBARA

ROSNER, SHARON ELLEN, actress, speech pathology/audiology services professional; b. Bklyn., Apr. 16, 1954; d. Herbert Paul and Linda (Kleiner) R. BS, Syracuse U., 1974; grad. program audiology, U. Ariz., 1975-76; MS, San Francisco State U., 1979; studied piano, San Francisco Conserv Music, 1979-84; acting degree, Drama Studio London, Berkeley, Calif., 1983. Audiologist Sonoma (Calif.) State Hosp., 1979-80; therapist Sch. for the Deaf, N.Y.C., 1984-86; speech-lang.-hearing specialist Home Therapists Assn., N.Y.C., 1988-93; tri-lingual cons., diagnostic/rehab. practitioner Comprehensive Network, N.Y.C., 1988-93; pvt. practice in speech, voice, comm. disorders and autism L.A., 1994—. Actor various off-Broadway and reg. theatre, film, TV, commls., and voiceovers; cons. Toward Rehab. Involvement by Parents of the Deaf (TRIPOD), L.A., 1993—; reader recorded books Jewish Guild for the Blind, N.Y.C., 1989-93; actor, dir., playmaking mentor Va. Ave. Project for At Risk Youth, L.A., 1996—. Actor: (solo theatrical piece) Family Matters: An Immigrant Memoir, 1986-91 (N.Y. Newsday Manhattan profile 1989); contbr. rsch. papers on psychophys. acoustics to profl. publs.; designer custom hearing protection for major rock bands; weekly columnist "Letters from L.A.," Athens, Greece; seminars on directing actors, faculty and film dept., N.Y. Coll., Athens, Greece, film dir's. and screenwriter's unions, Athens, Greece; dir. Theatre of the Deaf, Athens, Greece; journalist mags., Athens; tchr., actor, dir. workshops, Athens. Vol. Acad. Awards Silent Auction, AIDS Healthcare Found., L.A.; vol. John Huston Awards, Artists' Rights Found., L.A.; vol. Project Angel Food, L.A. Mem. AFTRA, SAG, Am. Speech-Lang.-Hearing Assn. (cert. of clin. competence), Actors Equity Assn., Women in Film (prodr. pub. svc. announcements 1994-96, vol. Crystal awards and Lucy awards), Ind. Feature Film Project/West (vol. programming), Women in Theater, Creative Women of the Arts. Avocations: piano, art, photography, weightlifting, yoga.

ROSNICK, KATHY CONRAD, mathematics educator; b. Mt. Pleasant, Pa., Jan. 19, 1951; d. James Fisher and Leah (Markle) Conrad; m. William A. Rosnick, Aug. 17, 1974; 1 child, Leeann. BA, W.Va. U., 1972; MEd, U. Pitts., 1976. Tchr. Somerset (Pa.) Area Schs., 1973-75, Yough Sch. Dist., Herminie, Pa., 1976-77; tutor Charleroi (Pa.) Area Schs., 1975-76; math. tchr. Mt. Lebanon Sch. Dist., Pitts., 1977—. Mem. Phi Beta Kappa. Avocations: piano, travel, aerobics, collectibles. Home: 195 Summit Dr Belle Vernon PA 15012-9688 Office: Mt Lebanon Sch Dist 155 Cochran Rd Pittsburgh PA 15228-1360

ROSOF, PATRICIA J.F., retired secondary school educator; b. N.Y.C., May 19, 1949; d. Sylvan D. and Charlotte (Fischer) Freeman; m. Alan H. Rosof, Sept. 13, 1970; children: Jeremy, Simon, Ali. BA, NYU, 1970, MA, 1971, PhD, 1978. Cert. tchr. social studies, N.Y. Instr. history Iona Coll., New Rochelle, N.Y., 1978-81; tchr. social studies Profl. Children's Sch., N.Y.C., 1981-82, Hunter Coll. H.S., N.Y.C., 1984—2003; ret., 2003. European history reader Advanced Placement Ednl. Testing Svcs.; adj. asst. prof. Sch. Edn., Pace U., 2003; coll. bd. cons.; adj. assoc. prof. history, Francis Coll., 2004. Co-editor Trends in History, 1978-84, Hunter Outreach, 1988-92; contbr. articles to profl. jours. Internat. Cultural Soc. Korea fellow, 1989; CUNY Women's Rsch. and Devel. Fund grantee, 1993-95; libr. resident rsch. fellow, Am. Philosophical Soc., 2004; Margaret Storrs Grieson scholar, 2006—. Mem. Am. Hist. Assn., Am. Assn. For History Medicine. Avocations: attending concerts, shows and dance performances.

ROSS, A. CATHARINE, biochemist, educator; BS in Zoology, U. Calif., Davis; MS, Cornell U., PhD, 1976. Prof. dept. biochemistry Med. Coll. Pa. State U., University Park, Dorothy Foehr Huck chair in nutrition, 1994—. Recipient Mead-Johnson award, Am. Inst. Nutrition. Mem.: NIH (mem. policy panel), AAAS, NAS (mem. policy panel), Fedn. Am. Socs. Exptl. Biology (mem. policy panel), Am. Soc. Cell Biology, Am. Soc. Nutritional Scis. (Osborne and Mendel award), Phi Kappa Phi, Sigma Xi. Office: Penn State Univ 126 Henderson South University Park PA 16802

ROSS, ALLYNE R., federal judge; b. 1946; BA, Wellesley Coll., 1967; JD cum laude, Harvard Law Sch., 1970. Assoc. Paul, Weiss, Rifkind, Wharton & Garrison, 1971-76; asst. U.S. atty. U.S. Dist. Ct. (N.Y. ea. dist.), 2nd circuit, Brooklyn, 1976-83, chief, appeals div., 1983-86, magistrate judge, 1986-94, dist. judge, 1994—. Mem. Fed. Bar Coun., Bar Assn. City N.Y. Office: US Dist Ct Ea Dist NY 225 Cadman Plz E Rm 252 Brooklyn NY 11201-1818

ROSS, ANNETTE LEE, educational consultant; b. Detroit, May 15, 1940; d. Jesse O. and Sylvia Irene Ross. BS Edn., Ctrl. Mich. U., Mt. Pleasant, 1963; M Edn., Wayne State U., Detroit, 1971. Cert. tchr. Mich. Tchr. Marian H.S., Bloomington, Mich., 1963—64, Macomb K-8 Sch., Mt. Clemens, Mich., 1964—71, Seminole K-8 Sch., Mt. Clemens, 1972—88; ednl. cons. Susan Kovalik & Assocs., Federal Way, Wash., 1988—2006, reflexologist Ctr. Integrative Therapy Spring Lake, Mich., 2006—. Girls basketball coach Seminole Middle Sch., 1978—88, girls volleyball coach, 1978—88, boys golf coach, 1978—88; varsity volleyball coach Mt. Clemens H.S., 1981—88; ptnr. Ctr. Reflexology Therapy, Spring Lake, 2005—. Author: The Way We Were The Way We Can Be, 1989, 2002. Recipient Slovak Republic award, Susan Kovalik & Assocs., 1997. Mem.: LWV. Home: 5970 Avalon Dr #211 Muskegon MI 49444

ROSS, ANNIE LEE, minister, counselor; b. Saluda, SC, Feb. 5, 1933; d. Alonzo and Daisy Bell (Stewart) Robinson; m. Robert L. Ross, Aug. 1957. Diploma, Washington Bapt. Sem., 1978, Automation Acad. Inc., Washington, 1979; DD (hon.), Gospel Ministry, Monicella, Ga., 1979; Doctrine in Ch., Bethany Baptist Ch., 2004. Ordained chaplain Nat. Chaplain Assn., 1979, lic. ministry lic. Christian Ch. Outreach, 1979. Minister New Bethany Bapt. Ch., Washington, 1966—, dir., Sunday sch. tchr., 1966—, tchr. Moments with the Children Sunday sch., 1992—2000; nurse asst. Jesuit Cmty. at Georgetown U., Washington, 1979—89; asst. Tobler Bookstore, Washington, 1986; owner Christian Books and Bibles, Washington, 1986—90. Author: The Works of Annie Lee Ross in the 90's to the Present, 2000. Chaplain Ward 6 Aging Planning Com., Washington, 1998—. Recipient Alumnus award, Washington Bapt. Sem., 1989. Mem.: Washington Bapt. Sem., So. Bapt. Assn. Women's Aux. (pres. Women's Aux. 1986, 1990), Abbey Place Block Club (chairperson 1985—). Democrat. Baptist. Avocations: writing, teaching, singing, preaching. Home: 1166 Abbey Place NE Washington DC 20002 Office: Christian Ch Outreach Ministry 1166 Abbey Place NE Washington DC 20002

ROSS, BEATRICE BROOK, artist; b. NYC, Mar. 31, 1927; d. Alexander and Ray (Tennenbaum) Brook; m. Alexander Ross, Dec. 23, 1945; children: Robert Alan, Kenneth Jay, Stefani Lynn. Student, Hunter Coll., 1943, CCNY, 1944, Bklyn. Mus. Art Sch., 1959-60, 64-65; pupil of Ruben Tam, Wang Chi Yuan, Leo Manso; scholar, Sch. Chinese Brush Work, 1973. Owner, operator Jean Rosenthal Bea Ross Gallery, Jericho, 1961-64; represented by Gillary Gallery, Jericho, N.Y., Patrician Gallery, West Palm Beach, Fla., Lawrence Gallery, Delray Beach, Fla. Founder Birchwood Art League, 1958-63; lectr. bd. edn., Ont., Can., 1972; ad hoc com. with Lucy Lippard Women in Art, 1970-74; presenter in field. Exhbns. include Women in Art, Huntington, NY, 1972, C.W. Post Coll., 1972, 73-76, Guild Hall Mus., East Hampton, 1969-72, Lever House, Inc., 1969-72, J. Walter Thompson Loan Show, 1970, Whitehouse Gallery, 1970, Park Ave. Synagogue, 1970, Locust Valley Ann., 1970, Nat. Arts Club, 1970, Loeb Student Ctr., NYU, 1969, Suffolk Mus., Stony Brook, NY, 1969, 71, Lynn U., Boca Raton, 1992, NAD, 1968, Audubon Artists, 1968, 70, Silvermine Guild, 1968, 71, Port Washington (NY) Libr., 1968, 70, 76, Profl. Artists Guild LI, 1968, Bklyn. Coll., 1968, Huntington Twp. Art League, Cold Spring Harbor, NY, 1967, Gillary Gallery, Jericho, NY, 1966, 68, 70, 72, 79, 83, Hecksher Mus., 1960, 63, 70, Ho. of Reps., 1965, Library of Congress, 1965, Merrick (NY) Gallery, 1963, North Shore Cmty. Art Ctr. ann., Roslyn, NY, 1959, 62, Birchwood Art League, Jericho, NY, 1958, 61-62, Hofstra U., 1960, City Ctr., NYC, 1960, Emily Lowe Gallery, 1960, Nassau Democratic County Com. ann., 1958, R.A.A. Gallery, NYC, 1969-70, 77, Roosevelt Field Art Gallery, Garden City, N., 1958, Boca Raton (Fla.) City Hall, 1991, Bryant Library, Roslyn, NY, 1973, Women's Interart Ctr., NYC, 1974, Wantagh (NY) Libr., 1975, LIU, 1976, NY Tech., 1974, C.W. Post Coll. Schwartz Libr., 1976, St. Johns U., 1976, Union Carbide, NYC, 1977, Harley U. Ctr. Gallery, Adelphi U., 1976, 82, Lincoln

Ctr., NYC, 1978, 82, Gallery 84, NYC, 1981, Jericho Libr., 1984, Donell Libr., NYC, 1991, Am. Properties Inc., Boca Raton, Fla., 1996; represented in pvt. collections, traveling shows in France, Italy and Japan; mus. curated show No. Trust Bank, Boca Mus., Fla., 1992, Nations Bank, Boca Raton Mus., Fla., 1995; author numerous poems. Recipient 1st prize oil Birchwood Art League, 1958; certificate award outstanding contbn. Mid Island Plaza Art League, Hicksville, N.Y., 1961, 2d prize oil, 1962; 1st prize oil, 1970; Benjamin Altman landscape prize N.A.D., 1968; 2d prize Heckscher Mus., Huntington, N.Y., 1970; Benjamin Altman Landscape prize Nat. award Nat. Acad. Design, N.Y.C., 1969, RAA Gallery, 1967-78, Harbor Gallery, Glen Cove, N.Y., 1983-85, Gillary Gallery Jericho, N.Y., 1984, Judge's Recognition award Boca Raton Mus., 1989, others; named to Nat. Women's Hall of Fame; MacDowell fellow, 1975, 80; selected for Unique and Universal South Fla. Artists Slide and Lctr., 1997. Mem. Profl. Artists Guild L.I. (v.p. admissions 1971-74, exec. v.p. 1975-77, 2d prize for group show 1990), Profl. Artists Guild Fla., Boca Raton Mus. Artist Guild, Easthampton Guild-Women in Arts, N.Y. Artists Equity, Nat. Mus. Women in Arts (charter), Gallery 84 (N.Y. 1979-85). Home: 5253 Bolero Cir Delray Beach FL 33484-1302 Office Phone: 561-495-4657.

ROSS, BECKY L., social studies educator; d. Wayne L. and Virigina L. Donaldson; m. Kyle T. Ross, Mar. 26, 1973. BSc, Morningside Coll., Sioux City, Iowa, 2000; BS of Art, Bendictine Coll., Atchison, Kans., 2002. Govt. & pub. rels. office Kans. Ins. Dept., Topeka, 1999—2001; social studies tchr. Sidney Cmty. Schools, Sidney, Iowa, 2002—05, Rock Port RII, Rock Port, Mo., 2006—. Recruitment adv. Theta Chi, Sioux City, Iowa, 2001. Democrat-Npl. Catholic. Avocations: coaching, softball, golf, travel. Office: Rock Port R-II Sch Dist 600 S Nebraska Rock Port MO 64482 Office Phone: 660-744-6296. Office Fax: 660-744-5539. E-mail: bross@rockport.k12.mo.us.

ROSS, BETSY R., psychotherapist; d. David G. Neustein and Reva R. Fischer; m. Lawrence I. Ross, Sept. 24, 1994; children: Adam, Emma. MSW, Fordham U., N.Y.C., 1992. Lic. clin. social worker (gen. practice) Mass., 1995, cert. group therapist Mass., 2004. Psychotherapist Norwood (Mass.) Hosp., 1995—99, HRI Psychiatric Hosp., Brookline, Mass., 1996—2000, Whitman (Mass.) Counseling Ctr., 2003—05. Pvt. practice, Mass., 1995—. Contbr. articles to profl. jours. Recipient Ann Walsh award, Fordham U. Grad. Sch. Social Work, 1992. Mem.: NASW, N.E. Soc. Group Psychotherapy. Office: PO Box 170 Sharon MA 02067 Office Phone: 781-784-0905. Business E-Mail: betsyross1@comcast.net.

ROSS, CONNIE L., music educator; b. Pratt, Kans., Nov. 5, 1952; d. Eugene Haile and Alta Ross. BA, Mid-Am. Nazarene U., 1975; MusM in Edn., Fort Hays State U., Kans., 1982. Vocal music tchr. USD 483, 1975—82; elem. vocal music tchr. USD 443, Dodge City, Kans., 1982—. Pvt. piano tchr. Ch. pianist & accompanist. Mem.: NEA, Music Edn. Nat. Conf., Delta Kappa Gamma (co-chmn. music com.). Home: 2805 Buffalo Dr Dodge City KS 67801

ROSS, DEBRA BENITA, marketing executive, jewelry designer; b. Carbondale, Ill., May 1, 1956; d. Bernard Harris and Marian (Frager) R. BS, U. Ill., 1978; MS, U. Wis., 1979. Dir. mktg. Ambion Devel., Inc., Northbrook, Ill., 1983-89, Fitness Horizons, Inc., Northbrook, 1989-91, v.p. mktg., 1991-97; owner Benita Ross Designs, Northbrook, 1992—. Home: 1853 Mission Hills Ln Northbrook IL 60062-5760

ROSS, DIANA (DIANA ERNESTINE EARLE ROSS), singer, actress, entertainer, fashion designer; b. Detroit, Mar. 26, 1944; d. Fred and Ernestine R.; m. Robert Ellis Silberstein, Jan. 1971 (div. 1976); children: Rhonda, Tracee, Chudney; m. Arne Naess, Oct. 23, 1985 (div. 2000, dec. 2004); children: Ross Arne, Evan Olaf. Pres. Diana Ross Enterprises, Inc., Anaid Film Prodns., Inc., RTC Mgmt. Corp., Chondee Inc., Rosstown, Rossville, music pub. Started in Detroit as mem. the Primettes; lead singer until 1969, Diana Ross and the Supremes; solo artist, 1969—; albums include Diana Ross, 1970, 76, Everything Is Everything, 1971, I'm Still Waiting, 1971, Lady Sings The Blues, 1972, Touch Me In The Morning, 1973, Original Soundtrack of Mahogany, 1975, Baby It's Me, 1977, The Wiz, 1978, Ross, 1978, 83, The Boss, 1979, Diana, 1981, To Love Again, 1981, Why Do Fools Fall In Love?, 1981, Silk Electric, 1982, Endless Love, 1982, Swept Away, 1984, Eaten Alive, 1985, Chain Reaction, 1986, Diana's Duets, 1987, Workin' Overtime, 1989, Red Hot Rhythm and Blues, 1987, Surrender, 1989, Ain't No Mountain High Enough, 1989, The Force Behind the Power, 1991, Stolen Moment: The Lady Sings.Jazz & Blues, 1993, Musical Memories Forever, 1993, The Remixes, 1994, A Very Special Season, 1994, Making Spirits Bright, 1994, Take Me Higher, 1995, Voice of Love, 1996, Gift of Love, 1996, The Greatest, 1998, The Real Thing, 1998, Every Day is a New Day, 1999, Love From.Diana Ross, 2001, The #1's, 2004, Complete Symphony, 2004, The Blue Album, 2006, I Love You, 2006; films include Lady Sings the Blues, 1972, Mahogany, 1975, The Wiz, 1978; NBC-TV spl., An Evening With Diana Ross, 1977, Diana, 1981, numerous others; TV movie Out of Darkness, 1994; author: Secrets of a Sparrow, 1993, Diana Ross: Going Back, 2002, Upside Down: Wrong Turns, Right Turns and the Road Ahead. Recipient citation V.P. Humphrey for efforts on behalf Pres. Johnson's Youth Opportunity Program, citation Mrs. Martin Luther King and Rev. Abernathy for contbn. to SCLC cause, awards Billboard, Cash Box and Record World as worlds outstanding singer, Grammy award, 1970, Female Entertainer Yr. NAACP, 1970, Cue award as Entertainer Yr., 1972, Golden Apple award, 1972, Gold medal award Photoplay, 1972, Antoinette Perry award, 1977, nominee as Best Actress Yr. Lady Sings the Blues Motion Picture Acad. Arts and Scis., 1972, Golden Globe award, 1972, BET (Black Entertainment Television) Walk Fame award, 1999, Heroes award, NARAS, NY Chpt., 2000; named to Rock and Roll Hall Fame, 1988. Office: c/o Motown Records 825 8th Ave New York NY 10019*

ROSS, DONNA DENICE, elementary school educator; b. Duncan, Okla., Sept. 18, 1957; d. Mac Bradley and LaDonna Yvonne McKinzie; children: Brett Matthew, Lindsay Michelle. BS, Kans. State U., Manhattan, 1980. Cert. tchr. Kans., 1980, Okla., 1996. Reading specialist Title 1, Custer Hill Elem. Sch., Ft. Riley, Kans., 1980—81; tchr. music Clarksville Acad., Tenn., 1989—92, tchr. 2d grade, 1992—95; tchr. music Sullivan Village Elem. Sch., Lawton, Okla., 1996—. Tchr. piano, Lawton, Okla., 1996; dir. spl. programs and performance groups Sullivan Village Elem., Lawton, Okla., 1996—; mem. Lawton Elem. showcase com. Lawton Pub. Schs., Okla., 2002—. Dir., choreographer numerous plays and musicals; singer: Cameron Singers, Cameron U. Mem.: Music Educators Nat. Conf., Shortgrass Artist Assn. (artist 1983—85), Sweet Adelines (singer 1985—87). Mem. Ch. Of Christ. Avocations: music, art. Office Phone: 580-355-0800.

ROSS, ELLYN N., educational association administrator, consultant; b. Hackensack, N.J., Apr. 2, 1949; d. Peter Henry and June Ellyn Naclerio; m. David Bradley Ross, Mar. 16, 1996; children: Joshua David, Jesse Deacon, Janie Dianne, Jonathan Dwain. BS, Fla. State U., Tallahassee, Fla., 1971; MS, Fla. Internat. U., Miami, Fla., 1976; PhD, U. Pitts., Pitts. Pa., 2000. Cert. Orientation and Mobility Specialist Acad. for Cert. of Vision Rehab. and Edn., 1999, profl. tchr., visually impaired Commonwealth of Pa., 2001. Tchr. of students with visual impairment(s) Dade County Pub. Sch., Miami, Fla., 1971—76, tchr. of students with learning disabilities, 1977—78, tchr. of students with visual impairment(s), 1978—88; ednl. specialist Dade-Monroe Diagnostic and Resource Ctr., Miami, Fla., 1976—77; coord., instrnl. resource svcs. Fla. Instrnl. Materials Ctr. for the Visually Impaired, Tampa, Fla., 1988—92; orientation and mobility specialist Susquehanna Assn. for the Blind and Vision Impaired, Lancaster, Pa., 1996—97; adj. faculty mem. Pa. Coll. of Optometry, Phila., 1996—2003; tchr. and orientation and mobility specialist/students with visual impairment(s) Lancaster-Lebanon Intermediate Unit 13, Lancaster, Pa., 1997—2000; ednl. cons. Pa. Tng. and Tech. Assistance Network, Harrisburg, Pa., 2000—. Orientation and mobility cert. bd. mem. Acad. for Cert. of Vision Rehab. and Edn. Profl., Tucson, 2001—02; profl. workshop presentation (invited speaker) Weekend with the Experts, Tampa, Fla., 2003; profl. presentation (juried) Coun. for Exceptional Children Ann. Conv., Charlotte, NC, 1999, Mpls., 98, Salt Lake City, 97, PA Spring Conf./Field of Visual Impairment, Grantville, Pa., 1996, numerous confs. in field. Author: (doctoral dissertation) Braille Reading Instruction for Beginning Readers: Perspectives Regarding Current Practice (Outstanding Dissertation of the Yr., 2000). Recipient Assoc. Master Tchr., State of Fla., 1984—87, Superlative Academic Performance, U. Pitts., Honors Convocation, 1996; Alumni Doctoral fellow, U. Pitts., 1995. Mem.: Assn. Direct Instruction, Assn. Direct Instrn., Coun. for Exceptional Children, Divsn. Visual Impairments (dir. exec. bd. 1991—93, student gov. 1993—95, dir. exec. bd. 1996—98, treas. 1998—2000, dir. exec. bd. 2000—02, pres.-elect 2004—), Internat. Dyslexia Assn., Assn. for Edn. and Rehab. of the Blind and Visually Impaired (south regional rep. (fla.) 1973—74), Coun. for Exceptional Children, Divsn. on Learning Disabilities. Avocations: piano, harp, travel, reading, needlecrafts. Home: 106 Stone Hedge Ct Lebanon PA 17042-7818 Office: PA Tng/Techl Assistance Network 6340 Flank Dr Ste 600 Harrisburg PA 17112-2764 Personal E-mail: ellynross@comcast.net.

ROSS, EUNICE LATSHAW, retired judge; b. Bellevue, Pa., Oct. 13, 1923; d. Richard Kelly and Eunice (Weidner) Latshaw; m. John Anthony Ross, May 29, 1943 (dec. Jan. 1978); 1 child, Geraldine Ross Coleman. BS, U. Pitts., 1945, LLB, 1951. Bar: Pa. 1952. Atty. Pub. Health Law Rsch. Project, Pitts., 1951-52; atty. jud. asst., law clk. Ct. Common Pleas Allegheny County, Pitts., 1952-70, dir. family divsn., 1970-72, judge, 1972-96, Commonwealth Ct. Pa., 1997—2004. Adj. law prof. U. Pitts., 1967-73; mem. Bd. Jud. Inquiry and Rev., Commonwealth of Pa., 1984-89, Gov's Justice Commn., 1972-78; mem. orphan's ct. rules com. Supreme Ct. Pa., 1998—2005. Author: (with others) Survey of Pa. Public Health Laws, 1952, Justice, 1995, Lötschers of Latterbach, Mennonite Heritage Mag., 2003; co-author: Will Contests, 1992; contbr. articles to law publs. Mem. exec. com. bd. trustees U. Pitts., 1980—86, bd. visitors Law Sch., 1985—, bd. visitors Sch. Health, 1986—98; mem. adv. bd. Animal Friends, Pitts., 1973—98; committeewoman for 14th ward, vice chmn. Pitts. Dem. com., 1972; bd. dirs. The Program, Pitts., 1983—87, Pitts. History and Landmarks Found., West Pa. Hist. Soc., West Pa. Conservancy. Named Girls Scouts Woman of Yr., Pitts. coun. Girl Scouts U.S.A., 1975, Alumni of Yr., U. Pitts. Law Sch., 2001; recipient Disting. Alumna award, U. Pitts., 1973, Medal of Recognition, 1987, Alumni award, U. Pitts. Sch. of Law, 2001, Susan B. Anthony award, Women's Bar Assn. Western Pa., 1993, Probate and Trusts award, 1994, cert. of achievement, Pa. Fedn. Women's Clubs, 1975, 1977. Mem.: ABA, Allegheny County Bar Assn. (vice chmn., exec. com. young lawyers sect. 1958—59), Pa. Trial Judges Conf., Scribes, Order of Coif. Home: 1204 Denniston Ave Pittsburgh PA 15217-1329 Personal E-mail: rossdent@comcast.net.

ROSS, GLORIA JEAN, artist; b. Terrell, Tex., June 24, 1943; d. John Frederick and Shirley Joe (West) Williams; m. Winston Byrd Ross, Aug. 24, 1963; 1 child, John Winston. BS, Tex. Woman's U., 1965; MS, U. North Tex., 1981, MFA, 1983. Cert. tchr. Art tchr. West Springfield H.S., Fairfax, Va., 1967-70, Tucker (Ga.) H.S., 1970-72, Westminster Sch., Atlanta, 1972-73; art/adult edn. tchr. San Jose (Calif.) Sch. Sys., 1973-74, Virginia Beach (Va.) Schs., 1975; adult edn. dir. Denton (Tex.) Pub. Schs., 1983-85; program dir. Children's Arts and Ideas Found., Dallas, 1985-88; continuing edn. coord. Tex. Woman's U., Denton, 1988-90; freelance artist Plano, Tex., 1990—. One person shows include U. North Tex. Art Gallery, Denton, 1983, Irving Cultural Ctr., Tex., 1986, Trammel Crow Ctr. Gallery, Dallas, 1988, Tex. Woman's U., Denton, Tex., 1990, Eleven East Ashland, Phoenix, 1991, Wichita Falls (Tex.) Art Assn. Gallery, 1992, Del Rio (Tex.) Arts Ctr., 1992; exhibited in group shows Irving (Tex.) Arts Ctr., 1985, Cedar Valley C.C., Cedar Hill, Tex., 1990, Paige-Hansen Art Gallery, Dallas, 1994, Arlington (Tex.) Mus. Art, 1995, Plano (Tex.) Cultural Arts Ctr., 1995, 96, Eastfield C.C., Mesquite, Tex., 1995; represented in collections Hyatt Hotel, Cancun, Mex., Renaissance Hotel, Washington, Harris Hosp., Ft. Worth, Bus. Interiors, Irving, EMSI, Dallas, Oracle Corp., Houston, Pitts Energy, Houston, The Mus. of Photography, Riverside, Calif., Pizza Inn Japan, Texins Credit Union, Richardson, Tex., Capstead Mortgage, Ft. Worth, Northern Telecom, Newark, Equitable Ins., Dallas, Ga. Street Hotel, Indpls., Fed. Depository Regional Office, Dallas, Harris Hosp., Ft. Worth, Butler and Binion, Dallas, MEPC, Dallas, Trinity Med. Ctr., Ft. Worth Gehad Investments, Dallas, Nat. Athletic Assn., Dallas, NCNB, Dallas, others. Founder, bd. mem. Dallas (Tex.) Women's Caucus for Art. 1983-90, first pres., 1983. Recipient Fellowship award Mid-Am. Arts Alliance, Kansas, Mich., 1992. Mem. So. Graphics Assn. Democrat.

ROSS, IVY, apparel executive, artist; Completed programs in indsl. design, Syracuse U. Sch. Design; completed programs in jewelry design, Fashion Inst. Tech.; profl. mgmt. development program, Harvard Bus. Sch. Positions with Coach, Liz Claiborne, Calvin Klein, Swatch Watch, Victoria's Secret, Bausch & Lomb; sr. v.p., design Mattel, Inc.; exec. v.p., product design and development, Old Navy Brand Gap, Inc., 2004—. Lectr. and workshops on a variety of topics RI Sch. Design, Phila. Coll. Art, Fashion Inst. Tech., Cooper-Hewitt Mus. and the Montreal Visual Arts Ctr. Artist, metal work in jewelry (permanent collections) Smithsonian Inst., Victoria and Albert Mus. London, Cooper-Hewitt Mus. NY; contbr. chapters to books. Named one of 25 Masters of Innovation, BusinessWeek; recipient Women in Design award, Diamond Internat. award; Nat. Endowment for the Arts grant. Office: Gap Inc Old Navy Divsn 2 Folsom St San Francisco CA 94105*

ROSS, JANE ARLENE, music educator; b. Uniontown, Pa., July 19, 1945; d. Earl Frank Diamond and Iva Jane Gower; m. Orval Jones Ross, June 17, 1967 (dec. Sept. 2003); 1 child, Elizabeth Jane. BS in Music Edn., Indiana U. of Pa., 1967; MusM in Music Edn., U. Akron, 1985, postgrad., Oberlin Coll., Ashland U., U. Akron. Music tchr. - elem. Fairview Park (Ohio) City Schs., 1967—70; music tchr.-jr. h.s. Medina (Ohio) City Schs., 1970—76, music tchr. - elem., 1979—2000; adj. prof. Ashland (Ohio) U., 2001—. Handbell choir cons. various area chs., Medina, 1994—99; guest clinician U. Akron, Ohio, 1986, Medina Coutny Schs., 1990; curriculum writer Medina City Schs., 1973. Contbr. articles to profl. jours. Organist, choir dir. Faith United Presbyn. Ch., Lakewood, Ohio, 1967—71, United Ch. of Christ, Congl., Medina, 1972—79, Mt. Zwingli United Ch. of Christ, Wadsworth, Ohio, 1983—93; dir. music ministries First Christian Ch., Wadsworth, 2001—. Grantee, Rockefeller Bros. Fund, N.Y.C., 1984; scholar, Martha Holden Jennings Found., Cleve., 1988. Mem.: Am. Guild Organists, Am. Guild English Handbell Ringers, Music Educators Nat. Conf. (nationally registered), Medina County Ret. Tchrs. Assn. (life), Ohio Ret. Tchrs. Assn. (life), Kappa Delta Pi, Delta Omicron (life). Democrat. Avocations: reading, collecting bells, old hymnals and music boxes, needlecrafts, travel. Office: First Christian Ch 116 E Boyer St Wadsworth OH 44281 E-mail: jross@wadsnet.com.

ROSS, JEAN M., think-tank executive; Grad., U. Calif., Santa Cruz; M in City and Regional Planning, U. Calif., Berkeley. Asst. rsch. dir. Svc. Employees Internat. Union, Washington; sr. cons. Assembly Human Svcs.; prin. cons. Assembly Revenue and Taxation Com.; exec. dir. Calif. Budget Project, Sacramento, 1994—. Mem. exec. com. Calif. Governance Consensus Project; bd. mem. Inst. on Taxation and Econ. Policy, Washington; mem. adv. com. Calif. Franchise Tax Bd.; spkr. in field. Contbr. articles to profl. jours. Sr. fellow, UCLA Sch. Pub. Policy and Social Rsch., 2000—01. Office: California Budget Project 1107 9th St Ste 310 Sacramento CA 95814-3608

ROSS, JEANNE NMI, psychologist; b. Chgo., Jan. 10, 1923; d. Joseph Pacwa and (Prendota) Tillie; m. Milton Jaeger (dec.); m. Gunther Rothenberg (dec.). BA with hons., U. Ill., 1952, MA, 1954; EdD, U. N.Mex., 1969. Lic. adminstr. Calif., 1977, Ariz., 1977, cert. sch. psychologist Calif., 1977. Tchr. Alamogordo (N.Mex.) Pub. Schs., 1954—55, Rantoul Pub. Schs., Ill., 1954—59; instr. So. Ill. U., Carbondale, Ill., 1960—63; clin. dir. N.Mex. Girl's Sch., Albuquerque, 1968—69; sch. counselor Albuquerque (N.Mex.) Pub. Schs., 1969—71; dir. project, head title III Am. Indian program Sacaton (Ariz.) Sch. Dist., 1972—73; sch. psychologist Vista (Calif.) Unified Sch. Dist., 1977—87, ret., 1987. Contbr. articles to profl. jours. Pvt. women's corps. U.S. Army, 1944—45. Recipient Chi Omega award, U. Ill., 1952, award, AAUW, 1967. Mem.: Calif. Ret. Tchrs. Assn., Phi Kappa Phi (scholarship 1952), Alpha Lambda Delta (scholarship 1950). Independent. Avocations: photography, painting, travel, theater, opera, music.

ROSS, JENNIFER JO, science educator; b. Detroit, Apr. 8, 1951; d. Joseph BoBo and Florence Honora Neal; m. Robert Ashton Ross, Jan. 29, 1972; children: Joseph Ashton, Daniel Adam. BLS magna cum laude, Hillsdale Coll., Hillsdale, Mich., 1973; MS, Kennesaw State U., Ga., 2002; postgrad., Brenau U., Gainsville, Ga., 2004—05. Cert. elem. tchr. Ga., 2006. 7th and 8th grade sci., reading, and math. tchr. Griffin Mid. Sch., Smyrna, Ga., 1984—88; 7th grade sci., social studies, english, and reading tchr. Pine Mt. Mid. Sch., Kennesaw, Ga., 1988—2000; 7th grade life sci. and social studies tchr. of gifted students Dodgen Mid. Sch., Marietta, Ga., 2000—01; hs phys. sci. and mid. sch. earth sci. tchr. Woodstock Mid. Sch., Ga., 2001—; assoc., adj. prof. Kennesaw State U., 2006—. Student mem. Kennesaw State Adv. Bd., Ga., 2001—02; coord. Sci. Olympiad, Woodstock, Ga., 2004—05; team leader Pine Mt. Mid. and Woodstock Mid. Sch., 1995—2005. Coord. at sch. United Way, Woodstock, 2005; sch. coord. Mar. of Dimes, Woodstock, 2001—06. Grantee, ESF, 2002, Celestial Sphere, GSTA, 2001, Cobb Co., 1999; scholar HOPE scholar, Ga., 1998—2002. Mem.: Kappa Deltat Pi. Avocations: sailing, walking, reading, travel, gardening. Home: 1209 Meadowbrook Ln Woodstock GA 30189 Office: Woodstock Middle School 2000 Towne Lake Hills S Dr Woodstock GA 30189 Business E-Mail: jennifer.ross@cherokee.k12.ga.us.

ROSS, JO ANN, media buyer; b. Bklyn., June 8, 1953; d. James Patrick and Rita Marie (McDonnell) R.; m. Michael Edward Zelman, Nov. 3, 1984. BA in Govt. and Pub. Adminstrn., Am. U., Washington, 1975. Negotiator Boxell & Jacobs, NYC, 1980-84; supr. Young & Rubicam, NYC, 1984; sr. negotiator Bozell, Jacobs, Kenyon & Eckhardt, NYC, 1984-85, v.p., 1985-88; sr. v.p. Bozell, Inc., NYC, 1988-89; account exec. ABC TV Network, NYC, 1989; v.p. Olympic sales CBS, 1992—2002, pres. network sales, 2002—. Named one of Most Powerful Women in Entertainment, Hollywood Reporter, 2005; recipient Woman of Yr. award, Women in Sports and Events, 2005. Mem. Am. Assn. Advt. Agencies (broadcast and program com. 1988—). Avocations: ballet, exercise. Office: CBS 51 West 52nd St New York NY 10019*

ROSS, JOAN STUART, artist, art educator; b. Boston, Sept. 21, 1942; d. John Stuart and Lulu Margery (Nelson) Ross. BA, Conn. Coll., 1964; postgrad., Yale U., 1964-65; MA, U. Iowa, 1967, MFA, 1968; Advanced Cert. in Poetry, U. Wash., 1996. Cert. tchr. Wash. Instr. painting, printmaking Seattle Art Mus., 1992, Edmonds (Wash.) C.C., 1992-96, Pratt Fine Arts Ctr., Seattle, 1992-96, North Seattle C.C., 1996—. Mem. artist in city program Seattle Arts Commn., 1979—81; mem. new proposals program King County Arts Commn., 1977, 80. One-woman shows include Seattle Art Mus., 1981, 1982, Karl Bornstein Gallery, Sant Monica, 1982, Surrey (B.C., Can.) Art Gallery, 1982, Lawrence Gallery, Portland, Oreg., 1987, 1988, Foster/White Gallery, Seattle, 1981, 1983, 1985, 1987, 1989, 1990, Skagit Valley Coll., Mt. Vernon, Wash., 1990, Green River CC, Auburn, Wash., 1985, 1990, 1004 Gallery, Port Townsend, Wash., 1993, Grover/Thurston Gallery, Seattle, 1991, 1993, 1995, Friesen Gallery, 1997, others, exhibited in more than 200 group and juried shows. Mem. Bumbershoot Festival Commn., Seattle, 1985—91, Seattle Arts Commn., 1981—85; bd. dirs. N.W. Women's Caucus Arts. Recipient Bowen award, Seattle Art Mus., 1981; Fulbright-Hays Travel grantee, Vietnam, 2005. Mem.: N.W. Inst. Architecture and Urban Studies Italy (Rome fellow 1993), Book Arts Guild, Seattle Print Arts, N.W. Print Coun. Office: North Seattle CC 3NC 2407 C/Art Dept 9600 College Way N Seattle WA 98103 Office Phone: 206-528-4536. Business E-Mail: jross@sccd.ctc.edu.

ROSS, JULIETTE, mathematics educator; b. Ogdensburg, N.Y. d. Ernie and Rosemarie Jeneault; m. Kevin C. Ross, July 2, 1994; children: Colin, Justin, Shelby. BA in Math., SUNY, Albany, 1991; M, Potsdam State U., N.Y., 1996. Tchr. math Adirondack H.S., Boonville, NY, 1992—96, Ogdensburg Free Acad., 1996—. Chair math. dept. Ogdensburg Free Acad. Mem.: Nat. Coun. Tchrs. Math.

ROSS, JUNE ROSA PITT, biologist, educator; b. Taree, NSW, Australia, May 2, 1931; came to U.S., 1957; d. Bernard and Adeline Phillips; m. Charles Alexander, June 27, 1959. BSc with honors, U. Sydney, New S. Wales, Australia, 1953, PhD, 1959, DSc, 1974. Rsch. assoc. Yale U., New Haven, 1959—60, U. Ill., Urbana, 1960—65, Western Wash. U., Bellingham, 1965—67, assoc. prof., 1967—70, prof. biology, 1970—2003, prof. emeritus, 2004—, chair dept. biology, 1989—90. Pres. Western Wash. U. Faculty Senate, Bellingham, 1984-85; conf. host Internat. Bryozoology Assn., 1986. Author (with others): A Textbook of Entomology, 1982, Geology of Coal, 1984; editor (assoc.): Palaios, 1985—89; contbr. 150 articles to profl. jours. Recipient J. Wolfensohn Award of Excellence Sydney U. Grad. Union of N.Am., 1995, P. and R. Olscamp Outstanding Rsch. award Western Wash. U., 1986; NSF grantee. Mem.: Internat. Bryozoology Assn. (pres. 1992—95), The Paleontol. Soc. (councillor 1984—86, treas. 1987—93), Australian Marine Scis. Assn., U.K. Marine Biol. Assn. (life). Avocations: hiking, classical music. Office: Western Wash U Dept Biology Bellingham WA 98225-9160 Office Phone: 360-650-3634. E-mail: ross@fire.biol.wwu.edu.

ROSS, KAREN, information technology executive; Founder, pres. Turn-Key Solutions, 1985—90; founder, prin. owner, pres., CEO Sharp Decisions, N.Y.C., 1990—. Office: Sharp Decisions 55 W 39th St 4th Fl New York NY 10018

ROSS, KAREN LEE HROMYAK, retired school psychologist; d. George Frank and Laina Dorothy (Luoma) Hromyak; m. Richard Ross (div.); m. William H. Uehlinger (div.); m. Carl Eugene Weiselberg (dec.); 1 child, Wendy Kay Weiselberg White. BS in Home Econs. Edn., Ohio State U., Columbus, 1961; MS in Edn., Westminster Coll., New Wilmington, Pa., 1963; postgrad., Ohio State U., Columbus, 1963—67, MS in Sch. Psychology, 1973; postgrad., Walden U., Mpls., 1974, Youngstown State U., Ohio, 1976—88, Ashland U., 2001. Cert. sch. psychologist. Home econs. tchr. Warren and Brookfield Schs., Ohio, 1961—63; prof. psychology Youngstown State U., 1968—78; owner antique and gift shop Karen's Store, 1989—2001; outpatient therapist David Lawrence Mental Health Ctr., Naples, Fla., 1990—91; psycholotist Collier County Pub. Schs., Naples, 1990—2000, Erie, Huron, Ottawa Edn. Svc. Ctr., Sandusky, Ohio, 2000—01, Covington Schs., Covington, Ky., 2001—02; counselor Franklin County Schs., Frankfort, Ky., 2002—03; ret., 2003. Mem. Ohio Educators Polit. Action Com., 1986—90; co-chmn. Dukakis Presdl. Campaign Hdqrs., Warren, Ohio, 1988; del. Nat. Dem. Confention, Atlanta, 1988. Recipient Action award, Northeastern Ohio Tchrs. Assn., 1989, Svc. award, Ohio Sec. of State Sherrod Brown, 1989. Mem.: NEA (del.), Ohio Edn. Assn. (life), Ohio State U. Alumni Assn. (chmn. exec. com. scholarship com. 1998—2000, Svc. award 1984—89), Phi Upsilon Omicron, Delta Kappa Gamma (pres., nat. del.), Psi Chi. Methodist. Avocations: antiques, growing orchids, travel, crafts. Home: 1156 Surrey Pointe Dr SW Warren OH 44484-2800

ROSS, KATHLEEN ANNE, academic administrator; b. Palo Alto, Calif., July 1, 1941; d. William Andrew and Mary Alberta (Wilburn) Ross. BA, Ft. Wright Coll., 1964; MA, Georgetown U., 1971; PhD, Claremont Grad. U., 1979; LLD (hon.), Alverno Coll. Milw., 1990, Dartmouth Coll., 1991, Seattle U., 1992, Pomona Coll., 1993, U. Notre Dame, 1999, Gonzaga U., 1999; LHD (hon.), Whitworth Coll., 1992, Coll. New Rochelle, 1998, Carroll Coll., 2003, Pacific Luth. U., 2004, U. Portland, 2006. Cert. tchr. Wash. Secondary tchr. Holy Names Acad., Spokane, Wash., 1964-70; dir. rsch. and planning Province Holy Names, Wash. State, 1972-73; v.p. acads. Ft. Wright Coll., Spokane, 1973-81; rsch. asst. to dean Claremont Grad. Sch., Calif., 1977-78; assoc. faculty mem. Harvard U., Cambridge, Mass., 1981; pres. Heritage U., Toppenish, Wash., 1981—. Cons. Wash. State Holy Names Schs., 1971-73; coll. accrediting assn. evaluator N.W. Assn. Schs. and Colls., Seattle, 1975—; dir. Holy Names Coll., Oakland, Calif., 1979—; cons. Yakama Indian Nation, Toppenish, 1975—; speaker, cons. in field. Author: (with others) Multicultural

Pre-School Curriculum, 1977, A Crucial Agenda: Improving Minority Student Success, 1989; Cultural Factors in Success of American Indian Students in Higher Education, 1978. Chmn. Internat. 5-Yr. Convocation of Sisters of Holy Names, Montreal, 1981, 96; TV Talk show host Spokane Coun. of Chs., 1974-76; mem. Nat. Congl. Adv. Com. on Student Fin. Assistance, 2002-06. Named Yakima Herald Rep. Person of Yr., 1987, MacArthur fellow, 1997; recipient E.K. and Lillian F. Bishop Founds. Youth Leader of Yr. award, 1986, Disting. Citizenship Alumna award, Claremont Grad. Sch., 1986, Golden Aztec award, Wash. Human Devel., 1989, Harold W. McGraw Edn. prize, 1989, John Carroll awrd, Georgetown U., 1991, Holy Names medal, Ft. Wright Coll., 1981, Pres.'s medal, Estern Wash. U., 1994, First Ann. Leadership award, Region VIII Coun. Advancement and Support Edn., 1993, Wash. State Medal of Merit, 1995, Lifetime Achievement award, Yakima YWCA, 2001, numerous grants for projects in multicultural higher edn., 1974—. Mem. Nat. Assn. Ind. Colls. and Univs., Soc. Intercultural Edn., Tng. and Rsch., Sisters of Holy Names of Jesus and Mary-SNJM. Roman Catholic. Office: Heritage U Office of Pres 3240 Fort Rd Toppenish WA 98948-9562 Office Phone: 509-865-8600.

ROSS, KATHRYN AMIE, psychologist; b. Miami Beach, Fla., Dec. 30, 1973; d. Nancy Lowenthal Ross-Bennett and Jonathan Michael Bennett (Stepfather), James Eli Ross; m. David Scully Jr., Apr. 6, 2002. BS with honors, U. of Fla., 1995; MS, Nova Southeastern U., Ft. Lauderdale, Fla., 1996; Psy. D., Nova Southeastern U., 2000. Lic. psychologist Fla., 2001. Psychology intern Dallas Child and Family Guidance Ctr., Dallas, 1999—2000; psychology resident Children's Psychology Assn., Weston, Fla., 2000—01, psychologist, assoc. dir., 2001—02; pvt. practice psychology Ft. Lauderdale, 2002—. Vol. Gilda's Club of South Fla., Ft. Lauderdale, Fla., 1997—99; mem. Pine Island Ridge Phase A-1 Condominiums, Davie, Fla., 2002—02. Recipient Hon. Mention, Gt. Women in Journalism, 1990. Mem.: APA (assoc.; mem. 1995—), Golden Key. Achievements include research in comparing symptoms of post-traumatic stress disorder and attention-deficit/hyperactivity disorder. Avocations: travel, exercise, yoga, sports. Office: Kathryn Ross PsyD PA PO Box 551363 Davie FL 33355 Office Phone: 954-801-3231. E-mail: drkathyross@yahoo.com.

ROSS, LESA MOORE, quality assurance professional; b. New Orleans, Jan. 25, 1959; d. William Frank and Carolyn West Moore; m. Mark Neal Ross, Nov. 30, 1985; children: Sarah Ann, Jacquelyne Caroline. BS in Engring., U. N.C., Charlotte, 1981; MBA in Quality and Reliability Mgmt., U. North Tex., 1991; MS in Reliability Engring., U. Md., 2004. Seismic qualification engr. Duke Power Co., Charlotte, N.C., 1981-82; quality assurance engr. Tex. Instruments Inc., Lewisville, Tex., 1982-91; compliance mgr. Am. Med. Electronics, Inc., 1992-93; owner Ross Quality Cons., 1993-95; customer quality assurance sect. mgr. Hitachi Semiconductor (Am.) Inc., 1995-96; v.p. quality Ross Networking Cons. Inc., Flower Mound, Tex., 1996—. Bd. dirs. Greater Lewisville YMCA, 2000—03. Recipient Nat. Sci. Found. Rsch. Grant, U. N.C., Charlotte, 1980. Mem. Am. Soc. Quality Control (cert. quality engr., quality auditor, reliability engr., cert. quality technician, cert. quality mgr., sec. Dallas sect. 1994-95, chair-elect Dallas sect. 1995-96, chair 1996-97), Zeta Tau Alpha (pres. 1984-85). Avocations: crafts, cross-stitching, reading, travel. Home and Office: 4925 Wolf Creek Trl Flower Mound TX 75028-1955 E-mail: Lross@rnc-inc.com.

ROSS, LISA SIMS, special education educator; b. Jackson, Miss., Feb. 14, 1952; d. Johnie Mack and Elizabeth Crane Sims; m. Richard C. Ross, Aug. 16, 1974 (div. Mar. 1996); children: Jason Conn, Robert Sims. BS, U. So. Miss., 1974, EdM, 1996. Cert. tchr. Miss. Spl. edn. tchr. Jackson County Sch., Wade, Miss., 1974—75, Holly Springs (Miss.) Sch., 1975—76, Lanar County Schs., Purvis, Miss., 1976—93, Richton (Miss.) City Sch., 1995—99; educator Ellisville (Miss.) State Sch., 1999—. Mem.: Miss. Assn. Educators, Kappa Delta Alumnae (pres. 1998—99), U. So. Miss. Alumni Assn. Baptist. Avocations: reading, exercise, shopping. Home: 2309 Adeline St Hattiesburg MS 39401 Office: Ellisville State Sch 1101 Hwy 11 South Ellisville MS 39437 Office Phone: 601-477-6245.

ROSS, LORI, radio personality; b. Delta, Ohio, May 14; Radio host Sta. WMBI-AM, Chgo. Avocations: photography, being outside, travel. Office: WMBI 820 LaSalle Blvd Chicago IL 60610

ROSS, MADELYN ANN, academic administrator, newspaper editor; b. Pitts., June 26, 1949; d. Mario Charles and Rose Marie (Mangieri) R. BA, Indiana U. of Pa., 1971; MA, SUNY-Albany, 1972. Reporter Pitts. Press, 1972-78, asst. city editor, 1978-82, spl. assignment editor, 1982-83, mng. editor, 1983-93, Pitts. Post-Gazette, 1993—2005; assoc. vice chancellor U. Pitts., 2005—. Bd. dirs. PG Pub. Co.; instr. Community Coll. Allegheny County, 1974-81; Pulitzer Prize juror, 1989, 90. Mem. Task Force Leadership Pitts., 1985-92; v.p. Old Newsboys Charity Fund; bd. dirs. Dapper Dan Charity. Mem. Am. Soc. Newspaper Editors, Press Club of Western Pa. (pres.), Internat. Women's Forum. Democrat. Roman Catholic. Avocations: tennis, piano, organ. Office: U Pitts 424 Craig Hall Craig St Pittsburgh PA 15260

ROSS, MARIE ELISA, elementary school educator; b. Flushing, N.Y., Aug. 20, 1954; d. Louis Joseph and Selma Irene (Burbank) Cafarchio; m. Philip J. Corman, Aug. 11, 1973 (div. Oct. 1990); children: Joshua, Marina, Meghan; m. Sherman P. Ross, July 28, 1991; children: Patrick, Peter, Tyler. BA in Elem. Edn., Notre Dame Coll., N.H., 1989. Tchr. Grace Christian Sch., Merrimack, N.H., 1985-87, Reeds Ferry Elem. Sch., Merrimack, 1989—. Sci. curriculum facilitator Reeds Ferry Elem., Merrimack, 1991-95; elem. sci. leadership team S.E. Regional Edn. Ctr., Derry, N.H., 1994-95. Support group leader Friendship Cmty. Ch., Hudson, N.H., 1992-94, Merrimack (N.H.) Christian Cmty. Ch., 1994-95. Named N.H. Elem. Sci. Tchr. of Yr., N.H. Excellence in Edn. Com., Concord, 1995. Mem. NSTA (Presdl. award for excellence in sci. tchg. 1994), N.H. Sci. Tchrs. Assn., Assn. Presdl. Awardees in Sci. Tchg. Office: Reeds Ferry Elem Sch 15 Lyons Rd Merrimack NH 03054-2821 Home: 23 Fairway Dr New Hampton NH 03256-4809

ROSS, MARILYN J., language and communications educator; BA in Am. Studies, U. Miami, Fla., 1969, MA in Am. Studies, 1971, PhD in Higher Edn. Leadership, 1995. Asst. prof. English Fla. Meml. Coll., 1971-84, assoc. prof. English and mass comm. arts, 1985-94, prof. higher edn., 1995—. Founder mass comm. arts program Fla. Meml. Coll., 1980, coord. modern langs., 1999—; presenter Round Table Oxford U., Eng., 2005, others. Author: Success Factors of Young African American Males at a Historically Black College, 1998, Success Factors of Young African American Women at a Historically Black College, 2002; prodr. over 100 hrs. African Am., Caribbean and Hispanic programming, WLRN-TV. Recipient Outstanding Svc. award Vets. Club, 1979, Outstanding and Dedicated Svc. in Behalf of FMC award Miami Cable Access Corp., 1987, award Fla. Meml. Coll./Black Archives History and Rsch. Found. of South Fla., Inc., 1999. Mem. MLA, AAUW, Assn. Ednl. Leadership, Nat. Coun. Tchrs. English, Nat. Assn. African Am. Studies, Am. Studies Aassn., Epsilon Tau Lambda, Kappa Delta Pi, Phi Lambda Pi, Delta Theta Mu, Phi Kappa Phi, Phi Alpha Theta. Address: Unit F-602 1121 Crandon Blvd Apt F602 Key Biscayne FL 33149-2781 E-mail: ross1848@bellsouth.net.

ROSS, MARION, actress; b. Albert Lea, Minn. children: Jim, Ellen. Grad., San Diego State U. Performed with Globe Theatre, San Diego, LaJolla Summer Theatre; Broadway debut in Edwin Booth; starred in touring prodns. of Never Too Late, Barefoot in the Park, The Glass Menagerie, Long Days Journey Into Night, Love Letter, Steel Magnolias, Over The River and Through The Woods, Barefoot in the Park, film debut in Forever Female, 1953; on woman show A Lovely Light, 1988—; TV series include Life with Father, 1953-55, Paradise Bay, 1965-66, Happy Days, 1974-84, Love Boat, 1985-86 (2 Emmy nominations), Bklyn. Bridge, 1991-93 (Emmy nomination for lead actress in a comedy 1992, 93), Hidden in Silence, 1995, Evening Star, 1996, The Great War, 1996, The Third Twin, 1997, About Search, 1998, The Lake, 1998, Drew Carey Show, 1998, That 70's Show, 1998, Touched By an Angel, 1999 (Emmy nomination 1999), The Ladies and the Champ, 2001, The Gilmore Girls, A Family of Strangers. Office: Dale Olson & Assocs 7420 Mulholland Dr Los Angeles CA 90046-1306 Office Phone: 323-876-9331.

ROSS, MOLLY OWINGS, jewelry designer, sculptor, small business owner; b. Ft. Worth, Tex., Feb. 5, 1954; d. James Robertson and Lucy (Owings) R. BFA, Colo. State U., 1976; postgrad., U. Denver, 1978-79. Graphic designer Amber Sky Illustrators and Sta. KCNC TV-Channel 4, Denver, 1977-79; art dir. Mercy Med. Ctr., Denver, 1979-83, Molly Ross Design, Denver, 1983-84; co-owner Deltex Royalty Co., Inc., Colorado Springs, Colo., 1981—, LMA Royalties, Ltd., Colorado Springs, 1993—; art dir., account mgr. Schwing/Walsh Advt., Mktg. and Pub. Rels., Denver, 1984-87, prodn. mgr., 1987-88; jewelry designer Molly O. Ross, Gold and Silversmith, Denver, 1988—. Coun. mem. feminization of poverty critical needs area coun. Jr. League Denver, 1989—90, chmn. children in crisis/edn. critical needs area, 1990—91, chmn. project devel., 1991—92, co-chmn. Done in a Day Cmty. Project 75th Anniversary Celebration, 1991—93, bd. dirs., 1993—94, co-chmn. project IMPACT, 1994—95, exec. v.p. external affairs, 1995—96, co-chmn. cmty. coalitions com., 1996—98; mem. steering com. Denver Urban Resources Partnership, 1995—2002, steering com. chmn., 1996—99; pres.-elect Jr. League Denver, 1989—99, pres., 1999—2000; mem. steering com. Internat. Conf. on Vol. Adminstrn., 2001—02; bd. dirs. Environ. Def. Regional Adv. Bd., 2003—; mem. nat. adv. bd. Am. Farmland Trust, 2005—; mem. Rachel's Network, 2005—; bd. dirs. ArtReach, 2001—; pres. Four Mile Hist. Pk. Vol. Bd., 1985—86; bd. dirs. Four Mile Hist. Pk. Assn., 1985—86, Hist. Denver, Inc., 1986—87, Denver Emergency Housing Coalition, 1989—90; co-founder, bd. dirs. Ctr. Ethics and Social Responsibility/PREP, 1994—2001, pres. bd. dirs., 1997—99, treas. bd. dirs., 1999—2000; bd. dirs. Jr. League Denver Found., 1998—2002, Excelsior Youth Ctr. Found., 2001—, Friends of Warren Village, 2000—01. Named Vol. of Month (March), Jr. League Denver, 1990, Vol. of Yr., Four Mile Hist. Pk., 1988; recipient Gold Peak Mktg. award-team design Am. Mktg. Assn., 1986, Silver Peak Mktg. award-team design Am. Mktg. Assn., 1986, Gold Pick award-art dir. Pub. Rels. Soc. Am., 1980-81, cert. Appreciation USDA, 1999, 2001. Mem. Natural Resources Def. Coun., Physicians for Social Responsibility, Am. Farmland Trust, Nat. Trust for Hist. Preservation, Environ. Def., Rachel's Network. Avocations: horseback riding, bicycling, hiking, backpacking, pastel drawing.

ROSS, NANCY G., lawyer; b. 1956; BA, U. Colo., 1978; JD, Loyola U., Chgo., 1985. Bar: US Supreme Ct., US Ct. Appeals (1st Cir.), US Ct. Appeals (2nd Cir.), US Ct. Appeals (5th Cir.), US Ct. Appeals (6th Cir.), US Ct. Appeals (7th Cir.), US Ct. Appeals (8th Cir.), US Ct. Appeals (9th Cir.), US Ct. Appeals (10th Cir.), US Dist. Ct. (No. Dist.) Ill., US Dist. Ct. (Ea. Dist.) Wis., US Dist. Ct. (Ea. Dist.) Mich., Ill. Ptnr., Trial Dept. McDermott Will & Emery, Chgo. Editor: Women's Law Reporter. Fellow: Am. Coll. Employee Benefits Counsel. Office: McDermott Will & Emery 227 West Monroe Chicago IL 60606 Office Phone: 312-984-7743. Office Fax: 312-984-7700. E-mail: nross@mwe.com.

ROSS, PATTI JAYNE, obstetrics and gynecology educator; b. Nov. 17, 1946; d. James J. and Mary N. Ross; m. Allan Robert Katz, May 23, 1976. BS, DePauw U., 1968; MD, Tulane U., 1972. Diplomate Am. Bd. Ob-Gyn. Asst. prof. U. Tex. Med. Sch., Houston, 1976—82, assoc. prof., 1982—98, prof., 1998—2004, dir. adolescent ob-gyn., 1976—, dir. student edn., dir. devel. dept. ob-gyn. Cons. in field; spkr. in field; appeared on Lifetime TV network. Contbr. articles to profl. jours. Mem. Rape Coun.; vol. Children's Miracle Network/Hermann's Children's Hosp.; Olympic torch relay carrier, 1996; founder Women's Med. Rsch. Fund, U. Tex. Med. Sch., Houston; bd. dirs. Am. Diabetes Assn., 1982—, Susan Komen Found. Recipient Patti Jayne Ross Professorship, 2004. Mem.: Profl. Women Execs., Orgn. Women in Sci., Am. Women's Med. Assn., AAAS, Soc. Adolescent Medicine, Assn. Profs. Ob-Gyn., Houston Ob-Gyn. Soc., Harris County Med. Soc., Tex. Med. Assn., River Oak Breakfast Club, Sigma Xi. Roman Catholic. Office: 6431 Fannin St #3278 Houston TX 77030-1501 Office Phone: 713-500-6431. Business E-Mail: patti.j.ross@mth.tmc.edu.

ROSS, ROBINETTE DAVIS, publisher; b. London, May 16, 1952; d. Raymond Lawrence and Pearl A. (Robinette) Davis; m. William Bradford Ross, III, Mar. 16, 1979; children: Nellie Tayloe, William Bradford IV. Student, Am. U., 1977-78. Asst. to editor The Chronicle of Higher Edn., Washington, 1978, advt. mgr., 1978-82, advt. dir., 1983-88, assoc. pub., 1988-94, The Chronicle of Philanthropy, 1988-94; publ. The Chronicle of Higher Edn., Washington, 1994—; pub. The Chronicle of Philanthropy, Washington, 1994—. Mem. Am. News Women's Club, City Tavern Club, Mt. Vernon Club. Episcopalian. Office: The Chronicle of Higher Edn 1255 23rd St NW Ste 700 Washington DC 20037-1146

ROSS, SALLY PRICE, artist, painter; b. Cleve., Oct. 25, 1949; d. Philip E. and Mimi (Einhorn) Price; m. Howard D. Ross, Mar. 3, 1979; children: Sasha, Emily. BFA, Kent State U., Ohio, 1971; MA, U. Iowa, Iowa City, 1974; MFA, U. Iowa, 1975; student, Art Students League, N.Y.C., 1976—78. Art cons. Art Options, Cleve., 1990—94; 1st and only woman artist to paint murals U.S. Capital/Ho. of Reps. corridors, 1978—79. One-woman shows include Humphrey Gallery, U. Hosps., Cleve., 2006, exhibitions include, Cain Park Art Gallery, Cleve., 1967, Jewish Cmty. Ctr. Cleve., 1967, 1986, Canton (Ohio) Art Inst., 1969, Studio Theatre, Iowa City, 1973, The Cleve. Playhouse Art Gallery, 2000, Fairmount Art Ctr., Russell, Ohio, 2001 (Best in Show); designed and executed murals, Montefiore Nursing Home, Cleve., designed and executed 2 murals, Rainbow Babies and Children's Hosp. New Bldg., Cleve., 1996—97, Menorah Pk. Nursing Home, Cleve., 1997, (bibl. mural) Hartzmark Libr., 1999, The Temple, Cleve., 1999, (commd. works), Solon (Ohio) Libr., 1998—99, (4 commd. murals) Hilton Garden Inn, Cleve., 2002; mural, Univ. Hosps., Cleve., 2002, Hilton Garden, 2002. Scholar Edwin Abbey, 1975—77, Fresco, Skowhegan Sch. Painting and Sculpture, 1977. Home: 5383 Golfway Ln Lyndhurst OH 44124

ROSS, SANDRA RAE, infection control practitioner, quality assessment manager; b. North Platte, Nebr., Jan. 11, 1947; d. Albert Henry and Evangeline Violet (Siewert) Hoerseh; 1 child, Heather Beth Ross. Diploma in nursing, Nebr. Meth. Coll., 1968. RN, Nebr.; cert. prof. in healthcare quality Healthcare Quality Cert. Bd. Staff nurse Nebr. Meth. Hosp., Omaha, 1968-69, staff nurse ICU, 1970-71, San Pedro Cmty. Hosp., Calif., 1969-70; dir. staff devel. Ea. Nebr. Cmty. Office Retardation, Omaha, 1976-83; staff devel. educator Douglas County Hosp., Omaha, 1971-76, quality assessment mgr., 1984—, infection control practitioner, 1992—, psychiat. ICU staff nurse, 2000—03; detox staff nurse Cath. Charities Campus of Hope, Omaha, 2003—05. Mem. Nebr. Coalition for Women, Omaha, 1971-76, Another Mother for Peace, 2003-, Code Pink, 2004-, Prog. Dems., 2004-, Move On, 2004-; adv. Nuc. Freeze, Omaha, 1972-80, Greater Assn. Retarded Citizens, Omaha, 1971-77, Greenpeace 1972—, Defenders of Wild Life, 1996—, Companion of Chalice Well, Glastonbury, UK, 1998—; edn. cons. YWCA, Omaha, 1978. Mem. ACLU, Nat. Assn. Healthcare Quality, Nebr. Assn. Healthcare Quality, Regional Nursing Quality Assurance Orgn. (treas. 1985, pres. 1987), Assn. for Profls. in Infection Control and Epidmiology, Union Concerned Scientists. Democrat. Avocations: reading, travel. Home: 1110 Ironwood Ct Apt 138 Bellevue NE 68005-4755 Personal E-mail: nanasandi2@animail.net.

ROSS, SUSAN E., elementary school educator; b. Rochester, NY, Nov. 27, 1978; d. Frederick S. and Joanne T. Marcellus; m. David W. Ross, June 21, 2003. B, John Carroll U., University Heights, Ohio, 2000. Tchr. reading Pub. Sch. Tchr., Hudson, Ohio, 2003—05, tchr. title 1 Manhattan, Kans., 2005—06.

ROSS, THERESA MAE, secondary school educator; m. Richard H. Ross, Sr.; 1 child, Gwendolyn Denise. BS, Eastern Mich. U., 1967, MS, 1970; PhD, U. Mich., 1981. Tchr. Jackson (Mich.) Pub. Schs., 1967—68, Ann Arbor (Mich.) Pub. Schs., 1968—69, 1971—; grad. intern Inkster (Mich.) Child Devel. Ctr., 1968—70. HEW Early Childhood fellow, 1969—70. Mem.: NEA, Internat. Platform Assn., Am. Bus. Women's Assn., Assn. Curriuclum and Supervision (curriculum cons.), World Orgn. Early Childhood Edn., Mich. Edn. Assn., Ann Arbor Edn. Assn. (lang. arts rep., multicultural coord., motivational spkr., life coach), Delta Kappa Gamma, Beta Sigma Phi, Phi Delta Kappa. Home: 1835 N Franklin Ct Ann Arbor MI 48103-2444 E-mail: rosst45@aol.com.

ROSS, VIOLET BICA, retired elementary school educator, retired psychologist; d. Ellie A. and Anna (Muresan) Bica; m. L. Clayton Ross, Oct. 23, 1976 (dec.). BS, Mount Union Coll., 1944; MA, Kent State U., 1952. Tchr. Alliance Bd. Edn., 1945—53; psychologist Maple Heights Bd. Edn., Ohio, 1954—56, Cleveland Heights Bd. Edn., 1956—61, Shaker Heights Bd. Edn., Ohio, 1961—76; ret., 1976. Psychologist chair Kent Area Sch., 1959—60, Cleve. Area Sch., 1962—63; editl. bd. Sch. Counselor Journal, 1962—64; del. nat. conventions. Named Dormitory at Mt. Union Coll. Bica-Ross Hall, 1999, Dormitory at Wash. Jefferson Coll. Bica-Ross Hall, 2004. Mem.: Kappa Delta, Kappa Delta Pi, Delta Kappa Gamma. Achievements include donations of scholarships to Mount Union College, Washington and Jefferson College. Avocations: reading, travel, golf. Home: 112 Royal Oak Dr Aurora OH 44202

ROSS, WENDY CLUCAS, retired newspaper editor, retired journalist; b. Balt., Apr. 15, 1942; d. Charles Max and Jean (Talbot) Clucas; m. David N. Ross, Sept. 5, 1964 (div. 1979). BA, Bradley U., 1964; MLA, Johns Hopkins U., 1999. Women's editor DeKalb Daily Chronicle, Ill., 1968-69; reporter Chgo. Tribune, Ill., 1969-70; copy editor, mag. editor Mpls. Tribune, Minn., 1970-72; copy editor Peoria Jour. Star, Ill., 1973-75, Miami Herald, Fla., 1975-77; asst. news editor Washington Post, 1977-83, dep. news editor, 1983-87, news editor, 1987-93, asst. mng. editor news desk, 1993-2000; design editor Internat. Herald Tribune, Paris, 1998—2003; art dir. Outlook Wash. Post, 2003—06; ret., 2006. Recipient award of excellence Soc. Newspaper Design, 1985, 87-91, Disting. Alumnae award Bradley U. Centurion Soc., 1994; Nieman fellow Harvard U., 1983-84. Avocations: skiing, sailing, reading, travel. Home: 2735 Olive St NW 4 Washington DC 20007 Personal E-mail: rossw1@verizon.net.

ROSSBACH, JANET B., art association administrator, not-for-profit fundraiser; b. N.Y.C., Mar. 17, 1971; BA cum laude, Georgetown U., 1993; MS in Nonprofit Mgmt., New Sch. U., 2002. Assoc. dir. Works of Art for Pub. Spaces, N.Y.C., 1993-95; acquisitions assoc. Voyager Co., N.Y.C., 1995-96; mktg. mgr. Kaufman Patric of Enterprises, N.Y.C., 1996; dir. devel. and alumni affairs Sch. of Visual Arts, N.Y.C., 1997-2001; dir. found. and govt. rels. Manhattan Theatre Club, N.Y.C., 2001—. Author, editor Visual Arts Jour., 1997-2001. Bd. dirs. Troika Ranch. Mem. Am. Assn. Museums, Blue Hill Troupe.

ROSSBACHER, LISA ANN, academic administrator; b. Fredericksburg, Va., Oct. 10, 1952; d. Richard Irwin and Jean Mary (Dearing) R.; m. Dallas D. Rhodes, Aug. 4, 1978. BS, Dickinson Coll., 1975; MA, SUNY, Binghamton, 1978, Princeton U., 1979, PhD, 1983. Cons. Republic Geothermal, Santa Fe Springs, Calif., 1979-81; asst. prof. geology Whittier (Calif.) Coll., 1982-84, Calif. State Poly. U., Pomona, 1984-86, assoc. prof. geol. sci., 1986-91, assoc. v.p. acad. affairs, 1987-93, prof. geol. sci., 1991-93; v.p. acad. affairs, dean faculty Whittier (Calif.) Coll., 1993-95; dean of coll., prof. geology Dickinson Coll., Carlisle, Pa., 1995-98; pres. So. Poly. State U., Marietta, Ga., 1998—. Vis. rschr. U. Uppsala, Sweden, 1984. Author: Career Opportunities in Geology and the Earth Sciences, 1983, Recent Revolutions in Geology, 1986; (with Rex Buchanan) Geomedia, 1988; columnist Geotimes, 1988—; contbr. articles to profl. jours. Recipient scholarship Ministry Edn. of Finland, Helsinki, 1984; grantee Sigma Xi, 1976, NASA, 1983-94. Fellow AAAS (geol. nominating com. 1984-87, chair-elect geology and geography sect. 1997-98, chair 1998-99, past chair 1999-00); mem. Geol. Soc. Am., Ga. Assn. Colls. (pres. 2005-06). Office: So Poly State U 1100 S Marietta Pkwy SE Marietta GA 30060-2855

ROSSEEL-JONES, MARY LOUISE, lawyer; b. Detroit, Apr. 19, 1951; d. Rene Octave and Marie Ann (Metcko) Rosseel; m. Mark Christopher Jones, Mar. 16, 1984; 1 child, Kathleen Marie. BA in French with honors, U. Mich., 1973, MA in French, 1976; JD, U. Detroit, 1981. Bar: Mich. 1982, U.S. Ct. Appeals (6th cir.) 1982, U.S. Dist Ct. (ea. dist.) Mich. 1982, U.S. Dist. Ct. (we. dist.) Mich. 1983. Tchg. fellow Wayne State U., Detroit, 1973—74; teaching asst. French U. Mich., Ann Arbor, 1974-76; law clk. Johnson, Auld & Valentine, Detroit, 1979-80; assoc. Monaghan, Campbell et al, Bloomfield Hills, Mich., 1981-82; lectr. law U. Clermont, Clermont-Ferrand, France, 1981-82; staff atty. Mich. Nat. Corp., Bloomfield Hills, 1983-85; litigation atty. Am. Motors Corp., Southfield, Mich., 1985-87; staff counsel Chrysler Corp., Auburn Hills, Mich., 1987-98; freelance designer, pvt. lang. and piano tutor, editor, writer; pvt. law counselor, 1998—; jr. h.s. homesch. tchr., 2002—. Editor: sequel One Life to Give. Recipient Mich. Competitive scholarship, 1969-70, Julia Emanuel scholarship, 1974-75, Henderson House scholarship, 1973; Wayne State U. fellow, 1973-74, U. Mich. fellow, 1974-76, U. Detroit fellow, 1981-82. Republican. Roman Catholic. Avocations: classical pianist, interior design.

ROSSELLINI, ISABELLA, actress, model; b. Rome, June 18, 1952; d. Roberto Rossellini and Ingrid Bergman; m. Martin Scorsese, Sept. 1979 (div. Nov. 1982); m. Jonathan Wiedemann (div.); 1 child, Elettra Ingrid. Student, Finch Coll., 1972, New Sch. for Social Research, N.Y.C. Model for Lancôme cosmetics, 1982—95. Actor (films) A Matter of Time, 1976, Il Pap'occhio, 1980, The Meadow, 1982, White Nights, 1985, Blue Velvet, 1986, Siesta, 1987, Red Riding Hood, 1987, Tough Guys Don't Dance, 1987, Zelly and Me, 1988, Cousins, 1989, Wild at Heart, 1990, Les Dames Galantes, 1990, Death Becomes Her, 1992, The Pickle, 1992, Fearless, 1993, Wyatt Earp, 1994, Immortal Beloved, 1994, The Innocent, 1995, The Funeral, Crime of the Century, 1996, Big Night, 1996, The Real Blonde, 1998, Empire, 2002, Roger Dodger, 2002, The Tulse Luper Suitcases: The Moab Story, 2003, The Saddest Music in the World, 2003, The Tulse Luper Suitcases, Part 2: Vaux to the Sea, 2004, King of the Corner, 2004, Heights, 2004, The Feast of the Goat, 2005, The Architect, 2006; (TV films) The Last Elephant, 1990, Lies of the Twins, 1991, Don Quixote, 2000, Monte Walsh, 2003, Earthsea, 2004; (TV miniseries) The Odyssey, 1997, Merlin, 1998, The Impostors, 1998, Left Luggage, 1998; (TV series) Napoléon, 2002; (TV appearances) Friends, 1996, Chicago Hope, 1997, The Simpsons, 1999, Alias, 2004, 2005; writer (films) My Dad is 100 Years Old, 2005; Author: Some of Me, 1997, In the Name of the Father, the Daughter and the Holy Spirits: Remembering Roberto Rossellini, 2006 Office: United Talent Agy 9560 Wilshire Blvd Ste 500 Beverly Hills CA 90212

ROSSER, ANNETTA HAMILTON, composer; b. Jasper, Fla., Aug. 28, 1913; d. Carlos Calvin and Jermai Reuben (Gilbert) Hamilton; m. John Barkley Rosser, Sept. 7, 1935 (dec. Sept. 1989); children: Edwenna Merryday, John Barkley Jr. BM, Fla. State U., 1932. Cert. tchr. Fla. Tchr. music Kirby-Smith Jr. High Sch., Jacksonville, Fla., 1932-35; 1st violinist Santa Monica (Calif.) Symphony, 1949-50; concertmaster Ithaca (N.Y.) Chamber Orch., 1948-56, Cornell Univ. Orch., Ithaca, 1948-56, soloist, 1957; 1st violinist Princeton (N.J.) Symphony, 1959-61; concertmaster Madison (Wis.) Symphony Orch., 1963-66, 1st violinist, 1967-82. Composer of over 100 vocal and instrumental compositions including Meditations on Cross, song cycle for 2 voices, flute and piano, 1976, An Offering of Song, book of 48 songs, 1977, Songs of a Nomad Flute, song cycle for soprano, flute and piano, 1978, Six Songs of the T'ang Dynasty for soprano and violin, 1983, Nocturne for violin and piano, 1989, Trio for flute, violin and piano, 1991, Scherzo for flute ensemble, 1991, (book of 21 songs) Another Offering of Song, 1998. Bd. dirs. Madison Opera Guild, 1972-86, Madison Civic Music Assn., 1983-85; past pres. Madison Symphony Orch. League, Ithaca Federated Music Club, Ithaca Composers Club; bd. dirs. Madison Art Ctr., 1979-83, Madison Woman of Distinction, 1980, Madison Civics Club, 1976-79, pres., 1977-78; pres. Art League Madison Art Ctr., 1980-82, Univ. League Scholarship Benefit Concert of Rosser Compositions, U. Wis., MMadison, 2003. Recipient Sr. Svc. award Rotary Club, 1994; original music manuscripts and programs were added to archives of U. Wis.-Madison Music Libr., 1996. Mem. AAUW, Wis. Acad. Scis., Arts, and Letters, Univ. League, Univ. League Bird Study Group, Madison Club, Wis. Acad. Scis., Arts, and Letters, PEO, Phi Kappa Phi, Pi Kappa Lambda, Sigma Alpha Iota. Republican. Presbyterian. Avocations: Chinese snuff bottles, English brass rubbings, birding. Home: 4209 Manitou Way Madison WI 53711-3703

ROSSETTI, ROSEMARIE, writer, publisher, speaker, consultant; b. Columbus, Ohio, Aug. 7, 1953; d. Fiorovante Dante and Rose (Mascari) R. BS, The Ohio State U., 1975, MS, 1979, PhD, 1982. Cert. interior horticulturist. Horticulture instr. Delaware (Ohio) Joint Vocat. Sch., 1975-78; interior horticulturist Stanford Interior Gardens, Columbus, 1978-86; teaching asst. The Ohio State U., Columbus, 1978-82; instr. Ohio State U., Columbus, 1986-87, vocat. edn. cons., 1987-90, asst. prof. tchr. edn., 1990-97; pres. Rosewell Pub., Inc., Columbus, 1991—2000, Rossetti Enterprises, Inc., 1994—. Trainer, spkr., cons. in field. Co-author: The Healthy Indoor Plant, 1992; researcher, author ednl. reports. Grantee Kellogg Found., 1990, Nat. FFA, 1990, Ohio State Dept. Edn., 1987, Springfield Vocat. Sch., 1989. Mem. Am. Assn. for Agrl. Edn. (com. chair 1988-90), Am. Vocat. Assn. (task force 1992), Am. Vocat. Edn. Rsch. Assn., Nat. Speakers Assn., Am. Soc. for Tng. and Devel., Nat. FFA Orgn. (mem. task force 1991-92), Nat. Vocat. Agr. Tchrs. Assn., Ohio FFA Alumni Coun. (chair, officer 1988-92, com. chair 1976-92). Avocations: gardening, photography, travel, skiing.

ROSSI, ALICE S., sociology educator, writer; b. N.Y.C., Sept. 24, 1922; d. William A. and Emma (Winkler) Schaerr; m. Max Kitt, Dec. 1941 (div. Sept. 1951); m. Peter H. Rossi, Sept. 29, 1951; children: Peter Eric, Kristin Alice, Nina Alexis. BA, Bklyn. Coll., 1947; PhD, Columbia U., 1957; 9 hon. degrees. Rsch. assoc. Cornell U., Ithaca, N.Y., 1951-52, Harvard U., Cambridge, Mass., 1952-55, U. Chgo., 1961-67, Johns Hopkins U., Balt., 1967-69; prof. sociology Goucher Coll., Balt., 1969-74, U. Mass., Amherst, 1974-91, prof. emerita, 1991—. Author/editor: 11 books; contbr. numerous articles to profl. jours. Founder, bd. mem. NOW, 1966-70; pres. Sociologists for Women in Soc., 1971-72. Career grantee NIMH, 1965-69, rsch. grantee Rockefeller Found., Ford Found., NIH, NSF, others; CommonWealth Disting. Scholarship award, 1988. Mem. Am. Sociol. Assn. (pres. 1983-84), Ea. Sociol. Soc. (pres. 1973-74). Avocations: design, sewing, gardening, creative writing. Home: 34 Stagecoach Rd Amherst MA 01002-3527

ROSSI, JENNIFER MICHELLE, athletic trainer; b. Lake Whales, Fla., June 17, 1976; d. Ronald Frederick and Yvonne Ruth Rossi; m. Justin Nelson Dupas, Apr. 4, 2004; 1 child, Madison Mae Rossi-Dupas. AA, Naugatuck Valley C.C., Waterbury, Conn., 1997; BS, Chowan Coll., Murfreesboro, N.C., 1999; MS, Ind. State U., Terre Haute, 2001. Cert. athletic trainer Nat. Athletic Trainers Assn., lic. Fla. Dept. Health. Athletic trainer, grad. intern Bathune Cookman Coll., Daytona Beach, Fla., 1999—2000; athletic trainer Rehabilitation Assoc., Stratford, Conn., 2002—03; head athletic trainer Osocola County H.S., Kissimee, Fla., 2003—04. Grad. intern Jour. of Sports Rehabilitation, Terre Haute, Ind., 2001. Contbr. articles to profl. jours. Mem.: Nat. Athletic Trainers Assn. Avocations: quilting, reading, singing, travel. Home: 2688 Shiprock Ct Deltona FL 32738

ROSSI, MARIANNE, financial analyst; b. Jan. 20, 1960; BA, NYU, 1982. Chartered fin. analyst. Analyst Kidder Peabody, N.Y.C., 1983-88, Prudential Inst. Co., Newark, 1988-91, Credit Suisse Asset Mgmt., N.Y.C., 1991—.

ROSSI, MARY ANN, classicist, researcher; b. Torrington, Conn., Jan. 25, 1931; d. George James and Virginia Angelina (Negri) R.; m. John Bruce Brackenridge, June 19, 1954 (dec.); children: Sandy Rossi (dec.), Lynn, Scot, Rob Brackenridge. BA in Classics, Conn. Coll. for Women, 1952; MA in Classics, Brown U., Providence, R.I., 1959; PhD in Classics, U. London, 1982. Asst. prof. English and classics Muskingum Coll., New Concord, Ohio, 1955-59; lectr. in classics and freshman studies Lawrence U., Appleton, Wis., 1959-71; lectr. in humanities U. Wis., Green Bay, 1973-76; lectr. in Greek and Latin City Lit. Inst., London, 1973-75, 80-81; asst. prof. classics Ball State U., Muncie, Ind., 1983-86; rsch. fellow Women's Studies Rsch. Ctr. U. Wis., Madison, 1989-95; ind. scholar London and Appleton, Wis., 1995—. Regional dir., reader Latin Exams. for Advancement Placement, 1986-88. Translator articles in field, also Principia. Pres. Fox Valley Human Rights Coun., Appleton, 1976-78; mem. exec. bd. Nat. Assn. Commns. for Women, 1978-80; founder Fox Cities chpt. NOW, 1973. NEH fellow Princeton U., 1979, Am. Acad. in Rome, 1983, Stanford U., 1986; grantee NEH, U. Wis., 1991. Mem. NOW, ACLU, Archaeol. Inst. Am. (founder Appleton chpt.), Am. Classical Assn. (treas. women's classical caucus 1980-85), Amnesty Internat., So. Poverty Law Ctr., Women's Ordination Worldwide. Democrat. Achievements include research on women's ordination. Fax: 920-730-1094. Office Phone: 920-284-7413. Personal E-mail: rossibrack@aol.com.

ROSSI, NORMA J., retired not-for-profit developer, advocate; b. Melrose, Mass., Dec. 10, 1929; d. Andrew Steven and Marie Eleanor (Nordbo) Scott; m. Bruce A. Rossi (dec. Dec. 1992); children: Robert, Barry, Max. Degree in Nursing, Peter Bent Brigham Hosp., Boston, 1952; grad. mediation skills, S.D. Mediation Ctr., 1992; completion 4-Day Diversity tng., 1998. RN, Mass., Calif. Emergency rm. nurse various hosps., Boston, Modesto, Calif., 1953-75, San Diego, 1962-73; founder, vol. exec. dir. San Diego Coalition for Homeless, 1988—2004; ret., 2004. Active Citizens Police Rev. Bd., San Diego, 1994—98; bd. dirs. City of San Diego Human Rels., 1991. Named Outstanding Citizen of Yr., Iota Chi chpt. Sigma Chi, 1995, hon. educator, St. Joseph's Indian Sch., 1997; recipient Seahorse award, City of San Diego, 1992, Appreciation of Svc. award, Uptown Interfaith, 1995, Leadership award, Channel 10, 1999—2000, San Diego Hunger Coalition, 2000, Spl. Commendation for continued commitment to make San Diego a better place to live, City Coun., 2001, Say award for making a difference in families in San Diego, 2001, Ranger Run Buddy Grey award, 2002—03, Juvenille Justice Accomadation, 2003. Personal E-mail: rossinorma@aol.com.

ROSSI, NORMA M., management consultant; b. N.Y.C., July 23, 1947; d. Attilio G. and Laura (Retsini) R. BA, CCNY, 1970; Masters, New Sch. Social Rsch., 1988. Dir. corp. quality Met. Life Ins. Co., N.Y.C., 1970—. Sec. Internat. Svc. Quality Assn., 1991—. Co-author: At the Service Quality Frontier, 1993; author: (chpts.) Service Quality Handbook, 1993, Total Quality Management, 1994; contbr. articles to profl. jours. Recipient Cert. of Appreciation, QUIS, 1994. Mem. ASTD, Human Resources Planning Soc. Roman Catholic. Avocations: opera, theater. Home: 260 Garth Rd Apt 8b4 Scarsdale NY 10583-4053 Office: Met Life Ins Co 1 Madison Ave New York NY 10010-3603

ROSSI, RUTH HARRIS, special education educator; d. Everett Tomlinson Harris and Clora Ethel Stanley; m. Raymond Anthony Rossi, Feb. 26, 1977; children: Hillary Niles, Tess Virginia, Anthony John. BA, U. R.I., 1967, postgrad., 1973; EdM, Seattle U., 1995. Spl. edn. tchr. Lakota Mid. Sch., Federal Way, Wash., 1989—, spl. edn. dept. chair, 2002—. Mem. post-secondary transition adv. com. Federal Way Sch. Dist., 1999—. Treas. PTA, Woodmont East Sch., Federal Way, 1982, 1996, 1997; leader, membership facilitator CampFire, Kent, Wash., 1982—86; mem. customer adv. com. Puget Sound Power, Renton, Wash., 1983, 1984. Grantee, Federal Way Edn. Found., 2003. Mem.: Assn. for Supervision and Curriculum Devel., ACLU, Audubon Soc. Avocations: reading, walking, gardening, cooking, needlepoint. Office: Lakota Mid Sch 1415 SW 314th St Federal Way WA 98023

ROSSITER, EILEEN, Canadian senator; b. Souris, Prince Edward Island, Can., July 14, 1929; m. Linus J. Rossiter (dec. Mar. 1987); children: Philip, Leonard, Kevin, Patricia, Colleen, Mary. Student, Prince of Wales Coll. Senator, The Senate of Can., 1986. Progressive. Avocation: Avocations: reading, knitting, swimming.

ROSSMAN, RUTH SCHARFF, artist, educator; b. Bklyn. d. Joseph and Elsie (Frankel) Scharff; m. Phillip Rossman; 1 dau., Joanne. Grad., Cleve. Inst. Art, 1934; BS, Case Western Res. U., 1934; postgrad., Kahn Inst. Art, 1947-50, UCLA, 1960. Art instr. Canton (Ohio) public schs., 1934-39, Canton Art Inst., 1937-45, Rustic Canyon Art Center, Los Angeles, 1978-81. One-woman shows at Heritage Gallery, L.A., 1963, 66, Canton (Ohio) Community Ctr., 1967, Marymount Coll., U. Judaism, 1980, L.A. Fedn. Bldg., 1981, 89, Platt Gallery, 1986, 93, 98, others; exhibited in group shows Mus. Modern Art, N.Y.C., Butler Mus., Washington and Jefferson Coll., Denver Mus., Space Mus., Mt. St. Mary's Coll., L.A., M.H. de Young Mus., San Francisco Mus. Art, Venice Art Walk, ann. 1981-94, 96-2000, Univ. Judaism, 1986, 93, Brand Art Gallery, 1987, Platt Gallery, 1998, others; represented in permanent collections Pa. Acad. Fine Arts, Phila., Brandeis-Bardin Inst., U. Redlands, Calif., Nat. Watercolor Soc., Ahmanson Collection, Rocky Mt. Nat., others; paintings included in book The California Romantics: Harbingers of Watercolor, 1987, Retrospective Art Exhibit U. Judaism Platt Gallery, 1998. Chair selection com. for Platt Gallery, U. Judaism, L.A., 1986—. Recipient purchase-cash awards Los Angeles All-City Art Exhbn. Mem. Nat. Watercolor Soc. (pres. 1974-75, juror 75th Ann. Exhbn. 1995).

ROSSMAN, TOBY GALE, molecular and genetic toxicology educator, researcher; b. Weehawken, N.J., June 3, 1942; d. Norman N. and Sylvia Betty (May) Natowitz; m. Neil I. Rossman, Sept. 16, 1962 (div. Sept. 1980); m. Gordon Rauer, Aug. 19, 1990. AB, NYU, 1964, PhD, 1968; postgrad., Brandeis U., 1964-65. Instr. Polytech. Inst. of N.Y., N.Y.C., 1968-69; postdoctoral dept. pathology NYU, N.Y.C., 1969-71; from asst. to assoc. prof. Inst. for Environ Medicine NYU Med Ctr, N.Y.C., 1974-85; prof. Inst. for Environ. Medicine, 1985—; dir. molecular and genetic toxicology Nelson Inst. Environ. Medicine, NYU Med. Ctr., N.Y.C., 1995—. Mem. editorial bd. Molecular Toxicology, 1989-91, Teratogenesis, Carcinogenesis, Mutagenesis, 1990-91, Environmental and Molecular Mutagenesis, 1994—, Mutation Research, 1994—; contbr. numerous articles to profl. jours. EPA grantee, NIH grantee. Mem. AAAS, Assn. for Women in Sci., Am. Assn. for Cancer Rsch., Environ. Mutagen Soc. (councilor 1990-93), Soc. Toxicology. Office: NYU Inst Environ Medicine 57 Old Forge Rd Tuxedo Park NY 10987-5007 E-mail: rossman@env.med.nyu.edu.

ROSSO DE IRIZARRY, CARMEN (TUTTY ROSSO DE IRIZARRY), finance executive; b. Ponce, P.R., Feb. 9, 1949; d. Jorge Ignacio and Carmen Teresa (Descartes) Rosso Castain; m. Alfredo R. Irizarry Sile, Aug. 29, 1967. BBA, U. P.R., Rio Piedras. Vice pres. Alcay Inc., San Juan, P.R., 1972—, also bd. dirs.; v.p. J.I.C. Corp., M.I.C. Corp. Bd. dirs., now pres. bd. Construcciones Urbanas Inc., Internat. Fin. Corp.; organizer Best of Saks Fifth Avenue 1990-2000. Troop leader Girl Scouts U.S.A., 1977-80; bd. dirs. PTA, San Juan, 1978-81, 86-88; activities coord. Colegio Puertorriqueño Niñas, San Juan, 1987-88; judge Miss P.R. Pageant, San Juan 1987-88, 93, 94, 95, Miss World P.R. Pageant, San Juan, 1987-88, Miss World of P.R., 1990; pres. fundacion dept. Oncologia Pediatrica Hosp. Universitario Dr. Antonio Ortiz, 1990-2005; organizer Best of Saks Fifth Avenue Benefit, 1991, 92, 93, 94, 95, pres. 1992, 94, 96, 2005; com. mem. Make a Wish Found. Colleccion Alta Moda, 1994; mem. com. Muceo Ponce Gala, 1994; mem. com. Museo Ponce Coala, 1994; luminaria J.C. Penney, 1994; destellos de la Moda, 1994, 95-96, 2005; pres. Best of Saks 5th Avenue Benefit, 1990-96; organizer Fundacion Oncologica Escada Spring and Summer, 2003. Named to Ten Best Dressed List, San Juan Star, 1986-87, Hall of Fame of Ten Best Dressed, 1989; recipient luminaria J.C. Penney, 1994, Club Damas Medal, 2005. Fellow Assn. Porcelanas; mem. Union Mujeres Americanas, Club de Leones (Garden Hills, P.R., Lady of Yr. award 1978), Club Avico Dama, Caparra Country Club (pres. 1985-86), Club de Presidentas, Altrusas, Bankers Club, Club Civicos Damas (judge hat show 1989, in charge spl. events 1992), Mu Alpha Phi. Republican. Roman Catholic. Avocations: china painting, boating, water-skiing. Office: Internat Fin Corp PO Box 8486 Santurce San Juan PR 00910-0486

ROSSON, ELIZABETH HANLE, artist, director; d. Edgar John and Catherine Sneden Hanle; m. Loren Herman Rosson Jr., Jan. 29, 1966; children: Loren Herman III, Holly Jane. BA in Art, Stetson U., Deland, Fla., 1963. Art therapist C.F. Menninger Meml. Hosp., Topeka, 1966—68, Souhegan Valley Assn. for Handicapped, Amherst, ND, 1980—83; art and spirituality retreat program dir. various locations, 1990—. Spiritual direction intern Jesuit Renewal Ctr., Milford, Ohio. One-woman shows include Nashua Pub. Libr., NH, exhibitions include Rivier Coll., Nashua. Mem.: Colored Pencil Soc. Am. Democrat. Home and Office: 49 Bowes Cir Hudson NH 03051

ROSS-PARSONS, DONNA MICHELLE, counselor, small business owner; b. Redwood City, Calif., Aug. 29, 1962; d. Fayne David Ross and Norma G. Moore, Francis Allen Moore (Stepfather); m. Eugene William Parsons, Nov. 4, 2000. MA, Sam Houston State U., Huntsville, Tex., 1995. Lic. profl. counselor Tex. State Bd. Examiners Profl. Counselors, 1998. Milieu activity therapist Ming Quong Children's Home, Los Gatos, Calif., 1988—90; mental health worker Sandstone Ctr., College Station, Tex., 1990—91; child protective services worker Tex. Dept. Protective & Regulatory Svcs., Centerville, 1992—94; social worker Gulf Coast Trade Ctr., New Waverly, 1995—96; therapist Ctrl. Plains Ctr. Mental Health, Mental Retardation & Substance Abuse, Plainview, 1996—99; clin. dir. Mesa Lake Residential Ctr., Zephyr, 1999—99; pvt. practice Donna M. Ross, LPC-S, Early, 1999—; therapist New Horizions Ranch & Ctr., Goldthwaite, 2001—02. Vol. ARC, Brownwood, Tex., 1996—98. Mem.: Tex. Counseling Assn., Am. Counseling Assn. Office: Donna M Ross LPC S Ste K 104 E Industrial Dr Early TX 76802 Office Phone: 325-649-9313. Home Fax: 325-643-2895; Office Fax: 325-643-4647. Personal E-mail: dparsons@bwoodtx.com.

ROST, CHRISTA VANDEZANDE, graphics and product designer; b. Fort Wayne, Ind., June 30, 1974; d. Barry Allen VandeZande and Patricia Anne Macy; m. Jacob Alexander Rost, Sept. 14, 2002. BA, Purdue U., 1997. Group sales mgr. Moguls Ski & Snow Tours, Boulder, Colo., 1997—99; sr. graphic designer Davis Design, Denver, 1999—2002; prin., creative dir. Figure 11 Studio, Denver, 2002—; designer, owner Lee Alexander Jewelry, Denver, 2004—. Cons. Creative Adoptions, Littleton, Colo., 2001—, McClain Finlon Advt., Denver, 2004—. Mem. adv. bd. Operation Frontline program Share Our Strength, Denver, 2002—, mem. TasteOfTheNation.com., 2004. Avocations: reading, cooking, bodybuilding, jewelry design. Office: Figure 11 Studio 411 Kalamath St Denver CO 80204

ROSTAD, LEE B., rancher, writer; b. Roundup, Mont., Oct. 28, 1929; d. Edward and Emma Gail (Haddock) Birkett; m. O. Phillip Rostad, June 29, 1952; children: Phillip, Carl Eric. BA with honors, U. Mont., 1951; LLD (hon.), Rocky Mountain Coll., Billings, Mont., 1995. Rancher Rostad and Rostad, Martinsdale, Mont., 1952—; tchr. Pub. Sch., Great Falls, Mont., 1953-54, White Sulphur Springs, Mont., 1967-68, Helena, Mont., 1968-72. Bd. dirs., fundraiser Mountainveiw Med. cTr., White Sulphur Springs, 1990—2000. Author: Honey Wine and Hunger Root, 1985, Fourteen Cents and Seven Green Apples, 1992, Mountains of Gold, Hills of Grass, 1994, Grace Stone Coates Her Life in Letters, 2004; illustrator, author Meagher County Sketchbook; newspaper columnist:. Trustee Mont. State Hist. Soc., 1997—; pres., exec. bd. Mont. chpt. Nat. Mus. Women in the Arts, 1992—2000; mem. County Study Commn., Meagher County, 1975; bd. dirs. Mont. Com. Humanities, 1989—96. Recipient Gov.'s Humanities award, 2001, Disting. Alumni award, U. Mont., 2004; scholar Fulbright, 1952. Mem.: Meagher County Archives Assn. (charter), Meagher County Hist. Assn. (fundraiser 1960—), Mont. Watercolor Soc. Republican. Avocations: pottery, art, writing. Home and Office: Rostad and Rostad 169 Bozeman Fork Rd Martinsdale MT 59053

ROSTOCIL, KELLY ANN, secondary school educator, coach; b. Cleve., Oct. 19, 1976; d. Robert Frank and Antoinette Mary Rostocil; m. Jason Allen Rutkowski, Nov. 11, 2006; m. Jason Allen Rutkowski, Nov. 11, 2006. BS in Edn., Ashland U., 1999; M in Gen. Edn., Marygrove Coll., 2002. Cert. tchr. Ohio, 1999. Acad. team leader Brunswick (Ohio) City Sch., 2004—. Women's varsity soccer team Ashland (Ohio) U., 1995—99, eagle mentor, 1998—99; track coach Brunswick City Sch., 2000—, soccer coach, 2004—; coach Brunswick Soccer Assn., 2004—05. Grantee, Brunswick Edn. Found., 2005; Leadership grantee, 1996. Independent. Roman Catholic. Avocations: running, reading, soccer, interior decorating.

ROSTOW, ELSPETH DAVIES, political science professor; b. NYC; d. Milton Judson and Harriet Elspeth (Vaughan) Davies; m. Walt Whitman Rostow, June 26, 1947 (dec. Feb. 2003); children: Peter Vaughan, Ann Larner. AB, Barnard Coll., 1938; AM, Radcliffe Coll., 1939; MA, Cambridge U., Eng., 1949; LHD (hon.), Lebanon Valley Coll.; LLD (hon.), Austin Coll., 1982, Southwestern U., 1988; LHD (hon.), Wheaton Coll., 2006. Mem. faculty various instns. Barnard Coll., N.Y.C. and MIT, Cambridge, 1939-69; mem. faculty U. Tex., Austin, 1969—, dean div. gen. and comparative studies, 1975-77, prof. govt., 1976—, dean Lyndon B. Johnson Sch. Pub. Affairs, 1977-83, Stiles prof. Am. studies, 1985-88, Stiles prof. emerita, 1988—. Mem. Pres.'s Adv. Com. for Trade Negotiations, 1978-82, Pres.'s Commn. for a Nat. Agenda for the Eighties, 1979-81; rsch. assoc. OSS, Washington, 1943-45; Geneva corr. London Economist, 1947-49; lectr. Air War Coll., 1963-81, Army War Coll., 1965, 68, 69, 78, 79, 81, Nat. War Coll., 1962, 68, 74, 75, Indsl. Coll. Armed Forces, 1961-65, Naval War Coll., 1971, Fgn. Svc. Inst., 1974-77, Dept. of State, Europe, 1973; bd. dirs. U.S. Inst. of Peace, vice chmn., 1991, chmn. 1991-92; co-founder The Austin Project, 1991; mem. Gov.'s Task Force on Revenue, Tex., 1991. Author: Europe's Economy After the War, 1948, (with others) American Now, 1968, The Coattailless Landslide, 1974; editor (with Barbara Jordan) The Great Society: A Twenty-Year Critique, 1986; columnist Austin Am. Statesman, 1985-92; contbr. articles to revs., poems to scholarly jours., newspapers, and mags. Trustee Nat. Acad. Pub. Adminstrn., 1989—95, Sarah Lawrence Coll., 1952—59, So. Ctr. for Internat. Studies, 1990—; bd. visitors and govs. St. Johns Coll., 1986—89; bd. dirs. Barnard Coll., 1962—66, Lyndon Baines Johnson Found., 1977—83, Salzburg Seminar, 1981—89, co-chair sr. fellows, 1997—2001; vis. scholar Phi Beta Kappa, 1984—85; bd. adv. to pres. Naval War Coll., Newport, RI, 1995—99; nat. advisor Commn. on Deliberative Polling, 1999—2001. Decorated Order of St. Joan D'Arc; named Fulbright lectr.; recipient Top Hand award, U. Tex. Ex-Students Assn., 1996, Presdl. citation, U. Tex., 1998, Disting. Alumna award, Barnard Coll., 1998, Dist. Svc. award, Tex. Exec., 2005, Disting. Svc. award, U. Tex., 2005, Civilian Svc. award, US Army, 2006; grantee, USIA, 1983—84, 1990. Mem.: Tex. Philos. Soc. (trustee 1989—95, 1997—2001), Headliners Found. (vice-chmn. 1996—2002), Phi Beta Kappa, Omicron Delta Kappa, Mortar Bd. (hon.), Phi Nu Epsilon (hon.). Home: 1 Wildwind Pt Austin TX 78746-2434 Office: U Tex PO Box Y University Station Austin TX 78713 Office Phone: 512-471-8909. Business E-Mail: elspeth.rostow@mail.utexas.edu.

ROTATCHKA, JANICE MARIE, medical/surgical and critical care nurse; b. Detroit, Apr. 8, 1958; d. John Robatchka and Marian M. Coatsworth; children: Shelaine Elizabeth, Vincent Thomas. AA, Wayne County Community Coll., Detroit, 1980; B in Applied Sci., Bus., Siena Heights Coll., 1986. Nursing supr. Heritage Hosp., Taylor, Mich.; RN supr. Associated Physicians Med. Ctr., Taylor, Mich.; clin. nurse staff asst. Sinai Hosp., Detroit. Nurse mgr. Henry Ford Hosp. Mem. Am. Heart Assn., Am. Assn. Office Nurses, ABWA. Home: 42263 Montroy Dr Sterling Heights MI 48313

ROTBERG, IRIS COMENS, social scientist; b. Phila., Dec. 16, 1932; d. Samuel Nathaniel and Golda (Shuman) Comens; m. Eugene H. Rotberg, Aug. 29, 1954; children: Diana Golda, Pamela Lynn. BA, U. Pa., 1954, MA, 1955; PhD, Johns Hopkins U., Balt., 1958. Research psychologist Pres.'s Commn. on Income Maintenance Programs, Washington, 1968-69, Office Planning, Research and Evaluation, Office Econ. Opportunity, Washington, 1970-73; dep. dir. compensatory edn. study Nat. Inst. Edn., Washington, 1974-77, dir. Office Planning and Program Devel., 1978-82; program dir. NSF, Arlington, Va., 1985-87, 89-91, 1993-96; tech. policy fellow Com. on Sci., Space and Tech., U.S. Ho. of Reps., Washington, 1987-89; sr. social scientist RAND, Washington, 1991-93; rsch. prof. edn. policy Grad. Sch. Edn. and Human Devel. George Washington U., Washington, 1996—. NSF fellow, 1956-58. Home: 7211 Brickyard Rd Potomac MD 20854-4808 Office Phone: 202-994-2735. Business E-Mail: irotberg@gwu.edu.

ROTE, NELLE FAIRCHILD HEFTY, management consultant; b. Watsontown, Pa. May 23, 1930; d. Edwin Dunkel and Phebe Hill (Fisher) Fairchild; m. John Austin Hefty, Mar. 20, 1948 (div. June 1970); children: Harry E. Hefty, John B. Hefty, Susan E. Hefty DeBartolo; m. Keith Maynard Rote, Dec. 16, 1983 (dec. Aug. 1985). Student, Bucknell U., 1961, Williamsport Sch. of Commerce, 1968-69, Pa. State U., 1971-72, 83, Susquehanna U., 1986. Typesetter, page designer Colonial Printing House, Inc., Lewisburg, Pa., 1970-76; account exec. Sta. WTGC Radio, Lewisburg, 1976-78; co-owner Colonial Printing Co., Lewisburg, 1978-83; temp. HATS-Temps, Lewisburg, 1986-89; artist, editor Create-A-Book, Inc., Milton, Fla., 1980-92; census crew leader, spl. svc. Dept. Commerce, Washington, 1990; cons. Create-A-Book, Inc., Gulf Breeze, Fla., 1991—99. Children's Playmate Mag., 1942; author: McGruff and Me, 1999, My Christmas Wish, 1999, School Fun Book, 1999, My Fishing Adventure, 1999, Nurse Helen Fairchild,World War I, 1917-1918, 2006; contbr., articles to profl. jours.; exhibitions include Union County Libr., Lewisburg, 2003. Proofreader Lewisburg Bicentennial Commn., Lewisburg, 1976; charter mem. Women's Art Mus., Washington; charter sponsor Women in Mil. Svc. Meml., Arlington, Va., 1991; founder, donor Nelle Fairchild Rote Book Fund, Union County Libr.; editor, poet Holiday Newspaper Bus. Assn., Lewisburg, 1987. Recipient Humanitarian recognition, Tri-County Fedn. Women's Clubs, Pa., 1965, Grand prize in Cooking, Milton Std., 1966, Most Profl. Photo award, Lewisburg Festival Arts, 1980, Hon. Mention award, Women in Arts, Harrisburg, Pa., 1981, Photo Contest award, Congressman Allen Ertel, 1981, 2d pl. Photo award, Union County Fair, 1981, 3d pl. Photo award, 1981, Hon. Mention Photo award, Susquehanna Art Soc., 1981, Silver award for Poetry, World of Poetry, 1990. Mem.: DAR (nat. def. reporter Shikelimo chpt. 1989—95, sec. 1992—95, regent 1995—2001, vice chmn. Pa. State Soc. DAR women vets com. 1998—2001, vice-regent 2001—04, Prize for safety poster 1942), Soc. Profl. Journalists, Warrior Run Heritage Soc., Western Front Assn., Marine Corps League Aux. (life), Civic Club Lewisburg (v.p. 1994—97), Am. Legion Aux. (sgt.-at-arms 2003, Unit 182). Achievements include Initiator for renaming bridge in Watsontown, PA. to "Nurse Helen Fairchild Meml. Bridge" (a WWI Reserve Army Nurse relative), 2002. Home: 1015 St Paul St Lewisburg PA 17837-1213 Personal E-mail: elle12@ptd.net.

ROTELL, CYNTHIA A., lawyer; BA, Barnard Coll., 1982; JD, Bklyn. Law Sch., 1990. Bar: Calif. 1990. With Latham & Watkins, L.A., 1990—, ptnr., 1997—. Mem.: L.A. County Bar Assn. (exec. com. bus. and corps. law sect.), State of Calif. Bar Assn. Office: Latham and Watkins LLC 633 W Fifth St Ste 4000 Los Angeles CA 90071

ROTH, AIMEE ELIZABETH, secondary school educator, athletic trainer; b. Buffalo, Mar. 24, 1978; d. Peter Thomas and Lorraine Adele (Dillon) Roth. AA in Math. & Sci., Erie CC, Orchard Park, NY, 1998; BA in Phys. Edn./Athletic Tng., State U. NYC, Brockport, 2001; MA in Athletic Tng., We. Mich. U., Kalamazoo, 2004. Cert. ATC/L. Athletic trainer sports medicine clinic We. Mich. U., 2002—04; surgery scheduler, athletic trainer Ctrl. Ind. Orthopaedics, Anderson, Ind., 2004—05; pys. edn. instr., athletic trainer Columbus East HS, Ind., 2005—. Contbr. articles to profl. jours. Mem.: Am. Alliance Physical Edn., Health, Recreation & Dance, Nat. Athletic Trainer's Assn. Avocations: soccer, reading, running, hiking.

ROTH, CAROLYN LOUISE, art educator; b. Buffalo, June 17, 1944; d. Charles Mack and Elizabeth Mary (Hassel) R.; m. Charles Turner Barber, Aug. 4, 1991. Student, Art Student's League N.Y., 1965, Instituto Allende, San Miguel de Allende, Mex., 1966; BFA, Herron Sch. Art, 1967; MFA, Fla. State U., 1969. Asst. prof. art U. Tenn., Chattanooga, 1969-72; lectr. art So. Ill. U., Carbondale, 1973-75; asst. prof. art U. Evansville, Ind., 1975-80; instr. art U. So. Ind., Evansville, 1984—. Exhbn. coord., gallery dir. Krannert Gallery, U. Evansville, 1977-79; exhbn. coord., conf. advisor Ind. Women in Arts Conf., Ind. Arts Commn., Evansville, 1978; reviewer in field. One-woman shows include Wabash Valley Coll., Mt. Carmel, Ill., 1994, So. Ind.

Ctr. for Arts, Seymour, Ind., 1996, Zionsville (Ind.) Muncie Art Ctr., 1997, Oakland City (Ind.) U., 1998, Women's Inst. and Gallery, New Harmony, Ind., 2005; exhibited in group shows Liberty Gallery, Louisville, 1992, Artlink Contemporary Art Gallery, Ft. Wayne, Ind., 1994, S.E. Mo. Coun. on Arts, Cape Girardeau, 1994, Lexington (Ky.) Art League, 1996, Mills Pond Horse Gallery, St. James, N.Y., 1996, SOHO Gallery, Pensacola, Fla., 1996, Indpls. Art Ctr., 1996, Artemesia Gallery, Chgo., 1997, DelMar Coll., Corpus Christi, Tex., 1998, La. State U., Baton Rouge, 1998, Woman Made Gallery, Chgo., 2002; works appeared in various publs.; represented by Creative Art Gallery, St. Louis, the New Harmony Gallery of Contemporary Art, New Harmony, Ind. Malone fellow visitor to Morocco and Tunisia, 1996. Mem. Nat. Mus. Women in Arts, Met. Mus. Art, Evansville Mus. Arts and Sci., New Harmony Gallery of Contemporary Art, Golden Key Honor Soc. (hon.). Democrat. Mem. Unity Ch. Avocation: travel to study art works in museums and galleries in europe and mex. Home: 10801 S Woodside Dr Evansville IN 47712-8422 Office: U So Ind 8600 University Blvd Evansville IN 47712-3534 Business E-Mail: croth@usi.edu.

ROTH, DARYL, theater producer; b. NJ; m. Steven Roth, 1969; children: Amanda, Jordan. Student, NYU. Prodr., owner Daryl Roth Prodns., N.Y.C.; owner Daryl Roth Theater, 1998—, DR2 Theater, 2002—. Co-anchor PBS show N.Y. Theatre Rev.; spkr. in field; guest lectr. Columbia U., NYU, Harvard Club, Women's Art Coalition. Prodr.: (N.Y. and London prodn.) Three Tall Women (Pulitzer prize, 1994), (Broadway prodn.) Twilight. Los Angeles.1992 (Tony nomination), Camping with Henry and Tom (Outer Critics Circle award, Lucille Lortel award), Defying Gravity, (off-Broadway) Snakebit, How I Learned to Drive (Best Play of Season, 1997, Pulitzer prize, 1998), Old Wicked Songs, 1996 (Pulitzer prize finalist for drama, 1996), Wit (Pulitzer prize for Drama, 1999), Bomb-itty of Errors; (plays) Closer Then Ever, 1987—1888, Nick & Nora, 1991, Proof, 2000—03 (Tony Award for Best Play, 2001), The Tale of the Allergist's Wife, 2000—02, Bea Arthur on Broadway, 2002, The Goat, or Who is Sylvia, 2002 (Tony Award for Best Play, 2002), Medea, 2002—03, Salome, 2003, Anna in the Tropics, 2003—04, Caroline, or Change, 2004—. Established (with husband) Roth Ctr. for Jewish Life, Dartmouth U., 1997; bd. dirs. Lincoln Ctr. Theater, Sundance Inst., Albert Einstein Coll. for Med. Rsch. Named award in her honor Daryl Roth Creative Spirit award, honored (with husband) with the Louis Marshall Award, Jewish Theological Seminary. Office: Daryl Roth Prodns 152 W 57th St Fl 21 New York NY 10019

ROTH, GLADYS THOMPSON, retired special education educator; b. N.Y.C., June 24, 1923; d. Meyer and Sarah (Siporin) Thompson; m. Martin Roth, Dec. 25, 1949; children: Jan Roth Hauptman, Lisa. BA, Bklyn. Coll., 1943; postgrad., Queens Coll., 1961-63; M in Spl. Edn., NYU, 1972. Cert. kindergarten tchr., health conservation tchr., tchr. grades K-6, N.Y.C. Bd. Edn. Tchr. Day Care Ctr. Mayor's Com., Bedford & Stuyvesant, N.Y., 1943-45; kindergarten tchr. N.Y.C. Bd. Edn., Red Hook, N.Y., 1945-62; spl. edn. tchr. N.Y.C. Bd. Edn.-St. Francis Hosp., 1962-64, N.Y.C. Bd. Edn.-Queens Gen. Hosp., 1964-65, N.Y.C. Bd. Edn.-St. Mary's Hosp., 1965-79; ednl. evaluator N.Y.C. Bd. Edn. Queens Dist., 1979-90; ret., 1990. Mem. exec. com. Coun. for Exceptional Children, Queens, 1962-64; spl. reading cons. St. Mary's Hosp., Queens, 1964-65. Contbr. articles to profl. jours.; exhibits stone and wood sculpture. Organizer parenting groups Pub. Sch. 84-Queens, Bayside, N.Y., 1979-90; dir. Womanspace in Great Neck, N.Y., 1989-96, dir. of outreach, 1996—; mem. adv. bd. Copay Hispanic Cmty., Inc., Great Neck, 1996—. Recipient Achievement award Soroptomist Soc., Nassau County, N.Y., 1992, Cmty. Achievement award Eleanor Roosevelt chpt. Am. Jewish Congress, Nassau County, 1992, Martin Fisher Post Harvest award Bklyn. Coll., 1997; named Outstanding Woman, Town of North Hempstead, 1994, Disting. Citizen, N.Y. State Assembly, Albany, 1995. Avocations: sculpture, tennis, music. Home: 13 Briar Ln Great Neck NY 11024-1720

ROTH, HARRIET STEINHORN, advocate, educator, public speaker; b. Lodz, Poland, Apr. 12, 1929; d. Pinkus Feldman and Brenda Rubinstein; m. Irving Hyman Steinhorn, Apr. 15, 1951 (dec. June 1981); children: Pauline-Sue, Allan Wrenn, Mark Paul; m. Marvin Roth, June 22, 1986; stepchildren: Linda Fern, Steve Howard. B in Hebrew Lit., Balt. Hebrew U., 1974. Tchr. Hebrew Shaare Tefila Hebrew Sch., Silver Spring, Md., 1964-84, ednl. dir., 1984-92. Author: Shadows of the Holocaust, 1983. Publicity chair Jewish Holocaust Survivors & Friends Greater Washington, Rockville, Md., 1990-99. Avocations: gardening, reading, swimming, theater, travel. Home: 10411 Burnt Ember Dr Silver Spring MD 20903-1337

ROTH, JANE RICHARDS, federal judge; b. Phila., June 16, 1935; d. Robert Henry Jr. and Harriett (Kellond) Richards; m. William V. Roth Jr., Oct. 9, 1965; children: William V. III, Katharine K. BA, Smith Coll., 1956; LLB, Harvard U., 1965; LLD (hon.), Widener U., 1986, U. Del., 1994. Bar: Del. 1965, U.S. Dist. Ct. Del. 1966, U.S. Ct. Appeals (3d cir.) 1974. Adminstrv. asst. various fgn. service posts US Dept. State, 1956-62; assoc. Richards, Layton & Finger, Wilmington, Del., 1965-73, ptnr., 1973-85; judge U.S. Dist. Ct. Del., Wilmington, Del., 1985-91, US Ct. Appeals (3d Cir.), Wilmington, Del., 1991—2006, sr. judge, 2006—. Adj. faculty Villanova U. Sch. Law. Hon. chmn. Del. chpt. Arthritis Found., Wilmington; bd. overseers Widener U. Sch. Law; bd. consultors Villanova U. Sch. Law; trustee Hist. Soc. Del. Recipient Nat. Vol. Service citiation Athritis Found., 1982. Fellow Am. Bar Found.; mem. ABA, Fed. Judges Assn., Del. State Bar Assn. Republican. Episcopalian. Office: US Court of Appeals 3rd Cirt Lock Box 12 5100 Fed Bldg 844 King St Wilmington DE 19801-1790*

ROTH, JUDITH SHULMAN, lawyer; b. NYC, Apr. 25, 1952; d. Mark Alan and Margaret Ann (Podell) Shulman; m. William Hartley Roth, May 30, 1976; children: Andrew Henry, Caroline Shulman. AB, Cornell U., 1974; JD, Columbia U., 1977. Bar: N.Y. 1978, U.S. Dist. Ct. (ea. dist.) N.Y. 1978, U.S. Dist. Ct. (so. dist.) N.Y. 1978, U.S. Ct. Appeals (2d cir.) 1993. Assoc. Phillips Nizer Benjamin Krim & Ballon, N.Y.C., 1978-87, ptnr., 1988—. Lectr. CLE Fordham Law Sch., N.Y.C., 1990. Mem.: Cosmopolitan Club. Jewish. Avocations: reading, tennis, golf, art, gardening. Office: Phillips Nizer Benjamin Krim & Ballon 666 5th Ave New York NY 10103-0001 Office Phone: 212-841-0543. Home Fax: 212-535-3617. E-mail: jroth@phillipsnizer.com.

ROTH, KATHLEEN C., dentist; m. Daniel H. Roth. BS, Univ. Wis.; DDS, Marquette Univ., Milw., 1974. Gen. dentist, West Bend, Wis., 1974—. Mem.: Am. Assn. Women Dentists, Internat. Coll. Dentists, Am. Coll. Dentists, Washington-Ozaukee Dental Soc., ADA (trustee, 9th dist. 2001—04, pres.-elect 2005—06, pres. 2006—, sr. trustee, Strategic Planning Com.), Wis. Dental Assn. (pres. 1998—99). Office: 1713 Vogt Dr West Bend WI 53095 Office Phone: 262-334-3070.*

ROTH, LISA MAE, writer; b. Quakertown, Pa., Apr. 13, 1963; d. Willard Leon Stoneback, Pauline D Stoneback; m. William Andrew Roth; children: Alison, Andrew. BA cum laude, Calif. U. Pa., 1985. Prodn. dir., copywriter WOVU-Radio Sta., Ocean View, Del., 1985—88; pub. rels. coord. Hist. Soc. Talbot County, Easton, Md., 1988—90; home day care provider Lisa Roth Daycare, McDaniel, 1990—2001; tchrs. aide St. Luke's United Meth. Ch. Pre-school, St. Michael's, 1999—2000; writer self-employed, McDaniel, 1998—. Author: (plays) Something to Chew On, 1999, Toying With History, 2000, The Golden Halo Awards, 2001, To Shine Or Not to Shine, 2001; actor(Tred Avon Players): (plays) Women and Children, 1992, Ten Little Indians, 1994, Habitat for Humanity/FOLLIES, 1996, The Man Who Came to Dinner, 1996, The Nerd, 1997, Later Life, 1997, Cat On a Hot Tin Roof, 1998, Neil Simon's Rumors, 2000, Royal Gambit, 2003, Design for Murder, 2004, (audiotape) St. Mary's Square Mus., 1999; singer: (audio drama) Chesapeake Bay Maritime Museum, 2005, (plays) Habitat for Humanity/Neviaser FOLLIES, 1999, 2001, 2003, Cabaret, 2000, Past to Present to Oxford: The Music of Broadway, 2003; actor: (plays) Broadway's Best in Oxford, 2005, Sondheim's Follies, 2005; asst. dir.: 1776, 1998; asst. state mgr. Twelve Angry Men, 2000. Bd. dirs. Tred Avon Players, 2001—02; dir., writer Christmas Pageants St. Luke's United Meth. Ch., St. Michael's, 1996—2002, comm. coord., 1997—98. Mem.: Ea. Shore Writer's Assn., Alpha Psi Omega (life). Avocations: acting, dance, swimming, boating, reading. Home: 23387 Sans Souci Dr Mcdaniel MD 21647 Personal E-mail: cooldeal@dmv.com.

ROTH, MARGARET AGNES, child development educator; b. Rockford, Ill., Oct. 18, 1921; d. Otto Garfield and Agnes Marie (Anderson) Beckstrand; m. Robert Paul Roth, June 17, 1943; children: Erik, Maren, Maarja, John, Sonja. BA, Carthage Coll., 1943. Cert. Elementary and Preschool Edn. Home and family child care instr. Luthergiri Seminary, Rajahmundry, India, 1947-48; dir. nursery sch. Ebenezer Luth. Ch., Columbia, S.C., 1954-58; head tchr. St. David's Episcopal Ch. Nursery Sch., Minnetonka, Minn., 1959-67; head tchr., dir. Jr. League Underpriviledged Sch., Mpls., 1963-67; tchr., adminstrv. asst. U. Minn. Lab. Nursery Sch., Mpls., 1967—. Cons. Midwest State Head Start, Chgo., 1965-68; tchr. Midwest Head Start, 1965-80, Kai Tak Refugee Sch., Hong Kong, 1983-84; tng. tchr. Minn. Migrant Schs., 1968-70; child devel. assoc. rep. Tchr. Assessments, Washington, 1974—. Author: Music for Young Children, 1973, Bible Times, 1973, Jesus Friend of Children, 1979; edit. asst. Areopagus Mag., 1990-91. Mem. Adv. Commn. for Preschool Edn., St. Paul, 1972-80, Gov.'s Commn. for Day Care, St. Paul, 1972, Commn. Com. for Childcare Lic. and Standards for Minn., Council for Childcare and Devel., St. Paul, 1972, Courage Ctr. Therapeutic Preschool Adv. Com., Mpls., 1979-82. Mem. Nat. Assn. for Edn. Young Children (bd. mem. 1977-81), Nat. Bd. Citation 1981), Midwest Assn. for Edn. Young Children (pres. 1976-79, Shirley Dean award 1984, Midwest Honor Ctation 1986), Minn. Assn. for Young Children Edn. (pres., 1972-74, Evelyn House award 1982). Lutheran. Avocations: swimming, skiing, sailing, sewing, music. Home: 4194 Hillcrest Ln Wayzata MN 55391-3604 Office: U Minn-ICD 51 E River Rd Minneapolis MN 55455-0365

ROTH, PAMELA JEANNE, intellectual property asset management consultant; b. Huntington, NY, Sept. 9, 1955; d. Julius Leo and Constance Abby (Gettenberg) R. BA with honors, New Coll. Hofstra U., 1975; MS, Rensselaer Poly. Inst., 1977; JD, New England Sch. Law, 1983; LLM, Franklin Pierce Law Ctr., 2005. Pres., CEO SPIRAL Comm., Inc., SPIRAL Group, SPIRAL Books, Bedford, NH, 1986—; conf. dir. Sensors Expo, 2001—03; CEO IP InSource, 2003—06; editor Consultants News, Kennedy Info., Petersborough, NH, 2006—. Presenter in field. Author: The First Book of Adam, 1984, The Second Book of Adam, 1984, Using the PFS Family, 1985; editor: Data Warehousing and Decision Support-The State of the Art, 1995, Data Warehousing and Decision Support, vol. 2, 1997; contbr. articles to profl. jours. Avocations: acting, travel, bicycling. Business E-Mail: proth@ipinsource.com.

ROTH, PAMELA SUSAN, lawyer; b. N.Y.C., Nov. 23, 1961; d. Edward Abraham and Susan Violet (Castro) R. BS in Biology, Adelphi U., 1982, MBA, 1986; JD, Pace U., 1990. Bar: N.Y. 1991, U.S. Dist. Ct. (ea. and so. dists.) N.Y. 1991, U.S. Ct. Appeals (10th cir.) 1993, Colo. 1995, U.S. Dist. Ct. Colo. 1995, U.S. Supreme Ct. 1995. Asst. gen. counsel N.Y.C. Dept. Probation, Bklyn., 1990-91; asst. dist. atty. Kings County Dist. Atty., Bklyn., 1992-93; assoc. Law Firm of Portales & Assocs., Denver, 1993-95; pvt. practice N.Y.C., 1995—. Gen. counsel Hispano Crypto-Jewish Rsch. Ctr., Denver, 1994—. Mem. ABA, Am. Soc. Internat. Law, Hispanic Nat. Bar Assn., Bklyn. Bar Assn., Internat. Assn. Jewish Lawyers and Jurists, Kings County Criminal Bar Assn. Avocations: aerobics, skiing, roller blading, gourmet cooking. Office: 26 Court St Ste 2003 Brooklyn NY 11242-1120 Address: 2361 E 71st St Brooklyn NY 11234-6511

ROTH, SUSAN BETSY, artist; b. N.Y.C., May 15, 1950; d. Samuel and Rene Roth; m. Darryl Leo Hughto, June 6, 1976; 1 child, Jeremy Roth Hughto. One-woman shows include Everson Mus. Art, Syracuse, N.Y., 1976, William Edward O'Reilly Gallery, N.Y.C., 1980, Salander-O'Reilly Gallery, N.Y.C., 1981, 82, 84, 86, 87, The Hett Gallery, Ltd., Edmonton, Alta., 1983, Martha White Gallery, Louisville, Ky., 1983, Robert Kidd Gallery, Birmingham, Mich., 1987, Gallery Elca London, Montreal, Quebec, Can., 1987, 88, 90, 91, Sangren Hall Gallery, We. Mich. U., Kalamazoo, 1987, Gallery One, Toronto, Ont., 1988, 90, 96, Rome (N.Y.) Art Ctr., 1995; exhibited in group shows including Everson Mus. Art, 1976, 78, Edmonton Art Gallery, 1977, Boston Mus. Fine Arts, 1977, William Edward O'Reilly, Inc. N.Y.C., 1980, Martha White Gallery, Louisville, Ky., 1981, Nicola Jacobs Gallery, London, 1982, Hirshorn Mus. and Scripture Gallery, Washington, 1982, 83, Rubiner Gallery, Royal Oak, Mich., 1982, Salander-O'Reilly Gallery, N.Y.C., 1984, 86, 90, Richard Brush Art Gallery, Canton, N.Y., 1985, Gallery 53, N.Y.C., 1985, Lowe Art Gallery, Syracusem N.Y., 1985, Picker Art Gallery, Hamilton, N.Y., 1986, Edmonton Art Gallery, 1987, 88, Mus. Art, Ft. Lauderdale, Fla., 1991, Mus. Art. Vero Beach, Fla., 1992, Wendy Hoff Gallery, N.Y.C., 1995, Gallery One, Toronto, 1996; represented in permanent collections including Art Council, Boston, Boston Mus. Fine Arts, Cabot Collection, Portland, Maine, Can. Imperial Bank of Commerce, Toronto, Castillejo Collection, Madrid, Comino Found., Vaduz, Lichtenstein, Corin Internat., Hong Kong, de Menil Family Trust, Paris, Elefant Collection, Montreal, Foley Hoag & Eliot, Boston, Surreal Holding, Inc., Toronto. Home: 8176 N Main St Rd Canastota NY 13032 Personal E-mail: sdstudios@earthlink.net.

ROTHAAR, SUSANNE ELISABETH, musician, educator; d. Walter Henry and Lore Rothaar; m. John Paul Haggard, Feb. 14, 2000. BA, U. Utah, Salt Lake City, 1990; MusM, Wichita State U., Kans., 1995. Violinist Utah Chamber Orch., Salt Lake City, 1990—93, Wichita (Kans.) Symphony Orch., 1993—98, Oklahoma City Philharm., 1997—98; mem. violin faculty Wichita State U., 1995—96; pvt. violin instr. Las Vegas, Nev., 1998—2000, Phoenix, 2001—. Lectr. violin pedagogy at various univs. and colls., 2001—; mem. summer music faculty Utah State U., 2000—02, U. Oreg., 2001—02. Author: Teaching Violin Technique, 2002. Mem.: Nat. Symphony Orch. Assn., Music Tchrs. Nat. Assn., Am. String Tchrs. Assn. Avocation: tennis. E-mail: derazy@aol.com.

ROTHAUSER, FLORENCE ARAX, artist; b. NYC, July 22, 1922; d. Harry Malcolm Raphaelian and Venus Aroosiag Kabakjian; 1 child, Diane Clark. Student, Pratt Inst., Bklyn., 1944. Asst. mural artist MmGreely Dept. Store, NYC, 1944—46; freelance mural painter, 1946—59. Color cons. NY Sch. Nursing, NYC, 1958. Avocation: cooking. Home: 206 Rock St Apt 41 Norwood MA 02062

ROTHBARD, BARBARA, allergy and dermatology nurse; b. Miami, May 20, 1943; Diploma, Mt. Sinai Hosp. Sch. Nursing, N.Y.C., 1964. Staff nurse Group Health Assocs., Takoma Park, Md.; head nurse physician's office, Washington; staff nurse Washington Hosp. Ctr.; head nurse physicians' office, Silver Spring, Md. Recipient Guggenheim medal, 1964. Mem. Dermatology Nurses Assn., Am. Acad. Allergy and Immunology.

ROTHBERG, JUDITH, elementary school educator, researcher; b. N.Y.C., Mar. 4, 1934; d. Louis and Esther (Charloff) Jablowsky; m. Lawrence Rothberg, Apr. 13, 1957; children: Richard, Loretta. BA, Bklyn. Coll., 1955, MS, 1960; cert. in guidance, L.I. U., 1969; cert. in adminstrn., Columbia U., 1988, PhD in Ednl. and Family Counseling. Tchr. grades 2 to 6, supr. Lindenhurst (N.Y.) Sch. System, 1955—. Pvt. practice ednl. counseling, Glen Cove, N.Y., 1990-92. Author: Meet Me in West Africa, 1992, Meet the Russian Historic Rivers Then and Now, 1992; co-host (cable program) Innersight; prodr. (cable program) Exploring Your Emotions. Mem., lectr. Bnai Zion, Glen Cove Chpt., 1989-93; bd. dirs. Innersight-Assn. for the Blind. Mem. Tchrs. Assn. Lindenhurst. Avocations: drama club, aerobics, writing, traveling to africa and asia, lecturing. Home: 1 Cedar Ln Glen Cove NY 11542-1320 Office Phone: 516-759-1779.

ROTHBERG-BLACKMAN, JUNE SIMMONDS, retired nursing educator, psychotherapist; b. Phila., Sept. 4, 1923; d. David and Rose (Protzel) Simmonds; m. Jacob Rothberg, Sept. 7, 1952 (dec. Feb. 2001); children: Robert Rothberg, Alan Rothberg; m. Stanley F Blackman, May 27, 2002 (dec. July 2005). Diploma in nursing, Lenox Hill Hosp., 1944; BS, N.Y. U., 1950, MA, 1959, PhD (NIH fellow), 1965; Diploma in Psychotherapy and Psychoanalysis, Adelphi U., Inst. for Advanced Psychol. Studies, 1987. USPHS traineeship N.Y. U., 1957-59; sr. public health nurse Bklyn. Vis. Nurse Assn., 1951-53; prin. investigator in nursing, homestead study project Goldwater Hosp. and N.Y. U., 1959-61; instr. N.Y. U., 1964-65, asst. prof., 1965-68, assoc. prof., 1968-69, project dir. grad. program rehab. nursing, 1964-69, prof., 1969-87, prof. emeritus, 1987—; dean Adelphi U., Garden City, NY, 1969-85, v.p. acad. adminstrn., 1985-86; pvt. practice West Hempstead, NY, 1993-97. Pres. David Simmonds Co. Inc., Med. Supply Co., 1982-89; dir., chmn. compensation com. Quality Care, Inc.; cons. region 2 Bur. Health Resources Devel., HHS.; audit com. Ipco Corp. (formerly Sterling Optical Corp.), 1991; cons., spkr. in field. Contbr. articles to profl. jours. Mem. pres's coun. N.Y. U. Sch. Edn., 1973-75; treas. Nurses for Polit. Action, 1971-73; trustee Nurses Coalition for Action in Politics, 1974-76; bd. visitors Duke Med. Ctr., 1970-74; mem. governing bd. Nassau-Suffolk Health Systems Agy., 1976-79; leader People-to-People Internat. med. rehab. del. to People's Republic of China, 1981; mem. com. for the study pain disability and chronic illness behavior Inst. Medicine, 1985-86, com. on ethics in rehab. Hastings Ctr., 1985-87; trustee Paget's Disease Found., 1987-89. Recipient Disting. Alumna award NYU, 1974, recognition award Am. Assn. Colls. Nursing, 1976, Achievers award Ctr. for Bus. and Profl. Women, 1980 Fellow Am. Acad. Nursing (governing coun. 1980-82); mem. Nat. League Nursing (exec. com. coun. of baccalaureate and higher degree programs 1969-73), Am. Nurses Assn. (joint liaison com. 1970-72), Commn. Accreditation of Rehab. Facilities, Am. Congress Rehab. Medicine (pres. 1977-78, chmn. continuing edn. com. 1979-86, 34th Ann. John Stanley Coulter Meml. lectr. 1984, Gold Key award 1984, Edward W. Lowman award 1990), Am. Assn. Colls. Nursing (pres. 1974-76), L.I. Women's Network (pres. 1980-81), Kappa Delta Pi, Sigma Theta Tau, Pi Lambda Theta. Achievements include having June S. Rothberg collection in Nursing Archives, Mugar Meml. Library, Boston U. Home and Office: 3941 Redondo Way Boca Raton FL 33487 Personal E-mail: stanleyb2@aol.com.

ROTHENBERG, ELEANORE, psychotherapist; d. Max and Dora (Kaplan) Dubin; children: David, Michael, Seth. BA cum laude, Bklyn. Coll., 1955; MPA, N.Y. U., N.Y.C., 1969, PhD, 1975; MSW, Yeshiva U., N.Y.C., 1992. Cert. group psychotherapist Am. Group Psychotherapy Assn.; LCSW Office of Professions N.Y. State Edn. Dept. Exec. dir. N.Y.C. Profl. Standards Rev. Orgn., 1974—80; dir. stds. and evaluation N.Y.C. HHC, 1981—83; social worker Cmty. Living Corp., Mt. Kisco, 1992—94; founder, exec. dir. and group leader Sibling Ctr. Sisters and Brothers of People with Disabilities, N.Y.C., 1994—. Chair bd. dir. Sibling Ctr.; adj. asst. prof. Columbia U. Sch. Pub. Health, 1980—2001; lectr. New Sch. U., 1984—86; preceptor King's Fund Coll., London, 1980; pro bono psychotherapist N.Y. Disaster Counseling Coalition, 2001—; conducted psychotherapy group with 9/11 survivors, NYC, 2002; conducted 9/11 commemorative art exhibit Am. Group Psychotherapy Assn./N.Y. Times/9/11 Fund, N.Y.C., NY, 2002—04; presenter to workshops and confs.; book reviewer. Contbr. scientific papers, articles to profl. jours. Vol. Physicians Social Responsibility, 1980. Fellow, NIH, 1965—75; grantee, W.T. Grant Found., 2002—03, Pettus Found., 2004. Mem.: Ea. Group Psychotherapy Soc. (co-chair mentoring com. 2002—), Am. Group Psychotherapy Assn., NYU Alumni Assn., Bklyn. Coll. Alumni Assn. Democrat. Jewish. Avocations: drawing, skiing, kayaking, cooking, dancing. Office: Sibling Ctr 525 E 89th St #4C New York NY 10128 also: 180 E 79th St Ste 1C New York NY 10021 Office Phone: 212-831-5586.

ROTHENBERG, KAREN H., dean, law educator; BA magna cum laude, Princeton U., 1973, MPA, 1974; JD, U. Va., 1979. Faculty mem. U. Md. Sch. Law, 1983—, founding dir. Law & Health Care Prog., Marjorie Cook Prof. Law, interim dean, 1999—2001, dean, 2001—. Assoc. Covington and Burling, Washington, DC; pres. Am. Soc. Law, Medicine and Ethics; spl. asst. to dir. Office Rsch. on Women's Health, NIH, 1995—96. Co-editor-in-chief Jour. Law, Medicine, and Ethics; co-editor: Women and Prenatal Testing: Facing the Challenges of Genetic Technology; contbr. articles to profl. jours. Named one of Md. Top Women, Daily Record; recipient Joseph Healey Health Law Tchr.'s award, Am. Soc. Law, Medicine and Ethics, 1996, Md. Leadership in Law Award, 2003. Mem.: ABA (coordinating group on bioethics and the law), NIH (sect. on prenatal care, recruitment & ret. of women in clin studies, sect. on ethical, legal and social implications of genetics), Nat. Inst. Child & Human Develop. (adv. coun.), Nat. Action Plan Breast Cancer, Ethics in Reproduction (nat. adv. bd.), Inst. Medicine's Com. (sect. legal and ethical issues for inclusion of women in clin. stud.). Office: U Md Law Sch Dean's Office 500 W Baltimore St Baltimore MD 21201 Office Phone: 410-706-2041. Fax: 410-706-4045. Business E-Mail: krothenberg@law.umaryland.edu.

ROTHENBERG, LARAINE S., lawyer; b. Bklyn., Feb. 20, 1947; BA, U. Pa., 1967; JD, Columbia U., 1971. Bar: N.Y. 1972. Atty. Proskauer Rose LLP, 1974—90; ptnr. McDermott, Will & Emery, N.Y.C., 1990—94, Fried Frank Harris Shriver & Jacobson LLP, N.Y.C., 1994—. Contbr. articles to profl. jour. Bd. dir. Wallace Found., Pig Iron Theatre Co.; mem. bd. vis. Columbia Law Sch. Recipient Tax Mmgt. Disting. Author award, 1997, Women of Power and Influence award, NOW-NYC, 2002, Disting. Svc. medal, Columbia U. Alumni Fedn., 2003, award for outstanding pro bono svc., Legal Aid Soc., 2005. Mem. N.Y. State Bar Assn. (mem. exec. com. 1981-89, co-chmn. continuing legal edn. 1988-89, problems of the profession 1987-88, chmn. employee benefits com. 1985-86, co-chmn. 1984-85, chmn. exempt orgns. com. 1982-84, mem.-at-large exec. com. 1981-82), Assn. Bar City N.Y. (mem. taxation of corporations com. 1990—, chmn. spl. com. on employee benefits 1987-88, mem. taxation com. 1979-82), Internat. Bar Assn., Internat. Fiscal Assn.; founding mem. Alumnae Columbia Law Sch. Office: Fried Frank Harris Shriver & Jacobson LLP 1 New York Plz New York NY 10004 Business E-Mail: rothela@friedfrank.com.*

ROTHENBERG, LINDA ANN, science educator; b. NYC, May 11, 1956; d. John and Muriel Angus; m. Thomas Charles Rothenberg, Apr. 23, 1977; children: Mark, Jason. BA in Elem. Edn., Queens Coll., 1978, MS in Spl. Edn., 1982. Cert. early childhood edn. tchr. Fla. Bd. Edn., elem. edn. tchr. Fla. Bd. Edn. Sci. tchr. Hernando County Sch. Bd., Spring Hill, Fla., 2004—, elem. tchr., 1988—, dist. sci. fair dir., 1995—2004, tchr. trainer ESL, 1993—98, exceptional student educator, 1988—93; adj. instr. St. Leo's Coll., Dade City, Fla., 1994; elem. tchr. NYC Bd. Edn., 1978—88. Chmn. Pine Grove Sch. Adv. Bd., Brooksville, Fla., 1990—92. V.p. Springstead H.S. Band Boosters, Spring Hill, Fla., 2001—03; chmn. of charity events Nature Coast Corvettes, Spring Hill, 2003; support group leader Internat. Waldenstrom's Macroglobulin Anemia Found., 2004—. Grant, Hernando County Edn. Found., 2004. Mem.: Nat. Sci. Teachers Assn. Achievements include established Hands On Sci. Mus. for Children at Pine Grove Elem. Sch; established first science lab for Westside Elementary School. Avocations: painting, music, swimming. Office: Westside Elem Sch 2400 Applegate Dr Spring Hill FL 34609

ROTHENBERG, MIRA KOWARSKI, clinical psychologist, psychotherapist; b. Wilno, Poland; came to U.S., 1938; d. Jacob and Rosa (Joffe) Kowarski; m. Tev Goldsman, Dec. 7, 1960 (div. June 1974); 1 child, Akiva. BA, Bklyn. Coll., 1943; MA, Columbia U., 1957, Yeshiva U., 1959, ABD, 1962. Lic. psychologist, N.Y. Therapist, tchr.ir. Hawthorne (N.Y.) Cedar Knolls, 1952-53, League Sch., Bklyn., 1953-58; founder, clin. dir. Blueberry Treatment Ctrs., Bklyn., 1958-90; staff psychologist L.I. Coll. Hosp., Bklyn., 1966—. Pioneer in working with autistic children; cons. Beachbrook Nursery, Bkyn., 1969-70, San Felipe Del Rio, Santa Fe, 1980—, Children's House Montessori Nursery, Bklyn., 1982-89, Austrlia Dept. Edn., Carynia, New South Wales, SOS Village, Vilnius, Lithuania, 1997—; adj. prof. L.I. U., Bklyn., 1976-78; internat. speaker in field; worker, lectr. and cons. with psychotic and autistic children, Croatia, 1994, Lithuania, 1994-99; cons. for movies on foster care, 1990—; clin. cons. Sierra Leone project, 2002. Author: Children with Emerald Eyes, 1977, 2003, (with others) Pet Oriented Psychotherapy, 1980, The Outsiders, 1989; contbr. to books and articles to profl. jours. and mags.; documentary movie based on work with autistic children, 1962; Lithuanian play based on book, 1999; Children with Emerald Eyes play based on book, 1999. Bd. dirs. Friends of Island Acad. Mem. APA, World

Fedn. Mental Health, N.Y. State Psychol. Assn., Inter. Soc. Child Abuse and Neglect (Hamburg, Germany), Physicians for Social Responsibility, N.Y. Acad. Scis., Amnest Internat., ACLU, NOW, Anti Defamation League, Yivo, Nat. Register Svc. Providers in Psychology. Avocations: writing, painting, sculpture, dance. Home and Office: 160 State St Brooklyn NY 11201-5610 Office Phone: 718-875-6890. E-mail: mirark@cs.com.

ROTHENBERG, PAMELA V., lawyer; b. Ft. Knox, Ky., Dec. 11, 1958; BA in History summa cum laude, Tufts U., 1981; JD, Northwestern U., 1984. Bar: Ill. 1984, DC 1985. Assoc. Rudnick & Wolfe, Chgo., 1984—85, Lane & Edson PC, Washington, 1985—86; assoc & prin. David, Hagner, Kuney & Davison, Washington, 1986—98; mem. Womble Carlyle Sandridge & Rice PLLC, Washington, 1998—, co-mng. mem. Washington, DC office, 2004—. Mem.: ABA, Women's Bar Assn. of DC, Phi Beta Kappa. Office: Womble Carlyle Sandridge & Rice PLLC 7th Fl 1401 Eye St NW Washington DC 20005 Office Phone: 202-857-4422. Office Fax: 202-261-0022. Business E-Mail: prothenberg@wcsr.com.

ROTHENBERGER, DOLORES JANE, legal association administrator, actress, singer; b. Blue Island, Ill., July 19, 1932; d. Ervin Louis and Emily Lorraine (Karafa) R. Grad. h.s., Chgo. Sec. claims dept. Continental Casualty Co., Chgo., 1950-51; legal sec. Rlwy. Express Agy., Chgo., 1951-59, Slovacek and Galliani, Chgo., 1959-69; actress, singer various theaters, 1967—; asst. to exec. dir. Internat. Assn. of Def. Counsel, Chgo., 1982-98. Mng. editor company newsletter, 1985-98. Active campaign Gov. Otto Kerner, Ill.; dir. ch. choir, writer, prodr., choreographer ch. shows. Recipient 1st Joseph Jefferson award for best Chgo. actress Joseph Jefferson Com., 1970, Svc. award Village of Calumet Park, 1983. Mem. Actors' Equity Assn. Roman Catholic.

ROTHERMICH, GAYLA, music educator, director; b. Denver, May 5, 1946; d. C. Stanley and Bessey Welsh; children: Stefan, Candace. B in Music Edn., Wichita State U., s, 1968; MusM, So. Ill. U., Edwardsville, 1973; student, Hamburg Musikhochschule, Germany, 1973—75. Cert. instrumental/vocal K-12. Dir. Rothermich Studio for violin and viola, Ballwin, Mo., 1976—, St. Louis Suzuki Edn. Program, 1976—81; dir. strings, Suzuki specialist Parkway Sch. Dist./Barretts, Manchester, 1983—; program dir. Barretts Voyage to Mars, Manchester, Mo., 1999—. Freelance spkr. Parkway Sch. Dist., St. Louis, 1997—, Barretts Voyage to Mars, 1999—2000, musician website design, 1999—, prodr. integrated arts and scis. program, 1999—. Named All-State Award winner, Nat. Federated Music Club, 1964. Mem.: NEA (workshop leader Mo. state convention 2001), Music Educators Nat. Conf. (curriculum coun.), Am. String Tchrs. Assn., Social Concerns Com. Presbyterian. Avocations: computer technology/graphic design, gardening, travel, research, exploring. Office: Barretts Elem Sch 1780 Carman Rd Ballwin MO 63021 Personal E-mail: GRothermic@aol.com. Business E-Mail: grothermich@pkwy.k12.mo.us.

ROTHERMUND, CATHY LOU, elementary school educator; b. Wheeling, W.Va., Oct. 9, 1955; d. Richard L. and Martha L. (Vance) Ging; m. James E. Rothermund, Jr., July 26, 1980; children: Derek James, Chad Garrett. BS in Edn., Ohio U., 1977; MA in Edn., W.Va. U., 1983. Cert. elem. tchr., W.Va. Elem. sch. tchr. Ohio County Schs., Wheeling, 1977—, also TESA instr., 1981-84, also bldg. chairperson, 1986—. Mem. W.Va. Edn. Assn., Ohio Valley Lang. Arts Council, AAUW (treas. 1989—), Jr. League of Wheeling (parliamentarian 1988-91), Phi Kappa Phi. Presbyterian. Avocations: reading, music, movies, literature.

ROTHERT, MARILYN L., dean, nursing educator; b. June 4, 1939; married; 3 children. BSN cum laude, Ohio State U., 1961; MA in Ednl. Psychol., Mich. State U., 1979, PhD in Ednl. Psychol., 1980. RN, Mich. Staff nurse Univ. Hosp., Columbus, Ohio, 1961; instr. sch. nursing Hurley Hosp., Flint, Mich., 1961-66; asst. instr. sch. nursing Mich. State U., East Lansing, 1967-77, grad. asst. dept. community health sci., 1977-80, asst. prof. Coll. Human Medicine, 1980-82, asst. prof., dir. lifelong edn. Coll. Nursing, 1982-84, asst. prof. Coll. Human Medicine, 1982-84, assoc. prof., dir. lifelong edn. Coll. Nursing, 1984-88, assoc. prof. Coll. Human Medicine, 1984-86, prof., dir. lifelong edn. Coll. Nursing, 1988-92, prof., assoc. dean outreach and profl. devel., 1992-96, prof., dean Coll. Nursing, 1996—. Cons. No. Ill. U., Ohio State U., Mich. State Dept. Natural Resources, Can. Nurses Assn., Mich. Judicial Inst., Med. Coll. Va., U. Wash., Kirtland Coll., Anderson Coll. Contbr. articles to profl. jours. Co-chmn. Capitol Health Event, 1987-88; mem. worksite health subcom. Mich. Dept. Pub. Health; mem. State 4-H Health Com. Coop. Extension Svc., 1972-75, 82—; mem. med. adv. com. Mich. Civil Svc. Health Screening Unit, 1984. Mem. ANA (mem. coun. continuing edn., nurse researchers), Mich. Nurses Assn. (chmn. continuing edn. adv. com. 1989), Soc. for Med. Decision Making, The Brunswik Soc., Soc. for Judgment and Decision Making, Soc. for Rsch. in Nursing Edn., Midwest Nursing Rsch. Soc., Am. Pub. Health Assn., Nat. Ctr. for Health Edn., Nat. League for Nursing, Mich. State U. Faculty/Profl. Women's Assn. (bd. dirs. 1989—), Capitol Area Dist. Nurses Assn. (mem. nom. com. 1984-86, continuing edn. com. 1984), Phi Kappa Phi. Office: Mich State U Coll Nursing A-230 Life Sci Bldg East Lansing MI 48824

ROTHFIELD, NAOMI FOX, physician; b. Bklyn., Apr. 5, 1929; d. Morris and Violet (Bloomgarden) Fox; m. Lawrence Rothfield, Sept. 18, 1954; children: Susan, Lawrence, John, Jane. BA, Bard Coll., 1950; MD, NYU, 1955. Intern Lenox Hill Hosp., N.Y.C., 1955-56; instr. NYU Sch. Medicine, 1956-62, asst. prof., 1962-68; assoc. prof. U. Conn. Sch. Medicine, Farmington, 1968-72, prof., 1972—, chief divsn. rheumatic diseases, 1972—99. Contbr. chpts. to books, articles to med. jours. Bd. dirs. Conn. Choral Artists, 1999—. Mem. Am. Soc. Clin. Investigation, Am. Rheumatism Assn., Assn. Am. Physics. Jewish. Home: 540 Deercliff Rd Avon CT 06001-2859 Office: U Conn Sch Medicine Divsn Rheumatic Diseases Farmington CT 06030-0001 Office Phone: 860-679-3604. E-mail: rothfield@nso.uchc.edu.

ROTH-KAUFFMAN, MICHELE M., dean; b. Cleve. d. John and Rita Roth; m. Mark Kauffman; children: Adam Kauffman, Kevin Kauffman. BS in Physician Asst., St. Francis U., 1990; JD, Duquesne U., 1996. Bar: Pa. 1996, Ohio 1997; cert. physician asst. NCCPA. Chair physician asst. dept. Gannon U., Erie, Pa., 1997—, assoc. dean Coll. Scis. Engring. and Health Scis., 2004—. Legal aide vol. atty. LAVA, Erie; cons. Ohio Bd. Regents, Columbus, 2004—. Fellow: Pa. Soc. Physician Assts. (co-chair student affairs com. 2001—), Am. Acad. Physician Assts. Office: Gannon U 109 U Sq Erie PA 16541 Office Phone: 814-871-5645. Office Fax: 814-871-5502. E-mail: rothkauf001@gannon.edu.

ROTHMAN, BARBARA KATZ, sociology educator; b. NYC, June 21, 1948; d. Marcia Katz Berken; m. Herschel M. Rothman; children: Daniel Colb, Leah Colb, Victoria Colb. BA, Bklyn. Coll., 1969, MA, 1972; PhD, NYU, 1979. Prof. sociology CUNY, 1979—. Author: Recreating Motherhood, 1989, The Tentative Pregnancy, 1986, In Labor: Women and Power in the Birthplace, 1982, Of Maps and Imaginations: Genetic Thinking and The Meaning of Life, 1998, The Book of Life, 2000, Weaving a Family: Untangling Race and Adoption, 2005; editor: Ency. of Childbearing, 1993. Mem. Soc. for Study of Social Problems (pres. 1993-94). Office: CUNY Sociology Dept 55 Lexington Ave New York NY 10010-5518 Office Phone: 646-387-4470. Business E-Mail: bkatzrothman@gc.cuny.edu.

ROTHMAN, ESTHER POMERANZ, social agency executive, psychologist; b. N.Y.C., Nov. 25, 1919; d. Max and Anne (Reiner) Pomeranz; m. Arthur M. Rothman, Apr. 13, 1946; 1 dau., Amy. B.A., Hunter Coll., 1942; M.A., Columbia U., N.Y.C., 1944; M.A., CCNY, 1946; Ph.D., NYU, 1958. Cert. psychologist, N.Y. Tchr., N.Y.C. Bd. Edn., 1944-57, prin., 1957-80; exec. dir. Glie Youth Program, N.Y.C., 1980-85; exec. dir. Correctional Edn. Consortium, 1985—91; pres. Correctional Edn. Consortium, 1991—; research psychologist Tchrs. Hot Line, N.Y.C., 1972-74. Author: Angel Inside Went Sour, 1972; Troubled Teachers, 1974; co-author: Disturbed Child, 1967. Mem. Citizens Com. for Children, N.Y.C., 1972—. Recipient Valley Forge Freedom award, 1976. Fellow Am. Assn. Orthopsychiatry (sec. 1976-79); mem. Am. Psychol. Assn. Home: 200 E 16th St New York NY 10003-3707 Office: Correctional Edn Consortium 500 8 Ave New York NY 10018

ROTHMAN, JULIET CASSUTO, social work educator, writer; b. Chgo., Jan. 29, 1942; m. Leonard A. Rothman; children: Susan R. Kolko, Deborah M. Rothman, Daniel M. (dec.). BA, Tufts U., 1962; MSW, CUNY, 1973; MA, St. John's Coll., Annapolis, Md., 1988; PhD, Am. U., 1990. Cert. social worker Md. Geriat. cons. Chesapeake Manor Extended Care Annapolis Convalescent Ctr., 1974-90; tri-county social svcs. coord. Nat. Multiple Sclerosis Soc., Balt., 1980-82; lectr. Sch. Social Welfare, U. Calif., Berkeley, 1998—, lectr. Sch. Pub. Health, 2003—; prof. devel. faculty NASW, 1998—. Tutor Italian, Annapolis, 1974—88; chair ethics com. Chesapeake Manor, Annapolis, 1986—90, chair adv. bd., 1987—90; lectr. Anne Arundel C.C., Arnold, Md., 1988—90; vis. asst. prof. Nat. Cath. Sch. Social Svc., Cath. U., Washington, 1990—98; mem. ethics com. Hospice Chesapeake, 1992—97; adj. faculty Sch. Social Work, San Francisco State U., 1999—2000. Author: Saying Goodby to Daniel, 1994, A Birthday Present for Daniel, 1995 (award Parent Coun. 1997), The Bereaved Parent's Survival Guide, 1997, German edit., Dutch edit., From the Front Lines: Student Cases in Social Work Ethics, 1998, 2d edit., 2004, Contracting in Clinical Social Work, 1998, The Self-Awareness Workbook for Social Workers, 1999, Stepping Out into the Field: A Field Work Manual for Social Workers, 2000, Social Work Practice Across Disability, 2002; edit.adv. bd. Jour. Religeon & Spirituality, 2000—, Jour. Disability and Rehab., 2005—; contbr. articles to jours. in field; series editor Internat. Healthcare, Bern, Switzerland, 1990-2000. Judge Bd. of Elections, Anne Arundel County, Md., 1985-90; sec. Anne Arundel County Cmty. Svcs. Coalition, Annapolis, 1992-93; pres. Friends of Annapolis Chorale, 1992-94; mem. San Francisco City Chorus; docent Nat. Park Svc., Calif. Acad. Sci., 2003-; inspector Bd. Elections San Francisco City and County, 2003-. Mem. NASW, Am. Philos. Assn. Avocations: travel, music, photography, arts and crafts, outdoor activities.

ROTHMAN, PATRICIA MARY, elementary school educator; b. N.Y.C., May 30, 1946; d. Henry J. and Katherine (Enright) Parker; m. Neil F. Rothman, Aug. 30, 1945; children: Eric Parker, Craig Lawrence. BA, Mt. St. Mary Coll., Newburgh, N.Y., 1968; MA, Kean Coll., 1974; postgrad. computer sci., Jersey City State Coll., 1984. Cert. elem. tchr., tchr. of handicapped, N.J. Learning disabilities tchr. Bd. Coop. Edn. Svcs., Westchester, NY, 1968-69; tchr. educable class Wanamassa Sch., Ocean, NJ, 1969-72; supplemental tchr. Wall Cen. Sch., NJ, 1972-79; tchr. handicapped Brielle Elem. Sch., NJ, 1979—, tchr. 2nd grade, 1999—. Mem. NEA, N.J. Edn. Assn., Brielle Edn. Assn. (sec. 1983-88), AAUW, Westlake Golf and Country Club, Atlantic Club Tennis Group. Democrat. Roman Catholic. Avocations: skiing, tennis, swimming, golf. Office: Brielle Elem Sch 68 Oakmont Ln Jackson NJ 08527

ROTHMAN-BERNSTEIN, LISA J., occupational health nurse; b. Toledo, Dec. 29, 1949; 1 child, Daniel Karvinen. Diploma, Mercy Hosp. Sch. Nursing, Toledo, 1974; B Individualized Studies magna cum laude, Lourdes Coll., Sylvania, Ohio, 1989; AS in Bus., U. Toledo, 1970; cert. in Italian lang., history, art, U. Florence, Italy, 1972. Cert. hypnotherapist 2003. Buyer Lamson's of Toledo, 1971; owner, designer FUNKtional Art, Inc., 1984—; owner, baker Tres Bon Cheesecakes, Inc., Margate, Fla., 1984; cruise ship nurse Costa Cruise Line, Miami, Fla., 1979; sales Chandris Cruise Line, Greece, 1980, Bahama Cruise Line, Miami, Fla., 1980; home health nurse Upjohn, Ft. Lauderdale, Fla., 1983; patient svcs. coord. Fla. Med. Ctr., Lauderdale Lakes, Fla., 1983; sales and entertainment Norwegian Cruise Line, Miami, Fla., 1984—87; vol. nurse in ob-gyn. Yoseftal Hosp., Eilat, Israel, 1976—78; staff nurse in ob-gyn. Mt. Sinai Med. Ctr., Miami Beach, Fla., 1974—76; staff nurse on eye svc., oper. rm. St. Vincent Mercy Med. Ctr., Toledo, 1990, nursing and healthcare recruiter, 1991—95, patient advocate, 1995—99. Co-chair Lourdes Coll. Red Cross Blood Drive, 1988, 89; publicity chair St. Vincent Med. Ctr. 1993 Nurses' Week. Mem. Phi Theta Kappa, Kappa Gamma Pi.

ROTHMAN-DENES, LUCIA BEATRIZ, biology educator; b. Buenos Aires, Feb. 17, 1943; came to U.S., 1967; d. Boris and Carmen (Couto) Rothman; m. Pablo Denes, May 24, 1968; children: Christian Andrew, Anne Elizabeth. Lic. in Chemistry, Sch. Scis., U. Buenos Aires, 1964, PhD in Biochemistry, 1967. Vis. fellow NIH, Bethesda, Md., 1967-70; postdoctoral fellow biophysics U. Chgo., 1970-73, rsch. assoc., 1973-74, from asst. prof. to assoc. prof., 1974-83, prof. molecular genetics and cell biology, 1983—. Mem. microbial genetics study sect. NIH, 1980—83, 1993—96, chair, 1994—96, mem. genetic basis of disease study sect., 1985—89, mem. coun. Ctr. for Sci. Rev, 2000—04; sci. adv. com. Damon Runyon and Walter Winchell, NYC, 1989—93; biochemistry panel NSF, 1990—92. Contbr. articles to profl. jours. Fellow AAAS, Am. Acad. Microbiology (bd. govs. 2000-03); mem. Am. Acad. Arts and Scis., Am. Soc. Microbiology (divsn. chair 1985, divsn. group II rep. 1990-92, vice chair GMPC 1995-99, chair GMPC 1999-2001, chair meetings. bd. 2003-), Am. Soc. Virology (councilor 1987-90), Am. Soc. Biochemistry and Molecular Biology. Office: Univ Chgo 920 E 58th St Chicago IL 60637-5415 Office Phone: 773-702-1083. E-mail: lbrd@midway.uchicago.edu.

ROTHS, BEVERLY OWEN, municipal official; b. Kansas City, Kans., Aug. 25, 1935; d. Edward Charles and Josephine Mary (Vogel) Owen; m. Robert L. Roths, Sept. 4, 1954; children: Karen Kay, Daniel Owen, Nancy Jo. AA with honors, Antelope Valley Coll., 1975. Sec. McDonnell Aircraft Co., St. Louis, 1955-58; exec. dir. Florissant (Mo.) Valley C. of C., 1976-86; pres. Poppy Reserve/Mojave Desert Interpretive Assn., Lancaster, Calif., 1988-2000. Pres. Soroptimist Internat., North St. Louis County, 1981-82; sec.-treas. St. Louis County League C. of C., Clayton, 1978; bd. dirs. Lake Shastina (Calif.) Cmty. Svcs. Dist., 2003—. Prodr. Small Bus. Profiles, condr. interviews Storer Cable TV, Florissant, 1983-86. Mem. Florissant City Coun., 1968-72; bd. dirs. Mo. Mcpl. League First Woman, Florissant, 1970-71; co-chair Bicentennial, Florissant, 1985-86, Police Bldg. Bond Issue, Florissant, 1980. Recipient Woman of Achievement award, Florissant Bus. and Profl. Women, 1979, Superior Achievement award, State Calif. Dept. Parks and Recreation, 1999; Inst. Orgn. Mgmt. scholar, C. of C. Jefferson City, Mo., 1980. Mem. Lancaster Woman's Club., Wildflower Preservation Found. (bd. dirs., treas. 1991-2000), League Calif. State Park Non-Profit Orgns. (bd. dirs., sec. 1994-98), Poppy Res./Mojave Desert Interpretive Assn. (pres. 1988-2000). Roman Catholic. Avocations: bird watching, gardening, golf, reading, genealogy.

ROTHSCHILD, AMALIE RANDOLPH, filmmaker, film producer, film director, photographer; b. Balt., June 3, 1945; d. Randolph Schamberg and Amalie Getta (Rosenfeld) R. BFA, R.I. Sch. Design, 1967; MFA in Motion Picture Prodn., NYU, 1969. Spl. effects staff in film and photography Joshua Light Show, Fillmore E. Theatre, N.Y.C., 1969-71; artist-photographer represented by Staley-Wise Gallery N.Y.C., 2004. Still photographer TWA Airlines Pub. Rels. Dept., Village Voice newspaper, Rolling Stone mag., Newsweek mag., After Dark, N.Y. Daily News, others, 1968-72; co-founder, ptnr. New Day Films, distbn. coop., 1971—; owner operator Anomaly Films Co., N.Y.C., 1971—; mem., co-founder Assn. Ind. Video and Filmmakers, Inc., N.Y.C., 1974; bd. dirs., 1974-78; instr. in film and TV, NYU Inst. of Film and TV, 1976-78; cons. in field to various organizations including Youthgrant Program of Nat. Endowment for Humanities, Washington, 1973-76. Exhibitions include Soho Triad Fine Arts Gallery, 1997, 2000, 2002, Gomez Gallery, 1998, 2000, VH-1 Mus. First Gallery, 1999, Govinda Gallery, 2001, Snap Galleries, Birmingham, Eng., 2005, SACI, Florence, Italy, 2005, Tate Gallery, Liverpool, England, 2005, Holden Luntz Gallery, 2005, Redferns Music Picture Gallery, London, 2006; (film): Woo Who? May Wilson, 1969, It Happens to Us, 1972, Nana, Mom and Me, 1974, Radioimmunoassay of Renin, Radioimmunoassay of Aldosterone, 1973, Conversations with Willard Van Dyke, 1981, Richard Haas: Work in Progress, 1984, Painting the Town: The Illusionistic Murals of Richard Haas, 1990 (Emily award Am. Film and Video Festival 1990); editor: Doing It Yourself, Handbook on Independent Film Distribution, 1977; author: Live at the Fillmore East: A Photographic Memoir, 1999; licensed photograph collections include Corbis/Bettmann Archive, 1994—, Star File Photo Agy., 1997-. Mem. Cmty. Planning Bd. 1, Borough of Manhattan, N.Y.C., 1974-86. Recipient spl. achievement award Mademoiselle mag., 1972; Ind. filmmaker grant Am. Film Inst. 1973; film grantee N.Y. State Coun. on the Arts, 1977, 85, 87, Nat. Endowment Arts, 1978, 85, 87, Md. Arts Coun., 1977, Ohio Arts and Humanities Couns., 1985. Mem.: AIVF, Ind. Documentary Assn., NY Women in Film, Univ. Film and Video Assn. Democrat. Address: 135 Hudson St New York NY 10013-2102 also: Via Carrand 22 Florence 50133 Italy E-mail: a.rothschild@agora.it.

ROTHSCHILD, GITA F., lawyer; b. 1950; BA, George Washington U., 1971; MS, Boston U., 1972; JD cum laude, Temple U. Sch. of Law, 1977. Bar: NJ 1977, NY 1984, US Ct. of Appeals, Second & Third Circuits, US Supreme Ct. Ptnr., insurance group McCarter & English, Newark. Chmn., dist. V fee arbitration com. NJ Supreme Ct., 1984—88; mem. Am. Law Inst., Defense Rsch. Inst.; faculty mem. Defense Trial Academy, 1996; ed. bd. mem. NJ Lawyer, 1996—99. Mem.: ABA, Internat. Assn. of Defense Counsel, Essex County Bar Assn., NJ State Bar Assn. Office: McCarter & English Four Gateway Ctr 100 Mulberry St Newark NJ 07102 Office Phone: 973-639-5959. Office Fax: 973-624-7070. Business E-Mail: grothschild@mccarter.com.

ROTHSCHILD, JENNIFER ANN, artist, educator; b. Mesa, Ariz., Aug. 16, 1948; d. Joe Dean and Frances Ann (McFarland) Johnston; m. Harry Ronald Rothschild, Feb. 14, 1981. Diploma, El Camino Jr. Coll., 1968; BA in Art Edn., Calif. State U., 1970. Cert. secondary sch. tchr., Calif. Arts and crafts specialist City of Hawthorne (Calif.) Parks and Recreation, 1966-67; portrait artist Disneyland, Anaheim, Calif., 1970-74; secondary sch. art tchr. Orange (Calif.) Unified Schs., 1972-80; freelance custom apparel designer Honolulu, 1982-94; sculptor, artist, 1994—. One woman show at Roy's Honolulu, 2001, Art Centre Gallery, Honolulu, 1997, Studio 1 Gallery, 2004; corp. artist Arts of Paradise Gallery, Honolulu, 1997—; exhibited in show at City of Manhattan Beach, Calif., 1966, Assn. of Hawaii Artists, 1996—, in book Encyclopedia of Living Artists, 10th edit., 1997. Bd. dirs. Hawaii Tennis Patrons, Honolulu, 1996—. Assn. of Hawaii Artists Show chairwoman, 2002. Recipient scholarship Chouinard Sch. Art Inst., 1965-66, 1st Place Stamp Design award Easter Seals, 1995-96, Hokele Artists award Hawaiian Airlines, 1996, Most Unique Art award Assn. of Hawaii Artists Aloha Show, 1997. Fellow Nat. Mus. Women in Arts; mem. AAUW, Honolulu Art Acad., Assn. Hawaii Artists (v.p. 1996-97, pres. 1999-2001), Hawaiian Pacific Tennis Assn. (rules chmn. 1997), mem. Windward Art Guild, 2002, Nat. League of Am. Pen Women, Hon., chapter, Alpha Omicron Pi. Republican. Presbyterian. Avocations: reading, writing, painting, sculpting, carving. E-mail: onoaloha@hawaii.rr.com.

ROTHSTEIN, BARBARA JACOBS, federal judge; b. Bklyn., Feb. 3, 1939; d. Solomon and Pauline Jacobs; m. Ted L. Rothstein, Dec. 28, 1968; 1 child, Daniel BA, Cornell U., 1960; LL.B., Harvard U., 1966. Bar: Mass. 1966, Wash. 1969, U.S. Ct. Appeals (9th cir.) 1977, U.S. Dist. Ct. (we. dist.) Wash. 1971, U.S. Supreme Ct. 1975. Pvt. practice law, Boston, 1966-68; asst. atty. gen. State of Wash., 1968-77; judge Superior Ct., Seattle, 1977-80, Fed. Dist. Ct. Western Wash., Seattle, 1980—, chief judge, 1987-94, dir. Fed. Jud. Ctr., 2003—. Faculty Law Sch. U. Wash., 1975-77, Hastings Inst. Trial Advocacy, 1977, N.W. Inst. Trial Advocacy, 1979—; mem. state-fed. com. U.S. Jud. Conf., chair subcom. on health reform; dir. Fed. Jud. Ctr.; bd. dirs. Inst. Jud. Adminstrn., NYU Sch. Law. Recipient Matrix Table Women of Yr. award Women in Communication, Judge of the Yr. award Fed. Bar Assn., 1989; King County Wash. Women Lawyers Vanguard Honor, 1995 Mem. Am. Judicature Soc. (mem. commn.), Nat. Assn. Women Judges, Fellows of the Am. Bar, Am. Law Inst. (bd. dirs.), Wash. State Bar Assn., Am. Law Inst., Phi Beta Kappa, Phi Kappa Phi. Office: Fed Jud Ctr 1 Columbus Cir NE Washington DC 20002-8003

ROTHSTEIN, LAURA, dean, law educator; BA, U. Kans., 1971; JD, Georgetown U. Law Ctr., 1974. Asst. prof. law Ohio No. U., 1976—79, dir. admissions, 1978—79; assoc. prof. law W.Va U., 1980—84, prof. law, 1984—86, U. Houston, 1985—96, assoc. dean Student Affairs, 1988—93, Law Found. prof., 1996—2000, assoc. dean Grad. Studies and Spl. Progs., 1999—2000; prof. law Brandeis Sch. Law, U. Louisville, 2000—, dean, 2000—. Vis. asst. prof. law U. Pitts., 1979—80; staff atty. Dept. Justice, Antitrust Div., Washington, DC, 1974—75, Ohio State Atty. Gen., Antitrust Sec., 1975—76, Devel. Disabilities Law Project, U. Pitts. Sch. Law, 1979—80; affiliated Appalachian Rsch. & Defense Fund, Inc., Charleston, W.Va., 1980—85; assoc. dir. devel. Health Law and Policy Inst., U. Houston, 1997—2000. Editor: Health Law News, 1993—98; contbr. articles to law jours. Bd. mem. Urban Montessori Sch., Louisville, 2001—; adv. bd. mem. Children's Organ Transplant Assn., 2000—. Mem.: ABA (mem. Diversity Com. 2002—), Soc. Am. Law Tchrs., Brandeis Inns Ct., Ky. Bar Assn., Ky. Bar Found., Louisville Bar Assn., River Oaks Women's Breakfast Club. Office: Louis D Brandeis Sch Law U Louisville Wilson W Wyatt Hall 2301 S Third St Louisville KY 40292 Office Phone: 502-852-6879. Office Fax: 502-852-0862. E-mail: laura.rothstein@louisville.edu.

ROTHSTEIN, RUTH M., county health official; Dir. Cook County Hosp., Chgo., to 1999; chief Cook County Bur. of Health Svcs., Chgo., 1999—. Office: Cook County Bur Hlth Svcs 1900 W Polk St Ste 220 Chicago IL 60612-3736

ROTH TAYLOR, LYNN E., gifted and talented educator; b. Chgo., Ill., Oct. 7, 1947; d. Robert James Roth and Eleanor Claire Norton; m. Lewis Jay Taylor, III, May 24, 1984; 1 child, Franklin Van Meter Taylor. BA, Coll. of Holy Names, Oakland, Calif., 1966—70; MEd, U. Calif., Berkeley, 1970—72; M in Elem. & Secondary Edn., Calif. State U., L.A., 1976—80; coursework in Gifted Edn., U.Va., Charlotteville, 1989—2006. Cert. Tchr., Gifted Endorsement. Mid. sch. tchr. Montebello Unified Sch. Dist., Calif., 1973—75, profl. staff devel. tchr., trainer on curriculum, 1975—79, gifted specialist, mid. sch., 1979—84; primary specialist Norfolk Pub. Schs., Va., 1984—86, gifted edn. specialist, 1986—97, sr. coord., gifted edn., 1997—2000; literacy specialist Va. State Dept. Edn., 2000—06, U. Va., 2000—06. Adj. prof. U. Va., 1989—2006; sec. Gifted Edn. Coun., Norfolk, 2003—; data analysis team leader, Norfolk, 2005—06; cons. & presenter in field. Precinct capt. Talbot Pk. Civic League, 2001—06, pres., 2003—06, Granby HS PTA, Norfolk, 2002—06; profl. senate Supt.'s Educator's Coun., 2003—06. Recipient Tchr. of Yr., 2002—04, Sch. Bell award, Coun. Gifted Children, 2002, Dist. Level Tchr. of Yr., 2004; grantee, Reader's Digest Found., 1995. Mem.: ASCD, Va. Assn. Gifted, Nat. Assn. Gifted Children. Independent. Avocation: playwriting. Home: 516 Oak Grove Rd Norfolk VA 23505 Office: Norfolk Pub Schs 800 City Hall Blvd Norfolk VA 23507

ROTHWARF, MARTA, lawyer; b. 1957; Degree, Rutgers U., 1979; diploma, U. London, 1984; JD, Temple U., 1990. Pvt. atty., 1990—94; asylum officer Dept. Homeland Security, Bureau Citizenship and Immigration Svc. (formerly INS), LA, 1994—97, Washington, 1997—2003; assoc. gen. council Office Gen. Council, Exec. Office Immigration Review, US Dept. Justice, 2003—. Mem.: DC Bar Assn., NY Bar Assn., NJ Bar Assn., Pa. Bar Assn. Office: US Dept Justice Exec Office Immigration Review Office Dir 5107 Leesburg Pike Ste 2600 Falls Church VA 22041

ROTHWELL, ELAINE B., artist; b. Mpls., May 8, 1926; d. Frederick Roscoe and Stella Frances (LaVallee) Bartholomew; m. William Stanley Rothwell, May 10, 1946; children: Suzanne, Amy Verrett, Wendy Rothwell-Lopez, Bart. BFA, San Jose State U., 1966; pvt. study, Woodbury Graphic Studio, Los Altos, Calif., 1975-76, Amaranth Intaglio Workshop, Los Altos, 1985. One-woman shows include Triton Mus. Art, Santa Clara, Calif., 1976, Palo Alto Civic Ctr., Calif., 1977, Stanford Art Spaces, Stanford U., Calif., 1985, 1988, 1989, West Valley Art Mus., Surprise, Ariz., 1996, Roseville Arts Ctr., Calif., 2003, exhibited in group shows at Carnegie Art Ctr., North Tonawanda, N.Y., 1995, 1996, N.J. Ctr. Visual Arts Internat., Summit, 1997, 1998, Brand Libr. and Art Ctr., Glendale, Calif., 1996, Internat. Exhbn. Art League Manatee County, Fla., 1996, Nat. Soc. Artists, 1997, Am. Color Print

Soc., 1997, Grand Exhbn. Nat. Competition, Akron, Ohio, 1998, Printwork '98, Barrett Ho., Poughkeepsie, N.Y., 1998, 73d Ann. Internat. Print Competition/Print Ctr., Phila., 1999, Manhattan Arts Internat., 1999, Chautauqua Nat. Exhbn. Am. Art, 1999, No. Colo. Ann. Nat. Exhbns., 1999, 2000, Stage Gallery, Merrick, N.Y., 2000, Pacific Prints, Palo Alto, Calif., 2006, retrospective exhbns., Gallery 9, Los Altos, Calif., 2002, Gallery II, Nevada City, Calif., 2002, Represented in permanent collections Newberry Libr., Chgo., Triton Mus. Art, Santa Clara, West Valley Art Mus., Brand Libr. Art Ctr., Glendale. Mem.: Am. Color Print Soc., Nat. Mus. Women in Arts (charter), Crocker Art Mus., Auburn Old Town Gallery, Triton Mus. Art. Home and Office: 3030 Eagles Nest Auburn CA 95603-5918

ROTOLO, SUSAN (SUZE), artist; b. N.Y.C., Nov. 20, 1943; d. Joachim Peter and Mary Teresa Rotolo; m. Enzo Bartoccioli; 1 child, Luca. Tchr. bookmaking; workshop leader in field. Illustrator, designer textiles, compact disc cover art, scenery and props for theater, Laugh the Blues Away Cookbook, 2001; solo exhbns. at Jefferson Market Libr., N.Y.C., 1997, 98, 99, NYU Casa Italiana Gallery, 1998, Donnell Libr. Ctr., N.Y. Pub. Libr., 2000, Ctr. for Book Arts, N.Y.C., 2001, 05; art exhibited in shows including Galleria Todini, Perugia, Italy, Ctr. for Book Arts, N.Y.C., ARC Gallery, Chgo., Spring Studio, N.Y.C., Columbia Coll. Gallery, Chgo., N.Y. State Mus., Albany, Left Bank Gallery, Bennington, Vt., Art Acad. Cin., Nat. Guild Bookworkers Traveling Exhbn., Harper Collins Exhbn. Space, N.Y.C., Corcoran Gallery, Washington, Nat. Mus. Women in Arts, Washington, Md. Fedn. Art, Balt., Medlalia Gallery, N.Y.C., many others; artist one-of-a-kind sculptural books; included in Book Arts Collection of L.I. U., Bklyn. Mus., Nat. Mus. Women in the Arts, Washington, Mus. Modern Art, Franklin Furnace, N.Y.C.; art appears in books pub. by Lark Books, Davis Publs.; featured in Somerset Studio Mag., 2005, other nat. and internat. art publs.; appearances (TV shows) No Direction Home: Bob Dylan, PBS, NY Voices: Big Town Groove (PBS). Recipient Spl. Mention award for tech. expertise combined with creative risk, Appearances and West Village Coalition for Parks and Playgrounds, 1995, First Pl. Jury prize Valdosta (Ga.) Fine Arts Gallery, Valdosta (Ga.) U. Mem. Ctr. for Book Arts, Am. Craft Coun., Guild of Bookworkers. Avocations: art, music, reading. Office: Suzart 682 Broadway New York NY 10012-2320 Office Phone: 212-254-5591. E-mail: suzarte@verizon.net.

ROUBIEU, AMANDA MARCELLE, elementary school educator; b. New Orleans, Mar. 5, 1956; d. Roger Jerome and Nancy C. Roubieu. BS in Elem. Edn., U. Louisville, Louisville, Ky., 1979, MA in Elem. Edn., 1981, student in Secondary Social Studies, 1998—2000, MA in History, 2000. Cert. tchr. Ky. Dept. Edn., 1979. Tchr. LaGrange Edn. Ctr., Louisville, 1984—2001, Carrithers Mid. Sch., Louisville, 2001—. Sec. faculty exec. com. Ky. Cmty. and Tech. Coll. Sys., Louisville, 2000—01, mem. peer rev. com., 2000—01; mem. adult edn. credentialing com. Ky., Frankfort, 2000—01; mem. state textbook com. Ky. Dept. Edn., Louisville, 2006—; coach cross-country Carrrithers Mid. Sch., Louisville, 2002—06; coach chess team Carrithers Mid. Sch., 2002—, coach track team, 2002—05, team leader, 2004—. Author: The Flame in Winter (named Outstanding Poem, Nat. Poetry contest, 2005); contbr. articles to profl. jours. Nominee Best Tchr. award, Nat. Hon. Soc., 2006; named Educator of the Year, LaGrange Edn. Ctr., 1985, 2000. Mem.: NEA. Avocations: reading, photography, history, movies, travel. Home: 9400 Doral Court 7 Louisville KY 40220 Office: Carrithers Middle School 4320 Billtown Road Louisville KY 40229 Office Phone: 502-485-8224. Personal E-mail: aroubieu@aol.com.

ROUECHE, SUANNE DAVIS, university administrator; b. Dallas, Aug. 6, 1942; d. Raymond Louis and Edna Sue (Leatherwood) Davis; m. Benjamin Frank Maca, June 12, 1964 (div. Feb. 1975); 1 child, Robin Sue; m. John Edward Roueche, May 22, 1976; children: Michelle, John III BA English, North Tex. State U., 1964, MA English, 1967; PhD, U. Tex., 1976. Tchr. English Sam Houston H.S., Arlington, Tex., 1964—65, MacArthur H.S., Irving, Tex., 1966—67; instr. El Centro Coll., Dallas, 1967—74; dir. cmty. coll. internship program U. Tex., Austin, 1976—82, dir. Nat. Inst. for Staff and Orgnl. Devel., 1982—. Cons. in field Co-author: Between a Rock and a Hard Place, 1993 (Disting. Rsch. award 1993-94), Strangers in Their Own Land, 1995 (Dist. Rsch. award 1995-96), Embracing the Tiger, 1997, The Company We Keep, 1995, High Stakes, High Performance: Making Remedial Education Work, 1998, In Pursuit of Excellence: The Community College of Denver, 2001, Practical Magic: On the Front Lines of Teaching Excellence, 2003; contbr. more than 50 articles to profl. jours Mem. Assistance League Austin, 2002—, v.p. resource devel., 2004—; mem. chancellor's coun. U. Tex. Sys.; mem. Pres.' Assocs., U. Tex., Austin Named Ky. Col., Ky. State Legis. and Gov., 1979; recipient Disting. Leadership award Fla. State Legis., 1989, Nat. Leadership award Am. Assn. Cmty. Colls., 1997, Disting. Svc. award Nat. Coun. Instrnl. Adminstrn., 2001, One of Ten Women On Their Toes, Ballet Austin, 2006. Mem. Littlefield Soc., Delta Gamma (pres. alumnae 1979-81) Avocations: needlepoint, reading, gardening, wildlife rehabilitation. Office: Nat Inst Staff/Orgnl Devel MLK/Speedway SZB 348 Austin TX 78712 Office Phone: 512-471-7545.

ROUGEMONT, DENISE, elementary school educator; b. La Plata, Md., Aug. 12, 1970; d. John and Sandra (Myatt) Hall; m. Calvin Rougemont, Aug. 1, 1999; children: Calie, Clay, Devin. MEd, Trevecca Nazarene, Nashville, 1998. 7th grade sci. tchr. Charlotte Mid. Sch., Tenn., 1987—. Recipient Apple for the Tchr. award, Channel 4 News, 2006. Home: 4965 Hwy 49 W Vanleer TN 37181 Office: Charlotte Mid Sch 250 Humphries St Charlotte TN 37036 Office Phone: 615-740-6060. Business E-Mail: drougemont@dcbe.org.

ROUGH, MARIANNE CHRISTINA, librarian, educator; b. Glen Cove, N.Y., June 27, 1941; d. Michael Anthony Scarangello, Ann Nancy (Kulka) Scarangello; m. Allan Conrad Rough; 1 child, William Johnson. AAS, SUNY, Farmingdale, 1976; BA, SUNY, Old Westbury, 1977; MLS, L.I. U., 1978; cert. in advanced librarianship, Columbia U., 1985. Art dir. Technamation, Inc., Port Washington, NY, 1962—68; dir. new product design Queens Lithography, Inc., L.I., NY, 1968—70; tech. specialist SUNY, Coll.at Farmingdale, 1970—78; dir. Libr. Learning Resources Ctr. SUNY, Coll. Old Westbury, 1978—82; prof., libr. Prince George's C.C., Largo, Md., 1983—. Mem. C.C. adv. group OCLC Online Computer Libr. Ctr., Inc., Dublin, 2001—. Contbr. chapters to books. Regional publicity coord. Audubon Soc., L.I., 1978—79; coordinating team mem. Sierra Club, Annual C&O Canal Hike, Washington, 1991—95; bd. dirs. Friends Pub. Libr., Port Washington, NY, 1980—81. Recipient award of merit, Md. Assn. Higher Edn., 1987; grantee Pathfinder grants, Prince George's C.C., 1999, 2001. Mem.: Assn. Coll. and Rsch. Librs. of ALA (sec. cmty. and jr. coll. sect. 2001—02, vice-chmn., chmn.-elect, past chmn. 2002—), Assn. Libr. Collections and Tech. Svcs. of ALA (sec. coun. regional groups 1999—2001, Md. rep. Potomac Tech. Processing Librs.). Methodist. Avocations: fine art, art history, history, historical preservation. Home: 1015 Danbury Dr Bowie MD 20721-3202 Office: Prince Georges CC 301 Largo Rd Upper Marlboro MD 20774-2199 Home Fax: 301-390-7824; Office Fax: 301-808-8847. Personal E-mail: mrough@pgcc.edu.

ROUGHIA, GINGER LOU, elementary school educator; b. Decatur, Ind., Feb. 5, 1955; d. Gail Alton Runyon and Doris Erlene Haines; m. Jon David Roughia, June 21, 1975; 1 child, Jill Elizabeth. BS, Bowie State Coll., Md., 1977; MS, St. Francis Coll., Fort Wayne, Ind., 1982. Cert. tchr. K-8 Ind. Dept. Edn., 1977. Tchr. sci. grade 6 South Adams Schs., Geneva, Ind., 1977—87, tchr. reading and spelling grade 6, 1987—97, tchr. social studies grade 6, 1997—. Vol. Jay County Hist. Soc., Portland, Ind., 2004—05, Jay County Genealogy Soc., 2004—05; mem. Redeemer Luth. Ch., Bryant, Ind., 1988—. Recipient Make a Difference Tchg. award, South Adams Student Coun., 2005. Mem.: East Ctrl. Reading Coun. Avocations: history, sewing, photography, knitting, crocheting. Home: 8931 N 125 W Bryant IN 47326 Office: South Adams Schs 105 W Line St Geneva IN 46740 Office Phone: 260-368-7256.

ROUKEMA, MARGARET SCAFATI, congresswoman; b. West Orange, N.J., Sept. 19, 1929; d. Claude Thomas and Margaret (D'Alessio) Scafati; m. Richard W. Roukema, Aug. 23, 1951; children: Margaret, Todd (dec.), Gregory. BA with honors in History and Polit. Sci, Montclair State Coll., 1951, postgrad. in history and guidance, 1951-53; postgrad. program in city and regional planning, Rutgers U., 1975. Tchr. history, govt., public schs., Livingston and Ridgewood, N.J., 1951-55; mem. U.S. Congress from 7th N.J. dist., Washington, 1981—83, U.S. Congress from 5th N.J. dist., Washington, 1983—2003; vice chair fin. svcs. com., chair housing and community opportunity subcom.; mem. banking com., edn. and the workforce com. Vice pres. Ridgewood Bd. Edn., 1970-73; bd. dirs., co-founder Ridgewood Sr. Citizens Housing Corp.; chairwoman Fin. Inst. and Consumer Credit Sub. Com. U.S. Congress; sponcer Family Med. Leave U.S. Congress; lectr. Rutgers Univ. Trustee Spring House, Paramus, N.J.; trustee Leukemia Soc. No. N.J., Family Counseling Service for Ridgewood and Vicinity; mem. Bergen County (N.J.) Republican Com.; NW Bergen County campaign mgr. for gubernatorial candidate Tom Kean, 1977; bd. mem. Children's Aid and Family Svcs., The Red Cross, Ramapo Coll. Mem. Bus. and Profl. Women's Orgn. Clubs: Coll. of Ridgewood, Ridgewood Rep. Republican.

ROULEAU, ANN F., retired elementary school educator; b. Rumford, Maine, May 15, 1939; d. Arthur J. and Gwendolyn Ferland; m. Robert J. Rouleau, July 1986; children: Jeffrey, Terrence, Wayne. BS, U. Maine, Farmington, 1978. Cert. tchr. Maine. Staffing supr. Rumford Cmty. Hosp., 1968—78; mid. sch. tchr. Mexico Sch. Adminstrv. Dist., Maine, 1978—2001; ret., 2001. Mem.: Red Hat Soc. Western Maine, Mexico Mothers' Club (sec.). Home: 1142 Rte 2 PO Box 662 Rumford ME 04276

ROULY, ELLIE ARCENEAUX, dancer, educator; b. New Iberia, La., Sept. 18, 1977; d. James and Paula Arceneaux; m. Karl Anthony Rouly, June 1, 2002; 1 child, Karrigan Elizabeth Andrea'. BA in Elem. Edn., U. La., Lafayette, 2001. Presch. tchr. ABC 123's Presch. Daycare, New Iberia, La., 1995—2001; dir., choreographer Dance Connection, 1998—; tchr. VB Glencoe Charter Sch., Franklin, 2001—. Lt. Mystic Krewe de Fou of Iberia, 1998. Scholar, Ladies Aux. Club, 1995. Office: VB Glencoe Charter School 4491 La 83 Franklin LA 70538 Office Phone: 337-923-6900.

ROUMBOS, MARIA K., elementary school educator; b. Flushing, NY, Nov. 22, 1970; d. Kostas J. and Alexandra K. Roumbos; m. Mark A. Cichon, July 2, 1995; children: Michael Roumbos Cichon, Marissa Roumbos Cichon. BS in Elem. Edn. summa cum laude, Adelphi U., 1991, MA in Secondary Edn. in Math. summa cum laude, 1993. Cert. tchr. early childhood edn., elem. edn., math. edn. Tchr. St. Nicholas Ch. Sch., Flushing, NY, 1986—, asst. dir., 1990—; tchr. Floral Park-Bellerose Sch. Dist., 1991—. Tutor in field, NY, 1991—2001. Recipient Pres.'s Achievement award, Queens Coll., 1989, Honors in Sci. and Math cert. merit, Soc. Women Engrs., 1991, Merit award, N.Y.C. Assn. Tchrs., 1988, Scholastic Achievement award, N.Y. Gov.'s Com., 1991, Merit award, Hellenic U. Club of N.Y., 1993, Outstanding Achievement award, Greek Lang. Inst., 1988, Internat. award for Striving for Peace on Earth, N.Y. Dist. of Kiwanis, 1987; Paul Douglas scholar, Empire State Challenger scholar, United Fedn. Tchrs. scholar, N.Y. State scholar. Mem.: Inst. for Math. and Sci. Studies (life), Internat. Baccalaureate Scholars (life), Nat. Honor Soc. (life; chpt. co-pres. 1987—88), Kappa Delta Pi (life). Democrat. Greek Orthodox. Avocations: reading, photography, painting, arts-n-crafts, gardening.

ROUMM, PHYLLIS EVELYN GENSBIGLER, retired literature educator, writer; b. New Alexandria, Pa., Jan. 1, 1927; d. Theodore Roosevelt and Daisy Isabelle (Patterson) Gensbigler; m. Milton Leonard Roumm, Nov. 23, 1946; children: David Lynn, Nikolyn, Dennis Eric, Janna Leigh. BS in English Edn., Indiana U. of Pa., 1945, MEd, 1963; postgrad., Ohio U., 1964, 65; PhD, Kent State U., 1977. Tchr. English Elders Ridge (Pa.) Joint HS, 1945-46, Apollo (Pa.) HS, 1946-47; tchr. English, speech Indiana (Pa.) Area Jr.-Sr. HS, 1959-67; tchg. fellow Kent (Ohio) State U., 1970-71; prof. English Indiana U. Pa., 1967-85, prof. emeritus, 1985—. Freelance writer, 1985—; mem. strategic planning steering com. Indiana Area Sch. Dist. Bd. dirs. Hist. and Geneal. Soc. Indiana County, 1984, Indiana Free Libr., 1988—91; mem. health promotion com. Aging Svcs., Inc., Indiana; mem. Last Stand, Key West, Fla., Friends of Libr., Key West. Mem.: AAUW, Pa. Assn. Sch. Retirees (Ind. County chpt.), Indiana Wordsmiths, So. Humanities Conf., Ligonier Valley Writers Assn., Coll. English Assn. (life), Pa. Sch. Retirees, Hadassah (life), Derry Hist. Soc. (life), Kent State Alumni Assn. (life), Pa. Ret. State Employees (v.p. Indico chpt. 1996—97, pres. 1997—98, bd. dirs. 1998—), Assn. Pa. State Coll. and Univ. Ret. Faculty (bd. dirs. 1998—), Am. Assn. Ret. People, New Century Club, Alpha Delta Kappa (pres. 1968—70, Silver Sister award 1991), Phi Delta Kappa. Avocations: reading, reviewing books, walking, writing. Home: 310 Poplar Ave Indiana PA 15701-3024

ROUNTREE, RUTHANN LOUISE, social worker, lecturer; b. Denver, Mar. 18, 1950; d. Charles Lindy and Marian Louise (Jenkins) R. BSW, U. Nebr., 1972; MSW, Denver U., 1973; MDiv, Fuller Theol. Sem., 1988; postgrad. social work studies, U. So. Calif., 1993—. Lic. clin. social worker, Calif.; ordained minister African Meth. Episcopal Ch. Asst. dir. Denver br. Virginia Neal Blue Resource Ctr. for Colo. Women, Denver, 1973-76; cons, edn. coord. Aurora (Colo.) Community Mental Health Ctr., 1976-78; program evaluator Castle Substance Abuse Program, L.A., 1978-81; program ops. mgr. Nat. Coun. on Aging, L.A., 1981-85; program mgr. gerontology out-patient facility Fuller Theol. Sem., Pasadena, Calif., 1985-89; mem. faculty, dir. of admissions, dept. social work Calif. State U., Long Beach, 1989-93, part-time faculty, 1993—; dir. tng. and edn. Martin Luther King Jr./Charles R. Drew Med. Ctr., 1997—. Vice chair San Gabriel Valley Elder Abuse Task Force, Pasadena, Calif., 1987-88; bd. dirs. Living at Home Project, Pasadena, 1988-89; mem. Black Aging Network, L.A., 1990-92; patr-time faculty Immaculate Heart Coll. Ctr., L.A., 1997—. Contbr. articles various profl. jours. Facilitator Diakanos-Inner Healing Workshops, Pasadena, 1987-88; adv. YWCA Rape Hotline, Pasadena, 1987-89; dir. westside counseling and tng. ctr., pastoral counselor Westminster Presbyn. Ch., 1991-93; trainer lay counselor and peer counselor; assoc. min. Holy Trinity AME Ch., Long Beach, 2002—. Recipient Gov.'s award State of Calif., 1987; named Outstanding Young Women of Am., 1987. Mem. ASTD, NASW (mem. editl. com. Calif. News 2001—), Am. Assn. Christian Counselors, Nat. Assn. Christian Social Workers, Assoc. Gerontology and Human Devel. Council on Social Work Education. Avocations: sewing, crafts, snorkeling, theater. Personal E-mail: rrukiya@peoplepc.com. Business E-Mail: rrountr@csulb.edu.

ROUP, BRENDA JACOBS, nurse, retired army officer; b. Petersburg, Va., July 8, 1948; d. Eugene Thurman and Sarah Ann (Williams) Jacobs; m. Clarence James Roup, May 8, 1976. BSN, Med. Coll. Va., Richmond, 1970; MSN, Cath. U. Am., 1977; PhD, U. Md., 1995. Commd. 2d lt. U.S. Army, 1970, advanced through grades to lt. col., 1986; infection control cons. 7th MEDCOM, Fed. Republic Germany, 1982-83; chief infection control Brooke Army MEDCEN, San Antonio, 1983-86; chief infection control Walter Reed MEDCEN, Washington, 1986-92, ret., 1992; Johnson & Johnson postdoctoral fellow Johns Hopkins U. Sch. Nursing, Balt., 1995-97; nurse cons. in infection control Md. Dept. Health and Mental Hygiene, 1999—; nurse cons. in infection control to U.S. Army Surgeon Gen., 1986-92. Contbr. articles to profl. jours. Mem. Assn. Profls. in Infection Control, Sigma Theta Tau. Avocations: reading, gardening, cooking. Office: Md Dept Health & Mental Hygiene Baltimore MD 21201 E-mail: broup@dhmh.state.md.us.

ROURKE, DIANE MCLAUGHLIN, librarian; d. Frank and Mary McLaughlin; m. Otto Porter Ream IV; children: Sunny Ream Spillane, Sarah Ream Gable. BA in English, U. Miami, Coral Gables, Fla., 1966; MS in Libr. Sci., Fla. State U., Tallahassee, 1968. Children's libr., br. libr. Miami Dade Pub. Libr., 1968—69; children's libr. Surfside Libr., Miami Beach, 1972; med. libr., mgr. libr. svcs. Bapt. Hosp., Miami, 1976—95; dir. libr. svcs. Bapt. Health, 1995—. Founding chair Miami Health Sci. Libr. Consortium, 1978—79; cons. and presenter in field. Mem.: Med. Libr. Assn. Democrat. Episcopalian. Avocations: reading, singing, classical music, gardening. Home: 9641 SW 77 Ave 204D Miami FL 33156 Office: South Miami Hospital Medical Library 6200 SW 73 St Miami FL 33143

ROUSE, DORIS JANE, physiologist, research scientist; b. Greensboro, N.C., Oct. 3, 1948; d. Welby Corbett and Nadia Elizabeth (Grainger) R.; m. Blake Shaw Wilson, Jan. 6, 1974; children: Nadia Jacqueline, Blair Elizabeth. BA in Chemistry, Duke U., 1970, PhD in Physiology and Pharmacology, 1980. Tchr. sci. Peace Corps, Tugbake, Liberia, 1970-71; rsch scientist Burroughs Wellcome Co., Rsch. Triangle Park, NC, 1971-76; sr. physiologist Rsch. Triangle Inst., Durham, 1976-83, ctr. dir., 1980-2000, also dir. NASA tech. application team, 1980-2000, dir. TB Tech. Transfer Program, 1999—, dir. Global Health, 2001—; portfolio project mgr. Global Alliance for Tb Drug Devel., 2002—. Adminstr. ANSI Tech. Adv. Group for Wheelchairs, N.Y.C., 1982-86; adj. asst. prof. U. N.C. Sch. Medicine, 1983-92; chair Instl. Rev. Bd., Profl. Devel. Award com., chair salary com. Rsch. Triangle Inst.; mem. adv. bd. Assistive Tech. Rsch. Ctr., 1994-96; portfolio project mgr. Global Alliance for TB Drug Devel., 2002—, bus. adv. Healthspot, 2004-05. Mem. adv. bd. Assn. Retarded Citizens, Arlington, Tex., 1981—88, Western Gerontology Soc., San Francisco, 1982—85; bd. dirs. Simon Found., Chgo., 1983—95; mem. spl. rev. com. small bus. applications Nat. Forum on Tech. and Aging; mem. fund steering com. Academy Venture, 2000—04. Recipient Group Achievement award NASA, 1979, 2000, President's award, RTI, 2003, 05. Mem.: Am. Soc. Microbiology, Assn. Fed. Tech. Transfer Execs., Licensing Execs. Soc., Rehab. Engring. Soc. N.Am. (chmn. wheelchair com. 1981—86). Home: 2410 Wrightwood Ave Durham NC 27705-5802 Office: Research Triangle Inst PO Box 12194 Durham NC 27709-2194 Office Phone: 919-541-6980. Personal E-mail: drouse@nc.rr.com. Business E-Mail: rouse@rti.org.

ROUSE, SANDRA HOWARD, writer; b. Newport, R.I., Sept. 29, 1947; d. John Francis and Ruth Virginia Kane; m. William Bradford Rouse, Sept. 8, 1968; children: Rebecca Kane, William Howard. BA in English, Social Sci., RI Coll., 1969; MA in English, Simmons Coll., 1971, MS in Libr. Sci., 1973. Fiction editor The Chattahoochee Review, Atlanta, 2000—03; ptnr., founder Intervals, Atlanta, 2002—03. Contbr. over 20 publs. to profl. and lit. jours.; author: 2 books. Home: Apt 113 4409 Northside Pkwy NW Atlanta GA 30327

ROUSEY, ANNE, social worker; b. Denison, Tex., Dec. 7, 1939; d. Lynden A. and Evelyn M. Hagans; m. Lelon M. Rousey (dec. Nov. 22, 1998); children: Sharon A. Rousey Ward, Lynda Lee Fields. BSE, Midwestern State U., Wichita Falls, TX, 1975. Editor The Frauen, USAF Officers Wives, Ramstein, Germany, 1970—70; art instr. Southside Girls Club Inc., Wichita Falls, Tex., 1973; organist St. Mark's United Meth. Ch., Wichita Falls, Tex., 1974, choir dir., 1975—77; exec. dir. Southside Girls Club Inc., Wichita Falls, Tex., 1975—2001. Sec. Bus. & Profl. Women, Wichita Falls, Tex., 1975; pres. Soroptimist Internat., Wichita Falls, Tex., 1981. Recipient Good Neighbor Award, TV Channel 3, 1990. Mem.: Family Self-Sufficiency Coordinating Com., Soroptimist Club Internat. (pres. 1981—2002). D-Liberal. Methodist. Achievements include Have helped approximately 20,000 deserving young children reach their potentials, many of whom have become nurses, teachers, social workers, business professionals, accountants and doctors. Avocations: piano, cooking, bridge. Home: 2249 Wranglers Retreat Wichita Falls TX 76310 Office: Southside Girls Club Incorporated 1205 Montgomery Wichita Falls TX 76302

ROUSH, MICHELLE BEASON, secondary school educator; d. Stephen and Barbara Beason; m. Aric Devin Roush, Mar. 23, 2002. BA, Ohio No. U., Ada, 2006; postgrad., No. Ky. U., Highland Heights, Ky., 2006—. Cert. health and phys. edn. tchr., adminstr. Ill. Tchr. Mt. Notre Dame, Cin., 1997—2000, Colerain HS, Cin., 2000—01, New Trier HS, Winnetka, Ill., 2001—. Presenter in field. Vol. Boys and Girls Club, Chgo., 2003—. Mem.: Am. Sch. Health Assn., Ill. Sch. Health Assn. (bd. dirs. 2005—). Office: New Trier HS 385 Winnetka Ave Winnetka IL 60093 Office Phone: 847-784-6563.

ROUSH, NANCY SCHMIDT, lawyer; b. Ottawa, Kans., Sept. 17, 1951; d. Raymond Stanley and Caroline Jeanne (Ward) Schmidt: m. John Mark Roush, Aug. 25, 1973; 1 child, Jessica Lynn. BA, Taylor U., Upland, Ind., 1973; JD, U. Kans., 1979. Bar: Kans. 1979, U.S. Dist. Ct. Kans. 1979, U.S. Ct. Appeals (10th cir.) 1980, U.S. Tax Ct. 1982. Jud. clk. U.S. Ct. Appeals (10th cir.), Olathe, Kans., 1979-80; lawyer Logan & Martin, Overland Park, Kans., 1980-85; ptnr. bus. planning and estate planning Shook, Hardy & Bacon LLP, Overland Park, 1986—. Editor and author: Kansas Estate Administration, 1986; contbr. articles to profl. jours. Mem. bd. govs. Kans. U. Law Sch., Lawrence, 1984-87; participant Midwest Bioethics Ctr., Kansas City, Mo., 1989-90. Fellow Am. Coll. of Trust and Estate Coun. (mem. Bus. Planning Com.); mem. ABA, Kans. Bar Assn. (pres. real estate probate and trust sect. 1984-86, pres. elect tax law sect. 1990-91, pres. 1991—, editor bd. edn. jour. 1982, Outstanding Svc. award 1985, 1991, 2001), Kansas City Met. Bar Assn., Mo. Bar Assn., Order of Coif. Office: Shook, Hardy & Bacon LLP 2555 Grand Blvd Kansas City MO 64108 Office Fax: 816-559-2501, 816-421-5547. E-mail: nroush@shb.com.

ROUSON, VIVIAN REISSLAND, alcohol/drug abuse services professional, journalist; b. New Orleans, July 18, 1929; d. Albert Isaac and Ophelia (Scott) Reissland; m. W. Ervin Rouson, June 22, 1953 (dec. May 1979); children: Lizette Hélène, Darryl Ervin, Brigette Maria, Janine Patrice, Damian William. BA, Xavier U., 1951; MS, Nova U., 1979; postgrad., U. Ky., 1965, U. South Fla., 1970. Tchr., cons. Gibbs Jr. Coll., St. Petersburg, Fla., 1958-60; tchr., cons. Pinellas County Schs., St. Petersburg, Clearwater, Fla., 1960-78; freelance opinion editorial columnist U.S. newspaper, 1976-82; columnist Evening Independent, Pinellas County, Fla., 1976-78, Palm Beach (County, Fla.) Post, 1979-82; tchr., cons. Palm Beach County Sch., Lake Worth, W. Palm Beach, Fla., 1978-82; editorial writer St. Petersburg Times, 1979, Cath. Standard, 1990—, Nat. Cath. Reporter, 1997—. In a Word mag., 2000—; program coord., interim dir. Women's Resource Ctr. Normandale C.C., Bloomington, Minn., 1986-89; interim dir. Women's Resource Ctr., Normandale Community Coll., Bloomington, Minn., 1989; vol., intern program coord. Inst. on Black Chem. Abuse, Mpls., 1989-90; assoc. editor Nat. Black Media Coalition, Washington, 1991—. V.I.P. coord. Inst. on Black Chem. Abuse, Mpls., 1989-90; writing and fgn. lang. cons. Pinellas County and Palm Beach County, fla., 1960-82; bd. dirs. Carroll Pub. Co.; tchr. French, St. Peter's Interparish Sch., 1999. Author: The Hummingbird Within Us, 1980, Like a Mighty Banyan, 1982, Alcohol and Drug Abuse in Black America, 1988; editor conf. proceedings; editorial writer-columnist; editorial bd. St. Petersburg Times, 1979. Bd. dirs. St. Petersburg Cath. High Sch., 1976, Minn, divsn. Am. Cancer Soc., Mpls., 1983-90, Ind. Sch. Dist. 191, Burnsville, Eagan, Savage, Minn., 1984-87, Minn. Valley YMCA, Dakota County, Minn., 1987-90; pres. D.C. chpt. Hook-Up Black Women, 1992—; sec., bd. dirs. Ionia Whipper Home, Inc., 1992-, Nat. Urban League, initiator and mem. Archdiocese of Wash. Sisters in the Spirit, 2001- Named Outstanding Journalist south Atlantic region Alpha Kappa Alpha, 1978, 79, 80; recipient Appreciation Pub. Svc. cert. Nat. Assn. Black Accts., 1992. Mem. AAUW, Twin Cities Black Journalists (co-chair 1985-86, v.p. 1989-90), Minn. Polit. Congress Black Women (charter), Minn. Elected Women Ofcls., Dakota County Soc. Black Women (founder 1983, v.p. 1983-84), Pinellas County Fgn. Lang. Tchrs. (treas., pres.), The Links (alumna mem. Capital City chpt.), Washington Urban League (life), Alpha Kappa Alpha (life). Roman Catholic. Avocations: oratory, poetry, civic volunteerism, floral arrangements, walking. Home and Office: Seminars/Workshops 2311 N Capitol St NE Washington DC 20002

ROUSSAKIS, DOROTHY FERGUSON, artist; b. Danbury, Conn., Apr. 24, 1914; d. Daniel Odell and Flora Ellwood Ferguson; m. Charles Roussakis, Dec. 15, 1944 (dec. Sept. 25, 1990); 1 child, Peter. Student, Fed. Art Sch., 1932—36; studied with Karl Anderson, 1943—45. Fashion illustrator Leavitts Dept. Store, 1963—64; dir. Am. Artists Profl. League, NY, 1965—66; tchr. Nichols Cmty. Ctr., Conn., 1969. One-woman shows include Rochester (N.H.) Libr., 1998, Ind. U., Kokomo, 2001, Burlington (Ind.) Libr., 2001. Recipient Best Portrait, Contemporary Arts and Crafts, 1953, Best Portrait award, Milford Conn. Art League, 1955, 1966, award for graphics, Acad. Artists, 1981, Sheffield Mass. Art Assn., 1981, Kent Art Assn., 1988. Mem.:

Am. Pen Women (pres. Conn. br. 1962—64, 1970—72, 1978—80, pres. Conn. state 1974—76, art chmn. Conn. state 1962—64, state sec. 1968—70). Home and Studio: 1101 S Jackson St Burlington IN 46915

ROUSSEAU, CHRISTINA JEANNIE, elementary school educator; b. Gardner, Mass., Jan. 18, 1951; d. Edward Patrick and Marjorie Forbes (Arey) O'Connor; m. Douglas Edward Rousseau, Aug. 11, 1973; children: Justin Douglas, Amanda Leigh. BSc, We. Conn. State U., Danbury, 1973, MSc, 1975; postgrad., L.I. U., Bklyn., 1986—88. Cert. tchr. Conn., 1973, N.Y., 1975. Tchr. Beacon City Sch. Dist., NY, 1973—. Sci. coord. Beacon Sch. Dist., 1987—88. Den mother Boy Scouts Am., Hopewell Junction, NY, 1984—85; participant holiday meal delivery Trinity Ch., Fishkill, NY. Named Sci. Tchr. of Yr., Ctrl. Hudson Corp., Poughkeepsie, N.Y., 1989; grantee, Area Fund Dutchess County, N.Y., 1990. Mem.: NEA, NSTA. Episcopalian. Achievements include selected for National Science Foundation program for exemplary teachers. Avocations: travel, exercise, reading, cooking, theater. Office: Beacon City Sch Dist Education Dr Beacon NY 12508 Personal E-mail: crousse44@optonline.net.

ROUSSEAU, IRENE VICTORIA, artist; children: Douglas, Scott. BA, Hunter Coll., N.Y.C.; MFA, Claremont (Calif.) Grad. Sch., 1969; PhD, N.Y. U., 1977. Tenured prof. William Paterson Coll., Wayne, NJ, 1970-74. Spkr. in field. Exhbns. include Betty Parsons Gallery, N.Y.C., Claremont Colls., State Mus. Sci. and Industry, L.A., Morris Mus. Arts and Scis., Morristown, N.J., The Bronx Mus. of Art, Galleri Sci. Agnes, Copenhagen/Roskilde, Denmark, Sculptors 5, Madison, N.J., Edmund Sci. Co., Barrington, N.J., AT&T World Hdqrs., Basking Ridge, N.J., N.J. Ctr. for Visual Arts, The Brotherhood Synagogue Holocaust Meml. Gramercy Pk. (mosaic), N.Y.C., 1986, 1st Internat. Art Biennale, Malta, 1995, U. Lausanne (Switzerland), 1997, Internat. Biennale Malta, 1997 (awards), Am. Inst. Archs., N.Y., 1998, Southwestern Coll., Kans., 1999, Lausanne, Switzerland, 2001, BRIDGES, Internat. Joint Conf., 2003, Math. Soc. France and Ministry of Culture Exhbn., 2004-05, Internat. Interdisciplinary Conf., Athens, Greece, 2005, Renaissance Banff, Alb., Can., 2005, travelling exhibit, Soc. Math. France and The Min. Culture, 2005, Yellow Bird Gallery, Newburg, N.Y., 2005; artist in residence Program Greece, 2000, Internat. Conf. Internat. Soc. Art, Math., Architecture, Freiburg, Germany, 2002, Internat. Conf. Connections in Math., Music, Art, Sci., and Arch., Granada, Spain, 2003, Internat. Soc. Arts, Math., and Arch. and BRIDGES (Math. Connections in Art, Music, and Sci.) Internat. Joint Conf., Granada, Spain, Inst. Math. Scis. Banff Ctr., Can. Math.Soc., Banff Internat. Rsch. Sta.; one woman shows Weston Gallery Sch. Arch., Newark, 2003, N.J. Inst. Tech. Sch. Arch., 2003, Weston Art Gallery Sch. Arch. NJIT, Newark, 2004; traveling exhibit Math. Soc., 2005; contbr. articles and works of art to jours., books and catalogues. Recipient seven 1st prize awards for creative work in N.J., ER Squibb and Sons Sculpture award, AIA N.J. Presentation Design award, 1995, Internat. Art Biennale Malta Installatin award, 1997, Traveling Exhibit throughout Europe and Middle East and Africa of Winners of the 1997 Biennale in Malta, 1997-99. Mem. AIA (profl. affiliate N.J., N.Y., chmn. architecture dialogue com. Presentation award 1995), Internat. Sculptors Assn., Am. Abstract Artists (exhbn. chmn. 1978-79, pres. 1979-82), Fine Arts Fedn. (bd. dirs.), Coll. Art Assn., Women's Caucus on Art (conf. spkr.), Phi Delta Kappa. Home: 41 Sunset Dr Summit NJ 07901-2322 Personal E-mail: mosaicartforms@comcast.net.

ROUSSEAU-VERMETTE, MARIETTE, artist; b. Trois-Pistoles, Que., Can., Aug. 29, 1926; d. Joseph-Herve and Corrinne (Belanger) Rousseau; m. Claude Vermette, Nov. 29, 1952; children: Marc, Jerome. Student, Ecole des Beaux Arts du Que., 1944-48, Studio Dorothy Liebes, San Francisco, 1948-49, Oakland Coll. Arts and Crafts, 1948-49; studied different tapestry techniques in Europe, 1952, 58. Head dept. fibre, visual arts Banff (Alta.) Sch. Fine Arts, Canada, 1979—85. Solo exhbns. include: Musée des Beaux-Arts de Montréal, 1961, Galerie Camille Hébert, Montréal, 1964, New-Design Gallery, Vancouver, B.C., 1964, Galerie Godard-Lefort, Montréal, 1969, Musée du Québec, 1972, Marlborough-Godard Gallery, Toronto, 1974, Centre Culturel Canadien, Paris, 1974, Centre Culturel Canadien, Brussels, 1974, Winnipeg (Man.) Art Gallery, 1976, Grace Borgenicht Gallery, N.Y., 1977, Galerie Alice Pauli, Lausanne, Switzerland, 1978, Brown Grotta Gallery, Wilton, Conn., 1993-2001, Galerie Bernard, Montreal, Can., 2004—, numerous others; group shows include: Nat. Gallery of Can., 1959, Biennale Internationale de la Tapisserie, Lausanne, Switzerland, 1962, 65, 67, 71, 77, Triennale de Milan, 1968, Mus. Modern Art, N.Y.C., 1968-69, Art Gallery of Windsor, Ont., 1977, 81, Musée d'Art Contemporain, Montréal, Mus. Modern Art, Kyoto, Japan, 1977, Mus. Modern Art, Tokyo, 1978, Musée d'Art Contemporain de Montréal, 1979, Biennale, Lodz, Poland, 1981, numerous others; theatrical works include: Théâtre Maisonneuve, Place des Arts, Montréal, 1967, Theatre of the Can. Ctr. of Arts, Ottawa, 1965-68, The JFK Ctr. for Performing Arts, Washington, 1970, Group de la Place Royal, 1968, 69, 73; permanent collections include: Nat. Gallery of Can., Art Gallery of Charlottetown, Can. Pavilion, Osaka, Japan, Québec Pavilion, Osaka, Palais de Justice, Montréal, Mus. Modern Art, Kyoto, Met. Mus., N.Y.C., Chgo. Art Mus., numerous others. Decorated officer Order of Can.; Can. Coun. grantee, 1968; recipient Honor certificate la Conférence Canadienne des Arts, 1974. Subject of numerous articles and books. Office: 373 Rue Morin Saint-Adele PQ Canada J8B 2P8

ROUSSEL, LEE DENNISON, economist; b. NYC, May 15, 1944; d. Ethan Allen and Frances Isabel (Ferry) Dennison; m. Andre Homo Roussel, Sept. 6, 1980; children: Cecilia Frances, Stephanie Anne. AB, Wellesley Coll., 1966; MA, Northeastern U., 1974. Mgmt. intern U.S. Dept. HEW, 1966-68; with Planning Office Commonwealth of Mass., 1968-70; exec. dir. Gov.'s Commn. Citizen Participation, Boston, 1973; with Boston area office U.S. Dept. HUD, 1970-78; fgn. svc. officer USAID, 1978-99, with housing and urban devel. office Washington and Tunis, 1978-82, chief housing and urban devel. office for C.Am. Honduras, 1982-87, asst. dir. office housing and urban programs Washington, 1987-91, country rep. for Czech and Slovak Fed. Rep., 1991-92, country rep. for Czech Rep., 1993-94; min. counselor, U.S. rep. to devel. assistance com. OECD, Paris, 1994-99; sr. advisor USAID, Panama, 1999—2002, chief, exec. mgmt. human resources, 2004—05, mgmt. advisor Office of Econ. growth, 2006—. Episcopalian. Home: 2333 N Oak St Falls Church VA 22046 E-mail: leeroussel@hotmail.com.

ROUSUCK, J. WYNN, theater critic; b. Cleve., Mar. 19, 1951; d. Morton I. and Irene Zelda (Winograd) R. BA summa cum laude, Wellesley Coll., 1972; MS, Columbia U., 1974. Assoc. editor, program guide, Sta. WCLV-FM, Cleve., 1972-73; theater and film reviewer Cleve. Press, 1973; gen. assignment arts reporter Balt. Sun, 1974-84, theater critic, 1984—. Instr. English Goucher Coll., Towson, Md., 1981; master critic O'Neill Critics Inst., Waterford, Conn., 1990—; theater critic Md. Pub. TV., 1986; faculty Nat. Endowment for Arts Journalism Inst. in Theater U. So. Calif., 2005; spkr. in field. Recipient Dog Writers Assn. Am. awards 1977, 79, Md. chpt. 1st Place Arts Reporting award Soc. Profl. Journalists, 1993, Front Page award, Disting. Criticism Washington-Balt. Newspaper Guild, 1997, 99, 2002, Bill Pryor Meml. grand prize for writing, 1999, Bernie Harrison Meml. award for commentary, 2002; NEH journalism fellow U. Mich., 1979-80, fellow O'Neill Critics Inst., 1982. Mem. Balt. Bibliophiles (bd. dirs. 1982-83), Octavo Plus, Walters Art Gallery, Balt. Wellesley Club (pres. 1978-79). Jewish. Avocations: rare books, art. Office: The Baltimore Sun 501 N Calvert St Baltimore MD 21278-0001

ROUTLY, TRACEY LAURENE, elementary school educator; b. Rochester, NY, Nov. 6, 1964; d. Frank Sampson and Judith Toombs Gilbert; m. Christopher M. Routly, Jan. 24, 2003; 1 child, Ethan T. BS in Mgmt. Sci., SUNY, Geneseo, NY, 1986; MS in Edn., Nazareth Coll., Rochester, 1992. Cert. Tchg. Elem. Edn. and Bus. and Distributive Edn. NY. Customer svc./claims Preferred Care, Rochester, 1987—95; substitute tchr. various sch. dists., Rochester, 1992—95; tchr. St. Helen Sch., Gates, NY, 1995—2002, St. Ambrose Sch., Irondequoit, NY, 2002, St. Louis Sch., Pittsford, NY, 2002—03, St. Helen Sch., Gates, NY, 2003—05, St. Margaret Mary Sch., Irondequoit, NY, 2005—. Vol. Special Olympics, Monroe County, 1987—2002. Office: St Margaret Mary Sch 400 Rogers Pkwy Rochester NY 14617

ROUTSON, MARY A., special education educator; b. Manhattan, NY, July 27, 1958; d. John F. and Rita K. Devine; m. Geoffrey L. Routson, Dec. 8, 1979; children: Ashley V., Rebecca L. BA in Sociology, Boston Coll., Chestnut Hill. Mass., 1980; MS in Spl. Edn., SUNY, New Paltz, 1996. Vol. ARC, Orange-Sullivan, NY; leader Girl Scouts Am., Orange County, NY, 1989—96; pres., team mom Stingrays Swim Team YWCA, Newburgh, NY, 1991—98; former coach ski, swim, cheerleader Spl. Olympics. Recipient Excellence in Leadership, Girl Scouts Am., 1995, Taking a Stand award, So. Poverty Law Ctr., Montgomery, 2005. Mem.: Stewart Park and Res. Coalition, Minnewaska Distance Swimmers Assn. (guide 2002—), Scott's Corners Ladies Golf League (pres. 2002—04). Avocations: cross country skiing, hiking, exercise, golf, reading.

ROVELSTAD, MATHILDE V(ERNER), retired library and information scientist, educator; b. Germany, 1920; came to U.S., 1951. m. Howard Rovelstad, 1970. PhD, U. Tubingen, 1953; MS in L.S, Catholic U. Am., 1960. Prof. libr. sci. Cath. U. Am., 1960-90, prof. emeritus, 1990—; ret., 1990. Vis. prof. U. Montreal, 1969 Author: Bibliotheken in den Vereinigten Staaten, 1974; translator Bibliographia, an Inquiry into its Definition and Designations (R. Blum), 1980, Bibliotheken in den Vereinigten Staaten von Amerika und in Kanada, 1988; contbr. articles to profl. jours. Research grantee German Acad. Exch. Svc., 1969, Herzog August Bibliothek Wolfenbüttel, Germany, 1995. Mem. Internat. Fedn. Libr. Assns. and Instns. (standing adv. com. on libr. schs. 1975-81), Assn. for Libr. and Info. Sci. Edn. Office: Cath U Am Sch Libr & Info Sci Washington DC 20064-0001

ROVIGO, CONNIE BRIGITTA, jewelry and fine arts retailer; b. Bklyn., Oct. 22, 1962; d. Louis and Marta Rovigo. AS in Biology, Queens Coll., 1982; BFA, N.Y. Inst. Tech., 1991. Accredited jewelry profl. Gemological Inst. Am., 2006. With N.Y.C. Emergency Med. Svcs., 1983-87; tech. illustrator Vantage Art Inc., Massapequa, N.Y., 1987-92; graphic artist Rovigo Graphics, Woodstock, NY, 1992—2000; jewelry designer, manufacturer Cavallo Fine Jewelry and Gifts, LLC, Red Hook, NY, 1998—. Instr. riding Silver Springs Ranch, Haines Falls, NY, 1992—98; graphic artist, advt. cons.; instr. of dressage and hunter, jumpers Green Heron Farm, Woodstock, 1992—2001. Designer fine jewelry 21st Century Fox, 1998, Star of Woodstock, 1998. Avocations: equestrian activities, alternative/herbal medicines, reading, jogging, exercise. Office: Cavallo Fine Jewelry and Gifts LLC 7486 S Broadway Red Hook NY 12571 Home: 7486 S Broadway Red Hook NY 12571 Office Phone: 845-758-0068. Business E-Mail: cavallojewelers@valstar.net.

ROVINSKI, HELEN THÉRÈSE, retired psychiatrist; b. Harrison, NJ, Dec. 15, 1916; d. Frank and Josephine Rovinski; children: Judith Stanley, Elizabeth Stanley, Richard Stanley, Paul Stanley, Michael Stanley. MD, George Washington U., Washington, 1943. Cert. Am. Bd. Phys. Medicine and Rehab. Staff psychiatrist VA Hosp., Phila., 1962, Coatesville, Pa., 1962—63, chief PM&R, 1965—70; staff psychiatrist Magee Rehab., Phila., 1963—65; chief PM&R VA Hosp., Topeka, 1971—80, Lebanon, Pa., 1980—84, chief of staff, 1987—88, dir. dept. phys. medicine and rehab. Washington, 1984—87, assoc. chief of staff extended care, 1988—93; ret., 1993. Mailing: PO Box 125 Cornwall PA 17016-0125

ROVNER, ILANA KARA DIAMOND, federal judge; b. Riga, Latvia, 1938; arrived in U.S., 1939; d. Stanley and Ronny (Medalje) Diamond. AB, Bryn Mawr Coll., 1960; postgrad., U. London King's Coll., 1961, Georgetown U., 1961—63; JD, Ill. Inst. Tech., 1966; LittD (hon.), Rosary Coll., 1989, Mundelein Coll., 1989; DHL (hon.), Spertus Coll. of Judaica, 1992. Bar: Ill. 1972, U.S. Dist. (no. dist.) Ill. 1972, U.S. Ct. Appeals (7th cir.) 1977, U.S. Supreme Ct. 1981, Fed. Trial Bar (no. dist.) Ill. 1982. Jud. clk. U.S. Dist. Ct. (no. dist.) Ill., Chgo., 1972—73; asst. U.S. atty. U.S. Atty.'s Office, Chgo., 1973—77, dep. chief of pub. protection, 1975—76, chief pub. protection, 1976—77; dep. gov., legal counsel Gov. James R. Thompson, Chgo., 1977—84; dist. judge U.S. Dist. Ct. (no. dist.) Ill., Chgo., 1984—92; cir. judge U.S. Ct. Appeals (7th cir.), Chgo., 1992—. Mem. Gannon-Proctor Commn. on the Status of Women in Ill., 1982—84; mem. civil justice reform act adv. com. 7th Cir. Ct., Chgo., 1991—95, mem. race and gender fairness com., 1993—; mem. fairness com. U.S. Ct. Appeals (7th cir.), 1996—, mem. gender study task force, 1995—96; mem. jud. conf. U.S. Com. Ct. Adminstrn. Case Mgmt., 2000—. Ctrl. and East European law initiative vol. ABA, 1997—; trustee Bryn Mawr Coll., Pa., 1983—89; mem. bd. overseers Ill. Inst. Tech./Kent Coll. Law, 1983—; trustee Ill. Inst. Tech., 1989—; mem. adv. coun. Rush Ctr. for Sports Medicine, Chgo., 1991—96; bd. dirs. Rehab. Inst. Chgo., 1998—; bd. visitors No. Ill. U. Coll. Law, 1992—94; vis. com. Northwestern U. Sch. Law, 1993—98, U. Chgo. Law Sch., 1993—96, 2000—03; chair Ill. state selection com. Rhodes Scholarship Trust, 1998—2000. Named Today's Chgo. Woman of the Yr., 1985, Woman of Achievement, Chgo. Women's Club, 1986; named one of 15 Chgo. Women of the Century, Chgo. Sun Times, 1999; named to Today's Chgo. Women Hall of Fame, 2002; recipient Spl. Commendation award, U.S. Dept. Justice, 1975, Spl. Achievement award, 1976, Ann. Nat. Law and Social Justice Leadership award, League to Improve the Cmty., 1975, Ann. Guardian Police award, 1977, Profl. Achievement award, Ill. Inst. Tech., 1986, ORT Women's Am. Cmty. Svc. award, 1987—88, commendation def. of prisoners com., Chgo. Bar Assn., 1987, Svc. award, Spertus Coll. of Judaica, 1987, Ann. award, Chgo. Found. for Women, 1990, Louis Dembitz Brandeis medal for Disting. Legal Svc., Brandeis U., 1993, 1st Woman award, Valparaiso U. Sch. Law, 1993, Hebrew Immigrant Aid Soc. Chgo. 85th Anniversary honoree, 1996, Arabella Babb Mansfield award, Nat. Assn. Women Lawyers, 1998, award, Chgo. Attys. Coun. of Hadassah, 1999, First Woman award, Chgo. Bar Assn. Alliance for Women and Women's Bar Assn. Ill., 2000, Georgetown U. Law Ctr., 2001, Chgo. Hist. Soc. Trailblazers Award, 2003, Lifetime Achievement award, Decalogue Soc. Lawyers, 2004, Vanguard award, Chgo. Bar Assn. and Lesbian and Gay Bar Assn. Chgo., 2004, Thurgood Marshall Career Achievement award, Assn. Corp. Counsel Chgo. chpt., 2005, Hero of Liberty award, Nat. Liberty Mus., 2005, Inaugural Judge Abraham Lincoln Marovitz Mentoring award, Chgo. Bar Assn. and Found. Lend-a-Hand Program, 2005. Mem.: Chgo. Bar Assn. (Justice John Paul Stevens award 2005), Jewish Judges Assn. Ill. (Lifetime Achievement award 2004), Decalogue Soc. of Lawyers (citation of honor 1991, Merit award 1997), Chgo. Coun. Lawyers, Women's Bar Assn. Ill. (ann. award 1989, 1st Myra Bradwell Woman of Achievement award 1994, 1st Woman Award (in conjunction with Chicago Bar Assn. Alliance for Women) 2000), Fed. Judges Assn., Fed. Bar Assn. (mem. selection com. Chgo. chpt. 1977—80, treas. 1978—79, sec. 1979—80, 2d v.p. 1980—81, 1st v.p. 1981—82, pres. 1982—83, 2d v.p. 7th cir. 1983—84, v.p. 7th cir. 1984—85), Kappa Beta Pi, Phi Alpha Delta (hon.). Office: 219 S Dearborn St Ste 2774 Chicago IL 60604-1803

ROVNER, MICHAL, video artist, photographer; b. Tel Aviv, Nov. 7, 1957; BA in cinema/television and philosophy, Tel Aviv U., 1981; BFA (hon.), Bezalel Acad. Art. Co-founder Camera Obscura Art Sch., Tel Aviv, 1978. Permanent Collections: Mus. Modern Art, Metrop. Mus. Art, Guggenheim Mus., Whitney Mus. American Art, NYC, Art Inst Chgo., Mus. of Contemporary Art, Chgo., Los Angeles County Mus. Art, Mus. Fine Arts Houston, Corcoran Gallery Art, Washington, D.C., Israel Mus., Jerusalem, MACRO: Museo d'arte contemporanea Rome, Musée de l'Elysée, Lausanne, Tel Aviv Mus., Israel.; Commissioned Works: Installation Tel/Hill (mural), Colonnade House, Tel Aviv, 95.; Installation Co-Existence (several murals overhanging Syrian-African break); Construct Process-Artist's Mus., Mitzpe-Ramon, Israel, 95.; Exhibitions: Sky Line, Tel Aviv Mus. Art, 88.; Video installations include: Overhang, Chase Manhattan Bank on Park Ave. NYC, 2000; Overhanging, Stedelijk Mus., Amsterdam, 1999; Mutual Interest, Tate Gallery, London, 1997, Stedelijk Mus., Amsterdam, 1997 and P.S.1, NYC, 1999; Over 40 solo exhibitions in video and film including: Tel Aviv Mus. Art, 90, Maison Cult Mercier, Montreal, 91, Art Inst Chgo. 93 & Israel Mus., Jerusalem, 94, Michal Rovner: The Space Between, Whitney Mus. of American Art, 2002, Against Order? Against Disorder?, Israeli Pavilion at the 50th Internat. Art Exhibition, Venice Biennale, 2003, Michal Rovner: in stone, PaceWildenstein Gallery, 2004. Office: PaceWildenstein Gallery 32 E 57th St 2nd Fl New York NY 10022

ROVNIAK, LIZA S., research scientist, educator; b. Vancouver, BC, Can., Dec. 12, 1973; arrived in US, 1997; d. Joe and Sheilah Rovniak. BA, McGill U., Canada, 1996; PhD, Va. Tech, Blacksburg, 2003. Instr., rsch. asst. Va. Tech, Blacksburg, 1997—2002; rsch. scientist, adj. asst. prof. San Diego State U., 2002—. Expert cons. Can. Insts. Health Rsch., Vancouver, 2004—. Contbr. articles to profl. jours. Recipient Rsch. award, Grad. Rsch. Devel. Program, Va. Tech, 2002; Doctoral Rsch. scholar, FCAR-Fonds pour la Formation de Chercheurs et l'Aide a la Recherche, 2001—02, Tobacco Related Disease Rsch. Program grant, U. Calif., 2003—, IDEA grantee, Universitywide AIDS Rsch. Program, 2004—. Mem.: APA, Soc. Behavioral Medicine (citation award 2002). Achievements include first to introduce concept of theoretical fidelity. Office: San Diego State U 9245 Sky Park Ct Ste 230 San Diego CA 92123 Office Phone: 858-505-4770 ext. 152.

ROWAN, CYNTHIA L. REEVES, accountant; b. Pomona, Calif., Sept. 30, 1957; d. Jack Harding and Ruth Evelyn Reeves; m. Jeffrey Wayne Rowan, Dec. 21, 1985; children: Alexander Roy Harding, Kathryn Elizabeth. BS, Calif. Poly. State U., Pomona, 1980; MS, Golden Gate U., 1987. CPA, Colo., Calif. Tax mgr. Fleming and Co., San Bernardino, Calif., 1980-93, Fleming and Co. formerly Lester Witte & Co., Colorado Springs, Colo., 1993—. Fundraising chair Kiwanis, Redlands, Calif., 1990-93; bd. dirs. Kiwanis Found., Redlands, 1990-93. Named Rookie of the Yr., Kiwanis, Redlands, 1993. Mem. AICPA, Colo. Soc. CPAs. Republican. Methodist. Avocations: water-skiing, puzzles, skiing, kids activities. Office: Fleming and Co #203 2975 Broadmoor Valley Rd Colorado Springs CO 80906-4466

ROWARK, MAUREEN, fine arts photographer; b. Edinburgh, Midlothian, Scotland, Feb. 28, 1933; came to U.S., 1960, naturalized, 1970; d. Alexander Pennycook and Margaret (Gorman) Prezdpelski; m. Robert Rowark, May 3, 1952 (div. July 1965). 1 child, Mark Steven. Student, Warmington Bus. Coll., Royal Leamington Spa, Eng., 1950-51, Royal Leamington Spa Art Sch.; diploma, Speedwriting Inst., N.Y.C., 1961; AS in Edn., St. Clair County Community Coll., Port Huron, Mich., 1977, AA, 1978. Supr. proof reading Nevin D. Hirst Advt., Ltd., Leeds, England, 1952-55; publicity asst. Alvis Aero Engines, Ltd., Coventry, England, 1955-57; adminstrv. asst. Port Huron Motor Inn, 1964-66; adminstrv. asst. pub. rels. dept. Geophysics and Computer Svcs., Inc., New Orleans, 1966-68; sales mgr. Holiday Inn, Port Huron, 1968-70; adminstrv. asst. Howard Corp., Port Huron, 1971-73; sales and systems coord. Am. Wood Products, Ann Arbor, Mich., 1973-74; systems coord. Daniels & Zermack Architects, Ann Arbor, 1974; systems coord., cataloger fine arts dept. St. Clair County Community Coll., Port Huron, 1976-79; freelance fine arts photographer Port Huron, 1978—. Photographer Patterns mag. front cover, 1978, Erie Sq. Gazette, 1979, Bluewater Area Tourism Bur. brochure, 1989, 92, 95, 97, 2000, 01, Corits Castle, Lexington, 2002, Port Huron, Can. Legion, Wyo., Ont. Br., 1987, 88—, Grace Episcopal Ch. Mariner's Day, Port Huron, 1987, 92-2001, Homes mag., 1989. Photographer (one-woman shows) Grace Episcopal Ch., 1995, Port Huron Mus., 1995, St. Clair River Remedial Action Plan, 1995 (Best in Landscape Category), Mich. Waterways Coun. Girl Scouts Exhibit, 1996; Exhibited in group shows at Ea. Mich. Internat. Juried Exhbn., 2000, 1981—98 (Award of Excellence, 1982, 1983, Best Photography award, 1995, 1996, 1997), Our Town Juried Exhbn., 1997, St. Clair County C.C., 1983, 1986 (Award of Excellence, 1986), Gallery Lambton, Sarnia, Ont., Can., 1983—92 (Best Photography, 1988), 1994, 1996—97, 2000, Bluewater Bridge, 1988, Kaskilaaksontie, Finland, 1991 (Par Excellence award), Swann Gallery, Detroit, 1996, St. Clair (Mich.) Art Gallery, Genesis Gallery, Lexington, Mich., others, Represented in permanent collections Royal Can. Legion, Wyo. Br. Centaph, Capac State Bank, Grace Episcopal Ch., Thomas Edison Inn, Port Huron Hosp., Front Cover Good Health News; costume design, manufacture and modelling Bluewater Art Assn., 2000—01, photographer Bluewater Percussion Brochure, 2001;, author short stories. Cons., buyer interior decor Grace Episcopal Ch., 1994; active Port Huron Mus., 1978; founder Bluewater les Chapeaux Rouge chpt. Red Hat Soc., 2001—; prodr., dir. calendar We Can Still Make Waves, 2005; prodr., designer parade float Rotary Internat., 2005 (1st pl. award). Recipient hon. mention Gallery Lambton, Sarnia, 1981, 2d pl. memoir writing women's history month St. Clair County C.C., 1999; winner 2d and 3d place awards Times Herald Newspaper, 1988, 1st place juried photography award Port Huron Art Festival, 1997, 1st place St. Patrick's Day Parade Float, 2005, 1st place Rotary Internat. Day Parade Float, 2005. Mem. St. Clair County C.C. Alumni Assn., Phi Theta Kappa, Lambda Mu. Democrat. Episcopalian. Avocations: costumes and interior design, travel, theater, memoir writing. Home and Office: 3512 Walnut St Port Huron MI 48060 Office Phone: 810-989-9192. E-mail: ha-penerth-of-tar@prodigy.net.

ROWBERRY, CONNIE, secondary school educator; b. Mora, Minn., Dec. 18, 1951; d. Earl Orlin and Karen Marie Johnsen; m. Hal Rowberry, June 17, 1975; children: Kristopher Cal, Raegan, Tyler, Ky Erik. BA, Brigham Young U., Provo, Utah, 1975. Edn. credential Dept. Edn., Idaho, 2006. Tchr. Sandcreek Mid. Sch., Idaho Falls, 1985—. Mem. Idaho Response Team for Accreditation of Madison Mid. Sch., Rexburg, Idaho, 1997—2000, State Response Team for Accreditation of Rigby H.S., Idaho, 2001—02. Tchr. Sunday sch., young women's pres., relief soc. counselor Ch. of Jesus Christ of Latter-day Saints, Idaho Falls, 1981—2006. Nominee Am. Tchr. award, Disney, 2000, 2002, 2005, 8 Who Make a Difference award, 2002, Tchr. award, Sylvan Learning Ctr., 1999, 2000, 2006; named one of Outstanding Young Women of America, 1991. Mem.: Idaho Edn. Assn. (assoc.; region 6 rep. 2000—01, 2006—, state del. 1997—2000, Membership Recruiter award 2001), Bonneville Edn. Assn. (assoc.; sec. 2000—01). Office: Sandcreek Mid Sch 2955 E Owen St Idaho Falls ID 83406 Office Phone: 208-525-4416.

ROWE, AUDREY, paralegal; b. Albuquerque, June 26, 1958; d. James Franklin Ringold and Geneva Doris (Jennings) Robinson. A in Specialized Bus. in Acctg., ICS Ctr. for Degrees, Scranton, Pa., 1988, A in Specialized Bus. in Fin., 1989; BSBA, Century U., 1991, MBA, 1995, cert. paralegal studies, 1996, A in Specialized Bus. in Paralegal Studies, 1999. Svc. rep. Mountain and Southwestern Bell Telephone Co., Albuquerque, Houston, 1978-83; clk., carrier U.S. Postal Svc. PS05, Bellaire, Sugar Land, Tex., 1983-86; supr. mails U.S. Postal Svc. EAS15, Sugar Land, 1986-87; officer-in-charge U.S. Postal Svc. EAS 18, Rosharon, Tex., 1987; from supr. mails EAS 15 to gen. supr. mails EAS 17 U.S. Postal Svc., Houston, 1987-89; relief tour supt. U.S. Postal Svc. EAS 21 (Detail Assignment), Houston, 1989; mgr. gen. mail facility U.S. Postal Svc. EAS22 (Detail Assignment), Capitol Heights, Md., 1989-90; mgr. mail processing U.S. Postal Svc. EAS21, Charlottesville, Va., 1990-91; MSC dir. city ops. U.S. Postal Svc. EAS23 (Detail Assignment), Roanoke, Va., 1991; mgr. gen. mail facility U.S. Postal Svc. EAS24, Washington, 1991-96; plant mgr. U.S. Postal Svc. EAS25, Dulles, Va., 1992; pvt. contractor, paralegal, 1996-98; paralegal Lenox, Biddinger & Conrad, P.C., Woodbridge, Va., 1997-99, Wilson Strickland & Benson P.C., Atlanta, 1999-2000, Chamberlain, Hrdlicka, White, Williams & Martin, 2000—03, Holland & Knight, LLP, 2003—. Mem. Nat. Fedn. Paralegal Assn., Nat. Assn. Legal Assts. Avocations: piano, violin, reading. Personal E-mail: allrowe@aol.com.

ROWE, JOYCE, principal; d. Willis J. and Mary W. Smith; m. Jim Rowe, June 12, 1970; children: James Grantland, Brandy Rowe Kennedy. M, Columbus State U., Ga., 2001—02. Tchr. Support Specialist Ga., 1992, Nat. Bd. for Profl Tchg. Stds. Ga., 2001, Ednl. Leadership Ga., 2003. Eligibility caseworker Dept. Family and Children Svs., Griffin, Ga., 1970—75; tchr. Barnesville Acad., Ga., 1982—87, Griffin Spalding Schools, Griffin, 1987—2003; learning support specialist Daughtry Elem. Sch., Jackson, 2003—05, prin., 2005—. Recipient Outstanding Student Award, Columbus State U., 2002. Mem.: ASCD, Ga. Assn. of Ednl. Leaders, PA of Ga.

Educators, McIntosh Reading Coun., Ga. Reading Assn., Internat. Reading Assn., Pi Lambda Theta, Kappa Delta Pi. Home: 464 Carter Rd Griffin GA 30224 Office: Daughtry Elem Sch 150 Shiloh Rd Jackson GA 30233 Office Phone: 770-504-2356.

ROWE, JULIE, theater educator, actress; b. Pocatello, Idaho, Oct. 24, 1967; d. Pat and Linda Rowe. BA in Theatre Arts, Idaho State U., 1990. Tchg. artist various regional theatres and Broadway productions, 1985—; music dir. Various Regional Theatres, various, 1985—, actress, 1990—; dir. edn. Am. Stage, St. Petersburg, Fla., 2003—. Author: (children's play) The Day the Gators Came Out to Play, Who Put the Sea Serpent in my Soup?, Folk Tale Plays for Children. Mem. artists task force Pinellas County Arts Coun., St. Petersburg, Fla., 2005—05; liaison com. chair Actors Equity Assn., Nashville, 2001. Named Vol. of Yr., United Way Tampa Bay, 2005; recipient Best Supporting Actress award, The Tennessean, 2001—02, Best Actress award, 2003, The Weekly Planet, 2004, Profl. Achievement award, Coll. Arts. and Scis. Idaho State U., 2005. Mem.: AFTRA, Actors Equity Assn. Democrat. Office Phone: 727-823-1600. Business E-Mail: julierowe@americanstage.org.

ROWE, KATHERINE L., former computer company executive; BSME, Purdue U.; MS in Mgmt. Tech., MIT. Engring. mgr. ELDEC Corp.; mfg. mgr., project mgr. Physio-Control Corp.; dir. mfg. Tera Computer Co., Seattle, 1994-96, v.p. mfg., 1996—2000. Office: Tera Computer Co 411 1st Ave S Ste 600 Seattle WA 98104-3847

ROWE, LISA DAWN, computer programmer/analyst, computer consultant; b. Kenton, Ohio, Feb. 2, 1966; d. Daniel Lee and Frances Elaine (Johnson) Edelblute; m. Jeffrey Mark Rowe, Feb. 13, 1982; children: Anthony David, Samantha Paige Elizabeth, Zane Thomas, Zachary Tyler. Student, Inst. of Lit., 1988-90, Acad. Ct. Reporting, 1988, Marion Tech. Coll., 1991-92; postgrad., Ohio State U., 1993—. Writer, model Newslife, Marion, Ohio, 1982-83; bookkeeper Nat. Ch. Residences, Columbus, Ohio, 1985, Insty-Prints, Columbus, 1985; asst. editor Columbus Entertainment, 1984-85; book reviewer, writer Columbus Dispatch, 1989-91; writer Consumer News, Delaware, Ohio, 1989-90; computer programmer, supr. Dyserv, Inc., Columbus, 1986-92; bookkeeper, acct., office mgr. Marion Music Ctr., Inc., 1990; computer programmer EBCO Mfg., Columbus, 1992-93; sr. programmer/analyst Borden, Inc., Columbus, 1993-94; computer cons. System X, Columbus, 1994-95, LDA Systems, Dublin, Ohio, 1995-96; pres. Rowe Techs. Inc., Marion, Ohio, 1996—. Editor newsletter Assn. System Users, 1989-90; contbr. articles and revs. to profl. jours. Mem. NAFE, MADD, DAV (chaplain 1990), Heart of Ohio Am. Cat Fanciers Assn. Cat Club (pres. 2002), Ragamuffin Cat Lovers Soc., Inc. (v.p. 2003). Republican. Mem. Lds Ch. Avocations: horseback riding, swimming, camping, fishing, reading. Home: 1150 Toulon Ave Marion OH 43302-6610 Office: Rowe Techs Inc 1150 Toulon Ave Marion OH 43302-6610 E-mail: Lisarowe@rowetech.com.

ROWE, MARIELI DOROTHY, media literacy education consultant, organization executive, editor; b. Bonn, Germany, Aug. 13; came to U.S., 1939; m. John Westel Rowe; children: Peter Willoughby, William Westel, Michael Delano. BA, Swarthmore Coll., Pa.; postgrad., U. Colo., Boulder; MA, Edgewood Coll., Madison, Wis., 1990. Interim exec. dir. Friends of Sta. WHA-TV, Madison, Wis., 1976; exec. dir. Nat. Telemedia Coun., Madison, 1978—. Project assoc. Loyola U., Chgo., 1989—92; bd. dirs. Sta. WYOU, Madison. Co-prodr., author TV documentary Kids Meet Across Space, 1983; editor Telemedium, Jour. of Media Lit., 1980—. Co-founder, bd. dirs., pres. Friends of Pub. Stas. WHA-TV, radio, Madison, 1968-78; v.p. bd. Nat. Friends of Pub. Broadcasting, N.Y. and Washington, 1970-76; pres., v.p. bd. Wis. Coun. and Am. Coun. for Better Broadcasts, Madison, 1963-75; commr. Gov.'s Blue Ribbon Commn. on Cable Comm., Wis., 1971-73; bd. dirs. Broadband Telecomm. Regulatory Bd., Madison, 1978-81. Recipient Spl. Recognition award Am. Coun. Better Broadcasts, 1981, Spl. award Joint Congress and World Meeting on Media Lit., Spain, 1995, Meritorious Svc. award Alliance for Media Literate Am., 2003, 50th Anniversary Lighting the Way Toward a Media Wise World award Nat. Telemedia Coun., 2003. Mem. Soc. Satellite Profls. Internat. (charter), Internat. Visual Lit. Assn., Zeta Phi Eta (1st v.p. 1992, pres. 1993, Marguerite Garden Jones award 1989). Unitarian Universalist. Avocations: skiing, hiking, travel, music. Home: 1001 Tumalo Trl Madison WI 53711-3024 Office Phone: 608-218-1182. Personal E-mail: ntelemedia@aol.com.

ROWE, MARY R., lawyer; AD, Blinn Jr. Coll., 1994; BS in Agribusiness, Tex. A&M U., 1996; JD, U. Mo.-Kansas City Sch. Law, 1999. Bar: Tex. 2000. Shareholder bus. sect. Cotton, Bledsoe, Tighe & Dawson, P.C., Midland, Tex. Named a Rising Star, Tex. Super Lawyers mag., 2006. Office: Cotton Bledsoe Tighe & Dawson PC 500 W Illinois Ste 300 PO Box 2776 Midland TX 79701 Office Phone: 432-684-3136. E-mail: mrowe@cbtd.com.*

ROWE, MELINDA GRACE, public health service officer; b. Decatur, Ala., Aug. 18, 1953; m. Dana Calvin Craig Jr., Jan. 1, 1994. MD, U. Ala., 1978, MPH, 1985, MBA, 1987. Bd. cert. Am. Bd. Pediatrics, Am. Bd. Preventive Medicine. Pediatrics intern U. Ky., Lexington, 1978-79; pediatrics resident Lloyd Nolan Hosp., Fairfield, Ala., 1979-81; physician Columbus (Miss.) Children's Clinic, 1981, pvt. practice, Winfield, Ala., 1982-84; preventive medicine resident U. Ala., Birmingham, 1984-85; asst. state health officer Pub. Health Area III, Pelham, Ala., 1985-95; dir. health Jefferson County Health Dept., Louisville, 1995—2001; dist. health officer Savannah (Ga.) East Health, 2001—03; commr. of health Lexington Fayette County Health Dept., Lexington, Ky., 2003—. Asst. prof. U. Ala., Birmingham, 1988—, U. Louisville, 1995—. Bd. dirs. Cahaba River Soc., Birmingham, 1988—95, U. Ala.-Birmingham Nat. Alumni Soc., 1988—93, Health Ky., Goodwill Industries; bd. dirs. Wilderness Road coun. Girl Scouts U.S., Lexington, 2006—. Mem.: Lexington Med. Soc., Ga. Med. Assn., Ky. Health Depts. Assn. (v.p.), Louisville/Jefferson County Primary Care Assn. (bd. dirs.), Jefferson County Med. Soc., Ky. Pediat. Soc., Ky. Pub. Health Assn. (pres.-elect), Ky. Med. Assn., Rotary of Lexington. Methodist. Avocations: reading, walking, travel, music. Home: 3557 Cornwall Dr Lexington KY 40503-4150 Office Phone: 859-288-2300. Business E-Mail: melindag.rowe@ky.gov.

ROWE, NANCIE E., director, minister; b. New Castle, Pa., Nov. 4, 1943; d. John Francis and Ellen Mae Gwin; m. Ronald Allen Rowe, June 10, 2001; m. Edward Dwight Sickels, Oct. 24, 1958 (div.); children: Teddy Edward Sickels, Terrie Ellen Wells. BA in Bus., M in Psychology, Dallas Bapt. Coll.; PhD, Salt Lake Bapt. U., Dallas, 2001. Sch. adminstr. Calvary Christian Acad., Desoto, Tex., 1991—99; CEO, sch. adminstr., pastor Cmty. Christian Acad., Glenn Heights, 1999—. Assoc. pastor Victory Bapt. Ch., Desoto, 1997—2005; pastor Soulspiration Outreach Ch., Dallas, 1997—. Dir.(writer, editor, actor, singer): over 30 drama/mus. prodns. for children. Chairwoman ways & means Desoto BiCenntennial, 1973—76; prayer ptnr., support troops Presedential Prayer Team, 2000—06. Fellow Assoc. Christian Sch. Internat., Am. Salesmasters, 1970—76. Mem.: Assn. Christian Sch. Adminstrs. (assoc.). Liberal. Achievements include design of Commercial/Residential Design Firm; 1976 -1990; development of Hands on Teaching program for at risk students; Counseling program for troubled or at risk youth. Avocation: interior decorating. Office: Cmty Christian Acad PO Box 762 1931 S Hampton Rd Glenn Heights TX 75154 Office Phone: 972-274-0015. Office Fax: 972-274-0078. Personal E-mail: ccaacademy137@sbcglobal.net.

ROWE, SANDRA MIMS, editor; b. Charlotte, NC, May 26, 1948; d. David Lathan and Shirley (Stovall) Mims; m. Gerard Paul Rowe, June 5, 1971; children: Mims Elizabeth, Sarah Stovall. BA, East Carolina U., Greenville, N.C., 1970; postgrad., Harvard U., 1991. Reporter to asst. mng. editor The Ledger-Star, Norfolk, Va., 1971-80, mng. editor, 1980-82, The Virginian-Pilot and The Ledger Star, Norfolk, Va., 1982-84, exec. editor, 1984-86, v.p., exec. editor, 1986-93; editor The Oregonian, Portland, 1993—. Mem. Pulitzer Prize Bd., 1994-2003, chair, 2003, Bd. visitors James Madison U., Harrisonburg, VA., 1991-95; chair journalism adv. bd. Knight Found.; mem. adv. bd. The Poynter Inst., Medill Sch. Journalism, Northwestern U.; chair bd. visitors Knight Fellowships, Stanford U. Recipient George Beveridge Editor of Yr. award Nat. Press Found., 2003; named Woman of Yr. Outstanding Profl. Women of Hampton Rds., 1987; inducted into Va. Journalism Hall of Fame, 2000. Mem. Am. Soc. Newspaper Editors (pres., bd. dirs. 1992-99), Va. Press Assn. (bd. dirs. 1985-93). Episcopalian. Office: The Oregonian 1320 SW Broadway Portland OR 97201-3499

ROWE, SHERLIE JEAN, writer; b. Houston, July 5, 1930; d. Nathan Cuthbert and Alta Lee (Bell) Thompson; m. John A. Rowe, Jr., Feb. 14, 1952; children: Gary W., Bonnie B., John D. Spkr. in field. Author: Mary, Handmaiden of God, 1976, Decisions I, 1983, Decisions II, 1983, Living with My Father, 1985, Teaching Teenage Girls, 1985, And God Sings, 1992, Behold the Man, 2000, Our Father, 2000; Exhibited in group shows; featured artist Draw mag., 1995. Recipient numerous awards, Colo. Art Show, 1993, People's Choice award, 1993. Mem.: Oil Pastel Assn. Avocations: bible school teacher, art teacher, choral singer. Home: PO Box 773 Ouray CO 81427-0773

ROWELL, BARBARA CABALLERO, retired academic administrator; b. New Orleans, Sept. 5, 1922; d. Albert Henry Wischnewske (stepfather) and Antoinette (Angelo) Caballero; m. J.C. Rowell, Dec. 17, 1941; children: Jerrie Carlene, Kerry Gene, Ricky Ray. AA in Bus. Adminstrn., Okaloosa Walton. Coll., 1972; BA in Social Sci., U. West Fla., 1987. Exec. sec. Bishop Enterprises, Ft. Walton Beach; office mgr. and real estate property mgr. Fred Cooke Real Estate, Ft. Walton Beach, Fla.; adminstrv. sec. to v.p. Okaloosa Walton Coll., Niceville, Fla. Leader brownie scouts Girl Scouts U.S., cub scouts Boy Scouts Am.; bd. dirs. U. West Fla. Ctr. for Life Long Learning; chair univ svc. com., pres., began Writing Lab; originator, implementor U. West Fla. Tutor Program, Career Fair, started scholarship program, Proctor Program; curriculum com. U. West Fla.Ctr. for Lifelong Learning, presenter S.E. Conf. Insts. of Learning in Retirement, Charleston, S.C.; gov.'s campaign vol.; state legislature campaign vol.; active Ctr. for Life Long Learning, U. West Fla. Mem. AAUW, DAV Aux., Order of Ea. Star (past matron). Avocations: travel, reading, gardening, dance.

ROWELL, VICTORIA, actress; b. Portland, Maine, May 10, 1960; m. Tom Fahey (div.); 2 children. Attended, Sch. Am. Ballet. Dancer Am. Ballet Theatre, Dance Theatre Harlem, Am. Ballet Theatre II. Actor: (TV series) The Young and the Restless, 1990—98, 2000, 2002— (Outstanding actress in daytime drama series, NAACP Image award, 2006), As the World Turns, 1988, The Cosby Show, 1989—90, The Fresh Prince of Bel-Air, 1990, Herman's Head, 1991, 1993, Deadly Games, 1995, Diagnosis Murder, 1997, Family Law, 2001; (TV films) Full Eclipse, 1993, Secret Sins of the Father, 1994, Feast of All Saints, 2001, Without Warning, 2002, A Town Without Pity, 2002; (films) Leonard Part 6, 1987, The Distinguished Gentleman, 1992, Dumb and Dumber, 1994, One Red Rose, 1995, Barb Wire, 1996, Eve's Bayou, 1997, Dr. Hugo, 1998, Secrets, 1998, A Wake in Providence, 1999, Fraternity Boys, 1999, Black Listed, 2003, Motives, 2004, Midnight Clear, 2005, A Perfect Fit, 2005. Mem.: Sigma Gamma Rho. Mailing: c/o CBS Television City 7800 Beverly Blvd Los Angeles CA 90036*

ROWEN, RUTH HALLE, musicologist, educator; b. N.Y.C., Apr. 5, 1918; d. Louis and Ethel (Fried) Halle; m. Seymour M. Rowen, Oct. 13, 1940; children: Mary Helen Rowen, Louis Halle Rowen. BA, Barnard Coll., 1939; MA, Columbia U., 1941, PhD, 1948. Mgmt. ednl. dept. Carl Fischer, Inc., N.Y.C., 1954-63; assoc. prof. musicology CUNY, 1967-72, prof., 1972—, mem. doctoral faculty in musicology, 1967—. Author: Early Chamber Music, 1948, reprinted, 1974; (with Adele T. Katz) Hearing-Gateway to Music, 1959, (with William Simon) Jolly Come Sing and Play, 1956, Music Through Sources and Documents, 1979, (with Mary Rowen) Instant Piano, 1979, 80, 83, Symphonic and Chamber Music Score and Parts Bank, 1996; contbr. articles to profl. jours. Mem. ASCAP, Am. Musicol. Soc., Music Library Assn., Coll. Music Soc., Nat. Fedn. Music Clubs (nat. musicianship chmn. 1962-74, nat. young artist auditions com. 1964-74, N.Y. state chmn. Young Artist Auditions 1981, dist. coord. 1983, nat. bd. dirs. 1989-2000, rep. UN 1991-2000), N.Y. Fedn. Music Clubs (pres.), Phi Beta Kappa Home: 115 Central Park West At 25D New York NY 10023-4153

ROWLAND, ANGELA KAY, education educator, consultant; b. Chillecothe, Ohio, Sept. 11, 1970; d. Cecil Clement Rowland and Sandra Kay Sparks. BA in Psychology, W.Va. U., 2002, MA in Corp. and Orgn. Comm., 2004. Cert. notary pub., tng. and devel. specialist. Asst. to exec. dir. W.Va. Conservation Agy., Charleston, 1993—97; desktop publ. specialist Ohio Univ., Athens, 1997—2000; records asst. W.Va. U., Parkersburg, 2001—02, English prof., 2004—; prof. speech, English and psychology Wash. State CC, 2005—. Trainer, spkr. stress mgmt. Wash. Co. Pub. Defender, Marietta, Ohio, 2004. Author: (poetry) Rays of Light Anthology, 1997 (Bronze medal, 1997), (short stories) Into the Mist Anthology, 2001 (Editor's Choice, 2001). Tchr. Literary Vols., Parkersburg, W.Va., 1994—99; mem. Nat. Dem. Comm., Parkersburg, W.Va., 1996—97; bd. dirs. Good Samaritan Low-Income Health Clinic, 2005—. Mem.: W.Va. Assn. Notary Publics. Avocations: writing, swimming, reading. Home: 2306 Pennsylvania Ave Parkersburg WV 26101 Personal E-mail: rowland@wirefire.com.

ROWLAND, DIANE, health facility administrator, researcher; b. Bridgeport, Conn., Oct. 14, 1948; m. Brian L. Biles, Sept. 17, 1977. BA, Wellesley Coll., 1970; MPA, U. Calif., L.A., 1973; SCD, Johns Hopkins U., 1987. Mem. staff U.S. House Rep., Washington, 1983—91; assoc. dir. Commonwealth Fund Commn. on Elderly People Living Alone, Balt., 1985—91; assoc. prof. Johns Hopkins U., Balt., 1987—93; exec. v.p. Kaiser Family Found., Washington, 1993—. Exec. dir. Kaiser Commn. on Future of Medicaid, Washington, 1991—98, Kaiser Commn. on Medicaid & the Uninsured, Washington, 1998—; pres. Assn. Health Svc. Rsch., Washington, 2000; mem. Sec. Task Force on Infant Mortality, Washington, 2000—. Contbr. articles to profl. jours. Fellow Brookdale Nat. fellow, Brookdale Found., 1987. Mem.: Inst. Medicine, 2004. Greek Orthodox. Avocations: travel, reading, sailing. Office: Henry J Kaiser Family Found 1330 G Street NW Washington DC 20005

ROWLAND, ESTHER E(DELMAN), retired dean; b. NYC, Apr. 12, 1926; d. Abraham Simon and Ida Sarah (Shifrin) Edelman; m. Lewis P. Rowland, Aug. 31, 1952; children: Andrew, Steven, Joy Rosenthal. BA, U. Wis., 1946; MA, Columbia U., 1948, MPhil, 1984; cert. in bioethics, Columbia U./Albert Einstein, 1996. Instr. in polit. sci. CCNY, 1947-51, Mt. Holyoke Coll., South Hadley, Mass., 1948-49; dir. health professions adv. bd. U. Pa., Phila., 1971-73; adviser to pre-profl. students Barnard Coll., N.Y.C., 1974-79, dean for pre-profl. students, 1980-93, assoc. dean studies, 1989-95; ret., 1995—. Proofreader Monthly Review, N.Y.C., 1997-2003. Mem. exec. com. Nat. Emergency Civil Liberties Com., N.Y.C., 1975-90; mem. exec. com. Women's Counseling Project, 1981-86. Mem. N.E. Assn. Health Professions Advisers (exec. com. 1973-74), N.E. Assn. Pre Law Advisors (exec. com. 1981-83, 85-86), Neurol. Inst. Aux., N.Y.C. Found. Sr. Citizens (ombudsman 1997-99), Aux. Am. Acad. Neurologists (exec. bd. 1999-2001). Home: 404 Riverside Dr New York NY 10025-1861 E-mail: eerowland@gmail.com

ROWLAND, KELLY (KELENDRIA TRENE ROWLAND), singer; b. Atlanta, Ga., Feb. 11, 1981; With Destiny's Child, 1992—2005; solo career, 2005—. Singer (with Destiny's Child): (albums) Destiny's Child, 1998, The Writing's on the Wall, 1999, Survivor, 2001 (Am. Music award for Favorite Pop Album, 2002), 8 Days of Christmas, 2001, Destiny Fulfilled, 2004 (Am. Music award for Favorite R&B Album, 2005), (songs) No, No, No, 1997, Say My Name, 1999 (2 Grammy awards, 2001, MTV Video Music award for Best R&B Video, 2000), Get on the Bus, 1999, Bills Bills Bills, 1999, Bug-A-Boo, 1999, Jumpin' Jumpin', 2000, Independent Woman, 2000, Survivor, 2001 (Grammy award, Best R&B Performance, 2002, MTV Video Music award for Best R&B Video, 2001), Bootylicious, 2001, Emotion, 2001, Lose My Breath, 2004, Soldier, 2005; singer: (solo career) (albums) Simply Deep, 2002, (songs) Stole, 2002, Can't Nobody, 2003, Train on a Track, 2003; singer: (with Nelly) Dilemma, 2002 (Grammy award for Best Rap/Sung Collaboration, 2003); actor: (films) Freddy vs. Jason, 2003. Recipient Favorite R&B Group, Am. Music Awards, 2001, 2002, 2005, BET award for Best Female Group, 2001, NAACP Image award for Outstanding Duo or Group, 2001, 2005, 2006, Choice Pop Group, Teen Choice Awards, 2001, Brit award for Best Internat. Group, 2002, World's Best-Selling Group, World Music Awards, 2002, World's Best-Selling Pop Group, 2002, 2006, World's Best-Selling R&B Group, 2002, 2006, Best-Selling Female Group of All Time, 2006. Address: 1505 Hadley Houston TX 77002 Office Phone: 713-772-5175.*

ROWLAND, PLEASANT T., toy company executive, publisher; m. Jerry Frautschi. Grad., Wells Coll., 1962. Elem. tchr. Mass., Calif., Ga. and N.J.; TV news reporter, anchor KGO-TV, San Francisco; v.p. Boston Ednl. Rsch. Co., 1971-78; pub. Children's Mag. Guide, 1981-89; creator Am. Doll Collection, 1985; founder, pres. Pleasant Co. (sold to Mattel and renamed American Girl, Inc.), 1986—98; vice chmn. Mattel, Inc., 1998—2000. Founder Pleasant T. Rowland Found., Aurora Found. LLC. Named one of 12 Outstanding Entrepreneurs, Inst. Am. Entrepreneurs, 1990, one of Am.'s Top 50 Women Bus. Owners, Working Women mag., 1993-98; recipient Best and Brightest in Mktg. award Advt. Age, 1993, Mem. Internat. Women's Forum, Com. of 200.*

ROWLAND, VICKI DIANE, home health nurse; b. Manchester, Ky., July 15, 1953; d. Roy and Eugenia (Baker) Isom; m. Wade Rowland, Dec. 19, 1970; children: Jason, Jennifer Student, Cumberland Coll., Williamsburg, Ky., 1976—77; LPN, Pineville Sch. Practical Nurse, Ky., 1979; ADN, Ea. Ky. U., 1986. RN, Ky. Charge nurse Meml. Hosp., 1979—80; staff nurse Manchester Clinic, 1980—88; home health nurse Cumberland Valley Dist. Health Dept., Manchester, 1988; staff nurse Laurel Creek Health Care Ctr., Manchester, 1989—91, DON, 1991—95; coord. home health quality assurance Meml. Hosp., Manchester, 1996—. Presdl. scholar Ea. Ky. U., 1984-86 Mem. Am. Soc. Long Term Care Nurses, Ky. Assn. Health Care Facilities (dep. registrar of vital stats.) Home: 276 Engine Branch Rd Manchester KY 40962 Office Phone: 606-598-1969. Personal E-mail: vrowland21@hotmail.com.

ROWLANDS, GENA, actress; b. Madison, Wis., June 19, 1936; d. Edwin Merwin and Mary Allen (Neal) R.; m. John Cassavetes, Apr. 9, 1954 (dec. Feb. 3 1989); 4 children. Student, U. Wis., Am. Acad. Dramatic Art, NYC. Theatrical appearance include The Middle of the Night, 1956; Actress: (films) including The High Cost of Loving, 1958, Lonely Are The Brave, 1962, A Child is Waiting, 1962, Spiral Road, 1962, Faces, 1968, At Any Price, 1970, Minnie and Moscowitz, 1971, A Woman Under the Influence, 1974 (Golden Globe award for Best Motion Picture Actress in a Drama, 1975), Two Minute Warning, 1976, Opening Night, 1977, The Brinks Job, 1978, One Summer Night, 1979, Gloria, 1980, Tempest, 1982, Love Streams, 1983, Light of Day, 1987, Another Woman, 1988, Once Around, 1990, Ted and Venus, 1991, Night on Earth, 1992, Silent Cries, 1993, Parallel Lives, 1994, Anything for John, 1995, Something to Talk About, 1995, The Neon Bible, 1995, Enfants de Salaud, 1996, Unhook the Stars, 1996, Hope Floats, 1997, She's so Lovely, 1997, The Mighty, 1997, Paulie, 1998, The Weekend, 1999, Taking Lives, 2004, The Notebook, 2004, The Skeleton Key, 2005, (TV movies) A Question of Love, 1978, Strangers, 1979, Thurday's Child, 1983, Early Frost, 1986, The Betty Ford Story, 1987 (Emmy award for Outstanding Lead Actress in a Miniseries or Special, 1987, Golden Globe award for Best Performance by an Actress in a TV Film, 1988), Montana, Face of a Stranger, 1991 (Emmy award, Leading Actress in a Mini-Series or Special, 1992), Parallel Lives, 1994, Best of Friends for Life, 1996, Ljuset häller mig sällskap, 2000, Color of Love: Jacey's Story, 2000, Wild Iris, 2001, Hysterical Blindness, 2002, (Emmy award best supporting actress in TV movie, 2003), Charms for the Easy Life, 2002, The Incredible Mrs. Ritchie, 2003 (Daytime Emmy award for Outstanding Performer in a Family Special, 2004); numerous other TV appearances. Mem. Actors Equity Assn., Screen Actors Guild, AFTRA, Am. Guild Variety Artists.

ROWLANDS, KATHLEEN DUDDEN, education educator; b. South Weymouth, Mass., Jan. 11, 1945; d. Arthur Power Dudden and Millicent Ruth (Hancock) Dillon; m. Dennis Earl Rowlands, July 5, 1997; children: Christopher J. Andrasick, Gregory O. Andrasick, Christopher, Jeffrey, Satia T-A. Wang, Jocelyn Vo, Jacquie Vo. AB in English, Conn. Coll., New London, 1966; MA in English, U. Hawaii, Honolulu, 1988; PhD in Composition, Indiana U. Pa., 2004. English tchr. Tottenville HS, NY, 1967—68, Weeks Jr. HS, Newton, Mass., 1969—71, St. Andrews Priorty Sch., Honolulu, 1978—81; English tchr., chmn. dept. Iolani Sch., Honolulu, 1981—92; instr. Montgomery CC, Conroe, Tex., 1998, Sam Houston State U., Huntsville, Tex., 1999—2000; asst. prof. Calif. State U., Northridge, 2004—. Co-dir Hawaii Writing Project, Honolulu, 1982—96, dir. literature inst., 1992, Honolulu, 1997—2003; dir. Reading Inst. Acadm. Preparation, Northridge, 2004—. Author: (as Kathleen D. Andrasick) Opening Tests: Using Writing to Teach Literature, 1990; contbr. articles to profl. publs. Named Master Tchr., Iolani Sch., 1990; recipient Excellence in Tchg. English award, English Speaking Union, 1989, award for ednl. contbns. to state of Hawaii, Hawaii State Senate, 1992. Mem.: Nat. Coun. Tchrs. English, Phi Kappa Phi. Avocations: reading, cooking, golf, tennis. Office: Calif State U Northridge Dept Secondary Edn 18111 Nordhoff St Northridge CA 91330-8265 Office Phone: 818-677-2556. Business E-Mail: krowlands@csun.edu.

ROWLEY, BEVERLEY DAVIES, sociologist; b. Antioch, Calif., July 28, 1941; d. George M. and Eloise Davies; m. Richard B. Rowley, Apr. 1, 1966 (div. 1983). BS, Colo. State U., 1963; MA, U. Nev., 1975; PhD, Union Inst., 1983. Social worker Nev. Dept. Pub. Welfare, Reno, 1963—65, Santa Clara County Dept. Welfare, San Jose, Calif., 1965—66; field dir. Sierra Sage coun. Camp Fire Girls, Sparks, Nev., 1966—70; program coord. divsn. health scis. Sch. Medicine U. Nev., 1976—78, program coord., health analyst office rural health, 1978—84, acting dir. office rural health, 1982—84; exec. asst. to pres. Med. Coll. of Hampton Rds., Norfolk, Va., 1984—87; rsch. mgr. Office Med. Edn. Info. AMA, Chgo., 1987—88, dir. dept. data systems, 1988-91; dir. med. edn. Maricopa Med. Ctr., Phoenix, 1991—99; pres. Med. Edn. and Rsch. Assocs., Inc., Phoenix, Chgo., 1999—, Med. Edn. & Rsch. Assocs., Tempe, Ariz., 1999—; vis. prof. Ariz. State U. East, Mesa, 1999—2000, profl. and personal coach, 2004—; pres., exec. dir. Maricopa Med. Found., Phoenix, 2004—. Various positions as adj. prof. and lectr. in health scis. U. Nev. Sch. of Medicine, 1972-75; lectr. dept. family and cmty. medicine U. Nev., 1978-84, asst. dir., evaluator Health Careers for Am. Indians Programs, 1978-84; cons. Nev. Statewide Health Survey, 1979-84; interim dir. Health Max, 1985-86; asst. prof. dept. family and cmty. medicine Med. Coll. of Hampton Rds., Norfolk, Va., 1985-87. Editor of five books; contbr. numerous articles to profl. jours. Mem. Am. Sociol. Assn., Nat. Rural Health Assn. (bd. dirs. 1986-88), Assn. Behavioral Sci. and Med. Edn. (pres. 1986), Assn. Am. Med. Colls. (exec. coun. 1993-95), Coun. Acad. Scis. (adminstrv. bd. 1992-97), Assn. Hosp. Med. Edn. (bd. dirs. 1997—), Delta Delta Delta. Achievements include development of three computer systems including AMA-FREIDA; four internet-based educational programs for physicians. Avocations: hiking, skiing, gardening, sewing, ceramics. Office: MERA Inc 1903 E Sarah Ln Tempe AZ 85284-3430 E-mail: BDR@MERAInc.com.

ROWLEY, JAN, secondary school educator; m. Robert Williamson. BA, Drake U., Des Moines. English tchr. Ralston H.S., Omaha, 1976—. Office: Ralston High School 8969 Park Dr Omaha NE 68127 Office Phone: 402-331-7373.

ROWLEY, JANET DAVISON, physician; b. NYC, Apr. 5, 1925; d. Hurford Henry and Ethel Mary (Ballantyne) Davison; m. Donald A. Rowley, Dec. 18, 1948; children: Donald, David, Robert, Roger. PhB, U. Chgo., 1944, BS, 1946, MD, 1948; DSc (hon.), U. Ariz., 1989, U. Pa., 1989, Knox Coll., 1991, U. So. Calif., 1992, St. Louis U., 1997, St. Xavier U., 1999, Oxford U., Eng., 2000, Lund U., Sweden, 2003, Dartmouth U., 2004. Diplomate Am. Bd. Med. Genetics. Rsch. asst. U. Chgo., 1949—50; intern Marine Hosp., USPHS, Chgo., 1950—51; attending physician Infant Welfare and Prenatal Clinics Dept. Pub. Health, Montgomery County, Md., 1953—54; rsch. fellow

Levinson Found., Cook County Hosp., Chgo., 1955—61; clin. instr. neurology U. Ill., Chgo., 1957—61; USPHS spl. trainee Radiobiology Lab. The Churchill Hosp., Oxford, England, 1961—62; rsch. assoc. dept. medicine and Argonne Cancer Rsch. Hosp. U. Chgo., 1962—69, assoc. prof. dept. medicine and Argonne Cancer Rsch. Hosp., 1969—77, prof. dept. medicine and Franklin McLean Meml. Rsch. Inst., 1977—84, Blum-Riese Disting. Svc. prof., dept. medicine and dept. molecular genetics and cell biology, 1984—, Blum-Riese Disting. Svc. prof. dept. human genetics, 1997—, interim dep. dean for sci. biol. scis. divsn., 2001—02. Bd. sci. counsellors Nat. Inst. Dental Rsch., NIH, 1972—76, chmn., 1974—76; mem. Nat. Cancer Adv. Bd., Nat. Cancer Inst., 1979—84, Nat. Adv. Coun. for Human Genome Rsch. Inst., 1999—2004; adv. com. Frederick Cancer Rsch. Facility, 1983—84; bd. sci. counsellors Nat. Human Genome Rsch. Inst., NIH, 1994—99, chmn., 1994—97; adv. bd. Howard Hughes Med. Inst., 1989—94, MD Anderson Cancer Ctr., 1998—2005; vis. com. dept. applied biol. scis. MIT Corp., 1983—86; bd. sci. cons. Meml. Sloan-Kettering Cancer Ctr., 1988—90; adv. com. Ency. Britannica U. Chgo., 1988—96; W. Jack Stuckey Jr. lectr. Tulane Career Ctr., 1996; Presdl. Symposium Am. Soc. Pediatric Hematology/Oncology, 1995; lectr. in field; mem. coun. adv. Internat. Geneminica Rsch. Inst., 2004—; mem. sci. adv. bd. Meml. Sloan-Kettering Cancer Ctr., 2004, Translational Genomics Rsch. Inst., Phoenix., 2004—; mem. sci. and med. adv. bd. Calif. Inst. Regenerative Medicine, 2005—. Co-founder, co-editor: Genes, Chromosomes and Cancer, mem. editl. bd.: Oncology Rsch., Cancer Genetics and Cytogenetics, Internat. Jour. Hematology, Genomics, Leukemia; past mem. editl. bd. Internat. Jour. Cancer, Blood, Cancer Rsch., Hematol. Oncology, Leukemia Rsch.; contbr. chapters to books, articles to profl. jours. Adv. com. for career awards in biomed. scis. Burroughs Wellcome Fund, 1994—98; selection panel for Clin. Sci. award Doris Duke Charitable Found., 2000—02, 2006; mem. Pres.'s Adv. Coun. on Bioethics, 2001—; mem. med. rsch. material command leukemia program U.S. Army, 2002—04; mem. selection com. Rosalind Franklin young investigator award, 2004; nat. adv. com. McDonnell Found. Program for Molecular Medicine in Cancer Rsch., 1988—98; adv. bd. Leukemia Soc. Am., 1979—84; selection com. scholar award in biomed. sci. Lucille P. Markey Charitable Trust, 1984—87; trustee Adler Planetarium, Chgo., 1978—; med. adv. bd. G&P Charitable Found., 1999—. Co-recipient Charles Mott prize, GM Cancer Rsch. Found., 1989; named Chicagoan of Yr., Chgo. mag., 1998; recipient First Kuwait Cancer prize, 1984, Esther Langer award, Ann Langer Cancer Rsch. Found., 1983, A. Cressy Morrison award in natural scis., N.Y. Acad. Scis., 1985, Past State Pres. award, Tex. Fedn. Bus. and Profl. Women's Clubs, 1986, Karnofsky award and lecture, Am. Soc. Clin. Oncology, 1987, Antoine Lacassagne Lique prize, 1987, Nat. Francaise Contre le Cancer prize, 1987, King Faisal Internat. prize in medicine (co-recipient), Nat. Francaise Contre le Cancer, 1988, Katherine Berkan Judd award, Meml. Sloan-Kettering Cancer Ctr., 1989, Steven C. Beering award, U. Ind. Med. Sch, 1992, Robert de Villiers award, Leukemia Soc. Am., 1993, Kaplan Family prize for cancer rsch. excellence, Oncology Soc. Dayton, 1995, Cotlove award and lecture, Acad. Clin. Lab. Physicians and Scientists, 1995, Nilsson-Ehle lecture, Mendelian Soc. and Royal Physiographic Soc., 1995, Gairdner Found. award, 1996, medal of honor, Basic Sci. Am. Cancer Soc., 1996, Nat. Medal of Sci., 1998, Lasker award for clin. scis., 1998, Woman Extraordinaire award, Internat. Women's Assocs., 1999, Golden Plate award, Am. Acad. Achievement, 1999, Women Achieving Excellence award, YWCA of Met. Chgo., 2000, Philip Levine award, Am. Soc. Clin. Pathology, 2001, Emile M Chamot award, State Microscopy Soc. Ill., 2001, Mendel medal, Villanova U., 2003, Benjamin Franklin medal, Am. Philos. Soc., 2003, Dist. Alumni Award, U. Chgo., 2003. Fellow: AAAS (nominating com. 1998); mem.: NAS (chmn. sect. 41 1995—99, mem. com. 2004), Chgo. Network, Inst. Medicine (coun. 1988—90), Cancer Rsch. (lectr. 2003, G.H.A. Clowes Meml. award 1989, Charlotte Friend award 2003, Dorothy P. Landon award 2005), Am. Soc. Hematology (lectr. Millenium Symposium 1999, Presdl. Symposium 1982, Dameshek prize 1982, Ham-Wasserman award 1995, Henry M. Stratton medal 2003), Genetical Soc., Am. Soc. Human Genetics (pres.-elect 1992, pres. 1993, Allen award and lectr. 1991, Disting. Sci. lectr. 2003), Am. Philos. Soc., Am. Acad. Arts and Scis. (nominating com. 1998), Alpha Omega Alpha, Sigma Xi (William Proctor prize for sci. achievement 1989). Episcopalian. Home: 5310 S University Ave Chicago IL 60615-5106 Office: U Chgo 5841 S Maryland Ave Rm 2115 Chicago IL 60637-1463 Office Phone: 773-702-6117. Business E-Mail: jrowley@medicine.bsd.uchicago.edu.

ROWLEY, KATHLEEN DOROTHY, elementary school educator; b. Spokane, Wash., June 21, 1941; d. Claude Karl and Kathleen Edith (Bailey) Irwin; m. George Waldo Rowley, Jr., July 18, 1964 (div. 1974); children: Kari KathleenMagill, Kelly Patricia Richardson; m. Raymond DeLoss Smith, Jan. 3, 1975 (div. 1984). BS in Edn., U. Idaho, 1963, MEd, 1986. Cert. tchr., Wash. Elem. tchr. Bellevue (Wash.) Schs., 1963-66; asst. mgr. resort Rowley Enterprises/Silver Pacific Co., Port Townsend, Wash., 1970-72; tchr. music and reading Issaquah (Wash.) Coop. Presch., 1969-70, 72-73; asst. farm mgr. R.D. Smith & Sons Farm & Ranch, La Cross, Wash. and Craig Mountain, Idaho, 1975-84; tchr. Chpt. I reading Pullman (Wash.) Schs., 1986-90; an owner The Ivy Profl. Ctr., Spokane, 1991—93; tchr. piano Music City, Spokane, 1991—94; substitute tchr. Spokane Schs. Dist 81, 1991—2002. Mgr. apt. rentals, Pullman, 1986-95, owner, pres. Rowley Rentals, 2000-. Leader LaCross All Purpose 4-H Club, 1975-84; sec. LaCrosse Sch. PTA, 1976-77. Mem. Tamarack Reading Coun. (membership officer 1987-90), Powderhorn Bay Water Assn. (pres. 1988—), Kappa Kappa Gamma (pres. Pullman 1986-91, reference officer 1991-92, pres. Spokane 1994—, Shyrock award 1989), Phi Delta Kappa, Kappa Kappa Gamma (pres. 1994-96, sec. 2005-). Avocations: snorkeling, gardening, dance, canoeing, travel. Home: 3904 S Alder Cir Spokane WA 99223-7300

ROWLEY, MAXINE LEWIS, retired home economics and consumer educator, retired department chairman; b. Provo, Utah, Sept. 23, 1938; d. Max Thomas Lewis and Illa Lewis Sanford; m. Arthur William Rowley, Sept. 23, 1960; children: Anne, Jenefer. BA (Ford Found. scholar), Brigham Young U., 1960, PhD in Edn. Adminstrn., 1989; BS, U. Utah, 1974; MA, Utah State U., 1980. Promotion writer Sta. ABC KCPX-TV, 1960; extension home economist USDA, 1961; mgmt. trainee Deseret Book Co., Salt Lake City, 1969; dept. chair Patricia Stevens Career Coll., Salt Lake City, 1970; chair consumer and homemaking dept. Sand Ridge Jr. H.S. Weber Sch. Dist., Roy, Utah, 1975, learning experience designer, 1976-78; consumer and home econs. faculty Utah State U., Logan, 1978-79; spl. appointee to Utah State U. by the Utah State Bd. Edn., 1978-86; intern Gladys Chalkley Brannegan Am. Home Econ. Assn., 1993; chair dept. family life and home econs. Brigham Young U., 1988, 1999—2002; ret., 2002. Instrumental writer Utah State U. Found., 1979; mem. faculty Brigham Young U., 1979; mem. women's legis. coun. State of Utah, 1992—2005. Author: NCFR Public Policy Handbook, 1997; (filmstrips, texts and tchrs. guide) CHECS, 1979; (curriculum guide) Operation: Free Enterprise, 1982, Curriculum of Food Sci., Nutrition, vol. I, 1990, vol. II, 1992, vol. III, 1993; co-author: Legacy, vol. I, 1998. Active ward, stake and region positions Ch. of Jesus Christ of Latter-day Saints; leader 4-H Club, coun. mem., adv. bd.; leader Girl Scouts U.S.A., Young Homemakers; active State Text Book Evaluation Com., 1978-86, U. Utah Evaluation Com., 1979; edn. and rsch. com. Am. Cancer Soc., State of Utah, 1993-94. Named Outstanding Leader Am. Edn., 1976, Nat. Tchr. of Yr., 1977, Outstanding Tchr. in Dept., Brigham Young U., 1984-94, Outstanding Voccat. Edn. Leader, State of Utah, 1996, Nat. Honor Roll in vocat. edn. Nat. Assn. Vocat. Family and Consumer Scis., 1999. Mem.: NEA, Internat. Fed. Home Econ. (nat. officer), Am. Edn. Rsch. Assn. (Nat. chair, HERSIG 2001—03), Utah Assn. Family and Consumer Scis. (disting. svc. award 2003), Worldwide Orgn. Women (women's legis. coun. State of Utah 1998—2004, internat. bd. dirs. 1999—2003), Vocat. Home Econs. Tchrs. (nat. chmn. public rels. and legis. coms. 1978), Home Econs. Edn. Assn., Am. Edn. Rsch. Assn (nat.chair Home Econs. Related Spl. Interest Group 2000—03, marriage, family & human devel. dept. 2002—), County Welfare Com., Utah Edn. Assn. (award for womens awareness task force project 1976), Utah Nutrition Coun. (chair 1995), Utah Coun. for Improvement Edn., Utah Vocat. Assn., Utah Home Econs. Assn., Am. Vocat. Assn., Am. Assn. Family and Consumer Scis. (nat. v.p., bd. dirs., chair ann. meeting, bd. liaison publs. 1995—97, nat. com. publs. 1999—), Am. Home Econs. Assn. (contbr., author yearbook 1984, Nat. Leadership award 1993), Nat. Assn. Vocat. Home Econs. Tchrs., Ellen H. Richards Cir., Spurs, White Key (pres. 1960), Alpha Delta Kappa, Gamma Phi Omicron, Phi Kappa Phi, Kappa Omicron Nu (advisor 1980—2005, Nat. award of excellence 1999, nat. endowment honoree 1989, nat. leadership endowment 2001). Home: 9801 Lampton Cir South Jordan UT 84095-9211

ROWLING, J.K. (JOANNE KATHLEEN ROWLING), writer; b. Gloucestershire, England, July 31, 1965; d. Peter and Anne Rowling; m. Jorge Arantes, Oct. 16, 1992 (div. Nov. 30, 1993); 1 child, Jessica; m. Neil Murray, Dec. 26, 2001; children: David, Mackenzie. BA in French & Classics, Exeter U., 1986; LittD (hon.), Napier U., 2000, Dartmouth Coll., 2000, U. Exeter, 2000; degree (hon.), U. St. Andrews, 2000, U. Edinburgh, 2004; LLD (hon.), Aberdeen U., 2006. Former rschr. Amnesty International; teacher Scotland, 1990—94. Author: (novels) Harry Potter and the Philosopher's Stone, 1997 (Children's Book of the Year, British Book Awards, 1998, Gold Winner, Smarties Book Prize, 1997, Birmingham Cable Children's Book Award, Young Telegraph Paperback of the Year, Sheffield Children's Book Award, Sorcieres Prix, 1999, Premio Cento per la Letteratura Infantile, 1998), Harry Potter and the Sorcerer's Stone (U.S. title), 1998 (Anne Spencer Lindbergh Prize in Children's Literature, 1998, ABBY Award, American Booksellers Assoc., 1999), Harry Potter and the Chamber of Secrets, 1998 (Gold Winner, Smarties Book Prize, 1998), Harry Potter and the Prisoner of Azkaban, 1999, Harry Potter and the Goblet of Fire, 2000, Quidditch Through the Ages, 2001, Fantastic Beasts & Where to Find Them, 2001, Harry Potter and the Order of the Phoenix, 2003, Harry Potter and the Half-Blood Prince, 2005 (Quills award for Book of Yr., 2005, Brit. Book of Yr. award, 2006). Named Officer of the Most Excellent Order of the British Empire (O.B.E.) by Charles, Prince of Wales, No. 2 on the list, "British Top 50 Movers and Shakers", BBC 3, Amazon.com's No. 1 of Top 10 authors, 1995—2005; named one of Most Powerful Women, Forbes mag., 2005. Office: Christopher Little Literary Agency 10 Eel Brook Studios 125 Moore Park Rd London SW6 4PS England

ROY, ANURADHA, statistician, educator, researcher; d. Nirmal Chandra and Biva Roy. BSc in Math. with honors, Calcutta U., 1978; M Stat. in Advance Probability and Math. Stats. with honors, Indian Statis. Inst., Calcutta, 1981; PhD in Applied Stats., Oakland U., 2002. Rsch. scholar Indian Statis. Inst., Calcutta, 1982—86; rsch. officer Govt. of India, 1986—98; tchg. assoc. Oakland U., Mich., 1998—2002; asst. prof. U. Tex., San Antonio, 2002—. Rsch. asst. Wayne State U. Sch. of Medicine, Detroit, 2000. Contbr. articles to profl. jours. Office: U Tex San Antonio Dept Mgmt Sci and Statistics San Antonio TX 78249 Office Phone: 210-458-6343. Business E-Mail: aroy@utsa.edu.

ROY, BETH, sociologist, mediator; b. NYC, Apr. 1, 1941; d. Ruth Rapfogel; life ptnr. Mariah Breeding, July 5, 1992; children: Tuhin, Joshua Walker. PhD, U. of Calif., Berkeley, 1991. Mediator, San Francisco, 1973—; lectr. Peace and Conflict Studies, U. Calif., Berkeley, 1993—. Chair Practitioners Rsch. and Scholarship Inst., Atlanta, 2000—. Author: (nonfiction book) Some Trouble with Cows: Making Sense of Social Conflict, 1994, Bitters in the Honey: Tales of Hope and Disappointment across Divides of Race and Time, 1999. Home: 270 Prospect Ave San Francisco CA 94110 Office: 270 Prospect Ave San Francisco CA 94110 Office Phone: 415-695-8119. Home Fax: 866-529-6964; Office Fax: 866-529-6964. Business E-Mail: broy@igc.org.

ROY, DARLENE, human services administrator; b. St. Louis, June 17, 1945; d. Robert and Ezora Gertrude Duncan; m. Lovell Swanson, June 17, 1967 (div. 1980); 1 child, Troy Anthony Swanson. BA, So. Ill. U., 1967; MSW, St. Louis U., 1971. Caseworker Ill. Dept. Pub. Aid, East St. Louis, 1967-72, supr., 1972-80, asst. adminstr. I, 1980-94, asst. adminstr. II, 1994-97, adminstr., 1997—. Mem., past pres. Child Care Resource and Referral Coun., Granite City, Ill., 1989—; mem. SIU Headstart Coun., East St. Louis, 1994—97, Social Svc. Task Force, East St. Louis, 1996—, St. Clair County Homeless Action Coun., 1996—. Assoc. editor: (literary jour.) Drumvoices Rev., 1994; contbr. articles to literary jours. Mem. Bi-State Arts in Transit, St. Louis, 1990; mem. Ct. Apptd. Spl. Advs. Bd. Dirs.; bd. dirs. Delta Child Devel. Ctr., v.p., 2001—. Recipient Black Women in Middlewest award Purdue U., 1986, Cmty. Svc. award Top Ladies of Distinction, 1987, Jail and Bail Fund Raising award Am. Cancer Soc., 1999. Mem.: NAACP, East St. Louis Pan Hellenic Coun. (v.p. 1999—), Arts Coun., Nat. Coun. Negro Women (charter), Sunday Jams Fund Raiser Club (v.p. 2001—), Eugene B. Redmond Writers Club (pres. 1986—), Delta Sigma Theta (life; pres. 1979—81). Baptist. Avocations: reading, modeling, dance. Office: Ill Dept Human Svcs 225 N 9th St East Saint Louis IL 62201-1706 Home: 282 Winchester Pl Fairview Heights IL 62208-3843

ROY, DELLA MARTIN, materials science educator, researcher; b. Merrill, Oreg., Nov. 3, 1926; d. Harry L. and Anna (Cacka) Martin; m. Rustum Roy, June 8, 1948; children: Neill R., Ronnen A., Jeremy R. BS, U. Oreg., 1947; MS, Pa. State U., 1949, PhD, 1952. Various rsch. positions Pa. State Univ., Univ. Park, 1952—60, sr. rsch. assoc. geochemistry, 1960—62, sr. rsch. assoc. materials sci. engring., 1962—69, assoc. prof. materials sci. engring., 1969—75, prof. materials sci. engring., 1975—92, prof. emeritus materials sci., 1992—; rsch. prof. Ariz. State U., 2005—. Cons. in field; chmn. status of cement, concrete materials adv. bd., Washington, 1977—80; spl. adv. concrete durability NRC, 1985—. Editor: Instructional Modules in Cement Science, 1985, Jour. Cement & Concrete Rsch., 1971—; contbr. articles to profl. jours. Fellow: AAAS, Am. Concrete Inst. (Keynote address 1980, Can. Ctr. Mineral and Energy Tech. award 1989), Mineral. Soc. Am., Inst. Concrete Tech. (hon.), Am. Ceramic Soc. (trustee 1990—, Jeppson Medal award 1982, Copeland award 1987, Bleininger award 2004); mem.: NAS (exec. com., transp. rsch. bd. 1991—), Internat. Acad. Ceramics, Nat. Acad. Engring. (acad. adv. bd. 1989—, membership policy com. 2001—), Coun. Materials Rsch. Soc. (chmn. cement symposia 1980—81, 1986—88, trustee 1988—90), Friends of Health (mem. bd.). Democrat. Office: Pa State U Hastings Rd 110 Materials Rsch Lab University Park PA 16802 Business E-Mail: dellaroy@psu.edu.

ROY, ELIZABETH MARY, secondary school educator; b. Colorado Springs, Colo., Feb. 10, 1973; d. Ellen and James Bollmeier; m. Patrick Roy, July 19, 1997; children: Julia, Brenden. BS, U. Ill., Champaign-Urbana, 1996. Sci. tchr. Mascoutah (Ill.) H.S., 1996—. Office: Mascoutah High Sch 1313 W Main St Mascoutah IL 62258 Office Phone: 618-566-8523.

ROY, JULIANA W., music educator; b. Bandung, West Java, Indonesia, July 28, 1969; d. Yusak and Hanna Wiriasantosa; m. Dean P. Roy, June 4, 1994; 1 child, Jaden P. MusM, Southwestern Bapt. Theol. Sem., Ft. Worth, Tex., 1996. Cert. tchr. music Tex., 1999. Elem. sch. music tchr. Lubbock Ind. Sch. Dist., Tex., 1999—2001, 2003—. Ch. accompanist Calvary Bapt. Ch., Lubbock, 1995—. Recipient music scholarship, Calif. Bapt. U., 1992, Academic Music award, 1992. Mem.: Tex. Music Educator Assn. Office: Arnett Elem Sch 701 E Queens St Lubbock TX 79403 Office Phone: 806-766-1644. Business E-Mail: jroy@lubbockisd.org.

ROY, NANCY LOU, science educator; b. N.Y.C., Aug. 7, 1950; d. Robert William and Harriet Elizabeth Betchtel; m. Cecil Clifford Roy, Nov. 14, 1973; 1 child, Clifford William. BS in Housing and Interiors, Auburn U., Ala., 1973; M of Secondary Edn., Auburn U., Montgomery, Ala., 1992. Salesperson Bishop Parker, Montgomery, Ala., 1973—74; bookkeeper/jr. acct. Eubank, Wade and Lyons, Montgomery, Ala., 1974—78; bookkeeper Franco Distributing, Montgomery, Ala., 1979—91; tchr. 7th grade sci. Millbrook Jr. H.S., Ala., 1993—. Mem. Ala. Sci. Adv. Bd.-McGraw Hill, 2004—05. Mem.: Elmore County Edn. Assn. (pres., sec., treas. 1990—). Office: Millbrook Mid/Jr HS 4228 Chapman Rd Millbrook AL 36054 Office Phone: 334-285-2124.

ROY, SUZANNE SCULLY, reading specialist; d. Paul V. and Caroline A. Scully; 1 child, Robert W. MS in Edn., Duquesne U., Pitts., Pa., 1981. Cert. tchr. Pa., 1972. Reading specialist North Allegheny Sch. Dist., Pitts., 1983—. Participant Gov.'s Inst. for English Lang. Arts Educators: Oral History, Valley Forge, Pa., 1999, Gov.'s Inst. for English Lang. Arts Educators, Selingsgrove, Pa., 2005; Ffulbright tchr. exch. US Dept. of State, Rapla, Estonia, 2006—. Sec. North Allegheny Fedn. of Tchrs., Pitts., 1992—96, treas., 1996—2000. With USN, 1973—76. Mem.: Internat. Reading Assn., Am. Legion. Office: Marshall Mid Sch 5145 Wexford Run Rd Wexford PA 15090 Office Phone: 724-934-6060. Business E-Mail: sroy@northallegheny.org.

ROYAL, SUSAN, classical musician, educator; b. Phila., July 21, 1955; d. Douglas David and Bette Royal; m. Wayne Arthur Jones, Aug. 13, 1988; children: Daria Jones, Ethan Jones. BMusic, Ithaca Coll., 1977; MMusic, Yale U., 1981; DMusical Arts, SUNY, Stony Brook, 1989. Instr. flute Tenn. Technol. U., Cookeville, 1981-83; flutist Erie (Pa.) Philharm., 1983—, We. N.Y. Chamber Orch., 1983—; substitute flutist Buffalo Philharm., 1984—; prof. flute SUNY Coll., Fredonia, 1983—. Performer/clinician Fredonia Woodwind Quintet Summer Camp, 1994—, Fredonia Woodwind Quintet, 1983—; artist performer Armstrong/Artley Flutes, 1991—. Concert soloist; performances on CD include Opera Sacra, 1994, Piorkowski, 1998, Buffalo Phil, 2003, 04. Elder First United Presbyn. Ch., Dunkirk, N.Y., 1987—. Recipient Pres.'s Excellence award, SUNY, 2004. Mem. Nat. Flute Assn. (performer/adjudicator/panelist 1977—), Niagara Frontier Flute Assn. Democrat. Avocations: sailing, gardening. Office: SUNY Fredonia Sch Music Fredonia NY 14063

ROYALL, MARY-JULIA C., church organist, historian; b. Donalds, S.C., Dec. 30, 1925; d. John McCants Campbell and Cordelia Bearden; m. Jervey DuPré Royall, Sept. 18, 1949; children: Julia C., Anne DuPré. BA, Erskine Coll., 1945; MA, U. S.C., 1948, performers cert. in organ, 1953. With Salem Coll. Organ Acad.; mem. staff Brevard Music Camp, 1946; music tchr. Montreat (N.C.) H.S. and Coll., 1946—47; pvt. piano tchr., 1953—66; dir. h.s. glee club Moultrie H.S., Mt. Pleasant, SC, 1960—62, Coll. Prep. Sch., Charleston, 1972—74; organist St. Mary's Cath. Ch., Charleston, 1979—. Author: Mt. Pleasant S.C.: The Victorian Village, 1997, Mt. Pleasant, S.C.: The Friendly Town, 2001. Historian Town of Mt. Pleasant, 1996—; mem. com. Charleston County SC Nat. Heritage Corridor, 1995—98; mem. Mt. Pleasant Presbyn. Ch., 1950—; pres. Confederate Meml. Assn., Mt. Pleasant, 1984—, Christ Ch. Parish Preservation Soc., Mt. Pleasant, 1994—. Named Tree Farmer of Yr., S.C., 1982—83; named to Order of the Gavel, Town of Mt. Pleasant, 1996; recipient Robert N. Pryor Svc. award, Confederation of Local Hist. Socs., S.C., 1997, Outstanding So. Citizen award, Sons of Confederate Vets., 2003. Mem.: S.C. Forestry Assn., Organ Hist. Soc. (editor newsletter S.C. chpt. 1979—84), Am. Guild Organists (S.C. state chmn., mem. Charleston chpt.). Home: 349 Bay View Acres Mount Pleasant SC 29464

ROYBAL-ALLARD, LUCILLE, congresswoman; b. Boyle Heights, Calif., June 12, 1941; d. Edward Roybal; m. Edward T. Allard; 4 children. BA in Speech, Calif. State U., L.A., 1965. Former mem. Calif. State Assembly, 1987—93; mem. U.S. Congress from 34th Calif. dist., 1993—; mem. appropriations com.; mem. Ho. Com. on Standards of Official Conduct. Recipient Madre y Mujer award, Kimberly-Clark, 2006. Democrat. Office: Ho of Reps 2330 Rayburn Bldg Washington DC 20515-0534 also: 225 E Temple St Ste 1860 Los Angeles CA 90012

ROYCE, CHRISTINE ANNE, primary school educator; b. Scranton, Pa., Jan. 4, 1968; d. Walford Harold Royce and Ann Marie Bernadette (Samuels) Royce Robinson. BS, Cabrini Coll., 1990; MEd, Del State U., 1994. Cert. mid. and elem. sci. tchr. Pa., Del. Adminstrv. specialist Valley Forge Mil. Acad., Wayne, Pa., 1989-90, asst. camp dir., 1988-92 summers; adminstrv. aide ARA Svcs., Wayne, 1990-91; tchr. St. Hedwigs Sch., Chester, Pa., 1990-91, Capital Sch. Dist., Dover, Del., 1991—. Environ. ednl. cons. Girl Scouts, Scranton, 1986-93; merit badge cons. Boy Scouts Am., Dover, 1991—; coach Cath. Youth Orgn., Dover, 1992-93. Rsch. fellowship Dept. Energy, 1993; recipient Comdrs. Award for Pub. Svc. Dept. of Army, 1990. Mem. NEA, Pa. Sci. Tchrs. Assn., Del. Sci. Tchrs. Assn., Nat. Sci. Tchrs. Assn., Capital Educators Assn. Avocations: music, outdoor activities, volleyball. Home: 429 S 9th Ave Scranton PA 18504-2801 Office: Ctrl Middle Sch Delaware Ave Dover DE 19901-3895

ROYCROFT, CHERYL, secondary school educator; b. Buffalo, N.Y., Mar. 11, 1961; d. Edward Stanley and Delphine Theresa Janusz; m. Henry Phillip Roycroft, Oct. 14, 1983. BS, Daemen Coll., 1993; MEd, Cambridge Coll., 2002. Cert. tchr. Payroll clerk Sellmore Industries, Buffalo, N.Y., 1984-85; acct. clerk Desiderio Produce, Buffalo, 1985-87, Fisher-Price, E. Aurora, 1987-90, Acme Electric, E. Aurora, 1993-94; tchr. Bryant & Stratton, Buffalo, 1994-96, Lake City H.S., S.C., 1996-97, Mt. Pleasant H.S., Elliott, S.C., 1997-2000, Lee Ctrl. H.S., Bishopville, S.C., 2000—. Mem. Assn. Career and Tech. Educators, S.C. Bus. Educators Assn., Coun. for Exceptional Children, Kappa Delta Pi (pres. 1992-95, historian 1991-92), Delta Mu Delta (v.p. 1991-92, pres. 1992-93), ASCD. Avocations: reading, swimming, dance. Office: Lee Ctrl HS 1800 Wisacky Hwy Bishopville SC 29010 E-mail: keyteacher77@hotmail.com.

ROYCROFT, ELIZABETH ANNE, elementary school educator; b. Durham, N.C., June 23, 1960; d. George Washington and Eula Elizabeth (Hux) Miller; m. Rodney Ross Roycroft, Oct. 22, 1983. BA, U. N.C., 1981, MEd, 1983. Edn. program coord. Family Svc. Ctr., Cecil Field, Fla., 1986-88; counselor Women's Ctr. Fla. Community Coll., Jacksonville, 1988-89; coord. Cmty. Drug and Alcohol Coun., 1990—92; mid. sch. tchr. Escambia County Sch. Dist., 2004—; self employed grant writeer, cons., 1992—. Mem. Phi Beta Kappa. Democrat. Methodist. Home: 3398 Valdor Pl Pensacola FL 32503-3436

ROYER, KATHLEEN ROSE, pilot; b. Pitts., Nov. 4, 1949; d. Victor Cedric and Lisetta Emma (Smith) Salway; m. Michael Lee Royer, June 6, 1971 (div. Aug. 1975). Student, Newbold Coll., 1968-69; BS, Columbia Union Coll., 1971; MEd, Shippensburg U., 1974; student, Lehigh U., 1974-75. Cert. tchr. Pa. Music. Music tchr. Harrisburg (Pa.) Sch. Dist., 1971-77; flight instr. Penn-Air, Inc., Altoona, Pa., 1977; capt., asst. chief pilot Air Atlantic Airlines, Centre Hall, Pa., 1977-80; capt., chief pilot Lycoming Air Svc., Williamsport, Pa., 1980-81; govs. pilot Commonwealth of Pa., Harrisburg, 1981-87; flight engr. Pan-Am, N.Y.C., 1987-91; pilot, 1st officer B737 United Airlines, Chgo., 1992-96, 1st officer B767 N.Y.C., until 1996, Washington, 1996-99; flight officer B747-400 JFK Internat. Airport, Jamaica, NY, 1999—2001, capt. Airbus 320, 2001—, airbus line check airman, 2005—. Frist woman pilot/engr. crew mem. on 747 Pan Am. Airlines, 1989—91, chief pilot, cons. Mem.: UAL-Airline Pilot Assn. (coord. critical incident stress program 1994—96), Flight Engrs. Internat. Assn. (scheduling rep. 1989, scheduling dir. 1990, 1st vice chmn., mem. bd. adjustments 1989, v.p. dir. scheduling 1991—92), Internat. Soc. Women Airline Pilots, Whirley Girls (Washington), 99's (local chair Ctrl. Pa. chpt. 1987—92). Republican. Avocations: owner/flying 1965 Cessna 180, golf, music, reading. Home: 34 Lazy Eight Dr Daytona Beach FL 32128 Office: San Francisco Intl Airport San Francisco CA Personal E-mail: royer17@bellsouth.net.

ROYLANCE, LYNN MICHELLE, electrical engineer; b. San Francisco, Nov. 27, 1951; d. Jack Clifton and Alice Helen (Gordh) R.; m. Julian Payne Freret Jr., June 21, 1979; children: Morgan Elizabeth Freret, Taylor Susanne Freret. BSEE, BS in Physics, MIT, 1972; MSEE, Stanford U., 1973, PhD in Elec. Engring., 1978. Instr. Stanford U., Stanford, Calif., 1974; mem. tech. staff Hewlett-Packard Labs., Palo Alto, Calif., 1977-81, project mgr., 1981-87, project mgr. Cir. Tech. Group R & D, 1987-89, sect. mgr. Integrated Circuits Bus. Divsn. R&D, 1989-96, program mgr., 1996—99; tech. contbr. Agilent Techs., Santa Clara, Calif., 2000—01, product engring. mgr. high speed networking divsn, 2001—. Mem. program com. Internat. Symposium on Very Large Scale Integration Tech., 1982-85. Contbr. articles to profl. jours. NSF fellow, 1972-75. Mem. IEEE, Am. Mgmt. Assn., Phi Beta Kappa,

Sigma Xi, Tau Beta Pi (program com., No. Calif. Electronic Material Symposium 1981, chmn. 1983-84, treas. No. Calif. section 1985-87). Avocations: woodworking, genealogy. Home: 1160 Laureles Dr Los Altos CA 94022-1012

ROYSTON, GINGER KNIERIM, secondary school educator; b. Boonville, Mo., Nov. 25, 1949; d. James Patrick and Helen Marie Knierim; 1 child, Daniel. BME, Ctrl. Meth. Coll., 1971. Vocal music tchr. Salisbury Sch., 1971—2006; pvt. voice instr. Mem.: Mo. Retired Teachers Assn., Mo. State Teachers Assn., Mo. Choral Assn. of Directors, Music Educators Nat. Conf. Home: 510 S Birch Dr Salisbury MO 65281 Office Phone: 660-388-6442.

ROYSTON, PAMELA JEAN, special education educator; b. Anchorage, Alaska, Sept. 26, 1958; d. Ralph Vedra Allen (Deceased) and Wilma Jean Daniels, Franklin Hicks Daniels (Stepfather); m. Randy Glenn Royston, June 23, 1977; children: Rusty Brandon, Bridgett Starr Vaughn. AA, Emmanuel Coll., Franklin Springs, Ga., 1990—91; BS edn., The U. of Ga., Athens, Ga., 1991—94. Severe/profound spl. edn. tchr. Madison County Mid. Sch., Danielsville, Ga., 1994—96; moderate/severe spl. edn. tchr. Hart County Mid. Sch., Hartwell, Ga., 1996—. Sch. beautification dir. Madison County Mid. Sch., Danielsville, Ga., 1994—96; peer tutor dir. Hart County Mid. Sch., Hartwell, Ga., 1996—, sch. beautification dir., 1996—, cmty.-based instrn. dir., 1996—; presenter in field. Rschr. (instrnl. procedures rsch.) Collaborated with Dr. Gast and Dr. Wall: Univ. of Ga., in conducting a rsch. study investigating the effectiveness of using constant time delay when tchg. leisure skills to students who are intellectually disabled. (Jour. of Devel. and Phys. Disabilities, 11l., 193-218., 1999), presenter Gave presentation to the Ga. State Adv. Panel for Spl. Edn. about my Peer Tutor and Cmty.-Based Instn. Program., (rsch.) Mid. Sch. Students Tchg. Leisure Skills to Peer with Disabilities. Paper presented at the 2001 Ann. Meeting of the Am. Assn. on Mental Retardation, Denver, Colo., Presented rsch. paper at the Nat. Inst. for People with Disabilities' 20th Ann. Internat. Conf., NYC, NY, Gave Power Point presentation for the pre-svc. spl. edn. students at Ga. So. Univ. Focus: Cmty.-Based Instrn. and classroom set-up., Presented paper concerning using e-mail as a way of increasing written lang. skills at the Conf. of the Tchr. Edn. Divsn. of the Coun. for Exceptional Children, Dallas, Tex., Presented paper concerning teachers and researchers at he Conf. of the Tchr. Edn. Divsn. of the Coun. for Exceptional Children, Savannah, Ga., (research-instructional procedues) Poster session presented at the Ann. Conf. of the Assn. for Persons with Severe Handicaps, New Orleans, La., (rsrch.-instructional procedures) Presented paper at the Ann. Meeting of the Assn. for Persons with Severe Handicaps, San Francisco, Calif. Assist in fundraising activities Congressman Charles Taylor, Asheville, NC, 2002—03. Recipient Honor Special Education Teacher for the State of Georgia, Atlanta Journal-Constitution, 2000. Mem.: Ga. Assn. of Educators, Coun. for Exceptional Children, The Assn. for Persons with Severe Handicaps, Golden Key Honor Soc., Kappa Delta Pi Ednl. Honor Soc., PA of Ga. Educators. Meth. Avocations: houseboating, painting, travel. Home: 196 Dove Hill Road Royston GA 30662 Office: Hart County Middle School 176 Drive Powell Drive Hartwell GA 30643 Office Phone: 706-856-7320. Personal E-mail: pa1ra1@aol.com. E-mail: proyston@hart.k12.ga.us.

ROZANTINE, GAYLE STUBBS, psychologist; b. Atlanta, Dec. 1, 1944; d. William L. and Louise (Cash) Stubbs; children: Kathryn Patricia, Webb Black III, Gregory William, Benjamin Stubbs, John Paul; m. Barry Rozantine. BA in Psychology, Agnes Scott Coll., 1965; MA in Tchg., Emory U., 1966; MA in Clin. Psychology, Western Carolina U., 1990; PhD, U. Tenn., 1995. Lic. psychologist, Ga.; diplomate Am. Acad. of Experts in Traumatic Stress; bd. cert. in stress mgmt. Tchr. Fulton Co. Bd. Edn., Ga., 1967-68; psychology resident Med. Coll. of Ga., Augusta, 1994-95, clin. fellow, 1995-96; rsch. psychologist Pain Evaluation and Intervention Program Dept. of VA Med. Ctr., Augusta, 1995-98; staff psychologist Compass Health Systems, Miami Beach, Fla., 1998, Charter Savannah Bevioral Health System, Ga., 1999-2000; CEO Ctr. Health and Well-Being, 2000—. Mem. critical incident stress debriefing team Med. Coll. Ga.; disaster mental health response team ARC; presenter in field. Mem. APA, Coastal Area Psychologists, Ga. Psychol. Assn., Ga. Breast Cancer Coalition and Fund, Nat. Assn. Forensic Counselors, Nat. Register Health Svc. Providers in Psychology. Office: The Ctr for Health and Well-Being PC 400 Commercial Ct Savannah GA 31406 Office Phone: 912-352-9500 ext. 105. Personal E-mail: gaylerozantine@yahoo.com. Business E-Mail: gaylerozantine@quietawakening.com.

ROZARIO STEWART, GWENDOLYN MICHELLE, elementary school educator; b. San Francisco, Dec. 13, 1954; d. James Calhoun and Annette Marie Miller; m. Stephen Michael Stewart, Jan. 1, 2000; children: Alicia Marie Rozario, Alexander Rozario Jr. BA, U. San Francisco, 1977; M in pub. admin., Coll. of Notre Dame, 1989; D in edn., U. San Francisco, 1995. Vice principal San Lorenzo (Calif.) Unified Sch. Dist., 1992—93; tchr. Martin Luther King Jr. Mid. Sch., Madera, Calif., 1993—2001; adj. faculty Merced Cmty. Coll., Merced, Calif., 1994—98; mentor tchr. Martin Luther King Jr. Mid. Sch., Madera, Calif., 1999—2000; principal Fresno Unified Alternative Edn., Fresno, Calif., 2000—01; tchr. Westside Intermediate Sch., Los Banos, Calif., 2001—04; English tchr. Los Banos (Calif.) HS, 2004—. Grant writing cons. self employed, Madera, Calif., 1992—; summer sch. principal Los Banos HS, 2006. Author: An Analysis of New Teacher Introduction Program in Madera Unified School District, 1995. Recipient Cmty. Svc. award, Martin Luther King Jr. Sch., 1991, Distg. Tchr. award, Madera Unified Sch. Dist. Com., 1994. Mem.: The Link, Inc., Fresno Cpt. (recording sec. 2004—05), Nat. Soc. of Philathropy, Madera County Food Bank (recording sec. 1999—2005). Avocations: writing poetry, exercise, reading, jazz. Office Phone: 559-474-6341.

ROZELL, LINDA JOY, art educator; b. Lindale, Tex., May 27, 1949; d. Henry P. and Eva (McArthur) Hall; m. Robert S. Rozell, Sr., Dec. 17, 1971; children: Robert S. Jr., Stephanie Bussell, Shannon Polk, Carrie Allen. AA, Tyler Jr. Coll., Tex., 1969; BA, Baylor U., Waco, Tex., 1971; MA, Stephen F. Austin U., Nacogdoches, Tex., 1974. Tchr. art Kilgore Jr. H.S., Tex., 1971—76; tchr. English, Lindale H.S., Tex., 1976—80; tchr. art Henderson H.S., Tex., 1987—91, Hardin-Jefferson H.S., Sour Lake, Tex., 1991—93, Nederland H.S., Tex., 1993—. Office: Nederland HS 220 N 17th St Nederland TX 77627-5029

ROZENBERG, LANA, cosmetic dentist; b. 1968; DDS, U. Pacific Sch. Dentistry, 1994. Dir. Dental Day Spa, NY. Named one of NY Top Cosmetic Dentists, NY Mag., 2002, 2004. Avocations: boating, golf, skiing, tennis, financial investments. Office: Dental Day Spa 45 W 54th St - Ste 1B New York NY 10019 Office Phone: 212-265-7724. Business E-Mail: office@rozenbergdds.com.*

ROZMUS, KAREN JANET, artist, porcelain doll maker; b. Chgo., Jan. 20, 1952; d. Clyde Anthony and Janet Lois (Barnes) Rudd; m. Thaddeus Michael Rozmus, July 26, 1972; children: Michael Vincent, Thaddeus Loree. Student, Triton Jr. Coll. Teller supr. Avenue State Bank, Oak Park, Ill., 1975-79; owner, artist Roz Dolls, Forest Park, Ill., 1980—; recycling coord. Forest Park, 1990-95, Oak Park, 1995—. Tchr. Dollmakers of Ill., Chgo., 1984-88, Doll Artisan Guild, Oneonta, N.Y., 1984. Author clothing patterns; contbr. articles to profl. jours. Recipient Best of Show award Dollmakers of Ill., 1981, Best of Show award Chgo. Ceramic Show, 1983, Top award small dolls Doll Artisan Guild, 1984. Mem. Doll Artisan Guild, Nat. Assn. Miniature Enthusiasts, United Fedn. Doll Clubs. Home and Office: 7659 Monroe St Forest Park IL 60130-1722

ROZOF, PHYLLIS CLAIRE, lawyer; b. Flint, Mich., Aug. 3, 1948; d. Eugene Robert and Loveta Lucille Greenwood; m. Robert James Rozof, July 17, 1970 (dec. Oct. 1995); children: Nathan, Zachary. AB with high distinction, U. Mich., 1970, JD magna cum laude, 1977. Bar: Mich. 1977, Fla. 1978. Assoc. Honigman Miller Schwartz and Cohn, Detroit, 1977-81, ptnr., 1982—. Mem. Comml. Real Estate Women Detroit (pres. 1992-93). Office: Honigman Miller Schwartz & Cohn LLP 2290 1st National Bldg Detroit MI 48226 Office Phone: 313-465-7532. Business E-Mail: prozof@honigman.com.

RUARK, SHEILA GAYE, elementary school educator; b. Vanceburg, Ky., Aug. 28, 1959; d. Ezra Davis and Anna Louella (Hauck) R. AA, Ky. Christian Coll., 1979; BA, Morehead (Ky.) State U., 1982, Rank II cert., 1987. Cert. tchr., Ky. Social rehab. counselor Vanceburg Health Care Ctr., 1983-84; tchr. Garrison (Ky.) Elem. Sch., 1984—, acad. coach, 1992—94. Resource tchr. Lewis County Bd. Edn., Vanceburg, 1990—; mem. Commonwealth Inst. for Tchrs., 1988. Sunday Sch. leader Fly Branch Ch. of Christ, 1977—; mem. Lewis County Area Improvement Com., 1990-92, treas., 1991-92; youth coord. Lewis County Young Rep. Com., 1992-93. Mem. Lewis County Edn. Assn. (bldg. rep. 1990—, officer treas. 1993, officer pres. 1992-95, trustee 1993, v.p. 1990-92). Avocations: singing, reading, playing omnichord, keyboard, piano. Home: HC 75 Box 700 Vanceburg KY 41179-9401 Office: Garrison Elem Sch Highway 10 Garrison KY 41141

RUBEL, LUCIA M., music educator; b. Chgo., Jan. 20, 1951; d. Irvin A. and Therese A. Szymanski; m. Arthur W. Rubel, July 11, 1986. B Music Edn., DePaul U., 1973; MA in Curriculum and Instrn., Loyola U., Chgo., 1981. Music tchr. Chgo. Pub. Schs., 1974—79; music coord. Access to Excellence, Chgo., 1979—80; music specialist Kirby (Ill.) Sch. Dist., Tinley Park, Ill., 1980—. Musician solo concert tour, Germany; performer: Glass House Players comedy troupe. Life mem. Hillside (Ill.) Hist. Commn., 2002—. Mem.: Am. Orff Schulwerk Assn., Ill. Edn. Assn. (mem. exec. bd., vice chmn. 1999—2005, regional chmn. 2005—). Roman Catholic. Avocations: guitar, bicycling, water-skiing, skiing, community theater. Office: Bannes Elem Sch 16835 S Odell Ave Tinley Park IL 60477 E-mail: lsings@comcast.net.

RUBELL, JENNIFER, writer, hotelier; d. Donald and Mera Rubell; life ptnr. Daniel Phillip Kim; 1 child, Stevie Kim-Rubell. BA in Art History, Harvard U., 1993. Concierge Royalton Hotel, NYC; cofounder Greenview Hotel, South Beach, Fla., 1994, Albion Hotel, South Beach, Fla., 1994, Beach House, Bal Harbour, Fla., 1994; food and entertaining editor, Home & Design mag. Miami Herald, Fla., 2002—, columnist Fla., sr. editor, Style & Entertaining mag. Fla.; contbg. food editor Domino mag., columnist, The Dish. Regular columnist LA Times Syndicate; contbr. Vogue, Harper's Bazaar, W mag., Better Homes and Gardens, Elle, NY Times, Every Day with Rachael Ray, Ocean Drive mag., Food and Wine mag. Creator (vis. artist series) Pillow Talk, 2001; author: Real Life Entertaining, 2006. Vol. Rubell Family Collection, NYC; chair cultural tourism com. Greater Miami Convention and Visitor's Bur., Fla.; vol. South Beach Wine & Food Festival, Fla. Mailing: Domino Magazine Conde Nast 4 Times Square New York NY 10036 Office Phone: 212-286-2860.*

RUBEN, IDA GASS, state senator; b. Washington, Jan. 07; d. Sol and Sonia E. (Darman) Gass; m. L. Leonard Ruben, Aug. 29, 1948; children: Garry, Michael, Scott, Stephen. Del. Md. Ho. of Dels., Annapolis, 1974-86; mem. Md. Senate, Annapolis, 1986—, majority whip, 1995-99, pres. pro-tem, 2000—. Chair Montgomery County House Delegation, 1981-86, Montgomery County Senate Delegation, 1987—; mem. house econ. matters com., 1974-85, house ways and means com., 1985-86, legis. policy com., 1991—, vice-chair senate budget and taxation com., 1997-99, joint budget and audit com., 1991—, exec. nominations com., 1991—, joint protocol com., 1991—, chair, senate budget and tax., subcom. on pub. safety, transp., econ. devel. and natural resources, 1995-99, mem. joint com. on spending affordability, 1995—, mem. capital budget subcom., 1995—; mem. Gov.'s Motor Carrier Task Force, 1989—; conv. chair Nat. Order Women Legislators, 1980. Chair Women Legislators Caucus Md., 1982-84; trustee Adventist Health Care Mid-Atlantic, Takoma Park, Md.; bd. dirs. Ctrs. for Handicapped, Silver Spring, Md.; former internat. v.p. B'nai Brith Women. Recipient Cert. Appreciation Ctrs. for Handicapped, 1987, Meritorious Svc. award Safety and Survival, 1989, Cover Those Trucks award AAA Potomac, 1989, Leadership Laurel award Safety First Club Md., 1989, Woman of Valor award B'nai B'rith Women, 1991, Pub. Affairs award Planned Parenthood Md., 1992, ESOL support recognition Montgomery County Pub. Schs., 1992, Appreciation award Fraternal Order Police, 1992, John Dewey award Montgomery County Fedn. Tchrs., 1992, ARC of Md., 1992, Safety Leader award Advocates for Hwy. and Auto Safety, 1993, Disting. Svc. award Gov.'s Commn. Employment of People with Disabilities, 1993, award Faculty Guild U. Md. for support of faculty and univ., 1993, Sincere Appreciation award for commitment to Md.'s youth Md. Underage Drinking Prevention Coalition, 1994, Faithful Svc. to citizens Montgomery County award Montgomery County Assn. of Realtors, 1994; named Most Effective Pub. Ofcl. by residents of Silver Spring, 1990, one of 100 Most Powerful Women in Washington Metro Area by Washingtonian Mag., 1994, 97, Legislator of Yr. award Nat. Commn. Against Drunk Driving, 1995, Legislator of Yr. award Montgomery County Med. Soc., 1995, Carmen S. Turner Achievement in Cmty. Svc. award Montgomery County Dept. Transp., 1995, Safety Leader award Advocates for Hwy. and Auto Safety, 1996, Legislator of Yr. award AAA, Potomac, Md., 1997, Vince and Larry award Md. Com. for Safety Belt Use, 1997, Legislative Leadership award Montgomery County, 1998, Leadership award Olney Theater Ctr., 1998, Legislator of Yr. award Greater Montgomery County C. of C., 1999, Hwy. Safety Herd award Advocates for Hwy. and Auto Safety, 1999, One of Md.'s Top 100 Women, The Daily Record, 1994, 97, 2001, 03, Am. Lung Assn. Appreciation award in protecting youth from tobacco industry, 2000, Olney Theater honoree contbns. Olney Theatre and arts in Md., 2000, Pub. Policy Leadership award Am. Cancer Soc., 2002; M.A.D.D. Award of Exellence, 2002, Disting. Pub. Svc. award Am. Lung Assn. of Md., 2003, Disting. Legislator award Md. Impaired Driver Coalition, 2003, S. Robert Cohen award Jewish Found. Group Homes, 2004, Arts Stars award Montgomery Coll., 2004, others; named to Washington, Md., Del., Pa. Svc. Sta. Assn. Hall of Fame, 1994, Suburban Md. Transp. Priorities outstanding leadership in transp. pub. policy adminstrn., 2000; Md. Coll. Art and Design honoree, 2000. Mem. Coun. State Govts. (com. on suggested legislation), Hadassah. Democrat. Jewish. Home: 11 Schindler Ct Silver Spring MD 20903-1329 Office: Md State Senate 422 Miller Senate Office Bldg 11 Bladen St Annapolis MD 21401-8012 Office Phone: 301-858-3634. Business E-Mail: ida_ruben@senate.state.md.us.

RUBENSTEIN, ATOOSA BEHNEGAR, editor-in-chief; b. Iran, 1973; arrived in U.S., 1978; m. Ari Rubenstein, 1998. BA in Polit. Sci., Barnard Coll., 1993. Fashion asst., assoc. fashion editor, fashion edit to sr. fashion editor Cosmopolitan Mag., 1993—95; founding editor-in-chief CosmoGirl! mag., 1998—2003; editor-in-chief Seventeen Mag., 2003—. Office: Seventeen Mag 1440 Broadway 13th Fl New York NY 10018 Office Phone: 917-934-6601. Office Fax: 917-934-6650.*

RUBENSTEIN, PAMELA SILVER, manufacturing executive; b. Lansing, Mich., May 12, 1953; d. Neil M. and Leah Rebecca (Coffman) Silver; m. Alec Robert Rubenstein. BA in Linguistics, U. Mich., 1974; MA in teaching English to spkrs. of other langs., Columbia U. Tchrs. Coll., 1976; MA in Linguistics, U. Ill., 1978, doctoral studies in linguistics, 1978-80. Instr. Columbia U. Tchrs. Coll., N.Y.C., 1976, U. Ill., Urbana, 1978, libr. Linguistic Dept., 1978-79; asst. libr. Ill. State Geol. Survey, 1979-80; tchr. Congregation Temple Israel, Springfield, Ill., 1980-81; adminstr., tchr. Springfield Bd. Jewish Edn., 1981-82; instr. Comm. Divsn. Lincoln Land C.C., Springfield, 1981-82; tchr. Cmty. Hebrew Sch., Charleston, SC, 1982-83; instr. The Citadel and Coll. of Charleston, 1983; legal sec. Gibbs & Holmes, Charleston, 1984, May, Oberfell & Lorber, South Bend, Ind., 1984-88; instr. U. Notre Dame, Ind., 1987; tchr. Triton Sch. Corp., Bourbon, Ind., 1988-89; v.p., asst. treas. Allied Splty. Precision, Inc., Mishawaka, Ind., 1989—2005, CEO, owner, 2005—. Contbr. articles to profl. jours. Mem. Temple Beth-El Sisterhood, South Bend, Ind., 1987—. Mem.: Nat. Tooling and Machining Assn. (mem. edn. team, audit team 2005—, bd. mem., Mich. chpt. 2004—), Hadassah (life). Office: Allied Splty Precision Inc 815 E Lowell Ave Mishawaka IN 46545-6480 Office Phone: 574-255-4718. Business E-Mail: pam.rubenstein@aspi-nc.com.

RUBIN, CATHY ANN, retired secondary school educator; b. Denver, July 17, 1948; d. Harry Phillip and Charlotte Ruth (Brinig) R. BA, Colo. State U., 1970; MA, U. No. Colo., 1971. Cert. tchr. Colo. Tchr. Adams County Dist. 50 Schs., Westminster, Colo., 1971-72; tchr. educationally handicapped Jefferson County Pub. Schs., Golden, Colo., 1972-98. Typist, bookkeeper Kenmark-Shaw's Jewelers, Denver, 1966—. Sec.-treas. Hillel Found., Denver, 1979-81; fundraiser Women's Am. Orgn. for Rehab. through Tng., Denver, 1979—; bookkeeper Religious Coalition for Abortion Rights, Denver, 1982-90; vol. TV PBS sta., Denver, 1978, Muscular Dystrophy Assn., Colo. AIDS Project; vol. usher DCTC, 1999—; vol. for the blind and dyslexic, 2005-. Democrat. Jewish. Avocations: music, reading, sailing, knitting, needlepoint. Home: 3500 S Ivanhoe St Denver CO 80237-1123

RUBIN, CHANDA, professional tennis player; b. Lafayette, La., Feb. 18, 1976; d. Edward and Bernadette Rubin. Grad., Episcopal Sch. Acadiana, 1993. Mem. USTA Jr. Devel. Team, 1989, USTA Nat. Team, 1990; prof. tennis player, 1991—. Mem. U.S. Pan Am. Team, 1995, U.S. Fed Cup Team, 1995—97, 1999, 2003—04, U.S. Olympic Team, Atlanta, 1996, U.S. Women's Olympic Tennis Team, Athens, 2004. Founder The Chanda Rubin Found. Recipient 3 U.S. Jr. Titles; winner U.S. nat. title and Rolex Orange Bowl 12s crown, 1988; named Most Improved Female Player, Tennis Mag., 1995, Female Athlete of Yr., U.S. Tennis Assn., 1995, Most Caring Athlete, USA Weekend Mag., 1997; finalist (with Testud) U.S. Open.; winner 7 Career Singles titles and 10 Career Doubles titles, WTA Tour. Office: USTA 70 W Red Oak Ln White Plains NY 10604-3602 also: Advantage International 1751 Pinnacle Dr Ste 1500 Mc Lean VA 22102-3833

RUBIN, DOROTHY MOLLY, language educator, writer; b. NYC, Feb. 11, 1932; d. Harry and Clara (Schweller) Schleimer; m. Arthur I. Rubin, Aug. 24, 1950; children: Carol Anne, Sharon Anne. Student, CUNY, 1949—51; BA, Rutgers U., 1959, MEd, 1961; PhD in Ednl. Psychology, Johns Hopkins U., 1968. Tchr. N.J. pub. schs., 1959—62; asst. prof. Coppin State Coll., Md., 1962—63, Towson State Coll., Md., 1963—66; adj. prof. Rollins Coll., Fla., 1968—69; assoc. prof. Ewing Coll. N.J., 1969—73, prof., 1973—. Cons. s.Harper & Row, 1983; cons., spkr., columnist. Author: Teaching Elementary Language Arts, 1975, 6th edit., 2000, Gaining Word Power, 1978, 7th edit., 2006, The Vital Arts-Reading and Writing, 1979, Reading and Learning Power, 1980, 3d edit., 1991, The Teacher's Handbook of Reading-Thinking Exercises, 1980, The Primary-Grade Teacher's Language Arts Handbook, 1980, The Intermediate Grade Teacher's Language Arts Handbook, 1980, Gaining Sentence Power, 1981, The Teacher's Handbook of Primary-Grade Reading/Thinking Exercises, 1982;: Vocabulary Expansion, 1982, A Practical Approach to Teaching Reading, 1982, 2d edit., 1993, Diagnosis and Correction in Reading Instruction, 1982, 4th edit., 2002, Teaching Reading and Study Skills in Content Areas, 1983;: 2d edit., 1991, Writing and Reading: The Vital Arts, 2d edit., 1983, Power English: Basic Language Skills for Adults, 1989, rev. edit., 1990, Power Vocabulary: Basic Vocabulary for Adults, 1992—93, Comprehension Strategies for an Integrated Language Arts Classroom, 1994, Mind Bind, Moon Master, Quick Scramble, endl. video games, Comprehension Strategies for an Integrated Language Arts Classroom, 1994, Teaching Elementary Language Arts: An Integrated Approach, 1995, 5th edit., 2000, Power Reading: Reading and Thinking Strategies for Adults, 1995, Phonics: Skills and Strategics in a Balanced Reading Program, 1998, Levels 1-4, Comprehension Skills and Strategies in a Balanced Reading Program, 1998, Vocabulary Skills and Strategies in a Blaanced Reading Program, 1998, Your Child Can Succeed in School: 100 Common-Sense Answers to Frequently Asked Questions, 1999, Writing and Thinking Skills: Sentence Writing, 2000, Writing and Thinking Skills: Paragraphs and Composition, 2000, Word Meaning & Reasoning Levels 1-3, 2000, Writing and Thinking Skills: Fun With Writing, 2001, One Year of Words: College Vocabulary Enhancement, 2004, Grammar and Usage: Simplified, 2005, (audio) Passport to Power English, 1987; contbr. articles to profl. jours.; syndicated columnist Word Games, columnist The Times, Trenton, N.J., Asbury Park (N.J.) Press. Recipient profl. awards. Mem.: Phi Kappa Phi, Nat. Coun. Tchrs. English, Internat. Reading Assn., Pi Lambda Theta, Kappa Delta Pi. Home and Office: 917 Stuart Rd Princeton NJ 08540-1212 E-mail: arthurirubin@aim.com.

RUBIN, JUDITH O., not-for-profit trustee; b. Phila., Feb. 3, 1941; d. Henry Oxenberg and Sylvia Marshak; m. Robert E. Rubin, Mar. 27, 1963; children: James Samuel, Philip Matthew. AB, Wellesley Coll., Wellesley, Mass., 1962; BA, Yale Univ. Graduate Sch., New Haven, Conn., 1964. Profl. singer/actress various, N.Y., 1963—67; trustee, v.p. Collegiate Sch., N.Y., 1984—90; trustee Playwrights Horizons, N.Y., 1985—, chmn., bd. trustees, 1992—; trustee Mt. Sinai Health Sys./ Mt. Sinai Sch. of Medicine, N.Y., 1993—. Pres. bd. dirs. 92nd St. YM-YWHA, N.Y., 1984—88, chmn. bd. dirs., 1988—91, dir., 1976—. Mem. adv. com. Am. Theatre Wing, N.Y., 2004—; mem. bd. overseers Calif. Inst. Arts, 2006—; mem. nominating com. Tony Awards, N.Y., 2001—04, mem. adminstrn. com., 2004—; coun. mem. N.Y. State Coun. on the Arts, N.Y., 1989—; commr. protocol City of N.Y., N.Y., 1990—93; coun. mem. Nat. Coun. on the Arts, Washington, 1994—2002; mem. cultural adv. commn. N.Y.C. Dept. of Cultural Affairs, N.Y., 2003—; mem. Yale Univ. Coun Com. on theatre at Yale, New Haven, 2004—; dir., vice chmn. Pub. Radio Internat., Mpls., 1992—2004; dir., v.p. Theatre Comm. Group, N.Y.C., 1997—2002. Democrat. Jewish. Office: New York NY 10021

RUBIN, MICHELE S., radiologist; b. Bklyn., Aug. 7, 1962; d. Philip L. and Charlotte (Susskind) R.; m. Floyd Martin, May 26, 1996; 1 child, Shane Perry. BA summa cum laude, NYU, 1983, MD, 1987. Diplomate in radiology and in neuroradiology Am. Bd. Radiology. Resident in pathology North Shore Univ. Hosp., Manhasset, N.Y., 1987-88; resident in radiology Nassau County Med. Ctr., East Meadow, N.Y., 1988-92; fellow in neuroradiology Montefiore Med. Ctr., Bronx, N.Y., 1992-94; neuroradiologist, asst. prof. radiology Jacobi Med. Ctr., Bronx, 1994—97, Albert Einstein Coll. Hosp., Bronx, 1994—97; owner, med. dir. Precision Radiology Svcs., Amityville, 1997—2004, Lynbrook, 2004—05, Rockville Centre, 2005—. Mem. AMA, Am. Soc. Neuroradiology, Am. Soc. Spine Radiology, Radiol. Soc. N.Am., Am. Roentgen Ray Soc., Phi Beta Kappa.

RUBIN, PHYLLIS GETZ, health association executive; b. N.Y.C., Aug. 6, 1937; d. Joseph and Sylvia (Rosenberg) Getz; m. James Milton Rubin, Oct. 28, 1961; children: Felicia Sue, Andrea Faith. BA, Syracuse U., 1959; MA, Columbia U., 1961, Adelphi U., 1975. Physical edn. tchr. Hicksville (N.Y.) Pub. Schs., 1959-93; bd. dirs., pres. Assoc. Am. Acad. Allergy, Asthma and Immunology; owner JP Med Fit, 1997—. Producer: (video) Aerobic Dancercise for Children, 1987. Bd. dir. COPAY, Great Neck, N.Y., 1986-91; v.p., sec. Pierpont Condominium Bd., 1986-90. Recipient Founder's Day award PTA, 1986. Mem.: N.Y. State Alliance for Health, Phys. Edn., REcreation and Dance (program spkr. 1984, 85, 93, v.p. Nassau zone 1987—2000, Zone Svc. award 1993). Avocations: tennis, reading, meditation, golf. Office Phone: 516-972-2342. E-mail: jpmedfit@aol.com.

RUBIN, RHEA JOYCE, library consultant; b. Chgo., June 14, 1950; d. Harold and Edith (Botkin) B.; m. Lawrence Berman, June 7, 1975; 1 child, Hannah Rubin Berman. BA, U. Wis., 1972, MA, 1973. Dir. Oreg. Regional Library for The Blind and Handicapped, Salem, 1976—78; libr. Nat. Coun. Aging, Inc., Washington, 1978—80; cons. Rubin Cons., Oakland, Calif., 1980—. Author: Using Bibliotherapy, 1978, Bibliotherapy Sourcebook, 1978; (with others) Challenge of Aging, 1983, (with others) Let's Talk About It: A Planners Manual, 1984, Working With Older Adults, 1987, 2d edit., 1988, 3d edit., 1990, Of a Certain Age: A Guide to Contemporary Fiction Featuring Older Adults, 1990, Intergenerational Library Programs: A How to Do It Manual, 1993, (with others) Librarian Inside: A Practical Guide for Prison Librarians, 1995, Humanities Programming: A How to Do It Manual, 1997, Defusing the Angry Patron: A How to Do It Manual, 2000, Planning Library Services for People with Disabilities, 2001, Demonstrating Results: Using Outcome Measurement, 2006; book reviewer Libr. Jour.; contbr. articles to profl. jours. Recipient Show Monroe award, 1992, Exceptional Svc. award,

ASCLA, 1993, 2006. Mem. ALA (chair numerous com. 1972—, Shaw award 1980). Office: 5860 Heron Dr Oakland CA 94618-2628 Office Phone: 510-339-1274. E-mail: rhea@rheajoycerubin.org.

RUBIN, SANDRA MENDELSOHN, artist; b. Santa Monica, Calif., Nov. 7, 1947; d. Murry and Freda (Atliss) Mendelsohn; m. Stephen Edward Rubin, Aug. 6, 1966. BA, UCLA, 1976, MFA, 1979. Instr. Art Ctr. Coll. Design, Pasadena, Calif., 1980, UCLA, 1981. One-woman exhbns. include L.A. Louver Gallery, 1982, 92, 2003, L.A. County Mus. Art, 1985, Fischer Fine Arts, London, 1985, Claude Bernard Gallery, NYC, 1987; group exhbns. include L.A. County Mus. Art, 1977, 82, 83, L.A. Mcpl. Art Gallery, 1977, 83, 93, L.A. Contemporary Exhbns., 1978, L.A. Inst. Contemporary Arts, 1978, Newport Harbor Art Mus., Newport Beach, Calif., 1981, Odyssia Gallery, NYC, 1981, Nagoya (Japan) City Mus., 1982, Long Beach (Calif.) Mus. Art, 1982, Brooke Alexander Gallery, NYC, 1982, Laguna Beach (Calif.) Mus. Art, 1982, Jan Baum Gallery, L.A., 1984, San Francisco Mus. Art, 1986, Claude Bernard Gallery, NYC, 1986, Struve Gallery, Chgo., 1987, Boise (Idaho) Mus., 1988, Judy Youen's Gallery, London, 1988, Tatistscheff Gallery, Inc., Santa Monica, Calif., 1989, Tortue Gallery, Santa Monica, 1990, Contemporary Arts Forum, Santa Barbara, Calif., 1990, San Diego Mus. Art, 1991, Fresno (Calif.) Met. Mus., 1992, Jack Rutberg Fine Arts, L.A., 1993, San Jose Mus. Art, 2003, Pasadena Mus. Calif. Art, 2004. Recipient Young Talent Purchase award L.A. County Mus. Art, 1980; Artist's Fellowship grant NEA, 1981, 91. Avocations: gardening, exercise, reading, singing. E-mail: smr@pacific.net.

RUBIN, SUSAN M., neurologist; b. N.Y.C., Aug. 14, 1956; BS in Speech Pathology, MS in Speech Pathology, Northwestern U.; MD, U. Ill., 1988. Diplomate Am. Bd. Neurology. Intern Luth. Gen. Hosp., Park Ridge, Ill., 1989—90, staff neurologist; resident in neurology Northwestern U. Med. Ctr., Chgo., 1990—93, fellow in neurophysiology, 1993—94; staff neurologist Highland Park (Ill.) Hosp., Holy Family Hosp.; dir., founder Women's Neurology Ctr., Dept. Neurology, Glenbrook Hosp., Glenview, 2001—. Clin. instr. dept. neurology Feinberg Sch. Medicine, Northwestern U., Chgo. Contbr. articles to profl. jours.; peer reviewer Headache jour., 2000. Named one of Chgo.'s Best Drs. in Neurology, Castle Connolly, 1999, 2000; recipient Edward R. Henderson Meml. Student award for geriat. rsch., Murer Health-care Consultants and Gerontology Ctr. U. Ill.-Chgo., 1988, E.A. Codman award for rsch., 1988. Mem.: Am. Epilepsy Soc., Am. Headache Soc., Am. Acad. Neurology, Alpha Omega Alpha. Office: Glenbrook Hosp 2100 Pfingsten Rd Glenview IL 60025

RUBIN, VERA COOPER, astronomer, researcher; b. Phila., July 23, 1928; d. Philip and Rose (Applebaum) Cooper; m. Robert J. Rubin, June 25, 1948; children: David M., Judith S. Young, Karl C., Allan. BA in Astronomy, Vassar Coll., 1948; MA, Cornell U., 1951; PhD, Georgetown U., 1954, DHL (hon.), 1997; DSc (hon.), Creighton U., 1978, Harvard U., 1988, Yale U., 1990, Williams Coll., 1993, U. Mich., 1996, Ohio State U., 1998, Smith Coll., 2001, Grinnell Coll., 2002, Ohio-Wesleyan U., 2004, Princeton U., 2005. From rsch. assoc. to asst. prof. Georgetown U., Washington, 1955-65; physicist U. Calif., LaJolla, 1963-64; astronomer Carnegie Inst., Washington, 1965—2001, sr. fellow, dept. terrestrial magnetism, 2001—. Chancellor's Disting. prof. U. Calif., Berkeley, 1981; vis. com. Harvard Coll. Obs., Cambridge, Mass., 1976—82, 1992—2002, Space Telescope Sci. Ins., 1990—92; Beatrice Tinsley vis. prof. U. Tex., 1988; Commonwealth lectr. U. Mass., 1991; Yunker lectr. Oreg. State U., 1991; Bernhard vis. fellow Williams Coll., 1993; Oort vis. prof. U. Leiden, The Netherlands, 1995; lectr. in field, Chile, Russia, China, Armenia, India, Japan, Europe; trustee Assoc. Univs., Inc., 1993—96; mem. Pres. Commn. to Select U.S. Nat. Medal Sci. Awardees, 1995—98, chair, 1997—98; Pres.'s disting. visitor Vassar Coll., 1987; Halley lctr. Oxford Univ., 1997; bd. dir. Sci. Service, 2002—; adv. bd. Lowell Observatory. Assoc. editor: Astrophys. Jour. Letters, 1977—82, mem. editl. bd.: Sci. Mag., 1979—87, mem. sr. editl. bd.:, 2001—, co-author several peer reviewed research papers. Named to Nat. Sci. Bd., 1996—2002; recipient U.S. Nat. Medal of Sci., 1993, Jansky Lectureship, Nat. Radio Astronomy Observatory, 1994, Gold medal, Royal. Astorn. Soc. London, 1996, Weizmann Women and Sci. award, 1996, Helen Hogg prize, Can. Astron. Soc., 1997, John Scott Award, City of Phila., 2001, Peter Gruber Internat. prize in cosmology, 2002, Bruce medal, Astron. Soc. of Pacific, 2003. Mem.: NAS (space sci. bd. 1974—77, chair sect. on astronomy 1992—95, James Craig Watson medal 2004), AAAS, Am. Philos. Soc., Assn. Univ. Rsch. in Astronomy (trustee 1973—76, 1994—96), Pontifical Acad. Scis. (Gold medal), Internat. Astron. Union (pres. commn. on galaxies 1982—85, chair U.S. nat. commn. 1999—2001), Am. Astron. Soc. (coun. 1977—80, Henry Norris Russell prize lectr. 1994), Phi Beta Kappa (scholar 1982—83). Democrat. Jewish. Achievements include being the first women permitted to observe at Palomar Observatory in California in 1965; being the first women since 1828 to receive the Gold Medal of the Royal Astronomical Society in London.

RUBIN-KATZ, BARBARA, sculptor, human services manager; b. Springfield, Mass., May 3, 1931; d. Samuel and Jane (Freeman) Kurn; m. Emanuel Rubin, Mar. 27, 1955 (div. Dec. 1984); children: Raphael, Jonathan, Daniel, Rebecca; m. Robert Nathan Katz, June 15, 1986. BA, U. Ariz., 1952; MSW, Simmons Coll., 1955; MPH, Columbia U., 1977; postgrad. in Sculpture Studies, Phila. Coll. Art, 1981-85. Rschr. Bellevue Hosp., N.Y.C., 1970-75; health svcs. coord. Fedn. Jewish Agencies, N.Y.C., 1977-79, assoc. dir. planning Phila., 1979-84; sculptor Brookline, Mass., 1985—. Prin. works include sculpture at Mass. Gen. Hosp., Villa Campana, Tucson, Worcester Poly. Inst., Regency Park, Brookline, Mass, Temple Emanuel, Tucson, St. Elizabeth's Hosp., Brighton, Mass.; exhibited in group shows at Copley Soc. Boston shows, 1990—, New Eng. Sculptors Assn. shows, 1987—, The Roxbury Latin Sch., 1991, Jr. League Boston Decorator's Showhouse, Walpole, Mass., 1994, Faneuil Hall, Boston, 1994, Prestige Gallery, Danvers, Mass., 1995, Michael Allen Gallery, Brookline, Mass., 1996, Festival Arts, Newton, 1997, Curtis Gallery, Lenox, Mass., 1997, 98, Worcester Poly. Inst., 1997-98, Bradford (Mass.) Coll., 1999; contbr. articles to profl. jours. Mem. Copley Soc. Boston (Copley Artist award 1992), New Eng. Sculptor's Assn. (bd. dirs. 1993), Brookline Coun. for Arts and Humanities. Home: 1731 Beacon St Apt 1403 Brookline MA 02445-5329 Personal E-mail: kate@wpi.edu.

RUBINO, JOELLE L., physical therapist, athletic trainer; b. Latrobe, Pa., Feb. 23, 1978; d. Dennis L. and Nancy D. Rubino. BA in Psychology, W.Va. Wesleyan Coll., Buckhannon, BS in Sports Medicine, 2000; D in Phys. Therapy, Creighton U., Omaha, 2003. Athletic trainer cert. NATABOC. Lab./tchg. asst. W.Va. Wesleyan Coll., Buckhannon, 1997—2000; tchg. asst. Creighton U., Omaha, 2002; clinician Brown and Assocs. PT, Dover, Del., 2003—. Presenter Sideline Sports Medicine. Vol. Sr. Olympics, Dover, 2004—06; life mem., vol. Girl Scouts US, Dover, 1996—2006; com. mem. Wyoming United Meth. Ch., Del., 2006; vol. Habitat for Humanity, 2000—06; vol. med. coverage DFRC, Newark, 2004—06. Recipient Most Creative Nat. Award, Nat. Athletic Tng. Month. Mem.: Del. Athletic Trainers Assn. (Del. Athletic Trainer of the Yr. 2005), Nat. Athletic Trainers Assn., Am. Phys. Therapy Assn., Kappi Phi (life; pres. 1999—2000). Republican. Office: Brown and Assocs Physical Therapy 1288 S Governors Ave Dover DE 19904 Office Phone: 302-677-0100. Personal E-mail: rubinoj_2000@yahoo.com.

RUBINSON, JILL LINDA, literature and language professor; b. Phila., Aug. 17, 1943; d. Harold Rubinson and Louise Sernoff; m. David Fenton, Aug. 16, 1981 (div.); 1 child, Anny Fenton. AB, Cornell U., Ithaca, NY, 1961—65; AM, Harvard U., Cambridge, Mass., 1965—66, PhD, 1965—83. English instr. Emmanuel Coll., Boston, 1967—69; founding dir. Cambridge Cmty. Learning Ctr. for Adults, 1971—75; dir. spl. svcs. U. Maine, Augusta, 1978—84, English prof., 1984—. Cons. Adult Literacy, Bournemouth, 1975—76; cons. adult edn. Cambridge Pub. Schs., 1976—78; spl. asst. to pres. U. Maine, Augusta, 1984—87; evaluator New Eng. Assn. Schs. & Colls., Boston; spkr. in field. Author: (book) From Page to Screen: Women Writers; contbr. articles to profl. jours. and pubs. Mem. Govs. Coun. on Youth, Augusta, 1980—82; bd. dirs. Maine Arts Coun., Augusta, 1988—91, Kennebec Montessori Sch., Fairfield, Maine, 1997—2001. Recipient Tchr. of Yr. award, U. Maine, 2001; fellow, Harvard U., 1965—67; scholar, Maine Humanities Coun., 1985—95. Mem.: MLA (assoc.), Jane Austen Soc. N.Am. (assoc.). Office: Univ Maine 46 University Dr Augusta ME 04330 Office Phone: 207-621-3454. Business E-Mail: jillr@maine.edu.

RUBINSTEIN, CHARLOTTE STREIFER, writer, art historian, educator; b. N.Y.C., Dec. 14, 1921; d. Aaron and Lillian (Kaufman) Streifer; m. William Rubinstein, May 31, 1941 (dec. Apr. 1991); children: Arthur, Joan, Elaine (dec.). BA, Bklyn. Coll., 1941; MA, Columbia U., 1946; MFA, Otis-Parsons Art Inst., 1969. Instr. West L.A. Coll., Fullerton Coll., Saddleback Coll., 1969-84. Author American Women Sculptors, 1990, American Women Artists, 1982 (Best Humanities Book of 1982 award); contbr. articles to art jours. Recipient Individual Rsch. grant AAUW, 1984. Mem. Coll. Art Assn., Women's Caucus for Art (nat. honor award 1994), Assn. Am. Art Historians. Home and Office: 31532 Flying Cloud Dr Laguna Niguel CA 92677

RUBINSTEIN, EVA (ANNA), photographer; b. Buenos Aires, 1933; d. Arthur and Aniela (Mlynarska) R.; m. William Sloane Coffin Jr., 1956 (div. 1968); children: Amy, Alexander (dec.), David. Ballet tng., Paris, N.Y.C., Calif., 1938-53; student, Scripps Coll., 1950-51, UCLA, 1952-53; student in photography, Lisette Model, 1969, Jim Hughes, 1971, Ken Heyman, 1970, Diane Arbus, 1971. Lectr. numerous workshops, seminars, confs.; instr. photo seminars Lodz Film Sch., Poland, 1986, 87. Dancer, actress: off-Broadway and Broadway, including original prodn. The Diary of Anne Frank, 1955-56; European dance tour, 1955; one-person shows of photographs include Underground Gallery, N.Y.C., 1972, Dayton Art Inst., Ohio, 1973, Arles Festival, France, 1975, Canon Photo Gallery, Amsterdam, 1975, Neikrug Gallery, N.Y.C., 1975, 79, 81, 82, 85, La Photogalerie, Paris, 1975, Friends of Photography, Carmel, Calif., 1975, Galerie 5.6, Ghent, Belgium, 1976, Gallery Trochenpresse, Berlin, 1977, Frumkin Gallery, Chgo., 1977, Galeria Sinisca, Rome, 1979, Hermitage Found. Mus., Norfolk, Va., 1982, Photographers Gallery, London, 1983, Galerie Forum Labo, Arles, France, 1983, Galerie Nicephore, Lyon, France, 1983, Image Gallery, Madrid, 1984, Muzeum Sztuki, Lodz, Poland, 1984, Il Diaframma/Canon Gallery, Milan, 1984, A.R.P.A. Gallery, Bordeaux, 1984, Chateau d'Eau, Toulouse, France, 1985, Galerie Demi-Teinte, Paris, 1985, Associated Artist Photographers galleries in Warsaw, Krakow, Lodz, Katowice and Gdansk, Poland, 1985-86, Foto/Medium/Art Gallery, Wroclaw, Poland, 1986, Visions Gallery, San Francisco, 1986, Canon Galerie, Paris, 1986, Salone Internat. SICOF, Milan, 1987, St. Krzysztof Gallery, Lodz, 1987, L'Image Fixe, Lyon, 1988, Artotheque, Grenoble, 1988, Neikrug Photographica, N.Y.C., 1989, Heuser Art Ctr. Gallery, Bradley U., Peoria, Ill., 1989, 3-os Encontros da Imagem, Braga, Portugal, 1989, Bibliotheque Nat. Galerie Colbert, Paris, 1989, Galerie Picto-Bastille, Paris, 1989-90, Portfolio Gallery, London, 1990, Vaison-La-Romaine, France, 1990, Hist. Mus. of City of Lodz, 1990, Galerie Artem, Quimper, France, 1993, Galerie F.N.A.C. Etoile, Paris, 1994, other F.N.A.C. galleries (France, Belgium, Spain), 1994-97, Galerie Augustus, Berlin, 1995, L'Imagerie, Lannion, France, 1995, Zacheta Gallery, Warsaw, 1996, Salon of Modern Art B.W.A., Bydgoszcz, Poland, 1997, Galleries of Polish Insts., Sofia, Bulgaria, Berlin, Moscow, Bratislava, Slovakia, I. Beszkova Gallery, Plewen, Bulgaria, 1997, Hungarian Mus. Photographic Art, Budapest, 1997, LTF Gallery, Lodz, Poland, 1998, Konfrontacje Fotograficzne, Gorzow Wielopolski, Poland, 1998, Centrum Kultury Zamek, Poznan, Poland, 1998, Mus. Regionalny, Wrzesnia, Poland, 1998, Galeria Korytarz, Jelenia Gora, Poland, 1998, Galeria Foto-Medium-Art, Wroclaw, Poland, 1998, Galeria Pusta, Centrum Kultury, Katowice, Poland, 1998, Teatr Wielki, Lodz, Poland, 2000, Gallery Europa Club, NY, 2003, Château de la Petite, Malmaison, France, 2004, Alliance Française, N.Y.C., 2006; numerous group shows since 1971 including most recently Zacheta Gallery, Warsaw, 2002, Lodz Photographic Soc., 2002, Polish/Am.Photographers, Polish Consulate, NY, 2003, Gutman Libr., Harvard, 2003, Floating Found. Photography, N.Y., 2004, XL, La Collection Photographique du Musée d'Arles, 2005; represented: in permanent collections Library of Congress, Washington, Met. Mus. Art, N.Y.C., Bibliotheque Nationale, Paris, Musee Reattu, Arles, France, Kalamazoo Inst. Arts, Israel Mus., Jerusalem, Fotografiska Museet, Stockholm, Muzeum Sztuki, Lodz, Poland, Histo Mus. of City of Lodz, others; author: Eva Rubinstein, 1974, Eva Rubinstein, I Grandi Fotografi, 1983, 2 ltd. edit. portfolios with introductions by John Vachon andAndré Kertész, Lodz: Brief Encounters, 1998, Eva Rubinstein: Fotografie 1967-1990, 2003; contbr. photographs in various books, mags., profl. jours.

RUBINSTEIN, NANCY G., social worker, consultant; b. New Haven, June 23, 1945; d. Louis and Florence (BLumenthal) Goodwin; m. Joel Franklin Rubinstein, June 18, 1967 (div. Mar. 1991); children: Sally Goodwin Rubinstein, Ann Goodwin Rubinstein. BA, Smith Coll., 1967; MSW, Boston U., 1973. Lic. Lic. ind. clin. social worker. Pub. health adminstrv. asst. Conn. State Dept. Health, New Haven, 1967-70; designer, rschr. cardiac care program study Maine Med. Ctr., Portland, 1970-71; clin. case worker depression study Mass. Gen. Hosp., Boston, 1973-74; dir. clin. svcs. Emmaus Inc., Haverhill, Mass., 1987—; psychotherapist North Essex Mental Health Ctr., Haverhill, 1990-95. Mem. med. rev. team, cons. social worker Mass. Dept. Pub. Health, Boston, 1998—. Mem. Newburyport (Mass.) Sch. Health and Safety Task Force, 1998-2000, Seacoast Affordable Housing Coalition, 2001-03; bd. dirs. Merrimack River Watershed Coun., 1979-90, now mem.; mem. Acad. of Women/Haverhill YWCA, 1997—, Civil Rights Commn., Haverhill, Mass., 2003—. Recipient Mass. Common Works award State of Mass. Dept. Welfare, 1991. Mem. NASW (mem. homeless com. Mass. chpt. 2003—), Smith Coll. Aumni ASsn., Andover Merrimack Valley Smith Coll. Club (pres. 1986-88). Jewish. Avocations: choral singing, ski touring, gardening, bicycling. Home: 29 Collins St Newburyport MA 01950-2138 Office: Emmaus Inc 127 How St Haverhill MA 01830-5615 Office Phone: 978-241-3414. E-mail: nancy@emmausinc.org, nrube@verizon.net.

RUBINSTEIN, ROSALINDA, allergist, medical association administrator; b. Buenos Aires, Jan. 3, 1942; arrived in US, 1967; MD, U. Buenos Aires, 1965. Residence Beth Israel Hosp., 1968-70; fellow in allergy-asthma Harvard Med. Sch., Boston, 1970-71; allergy-asthma asst. pediatrician Columbia Presbyn., N.Y.C., 1971—, Mt. Sinai Med. Ctr., N.Y.C., 1972—. Bd. dirs. N.Y. Women's Agenda, Argentina Am. Med. Soc.; pres. elect Nat. Coun. Women's Health, 1998-2000, pres., 2000-2002; pres. Women's Med. Assn., N.Y.C., 1995-97. Recipient Recogition award N.Y. Women's Agenda, 1997, Women's Med. Assn., N.Y.C., 1996, Community award Am. Med. Women's Assn., 1998. Mem. AMA, Am. Coll. Allergy-Asthma, Am. Acad. Allergy-Asthma, N.Y. County Med. Soc., Columbia Presbyn. Club, N.Y. Harvard Club. Avocation: women's health issues. Home and Office: 1016 5th Ave New York NY 10028-0132 Office Phone: 212-737-2996.

RUBIN-VEGA, DAPHNE, actress; b. Panama City, Panama, Nov. 18, 1969; m. Tommy Costanzo, 2002; 1 child. LHD (hon.), Kean U., 2005. Mem. Pajama Party (pop trio), DRV (rock band). Actress (films) The Occultist, 1987, I Like It Like That, 1994, Lotto Land, 1995, Wild Things, 1998 (Blockbuster award best supporting actress in a suspense thriller), Flawless, 1999, Skeleton Woman, 2000 (Best Actress in a feature film, NY Independent Film and Video Festival), Justice, 2003, Virgin, 2003, Alchemy, 2005, Life on the Ledge, 2005, (TV series) NY Undercover, 1996, Hey Joel, 2003, (Broadway plays) Rent, 1996—97 (Theatre World award best actress in musical, Tony award nomination best actress in a musical, Drama Desk award nomination), (plays) Rocky Horror Picture Show, 2001, Anna in the Tropics, 2004 (Tony award nomination best featured actress in a play), Two Sisters and a Piano, Gum, Between Us (Outstanding Female Performance Rutgers U.), The House of Bernarda Alba, 2006, Everything's Turning into Beautiful, 2006. Mailing: c/o Cathexis Inc ATTN Juan Azize PO Box 778 New York NY 10013 E-mail: daphnespeaks@att.net.*

RUBLEY, CAROLE A., state legislator; b. Bethel, Conn., Jan. 18, 1939; d. George B. and Evelyn M. (Maloney) Drumm; m. C. Ronald Rubley, Aug. 25, 1962; children: Lauren M. Rubley Simpson, Stephen R., Kristin Rubley Vaughan. BA in Biology, Albertus Magnus Coll., 1960; MS in Environ. Health, West Chester U., 1988. Tchr. biology Danbury (Conn.) High Sch., 1960-62, Waltham (Mass.) High Sch., 1962-63; real estate salesperson Henderson-Dewey, Wayne, Pa., 1976-81; solid waste coord. Chester County Health Dept., West Chester, Pa., 1981-88; environ. cons. Environ. Resources Mgmt., Exton, Pa., 1988-92; mem. Pa. Ho. Reps., Valley Forge, 1992—. Mem. environ. resources, energy, consumer affairs, fin. and children and youth com. House of Reps.; mem. Pa. 21st Century Environ. Commn.; former chair energy and elec. utilities com. NCSL, task force on protecting Democracy. Author: (with others) Leading Pennsylvania into 21st Century, 1990. Chmn. Ea. Chester County Regional Planning Commn., 1976-85; vice chmn. planning commn. Tredyffrin Twp., Berwyn, Pa., 1976-86, mem. bd. suprs., 1987-92; bd. dirs. Pa. Resources Coun., exec. v.p., 1988-92. Recipient Outstanding Legislator award, Pa. Planning Assn., 2004. Mem. LWV (pres. Upper Main Line chpt. 1976-78, Involved Voter of Yr. award 1993), Pa. Environ. Coun., Green Valleys Assn., Open Land Conservancy. Republican. Roman Catholic. Avocations: aerobics, tennis, hiking, reading, travel. Home: 621 Vassar Rd Wayne PA 19087-5312 Office Phone: 610-640-2356. Business E-Mail: carole.rubley@verizon.net.

RUBRUM, ERICA COURTNEY, family therapist, school counselor; b. N.Y.C., Feb. 20, 1965; d. Walter and Rhoda (Metviner) Rubrum; m. Todd Schaffhauser, Sept. 29, 1996; children: Olivia Morgan, Maxwell Drew. BA, U. Mass., 1987; MS in Edn., L.I. U., 1990; MS in Counseling, Queens Coll., 1992. Registered sch. counselor, N.Y.; lic. marriage and family therapist, NY, 2006. Mgr. Am. Leisure, N.Y.C., 1988-90; family therapist Counseling and Psychotherapy Group, Merrick, NY, 1990-94; sch. counselor Herricks Pub. Schs., New Hyde Park, NY, 1992-94; pvt. practice family therapy Roslyn, NY, 1994—; social worker Big Bros./Big Sisters, Levittown, NY, 1995-96; supervising therapist New Image Med., Huntington, NY, 1995-96; sch. counselor Carle Place Pub. Schs., 1996-2000, Half Hollow Hills Pub. Schs., 2000. V.p. One to One: L.I.'s Disability Support and Outreach Group, Islip, N.Y., 1993—; family therapist Family Wellness Ctr., Smithtown, N.Y., 2000-03. Mem. ACA, Am. Assn. Marriage and Family Therapists (clin. mem.), Am. Psychotherapy Assn., Nassau Counselors Assn. (exemplary practice award 1992, 95). Office: 56 Sherrard St Roslyn Heights NY 11577-1713

RUCK, ROSEMARIE ULISSA, retired social worker, freelance/self-employed writer; b. Buffalo, Aug. 24, 1939; d. Stanley Joseph Ren and Bertha Sosnowski; m. Donald Neil Ruck, Nov. 8, 1958; children: Theresa Dorene Ruck Novak, Donna Rose Ruck Seyler, Michael Donald. AS, Genesee C.C., 1970—72; BS, SUNY Brockport Coll., 1972—75. Chemical Dependency Counselor Pk. Ridge Unity Health Sys. & Brockport Coll., NY, 1999, Basic Reading and ESL Tutor Literacy Volunteers of Am., Inc., NY, 1984. Sr. caseworker/counselor Assn. for Retarded Citizens, Batavia, NY, 1975—79; dir. Literacy Volunteers of Am. - Genesee County Chpt., Batavia, NY, 1983—89. Exec. dir. Literacy Volunteers of Am. - Orleans County Chpt., Albion, NY, 1989—98; chem. dependency counselor Pk. Ridge- Unity Health Sys., Rochester, NY, 1998—99; social worker Lakeside Beikirch Care Ctr., Brockport, NY, 1999—2002; writer Freelance -, Holley, NY, 2002—. Mem. of Genesee c.c. steering com. Genesee County Legislature, Batavia, NY, 1967—68; mem. of com. responsible for devel. of Genesee county registry Genesee County Inter-Agy. Coun., Batavia, NY, 1975—77; grant writer & mem. of program com. for domestic violence program YWCA, Batavia, NY, 1980—81; mem. of steering com. for regional action phone Genesee County Inter-agency Coun., Batavia, NY, 1985—86; mem. of steering com. for vol. connection registry United Way of Genesee County, Batavia, NY, 1983—84; program chair person YWCA, Batavia, NY, 1980—82; voluneer leadership chairperson Young Women's Christian Associaiton, Batavia, NY, 1983—84; strategic planning com. chairperson United Way of Ea. Orleans County, Albion, NY, 1999—2001. Recipient Friends of Edn., Albion Ctrl. Sch. Bd. of Edn., 1991, Recognition of Outstanding Leadership, Literacy Volunteers of Am. - Genesee County Chpt., 1989, Literacy Volunteers of Am. - Orleans County Chpt., 1992, 1993, 1994, 1995, 1996, 1997, 1998, Genesee County Chpt. of Assn. for Retarded Citizens, 1979, Quality Recognition award, Lakeside Beikirch Care Ctr., 2001. Mem.: Literacy Volunteers of Am., Holley's Writers Club. Catholic. Achievements include Revived rural literacy organization and became number one in national organizations from over 450 affiliates; development of first workplace literacy program in Western NY state. Avocations: reading, writing, travel, art, exercise. Home: 5314 Upper Holley Rd Holley NY 14470 Personal E-mail: ruruck@juno.com.

RUCKER, MARGARET RICKENBACKER, psychologist, special education educator; b. Simpsonville, S.C., July 2, 1972; d. Douglas Randolph and Emily Gressette Rucker. BS, Coll. of Charleston, 1994; EdS, Citadel, 2002. Cert. tchr. S.C. Bd. Edn., Nat. Cert. Sch. Psychologist Nat. Assn. Sch. Psychologists. Spl. edn. tchr. Calhoun County Sch. Dist., St. Matthews, SC, 1994—97, Charleston County Sch. Dist., 1997—99; sch. psychologist Cherokee County Sch. Dist., Gaffney, 2001—05. Contbr. articles to profl. jours. Mem.: Nat. Assn. Sch. Psychologists (award 2004), Palmetto State Tchrs. Assn. Avocations: kayaking, reading, hiking. Home: 648 Cotton Branch Dr Boiling Springs SC 29316

RUCKERT, ANN JOHNS, musician, singer; b. N.Y.C., Mar. 12, 1945; d. G. Wallace and Elizabeth (Johns) R. Student, Julliard Sch., 1961-69, NYU, 1969-70, Royal Acad. Music, London, 1972; studies in composition with Nadia Boulanger, Paris, 1972-73; studies with Helen Hobbs Jordon, N.Y.C., 1973-75; studies with David Sorin Collyer, 1975-78. Profl. musician over 3,000 commercially released records, 1960—; owner, pres. Ann Ruckert Music, N.Y.C. and Los Angeles, 1980—. Cons., spkr. Platinum Record Industry seminars; chairperson N.Y. Jazz Mus., N.Y.C., 1977-79; bd. dirs. Jazzmobile, N.Y.C., 1983-89, 92—; TV com. Grammy awards, 1985-87; mem. creative staff Lifetime Achievement awards show, 1987; adv. Universal Jazz Coalition, N.Y.C., 1979-87; cons. rec. industry including: Zero House Records, Warner Group, bd. dirs. ASCAP; also individual artists: Roberta Flack, Diane Schnur, Morgan Ames, over 300 clients; performance Ann Ruckert Choir, Macy's 4th of July Show, 1996; lectr. NYU, SUNY, Harvard, 1996-97. Musician, singer: (recs.) Strawbs, Greatest Hits (Gold Record award, 1975); music contractor: (film) Housesitter, 1993, Boys on the Side, 1994; performed at Hudson Theatre, 1994, Shea Stadium, 1994, Lincoln Ct., 1994; producer albums: Jane Jarvis, Jazz, Mike Longo, Jazz, 1996-97. Commr. Deed, N.Y., 1986—, Schomberg Collection N.Y.C. Pub. Library; mem. county com. Westside Manhattan, 1980-89; co-chair and chair edn. com. Grammys in the Schs., N.Y.C. Mem. NARAS (Named Most Valuable Player 1982, 89, trustee, gov., v.p. N.Y. chpt., bd. trustees 1989—, bd. dirs. World Hunger Yr.), Soc. Singers (bd. dirs. N.Y.C. chpt.), Songwriters Guild Am. (bd. dirs., concert, Pres.'s award 1997). Democrat. Episcopalian. Avocations: arts, music, visual arts. Home and Office: 119 W 71st St New York NY 10023-3876

RUCKLE, BARBARA ANN, science educator; b. Pontiac, Mich., Oct. 2, 1951; d. Adolph Edward and Lucille Eustice Walter; children: Jarrod, Michael, Trevor. BS, Ctrl. Mich. U., Mt. Pleasant, 1973, EdS, 1999; MEd, Saginaw Valley State U., Univ. Ctr., Mich., 1991. Mid. sch. tchr. Caro Cmty. Schs., Mich., 1976—. Bd. mem. Habitat for Humanity, Caro, 2006. Recipient Environ. award, Phillips Petroleum Co., 1993, Presdl. award for Sci. Tchg., Mich., 1994, Tchr. of Yr., VFW Post 4164, 2001—02. Home: 1610 S Ringle Rd Caro MI 48723 Office: 301 Hooper Caro MI 48723

RUDACILLE, SHARON VICTORIA, medical technician; b. Ranson, W.Va., Sept. 11, 1950; d. Albert William and Roberta Mae (Anderson) Rudacille. BS cum laude, Shepherd Coll., 1972. Med. technologist VA Ctr., Martinsburg, W.Va., 1972—. Instr. Sch. Med. Tech., 1972—76, assoc. coord. edn., 1976—77, edn. coord., 1977—78, quality assurance officer clin. chemistry, 1978—80, lab. svc. quality assurance and edn. officer, 1980—84, clin. chemistry sect. leader, 1984—86, staff med. technologist, 1986—94, supervisory med. technologist, 1994—95, sr. med. technologist, 1995—; adj. faculty mem. Shippensburg (Pa.) State Coll., 1977—78, Shepherd Coll.,

1977—78. Mem.: Shepherd Coll. Alumni Assn., W.Va. Soc. Med. Technologists, Am. Soc. Clin. Pathologists, Am. Soc. Med. Tech., Sigma Pi Epsilon. Bapt. Home: PO Box 14 Ranson WV 25438-0014

RUDAVSKY, DAHLIA C., lawyer; b. NYC, Sept. 9, 1951; d. Benjamin Zev and Malka B. (Liben) R.; m. Robert R. Jampol, Oct. 31, 1971; children: Malka, Noah. BA magna cum laude, Yale U., 1972; JD, U. Calif., Berkeley, 1978. Bar: Calif. 1979, Mass. 1980, U.S. Dist. Ct. (no. dist.) Calif. 1979, U.S. Dist. Ct. Mass. 1981, U.S. Ct. Appeals (1st cir.) 1984, U.S. Supreme Ct. 1990. Assoc. Angoff, Goldman, Manning, Pyle, Wanger & Hiatt, Boston, 1980-84, Avery & Friedman, Boston, 1984-86, McDonald Noonan & Kaplan, Newton, Mass., 1986-88; ptnr. Shilepsky, Messing & Rudavsky, P.C., Boston, 1988-93, Messing and Rudavsky, P.C., Boston, 1993—, Messing, Rudavsky & Weliky PC, Boston. Cons. in field. Named one of top Boston lawyers, Boston Mag., 2004; recipient Georgina Smith Award, AAUP, Washington, 1990. Mem. AFL-CIO (lawyers coordinating com., nat. adv. bd. 1983-84), Nat. Lawyers Guild, Mass. Bar Assn. Fluent in french & Hebrew. Office: Messing Rudavsky & Weliky PC 50 Congress St Boston MA 02109 E-mail: drudavsky@mrwemploymentlaw.com.

RUDD, ANN TALTON, psychologist, artist; b. Raleigh, N.C., Mar. 29, 1960; d. Fred Wesley and Margaret Baucom Talton; m. James Robert Rudd, Mar. 22, 1986; 1 child, Holden. BA Psychology, East Carolina U., Greenville, N.C., 1982; MS Applied Psychology, Va. Tech, Blacksburg, 1984; postgrad., Art Inst. Charlotte, N.C. Lic. Psychol. Assoc. N.C. Psychology Bd., 1985, cert. Psychologist N.C. Psychology Bd., 1999. Staff psychologist Murdoch Ctr., Butner, NC, 1984—86; post-disaster counselor d Mental Health Roanoke Valley, Va., 1986; behavior cons. Behavior Therapy and Learning Ctr., Signal Hill, Calif., 1987—88; devel. disabilities specialist Mecklenburg County Area Mental Health/Devel. Disabilities Svcs., Charlotte, 1988—91; psychologist St. Marks Residential Svcs. and Luth. Family Svcs. Group Homes, Charlotte, 1989—94; staff psychologist Mecklenburg County Area Mental Health/Devel. Disabilities Svcs., Charlotte, 1994—99; psychologist Rudd Psychol. Svcs., Charlotte, 2003—. Mem.: Charlotte Art League, Psi Chi (sec. 1980—82), Chi Beta Phi Sci. Honor Soc. (sec. 1981—82), Mensa. Avocations: painting, drawing, graphic design, piano, reading.

RUDD, CHERYL KAI, language educator; b. Spokane, Wash., May 17, 1964; d. Howard James and Sharon Dorothy Rudd. BA in History, Ea. Wash. U., 1990, BEd., 1991, MA, 2000. Cert. edn. tchg. Office Supt. Pub. Instrn. Firefighter, fire lookout Wash. State Dept. Natural Resources, Colville, 1986—98; rsch. asst. Archeol., Hist. Svcs., Cheney, Wash., 1988—91; social studies, humanities, Japanese lang. tchr. Colville (Wash.) HS, 1991—. Classroom based assessment trainer Office Supt. Pub. Instrn., Olympia, Wash., 2002—. Contbr. NEH teacher curriculum units. Named Tchr. of Yr., Colville HS; scholar, Fulbright, Rotary. Mem.: NEA (corr.), Nat. Coun. Japanese Lang. Tchrs. (corr.), Wash. Assn. Japanese Lang. Tchrs. (corr.), Wash. Assn. Fgn. Lang. Tchrs. (corr.), Colville Edn. Assn. (corr.), Wash. Ednl. Assn. (corr.). Democrat-Npl. Buddhist. Avocations: travel, hiking, sailing. Home: 810 S Pine St Colville WA 99114-3443 Office: Colville HS 154 Hwy 20 E Colville WA 99114

RUDD, SUSAN, retail executive; b. Rolla, Mo., Jan. 25, 1961; d. Wayne LeRoy and Chie Owada Schwatka; m. Edward Thomas Rudd, Oct. 27, 1947. BBA, Fontbonne U., 1999. Exec. sec. McDonnell Douglas Astronautics, St. Louis, 1981—90; sr. exec. office adminstr. Anheuser-Busch Cos. Inc., St. Louis, 1990—2000, corp. rels. mgr. Asian Pacific Am. market, 2000—02; mgr. nat. retail sales Anheuser-Busch Inc., St. Louis, 2002—. Bd. dirs. Asian Pacific Am. Women's Leadership Inst., Denver. Recipient Women's Bus. Leadership award, Columbia Coll.-Ctr. Asian Arts and Media, 2001. Mem.: NAFE. Office: Anheuser-Busch Inc One Busch Pl Saint Louis MO 63118 Office Phone: 623-551-2408. Business E-Mail: susan.rudd@anheuser-busch.com.

RUDDELL, ALYSA ANN, clinical psychologist; b. Ellensburg, Wash., Nov. 11, 1949; d. Clyde Ruddell and Helen May (Ponath) Bostrom; m. Abdelmajid Azzedine, Sept. 15, 1989; children: Mostefa Azzedine. BA, Western Wash. U., 1972; MA, U.S. Internat. U., 1982, PhD, 1986. Counselor Salvation Army, Door of Hope, San Diego, 1982-84; psychology intern Cuyamaca Outpatient Clinic, San Diego, 1984, Southwood Adolescent Psychiat., San Diego, 1985; counselor Community Rsch. Found., San Diego, 1984-87; sexual assault counselor Women's Resource Ctr., San Luis Rey, Calif., 1986-87; mental health specialist Evergreen Counseling Ctr., Aberdeen, Wash., 1987-88; clin. psychologist Ruddell & Assocs., Aberdeen, 1988-96, Federal Way, Wash., 1988—, Federal Way Psychology Clinic, 1996—. Clin. cons. health dept. St. Joseph Hosp. Aberdeen, 1987-90; clin. supr. Cath. Community Svcs., Tacoma, Wash., 1992-94; expert witness Tech. Adv. Svc. for Attys., 1988—; guest radio talk shows, 1987-94. Dir. Camps Farthest Out, Wash., 1990, 96; pres. of bd. Grays Harbor Rape Crisis, Aberdeen, 1987-90. Named for Spl. Contbns., Bellingham (Wash.) C. of C., 1979, for Outstanding Svc., YWCA, Bellingham, 1974. Mem. APA, Wash. State Psychol. Assn., Internat. Soc. for the Study of Dissociation, Child Abuse Prevention Resources. Office: Federal Way Psychology Clinic 801 S 336 St Federal Way WA 98003-6310 Home: 431 Lake Louise Dr SW Lakewood WA 98498-3149

RUDDIMAN, JOAN, elementary school educator; b. Trenton, NJ, Dec. 24, 1953; d. Joseph Howard and Mary Evelyn (Gould) Runner; m. John Alexander Ruddiman, July 5, 1975; children: John Anthon7, Jillian Mary, Jayne Irene. BA in English, Rutgers U., New Brunswick, NJ, 1975, MEd, 1981; EdD, Columbia U., NYC, 2004. English tchr. McCorristan HS, Hamilton, NJ, 1975—78; pvt. tutor Allentown, N.Mex., 1978—87; mid. sch. reading tchr. West Windsor-Plainsboro Schs., Princeton Junction, NJ, 1987—99, tchr. gifted and talented students, 1999—. Cons., trainer, presenter in field. Contbr. articles to profl. publs., anthology. Pres. bd. dirs. Allentown Pub. Libr., NJ, 1980—94; leader Girl Scouts USA, Allentown, 1976—80; mem. com., advocate St. Gregory the Gt., Hamilton, NJ, 1980—. Named Nat. History Day Educator of Yr., NJHD, 2005. Mem.: Nat. Coun. Tchrs. Englisy, Internat. Reading Assn., PTSA, NEA (team leader), NJ Edn. Assn. (mem. com.), NMSA (founding mem.), NJAMLE, NJ Assn. Gifted Children (bd. dirs. 2004—, Educator of Yr. 2005), Kappa Delta Pi. Republican. Roman Catholic. Office: Thomas R Grover Mid Sch 14 Southfield Rd Princeton Junction NJ 08550

RUDDOCK, ELLEN SYLVES, management consultant; b. Pitts., May 9, 1944; d. Clyde Lysle and Margaret Beck (Tilley) Sylves; m. Rodney David Ruddock, Apr. 2, 1966; children: Dana William, Darin Willis. BS, Indiana U. Pa., 1966; cert. in entrepreneurial mgmt., Carnegie Mellon U., 1995. Lic. real estate agt. Pa., cert. facilitator Leadership Mgmt. Inc. Tchr. Penn Hills H.S., Pitts., 1966; adminstrv. asst. Utah-Martin-Day, Bangkok, 1967-68, COMUS-MACTHAI, Bangkok, 1968-69; tchr. United H.S., Armagh, Pa., 1969-70; owner Swing Set Children's Store, Indiana, 1975-80; radio cons. RMS Media Mgmt., Indiana, 1980-89; owner Career Dynamics, Pitts., 1989—2002. Pres. PowerLink, Pitts., 2000—01; initiator partnership between PowerLink and Athena Internat. to aid women-owned bus. Initiator 100-mem. vol. strategic planning group Indiana County for 2020 Greater Indiana Strategic Planning Commn., revitalization program Indiana for the 80s, also fundraisers; chairperson New Growth Arts Festival, Indiana, 1984—85, 1995—2001, PNC Adv. Bd., Indiana, 1986—2000; bd. dirs. ATHENA Internat., Lansing, Mich., 1998—2006, chmn. bd. dirs., 2003—05; bd. dirs., now emeritus Downtown Indiana, 1975—, pres., 1979—81; campaign mgr. Found. Indiana U. Pa., 2001—05; bd. dirs. Indiana U. Pa. Alumni Assn., 2001—. Named World Sales Leader of Assessments, Leadership Mgmt. Inc., 2001, Retailer of Yr., Kids Mag., N.Y.C., 1978, Ind. County Civic Leader of Yr., 2000; named one of Pa. 50 Best Women in Bus., 1999; recipient Athena award, ATHENA Found., 1987, Svc. award, Alice Paul Ho., Ind., Pres.'s Club award, Leadership Mgmt., Inc., Waco, Tex., 1997, Golden Eagle award, 1997, Distbr. of Yr. award, Leadership Mgmt. Inc., 2000, Outstanding Civilian Svc. award, USAR, Pitts., 1997, 2000. Mem.: Indiana County C. of C. (bd. dirs. 1997—2003), Quota Club (pres. 1986—88, Svc. award 1986). Republican. Methodist. Avocations: reading, walking, community service. Home: 465 Edgewood Ave Indiana PA 15701 E-mail: eruddock@adelphia.net.

RUDDY, STACEY ANN, literature and language educator; d. Mark and Joyce Stack; m. Joseph Ruddy, Aug. 24. BS, Villanova U., Pa.; MS in Edn., Wilkes U., Wilkes-Barre, Pa. Tchr. English Lake-Lehman H. S., Lehman, Pa., 1999—. Office: Lake Lehman Jr Sr HS PO Box 38 Lehman PA 18627-38

RUDE, DEBRA MARIE, music educator; b. Peoria, Ill., Sept. 17, 1966; d. Dennis Albert and Dolores Frances Miller; m. Dennis Michael Rude, Aug. 13, 1988; children: Craig Edward, Carolyn Eylene. BSc in Music Edn., Ill. Wesleyan U., 1988. Music tchr. Peoria Christian Sch., Ill., 1996—2004, Peoria Pub. Schs., 2004—. Dir., condr.: (community theatre productions) Corn Stock Theatre; Peoria Players Theatre; singer, production chair: Peoria Area Civic Chorale. Pianist Fellowship Bible Ch., Peoria, 1990—2005. Mem.: Am. Choral Dirs. Assn., Music Educators Nat. Conf. Home: 1289 North Woodland Ln Metamora IL 61548 Personal E-mail: dmrude@ocslink.com.

RUDEL, BARBARA ELIZABETH, elementary school educator; b. Chgo., Mar. 15, 1964; d. Alfred and Elizabeth Kocialkowski; m. Richard Rudel, Dec. 21, 1986; children: Anna, Cecylia. BA, Concordia U., River Forest, Ill., 1986. Cert. Standard Tchg. Ill. Primary tchr. Union Ridge Sch., Harwood Heights, Ill., 1986—. Mentor tchr. Union Ridge Sch., 2003—05, cooperating tchr., 1986—, yearly com. cons., 1986—. Tchr. rep. PTA, Sch. Dist. 86, 1987. Mem.: NEA (union treas. 1989), Nat. Coun. Tchrs. Math., Internat. Reading Assn., Phi Delta Kappa. Avocations: travel, reading, landscape design. Office: Union Ridge Sch 4600 Oak Pk Ave Harwood Heights IL 60706

RUDER, DIANE G., not-for-profit fundraiser; b. Pasadena, Tex., Feb. 3, 1941; d. David A. and Gladys S. (Cook) Garrett; m. Melvin P. Ruder, Nov. 11, 1961; children: N. Christine, M. Shawn, M. Kirk, Heather M., Eric R. AB, Miami U., Oxford, Ohio, 1984; MBA, Xavier U., Cin., 1992. News writer The Jour. News, Hamilton, Ohio, 1972-76; alumni dir. Wilmington (Ohio) Coll., 1985-88, dir. alumni rels. and ann. fund progs., 1988-89, dir. ann. fund, 1989-90; exec. dir. Middletown (Ohio) Regional Hosp. Found., 1990-92; asst. dir. devel. Episcopal Retirement Homes, Cin., 1992-93; dir. devel. United Cerebral Palsy of Cin., 1993-94, Otterbein Retirement Living Cmtys., Lebanon, Ohio, 1994—; v.p. devel. OtterbeinHomes, 2005—. Mem. Ctrl. Com., Rep. Party, 1968-84; bd. dirs. Am. Heart Assn. Butler County; bd. dirs. Sr. Citizens Assn. Middletown, Friends of Chrisholm; bd. dirs. Warren County Social Svcs., Lebanon, Ohio, 2004-, Holy Spirit Comms., Dayton. Ohio. Recipient May Cup award of spl. recognition, Am. Mktg. Assn., 1989, Cert. of Merit, Admissions Mktg. Report, 1989. Mem. Ohio Assn. Hosp. Devel., Nat. Assn. Hosp. Devel., Nat. Soc. Fund Raising Execs. (cert. fund raising exec.), Nat. Assn. Fundraising Profls., Leadership Middletown, Nat. Planned Giving Coun. Roman Catholic. Home: 5660 Headgates Rd Hamilton OH 45011 Office: Otterbein Homes 580 N St Route 741 Lebanon OH 45036-8839 E-mail: ruder@otterbein.org, lmcfre@aol.com.

RUDER, TIA L., music educator; d. Judy K and Duane F Ruder. MusB cum laude in Edn., Wichita State U., 1992, MusB cum laude in Performance, 1992, BA cum laude, 1993, MusM in Edn., 1999. K-12, Vocal and Instrumental Music Kans. State Bd. of Edn., 1992, nat. bd. cert. in early adolescent and young adult. Instrumental music tchr. Wichita Pub. Schools, Kans., 1992—. Summer instrument cleaning and repair Wichita Pub. Schools, Kans., 2000—05; asst. dir. all-city band Wichita Pub. Schs., 1993—; pvt. music tchr., Wichita, 1992—2003; soprano soloist and instrumental music dir. Mt. Vernon Presbyn. Ch., Wichita, Kans., 1992—2001; summer sch. tchr. Oakley Pub. Schools, Oakley, Kans., 1992—97, Wichita Pub. Schools, 2000—04. State forensics championships adjudicator Kans. State H.S. Activities Assn., Wichita, 1992—2005. Recipient Honors Program Grad., Wichita State U., 1992, Mortar Bd. Scholar, 1991; U. Leader Scholar, 1992—96. Mem.: NEA, Kans. Bandmasters Assn., Fedn. of Teachers, Kans. Music Educators Assn., Music Educators Nat. Conf. Avocations: cooking, home improvement, science fiction, theater. Personal E-mail: tiaruder@email.com, tia.ruder@cox.net.

RUDIN, ANNE, retired mayor, nursing educator; b. Passaic, NJ, Jan. 27, 1924; m. Edward Rudin, June 6, 1948; 4 children. BS in Edn., Temple U., 1945, RN, 1946; MPA, U. So. Calif., 1983; LLD (hon.), Golden Gate U., 1990. RN, Calif. Mem. faculty Temple U. Sch. Nursing, Phila., 1946-48; mem. nursing faculty Mt. Zion Hosp., San Francisco, 1948-49; mem. Sacramento City Council, 1971-83; mayor City of Sacramento, 1983-92; ind. pub. policy cons. Pres. LWV, Riverside, 1957, Sacramento, 1961, Calif., 1969-71, Calif. Elected Women's Assn., 1973—; trustee Golden Gate U., 1993-96; mem. adv. bd. U. So. Calif., Army Depot Reuse Commn., 1992-94; bd. dirs. Sacramento Theatre Co., 1992-99, Japan Soc. No. Calif., Sacramento Symphony, 1993-96, Calif. Common Cause, 1993 -96, Sacramento Edn. Found., 1993-2006; v.p. Sacramento Traditional Jazz Soc. Found.; pres. bd. dirs. Natomas Basin Conservancy; foreman Sacramento County Grand Jury, 2000-01. Recipient Women in Govt. award U.S. Jaycee Women, 1984, Woman of Distinction award Sacramento Area Soroptimist Clubs, 1985, Civic Contbn. award LWV Sacramento, 1989, Woman of Courage award Sacramento History Ctr., 1989, Peacemaker of Yr. award Sacramento Mediation Ctr., 1992, Regional Pride award Sacramento Mag., 1993, Humanitarian award Japanese Am. Citizen's League, 1993, Outstanding Pub. Svc. award Am. Soc. Pub. Adminstrn., 1994, Cmty. Svc. Recognition award, Japanese Am. Citizens League, 1999, Contbr. to Pub. Art award Am. Soc. for Pub. Admin., 2004, Robert T. Malsui award Pub. Svc., Town & Country Dem. Club, 2005; named Girl Scouts Am. Role model, 1989; named to Sacramento Traditional Jazz Soc. Hall of Fame, 2000. Mem.: Calif. Med. Alliance (Mem. of Yr. 2005).

RUDINGER, JENNIFER IRENE, legal association administrator; b. Sandusky, Ohio, Nov. 10, 1968; d. Joel Douglas Rudinger and Honey Christian, Anthony Darryl Christian (Stepfather). AB, Duke U., 1991; JD, Ohio State U. Coll. of Law, 1996. Bar: Ohio 1996. Polit. canvasser/crew mgr. Ohio Citizen Action, Columbus, Ohio, 1991—93; law clk. John S. Marshall Atty. at Law, Columbus, Ohio, 1995—97; exec. dir. Alaska Civil Liberties Union, Anchorage, 1997—2004, ACLU N.C., Raleigh, NC, 2004—. Asst. legislative coord. Nat. Orgn. for Women Ohio Chpt., Columbus, 1994—94, ACLU of Ohio, 1995—95; jud. extern Hon. Alice Robie Resnick, Supreme Ct. of Ohio, 1995—95; coord., voter registration dr. Nat. Lawyers Guild, 1994—94; vol. Columbus Bar Assn. Homeless Project, 1994—96. Vol. organizer Murray for Congress, Sandusky, Ohio, 1988. Recipient award, Phi Eta Sigma, Golden Key award, Golden Key Nat. Honor Soc., Paul Edwin Harner Svc. award, Associated Students of Duke U., 1991, Nat. Achievement award, Citizen Action; Robert C. Byrd scholar, Senator Robert C. Byrd, 1987. Avocations: theater, travel. Office: ACLU of NC P O Box 28004 Raleigh NC 27611-8004 Office Phone: 919-834-3466. Office Fax: 919-828-3265.

RUDMAN, MASHA KABAKOW, education educator, author, consultant; b. N.Y.C., Jan. 16, 1933; d. Benedict and Rose (Wolf) Kabakow; m. Seymour L. Rudman, June 14, 1953; children: Rachel, Reva, Deborah. AB, CUNY, 1953, MS, 1956; EdD, U. Mass., 1970. Tchr. elem. N.Y.C. Pub. Schs., 1953—58; lectr. edn. Hunter Coll. CUNY, N.Y.C., 1964; mem. faculty Sch. Edn. U. Mass., Amherst, 1965—. Author: Children's Literature: An Issues Approach, 1984, Children's Literature: Resource for the Classroom, 1989; co-author: (with J. Bernstein) Books to Help Children Cope with Separation and Loss, 1989, (with A. Pearce) For Love of Reading, 1988; contbr. numerous articles to profl. jours. Recipient Disting. Tchr. award U. Mass., 1973; Noyes Found. Fellowship grantee, 1982-83, Nat. Endowment for the Humanities grantee, 1983. Mem. ASCD, Profs. Curriculum, Internat. Reading Assn., Nat. Coun. Tchrs. English, Phi Delta Kappa Avocations: travel, reading, family, writing. Office: U Mass 224 Furcolo Hall Amherst MA 01003

RUDNER, SARA, dancer; b. Bklyn., Feb. 16, 1944; d. Henry Nathaniel and Jeannette (Smolensky) R.; 1 child, Edward Eli Rudner Marschner. AB in Russian Studies, Barnard Coll., 1964; MFA in Choreography, Bennington Coll., 1999. Dancer Sansardo Dance Co., N.Y.C., 1964-65, Am. Dance Co. at Lincoln Ctr., N.Y.C., 1965, Shakespeare Festival Touring Children's Show, N.Y.C., 1966; featured dancer Twyla Tharp Dance Found., N.Y.C., 1966-85; artistic dir., dancer Sara Rudner Performance Ensemble, N.Y.C., 1977—; guest dancer Joffrey Ballet, N.Y.C., 1973, Pilobolus Dance Theatre, N.Y.C., 1975, Lar Lubovitch Dance Co., N.Y.C., 1975-76; guest lectr., choreographer grad. dance dept. UCLA, 1975. Dir. dance Sarah Lawrence Coll.; tchr. master workshop NYU Theater Program, 1988-90; pres., artistic dir. Heart Dance, Inc. Choreographer: Palm Trees and Flamingoes, 1980, Dancing for an Hour or So, 1981, Minute by Minute, 1982, Eight Solos, 1991, Heartbeats, Inside Out, 1993; (with Jennifer Tipton and Dana Reitz) Necessary Weather, 1994; (with Rona Pondick, Robert Feintuch and Jennifer Tipton) Mine, 1996, Alley Theater-The Greeks part I and II, 1997, Heartbeat/mb with Christopher Janney and Mikhail Barysnikov, 1998. Choreographer Dancing-on-View St. Mark's Ch., N.Y.C., 1999, Santa Fe Opera. Grantee Creative Artists Pub. Svc. Program, N.Y., 1975-76, N.Y. State Coun. on Arts, 1975-78, Nat. Endowment for Arts, 1979-81, 91-92, 94-97; Guggenheim fellow, 1981-82; recipient N.Y. Dance and Performance award, 1984. Business E-Mail: srudner@slc.edu.

RUDNICK, ELLEN AVA, health facility administrator; b. New Haven; d. Harold and C. Vivian (Soybel) R.; children from previous marriage: Sarah, Noah; m. Paul W. Earle. BA, Vassar Coll., 1972; MBA, U. Chgo., 1973. Sr. fin. analyst Quaker Oats, Chgo., 1973-75; from with to pres. Baxter Internat., Deerfield, Ill., 1975—83; pres. Baxter Mgmt. Svcs., 1983-1990, HCIA, Balt., 1990-92, CEO Advs., Northbrook, Ill., 1992—; prin., chmn. Pacific Biometrics, Lake Forest, Calif., 1993-99; exec. dir., clin. prof. Polsky Ctr. for Entrepreneurship U. Chgo., 1999—. Bd. dirs. Liberty Mut. Ins., Pattrson Dental Co., First Midwest Bank. Chief crusader Met. Chgo. United Way, 1982—85; mem. cir. friends Chgo. YMCA, 1985—89; bd. dirs. Evanston Northwestern-Highland Park Hosp., 1990—99, 2003—, Health Mgmt. Sys., 1997—, Evanston-Northwestern Hosp., 2000—02; pres. coun. Nat. Coll. Edn., Evanston, Ill., 1983—93. Office: Univ Chgo Grad Sch Bus 5807 S Woodlawn Chicago IL 60637

RUDNICK, IRENE KRUGMAN, lawyer, educator, former state legislator; b. Columbia, SC, Dec. 27, 1929; d. Jack and Jean (Getter) Krugman; m. Harold Rudnick, Nov. 7, 1954 (dec.); children: Morris, Helen Gail. AB cum laude, U. S.C., 1949, JD, 1952. Bar: (S.C.) 1952. Individual practice law, Aiken, SC, 1952—; now ptnr. Rudnick & Rudnick; instr. bus. law U. S.C., Aiken, 1962—; tchr. Warrenville Elem. Sch., 1965-70; supt. edn. Aiken County, 1970-72; mem. S.C. Ho. of Reps., 1972—78, 1980—84, 1986—94. Pres. Adath Yeshurun Synagogue; active Aiken County Dem. Party, S.C. Dem. Party; hon. mem. Aiken Able-Disabled. Recipient Citizen of Yr. award, 1976-77, Bus. and Profl. Women's Career Woman of Yr., 1978, 94, Aiken County Friend of Edn. award, 1985, 93, Outstanding Legis. award Disabled Vets., 1991, Citizen of Yr. award Planned Parenthood, 1994, Sertoma Svc. to Mankind award, 1996, Pickens Salley So. Woman of Distinction award, 2005; named Aiken County C. of C. Woman of Yr., 2005. Mem. AAUW, Aiken Able-Disabled (hon.), Aiken Hist. Soc., Hist. Aiken Found., Alpha Delta Kappa, Order Eastern Star, Hadassah Sisterhood, Am. Legion Aux. Office: PO Box 544 135 Pendleton St NW Aiken SC 29801-3859

RUDNICK, PESHA EVA, theater director; b. Amherst, Mass., Dec. 15, 1973; d. Philip Tim Rudnick and Robin Lithgow. BA, U. Calif., Berkeley, 1996; MA in Theater Edn., NYU, NYC, 2005. Theater edn. prodr. Cornerstone Theater, LA, 1999—; freelance dir. Kennedy Ctr., Washington, 2005, Hanger Theater, NYC, 2005—06, Vital Theater, NYC, 2006. Home: 653 Broadway St Venice CA 90291-3403

RUDOLPH, CAROL ANN GREENBERG, human resource education consultant; Tchr. N.Y.C. Pub. Schs., 1964, DC Pub. Schs., 1965—66, Georgetown Children's House, Washington, 1966—67; dir. Focus Child Care Ctr., Fairfax, Va., 1973—74, NIH Child Care Ctr., Bethesda, Md., 1974—77; regional child devel. tng. specialist U. Md., College Park, 1977—81; cons. Child Care Mgmt. Resources, Bethesda, 1981—96, Family Care Resources, Bethesda, 1996—, prin. Pres. Huntington Terr. Citizen's Assn., Bethesda, 1978—79; v.p. Concert on Beach, 2006—. Mem.: Am. Counseling Assn., Am. Assn. Ret. Persons. Democrat. Jewish. Avocations: tennis, swimming, travel, art, music. Office: Family Care Resources 5620 Greentree Rd Bethesda MD 20817 Office Phone: 301-897-8272. E-mail: ccmrfcr@aol.com.

RUDOLPH, LISA BETH, news correspondent; b. Oceanside, Calif., Dec. 7, 1957; d. Jerome Howard and Suzanne (Garber) R.; m. Richard Hurwitz, Sept. 23, 1989; children: Kyra Rachael, Gabriel Jerome. BA in History, Wellesley (Mass.) Coll., 1979; MA in Internat. Affairs, Columbia U., 1984. Children's news show writer WXXI-TV PBS, Rochester, N.Y., 1979-80; reporter WOKR-TV, ABC affiliate, Rochester, 1979-82; news writer WCBS-TV, CBS affliate, 1983-86; anchor, reporter KSAT-TV, ABC affiliate, San Antonio, 1986-87, WCBS-TV, CBS affiliate, N.Y.C., 1987-93; corr. Dateline NBC, N.Y.C., 1994—. Recipient 3 Emmys, 1990-92, Media award N.Y. State Bar Assn., 1991, 19th Ann. Eddy award, 1992, Clarion, Gabriel awards, 1997, 98. Mem. Phi Beta Kappa. Office: Dateline NBC 30 Rockefeller Plz Fl 2 New York NY 10112-0044

RUDOLPH, MAYA, actress, comedienne; b. Gainesville, Fla., July 27, 1972; d. Richard and Minnie (Riperton) Rudolph. BA in photography, U. Calif., Santa Cruz, 1994. Former backup singer The Rentals. Actor: (TV series) Saturday Night Live, 2000—, City of Angels, 2000, (guest star) Chicago Hope, 1996—97,: (TV films) The Devil's Child, 1997, True Love, 1999; (films) Gattaca, 1997, Chuck & Buck, 2000, Duets, 2000, Duplex, 2003, 50 First Dates, 2004, A Prairie Home Companion, 2006, Idiocracy, 2006.*

RUDOLPH, NANCY K., photographer, writer; b. N.Y.C., Dec. 26, 1923; d. Morris and Eva (Cohn) Kallman; m. Alan Goldsmith Rudolph, div. 1970. BA, Union Inst., 1989. Pub. rels. asst. Mus. Modern Art, N.Y.C., 1947-48; press attaché Econ. Cooperation Adminstrn., Rome, 1948-49; photography workshops Elizabeth Irwin H.S., 1969-70; pvt. instr.; tchr. New Sch. of Social Work, N.Y.C., 1978, guest lectr. Author: New Neighborhoods, New Lives, 1964, Workyards, Playgrounds Planned for Adventure, 1974; contbr. articles to profl. jours.; one-woman shows include Menemsha Gallery, Martha's Vineyard, Mass., 1962, Bank St. Coll. Edn., N.Y.C., 1962, Parents Mag. Gallery, N.Y.C., 1969, City Hall, Boston, 1970, Met. Mus. Art, N.Y.C., 1971, Dept. Interior, Washington, 1971, Jefferson Mkt. Br. of the N.Y. Pub. Libr., N.Y.C., 1975, 209 Photo Gallery, N.Y.C., 1976, Carver Cultural Cmty. Ctr., San Antonio, Tex., 1977, Photo Ctr. Gallery N.Y.U., 1981, Open Ctr. SOHO, N.Y.C., 1984, Seacliff Gallery, N.Y., 1989, Espacio Y Eventos, Valenzia, Venezuela, 1992; group shows include Neikrug Gallery, N.Y.C., 1975, Cooper Hewitt Mus., 1979, Foto Gallery, N.Y.C., 1981, Mus. of the City of N.Y., 1984, 88, Visual Arts Mus., N.Y.C., 1989, Nikon House, N.Y.C., 1991, U.N., N.Y.C., Copenhagen, Beijing, 1994-95, Children of the World, Vienna, 1997, others; represented in permanent collections at Ministry of Health, Mex. City, Mex., The Schomburg Collection of the N.Y. Pub. Libr., Phila. Mus. Art, Mus. of the City of N.Y., Union Inst., Cin., Helen Keller Internat., N.Y.C., The Ctr. for Creative Photography, Tucson, Ariz. Mem. Citizen's Com. for Children of N.Y.C., 1970—, bd. dirs., 1972-81; mem. Citywide Headstart Com., 1974. Recipient Excellence in Photography award Comm. Arts, Excellence in Photography award Am. Inst. Graphic Arts, award Internat. Assn. Bus. Comm., 1996. Mem. Am. Soc. Media Photographers (dir. 1974-76, dir. N.Y. chpt. 1986-87), Dronmenon. Home: PO Box 244 Clinton Corners NY 12514-0244

RUDY, ELAINE KIM, elementary school educator; b. Meadville, Pa., Nov. 5, 1951; d. George David Matteson and Marie Alta Webster; m. Joseph G. Rudy, May 8, 1976; children: Angela Crawford, Julie Riley, Tamara Zwick. AS Early Childhood, Edinboro U., Pa., 1986; BS Edn., Edinboro U., 1987, M Edn. Reading, 1988. Tchr. Penncrest Sch. Dist., Townville, Pa., 1977—88, tchr. Title I, Reading Recovery Cambridge Springs, Pa., 1991—. Tchr. adult edn. Penncrest Sch. Dist., Townville, 1986—, coord. literacy, 2004—, mentor Title I, Cambridge Springs, mem. program improvement team, Saegertown, Pa., mem. strategic planning com.; leader Maplewood Elem. Literacy Leadership Team, 2004—. Named Outstanding Educator, Crawford County Headstart, 1990; named to Chancellor's List, Ednl. Comm. Inc., 2004—05, 2005—06. Avocations: reading, camping. Home: 31150 State Hwy 27 Guys Mills PA 16327 Office: Maplewood Elem Sch 32695 Hwy 408 Townville PA 16360

RUDY, JANET FAYE WALKER, science educator; b. Meridian, Miss., Feb. 26, 1963; d. John Edwin and Pam Anne Walker (Stepmother); life ptnr. Jonathan Mark Gray; children: Tasha Brooks Edwards Veazey, Zachory Adam Edwards, Crystal Faye. AD, Ark. State U., 1989; B in Edn., U. Ctrl. Ark., 1991. Cert. profl. educator Ark., 1991. Tchr. 4th grade Cabot Sch. Dist., Ark., 1992—2001, 2003—04, tchr. 3d grade, 2001—03, sci. lab. specialist, 2004—. Educator art, health, literacy, math, and counseling Twenty First Century Cmty. Learning Coll. Yale U., Cabot, Ark., 2002—. Mem.: Cabot Tchrs. Assn. (v.p. 2005—06, pres. 2006—), NEA, Ark. Edn. Assn. (assoc.; v.p., pres. 2005—). Baptist. Achievements include development of science curriculum. Home: 23 Timber Ln Cabot AR 72023 Office: Ward Ctrl 1570 Wilson Loop Ward AR 72176 Office Phone: 501-843-9601. Business E-Mail: janet.rudy@cps.k12.ar.us.

RUDY, KATHLEEN VERMEULEN, small business owner; b. Grand Rapids, Mich., Dec. 29, 1931; d. John Weston and Geneva (Swiet) Vermeulen; m. Fredrick Albers Yonkman, June 9, 1953 (div. Sept. 1980); children: Sara Yonkman Davis, Margriet Yonkman Finnegan, Nina Yonkman Tower; m. Raymond Bruce Rudy, Nov. 14, 1981. BA, Hope Coll., 1953. Owner Kate's Antiques, 1974—2000. Editor mag. Jr. League of Boston, 1960's, Scarsdale Jr. League, 1960's. Bd. dirs. Jr. League of Boston, 1960s, Greenwich Cmty. for Human Svcs., 1970s-80s, Neighbor to Neighbor, Greenwich, 1980-98; trustee Hope Coll., 1986-96; chmn. Mary Fund com. Ladies Golf Tournament, 1985; mem. Women's Nat. Rep. Club, N.Y.C., 1995—, bd. govs., 1997-2004, 06—; mem. Hope Coll. Pres.'s Task Force, 1997-99; treas. Women's Nat. Rep. Club, 2000-02, chmn. nominating com. 2000—, 2d v.p., 2002-04, mem. internat. affairs com., 2004—. Mem. Jr. League of Phoenix, Greenwich Country Club, Boulders Golf Club (Scottsdale), Dorset Field Club, Doubles Club, Kappa Alpha Theta. Republican. Congregationalist. Avocations: tennis, golf, antiques, travel, art. Home and Office: 37 Lismore Ln Greenwich CT 06831-3741 Personal E-mail: RayRudy@worldnet.att.net.

RUDY, RUTH CORMAN, former state legislator; b. Millheim, Pa., Jan. 3, 1938; d. Orvis E. and Mabel Jan (Stover) Corman; m. C. Guy Rudy, Nov. 21, 1956; children: Douglas G., Donita Rudy Koval, Dianna F. Degree in x-ray tech., Carnegie Inst., 1956; student, Pa. State U., 1968-71. Clk. of cts. County of Centre (Pa.), Bellefonte, 1976-82; rep. Pa. Gen. Assembly, Harrisburg, 1982-96. Mem. Dem. Nat. Com., 1980—, chair women's caucus, 1989-91; past pres. Pa. Fedn. Dem. Women, Harrisburg; pres. Nat. Fedn. Dem. Women, 1987-89; mem. exec. com. Dem. Nat. Com., 1987-89; candidate U.S. Congress, 5th Dist., 1995-96; rep. Nat. Dem. Inst. for Internat. Affairs, 1997—; rep. to Yemen, 1997. Mem. Gov. Rendell's Transition Team on Agr., 2003. Named Woman of Yr. Pa. Fedn. dem. Women, 1982, Centre County Living Legend, 2000. Methodist. Achievements include patent for hair spray face shield.

RUDZIK, LYNNE A., musician, educator; b. Concord, NH, June 28, 1963; d. Richard R. and Camille E. Ashland; m. John A. Rudzik, July 19, 1988; children: Thomas J., Michael R., Daniel R. MusB Edn., Fla. State U., Tallahassee, 1986. Profl. tchg. cert. Fla., 1986, cert. levels 1A, 1B, 2, 3 Suzuki Assn. of the Ams. Tchr. Orange County Pub. Schs., Orlando, Fla., 1986—2002; orch. dir. Gotha Mid. Sch., Windermere, Fla., 2002—. Musician St. Luke's United Meth. Ch., Windermere, 1990—2006. Mem.: Fla. Orch. Assn. (assoc.). Methodist. Avocations: reading, practicing instruments, swimming, camping. Office: Orange County Public Schools-Gotha Middl 9155 Gotha Rd Windermere FL 34786 Office Phone: 407-521-2360. Personal E-mail: jru1053016@aol.com. Business E-Mail: rudzikl@ocps.net.

RUEB, SHEREE A., social services administrator; b. Lincoln, Nebr., Aug. 23, 1960; d. Larry Hawkins, Annette Hawkins; m. Brent G. Rueb, July 7, 1985. BA, Hastings Coll., 1979—83; MA, Witchita State U., 1989—91. V.p. Mental Health Assn. South Ctrl. Kans., Wichita, 1991—95; state dir. Green Thumb, In.c, Arlington, Va., 1995—97; dir. sr. work experience ARC, Wichita, 1997—. Adv. bd. Reno County Workforce, Hutchinson, Kans., 1998—; bd. dirs. Kans. Workforce Investment, Hays, 1997—; adv. bd. Sedgwick County Workforce Partnership, Wichita, 1998—. Vice chair Older Workers Task Force State of Kans., 1997—. Mem.: Harvey County Archl. Assn. (sec., treas. 1995—, pres. 1996—98). Avocation: historic architecture, historic preservation. Office: ARC Midway KS Chpt 707 N Main Wichita KS 67203

RUECKER, MARTHA ENGELS, retired special education educator; b. South Gate, Calif., Sept. 22, 1931; d. Eugene and Minna (Wilhelm) Engels; m. Geert Frank Ruecker, Aug. 10, 1959 (div. 1964); 1 child, Ann. MusB, U. So. Calif., 1954, Calif. tchr. credential, 1955. Cert. tchr. for non-English speaking students, Calif. Tchr. educationally handicapped Downey (Calif.) Unified Schs., 1964-92; tchr. 2d grade Lynwood (Calif.) Unified Schs., 1992-97, 1997—2001; ret. Recipient award for work with mentally gifted Johns Hopkins U., 1992; South Gate Kiwanis scholar U. So. Calif., 1949-54. Mem. NEA (life), Los Angeles County Art Mus. Republican. Methodist. Avocations: interior design, gardening, music, travel. Home: PO Box 630 Downey CA 90241-0630

RUEHL, MERCEDES, actress; b. Queens, NY, Feb. 28, 1948; BA in English, Coll. of New Rochelle; studied acting with Uta Hagen, Tad Danielewski. Appearances include (theatre) Vanities, 1977-78, Billy Irish, 1980, Much Ado About Nothing, Misalliance, Androcles and the Lion, Tartuffe, Medea, 1980-82, Three Sisters, 1982-83, The Day They Shot John Lennon, 1982-83, Flirtation, 1983, June Moon, 1983-84, Monday After the Miracle, 1983-84, Coming of Age in Soho, 1985, The Marriage of Bette and Boo, 1985, I'm Not Rappaport, 1985 (Obie Award, Village Voice, 1985), American Notes, 1988, Other People's Money, 1989, Lost in Yonkers, 1991 (Tony award, 1991, Drama Desk award, 1991, Outer Critics Circle award 1991), The Shadow Box, 1994 (Tony nominee - Featured Actress in a Play, 1995), The Rose Tattoo, 1995, Woman Before a Glass, 2005 (Obie award, Village Voice, 2005); (film) The Warriors, 1979, Four Friends, 1981, Heartburn, 1986, 84 Charing Cross Road, 1987, Leader of the Band, 1987, The Secret of My Success, 1987, Radio Days, 1987, Big, 1988, Married to the Mob, 1988, Slaves of New York, 1989, Crazy People, 1990, Another You, 1991, The Fisher King, 1991 (Academy award Best Supporting Actress 1991), Lost in Yonkers, 1993, Last Action Hero, 1993, Roseanna's Grave, 1996, Out of the Cold, 1999, More Dogs Than Bones, 1999, The Minus Man, 1999, What's Cooking, 2000, Spooky House, 2000; (TV movie) Indictment: The McMartin Trial, 1995, Subway Stories: Tales From the Underground, 1997, Gia, 1997, Mary Kay Letourneau Story: The All-American Girl, 2000, The Lost Child, 2000, The Amati Girls, 2000, Guilt by Association, 2002; (TV mini-series) Widows, 2002, (TV series) Frazier, 1996, Spooky House, 1999. Recipient Nat. Film Critics Circle award, 1988, Clarence Derwent award, 1989.

RUEHLE, DIANNE MARIE, retired elementary education educator; b. Detroit, Aug. 14, 1943; d. Richard Francis and Luella Mary (Kopp) R. BS, Ea. Mich. U., 1966, MA, 1971, adminstrv. cert., 1990, renewed adminstrv. cert., 1995. Cert. tchr., adminstr., Mich. Tchr. Cherry Hill Sch. Dist., Inkster, Mich., 1966-85; tchr. elem. sch. Wayne-Westland (Mich.) Community Schs., 1985-95; retired. Dist. com. Pub. Act 25 for State of Mich., Westland, 1990-93, chair bldg., 1991-95. Improvement Instrn. grantee Wayne Westland Found., 1992-94. Mem. ASCD, NEA, Mich. Edn. Assn. Avocations: reading, golf, photography, travel. Home: 13385 N Heritage Gateway Ave Marana AZ 85653-4013

RUEMMLER, KATHRYN H., prosecutor; b. Richland, Wash., 1972; BA cum laude, U. Wash., Seattle, 1993; JD, Georgetown U., 1996. Def. atty. Zuckerman Spaeder LLP, Washington; litig. atty. Latham & Watkins, Washington; prosecutor, US Atty's Office US Dept. Justice, Washington, 2001—. With Enron Task Force, US Dept. Justice, 2003—, dep. dir., 2005—.*

RUESTERHOLZ, VIRGINIA P., telecommunications industry executive; m. Kevin Ruesterholz; 2 children. B in Chem. Engring., Stevens Inst. Tech., 1983; MS in Telecom. Mgmt., Bklyn. Poly. Inst., 1991. Mgr. NY Tel., 1984, market area v.p., gen. mgr. svc. delivery and field ops., 1993; v.p. complex installation and maintenance for network svcs. Bell Atlantic, v.p. ops. assurance, sr. v.p. wholesale markets; pres. Verizon Ptnr. Solutions Verizon Comm., pres. Verizon Telecom. Mem. bus. and tech. bd. Stevens Inst. Tech. Bd. dirs. Manhattan Theater Club. Recipient 40 Under 40 award, Crain's NY Bus., Rising Star award, NY Women's Agenda. Mem.: Edwin A. Stevens Soc. (chair). Office: Verizon Comm 140 West St New York NY 10007*

RUFE, LAURIE J., museum director; b. Pa. m. Mike Rufe. BA in Art History, Va. Commonwealth U. Intern Valentine Mus., Hist. Ho. Mus.; with Mercer Mus., Doylestown, Pa., 1973—80; Big Horn Basin Project Wyo., 1981—85; with Douglas County Coun. for the Arts and Humanities, Castle Rock; dir. Custer County Art Ctr., Mont., 1986—87; asst. dir. Roswell (N.Mex.) Mus. and Art Ctr., Roswell, 1987—98, dir., 1998—2002, Tucson Mus. Art, 2002—05. Office: Tucson Mus Art 140 N Main Ave Tucson AZ 85701 Office Phone: 520-624-2333 ext. 101. Business E-Mail: lrufe@tucsonarts.com.

RUFFALO, MARIA THERESE, secondary school educator; b. Seattle, Feb. 26, 1963; d. Patrick and Helen (Eckhardt) Ruffalo; m. Joseph Patrick Otterbine, May 5, 1987. BSME, U. Rochester, 1985. Proj. engr. Polycast Tech. Corp., Hackensack, NJ, 1985-86, sr. project engr., 1986-87, cons., 1987; project engr. ink divsn. J.M. Huber Corp., Edison, NJ, 1987-89; sr. engr. Himont USA, Inc., East Brunswick, NJ, 1990-93; engring. team leader Anchor Glass Container, Cliffwood, NJ, 1993-95; real estate developer, 1995—2001; tchr. math. Lacey Twp. (N.J.) HS, 2002—. Avocations: reading, gardening.

RUFFING, ANNE ELIZABETH, artist; b. Bklyn. d. John Paul and Ruth Elizabeth (Price) Frampton; m. George W. Ruffing, Mar. 29, 1967; 1 dau., Elizabeth Anne. BS, Cornell U., 1964; postgrad., Drexel Inst. Tech., 1966. One-woman exhbns. include, IBM, 1966, Hall of Fame, Goshen, N.Y., 1971, group exhbns. include, Internat. Women's Arts Festival, World Trade Center, N.Y.C., 1975-76, Berkshire Mus., Pittsfield, Mass., 1965, 76, Cooperstown (N.Y.) Mus., 1969; represented in permanent collections, Met. Mus. Art, Bklyn. Mus., Library of Congress, Harvard U., Smithsonian Instn., N.Y. Hist. Soc. Johnston Hist. Mus., Atwater Kent Mus., Albany Inst. History and Art, Whitney Mus. Am. Art, Boston Public Library. Recipient 1st place Eric Sloane award, 1974; Internat. Women's Year award Internat. Women's Art Festival, 1976 Address: 1031 Lewis Farm Rd Zebulon NC 27597

RUFFING, JANET KATHRYN, spirituality educator; b. Spokane, Wash., July 17, 1945; d. George Benjamin and Dorothy Edith (Folsom) R. BA, Russell Coll., 1968; M of Applied Spirituality, U. San Francisco, 1978; lic. in Sacred Theology, Jesuit Sch. Theology, 1984; PhD in Christian Spirituality, Grad. Theol. Union, 1986. Joined Sisters of Mercy Congregation, Roman Cath. Ch., 1963. Tchr. reading and English Mercy High Sch., Burlingame, Calif., 1968-72, 75-77, San Francisco, 1972-75; tchr., dept. head Marian High Sch., San Diego, 1978-80; faculty and originating team mem. Fully Alive, Burlingame, 1980-86; faculty, facilitator Permanent Diaconate Formation Program, Oakland, Calif., 1984-86; faculty Internship in Art of Spiritual Direction, Burlingame, 1984, 85, 87; prof. spirituality and spiritual direction Fordham U., Bronx, NY, 1986—, prof., 2000—. Spkr. Villanova Theol. Inst., 1995, Roger Williams Symposium, Pullman, Wash., 1985; vis. faculty Australian Cath. U., Brisbane, summer 1994, San Francisco Theol. Sem., summer 1993, U. San Francisco, summer 1991, St. Michael's Coll., Vt., summer 1990, Fordham at Limerick, Ireland, 1996-97,, CERFAC, Chennai, India, 1999, Colston Symposium, Bristol, Eng., 2000, San Francisco Theol. Sem., 2001, Gettysburg Luth. Sem., 2001, Inner Sabbath, Leuven, Belgium, 2002, Redemptionist Spirituality Inst., Thailand, 2002, 04; Holy Wisdom lectr. Washington Theol. Union, 2003, Retreats Internat., Chgo., 2005, 06, Maryknoll Mission Inst., 2006; presenter in field. Author: Uncovering Stories of Faith, 1989, Spiritual Direction: Beyond the Beginnings, 2000; contbg. author, editor: Mysticism and Social Transformation, 2001; assoc. editor The Way; mem. editl. bd. Presence; transl. Elisabeth Leseur: Selected Writings, 2005; contbr. articles to profl. jours. Mem. Cath. Theol. Soc. Am. (seminar moderator 1987-90), Am. Acad. Religion (chairperson mysticism group 1994-98), Mercy Assn. in Scripture and Theology (treas. 1987-96, mem. editorial bd. MAST jour.), Spiritual Dirs. Internat. (founding coord. com. mem. 1990-93, coord. of regions 1990-93), Women's Ordination Conf. Democrat. Avocations: cooking, swimming. Office: Fordham U Grad Sch Religion and Religious Bronx NY 10458 Office Phone: 718-817-4816.

RUFFNER, GINNY MARTIN, artist, glassblower; BFA cum laude, U. Ga., 1974, MFA summa cum laude, 1975. Instr. Université d'été, Sars-Poteries, France, 1990, Penland Sch. Crafts, N.C., 1987, vis. scholar, 1979, 83, Summervail Craft Sch., Vail, Colo., 1983; workshop instr. Calif. Coll. Arts and Crafts, Oakland, 1982, Tyler Sch. Art, Phila., 1984, N.Y. Experimental Glass Workshop, 1985, 86, 90, Pratt Fine Arts Ctr., Seattle, 1985, 86, Ausglas Conf., Melbourne, Australia, 1989; adj. instr. art dept. Dekalb Coll., 1977; artist in residence N.J. State Arts Commn., Wheaton Village, 1987; lectr. in field. Solo exhbns. include Ga. Tech. Gallery, 1984, David Bernstein Gallery, Boston, 1985, Fay Gold Gallery, Atlanta, 1985, 91, Habatat Gallery, Detroit, 1985, 87, 89, 97, Heller Gallery, N.Y.C., 1987, 88, 90, 93, 97, Huntington (W.Va.) Mus., 1988, Brendan Walter Gallery, L.A., 1990, Linda Farris Gallery, Seattle, 1991, 94, 95, Renwick Gallery of Nat. Mus. Am. Art, Smithsonian Instn., Washington, 1990, Bellevue (Wash.) Mus. Art, 1994, Meyerson/Nowinski Art Assocs., Seattle, 1996, others; group exhbns. include LaGrange Mus., Ga., 1975, Horizons Gallery, Mill Valley, Calif., 1982, Macon Mus. Arts and Scis., 1984, Leigh Yawkey Woodsen Art Mus., Wausau, Wis., 1981, 84, Traver-Sutton Gallery, Seattle, 1985, 87, 88, 89, Cooper-Hewitt Mus., NY.C., 1985, Kultur-huset, Stockholm, 1985, Bellevue (Wash.) Mus., 1986, 88, Louisville Art Gallery, 1986, Galerie Rob van den Doel, Hague, Netherlands, 1987, Darmstadt (W. Ger.) Mus. 1987, Mus. Modern Art, Hokkaido, Japan, 1988, 91, Fla. State U. Mus., 1988, Am. Embassy, Prague, 1988, The Louvre, Paris, 1989, High Mus., Atlanta, 1989, Blum Helman Gallery, N.Y.C., 1990, Am. Craft Mus., N.Y.C., 1990, 95, West End Gallery, N.Y.C., 1991, Nat. Mus. Ceramic Art, Balt., 1991, Detroit Inst. Arts, 1991, Internat. Exhbn. Contemporary Glass, Rouen, France, 1991, N.J. Ctr. Visual Arts, 1992, Betsy Rosenfield Gallery, 1992, Bellevue Mus. Art, 1994, Mus. Correr, Venice, 1996, Met. Mus. Art, N.Y., 1996, many others; represented in collections Am. Craft Mus., Bergstrom Mahler Mus., Cooper-Hewitt Mus., Corning Mus., Detroit Inst. Arts, High Mus., Hokkaido Mus. Modern Art, Kunstmus., L.A. County Mus. Art, Met. Mus. N.Y., Musée des Arts Décoratifs, Queensland Art Gallery, Renwick Gallery of Nat. Mus. Am. Art, Smithsonian Instn., Seattle Art Mus., Toledo Mus. Art, Cathedral St. Denis, Philip Morris Collection, Wash. State Art Commn.; edit. adv. bd. Glass Mag., 1989-91. Commr. Seattle Arts Commn., 1991; trustee Pilchuck Sch., 1991, artist in residence, 1988, instr., 1984-90. Recipient Ga. Bus. Com. for Arts award 1985, Urban Glass award for Outstanding Contbn., 1995; named Woman of Yr., Palm Springs Desert Mus., Calif., 1996;; NEA So. Arts Fedn. grantee, 1985, NEA Visual Artist fellow, 1986; Glass Eye scholar, 1993. Mem. Glass Art Soc. (bd. dirs. 1988-90, pres. 1990-91, coord. annual conf. 1990). Home: 5006 20th Ave Nw Seattle WA 98107-4807

RUGENSTEIN, CARRIE L., secondary school educator; b. Royal Oak, Mich., Jan. 15, 1978; m. Jeremy Rugenstein, Feb. 14, 2004. BS in Math., U. Detroit Mercy, 2000. Secondary Tchg. cert. Mich. Dept. Edn. Math tchr. Oak Pk. (Mich.) Schs., 2002—04, Owosso (Mich.) Pub. Schs., 2004—. Varsity tennis coach Dondero HS, Royal Oak, Mich., 1999—2004. Mem.: Gamma Phi Beta. Office: Owosso HS 765 East North St Owosso MI 48867 Office Phone: 989-729-5521.

RUGGIE, MARY, humanities educator; b. Toronto, Canada, Aug. 1, 1945; m. John Gerard Ruggie, May 21, 1965; 1 child, Andreas John. BA in Sociology, U. Calif., Berkeley, MA in Edn., PhD in Sociology, 1980. Asst. prof. Barnard Coll., NYC, 1981—87; assoc. prof. U. Calif. San Diego, La Jolla, Calif., 1987—91; prof. Columbia U., NYC, 1991—2001, Kennedy Sch., Harvard U., Cambridge, Mass., 2001—. Chair dept. sociology Columbia U., NYC, 1994—97. Author: (books) The State and Working Women: A Comparative Study of Britain and Canada, Realignments in the Welfare State: Health Policy in the United States, Britain and Sweden, From Marginal to Mainstream: Alternative Medicine in America. Mem. Health Care for Mass. Campaign, Boston, 2004—06. Rsch. grantee, German Marshall Fund, 1986—87, Can. Embassy, 1988—91, Nat. Inst. Medicine, 2002—05. Mem.: Am. Sociol. Assn. Office: Kennedy Sch Harvard Univ 79 JFK St Cambridge MA 02138

RUGGLES, SANDRA WAUGH, biophysicist; BS in Physics, U. Calif., San Diego; PhD in Biophysics, U. Calif., San Francisco, 2002. Co-founder Quicksilver Genomics, Inc., 2000, Catalyst Biosciences, Inc., 2002; postdoctoral rschr. U. Calif., San Francisco, 2002—. Named one of Top 100 Young Innovators, MIT Tech. Review, 2004. Office: Catalyst Biosciences Inc 209 Utah Ave South San Francisco CA 94080

RUHE, SHIRLEY LOUISE, government official; b. Des Moines, Mar. 20, 1943; d. Merritt Elton and Grace Alberta (Crabtree) Bailey; m. Jonathan Mills Ruhe, Feb. 28, 1970; children: Alix-Nicole, Jonathan G.B. BS, Iowa State U., 1965, MS, 1969. Wire editor, photographer Ames (Iowa) Daily Tribune, 1968—69; legis. asst. Congressman John Culver, 1969—72; staff asst. Congressman John Blatnik, 1973—75; dep. dir. budget process and ops. Ho. of Reps., Washington, 1978—82, assoc. dir., 1983—86, dir. budget policy, 1987—94; co-staff dir. Reconciliation Task Force, 1981—. Adviser spl. rules com. Task Force on Budget Process, 1982—83. Social action bd. Rock Spring Congl. Ch.; chmn. bd. dirs. Le Neon French-Am. Theatre. Resource Coun. Inst. Ednl. Policy. Ford Found. grant, 1969. Mem.: Phi Kappa Phi, Delta Sigma Phi. Democrat. Home: 3915 N Woodstock St Arlington VA 22207-2941 Office: Budget 203 Oneill House Office Bldg Washington DC 20515-0001

RUHL, MARY B., lawyer; BA, Wilson Coll., 1971; MA, U. Wis., 1973, JD, 1977. Bar: Calif. 1977, Wis. 1977. With Latham & Watkins, L.A., 1977—, ptnr. Mem.: Wis. State Bar Assn., Calif. State Bar Assn. Office: Latham and Watkins LLP 633 W Fifth St Ste 4000 Los Angeles CA 90071

RUHL, SARAH, playwright; b. 1974; m. Tony Charuvastra; 1 child, Anna Beatrice Ruhl Charuvastra. BA in English, Brown U., 1997, MFA in Playwriting, 2001. Author: (plays) Melancholy Play, 2002, Eurydice, 2003, Late: A Cowboy Song, Orlando, 2003, The Clean House, 2004 (Susan Smith Blackburn Prize, 2004, Pulitzer Prize finalist, 2005), Dead Man's Cell Phone, 2005, Passion Play: A Cycle, 2005. Recipient Helen Merrill award, 2003, Whiting Writers' award, 2003; Kennedy Ctr. Fellow, Sundance Theatre Lab., 2000, MacArthur Fellow, John D. and Catherine T. MacArthur Found., 2006. Office: c/o Bruce Ostler Bret Adams Ltd Artists' Agency 448 W 44th St New York NY 10036*

RUHLIG, SHELBY MARIA, secondary school educator; d. Robert J. and Deborah L. Males; m. Jon W. Ruhlig, July 29, 2005. BS in Secondary Edn., Ctrl. Mich. U., Mount Pleasant, 2002. Tchr. Riverveiw Cmty. H.S., Riverview, Mich., 2003—. Office Phone: 734-285-7361.

RUIZ, COOKIE, performing company executive; BA in English, Spanish, Wright St. U., Dayton, Ohio. Cert. Fund Raising Executive, 2002. Pres. Jr. League, Austin, Tex.; dir. fund devel. Ballet Austin, 1996-97, gen. mgr., 1997—99, exec. dir., 1999—. Recipient American Red Cross Clara Barton Medal of Honor. Mem.: bd. Austin Convention & Visitors Bureau, Assoc. of Fundraising Professionals, bd. trustees, Dance USA. Office: Ballet Austin 3002 Guadalupe St Austin TX 78705-2818

RUIZ, MICHELE ILENE, lawyer; b. Washington, Nov. 3, 1969; BS, Cornell U., 1991; JD, U. Chgo., 1994. Bar: U.S. Dist. Ct. (no. dist.) Ill. 1994. Assoc. McDermott, Will & Emery, Chgo., 1994—96; ptnr. Sidley Austin LLP, Chgo., 1996—. Office: Sidley Austin LLP One S Dearborn Chicago IL 60603 E-mail: mruiz@sidley.com.

RUIZ, MIRIAM, secondary school educator; b. San Lorenzo, Puerto Rico, May 15, 1968; d. Margaro Ruiz and Salvadora Vázquez; m. Pedro J. Mañón, Dec. 1995. B in Edn. and secondary Spanish (magna cum laude), U. Puerto Rico, 1992, M in Edn. Adminstrn. and Supervision, 2005. Lic. secondary edn. Tex. Tchr. Spanish Nuestra Senora la Providencia Acad., Rio Piedras, PR, 1992—94, Panamerica Lang. Inst., Guaynabo, PR, 1992—98, Caribbean Preparatory Sch., Hato Rey, PR, 1994—2004, Sam Rayburn HS, Pasadena, Tex., 2004—. Com. mem. sch. accreditation Middle State Assn., Hato Ray, PR, 2003—04. Mem.: Curriculum and Supr. Assn., Nat. Tchrs. Assn., Tex. State Tchrs. Assn., Fgn. Lang. Tchrs. Assn. Avocations: diving, reading, music, travel, writing. Home: 103 Marina Oaks Dr Kemah TX 77565 Office: Sam Rayburn HS 2121 Cherrybrook Pasadena TX 77502 Office Phone: 713-477-3601.

RUIZ, VANESSA, judge; b. San Juan, P.R., Mar. 22, 1950; d. Fernando and Irma (Bosch) Ruiz-Suria; married; m. David E. Birenbaum, Oct. 22, 1983; stepchildren: Tracy, Matthew. BA, Wellesley Coll., 1972; JD, Georgetown U., 1975. Bar: D.C. 1972. Assoc. Fried, Frank, Harris, Shrives & Kampelman, Washington, 1975—83; sr. mgr., counsel Sears World Trade Inc., Washington, 1983—87; founding ptnr. Sloan, Lehner & Ruiz, Washington, 1987—89; ptnr. Pepper, Hamilton & Scheetz, Washington, 1989—91; dep. corporation counsel, legal counsel div. D.C., Washington, 1991—93, prin. dep. corporation counsel, 1993—94, corporation counsel, 1994; assoc. judge D.C. Ct. of Appeals, Washington, 1994—. Spkr. in field; adjunct prof. Georgetown U. Co-author: Europe Without Frontiers: A Lawyers' Guide, 1989. Recipient Judge of the Yr. award, Hispanic Bar Assn., 2001. Mem.: ABA, Hispanic Bar Assn., DC, Am. Law Inst., Coun. for Ct. Excellence, Nat. Assn. Women Judges (pres.-elect), Inter-Am. Bar Assn. Office: DC Ct of Appeals 500 Indiana Ave NW Fl 6 Washington DC 20001-2131 Office Fax: 202-626-8868.*

RUIZ-BRAVO, NORKA, federal agency administrator; B in biology, Goucher Coll., Towson, Md., 1975; M in biology, Yale U., PhD in biology, 1983. Post-doctoral fellow in physiol. chemistry Johns Hopkins U.; post-doctoral fellow in biochemistry and molecular biology U. Tex. MD Anderson Cancer Ctr., mem. faculty, 1983—89, Baylor Coll. Medicine, Houston, 1983—89; sci. rev. adminstr. Office Rev. Activities Nat. Inst. Gen. Med. Sciences, NIH, 1990, program dir. Divsn. Genetics and Biology, 1992, acting dep. dir. Divsn. Minority Opportunities in Rsch., spl. asst. Office Extramural Activities; sci. rev. adminstr. Nat. Ctr. Human Genome Rsch., NIH; dep. dir. Divsn. Cancer Biology Nat. Cancer Inst., NIH, 1997—98, acting dir. Divsn. Cancer Biology, 1998—99; dep. assoc. dir. extramural activities Nat. Inst. Gen. Med. Sciences, NIH, 1999—2000, assoc. dir. extramural activities, 2000—03; dep. dir. extramural rsch. NIH, 2003—. Mem.: AAAS, Soc. Devel. Biology, Am. Soc. Cell Biology. Office: NIH 9000 Rockville Pike Bethesda MD 20892 Office Phone: 301-496-1096. Office Fax: 301-402-3469. E-mail: nb9b@nih.gov.

RUIZ DIAZ, CAROLYN ANN, secondary school educator; b. San Francisco, Oct. 10, 1970; d. Michael and Dolores Goding; m. Fermin Ramiro Ruiz Diaz, Feb. 3, 2001; 1 child, Jeremiah. BA in Edn., Coll. of Ozarks, Point Lookout, Mo., 1996; MA in TESOL, SE Mo. State U., 2005. Cert. tchr. Mo. Spanish tchr. Cabool HS, Mo., Strafford HS, Mo., 1998—99; apiculture vol. Peace Corps, Fulgencio Yegros, Caazapa, Paraguay, 1999—2001; Spanish/ESOL tchr. Verona HS, Mo., 2001—. Mem.: NEA (assoc.). Roman Catholic. Office Phone: 417-498-6775.

RUIZ-VARGAS, YOLANDA, finance educator; b. Mayagüez, P.R., Apr. 24, 1968; d. Samuel Ruiz and Isabel Vargas. BSBA cum laude, U. P.R., Mayagüez, 1990, MBA, 1994; PhD, U. of Tex., Edinburg, 2000. Acctg. officer Calzados HQ, Inc, Mayagüez, 1990—93; planner trainee Cutler Hammer of PR, Cabo Rojo, PR, 1994; tchg. asst. U. of Texas-Pan Am., Edinburg, 1996—99; instr. U. P.R., Mayagüez, 1994—96, asst. prof., 2000—03, assoc. prof., 2003—, assoc. dean for rsch. and grad. affairs, 2004—. Co-coordinator UPR- Ctr. for Profesional Enhancement, Mayagüez, PR, 2002—02; faculty rep. Grad. Coun. - UPR Mayagüez, Mayagüez, PR, 2001—03; faculty advisor 2002 Ph.D. Project Fin. Doctoral Students Assn. Conf., San Antonio, —, 2001 Ph.D. Project Fin. Doctoral Students Assn. Conf., Toronto, Canada; liaison 2000 PhD Project Fin. Doctoral Students Assn. Conf., Seattle; planning com. mem. 1999 PhD Project Fin. Doctoral Students Assn. Conf., Orlando; mem. 2002 FMA Ann. Meeting Program Com., San Antonio; vis. asst. prof. Tex. A&M Internat. U., Laredo, 1999—2000. Scholar acad. scholar, U. P.R., 1996—2000. Mem.: Am. Fin. Assn., Internat. Coun. for Small Bus., Fin. Mgmt. Assn. Internat., Alpha Delta Kappa, Beta Gamma Sigma. Avocations: reading, travel. Office: U PR COBA - PO Box 9009 Mayaguez PR 00681-9009 Business E-Mail: yruiz@caribe.net. E-mail: yruiz@uprm.edu.

RULE, ANN, author; 4 children. Degree in English, U. Washington, 1958, PhD in Humane Letters, Willamette U., 2004, postgrad. in police sci. Former policewoman, Seattle; speaker on subject of serial killers. Author (non-fiction books): The Stranger Beside Me, 1980, The I-5 Killer, Want-Ad Killer, Lust Killer, Beautiful Seattle, 1984, Small Sacrifices, 1987, If You Really Loved Me, 1991, Everything She Ever Wanted, 1992, (novel): Possession, 1983, A Rose for Her Grave, 1993, You Belong to Me, 1994, Dead by Sunset, 1995, A Fever in the Heart, 1995, Green River, Running Red, 2004, Kiss Me Kill Me: And Other True Cases, 2004; exec. prodr. ABC mini-series Small Sacrifices, 1989 (Peabody award), NBC mini-series Dead by Sunset, 1995, CBS mini-series And Never Let Her Go, 2000, USA Network mini-series The Stranger Beside Me, 2003; contbr. over 1400 articles to newspapers and mags. including True Detective, Cosmopolitan, and others. Vol. Seattle Crisis Clinic. Recipient: Washington State Governor's award. Address: PO Box 98846 Seattle WA 98198-0846

RULE, MOLLY MCCORKLE, music educator; d. Leon Marshall McCorkle Jr. and Patricia Esther Rengert; m. Benjamin William Rule, July 15, 2005. MusB, Capital U., Columbus, Ohio, 1998, M Music Edn., 2006. Tchr. Burbank Early Childhood Sch., Columbus, 1998—99; music tchr. We Joy Sing, Columbus, Pickerington Local Schs., Columbus, 2002—; English tchr. Divsn. Global Missions, Kosice, Slovakia, 2000—01. Condr. Satellite of Columbus Children's Choir, 2004—. Vol. youth programs Hilltop Luth. Ch., Columbus, 2006—. Named Tchr. of Yr., Fairfield Elem. Sch., 2005. Mem.: Orgn. Am. Kodaly Educators, Am. Choral Dirs. Assn., Phi Delta Kappa.

RUMFOLO, MARILU, financial analyst, non-profit corporation executive; b. Houston, July 19, 1953; d. Walter John and Lucille (Jones) R. Grad., Arrons Sch. Real Estate, 1978; student, U. Houston, 1979. Lic. real estate agt. Jr. acct. Gen. Leisure Corp., Houston, 1973-75; security cons. Burns Internat. Security, Houston, 1975-77; founder, dir. govt. affairs Time Energy Systems, Inc., Houston, 1977-83; founder, exec. dir., chmn. bd. trustees The Children's Drug Abuse Network, Houston, 1983—; founder, pres. Sun Am. Fin., LLC, 2000; general securities, principal, pres. founder Rumfolo & Assocs., Securities, LP, 2000—; founder, pres. Tex. Capital Securities, LLC, 2002. Bd. dirs. Eliza Johnston Home for Aging, Houston, 1981-82; chmn. bd. Citizens United for Pub. Edn., Houston, 1980-82; candidate city council, Houston, 1981, 83; team capt. Am. Heart Assn. Houston, 1982. Recipient Drugbuster award Children's Drug Abuse Network, 1985; honoree ann. appreciation breakfast for outstanding work in community, County Commr. Houston, 1986; named Rep. of Yr., Tex., 2001. Mem.: Order Eastern Star (officer 1986-87). Republican. Avocations: swimming, reading, poetry, walking.

RUNDIO, JOAN PETERS (JO RUNDIO), retired public information officer; b. Dearborn, Mich., Mar. 17, 1941; d. Joe and Donna (Sells) Peters; m. Florian (Pug) Frank Rundio Jr., Sept. 8., 1971; children: Jeffrey Daniel, David Eric. Diploma, Bronson Meth. Sch. Nursing, 1962; BA, U. Redlands, 1978; MPA, U. South Ala., 1987. RN, Mich. Emergency nurse Bronson Meth. Hosp., Kalamazoo, 1962-63, Queen's Med. Ctr., Honolulu, 1963-65; orthopaedic nurse Honolulu Med. Group, 1965-72; sch. nurse Corpus Christi Sch. Dist., Tex., 1979-81; pub. health nurse Tri-County Health Dept., Traverse City, Mich., 1983-85; adminstrv. intern City of Troy, Mich., 1987-88; acting econ. devel. dir. City of Traverse City, 1988-89, asst. city mgr., 1990-98; mgr. personal health svcs. Tri-County Health Dept., Traverse City, 1989; ret., 1998. Mediator Conflict Resolution Svc., 1998—, pres., 2000—02, exec. com., 2002—04. V.p. Women's Econ. Devel. Orgn., Traverse City, 1993-95, mem., 1984-2002; mem. Traverse City Planning Commn., 1995-97; rep. Traverse City Schs. Adv. Com., 1982-85, 88-89; trustee Nat. Cherry Festival, 1996-98; bd. mem. Conflict Resolution Svc., 1999-2004. Recipient James H. Boyd award U. South Ala., Mobile, 1987. Mem. AAUW (sec. Traverse City br. 2000—02), NOW (founding mem. Meridian, Miss. chpt. 1973), Michigan City. Mgmt. Assn. (bd. dirs. 1996-98), Internat. City Mgmt. Assn., Cherryland Humane Soc., Pi Sigma Alpha. Avocations: travel, reading, canoeing, cross country skiing.

RUNDQUIST, ELIZABETH ANN, art therapist; b. Bklyn, June 17, 1933; d. Carl Edgar and Margaret Langford Rundquist; children: Arthur L. Porter Jr., Karl L. Porter, Edward S. Porter, Elizabeth S. Cohen. BS, CUNY, N.Y., 1988; MA, NYU, N.Y., 1991. Bd. cert. art therapist. Art therapist supr. N.Y. City Health & Hosp. Corp., N.Y., 1992—98; art therapist Vantage Health System, Dumont, NJ, 2000—. Psychotherapist pvt., Teaneck, NJ, 2003—. Contrbg. author Tuning the Therapeutic Instrument, 2000; clergy vestments, St. Ann & The Holy Trinity Episc. Ch., Bklyn., N.Y.; prodr.: Not 1984 Film Festival, 2005. Vol. Peace Corps., Malaysia, 1971—74; curator/prod. film festival St Ann & the Holy Trinity Episc. Ch., Bklyn., 1984. Scholar, Art Students League, 1978, Provincetown Art Assn., 1985, CUNY, 1988. Mem.: Am. Group Psychotherapy Assn., Am. Art Therapy Assn.

RUNFOLA, SHEILA KAY, nurse; b. Canton, Ohio, Feb. 8, 1944; d. Benjamin and M. Suzanne (deBord) Suarez; m. Steven Joseph Runfola, Aug. 17, 1968; children: Michael, Janine, Christine; stepchildren: Stephanie Bufalini, Darlene Teran. BS in Nursing, St. John Coll. Cleve., 1966; teaching credential jr. coll. nursing, UCLA Ext., San Diego, 1973. RN, Calif.; cert. occupational health nurse, cert. pub. health nurse. Staff nurse emergency rm. Leland Meml. Hosp., Riverdale, Md., 1966-67; staff nurse/team leader med./surg. Mercy Hosp., San Diego, 1967-68; staff nurse, charge nurse emergency dept., dept. radiology U. Calif.-San Diego Med.Ctr., 1968-76; staff devel./asst. dir. nurses TLC Nursing Home, El Cajon, Calif., 1978-80; staff nurse/charge nurse emergency dept. Kaiser Permanente Hosp., San Diego, 1980-89, staff nurse emergency dept. Sacramento, Calif., 1989-90, house supr., 1992-94, case mgr. occupational medicine, 1995—; health svcs. nurse U.S. Automobile Assn., Sacramento, 1990-95. Contbr. articles to profl. jours. Leader Girls Scouts Am., San Diego and Sacramento, 1982-91, treas., local svc. team, 1986-89, 90; parent rep. Elk Grove (Calif.) Sch. Bd. for Elk Grove H.s., 1994, co-chair Sober Grad. Night, 1993-95. Mem. Sacramento Valley Occupational Health Nurses (v.p. 1992-95, sec. 1998—, election chair 1998), Newcomers Club, Calif. State Assn. Occupl. Health Nurse (bd. dirs. 1998—, newsletter editor). Democrat. Roman Catholic. Avocations: crafts (quilting), piano, reading, cooking, boating. Office: Kaiser Permanente Dept Occupl Med 6600 Bruceville Rd Sacramento CA 95823-4671 Home: 260 Tall Spruce Cir Brighton CO 80601-5356

RUNGE, KAY KRETSCHMAR, library director; b. Davenport, Iowa, Dec. 9, 1946; d. Alfred Edwin and Ina (Paul) Kretschmar; children: Peter Jr., Katherine. BS in History Edn., Iowa State U., Ames, 1969; MLS, U. Iowa, Iowa City, 1970. Pub. svc. libr. Anoka County Libr., Blaine, Minn., 1971-72; cataloger Augustana Coll., Rock Island, Ill., 1972-74; dir. Scott County Libr. Sys., Eldridge, Iowa, 1974-85, Davenport (Iowa) Pub. Libr., 1985—2001, Des Moines Pub. Libr., 2001—. V.p. Quad-Cities Conv. and Visitors Bur., 1992—97, Quad-Cities Grad. Study Ctr., 1992—2001, Downtown Davenport Devel. Corp., 1992—2000, Hall of Honor Bd., Davenport Ctrl. H.S., 1992—95, Brenton Bank Bd., 1995—2001, Wells Fargo Bank Bd., 2001; steering com. Quad-Cities Vision for the Future, 1987—91, Humanities Iowa, 1993—2000, chair, 1998—99; bd. govs. Iowa State U. Found., 1991—; citizens adv. coun. Iowa State U., 1998—2000, Leadership Iowa, 1998—99; adv. bd. U. Iowa Sch. Libr. Sci., 1999—, adj. prof., 2000—01; devel. bd. Iowa State U. Found., 2000—; active Greater Des Moines Leadership, 2002—03; dean's adv. bd. Liberal Arts and Sci. Coll. Iowa State U., 2004—; bd. regents Iowa Pub. Radio Exec. Coun., 2005—; bd. dirs. River Ctr. for Performing Arts, Davenport, 1983—97, Iowa State U. Rsch. Pk., 1998—2000, Hamilton/Kaplan U., 2002—, Davenport One, Downtown Devel., 2000—01, Des Moines Operation Downtown, 2004—; chmn. bd. dirs. Am. Inst. Commerce, 1989—98. Recipient Svc. Key award Iowa State U. Alumni Assn., 1979, ALA/ALTA Nat. Advocacy Honor Roll award, 2000, Des Moines Women of Influence award, 2004, Carrie Chapman Catt Pub. Advancement award Iowa State U. Alumni Assn., 2006; named Quad City Panhellenic Woman of Yr., 1998. Mem. ALA (chmn. libr. adminstrs. and mgrs. div., fundraising sect. 1988, bd. dirs., Exhibits Round Table 2003-), Iowa Libr. Assn. (pres. 1983, Mem. of Yr. award 2000), Pub. Libr. Assn. (bd. dirs. 1990-99, pres. 2000-01), Iowa Edn. Media Assn. (Intellectual Freedom award 1984), Alpha Delta Pi (alumni state pres. 1978). Lutheran. Office: Des Moines Pub Libr 1000 Grand Ave Des Moines IA 50309-3027 Address: 126 Forest Rd Davenport IA 52803 Office Phone: 563-355-7667.

RUNGE, LINDA JACOB, university administrator; b. Nashville, Dec. 10, 1947; d. William G. and Margaret (Long) Jacob; m. Roger Robinson Runge, Feb. 19, 1981; children: Scott Jacob, Christopher Daniel. BS in BA, U. Tenn., 1977; MBA in Mgmt., U. Tenn./Tenn. State U., 1984; MA in Mgmt. and Health Care, Cen. Mich. U., 1983. Adminstrv. sec. St. Thomas Hosp., Nashville, 1969-73; exec. sec. Commerce Union Bank, Nashville, 1973-74; exec. asst. Stanley D. Lindsey & Assocs., Ltd., Nashville, 1974-77; office svcs. mgr. No. Telecom, Nashville, 1978-80; office mgr. Pediatric Assocs. of Savannah, P.C., Ga., 1980-82; mgr. operational svcs. The Great Savannah Exposition, 1983-85; dir. retention The Savannah Coll. of Art and Design, 1985-93, registrar, 1993—97, admission counselor, 1997—. Vol. March of Dimes, Savannah, 1991—, Oatland Island Edn. Ctr., Savannah, 1990-91; usher, vol. Savannah Theatre, 1998-2000, Savannah Music Festival, 2005, 2006, Savannah Film Festival, 2004, 05, 06; lt. col. Med. Svcs. Corps, USAR, 1975—. Decorated Army Commendation medal, Army Achievement medal. Mem. Oglethorpe Bus. and Profl. Women (sec. 1991, 2004-06, 1st v.p. 1992, 2d v.p. 1993). Mem. Ch. of Christ. Avocations: travel, reading, sports, party planning, photography. Home: 107 Junco Way Savannah GA 31419-9090 Office: Savannah Coll Art & Design 342 Bull St Savannah GA 31401-4354 Office Phone: 912-525-5954. Business E-Mail: lrunge@scad.edu.

RUNKLE, BEATRIZ PAMELA, pediatrician, educator; AB, Radcliffe Coll., Cambridge, Mass., 1969; MD, Georgetown U., 1975. Diplomate Am. Bd. Pediat., 1983. Resident pediat. Georgetown Univ. Med. Ctr., 1975—79; fellow neonatal-perinatal medicine Univ. Miami, 1980—83; asst. prof. pediat. Emory U. Sch. Medicine, Atlanta, 1983—86; clin. asst. prof. pediat. Georgetown U. Sch. Medicine, Washington, 1986—; neonatologist Va. Hosp. Ctr., Arlington, 1986—, med. dir. nurseries, 1991—2004. Fellow: Am. Acad. Pediat. Office: Va Hosp Ctr 1701 N George Mason Dr Arlington VA 22205 Office Phone: 703-558-6675.

RUNKLE, ETHEL MONA, artist; b. Davenport, Iowa, Dec. 4, 1921; d. Louis and Agnes (Jungjohann) Behrens; m. Karl Ehresman Runkle, Jan. 25, 1947; children: Carol Ann, Richard Louis. Grad., Shimer Coll., Ill., 1942; student, St. Ambrose Coll., Davenport, Iowa, 1943, Chgo. Art Inst., 1945, N.Y. Sch. Interior Design, 1955. Illustrator Rock Island (Ill.) Arsenal, Huntington Hist. Soc. Color, San Diego, 1942-44; stewardess United Air Lines, Chgo., 1944-46; craft dir. Westbury (N.Y.) Country Club, 1967; owner, operator Polynesian Fashions, Huntington, N.Y., 1967-71, The Woodshed, Escondido, Calif., 1975-77; art dir. Holland-Am. Lines, Seattle, 1986-87; artist San Diego, 1983—. Operator Hawaii Condo Rentals, San Diego, 1964—; art demonstrator San Marcos Art Assn., Calif., 1987, Escondido Art Assn., Calif., 1987, La Jolla Art Assn., La Jolla, Calif., 1986, So. Calif. Executed mural, 1987; represented in pvt. artist collections; exhibited in Nat. Watercolor Soc., L.A., 1987. Historian Clipped Wings, San Diego, 1985-86, Lloyd Harbor Hist. Assn., N.Y., 1966-71, Huntington Hist. Soc., N.Y., 1963-71, Soc. Preservation L.I. Antiquities, N.Y., 1967-70. Recipient Pres.'s Citation of Merit, Nat. Soc. Paint Casein & Acrylic, N.Y., 1988, Am. Watercolor Soc., Am. Soc. Marine Painters, San Bernadino Art Mus., award Escondido Art Assn., 1987. Mem.: Nat. Watercolor Soc. (cert., regional rep.), San Diego Watercolor Soc. (pres.), North County Vallecitos Art Assn. (pres.), Am. Soc. Marine Artists (bd. dirs.). Republican. Lutheran. Avocations: marine biology, snorkeling, travel, reading, history.

RUNNER, KATHLEEN KAHLE, secondary school educator; b. Lima, Ohio, Mar. 6, 1955; d. John H. and Catherine M. Kahle; m. Jack C. Runner, July 15, 1978; children: Kristen, Kelly. BS, Bowling Green State U., 1977; postgrad., Toledo U., Ashland U. Tchr. Ft. Jennings (Ohio) Sch., 1977—78, Holy Angels Sch., Sandusky, Ohio, 1978—81, St. Mary Ctrl. Cath. H.S., Sandusky, Ohio, 1989—. Mem. Erie County Eating Disorder Task Force, 1995—; mem. Tri County Student Svcs., 1990—2000. Mem. exec. bd. U.S. Power Squadron, Sandusky, 2000—. Mem.: NEA, Ohio Cath. Educator Assn., Ohio Edn. Assn. Home: 620 Marshall Ave Sandusky OH 44870 Office: St Mary Ctrl Catholic HS 410 W Jefferson St Sandusky OH 44870

RUNOLFSON, ANNE, soprano, actress; m. Tony Adams (dec. 2005). Performer: (albums) At Sea, (concerts) The Orch. of St. Lukes, The Dutch Metropole Orch., The St. Louis Symphony, The Utah Symphony, The Milwaukee Symphony, The Indianapolis Symphony, (concert) The Long Island Philharmonic; actress (Broadway plays) Les Misérables, The Phantom of the Opera, Aspects of Love, 1990, Cyrano-The Musical, 1993, Victor/Victoria, 1995, James Joyce's The Dead, 2000, (Off-Broadway plays) Listen to My Heart, Jack's Holiday, Cather Country, (regional plays) A Little Night Music, Show Boat, Funny Girl.*

RUNOLFSON, MARILYN DOLORES, special education educator; d. Frances (Baier) MacDonald, Margaretta MacDonald (Stepmother), Clifford MacDonald; m. Randall Runolfson, Aug. 8, 1981; children: Samuel, Simon, Shaina. BS in Elem. Edn., Weber State U., 1995; MEd in Spl. Edn., Utah State U., 2001. Cert. tchr. spl. edn. Utah State Office of Edn., 1995. Reading specialist Ogden (Utah) City Sch. Dist., 1996; spl. edn. tchr. Weber County Sch. Dist., Ogden, Utah, 1996—2002, mentor, cooperating tchr., behavior specialist, 2000—03, spl. edn. coord., 2003—. Mem mentor and induction com. Weber County Sch. Dist., Ogden, Utah, 2002—; mem. mentor and induction com. Utah Signal Project, Mentor and Induction Com., Salt Lake City, 2002—; presenter in field. Author: A Mentor's Handbook, (calendar) The Art and Soul of Tching.: A Weekly Calendar for New Spl. Edn. Tchrs., 2003. Mem.: Coun. for Exceptional Children. Roman Catholic. Avocations: reading, gardening, needlecrafts. Office: Weber School District 5320 S Adams Avenue Ogden UT 84405 E-mail: mrunolfson@weber.k12.ut.us.

RUNOWICZ, CAROLYN DILWORTH, physician; b. Willimantic, Conn., May 1, 1951; d. S. Robert and Aline (Bergeron) Dilworth. BA, U. Conn., 1973; MD, Jefferson Med. Coll., 1977. Diplomate in ob-gyn. and gynecol. oncology Am. Bd. Ob-Gyn. Resident in ob-gyn. Mt. Sinai Hosp., NYC, 1977-81, fellow gynecol. oncology, 1981-83; instr., dir. divsn. ob-gyn. Albert Einstein Coll. Medicine, NYC, 1983-88, asst. prof. dept. ob-gyn., 1988-93, assoc. prof., 1993—98; dir. gynecologic and oncology, divsn. ob-gyn. Our Lady of Mercy, Bronx, NY, 1988; prof., dir. gynecol. oncology dept. ob-gyn. Montefiore Med. Ctr., NYC, 1998—2001; prof. Columbia U. Coll. Physicians and Surgeons, 2001—03; vice chmn. ob-gyn. St. Luke's Roosevelt Hosp., 2001—03; dir. Carole and Ray Neag Comprehensive Cancer Ctr., prof. ob-gyn., NE chair exptl. oncology U. Conn. Health Ctr., Famington, NY, 2003—. Presdl. appointee Nat. Cancer Adv. Bd., 2004—, presdl. appointee chair, 2006—; lectr. in field. Author: Menopause Book, 1994, To Be Alive, 1995, Woman and Cancer, 1999, Answer to Cancer, 2004; contbr. chapters to books, articles to profl. jours. Galloway fellow Sloan Kettering Meml. Hosp., NYC, 1980. Fellow: Am. Coll. Ob-Gyn.; mem.: AMA, ACS (pres. 2005), Am. Gynecol. Club, Am. Cancer Soc. (pres. 2005—06), NY Obstet. Soc., Am. Gynecol. Obstetrics Soc., Soc. Gynecologic Oncologists, Am. Med. Women's Assn. Office: U Conn Health Ctr 263 Farmington Ave Farmington CT 06032 Office Phone: 860-679-2809. Business E-Mail: crunowicz@uchc.edu.

RUNQUIST, LISA A., lawyer; b. Mpls., Sept. 22, 1952; d. Ralf E. and Violet R. BA, Hamline U., 1973; JD, U. Minn., 1976. Bar: Minn. 1977, Calif. 1978, U.S. Dist. Ct. (ctrl. dist.) Calif. 1985, U.S. Supreme Ct. 1995. Assoc. Caldwell & Toms, L.A., 1978-82; ptnr. Runquist & Flagg, L.A., 1982-85; pvt. practice Runquist & Assocs., L.A., 1985-99, 2005—, Runquist & Zybach LLP, L.A., 1999—2005. Mem. adv. bd. Exempt Orgn. Tax Rev., 1990—, Calif. State U. L.A. Continuing Edn. Acctg. and Tax Program, 1995—. Mem. editl. bd.: ABA Bus. Law Today, 1994—2002; author: The ABCs of Nonprofits, 2005; contbr. chapters to books. Recipient Outstanding Lawyer award, ABA Bus. Law Sect., 1999. Mem. ABA (bus. law sect. coun. 1995-99, com. on nonprofit corps. 1986—, chair 1991-95, subcom. current devels. in nonprofit corp. law 1989—, chair 1989-91, subcom. rels. orgns. 1989—, chair 1987-91, 95-98, subcom. legal guidebook for dirs. 1986—, subcom. model nonprofit corp. act, partnerships and unincorp. bus. orgns. com. 1987—, sec. of taxation exempt orgns. com. 1987—, subcom. religious orgns. 1989—, chair 1995-97, 2005—, state regulation of securities com. 1988-99, ad hoc com. info. tech. 1997-2003, chmn., 1997-98, co-chmn. 1998-2002, sect. liaison to tech. coun. 1997-2000, co-chmn. subcom. non-exempt orgns. 1997-2003, corp. laws com. 1999-2005, subcom. guidebook for dirs. of closely held corps. chair 2000-04, liaison ALI/ABA principles of law of nonprofit orgns. project 2003—, standing com. solo and small firm practitioners 2004-05, co-chair state and local regulation subcom. 2003-05), Calif. Bar Assn. (bus. law sect., nonprofit and unincorp. orgns. com. 1985-92, 93-96, 97—, chair 1989-91, 2006—), Christian Legal Soc., Ctr. Law and Religious Freedom, Christian Mgmt. Assn. (dir. 1983-89). Office: 17554 Community St Northridge CA 91325 Office Phone: 818-760-8986. Business E-Mail: lisa@runquist.com.

RUNTE, ROSEANN, academic administrator; b. Kingston, NY, Jan. 31, 1948; arrived in Can., 1971, naturalized, 1983; d. Robert B. and Anna Loretta O'Reilly; m. Hans-Rainer Runte, Aug. 9, 1969. BA summa cum laude, SUNY, New Paltz, 1968; MA, U. Kans., 1969, PhD, 1974; DLitt (hon.), Acadia U., 1989, Meml. U., 1990, U. Vest Timisoara, 1996, U. Arad, 2001; Assoc. (hon.), Moraine Valley C.C., 2003. Lectr. Bethany Coll., W.Va., 1970—71; lectr. adult studies St. Mary's U., Halifax, N.S., Canada, 1971—72; from lectr. to assoc. prof. Dalhousie U., Halifax, N.S., Canada, 1972—83, asst. dean, 1980—82, chmn. dept. French, 1980—83; pres. U. Sainte-Anne, Pointe-de-l'Eglise, N.S., Canada, 1983—88; prin. Glendon Coll., Toronto, Canada, 1988—94; pres. Victoria U., 1994—2001, Old Dominion U., 2001—. Bd. dirs. Banque Nat., Va. Advanced Carrier and Shipbldg. Integration Ctr., Le Groupe Jean Coutu, 2003—06, Va. Nat. Def. Indsl. Authority. Author: Brumes Bleues, 1982, Faux-Soleils, 1984, Birmanie Blues, 1993; editor: Studies in 18th Century Culture, vols. VII, VIII, IX, 1977—79, A Canadian in Love, 2000, The Passionate Mind, 2000; lit. rev. editor: French Rev., 1988—94; editor: Lit. Rsch., 1994—97; co-editor: Man and Nature, 1982, Le Development Regional, 1986—87, From Orality to Literature, 1991, Lectures Canadiennes, 1993, Visions of Beauty, 1995, The Foundation for International Training: 25 Years of International Development, 2001; co-translator: Local Development, 1987; mem. editl. bd. Purdue Romance Lang. Series, 2001—. V.p. Can. commn. UNESCO, 1991—92, pres., 1992—96; vice-chair exec. bd. Found. for Internat. Tng., 1994—95, chair bd., 1995—2000; internat. adv. bd. Expo 2000, 1995—2000; v.p. Assn. Internat. des études québecoises, 1999—2001; mem. Internat. Women's Forum, 1998—; chair comm. internat. edn. Am. Coun. on Edn., 2004—06; chair accreditation com. visit NCAA, 2004—, 2005, 2006; commr. Southeastern Accreditation Commn., 2004—; chair Gottschalk Prize Com., 1994; chair publs. com. Hannah Found., 1989—92; vice-chair bd. Gardiner Mus., 1994—2001; mem. Commn. Langs. Instrn., Ontario, Canada, 1999—2001; chair prix du salon Livre Com., 1998; hon. life mem. UNESCO, 2003; bd. dirs. Assn. Med. Svcs., 1989—92; adv. bd. Nat. Libr., 1984—91; bd. dirs. Urban League, United Way, Va. Stage Co., Second Wind Dance Co., Hampton Roads Partnership, Greater Norfolk Corp. Decorated Order of Can., Ordre du Mérite France, Order Acad. Palmes; recipient Fr. Coppée award, French Acad., 1989, Queen Elizabeth Jubilee medal, 2002, Woman of Distinction award, Zonta Group, 2004, Environ. award, Norfolk Environment Commn., 2004, WFXN Trailblazer award, 2004, Lighthouse award, Elizabeth River Project, Tidewater Humanitarian award, Nat. Conf. Cmty. and Justice, 2006, Women of Distinction award, YWCA, 2006, Humanitarian award, NCCJ, 2006, Billbro award Servant Leadership, 2006; Regents scholar, SUNY, 1965, Title IV grantee, NDEA, 1968. Fellow: Royal Soc. Can., Soc. Study Values in Edn., World Acad. Arts and Scis.; mem.: Royal Coll. Physicians and Surgeons (exec. com. 1998—2002), Soc. for Study Higher Edn. (bd. dirs. 1988—90), Can. Soc. 18th Century Studies (pres. 1975—76), Atlantic Soc. 18th Century Studies (pres. 1972—76), Can. Fedn. Humanities (pres. 1982—84), Internat. Assn. of Comparative Lit. (treas. 1985—91, sec. 1991—94), Internat. Soc. 18th Century Studies (assoc. treas. 1983—87), World Parliament of Cultures, Club of Rome (exec. com. 1999—2006), Knights of Malta (grande dame 1991—), Phi Delta Kappa, Delta Kappa Gamma. Home: 5000 Edgewater Dr Norfolk VA 23508 Office: Old Dominion U Norfolk VA 23529 Office Phone: 757-683-3159. E-mail: rrunte@odu.edu.

RUNYON, MELISSA K., psychologist, educator; b. Rockford, Ill., May 8, 1967; d. Homer and Yvonne Runyon. BS, Ea. Ky. Univ., 1989, MS, 1991, Nova Southeastern Univ., 1994, PhD, 1996. Lic. Psychologist Fla., 1998, N.J., 2000. Psychologist intern Stanford Univ. Med. Sch., Palo Alto, Calif., 1995—96; post doctoral fellow Univ. Miami Sch. of Medicine, Miami, Fla., 1997—98, rsch. assoc., 1998—99; asst. prof. UMDNJ, 1999—2001, asst. prof. psychiatry, 2001—04, assoc. prof., 2004—. Contbr. articles pub. to prof. jour., chapters to books, scientific papers. Mem.: APA, Am. Profl. Soc. on Abused Children, Phi Theta Kappa, Psi Chi.

RUPERD, THERESA, music educator; b. Kansas City, Kans., Nov. 1, 1972; d. Walter Raymond and Karen Lorene R. BA, U. Mo., 1995. Freelance musician, ind. music tchr., Kans. City, Kans., 1991—. Singer Madrigalia Bar Nonne, Overland Park, Kans., 1996—, Carolers of Note, Overland Park, 1996—; mgr. JW Pepper WJ Music and Gifts Divsn., Overland Park, 1996—2006, Independence, Mo., 1999—2001; mem. U. Mo.-Kansas City Conservatory Women's Com., 1998—; singer Musica Sacra, Kans. City, 2003—; mgr. Music divsn. JW Pepper Wingert Jones, Kansas City, Mo., 2006—. Author: (newsletter) KCFA Newsletter, 1991-96; editor: (newsletter) Pieces of Pi, 1996-97; contbr. articles to profl. jours. Founder, v.p. Kansas City Met. Opera. Mem. Fedn. Music Tchrs., Music Tchrs. Nat. Assn., Kansas City Music Tchrs. Assn., Kansas City Flute Assn., Nat. Flute Assn., Sigma Alpha Iota, Mortar Board, Omicron Delta Kappa, Golden Key. Avocations: gardening, cooking, travel, reading. Office: JW Pepper Wingert Jones Music Divsn 11225 Colorado Ave Kansas City MO 64137 Personal E-mail: truperd@juno.com. E-mail: truperd@kcmetroopera.com.

RUPERT, ELIZABETH ANASTASIA, retired dean; b. Emlenton, Pa., July 12, 1918; d. John Hamilton and Eva Blanche (Elliott) R. Diploma, Altoona Sch. Commerce, 1936; BS in Edn., Clarion State Coll., 1959; MSLS, Syracuse U., 1962; PhD, U. Pitts., 1970. Sec. Quaker State Oil Refining Corp., 1939-56; tchr., libr. Oil City Area Schs., 1959-61; libr. Venango campus Clarion (Pa.) U., 1961-62, prof. Sch. Libr. Sci., 1962-70, dean Sch. Libr. Sci., Coll. Libr. Sci., 1971-85; prof. emeritus, 1994. Interim pres. Clarion U., spring, 1977; acct. William Rupert Mortuary, Inc., 1948—88.

Author: Pennsylvania Practicum Program for School Librarians: An Appraisal, 1970; mem. ad hoc edit. com. Pa. Media Guidelines, Pa. Dept. Edn., 1976, author (with others) Encylopedia of Library and Information Science, 1984. Bd. dirs. Knox Pub. Libr., 1991-97; mem. Abscurf; mem. numerous bds. and couns. Church of God. Recipient Disting. Faculty award Clarion U. Alumni Assn., 1976, Disting. Svc. award, 1986, Disting. Alumni award, 1987, Zonta Internat. Women of Achievement award, 1987. Mem. Beta Phi Mu, Pi Gamma Mu. Republican. Home: PO Box H Knox PA 16232-0608

RUPNICK, MARIA ANN, internist; b. Phila., Jan. 25, 1962; PhD, Thomas Jefferson U., 1987; MD, Harvard U., 1991. Diplomate Am. Bd. Internal Medicine. Intern Brigham and Women's Hosp., Boston, 1991—92, resident in internal medicine, 1992—94, fellow in cardiology, 1994—98, instr., internist. Contbr. articles to profl. jours. Recipient Young Investigators award, Am. Heart Assn. Achievements include patents in field. Office: Brigham and Women's Hosp Cardiovascular Divsn 75 Francis St Boston MA 02115

RUPP, NAOMI NAKANO, science educator; b. L.A., Dec. 10, 1974; d. Kazuyuki and Ayako Nakano; m. Michael Richard Rupp, July 27, 1996. BSChemE with an emphasis in Environ. Engring., U. So. Calif., 1996; MEd in Crosscultural Tchg., Nat. U., 1999. Tchr. sci. Sherman Oaks Ctr. for Enriched Studies, Reseda, Calif., 1996—2000; tchr. physics Pearland HS, Tex., 2000—04; tchr. physics and chemistry Madison Ctrl. HS, 2004—. Girls' tennis coach Sherman Oaks Ctr. for Enriched Studies, 1997—2000, golf coach, 1999—2000; sci. quiz bowl team sponsor Pearland HS, 2001—04, tech. com. dept. rep., 2000—04, co-sponsor, nat. sci. honor soc., 2002—04, mem. pre-engring. adv. com., 2003—04; swim team coach Madison Ctrl. HS, 2004—, girls' golf coach, 2006—. Actor: (movie) Come See the Paradise; musician (pianist): (HS musical) Once Upon a Mattress; musician: (pianist and musical dir.) (cmty. theater) School House Rock, Live!, CLUE, The Musical. Sec. Ctr. Players, Madison, Miss., 2005—06. Mem.: SAG, Am. Assn. Physics Tchrs., Nat. Sci. Tchrs. Assn. Church Of Jesus Christ Of Latter-Day Saints. Avocations: golf, piano, swimming. Office: Madison Ctrl HS 1417 Highland Colony Pkwy Madison MS 39110 Office Phone: 601-856-7121. Office Fax: 601-853-2712. Personal E-mail: nnrupp@gmail.com. Business E-Mail: nrupp@madison.k12.ms.us.

RUPP, SHERON ADELINE, photographer, educator; b. Mansfield, Ohio, Jan. 14, 1943; d. Warren Edmund Rupp and Frances (Hanson) Christian. BA in Sociology and Psychology, Denison U., 1965; MFA in Photography, U. Mass., 1982. Teaching asst. in photography Hampshire Coll., Amherst, Mass., 1981; instr. photography Northfield (Mass.) Mt. Hermon Sch., 1982-83, U. Mass., Amherst, 1984, Holyoke (Mass.) Community Coll., 1986, 87-88; vis. asst. prof. photography Hampshire Coll., 1985, 87; vis. lectr. photography Amherst (Mass.) Coll., 1994. Guest artist, lectr. Boston Mus. Sch., Portland (Maine) Sch. Art, NYU, U. Mass., Deerfield (Mass.) Acad., Hartford Sch. Art/U. Hartford-Conn., Springfield Mus. Fine Arts, Mass., Bard Coll, N.Y., Mass. Coll. Art, Boston, others; guest lectr. Carpenter Ctr., Harvard U., Cambridge, Mass., 2000. One-woman shows include Tisch Sch. Arts NYU, 1987, Portland Sch. Art, 1989, Hart Gallery, Northampton, Mass., 1992, O.K. Harris Gallery, N.Y.C., 1992, Cleve. Mus. Art, 2000; two-person shows include Columbus (Ohio) Mus. Art, 1997—98, Springfield (Mass.) Tech. C.C., 1997; Exhibited in group shows at Mus. Modern Art, N.Y.C., 1991, 1999—, Springfield Mus. Fine Art, 1993, U. Mass., Amherst, 1993, Dirs. Guild, L.A., 1994, Manchester (N.H.) Inst. Arts and Scis., 1995, Weber State U., Utah, 1995, Grand Ctrl. Terminal, N.Y.C., 1995, Photog. Resource Ctr. 3d Biennial, Boston, 1995, DeCordova Mus., Lincoln, 2000—, Smithsonian Arts and Scis., Washington, 2001, Denison U. Art Gallery, Granville, Ohio, 2002, Around the House, A.N. Bush Gallery, Salem, Oreg., 2002, Boston Mus. Fine Arts, 2002—03, Guild Hall, East Hampton, N.Y., 2003, Smith Coll. Mus. Art, Northampton, Mass., 2004, Represented in permanent collections De Cordova Mus., Mus. Modern Art, N.Y.C., Fogg Art Mus. at Harvard U., Hallmark Collection of Photography, Kansas City, Columbus Mus. Art, The J. Paul Getty Mus., L.A., Mus. Fine Arts, Boston, Rose Art Mus. Brandeis U., Mead Art Mus. Amherst Coll., Smith Coll. Mus. Art, Danforth Mus. Art, Springfield Tech. C.C. Found., Carpenter Ctr. for Visual Arts Harvard U., The Smithsonian, Corcoran Galley of Art, Washington; photographs (including cover photo) in Double-Take Mag., winter 1998. Bd. dirs. Zone Art Ctr., 1987-94. Recipient Mass. Fellowship award in photography Artist Found., 1984, 87; visual artist fellow Nat. Endowment for the Arts, 1986, 94, Guggenheim fellow, 1990. Avocations: hiking, bicycling, writing. Home and Office: 364 Hatfield St Apt C Northampton MA 01060-1541 also: 3 The Lope Haydenville MA 01039 E-mail: sheron@crocker.com.

RUPPRECHT, ELIZABETH, art educator; b. Paris, Mar. 28, 1932; came to U.S., 1932; d. Edgar Arthur and Isobel Steele (MacKinnon) R. BFA, Inst. Chgo., 1954, MFA, 1965. Designer Marshall Field's, Chgo., 1957; dir. gallery Old Town Art Ctr., Chgo., 1958-59; sch. dir. Summer Sch. Painting, Saugatuck, Mich., 1958-63; from instr. to prof. Sch. of The Art Inst. Chgo., 1960—. Cons. in field; color cons. Portrait painter. Bd. dirs. Oxbow Sch. of Art, Saugatuck, 1957—. Recipient Key to the City, Iron River (Mich.) City Coun., 1980; John Quincy Adams Fgn. Travel fellow, 1954. Office: Sch of The Art Inst Chgo 37 S Wabash Ave Chicago IL 60603-3002

RUPPRECHT, NANCY ELLEN, historian, educator; b. Coeur d'Alene, Idaho, Sept. 23, 1948; d. George John and Nancy Berneeda (Baird) R. BA with honors, U. Mo., 1967, MA, 1969; PhD, U. Mich., 1982. Acad. dir. pilot program U. Mich., Ann Arbor, 1971-73, lectr. in women studies, 1973-75; vis. lectr. history U. Mo., St. Louis, 1976-77; vis. instr. of history Wash. U., St. Louis, 1977-79, Grinnell (Iowa) Coll., 1979-81; asst. prof. Oakland U., Rochester, Mich., 1981-83; asst. prof. of history Mid. Tenn. State U., Murfreesboro, 1985-91, assoc. prof., 1991-97, prof. history, 1997—. Dir. women's studies program Middle Tenn. State U., 1988—, publicity dir. women's history month, 1989-92, mem. faculty senate, 1992-95; bd. dir. Remember the Women. Mem. editl. bd. German Studies Rev., 1999—; contbr. articles to profl. jours. Bd. adv. Remember the Women Found. Mem.: NOW, AAUW, AAUP (chpt. v.p. 1988—89, pres. 1989—93), Remember the Women (bd. mem.), Assn. Faculty and Adminstrv. Women (chpt. pres. 1995—), Concerned Faculty and Adminstrv. Women (chpt. v.p. 1993—95, chpt. pres. 1995—96), Women in Higher Edn. in Tenn., German Studies Assn., Mid Tenn. Women's Studies Assn., Holocaust Studies Assn., So. Humanities Assn., So. Hist. Assn. (chair nominating com. European divsn. 1996—97, mem. exec. com. 1996—, mem. program com. 1997—2000, chmn. program com. 2001—02, vice chair European divsn. 2002—03, chair European divsn. 2003—), S.E. Women's Studies Assn., Am. Hist. Assn. Home: 1106 Jones Blvd Murfreesboro TN 37129-2310 Office: Middle Tenn State U 275 Peck Hall Murfreesboro TN 37132-0001

RUPRECHT, SUSAN ELIZABETH, art educator; b. Boston, Apr. 11, 1950; d. Charles Warren and Ruth Elizabeth Kline; m. William Michael Ruprecht, Sr., June 26, 1993; 1 child, William Michael Jr. Assoc. in Art, Vernon Ct. Jr. Coll., Newport, RI, 1970; BS in Art Edn., Tufts U., Medford, Mass., 1974. Art tchr. K-12 Haverford (Pa.) Township Sch. Dist., 1979—93; art tchr. K-12, edn. technician I and II Rangeley Lakes Regional Sch., Rangeley, Maine, 1996—. Republican. Avocations: painting, drawing. Home: McCard Rd # 61 PO Box 766 Rangeley ME 04970

RUSAW, SALLY ELLEN, librarian; b. Potsdam, N.Y., Apr. 24, 1939; d. Ralph Clinton and Marion Ellen (Jenack) R. BS in Edn., Potsdam Coll., 1964; MLS, SUNY, Albany, 1975. Cert. libr. media specialist, pub. libr., permanent tchr. N-6, N.Y. Tchr. grade 7th-9th Diocese of Ogdensburg, NY, 1960-74, cons. office edn. NY, 1975-78, archivist NY, 2005—; assoc. libr. Mater Dei Coll., Ogdensburg, 1974-89, head libr., 1989-99, SUNY, Potsdam, 2000—04. Vol. Ogdensburg Correctional Facility, 1982-95, Riverview Correctional Facility, Ogdensburg, 1987—; lector, Eucharistic min. Rite for Christian Initiation of Adults catechist St. Mary's Cathedral; vol. Ogdensburg Cath. Ctrl. Sch., sch. bd., 1995-2000; commd. lay minister Diocese of Ogdensburg, 2005—. Named Vol. of Yr. Ogdensburg Correctional Facility, 1985, Outstanding Vol. Riverview Correctional Facility, 1991; Nat. Def. Edn. Act grantee, 1965. Mem. ALA, N.Y. Libr. Assn., North Country 3Rs Coun., North Country Ref. and Rsch. Resources Coun. (trustee 1994-99). Roman Catholic. Avocations: music, reading, berrying, outdoor activities, swimming.

RUSE, KATHLEEN DIANE, elementary school educator; b. Toledo, Ohio, June 22, 1953; d. Richard William and Gloria Marcia Ruse. BEd, U. Toledo, 1988. ESOL tchr., sci. tchr., tchr. facilitator Broward County Schs., Ft. Lauderdale, Fla., 2003—. Recipient Environ. Tchr. award, Fla. Tchrs. Assn., 1993. Mem.: Sierra Club. Democrat. Roman Catholic. Home: 1222F St Westlake Blvd Westlake Village CA 91361 Office: OUr Lady of Mailbu 3625 S Winter Canyon Malibu CA 90265 E-mail: kruse@olmalibuschool.org.

RUSH, ANNE KENT, writer, illustrator; b. Mobile, Ala., July 28, 1945; BA, Wayne State U., Detroit, 1967. Writer Little, Brown Pubs., Boston, 1968; advt. designer Bookworks Pubs., Berkeley, Calif., 1970-73; tchr. Alyssum Therapy Inst., San Francisco, 1973-75, Esalen Inst., San Francisco, 1971-76; founding ptnr., mng. editor Moon Books Pubs., Berkeley, 1976-79. Author: Getting Clear, 1972, Feminism as Therapy, 1974, Moon, Moon, 1976, The Basic Back Book, 1979, Greta Bear Goes to Yellowstone National Park, 1981, The Back Rub Book, 1985, Romantic Massage, 1989, The Modern Book of Massage, 1994, Modern Book of Yoga, 1996, Modern Book of Stretching, 1997, The Way of Stretching: Flexibility for Body and Mind, 2005; illustrator: The Massage Book, 1971. Avocations: piano, travel. Office: PO Box 2498 Daphne AL 36526-2498 Mailing: c/o Katinka Matson Brockman Inc 5 East 59th Street New York NY 10022

RUSH, DEBORAH, actress; b. Chatham, NJ, Apr. 10, 1954; m. Walter Cronkite, III; 2 children. Actress (TV series) Ryan's Hope, 1985, Stir Crazy, 1985, (TV films) A Midsummer Night's Dream, 1982, Alice at the Palace, 1982, Earthly Possessions, 1999, Tempting Adam, 2004, (miniseries) John Jakes' Heaven and Hell: North and South, Part III, 1994, Unnatural Pursuits, 1994, (films) 10, 1979, The Purple Rose of Cairo, 1985, Heat, 1987, Big Business, 1988, Family Business, 1989, Parents, 1989, She-Devil, 1989, My Blue Heaven, 1990, Passed Away, 1992, Reckless, 1995, In and Out, 1997, You've Got Mail, 1998, Advice from a Caterpillar, 1999, Three to Tango, 1999, The Good Girl, 2002, Bad Company, 2002, American Wedding, 2003, Strangers with Candy, 2005, Half Nelson, 2006; numerous stage appearances include The Taming of The Shrew, 1978, A Midsummer Night's Dream, 1982, Hay Fever, 1985-86, Two Gentlemen of Verona, 1987, Twice Removed, 1995, The Largest Elizabeth in the World, 1996, The Revelers, 1996, Arms and the Man, 1997, Absurd Person Singular, 2005. Nomination Antoinette Perry award for Noises Off, 1984.*

RUSH, DORIE MAE, nursing educator; b. Assiniboia, Sask., Can., May 3, 1970; d. June and Steve Yorga (Stepfather); m. Tark Morgan Rush, Mar. 22, 2003; children: Hailey Madison Caragata, Stone Morgan, Brooke Ashlyn Caragata, Austin Talon. DON, Sask. Inst. Applied Arts and Sci., Regina, 1990; BSN, U. Phoenix, Tucson, 2003; postgrad., U. Phoenix, Yuma, Ariz., 2004—. Cert. inpatient OB, NCC, Ariz., fetal monitoring, NCC, Ariz. Unit-based educator Yuma Regional Med. Ctr., 2000—, resource coord., 1997—2000, staff nurse, 1993—97; OB flight nurse Suncare Air Ambulance, Yuma, 1999—2002; part-time Ariz. Western Coll., Yuma, 2002—. Fetal monitor instr. Assn. Women's Health Obstetric and Neonatal Nurses, Yuma, 2003—. Author: (poster presentation) Dynamic New Grad Orientation to Labor and Delivery. Named Yuma's Best Nurse, City of Yuma, 2002. Mem.: AWHONN. Office: Yuma Regional Med Ctr 2400 S Ave A Yuma AZ 85364-7127 Office Phone: 928-336-3020. Home Fax: 928-329-7706; Office Fax: 928-336-7453. Personal E-mail: dmrush@adelphia.net. E-mail: drush@yumaregional.org.

RUSH, JULIA ANN HALLORAN (MRS. RICHARD HENRY RUSH), artist, writer; b. St. Louis, Oct. 25, 1927; d. Edward Roosevelt and Flavia Hadley (Griffin) Halloran; m. Richard Henry Rush, Aug. 15, 1956; 1 child, Sallie Haywood. Student Washington U., St. Louis, 1945-47; B.A., George Washington U., 1949. One-woman shows: Fort Amador Officers Club, Panama Canal Zone, El Panama Hotel, Panama, George Washington U., Statler Hotel, Roosevelt Hotel, Washington, Newspaper Women's Club, Washington, Waukegan Library, Ill., Epworth Heights Hotel, Ludington, Mich.; exhibited in group shows: Panama Art League, Corcoran Gallery; represented in permanent collections: U. Panama; also pvt. collections; model John Robert Powers Agy., 1950; sec.-treas., dir. N.Am. Acceptance Corp., 1956-58; v.p. Rush and Halloran, Inc., 1957-58, ptnr., 1954-57; research asst. to husband's bi-weekly newsletter Art/Antiques Investment Report, 1973—, articles in Wall St. transcript, 1971—. Illustrator: Antiques As An Investment (author Richard H. Rush), 1968; research asst.: Investments You Can Live With and Enjoy (author: Richard H. Rush), 1974, 2d, edit., 1975, 3d edit., 1976; Photographer: Automobiles as an Investment, 1982; Investing in Classic Cars, 1984. Recipient 1st prize (Panama) Newspaper Women's Club, 1953; First Prize Panama Art League, 1953. Mem. DAR, Nat. League Am. Penwomen, Florence Crittenton Circle (rec. sec. 1968-69), Kappa Kappa Gamma. Club: Washington, Royal Palm Yacht (No. Ft. Myers, Fla.), Boca West Golf and Country (Boca Raton, Fla.)

RUSH, KATHRYN ANN, psychotherapist; b. McKeesport, Pa., Aug. 3, 1954; d. Steve and Mary (Lehman) R. BA in Psychology, Villa Maria Coll., 1976; MEd in Counseling, Calif. Univ. of Pa., 1978. Nat. cert. counselor; cert. sch. guidance and counseling, Pa.; lic. profl. counselor, 2002. Out-patient adult psychotherapist, adult unit psychotherapist Chestnut Ridge Counseling Svcs., Inc., Uniontown, Pa., 1981—91, 1999—, adult partial hospitalization program psychotherapist, 1991—99, supr. on site grad. student practicum, 1982—2004. Expert witness Pa. ct., 1990. Mem. Am. Counseling Assn., Assn. Adult Devel. and Aging, Chi Sigma Iota. Byzantine Catholic. Avocations: reading, baseball, crafts, walking, movies.

RUSH, LEE A., marketing executive; b. Manhattan, N.Y., Dec. 20, 1968; d. Irene C. and Roger Giles Rush. BA, Roger Williams Coll., Bristol, R.I., 1990. Mgr. mktg. UNICOM, Providence, 1997—2000, Mediaweave, Woonsocket, RI, 2000—03; mgr. global mktg. Numark Industries LLC, Cumberland, RI, 2003—. Actor, dir.: Various Roles. Mem. Therapy Dogs Internat., RI, 2004—06. Mem.: Mensa. Office: Numark Industries LLC 200 Scenic View Drive Cumberland RI 02864 Office Fax: 401-658-4921. Personal E-mail: aroough1@gmail.com. E-mail: lrush@numark.com.

RUSH, PATRICIA ANNE, pastor, music educator; b. Washington, Pa., Nov. 29, 1935; d. James David and Joanna Nell (Porter) McClay; m. Merle Lee Rush, Dec. 27, 1966 (dec. 1987); children: Christopher, Cheryl. B in Music Edn., U. Ctrl. Ark., 1965; M in Religious Edn., Evang. Bible Coll., Lake Worth, Fla., 1988, D in Religious Edn., 1989; DTh, Evang. Bible Sem., 2000, D in Sacred Music, M in Sacred Music, 2002. Music edn. tchr. Gillette (Ark.) Pub. Schs., 1965, Orange County, 1966-67; prin., music tchr. Faith Christian Acad., Tulsa, 1983-84; tchr. Agape Faith Christian, Tulsa, 1984-85; traveling psalmist Sch. of Psalmisi, Fort Worth, 1985-88; traveling missionary Pat Rush Ministries, Inc., Tulsa, 1985-88; pres., tchr. Agape Bible Tng. Outreach, Titusville, Fla., 1989; pastor, tchr. Spirit Fire World, Titusville, Fla., 1995—. Founder Agape Bible Tng., Spirit Fire World Outreach; voice, piano, theory and composition tchr., 1970-96; instr. developing workshops, manual writing, and vision devel. and practical tng.; internat. spkr. ch. music svcs., cmty. outreach, classes and sems. for overcoming fear, overcoming stress, anxiety and depression, and getting/staying free from addictions. Composer: Sacrifice, 1999, Celebrate, 1999; author: Joy fro Psalms, 1990, Champions in Spirit, 1992, Building Relationships, 1993. Founder, pres. Hope Found., Inc., 1981-83; choir dir. Indian River City Meth., Titusville, 1970-73, St. Andrew Meth. Ch., Titusville, 1973-74. Mem. NAFE, Nat. Guild Piano Tchrs., Nat. Assn. Music Tchrs., Spirit Fire Evangelistic Assn., Brevard County Ministerial Assn., Internat. Charismatic Bible Ministries. Avocations: music, writing, travel, studying, folk music. Office: Spirit Fire World Outreach 150 Country Club Dr Titusville FL 32780-8607

RUSH, SOPHIA, law educator; b. Stroudsburg, Pa., Mar. 2, 1964; d. Robert and Karen; life ptnr. Brian Lank; children: Eric, Thomas. BS in Criminal Justice, Pa. State U., University Park, 1982; MS in Crime, Law and Justice, Louisville U., 1985; JD, NYU, 1989. Bar: NY 1990. Asst. prof. law Queen's Coll., NY, 1985—88, Kingston Law Sch., NY, 1989, assoc. prof. law NY, 1990—95; prof. law Pace Law Sch., NY, 1996—. Vis. prof. Kingston Sch. Law, London, 1998, Preston Sch. Bus. and Adminstrn., England, 1999, Duke U., 2002; various pro bono cases. Author: Criminal and Civil Law: Preparing Post Conviction Civil Suits, 2006. Active PTA, 1996—2001. Named one of Pace Law Schs. Most Liked Tchrs., 2000; recipient Disting. Prof. award, Pace Law Sch., 2006. Mem.: ASPCA, ABA, NY Bar Assn. Conservative. Roman Catholic. Avocations: swimming, horseback riding, cliff diving, skydiving. Office Phone: 800-473-7020.

RUSHER, MARY NASH KELLY, lawyer; b. Norfolk, Va., May 25, 1958; BA in Polit., German, magna cum laude, Wake Forest Univ., 1980; JD, Univ. Va., 1984. Bar: NC 1985. Law clk., Hon. John D. Butzner, Jr. U.S. Court of Appeals, 4th Cir., 1984—85; with Hunton & Williams LLP, Raleigh, NC, 1985—, ptnr., capital fin., real estate, 1993—, and mem. exec. com., 2002. Mem.: ABA, NC Bar Assn., Nat. Assn. Bond Lawyers, Mortar Board, Omicron Delta Kappa, Phi Beta Kappa, Order of Coif. Office: Hunton & Williams LLP Ste 1400 421 Fayetteville St Mall Raleigh NC 27601 Office Phone: 919-899-3066. Office Fax: 919-899-3160. Business E-Mail: mnrusher@hunton.com.

RUSHFORTH, ANN FAY, artist, educator; b. Tampa, Fla., July 17, 1944; d. Robert George Rushforth and Alla Petrovna Riordan; m. Reid Johnson Perryman, May 13, 2000; m. John William Semko, Nov. 11, 1971 (div.); 1 child, Tao Alexandre Semko. BA, George Wash. U., 1966—66; MFA, Antioch U., 1980. Asst. to dir. of film and broadcasting Smithsonian Instn., Washington, 1967—68; adminstrv. asst. Am. Craft Council-Bennington Exhbns., Bennington, Vt., 1972; asst. mgr. Am. Craft Council-Rhinebeck Exhbns., Rhinebeck, NY, 1973—74; dir. pub. rels. Scope Gallery, Torpedo Factory, Alexandria, Va., 1975, pres., 1976—77, bd. dirs., 1978; chmn. dept. art Stoneridge H.S., Bethesda, Md., 1981—84; v.p. Foundry Gallery, Washington, 1986; dir. Pavo Real Gallery, Washington, 1987—88; gallery dir. Arise Gallery of Asian Art and Antiques, Washington, 1988—90; spl. projects photographer Woodrow Wilson Ho. Mus., Washington; arts instr. Duke Ellington Sch. of Arts, Washington, 1990—91, Visual Systems, Rockville, Md., 1991, Fillmore Art Ctr., Washington, 1991; executive dir. The Art Barn Assn., Washington, 1991—93; freelance master paintings copyist Nat. Gallery of Art, Washington, 1993—94; arts instr., 2005—. Rep. Dupont Cir. Consortium of Galleries, Washington, 1986; art instr. Md. Coll. of Art and Design, Dept. Continuing Edn., Rockville, 1990—91; dir., devel. officer R St. Gallery, Washington, 1992—93; conservator, appraiser Artsserve, Ltd., Newnan, 1995—; co-founder Contemporary Arts Alliance, Newnan, 2003—; art instr. The Pottery Wheel, Newnan, Ga., 2005—. Dir.: Carrollton Arts Guild Exhbns.; art critic: Eyewash Newpaper, 1990—91; editor: (exhibition catalog) Sculpture to Touch: For the Sight Impaired, 1987, Md. Craft Coun. News, 1976—78; Wash. Post Mag., 1977, Woodrow Wilson House Mus. Annual Report, Nat. Trust Hist. Preservation, 1987, Greater Chattanooga Artists, The Bureau, 1999, CABIA Arts Calendar, 1999, one-woman shows include Everson Mus. Art Gallery, Syracuse, NY, 1978, Montpelier Cultural Ctr., Md., 1981, Foundry Gallery, Washington, DC, 1986, In Town Gallery, Chattanooga, 2000, exhibited in group shows at NE Juried Exhbn. 12, Rhinebeck, NY, 1974—77, Frederick Wholesale Fair 3, Md., 1975—77, Fairtree Gallery, NYC, 1976, Inc. Gallery, 1976, Concepts Gallery, Ridgewood, NJ, 1976, Scope Gallery, Alexandria, Va., 1976 (Best in Show), 1977, 1984, Montgomery Coll. Gallery, Rockville, Md., 1977, US Govt. Svc. Adminstrn. Invitational Exhbn., Washington, DC, 1977, Westlake Gallery, White Plains, NY, 1977, 1980, 1983, Coqui Galleries, Westport, Conn., 1977, 1978, 1979, Fredericksburg Gallery of Modern Art, Va., 1977, Jelly Mill Gallery, Manchester, Vt., 1981, Md. Nat. Capitol Park and Planning Commn., 1980, VAC Gallery, Columbia, Md., 1981, Visual Arts Ctr., 1982, WWAC Gallery, Washington, DC, 1982, 1985, 1985, 1986, Nat. Capital AMCCAP Festival, 1984 (Second Place, Hon. Mention in Sculpture), 1993, Design Ctr., 1984, Art League Gallery, Alexandria, 1985, Art Barn Gallery, Washington, DC, 1985, 1992, 1992, 1993, Signature Galleries Invitational, Boston and Hyannis, Mass., 1985, Concepts '85, Margate, NJ, 1985, Martin Luther King Libr. Gallery, Washington, DC, 1986, R St. Gallery, 1989, Rockland Ctr., Ellicott City, Md., 1989, Foundry Gallery, Washington, DC, 1989, Jackson Sch. Studios, 1990, 1991, 1992, 901 E St. Gallery, 1991, 1993, Capital Arts Inc. Georgetown Visitation Sch., 1992, 1993, Georgetown Holiday Inn, 1992, The Spy Club, 1993, Universal N. Gallery, 1993, 1993, Washington Project for the Arts, 1993, Jackson Art Ctr., Studio #21, 1993, Gallery West, Alexandria, 1993, Corcoran Sch. Gallery, Washington, DC, 1993, Avery Gallery, Atlanta, Ga., 1995, Blair Voltz Exhbns., Atlanta, 1997, The Stalls, Bennett St., 1997, Grandview Gallery, 1997, Waterhouse Pavilion, Chattanooga, 1998, AVA Gallery, 1998, 1999, Urban Art Inst., 2000, Panoply Showhouse, Newnan, Ga., 2001, Tenn. Valley Art Mus., Tuscumbia, Ala., 2002, Arts Clayton Gallery, Jonesboro, Ga., 2002, Atlanta Arts Club, 2002, Forum Gallery at Defoor Centre, Atlanta, 2002, 2004, Atlanta Col. Art, Coweta County, Ga., 2003, Keptever Gallery, Peachtree City, Ga., 2004, Mandeville Gallery, Carrollton, Ga., 2004, Jackalope's Gallery, Carrollton, 2004, MECCA Festival for the Arts, 2004, Carrollton Artists Guild, 2004, Carrollton Arts Ctr., 2005, exhibitions include HMR Engring. Inc., Alexandria, 1993, Meml. Hosp. Foyer, Chattanooga, 1999, UTC Faculty Club, 1999, Ga. State Fair, Perry, 2001, prin. works include St. John the Wonderworker, Patron St. Altarpiece and Icon of St. Brigid, Abess & Healer, St. John the Wonderworker Ea. Orthodox Ch., Atlanta, 1996, Christus Rex, Ceramic bas Relief Altarpiece, St. Paul's Episc. Ch., Newnan, 2006. Lector St.Paul's Episcopal Ch., Newnan, 2004—06. Mem.: Am. Ceramic Soc. Potter's Coun., Womens Caucus for Arts, Portrait Soc. Atlanta (edn. dir. 2005), Nat. Coun. Edn. for Ceramic Arts, Newnan-Coweta Artist Assn., Carrollton Artist Guild (exhbn. dir. 2005). Libertarian. Episcopalian. Avocations: physical fitness, dog shows, travel, art history. Office Phone: 678-634-6360. E-mail: annfayrushforth@hotmail.com.

RUSHING, ANNETTE, elementary school educator; d. Mack and Sue (Sims) Johnson; m. David Wayne Rushing, Aug. 21, 1970; 1 child, Jon R. BA in Music Edn., U. Ark., Monticello, 1988. Music tchr. Warren Elem., Ark., 1988—90; choral dir. White Hall Jr. High, Ark., 1990—. Pvt. voice instr., White Hall, 1988—; guest clinician, dir. Dist. I Jr. High Honors Choir, 2003. Named S.E. Region Jr. High Dir. of Yr., 1996—97, 2000—01, 2005—06. Mem.: Am. Choral Dirs. Assn., Ark. Choral Dirs. Assn. Avocations: quilting, hunting, fishing. Office: White Hall Jr High 8106 DoHarway Rd White Hall AR 71602 Home: 1502 Discovery Cove White Hall AR 71602

RUSHING, DOROTHY M., retired historian, writer; b. Bonham, Tex., Aug. 28, 1925; d. Van Bain and Ada (Price) Hawkins; m. J. E. Rushing, Aug. 6, 1960 (dec. 1985); children: Charles Maret, Bill Maret, Bob Maret, Charles Rushing, Martha Rushing Sosebee. BA, Tex. Woman's U., 1972; MA, Tex. A&M Commerce, 1974; PhD, U. North Tex., Denton, 1981. Instr. Tex. A&M Commerce, Commerce, 1972-74, 80-81, U. North Tex., Denton, 1975-76; prof. Richland Coll., Dallas, 1975-98, Collin County Community Coll., McKinney, Tex., 1985-88; historian-archivist J.C. Penney, Inc., Dallas, 1988-95. Vis. prof. Johns Hopkins U., 1985, U. Va., 1989; statis. analyst Dallas County C.C., 1982; lay rep. N.E. Tex. Libr. System, 1982-90. Contbg. author: Handbook of Texas, 1986. Named Outstanding Instr., Richland Coll., 1987, Disting. Alumni, Denison H.S., 2001; postdoctoral fellow NEH, 1985, 89, Outstanding Hist. Instr. award Dallas County Cmty. System, 1988. Mem. Phi Kappa Phi, Sigma Tau Delta, Phi Alpha Theta. Avocations: genealogy, literacy, U.S. history. Home: 498 Lockloma Ct Denison TX 75020-3668

RUSHING, TONNIE AUSTIN PAGE, musician, educator; b. Hartwell, Ga., Mar. 6, 1940; d. George Wilson and Ruth Smith Page; m. Roger Kendall Vichery, June 18, 1960; children: George Kendall, Carol Page; m. Charles Maynard Rushing, Aug. 18, 1979; stepchildren: Joan E., Brian C., Susanne E. BS in Edn., Athens State Coll., Ga., 1973; cert. in Computer Tech., Trident Tech. Coll., 1992, Sylvan Learning Ctr., 1996; cert. in Sign Lang., Trident

Tech. Coll., 1997. Musician, Ga., 1958—; prin., owner Opus 11 George Bed & Breakfast, 1988—97; afternoon activities dir. O'Quinn Preschool-Kindergarten, 2001. Dir. music Summer Stock Theater, Morristown, Tenn., 1969; music educator Covenant Sch. Fine Arts Enrichment, 1976—79; music dir. Young Charleston Theatre Co., 1988, 96; mem. founding com. Covenant Fine Arts Enrichment Sch., Decatur, 1976; mem. adv. com. Coun. Arts John C. Calhoun State Coll., Decatur. Singer: North Ala. Charleston Symphony, St. Micheal's Ch., Grace Episc. Ch., Choir Eng. Tour, 1981—2002; musician: French Protestant Ch., 1988—96; author: Huguenots and the Legacy, 1994; dir.: (recording) Huguenot Psalter, 1991; jacket cover, Huguenot Psalter, 1991. Pres. Decatur (Ala.) Civic Chorus; vol. Crisis Ctr. Mental Health Ctr., Decatur, 1971—79; mem. comprehensive planning com. City Hartwell, Ga., 2003; bd. dirs. Preservation Soc., 2004, Hart County Hist. Soc., 2004; music asst. 2d Presbyn. Ch., Charleston, SC, 1988; sect. leader St. Michaels Ch., Charleston, 1998—2001; elder Hartwell 1st Presbyn. Ch., 2004; bd. dirs. Charleston (S.C.) Symphony Orch. Chorus and Chamber Choir. Mem.: PTA, Am. Guild Organists, Presbyn. Assn. Musicians, Charleston (S.C.) County Med. Auxilliary, Nat. assn. Mental Illness, Hartwell Women's Club, Sigma Alpha Iota. Republican. Home: 175 E Johnson St Hartwell GA 30643 Personal E-mail: cmandtpr@hartcom.net.

RUSINKO, ELAINE, language educator; b. Coaldale, Pa., Aug. 7, 1949; d. Wasyl Rusinko and Anastasia Gauronsky; m. Stuart Rothenberg, July 14, 1980; children: Benjamin Samuel Rothenberg, Julia Anna Rothenberg. BA, U. Md., 1971; PhD, Brown U., Providence, 1976. Info. officer USIA Fgn. Svc., Washington; asst. prof. Russian Bucknell U., Lewisburg, Pa., 1977—80; assoc. prof. Russian U. Md. Baltimore County, 1980—. Author: Straddling Borders: Literature and Identity in Subcarpathian Rus', 2003; translator: Virtue is More Important than Riches (Aleksander Dukhnovych), 1994; contbr. articles to profl. jours. V.p. Carpatho-Rusyn Rsch. Ctr., Ocala, Fla., 2002; v.p. Nat. Capital chpt. Carpatho-Rusyn Soc., Washington. Fellow, IREX, 1977, NEH, 1979, Am. Coun. Learned Socs., 1984; Provost's Rsch. fellow, U. Md. Baltimore County, 1977—78. Byzantine Catholic. Home: 13305 Morning Field Way Potomac MD 20854 Office: U Md Baltimore County 1000 Hilltop Cir Baltimore MD 21250 Personal E-mail: rusinko@umbc.edu.

RUSKAI, MARY BETH, mathematics professor; b. Cleve., Feb. 26, 1944; d. Michael J. and Evelyn (Gortz) R. BS, Notre Dame Coll., Cleve., 1965; MA, PhD, U. Wis., 1969. Battelle fellow in theoretical physics U. Geneva, 1969-71; rsch. assoc. in math. MIT, Cambridge, Mass., 1971-72; rsch. assoc. in physics U. Alta., Edmonton, Can., 1972-73; asst. prof. math. U. Oreg., Eugene, 1973-76; asst. prof. U. Lowell, Mass., 1977-82, assoc. prof. Mass., 1982-86, prof. dept. math. Mass., 1986—2002, emeritus, 2002—, pres. faculty senate Mass., 1990-91; rsch. prof. Tufts U., 2003—. Sci. scholar Bunting Inst., Cambridge, Mass., 1983-85; rsch. prof. MSRI, Berkeley, 2002; vis. prof. Rockefeller U., N.Y.C., 1980-81, U. Vienna, Austria, 1981, Rome, 1988, Ga. Tech., Atlanta, 1997, Walton vis. prof. Dublin Inst. Tech., 2003; faculty rsch. assoc. Naval Surface Warfare Ctr., Silver Springs, Md., 1986; vis. prof. math. U. Mich., Ann Arbor, 1991-92; vis. mem. Courant Inst. Math. Sci., NYU, 1988-89; cons. Bell Labs., Murray Hill, N.J., 1972, 83, 88-89; conf. dir. NSF/CBMS Conf. on Wavelets, 1990; Flora Stone Mather vis. prof. Case Western Res. U., Cleve., 1995; vis. prof. Ga. Inst. Tech., 1997, U. Reims, France, 1998, Tech. U. Berlin, 2000; cons. Microsoft Rsch., 1999. Editor-in-chief Wavelets and Their Applications, 1990-92; mem. editl. bd. Notices of Am. Math. Soc., 1994-99, Jour. Math. Physics, 2001-; mem. editl. adv. bd. Internat. Jour. Quantum Chemistry, 1996-2000; contbr. articles to profl. jours. NSF predoctoral fellow, 1965-69; recipient NSF Career Advancement award, 1988-89. Fellow AAAS (symposium organizer 1991, 94, nominating com. math. sect. 1991-94, mem.-at-large math. sect. 2004—); mem. Internat. Union Pure & Applied Physics (vice chair commn. on math. physics, U.S. liaison com. 1999-2005), Internat. Assn. Math. Physicists, Am. Math. Soc. (reviewer, session chmn., com. 1987—, com. chmn., coun. mem. at-large 1998-2000), Math. Assn. Am. (com.), Am. Phys. Soc. (reviewer), Assn. Women in Math., Assn. Women in Sci. (pres. New Eng. chpt. 1986-87), Appalachian Mountain Club (Boston; winter leader 1979-97), Sigma Xi. Office: Tufts U Dept Math Medford MA 02155 E-mail: marybeth.ruskai@tufts.edu.

RUSKIN, RUTH ZAFREN, social worker; b. Washington, May 23, 1953; d. Frank and Rose (Charkin) Zafren; m. Jonathan S. Ruskin, June 12, 1976; children: David Frank, Diana Beth. BA cum laude, Cornell U., 1975; MSW, Cath. U. Am., 1977. Lic. clin. social workers, Va. Social worker Arlington (Va.) County Dept. Social Svcs., 1977-85; clin. social worker, supr., dir. hypnotherapy program Roundhouse Sq. Psychiat. Ctr., Alexandria, Va., 1985—. Pres. Ruskin-Zafren Found., 2002—. Mem. NASW. Home: 5905 6th St Falls Church VA 22041-2535

RUSNAK, CYNDI MOSS, lawyer; b. Fairfax, Va., Oct. 19, 1970; d. Robert Earl and Grace Marie Moss; m. Gary Lee Rusnak, July 29, 2005; children: Connor Sutton, Taylor Paige. BA, U. Tex., Austin, 1993; JD, South Tex. Coll. Law, Houston, 1997. Bar: Tex. 1998, cert.: Tex. (legal asst.) 1994. Atty. Williamson and Sears, Houston, 1997—2002; asst. county atty. Angelina County Atty.'s Office, Lufkin, Tex., 2002—05; atty., ptnr. Williamson and Rusnak, Houston, 2005—. Bd. dirs., sec. Angelina Alliance for Children, Lufkin, 2002—05. Sec., prosecutor Angelina Alliance for Children, Lufkin, 2002—05. Office: Williamson & Rusnak 4310 Yoakum Blvd Houston TX 77006 Office Phone: 713-223-3330. Office Fax: 713-223-0001. Business E-Mail: crusnak@jimmywilliamson.com.

RUSNAK, MARTHA HENDRICK, reading education educator; b. Boston, Jan. 15, 1938; d. Ives and Marie (McClung) Hendrick; m. Robert J. Rusnak Sr., Nov. 14, 1964; children: Robert J. Jr., Jennifer Marie. AB, Mills Coll., 1959; MSEd, No. Ill. U., 1978, EdD, 1983. Primary tchr., Hawaiian Gardens, Calif., 1961-63; intermediate tchr. Mill Valley, Calif., 1963-65; jr. high tchr. Santa Barbara, Calif., 1965-68; intermediate tchr. Bensenville, Ill., 1974-77; instr. reading No. Ill. U., DeKalb, 1978-80; prof. Lewis U., Romeoville, Ill., 1980—, dir. graduate reading, 1983—. Cons. in field. Contbr. articles to profl. jours. Mem. Internat. Reading Assn., Nat. Coun. Tchrs. English, No. Ill. Reading Coun. (exec. bd. 1988—), Ill. Reading Coun. (editorial bd. 1989—). Avocations: reading, guitar, travel, pottery. Office: Lewis U One Univ Pky Romeoville IL 60446

RUSS, FENEE L., principal, consultant; d. Charles and Hassie Russ. BA in Bus. Adminstr. and Mktg., Clark-Atlanta U., 1991; MS in Ednl. Leadership, Nova Southeastern U., 1998, EdD, 2005. Cert. profl. educator Fla. Dept. Edn., 1993. Tchr. Sch. Dist. Palm Beach County, West Palm Beach, Fla., 1993—98, asst. prin., 1998—. Named Tchr. of Yr., Boca Raton Rotary Club, 1995; recipient, Palm Beach County Vocat. Assn., 1995. Mem.: LWV, AAUW (assoc.), Nat. Mus. Women Arts (assoc.), Toastmasters Internat. (assoc.), Phi Delta Kappa (assoc.). Avocations: piano, reading, travel. Office: Sch Dist PBC/Eagles Landing 19500 Coral Ridge Dr Boca Raton FL 33498 Office Phone: 561-470-7022.

RUSS, JOANNA, author; b. N.Y.C., Feb. 22, 1937; d. Evarett and Bertha (Zinner) R. BA English high honors, Cornell U., 1957; MFA Playwriting and Dramatic Lit., Yale U., 1960. Lectr. English Cornell U., 1967—70, asst. prof., 1970—72; asst. prof. English Harpur Coll. SUNY Binghamton, 1972—75; asst. prof. English U. Colo., 1975—77; assoc. prof. English, U. Wash., 1977—90, prof., 1984—90. Author: Picnic on Paradise, 1968, And Chaos Died, 1970, The Female Man, 1975, We Who Are About To, 1977, Kittatinny: A Tale of Magic, 1978, The Two of Them, 1978, On Strike Against God, 1980, The Adventures of Alyx, 1983, The Zanzibar Cat, 1983, How To Suppress Women's Writing, 1983, Extra (Ordinary) People, 1984, Magic Mommas, Trembling Sisters, Puritans and Perverts: Feminist Essays, 1985, (collection) The Hidden Side of the Moon, 1987, To Write Like a Woman, 1995, (nonfiction) What Are We Fighting For, 1998; also numerous short stories Mem. Sci. Fiction Writers Am. (Nebula award Best Short Story 1972, Hugo award for Best Novella 1983)

RUSSAKOFF, NINA L., lawyer; b. New Haven, Conn., 1972; BA, Columbia Coll., 1996; M in Studies, Oxford U., 1997; JD, Columbia U., 2002. Bar: Pa. 2002, NJ 2002, Supreme Ct. Pa., Supreme Ct. NJ, US Dist. Ct. (ea. dist., middle dist.) Pa., US Dist. Ct., NJ. Legis. asst. to Rep. Peter J. Visclosky of Ind.; assoc. litig. Hangley Aronchick Segal & Pudlin, P.C., Phila. Contbr. articles to law jours. Mem.: ABA, Pa. Bar Assn. Office: Hangley Aronchick Segal & Pudlin One Logan Sq, 27th Fl 18th & Cherry Streets Philadelphia PA 19103 Office Fax: 215-496-7370, 215-568-0300. E-mail: nrussakoff@hangley.com.*

RUSSELL, ANNE M., editor-in-chief; Editor book divsn. Billboard Publ.; editor Photo Dist. News; reporter Adweek; assoc. editor Am. Photographer; sr. editor Working Women; exec. editor Folio: Pub. News, editor-in-chief, 1992—97, Living Fit, 1997—99, Vegetarian Times, 1999; editl. dir. Fox TV's Health Network, Shape mag., 2001—03, editor-in-chief, 2003—. Office: Shape 21100 Erwin St Woodland Hills CA 91367*

RUSSELL, ANNE WRENN, property manager; b. Greensboro, NC, Mar. 2, 1934; d. Oscar Ivey and Lucy (Lula) Elinor (Wright) Wrenn; children: Elinor Russell Ball, Martha Anne Russell Martin, John Leon, Barbara Russell Richardson. BA in French, U. NC, Chapel Hill, 1956. Cert. N.C. Real Estate Bd., paralegal Atlanta Paralegal Inst., 1991. Camp counselor, Mass., 1954; with acctg. dept. Bank Greensboro, 1955; sec. Meth. Bd. Edn., Durham, NC, 1957—59; real estate sales person Geraci and Preston, Greensboro, 1991—92; property mgr. Wrenn-Zealy Properties, Inc., Greensboro, 1992—. Active Greensboro Opera Guild, Greensboro Opera Co., 1981—90; opera chorus mem. Greensboro Opera Co., 1981—85; active Greensboro Symphony Guild, 1981—90; com. correspondent Ch. Missions, 2005—; bd. mem. Ea. Music Festival, Greensboro, 1985—86. Mem.: U. N.C. Greensboro Musical Arts Guild (bd. mem. 2003—), English Speaking Union, Greensboro Choral Soc. (mem. steering com.), U. N.C. Chapel Hill Alumni Assn. (life), Greensboro Hist. Book Club (life). Republican. Methodist. Avocations: piano, singing, painting, sewing, tennis. Office: Wrenn-Zealy Properties 1403 Sunset Dr Greensboro NC 27408 Office Phone: 336-272-3183. Personal E-mail: nannebird@hotmail.com.

RUSSELL, ANNIKA RENEE, secondary school educator, financial consultant; d. Sondra Kay and Steve Lynn Russell. BA, Dakota Wesleyan U., 1996; MEd, U. Nebr., Lincoln, 2002. Lic. Securities SD, 2003. HS tchr., coach Sanborn Ctrl. Sch., Forestburg, SD, 1996—2005, Wessington Springs Schs., SD, 2005—; fin. rep. Primerica Fin. Svcs., Mitchell, SD, 2000—. Tech. instr. cons. State of SD, Spearfish, 1998—99; SD team coach Internat. Sports Specialist, Inc., North Logan, Utah, 1999—. Youth group leader United Meth. Ch., Mitchell, SD, 1999—2001. Mem.: ACTE, NEA, ASCD, SD Edn. Assn., SD Volleyball Coaches Assn., SD Coaches Assn., Nat. Bus. Edn. Assn. Methodist. Avocations: running, reading, crafts, skiing, biking. Home: 301 W 12th Ave Mitchell SD 57301

RUSSELL, CHARLOTTE SANANES, biochemistry professor, researcher; b. NYC, Jan. 4, 1927; d. Joseph and Marguerite (Saltiel) Sananes; m. Joseph Brooke Russell, Dec. 20, 1947; children: James Robert, Joshua Sananes. BA, Bklyn. Coll., 1946; MA, Columbia U., 1947, PhD, 1951. Asst. prof. chemistry CCNY, N.Y.C., 1958-68, assoc. prof., 1968-72, prof., 1972—, prof. emerita, 2001—. Peer reviewer NSF, NIH; ad hoc reviewer sci. jours. including Jour. Bacteriology, Biochemistry. Contbr. articles to profl. jours. Mem. AAAS, Am. Soc. Biochemistry and Molecular Biology, Am. Chem. Soc., Amnesty Internat., Sigma Xi. Office: CCNY Dept Chemistry 138th St & Convent Ave New York NY 10031 Office Phone: 212-650-6681. Business E-Mail: chrcc@sci.ccny.cuny.edu.

RUSSELL, CLARA B., information technology manager; b. Washington, Mar. 20; d. Gilbert L. Sr. and Emma Howard Bullock; m. William A. Russell. BA, Howard U., 1971. Cert. arbitrator. Info. tech. specialist U.S. Govt., Washington, 1971—. Arbitrator Better Bus. Bur., Atlanta. Mem. Am. Bus. Women's Assn., Am. Pub. Welfare Assn., Am. Arbitration Assn., Howard U. Alumni Assn., Order of Ky. Colonels. Avocations: travel, gardening.

RUSSELL, DAWN ANN, dean; BA, St. Thomas U., 1977; LLB, Dalhousie U., 1981; LLM, Cambridge U., 1985. Bar: N.B. 1982, N.S. 1983. Assoc. lawyer Halifax (Can.) Stewart McKelvey Stirling Scales, 1983-87, part-time assoc., 1987-95; asst. prof. law Dalhousie Law Sch., Halifax, 1987-92, assoc. prof., 1992—, dean, 1995—2005. Pres. Nova Scotia Law Reform Commn., 1995-2002; chmn. selection com. Maritime Can. Rhodes Scholarship; bd. dirs. Oxford Frozen Foods Ltd., The Canadian Investors Protection Fund, Canadian Inst. Resources Law, Heritage Gas. Contbr. articles to profl. jours. Mem.: N.S. Barristers Soc., Bar Coun. Office: Dalhousie U Law Sch 6061 University Ave Halifax NS Canada B3H 4H9 Office Phone: 902-494-3495. Business E-Mail: dawn.russell@dal.ca.

RUSSELL, DEBORAH LOUISE, psychologist, researcher; b. Portland, Oreg., Dec. 28, 1977; d. James Monroe and Patricia Ray Russell. BS, Albertson Coll. of Idaho, 2000; MS in Early Intervention/Early Childhood Spl. Edn., U. Oreg., 2003, PhD in Spl. Edn., 2006. Cert. spl. educator early childhood/elem. Oreg. Devel. specialist Western Idaho Tng. Co., Caldwell, 2000; youth rehab. specialist Diamond Ranch Acad., Hurricane, Utah, 2001; field staff Obsidian Trls. Wilderness Therapy Program, Bend, Oreg., 2001; program specialist, vocat. coord. Inclusion Vocat. Support, Inc., Meridian, Idaho, 2002; practicum supr. U. Oreg., Eugene, 2003—05, rsch. coord., 2004—, grad. tchg. fellow, 2005. Named Outstanding Jr. in Psychology, Albertson Coll. of Idaho, 1999, Outstanding Sr. in Psychology, 2000, Collegiate Nat. All-Am. Giant Slalom, US Collegiate Ski Assn., 1999, Collegiate Nat. All- Am. Slalom, 1999, Collegiate Regional Overall Champion Downhill Skiing, 1999; named to Acad. All-Am. 1st Team, 1999; scholar, Choctaw Nation of Okla., 2000, 2003, 2004, 2005, Oreg. Student Assistance Commn., 2003, 2004, 2005; Athletic scholar, Albertson Coll. of Idaho, 1996—2000, Honor Student scholar, 1996—2000, J.L. Scott scholar, 1996—2000, Ray Hickey scholar, 1998, W.G. Bill & Una Shannon Meml. scholar, 1999, Fergusson, Wellman, Rudd, Purdy & Van Winkle, Inc. scholar, 1999, Ray Hickey scholar, 1999, 2000, Columbia Region scholar, Inland Boatmen's Union of the Pacific, 1998, Rhodes Scholarship regional finalist, 1999, Bur. of Indian Affairs grantee, Choctaw Nation of Okla., 1999, Helena DeGnath Wessala scholar, U. Oreg., 2003, 2004, Leon Culbertson scholar, 2004, 2005. Mem.: APA, NEA, Western Psychol. Assn., Oreg. Edn. Assn., Coun. for Exceptional Children, Assn. for Positive Behavior Support, Phi Eta Sigma, Psi Chi, Scarab. Business E-Mail: deborah.russell@unlv.edu.

RUSSELL, DIANE ELIZABETH HENRIKSON, career counselor; b. Chgo., July 18, 1952; d. Arthur Allen and Lois Elizabeth (Wessling) H.; m. Darrell Lee Slider, May 31, 1975 (div. Dec. 1992); m. Thomas Lee Russell, July 27, 1999. BA in Spanish, U. Ill., 1974; MA in Counselor Edn., U. South Fla., 1996. Employment counselor Crown Personnel Inc., Mt. Prospect, Ill., 1974-75; bilingual tchr.'s aide Sch. Dist. #21, Wheeling, Ill., 1975; sec., asst. registrar Yale U., New Haven, 1975-77; asst. to personnel dir., personnel coord. Housing Authority New Haven, 1977-79; benefits specialist Profl. Pensions Inc., New Haven, 1980-81, Chloride Inc., Tampa, Fla., 1981-83; personnel technician II human resources dept. U. South Fla., Tampa, 1984-86, personnel technician III, personnel svcs. specialist, 1986-90, coord. human resources dept., 1990-96, career specialist Career Ctr., 1996—2002, 2004—, counselor, advisor honors coll., 2002—04. Mem. choirs St. Mark United Ch., Valrico, Fla., 1987-99, 2003-, dir. Caregivers, 2001-2003; mem. chorus U. South Fla., 1986-88, women's chorale, 1993-95. Mem. AAUW (treas. 1976-78, 80-81), Am. Assn. Employment in Edn., Fla. Career Profls. Assn., Phi Kappa Phi, Phi Beta Kappa, Alpha Lambda Delta, Lambda Delta, Zeta Tau Alpha Soc. Avocations: singing, theater, going to theme parks, travel. Home: 723 Herlong Ct Brandon FL 33511-7920 Office: U South Fla Fla Career Ctr 4202 E Fowler Ave Stop SVC 2088 Tampa FL 33620-6930 E-mail: dhenrik718@aol.com.

RUSSELL, EILEEN MEYER, music educator; b. Detroit, May 20, 1964; d. Richmond George Meyer and Eleanor Elizabeth Seidl; m. Andrew Milo Russell, Dec. 21, 1998. MusB, Ind. U., Bloomington, 1987; MusM, U. No. Iowa, Cedar Falls, 1989; MusD, Ind. U., Bloomington, 1996. Asst. prof. music Vincennes U., Ind., 1989—93; instr. music Austin Peay State U., Clarksville, Tenn., 1993—94; assoc. prof. music Del Mar Coll., Corpus Christi, Tex., 1995—2006, Southwestern U., Georgetown, Tex., 2006—. Euphonium instr. Blue Lake Fine Arts Camp, Twin Lake, Mich., 2004—; presenter in field. Contbr. articles to profl. jours. Mem.: Internat. Tuba Euphonium Assn. (asst. membership coord. 2005—). Office: Southwestern Univ Sarafin Sch Fine Arts Georgetown TX 78626 E-mail: russelle@southwestern.edu.

RUSSELL, ELISE BECKETT, piano educator; b. Misawa AFB, Japan, June 16, 1955; d. George Stanley and Jettie Louise (Thomas) Beckett; m. Michel Gene Russell, Jan. 31, 1981; 1 child, Sean Michael. BMusic, U. Miss., 1976. Tchr. English and music Millington (Tenn.) H.s., 1977-79; tchr. music Port Sulphur (La.) Elem., Middle and High Schs., 1979-80; piano lab., pvt. piano tchr., accompanist self employed, Bay St. Louis, Miss., 1980-81, pvt. piano tchr. Kenner, La., 1981-86, Sugar Land, Tex., 1987—. Adjudicator Nat. Guild Piano Tchrs.; mem. The Piano Curriculum Series, LLC. Asst. youth councilor United Meth. Ch., Bay St. Lois, 1980; PTO bd. dirs. Colony Bend Elem. Sch., Sugar Land, 1989-90; founder Bay St. Louis Fine Arts Coun., mem., dir. players; soloist St. Charles Christian Ch. Named to Outstanding Young Women of Am., 1981. Mem. Tex. Music Tchrs. Assn. (theory coord., presenter, nominations mem., dist. asst., bd. dirs. 2001, chmn. cmty outreach and edn., 2001, pres. ind. music tchrs. assn., 2001—), Ind. Music Tchrs. Assn. (founder, charter mem., pres. 2001). Methodist. Avocations: gardening, sewing, home renovation. E-mail: pianolesson@mylinexisp.com.

RUSSELL, FLORENCE L., elementary school educator; d. Helmer Russell, Jr. and Alma D. Russell. BS, Albany State Coll., Ga., 1972; MS, Nova U., Fort Lauderdale, Fla., 1995. Cert. tchr. Fla., 1972. Tchr. Lee County Sch. Dist., Fort Myers, Fla., 1972. Orgn. head Boy Scout #217, 2005—; recording sec. St. Mary's Program M.B. Ch., 1980—2005; grade level chmn./team leader Tanglewood Riverside Sch., Fort Myers, Fla., 1977—2003; dir. Tanglewood Riverside After Sch. Program, Fort Myers, Fla., 1988—96; pres. Tanglewood Riverside Sch. PTA, Fort Myers, Fla., 2002—04; chmn. sch. adv. com. Tanglewood Riverside Sch., Fort Myers, Fla., 2004—06, environ. edn. tchr. laison Fla., 1973—2006. Recipient Outstanding Vol. award, Tanglewood Riverside PTA, 2004. Mem.: Fla. PTA, Nat. PTA. Democrat. Office Phone: 239-936-0891. Personal E-mail: florenrss@aol.com.

RUSSELL, FRANCIA, ballet director, educator; b. LA, Jan. 10, 1938; d. W. Frank and Marion (Whitney) R.; m. Kent Stowell, Nov. 19, 1965; children: Christopher, Darren, Ethan. Studies with, George Balanchine, Vera Volkova, Felia Doubrouska, Antonina Tumkovsky, Benjamin Harkarvy; student, NYU, Columbia U.; degree (hon.), Seattle U., 2003. Dancer, soloist N.Y.C. Ballet, 1956-62, ballet mistress, 1965-70; dancer Ballets USA/Jerome Robbins, N.Y.C., 1962; tchr. ballet Sch. Am. Ballet, N.Y.C., 1963-64; co-dir. Frankfurt (Fed. Republic Germany) Opera Ballet, 1976-77; dir., co-artistic dir. Pacific N.W. Ballet, Seattle, 1977—; dir. Pacific N.W. Ballet Sch., Seattle. Affiliate prof. of dance U. Wash. Dir. staging over 100 George Balanchine ballet prodns. throughout world, including Russia and China, 1964—. Named Woman of Achievement, Matrix Table, Women in Comm., Seattle, 1987, Gov.'s Arts award, 1989, Dance Mag. award, 1996, Brava award Women's U. Club, 2003. Mem. Internat. Women's Forum. Home: 2833 Broadway E Seattle WA 98102-3935 Office: Pacific NW Ballet 301 Mercer St Seattle WA 98109-4600

RUSSELL, HARRIET SHAW, social worker; b. Detroit, Apr. 12, 1952; d. Louis Thomas and Lureleen (Hughes) Shaw; m. Donald Edward Russell, June 27, 1980; children: Lachante Tyree, Krystal Lanae. BS, Mich. State U., 1974; AB, Detroit Bus. Inst., 1976; BA in Pub. Adminstrn., Mercy Coll., Detroit, 1988; MSW, Wayne State U., 1992. Factory staff Gen. Motors Corp., Lansing, Mich., 1973; student supr. tour guides State of Mich., Lansing, Mich., 1974; mgr. Ky. Fried Chicken, Detroit, 1974-75; unemployment claims examiner State of Mich. Dept. Labor, Detroit, 1975-77, asst. payment worker, 1977-84, social svcs. specialist, 1984-90; pres. Victory Enterprises, 1991; social worker Detroit Bd. Edn., 1992—. Ind. contractor Detroit Compact; moderator Mich. Opportunity Skills and Tng. Program, 1985-86. Vol. Mich. Cancer Soc., East Lansing, 1970-72, Big Sisters/Big Bros., Lansing, 1972-73; elected rep. Mich. Coun. Social Svcs. Workers; spkr. Triumph Bapt. Ch., Detroit, 1976-80; chief union steward Mich. Employees Assn., Lincoln Park, 1982-83; leader Girl Scouts U.S.; area capt. Life Worker Project Program; bd. dirs. Neighborhood Found., 1995-97. Wayne State U. scholar, 1990-91, Deans scholar, 1991-92; recipient Outstanding Work Performace Merit award Mich. Dept. Social Svcs., 1979, Unsung Hero award Neighborhood Found., 1995; elected to Wayne State Sch. Social Work Bd., 1992-98. Mem. NAFE, Am. Soc. Profl. and Exec. Women, Assn. Internat. Platform Spkrs., Mich. Coun. Social Svcs. Workers, Nat. fedn. Bus. and Profl. Womens Clubs Inc. U.S.A. (elected del. to China), Nat. Assn. Black Social Workers, Wayne State U. Social Work Alumni Assn. (bd. dirs. 1992-98), Delta Sigma Theta. Democrat. Baptist. Office: PO Box 361 Lincoln Park MI 48146-0361 E-mail: harrietblessed@aol.com.

RUSSELL, JACQUELINE ANNETTE, recreation director; b. N. Attleboro, Mass., Mar. 5, 1936; d. Fernod and Bella Viola (Dion) Dupuis; m. Donald Paine Russell (div.); children: Michael Robert, Mark Donald, Mark Donald, Nancy Jennifer Russell O'Connor, Matthew George. AA, Quinsigamon Cmty. Coll., Worchester, Mass., 1977; BS magna cum laude, Fitchburg State Coll., Fitchburg, Mass., 1981. Svc. rep. New Eng. Tel. & Tel. Co., Fitchburg, Mass., 1953—61; exec. dir. and downtown mgr. Clinton Area C. of C., Clinton, Mass., 1980—81, exec. dir., 1980—88. Editor: Know Your Town, 1969, Clinton, 1982; contbr. articles pub. to profl. jour. Fund raiser Pub. TV Boston Channel 2, Boston, 1965—67; pres. League of Women Voters, Clinton, 1969—71; v.p., bd. mem. Clinton Cmty. Devel. Corp., Bolton, 1970—73; adv. bd. Clinton Pub. Sch., Clinton, Mass., 1970; bd. dirs. Clinton Area Cmty. Chest, Clinton, 1980—83. Mem.: AARP, Nat. Arbor Found., Womens History Mus. Avocations: gardening, golf, painting, knitting.

RUSSELL, JOY R., computer scientist, educator; d. L.J. and Barbara P. Russell. AAS, Jones County Jr. Coll., Ellisville, Miss., 2001; BS, William Carey Coll., Hattiesburg, Miss., 1998; MS, USM, Hattiesburg, Miss., 2002. Instr. Meridian Cmty. Coll., Miss., 2002—. Mem.: Phi Beta Lambda. Avocations: camping, hiking. Office: Meridian CC 910 Hwy 19 N Meridian MS 39307 Office Fax: 601-484-8704. E-mail: jrussell@meridiancc.edu.

RUSSELL, JOYCE ANN, secondary school educator, librarian; b. Nashville, Mich., May 15, 1940; d. Lawrence Kern and Beatrice Laurine Russell. BA in Edn., Mich. State U., East Lansing, 1962; MLS, Western Mich. U., Kalamazoo, 1972. Tchr. Grand Rapids Pub. Sch., Mich., 1962—70, Northview Pub.Sch., Mich., 1970—72; libr., media specialist Shaker H.S. City Sch., Ohio, 1972—95; ret. Editor, tchr. Summer Sunday Sch. Curriculum, 2002; editor Jr. Ch. Curriculum, 2004; summer sch. tchr. Shaker Heights City Sch., Ohio, 1984—85; esol tutor Shaker Heights, 1996—99. Vol. tchr. Cleve. Heights Sch., Ohio, 1997—99; singer Met. Choir of Praise, Grand Rapids, Mich., 1970—72; sec., v.p. Chalfant Condo Bd., 1980—99. Recipient Star award, United Meth. Women, 2003, Cert. of Appreciation, 1999—2000. Mem.: Eaton County Retired Sch. Personnel, Bellevue Hist. Soc., Delta Kappa Gamma, Kappa Delta Pi. Meth. Avocations: cooking, flower arranging, crafts, reading.

RUSSELL, JOYCE ANNE ROGERS, retired librarian; b. Chgo., Nov. 6, 1920; d. Truman Allen and Mary Louise (Hoelzle) Rogers; m. John VanCleve Russell, Dec. 24, 1942; children: Malcolm David, John VanCleve. Student, Adelphi Coll., 1937; BS in Chemistry, U. Ky., 1942; M.L.S., Rosary Coll., 1967; postgrad., Rutgers U., 1970-71. Research chemist Sherwin Williams Paint Co., Chgo., 1942-45; reference librarian Chicago Heights (Ill.) Pub.

Library, 1959-61; librarian Victor Chem. Works, Chicago Heights, 1961-62; lit. chemist Velsicol Chem. Corp., Chgo., 1964-67; chemistry librarian U. Fla., Gainesville, 1967-69, interim assoc. prof., 1967-69; librarian Thiokol Chem. Corp., Trenton, N.J., 1969-73; supr. library operations E.R. Squibb Co., Princeton, N.J., 1973-80, sr. research info scientist, 1980-91. Mem. library adv. commn. Mercer Community Coll., 1979—; adv. asso. Rutgers U. Grad. Sch. Library and Info. Scis., 1978— Editor: Bibliofile, 1967—69; contbr. articles to profl. jours. Mem. PTA, 1950-66; den mother Cub Scouts, 1952-59. Mem. Spl. Libraries Assn. (sec., dir., v.p., pres. Princeton-Trenton 1971, 75-80), Am. Chem. Soc. (bus. mgr., sec., dir. Trenton sect. 1969-78), AAUW, Mortar Board, Beta Phi Mu, Sigma Pi Sigma, Chi Delta Phi, Pi Sigma Alpha. Home: 1189 Parkside Ave Trenton NJ 08618-2625

RUSSELL, JUDITH KAY, educator, researcher; b. Unionville, Tenn., July 23, 1952; d. Johny Dual South and Treva Opal Stephens; m. Gether Dale Russell; 1 child, Melissa Rhea. AS, Motlow State C.C., Lynchburg, Tenn., 1990; BA, MA, Mid. Tenn. State U., Murfreesboro, 1994, DA, 2000. Asst. prof. Motlow Coll., Lynchburg, Tenn., 2000—. Moderator Women and Power Conf., 2002, 03; rsch. in field. Recipient Faculty Excellence award, Matolow Coll., 2001—04. Mem.: Rotary, Sigma Tau Delta (life). Democrat. Avocations: gardening, white water rafting. Office: Motlow State CC Dept Edn Murfreesboro TN

RUSSELL, JUDY C., government agency administrator; children: Christopher, Michael, Catherine. BA cum laude, Dunbarton Coll. of the Holy Cross, Washington; MLIS, Cath. U. Am., Washington. Libr. Office of Tech. Assessment; staff mem. program of policy studies in sci. and tech. George Washington U., Washington; staff mem. COMSAT Labs.; dir. fed. depository libr. program Govt. Printing Office, Washington, dir. office of electronic info. svcs., 1991—96, supt. documents, 2003—; dir. govt. svcs. divsn. IDD Ent., 1996—98; dep. dir. Nat. Commn. on Librs. and Info. Scis., 1998—2003. Cons. in field. Recipient Spl. award, Fed. Computer Week's Fed. 100: The Readers' Choice awards, 1993. Office: Govt Printing Office 732 N Capitol St NW Washington DC 20401

RUSSELL, JUDY D., mathematics educator; b. Memphis, Mar. 9, 1953; BS, U. Tenn., 1975; MS, Memphis State U., 1986. Profl. and career ladder II, Tenn. Tchr. math. Memphis City Schs., 1975—. Recipient Outstanding Tchr. award Tandy Tech. Scholars, 1992. Mem. Memphis Urban Math. Collaborative, Nat. Coun. Tchrs. Math. Office: Raleigh Egypt High Sch 3970 Voltaire Ave Memphis TN 38128-2298

RUSSELL, KAREN SUE, musician, educator; b. Hartford, Conn., Oct. 27, 1961; d. Olga Y and Thomas Walter Bowry; m. Trent Justin Russell; children: Taylor, Jake. B in Music Edn. and Performance, Ithaca Coll., 1984; MSc in Edn., Coll. St. Rose, 1989. Cert. perm. tchr. in music K-12, adjudicator N.Y. State Sch. Music Assn. Prin. second violin Schenectady Symphony Orch., Schenectady, NY, 1985—95; orch. dir./strings tchr. Niskayuna Ctrl. Schs., Niskayuna, NY, 1989—2000; adj. music faculty Coll. St. Rose, Albany, NY, 1990—2003; sect. violinist Glens Falls Symphony Orch., Glens Falls, NY, 1991—2000; orch. dir., strings tchr. Burnt Hills-Ballston Lake Ctrl. Schs., Burnt Hills, NY, 2000—. Guest conductor Dutchess County Music Educators Assn., Poughkeepsie, NY, 1990, Saratoga/Warren County Music Educators Assn., Burnt Hills, NY, 1991, Saratoga Warren County Music Educators Assn., Queensbury, NY, 1997, Shenendehowa Ctrl. Schs. Dist. String Festival, Clifton Park, NY, 2001; adj. prof. music theory SUNY, Albany, NY, 2002—. Recipient Performance award, N.Y. State Sch. Music Assn. 60th Ann. Conf., 1996. Mem.: Am. Fedn. Musicians, N.Y. State Tchr.'s Union, N.Y. State Sch. Music Assn. Conservative. Avocation: travel. Office: Burnt Hills-Ballston Lake CSD 88 Lakehill Rd Burnt Hills NY 12027 Office Phone: 518-399-9141 3184. Business E-Mail: krussell2@nycap.rr.com.

RUSSELL, KERI, actress; b. Fountain Valley, Calif., Mar. 23, 1976; Actress in films: Honey, I Blew Up the Kids, 1992, Dead Man's Curve, 1998, Mad About Mambo, 2000, We Were Soldiers, 2002, The Upside of Anger, 2005; TV series include: MMC, 1989, Mickey Mouse Club, 1991-93, Emerald Cove, 1993, Daddy's Girls, 1994, Malibu Shores, 1996, Roar, 1997, Felicity, 1998-2002 (Golden Globe for Best Performan by an Actress in a TV series 1999); TV films include: MMC in Concert, 1993, Clerks, 1995, The Babysitter's Seduction, 1996, The Lottery, 1996, When Innocence is Lost, 1997, Eight Days a Week, 1997, Cinderelmo, 1999; TV guest appearances include: Boy Meets World, 1993, Married.with Children, 1987, 7th Heaven, 1996, Roar, 1997. Winner Golden Globe for best performance by an actress in a TV series for Felicity, 1999. Office: The Gersh Agy 232 N Canon Dr Beverly Hills CA 90210-5302

RUSSELL, LOUISE, education educator; b. Stratford, Okla., Aug. 9, 1931; d. Virgel Wylie and Louise J. (Hayden) R. BA magna cum laude, Oklahoma City U., 1953; MA, Northwestern U., 1955; PhD, Ind. U., 1977; postgrad., Colo. State U., 1981-82. Tchr. pub. schs., Sterling, Colo., 1958-59, Washington-Lee H.S., Arlington, Va., 1959-62, John Handley H.S., Winchester, Va., 1962-63, Weld Sch. Dist. No. 6, Greeley, Colo., 1963-68, 72-87, Colegio Internat., Valencia, Venezuela, 1968-69, Holmdel Schs., N.J., 1971-72; chmn. staff devel. team, English and basic skills Northland Pioneer Coll., Holbrook, Ariz., 1987-91, also subject specialist, 1987-91; instr. English humanitiea Ea. N.Mex. U., 1992-93; grant dir. Title V Indian edn. Dulce Ind. Sch. Dist., 1994-96; chmn. English dept. Santa Rosa Consol Schs., 1996-98. Adj. faculty Otero Jr. Coll., La Junta, Colo., 1999-2000. Author: Understanding Folklore, 1975, Understanding Folk Music, 1977; also articles. Named Tchr. of Yr., Masons. Mem. MLA, Am. Anthrop. Assn., Am. Folklore Soc., Nat. Coun. Tchrs. English, Phi Delta Kappa.

RUSSELL, LOUISE BENNETT, economist, educator; b. Exeter, N.H., May 12, 1942; d. Frederick Dewey and Esther (Smith) B.; m. Robert Hardy Cosgriff, May 3, 1987; 1 child, Benjamin Smith Cosgriff. BA, U. Mich., 1964; PhD, Harvard U., 1971. Economist Social Security Adminstrn., Washington, 1968-71, Nat. Commn. on State Workmen's Compensation Laws, Washington, 1971-72, Dept. Labor, Washington, 1972-73; sr. economist Nat. Planning Assn., Washington, 1973-75; sr. fellow Brookings Instn., Washington, 1975-87; rsch. prof. Inst. for Health, Health Care Policy and Aging Rsch. Rutgers U., New Brunswick, N.J., 1987—, prof. econs., 1987—. Chmn. health care policy divsn. Rutgers U., 1988—. Author: Technology in Hospitals, 1979, The Baby Boom Generation and the Economy, 1982, Is Prevention Better Than Cure, 1986, Evaluating Preventive Care: Report on a Workshop, 1987, Medicare's New Hospital Payment System: Is It Working, 1989, Educated Guesses: Making Policy About Medical Screening Tests, 1994, (with MR Gold, JE Siegel and MC Weinstein) Cost-Effectiveness in Health and Medicine, 1996, also numerous articles; assoc. editor Med. Decision Making, 2004—. Mem. U.S. Preventive Svcs. Task Force, 1984-88; co-chair Panel on Cost Effectiveness in Health and Medicine DHHS, USPHS, 1993-96. Mem. Inst. Medicine of NAS (elected mem., com. to study future pub. health 1986-87, bd. on health scis. policy 1989-91, com. on clin. practice guidelines 1990-91, com. on setting priorities for practice guidelines 1994, nat. cancer policy bd. 2001-05). Office: Rutgers U Inst for Health Care Policy 30 College Ave New Brunswick NJ 08901-1293 Business E-Mail: lrussell@rci.rutgers.edu.

RUSSELL, MARGARET JONES (PEG RUSSELL), retired secondary school educator, writer; b. Durham, N.C., Apr. 25, 1938; d. Roderic O. and Margaret (Moore) Jones; m. Michael Morgan Russell; children: Lauren Skinner, Carol Martin, Seth Russell, Jay Russell. BA, Muskingum Coll., 1961. Ordained deacon Presbyn. Ch., 1970. Tchr. Sarasota (Fla.) County Sch. Bd., 1962-97, Sarasota H.S., 1982-96, ret., 1997. Sponsor literary mag. Quest, 1988-1997, contbg. writer Cherokee Scout. Editor: (newsletter) The Mainsail, 1992-95; contbr. poems to profl. pubs. ARC vol. Sarasota Meml. Hosp., 1966-83, aux. vol., 1994-2005; reader Fla. Studio Theatre, Sarasota, 1980-2005. Sarasota Herald Tribune scholar, 1993; Fla. Writing Project fellow, 1990. Mem. Nat. Coun. Tchrs. English, Mystery Writers Am., Fla. Coun. Tchrs. English, N.C. Writer's Network, Light Verse Workshop (co-chair 1995, chair 1998-2004), Sarasota Fiction Writers, Selby Poets, Sarasota Genealogical Soc., Alpha Gamma Delta. Presbyterian. Home: PO Box 1651 Murphy NC 28906-1651

RUSSELL, MARY ANN, secondary school educator; b. Murray, Ky., Oct. 12, 1932; d. Elginn Newton Underwood and Mary Louise Orr Underwood; m. Allen Wells Russell, Aug. 6, 1953; children: Mark Allen, Lisa Louise. BA, Murray State U., 1954, MA, 1956; cert. Rank 1, U. Colo., 1958; PhD, Vanderbilt U., 1970. Cert. Tchr. Ky. Dept. Edn., 1955. Tchr. English Murray City Sch., Murray, Ky., 1955—65, Paducah C.C., Paducah, Ky., 1965—66, Martin Jr. Coll., Pulaski, Tenn., 1968, Murray H.S., Murray, 1970—95; ret., 1995. Com. mem. Cmty. Edn., Murray, 1999—2000, Calloway 2020, Murray, 1999—2002, Cmty. United Benevolance Svc., Murray, 2001—02. Recipient Ky. Shakespeare Tchr. of Yr. award, State Shakespeare Festival, 1987, Golden Tchr. award, Ashland Oil, 1992, Tchr. of Yr. award, Kiwanis Club, 1992. Mem.: Calloway County Tchrs., Ky. Retired Tchrs., Murray Women's Club (pres. 1999—2002, Outstanding Clubwoman award 2001). Republican. Baptist. Avocations: reading, bridge, travel, cooking. Home: 1503 Sycamore Street Murray KY 42071

RUSSELL, MARY RHODES, state supreme court justice; b. Hannibal, Mo., July 28, 1958; d. Cleveland Jerome and Mary Elisabeth (Stewart) Rhodes; m. James Lowell Russell, Nov. 25, 1995. BA in Mass. Comms., BS in Home Econs., Truman State U., 1980; JD, U. Mo., Columbia, 1983. Bar: Mo. 1983, Ill. 1984, U.S. Dist. Ct. (ea. dist.) 1984, U.S. Supreme Ct. 1992. Adminstrv. asst. Mo. Senate, Jefferson City, 1980-83, law clk., 1983-84; ptnr. Clayton & Rhodes, Hannibal, 1984-95; judge Mo. Ct. Appeals (ea. dist.), St. Louis, 1995—2004, Mo. Supreme Ct., 2004—. Author: Enforcement of Discovery Sanctions, 1994. Bd. dirs. Comm. on Ret., Removal and Discipline of Judges, St. Louis, 1994-95, Matthews-Dickey Boys & Girls Club; mem. urban campout project Girl Scouts USA, St. Louis, 1996; mem., past pres. PEO, Hannibal, 1993-95, Jefferson City, 1995—. Recipient Equal Justice award Legal Svcs. Ea. Mo., 1994, Citation of Merit award U. Mo. Sch. Law, 1997; Henry Toll fellow, 1997. Mem. Bar Assn. St. Louis (chair bench/bar rels. 1996-97), Woman Lawyers Assn. St. Louis, Nat. Assn. Women Judges, Kansas City Met. Bar Assn., Mo. Lawyer Trust Account Found. (vice chmn., bd. dirs. 1990-95), Rotary (program chmn. 1996-97). Episcopalian. Avocations: cardinal baseball, travel, cooking. Office: Supreme Ct Mo PO Box 150 Jefferson City MO 65102 Office Phone: 573-751-6880. Business E-Mail: mary.russell@courts.mo.gov.*

RUSSELL, MARYANNE, photographer; Grad., NYU; student, Internat. Ctr. Photography. Staff photographer Time Inc.; owner Maryanne Russell Photography Inc., 1986—. Photographer (works appeared at) Acad. Art Coll., San Francisco, Lobet Gallery, NYC, Grant Gallery, Chelsea Art Gallery, (group exhbns.) Sephora's Flagship store. Mem.: Am. Soc. Media Photographers, NY Women in Comm. (Liz Hoover award 1994). Achievements include photography clients AT&T, Christian Dior, HBO, NY Giants, Paramount Pictures, People mag., Time Warner Inc., Viacom, and many others. Office: Maryanne Russell Photography Inc 230 E 52nd St Ste 1B New York NY 10022 Office Phone: 212-308-8722.

RUSSELL, MAXINE, poet, writer; b. St. Paul, Feb. 17, 1912; d. Maximilian Karl Kaiser and Klara Treubert; m. Robert Lee Russell, Oct. 2, 1946; children: James Max, Roberta Russell Fraser. BA, U. Minn., 1932. Retail mgr. Merriam Pk. Floral, St. Paul, 1932—46. Poetry reader, spkr. Career Day Cmty. Leaders, 1990; poetry reader Arts in the Pk., Brainerd, Minn., 1995—99. Author: (book) Leaves from a Greenhouse, 1984, Honey in the Heart, 1987, Jungle Angel: Bataan Remembered, 1988, (poems) Searching for Star Trillium, 1997, Crossing Wild Moccasin Trails, 2001; contbr. articles and poems to local mags. and newspapers. Chmn. UNICEF Halloween Dr., Brainerd, 1973—76. Recipient Appreciation cert., U. Minn. Alumni Assn., 1980, 1981, award of Merit, Minn. State Horticulture Soc., 1990. Mem.: AAUW, Heartland Poets, League Minn. Poets (Minn. Poet laureate 2001—), Nat. Fedn. State Poetry Socs. Republican. Roman Catholic. Avocations: gardening, beekeeping. Home: 15277 Russell Rd N Brainerd MN 56401

RUSSELL, MELINDA FARRAR, music educator; b. Arlington, Va., Oct. 30, 1954; d. Wallace and Kathryn Farrar; m. John Wallace Russell Jr., July 9, 1977; children: John, Charles, Elizabeth. BMus in Edn., Shenandoah Conservatory Music, Winchester, Va., 1976; MMus in Edn., Shenandoah U., Winchester, Va., 1994. Tchr. music Page County Pub. Schs., Luray, Va., 1979—83; youth choir dir. Front Royal United Meth. Ch., 1983—87; dir. music and choral Rappahannock County Pub. Schs., Sperryville, Va., 1990—96, Frederick County Pub. Schs., Winchester, Va., 1996—; dir handbell First United Meth. Ch., 2001—. Mem.: NEA, Frederick County Edn. Assn., Va. Edn. Assn., Music Edn. Nat. Conf., Va. Music Educators Assn. Avocations: reading, gardening. Home: 820 Parishville Rd Gore VA 22637 Office: Redbud Run Elem Sch 250 First Woods Dr Winchester VA 22603

RUSSELL, PAMELA REDFORD, scriptwriter, educator; b. Long Beach, Calif., June 11, 1950; d. George Martin and Helen Glyn (Brewen) R.; children: Caitlin, Maggie, Tess. Student, UCLA, 1970-74. Field prodr. Santa Fe Comm., L.A., 1983-84; exec. prodr. Guiding Star Prodns., L.A., 1994-96. Writer-in-residence San Fernando (Calif.) Valley Profl. Sch., 2005—. Author: The Woman Who Loved John Wilkes Booth, 1978, Wild Flowers, 1982, (screenplay) Am American Woman, 1993; writer for Mary Tyler Moore Show, 1974, Touched By An Angel, 1997, also 14 scripts for Sears and Mut. Radio Theater, 1980-81, (TV show) Touched by An Angel, 1997, (book) Have You Seen Me, 1998. Mem. Nat. Trust for Hist. Preservation, Civil War Trust., Pacific Grove Heritage Soc. Mem. PEN, Authors Guild, Writers Guild Am. West, PEN Ctr. USA West., UCLA Alumni Assn., Nat. Mus. Women in Arts, Nat. Women's History Mus. Avocation: historic preservation.

RUSSELL, PAMELA RUTH, music and theater educator, singer, entertainer; b. Bristol, Tenn., May 5, 1964; d. Edward G. and Mary Ruth Russell. BS in Music Edn., East Tenn. State U., Johnson City, 1988. Choir dir. Chinguapin Grove Baptist Ch., Bluff City, Tenn., 1987—88; choral dir. Cosby HS, Tenn., 1988—2001, Pigeon Force Mid. Sch., Tenn., 2001—04; choral dir., theater arts dir. Pigeon Force HS, 2004—. Choir dir. First Assembly of God Ch., Sevierville, Tenn., 1994—2000; exec. bd. mem. West Prodns., Sevierville, 2000—; singer, entertainer Oldies Show Place Dinner Theatre, Pigeon Force, 2004—. Mem.: Theatre Tchrs. Assn., East Tenn. Vocal Assn., Music Educators Nat. Conf., Daughters of Am. Revolution, Delta Sigma Pi, Delta Omicron. Republican. Protestant. Avocations: swimming, singing, travel. Office: Pigeon Force HS 414 Tiger Dr Pigeon Forge TN 37863

RUSSELL, PEGGY TAYLOR, soprano, educator; b. Newton, N.C., Apr. 5, 1927; d. William G. and Sue B. (Cordell) Taylor; m. John B. Russell, Feb. 23, 1953; children: John Spotswood, Susan Bryce. MusB in Voice, Salem Coll., 1948; MusM, Columbia U., 1950; postgrad., U. N.C., Greensboro, 1977; student, Am. Inst. Music Studies, Austria, 1972, student, 1978; student of Clifford Bair, Nell Starr (hon.), Salem Coll., Winston-Salem, N.C.; student of Edgar Schofield, Chloe Owen, N.Y.C.; student opera-dramatics, Boris Goldovsky, Southwestern Opera Inst.; student of Ande Andersen, Max Lehner, Graz, Austria. Mem. faculty dept. voice Guilford Coll., Greensboro, NC, 1952—53, Greensboro Coll., 1971—72; pvt. tchr. voice Greensboro, 1963—. Co-founder, v.p. sales, mktg. Russell Textiles, Inc., Greensboro, 1988; vis. instr. in voice U. N.C., Chapel Hill, 1973—77; founding artistic dir., gen. mgr. Young Artists Opera Theatre, Greensboro, 1983, staged and produced 18 operatic prodns., 1983—91; gues lectr. opera workshop U. N.C., Greensboro, 1990—91; lectr. opera Friends of Weymouth, Southern Pines, NC, 1994; lectr. on music history and opera, High Point, NC, Ctr. Creative Leadership, Greensboro, 1979—80, 1st Presbyn. Ch., 1982. Singer: debut in light opera as Gretchen in The Red Mill, 1947; singer: (debuts) Rosalinda in Die Fledermaus, 1949, Lola in Cavalleria Rusticana, 1951, Violetta in La Traviata, 1953, Fiordiligi in Cosi fan Tutte, 1956; singer: Marguerite in Faust, 1967, First Lady in The Magic Flute, 1972, mem. Greensboro Orotario Soc., 1955—59; singer: (soprano soloist) The Messiah, 1952, 1958, The Creation, 1955, Solomon, 1958, Presbyn. Ch. of the Covenant, 1958—71; singer: guest appearances Sta. WFMY-TV, 1958—62; singer: (soprano soloist) Greensboro Symphony Orch., 1964, 1980, Ea. Music Festival Orch., 1965, Greensboro Civic Orch., 1980; singer: (soloist in numerous recitals). Judge Charlotte Opera Guild Auditions, 1994; mem. Friendship Force of Guilford County, Netherlands, 1985, Germany, 1987; bd. dirs. Music Theater Assocs., Greensboro Friends of Music, N.C. Lyric Opera, Piedmont Opera Theatre. Grantee N.C. Arts Coun. and NEA, 1991. Mem.: Piedmont Triad Coun. Internat. Vis. (Appreciation award Nat. Coun. Internat. Visitors 1994), N.C. Symphony Soc., Civic Music Assn. (chmn. 1963—64), Atlanta Opera Guild, Broadway Theater League (chmn. 1961—63), Symphony Guild (dir. 1977—78), Greensboro Music Tchrs. Assn. (pres. 1966—67), Music Educators Nat. Conf., N.C. Fedn. Music Clubs (dir. 1956—58), Nat. Assn. Tchrs. of Singing (state gov. 1976—82, coord. Regional Artist Contest 1982—84), Ctrl. Opera Svc., Nat. Opera Assn. (chmn. regional opera cos. com. 1985—91, judge vocal competition auditions 1991, 1992, 1994, chmn. trustees Cofield Endowment 1991), Weatherspoon Art Mus. Guild, English Speaking Union (bd. dirs. Greensboro chpt., chmn. Shakespeare competition 1995), Guilford County Planning/Devel. Office (Forecast 2015 com.), Greensboro Preservation Soc., Greensboro City Club. Home: 3012 W Cornwallis Dr Greensboro NC 27408-6730

RUSSELL, RHONDA CHERYL, piano educator, recording artist, talent scout; b. Ada, Okla., May 19, 1947; d. Joe Roy and Vina Olive (McEntire) Sammons; 1 child, Christopher Nathaniel. BFA in Music, U. Okla., Norman, 1969, postgrad., 1970—71; M of Ch. Music, Performance, Golden Gate Bapt. Theol. Sem., 1984; postgrad., U. Ariz., Tucson, 1986. Tchr. piano, various states, 1969—; music evangelist So. Bapt. Conv., 1969—; asst. choral dept. Elk City H.S. Elk City Pub. Schs., Okla., 1975—78; supr. banking ops. Alaska Statebank, Anchorage, 1978—82; tchg. asst. to piano prof. Golden Gate Bapt. Theol. Sem., Mill Valley, Calif., 1982—83, adj. faculty, 1984—85; touring accompanist, ednl. tutor Tucson Ariz. Boys Chorus, 1985; choral dir., program founder fine arts dept. Buckingham Charter Sch., Vacaville, Calif., 1994—2001; rec. artist, 2002. State music cons. Calif. Bapt. Conv., Fresno, 1984-01; music dir., artistic dir. Solano Childrens Chorus, Fairfield, Calif., 1993-94; music dir. Playground Prodns. Theatre, Vacaville, 1994-96; music conf. clinician Nev. Bapt. Conv., Reno and Las Vegas, 1995-96; con. pianist N.Am. Mission Bd., So. Bapt. Conv., Santa Clara, Calif., 1995; accompanist Anchorage Civic Opera, 1979-81, So. Ariz. Light Opera Co., 1985; minister of music Internat. Bapt. Ch., 1999-2000, Garland Rd. Bapt. Ch., Enid, Okla., 2001-03. Author numerous poems, 4 original songs to CD You're Not Alone, 2003. Pres. Decent Lit. Coun., Ponca City, Okla., 1977-78; campaign office helper Dem. Party of Okla., Oklahoma City, 1968; music dir. nursing home; beauty pageant coach, cons. Miss Am. Pageant Scholarships, Okla. and Calif., 1969—; min. music Bethany United Meth. Ch., Enid, Okla., 2006—. Scholar Calif. Singing Churchwomen and Calif. Bapt. Conv., 1983; Greater Enid Arts Coun. scholar, 2006. Mem. Nat. Guild Piano Tchrs., Music Ednl. Nat. Conf., Music Tchr. Assn. of Calif. (past treas. 1987-89), Calif. Profl. Music Tchrs. Assn. (program chair 1996), U. Okla. Alumni Assn. (life), Tau Beta Sigma (life, treas., v.p., pres. 1965-69, Outstanding Mem. 1965). Democrat. Southern Baptist. Avocations: writing, composing, travel, reading. Home and Office: 1710 E Locust Ave Enid OK 73701-2618 Office Phone: 580-233-1092.

RUSSELL, ROBIN J., broadcast executive; Sr. exec. v.p., gen. mgr. Columbia TriStar Home Enertainment; sr. exec. v.p., gen. mgr. bus. Sony Pictures Home Entertainment. Office: Sony Pictures Home Entertainment 10202 West Washington Blvd Culver City CA 90232*

RUSSELL, SHARON LYNN, educational consultant; d. James C. and Shirley J. Russell. BS in Edn. and Early Childhood, Millersville U., Pa., 1989; MEd in Tchg., Curriculum and Reading, Pa. State U., 2000; PhD in Curriculum and Literacy, U. Md., 2005. Lit. coord. U. Md., College Park, 2002—04, rschr. reading instrn., 2002—03; lit. instr. Loyola Coll., Balt., 2003—05, reading clinic supr., 2004—05; sr. rsch. asst. U. Mich., Ann Arbor, 2005—06. Presenter in field. Recipient Excellence in Tchg. award, U. Md., 2003. Mem.: Am. Ednl. Rsch. Assn., Nat. Reading Conf., Internat. Reading Assn. (Dissertation of Yr. Disting. finalist 2006). Business E-Mail: slrussel@umich.edu.

RUSSELL, STELLA PANDELL, artist, author, educator; b. N.Y.C., June 14, 1927; d. James C. and Dorothy (Ross) Pandell; m. George Russell, Aug. 10, 1951 (dec.); children: Janna, Jonathan, Loriann. BA, Hunter Coll., 1948; MA, Columbia U., 1950, PhD, 1972; M in Comml. Arts, N.Y. Inst. Tech., 1986. Animator, Loucks and Norling Co., 1948; dir. art Alexander's Dept. Stores, N.Y.C., 1948-51; tchr. art pub. schs., N.Y.C., 1951-53; co-dir. Russell-Pandell Art Studies, N.Y.C., 1953-61; lectr. art Hunter Coll., N.Y.C., 1961-65; chmn. art Nassau Community Coll., N.Y., from 1965; one-woman shows include: Oyster Bay Library (N.Y.), 1962, 63, Huntington Library, 1970, Nassau Community Coll., 1971, South Nassau Library, 1973, 83, Firehouse Gallery, 1975, 84, Country Art Gallery, 1977; group shows include: N.Y. State U. traveling exhbn., 1969, St. John's U., 1975, Central Hall Gallery, 1976, C.W. Post Coll., 1977, Royal Acad., Stockholm, 1978, 82, Islip Mus., 1985, Fine Art Mus. of Lit., 1987; represented permanent collections Hunter Coll., Sallskapet, Sweden, Zimmerli Coll., Rutgers U.; host Art in World sta. WHPC, Garden City, 1972—, Art and Religion, 2005- . Author: Art in the World, 1975, 84, 89, 94; contbr. articles to profl. jours. Winner Chancellor's award excellence in teaching, 1982. Mem. Profl. Artists Guild, N.Y. State Ann. Jr. Colls., Nat. Assn. Women Artists, N.Y. State African Studies Assn. Unitarian. Club: Mensa. Home: 29 Tiffany Rd Oyster Bay NY 11771-1907 also: 190 Lawton Rd Hilton Head Island SC 29928 Office: Stewart Ave Garden City NY 11530 Personal E-mail: drstellarrussell@aol.com.

RUSSELL-LOVE, ZELDA M., special education educator; b. Idabel, Okla., Feb. 10, 1942; d. Jeffrey Henson and Ruby Faye (McDonald) Smith; m. Samuel D. Russell, May 14, 1960 (div.); children: Shelley Jaynes, Susan Vogel; m. Charles R. Love, June 24, 1998 BS in History and Generic Spl. Edn., U. Tex., Dallas, 1979, MA in Sci. Edn., 1982. Cert. tech. applications specialist. Secondary spl. edn. tchr. Dallas Ins. Sch. Dist., 1979—. Tchr. hosp./homebound students. Contbr. articles to Leadership mag. Mem. Assn. Tex. Profl. Educators, Dallas Assn. Profl. Educators. Achievements include All-State Basketball player 1960. Avocations: travel, walking, reading, computers. Home: 8328 Bocowood Dr Dallas TX 75228-5919 Office Phone: 972-581-4645.

RUSSELL-TYSON, PEARL LEONIE, elementary school educator; b. Kingston, Jamaica, July 10; d. Claudius Sylvester and Daisy Ann Cox; m. Kenneth Lee Tyson; children: Jermeth Angella Fothergill, Rosemary Tyson, Cheryl Andrea Russell, Laurel Emansea Robinson. BA, Mico U., Jamaica, 1977; BS, NSU, Davie, Fla., 1997, MS, 1999; EdD, Nova Southeastern U., Ft. Lauderdale, Fla., 2005. Cert. nurse, Fla. State Bd. Nursing, 1986; personnel mgmt. U. of Arts, Sci. & Tech., 1978. Literacy facilitator Palm Beach Schol Dist./ Belle Glade Elem. Sch., Fla., 1999—; pres. Tyson Ednl. & Cmty. Resources, Inc., Loxahatchee, Fla., 2000—. Tchr. Ministry Edn., Kingston, Jamaica, 1970—85; presenter in field. Pres. Home Owners' Assn., St Catherine, Jamaica, 1972—80; Cub Scout leader Jamaica, 1972—78; Sunday sch. tchr. Hope of the World Christian Ctr. Ministries, 1990—92; min. Hope of the World Christian Ctr. Ministry, Pembroke Pines, Fla., Hope of the World Christian Ctr. Ministries, Loxahatchee, Fla. Recipient Distinction in Edn., Mico U., 1973—76. Mem.: Internat. Reading Assn. Conservative. Avocations: travel, evangelism, reading. Office: Tyson Ednl & Cmty Resources I 16218- 83 Pl N Loxahatchee FL 33470 Office Phone: 561-386-8929. Personal E-mail: leonie710@aol.com.

RUSSMAN, IRENE KAREN, artist; b. Chgo., Mar. 10, 1942; d. Andrew Earl and Irene Margaret Kane (Barthley) James; m. James Ora Duffy, Jan. 27, 1963 (div. Oct. 20, 1993); children: Dawn Ann Duffy, James Sean Duffy,

Maureen Marie Duffy; m. Stephen George Russman, Aug. 10, 2002. BA, Wash. State U., 1985, MFA, 1989; student summer workshops, Red Deer Coll., 2001, Pitchuk Sch. of Glass, 2001. Exhibitions include Galeria 5, Caracas, Venezuela, 1989, Acad. Arts, Riga, Latvia, 1990, Union Gallery, Pullman, Wash., 1991, Chase Gallery, Spokane, Wash., 1992, Virginia Inn, Seattle, 1993, Wash. State U./U. Ill., 1994, Gallery X "Out of the Box", Art Inst. Chgo., 1995, juried summer workshop, Pilchuck Glass Sch., Seattle, 2001, Represented in permanent collections Johanna Bur. Handicapped, Chgo., Gordon Gilkey Collection, Portland Art Mus., Modern Art Gallery, Leningrad, Russia, Neill Pub. Libr., Vetreria 2001, S.R.L., Murano, Italy, The Nat. Marble Mus., Yreka, Calif., The National Marble Museum. Bd. dirs. Pullman/Moscow Regional Airport; mem. Global Vols. Project, Ostuni, Italy, 1998, Passport Time Forest Svc., 2000. Recipient Civic Appreciation award, City of Pullman Mayor Pete Butkus, 1984. Mem.: Red Hat Soc., Palouse Folklore Soc., Bella Vita Lodge Number 2285. Avocations: folk dancing, flying, travel, gardening. Home: 80 E Ballantrae Dr Shelton WA 98584 Personal E-mail: irussman@hotmail.com.

RUSSO, CHRISTINE FIORELLA, language educator; b. N.Y.C., July 24, 1931; d. Anthony Joseph and Assunta Mary (Moroni) Fiorella; m. Victor Donald Russo, Jr., Apr. 30, 1960. BA, Marymount Manhattan Coll.; MS, Fordham U., 1959; diploma in reading, Hofstra U., 1978, PhD, 1987, postgrad., 1987—; cert. in litigation, Adelphi U. and Nat. Ctr. for Paralegal Tng., 1980. Cert. elem. and secondary English tchr., N.Y., reading specialist, N.Y. Tchr. St. Margaret's Sch., Bronx, N.Y., 1955-56, Sacred Heart, N.Y.C., 1956-57, Bd. Edn., N.Y.C., 1957-60, Harborfields Dist. 6, L.I., 1960—; instr. English, Marymount Manhattan Coll., 1990-96, mem. alumni adv. coun., 1985-96, 1st v.p., bd. dirs., 1995-97, L.I. rep. recruitment program, 1992. Bd. dirs. Sch. Edn., Fordham U., 1995—. Bd. dirs. president's coun. Fordham U., Bronx, 1985-87, active recruitment program, 1983-87, mem. alumnae/i adv. bd. coun., 1994—; campaign worker Dem. Party, N.Y.C., 1990, 92; Marymount rep. N.Y. State Bundy/Affairs Fund, 1982-83; chmn. Ft. Salong Assn., L.I., 1979-83; vol. St. John's Hosp., L.I.; co-dir. Just Say No, Thomas J. Lahey Sch. Recipient Tchr.-Student Participation award Suffolk Reading Coun., 1991—, Tchr.-Student Participation award N.Y. Senate Earth Day Competitions, 1994—, Alumni Achievement award Fordham U., 1998, cert. of participation reflections progam in humanities N.Y. State PTA, 1996-98. Mem. APA, Guilford Internat. Soc. Intelligence Edn. (v.p. 1991—, bd. dirs. 1990—), N.Y. Acad. Scis., N.Y. Orton Dyslexia Soc., Nat. Dyslexia Rsch. Found., Coun. for Exceptional Children, World Coun. for Gifted and Talented Children, Children and Adults with Attention Deficit Disorder, Am. Assn. Higher Edn., Marymount Manhattan Coll. (1st v.p. 1995-97), Fordham U. Alumni Assn. (bd. dirs. adv. coun. Sch. Edn. 1995—), Phi Delta Kappa (1st v.p. chpt. 1995-97). Roman Catholic. Home: 7 Bonnie Dr Northport NY 11768-1448

RUSSO, GINA MARIE, music educator; d. Joseph and Marcia Russo. MusB in Music Edn., SUNY, Fredonia, 2002. Cert. tchr. NY, 2002. Music tchr. Craig Hill Elem. Sch., Greece Ctrl. Sch. Dist., Rochester, 2002—, Bread of Life Christian Acad., Penfield, NY, 2002—. Mem.: Am. String Tchrs. Assn. (student chpt. pres. 2000—01).

RUSSO, IRMA HAYDEE ALVAREZ DE, pathologist; b. San Rafael, Mendoza, Argentina, Feb. 28, 1942; came to U.S, 1972; d. Jose Maria and Maria Carmen (Martinez) de Alvarez; m. Jose Russo, Feb. 8, 1969; 1 child, Patricia Alexandra. BA, Escuela Normal MTSM de Balcarce, 1959; MD, U. Nat. of Cuyo, Mendoza, 1970. Diplomate Am. Bd. Pathology. Intern Sch. Medicine Hosps., Argentina, 1969-70; resident in pathology Wayne State U. Sch. Medicine, Detroit, 1976-80. Rsch. asst., instr. Inst. Histology and Embryology Sch. Medicine U. Nat. of Cuyo, 1963-71, assoc. prof. histology Faculty Phys., Chem. and Math. Scis., 1970-72; rsch. assoc. Inst. Molecular and Cellular Evolution U. Miami, Fla., 1972-73; rsch. assoc. exptl. pathology lab. divsn. biol. scis. Mich. Cancer Foun., Detroit, 1973-75, rsch. scientist, 1975-76, vis. rsch. scientist, 1976-82, asst. mem., pathologist, 1982-89, assoc. rsch. mem., 1989-91, co-dir. pathology reference lab., 1982-86, chief exptl. pathology lab., 1989-91; co-dir. Mich. Cancer Found. Lab. Svcs., 1986-91; mem. Fox Chase Cancer Ctr., 1991—, active staff mem. dept. surgery med. scis. divsn., 2004—; dir. anatomic pathology Am. Oncologic Hosp. Dept. Pathology, 1991-92; dir. Lab. Svcs., 1992-94; chief molecular endocrinology sect. Breast Cancer Rsch. Lab. Fox Chase Cancer Ctr., 1994—; chief resident physician dept. pathology Wayne State U. Sch. Medicine, 1978-80, asst. prof., 1980-82; mem. staff Harper-Grace Hosps., Detroit, 1980-82; adj. prof. Pathology and Cell Biology Jefferson Sch. Medicine/Thomas Jefferson U., 1992—, chairperson Basic Breast Biology Study Sect. U. Calif. Breast Cancer Program, 1997, mem. endocrinology panel peer rev. com. breast cancer rsch. program U.S. Army R & D Command, 1994, 95, 96, 2002, 03, chairperson endocrinology peer rev. com., 1996; ad-hoc mem. biochem. endocrinology study sect. NIH, DHHS, 1994, metabolic pathology study sect., 1996-97; mem. European Commn. Cancer Prevention, 1994—; mem. bd. sci. counselor, sec. health and human svcs. Nat. Toxicology Program Bd., 1994-98; mem. Internat. Life Scis. Inst.-Risk Sci. Inst. Mammary Working Group, 1992—; pres., founder League of Women Against Cancer, Rydal, Pa., 1994—; guest lectr. dept. obstetrics Sch. Medicine U. Nat. of Cuyo, 1965-71; mem. resource devel. subcommittee of the profl. advisory com., Latinas Living Beyond Breast Cancer, 2000—; mem. Breast Cancer Res. Sci. Review Panel, N.J.commr. on cancer rsch., Trenton, N.J., 1997, 2000. Editor-in-chief Jour. Women's Cancer, 1997—; contbr. articles to profl. jours. Rockefeller grantee, 1972-73; Nat. Cancer Inst. grantee, 1978-81, 84-87, 94-99, 2003—, Am. Cancer Soc. grantee 1988-89, 91-94, U.S. Army Med. R&D Command grantee, 1994-99, 2003—; recipient Shannon award Nat. Cancer Inst./NHHSS, 1992-94, Gold medal Inst. U. Dexeus, Barcelona, Spain, 2000. Mem. AAAS, Soc. Española Senología y Patología Mamaria, Nat. Cancer Inst. (breast cancer working group, breast cancer program 1984-88), Nat. Alliance Breast Cancer Orgns. (med. adv. bd. N.Y.C. chpt. 1986—), Ea. Coop. Oncology Group, Coll. Am. Pathologists, Am. Soc. Clin. Pathologists, Am. Assn. Cancer Rsch., Am. Assn. Clin. Chemistry, Internat. Coll. Physicians and Surgeons, Women in Cancer Rsch., The Endocrine Soc., Internat. Assn. Against Cancer, Sigma Xi, Food Quality Protection Act, Sci. Review Bd., Fed. Insecticide Fungi and Rodenticide Act, Adivsory Panel, EPA. Roman Catholic. Office: Fox Chase Cancer Ctr 333 Cottman Ave Philadelphia PA 19111 Office Phone: 215-728-4781. Personal E-mail: Lowac@msn.com. Business E-Mail: Irma.Russo@fccc.edu.

RUSSO, JOAN MILDRED, special education educator; b. New Haven, Aug. 23, 1933; d. Stanley Alfred and Mildred Mary (Burns) Marcotte; div.; children: David C., Thomas E., Mary Russo Herrmann, Elizabeth Russo Sant, Robert J., James E. Goeth. AA, Coll. DuPage, 1975; BS in Edn., No. Ill. U., 1977; MEd, Lewis U., Evanston, Ill., 1985. Cert. K-12 educable mentally handicapped, K-12 learning disabilities, K-12 Trainable mentally handicapped, K-9 elem tchg., Ill. Tchrs. aid Pioneer Sch., West Chgo., 1977-78; pvt. practice Wheaton, Ill., 1978—. Co-editor: Yes, You Can, 1994. Active Dem. political campaigns, Ill., 1960—; sec. Winfield Libr. Assn., 1963-68; bd. dirs. Orton Dyslexia Soc., Ill., 1980-81, sec., 1981-82. Mem. LWV (con-con com., 1972), Orton Dyslexia Soc. (bd. dirs. 1980-81, sec. 1981-82), Nat. Assn. Learning Disabilities, Nat. Ctr. Learning Disabilities. Avocations: music, theater, reading, art, travel. Home and Office: 10 Old Blue Point Rd Scarborough ME 04074-7600 Office Phone: 207-883-3621.

RUSSO, JUDITH A., paralegal, writer; b. Vancouver, Wash., Aug. 24, 1960; d. Michael Haley Russo and Bonnie Marie Blevins. BA, Mt. Holyoke Coll., South Hadley, Mass., 1994. Editl. asst. AP, Seattle, 1981—92; dir. edn. Rape Crisis Ctr. Berkshire County, Pittsfield, Mass., 1995—97; personal fin. advisor Portland, 1998—99; dir. corp. rels. Vancouver Hist. Res., Wash., 2000—01; paralegal Sam Hochberg & Assocs., Portland, 2003—. Vol. Trauma Intervention Program, Portland, Neighborhood Emergency Team. Mem.: Oreg. Trial Lawyers Assn. Avocations: remodeling/rehabilitating properties, writing. Office Phone: 503-775-2588.

RUSSO, LISA ANN, registrar; b. Encino, Calif., Dec. 20, 1961; d. Edmund Severo and Lucille Delores Russo. AA in Politics, Coll. San Mateo; BS, UCLA, 1985, postgrad. Fin. dir. So. Calif. Inst. Architecture, Santa Monica, 1988-92, registrar L.A., 1992—, chief adminstrv. officer, 2003—. Con. Exec. Search Solutions, Newport Beach, Calif., 1999—. Mem. Chgo. Art Inst., 1996—; activist World Wildlife Fund, 1997—, Nature Conservancy, 1998—, Nat. Mus. Women Arts, 1998—, Natural Resources Def. Coun., 1999—. Mem. AAUW, Am. Assn. Collegiate Registrars and Admissions Officers, Nat. Assn. Fgn. Student Admin. Roman Catholic. Avocations: skiing, mountain biking, travel, language, politics. Office: So Calif Inst Architecture 970 E Third St Los Angeles CA 90013 E-mail: lisarusso@sciarc.edu, lrusso3626@earthlink.net.

RUSSO, PATRICIA F., telecommunications company executive; b. Trenton, NJ, June 12, 1952; m. Frank Russo. BA, Georgetown U., 1973; postgrad. in advanced mgmt., Harvard U., 1989; DEng (hon.), Steven Inst. Tech.; D in Entrepreneurial studies (hon.), Columbia Coll., SC. Sales and mktg. mgmt. exec. IBM, 1973-81; with AT&T (now Lucent Techs. Inc.), 1981; pres., Bus Comm. Sys. Unit AT&T (now Avaya Inc.), 1992-96; pres., COO Eastman Kodak Co., 2000—02; exec. v.p. strategy bus. devel. and corp. ops. Lucent Techs. Inc., Murray Hill, NJ, 1997-99, exec. v.p., CEO svc. provider networks Warren, NJ, 1999—2000, pres., CEO Murray Hill, NJ, 2002—03, chmn., CEO, 2003—. Bd. dirs. Lucent Techs. Co., 2002—, Schering-Plough Corp., NJ Mfrs. Ins. Co., Avaya Inc.; chair Nat. Security Telecom. Adv. Com., 2004—. Bd. dirs. Georgetown U.; mem. Network Reliability Interoperability Coun.; mem. appointed by Gov. James McGreevey NJ Commn. on Jobs Growth and Econ. Develop. Named one of 100 Most Powerful Women in Bus., Fortune mag., 1998—2006, 100 Most Influential People, Time mag., 2006, 10 Most Powerful Women in NJ Bus., Star-Ledger, 2006. Office: Lucent Techs Inc 600 Mountain Ave New Providence NJ 07974*

RUSSO, RENE, actress; b. Burbank, Calif., Feb. 17, 1954; m. Dan Gilroy, Mar. 14, 1992; 1 child, Rose. Fashion model Eileen Ford Agy. Actor: (films) Major League, 1989, Mr. Destiny, 1990, One Good Cop, 1991, Freejack, 1992, Lethal Weapon 3, 1992, In the Line of Fire, 1993, Major League 2, 1994, Outbreak, 1995, Get Shorty, 1995, Tin Cup, 1996, Ransom, 1996, Buddy, 1997, Lethal Weapon 4, 1998, The Thomas Crown Affair, 1999, The Adventures of Rocky and Bullwinkle, 2000, Showtime, 2002, Big Trouble, 2002, Two for the Money, 2005, Yours, Mine and Ours, 2005, (TV series) Sable, 1987-88. Address: 8046 Fareholm Dr Los Angeles CA 90046

RUSSO, SABRINA, architect; b. Montreal, Can., Jan. 4, 1982; BS in Arch. cum laude, Ariz. State U., 2004. Student intern OWP/P, 2002—04; arch. intern RNL Design, 2004—. Author of poems. Pell grantee, Ariz. State U., Tempe, 2002, 2003. Avocations: scrapbooks, dance, creative writing, poetry.

RUST, MILDRED D., retired psychiatrist; b. Summit, N.J., Feb. 14, 1928; d. Jared Blanchard and Mildred (Downs) Moore; m. Wallace Richard Rust (div.); children: Paula, Lynn. AB, Barnard Coll., N.Y.C., 1950; MA, Mt. Holyoke Coll., South Hadley, Mass., 1952; MD, Weill Cornell Med. Coll., N.Y.C., 1956. Bd. cert. neurology and psychiatry Am. Bd. Psychiatry and Neurology. Psychiatrist I, II, III Rochester Psychiat. Ctr., 1965—79; pvt. practice Rochester, NY, 1969—98; med. dir. Western Monroe Mental Health Ctr., Rochester, 1980—86; staff psychiatrist Wilson Health Ctr., Rochester, 1986—92; ret. Lectr. Cath. Family Svcs., Rochester, 1980—85. Author: (book) A Unique Life, 2005. Mem. Unitarian-Universalist Svc. Com., 1959—; 1st pres. Rochester Meml. Soc., 1960—63; cons. La Leche League, Rochester, 1959—64; founders PARTNERS, Rochester, 1964—68. Mem.: Nature Conservancy (legacy mem.), Am. Assn. Ret. Persons. Democrat. Unitarian. Avocations: classical music, reading, reading the news, spending time with friends. Home: Sunrise Assisted Living Apt 251 190 Summerhill Rd East Brunswick NJ 08816-4908

RUSTAND, KAY, lawyer; Ptnr. Lawler, Felix & Hall, Arter & Hadden LLP, 1989—2001; v.p., gen counsel Reliance Steel & Aluminum Co., Los Angeles, 2001—. Office: Reliance Steel & Aluminum Co 350 S Grand Ave Ste 5100 Los Angeles CA 90071 Office Phone: 213-687-8792.

RUSTAY, JENNIFER BETH, lawyer; b. Kansas City, Mo., Jan. 30, 1973; m. Allen Harrington Rustay, Sept. 29, 2001. BA, Baylor U., 1995, JD, 1997. Bar: Tex. 1997, U.S. Dist. Ct. (all dists. Tex.), US Dist. Ct. (dist. Colo.), US Ct. Appeals (5th cir.). Law clk. Hon. Sam Johnson US Ct. Appeals (5th cir.), Austin, Tex., 1997—98; atty. Bracewell & Patterson, Houston, 1998—2001, Hagans Burdine Montgomery Rustay & Winchester P.C., Houston, 2001—. Mem. bd. trustees Houston Lawyer Referral Svc. Notes and comments editor: Baylor Law Rev., 1996—97. Named a Rising Star, Tex. Super Lawyers mag., 2006. Fellow: Houston Bar Assn.; mem.: Assn. Women Lawyers (chair jud. screening com.), Houston Trial Lawyers Assn., Assn. Trial Lawyers of Am., Tex. Trial Lawyers Assn., Houston Young Lawyers Assn. Office: Hagans Burdine Montgomery Rustay & Winchester PC 3200 Travis 4th Fl Houston TX 77006*

RUSTGI, EILEEN BOYLE, clinical psychologist; b. N.Y.C., Apr. 4, 1955; d. Francis Edward and Eileen Mary (Meagher) Boyle; m. Vinod Kumar Rustgi, Nov. 5, 1983; children: Sheila, Nina, Neil. BA, Yale U., New Haven, 1977; MA, Cath. U. Am., Washington, 1980, PhD, 1986. Lic. psychologist Md. Intern Pacific Med. Ctr., San Francisco, 1982-83; psychologist Chestnut Lodge Hosp., Rockville, Md., 1995—2001; pvt. practice, 1997—2004; psychologist NIMH, Bethesda, 2004—. Mem.: APA. Roman Catholic. Avocations: travel, aerobics, sailing. Office Phone: 301-435-1553. E-mail: rustgi@mail.nih.gov.

RUTENBERG-ROSENBERG, SHARON LESLIE, retired journalist; b. Chgo., May 23, 1951; d. Arthur and Bernice (Berman) Rutenberg; m. Michael J. Rosenberg, Feb. 3, 1980; children: David Kaifel and Jonathan Reuben (twins), Emily Mara. Student, Harvard U., 1972; BA, Northwestern U., 1973, MSJ, 1975; cert. student pilot. Reporter-photographer Lerner Home Newspapers, Chgo., 1973—74; corr. Medill News Svc., Washington, 1975; reporter-newsperson, sci. writer UPI, Chgo., 1975—84; ret., 1984. Interviewer: exclusives White House chief of staff, nation's only mother and son on death row; others. Vol. Chgo.-Read Mental Health Ctr. Recipient Peter Lisagor award for exemplary journalism in features category, 1980, 81; Golden Key Nat. Adv. Bd. of Children's Oncology Svc. Inc., 1981; Media awards for wire svc. feature stories, 1983, 84, wire svc. news stories, 1983, 84, all from Chgo. Hosp. Pub. Rels. Soc. Mem. Profl. Assn. Diving Instrs., Nat. Assn. Underwater Instrs., Hon. Order Ky. Cols., Hadassah, Sigma Delta Chi, Sigma Delta Tau Home: 745 Marion Ave Highland Park IL 60035-5123

RUTER, RUTH EVELYN, elementary school educator; b. Louisville, Apr. 24, 1923; d. Thurston Lowell and Ida Lee (Shaw) Wise; m. Charles M. Ruter, Apr. 15, 1944. BA, We. Ky. U., Bowling Green, 1948; MA, George Peabody, Nashville, 1953. Tchr. elem. Bullitt County Pub. Schs., Sheperdsville, Ky., 1943, Jefferson County Pub. Schs., Louisville, 1943—79. Pres. 15th Dist. PTA, Louisville, 1981—83; pres. Fern Creek Women's Club, Ky., 1983—85, 1991—93, 2000—02; worthy matron Order Ea. Star, Louisville, 1962—63, 1984—85, 1987—88; coord. meals Ky. Fedn. Women's Club, Louisville, 1994—2006. Named to Hall of Fame, Heritage Festival, 2000, Fern Creek Traditional H.S., 2005. Presbyterian. Home: 9801 Hillock Dr Louisville KY 40291

RUTGARD, LORRAINE LEVIN, hearing impaired educator; b. Chgo., May 29, 1925; d. Sam and Rhea (Schneiderman) Levin; m. Meyer David Rutgard, July 4, 1947; children: Marlan Beth Globerson, Jeffrey Jay. BA, U. Wis., 1946; MA in Spl. Edn., Northeastern Ill. U., 1974. Social worker Hebrew Immigrant Aid Soc. (HIAS), Chgo., 1946-50; tchr. Chgo. Bd. Edn., 1959-72; adminstr. pvt. practice physician Med. Office, Skokie, Ill., 1972-81; ret., 1981. Vol. St. Mary's/Westside Food Bank Alliance, Area Agy. on Aging; docent West Valley Art Mus.; mem. Planned Parenthood; charter mem. Holocaust Mus., Washington. Mem. NOW, Hadassah, Temple Beth Shalom and Sisterhood (mem. CARE com.). Avocations: yoga, hiking, aerobics, snorkeling, sports.

RUTH, DEBORAH ANN, music educator; b. Brookline, Mass., July 25, 1950; d. Neil J. and Mary E. Valerio; m. Gregory J. Ruth, May 1, 1971; children: Melissa, Geoffrey, Jonathan, Stephen, Jennifer. MusB summa cum laude, Columbia Coll., Columbia, SC, 2000. Cert. tchr. of music in piano MTNA, 2001. Pianist, music ministry assoc. Fellowship Baptist Ch., Lexington, SC, 1995—; instr. piano Columbia Coll., Columbia, SC, 2001—. Adjudicator keyboard auditions Richland Sch. Dist. II Tri-Dist. Arts, Columbia, SC, 2003—05. Co-dir. summer music camp Fellowship Baptist Ch., Lexington, SC, 2001—04. Mem.: Columbia Music Tchrs. Assn. (mem. exec. bd. 2000—, corr. sec. 2001—03, adjudicator keyboard auditions 2002—05, v.p. programs. 2003—04, pres.-elect. 2005—), SC Music Tchrs. Assn., Music Tchrs. Nat. Assn. Office: Musical Arts Studios Columbia Coll 1301 Columbia College Dr Columbia SC 29203-5949

RUTH, DIANNE, counselor; b. Flint, Mich., Apr. 28, 1939; AA, L.A. City Coll., 1982; BA in Psychology, Antioch U., Marina Del Rey, Calif., 1983; MA in Counseling Psychology, Sierra U., Santa Monica, Calif., 1985; PhD in Clin. and Counseling Psychology, Union Inst. and U., Cin., 1989; cert., Inst. Life Coach Tng., Ft. Collins, Colo., 2000. Founder, exec. dir. The Healing Tree, Inc., San Diego, Dynamic Resources Internat. Home and Office: Dynamic Resources Internat 1081 Camino del Rio South Ste 202 San Diego CA 92108-3544 Office Phone: 619-546-5309. Personal E-mail: drruth@dynamicresources.net.

RUTHCHILD, GERALDINE QUIETLAKE, training and development consultant, writer, poet; d. Nathan and Ruth (Feldman) Stein; m. Neil Wolinsky, Dec. 31, 1993; 1 child, Nathaniel Gideon Wolinsky. BA summa cum laude, Queens Coll., 1977; MA in Am. Lit., Johns Hopkins U., 1980, PhD in Am. Lit., 1983. Asst. prof. Albion (Mich.) Coll., 1982-84; assoc. Investor Access Corp., N.Y.C., 1984-85; program dir. Exec. Enterprises, Inc., N.Y.C., 1985-86; pres. Ruthchild Assocs., N.Y.C., 1987-90, Exemplar, N.Y.C., 1991-95, Exemplar, Ltd., NY, 1995—. Cons. J.P. Morgan & Co., Inc., MetLife, U.S. Army, Bankers Trust Co., MasterCard Internat., GreenPoint Bank, Koch Industries, Inc., Chase Manhattan Bank N.A., Merrill Lynch, TIAA-CREF, Drake Beam Morin, Trans Union Corp, NatWest Bank, U.S.A., Citibank N.A., Robert Morris Assocs., Goldman, Sachs & Co., Dean Witter Reynolds, Inc., also others, 1987—. Contbr. articles, poems to profl. and lit. jours. Vol. handicapped children N.Y. Foundling Hosp., N.Y.C., 1988-90, Fgn. Visitors Desk, Met. Mus. Art, N.Y.C., 1989-97. Hopkins fellow Johns Hopkins U., 1979-80, Andrew Mellon Found. fellow, 1980-81, 81-82. Mem. ASTD, Internat. Soc. Philos. Enquiry, Phi Beta Kappa. Avocations: foreign languages, needlecrafts, gardening. Office: Exemplar Ltd Ste 9 One Alderwood Syosset NY 11791-4711 Business E-Mail: GQR@exemplar-ltd.com.

RUTHERFOORD, REBECCA HUDSON, computer scientist, educator; b. Elkhart, Ind., Feb. 24, 1948; d. Charles Melvin Hudson and Eunice Klaire (Lund) Edmonds; m. James Kincanon Rutherfoord, Aug. 31, 1968; children: James Kincanon Jr., Charles Penn. BS, Ind. State U., Terre Haute, 1971, MS, 1972, EdD, 1975; MS Computer Sci., So. Poly. State U., Marietta, Ga., 1995. Cert. data processor. Staff asst. Ind. State U., Terre Haute, 1969—71; tchr. vocal music S.W. Parke Schs., Rockville, Ind., 1971—73; fellowship asst. Ind. State U., Terre Haute, 1974—75; tchr. vocal music Slidell H.S., La., 1977—78; programmer, analyst La. State U., Baton Rouge, 1978—79, dir. computer rehab. program, 1979—80; programmer, analyst Hanes Corp., Atlanta, 1980—91; acting dept. chair So. Poly. State U., Marietta, 1989—92, prof. computer sci., 1993—. Cons. Assocs. Group, Inc., Roswell, Ga., 1986—88, Crawford Comm., Atlanta, 1987; adj. prof. Cobb County Bd. Edn., Marietta, 1985—87, Joseph T. Walker Sch., Marietta, 1985—86; asst. prof. Devry Inst., Atlanta, 1981—83; vis. prof. Leicester Poly., 1990; coord. computer sci. grad program So. Poly. State U., Marietta, 1996—97, asst. to pres., 1997—98, interim dean arts and scis., 1998—99, chair MSIT program, 1999—, acting head computer sci. dept., 2000—01, chair, grad. coord. Info. Tech. dept., 2001—, campus liaison So. Assn. Coll. and Schs., 2004—. Bd. dirs., mem. Cherokee Cmty. Habitat for Humanity, 1994—98; choir dir. St. Peter and Paul Episcopal Ch., Marietta, 1981—85, choir mem., 1992—2001, bd. dirs., 1998—2001; Christian edn. dir. St. Francis Episcopal Ch., Denham Springs, La., 1978—80; choir mem. St. David's Episcopal Ch., Roswell, 1985—92; choir dir. Ch. of the Messiah, 2001—. Mem.: Info. Tech. Edn. (spl. interest group), Computer Sci. Edn. (spl. interest group), Nat. Assn. Women Edn., Assn. Computing Machinery, Assn. Info. Tech. Profls., Sigma Alpha Iota, Delta Kappa Gamma. Republican. Avocations: boating, reading. Office: So Poly State Univ 1100 S Marietta Pky Marietta GA 30060-2855 Office Phone: 678-915-7400. Business E-Mail: brutherf@spsu.edu.

RUTHERFORD, DOREEN, artist, construction executive; b. Newton, N.J., Dec. 12, 1966; m. Daniel Grey Rutherford, Aug. 30, 1986; children: Lillian, Julia. Diploma in computer programming, Warren Vocat. Sch., N.J., 1986; pvt. studies in art, with Howard Carr and Charles Slovek. CEO, Rutherford's Excavating, Bend, Oreg., 1992—. Art cons. Gallery Haleiwa, Hawaii, 1988-89, Fettiq Gallery, Haleiwa, 1989-90, Where Eagles Soar Gallery, Sun River, Oreg., 1991-92; mem. adv. bd. Humane Soc. Art Show, Bend, 1992; distbr. lit. Living Waters, Beijing and Canton, 1987, Taipei, Taiwan, 1987. Illustrator: (book) Bend Business Woman's Association, 1994; one-woman shows Rix of Hawaii, Haleiwa, Oahu, 1987, Sun River (Oreg.) Coffee Co., 1999, Wind River Gallery, Bend, Oreg., 1997, Charlotts Fine Art Gallery, 2001, Artscape Gallery, 2004, 05, 06. Contbr. Sara Fisher Cancer Rsch. Auction, Bend, Oreg.; sole contbr. SunRiverDance Acad. Ann. Presentation, 2002. Mem. OPA, Oreg. C. of C. Avocations: skiing, equestrian sports, antiques, writing. E-mail: ddlj@cmc.net.

RUTHERFORD, GUINEVERE FAYE, surgeon; b. Cleve., Sept. 17, 1955; d. Alex and Alice Rose Watson; m. La Juane Edward Rutherford, Apr. 23, 1999. Grad. liberal arts, Highland Park C.C., Highland Park, Mich., 1981; BS Allied Health, Madonna U., 1983; MA Bus. Sci., Ctrl. Mich. U., 1991. Surg. technologist Children Hosp. Mich., Detroit, 1981—85; clin. and classroom instr. Madonna U., Livonia, Mich., 1983; surg. unit specialist Botsford Gen. Hosp., Farmington Hills, Mich., 1985—87, surg. technologist, 1985—95; clin. and classroom instr. Detroit Bd. Edn., 1986, Highland Park (Mich.) C.C., 1992—94; surg. technologist various hosps., 1995—, St. John Hosp., Detroit, 1998—99. Mem.: Am. Bus. Women Assn., Assn. Surg. Tech. Office: Surg Helping Hand Inc PO Box 47317 Oak Park MI 48237

RUTHERFORD, VICKY LYNN, special education educator; b. Florence, SC, Sept. 12, 1947; BS, Hampton U., 1969, MA, 1971; PhD, Mich. State U., 1991. Cert. tchr. French, spl. edn., reading specialist, Va., tchr. spl. edn., S.C. Social worker day care Hampton (Va.) Dept. Social Svc., 1970-72; reading therapist, asst. dir., dir. Bayberry Reading Clinic, Hampton, 1973-77; tchr. reading, English, counselor York County Schs., Yorktown, Va., 1977-85; staff advisor, asst. to course coord. Mich. State U., East Lansing, 1985-90; tchr. autism/emotionally impaired Florence (S.C.) Dist. 1 Sch. Sys., 1996—2004; tchr. emotionally impaired Long Beach Unified Sch. Dist., 2004—. Instrnl. designer: Addiction Severity Index #1, 1987, #2, 1988, Managing a Diverse Workforce, 1990; designer, trainer: Project Teach, 1991; designer, developer: (video) Camp Takona Summer Experience, 1992. Bass guitarist, Sunday sch. sec., youth worker, Sun. sch. supt. Progressive Ch. of Jesus, Florence, 1992-98, Greater Zion Tabernacle Apostolic Ch., Florence, 1998-2004, City of Refuge Gardena, Calif., 2004-. Fellow Mich. Dept. Edn., 1987-89. Mem. Internat. Reading Assn. Office: Rogers Mid Sch 365 Monrovia Ave Long Beach CA 90803

RUTLEDGE, DEBORAH JEAN, secondary school educator; b. St. Louis, Mar. 13, 1954; d. George Roosevelt and Morie Louise Albin; m. Mark H. Rutledge, Mar. 12, 1978 (div. July 28, 1997); children: Mary-Esther, Martha-Ann, Joanna-Ruth, Susanna-Rachel, Sarah-Naomi. MusB, So. Meth.

U., 1976; MEd, U. No. Tex. Cert. tchr. reading, elem., ESL, music, English lang., arts and English Tex. Reading tchr.'s aide Sam Houston Mid. Sch., Irving, Tex., 1994—95; reading tchr. Irving H.S., 1995—2002; reading and ESL tchr. Lorenzo de Zavala Mid. Sch., Irving, 2002—03, counselor, 2002—03. Reading tutor, Irving; piano tchr., Irving. Pianist The Ch. in Oklahoma City, 1976—81. Grantee, Irving Schs. Found., Tex. Pub. Edn., U. North Tex. Mem.: Irving Music Tchrs. Assn., Internat. Reading Assn., Assn. Tex. Profl. Educators, Tex. Counselling Assn., Tex. Music Tchrs. Assn., Nat. Guild Piano Tchrs., Nat. Music Tchrs. Assn., Phi Delta Kappa. Home: 2008 Addington St Irving TX 75062

RUTLEDGE, JOANNE, artist, consultant; b. Indpls., Dec. 17, 1941; d. Edward John and Dorothy Louise (Bachelor) Underwood; m. Kenneth Clay Smith, Sept. 7, 1963 (div. May 1990); children: Elizabeth, Kenneth Clay, Jr., Andrew; m. Mark Alan Rutledge, July 31, 1993. RN, St. Vincent's Sch. Nursing, Indpls., 1962; BSN, Ind. U., Indpls., 1979. RN Ind. Staff RN Children's Hosp., Washington, 1962—63, St. Vincent's Hosp., Indpls., 1963—64, Women's Hosp. Spl. Care Nursery, Indpls., 1990—97; nurse cons. Hosp. Care for Indigent Ind. State Program, Indpls., 1995—. Exhibitions include Ind. State Fair, Ind. Heritage Arts, Southside Art League Regional Show. Docent Indpls. Mus. Art, 1983—; reading tutor Kiwanis Project, 2002—; active various coms. Children's Mus. Guild, 1975—; v.p. Indpls. Athletic Club Art Bd. Found., 1990—. Recipient Billy Cothran Landscape award, Indpls. Art Ctr., 1985. Mem.: Ind. Plein Art Painters Assn., Stutz Artist's Assn., Ind. Artist's Club (assoc.), Proctor Club (pres. 1994—95). Roman Catholic. Avocations: travel, photography, hiking, attending concerts and theater, scuba diving. Home: 1019 W 75th St Indianapolis IN 46260-3408 Office: Ind Hosp Care for the Indigent 402 W Washington St Indianapolis IN 46204

RUTLEDGE, KATHERINE BURCK, artist; b. La., Mar. 16, 1949; d. Cyril Büsing and Sarah Marlette Burck; m. Clayton Fenton Rutledge, Apr. 24, 1982. BFA, La. State U., 1971; postgrad., New Orleans Acad. Fine Arts, 1988—90. Represented in permanent collections McIlhenny Collection of Natural Sci., La. State U., New Orleans Zoo. Fellow La. State Mus. Natural Sci., Baton Rouge, 1979—82. Scholar, Audubon Soc., Baton Rouge Chpt., 1980. Mem.: The Pocahontas Found., Magna Carta Dames, Jamestown Soc. (life). Republican. Avocations: gardening, birdwatching. Home: 238 Ship Dr Baton Rouge LA 70806

RUTLEDGE, MARY ELIZABETH, cultural organization administrator; b. Denver, Oct. 20, 1923; d. Frederick Edwin Tibbetts and Mary Frances Tibbetts-Wallace, Robert John Wallace (Stepfather); m. Albert Francis Rutledge, May 1, 1948 (dec.); children: John, James, Frances. BA in Sociology, Wells Coll., 1945. Field mgr. Seal Ohio Girl Scout Coun., Columbus, 1967—80, publs. mgr., 1980—95; exec. staff Assn. Girl Scouts, 1968—. Editor Cook Book for a Water Tank, Cook Book for Hunger. Instr., trainer CPR Am. Red Cross, Am. Heart Assn.; with Columbus Girl Scout Coun., 1967—95; mem. Diocesan Coun. Cath. Women, Columbus, 1960—; pres. Diocesan Coun. of Coun. Women, Columbus, 1984—86. Mem.: Norwester Women's Club (pres. 2001—), Ft. Monroe Wines Club (v.p., officer 1956), St. Agatha Womens Club (pres. 1966). Roman Catholic. Avocations: gardening, cooking, travel.

RUTLEDGE, PATSY LEITH, educational specialist; b. Longview, Tex., Mar. 3, 1951; d. George Edgar and Vivian Laverne (O'Keefe) Leith; m. Thomas Wendell Rutledge, Jan. 26, 1985; children: Erin, John. BSEd summa cum laude, Abilene Christian U., 1973; MEd, Stephen F. Austin State U., 1977. Cert. Irlen screener, Ednl. Supr. U. Tex. at Tyler, 1996. Tchr. spl. edn., learning disabilities Longview (Tex.) Ind. Sch. Dist., 1973-76, diagnostic tchr., cons., 1976-78, ednl. diagnostician, 1978—93, spl. edn. supr., 1993—2003, ednl. diagnostician, 2003—. Presenter state conf. Tex. Council for Exceptional Children, San Antonio, 1984; test adminstr. Stanford Binet Intelligence Scale IV norming study, Longview, 1985. Mem. NEA (del. nat. conv. 1983), Tex. State Tchr. Assn. (del. state conv.), Tex. Ednl. Diagnostician Assn. (sec. 1982-83, publicity chair state conv. 1987-88), Longview Educators Assn. (sec. 1982-83), Women for Abilene Christian U. (publicity chair 1988-90, treas. 1992-93). Mem. Ch. of Christ. Avocations: outdoors activities, ch. activities.

RUTSCHKE, ANNAMARIE, artist; b. Santa Barbara, Calif., June 29, 1965; d. Benjamin Wiley Jordan and Jeannette Irene Rutschke; m. Robert Allan Bryant, July 31, 1988 (div. 1996); child: Phillip Dale Dodge Jr. File clk. San Luis Welding Supply, San Luis Obispo, Calif., 1983; customer svc. clk. The Living Picture, Alameda, Calif., 1984, 7-11, Alameda, 1985-86; clk. Def. Subs. Reg. Pacific, Alameda, 1987-88; pers. clk. Def. Depot Tracy, Alameda, 1988-90; adminstrv. clk. Gen. Svcs. Adminstrn., San Francisco, 1990, purchasing agt., 1990-96, adminstrv. technician, 1996-99; legal clk. IRS Dist. Counsel, San Francisco, 1999-2000. Freelance artist. Co-coord. Fed. Recycling Coun., 1992, 93; operator Muscular Dystrophy Assn., Arroyo Grande, Calif., 1980. Republican. Lutheran. Avocations: art, writing, computer programming, web design, cooking. E-mail: mommyofanangel38@aol.com.

RUTSTEIN, ELEANOR H., psychologist; b. N.Y., Dec. 26, 1933; d. Louis Morris and Sarah Rutstein; m. Gilbert Sussman, Aug. 17, 1971; 1 child, Susanna Beth Sussman. BA in psychology summa cum laude with honors, Cornell U., Ithaca, NY, 1955; MA with honors, Boston U., 1956; PhD in Clin. Psychology, NYU, 1970. Lic. psychologist 1971. Training fellow Rsch. Ctr. for Mental Health, N.Y., 1965—66; psychologist Bronx Psychiatric Ctr., Bronx, NY, 1966—70; clin. psychologist Beth Israel Hosp., N.Y., 1970—72; clin. asst. prof. Cornell Univ. Med. Coll., White Plains, NY, 1980—89; vis. asst. prof. Albert Einstein Coll. of Medicine, Bronx, NY, 1987—91; adj. clin. supr. Yeshiva Univ., Bronx, NY, 1991—; pvt. practice New Rochelle, NY, 1971—. Contbr. scientific papers pub. to profl. jour. Group facilitator Group Mothers of Pre-Schoolers, recently div. woman, White Plains, 1976—; mem. Move On, 2004—. Mem.: APA, N.Y. State Psychol. Assn., Psi Chi, Phi Kappa Phi, Phi Beta Kappa. Democrat. Avocations: piano, photography, theater, music, gourmet cooking. Home and Office: 597 Pinebrook Blvd New Rochelle NY 10804 Office Phone: 914-576-4866. Personal E-mail: eleanorhrutstein@aol.com.

RUTSTEIN, REBECCA ANNE, painter; b. Phila., June 25, 1971; Studied art history and studio art, Wash. U., St. Louis, 1989—90; BFA, Cornell U., 1993; MFA, U. Pa., 1997. Artist-in-residence Vt. Studio Ctr., Johnson, 1997, Banff Centre for the Arts, Canada, 2003, 2004. Solo exhibitions include, Painting and Drawings, Tjaden Gallery, Ithaca, NY, 1993, Painting and Collages, Morgan Print Gallery, U. Pa., Phila., 1996, Small Works/Sacred Spaces, 1997, Recent Works, Lockjaw Gallery, Phila., 1999, Paintings, Drawings & Illuminations, 2000, Erasure, Tribes Gallery, NYC, 2000, Second Skin, In Rare From Gallery, Lambertville, NJ, 2000, Shifting Images, Bridgette Mayer Gallery, Phila., 2002, Love & Subduction, 2004, Underworld, Fleisher Art Meml., Phila., 2002, Breaking Boundaries, Phila. Mus. Art Mus. Restaurant, 2004, Canopy Adventures, List Gallery, Swarthmore Coll., PA, 2004. Bd. dirs. Grad. Sch. Fine Arts (now Sch. Design) Assn. U. Pa., 2001—04. Named Degree Marshall (Valedictorian), Fine Arts Dept., Cornell U., 1993; recipient Piero Dorazio Color Award, Grad. Sch. Fine Arts, U. Pa., 1996, Charles Addams Meml. Prize, 1997, Natvar Bhavsar Prize for group exhbn. East/West Visions In Between, Arthur Ross Gallery, Phila., 1997; Overseers Scholar Fellowship, U. Pa., 1995—96, Artist's Grant, Vt. Studio Ctr., 1997, Pew Fellowship in the Arts, 2004.

RUTSTEIN, SEDMARA ZAKARIAN, concert pianist, educator; b. Kazan, Russia, Oct. 18, 1937; came to U.S., 1974; d. Suren and Ekaterina (Todorovskaya) Zakarian; m. Alexander Rutstein, Aug. 29, 1958; 1 child, Alla. D in Music, Leningrad State Conservatory, USSR, 1961, diploma (hon.), 1959. Prof. Leningrad State Conservatory, 1961-73; artist-in-residence Grinnell (Iowa) Coll., 1974—76; prof. Oberlin (Ohio) Conservatory, 1976—. Recording artist, classical piano music XVIII through XX centuries, 1972—. Grantee Oberlin Coll., 1984-98. Mem. Am. Music Tchrs. Assn. Avocations: reading, music, travel. Home: 226 N Prospect St Oberlin OH 44074-1035 Office: Oberlin Coll Conservatory of Music Oberlin OH 44074 Office Phone: 440-775-8250. Business E-Mail: sedrut@oberlin.edu.

RUTTAN, SUSAN, actress; b. Oregon City, Oreg., Sept. 16, 1948; d. Daryl and Helen Dunrud; m. Randy McDonald, 1986 (div. 1992); 1 adopted child, Jackson. BA, U. of Oregon; MA, U of Calif., Santa Cruz. Formerly with prodn. dept. Universal Studios Casting. Appeared in Hot L Baltimore (Staircase Repertory Prodn.), Santa Cruz, Calif.; (TV series) L.A. Law, 1986-1993, guest appearance in Popular, 2000, Yes, Dear, 2001, LA Law, 2002, CSI: NY, 2004, Boston Legal, 2005, Monk, 2005; (TV movies) Triumph of the Heart: The Ricky Bell Story, 1991, Without Warning: Terror in the Towers, 1993, Jack Deed: Badge of Honor, 1993, Jack Reed: A Search for Justice, 1994, Justice for Annie: A Moment of Truth Movie, 1996, Touched by Evil, 1997, Life of the Party: The Pamela Harriman Story, 1998; (films) include Bad Dreams, 1988, Chances Are, 1989, Funny About Love, 1990, Love Kills, 1998, Krippendorf's Tribe, 1998, The Sure Hand of God, 2004; TV movies include All My Darling Daughters, Bay Coven, 1987, Second Sight, Packing It In, Kicks, Life of the Party: The Pamela Harriman Story, 1998, L.A. Law: The Movie, 2002, The Legend of Butch and Sundance, 2004. Nominated for several Emmy and Golden Globe awards. Office: Gold Harry Talent Agency 3500 W Olive Ave Burbank CA 91505

RUTTENBERG, RUTH A., economist; b. Washington, Feb. 16, 1948; d. Stanley Harvey and Gertrude Leah Bernstein Ruttenberg; children: Estye Ross, Jack Ross. BA in Econs. with honors, U. Wis., 1969; M in City Planning, U. Pa., 1971, PhD in City Planning, 1981. Prof. Bradford Coll., 1972—73; sr. assoc. Ruttenberg, Kilgallon & Assocs., Inc., Washington, 1973-86; pres. Ruth Ruttenberg & Assocs., Bethesda, Md., 1986—; prof. Nat. Labor Coll., 2001—. Sr. lectr. Am. U., Washington, 1973—75; asst. prof. Howard U., Washington, 1975—82; adj. faculty U. Md., College Park, Md., 1974—; mem. Bd. Equalization and Rev., Washington, 1981—82; sr. economist Occupl. Safety and Health Adminstrn., Washington, 1979—80; dir. Nat. Clearinghouse for Worker Safety and Health Tng., Bethesda, 1995—2000; co-chair instl. rev. bd., Ctr. Protect Workers Rights CPWR, Washington, 1996—, mem. constrn. econ. rsch. network, 2000—; peer rev. mem. U.S. Dept. Energy, Washington, 1996, 97; mem. DOE adv. bd. Hazardous Materials Tng. Inst., 2004—, terrorism adv. bd., 2004—05, Newspaper Guild-Comms. Workers Am., 2001—; mem. tng. program rev. group NIOSH, 2005—. Author: Occupational Safety and Health in the Chemical Industry, 1981; mem. editl. rev. bd. Labor and Employment Rels. Assn., 2002—. Bd. dirs. Group Health Assn., Washington, 1982-88, 90-94; bd. dirs., Consumer Health Found., Washington, 1994—. Woodrow Wilson fellow, 1969-70; Bicentennial grantee Govt. Sweden, 1978. Democrat. Avocations: reading, kayaking, travel. Office: Ruth Ruttenberg & Assocs Inc 5107 Benton Ave Bethesda MD 20814-2807 Business E-Mail: rruttenberg@nlc.edu. E-mail: rruttenberg@comcast.net.

RUTTENBERG, SUSANN I., health sciences administrator; b. Chgo., Apr. 7, 1943; d. William and Audrey A. Kray; m. Harold Seymour Ruttenberg, Aug. 11, 1963 (div. Oct. 1977); children: Adam, Michael, Leslie. BS, Northwestern U., 1964; MBA, U. Calif., Irvine, 1993. Writer, prodr. Kragie Newell & Assocs., Des Moines, 1977-80, Nat. Cable Prodns. and Telesshopper, 1980-81; owner, mgr. Rib Joint, Des Moines, 1978-81; gen. mgr. Stuart Anderson's Black Angus, Ariz. and Calif., 1982-87; various adminstr. positions in pediats. U. Calif., Irvine, 1988-93, adminstr. child devel. ctr., 1997-98, adminstr. dermatology, 1996—, adminstr. phys. medicine and rehab., 1999—. V.p. U. Calif. Irvine GSM Healthcare Alumni, 1995—2002; mem. exec. bd. Acad. Bus. Officers Group, 2000—03, chair exec. bd., 2000—01, ADA/M bd. dirs., 2000—04, chair IT com., 2003—04. Editor, contbr.: (cookbook) Child's Play, 1989; editor, writer newsletter UCInsights on Pediatrics, 1995; author: Never Let'em Catch You With Your Bed Rails Down, 2003; contbr. Executive Decisions in Dermatology, 2000—04. Women's chair United Jewish Appeal, Des Moines, 1975; bd. dirs. Child Guidance Ctr., Des Moines, 1976-77, Cmty. Telephone Coun., Des Moines, 1978-81; mem. dir.'s coun. U. Calif. Irvine Chao Family Comprehensive Cancer Ctr., 1998—; vol. rep., sec. bd. dirs. Rancho Mirage, Calif. C. of C., 1984-86. Northwestern U. scholar, 1963-64; U. Calif. Irvine Coll. Medicine Career Devel. award, 1992-93, Healthsci. Adminstr. of Yr. award, U. Calif. Chancellor. Mem.: Assn. Dermatology Adminstrs./Mgrs. (chair newsletter com. 2001, chair comms. com. 2002—03, bd. dirs. 2002—), Assn. Profs. Dermatology, Med. Group Mgmt. Assn. Avocations: cooking, reading, literacy tutoring, dance, travel. Office: U Calif Irvine C340 Med Scis I Irvine CA 92697-0001

RUTTER, FRANCES TOMPSON, retired publisher; b. Arlington, Mass., Apr. 12, 1920; d. Harold F. and Mildred F. (Wheeler) Tompson; m. John H. Ottemiller, Mar. 24, 1943; children: Joan Tompson Gillum, John Tompson Ottemiller; m. William D. Rutter, Oct. 26, 1970. AB magna cum laude, Pembroke Coll., Brown U., 1941; postgrad., Mt. Holyoke Coll., 1942—43. Res. book librarian Brown U., 1941-42; annotator ship's papers John Carter Brown Library, Providence, 1943-44; librarian Sci. Service, Washington, 1944-45; ptnr. Shoe String Press, Hamden, Conn., 1952-58; sec., treas. Shoe String Press, Inc., 1958-68, pres., treas., 1968-80, also bd. dirs.; sec.-treas., dir. Tompson-Malone, Inc., book mfrs., 1967-80; pres., treas., dir. Tompson & Rutter, Inc., 1980-89; ret., 1989. V.p. class 1941 Pembroke Coll., 1967-73, 76-91, pres., 1973-76, head class agt., 1979-85, bequests and trust chmn., 1979-90, 40th reunion gift com., 1980, co-chair 50th reunion gift com., 1990-91, 55th reunion gift com., 1995-96; spl. projects adv. panel N.H. Commn. on Arts, 1980-84; mem. natural resources com. Grantham, 1980; mem. Grantham Planning Bd., 1981-87, sec., 1981-83, chmn., 1985-87; chmn. Grantham Recycling Com., 1988-89, Grantham Hist. Soc., 1992-96, Habitat for Humanity-Kearsarge/Sunapee chpt., 1989-94; mem. Diocesan Altar Guild Bd., 1990-93, sec., 1991-92; vol. Mary Hitchcock Meml. Hosp. Aux., 1991-2003; mem. vestry St. Paul's Episc. Ch., 1997-2000, jr. warden, 1998-2000; assoc. Holy Cross Monastery, West Park, N.Y. Mem. Friends of Fernald Libr. of Colby-Sawyer Coll., ACLU (life), LWV (editor newsletter 1987-89), Assoc. Alumni Brown U. (bd. dirs. 1981-83), Nicholas Brown Soc., Pembroke Ctr. Assocs. (coun. 1984-86), Soc. for Preservation N.H. Forests, Episcopal Peace Fellowship, Phi Beta Kappa. Episcopalian. Home: Apt 203 Valley Terrace 2820 Christian St White River Junction VT 05001 Personal E-mail: franbill@valley.net.

RUTTER, MARIE E., music educator; b. Bklyn., Nov. 6, 1939; d. Edward George de Beaumont and Lela Dean Graham; m. Stuart Mishler Rutter, Aug. 26, 1961; children: Deborah Gulliver, Jeanne Meister, Suzanne Cook, Caryn Einsweiler. BA, Albion Coll., 1961. Profl. cert. in piano Music Tchrs. Nat. Assn. Pub. sch. music tchr. Mona Shores Sch. Dist., Muskegon, Mich., 1961-63; pvt. piano tchr. Muskegon, 1962-63, Ft. Wayne, Ind., 1963-73, Lincoln, Nebr., 1973-74, Elk Grove Village, Ill., 1974-76, Hickory, N.C., 1976-84, Schaumburg, Ill., 1984—. Elder Ch. of the Cross, Hoffman Estates, Ill., 1995—96, mem. Christian edn. com., 1996—2000, dir. handbell choir, 2002—04, deacon, 2006—. Mem. Ill. State Music Tchrs. Assn. (profl. cert. in piano, state syllabus performance chair 1994—), N.W. Suburban Music Tchrs. Assn. (syllabus chair, 2nd v.p., 1st v.p., pres.). Presbyterian. Avocations: quilting, reading, sewing, gardening.

RUUD, RUTH MARIE, science educator; b. Cleve., Aug. 1, 1944; d. William and Mary (Kastellic) Weizer; m. James Ruud; children: James, David, Karen. BA in Edn., Villa Maria Coll., 1978; MEd, Edinboro U., 1983, cert. reading specialist, 1983, elem. adminstr. cert., 1988. Cert. elem. tchr. Elem. tchr. Diocese of Erie, Pa., 1978-79, Millcreek Schs., Erie, 1979-93, tchr. sci., 1993—. Adv. bd. mem. Gannondale, Erie, 1991—. Recipient STAR award Am. Gas Assn., 1991, Catalyst award Chem. Soc., 1994. Mem. ASCD, NSTA (presdl. award for excellence in sci. tchg. 1993), Coun. Elem. Sci. Instrn., Pa. State Tchrs. Assn. (bd. dirs., northwest rep.), Millcreek Edn. Assn., Phi Delta Kappa. Avocations: tennis, walking, golf, bridge. Home: 5432 W 50th St Fairview PA 16415-2339 Office: Walnut Creek Sch 5901 Sterrettania Rd Fairview PA 16415-3201

RUVIELLA-KNORR, JEANNE L., music educator, consultant, clinician; d. Jean and Marion Post Ruviella; m. H. Richard Knorr, May 26, 1962 (div. Dec. 24, 1993); children: Richard Post Knorr, Michelle Renee Mitchell. MusB, Boston U., 1962; MA, U. So. Calif., 1966; PhD, U. Md., 2004. Cert. advanced profl. cert. tchg. Md., Dalcroze cert. Longy Sch., Dalcroze-Orff-Kodaly cert. Manhattan Sch. Music. Music tchr. L.A. Pub. Schs., 1962—66, Burlington Pub. Schs., Vt.; prof. music edn. Shelton Coll., Cape Canaveral, Fla., 1968—74; music tchr., cons. Anne Arundel County Pub. Schs., Severna Park, Md., 1974—79; prof. music edn. Towson (Md.) U., 1979—97, prof. emerita, 1997—; prof. music edn. Frostburg (Md.) State U., 1999—2000; tchr. music Harford County Schs., Abingdon, Md., 2000—06. Clinician Towson U., 1994—, developer Grad. Dalcroze-Orff-Kodaly Cert. program, co-dir. Dalcroze-Orff-Kodaly Cert. program, 1981—97, adj. faculty Dalcroze-Orff-Kodaly Cert. program, 1997—; cons. in field. Contbg. author: music series Share the Music, Grades 7-8, 1996—2005, Music and You, Grades 7-8, 1989—2005, co-compiler: keyboard proficiency packet for Towson U., rev. Leader women's support groups Chapelgate Ch., Marriottsville, Md., 2000—. Mem.: Md. Music Educators Assn., Music Educators Nat. Conf. (clinician 1983—87, 2000). Avocations: travel, music. Personal E-mail: ruviella@comcast.net.

RUYLE, LYDIA MILLER, artist, educator; b. Denver, Aug. 4, 1935; d. David Jacob and Lydia (Alles) Miller; m. Robert A. Ruyle, Sept. 15, 1957; children: Stephen Robert, Margaret Lee, Robin Lee. BA magna cum laude, U. Colo., 1957; MA, U. No. Colo., 1972; postgrad. Syracuse U., 1986, 88, Art Inst. Chgo., 1991. Rsch. assoc. Bur. State and Cmty. Svc., U. Colo., Boulder, 1957-59; paralegal Miller and Ruyle Law Offices, Greeley, Colo., 1968-70; instr. Creative Arts Ctr., Greeley, 1970-75; artist-in-residence, instr. printmaking U. No. Colo., Greeley, 1980-82, adj. faculty art history, 1984—; freelance artist, Greeley, 1965—; owner Goddess Tours/Ya-Ya Journeys, Women's Pilgrimages, 1993-2004; dir., v.p. Weld County Dist. Six Bd. Edn., Greeley, 1975-77; mem. Colo. Coun. Arts and Humanities, Denver, 1977-83; chmn. Art in Pub. Places, 1979-82; chmn. Cmty. Arts Couns. of Colo., 1980-81, chmn. grants-in-aid, 1981-82; commr. Colo. Commn. Higher Edn., Denver, 1983-85; bd. dirs. No. Colo. Found., 1984-90, Colo. Found. Arts, 1984-92; organizing com. Colo. Group Nat. Mus. Women Arts, Washington, 1984-90. Author: Goddess Icons, Spirit Banners of the Divine Feminine, 2002, China, Goddess Icons, Spirit Banners of the Divine Feminine, 2004, Mexico, Spirit Banners of the Divine Feminine, 2004, Lydia Ruyle, Fifty Years of Her Story in Art, 1955-2005, Turkey Goddess Icons, Spirit Banners of the Divine Feminine, Istanbul, 2005; illustrator Turkey Godess Icons, Spirit Banners of the Divine Feminine, Istanbul, Making Place, Making Self (cover), 2005, Prayers and Seven Contemplations of the Sacred Mother (cover), 2004, Küche Kochen cookbook, 1973, Layering: Society of Layerists in Multi-Media, 1991, Bridging Time and Space, 1998, Dark Mother: African origins, 2002, (cover) The Great Goddess. An Introduction to Her Many Names, 1992; sculptor bronze armillary sundial Rutherford Hill Winery Napa Valley, Calif., 1972; exhibitor UN Conf. on Women, Nairobi, Kenya, 1985, Huarou, China, 1995; contbr. The Birth Project, Judy Chicago, 1985; one women shows include Women's Libr., Istanbul, Turkey, 1995, Ephesus Mus., 1995, 2005, Ecumenent Kalmik Mus. and Anacultur Conf., Istanbul, 1998, Woman and Earth, St. Petersburg, Russia, 1997, 2003, Montpeyroux, Castelfranc, 1996, Gordes, France, 2000, Valletta, Malta, 1997, Women's Caucus for Art 25th Ann. Conv., Phila., 1997, Ghost Ranch, N.Mex., 1997, The Desert Mus., Palm Springs, 1999-2002, FrauenMusuem, Wiesbaden, Germany, 1998, Goddess Confs., Glastonbury, Eng., 1999-2006, Melbourne, Australia, 2003, Czech Republic, 2004, Archeomythology Confs., Greece, 1998, Novi Sad, Serbia, 2004, Rila Monastery, Bulgaria, 2004, Machu Picchu, Peru, 1999, 2001, Patan Mus., Kathmandu, Nepal, 2000, Mexico City, 1999, 2000, 2002, Kauai Mus., Hawaii, 2001, Uisneach, Ireland, 2001, Santa Reparata Internat. Sch. Art, Florence, Italy, 2002, China, Beijing, Pu'tu'oshan, 2003, Dairy Ctr. for Arts, Boulder, Colo., 2003, Sun Valley Idaho Arts Ctr., 2003, Ft. Mason, San Francisco, 2004, San Antonio, Tex. Mus. Art, 2004, Ball State U., 2004, Gathering the Women, Dallas, 2004, Sanctuary Retreat Cer., Beallsville, Md., 2005, Morgenlicht Retreat Ctr., Brazil, 2005, Women of Wisdom Conf., Seattle, 2005, U. Colo., Boulder, 2005, 26d ann Women's Studies Nat. Conf., Orlando, Fla., 2005, Black Madonna Conf., Berkeley, 2005, 2d World Congress on Matriarchal Studies, Austin, Tex., 2005, Goddess Conversations, Florence, Italy, 2005, Union Colony Civic Ctr., Greeley, Colo., 2005, Mich. Festival Sacred Music, Kalamazoo, 2005, Woman of Wisdom Conf., Seattle, 2006, Cerritos C.C., Norwalk, Calif., 2006, Leedy Voulkos Art Ctr., Kansas City, Mo., 2006, Aurora U., Williams Bay, Wis., 2006, Gather the Women, Sydney, Australia, 2006, Casa Internazionale Della Donna, Rome, 2006, Inst. Archaeomythology, Bulgaria, 2006, Goddess Confs., Istanbul, Turkey, 2006, Budapest, Hungary, 2006, Glastonbury, Eng., 2006, Seventh Ann. Magdalene Celebration, Atlanta, 2006, Sekmet Festival, Indian SpringsNev., 2006, Healing Retreats, Machu Picchu, Peru, 2006, Mysteries of Ancient Greece, 2006, Goddess Conversations, Paris, 2006. Chair Citizens Task Force Cultural Affairs, Greeley, 1977-80, Residential Ch., United Way, Weld County, 1972-73; vice chmn. Weld County Dem. Cen. Com., Greeley, 1968-72. Recipient Jurors award Manhattan Nat. Print Exhbn., 1984, Cmty. Svc. award, 1985, Arts Alive! award City of Greeley, 2005; named Parent of Yr., U. Colo. Alumni Assn. 1983; Boettcher Found. scholar 1953-57. Mem. AAUW (chmn. Nat. Art Mart Greeley br. 1970, 82-85), Artists Equity Assn., Nat. Assn. Women Artists (Printmaking award 1986), L.A. Printmaking Soc., World Print Coun., Soc. Layerists in Multi Media, Phi Beta Kappa. Home: 2101 24th St Greeley CO 80631-8129

RUYLE-HULLINGER, ELIZABETH SMITH (BETH RUYLE), municipal financial advisor, consultant; b. Oct. 26, 1946; d. Daniel Lester and Mae (Coley) Smith; m. Craig Harlan Hullinger, Oct. 24, 1985; children: Leigh Ann Ruyle, Clint (dec.), Bret AA, St. Petersburg Jr. Coll., Fla., 1966; BA English, U. Fla., Gainesville, 1968; MPA, U. Ga., Athens, 1975. Rsch. asst. Emory U., Atlanta, 1969—70; health planner Met. Coun. for Health, Atlanta, 1960—72; coord. govtl. rels. Atlanta Regional Commn., 1972—76, coord. govtl. affairs, 1976—78; exec. dir. South Suburban Mayors' and Mgrs. Assn., East Hazel Crest, Ill., 1978—2000; pres. Chgo. Southland Econ. Devel. Alliance, 1999—2000; exec. v.p., dir. Ehlers & Assocs., Lisle, Ill., 2000—. Exec. dir. South Towns Agy. Risk Mgmt., 1980-98, South Towns Area Benefits Coop., 1983-89, South Towns Bus. Growth Corp., 1983-90; cons. Planning Devel. Svc., Tinley Park, Ill., 1986—. Contbr. articles to profl. and devel. mags Mem. World's Fair Adv. Com., Chgo., 1986, Met. Planning Coun., 1990-2000, Cook County Tax Reform adv. coun., South Suburban Arts Coun., 1987, Coun. Urban Econ. Devel., 1986; adv. coun. Urban Innovations, Chgo., 1995-2000, Chgo. Assembly Project, 1995-2000; mem. Regional Partnership, 1985-2000; bd. dirs. South Suburban Hosp., 1987-96, mem. governing coun., 1999—; bd. dirs. Fin. Cmty. Devel. Corp., 1998-2000 Mem. Internat. City Mgmt. Assn., Ill. City Mgmt. Assn., Met. City Mgrs. Assn., Ill. Govtl. Fin. Officers Assn., Ill. Tax Increment Assn., Lambda Alpha Methodist. Office: Ehlers & Assocs 550 Warrenville Rd Ste 220 Lisle IL 60532-5500 Office Phone: 630-271-3330. Business E-Mail: bruyle@ehlers-inc.com.

RUYTER, NANCY LEE CHALFA, dance educator; b. Phila., May 23, 1933; d. Andrew Benedict Chalfa and Lois Elizabeth (Strode) McClary; m. Ralph Markson (div.); m. Hans C. Ruyter, Dec. 7, 1968 (dec. Jan. 1998). BA in History, U. Calif., Riverside, 1964; PhD in History, Claremont Grad. Sch., 1970. Tchr. theater dept. Pomona Coll., 1965-72; instr. dance program U. Calif., Riverside, 1972-76, acting chair dance program, 1974-75; instr. dance dept. UCLA, 1976; instr. phys. edn. dept. Orange Coast Coll., 1976-77; asst. prof. dept. phys. edn. and dance Tufts U., 1977-78; asst. prof. phys. edn. dept. Calif. State U., Northridge, 1978-82; from asst. prof. to full prof. dance dept. U. Calif., Irvine, 1982—, assoc. dean Sch. Fine Arts, 1984-88, 95-96, chair dept. dance, 1989-91. Presenter in field. Appeared with Jasna Planina Folk Ensemble, 1972-77, 78-79, Di Falco and Co., 1955-57; choreographer, dir. numerous coll. dance prodns.; contbr. articles, revs. to profl. publs.; author: Reformers and Visionaries: The Americanization of the Art of Dance, 1979, The Cultivation of Body and Mind in Nineteenth-Century American Delsartism, 1999. Mem. Am. Soc. Theatre Rsch., Bulgarian Studies Assn., Congress on Rsch. in Dance (bd. dirs. 1977-80, 2003-, pres. 1981-85), Folk Dance Fedn., Internat. Fedn. Theatre Rsch., Soc. Dance Rsch., Soc. Ethnomusicology, Soc. Dance History Scholars (steering com. 1980-81), Spanish Dance Soc., Theatre Libr. Assn. Office: U Calif Dept Dance Irvine CA 92697-2775 Office Phone: 949-824-7284. Business E-Mail: nlruyter@uci.edu.

RYALL, JO-ELLYN M., psychiatrist; b. Newark, May 25, 1949; d. Joseph P. and Tekla (Paraszczuk) R. BA in Chemistry with gen. honors, Rutgers U., 1971; MD, Washington U., St. Louis, 1975. Diplomate Am. Bd. Psychiatry and Neurology. Resident in psychiatry Washington U., St. Louis, 1975-78, psychiatrist Student Health, 1978-83, asst. prof. clin. psychiatry, 1983—2003, assoc. prof. clin. psychiatry, 2003—. Inpatient supr. Malcolm Bliss Mental Health Ctr., St. Louis, 1978-80, pvt. practice medicine specializing in psychiatry, St. Louis, 1980—. Bd. dirs. Women's Self Help Ctr., St. Louis, 1980. Fellow: APA (pres. ea. Mo. dist. br. 1983—85, sect. coun. AMA 1986—99, dep. rep. to assembly 1994—97, rep. 1997—2001, chair bylaws com. 2000—03, dep. rep. area 4 2001—06, rep. area 4 2006); mem.: AMA (alt. del. Mo. 1988—90, 1993—94, del. 1995—, mem. coun. on constn. bylaws 1998—2006, vice chair 2002—04, chair 2004—06), Manic Depressive Assn. St. Louis (chmn. bd. dirs. 1985—89), Mo. State Med. Assn. (vice spkr. ho. of dels. 1986—89, spkr. 1989—92), St. Louis Met. Med. Soc. (del. to state conv. 1981—86, councilor 1985—87, v.p. 1989, del. to state conv. 1993—), Am. Med. Women's Assn. (pres. St. Louis dist. br. 1981—82, regional gov. VIII 1986—89, pres. St. Louis dist. br. 1992, spkr. ho. of dels. 1993—96), Washington U. Faculty Club. Office: 12166 Old Big Bend Rd Ste 210 Saint Louis MO 63122 Office Phone: 314-909-0121.

RYALLS, BARBARA TAYLOR, freelance/self-employed editor, critic; b. Akron, Ohio, Apr. 13, 1940; d. Robert Hull and Rosemary Resch Taylor; m. Frederick Ryalls, Sept. 14, 1963; children: Christopher Hull, Jordan Lee. BA, Beaver Coll. (now Arcadia U.), 1962. Food critic Bucks County Courier Times, Bristol, Pa., 1976—; project editor Lippincott Williams & Wilkins, Phila., 1992—96, mng. editor, 1996—2001; freelance editor, 2001—. Author: Dining Out in Bucks County, 1984; co-author: $ave Bucks in Buck$, 1977, 1979. Pres. LWV, Newtown, Pa., 1970—72; tour guide Walk Phila.; bd. mem. Famly Svcs., Bucks County, 1977—79, Delaware Valley Philharm. Orch., Bucks County, 1993—95. Avocations: architecture, gardening, travel. Home: 490 Rocksville Rd Holland PA 18966

RYAN, CANDACE I., writer, director, editor; d. Lilburn Terry and Maureen Adell Ryan; children: Elizabeth Maureen Solomon, Virginia Violet Hildenbrand. AA in human rels., Bridgeport U., 1976—79; BBA in journalism, Rice U., 1965—68. Human Relations-Death & Life. Abused Woman & Children of CT, 1978. Adv. bd. Barrington Rev. of the Arts, Westport, Conn., 1976—85; councilor Inner Cities Volunteers of CT., Stamford, Conn., 1976—89; asst dir. & advisor CT. Commn. on the Arts, Westport, Conn., 1977—89. Roving writer Family & Moral Issues, Sacremento, Calif., 1993—. Author: Detecting! The Midnight Tattler, over 20 novels, 14 short stories. Travel industry rep. State Dept. Amb. of Peace, India, Africa, China, numerous countries, Madagascar, 1978—89; sec. World Wildlife Found., San Diego, 1990—93; asst. advisor Women & Children Outreach Org., Sacramento, 1991—2003; asst. editor Wolferts Retreat Ctr. for the Arts, Stamford, Conn., 1980—90. Recipient Journalism Excellence, Fairfield U., 1982, 6 Poetry awards, 1976—2004; Louis Webber grant, Century Acceptance Assoc., 1990—92. Fellow: Mystery Writers Assoc. (corr.; sr. writer 2000); mem.: Beta Corp. Agy. Consortium (v.p. 1981—91), US Travel Industry (rep. China 1984, Israel 1985, France 1986), Quota Club Internat. (sec. 1984—88), Eagles Club of Am. (corr.; mem. 2000, Volunteers above and Beyond the Call of Duty 2001). Republican. Bapt. Achievements include research in Human Relations-Death & Survivors. Avocations: writing, reading, camping, travel. Home: 1419 Eckman Ave Chula Vista CA 91911 Office: Ghost & Creative Writers Co 1419 Eckman Ave Chula Vista CA 91911

RYAN, CAROL J., educational administrator; b. Niagara Falls, N.Y., June 13, 1939; d. Samuel Battaglia and Josephine Latona; m. John W. Ryan, Sept. 17, 1960; children: James, Kathleen, John Jr., Michael. BA, Niagara Univ., 1960; MEd, George Mason U., 1980. Cert. reading specialist emotional distbr., mental retardation K-12, specific lang. disabilities pre-K-12. Special edn. cons. Mass. Dept. of Youth Svcs., Worcester, Mass., 1982—84; edn. liaison Bureau of Instl. Sch., Westboro, Mass., 1986—87; edn. coord. Univ. Mass Med. Ctr., Westboro, Mass., 1987—98; edn. dir. Found. Sch., Alexandria, Va., 1998—2003, Largo, Md., 2003—. Mem.: Coun. of Exceptional Children. Office: The Found Sch 1330 McCormick Dr Largo MD 20774

RYAN, CYNTHIA RHOADES, lawyer; b. Wilmington, Del., Feb. 6, 1954; d. Harry Edris and Patricia Irene (Dux) Rhoades; m. John G. Christfield, Aug. 6, 1977 (div. 1984); m. Matthew C. Ryan, Oct. 10, 1993. BA in Polit. Sci., U. Del., 1976; JD, Widener U., 1979. Bar: Del. 1979, U.S. Supreme Ct. 1989. Dep. atty. gen. State of Del., Wilmington, 1979-85; staff counsel permanent subcom. investigations U.S. Senate, Washington, 1985-87; trial atty. criminal div. U.S. Dept. Justice, Washington, 1987-88, sr. atty. DEA, 1988-91, assoc. chief counsel internat. law sect., 1991-96; chief counsel Office of the Chief Counsel, Drug Enforcement Adminstrn., 1996—. Mem. ABA, Del. Bar Assn., Internat. Assn. of Chiefs of Police, Alpha Sigma Alpha. Avocations: sports, gardening, gourmet cooking, piano, tenor banjo. Business E-Mail: cynthia.r.ryan@usdoj.gov.

RYAN, ELLEN BOUCHARD, psychology professor, gerontologist; b. Holyoke, Mass., 1947; arrived in Can., 1982; d. Raoul Rosario and Etiennette Marie Bouchard; m. Patrick J. Ryan, July 12, 1969; children: Lorraine Yvette, Dennis Patrick, Kevin Myles. BA, MA, Brown U., 1968; PhD, U. Mich., 1970. From asst. prof. psychology to prof. U. Notre Dame, 1970—82, chmn. dept., 1978-82; prof. psychiatry McMaster U., Hamilton, Ont., Canada, 1982—, dir. Ctr. for Gerontol. Studies, 1985-95, prof. gerontology, 1987—. Editor: Attitudes Toward Language Variation, 1982, Language Communication and The Elderly, 1986, Intergenerational Communication, 1994, Language Attitudes, 1994, Communication, Aging and Health, 1996. Grantee NICHD, 1972-75, NSF, 1976-79, Nat. Inst. Edn., 1979-82, Natural Scis. and Engring. Rsch., 1983-89, Gerontol. Rsch. Coun. of Ont., 1983-85, Ont. Ministry Health, 1986-89, Soc. Sci. and Humanities Rsch. Coun., 1986—. Fellow APA, Gerontol. Soc. Am., Can. Psychol. Assn.; mem. Internat. Assn. of Lang. and Social Psychology, Can. Assn. Gerontology. Roman Catholic. Home: 71 Sulphur Springs Rd # 14 Ancaster ON Canada L9G 5C1 Office: McMaster U Dept Psychiatry 1200 Main St W Hamilton ON Canada L8N 3Z5 Office Phone: 905-525-9140 ext. 24449. Business E-Mail: ryaneb@mcmaster.ca.

RYAN, GRETCHEN MARGARETE FRIEDA, art educator; b. Niederschona, Saxony, Germany, Nov. 2, 1929; arrived in U.S., 1952; d. Paul Robert Lutzner and Frieda Gertrud Lutzner-Kupsch; m. Raymond Andrew Ryan, May 12, 1952; children: Michael D., Ralph T., Robert P., Ronald J., Rex W., Renee G. Student, Berlin Art Acad., 1970; AA, Am. River Coll., Sacramento, 1975. Instr. art McClellan AFB, Sacramento, 1967—68, Am. Women's Club, Berlin, 1969—72, Edwards AFB, Calif., 1972—74, Am. River Coll., Sacramento, 1975—2005, Gretchen's Studio, Carmichael, Calif., 1986—. Tchr. art San Juan Sch. Dist., Sacramento, 1975—95; instr. art City of Sacramento, 1980—2006. California's Gold, 2000, Ancient Book of Future, 2002, Decorating 2 Life size Elk, Elk Grove, Calif., 2002, Decorating 1 Life size Lion, Sacramento, 2004. Recipient Restoring Meml. Auditorium resolution, Sacramento City Coun., Recognition award, Shriners Children's Hosp. Sacramento, Purchase award, USAF, 1976, award, Berlin Air Force, 1971, Cmty. Svc. award, Comdr. Air Force Berlin, 1972. Mem.: Sacramento Fine Arts Ctr., Valley Sculpture Artists (bd. dirs., v.p. 1998—), No. Calif. Arts Assn. (bd. dirs.). Avocations: crafts, exercise. Home and Studio: 6225 Luna Ln Carmichael CA 95608

RYAN, IONE JEAN ALOHILANI RATHBURN, retired education educator, counselor; b. Honolulu, Oct. 18, 1926; d. William Alexander and Lilia (Nainoa) Rathburn; m. Edward Parsons Ryan, June 23, 1962 (dec.); children: Ralph M., Lilia K. BEd, U. Hawaii, 1948; MS in Pub. Health, U. Minn., 1950; EdD, Stanford U., 1960. Lic. marital and family therapist, N.C. Tchr. W.R. Farrington High Sch., Honolulu, 1948; instr. to asst. prof. U. Hawaii, Honolulu, 1950-66; assoc. prof. to prof. East Carolina U., Greenville, 1966-90, prof. emerita, 1990—. Contbr. articles to profl. publs. Recipient first scholarship Honolulu C. of C., 1948-50.

RYAN, JEANNE VANYO, music educator; b. Bklyn., July 30, 1930; d. John Joseph Vanyo and Veronica Zupko; m. Joel Kenneth Ryan, Oct. 21, 1961 (dec.); children: Vanessa, Joel Bradley, Darrell. Student, NYU, 1951, Queens Coll., 1958—61. Pvt. piano tchr., Bklyn., 1948—62, Bowie, Md., 1972—. Musician: (piano debut) Steinway Concert Hall, 1951, WNYC Radio Young Am. Artists Series, 1955—56, Bd. Concert Pianists League. Pres. Whitehall PTA, Bowie, 1975—77; leader Girl Scouts USA, Boys Scouts Am., 1970—80; election judge Rep. Party, Bowie, 1992—2002. Mem.: Bowie Music Tchrs. (pres. 1992—94), Md. State Music Tchrs. (chmn. theory 1995, chmn. spring festival 1995—97, chmn. theory 2002, 2004), Kenilworth Women's Club (pres.). Avocations: bridge, reading, crossword puzzles, music, games.

RYAN, JOANNE WINONA, art administrator, artist, consultant, educator; b. Jersey City, May 24, 1932; d. James Joseph and Josephine Veronica (Di Blasi) R. BA, Caldwell Coll., 1963; MA, U. Notre Dame, 1969; PhD, NYU, 1981. Elem. tchr. Archdiocese of Newark, Newark and West Orange, NJ, 1951-60; secondary tchr., chmn. art dept. Mount St. Dominic Acad., Caldwell, NJ, 1960-70; instr., dir. art edn. Caldwell Coll., NJ, 1972-75, acad. dean, 1975-78, assoc. prof., 1975-81; dean acad. affairs, prof. Phila. Colls. Arts, 1982—87, v.p. dean acad. affairs, 1984—86, acting pres., 1983; pres. Creative Enterprises, 1987—2003. Exec. dir. Internat. Soc. for Advancement of Living Traditions in Arts, Mid. Atlantic region, N.Y.C., 1981-1990; prof., Caldwell Coll., N.J., 2003—. Author: The Aesthetic Dimension of Process Philosophy, 1982; one-woman shows include Caldwell Coll., 1972, Muhlenberg Coll., Pa., 1973, 80, Washington Square East Galleries, NYC, 1980-81; exhibited in group shows at U. Notre Dame, 1969, Nutley Art Festival, NJ, 1972, Cath. Fine Arts Soc., 1972, Miniature Art Soc., 1972 (1st prize), Art Ctr. of Oranges, NJ, 1972, Caldwell Coll. Faculty Show, 2003; artist, writer in residence W.S. Davis Estate, Orient, NY, 1972-73. Mem. Pa. Humanities Coun., Phila., 1984-1988; mem. bd. advisors Art and Cmty. Inst., New Sch., N.Y.C., 1975-83. Research grantee NYU/John D. Rockefeller III Fund, N.Y.C., 1972. Visceglia Found., Raritan, N.J., 1982. Mem. AAUW, Coll. Art Assn., Women's Caucus for Art, Cath. Fine Arts Soc. (sec.-treas. 1970-72). Office: Caldwell Coll Caldwell NJ 07006 Office Phone: 973-618-3254. Business E-Mail: jryan@caldwell.edu.

RYAN, JOYCE ETHEL, writer, artist; b. Atlanta, Aug. 29, 1949; m. Jim Cyril Klar, Apr. 5, 1975 BFA, U. Ga., 1972. Instr. Marsh Draughon Coll., Atlanta, 1972—73; mgr. retail store Army & Air Force Exch. Svc., Dallas, 1974; illustrator U.S. Army Logistics Ctr., Ft. Lee, Va., 1975—77; mgr. graphics Ecosystems Internat., Millersville, Md., 1980—82; dir. freelance art studio Seoul, 1983—85; pres. Butterfly Books, Ariz., 1985—. Instr. Cochise Coll., Sierra Vista, 1986 Illustrator, author: Seoul Sketches, 1985, Scenes of Southern Arizona, 1986, Seoul Travel Guide, 1987, Traveling with Your Sketchbook, 1990, The Happy Camper's Gourmet Cookbook, 1992, Calligraphy: Elegant and Easy, 1994, Drawing at Home, 1996, America's Best Cheesecakes, 1998, Fifty Years of Excellence: Texas Watercolor Society, 1999, America's Best RV Cookbook, 2003; contbr. to RV America mag., 2003— Mem.: Art Ctr. Corpus Christi, San Antonio Watercolor Group. Avocations: drawing, painting. Office Phone: 210-494-0077. Personal E-mail: texaswavelady@hotmail.com.

RYAN, JUDITH ANN, dean; d. Thomas Patrick and Ann Patricia Ryan. BA, Queens Coll., Flushing, NY, 1993; MS, Coll. Mt. St. Vincent, Riverdale, 1998. Cert. English 7-12 NY, Sch. Dist. Adminstr. NY. Coom. art tchr. IS204 NYC Bd. Edn., Long Island, NY, 1993—96, title I reading specialist, 1996—2000, title I dept. coord. Jackson Heights, 2000—03, dean of students, 2003—. Advisor liaison IS230, Jackson Heights, NY, 2004—06, fin. officer, 2006. Mem. NYC 2012 Campaign, NYC, 2003—05. Mem.: Nat. Coun. Tchrs. English, Assn. for Supr. and Circculum Devel. Office: IS230 73-10 34th Ave Jackson Heights NY 11372

RYAN, JUDITH W., geriatrics nurse, educator; b. Waterbury, Conn., Dec. 8, 1943; d. James Patrick Ryan and Edna (Swanson) Billings. BS, U. Conn., 1965; MS, Boston U., 1967; PhD, U. Md., 1984. RN, Md., Conn.; cert. adult nurse practitioner ANCC. Instr. U. Conn., Storrs, 1967-69; asst. prof. Ind. U., Purdue U., Indpls., 1969-73, U. Md., Balt., 1973-82, dir. primary care adult nurse practitioner cert. program, dept. medicine, supportive care project, 1985-87, asst. prof. sch. nursing, 1987-95, asst. prof., 1976-82; clin. dir. EverCare, Balt., 1995-99; pres. Nurse Practitioners and Cons., P.C. of Prime Health Group, 2000—. Arbitrator Health Claims Arbitration Program, Md., 1976—; bd. mem. Md. Bd. Nursing, Balt., 1991-98, pres., 1993-96; trustee Md. Nurses Assn. Polit. Action Com., Balt., treas., 1989-91. Contbr. articles to profl. jours. Named Distinguished Practitioner Nursing, Nat. Acad. Practice, 1984-99. Mem. Am. Coll. Nurse Practitioners, Md. Nurses Assn. (2d v.p. 1986-88), Nurse Practitioner Assn. Md., Sigma Theta Tau, Phi Kappa Phi. Office: 20 New Plant Ct Ste 204 Owings Mills MD 21117 Home: 1514 Woodside Ave Baltimore MD 21227 Office Phone: 410-654-8602. Personal E-mail: jwryan128@comcast.net.

RYAN, KELLI LORRAINE, ballerina, educator; b. Merced, Calif., June 26, 1957; d. Howard Fredrick Burley Adcock and Lorraine Cervantes-Adcock; m. Riley Ray Ryan III, May 1, 1999; 1 child, Victoria Alyn Bommarito Salda. M. in Psychology, San Jose State U., 1988. Ballerina Vaganova Choreographic/Kirov Ballet, USSR, 1977, Paris Opera Ballet, France, 1977, Diplomat of Elem., Intermediate and Advanced Cecchetti Syllabus Cecchetti Coun. Am., Calif., 1970, cert. hypnotherapist A.C.H.E., Calif., 1988. Instructress ballet/jazz for the deaf Berkley Sch. for Deaf, 1972—74; corps de ballet San Francisco Ballet, 1975—82; soloist Ballet Lausanne, Brussels, 1976—77; artistic dir. Alameda Dance Repertory Theater, Calif., 1978—82; soloist Ballet de Toscano, Florence, Italy, 1998—99; vol. instructress, ballet/movement for the developmentally disabled Calif., 1982—. Regional del. Nat. Dance Week, Calif., 2003—; mem. Nat. Dance Assn., Reston, Va., 2004—, Am. AAHPERD, Reston, 2004—. Solo performer (TV spl. - ballet) Isadora by Bejart; oil painting series for Valican Coll., As It Is In Heaven (In the Vatican's permanent collection, 1998), watercolor series (aquarelli), Garden in the Rain (In the Vatican's permanent collection, 1999); ballerina (performance L.A. Times Book Fest) Celebrate Nat. Dance Week. Mem. Atwater C. of C.; chmn. bd. Am. Ballet Conservatory, Atwater, Calif., 2003—05. Recipient Commendation of Pub. Svc., U.S. Congress, 18th Dist., 2004, cert. of recognition, Merced County Bd. Suprs., 2004. Mem.: Internat. Dance Coun., Kiwanis (Greater Atwater). Conservative. Catholic. Achievements include founding American Ballet Conservatory; creation of tax-exempt ballet/music/art conservatory which provides scholarships to Central Calif.'s dance, art, music, photography, writing students; creating a ballet school which provides a comprehensive ballet conservatory education regardless of students ability to pay; development of method of instructing toddlers in Ballet and foreign languages; a no fail smoking cessation method. Avocations: teaching piano, painting, sculpting to underprivilaged children, volunteer teaching art/dance to the developmentally disabled, photography. Home: 1301 Fruitland Ave Atwater CA 95301 Office: American Ballet Conservatory 1175 Broadway Atwater CA 95301 Office Phone: 209-356-1401. Office Fax: 209-357-8812. Personal E-mail: kellryan@pacbell.net.

RYAN, MARLEIGH GRAYER, language educator; b. NYC, May 1, 1930; d. Harry and Betty (Hurwick) Grayer; m. Edward Ryan, June 4, 1950; 1 child, David Patrick. BA, NYU, 1951; MA, Columbia U., 1956, PhD, 1965; Cert., East Asian Inst., 1956; postgrad., Kyoto U., 1958-59. Research assoc. Columbia U., NYC, 1960-61, lectr. Japanese, 1961-65, asst. prof., 1965-70, assoc. prof., 1970-72; vis. asst. prof. Yale U., New Haven, 1966-67; assoc. prof. U. Iowa, Iowa City, 1972-75, prof., 1975-81, chmn. dept., 1972-81; prof. Japanese SUNY, New Paltz, 1981-98, dean liberal arts and scis., 1981-90, prof. emeritus, 1999—; assoc. in rsch. Reischauer Inst. for Japanese Studies, Harvard U., Cambridge, Mass., 1999—, chair study group on Asian Am. Lit., 2000—02; retirement study group leader Harvard Inst. Learning, 2003—06. Vice chmn. seminar on modern Japan, Columbia U., 1984-85, chmn., 1985-86; co-chmn. N.Y. State Conf. on Asian Studies, 1986, editor, 1993-99, mem. exec. com., 1993-96, sec., 1993-99, co-chmn., 1998. Co-author: (with Herschel Webb) Research in Japanese Sources, 1965; author: Japan's First Modern Novel, 1967, The Development of Realism in the Fiction of Tsubouchi Shoyo, 1975; assoc. editor: Jour. Assn. Tchrs. Japanese, 1962-71, editor, 1971-75. East Asian Inst. fellow Columbia U., 1955; Ford Found. fellow, 1958-60; Japan Found. fellow, 1973, Woodrow Wilson Ctr. Internat. Scholars fellow, 1988-89; recipient Van Am. Disting. Book award Columbia, 1968 Mem. MLA (sec. com. on teaching Japanese Lang. 1962-68, mem. del. assembly 1979-87, mem. exec. com. div. Asian lit. 1981-86), Assn. Tchrs. Japanese (exec. com. 1969-72, 74-77), Assn. Asian Studies (bd. dirs. 1975-78, N.E. asian coun. 1975-78, coun. of confs., 1993-96), Midwest Conf. Asian Studies (pres. 1980-81) Personal E-mail: marleighryan@earthlink.net.

RYAN, SISTER MARY JEAN, health facility executive; LHD, Webster U., 1994, U. Mo., St. Louis, 2003, Lindenwood U., 2003. Pres., CEO SSM Health Care, 1986—. Presenter in field. Co-author: CQI and the Renovation of an American Health Care System: A Culture Under Construction, 1997. Mem. Excellence in Mo. Found.; chair Taking Care/A Health Forum for Women Religious, Madison, Wis.; bd. dirs. Inst. for Healthcare Improvement, United Way of Greater St. Louis; sec. Hawthorn Found. of Mo.; mem., treas., bd. dirs. St. Louis Regional Chamber and Growth Assn.; bd. dirs. SSM Health Care of Okla., SSM Health Care of Wis., SSM Health Care-St. Louis. Named one of 20 Disting. Women/St. Louis Area, 25 Most Influential Women in Bus. in St. Louis; recipient Brotherhood/Sisterhood award, Nat. Conf. Cmty. and Justice, Gov.'s Quality Leadership award, State of Mo., Corp. that Makes a Difference award, Internat. Women's Forum. Office: SSM Health Care Sys Inc 477 N Lindbergh Blvd Saint Louis MO 63141

RYAN, MEG (MARGARET MARY EMILY ANN HYRA), actress, film producer; b. Fairfield, Conn., Nov. 19, 1961; m. Dennis Quaid, Feb. 14, 1991 (div. July 16, 2001); 1 child, Jack Henry; 1 adopted child, Daisy True. Student, NYU. Established Fandango Films (then called Prufrock Pictures), 1994—2000. Mem. of jury Festival Internat. de Cannes, 2003. Appearences include (TV) One of the Boys, 1982, As The World Turns, 1982-84, Wild Side, 1985, (films) Rich and Famous, 1981, Amityville 3-D, 1983, Top Gun, 1986, Armed and Dangerous, 1986, Innerspace, 1987, Promised Land, 1987, D.O.A., 1988, The Presidio, 1988, When Harry Met Sally, 1989, Joe Versus the Volcano, 1990, The Doors, 1991, Prelude to a Kiss, 1992, Sleepless in Seattle, 1993, Flesh and Bone, 1993, When a Man Loves a Woman, 1994, Restoration, 1994, I.Q., 1994, French Kiss, 1995 (also prodr.), Two for the Road, 1996 (also prodr.), Courage Under Fire, 1996, Addicted to Love, 1997, Anastasia (voice), 1997, City of Angels, 1998, Hurlyburly, 1998, You've Got Mail, 1998, Hanging Up, 2000, Proof of Life, 2000, Kate & Leopold, 2001, In the Cut, 2003, Against the Ropes, 2004; prodr. Lost Souls, 2000, Desert Saints, 2002; exec. prodr. Northern Lights, 1997, The Wedding Planner, 2001. Vol. CARE humanitarian orgn. Recipient Golden Apple award Hollywood Women's Press Club, 1989, Woman of Yr. award Hasty Pudding Theatricals, 1994, ShoWest Conv. Actress of Yr. award, 1999, Am. Comedy Award, 1990, 1994, Women in Film Crystal Award, 1995; named one of the Top 100 Movie Stars of All Time, Empire (UK) Magazine, 1997, The Most Powerful People in Hollywood, Premiere (USA) Magazine, 1999, Most Powerful People in Hollywood, Entertainment Weekly's, 1998. Office: Creative Artists Agy 9830 Wilshire Blvd Beverly Hills CA 90212*

RYAN, MELBAGENE T., retired food service and nutrition director; b. Arkadelphia, Ark., Jan. 6, 1927; d. Horace Samuel and Eunice Bridges (Moorman) Tull; m. Wayne Stuart Ryan, Dec. 26, 1954. BS in Edn., Henderson U., 1948; M in Edn., Tex. Women's U., 1951. Tchr. Eudora Pub. Schs., Ark., 1948-52; dir. food services Tex. Christian U., Ft. Worth, 1952-53, Tex. Women's U., 1953-58; dir. food and nutriton service Irving Ind. Sch. Dist., Tex., 1958-85. Project dir. to develop stds. excellence with a self study and evaluation Tex. Sch. Food Svc. Assn., 1985-88; cons. in field. Co-author and project dir.: (with others) Youth Advisory Council Resource Manual, 1978-79, Effective Food Service Management Using Computers, 1982. With child nutrition Tex. Sch. Food Svc. Assn., Washington, 1974-79; with legis. Am. Sch. Food Svc. Assn., Irving, 1980-85; mem. Denton Co. Hist. Commn., 1997—, Denton Co. Courthouse-on-the Square Mus., chmn. 1998—; mem. adv. bd. Lake Forest Good Samaritan Village, 1998—, Tex. Woman's U. Centennial Celebration, 2001, planning com., 1998-99, Denton Good Samaritan Village, 2003; chmn. Bayless Selby House Mus., 2002—. Recipient Food Facilities Design award Instns. Volume Feeding Awards Program, New Orleans, 1977, Trend Setter award, North Tex. Brokers Assn., Dallas, 1978; Melbagene Ryan Scholarship named in her honor by Dallas Profl. Friends, 1985. Mem. Denton Dietetic Assn. (pres. 1977-78), Tex. Dietetic Assn., Am. Dietetic Assn. (chmn. joint com. 1979-82), Tex. Sch. Food Svc. Assn. (pres. 1975-76, nutrition edn. 1975), Am. Sch. Food Svc. Assn. (conf. com. 1977-78, 1982-83), Tex. Women's U. Alumni Assn. Methodist. Home and Office: 1121 Ryan Rd Denton TX 76210-5539

RYAN, MICHELE KING, marketing professional; b. Connellsville, Pa., Nov. 25, 1939; d. Francis Joseph and Ella Elizabeth (Hoffman) King; m. Charles Joseph Ryan Jr. (dec Jan. 1994); children: Charles J. Ryan III, Kimberly Ryan Winchester; m. Ernest Bayard Crofoot, Jan. 6, 1996; 6 stepchildren. Student, Georgetown U., 1958. Lic. real estate broker, Md. Adminstr. Corridor Info. Ctrs., Laurel, Md., 1977; devel. dir. Resource Realty, Inc., Laurel, 1977-81, v.p., 1981-88; exec. v.p. Resource Enterprises LLC, 1988-95; dir. mkgt. Balt./Washington Corridor C. of C., 1997-2000; pres. The Ryan Group, Annapolis, Md., 2000—. Bd. dirs. Citizens Nat. Bank, Laurel; commr. Md. Aviation Commn., Annapolis, 1995—, Md. Commn. on Transp. Investment, Annapolis, 1999; v.p. Gtr. Laurel Nursing Home, 1980-93 Author, co-editor: Travel Patterns in Baltimore/Washington Corridor, 1977. Bd. dirs. Balt./Wash. Internat. Airport Devel. Coun. Named Bus. Woman of Yr. Bowie Crofton BPW, 1981. Mem.: Balt.-Washington C. of C. (chmn. bd. 1991—92), Soroptimist Internat. (treas. 1976), Bowie Women's Club (pres. 1966—68), Bowie Bus. Profl. Women's Club (pres. 1976). Roman Catholic. Avocations: music, reading, travel. Home: 910 Boom Way Annapolis MD 21401-6889 Office: The Ryan Group 910 Boom Way Annapolis MD 21401

RYAN, PRISCILLA E., lawyer; AB, Marquette U., 1969; JD, Loyola U., Chgo., 1982. Bar: Ill. 1982. With IRS, 1986-87; atty.-advisor Office Tax Policy, U.S. Treasury Dept., Washington, 1988-89; ptnr. Sidley & Austin, Chgo. Frequent spkr. on employee benefits. Contbr. articles to profl. jours. Mem. ABA. Office: Sidley & Austin 1 S First National Plz Chicago IL 60603-2000 Fax: 312-853-7036.

RYAN, RITA MARIE, science educator; d. Chester George and Mildred Marie (Means) Sandman; m. Stewart Richard Ryan, July 9, 1966; children: Kathleen, Beth Colleen, Ellen Mary. BA in Edn., U. N.C., Chapel Hill, 1964; MA in English Edn., U. Mich., Ann Arbor, 1965; reading cert., U. Okla., Norman, 1981. Humanities tchr. Livonia H.S., Mich., 1965; reading tchr. Irving Mid. Sch., Norman, Okla., 1982—96; sci. tchr. Alcott Mid. Sch., Norman, Okla., 0197—. Mem. std. setting com. Nat. Bd. for Profl. Tchg. Stds., U. N.C.; mem. Okla. Commn. for Tchr. Prep. Named Tchr. of Yr., Norman Pub. Sch. Mem.: NEA, Nat. Sci. Tchrs. Assn. Avocations: travel, reading, gardening, cooking.

RYAN, SHEILA A., retired dean, nursing educator; Diploma in nursing, Creighton Meml. St. Joseph's Hosp. Sch. Nursing, 1967; BSN, U. Nebr., 1969; MSN in Psychiat. Nursing, U. Calif., San Francisco, 1971; PhD in Clin. Nursing Rsch., U. Ariz., 1981. Asst. prof. nursing Creighton U., Omaha, 1971—76, dean nursing, 1977—86; dean Sch. Nursing, dir. Med. Ctr. Nursing U. Rochester, NY, 1986—99; prof., Charlotte Peck Lienemann and Alumni Disting. Chair Coll. Nursing U. Nebr. Med. Ctr., Omaha. Fellow: Am. Acad. Nursing; mem.: Inst. for Healthcare Improvement, Nat. League Nursing (treas. 1993, pres. 1996—97), Inst. Medicine (treas.-sec.), Am. Internat. Health Alliance (bd. dirs. 1999—). Office: UNMC Coll Nursing Rm 4030 985330 NE Medical Ctr Omaha NE 68198-5330

RYAN, SHELLI ANN, public relations executive; b. Blair, Nebr., Dec. 8, 1968; d. Gorlyn Lew and Ruthie Ann Hagerbaumer; m. Mark Anthony Ryan, Sept. 26, 1992. BS, Bellevue U., 1992; MPA, U. Okla., 1997. Accredited Pub. Rels., Pub. Rels. Soc. Am. Mgr. mktg. svcs. Electronic Display Sys., Grand Island, Nebr., 1988-90; mktg. rep. Keeler/Raynor/Hinz, Bellevue, Nebr., 1990-92; mktg. coord. Accent Svc. Co., Omaha, 1992-95; corp. comm. specialist Applied Comm., Inc., Omaha, 1995-96; prin. Ryan Designs, Omaha, 1996-98; pres. Ad Hoc Comm. Resources, Omaha, 1999—. Media spokesperson Am. Heart Assn., Omaha, 1990-95; pub. rels. judge Jr. Achievement, Omaha, 1990, 96. Recipient 40 under 40 award Midlands Bus. Jour., 2002; named Woman Yr. Am. Women's Bus. Assn., Omaha, 1996, Gold Citation of Excellence, Am. Mktg. Assn., 2004, Best of Show and Pinnacle award Am. Mktg. Assn., 2002, Profl. Achievement award Am. Women's Assn., 2005, Bronze award Vision awards League Am. Comms. Profls., 2005. Mem. Pub. Rels. Soc. Am. (sec. 1998, treas. 1997, pres. 2001, dir. 1996—), Am. Bus. Women's Assn. (pres. 1995-96, Profl. Achievement award 2005). Avocations: weightlifting, bicycling. Home: 9030 Raven Oaks Dr Omaha NE 68152-1759

RYAN, SHERRY LYNN, executive administrator; b. South Bend, Ind., June 21, 1944; d. Charles Roscoe and Barbara Jeanne (Westfall) Jones; m. James J. Ryan, Dec. 18, 1971 (div. May 1984); children: Christopher Jeffrey, Jennifer Leigh, Cameron James. AA, Va. Intermont Coll., Bristol, Va., 1964. Med. sec. Drs. Montgomery, Greer & Howard, White Plains, N.Y., 1964; exec. sec. Mobil Oil Corp., N.Y., 1964-69; office mgr. Allen M. Ross, M.D., Darien, Conn., 1969; exec. sec. to pres. The Norwalk Co., Norwalk, Conn., 1969-70; exec. sec. Xerox Data Systems, Hackensack, N.J., 1971-73; from exec. asst. to asst. v.p. Capital Assocs., Inc., Redondo Beach, Calif., 1980-90; adminstr. Held Properties, L.A., 1991—92; asst. to the chmn. Total Pharm. Care, Inc., 1992—96; asst. to the chmn., mgr. adminstrn. Total Renal Care, Inc., Torrance, Calif., 1996—2000. Pres. mother's group Nat. Assn. for Retarded Children, 1976-77; vol. Torrance (Calif.) Meml. Med. Ctr. Mem. NAFE, Nat. Mothers of Twins Club. Methodist. Avocations: gourmet cooking, sewing, knitting, dart tournaments, camping. Home: 12061 Caminito Campana San Diego CA 92128-2061

RYAN, THERESA ANN JULIA, accountant; b. N.Y.C., Mar. 1, 1962; d. John Patrick and Diane Elizabeth Ryan. BA in Math. and Econs., Fordham U., Bronx, N.Y., 1984, MBA in Profl. Acctg., 1989. CPA, N.Y., F.L.M.I. With sales dept. Abraham & Straus, White Plains, N.Y., 1980-84; adminstrv. asst. Companion of N.Y., Rye, 1984-86, asst. fin. analyst, 1986-87; with tech. ctr. Fordham U., N.Y.C., 1987-88; staff acct. Konigsberg Wolf & Co., N.Y.C., 1989-91; sr. audit assoc. Coopers & Lybrand, L.L.P., N.Y.C., 1992-95; internal auditor N.Y. Power Authority, White Plains, 1996-99; circulation acctg. analyst Gannett Corp., White Plains, 2000-2001; sr. acct. Time Warner Cable, 2001—05; acct. Coll. of Mt. St. Vincent, 2005—. Mem. Inst. Internal Auditors (cert.), Beta Gamma Sigma. Avocations: music, biking, writing, travel, psychology. Home: 5 Clare Ter Yonkers NY 10707-3201 Office: 6301 Riverdale Ave Bronx NY 10471

RYAN, UNA SCULLY, health science association administrator, medical educator; b. Kuala Lumpur, Malaysia, Dec. 18, 1941; d. Henry and Amy (Yee) Scully; m. Allan Dana Callow, May 26, 1989; children: Tamsin Randlett, Amy Jean Susan Ryan. BSc in Zoology, Chemistry & Microbiology, Bristol (Eng.) U., 1963; PhD in Cell Biology, Cambridge (Eng.) U., 1968. Fellow dept. biology U. Va., Charlottesville, 1964-66; fellow dept. medicine U. Miami, Fla., 1966-67, adj. asst. prof. biology Fla., 1968-71; dir. lab. for ultrastructure studies Howard Hughes Med. Inst., Miami, 1967-71; from instr. to assoc. prof. medicine U. Miami Sch. Medicine, 1967-80, prof. medicine, 1980-89; sr. scientist Papanicolaou Cancer Rsch. Inst., Miami, 1972-77; rsch. prof. surgery Washington U. Sch. Medicine, St. Louis, 1990—; dir. health scis. Monsanto Co., St. Louis, 1990-93; pres., CEO T Cell Scis., Needham, Mass., 1993-98; rsch. prof. medicine Boston U. Sch. Medicine, 1993—; pres., CEO AVANT Immunotherapeutics, Needham, Mass., 1998—. Dir. course W. Alton Jones Cell Sci. Ctr., 1979-81; dir. Hybridoma Facility, U. Miami, 1986-89; chair local organizing com. Internat. Coun. on Thrombosis and Hemostasis, 1984; chair Rev. Com. for Extracellular Matrix Interactions in Lung, 1983; chair various revs. NHLBI; chair Mass. Biotech. Coun., 2004-06; mem. various rev. and adv. coms.; bd. dirs. Albany Molecular Rsch. Inc., 2006- Author: J. Tissue Culture Methods, 1987, Pulmonary Endothelium in Health Disease, 1987, Endothelial Cells, 1988, Vascular Endothelium: Receptors and Transduction Mechanisms, 1989; editor: Tissue & Cell, 1981-87; rev. editor: In Vitro, 1986; reviewer profl. jours.; contbr. articles to profl. jours. UK state scholar, 1960, Country Major scholar, 1960; D.S.I.R. rsch. fellow, 1964, 65, Ethel Sargant Rsch. fellow, 1964-65, Sci. Rsch. Coun. fellow, 1966; recipient Louis and Artur Lucian award for rsch. in circulatory diseases, 1984, Merit award Nat. Heart, Lung and Blood Inst., 1986, Lillie award Woods Hole, Marine Bill. Lab., 1989, Order of Brit. Empire, 2002. Mem. Am. Soc. Cell Biology, Soc. Neurosci., Tissue Culture Assn., Internat. Soc. Heart Rsch., Am. Heart Assn. (coun. on basic rsch., coun. on circulation, cardiopulmonary coun.), Am. Physiol. Soc., Am. Microcirculatory Soc., European Soc. Microcirculation, Am. Thoracic Soc. (dir. course on culture of pulmonary endothelial cells), Internat. Soc. Applied Cardiovascular Biology, N.Y. Acad. Scis., Fla. Soc. Electron Microscopy, Sigma Xi. Office: AVANT Immunotherapeutics 119 4th Ave Needham MA 02494-2725

RYAN-GRIFFITH, MARY KATE, special education educator; b. Balt., Oct. 9, 1957; d. Charles Ambrose Ryan and Elizabeth Joan Ebert; m. George Vintin Griffith Jr., June 29, 1991; 1 child, Virginia Elizabeth Griffith; m. Ronald Hemmerick, Apr. 24, 1982 (div. 1988). BS, Vanderbilt U., 1980; MA, Gallaudet U., Washington, 1984. Cert. advanced profl. tchr. Md. Interpreter, tutor Montgomery County Pub. Schs., Wheaton, Md., 1986—87, spl. edn. instrln. asst. Rockville, Md., 1987—89, 3d-4th gr. tchr. Tacoma Park, Md., 1989—91, spl. edn. tchr. Gaithersburg, Md., 1991—2005, Loiederman Mid. Sch., Silver Spring, Md., 2005—. Presenter in field. Contbr.: textbook Exceptional Children - An Introduction to Special Education, 2003, 2005. Pres. Lovettsville Cmty. Ctr., Va., VSA Arts Bd., 2000; mem. Lovettsville ES PTO, Va., Resnik E.S. PTA, Gaithersburg, Va. Named Outstanding Woman of Loudoun County, Loudoun Commn. on Women, 2003, Outstanding Spl. Educator, PTA Mont. chpt. Mem.: NEA, Coun. for Exceptional Children, Md. State Tchr.'s Assn., Delta Kappa Epsilon. Achievements include being named Ms. Wheelchair, Md., 1987. Avocations: performing with very special arts, drawing, making jewelry, writing, stained glass. Home: 12942 Axline Rd Lovettsville VA 20180

RYAN-HALLEY, CHARLOTTE MURIEL, oncology clinical specialist, family practice nurse practitioner; b. Beedeville, Ark., Sept. 2, 1939; d. Eugene Sanford and Edith Elizabeth (Goforth) Breckenridge; m. Alexander Halley; children: Russell Kent Ryan, Cary Randall Ryan, Molly Reneé Ryan Nankervis. BSN cum laude, Calif. State U., Fresno, 1991, MSN, clin. specialist, 1997. RN Calif., cert. pub. health nurse, cert. advanced oncology nurse. Psychiat. technician Porterville (Calif.) State Hosp., 1959-67; tchr. developmentally disabled Ariz. Tng. Ctr., Coolidge, 1967-71; Montessori tchr. Tucson, 1972-77; tchr. developmentally disabled Heartland Opportunity Ctr., Madera, Calif., 1977-79; med. office mgr. office of orthopedic surgeon, Madera, 1979-83, office mgr., x-ray technician, 1983-87; staff nurse in oncology St. Agnes Med. Ctr., Fresno, 1991—99, 2002—06; oncology clin. nurse specialist Kaweah Delta Hosp., Visalia, Calif., 1999—2002. Instr. nursing dept. Calif. State U., Fresno, 1992-93, 95-98; clin. instr. paradigm nursing program Fresno City Coll., Fresno, Calif., 2003-05; nursing instr. Coll. Sequoias Visalia, Calif., 2005, 06; Calif. nurse del. to China, People to People Am. Program, 2005. Treas. Hospice of Madera County, 1990-92, bd. dirs., 1992; peer counselor Calif. State U., Fresno, 1989-91; pres. bd. dirs. Easter Seals Soc., Madera, 1981. Mem. Nat. Oncology Nursing Soc. (on-line forum moderator, item writer cert. test 1998-2002), Nightingale Soc., Golden Key, Sigma Theta Tau (chmn. pub. com., editor MUNEWS newsletter 1994-95). Republican. Avocation: reading. Office Phone: 559-458-3222. Personal E-mail: rx4hugs@aol.com.

RYAN-KNUPPEL, BETTE L., nurse, educator; b. N.J., July 28, 1936; d. William and Mathilde Lynn (Bendlin) Wagner; children: Steven, Bonnie. AAS, Bergen Community Coll., 1979; BSN summa cum laude, Dominican Coll., Orangeburg, N.Y., 1981. Cert. RNC inpatient obs. RN NAACOG, childbirth educator ASPO-Lamaze. Instr. adult edn. Riverdell Bd. Edn., Oradell, NJ; organizer, instr. New Milford Bd. Edn., NJ; educator, staff OB. labor and delivery Barnert Hosp., Paterson, NJ; educator, staff labor and delivery Englewood Hosp., NJ; obstet. staff nurse Arrowhead Community Hosp., Glendale, Ariz.; retired. Guest lectr. sr. seminar Ramapo Coll.; presenter NAACOG study tours of USSR, Kenya; instr. Computers West. Pres. West Valley Affiliate of the Nat. Alliance on Mental Illness. Profl. Women's scholar, Bergen Community Merit scholar. Mem. No. N.J. ASPO (exec. bd. perinatal edn. planning com.), Sigma Theta Tau. Home: 12346 W Cougar Dr Sun City West AZ 85375-3345

RYBERG, BRIDGET FAY, literature and language educator; d. Kim and Joanne Fay Sorum; m. J.R. William Ryberg, July 13, 2002. BS in English Edn., U. Mary, Bismarck, ND, 2002. English tchr. Shanley HS, Fargo, ND, 2002—03, Grand Forks Sch. Dist., ND, 2003—. Office: Ctrl HS 115 N 4th St Grand Forks ND 58203-3709

RYDALCH, ANN, federal agency administrator, former state senator; m. Vernal Rydalch. BS in Business Educ., Idaho State U. Mem. Idaho Senate, 1983—1990, chmn. Fed. Lab. Consortium Tech. Transfer, 2001-, state repr. Idaho, 2004-. Past mem. Idaho Bicentennial Commn.; former vice chmn. Idaho Republican Com. Office: ID Natl Energy & Envrn Lab PO Box 1625 MS 3810 2525 N Fremont Ave Idaho Falls ID 83415-3810

RYDELL, CATHERINE M., medical association administrator, former state legislator; b. Grand Forks, ND, May 8, 1950; d. Hilary Harold and Catherine F. (Ireland) Wilson; m. Charles D. Rydell, 1971; children: Kimberly, Jennifer, Michael. BS, U. N.D., 1971. Mem. N.D. Ho. of Reps., 1985—, mem. supreme ct. judicial planning, govt., vet. affairs com., past rep. caucus leader; now exec. dir. Am. Acad. Neurology, St. Paul. Coord. cmty. svc. Bismarck Jr. Coll.; bus. mgr. surg. svc. St. Alexius Med. Ctr. Bd. dirs. Mission Valley Family, YMCA, N.D. Early Childhood Tng. Ctr., Ronald McDonald Found., CHAND; mem. state adv. bd. Casey Family Program, Juvenile Justice; mem. lay adv. bd. St. Alexius; mem. regional adv. bd. Luth. Social Svcs.; mem. N.D. State Centennial Com., N.D. State Mus. Art. Recipient Outstanding Svc. award Tobacco Free N.D., Legislator of Yr. award Children's Caucus, Guardian of Bus. award Nat. Fedn. Ind. Bus. Mem. Philanthropic and Edn. Orgn. Sisterhood, N.D. Med. Assn. (v.p.), Gamma Phi Beta. Office: Am Acad Neurology 1080 Montreal Ave Saint Paul MN 55116-2386*

RYDER, ANNE, newscaster; m. Kevin O'Keefe. Grad., U. Mo.; LHD (hon.), Marian Coll., U. Indpls. Creator, prodr. Hope to Tell series WTHR-TV, Indpls., reporter, anchor, 1984—. Columnist: Indpls. Women mag. Named Best Female News Anchor, The Indpls. Star and Indpls. Monthly Mag.; recipient Gabriel award, Wilbur award, Edward R. Murros award, Emmy awards. Office: WTHR-TV 1000 N Meridian St Indianapolis IN 46204

RYDER, BEVERLY, utilities executive; BA in Econs., Stanford U., Calif.; MBA in Fin., U. Chgo. From dir. strategic alliances So. Calif. to corp. sec. Edison Internat., Rosemead, Calif., 1972—96, corp. sec., 1996—, v.p. cmty. involvement, 2000—. Trustee Stanford (Calif.) U.; commr. LA (Calif.) City Employees' Retirement Bd. Bd. dir. United Way, LA. Office: Edison International 2244 Walnut Grove Ave Rosemead CA 91770

RYDER, ELIZABETH GODBEY, psychiatric nurse consultant, missionary; b. Atlanta, Sept. 19, 1943; d. Merle Harrison and Ida Myrtis (Davis) Godbey; m. Thomas Van Brakle Ryder, June 19, 1965; children: Paul, Peter. BA in English, U. Ga., 1965; AA in Nursing, Anne Arundel Community Coll., Arnold, Md., 1983; MA in Edn., Cen. Mich. U., 1987. Cert. psychiat. mental health nurse. Staff nurse Shock Trauma, Balt., 1983-85; adj. faculty Anne Arundel C.C., Arnold, Md., 1985-87; geropsy nurse Sheppard Pratt Hosp., Balt., 1987-89; clin. triage nurse Francis Scott Key Hosp., Balt., 1989-92; psychiat. nurse therpist ACT Team U. Md., Balt., 1992-94; interim dir. English Speaking Sch. Lubumibashi, 1995-98; med. missionary coord. North Katanga Conf., 1998—, dir. cmty. based health care sys., 1998—; dir. Kamina Nursing Sch., 1998—. Instr., cons. Dept. of Aging, Annapolis, Md., 1985-94; speaker Cult Awareness Network, Chgo., 1989-94; health care cons. So. Congo Conf. Dice-chmn. U.S. Swimming/Md., 1985-89; missionary to People's Dem. Republic of the Congo U. Meth. Ch. Gen. Bd. Global Ministry, 1994—. Recipient Nat. Svc. award U.S. Swimming, 1985. Mem. AAUW (book chmn. 1991), Severn River Swim Club (v.p. 1978-80), Annapolis Chorale. Methodist. Avocations: white water rafting, scuba diving. Home and Office: L eglise Methodiste PO Box 22037 Kitwe Zambia

RYDER, LOIS IRENE, artist; b. Pittsfield, Mass., Dec. 5, 1932; d. George Iver and Marion Irene (Allen) Kisselbrock; married, Jan. 19, 1952; children: Sharon, Karen, Charlene, Shawn, Scott. Instr. Westenhook Art Gallery, 1983. Exhibited in group shows at Redwood Arts, Gualala, Calif., 1992, Allentown Arts Festival, Buffalo, 1993, Trinity Ch., Lime Rock, Conn., 1986, 87, 88, Art in the Yard, Norman Rockwell Mus., Stockbridge, Mass., Crafts Expo, Hartford Civic Ctr., Conn., Marietta Mus. Art, Ga., Valley Forge Conv. Ctr., Pa., 1988, Kent art Assn., Conn., Berkshire Mus., Pittsfield, Mass., Albany Profl. Crafts, NY, 1987, 88, 89, New Eng. Profl. Show, Northampton, Mass., St. Timothy's Ch., West Hartford, Conn., Welles Gallery, Lenox, Mass., Santarella Gallery, Tyringham, Mass., Artist's Showcase, New England; author: The Best of Sketching in Drawing, 1998. Active Sheffield (Mass.) Art League, 1973-91, chair juried art show, 1982-83, chair country arts and crafts show, 1984-86, chair art league membership show, 1991, adv. bd., 1991, chair scholarship com., 1987—, Pittsfield Art League, 1976—, com. bd. mem. league coop., 1991, Springfield Art League, 1981—, Kent Art Assn., 1986—, bd. dirs., active artist status, v.p. Copley Soc. Boston, 1992—. Recipient Excellence award Sheffield Art League (2) 1987, (2) 1989, 1st in grapics, 1988, Art award, 1993, Graphics award, 1993, Merit award in graphics, 1995-96, Best in Fine Arts award Westfest, 1990, Cert. of Merit, Kent Art Assn., 1993, 1999, Graphics award, 1993, 99, 1st in graphics, 1997, Excellence award, 2004, 1st in Oil award Pittsfield Art League, 1994, Excellence award Nat. Parks Wyo., 1997, Top award, Copley Art Soc., Boston. Mem. Nat. Mus. Women in Arts (charter), Acad. Artists Assn., Miniature Art Soc. Mont., Miniature Art Soc. Fla., Miniature Art Soc. N.J., Miniature Art Soc., Miniature Painters, Sculptors and Gravers Soc. of Washington. Republican. Home: Creative Artworks 195 Main Rd Monterey Great Barrington MA 01230-8418

RYDER, TERESSA KAI, retired protective services official; b. Lansing, Mich., Aug. 1, 1960; d. Donald C. Patterson and Carole Dae Swain; divorced; 1 child, Erik Zar. AA, Lansing Cmty. Coll., 1999; student, Siena heights U., 1999—. EMT, Mich.; cert. fire svc. instr. Mich. Firefighters Tng. Coun. Firefighter, engr., paramedic, EMT Lansing Fire Dept., 1985-99. Fire svc. instr. Lansing C.C., 1996-01; instr. Lansing Fire Dept., 1996-99; cons., instr. Mich. State U., East Lansing, 1999-00; tutor Grand Rapids Pub. Sch., 2003-04. Founder Meridian Residents Responsible Govt., Haslett, Mich., 1996-97. Recipient Cert. Recognition, Mayor Terry McKane, City of Lansing, 1986. Avocations: drawing, writing, walking, reading, knitting.

RYERSON, LISA M., academic administrator; BA in English cum laude, Wells Coll., Aurora, N.Y., 1981; MS, SUNY. Asst. dir. admissions Wells Coll., Aurora, NY, 1981—84, assoc. dean of students, 1984—87, dean of students, 1991—94, v.p. to exec. v.p., 1994—95, pres., 1995—. Vice chair bd. of mng. dir. Ind. Coll. Funf of N.Y.; chair exec. bd. Pub. Leadership Edn. Network, Washington; bd. mem. Women's Coll. Coalition, Washington. Mem. exec. com. Cayuga County C. of C., Auburn, NY. Office: Wells Coll 170 Main St Aurora NY 13026

RYLANT, CYNTHIA, writer; b. Hopewell, Va., June 6, 1954; d. John Tune and Leatrel (Rylant) Smith; 1 child, Nathaniel. BA, U. Charleston, 1975; MA, Marshall U., 1976; MLS, Kent State U., 1981. English instr. Marshall U., Huntington, W.Va., 1979-80, U. Akron, Ohio, 1983-84; children's libr. Akron (Ohio) Pub. Libr., 1983. Part-time lectr. Northeast Ohio Univs. Coll. Medicine, Rootstown, Ohio, 1991—. Author: (picture books) When I Was Young in the Mountains, 1982 (Caldecott Honor book, 1983, English Speaking Union Book-Across-the-Sea Amb. of Honor award, 1984, Am. Book award nom., 1983), Miss Maggie, 1983, This Year's Garden, 1984, Waiting to Waltz: A Childhood (verse), 1984 (Nat. Coun. for Social Studies Best Book, 1984), A Blue-Eyed Daisy (in U.K. as Some Year for Ellie), 1985 (Children's Book of Yr., Child Study Assn. Am., 1985), The Relatives Came, 1985 (Horn Book Honor book, 1985, Children's Book of Yr., Child Study Assn. Am., 1985, Caldecott Honor book, 1986), Every Living Thing (stories), 1985, A Fine White Dust, 1986 (Newbery Honor Book, 1987), Night in the Country, 1986, Birthday Presents, 1987, Children of Christmas (in U.K. as Silver Packages and Other Stories), 1987, All I See, 1988, A Kindness, 1989, Mr. Grigg's Work, 1989, Soda Jerk (verse)1990, A Couple of Kooks (stories), 1990, Appalachia: The Voices of Sleeping Birds, 1991 (Boston Globe/Horn Book Honor book for nonfiction, 1991), Best Wishes, 1992, An Angel for Solomon Singer, 1992, Missing May, 1992 (Newbery Medal, 1992), The Dreamer, 1993, I Had Seen Castles, 1993, The Everyday Books, 1993, The Old Lady Who Named Things, 1996, Whales, 1996, Bookshop Dog, 1996, Blue Hill Meadows, 1997, Poppleton, 1997, Poppleton and Friends, 1997, Cat Heaven, 1997, Blue Hill Meadows and the Much-Loved Dog, 1997, Scarecrow, 1998, Bear Day, 1998, Tulip Sees America, 1998, Poppleton Everyday, 1998, Poppleton Forever, 1998, Bird House, 1998, Islander, 1998, Bless Us All, 1998, Cobble Street Cousins in Aunt Lucy's Kitchen, 1998, Bunny Bungalow, 1999, Cookie-Store Cat, 1999, Poppleton in Spring, 1999, Cobble Street Cousins: Some Good News, 1999, Cobble Street Cousins: Special Gifts, 1999, Poppleton in Fall, 1999, Give Me Grace, 1999, Heavenly Village, 1999, Poppleton Through and Through, 2000, Wonderful Happens, 2000, Thimbleberry Stories, 2000, Let's Go Home, 2000, Little Whistle, 2000, In November, 2000, Poppleton Has Fun, 2000, Little Whistle's Dinner Party, 2001, Little Whistle's Medicine, 2001, Ticky-Tacky Doll, 2001, The Great Gracie Chase, 2001, Poppleton in Winter, 2001, Summer Party, 2001, Good Morning Sweetie Pie and Other Poems for Little Children, 2002, Old Town in the Green Groves, 2002, Wedding Flowers, 2002, Long Night Moon, 2004, (Mr. Putter and Tabby series) Walk the Dog, 1994, Bake the Cake, 1994, Pour the Tea, 1994, Pick the Pears, 1995, Fly the Plane, 1997, Row the Boat, 1997, Toot the Horn, 1998, Take the Train, 1998, Paint the Porch, 2000, Feed the Fish, 2001, (The High-Rise Private Eyes series) Case of the Climbing Cat, 2000, Case of the Missing Monkey, 2000, The Case of the Puzzling Possum, 2001, The Case of the Troublesome Turtle, 2001, (Henry and Mudge Series) Henry and Mudge, 1987, Henry and Mudge in Puddle Trouble, 1990, Henry and Mudge Take the Big Test, 1991, Henry and Mudge in the Green Time, 1992, Henry and Mudge under the Yellow Moon, 1992, Henry and Mudge in the Sparkle Days, 1993, Henry and Mudge and the Forever Sea, 1993, Henry and Mudge Get the Cold Shivers, 1993, Henry and Mudge and the Happy Cat, 1994, Henry and Mudge and the Bedtime Thumps, 1991, Henry and Mudge and the Long Weekend, 1992, Henry and Mudge and the Wild Wind, 1992, Henry and Mudge and the Careful Cousin, 1994, Henry and Mudge and the Best Day of All, 1995, Henry and Mudge in the Family Trees, 1997, Henry and Mudge and the Sneaky Crackers, 1998, Henry and Mudge and the Starry Night, 1998, Henry and Mudge and Annie's Good Move, 1998, Henry and Mudge and the Snowman Plan, 1999, Henry and Mudge and Annie's Perfect Pet, 1999, Henry and Mudge and the Funny Lunch, 1999, Henry and Mudge and the Tall Tree House, 1999, Henry and Mudge and Mrs. Hopper's House, 1999, Henry and Mudge and the Great Grandpas, 1999, Henry and Mudge and a Very Special Merry Christmas, 1999, Henry and Mudge and the Wild Goose Chase, 1999, Henry and Mudge and the Big Sleepover, 1999, Henry and Mudge and the Tumbling Trip, 1999, Henry's Puppy Mudge Has a Snack, 2001, Henry's Puppy Mudge Takes aBath, 2001, Henry and Mudge and the Great Grandpas, 2005 (Am. Libr. Assn.'s Theodor Seuss Geisel Medal, 2006). Office: Simon & Schuster Children's 4th Floor 1230 Ave of The Americas New York NY 10020*

RYLEE, GLORIA GENELLE, music educator; b. Commerce, Ga., Nov. 26, 1947; d. John Otis Sr. and Genelle Byrd Rylee. BS in Edn., Ga. So. Coll., 1969; MusM, Southwestern Bapt. Theol. Sem., 1973. Tchr. Banks County Bd. Edn., Homer, Ga., 1969-71; piano tchr. Ft. Worth, 1972-73; min. music, ch. sec. Mt. Olive Bapt. Ch., Commerce, Ga., 1974-81; sec. Ga. Bapt. Conv., Atlanta, 1981-86; parapro Banks County Bd. Edn., Homer, 1986-87, tchr. music, 1987—. Tchr. piano, Homer, 1975-81, 89-96; staff mem. Youth II Music Camp, Norman Park, Ga., 1996-98. Pianist Webbs Creek Bapt. Ch., Commerce, 1991—. Active Grassroots Arts Coun., Gainesville, Ga., 1994—, State Bapt. Women's Choral Group, 1979-86, 1996-2001, Messiah Singers, Khabarovsk, Russia, 2003; team mem. Vol. Missions-Ga. Bapt. Conv., Seoul, Korea, 1998-2000; mem. Messiah singers Kahbarovsk, Russia, 2003. Mem. Nat. Mus. Educators Assn., Music. Tchrs. Nat. Assn., Ga. Music Educators Assn., Profl. Assn. Ga. Educators. Home: 1785 Wilson Bridge Rd Homer GA 30547-2911 Office: Banks County Elem Sch 335 Evans St Homer GA 30547

RYMER, ILONA SUTO, artist, retired educator; b. NYC, Dec. 1, 1921; d. Alexander and Elizabeth (Komaromy) Suto; m. Robert Hamilton Rymer, Mar. 27, 1944 (dec. Dec. 1999); children: Thomas Parker, Shelley Ilona. BA, Long Beach State U., 1953, MA, 1954. Tchr., cons. Long Beach (Calif.) Sch. Dist., 1953-56; tchr. Orange (Calif.) Sch. Dist., 1956-58; tchr., cons. Brea (Calif.)-Olinda Sch. Dist., 1958-80; ind. artist, designer Graphic House Studio, Solvang, Calif., 1980—, Stampa-Barbara, Santa Barbara, Calif., 1990—. Lectr. folk art Brea Sch. Dist., 1975—80; co-founder and mem. Gallery Los Olivos, pres, 1993—. Author: (instrn. book) Folk Art U.S.A., 1975 (Proclamation City of Brea, 1975); art editor, feature writer, illustrator: Arabian Conneciton mag., 1985—86; needlepoint designer Backsticth Store, Solvang, Calif., 1982—83; one-woman shows include Liberty Bell Race Track, Pa., 1970, Gallery Los Olivos, Calif., 2004, exhibited in group shows at Dennas Mus. Ctr., Northwestern Mich. Coll., 2001, Nat. Exhbn. Am. Watercolor, 2002, Adirondack's Nat. Exhbn. of Am. Watercolors, Old Forge, N.Y., 2002—, commission, Pres. Reagan's portrait on his stallion, Reagan Libr., Simi Valley, Calif., Khemosabi and Ruth, 1995. Artist and donor City of Solvang, Calif., 2005. Recipient 1st pl. Seminar award, Rex Brandt, 1961, Affiliate award, Laguna Art Mus., 1967, Best of Watercolor award, Orange County Fair, 1969, Bicentennial trip to France, Air France, 1975, Proclamation for Tchg., City of Brea, 1980, Theme award, Santa Barbara County Fair, 1991. Mem.: Mendocina Art Assn., Collage Artists Am., Artist Guild Santa Ynez Valley, Ctrl. Coast Art Assn., Santa Barbara Art Assn., Calif. Gold Coast Watercolor Soc. (signature). Presbyterian. Studio: 1887 Augustenburg Pl Solvang CA 93463 Personal E-mail: ilonarymer@comcast.net.

RYMER, PAMELA ANN, federal judge; b. Knoxville, Tenn., Jan. 6, 1941; AB, Vassar Coll., 1961; LLB, Stanford U., 1964; LLD (hon.), Pepperdine U., 1988. Bar: Calif. 1966, U.S. Ct. Appeals (9th cir.) 1966, U.S. Ct. Appeals (10th cir.), U.S. Supreme Ct. Dir., polit. rsch. and analysis Goldwater for President Com., 1964; v.p. Rus Walton & Assoc., Los Altos, Calif., 1965—66; assoc. Lillick McHose & Charles, L.A., 1966—75, ptnr., 1973—75, Toy and Rymer, L.A., 1975—83; judge U.S. Dist. Ct. (cen. dist.) Calif., L.A., 1983—89, U.S. Ct. Appeals (9th cir.), L.A., 1989—. Faculty The Nat. Jud. Coll., 1986-88; mem. com. summer ednl. programs Fed. Jud. Ctr., 1987-88, mem. com. appellate judge edn., 1996-99; chair exec. com. 9th Cir. Jud. Conf., 1990; mem. com. criminal law Jud. Conf. U.S., 1988-93, Ad Hoc com. gender-based violence, 1991-94, fed.-state jurisdiction com., 1993-96; mem. commn. on structural alternatives Fed. Cts. Appeals, 1997-98. Mem. editorial bd. The Judges' jour., 1989-91; contbr. articles to profl. jours. and newsletters. Mem. Calif. Postsecondary Edn. Commn., 1974-84, chmn., 1980-84; mem. L.A. Olympic Citizens Adv. Commn.; bd. visitors Stanford U. Law Sch., 1986-99, trustee, 1991-2001, chair, 1993-96, exec. com., chmn. bd. trustees com. acad. policy, planning and mgmt. and its ad. hoc. com. athletics, chmn. bd. visitors Sch. Law, 1987—; bd. visitors Pepperdine U. Law Sch., 1987—; mem. Edn. Commn. of States Task Force on State Policy and Ind. Higher Edn., 1987-89, Carnegie Commn. Task Force Sci. and Tech. Jud. and

Regulatory Decisionmaking, 1990-93, Commn. Substance Abuse Coll. and Univ. Campuses, 1992-94, commn. substance abuse high schs. Ctr. Addiction and Substance Abube Columbia U.; bd. dirs. Constnl. Rights Found., 1985-97, Pacific Coun. Internat. Policy, 1995—, Calif. Higher Edn. Policy Ctr., 1992-97; Jud. Conf. U.S. Com. Fed.-State Jurisdiction, 1993, Com. Criminal Law, 1988-93, ad hoc com. gender based violence, 1991-94; chair exec. com. 9th cir. jud. conf., 1990-94. Recipient Outstanding Trial Jurist award L.A. County Bar Assn., 1988; named David T. Lewis Disting. Jurist-in-Residence U. Utah, 1992. Mem. ABA (task force on civil justice reform 1991-93, mem. coord. com. agenda civil justice reform in Am. 1991), State Bar Calif. (antitrust and trade regulation sect., exec. com. 1990-92), L.A. County Bar Assn. (chmn. antitrust sect. 1981-82, mem. editl. bd. The Judges Jour. 1989-91, mem. com. professionalism 1988—, numerous other coms.), Assn. of Bus. Trial Lawyers (bd. govs. 1990-92), Stanford Alumni Assn., Stanford Law Soc. Soc. Calif., Vassar Club So. Calif. (past pres.). Office: US Ct Appeals 9th Cir US Court of Appeals Bldg 125 S Grand Ave Rm 600 Pasadena CA 91105-1621*

RYPCZYK, CANDICE LEIGH, employee relations executive; b. Norman, Okla., Apr. 24, 1949; d. John Anthony and Lee (Brunswick) Wirth; m. Peter Charles Rypczyk, Nov. 27, 1976. BA, Kalamazoo Coll., Mich., 1971; cert. labor studies extension program, Cornell U., N.Y. Sch. Indsl., Labor Relations, Middletown, 1985. Personnel asst. PFW divsn. Hercules Inc., Middletown, 1973-77, asst. personnel mgr., 1977-79, mgr. employee relations, 1979-92; mgr. human resources Huck Internat., Kingston, N.Y., 1992-2000; human resources cons., 2000—04. Mem. DAR, Soc. for Human Resource Mgmt. (v.p. Mid-Hudson Valley chpt. 1985, pres. 1986, treas. N.Y. State coun. 1986, dist. bd. dirs. 1988-90, cert.). Avocations: photography, reading, genealogy.

RYSER, CAROL PIERSON, psychologist; b. Orange, N.J., May 1, 1932; d. Malcolm Gregory Pierson and Evelyn (Maffitt) Goodrich; m. Hughes Jean-Paul Ryser, June 10, 1961; children: Marc, Jeannine, Eve, Warren. AB, Boston U., 1957, MA, 1958; PhD, Harvard U., 1967. Lic. psychologist, Mass. Dir., founder Affiliates for Adult Devel., Bedford, Mass., 1976-91, clin. psychologist, 1978—. Faculty cons. seminar Wellesley (Mass.) Coll., 1976-77, cons. to adminstrn., 1973-77; lectr. sociology Harvard Grad. Sch. of Edn., Cambridge, 1976-77; rsch. assoc. Harvard Med. Sch., Boston, 1967-73; lectr. Emmanuel Coll., Boston, 1967-69. Author: (monograph) Problems of Retirement, 1972, (book chpt.) Arts in Society, 1964; contbr. numerous articles to profl. jours. Mem. Back Porch Dance Co., Cambridge, Mass., 1993—, LAWS, Concord, Mass., 1975-80; dir. Women's Equity Action League, Boston, 1975-78; bd. dirs. various local social and svc. orgns., 1972-82. Democrat. Home: 503 Annursnac Hill Rd Concord MA 01742-5414 Office: Affiliates for Adult Devel 330 South Rd Bedford MA 01730-2523 Office Phone: 781-275-2122. Personal E-mail: ryser5@juno.com.

RYSER, ROBYN CAREY, elementary school educator; b. Dodgeville, Wis., Feb. 11, 1970; d. Robert and Janice Carey; m. Jerry Ryser, Dec. 31, 1997; children: Alex Carey, Hannah Carey, Addison Carey. Degree in Elem. Edn., Edgewood Coll., Madison, Wis., 1993; MEd, Viterbo U., LaCrosse, Wis., 1997. Tchr. Pecatonica Area Schs., Blanchardville, Wis., 1993—. Instr. U. Wis., Platteville, 2005—. Pres. Pecatonica Christian Presch., Blanchardville, 2004—05, mem., 2005—. Office: Pecatonica Area Schs 704 Cross St Blanchardville WI 53516 Office Phone: 608-523-4285. Office Fax: 608-523-4286. Business E-Mail: rryser@pecatonica.k12.wi.us.

SA, LILY, artist, educator; b. St. Petersbourg, Russia, Sept. 26, 1909; came to the U.S., 1970; d. Yin-Tu Sa and Lan-Hsing Wang; m. Tan-Chi Sang, June 6, 1945 (dec. Aug. 1987); children: Barbara Liang Sang, Rebecca Liang Sang, Mildred Liang Sang. BS, Coll. S.I., 1984; MFA, CUNY, 1991; postgrad., NYU, 1993—. Recipient Women of Excellence award CUNY Women's Coalition, N.Y.C., 1992. Mem. Pi Lambda Theta (Rho chpt.), Golden Key Nat. Honor Soc.

SAAB, DEANNE KELTUM, real estate broker, appraiser; b. Allentown, Pa., Jan. 27, 1945; d. James A. and Agnes G. (Hanzlik) S. BA, Cedar Crest Coll., 1966; MS, U. Calif., Santa Barbara, 1973; realtors cert., Pa. State U., 1978. Cert. appraiser Assoc. Appraisal Inst., Pa., 1991; cert. sales profl. Nat. Assn. Home Builders, 1994. Tchr. Ojai (Calif.) Unified Sch. Dist., 1966-74; pvt. practice Allentown, 1978—; owner Heritage Gardens, Allentown, 1981—; pres., treas. DeAnne & Assoc., Inc., Allentown, 1987—. Co-founder, treas. performance group Lehigh Valley Folk Music Soc., 1996. Mem. AAUW (various offices, Best State Newsletter award 1987), Nat. Assn. Realtors, Pa. Assn. Realtors, Allentown Lehigh Valley Assn. Realtors, Cedar Crest Coll. Alumnae Assn. (class rep., various offices), Lehigh Valley Guild Craftsmen (various offices). Avocations: gourd, herbal crafting, painting, folk music performance. Home and Office: 1360 Dorney Ave Allentown PA 18103-9731 Personal E-mail: dksaab@ptd.net.

SAAB, MAUREEN WILSON, social worker, consultant; b. Lackawanna, NY, Nov. 7, 1940; d. Martin Francis Wilson and Alice Joan Conmy; m. Richard Joseph Saab, June 12, 1965; children: Alice Joan, Joseph Richard, Bridget Jane Saab Van Sickle. BA, Marymount Coll., 1962; MSW, SUNY, Buffalo, 1964. Family counselor Family Svc. Soc., Buffalo, 1964—66; sch. social worker Zenia (Ohio) Schs., 1974; devel. dir. Nichols Sch., Buffalo, 1989—95; devel. coord. Arts Coun. Buffalo and Erie County, Buffalo, 1996—98; devel. cons. Buffalo, 1995—2000. Pres. Jr. League Buffalo, 1983—84; pres., chmn. bd. Hibert Coll., Hamburg, NY, 1999—2000; vice chmn. United Way of Buffalo and Erie County, 1986—88; vice chair cmty. bd. WNED, Western N.Y. Pub. Broadcasting Assn.; mem. cmty. bd. Theodore Roosevelt Inaugural Site; trustee Nichols Sch. Bd., Hibert Coll.; mem. SUNY Buffalo Friends of Sch. Architecture; vol. Albright-Knox Fine Arts Acad.; bd. dirs. Hopevale Home for Girls; mem. alumnae bd. Marymount Coll.; chair, pres. Presbyterian Homes and Sr. Care Found. Recipient Gloria Gaines award, Marymount Coll., Tarrytown, NY, 1997, Pres.' medal, Hilbert Coll., 2002, Susan Reid Greene Russell award, Jr. League Buffalo, 2004. Mem.: Garret Club (bd. dirs. 1998—2001). Roman Catholic. Avocations: reading, golf, walking. Home: 47 Hallam Rd Buffalo NY 14216

SAARI, JOY ANN, family practice nurse practitioner, geriatrics nurse, medical/surgical nurse; b. Chippewa Falls, Wis., July 14, 1953; d. Harry R. and Hilda R. (Christianson) Harwood; m. Allan A. Saari, Dec. 31, 1973 (dec.); children: Christopher, Erik. BSN summa cum laude, U. Wis., Eau Claire, 1978; postgrad., Blue Ridge Community Coll., Verona, Va., 1987; MSN, FNP, George Mason U., 1995; MSN. RN, Mich., Wis., Va.; FNP, Va.; cert. BLS instr., ACLS. Staff nurse Portage View Hosp., Hancock, Mich., 1979-80; evening supr., asst. dir. nursing Chippewa Manor, Chippewa Falls, 1980-86; staff nurse Bridgewater Home, Inc., Va., 1986-90; p.m. charge nurse Medicalodge Leavenworth, Kans., 1990-91; outdoor edn. nurse Montgomery County Schs., Md., 1991-93; FNP Leesburg/Sterling Family Practice, 1995—; active duty head nurse Ft. Knox Med. Unit, 2004—06. Affiliate faculty George Mason U., 2003—. Maj. USAR Nurse Corps, 1989—. Mem. Am. Acad. Nurse Practitioners, Nat. League of Nursing, No. Va. Nurse Practitioner Assn., Res. Officer Assn., Am. Legion Aux., Phi Kappa Phi. Office Phone: 703-777-1612. Personal E-mail: saarinp@aol.com.

SABAJ, NANCY J., secondary school educator; b. Chgo., Mar. 23, 1969; d. Eugene A. and Florence M. Sabaj. BS in Music Edn., U. Ill., 1992; M in Music Edn., Vander Cook Coll. Music, Chgo., 1997. Cert. tchr. Ill. Band dir. St. John Luth. Sch., Champaign, Ill., 1992—94, Iuka (Ill.) Cmty. Consolidated Dist. 7, 1994—96, Odin (Ill.) Pub. Schs., 1997—2000, Roxana (Ill.) Cmty. Unit Sch. Dist. 1, 2000—. Mem.: Madison County Band Dirs. Assn., Ill. Music Educators Assn., Music Educators Nat. Conf. Avocations: church, exercise, sports. Home: 608 Hillside Bethalto IL 62010

SABATELLA, ELIZABETH MARIA, clinical therapist, educator, mental health facility administrator; b. Mineola, N.Y., Nov. 9, 1940; d. D. F. and Blanche M. (Schmetzle) S; 1 child, Kevin Woog. BS, SUNY, Brockport, 1961; MA, SUNY, Stony Brook, 1971, MSW, 1983; postgrad., Univ. Calif., San Diego, 1999. Lic. social worker N.Y., N.Mex., Oreg.; tchr., sch. counselor Oreg., N.Y., cert. pupil pers. credential, sch. counselor, registered clin. social worker Calif., Oreg. Tchr. physical edn. Comseqogue Sch. Dist., Port Jefferson, N.Y., 1968-73, 84-87, 88-91; sch. counselor, 1975—84; clin. therapist Cibola Counseling Svcs., Grants, N.Mex., 1991-95, regional dir., 1993-95; clin. therapist Family Growth Counseling Ctr., Encinitos, Calif., 1995-96; clin. social worker Family Advocacy, San Diego, 1995-99; sch. counselor San Diego, 1999-2000; counselor Navy Coll., 2000—01; sch. counselor Redmond (Oreg.) Sch. Dist., 2001—, 2001—. Therapist for abused children Farmingville Mental Health Clinic; therapist for adolescents Comsewogue Sch. Dist.; therapist for alcoholics Lighthouse Ctr.; mem. Family Systems Network for Continuing Edn., Calif., Colo., 1978-80; mem. biofeedback and mediation com. McLean Hosp., Boston, 1978; mem. therapeutic touch team East and West Ctr., N.Y.C., 1980-84, sexual abuse treatment coord., 1992-95. Art and photographs exhibited at group show N.Mex. Art League, 1991; author: Stop Before You Blow Your Top, 1998, We Want You To Stop. Children Who Witness Domestic Violence, 1998, Children at Play: Tales of Gang Boys in Treatment, 1999; contbr. poetry and children's story to various publs. Recipient Editor's Choice award and Best New Poet award Nat. Libr. Poetry, 1988, Merit award and Place Winner for Poetry, Iliad Press, 1993. Mem.: NASW, Oregon Ed. Assn., Writers Assn., Oreg. Tchrs. Assn., Acad. Cert. Social Workers, N.Y. State United Tchrs., Sierra Club. Avocations: travel, bicycling, yoga, dance, photography. Home: 826 NE Providence Dr Bend OR 97701 E-mail: LIZSABOR@MSN.com.

SABAU, CARMEN SYBILE, retired chemist; b. Cluj, Romania, Apr. 24, 1933; naturalized U.S. citizen; d. George and Antoinette Marie (Chiriac) Grigorescu; m. Mircea Nicolae Sabau, July 11, 1956; 1 child, Isabelle Carmen. MS in Inorganic and Analytical Chemistry, U. C.I. Parhon, Bucharest, Romania, 1955; PhD in Radiochemistry, U. Fridericiana, Karlsruhe, Fed. Republic of Germany, 1972. Chemist Inst. Atomic Physics, Bucharest, Romania, 1956—74, Joint Inst. of Nuclear Rsch., Dubna-Moscow, 1974—75, Argonne (Ill.) Nat. Lab., 1976-98; ret., 1998. Author: Ion-exchange Theory and Applications in Analytical Chemistry, 1967; contbr. articles to profl. jours. Active Romanian World Coun.; del. NGO/DPI Conf. on Human Rights. Internat. Atomic Energy Agy. fellow, 1967-68, Humboldt fellow, 1970-72. Mem. Am. Romanian Acad. Arts and Sci., Internat. Soc. Intercomm. of New Ideas, Alexander von Humboldt Assn. Am., Alpha Friends of Antiquity, Rocky Mountain MLA. Home: 689 Banbury Way Bolingbrook IL 60440-1057 Personal E-mail: carmen_sabau@hotmail.com.

SABELHAUS, MELANIE R., government agency administrator; b. Cleve. m. Bob Sabelhaus; 2 children. BS in Journalism, Ohio U. With IBM, 1972—86; founder, CEO Exclusive Interim Properties Ltd., Balt., 1986—97; v.p. global sales Bridgestreet Accommodations, 1997—98; dep. adminstr. SBA, Washington, 2002—. Co-chair Nat. Summit on Women in Philanthropy; bd. dirs. United Way, Alzheimer's Assn. of Ctrl. Md. Recipient Outstanding Vol. Fundraiser of the Yr. award for Md., Assn. of Fundraising Profls., 2002.

SABINI, BARBARA DOROTHY, artist, educator; b. Bklyn., June 11, 1939; d. Joseph and Fannie (Ciazzia) Gugliucci; m. John Sabini Jr., June 22, 1957 (div. 1982); children: Michael, John, Gerald, Barbara-Jo. AAS in Psychology, Orange County C.C., Middletown, N.Y., 1979; BFA in Painting, SUNY, New Paltz, 1984, MFA in Painting, 1988. Cert. tchr. art edn. Tchg. asst. drawing and design SUNY, New Paltz, 1986; art tchr. Newburgh (N.Y.) Free Acad. H.S., 1987—. Lectr. freshman drawing SUNY, NW Paltz, 1990; painting instr. Orange County C.C., 1991; instr. collage Coll. New Rochelle, N.Y., 2001; faculty supr. teen art projects Newburgh Free Acad. H.S., 1990-99; instr. Kosciuszko Found./UNESCO, Poland, 1995, 96, 97; mem. China Study Tour, 1998; lead tchr. Travel & Tourism Acad., 1999. One-woman shows include White Herron Lounge, Virginia Beach, Va., 1986, Ave. A Cafe, N.Y.C., 1987, Pumpkin Eater, N.Y.C., 1989, Painters Tavern, Cornwall-on-Hudson, N.Y., 1992; exhibits include Hammerquist Gallery, N.Y.C., 1984, Ariel Gallery, N.Y.C., 1985, James Callahan Gallery, Palm Springs, Calif., 1985, The Real Gallery, Cornwall, N.Y., 1986, Cork Gallery, Lincoln Ctr., N.Y.C., 1986, Mid Hudson Arts and Sci. Ctr., Poughkeepsie, N.Y., 1986, Ledo Gallery, N.Y.C., 1987, Outer Space Gallery, N.Y.C., 1989, 91, Wall Gallery, N.Y.C., 1989, 90, Women in the Arts Found. Gallery, N.Y.C., Ledger DeMain Gallery, N.Y.C., China Phoenix Gallery Store, Albuquerque, 1995, West Point (N.Y.) Art Gallery, 2005, Am. Artists for Tsunami Victimms, 2005, Aarden House, Harriman, N.Y., 2005; group exhbns: Orange County Art Fedn. Recipient Appreciation cert. N.Y. State Art Tchrs. Assn., 1st pl. award Most Creative Olympics of Visual Arts. Mem. Nat. Art Tchrs. Assn., N.Y. State Tchrs. Assn., N.Y. State Art Tchrs. Assn., Orange County Art Soc. Avocations: travel, cross country skiing, reading, arts. Office: Newburgh Free Acad 201 Fullerton Ave Newburgh NY 12550-3798

SABINO, CATHERINE ANN, magazine editor; b. NYC, May 6, 1952; d. Joseph A. and Frances (Phelan) S. AB, Barnard Coll., 1973. Beauty editor, editor-at-large Harper's Bazaar, Italia, Men's Bazaar, 1976-79; beauty editor Seventeen mag. Triangle Comms., 1979-83; N.Y. editor Linea Italiana Mondadori, 1983-85; N.Y. editor Moda RAI, 1985-86; editor in chief Worldstyle The Aegis Venture Group, 1987-88; editor in chief In Fashion Murdoch Mags., 1988-89; editor mag. devel. European Home, 1989-91; cons. Hachette Mags., 1992; editor in chief Woman's Day Beauty Hachette Mags., 1993; editor-in-chief, group editor N.Y. Times Custom Pub., N.Y.C., 1993-97; editor-in-chief, group editor, v.p. Forbes C.M., N.Y.C., 1997—; editor-in-chief Brit. Living and Style, 2000—02, Forbes Finest Luxury Real Estate, Four Seasons Mag., 1995—. Author: Italian Style, 1985, Italian Country, 1988. Recipient Folio award 1994, Clarion award 1998-2000, 02, 04. Mem. Am. Soc. Mag. Editors, Barnard-Columbia Club N.Y. (dir. at large 1991-93), Yale Club. Office: 90 Fifth Ave New York NY 10011 Office Phone: 212-367-4114. Business E-Mail: csabino@forbes.com.

SABIO, DOROTHY, elementary school educator; b. Paterson, N.J., Aug. 18, 1963; d. Vincent Anthony and Loretta Grace Sabio. BA in Comm., William Paterson U., Wayne, N.J., 1986, M in Elem. Edn., 1991. Cert. elem. edn. N.J., 1991. Tchr. visual and performing arts Belmont Runyon Sch., Newark, 1992—. Cooperating tchr. Kean U., Union, NJ, 1996—97; sch. liaison N.J. Performing Arts Ctr., Newark, 1998—; mentor tchr. Belmont Runyon Sch., Newark, 2006—; judge N.J. state forensics tournament N.J. Speech and Theatre Assn.; presenter in field. Named Newark Pub. Schools Tchr. of Yr., State Supt. Beverly Hall, 1999; recipient Dr. Martin Luther King, Jr. award, Gov. Christine Todd Whitman and the N.J. Dept. State, 1998; VH-1 Music In Our Schools grantee, Pres. Bill Clinton, 2001. Mem.: Newark Tchrs. Union (assoc.). Avocations: ballet, piano, theater, travel. Home: 1408 Magnolia Ln Branchburg NJ 08876-6100 Office: Belmont Runyon School One Belmont Runyon Way Newark NJ 07108 Office Phone: 973-733-6920. Business E-Mail: dorothys@nps.epals.com.

SABISTON, KELLI BREWER, athletic trainer, consultant; b. Hampton, Va., Aug. 3, 1964; d. William Dennis and Sandra Bright Brewer; m. Paul Sabiston, May 26, 1990; children: Natalie Clare, Eric Brewer. BS cum laude, Wake Forest U., Winston-Salem, NC, 1986; MA in Athletic Tng., U. NC, Chapel Hill, 1990. Cert. athletic trainer Nat. Athletic Trainers' Assn., Tex., 1988, lic. Ga. Bd. Athletic Tng., 1990, Fla. Dept. Health, 2002, NC Bd. Athletic Trainers, 2005, cert. CPR, standard first aid, AED ARC, 2006. Health club mgr. Corp. Sports Unlimited, Atlanta, 1986—88; phys. edn. instr., grad. asst. athletic trainer U. NC, 1988—90; head athletic trainer Marietta H.S., Ga., 1990—2002; founder, cons. Coastal Athletic Tng. Svcs., Panama City, Fla., 2003—; cons. Am. Splty. Health, San Diego, 2006—. Staff athletic trainer Crosby Celebrity Golf Tournament, Bermuda Run, NC, 1984—2001, Ga. State Games, Atlanta, 1991—97, US Track & Field Championships, 1992—93, North-South Ga. HS All-Star Football Games, 1992—94, Profl. Football Regional Combine Testing Camp, Atlanta, 1992—94, Atlanta Olympic Com., 1996—96; panelist Women Athletic Tng. Com., 2004—04; examiner Nat. Athletic Trainers' Assn. Cert. Exam., Marietta, 1994—95; presenter Nat. Athletic Trainers' Assn., Nashville, 2000, Nat. Athletic Trainers Assn., Dallas, 2002; chmn. dist. 9 women in athletic tng. com. Nat. Athletic Trainers' Assn., 2002—05; presenter NC Med. Soc., Wrightsville Beach, 2005—06. Vol. Union Elem. Sch., Shallotte, NC, 2005—06. Recipient Tchg. Excellence award, U. NC, 1989—90, HS Athletic Trainers of Yr. award, SE Athletic Trainers' Assn., 1999, NATA Svc. award, Nat. Athletic Trainers' Assn., 2005. Mem.: Ga. Athletic Trainers Assn. (pres. 1997—2001, keynote spkr. 2004), S.E. Athletic Trainers Assn. (v.p. 2004—05), NC Athletic Trainers Assn., Mid-Atlantic Athletic Trainers Assn., Nat. Athletic Trainers Assn. Protestant. Avocations: water-skiing, golf, camping, running. Office: Coastal Athletic Tng Svcs 19 Fairway Dr Shallotte NC 28470

SABLE, BARBARA KINSEY, retired music educator; b. Astoria, NY, Oct. 6, 1927; d. Albert and Verna (Rowe) Kinsey; m. Arthur J. Sable, Nov. 3, 1973. BA, Coll. Wooster, 1949; MA, Tchrs. Coll. Columbia U., N.Y.C., 1950; DMus, U. Ind., 1966. Office mgr., music dir. Sta. WCAX, Burlington, Vt., 1954; instr. Cottey Coll., 1959-60; asst. prof. N.E. Mo. State U., Kirksville, 1962-64, U. Calif., Santa Barbara, 1964-69; prof. music U. Colo., Boulder, 1969—, prof. emeritus, 1992—. Author: (novels) The Vocal Sound, 1982; contbr. poetry and short stories to lit. jours. Mem.: Colo. Music Tchrs. Assn., AAUP, Nat. Assn. Tchrs. Singing (past state gov., assoc. editor bull.). Democrat. Avocation: poetry. Home: 3430 Ash Ave Boulder CO 80305-3432 Office: U Colo PO Box 301 Boulder CO 80309-0301 Business E-Mail: bks@sable-boulder.com.

SACCO, GAIL ALTER, librarian; b. Stamford, Conn., Nov. 12, 1953; d. Harry Philip and Minnie (Wunsch) Alter; m. Joseph Dominic Sacco, Aug. 19, 1979. BA, Boston U., 1975; MA, U. Chgo., 1977. Libr. Computer Processing Inst., East Hartford, Conn., 1978; reader's advisor Bristol (Conn.) Pub. Libr., 1979-83; br. mgr. Albany (N.Y.) Pub. Libr., 1983-88; dir. Voorheesville (N.Y.) Pub. Libr., 1988—. Recipient Poets-in-Person award Modern Poetry Assn., 1991; NEH poetry grantee, 1993—. Mem. ALA, N.Y. Libr. Assn. (editor bull. 1991-92, chair pub. editorial bd. 1989-91, pres. pub. libr. section, 2004-2005). Office: Voorheesville Pub Libr 51 School Rd Voorheesville NY 12186-9609

SACCOCCIO, JACQUELINE, artist; b. Providence, 1963; BFA in painting, RI Sch. Design, 1985; MFA in painting, Sch. of the Art Inst. of Chgo., 1988; student, L'Universita per Stranieri, Perugia, Italy, 1990. Adj. faculty RI Sch. Design. Solo exhibitions include, Lauren Wittels Gallery, NYC, 1997, White Columns, NYC, 2001, Portage, Galerie Michael Neff, Frankfurt, Germany, 2003. Edward L. Ryerson Traveling Fellowship, 1988, Fulbright-Hays Found. Grant/Miguel Vinciguerra Award, 1990—91, John Simon Guggenheim Meml. Found. Fellowship, 2000, Harold M. English/Jacob H. Lazarus-Met. Mus. Art Rome Prize Fellowship, Am. Acad. in Rome, 2004—05. Mem.: Coll. Art Assn.

SACHAR, EMILY M., editor; b. St. Louis, Apr. 12, 1958; d. Byron David and Nancy (Adler) S.; children: Amy, Caroline. BA in Econs., Stanford U., 1980; postgrad., NYU. Reporter, columnist Newsday, NYC, 1982-95; editl. dir. Scholastic, Inc., NYC, 1996; exec. editor, web sites Meredith Corp.; group site dir., digital bus. group Reader's Digest Online (RD.com), 2005—. Adj. prof. Sch. Journalism Columbia U., NYC, 1995-96; 8th grad. math. tchr. Walt Whitman Intermediate Sch., Bklyn., 1988-89. Author: Shut Up and Let the Lady Teach, 1991 (Pulitzer prize nominee); contbr. articles to profl. publs. Trustee Berkeley Carroll Sch., Bklyn., past pres. PTA, 1994-96; troop leader Girl Scouts USA, 1993—. Named Woman of Distinction YWCA, 1994. Jewish. Avocations: bridge, tropical fish, computing, piano. Office: RD Online Reader's Digest RD Pleasantville NY 10570-7000

SACHS, MARILYN STICKLE, writer, educator, editor; b. N.Y.C., Dec. 18, 1927; d. Samuel and Anna (Smith) Stickle; m. Morris Sachs, Jan. 26, 1947; children: Anne, Paul. BA, Hunter Coll., 1949; MSLS, Columbia U., 1953. Children's libr. Bklyn. Pub. Libr., 1949-60, San Francisco Pub. Libr., 1961-67. Author: Amy Moves In, 1964, Laura's Luck, 1965, Amy and Laura, 1966, Veronica Ganz, 1968, Peter and Veronica, 1969, Marv, 1970, The Bears' House, 1971 (Austrian Children's Book prize 1977, Recognition of Merit award George G. Stone Ctr. for Children's Books 1989), The Truth About Mary Rose, 1973 (Silver Slate Pencil award 1974), A Pocket Full of Seeds, 1973 (Jane Addams Children's Book Honor award 1974), Matt's Mitt, 1975, Dorrie's Book, 1975 (Silver State Pencil award 1977, Garden State Children's Book award 1978), A December Tale, 1976, A Secret Friends, 1978, A Summer's Lease, 1979, Bus Ride, 1980, Class Pictures, 1980, Fleet Footed Florence, 1981, Hello.Wrong Number, 1981, Call Me Ruth, 1982 (Assn. Jewish Librs. award 1983), Beach Towels, 1982, Fourteen, 1983, The Fat Girl, 1984, Thunderbird, 1985, Underdog, 1985 (Christopher 1986), Baby Sister 1986, Almost Fifteen, 1987, Fran Ellen's House, 1987 (award Bay Area Book Reviewers Assn. 1988, Recognition of Merit award George C. Stone Ctr. for Children's Books 1989), Just Like A Friend, 1989, At the Sound of the Beep, 1990, Circles, 1991, What My Sister Remembered, 1992, Thirteen, 1993, Ghosts in the Family, 1995, Another Day, 1997, Suprise Party, 1998, Jo Jo & Winnie, 1999, Jo Jo & Winnie Again, 2000, The Four Ugly Cats in Apartment 3D, 2002, Lost in America, 2005, First Impressions, 2006; co-editor: (with Ann Durell) Big Book for Peace, 1990 (Calif. Children's Book award 1991, Jane Addams Children's Book prize 1991); reviewer San Francisco Chronicle, 1970—. Mem. PEN, ACLU, Sierra Club, Authors' Guild. Democrat. Jewish. Avocations: reading, walking, baseball. Home: 733 31st Ave San Francisco CA 94121-3523

SACHSE, DOMINIQUE, newscaster; b. Miami, Fla. m. Scott Credeur, 1999. BA in Radio/TV Journalism, U. Houston, 1990; postgrad., Richmond Coll., Eng. Anchor Sta. KPRC-TV, Houston, 1993—. Named Best TV Personality, Am. Women in Radio and TV, Houston, Outstanding Young Comm. Alumnus, U. Houston, 1996; recipient Disting. Alumni award, 2002, AP award, Houston Press Club award. Office: Sta KPRC-TV PO Box 2222 Houston TX 77252-2222

SACKELLARES, DALMA KALOGJERA, psychologist; b. Zagreb, Croatia, Feb. 11, 1954; came to U.S., 1973; d. Jaksa Martin and Biserka (Erak) Kalogjera; m. James Chris Sackellares, Dec. 14, 1991; 1 child, Chiara. BA summa cum laude in Exptl. Psychology, Western Mich. U., Kalamazoo, 1977; MA in Clin. Psychology, Loyola U., Chgo., 1983, PhD in Clin. Psychology, 1986. Lic. clin. psychologist, Ill., Mich., Fla. Staff psychologist neuropsychology program U. Mich. Med. Ctr., Ann Arbor, 1988-89, clin. psychologist, 1989-92, rsch. assoc., 1992-93; clin. asst. prof. clin. and health psychology U. Fla., Gainesville, 1993-96, rsch. psychologist dept. neurosci., 1996—2005; clin. psychologist Arbor Psychological Svcs., 2005—. Author, Psychodynamics and Psychotherapy of Pseudoseizures, 2004; Contbr. articles to profl. jours., chpts. to books. NIMH fellow Older Adult Program, Inst. Psychiatry Northwestern U. Med. Sch., Chgo., 1986-87. Mem.: APA. Roman Catholic. Avocations: occupational safety and health, protection of animal species, history of medicine. Home: 9841 SW 55th Rd Gainesville FL 32608-4336 Office: Haile Vill Ctr 9116 S W 51st Rd Ste 103C Gainesville FL 32608

SACKETT, DIANNE MARIE, city treasurer, accountant; b. Oil City, Pa., Dec. 29, 1956; d. Clarence Benjamin and Donna Jean (Grosteffon) Knight; m. Mark Douglas Sackett, May 26, 1984 (dec. May 2004); children: Jason Michael, Cory James. BBA, Ea. Mich. U., 1979, MBA, 1986. Cert. pub. fin. adminstr. Accounts payable supr. Sarns, Inc., Ann Arbor, Mich., 1979-81; cost acct. Simplex Products Divsn., Adrian, Mich., 1981-83, gen. acctg. supr., 1983-88; city treas. City of Tecumseh, Mich., 1991—. Mem. Mich. Mcpl. Treas.' Assn., Mich. Govt. Fin. Officers Assn., Assn. Pub. Treas.' of the U.S. and Can. Pentecostal. Office: 309 E Chicago Blvd Tecumseh MI 49286-1550 E-mail: dsackett@tecumseh.mi.us, dsackett56@comcast.net.

SACKETT, SUSAN DEANNA, writer; b. NYC, Dec. 18, 1943; adopted d. Maxwell and Gertrude Selma (Kugel) S. BA in Edn., U. Fla., 1964, MEd, 1965. Tchr. Dade County Schs., Miami, Fla., 1966-68, L.A. City Schs., 1968-69; asst. publicist, comml. coord. NBC-TV, Burbank, Calif., 1970-73; asst. to Gene Roddenberry, creator Star Trek, 1974-91; prodn. assoc. TV series Star Trek: The Next Generation, 1987-91, writer, 1990-91. Lectr. and guest spkr. Star Trek convs. in U.S., Eng., Australia, 1974-. Author, editor: Letters to Star Trek, 1977; co-author: Star Trek Speaks, The Making of Star Trek--The Motion Picture, 1979, You Can Be a Game Show Contestant and Win, 1982, Say Goodnight Gracie, 1986; author: The Hollywood Reporter Book of Box Office Hits, 1990, 2d edit., 1996, Prime Time Hits, 1993, Hollywood Sings, 1995, Inside Trek: My Secret Life with Star Trek Creator Gene Roddenberry, 2002. Mem. ACLU, Writers Guild Am., Am. Humanist Assn., Humanist Soc. Greater Phoenix (pres. 2000—), Mensa, Sierra Club, Am. Humanist Assn. (bd. dir., 2005—). Democrat.

SACKIN, CLAIRE, retired social work educator; b. N.Y.C., Oct. 1, 1925; d. Harry and Diana (Mednick) Gershfeld; m. Milton Sackin, Feb. 4, 1955; children: William, Daniel, David. BA, Hunter Coll., 1946; MEd, U. Pitts., 1968, MSW, 1972, PhD, 1976. Tenured tchr. jr. high sch., Bronx, N.Y., 1947-57; rsch. asst. U. Pitts., 1973, instr. dept. urban mgmt., 1974; rsch. assoc. U. Pitts. Sch. of Social Work, 1975-76, Health & Welfare Planning Assn., 1974; prof. social work, dir. social work program St. Francis U., Loretto, Pa., 1976-97, prof. emerita, 1997—. Registered trainer alcoholism specialists cert. program; mem. adv. bd. Cedar Manor Treatment Ctr., Cresson, Pa., 1994-95; mem. Pa. Gov.'s Coun. Alcoholism, 1980, Nat. Assn. People with AIDS; presenter in field. Contbr. articles to jours. Mem. NASW (social action com. Pa. chpt. 1983-85, mem. Del. Assembly 1984, eastern regional coalition liaison 1984), Coun. on Social Work Edn., Amyotrophic Lateral Sclerosis Assn., Alpha Delta Mu (nat. bd. dirs.). Avocations: reading, crossword puzzles, opera, gardening, travel. Home: 531 Sandrae Dr Pittsburgh PA 15243-1727 Office: St Francis U Loretto PA 15940 E-mail: sackin.dsl@verizon.net.

SACKLOW, HARRIETTE LYNN, advertising agency executive; b. Bklyn., Apr. 12, 1944; d. Sidney and Mildred (Myers) Cooperman; m. Stewart Irwin, July 2, 1967; 1 child, Ian Marc. BA, SUNY, Albany, 1965, postgrad., 1967-69, Union Coll., 1969-70, Telmar Media Sch., N.Y.C., 1981. Tchr. math. Guilderland (N.Y.) Cen. Schs., 1967-76; v.p., COO Wolkcas Comm. Group, Inc., Albany, NY, 1975—2004; supr. internship programs Coll. St. Rose, 1981; ret. Lectr. to area colls., Albany, 1981-83. Key market coord. Partnership for a Drug Free Am., 1994—2000; advisor Ronald McDonald Ho.; v.p. sisterhood Congregation Ohav Sholom, Albany, 1983—86; bd. dirs. Northea. N.Y. chpt. Arthritis Found., Takundewide Homeowners Assn. Recipient Disting. Svc. award Northeast Assn. Profl. Communicators, 1998. Mem. NAFE, Am. Mktg. Assn., Am. Women in Radio and TV (pres. 1982-84, chmn. task force for new mem. acquisition, v.p. N.E. area 1987-89, chmn. area conf. 1987, pres. 1982-84, speaker, dist. dir.), N.Am. Advt. Agy. Network (bd. dirs. 1992—), Advt. of the Capital Dist., Capital Region C. of C. (Disting. Svc. award 1997-98), Albany (N.Y.) Yacht Club. Office: 716 St Marks Ln Schenectady NY 12309-4843

SACKMANN, PAMELA JAYNE, lawyer; b. Naperville, Ill., Nov. 30, 1965; d. Jacob and Paulina Alison (Quigley) S. BS in Biology and Psychology summa cum laude, U. Ill., 1987; JD, Stanford U., 1991. Bar: NY 1992. Assoc. Fried Frank Harris Schriver, NYC, 1991—95, Debevoise & Plimpton, NYC, 1995—97; atty. Deutsche Bank/Bankers Trust, NYC, 0998—1999, Donaldson, Lufkin & Jenrette, NYC, 1999—2000, Lehman Brothers Inc., NYC, 2000—01; counsel Mayer, Brown, Rowe & Maw LLP, NYC, 2001—. Assoc. mng. editor Stanford Jour. Internat. Law; editor: Stanford Environ. Law Jour. Office: Mayer Brown Row & Maw 1675 Broadway New York NY 10019-5820 Office Phone: 212-506-2640. Office Fax: 212-262-1910. Business E-Mail: psackmann@mayerbrownrowe.com.

SACKS, PATRICIA ANN, librarian, consultant; b. Allentown, Pa., Nov. 6, 1939; d. Lloyd Alva and Dorothy Estelle (Stoneback) Stahl; m. Kenneth LeRoy Sacks, June 27, 1959. AB, Cedar Crest Coll., 1959; MS in Libr. Sci., Drexel U., 1965. News reporter Call-Chronicle, Allentown, 1956-59, 61-63; reference libr. Cedar Crest Coll., Allentown, 1964-66, head libr., 1966-73; dir. librs. Muhlenberg and Cedar Crest Colls., Allentown, 1973-94; dir. libr. svcs. Cedar Crest Coll., 1994; sr. fellow Lehigh Valley Assn. Ind. Colls., 1994-97, Ctr. Agile Ptnrs. in Edn., 1997-98; info. svcs. cons., 1998—. Del. On Line Computer Library Ctr. Users Council, Columbus, Ohio, 1977-84; cons. colls./health care orgns., libr. orgns. 1981—. Author: (with Whildin Sara Lou) Preparing for Accreditation: A Handbook for Academic Librarians, 1993; mem. editl. bd. Jour. Acad. Librarianship, 1982-84. Mem. United Way Lehigh Valley Coms., 1993—97; trustee Cedar Crest Coll., 1985—89; bd. dirs. John and Dorothy Morgan Cancer Ctr., 1994—96; mem. bd. Allentown Cmty. Concert, Pa., 2003—06. Named Outstanding Acad. Woman, Lehigh Valley Assn. Acad. Women, 1984, Muhlenberg Coll. Outstanding Adminstr., 1987, Alumni Tricorn award Muhlenberg Coll., 1989, Alumnae Achievement award Cedar Crest Coll., 1994. Mem. ALA (chmn. copyright com. 1985-87), Assn. Coll. and Rsch. Librs. (chmn. stds. and accreditation com. 1976-78, 81-84), Lehigh Valley Assn. Ind. Colls. (chmn. librs. sect. 1967-81, 88-92), AAUW, LWV, Wildlands Conservancy, Appalachian Mountain Club (Echo Lake naturalist 1997—), Phi Alpha Theta, Phi Kappa Phi, Beta Phi Mu. Democrat. Home: 2997 Fairfield Dr Allentown PA 18103-5413 Personal E-mail: sackspa@ptd.net.

SACKS, TEMI J., public relations executive; b. Phila. d. Jule and Adeline (Levin) S. BA, Temple U. Pubs. editor Del. Valley Regional Planning Commn., Phila.; comms. assoc. Fedn. Jewish Agys., Phila.; exec. v.p., mng. dir. consumer and healthcare divsns. Lobsenz-Stevens Inc., N.Y.C.; exec. v.p., dir. nat. healthcare practice Shandwick, N.Y.C.; sr. v.p. Noonan-Russo, N.Y.C.; pres. T.J. Sacks & Assocs. Inc., N.Y.C. Mem. Healthcare Business-women's Assn., Healtcare Mktg. Assn., Women Execs. in Pub. Rels. Avocations: painting, skiing, jewelry design, antiques. Office Phone: 212-787-0787. Personal E-mail: tjsacks@tjsacks.com.

SADAK, DIANE MARIE, director, performing arts educator; d. John Charles and Dolores Hope (Salvi) Sadak; m. Barry Kendall Smith, Oct. 18, 1999; children: Noel Kendall Smith-Sadak, Sage Noelle Smith-Sadak. MFA in Directing, Fla. State U., 1989; BA in Polit. sci. and Econs., Union Coll., 1985; studied with R. Armstrong, 2000—; student in Advanced Voice Intensives, Banff Ctr. Arts, 2001, student in Advanced Voice Intensives, 2003—04; student, Roy Hart Internat. Voice Intensive, Malerargues, France, 2005. Staff artist Calif. Young Playwrights Project, San Diego, 1989—93; vis. prof. voice and acting Korean Nat. U. of Arts, Seoul, Sokkwan-dong, Republic of Korea, 1997—98; guest artist Union Coll. and Schenectady County C.C., Schenectady, NY, 1998—99; asst. prof. acting and directing Towson (Md.) U., 1999—2005, assoc. prof., 2005—, head Acting Program Dept. Theatre Arts, 2000—04, program dir. MFA in Theatre Dept. Theatre Arts, 2004—06. Cons. in field; presenter in field; guest artist Union Coll., Schenectady, NY, 1998—99, Schenectady (N.Y.) County C.C., 1998—99; artist-in-residence Laurel Elem. Sch., San Diego, 1990—92; artist-in-residence Comprehensive Adolescent Treatment Ctr. Ensemble Arts Theatre, San Diego, 1991; adj. faculty Grossmont Coll., Calif., 1992. Actor(Janis Joplin): (theatre) LEGENDS; author: (playscript: one-woman show) It's Not Funny, I'm Only Laughing; contbr. mgmt., prodr. Actors Alliance of San Diego; singer: (cabaret show) You're Gonna Hear From Me; actor(Lula): (theatre) Dutchman; dir.: The Cultural Hyphen; actor: A Cave In The Sky; dir.: Cabaret, Evita, Three Sisters, Hot 'N Throbbing, (theatre production) How To Succeed In Business Without Really Trying, (theatrical prodn.) Our Country's Good; actor: (indsl. video series) ACT Training Series; prodr.(dir. pub. rels.): San Diego Actors Festival; contbr. chapter to book. Grantee Artist-In-Residence Funding, Calif. Arts Coun., 1990—92. Mem.: Internat. Alliance of Tchrs. and Scholars, Actors Equity Assn., Internat. Fedn. of Theatre Rsch. (convener of working group 2002—). D-Liberal. Buddhist. Avocations: cooking, gardening, travel, yoga, reading. Office: Towson U Dept Theatre Arts 8000 York Rd Rm 3027 Baltimore MD 21252 Office Phone: 410-704-4970. Business E-Mail: dsadak@towson.edu.

SADD, WENDY MARIE, science educator; d. Jan Claire and Charles Elmer Willis; m. Ryan Charles Sadd, Aug. 9, 2001. BS, W.Va. U., Morgantown, 1998; MEd (hon.), U. Akron, Ohio, 2002. Cert. tchr. Ohio, 1999. Tchr. math. St. Rita Sch., Solon, Ohio, 1999—2000; tchr. sci. Brunswick City Sch. Dist., Ohio, 2000—. Track and field coach Brunswick City Schs., Ohio, 2001—, Brunswick staff devel. com., 2003—; trainer Assessment Tng. Inst., Portland, Oreg., 2004—; Ohio Sci. Inst. facilitator Ohio Dept. of Edn., Columbus, 2005—06. Health and safety instr. ARC, Medina, Ohio, 2002—06. Recipient Tchr. of Yr. award, Medina County Soil and Water Conservation Dist., 2005-2006, Willetts Mid. Sch., 2005-2006; grant, Martha Holden Jennings Found., 2003. Mem.: NSTA (corr.), Environ. Edn. Coun. of Ohio (corr.), Nat. Honor Soc. (life), Alpha Phi Sorority (hon.). Achievements include design of meaningful and engaging instruction for adults and childern throughout the state of Ohio. Office: Willetts Mid Sch 1045 Hadcock Rd Brunswick OH 44212 Office Phone: 330-273-0498. E-mail: wsadd@bcsoh.org.

SADDLEMYER, ANN (ELEANOR SADDLEMYER), humanities educator, critic, theater historian; b. Prince Albert, Sask., Can., Nov. 28, 1932; d. Orrin Angus and Elsie Sarah (Ellis) S. BA, U. Sask., 1953, DLitt, 1991; MA, Queen's U., 1956, LLD (hon.), 1977; PhD, U. London, 1961; DLitt (hon.), U. Victoria, 1989, McGill U., 1989, Windsor U., 1990, U. Toronto, 1999, Concordia U., 2000. Lectr. Victoria Coll., BC, 1956-57, instr. BC, 1960-62, asst. prof. BC, 1962-65; assoc. prof. U. Victoria, 1965-68, prof. English, 1968-71, Victoria Coll. U. Toronto, 1971-95; prof., dir. Grad. Ctr. for Study of Drama, U. Toronto, 1972-77, 85-86, prof. emerita Dept. English, Comparative Lit., 1995—; sr. fellow Massey Coll., 1975-88, master, 1988-95, master emerita, 1995—; Berg prof. NYU, 1975. Adj. prof. U. Victoria; dir. Hedgerow Press; mem. heritage adv. commn. North Saanich, 2004—06. Dir. Theatre Plus, 1972-84; dir. Colin Smythe Pubs.; author: (with Robin Skelton) The World of W.B. Yeats, 1965, In Defence of Lady Gregory, Playwright, 1966, Synge and Modern Comedy, 1968, J.M. Synge Plays Books One and Two, 1968, Lady Gregory Plays, 4 vols., 1970, Letters to Molly: Synge to Maire O'Neill, 1971, Letters from Synge to W.B. Yeats and Lady Gregory, 1971, Collected Letters of John Millington Synge, Vol. 1, 1983, vol. II, 1984, Theatre Business, The Correspondence of the First Abbey Theatre Directors, 1982, (with Colin Smythe) Lady Gregory Fifty Years After, 1987, Early Stages: Theatre in Ontario, 1980-1914, 1990, J.M. Synge: The Playboy of the Western World and Other Plays, 1995; (with Richard Plant) Later Stages: Theatre in Ontario, 1914-1970s, 1997, Becoming George--The Life of Mrs. W.B. Yeats, 2002; co-editor Theatre History in Canada, 1980-86, Selected Irish Drama; co-gen. editor Cornell Yeats series; editorial bds. Modern Drama, 1972-82, English Studies in Can., 1973-83, Themes in Drama, 1974-93, Shaw Ann., 1977—, Research in the Humanities, 1976-90; Irish Univ. Rev., 1970—, Yeats Ann., 1982-86; Studies in Contemporary Irish Lit., 1986—, Irish Studies Rev., 1997—; contbr. articles to profl. jours. Recipient Brit. Acad. Rose Mary Crawshay award, 1986, Disting. Svc. award Province of Ont., 1985, U. Toronto Alumni award of excellence, 1991, award yeats Soc. NY 2001; named Disting. Dau. of Pa., 1992, Woman of Distinction in Letters, Toronto, YWCA, 1994; Officer of Order of Can., 1995; Can. Coun. scholar, 1958-59, fellow, 1968, Guggenheim fellow, 1968, 77, sr. rsch. fellow Connaught, 1985. Fellow Royal Soc. Can., Royal Soc. Arts; mem. Internat. Assn. Study Irish Lit. (chmn. 1973-76), Assn. Can. Theatre Rsch. (pres. 1976-77), Can. Assn. Irish Studies, Assn. Can. Coll. and Univ. Tchrs. English. Home: 10876 Madrona Dr North Saanich BC Canada V8L 5N9 Personal E-mail: saddlemy@uvic.ca.

SADDLER, PEGGY CHANDLER, counselor; b. Paducah, Ky., June 16, 1955; d. Joe Paul and Nell (Garrett) Chandler. BS in Psychology and Sociology, Union Coll., Barbourville, Ky., 1977; M of Pub. Svc. in Counseling, Western Ky. U., 1977; postgrad., U. South Fla. Cert. in guidance and counseling Fla. Dept. Edn., in secondary guidance and counseling Va. Dept. Edn. Instr. U. Ky. S.E. C.C., Cumberland, 1979; guidance counselor Northampton H.S., Eastville, Va., 1980-85; dist. intake counselor Dept. Health and Rehabilitative Svcs., Wauchula, Fla., 1986; guidance counselor McLaughlin Jr. H.S., Lake Wales, Fla., 1986-87, Hardee Sr. H.S., Wauchula, 1987—. Acad. team coach Northampton H.S., Eastville, 1981-85, Hardee Sr. H.S., Wauchula, 1992—, coach, State championship team divsn.3, 2004, coach team Fla., 2004; counselor summer youth employment program Ea. Shore C.C., Melfa, Va., 1982-85; bd. mem., exec. com. mem. Hardee County Juvenile Justice Bd., Wauchula, 1993-98; mem. adv. bd. Hardee County 4-H, Wauchula, 1993-98. Editor: Food for Thought, 1985. Coun. mem. Alcohol, Drug Abuse and Mental Health Planning Coun., 1991-93; vice-chmn. Dist. 14 Health and Human Svcs. Bd., 1992-96; chmn. strong families and cmtys. com. Health and Human Svcs. Bd., 1993-96, mem. dist. 14 Ptnr. in Crisis Bd., 2000-. Recipient Vol. Svc. award Fla. Dept. Corrections, Wauchula, 1993, Cmty. Svc. award Ctrl. Fla. Human Svcs. Ctrs., Lakeland, 1994; named Outstanding Young Women of Am., Jaycees, 1984. Mem. Fla. Counselor's Assn., Fla. Sch. Counselor's Assn., Fla. Assn. for Humanistic Edn. and Devel., Hardee Optimist Club (bd. dirs. 1995-96). Democrat. Avocations: audiophile, ailurophile, bibliophile. Home: PO Box 172 Wauchula FL 33873-0172 Office: Hardee Sr HS 830 Altman Rd Wauchula FL 33873-9453 Office Phone: 863-773-3181. E-mail: saddlep@hotmail.com.

SADE, (HELEN FOLASADE ADU), singer, lyricist; b. Ibadan, Nigeria, 1959; d. Adebisi Adu and Anne Adu, BA, St. Martin's Coll. of Art, London, 1979. Mem. band Sade; recording artist Epic, A Division of Sony Music, N.Y.C. Albums include Diamond Life, 1984, Promise, 1985, Stronger Than Pride, 1988, Love Deluxe, 1992, The Best of Sade, 1994, Lovers Rock, 2000, Lovers Live, 2002; singles include Smooth Operator, 1984. Recipient Grammy award Best New Artist, 1986, Best R&B duo or group performance for "No Ordinary Love", 1994.

SADEK, NOHA, psychiatrist; arrived in U.S., 1997; BS in Biology, Am. U. of Beirut, Lebanon, 1996; MD, Am. U. of Beirut. Attending psychiatrist Fairmont Med. Ctr., Minn., 2002—. Pres. Am. U. of Beirut-Alumni, Psychiatry Chpt., NYC, 2002—; mem. Am. Psychiat. Assn.-Council on Global Psychiatry, Washington. Recipient Emory President's Writing award, Emory U., 2001, Julian Gomez award, Atlanta Psychoanalytic Soc., 2001, Skobba Hope award, Ga. Psychiat. Assn., Outstanding Women Psychiatry Resident award, Wyeth-Ayrest, 2001, Colloquium-Junior Investigator award, Am. Psychiat. Assn., 2001. Mem.: Am. Psychiat. Assn. (coun. on global psychiatry 2000—05). Office: Fairmont Med Ctr 800 Medical Ctr Dr Fairmont MN 56031 Office Phone: 507-238-8598.

SADER, CAROL HOPE, former state legislator; b. Bklyn., July 19, 1935; d. Nathan and Mollie (Farkas) Shimkin; m. Harold M. Sader, June 9, 1957; children: Neil, Randi Sader Friedlander, Elisa Sader Waldman. BA, Barnard Coll., Columbia U., 1957. Sch. tchr. Bd. Edn., Morris, Conn., 1957-58; legal editor W. H. Anderson Co., Cin., 1974-78; freelance legal editor Shawnee Mission, Kans., 1978-87; mem. Kans. Ho. of Reps., 1987-94. Chair Ho. Pub. Health and Welfare Com., 1991-92; chair Joint Ho. and Senate Com. on Health Care Decisions for the 90's, 1992; vice chair Ho. Econ. Devel. Com., 1991-92; policy chair Ho. Dem. Caucus, 1993-94; appointee Kans. jud. qualifications commn. Kans. Supreme Ct., 1995-2004; apptd. Kans. Racing and Gaming Commn., 2003-, chmn., 2005—, Kans. State Bd. Healing Arts, 2003—. Pres. LWV, Johnson County, 1983—85; mem. State of Kans. LWV Bd., 1986—87; pres. Johnson County Found. Aging, 2002—04; mem. Johnson County Charter Commn., 1999; mem. exec. bd. Johnson County C.C. Found., 2000—03; mem. adv. group Kans. Gov.'s B.E.S.T. Team, 2002—; cmty. adv. com. Kans. REACH Found., 2003—; Dem. candidate for Kans. Lt. Gov., 1994; mem. Jewish Cmty. Rels. Bd., 1999—; chmn. bd. trustees Johnson County C.C., Overland Park, Kans., 1984—86, trustee, 1981—86; bd. dirs. United Cmty. Svcs. of Johnson County, Shawnee 1981—86; bd. dirs. Jewish Vocat. Svc. Bd., 1983—92, House of Menuha, Mission, 1984—92, Jewish Vocat. Svc. Bd., 1983—92, House of Menuha, 1998—99, Appleseed Found. Kans., 1999—2001, Midwest Ctr. Holocaust Edn., 1999—2004, 2006—, exec. bd., 1999—2004, 2006—; chmn. Kans. State Holocaust Commn., 1991—94; pres. MAINstream Coalition, 1995—97, vice chair, 1998—2003; v.p. Kans. Advocates for Better Care, 1998—2001. Recipient Trustee award Assn. of Women in Jr. and C.C., 1985, awards Kans. Pub. Transit Assn., 1990, AARP, 1992, Assn. Kans. Theater, 1992, Nat. Coun. Jewish Women, 1992, Kans. Assn. Osteo. Medicine, 1992, Kans. Chiropractic Assn., 1992, United Com. Svcs. Johnson County, 1992, Disting. Pub. Svcs. award Johnson County, 1993, Hallpac Kans. Pub. Svc. award Hallmark Cards, Inc., 1993, Eddie Jacobsen award B'nai B'rith, 1994, Cmty. Svc. award House of Menuha, 1998, The Pillar award Greater K.C. Women's Political Caucus, 2003, Stand-Up, Speak-Out award Mainstream Coalition, 2003. Mem.: Phi Delta Kappa. Democrat. Avocations: lakehouse, theater, travel. Home: 8612 Linden Dr Shawnee Mission KS 66207-1807

SADIK, NAFIS, United Nations administrator; b. Jaunpur, India, Aug. 18, 1929; d. Iffat Ara and Mohammad Shoaib; m. Azhar Sadik, 1954; 5 children. Student, Loretto Coll., Calcutta, India, Dow Med. Coll., Karachi, Pakistan, Johns Hopkins U., LHD (hon.), 1989, Brown U., 1993, Duke U., 1995; LLD, Wilfrid Laurier U., 1995; DSc (hon.), U. Mich., 1996, Claremont U., 1996; LHD (hon.), Philippines U., 1997; DSc (hon.), Long Island U., 1997; LHD (hon.), Nepal Tribhuvan U., 1998; DSc, Tulane U., 1999. Intern ob-gyn. City Hosp., Balt., 1952-54; civilian med. officer in charge of women's and children's wards various Pakistani armed forces hosps., 1954-63; resident physiology Queens U., Kingston, Ont., Can., 1958; head health sect. Planning Commn. on Health and Family Planning, Pakistan, 1964; dir. planning and tng. Pakistan Ctr. Family Planning Coun., 1966-68, dep. dir.-gen., 1968-70, dir.-gen., 1970-71; tech. advisor UN Fund for Population Activities, 1971-72, chief programme divsn., 1973-77, asst. exec. dir., 1977-87, exec. dir., 1987—; under-sec.-gen. UN, 1987—. Sec.-gen. Internat. Conf. on Population and Devel., 1994, Soc. for Internat. Devel. (pres. 1994-97). Writings include: Population: National Family Planning Programme in Pakistan, 1968, Population: the UNFPA Experience, 1984, Population Policies and Programmes: Making a Difference: Twenty-five Years of UNFPA Experience, 1994, Lessions learned from Two Decades of Experience, 1991, Making a Difference: Twenty-Five Years of UNFPA Experience, 1994; contbr. articles to profl. jours. Recipient Hugh Moore award; Paul Harris fellow Rotary, 1997. Fellow Royal Coll. Ob-Gyn. Avocations: bridge, reading, theater, travel. Office: UN Population Fund 220 E 42nd St Fl 19 New York NY 10017-5806

SADLER, MARION HANSON, retired art educator; b. Owynee, Nev., Nov. 4, 1937; d. Lewis William Hanson and Helen Brown Morton; m. Alf Sadler, Jan. 20, 1957; children: Lisa, Scott(dec.), Dale, Seán. AS in journalism, Murray State Coll., Okla., 1967; BA in Art Edn., So. State U., Okla., 1970; MEd and learning disabilites, Okla. U., 1976. Cert. pvt. and pub. music. Operator Bell Telephone, Ardmore, Okla., 1957—63; spl. edn. art and music tchr. Ardmore City Schs., Okla., 1968—96. Active Presbyn. Ch. Avocation: travel. Home: 516 Regent St Ardmore OK 73407-1764

SADOWSKI, CAROL JOHNSON, artist; b. Chgo., Mar. 20, 1929; d. Carl Valdamar Johnson and Elizabeth Hilma (Booth) Johnson Chellberg; m. Edmund Sadowski, July 9, 1949; children: Lynn Carol Mahoney, Christie Sadowski Cortez. AAS, Wright Coll., Ill., 1949. Tchr. art Malverne H.S., NY, 1968-69; artist Valley Stream, NY, 1968-76, Hollywood, Fla., 1976—. Guest spkr. Mus. Art, Ft. Lauderdale, Fla., 1991; Libr. League, Oakland Park, 1985; Boca Raton, Fla. Mus., others; TV appearances on WCGB, Gainesville; WSVN, Miami; Storer and Hollywood Cable; Artist Guild, Boca Raton Mus.; Broward C.C., Hollywood, Fla. One woman shows include Mus. Fla. History, Tallahassee, 1984-85, 87; Hist. Mus. South Fla., Miami, 1986; Thomas Ctr. Arts, Gainesville, Fla., 1985, 87; Elliott Mus., Stuart, Fla., 1987; Hemingway Mus. and Home, Key West, Fla., 1986; I.G.F.A. Fishing Hall of Fame Mus., Dania, Fla., 1999, Alliance Francaise de Miami, 1995; commd. painting St. Agustin Antigua Found., St. Augustine, Fla., 1985, Atlantic Bank, Ft. Lauderdale, Fla., Bonnet House Fla. Trust, Ft. Lauderdale, Hollywood Art & Culture Ctr., Hemingway Mus., San Francisco de Paula, Presdl. Palace, Havana, Tropical Art Gallery, Naples, Fla., 1981-83, Tequesta (Fla.) Art Gallery, 1985-89, Gingerbread Square Gallery, Key West, 1990—, Wally Findlay Galleries, Inc., Palm Beach and N.Y.C., DeBruyne Fine Arts Gallery, Naples, 1998—, Patricia Cloutier Gallery, Tequesta, Fla., 1992-. Mem. Ft. Lauderdale Mus. Art; Hollywood Art and Culture Ctr. Recipient Hemingway medal, Ernest Hemingway Mus., Cuba, 1990; appreciation award City of Hollywood; Chgo. Art Inst. scholar; Salmagundi Club N.Y. scholar. Mem. Internat. Platform Assn., Broward Art Guild, Fla. Hist. Assn., Ernest Hemingway Soc., Chopin Found., Am. Inst. for Polish Culture, Alliance Francaise de Miami, Women in the Arts Nat. Mus. (charter mem.), Nat. Women's History Mus. (charter mem.). Avocations: travel, bicycling, swimming, reading. Home: 1480 Sheridan St Apt B 17 Hollywood FL 33020-2295 Office Phone: 954-925-7482. Personal E-mail: esadowski@msn.com.

SAEED, FAIZA J., lawyer; BA with highest distinction, U. Calif., Berkeley, 1987; JD magna cum laude, Harvard Law Sch., 1991. Bar: NY 1992, Calif. 1993, DC 1993. Assoc. Cravath, Swaine & Moore LLP, 1991—98, ptnr., corp., 1999—. Named a Young Global Leader, World Econ. Forum, 2006; named one of 45 Under Forty-Five, Am. Lawyer, 2003, Top 40 Lawyers Under 40, Nat. Law. Jour., 2005. Mem.: Harvard Law Sch. Vis. Com., Calif. State Bar Assn., Internat. Bar Assn., ABA, NY State Bar Assn., Assn. Bar City of NY, Phi Beta Kappa. Office: Cravath Swaine & Moore LLP Worldwide Plaza 825 Eighth Ave New York NY 10019-7475 Office Phone: 212-474-1454. Office Fax: 212-474-3700. Business E-Mail: fsaeed@cravath.com.

SAEGER, REBECCA, advertising executive; B in Psychology and Polit. Sci., Muhlenberg Coll., 1976; MBA, U. Pa., 1980. Various positions including sr. v.p., group dir. for Lever Bros. and Am. Express Ogilvy & Mather, NY, 1980—91; sr. v.p., group mgmt. supr., dir. account mgmt. Foote, Cone & Belding, San Francisco, 1991—97; exec. v.p. advt. and brand mktg. svcs. Visa USA, 1997—2001; exec. v.p. brand mgmt. and mktg. comm. Charles Schwab Corp., San Francisco, 2004—. Mem. exec. mgmt. com. Visa USA. Mem. mktg. com. San Francisco Symphony; mem. adv. bd. World Congress Sports. Mem.: Assn. Nat. Advertisers (bd. dirs.). Office: The Charles Schwab Corp 101 Montgomery St San Francisco CA 94104

SAEGESSER, MARGUERITE M., artist; b. Bern, Switzerland, May 27, 1922; came to U.S., 1974; d. Wilhelm and Fanny (Kuepfer) Ruefenacht; m. Max Saegesser, May 27, 1952; 1 child, Francisca Marguerite; stepchildren: Anne-Marie Logan, Elisabeth, Barbara, Ursula L'Eplattenier. Solo exhbns. include De Saisset Mus., Santa Clara, Calif., 1995, Smith Andersen Gallery, Palo Alto, Calif., 1981, 85, 89, 91, 92, 95, Galerie Schindler, Bern, 1968, 90, Art Fair, Basel, Switzerland, 1990, many others; group exhbns. include Long Beach, Calif., 1971, Bienne Open Air Sculpture Show, Switzerland, 1958, 62, 66, Soc. Painters & Sculptors, Bern, 1945-46, 52, 56. Grantee Swiss Endowment Arts, 1995. Mem. South Bay Area Women's Caucus for Arts. Democrat.

SAENZ, CECILIA SONIA, education educator; d. Justo Valdez and Ruth Martinez Molina; m. Lloyd Neal Smith, Sept. 14, 1984; 1 child, Michael Robert. BS, Sam Houston U., 1964; MEd, U. Houston, 1975; student, Tex. So. U., 1989; PhD Capella U., 2005—. Adminstrv. cert. 1977, supt. cert. Ariz., Tex., 2003. Second grade tchr. Houston I.S.D., 1972—78, prin., 1978—98, dir. dist. 13, 1989—91; asst. supt. Phoenix Elem. Sch. Dist. 1, Phoenix, 1998—2003; master tchr. U. Houston, 1974—78; prof. online U. Phoenix, 2004—. Prin. ACET (Assn. Compensating Edn.) Conf., Houston, 1995—98; state mem. Tex. Sch. Improvement Initiative Tex. Edn. Agy., 1997—99; asst. supt. Proposition 301 P.E.S.D., Phoenix Elem., Phoenix, 2002—03; dir./cons. Montessori Magnet Program Com., Phoenix, 2003; spkr. and presenter in field. Lobbyist Phoenix Elem., 2002—03, advocate/legis., 2003, spirit program coord., 2003. Named Helping Schs. Outstanding Prin., Tex. Soc. Cert. Pub. Accountants, 1996, Houston Prin. of Yr., Cert. Pub. A Schs., 1996; recipient Tex. Prin. of Yr., 1996, Best Prin. in Tex. award, 1997, Hispanic Prin. of Yr., Houston Independetn Sch. Dist., 1996, Tex. Assn. Hispanic Adminstrv. Exemplary Educator award, Houston Independent Sch. Dist., 1998, Edn. Recognition award, Tex. Assn. Hispanic Adminstrs., 1998, Spirit 2006 award, City of Phoenix, 2004. Mem.: Tex. Retirement System, Ariz. Sch. Adminstr., Am. Assn. U. Women. Democrat. Roman Catholic. Achievements include created, developed, structured Montessori Program for public schools; implemented school improvement process "Eight Steps" as trainer; initiated school reform process "Success for All" Alignment. Avocations: hiking, camping, gardening, travel, tree triming. Office Fax: 623-572-4219. Personal E-mail: soniamaui@aol.com.

SAENZ, NANCY ELIZABETH KING (MRS. MICHAEL SAENZ), civic worker; b. Greenville, Tex., Jan. 28, 1930; d. Henry M. and Vallie (Wheatley) King; m. Michael Saenz, July 28, 1950; children— Michael King, Cynthia Elizabeth. Saenz Ward. A.B. with honors, Tex. Christian U., 1950, B.S. magna cum laude, 1952; postgrad. Hartford Sem. Found., 1952-53, Escuela de Idiomas, 1953, Lexington Theol. Sem., 1953. Missionary, United Christian Missionary Soc., Indpls., serving in P.R., 1954-65; bd. dirs. Adminstrv. Bd. Christian Chs., P.R., 1950-65; chmn. dept. Christian edn. Christian Chs., P.R., 1962-64, sec., 1959-61, state dir., 1963; dept. Christian edn. P.R. Council Chs., 1959-64, sec., 1959-60; sec. and counsellor State Christian Women Fellowship of Christian Chs., P.R., 1955-57, 59-63, dist. chmn. Ind. and Tex., 1968-75, adminstrv. com. Tex., 1971-74; mem. Internat. Christian Women's Fellowship Quadrennial Coms., 1974-82; mem. gen. bd. Christian Ch. in U.S. and Can., 1974-78, 80; pres. Christian Ch. in S.W., 1976-78. Sec., Disciples of Christ Acad. PTA, Bayamon, P.R., 1962-63; mem. state com. Home for Aged, United Ch. Women, P.R., 1963; women's com. Ind. State Symphony Soc., 1967—; women's com. Internat. Christian U. Japan, 1962-64, 65-72, pres. Indpls. chpt. 1967-68; mem. vocational-tech. adv. council Laredo Ind. Sch. Dist., 1971—; vol. coordinator Am. Bible Soc., 1971—; dir. Vol. Center Met. Tarrant County, 1982-93. Bd. dirs. Greater Indpls. Fedn. Chs., 1970-71; bd. dirs. Planned Parenthood Assn. Webb County, 1972-74, pres.-elect, 1974-75; bd. dirs. Civic Ballet Laredo, 1972-75; mem. adv. com. Tarrant County Vol. Center, 1976-81, chmn., 1980; mem. Mercy Hosp. Aux., 1973-75, pres.-elect, 1974-75; interim dir. Ft. Worth Council Chs., 1979, pres., 1981; pres. Ch. Women United, Fort Worth, 1980; bd. dirs. ch. fin. council Christian Ch. (Disciples of Christ) U.S. and Can., 1979-83. Mem. Irvington Union of Clubs (exec. bd. 1966—, 2d v.p. 1968-70), Young Mothers Club Irvington (v.p. 1965, pres. 1967), Marion County Guardian Home Guild (pres. 1968-70), Art Assn. Indpls., Art League, Civic Music Laredo, AAUW, Laredo and Fort Worth Pan Am. Roundtable, Thistle Hill, Docent Guild, Tex., Tex. Christian U., Tex. Christian U. Alumni Assn. (life), Ft. Worth Women's Club, Assn. Vol. Ctrs. (pres. 1990-91), Alpha Chi, Phi Sigma Iota. Clubs: Rotary Anns, Women's College (R.P.); Irvington Women's Laredo Tuesday Music and Lit. (pres. 1973-74), Women's City. Author: Winds of Change, 1968; Step by Step, 1984. Home: 4427 Tamworth Rd Fort Worth TX 76116-8127

SAENZ, SILVIA PATRICIA, special education educator; b. Chihuahua, Mexico, Mar. 8, 1980; arrived in U.S., 1999; d. Alvaro Saenz and Patricia Wong De Saenz. BA, U. Tex., El Paso, 2003. Cert. classroom tchr., spl. edn. grades earlychildhood-12th Tex., 2005, bilingual generalist, generalist early childhood-4th Tex. Rsch. asst. U. Tex., El Paso, 2002—04; spl. edn. tchr. El Paso Ind. Sch. Dist., 2004—. Contbr. articles to profl. jours. Recipient Outstanding Rsch. award, U. Tex. El Paso, 2003, Oustanding Student Achievement award, 2004; Benito Juarez scholar, Marguerite Loya Pearson Scholarship Fund for the Arts, 2000—01, EPCF-Marguerite Pearson scholar, 2001—03. Mem.: Golden Key (life), Psi Chi (life). Roman Catholic. Avocation: photography. Office Phone: 915-231-2820. Personal E-mail: pattysanz@yahoo.com.

SAFFELS, ANNA WAYNE BROTHERS, retired mathematician, educator; b. Gallant, Ala., Nov. 6, 1928; d. Homer Ervin and Bertie Galloway Brothers; m. George Aaron Saffels (dec.); children: Michael Aaron, Elisabeth Anne. BS in Secondary Edn., Jacksonville State U., 1949; MA in Secondary Edn., U. Ala., Birmingham, 1973. Cert. tchr. Ala., 1949. Tchr. Ivalee Sch., Attalla, Ala., 1949—53, 1956—61, 1964—66; tchr. math. Etowah H.S., Attalla, Ala., 1966—86, ret., 1986. Pres. Etowah County Classroom Tchrs. Assn., 1967—68. Pianist Ivalee Bapt. Ch., 1950—2006, Sunday sch. tchr., 1950—97, dir. sr. activities, 2000—06. Nominee Jacksonville State Tchr. Hall of Fame, 1972, Presdl. award for excellence in math. tchg. Mem.: NEA, Ala. Edn. Assn., Alpha Delta Kappa (past pres. Ala. Alpha Xi chpt.), Kappa Delta Pi. Avocations: genealogy, stamp collecting/philately, photography, music, flower gardening. Home: 3194 Hwy 77 Attalla AL 35954-7140 Personal E-mail: awbsaffels@aol.com.

SAFFER, AMY BETH, foreign language educator; b. NYC, Apr. 19, 1950; d. William and Evelyn (Yankowitz) S. BA, Fairleigh Dickinson U., 1972, MA, 1983; postgrad., Jersey City State Coll., 1983—84. Cert. tchr. Spanish K-12, N.J. Tchr. Madison (N.J.) High Sch., 1973, Livingston (N.J.) High Sch., 1973—. Mem. faculty and dist. coms. Livingston Sch. Dist., 1975—; advisor to class of 1977, Livingston High Sch., 1975-77, chair mid. states subcom., 1990; tchr. mentor. Inducted Livington H.S. Alumni Hall of Fame, 1993. Mem. NEA, Am. Assn. Tchrs. of Spanish and Portuguese, N.J. Edn. Assn., Fgn. Lang. Educators of N.J., Livingston Edn. Assn. (negotiations rep. 1980—), Essex County Edn. Assn. Office: Livingston High Sch Livingston NJ 07039

SAFFIOTE, LINDA, secondary school educator; b. Hollywood, Calif., Sept. 5, 1958; d. Trudy Griffin; m. Rich Saffiote, July 2, 1999; children: Alex, Adam. BA, Bethany Coll., Scotts Valley, Calif., 1992. Cert. tchr. Calif., 2005. Tchr. English Monte Vista Christian Sch., Watsonville, Calif., 1992—96, Valley Ctr. HS, Calif., 1998—; tchr. Escondido Chart HS, 1996—98. Airman first class USAF, 1980—82. Mem.: Tchrs. Union (site rep. 2005—06). Home: 28610 Sunset Rd Valley Center CA 92082 Office: Valley Center High School 31322 Cole Grade Rd Valley Center CA 92082 Office Phone: 760-751-5500. Office Fax: 760-751-5509. Business E-Mail: saffiote.li@vcpusd.net.

SAFFIOTTI, PAOLA, retired music educator, performing arts association administrator; b. Milan, Aug. 19, 1925; arrived in US, 1960; d. Alfredo Amman and Margherita Cerletti; m. Umberto Saffiotti, June 21, 1958; children: Luisa M., Maria F.P. Diploma in pianoforte, Conservatorio G. Verdi, Milan, 1948. Tchr. pvt. piano lessons, Milan, 1949—51; asst. mgr. Internat. Concert Orgn., Milan, 1952—60; piano instr. pvt. lessons Chgo., 1963—66; personal sec. to music dir. Chgo. Symphony Orch., 1966—68; co-founder, assoc. music dir. Chamber Music Series Found. for Advanced Edn. in Scis., Bethesda, 1968—. Adminstrv. coord. Marlboro Recording Soc., Bethesda, Md. and Marlboro, Vt., 1971—91, overseer Libr. of Congress Marlboro Archives, 1974—. Vol. reader Recording for the Blind and Dyslexic, Washington, 1993—; bd. trustees Marlboro Sch. Music, 1991—. Roman Catholic. Home: 5114 Wissioming Rd Bethesda MD 20816-2259

SAFFORD, FLORENCE VIRAY SUNGA, travel agent, consultant; b. Masantol, Pampanga, Luzon, Philippines, Mar. 19, 1932; came to U.S., 1953; d. Filomeno Garcia and Dominga (Viray) Sunga; m. Francis Ingersoll Safford, Aug. 4, 1979; children: H. Robert, Erlinda Ann, Ruben Michael. BS in Edn., Adamson U., Manila, 1952; student Hotel Mgmt. and Polit. Sci., Kapiolani C.C., Honolulu, 1975; student, Am. Travel Sch., Honolulu, 1977. Tchr. Cecilio Apostles Elem. Sch., Manila, 1949-51, St. Michael Acad., Masantol, 1951-52; social worker Cath. Social Svc., Honolulu, 1970-77; cons. Travel Cons. of the Pacific, Honolulu, 1977—; social worker Kapiolani C.C., Honolulu. Mem. exec. bd. dirs. Oahu Cmty. Coun., 1994—; elected to Neighborhood Bd., 1982—84, 1993—95; apptd. by mayor of Honolulu to Ethics Commn., 1986—95; v.p. Marbella Home Owners Assn. at Summerlin Resorts, 2001—; bd. dirs., del. Summerlin Resorts Homeowners Assn., 2004—; bd. dirs. C. of C. of Hawaii. Named Most Outstanding Leader of the Community, Filipino Jaycees of Honolulu, 1976. Mem.: Aloha Bus. and Profl. Women's Club (treas., Outstanding award 1981—89), Filipino C. of C. of Hawaii (treas., bd. dirs. 1994, Outstanding award 1991—92), Women's Cmty. Action League of Hawaii (pres. 1972—2001, Outstanding Pres. 1992). Republican. Roman Catholic. Avocation: dance. also: 10849 Carbonia Ct Las Vegas NV 89144-4508

SAFIAN, GAIL ROBYN, public relations executive; b. Bklyn., Dec. 12, 1947; d. Jack I. and Harriet S.; m. Jay Mark Eisenberg, Jan. 6, 1979; children: Julia, Eric. BA, SUNY, Albany, 1968; MBA, NYU, 1982. Reporter Albany (N.Y.)-Knickerbocker News/Times-Union, 1969, Athens (Ohio) Messenger, 1969-71; pub. relations asst. Mountainside Hosp., Montclair, N.J., 1971-74; dir. pub. relations Riverside Hosp., Boonton, N.J., 1974-78; consumer affairs coordinator Johnson & Johnson Personal Products Div., Milltown, N.J., 1978-79; v.p., group mgr. Harshe Rotman & Druck, N.Y.C., 1979-82; exec. v.p., dir. Health Care Div. Ruder Finn & Rotman, N.Y.C., 1982-84; v.p., mgr. client services Burson-Marsteller, N.Y.C., 1984-86; v.p., group mgr. health care Cohn & Wolfe, N.Y.C., 1986-90; exec. v.p., gen. mgr. MCS, Summit, N.J., 1990-94; pres. Safian Comm. Inc., Maplewood, N.J., 1994—. Mem. devel. com. Cancer Care, N.Y.C., 1985—. Recipient MacEachern award Am. Hosp. Assn., 1974, Communications Award Internat. Assn. Bus. Communicators, 1976, Creativity in Pub. Rels. award Inside PR, 1992, 93, Big Apple award 2005 Mem. Healthcare Businesswomen's Assn. (mem. bd. dirs.), N.Y. Acad. Scis., Women in Comm. (Clarion award 1974). Jewish. Home and Office: Safian Comm Inc 31 Hickory Dr Maplewood NJ 07040-2107 E-mail: gsafian@safianhealth.com.

SAFIAN, SHELLEY CAROLE, advertising executive; b. Bklyn., May 29, 1954; d. Jack Israel and Harriet Sara (Cohen) S. BFA, Parsons Sch. Design, 1975; MA, U. Phoenix, 2002. Cert. coding specialist; in health svcs. mgmt. Keller Grad. Sch. Bus., 2005. Asst. art dir. Axelrod and Assocs., N.Y.C., 1975-77; art dir. Sta. WDBO-TV-AM/FM, Orlando, Fla., 1978-80; owner, pres. Safian Comm. Svcs., Inc., Winter Park, Fla., 1981—, Bonté Sportswear, Winter Park, Fla., 1993-97; chair allied health dept. Herzing Coll., Winter Park, Fla., 2004—. Mem. adv. com. Career Edn., Orange County, Fla., 1981—88, chmn., 1982—83; adj. prof. Internat. Acad. Design and Tech., 2000—; adj. prof. City Coll., Casselberry, Fla., 2000—. Author: Insurance Coding & Electronic Claims for the Medical Office, 2005. Exec. producer/dir. March of Dimes Telethon, Orlando, 1984; bd. dirs. Boy Scouts Am., 1987-91; exec. dir. United Cerebral Palsy Telethon, Orlando, 1982-83; pub. rels. liaison United Cerebral Palsy, Orlando, 1983-84; founder Career Dir. for Deaf, Orlando, 1985; trustee, pub. rels. chair Nat. Multiple Sclerosis Soc., 1991-92, bd. dirs., 1990, 91. Recipient 1st pl. Addy awards Orlando ADvt. Fedn., 1981, 87, 88, 89, 1st pl. Addy award, 2d pl. awards, merit awards, 1982, 84, 85, 87, 88, Nat. Telly award Bronze Statue, 1988, Up and Coming award Price Waterhouse/Orlando Bus. Jour., 1988, Pro-Mark 1st pl. awards Fla. Coun. Shopping Ctrs., 1989, 90, merit award, 1990, Telly award Bronze finalist, 1989, 91; named Tchr. of the Quarter, 2001. Mem. Broadcast Promotion and Mktg. Execs. Assn. (Silver Medalion 1983, nat. finalist 2 Silver Microphone awards 1986, 87), Broadcast Designer's Assn. (bd.d irs. 1980-82), Am. Women in Radio and TV (bd. dirs. 1980-81). Republican. Avocation: horseback riding.

SAFIER, REGAN S., lawyer; b. Randolph, NJ, Aug. 12, 1971; BA magna cum laude, Lehigh U., 1993; JD, U. Va., 1996. Bar: Pa. 1996, NJ 1996, US Dist. Ct. (ea. dist.) Pa., US Dist. Ct., NJ, US Ct. Appeals (3rd cir.). Ptnr. med. profl. liability Weber Gallagher Simpson Stapleton Fires & Newby LLP, Phila. Contbr. articles to law jours. Mem.: Pa. Bar Assn., Phila. Bar Assn. Office: Weber Gallagher Simpson Stapleton Fires & Newby 2000 Market St, Ste 1300 Philadelphia PA 19103 Office Phone: 215-972-7925. Office Fax: 215-564-7699. E-mail: rsafier@wglaw.com.*

SAFIRA, BARABARA, science educator; b. Kaprzewnica, Poland, Feb. 18, 1959; d. Regina and Jon Pielecha; m. Hertzel Safira, Jan. 11, 1990; children: Arthur Dov, Ariela. Masters, Acad. Of Mining & Metallurgy, Kracov, Poland, 1986. Cert. phys. sci. tchr. N.J., 2001. Chem. engr. Cement Plant, Ozarow, Poland, 1986—87; rsch. chemist Sika, Lyndhurst, NJ, 1989—98; tchr. phys. sci. Wallington H.S., NJ, 2001—. Head instr. of engring. club Wallington H.S., NJ, 2002—06; asst. math. team Bergen County Acad., Hackensack, NJ, 2004—06. Office: Wallington HS 234 Main Ave Wallington NJ 07057 Office Phone: 973-777-0808. E-mail: safira@wboe.org.

SAFRAN, CLAIRE, writer, editor; b. N.Y.C. d. Simon and Flora (R) S.; m. John Milton Williams, June 8, 1958; 1 son, Scott Edward. BA in English cum laude, Bklyn. Coll., 1951. News editor Photo Dealer mag., 1951-53; assoc. editor TV Radio Mirror, 1954-58; mng. editor Photoplay mag., 1958-61; editor TV Radio Mirror, 1961-65, IN mag., 1965-67; assoc. editor Family Weekly mag., 1967-68; editor Coronet mag., 1968-71; contbg. editor Redbook, 1974-77; exec. editor, 1977-78; contbg. editor, 1979-81; roving editor Reader's Digest, 1983-88; contbg. editor Woman's Day, 1988-91. Author: New Ways to Lower Your Blood Pressure, 1984, Secret Exodus, 1987, Looking for Lost Bird, 1999; contbr. to maj. nat. mags., 1972—. Recipient Media award Am. Psychol. Found., 1977; finalist Penney-Missouri Mag. Awards, 1977, Merit award in journalism Religious Pub. Rels. Coun., 1978, hon. mention journalism awards Am. Acad. Pediatrics, 1979, 1st pl. nat. editorials Odyssey Inst. Media Awards, 1979, 80, 86, Matrix award Women in Comm., 1982, 83, 84, William Harvey award, 1984, 91, Journalism award Am. Acad. Family Physicians, 1984, Investigative Journalism citation Deadline Club, 1993, Cert. of Merit Cmty. Action Network, 1995, PASS award Nat. Coun. on Crime and Delinquency, 1996. Mem. Am. Soc. Journalists and Authors (Outstanding Mag. Article award 1984, pres. 1996-98). Home: 53 Evergreen Ave Westport CT 06880-2563

SAFRAN, FRANCISKA KUHAROVITS, retired librarian, curator; b. Ujkécske, Hungary, Aug. 22, 1935; arrived in U.S., 1957; d. Janos Kuharovits and Franciska Bartucz; m. Karl Safran, Jan. 7, 1956 (div. 1973); children: Melinda, Aniko. AB in Am. Lit., Syracuse U., NY, 1965, MS in Libr. Sci., 1966; MA in Am. History, SUNY, 1983. Acquisitions libr. Guggenheim Meml. Libr. Monmouth Coll., West Long Br., NJ, 1966—70; chief bibliographer Alderman Libr. U. Va., Charlottesville, Va., 1970—72; libr. Reed Libr. SUNY, Fredonia, NY, 1973—2000, ret., 2000. Chmn. disaster preparedness in librs. com. We. N.Y. Libr., Buffalo, 1988—92; chmn. disaster preparedness Reed Libr., 1989—2000; curator Holland Land Co. Records, 2000. Editor: Inventory of the Stefan Zweig Collection, 1993, (microfilm) Archives of the Holland Land Co. 1789-1869, 1982—95; contbr. scientific papers. Recipient Rsch. and Creativity award, SUNY, 1984, Excellence in Librarianship award, Chancellor NYU, 1985, Quality Working award, NYU, 1985, 1998. Mem.: ALA (com. mem. 1989—94), Assn. for the Bibl. of History (com. mem. 1987—92, chair 1990—92), Am. Coll. and Rsch. Libr., SUNY Libr. Assn. (2d v.p. 1979—81), N.Y. Libr. Assn. (com. chmn. 1979—81), Phi Alpha Theta, Beta Phi Mu. Roman Catholic. Avocations: gardening, cooking, reading, classical music. Home: 146 Erie St Brockport NY 14420

SAFRAN, JOAN SCHULMAN, education educator, researcher; b. Jersey City, Oct. 5, 1951; d. Arthur and Henrietta R. (Schindler) Schulman; m. Stephen P. Safran, Feb. 13, 1974; children: Adam, Elisa. BA, Conn. Coll., 1973; MEd, Rutgers U., 1975; PhD, U. Va., 1980. Tchr. Highland Park (N.J.) Schs., 1975-77; evaluator Ctr. for Human Devel., Athens, Ohio, 1980-81; asst. prof. edn. Ohio U., Athens, 1981—. Coord. master's programs Ohio U., Zanesville, 1983-85, 90—; cons., Va., Ohio, 1978—. Editor Athens Assn. for Gifted Children Newsletter, 1991—; contbr. articles to profl. jours. Vol., rschr. Child Assault Prevention Program, Athens, 1990—; apptd. Children's Trust Fund Bd., 1993—. Recipient community recognition award Spl. Edn. Parent Advocacy Network, 1992, also community svc. awards, 1980—; rsch. grantee Ohio U., 1982—. Mem. Coun. for Exceptional Children. Achievements include research in Asperger Syndrome. Home: 7889 N Coolville Ridge Rd Athens OH 45701-9432 Office Phone: 740-593-0840. E-mail: safran@ohio.edu.

SAFREN, CHERYL, art educator, artist; d. Abraham Rothberg and Marilyn Pearl Finchler; m. Martin Safren, Jan. 19, 1975; children: Aviva Einhorn, Nathaniel Isaac. BFA, Pratt Inst., 1973; MSc, Hofsta U., 1996. Cert. tchr. N.Y. Edn. Dept., 1997. Tchr. art North Shore Hebrew Acad., Great Neck, NY, 1996—2005, Manhasset (N.Y.) Union Free Sch. Dist., 2005—. Instr. Hofstra U., Hempstead, NY, 1998. One-woman shows include Lawrence Inst. Tech., AAAS, Washington, Great Neck Art Ctr., NY, Discovery Mus., Bridgeport, Conn., Represented in permanent collections City of Aurora, Colo., City of Balatonfored, Hungary, Teleflex Internat., Thyssen Industries, Germany, U. Ga., Athens, U. Maine, Orono, Wyeth Pharms. Recipient Kufeld award, North Shore Hebrew Acad., 2000; grantee, N.Y. State Coun. Arts, 1992, 2005. Mem.: Williamburg Art and Hist. Ctr. (assoc.), L.I. (N.Y.) Arts Coun. Freeport (assoc.), N.Y. State Art Tchrs. Assn. (assoc.), Art and Sci. Collaborations, Inc. (assoc.), N.Y. Artists Equity (assoc.). Achievements include development of chemistry on metals art techniques and processes. Office Phone: 516-792-0962. Home Fax: 516-285-8433. Personal E-mail: tzayaret@artlover.com.

SAFRO, MILLICENT, small business owner, decorative arts scholar, writer; Co-owner Tender Buttons, N.Y.C. and Chgo., 1964—. Lectr., appraiser in field; collector, dealer antique buttons. Co-author: Buttons, 1991; contbr. articles to mags., periodicals; exhibitions include Cooper-Hewitt Mus., N.Y.C., Smithsonian Instn., Washington, Atheneum, La Jolla, Calif., L.A. County Mus. Art, Henry Flagler Mus., Palm Beach, Fla., Shiseido Art Gallery, Tokyo. Avocation: dealer and collector of antique buttons. Office: Tender Buttons 143 E 62d St New York NY 10021 Office Phone: 212-980-3540.

SAGAL, KATEY, actress; b. L.A., Jan. 19, 1954; d. Boris Sagal and Sara Zwilling; m. Jack White, 1993 (div. 2000), m. Kurt sutter, Oct. 2, 2004. Student, Calif. Sch. of the Arts. Former back-up singer for various performers including Bob Dylan, Etta James; (with Bette Midler) former mem. The Harlettes. Actress: (stage prodns.) Martha Rose and the Miners, 1982, My Beautiful Lady, (TV series) Mary, 1986, Imagine That, 2002, (TV movie) The Failing of Raymond, 1971, Mother Goose Rock 'n' Rhyme, 1990, She Says She's Innocent, 1991, Trail of Tears, 1995, Mr. Headmistress, 1998, Chance of a Lifetime, 1998, God's New Plan, 1999, Smart House, 1999, (films) Maid to Order, 1987, The Good Mother, 1988, Following Tildy, 2002; regular (TV series) Married.With Children, 1987-97, (voice) Recess, 1997, (voice) Futurama, 1999, Tucker, 2000, 8 Simple Rules.for Dating My Teenage Daughter, 2002—. Mem. Actors' Equity Assn., Assn. TV and Radio Artists. Office: Progressive Artists Agy Inc 400 S Beverly Dr Ste 216 Beverly Hills CA 90212-4404

SAGANICH, BONNIE SUE, medical/surgical nurse; b. Lancaster, Pa., Apr. 30, 1956; d. Gerald Charles and Reta Ruth (Rupp) Hake; m. David Anthony Saganich, Aug. 30, 1980. BSN, Temple U., 1988; MSN, U. Pa., 1991. RN, Pa.; bd.cert. med.-surg. nurse. Med.-surg. nurse Lancaster Gen. Hosp., 1988-90, renal dialysis nurse, 1991-93; med.-surg. nurse York (Pa.) Hosp., 1993-94; staff nurse Vis. Nurse Assn., Lancaster, 1994-95, nurse long term care, 1996; neurology and step-down trauma nurse Lancaster Gen. Hosp., 1997-2000, step-down nurse open heart surgery, 2000—05; agy. nursing Medi Quest Staffing, 2005—. Contbr. profl. jours. Mem. Sigma Theta Tau. Avocations: gardening, photography, walking, travel. Home: 75 Silver Mine Rd Conestoga PA 17516-9732 Office: MediQuest Staffing 600-E Eden Rd Lancaster PA 17601

SAGAWA, SHIRLEY SACHI, lawyer; b. Rochester, NY, Aug. 25, 1961; d. Hidetaka H. and Patricia (Ford) S.; m. Gregory A. Baer; children: Jackson Ford Baer, Matthew Sagawa Baer, Thomas Arthur Baer. AB, Smith Coll., 1983; MSc, London Sch. Econs., 1984; JD, Harvard U., 1987. Bar: Md. 1988. Chief counsel youth policy, labor and human resources com. U.S. Senate, Washington, 1987-91; sr. counsel and dir. family and youth policy Nat. Women's Law Ctr., Washington, 1991-93; spl. asst. to Pres. Clinton for domestic policy, 1993; exec. dir., mng. dir., exec. v.p. Corp. for Nat. and Comty. Svc., Washington, 1993-97; exec. dir. Learning First Alliance, Washington, 1997-98; dep. asst. Pres. Clinton, dep. chief staff First Lady The White House, Washington, 1998-2001; ptnr. sagawa/jospin, 2001—. Co-author: Common Interest, Common Good, Creating Value Through Business and Social Sector Partnership, 1999. Exec. bd. Orgn. for Pan-Asian Am. Women, Washington, 1987-89; mem. Women of Color Leadership Coun., 1991-92; vice-chair, bd. dirs. Nat. Cmty. Svc. Commn., 1991-93; trustee Am. Folklife Ctr., Libr. Congress, 1996-97; commr. Head Start Fellowships Commn., 1996-97; bd. dirs. My Sister's Place, 1996-98, Jumpstart, 1998, Campus Outreach Opportunity League, 1997-98, Nat. Inst. Dispute Resolution, 1997-98, Nat. Womens Law Ctr., 2003—, Nat. AmeriCorps Assn., 2004—, Nat. Assn. Childcare Resource and Referral Agencies, 2004—. Recipient Philip V. McGance award Coun. for Advancement of Citizenship, 1991, cert. of recognition Nat. Coun. Jewish Women, 1989, Alexandrine medal Coll. St. Catherine, St. Paul, 1995, Alec Dickson Servant Leader award Nat. Youth Leadership Coun., 2002; named one of 25 most influential working women Working Mother Mag., 1999; recipient Alec Dickson Servant Leader award, National Youth Leadership Council, 2002; Harry S. Truman scholar, 1981; Smith Coll. Alumnae Assn. fellow, 1983, AAUW fellow, 1986. Mem. Md. Bar Assn. Democrat. Episcopalian.

SAGE-GAVIN, EVA MARIE, retail executive; b. Boston, Sept. 26, 1958; d. Ross Francis and Theresa Veronica (Bufalo) S.; m. Dennis Gavin. BS in Indsl. Relations, Cornell U., 1980. Affirmative action personnel specialist Xerox Corp., Washington, 1980-81; compensation analyst Xerox Corp, Rochester, N.Y., 1981-82, sales recruiter Boston, 1982, employment mgr., 1983, systems mktg. rep., 1983-85; personnel mgr. Xerox Corp., L.A., 1985—86; human resources mgr. Xerox Corp, Irvine, Calif., 1986; dir. human resources Pepsi Co., 1991, v.p. corp. human resources, Taco Bell; sr. v.p. human resources Disney Consumer Products, 1997—2000, Sun Microsystems, Inc., 2000—03; exec. v.p. human resources Gap Inc., 2003—. Mem. career adv. bd. Emmanuel Coll., Boston, 1983-85. Named one of Top 25 Most Powerful Women in HR, HR Exec. mag., 2005. Mem. Am. Soc. Personnel Adminstrn., Women in Mgmt., Xerox Women's Network (edn. com. 1988), Kappa Kappa Gamma. Democrat. Roman Catholic. Avocations: skiing, travel, boating, sailing, aerobics. Office: Gap Inc 2 Folsom St San Francisco CA 94105 Office Phone: 650-952-4400. Office Fax: 415-427-2553.

SAGIANI, FREDERICA, science educator; b. Pontikates, Janina, Epiros, Oct. 8, 1953; arrived in U.S., 1967; d. Manthos and Polixeni Sagianis; m. George Panagiotakis, July 13, 1986; 1 child, Stephan Panagiotakis. BA in Biology, Hunter Coll., N.Y.C., 1976, MS in Guidance and Counseling, 1981; EdM in Curriculum and Tchg., Tchrs. Coll., N.Y.C., 1984. Sci. tchr. St. Demetrios Sch. Sys., N.Y.C., 1978—81, guidance counselor, 1980—81; cons. Ford Found., Tchrs. Coll., N.Y.C., 1982—84; prin. A. Fantiso Par. Sch., Bklyn., 1984—90, St. Demetrios/Jamaica Day Sch., Queens, NY, 1990—98; sci. tchr. MS 216 Q, N.Y.C., 1998—2006. Mem. Sch. Around the World, 2004—05. Mem.: Phi Delta Kappa. Avocations: reading, gardening, travel, history. Home: 23-28 Crescent St Astoria NY 11105 Office Phone: 718-358-2005. E-mail: paidea218@yahoo.com.

SAGNER, DIANNE R., lawyer; m. Menn Julius Sagner. BA, Am. U., 1967; KD, U. Ma., 1973; LLM, Washington U., 1974. Corp. assoc. Bryan Cave, St. Louis; with gen. counsels office Washington U.; in-house lawyer U. Ill., Howard Hughes Med. Ctr., Chevy Chase, Md., 1987—94; gen. counsel Peak Technologies Group, Columbia, 1994—2000, OAO Tech. Solutions, Greenbelt, 2000—02, FTI Cons. Inc., Annapolis, 2002—. Office: FTI Cons 900 Bestgate Rd # 100 Annapolis MD 21401

SAGO, JANIS LYNN, photography educator; b. St. Louis, Nov. 27, 1948; d. Bernard William and Eunice Alberta (Henry) Osthof; m. William Leo Sago Jr., Feb. 18, 1967 (dec. Mar. 1989); children: Brian William, Shelley Lynn, Carrie Renee. AA, St. Louis C.C., 1990; BA cum laude, Webster U., St. Louis, 1993. Office mgr. C.B. Smith Co., St. Louis, 1989—2004; free-lance photographer St. Louis, 1990—. Interim staff photographer St. Louis C.C., 1990, adj. instr. photography, 1993—; adj. faculty photographer St. Charles County C.C., 1998-2003; gallery asst. Webster U., St. Louis, 1993; adj. faculty photography St. Louis C.C., 1993—, coord. photography program, 2006—; photography instr. Mo. Bot. Gardens, 1999—. Photographer The Webster Jour., 1992-93; photos exhibited at May Gallery, 1993, Campus Gallery, 1996—, Martin Schweig Gallery, 1996, St. Charles County C.C., 1998-2003, St. Peters Cultural Art Ctr., 2002—, St. Louis CC. Mem. St. Louis Art Mus., 1994—, St. Louis Sci. Ctr., 1996-97, Mo. Bot. Gardens, 1997—; officer, asst. chief YMCA Indian Guides, St. Louis, 1989-97; vol./chair Mothers' Club, Lindbergh Schs., St. Louis, 1974-90, PTO, 1974-90. Mem. AAUW, Greater St. Louis Orchid Soc., Phi Theta Kappa. Avocations: gardening, reading, travel, music. Office: St Louis C C 11333 Big Bend Rd Saint Louis MO 63122-5720 Office Phone: 314-984-7632.

SAHAGIAN, LUCILLE BEDROSIAN, gasoline company executive; b. Chgo., Mar. 27, 1927; d. KEsrow and Rebecca (Babian) Bedrosian; m. John Sahagian, Jan. 10, 1953 (dec. Sept. 1993); 1 child, Rebecca Jan. Grad. exec.

sec. and bus. acctg., Bryant and Stratton Bus. Sch., Chgo., 1944. Exec. sec. William Morris Theatrical Agy., Chgo., 1944-46, Goldblatts Dept. Store/Retail Advt., Chgo., 1946-53, Ross Roy Advt. Agy., Chgo., 1953-54; dealer, ptnr. John Sahagian Svc. Stas., Conn. Turnpike East, Fairfield, 1958-64, Darien, 1966-72, lessee, ptnr. East and West, 1972-84; treas., owner John Sahagian, Inc., Fairfield, Conn., 1976-85; lessee, ptnr. N.Y. State Thruway Authority John Sahagian Svc. Stas., Ramapo, Sloatsburg, N.Y., 1978-84, lessee, ptnr. Paliades Pkwy., N. & S. Interstate Pkwy. Englewood Cliffs, N.J., 1981-86; account exec. Sebastian Gangemi Svc. Stas., Conn. Turnpike, Darien, 1984-88, Trumbull (Conn.) Shell, 1988—; travel cons. Etna Travel Bur., Inc., Stratford, Conn., 1944—. Treas. Ladies Prelacy Guild of Armenian Apostolic Ch., N.Y.C., 1981—; dir. Fairfield County Charity for Austic Children, 1961-64; pres., treas. Armenian Relief Soc., 1970. Mem. Gasoline Retailers Assn., Internat. Airlines Travel Agt. Network, Shorehaven Golf Club (bd. mem. 1966, treas. ladies golf 1990). Avocations: golf, travel, music and religious studies. Home: 168 Spring Hill Rd Fairfield CT 06430-1949 Office: Etna Travel Bureau Inc 3241 Main St Stratford CT 06614-4850

SAHAKIAN, LILLIAN ZAROUHI, artist, designer; d. Archak Agapov Sahakian and Mariam Zarouhi Zahrbhanelian-Sahakian. Secretarial pool First Nat. City Bank, N.Y.C., 1954—55; sec., sales & mktg. Walker Mktg. Corp., Racine, Wis., 1958—59; typist, purchasing Kollsman Instrument Corp., Elmhurst, NY, 1963—70; supv. stenographer City Hosp. Ctr., 1974—78; exec. sec. Racine/Kenosha Cmty. Action Agy., 1979—80, Butter Buds Corp., Racine, 1989—91; mktg. specialist Johnson Internat., Inc., Racine, 1994—2003. Oil portrait - copy, Victor Choque (2nd Prize, 1955), exhibition, Early Oil Paintings-American Artist, Smithsonian, 1957, altar piece, Madonna & Child, St. Sarkis Ch., 1960, graphite rendering, Viet Nam Refugees - Grandmother & Grandson, 1964, watercolor painting, After Matisse, 1990, graphics logo, Lili Archak Studios, 2004, lifestyle interior designs, Interior Designs LLC. Choir mem. St. Hagop Ch., Wis., 1958—59. Scholar Entrepreneurial Incentive award, State of Wis., 2004. Mem.: NAMI Racine (bd. dirs. 1985—2006), Soc. for Tech. Comm., Kenosha Art Assn., Am. Inst. Graphic Artists (assoc.). Independent. Avocations: reading, do it yourself home repairs, research on the internet & other, computer generated art, cooking. Office: Lili Archak Studios LLC 1117 Saxony Dr Racine WI 53402 Office Phone: 262-898-9351.

SAHATJIAN, MANIK, retired nurse, retired psychologist; b. Tabris, Iran, July 24, 1921; came to U.S., 1951; d. Dicran and Shushanig (Der-Galustian) Mnatzaganian; m. George Sahatjian, Jan. 21, 1954; children: Robert, Edwin. Nursing Cert., Am. Mission Hosps.-Boston U., 1954; BA in Psychology, San Jose State U., 1974, MA in Psychology, 1979. RN Calif. Head nurse Am. Mission Hosp., Tabris, 1945-46; charge nurse Banke-Melli Hosp., Tehran, 1946-51; vis. nurse Vis. Nurse Assn., Oakland, Calif., 1956-57; research asst. Stanford U., 1979-81, Palo Alto (Calif.) Med. Research Found., 1981-84; documentation supr. Bethesda Convalescent Ctr., Los Gatos, Calif., 1985-86; sr. outreach worker City of Fremont (Calif.) Human Svcs., 1987-90, case mgr., 1990-97; ret., 1997. Guest rsch. asst. NASA Ames Lab., Mountain View, Calif., summers 1978, 79. Author (with others) psychol. research reports. Mentor elem. sch. children, 1997-2002; pro bono tchg./counseling for srs. who are home bound, Bay Area, Calif., 1999—; pro bono tchr. peer counseling trainers for srs. Armenian Cmty. Santa Clara, Calif., St. Andrew Ch. Fulbright scholar, 1951; Iran Found. scholar, 1953; Morgan-Segal scholar for peer counseling tng., 1998. Mem. AAUW, Western Psychol. Assn., Am. Assn. Sr. Counseling. Democrat. Mem. St. Andrew Armenian Church. Achievements include fluency in Armenian, Farsi, Turkish; familiarity in Spanish, Russian, French langs. Avocations: painting, classic dance. Home: 339 Starlite Way Fremont CA 94539-7642

SAHLBERG, ANNE KISZKA, secondary school educator; d. Richard Edward Kiszka and Sharon Marie Hane. BA in English Lit., Calif. State U, Chico, 1994. Cert. tchr. Calif., 2002. Hons. English tchr. McKinleyville H.S., Calif., 2004—, journalism adviser, 2002—06; class adviser class of 2007 McKinleyville H.S, Calif., 2003—; dist. literacy team mem. McKinleyville H.S., Calif., 2004—, literacy site co-chairperson Calif., 2004—, asst. track and field coach Calif., 2003—04. Case study cons. Reading Inst. for Acad. Preparation, Humboldt State U., Arcata, Calif., 2003—. Named MHS Staff Mem. of the Yr., MHS student body, 2004; recipient Wells Fargo Stagecoach Legacy award, Humboldt County, 2005. Mem.: Calif. Assn. Tchrs. English (pres. Redwood coun.). Office: McKinleyville HS 1300 Murray Rd Mckinleyville CA 95519 Office Phone: 707-839-6400. Office Fax: 707-839-6407. E-mail: asahlberg@nohum.k12.ca.us.

SAHLENE, singer; b. Soderhamn, Sweden, 1976; Rep. for Estonia Eurovision Song Contest, 2002. Child actress (TV series) The Children of Bullerbyn; singer: (albums) 12 Steps Down the Avenue, 1997, It's Been A While, 2003. Recipient 3rd Place for the song "Runaway", Eurovision Song Contest, 2002. Mailing: Comino Productions Inc 1648 10th Ave Brooklyn NY 11215 E-mail: sahlene@sahlene.com.

SAIA, DIANE PLEVOCK DIPIERO, nutritionist, educator, legal administrator; b. Oct. 2, 1941; d. Charles and Monica (Alexandravich) Plevock; married; 1 child, David. BS, Framingham State Coll., Mass., 1962; MS, Simmons Coll., Boston, 1969; doctoral candidate, U. Mass., 1974—75. Field nutritionist Mass. Dept. Edn., Boston, 1962—64; sch. program coord. New Eng. Dairy and Food Coun., Boston, 1964—67, sr. staff Springfield, Mass., 1970—83; tchr. Weymouth (Mass.) Schs., 1967—70; adj. prof. Springfield Coll., 1970—80. Nutrition tchr. Baystate Med. Ctr., Springfield; adj. faculty Western New Eng. Coll., 1982—84; legal adminstr. Saia Law Firm, LLC, 1984—; host radio show Law Talk, 1997—; prodr. TV shows, radio and consumer edn. programs. Fund raiser Am. Heart Assn., 2000—02. Mem.: ATLA, Assn. Legal Adminstrs., Sales and Mktg. Execs., Assn. Family and Consumer Econs. (exec. bd. 1972—, pres. 1978—79), New Eng. Pub. Health Assn., Mass. Bar Assn., Valley Press Club (assoc. dir. 1976—79, chmn. scholarship ball 1977—79). Roman Catholic. Home: 502 Frank Smith Rd Longmeadow MA 01106-2928 Office: 106 State St Springfield MA 01103

SAIBLE, STEPHANIE IRENE, magazine editor; b. Mobile, Ala., Sept. 11, 1954; d. Lewis J. Slaff and Phoebe-Jane (Berse) Meiss. Student, Va. Commonwealth U., 1972—75. Editorial asst. Woman's World Magazine, Englewood, NJ, 1980—81, service copywriter, 1981—83, assoc. articles editor, 1983—84, articles editor, 1984—85, sr. editor features dept., 1985—86, sr. editor services dept., 1986, now editor-in-chief, 1994—. Contbr. articles to Woman's World, Modern Bride, New Body, Celebrity Beauty, Trim and Fit, Ladies Home Jour. Named Wonder Woman of the Yr., Bus. Jour., N.J., 1986. Mem.: Women in Comms. Office: Woman's World Mag 270 Sylvan Ave Englewood Cliffs NJ 07632-2521*

SAID, NAIMA, lawyer; LLB, U. Nairobi, 1979; LLM, Harvard U., 1990. Bar: Md., NY 1991. Assoc. Bryson, Inamdar, and Bowyer, Mombasa, Kenya, 1980—84; atty. Civil and Govt. Litig. Dept. SC Atty. Gen. Office, 1980—84; assoc. Kirkpatrick & Lockhart, Washington, DC, 1986—89; pvt. practice Naima Said & Associates, P.C., 1991—. Pro bono liaison officer Immigration Ct., Baltimore, 1999—2000. Mem.: ABA, Am. Immigration Lawyers Assn., NY State Bar Assn., Md. State Bar Assn. Office: Naima Said & Assocs 5513 Twin Knolls Rd Columbia MD 21045 Office Phone: 410-992-6602. E-mail: naima@naimasaid.com.

SAIDENS, SUSAN M., accountant, consultant; d. Julius and Bella Mendick; m. Gary L. Saidens, June 3, 1979; 1 child, Lindsay. BA, Douglass Coll., New Brunswick, 1973. CPA Pa. Inst CPAs, 1991, cert. valuation analyst, Nat. Assn. Cert. Valuation Analysts, accredited in bus. valuation, AICPA, cert. fraud examiner, Assn. Cert. Fraud Examiners, 2004. Sportswear buyer Macy's, N.Y.C., 1973—78; divsional mdse. mgr. Abraham and Straus, Bklyn., 1978—80; auditor KPMG, Phila., 1989—94; asst. contr. Home Health Corp. of Am., King of Prussia, Pa., 1994—96; dir. Smart & Assocs., LLP, Paoli, Pa., 1996—2000; dir., shareholder Asher & Co., Ltd., Phila., 2000—05; founder SMS Valuation and Forensic Svcs., LLC, Exton, Pa., 2005—. Bd. mem. adv. bd. Chester County Mental Health/Mental Retardation, West Chester, Pa., 1999—2001. Author: The Challenge: Educating Clients on the Valuation Process, 2002. Steering com. United Way of Chester County, West Chester, Pa., 1995—2001; vol. Pew Charitable Trusts. Named a Instr. Great Distinction, Nat. Instrs. Bus. Valuations, 2006. Mem.: Appraisal Issues Task Force, Assn. Cert. Fraud Examiners, Nat. Assn. Female Execs., Pa. Inst. CPAs. (com. mem. 1998—), Am. Inst. CPAs., Nat. Assn. Cert. Valuation Analysts (mentor 2000—, chair valuation credentialing bd., bd. mem. 2002—05, exec. adv. bd. 2005—). Avocations: music, reading. Office Phone: 484-875-3068. Business E-Mail: sms@valuationforensics.com.

SAIDI, PARVIN, hematologist, medical educator; b. Teheran, Iran, Mar. 21, 1932; came to U.S., 1946; d. Ahmad and Fatemeh (Ashouri) S.; m. Allahverdi Farmanfarmaian, May 27, 1958; children: Dellara Farmanfarmaian Terry, Kimya Farmanfarmaian Harris. BS, Smith Coll., Northampton, Mass., 1952; MD, Harvard U., 1956. Diplomate Am. Bd. Internal Medicine, subspecialty hematology and med. oncology. Intern medicine UCLA Med. Ctr., 1956-57; resident internal medicine U. Calif., San Francisco, 1957-59; NIH rsch. fellow hematology U. Calif. Hosps. and Children's Med. Ctr., San Francisco, 1959-61, 63-64; asst. prof. medicine U. Medicine & Dentistry N.J.-Rutgers Med. Sch., New Brunswick, 1968-71, assoc. prof., 1971-74; prof. U. Medicine & Dentistry N.J.-Robert Wood Johnson Med. Sch., New Brunswick, 1974—, chief divsn. hematology and oncology, dept. medicine, 1972—, Robert Wood Johnson U. Hosp., New Brunswick, 1981—, Melvyn H. and AB Motolinsky chair hematology, 2000—. Cons. internist, hematologist, oncologist St. Peter's Med. Ctr., New Brunswick, Douglass Coll., Rutgers U., New Brunswick, VA Hosp., Lyons, N.J., Muhlenberg Hosp., Plainfield, N.J., Princeton (N.J.) Med. Ctr.; dir. Melvyn H. Motolinsky Lab. Hematology Rsch., N.J. Regional Comprehensive Hemophilia Care Program; mem. Gov.'s Adv. Coun. on AIDS; chmn. N.J. Regional Comprhensive Hemophilia Care Program Adv. Bd.; chmn. HHS region II Comprehensive Hemophilia Diagnostic and Treatment Ctrs., 1984-85, 89-90, 94-95, 99-2000; chmn. med. adv. bd. Hemophilia Found. N.J.; mem. med. adv. exec. com. N.J. Blood Svcs. Cons. editor Am. Jour. Medicine; contbr. articles to profl. jours. Recipient disting. svc. award for rsch. in leukemia Melvyn H. Motolinsky Rsch. Found., 1977, Humanitarian award Hemophilia Assn. No. N.J., 1978. Fellow ACP (mem. sci. program com. N.J. region), Acad. Medicine N.J.; mem. Am. Soc. Hematology (edn. com.), N.J. Hemophilia Assn. (chmn. med. adv. com., spl. award, Dr. L. Michael Kuhn Meml. award 1996), Coop. Oncology Group N.J. (exec. com., chairperson subcom. on lymphoma), Am. Heart Assn. (coun. on thrombosis), Am. Fedn. Clin. Rsch., Royal Soc. Medicine (affiliate), Am. Soc. Clin. Oncology, World Fedn. Hemophilia, Alpha Omega Alpha, Phi Beta Kappa, Sigma Xi. Office: Robert Wood Johnson Med Sch 1 Robert Wood Johnson Pl New Brunswick NJ 08901-1928

SAIF, LINDA J., veterinary scientist, virologist, immunologist; BA, Coll. Wooster, 1969; MA, Ohio State U., 1971, PhD in Microbiology/Immunology, 1976; PhD (hon.), Ghent U., Belgium, 2003. Prof. OARDC Ohio State U., Wooster, 1979—, disting. univ. prof., 2002—. Contbr. articles to profl. jours. Mem.: NAS. Office: Food Animal Health Rsch Program OARDC/OSU 1680 Madison Ave Wooster OH 44691

SAIGAL, ASHIMA, not-for-profit developer; d. Romesh and Veena Saigal; m. David Jerry Fridsma. BS, Mich. State U., East Lansing, 1991. Sr. software engr. Cardiff Software, Grand Rapids, Mich., 2000; sr. application engr. Steelcase Inc., Grand Rapids, 2001—02; dir. svcs. for West Mich. NPower Mich., Grand Rapids, 2002—04; dir. Nonprofit Good Practice Guide Johnson Ctr. for Philanthropy at GVSU, Grand Rapids, 2005—. Mem. exec. com. Grand Rapids Cmty. Media Ctr., 2005. Recipient Mich. Best Small Bus. award, Mich. Small Bus. Devel. Ctr., 1998. Mem.: AAUW. Office: Johnson Ctr for Philanthropy at GVSU 401 W Fulton St 288C Grand Rapids MI 49503 Office Phone: 616-331-6412. E-mail: saigalas@gvsu.edu.

SAIKI, KIM, professional golfer; b. Inglewood, Calif., Jan. 24, 1966; Degree in pub. admin., U. Calif. Winner Wegmans Rochester LPGA Championships, 2004. Four-time All-PAC 10 honoree; NCAA All-Am., 1986; winner Jr. World Championships, USGA Jr. Girls Championships; five-time winner Players West Golf Tour; two-time winner Futures Tour. Achievements include earning 20 career top-ten finishes. Avocations: fitness, cooking, music. Office: c/o LPGA 100 International Golf Dr Daytona Beach FL 32124-1092

SAIKI, PATRICIA (MRS. STANLEY MITSUO SAIKI), federal agency administrator, congressman; b. Hilo, Hawaii, May 28, 1930; d. Kazuo and Shizue (Inoue) Fukuda; m. Stanley Mitsuo Saiki, June 19, 1954; children: Stanley Mitsuo, Sandra Saiki Williams, Margaret C., Stuart K., Laura H. BA, U. Hawaii, 1952. Tchr. U.S. history Punahou Sch., Kaimuki Intermediate Sch., Kalani High Sch., Honolulu, 1952-64; sec. Rep. Party Hawaii, Honolulu, 1964-66, vice chmn., 1966-68, 82-83, chmn., 1983-85; rsch. asst. Hawaii State Senate, 1966-68; mem. Hawaii Ho. of Reps., 1968-74, Hawaii State Senate, 1974-82, 100th-101st Congresses from 1st Hawaii dist., Washington, 1987-91; adminstr. SBA, Washington, 1991-93. Mem. Pres.'s Adv. Coun. on Status of Women, 1969-76; mem. Nat. Commn. Internat. Women's Yr., 1969-70; commr. We. Interstate Commn. on Higher Edn.; fellow Eagleton Inst., Rutgers U., 1970; fellow Inst. of Politics, Kennedy Sch. Govt., Harvard U., 1993; bd. dirs. Bank of Am.-Hawaii, Landmark Systems Corp., Internat. Asset Recovery Corp.; mem. nat. selection com. Innovations in Am. Govt., Ford Found., Harvard U., 1999-2002. Mem. Kapiolano Hosp. Aux.; sec. Hawaii Rep. Com., 1964-66, vice chmn., 1966-68, chmn., 1983-85; del. Hawaii Constl. Conv., 1968; alt. del. Rep. Nat. Conv., 1968, del., 1984, Rep. nominee for lt. gov. Hawaii, 1982, for U.S. Senate, 1990, for. gov. Hawaii, 1994; mem. Fedn. Rep. Women; trustee Hawaii Pacific Coll.; past bd. govs. Boys and Girls Clubs Hawaii; mem. adv. coun. ARC; bd. dirs. Nat. Fund for Improvement of Post-Secondary Edn., 1982-85; past bd. dirs. Straub Med. Rsch. Found., Honolulu, Hawaii's Visitors Bur., Honolulu, Edn. Commn. of States, Honolulu, Hawaii Visitors Bur., 1983-85; trustee U. Hawaii Found., 1984-86, Hawaii Pacific Coll., Honolulu; bd. govs. East West Ctr., 2003—. Republican. Episcopalian. Avocation: golf. Home: 784 Elepaio St Honolulu HI 96816-4710 E-mail: pfsaiki@cs.com.

SAILA, COLLEEN G., special education educator; b. Westerly, Ri, Feb. 15, 1970; d. Paul and Rose Harkins Gencarella; m. Karl Erik Saila, July 5, 1997; children: Connor Kalervo, Kevin Paul. BS in Elem. Edn., St. Bonaventure U., NY, 1992; MS in Spl. Edn., SUNY, Albany, 1993. Nat. bd. cert. tchr. Nat. Bd. Profl. Tchr. Stds., 2002. Spl. edn. tchr. Norwich Pub. Schs., Conn., 1993—2001, Westerly Pub. Schs., 2001—. I-plan scorer State Dept. Edn., Providence, 2001—03; ednl. tutor Dunn's Corners Sch., Westerly, 2002—, evaluation team chairperson, 2004—; chairperson Sch. Improvement Team, Westerly, 2005—. Grantee, Bell Grant, 1998. Democrat. Roman Catholic. Avocations: running, hiking, reading, travel. Home: 8 Matarese Hills Westerly RI 02891 Office: Dunns Corners School 8 1/2 Plateau Rd Westerly RI 02891 Office Phone: 401-348-2321. Personal E-mail: csaila@westerly.k12.ri.us.

SAINCLIVIER, ANNAMARIA TAMBONE, elementary school educator; b. Taranto, Italy, Jan. 1, 1978; d. Michele and Rosa Tambone; m. Frederic Julien Sainclivier. BA in English and Italian, Rutgers U., New Brunswick, N.J., 2000; JD, Seton Hall U., Newark, N.J., 2004. Assoc. Lexis Nexis, Newark, 2001—03; rsch. asst. Sch. Law Seton Hall U., 2003—04; tchr. literature Bergen Cath. H.S., Oradell, NJ, 2004—. Coach, moderator mock trial Bergen Cath. H.S., 2004—, tchr. music theory, 2004—05. Contbr. poems to anthologies. Avocations: guitar, piano, clarinet, writing, running.

SAINT, EVA MARIE, actress; b. Newark, July 4, 1924; d. John Merle and Eva Marie (Rice) S.; m. Jeffrey Hayden, Oct. 28, 1951; children: Darrell, Laurette. BA, DFA, Bowling Green State U., 1946; student, Actors Studio, 1950. Appeared in various radio and TV dramatic shows, N.Y.C., 1947—; theater roles include The Trip to Bountiful, 1953 (Outer Circle Critics award, N.Y. Drama Critics award 1953), The Rainmaker, 1953, Winesburg, Ohio, 1970, The Lincoln Mask, 1972, Summer and Smoke, 1973, Desire Under the Elms, 1974, The Fatal Weakness, 1976, Candida, 1977, Mr. Roberts, First Monday in October, 1979, Duet for One, 1982-83, The Country Girl, 1986 (L.A. Dramalogue award 1986), Death of a Salesman, 1994, Love Letters, 1994-2005, On the Divide, 1994-2004, Touch the Names, 2005; appeared in films On the Waterfront, 1954 (Acad. Award for best supporting actress 1955), That Certain Feeling, 1956, Raintree Country, 1957, A Hatful of Rain, 1957, North by Northwest, 1959, Exodus, 1961, All Fall Down, 1962, 36 Hours, 1963, The Sandpiper, 1964, The Russians are Coming, The Russians are Coming!, 1965, Grand Prix, 1966, The Stalking Moon, 1969, Loving, 1970, Cancel My Reservation, 1972, Nothing in Common, 1986, Mariette in Ecstacy, 1995, I Dreamed of Africa, 2000, Because of Winn-Dixie, 2005, Don't Come Knocking, 2005, (feature film) Superman Returns, 2006; TV dramas include The Macahans, 1976 (Emmy nom.), The Fatal Weakness, 1976, Taxi!!, 1978 (Emmy nom.), A Christmas to Remember, 1978, When Hell Was in Season, 1980, The Curse of King Tut's Tomb, The Best Little Girl in the World, 1981, Splendor in the Grass, 1981, Love Leads the Way, 1983, Jane Doe, 1983, Fatal Vision, 1984, The Last Days of Patton, 1986, A Year in the Life, 1986, Breaking Home Times, 1987, I'll Be Home for Christmas, 1988, Voyage of Terror: The Achille Lauro Affair, 1990, People Like Us, 1990 (Emmy award 1990), Palomino, 1991, Kiss of the Killer, ABC, 1992, My Antonia, 1994, After Jimmy, 1996, Time to Say Goodbye, 1997, Titanic, 1997; (documentary) Primary Colors: The Story of Corita, 1991; (with Bill Moyers) Children in America's Schools, 1997, Papa's Angels, 2000, Open House, TV-CBS, 2003; prodr. Fences, 2006.

ST. AMAND, JANET G., government relations lawyer; b. N.Y.C., Feb. 27, 1953; d. Leonard Marsh and Glenda Weaver St. A.; children: Nikolai, Peter. BA, Arcadia U., 1975; JD, Georgetown U., 1980. Bar: D.C. 1981, N.Y. 1989. Legis. counsel Congressman Jim Coyne, Washington, 1981-83, Congressman Tom Carper, Washington, 1983-85, Sen. John Heinz, Washington, 1985-86, Am. Bankers Assn., Washington, 1986-87; asst. resident counsel J.P. Morgan, N.Y.C., 1987-90; counsel Fin. Svcs. Coun., Washington, 1990-93; fed. dir., counsel HSBC N.Am. (formerly Household Internat.), Washington, 1993—. Mem. Leadership Coun., Salvation Army, 1994—; trustee Arcadia U. (formerly Beaver Coll.), Glenside, Pa., 1999-2002, alumni bd. dirs., 1995-2002; trustee Women in Housing and Fin. Found.; mem. Tax Coalition, 1999—. Recipient Mary Armstrong Wolf award Arcadia U., 1999. Mem. Women in Housing & Fin. (bd. dirs. 1991-95, mem. of yr. 1993), Univ. Club, Columbia Country Club, Exchequer Club, Tax Coalition. Presbyterian. Avocations: reading, travel, jogging, politics. Home: 5423 33rd St NW Washington DC 20015 Office: HSBC NAm 1401 I St NW # 520 Washington DC 20005 E-mail: janet.g.st.amand@us.hsbc.com.

ST. CLAIR, GLORIANA STRANGE, librarian, dean; b. Tonkawa, Okla., Dec. 13, 1939; d. Glen Leroy and Doris Mildred (Furber) Strange. BA in English, U. Okla., 1962, PhD in Literature, 1970; MLS, U. Calif., Berkeley, 1963; MBA in Mgmt., U. Tex., San Antonio, 1980. Rsch. asst. U. Calif., Berkeley, 1962-63, asst. libr., 1963-65; cataloguer U. Okla., Norman, 1965-68; supervising libr. San Antonio Pub. Libr., 1980-84; head acquisitions divsn. Tex. A&M U. Librs., College Station, 1984-87, humanities bibliographer, 1985, head pers. ops., 1986; asst. dir. tech. automation and adminstrv. svc. Kerr Libr., Oreg. State U., Corvallis, 1987-90; assoc. dean, head info. access svcs. Pa. State U. Librs., University Park, 1990-98; dean univ. libr. Carnegie Mellon U., Pitts., 1998—. Editor Coll. & Rsch. Librs., 1990-96, Jour. Academic Librarianship, 1996—. Bd. dirs. Towers Condo. Bd., State College, 1993-94; mem. vestry, mem. book discussion group St. Andrew's Episcopal Ch., State College, 1991-98; examiner Pa. Quality Leadership, 1994. Sr. fellow UCLA, 1991. Mem. Assn. Coll. and Rsch. Librs. (chair editl. adv. bd. 1990-96). Home: 154 N Bellefield Ave Apt 45 Pittsburgh PA 15213-2640 Office: Univ Librs Carnegie Mellon U 4909 Frew St Pittsburgh PA 15213-3890 Office Fax: 412-268-2793.*

ST. CLAIR, JANE ELIZABETH, health science association administrator, consultant; b. Concord, Mass., Aug. 15, 1944; d. James F. and Mary E. (Clyne) Connell. BA, Salem State Coll., 1969; MPH, Columbia U., N.Y.C., 1990. Field rep., safety program Am. Red Cross of Greater N.Y., 1971-72; program dir. Bronx Community Coll., N.Y., 1973-75; dir. edn. Council N.Y.C., Inc., 1975-77, asst. exec. dir., 1978; exec. dir. Regional Emergency Med. Services, N.Y., 1979-91; dir. Peace Corps, Kenya, 1991-94, Gulfcoast South Area Health Edn. Ctr., Sarasota, Fla., 1995—96; cons. Dept. Anesthesiology Boston Med. Ctr., 1996—99; exec. dir. Mid/Upper Cape Cmty. Health Ctr., Hyannis, Mass., 2000—02; cons. Coll. Medicine Charles Drew U. Medicine and Sci., L.A., Calif., 2002—. Adjunct asst. prof., Hunter Coll. N.Y., 1973-91. Contbr. articles to profl. jours. Mem. Emergency Cardic Care Com. N.Y., Heart Assn., Am. Soc. Safety Engrs., Profl. Edn. Com., Am. Red Cross, First Aid Com. Home: 182 Thacher Shore Rd Yarmouth Port MA 02675-1130 E-mail: jstclair@earthlink.net.

ST. CLAIR, MARY ANN WALKER, secondary school educator, small business owner; d. Larry K. Walker and Margaret A. Bye; m. Mark Edward St. Clair, July 11, 1987; 1 child, Kelsey; 1 child, Kallie. EdB in History and Psychology, Iowa State U., Ames, 1987; MS, William Woods U., Fulton, Mo., 2004. Cert. sch. adminstr. Mo. Tchr. Hannibal Pub. Schs., Mo., 1987—; owner Quixtar, Hannibal, 1993—. Presenter in field. Sunday sch. tchr. Arch Meth., Hannibal, Mo., 2000. Republican. Methodist. Avocations: athletics, coaching volleyball, travel. Office: Hannibal Pub Schs 4500 McMasters Hannibal MO 63401 Business E-Mail: mstclair@hannibal.k12.mo.us.

ST. CLAIR, MIRIAM MACLEOD, biology professor; b. Pitts., Mar. 19, 1951; d. George Stuart and Patricia Ryan Macleod; m. Munsell Winfield St. Clair, June 8, 1991. BS in Natural Sci., U. Pitts., 1982; MS in Molecular Biology, John Hopkins U., Balt., 1994; MS in Forensic Toxicology, U. Fla., Gainesville, 2006. Rsch. asst. U. Pitts., 1980—82; rsch. asst., Med. Sch. U. Tex., Houston, 1982—86, 1987—91, rsch. asst., M.D. Anderson, 1986—87; biologist NIH, Bethesda, Md., 1994—95; instr. No. Va. C.C., Woodridge, Va., 1999—. LAS coord. George Mason U., Fairfax, Va., 2001—03. Vol. Castle Cat Rescue, Fairfax, 2003—. Nominee Faculty of Yr., No. Va. CC Alumni Fedn., 2005, 2006; recipient Achievement award, NIH, 1995, Honor award, 1995. Mem.: AAUW, Am. Assn. Women in Sci. Avocations: painting, sculpting, cooking, crocheting. Home: 6526 Byrnes Dr Mc Lean VA 22101 Office: No Va Cmty Coll 15200 Neabsco Mills Rd Woodbridge VA 22191 Office Phone: 703-878-5652. Business E-Mail: mstclair@nvcc.edu.

ST. GEORGE, ELAINE, art educator; b. Wilkes Barre, Pa., Mar. 11, 1948; d. John and Hilda St. George; m. Jeffrey Michael Roblyer (div.); children: Ginevra Gwen Wilson, Julia Gia Roblyer. BFA, U. Miami, 1970, MEd, 1972; MFA, U. NC, 1972. Prof. Broward CC, Darie, Fla., 1979—99; art tchr. Broward County Sch. Bd., Ft. Lauderdale, Fla., 1988—92; Prof. Palm Beach CC, Lakworth, Fla., 1999—. Restoration appraiser Harvey Brown Ins. Agy., Delray Beach, Fla., 2004—. Paintings, original printmaking, pastel drawings, one-woman shows include Bailey Hall Broward CC, 1966. Mem.: Broward Ctr. Performing Arts, NYC Mus. Modern Art, Boca Raton Mus. Art, Ft. Lauderdale Mus. Art. Republican. Avocations: deep sea diving, tennis, horseback riding. Home and Office: 5095 Van Buren Rd Delray Beach FL 33484

ST. GEORGE, JUDITH ALEXANDER, writer; b. Westfield, N.J., Feb. 26, 1931; d. John Heald and Edna (Perkins) Alexander; m. David St. George, June 5, 1954; children: Peter, James, Philip, Sarah Anne. BA, Smith Coll., 1952. Author: Turncoat Winter, Rebel Spring, 1970, The Girl with Spunk, 1975, By George, Bloomers!, 1976, The Chinese Puzzle of Shag Island, 1976, The Shad Are Running, 1977, The Shadow of the Shaman, 1977, The Halo Wind, 1978, The Halloween Pumpkin Smasher, 1978, Mystery at St. Martin's, 1979, The Amazing Voyage of the New Orleans, 1980, Haunted, 1980, Call Me Margo, 1981, The Mysterious Girl in the Garden, 1981, The Brooklyn Bridge: They Said It Couldn't Be Built, 1982 (Am. Book award, N.Y. Acad. of Sci. award), Do You See What I See?, 1982, In The Shadow of the Bear, 1983, What's Happening to My Junior Year?, 1983, Who's Scared? Not Me!, 1984, The Mount Rushmore, 1985 (Christopher award), Panama Canal: Gateway to the World, 1989 (Golden Kite award), The White House,

1990, Mason and Dixon's Line of Fire, 1991, Dear Dr. Bell.Your Friend Helen Keller, 1992, Crazy Horse, 1994, To See With the Heart: The Life of Sitting Bull, 1996, Betsy Ross: Patriot of Philadelphia, 1997 (N.Y. Sons of the Am. Revolution award), Sacagawea, 1997, In the Line of Fire: President's Lives at Stake, 1999, So You Want To Be President?, 2001 (Caldecott medal, 2001), John and Abigail Adams: An American Love Story, 2001, So You Want to be an Inventor?, 2002, You're On Your Way, Teddy Roosevelt, 2004, Take the Lead George Washington, 2005, So You Want to Be an Explorer?, 2005, Take the Lead. George Washington, 2005;: The Journey of the One and Only Declaration of Independence, 2005, So You Want to be an Explorer?, 2005, Haunted, 2005. Adv. coun. on children's lit. Rutgers U., 1977-94; chmn. ednl. com. Bklyn. Bridge Centennial Commn., 1981-83; tchr. creative writing York Correctional Instn., Niantic, Conn. Mem. Soc. Children's Book Writers, Author's Guild. Episcopalian. Avocations: tennis, hiking, travel. Home: 8 Binney Rd Old Lyme CT 06371-1445

ST. GERMAIN, CAROL ANN, secondary educator; b. Lowell, Mass., Sept. 28, 1941; d. Thomas E. and Angela (Mullen) Connolly; m. Thomas A. St. Germain, Aug. 22, 1964; children: Elizabeth, Thomas A. Jr., Suzanne, Daniel. BA in Math., Merrimack Coll., North Andover, Mass., 1963; grad. degree, U. Mass.-Lowell, 1993. Tchr. math. Dracut Jr. HS, Mass., 1963-65, Westford Acad., Mass., 1983-84, John Wynn Mid. Sch., Tewksbury, 1992—94, Tewksbury Meml. HS, Mass., 1985-92, 1994—97. Mem. bd. Mass Soc. for the Prevention of Cruelty to Children, Merimack Valley. Mem. adv. bd. Camp Paul for Handicapped, Chelmsford, Mass., 1974—; tchr. religion St. Mary's Ch., Chelmsford, 1965-80, vol. blood program ARC, Lowell, Mass., 1970-90. Mem. Mass. Tchrs. Assn., Tewksbury Tchrs. Assn. Avocations: hiking, reading, gardening.

ST. GERMAIN, JEAN MARY, medical physicist; b. N.Y.C. BS, Marymount Manhattan Coll., N.Y.C.; MS, Rutgers U. Cert. Am. Bd. Health Physics; lic. med. physicist, N.Y.; cert. Am. Bd. Med. Physics. USPHS fellow radiol. health Rutgers U., New Brunswick, NJ; fellow dept. med. physics Meml. Hosp., N.Y.C.; asst. physicist Cornell U. Med. Coll., N.Y.C., 1968—71, instr. radiology (physics), 1971—78, clin. asst. prof., 1979—94; assoc. attending physicist Meml. Sloan-Kettering Cancer Ctr., 1993—2006, attending physicist, 2006—. Vice chair Am. Bd. Med. Physics, 2004—, chair panel med. health physics, 1993—2000; cons. in field. Author: The Nurse and Radiotherapy, 1978; contbr. articles, chpts. to med. jours Fellow: Health Physics Soc. (Failla Meml. lectr. 1999, pres. N.Y. chpt., pres. med. health physics sect.), Am. Assn. Physicists in Medicine (sec., bd. dirs.); mem.: Nat. Soc. Arts and Letters (regional dir., pres. N.Y. chpt., nat. music chair, nat. career awards chair), Radiol. and Med. Physics Soc. N.Y. (past pres.), Am. Acad. Health Physics (treas. 1996—99), Am. Inst. Physics (govs. bd.), Iota Sigma Pi (treas., pres. V chpt.). Office: 1275 York Ave New York NY 10021-6007

ST. GERMAIN, SHARON MARIE, writer; b. Mpls., Nov. 14, 1938; d. John Benjamin and Esther Lenoria Vandermyde; m. Donald Joseph St. Germain, June 17, 1961; children: Kim, Michael, Beth. BE, Hamline Univ., St. Paul, Minn., 1960. Co-dir. Writers Unlimited, White Bear Lake, Minn., 1969—; writing tchr. Hamline Univ., St. Paul, 1978—84, Mpls. Cmy. & Tech. Coll., Mpls., 1981—, Century Coll., White Bear Lake, Minn., 1994—, Cmty. Edn. programs, Mpls., St. Paul, Rochester Cmty. Edn., Minn., 1997—, St. Cloud Cmty. Edn., Minn., 1997—. Writer-in -the-sch. Mid. Sch., Mpls., St. Paul, 1980—85; faculty presenter Midwest Writers Conf., River Falls, Wis., 1979; guest spkr. pub. sch., libr. and writing organizations, Mpls., St. Paul, 1980—. Author: (childrens book) The Terrible Fight, 1990, several children's books; contbr. mag. story Boys' Life, 1975, sport series book Highlights for Children, 1975, articles to numerous profl. jours. Mem.: So. of Children's Book Writers and Illustrators, Writers Unlimited, World Wildlife Fund, Minn. Sr. Fedn., Am. Assn. of Retired People. Avocations: reading, travel, bicycling, swimming. Home: 2555 Upper Afton Rd Maplewood MN 55119 E-mail: donstg@netzero.com.

ST. HILAIRE, CAROLINE, legislator; b. Longueuil Pierre-Boucher, Can., Nov. 16, 1969; children: Etienne, Louis-Félix. BA in Adminstrn., U. Québec, 1993. With Soc. du droit de reproduction des auteurs, compositeurs et éditeurs du Can.; M.P. for Bloc Quebecois House of Commons, spokesperson for transports. Founder Soc. de Promotion Pour La Releve Musicale de l'espace Francophone. Avocation: competitive figure skating. Office: House of Commons 209 Justice Bldg Ottawa ON Canada K1A 0A6

ST. JEAN, CATHERINE AVERY, advertising executive; b. Dubuque, Iowa, Oct. 10, 1950; d. Harvey Dale and Mary Theresa (Heinz) Avery; m. Kenneth R. St. Jean, June 24, 1978 (div. May 1983); m. Paul J. Frahm, Mar. 7, 1987; children: Ian, Christian. BA in Comm., Loyola U., Chgo., 1977. Video editor Needham, Harper & Steers, Chgo., 1978, creative coord., 1979—80; presentations svcs. mgr. Needham, Harper & Steers/USA, Chgo., 1980—82; v.p., corp. dir. comm. svcs. Needham, HarperWorldwide, Inc., NYC, 1982, v.p., 1983, v.p., asst. dir. creative svcs., 1985—86; v.p., dir. creative svcs. DDB Needham Worldwide, 1986—91; sr. v.p., dir. creative svcs. Lintas, NYC, 1991—. Author (brochure): How to Keep the Heart in NY, Tri-State United Way, 1982 (Merit award, 1982, Bronze medal NY Internat. Film and TV Festival, 84). Chmn., fundraiser for homeless Cannes Gala at Lincoln Ctr., 1986—. Recipient Crystal Prism award, Am. Advt. Fedn, 1987, Women Achievers award, WYCA, 1990. Mem.: Advt. Women in NY (chmn. 1984, bd. dirs. 1985—86, 2d v.p. 1987, 1990, Pres.'s award 1990, Addy award). Avocations: photography, writing. Office: Lintas: N Y 1 Dag Hammarskjold Plz Fl 2 New York NY 10017-2279

ST. JOHN, JULIE, mortgage company executive; BA in English, U. Mich.; MBA, Fla. State U. CPA, Fla. Prin. Arthur Young & Co.; v.p. info. systems Residence Inn divsn. Marriott; joined Fannie Mae, Washington, 1990, sr. v.p. mortgage bus. tech., now exec. v.p., chief info. officer enterprise systems and ops. divsn. Mem. exec. bd. Boys & Girls Club of Greater Washington. Named one of Premier 100 IT Leaders, Computerworld, 2005. Mem.: AICPA, Women of Washington, Women in Housing and Fin. Office: Fannie Mae 3900 Wisconsin Ave NW Washington DC 20016-2892*

ST. JOHN, MARGIE See GABRIELE, MARGUERITE

ST. JOHN, MARIA ANN, nurse anesthetist; b. Rochester, Pa., Dec. 15, 1953; d. James Edward and Evelyn Marie (Sayers) St. J.; m. Paul David Dworsky, Aug. 19, 1978 (div. Dec. 13, 1991); children: Lauren Marie Dworsky, Michael David Dworsky. BSN, U. Pitts., 1975; cert. reg. nurse anesthetist, U. Health Ctr. Pitts. Sch. Anesthesia for Nurses, 1984. Advanced RN practitioner Fla., Ohio; cert. RN anesthetist, Pa., Ohio, N.C., Ky. Nurse Presbyn. U. Hosp., Pitts., 1975-77, VA Hosp., Pitts., 1977-82; nurse anesthetist Anesthesia Assocs. of Hollywood, Fla., 1984-87, North Hills Anesthesia Assocs., Pitts., 1987-98, Queen City Anesthesiologists, Inc., Cin., 1998—. Vol. tchr. art history, fundraiser St. Alexis Sch., Wexford, Pa., 1991-97, recording sec. PT6 Bd., 1996-97, v.p. PT6 Bd., 1997-98; mem. Cranberry Twp. Athletic Assn., 1991-98, Oak Hills PTA, Cin., 1998-99, Oak Hills Athletic Boosters, 1999, PTG Springmeyer Sch. and Bridgetown Jr. H.S., Cinn., 1998-99, PTG and Athletic Boosters, Bridgetown Middle Sch., 1999—. Recipient scholarship March of Dimes, Beaver County, Pa., 1971, Pitt. scholarship, 1971-75. Mem. DAR, Am. Assn. Nurse Anesthetists, Pa. Assn. Nurse Anesthetists, Ohio Assn. Nurse Anesthetists, Fla. Assn. Nurse Anesthetists, Ky. Nurse Anesthetists, N.C. Nurse Anesthetists. Avocations: playing piano, reading, travel, school volunteering, swimming. Home: 6073 Werk Rd Cincinnati OH 45248-4043

ST. JOHN, TERRI, secondary school educator; b. Battle Creek, Mich., July 17, 1953; d. Donald George and Virginia Beth Kelley. AA, Kellogg CC, 1975; BA, U. Central Fla., 1981; MA in Edn., U. Sarasota, 1995, EdD, 2001. Cert. tchr. Fla. Tchr., debate coach Forest Hill HS, West Palm Beach, Fla., 1983—85; tchr., theatre dir. Lake Weir HS, Ocala, Fla., 1985—89; tchr., debate coach Lake Highland Prep Sch., Orlando, Fla., 1991—97, Sarasota (Fla.) HS, 1997—. Presenter in field. Supporter St. Labre Indian Sch., Ariz., 2001—, Mayo Clinic Rsch., Minn., 2002—. Named Diamond Coach, Nat. Forensic League, 2005, Regional Coach of Yr., Fla. Forensic League Region III, 2005. Mem.: ASCD, Fla. Forensic League (v.p. ops. 2004—, 2d v.p. 2000—, mem. com. 2003—, named Region III Coach of Yr. 2005, 2006, named State Coach of Yr. 2006), Cath. Forensic League, Fla. Comm. Assn., Nat. Comm. Assn., Nat. Coun. Tchrs. English. Avocations: movies, golf, reading, theater. Office: Sarasota HS 1000 S Sch Ave Sarasota FL 34237 Business E-Mail: terri_st_john@sarasota.k12.fl.us.

ST. JULIEN, THAIS MARY, soprano, musician; d. George W. St. Julien Jr. and Rosemary Gloria Bourda. Pvt. vocal studies, Charles Paddock, New Orleans, 1973—81, Virginia Mac Watters, Bloomington, Ind., 1978—81, Norma Newton, Houston, 1981—88, Andrea von Ramm, New Orleans, 1986; pvt. recorder studies, Milton G. Scheuermann, Jr., 1975—80; apprentice, Des Moines Metro Opera Festival, Indianola, Iowa, 1987; Opera Workshop, Loyola U., New Orleans, 1977—78; Baroque performance practice, Skip Sempe, 1995. Asst. season ticket sales mgr. New Orleans Opera Guild, 1974—77; ensemble singer New Orleans Musica da Camera, 1974—78, principle vocal soloist, 1978—, asst. music dir., 1980—91, asst. instrument builder, 1981—, co-artistic dir., 1991—, founder/dir. Vox Feminae (women's vocal ensemble), 1994—, chief adminstr., 1999—; mgr. single ticket sales New Orleans Philharm. Orch., 1977—79; founder, soloist Banquette Opera, New Orleans, 1979—84; founding mem., calligrapher Scriptease Calligraphy, New Orleans, 1980—92; founding mem., soloist Ezcudantza (voice/guitar duo), New Orleans, 1982—85; part- time libr. technician Tulane U., Maxwell Music Libr., New Orleans, 1989—2005. Musical advisor Hermann Grima Ho. Mus., New Orleans, 1980—84; sec., adv. bd. Entergy Arts Bus. Ctr., New Orleans, 1997—2002; adv. bd. New Orleans Internat. Music Colloquium, 1998—2001; musical advisor Musica Antiqua, Albany, Oreg., 1998—2005; founding dir. music series Belle Alliance Hist. Plantation, Donaldsonville, La., 2002—; bd. pres. New Orleans Musica da Camera, New Orleans; instr. vocal masterclass S.W. Mo. State U.; presenter in field; founding artistic dir. Thursdays at Twilight Concert Series New Orleans Bot. Garden, 2003—. Musician (co-dir.): (albums) Satires, Desires and Excesses: Songs from the Carmina Burana, Natus Est: A Christmas Celebration, The Cross of Red: Music of Love and War from the Time of the Crusades, Maiden, Mother, Muse: The Women of the Cantigas of Alfonso X, Les Motets d'Arras: Songs and Dances of Medieval Arras, The Play of Robin and Marion, A Christmas Offering (Early Music Am./Millenium of Music Nat. Radio Competition, 1996), Natus Est, 1994, 1995, Now Make We Mirthe; musician: (co-dir., host) Alone of All Her Sex; musician: A Voice Still Heard, Early Jewish Music, (radio spl.) Praises from the Heart, Tristan et Iseult, on Cathedral, Court and Countryside Series, 1981; musician: (dir.) (albums) Medee; musician: Moonrise, Circles, Tristan et Iseult, on Cathedral, Court and Countryside Series, 1982, The Garden of Love; hist. music adv. (films) Interview with the Vampire; musician: Creole Cameos: Music of New Orleans Creoles of Color, Performances throughout the U.S.; prodr.(co-host): Continuum-WWNO2, Continuum; editor, contbr.: newsletter The Cypher (Am. Guild Organists, New Orleans); contbr. articles to profl. jours. Founding mem., pres. bd. dirs. St. Charles Ave. Com., New Orleans, 1972—75. Named Vis. Artist in Residence with Musica da Camera, The Hist. Nat. Shrine of Our Lady of Prompt Succor, New Orleans, 1989—; recipient Lifetime Achievement award, Gambit Newspaper, Tribute to the Classical Arts, 1997, Pioneer in Preservation Honor award, Hist. Dist. Landmarks Commn., 1997, Cert. of Appreciation in Thankfulness for Contributions to the City, City of New Orleans, 2001. Mem.: Soc. Am. Magicians (v.p. local assembly), La. Partnership for the Arts, Southeastern Medieval Assn., Entergy Arts Bus. Ctr., Am. Musicological Soc., Knights of Slights, Internat. Brotherhood Magicians (pres. local ring), Mensa. Avocations: magic, reading, drawing, photography. Office: New Orleans Musica da Camera 1035 Eleonore St New Orleans LA 70115 Business E-Mail: mdc@nomdc.org.

ST. MARIE, SATENIG, writer; b. Brockton, Mass., June 2, 1927; d. Harry and Mary K. Sahjian; m. Gerald L. St. Marie, Dec. 26, 1959. BS, Simmons Coll., Boston, 1949; MA, Columbia U., 1959; LL.D. (hon.), N.D. State U., 1976. Extension home economist U. Mass. Extension Service, 1949-52, U. Conn. Extension Service, 1953-56; with J.C. Penney Co., Inc., 1959-87, mgr. endl. and consumer relations, 1967-73, dir. consumer affairs, 1973-87, div. v.p., 1974-87. Dir. Nat. Reins. Co.; mem. U.S. Metric Bd. Author: Homes Are For People, 1973, Romantic Victorian Weddings: Then and Now, 1992; pub. J.C. Penney Consumer Edn. Services, 1981-87; lifestyles editor: Victorian Homes Mag., 1987—. Mem. Am. Home Econs. Assn. (past pres.), Antiques Dealers Assn. Am. (exec. dir. 1987—). Office: PO Box 335 Greens Farms CT 06436-0335

ST. MARTIN, CHARLOTTE, trade association administrator; b. 1945; BS, U. North Tex., 1967. Office mgr. to rep. James M. Collins U.S. Ho. of Reps., 1970; mgr. sales and catering The Fairmount Dallas, 1971—77; dir. sales and mktg. Loews Anatole Hotel, Loews Corp., 1977—82, pres., CEO, 1989—95; regional v.p. sales and mktg. Loews Hotels, Loews Corp., 1982—87, exec. v.p. sales and mktg., 1996—2005; pres. Dallas Convention and Visitors Bur., 1987—89; pres., CEO Charlotte St. Martin Enterprises, 2005—06; exec. dir. League of Am. Theatres and Producers, Inc., 2006—. Office: League Am Theatres and Producers Inc 226 W 47th St New York NY 10036-1487 Office Phone: 212-764-1122. Office Fax: 212-398-2409. E-mail: league@broadway.org.*

ST. MARTIN, JO-MARIE, lawyer; b. Feb. 10, 1960; BS, Mary Washington Coll., 1982; JD, Univ. Tenn., 1985. Atty. U.S. Dept. Labor, 1985—86; minority edn. counsel Com. Edn. & Workforce, U.S. Ho. Rep., Washington, 1986—92, parliamentary counsel, 1995—98, gen. counsel, 1998—. Office: Com on Edn and Workforce Rm 2181 Rayburn Ho Office Bldg Washington DC 20515-6100

ST. ONGE, MARY FRANCES BURKETT, retired art education educator; b. Indiana, Pa., Feb. 24, 1939; d. George Kelly and Bertha (Ness) Burkett; m. Peter St. Onge, May 20, 1972; 1 child, Anne. BS in Art Edn., Indiana U. Pa., 1961; MEd in Art Edn., U. Pitts., 1964; PhD in Art Edn., Pa. State U., 1977. Cert. K-12 art tchr., Pa. Tchr. art S.W. Butler Sch. Dist., Evans City, Pa., 1961-64, Penn Hills (Pa.) Sch. Dist., 1964-65; grad. asst. U. Pitts., 1965; asst. prof. Kutztown U. Pa., 1966-72, assoc. prof., 1972-77, mem. grad. faculty, 1975—, prof., 1977—, chmn. dept. art edn. and crafts, 1985—99. Recipient numerous grants. Mem. ASCD, Nat. Art Edn. Assn., Pa. Art Edn. Assn. (co-edditor newsletter 1986-92, bd. dirs. 1986-92, Outstanding Art Educator award 1991). Avocations: photography, gardening. Personal E-mail: ongem@hotmail.com.

SAINT-OUEN LEUNG, BRIGITTE, art dealer, consultant; arrived in U.S., 1993; d. Rene-Gerard Saint-Ouen and Christiane; m. John Leung, May 31, 1999. BA of Bus., Paris VIII, 1984; degree in art history, The Louvre, Paris, 1993. Mktg. dir. Wally Findlay, Paris, 1989—93; mktg. dir., art cons. Wally Findlay Galleries, N.Y.C., 1993—2000; pres., owner Gramercy 32 Fine Arts, N.Y.C., 2000—; art, art cons. 19th Century to Outsider and Photography, European and Am. artists. Office: Gramercy 32 Fine Arts Ste 15 D-B 32 Gramercy Park S New York NY 10003 Office Phone: 212-780-0932. E-mail: gramercy@32finearts.com, infowhowho@32finearts.com.

ST. PIERRE, MARY SHARON, literature educator; b. Hamilton, N.Y., Aug. 27, 1964; d. Sigmund Ernest Urben and Sharon Ruth Stratton; m. David Michael St. Pierre, Oct. 25, 1986; children: Christopher, Katherine. Student, SUNY Oneonta, 1985; AS, Cazenovia Coll., N.Y., 1985; BS, SUNY Cortland, 1987. Tchr. asst. Kindergarten Stockbridge Valley Sch., NY, 1991—92; tchr. 3d grade Hamilton Ctrl. Sch., 1992—93; tchr., lang. mid. sch. and HS New Life Christian Sch., Hamilton, 1999—2006, student adviser student coun., 2001—06. Vol. libr. New Woodstock Free Libr., NY, 2002—, vol. children's summer program, 2005, 06. Avocations: gardening, reading, travel.

SAIYED, HUMAIRA, psychiatrist, director; arrived in U.S., 1981; d. Hamid and Zubeda; m. Shahid Saiyed, Aug. 21, 1987; children: Natasha, Rehan. Pre-med, St. Francis Coll., India; MBBS, Ghandhi Med. Coll., India; MD, Loyola U. Med. Ctr., Maywood, Ill. Cert. in psychiatry Am. Bd. Psychiatry and Neurology, 1998. Dir. Riverside Psychiatry and Counseling, Ill., 1988—98, Midwest Psychiatry and Counseling, 1998—; clin. dir. Riveredge Hosp., Forest Park, 1998—; clin. faculty Loyola U. Med. Ctr., Maywood, 1998—; med. dir. Good Samaritan Hosp., Downers Grove, 2005—. Named one of Am.'s Top 100 Psychiatrists, Consumer Rsch. Coun. Am., 2005. Mem.: Am. Psychiatry Assn. Avocations: tennis, golf, exercise, music, interior decorating. Office: Riveredge Hosp 8311 W Roosevelt Rd Forest Park IL 60130 Office Phone: 630-915-1410.

SAIYED, SEEMA, education educator, researcher; b. Karachi, Pakistan, Jan. 1, 1962; d. Saiyed Ahmed and Nafeesa Khatoon; m. Alif Hussain Siddiqui, Sept. 14, 1983; children: Alif Hussain, Adeel Hussain. BS (hons.), Karachi U., Pakistan, 1987, MS, 1988, U. of Tex., Richardson, 2004. Lectr. Shi Khalifa Bui Zayed Arab Pakistani Coll., Abu Dhabi, United Arab Emirates, 1995—2000; tchg. asst. U. Tex., Richardson, 2002—04, U. North Tex., Denton, 2002—. Office: Univ North Tex Chemistry Dept PO Box 305070 Denton TX 76203-5070

SAIZAN, PAULA THERESA, business consultant; b. New Orleans, Sept. 12, 1947; d. Paul Morine and Hattie Mae (Hayes) Saizan; m. George H. Smith, May 26, 1973 (div. July 1976). BS in Acctg. summa cum laude, Xavier U., 1969. CPA Tex. Sys. engr. IBM, New Orleans, 1969—71; acct., then sr. acct. Shell Oil Co., Houston, 1971—76, sr. fin. analyst, 1976—77, fin. rep., 1977—79, corp. auditor, 1979—81, treasury rep., 1981—82, sr. treasury rep., 1982—86; asst. treas. Shell Credit Inc., Shell Leasing Co., Shell Fin. Co., Houston, 1986—88, sr. pub. affairs rep., 1988—89, sr. staff pub. affairs rep., 1990—91, program mgr., 1991—96, sr. program mgr., 1996—97, mgr. constituent rels. and edn. support, 1997—2000, mgr. nat. and cmty. outreach, 2000—03, mgr. stakeholder mgmt., 2003—04, sr. advisor corp. affairs, 2005; pres. PTBS, Inc., Houston, 2006—. Bd. dirs. Greater Houston Conv. and Visitors Bur., Xavier U.; vice-chair Nat. Coun. Negro Women, Inc.; adv. bd. Sch. Engring, Tex. So. U.; del. White House Conf. on Small Bus., 1995. Mem. AICPA, NAACP (life mem., bd. dirs., trustee spl. contribution fund), Tex. Soc. CPA, Leadership Houston, LWV Houston, Xavier U. Alumni Assn., Nat. Assn. Black Accts., Links, Inc., Nat. Coun. Garden Clubs (life), Nat. Congress Black Women, Alpha Kappa Alpha, Phi Gamma Nu, Kappa Gamma Phi. Roman Catholic. Home: 7601 Oak Fern Houston TX 77040-4407 Office: PTBS Inc Ste 1000 5740 W Little York Rd Houston TX 77091 Business E-Mail: ptbs3@aol.com.

SAKARA, MARILYN JUDITH, retired social worker; b. Youngstown, Ohio, Nov. 21, 1949; d. Michael Joseph and Mary Jane (Makar) S. AB, Youngstown State, 1967-71; MSW, La. State, 1973. Lic. ind. social worker. Social worker Los Lunas (N.Mex.) Hosp. and Tng. Sch., 1977-78, Dept. Human Services, Albuquerque, 1978-79, Santa Fe, 1979-80, Child Devel. Ctr., Santa Fe, 1980-83; social worker supr. Children's Med. Svcs., Santa Fe, 1983-89, program mgr., 1989-99, chief Family Health Bur., 1999—2003, ret., 2003. Pres. Field Rsch., Inc., Santa Fe, 1978-1984; clin. co-dir. N.Mex. Critical Incident Stress Debriefing Team, 1988-90. Mem. NASW, Acad. Cert. Social Workers. Democrat. Avocations: gardening, cooking. Home: 251 Plaza Canada Santa Fe NM 87501-2374

SAKIHARA, SANDRA I., middle school educator; d. Yoshio and Hisayo Fujinaga; m. Lorrin Sakihara, Aug. 5, 1972; children: Mark S, Randi Gm. BA in Math., U. Hawaii, Honolulu, 1971. Math. tchr. Waianae Intermediate Sch., Hawaii, 1971—98, curriculum coord., 1998—2006, registrar, 2004—, design coach, 2000—. Mem. Oahu Jr. Golf Assn., Honolulu, 1992—97. Office: Waianae Intermediate School 85-626 Farrington Hwy Waianae HI 96792 Office Phone: 808-697-7131.

SAKSENA, MARIAN E., lawyer; BA in Polit. Sci., Grinnell Coll., Iowa, 1993; cert. with high distinction, U. Minn. Grad. Sch. Social Work, 1998; JD, U. Minn. Law Sch., Mpls., 1998. Bar: Minn. 1999, White Earth Band of Chippewa Tribal Ct. 2001. Crisis care provider Mpls. Crisis Nursery, 1993—94; child adv. Cornerstone, Bloomington, Minn., 1993—95; summer law clk. Children's Law Ctr. Minn., 1996; Mansfield fellow, summer law clk. Legal Aid Soc. Mpls., 1997; vol. guardian ad litem Ramsey County Guardian ad Litem Prog., 1997—99; law clk. Office of the Hennepin County Atty., 1998—99; atty. Children's Law Ctr. Minn., 1999—2002, Fredrikson & Byron, P.A., 2002—04; assoc. Walling, Berg & Debele, P.A., Mpls., 2004—. Mem. transitioning from adolescence task force Casey Found./VOA, 2000; mem. juvenile rules com. Minn. Supreme Ct., 2001—, mem. guardian ad litem rules com., mem. adoption rules com.; mem. Uniform Parentage Act Task Force, 2001—02, Statewide Adv. Com. on Long-Term Foster Care, 2002. Youth Support Grp. Facilitator Cornerstone, Bloomington, Minn., 1995—96; bd. dirs. Legal Advocacy for West Bank Women, Mpls., 1995—97. Named Rising Star, Minn. Super Lawyers mag., 2006. Mem.: Nat. Assn. Counsel for Children, Children's Justice Initiative (mem. Hennepin County, state wards subcommittee 2002), Minn. State Bar Assn. (chair children & the law sect. 2001—). Office: Walling Berg & Debele PA 121 S 8th St Ste 1100 Minneapolis MN 55402 Office Phone: 612-335-3233. E-mail: Marian.Saksena@wbdlaw.com.*

SALAM, HALIDE, artist, educator; b. Calcutta, India, Sept. 25, 1951; came into U.S., 1971; d. Badi Us and Fatema Reza Salam; m. Timothy Edward Archer, May 31, 1980. BA in Psychology, Chittagong (Bangladesh) Girls Coll., 1965; MA in Painting, N.Mex. Highland U., 1973; PhD in Fine Arts, Tex. Tech. U., 1977. Prof. art Radford (Va.) U., 1977—. Curator non western art Radford (Va.) U., 2000—; curator StudioAmbiance, Blacksburg, Va., 2004—; curator numerous exhbns.; presenter in field. One-woman shows include Danville (Va.) Mus., 1986, Bangladesh Art Acad., 1988, Greensboro (N.C.) Artist's League, 1989, Ircica Yildiz Sarayi, Turkey, 1992, 100 Yil Sanat Galerisi, Turkey, 1992, Izmir Resim Ve Heykel Muzesi, Turkey, 1992, Devlet Guzel Sanatlar Galerisi, Turkey, 1993, Flossie Martin Gallery, Radford, Va., 1993, Art Inst. and Gallery, Salisbury, Md., 1995-96, Internat. Vistion The Gallery, Washington, 1998-2001, Artemisia Galler, Chgo., 2001, Radford (Va.) Art Mus., 2002, Artspace Richmond, Va., 2004, Internat. Visions The Gallery, Washington, 2006; exhibited in group shows at Radford U., 1978, Radford U. Kent Gallery, 1977-87, James Madison U., Harrisonburg, Va., 1979, Roanoke Mus., 1981, 82, Danville Mus. Art, 1982, numerous other nat. and internat. group shows; numerous pub. and pvt. collections; subject numerous revs. Mem. Architecture and Design Assn. (bd. dirs. 1990—). Avocations: travel, hiking, gardening. Home: 335 Deercroft Dr Blacksburg VA 24060-0261 Office: Radford Univ Dept Art Radford VA 24142 Office Phone: 540-831-5032. Business E-Mail: hsalam@radford.edu.

SALAMAN, MAUREEN KENNEDY, writer, nutritionist; b. Glendale, Calif., Apr. 4, 1937; d. Ted and Elena (Peters) Kennedy; 1 child, Sean. With Making Healthy Choices, 1980—; hostess Le Sea Broadcasting, Sky Angel Satellite Worldwide Direct TV with Maureen Kennedy Salaman; pres. Nat. Health Fedn., Monrovia, Calif., 1982—. Cons., lectr., rschr. on cancer rsch. and metabolic medicine, nutrition; lobbyist for freedom of choice. Author: Foods That Heal, Nutrition: The Cancer Answer, 1983, 2d edit., The Diet Bible, The Light at the End of the Refrigerator, All Your Health Questions Answered, Naturally I and II, Achieving Super Immunity, How to Renew You; editor: Nosy News, Health Freedom News, 1982—2004; contbr. articles to profl. jours. Office: Nat Health Fedn PO Box 688 Monrovia CA 91017-0688 also: Maureen Kennedy Salaman Inc 1259 El Camino Real Ste 1500 Menlo Park CA 94025-4227

SALAMON, LINDA BRADLEY, English literature educator; b. Elmira, N.Y., Nov. 20, 1941; d. Grant Ellsworth and Evelyn E. (Ward) Bradley; divorced; children: Michael Lawrence, Timothy Martin. BA, Radcliffe Coll., 1963; MA, Bryn Mawr Coll., 1964, PhD, 1971; Advanced Mgmt. Cert., Harvard U. Bus. Sch., 1978; D.H.L., St. Louis Coll. Pharmacy, 1993. Lectr., adj. asst. prof. Eng., Dartmouth Coll., Hanover, NH, 1967-72; mem. faculty lit. Bennington Coll., Vt., 1974-75; dean students Wells Coll., Aurora, NY, 1975-77; exec. asst. to pres. U. Pa., Phila., 1977-79; assoc. prof. English Washington U., St. Louis, 1979—88, prof., 1988-92, dean Coll. Arts and Scis., 1979-92; prof. English George Washington U., Washington, 1992—. Mem. faculty Bryn Mawr Summer Inst. Women, 1979—99; dean Columbian Coll. Arts and Sci., Washington, 1992—95, interim v.p. acad. affairs, 1995—96. Author, co-editor: Nicholas Hilliard's Art of Limning, 1983; co-author: Integrity in the College Curriculum, 1985; contbr. numerous articles to literary and ednl. jours. Bd. dir. Assn. Am. Colls., vice chmn., 1985, chmn., 1986; bd. dir. Greater St. Louis council Girl Scouts U.S.A.; trustee Coll. Bd., St. Louis Coll. Pharmacy. Fellow Radcliffe Inst., 1973-74, Folger Shakespeare Libr., 1986, NEH Montaigne Inst., 1988, Fulbright fellow, Taiwan, 2003, Ringler fellow Huntington Libr, 2004; Am. Philos. Soc. Penrose grantee, 1974. Mem.: MLA, Cosmos Club, Phi Beta Kappa. Office: George Washington U Dept of Eng Rome Hall 760 801 22D St NW Washington DC 20052-0001 Business E-Mail: lbs@gwu.edu.

SALAMON, RENAY, real estate broker; b. NYC, May 13, 1948; d. Solomon and Mollie (Friedman) Langman; m. Maier Salamon, Aug. 10, 1968; children: Mollie, Jean, Leah, Sharon, Eugene. BA, Hunter Coll., 1969. Licensed real estate borker, N.J. Mgr. office Customode Designs Inc., N.Y.C., 1966-68; co-owner Salamon Dairy Farms, Three Bridges, NJ, 1968-86; assoc. realtor Max. D. Shuman Realty Inc., Flemington, NJ, 1983-85; pres., chief exec. officer Liberty Hill Realty Inc., Flemington, NJ, 1985—. Cons. Illva Saronna Inc. (Illva Group), Edison, N.J. 1985—; real estate devel. joint venture with M.R.F.S. Realty Inc. (Illva Group), 1986—; bd. dirs. Anderson House. Mem. Readington twp. Environ. Commn., Whitehouse Sta., N.J., 1978-87, N.J. Assn. Environ. Commrs., Trenton, 1978—; fundraiser Rutgers Prep. Sch., Somerset, N.J., 1984-95; bd. dirs. Hunterdon County YMCA, 1987-95, Anderson House, 2000-04; mem. N.J.-Israel Commn., 1998—; bd. trustees Rutgers Prep. Sch., 2000—; chair Hunterdon County Bd. Social Svc., 2002, 2004; chair Hunterdon County Health and Human Svcs. Commn., 2004—. Named N.J. Broker Record, Forbes Inc., N.Y.C. 1987. Mem.: Realtors Land Inst. Republican. Jewish. Office: Liberty Hill Realty Inc 415 US Highway 202 Flemington NJ 08822-6021 Office Phone: 908-782-1919.

SALAMONE-KOCHOWICZ, JEAN GLORIA, retired bank executive; b. White Deer, Pa., Dec. 28, 1929; d. Dewey and Pearl Viola (Bastian) Smith; m. Daniel W. Salamone, Nov. 2, 1946 (div. 1977); children: Daryl Joseph, John Daniel; m. John T. Kochowicz, Feb. 10, 1990 (dec. 1993). Student, Bloomsburg State Coll., 1946, Am. Inst. Banking, 1974-85. Sec. Chef Boy-ar-Dee Foods, Milton, Pa., 1946-48, Arthur Andersen & Co., Washington, 1948-58; exec. sec. Citizens Bank and Trust Co., Riverdale, Md., 1970-74, asst. treas., 1974-77, asst. v.p., 1977-84; v.p. Citizens Bank, Laurel, Md., 1984-97; corp. sec. Citizens Bancorp (holding corp. for Citizens Bank), Laurel, 1982-96; ret. CRESTAR, 1997. Trustee Prince George's Arts Coun., Riverdale, 1983-98, treas., 1983-89, pres. 1990-91. Mem. Fin. Women Internat. (pres. met. Md. group 1977-78), Chesapeake Cancer Alliance. Roman Catholic. Avocations: travel, photography, art collecting, volunteering. E-mail: salakoch@aol.com.

SALAND, DEBORAH, psychotherapist, educator; b. Val Dosta, Ga., July 25, 1954; d. Charles and Audrey (Horan) Gianniny. B in Profl. Studies, Barry U., 1990, MSW, 1992; D in Psychology, So. Calif. Sch. Profl. Studies, 1996. Lic. clin. social worker, Fla.; cert. addictions profl.; cert. master addiction specialist; diplomat Am. Psychotherapy Assn.; cert. forensic sentence mitigation specialist; cert. forensic addictions specialist; cert. group psychotherapist. Substance abuse counselor Spectrum Programs, Ft. Lauderdale, Fla., 1974—79; owner Obsession in Time, Miami, Fla., 1984—88; asst. clin. dir. Interphase Recovery, Miami, 1988—89; substance abuse counselor Transitions Recovery, Miami, 1989—91; clin. dir. level II Pathways Treatment, Miami; pvt. practice Inst. Human Potential, Miami, 1993—; founder Eating Disorder Tex. Program, 1997—. Lectr. Addiction Traingin Inst. U. Miami, 1992, mem. faculty, 1993—; clin. supr. Transitions Recovery, Miami, 1993—, Treatment Resources, Miami, 1993-94; adj. faculty N.Y. Inst. Tech., Boca Raton, Fla., 1997—; dir. Am. Family Eating Disorder Tract, 1997-98. Contbr. articles to profl. jours. Named Spl. Alumni Barry U., 1996. Mem. NASW, APA, Am. Group Psychotherapy Assn. (clin.), Med. Psychotherapist Am. (assoc. clin.) Nat. Bd. Cert. Counselors (counselor), Broward County Mental Health Assn. Office: Inst Human Potential 19501 NE 10th Ave Ste 305 Miami FL 33179-3502 Office Phone: 305-653-1716.

SALAND, LINDA CAROL, anatomist, educator, neuroscientist; b. NYC, Oct. 24, 1942; d. Charles and Esther (Weingarten) Gewirtz; m. Joel S. Saland, Aug. 16, 1964; children: Kenneth, Jeffrey. BS, CCNY, 1963, PhD in Biology, 1968; MA in Zoology, Columbia U., 1965. Rsch. assoc. dept. anatomy Columbia U. Coll. Physicians and Surgeons, N.Y.C., 1968-69; sr. rsch. assoc. dept. anatomy Sch. Medicine U. N.Mex., Albuquerque, 1971-78, asst. prof. anatomy, 1978-83, assoc. prof., 1983-89, prof., 1989-97, prof. dept. neuroscis., 1997—. Ad hoc reviewer study sect. NIH, 1994, 1995, 1997, 2000, 2005, 2006, mem. site visit team. Mem. editl. bd. Anat. Record, 1980-98; contbr. articles to profl. jours. Recipient Khatali Tchg. Excellence award, U. N.Mex. Med. Class of 2001; fellow NDEA, 1966—68. Mem. AAAS, Soc. for Neurosci., Women in Neurosci. (chmn. steering com. 1991-93). Office: U New Mex Sch Medicine Dept Neurosics MSC 084740 Albuquerque NM 87131-0001 Business E-Mail: lsaland@salud.unm.edu.

SALAT, CRISTINA, writer; b. NYC; Student, L.I. U. Founder Shark Prodns., 1998—, Kulana Affordable Artists Sanctuary, Hawaii, 1999—. Freelance editor, 1987—; author, editor, manuscript cons., workshop facilitator, 1985—. Author: Living in Secret, 1993, Alias Diamond Jones, 1993, Min Mors Koereste hedder Janey, 1995, Peanut's Emergency, 2002; contbr. to anthologies including Sister/Stranger, 1993, Am I Blue, 1994, Once Upon A Time, 1996, Higher Learning, 2001; contbr. to popular publ. Office Phone: 808-985-9055. E-mail: discoverkulana@yahoo.com.

SALAY, CINDY ROLSTON, systems engineer; b. Roanoke, Va., July 18, 1955; d. Gilbert Wilson and Elinor Patterson (Sandridge) Rolston; m. John Matthew, July 7, 1988; 1 child, David. AAS, Va. Western Community Coll., 1976; AS, J. Sargeant Reynolds Community Coll., 1982; BS, Va. Commonwealth U., 1984. RN. Operating room RN Henrico Doctors Hosp., Richmond, Va., 1979-80; nursing supr. Johnston Willis Hosp., Richmond, 1980-87; systems analyst, coord. Health Corp Va., Richmond, 1983-87, sr. project leader, 1987-88; sr. systems analyst Hosp. Corp. Am., Nashville, 1987; sr. systems cons. IBAX Healthcare Systems, Reston, Va., 1988-94; sys. analyst MCV Hosps. Info. Sys., Richmond, Va., 1994-95; sr. sys. engr. McKesson, Atlanta, 1995—. Methodist. Avocations: reading, plants, pets, exercising. Home: 13800 Sunrise Bluff Rd Midlothian VA 23112-2512 Office: McKesson 5995 Windward Pkwy Alpharetta GA 30005-4184 Office Phone: 804-639-1070. E-mail: cindy.salay@mckesson.com.

SALAZAR, JOSEPHINE M., behavioral health specialist; b. Big Spring, Tex., Apr. 30, 1952; d. Juan Flores and Maria Campas Moreno; 1 child, Tina S. Amaya. AA, Howard Coll., Big Spring, 1976; BA, U. Tex. of Permian Basin, Odessa, 1980; MSW, U. Houston, 1999. LCSW Tex.; lic. tchr. secondary edn. Legal guardian Harris County Social Svcs., Houston; med. social worker, case mgr. U. Tex. Health Sci. Ctr., Houston; mgr. childrens support svcs. Harris County Dept. Edn., Houston; social worker II Harris County Hosp. Dist., Houston; behavioral health specialist El Centro de Corazon, Houston. Contbr. poetry to anthologies (1st pl. award);, author documentary. Bd. dirs. YMCA, Big Spring, 1985—86, Dora Roberts Rehab. Ctr., Big Spring, 1985—86, Big Spring Head Start, 1985—86; grad. Leadership Big Spring C. of C. Recipient Best Poem award, Howard Coll., 1976. Avocation: reading. Office: El Centro de Corazon 412 Telephone Rd Houston TX 77023

SALCETTI, MARIANNE, newswriter, educator; d. Robert Anthony Salcetti and Mary Jane Lusher; m. Michael Mrkvicka, May 21, 1977 (div. Mar. 1985); 1 child, Jacob Gene Mrkvicka; m. Dale Rhines, Mar. 18, 1989 (div. June 1995); 1 child, Amalia Margaret Rhines. BA in Polit. Sci., Ohio State U., 1972, MA in Journalism, 1975; PhD in Mass. Comm., U. Iowa, 1992. Editor Franklinton News, Columbus, Ohio, 1974—76; beat reporter Chillicothe (Ohio) Gazette, 1976—77; investigative and health reporter Colorado Springs Gazette Telegraph, 1977—78; editor, co-owner The Weekly News, Johnson County, Iowa, 1980—82; instr. U. Iowa Sch. Journalism and Mass Comm., Iowa City, 1982—87; adj. faculty John Carroll U. and Ursuline Coll., Cleve., 1988—89; asst. prof. dept. comm. John Carroll U., Cleve., 1990—2000; contbg. writer The Cleve. Free Times, 1995—98; spl. projects editor The Garden City (Kans.) Telegram, 2000—02; comm. cons. Water Preservation Com., Finney County, Kans., 2002; investigator-rschr. Rebein & Bangerter, Attys. at Law, Dodge City, 2002—. Editl. radio commentator KSUI/WSUI, 1984—87; Presdl. election commentator WHK, Cleve., 1992; legis. prodr.-reporter State Capitol Update High Plains Pub. Radio, 2003; asst. prof. journalism Keene (N.H.) State Coll., 2003—; lectr. and presenter in field. Contbr. articles to profl. jours. V.p. Greater Cleve. Labor History Soc., 1997—99. Recipient Investigative Reporting award, Inland Daily Press Assn., 1977, Best News Story of the Yr. award, Iowa Press Assn., 1980, Silver Gavel award, ABA, 1981, Nat. Scholar award, Gannett Found., 1986, 1st pl. consumer reporting, Ohio Soc. Profl. Journalists, 1998, 2nd pl. best explanatory journalism, 1998, two honorable mentions, Enterprise News, 2001, honorable mention, Spot News, 2001, Bus. Reporting, 2002; Grauel Faculty fellow, John Carroll, 1995, John F. Murray Dissertation Rsch. grantee, George Meany Meml. Archives, AFL-CIO, 1987. Mem.: Kappa Tau Alpha. Avocations: reading, kayaking, gardening. Home: 272 South St Troy NH 03465 Office: Keene State Coll 229 Main St Keene NH 03435 Office Phone: 603-358-2724. Business E-Mail: msalcetti@keene.edu.

SALCIDO, DEBRA KAY, elementary school educator; b. Port Lavaa, Tex., Oct. 14, 1951; d. Zane Rex Dooley and Alpha Omedia Floyd-Dooley; children: Justen Rex, Jennifer Kay. BS in Interdisciplinary Studies, Stephen F. Austin State U., Nacogdoches, Tex. Cert. tchr. Tex., 1992. Elem. tchr. Lewisville (Tex.) Ind. Sch. Dist., 1992—96, Gause (Tex.) Ind. Sch. Dist., 1996—2002; jr. high tchr. Gause Jr. H.S., 2002—. Chair sci. fair com. Robertson County Fair Assn., Hearne, Tex., 1999—2006; children's choir First Bapt. Ch., Franklin, Tex., 2004—05; leader Boy Scouts Am., Crockett, Tex., Girl Scouts Am., Santa Fe, 1982—84, 4-H Riding Club, Franklin, 1997—2003. Mem.: Kappa Delta Pi. Home: 754 Mt Calvary Rd Hearne TX 77859 Office: Gause Independent School District PO Box 38 Gause TX 77857 Office Phone: 979-279-5891. Personal E-mail: dsalcido@gauseisd.net.

SALCUDEAN, MARTHA EVA, mechanical engineer, educator; b. Cluj, Romania, Feb. 26, 1934; arrived in Can., 1976, naturalized, 1979; d. Edmund and Sarolta (Hirsch) Abel; m. George Salcudean, May 28, 1955; 1 child, Septimiu E. BEng, U. Cluj, 1956, postgrad., 1962; PhD, U. Brasov, Romania, 1969; DSc (hon.), U. Ottawa, Ont., Can., 1992, U. B.C., Can., 2001. Mech. engr. Armatura, Cluj, 1956-63; sr. rsch. officer Nat. Rsch. Inst. Metallurgy, Bucharest, 1963-75; part-time lectr. Inst. Poly., Bucharest, 1967-75; sessional lectr. U. Ottawa, 1976-77, from asst. prof. to assoc. prof. to prof., 1977-85; prof., head dept. mech. engring. U. B.C., Vancouver, 1985-93, assoc. v.p. rsch., 1993-95, acting v.p. rsch. pro-tem, 1995, Weyerhausen Indsl. Rsch. chair computational fluid dynamics, 1996—2002, prof., Weyerhausen indsl. chair emerita dept. mech. engring., 2002—. Mem. grant selection com. for mech. engring. Natural Scis. and Engring. Rsch. Coun. Can.; mem. Nat. Adv. Panel to Min. Sci. and Tech. on advanced indsl. materials, Can., 1990; mem. governing coun. NRC; mem. def. sci.e adv. bd. Dept. Nat. Def.; chair Sci. Coun. B.C. Contbr. numerous articles to profl. jours. Decorated Order of B.C., 1998; recipient Gold medal B.C. Sci. Coun., Killam Rsch. prize U. B.C.; Rsch. Coun. Can. grantee, 1978—, Commemorative medal 125th anniversary Can. Confederation, 1993, Julian C. Smith medal Engring. Inst. Can., 1994-95, Meritorious Achievement award Assn. Profl. Engrs. & Geoscientists B.C., 1996, Killam Meml. prize engring., 1998. Fellow CSME, Can. Acad. Engring., Royal Soc. Can.; mem. ASME, Assn. Profl. Engrs. Ont., Order of Can. (apptd. officer 2004). Home: 1938 Western Pkwy Vancouver BC Canada V6T 1W5 Office Phone: 604-822-2732. Business E-Mail: msal@interchange.ubc.ca.

SALEH, FARIDA YOUSRY, chemistry professor; b. Cairo, June 17, 1939; came to U.S., 1968; d. Michael Yousry and Fakiha Yousef (Badawy) Wassif; m. Hosny Gabra Saleh, Oct. 8, 1959; children: Magda, Nagwa. BS, Ain Shams U., 1959; MS, Alexandrial U., Egypt, 1967; PhD, U. Tex., 1976. Postdoctoral rsch. assoc. Tex. A&M U., College Station, 1977-78; rsch. scientist II U. North Tex., Denton, 1978-83, asst. prof. chemistry, 1980-83, assoc. prof., 1985-94, prof., 1994—2005; ret., 2005. Cons. Stanford Rsch. Inst., Menlo Park, Calif., 1983-84, Allied Chems. Co., Hackettstown, N.J., 1985-86, Am. Chrome Chems., Corpus Christi, Tex., 1988-89, USEPA Rev. Panel, Washington, 1986—. Contbg. author book chpts. in field; contbr. more than 60 articles to profl. jours. Recipient Svc. award U.S. EPA, Washington, 1993; recipient numerous grants in field. Mem. Am. Chem. Soc., Internat. Union of Pure and Applied Chemistry, Internat. Humic Substances Soc., Assn. Women in Sci. Avocations: music, swimming, tennis. Office Phone: 972-436-2944. Personal E-mail: f.saleh@verizon.net.

SALEM, KAREN E., information technology executive; BS in indsl. engring., Penn. State U.; MBA, U. Cin. Sr. cons. Anderson Consulting; dir. bus. solutions Burger King; v.p. info. tech. Rexall Sundown; IT head AFC Enterprises; sr. v.p. and CIO Corning Cable Sys.; former sr. v.p. and CIO Winn-Dixie Stores, Inc., Jacksonville, Fla., 2002, Ingram Micro, 2005. Office: Ingram Micro PO Box 25125 1600 E St Andrew Pl Santa Ana CA 92799-5125

SALEMBIER, VALERIE BIRNBAUM, publishing executive; b. Teaneck, N.J. d. Jack and Sara (Gordon) Birnbaum; m. Paul J. Block, Dec. 9, 1990. BA, Coll. New Rochelle, 1973. Advt. dir. Ms. Mag., N.Y.C., 1976-79, assoc. pub., 1979-81; pub. Inside Sports Mag., N.Y.C., 1982; sr. v.p. advt. USA Today, 1983-88; pub. TV Guide, Radnor, Pa., 1988; pres. N.Y. Post, N.Y.C., 1988—90; pub. Family Circle Mag., N.Y.C., 1991-93; sr. v.p. advt. N.Y. Times, 1993-95; v.p., pub. Esquire Mag., 1996—2003; sr. v.p., pub. Harper's Bazaar, N.Y.C., 2003—. Lectr. in field. Author: (book) Rotissereie League Baseball, 1982; freelance mag. writer:. Chmn. N.Y.C. Police Found.; bd. dirs., past pres. Nat. Alliance Breast Cancer Orgns., former bd. dirs.; bd. dirs., past pres. Beneficial Orgn. Aid Ex-Fighters; former trustee Ctrl. Synagogue, Coll. New Rochelle; trustee N.Y.C. Sports Devel. Corp. Mem.: Women in Comm., Com. 200, Womens Forum. Office: Harpers Bazaar 1700 Broadway New York NY 10019

SALERNO, CHERIE ANN (C. S. MAU), artist; b. Chgo., Nov. 21, 1948; d. Henry Jasper and Helen (Polyak) Mau; m. Kenneth Daniel Salerno; children: Nick Anthony, Brittney Ann. AAS in Advt., Triton Coll., River Grove, Ill., 1985; BFA, Art Inst. Chgo., 1999. Freelance comml. artist, Chgo., 1986—90, 2000—; artist Chgo. Fine Arts Exch., 1994—98; artist, owner C.S. Mau Studio, River Grove, Ill., 1992—; art dir., bd. dirs. Harrison St. Coop. Gallery, Oak Park, Ill., 1999—2002; art tchr. grades 3-7, 2000—03, Bethlehem Luth. Sch., River Grove, 2002—; represented by Anav Art Gallery, Ill. Designer Centennial Quilt, River Grove Libr., 1988; logo designer, River Grove Sch., 1984. Designer stained glass window Bethlehem Luth. Ch., River Grove, Ill., 1999, Celebrating Diversity art exhibit, Chgo., 2002; cover designer Louie Records, Corvallis, Oreg., 1998-99, MSS Pub., Jefferson, Oreg., 2002, A440 Music Group, Chgo., for Henry Johnson and Nancy Wilson, 2003; cover artist Aim Mag., 2003-04, Chicagoland Tails, 2005, Indy Tails, 2005. Vol. tchr. art Bethlehem Luth. Sch., River Grove, Ill., 1996-2002; vol. ElderCare, 1990-94. Fellow: West Suburban Art League (Excellences honor award 1990—2005, excellences awards 1990—), Glenview Art League (Excellence award 1996), Chgo. Artist Coalition; mem.: Oak Park Art League (bd. dirs. 1989—, arts and stds. judge 1991—93, sch. bd. 1993—94, active fundraising 1994, stds. judge 2000—, juror of artist stds., Excellences merit 1990—94). Lutheran. Avocations: gardening, reading, weightlifting, sewing, gourmet cooking. Personal E-mail: cheriesart@salerno.com.

SALERNO, LAURA ANN, elementary school educator; d. John and Camille Cahill; m. James Salerno, July 11, 1997; children: Tara Paige, Ryan James. BA in Humanities, Georgian Ct. U., Lakewood, NJ, 1992, MA in Elem. Edn., 1998. Tchr., reading specialist Brick Twp. Bd. Edn., NJ, 1993—. Avocations: scrapbooks, reading.

SALERNO, SISTER MARIA, advanced practice nurse, educator; b. Syracuse, N.Y. d. Joseph and Josephine (Ostrowski) S. Diploma in nursing, St. Joseph's Hosp., Syracuse, 1962; BSN summa cum laude, Cath. U. Am., 1974, MS in Nursing, 1976, PhD in Nursing, 1981; cert. nurse practitioner, U. Rochester, 1984. RN, N.Y., Md., Washington; cert. adult, geriatric nurse practitioner ANCC; joined Sisters of Third Franciscan Order, Roman Cath. Ch., 1963. Staff nurse St. Joseph Hosp. Health Ctr., Syracuse, 1962-63; sr. charge nurse ICU, gen. med. and surg. units St. Elizabeth Hosp., Utica, NY, 1965-66, head nurse pediat. unit, 1966-69; head nurse ECF Loretto Geriatric Ctr., Syracuse, 1969-72; lectr. Cath. U. Am., Washington, 1977—78, 1980—81, asst. prof. nursing, 1978-79, 81-92, assoc. prof., 1992—, dir. primary care adult/geriatric nurse practitioner programs, 1984—, co-dir. FNP program, 1994-97; dir. Adult CNS Nurse Educator Program, 2004—. Contbr. chpts. to books; contbr. articles to profl. jours. Vol. nurse practitioner Cmty. of Hope, Washington; instl. animal care and use com. George Washington U., 1996-, Cath. U. Am. 2000-, Veteran's Adminstrn. Med. Ctr., 2004-; scholarship com. Franciscan Found. for the Holy Land, 1996-. Grantee NIH, 1984-89, Cath. U. Am., 1989-90. Mem.: AAUP, ANA, D.C. League for Nursing (bd. dirs. 1995—97, 1999—), D.C. Nurse Practitioners Assn. (nom. com. 2006), N.Y. Acad. Scis., Nat. League for Nursing, Nat. Orgn. Nurse Practitioner Facilities, Nat. Gerontol. Nurses Assn., Am. Coll. Nurse Practitioners, Am. Acad. Nurse Practitioners, Am. Assn. for History of Nursing, Cath. U. Am. Nursing Alumni Assn. (pres. 1986—87, chpt. exec. bd. 1992—2003, treas. 1998—2003), Nat. Italian Am. Found. (assoc.), Sigma Theta Tau (grad. counselor Kappa chpt. 1985—87, awards com. 1987—89, grad. counselor Kappa chpt. 1991—97, eligibility com. 1991—97, 2002—03). Office Phone: 202-319-6545. Office Fax: 202-319-6485. Business E-Mail: salerno@cua.edu.

SALERNO-SONNENBERG, NADJA, violinist; b. Rome, Jan. 10, 1961; arrived in U.S., 1969; d. Josephine Salerno-Sonnenberg. Grad., Curtis Inst. Music, 1975, Juilliard Sch., 1982; D (hon.), N.Mex. State U., 1999. Profl. debut Phila. Orch., 1971; appeared with Am. Symphony Orch., Balt. Symphony, Chgo. Symphony, Colo. Symphony, Cin. Symphony, Detroit Symphony, Houston Symphony, Indpls. Symphony, Milw. Symphony, Montreal Symphony, N.J. Symphony, Pitts. Symphony, San Diego Symphony, Seattle Symphony, St. Louis Symphony, Utah Symphony, Boston Symphony, Dallas Symphony, Minn. Orch., Phila. Orch., L.A. Philharm.; appeared Cabrillo Festival, Ravinia Festival, Blosson Festival, Meadow Brook Festival, Gt. Woods Festival, Caramoor Festival, Hollywood Bowl Festival; internat. appearances Vienna, Munich, Stuttgart, Franfurt, Liverpool, England, Geneva, Rotterdam, Netherlands, Lisbon, Portugal, Tokyo. Founder, rec. artist Capital Classics and Jazz Records, 1987—, Nonesuch, 1996—, NSS Music, 2005—. Performer: (recitals) with Anne Marie McDermott, with Regina Carter, with Eileen Ivers, with The Assads; appearances: TV 60 Minutes, CBS Sunday Morning, NBC Nat. News, PBS Live from Lincoln Ctr., CNN Newsstand, Charlie Rose Show, Sesame Street; appearances (TV) The Tonight Show with Johnny Carson, subject (documentaries) Speaking in Strings, 1999 (Oscar nomination, 2000). Recipient 1st prize, Naumburg Violin Competition, N.Y.C., 1981, Avery Fisher prize, 1999; Avery Fisher Career grantee, 1983. Mem.: SAG, AFTRA. Office: care M L Falcone Pub Rels 155 W 68th St Ste 114 New York NY 10023-5808

SALES, CATHERINE, special education educator; b. N.Y.C., July 30, 1966; d. Nicholas Sales and Carol Ann Romano. BS in Spl. Edn. magna cum laude, Manhattan Coll., 1988; MS in Spl. Edn., Fordham U., 1991; EdM in Instrnl. Practices, Columbia U., 1997, EdD in Spl. Edn., 1998. cert. spl. edn. tchr. Sch. Adminstrn. and Supervision. Spl. edn. tchr Fred S. Keller Sch., Yonkers, N.Y., 1988-92, asst. behavior analyst, 1992-93, curriculum coord., 1993-94, individualized edn. plan coord., 1994-97, spl. edn. itinerant tchr. coord., 1997—2001; tchr. Rye City Sch. Dist., 2001—04, chairperson on spl. edn., 2004—. Adj. prof. Fordham U., 2002—, Pace U., 2006—. Mem. Assn. for Behavior Analysis, Calif. State Assn. for Behavior Analysis, N.Y. State Assn. for Behavior Analysis, Coun. Exceptional Children, Epsilon Sigma Pi, Kappa Delta Pi. Democrat. Avocations: photography, Karate. Office Fax: 914-967-2764. E-mail: dancingcat@msn.com.

SALES, MITZI S., science educator; b. Toronto, Ontario, Canada, Feb. 1, 1978; d. Argeo Cadiz and Milagros Albano Sales. BA in Sci., Brown U., 2000, MA in Secondary Biology, 2003. Tchr., sci. dept. E. W. Thurston Mid. Sch., Westwood, Mass., 2003—06, Rye Country Day Sch., Rye, NY, 2006—. Choreographer, musical E. W. Thurston Mid. Sch., 2005—06, dir., honoring our voices, 2005—06. Mem.: Nat. Sci. Tchrs. Assoc. Achievements include development of honoring our voices curriculum. Office: Rye Country Day Sch 1 Cedar St Rye NY 10580 Office Phone: 914-967-1417. Personal E-mail: mitzi1000@hotmail.com.

SALETTA, MARY ELIZABETH (BETTY SALETTA), sculptor; b. Miami, Fla., Sept. 30, 1941; d. Earl Robert and Alta Florence Cotner; m. Albert Michael Saletta, July 1, 1959; children: Tia Suzanne, Kamber Ann. Graphic artist Moore Bus. Forms Inc., Modesto, Calif., 1960-67, Live Oak Pub. Co., Oakdale, Calif., 1977-80; freelance artist U.S. Forest Svc., Modesto Irrigation Dist., Stanislaus Schs., New Don Pedro Dam Project, Calif., 1967-77; sculptor Saletta Sculpture, Oakdale, 1980—. Mem. adv. bd. Calif. State U. Coll. Arts, Letters and Sci., Turlock, 1999-2002; charter mem., dir. Downtown Arts Project, Modesto, 1992-96. One-woman shows City of Oakdale Redevel. Agy., 1990, Modesto C. of C., 1996; group shows include Calif. State U. Stanislaus, Turlock, 1986, Cowboy Artist Am. Mus., Kerrville, Tex., 1988, Benson Park Sculpture Garden, Loveland, Colo., 1989, 90, 93, Danada Sculpture Garden, Chgo., 1991, 93, Tucson Mus. Art, 1995; represented in permanent collections Tucson Mus. Art, Buckaroo Hall of Fame, cities of Modesto, Oakdale, Ripon, Calif., Stockton, Los Banos, Montery, San Leandro, Calif.; sculptures include life-size pub. sculptures Yesterday Is Tomorrow, 1991, Paperbohy, 1995, Am. Graffiti, 1997, Stockton Firefighters Meml., 1998, World War II Meml., 1999, Nursing, the Finest Art, 2001, Chief Estanislao, 2001, Firefighter Sculpture produced at Laguna Beach Pageant of the Masters, 2002. Recipient Excellence in Fine Art award Bank Am., Stockton, Calif., 1959, Best of Show award Western Art Roundup, Winnamucca, Nev., 1987, 88, Excellence in Visual Arts award Stanislaus Arts Coun., Modesto, 1999. Mem. Nat. League Am. Pen Women, Ctrl. Calif. Art League (advisor 1991, Best of Show award 1987), Rotary (bd. dirs. Oakdale 1997-99). Democrat. Avocations: horses, skiing, mountain climbing, fishing. Home: 4255 Wellsford Rd Oakdale CA 95361-7930 Fax: 209-572-4089. E-mail: salettasculpture@aol.com.

SALHANY, LUCILLE S. (LUCY SALHANY), broadcast executive; b. 1946; married; 2 children. LHD (hon.), Emerson Coll., 1992. Program dir. WKBF-TV, Cleve., 1967; program mgr. WLVI-TV, Boston, 1975—79; v.p. television & cable programming Taft Broadcasting Co., 1979—85; pres. Paramount Domestic TV, 1985—91; chmn. 20th Century Television, 1991—93, Fox Broadcasting Co., 1993—94; pres. United Paramount Network (UPN), 1994-97; pres., CEO JH Media, Boston, 1998—2004, HJ Media, LifeFX Networks Inc., 2002—04; co-founder, mng. ptnr. Echo Bridge Entertainment, Needham, Mass., 2004—. Bd. dirs. Hewlett-Packard Co., Am. Media Co., Inc., ION Media Networks, Inc., 2006—. Bd. trustees Emerson Coll.; profl. adv. bd. ALSAC/St. Jude Children's Rsch. Hosp. Named Exec. of Yr., Caucus for Prodrs., Writers & Dirs.; recipient Sherrill C. Corwin Human Rels award, Am. Jewish Com., 1995, Silver Satellite award, Am. Women in Radio and TV, 1995, HELP Humanitarian award, 1997, Avatar award, Cable

Fin. Mgmt. Orgn., Silver Circle award, Nat. Acad TV Arts and Sci. Achievements include becoming the first woman to manage an American broadcast television network, 1993. Office: Echo Bridge Entertainment Ste 500 75 Second Ave Needham Heights MA 02494 Office Phone: 781-444-9680.*

SALI, AMANDA LEIGH, choral director; d. Nanci and Steven Hostetter; m. Juan Jose Sali, May 26, 2001. B in Music Edn., Stetson U., 2002—02; MusM, U. North Tex., 2004. Teaching Certificate Ga., 2004. Rehearsal asst. Gwinnett Young Singers, Duluth, Ga., 1997—98; guest dir. First Presbyn. Ch., DeLand, Fla., 1999, Stetson U. Children's Choir, DeLand, Fla., 2001; student tchr. DeLand H.S., Fla., 2001—02; music intern Stetson Bapt. Ch., DeLand, Fla., 1999—2002; condr. U. of North Tex. Women's Chorus, 2002—04; staff singer Oreg. Bach Festival, 2004—; choral dir. South Gwinnett H.S., Snellville, Ga., 2004—; interim artistic dir. Atlanta Youth Choir, Snellville, Ga., 2005—. Singer North Metro First Bapt. Ch. Choir, Lawrenceville, Ga., 2004—05. Finalist Nat. Conducting Competition, Am. Choral Director's Assn., 2001; recipient Outstanding Grad. Student in Conducting and Ensembles, Sch. of Music (U. of North Tex.), 2004, Outstanding Freshman Music Maj., Sch. of Music (Stetson U.), 1999, Rookie of the Month, South Gwinnett H.S., 2004; Conducting fellowship, U. of North Tex., 2002—04, Toulouse fellowship, 2002—04, Tex. Pub. Edn. grant, 2003—04. Mem.: Georgia Music Educator's Assn., Am. Choral Director's Assn. (student chpt. pres. 1999—2002), Phi Eta Sigma, Omicron Delta Kappa, Pi Kappa Lamba. Christian. Office: South Gwinnett H S 2288 East Main St Snellville GA 30078 Office Phone: 770-972-4840. Business E-Mail: amanda_sali@gwinnett.k12.ga.us.

SALICRUP, MADELINE, nurse; b. Bronx, N.Y., Jan. 16, 1968; d. Natanael and Mirriam (Echevarria) S. BS cum laude, Coll. Mt. St. Vincent, 1990. Specialized clin. asst. Albert Einstein Coll. Medicine, Bronx, 1988-90; RN Mt. Sinai Hosp., Bronx, 1990-91, Bronx (N.Y.) Lebanon Hosp., 1991—; del., 1993—. Recipient Woman of Yr. award Nat. Ferrek Assocs., 1996. Mem. ANA, N.Y. State Nurses Assn., Sigma Theta Tau, Delta Epsilon Sigma. Democrat. Avocations: reading, fishing. Home: 1530 Gillespie Ave Bronx NY 10461 Personal E-mail: modelinzzz@aol.com.

SALIER, EVA, artist, writer; m. Max Salier, Dec. 23, 1947; children: Edward, Ralph. Paintings, watercolors; author: Survival of a Spirit. Bd. dirs., play reader Little Theater, Vineland, NJ, 1998—2004. Avocation: travel.

SALIERS, EMILY, singer, musician; b. New Haven, Conn., July 22, 1963; d. Don Saliers; life ptnr. Leslie Zweben. Student, Vanderbilt U.; BA, Emory U., 1985. Mem. folk rock duo Indigo Girls, 1983—; represented by Epic Records, 1988—2006, Hollywood Records, 2006—. Co-owner Watershed Restaurant, Decatur, Ga.; co-founder Flying Biscuit Cafe, Atlanta. Singer (with Amy Ray): (albums) Early 45, 1985, Strange Fire, 1987, Indigo Girls, 1989 (Grammy award for Best Contemporary Folk Album, 1990), Nomads Indians Saints, 1990, Rites of Passage, 1992, Swamp Ophelia, 1994, Touch Me Fall, 1995, 1200 Curfews, 1995, Shaming of the Sun, 1997, Come on Now Social, 1999, Retrospective, 2000, Become You, 2002, All That We Let In, 2004, Rarities, 2005, Despite Our Differences, 2006, (songs) Closer to Fine, 1989, Hammer and Nail, 1990, Galileo, 1992, Least Complicated, 1994, Shame on You, 1997; composer: (films) One Weekend a Month, 2004; co-author (with Don Saliers): A Song to Sing, A Life to Live: Reflections on Music as Spiritual Practice, 2004; appearances include (films) Boys on the Side, 1995, (documentaries) Wordplay, 2006. Mem.: Phi Beta Kappa. Office: c/o Russell Carter Artist Mgmt Ste 755 315 W Ponce de Leon Ave Decatur GA 30030 Office Phone: 404-377-9900. E-mail: igfan@rcam.com.*

SALINAS, MARÍA ELENA, newscaster, columnist; b. LA, 1956; d. Jose Luis Cordero Salinas and Luz Tiznado; m. Eliott Rodriguez, Mar. 1993; children: Julia Alexandra, Gabriela Maria stepchildren: Erica, Bianca. Reporter KMEX-34 TV, LA, 1981—87; co-anchor Noticiero Univisión, Miami, Fla., 1987—; columnist King Features Syndicates. Co-anchor (TV series) Noticiero Univisión, 1987—, co-host Aquí y Ahora, 2000—; author: I Am My Father's Daughter: Living a Life Without Secrets, 2006. Founding mem. Nat. Assn. Hispanic Journalists; active in Nat. Assn. Latino Elected & Apptd. Officials; established Maria Elena Salinas Scholarship for Excellence in Spanish-Language News, 2002—. Named Journalist of Yr., Hispanic Media 100, 2002; named one of 100 Most Influential Hispanics, Hispanic Mag., 1999; named to Nat. Assn. Hispanic Journalists' Hall of Fame, 2006; recipient Edward R. Murrow award, 1997, 2 Nat. News Emmy awards, Nat. Acad. TV Arts & Sciences, 1999, LA Area Emmy award, 2002, Pride award, Hispanic Fedn., 2006, President's award, Nat. Assn. Latino Elected & Apptd. Officials, 2006. Mem.: Nat. Assn. Hispanic Journalists (former v.p.). Office: Univision Communications Inc 9405 NW 41st St Miami FL 33178 also: King Features 15th Fl 300 W 57th St New York NY 10019 Office Phone: 305-471-3900. Office Fax: 305-471-4346.*

SALISBURY, HELEN HOLLAND, education educator; b. Bedford, Ind., Dec. 15, 1923; d. Deward Julius and Zella (Kinser) Holland; m. Charles Jackson Salisbury, Jan. 10, 1942; children: Creggie Helen Salisbury Henderson, Andrew Jackson Salisbury Henderson. BS in Home Econs., Ind. U., 1957; MEd, U. Va., 1967; EdD, Temple U., 1979. Plating chemist Curtiss-Wright, Indpls., 1943; supr. sch. lunch program Charlottesville Pub. Sch., Va., 1963—65; dir. Harcum Jr. Coll. Lab. Sch., Bryn Mawr, Pa., 1966—68, prof. edn., 1965—73; tchg. assoc. Temple U., Phila., 1974; early childhood cons., 1979—. Prof. edn. Harcum Jr. Coll., 1982—94, dir. infant devel. practice, 1982—94; early childhood cons. Head Start, 1965; instr. Child Care Tng. Project, Pa., 1992—94. Co-author: Diagnosing Individual Needs for Early Childhood Education, 1975. Mem.: DAR, ASCD, Orgn. Mondiale pour L'Education Prescolaire, Delaware Valley Assn. Edn. Young Children, Nat. Assn. Edn. Young Children, Kappa Alpha Theta. Episcopalian. Home: 3915 Nimit Dr Bloomington IN 47401-8964 Office: Harcum Jr Coll Montgomery Ave Bryn Mawr PA 19010

SALJINSKA-MARKOVIC, OLIVERA T., oncology researcher, educator; b. Skopje, Macedonia; d. Trajko and Radmila; m. Nenad Markovic, July 9, 1961; 2 children. MD, Med. Faculty, Skopje, 1962; PhD, Med. Faculty, Belgrade, 1977; Specialist Med. Biochemistry, U. Kiril and Metodij, Skopje, 1969. Asst. prof. Med. Faculty, Skopje, 1964-79, assoc. prof., 1979-84; dir. clin. lab. U. Children's Hosp., Skopje, 1974-84; sr. rsch. assoc. Pa. State U., State College, 1984-85; sr. fellow U. Pa., Phila., 1985-88; prof. U. Belgrade, 1988-93. Adj. prof. Med. Coll. of Pa., 1993-95, Columbia Union Coll., Tacoma Park, Md., 2003—; vis. scientist NIAMDD, NIH, Bethesda, 1976-77; vis. scientist Am. Type Culture Collection, Rockville, Md., 1995-96; dir. BioSciCon, Md., 1996—; primarius Univ. Children's Hosp., Skopje, 1983-86; head lab. for rsch. and devel., Clin. Ctr., Belgrade, 1990-93; mem. exam. com., State of Macedonia, 1980-90; adj. prof. U. Md. U. Coll., 1998, Am. U., Washington, 1999-2002, Columbia Union Coll., Takoma Park, Md., 2003-; vis. prof. Georgetown U., Washington, 2000. Author: Quantitative Cytoch of Enzymes, 1986; contbr. articles to profl. jours., publs. Postdoctoral intern rsch. fellowship Fogarty Internat. Ctr., NIH, Bethesda, 1971-73; recipient several rsch. grants NIH, Pharm. Co. Mem. Histochem. Soc., Am. Assn. Clin. Chem., NY Acad. Scis., Am. Assn. Cell Biology, Am. Soc. Investigative Pathology. Achievements include development of new concepts and methods in cancer diagnosis and treatment; patents for CAP-PAP test for cervical cancer screening, and Inosinic Acid Dehydrogenase Assay; inventor, principle investigator of translational research and sponsor of MarkPap technology for more efficient cervical cancer screening; research on the improvement of mass cervical cancer screening. Office: BioSciCon Inc Rockville MD 20852

SALKIN, BARBARA RUTH, social worker; b. Washington, Sept. 16, 1938; d. David and Bess Marguerite (Adelman) S. BA, UCLA, 1960; MSW, U. Calif., Berkeley, 1962. Lic. clin. social worker, Calif. Clin. social worker Neuropsychiat. Inst. UCLA, 1962-79, Kaiser-Permanente, Woodland Hills, Calif., 1979—2004; pvt. practice San Fernando, Calif., 2004—. Contbr. articles to profl. jours. Mem. Nat. Assn. Social Work (cert.), Soc. Clin. Social Work, So. Calif. Blues Soc. (treas. 1986—). Democrat. Jewish. Avocations: travel, music, dance. Office: Nagar Psychology Ctr 11273 Laurel Canyon Blvd San Fernando CA 91340-4300 Office Phone: 818-361-7717.

SALLEE, WANDA JEAN, music educator; b. Seminole, Okla., Nov. 30, 1929; d. John Mordecai Cooper and Mary Blanche Jenkins-Cooper; m. William J. Sallee, Jan. 6, 1951; children: Susan Dwan, Martha Jean. MusB in Piano Theory, Okla. State U., 1950; student in Edn. and Pedagogy, Levine Sch. Music, 1990. Cert. tchr. music Am. Coll. Musicians. Tchr. music Hobart (Okla.) Elem. Schs., 1950—51, Mangum (Okla.) Elem. Schs., 1951—52; dir. ch. music First Bapt. Ch., Mangum, 1952—57, Westover Bapt. Ch., Arlington, Va., 1959—72; pvt. piano tchr. Mangum, 1952—58; tchr. Sallee Music Studio, Arlington, Va., 1959—94, Dallas, 1994—. Dir. music Bapt. Ch., Arlington, 1959—72; bd. trustees Oak Hill Acad., Va., 1965—68; presenter in field. Vol. Reagan-Bush Campaign, Arlington, 1980. Mem.: Music Tchrs. Nat. Assn., Am. Coll. Musicians (adjudicator, nat. guild judge), Richardson (Tex.) Music Tchrs. Assn. (pres., v.p., corr.sec.), Tex. State Music Tchrs. Assn. (chmn. practice student affiliate 2003—, named Piano Tchr. of Yr. 2002), Sigma Alpha Iota (life). Avocations: poetry, writing, reading, painting, eggery. Home and Office: Sallee Music Studio 7615 Cliffbrook Dr Dallas TX 75254-8101 Personal E-mail: wjs6214@airmail.net.

SALLOWAY, JOSEPHINE PLOVNICK, psychologist, educator, marriage and family therapist, mental health counselor; b. Brookline, Mass., July 30, 1944; d. Isadore B. and Gladys J. (Press) Plovnick; m. Richard B. Salloway, July 4, 1967; 1 child, Matthew. AB in History, Boston U., 1965, EdM in Counseling, 1966; cert. in human resource mgmt., Bentley Coll., 1980. Cert. sch. psychologist, sch. adjustment counselor, history and social studies tchr.; clinically cert. forensic counselor; clinically cert. domestic violence counselor; lic. mental health counselor; lic. marriage and family therapist; nationally cert. psychologist. Counselor Boston Pub. Schs., 1966-78; counselor, psychologist ednl. enrichment program Milton (Mass.) Acad., 1970-71; psychologist Braintree (Mass.) Pub. Schs., 1983-89; psychologist, adjustment counselor Norwood Pub. Schs., 1990-92; sch. adjustment counselor Stoughton, Mass., 1993-94; cons. psychologist Waltham (Mass.) Schs., 1997—2000; pvt. practice Braintree, 1997—; prof. faculty in psychology and early childhood edn. Quincy (Mass.) Coll., 1997—2004, head counselor student support advisor, 1997—2003; faculty in psychology Curry Coll., Milton, Mass., 1999—. Faculty psychology and early childhood edn. and devel., faculty advisor Massasoit C.C., 1999—, psychology Curry Coll., Milton, Mass., 1999—; field supr. dept. counselor edn. Harvard U., Cambridge, Mass., Northeastern U., Boston; del. Coastline Coun. for Children, Mass., 1985-2000, del. Mass. Soc. for Prevention of Cruelty to Children, 1998—; psychometrist Mass. Gen. Hosp., Boston; asst. coord. Boston U. Counseling Clinic; diagnostic tchr. Braintree, Mass., 1999-2002, Mass. Edn. Reform, Tutor, Canton Pub. Schs., 2000; mem. edn. reform Mass. Comprehensive Assessment Sys., 2000; commn. on child advocacy and domestic violence Dist. Atty.'s Office, 2000-02; lectr., presenter in field; provider seminars, workshops and groups on women's issues, parenting, children and adolescents, child development, positive psychology, multiculturalism and stress reduction. Pub. dir. Curtain Call Theatre, 1997; contbg. editor Gazette newsletter, 1996— Class agt. Boston U. Alumni Assn., 1996—2006; del. Braintree Fair Housing Commn., 1994—2000, Braintree Multicultural Com., 1994—2000; pres., bd. chmn. Cmty. Friends for Human Svcs., Inc., Boston, 1995—, chmn. edn. bd.; vol. Genesis Fund Telethon; ednl. dir. Ho. of Worship, Braintree, 1994—. Recipient Presdl. award, Cmty. Friends for Human Svcs., Inc., 1996—97, 2001, Svc. award, 1998, 1999, 2001, 2003, Cmty. Mass. Senatorial award, 1998, award for contbn. to svcs. for children, Mass. Soc. Prevention of Cruelty to Children, 1998, 1999, Senatorial award for outstanding contbn. to mental health, Mass. Senate, 1998, award for contbn. to adult and familly edn., 2003, Contbr. Edn. award, NE Educators Assn., 2003, award, Plymouth (Mass.) County Dist. Atty.'s Office, 2005, award in recognition of outstanding contbn. to educating students, Massasoit C.C., 2006. Mem. APA, AAUP, ACA (clin.), NASP, NAMP, Nat. Assn. Cert. Forensic Counselors, Am. Assn. Marriage and Family Therapists (clin.), N.E. Assn. Coll. Educators, Mass. Assn. Sch. Adjustment Counselors, Mass. Assn. Marriage and Family Therapists, Mass. Assn. Mental Health Counselors, Mass. Tchrs. Assn., Pi Lambda Theta, Scarlet Key. Avocations: antiques, reading, travel, theater. Home: 57 Cochato Rd Braintree MA 02184-4628 E-mail: jsallowa@curry.edu.

SALMELA, LYNN MARIE, clinical nurse specialist; b. Albert Lea, Minn., Mar. 29, 1960; d. Melvin Raymond and Patricia Lou (Bushey) Salmela. BSN, Winona State U., Minn., 1982; MA, Coll. St. Scholastica, Duluth, Minn., 2000; compliant documentation mgmt. course, J.A. Thomas & Assocs., 2000; cert. emergency dept. electronic med. record tng., Epic Sys. Corp., 2004. RN Minn., Wis., cert. pub. health nurse, Minn., intravenous therapy nurse, 1997, in ambulatory electronic med. record application, Epic Sys. Corp., 2004. Staff nurse Milw. Children's Hosp. (now Children's Hosp. of Wis.), 1982—83, Mpls. Children's Hosp., 1983—86, St. Mary's Duluth (Minn.) Clinic, 1986—2001; adj. faculty mem. Coll. of St. Scholastica, Duluth, 1998—99; utilization mgmt./compliant documentation coord. St. Luke's Hosp., Duluth, 2000—03; clin. informatics analyst St. Mary's Duluth Clinic Health Sys., 2003—05, nurse clinician, nurse-on-line, 2005, EpicCare edn. specialist, 2005—. Author: (newsletter) Volunteer Link, St. Mary's Grief Support Ctr., 1993, 1995—96; contbr. articles to profl. pubs. and newspapers. Vol. presch. screening programs, Winona, Minn., 1981—82; vol. blood screening clinic, Milw., 1982; vol. med. staff Grandma's Marathon, Duluth, 1989; vol. St. Mary's Grief Support Ctr., Duluth, 1993—97, Children's Asthma Camp, 1988. Recipient 1st Pl. award, Amateur Still Life Category, photography contest, 2001, 1st Pl. award portrait category, Photography Contest, 2002; scholar Presdl. scholar, Winona State U., 1978. Mem.: Nat. Assn. Clin. Nurse Specialists, Sigma Theta Tau. Republican. Avocations: walking, music, photography, writing, cooking, camping. Home: 110 S 58th Ave E Duluth MN 55804 Office Phone: 218-786-4646. Business E-Mail: lsalmela@smdc.org.

SALMI, ELLABLANCHE, retired literature and language professor, artist, writer; b. Warren, Minn., Sept. 16, 1928; d. Erwin Riley and Olga Viola (Ehaust) Kezar; children from previous marriage: Carlynne Hernandez, Becky Leyse, Roxanne Flom. BA, San Diego State U., 1970, MA, 1977. Instr. Southwestern Coll., Chula Vista, 1978—91; ret., 1991. Author: (poems) Homeland, 2000, Raindrops, 2003. Mem.: Carlsbad Oceanside Art League, San Diego Art Guild.

SALMON, BETH ANN, magazine editor in chief; b. Syracuse, NY, Oct. 1, 1969; d. Richard George and Sharon Dian (Clark) S. BFA, Emerson Coll., 1991. Editl. asst. Let's Live mag., L.A., 1994, asst. editor, 1994-95, editor in chief, 1995—. Author: (screenplays) Postcards, 1994, Watch Me, 1995. Office: Lets Live Magazine 11050 Santa Monica Blvd Los Angeles CA 90025-3594

SALMON, MARGARET BELAIS, nutritionist, dietician; b. N.Y.C. m. Douglas A. Salmon; children: Robert, Betty Lynn, Donald. BS in Food Chemistry, Dietetics and Nutrition, U. Calif., Berkeley, 1941; MS in Human Nutrition, Columbia U., 1964, MS in Sci. Nutrition, 1982. cert. Hosp. Dietetics, Duke U. Hosp., 1943; specialist Nutrition Edn., Columbia U., 1967. Clin. dietitian Columbia-Presbyn. Med. Ctr., N.Y.C., 1943-44, research dietitian, 1956-66; teaching and therapeutic dietitian Englewood (N.J.) Hosp., Hackensack (N.J.) Hosp. and Holy Name Hosp., 1954-57; adminstrv. and therapeutic dietitian St. Luke's Hosp. Ctr., N.Y.C., 1966-70; chief dietitian, dir. dietetic traineeship program St. Joseph's Hosp. and Med. Ctr., Paterson, N.J., 1971-82; pres. Salmon Cons., Harrington Park, N.J., 1970—. Assoc. dir. dietary dept. Bronx (N.Y.)-Lebanon Hosp. Ctr., 1970-71; lectr. in field. Author: Soy Discoveries: Over 700 Quick Soy Recipes, 2001, Diabetic Diet Handbook, 1998, Food Facts for Teenagers, 1965, 2d edit., 2003, (with A. Colby) Physician's Diet Handbook, 1975, rev., 1978, The Joy of Breastfeeding, 1977, 2d rev. edit., 1979, Diabetic Diet Handbook, 1977, Dieta Diabetica Para Buena Salud, 1979, Diabetic Diet Handbook for Low Sodium Diets, 1980, Breast Milk: Nature's Perfect Formula, 1994, Soy Expressions: Common Sense Way to Small Food Bills, 1999, Soy Discoveries: Over 700 Quick Soy Recipes, 2001; editor: Enjoying Your Restricted Diet, 1972, St. Joseph's Hosp. & Med. Ctr. Diet Man., 1977, rev., 1981; contbr. Career Guidance for Young Women, 1974, Easy and Delicious Rice Flour Recipes, 1974, A Professional Dietitian's Natural Fiber Diet, 1987, La Alegria De Alimentacion A Pecho (Joy of Breastfeeding, in spanish), 1987; contbr. articles profl. books and jours.; numerous TV appearances. Mary Swarz Rose scholar, 1961. Mem. Am. Dietetic Assn., Pi Lambda Theta, Omicron Nu, Kappa Delta Pi. Home: 435 Lynn St Harrington Park NJ 07640-1131 Office: Salmon Cons 435 Lynn St Harrington Park NJ 07640-1131

SALMON, MARLA E., nursing educator, dean; b. Vermillion, SD, May 2, 1949; d. Everett Lloyd and Marceline Louise (Adamson) Salmon; m. Jerry Steven Anderson, Aug. 1, 1984; children: Jessica Louise White, Matthew Lawrence White. BA cum laude, U. Portland, 1971, BSN cum laude, 1972; MSN, 1999; ScD, Johns Hopkins U., 1977; DSc (hon.), UNMC, 2003. Dir. patient advocacy program Johns Hopkins U., Balt., 1974-75, instr., 1975-78; asst. prof. U. Minn., Mpls., 1978-82, asst. dir. PRONA, 1978-79, acting dir. PRONA, 1978-80, dir. pub. health nursing programs, 1980-85, assoc. prof., 1982-86; prof. pub. health nursing, chmn. dept. U. N.C., Chapel Hill, 1986-92; dir. nursing div., Bureau Health Professions HHS, Rockville, 1991-97; prof., dean Grad. Sch. Nursing U. Pa., Phila., 1997-99, dir. grad. studies; dean, prof. Nell Hodgson Woodruff Sch. Nursing Emory U., Atlanta, 1999—. Cons. in field. Co-editor: News Outlook, 1989—91; contbr. articles to profl. jours. Trustee Robert Wood Johnson Found., 2002—; mem. Presdl. Task Force Health Care Reform, Washington, 1993; U.S. del. WHO, Geneva, 1995. Recipient Recognition award, Assn. State Territorial Dirs. Nursing, 1993, Achievement award, Nat. Black Nurses Found., 1994, Presdl. award for Meritorious Exec., The White House, 1995; Fulbright scholar, 1972—73, W. K. Kellogg fellow, 1984—87, Reflective Leadership fellow, 1985—86, Rsch. grantee, 1975—78. Mem.: APHA, ANA (v.p. coun. cmty. health nursing 1988—, mem. task froce credentialing 1989), Women's Health Leadership Trust, Assn. Cmty. Healgh Nurses Educators, N.C. Nurses Assn., N.C. Pub. Health Assn., N.C. League Nursing, Nat. League Nursing, Am. Tae Kwon Do Assn., Am. Acad. Nursing, Sigma Xi, Delta Omega, Sigma Theta Tau. Avocations: athletics, gardening. Office: Emory U Nell Hodgson Woodruff Sch 1520 Clifton Rd Ste 402 Atlanta GA 30322-4207 Office Phone: 404-727-7976. Business E-Mail: msalmon@emory.edu.

SALO, ANN SEXTON DISTLER, lawyer; b. Indpls., Sept. 2, 1947; d. Harry W. and Ann (Malloy) Distler; m. Donald R. Salo, June 3, 1972 (div. Feb. 1983); 1 child, Eric V.; m. Phillip G. Clark, May 5, 1990; children: Ann Potter Clark, Phillip Gray Clark. BA, Purdue U., 1969; JD, George Washington U., 1972; LLM in Taxation, Emory U., 1976. Bar: Ga. 1973, U.S. Dist. Ct. (no. dist.) Ga. 1974. Assoc. Hansell & Post, Atlanta, 1972-78, mng. ptnr., 1978-89; ptnr. Grenwald and Salo, Atlanta, 1989-92, Long, Aldridge & Norman, Atlanta, 1992-95, Salo & Walker, Atlanta, 1995—. Adj. prof. law Emory U., 1983—86; mem. fin. planning adv. bd. Warren Gorham & Lamont, 1988—2000. Author: Estate Planning, 1988. Bd. dirs. Auditory Edn. Ctr., Atlanta, 1987—93, 1998—2001; pres. Planned Parenthood, Atlanta, 1984—88, Atlanta Humane Soc., 1990—93. Fellow: Am. Coll. Trust and Estate Counsel (state chair 2001—); mem.: Atlanta Estate Planning Coun. Office: Salo & Walker 2968 Lookout Pl NE Atlanta GA 30305-3272 Office Phone: 404-264-4555. Personal E-mail: adsalo@bellsouth.net.

SALO, PATRICIA ANN, elementary school educator; b. Chgo., Dec. 6, 1953; d. Valentin Frank and Vivian Jean Bruner; m. Brad S. Salo, June 26, 1976; children: Eric Michael, Aili Victoria Heintz. BA in History, St. Norbert Coll., DePere, Wis., 1975, BA in Elem. Edn., 1975; MA in Edn., Viterbo U., LaCrosse, Wis., 1991. Cert. tchr. Wis. Dept. Edn., 1975. Tchr. S.S. Peter and Paul Sch., Green Bay, Wis., 1975—80, St. Joseph Sch., Green Bay, 1983—85; tchr. Franklin Mid. Sch. Green Bay (Wis.) PUb. Schs., 1985—. Recipient Golden Apple award, Ptnrs. Edn., Green Bay, 1999. Mem.: NEA. Office: Franklin Middle School 1234 West Mason Green Bay WI 54393 Office Phone: 920-492-2670. Business E-Mail: psalo@greenbay.k12.wi.us.

SALOMON, JOHANNA, artist; b. Passaic, N.J., Jan. 29, 1944; d. Anthony Locicero and Antoinette Marie (Sanna) Patti; m. William John Blomquist, Nov. 3, 1963 (div. 1980); 1 child, Kim Marie Blomquist Manning; m. Martin Eugene Salomon, Aug. 28, 1983; stepchildren: David, Lisa, Jeffrey Student, Arts Ctr. No. N.J., 1986—92, Bergen C.C., 1987, Art Students League, 1990—91. Exhibit coord. N.Y. Theol. Sem. Gallery, 1993-2000, Mary Poulos Gallery, Paramus Cmty. Sch., N.J., 1994-99; chair Art Ctr. No. N.J., Nat. Juried Show, 1993-94; art judge various art show, 1991-2005 Exhibited in one-woman and group shows including Nat. Arts Club, N.Y., 1990, 92, Art Student's League Gallery, N.Y.C., 1991, William Carlos Williams Ctr. for Arts, Rutherford, N.J., 1991-92, 94, Cmty. Arts Assn. Tri-State Show, Ridgewood, N.J., 1990, 94, Vineyard Theatre Gallery, N.Y.C., 1990, Art Ctr. No. N.J., New Milford, 1989-2006, Stable Gallery, Ridgewood, 1990-2003, Hackensack (N.J.) Women's Club, 1987-92, Westwood (N.J.) C. of C. Art Festival, 1990, Hackensack C. of C., 1987-91, Pascack Art Club, 1989-91, Norfield Ch., Weston, Conn., 1990, Interchurch Ctr., N.Y., 1990, 92, 94, 2004, Bergen County Mus. Art, Paramus, 1991, So. Vt. Artists Nat. Exhibit, 1991, Little Firehouse Theatre, Oradell, N.J., 1992, Nathan's Gallery, West Paterson, N.J., 1992, Essex Fine Art Gallery, Monclair, N.J., 1992, Paramus Cmty. Sch., 1992, The Women's Rights Info. Ctr., Englewood, N.J., 1991-92, Nabisco Corp., Hanover, N.J., 1992, N.Y. Theol. Sem., 1993, Paterson Mus., 1993, Lever House, 1993, Old Ch. Cultural Ctr., Demerest, N.J., 1993, YM-YWHA, Washington Twp., N.J., 1994, 2003, 06, Cork Gallery, Lincoln Ctr., N.Y.C., 1994, Ceres Gallery, N.Y., 1994, Ringwood Manor Mus., N.J., 1994, Belskie Mus. Art and Sci., 2002, 06, others Art judge Substance Abuse Group Emerson, N.J., 1991 Mem. Art Ctr. Watercolor Affiliates (pres. 1990—), Hackensack Art Club (chair membership 1985-92, Winsor and Newton award 1985, Grumbacher award 1989), Art Ctr. No. N.J. (bd. dirs. 1990-94), Salute to Women in Arts, Art Ctr. Painting Affiliates, Cmty. Arts Assn Avocations: painting, drawing.

SALOMON, LAUREN MANNING, psychologist; b. Houston, Jan. 28, 1970; d. Diane and Arthur Abraham Manning; m. Miguel Roberto Salomon, June 7, 1998; children: Analia Nicole, Layla Michelle. BS Psychology, Tex. A&M U., College Station, 1992; MA Psychology, U. Houston, 1997, PhD Indsl. Orgnl. Psychology, 2000. Intern Andersen Cons., Houston, 1995; assoc. cons. Mgmt. & Pers. Sys., Houston, 1995—97; cons. Aon Cons., Houston, 1997—99; orgn. devel. specialist MD Anderson Cancer Ctr., Houston, 2000—04; cons. Salomon Solutions, Houston, 2005—. Adj. prof. U. Houston, Clear Lake, Tex., 2005—, U. Phoenix, Houston, 2005—; presenter in field. Interview coord. Bellaire Young Mothers, Houston, 2005; sec. Mothers for Clean Air, Houston, 2004. Recipient Trammel Tuition award, Tex. A&M U., 1988—92, Oustanding Jr. award, 1991; scholar, Bus. & Profl. Womens Club, 1995, Burnett Pers., 1988, Grocers Assn., 1988. Mem.: APA, Houston Area Indsl. Orgnl. Psychologists (newsletter editor 1996), Soc. of Indsl. Orgnl. Psychologists. Democrat. Jewish. Avocations: Karate, bicycling, yoga. Home: 6620 Community Houston TX 77005 Personal E-mail: laurensalomon@sbcglobal.net.

SALOMON, MARILYN, artist; b. Ann Arbor, Mich., Jan. 30, 1943; d. William Iane and Sarah Sheon; m. Charles Sam. Salomon, Dec. 22, 1962; children: Teri(dec.), Alicia, Cliff. BA, UCLA, 1965; postgrad., Calif. State U., Northridge, 1969-70, 88, Miriam Ariav, Israel, 1970. Elem. edn. tchr., Simi Valley, Calif., 1966-69; artist, 1970—. Guest lectr. Internat. Batik Conf., Ghent, Belgium, 1999, Scottsdale Art League, 2003, Payson Art League, 2005; asst. art curator mus. show, Lancaster, Calif., 1993; leader workshop Surface Designer Nat. Conf., Calif. State U., Northridge, 1988; represented by Judith Hale Gallery, Los Olivos, Calif., Feats of Clay, Idyllwild, Calif., La Fuente, Sedona, Ariz., Pepper Tree Show, Santa Ynez, Calif., 2003, 40, 05, 06; participant Internat. Batik Exhibit, Hanover, Germany, 2002, Internat. Batik Exhibit, Cologne, Germany, 2002, Internat. Batik Exhibit, Dortmund, Germany, 2002, Ryman Found. show, 2000-05, 06, Koln, Germany, 2002, Dortmund, 2003, World Batik Exbhn., Boston, 2005, Stone Ave. Gallery, Tucson, 2006; lectr. in field; subject of TV interview Process of Batik, 2001. One-woman shows include Ranch House, Ojai, Calif., 1975-78, Gallerie 507,

Carlsbad, Calif., 1984, Sun West Gallery, Prescott, Ariz., 1986, Art Beat Gallery, Agoura, Calif., 1987, Jewish Cmty. Ctr., Long Beach, Calif., 1985; exhibited in group shows at Cygnet Gallery, Santa Rosa, Calif., 1981, Jewish Fedn. Bldg., Olympic Exhbn., L.A., 1984, La Quinta Arts Found., 1985-91, Thousand Oaks Mus., 1988-89 (1st pl. 1988, Purchase award 1989), Calif. Luth. U., 1989, Nat. Mus. History, Santa Barbara, Calif., 1990, City of La Quinta, 1991 (Purchase award), Lancaster Mus., 1992-93, 98, Conejo Valley Mus., 1992 (2d pl. award), Riverside Mus. Art, 1998, Walt Disney Ryman Found., Burbank, Calif., featured artist, 1997-99, Horizen Fine Arts, Jackson, 2002; represented in permanent collections City of Tempe, City of Thousand Oaks, City of La Quinta, Taft Entertainment, 1983, Cancer Inst. Ariz., 1983 (Phippen Art Mus. 1st Pl. Mixed MEdia award 2006); featured in TV interview KTVK, Ariz., 2000, featured artist, 2000-05; works appear in Batik for Artists & Quilters, 2000. Workshop leader Surface Designer's Nat. Conf., Calif. State U., Northridge, 1988; studio home tour Westlake Art Guild, Calif., 1989, Pan Hellenic Home Tour Riverside featured Salomon's Art, 1986; home studio tour Payson Art League, 2004, 05, 06. Recipient purchase award City of Tempe, Ariz., 1983, City of Thousand Oaks, Calif., 1989, City of La Quinta, 1991. Mem. (elected charter mem.) Women's Nat. Mus., Phoenix Art Mus. Avocations: hiking, yoga, reading, music, gardening. Home: HC 2 Box 261D Payson AZ 85541-9418 Personal E-mail: mcsalomon@earthlink.net.

SALOMON, MARYLOU ANN, elementary school educator; b. Scottsbluff, Nebr., May 11, 1972; d. James Arthur and Bonnie Lou Arends; m. Matthew Eric Salomon, Aug. 10, 1996; children: Sarah Lou Ann, Michael Alan. BS in Edn., U. Nebr., Kearney, 1996. Tchr. 8th grade math, algebra Bluffs Mid. Sch., Scottsbluff, Nebr., 1997—. Sponsor Thinking Cap Quiz Bowl, Scottsbluff. Mem. Westway Christian Ch., Scottsbluff, 1995—2006. Mem.: Scottsbluff Edn. Assn. Office: Bluffs Middle School 23rd & Broadway Scottsbluff NE 69361 Office Phone: 308-635-6270. E-mail: msalomon@sbps.net.

SALONGA, LEA, actress, singer; b. Manila, Feb. 22, 1971; d. Feliciano Genuino and Maria Ligaya (Imutan) Salonga; m. Robert Charles Chien, Jan. 10, 2004. Attended, Ateneo De Manila U., 1988-89. Actress, singer The King and I, Manila, 1978, Annie, Manila, 1980, The Rose Tattoo, Manila, 1980, The Bad Seed, Manila, 1981, The Goodbye Girl, Manila, 1982, Paper Moon, Manila, 1983, The Fantasticks, Manila, 1988, Miss Saigon, London, 1989-90 (Outstanding Performance by Actress in Musical Olivier award 1990), Broadway, 1991-92 (Best Actress in Musical Tony award 1991, Best Actress in Musical Drama Desk award 1991, Best Actress in Musical Outer Critics Circle award 1991, Outstanding Debut Theatre World award 1991), Les Miserables, Broadway, 1993, My Fair Lady, Manila, 1994, Into the Woods, Singapore, 1994, Les Miserables, London, 1996, 3rd nat. tour, 1996, also The Sound of Music, Manila, Fiddler on the Roof, Manila, Cat on a Hot Tin Roof; Philippine films include Bakit Labis Kitang Mahal?, Dear Diary, Pik Pak Boom, Captain Barbell, Ninja Kids, Like Father, Like Son, Tropang Bulilit; Philippine TV: (host) Kulit Bulilit, Love Lea, Naku, Ha!, Sunday Special, Iba Ito!, That's Entertainment!, This is It!, (co-host) Patok Na Patok!; opening act for Stevie Wonder, Menudo; concerts: The Filipinos of Miss Saigon, A Miss Called Lea, Lea Salonga in Concert, L.A., San Francisco, Les Miserables 10th Anniversary Concert, London, 1995; recs. include Small Voice, 1981 (gold record), Lea, Happy Children's Club, Christmas Album, We are the World, (debut album) Lea Salonga, 1993, Miss Saigon original London cast rec. (gold record), The King and I, Aladdin, 1992 (singing voice Princess Jasmine, motion picture soundtrack), Les Miserables 10th Anniversary Concert Album, 1996, Royal Couyabyab: The Silver Album, 1996, The Little Tramp, (singing voice) Mulan, 1998, (Broadway) Flower Drum Song, 2002; TV films include: Redwood Curtain, 1998, (TV series) As the World Turns, 2001, 03; concert, Carnegie Hall, 2005. Recipient AWIT award outstanding svc. Philippings Recording Industry, 1993, ASEAN Industry award performing arts, 1992, Ten Outstanding Young Men award outstanding debut, 1991, AWIT award outstanding performer, 1990, Presdl. Award of Merit Pres. Aquino, 1990, Laurence Olivier award best actress musical, 1990, Cecil award best recording by a child, 1984, Tinig award one of 10 outstanding singers, 1983, 94, 92, ALIW award best child performer, 1980, 81, 82; named Outstanding Manilan by Govt. City of Manila, 1990. Mem.: Screen Actors' Guild, Actors' Equity Assn., AFTRA. Roman Catholic. Avocations: music, reading, collecting raised-trunk elephants, collecting swatches, working on computers. Office: c/o Jeff Hunter 1325 Avenue Of The Americas New York NY 10019-6026 Home: 1926 Caminito Del Pilar Glendale CA 91208-3051

SALSBURY, DONNA DENISE, elementary school educator; b. St. Louis, May 28, 1954; d. Oliver Dennis Hensley and Lois Laconia Parks - Stuck; children: Douglas Lemoine, Matthew Stuart, Justin Curtis. BA in Elem. Edn., NE La. U., 1984. 4th grade tchr. Waxahachie (Tex.) Ind. Sch. Dist., 1984—88; patient edn./liason Garst Med. Clinic, Mountain View, Ark., 1988—90; 5th & 6th grade tchr. Leslie (Ark.) Pub. Sch. Dist., 1991—2002; 6th grade sci. tchr. Fayetteville (Ark.) Pub. Schs., Holt Mid. Sch., 2002—03; 5th grade tchr. Point Isabel (Tex.) Ind. Sch. Dist., Derry Elem., 2003—04, Okaloosa County Sch. Dist., Valparaiso Elem., Fort Walton Beach, Fla., 2004—. Math stds. com. Ark. Dept. Edn., Little Rock, 1996—2002. Coach jr. olympics swim team Ark. AAU, 1992—95; facilitator world leadership forum People To People Amb. Program, Washington, 2006; swim team coach Boston Mountains Swim Team, Stone County Swim Team, Marshall and Mountain View, Ark., 1991—2001; water safety instr., lifeguard Red Cross, Marshall and Mountain View, Ark., 1992—2001; scout leader, awards chmn. Boy Scouts of Am., Mountain View and Leslie, Ark., 1988—2001; organizer Jump Rope for Heart Am. Heart Assn., Leslie, 1998—2001; pres. swimming Ark. AAU, 1992—94. Mem.: NEA. Avocations: reading, travel, swimming. Office: Valparaiso Elementary School 379 Edge Ave Valparaiso FL 32580 Office Phone: 850-833-4120. Office Fax: 850-833-4177. Business E-Mail: salsburyd@mail.okaloosa.k12.fl.us.

SALTER, ELIZABETH MARY, academic administrator; d. Robert William Salter; m. John Carl Kolar, June 14, 1980; children: Victoria, Ian. BA, U. Toronto, Ont., 1971, M of Mus. Studies, 1972; MA, U. Calgary, Alta., Can., 1974; PhD, U. Toronto, Ont., 1984. Asst. prof. U. Toronto, 1985—87; asst. to dean U. Tex., Dallas, 1994—95, assoc. undergrad. dean, 1997—99, asst. dean, 1995—2000, assoc. dean, 2000—. Elected mem. acad. senate U. Tex.-Dallas, Richardson, 2000—07, chair student scholarship com., 2005—06. Co-author: Craniofacial Anthropometry, 1996. Named Best Tchr. Social Scis., U. Toronto, 1998; recipient Praxis award, Wash. Assn. Profl. Anthropologists, 1997. Avocations: reading, pets. Office: U Tex-Dallas Gen Studies GR26 2601 N Floyd Rd Richardson TX 75083

SALTER, LINDA LEE, security officer; b. Garden City, Mich., Oct. 10, 1953; d. Bertram Edward and Gertrude Thersa (Barnes) S.; children: Korina Reshell Irene Miller, Terry Wayne Tomlin II. Grad., Henry Ford C.C., 1998; student, U. Detroit, 1999. Security supr. Guardsmark, Memphis, 1979-86, security officer, 1986-96, Detroit, 1998—, Detroit Newspapers, 1986-96, advt. officer, 1996—. Emergency first aid specialist ARC, Dearborn, Mich., 1993—. Mem. St. Anne's Cath. Ch.; pres. Downriver/Monroe County Women Involved Wings, South Rockwood, Mich., 1991—; mem. Lupus Found., 1995—, Monroe County Humane Soc., 1993—, Ladies Aux., 1971—; reunion class tchr. Carlson HS, Gibraltar, Mich., 1971. Mem.: Mich. Humane Soc. Roman Catholic. Avocations: reading, travel, horses, sports, gardening. Home: 22033 Verdun St Romulus MI 48174-9533 Office: Detroit Newspapers 615 W Lafayette Blvd Detroit MI 48226-3197 Office Phone: 313-303-6181. E-mail: llsalt@prodigy.net.

SALTER, MARY JO, poet; b. Grand Rapids, Mich., Aug. 15, 1954; d. Albert Gregory and Lormina (Paradise) S.; m. Brad Leithauser, 1980; children: Emily Salter, Hilary Garner. BA cum laude, Harvard U., 1976; MA, Cambridge U., 1978. Instr. Harvard U., 1978-79; instr. English conversation Japan, 1980-83; lectr. English Mt. Holyoke Coll., South Hadley, Mass., 1984—, Emily Dickinson sr. lectr. in humanities, 1995—. Staff editor Atlantic Monthly, 1978-80; poet-in-residence Robert Frost Place, 1981; poetry editor The New Republic, 1992-95. Author: Henry Purcell in Japan, 1985, Unfinished Painting, 1989 (Lamont prize in poetry 1988), The Moon Comes Home, 1989, Sunday Skaters: Poems, 1994 (Nat. Book Critics Circle award nomination 1994), A Kiss in Space: Poems, 1999, Open Shutters: Poems, 2003; co-editor: Norton Anthology of Poetry, 5th edit., 2005; contbr. to periodicals including New Yorker, New Republic, Kenyon Rev. Amy Lowell scholar, 1995; recipient Discovery prize Nation, 1983; Nat. Endowment for Arts fellow, 1983-84, Guggenheim fellow, 1993. Mem. Internat. P.E.N. Office: care Alfred A Knopf Inc 1745 Broadway New York NY 10019

SALTER, PHYLLIS JEAN, counselor; b. Jackson, Miss., Nov. 15, 1959; d. John Emmette and Sarah Kathryn (Dilworth) Lang; m. Eric Todd Salter, Aug. 2, 1986; children: Eric Todd II, Rekia. BS in Zoology, Ohio State U., 1981; M Rehab. Counseling, Wright State U., 1983. Lic. counselor, Ohio. Counseling intern Greene Hall Rehab. Ctr., Xenia, Ohio, 1982, Bur. Vocat. Rehab. Svcs., Dayton, Ohio, 1983; instr., counselor Sinclair Community Coll., Dayton, 1984—. Tutor Wright State U., Dayton, 1982-83, counselor grad. asst., 1982-84, spl. svcs. project counselor, 1983-84. Mem. Nat. Assn. Developmental Edn., Ohio Assn. Developmental Edn. (pres. 1990-91), Ohio Coll. Personnel Assn., Alpha Kappa Alpha (life). Democrat. A.M.E.

SALTIEL, NATALIE, accountant; b. Chgo., Mar. 19, 1927; d. Henry Carl and Dorothy (Maremont) S.; m. Sidney D. Levin, Oct. 13, 1963; 1 chld, Erica Saltiel Levin. BBA with highest distinction, Northwestern U., 1948. CPA, Ill. Mem. staff acctg. firm, Chgo., 1948-52; pvt. practice acctg. Chgo., 1952—. Bd. dirs., mem. exec. com., chmn. com. United Way Chgo., 1979-85, United Way/Crusade of Mercy, 1979-86; mem. adv. coun., chmn. com. Sta. WBEZ Chicagoland Pub. Radio, 1981-91; bd. dirs. Chgo. Fin. Exch., 1989-90; bd. dirs., treas., v.p., Jewish Coun. Urban Affairs, 1992-98. Mem. AICPA, Ill. CPA Soc., Am. Women's Soc. CPAs, ACLU (Ill. bd. dirs., 1961-1978, Vol. Svc. award, 2003), Beta Gamma Sigma. Office: 105 W Madison St Ste 401 Chicago IL 60602-4603 Office Phone: 312-332-7405.

SALTMAN, JULIET A., retired sociology educator; b. Haifa, Israel, Apr. 30, 1923; d. Samuel Herman and Bertha Zion; m. William M. Saltman, Feb. 14, 1943; children: David, Nina, Daniel. BA, Rutgers U., New Brunswick, NJ, 1943; MA, U. Chgo., 1948; PhD, Case Western Res. U., Cleve., 1971. Prof. emerita sociology Kent State U., 1988—. Cons. fair housing and neighborhood stabilization for govt. and pvt. agys.; mem. adv. bd. intergroup rels. grant program Mott Found. Author: 3 books in field; contbr. articles to profl. publs. Founder Akron Fair Housing Contact Svc., 1965, West Side Neighbors, 1967. Recipient Nat. Vol. award, 1970, Akron Area Brotherhood award, 1977, Douglass Soc. Alumna award, Rutgers U. Home: 12973 Candela Pl San Diego CA 92130

SALTUS, PHYLLIS BORZELLIERE, music educator; b. Rochester, N.Y., Jan. 17, 1931; d. Nicholas and Sadie Veronica (Leone) Borzelliere; m. William Thomas Saltus, Aug. 21, 1965 (div. Apr. 1991); children: Julie Marie Nicole, William Nicholas. AA, Burlington County Coll., Pemberton, N.J., 1987; MEd in Measurement and Guidance, U. Maine, Orono, 1963; BS in Music Edn., SUNY, 1953, MS, 1957. Cert. student personnel svcs., music and guidance, N.J., N.Y., Me. Music tchr., choral dir. Rochester Pub. Schs., 1953-56, 62-63, 1969-70, high sch. guidance counselor, 1963-65; asst. prof. music edn. SUNY, Geneseo and Fredonia, 1956-62; music tchr, choral dir. Concord (Mass.) Pub. Schs., 1965-66; owner, dir. Saltus Music Studio, Medford, N.J., 1982-94. Music tchr., choral dir. Delanco (N.J.) Pub. Schs., 1984-86; prof. voice N.J.Dept. Edn. Sch. Arts, Rowan Univ., Glassboro (N.J.) State Coll., 1987-89; sr. adj. prof. & coordn., piano lab Burlington County Coll., Pemberton, N.J. and Ft. Dix Mil. Post, Cmty. Coll. of the Air Force at McGuire AFB, 1989—, Interactive Classroom Program, 1995—, Power Package Accelerated Program, 1995—, Telecourse for Distance Learners Program WBZC, 1995—; music coord., dist. tchr. for gifted and talented program Mt. Laurel (N.J.) Pub. Schs., 1989-94; music dir., founding mem. Triple Threat Prodns., Cherry Hill, N.J., 1991—, Burlington County Cmty. Chorus, N.J., 1995—, Kosciusko Boys Choir, Rochester, 1959-60, Young Adults Cath. Youth Orgn. Choir, Dunkirk, N.Y., 1960-62; faculty adv. N.Y. Province of Newman Clubs Fedn. SUNY, 1957-62, lectr., researcher in field. Artist: The Fredonia Main Street Diner, 1952-53, Clarence Welcome Wagon Gourmet Cook Book, N.Y., 1973; contbr. poems to various publs.; soloist Rochester Philharm. Orch. Concert Series, Songsters, Inc., 1953-59. Choir dir., organist, soloist St. Philip Neri R.C. Ch., Rochester, 1949-65, St. Peter's Episc. Ch., Medford, 1989-90; choir dir., accompanist Thessalonia Baptist Ch. Sr. and Jr. Choirs, Willingboro, N.J., 1990-91; vocal dir., accompanist Pineland Players of South Jersey Community Theatre, Medford, 1987-89, Cherry Hill East High Sch., N.J., 1991—; team capt. United Way, Rochester, 1953-56; membership chair Rochester Community Theater, 1955-56; founding mem. Sta. WCVF, 1952-58; bd. dirs., founding mem. Rochester Chamber Orch., 1964-65, Medford (N.J.) Newcomers Club, 1977—; vol. Cmty. Companions of Erie County Office of the Aging, N.Y., 1972-76, Medford PTO, 1976-85; judge preliminary Miss Am. contest Jr. C. of C., Jamestown, N.Y., 1962, vocal dir., accompanist Miss Dunkirk (N.Y.) pageant, 1962, vocal coach Miss Burlington County Pageant, Jr. C. of C., 1989,97-99; active Welcome Wagon, Inc., Clarence, N.Y., pres., 1974, historian, 1981; chair Medford (N.J.) Evening Book Review Group, 1978-80; mem. Medford Morning Book Review Group, 1980—; active Meml. Health Alliance, Burlington County Women's Health Network. NDEA grantee, 1964; EEOC scholar, 1986-87; recipient Jr. County Rifle Championship award Monroe County Dept. Health and Recreation, 1948, Womens Student Table Tennis Championship award SUNY, 1952, Outstanding Scholarship award Charlotte Putnam Landers Outstanding Scholarship award SUNY, 1953. Mem. AAUP (treas. 1960-62, state del. 1961), Music Educators Nat. Conf., Am. Personnel and Guidance Assn., South Jersey Music Tchrs. Assn., Meml. Health Alliance, Women's Health Network, AARP Medford chpt. of Deborah heart & lung hosp. foudn.,Red Lion wildlife Refuge, Vincetown, N.J., Cedar Run Wildlife Refuge, Medford, N.J., Order Sons of Italy in Am., Kappa Delta Pi (del. Barnard Coll., N.Y., 1952, state del., Atlantic City, N.J., 1953). Roman Catholic. Avocations: reading and research, creative writing, golf, painting, crossword puzzles, gourmet cooking. Home: 77 Finchley Ct Southampton NJ 08088-1006

SALTZ, AMY, theater educator, director; b. Bklyn. d. Jerome Lawrence and Florence Zunser Saltz. BA, Univ. Wis. Staff repertory dir. The Acting Co., NYC, 1976—79; adj. assoc. prof. theater arts Columbia U., NYC, 1986—87; adj. prof. directing Rutgers U., New Brunswick, NJ, 1987—2000; adj. assoc. prof. drama Yale U., New Haven, 1991—. Assoc. artistic dir. Napa Valley Theater Co., St. Helena, Calif., 1970—73; theater auditor NY State Coun. Arts, NYC, 1970—79; dir. Eugene O'Neill Nat. Playwright's Conf., Waterford, Conn., 1981—; Tony Award voter Am. Theater Wing Soc. Stage Dirs. & Choreographers, NYC, 1985—93; final selection com. O'Neill Nat. Playwrights' Conf., Waterford, 1990—99; adv. bd. 7 Devils Playwright's Conf., McCall, Idaho, 2001—; artistic dir. InHouse Theater Co., NYC, 2001—; individual artist, new works panelist Mass. Cultural Coun., Boston, 2001, 2005—; dirs. project panelist The Drama League, NYC, 2005—; directing fellowship panelist Nat. Endowment Arts, Theater Comm. Group, NYC; plays in process selection com. panelist Theatre Comm. Group, NYC; playwright, dirs. panel Theater Comm. Group, NYC; artistic dir. InHouse Theater Co., NYC; award panelist Edith Oliver award; award panelist Eric Kocher award; award panelist Herbert Brokin award; award panelist Charles MacArthur award; theatre panelist, on-site evaluator Mass. Cultural Coun., Boston; guest dir. NYU, Tisch Sch. of the Arts, NYC, The Juilliard Sch., NYC; asst. dir. NY Shakespeare Festival, NYC; head mfa dir. program Rutgers U. Dir.: (play) Brave New World: A Response To 9/11; (plays) The Scottish Play, Verily, Verily, The Buriel Society, Something Unspoken: One Act Plays by Tennessee Williams, A Midsummer Night's Dream, Fishing, Final Placement, Something Unspoken: An evening of Tennessee Williams One Act Plays; dir., dir.: (plays) A Delicate Balance, Man and Superman, A Case of You, Arms and the Man, Fuente, Hedda Gabler (Time Out Best Area Play of Season, 1994), The Find, Heidi Chronicles (Handy award, Best dir. & best prodn., 1991), Funeral March for a One-Man Band (Joseph Jefferson award for Best Dir. & Best Prodn., 1980), A Voice of My Own (NY Times Top 10 Off Broadway Shows, 1980), Tiny Mommy; (TV series) Search for Tomorrow, Another World; author: (plays) Touch (Grammy Award Nominee, 1970); dir.: (theater) To Kill A Mockingbird. Mem.: Am. Dirs. Inst. (adv. bd. mem.), Soc. Stage Dirs. & Choreographers (exec. com. mem.), Am. Theatre Inst. (panelist), Am. Assn. Theatre in Higher Edn. (panelist), Dirs. Guild Am., League Profl. Theater Women, Soc. Stage Dirs. & Choreographers (exec. bd. 1984—93). Achievements include aided in the development of new work by numerous prestigious writers including Neal Bell, Lee Blessing, Adam Rapp, John Patrick Shanley and August Wilson; directed at major theatres across the country including The Public Theatre, NYC, Playwrights Horizons, NYC, The Second Stage, NYC and Theatre for a New Audience, NYC; Yale Repertory Theatre, Seattle Rep, Actor's Theater of Louisville, Ivanhoe Theatre, Chicago, St. Nicholas, Chicago, Syracuse Stage, Great Lakes Theatre Festival, Cincinatti Playhouse. Home: 108 Fifth Ave #8B New York NY 10011 Office: Rutgers U Theatre Arts Dept 2 Chapel Dr New Brunswick NJ 08901 Home Fax: 212-924-5009; Office Fax: 732-932-1409. Personal E-mail: ascl594@aol.com. Business E-Mail: asaltz@rci.rutgers.edu.

SALTZMAN, BOBBIE, theater educator; b. Paterson, N.J., Sept. 29, 1960; d. Samuel S. and Lenore (Friedman) Saltzman. BA magna cum laude, Montclair State Coll., N.J., 1982; MA, Montclair State Coll., 1987; MFA, U. Calif. Davis, 1995. Stage performer Nat. Touring Co. Happy Times Children's Co., 1983—86; dir. conservation Am. Stage Co., Teaneck, NJ, 1987—90; exec. dir. Hadassah, San Francisco, 1990—93; prof. Theatre South Suburban Coll., South Holland, Ill., 2001—. Adj. prof. numerous colls., 1987—2000; bd. dirs. Evanston Arts Coun., Ill., 1999—2003, mem. cultural diversity com., 1999—2003. Author (performer): Fanny: Remembering, 1982—87. Mem., donor WTTW Pub. TV, Chgo., 1999—, Guide Dogs for Blind, San Rafael, Calif., 1999—, Broadway Cares, N.Y.C., 1999—. Fellow, Montclair State Coll., 1986—87, U. Calif. Davis, 1993—95. Democrat. Jewish. Avocations: art, architecture. Home: 10418 S Walden Pkwy Chicago IL 60643 Office: South Suburban Coll Theatre Dept 15800 S State St South Holland IL 60473

SALTZMAN, IRENE CAMERON, consumer products company executive; b. Cocoa, Fla., Mar. 23, 1927; d. Argyle Bruce and Marie T. (Neel) Cameron; m. Herman Saltzman, Mar. 23, 1946 (dec. May 1986); children: Martin Howard (dec.), Arlene Norma Hanly. Owner Irene Perfume and Cosmetics Lab., Jacksonville, Fla., 1972—. Mem. Cummer Mus. Art, Jacksonville, 1972-. Mem. NAFE, Ret. Judge Advocates Assn. of USAF (hon.), Mil. Officers Assn. Am., Aircraft Owners and Pilots Assn., Trade, Cosmetic, Toiletry and Fragrance Assn., Ret. Officers Assn., Soc. Cosmetic Chemists (affiliate), Ponte Vedra Club. Democrat. Episcopalian. Avocations: aviation, painting, travel, swimming, golf. Home: 2701 Ocean Dr S Jacksonville Beach FL 32250 Office Phone: 904-641-5171. Business E-Mail: irene@ireneparfums.com.

SALTZSTEIN, SUSAN L., lawyer; b. N.Y., 1965; BA, U. Pa., 1987; JD magna cum laude, Columbia U., 1991. Bar: N.Y. 1992. Atty. Skadden, Arps, Slate, Meagher & Flom LLP, N.Y., 1992—. Office: Skadden Arps Slate Meagher & Flom LLP Four Times Sq New York NY 10036

SALVATORE, DIANE J., editor-in-chief; BA in Journalism, Pa. State U.; MA in English and Creative Writing, NYU. Rschr., reporter The Soho News, NYC; editl. asst. Met. Home, NYC, Cosmopolitan, NYC; sr. assoc. editor Ladies' Home Jour., NYC, 1985—88; articles assoc. editor Glamour, NYC, 1988—89; sr. editor Redbook, NYC, 1989—94; dep. editor Good Housekeeping, NYC, exec. editor, 1994—99; editor in chief YM, NYC, 1998—2002; exec. dir. Marie Claire, 2001; editor in chief Ladies Home Jour., NYC, 2002—; dir. editl. ops. Hearst Mag., 2002. Contbr. articles and short stories in various nat. periodicals. Mem.: Am. Soc. Mag. Editors. Office Phone: 212-455-1025. Office Fax: 212-455-1313. E-mail: diane.salvatore@meredith.com.*

SALVATORE, NANCY BAKER, elementary school educator; b. Bristol, Conn., Sept. 9, 1955; d. Edward Paul and Marcia Veitch Baker; m. Anthony Joseph Salvatore, Dec. 23, 1977; children: ELizabeth Ann, Michael Baker. BS in Biology, Ctrl. Conn. State U., 1977, MS in Adminstrn. and Supervision, 1982. Tchr. sci. Sunset Ridge Sch., East Hartford, Conn., 1977—78, Meml. Blvd. Sch., Bristol, 1978—83; tchr., sci. team leader Hbr-Bur Mid. Sch., Burlington, 1994—98; team leader King Philip Mid. Sch., West Hartford, 1998—. Presenter in field. Mem.: West Hartford Edn. Assn., Nat. Sci. Tchrs. Assn., Phi Delta Kappa. Office: King Philip Mid Sch 100 King Philip Dr West Hartford CT 06117 Office Phone: 860-233-8236 ext 1308. Personal E-mail: nbsalvatore@yahoo.com. Business E-Mail: nancy_salvatore@whps.org.

SALVESEN, B. FORBES, artist; b. Elgin, Ill., Nov. 6, 1944; d. Donald Behan and Helen Elaine (Krajacik) Forbes; m. Bruce Michael Salvesen, Sept. 3, 1966. Studied with Elvira Spivey, Barrington, Ill., 1972-74; studied with Peter Schoelch, Cary, Ill., 1975-82; student, Am. Acad. Art, 1976, Sch. Art Inst. Chgo., 1980-82, Kulick-Startk Byzantine Jewelry Sch., 1983. Asst. to purchasing agt. Harnischfeger, Crystal Lake, Ill., 1962-64; rec. sec. Electric Mfrs. Credit Bur., Cary, Ill., 1964-66; student and practicing artist, 1968—. Illustrator: (book) There were Reasons, 1983. Recipient Award of Excellence, Ill.-Arlington Heights Fine Arts Festival, 1995, Best of Show award 20th Ann. Cambridge Art Fair, 1995, 19th Ann. Fine Arts Festival, Downers Grove, Ill., 1995. Democratic. Roman Catholic. Avocations: writing, poetry, jewelry crafting, cross country skiing, hiking. Home: 1312 Whippoorwill Dr Crystal Lake IL 60014-2614 Studio: 1311 Behan Rd Crystal Lake IL 60014 Office Phone: 815-455-0089.

SALZGEBER, KAREN A., secondary school educator; b. Cleve., Oct. 19, 1953; d. Frederick Robert and Carol Grace Petersen; m. Alan Joseph Salzgeber, May 6, 1978; children: Kristen, Kurt. BE cum laude in Math., Kent State U., 1976; MEd in Curriculum & Instr., Cleve. State U., 1993. Permanent cert. tchr. Ohio, 1998. Tchr. math. & journalism Cleve. Pub. Schs., Cleve., 1976—79; presch. tchr. Ridgewood Presch., Parma, Ohio, 1989—91; tchr. H.S. math. Parma City Sch., Parma, 1991—. Math. chairperson Parma Sr. H.S.; co-chmn. Action Com. for Essential Schs., Parma, 1999—; mem. various coms. Parma City Schs. Mem.: Parma Edn. Assn., Ohio Edn. Assn., Nat. Edn. Assn., Ohio Coun. Tchrs. Math., Nat. Coun. Tchrs. Math. Avocations: reading, travel, counted cross stitch, skiing, gardening. Office: Parma Sr High School 6285 W 54th St Parma OH 44129 Office Phone: 440-885-2363. Business E-Mail: salzeberk@parmacityschools.org.

SALZMAN, ANNE MEYERSBURG, retired psychologist; b. N.Y.C., Feb. 25, 1928; d. Reuben and Dorothy (Steinberg) Meyersburg; m. Paul Salzman, Sept. 11, 1952; children: Carol, Harold, Richard. BA, U. N.Mex., 1949; MA, NYU, 1950. Lic. psychologist. Psychologist, field instr. UCLA Psychology Clinic Sch., L.A., 1952-55; psychologist Temple Beth Am, L.A., 1956-60; psychologist, co-dir. Acad. Guidance Svcs., L.A., 1960-76; psychologist, dir. The Guidance Ctr., Santa Monica, Calif., 1976—2006; ret., 2006. Mem. Am. Psychol. Assn., Fedn. Am. Scientists, Calif. State Psychol. Assn., L.A. County Psychol. Assn., Greenpeace. Democrat. Jewish. Avocations: gardening, cooking, sculpting.

SAMAMRA, ELIZABETH PRESTWOOD, literature educator; b. Hickory, NC, Feb. 10, 1978; d. David and Elizabeth Prestwood; m. Raed Rasmi Samamra. BA in Journalism, U. NC, Chapel Hill, 2000; MA in English, NC State U., Raleigh, 2003. English instr. Catawba Valley C.C., Hickory, 2004—. Mem.: Soc. Profl. Journalists. Democrat. Achievements include research in Palestinian literature in occupied Palestine, in exile, and in Israel. Office: Catawba Valley Community College 2550 Hwy 70 SE Hickory NC 28602 Office Phone: 828-327-7000. Personal E-mail: esamamra@cvcc.edu.

SAMANS, ELAINE MAE, education counselor, human services educator; b. Phila. m. Edward W. Samans; children: Deborah, Judith Samans-Dunn, Susan Samans Robinson. BS, Temple U., 1946; MA, Villanova U., 1969; EdD, U. Pa., 1983. Nationally cert. sch. counselor; Pa. cert. sch. counselor, asst. supt., elem. sch. adminstr., supr. I, sch. guidance, instr. II, guidance counselor, social studies tchr., English tchr. Sch. counselor Kennett Consolidated Sch. Dist., Kennett Square, Pa., 1969-74; elem. sch. counselor West Chester (Pa.) Area Sch. Dist., 1974-92; part-time faculty Edn. and Human Svcs. Villanova U., 1990-93. Formerly bd. dirs., treas. Chester County Head Start; presenter numerous workshops; guest lectr. West Chester U.; mem. evaluation team elem. sch. guidance counseling programs Chester County Intermediate Unit #25, 1969-92; counselor edn. advisor on edn. dept. adv. com. West Chester U.; mem. long range planning com. Marie-Newton Sch. Dist., Del. County C.C. Nursery Sch. Asst. Program Adv. Com., ctrl. admissions com. Camp Sunshine for underprivileged children, Del. County. Contbr. articles to profl. jours. and newsletters. Charter mem., past pres., adminstr. Hillview-Trout Run Assn., Inc. (non-profit nursery sch./kindergarten); mem. strategic planning com. Marple Newtown Sch. Dist., Newtown Square, Pa., 1994-95, mem. caring coalition's com. Family Resource Ctr., Marple Newtown; mem. youth aid panel Marple Township, Del. County. Recipient Cert. of Honor, Area Coun. for Econ. Edn., 1985, Joint Coun. Econ. Edn., 1985, Plaque for Outstanding Svc., 1996-2003, Cert. of hon. Del. County. Mem. NEA, ACA, Am. Sch. Counselors Assn., Pa. Student Assistance Program, Pa. Sch. Counseling Assn. (exec. bd., treas. 1985-91, spl. edn. com. chair 1988-92, Elem. Sch. Counselor of Yr. 1989), Pa. Edn. Assn. (S.E. regional counselor sect. steering com., profl. devel. coun., stds. com. chair, adv. bd.), Pi Gamma Mu, Kappa Delta Epsilon, Hist. Honor Soc. Temple U., Phi Delta Kappa, Pi Lambda Theta. Avocations: travel, crossword puzzles, walking, music, theater. Home: 2735 Brierwood Rd Broomall PA 19008-1720

SAMEC, DIANE PATRICIA, retired elementary school educator; b. Oak Pk., Ill., Mar. 17, 1942; d. Albert Vincent Samec and Helen Hrubec. BA, Hope Coll., Holland, Mich., 1964; MSc in edn., No. Ill. U., DeKalb, 1988. Tchr. Interboro Schools, Glenolden, Pa., 1964—65, Sch. Dist. u-46, Elgin, Ill., 1966—2004; ret., 2004. Vol. and mem. Willow Creek Cmty. Ch., South Barrington, 1986—, Sherman Hosp. Aux. Ch., Elgin, 2004—. Mem.: Nat. Audubon Soc., Elgin Ret. Teachers Assn., Elgin Edn. Assn., Ill. Edn. Assn., Nat. Edn. Assn., Willow Creek Comm. Ch., Nat. Wildlife Assn., Environ. Def., Sierra Club, Fox Valley Beaux Arts Women's Club. Avocations: travel, reading, photography.

SAMELSON, JUDY, editor; Editor Playbill, N.Y.C., 1993—.

SAMET, DEE-DEE, lawyer; b. Greensboro, NC, Sept. 18, 1940; BA, U. Ariz., 1962, JD, 1963. Bar: Ariz. 1964. Pvt. practice, Tucson, 1974—; ptnr. Samet & Gage, P.C., Tucson, 2001. Arbitrator U.S. Dist. Ct. Ariz., Gender Equality Task Force, 1993; judge pro tem Pima County Superior Ct., 1985—; Ninth Cir. Lawyer rep., 1990-93; mem. Jud. Performance Rev. Commn., 1996-99; pres. Casa de los Ninos, 2003-05. Mem. Fed. Bar Assn. (pres. Tucson chpt. 2004—), State Bar Ariz. (family law sect., workers compensation sect., trial law sect., co-chair workers compensation sect. 1988-89, gender bias task force, bd. govs. 1994-97, pres. 1999-2000, chmn. elect worker's compensation sect. 2004, chair alternative dispute resolution sect. 2005-), Am. Arbitration Assn. (nat. panel arbitrators, com. on exams., supreme ct. state Ariz. 1984-91), Pima County Bar Assn. (bd. dirs. 1994—), Nat. Assn. Counsel for Children, Ariz. Assn. Counsel for Children, So. Ariz. Women Lawyers Assn. (bd. dirs. 1990, pres. 1994-95, treas. alt. dispute resolution sect. 2003-04, chmn. 2005—), Nat. Orgn. Social Security Claimants' Reps. Office: Dee-Dee Samet PC 717 N 6th Ave Tucson AZ 85705-8304 Office Phone: 520-624-8595. Business E-Mail: dee-dee@samet.psemoil.com.

SAMFORD, KAREN ELAINE, small business owner, consultant; b. Houston, Aug. 14, 1941; d. George C. and Agnes M. (Phillips) Sanford; m. Jeff E. Samford, Aug. 18, 1938; children: Jeffrey Barton, Keri Lynn. BA in English, History, Tex. Christian U., 1964. Cert. secondary tchr., Tex. Tchr. secondary schs., Tex., La., Mo., 1964-74; saleswoman, 1974-83; corp. trainer, 1983-86; owner Karen E. Samford Tng. Cons., Plano, 1986—. Republican. Home and Office: 3409 Haversham Dr Plano TX 75023-6109

SAMFORD, SHARON ANNETTE, elementary school educator, researcher; b. Center, Tex., Nov. 30, 1951; d. Lem Herrin and Tommie Jean Hudson; m. Roy Mac Samford, Nov. 30, 1968; children: Crystallyn Brandi Samford Edwards, Jason Mac. Med, Stephen F. Austin State U., Tex., 1990. Cert. Tchr. Tex. Edn. Agy., 1979. Educator Nacogdoches County Schs. Spl. Edn. Coop., Garrison, Tex., 1979—80, Garrison Ind. Sch. Dist., Tex., 1980—88, Timpson Ind. Sch. Dist., Tex., 1988—2006; 7th & 8th grade math. educator Gary Ind. Sch. Dist., Tex., 2006—. In-svc. presenter Timpson Ind. Sch. Dist., Tex., 2000—, dist. math coord., 2003—. Mem. Garrison Heritage Soc., Tex., 1981—2006, Mt. Olive Bapt. Ch., Timpson, Tex., 1979—2006. Recipient Tchr. of Yr., Shelby County C. of C., 2003; grantee Minorities Math. and Sci. Ednl. Coop., Stephen F. Austin State U., 1993—95. Mem.: Tex. Classroom Tchrs. Assn., Delta Gamma Chpt. of the Delta Kappa Gamma Soc. Internat. (com. chairperson 2004—06). Conservative. Baptist. Avocations: photography, scrapbooks, ATV riding, travel, reading. Home: 7783 Rm 415 Timpson TX 75975

SAMMARTINO FRESE, JENNIFER M., telecommunications industry executive; b. Belleville, N.J., Sept. 5, 1971; d. Joseph Sammartino and Patricia Rose Bedigian, Michael Bedigian (Stepfather); m. Brian S. Frese, Nov. 8, 2003. BS, Ithaca Coll., NY, 1993. Carrier account mgr. TotalTel, Little Falls, NJ, 1994—99; carrier account exec. Compass Global Comm. (Formerly Forval USA), Woodcliff Lake, 1999—2004, Reach Global Svcs., Morristown, 2004—. Music min. Roman Cath. Ch., NJ, 1987—2006. Mem.: Mensa, Republican. Roman Catholic. Avocations: singing, theater, dogs, reading, travel.

SAMMET, JEAN E., computer scientist; b. NYC; d. Harry and Ruth S. BA, Mt. Holyoke Coll., Sc.D. (hon.), 1978; MA, U. Ill. Group leader programming Sperry Gyroscope, Great Neck, NY, 1955-58; sect. head, staff cons. programming Sylvania Electric Products, Needham, Mass., 1958-61; with IBM, 1961-88; adv. program mgr. Boston, 1961-65; program lang. tech. mgr. IBM, 1965-68; programming tech. planning mgr. Fed. Systems div., 1968-74, programming lang. tech. mgr., 1974-79, software tech. mgr., 1979-81, div. software tech. mgr., 1981-82, programming lang. tech. mgr., 1983-88; programming lang. cons. Bethesda, Md., 1989—. Chmn. history of computing com. Am. Fedn. Info. Processing Socs., 1977-79; mem. exec. com. Software Patent Inst., 1991—, edn. com., 1992—, chair edn. com., 1992-93; bd. dirs. Computer Mus., 1983-93. Author: Programming Languages: History and Fundamentals, 1969; editor-in-chief: Assn. Computing Machinery Computing Revs, 1979-87; contbr. articles to profl. jours. Recipient Fellow award, Computer History Mus., 2001. Fellow Assn. for Computing Machinery, 1994, (charter; pres. 1974-76, Disting. Svc. award 1985), Computer History Mus.; mem. NAE, Upsilon Pi Epsilon. Home and Office: 3124 Gracefield Rd Apt 311 Silver Spring MD 20904-5818

SAMMLER, ANNE MICHELLE, healthcare educator; b. Binghampton, NY, Oct. 1968; d. Robert (Stepfather) and Carol Anne Roach, Fredrick Thaddeus Mastine; m. Sean Edward Sammler, May 2, 1992; children: Aleni, Alexis. BS in Health Edn. summa cum laude, SUNY, Brockport, 2003. CERT coord. Rochester City Fire Dept., cert. instr. ARC, tchr. NY. Co-chmn. Reading is Fundamental, Rochester, NY, 1998—2002; religious edn. instr. Sacred Heart Cathedral, Rochester, 1999—2002; health educator Aquinas Inst, Rochester, 2003—. Team leader breast cancer walks Am. Cancer Soc., Rochester, 2004; team leader, vol. Spl. Olympics, Rochester, 2000; team leader, fund raiser Am. Heart Assn., Rochester, 2005. Scholar, Health Sci. Dept., Brockport State U., 2003. Mem.: AAHPERD (corr.), Eta Sigma Gamma (corr.), Alpha Chi (life). Avocations: running, reading, canoeing. Office: Aquinas Inst 1127 Dewey Ave Rochester NY 14613 Office Phone: 585-254-2020 1048. Business E-Mail: asammler@aquinasinstitute.com.

SAMMONS, ELAINE D., manufacturing executive; m. Charles A. Sammons (dec. 1988). Chmn. Sammons Enterprises, Inc., Dallas, 1988—. Chmn. bd. Sammons Ctr. for the Arts, Dallas, 1988—. Office: Sammons Enterprises Inc 5949 Sherry Ln Ste 1900 Dallas TX 75225-8015

SAMMONS, MARY F., retail executive; b. Portland, Oreg., Oct. 12, 1946; d. Lee W. and Ann (Cherry) Jackson; m. Nickolas F. Sammons, Sept. 12, 1967; 1 child, Peter. BA, Marylhurst Coll., 1970. Buyer Fred Meyer Inc., Portland, 1975-80, v.p., merchandiser, 1980-85, sr. v.p., softgoods div. mgr., from 1986, sr. v.p., apparel & home electronics group, 1996, exec. v.p., apparel, home & home electronics group, 1997—98; pres. Fred Meyer Stores, Portland, 1998, pres., CEO, 1999; pres., COO Rite Aid Corp., Camp Hill, Pa., 1999—2003, pres., CEO, 2003—. Bd. dirs. First Horizon Nat. Corp., Rite Aid Found., Rite Aid Corp., 1999—; chmn. Nat. Assoc. Chain Drug Stores. Named Woman of Achievement, YWCA, Portland, 1987; named one of 100 Most Powerful Women, Forbes mag., 2005—06, 50 Most Powerful Women in Bus., Fortune mag., 2006. Mem. Am. Mgmt. Assn. Office: Rite Aid Corp 30 Hunter Ln Camp Hill PA 17011*

SAMPEY, DEBRA A., middle school principal; b. Chgo., Apr. 10, 1961; d. John Francis and Geri Ann Sampey; m. Timothy Collins Cronister, July 1, 1995; 1 child, Catherine Taylor Cronister. BS, George Williams Coll., Downers Grove, Ill., 1983; MS, U. Wis., 1985. Tchr. phys. edn., athletic dir. St. Teresas and St. Priscillas, 1985-86; tchr. phys. edn./health, coach track, volleyball, basketball Latin Sch., Chgo., 1986—. also Middle Sch. dean of students, Middle Sch. prin., varsity volleyball coach. Named Coach of Yr., Ind. Sch. League, 1995, 97; Klingenstein summer fellow, 1989. Mem. AAUW, Nat. Mid. Sch. Assn., Nat. Assn. Ind. Schs., Nat. Assn. Secondary Sch. Prins., Phi Beta Kappa. Democrat. Roman Catholic. Avocations: ethnic cooking, reading, tennis. Office: Latin Sch Chgo 59 W North Blvd Chicago IL 60610-1403

SAMPLE, ALTHEA MERRITT, secondary education educator, conductor; b. Miami, Fla., Apr. 6, 1937; d. Otis and Alma (Carter) S. BS in Music Edn., Fla. A&M, 1960; Master in Music Edn., U. Miami, 1971. Tchr. elem. music edn. Dade County, Miami, 1960-65, dir. jr. hs orch., 1965-84, dir. orch. sr. hs, 1984—; dir. orch. Miami Northwestern Performing Arts Ctr., 1984—. Clin. tchr. internship program U. Miami, 1988-90; clinician Broward County Orch. Evaluation, 1986, 87; participant workshops in field, 1965—. Coord. North Area Festival, 1988; conducted Supt.'s Honors Orch., 1988, 92, South Area Festival Orch., 1989, tribute Dr. George Bornoff Concert, 1994, Gov. Fla. Inaugural Concert, 1991; performed Nat. Educator Reception, 1993; sponsor Miami Herald Silver Knight Award winners, 1988, 90, 92. Recipient Black Music Achievement award, 1992, Outstanding Educator award US Rep. Dante Fussell, 1992, Disting. Alumnus award Fla. A&M U., 1997; named Area III Tchr. of Yr., Dade County, 1992; named to Dade County Schs. Music Educators Hall of Fame, 2006. Mem. United Tchrs. Dade, Fla. Orch. Assn., Fla. Music Educators, Dade Music Educators, Nat. Alliance Educators, Eta Phi Beta. Democrat. Episcopalian. Avocations: reading, playing flute, violin, organ, tennis. Home: 15720 E Bunche Park Dr Opa Locka FL 33054-2020

SAMPSON, DONNA RENE, mathematics educator; b. Columbia, SC, Mar. 26, 1957; d. James Bradford and Celia Meetze Sampson; children: Shoshone Sampson Willis, Shuyon Sampson Willis. BA in Math., Lehman Col., Bronx, NY, 1979; MA in Edn., U.S. Internat. U., San Diego, Calif., 1991. Math. tchr. John Philip Sousa Jr. HS, Bronx, 1979—81, Luther Burbank Jr. HS, Burbank, Calif., 1981—95, Carver Mid. Sch., Sanford, Fla., 1995—96, Croons Acad., Sanford, 1996—98, Southern HS, Guam, 1998—99, North HS, Phoenix, 1999—2005. Mem.: NEA, Tchr. Assn. Avocations: dance, kickboxing, weightlifting, reading, skating.

SAMPSON, EARLDINE ROBISON, education educator; b. Russell, Iowa, June 18, 1923; d. Lawrence Earl and Mildred Mona (Judy) Robison; m. Wesley Claude Sampson, Nov. 25, 1953; children: Ann Elizabeth, Lisa Ellen. Diploma, Iowa State Tchrs. Coll., 1943, BA, 1950; MS in Edn., Drake U., 1954; postgrad., No. Ill. U., Iowa State U., 1965-66, 74. Cert. tchr., guidance counselor, Iowa. Tchr. elem. sch. various pub. sch. sys., 1943-48; cons. speech and hearing Iowa Dept. Pub. Instrn., Des Moines, 1950-52; speech therapist Des Moines Pub. Schs., 1952-54, 55; lectr. spl. edn. No. Ill. U., DeKalb, 1964-65; tchr. of homebound Cedar Falls (Iowa) Pub. Schs., 1967-68; asst. prof. edn. U. No. Iowa, Cedar Falls, 1968; asst. prof., counselor Wartburg Coll., Waverly, Iowa, 1968-70; instr. elem. edn., then head of advising elem. edn. Iowa State U., Ames, 1972-82; field supr. elem. edn. U. Toledo, 1988, 89; ind. cons. Sylvania, Ohio, 1989—. Cons. Des Moines Speech and Hearing Ctr., 1958-59; cons. Sartori Hosp., Cedar Falls, 1967-69. Fellow, NDEA, 1965. Methodist. Avocations: public speaking on preservation of prose and poetry, reading, music, photography. Home: 4047 Newcastle Dr Sylvania OH 43560-3450

SAMPSON, JEANNE LOUISE, retired special education educator; b. Boise, Idaho, May 1, 1938; d. Wayne Ira and Fern Marie (Paulsen) Stokes; m. R. Neil Sampson, June 7, 1960; children: Robert Wayne, Eric Scott, Christopher Brent, Heidi Lynne. BS in Edn., U. Idaho, 1960; MEd in Early Childhood Spl. Edn., George Washington U., 1980. Tchr. Cassia County Pub. Schs., Burley, Idaho, 1960-62, Clearwater County Pub. Schs., Orofino, Idaho, 1963-64, Idaho Falls (Idaho) Pub. Schs., 1967-68; tchr.-aide Fairfax County Pub. Schs., Fairfax, Va., 1977-79, tchr. spl. edn., 1980—2003, ret., 2003. Mem. Coun. on Exceptional Children, P.E.O. Democrat. Presbyterian. Avocations: sewing, travel, music, singing. Home: 5209 York Rd Alexandria VA 22310-1126

SAMPSON, LYNETTE DIANE, secondary school educator; b. Fresno, Calif, June 15, 1957; d. Cecil and Louise Clements; m. Bryan Sullivan, Aug. 2005; children: Matthew, Tracy 1 stepchild, Bryan. BA in Theater, UCLA, 1973; tchg. credential, Hayward State U., Calif., 1974; postgrad., U. LaVerne, Calif., 1990. Tchr. literature, composition, theatre, dance, art Foothill HS, Pleasanton, Calif., 1974—76, Lincoln HS, Stockton, Calif. Mentor tchr. Lincoln Unified Sch. Dist., Stockton; cons. assoc. Learning Record Literacy, San Diego; mem. Calif. state bd. Internat. Thespians. Dir., prodr. Lincoln Summer Theatre, 2004—05; prodr. Italian St. Painting Festival, Stockton, 2004—05. Mem.: Calif. Tchrs. Assn. Avocations: tennis, kayaking, travel, painting, weaving. Office: Lincoln HS 6844 Alexandria Pl Stockton CA 95207-2498

SAMPSON, MARTHA FRAY, portrait artist, educator; b. Clarks Summit, Pa., May 4, 1928; d. Willard H. and Isabel (Holden) Fray; m. Thomas Henry Longmore, Aug. 27, 1950 (dec. Dec. 1963); children: Robert W., David T., John W.; m. Verlin Eugene Sampson, Dec. 20, 1974. BS in Art Edn., Kutztown U., 1950; MFA in Painting and Drawing, Marywood Coll., 1988. Cert. tchr., Pa. Art supr., tchr. Union Sch. Dist., Honesdale, Pa., 1950-52; art tchr. Dallas (Pa.) Area Sch. Dist., 1964-68, Wyoming Valley West, Kingston, Pa., 1968-76; lectr. Marywood Coll., Scranton, Pa., 1987-89, U. Scranton, Pa., 1989-95. Exhibited in many local and nat. exhibits. Mem. Endless Mountains Coun. of the Arts (pres., founder 1993-97, sec. 1997-98, bd. dirs. 1993-2006).

SAMPSON, MARY POND, special education educator; b. Memphis, Apr. 16, 1944; d. Ralph Andrew and Vestelle Cleo (James) Pond; m. Carlton Ray Sampson, Dec. 14, 1963; children: Tobee Lee Sampson Firebaugh, Vicki Lyn Sampson Clark. BS cum laude, Va. State U., Petersburg, 1985; MS, Longwood U., Farmville, Va., 1993. Electronic fabricator Stranberg Engring. Lab., Greensboro, NC, 1967—71; audit clk.-typist Sheet Metal Workers Internat., Washington, 1962—64; tutorial aide Robeson County Schs., Lumberton, NC, 1972—75, Chesterfield County Schs., Chester, Va., 1976—85; spl. edn. tchr. Amelia County Schs., Amelia, Va., 1985—, 2001—02; hospitality coord. mid. sch., 1985—2005; yearbook advisor mid. sch., 1998—2002. Lectr. in field; mentor student tchrs., 1999—, Pathwise, 2004. Poll worker Dem. Party, Robeson County, NC, 1970. Named Tchr. of the Yr., Amelia County Mid. Sch., 1998; named to Wall of Tolerance, 2003. Mem.: NEA, Va. Edn. Assn., Nat. Mus. Native Ams., Internat. Reading Assn., Va. Ret. Tchrs. Assn. (life). Democrat. Baptist. Avocations: reading, crafts. Home: 7131 Buckskin Creek Rd Amelia Court House VA 23002 Office: Amelia County Middle School 8740 Otterburn Rd Amelia Court House VA 23002

SAMPSON, SUSAN AUDREY, private school educator; d. Ray G. Sampson and Sylvia Johanna Ruohonen; children: Alexander, Grant, Olivia, Chase, Irving Jr. BA, Western Ill. U., 1995; MA, No. Mich. U., 1999. Cert. screener Irlen Inst. Calif., dyslexic tutor Mich. Dyslexia Inst. Dir. Lincoln Learning Ctr., Hancock, Mich., 1993—; instr. Gogebic C.C., Ironwood, Mich., 2000—03, Finlandia U., Hancock, 2002—04. Lead comm. instr. N.E. Tex. CC, Mt. Pleasant, 2000—01. Author: (textbook) 6 Continents, 1997, Avalon Across the Plains, 2004, (poetry) Harpweaver, 2001, Karmanu, 2002; illustrator: Tommy Trapper and the Muskrat Swamp, Working Person's Cookbook. Bd. dirs. Keweenaw Coop., Hancock, 1994; writer, illustrator Vol. Ctr., Hancock, 1997; art instr. Cmty. Arts Coun., Hancock, 2000; artist, designer 99's Women in Aviation, 2005. Recipient Matt Clark Lit. prize, New Delta Rev., 2005. Mem.: Writers Guild East, Acad. Am. Poets. Home: 921 S Lincoln Dr Hancock MI 49930 Office: Lincoln Learning Ctr 921 S Lincoln Dr Hancock MI 49930

SAMPSON, ZORA J., librarian; b. Norman, Okla., Feb. 24, 1951; d. Ephraim Leon and Imogene Gay (Garland) Lobaugh; m. Kenneth Gene Sampson, Nov. 20, 1984; children: Aaron Lee, Sarah Kay. BFA, U. Okla., 1972; postgrad., U. Wis., 1974, U. Sci. Arts Okla., 1982-83; MLIS, U. Okla., 1992. Libr. assoc. State Hist. Soc. Wis., Madison, 1974-80; libr. asst. Hist. Sci. Coll., Norman, 1983; br. supr. Art and Drama Librs., Norman, 1984-85; br. supr. Physics, Astronomy Libr. U. Okla., Norman, 1986—96; dir. libr. info. and instructional tech. U. Wis.-Barron County, Rice Lake, Wis., 1996—. Home: 911 W Marshall St Rice Lake WI 54868-1445 Office: U Wis-Barron County 1800 Coll Dr Rice Lake WI 54868-1445

SAMS, ROBIN DAHL, artist; b. Perth Amboy, N.J., Mar. 2, 1950; d. George Martin and Lillian Dorothy (Farr) Dahl; m. John Lawrence Sams, Aug. 3, 1973. BFA, R.I. Sch. Design, Providence, 1972. Illustrator U.S. Army, Vaihingen, West Germany, 1985-88; sole proprietor Peace & Plenty Studio, Tyner, N.C., 1993—; owner Edenton (N.C.) Art Gallery, 1998—, Robin Sams Gallery, 2001. Exhbns. include Pasquotanic Arts Coun., 1995, Beaufort County Arts Coun., 1997, Chowan Arts Coun., 1998. Head conservation Gen. Fedn. Women's Clubs, 1998; rep. candidate Chowan County Commr., 1998; bd. dirs. Chowan Arts Coun. Grantee N.C. State Arts Coun., 1997, 99. Mem. Watercolor Soc. N.C., Psquotank County Arts Coun., Dare County Arts Coun., Edenton Womans Club (pres. 1997-99). Home: 315 S Broad St Edenton NC 27932-1933

SAMSON, LEONA D., biological engineering educator, research center director; BSc in Biochemistry, Aberdeen U., Scotland, 1974; PhD, London U., 1978. Postdoctoral rschr. U. Calif., San Francisco, Berkeley; from asst. prof. to full prof. dept. molecular and cellular toxicology Harvard Sch. Pub. Health, 1983—2001; prof. biol. engring. and toxicology MIT, 2001—, dir. MIT Ctr. for Environ. Health Scis., MIT Toxicogenomics Rsch. Program, 2001—. Mem. exec. com. Computational and Systems Biology Initiative MIT; mem. bd. sci. counselors NIEHS; mem. coun. for extramural grants ACS. Named Am. Cancer Soc. Rsch. Prof., 2001; recipient Burroughs Wellcome Toxicology Scholar award, 1993, Charlotte Friend Women in Cancer Rsch. award, 2000. Mem.: Inst. Medicine. Office: Ctr for Environ Health Scis MIT Bldg 56-235 Cambridge MA 02139 Business E-Mail: lsamson@mit.edu.*

SAMSON, LINDA FORREST, nursing educator, nursing administrator; b. Miami, Dec. 7, 1949; d. Alvin S. and Grace (Kanner) Forrest; m. Mark I. Samson, Jan. 29, 1972; children: Amy, Josh. BSN, Emory U., 1972, MN, 1973; PhD, U. Pa., 1989. RN, Fla., Ga., N.J., Pa., Ill. Nursing instr. Ga. State U., Atlanta, 1974-78; neonatal intensive care nurse Northside Hosp., Atlanta, 1976-78; perinatal clin. specialist Our Lady of Lourdes Med. Ctr., Camden, N.J., 1978-82, per diem staff nurse, ICU nursery, labor and delivery, 1982-88; asst. prof., nursing Kennesaw Coll., Marietta, Ga., 1988-89; asst. prof. Clayton Coll. and State U., Morrow, Ga., 1989-92, assoc. prof., 1992-98, prof., 1998—, head baccalaureate nursing dept. Morrow, Ga., 1991-94, acting dean Sch. Health Scis., 1992-94, dean Sch. Health Scis., 1994—2002; dean Coll. Health Professions, Govs. State U., University Park, Ill., 2002—. Adj. faculty Gloucester County Coll., 1981-83; adj. clin. preceptor U. Pa. Sch. Nursing, 1981-83, lectr. in perinatal nursing, 1983-88; nursing dir. So. N.J. Perinatal Coop., 1982-84; researcher and lectr. in field. Mem. editorial rev. bds.; contbr. chpts. to textbooks, articles to profl. jours. Bd. dirs., chmn. profl. adv. com. South Jersey chpt. March of Dimes, 1980-85. Named Nurse of Yr. N.J. State Nurses Assn., 1985; recipient Network Edn. grant N.J. State Dept. Health, 1982-84, numerous grants for rsch., 1983-89, Outstanding Svc. award March of Dimes, 1983, Disting. Leadership award March of Dimes, 1984; grantee Fuld Inst. Post Secondary Edn., 1997—, Nursing Workforce Diversity Grant, 2000-03, NCMHD, 2003—, Samhsa CSAP, 2002—. Mem. ANA (cert. advanced nursing adminstrn., RNC high risk perinatal nursing), AACN (program com. 1987-88, rsch. com. 1988-89, project devel. task force 1989, strategic planning com. 1989, bd. dirs. 1987-90, bd. dirs. certification corp. 1987-90, chair neonatal and pediatric appeal panels 1992), Am. Orgn. Nurse Execs. (planning com. 1994-95), Nat. Assn. Neonatal Nurses (pub. policy and legis. com. 1994-96), Assn. Women's Health, Obstetrics and Neonatal Nurses, Nat. Perinatal Assn. (program planning com. 1983-85, resolutions com. 1984-88, stds. devel. com. spl. interest group task force 1985-88, bd. dirs. 1985-89, chmn. resolutions com. 1988, fin. com. 1989, pub. health policy com.), Ill. Nurses Assn., Ga. Perinatal Assn. N.J. (pres. 1982-86), Sigma Theta Tau (bylaws com.). Home: 20676 Francisca Way Frankfort IL 60423 Office: Govs State U Coll Health Professions 1 University Pkwy University Park IL 60466-0975 Office Phone: 708-534-4389.

SAMSON, VALERIE J., elementary school educator, consultant; b. Mar. 28, 1948; EdB, U. Mont., 1986; EdM, Mont. State U., 1995. Nat. bd. cert. tchr. 2001. Facilitator Project Water Edn. for Tchrs. Mont., Bozeman, 1994—2001; elem. sch. tchr. Kalispell Sch. Dist. # 5, Mont., 1986—2001; edn. cons., 2002—; elem. tchr. Pensacola, Fla., 2004—06. Cons. Ensley Elem. Sch., Pensacola, 2003—. Recipient Presdl. award, Project Water Edn. for Tchrs. Mem.: NSF, ASCD, NEA (State Presdl. award for excellence in sci. and math. tchg. 1999, Nat. Presdl. award for excellence in sci. and math. tchg. 2000), Nat. Assn. Edn. Young Children, Nat. Sci. Tchrs. Assn., Nat. Coun. Tchrs. Math., Phi Delta Kappa (exec. bd. 2003—05, sec. 2003—04). Home: 437 S Cass Newport WA 99156

SAMSON, WANDA KAY, retired secondary school educator, consultant; b. Shenandoah, Iowa, July 1, 1950; d. Carl Frederick and Margaret Ann (Vette) Sickman. BA, Midland Luth Coll., Fremont, Nebr., 1972; MA in Bus. Edn., U. Nebr., 1983. Cert. tchr., Nebr. Tchr. bus. edn. Fremont (Nebr.) H.S., 1972—2005, ret., 2005. Cons. Cortez Peters Keyboarding, 1991—. Bd. dirs., coord. bloodmobile ARC of Dodge County, Fremont, 1990—. Recipient Belong Excel Study Travel award Nebr. Dept. Edn., 1991—. Mem. NEA, Internat. Soc. Bus. Edn., Am. Vocat. Assn., Nat. Assn. Classroom Educators Bus. Edn., Nebr. Edn. Assn., Fremont Edn. Assn., Nat. Bus. Edn. Assn., Mountain-Plains Bus. Edn. Assn. (legis. chmn. 1997-2002, treas. 2003—, 2003-2005, newsletter editor, 2005—), Nebr. Bus. Edn. Assn. (met. rep. 1990-91, pres.-elect 1993-94, pres. 1994-95, past pres. 1995-96, sec. 1999-2002, treas. 1999-2003), Delta Pi Epsilon (rec. sec., newsletter editor). Lutheran. Avocations: working on computer, reading, counted cross-stitch.

SAMUEL, MAY LINDA, environmental scientist; d. Joe and Elvira Dixon; m. Earl Samuel; children: Annette Heyward, April Heyward. BS in Biology and Chemistry magna cum laude, Benedict Coll., 1977; MPH in Environ. Health Sci., U. SC, 1982; DD, Inst. Christian Works Coll. and Sem., 1996, PhD, ThD, 1999. Broadcaster Radio Sta. WGCV, Columbia, SC, 1984—86; asst. dir. environ. health scis. Benedict Coll., Columbia, 1990—; exec. dir. SC Environ Econ. Justice Network, Columbia, 2003—. Prof. biology Allen U., Columbia, 1984—86; cons. Inst. for Energy and Environ. Rsch., Tacoma Park, Md., 1999—2004. Contbr. articles to profl. jours. Founder, pastor Light of the World Ch., Winnsboro, SC, 1995—. Recipient SC Dept. Health and Environ. Control award, 1990, SC Dept. Corrections award, 1990; grantee,

Dept. of Energy, 1995—97, EPA, 1996—99, Assn. Environ. Health, 2002—03, Sierra Club, 2003. Avocations: travel, reading. Office: Benedict Coll 1600 Harden St Columbia SC 29204-1058 Business E-Mail: samuelm@benedict.edu.

SAMUELS, LINDA S., science administrator, consultant; b. Mansfield, Ohio, Feb. 15, 1947; d. Robert Lloyd and Esther Sophia (Schwob) Garber; children: Marilyn L., Charles L. AB in Biology-Zoology, U. Cin., 1969, MS in Population Biology, 1971; MBA, Suffolk U., 2003. Anatomy and physiology instr. U. Cin., 1969—70; biology, chemistry, physics, algebra instr. Cambridge (Mass.) Acad., 1971—72; instr. biology Simmons Coll., Boston, 1972—73; instr. advanced biology, life sci., dance sci. Dana Hall Sch., Wellesley, Mass., 1972—2002; founder, CEO Sci. of Learning Ctr., Boston, 2001—, Premier Capitol by the Sea, 2005. Rap Around: Discussion Dissection in the Classroom, WBZ-TV, Boston, 1996-97; liaison com. to head of sch. Dana Hall Sch., Wellesley, Mass., 1995-98, developer dance sci. curriculum, 1998—; cons. NSF summer project Girls in Engring. engring. adv. com. Tufts U., 1997; com. to study physiology of learning Harvard Med. Sch, 1998—; neurosci. com. minority faculty devel. program, 1995 Author: Girls Can Succeed in Science, 1999; contbr. articles to sci. jours. Active Bar/Bat Mitzah Com. Temple Israel, Boston, 1995, adult choir, 1997; parent rep., Buckingham, Browne and Nichols Sch., Cambridge, 1995-98; parking com. Back Bay Assn. Recipient Sci. Tchr. of Yr. award Norfolk County, 1994, sabbatical grant Dana Hall Sch., 1995, Disting. Alumni award U. Cin., McMicken Coll. Arts and Scis., 1996, H. Dudley Wright Fellowship for Innovative Sci. Edn. Tufts U., Medford, Mass., 1996-97; named Linda S. Samuels Animal Behavior Lab. in her honor at Dana Hall; named to Mass. Hall of Fame Educators, Boston, 1999 Mem. Nat. Assn. Biology Tchrs. (presenter 1986—, award for excellence in encouraging equity sect. on women 1997-98, Outstanding Biology Tchr. Mass. 1994), Nat. Sci. Tchrs. Assn. (presenter 1986—, Tchr. of Yr. award 1994), New Eng. Sci. Tchrs., Mass. Assn. Biology Tchrs. (v.p. 1997, pres. 1998), Mass. Assn. Sci. Tchrs. (presenter 1986-95, 99, Presdl. award state finalist Sec. Sch. Sci., Mass). Avocation: exercise. Office Phone: 617-908-9660. Business E-Mail: lsamuels@learnscience.net. E-mail: lsamuels@premiercapital.biz.

SAMUELSON, BILLIE MARGARET, artist; b. Long Beach, Calif., Apr. 11, 1927; d. William Christian and Gladys Margaret (Caffrey) Newendorp; m. Fritz Eric Samuelson, Aug. 12, 1950 (div. 1985); children: Craig Eric, Clark Alan, Dana Scott. Student, Long Beach City Coll., 1945—46. Pvt. art tchr., Wycokoff/Allendale, NJ, 1985. Workshop instr. Jane Law Studio, Long Beach Island, NJ, 1990—. One-woman shows at Ridgewood (NJ) Art Inst., 1985, West Wing Gallery, 1991, Chas. Austin Gallery, Saddle River, NJ, 1997; group shows include Craig Gallery, Ridgewood, 1979, Charisma Gallery, Englewood, NJ, 1981-83, Custom Gallery, Waldwick, NJ, 1985, Wyckoff (NJ) Gallery, 1987-90, West Wing Gallery, Ringwood State Park, NJ, 1991, Union Camp Corp., 1992, Eisenhauer Gallery, Block Island, RI, 1996—; featured in Am. Artists Mag., 2001. Recipient 1st in State N.J. Womens Clubs, 1978-80, Watercolor award N.J. Painters and Sculptors, 1981. Mem. DAR, Cmty. Arts Assn. (pres. 1978-79), Am. Artists Profl. League (bd. dirs. 1985-87, Watercolor prize 1992), Ringwood Manor Arts Assn. (sr. profl.), Catherine Lorillard Wolfe Art Club (cash award 1993), Salute to Women in the Arts, Art Ctr. Watercolor Affiliates, Nat. Mus. Women in the Arts. Avocations: bridge, travel, museums, theater, reading. Home: 1-3 Chestnut Pl Waldwick NJ 07463-1113

SAMUELSON, EMILY MEG, psychologist; b. Balt., May 5, 1952; divorced; 1 child, Allison Kara. BA, Tufts U., 1970; MEd, Temple U., 1978, PhD, 1989. Coord. creative arts therapy Thomas Jefferson U. Hosp., Phila., 1978-85; pvt. practice in psychotherapy Balt., 1982—; dir. day treatment svcs. for children and adolescent Vance, Franklin, Warren & Granville Counties, N.C., 1985-87; pvt. practice consultation, 1987—; sr. psychologist Children's Guild, Balt., 1989-90, therapy supr., 1990-94. Faculty Thomas Jefferson U., Phila., 1980-85; adj. faculty Antioch New England, Vt., 1980-83; sr. clin. faculty Hahnemann U., Phila., 1980-85; cons., expert witness, lectr. on child sexual abuse, Balt., 1993—; dir. traveling oral history/photography project Soaring Above the Ashes, Balt., 1996—. Mem. Am. Psychol. Assn. Office: 28 Allegheny Ave Ste 1305 Baltimore MD 21204-1379

SAMUELSON, JOAN BENOIT, professional runner; b. Cape Elizabeth, Maine, May 16, 1957; d. André and Nancy Benoit; m. Scott Samuelson; children: Abigail, Anders. Student, Bowdoin Coll., N.C. State U. Long-distance coach Boston U.; runner; Runner 10K L.L. Bean Run, July 4, 1997. Bd. dirs. Gulf of Maine Aquarium, Found. for Advancement Edn., Internat. Amateur Athletic Fedn. Coun.; active Maine Lung Found., Natural Resources Coun. Main, Alzheimer's Found., Multiple Sclerosis Soc., Spl. Olympics. Gov.'s Coun. Phys. Edn. and Sports, 1995—; Gov.'s Exec. Coun., Communities for Children, 1997—; founder and chmn. Peoples Heritage Bank Beach to Beacon 10K, 1997—. Recipient Gold medal Olympic Games, 1984 (set world record); won Boston Marathon, 1983 (set world record). Office: Edwin P Whittemore 114A Massachusetts Ave Arlington MA 02474-8624 also: Roadrunners Club of America 1150 S Washington St Ste 205 Alexandria VA 22314-4493

SAMUELSON, LINDA J., special education educator; d. John William Powley and Lillian Mae Frank-Powley; m. Eric J. Samuelson, Aug. 3, 1979; children: Christina M., Jessica L. Harrel-Samuelson. BA in Spl. Edn., Ariz. State U. West, Glendale, 2002; M in Curriculum Develop., Ariz. State U., Tempe, 2005. Spl. edn. tchr. Cartwright Sch. Dist., Phoenix, 1994—. Co-chair, spl. edn. dept. Cartwright Sch. Dist., 2002—03. Mem. Nat. Orgn. Mothers of Twins, Ariz., 1986—99; mem., bd. dirs. Ariz. State Mothers of Multiples Orgn., Tucson, 1986—99, Phoenix Mothers of Multiples Orgn., 1986—99. Named Lifetime Mem., Ariz. State Parent Tchr. Assn., 1987—. Office Phone: 602-618-0870. Personal E-mail: speced4me@cox.net.

SAMUELSON, PAMELA ANN, law educator; b. Seattle, Aug. 4, 1948; d. Peter David and Margaret Susanne (Green) S.; m. Robert J. Glushko, May 7, 1988; 1 child, Robert M. BA in History, U. Hawaii, 1971, MA in Polit. Sci., 1972; JD, Yale U., 1976. Bar: NY 1977, US Dist. Ct. (so. dist.) NY 1977. Rsch. assoc. Vera Inst. of Justice, NYC, 1976-77; assoc. Willkie Farr & Gallagher, NYC, 1977-81; prin. investigator Software Engring. Inst., Pitts., 1985-86; asst. prof. Law Sch. U. Pitts., 1981-84, assoc. prof. Law Sch., 1984-87, prof. Law Sch., 1987-96; prof. law and info. mgmt. U. Calif. Law Sch./Sch. Info. Mgmt. and Sys., Berkeley, 1996—, chancellor's prof. info. mgmt. & law, 2001—06, Richard M. Sherman prof. law & info. mgmt., 2005—. Dir. Berkeley Ctr. for Law & Tech./U. Calif. Berkeley, 1997-; advisor Samuelson High Tech. Law & Pub. Policy Clinic, U. Calif. Berkeley; mem. adv. bd. Electronic Privacy Info. Ctr.; vis. prof. Emory Law Sch., Atlanta, 1989-90, Cornell Law Sch., Ithaca, 1995-96; hon. prof. U. Amsterdam, Netherlands, 2002-; mem. Nat. Rsch. Coun. Study Com. on Intellectual Property Rights and Info. Infrastructure, 1998-2000. Contbr.: articles to profl. jours, chapters to books; co-author: Software & Internet Law, 2000; author: The Future of the Information Society & the Role of Copyright In It, 1998. Bd. dirs. ACLU Greater Pitts., 1983-88, Electronic Frontier Found., 2000—. John D. and Catherine T. MacArthur Found. fellow, 1997-2002, Pub. Policy fellow Electronic Frontier Found., 1997—; recipient Pioneer award, Berkeley Tech. Law Jour., 1999, Disting. Alumni award U. Hawaii, 2000, World Tech. Network award for Law, 2004, Women of Vision award for Social Impact, Anita Borg Inst., 2005. Mem. ABA (sci. and tech. sect.), Am. Intellectual Property Law Assn. (subcom. chair 1988-89), Assn. Am. Law Schs. (intellectual property sect.), Am. Law Inst., Assn. Computing Machinery (contbg. editor comm.), Open Source Application Found. (bd. dirs., 2002-). Democrat. Avocations: gardening, reading. Office: U Calif Berkeley Sch Info Mgmt and Sys 102 South Hall #4600 Berkeley CA 94720-4600 E-mail: pam@sims.berkeley.edu.*

SAN AGUSTIN, MUTYA, pediatrician; b. Manila, Nov. 25, 1934; d. Dionisio and Trinidad (Tolentino) San A.; m. Barry Shaw, July 27, 1969; children: Noel, Ariel, Angela, Joanna. MD, U. Philippines, 1957. Diplomate Am. Bd. Pediats. Intern, resident Sinai Hosp., Balt., 1960, chief resident in pediats., 1961; chief phys. devel. rsch. divsn. Nat. Coordinating Rsch. Ctr., Philippines, 1962-64; dir. Montefiore-Morrisania Comprehensive Health Care Ctr., Bronx, N.Y., 1968-76; dir. ambulatory care medicine North Ctrl. Bronx Hosp.- Montefiore Med. Ctr., Bronx, 1976-97; dir. dept. primary care medicine Montefiore Med. Ctr., Bronx, 1997—. Cons. internat. ednl. br. HEW, 1969-74; cons. health com. U.S. China People's Friendship Assn., 1975-81; cons. to pres. N.Y.C. Health and Hosps. Corp., 1979-89; dir. primary care residency in pediats. and internal medicine Albert Einstein Coll. Medicine, 1979-92, prof. pediat.- clin. epidemiology and social medicine, 1993; vis. prof. UCLA, 1985, Ben-Gurion U., Beer-Sheva, Israel; mem. N.Y. State Coun. Grad. Med. Edn., 1988-90, N.Y. State Hosp. Rev. and Planning Coun., 1990-95, N.Y. State Gov.'s Health Adv. Bd., 1991-95; mem. residency tng. rev. com. divsn. medicine Bur. Health Profls., HHS, 1990-94; project dir. internat. pediat. fellowship program Montefiore Med. Ctr., Albert Einstein Coll. Medicine, 1989—; adj. prof. NYU A/P/A studies program and inst.; lectr. cultural diversity and cmty. health; vis. faculty dept. pediats. U. Philippines Coll. Medicine; lectr. in field. Pediats. fellow John Hopkins U., 1960-61; Grantee NIH, 1967, NIMH, 1990-92; Atram Found. scholar, 1980; recipient Hon. Fellow award Philippine Pediat. Soc., Inc., 1996. Mem. APHA, Am. Acad. Pediat., Am. Pediat. Soc., Royal Soc. Medicine, Soc. Gen. Internal Medicine, Ambulatory Pediat. Assn., N.Y. Acad. Medicine, Philippine Ambulatory Pediat. Assn. (founding pres. 1995).

SANBORN, ANNA LUCILLE, pension fund administrator, consultant; b. Bklyn., Mar. 29, 1924; d. Peter Francis and Matilda M. (Stumpp) Galligen; 1 son, Dean Sanborn. BA. Bklyn. Coll., 1945. Head dept. benefit and estate planning Union Ctrl. Life Ins. Co., N.Y.C., 1949—51; adminstr. employee benefits Seaboard Oil Co., N.Y.C., 1952—56; with Frank J. Walters Assocs., Inc., N.Y.C., 1957—, pres., 1982—. Mem. Am. Acad. Actuaries. Republican. Roman Catholic. Office: Frank J Walters Assocs 58-13 Seabury St Flushing NY 11373-4825 E-mail: fjwainc@aol.com.

SANBORN, DOROTHY CHAPPELL, retired librarian; b. Apr. 26, 1920; d. William S. and Sammie Maude (Drake) Chappell; m. Richard Donald Sanborn, Dec. 1, 1943; children: Richard Donald, William Chappell. Asst. cataloger El Paso (Tex.) Pub. Libr., 1954-55, 57-59, Stanford Rsch. Inst., Menlo Park, Calif., 1955-57; libr. Auburn (Calif.) Pub. Libr., 1959-62; cataloger Sierra Coll., Rocklin, 1962-64; reference libr. Sacramento (Calif.) City Libr., 1964-66; county libr. Placer County (Calif.), Auburn, 1966-89, ret., 1989. Chmn. Mountain Valley Libr. Sys., 1970-71, 75-76, 1984-85; cons. county libr. Alpine County Libr., Markleeville, Calif., 1973-80. Mem. Auburn Friends of Libr., 2005—, pres., 1995-97; vol. Peace Corps., Thailand, 1991-93. With WAVES, 1944-46. Mem. AAUW (pres. chpt. 1982-84), Calif. Libr. Assn., Auburn Friends of Libr., Soroptimists. Democrat. Mem. United Ch. Christ. Home: 135 Midway Ave Auburn CA 95603-5415

SANCHEZ, ALITA CASSANDRA, physical education educator, personal trainer; d. John Phillip and Florinda Lou Sanchez; m. Christopher Brendan McManus, July 31, 2006; 1 child, Sarah. BA in English Lit., U. Calif., Santa Cruz, 1991; tchg. credential, San Francisco State U., 1997. Adapted phys. edn. specialist Hayward Unified Sch. Dist., Calif., 1997—98, Oakland Unified Sch. Dist., Calif., 1998—. Vol. adult leader Family Resource Network, Oakland, 2001—05; vol. coach/capt. Students Run Oakland, 2002—05. Mem.: Calif. Assn. Health, Phys. Fitness, Recreation and Dance, Am. Coll. Sports Medicine (cert. health and fitness instr.).

SANCHEZ, CINDI ASBURY, physical education educator; d. Edgar Allen and Idabell Rogers Asbury; m. Sonny Anthony Sanchez, July 12, 1980; children: Erin, Sonny. BS, North Tex. State U., Denton, 1976. Tchr. phys. edn. Poteet (Tex.) Ind. Sch. Dist., 1976—78; tchr. phys. edn., coach Schertz (Tex.), Cibilo, and Universal City Ind. Sch. Dist., 1978—81; tchr. phys. edn. St. Mary's Episcopal Sch., Edmond, Okla., 2000—. Bd. dirs. Parents Helping Parents, Edmond, 2002—. Named Mathews Elem. Vol. of Yr., Plano Ind. Sch. Dist., 1993, Small Sch. State Champion, Pres.' Phys. Fitness Challenge, 2004, 2005. Mem.: AAHPERD, Okla. Alliance for Health, Phys. Edn., Recreation, and Dance. Avocations: softball, soccer, woodworking, landscaping. Office: St Mary's Episcopal Sch 505 E Covell Edmond OK 73034 Office Phone: 405-341-9541. E-mail: cindi427@aol.com.

SANCHEZ, EVELYN FORD, retired humanities educator; b. Bowling Green, Fla., Jan. 18, 1929; d. Lewis Earl and Ruth Annie (Futch) Ford; m. Robert Edward Sanchez, Nov. 1, 1947; children: Diane Petteway, Sandra LaCost, Krystal Bottom. BA, U. South Fla., Tampa, 1964, MA, 1969. Cert. tchr. Fla. Tchr. humanities Brandon Acad., Fla.; tchr. art and humanities East Bay HS, Riverview, Fla., 1965—67, Hillsborough Coll., Brandon, 1970—76; ret. Author: numerous poems. Treas. Pres. Roundtable, Brandon, 1973—92; pres., com. me. PTA, Tampa, Fla., 1955—65; bd. dirs. Brandon Outreach Clinic, Brandon, 2000—03. Recipient Appreciation award, Pres. Roundtable, 1986, Alice B. Tomkins Cmty. Svc. award, 1995. Mem.: AAUW (pres. 1974—76, 1980—82, 1988—92, chair 1998—2006, Appreciation award 1980). Republican. Avocations: drawing, painting, writing, gardening, stained glass. Home: 401 N Bryan Cir Brandon FL 33511 also: PO Box 17 5079 Spring Cove Ext Blairsville GA 30512

SANCHEZ, KARLA ANN, language educator; m. Steven Alfred Sanchez, Aug. 17, 1991; 1 child, Lydia. AA, Colo. Mountain Coll., 1984—86; BS in environ. sci., Prescott Coll., 1986—89. Colorado State Professional Teacher License State of Colo., 2002. Field instr. Keystone Sci. Sch., Dillon, Colo., 1989—90; outdoor edn. instr./counselor Farm and Wilderness, Plymouth, Vt., 1989; seasonal naturalist Pueblo State Recreation Area, Colo., 1991; summer sci. instr. Marine Sci. Ctr., Poulsbo, Wash., 1992; after sch. sci. acad. instr. Pueblo Sch. Dist. 60, Colo., 1995; student tchr. Minnequa Elem., Pueblo, Colo., 1998; mid. and h.s. lang. arts tchr. Mountain Valley Sch., RE-1, Saguache, Colo., 1999—. Chair Cadre, Bully Proofing Your Sch., Saguache, Colo., 2001—, SPOT Intervention Team, Saguache, Colo., 2001—. Author: (anthology of poetry) Celebrate! Poets Speak Out (Poet of High Merit, 2002). Svc. mem. AmeriCorps, Saguache, Colo., 2004—05; vol. Beyond Fishing, Saguache and Pueblo, Colo., 1992—2005; docent N.Mex Mus. of Natural History, Albuquerque, 1991—92, Prescott Animal Pk., Ariz., 1988—99; religious educator Cmty. of Christ, Pueblo, Colo., 1996—98. Named Outstanding Tchr. of Yr., Mountain Valley Sch. Dist., 2004—05; recipient Outstanding Vol., Pueblo Greenway and Nature Ctr., 1998, Outstanding Educator in Youth Services, Concerned Parents of Pueblo and Pueblo Youth Naturally, 1991. Mem.: Tchrs. Edn. Assn. (Outstanding mem. 1997, 1998), Mountain Valley Edn. Assn., Colo. Edn. Assn., Nat. Coun. of Teachers of English, ASCD, So. Poverty Law Ctr., Friends of the Ctr. D-Liberal. Cmty. Of Christ. Avocations: fishing, camping, walking, reading. Office: Mountain Valley Sch RE-1 PO Box 127 403 Pitkin Ave Saguache CO 81149-0127 Office Phone: 719-655-2578. Office Fax: 719-655-0269. E-mail: sanchezk@valley.k12.co.us.

SANCHEZ, KARLA G., lawyer; AB in History, Columbia U., 1992; JD cum laude, Fordham U., 1995. Bar: NY, US Dist. Ct. (So. Dist. NY), US Dist. Ct. (Ea. Dist. NY). Law clk. to Hon. Deborah A. Batts US Dist. Ct. (So. Dist. NY); ptnr. Patterson, Belknap, Webb & Tyler LLP, NYC. Dean's planning coun. Fordham U. Sch. Law, bd. adv. minority mentorship program; bd. dir. Puerto Rican Legal Defense and Edn. Fund. Named one of 40 Under 40, Crain's NY Bus., 2006, 100 most influential Hispanics in US, Hispanic Bus. mag., 2006; recipient Lucero award, Puerto Rican Legal Defense and Edn. Fund, 2004, Andrew J. Rivera Alumni Achievement award, Fordham U. Sch. Law, 2005, Rising Star award, NY Women's Agenda, 2005. Mem.: Fed. Bar Coun. Inns of Ct., Hispanic Nat. Bar Assn., ABA, Assn. Bar City NY, Order Coif. Office: Patterson Belknap Webb & Tyler LLP 1133 Avenue of the Americas New York NY 10036 Office Phone: 212-336-2785. Office Fax: 212-336-2788. E-mail: kgsanchez@pbwt.com.*

SANCHEZ, LINDA T., congresswoman; b. Orange, Calif. m. Mark Sanchez. BA in Spanish Lit., U. Calif., Berkeley; JD, UCLA, 1995. Bar: Calif. 1995. Clk. to Hon. Chief Justice Terry Hatter, Jr. Ctrl. Dist. Ct., Calif.; compliance officer Nat. Elec. Contractors Assn. and Internat. Brotherhood Elec. Workers, 1998—2002; mem. US Congress from 39th Calif. dist., 2003—; mem. judiciary com.; mem. govt. reform com., small bus. com. Lectr. Nat. Assn. Elected and Apptd. Ofcls., 1998—. Exec. sec.-treas. Orange County ctrl. labor coun. AFL-CIO; campaign worker Loretta Sanchez for U.S. Congress, 1996, 1998. Mem.: Internat. Brotherhood Elec. Workers (Local 441). Democrat. Office: US Ho Reps 1007 Longworth Office Bldg Washington DC 20515-0539 also: Dist Office Ste 106 4007 Paramount Lakewood CA 90712

SANCHEZ, LORETTA, congresswoman; b. Lynnwood, Calif., Jan. 7, 1960; BA, Chapman U., 1982; MBA, Am. U., 1984. With Orange County Transp. Authority, 1984-87, Fieldman Rolapp & Assocs., 1987-90; strategic mgmt. cons. Booz Allen & Hamilton; owner, operator AMIGA Advisors Inc.; mem. U.S. Congress from 47th Calif. dist., 1997—; former mem. edn. and the workforce com., mem. armed svcs. com.; mem. House Select Com. on Homeland Security, House Blue Dogs. Mem. Anaheim Rotary Club. Democrat. Office: US Ho Reps 1230 Longworth Ho Office Bldg Washington DC 20515-0547 also: Dist Office Ste 101 12397 Lewis St Garden Grove CA 92840 Office Phone: 202-225-2965. E-mail: loretta@mail.house.gov.

SANCHEZ, LUPITA A., elementary school educator; b. Antonito, Colo., Mar. 17, 1949; d. Manuel Lucas and Isabel Evangeline Sanchez. BA, Adams State Coll., 1972. Cert. Teacher Colo., 1986. Sub. tchr. South Sch. Dist., Antonito, Colo., 1975—85; elem. bilingual tchr. Haskin Elem. Sch., Center, Colo., 1988—2005. Tchr. rep. Dist. Accountability Com., Center, Colo., 1996—99. Vol. San Luis Valley Care Ctr., Alamosa, Colo., 2003—06. Mem.: NEA. Republican. Cath. Avocations: painting, ceramics, gardening, arts and crafts. Home: 300 13th St Alamosa CO 81101

SANCHEZ, MARLA RENA, communications executive; d. Tomas Guillermo and Rose Sanchez; m. Bradley D. Gaiser. BS, MS, Stanford U., 1979; MBA, Santa Clara U., 1983. Rsch. biologist Syntex, Palo Alto, Calif., 1980-81; fin. analyst Advanced Micro Devices, Sunnyvale, Calif., 1983-85; fin. mgr. ultrasound divsn. Diasonics, Inc., Milpitas, Calif., 1985-86, contr. therapeutic products divsn., 1989-93, contr. internat. divsn., 1992-93; contr. Ridge Computers, Santa Clara, Calif., 1986-88; dir. fin. VLSI Tech., Inc., San Jose, Calif., 1993-98; corp. contr. SDL, Inc., San Jose, 1999—2001, interim CFO, 2005; sr. v.p., CFO Avanex Corp., Fremont, Calif., 2006—. Office: Avanex Corp 40919 Encyclopedia Cir Fremont CA 94538*

SANCHEZ, MARTA, music educator; b. Vina del Mar, Chile; came to U.S., 1957; d. Julian and Mary (Cerani) S.; m. Segio Carvajal. Diplome eurhythmics, Inst. Jaques-Dalcroze, Geneva, 1955; PhD in Musicology, U. Pitts., 1978. Tchr. high sch., Vina del Mar, 1952-53; prof. music Nat. Conservatory, Santiago, Chile, 1953-54; faculty Pittsfield (Mass.) Community Sch., 1955-56, Los Angeles Conservatory, 1956-57; prof. Carnegie-Mellon U., Pitts., 1957—, head. dept., 1985-87, dir. Dalcroze Tng. Ctr., 1968—. Piano tutor rsch. project to teach beginning piano with aid of computer and videodisk; cons., supr. Pitts. Pub. Sch., 1966-69; faculty Cleve. Inst. Music, 1972-73, Inst. Jaques Dalcroze, Geneva, 1979-80, Biel (Switzerland) Konservatorium, 1979-80, New South Wales State Conservatorium, Sydney, Australia, 1981, 86; worldwide lectr.; cons. McMillan Publ. Co. Author: Spanish Villancicos of the 18th Century, 1987; contbr. articles to profl. jours. Inst. Jaques-Dalcroze fellow, 1954-55, U. Pitts. fellow, 1964-65, 75-76. Mem. Music Educators Nat. Conf., Internat. Soc. for Music Educators, Ctr. Internat. de Documentation Jaques-Dalcroze (bd. dirs.), Pitts. Fund for Arts Edn. (bd. dirs.), Latinam. Literary Rev. Editorial (bd. dirs.), Pitts. Oratorio Soc. (bd. dirs.). Avocations: nature, animals.

SÁNCHEZ, PATSY Y., bilingual educator; b. Denton, Tex., Oct. 9, 1965; d. Francisco and Elizabeth M. Sosa; m. Reymundo S. Sánchez, Aug. 4, 1990; children: Jessica Y., Christina P., Reymindo F. BS, Tex. Women's U., Denton, 2004, EdM specialation in Bilingual Edn., 2006. Cert. TEA tchr. Tex. Tchr. bilingual edn. Denton Ind. Sch. Dist., Tex., 2003—. Sales cons. Mary Kay Cosmetics, Dallas, 1990—; artistic dir. Ballet Folklorico de Woodrow Wilson, Denton, 2004—; co-chmn. dual implementation team Woodrow Wilson Sch., 2005—, presenter dual lang. staff devel., 2005—. Coach Denton Soccer Assn., Tex., 1998—, commissioner, 1998—; tchr. Sunday sch. Immaculate Conception Cath. Ch., 1998—, lector, 2004—. Mem.: Tex. State Tchrs. Assn., Tex. Assn. Bilingual Edn., Nat. Assn. Bilingual Edn., Tex. State Reading Assn., Phi Delta Kappa. Avocations: reading, dance, research, cooking, sewing. Office: Woodrow Wilson Elem 1306 E Windsor Dr Denton TX 76209-1211 Home: 8200 Stallion St Denton TX 76208 Office Phone: 940-369-4500.

SANCHEZ, RITA B., humanities educator, writer; b. San Bernardino, Calif., May 20, 1937; d. Leonidas Nicolas Sanchez and Macedonia Acuña; m. Richard Griswold del Castillo, June 29, 1996; m. Donald Gene Fink (div.); children: Lisa Fink La Rossa, Teyana Fink Viscarra, Mario Torero Acenedo, Lucin Acenedo, Acenedo Palilo. BA in English, Stanford U., Calif., 1972, MA in English, 1973, MA in English, 1974; student, U. Calif., 1976—82. Student tchr. Forthill C.C., Palo Alto, Calif., 1972; tchr. Stanford U., 1973; tchr. English Cañuda C.C., Redwood City, Calif., 1973; prof. English San Diego State U., 1974—84; prin., owner Acenedo Gallery, San Diego, 1983—90; prof. English San Diego Mesa Coll., 1990—. Chmn. com. against racism Mesa Coll.; presenter in field; spkr. in field. Editor: Jour. Chicana Writings, 1973, Vision; author: Cochise Remembers My Great-Grandfather, 2000; contbr. articles to profl. jours. Fellow, Ford Found., 1976—81. Office: Sch Humanities and Langs San Diego Mesa Coll 7250 Mesa Coll Dr San Diego CA 92111-1999

SANCHEZ, SUSIE RIOJAS, elementary school educator; b. San Antonio, Dec. 25, 1937; d. Lorenzo and Juanita (Cisneros) Riojas; m. Edward R. Sanchez, Aug. 28, 1960; six children. BA, St. Mary's U., San Antonio, 1984; cert., Our Lady of the Lake, 1985; MS, A&I U., 1990. Tchr. San Antonio Ind. Sch. Dist.; ret. Mem. PTC bd. Ursuline Acad. Mem. NEA, ASCD, San Antonio Tchrs. Coun., Tex. Tchrs. Assn. Home: 1326 Stetson Grn San Antonio TX 78258-7288 Office Phone: 210-977-9301.

SANCHEZ, VICTORIA WAGNER, science educator; b. Milw., Apr. 11, 1934; d. Arthur William and Lorraine Marguerite (Kocovsky) Wagner; m. Rozier Edmond Sanchez, June 23, 1956; children: Mary Elizabeth, Carol Anne, Robert Edmond, Catherine Marie, Linda Therese. BS cum laude, Mt. Mary Coll., 1955; MS, Marquette U., 1957; postgrad., U. N.Mex., 1979-86, U. Del., 1990. Cert. secondary tchr., N.Mex. Chemist Nat. Bur. Standards, Washington, 1958-60; tchr., chmn. sci. dept. Albuquerque Pub. Schs., 1979-94. Chmn. pub. info. area conv. Nat. Sci. Tchrs. Assn., 1984, mem. sci. rev. com. Albuquerque Pub. Schs., 1985-86, 92-93, dedication of N.W. Regional Sci. Fair, 1994, Gov.'s Summit on Edn., 1991, 92, Gov.'s Steering Com. Systemic Change in Math. and Sci. Edn.; panel mem. NSF, 1991-93. Bd. dirs. Encino House, Albuquerque, 1976-92, treas., 1977-79; leader Albuquerque troop Girl Scouts U.S., 1966-77; cmty. interpreter Environ. Open Space Divsn. City Albuquerque, N.Mex., 2000—. Named Outstanding Sci. Tchr., NW Regional Sci. Fair, Albuquerque, 1983, 88, 90, N.Mex. Parents of Yr., 2001; recipient St. George's award N.Mex. Cath. Scouting Com., 1978, Focus on Excellence award ASCD, Albuquerque, 1985, 89, Presdl. awards for excellence in sci. and math., 1989. Mem. AAUW (officer Albuquerque br. 1976-77, N.Mex. divsn. 1977-78), NSTA, N.Mex. Sci. Tchrs. Assn. (treas. 1988-90), Albuquerque Sci. Tchrs. Assn. (treas. 1984-85, v.p., pres.-elect 1986-87, pres. 1987-88, Svc. to Sci. award 1994), N.Mex. Acad. Sci., Am. Coun. on Edn. (math. and sci. edn. nat. com. 1990-92), DuPont Honors Workshop for Tchrs., Albuquerque Rose Soc. (sec. 1962-63). Democrat. Roman Catholic. Avocations: reading, fishing, hiking, needlecraft, camping. Home: 7612 Palo Duro Ave NE Albuquerque NM 87110-2315

SANCHEZ MILLS, PEGGY, women's association executive; b. Roswell, N.Mex., Aug. 1, 1953; d. Myron and Gloria Carson; children: Jennifer, Jason. BA in Sociology and Psychology, U. South Fla.; MPA, Golden Gate U. Reading specialist Girl's Clubs Pinellas County, Clearwater, Fla., 1979-80, ctr. supr. St. Petersburg, Fla., 1980-81; project adminstr. YWCA St. Petersburg, 1981-84; exec. dir. YWCA Tampa Bay, St. Petersburg, 1984—2004; CEO YWCA USA, Washington, 2004—. Mem. adv. com. Riviera Mid. Sch., Lealman Discovery. Chair edn. com. Community Alliance, 1989-91; chair Dist. Task Force on Child Abuse Prevention, 1988-91; pres. Leadership St. Pete Assn., mem. planning coun., United Way; pres. Coun. of Exec. Dirs.; sec., bd. dirs. Suncoast Tiger Bay Club; mem. steering com. Teen Parent Self Sufficiency Task Force for Pinellas County; mem. Abuse, Neglect, and Dependency Com., Coalition for Homeless/Affordable Housing. Fla. Ctr. for Children and Youth, Human Svc. Coalition; mem. adv. com. Jr. League of St. Petersburg; apptd. to state coord. coun. early childhood svcs. Recipient Up and Comers award Price-Waterhouse, 1990. Office: YWCA USA 1015 18th St NW Ste 1100 Washington DC 20036 Business E-Mail: jsanchezmills@ywca.org.

SANCHEZ-SILKMAN, JENNIFER CHRISTINE, elementary school educator; b. Bronx, N.Y., Sept. 11, 1974; d. George Peter Sanchez and Lucille Ann Ramirez; m. Jeffrey Howard Silkman, Dec. 22, 2000; 1 child, Julian Michael Silkman. BS in Elem. Edn., Iona Coll., New Rochelle, N.Y., 1996; MS in Early Childhood Edn., Coll. New Rochelle, 2000; post grad. in curriculum and tchg., Tchrs. Coll. Columbia U., N.Y.C., 2002—04. Lic. (permanent) tchr. K-6 N.Y. State and N.Y.C., spl. edn. K-12 N.Y. State and N.Y.C. Tchr. grade 3 St. Francis de Chantal Sch., Bronx, NY, 1998—2002; tchr. grade 4 Pub. Sch. 182, 2002—. Tchr. rep. St. Francis de Chantal Sch. PTA, 2000—01. Mem.: ASCD. Roman Catholic. Avocations: walking, exercise, dance, music. Home: 737 Hollywood Ave Bronx NY 10465-2303 Office: PS 182 601 Stickball Blvd Bronx NY 10473

SANCHEZ-WAY, RUTH DOLORES, public health administrator; b. NYC, Aug. 8, 1940; d. Manuel and Cruz Maria (Rivera) Sanchez; m. Harley Milton Dirks, Feb. 9, 1974 (dec. Aug. 1986); stepchildren: Timothy, Darcy Kimmel, Marcine Thomas, James, David, Dale; m. David Vincent Way, Apr. 16, 1988. BS, St. John's U., 1962; MSW, Fordham U., 1965; PhD, NYU, 1978; postgrad., Emory U., Geroge Washington U. Cert. social worker, Md.; cert. prevention profl. Spl. asst. to dir. Nat. Inst. Alcohol Abuse and Alcoholism, U.S. Dept Health, Edn. and Welfare, Rockville, Md., 1971-79; assoc. dep. adminstr. Equal Employment Opportunity Office Asst. Sec. Health, U.S. Dept. HEW, 1979-83; dep. dir. Office Adolescent Pregnancy Programs Health and Human Svcs., Washington, 1983-91; assoc. adminstr. minority health concerns Substance Abuse & Mental Health Svcs. Adminstrn., Health and Human Svcs., Rockville, 1993-96, divsn. dir. Ctr. for Substance Abuse Prevention, 1991-96, acting dep. dir. Ctr. for Substance Abuse Prevention, 1997, acting dir., 1997—2000, dir., 2000—02; assoc. dir. Ctr. for Faith-Based and Cmty. Initiatives, HHS, 2002—03; v.p. health and cmty. initiatives Mgmt. Scis. for Devel., 2003—. Bd. dirs. Nat. Health Coun., Washington, 1987-94, Nat. Coun. on Alcoholism and Drug Dependence, N.Y.C., 1979-91, Nat. Orgn. Adolescent Pregnancy Parenting and Prevention, Washington, 1991-93. Vol. Girl Scouts U.S.A., N.Y.C., 1996—. Recipient Excellence in Govt. Svc. award Mex.-Am. Legal Def. and Ednl. Fund, 2000, Presdl. Meritorious Exec. Rank award SES, 1998, Sec.'s award for disting. svc. HHS, 2001; primary care policy fellow USPHS. Mem. NASW, APHA, Chesapeake Crusing Multihull Assn. (past commodore, Kilmon award 1996). Roman Catholic. Avocations: sailing, skiing, jazzercise. Office: Mgmt Scis for Devel 4455 Connecticut Ave NW Ste A100 Washington DC 20008 Office Phone: 202-537-7410. Personal E-mail: rsanchez@msdglobal.com.

SANDAGE-MUSSEY, ELIZABETH ANTHEA, retired market research executive; b. Larned, Kans., Oct. 13, 1930; d. Curtis Carl and Beulah Pauline (Knupp) Smith; m. H.I. Danner, 1948 (div. 1956); children: Dianna Louise Danner Wilson, David Alan Danner; m. Charles Harold Sandage, July 18, 1971; m. Robert D. Mussey, Oct. 21, 2000. BS, U. Colo., 1967, MA, 1970; PhD in Comms., U. Ill., 1973. Pub. rels. rep., editor Martin News Martin Marietta Corp., Denver, 1960-63, 65-67; retail advt. salesperson Denver Post, 1967-70; instr. advt. U. Ill., 1970-71, vis. lectr. advt., 1977-84; v.p., corp. sec., dir. Farm Rsch. Inst., Urbana, Ill., 1984-95; ret., 1995. Editor: Advertising as a Social Force: Selected Speeches and Essays by Charles H. Sandage, 1998, Occasional Papers in Advertising, 1971, The Sandage Family Cookbook, 1976, 3d edit., 2002, The Inkling (Carle Hosp. Aux. Newsletter), 1975-76. Bd. dirs. U. Ill. Libr. Friends, 1991-95; exec. dir. Sandage Charitable Trust, 1986—. Mem. U. Ill. Alumni Assn. (pres.'s coun.), Champaign Social Sci. Club, The Book Club, Moneymakers Investment Club, Kappa Tau Alpha.

SANDAHL, BONNIE BEARDSLEY, nursing administrator; b. Washington, Jan. 17, 1939; d. Erwin Leonard and Carol Myrtle (Collis) Beardsley; m. Glen Emil Sandahl, Aug. 17, 1963; children: Cara Lynne, Cory Glen. BSN, U. Wash., 1962, MN, 1974; cert. pediat. nurse practitioner, 1972. Dir. Wash. State Joint Practice Commn., Seattle, 1974-76; instr. pediatric nurse practitioner program U. Wash., Seattle, 1976, course coord. quality assurance, 1977-78; pediatric nurse practitioner/health coord. Snohomish County Head Start, Everett, Wash., 1975-77; clin. nurse educator (specialist), nurse mgr. Harborview Med. Ctr., Seattle, 1978-97, dir. child abuse prevention project, 1986-97; mgr. Children's Ctr., Providence Health Sys. Northwest, 1997-2000; v.p. clin. svcs. and ops., COO Seattle Children's Home, 2000—03, exec. dir., 2003—05; sch. nurse Seattle Pub. Schs., 2006—. Spkr. legis. focus on children, 1987; clin. assoc. dept. pediatrics U. Wash. Sch. Medicine, 1987—; clin. faculty U. Wash. Sch. Nursing, 1987—97; mgr. Providence Gen. Children's Ctr., Everett, 1997—2000; gov. appointee State Interagy. Coord. Coun., 1998—, gov. appointee chair, 2003—. Interim chair nat. coun. health planning and devel. HHS, 1980—87; mem. task force pharmacotherapeutic courses Puget Sound Health Sys. Agy., 1975—88, pres., 1980—82; mem. task force pharmacotherapeutic courses Wash. State Bd. Nursing, 1985—86; mem. child devel. project adv. bd. Mukiteo Sch. Dist., 1984—85; mem. parenting adv. com. Edmonds Sch. Dist.; chmn. hospice-hom health task force Snohomis County Hospice Program, Everett, 1984—85, bd. dirs. hospice, 1985—87, mem. adv. com., 1986—88; mem. Wash. State Health Coordinating Coun., 1977—82, chmn. nursing home bed projection methodology task force, 1986—87; mem. adv. com. uncompensated care Wash. State Legislature, 1983—84; mem. joint select com. Tech. Adv. Com. Managed Health Care Sys., 1984—85; pres. Alderwood Manor Cmty. Coun., 1983—85; treas. Wash. St. Women's Polit. Caucus, 1983—84; mem. com. examine changes in Wash. State Criminal Sex Law, 1987; appointee county needs assessment com. Snohomish County Govt. United Way, 1989, 1994; chair human svcs. adv. coun. Snohomish County Human Svcs. Dept., chmn. adv. com., 1998—; gubernatorial appointee state interagency coordinating coun. Health Svcs. Adv. Com. Wash. State, 1995—97. Recipient Golden Acorn award, Seattle-King County PTA, 1973, Katherine Rickey Vol. Participation award, 1987. Mem.: ANA (chair com. examiners maternal-child nursing practice 1988—90), King County Nurses Assn. (1st v.p. 1992—96, pres. 1996—97, Nurse of the Yr. 1985), Wash. State Nurses Assn. (chair healthcare reform task force 1992—96, Hon. Leadership award 1981), Sigma Theta Tau. Home: 1814 201st Pl SW Lynnwood WA 98036-7060 Office: Seattle Childrens Home Seattle WA 98119-2899

SANDALL, JOANN MARY, mathematics educator; b. Breese, Ill., Apr. 24, 1949; d. Harold John and Josephine Mary Kapp; m. Steven John Sandall, Sept. 6, 1975; children: Justin, Jana, Jeremy. BS in Math., Ill. State U., Normal, 1979; MS in Counseling and Sch. Psychology, Wichita State U., Kans., 1983. Tchr. math., dept. chair Peoria Heights H.S., Ill., 1973—75; tchr. math. Maize H.S., Kans., 1975—76, Goddard H.S./Mid. Sch., Kans., 1976—82, Wichita West H.S., Kans., 1983—90, counselor, dept. chair, 1990—2003; tchr. math. Metro Midtown Alt. H.S., Wichita, Kans., 2003—04, Goddard H.S., Kans., 2004—. Tutor Town East Resource Ctr. and USD 259, Wichita, Kans., 1999—2005. Recipient Staff Mem. of Yr. award, Wichita West H.S., 1990, 1995, 1999, 2005, Support Staff of Yr. award, USD 259, 1993, Tchr. of Yr. award, Goddard H.S., 2005—06. Mem.: NEA, ASCD, Kans. Ednl. Assn., Nat. At-Risk Edn. Network, Nat. Coun. Tchrs. Math. Avocations: cooking, reading, hiking, crafts. Home: 19911 Amity Ct Goddard KS 67052 Office: Goddard HS 2500 S 199th St W Goddard KS 67052 E-mail: jsandall@goddardusd.com.

SANDBERG, ANNETTE M., federal agency administrator; MBA magna cum laude, City U., Bellevue, Wash., 1988; JD, U. Puget Sound, 1993. Atty. Maple Valley Law Group; chief Wash. State Patrol, 1995; dep. adminstr. Nat. Highway Traffic and Safety Adminstrn., US Dept. Transp., Washington, Fed. Motor Carrier Safety Adminstrn., Washington, 2002—03, acting adminstr., 2003, adminstr., 2003—. Named Women of Achievement, Women in Comm., Inc., 1996; recipient Nat. Pub. Svc. Award, Am. Soc. for Pub. Adminstrn. and Nat. Acad. Pub. Adminstrn., 1999. Office: Fed Motor Carrier Safety Adminsrn 400 7th St SW Washington DC 20590 Office Phone: 800-832-5660.

SANDBERG, MARILYN LEE, special education educator; b. Indpls., May 7, 1936; d. Chester Lee and Florence A. (Wilkens) Hughes; m. Donald Lawrence Sandberg, June 14, 1958; children: Robert Lawrence, Gregory Lee, Steven Lawrence. BS, Butler U., 1958; MS, Ind. U., 1971; endorsement learning disabilities edn., Indpls. U., 1985; endorsement mentally handicapped edn., Butler U., 1987. Tchr. elem. edn. Klondike (Ind.) Schs., 1958, Indpls. Pub. Schs., 1959; tchr. 1st grade M.S.D. Warren Twp. Schs., Indpls., 1971-74, tchr. kindergarten, 1974-85, tchr. spl. edn., 1985—96. With Reach Out and Read Wischard Hosp. Primary Care children. Mem.: Alpha Delta Kappa (chaplain 1991—93, historian 1995—97, pres. elect 2005—), Delta Delta Delta (chmn. 1952, rush asst. chmn. 1955, v.p. 1958). Avocations: antiques, stained glass, craft work, church work. Home: 2540 Andrews Ct Indianapolis IN 46203-5619 E-mail: dsandb@mibor.com.

SANDBERG, SHERYL, information technology executive; BA summa cum laude, Harvard U., MBA. Economist World Bank; mgmt cons. McKinsey & Co.; chief of staff to sec. of treasury US Dept. Treasury, 1999—2001; joined Google Inc., Mountain View, Calif., 2001, v.p. global online sales and ops. Bd. mem. Ad Coun., Leadership Pub. Schs. Office: Google Inc 1600 Amphitheatre Pkwy Mountain View CA 94043 Office Phone: 650-253-0000. Office Fax: 650-253-0001.*

SANDBERG-MORGAN, BARBARA, retired communication and women's studies educator; b. McAllen, Tex., Dec. 19, 1934; d. Dean M. and Katherine (Hurlbert) Baer; m. Robert Morgan, July 31, 1976 (dec. Nov. 1994); 1 chld, Allison Morgan. BS, Ind. U., 1959; MA, Columbia U., 1963, EdD, 1974. Registered drama therapist. Prof. William Paterson U., Wayne, N.J., 1963-2000, prof. emerita, 2000—. Instr. Tchrs. Coll./Columbia U., N.Y.C., 1971-77; drama therapist, 1979—; mem. adv. bd., drama cons. Jersey Shore Arts Ctr., Ocean Grove, N.J., 1996—; dir. edn. Inner City Ensemble, Paterson, N.J., 1984-89; dir. Washington St. Gallery, Paterson, 1989-93. Dir. Paterson Bicentennial Pageant, Hist. Commn., 1992; dir. Washington St. Cultural Activities Assn., Paterson, 1990-93. Recipinet Heritage Citizen award Paterson, 1993, citation for tchg. excellence William Paterson U., 1994; named Woman of Yr., World of the Arts-Girl Scout Coun., 1995. Mem. Nat. Assn. for Drama Therapy (founding; bd. dirs.). Avocations: acting, directing, gardening. Home: Santander 400 Deal Lake Dr Apt 2J Asbury Park NJ 07712-5174 E-mail: millik@sedona.net, barbara.sandberg@verizon.net.

SANDBURG, HELGA, author; b. Maywood, Ill., Nov. 24, 1918; d. Carl and Lilian (Steichen) S.; m. George Crile, Jr., Nov. 9, 1963; children by previous marriage: John Carl Steichen, Paula Steichen Polega. Student, Mich. State Coll., 1939-40, U. Chgo., 1940. Dairy goat breeder, also personal sec. to father, 1944-51; sec. manuscripts div., also for keeper of collections Library of Congress, 1952-56; adminstrv. asst. for papers of Woodrow Wilson, 1958-59; writer, lectr., 1957—. Author: (novels) The Wheel of Earth, 1958, Measure My Love, 1959, The Owl's Roost, 1962, The Wizard's Child, 1967; (non-fiction) Sweet Music, A Book of Family Reminiscence and Song, 1963; (with George Crile, Jr.) Above and Below, 1969; (poetry) The Unicorns, 1965; To A New Husband, 1970, The Age of the Flower, 1994; (young adult novels) Blueberry, 1963; Gingerbread, 1964; (juveniles) Joel and the Wild Goose, 1963; Bo and the Old Donkey, 1965, Anna and the Baby Buzzard, 1970; Children and Lovers: 15 Stories by Helga Sandburg, 1976; (biography) A Great and Glorious Romance: The Story of Carl Sandburg and Lilian Steichen, 1978; ".Where Love Begins", 1989, (recorded poems) From in the Dream: Helga Sandburg Reads her Poems, 2001; also numerous short stories; rep. in collections.; contbr.short stories, poems, articles to popular mags. including Seventeen. Recipient Va. Quar. Rev. prize for best short story, 1959, Borestone Mountain poetry award, 1962, Poetry award Chgo. Tribune, 1970; 2d prize 7th Ann. Kans. Poetry Contest, Florence Roberts Head Ohioana Book award, 1990; grantee Finnish Am. Soc. and Svenska Inst., 1961 Mem. Authors Guild, Poetry Soc., Am. Milk Goat Record Assn., Am.-Scandinavian Found., Nat. Nubian Club, Coun. Save the Dunes, Am. Luxembourg Soc., Acad. Am. Poets. Address: 2060 Kent Rd Cleveland Heights OH 44106-3339 E-mail: helgacrile@steichen.ws.

SANDERS, AUGUSTA CAROLYN, school librarian, educator; b. Middletown, Ohio, Sept. 7, 1945; d. Clarence Marvin Reynolds and Sarah Inell Gary; m. Charles Walton Sanders, Dec. 23, 1972. BS, Miami U., Oxford, Ohio, 1968, MEd, 1972; MLS, Ind. U., Bloomington, 1994. Cert. elem. tchr. Ohio, 1979, spl. edn. tchr. Ohio, 1983, reading tchr. Ohio, 1989, tchr. ednl. media Ohio, 1998, ednl. adminstv. specialist svcs. Ohio, 1989, specialist-reading supr. Ohio, 1995, ednl. adminstrv. specialist exceptional children Ohio, 1989. Tchr., libr., coord. Middletown (Ohio) City Schs., 1967—97; asst. prof., media svcs. and curriculum reference libr., prodn. lab dir. Ctrl. State U., Wilberforce, 1998—. Coord. gifted & talented edn. Middletown City Schs., 1980—81; presenter in field. Prodr., writer: (videos) Electronic Educational Portfolio: An Outline, 2000; Electronic Educational Portfolio: Digitizing, 2004; prodr., editor Civil Rights Sites Revisited 2000, 2001; Desert Storm Military Equipment, 2000. Singer Lebanon Cmty. Choir, Ohio, 1976, Bridges of Song Choir Internat., Tallin, Estonia, 1991; pres. Waynesville Prog. Women's Club, 1994—95, mem., 1989—; charter com. Village of Waynesville, 1995, 2005; dir. Christian edn. United Missionary Bapt. Ch., Middletown, 1967—72; singer People Relating Our Mission In Svc., Ext. and Study, 1970—72; pres. Mary L. Cook Pub. Libr., Waynesville, 1997, 1998, mem., 1992—. Mem.: AAUP, ALA (black caucus), Ohio Libr. Coun. Home: PO Box 637 Waynesville OH 45068 Office: Ctrl State Univ Box 1006 1400 Brush Row Rd Wilberforce OH 45384-1006 Office Phone: 937-376-6213. Home Fax: 513-897-1456; Office Fax: 937-376-6132. Business E-Mail: csanders@centralstate.edu.

SANDERS, BARBARA BOYLES, secondary school educator; b. Charleston, Miss., May 4, 1950; d. Marion Enoch and Bettye Wright Boyles. BA, Miss. Coll., Clinton, 1970; MA, Delta State U., Cleveland, Miss., 1972, MEd, 1975. Nat. exec. dir. Nat. Assn. EMTS, Clinton, 1994—98; secondary sch. tchr. Puckett HS, Miss., 1999—. Dir. regional svcs. Am. Heart Assn., Little Rock, 1977—81; v.p. Boyles Enterprises, Jackson, Miss., 1981—84; exec. dir. Nat. Multiple Sclerosis Soc., Jackson, 1984—93. Named Star Tchr., Miss. Econ. Coun., 1973, 1974; recipient, 2004, 2005. Republican. Full Gospel. Avocations: travel, history, missions work. Home: 242 Terrace Dr Brandon MS 39042 Office: Puckett HS 6382 Highway 18 Puckett MS 39151 Office Phone: 601-825-5742. Home Fax: 601-825-9838; Office Fax: 601-825-9838. Business E-Mail: bsanders@rcsd.ms.

SANDERS, BARBARA FAYNE, artist, educator; b. Draper, N.C., Apr. 20, 1936; d. Elwood Oris and Gladys (Martin) Fayne; m. Joseph J. Sanders, June 11, 1960; children: J. Gregory, Kimberly Ann. Student., Rockingham C.C., Wentworth, N.C., 1970—92. Jr. designer Design Dept., Karastan Rug Mill, Eden, NC, 1954—60; art instr. Rockingham C.C., Wentworth, 1985—2000; pvt. instr./condr. workshops, 1985—. Art coord. Eden Pub. Libr., 1985—90, Eden City Hall, 1995—. One-woman shows include Eden (N.C.) Pub. Libr., Eden City Hall Gallery, Rockingham County Govtl. Ctr., Wentworth, N.C., Forum VI, Greensboro, N.C., Stokes County Arts Coun. Gallery, Danbury, N.C., Chinqua Penn Plantation, Reidsville, N.C., Women's Club Gallery, Reidsville, Mt. Airy (N.C.) Art Guild, others, exhibited in group shows at Rockingham County Fine Arts Festival, Wentworth, Arts Davidson County Mus., Lexington, N.C., Carolina Craftsmen, Greensboro, Southeastern Artists Assn., Benton Conv. Ctr., Winston-Salem, N.C., Sawtooth Gallery, Winston-Salem, Art in the Pk., Blowing Rock, N.C., High Point (N.C.) Theatre Art Galleries, Carolina St. Scene, Winston-Salem, Arts Coun. Gallery, Cary, N.C., Piedmont Arts Assn. Gallery, Martinsville, Va., Danville Mus. History and Art, Capt.'s Ho. Gallery, others, Represented in permanent collections NationsBank, Wachovia Bank, First Nat. Bank, Home Savs. Bank., Miller Brewing Co., RJR Nabisco, Gem Dandy, Inc., Rockingham Arts Coun., Rockingham CC, Rockingham County Pub. Libr., Morehead Meml. Hosp., Steamway Internat., Gov. James Martin, N.C. U.S. area dir. Y's Menettes YMCA, Geneva, 1995—96, regional dir. Kannapolis, NC, 1993—95; pres. Draper Y's Menettes, Eden, 1978—2001. Named Y's Menette of the Yr., Draper Y's Menettes, 1984; recipient Vis.'s Favorite award, Fine Arts Festival Rockingham County, 1975, Best in Show, Rockingham County Fine Arts Festival, 1980, 1st pl., Sr. Art Expo, 1996, award of distinction, Danville Artists League, 1998, Piedmont Arts Assn., 2000, 2001, others. Mem.: Studio Group of Rockingham County (pres. 1996—97), High Point Art Guild (RECEPTION COORD. 1992—), Watercolor Soc. N.C. Avocations: reading, music, writing poetry and stories. Home: 135 River Ridge Rd Eden NC 27288-8004

SANDERS, BESSIE ELAINE, secondary school educator; b. Cabool, Mo., May 31, 1960; d. Donald Everett Miller and Billie Mae Shelley; children: Jeremy Donald, Amy Elizabeth Dyer, Sarah Mae. BS in Comprehensive Agr. with Minor in Geography, SW Mo. State, 1994, M in Edn., 2002. Mid. sch. sci. tchr. Raymondville Schs., Mo., 2000—03; HS sci. tchr. Salem R-80, Mo., 2004—. Scoutmaster BSA Troop 1763, Houston, Mo., 1994—97; rep. Relay For Life, Houston, Mo., 2002—06. Grantee Outdoor Classroom Grant, Mo. Dept. of Conservation, 2002. Mem.: Delta Tau Alpha (life; v.p. 1993—94). Avocations: gardening, camping, bowling, quilting. Office Phone: 573-729-6642.

SANDERS, COYETTA TRESHAY, accountant; b. Sarasota, Fla., Jan. 14, 1977; d. Calvin Otis Gibbons and Cynthia Elaine Brown; m. Tony Latroy Sanders, Mar. 18, 2006; children: Amauri Latroy, Amaya Lashay, Amani Treshay. A in Acctg., Manatee CC, Bradenton, Fla., 2000; B in Mgmt., Internat. Coll., Naples, Fla., 2006. Dispatcher, travel counselor AAA Auto Club S., Sarasota, 1997—2000; records technician Sarasota Police Dept., 2000—03, jud. liaison, 2003—06; acctg. specialist City of Sarasota- Pub. Works, 2006—. Rep. United Way, Sarasota, 2003—05. Scholar, Sarasota Cmty. Found. and Women's Resource Ctr., 2005—06. Home: 1835 31st St Sarasota FL 34234 Office Phone: 941-955-2325.

SANDERS, DORIS JEAN, mental health therapist; d. Ralph and Ruby Lee Petermon; m. Victor J. Sanders, Sr., Jan. 6, 1966 (dec. July 22, 1981); children: Victoria Jenine(dec.), Victor J. Jr. AAS, Harold Washington Coll., Chgo., 1997; BS, Roosevelt U., Chgo., 1999; MS in Mental Health Counseling, Roosevelt U., 2006. Life skills and mental health therapist Ascend and Assocs., Blue Island, Ill.; employment specialist IDOC and Roosevelt U., Chgo.; domestic violence counselor Neopalitan Lite House, Chgo.; substance abuse counselor Womens Treatment Ctr., Chgo.; exec. svc. provider In His Hands, Chgo., 1998—. Active Father and Families in Transition, Faith Inc. Avocations: music, outdoors, writing. Home: 6806 S Talman Ave Chicago IL 60629-1824 Office: In His Hands 6806 S Talman Ave Chicago IL 60629-1824

SANDERS, ELIZABETH ANNE WEAVER (BETSY SANDERS), management consultant, writer; b. Gettysburg, Pa., July 25, 1945; Student, Gettysburg Coll., 1963—65; BA in German Lang. and Linguistics, Wayne State U., 1967; MEd, Boston U., 1970; postgrad., U. Wash., 1976—78. With Nordstrom, 1971—90, v.p., gen. mgr., 1978—90; prin. The Sanders Partnership, Sutter Creek, Calif., 1971-90, prin., owner, 1990—; founder, dir. Nat. Bank So. Calif., 1971-90. Bd. dirs. Wal Mart Stores, Inc., Washington Mut., Wellpoint Health Sys., Inc., Wolverine Worldwide, Inc., Denny's Inc., H.F. Ahmanson Co., Carl Karcher Enterprises, Sport Chalet, St. Joseph Health Sys., spkr. in field. Author: Fabled Service, 1995. Trustee Gettysburg Coll.; coach; mentor. Recipient Woman of Achievement in Bus. award YWCA South Orange County, Director's Choice award, 1997; named Woman of Yr. Bus. and Industry YWCA North Orange County, Humanitarian of Yr. NCCJ, Author of Yr., 1996, Dir. of Yr., Corp. Gov. Forum for Corp. Dirs., 2002. Mem. Internat. Women's Forum. Office: The Sanders Partnership PO Box 14 Sutter Creek CA 95685-0014 Office Phone: 209-267-5400. E-mail: betsanders@aol.com.

SANDERS, ELIZABETH GREY, English and history professor; d. Michael Raleigh and Phyllis Elizabeth Sanders. MA English, U. NC Greensboro, 2002. English/history prof. Randolph CC, Asheboro, NC, 2003—. Coord. humanities/fine arts program Randolph C.C., Asheboro, 2006—. Dir.: (theater co.) Dorothy Meets Alice. Mem.: N.C. Faculty Assn. (assoc.). Avocations: reading, Tex. hold'em.

SANDERS, GINA SUSAN, publishing executive; d. Arnold R. and Joyce S.; m. Steven Oliver Newhouse, Feb. 28, 1993; 2 children. BA magna cum laude, Tufts Univ. Account mgr. House & Garden Condé Nast, 1988, advt. dir. Details mag., 1993—94, pub. Details mag., 1994—97, pub. Gourmet mag., 1997—2002, v.p. Gourmet mag., 2000—02; founding pub. & v.p. Teen Vogue, 2003—. Named Pub. of Yr., Condé Nast, 2005. Office: Teen Vogue Condé Nast 4 Times Sq New York NY 10036 Office Phone: 212-286-4316.*

SANDERS, HEATHER JO, elementary school educator; b. Davenport, Iowa, May 19, 1970; d. Joseph Fred Sanders and Mary Louise Veerhusen. BS, Western Ill. U., 1992; lic. tchr., Iowa State U., 1996, MS, 2002. Sci. tchr. Canton (Mo.) Schs., 1996—97, Ankeny (Iowa) Cmty. Schs., 1997—. Mem.: NEA, NSTA (Ohaus award for excellence in sci. tchr. 2002), Ankeny Citizens Police Acad. Alumni Assn. (pres. 2004—05), Iowa State Tchrs. Assn. Presbyterian. Avocations: ceramics, pottery, crafts, videography. Home: 1018 NE 9th Ankeny IA 50021 Office: Parkview Mid Sch 105 NW Pleasant Ankeny IA 50021 E-mail: hsanders0519@aol.com.

SANDERS, JACKIE WOLCOTT, ambassador; married. BA, Bowling Green State U., 1976. Spl. asst. Congl. affairs Bur. Near Eastern and South Asian Affairs US Dept. State, Washington, 1984—85, White House liaison, 1985—87, dep. asst. sec. for polit. affairs, 1987—89, dep. asst. sec. state Bur. Internat. Orgn. Affairs, 2001—03; assoc. dir. NSC, Washington, 1987—89; US rep. to Conf. on Disarmament, spl. rep. of Pres. of the US for Non-proliferation of Nuclear Weapons Geneva, 2003—; spl. rep. of Pres. for Non-Proliferation of Nuclear Weapons The White House, Washington, 2003—; alt. US rep. spl. polit. affairs, US Mission to UN US Dept. State, NYC, 2006—. Office: US Dept State 2201 C St NW Washington DC 20520*

SANDERS, JACQUELYN SEEVAK, psychologist, educator; b. Boston, Apr. 26, 1931; d. Edward Ezral and Dora (Zoken) Seevak; 1 child, Seth. BA, Radcliffe Coll., 1952; MA, U. Chgo., 1964; PhD, UCLA, 1972. Counselor, asst. prin. Orthogenic Sch., Chgo., 1952—65; rsch. assoc. UCLA, 1965—68; asst. prof. Ctr. for Early Edn., LA, 1969—72; assoc. dir. Sonia Shankman Orthogenic Sch., U. Chgo., 1972—73, dir., 1973—93, dir. emeritus, 1993—; curriculum cons. day care ctrs. LA Dept. Social Welfare, 1970—72; instr. Calif. State Coll., LA, 1972; lectr. dept. edn. U. Chgo., 1972—80, sr. lectr., 1980—93, clin. assoc. prof. dept. psychiatry, 1990—93, emeritus, 1993—; instr. edn. program Inst. Psychoanalysis, Chgo., 1979—82. Cons. Osawatomie State Hosp., Kans., 1965—68; reading cons. Foreman HS, Chgo.; treas. Chgo. Inst. Psychoanalysis, 2003—. Author: Greenhouse for the Mind, 1989; editor (with Barry L. Childress): Psychoanalytic Approaches to the Very Troubled Child: Therapeutic Practice Innovations in Residential & Educational Settings, 1989; editor: Severely Disturbed Children and the Parental Alliance, 1992; editor: (with Jerome M. Goldsmith) Milieu Therapy: Significant Issues and Innovative Applications, 1993; editor: The Seevak Family, The Zoken Family; contbr. articles to profl. jours. Mem. vis. com. univ. sch.

rels. U. Chgo.; bd. dirs. KAM Isaiah Israel Congregation, 1997—2001; bd. dirs., treas. Chgo. Inst. for Psychoanalysis. Recipient Alumna award, Girls' Latin Sch., Boston, Bettelheim award, Am. Assn. Children's Residential Ctrs., Disting. Svc. award, Radcliffe Assn., 2002; scholar Radcliffe Coll. scholar, 1948—52; Univ. fellow, UCLA, 1966—68. Mem.: Chgo. Inst. for Psychoanalysis, Assn. Children's Residential Ctrs. (past pres.), Harvard Club (bd. dirs. 1986—2001, Chgo.), Radcliffe Club (sec.-treas. 1986—87, pres. 1987—89, Chgo.). Home: 5842 S Stony Island Ave Apt 2G Chicago IL 60637-2033

SANDERS, JAN W., librarian; b. Kansas City, Kans., Sept. 20, 1947; d. Joseph A. and Esther Knierim Wilkes; m. Merritt V. Sanders, Apr. 15, 1972 (div. Apr. 1989); 1 child, Sara Kay. BSEd, N.W. Mo. State U., 1969; MLS, Ind. U., 1970. Libr. S.E. Mo. Libr. System, Cape Girardeau, Mo., 1970-73, Memphis (Tenn.) Shelby County Libr., 1973-78; instr. N.W. Ark. C.C., Harrison, 1978-82; mgr., libr. Springfield (Mo.) Greene County, 1982-87, Pioneer Libr. System, Norman, Okla., 1987-91; dir. libr. City of Bartlesville, Okla., 1991—2001; dir. Spokane Public Libr., 2001—05, Pasadena (Calif.) Public Libr., 2005—. Cons./trainer in field, Bartlesville, 1991—2001. Contbr. articles to profl. jours. Vice-pres. Allied Arts/Humanities Coun., Bartlesville, 1991—2001; bd. dirs. Boy Scouts Am., Bartlesville, 1997—2001, YWCA; active Heart of Town Advocates, Cert. Cities. Recipient Wall of Honor award Office of Intellectual Freedom, ALA, Chgo., 1999. Mem. Okla. Libr. Assn. (various offices, including pres. 1987—2001), Rotary (v.p. Daybreak Club 1999—2001), Bartlesville Leadership. Episcopalian. Office: Pasadena Public Libr 285 E Walnut St Pasadena CA 91101 Office Phone: 626-744-4066.*

SANDERS, JANET RUTH, elementary school educator; b. Spokane, Wash., Apr. 6, 1958; d. William Sylvester and Margaret Louise Boyd; m. Ralph Lee Sanders, Mar. 17, 1979; children: Jacob Lee, Jessica Lynn. AA in Mktg., West Ga. Coll., 1981, BBA, 1983, cert. in Tchg., 1985. Cert. tchr. Ga. Mgr. Milliken Textile Co., LaGrange, Ga., 1983—85; tchr. Carroll County Schs., Carrollton, Ga., 1985—. Named Tchr. of Yr., Bowdon Elem. Sch., 1999. Methodist. Avocations: reading, crafts, sports. Office: Jonesville Middle Sch 129 North Jonesville Rd Bowdon GA 30108

SANDERS, JOAN SKOGSBERG, artist; b. Portland, Oct. 18, 1930; d. George and Dorothy (Myers) Skogsberg; m. Milford P. Cooper, Oct. 17, 1953 (div. 1972); children: Chapman J., Kristin D. Cooper-Segal; m. Salvador L. Sanders, June 12, 1983. BA, Calif. State U., 1988. One-woman shows include World Trade Ctr., Long Beach, Calif., 1994; group shows include Legal Aid Found., 1995, Long Beach Mus. Art, 1996, Goldenwest Coll. Fine Arts Gallery, 1997, JCC Gallery, Long Beach, 1997, 98, Art Auction 6, Long Beach, 1998, MWP Prodn. House, L.A., 1998, Orlando Gallery, Sherman Oaks, Calif., 1999, Macy Gallery, Valhalla, N.Y., 1999, Black Sheep Gallery, England, 1999, others; represented in permanent collections Mr. and Mrs. George Ryder, Ont., Can., Mr. and Mrs. Robert Kendrick, Ashland, Oreg., Mr. and Mrs. Elliot Segal, Laguna Hills, Calif., Mrs. Donna Lemmon, Las Vegas, Mr. and Mrs. Paul Casselman, San Juan Capistrano, Calif., Mr. Howard Harris, Mercer Island, Wash., Mr. William Beahm, Rolling Hills Estates, Calif., Mr. Chap Cooper, Long Beach, Calif., Mr. and Mrs. Henry Trujillo, Pueblo, Colo., Mr. and Mrs. Rich Darling, Long Beach, Ms. Barbara Ross, Hermosa Beach, Calif., Ms. Jacqueline Thompson, Manhattan Beach, Calif., Mr. and Mrs. Robert Langslet, Long Beach. Republican. Home: 3156 Stevely Ave Long Beach CA 90808-4439

SANDERS, KATHRYN A., lawyer; b. Fresno, Calif., 1958; BA in Bus. and Econs., U. Calif., Los Angeles, 1980; JD, U. So. Calif., 1985. Bar: Calif. 1985. Ptnr. O'Melveny & Myers LLP, LA, co-chair private equity fund practice, mem. policy com. Mem. So. Calif. Law Review, 1983—85. Past pres. Nat. Women's Political Caucus, LA Metro Chpt. Mem.: Inst. for Corp. Counsel, Bd. of Govenors, Calif. State Bar Assn., LA Bar Assn., ABA, Order of the Coif. Office: O'Melveny & Myers LLP 400 S Hope St Los Angeles CA 90071-2899 Office Phone: 213-430-6376. Office Fax: 213-430-6407. Business E-Mail: ksanders@omm.com.

SANDERS, LINDA E., psychologist, educator; d. James E. and Madonna Elaine Hoelscher; m. Jim R. Sanders, June 3, 1973; 1 child, Jason R. BA in English and Journalism, U. Ark., 1976; MEd, Northeastern State U., Tahlequah, Okla., 1988; PhD, U. Okla., 2005. Nat. cert. sch. psychologist Nat. Sch. Psychology Certification Bd., 2005. Tchr. Jenks Pub. Schs., Jenks, Okla., 1985—96, psychologist, 1996—; adj. prof. psychology, asst. prof. Northeastern State U., Broken Arrow, Okla., 2003—. Ednl. cons. and reviewer Holt, Rinehart & Winston Pub. Co., Austin, Tex., 1993—98. Team co-leader home bldg. Habitat for Humanity, Nuevo Progreso, Mexico, 1994—95; adult vol. Day Ctr. for the Homeless, Tulsa, Okla., 1993; team leader Asbury United Meth. Ch., Tulsa, 1993—96. Recipient Pioneer in Edn. award, Nat. Bd. for Profl. Tchg. Standards, 1994, Mortar Bd., U. Ark., 1974. Mem.: APA, ASCD, NASP (regional leader 1997—99, Exemplary Mental Health Programs recipient 1997-1998), Okla. Ednl. Studies Assn., Coun. for Exceptional Children, Okla. Sch. Psychol. Assn. (pres. elect 1997—98, state pres. 1998—99, Past Pres. award 1999). Methodist. Avocations: reading, gardening, writing, travel. Office Phone: 918-299-4415 ext. 5507.

SANDERS, LISA GAIL, mathematics educator; d. Gale Herman and Nancy Marie Hanson, Sally Grace Hanson (Stepmother); m. Kelly Scot Sanders, Jan. 1, 2006. BS, U. N. Tex., Denton, 1996. Cert. tchr. Tex., 1996. Math tchr. Lewisville ISD, Flower Mound, Tex., 1997—. Scholar Nat. Merit scholar, 1987, MBNA, 1994. Mem.: ATPE. Office: Downing Middle School 5555 Bridlewood Blvd Flower Mound TX 75028 Office Phone: 972-450-1455.

SANDERS, MARION YVONNE, retired geriatrics nurse; b. St. Petersburg, Fla., Dec. 4, 1936; d. Ira Laurey and Maude Mae (Cherry) Sanders; children: Dwayne Irwin, Princess Charrie. BS, Fla. A&M U., 1959; MS, Nova U., Ft. Lauderdale, Fla., 1992. RN Fla. Staff nurse Lantana (Fla.) TB Hosp., 1960-61, Mercy Hosp., St. Petersburg, 1961; gen. duty nurse VA, Tuskegee, Ala., 1961-62; staff nurse John Andrews Hosp., Tuskegee, 1962-63; gen. duty staff nurse Brewster Meth. Hosp., Jacksonville, Fla., 1963-65, Duval Med. Ctr., Jacksonville, 1965-66; pvt. duty nurse Dist. 2 Registry, Jacksonville, 1966-70; supr. Eartha White Nursing Home, Jacksonville, 1970; staff nurse Bapt. Hosp., Jacksonville, 1971-73, City-County Methadone Clinic, Jacksonville, 1976-78; pvt. duty nurse Home Nursing, Jacksonville, Fla., 1982-86, pvt. duty geriatric nursing and gerontology specialist, 1995—2001, Sr. Companion Svc. Corp., 1997-98; ret., 2001. Mem. Ideas for Am.'s Future, 1997, 1998, NAACP, 1997—98; vol. shelter mgr. ARC, Miami, Fla., 1992—94; vol. cmty. activist, 1994; respite and relief sr. companion vol. Urban Jacksonville Cathedral Found., 1996—98, 2005—06; vol. Jacksonville Cmty. Rels. Bd., 1996, Jacksonville Inc. Cathedral Found., 1997—2006; sr. companion Svc. Corp., 1997—98, 1999, 2005, 2006; mem. Brewseter's and Cmty. Nurses Alumni, 1998—2000, 2001—02; vol. cmty. svcs., elem. grades tutor, polit. campaigns, tchr. health edn.; vol. Rep. Nat. Com., 1997—2000, 2001—02, 2005, Rep. Senatorial Com., 1999, Rep. Com. Fla., 1997—98, Northside Rep. Club, 1997, 1998, 1999; active St. Stephen AME Ch., Jacksonville, tch. Bible studies for youth, advocate for poor, homeless and prisoners. Recipient cert. of Recognition, Rep. Party, Fla. and Washington, 1990, Rep. Congl. Orgn., 1988, 1990, 1999. Mem.: ANA (mem. polit. actions com.), Nova Southeastern U. Alumni Assn., Fla. A&M U. Alumni Assn., Fla. Sheriff's Assn., Fla. Nurses Assn., Women's Missionary Soc. (life). Republican. Methodist. Avocation: reading. Home: 4832 N Main St Apt 14 Jacksonville FL 32206-1458

SANDERS, MARLENE, news correspondent, journalism educator; b. Cleve., Jan. 10, 1931; d. Mac and Evelyn (Menitoff) Sanders; m. Jerome Toobin, May 27, 1958 (dec. Jan. 1984); children: Jeff, Mark. Student, Ohio State U., 1948—49. Writer, prodr. Sta. WNEW-TV, N.Y.C., 1955-60, P.M. program Westinghouse Broadcasting Co., N.Y.C., 1961-62; asst. dir. news and pub. affairs Sta. WNEW, N.Y.C., 1962-64; anchor, news program ABC News, N.Y.C., 1964-68, corr., 1968-72, documentary prodr., writer, anchor, 1972-76, v.p., dir. TV documentaries, 1976-78; corr. CBS News, N.Y.C., 1978-87; host Currents Sta. WNET-TV, N.Y.C., 1987-88; host Met. Week in Rev., 1988-90; host Thirteen Live Sta. WNET-TV, 1990-91; prof. dept. journalism NYU, N.Y.C., 1991-93, adj. prof. journalism, 1996—; adj. prof. journalism, adminstr. Columbia U. Grad. Sch. Journalism, N.Y.C., 1994-95. Profl.-in-residence Freedom Forum Media Studies Ctr., 1997-2000; freelance broadcaster, narrator; bd. dirs. womensenews.org.; chair RSVP, Inc., 1997-. Co-author: Waiting for Prime Time: The Women of Television News, 1988. Mem. N.Y.C. Commn. on Women's Issues, 2003—. Recipient award N.Y. State Broadcasters Assn., 1976, award Nat. Press Club, 1976, Emmy awards, 1980, 81, others. Mem. Am. Women in Radio and TV (Woman of Yr. award 1975, Silver Satellite award 1977), Women in Comm. (past pres.), Coun. Fgn. Rels. Office Phone: 212-877-1250. Personal E-mail: sanders110@aol.com.

SANDERS, MARY ELIZABETH, writer, historian; b. Baton Rouge, May 25, 1923; d. Jared Young and Mary (Briggs) S. BA, La. State U., 1944, MA, 1955. Adminstrv. asst. Congressman J.Y. Sanders, Washington, 1942-43, Sanders, Miller, Downing, Rubin & Kean, Baton Rouge, 1946-48; librarian, archivist New Orleans Pub. Libr., 1955-57. Appeared on Restore Am.-La. program Home & Garden TV, 1999. Author: Avoca Plantation Receipts and Other Family Favorites, 1995; editor: Letters of a Southern Family, 1816-1941, 2001, Diary in Gray: Civil War Journal of J. Y. Sanders, 1994; compiler Records of Attakapas District, La., 1739-1811, 1962, Records of Attakapas District, La., Vol II: St. Mary Parish, 1811-1860, 1963, Records of Attakapas District, La., Vol. III: St. Martin Parish, 1808-1860, 1974, St. Mary Parish, Louisana, Heirship Series: Vol. I—Annotated Abstracts of the Successions, 1811-1834, 1972, Vol. II—Selected Annotated Abstracts of Marriage Book 1, 1811-1829, 1973, Vol. III—Selected Annotated Abstracts of Court Records, 1811-1839, 1978. Mem. La. Hist. Records Adv. Commn., Baton Rouge, 1981-85; charter mem., pres. La. Genealogy and Hist. Soc., 1954-56, editor, 1957-58; hon. mem. Morgan City (La.) Arch. Commn., 1985—; co-trustee J. Y. Sanders Found., Baton Rouge, 1988—; pres. La. Archives Found., Baton Rouge, 1988-96, Young-Sanders Ctr. Found., Morgan City, 1998—; mem. La. State U. Found., Baton Rouge, 1988-92; mem. nat. bd. Coun. Conservative Citizens, St. Louis, 1997—; hon. chmn. La. Sovereignty Party, Baton Rouge, 1999. Named Hon. Citizen Morgan City, La., 1985; recipient award of commendation La. State Dept. Archives, Records Mgmt. and History, 1988, cert. of appreciation Coun. Conservative Citizens, 1996, cert. of honor Jud. Watch, 1999. Mem. DAR (registrar La. soc. 1983-86, nat. vice chmn. flag com. 1986-89, corr. sec. 1992-95), United Daus. of the Confederacy (divsn. corr. sec. 1989-91, divsn. pres. 2000-2002, Gen. Grave Markers com. 2002-), Jefferson Davis medal 1989, cert. of merit 1998), Huguenot soc. of Founders of Mamakin in Colony of Va. (nat. registrar 1979-85), Colonial Dames Am. Republican. Christian Scientist. Avocations: genealogy, preservationist, cooking. Home: 2332 Wisteria St Baton Rouge LA 70806-5352

SANDERS, PATRICIA SMITH, language educator, consultant; b. St. Louis, Nov. 28, 1944; d. Maudeva (Williams) and John Bert Smith; m. Melvin Leon Sanders, Jan. 20, 1967; children: Darren Anthony, Marlon Chadley. BA Edn., Harris Tchrs. Coll., St. Louis, 1966. Tchr. elem. St. Louis Pub. Schs., 1966—67; tchr. lang. arts, soc. studies Knob Noster Sch. Dist., Mo., 1968—70; tchr. lang. arts Parkway Sch. Dist., St. Louis, 1970—72, Ladue Sch. Dist., St. Louis, 1973—2005; ednl. cons. St. Louis, 2005—. Coach h.s. dance squad Ladue Sch. Dist., St. Louis, 1976—2000; chair English dept. Ladue H.S., St. Louis, 2000—05; tchr. Mo. Scholar Acad., Columbia, 1988—91; ednl. cons. Cooperating Sch. Dists. St. Louis, 1999—2005. Pres. Archway chpt. The Links, Inc., St. Louis, 2004—; fin. sec. St. Louis chpt. The MOLES, Inc., 2006—; mem. St. Louis Alumnae chpt. Delta Sigma Theta Sorority, Inc., 1964—2006; bd. dirs. Harris Stowe State U. Alumni Assn., St. Louis, 2006—; rec. sec. exec. bd. Mo. Dance Team Assn., St. Louis, 1990—2006. Named Tchr. of Yr., Ladue H.S., 2001—02; named to Who's Who Among America's Tchrs., 1994, Who's Who Among Black St. Louis, 2005—06; recipient Spirit of Inclusion Scholarship named in my honor, Ladue H.S., 2005. Fellow: Ednl. Policy Fellowship Program; mem.: Greater St. Louis English Tchrs. Assn. (pres. 1995—98). Avocations: travel, reading, dance, writing, exercise. Office Phone: 314-205-1422.

SANDERS, PHYLLIS MAY, musician; b. Cleve., Aug. 7, 1922; d. Charles Lester and Marjorie (Roof) Flick; m. Roger Fred Sanders, Aug. 3, 1946 (div. 1986); children: William Paul, Richard Allen, Bruce Edward, Patricia Ann. MusB in Edn., Drake U., Des Moines, 1944. Music tchr. Jefferson (Iowa) jr. high schs., 1944-45, Des Moines jr. high schs., 1945-46; organist, choir dir. Columbia U. Meth. Ch., Columbia Station, Ohio, 1963-83; organist Magyar United Ch. of Christ, Elyria, Ohio, 1984—. Dir. Lorain County Community Messiah Chorus, Elyria, 1981, 88-91; dir., founder Choraliers, Columbia Station, 1975-80. Mem. Southwest Chorus, Berea, Ohio, 1988-90, Berea Sr. Ctr. Chorus, 1978—; pres. Columbia Rep. Women, Columbia Station; mem. Columbia Mothersingers, Cleve. Messiah Chorus, 1991—. Mem. Sigma Alpha Iota, Beta Gamma Kappa. Republican. Mem. Christian Ch. (Disciples Of Christ). Avocations: ceramics, needlecrafts. Home: Apt 528 55 Barrett Rd Berea OH 44017-1699

SANDERS, ROBIN RENEE, former ambassador; b. Hampton, Va., July 5; d. Robert M. and Geneva (Machoney) Sanders. B.A., Hampton Inst.; M.A., Ohio U., 1979, M.S., 1979. Broadcast lic. FCC 3d class. Editoral assts. Essence Mag., N.Y.C., 1974-76, Fgn. Broadcast Info. Service, Washington, 1976-77; intern account exec. Burson-Marsteller Co., N.Y.C., 1977-78; pub. relations assoc. Seventeen mag., N.Y.C., 1979-80; polit. and counselor officer Am. embassy, Dominican Republic, 1980-83, consular officer Am. consulate, Oporto, Portugal, 1983-86, dep. polit. sect. chief Am. Embassy Khartoum, Sudan, 1986-88; spl. asst. AF Bur., 1989; dir. for pub. diplomacy for Africa, State Dept.; dir. for Africa, Nat. Security Coun. at the White House, 1988-89, 97-99; spl. asst. for L.Am., Africa and internat. crime for the under sec. for polit. affairs Dept. State, Washington; chief of staff, sr. fgn. policy Mem. Ho. Internat. Rels. Com.; U.S. amb. to Republic of Congo, 2002-2006; cons. Profl. Women's Seminar, 1983, 84; speaker U. Oporto, 1983; researcher dept. internat. relations Ohio U., 1978; TV producer dept. gerontology Hampton Inst., 1976-77. Recipient 1st place award for painting Two Faces, Scholastic Art Bd., 1981, Dept of State Meritorious award, 1989, three State Dept. Superior Honor awards, three State Dept. Meritorious Honor awards; journalism scholar Syracuse U, 1970. Dir. Nat. Security Coun., 1989; political Econ. Officer Namibia, 1989. Mem. Women in Communications, Pub. Relations Soc. Am., Am. Fgn. Service Assn., Nat. Council Negro Women, Black Caucus, Mus. African Art, Coun. on Fgn. Rels., D.C. C. of C.; Alpha Kappa Alpha, Alpha Kappa Mu. Consular Corps (Oporto); Diplomatic (Santo Domingo), Thursday Luncheon Group, Capital Press (Washington).

SANDERS, SARAH LYNNE, small business owner, director; b. Bryan, Tex., Aug. 21, 1978; d. Howard M. and Debra L. Monroe; m. Chad W. Sanders. B in Dance, Tex. State U., San Marcos, 2001, MEd, 2002. Dir. dance Connally HS, Austin, 2002—; owner Sanders Dance Acad., Hutto, Tex., 2005—. Choreographer (dance performance) Making Magic. Roman Catholic. Avocations: travel, reading, scrapbooks, photography, boating. Office: Sanders Dance Acad 636 W Front St Ste 300 Hutto TX 78634 Office Phone: 512-680-1801. Business E-Mail: sandersdance@hotmail.com.

SANDERS, SUMMER, Olympic athlete, news correspondent, newscaster; b. Oct. 13, 1972; d. Bob and Barbara Sanders; m. Mark Henderson, July 1997. Student, Stanford U. Olympic swimmer, Barcelona, 1992; ret. from profl. swimming, 1993; returned but did not qualify for Olympics, 1995—96; hostess, Sandblast MTV, 1994—95; host game show for children Figure It Out Nickelodeon, 1997—99; broadcaster WNBA Lifetime TV, 1997—98; co-host NBA Inside Stuff, 1997—; host Beg, Borrow or Deal ESPN 2, 2002—. Co-author (with Melinda Marshall): Champions are Raised, Not Born: How my Parents made me a Success, 1999. Achievements include gold medal 200-meter butterfly, 400-meter medley relay preliminaries; silver medal, 200-meter individual medley and bronze medal 400-meter individual medley, 1992 Olympic Games, Barcelona, Spain. Office: NBA Inside Stuff care NBA Entertainment Inc 450 Harmon Meadow Blvd Secaucus NJ 07094-3618

SANDERS, VIRGINIA HINCKLEY, music educator; b. Greenfield, Mass., Feb. 19, 1945; d. Edwin Gager and Harriet Manning Hinckley; m. J. Lloyd Sanders Jr., Nov. 24, 1988. MusB, Boston U., 1967; MS, U. Ill., 1973. Cert. tchg. cert. music K-12 Md. Music tchr. South Hadley Pub. Schs., Mass., 1967—70, Omaha Pub. Schs., 1970—71; instrumental music tchr. Harford County Pub. Schs., Bel Air, Md., 1973—2003; dist. office mgr. Congressman Wayne T. Gilchrest, 2004—. Bd. dirs., sec. Susquehanna Symphony Orch., Bel. Air., 1977—86. Chmn. Reagan for Pres. Campaign, 1980, 1984; elected mem. Rep. Nat. Convention, 1980, 1984; founder, pres. Harford County Rep. Women, Bel Air, 1978—86; mem., chair Harford County Rep. Ctrl. Com., 1982—88; mem., pres. Cecil County. Rep. Club, Cecil County, Md., 1991—98. Mem.: Internat. Horn Soc., Music Educators Nat. Conf. Republican. United Church Of Christ. Home: 55 Lake Dr Rising Sun MD 21911 Office: US Rep Wayne T Gilchrest 112 West Pennsylvania Ave Bel Air MD 21014 Office Phone: 410-838-2517.

SANDERSFELD, LAVONNE LUCILLE, elementary school educator; b. Gaylord, Minn., July 1, 1937; d. Herbert Paul Martin and Adella Rose Louise (Laabs) Spiering; m. Dennis Arnold Sandersfeld, July 9, 1960. AA, Concordia Coll., St. Paul, 1957; BS, Concordia Tchrs. Coll., Seward, Nebr., 1963. Cert. elem. tchr., Iowa. Tchr. K-4 St. John Luth. Sch., Victor, Iowa, 1957—60; tchr. 4-6 St. Paul Luth. Sch., Williamsburg, Iowa, 1960—66; tchr. 2d grade Luth. Inter-parish Sch., Williamsburg, 1968—2000; ret., 2000. Sec. Iowa County Hist. Soc., Marengo, 1980-93 Mem. Internat. Reading Assn., Wally Byan Caravan Club Internat. (Iowa unit sec. 1994, pres. 2005), Delta Kappa Gamma (sec. 1982, treas. 1994-2000) Republican. Lutheran. Avocations: reading, history, travel, genealogy. Home: 1042 Chatham Dr Williamsburg IA 52361-9419 Office: Luth Interparish Sch 804 Court Williamsburg IA 52361

SANDERSON, CHRISTINE GRAVES, literature and language educator; b. Bad Cannstadt, Germany, Sept. 8, 1955; d. James Clarence and Emma Schneider Graves; children: James Edward, Gregory Lawrence, Sean William, Thomas Patrick. BA in English, Spring Hill Coll., 1977; MA in English, La. State, 1980. Cert. Tchr. La., 1983. Tchr., tech. coord. Archbishop Chapelle HS, Metairie, La., 1980—. Cons. Coll. Bd., Atlanta, 2001—. Reviewer: magazine VOYA, 2001—; contbr. articles in field. Mem.: Nat.Cath. Edn. Assn. Roman Catholic. Avocations: reading, computers. Office: Archbishop Chapelle HS 8800 Veterans Blvd Metairie LA 70003 Office Phone: 504-467-3105 171. Office Fax: 504-466-3191. Business E-Mail: csanderson@archbishopchapelle.org.

SANDERSON, JANET A., former ambassador; b. Tucson, Ariz., Apr. 1955; Diploma, Coll. of William and Mary, 1977; MA in Nat. Security Studies, Naval War Coll., 1993. Econ. officer U.S. Fgn. Svc., 1978; various govt. positions, including energy and petroleum advisor Bur. of European Affairs (OECD), 1986—88; various state dept. positions to dept. econ. counselor to min./counselor for econ. affairs U.S. Embassy, Cairo, dept. chief of mission Amman, Jordan, 1997—2000; U.S. amb. to Algeria US Dept. State, Algiers, 2000—03. Recipient Herbert A. Salzman award for Internat. Econ. Performance, U.S. Dept. of State, 1996, numerous honor awards.

SANDERSON, MARY LOUISE, medical association administrator; b. Fairmont, W. Va., Oct. 29, 1942; d. Lawrence Oliver and Frances Evelyn (Shuttleworth) Shingleton; m. William W. Olmstead III, Dec. 1966 (div. June 1974); children: William W. IV, Happy; m. Lester F. Davis, III, Oct. 1979 (div. Dec. 1986); m. David S. Sanderson, Sept. 1992. Student, Vassar Coll., 1960-62, Carnegie Mellon, 1962-63. Real estate broker, N.C. Exec. sec. Creative Dining, Raleigh, NC, 1980-83, Sea Pines Plantation Co., Hilton Head, SC, 1973-79; adminstr. Am. Bd. Neurological Surgery, Houston, 1983—. Vol. Interact, Raleigh, 1984-86, M.D. Anderson Cancer Ctr./Camp Star Trails, 1994-96; docent Mordecai House Hist. Preservation, Raleigh, 1981-83; mem./vol. Reach to Recovery, 1995-2001, Houston Symphony, 2002-, Mus. of Fine Arts, Houston, 1999-. Recipient Vol. award N.C. State Gov., 1986. Mem. Am. Soc. Assn. Execs. Democrat. Episcopalian. Office: Am Bd Neurol Surgery 6550 Fannin St Ste 2139 Houston TX 77030-2718*

SANDFORD, JUANITA DADISMAN, sociologist, educator, writer; b. Wichita, Kans., June 20, 1926; d. Carl Orville and Mabel Bernice (Stearman) Dadisman; m. Herman Prestridge Sandford, Dec. 22, 1946; children: Susan Jane, Linda Ann, Mary Kaye. BA, Baylor U., 1947, MA, 1948; LLD (hon.), Hendrix Coll., 1991. Instr. sociology Wayland Bapt. Coll., Plainview, Tex., 1948-49, Ft. Smith (Ark.) Jr. coll., 1959, Ouachita Bapt. U., Arkadelphia, Ark., 1960-68, adj. prof., 1996—; asst. prof. sociology Henderson State U., Arkadelphia, Ark., 1968-89, coord. women's studies, 1975-89; ret., 1989; adj. tchr. Ouachita Bapt. U., 1996—. Chmn. bd. Coll. Cmty. Action, Inc., 1974-78; cons. human rels. Ark. Tech. Assistance & Consultative Ctr., 1964-78; mem. Gov. Ark. Commn. on Status of Women, 1975-80, Atty. Gen. Consumer Adv. Bd., 1977-79. Author: I Didn't Get a Lot Done Today, 1974, Poverty in the Land of Opportunity, 1978, Sunbonnet Sue: The Crone, 1996; contbg. author Women & Religion: Images of Women in the Bible, 1977, Arkansas: State in Transition, 1981, Arkadelphia: 2000 AD, 1982. Bd. dirs. Ctrl. Ark. Devel. Coun., 1975-80, Ark. Hunger Project, 1983-86, Ark. Advs. for Children and Families, 1986-89. Recipient Ark. Woman of Achievement award Ark. Womens Polit. Caucus, 1975. Mem. NOW, Ark. Sociolog. & Anthropolog. Assn. (pres. 1991-92), Inst. Noetic Sci. Avocations: quilting, flower gardening. Home: 959 N 8th St Arkadelphia AR 71923-3201 E-mail: hermanpsandford@cox.net.

SANDHAAS, JILL T., lawyer; b. Manhasset, NY, July 13, 1961; BA, SUNY, Albany, 1983; JD, St. John's U., 1990. Bar: NY 1991. Ptnr. Wilson, Elser, Moskowitz, Edelman & Dicker LLP, Albany, NYC. Past counsel to chmn. NY State Senate Health Com. Mem.: NY State Bar Assn., Nassau County Bar Assn. Office: Wilson Elser Moskowitz Edelman Dicker Ll 677 Broadway Ste 901 Albany NY 12207-2989 Office Phone: 519-449-8893. Office Fax: 518-449-8927. Business E-Mail: sandhaasj@wemed.com.

SANDIDGE, KANITA DURICE, retired communications executive, consultant; b. Cleve., Dec. 2, 1947; d. John Robert Jr. and Virginia Louise (Caldwell) S. AB, Cornell U., 1970; MBA, Case Western Res. U., 1979. Supr. assignments service ctrs. and installation AT&T, Cleve., 1970-78, chief dept. data processing and acctg., 1979-80, adminstrn. mgr. exec. v.p. staff N.Y.C., 1980-83, sales forecasting and analysis mgr. resources planning Newark, 1983-86; planning and devel. mgr. material planning and mgmt. AT&T Network Systems, Morristown, N.J., 1986-87, dir. adminstrv. services Lisle, Ill., 1987-89, dir. divsn. staff customer support and ops. Morristown, 1990-94; dir. global procurement minority and women bus. enterprises AT&T, Basking Ridge, N.J., 1994-98; prin. Sandidge Cons. Group, Randolph, N.J., 1999—. Mem black exchange program Nat. Urban League, N.Y.C., 1986-98. Named Black Achiever in Industry, Harlem YMCA, 1981; recipient Tribute to Women and Industry Achievement award YWCA, 1985; one of Minority Bus. News USA's Women Who Mean Business; named Nat. Minority Supplier Devel. Coun. MBE Coord. of the Yr., 1996; recipient Nat. Fedn. of Black Women Bus. Owners Black Women of Courage Woman Owned Bus. Advocate award, 1997. Mem. Nat. Black MBA's, Alliance Black AT&T Mgrs., Am. Mgmt. Assn., Nat. Assn. for Female Execs., NAACP, Beta Alpha Psi. Mem. African Meth. Episcopal Ch. Home and Office: 10 Trade Winds Dr Randolph NJ 07869-1238 E-mail: kdsandidge@att.net.

SAND LEE, INGER, artist, interior architect; came to U.S., 1960; d. Inge Sigvald and Johanne Elise (Hamre) Sand; m. Charles Allen Lee Jr., Aug. 28, 1981 (dec.). Cert. in decorative art, N.Y. Sch. Interior Design, 1968; BFA, Marymount Manhattan Coll./N.Y. Sch. Interior Design, 1980; cert. completion, Art Students League, 1993; postgrad., Nat. Acad. Design, 1993-94. Auction benefit ASID 85th Anniversary, 2001; juror small works Wash. Sq. East Galleries Dept. or N.Y.U., 2002. One-woman shows include Art 54, N.Y.C., 1988, Pyramid Gallery, 1990, Exhbn. Space, 1991, Denise Bibro Fine Art, 1993, 1995, 1997—2001, DYN-CORP, Oak Ridge, Tenn., 1998, En Vogue Gallery, Knoxville, 1999, exhibitions include Lincoln Ctr., N.Y.C., 1988, Avery Fisher Hall, 1988, Mus. Atheism and Realism, Lviv, USSR,

1990, Lever House, N.Y.C., 1991, Nat. Acad. Mus., 1994, Albright-Knox Mus., Buffalo, N.Y., 2000, exhibited in group shows at Pyramid Gallery, N.Y.C., 1989—91, Ariel Gallery, 1991, Broome St. Gallery, 1992—93, Ward-Nasse Gallery, 1992, Hudson Guild Art Gallery, 1992, Denise Bibro Fine Art, 1992, 1994—95, 1997, 1999—2001, 2003—05, Frank Bustamante Gallery, 1993, So. Alleghenies Mus. Art, Loretto, Pa., 1994, Edward WilliamGallery, 1996, Knoxville (Tenn.) Opera Guild, 1996, Fairleigh Dickinson U., 1996, N.Y. Internat. Film and Video Festival, 1998, Gramercy Pk. Armory, N.Y.C., 1998, Jacob K. Javits Conv. Ctr., 1998, DYN Corp., Oakridge, Tenn., 1998, En Vogue Gallery, Knoxville, Tenn., 1999, Art at the Mill, Millwood, Va., 1999, Adventures in Art, The Women's Nat. Rep. Club, 2001, Cambridge Fin., Knoxville, 2000, others. Mem. presdl. victory team Republican Nat. Com., 2001. Grantee Cork Gallery, Lincoln Ctr., N.Y.C.; recipient Alumni award N.Y. Sch. Interior Design, 1979; merit scholar Art Student's League, 1991. Mem. Archtl. League N.Y., Friends N.Y. Libr., Ams. Soc. (N.Y.), Nat. Geog. Soc., Nat. Mus. Women in the Arts, Pres.'s Cir. Smithsonian Nat. Mus. Am. History (charter, name inscribed on wall of Am. history patrons), Frick Mus., Guggenheim Mus, The Women's Nat. Republican Club. Address: PO Box 2036 New York NY 10021-0051 Office Phone: 212-560-2481.

SANDLER, ANITA, singer, artist; d. Harry W. Goldstein and Esther N. Gilman. BFA, Mass. Coll. Art, 1967. Art dir. Boston After Dark, Boston; singer, songwriter, entertainer Shawmut Minstrel Tribe, West Rupert, Vt., 1973—80; advt., design agy. owner Ideas into Images, Manchester, Vt., 1980—87; traveling artist Graphic Images of Vt., Manchester, 1987—2000; gallery/studio owner Touche', Manchester Village, Vt., 2002—; cabaret singer Village Country Inn, Manchester Center, 2004—. Cons. Cave in The Sky Press, Montclair, NJ, 2000—, Lizanne Degen Designs, Manchester Village, 1987—. Singer, composer, prodr.: CD I'm A One Of A Kind I'm Told, Waiting For A Unicorn, musician, composer: cabaret series Poetry as Music: Music as Poetry; exhibitions include Silverhawk On-line Gallery, 2000. Mem.: So. Vt. Arts Ctr., Mus. Women Artists. Avocations: writing, reading, travel, tai chi. Home: PO Box 1124 Manchester Center VT 05255 Personal E-mail: nitasarts@yahoo.com.

SANDLER, BARBARA S., artist; b. N.Y.C. d. Sidney and Josephine S. One-woman shows include, Danenberg Gallery, N.Y.C., 1973, Gimpel Weitzenhoffer, N.Y.C., 1975, 1st Woman's Bank, N.Y.C., 1975, Segal Gallery, N.Y.C., 1981-85, Mary Martin Gallery, Aspen, Colo., 1982, Trabia MacaFee Gallery, 1988,89, group shows include, Lehigh U., 1975, Alex Rosenberg Gallery, N.Y.C., 1978, Segal Gallery, N.Y.C., 1981, Futura Gallery, Stockholm, Sweden, 1983, Bruce Mus., Conn., 1985, Zeus Trabia Gallery, 1986; Art in General, 1987; represented in permanent collections, Hirshhorn Mus. Collection, Mus. Modern Art, Chgo. Art Mus., Smithsonian Inst., Chase Manhattan Bank, Mfrs. Hanover Trust, Hearst Corp.; illustrator mags., record covers, book jackets. Elizabeth T. Greenshield Meml. grantee, 1975 Office: 10 W 23rd St New York NY 10010-5202

SANDLER, BERNICE RESNICK, women's rights specialist; b. N.Y.C., Mar. 3, 1928; d. Abraham Hyman and Ivy (Ernst) Resnick; children: Deborah Jo, Emily Maud. BA cum laude, Bklyn. Coll., 1948; MA, CCNY, 1950; EdD, U. Md., 1969; LLD (hon.), Bloomfield Coll., 1973, Hood Coll., 1974, R.I. Coll., 1980, Colby-Sawyer Coll., 1984; LHD (hon.), Grand Valley State Coll., 1974; Dr. Pub. Svc. (hon.), North Adams State Coll., 1985; LLD (hon.), Goucher Coll., 1991; LHD (hon.), Plymouth State Coll., 1992, Wittenberg U., 1993, Ripon Coll., 1998; LLD (hon.), U. St. Thomas, 2006. Rsch. asst., tchr. nursery sch., employment counselor, adult edn. instr., sec.; psychologist HEW, 1970; tchr. psychology Mt. Vernon Coll., 1970; head Action Com. for Fed. Contract Compliance, Women's Equity Action League, 1970—71; edn. specialist U.S. Ho. Reps., Washington, 1970; dep. dir. Womens Action program, HEW, Washington, 1971; dir. project on status and edn. of women Assn. Am. Colls., Washington, 1971—91; sr. assoc. Ctr. for Women Policy Studies, 1991—94; sr. scholar in residence Nat. Assn. Women in Edn., Washington, 1994—2000; sr. scholar Women's Rsch. and Edn. Inst., 2000—. Cons., 1991—; expert witness, 1990—; writer, 1971—; vis. lectr. U. Md., 1968-69; adv. bd. Women's Equity Action League Ednl. and Legal Def. Fund, 1980—, trustee, 1974-80, Women's Equity Action League, 1971-78; adv. com. Math./Sci. Network, 1979, Wider Opportunities for Women, 1978-85, Women's Legal Def. Fund, 1978-84; Nat. Coun. for Alternative Work Patterns Inc., 1978-85, Women's Hdqs. State Nat. Bank for Women's Appointments, 1977-78, and others. Mem. adv. bd. Jour. Reprints Documents Affecting Women, 1976-78, Women's Rights Law Reporter, 1970-80; editor: (newsletters) On Campus With Women, 1971-91, About Women on Campus, 1991-99; contbr. articles. Mem. bd. overseers Wellesley Coll. Ctr. for Rsch. on Women, 1975-87; bd. dirs. Ctr. for Women's Policy Studies, 1972-75; mem. exec. com. Inst. for Ednl. Leadership, 1982-87, mem. program adv. com., 1987-88, chair bd. dirs., 1981, chair adv. com., 1975-81; mem. affirmative action com., task force on family, nat. affairs commn. Am. Jewish Com., 1978, bd. dirs. D.C. chpt.; tech. adv. com. Nat. Jewish Family Ctr., 1980-89; adv. coun. Ednl. Devel. Ctr., 1980-85; adv. bd. Urban Inst., 1981-85, Women Employed Inst., 1981-84, Ex-New Yorkers for N.Y., 1978-79; mem. adv. com. Arthur and Elizabeth Schlesinger Libr. History of Women in Am., 1981-85; nat. adv. com. Shelter Rsch. Inst., Calif., 1980-82; chair adv. panel project on self-evaluation Am. Insts. for Rsch., 1980-82; bd. dirs. Equality Ctr., 1983, Evaluation and Tng. Inst., Calif., 1980, Inst. for Studies in Equality, 1975-77; exec. v.p. Bd. Women for Women, 1997—. Recipient Athena award Intercollegiate Assn. Women Students, 1974, Elizabeth Boyer award Women's Equity Action League, 1976, Rockefeller Pub. Svc. award Princeton U., 1976, Women Educators award for activism, 1987, Anna Roe award Harvard U., 1988, Readers Choice honors Washington Woman Mag., 1987, Woman of Distinction award Nat. Assn. Women in Edn., 1991, Georgina Smith award AAUP, 1992, Woman of Achievement Turner Broadcasting System, 1994; named one of 100 Most Powerful Women Washingtonian Mag., 1982, one of the nation's 100 Most Important Women, Ladies Home Jour., 1988, Leadership Matters award Inst. Ednl. Leadership, 1997, Medal of Honor, Vet. Feminists, 2001, Donna Shavlik award Am. Coun. Edn., 2003, Mary Keetz award Women's Consortium Pa. State Sys., 2004, Am. Fedn. Tchrs. Women's Rights award Mem. Assn. for Women in Sci. Found. (bd. dirs. 1977—), Am. Soc. Profl. and Exec. Women (adv. bd. 1980). Avocations: birding, music, swimming, hiking. Office: Women's Rsch and Edn Inst 1350 Connecticut Ave NW Ste 850 Washington DC 20036-1740

SANDLER, LUCY FREEMAN, art history educator; b. NYC, June 7, 1930; d. Otto and Frances (Glass) Freeman; m. Irving Sandler, Sept. 4, 1958; 1 child, Catherine Harriet. BA, Queens Coll., 1951; MA, Columbia U., 1957; PhD, NYU, 1964. Asst. prof. NYU, 1964-70, assoc. prof., 1970-75, prof. fine arts, 1975-86, Helen Gould Sheppard prof. art history, 1986—2003, chmn. dept., 1975-89; editorial cons. Viator, UCLA, 1983-97; Helen Gould Sheppard prof. emerita, 2003—. Author: The Peterborough Psalter in Brussels, 1974, The Psalter of Robert De Lisle in the British Library, 1983, new edit., 1999, Gothic Manuscripts 1285-1385, 1986, 'Omne Bonum': A Fourteenth-Century Encyclopedia of Universal Knowledge, 1996, The Ramsey Psalter, 1999, Der Ramsey-Psalter (Glanzlichter der Buchkunst 12), 2003, Der Bestiarium aus Peterborough/The Peterborough Bestiary, 2003, The Lichtenthal Psalter and the Patronage of the Bohun Family, 2004, (with Jonathan J.G. Alexander and James H. Marrow) The Splendor of the Word, Medieval and Renaissance Illuminated Manuscripts, NY Pub. Libr., 2005; editor: Essays in Memory of Karl Lehmann, 1964, Art the Ape of Nature: Studies in Honor of H.W. Janson, 1981, Coll. Art Assn. Monograph Series, 1970-75, 86-89, Gesta, 1991-94; asst. editor Art Bull., 1964-67, mem. editl. bd., 1994; mem. editl. bd. Jour. Jewish Art, 1978, Speculum, 1994. Trustee Godwin-Ternbach Mus., Queens Coll., 1982-94; chair dels. exec. com. Am. Coun. Learned Socs., 2002-04. NEH fellow, 1967-68, 77; fellow Pierpont Morgan Library; Guggenheim fellow, 1988-89. Fellow: Medieval Acad. Am. (councillor 2002—05), Soc. Antiquaries (London); mem.: AAUP, Coll. Art Assn. (pres. 1981—84), Internat. Ctr. Medieval Art (adv. bd., bd. dirs. 1976—80, 1984—87, 1989—92, 1995—2001). Home: 60 E 8th St Apt 19E New York NY 10012 Office: NYU Dept Fine Arts New York NY 10003 Office Phone: 212-998-8181.

SANDLER, MARION OSHER, bank executive; b. Biddeford, Maine, Oct. 17, 1930; d. Samuel and Leah (Lowe) Osher; m. Herbert M. Sandler, Mar. 26, 1961. BA, Wellesley Coll., 1952; postgrad., Harvard U.-Radcliffe Coll., 1953; MBA, NYU, 1958; LLD (hon.), Golden Gate U., 1987. Asst. buyer Bloomingdale's (dept. store), NYC, 1953-55; security analyst Dominick & Dominick, NYC, 1955-61; sr. fin. analyst Oppenheimer & Co., NYC, 1961-63; sr. v.p., dir. Golden West Fin. Corp. and World Savings Bank, Oakland, Calif., 1963-75, vice chmn. bd. dirs., CEO, mem. exec. com., dir., 1975-80, pres., co- chief exec. officer, dir., mem. exec. com., 1980-93, chmn. bd. dirs., CEO, mem. exec. com., 1993—2006; pres., chmn. bd. dirs., CEO Atlas Assets, Inc., Oakland, 1987—, Atlas Advisers, Inc., Oakland, 1987—, Atlas Securities, Inc., Oakland, 1987—. Mem. adv. com. Fed. Nat. Mortgage Assn., 1983-84. Mem. Pres.'s Mgmt. Improvement Coun., 1980, Thrift Insts. Adv. Coun. to Fed. Res. Bd., 1989-91, v.p., 1990, pres., 1991; mem. policy adv. bd. Ctr. for Real Estate and Urban Econs. U. Calif., Berkeley, 1981—, mem. exec. com. policy adv. bd., 1985—; mem. ad hoc com. to rev. Schs. Bus. Adminstrn. U. Calif., 1984-85; vice chmn. industry adv. com. Fed. Savs. and Loan Ins. Corp., 1987-88, Ins. Corp., 1987-88; bd. overseers NYU Schs. Bus., 1987-89; mem. Glass Ceiling Commn., 1992-93; bd. dirs. Success for All Found., 1997-2005, Manpower Demonstration Rsch. Corp., 1998-2004, Ctr. Am. Progress, 2003-. Named Morningstar's CEO of Yr., 2004; named one of 50 Women to Watch, Wall St. Jour., 2005; recipient Corp. Inventor award, Com. 200 Found., 2005, Lifetime Achievement award, US Banker, 2005. Mem. Phi Beta Kappa, Beta Gamma Sigma. Office: Golden W Fin Corp 1901 Harrison St Fl 6 Oakland CA 94612-3588*

SANDMEYER, E. E., toxicologist, consultant; b. Winterthur, Zurich, Switzerland, Aug. 9, 1929; came to U.S., 1955; BSChemE, Technikum, Winterthur, 1951; MS in Organic Chemistry, Ohio State U., 1960, PhD in Biochemistry, 1965. Cert. civil svc. chemist II, Nev., biochemist II, Pa., clin. lab. dir. Ctrs. for Disease Control. Asst. prof. sci., gen. chemistry, organic chemistry Friends U., Wichita, 1965-66; asst. prof. biochemistry, labs., and rsch. U. Nev., Reno, 1966-71; head corp. toxicology Gulf Oil Corp., Pitts., 1971-76; divsn. head organic analysis Barringer Labs., Denver, 1987-88; pres., toxicologist, owner Transcontec, Inc., Kelseyville, Calif., 1976—. Div. head organic analysis Barringer Labs., Denver, 1986-88. Contbg. author: Patty's Industrial Hygiene and Toxicology, 1981, A Guide to General Toxicology, 1983. Mem. AAAS, Am. Chem. Soc., Soc. Environ. Health, Sigma Xi, Sigma Delta Epsilon. Office: Transcontec Inc 7305 Live Oak Dr Kelseyville CA 95451-7862

SANDOR, ELLEN RUTH, artist; b. N.Y.C., Apr. 22, 1942; d. Julius and Matilda (Greene) Simon; m. Richard L. Sandor, June 27, 1963; children: Julie, Penya. BA, Bklyn. Coll., 1963; postgrad., U. Calif., Berkeley, 1968-72; MFA, Sch. of Art Inst. of Chgo., 1975. Dir., founder (Art)n Lab. Northwestern U., Evanston, Ill., 1982—. Adj. artist Nat. Ctr. for Supercomputing Applications, Urbana-Champaign, Ill., 1987—; grad. advisor Sch. of Art Inst. Chgo., 1989; adj. assoc. prof., grad. advisor U. Ill. at Chgo., 1988—; speaker, lectr., presenter in field. Patentee for computer-generated autostereography method apparatus Barrier-Strip and Lenticular Autostereogram; co-inventor PHSColograms and Stealth Negative PHSColograms—3D imaging press supporting large-scale full color images with depth; exhbns. include Imaging Antarctica, Linz, Austria, 1986, High Technology and Art, Chunichi Shimim Kaka-ku Mus., Tokyo, 1986, Cinderella Rockefeller Feature, N.Y.C., 1989, Beautiful Stranger Feature, N.Y.C., 1989, Dorothy, Ctr. for Contemporary Art, Chgo., 1989, SIGGRAPH '89 Travelling Art Show, Boston, 1989, Strange Attractors: Signs of Chaos, The New Mus. of Contemporary Art, N.Y.C., 1989, Daydreams to Bitstreams, NAS, Washington, 1989, Photography: Inventions and Innovations, Art Inst. Chgo., 1989-90, A New Generation Part I: Chicago Artists, Carnegie-Mellon Art Gallery, Pitts., 1990, SIGGRAPH '90 Travelling Art Show, Dallas, 1990, Art Futura, Barcelona, Spain, 1991, The Third Emerging Expression Biennial: The Third Dimension and Beyond, Bronx Mus., N.Y.C., 1991, Matter Over Mind = Sculpture, Fermilab, Batavia, Ill., 1991, Retretti Art Centre, Punkaharju, Finland, 1991, Exploratorium, San Francisco, 1991, SIGGRAPH '91 Travelling Art Show, Las Vegas, Nev., 1991, From Media to Metaphor 1991—; Art and the Computer, Idmi-Istituto Dalle Molle di Metodologie Interdisciplinari, Lugano, Switzerland, 1991, La Cité des Arts et des Nouvelles Technologies de Montréal, Que., 1991, Science in Depth travelling PHSCologram exhbn., NASA/AMES Rsch. Ctr., Moffett Field, Calif., 1991—, Computer Mus., Boston, 1991, Mus. Sci. & Industry, Chgo., 1990-91, From Media to Metaphor: Art About Aids, Emerson Gallery, Clinton N.Y., 1992, Ctr. Contemporary Art, Seattle, 1992, Sharadin Art Gallery, Kutztown (Pa.) U., 1992, 3Dmt, Montreal, 1992, CyberArts, Pasadena, Calif., 1992, SIGGRAPH '92 Art Show, Chgo., 1992, Computer Art Pushing the Boundries, State Ill. Gallery, 1992, New Work Feature, N.Y.C., 1992, Images Du Futur '92, Montreal, 1992, Spain Today, Spanish Pavilion Expo '92, Seville, Spain, 1992, Entourage: Exhibitions, Rosenwald-Wolf Gallery, U. of Arts, Elkins Park, Pa., 1992, Electronic Expressions.2, Allegheny Coll., Meadville, Pa, 1992, Musee d'Art Contemporian de Montreal, 1992-93, Grey Art Gallery, N.Y.U., 1993, Tomorrow's Realities, SIGGRAPH '93, Anaheim Calif., 1993, The New Image Montage '93, Rochester, N.Y., 1993, Digital Art/Digital Design, Saatchi and Saatchi, N.Y.C., 1993, Sony Gallery Chgo., 1993, (Art)n: Virtual Photography, 1993, Rhona Hoffman Gallery, Chgo, 1993, Editions Rhona Hoffman Gallery, Chgo., 1993, Gahlberg Gallery-The Coll. of DuPage, Ill., 1994, The Martin Luther King Jr. Performing and Cultural Arts Complex, Columbus, Ohio, 1995, Triennale di Milano, Italy, 1995, Art Chgo., 1995, Oskar Friedl Gallery, Chgo., 1995; exhibited in collections AT&T Bell Labs., Murray Hill, N.J., Eastman Kodak Co., Rochester, N.Y., Electronic Visualization Lab., U. Ill. at Chgo., IBM TJ Watson Rsch. Ctr., Yorktown Heights, NASA/AMES Rsch. Ctr., Moffett Field, Nat. Ctr. for Supercomputing Applications, Urbana-Champaign, Rsch. Inst. of Scripps Clinic, La Jolla, Calif., Monsanto Corp., St. Louis, McDonald's Corp., Northbrook, Ill., Fla. State U., Tallahassee, U. Chgo., Northwestern U., Chgo., Lockheed Aero. Systems Co., So. Calif., Anheuser Busch., St. Louis, Ont. Sci. Ctr., Toronto, Idaho Nat. Engring. Lab., Idaho Falls, and numerous others; subject in numerous publs., articles, revs.; co-author tech. papers. Bd. dirs. Soc. for Outsider, Intuitive and Visionary Art, Chgo., 1991, Randolph Street Gallery, Chgo., New Art Examiner, Chgo., 1985—, The Body Politic, Chgo., NOW, Berkeley, Calif., 1970-72; bd. mem. devel. com. Sch. of Art Inst. of Chgo., 1980-85. Grantee IPP Lithocolor, Chgo., 1985-91, Eastman Kodak Co., Rochester, N.Y., 1987-89, ACM Siggraph, N.Y.C., 1990. Mem. IEEE, Arts Club of Chgo. Democrat. Jewish. Avocation: art collection. Home: 1301 N Astor St Chicago IL 60610-2186 Office: (Art)n Lab IIT BIRL Northwestern U 1801 Maple Ave Evanston IL 60208-0001

SANDOR, JOCELYN R., artist; b. Stamford, Conn., Mar. 4, 1957; d. Edward Albert and Rita Malyndziak Sandor; m. Richard Bruce Urban, Dec. 30, 1989; 1 child, Nicholas Vincent. BS in Fine Art, Skidmore Coll., 1979; MFA, U. Mass., 1981. Owner Jocelyn Sandor Fine Animal Portraits, Sherman, Conn., 1982—; v.p. FurSure Enterprises, Inc., Sherman, 1989-94, pres., 1994—. Artist Sherman Sentinel/Hist. Soc., 1999—. Selected exhbns. include N.C. Print and Drawing Soc., Charlotte, 1983, John Cusano Fine Art, South Norwalk, Conn., 1984, 86, 88, Mary Ryan Gallery, N.Y.C., 1985, Wenniger Graphics, Boston, 1985, Miriam Perlman Gallery, Chgo., 1985, Gallery on the Green, Lexington, Mass., 1987, U. Mass. Med. Ctr. Gallery, Worcester, 1987, Jocelyn Sandor/Cathrin Cammett/James Leslie Parker, Clayton and Liberatore Gallery, Bridgehampton, N.Y., 1991, Burnham Libr., Bridgewater, 1994, No. Westchester Ctr. for the Arts, Mt. Kisco, N.Y., 1998, 99, Sherman Libr., 1999, Hartford (Conn.) Fine Art and Framing, 1999, Bruce Mus., Greenwich, Conn., 1999; represented in permanent collections E.F. Hutton & Co., Inc., N.Y.C., Am. Nat. Bank and Trust, Chgo., Reader's Digest Assn., Inc., Pleasantville, N.Y., Exxon Corp., N.Y.C., World's Finest Chocolate, Inc., Chgo., Irving Trust, Westport, Conn., Ill. Bell Tel., Chgo., Ency. Brittanica, Chgo., Skadden, Arps, Meagher and Flom, N.Y.C., Skidmore Coll., Saratoga Springs, N.Y., Ky. Derby Mus., Louisville, Shearson Lehman, Chgo., Salomon Bros., Inc., N.Y.C., Chgo., Conn. Bank and Trust Co., Mktg. Corp. Am., Westport, Prudential Ins. Co., Boston, Mfrs. Bank Detroit, Reliance Nat. Ins. Co., N.Y.C., Westinghouse Corp., Chgo., Stonebridge Ptnrs., N.Y.C., others. Mem. varsity tennis team Skidmore Coll., 1975-79. Named Best in Show, Bruce Mus. Outdoor Art Festival, Greenwich, Conn., 1988; Rotary Found. fellow Rotary Club Fairfield, Conn., 1981. Mem. Quaker Hill Country Club (Pawling, N.Y.). Republican. Roman Catholic.

SANDORSEN, CASSIOPEIA, public health service officer; b. East Chicago, Ind., July 30, 1958; Health info. mgmt. cons. Wash. U. Sch. Medicine, St. Louis, 2001—; clin. analyst cons. Sisters Saint Mary DePaul Health Ctr., Bridgeton, Mo., 2002—; special corr. Pulitzer, Inc., St. Louis, 2004—. Clin. analyst cons. Gateway Health Info. Mgmt. Project, St. Louis, 2002—. Audio tape and cd series, Sound of Poetry, poetry, Half-Dimension, anthology, Essence of a Dream, Diamonds and Pearls, The Fourth Dimension, New Dawnings, Dreams Gone By, Theatre of The Mind, 2003, Autumn Necklace, Best Poems and Poets of 2003, 2004. Founder Nat. Law Enforcement Mus., Washington, 2003—03; mem. Republican Presdl. Task Force, 2003—04. Recipient Poetic Achievement award, Creative Arts and Sci. Enterprises, 1997, Amherst Soc., 1998, Malcolm Baldridge Nat. Quality award, Bush Adminstrn., 2002, award, Robert Wood Johnson Found., 2003; scholar, Esperanto League of N.Am., 2003. Mem.: Am. Acad. Poets, Internat. Soc. Poets, Mo. Bot. Garden, St. Louis Art Mus., Mo. Hist. Soc., Am. Mus. Natural History, St. Louis Symphony Orch. Vivaldi Soc. Republican. Avocations: nature walks, gardening, fiber arts, travel.

SANDOVAL, ARLENE R., elementary school educator; d. Pete Manuel and Alicia Cardenas Rubi; m. Noé Constantino Sandoval, Dec. 14, 1984. B in Bilingual Elem. Edn., U. Ariz., Tucson, 1996. Cert. ESL Ariz. Dept. Edn. Project cost analyst Hughes Aircraft Co., Tucson; paralegal Keefe & Rubi Law Offices, Tucson; head, bilingual dept. Sunnyside Sch. Dist., Tucson. Office: Challenger Mid Sch 100 E Elvira Tucson AZ 85706

SANDOVAL, ISABELLE MEDINA, education educator; b. Laramie, Wyo., Sept. 30, 1948; d. John Ben and Ida Medina Sandoval; 1 child, Tomas Andres Duran. BA, U. N.Mex., 1970; MA, U. Mo., 1976; EdD, U. Wyo., 1982. Cert. Spanish, reading, English, adminstrn. Tchr. Spanish and English Menaul Sch., Albuquerque, 1971-73; tchr. bilingual edn. and reading Kansas City, Mo., 1973-78; tchr. title I Sch. Dist. #60, Pueblo, Colo., 1978-83, adminstr., 1983-88, Acad. Dist. 20, Colorado Springs, Colo., 1988-95; human resources coord. Harrison Dist. 2, Colorado Springs, 1995-98; prof. edn. Coll. of Santa Fe, N.Mex.; dir. bilingual edn. Santa Fe Pub. Schs. V.p. Hispano Crypto Jewish Resource Ctr., Denver. Author numerous poems. Pres. South Holman Domestic Water Assn. Mem. Geneal. Soc. Hispanic Am., Hispanic Geneal. Rsch. Ctr. N.Mex., Mana del Norte, Olibama Lopez Tushar Hispanic Legacy Rsch. Ctr., N.M. Jewish Hist. Soc. (bd. dirs.), N.Mex. Acequia Assn., N.Mex. Land Grant Forum, Soc. for Crypto Judaic Studies, Nat. Assn. Sephardic Artists, Writers and Intellectuals, LaSallian Leadership (bd. dirs.), Phi Kappa Phi, Kappa Delta Phi, Phi Delta Kappa. Jewish. Avocations: poetry, researching family history and hispano jewish materials. Home: 4358 Lost Feather Santa Fe NM 87507-2580 Office: Santa Fe Pub Schs 1300 Camino Sierra Vista Santa Fe NM 87505 Business E-Mail: isandoval@sfps.info.

SANDRA, CHARLENE GREER, educator; d. Charles Williams and Sarah Louise Thomason; life ptnr. Ruth E. Fassinger; children: Andrew S. Greer children: Michael G. Greer. BS, Furman U., Greenville, SC, 1966; PhD, U. Chgo., 1969. Rsch. chemist Nat. Bur. Stds., Gaithersburg, Md., 1969—78; assoc. prof. U. Md., College Park, 1978—83, prof., 1983—; program dir. NSF, Washington, 1985—86. Adv. bd. Com. Advancement Women Chem. Scis., Eugene, Oreg., 1998. Fellow: AAAS, Am. Phys. Soc.; mem.: Assn. Women Sci., AICE, Biophysical Soc., Am. Chem. Soc. (Francis P. Garvan-John M. Olin medal 2004), Phi Kappa Phi, Phi Beta Kappa. Office: University of Maryland College Park Dept Chemical & Biomolecular Engineering College Park MD 20742 Office Phone: 301-405-1895. E-mail: sgreer@umd.edu.

SANDS, CHRISTINE LOUISE, retired English educator; b. Johnstown, Pa., Oct. 13, 1947; d. Joseph and Margaret (Kocsis) Migut; m. Angelo Joseph Sands, Dec. 28, 1968 (div. Nov. 1989); children: Vincent, Linda. BS in German, Indiana U. Pa., 1969, BS in English, 1975; postgrad., Slippery Rock U., 1971-76. Tchg. cert. Pa. Tchr. New Castle (Pa.) Schs., 1969—2004. Student advisor, judge Forensics, New Castle, 1981-96, Youngstown (Ohio) Reading Festival, 1981-95. Pres. New Castle City Coun., 1996, 2004-05; mem. parish coun. St. Vitus Ch., New Castle, 1986-92; basketball referee PIAA, Mechanicsburg, Pa., 1972-91; coach New Castle H.S. Bowling, 1986-97, cheerleading adv., 1993-94, adv. sch. tv studio, NC-TV, 1991-96. Democrat. Roman Catholic. Avocations: reading, travel, sports, cooking, politics. Home: 819 E Hillcrest Ave New Castle PA 16105-2256

SANDS, DAWN M., lawyer; BA magna cum laude, Univ. Wis., Eau Claire, 1985; JD cum laude, William Mitchell Coll. Law, 1993. Aide to U.S. Senator Robert Kasten, Wis., Washington; aide to U.S. Senate Fgn. Rels. Com.; mem. exec. staff. Nat. Rep. Senatorial Com.; adminstr. Campaign America PAC; v.p., gen. counsel Menard Inc., Eau Claire, Wis., 1999—. Office: Menard Inc Legal Dept 4777 Menard Dr Eau Claire WI 54703-9604

SANDS, DEANNA, editor; BA in Journalism, U. Nebr., Lincoln, 1972; grad., Ioaw State U., 1974. Intern Nebr. City News Press, 1974; night copy desk editor Omaha World Herald, 1974, night mng. editor, 1990—93, mng. editor, 1993—, 1995—. Office: Omaha World-Herald 1334 Dodge St Omaha NE 68102-1138 Office Phone: 402-444-1000. E-mail: deanna.sands@owh.com.

SANDS, ROBERTA ALYSE, real estate investor; b. N.Y.C., Oct. 7, 1937; d. Harry and Irene (Mytelka) S. BEd, U. Miami, 1960; postgrad., U. Oslo, 1960. Cert. secondary educator biology, Mass. Phys. edn. instr. Key Biscayne and Ludlam Elem. Sch., Miami, 1961-63; sci. tchr. Plantation (Fla.) Mid. Sch., 1969-71, Rickards Middle Sch., Ft. Lauderdale, Fla., 1972-76. Founder U. Miami Diabetes Rsch. Inst., 1989. Author: Biology on the Secondary Level, 1970. Vol. Douglas Garden Retirement Home, Miami, 1988-92, Mus. of Art, Ft. Lauderdale, 1988-92, Imperial Point Hosp., Ft. Lauderdale, 1981-83. Mem. AAUW (Ft. Lauderdale br. rec. sec. 1988-92, cultural chair 1993-94, legis. chair 1994-95, women's issue chair 1994-2005, 1994-96, corr. sec. 2005, Recognition of Significant Svc. award 1983). Avocations: painting, golf, embroidery, travel. Home: 4250 Galt Ocean Dr Apt 8S Fort Lauderdale FL 33308-6113

SANDS, SHARON LOUISE, art director, publishing executive, artist; b. Jacksonville, Fla., July 4, 1944; d. Clifford Harding Sands and Ruby May MacDonald; m. Jonathan Michael Langford, Feb. 14, 1988. BFA, Ctrl. Washington U., 1968; postgrad, UCLA, 1968. Art dir. East West Network, Inc., L.A., 1973-78, Daisy Pub., L.A., 1978; prodn. dir. L.A. mag., 1979-80; owner, creative dir. Carmel Graphic Design, Carmel Valley, Calif., 1981-85; creative dir., v.p. The Video Sch. House, Monterey, Calif., 1985-88; graphic designer ConAgra, Omaha, 1988; owner, creative dir. Esprit de Fleurs, Ltd., Carmel, Calif., 1988-99; owner Sweden by the Sea, Carmel, Calif., 1999—2001; owner, dir. Sands Art Studios, 1999—. Lectr. Pub. Expo, LA, 1979; panelist Women in Mgmt., LA, 1979; designer corp. ID Carmel Valley CC, 1981, 90; redesign of local newspaper, Carmel, Calif., 82. Contbr. articles to profl. mags.; one-woman shows include Ananda Retreat Ctr., Nevada City, Calif., 2004, Nevada City Winery, 2004. Recipient 7 design awards, Soc. Pub. Designers, 1977, 1978, Maggie award, LA, 1977, 5 Design awards, Ad Club Monterey Peninsula, 1983, 1985, 1987, Design awards, Print Mag. N.Y., 1986, Desi awards, N.Y., 1986, 1988, Oil Painting awards, Monterey Jazz Festival, 1999. Mem.: Sierra Club. Democrat. Avocations: oil painting, interior decorating, hiking, kayaking. Home and Studio: Lake Wildwood 18807 Chaparral Dr Penn Valley CA 95946-9688

SANDS, VELMA AHDA, lawyer; d. John T. and Thelma Jane (Davis) Carlisle BS, Calif. State U., Dominguez Hills, 1976; JD, Southwestern U., 1985. CPA. Cons. KPMG Peat Marwick Main, L.A., 1980—81; v.p. Security Pacific Bank, L.A., 1981—86; contr. L.A. Investors, 1986; mgr. IRC divsn. FN Realty Svcs., Pasadena, Calif., 1986—88; mgr. fin. reporting Luz Internat. Ltd., L.A., 1988—89; pvt. practice law L.A., 1990—; temp. judge L.A.

Superior Ct., 1996—. Instr. Fame Entrepreneurial Tng. Program; co-pres. Multicultural Bar Alliance, 2001-02 Participant career day programs for local high schs.; mem. United We Stand Scholar Black Woman Lawyers Assn., 1982; recipient Commendation City of L.A., 2001, Cert. of Commendation, Gov. Calif. 2001, U.S. Senate 2001, Cert. of Recognition, Calif. State Assembly, 2001, Cert. Spl. Recognition, U.S. Rep. 2001, Cert. Congratulations Black Woman Lawyers Assn., 2002; Cert. Appreciation, Superior Ct. Calif., RBD Comm., Inc. award - 1st Ann., Samuel L. Williams Spirit of Law award for outstanding contbn. in field of law, 2001 Mem. ABA, NAFE, Nat. Assn. Bank Women (chair ways and means com. of scholarship fund 1986, scholar 1984), So. Calif. Chinese Lawyers Assn., L.A. County Bar Assn., John M. Langston Bar Assn. (pres. 2000, Pres.' Spl. Recognition award 1997, Appreciation award 2000, 2002), L.A. Bench and Bar Affiliates (scholarship com., meeting host, scholar 1983), Am. Bridge Assn., Phi Alpha Delta Office: 300 E Esplanade Dr 9th Fl Oxnard CA 93036 Home: 154 E Carmel Green Port Hueneme CA 93041 Office Phone: 800-281-1622.

SANDSTEAD, AURIEL J., retired secondary school educator, researcher, historian; d. Charles Ford and E. Fae (Stanley) Oram; m. Willard W. Sandstead, Mar. 16, 1946; children: Vicki Jo, Margo Dale, Shauna Gae. BA, Colo. State Coll. (now U. Northern Colo.), 1957, MA, 1961. Emergency tchg. certificate WWII Colo. Tchr. Weld County Dist. #93, New Raymer, Colo., 1942—44; tchr. classroom/gymnasium Logan County Jr. HS, Sterling, Colo., 1956—60; instr. English & Sports Northeastern Jr. Coll., Sterling, 1960—68; social worker, family & children svcs. Logan County Social Svcs., Sterling, 1969—77; ret., 1977. Local historian Keota, Along the Burlington R.R. Sterling to Cheyenne, Homesteaders, Schs., etc., Mary Stanley (1869-1955), quilt collection embodying three generations. Author: (poem) Fifty-one Syllables of Spring, in Best Poems of the 90s, 1995, Boundless, in Best Poems of the 90s, 1996; publisher A Cartouche Collection, 2000, A Cartouche Collection, 6th edit., 2004. Charter mem. Nat. Mus. Women in the Arts, 1987; charter pres. Colo. Quilting Coun., 1979. Named to Hall of Fame (1st inductee), Colo. Quilting Coun., 1988; recipient Heritage award, Colo. Coun. on the Arts, Denver, 2000. Mem.: Am. Quilt Study Group, High Plains Heritage Quilters (life), Alpha Delta Kappa. Avocations: reading, writing, quilting.

SANDSTROM, ALICE WILHELMINA, accountant; b. Seattle, Jan. 6, 1914; d. Andrew William and Agatha Mathilda (Sundius) S. BA, U. Wash., 1934. CPA, Wash. Mgr. office Star Machinery Co., Seattle, 1935—43, Howe & Co., Seattle, 1943—46; pvt. practice acctg. Seattle, 1945—85; ret., 1985. Contr. Children's Orthop. Hosp. and Med. Ctr., Seattle, 1948-75, assoc. adminstr. fin., 1975-81; lectr. U. Wash., Seattle, 1957-72 Mem. Wash. state Title XIX Adv. Com., 1975-82, Wash. State Vendors Rate Adv. Com., 1980-87, Mayor's Task Force for Small Bus., 1981-83; bd. dirs. Seattle YWCA, pres., 1986-88; bd. dirs. Sr. Svcs. Seattle King Co., 1985, 1989-95, 2003, treas., 1986, pres., 1988-90; bd. dirs. Children's Orthop. Hosp. Found., 1982-90; rsch. team Children's Hosp., Seattle, 2003 Recipient Jefferson award for vol. svcs., 1997, Alumnus award, U. Wash. Bus. Sch., 2002, Leadership award, 2002—03, Isabel Coleman Pierce award, YWCA, 2003. Fellow Hosp. Fin. Mgmt. Assn. (charter, state pres. 1956-57, nat. treas. 1963-65, Robert H. Reeves Merit award 1970, Frederick T. Muncie award 1985; mem. LWV, Wash. State Hosp. Assn. (treas. 1956-70), Am. Soc. Women Accts. (pres. Seattle chpt. 1946-48), Am. Soc. Women CPA, Wash. Soc. CPA, Seattle Women's Voters League, Women's Univ. Club (Seattle), City Club (Seattle, charter), Beta Alpha Psi (Outstanding Alumnus award 2001) Home and Office: 5725 NE 77th St Seattle WA 98115-6345 Personal E-mail: sandstromaw@hotmail.com.

SANDWEISS, MARTHA ANN, writer, history professor; b. St. Louis, Mar. 29, 1954; d. Jerome Wesley and Marilyn Joy (Gilk) S. BA magna cum laude, Radcliffe Coll., 1975; MA in History, Yale U., 1977, MPhil in History, 1981, PhD, 1985. Smithsonian-Nat. Endowment Humanities fellow Nat. Portrait Gallery, Washington, 1975-76; curator photographs Amon Carter Mus., Ft. Worth, 1979-86; adj. curator photographs, 1987-89; dir. Mead Art Mus. Amherst Coll., 1989-97, adj. assoc. prof. of fine arts and Am. studies, 1989-94, assoc. prof. Am. studies, 1994-97, assoc. prof. Am. studies and history, 1997-2000, prof. Am. studies and history, 2000—. Author: Carlotta Corpron: Designer with Light, 1980, Masterworks of American Photography, 1982, Laura Gilpin: An Enduring Grace, 1986, (catalogue) Pictures from an Expedition: Early Views of the American West, 1979, Print the Legend: Photography and the American West, 2002; co-author: Eyewitness to War: Prints and Daguerreotypes of the Mexican War, 1989; editor: Historic Texas: A Photographic Portrait, 1986, Contemporary Texas: A Photographic Portrait, 1986, Denizens of the Desert, 1988, Photography in Nineteenth Century America, 1991; co-editor: Oxford History of the American West, 1994. Fellow Ctr. for Am. Art and Material Cultures, Yale U., 1977-79, NEH, 1988, 2000-01, Am. Coun. Learned Socs., 1996-97, Weatherhead, 2000-01; Beinecke fellow Yale U., 2004-05. Office: Amherst Coll Am Studies Dept Box 2225 Amherst MA 01002-5000

SANDWELL, KRISTIN ANN, special education educator; b. Topeka, Kans., Jan. 13, 1955; d. Edwin C. and E. Maxine (Nelson) Henry; m. Steve Sandwell, Dec. 27, 1997; children: Dustin Grimm, Chris Creek, Brandon Grimm, Sarah Sandwell, Paul Sandwell. AA, Hutchinson (Kans.) C.C., 1986; BS, McPherson (Kans.) Coll., 1989; MEd, Wichita State U., 1992. Cert. tchr. elem., gifted. Math/parenting tchr. Flint Hills Job Corps Ctr., Manhattan, Kans., 1992; gifted facilitator Unified Sch. Dist. 353, Wellington, Kans., 1993-94, Unified Sch. Dist. 260, Derby, Kans., 1995-97; tchr. City of Wichita Summer Youth Employment Program-Edn., 1997—98; gifted facilitator Unified Sch. Dist. 259, 1998—. Head injury counselor, life skills trainer Three Rivers Ind. Living Ctr., Wamego, Kans., 1992; facilitator Summer Youth Employment Edn. Program, 1997-98. Epiphany Festival prodr. Trinity Luth. Ch., McPherson, 1991, 93; CASA organizer McPherson Coll., 1988-89; vol. Coun. on Violence Against Persons, McPherson, 1990-92. Mem. ASCD. Avocations: reading, travel, working with disability issues. Office Phone: 316-973-6450. Personal E-mail: ksandwell@yahoo.com.

SANDWELL, STEPHANIE ANNETTE, mathematics educator; b. Alexandria, La., Jan. 4, 1973; d. Stephen David and Annette Coon Richardson; m. Chad Michael Sandwell, June 7, 1972; 1 child, Eryn Elizabeth. BS in Math. Edn., Northwestern State U., Natchitoches, La., 1994. Math. tchr. Rapides Parish Sch. Bd., Alexandria, 1994—97, Port Neches (Tex.) Ind. Sch. Dist., 1997—99, LaFeria (Tex.) Ind. Sch. Dist., 1999—2000; staff devel. specialist Tech Prep of the Rio Grande Valley, Harlingen, Tex., 2000—01; math. tchr. Harlingen (Tex.) Consol. Ind. Sch. Dist., 2001—. Math. cons. Coll. Bd. SW Region, Austin, Tex., 2002—. Advanced Placement Strategies, Dallas, 2004—. Dir. Sunday sch. adult 7 dept. First Bapt. Ch., Harlingen, 2002—. Mem.: Rio Grande Valley Coun. Tchrs. Math. Republican. Baptist. Avocations: scrapbooks, exercise, crossword puzzles, card making. Home: 2105 Summerfield Ln Harlingen TX 78550 Office: Harlingen HS 1201 E Marshall Harlingen TX 78550 Office Phone: 956-427-3600. Personal E-mail: 4caster@sbcglobal.net. Business E-Mail: sandwell@harlingen.isd.tenet.edu.

SANDY, CATHERINE ELLEN, librarian; b. Italy; d. Felice Antonio and Guglielma Elena Santaniello; student Rosary Coll., 1933-34, U. Florence, Italy, 1951; B.S., Columbia U., 1953. Librarian, Port Washington (N.Y.) Pub. Library, 1926-73. Bd. dirs. Art Adv. Council, Port Washington Pub. Library; trustee, charter mem. Cow Neck Peninsula Hist. Soc. Recipient Alumni medal Columbia, 1970. Mem. Am., N.Y., N.C. library assns., UN Assn., Gen. Studies Alumni Assn. Columbia. Catholic. Editor: Cow Neck Peninsula Hist. Jour.

SANDY, SANDRA V., psychologist; d. Eugene Leon and Ruby Elizabeth Sandy. BA, W.Va. U., 1967; MA, New Sch. U., 1974; MPhil, Columbia U., 1983, PhD, 1985. Evaluation assoc. NYC Bd. Edn., Bklyn., 1985—87; sr. rsch. assoc. Cornell U. Med. Coll., NYC, 1987—94; dir. rsch. Internat. Ctr. Coop. & Conflict Resolution Columbia U., NYC, 1995—2001; dir. rsch. Ctr. Social & Emotional Edn., NYC, 2001—06; dir. Educating Com. Social Emotional Learning Inst., New York, NY. Cons. NY Acad. Medicine, NYC, 1995—2000, NJ Health Decisions, Verona, NJ, 2000—02; presentations, workshops in field. Author: (curriculum manual) Peaceful Kids Educating Communities in Social Emotional Learning, 2000; contbr. chapters to books. Grantee Homeless Children co-grant, Willliam T. Grant Found., 1988—91, Parent Child Conflict Resolution grant, William & Flora Hewlett Found., 1996—99, Peaceful Kids ECSEL grant, 1999—2002. Mem.: APA, Internat. Assn. Conflict Mgmt., Assn. Conflict Resolution (editl. bd. 2001—). Office: Ctr Social & Emotional Edn 1841 Broadway New York NY 10023 Personal E-mail: sandrasandy@earthlink.net.

SANDZA, ELIZABETH BARRY, lawyer; b. Duluth, Minn., Aug. 26, 1951; d. Thomas Gerald and Marguerite Mary (Collins) Barry; m. Richard William Sandza, Feb. 14, 1976; children: Anne Elizabeth, Allison Barry, Richard William, Mary Molly Rose. BS, U. Minn., 1973; MA, Northwestern U., 1974; JD, Temple U., 1979. Bar: Del. 1979, Calif. 1981, Md. 1988, D.C. 1988, U.S. Dist. Ct. Del., U.S. Dist. Ct. (so. dist.) N.Y., U.S. Dist. Ct. (no. and ctrl. dists.) Calif., U.S. Dist. Ct. D.C., U.S. Ct. Appeals (9th cir.). Dep. atty. gen. Del. Dept. Justice, Wilmington, 1979-81; assoc. atty. Gordon & Rees, San Francisco, 1981-86, LeBoeuf Lamb Greene & MacRae LLP, Washington, 1986-89, ptnr., co-chmn. Casualty/Arbitration/Litig. Practice Group, 1989—, chmn. litig. dept. Formerly gen. counsel Discovery Creek Children's Mus., Washington. Past pres. Intown Play Group, Inc., Washington, 1990-94. Mem. Fedn. Ins. and Corp. Counsel, Def. Rsch. Inst. Democrat. Roman Catholic. Office: LeBoeuf Lamb Greene & MacRae LLP 1875 Connecticut Ave NW Washington DC 20009-5728 Office Phone: 202-986-8036. Office Fax: 202-986-8102. Business E-Mail: ebsandza@llgm.com.

SANFORD, JANE AGNES, music educator; b. Ft. Madison, Iowa, Mar. 24, 1947; d. Bernard Herman and Genevieve Catherine (Koellner) Klesener; m. Richard Lee Sanford, Aug. 18, 1973; children: Cynthia Lee, Jennifer Lyn. MusB, Alverno Coll., Milw., 1969. Cert. tchr. Iowa, Wis. Elem. music tchr. Milw. Pub. Schs., 1969—72, Burlington Cmty. Schs., Iowa, 1973—78, Ft. Madison Cath. Schs., Iowa, 1983—2005; music tchr. Holy Trinity Cath. Elem. Sch., Ft. Madison, 2005—. Membership chair Ft. Madison Cmty. Concert Assn., 1977—84, pres., 1984—88; choir dir. St. Joseph's Ch., Ft. Madison, 1980—85; choir Sts. Mary and Joseph Ch., 1999—2006. Mem.: Music Educators Nat. Conf. Roman Catholic. Avocations: needlecrafts, reading, walking, travel, papercutting. Office: Holy Trinity Cath Schs 24th and Ave A Fort Madison IA 52627

SANFORD, LINDA S., information technology executive; b. Jan. 21, 1953; d. William J. and Catherine A. Sanford; 2 children. BA, St. John's U.; MS in Ops. Rsch., Rensselaer Poly. Inst. From mem. staff to gen. mgr. IBM, Westchester, NY, 1975—98, gen. mgr., global industries, 1998—2000, sr. v.p., group exec., storage systems group, 2000—03, sr. v.p. enterprise on demand transformation and info. tech. Somers, 2003—. Mem. bd. dirs. ITT Industries, 1998—. Bd. dirs. St. John's U., Rensselaer Poly. Inst., The Bus. Coun. of N.Y. State. Named one of 50 Most Influential Women in Bus., Fortune Mag., Top 10 Innovators in Tech. Industry, Info. Week Mag., 10 Most Influential Women in Tech., Working Woman Mag.; named to Women in Tech. Internat. Hall of Fame. Mem.: NAE. Office: IBM Corp Rte 100 Somers NY 10589

SANFORD, SARAH J., healthcare executive; b. Seattle, July 20, 1949; d. Jerome G. and Mary L. (Laughlin) S. BS in Nursing, U. Wash., 1972, MA in Nursing, 1977. Cert. in advanced nursing adminstrn. Critical care staff nurse Valley Gen. Hosp., Renton, Wash., 1972-75, Evergreen Gen. Hosp., Kirkland, Wash., 1975-76; instr. nursing Seattle Pacific U., 1977-79; with Overlake Hosp. Med. Ctr., Bellevue, Wash., 1979-88, critical care coord., 1979-80, dir. acute care nursing, 1980-82, assoc. adminstr., 1982-83, sr. v.p. patient care, 1983-88; exec. dir. AACN, Aliso Viejo, Calif., 1988-90, CEO, 1990-99; exec. dir. Actuarial Found., Schaumburg, Ill. Bd. dirs. Partnership for Organ Donation, Boston, Am. Soc. of Assn. Execs. Found., Washington. Co-editor: Standards for Nursing Care of the Critically Ill, 1989; contbr. articles to books and jours. Fellow Am. Acad. Nursing; mem. AACN (pres. 1984-85, bd. dirs. 1981-83), ANA, Am. Coll. Healthcare Execs., Soc. for Critical Care Medicine, Am. Orgn. Nurse Execs., Sigma Theta Tau.

SANG, BARBARA ELLEN, psychologist; b. NYC, Mar. 18, 1937; d. Alfred David and Kitty Betty (Spector) S BA, Bard Coll., 1958; MA, Yeshiva Coll., 1960, PhD, 1970. Rsch. asst. Mus. Natural History, N.Y.C., 1958—60; counselor Hillside Hosp., N.Y.C., 1960—62; rsch. asst. NYU, 1962—64; clin. psychologist Dept. Social Svcs., N.Y.C., 1966—74; faculty NYU, 1976—79; pvt. practice psychotherapist N.Y.C., 1972—. Adj. prof. Union Grad. Sch., N.Y.C., 1973-90; guest lectr. New Sch., CUNY, and others, 1968—; cons. Office of Disability, Dept. Social Svcs., N.Y.C., 1987— Editor: (with J. Warshow and A. Smith) Lesbians at Midlife: The Creative Transition. Contbr. articles to profl. jours Recipient Cmty. Svc. award Nat. Lesbian and Gay Health Found., Calif., 1989, Leadership scholarship APA Com. on Gay and Lesbian Concerns, Calif., 1991 Mem. APA, Assn. for Women in Psychology (regional coord.), Orton Dyslexia Soc Avocations: sports, nature photography, painting, indoor gardening. Home: 200 E 16th St New York NY 10003-3707

SANGER, CAROL, law educator; BA, Wellesley Coll., 1970; JD, U. Mich., 1976. Atty., San Francisco; tchr. U. Oreg., 1979—81, Santa Clara U. Law Sch., 1985—94; vis. prof. Columbia Law Sch., NYC, 1994—96, faculty mem., 1996—, Barbara Aronstein Black prof. law. Vis. scholar, Inst. Rsch. on Women and Gender Stanford U., 1990—91, vis. prof. law, 1991—92; mem. exec. bd. Inst. Rsch. on Women and Gender. Co-editor: Cases and Materials on Contracts, 2001. Fellow, Program on Law and Public Affairs, Princeton U., 2003—04. Office: Columbia Law Sch Jerome Greene Hall, Rm 818 Mailbox D-13 New York NY 10027 Office Phone: 212-854-5478. E-mail: csanger@law.columbia.edu.

SANGER, HAZEL A D, investment company executive; b. Glasgow, United Kingdom, Feb. 1, 1941; came to U.S., 1966; d. Paul Cedric Douglas Archer and Marian Reid Carmichael; m. Paul Weldon Sanger, Jul. 23, 1965; children: Georgina, Christopher. MA, Oxford U., England, 1962. CFA. With JF Chown & Co., London, 1963-66; v.p. TDP & L (name now Wellington Mgmt.), Atlanta, 1967-83; dir., managing dir. Atlanta Capital Management, 1983-93; dir. The Arden Group, Inc., Atlanta, 1994—2003; sr. dir. account mgmt. Mellon, 2003—. Co-author (with Prof. J. Peter Williamson): section on endowment fund mgmt., Investment Manager's Handbook, 1980. Hon. mem. adv. bd. dirs. Trust for Pub. Lands, Ga.; chmn. adv. coun. Lady Margaret Hall, Oxford U.; hon. bd. dirs. Atlanta Opera; bd. visitors, vice-chmn. fin. com. CDC Found., Atlanta; trustee Hambridge Ctr. Fellow Royal Soc. Arts and Commerce, London, U.K.; mem. Assn. for Investment Mgmt. and Rsch. Avocations: reading, travel, opera, theater, countryside. Office: The Arden Group Inc 3495 Piedmont Rd NE Atlanta GA 30305-1773

SANGER, PRIYA SESHACHARI, lawyer; d. Candadai Seshachari and Neila C. S. BA in Classics, Smith Coll., Northampton, Mass.; JD, Univ. Utah, 1990. Bar: NY, Calif., Utah, US Ct. Appeals (9th cir.), US Supreme Ct. Former litigator; now sr. counsel Wells Fargo Bank NA, San Francisco. Staff: Utah Law Rev. Apptd. to San Francisco Human Rights Commn. Disadvantaged Bus. Com.; adv. com. Minority/Women/Local Bus. Enterprise Cmty. Named one of Best Lawyers Under 40, Nat. Asian Pacific Am. Bar Assn., 2004. Mem.: Lawyers for One Am. (founding mem.), Korean Am. Bar Assn., San Francisco Bank Attys. Assn. (pres.-elect 2004), Bar Assn. San Francisco (bd. dir. 2003—04), Barristers Club San Francisco (past pres.). Office: Sr Counsel Wells Fargo Bank NA 5th Fl 633 Folsom St San Francisco CA 94107 Office Phone: 415-396-4113. Office Fax: 415-975-7861. Business E-Mail: sangerps@wellsfargo.com.

SAN GIACOMO, LAURA, actress; b. Hoboken, NJ, Nov. 14, 1962; Appeared in films Vital Signs, 1990, Pretty Woman, 1990, Quigley Down Under, 1990, Once Around, 1991, The Other Woman, 1993, Nina Takes A Lover, 1993, The Stand, 1994, Stuart Saves His Family, 1995, Right to Remain Silent, 1996, Suicide Kings, 1997, Apocalypse, 1997, With Friends Like These., 1998, Eat Your Heart Out, 1997, Apocalypse, 1997, A House on a Hill, 2003, Checking Out, 2005, Havoc, 2005,; appeared in TV series Gargoyles, 1994, Gargoyles: The Goliath Chronicles, 1996-97, Just Shoot Me, 1997-2003.; guest appearances include: The Equalizer, 1985, Crime Story, 1986, Spenser: For Hire, 1985. Office: More Medavoy Mgmt 7920 W Sunset Blvd Ste 401 Los Angeles CA 90046-3300*

SANGIOVANNI, MARY ELIZABETH, writer, freelance manager; b. Orange, NJ, Jan. 28, 1976; d. Michael Louis and Suzanne Kathleen SanGiovanni; 1 child, Adam Joseph. BA in English, Fairleigh Dickinson U., 1998. Asst. editor Marquis Who's Who, New Providence, NJ, 1998—99, from freelance coord. to freelance supr., 1999—2001, freelance mgr., 2002—. Author: (short stories) Under Cover of Night, 2002; contbr. short stories to various periodicals, articles to various periodicals. Mem.: Garden State Horror Writers (v.p. 2001, pres. 2002—03), Horror Writers Assn. (internet mailer editor 2003—), Mid Atlantic Horror Profls., Nat. Assn. Women Writers. Roman Catholic. Avocations: reading, movies, model building, video games, computer art. Office: Marquis Whos Who 630 Central Ave New Providence NJ 07974

SANGIULIANO, BARBARA ANN, tax consultant; b. Bronx, N.Y., Dec. 28, 1959; d. Patrick John and Mildred (Soell) Gallo; m. John Warren Sangiuliano, Aug. 28, 1982. BA, Muhlenberg Coll., 1982; MST, Seton Hall U., 1989, JD, 1997. Bar: N.J. 1997, N.Y. 2006; CPA, N.J., 1987; CMA. Sr. tax mgr. KPMG Peat Marwick, Short Hills, N.J., 1988-92; sr. tax analyst Allied Signal, Morristown, N.J., 1992-93; tax mgr. AT&T, Morristown, 1993-96, Lucent Techs., Morristown, 1996-97; tax atty. Witman, Stadtmauer & Michaels, Florham Park, NJ, 1997-98; tax cons. Ernst & Young LLP, Iselin, NJ, 1998—2003, Deloitte Tax LLP, Parsippany, NJ, 2003—06, Smolin, Lupin & Co. PA, Fairfield, NJ, 2006—. Mem. AICPA, ABA, N.J. Soc. CPAs (past pres. Union County chpt.), N.J. Bar Assn., Inst. Mgmt. Accts., Mensa, Omicron Delta Epsilon, Phi Sigma Iota. Republican. Roman Catholic. Avocations: reading, bicycling, fencing. Home: 340 William St Scotch Plains NJ 07076-1430 Office: Smolin Lupin and Co PA 165 Passaic Ave Fairfield NJ 07004 Office Phone: 973-439-7200.

SANKAR, LAKSHMI, special education educator; b. Calcutta, India, July 5, 1955; d. Pichu and Chintamani (Ramaswamy) Jayaraman; m. Chetan Sankar, Mar. 6, 1977; chldren: Akila, Shiva BA honors, Calcutta U., 1974; MA, Jadavpur U., Calcutta, 1977; MEd, Temple U., 1981; EdS, U. West Ga., 2005. Cert. spl. educator, Ala., N.J., Pa. Resource tchr. Home of the Merciful Savior, Phila., 1981—82; tchr. Growth and Devel., Phila., 1984—85, Crighton Sch., Matawan, NJ, 1985—86, United Ctrl. Palsy, Long Branch, NJ, 1986—89, Auburn Schs., Ala., 1989—2003; rep. local edn. agy. Fayette County Bd. Edn., Ga., 2003—05; dir. Exceptional Children Troup County Bd. Edn., Ga., 2005—. Rep. Auburn City Schs., 1989-91, mentor, 1991—, advisor, 1992—, instnl. leader, 1994—; reviewer State Dept. Edn., Montgomery, Ala., 1990-91, tchr. trainer, 1993; tchr. trainer Auburn U., 1992— Contbr. articles to profl. jours Program v.p. PTA, Carywood, 1991-92; coord. Program-Drake Mid. Sch., Auburn, 1992-93, Carywood Sch., Auburn, 1992-93; mentor Adult Lit. Ctr., Phila., 1978-81 Recipient Woodhaven fellowship Temple U., 1979-81; named Outstanding Spl. Edn. Tchr. of Yr., State of Ala., 1993 Mem. Coun. for Exceptional Children (Nat. Bd. cert. 2002), Coun. Spl. Educators, Ga. Assn. Ednl. Leaders (cert.), East Ala. Indian Assn. (pres. 1995-96) Democrat. Hindu. Avocations: reading, writing, aerobics, music, acting. Home: 241 Oid Pond Rd Lagrange GA 30241 Office: Troup County Bd Edn Exceptional Children Ctr 1712 Whitesville Rd Lagrange GA 30240

SANKOFF, TINA M., foundation administrator; d. Suby and Boyka (Rice) Sankoff; 1 child, Sabrina Ohnemus. Cert., Golden Gate Coll., San Francisco, Heald Coll. V.p. Lam Rsch. Inc., Fremont, Calif.; pres. Tina M. Sankoff FUN-DATION, Livermore, Calif., 1999—. Bd. dirs. San Jose Mus. of Art, The Tech Mus. of Innovation, San Jose, Wash. Hosp. Found., Fremont, San Francisco 49er Acad., East Palo Alto, Calif., San Francisco Bay Area Sports Hall of Fame. Cir. of care Lucile Packard Stanford Children's Hosp., Palo Alto, Calif.; mem. Girl Scouts of Am., San Jose, Calif., YWCA, San Jose, Calif. Recipient Senator Liz Figueroa Domestic Violence Prevention award, Safe Alternatives to Domestic Violence, 2002, Tribute to Women in Industry award. Mem.: Bulgarian Macedonia Soc. Bd.

SAN MIGUEL, LOLITA, artistic director; Student, Sch. Am. Ballet. Performer Robert Joffrey Co., Benjamin Harkarvy Co., Slavenska-Franklin Ballet; soloist Met. Opera Ballet; founder Puerto Rican Dance Theatre, N.Y., 1970; artistic dir., founder Ballet Concierto de P.R., Santurce, 1978—. Tchr., ballet mistress Ballet Hispánico, N.Y.; tchr. Dance Theatre Harlem, Performing Arts H.S., Adelphi Coll., Hofstra U., L.I. U., Clark Ctr., Met. Opera.

SANO, EMILY JOY, museum director; b. Santa Ana, Calif., Feb. 17, 1942; d. Masao and Lois Kikue (Inokuchi) S. BA, Ind. U., 1967; MA, Columbia U., 1970, MPhil, 1976, PhD, 1983. Lectr. Oriental Art Vassar Coll., Poughkeepsie, NY, 1974-79; curator Asian Art, asst. dir. programs Kimbell Art Mus., Ft. Worth, 1979-89; dep. dir. collections and exhbns. Dallas Mus. Art, 1989-92; dep. dir., chief curator Asian Art Mus., San Francisco, 1993-95, dir., 1995—. Author: Great Age of Japanese Buddhist Sculpture, 1982; editor: The Blood of Kings, 1986, Weavers, Merchants and Kings, 1984, Painters of the Great Ming, 1993. Active Assn. Art Mus. Dirs.; vis. com. Harvard U. Art Mus. Woodrow Wilson Fellow, 1966-67; grantee Carnegie, 1963-64, Fulbright-Hays, 1977-78. Office: Asian Art Museum 200 Larkin St San Francisco CA 94102-4734

SANONA, NUNO ALEXANDRE FERNANDES RORIGUES, financial consultant; b. Lisbon, Portugal, Oct. 13, 1965; arrived in Spain, 1969; d. José Rodrigues Sanona and Maria Celestina Fernandes Rodrigues-Sanona. B Fin. Mktg., Essen U., Madrid, 1991; B Corp. Law, Buxton U., London, 1994, BS in Econ., 1994, DBA, 2000. Coml. dir. OMEC Orgn., Madrid, 1990—92, Dunbar Fin. Svcs., Madrid, 1992—94, Eagle Star Fin. Svcs., Madrid, 1994—96; exec. pres. Clifford Overland Cons., Madrid, 1996—. Mem. adv. bd. Harold Madeley Fin. Svcs., Madrid, 2000—, Internat. Property Fund, Madrid, 2000—, McKenzie Fin. Svcs., Madrid, 2000—. Hon. sen. Old San Francisco, 2005; hon. amb. United World Authority, NY, 2005. Named Hon. Admiral, Confederate Navy Assn., 2005, Hon. Adm., 2005, Hon. Col., Confederate Army Assn., 2005, Hon. Sheriff, Confederate Sheriff's Assn., 2005, Knight Grand Comdr., Order Richard Lion Heart of Jerusalem, 2005, Laird of Glenairn, Scotland, 2005. Mem.: Laird of Glenairn. Avocations: Karate, kickboxing, power lifting. Office: Clifford Cons Calle Rios Rosas 46-60A 28003 Madrid Spain

SAN PEDRO, SYLVIA P., mathematics educator, department chairman; b. Modesto, Calif., Feb. 26; d. Alfredo D. and Carmen R. Perez; m. Ramon I. San Pedro, Nov. 25, 1988; children: Alyssa P., Enrique P. BS in Math., U. Houston, 1993; EdM, U. St. Thomas, Houston, 1997. Cert. secondary math. tchr. Tex. Edn. Agy., 1996. Math. tchr. Booker T. Washington H.S., Houston, 1993—2002; math. tchr., dept. chair Cypress Ridge H.S., Houston, 2002—. Girl scout leader San Jacinto Girl Scout Coun., Houston, 1996—2006. Named Tchr. of Yr., SECME, Inc., 2000. Office: Cypress Ridge High School 7900 North Eldridge Pkwy Houston TX 77041 Office Phone: 281-807-8000. Business E-Mail: sylvia.sanpedro@cfisd.net.

SANT, VICTORIA P., museum administrator; BA, Stanford U. Docent Nat. Gallery Art, Washington, DC, 1983—85, chmn. trustees coun., 2001—02, immediate past chmn., The Phillips Collection, pres., 2003—. Co-founder, pres. The Summit Found., The Summit Fund of Washington. Bd. mem. Stanford U., Cmty. Found. for Nat. Capitol Region, Nat. Campaign to Prevent Teen Pregnancy, DC Campaign to Prevent Teen Pregnancy, Population Action Internat., Vital Voices for Global Partnership. Office: The Summit Found Ste 525 2100 Pennsylvania Ave, NW, Washington DC 20037 Office Phone: 202-912-2900.

SANTAELLA, IRMA VIDAL, retired state supreme court justice; b. N.Y.C., Oct. 4, 1924; d. Rafael and Sixta (Thillet) Vidal; children: Anthony, Ivette. Acctg. degree, Modern Bus. Coll., 1942; BA, Hunter Coll., 1959; LLB, Bklyn. Law Sch., 1961, JD, 1967; LLD, Sacred Heart U., Conn., 1990. Bar: N.Y. 1961. Sole practice, N.Y.C., 1961-63; with ptnr., 1966-68; dep. commr. N.Y.C. Dept Correction, 1963-66; mem. N.Y. State Human Rights Appeal Bd., N.Y.C., 1968-83, chmn., 1975-83; justice N.Y. State Supreme Ct., N.Y.C., 1983-94, ret., 1994. Mem. N.Y.C. Adv. Council on Minority Affairs, 1982—, N.Y.C. Commn. on Status of Women, 1975-77. Founder, chmn. Legion of Voters, 1962-68; nat. del. Presdl. Democratic Convs., 1968, 72, 76, 80; vice chmn. N.Y. State del. 1976 Conv.; founder Nat. Assn. for Puerto Rican Civil Rights, 1962, Hispanic Community Chest Am., 1972; chmn. bd. dirs. Puerto Rican Parade, 1962-67; bd. dirs. Catholic Interracial Council, 1968-81; nat. co-chmn. Coalition Hispanic People, 1970; fund raiser Boy Scouts Am., 1962-63; chmn. Children's Camp, South Bronx (N.Y.) 41st Police Precinct, 1967; active City-Wide Steering Com. for Quality Edn., 1962-64, Community Service Soc., 1972-74, Talbott Perkins Children's Services, 1973-75, Planned Parenthood Assn., 1968-69, Puerto Rican Crippled Children's Fund, 1965-69; founder N.Y. chpt. Clinica Grillasca, P.R. Cancer Assn., 1974—. Recipient citations for civic work Gov. Rockefeller, 1972, Gov. Carey, 1982, First Puerto Rican woman to be elected to the N.Y. State Supreme Ct., County of Bronx, 1983; recipient Recognition award Gov. Mario M. Cuomo, 1990, Nat. Puerto Rican Coalition Life Achievement award, 1990, Life Achievement award Pres. of Dominican Republic, 1991, Life Achievement award Nat. Coun. Hispanic Women, 1991, others; inducted to N.Y. City Hunter Coll. Hall of Fame, 1998. Mem. Am. Judicature Soc. Roman Catholic. Home: 853 7th Ave New York NY 10019-5215

SANTAMARIA, JOANNE C., psychologist; b. Springfield, Mass., Oct. 2, 1949; d. Rinaldo Leonardo and Dorothy Margaret (Sousa) Santamaria; m. James D Freihaut, Aug. 4, 1973; children: Sara S Kelly, Nathaniel Freihaut. BA, Coll. of New Rochelle, 1971; MA, U. Mo., 1974; MS, U. Hartford, 1994. Sch. psychologist So. Windsor Bd. Edn., 1997—; adj. prof. U. Hartford, West Hartford, 1994—95. Presenter in field. Grantee, So. Windsor Pub. Schs., 2000—05. Mem.: Nat. Assn. Sch. Psychologists, Conn. Assn. Sch. Psychologists, Psi Chi, Kappa Gamma Pi.

SANTANA, LYMARI JEANETTE, lawyer; b. Augusta, Ga., 1968; married. BA with honors in Polit. Sci., U. PR, Rio Piedras, 1991; JD with honors, Mich. State U. Detroit Coll. Law, 1994. Bar: Mich. 1994, Minn. 2000. With James M. Hacker, P.C., Mt. Clemens, Mich.; asst. prosecutor Village of New Haven, Mich.; asst. US atty. No. Dist. Ala.; founding shareholder Mack & Santana Law Offices, P.C.; of counsel Mansfield, Tanick & Cohen, P.A., Mpls. With Judge Adv. Gen. Corps U.S. Army, 1995—2000, criminal trial def. counselor 82nd Airborne Divsn. U.S. Army, 1998. Decorated Meritorious Svc. medal; named a Rising Star, Minn. Super Lawyers mag., 2006. Mem.: Nat. Hispanic Bar Assn., Minn. Hispanic Bar Assn. (pres. 2004—05, sec. 2001—03), Hennepin County Bar Assn. Avocations: reading, sports, movies. Office: Mack & Santana Law Offices PC 1700 US Bank Plz South 220 S 6th St Minneapolis MN 55402 Office Phone: 612-605-0967. E-mail: lymari@macksantanalaw.com.*

SANTANA, NIURKA MARIBEL, neuropsychologist, educator; b. NY, Dec. 5, 1969; d. Angel M. and Idalia L. Santana. BA, Fla. Internat. U., 1991; MS, Miami Inst. of Psychology, 1993; PhD, Carlos Albizu U., 2000. Adj. faculty Carlos Albizu U., Miami, Fla., 1997—; case mgr. United Behavorial Health, Miami, 2001—03; lic. psychologist Pinecrest Rehab Hosp., Delray Beach, Fla., 2002—06; neuropsychologist Rehab without Walls, Ft. Lauderdale, 2003—06; pvt. practice, 2006—. Presenter in field. Mem.: Am. Psychological Assn. Avocations: writing, dance, poetry. Office Phone: 786-277-3100. Personal E-mail: DrSantanal@hotmail.com.

SANTI, KRISTI L., special education educator, researcher; b. Des Moines, Apr. 16, 1969; d. Joseph L. and Lois A. Santi. PhD, Fla. State U., 2002; M in Spl. Edn., Drake U., 1995, MA, 1993. Tchg. Cert. Iowa, 1993. Asst. prof. U. Tex. Houston, 2001—; adj. prof. Fla. State U., Tallahassee, 2000—02. Author: (jour. article) Remedial and Spl. Edn (Publ., 2004). Mem.: Am. Ednl. Rsch. Assn., Coun. for Exceptional Children. Home: PO Box 20766 Houston TX 77225 Office: University of Texas Houston 7000 Fannin Street UCT 2443 Houston TX 77030 Personal E-mail: kristisanti@netscape.net.

SANTIAGO, IRMA, science educator, department chairman; b. Luquillo, P.R., Oct. 2, 1947; d. Julio Santiago and Pillar Casillas; m. Carlos A. Cerra (div.); children: Aurelio Cerra, Arnaldo Cerra, Veronica Cerra, Julio Cerra, Barbara Caraballo. BA in Social Work, Inter Am. U., P.R., 1974; BA in Elem. and Secondary Edn., Mary Hardin Baylor U., Belton, Tex., 1987; EdM in Mgmt., Sul Ross State U., Alpine, Tex., 1993; grad., Adminstrs. Leadership Acad. El Paso Ind. Sch. Dist. Cert. social worker Tex.; elem. and secondary edn. Tex., ESL Tex., mid mgmt.in edn. Tex. Program supr. Headstart, PR, 1969—73; tchr. secondary edn. P.R. Dept. Edn, 1974—79; elem. tchr. San Elizario Ind. Sch. Dist., Tex., 1986—89, Gadsden Ind. Sch. Dist., Anthony, N.Mex., 1989—90, El Paso Ind. Sch. Dist., Tex., 1990—2001; sci. coord. and leader Rusk Elem. Sch. El Paso Ind. Sch. Dist., 2001—. Art editor: The Baylorian, 1983—87. Literacy vol. Recipient Svc. award, El Paso Ind. Sch. Dist. PTA, 1991, 20 yr. award, El Paso Ind. Sch. Dist., 2005. Mem.: Tex. Prins. Assn., Tex. State Tchrs. Assn. Roman Catholic. Avocations: swimming, reading. Office: Rusk Elem Sch 3601 N Copia El Paso TX 79930-4796

SANTINA, DALIA, nutritionist, writer, skin care specialist; b. Amman, Jordan, Sept. 24, 1954; d. Mahmoud Dauod Abbasi, Widad Abbasi; m. Mohammed Shafiq Santina. BA in English Lit., U. Riyadh, Saudi Arabia, 1977; diploma in computer programming, Western Bus. Coll., 1980; diploma in Skin Aesthetics, Career Acad. Beauty, 1989; PhD in Holistic Nutrition, Clayton Coll. Natural Health, 1994. Cert. paramedical acne 1990, glycolic acid services 1991, mgmt. aging and sun-damaged skin 1992, natural pharmacology 1992, aesthetic peeling 1992, oxygenation of the skin 1993, lymphatic drainage massage techniques 1994, homeopathic estheticology 1994, iridology diploma 1995, cert. chem. peels 1996, hydrotherapy 1997, glycolic treatments 1998, diploma in iridology 2003, cert. in herbology 2003. Exec. asst. to v.p. Am. Health Ctr., Newport Beach, Calif., 1988—89; skin care co. Skinclub, Huntington Beach, Calif., 1991—96; lectr. holistic nutrition/skin health issues, 1999—. Translator computer sys. tng. manuals, Dallas, 1983—84; tech. translator England and No. Ireland, 1984. Author: Holistic Skin Is.In, 2001, Super Supplements for Skin, Body & Mind, 2004; contbr. articles to profl. jours. Recipient Gold medal in Table Tennis, Sports Bd., Kuwait, 1972. Avocations: horseback riding, reading, antiques. Personal E-mail: dalia4skin@msn.com.

SANTONA, GLORIA, lawyer; b. Gary, Ind., June 10, 1950; d. Ray and Elvira (Cambeses) S.; m. Douglas Lee Frazier, Apr. 12, 1980. BS in Biochemistry, Mich. State U., 1971; JD, U. Mich., 1977. Bar: Ill. 1977. Atty. McDonald's Corp., Oak Brook, Ill., 1977-82, dir., 1982-86, assoc. gen. counsel, 1986-92, asst. v.p., 1989-93, v.p., sec., dep. gen. counsel, 1996-99, v.p., U.S. gen. counsel, sec., 1999-2001, sr. v.p., gen. counsel, sec., 2001—03, exec. v.p., gen. counsel, sec., 2003—. Mem. ABA, Chgo. Assn., Am. Corp. Counsel Assn., Am. Soc. Corp. Secs. Office: McDonalds Corp 1 McDonalds Plz Oak Brook IL 60523-1911

SANTORELLY, ANNMARIE, special education educator; b. Bklyn., Dec. 1, 1955; d. Thomas Paul Barry, Marie Assumpta Barry; m. William Michael Santorelly; children: Michael, Christopher. BA, Marywood U., 1977; M, Austin Peay State U., 1981. Cert. spl. edn. tchr. N.Y. Tchr. Monroe-Woodbury Mid. Sch., Central Valley, NY, 1981—85; tchr., dept. chair Monroe-Woodbury H.S., Central Valley. Mem.: Coun. Exceptional Children (Named Profl. Spl. Edn. Tchr. 2000), Delta Kappa Gamma. Roman Catholic. Avocation: outdoor activities. Home: 41 Rye Hill Rd Monroe NY 10950

SANTOS, ADÈLE NAUDÉ, architect, educator; b. Cape Town, South Africa, Oct. 14, 1938; came to U.S., 1973; d. David Francois Hugo and Aletta Adèle Naudé. Student, U. Cape Town, South Africa, 1956-58; diploma, Archtl. Assn., London, 1961; MArch in Urban Design, Harvard U., 1963; MArch, M in City Planning, U. Pa., 1968. Registered arch., Pa., Mass. Pvt. practice architecture with Antonio de Souza Santos, 1966-73; ptnr. Interstudio, Houston, 1973-79; assoc. prof. architecture Rice U., Houston, 1973-78, prof., 1979; prof. architecture, grad sch. design Harvard U., Cambridge, Mass., 1979—81; prof. architecture and urban design, dept. architecture U. Pa., Phila., 1981-90; founding dean Sch. Architecture U. Calif., San Diego, 1990-94; pvt. practice architecture and urban design Adele Naude Santos, Arch., Phila., 1979-90, Adele Naude Santos and Assocs., San Diego and Phila., 1991—2002; prof. architecture Coll. Environ. Design U. Calif., Berkeley, 1994—2003; dean Sch. Architecture and Planning, MIT, Cambridge, 2004—. Project dir., co-filmmaker for 5 part series, 1979-80; works include Albright Coll. Ctr. for the Arts, Reading, Pa., 1991, Franklin-LaBrea Housing, Hollywood, Calif., 1995, Inst. of Contemporary Art, Phila., 1991, Yerba Buena Gardens, San Francisco, 1998. Wheelwright Travelling fellow, Harvard U., 1968; NEA grantee, 1976, Tex. Com. for Humanities grantee, 1979; recipient (with Hugo Naudé) Bronze medal for House Naudé Capt. Inst. South African Architects, 1967, award for public TV program So. Ednl. Communications Assn., 1980, 3d place award Inner city Infill Competition, 1986; winner Internat. Design Competition, Hawaii Loa Coll., hon. mention Cin. Hillside Housing Competition and City Visions, Phila., 1986; winner competition for Franklin/La Brea Affordable Housing Project Mus. Comtemporary Art and Community Redevel. Agy. City L.A., 1988, Pa. Soc. Architects design award for Franklin/La Brea Multi-Family Housing, 1988; winning entry collaborative competition for amphitheater, restaurant and natural history mus., Arts Pk., La., 1989; winner competition for 24-unit residential devel., City of Camden, N.J., 1989, for New Civic Ctr., City of Perris, Calif., 1991, children's mus. The Zeum, 1998, child care facility Yerba Buena Gardens, San Francisco, 1998, Please Touch Mus., Phila., 1998, winner design competition ChildCare Ctr. U. Pa., 1999. Fellow Am. Inst. Archs.; mem. Pa. Soc. Archs., Archs. Registration Coun. (U.K.). Office: Dean Sch Architecture 77 Massachusetts Ave Cambridge MA 02139-4307

SANTOS, NADINE, music director; Grad., Full Sail Coll. Phone op. WWPR-FM Clear Channel Comm., 2002—03, programming asst., 2003—05; exec. asst. Warner Music Group, Atlantic Records, 2005—06; music dir. WWPR NY (Power 105.1) Clear Channel Comm., 2006—. Office: Power 105.1 FM 11206th Ave New York NY 10036 Office Phone: 212-704-1051.*

SANTOS, SHARON LEE, parochial school educator; b. Perth Amboy, N.J., June 23, 1955; d. John Anthony Santos and Dolores Estelle Barrett. BA in History, Kean U., 1978, MA in Guidance and Counseling, 1985; MA in Systematic Theology, Seton Hall U., 1998. Religious sr. Franciscan of Our Lady of Guadalupe; cert. tchr. K-12, guidance counelor N.J., religion tchr. Diocese of Metuchen, N.J. Tchr. Archdiocese of Newark, Diocese of Metuchen, Perth Amboy, Fords, NJ, Woodbridge, NJ; dir. religious edn. Vicariate of Perth Amboy, St. Mary Parish, New Monmouth, NJ. Guest spkr. on biblical and doctrinal topics various cities in NJ, 1993—; adv. bd. on evangelization Diocese of Meetuchen, 1999. Mem.: Fellowship of Cath. Scholars, St. Edith Stein Guild (life), Kappa Delta Phi. Avocations: astronomy, gardening. Office: St Mary Cath Ch 26 Leonardville Rd New Monmouth NJ 07748 Home: 355 Carr Ave Keansburg NJ 07734-1419 Office Phone: 732-671-8550.

SANTOS DE ALVAREZ, BRUNILDA, lawyer; b. 1958; BSFS, Georgetown U.; JD, Boston Coll. Bar: P.R. 1983. Gen. counsel Popular, Inc., San Juan, PR, 1997—. Sec. of bd. Popular Internat. Bank, Inc., Banco Popular N. Am., Popular Cash Express, Inc., Banco Popular, Popular Insurance, Inc., Popular Securities, Inc., Levitt Mortgage Corp., Popular Insurance Agy. USA, Inc., Popular Mortgage, Inc., P.R. Investor Tax Free Fund, Inc., P.R. Tax Free Target Maturity Fund, Inc., P.R. Investors Flexible Allocation Fund, Inc., Popular Fin. Holdings; asst. sec. of bd. Popular Auto, Inc., Popular Finance, Inc.; mem. bd. of regents Colegio Puertorriqueno de Ninas, 2002—. Office: Popular Inc Popular Ctr Bldg 209 Munoz Rivera Ave San Juan PR 00918

SANTOSO, MICHELLE JO, music educator, pianist; b. Surabaya, Indonesia, Sept. 8, 1968; arrived in U.S., 1993; d. Kim Man Jo and Kiem Ing Tio; m. Peter Santoso, July 10, 1994; children: Hillary Lin, Herbert Lin. BA cum laude, IKIP, Jakarta, Indonesia, 1992; MA, Calif. State U., L.A., 1998. Music dir. Yip's Children Choir, San Marino, Calif., 1994—96; dir., tchr. piano Master Artists Piano Performing Studio, Alhambra, 1996—. Performer: Chopin's Nocturne, 1992 (Best Performance and Interpretation award, 1992), Bratislava Chamber Orch., Austria, 2001, Internat. Chamber Music Festival, Italy, 2002, Internat. Chamber Music Festival, Prague, 2003. Vol. Tiu Chi Orgn. Recipient prize, Yamaha Piano Competition, 1992, L.A. Liszt Piano Competition, 2000; scholar Inez Schubert scholarship, Calif. State U., L.A., 1996. Mem.: Southwestern Youth Music Festival, Nat. Guild Piano Tchrs., Calif. Assn. Profl. Music Tchrs., Music Tchrs. Assn. Calif., Nat. Fedn. Music Clubs. Home: 1475 Rubio Dr San Marino CA 91108

SANTUCCI, L. MICHELLE, adult nurse practitioner, nutritionist, consultant; b. Denville, N.J., Oct. 11, 1956; d. Anthony Jr. and Raymonde (Cloitre) Santucci. BS in Biology, U. Bridgeport, 1977; AAS, Cumberland County Coll., Vineland, N.J., 1982; MSN, U. Medicine/Dentistry N.J., 1997; PhD in Holistic Nutrition, Clayton Coll. Natural Health, Birmingham, Ala., 1998. RN; cert. critical care nurse, intravenous therapy nurse, adult nurse practitioner. Staff nurse South Jersey Hosp. System, Bridgeton Divsn., N.J., charge nurse Bridgeton, N.J., nurse educator, adminstrv. nursing supr. Millville, N.J.; adult nurse practitioner Regional Med. Assocs., Millville, N.J., 1997-99; adult nurse practitioner, nutrition cons. Cumberland Med. Assocs., Millville, NJ, 1999—2001; prin., owner The Wholistic Ctr. for Wellness, Inc., 2001—. Clin. faculty assoc. U. Medicine and Dentistry N.J., Wilmington Coll.; cons. South Jersey AIDS Alliance, Bridgeton, N.J., 2003— Mem. Am. Acad. Nurse Practitioners. Home: 3284 Swan Dr Vineland NJ 08361-7367 Office Phone: 856-690-0627. Personal E-mail: lmsnp@aol.com.

SANUSI, MARINA THERESIA, retired psychiatrist; b. Surabaya, Java, Indonesia, June 15, 1931; arrived in U.S., 1970; d. Sing Gwan Oen and Siong Nio Tjio; m. Irwan Daniel Sanusi, Sept. 18, 1960; children: Hani David, H. August, Monica Sanusi Gelé. MD, Airlangga U. Sch. Medicine, Indonesia, 1959. Diplomate Am. Bd. Psychiatry and Neurology. Resident psychiatry and neurology Airlangga U. Sch. Medicine, Surabaya, 1959—63; resident psychiatry Confederate Meml. Hosp., Shreveport, La., 1971—74; staff psychiatrist Sch. Medicine La. State U., Shreveport, 1974—76; psychiatrist Shreveport Mental Hosp. Ctr., 1976—2000; ret., 2000. Home: 3148 Turnberry Cir Charlottesville VA 22911

SANZONE, DONNA S., publishing executive; b. Bklyn., Apr. 4, 1949; d. Joseph J. Seitz and Faye (Brooks) Rossman; m. Charles F. Sanzone, Jan. 2, 1972; children: Danielle, Gregory. BA magna cum laude, Boston U., 1970; MA, Northeastern U., 1979. Grad. placement specialist Inst. Internat. Edn., NYC, 1970-72; adminstr. AFS Internat. Scholarships, Brussels, 1972-74; editor Internat. Ency. Higher Edn., Boston, 1974-76, G.K. Hall & Co., Pubs., Boston, 1977-81, exec. editor, 1981-91, editor-in-chief, 1991-96; v.p. Oryx Press, Boston, 1996-2000; editor-in-chief Grolier Acad. Reference, Danbury, Conn., 2000—04; exec. editor Collins Reference, Harper Collins, NYC, 2004—. Contbg. author: Access to Power, 1981. Mem.: ALA, Libr. and Info. Tech. Assn., Assn. Coll. and Rsch. Librs., Soc. for Scholarly and Profl. Pub., Assn. Am. Pubs. Office: Collins Reference 18 Pine St Weston MA 02493-1116

SAPINSLEY, LILA MANFIELD, state official; b. Chgo., Sept. 9, 1922; d. Jacob and Doris (Silverman) Manfield; m. John M. Sapinsley, Dec. 23,1 942; children: Jill Sapinsley Mooney, Carol Sapinsley Rubenstein, Joan Sapinsley Lewis, Patricia Sapinsley Levy. BA, Wellesley Coll., 1944; D in Pub. Svc., U. R.I., 1971; D in Pedagogy, R.I. Coll., 1973; LHD, Brown U., 1993. Mem. R.I. Senate, 1972-84, minority leader, 1974-84; dir. R.I. Dept. Cmty. Affairs, 1985; chmn. R.I. Housing and Mortgage Fin. Corp., 1985-87; commr. R.I. Pub. Utilities Commn., 1987-93. Bd. dirs. Lifespan Corp.; mem. R.I. Gov.'s Commn. on Women; commr. Edn. Commn. of States. Pres. bd. trustees Butler Hosp., 1978-84; trustee R.I. State Colls., 1965-70, chmn., 1967-70; trustee U. R.I., R.I. Coll. Found.; bd. dirs. Hamilton House, Trinity Repertory Co., Lincoln Sch., Wellesley Ctr. for Rsch. on Women, 1980, Providence Pub. Libr. Recipient Alumnae Achievement award Wellesley Coll., 1974, Outstanding Legislator of Yr. award Rep. Nat. Legislators Assn., 1984. Republican. Jewish. Home: 355 Blackstone Blvd Apt 402 Providence RI 02906-4951

SAPIRO, VIRGINIA, academic administrator, political science professor; b. East Orange, N.J., Feb. 28, 1951; m. Graham K. Wilson; 1 child, Adam. AB, Clark U., 1972; MA in Polit. Sci., PhD in Polit. Sci., U. Mich., 1976. Asst. prof. polit. sci. and women's studies program U. Wis., Madison, 1976-81, assoc. prof., 1981-86, prof., 1986—, Sophonisba P. Breckinridge prof., 1995—, assoc. vice chancellor teaching and learning, 2002—, interim provost, vice chancellor academic affairs, 2005—06. Vis. lectr. dept. govt. U. Essex, 1979-80, lectr., 1981, 82-83, vis. prof., 1989. Author: Women in American Society: An Introduction to Women's Studies, 1986, 3d edit., 1994, Women, Biology and Public Policy, 1985, The Political Integration of Women: Roles, Socialization and Politics, 1983, A Vindication of Political Virtue: The Political Theory of Mary Wollstonecraft, 1992; contbr. articles to profl. jours. Mem. bd. trustees Clark U., Worcester, Mass., 2001—. CIC Academic Leadership fellowship, 2003-04. Mem. Am. Acad. Arts and Scis., Am. Polit. Sci. Assn. (v.p. 1999-2000, pres. sect. elections, pub. opinion, voting behavior), Midwest Polit. Sci. Assn. (exec. coun. 1984-86), Internat. Soc. Polit. Psychology (governing coun. 1988-90, 2000-03), Phi Beta Kappa. Office: Univ Wisconsin 117 Bascom Mall 500 Lincoln Dr Madison WI 53706-1380 Office Phone: 608-262-5246. Office Fax: 608-265-3353. E-mail: vsapiro@wisc.edu.

SAPP, BRENDA, elementary school educator; b. Fuquay-Vanna, NC, Oct. 12, 1945; d. Isaac Sr. and Bertha Bell Sapp. BA in Social Studies, St. Augustine's Coll., Raleigh, NC, 1972; MEd cum laude, NC Ctrl. U., Durham, 1995. Reading tchr. Wake County Pub. Schs., Raleigh; part-time reading tchr. Holly Springs Elem. Sch., NC. Recipient Swift Creek Tchr. of Yr., Wake County Pub. Schs., 1999, Leadership award, Nat. Coun. Negro Women, 1993; grantee, Wake County. Mem.: NC Ret. Tchrs. Assn., Internat. Reading Assn. Democrat. Avocations: reading, gardening, poetry. Home: PO Box 1185 Apex NC 27502-3185

SAPP, EVA JO, writer, editor, educator; b. San Antonio, Feb. 4, 1944; d. Herschel Barnhill Jr. and Ada Rasdon; m. David Paul Sapp, July 6, 1968; children: Lesley Jeanne, Michael David. BA in English with honors, U. Mo., 1976, MA in English, 1982, postgrad., 1985. Assoc. editor Mo. Rev., Columbia, 1978-97; lectr. U. Mo., Columbia, 1985-87; instr. UCLA, 1999—. Editl. cons. Martin Luther King Jr. Program, Columbia, 1993; cons. Internat. Islamic U., Petaling Jaya, Malaysia, 1995; bd. dirs. CAT3 TV. Co-editor: (online) Mo. Rev. Online, 1986-88; (book) The Best of Missouri Review, 1992, Conversations with American Novelists, 1997; contbg. author: Norton Anthology of Short Fiction, 1994. Membership chair Arts & Crafts Guild Kuala Lumpur, Malaysia, 1994—95; coord. Boone County Clinton/Gore Vols., Columbia, 1996; mem. Boone County Hist. Soc., 1997—, Daniel Boone Regional Libr. Bd., 1998—, pres., 2000—, maintenance chair, 2003—; v.p. Columbia Pub. Libr., 1999—; chair Columbia Commn. on the Arts, 1988—93; pres. Columbia Pub. Libr. Bd., 2001—02; Editor Boone County Dems., Columbia, 1990—91; events coord. Vogt for Congress, Mo., 1998; v.p. publicity Boone County Dem. Women, 1998—99; 1st. v.p. League of Women Voters, Columbia-Boone County, 2003; mem. Mo. League of Women Voters governing bd., 2003; pres. League of Women Voters, Columbia-Boone County, 2004—. Recipient Creative Artists Project award Mo. Arts Coun., 1988, Author Recognition award Mo. Ctr. Book, 1993. Mem. LWV (pres. Columbia-Boone County chpt. 2004—, chmn. libr. boundries study 2003-05), Boone County Muleskinners (editor newsletter 1990-91). Home: 1025 Hickory Hill Dr Columbia MO 65203-2322 Personal E-mail: djsapp2@yahoo.com.

SAPP, GINA LEANN, music educator; b. Chillicothe, Mo., Dec. 6, 1964; d. Marvin Lee and Shirley Ann Arbuckle; m. Jeffrey Dean Sapp, Sept. 7, 1991. B in Music Edn., Mid Am. Nazarene U., Olathe, Kans., 1989; M in Music Edn., U. Mo., Kansas City, 2005. Cert. K-12 vocal/instrumental music tchr. Kans., Mo. Music educator K-5 Kans. City (Mo.) Sch. Dist., 1990—94; music educator K-6 Shawnee Mission Sch. Dist., Prairie Village, Kans., 1994—. Mem. faculty adv. com., student coun. sponsor Leroy Satchel Paige Classical Greek Magnet, Kansas City, 1992—93; AAA safety patrol sponsor Briarwood Elem., Prairie Village, 1994—99, mem. quality performance accreditation reading com., 6th grade musical co-dir., 5th and 6th grade choral dir., 1994—; East Area Choral Festival chairperson Shawnee Mission Sch. Dist., 2000; Lyric Opera Express in conjunction with 5th grade choir participants Lyric Opera, Kansas City, Mo., 1994—. Active Project WILD, Pratt, Kans., 1997, Borders Book Benefit for Edn., Overland Park, Kans., 2002, 2004, Johnson County and Shawnee Mission East H.S. Earth Day Fair, Prairie Village, 2003—05; worship team soprano singer Westside Family Ch., Shawnee, Kans., 2001—03. Recipient Outstanding United Way Student Campaign award tchr. sponsor, 2003; grantee, Shawnee Mission Sch. Dist., 2003, 2005. Mem.: NEA, Music Educators Nat. Conf., Nat. Riviera Owners Assn., Nat. Gran Sport Club Am., Nat. Buick Club Am., Phi Delta Lambda, Phi Theta Kappa, Pi Kappa Lambda. Avocations: antiques, Victorian architecture photography, classic automobiles, motorcycling, travel. Business E-Mail: ginasapp@smsd.org.

SAPP, NANCY L., director; b. Joplin, Mo., July 22, 1951; d. Jim L. and Leah (Smith) Hayes; children: Michael A., Julie D. B in Music Edn., Pittsburg (Kans.) State U., 1973; MEd in Psychology, Wichita State U.; cert. in elem./secondary sch. adminstrn., Emporia State U., 1994. Cert. elem./secondary vocal/instrumental music tchr., learning disabled tchr., behavior disorder tchr., adminstr., dist. level adminstrn. dir. spl. edn. Vocal and instrumental music instr., Cherokee, Kans., 1973-75, Holy Cross Grade Sch., Hutchinson, Kans., 1980-85, Trinity H.S., Hutchinson, 1980-82; learning disabilities tchr. Unified Sch. Dist. # 308, Hutchinson, 1987-89, behavior disorder tchr., 1989-95, behavior cons., 1990-95; asst. sch. prin. Unified Sch. Dist. 308, Hutchinson, 1995-97; prin., coord. student svcs. Unified Sch. Dist. 443, Dodge City, Kans., 1997-99; asst. dir. spl. edn. Southwest Kans. Area Coop. Dist., Dodge City, 1999—. Prin. second violin Hutchinson Symphony, 1991-97; pres. exec. bd. Hutchinson Regional Youth Symphony, 1994-95; bd. dirs. Reno Choral Soc., Kans. Youth Soc. Grantee Southwestern Bell Tel., Hutchinson, 1992. Mem. Internat. Reading Assn., NEA, Kans. NEA, Kans. Reading Assn., Hutchinson NEA (bldg. rep. 1992-94), Ark Valley Reading Assn. (pres. 1994-95), Phi Delta Kappa. Republican. Methodist. Avocations: theater, music, cross stitch, quilting. Home: 108 La Vista Blvd Dodge City KS 67801-2848

SAPP, PEGGY G., pastor, editor, writer, speech professional; d. Arthur Charles and Mae Belle (Graves) Gibby; m. Roger W. Sapp, Sr., Sept. 4, 1965 (dec.); children: Roger Warren II, LaDonna Hope Sapp Ranke, Jonathan T., Angela Faith Sapp Little. Degree in Bus. Adminstrn., Marsh Bus. Coll., Atlanta, 1963; degree in Theology/Missions, Pentecostal Bible Inst., Jackson, Miss., 1966; degree in Bus. Adminstrn., Mid. Ga. Coll., Cochran, 1968; degree in Theology, Moody Bible Inst., Chgo., 1985. Dean students Inst. Biblical Studies, Dublin, Ga., 1978—83; radio bible tchr. Voice of Truth Ministries, Dublin, 1985—, Bible instr.-tchr., 1985—; adminstr. Ch. Jesus Christ Christian Sch., Dublin, 1986—94; editor Ch. Jesus Christ Orgn., Kingsport, Tenn., 1991—, ordained minister, 1971—, motivational spkr., 1991—; sr. pastor Ch. Jesus Christ Full Gospel, Dublin, 1994—; cert. correctional assoc. Johnson State Prison, Wrightsville, Ga., 2000—, spkr., counselor, 2000—. Author: (books) Anointed Leadership Series, 1985, Institute of Biblical Studies, 1994, (periodical) The Broken Vessel, 2001;

editor: (mag. periodicals) The Messenger, 1991. Mem.: Assn. Christian Counselors. Achievements include assisted in providing curriculum for founding of Inst. Biblical Studies, Cebu, Philippines. Office: Ch Jesus Christ Full Gospel 759 Vernon Woodard Rd Dublin GA 31027

SAPP, R. LACHANZE See LACHANZE

SAPPENFIELD, MAEDEANE L., piano and organ educator; b. Belmond, Iowa, Nov. 1, 1927; d. Henry Gerhard and Lucille Bernice (Legge) Mennenga; m. David Reddick Sappenfield, May 14, 1948 (dec. Apr. 1997); children: Valoris Jane, Linda Jo-Anne, David Clark. Lic. pvt. pilot. Sec. at airport Bram Air Svc., Clarion, Iowa, 1947-48; sec. to sec. C. of C., Clarion, 1948-49; sales, demonstrator, tchr. Jones Piano and Organs, Mason City, Iowa, 1970-85. Tchr. piano and organ. Composer organ solo (state winner Adult Composer, Fed. Music Club 1987). Leaders chair Campfire Girls Am., Belmond, 1959-61; pres. Women's Missionary Fedn., Belmond, 1963-64; pres. Luth. Ch. Women, Osage, Iowa, 1967-69, sec. Mason City conf., 1970-75; organist various chs., presently at Ch. of Christ Scientist, Clear Lake, Iowa. Mem. Music Tchrs. Nat. Assn., North Iowa Music Tchrs., Matinee Musicale Club (pres. 1989-90), Am. Guild Organists (dean 1975-78). Avocations: creative design/sewing, composing, photography, gourmet cooking. Home: One S Taylor Mason City IA 50401

SAPPINGTON, SHARON ANNE, retired school librarian; b. West Palm Beach, Fla., Sept. 15, 1944; d. A.D. and Laura G. (Jackson) Chambless; m. Andrew Arnold Sappington III, June 11, 1966; children: Andrew Arnold IV, Kevin Sean. Student, Fla. So. Coll., 1962—64; BA in Edn., U. Fla., 1966; postgrad., U. Ala., 1980. Tchr. 5th grade Tates Creek Elem., Lexington, Ky., 1966—68; tchr. 4th grade Sadieville Elem., Ky., 1968—69; libr. media specialist A.H. Watwood Elem., Childersburg, Ala., 1980—98, ret., 1998. Guest storyteller Young Author's Conf., Winterboro, Lincoln, Sylacauga, and Fayetteville, Ala., 1982-94; vis. com. Southeastern Accreditation Assn.; program presenter Internat. Reading Assn., Birmingham, Ala., 1983; guest spkr. rare children's books By the Way TV talk show, 1983; pres. Tale Tellers of St. Augustine, 2003—05; chmn. RSVP Read Aloud Program, 2002-04. Creator, presenter: (slide presentation) Tellers of Tales and Sketchers of Dreams, 1983, (multimedia programs) Dinosaurs, Teddy Bears, and Wild Things, 1990, Shanghaied in the Beijing Airport, 1994. Circle chmn., Sunday tchr. Grace United Meth. Ch., Birmingham, 1973, 92-95; delivery mem. Meals on Wheels, Birmingham, 1975-76; radio reader for the blind WBHM Pub. Broadcasting, Birmingham, 1980; guest spkr., program presenter Jaycees, Kiwanis, and C. of C., Childersburg, 1993-94. Grantee Title I grantee, 1991, Stutz Bearcat grantee, 1992. Mem. AAUW (lit. chmn. St. Augustine chpt., 2005-), ALA, Internat. Platform Assn., Am. Assn. Sch. Librs., Ala. Libr. Assn. (children's and sch. divsn. publicity chmn. 1991-93, chmn. Nat. Libr. Week in Ala. 1993-94, Outstanding Youth Svcs. award 1989), People to People Internat. (libr. del. to China 1993), Kappa Delta Pi. Democrat. Methodist. Avocation: book collecting. Home: 5131 Shore Dr Saint Augustine FL 32086-6473

SARA, ELIZABETH CLORINDA, marketing professional; b. NYC, Mar. 19, 1957; d. Robert and Joan Nanni. BA in Comms., SUNY, 1979; MA in Journalism, U. Md., 1980. Chief mktg. officer Info. Industry Assn., Washington, 1984-86, Mead Data Ctrl./Lexis Nexis, Washington, 1986-88; dir. corp. mktg. UPI, Washington, 1988-90; pub. rels. counsel America Online, Vienna, Va., 1991-92; co-founder, v.p. mktg. Space Works, Rockville, Md., 1993—2001; mng. dir. Best Mktg., Washington, 2001—. Founding mem. organizing bd. No. Va. Tech. Coun., CEO Mindshare, Vienna, Va., 1997—. Mem. editl. adv. bd. Potomac Tech Jour. Vice chmn. Summer Opera Theatre Co., 2000—; adv. bd. mem. Leap Frog, Inc., 2000—, INFE, Inc., 2000—. Mem. Am. Electronics Assn. (exec. com. Potomac Coun. 1999). Republican. Roman Catholic. Avocations: theater, arts, international travel, gourmet cooking. Home: The Watergate 700 New Hampshire Ave NW Washington DC 20037

SARACHIK, MYRIAM PAULA MORGENSTEIN, physics professor, condensed matter physicist; b. Antwerp, Belgium, Aug. 8, 1933; arrived in US, 1947; d. Solomon and Sarah (Segal) Morgenstein; m. Philip Sarachik, Sept. 6, 1954; 1 child, Karen Beth. AB, Barnard Coll., 1954; MS, Columbia U., 1957, PhD, 1960. Rsch. assoc. IBM Watson Labs., Columbia U., N.Y.C., 1960-61; mem. tech. staff Bell Telephone Labs., Murray Hill, NJ, 1962-64; asst. prof. physics CCNY (CUNY), 1964-67, assoc. prof., 1967-70, prof., 1971—, Disting. prof. physics, 1995—. Advisor NSF, NRC. Contbr. articles to profl. jours. Recipient NYC Mayor's award for excellence in sci. and tech., 1995, Sloan Pub. Svc. award, 2004, Oliver E. Buckley prize in Condensed Matter Physics, 2005, L'Oreal/UNESCO for Women in Sci. (N.Am.) Laureate, 2005. Fellow AAAS, Am. Phys. Soc. (pres. 2003), N.Y. Acad. Scis.; mem. NAS, Am. Acad. Arts and Scis. Office: CCNY (CUNY) Divsn Sci MR429 Physics Dept Convent Ave and 138 St New York NY 10031 Office Phone: 212-650-5618. Business E-Mail: sarachik@sci.ccny.cuny.edu.

SARACHO, TANYA SELENE, performing company executive, playwright; d. Ramiro Alfonso Saracho and Rosalina Armenta; life ptnr. Malik Ahmad Carroll. BFA, Boston U., 1998. Co-artistic dir. Teatro Luna, Chgo., 2000—. Author: (plays) Kita y Fernanda, 2003. Recipient runner-up, METLife Nuestras Voces Playwriting Competition, 2003, Ofner prize, Goodman Theatre, 2005. Mem.: AFTRA, SAG. Office: Teatro Luna Ste 210 5215 N Ravenswood Chicago IL 60640 E-mail: teatroluna@aol.com.

SARAH, PEARSON LYNN, elementary school educator; b. Altoona, Pa., June 23, 1982; d. Lynn Robert and Mary Jo Pearson. B, Ind. U. of Pa. 5th grade tchr., Culpepper, Va. Mem. salary & benefits com., Culpepper, 2004—05; extended day tchr., tutor, Culpepper, 2004—05. Mem.: NEA, Pa. Sci. Edn. Assn., Va. Edn. Assn., Kappa Delta Pi. Roman Catholic. Home: 316 Dennison Ct Culpeper VA 22701 Office: Emerald Hill Elem 11245 Rixeyville Rd Culpeper VA 22701

SARALEGUI, CRISTINA MARIA, Spanish language television personality, journalist; b. Havana, Cuba, Jan. 29, 1948; came to U.S., 1960; d. Francisco and Cristina (Santamarina) Saralegui; m. Marcos Avila, June 19, 1984; 3 children. Student mass comm., U. Miami. Features editor Vanidades Continental, Miami, Fla., 1970-73; editor Cosmopolitan Spanish, Miami, 1973-76, editor-in-chief, 1979-89; dir. enterntainment Miami Herald, 1976-77; editor-in-chief Intimidades mag., Miami, 1977-79, TV y Novelas mag., 1986-89; hostess The Cristina Show Univision Network, 1989—; publisher Cristina the Magazine; hostess Cristina Opina, ABC radio program. Keynote spkr. Union Am. Women, P.R., 1981, Legendary Women of Miami. Featured in bestseller Latin Beauty, 1982; author autobiography My Life as a Blonde, 1998. Mem. internat. jury Miss Venezuela Pagent, 1982, Miss Columbia Pagent, 1987; bd. dir. Nat. Council of La Raza, Mus. TV & Radio; mem Nat. Council, AmFar. Recipient 10 Emmy awards; Keys to City Cartagena, Colombia, 1987; award of Distinction for Leadership, AmFar, 1995; Outstanding Communicator of the Year award, Nat. Org. for Women in Comm., 1996; Star on the Walk of Fame, 1999; Cmty. Svc. award, Nat. Council La Raza, 2000; Corp. Leader award, Nat. Network of Hispanic Women; VIP Honoree of the Year, Am. Cancer Soc., 2000; Gracie Allen Tribute award, Found. of Am. Women in radio & TV, 2001; Lifetime Achievement award, Imagen Found., 2002. Named one of the 25 Most Influential Hispanics, Time Mag., 2005. Mem. NAFE, Women in Comm. (key note spkr. 1986), Am. Soc. Profl. and Exec. Women, Am. Mgmt. Assn., Nat. Network Hispanic Women (Corp. Leader award), Latin Bus. and Profl. Women's Club. Republican. Roman Catholic. Office: The Christina Show 9405 NW 41st St Miami FL 33178-2301

SARANA, SHIREE, writer; b. L.A., Dec. 15, 1965; d. Annette (Lang) Rockey. Student, U. So. Calif., 1984-85, Santa Monica Jr. Coll., 1985-87. Featured poet Anansi Writers Workshop, 1993, Watts Summer Festival, 1994, Santa Monica Jr. Coll., 1995, Eso Won Bookstore, 1996, No Holds Barred Writer's Series, 1996, Jazz Speak, 1996. Author: Essence of Life, 1993, Mighty Is the Blackness, 1993; contbr. poems to profl. publs. Recipient 1st Pl. Short Story award U. Calif., Santa Barbara, 1983, Hon. Mention award U. Calif., Santa Barbara, 1984, Tommy award U.So. Calif., 1985, Best New Poet award Am. Poetry Anthology, 1985-87. Mem.: Acad. Am. Poets.

SARANAC, WINNIE B., special education educator; b. N.Y.C., Jan. 30, 1929; d. Jack and Pauline (Weisman) Brokaw; m. George Eugene Saranac, Sept. 30, 1949; 1 dau., Paula Beth. B.S. in Journalism, Ohio U., 1949; M.S., C.W. Post Coll., 1978. Tchr. Farmingdale Schs., N.Y., 1969-78, tchr. spl. edn., 1978—. Mem. Spl. Edn. Parent-Tchr. Assn., Theta Sigma Phi. Avocations: skiing; tennis; biking; traveling.

SARANDON, SUSAN ABIGAIL, actress; b. NYC, Oct. 4, 1946; d. Phillip Leslie and Lenora Marie (Criscione) Tomalin; m. Chris Sarandon, Sept. 16, 1967 (div. 1979); children: Eva Maria Livia Amurri, Jack Henry Robbins, Miles Guthrie Robbins. BA in Drama and English, Cath. U. Am., 1968. Actress: (plays) include An Evening with Richard Nixon, 1972, A Coupla White Chicks Sittin' Around Talkin', 1980-81, A Stroll in the Air, Albert's Bridge, Private Ear, Public Eye, Extremities, 1982, (films) Joe, 1970, Lady Liberty, 1972, The Rocky Horror Picture Show, 1975, Lovin' Molly, 1974, The Front Page, 1974, The Great Waldo Pepper, 1975, Dragon Fly, 1976, Crash, 1976, The Other Side of Midnight, 1977, The Last of the Cowboys, 1978, Checkered Flag or Crash, 1978, Pretty Baby, 1978, King of the Gypsies, 1978, Something Short of Paradise, 1979, Loving Couples, 1980, Atlantic City, 1980 (Prix Genie Best Fgn. Actress award 1981, Acad. award nominee 1981), Tempest, 1982 (Best Actress award Venice Film Festival 1982), The Hunger, 1983, Buddy System, 1984, Compromising Positions, 1985, The Witches of Eastwick, 1987, Bull Durham, 1988, Sweet Hearts Dance, 1988, A Dry White Season, 1989, The January Man, 1989, White Palace, 1990, Thelma and Louise, 1991 (Acad. award nominee for best actress 1992, Golden Globe award nominee 1992), The Player, 1992, Light Sleeper, 1992, Bob Roberts, 1992, Lorenzo's Oil, 1992 (Acad. award nominee 1993), The Client, 1994 (Acad. award nominee for best actress), Little Women, 1994, Safe Passage, 1994, Dead Man Walking, 1995 (Golden Globe award nominee for best actress 1996, Acad. award for best actress 1996), James and the Giant Peach (voice), 1996, 187 (voice), 1997, Illuminata, 1998, Twilight, 1998, Stepmom (also producer), 1998, Joe Gould's Secret, 1999, Baby's in Black, 1999, Cradle Will Rock, 1999, Anywhere But Here, 1999, (voice) Rugrats in Paris: The Movie - Rugrats II, 2000, Moonlight Mile, 2002 (also exec. prodr.), The Banger Sisters, 2002, Igby Goes Down, 2002, Noel, 2004, Shall We Dance?, 2004, Alfie, 2004, Jiminy Glick in La La Wood, 2004, Elizabethtown, 2005; TV appearances: The Haunting of Rosalind, 1973, F. Scott Fitzgerald and The Last of the Belles, 1974, Who Am I This Time, 1982, A.D., 1985, Mussolini: The Decline and Fall of Il Duce, 1985, Earthly Possessions, 1999, Friends, 2001 (Emmy nominee), Malcolm in the Middle, 2002 (Emmy nominee), Ice Bound, 2003., The Exonerated, 2005; (TV series) A World Apart, 1970-71, Search for Tomorrow, 1972-73; TV miniseries: Children of Dune, 2003. Mem. AFTRA, Screen Actors Guild, Actors Equity, Acad. Motion Picture Arts and Scis., NOW, MADRE, Amnesty Internat., ACLU Office: Internat Creative Mgmt care Samuel Cohen 40 W 57th St New York NY 10019-4001

SARD, SUSANNAH ELLEN, non-profit executive; b. Boston, May 10, 1944; d. Russell Ellis and Miriam Clark Sard. AB, Bryn Mawr Coll., 1966. Devel. adminstr. Ky. Ednl. TV, Lexington, 1978—88; dir. found. and corp. rels. Sarah Lawrence Coll., Bronxville, NY, 1991—96; dir. devel. The Town Hall, NYC, 1998—2002; exec. dir. Women's City Club NY, NYC, 2002—04; edn. liaison R.J. & S.H. Kaplan Family Found., NYC, 2004—. Alumni bd. Rippowam Cisqua Sch. Mem.: Blue Hill Troupe. Office: Kaplan Family Found 866 UN Plz Ste 306 New York NY 10017 Business E-Mail: owlkap@aol.com.

SARDI, ELAINE MARIE, special education educator; b. Shippenville, Pa., Dec. 2, 1952; d. Willis Henry and Genevieve Evelyn (Hanby) Etzel; m. Michael James Sardi, Dec. 28, 1974; children: Jason Michael, Justin James. BS in Spl. Edn., Clarion State Coll., 1974; MEd in Reading, Clarion U., 1991. Tchr. spl. edn. North Clarion Sch. Dist., Leeper, Pa., 1974-75, Riverview Intermediate Unit, Shippenville, 1986-92; tchr. learning support Keystone H.S., Knox, Pa., 1992-97; lead tchr. Riverview Intermediate Unit, Shippenville, 1991-92; cross-categorical tchr. Louisburg (N.C.) H.S. Franklin County Sch. Sys., 1998; learning disabilities specialist Wake Tech. C.C., Raleigh, NC, 1998—2004, learning disabilities/ADD coord., 2005—. Clin. field supr. Clarion (Pa.) U., 1988-97; Lamaze instr. Clarion Orgn. Parent Edn., 1976-83; mentor tchr. Keystone Sch. Dist., 1993-94. Sunday sch. tchr. 1st United Meth. Ch., Clarion, 1977-86; treas. Clarion County Spl. Olympics, 1986-93. Mem. DAR, Nat. Coun. Tchrs. English, Coun. Exceptional Children, Internat. Reading Assn., Learning Disabilities Assn. Wake County, Daus. Union Vets., Kappa Delta Pi. Republican. Avocations: reading, cooking, travel. Home: 8812 Valley Springs Pl Raleigh NC 27615-8120 Office Phone: 919-662-3407. Business E-Mail: emsardi@waketech.edu.

SARGENT, ANNEILA ISABEL, astrophysicist; b. Kirkcaldy, Fife, Scotland; came to US, 1964; d. Richard Anthony and Annie (Blaney) Cassells; m. Wallace Leslie William Sargent, Aug. 5, 1964; children: Lindsay Eleanor, Alison Clare. BSc with honors in Physics, U. Edinburgh, 1963; MS, Calif. Inst. Tech., 1967, PhD in Astronomy, 1977. Postdoctoral rsch. fellow Calif. Inst. Tech., Pasadena, 1977-80, mem. profl. staff, 1980-88, sr. rsch. fellow, 1988-90, sr. rsch. assoc., 1990—98; assoc. dir. Owens Valley Radio Obs., 1992—96, exec. dir., 1996—98, dir., 1998—, prof., assoc. dir. 1998—, Benjamin M. Rosen prof. astronomy, 2004—. Dir. Michelson Interferometry Sci Ctr., 2000—03, dir. combined array for rsch. in millimeter wave astronomy, 2003—. Contbr. articles to profl. jours. Recipient NASA Pub. Svc. medal, 1998, Alumna of Yr., U. Edinburgh, 2002; grantee, NASA, NSF. Fellow Am. Acad. Arts & Scis.; Mem. Royal Astron. Soc. (assoc.), Am. Astron. Soc. (pres. 2000-02), Internat. Astron. Union Roman Catholic. Office: Dept Astronomy Calif Inst Tech MC 105-24 1200 E Calif Blvd Pasadena CA 91125 E-mail: afs@astro.caltech.edu.*

SARGENT, ARLENE ANNE, nursing educator; b. Little Falls, Minn, Jan. 11, 1944; d. Anton Clarence and Eleanor Anne (Buerman) Hondl; m. Ken William Sargent, June 16, 1972; children: Lisa, Michelle. BSN, Coll. St. Catherine, 1969; MSN, U. Minn., 1972; EdD, No. Ill. U., 1980. Staff nurse U. Wash., Seattle, 1969-70, U. Minn. Hosp., Mpls., 1970-72; instr. Loyola U., Chgo., 1972-75; asst. prof. U. Dubuque, Iowa, 1975-76, assoc. prof., chairperson, 1976-79; assoc. prof. No. Ill. U., DeKalb, 1979-83; prof., chairperson Holy Names Coll., Oakland, Calif., 1983-98; assoc. dean St. Mary's-Samuel Merritt Intercollegiate Nursing Program, Oakland, Calif., 1999—2004, dean nursing program, 2000—04; mng. dir. for edn. and workforce Kaiser Permanente, Oakland, Calif., 2004—. Bd. mem. Calif. Strategic Planning Commn., 1993—. Mem. Sigma Theta Tau (mem. heritage com. 1994—), Pi Lambda Theta, Kappa Delta Pi. Presbyterian. Avocations: playing piano, hiking. Office: Samuel Merritt Coll 435 Hawthorne Ave Oakland CA 94609 E-mail: asargent@samuelmerritt.edu, sargentak@earthlink.net.

SARGENT, JANE DIANE ROBERTSON, mathematician, educator; b. Savannah, Ga., Jan. 9, 1942; d. Augustus John Robertson III and Jayne Evelyn (Winter) Robertson; m. George Blackburn Sargent, Aug. 14, 1976; 1 child, Debra Paige. AA, Orlando Jr. Coll., 1962; B in Gen. Studies, Rollins Coll., 1970; specialist in Edn., Ga. Coll. & State U., 1991, MEd, 1977. Cert. tchr. Fla., 1963, Tchr. Ga., 1972. Tchr. St. Mary Magdalen, Altamonte Springs, Fla., 1963—72, Lakeview Acad., Gainesville, Ga., 1972—76; middle sch. sci. tchr. Gatewood Acad., Eatonton, Ga., 1976—85; 7th grade math. & sci. tchr. John Millege Acad., Milledgeville, Ga., 1985—87; 6th grade math. tchr. Ga. Military Coll., Milledgeville, 1987—, team leader 6th grade, 2004—05, chair mid. sch. math., 2004—05. Instr. Ga. Coll. & State U., Milledgeville, 1991—2000; mem. Ga. Coun. Math. Tchrs., 1995—. Pres. Am. Heart Assn., Baldwin County, Ga., 1983—85, Pink Ladies Baldwin County Hosp., Milledgeville, 1978—82, Dem. Women, Baldwin County, 1980—. Named Tchr. of the News, Channel One News, N.Y., 1999. Mem.: AAUW (pres. 1988—2001, state sec. 1988—2001), Ga. Mid. Sch. Assn., Delta Kappa Gamma (treas. 1995—2000). Democrat. Roman Catholic. Avocations: reading, travel, volunteer work. Home: 215 Lakeshore Dr Milledgeville GA 31061 Office: Ga Military Coll Middle School 201 E Greene Str Milledgeville GA 31061 Office Phone: 478-445-2724.

SARGENT, MOLLY ANNE, literature and language educator; b. Redding, Calif., June 19, 1958; d. Jack Eldon and Marjorie Joyce Beebe; m. James Marshall Sargent, May 31, 1981; children: Wendy Moullet, Paul, Mary. BA in Comms., Biola U., La Mirada, Calif., 1980. Cert. tchr. Calif., Assn. Christian Schs. Publicist, journalism tchr. Victory Christian Sch., Carlsbad, Calif., 1980—84; English tchr. Capistrano Valley Christian HS, San Juan Capistrano, Calif., 1984—88, Whittier Christian HS, La Habra, Calif., 1990—92; 7th grade core tchr. Hawthorn Christian Sch., Fountain Valley, Calif., 1988—90; chmn. English dept., girls counselor Fresno Christian HS, Calif., 1993—. Office: Fresno Christian Sch 7280 N Cedar Ave Fresno CA 93720-3633

SARGENT, PAMELA, writer; b. Ithaca, N.Y., Mar. 20, 1948; BA, SUNY, Binghamton, 1968, MA, 1970. Mng. editor, Binghamton, 1970-73; asst. editor, 1973-75; Am. editor Bull. Sci. Fiction Writers Am., Johnson City, NY, 1983-91. Author: Cloned Lives, 1976, Starshadows, 1977, The Sudden Star, 1979, Watchstar, 1980, The Golden Space, 1982, The Alien Upstairs, 1983, Earthseed, 1983, Eye of the Comet, 1984, Homesmind, 1984, Venus of Dreams, 1986, The Shore of Women, 1986, The Best of Pamela Sargent, 1987, Alien Child, 1988, Venus of Shadows, 1988, Ruler of the Sky, 1993 (Nebula best novelette award 1992, Locus best novelette award 1993, Electric Sci. Fiction award 1993), Climb the Wind: A Novel of Another America, 1999, (with Ron Miller) Firebrands: The Heroines of Science Fiction and Fantasy, 1998, Child of Venus, 2001, Behind the Eyes of Dreamers and Other Short Novels, 2002, The Mountain Cage and Other Stories, 2002, Eye of Flame: Fantasies, 2003, Thumbprints, 2004; editor: (anthology) Women of Wonder, 1975, Bio-Futures, 1976, More Women of Wonder, 1976, The New Women of Wonder, 1978, (with Ian Watson) Afterlives, 1986, Women of Wonder, The Classic Years, 1996, Women of Wonder, The Contemporary Years, 1995, Nebula Awards 29, 1995, Nebula Awards 30, 1996, Nebula Awards 31, 1997, Conqueror Fantastic, 2004. Office: care Richard Curtis Assocs Inc 171 E 74th St New York NY 10021-3221 Personal E-mail: psdel2003@yahoo.com, pamsargent@gmail.com.

SARICKS, JOYCE GOERING, librarian; b. Nov. 8, 1948; d. Joe W. and Lovella Goering; m. Christopher L. Saricks, Aug. 21, 1971; children: Brendan James, Margaret Katherine. BA with highest distinction in English and German, U. Kans., 1970; MA in Comparative Lit., U. Wis., 1971; MA/MAT in LS, U. Chgo., 1977. Reference librarian Downers Grove Pub. Library, Ill., 1977-80, head tech. svcs., 1980-83, coord. lit. and audio svcs., 1983—2004; ret., 2004. Columnist Booklist Mag.; adj. prof. Dominican U., River Forest, Ill; lectr., presenter workshops in field. Author: (with Nancy Brown) Readers' Advisory Service in the Public Library, 1989, revised edit., 1997, 3d edit., 2005, The Readers' Advisory Guide to Genre Fiction, 2001. Mem. Read Ill. adv. com., 1990-91. Woodrow Wilson fellow, 1970; recipient Allie Beth Martin award Pub. Library Assn., 1989, No. Ill. Libr. of Yr. award Windy City Romance Writers, 1995, Libr. of the Yr. award Romance Writers of Am., 2000. Mem. ALA, Ill. Library Assn., Adult Reading Round Table (founder), Phi Beta Kappa, Delta Phi Alpha, Pi Lambda Theta, Beta Phi Mu. Home: 1116 61st St Downers Grove IL 60516-1819 E-mail: saricksj@juno.com.

SARINANA, SILVIA, art educator; b. Mexico City, Aug. 12, 1954; came to U.S., 1989; d. Carlos and Sara Carmela (Flores) Sarinana. Interpreter, translator, Berlitz Sch. Langs., Mexico City, 1973; TESOL, U. Autonoma de Mexico, Mexico City, 1978; BA in Edn., Incarnate Word Coll., 1993; MA in Edn., Tex. Tech. U., 1998. Lic. art tchr. Interpretation and transl. instr. Berlitz Sch. Langs., Mexico City, 1973-74; H.S. English tchr. Ignacio L. Vallarta H.S., Mexico City, 1976-82; head elem. English dept. Colegio del Bosque, Mexico City, 1984-87, head jr. H.S. English/Spanish dept., 1987-89; tchr. art St. Luke's Episcopal Sch., San Antonio, 1993—. Roman Catholic. Avocations: collage, ceramics. Office: St Lukes Episcopal Sch 15 Saint Lukes Ln San Antonio TX 78209-4445 Home: 3459 Monterrey Oak San Antonio TX 78230-2597

SARIS, PATTI BARBARA, federal judge; b. 1951; BA magna cum laude, Radcliffe Coll., 1973; JD cum laude, Harvard U., 1976. Law clerk to Hon. Robert Braucher Mass. Supreme Judicial Ct., 1976-77; atty. Foley Hoag & Eliot, Boston, 1977-79; staff counsel U.S. Senate Judiciary Com., 1979-81; atty. Berman Dittmar & Engel, Boston, 1981-82; chief civil divsn. U.S. Atty.'s Office, 1984-86; U.S. magistrate judge U.S. Dist. Ct. Mass., 1986-89; assoc. justice Mass. Superior Ct., 1989-94; dist. judge U.S. Dist. Ct. Mass., 1994—. Bd. overseers, chair com. on defender svcs. judicial conf. Harvard. Bd. trustees Beth Israel Hosp.; active Wexner Heritage Found. Recipient award Haskell J. Cohn Disting. Jud. Svc. award Boston Bar Assn.; Nat. Merit scholar, 1969. Mem.: Phi Beta Kappa. Office: US Courthouse Courthouse Way Ste 6130 Boston MA 02210

SARKISIAN, CHERILYN See CHER

SARKISIAN, PAMELA OUTLAW, artist; b. Spokane, Sept. 26, 1941; d. Willard Clinton and Frances (Montieth) Outlaw; m. Ronald Edward Sarkisian, Nov. 11, 1960; children: Ronald Abraham, Michelle Suzanne. Grad. h.s., Stockton, Calif. Art student, Oceanside, Calif., 1972-80; founder Palette 'N Easel Studio, Oceanside, 1980—2005, operator, mgr., 1980—2005, art tchr. in residence, 1985—; ret., 2004. Publisher greeting cards Polytint, Ltd., Eng., 1995, 96; fine art prints pub. by Bentley House, Ltd., Walnut Creek, Calif., 1994-97. Designer collector plate series Danbury Mint/MBI, Inc., gift items Enesco Internat. Gift Co.; represented by Casay Gallery, Kailau, Kona, Hawaii, 1991, Galeria Jean Lammelin, Paris, 1991, 2d St. Gallery, Encinitas, Calif., 1991, Blondes Gallery, San Diego, 1992, Valentine-Owens Gallery, Santa Monica, Calif., 1992, Sodarco Gallery, Montreal, 1993, Surtex, 1993, Jacob G. Javity Conv. Ctr., NYC, 1993, Laura Larkin Gallery, Del Mar, Calif., 1993-94, Charles Hecht Galleries, Tarzana and Palm Desert, Calif., 1993-96, Lou Martin Gallery, Laguna Beach, Calif., 1994, Charles Hecht Gallery, La Jolla, Calif., 1995-96, Calif. Art Gallery, Laguna Beach, 1996, Hunter Gallery, Tucson, 1996, Cottage Gallery at Carmel, Calif., 1996, Dy'ans-Branham Gallery, Laguna Beach, 1997-99, Aka'mai Gallery, Del Mar, 1998-99, Gallery Adrienne, La Jolla, 1998, Cosmopolitan Gallery, La Jolla, 1998-99, The Lillian Berkley Collection, Escondido, Calif., 1999-2003, Waters Edge Gallery, Rancho Mirage, Calif., 2003; one-woman shows include AKA Mai Gallery, 1999, Lillian Berkeley Collection, 2001, Four Seasons-Aviara, La Costa, Calif., 2001, Waters Edge Gallery, Rancho Mirage, 2003, Calix Gallery, 2005. Pres. Zonta Internat., Oceanside, 1980-81; mem. Emblem Club #177, Oceanside, 1971-2003; princess Daughters of the Nile, San Diego, 1974; bd. dirs. Oceanside Girls Club, 1980. Recipient 1st Pl. award San Dieguito Art Guild, 1978, 85, 2nd Pl. award, 1983, 89, 3rd Pl. award, 1983, 1990; winner People's Choice award Internat. Show of Women Artists of the West, Las Vegas, 1992. Mem. North County Art Assn. (founder), Carlsbad Oceanside Art League, 1978, San Dieguito Art Guild, Fallbrook Art Assn., San Diego Art Inst., Assn. pour Promotion Artiste Français, Artisphere. Avocations: ceramics, sculpture, swimming. E-mail: pamiwigle@msn.com.

SARKODIE-MENSAH, AIMIE, physical education educator; b. Syracuse, NY, Mar. 6, 1979; d. Dany and Jill Sarkodie-Mensah. BS in Exercise Sci., SUNY, Buffalo, 2001; MS in Phys. Edn., Canisius Coll., Buffalo, N.Y., 2002. Cert. athletic trainer Nat. Athletic Trainers Assn., phys. edn. tchr. NY. Athletic trainer Cath. Health Systems, Buffalo, 2002—05; tchr. phys. edn. Holy Angels Acad., Buffalo, 2003, Christ the King Sch., Snyder, NY, 2003—04, Cheektowaga Ctrl., Cheektowaga, NY, 2004—05, Byram Hills Schs., Armonk, NY, 2005—; athletic trainer, health and performance coach Altheus, Rye, NY, 2005—. Home: 226 S Ridge St Rye Brook NY 10573-3410

SARNA, HELEN HOROWITZ, retired librarian, educator; b. London, Aug. 3, 1923; came to U.S., 1951; d. Elisha and Rachel Leah (Landau) Horowitz; m. Nahum M. Sarha (dec.); children: David E.Y., Jonathan D. BS, Columbia U.; B in Hebrew Lit., Jewish Theol. Sem.; M in Hebrew Lit., Hebrews Coll.; MLS, Simmons Coll. Libr. Asst. dir. Hebrew Coll., Brookline, Mass., 1965-90; libr. dir. Hist. Soc., Waltham, Mass., Am. Jewish Hist. Soc., Boston, 1992-95, Fla. Atlantic U., Boca Raton, Fla., 1995-96; ret., 1996. Mem. Assn. Jewish Librs. Democrat. Jewish. Avocations: reading, studying. Home: 1215 Commonwealth Ave West Newton MA 02465

SARNOFF, ANN M., publishing executive, former sports association executive; b. Nov. 2, 1961; m. Richard I. Sarnoff; 2 children. BS in Mktg., Georgetown Univ., 1983; MBA, Harvard Bus. Sch., 1987. Strategic consul. Marakon Assoc., Stamford, Conn., 1987—93; v.p. bus. develop. Nickelodeon, 1994, exec. v.p. consumer products, bus. develop.; dir. corp. devel. Viacom, 1993—94, COO, VH1, Country Music Television, 2001—04; COO WNBA, 2004—05; pres. Dow Jones Ventures, NYC, 2006—. Mem. bd. trustees Georgetown Univ. McDonough Sch. Bus. Office: Dow Jones & Co 1 World Fin Ctr 200 Liberty St New York NY 10281*

SARNOFF, LILI-CHARLOTTE (LOLO SARNOFF), artist; b. Frankfurt, Germany (as Swiss citizen), Jan. 9, 1916; arrived in U.S., 1940; d. Willy and Martha (Koch von Hirsch) Dreyfus; m. Stanley Jay Sarnoff, 1948; children: Daniela Martha Bargezi, Robert L. Grad., Reimann Art Sch., Germany, 1936, U. Berlin, 1938; student, U. Florence, Italy, 1936—38; DFA (hon.), Corcoran Coll. Art & Design, 2003. With Red Cross Swiss Motor Corps, 1939—40; Red Cross nurse Bellevue Hosp., N.Y.C., 1942—47; rsch. asst. Harvard Sch. Pub. Health, 1950—54; rsch. assoc. cardiac physiology Nat. Heart Inst., Bethesda, Md., 1954—59; pres. Rodana Rsch. Corp., Bethesda, 1959—61; v.p. Catrix Corp., Bethesda, 1959—61; prin., owner Dara's Sr. Pets for Srs., 2003. Inventor Flolite light sculptures under name Lolo Sarnoff, 1968—; one-woman shows include Agra Gallery, Washington, 1969, Corning (N.Y.) Glass Ctr. Mus., 1970, Gallery Two, Woodstock, Vt., 1970, Gallery Marc, Washington, 1971, 1972, Franz Bader Gallery, 1976, Gallery K, 1978, 1981, 1985, 1987, 1991, Retrospective Show, 1995, Alwin Gallery, London, 1981, Galerie von Bartha, Basel, Switzerland, 1982, La Galerie L'Hotel de Ville, Geneva, 1982, Pfalzgalerie, Kaiserslautern, Germany, 1985, Galerie Les Hirondelles, Geneva, 1988, Represented in permanent collections. Founder, chmn. bd. Arts for Aging, Inc., Bethesda, 1988—; chmn. bd. Dara's Canine Found., Inc., 1999—. Recipient Golda Meir award, 1995, Life Commitment to Arts award, Swiss Am. Cultural Exch., 1999, Path of Achievement award for Arts and Humanities, Montgomery County, Md., 2000, Outstanding Citizen award, Iona Sr. Citizen Svcs., Washington, 2002, Chevalier de L'Ordre des Arts et Des Lettres, République Française, 2006. Home: 7507 Hampden Ln Bethesda MD 20814-1331 Personal E-mail: lolos@erols.com.

SAROFIM, LOUISA STUDE, art patron, philanthropist; m. Fayez S. Sarofim (div. 1990); 1 child, Allison. Co-author (with Matthew Drutt and Anna Gaskell): Anna Gaskell: Half Life, 2003. Chair Houston Grand Opera Studio; pres. bd. trustees Menil Collection; trustee adv. Rice U.; hon. chair The Drawing Ctr., NYC. Named one of top 200 collectors, ARTnews mag., 2006. Avocation: collecting American and European paintings.*

SARRAF, SHIRLEY A., secondary school educator; BA in polit. sci., U. Calif., Davis, 1968; MEd, Idaho State U., 1976, postgrad., 1976—. Cert. Educator Nat. Bd. Edn., 2001. Asst. psychometrist U. Wash., 1969-72; asst. prof. dept. fgn. lang. Farah Pahlavi U., Teheran-Vanek, Iran, 1978-79; tchr. presch. program T.L.C. Child Care Ctr., Pocatello, Idaho, 1980-82; dir. of curriculum for English as a second lang. Idaho State U., Pocatello, Idaho, 1982-85; tchr. English, Math, History, Computers Highland High Sch. Sch. Dist. 25, Pocatello, Idaho, 1986—2001; tchr. English Folsom H.S., Folsom, Calif., 2001—. Recipient Tchr. of the Year award State of Idaho, 1994-95. Home: PO Box 6001 Folsom CA 95763-6001

SARREALS, SONIA, data processing executive, consultant; b. NYC, Sept. 17, 1938; d. Espriela and Sadie Beatrice (Scales) Sarreals; m. Waldro Lynch, Sept. 18, 1981 (div. Oct. 1983). BA in Langs. summa cum laude, CCNY, 1960; cert. in French, Sorbonne, Paris, 1961. Systems engr. IBM, N.Y.C., 1963-69; cons. Babbage Systems, N.Y.C., 1969-70; project leader Touche Ross, N.Y.C., 1970-73; sr. programmer McGraw-Hill, Inc., Hightstown, NJ, 1973-78; staff data processing cons. Cin. Bell Info. Systems, 1978-89; sr. analyst AT&T, 1989-92; lead tech. analyst Automated Concepts Inc., Arlington, Va., 1992-96; tech. cons. Teksystems, Reston, Va., 1996—. Elder St. Andrew Luth. Ch., Silver Spring, 1992-96. Downer scholar CUNY, 1960; Dickman Inst. fellow Columbia U., 1960-61. Mem.: Assn. for Computing Machinery, Phi Beta Kappa. Democrat. Avocations: needlecrafts, sewing. Home: 13705 Beret Pl Silver Spring MD 20906-3030 Office: Teksystems 12343 Sunrise Valley Dr Reston VA 20191 Business E-Mail: ssarreals@teksystems.com.

SARRIS, JEAN ADAMS, retired psychologist; b. Arlington, Mass. m. George Sarris (dec.). BA, Harvard U., Cambridge, Mass., 1964; MA, San Francisco State U., 1971; PhD, Calif. Sch. Profl. Psychology, San Francisco, 1975. Lic. psychologist Calif. Staff rsch. assoc. U. Calif. Med. Ctr., San Francisco, 1965—77; staff psychologist, tng. dir. Sunset Mental Health Svcs. Ctr., San Francisco, 1977—2002; ret., 2002. Bd. dirs. Friends of Sunset Mental Health Svcs., San Francisco.

SARRY, CHRISTINE, ballerina; b. Long Beach, Calif., May 25, 1946; d. John and Beatrice (Thomas) S.; 1 child, Maximilian Sarry Varriale. With Joffrey Ballet, 1963—64, Am. Ballet Theatre, 1964—68, prin. dancer, 1971—74; leading dancer Am. Ballet Co., 1969—71; ballerina Eliot Feld Ballet, 1974—81. Dir. faculty Ballet Tech., N.Y.C.; also freelance guest tchr. Performed ballets for Agnes DeMille, Antony Tudor, Jerome Robbins, Twyla Tharp, Eliot Feld; appeared at White House, 1963, 67; U.S. Dept. State tours include, Russia, 1963, 66, S.Am., 1964, 76, various tours of N.Am., Orient, Europe, various appearances U.S. nat. TV; partnered by Mikhail Baryshnikov. Office Phone: 212-777-7710 x 307. E-mail: csarry@ballettech.org.

SARSON, EVELYN PATRICIA **See KAYE, EVELYN**

SARTAIN, LIBBY, human resources specialist; BA, So. Methodist U.; MBA, U. North Tex. Various positions Southwest Airlines, 1988—98, v.p. people, 1998—2001; sr. v.p. human resources, chief Yahoo!, Inc., Sunnyvale, Calif., 2001—. Fellow: Nat. Acad. Human Resources; mem.: Soc. Human Resource Mgmt. (former chmn.). Office: Yahoo Inc 701 1st Ave Sunnyvale CA 94089 Office Phone: 408-349-3300. Office Fax: 408-349-3301.

SARTOR, VIVIAN JUANITA, nursing administrator; b. Mount Enterprise, Tex., Apr. 13, 1937; d. Rochelle Williams and Verline Chambers; children: Renita Starr Yvette Cleary, La Dorsia Parks-Jones. AA, L.A. S.W. Coll., 1971; BA, Calif. State U., L.A., 1973; cert. in pub. health, Long Beach State Coll., 1975; M Health Adminstrn., Chapman Coll., 1994. RN Calif., cert. diabetic educator. Med./surg. staff nurse Martin Luther King Med. Ctr., L.A., 1972—74; emergency triage nurse Cedars Sinai Med. Ctr., L.A., 1975—80; pub. health nurse L.A. County Health Svc., L.A., 1981—91; pvt. duty nurse L.A. Nurses Assn., 1992—95; health care mgr. L.A., 1995—98; asst. adminstr. Oak Car Med. Group, Oakland, Calif., 2001—02; asst. dir. nurses Oakridge Care Ctr., Oakland, 2003—. Med./legal cons. Lancaster (Calif.) Legal, 1990—99; founder WASP Home Health Mgmt. Student recruiter LA Sch. Nursing, 1992—; mem., minister spl. tutoring Allen Temple Missionary Baptist Ch. Fellow: Prince Hall Ea. Star (doorkeeper 1997); mem.: LA Nurses Alumni Assn. (sec. 1975). Avocations: reading, travel, sailing, fishing. Office: Oakridge Care Ctr 2919 Fruitvale Avew Oakland CA 94602 Home: PO Box 27531 Oakland CA 94602-0531 E-mail: taddy07@earthlink.net.

SARTORI, BRIDGET ANN, home health care nurse; b. Plattsburg, N.Y., July 17, 1957; d. Francis McCarthy and Phyllis (Harvey) McCarthy/Haegler; m. Robert S. Sartori, May 20, 1978; children: Robert F., Ryan R. BSN, Mt. St. Mary's Coll., Newburgh, N.Y., 1990. RN, N.Y. Staff nurse CCU White Plains (N.Y.) Hosp., 1990-91; nurse in home care divsn. Putnam Hosp. Ctr., Carmel, N.Y., 1991—, acting long term home health cert. program coord. home care divsn., 1995-97; supr. clin. svcs. Homecare, Inc., Brookfield, Conn., 1997-98; intravenous therapy nurse Anytime Home Care, Poughkeepsie, N.Y., 1992-93; substitute tchr., nurse Dover Union Free Sch. Dist., 1994—; homecare nurse, billing coord. Putnam Hosp. Ctr., Carmel, 2005—. Children's adv. Astor Head Start, Dover Plains, N.Y., 1989-92; pres. J.H. Kethcam Hose Co., 1998. Mem. rescue squad J.H. Ketcham Hose Co., Dover Plains, 1978—, mem. ladies aux., 1978—, fire prevention officer, 1994—, corp. sec., 1996-97, bd. dirs., 2001—; 1st v.p. J.H. Ketcham Hose Co. Fire Police, 1994—, pres., 1998; coach Dover Little League, 1994, 95; pres. J.H. Ketcham Hose Co., 1998, 2000, 2001, bd. dirs., 2002—; 1st v.p. Dutchess County Assn. Fire Dist., 2000-02, pres. 2002; mem. Dutchess County Fire Adv. Bd., 1998—, sec., 2004—. Recipient Army Nurse Perseverance award U.S. Army, 1990. Republican. Roman Catholic. Avocations: reading, bicycling. Office: Putnam Hosp Ctr Homecare Bldg 121 Clocktower Commons Brewster NY 10509 Office Phone: 845-278-4068. E-mail: bsartori@aol.com.

SARTORI, MARILEE A., space designer; b. Paducah, Ky., June 23, 1942; d. Paul Dean Bynum and Nell Catherine Roberts; m. Donald Joseph Sartori; children: Suzanne, Joseph. BA magna cum laude, DeSales U., Allentown, Pa., 1985. CEO, pres. Occasional Displays, Kintners, Pa., 1990—. Chair spring art exhibit, Beaufort, SC. Mem.: Beaufort Art Assn. (v.p. 2005—06, Excellence award in acrylic painting 2005), Lydia's Guild, Delta Epsilon Sigma. Republican. Roman Catholic. Avocation: sculpting. Home: 5365 Harrow Rd Rt 412 Kintnersville PA 18930 E-mail: mas55@yahoo.com.

SARWAR, BARBARA DUCE, educational consultant; b. Mpls., Aug. 9, 1938; d. Harold Taylor and Barbara (Thayer) Duce; m. Mohammad Sarwar, Dec. 28, 1972; 1 child, Barbara Sarah Franklin. BS, U. Colo., 1972; M Spl. Edn., Ea. N.Mex. U., 1975, Edn. Specialist, 1979. Cert. tchr., adminstr., N.Mex. Tchr. 2d grade, English as 2d lang. Lake Arthur (N.Mex.) Mcpl. Schs., 1972-74; tchr. spl. edn. Artesia (N.Mex.) Pub. Schs., 1974-79, ednl. diagnostician, 1979-88, dir. spl. edn., 1988-97; cons. Edn. Diagnosis, Artesia, 1998—; owner Barbara's Diagnostic Svcs., Artesia, 1998—. Contbr. to profl. publs. Pres. Altrusa Club Artesia, 1981-82, 86-87, The Arc of Artesia, 1990-92; bd. dirs. Zia Girl Scout Coun., 2002—. Named Employee of Yr. Arc of N.Mex., 1994. Mem.: Coun. for Exceptional Children (professionally recognized spl. educator in ednl. diagnosis), Nat. Assn. Sch. Psychologists, Internat. Reading Assn. (pres. Pecos Valley chpt. 1975—76, sec. N.Mex. unit 1977—78), Artesia Edn. Assn. (pres. 1978—79), Phi Delta Kappa, Phi Kappa Phi. Avocations: reading, sewing, golf. Home: 2625 N 24th St Unit 26 Mesa AZ 85213-1469

SAS, ELLEN, bank executive; 2 children. CPA. Ptnr., CPA firm, 1989—2000; pres. Fremont First Nat. Bank, 2000; chmn., pres., CEO NorthStar Bank (bought by Frontier), Seattle, 2000—05; exec. v.p. Frontier Bank, Seattle, 2005—. Named one of Most Powerful Women in Banking, USBanker Mag., 2005. Mem.: We. Independent Bankers (bd. dir., chmn., svc. corp.). Office: NorthStar/Frontier Bank 5602 15th Ave NW Seattle WA 98107 Office Phone: 206-783-0300.

SASEK, GLORIA BURNS, English language and literature educator; b. Springfield, Mass., Jan. 20, 1926; d. Frederick Charles and Minnie Delia (White) Burns; m. Lawrence Anton Sasek, Sept. 5, 1960. BA, Mary Washington Coll. of U. Va., 1947; student, U. Paris, 1953, U. Stranieri, Perugia, Italy, 1955; MA, Radcliffe Coll., 1954; EdM, Springfield Coll., 1955. Tchr., head dept. jr. and sr. hs English, Pub. Schs., Somers, Conn., 1947—59; tchr. English, Winchester (Mass.) Pub. Schs., 1959—60; mem. faculty La. State U., Baton Rouge, 1961—, asst. prof. English, 1971-96, chmn. freshman English, 1969-70. Named La. State U. Yearbook Favorite Prof., 1978; recipient George H. Deer Disting. Tchg. award, La. State U., 1977, Disting. Undergrad. Tchg. award, Amoco Found., 1994, commendation, La. Ho. of Reps., 1996. Mem. MLA, AAUP (chpt. v.p. 1981-84), South Ctrl. MLA, South Ctrl. Renaissance Soc., South Ctrl. Conf. on Christianity and Lit. Office: 1458 Kenilworth Pkwy Baton Rouge LA 70808

SASKO, NANCY ANN, insurance agent; b. Camp Lejeune, NC, Nov. 22, 1956; d. George Michael Jr. and Margaret (Simons) S. BA in English Lit., Ind. U., 1981. Customer svc. rep. Apple Computer, Inc., Denver, 1982—89; owner Monitor Systems, Inc., Denver, 1992—; long term care ins. sales rep. Sr. Ins. Svs., 2003—. Substitute tchr. Ft. Wayne (Ind.) Cmty. Schs., 2003—. Cath. Avocations: classical music, art, reading, gardening, cooking.

SASMAN, IRENE DEAK HANDBERG, publishing executive; b. Jamaica, N.Y. d. Paul and Irene (Dyroff) Deak; children: Roger B. Handberg III, Ryan Paul Handberg; m. Timothy Carl Sasman. BS, Fla. State U.; MEd, U. N.C., 1970. Cert. tchr. in reading and math., N.C. Lead tchr., reading specialist Chapel Hill (N.C.) City Schs., 1966-69; dir. learning lab. Seminole Community Coll., Sanford, Fla., 1974-78; basic skills cons. EDL/McGraw-Hill Book Co., Orlando, Fla., 1978-82; regional dir. EDL/Arista Pub., Orlando, 1982-84; mktg. mgr., product mgr. Arista/Regents/EDL-Hachette, N.Y.C., 1984-85; v.p. mktg. and sales Raintree Pubs., Milw., 1985, gen. mgr., pub., 1985-87; dir. spl. projects Simon & Schuster, Englewood Cliffs, NJ, 1987-88, v.p. corp. devel. N.Y.C., 1988-90, sr. v.p., 1990-91; chmn. Irene Handberg Internat., N.Y.C., 1991—; pres. The Learning Connection, New York, NY, 1991—. Co-author: EDL/McGraw-Hill Teacher's Guide. Elected precinct woman com. Dem. County Com., Fla.; capt. Nat. Cancer So., Fla., chmn. Sch. Adv. Com., Fla. NSF fellow U. N.C., 1969; recipient Svc. award Jr. Achievement. Mem. Chief Exec. Officers Group (coun. small bus. execs.), Sales and Mktg. Execs., Profl. Dimensions, Chief Exec. Officers Club. Lutheran. Avocations: spectator sports, art, music, skiing. Office: The Learning Connection 300 E 93rd St Apt 29C New York NY 10128-6109

SASS, CANDACE ELAINE, chemist, researcher; b. Mar. 16, 1960; d. Robert Ernest and Dolores LaRue Truscott; m. Craig Steven Sass, May 5, 1959; 1 child, Christine Elizabeth. BSChem, Muskingum Coll., 1982; MSChem, PhDChem, U. Cin., 1986. Postdoctoral fellow U. Houston, 1986-88; rsch. chemist Eastman Chemical Co. Rsch., Kingsport, Tenn., 1988-91; sr. chemist Tenn. Eastman Divsn., Kingsport, 1991-94; principal chemist Eastman Chemical Co., Kingsport, 1994-98, rsch. assoc., 1998—. Contbr. to profl. jours. Bd. dir. Waverly Road Child Care Ctr. (v.p., 1997, sec., 1996); mem. Am. Chemical Soc., An. Lab. Mgrs. Assocs. Home: 430 Harding Rd Kingsport TN 37663-2557 Office: Eastman Chemical Co PO Box 1972 Kingsport TN 37662-1972

SASS, MARY MARTHA, freelance writer, artist; b. Chgo. d. George James and Arbutus Laraine (Schwartz) Harles; m. Roger Edward Sass, June 29, 1968. BS in Edn., U. Ill., 1965; MA in Guidance and Counseling, Northeastern Ill. U., 1977. Cert. secondary educator, guidance counselor, Ill. Tchr. English Kelvyn Park High Sch., Chgo., 1965-83; freelance writer, Skokie, Ill., 1983—. Lectr. North Suburban Libr. Sys., Chgo., 1992; author radio scripts Chgo. Pub. Libr. Broadcasting Sys.; author short stories, essays and articles; illustrator short stories and essays. Author (and illustrator): (novels) The Katy Ornament, 2002; exhibitions include Oakton C.C., 1993, All Chgo. Juried Art Show Skokie Pub. Libr., 1993, 1994, 1995, 1996, 1997 (hon. mention), 1998, 1999, 2000, 2001, Woman's Club Evanston Ann. Art Exhibit, 1994, 1995, 1996, 1997, 1998, 1999, 2000, Skokie Hist. Soc., 1993, 1994 (hon. mention), 1995, 1996, 1997, 1998, 1999, 2000 (First prize, 2000), 2001, 2002, 2003 (First prize), Allstate Ins., 1995, 1996, 1997, Blue Moon Art Gallery, 1999, Devonshire Cultural Ctr., 2002, Morton Grove Pub. Libr., 2002, 2004, Lincolnwood Village Hall Gallery, 2005, Emily Oaks Nature Ctr, 2006, South Shore Cultural Ctr., 2006, Represented in permanent collections Artists Archives, Chgo. Pub. Libr. Vol. Emily Oaks Nature Ctr. Skokie Park Dist., Ill. Recipient Radio Script hon. mention award Take One Nat. Radio Theatre Competition, 1994, Women in Cable award for cable TV documentary; Nat. Pub. Radio scholar, 1984. Mem. Mystery Writers Am., Mystery Writers Am. Spkr.'s Bur., Chgo. Artist's Coalition, Nat. Parks & Conservation Assn., Greenpeace, Nature Conservancy, Park Activist Network, Sr. Artists' Network, Ocean Conservancy, World Wildlife Fund Avocations: classical guitar, sculpting, cable television writing and production, gardening. Office Phone: 847-674-7118. Personal E-mail: maryhsass@aol.com.

SASSEN, SASKIA, urban planner, educator; b. The Hague, The Netherlands, Jan. 5, 1949; came to U.S., 1970; d. Willem S. and Mara (Van de Voort) Van Elsloo; m. Daniel J. Koob, Aug. 30, 1973 (div. 1982); 1 child, Hilary Koob-Sassen; m. Richard Sennett, Oct. 23, 1987. Maitrise, U. Poitiers, France, 1973; PhD in Econs. and Sociology, U. Notre Dame, 1974. Postdoctoral fellow Ctr. Internat. Affairs Harvard U., Cambridge, Mass., 1974-75; from asst. to full prof. Queens Coll. CUNY, 1976-85; prof. dept. urban planning Columbia U., N.Y.C., 1985—, chair divsn. planning, preservation and real estate, 1988-91, chair PhD program in urban planning, 1989—92, 1994—98, U. Chgo., 1998—. Mem. faculty Sch. Internat. and Pub. Affairs Columbia U.; past mem. non-govtl. internat. planning com. on yr. of shelter for homeless UN; former mem. Queens Borough Pres. Claire Shulman's Blue Ribbon Panel on Govt., N.Y. State Indsl. Corp. Coun.; mem. Social Sci. Rsch. Coun. working group on N.Y.C. Russell Sage Found., 1985-90, mem. immigration and econ. sociology project; mem. Social Sci. Rsch. Coun. com. Hispanic pub. policy Ford Found., 1987-91; mem. econ. restructuring in U.S. and Japan UN Ctr. on Regional Devel. and MIT, 1988-90; mem. N.Y.-London comparative study Econ. Social Rsch. Coun. of U.K.; mem. comparative urban studies project Woodrow Wilson Ctr., Washington; mem. group of Lisbon Sci. Program of EC and Gulbenkian Found., Portugal; advisor Ctrl. European U.; disting. lectr. Inst. Advanced Studies, Vienna, Austria; Henry Luce lectr. Clark U., 1995-2000, Theodore Hesbaugh lectures on politics and ethics, Yale Law Sch. Sherril Lecture, 2005; co-curator Trade Rts. exhbn. New Mus. Contemporary Arts, N.Y.C., 1993; cons. UN, PBS, Ford Found., Nat. Urban League N.Y.C. Office Econ. Devel., Ralph Lewis prof. sociology, mem. faculty law sch., com. internat. affairs; centennial visl prof. London Sch. Econs., 2000-, others; lectr. in field. Author: The Mobility of Labor and Capital, 1988, The Global City: New York, London, Tokyo, 1991, 2d edit., 2001, Cities in a World Economy, 1994, 2d edit., 2000, Losing Control, 1996, Globalization and its Discontent, 1998, Guests and Aliens, 1999, Global Nations/Limited Cities, 2002, Territory: Authority and Rights, 2005; mem. editl. bd. Urban Affairs Rev., Competition and Change, Internat. Planning Studies, others; reviewer Times Lit. Supplement, several acad. jours.; contbr. articles to profl. jours; comments published in N.Y. Times, Fin. Times, The Guardian, Internat. Herald Tribune, others. Rsch. grantee Chgo. Inst. Architecture and Urbanism, 1988-89, Twentieth Century Fund, 1994—, others; fellow Robert F. Kennedy Found., 1970-71, Ford Found., 1972-73, Social Sci. Rsch. Coun., 1977-78, Ford and Tinker Founds., 1980-81, N.Y. Inst. Humanities, 1982-90, Tinker Found., 1982-83, Wissenshaftszentrum, Berlin, 1991-92; scholar Russell Sage Found., 1992-93, Woodrow Wilson Internat. Ctr. Scholars, Ctr. for Advanced Study, summer 1993; fellow World Econ. Forum, 1997-. Office Phone: 773-702-7279. Business E-Mail: s-sassen@uchicago.edu.

SASSER, BRENDA GLENN, elementary school educator; b. Kinston, NC, Apr. 2, 1957; d. Frances Louise Sutton; children: Melissa Anne Gray, Frances Michelle. Degree in criminal justice, Mt. Olive Coll. Cert. tchr. NC. Tchr. Lenoir County Schs., Kinston, NC, 2003—. V.p. women's aux. Free Will Bapt. Ch., La Grange, NC. Democrat. Baptist. Avocations: gardening, travel, outdoor activities. Home: 1566 Hardy Bridge Rd La Grange NC 28551 Office Phone: 252-527-4432.

SASSO, RUTH MARYANN, educator; b. Bridgeport, Conn., Dec. 9, 1928; d. Angelo Nicholas and Mildred Rita (Hayes) Sasso BS in Edn., St. Joseph Coll., 1957, MA, 1968. Tchr. Catholic Schs. of Conn., 1950-68; founder, dir. Berkeley Primary Sch., Waterbury, Conn., 1969-71; from assoc. prof. to prof. early childhood edn., coordinator child care program Naugatuck Valley Community-Tech. Coll., Waterbury, 1971—, dir. early childhood edn., coordinator child care program, 1971—, founder, dir. early childhood child devel. ctr., 1976—. Mem. adv. council on early childhood edn. Conn. Dept. Edn.; cons. in field; adv. council Waterbury YMCA Day Care Ctr., 1980—; mem. adv. com. to Magnet Sch., Waterbury, Infant/Toddler Day Care, Wilson Sch., Waterbury; mem. adv. com. home cons. high sch. curriculum Conn. State Dept. Edn. Author: Field Placement Manual for Student Teachers, 1971, rev., 1980; Observation Manual in Early Childhood Edn., 1979. Bd. dirs. Child Care Ctr. Abused Children, Waterbury, 1971—; pres. St. Francis Sch. Bd., Naugatuck, 1989; chair Prek com. Office of Cath. Schs., Archdiocese of Hartford, Conn., 1990-91, mem. Office of Cath. Schs., 1992—. Recipient Service award Head Start Policy Com., Danbury, Conn., 1973, YWCA Women in Leadership award, 1992, Twenty Yr. Appreciation award Naugatuck C.C., 1992. Mem. Nat. Assn. Edn. Young Children (validator), Soc. Nutrition Edn., Action Children's TV, Nat. Council Campus Child Care Centers. Democrat. Roman Catholic. Home and Office: 93 Barn Finch Cir Naugatuck CT 06770-4879

SASSOON, JANET, ballerina, educator; b. Sorabaya, Indonesia, Sept. 2, 1936; came to U.S., 1937; d. Edward and Flora (Bar) S.; m. John Roland Upton Jr., Aug. 7, 1983. Began training with Christensen brothers, Ruby Asquith, and Gisella Caccialanza, San Francisco; Studied with Leo Staats, Lubov Egorova, Olga Preobrajenska, Mathilde Kshessinskaya, Paris, 1951. Dancer Grand Ballet du Marquis de Cuevas, Paris, 1952-55, Chgo., Utah and San Francisco Ballets, 1955; prima ballerina Berlin Ballet, 1956; dir. Acad. of Ballet, San Francisco, 1974-89, assoc. dir., 1989-97. Coach master classes in ballet, profl. dancers including Natalia Makarova, Karen Averty, Wes Chapman, Jean Charles Gil, others; coached principle dancers, Cin. Ballet; guest coach for Ballet Camille-Boston Ballet. Avocations: cooking, gardening, writing. Home (Summer): 1112 Pine St Calistoga CA 94515-1734

SASTROWARDOYO, TERESITA MANEJAR, nurse; b. Iloilo, Philippines; came to U.S., 1960; d. Timoteo and Monica (Casianan) Manejar; m. Sumarsongko H. Sastrowardoyo, June 8, 1962; children: Timoteo, Daniel (dec.), Benjamin. BSN, Ctrl. Philippine U., Iloilo, 1957; cert. operating rm. and surgical nursing, St. Luke's Hosp Ctr., N.Y.C., 1960-61. Head nurse med. unit Emmanuel Hosp., Roxas City, Philippines, 1957-58; supr. oper. rm. Brent Hosp., Zamboanga City, Philippines, 1958-60; staff nurse oper. rm. Jewish Meml. Hosp., N.Y.C., 1961-62; evening staff nurse oper. rm. Flower and Fifth Ave Hosp., N.Y.C., 1963-65; staff nurse oper. rm., charge nurse night shift St. Lukes Hosp. Ctr., N.Y.C., 1966-76; staff nurse oper. rm. South Side Hosp., Bayshore, NY, 1976—, asst. head nurse operating room, 2003—. Mem.: N.Y. State Nurses Assn., Ctrl. Philippine U. Alumni Assn. N.Y., N.J. and Conn. (bd. dirs. 1994—95, 1995—97). Baptist. Avocations: gardening, reading.

SATER, BEVERLY, music educator; b. Lancaster, Ohio, Aug. 29, 1946; d. Harold R. and Maxine T. Sater. BFA, Ohio U., Athens, 1969, MusM, 1971. Tchr. Cleve. Mcpl. Sch. Dist., Cleve., 1971—; instr. voice Beck Ctr. Arts, Lakewood, Ohio, 1999—. Singer: Cleve. Orch. Chorus, 1971—88, Cleve. Opera, 1982—89, Robert Page Singers, 1989—99. Trustee Luth. Children's Aid and Family Svcs., Cleve., 1997—2003. Martha Holden Jennings Fund scholar, 1999. Mem.: Cleve. Tchrs. Union (trustee, exec. bd. 2002—06), Sigma Alpha Iota (province officer 1995—2003, Rose of Honor 2003). Avocations: travel, gardening, reading.

SATER, DENISE M., journalist, editor; b. Spangler, Pa. d. Harry Edward Murphy and Mary Louise Valeria. BA, Pa. State U., 1974. Counselor Devereaux, Devon, Pa., 1974-75; editor Antiques & Auction News, Marietta, Pa., 1975-82, Mount Joy, Pa., 1995—. Mem. Phi Beta Kappa. Avocation: antiques. Office: Antiques & Auction News PO Box 500 Mount Joy PA 17552-0500

SATHER, SYLVIA CAROLYN, science educator, consultant; b. Morris, Minn., Feb. 27, 1944; d. Ralph Jennings and Clara Randina (Morseth) S. BA, Augusburg Coll., Mpls., 1966; MS, U. No. Colo., Greeley, 1976. Cert. elem. edn., phys. edn., gifted and talented, sci. and health endorsements. 3rd grade tchr. Mpls. Pub. Schs., 1966-68; tchr. grades 1-6 gifted/talented Denver Pub.

Schs., 1968—, tchr. mid. sch. sci., math., 1987-92, tchr. biology H.S., 1992—; tchr. Denver Sch. Arts, 1997—2000. Cons. Energy & Mans Environ., Salt Lake City, 1970-82; prof. Colo. Sch. Mines, Golden, 1975-90; grad. asst. U. Denver, 1980-81; adj. prof. Wartburg Coll., 2000—. Author: Best of Energy, 1977, Energy Man's Environment, 1971-76. Mem. Nat. Sci. Tchrs. Assn., Phi Delta Kappa. Democrat. Avocations: potter, furniture maker, naturalist, ornithologist, travel. Home: 2795 S Ingalls Way Denver CO 80227-3825

SATIN, CLAIRE JEANINE, sculptor, artist; b. Bklyn., Jan. 9, 1942; BA, Sarah Lawrence Coll., 1956; MFA, Pratt Inst., 1968. Instr. art edn. dept. edn. Bklyn. Mus., 1958-59; instr. dept. edn. and dept. Fine Arts Broward Cmty. Coll., Ft. Lauderdale, Fla., 1971-83; dir. Broward Cmty. Coll. Gallery, Ft. Lauderdale, 1975-76. Artist rep. Gabriela Herrera, N.Y.C., Art Vitam, Wynwood, Miami, Priscilla Juvelis, Maine, Vamps and Tramps, Birmingham, Ala. Collections include Libr. Congress, Rare Books Collection, Victoria and Albert Mus., London, Getty Ctr. Hist. Art and Humanities, L.A., Mus. Modern Art, N.Y.C., Mus. Art, Ft. Lauderdale, King Stephen Mus., Szekesfeherdr, Hungary, Ruth and Marvin Sackner Archive of Concrete and Visual Poetry, others; commd. works include: Chapman Chronicles, State of Alaska, U. Alaska, Fairbanks, 1992, Alphawalk, New Tampa Regional Libr., Hillsborough County, Tampa, Fla., 1997 (catalog); Alphastory, Pembroke Pines Libr., Pembroke Pines, Fla., Broward County Art in Pub. Places Program (brochure), Am. Ctrs., New Delhi, Bombay, India. Hon. chair Broward County Cultural Affairs Coun., Ft. Lauderdale, 1981-, bd. dirs., 1975-83, Meml. Found. Jewish Culture, N.Y.C. Recipient S. Fla. Cult Consortium award Miami Art Mus., Fla., 1997-98; So. Arts Fedn./NEA Regional Visual Arts fellow, 1996; Fla. State Individual Artist fellow Statewide Exhbn., 1978, 97-98; Cult Consortium fellow Miami Art Mus., 1997-98; Tiffany Found. grantee, 1968-69, Meml. Found. for Jewish Culture, 2001-02. Mem. Internat. Sculpture Ctr., Am. Craft. Coun., Ctr. Book Arts, Fonteneda Soc. (bd. dirs. 1997—). Office: c/o Artworks/Artspace 101 SW 1st St Dania Beach FL 33004-3628 Office Phone: 954-923-9117.

SATIN, ELAINE, educator; b. Wilmington, Del. 1 child, Jenny BA, Fairleigh Dickinson U., Teaneck, N.J., 1969; MS, Columbia U., 1975. Dental hygienist, various locations, 1969—; rsch. cons. Hilltop Rsch., East Brunswick, NJ, 1981—85; prof. Bergen C.C., Paramus, NJ, 1973—. Mem Am. Assn. Dental Hygiene, N.J. Edn. Assn., Columbia Alumni Assn Office: Bergen Community Coll 400 Paramus Rd Paramus NJ 07652-1508 Home: Apt 5H 345 Prospect Ave Hackensack NJ 07601-7750

SATIR, BIRGIT H., medical educator, researcher; b. Copenhagen, Mar. 22, 1934; Magistra in Biochemistry, U. Copenhagen, 1961. Rsch. assoc. dept. zoology U. Chgo., 1962-66; asst. rsch. physiologist U. Calif. Dept. Physiology-Anatomy, Berkeley, 1967-74, assoc. rsch. physiologist, 1974-76, adj. assoc. prof., 1976-77; sci. dir. Analytical Ultrastructure Ctr., Cancer Rsch. Inst. Albert Einstein Coll. of Medicine, Bronx, NY, 1977-84, prof. dept. anatomy and structural biology, 1977—. Rschr. Phys.- Chem. Inst. Copenhagen, 1956-57, Biol. Inst., Copenhagen, 1958-61; mem. Cellular and Molecular Basis of Disease Rev. Com., Nat. Inst. Gen. Med. Scis., 1977-79; vis. prof. divsn. biology Calif. Inst. Tech., 1984-85. Mem. editl. bd. Jour. Ultrastructural Rsch., 1975-80, Jour. Cell Biology, 1979-81, Modern Cell Biology, 1980-90, Jour. Eukaryotic Microbiology, 1989-95. Rsch. fellow U. Geneva, 1965-66, Spl. fellow USPHS, 1972-73; recipient Outstanding Women Scientist award N.Y. chpt. Assn. Women in Sci., 1990, Rsch. award Am. Diabetes Assn., 1995. Fellow AAAS, Royal Danish Acad. Sci. and Letters; mem. Am. Soc. Cell Biology (coun. 1975-78, minority affairs com. 1987-90, fin. com. 1993—), Am. Assn. Anatomists, Am. Soc. Biochemistry and Molecular Biology, Electron Microscopy Soc. Am. (program vice-chairperson 38th Meeting 1980, program chairperson 39th Meeting 1981), NYSEM (pres. 1979-80), N.Y. Acad. Sci., Biophys. Soc. Office: Albert Einstein Coll of Medicine Jack and Pearl Resnick Campus 1300 Morris Park Ave Bronx NY 10461-1926 E-mail: bsatir@aecom.yu.edu.

SATISH, SUSANY, biology educator; d. Baboo Werghees Kunbalaseriyil and Lilly Baboo; m. Chandran Satish, Oct. 19, 1994; children: Roshan, Ethan, Steven. BS, Bangalore U., 1992, MS, 1994; MA, Nat. Lewis U., Chgo., 2006—. Microbiologist Internat. Fruits Ltd., Bangalore, India, 1994, Nat. First Grade Coll., Bangalore, India, 1994—99; tchr. Fenger HS, Chgo., 2001—. Achievements include invention of in astrobiology. Avocations: gardening, reading. Office: Fenger HS 11220 S Wallace Chicago IL 60628 Personal E-mail: susanysatish@yahoo.com.

SATO, EUNICE NODA, former mayor, consultant; b. Livingston, Calif., June 8, 1921; d. Bunsaku and Sawa (Maeda) Noda; m. Thomas Takashi Sato, Dec. 9, 1950; children: Charlotte Patricia, Daniel Ryuichi and Douglas Ryuji (twins). AA, Modesto Jr. Coll., 1941; BA, U. No. Colo., 1944; MA, Columbia U., 1948. Pub. sch. tchr. Mastodon Twp. Schs., Alpha, Mich., 1944-47; ednl. missionary Reformed Ch. Am., Yokohama, Japan, 1948-51; coun. mem. City of Long Beach, Calif., 1975-86; mayor, 1980-82. Sec. corp. bd. Los Angeles County Health Systems Agy., 1978-79 Monthly contbr. articles to 2 neighborhood papers, 1975-86. Bd. dirs. Long Beach chpt. ARC, 1975-2000, mem. exec. com., 1978-91, 93-99, past pres. and v.p., mem. Calif. state svc. coun., A.R.C., 1995-2001; bd. dirs. Goodwill Industries, 1978-82; trustee St. Mary's Bauer Med. Ctr., 1977—; pres. Industry Edn. Coun., Long Beach, 1984-86, mem. exec. bd., 1984—; bd. dirs. Industry Edn. Coun. of Calif.; treas. So. Calif. Consortium of I.E.C., 1984-86, pres., 1988-89; mem. State Adv. Group on Juvenile Justice and Delinquency Prevention, 1983-91, Calif. Coun. Criminal Justice, 1983-92, legis. com. Girl Scout coun. Calif., 1986-92, chair, 1991-92; bd. dirs. Long Beach coun. Girl Scouts U.S., 1986-92, Region III United Way, 1974-88; mem. Asian Pacific adv. com. Calif. Dept. Rehab., 1985-87, recreation commn. City of Long Beach, 1985-86, pub. safety policy com. League Calif. Cities, 1981-86, cmty. econ. and housing devel. com. So. Calif. Assn. Govts., 1976-86, Calif. Task Force to Promote Self-Esteem and Personal and Social Responsibility, 1987-90; Long Beach chpt. pres. NCCJ, 1987-88; pres. Internat. Cmty. Coun., 1986-87, bd. dir. 1986-2001, pres. Japanese Am. Reps., 1987, 88, exec. bd. mem. 1987-2003, 2004—; presdl. appointee Nat. Adv. Coun. Ednl. Rsch. and Improvement, 1991-94; pres. Aux. to Sch. Theology, Claremont, 1990-91, exec. bd. 1989-91, nat. selective svc. sys. local bd. 138, 1990-2001, SCA Edison Co. Equal Opportunity adv. coun., 1990-94; chair selection com. Leadership Long Beach, 1990-91, sec. exec. bd., 1991-92, bd. govs. 2003—; chair adv. bd. AIESEC, 1990-92; chmn. Long Beach Area Rep. Party, 1990-92; asst. sec. cen. com., L.A., 1990-92; sec.-gen. coun. on fin. and administrn. United Meth. Ch., 1992-2000; appointed by Gov. to commn. on tchr. credentialing State Calif., 1994, L.A. coun. svc. coun. A.R.C., 1995-99; chair adminstrv. bd. Leisure World Cmty. Ch., 1996-2002; rep. to South Coast Ecumenical Coun., 1993-2002, chair pastor parish rels. com., 2000; chair Parents Day Festival com. greater L.A. county, 1996-2000, Blue Ribbon Com. for Effective Parenting in Long Beach, 1997-99; mem. adult and elder care adv. com. Long Beach (Calif.) City Coll., 2004—; caregiver Grace First Presbyn. Ch., 2005—. Recipient Outstanding Svc. award Long Beach Coord. Coun., 1969, Mother of Yr. award Silverado United Meth. Ch., 1973, Hon. Svc. award Calif. PTA, 1963, Continuing Svc. award, 1974, hon. life membership award Nat. PTA, 1974, Outstanding Laywoman of Yr. award Long Beach Area Coun. Chs., 1976, Woman of Yr. award State Women's Coun.-C. of C., 1979, Long Beach Internat. Bus. and Profl. Women's Club, Nat. Merit award DAR, 1982, Citizen of Yr. award Los Altos YMCA, 1982, Calif. Cmty. Pool for Handicapped, 1982, Outstanding Citizen award Torch Club of Long Beach, 1983, W. Odie Wright award Industry Edn. Coun., 1990, Humanitarian award NCCJ, 1992, Vol. of Yr. award ARC, 1995, 1st Life Membership award Long Beach chpt. UN Assn., Kunsho award of Order of the Sacred Treasure, Gold Rays with rosette from Japanese Govt., 1996, Sr. Vol. of Yr. Long Beach C.C., 1999, Al Taucher Rep. of Yr. award, 2001, Excellence in Leadership award Leadership Long Beach, 2004, Ann. Hall of Fame honoree Long Beach Century Club, 2006. Mem. Industry Edn. Coun. Long Beach (hon. life), Long Beach C. of C. (Dewey Smith cmty. svc. award), Lions Club (hon. life), Soroptimist Internat. (Woman of Distinction in Econ. and Social Devel. 2001), Alpha Iota. Republican. Presbyterian. Home: Bixby Village 551 Pittsfield Ct Unit 101 Long Beach CA 90803-6355

SATTER, MARY ANN, literature and language educator; b. Rochester, N.Y., Apr. 8, 1950; d. Genevieve and Andrew Satter. BA in English, U. Rochester, N.Y., 1972, MA in English, 1976. Cert. English Tchr. grades 7-12 N.Y., 1976. English tchr. Nazareth Acad., Rochester, NY, 1972—83, Brighton HS, Rochester, NY, 1983—; adj. faculty Rochester Inst. of Tech., NY, Nazareth Coll. of Rochester, NY. Mem. ACLU, NY. Recipient Adviser of Yr., Empire State Sch. Press Assn., 1998. Mem.: Nat. Coun. Tchrs. of English, N.Y. State English Coun. (English Tchr. of Excellence 2004). Avocations: reading, writing, films. Office: Brighton HS 1150 Winton Rd S Rochester NY 14618 Office Phone: 585-242-5036. Business E-Mail: maryann_satter@bcsd.org.

SATTERFIELD-HARRIS, RITA, financial analyst; b. Bklyn., Oct. 14, 1949; d. Wilton Anthony and Hattie Eva (Tunstall) Satterfield; m. Sidney Harris, Jan. 5, 1973; 1 child, Marcial A.H. BA in Psychology, Bernard Baruch Coll., N.Y.C., 1983; student, CCNY, 1971-74; Cert. in Paralegal Studies, L.I. U., Bklyn., 1982; cert. unemployment ins. benefits law, Cornell U., 1984. Lic. workers' compensation rep. N.Y.; registered agt. N.Y. State Unemployment Ins. Dir. social svcs. Lincoln Sq. Neighborhood Ctr., N.Y.C., 1979-88; pvt. practice N.Y.C., 1988—. Writer of proposals funded by N.Y.C. Dept. for Aging Inc., 1980-82, and N.Y.C. Cmty. Devel. Agy., 1984-88. Recipient Cert. of Appreciation for participation in vol. income tax assistance program Dept. Treasury, IRS, 1985, 86, Ptnrs. in Change award Nat. Displaced Homemakers Network, 1991. Mem. Workers' Def. League, Nat. Orgn. Social Security Claimant's Reps. Avocations: rollerskating, music, gourmet cooking. Office: 141 Livingston St Brooklyn NY 11201-5133 Office Phone: 718-403-9041.

SATTERLEE, TERRY JEAN, lawyer; b. Kansas City, Mo., Aug. 28, 1948; d. Charles Woodbury and Francis Jean (Shriver) Satterlee; m. William W. Rice, Jan. 9, 1982; children: Cassandra Jean Rice, Mary Shannon Rice. BA, Kans. U., 1970; JD, U. Mo., 1974. Bar: Mo. 1974. Lawyer Arthur Benson Assocs., Kansas City, 1974—77, Freilich & Leitner, Kansas City, 1977—78, U.S. EPA, Kansas City, 1978—83; of counsel Lathrop & Norquist, Kansas City, 1985—87, ptnr., 1987—, Shook Hardy & Bacon LLP, Kansas City, 2006—. Exec. com. Lathrop & Norquist, Kans. City, 1997—2002. Contbr. articles to profl. jours. Chmn. Bd. Zoning Adjustment, Kansas City, 1983—87, Mo. State Pks. Adv. Bd., 1997—2002; mem. hazardous materials com. Kansas City; mem. steering com. COMPASS Met. Planning, Kansas City, 1990—93. Mem.: Kansas City Bar Assn. (environ. com. chmn. 1986—90, chair 2001), Mo. Bar Assn. (chair environ. com. 1990—93), Nat. Assn. Clean Water Agys. (legal affairs com. 1992—, vice chair 2005—06), Women's Pub. Svc. Network (named Top 25 U.W. Women in Bus. 2000), Kansas City C. of C. (environ. com. chmn. 1992), Mo. C. of C. (mem. natural resource coun. 1990—2002, chair 1998—2002, bd. dirs. 1999—2002). Democrat. Episcopalian. Office: Shddk Hardy & Bacow LLC 2555 Grand Blvd Kansas City MO 64108 Office Phone: 816-292-2000, 816-474-6550. Business E-Mail: tsalterlee@shb.com.

SATTERTHWAITE, HELEN FOSTER, retired state legislator; b. Blawnox, Pa., July 8, 1928; d. Samuel J. and Lillian (Schreiber) Foster; m. Cameron B. Satterthwaite, Dec. 23, 1950 (div. July 1979); children: Mark Cameron, Tod Foster, Tracy Lynn, Keith Alan, Craig Evan (dec.). BS in Chemistry, Duquesne U., 1949. Rsch. asst. Gulf R & D, Harmarville, Pa., 1950; rsch. chemist E.I. duPont de Nemours & Co., Wilmington, Del., 1951-53; biol. technician USDA, 1967-68; lab. technician U. Ill. Coll. Agr., 1968-70; rsch. asst. Iowa State U. Coll. Agr., 1971; technician Nat. Sci. Lab., U. Ill. Coll. Vet. Medicine, 1971-74; rep. Ill. Ho. of Reps., Springfield, 1974-92, majority leader, 1991-92, mem. sch. fin. task force, 1990-92, chmn. com. on higher edn., 1983-91, vice chmn. elem. and secondary edn., 1983-91; ret., 1993. Mem. Commn. on Mental Health and Devel. Disabilities, 1975-85, mem. exec. com., 1977-85, vice chmn., 1979-85; mem. Commn. to Visit and Examine State Instns., 1977-85; mem. Task Force on Global Climate Change, 1991-96; treas. LWV, 1995-98, sec., 1998-2001; treas. Bus. and Profl. Women's Club, 1993-94, sec., 1994-95; bd. dirs. East Ctrl. Ill. Health Sys. Agy., 1977-79, Champaign County Mental Health Ctr., 1993-2002, Univ. YWCA, U. Ill., 1987—, Girls Inc., 1992-96; bd. dirs. Champaign County United Way, 1970-74, mem. budget com., 1973-74, mem. joint rev. com. on funding Champaign County mental health programs, 1973; co-chmn. task force on mental retardation Champaign County Mental Health Bd., 1973; mem. Ill. Devel. Disability Advocacy Authority, 1977-85, vice chmn., 1979-80; chmn. Ill. House Dem. Study Group, 1979-81; mem. Edn. Commn. on States, 1985-92, Nat. Conf. State Legis. Commn. on Labor and Edn., 1985-92; bd. govs. U. YMCA, 1995-2003. Recipient Freshman Legislator of Yr. award Ill. Edn. Assn., 1975, commndation Ill. State's Attys. Assn., 1975, Best Legislator award Ind. Voters Ill., 1976, 78, 80, 82, 84, 86, 88, 90, cert. of honor Assn. Student Govts., 1977, Disting. Svc. cert. AMVETS, 1977, Environ. Legislator of Yr. award Ill. Environ. Coun., 1977, 79, 81, 83, Meritorious Svc. award Champaign County Coun. on Alcoholism, 1978, Ill. C.C. Trustees ASsn., 1986, Perfect Voting Record award Ill. Credit Union League, 1979, Ill. Wildlife Fedn., 1979, cert., of spl. recognition Ill. Women's Polit. Caucus, 1979, 80, Pub. Svc. award Izaak Walton League, 1980, Friend of Edn. award Ill. Bd. Edn., 1985, cert. of appreciation Champaign County Urban League, 1987, Resolution of Honor, Ill. Libr. Assn., 1987, 100 Percent award Ill. Coun. Sr. Citizens Orgns., 1989, Dare To Be Great award Ill. Women Adminstrs., 1989; named Person of Yr., Champaign County Mental Health Assn., 1981, Pub. Citizen of Yr., Illino Dist. and Ill. chpt. NASW, 1981, Legislator of Yr., Ill. Assn. Sch. Social Workers, 1989. Mem. Ill. Conf. Women Legislators (co-convenor 1981-83), Nat. Order Women Legislators (bd. dirs. region IV 1982, treas. 1983-84), State Univs. Annuitants Assn. (exec. com. U. Ill. Urbana Champaign chpt. 2003—), Champaign County League Women Voters, Delta Kappa Gamma. Mem. Soc. Of Friends.

SATTERTHWAITE, JANET F., lawyer; b. Washington, Apr. 29, 1960; BA, Yale Univ., 1982; attended, Christ's Coll., Cambridge Univ.; JD, Univ. Va., 1986. Bar: Va. 1986, DC 1988, Wash. 1993. Ptnr., Trademark & Domain Name practice Venable LLP, Washington, 2001—. U.S. corr. Marques newsletter, Assn. European Trademark Owners. Contbr. articles to profl. jours. Office: Venable LLP 575 7th St NW Washington DC 20004 Office Fax: 202-344-4974, 202-344-8300. Business E-Mail: jfsatterthwaite@venable.com.

SATTLER, NANCY JOAN, educational association administrator; b. Toledo, July 14, 1950; d. Thomas Joseph and Margaret Mary (Linenkugel) Ainsworth; m. Rudolph Henry Sattler, June 17, 1972; children: Cortlund, Clinton, Corinne. BS, U. Toledo, 1972, MEd, 1988, PhD, 2004. Office worker/bookkeeper Gilbert Mail Svc., 1967-71; computer typesetter Quality Composition, Toledo, 1971-89; instr. Terra Tech. Coll. (now Terra C.C.), Fremont, Ohio, 1988-89; dept. head Terra Tech. Coll., Fremont, Ohio, 1989-95, curriculum chair bus., social scis., math. and arts, 1995-99, assoc. dean curriculum, 1999—2003, dean arts and scis., 2003—. Adj. instr. Terra Tech. Coll., Fremont, 1982-88, Terra Cmty. Coll., 1998—, U. Toledo, 1988, Lucas County Bd. Edn. Gifted Program, Toledo, 1988-92; computer coord. St. Joseph Elem. Sch., Fremont, 1987-94, coord. quiz bowl, 1993; extern in quality control Atlas Crankshaft, Fostoria, Ohio, 1990; instr. devel. math. A.O. Smith, Bellevue, Ohio, 1991, 93, 94; adult edn. computer instr. St. Joseph Ctrl. Cath. Sch., Fremont, 1990-92, sec. sch. bd., 1989-94, pres., 1991-94; instr. devel. math. and sci. Whirlpool Corp., Findlay, Ohio, 1992; presenter Am. Math. Assn. Two-Yr. Colls., 1991-2005, Nat. Coun. Tchrs. Math. Conf., 1993, 95, 98, 99; co-presenter Continuous Improvements Through Faculty Externship, League for Innovation, 1992; co-chmn. Ohio Gt. Tchrs. Seminar, 1993—; chmn. Kids Coll., Fremont, 1993-95; facilitator Mo. Gt. Tchrs. Seminar, 1993, Ohio Gt. Tchrs. Retreat, 1994-2006, N.Y. Gt. Tchrs. Seminar, 1994, Inventing Our Future, 1995-2002; co-chmn., presenter Ohiomatyc Winter Inst., 1994-98, 2000, 02, 03, 05; TOM trainer Terra C.C., 1994-96; mem. Math. Scis. Edn. Bd, Washington, 2004—. Author: The Implication of Math Placement Testing in the Two Year College, 1988, Applied Math for Industrial Technology, 1989; co-author: Math and Science Made Easy, 1992, The Metric System, Preparing for the Future, 1992, Workplace Literacy, 1994, The Basics of Using the TI-85 Graphing Calculator, 1995, Using the TI-85 Calculator to Solve Practical Application Problems for Business and Engineering Technologies. Clk. Sandusky County Fair, 1977—; parliamentarian Welcome Wagon, 1980; mem. MSEB; advisor Distributed Learning Workshop, 2001—; Sunday sch. dir. St. Joseph Ch., Fremont, 1977—87; Eucharist min., 1991—; sec. St. Joseph Ctrl. Cath. Sch. Bd., 1989—94, pres., 1991—94, Plant 'N Bloom Garden Club, Fremont, 1977—79, 2004—05; chair comm. Inventing Our Future, 1996—2003; mem. adv. bd. Ohio Resource Ctr.; coun. bd. mem. Family and Children First, 2002—, Prevention Partnership, 2000—, chair, 2005—; rep. for deanery Early Childhood Devel., 1982—84. Named to Hall of Fame, Notre Dame U., 2005. Mem. Ohio Math. Assn. Two-Yr. Colls. (pres. 1992-95, historian 1997-, NSF grant com. 1992), Am. Math. Assn. Two-Yr. Colls. (assessment com. 1990—, chmn. 1993-97, program com. 1993, chmn. distance edn. task force 1998-2000, chmn. distance learning com. 2001-2005, treas. 2005-), Ohio Assn. Garden Clubs, Ohio Math. and Sci. Coalition (co-chmn. collaboration com. 1996-98, chmn. 1998—, mem. exec. bd. 1998—, chmn.-elect 2003-2004, chair 2005—). Democrat. Roman Catholic. Avocations: quilting, gardening, canning, sewing. Home: 712 Hayes Ave Fremont OH 43420-2914 Office: Terra Cmty Coll 2830 Napoleon Rd Fremont OH 43420-9814 Office Phone: 419-559-2179. Business E-Mail: nsattler@terra.edu.

SAUCERMAN, ALVERA ADELINE, elementary school educator; b. Colorado Springs, Nov. 29, 1932; d. Alva Arthur and Delpha Adeline (Cole) Gieck; m. James Ray Saucerman; 1 child, James Randall. Student, Stephens Bus. Sch., Denver, 1950-51; AA, Scottsbluff Coll., 1961; BEd, NW Mo. State U., 1965, MEd, 1971. Cert. French, reading specialization and learning disabilities tchr. Tchr. Lake Alice (Nebr.) Sch., 1961-62, West Nodaway Sch., Clearmont, Mo., 1965-67; remedial reading tchr. Maryville (Mo.) R II, 1968-74, dir. learning lab., 1975-88, tchr. learning disabilities, 1974-97; ret. Lectr. spl. edn. N.W. Mo. State U., Maryville, 1978—97. Mem. Maryville State Tchrs. Assn. (sec. 1978-79), AAUW (life, pres. 1981-83 Maryville Br.), Mo. State Tchrs. Assn. (life), Delta Kappa Gamma, Kappa Delta Pi (life). Avocations: travel, photography, reading, dance. Home: 1331 NW 107th Ter Gainesville FL 32606-5489

SAUCIER, GUYLAINE, corporate financial executive; b. Noranda, Que., Can., June 10, 1946; d. Gérard and Yvette (Thiffault) S. Chartered acct., École Hautes Etudes Commls., Montreal, Can., 1971. Formerly chair Joint Com. on Corp. Governance. Bd. dirs. Petro-Can., Axa Assurances Inc., Bank Montreal, Altran Techs., CHC Helicopter Corp., Areva Group. Fellow Inst. Chartered Accts., Inst. Corp. Dirs.; mem. Order Can. Avocation: tennis. Office Phone: 514-397-5494. Business E-Mail: gsaucier@gsaucier.com.

SAUDEK, MARTHA FOLSOM, artist, educator; b. Palo Alto, Calif., Nov. 27, 1923; d. David Morrill and Clinton Erwin (Stone) Folsom; m. William Morrison Kingsley, Dec. 3, 1943 (div. 1971); 1 child, Lucy Clinton Kingsley; m. Victor Mead Saudek, Aug. 18, 1973. BA, Pomona Coll., 1947. Tchr. Concord (Calif.) Sch. Dist., 1949-51, Hermosa Beach (Calif.) City Schs., 1966-76, adminstrv. asst. to supt., 1977-81. Contbg. artist: (books) Painting With Passion, 1994, How to Paint Trees, Flowers, and Foliage, 1995, How to Paint Water, 1996. Sch. bd. dirs. Manhattan Beach (Calif.) Sch. Dist., 1964-72, pres., 1965. Named to Top 100, Arts for the Parks, 1994, 96, Region III winner, 2001, One of Nat. Gold Winners, Grumbacher Hall of Fame, 1995. Fellow Am. Artists' Profl. League, Calif. Art Club (signature mem.), Oil Painters of Am. (signature). Democrat. Avocations: photography, cooking, reading, gardening. Home: 900 East Harrison Ave D 35-36 Pomona CA 91767 Office Phone: 909-624-6160. Personal E-mail: msaudek@verizon.net.

SAUER, ELISSA SWISHER, nursing educator; b. Williamsport, Pa., Jan. 9, 1935; d. Oliver S. and Emily Louisa (Gehron) Swisher; m. Raymond James Sauer, Nov. 27, 1964. Diploma, Reading (Pa.) Hosp. Sch. Nursing, 1957; BS, Albright Coll., Reading, 1958; MSN, U. Pa., 1964. Instr. Reading Hosp. Sch. Nursing, 1957—60, 1964—66, 1969—70, Abington Meml. Hosp. Sch. Nursing, 1960—63; nurse Cmty. Health and Civic Assn., Ardmore, Pa., 1966-67; pub. health coord. Albert Einstein Med. Ctr., 1967-68; pvt. duty nurse, 1968-73; clin. faculty Schuylkill County AVTS, 1973-74; prof. nursing Reading Area CC, 1975-80, dir. nursing programs, asst. dean health svcs., 1989-2000, asst. dean emerita, 2001—, adj. instr. nursing, 2003—; oncology nurse adminstr.-educator Comprehensive Cmty. Cancer Ctr., Allentown, Pa., 1981-85; exec. dir. Holy Family Home Health Care, Orwigsburg, Pa., 1985-89. Cons. nursing edn. and continuing edn.; evaluator for nat. nurse aide cert. assessment program, 2000—; adj. instr. nursing Reading Area C.C., 2003—. Author: Procedure Manual to accompany Fundamentals of Nursing: Human Health and Function, 3d edit., 2003. Mem.: Sigma Theta Tau. Home: 1114 Pepper Ridge Dr Reading PA 19606-3803 E-mail: esauer@ptd.net.

SAUER, ELIZABETH MASON, school social worker; b. Chgo., Aug. 1, 1933; d. George Allen Jr. and Louise Townsend (Barnard) Mason; m. Louis Sauer, June 7, 1956 (div. Aug. 1990); children: Christopher G., Kathryn Sauer Chandler. BS in Speech/Theatre, Northwestern U., Evanston, Ill., 1955; MSW, U. Pa., 1961; Diploma in Edn. for Ministry, Theol. Sch. of the South, Sewanee, Tenn., 1992. Lic. social worker, Pa.; cert. home and sch. visitor, Pa. Social worker, supr. Dept. of Welfare City of Phila., 1958-65; social work supr. Child Care Ctrs. Sch. Dist. of Phila., 1965-69; social worker St. Peter's Child Devel. Ctrs., Pitts., 1982-84; supr. run-away-youth program Youth Emergency Svcs./Youth Svc., Inc., Phila., 1984-87; foster care social worker Residential Treatment/Silver Springs-Martin Luther Sch., Plymouth Meeting, Pa., 1987-89; sch. social worker Martin Luther Sch., Plymouth Meeting, Pa., 1989—. Cons. Child Care Ctrs., Phila., 1970—72. Actor The Playhouse, Eagles Mere, Pa., 1954, 55. Bd. dirs. Northwest Cmty. Coun., Phila., 1976-79; mem. outreach com. Ch. of St. Martin's In the Fields, Phila., 1993-96, Liturgist, 1995-2002; mem. Phila.-Chestnut Hill Cmty. Assn., 1970-79, 84—; mem. Water Tower Adv. Coun., Phila. Dept. Recreation, Move On and Neighborhoods Networks, Phila. Mem. NASW, ACSW, Pa. Assn. Sch. Social Work Personnel. Democrat. Episcopalian. Avocations: gardening, reading, quilting, travel, needlecrafts. Office: Martin Luther Sch 512 Township Line Rd Plymouth Meeting PA 19462-1001

SAUER, KARIN, microbiology educator; PhD, Philipps U., Marburg, Germany, 1999, diploma, 1996. Postdoctoral assoc. Max-Planck-Inst. Terrestrial Microbiology, Marburg, Germany, 1999, Ctr. Biofilm Engring., Bozeman, Mont., 2000—01; asst. prof. microbiology Binghamton U., NY, 2003—. Vis. asst. prof. Binghamton U., 2002—03. Office: Binghamton University Vestal Parkway East Binghamton NY 13902 Office Phone: 777-3157.

SAUER, MARY JULIA, special education educator; b. Pitts., Oct. 10, 1949; d. Edward Henry and Julia Ann (Polkabla) Sauer; 1 child, Jason Michael Sauer; m. John Harold Moore, Oct. 27, 1990 (div.); 1 adopted child, Jocelyn Quan. BS in Art Edn., Edinboro State Coll., 1971; MS in Spl. Edn., Clarion State Coll., 1980; postgrad. U. Pitts., 1988—. Cert. art tchr., spl. edn. tchr. for mentally retarded. Tchr. Polk (Pa.) State Sch. & Hosp., 1971-72; vol. VISTA, Bath, NY, 1972-73; tchr. Polk Ctr., 1973-80, program specialist, 1980-92; residential svc. supr., qualified mental retardation profl. Polk (Pa.) Ctr., 1992—. Lectr., speaker, video on local TV on history of Polk Ctr., 1987. Patentee beer bottle shaped cake pan; cakes displayed in TV videos and in various mags.; creator history video Polk Ctr., Some Leaky Boot Statues, Polk Center--100 Years; creator video A Century of Care-The History of the Evolution of Institional Care of the Devlopment Disabled. Past vol. Big Bros./Big Sisters. Democrat. Roman Catholic. Avocations: cake decorating, reading. Home: PO Box 97 Franklin PA 16323

SAUERBREY, ELLEN ELAINE RICHMOND, federal agency administrator, former ambassador; b. Balt., Sept. 9, 1937; d. Edgar Arthur and Ethel Frederika (Landgraf) Richmond; m. Wilmer John Emil Sauerbrey, June 27, 1959. AB summa cum laude in Biology and English, Western Md. Coll., 1959. Biology instr., chmn. sci. dept. Baltimore County Sch. System, 1959-64; dist. mgr. Baltimore County U.S. Census, 1970; mem. Md. Ho. of Dels., Annapolis, 1978-94, minority leader, 1986-94; radio talk show host Sta. WBAL, Balt., 1996; US amb. to Commn. on the Status of Women UN, 2002—05; asst. sec. Bur. Population, Refugees & Migration US Dept. State, Washington, 2006—. Rep. nominee for Gov., 1994, 98; U.S. del. commn.

human rights UN, 2001, 03; head U.S. del. Baltic states conf., 03; U.S. del econ. commn. Latin Am. and Caribbean, 04; mem. adv. com. women in svcs. US Dept. Def., 2004—06. Nat. chmn. Am. Legis. Exec. Coun., 1990—91; trustee Md. Coun. Econ. Edn., Franklin Sq. Hosp.; founder United Citizen's for Md.'s Future; bd. advisors Yorktown University; Rep. Nat. Com. Woman Md., 1996—2003; Rules com., 1996; del. Rep. Nat. Convs., 1968, 1976, 1984, 1988, 1992, 1996, 2000, platform com., chmn. subcom. on economy, 1977; nat. adv. bd. Nat. Conservative Campaign Fund; mem. credentials com. Rep. Nat. Convs., 1984; vice chmn. Rep. State Ctrl. Com. of Balt. County, 1966—71; state chmn. Md. chpt. George W. Bush for Pres., 1999—2000. Recipient Pvt. Property award Greater Balt. Bd. Realtors, 1984; named Legislator of Yr., Md. Assn. Builders and Contractors, 1982, Am. Legis. Exec. Coun., 1986, Western Md. Coll. Alum of Yr., 1988, Outstanding Legis. Leader, Am. Legis. Exec. Coun., 1992, Rep. Woman of Yr., Md. Rep. Party, 1995, Nat. Fedn. Ind. Bus., Guardian of Small Bus. award, 1989, Lifetime Svc. award Baltimore County Rep. Party, 2003, Md. State of Mind award, 2004; named one of top 100 Md. Women, The Daily Record, 1998. Mem. DAR, Nat. Fedn. Rep. Women (Margaret Chase Smith award 1995, Md. State of Mind award 2004), Md. Fedn. Rep. Women, Am. Legis. exch. Coun. (chmn. emeritus), Md. Farm Bur., Md. Conservative Union, Beta Beta, Beta, Phi Beta Kappa. Presbyterian. Avocations: gardening, travel. Office: US Dept State Harry S Truman Bldg 2201 C St NW Rm 5824 Washington DC 20520 Personal E-mail: Ellen99@erols.com.

SAUERESSIG-RIEGEL, SUZANNE, veterinarian, writer, columnist; b. Nuremberg, Germany, Feb. 4, 1925; arrived in US, 1955; d. Josef and Elizabeth (Walsch) Saueressig; m. Richard T. Riegel, Dec. 26, 1955. DVM, Munich U., 1954. Staff veterinarian Humane Soc. Mo., St. Louis, 1955—65, chief of staff, 1965—. Author:: Salmonella in Shellfish, 1954; columnist Ask the Pet Doctor, St. Louis Globe Democrat, 1980—85; contbr. articles to popular mags. With German Army, 1943—49. Recipient Spl. Leadership award, YWCA, St. Louis, 1983. Mem.: AVMA, Mo. Vet. Med. Assn., Mo. Control Officers Assn., Am. Vet. Cardiology Soc., Vet. Oncology Soc., Am. Assn. Lab. Animal Sci., Mo. Acad. Vet. Medicine, Assn. Feline Practitioners, Assn. Woman Veterinarians (Woman Vet. of Yr. 1972), Am. Animal Hosp. Assn. Roman Catholic. Office: Humane Soc of Mo 1210 Macklind Ave Saint Louis MO 63110-1432

SAUFLEY, LEIGH INGALLS, state supreme court chief justice; b. Portland, Maine, June 21, 1954; m. William Saufley; 2 children. BA, U. Maine, Orono, 1976; JD, U. Maine Sch. of Law, 1980. Pvt. practice, Ellsworth; asst. counsel U.S. VA; asst., then dep. atty. gen. Maine, 1981-90; judge Maine Dist. Ct., 1990—93; justice Maine Superior Ct, 1993—97; assoc. justice Maine Supreme Judicial Ct., 1997—2001, chief justice, 2001—. Mem.: ABA. Maine's first female chief justice. Office: Cumberland County Courthouse PO Box 368 142 Federal St Portland ME 04112-0368 E-mail: amanda.j.martin@maine.gov.

SAUL, JENNIFER ANN, therapist; b. El Centro, Calif., June 2, 1972; d. Roy John Schoolcraft and Kukya Yi (Lee) Marshall; m. Mark Kahiona Saul, Feb. 10, 1996. BS in Occupl. Therapy, Tex. Womans U., 1995. Occupl. therapist Rehability/Am. Therapy Svcs., Arlington, Tex., 1995-97, Walls Regional Hosp., Cleburne, Tex., 1997—. Restraint reduction cons. Rehability, Alvarado, Tex., 1995-97; spkr. in field. Mem. Am. Occupl. Therapy Assn., Tex. Occupl. Therapy Assn. Democrat. Baptist. Avocations: walking, reading, cross-stitch, water sports, family. Office: 201 Walls Dr Cleburne TX 76033-4008 Home: 350 NE James Cir Burleson TX 76028-2674

SAULS, ALLISON HOUSTON, art educator; b. Columbus, Ohio, Aug. 4, 1949; d. Loren Charles and Beulah Mae (Veal) Miller; m. James Mack Sauls, Aug. 31, 1979; children: Zachary Houston, Christopher Bennett. BA, Huntingdon Coll., 1971; MA, U. Ga., 1981; PhD, Emory U., 1993. Instr. U. Ga., Athens, 1982-85; asst. prof. U. Tenn., Chattanooga, 1985; libr. cons. Nat. Park Svc. Regional, Atlanta, 1987-89; assoc. prof. Mo. Western State U., St. Joseph, 1993—, chair dept. art, 1996—. Co-author: Historic Places in Central Alabama: A Preliminary Inventory, 1973; rsch. asst. (book) Frederic Guitheim at 80-A Festschrift, 1988, (film) The Making of Atlanta, 1989-90, Emmy nomination, 1990; editl. asst. About Atlanta: A Research Guide, 1988. Commr. Landmarks Commn., St. Joseph, 1995—. Grantee Nat. Endowment Arts, 1985, Dept. Interior, 1972-73; Mary Wallace Kirk scholar Agnes Scott Coll., Decatur, Ga., 1987-89. Mem. Coll. Art Assn., Soc. for Cinema Studies. Democrat. Episcopalian. Home: 1308 N 11th St Saint Joseph MO 64501-1204 Office: Mo Western State Coll 4525 Downs Dr Saint Joseph MO 64507-2246 Office Phone: 816-271-4422.

SAULSBURY, GLYNIS ELLIOTT, elementary school educator; d. Frank Verocian and Juanita Elliott; m. Joseph Garfield Saulsbury, Apr. 3, 1993; 1 child, Joseph (Alex) Alexander. B Early Childhood Edn., Clark Atlanta U., 1991; MEd, Cumberland U., Lebanon, Tenn. Tchr. 4th grade Bethune Elem., Atlanta, 1991—94; tchr. 2nd grade Carter Elem., Knoxville, 1994—95; tchr. 5th grade Strathmore Elem., Silver Spring, Md., 1995—98; tchr. West Manor Elem., Atlanta, 1998—99; tchr. 2nd grade Lakeside Elem., Chattanooga, 1999—2002; tchr. 4th grade Crabapple Ln. Elem., Peachtree City, Ga., 2002—. Leadership team Crabapple Ln. Elem., Peachtree City, 2003—04. Mem.: Jack & Jill Club (assoc.; advisor 2004—05). Democrat. Methodist. Office: Fayette County Schools 450 Crabapple Lane Peachtree City GA 30269 Office Phone: 770-487-5425.

SAULS RAINS, AMY, elementary school educator; b. Gadsden, Ala., Aug. 9, 1980; d. Jeffrey David Sauls and Deborah Gail McDaniel Sauls; m. Kenneth Scott Rains, Aug. 7, 1999; 1 child, Wesley Scott. MusB in Edn., U. Miss., 2003. Tchr. music Livingston Elem. Sch., Covington, Ga., 2003—. Dir. Cardinal Chorus Livingston Elem. Sch., 2003—. Scholar, U. Miss., 1998—2003. Mem.: Am. Orff Schulwerk Assn. (cert.), Music Educators Nat. Conf., Profl. Assn. Ga. Educators, Sigma Alpha Iota (life; pres. chpt. 2003—). Bapt. Avocations: music, scrapbooks, collecting precious moments. Office: Livingston Elem Sch 3657 Hwy 81 S Covington GA 30016

SAUM, ELIZABETH PAPE, community volunteer; b. Evanston, Ill., Aug. 7, 1930; d. Karl James and Catherine (Schwall) Pape; m. William Joseph Saum, Dec. 31, 1960; children: JeanMarie, Katherine Anne, Mary Elizabeth. BA in English cum laude, Fontbonne Coll., 1952; MA in English, Northwestern U., 1958. Cert. tchr., Ill. Tchr. Our Lady of Perpetual Help, Glenview, Ill., 1952-55, Wilmette (Ill.) Jr. High Sch., 1955-61; dir. religion edn. St. Paul's Ch., Valparaiso, Ind., 1972-76; activities dir. Heritage Manor Nursing Home, Plano, Tex., 1982-84; exec. dir. Jessamine County Assn. Exceptional Citizens, Nicholasville, Ky., 1985-89; ret., 1989. Pres. bd. dirs. Women's Neighborly Orgn., Lexington, 1977-81; mem. Bluegrass Long-Term Care Ombudsman, Lexington, 1984-89; bd. dirs. Women's History Coalition Ky., Midway, 1985-90, Sr. Citizens East, Louisville, 1991-93, treas., 1992-93; creator, pres. Ky. Women's Heritage Mus., Lexington, 1986-90; adminstrn. coord. Transfiguration Ch., Goshen, Ky., 1991-93; liturgy coord. St. Stephen's Ch., Cadiz, Ky., 1996—; pres. Friends of the Libr., Trigg County, Ky., 1997-2000; vol. quilt tchr., 1997-; lectr. St. Mary Ch., 2005 Mem. AAUW (bd. dirs. Ky. br. 1977-81, 85-96, named gift honoree 1988, v.p. Ednl. Found. 1988-94, 95-96, co-pres. Ky. br. 1994-96, named gift honoree Lexington br. 1987, pres. 1984-86, 88-90, Louisville br. editor newsletter 1990-93, treas. 1991-93, v.p. Ednl. Found. 1991-93, mem. br.-state adv. bd. Ednl. Found. 1996-98), Lexington Newcomers (editor newsletter 1976-78), Trigg County Quilter's Guild (pres. 1995-97). Democrat. Roman Catholic. Home: 7709 Paige Dr Newburgh IN 47630 Personal E-mail: bills31@sbcglobal.net.

SAUNDERS, ANTOINETTE MERCIER, psychologist, educator; b. Detroit, Sept. 30, 1947; d. Frank Breckenridge and Barbara (Shuell) S.; m. Terrence Joseph, Nov. 26, 1986; 1 child, Annie. BS, St. Louis U., 1969; MEd, U. Tex., El Paso, 1970; PhD, St. Andrews U., Dundee, Scotland, 1972. Lic. psychologist, Ill. Postdoctoral fellow Loyola U., Chgo., 1972-74; asst. prof. psychology U. Ill. Med. Sch., Chgo., 1974-80; dir., founder Stress Edn. Ctr. (now Capable Kid Ctrs.), Evanston, Ill., 1980—93, Transformations Inst. Psychol. and Spiritual Devel., 1996—. Faculty family studies Northwestern U., Evanston, 1978—. Author: Stress Proof Child, 1984, (curriculum) Capable Kid Program, 1980, Step Family Program, 1991, Capable Parent Program, 1992, Focus on Children, 1995. Mem. Am. Psychol. Assn., Ill. Psychol. Assn., Nat. Coun. on Self Esteem. Avocations: scuba diving, skiing, tennis. Office Phone: 847-853-0601.

SAUNDERS, ARLENE, opera singer; b. Cleve., Oct. 5, 1935; MusB, Baldwin-Wallace Coll., 1957. Kammersaengerin German Govt., 1970—; tchr. voice Rutgers U., New Brunswick, N.J., 1987-88; tchr. classical vocal repertoire Abraham Goodman Sch., N.Y.C., 1987-88; advisor; tchr. vocal dept. NYU, 1990-96, tchr. master classes, head opera dept., 1990-96. Tchr. master classes Baldwin Wallace Coll., Santa Fe Opera Co., etc.; founder, dir. Opera Mobilé, Inc., N.Y.C., 1991-97; adjudicator Met. Opera Regional Auditions, Liederkranz Voice Auditions, etc. Debut Milan Opera, 1961; Met. Opera debut in Die Meistersinger, 1976; specializes in Strauss and Wagner; performer with Phila. Opera, Lyric Opera, Houston Opera, Covent Garden, London, Teatro Colon, Buenos Aires, San Francisco Opera, Vienna Staatsoper, Paris Opera, Australian Opera, Sydney, Berlin Deutsche Opera, Munich Staatsoper, Hamburg State Opera, 1963-86, Rome Opera, Brussels Opera, Maggio Musicale, Florence, Italy, Geneva (Switzerland) Opera, Berlin Festival, Lisbon Opera, Glyndebourne Festival Opera, Eng., English Opera North, Boston Opera, N.Y.C. Opera; performed world premieres of Beatrix Cenci, 1971, Jakobowsky und der Oberst, 1965, Help, Help, The Globolinks, 1968, Ein Stern Geht Auf Aus Jaakob, 1970 (Gold medal Vercelli (Italy) voice competition); appeared in opera films including Arabella (title role), Meistersaenger (Eva), Marriage of Figaro (Countess), Help, Help the Globolinks (Mme. Euterpova), Der Freischuetz (Agathe), Gasparone (Carlotta); recs. for Philips and Victor. N.Y.C. Mayor's award, 1962; Kammersängerin Hamburg, 1967 Mem. Pi Kappa Lambda (Epsilon Phi chpt.) Address: 535 E 86th St Apt 7A New York NY 10028-7533 E-mail: Divasaund@aol.com.

SAUNDERS, DANIELLE, lawyer, telecommunications industry executive; BA magna cum laude, George Washington U., JD. Atty. Hunton & Williams, Shaw Pittman; sr. counsel Teleglobe Internat.; v.p. bus. devel. Primus Telecom. Group, Inc., McLean, Va., 1999—, exec. v.p., gen. counsel, 2001—. Office: Primos Telecommunications Group Inc 7901 Jones Branch Dr # 9 Mc Lean VA 22102-3338 Office Phone: 703-902-2800.

SAUNDERS, DONNA M., accountant; b. Washington, July 23, 1969; d. Ellridge Everette Carey and Joyce Bernice Ramey; m. Gary Roland Saunders, June 10, 2000. BS, U. Md., 1991. Market rschr. Nat. Rsch. Inc., New Carrollton, Md., 1986-87; clk.-typist USN, Washington, 1987; student asst. U. Md. College Park, Washington, 1987-91; sr. acct. Bert Smith & Co., Washington, Va., 1992-94; staff acct. Arrow Gen., Alexandria, Va., 1994; accts. payable supr. Franklin Acceptance, Greenbelt, Md., 1994-96; acctg. mgr. Rental Tools, Upper Marlboro, Md., 1996-99; sr. acct. FTI Cons., Annapolis, Md., 1999; acctg. mgr. Safeware, Inc., Largo, Md., 1999—2004; sr. acct. AES Corp., 2004—. Bd. dirs., asst. sec./treas. Safeware, 2003. Mem. AICPAs, Md. Assn. CPAs. Democrat. Baptist. Avocation: missionary youth work.

SAUNDERS, JUDITH P., literature and language professor, writer; b. Chgo. AB, U. Calif., Berkeley, 1968, MA, 1969; PhD, U. Calif., San Diego, 1975. Instr. English Wellesley Coll., Mass., 1973—77; asst. prof. English Vassar Coll., Poughkeepsie, NY, 1977—82; assoc. acad. dean Marymount Coll., Tarrytown, 1983—86; prof. English Marist Coll., Poughkeepsie, 1986—. Dir. honors program Marist Coll., 1994—2000. Author: (poetry) Check-out Counter Suite (winner, Panhandler Poetry Chapbook Competition, 1992), The Poetry of Charles Tomlinson: Border Lines (Fairleigh Dickinson U. Press, 2003); contbr. articles to lit. jours. Mem.: Human Behavior And Evolution Soc., Edith Wharton Soc., Phi Beta Kappa. Office: Marist College 3399 North Rd Poughkeepsie NY 12601 Office Phone: 845-575-3000.

SAUNDERS, LESLIE, insurance company executive, marketing professional; Pres., CEO Leslie Saunders Ins. and Mktg. Internat., Lutz, Fla., 1988—. Adv. Travel Safety Programs for Women Bus. Travelers; supporter Diversity in the Workplace, Minority and Women Supplier Devel. Office: Leslie Saunders Ins and Mktg Internat 1535 N Dale Mabry Lutz FL 33549

SAUNDERS, LONNA JEANNE, lawyer, newscaster; b. Cleve. d. Jack Glenn and Lillian Frances (Newman) Slaby. Student, Dartmouth Coll.; AB in Polit. Sci. with honors, Vassar Coll.; JD, Northwestern U., 1981; cert. advanced study in Mass Media, Stanford U., 1992. Bar: Ill. 1981. News dir., morning news anchor Sta. WKBK-AM, Keene, NH, 1974-75; reporter Sta. KDKA-AM, Pitts., 1975; pub. affairs dir., news anchor Sta. WJW-AM, Cleve., 1975-76; helicopter traffic reporter WERE-AM Radio, Cleve., 1976-77; morning news anchor Sta. WBBG-AM, Cleve., 1978; talk host, news anchor Sta. WIND-AM, Chgo., 1978-82; atty. Arvey, Hodes, Costello & Burman, Chgo., 1981-82; host, "The Stock Market Observer", news anchor WCIU-TV, Chgo., 1982-85; staff atty. Better Govt. Assn., Chgo., 1983-84; news anchor, reporter Sta. WBMX-FM, Chgo., 1984-86; pvt. practice law Chgo., 1985—; news anchor Sta. WKQX-FM, Chgo., 1987; arbitrator Cir. Ct. 17th Jud. Dist., Ill., 2005—; tchr. Rockford Pub. Schs., Ill., 2005—, Allen County Pub. Schs., Ohio, 2005—. Instr. Columbia Coll., Chgo., 1987-90; guest talk host Sta. WMCA, N.Y.C., 1983, Sta. WMAQ, Chgo., 1988, Sta. WLS, Chgo., 1989, Sta. WWWE, Cleve., 1989, Sta. KVI, Seattle, 1994, WCBM-AM, Balt., 1996, WRC-AM, Wash., D.C., 1997; host, prodr. The Lively Arts, Cablevision Chgo., 1986; talk show host The Lonna Saunders Show, Sta. KIRO-AM, Seattle, 1995-96; news anchor, WTOP-AM Radio, Washington, D.C., 1996-97; talk host, "Today and Tomorrow show", WMAL-AM radio, Washington, D.C., 1997, freelance reporter, CBS Radio Network, N.Y.C., 1975—; atty. Lawyers for Creative Arts, Chgo., 1985-91; guardian Ad litem and child rep., 2005—. Mem. editl. bd. Jour. Criminal Law and Criminology, 1979-81; creator pub. affairs program WBBM-AM, Chgo., 1985; law columnist Chgo. Life Mag., 1986-99; sports columnist (Cleve.) Indians Ink mag., 1998-2000; writer Rock River Times newspaper, 2004; guest columnist Gainesville Sun, Fla., 1998-99, Rockford Register Star newspaper, 1998-2006; contbr. articles to profl. jours.; contbr. columns to mags. and newspapers. Atty., county counsel voter protection project Kerry-Edwards 2004, Inc.; mem. women's action coun. Amnesty Internat., 2000—. Recipient Akron Press Club award for best pub. affairs presentation, 1978; grantee Scripps Howard Found., 1978-81; AFTRA George Heller Meml. scholar, 1980-81. Fellow Am. Bar Found.; mem. ABA (mem. exec. coms. Lawyers and the Arts, Law and Media 1986-92, chmn. exec. com. Law and Media 1990-91, 91-92, Young Lawyers divsn. liaison to Forum Com. on Comm. Law 1991-93, Commn. for Partnership Programs 1993-94, regional divsn. chair Forum on Comm. Law 1995-96). Roman Catholic. Avocations: theater, piano, baseball. Office Phone: 815-218-9773. Personal E-mail: lonnasaunders@yahoo.com.

SAUNDERS, LUCILLE MAE, elementary education educator, librarian; b. Sioux City, Iowa, Sept. 30, 1930; d. Merwin B. and Frances (Sapienza) S. BA, Clarke Coll., 1952; MA, Ft. Wright Coll., 1970; postgrad., U. Nebr., 1980. Dir., tchr. Sisters of Charity of the Blessed Virgin Mary, Dubuque, Iowa, 1952-70, Children's Discovery Ctr., Omaha, 1970-81, Open Elem. Sch., Omaha, 1981-82; head tchr. Friedel Jewish Acad., Omaha, 1982-93; libr. media specialist Minne Lusa Sch. Omaha Pub. Schs., 1993—. Mem. libr. com. Omaha Together One Cmty.; active Omaha Orgn. for Purpose of Storytelling. Mem. Nebr. Assn. for Edn. of Young Children (officer, sec. 1970—), Nebr. Libr. Assn. (Golden Sower com.), Metro. Reading Coun. Avocations: sewing, hiking, camping, writing. Home: 7011 S 142nd St Omaha NE 68138-6244 Office: Minne Lusa Sch Libr Media Ctr 30th and Ida Omaha NE 68112

SAUNDERS, MARI PITTMAN, psychologist; b. Newark, May 13, 1935; d. Tillmon Ulysses Pittman and Christine Lisabeth Von Heiskell; m. David Milton Saunders Jr., Apr. 10, 1960; children: Phillip Michael, Leslie Beth. BS, CUNY, 1958, MA, 1962, MS, 1964; Doctorate, Fordham U., 1976. Cert. tchr., guidance counselor, N.Y.; Nat. Assn. Forensic Counselors cert. psychopathologist, psychotherapist, and addictions counselor. Tchr. elem. edn. Pub. Sch. 161, N.Y.C., 1961-62; tchr. jr. h.s. Jr. H.S. 43, N.Y.C., 1962-65; tchr. h.s. English, guidance counselor Taft H.S., Bronx, N.Y., 1965-70; clin. counselor H.H. Lehman, CUNY, Bronx, 1970-75; psychologist, therapist Edupsych Assocs., N.Y.C., 1975—; pvt. practice Urban League, Bklyn. and N.Y.C., 1981—, Addicts Rehab. Ctr., N.Y.C., 1984—. Clin. supr. Samaritan Women's Project, Rikers Island, N.Y., 1988-90; therapy cons. Assn. for Interpersonal Dynamics, N.Y.C., 1980-88; asst. supr. for cmty. guidance and edn. Bd. Edn., Bklyn., 1970-73; social worker NY Dept. Welfare N.Y.C. Social Svcs., Bronx, 1959-60. Author: (book) Marry Yes, Marry No, 1999; contbr. articles and book revs. to profl. publs. Psychologist, treas. Inst. for Interracial Harmony, Bklyn., 1982—; host telequest radio program WMCA, N.Y.C., 1983; appeared on several TV shows. Mem. Les Vivantes Noires (v.p. 1978, 2000—, pres.), Vanguard Coalition (psychologist 1999, 2000—). Personal E-mail: msaun4753@aol.com.

SAUNDERS, MARTHA DUNAGIN, academic administrator; m. Joseph Bailey; 7 children. BA, U. So. Miss., 1969; MA, U. Ga.; PhD in comm. theory, Fla. State U. Asst. prof. comm. U. West Fla., dir. Univ. Honors Prog., dean Coll. Arts and Scis., 1999; v.p. Academic Affairs Columbus State U.; chancellor U. Wis., Whitewater, 2005—. Author: Eastern's Armageddon: Labor Conflict and the Destruction of Eastern Airlines, 1992. Mem.: Pub. Relations Soc. Am. (Silver Anvil award). Avocations: fishing, gardening. Office: U Wis 800 W Main St Whitewater WI 53190 Office Phone: 262-472-1918. Office Fax: 262-472-1518.

SAUNDERS, MARY JANE, lawyer; b. Waltham, Mass., Oct. 15, 1956; BA, Va. Polytech. Inst., 1978; JD, Mercer Univ., 1981. Bar: Va. 1982, DC 1993, US Supreme Ct. 1992. Ptnr., Copyright & Unfair Trade, Nonprofit Org. practices Venable LLP, Washington. Mem.: DC Computer Law Forum (past pres.). Office: Venable LLP 575 &th St NW Washington DC 20004 also: Venable LLP Suite 300 8010 Towers Crescent Dr Vienna VA 22182 Office Phone: 202-344-8108, 703-760-1950. Office Fax: 202-344-8300. Business E-Mail: mjsaunders@venable.com.

SAUNDERS, PATRICIA GENE KNIGHT, freelance writer, editor; b. Tulsa, Okla., Nov. 29, 1946; d. Eugene Merritt and Patricia May (Hough) Knight; m. Joseph Eugene Saunders, June 24, 1989. BA, Baylor U., 1969. Nat. advt. sec. KTVT-TV, Ft. Worth, 1969-71; tchr. Arlington (Tex.) Ind. Sch. Dist., 1971-77, Garland (Tex.) Ind. Sch. Dist., 1977-79; payroll, spl. projects assoc. Electronic Data Systems, Dallas, 1979-81; adminstrv. asst. Diversifield Innovators, Dallas, 1981-82; system ops. mgr. Span Instruments, Plano, Tex., 1982-86; data processing mgr. Claire Mfg., Addison, Ill., 1986-87, Everpure, Inc., Westmont, Ill., 1987-88; software cons. Software Alternatives, Inc., Downers Grove, Ill., 1988-89; sys. ops. asst., cons. J&J Maintenance, Inc., Austin, Tex., 1989-90; pres., computer cons. Cardinal Software Solutions, Inc., Austin, 1990-93; editor Holt, Rinehart & Winston, Austin, 1993-99. Mem.: Writers' League of Tex., Soc. of Children's Book Writers and Illustrators, N.Y. Met. Mus. Fine Art, Smithsonian Instn., Nat. Mus. Women in the Arts, Nat. Arbor Day Found., Nat. Wildlife Fedn. Republican. Baptist. Avocations: cats, gardening, travel, movies, reading. Home: 410 Teal Ln Kyle TX 78640-8888 Office Phone: 512-262-2062. Office Fax: 512-268-1625. Personal E-mail: pgs2508@austin.rr.com.

SAUNDERS, SALLY LOVE, poet, educator; b. Bryn Mawr, Pa., Jan. 15, 1940; d. Lawrence and Dorothy (Love) S. Student, Sophia U., Tokyo, Japan, 1963, U. Pa., Columbia; BS, George Williams Coll., 1965. Tchr. Shipley Sch., Bryn Mawr, 1962-65, Agnes Irwin Sch., Wynnewood, Pa., 1964-65, Montgomery County Day Sch., Wynnewood, 1962, Miquon (Pa.) Sch., Waldron Acad., Merion, Pa., 1965-66, Phelps Sch., Malvern, Pa., 1965-70, Frankford Friends Sch. Phila., 1965-66, Haverford (Pa.) Sch., 1965-66, Friends Sem. Sch., N.Y.C., 1966-68, Ballard Sch., N.Y.C., 1966-67, Lower Merion Sch., Ardmore, Pa., nights 1967-71, Univ. Settlement House, Phila., 1961-63, Navajo Indian Reservation, Fort Defiance, Ariz., 1963, Young Men's Jewish Youth Center, Chgo., 1964-65, Margaret Fuller Settlement House, Cambridge, Mass., 1958-61; poetry therapist Pa. Hosp. Inst., 1969-74, also drug rehab. house Phila.; poet in residence Tyrone Guthrie Ctr., Newbliss, Ireland, Aug. 1988; poetry workshop leader Pendle Hill Quaker Ctr., Wallingford, Pa., Apr. 1988; poetry week leader Ferry Beach, Saco, Maine, summer 1988. Pioneer in poetry therapy. Poet, 1946—; poems pub. in periodicals including others; author: Past the Near Meadows, 1961, Pauses, 1978, Fresh Bread, 1982, Random Thoughts, 1992, Patchwork Quilt, 1993, Quiet Thoughts and Gentle Feelings, 1996, Word Pictures, 1998, Bits of Thought, 2006; contbr. poems to newspapers. Mem. Acad. Am. Poets, Nat. Fedn. State Poetry Socs., Am. Poetry League, Nat. League Am. Pen Women, Poetry Therapy Assn. (v.p.), Avalon Orgn., Authors Guild, Nat. Writers Club, Pen and Brush Club, N.H.Poetry Soc., Pa. Poetry Soc., Cath. Poetry Soc. (asso.), Fla. State Poetry Soc. (asso.) Episcopalian. Home: 2030 Vallejo St Apt 501 San Francisco CA 94123-4854 Office: 609 Rose Hill Rd Broomall PA 19008-2254 Office Phone: 610-356-0849. E-mail: slovesndrs@aol.com.

SAUNDERS, VIRGINIA FOX, psychology educator; b. Roanoke, Va., May 31, 1938; d. William Alexander and Mary Elizabeth (Gray) Fox; children: Evan Keith, Kari Jennifer. BA with honors, U. Mich., 1960; PhD in Psychology and Neurophysiology, Ind. U., 1965. Postdoctoral fellow U. Calif. Med. Ctr., San Francisco, 1965—67; prof. psychology San Francisco State U., 1967—; Hebrew tchr., 2001—. Presenter workshops on psychoneuroimmunology, Calif.; reviewer textbooks and psychol. fiction. Mem. editorial bd. Ann. Edits. in Psychology, 1986—. Bd. dirs. Del Norte Oaks Homeowners Assn., San Rafael, Calif., 1991; v.p. Campus Ecumenical Ministry, San Francisco, 1982-85. Mem. Calif. Tchrs. Assn. Avocations: hiking, tennis. Office: San Francisco State U Dept Psychology 1600 Holloway Ave San Francisco CA 94132-1722

SAURER, MARY MARCELLE, minister; d. Ben Wiley and Gladys Magalene (Williamson) Lester; m. Gil Leroy Saurer, Apr. 9, 1988; children: Kenneth Wiley Hines, Gina Marie Buckner. BA in Interior Design, LaSalle U., 1975. Lic. tchr. Unity, Tulsa, Okla., 1984—; min., tchr., spiritual counselor, co-founder Soc. Christian Mystics and Metaphysicians, Tulsa, Okla., 1990—. Silent unity supr., trainer Unity, Unity Village, Mo., 1982—87; asst. activities dir. Southpark Nursing Home, Kansas City, Mo., 1988; dir., vol. program, coord. bereavement and chaplain's programs Hospice of Green Country, Tulsa, 1990—2001. Author: Windows of Life and Death, 1998, What Jesus Taught, 1999, Your Master Teacher Within, 1999, A Comparison of World Religions, 2005. Recipient Cert. in Vol. Mgmt., Boulder, Colo., 1994. Avocations: writing, yoga, dance, gardening, aromatherapy. Home: 5151 S Madison Ave Tulsa OK 74105 Personal E-mail: marysaurer@sbcglobal.net.

SAUSEDO, SASHA A., social studies educator; d. Paul Joseph and Valrie Jean Sausedo. BS in History, Ill. State U., Normal, 1998. Social studies tchr. Moline Sch. Dist. #40, Ill., 1999—. Office: Moline Sch Dist # 40 3600 Ave of the Cities Moline IL 61265 Personal E-mail: ssausedo@molineschools.org.

SAUSMAN, KAREN, zoological park administrator; b. Chgo., Nov. 26, 1945; d. William and Annabell (Lofaso) S. BS, Loyola U., 1966; student, Redlands U., 1968. Keeper Lincoln Park Zoo, Chgo., 1964-66; tchr. Palm Springs (Calif.) Unified Sch., 1968-70; ranger Nat. Park Svc., Joshua Tree, Calif., 1968-70; zoo dir. The Living Desert, Palm Desert, Calif., 1970—. Natural history study tour leader internat., 1974—; part-time instr. Coll. Desert Natural History Calif. Desert, 1975-78; field reviewer conservation grants Inst. Mus. Svcs., 1987—, MAP cons., 1987—, panelist, 1992—; internat. studbook keeper for Sand Cats, 1988-2001, for Cuvier's Gazelle, Mhorr Gazelle, 1990-2000; co-chair Arabian Oryx species survival plan propogation group, 1986-95; spkr. in field. Author Survival Captive Bighorn Sheep, 1982, Small Facilities- Opportunities and Obligations, 1983; wildlife illustrator books, mags, 1970—; editor Fox Paws newsletter Living Desert, 1970—, ann. reports, 1976—; natural sci. editor Desert Mag., 1979-82;

compiler Conservation and Management Plan for Antelope, 1992; contbr. articles to profl. jours. Past bd. dirs., sec. Desert Protective Coun.; adv. coun. Desert Bighorn Rsch. Inst., 1981-85; bd. dirs. Palm Springs Desert Resorts Convention and Visitors Bur., 1988-94; bd. dirs., treas. Coachella Valley Mountain Trust, 1989-92. Named Woman Making a Difference Soroptomist Internat., 1989, 93, 97, Woman of Distinction, Riverside Bus. Press, 2000. Fellow Am. Assn. Zool. Parks and Aquariums (bd. dirs., accredation field reviewer, desert antelope taxon adv. group, caprid taxon adv. group, felid taxon adv. group, small population mgmt. adv. group, wildlife conservation and mgmt. com., chmn. ethics com. 1987, mem. com., internat. rels. com., ethics task force, pres'. award 1972-77, outstanding svc. award 1983, 88, editor newsletter, Zool. Parks and Aquarium Fundamentals 1982); mem. Internat. Species Inventory System (mgmt. com., policy adv. group 1980-96, trustee 1997-2004), Calif. Assn. Mus. (v.p. 1992-96), Calif. Assn. Zoos and Aquariums, World Assn. Zoos and Aquariums (coun. 2002-, governing coun. 200—, pres. 2005—), Western Interpretive Assn. (so. Calif. chpt.), Am. Assn. Mus., Arboreta and Bot. Gardens So. Calif. (coun. dirs.), Soc. Conservation Biology, Nat. Audubon. Soc., Jersey Wildlife Preservation Trust Internat., Nature Conservancy, East African Wildlife Soc., African Wildlife Found., Kennel Club Palm Springs (past bd. dirs., treas. 1978-80), Scottish Deerhound Club Am. (editor Scottish Deerhounds in N.A., 1983, life mem. U.K. chpt.), Internat. Bengal Cat Soc. (pres. 1994-96). Avocations: pure bred dogs, cats, dressage, painting, photography. Office: The Living Desert 47 900 Portola Ave Palm Desert CA 92260 E-mail: kastld@aol.com.

SAUVÉ, CAROLYN OPAL, writer, journalist, poet; b. Columbus, N.C., Apr. 30, 1934; d. Anthony Floyd and Nina Morris Pittman; m. Joseph Ernest Sauvé, Mar. 31, 1953; children: Floyd, Kenneth, Timothy. Student, Spartanburg Meth. Coll., 1952—53; AAS, Isothermal C.C., 1976. Editor, author, photographer: History of Polk County, 1983; author, photograph APP Jour., 1999; author: Spirit of the Age, 1996. Trustee Isothermal C.C., Spindale, N.C., 1985-93; bd. dirs. Area Mental Health Bd., Spindale, 1985-91; v.p., sec., edn. chmn. Am. Cancer Soc., Polk County, N.C., 1975-79; bd. dirs. Juvenile Justice Bd., Rutherfordton, N.C., 1978-82; chmn. Polk County Commn., Columbus, 1978-82; chmn. Polk County Rep. Party, Columbus, 1984-86, 95-98; vice chmn., dist. chmn. N.C. Rep. Women's Club, Raleigh, 1975-79; chmn. World Missions Com., 1994-2000; chmn. bd. Polk County Dept. Social Svcs., 2003—. Mem. Polk County Hist. Assn. (pres. 1984-86, v.p. 1996-2000). Presbyterian. Avocations: creative writing, boating, cake decorating. Home: 165 Landrum Rd Columbus NC 28722-9545

SAVAGE, CARLA LEE, insurance agent; b. Howell, Mich., Dec. 12, 1963; d. Evert and Gloria Jean (Andrews) Van Raden; m. Matthew Paul Savage, Apr. 9, 1994; 1 child, Trevor MacKenzie. AA, Yakima Valley C.C., Yakima, Wash., 1984; BA cum laude, Ctrl. Wash. U., 1986. Asst. mgr. Jay Jacobs, Yakima, Wash., 1983-85; probation counselor Kittitas Co. Probation Svc., Ellensburg, Wash., 1985-86; staff asst. N.W. Adminstr., Inc., Seattle, 1986-89; svc. rep., agent Sedgwick Noble Lowndes, Yakima, 1989-94; sales exec., agent Marsh Advantage America/Seabury & Smith, Yakima, 1995—. Mem. adv. bd. health care reform Yakima Herald Republic, 1996. Vol. phone lines Crisis Line, Ellensburg, 1985, ARC, YMCA, Yakima Greenway, Pub. TV, Yakima C. of C., Kiwanis. Recipient Bus. Edn. award U.S. Achievement Acad., 1982. Avocations: boating, fishing, camping, sewing, furniture refinishing. Office: Marsh Advantage Amer/Seabury & Smith Lake Aspen Office Park 1430 N 16th Ave Yakima WA 98902-1381 E-mail: carla.l.savage@seabury.com.

SAVAGE, CLARE LEAVY, school psychologist; b. NYC, Mar. 20, 1953; d. Charles Joseph Leavy and Catherine Theresa Frary; m. Paul Jonathan Savage; children: Stephanie, Matthew. BA, Marymount Manhattan Coll., 1975; MSc, Hunter Coll., 1977; Advt. Cert. in Sch. Psychology, CUNY, 1986; PhD, Kennedy Western U., 2003. Cert. sch. psychologist NY, tchr. K-6 NY. Sch. psychologist, spl. edn. tchr. Western Suffolk Bd. Coop. Ednl. Svcs., 1986—99; sch. psychologist Babylon Union Free Sch. Dist., 1999—. Extraordinary min. Eucharist Ch. St. Mary, Manhasset, 1999—; extraordinary min. of Eucharist North Shore Univ. Hosp., Manhasset, 1999—2001; catechist religious edn. program Ch. St. Mary, 1999—2005. Mem.: NY State United Fedn. Tchrs., Nat. Assn. Sch. Psychologists. Roman Cath. Avocations: calligraphy, reading, theater, writing. Home: 24 Stuart Pl Manhasset NY 11030 Personal E-mail: clsavage@optonline.net.

SAVAGE, KIM L., academic administrator; d. William T. and Sylvia V. Savage; 1 child, Nicholas. BA, North Ctrl. Coll., 1977; MEd, Oreg. State U., 1980. Asst. dir., Hermann Hall Ill. Inst. Tech., Chgo., 1977—78; program advisor Oreg. State U., Corvallis, 1978—80; asst. program dir. Ohio State U., Columbus, 1980—81; various positions in student centers adminstrn. U. Ill., Chgo., 1981—2001, campus aux. svcs., 2001—05, asst. to vice chancellor student affairs, 2005—. Contbr. articles to profl. jours. Vice chmn. Downers Grove Twp. Dem. Orgn., Ill., 2004—06, precinct committeeman, 2000—06; mem. Ill. Dem. Women, Springfield; dir. Alford Am. Family Assn., Florrissant, Mo., 2001—04. Mem.: AAUW, LWV, Assn. Coll. Unions Internat. (various regional and nat. leadership positions 1980—2003, pub. policy liaison 2005—), Woodridge Toastmasters (v.p. 2005—).

SAVAGE, LINDA EILEEN, psychologist; b. Boston, Apr. 18, 1945; d. E. Linwood and Helen (Mills) Savage; m. Jerry Allen Spiegel, Jan. 26, 1973 (div. Aug. 29, 1979); 1 child, Sarah Orion; m. Gary Lee Reinhardt, Mar. 23, 1986; 1 child, Jamie Linn Reinhardt. BA, Mount Holyoke Coll., 1967; MA, U. Mass., Amherst, 1970; PhD, Internat. Coll., L.A., 1983. Lic. marriage and family therapist Calif., psychologist Calif., cert. Am. Bd. Sexology. Tchg. asst. U. Mass., Amherst, 1967—69; counselor Miami Dade C.C., Fla., 1970—72; co-dir., cons. Lakeview Ednl. Assn., Chgo., 1973—79; clin. dir. Astarte Comm. Ctr., Leucadia, Calif., 1983—85; pvt. practice clin. psychologist Linda E. Savage PhD, Vista, Calif., 1985—. Speaker, seminar leader Goddess Seminars, 1999—. Author: Reclaiming Goddess Sexuality, 1999. Mem. Found. for Women, San Diego, 2001—. Mem.: San Diego Psychol. Assn., Soc. for Sci. Study of Sexuality, Am. Assn. Marriage and Family Therapists, Am. Assn. Sex Educators, Counselors and Therapists (cert. sex educator 2000), Phi Beta Kappa. Office: Family Counseling Ctr 630 Alta Vista Ste 206 Vista CA 92084 Office Phone: 760-758-3308. Business E-Mail: lindasavagephd@goddesstherapy.com.

SAVAGE, MARTHA, art educator; b. N.Y.C., May 28, 1951; d. Richard and JoAnn Osherow Savage; 1 child, Adam. BFA, San Francisco Art Inst., 1973; BS, Boston U., 1981; MFA, Vermont Coll., 1994. RN N.Mex., Mass., Conn. Horticultural asst. Harvard U., Cambridge, Mass., 1973—78; RN Yale New Haven Hosp., New Haven, 1982—86; art educator Area Coop. Ednl. Svcs., North Haven, Conn., 1986—; art coord. Betsy Ross Summer Art Camp, New Haven; tchr. Creative Arts Workshop, New Haven, 1991—. Fellow Yale-New Haven Tchrs. Inst., 1992, 93, 98; art coord. Creative Art Workshop PACK program, New Haven, 2000—; mentor Grad. Inst., Milford, Conn., 2005—; coord. City-Wide Open Studios, New Haven, 2004—05. Contbr. articles various profl. jours. Grantee New Haven Found. Greater New Haven, Southern Poverty Law Ctr., City New Haven. Mem.: Conn. Women Artists, Conn. Assn. Art Edn. Personal E-mail: msavage2@comcast.net.

SAVAGE, RUTH HUDSON, poet, writer, speaker; b. Childress, Tex., Apr. 29, 1932; d. John Floyd and Eula Jemima (Cornelius) Hudson; m. Robert Berkes, Nov. 6, 1950 (div. June 1963); children: Donna, Mike, Kelly, Rex; m. Martin Thomas Savage, Sept. 18, 1965. Pres. Poets of Tarrant County, 1992—94; founder, pres. New Millennium Poets, Arlington, Tex., 2000; judge local, nat. and state poetry contests; featured spkr., writer, Tex.; sponsor poetry contests; cores. poet Arlington Arts Advocate. Author: (poetry) Voices in the Wind, 1982, (CD) Savage Whispers, 1999, Texas Tuff, 2001, (plays) Tumbleweed Christmas, 1989, (cassette) Simply Savage, 1992, numerous poems, Impersonations of Eleanor Rossevelt Resumed. Judge various chpts. Poetry Soc. Tex. and Tex. Students, 1987—. Recipient numerous awards for poetry. Mem.: Poetry Soc. Tex. (judge various chpts. 1987—, councilor 2000—, sch. liaison 2000—, rec. sec. 2000—, sec. 2000—), Nat. Fedn. State Poetry Socs. Avocations: art, speaking, writing. Home: 1700 Ocho Rios Ct Arlington TX 76012-2023

SAVAGE, SUSAN M., state official, former mayor; b. Tulsa, Okla., 1936; married; 2 children. Student, U. Aix-Marseilles, Aix-en-Provence, France, 1969, City of London Poly., Eng., 1972; BA in Sociology with honors, Beaver Coll., 1974. Pre-trial rep. Phila. Ct. Common Pleas, 1974-75; criminal justice planner Montgomery County Criminal Justice Unit, 1975-77; exec. dir. Met. Tulsa Citizens Crime Com., 1977-87; vol. coord. Vote Yes For Tulsa, 1987; chief of staff to mayor City of Tulsa, 1988-92, mayor, 1992—2002; sec. of state State of Okla., Oklahoma City, 2003—. Active Lee Elementary Sch. PTA; bd. dirs., treas. Okla. Crime Prevention Assn.; bd. dirs. Youth Svcs. of Tulsa County, 1984-88, pres., 1986-87; co-chair Safe Streets/Enhanced 911 Steering Com., 1987; mem. C. of C. Task Force/Community Edn. Network, 1983. Mem. U.S. Conf. Mayors (chmn. com. energy and environment). Democrat. Office: Office Sec of State State Capitol Rm 101 Oklahoma City OK 73105 Home: 224 NW 33rd St Oklahoma City OK 73118-8614 Office Phone: 405-521-3911. Office Fax: 405-521-3771. Business E-Mail: susan.savage@sos.state.ok.us.*

SAVAGEAU, ANN ELISA, artist; b. Bloomington, Ind., Feb. 13, 1945; d. Carl William and Pauline Elizabeth (Livengood) Birky; m. Michael Antonio Savageau, July 22, 1967; children: Mark Edward, Patrick Daniel, Elisa Marie. AB with great distinction, Stanford U., Palo Alto, Calif., 1967; MFA, Wayne State U., Detroit, 1978. Lectr. in studio art U. Mich. Resdl. Coll., Ann Arbor, 1978—2002; assoc. prof., dept. design U. Calif. Davis, 2005—. One-woman shows include Lincoln Cmty. Ctr. Gallery, Ft. Collins, Colo., 1981, Ann Arbor (Mich.) Art Assn., 1982, Edits. Gallery, Perth, We. Australia, 1984, Clare Spitler Works of Art, Ann Arbor, 1992, Inst. Humanities, U. Mich., Ann Arbor, 1997; exhibited in group shows at Craftsmen's Guild of Miss., 1976, 17th Annual Mid-Mich. Exhbn., Midland, 1976, Pontiac (Mich.) Ctr. for Arts, 1976, Loretta Heights Coll., Denver, 1978, Seventh Marietta (Ohio) Coll. Crafts Nat., 1978, Hera Gallery, Wakefield, R.I., 1979, Textile Workshops, Santa Fe, N.Mex., 1979, Detroit Inst. Arts, 1981, 85, Birmingham/Bloomfield Art Assn., Birmingham, Mich., 1982, U. Wis., Madison, 1983, Wayne State U., Detroit, 1987, 2006, Detroit Artists Market, 1988, Art Link Gallery, Ft. Wayne, Ind., 1989, Ea. Mich. U. Art Gallery, 1992, 2000, Oakland C.C., 1993, Detroit Artists Market, 1993, Art Ctr. Battle Creek, 1993, Ann Arbor Art Assn., 1995, Buckham Gallery, Flint, Mich., 1995, The Anderson Gallery, Pontiac, 1996, Cranbrook Art Mus., Bloomfield Hills, Mich., 1998, Gualala Art Ctr., Calif., 2005, Long Beach Arts, 2005, and numerous others. Mem. AAUP, Surface Design Assn., Phi Beta Kappa. Home: 5418 Cowell Blvd Davis CA 95618 Business E-Mail: aesavageau@ucdavis.edu.

SAVALA, LINDSAY KAYE, athletic trainer; b. Temple, Tex., Feb. 20, 1980; d. Verl Otho and Mary Elizabeth Childers; m. Joe Angel Savala, Nov. 8, 2003; 1 stepchild, Joe Angel Jr. BSc, Tex. Christian U., Ft. Worth, 2002. Asst. athletic trainer U. Dallas, 2002—03; athletic trainer Joshua H.S., Tex., 2003; head athletic trainer John F. Kennedy H.S., San Antonio, 2003—. Athletic trainer Slam Dunk for Life Camps, San Antonio, 2005, TCU Soccer, Ft. Worth, 2000, TCU Volleyball, Ft. Worth, 2001. Presbyn. Office: John F Kennedy H S 1922 S General McMullen San Antonio TX 78226

SAVANNAH, MILDRED THORNHILL, public school educator; b. Lynchburg, Va., Aug. 10, 1951; d. Norman Nemrod and Ruby (Brown) Thornhill; m. Ronald L. Savannah, June 17, 2000. BS in Intermediate Edn., Elizabeth City State U., 1973; postgrad., U. Va., 1974—82, U. Tex., 1986—87; M in Ednl. Adminstr., U. North Tex., 1994. Cert. tchr., Va., Tex. Tchr. Campbell County Pub. Sch., Rustburg, Va., 1973-84; leader recreation City Lynchburg, Va., 1976-77; tchr. Dallas Ind. Sch. Dist., 1984—99, instrnl. specialist for mid. schs. math. dept., 1999—. Mem. cert. com. grades 4-8 math., 4-8 math./sci., 4-8 gen. studies, master math. tchr. Tex. State Bd. Educators, 2000; mem. assessment com. for 8th grade Tex. Assessment of Knowledge and Skills Tex. Edn. Agy., 2000—; dir. Dealey After Sch. Tutoring Program, mem. tchr. cert. coms. Adult leader Campbell County 4-H Clubs, 1973—83; officer NAACP, Campbell County, Va., 1980—84; sch. coord. March of Dimes; mem. Task Force Excellence in Edn., Richmond, 1982—84; charter mem. leadership edn. com. S.W. Edn. Devel. Labs., Austin, 1985—86; appointee Tex. Edn. Agy. Grant Reader Rev. Com., Tex.; amb. to People's Republic of China People to People, 2001, amb. to China, 2001; dir. youth dept. devel. programs Bethany Bapt. Ch., 1974—83; chaplain, tchr. Missionary Soc.-1st Bapt. Ch., Hamilton Park; pres. mission min., deaconess, mem. ushers' min. South Oak Cliff Bapt. Ch., 2001—. Named Outstanding Young Woman Am., 1981. Mem.: NEA, Tex. State Tchrs. Assn. (cert. trainer for profl. staff devel. 1984—, bd. dirs. 1999—2002, campus coord. Project Early Options, pres. Region 19 bd. dirs., chair, regional rep. to state instrnl. advocacy com.), Campbell County Edn. Assn. (pres. 1982—83), Va. Edn. Assn., Classroom Tchrs. Dallas (minority affairs chair, Black caucus chair, instrnl. and profl. devel. chair, v.p. region 19 exec. bd.), Nat. Coun. Supr. Math., Nat. Coun. Tchrs. Math., Nat. Mid. Sch. Assn., Elks, Phi Delta Kappa, Zeta Phi Beta Sorority, Inc. (Kappa Zeta chpt. Zeta Amicae sponsor 1998—, chair, 3d v.p. Kappa Zeta chpt.). Baptist. Home: 1207 Shady Ln Lancaster TX 75146 Office: PO Box 77 3700 Ross Ave Dallas TX 75204 Office Phone: 972-749-2474. Business E-Mail: msavannah@dallasisd.org.

SAVARD, TAMARA RENEE, music educator; b. Grand Rapids, Mich., Aug. 8, 1960; d. Donald Charles and Beverly LaVonne Jupstrom; children: Thomas Michael, Julie Michele. Assoc. Vet. Tech., Penn Foster Coll.; BS in Edn., Ctrl. Mich. U., Mount Pleasant, 1983; MusM, Wright State U., Dayton, Ohio, 1999. Music tchr., band dir. Ramstein Elem. Sch., Ramstein Air Base, Germany, 1984—87; music tchr. New Lebanon Elem. Sch., Ohio, 1989—92; elem. band dir. Xenia Cmty. Schs., Ohio, 1992—. Mem.: Music Educators Nat. Conf. Office: Xenia Cmty Schs 578 E Market St Xenia OH 45385

SAVEDRA, JEANNINE EVANGELINE, artist, educator; b. Montebello, Calif., Dec. 21, 1965; d. Robert Anthony Savedra and April Baroth Student, Pasadena C.C., Calif., 1985—87, Parsons Sch. Design, 1987—88; BA Studio Art, Calif. State U., L.A., 1991; MA Humanities and Art, Calif. State U., Dominguez Hills, 2000; postgrad. IMMEX Inst., UCLA, 1999; postgrad., Otis Sch. Art and Design, 2001—02. Cert. art tchr., Calif. Children's counselor Salvation Army, Pasadena, 1987—88; graphic artist Calif. State U., L.A., 1989; pvt. investigator Larry J. Larsen Investigations and Trial Preparations, L.A., 1990—93; instr. studio art Visual Arts and Design Acad., Pasadena, 1995—2001; tchg. supr. Dept. Edn. Mount St. Mary's Coll., 2002—; restoration artist, painter St. Gaudens Fine Art Restoration and Conservation, Pasadena, 1999—; visual arts edn. specialist Calif. Living History, Pasadena, Calif., 2005—. Supr. mural Pasadena Playhouse Improvement Assn., 1995-96; mentor Puente program U. Calif., Berkeley, 1995-2000; educator Nat. Conf. Human Rels., Temescal Canyon, Calif., 1996, Annenberg Inst. Sch. Reform, Brown U., 1998-2000; apptd. to ednl. adv. com. Jack Scott Cultural Master Plan, Sierra Madre; mem. Assembly, Calif. State Legislature, 1997-99; apptd. to Sierra Madre Arts Commn., 1999-2006, chairperson, 2002-06; ofcl. assessor tchg. performance Calif. Commn. on Tchr. Credentials Author: (art curriculum) Me, Myself and Eye, 2006; author, illustrator Art Heals, 2003 Bd. dirs. Calif. Living Histories, Pasadena; mem. Nat. Campaign for Tolerance, Montgomery, Ala. Calif. Partnership Acad. grantee, 1996—, NEH, 2004; recipient Excellence in Visual Arts award Calif. State U., 1990, VIP award Pntrs. Edn. Pasadena Unified Sch. Dist., 2004 Mem. L.A. County Mus. Art, Arboretum and Botanic Garden E-mail: jeanninesavedra@yahoo.com.

SAVELLA, BARBARA MARIA, educational association administrator; b. Providence, Apr. 30, 1960; d. Thomas Edward and Concetta Ann Caputo; m. George Henry Savella, Oct. 22, 1988; children: Francesca, Thomas. BA, Providence Coll., 1982, MEd, 1986. English tchr. Pawtucket Sch. Dept., RI, 1985—2003, literacy coach, 2003—05, spl. programs coord., 2005—. Mem. Gifted/Talented Adv., Providence, 2005—, RI Skills Commn., Providence, 1998—. Tel. vol. Providence Coll., 2000—. Avocations: sports, gardening, reading, music, theater. Home: 50 Bakewell Ct Cranston RI 02921 Office: Pawtucket Sch Dept 286 Main St Pawtucket RI 02860

SAVENOR, BETTY CARMELL, painter, printmaker; b. Boston, Sept. 2, 1927; d. Harry Hyman and Sally Carmell; m. Jack Savenor, June 1, 1948; children: Alan, Barry, Ronald. Student, Jackson Van Ladau Sch. Fashion, Brandeis U., DeCordova Mus.; BFA, Mass. Coll. Art, 1993. Represented by Art 3, Inc., Manchester, NH, Diane Levine, Boston, Gallery 333, Falmouth, Mass., So.Watercolor Soc. Exhibited in group shows at Guild of Boston Artists, Salmagundi Club, N.Y., Boston Printmakers, U. Mass., Harvard U., Okla. U., Brandeis U., Purdue U., Ind., Attleboro (Mass.) Mus., Western N.Mex. U., Montclair Art Mus., N.J., Duxbury Art Complex, Mass., Morris Mus. Arts & Scis., N.J., George Walker Vincent Smith Mus., Mass., Nat. Gallery, N.Y., Fairleigh Dickinson U., N.J., Fitchburg Art Mus., Mass., Boston C. of C., Fed. Res. Bank of Boston, Adelphi U., N.Y., Stonehill Coll., Cahoon Mus. Am. Art, Midwest Mus. Art, Ind., Allied Artists Am., N.Y., Bentley Coll., Mass.; represented in permanent collections Fairfield Med. Assn., Vackerville, Calif., Bank of Boston, Data Products, NEC Info. Sys., Inc., Skowhegan Bank, Maine, Sheraton Corp., Hollywood, Calif., Tex. A&M U., and New Orleans, Meadows Country Club, Fla., U. Tampa, First Bank of Concord, N.H., Indian Head Bank, N.H., New Eng. Life Ins. Co., Conn. Mut. Ins. Co., Liberty Mut. Ins. Co., Velcro Mgmt., Jo-Ann Fabrics, Tampa Energy Corp., Fla., Weisner Assocs., Fla.; pubs. include Collograph Printmaking, Best of Watercolor, Painting Textures, Best of Watercolor, The Collected Best of Watercolor. 2002. Juror for numerous art shows, Mass.; demonstrator for many art socs. Recipient Nicholas Reale Meml. award for graphics Allied Artists Am., First Frontier Collage Soc., Guiller Gall. Awd., TX, 1999, Sarasota Visual Art Ctr., First Prize, 1999-00, FL, Art League of Manatee, FL, Printmaker Awd., 2000. Mem. Nat. League of Am. Pen Women (award of excellence 1998), New Eng. Watercolor Soc. (sec. 1983-93, Best Contemporary Watercolor prize 1990, Pelikan Disting. award 1997, Bronze medal 1998), New Eng. Watercolor Soc. (Excellence in Abstraction 2002), Nat. Assn. Women Artists (prize 1982, 87, 89, 1st prize 2002), Northwest Watecolor Soc. (signature mem.), Cape Cod Art Assn. (Jurors Merit award 1992-94, 1st prize in graphics 1993-95, 97, 2002), Nat. League Am. PEN Women (Best in State award 1983-95, 39th Nat. Exhbn. award of excellence 1998), Concord Art Assn. (Gold medal 1985, 1st prize 1991, Yarmouth Art award 1998), Falmouth Art Guild (best in show 1997), Catamet Art Ctr. (1st prize 2002), Teco Co. (Hon. Mention 2003), Tampa, Women's Contemporary Artists, Art Ctr., Long Boat Key Art Ctr., N.W. Watercolor Soc., So. Watercolor Soc., New Eng. Watercolor Soc., Internat. Soc. Experimental Artists, Southern Watercolor Soc., Northwestern Watercolor Soc., New England Watercolor Soc. Democrat. Jewish. Avocations: tennis, swimming, decorating.

SAVERCOOL, SUSAN ELISABETH, elementary school educator; b. La Grande, Oreg., Aug. 1, 1947; d. Edwin Gilbert and Francis Gwynne Kirby; m. Niles Seymour Duncan, June 21, 1971 (div. Sept. 1976); m. Lawrence Yeldham Savercool, Aug. 6, 1983; 1 child, David R. BA in Theater/English, Calif. State U., Northridge, 1969; MA in Elem. Edn., No. Ariz. U., 1988. Cert. elem. tchr. Calif., Ariz. Elem. tchr. St. Catherine of Siena Sch., Reseda, Calif., 1969—71; presch. tchr. La Palma E. Preschool, Anaheim, Calif., 1973—74; elem. tchr. Egremont Sch., Encino, Calif., 1977—80, Ganado Intermediate, Ariz., 1980—84, Blue Ridge Elem., Lakeside, Ariz., 1986—98; freelance writer Penn Yan, NY, 2000—03. Presenter poetry for tchrs. workshop Blue Ridge Elem., Lakeside, 1991—96; instr. elem. lang. arts No. Ariz. U., Flagstaff, 1992. Editor: Mountains of Time, vols. 1-5, 1992—97, Saint Bobo and Other Contemporary Short Stories, 1994. Actress, make-up head Theater Mountain, Lakeside, 1993—97; contbg. author Oliver House Mus., Penn Yan, 2000—03; contbr. Internat. Libr. Poetry, Famous Poets Soc., Noble House, 2005. Scholar, Arts Coun., 1968. Mem.: Nat. Acad. Songwriters, Nat. Homer Poet Famous Poets Soc. (outstanding poet/contbr., internat. libr. poetry editions 2004, 2005, 2006), Phi Kappa Phi. Democrat. Unitarian Universalist. Achievements include development of PhotoLit Posters gift lines; freelance writing (as Glenna MacCauley). Avocations: reading, fishing, community chorus, community theater, writing.

SAVILLE, PAT, state senate official; b. Marysville, Kans., Sept. 10, 1943; Sec. Kans. Senate, Topeka, 1991—. Mem.: Nat. Conf. State Legis. Exec. Com., Am. Soc. Legis. Clks. and Secs. (past pres.). Office: Kans Senate State House 374 E Topeka KS 66612 Office Phone: 785-296-2456. E-mail: pats@senate.state.ks.us.

SAVIO, FRANCES MARGARET CAMMAROTTA, music educator; b. Phila., Oct. 2, 1936; d. Frank Cammarotta and Margaret Eleanor Cammarotta Parilla; m. Savio, Sept. 12, 1959; 1 child, Margaret Mary. B Music Edn., Immaculata Coll., 1958; M Music Edn., Trenton State U., 1976. Music and English tchr. East Lansdowne (Pa.) schs., 1958—59; music tchr. Mary Calcott Elem. Sch., Norfolk, Va., 1959—61; music and English tchr. Northside Jr. High, Va., 1961—63; kindergarten tchr. Bar H. Crocker Country Day Sch., Oceanside, NY, 1965—68; gen. music tchr. K-8, drama dir. St. Bartholomew Sch., NJ, 1968—. Leader Girl Scouts U.S.A.; music dir., counselor, music coord. summer camps, Pa., N.J., Va.; organist, pastoral musician St. Bartholomew Ch., East Brunswick, 1968—90; mem. curriculum com. Diocese of Trenton, 1977; organist adult choir, dir. folk group St. Bartholomew Ch., East Brunswick, NJ; mem. profl. day com., mem. com. for outstanding Cath. educator Metuchen Diocese; mem. Altar Rosary Soc. Named Tchr. of Excellence, Diocese of Metuchen, 1995. Mem.: Nat. Music Honor Soc., Pi Kappa Lambda. Home: 14 Hershey Rd East Brunswick NJ 08816 Office Phone: 732-390-9691.

SAVITZ, MAXINE LAZARUS, aerospace transportation executive; b. Balt., Feb. 13, 1937; d. Samuel and Harriette (Miller) Lazarus; m. Sumner Alan Savitz, Jan. 1, 1961; children: Adam Jonathan, Alison Carrie. BA in Chemistry magna cum laude, Bryn Mawr Coll., 1958; PhD in Organic Chemistry, MIT, 1961. Instr. chemistry Hunter Coll., N.Y.C., 1962-63; sr. electrochemist Mobility Equipment Rsch. and Devel. Ctr., Ft. Belvoir, Va., 1963-68; prof. chemistry Federal City Coll., Washington, 1968-72; program mgr. NSF, Washington, 1972-74; dir. FEA Office Bldgs. Policy Rshc. U.S. Dept. Energy, Washington, 1974-75, dir. div. indsl. conservation, 1975-76, from dir. div. bldgs. and community systems to dep asst sec., 1975-83; pres. Lighting Rsch. Inst., 1983-85; asst. to v.p. engrng. Ceramic Components div. The Garrett Corp., 1985-87; gen. mgr. ceramic components divsn. AlliedSignal Inc., Torrance, Calif., 1987-99; gen. mgr. tech. partnerships Honeywell, Torrance, Calif., 1999—2001, ret., 2001; prin. Washington Adv. Group. Bd. dirs. Am. Coun. for Energy Efficient Economy, Draper Corp.; bd. dirs. divsn. engrng. and phys. sci. NRC; cons. State Mich. Dept. Commerce, 1983, N.C. Alternative Energy Corp., 1983, Garrett Corp., 1983, Energy Engrng. Bd., Nat. Rsch. Bd., 1986—93, Office Tech. Assessment, U.S. Congress Energy Demand Panel, 1987—91; nat. materials adv. bd. NRC, 1989—94, adv. bd. on energy and environ. systems, divsn. of engrng. and physical sci., 2002—; chmn. U.S. Advanced Ceramic Assn., 1992; adv. com. divsn. ceramics/materials ORNL, 1989—92, adv. com. dir., 1992—96; mem. lab. adv. com. Pacific N.W. Nat. Lab., 2000—; adv. bd. Sec. Energy, 1992—2002; mem. Def. Sci. Bd., 1993—96; vis. com. adv. tech. Nat. Inst. Stds. and Tech., 1993—98, Nat. Sci. Bd., 1999—2004; mem. bd. on energy and environ. sys. NRC, 2002—, mem. divsn. on engrng. and phys. sci., 2003—; bd. dir. Fedn. Am. Scientists, Am. Coun. for an Energy Efficient Economy; mem. adv. bd. Sandia Sci., 2006—. Editor Energy and Bldgs.; contbr. articles to profl. jours. Mem. policy com. NAE, 1994—98. NSF postdoctoral fellow, 1961, 62, NIH predoctoral fellow, 1960, 61. Mem. NAE (v.p. 2006—), AAAS. Office Phone: 310-271-0874. E-mail: maxinesavitz@aol.com.

SAVOCCHIO, JOYCE A., former mayor; b. Erie, Pa. d. Daniel and Esther Savocchio. BA in History, Mercyhurst Coll., 1965; MEd, U. Pitts., 1969; cert. secondary sch. adminstrn., Edinboro U., 1975; LLD (hon.), Gannon U., 1990. Tchr. social studies Erie Sch. Dist., 1965-85, asst. prin. Strong Vincent High Sch., 1985-89, tchr. coord. high sch. task force, 1971-75; pres. Erie Edn. Assn., 1975-76; mem. coun. City of Erie, 1981-90, pres. coun., 1983, mayor,

1990—2001. Mem., past pres. Pa. League League of Cities and Municipalities, Northwestern Pa. Mayors' Roundtable; mem. subcoms. on transp. and comms. U.S. Conf. of Mayors; mem., sec. Electoral Coll. for Commonwealth of Pa.; v.p. Christopher Columbus Found.; past pres., mem. Coun. of Govts. of the Greater Erie Area. Past pres. Erie Hist. Mus.; mem. Pa. Gov.'s Flagship Commn., Cmty. Task Force on Drug and Alcohol Abuse; treas., v.p., pres. Erie Area Job Partnership Tng., Inc. Named Woman of Yr., Dem. Women Erie, 1981, Italian Am. Women's Assn., 1987, Outstanding Citizen of Yr., MECA United Cerebral Palsy, 1991; recipient Disting. Alumna award Mercyhurst Coll., 1990, Disting. Citizen award French Creek coun. Boy Scouts Am., 1991, Tree of Life award Jewish Nat. Fund, 1995; named to Pa. Honor Roll of Women. Roman Catholic.

SAVOIA, MARIA CHRISTINA, vice dean; BA with highest honors, Wellesley Coll., 1972; MD, Harvard U., 1976. Diplomate Am. Bd. Internal Medicine. Med. intern U. Calif., San Diego, 1976-77, med. resident, 1977-79, fellow divsn. infectious diseases, 1980-84, clin. instr. medicine, 1980-84, asst. adj. prof. medicine, 1984-90, acting vice-chair dept. medicine, 1987-89, assoc. prof. clin. medicine, 1990-96, assoc. dean curriculum and student affairs sch. medicine, 1990—2003, vice dean med. edn., 2003—, acting dir. office learning resources sch. medicine, 1991-95, acting assoc. dean admissions sch. medicine, 1991, chief acad. officer sch. medicine, 1994—, prof. clin. medicine, 1996—; sr. fellow in med. edn. Harvard Macy Inst., Boston, 1996-97; assoc. investigator VA Med. Ctr., San Diego, 1981-84, asst. chief to acting chief med. svc., 1984-90, 87-89. Author: (with others) Medical Microbiology and Infectious Diseases, 1986, Infectious Disease, 1986, Principles and Practice of Infectious Diseases, 1989, Infections in Urology, 1990, Medical Complications During Pregnancy, 1995, and others; contbr. numerous articles and abstracts to profl. jours. Recipient Calif. Women in Govt. award, 1987; NSF grantee, 1972; Durant scholar Wellesley (Mass.) Coll., 1968-72. Fellow Infectious Diseases Soc. Am.; mem. Am. Soc. Microbiology. Office: Univ Calif Sch Medicine Vice Dean for Med Edn 9500 Gilman Dr La Jolla CA 92093-0602

SAVOIE, ALLISON MARIE, secondary school educator; d. James Phillip Thibodeaux and Dannie Jo Broussard, Thomas G. Broussard (Stepfather); m. Robby Dean Savoie, Aug. 22, 2000; children: Alec Dean, Carson Maxx. BS, McNeese State U., Lake Charles, La., 1990—99. Cert. tchr. La., 1999. Tchr. A.M. Barbe HS, Lake Charles, 2000—. Sponsor student coun. A.M. Barbe HS, 2000—; co-sponsor Youth Art Coun., Lake Charles, 2000—; sponsor Key Club, Lake Charles, 2004—05. Drew grant, 2001. Mem.: NEA. Independent. Baptist.

SAVOIE, BRIETTA DOLORES, librarian; b. Milw., Aug. 28, 1933; d. Walter and Vera Margaret (Rueger) Giger; m. Edmond Albert Savoie, Oct. 11, 1959; children: Philip Edmond, Raymond Walter, Anne-Marie Margaret. BA, Ohio State U., 1955; MSLS, Columbia U., NYC, 1957. Profl. librarian's cert., NY, NJ Libr., Bklyn. Pub. Libr., 1957-59; cataloger, reference libr. New Sch. Social Rsch., NYC, 1959-60; children's libr. Teaneck Pub. Libr., NJ, 1981-86; asst. reference and circulation libr. River Edge Pub. Libr., NJ, 1986-92, libr. adult svcs., 1992-2002, ret., 2002. Substitute reference libr. Glen Rock Pub. Libr., NJ, 2005-; V.p. United Way of Ridgewood, Glen Rock, Hohokus and Midland Park, NJ, 1980-81; pres. Ridgewood chpt. UN Assn., 1981-85; mem. Fair Housing Coun. Northern NJ. Mem. LWV (chmn. voter registration Glen Rock chpt. 1978-81, chmn. membership Glen Rock chpt. 2004—, co-pres. Glen Rock chpt. 2005—), Am. Libr. Assn., Nat. Arbor Day Soc., So. Poverty Law Ctr. Klanwatch Project, UN Assn., LWV, Native Am. Rights Fund, Sierra Club. Democrat. Unitarian. Avocations: international relations, social justice, environmental protection, bicycling, gardening. Home: 654 Doremus Ave Glen Rock NJ 07452-2033

SAVORY, ELAINE, education educator; arrived in U.S., 1990; m. Robert W. Jones; children: Stacy Jones Buracqua, Todd Jones; m. Martin Fido (div. 1981); 1 child, Austin Fido. BA, U. Leeds, Eng., 1969, MPhil, 1975; PhD, U. West Indies, Barbados, 1994. Asst. prof. U. Ghana, 1970; assoc. prof. U. West Indies, Barbados, 1974—88, New Sch. U., NYC, 1996. Author over 100 articles, essays and and poems. Mem.: Carrabean Women Writers Assn., Modern Lang. Assn.

SAVOY, SUZANNE MARIE, nursing educator; b. NYC, Oct. 18, 1946; d. William Joseph and Mary Patricia (Moclair) Savoy. BS, Columbia U., 1970; M in Nursing, UCLA, 1978; PhD in Nursing, Loyola U., 2004—. RN, cert. clin. nurse specialist, critical care nurse. Staff nurse MICU, transplant Jackson Meml. Hosp., Miami, 1970-72; staff nurse MICU Boston U. Hosp., 1972-74, VA Hosp., Long Beach, Calif., 1974-75; staff nurse MIRU Cedars-Sinai Med. Ctr., L.A., 1975-77; critical care clin. nurse specialist Anaheim (Calif.) Meml. Hosp., 1978-81; practitioner, instr. Rush-Presbyn.-St. Luke's Med. Ctr. Coll. Nursing, Chgo., 1982-88; rsch. assoc. dept. neurosurgery Rush U., 1984-88; clin. rsch. assoc. Medtronic, Inc. Drug Adminstrn. Sys., Mpls., 1988-91; staff nurse crit. care Harper Hosp., Detroit, 1992-93; clin. nurse specialist, surg./trauma crit. care Detroit Receiving Hosp., 1993-95; clin. instr. Wayne State U. Coll. of Nursing, Detroit, 1991-96; adult crit. care clin. nurse specialist Saginaw (Mich.) Gen. Hosp., 1996—98; cardiac clin. nurse specialist Covenant Healthcare Sys., Saginaw, 1998—2005; asst. prof. Saginaw Valley State U. Coll. Nursing, 2005—. Adj. faculty Wayne State U. Coll. Nursing, 1996—98, program coord. Crit. Care ACNP-CC MSN, 1993—96; neurosci. clinician acute stroke unit Harper Hosp., Detroit, 1989; edn. cons. Critical Care Svcs., Inc., Orange, Calif., 1979—81; mem. staff Constant Healthcare, 2005—. Contbr. articles to profl. jours. Mem.: Am. Assn. Spinal Cord Injury Nursing (mem. rsch. com. 1993—95), Assn. Health Care Quality (treas. 2002—04), Am. Assn. Crit. Care Nurses (bd. dirs. Long Beach chpt. 1981—82, treas. NEMC chpt. 1999—2001), Am. Assn. Neurosci. Nurses (treas. Ill. chpt. 1983—85, pres. 1986—87, SE Mich. chpt. 1992—96, bd. dirs., treas., program chair), Sigma Theta Tau, Lambda and Gamma Phi (bd. dirs. 1994—96). Roman Catholic. Office Phone: 989-964-7026. Personal E-mail: cardiopn@aol.com. Business E-Mail: smsavoy@svsu.edu.

SAVVA, ANDREA, financial advisor; b. Nicosia, Cyprus, Apr. 30, 1955; arrived in U.S., 1964; d. Michael and Efrosine Savva; children: Paul E. Papapetrou, Michael G. Papapetrou. A in Occupl. Studies, Lab. Inst. Merchandising, N.Y.C., 1976. Lic. Series 7, 6, 63, 65 Nat. Assn. Securities Dealers, life and health lic./prodr. N.J., N.Y., Fla. Account rep., broker Mokrynsky & Assocs., Hackensack, NJ, 1993—97; fin. cons. Fin. Network Investment Corp., Florham Park, NJ, 1997—98, Hudson Trader Investment Svcs., Clifton, NJ, 1998—2001; sr. fin. cons. Quick & Reilly/Fleet Fin., Hackensack, NJ, 2001—. Greek Orthodox. Avocations: gardening, reading, physical activities, music, movies. Office: Banc of Am Investment 152 Blvd Hasbrouck Heights NJ 07604 Office Phone: 201-288-0216.

SAWAI, DAHLEEN EMI, language educator; b. Honolulu, Mar. 13, 1954; d. Kiyoto and Aiko Sawai. BA, U. Hawaii, Manoa, 1975, diploma in elem. edn., 1977, diploma in secondary edn., 1981, MEd, 1984. Cert. tchr. Hawaii. English tchr. Tokyo Family Court, 1977—78; Japanese tchr. Kailua H.S., Honolulu, 1978—80; English tchr. Family Ct. Probation Officer Tng. Sch., Tokyo, 1983—84; Japanese tchr. W. R. Farrington H.S., Honolulu, 1985—; educator Consortium for Tchg. Asia and the Pacific in the Schs., Honolulu, 1989—95; mentor tchr., 1995—. Instr. Sch. Cmty. Based Mgmt., Honolulu, 2000—04; interpreter Star Tanjo, 1976; chmn. dept. world langs. W.R. Farrington H.S., Honolulu, 2001—. Dir. Moanalua Gardens Cmty. Assn., Honolulu, 1976—77, sec., 1978—80; ad hoc com. mem. Sch. Cmty. Coun., 2005. Scholar, Keio Gijuku Daigaku, 1982—84. Mem.: Hawaii Assn. Tchrs. Japanese, Nat. Coun. Japanese Lang. Tchrs., Farrington Alumni and Cmty. Found., Japanese Cultural Ctr. Hawaii, Alliance Drama Edn., Temari Ctr. for Asian and Pacific Arts, Pi Lambda Theta.

SAWHILL, ISABEL VAN DEVANTER, economist; b. Washington, Apr. 2, 1937; d. Winslow B. and Isabel E. Van Devanter; m. John C. Sawhill, Sept. 13, 1958; 1 son, James W. BA, NYU, 1962, PhD, 1968. Asst. prof. econs. Goucher Coll., Balt., 1969—73; sr. rsch. assoc. Urban Inst., 1973—77, program dir., sr. fellow, 1980—93; dir. Nat. Commn. Employment Policy, Washington, 1977—79; program assoc. dir. Office Mgmt. and Budget, 1993—95; sr. fellow and Arjay Miller chair in pub. policy Urban Inst., 1995—97; sr. fellow Brookings Instn., Washington, 1997—, v.p., dir. econ. studies, 2003—06. Vis. prof. Georgetown U. Law Ctr., 1990-91; chairperson rsch. adv. bd. Com. for Econ. Devel., 1995-98; bd. dirs. Greenhill & Co., Inc. Author: Getting Ahead, 1998, One Percent for the Kids, 2003, Restoring Fiscal Sanity, 2004, 05. Bd. dirs. Manpower Demonstration Res. Corp.; pres. Nat. Campaign Prevent Teen Pregnancy, 1996—. Mem. Am. Econ. Assn., Assn. Pub. Policy Analysis and Mgmt. (pres. 1988), Phi Beta Kappa. Office: Brookings Inst 1775 Massachusetts Ave NW Washington DC 20036-2103

SAWIN, NANCY CHURCHMAN, educational consultant; b. Wilmington, Del., June 21, 1917; d. Sanford W. and Ellen (Quigley) S. BA, Principia Coll., 1938; MA, U. Del., 1940; EdD, U. Pa., 1962; PhD (hon.), Golden Beacom Coll., 1987. With Sanford Sch., Hockessin, Del., 1938-74, dean girls, 1945-62, head sch., 1962-74; coordinator student services U. Del. Div. Continuing Edn., Newark, 1974-77; ednl. cons. DuPont Co., ICI Ams., 1976-80. Chmn. Del. State Sci. Fair com., 1962; mem. com. Jr. Sci. and Humanities Symposium, 1962-76; mem. English, lang. arts adv. com. State Del., 1965-68; sec., dir. Recreation, Promotion and Service, Inc., 1963-74; mem. All-Am. Hockey Team, 1948-59. One-person shows include Ctr. for Creative Arts, 1993—, others; editor: The Eagle, 1961-62; co-pub., illustrator: Between the Bays, 1977, Delaware Sketchbook, 1976, Backroading Throuth Cecil County, 1977, Brick and Ballast, Canal Town Historic Chesapeake City, 1985; author, illustrator: Man-O-War My Island Home, 1978, Up the Spine and Down the Creek, 1982, Locks Traps and Corners, 1984, China Sketchbook, 1985, A Hockessin Diary, 1987, Privy to the Council, 1987, The Oulde King's Roade, 1989, North from Wilmington by Oulde Roads and Turnpikes, 1992, Once Upon a Time in the Country, 1994, Sketches of Early Delaware Main Streets, 1997, The Vanishing Countryside-Ghosts on the Landscape, 1998, Delaware USA - My hometown, 1999, Delaware Lacrosse Hall of Fame, 1999. Trustee Goldey Beacom Coll., pres., 1974-81, 97-98, mem. safety coun., 1964-74, trustee emeritus, 1999—; pres. Del. Sports Hall of Fame, 1982—; pres. bd. dirs. Del. Soc. for Preservation of Antiquities, 1986-88, chair, 1990—; chair fundraising com. Hockessin County Libr., 1989-94, chair fundraising com. for creative arts, 1997—; bd. dirs. Preservation Del., 1996—; trustee emeritus Sanford Sch., Hockessin, 1997—. 2d lt. CAP, 1942-45. Named to U.S. Field Hockey Hall of Fame (charter mem.), 1988, Del. Sports Hall of Fame, 1977, Hall of Fame of Del. Women, 1991, Wall of Fame, U. Del., 1991, Del. Lacrosse Hall of Fame, 1999, Nat. Mus. Women in the Arts (elected), 2001; recipient medal of merit, U. Del., 1989, History medal, DAR, Hist. Preservation award, New Castle County, 1996, Gold medal, Del. Sr. Olympic Swimming, 1994, 1995, 1996, 2 Gold medals, U.S. Sr. Olympics, 1997, 2000, Disting. Svc. award, Ctr. for Creative Arts, 1997, Pathfinder award, State of Del., Nat. Assn. Girls' and Women's Sports, 1998, She Knows Where She Is Going award, Girls Inc. of Del. and Wilmington Women in Bus., 1998, Sanford Sch. Alumni award, 2000. Mem. AARP, Headmistress Assn. East, Del. Art Mus., Rehoboth Art League, Middle Atlantic States Assn. Colls. and Secondary Schs. (past pres.), Commn. on Secondary Schs., Red Clay Creek Assn., Internat. Fedn. Women's Hockey Assns. (past pres.), U.S. Field Hockey Assn. (past pres., named to Sports Hall of Fame 1987), Del. Field Hockey Assn. (past pres.), Nat. League Am. Pen Women, DAR (History medal), Daus. of Founders and Patriots, Nat. Soc. New Eng. Women, Daus. Colonial Wars, Del. Greenbank Questars (pres. 1993-94), Hockessin Cmty. Club, Delta Kappa Gamma (past pres.), Pi Lambda Theta. Republican. Presbyterian (elder). Club: Quota (pres. Wilmington 1971-73, gov. 10th Dist. 1979-80). Home: PO Box 1228 Hockessin DE 19707-5228 Office Phone: 302-239-2416.

SAWIN, THERESE LYNN, elementary school educator; d. Jim and Mary Sawin. BS with hons. in Edn., U. Del., Newark, Del., 2004. Cert. tchr. elem. edn. Pa. Dept. Edn., 2004, tchr. mid. sch. math. Pa. Dept. Edn., 2004. Tchr. math. mid. sch. Downingtown Area Sch. Dist., Pa., 2004—. Mem.: Nat. Coun. Tchrs. Math. Office Phone: 610-518-0685 2292.

SAWYER, BETSY (ROSEMARY) E., elementary school educator; b. Fitchburg, Mass., June 14, 1955; d. Leonardo Mario Guercio and Mary Winnifred Ward; m. Charles Eugene Sawyer, Jan. 22, 1978; children: Mary Katherine, Alison Ann, Bryan Barnum. AS in Culinary Arts, Culinary Inst. Am., Hyde Park, NY, 1975; BA in Elem. Edn. and English Lit. (hon.), Fitchburg State Coll., Mass., 1997; MA in English Lit., U. Mass., Boston, 1998. Tchr. first grade Country Day Sch. Holy Union, Groton, Mass., 1993—2000; tchr. McKay Campus Sch., Fitchburg, 2000—03; tchr. lang. arts Groton-Gunstable Mid. Sch., 2003—. Dir. waterfront Camp Wanocksett, Jaffrey, NH, 1996—97. Dir., club leader Bookmaker's And Dreamer's Club For Peace, Groton, 2004—06. Democrat. Avocations: poetry, reading, swimming, travel. Office: Groton/Dunstable Middle School 727 Main Street Groton MA 01450 Office Phone: 978-448-6155. Personal E-mail: bsawyer60@aol.com. E-mail: bsawyer@gdrms.org.

SAWYER, CHERYL LYNNE, foundation administrator, consultant; b. Balt., Mar. 8, 1954; d. Carolyn (Brooks) Bulcken; m. Gary W. Sawyer, July 16, 1976; children: Jesse, Stacy. BA in English, Sam Houston State U., 1976; MA in Behavioral Scis., U. Houston, Clear Lake, 1984; EdD in Adminstrn. and Supervision, U. Houston, University Park, 1993. Lic. psychol. assoc. Tex., specialist sch. psychology., cert. trauma cons., tchr. English, history, psychology, chemistry, learning disabilities Tex., diagnostician, counselor, spl. edn. counselor, assoc. sch. psychologist, crisis prevention intervention instr. Tex., elem. tchr. Tchr. Alvin (Tex.) Ind. Sch. Dist., 1976-84, LaMarque (Tex.) Ind. Sch. Dist., 1985-90; ednl. cons. Dickinson, Tex., 1992—; from vis. asst. prof. to adj. prof. U. Houston, 1990—99; dir. acute children's programs Devereux Found., League City, Tex., 1994-97; counselor LaMarque (Tex.) Ind. Sch. Dist., 1997-98; tchr. Dickinson Ind. Sch. Dist., 1998—2000; asst. prof. counselor edn. U. Houston, Clear Lake, 2000—, coord. counselor edn., 2000—. Mem. adv. bd. spl. edn. Santa Fe Sch. Dist., 1993, 94, 95; mem. adv. bd. drug and alcohol prevention LaMarque Sch. Dist., 1989, 90, 91, 92; spkr. child-related psychol. issues; presenter in field. Contbr. articles to profl. jours. Mem. Am. Counseling Assn., Tex. Counseling Assn., Nat. Assn. for Gifted, Coun. for Exceptional Children, Dickinson Civic Assn. (bd. dirs. 1996-99, 2002-4), Beta Sigma Phi, Phi Delta Kappa, Chi Sigma Iota. Home: 12308 Marion Ln Dickinson TX 77539-9224 Business E-Mail: sawyer@cl.uh.edu.

SAWYER, DIANE (L. DIANE SAWYER), newscaster, journalist; b. Glasgow, Ky., Dec. 22, 1945; d. E. P. and Jean W. (Dunagan) Sawyer; m. Mike Nichols, Apr. 29, 1988. BA, Wellesley Coll., 1967. Reporter Sta. WLKY-TV, Louisville, 1967—70; adminstr. press office White House, 1970—74; rschr. Richard Nixon's memoirs, 1974—78; gen. assignment reporter, then Dept. State corr. CBS News, 1978—81; co-anchor Morning News CBS, 1981—, co-anchor Early Morning News, 1982—84; corr., co-editor 60 Minutes CBS-TV, 1984—89; co-anchor PrimeTime Live (now known as PrimeTime Thursday) ABC News, 1989—; co-anchor Day One, 1995, Turning Point, 1996, Good Morning Am. ABC News, N.Y.C., 1999—. Co-recipient George B. Polk award for TV reporting, 2005; named one of 100 most powerful women, Forbes mag., 2005; named to TV Hall of Fame, 1997; recipient 2 Peabody awards for pub. svc., 1988, Robert F. Kennedy award, 13 Emmy awards, 2 Dupont awards (one Spl.), IRTS Lifetime Achievement award. Office: Good Morning America Fl 10 147 Columbus Ave New York NY 10023-5900*

SAWYER, DIANE JANE, education educator; b. Buffalo, Feb. 26, 1940; d. Michael John and Camile Victoria (Subbie) S. BS, Geneseo State Coll., 1960; MS, Buffalo State Coll., 1963; MA in Edn., Columbia U., 1965; PhD, Cornell U., 1971. Elem. tchr. Alexander (N.Y.) Cen. Sch., 1960-62, jr. high sch. tchr., 1962-64; asst. prof. edn. Frostburg (Md.) State Coll., 1965-67; coordinator tchr. ctr. Howard County (Md.) Schs., 1967-68; prof. reading edn. Syracuse (N.Y.) U., 1971—90; prof. chair of excellence in Dyslexic studies Middle Tenn. State U., Murfreesboro, 1990—. Cons. various elem. reading programs throughout U.S., 1971—. Author lang. test, numerous articles and revs. Recipient Garcia Prize for Scholarship Internat. Assn. of Logopedics and Phoniatrics, 1989. Mem. Internat. Reading Assn., Am. Ednl. Research Assn., internat. Diplexia Assn., Internat. Assn. Rsch. in Learning Disabled. Roman Catholic. Avocations: skiing, bicycling, horseback riding, reading. Business E-Mail: dsawyer@mtsu.edu.

SAWYER, DOLORES, motel chain executive; b. Shreveport, La., Oct. 16, 1938; d. Orlan B. Greer and Doris Lucile (Sanders) Eckman; m. Raymond Lee Sawyer Jr., June 11, 1960; children: Lisa Kay, Linda Faye. BSN, Northwestern State Coll., 1960; MSN, Tex. Woman's U., 1975. Supr. obstetrics dept. Highland Hosp., Shreveport, La., 1962-64; head nurse (3-11 shift) Scott and White Meml. Hosp., Temple, Tex., 1966-71, dir. of nursing edn., 1975-76; sch. nurse Temple Ind. Sch. Dist., 1971-72; instr. Mary-Hardin Baylor Coll., Belton, Tex., 1972-74; asst. prof., clin. specialist U. Tex. Arlington, 1976-86; v.p. Budget Host Internat., Arlington, Tex., 1986-96, sr. v.p., 1996—, also bd. dirs. Recipient Amoco Outstanding Tchg. award, 1981. Mem. Sigma Theta Tau. Republican. Methodist. Avocations: reading, tole painting, gardening, crafts, piano. Office: Budget Host Internat Ste B 2307 Roosevelt Dr Arlington TX 76016-5865 Office Phone: 817-861-6088. Personal E-mail: rsawyerl@airmail.net. Business E-Mail: dsawyer@budgethost.com.

SAWYER, LORRAINE MCPHERSON, secondary school educator; b. L.A., Aug. 25, 1940; d. Harold Arthur and Helen B. (Trein) McP.; m. Morris Edward Sawyer, Sept. 1, 1967. AA, Pasadena City Coll., 1960; BA, Calif. State U., L.A., 1963; MA, U. Redlands, 1977. Cert. secondary tchr., Calif. Tchr. Whittier High Sch., Calif., 1964—2001, chair bus. edn. dept., 1975—2001. Editor: Shelters Right Hand Newsletter, 1999—. Vol. Presbyn. Intercommunity Hosp., Whittier, 1965-72. Mem. AAUW, Calif. Bus. Edn. Assn. (pres. So. sect. 1991-92), Whittier Hist. Soc., Delta Kappa Gamma Soc. Internat. (dir. area XIV 1985-87, chmn. state scholarship 1989-91, internat. scholarhsip com. 1992-94, recording sec. 1997-99, 1st v.p. 1999-2001, Calif. pres. 2001-03, internat. membership com. 2004—), Theta Alpha Delta (pres. 1974-75) Republican. Avocations: reading, gardening, exercise, travel.

SAWYER, MARGO LUCY, artist, educator; b. Washington, May 6, 1958; d. Eugene Douglas and Joan Imogen (Alford) S. BA hons., Chelsea Sch. Art, London, 1980; MFA, Yale U., 1982. Prof. U. Tex., Austin, 1988—. Vis. artist Chelsea Sch. Art, London, 1982—. One-person shows include Brit. Coun., Bombay, India, 1983, Barbara Toll Fine Arts, N.Y.C., 1989, 91, Sagacho Exhibit Space, Tokyo, 1996, Gallery Gallery, Kyoto, Japan, 1996, Internat. House of Japan, Tokyo, 1996, Austin (Tex.) Mus. Art, 1998, Artplace, 2000, Mattress Factory, Pitts., 2003, Blatter Gallery, Houston, 2004, others; group shows include Whitechapel Gallery, London, 1979, ICA, London, 1979, 80, Leo Castelli Gallery, N.Y.C., 1986, Portland (Maine) Mus. Art, 1987, U. Md. Art Gallery, Balt., 1988, Meyers/Bloom Gallery, Santa Monica, Calif., 1989, Archer M. Huntington Art Gallery, Austin, Tex., 1990, 91, 92, 93, 94, Harn Mus. Art, Gainesville, Fla., 1992, Laguna Gloria Art Mus., Austin, 1994, Abilene (Tex.) Outdoor Sculpture exhbn., 1995-96, Artspace A Found. for Contemporary Art, 2000, Finesilver Gallery, San Antonio, 2002; permanent collections include Hyde Park, London, Cityarts Workshop, Portland Mus. Art, Samuel O. Harn Mus. Art, U. Fla., Prudential Ins., Chem. Bank, Champion Paper, and various pvt. collections. Recipient Louis Comfort Tiffany Found. award, 2001; Am. Acad. Rome fellow, 1986-87, Japan Found. visual arts fellow, 1996; Travel grantee Ford Found., 1981, Fulbright rsch. grantee, India, 1982-83, Japan, 1995-96, N.Y. State Coun. on Arts grantee, 1987, Travel grantee NEA, 1994. Office: U Tex Dept Art and Art History Austin TX 78712-1104

SAWYER, TONI, actress; d. Howard White and Alice Prince (Woodruff) Smith; m. Arleigh Curtis Sawyer, Aug. 9, 1952 (dec.); children: A. Curtis, Roland Woodruff. Degree, Vermont Coll., 1949, Coll. of Marin, 1969, Am. Conservatory Theatre, 1974. Tchr. Springfield Day Nursery, Mass., 1949—52; publicist Actors' Enterprise Theatre, San Francisco, 1972—73, LA Actors' Theatre, 1977—79. Prodr. LA Actor's Theatre, 1977; prodr., dir. Ensemble Studio Theatre, 1987; casting com. SAG, 1987—91. Actor: (films) Goodbye, Norma Jean, 1976, Hughes & Harlow, 1977, (film, with Cher) Mask, 1985, (film with Jessica Lange) Sweet Dreams, 1985, (film with George Burns) 18 Again!, 1988, (film with Jim Carey) High Strung, 1991, (film with Nicole Kidman) My Life, 1993; (films) The Thirteenth Floor, 1999, Wildly Available, 1999, The Sky is Falling, 2000, numerous TV appearances, numerous stage prodns. Founder, pres. Zero Population Growth, Marin County, Calif., 1970—71; mem. Eco Earth Commn., LA, 1984—90, Women in Film, LA, 1985—95; Ovation Awards voter LA Stage Alliance, 2004—07. Recipient Outstanding Cooperation award, Coll. of Marin, Drama Dept., 1967—68, Outstanding Achievement in Theatre award, Drama-Logue Critics, 1991. Mem.: Film Ind., Colony Theatre. Office: c/o Schiowitz Connor Ankrum Wolf 1680 N Vine St Ste 1016 Los Angeles CA 90028

SAWYER-MORSE, MARY KAYE, nutritionist, educator; b. Ft. Stockton, Tex. BA in Psychology, S.W. Tex. State U., 1978; MS in Nutrition, Incarnate Word Coll., 1987; PhD, U. Tex., 1997. Lic. dietitian. Nutrition svcs. con. Christian Sr. Svcs., 1985-87, exec. dir., 1987-90; nutrition svcs. cons. Alternative Adult Day Care Ctr., 1989-90; pvt. cons. dietitian, 1990—; cmty. dietitian Health Enhancement Ctr. Humana Hosp. Met., 1990-91; assoc. prof., dietetic program dir. U. Incarnate Word, San Antonio, 1991—2004; clin. coord. Avidyn Health, 2004—. Presenter Innovative Nutrition Svc. Model S.W. Tex. Gerontol. Soc. Ann. Meeting, 1988, Diabetic Homebound Svcs. Nat. Conf. Meals-On-Wheels Am., 1989; spkr. in field. Contbr. articles to profl. jours. Named Tex. Dietetic Educator, 2003; recipient Disting. Rsch. award, 1977, 1978, Acad. Excellence award, 1978, Women's Leadership award, YWCA, 1988, Creative Tchg./Rsch. award, 1994; grantee, U.S. Dept. Edn., 1997—2000; Carnation Corp. scholar, 1995. Mem.: Nat. Spkrs. Assn. (devel. dir. 2000—01, Tex. Dietetic Educator of the Yr. 2003), San Antonio Dist. Dietetic Assn., Tex. Dietetic Assn., Am. Dietetic Assn. (sec. 1990—92, mem. nominating com. 1993—94, dietetic educators practice group). Office Phone: 830-997-1552. Personal E-mail: morsemk@msn.com. Business E-Mail: marykaye@thecenterforsuccess.com.

SAWYERS, CLAIRE ELYCE, arboretum administrator; b. Maryville, Mo., May 30, 1957; d. Scott Kirkir and Jane (Alexander) Sawyers. BS with distinction, Purdue U., 1978, MAg., 1981; MS, U. Del., 1984. Dir. Scott Arboretum of Swarthmore (Pa.) Coll., Swarthmore, Pa., 1990—. Recipient Disting. Alumna award, U. Del., 2001, Purdue U. Dept. Horticulture, 1999. Office: Scott Arboretum 500 College Ave Swarthmore PA 19081-1306 Office Phone: 610-328-8025. E-mail: csawyer1@swarthmore.edu.

SAWYERS, ELIZABETH JOAN, librarian, director; b. San Diego, Dec. 2, 1936; d. William Henry and Elizabeth Georgiana (Price) S. AA, Glendale Jr. Coll., 1957; BA in Bacteriology, UCLA, 1959, M.L.S., 1961. Asst. head acquisition sect. Nat. Library Medicine, Bethesda, Md., 1962-63, head acquisition sect., 1963-66, spl. asst. to chief tech. services div., 1966-69, spl. asst. to assoc. dir. for library ops., 1969-73; asst. dir. libraries for tech. services SUNY-Stony Brook, 1973-75; dir. Health Scis. Library Ohio State U., Columbus, 1975-90, spl. asst. to dir. Univ. librs., 1990—. Mem. Assn. Acad. Health Scis. Library Dirs. (sec./treas. 1981-83, pres. 1983-84), Med. Library Assn., Am. Soc. for Info. Sci., Spl. Libraries Assn., ALA Office: Ohio State Univ Librs 1858 Neil Ave Columbus OH 43210-1225 Office Phone: 614-292-4491. E-mail: sawyers.1@osu.edu.

SAWYERS, LORRIE BROWN, social studies educator; b. Winston Salem, NC, Mar. 25, 1967; d. Edward and Brenda Dezern Brown; m. Gregory Sawyers, Mar. 30, 1991; children: Jacob, Joshua. BA, Wake Forest U., Winston Salem, NC, 1989. Tchr. exceptional children Dobson Elem. Sch., NC, 1989—90, Ctrl. Mid. Sch., 1990—91; tchr. social studies East Surry H.S., PIlot Mountain, 1991—. Office: East Surry High School 805 West Main Street Pilot Mountain NC 27041 Office Phone: 336-368-2251. Office Fax: 336-368-3035.

SAX, MARY RANDOLPH, speech and language pathologist; b. July 13, 1925; d. Bernard Angus and Ada Lucile (Thurman) TePoorten; m. William Martin Sax, Feb. 7, 1948. BA magna cum laude, Mich. State U., 1947; MA, U. Mich., 1949. Cert. clin. competence in speech and lang. pathology. Supr. speech correction dept. Waterford Twp. Schs., Pontiac, 1949—69; lectr. Marygrove Coll., Detroit, 1971-72; pvt. practice in speech and lang. pathology Wayne and Oakland Counties, Mich., 1973—. Co-investigator Support Pers. Profl. Practice of Speech-Lang. Pathology; counselor to divsn. stroke liaisons Am. Heart Assn. Mich.; liaison between Am. Heart Assn. of Mich. and Am. Heart Assn., Dallas, 1996—98; adj. speech pathologist, Southfield, Mich.; lectr. on stroke Mich. Spkrs. Bur., Am. Heart Assn., 1990—; pub. spkg. coach, 1989—; mem. adj. faculty SS Cyril and Methodius Sem., Orchard Lake, Mich., 1989—90; adj. St. Mary's Prep. Sch., Orchard Lake, 1990—; mem. Met. Detroit Operation Stroke com. Am. Stroke Assn., 1999—2004, mem. med. subcom. to move area hosps. to become primary stroke ctrs. with active stroke teams, 2001—; founder, mem. Stroke Project Task Force for Detroit, 1993—98; com. mem. Charette, study Arch. and Design for phys. restructuring Franklin, Mich., 1993; invited speech pathology del. Internat. Health Programs People to People Citizen Amb. Program, 1996; mem. sci. coun. on stroke Am. Heart Assn., 1980—2002; invited U.S. rep. speech and lang. pathology (cancelled because of 9/11) Med. People to People Amb. Program, neurol. ctrs., Czech Republic, Hungary and Austria; mem. quality improvement and med. edn. subcom. Am. Heart Assn. New Heart and Stroke Network Metro Detroit, 2005—; mem. stroke adv. com./stroke advocacy com. Midwest affiliate Am. Heart Assn., 1995—2005; mem. stroke adv. com./stroke advocacy com. Greater Midwest Affiliate Mich., Ind., Ill., Wis., ND, SD, Minn. Am. Heart Assn., 2005—. Contbr. articles to profl. jours. including Lang. and Lang. Behavior Abstracts, Lang. Speech and Hearing Svcs., Speech Lang. Hearing Jour. Active Franklinites for Responsible Govt.; mem. stroke com. Mich. Heart Assn., 1982—99. Recipient Svc. Recognition award Coll. Edn. Mich. State U.; grantee Inst. Articulation and Learning, 1969, others; Christian svc. commn. St. Owen, Birmingham co-chmn. blood dr. Red Cross, Franklin, Mich., 1991—. Mem.: Founders Soc. of Detroit Inst. Arts, Franklin Found. (mem. natural resources adv. coun. 1991—99, bd. dirs. 1994—98), Pvt. Practitioners Speech-Lang. Pathology (co-founder), Internat. Assn. Logopedics and Phoniatrics (Switzerland), Am. Heart Assn. Mich. (mem. stroke awareness seminars, continuing edn. for physicians and other profls., planning and operation edn.), Mich. Speech-Lang.-Hearing Assn. (pvt. practitioner liaison 1991—, developer structural parameters for State Clin. Svc. award 1999—, com. comty. and hosp. svcs., mem. state award selection com.), Am. Speech-Lang.-Hearing Assn. (clin. competence cert.), Mich. Humane Soc., Gamma Phi Beta, Kappa Delta Pi, Phi Kappa Phi, Theta Alpha Phi. Achievements include research in language and speech acquisition in children in reference to the development of and prediction of biological speech change; research interests in developmental phonatory voice disorders, and in adult acquisition of language and speech relative to central and autonomic nervous systems. Office: 31320 Woodside Dr Franklin MI 48025-2027

SAXE, DEBORAH CRANDALL, lawyer; b. Lima, Ohio, July 23, 1949; d. Robert Gordon and Lois Barker (Taylor) Crandall; m. Robert Saxe, June 3, 1989; children: Elizabeth Sara, Emily Jane. BA, Pa. State U., 1971; MA, UCLA, 1973, JD, 1978. Bar: Calif. 1978, D.C. 1979, U.S. Dist. Ct. D.C. 1979, U.S. Dist. Ct. (ea. dist.) Calif. 1981, U.S. Dist. Ct. (ctrl. dist.) Calif. 1982, U.S. Dist. Ct. (no. and so. dists.) Calif. 1987, U.S. Ct. Appeals (4th and D.C. cirs.) 1979, U.S. Ct. Appeals (6th cir.) 1985, U.S. Ct. Appeals (8th and 9th cirs.) 1987, U.S. Ct. Appeals (2nd cir.) 1990, U.S. Supreme Ct. 1982, U.S. Dist. Ct. (no. dist.) Ill. 2001, U.S. Ct. Appeals (7th cir.) 2001. Assoc. Seyfarth, Shaw, Fairweather & Geraldson, Washington, 1978-83, Jones, Day, Reavis & Pogue, Washington, 1983-85, L.A., 1985-87, ptnr., 1988-97; shareholder Heller Ehrman LLP, 1997—2005; ptnr. Jones Day, L.A., 2006—. Judge pro tem, Small Claims Ct., L.A., 1985-88. Co-author: Advising California Employers, 1990, 3d edit., 2005; contbg. editor Employment Discrimination Law, 1989. Bd. dirs. Constitutional Rights Found., 1997—2002; chair Eisner Pediatric and Family Med. Ctr., L.A., 1996—98, bd. dirs., 1990—2003, Los Angeles County Bar Found., 1997—99. Fellow: Coll. Labor and Employment Lawyers; mem.: ABA (labor law sect. 1978—), L.A. County Bar Assn. (labor and employment law sect. 1985—, mem. exec. com. 1988—, chair 2002—03, trustee 2005—), Calif. Bar Assn. (labor law sect. 1985—), Phi Beta Kappa, Pi Lambda Theta. Office: Jones Day 555 S Flower St 50th Fl Los Angeles CA 90071 Office Phone: 213-489-3939. Office Fax: 213-243-2539. Business E-Mail: dsaxe@jonesday.com.

SAXE, THELMA RICHARDS, secondary school educator, consultant; b. Ogdensburg, N.J., Apr. 21, 1941; d. George Francis and Evelyn May (Howell) Richards; m. Kenneth Elwood Meeker, Jr., June 22, 1957 (div. 1965); children: Sylvia Lorraine Meeker Hill, Michelle Louise Meeker Aromando, David Sean (dec.); m. Frederick Ely Saxe, Feb. 18, 1983 (dec. Oct. 9, 2003); stepchildren: Jonathan Kent, Holly Harding Schenker. BA, William Paterson Coll., Wayne, N.J., 1972, MEd, 1975, postgrad., 1983-84; Dyslexia cert., Fairleigh Dickinson U., 1994; organ student with, Rick Roberts; voice student, Dr. Roberta Moger. Cert. paralegal. Tchr. handicapped Sussex (N.J.)-Wantage Regional Sch. Dist., 1972-75; resource rm. tchr. Sussex County Vo-Tech Sch., Sparta, N.J., 1975-77, learning cons., 1977-83; learning specialist Bennington-Rutland Supervisory Union, Manchester, Vt., 1986-87; learning cons. Stillwater (N.J.) Twp. Sch., 1987-88, Independence Twp. Cen. Sch., Great Meadows, N.J., 1989; learning cons., tutor in pvt. practice specializing dyslexia Sparta, 1986-97; asst. prin. Harmony Twp. Sch., Harmony, N.J., 1989-92; learning cons. Montague (N.J.) Elem. Sch., 1996-98; coord. gifted/talented Sussex Vo-Tech, 1980-83; coord. child study team Stillwater Twp. Sch., 1987-88, Montague Twp. Sch., 1996-98; ret., 1998; learning cons. Sandyston-Walpack Consolidated Sch., 1997-98. Soprano mem. Nature Coast Festival Singers, Spring Hill, Fla. Mem.: Kappa Delta Pi. Democrat. Mem. Unity Ch. Avocations: piano, travel. Home: 24098 Martin Dr Brooksville FL 34601

SAXTON, CATHERINE PATRICIA, public relations executive; b. Sheffield, Eng., July 5, 1944; d. Clifford and Kate Ann Saxton. BA cum laude, Fordham U., 1978. Mgr. corp. comms. Westinghouse Broadcasting & Cable Co., N.Y.C., 1981-82; prin., pres. Saxton & Assocs., N.Y.C., 1983—; CEO Potter/Saxton Assocs., Inc., N.Y.C., 1985-90, The Saxton Group Ltd., 1990—, co-founder, co-chair A-List Strategic affiliate, 2003—. Prof. pub. speaking Katharine Gibbs Coll., N.Y.C., 1977—. Mem. exec. com. Mayor's Commn. for a Vietnam Vets. Meml., 1982-90. Roman Catholic. Home: 325 E 90th St New York NY 10128-5260 Office Phone: 212-672-0509. Business E-Mail: cpsaxton@hotmail.com.

SAXTON, JUDITH ANN, musician, educator; d. Ada Mae Saxton. MusB in Edn., Mansfield U., Pa., 1986; MusM, Northwestern U., Evanston, Ill., 1987. Trumpet prof. Hong Kong Acad. for Performing Arts, Hong Kong, China; adj. prof. Northeastern Ill. U., Chgo., 1999; instr. of trumpet Ill. Wesleyan U., Bloomington, 1995—99; assoc. prof. of trumpet Wichita State U., Kans., 1999—2006; full-time artist/tchr. of trumpet N.C. Sch. of the Arts, Winston-Salem, 2006—. Prin. trumpet Wichita Symphony Orch., 1999—2006; trumpet Monarch Brass Ensemble, St. Louis, 2000—, Millar Brass Ensemble, Evanston, Ill., 1987—90; prin. trumpet Key West Symphony Orch., Key West, 2002—; third/assoc. prin. trumpet Ea. Music Festival, Greensboro, NC, 1997—; prin. trumpet Shenandoah Valley Bach Festival, Harrisonburg, Va., 2000—; prin. trumpet/soloist Chgo. Chamber Orch., 1995—99; prin. trumpet Ill. Symphony/Ill. Chamber Orch., Springfield, 1993—95; second/prin. trumpet South Bend Symphony, Ind., 1993—95; prin. trumpet Hong Kong Philharm. Orch., 1990—93, Wichita Brass Quintet, 1999—2006. Musician: (recordings) Monarch Brass Ensemble, (recording) Millar Brass Ensemble Music of Carlos Franzetti; musician: (millar brass ensemble) A Chicago Brass Tradition; musician: Millar Brass Ensemble Music of Louis Vierne, Millar Brass Ensemble; dir.: (competition) National Trumpet Competition (Semi-finals, 2006); composer: (musical composition for trumpet ensemble) Tribute for Maleah; musician: (solo recitalist) Kansas Arts Commission Touring Roster, (clinician/recitalist) Bach Selmer Artist Clinician. Com. mem. Internat. Women's Brass Conf., St. Louis, 2003—06. Named to Music Alumni Honor Role, Mansfield U., 2002; grantee Eckstein grantee, Northwestern U., 1986, Chpt. grantee, Internat. Trumpet Guild, 2006, Kans. Cultural Trust, 2004, 2006. Mem.: Music Educators Nat. Conf., Kans. Music Educators, Am. Fedn. of Musicians, Internat. Trumpet Guild, Internat. Women's Brass Conf., Pi Kappa Lambda, Kappa Delta Pi, Sigma Alpha Iota. Avocations: singing, hiking, travel, jazz. Home: 2536 Alderney Ln Winston Salem NC 27103 Office: NC Sch of the Arts 1533 South Main St Winston Salem NC 27127 Office Phone: 336-734-2191. Personal E-mail: judith.saxton@gmail.com.

SAYER, RUTH P., realtor; b. Washington, Sept. 15, 1942; d. Emory Charles and Ruth Bauman Pharr; m. John Dorsey Sayer, Aug. 21, 1965; children: Lorena O'Brien, Dorsey, Peter. BA in Psychology, Mary Washington Coll. of U. Va., Fredericksburg, 1964. Lic. realtor N.J., 1985. Tchr. 6th grade Fairfax County Bd. Edn., Va., 1964—65, North Kingstown Sch., RI, 1965—66; tchr. 3d grade Portsmouth Sch., RI, 1966—68, Newport Sch., RI, 1968—70; tchr. dir. Little Leisure Pre-Sch., Pennington, NJ, 1971—79; realtor Stewardson-Dougherty, Lawrenceville, NJ, 1985—88, Gloria Nilson Realtors/GMAC, Princeton, NJ, 1988—. Founder Little Leisure Pre-Sch., 1971, Hopewell Historic Preservation Soc., Pennington, 1975; pres. Jr. League Greater Princeton, 1986—88; chmn. Hopewell Township Historic Sites Ctr., NJ, 1989—93. Named Woman of Yr., YWCA, 2004; named to Cir. of Excellence, N.J. Assn. Realtors, 1994—2005. Mem.: Mercer County Top Prodrs. Assn. Independent. Episcopalian. Avocations: tennis, paddle tennis, golf, yoga, travel. Office: Gloria Nilson Realtors/GMAC 33 Witherspoon St Princeton NJ 08542 Home: 101 Library Pl Princeton NJ 08540 Business E-Mail: rsayer@gnrgmac.com.

SAYERS, KARI, literature and language professor, journalist; arrived in US, 1966; d. Theodor Haugsten and Solveig Wisur; m. Harry P. Sayers, Oct. 29, 1966; children: Thomas, Angela, Caroline. BA in English, Calif. State U., Long Beach, 1980, MA in Linguistics, 1984. Tchg. credential K-12 Calif., 1981. Tchr. English as 2d lang. Calif. State U., Long Beach, 1981—84; lectr. Long Beach City Coll., 1984—88; tchr. Torrance Adult Sch., 1984—95; asst. prof. Marymount Coll., Palos Verdes, 1986—. Free-lance writer Daily Breeze, Torrance, 1998—, Palos Verdes Peninsula News, Rolling Hills Estates, 1989—, Easy Reader, Hermosa Beach, 1995—. Democrat. Lutheran. Avocation: music. Office: Marymount Coll 30800 PV Dr E Rancho Palos Verdes CA 90275 Office Phone: 310-377-6501. Business E-Mail: ksawyers@marymountpv.edu.

SAYERS BUTLER, PATRICIA ANN, secondary school educator; b. Lebanon, Oreg., May 28, 1952; d. Earl Harold and Geraldine Mae (McCabe) Sayers; m. Joseph K. Butler, June 18, 1977; children: Christopher John, Kadiatu Marie. Student, N.C. Wesleyan Coll., 1970-72; BS in Edn., U. Ark., 1974; MS in Math., Ball State U., 1981; postgrad., Purdue U., 1987, postgrad., 1994, Ind. U., 1990, Ind. Wesleyan U., 1998. Vol., tchr. math. Peace Corps, Pendembu, Sierra Leone, 1974-76; tchr. math. Stuttgart (Ark.) Jr. High Sch., 1976-77; tchr., coach Frankfort (Ind.) Jr. High Sch. and Mid. Sch., 1978—. Religion instr. St. Mary's Cath. Ch., Frankfort, 1986—; leader troop 336, Girl Scouts U.S.A., Frankfort, 1986-1995 Mem. NEA, Nat. Coun. Tchrs. Math., Ind. Tchrs. Math., Ind. Tchrs. Assn., Frankfort Edn. Assn., Ind. Coaches Girls Sports Assn., NRA. Avocations: reading, sewing, handicrafts, sports, camping. Home: 903 S Jackson St Frankfort IN 46041-3035 Office: Frankfort Mid Sch 329 N Maish Rd Frankfort IN 46041-2800 E-mail: butlerp@frankfort.k12.in.us.

SAYLES, EVA, artist; b. N.Y.C., June 10, 1928; BA, Bklyn. Coll., 1949. Mem. coop. Amos Eno Gallery, N.Y.C., 1989—. One-woman shows include Pen and Brush Club, N.Y.C., 1971 (1st prize in mems. oil exhibit), St. Bartholomew's Ch., N.Y.C., 1970, Amos Eno Art Gallery, 1992, Port Chester Coun. for Arts, 1992; exhibited in group shows at Queens Mus., N.Y.C., 1983, Knickerbocker Artists Exhibit, N.Y.C., 1970, Pen and Brush Club, 1970, Marcolio Ltd., 1969, Vera Lazuk Galler, Cold Springs Harbor, 1966, Greenwich (Conn.) Art Soc., 1987; represented in private collections; appearances on TV and radio; contbr. articles (newspapers) Greenwich Time, Conn. Westchester, N.Y.; contbr. poetry to anthologies. Bd. dirs. Port Chester (N.Y.) Coun. Arts, 1989—. Mem. Nat. Assn. Women Artists (prize for oil painting called 'Life', publicity and advt. chairwoman), Pen and Brush Club (publicity chairwoman), Greenwich Arts Coun., Greenwich Art Soc., Oratorio Soc. (choir mem.). Avocations: music, writing, dance, philosophy. Studio: PO Box 510 Port Chester NY 10573-0510

SAYLES BELTON, SHARON, former mayor; b. St. Paul, Minn., May 13, 1951; m. Steve Belton, Aug. 29, 1981; 3 children. Student, Macalester Coll., 1969-1973; Doctorate (hon.), Walden U. Asst. dir. Minn. Program for Victims of Sexual Assault; parole officer Minn. Dept. Corrections; city coun. mem., 1983-93; coun. pres., 1989-93; mayor City of Mpls., 1994—2001; sr. fellow Roy Wilkins Ctr. Human Rels. and Social Justice U. Minn., 2001—. Pres., co-founder Nat. Coalition Against Sexual Assault; co-founder, pres. Harriet Tubman Shelter for Battered Women; trustee U.S. Conf. of Mayors, chair Youth Violence Task Forum; bd. dirs. Bush Found., Search Inst., Youth Coordinating Bd., Neighborhood Revitalization Program, Clean Water Partnership, Children's Healthcare and Hosp., Bush Found., U.S. Conf. Mayors, Nat. League Cities. Recipient Gertrude E. Rush Disting. Svc. award, Nat. Bar Assn., Rosa Parks award, Am. Assn. Affirmative Action. Office: U Minn Herbert Humphrey Inst Pub Affairs 301 19th Ave S Minneapolis MN 55455 E-mail: ssayles-belton@hhh.umn.edu.

SAZAMA, KATHLEEN, pathologist, lawyer; b. Sutherland, Nebr., May 8, 1941; d. Roger William and Esther Mary (Reitz) Paulman; m. Franklin Jed Sazama, Aug. 26, 1962; children: Clare Ann, Jill Patrice. BS, U. Nebr., 1962; MS, Am. U., 1969; MD, Georgetown U., 1976; JD, Cath. U. Am., 1990. Diplomate Am. Bd. Pathology; lic. pathologist Mich., Va., Md., D.C., Calif., Pa., Tex.; bar: Md. Intern and resident Georgetown U. Med. Ctr., Washington, 1976-78; resident NIH, Bethesda, Md., 1978-79; clin. asst. prof. pathology Uniformed Svcs. U. Health Scis., Bethesda, 1981-89; clin. affiliate Ferris State Coll., Big Rapids, 1985-86; chief lab. of blood bank practices FDA Ctr. for Biologics Evaluation and Rsch., Bethesda, 1986-89; cons. Ober, Kaler, Grimes & Shriver, Balt., 1989-90; assoc. med. dir. Sacramento (Calif.) Med. Found. Blood Ctr., 1990-92; asst. clin. prof. pathology U. Calif., Davis, 1990-92, assoc. prof., dir. clin. pathology, 1992-93; prof. pathology and lab. medicine Allegheny U. of the Health Scis., Phila., 1994—99; v.p. for faculty acad. affairs U. Tex./M.D. Anderson Cancer Ctr., Houston, 2000—02, prof. lab. medicine, 2000—. V.p. bd. Met. Washington Blood Banks, Inc., 1981-84; pres. bd. Am. Assn. Blood Banks, 2003-04; spkr. in field. Author: (with others) Stat: The Laboratory's Role, 1986; contbr. numerous articles to profl. jours. Comdr. USPHS, 1986-89. Fellow Coll. Am. Pathologists, Am. Soc. Clin. Pathologists; mem. ABA, Am. Health Lawyers Assn. (bd. dirs.), Health Lawyers Assn., Soc. Advancement Blood Mgmt. (bd. dirs.), Phi Kappa Phi, Beta Beta Beta. Avocations: tennis, playing bridge. Address: Univ of Texas MD Anderson Cancer Center 1515 Holcombe Blvd # 800 Houston TX 77030-4009 Office Phone: 713-792-7791. Business E-Mail: ksazama@mdanderson.org.

SCACCHI, GRETA, actress; b. Milan, Feb. 18, 1960; m. Vincent D'Onofrio, 1991 (div. 1993); 2 children. Films include Das Zweite Gesicht, 1982, Heat and Dust, 1982, Defence of the Realm, 1985, The Coca-Cola Kid, 1985, White Mischief, 1987, Un Homme Amoureux, 1987, Good Morning, Babylon, 1987, Paura e Amore, 1988, La Donna della Luna, 1988, Presumed Innocent, 1990, Turtle Beach, 1991, Fires Within, 1991, The Player, 1992, Desire, 1993, Country Life, 1994, The Browning Version, 1994, Jefferson in Paris, 1995, Emma, 1996, Bravo Randy, 1996, The Serpent's Kiss, 1997, Tom's Midnight Garden, 1998, The Red Violin, 1998, Ladies Room, 1999, The Manor, 1999, Looking for Alibrandi, 2000, Festival in Cannes, 2001, Baltic Storm, 2003, Beyond the Sea, 2004, Syriana, 2005, The Book of Revelation, 2005; TV movies include The Ebony Tower, 1984, Camille, 1984, Dr. Fischer of Geneva, 1985, Rasputin, 1996 (Emmy award), The Odyssey, 1997, Macbeth, 1998; (TV mini series) Waterfront, 1984, The Farm, 2001, Daniel Deronda, 2002. Office: c/o Susan Smith & Assocs 121 N San Vicente Blvd Beverly Hills CA 90211-2303

SCAFURO, LISA A., writer, journalist, poet; b. Ridgewood, N.J., Apr. 22, 1958; d. Angelo C. Scafuro and Barbara A. Purdy; m. Samuel C. Ilechuku, May 21, 1981 (div. Apr. 0, 2001); 1 child, Samantha Elise Ilechuku. BS in Design Scis., Ariz. State U., Coll. Architecture, 1981; at, Art Students League N.Y., 1975—76, at, 1987; postgrad., CCNY, 1988—89; at, Ridgewood Sch. Photography, 1977. Project designer The Kling Partnership, Phila., 1981—83, Ballinger Architects, 1983—85; project mgr. NY Hosp., Cornell Med. Ctr., 1987—88; project mgr., constrn. Columbia U./Columbia Presbyn. Med. Ctr., 1988—90; archtl. cons. pvt. practice, Saddle River, NJ, 1990—. Student Paolo Soleri: arch./visionary/philosopher, Paradise Valley, Ariz., 1996—; freelance journalist. Author (illustrator): Adventures at Cedar Hollow: Tigre Encounters the Great Horned Owl; prodr.(and writer): (documentaries); contbr. articles to mags. Office Phone: 602-531-8864. Personal E-mail: lasarizona@aol.com.

SCAIRPON, SHARON CECILIA, retired information scientist; b. New Brunswick, N.J., May 7, 1946; d. Eric Christian and Erica Cecile Schreiber Student, Trenton Jr. Coll., 1965—67; BSBA, Rider Coll., 1991. Various clerical positions E.R. Squibb & Sons, Princeton, NJ, 1967—87, sr. interlibr. loan and reference technician, 1987—88; lit. resource assoc., lan adminstr. Bristol-Myers Squibb, Princeton, 1988—91, info. scientist, 1991—2001; ret., 2001. Mem. Newcomers Club (newsletter editor 2003-06), Olympic Theater Arts, Audobon Soc., U.S. Lighthouse Soc Avocations: volunteer work, crafts, art, reading, computers. Home: PO Box 335 Carlsborg WA 98324-0335

SCALESE, ELLEN RENEE, maintenance company executive; b. Newton, Mass., Aug. 31, 1954; d. Anthony J. and Evelyn (Spicer) Cardarelli; m. Fred J. Scalese, Jr., June 2, 1973; children— Leah, Michael, Jenna. B.A., U. Mass., 1974; cert. U. Perugia, Italy, 1969. Comml. loan officer Shawmut Bank, Waltham, Mass., 1974-78; co-owner, pres. Coastal Cleaning Service, Plymouth, Mass., 1978—; pres., co-owner Coastal Cleaning Service, Kingston, Mass., 1978—, Daytime Domestics, 1986—, owner, pres., 1986—; bd. dirs. Cardarelli Coast. Editor: Handicap Directory U. Mass., 1974. V.p. adv. bd. Sacred Heart South Shore Cafe, 1986—, South Shore Cafe, 1986—; ccounselor, U. Mass., Amherst, 1972-74, handicap counselor, 1972-74. Mem. Bldg. Service Contractors, Plymouth C. of C. (bd. dirs. 1984-85), Greater Boston C. of C., Small Bus. Assn., South Shore C. of C. Office: Coastal Cleaning Service 19 Green St Kingston MA 02364-1443

SCALETTA, HELEN MARGUERITE, volunteer; b. Sioux City, Iowa, Apr. 13, 1927; d. Ralph J. and Ruth Cora (Coyle) Beedle; m. Phillip Jasper Scaletta, May 21, 1946; children: Phillip Ralph, Cheryl Diane Kesler. AA in Bus., Edwards Coll. Bus., Sioux City, 1946. Acct. Towners Dept. Store, Iowa City, 1947—48; legal sec. Phillip Scaletta, Sioux City, 1950—74; svc. chmn. Easter Seal Soc., Lafayette, Ind., 1970—88; rec. sec. Home Hosp. Aux., Lafayette, 1989. Danced in Civic Theatre Follies, 1962. Orch. mem. June's All-Girl Ensemble, 1943-50. Pres. Newcomers club YWCA, Lafayette, 1967-68, mem. chmn., bd. dirs., 1979; leader Girl Scouts Am., Ft. Wayne, Ind., 1960-63; chmn. Mental Health Inc., Ft. Wayne, 1960-61, Cancer Crusade, West Lafayette, 1973-74; precinct worker Rep. Cen. Com., West Lafayette, 1974-76; Nat. Missions sec. 1st Presbyn. Ch., 1957. Recipient Citation Easter Seal Soc., 1981, Ernestine Duncan Collins Pearl Ct. award Sigma Kappa, 1997. Mem. Purdue U. Women's Club (pres. 1973-74), Lafayette Country Club (golf chmn. 1971, 90, bowling pres. 1992-93, golf co-chair Battleground 9-hole group 1996), Purdue Women's Bowling League (treas. 1978-79), Cosmopolitan Club, YWCA (Diamond award, 2005), Sigma Kappa (corp. bd., sec., treas. 1971-99), Kappa Kappa Sigma (pres. 1972), Sigma Kappa Lafayette Alumnae (pres. 1970, 1988-93, Ernestine Duncan Collins Pearl Court award 1997). Avocations: collecting dolls, bowling, golf, sports. Home: One Via Verde Lafayette IN 47906

SCANGARELLO, DANIELLE LYNN, music educator; b. Elmwood Park, N.J., Apr. 8, 1979; d. Peter John and Irene Scangarello. BSc in music edn., West Chester U., 1997—2002. Teaching Certificate Music K-12 Md., 2003, Pennsylvannia, 2002. Music tchr. and band dir. Balt. City Pub. Sch. Sys., 2002—; instr. Lebanon (Pa.) Cath. H.S., 1998—. Dir. Hampstead Hill Acad. Bands, Balt., 2002—, Cross Country Elem. Sch. Bands, Balt., 2003—; co-chairperson Balt. City Pub. Schools Honor Band, 2005—; color guard designer Lebanon Cath. H.S. Marching Band Color Guard, Pa., 2004—. Save the Music grant, VH-1, 2002, Big Ed's Band Found., 2005—. Mem.: Md. Music Educators' Assn., Music Educators' Nat. Conf., Kappa Kappa Psi, Tau Beta Sigma (hon.). Roman Catholic. Avocations: drum and bugle corps, color guard, Ukrainian folk dance, clarinet. Home: 51 Willow Creek Ct Baltimore MD 21234 Personal E-mail: dlscangarello@yahoo.com.

SCANLAN, ALICIA RAE, music educator; b. Eugene, Oreg., Nov. 28, 1975; d. Ronald Dean Wright and Barbara Joyce Cook; m. Cavan Reed Scanlan, June 26, 2005. MusB in Vocal Performance cum laude, Willamette U., Salem, Oreg., 1997; MusM in Music Edn. in Choral Conducting summa cum laude, Ariz. State U., Tempe, 2000. Cert. K-12 music Ariz. Tchr. K-8 music and phys. edn. Soto Acad., Honolulu, 2001; tchr. 7-8 choral and gen. music Punahou Sch., Honolulu, 2001—, head K-8 music dept., 2005—. Pvt. voice instr. Punahou Sch., Honolulu, 2001—, mus. dir. for musicals, 2005—. Recipient All-Am. scholarship, NAIA Athletic Bd., 1995, 1996. Mem.: Am. Choral Dirs. Assn. (R&S chair mid. sch. 2005—06), Outrigger Canoe Club, Alpha Chi Omega. Independent. Avocations: beach volleyball, singing, performing, reading, travel. Home: 111 B Kalaiopu Pl Honolulu HI 96822 Office: Punahou Sch 1601 Punahou St Honolulu HI 96822

SCANLON, DOROTHY THERESE, history professor; b. Bridgeport, Conn., Oct. 7, 1928; d. George F. and Mazie (Reardon) Scanlon. AB, U. Pa., 1948, MA, 1949, Boston Coll., 1953; PhD, Boston U., 1956; postdoctoral scholar, Harvard U., 1962—64, postdoctoral scholar, 1972. Tchr. history and Latin Marycliff Acad., Winchester, Mass., 1950—52; tchr. history Girls Latin Sch., Boston, 1952—57; prof. Boston State Coll., 1957—82, Mass. Coll. Art, Boston, 1982—95, prof. emerita, 1995—; lectr. Cape Mus. Fine Arts, Dennis, Mass., 1997—. Author: Instructor's Manual to Accompany Lewis Hanke, Latin America: A Historical REader, 1974; contbr. Biographical Dictionary of Social Welfare, 1986. Recipient Disting. Svc. award, Boston State Coll., 1979, Faculty award of excellence, Mass. Coll. Art, 1985, Faculty Disting. Svc. award, 1987. Mem.: AAUW, AAUP, History of Sci. Soc., Am. Assn. History of Medicine., Am. Studies Assn., Orgn. Am. Historians, Am. Hist. Assn., L.Am. Studies Assn., Pan-Am. Soc., Delta Kappa Gamma, Phi Alpha Theta. Home: 23 Mooring Ln Dennis MA 02638-2321 Office: Mass Coll Art Dept History 621 Huntington Ave Boston MA 02115-5801

SCANLON, JANE CRONIN, mathematics professor; b. NYC, July 17, 1922; d. John Timothy and Janet Smiley (Murphy) Cronin; m. Joseph C. Scanlon, Mar. 5, 1953 (div.); children: Justin, Mary, Anne, Edmund. Student, Highland Park Jr. Coll., 1939-41; BS, Wayne State U., 1943; MA, U. Mich., 1945, PhD, 1949. Mathematician Air Force Cambridge Research Center, 1951-54; instr. Wheaton Coll., Norton, Mass., 1954-55; asst. prof. Poly. Inst. Bklyn., 1957-58, asso. prof., 1958-60, prof., 1960-65; prof. math. Rutgers U., New Brunswick, N.J., 1965-91, prof. emerita, 1991—. Cons. Singer-Kearfott Div., Naval Research Lab. Office Naval Research Fellow Princeton, 1948-49; Horace H. Rockham Postdoctoral fellow U. Mich., 1950-51, Rutgers Research Council fellow, 1968-69, 72-73; NSF vis. professorship for women Courant Inst., NYU, 1984-85. Author: Fixed Points and Topological Degree in Nonlinear Analysis, 1964, Advanced Calculus, 1967, Differential Equations: Introduction and Qualitative Theory, 1980, 2d edit., 1994, Mathematics of Cell Electrophysiology, 1980, Mathematical Aspects of Hodgkin-Huxley Neural Theory, 1987; editor: Analyzing Multiscale Phenomena Using Singular Perturbation Methods, 1999. Mem. Am. Math. Soc., Soc. for Indsl. and Applied Math., Internat. Soc. Chronobiology. Home: 110 Valentine St Highland Park NJ 08904-2106 Office: Rutgers U Dept Math New Brunswick NJ 08903 Personal E-mail: croninscanlon@optonline.net.

SCANLON, JANICE LYNN, retired gifted and talented educator; b. Goodland, Kans., July 28, 1940; d. Milton Parish Jr. and Bertha May Adams Parish. BS, Ft. Hays State U., 1962; MA, U. Denver, 1980. Tchr. kindergarten, music Brewster Pub. Schs., Kans., 1962—63; tchr. kindergarten Jefferson County Pub. Schs., Lakewood, Colo., 1963—81; tchr. gifted Washington Twp. Pub. Schs., Sewell, NJ, 1983—98; ret., 1998. Del. gifted tchrs. to visit China with People to People, 1990; sec. N.J. Tchrs. Gifted, 1990—92; pres. Jefferson County Kindergarten Tchrs. Assn., Lakewood, Colo., 1964—65. Author: Jefferson County Kindergarten Curriculum, 1974; actor: (films) Teaching Children in Remote Areas, 1968; contbg. author (lessons in book) Teaching Children in Remote Areas, 1968; author: Guides for Washington Twp. Schs., 1983—98; co-author: Ruleton and Its School, 2005, Adams and Parrish Family, 2005. Fund raiser Palm Aire Women's Club, Sarasota, Fla., 1999—; pres. Palm Aire Nine Hole Golf, 2000—03, assoc., 2002—03; presenter Indian hist. Ch. of Incarnation Sch., 2001—; active Clare's Sewing Angels; mem Dem. Party, S.E. Manatee County, Sarasota, Fla., 2003—. Nominee N.J. Sci. Tchr. of Yr.; scholar, Kiwanis Club, Goodland, Kans., 1958, Tuition grant, U.S. Edn. Office, U. Denver, 1978—80. Mem.: N.J. Ret. Tchrs. Assn., Alpha Delta Kappa (treas.). Democrat. Roman Catholic. Avocations: travel, painting, quilting, genealogy, golf. Home: 7222 Coachlight St Sarasota FL 34243 Personal E-mail: josescan@aol.com.

SCANLON, VICKI E., secondary school educator; b. Atlanta, Oct. 25, 1950; d. William Windsor and Martha King Evans; m. Stephen William Scanlon, June 18, 1971. BA, U. Kans., 1974, MA, 1981. Cert. tchr. Kans. Art tchr. K-6 Shawnee Mission (Kans.) Schs., 1974—89, art tchr. 7-8, 1989—2000, art tchr. 9-12, 2000—. Excellence in tchg. mentor Avila Coll., Kansas City, Mo., 1993—; mem. curriculum coun. Shawnee Mission Schs. Kans. Cow: Grazing, 2000. Pres. Morningside Homes Assn., Kansas City, 1989—93; v.p. Countryside Homes Assn., Kansas City, 1987—89; vol. Salvation Army, Kansas City, 1999—; art cons. Friends of Children's Ctr. for Visually Impaired, 2001—; bd. dirs. Leawood Homes Assn., 2004—. Recipient Purchase award for painting, McEachen Adminstrn. Ctr., 1986, Mayor's Proclamation for cmty. improvements, 1993; scholar, Pi Beta Phi, 2000, Kansas City Art Inst., 2003; Tchr. Inst. scholar, Sch. of Art Inst. Chgo., 2003, Excellence in Edn. grantee, Southwestern Bell, 1988. Mem.: NEA (rep. 1974—2000), Friends of Art, Delta Gamma (scholarship chmn. 1969—72). Democrat. Avocations: piano, drawing, painting, gardening, hiking. Home: 2012 W 96th St Leawood KS 66206 Office: Shawnee Mission NW HS 12701 W 67th St Shawnee KS 66216 Office Phone: 913-993-7270. Business E-Mail: vickiscanlon@smsd.org.

SCANNELL, ANN ELIZABETH, nurse, educator; b. Evanston, Ill., Sept. 23, 1953; BSN, Villanova U., 1975; MS in Community Health, Cath. U., 1977; ND, Case Western Reserve U., 1996. Staff nurse emergency rm. Rahway (N.J.) Hosp., 1975-76; staff nurse med. ICU Georgetown U. Med. Ctr., Boston, 1977-78; continuing care nurse Mass. Rehab. Hosp., Boston, 1977-78; skills coord. dept. nursing Coll. Health Professions U. Lowell, Mass., 1978-79; clin. supr. Melrose (Mass.) Vis. Nurse Svc., 1979-80, exec. dir., 1980-87; dir. coords. and continuing care VNA of Greater Lowell, 1988-89; child and adolescent psychiat. nurse Brookside Hosp., Nashua, N.H., 1989-93; instr. community health nursing St. Anselm Coll., Manchester, N.H., 1991-96; asst. prof., comm. health nurse Fitchburg State Coll., Fitchburg, Mass., 1996—. Mem. ANA (cert. community health, home health and nursing adminstrn.), Sigma Theta Tau (treas. Eta Omega chpt.). Home: 271 Sanders Ave Lowell MA 01851-3418 Office: Dept Nursing Fitchburg State Coll 160 Pearl St Fitchburg MA 01420-2631 E-mail: ascannell@fsc.edu.

SCANNELL, VICKI, humanities and language educator, consultant; b. Detroit, 1954; 1 child, Erin James. MA in Creative Writing, U. Wash., Seattle, 1979—85. English & humanities instr. Pierce Coll., Lakewood, Wash., 1986—. Freelance writer, editor, 1978—; editor, cons., facilitator Neighbors of Onondaga Nation, Syracuse, NY, 1999—2003; multicultural leadership inst., weekend intensive co-facilitator Pierce Coll., Lakewood, Wash., 2005—; editor, cons. Global Majority, Monterey, Calif., 2005—. Mem.: AAUP. Office: Pierce Coll 9401 Farwest Dr SE Lakewood WA 98498 Business E-Mail: vscannel@pierce.ctc.edu.

SCANTLEBURY, VELMA PATRICIA, surgeon; b. Barbados, West Indies, Oct. 6, 1955; came to U.S., 1970; d. Delacey Whitstanley and Kathleen (Jordan) S.; 2 children. BS, LI U., 1977; MD, Columbia U., 1981; DS (hon.), LI U., 1998, Seton Hall Coll. PA. Intern in surgery Harlem Hosp. Ctr., N.Y.C., 1981-82, resident in surgery, 1982-86; fellow in transplantation U. Pitts., 1988, assoc. prof. surgery, 1998—2002; prof. surgery, dir. transplantation U. South Ala. Med. Ctr., Mobile, 2002—. Mem. med. advisory bd. Nat. Kidney Found. Vol. King County Hosp., Bklyn., 1972. Recipient Martin Luther King Sch. award, 1973-74, Am. Fedn. Tchrs. Sch. award, 1973-75, Nat. Med. Found. award 1977-78, Joseph Collins Found. Sch. award 1978, Gift of Life award Nat. Kidney Found., OMNI Life Models award, Women of Spirit award Carlow Coll.; named Outstanding Young Women of Am. 1988. Fellow, ACS; mem. AMA (listed by AMA as nation's first African-Am. female transplant surgeon), P&S Alumni Assn., Black and Latin Students Orgn. (treas. N.Y.C. 1979-80), Slpha Epsilon Delta, Phi Sigma Soc. (sec. Bklyn. chpt. 1976-77), Am. Soc. Transplantation, Am. Soc. Transplant Surgeons, Soc. Black Academic Surgeons, Am. Soc. Minority Health and Transplant Professionals (bd. dirs.), Internat. Women's Forum We. Pa., Nat. Assn. Negro Bus. and Profl. Women. Democrat. Office: Univ S Ala Med Ctr 2451 Fillingim St Mobile AL 36617-2293*

SCARBOROUGH, ANN BARLOW, secondary school educator; Tchr. sci. Farmville (N.C.) Mid. Sch., South Ctrl. HS, Winterville, NC. Recipient Outstanding Earth Sci. Tchr. award, 1992. Mem.: N.C. Sci. Tchrs. Assn. (pres. 2003).

SCARBOROUGH, MARION NICHOLS, nutritionist, recreational facility executive; b. Enosburg Falls, Vt., July 26, 1915; d. George Leonard and Clara May (Woodward) Nichols; m. Mat. Scarborough, Aug. 30, 1950 (dec. Mar., 1960); 1 child Mary Anne Scarborough O'Donnell Adams. ASS, Green Mountain Coll., Poultney, Vt., 1935; BS, Kans. State U., 1937; MPH, Harvard U., 1947. Chief dietitian Newton (Mass.) Wellesley Hosp., 1938-43, 182d Gen. Hosp., U.S. Army, 1943-45; nutritionist, author food exch. list U.S. Pub. Health Diabetes Sect., Boston, 1947-50; nutritionist Fla. Bd. Health, Jacksonville, 1950-52; owner Happy Acres Ranch, Inc., Jacksonville, 1953—. Sec. Fla. Assn. Children Under Six ECA, 1965, pres., 1966, 67. Commd. officer USPHS, 1948-50. Mem. APHA, Am. Dietetic Assn., Am. Camping Assn., Nat. Assn. Edn. of Young Children. Episcopalian. Avocations: childrens' day care, summer camp. Home and Office: Happy Acres Ranch Inc 7117 Crane Ave Jacksonville FL 32216-9012 Office Phone: 904-725-1410.

SCARBROUGH, GLENDA JUDITH, elementary school educator; b. Hill County, Tex., July 17, 1940; d. Roland Leon and Bessie Bell (Ferguson) Blocker; m. Johnny Ray Scarbrough, Feb. 20, 1959; 1 child, Deborah Lynn Randolph BS, Coll. Southwest, Hobbs, N.Mex., 1969; MEd, Sul Ross State U., Alpine, Tex., 1985. Tchr. elem. Andrews Ind. Sch. Dist., Tex., 1969—86, reading specialist, 1986—2003; ret., 2003. Mem. Tex. Gov.'s Tchrs.' Profl. Practices Commn., 1991-93; mem. Tex. State Textbook Selection Com., 1993 Mem. Assn. Tex. Profl. Educators (campus rep., chpt. pres. 1982-84, regional v.p. 1983-84, pres. 1984-86, state bd. dirs. 1986-90, regional com. for dyslexia guidelines 1987), Delta Kappa Gamma Home: 306 SW 12th St Andrews TX 79714-6705

SCARBROUGH, SARA EUNICE, librarian, archivist, consultant; b. Houston, Jan. 8, 1933; d. George Washington Johnson and Frances Elizabeth Evans; m. Henry Lester Scarbrough Sr., July 5, 1953 (dec. Mar. 1993); children: Henry Lester Jr., Sarita. BA, Talladega Coll., 1953; MLS, U. Tex., 1968; PhD, Columbia State U., 1998. Cert. tchr., libr., media specialist, adminstr. Music tchr. Brazos County Pub. Schs., Bryan, Tex., 1954-58; English tchr. Edgewood Sch. Dist., San Antonio, 1958-62; head libr. Houston Ind. Sch. Dist., 1962-92; dir. Hope Resource Ctr., Houston, 1992—. Exec. bd. Friends of the Houston Pub. Libr., 1994-99. Author: History of a Black Family on the Brazos, 1998. Treas. West McGregor Civic Assn., Houston, 1995—96; pres. Women's Missionary Soc., Houston, 1994—97, pres. Sr. Adult Ministry, 1999. Named Churchman of the Yr., Good Hope Ch., Houston, 1993. Mem. AAUW, Tex. Libr. Assn., U. Tex. Alumni Assn., Order of the Ea. Star (worthy matron, Outstanding Contbn. award 1995), Zeta Phi Beta (Lambda Zeta chpt. exec. bd., sec., chmn. econ. devel. 1998, Outstanding Contbn. to Econ. Devel. award 1999). Avocations: music, travel, genealogy, bibliotherapy. Home: 3901 Fernwood Dr Houston TX 77021-1521

SCARBROUGH-CLAY, LINDA KATHLEEN, mathematician, educator; d. Eugene Sylvanus Scarbrough and Doris Kathleen Vest; m. Brinton Roxbury Clay, Jan. 23, 1970; children: Kimberly Brineen Clay-Bartley, Jennifer Lynne Clay. MA in Technol. and Occupl. Edn., U. N.Mex., Albuquerque, 2001. Instr. math. Ctrl. N.Mex C.C., Albuquerque, 1979—; online math instr. Butler C.C., El Dorado, Kans., 2005—; pvt. contractor for pub. co. Brooks Cole - Thomas Higher Edn., Belmont, Calif. Girl scout leader Girl Scouts of Am., Albuquerque, 1981—88. Recipient Excellence award, Ctrl. N.Mex C.C., 2000, 2002. Mem.: Nat. Assn. of Devel. Edn. Avocations: spending time with grandchildren, exercise, reading, travel. Office Phone: 505-224-5698.

SCARCELLA, KARYN ALLEE, staff developer, instructional coach; b. Riverside, N.J., Mar. 26, 1972; d. Roger Gene and Kathleen Karen Allee; life ptnr. Lisa Anne Scarcella. BA in Edn., U. Fla., 1993, MEd, 1994. Cert. early childhood generalist Nat. Bd. Profl. Tchg. Stds., cert. primary (K-3), elem. (1-6), and ESOL (K-12) tchr. Fla. Early childhood, primary grades tchr. Orange County Pub. Schs., Orlando, Fla., 1995—2003, instrnl. coach, 2001—. Nat. bd. candidate mentor, mem. mentor adv. coun. Orange County Pub. Schs., 2000—, trainer Gt. Beginnings (new tchr. induction tng.), 2002—; supervising tchr. for pre-svc. coll. interns Orange County Pub. Schs./U. Ctrl. Fla., Orlando, 2001, mem. supt.'s adv. coun. on advanced studies/profl. devel. Mem. Rainbow Dem. Club, Orlando, 2001. Mem.: NSDC, ASCD, NEA, U. Fla. Sch. Tchg. and Learning Alumni Assn. (life), Pi Lambda Theta. Episcopalian. Avocations: travel, gourmet cooking, outdoor leisure activities, reading. Home: 353 Coventry Estates Blvd Deltona FL 32725 Office: Orange County Pub Sch McCoy Elem 5225 S Semoran Blvd Orlando FL 32822 Office Phone: 407-249-6370 ext. 224. Personal E-mail: halcyongrl@aol.com. E-mail: scarcek@ocps.net.

SCARCHUK, LYNN NETTLETON, music educator; b. Hartford, Conn., July 25, 1950; d. Russell Chaffee Nettleton and Katharine Risley Chaffee; 1 child, James Paul. BS, Western Conn. State U., 1968—72; MS, Ctrl. Conn. State U., 1978. Tchr. Meriden Bd. Edn., Meriden, Conn., 1972—, Jefferson Mid. Sch., Meriden, 1972—84, Washington Mid. Sch., Meriden, 1984—87; choral dir., tchr. Maloney H.S., Meriden, 1988—. Dir.(and prodr.): (sch. prodn.) Oklahoma, 1990, My Fair Lady, 1992, Anything Goes, 1994, South Pacific, 1996, 42d St, 1998, Hello Dolly, 2000, Crazy for You, 2002, Footloose, 2004 (hon. mention for set building, Mag.). Music dir. Kiwanis Club Kapers, Meriden, Conn., 2000—01. Mem.: Conn. Music Educators Assn. (25 Yrs. Svc. award). Avocations: travel, bicycling.

SCARDINO, DAME MARJORIE MORRIS, publishing executive; b. Flagstaff, Ariz., Jan. 25, 1947; d. Robert Weldon and Beth (Lamb) Morris; m. Albert James Scardino, Apr. 19, 1974; children: Adelaide Katherine Morris, William Brown, Albert Henry Hugh. BA, Baylor U.; JD, U. San Francisco. Ptnr. Brannen Wessels & Searcy, Savannah, Ga., 1976-85; pub. Ga. Gazette Pub. Co., Savannah, 1978-85; pres. The Economist Newspaper Group, Inc., NYC, 1985-93; chief exec. The Economist Group, London, 1993-97, Pearson P.L.C., London, 1997—. Non-exec. dir. Nokia Corp. Trustee Carter Ctr.; bd. dir. The Bus. Coun., MacArthur Found., Atlantic Council of U.S.; trustee Victoria and Albert Mus. Named Dame Comdr. British Empire, 2002; named one of Most Powerful Women, Forbes mag., 2005, 50 Women to Watch, Wall St Journal, 2005, 50 Most Powerful Women in Global Bus., Fortune mag., 2005. Office: Pearson PLC 80 Strand London WC2R ORL England

SCARF, MARGARET (MAGGIE SCARF), author; b. Phila., May 13, 1932; d. Benjamin and Helen (Rotbin) Klein; m. Herbert Eli Scarf, June, 1953; children: Martha Samuelson, Elizabeth Stone, Susan Merrell. BA, South Conn. State U., 1989. Contbg. editor New Republic, Washington, 1978—, Self Mag., N.Y.C., 1991—; writer-in-residence Jonathan Edwards Coll., 1995—. Assoc. fellow Jonathan Edwards Coll. Yale U., New Haven, 1979—; sr. fellow Bush Ctr. in Child Devel. and Social Policy, Yale U., 1991—; mem. adv. bd. Am. Psychiat. Press, Poynter Fellowship Journalism Yale U., 1995-96. Author: Meet Benjamin Franklin, 1968, Antarctica: Exploring the Frozen Continent, 1970, Body, Mind, Behavior, 1976 (Nat. Media award Am. Psychological Assn. 1977), Unfinished Business: Pressure Points in the Lives of Women, 1981, Intimate Partners: Patterns in Love and Marriage, 1987, Intimate Worlds: Life Inside the Family, 1996, Secrets, Lies, Betrayals: The Body/Mind Connection, 2005; contbr. numerous articles to jours. including N.Y. Times mag. and book rev., Psychology Today; TV appearances include: David Letterman Show, Oprah Winfrey Show, CBS News, Good Morning Am., Today Show, Phil Donahue, numerous others. Recipient Nat. Media award Am. Psychol. Found., 1971, 74, 77, Conn. UN award Outstanding Conn. Women, 1987, cert. commendation Robert T. Morse Writers Competition Am. Psychiat. Assn., 1997, Disting. Svc. award Am. Psychiat. Assn., 1999, cert. of recognition N.Y. State Soc. Clin. and Social Work, 1998; grantee Smith Richardson Found., 1991-94; Ford Found. fellow, 1973-74, Neiman fellow Harvard U., 1975-76, Ctr. Advanced Study in Behavioral Scis. fellow, 1977-78, 85-86, Alicia Patterson Found. fellow, 1978-79. Mem. Conn. Soc. Psychoanalytic Psychologists, Am. Psychiat. Press (mem. adv. bd. 1992), Lawn Club, Elizabethans, PEN Writer's Assn. Avocations: reading, hiking, swimming. Office: Jonathan Edwards Coll Yale U 68 High St New Haven CT 06511-6643 Business E-Mail: maggie.scarf@yale.edu.

SCARLETT, LYNN (PATRICIA LYNN SCARLETT), federal agency administrator; b. Pitts., Dec. 8, 1949; d. James Miles and Virginia (Young) S.; m. James R. Trotter, May 6, 1978; 1 child, Rachel Scarlett Trotter. BA, U. Calif., Santa Barbara, 1970, MA, 1972. Vis. lectr. U. Calif., Santa Barbara, 1980-81; book rev. editor Reason Mag., Santa Barbara, 1982-85; dir. rsch. Reason Found., Santa Monica, Calif., 1985-89, v.p. rsch., 1990—2001, pres., CEO, 2001; asst. sec. policy, mgmt. & budget US Dept. Interior, Washington, 2001—05, dep. sec., 2005—, acting sec., 2006. Mem. task force Calif. Joint Legis. Com. on Surrogate Parenting, Calif., 1989-90; panel reviewer Project 88 Phase II, 1990; chmn. issues com. Citizens for Balanced Community, Santa Barbara, 1989—; chmn. "How Clean Is Clean" Working Group, Nat. Environmental Policy Inst., 1993-98; bd. dirs. Laguna Blanca Sch., Santa Barbara. Author: (chpt.) Food Politics, 1982; contbr. articles to profl. jours. Chmn. Jim Trotter for City Coun., Carpinteria, Calif., 1990—; mem. parents aux. Laguna Blanca, 1986-88. Geneva Inst. of Internat. Studies fellow, 1974-75. Mem. Friends of Girls Club Corp. (2d v.p. 1986-87). Republican. Avocations: birdwatching, drawing, swimming. Office: US Dept Interior 1849 C St NW Rm 5110 Washington DC 20240

SCARLETT, NOVLIN ROSE, occupational health nurse, educator; b. Jamaica, West Indies, Jan. 11, 1938; d. Cyrus Freeman and Sylvia Belafonte; m. Sherlock Anthony Scarlett, Dec. 19, 1964 (dec. Jan. 8, 1970); children: Douglas, Anne. Nursing degree, Queensboro C.C., 1978, York Coll., 1984. RN N.Y. Staff nurse City Hosp., Elmhurst, NY, 1978—82; asst. head nurse Margaret Tietz, NY, 1982—86, head nurse, 1986—97; public health nurse City of N.Y., 1997—.

SCARNECCHIA, SUELLYN, dean, law educator; BA, Northwestern U., 1978; JD, U. Mich., 1981. Bar: Mich. Ptnr. McCroskey, Feldman, Cochrane & Brock, Battle Creek, Mich.; clin asst. prof. U. Mich. Sch Law, 1987, clin. prof. law, 1993, clin. coord., 1994—96, assoc. dean clin. affairs, 1996—2002, assoc. dean adminstrn., 1999—2001, asst. provost academic and faculty affairs, 2002; dean, prof. law U. N.Mex, 2003—; chair Jud. Nominating Commn. Govt. N.Mex. Atty. U. Mich. Child Advocacy Law Clinic, 1987; bd. dirs. Clin. Legal Edn. Assn.; panelist Mich. Atty. Disciplinary Bd.; tech. adv. Mich. Supreme Ct. Task Force on Gender and Race Bias. Mem.: Women Lawyers Assn. Mich. (past pres.), Battle Creek Area Orgn. Against Domestic Violence (past bd. pres.). Office: U NMex Sch Law 1117 Stanford NE Albuquerque NM 87131-1431 Office Phone: 505-277-4700. Home Fax: 505-277-0068. E-mail: scarnecchia@law.unm.edu.

SCARR, SANDRA WOOD, retired psychology educator, researcher; b. Washington, Aug. 8, 1936; d. John Ruxton and Jane (Powell) Wood; m. Harry Alan Scarr, Dec. 26, 1961 (div. 1970); children: Phillip, Karen, Rebbecca, Stephanie; m. James Callan Walker, Aug. 9, 1982 (div. 1994). AB, Vassar Coll., 1958; AM, Harvard U., 1963, PhD, 1965. Asst. prof. psychology U. Md., College Park, 1964-67; assoc. prof. U. Pa., Phila., 1967-71; prof. U. Minn., Mpls., 1971-77, Yale U., New Haven, 1977-83; Commonwealth prof. U. Va., Charlottesville, 1983-95, chmn. dept. psychology, 1984-90; CEO, chmn. bd. dirs. KinderCare Learning Ctr., Inc., 1995-97; ret., 1997. Mem. nat. adv. bd. Robert Wood Johnson Found., Princeton, N.J., 1985-91; coord. coun. psychology SUNY Bd. Regents, N.Y.C., 1984-92; prof. Kerstin Hesselgren, Sweden, 1993-94. Author: Race, Social Class and Individual Differences in IQ, 1981, Mother Care/Other Care, 1984 (Nat. Book award APA 1985), Caring for Children, 1989; editor Jour. Devel. Psychology, 1980-86, Current Directions in Psychol. Sci., 1991-95. Fellow Ctr. for Advanced Studies, Stanford U., Calif., 1976-77; grantee NIH, NSF, others, 1967-95. Fellow AAAS, APA (chmn. com. on human rsch. 1980-83, coun. of reps. 1984-89, bd. dirs. 1988-90, Award for Disting. Contbn. to Rsch. on Pub. Policy 1988), Am. Psychol. Soc. (bd. dirs. 1992—, pres. 1996-97, James McKeen Cattell award 1993); mem. Am. Acad. Arts and Scis. (coun. mem. 1995-2000), Behavior Genetics Assn. (pres. 1985-86, exec. coun. 1976-79, 84-87, Dobzhansky award 2004), Soc. for Rsch. in Child Devel. (governing coun. 1974-76, 87-93, chmn. fin. com. 1987-89, pres. 1989-91), Internat. Soc. for Study of Behavioral Devel. (exec. bd. 1987-94). Avocations: dogs, gardening. Home: 77-6222 Kaumalumalu Dr Holualoa HI 96725-9757 Office Phone: 808-322-9445. Personal E-mail: sandrascar@aol.com.

SCARWID, DIANA ELIZABETH, actress; b. Savannah, Ga. d. Anthony and Elizabeth Scarwid. Grad., Am. Acad. Dramatic Arts, 1975; degree in Theater Arts, Acting, Pace U., 1975. Appeared in films including Pretty Baby, Honeysuckle Rose, Inside Moves, (Oscar award nomination Best Supporting Actress), Mommie Dearest, Rumble Fish, Strange Invaders, Silkwood, Psycho III, Extremeties, Heat, Neon Bible, The Cure, Gold Diggers: The Secret of Bear Mountain, What Lies Beneath, The Angel Doll, A Guy Thing, Party Monster, The Clearing; TV films include Thou Shalt Not Kill, Studs Lonigan, Guyana Tragedy: The Story of Jim Jones, Desperate Lives, A Bunny's Tale, After the Promise, Night of The Hunter, Critical Choices, Bastard Out of Carolina, Angel of Pennsylvania Avenue, Truman (Emmy nomination), If These Walls Could Talk, Ruby Bridges Story, also mini-series From the Earth to the Moon, Before He Wakes; theater prodns. include Key Exchange, Toronto, Can., A Thousand Clowns, Jupiter, Fla., Gethsamanie Springs, Mark Taper Forum, LA, Spoon River Anthology, Ring 'round the Moon, NYC, Nat. Shakespeare Conservancy, NY; (TV films) Down Will Come Baby, Dirty Pictures, Path to War, (series) WonderFalls. Avocations: reading, bicycling, crabbing, walking.

SCATENA, LORRAINE BORBA, retired rancher, women's rights advocate, researcher; b. San Rafael, Calif., Feb. 18, 1924; d. Joseph and Eugenia (Simas) de Borba; m. Louis G. Scatena, Feb. 14, 1960, dec. Nov. 1995; children: Louis Vincent, Eugenia Gayle. BA, Dominican Coll., San Rafael, 1945; postgrad., Calif. Sch. Fine Arts, 1948, U. Calif., Berkeley, 1956—57. Cert. elem. tchr. Calif. Tchr. Dominican Coll., 1946; tchr. of mentally handicapped San Anselmo (Calif.) Sch. Dist., 1946; tchr. Fairfax (Calif.) Pub. Elem. Sch., 1946—53; asst. to mayor Fairfax (Calif.) City Recreation, 1948—53; tchr., libr. U.S. Dependent Schs., Mainz am Rhine, Germany, 1953—56; translator Portugal Travel Tours, Lisbon, 1954; bonding sec. Am. Fore Ins. Group, San Francisco, 1958—60; rancher, farmer Yerington, Nev., 1960—98. Hostess com. Caldecott and Newbury Authors' Awards, San Francisco, 1959; mem. Nev. State Legis. Commn., 1975; coord. Nevadans for Equal Rights Amendment, 1975-78, rural areas rep., 1976-78; testifier Nev. State Senate and Assembly, 1975, 77; mem. adv. com. Fleischmann Coll. Agr. U. Nev., 1977-80, 81-84; speaker Grants and Rsch. Projects, Bishop, Calif., 1977, Choices for Tomorrow's Women, Fallon, Nev., 1989. Poetry presenter World Congress on Arts and Comm., Lisbon, Portugal, 1999, Washington, 2000, St. John's Coll.-Cambridge U., 2001, Vancouver, B.C., Can., 2002. Trustee Wassuk Coll., Hawthorne, Nev., 1984-87; mem. Lyon County Friends of Libr., Yerington, 1971—, Lyon County Mus. Soc., 1978—; sec., pub. info. chmn. Lyon County Rep. Women, 1968-73, program v.p., 1973-75; mem. Lyon County Rep. Ctrl. Com, 1973-74, Marin County Soc. Artists, San Anselmo, Calif., 1948-53; charter mem. Eleanor Roosevelt Edn. Fund for Women and Girls, 1990, sustaining mem., 1992—; Nev. rep. 1st White House Conf. Rural Am. Women, Washington, 1980; participant internat. reception, Washington, 1980; mem. pub. panel individual presentation Shakespeare's Treatment of Women Characters, Nev. Theatre for the Arts, Ashland, Oreg., Shakespearean Actors local performance, 1977; mem. Nev. Women's History Project, U. Nev., 1996—; mem. pres.'s circle Dominican U. Calif., 1997-; mem. Bancroft Libr.'s coun. U. Calif., Berkeley, 2002-. Recipient Outstanding Conservation Farmer award Mason Valley Conservation Dist., 1992, Soroptimist Internat. Women Helping women award 1983, invitation to first all-women delegation to U.S.A. from People's Republic China, U.S. House Reps., 1979; Public Forum Travel grantee Edn. Title IX, Oakland, Calif., 1977; Internat. Biog. Ctr. (Cambridge) fellow World Lit. Acad., 1993. Mem. AAUW (life mem. nat. br. 1975—, Leaders Circle 1998-), Lyon County Ret. Tchrs. Assn. (unit pres. 1979-80, 84-86, v.p. 1986-88, Nev. State Outstanding Svc. award 1981, state conv. gen. chmn. 1985), Rural Am. Women Inc., AAUW (br. pres. 1972-74, 74-76, chair edn. found. programs 1983—, state conv. gen. chmn. 1976, 87, state sec. 1970-72, state legis. program chmn. 1976-77, state chmn. internat. rels. 1979-81, state pres. 1981-83, br. travelship, discovering women in U.S. history Radcliffe Coll. 1981, State Humanities award 1975, Future Fund Nat. award 1983, Lorraine Scatena endowment gift named in her honor for significant contbns. to AAUW Ednl. Found. 1997), Mason Valley Country Club, Italian Cath. Fedn. (pres. 1986-88), Uniao Portuguesa Estado da Calif., Nat. Mus. of Women in the Arts (charter mem., 1987, assoc., mem. mus. coun. 2000—). Roman Catholic. Avocations: writing, photography, travel, history. Home: PO Box 247 Yerington NV 89447-0247

SCATES, ALICE YEOMANS, retired federal official; b. Pitts., Jan. 21, 1915; d. William E. and Georgiana L. (Lloyd) Yeomans. BS, State Tchrs. Coll., Glassboro, N.J., 1936; MEd, Duke U., 1949; EdD, George Washington U., 1963. Tchr. elem. sch., Haddon Heights, N.J., 1937-43; civilian personnel officer Sedalia Army Airfield, Mo., Greenfield Army Airfield, S.C., 1944-46; pers. tng. officer VA Ctr., Dayton, Ohio, 1947—48; rsch. assoc., dir. Am. Coun. on Edn. Staff for Office Naval Rsch. Projects, 1949-53; asst. dir. Nat. Home Study Coun., 1954; editor, rsch. asst. Office of Edn. HEW, 1955, rsch. analyst, coord. coop. rsch. program, 1956-64, program planning officer occupl. rsch. program, 1965-66, dir. basic rsch. br. secondary edn., 1967-69; program planning and eval. officer Nat. Ctr. Ednl. R & D, 1969-71; eval. specialist Office Program Eval., 1971-80; eval. officer Office of Mgmt. U.S. Dept. Edn., 1980-82, cons., 1982-91; mem. continuing care adv. com. Md. State Office on Aging, 1994-99. Contbr. articles to profl. jours.; editor: Life Line, 1998—. Mem. Nat. Continuing Care Residents Assn.; bd. dirs. Town Ctr. Cmty. Assn., Columbia, Md., 1997-2001. Capt. U.S. Army, 1943-46. Fellow AAAS; mem. LWV, Am. Sociol. Assn., Am. Ednl. Rsch. Assn., Adult Edn. Assn., Kappa Delta Pi, Phi Delta Gamma. Home and Office: Vantage House # 1006 5400 Vantage Point Rd Columbia MD 21044-2667 Personal E-mail: ayscates@msn.com.

SCATTERGOOD, FLORENCE GASSLER, music educator; b. Waco, Tex., Oct. 15, 1954; d. Robert Karl and Lois Conrad (Conrad) Gassler; m. Robert Alan Scattergood, May 30, 1987; children: Kenneth Edward, Kendra

Ann. MusB, Baylor U., 1976, MusM, 1983. Cert. gen. elem. and music tchr. Tex. Choral music tchr. St. Albans Mem. Sch., Waco, 1976—78, Clifton Indep. Sch. Dist., Tex., 1979—83, Waco Indep. Sch. Dist., 1984—86, 1999—, Grand Prairie Indep. Sch. Dist., Tex., 1986—89, Irving Indep. Sch. Dist., Tex., 1990—99. Recipient Model of Unity award, Com. Race Rels., Waco, 2004—05. Mem.: Tex. Music Educators Assn., Tex. Music Adjudicators Assn. (adjudicator 1999—). Achievements include mentoring 40 new educators and cooperating teacher totaling 34. Avocation: travel. Office: Waco HS 2020 N 42d Waco TX 76710 E-mail: fscattergood@wacoisd.org.

SCAVUZZO, TRACY TRUESDELL, mathematics educator, department chairman; d. Keith Norman and Doris Marie Truesdell; m. Christopher Scavuzzo, June 30, 1979 (dec. July 26, 1996); 1 child, Raghela Marie. BS in Edn., Southwestern Mo. State U., Springfield, 1979; post grad., Kansas City, Mo. Lic. secondary math. Mo. Dept. Elem. and Secondary Edn. Math tchr. Harrisonville H.S., Harrisonville, Mo., 1983—, chair math. dept., 2003—. Credit recovery summer sch. tchr. Harrisonville H.S., Harrisonville, Mo., 1995—; presenter math.- sci. interface conf. Mo. Dept. Elem. and Secondary Edn., Osage Beach, 1995—98, presenter bridges conf., 2001; tchr. comty. edn. Cass R-IX Sch. Dist., Harrisonville, 2000—; math cons. Cass Career Ctr., 2005—. Troop leader and svc. unit cons. Girl Scouts USA, Harrisonville, Mo., 1993—; sec. Academic Booster Club, Harrisonville, Mo., 2005—06; chalice bearer St. Peter's Episcopal Ch., Harrisonville, Mo., 2002—. Named one of Nat. Math., Sci., and Tech. Tchrs. of Yr., Radio Shack, 2003; recipient Breaking the Mold Educator award, KCPT TV, Kans. City Star and McDonalds, 1994, Hon. Mention Pres.'s Excellence in Math. Edn. award, U.S. Dept. Edn., 1995, Svc. Learning Educator of Yr., Cass R-9 Sch. Dist., 1996, 2000, Golden Apple Tchr. of Month, Harrisonville H.S., 2004; grantee Environ. Learning Project Display, Wal Mart, 2001. Mem.: NEA, Mo. Educators Assn., Nat. Coun. Tchrs. Math. Episcopalian. Avocations: reading, boating. Office: Harrisonville HS 1504 E Elm Harrisonville MO 64701 Office Phone: 816-380-3273. Office Fax: 816-380-5853. E-mail: scavuzzot@harrisonville.k12.mo.us.

SCEARSE, PATRICIA DOTSON, nursing educator, dean; b. Wabash, Ind., Sept. 4, 1931; d. Claude Richard and Lilly Etta (Colvill) D.; m. Vernon Quinton Scearse, June 26, 1955 (dec. Mar. 1990); 1 child, Victoria Lynn Lenderman. BS, Earlham Coll., 1955; MS, U. Colo., 1968; D in Nursing Sci., U. Calif., San Francisco, 1974. RN. Staff nurse Reid Meml. Hosp., Richmond, Ind., 1954-55; head nurse, instr. Hillcrest Bapt. Hosp., Waco, Tex., 1955-56; instr. Sch. Nursing Candler Hosp., Savannah, Ga., 1956-60; adminstrv. asst., edn. cons. Wyo. State Bd. Nursing, Cheyenne, 1964-68; asst. prof. San Diego State U., 1969, Ball State U., Muncie, Ind., 1969-71; assoc. prof., area chairperson U. Mich., Ann Arbor, 1974-80; prof., dean Coll. Nursing Tex. Christian U., Ft. Worth, 1980-95, emeritus dean, prof., 1995—. Pub. policy editor Jour. Profl. Nursing, Phila., 1986-89; editorial cons. Jour. Pub. Health Nursing, New Haven, 1984-89; contbr. articles to profl. jours. Recipient Outstanding Nurse award Sigma Theat Tau, Beta Alpha, Ft. Worth, 1986; Kennedy Inst. Ethics postdoctoral fellow, Georgetown U., 1978. Mem. ANA, APHA (bd. govs. 1976), Am. Assn. Colls. of Nursing (bd. dirs. 1982-84, 85-87), Nat. League for Nursing, Coun. Baccalaureate and Higher Degree Programs (bd. rev.), Assn. Community Health Nurse Educators (named Great 100 Nurses 1992). Home: 3301 Quail Run Dr High Point NC 27265-2589

SCEERY, BEVERLY DAVIS, genealogist, writer, educator; b. Hartford, Conn. d. Howard Coe and Gladys (Cotton) Davis; m. Walter Raymond Sceery; children: Nancy Bazar, Edward Sceery, Walter Sceery Jr., Martha Creed, Mary Heaton. BS magna cum laude, U. Md., 1975, MS, 1977, postgrad., 1977-82. Fin. counselor U. Md., College Park, 1975-77, lectr., 1977-82; realtor Washington, 1982-95; genealogist DAR, Washington, 1992—. Dir. handicapped program U. Md., College Park, 1975—77. Editor Capital Gardener mag., 1980-84; contbr. articles to profl. jours. Leader Girl Scouts Am., Potomac, Md., 1963—73, chmn., 1970—73; dir. Camp Tuckerman, Bethesda, Md., 1973; Stephen min. deacon Warner Meml. Presbyn. Ch., 2001—, deacon, 2004—. Mem.: DAR (mus. docent Nat. Soc. 1989—, chmn. Am. History 1991—94, spkrs. staff, organizing regent Potomac Hundred chpt. 1992—, state registrar 1994—97, hon. regent Great Falls chpt. 1996—, nat. vice chmn. vol. genealogists, state chmn. 1997—2000, historian Mary Washington chpt. 2001—, regent Mary Washington chpt. 2002—04, D.C. state chaplain 2004—, hon. regent), AAUW (chmn. nomination com. 1991), Hereditary Order Descs. Colonial Govs., Nat. Soc. New Eng. Women (Va. Colony pres. 1999—2002, registrar gen. 2002—05), Colonial Dames 17th Century (registrar Va. Colony chpt. 1997—99, genealogist Nat. Soc. 1997—, parliamentarian 2002—04, chaplain 2005—), Nat. Soc. Old Plymouth Colony Descs., Nat. Soc. Women Descs. Ancient and Hon. Arty. Co. (Va. sec. 1999—, nat. registration and credentials chmn. 2001—04, nat. rec. sec. 2004—, rec. sec. gen.), Women's Club Chevy Chase (chmn. thrift shop 1997—2004), Fernwood Garden Club (pres. 1996—98), Nat. Capital Area Fedn. Garden Clubs (master judge flower shows, landscape design 1972—, chmn. flower show sch. 1989—91), Omicron Nu, Alpha Lambda Delta, Phi Kappa Phi. Avocation: genealogy. Home: 10307 Riverwood Dr Potomac MD 20854-1539 E-mail: bsceery@yahoo.com.

SCEGO, MEGAN ELAINE, music educator; d. John Douglas and Elaine Lee Scego. B of Music Edn., U. Mo., Kansas City, 1998—2003. Tchr. Indian Woods Mid. Sch., Overland Pk., Kans., 2003—. Mem. PTA. Office Phone: 913-993-0675. Personal E-mail: meganscego@hotmail.com.

SCHAAL, BARBARA ANNA, evolutionary biologist, educator; BS in Biology with honors, U. Ill., Chgo., 1969; MPhil in Population Biology, Yale U., 1971, PhD in Population Biology, 1974. spkr. in field. Assoc. prof. biology Washington U., St. Louis, 1980-86, prof., 1986—; prof. genetics Wash. U. Sch. Medicine, Spencer T. Olin prof. biology in arts and scis., chair dept. biology, 1993-97, mem. various coms. Assoc. editor Molecular Biology and Evolution, Am. Jour. Botany, Molecular Ecology, Conservation Genetics. Trustee St. Louis Acad. Scis. Fellow AAAS, Am. Acad. Arts & Sciences; mem. NAS (v.p. 2005-), Bot. Soc. Am. (pres. 1995-96, Merit award 1999), Nature Conservancy (trustee Mo. chpt.). Achievements include research on the evolutionary process within plant populations.*

SCHAAR, SUSAN CLARKE, legislative staff member; b. Lawrenceville, Va., Dec. 21, 1949; d. Garland Lewis and Frances Virginia (Matthews) Clarke; m. William Berkley Schaar, Jr., Nov. 24, 1990. BA, U. Richmond, 1972. Engrossing clk. Senate of Va., Richmond, 1974, legis. rsch. analyst, 1974-77, asst. to the clk., 1977-83, asst. clk., 1983-90, clk., 1990—. Vice chair legis. effectiveness com. Nat. Conf. State Legis., 1996—98, chair, 1998—99, mem. exec. com., 1999—2002, staff vice chmn. standing com., 2002—03, staff vice chair, 2004—05, staff chair, 2005—06; exec. com. Mason's Manual Commn. Mem. model gen. assembly adv. com. YMCA, Richmond, 1990—; trustee U. Richmond, 1990—94; pres. Richmond Club Westhampton, 1988—90; bd. dirs. Spider Club Athletic Club, Richmond, 1988—90; govt. counselor Va. Girls State, bd. dirs.; mem. Va. Capitol Found., 2004—; bd. assocs. U. Richmond, 1995—2005. Mem.: Coun. Preservation Capitol Sq., Am. Soc. Legis. Clks. and Secs. (mem. exec. com. 1995—99, sec.-treas. 1996, pres.-elect 1997, pres. 1997—98, past pres. 1998—99), Pi Sigma Alpha, Omicron Delta Kappa. Baptist. Office: Senate of Va PO Box 396 Richmond VA 23218-0396 Business E-Mail: sschaar@sov.state.va.us.

SCHABACKER, BETTY BARCHET, artist; b. Balt., Aug. 14, 1925; d. Stephen George and Louise (Lankford) Barchet; m. Robert Bailey Schabacker, June 8, 1945; 1 child, Elizabeth M Student, Conn. Coll. Women, 1946. Freelance artist, Santa Fe, 1950—. Mem. Soc. Animal Artists, Nat. Water Color Soc., Audubon Artists, Inc., Coll. Artists Am.

SCHABERT, LEAH CHRISTINE, dance instructor; b. St. Paul, Apr. 4, 1982; d. Cynthia Marie and Edward Neil Schabert. Grad., Forest Lake H.S., Minn., 1996. Cert. human performance and fitness instr. N.D. State U., 2005. Instr. dance Fargo Pub. Schs., ND, 2002—; owner/dir. Galaxy Dance Studio, Fargo, ND, 2005—. Instr. dance West Fargo H.S., Fargo South H.S., N.D. State U., 2000. Captain, coach (dance) N.D. State U. Dance Team. Bd. dirs. N.D. Assn. of Dance and Drill, 2002. Recipient Most Valuable Dancer, N.D. State Dance Team, 2001, 2002, 2003, State Champion, N.D. Assn. of Dance and Drill, 2004, 2006, Nat. Ranked (5th), Universal Dance Assn., 2004, Nat. Grand Champions, United Performing Assn.- Discovery Jr. H.S., 2005, 2006, Nat. Divsn. Title, 2005, 2006. Home: 5301 Amber Valley Pky #18 Fargo ND 58104 Office: Galaxy Dance Studio 3019 13th Ave Fargo ND 58103 Office Phone: 701-293-6338. Personal E-mail: galaxydance@aol.com.

SCHABNER, DAWN FREEBLE, artist, educator; b. Mercer, Pa., Jan. 30, 1933; d. Benjamin Frederick and Mary Emma (McElheny) Freeble; m. Donald Russell Schabner, Jan. 5, 1954; children: Donald Russell Jr., Dean Aaron. Student, Phila. Mus. Sch. Art, 1950-52; BA in Fine Arts with honors magna cum laude, Hofstra U., 1971; student, Cleve. Inst Art., 1952-53; MA in Liberal Studies, SUNY, Stony Brook, 1976. Designer Am. Greetings, Cleve., 1953; art educator Islip (N.Y.) Pub. Schs., 1967-95, Dowling Coll., Oakdale, NY, 1991—. One-woman shows include East Islip (N.Y.) Pub. Libr., 1977, 1988, Unitarian Bay Gallery, Bellport, N.Y., 1997, L-Art Gallery, Kiev, Ukraine, 1999, exhibited in group shows at Hofstra U., 1970, Patchogue-Medford Pub. Libr., 1983, East End Arts & Humanities Coun., Riverhead, N.Y., 1984, Islip Art Mus. Juried Exhibit, 1985, 1987, 1988, 1999, 2000, 2002, 2006, Suffolk County Legis. Bldg., Hauppage, N.Y., 1988, Bennington Coll., 1989, 2006, Goat Alley Gallery, Sag Harbor, N.Y., 1989, Canio's Books, Sag Harbor, 1990, South County Libr., Bellport, N.Y., 1991, The Parrish Art Mus., Southampton, N.Y., 1999, Stage Gallery, Merrick, N.Y., 2001; featured artist East End Arts and Humanities Coun., Riverhead, 1986, Clayton Liberatore Art Gallery, Bridgehampton, N.Y., 1994, 1995, 1997, 2001, 2002, Spinnato Art Gallery, East Setauket, NY, 2005, Mus. Modern Art, N.Y.C., Phoenix Fine Arts Gallery, Bellport, N.Y., 2005, 2006. Mem. Nat. League Am. Pen Women Inc. (past pres. Suffolk County chpt.), Met. Mus. Art, East End Arts Coun., Parrish Art Mus., Mus. Modern Art. Avocations: golf, bicycling, weight training, reading, attending concerts & ballet.

SCHABOW, NANCY A. DEXTER, music educator; b. Green Bay, Wis., Feb. 1, 1970; d. David John and Dianne Marie (Hein) Dexter; m. Jeremy Jon Schabow, July 31, 1993. MusB, Alverno Coll., 1992. Registered music therapist, Wis. Music therapist Kindcare, Inc., Milw., 1993-94; music therapist in pvt. practice Hartland, Wis., 1993-98; owner, dir. Music Therapy Svcs. Waukesha County LLC, Hartland, 1999—. Bd. dirs. Wis. Dept. Regulation and Licensing: Music Art Dance Therapy, Madison. Mem. Am. Music Therapy Assn. (treas. Wis. chpt. 1994-96, govt. rels. 1996—; Gt. Lakes regional chpt. alt. del. 1999—). Avocations: cooking, reading, movies. Office: Music Therapy Assn Waukesha County LLC Hartland WI 53029

SCHACHTEL-GREEN, BARBARA HARRIET LEVIN, retired epidemiologist; b. May 27, 1921; d. Lester and Ethel (Neiman) Levin; m. Hyman Judah Schachtel, Oct. 15, 1941 (dec. Jan. 1990); m. Louis H. Green, Feb. 26, 1995; children: Bernard, Ann Molly. Student, Wellesley Coll., 1939—41; BS, U. Houston, 1951, MA in Psychology, 1967; PhD, U. Tex., Houston, 1979. Psychol. examiner Meyer Ctr. for Devel. Pediat., Tex. Children's Hosp., Houston, 1967-81; instr. dept. pediat. Baylor Coll. Medicine, Houston, 1967-81, asst. prof. dept. medicine, 1982—2005; ret., 2005. Asst. dir. biometry and epidemiology Sid W. Richardson Inst. for Preventive Medicine, Meth. Hosp., Houston, 1981-88, dir. quality assurance, 1988-93; instl. rev. bd. for human rsch. Baylor Coll. Medicine, Houston, 1981-87, 97—; devel. bd. U. Tex. Health Sci. Ctr., Houston, 1987-97; dean's adv. bd. Sch. Arch., U. Houston, 1987-89. Contbr. articles to profl. jours. V.p., bd. dirs. Houston-Harris County Mental Health Assn., 1966—67; vice-chmn. bd. mgrs. Harris County Hosp. Dist., Houston, 1974—90, chmn., 1990—92, bd. dirs., 1970—93; trustee Inst. Religion in Tex. Med. Ctr., 1990—, vice chmn., 2000—; sec. Bo Harris County Hosp. Dist. Found. Bd., 1993—; bd. dirs. Congregation Beth Israel, 1993—95, Planned Parenthood of Houston, Inc., 1994—2000, Houston Ind. Sch. Dist. Found., 1993—2001, Crisis Intervention, 1994—96. Named Great Texan of Yr., Nat. Found. for Ilietis and Colitis, Houston, 1982, Outstanding Citizen, Houston-Harris County Mental Health Assn., 1985; recipient Good Heart award B'nai Brith Women, 1984, Women of Prominence award Am. Jewish Com., 1991, Mayor's award for outstanding vol. svc., 1994. Mem. APA, APHA, Wellesley Club of Houston (pres. 1968-70). Avocations: golf, tennis, books. Home: 2527 Glen Haven Blvd Houston TX 77030-3511

SCHACHTER, BERNICE, sculptor, educator, writer; b. Elizabeth, N.J., Jan. 21, 1925; d. Samuel Naiman and Nettie (Cohen) Nodelman; m. Saul Schachter, Dec. 22, 1946 (dec. Nov. 1993); children: Shari E. Schachter Canepa, Steven M. BS, Goddard Coll., 1973, MA, 1974; postgrad., UCLA, 1974. Art dir. Artist and Craftsmen Guild, Cranford, N.J., 1966-73; instr. sculpture Everywoman's Village, Van Nuys, Calif., 1973-99; owner, dir. Sculpture Source, Culver City, Calif., 1975—. Dir. Summer Stone Carving Workshop, Pietrasanta, Italy, 1973-97. Author: 20th Century American Sculpture, 1974, Masks of the Muses, 1986, (screenplays) Morris, 1980, 100 Years from Now, 1995. Recipient Carducci Cultural medal Commune of City, Pietrasanta, 1990. Mem. AAUW, Internat. Sculptures Soc., Nat. Sculptors Soc., Golden West Sculptors, Am. Pen Women (pres. 2000). Democrat. Jewish. Avocations: golf, bridge, lawn bowling, travel. Home: 5263 Miembro Laguna Hills CA 92653-1821

SCHADEGG, AMY RACHELLE, language educator; b. Kimball, Nebr., Nov. 10, 1971; d. Jerry Lee and Karen Lee Beguin; m. Michael Shawn Schadegg, May 20, 1995; children: Haley Marie, Carley Rae. BE, U. Nebr., Kearney, 1995. 9-12 English tchr. Banner County Sch., Harrisburg, Nebr., 1996—2006; English tchr. Haxton County schs., 2006—. Assn. edn. Banner County Edn. Assn., Harrisburg, Nebr. Mem.: NSEA. Republican. Roman Cath. Avocations: travel, reading.

SCHADLER, FLORENCE, artist, educator; b. Phila., Mar. 13, 1941; d. Clayton and Elva Elizabeth (Hodges) Ashton; m. Gary Lane Schadler, July 14, 1962 (dec. Apr. 1983); children: Cynthia Lynne, Craig Raymond; m. J.M. Harrison, May 25, 1990 (div. May 1998). BFA magna cum laude, Kutztown State U.; cert., Moore Inst. Art Phila. Art educator Parkland Sch. Dist., Allentown, Pa., Pa. State U., Allentown, Baum Sch. Art, Allentown, Jacksonville (Fla.) Art Mus., 1994-95; adj. prof. Fla. C.C. Jacksonville, 1995-97. Exhibited in group shows at Cummer Mus., Jacksonville; represented in permanent collections. Mem. Fla. Watercolor Soc. (life), Jacksonville Watercolor Soc. (pres. 1994-95), Orange Park (Fla.) Fine Art Guild (v.p.), St. Augustine (Fla.) Art Assn., Kutztown U. Alumni Assn., Lehigh U. Alumni Assn. Republican. Home: 914 Bridgetown Pike Langhorne PA 19053-7218 E-mail: floschadler@comcast.net.

SCHADOW, KAREN E., public speaking trainer, educator; b. Mar. 1949; 1 child, Kelby. BA in comm. and humanities magna cum laude, Fla. State U., 1971, MA in theatre magna cum laude, 1973. Previous cameraperson numerous programs, ABC TV, previous prodn. staff mem.; pres. The Voice of Success!, NYC. Adj. asst. prof. NYU, 1990—; instr. Bergen Cmty. Coll., NJ; creator, presenter various lectures and seminars for sch. and orgn. including Nat. Acad. TV Arts & Scis., NY Coalition Women in Arts and Media, Ctr. Arts Edn., The Learning Annex, nationwide; prodr. student career conf. NY Women in Comm., 2002—05; nominating judge Drama League. Mem.: Nat. Acad. TV Arts & Scis. (past mem. bd. govs., Emmy award 1984), Fla. State U. Theatre Project, New England Soc., Univ. Film & Video Assn., Screen Actors Guild, Actors' Equity, NY Women in Comm. (v.p. student affairs). Office Phone: 212-563-2615. Business E-Mail: karen@thevoiceofsuccess.com.

SCHAEF, ANNE WILSON, writer, consultant; b. Siloam Springs, Ark., Mar. 22, 1934; d. Virgil Eustace and Manilla (Longan) Willey; m. Paul Wilson; 1 child, Beth Anne; m. Robert Schaef; 1 child, Rodney Walter. AB in psychology, Washington U., St. Louis, 1956, MA; PhD, Union Inst., 1986; HHD (hon.), Kenyon Coll., 1992. Pvt. practice psychologist, Mo., Ill., 1960-68; pvt. practice psychotherapist Colo., 1968-84; pres. Wilson-Schaef Assoc., Boulder, Colo., 1984—. Cons. drug & alcohol treatment ctrs., co-dependency treatment ctrs.; adj faculty San Francisco Theol. Sem.; lectr. in field. Author: Women's Reality, 1981, Co-dependence: Misunderstood/Mistreated, 1986, When Society Becomes an Addict, 1987, Escape From Intimacy/Untangling the Love Addictions: Sex, Romance, Relationships, 1989, Meditations for Women Who Do Too Much, 1990, Laugh, I Thought I'd Die.If I Didn't, 1990, Living in Process, 1999, Meditations For Living in Balance, 2000, Meditations for Women Who Do Too Much (revised edit. 2004); Author: (with D. Fassel) The Addictive Organization, 1988, Beyond Therapy, Beyond Science: A New Model for Healing the Whole Person, 1992. Nat. Honor fellow Washington U., Danforth Grad. fellow, Danforth Spl. fellow, NIMH fellow; Spl. grantee Union Theol. Sem. Office: Wilson-Schaef Assoc Inc PO Box 990 Boulder MT 59632-0990

SCHAEFER, BONNIE (E. BONNIE SCHAEFER), retail executive; b. Chgo., Mar. 16, 1963; d. Rowland Schaefer. From sales assoc. to store mgr. Claire's Stores, Inc., 1987—90, v.p. real estate, 1994—2002, co-vice chmn., 1999—2002, co-chmn., 2002—, co-CEO, 2002—. Bd. dirs. Claire's Stores, Inc., 1998—, Claire's Nippon. Office: Claires Stores Inc 3 SW 129th Ave Pembroke Pines FL 33027 Office Phone: 954-433-3900. Office Fax: 954-433-3999.*

SCHAEFER, ELEANOR MONTVILLE, retired publishing executive; b. Worcester, Mass., June 27, 1926; d. Joseph Samuel and Monica Savage Montville; m. Charles James Schaefer; 1 child, Charles James IV. AB, Trinity U., 1949. Radio/tv dept. Sullivan Staufer Colwell & Bayles, Inc., NYC, 1949—50; promotion dept. staff Life Mag., NYC, 1951—52; asst. promotion mgr. Sports Illustrated, NYC, 1953—59; promotion mgr. Glamour mag., NYC, 1960. V.p. League Women Voters, 1971—77; found. dir. Summit Coll. Club; vol. auxilliary mem. Assn. U. Women, Summit, NJ, 1998—99. Mem.: Trinity U. Alumni Assn. (past pres. 1959—60), Summit Coll. Club, Canoe Brook Country Club. Achievements include being first woman staffer on "Project X" which eventually became Sports Illustrated. Avocations: golf, interior decorating. Home: 307 Hobart Ave Short Hills NJ 07078 E-mail: montvilles@aol.com.

SCHAEFER, ELZBIETA A., music educator; b. Warsaw, May 8, 1938; came to the U.S., 1967; d. Roman and Janina Pierzchalski; m. Vladimir S. Levitski, 1962 (div. 1981); children: Konstanzia, Teresa, Alexander; m. Dean H. Schaefer, June 27, 1998. MusM, Warsaw Conservatory Music, 1963. Choir dir. Holy Cross ch., Mpls., 1990—. Author: (musical programs) Fr. Chopin in His Music and Letters, R. Schumann and His Letters. Mem. Minn. Music Tchrs. Assn. Roman Catholic. Avocations: tennis, skiing, cooking, gardening, art. Home: 9475 161st St W Lakeville MN 55044-8778

SCHAEFER, JOANN, public health service officer; MD, Creighton Univ., 1995. Cert. family medicine. Private practice, Omaha, 1995—2002; instr. Creighton Univ. Sch. Med., Omaha, 1997—2003, assoc prof., 2003; dep. chief med. officer Nebr. Dept. Health & Human Svc., Lincoln, 2002—05, chief med. officer, dir. regulation & licensure, 2005—. Named a Local Legend, Am. Med. Women's Assn. Mem.: Am. Acad. Family Physicians, AMA, Nebr. Acad. Family Physicians, Metro Omaha Med. Soc., Nebr. Med. Assn. (Physician of the Yr. 2004). Office: Dept Health & Human Svc 301 Centennial Mall S Lincoln NE 68509 Mailing: Dept Health & Human Svc PO Box 95007 Lincoln NE 68509-5007*

SCHAEFER, LOIS ALMA, special education educator; b. Mt. Vernon, NY, Aug. 16, 1934; d. Alfred William and Evelyn Bland Clater; m. James Matthew Schaefer, June 18, 1960; children: Scott Hollenbeck, Lucinda Dye, Stephen Hollenbeck, Shelley Krystowiak, Daniel, Mark, Ruth Potter, Julia Burleson, Paul. BS in Elem. Edn., Bob Jones U., Greenville, S.C., 1957, M of Christian Edn., 1959; MEd in Spl. Edn., U. of North Fla., Jacksonville, 1990; LittD (hon.), Trinity Bapt. Coll., Jacksonville, Fla., 2002. Cert. profl. educator Fla. Tchr. Hollis Elem. sch., Greenville, 1957—59; prof. Trinity Bapt. Coll., Jacksonville, 1978—. Cons. Trinity Christian Acad., Jacksonville, 1979—, coord., contbg. designer spl. edn. resource dept. Mem.: Kappa Delta Pi. Republican. Baptist. Avocations: reading, writing.

SCHAEFER, M. ELAINE, music educator, conductor; b. Frederick, Okla., Apr. 13, 1945; d. Arthur Lloyd and Mary Ellen Bush; m. Edward T. Vrable, July 28, 2001; children: Joel, Anne Marie, Scott Patrick Gillespie. Student, Diablo Valley Coll., Pleasant Hill, Calif., 1961—63, Chico State Coll., Calif., 1963—64; BA, Calif. State U. Hayward, 1967; MusM, U. Regina, Sask., Can., 1988. Tchrs. cert. Calif., 1967. Instrumental music tchr. Kenilworth Jr. HS, Petaluma, Calif., 1967—72; music tchr. Incline Village HS, Nev., 1972—78; instrumental and choral tchr. Humboldt HS, Sask., Canada, 1978—86; music tchr. Balgonie HS, Sask., Canada, 1988—96; music instr., condr. Coll. Siskiyous, Weed, Calif., 1996—. Adjudicator Sask. Music Festivals, 1985—96; condr. Holy Rosary Cathedral Choir, Regina, Sask., 1987—96, Royal Can. Mounted Police Choir, 1987—89; pres. Sask. Choral Dirs., 1989—90. Bd. mem. Sask. Coun. Cultural Orgns., 1990—96. Sgt. U.S. Army, 1974—78. Named Tchr. of Yr., Col. of the Siskiyans, 2006, Faculty Mem. of Yr., 2006; recipient award of Appreciation, Sask. Music Educators, 1982. Fellow: Nat. Assn. Jazz Educators, Calif. Music Educators Assn., Am. Choral Dirs.; mem.: Internat. Fedn. Choral Music, Assn. Can. Choral Dirs. (bd. mem.), Nat. Assn. Jazz Educators, Calif. Music Educators Assn., Am. Choral Dirs. Roman Catholic. Home: 5925 Mule Deer Ct Weed CA 96094 Office: College Siskiyous 800 College Ave Weed CA 96094 Office Phone: 530-938-5315. Business E-Mail: schaefer@siskiyous.edu.

SCHAEFER, MARGARET F., secondary school educator; b. Amherst, Tex., Oct. 27, 1945; d. Rudolph William and Clara Adeline Schaefer. BS, Concordia Tchr.'s Coll., Seward, Nebr., 1968. Luth. sch. tchr. Nebr. Tchr. grades 2-6 St. Paul's Luth. Sch., San Antonio, 1968—73; tchr. grades 6-8 lang. arts Topeka Luth. Sch., 1973—. Mem. Friends of the Topeka Zoo, 1980—2006. Mem.: Luth. Edn. Assn. Personal E-mail: mars1045@sbcglobal.net.

SCHAEFER, MARILYN LOUISE, artist, writer, educator; b. Cedar Rapids, Iowa, Apr. 22, 1933; d. Henry Richard and Maria Augusta (Dickel) S. AA, Monticello Coll. for Women, 1953; BFA, Cranbrook Acad. Art, 1956, MFA, 1960; MA cum laude, U. Chgo., 1958; MA, St. John's Coll., Santa Fe, 1979. Rsch. asst. editor Encyclopaedia Britannica, Chgo., 1960-63; humanities editor Encyclopedia Americana, NY, 1964-68; acquisitions editor Litton Ednl. Pub., NY, 1968-70; from instr. to prof. emeritus art and advt. design dept. N.Y.C. Tech. Coll. CUNY, 1970—. Contbg. editor Encyclopedia Americana, 1979—, Coll. Teaching jour., 1979. Contbr. articles to profl. jours. including Art and Auction mag., Art and Antiques mag., Am. Artist mag., Encyclopedia Americana, 1970—. Luce Found. postgrad. study fellow St. John's Coll., 1976-79; Ingram Merrill Found. grantee, 1983-84. Mem. AAUW, CUNY Acad. Arts and Scis. Home: 306 W 76th St New York NY 10023-8065 Office: NYC Tech Coll CUNY 300 Jay St Brooklyn NY 11201-1909

SCHAEFER, MARLA L., retail executive; b. Chgo., May 19, 1949; d. Rowland Schaefer; 2 children. BA, Fla. Internat. U., 1973; MA in Orgnl. Psychology, Columbia U., 2003. Resident buyer NY Office Claire's Boutiques, 1986, v.p. fashion merchandising, 1990—98, sr. v.p., 1998—, sec., 2002—; vice chmn. bd. dirs. Claire's Stores Inc., Pembroke Pines, Fla., 1998—99, co-vice chmn., 1999—2003, acting co-chmn., co-CEO, 2002—03, co-chmn., co-CEO, 2003—. Office: Claire's Stores, Inc 3 SW 129th Ave Pembroke Pines FL 33027 Office Phone: 954-433-3900. Office Fax: 954-433-3999. E-mail: marla.schaefer@claires.com.*

SCHAEFER-WICKE, ELIZABETH, reading consultant, educator; b. Bridgeport, Conn., Mar. 30, 1941; d. William Joseph and Loretta Schaefer; m. Frederick Paul wicke, July 3, 1976. BS, U. Conn., 1963; MA, Columbia U., 1966; 6th yr. profl. diploma, U. Bridgeport, 1975. Cert. reading cons. Elem. sch. tchr. Miles Ave. Sch., Huntington Park, Calif., 1963-64, Eli Whitney Sch., Meriden, Conn., 1966-68; supr. student tchg. interns Tracey Sch.,

Norwalk, Conn., 1968-70; reading splst. Wolfpit Sch., Norwalk, 1970-81; remedial reading and math tchr., cons. Rowayton (Conn.) Sch., 1981—2003. Mentor tng. program BEST, 1987-94, tchr. reading recovery, 1994-2003. Grantee Norwalk Fund for Excellence, 1986-87; named to honor roll, Conn. Fedn. Ednl. & Profl. Employees, 2003. Mem. Norwalk Fedn. Tchrs. (bldg. steward 1981-2003), Internat. Reading Assn., Reading Recovery Coun. Am., So. Fairfield County Ret. Tchrs. Assn., Delta Kappa Gamma, Phi Delta Kappa, Pi Beta Phi. Democrat. Roman Catholic. Avocations: writing short stories, worldwide ednl. rsch., photography, scuba diving, bicycling. Home: 41 Lakeview Dr Norwalk CT 06850-2003 also: 535 Broad Ave S Naples FL 34102-7159

SCHAEFFER, BRENDA MAE, psychologist, author; b. Duluth, Minn. d. Ralph J. Bernice M. (Johnson) Furtman; children: Heidi, Gordon III. BA in Sociology, Psychology and English cum laude, U. Minn., 1962; MA in Human Devel., St. Mary's Coll., Winona, Minn., 1976; D of Ministry, U. Creation Spirituality, Oakland, Calif., 2000. Lic. psychologist, Minn.; cert. addictions specialist. Mem. faculty Coll. St. Scholastica, Duluth, 1976—; trainer, therapist, communications cons. Transactional Analysis Inst., Mpls., 1984-88; owner, clin. dir. Brenda M. Schaeffer and Assocs., Inc., 1985—, Healthy Relationships, Inc., 1991—; continued edn. instr. St. Thomas U., 1995—. Vis. prof. U. Minn., Duluth, 1976—; guest lectr. dep. counseling U. Wis., Superior, 1980—81; founder, bd. dirs. Inst. for Indigenous Healing Practice, Inc.; nat. and internat. lectr. in field. Author: Is It Love or Is It Addiction, 1987, 97, Loving Me, Loving You, 1991, Signs of Healthy Love, Signs of Addictive Love, Power Plays, Addictive Love, Help Yourself Out, Loves Way, 2001; mem. editorial bd. Transactional Analysis Jour.; editor Healthy Relationships newsletter. Planner Lake Superior Task Force, Duluth, 1980-83; bd. dirs., sec. Nat. Coun. Sexual Addictions/Compulsions, 1992—, sec. 1994-95; v.p. H. Milton Erickson Inst. Minn., 1992-93. Mem. Internat. Transactional Analysis Assn. (1975), Transactional Anaylsis Inst. Minn. (founder, pres. 1984-86), U.S. Assn. Transactional Analysis, Northeast Minn. Transactional Analysis Seminar (founder and chairperson 1977-83). Home and Office: 15798 Venture Ln # 101 Eden Prairie MN 55344-5729 Office Phone: 953-944-4046.

SCHAEFFER, SUSAN FROMBERG, writer, educator; b. Bklyn., Mar. 25, 1941; d. Irving and Edith (Levine) Fromberg; m. Neil J. Schaeffer, Oct. 11, 1970; children: Benjamin Adam, May Anna. BA, U. Chgo., 1961, MA with honors, 1963, PhD with honors, 1966. Instr. English Wright Jr. Coll., Chgo., 1964—65; asst. prof. Ill. Inst. Tech., Chgo., 1965—67; from asst. prof. to prof. Broeklundian, Eng., Bklyn. Coll., 1967—95. Guest lectr. U. Chgo., Cornell U., U. Ariz., U. Maine, Yale U., U. Tex., U. Mass. Author: Falling, 1973, Anya, 1974, Time In Its Flight, 1978, Love, 1981, The Madness of a Seduced Woman, 1983, Mainland, 1984, The Injured Party, 1986, The Dragons of North Chittendon, 1986, The Four Hoods and Great Dog, 1988, Buffalo Afternoon, 1989, First Nights, 1993;: The Golden Rope, 1996;; author: (poetry) The Witch and the Weather Report, 1972, Alphabet For the Lost Years, 1976, Granite Lady, 1974, Rhymes and Runes of the Toad, 1975, The Bible of the Beasts of the Little Field, 1980; author: (short stories) The Queen of Egypt and Other Stories, 1980. Recipient E.L. Wallant award, Friends of Lit. award, Prairie Schooner's Lawrence award, O. Henry award, Poetry award, Centennial Rev.; John Simon Guggenheim fellow. Mem.: PEN, Poetry Soc. Am., Authors Guild. Democrat. Jewish.

SCHAEFFER-YOUNG, JUDITH, library director; b. York, Pa., Aug. 26, 1944; d. Robert Jackson and Helen Josephine (Chiappy) Schatz; m. Karl Schaeffer, Jan. 28, 1967 (div. Sept. 1981); children: Stephen Matthew, Elizabeth Chatten; m. Harrison H. Young Jr., Dec. 29, 1990. BA, Barnard Coll., 1966; MLS, Columbia U., 1968. part-time reference libr. Hewlett-Woodmere Pub. Libr., Hewlett, 1971-78; part-time reference libr. Chestnut Hill Hosp. Sch. Nursing, Phila., 1981-85; interim reference libr. Pa. State U., Abington, 1986. Editor std. catalog dept. H.W. Wilson Co., Bronx, N.Y., 1968-69; cataloger Hewlett-Woodmere (N.Y.) Pub. Libr., 1970-71, Merrick (N.Y.) Pub. Libr., 1972-78; sr. sch. libr. Chestnut Hill Acad., Phila., 1978-81; mgr. tech. svcs. Med. Coll. of Pa., Phila., 1981-83; libr. Sch. Nursing Albert Einstein Med. Ctr., Phila., 1983-86; coord. rsch. alerts Inst. for Sci. Info., Phila., 1986-89, mgr. editorial svcs., 1989-91; dir. med. libr. Wills Eye Hosp., Phila., 1991—. Cataloger St. Paul's Episcopal Ch., Phila., 1985—. Author: Index to Song Collections in the Hewlett-Woodmere Pub. Libr., 1974; contbr. articles to profl. jours. Bd. dirs. Friends of Glenside (Pa.) Libr., 1992—; mem. libr. com. St. Paul's Ch., Chestnut Hill, Pa., 1985—. Mem. Med. Libr. Assn., Acad. Health Info. Profls., Assn. Vision Sci. Librs. (sec.1996-97, chmn. 1998-99, treas. 2000—). Home: 529 Custis Rd Glenside PA 19038-2011 Office: Wills Eye Hosp 840 Walnut St Philadelphia PA 19107-5599 Office Phone: 215-928-3288. E-mail: jyoung@willseye.org.

SCHAFER, ALICE TURNER, retired mathematics professor; b. Richmond, Va., June 18, 1915; d. John H. and Cleon (Dermott) Turner; m. Richard Donald Schafer, Sept. 8, 1942; children: John Dickerson, Richard Stone. AB, U. Richmond, 1936, DSc, 1964; MS, U. Chgo., 1940, PhD (fellow), 1942. Tchr. Glen Allen (Va.) High Sch., 1936-39; instr. math. Conn. Coll., New London, 1942-44, asst. prof., 1954-57, assoc. prof., 1957-61, prof., 1961-62; prof. math. Wellesley Coll., 1962-80, Helen Day Gould prof. math., 1969-80, Helen Day Gould prof. math. emerita, 1980—, affirmative action officer, 1980-82; prof. math. Marymount U., Arlington, Va., 1989-96; ret., 1996. Instr. U. Mich., Ann Arbor, 1945-46; lectr. Douglass Coll., New Brunswick, N.J., 1946-48; asst. prof. Swarthmore (Pa.) Coll., 1948-51, Drexel Inst. Tech., Phila., 1951-53; mathematician Johns Hopkins Applied Physics Lab., Silver Spring, Md., 1945; lectr. Simmons Coll., Boston, 1980-88, Radcliffe Coll. Seminars, Cambridge, Mass., 1980-85; U.S. chair postsecondary math. edn. U.S./China Joint Conf. on Edn., 1992, co-chair Citizen Amb. program People to People U.S. and China Joint Conf. on Women's Issues, 1995, session women in sci. and math. Contbr. articles on women in math. and other articles to math. jours. Recipient Disting. Alumna award Westhampton Coll., U. Richmond, 1977; NSF sci. faculty fellow Inst. for Advanced Study, Princeton, N.J., 1958-59. Fellow AAAS (math. sect. A nominating com. 1979-83, mem.-at-large 1983-86, chair-elect sect. A 1991, chair 1992, retiring chair 1993, Assn. for Women in Math. rep., 1993—), AAUP (chmn. nat. com. W 1980-83, mem. nat. coun. 1984-87), Am. Math. Soc. (chmn. postdoctoral fellowship com. 1973-76, affirmative action procedures com. 1980-82, chair com. on Human Rights of Mathematicians 1988-94), Soc. Indsl. and Applied Math., Am. Statis. Assn., Inst. Math. Stats., Nat. Coun. Tchrs. of Math. (chair com. on women 1976-81), Math Assn. Am. (adv. com. for Women and Math. program 1987-89, dir. fund raising 1989-92, lectr. 1982—, chair devel. com. 1988-92, Yueh-Gin Gung and Charles Y. Hu disting. svc. to math. award 1998), Internat. Congress Mathematicians (mem. fund raising com. 1986), Assn. for Women in Math. (pres. 1973-75, Alice T. Schafer Prize established 1989, chair fund raising com. 1992-94, leader math. del. women mathematicians to China 1990, Disting. Svc. award 1996), Emily's List (mem. majority coun.), Cosmos Club, Phi Beta Kappa, Sigma Xi, Sigma Delta Epsilon. Achievements include first study of singularities of space curves in projective differential geometry; research on undulation point of a space curve. Home: 1010 Waltham St Apt A404 Lexington MA 02421-8064

SCHAFER, AMY ELISABETH, public relations executive; d. George E. and Mary E. Schafer. B in Theatre, Ball State U., 1990; MA in Arts Adminstrn., Ind. U., 1998; MA in Theatre, S.W. Mo. State U., 1992. Adminstrv. asst. Cox Gallery Drury Coll., Springfield, Mo., 1992—96; mktg. dir. Fla. Studio Theatre, Sarasota, Fla., 1999—. Author: (original one-act) Roses in the Spring (Winner, Ball State Original One-Acts, 1988). Mem.: Young Professionals Group. Achievements include Founding Member/FST Improv Company. Office: Fla Studio Theatre 1241 North Palm Ave Sarasota FL 34236 Office Phone: 941-366-9017 313. E-mail: amy@fst2000.org.

SCHAFER, ELIZABETH DIANE, historian, writer; b. Opelika, Ala., Sept. 26, 1965; d. Robert Louis and Carolyn Louise (Henn) S. BA in History cum laude, Auburn U., 1986, MA in History of Sci., 1988, PhD in History of Tech. magna cum laude, 1993; MA magna cum laude, Hollins Coll., 2003; MFA, Hollins U. Archivist Lee County Hist. Soc. Mus., 1988—. Ind. scholar, 1993—; presenter in field. Author: Exploring Harry Potter, 2000, Lake Martin: Alabama's Crown Jewel, 2002, Auburn: Plainsmen, Tigers and War Eagles, 2003, Auburn Football, 2004; co-author: Women Who Made A Difference in Alabama, 1995; cons. editor Ency. of Sci., 1998; freelance editor various tech. docs.; editl. asst. Proceedings of the We. Soc. for French History, 1988-91, Nat. Forum: The Phi Kappa Phi Jour., 1990-91; contbr. History News Svc.; reviewer Children's Lit. database; contbr. articles to profl. jours., encys., mags., chpts. to books. Recipient hon. mention poetry Writer's Digest, 1994 hon. mention children's non-fiction, 1997, children's non-fiction and fiction, 1998, Writer's Digest, Shirley Henn Meml. award Critical scholar, Hollins Coll., 1998. Mem. AAAS, AAUW, Am. Hist. Assn., Orgn. Am. Historians, Soc. History Tech., History Sci. Soc., Women's History Network, N.Y. Acad. Scis., So. Hist. Assn., Soc. Children's Book Writers and Illustrators, Children's Lit. Network, Ala. Poetry Soc., Children's Lit. Assn., Ala. Writer's Forum, Authors Guild, Lancaster Mennonite Hist. Soc., Lee County Hist. Soc. (life mem.), Auburn U. Alumni Assn. (life), Descs. Mex. War Vets., DAR (chpt. historian), Phi Alpha Theta. Home and Office: PO Box 57 Loachapoka AL 36865-0057 Personal E-mail: Elizabeth_D_Schafer@yahoo.com.

SCHAFER, JACQUELINE ELLEN, federal agency administrator; b. Greenport, NY; AB, Middlebury Coll., 1967. Analyst, rsch. asst. Fed. Reserve Bank NY, 1967—70; legis. asst. to Sen. James L. Buckley U.S. Senate, 1971—76; asst. sec. installations and environ. U.S. Navy; regional adminstr. region 2 U.S. Environ. Protection Agy., 1982—93; dir. Calif. Dept. Fish and Game, 1993—99, Ariz. Dept. Environ. Quality, 1999—2002; dep. asst. adminstr. bur. econ. growth USAID, 2002—05, asst. adminstr. for econ. growth agrl. & trade, 2005—.*

SCHAFER, LORRAINE, psychologist, researcher; b. Glendive, Mont., July 2, 1957; d. Ryland Norris and Marlene Joanne Chaska; m. David James Schafer, Aug. 24, 1979; 1 child, Daniel Rylie. BS in Psychology/Sociology, N.D. State U., 1979, MS in Clin. Psychology, 1981; PhD in Counseling Psychology, Colo. State U., 1989. Rsch. assoc. N.D. State U., U. N.D., Fargo, 1981-84; assoc. cons., asst. prof. psychology Mayo Clinic, Rochester, Minn., 1991-92; lic. psychologist Marshfield (Wis.) Clinic, 1992—. Reviewer Diabetes Care, 1990—; mem. instnl. rev. bd. Marshfield Clinic, 1994—. Contbr. articles to profl. jours. Biomed. Rsch. Support grantee Colo. State U., 1984, Outstanding Grad. scholar, 1986, Mayo Clinic grantee, 1990, Postdoctoral fellow in Med. Psychology, 1991. Mem. APA (lic., Dissertation Rsch. award 1988), Am. Diabetes Assn. (profl., behavioral scientists rep. nonperiodical pubs. com. Alexandria, Va. 1990-92), Soc. Pediatric Psychology, Soc. Tchrs. Family Medicine (assoc.). Roman Catholic. E-mail: schafer@mfldclin.edu.

SCHAFER, SHARON MARIE, anesthesiologist; b. Detroit, Mar. 23, 1948; d. Charles Anthony and Dorothy Emma (Schweitzer) Pokriefka; m. Timothy John Schafer, Nov. 12, 1977; children: Patrick Christopher, Steven Michael. BS in Biology, Wayne State U., 1971, MD, 1975; MBA in Practice Mgmt., Madonna U., 2000. Diplomate Am. Bd. Anesthesiology. Intern, resident Sinai Hosp. Detroit, 1975-78; pvt. practice anesthesiology Troy, Mich., 1988—. Mem. AMA, Am. Soc. Anesthesiologists. Roman Catholic. Home and Office: 5741 Folkstone Dr Troy MI 48085-3154 Office Phone: 248-879-6246.

SCHAFF, BARBARA WALLEY, artist; b. Plainfield, NJ, May 6, 1941; d. Miron M. and Silvia S. (Solott) Walley; m. John A. Schaff, Apr. 10, 1963 (div. 1992); children: Elizabeth A., Joshua L. BA, Syracuse U., 1963; grad., Pa. Acad. Fine Arts, 1994; cert., China Nat. Acad. Fine Art, Hangzhou, 1994. Clay artist, Stockton, NJ, 1968-88; advisor to faculty BFA program Kean Coll., Union, NJ, 1987—; painter Phila., 1990—; mem. fellows coun. Va. Ctr. for the Creative Arts, 2005. Mem. adv. bd. Hunterdon Art Ctr., Clinton, NJ, 1988, 89; workshop leader, U.S. and Can. One-man shows include NJ State Mus, Trenton, 1985, NJ State Mus., 1997, Lee Sclar Gallery, Morristown, NJ, 1986, Howe Gallery, Kean Coll., Union, 1989, ITT Boston Sheraton, 1995, Thos. Moser Cabinetmakers, Phila., 1995, Ciboulette, 1997, So. Vt. Art Ctr., Manchester, 1997, Questar Libr., New Hope, Pa., 1998, Restaurant Phila. Mus. Art, 1999, Cafe Gallery, Phila., 1999, Grounds for Sculpture, Hamilton, NJ, 2003, Shipley Sch., Bryn Mawr, Pa., 2005, exhibited in group shows at Newark Mus., 1973, 1977, Morris Mus., Morristown, NJ, 1973, 1977, Carnegie Ctr., Princeton, NJ, 1984, Newman Galleries, Phila., 1986, Ednl. Testing Svc., Princeton, 1987, Monarch Title Nat. San Angelo Mus. Art, Tex., 1989, US Artists, Phila., 1992, 1993, China Nat. Acad. Fine Art, 1994, Morris Gallery Mus. Am. Art, Phila., 1994, Am. Drawing Biennial V Muscarelle Mus. Art, Williamsburg, Va., 1996, Restaurant Phila. Mus. Art, 1996, 1999, Fellowship of Pa. Acad. Fine Arts, Woodmere Mus., 1996, Peng Gallery, Phila., 2000, Carspecker-Scott Gallery, Wilmington, Del., 2001—, Walker-Kornbluth Gallery, Fair Lawn, NJ, 2003, Wayne (Pa.) Art Ctr., 2003, Berman Mus. Art., Collegeville, Pa., 2004, 6th Biannial A.I.R. Gallery, N.Y.C., 2005, Ctr. for Emerging Visual Artists, Phila., 2005, Perkins Ctr. for the Arts, Moorestown, N.J., 2005 (Jurors award), Phila. Sketch Club, 2005, 2006 (Third prize Prints and Drawing Exhbn.), Woodmere Art Mus., Phila., 2006, Ctr. for Emerging Artists, 2006, Represented in permanent collections Linda Lee Aeter collection Art by Women, NJ State Mus., Trenton, Fuller Meml. Art Mus., Brockton, Mass., Pfizer Internat., NYC, Atlantic Richfield Corp., Phila., Towers Perrin, NYC, Independence Found., Phila., Temple U. Sch. Law, McGraw Hill, NYC, Chubb Corp., Warren, NJ, Sta. WHYY and WHYY-TV, Phila., Marriott Corp., Princeton, Prince Music Theater, Phila., BristolMeyers Squibb Co., Hopewell, NJ, Va. Ctr. for the Creative Arts, Sweet Briar, Montgomery Hosp., Norristown, Pa., Newark Mus., commns., NJ Natural Gas, Wall, 1983, Bell Comm. Rsch., Red Bank, NJ, 1985, Kenneth Endick, Boca Raton, Fla., 1987, McGraw Hill, 1998, works featured in, NJ Mag., Star Ledger, NY Times, Am. Artists, An Illustrated Survey of Leading Contemporaries, 2000 Outstanding artists and designers of the 20th Century. Recipient Medal of Excellence for promotion and design Art Dirs. Club NJ, 1986, medal for Outstanding Achievement, Long Beach Island Found. of the Arts and Scis., Harvey Aders, NJ, 1998, 99, Gold award Appleton Paper Corp., 2003, Newark Mus. Purchase award; fellow NJ State Coun. on Arts, 1984-85, resident fellow Va. Ctr. Creative Arts, 1996, 98, 99, 2001, 03, 04, 05; fellow Pa. Coun. on the Arts, 2004. Mem. Fellowship of Pa. Acad. Fine Arts (com. mem., exhibitor 1986, 87, 94, Mable Wilson Woodrow Meml. award 1994), Artist Equity, Nat. Arts Club. Avocations: gardening, cooking, music. Home: 1520 Spruce St Apt 906 Philadelphia PA 19102-4507 Studio: Barbara Schaff Studio 1627 N 2d St Philadelphia PA 19122 Office Phone: 215-829-0480. E-mail: babascha@aol.com.

SCHAFFER, BONNIE LYNN, psychologist; b. N.Y.C., Mar. 25, 1957; d. Leonard Harry and Lillian Clara (Simon) Grossflam; m. Neil Leonard Schaffer, May 15, 1988; childen: Beth Erin, Michael Lennon. BA, U. Rochester, 1978; MS, Kans. State U., 1981, PhD, 1983. Psychologist Ruston State Sch., LA, 1983-85; psychologist Rome Devel. Ctr., NY, 1985-87, O.D. Heck Devel. Ctr., Schenectady, NY, 1987—89; svc. coord. supr. Special Needs Program, Hudson, NY, 1997—2004; program rsch. specialist NYS Health Dept., Albany, NY, 2004—. Democrat. Jewish. Avocations: sewing, needlecrafts, reading.

SCHAFFER, SANDRA SUE, artist, educator; b. Kansas City, Mo., Jan. 12, 1947; d. Robert William and Marian Frances Effertz; m. Larry Alan Schaffer, Nov. 10, 1972; children: Kristen Noelle, Scott David. BA in Psychology, U. Mo., 1969; MSEd in Learning Disabilities, Ctrl. Mo. State U., 1974. Diagnostician and learning disabilities specialist Cenl. Mo. State U. Artist, Kansas City, Mo., 1997—. Diagnostician, spl. edn. coord. The Plaza Acad., Mercier, Mo., 2003—. One-woman shows include Corridor Gallery, 2005, Park Ctrl. Gallery, 2006, exhibitions include Finding the Extraordinary in the Ordinary: Works from Peru, Nepal and other Travels, Nepali Matron (MKEC Engring. award Kans. Watercolor Soc. Regional Show, 2004), Ledgemates (Excellence award Red River Watercolor Soc. Nat. Show, 2004), Rooftop Perspective (Past Pres.'s award N.W. Watercolor Soc. Nat. Show, 2001), Village Life (Friends Cash award Miss. Watercolor Soc. Nat. Show, 2001). Newsletter editor Watercolor Honor Soc., Springfield, Mo., 2004—05; bd. dirs. Mattie Rhodes Arts Ctr., Kansas City, Mo., 1994—95. Recipient First Pl. award, Wyo. Watercolor Soc. Nat. Exhbn., 2001, New Orleans Sch. of Fine Art and Daler-Rowney award, La. Watercolor Soc. Internat. Show, 2002, Nielsen-Bainbridge award, Western Colo. Watercolor Soc. Nat. Show, 2001, Pacific Gallery Artists' award, Pensicola Art League Nat. Show, 2004, Colvin Cash award, Baker Arts Ctr. Nat. Show, 2003, Catherine M. Mulkare Cash award, RI Watercolor Soc., 2005, George Latta Cash award, Mo. Watercolor Soc., 2005, Merit award, Watercolor Art Soc. Houston, 2005, Juror's Art award, Ctr. Nat. Show, 2005, Merit award, Red River Watercolor Soc., 2005, Honorable Mention, Watercolor Art Soc. Houston, 2006, numerous others. Mem.: Watercolor West Watercolor Soc., N.W. Watercolor Soc. (signature mem.), Tex. Watercolor Soc. (Purple Sage award, signature mem.), Watercolor Honor Soc. (assoc.; bd. dirs. 2004—05, Winsor-Newton award 2004, signature mem.). Democrat. Unitarian-Universalist. Avocations: international travel, bicycling, reading. Home: 12700 E 64th Ct Kansas City MO 64133 Office: The Plaza Acad 4232 Mercier Kansas City MO 64111 Office Phone: 816-561-0770. Home Fax: 816-373-2112; Office Fax: NA. Personal E-mail: lschaffer@kc.rr.com. E-mail: na.

SCHAFFNER, CYNTHIA VAN ALLEN, writer, educator, curator; b. Washington, Jan. 28, 1947; d. James Alfred and Abigail Fifthian (Halsey) Van Allen; m. Robert Todd Schaffner, June 11, 1972; 1 child, Hilary Van Allen. BA, Western Coll., 1969; MAT, Simmons Coll., 1971; MA in History of Decorative Arts, Cooper Hewitt Smithsonian Instn., N.Y.C., 1999. Editor Mademoiselle mag., N.Y.C., 1972-79; dir. devel. Am. Acad. in Rome, N.Y.C., 1987-89; curator Phila. Antiques Show, 1997-98; rsch. asst. Metropolitan Mus. Art, New York, 1999—; curator Halsey House, Southampton, N.Y., 1999—. Lectr. Am. Folk Art Inst., N.Y.C. Author: Discovering American Folk Art, 1991; co-author: Folk Hearts, 1984, American Painted Furniture, 1997; contbr. articles to popular mags. Co-chair Fall Antiques Show, N.Y.C., 1979-93; trustee Mus. Am. Folk Art, N.Y.C., 1980-95. Lisa Taylor fellow, 1995-96; Smithsonian Instn. Grad. Student fellow, 1998. Mem. Coll. Art Assn., Decorative Arts Soc., Cosmopolitan Club, Victorian Soc., Lenox Hill Hosp. Aux., Southampton Hist. Mus. (trustee 1996-2002). Avocations: canoeing, gardening, antiques. Home: 850 Park Ave New York NY 10021-1845 Office: Met Mus Art Dept Am Arts 100 Fifth Ave New York NY 10028 Personal E-mail: cvanschaf@aol.com. E-mail: cynthia.schaffner@metmuseum.org.

SCHAFFNER, KAREN ANN See FIELD, KAREN

SCHAFFNER, ROBERTA IRENE, retired medical/surgical nurse; b. Vero Beach, Fla., Oct. 5, 1926; d. Robert Wesley and Harriett Louise (Davis) Routh; m. David Leonard Schaffner, Apr. 25, 1947 (div. July 1975; dec.); children: Penny Routh S. (dec. July 1999), David Leonard II (dec. Jan. 1999). Mem. cadet nurse corps, Charity Hosp., New Orleans, 1944-45; ADA, Montgomery County C.C., Blue Bell, Pa., 1978; BSN, Gwynedd (Pa.) Mercy Coll., 1982, MSN, 1984. RN Pa. Med.-surg. nurse Chestnut Hill Hosp., Phila., 1978-2000, ret., 2000. Mem. delegation to study health care delivery sys., Moscow, Tbillisi, Azerbeijan, Kiev, 1981, Shanghai, Beijing, Nanjing, Hong Kong, 1984, Milan, Pisa, Bologna, Florence, Rome, Sorento, Naples, 1985. Cadet U.S. Nurse Corps, 1945. Mem. Oncology Nursing Soc., Sigma Theta Tau. Republican. Home: 1600 Church Rd Apt A214 Wyncote PA 19095-1929 E-mail: robertars4@aol.com.

SCHAIBLEY, ANN M., lawyer; b. St. Cloud, Minn. BA in Politics, Cornell Coll., Mt. Vernon, Iowa, 1994; JD, Hamline U. Sch. Law, St. Paul, 1997. Bar: Minn. 1997. Law clk. to Hon. Mary L. Davidson Hennepin County Dist. Ct., Family Ct. Divsn., 1997—99; assoc. pvt. practice, 1999—2002; ptnr. Schaibley & Vicchiollo, L.L.C., Edina, Minn., 2001—. Named a Rising Star, Minn. Super Lawyers mag., 2006. Mem.: Internat. Acad. Collaborative Profls., Collaborative Law Inst. Minn. (bd. dirs. 2004—), ABA, Minn. State Bar Assn., Ramsey County Bar Assn. (mem. family law sect.). Office: Schaibley & Vicchiollo LLC Edinborough Corp Ctr 3300 Edinborough Way Ste 550 Edina MN 55435 Office Phone: 612-333-0803. E-mail: ann@mnlaw.us.*

SCHAIR, ROBIN A., lawyer; b. Bronx, NY, Sept. 30, 1961; BA, SUNY, Binghamton, 1982; JD, Albany Law Sch., Union Coll., 1985. Bar: NY 1986, US Dist. Ct. Ea. Dist. NY, US Dist. Ct. So. Dist. NY. Asst. dist. atty. Bronx Dist. Atty.'s Office, NY, 1985—93; ptnr. Wilson, Elser, Moskowitz, Edelman & Dicker LLP, NYC. Office: Wilson Elser Moskowitz Edelman & Dicker LLP 150 E 42nd St 23rd Fl New York NY 10017-5639 Office Phone: 212-490-3000 ext. 2209. Office Fax: 212-490-3038. Business E-Mail: schairr@wemed.com.

SCHAKOWSKY, JANICE, congresswoman; b. Chgo., May 26, 1944; d. Irwin and Tillie (Cosnow) Danoff; m. Harvey E. Schakowsky, Feb. 17, 1965 (div. 1980); children: Ian, Mary; m. Robert B. Creamer, Dec. 6, 1980; 1 stepchild, Lauren. BS, U. Ill., 1965. Cert. elem. tchr., Ill. Tchr. Chgo. Bd. Edn., 1965-67; organizer Ill. Pub. Action Coun., Chgo., 1976-85; exec. dir. Ill. State Coun. Sr. Citizens, Chgo., 1985-90; mem. Ill. Ho. Reps., 1990-98, US Congress from 9th Ill. dist., 1999—; mem. banking and fin. svcs. com., 1999—2000; mem. govt. reform com., 1999—2000; Ho. Dem. leadership team-deputy whip; mem. energy and commerce Com. Bd. dirs. Ill. Pub. Action, 4 C's Day Care Coun., Evanston, Ill.; steering com. mem. Cook County Dem. Women, 1986-90; del. Nat. Dem. Conv., 1988; governing coun. Am. Jewish Congress, 1990—. Named Outstanding Legislator Interfaith Coun. for Homeless, 1993, Legislator of Yr. Ill. Nurses Assn., 1992, Ill. Assn. Cmty. Mental Health Agys., 1994, Coalition of Citizens with Disabilities and Ill. Coun. Sr. Citizens, 1993, Cmty. Action Assn., 1991, Champaign County Health Care Assn., 1992, Rookie of Yr. Ill. Environ. Coun., 1991. Mem. ACLU, NOW, Nat. Coun. Jewish Women, Ill. Pro-Choice Alliance, Evanston Mental Health Assn., Evanston Hist. Soc., Evanston Friends of Libr., Rogers Park Hist. Soc. Democrat. Jewish. Avocations: travel, horsebackriding, reading. Office: US Ho Reps 1027 Longworth Ho Office Bldg Washington DC 20515-1309 also: Dist Office 5533 Broadway St Chicago IL 60640 Office Phone: 202-225-2111.

SCHALLER, CHRISTINA C., editor; b. Nashua, NH, Jan. 13, 1974; d. John N. and Valerie J. Lamb. BA, Eckerd Coll., 1995. Microsoft cert. profl.; cert. BCLS. Mng. editor Network Publs., Nashua, 1997—2000; tech. writer MicroData Group, Topsfield, Mass., 2000—01, E-Nable, Westwood, Mass., 2001—02; med. asst. Access Sports Medicine and Orthopaedics, Exeter, NH, 2003—04; mng. editor Application Devel. Trends, Framingham, Mass., 2004—06, T.H.E. Jour., Chatsworth, Calif., 2006—. Cons. Unified Bus. Tech., Amherst, NH, 2001—02; editor Taking a Health Byte Out of the Tech. Knowledgy Pie, Consultancy. Editor: Taking a Health Byte Out of the Tech. Knowledgy Pie, 2002, The Consultancy, 2002, Refined to Real Food, 2003, Lebanon 123, 2004, The Story of Peter Little Bear, 2004. Mem.: Internat. High IQ Soc., Mensa. Democrat. Mem. Unity Ch. Avocation: walking.

SCHALLER, JANE GREEN, pediatrician; b. Cleve., June 26, 1934; d. George and May Alice (Wing) Green; children: Robert Thomas, George Charles, Margaret May. AB, Hiram Coll., Ohio, 1956; MD cum laude, Harvard U., 1960. Diplomate Am. Bd. Pediat., Am. Bd. Med. Examiners. Resident in pediat. Children's Hosp.-U. Wash., Seattle, 1960-63; fellow immunology Children's Hosp. U. Wash., 1963-65; faculty U. Wash. Med. Sch., 1965-83, prof. pediat., 1975-83; head divsn. rheumatic diseases Children's Hosp., Seattle, 1968-83; prof., chmn. dept. pediat., pediatrician-in-chief Tufts U. Sch. Medicine/New Eng. Med. Ctr., 1983-98; Karp prof. pediat. Tufts U. Sch. Medicine, Boston, 1983—, disting. prof., 1995—. Vis. physician Med. Rsch. Coun., Taplow, Eng., 1971-72; adj. prof. diplomacy The Fletcher Sch. Law and Diplomacy, Tufts U., 1998-2000. Contbr. articles to profl. jours. Bd. dirs. Seattle Chamber Music Festival, 1982-85; trustee Boston Chamber Music Soc., 1985—; mem. Boston adv. coun. UNICEF, tech. advisor UN Study on the Impact of Armed Conflict on Children, 1995-97; chmn., adv. com. children's rights divsn. Human Rights Watch, 1995—; mem. adv. com. Middle East divsn., 1998—; exec. com. Women's Commn. for Refugee Women and Children Internat. Rescue com., 1989-94, adv. coun. 1994—. Mem.: AAAS, Royal Coll. Pediats. U.K., Internat.

Women's Forum, Mass. Women's Forum, Harvard U. Med. Sch. Alumni Coun. (v.p. 1977—80, pres. 1982—83), Physicians for Human Rights (founding pres. 1986—89, exec. com. 1986—), Com. Health in So. Africa (exec. com. 1986—92), Assn. Med. Sch. Pediat. Chmn. (exec. com. 1986—89, rep. to coun. on govt. affairs and coun. acad. socs.), New Eng. Pediat. Soc. (pres. 1991—93), Am. Coll. Rheumatology, Internat. Pediat. Assn. (pres.-elect 1998—2001, pres. 2001—04, exec. dir. 2004—), Am. Acad. Pediat. (exec. com. sect. on internat. child health, head children's rights program, rep. to UNICEF), Am. Pediat. Soc., Soc. Pediat. Rsch., Inst. Medicine of NAS, Saturday Club, Tavern Club, Aesculapian Club (pres. 1988—89). Office: Floating Hosp for Children 750 Washington St # 8683 Boston MA 02111-1526 Business E-Mail: jschaller@tufts-nemc.org.

SCHAMBURG, TRACY MARIE, professional counselor; b. Amarillo, Tex., Nov. 20, 1964; d. William Edward and Dorothy Dean (Lehman) Chavey; m. Theodore Gene Schamburg, Jr., July 4, 1992; 2 children. B of Gen. Studies, West Tex. A&M, 1989, MEd, 1991. Nat. cert. counselor; lic. profl. counselor, Mo. Dir. social skills tng. Tex. Panhandle Mental Health Authority, Amarillo, 1990-91; profl. counselor Human Support Svcs., Waterloo, Ill., 1992—2003; pvt. practice St. Louis, 2003—. Singer GSP Band; author: (childern's book) Catie the Caterpillar, 2006—. Lectr., commentator St. Paul's Cath. Ch., St. Louis, 1994—. Republican. Roman Catholic. Avocations: cooking, gardening, entertaining, football, running. Office Phone: 314-487-5127.

SCHANDEL, SUSAN, professional sports team executive; Corp. controller Internat. Speedway Corp., Daytona Beach, Fla., 1992—96, CFO, 1996—, v.p. adminstrv. svcs. Office: ISC 1801 W International Speedway Blvd Daytona Beach FL 32114

SCHANFIELD, FANNIE SCHWARTZ, community volunteer; b. Mpls., Dec. 25, 1916; d. Simon Zouberman and Mary (Schmilovitz) Schwartz; m. Melvin M. Stock, Oct. 27, 1943 (dec. Apr. 1944); 1 child, Moses Samuel Schanfield; m. Abraham Schanfield, Aug. 28, 1947; children: David Colman, Miriam Schanfield Kieffer. Student, U. Minn., 1962-75. Author: My Thoughts, 1996, Son, I Have Something to Tell You, 1997, Ma, I Wrote It Down, 1997, 20 April 44 WWII, 2001, The Other Family's Kids, 2004, The Duplex: Fran and Dan Lived Upstairs, 2004. Bd. dirs. Jewish Cmty. Ctr., Mpls., 1975-96, chairperson older adult needs, 1982-88; past pres. Bnai Emet Women's League, Mpls., 1988-90; rschr., advocate Hunger Hennepin County, Mpls., 1969-75; sec. Joint Religious Legis. Coalition; v.p., bd. dirs. Cmty. Housing Svc., Mpls., 1971-85. Recipient Citation of Honor, Hennepin County Commn., 1989, Lifetime Achievement award Jewish Comty. Ctr. Greater Mpls., 1995. Mem. NOW, Lupus Found. Minn., Internat. Soc. Poets, Hadassah (pres. 1967-69, Citation 1969, Nat. Leadership award 2006). Jewish. Avocations: needlepoint, rug hooking, writing.

SCHANZENBACH, DIANE WHITMORE, economist; b. St. Louis, Nov. 13, 1972; d. William Whitmore and Mardelle Grimm; m. Max Schanzenbach, June 25, 2005. AB, Wellesley Coll., Mass., 1995; PhD, Princeton U., NJ, 2002. Rsch. asst. Coun. Econ. Advisers, Washington, 1995—97; asst. prof. U. Chgo., 2004—. Vis. rschr. Fed. Res. Bank Chgo., 2005—. Fellow, U. Calif., Berkeley, 2002—04. Office: Harris School of Public Policy 1155 E 60th Street Chicago IL 60637 Office Phone: 773-834-0207. E-mail: whitmore@uchicago.edu.

SCHAPIRA, DORIS R., UN observer; d. William H. Schwartz and Ida Silverman Schwartz; m. Alexander D. Schapira, Apr. 2, 1967; 1 child, Joan Schapira Conwell. BS, SUNY, New Paltz, 1964; MS in Computer Sci., Sch. of Engring. Pratt Inst., Bklyn., 1968. Ind. computer cons., Montclair, NJ, 1976—80; alt. UN observer LWV of U.S., Washington, 1991—2000, main UN observer, 2000—. Steering com. working group on girls UNICEF Non Govtl. Orgn., N.Y.C., 1994—; nat. coun. mem. UN Assn. USA, 2001—; vice chair exec. com. Dept. Pub. Info. Non Govtl. Orgn., 2004—; officer at large Coun. Orgns. UN Assn. USA, 2004—. Bd. mem. LWV Montclair Area, NJ, 1974—2005; county polit. party com. Montclair, NJ, 1982—90. Recipient Disting. Svc. award, LWV of N.J., 2003.

SCHAPIRO, KAREN LEE, language educator; b. Cleve., June 11, 1947; d. George and Lena Keserich; m. Ross Harley Schapiro, Aug. 17, 1991; 1 child, Trevor Ross. BA in Span. and French, Oberlin Coll., 1969; MA in Span. Lang. Lit., Ohio State U., 1971; doctoral studies, U. Mass., 1971—73; attended, U. Calif. Berkeley, 1975, U. Guadalajara, Mex., 1974. Tchg. asst. Ohio State U., Columbus, 1969—71; assoc. tchr. U. Mass., Amherst, 1971—73; lang. and dance tchr. Wooster Sch., Danbury, Conn., 1973—76, Carmel (Calif.) HS, 1976—81, Soledad (Calif.) Union Sch. Dist., 1981, Pacific Grove (Calif.) HS, 1981—. Named Calif. Span. Tchr. of Yr., Span. Heritage, 1986; recipient Travel Scholarship award, Mary Dufort, 1988. Avocations: travel, films, theater, reading, dance. Office: Pacific Grove HS 615 Sunset Pacific Grove CA 93950

SCHAPIRO, MARY L., financial regulatory service executive; b. NYC, June 19, 1955; d. Robert D. and Susan (Hall) S.; m. Charles A. Cadwell, Dec. 13, 1980, 2 children BA, Franklin and Marshall Coll., 1977; JD, George Washington U., 1980. Bar: D.C. 1980. Trial atty., 1980-81; counsel to chmn. Commodity Futures Trading Commn., 1981-84; sr. v.p. Futures Industry Assn., 1984, gen. counsel, 1984-88; commr. SEC, Washington, 1988-94, acting chmn., 1993—94; chmn. Commodity Futures Trading Commn. (CFTC), Washington, 1994-96; pres. Nat. Assn. Securities Regulation, Inc., Washington, 1996—2002; vice chmn., pres., regulatory policy oversight divsn. Nat. Assn. Securities Dealers, Washington, 2002—06, chmn., CEO, 2006—. Mem. Tech. Com. and the Develop. Markets Com. of the Internat. Org. of Securities (IOSCO); chmn IOSCO Cons. Com., 2001—. Mem. bd. trustees, vice chmn. audit com. Franklin and Marshall Coll.; bd. dirs. Cinergy Corp., 1999—, Kraft Foods. Named Fin. Women's Assn. Pub. Sector Woman of the Yr., 2000. Office: Nat Assn Securities Dealers 1735 K St NW Washington DC 20006-1516*

SCHAPIRO, MIRIAM, artist; b. Toronto, Ont., Can., Nov. 15, 1923; d. Theodore and Fannie (Cohen) S. BA, State U. Iowa, 1945, MA, 1946, MFA, 1949; doctorate (hon.), Wooster Coll., 1983, Calif. Coll. Arts Crafts, 1989, Mpls. Coll. Art Design, 1994, Miami U., 1995, Moore Coll. Art, Phila., 1995. Co-originator Womanhouse, Los Angeles, 1972, Heresies mag., N.Y.C., 1975; co-originator feminist art program Calif. Inst. Arts, Valencia, 1971; founding mem. Feminist Art Inst., N.Y.C.; mem. adv. bd. Women's Caucus for Art; assoc. mem. Heresies Collective; lectr. dept. art history U. Mich., 1987. Works in numerous books and catalogues; numerous one-woman shows including, Galerie Liatowitsch, Basel, Switzerland, 1979, Lerner Heller Gallery, N.Y.C., 1979, Barbara Gladstone Gallery, N.Y.C., 1980, Spencer Mus. Art, Lawrence, Kans., 1981, Everson Mus., Syracuse, N.Y., 1981, Galerie Rudolf Zwirner, Cologne, Fed. Republic Germany, 1981, Staatagalerie, Stuttgart, Fed. Republic Germany, 1983, Dart Gallery, Chgo, 1984, Bernice Steinbaum Gallery/Steinbaum Krauss Gallery, N.Y.C., 1986, 88, 90, 91, 94, 97, Brevard Art Ctr. and Mus., Melbourne, Fla., 1991, Guild Hall Mus., East Hampton, N.Y., 1992, ARC Gallery, Chgo., 1993, James Madison U., Harrisburg, Va., 1996, Nat. Mus. Am. Art Smithsonian Inst., Washington, 1997. others; retrospective exhbn., Wooster (Ohio) Coll. Art Mus., 1980; exhibited in numerous group shows, including, Palais de Beaux Arts, Brussels, 1979, Inst. Contemporary Art, Phila., 1979, Delahunty Gallery, Dallas, 1980, Indpls. Mus., 1980, Va. Mus., Richmond, 1980, Laguna Gloria Mus., Austin, Tex., 1980, R.O.S.C., Dublin, Ireland, 1980, Biennale of Sydney, Australia, 1982, Zurich, Switzerland, 1983, Sidney Janis Gallery, N.Y.C., 1984, Am. Acad. Arts and Letters, N.Y.C., 1985, Mus. Modern Art, N.Y.C., 1988, Whyte Mus. Can. Rockies, Banff, Alta., 1991, Nat. Mus. Women in Arts., Wash., 1993, Jane Voorhees Zimmerli art mus. Rutger's U., New Brunswick, N.J., 1994, Mus. of F.A. Boston, 1994, Santa Barbara Mus. of Art, 1994, Hudson River Mus. of Westchester, Yonkers, N.Y., 1995, Mus. of Contemporary Arts, Los Angeles, Calif. Bronx Mus. of the Arts, N.Y., 1995, Columbus (Ga.) Mus., 1996, Parrish Mus., Southampton, N.Y., 1997, Austin (Tex.) Mus., 1997, Whitney Mus., 2000; represented in permanent collections, Hirshhorn Mus., Washington, Bklyn. Mus., Met. Mus. Art, N.Y.C., Mus. Contemporary Art, San Diego, Mpls. Inst. Art, Mulvane Art Center, Topeka, Nat. Gallery Art, Washington, N.Y.U., Peter Ludwig Collection, Aachen, Germany, Stanford U., Palo Alto, Calif., Univ. Art Mus., Berkeley, Calif., Whitney Mus., N.Y.C., Worcester (Mass.) Art Mus., Santa Barbara (Calif.) Mus. Art. Nat. Mus. Am. Art Smithsonian Inst., Washington, also others; author: (books) Women and the Creative Process, 1974, Rondo: An Artists Book, 1988; sculpture Anna and David, Rosslyn, Va., 1987. Guggenheim fellow, 1987, Nat. Endowment for Arts fellow; grantee Ford Found.; recipient numerous other grants and fellowships. Mem. Coll. Art Assn. (past dir.). Office: Elly Flomenhaft Gallery 547 W 27th St Ste 308 New York NY 10001

SCHAPPELL, ABIGAIL SUSAN, retired speech, language and hearing specialist, massage therapist, Reiki master; b. York, Pa., May 25, 1952; d. Felix and Ann (Getty) DeMoise; m. Gery Mylan Schappell, Oct. 20, 1979; 1 child, Jonathan Michael. BS with Master's equivalency, Longwood Coll., 1974; postgrad., Bloomsburg U., 1975—77; cert., Lehmann Sch. Massage and Muscle, 1991, East-West Sch. Massage Therapy, 1995—. Lic. speech-lang. pathologist, Pa. Speech-lang.-hearing specialist dept. pub. welfare Hamburg (Pa.) Ctr., 1975—2004; ret., 2004. Judge deaf posters and essays Virginville (Pa.) Grange, 1990—, judge Pa. State Grange Conv., 1997, tchr. emergency pers. on communicating with deaf and hard of hearing, 1991, 92; leader demonstrations and workshops on sign lang. and dysphagia, non-verbal comm., active listening to various orgns., 1978—; instr. ARC, 1999-2002; bd. dirs. Berks Deaf and Hard of Hearing Svcs., 2000-06, sec., 2006—; presenter in field. Pub: (Boy Scouts Coun. manual), Scouting for the Handicapped, Hawk Mountain, 1981-82. Sign/del. to conf. Bible Sch. dir., mem. Zion's United Ch. of Christ, Windsor Castle, Pa., 1985—; rep. nat. triann. conv. Penn Laurel coun. Girl Scouts U.S., 1975; vol. residential monitoring project Berks County ARC, 1998-99. Named Virginville Grange Cmty. Citizen of Yr., 1994—95; named one of Outstanding Young Women of Am., 1984. Mem.: AAUW, Schuykill Haven Bus. and Profl. Women (Young Careerist local, dist. and state honors 1980—81, pres. 1983—84, asst. dir. dist. 9 1997—99, dist. 9 dir. 1999—2001, state mentoring com. 2001—03, dist. 9 parliamentarian 2002—04, state edn. and svc. funds com. 2003—05, state chair edn. and svc. funds 2005—06, individual devel. leadership program facilitator 2005—, state PAC com. 2006—, involvement on dist. and state level, presenter local, dist. and state level workshops, Eleanor Briner award as dist. 9 dir. 2000), Pa. Speech and Hearing Assn., Yorktown chpt. DAR, Young Careerist Alumni Assn. (life), Hamburg Area Soccer Assn. (sec. 1989—94), Order Ea. Star (chaplain Blue Mountain chpt. 1981, 1982, assoc. conductress 2005—06, conductress 2006—). Republican. Avocations: massage, signing, music. Home: 531 S 4th St Hamburg PA 19526-1307

SCHARBER, SUSAN ELIZABETH, music educator, director; b. Nashville, Jan. 6, 1981; d. Faye B. and Wayne K. Scharber. MusB Edn., U. N.C., Greensboro, 1999—2003. Band dir. Jere Baxter Mid. Sch., Nashville, 2003—04; asst. band dir. Sta. Camp HS, Gallatin, Tenn., 2004—; band dir. Knox Doss Mid. Sch., Gallatin, 2004—. Scholar scholarship, A.J. Fletcher Found., U. N.C., Greensboro, 1999—2003. Mem.: Music Educators Nat. Conf., Tenn. Music Educators Assn., Mid. Tenn. Sch. Band and Orch. Assn., Sigma Alpha Iota (psi b province officer 2004, Sword of Honor 2002, Coll. Honor award 2002, Province Leadership award 2003). Office Phone: 615-206-0116. Business E-Mail: scharbers@k12tn.net.

SCHARDINE, HEIDI FAE, choral educator; b. Miami, Fla., Nov. 15, 1973; d. Larry and Judith Ann Parcharsky; m. Daniel Thomas Schardine, Mar. 9, 2001. B.Mus.Edn., U. Ga., Athens, 1998; M.Mus.Edn., Boston U., 2006. Band tchr. The Lovett Sch., Atlanta, 1998—99; gen. music tchr. LaBelle Elem. Sch., Smyrna, Ga., 1999—2000; choral/mus. dir. Sandy Springs Mid. Sch., Atlanta, 2001—06; choral dir. Sprayberry H.S., Marietta, Ga., 2006—. Mus. dir. Sandy Spring Theater, Atlanta, 2001—06. Author: (poetry) Denial, 1995. Mem. PETA, Atlanta, 1994—. Named Tchr. of the Yr., 2003—04, Best Marimbist, Villa Rica, 1990—92; recipient winner piano competition, Kennesaw Coll., Ga., 1983—92. Mem.: Ga. Music Educators Assn., Am. Choral Assn. Avocations: music composition, animals.

SCHARF, MEGAN JEAN, mathematics educator; BA in Math., Hofstra U., N.Y., 1995; MS, Stony Brook U., N.Y., 1998. Tchr. math. Lindenhurst H.S., NY, 1995—. Named Region II Adviser of the Yr., NASC, 2006. Office: Lindenhurst High School 300 Charles St Lindenhurst NY 11757 Office Phone: 631-226-6445. Personal E-mail: mschar@lindenhurstschools.org.

SCHARF, STEPHANIE A., lawyer; m. Jeffry Mandell; children: Meredith, Jonathan. BA, Rutgers U.; MA, Stanford U.; PhD, U. Chgo., 1978, JD, 1985. Bar: Ill. 1985, US Dist. Ct. (no., ctrl. and so. dists.) Ill., US Dist. Ct. (no. dist.) Ind., US Dist. Ct. (we. dist.) Mich., US Ct. Appeals (first cir.). Sr. study dir. Nat. Opinion Rsch. Ctr., Chgo.; ptnr. Jenner & Block, Chgo. Author: Consumer Fraud Litigation: Law and Defenses in Illinois, 2004, The Business of Drug Development, 2004, Direct-to-Consumer Advertising of Prescription Pharmaceuticals and Medical Devices, 2004, Through the Glass Ceiling: Best Practices for Women Lawyers and Their Firms, 2004, Benchmarking for Success: Introducing NAWL Assessment Questionnaire, 2004, A Business Approach to Minimizing Product Liability Litigation, 2005; co-author: The Media and Products Litigation, 1996, Communications Specialists Help With Damage Control, 1997, Marketing Pharmaceutical Products on the Internet: Managing Risks and Limiting Liabilities in the World of E-Commerce, 2001, Post-Sale Duties to Warn, Recall, and Retrofit Defective Products in Illinois, 2003, The Evidentiary Impact of Regulatory Action on Product Litigation in the United States, 2004, Immigration Reform and the Federal Law of Employment Discrimination;; FDA's Comments Herald New Strength for Preemption Defense in Drug Product Litigation, 2006;; editor: The Use of Epidemiology in Tort Litigation: A Survey of Federal and State Jurisdictions, 2003; co-editor: The Use of Toxicology in Tort Litigation, 2005; contbr. articles in prof. jour. Bd. mem. The Youth Campus, Chgo.; chair, Best Interest of the Child Subcommittee Cir. Ct. Cook County, mem. Chief judge's Pub. Guardian Com. Harper Fellow, Univ. Chgo. Mem.: ABA (co-editor Product Liability newsletter 1997—2000, editor Mass Torts newsletter 2001, co-chair sect. litig. products liability com. 2005—, mem. mass torts com., bd. dirs., mem. spl. com. bioethics), Spl. Com. Bioethics, Pub. Guardian Com., Best Interest of Child Subcom. of Child Protection Adv. Com. (chair 1995—96), Circuit Ct. Cook County, Def. Rsch. Inst., Ill. Bar Found. (bd. mem. 2005—), Univ. Chgo. Women's Bus. Group, Products Liability Adv. Coun. (mem. case selection com.), Nat. Assn. Women Lawyers (exec. bd. 2000—, bd. dir. 2002—, pres. 2004—05, founding chair NAWL com. evaluation Supreme Ct. nominees, founding chair, com. for evaluation of Supreme Ct. nominees, Outstanding Mem. award 2002). Office: Jenner & Block One IBM Plz Chicago IL 60611 Office Phone: 312-923-2884. Business E-Mail: sscharf@jenner.com.

SCHAROLD, MARY LOUISE, psychoanalyst, psychiatrist, educator; b. Wichita Falls, Tex., Mar. 3, 1943; d. Walter John and Louise Helen (Hartmann) Baumgartner; m. William Ballew McCollum, Aug. 23, 1964 (div. 1981); m. Harry Karl Scharold, June 19, 1982; children: Margaret Louise, Walter Ballew. BA with highest distinction, U. Kans., 1964; attended, U. Kans. Sch. Medicine, 1964—66; MD, Baylor Coll. Medicine, 1968; attended, Houston-Galveston Psychoanalytic Inst., 1974—76; postgrad., Topeka Inst. Psychoanalysis, 1981. Diplomate Am. Bd. Psychiatry and Neurology, 1975, cert. adult psychoanalysis Am. Psychoanalytic Assn., 1982. Intern Meml. Bapt. Hosp., Houston, 1968-69; resident in psychiatry Baylor Coll. Medicine, Houston, 1969—72, chief resident, 1971-72; psychoanalyst Houston, 1972—. Asst. prof. Baylor Coll. Medicine, Houston, 1973-76, asst. clin. prof., 1981-84, assoc. clin. prof., 1984—; dir. Baylor Psychiat. Clinic, Houston, 1973-76; co-dir. Rice U. Psychiat. Svc., Houston, 1981-82; asst. clin. prof. U. Kans. Sch. Medicine, Kansas City, 1977-81; tchg. assoc. Topeka Psychoanalytic Inst., 1984-86; tchg. analyst, Houston-Galveston Psychoanalytic Inst., 1986-90, tng. and supervising analyst, 1990—, v.p., 1994-96, pres., 1996-01, bd. dirs., 2001-04; pres. bd. trustees Child Devel. Ctr., 2005. Adv. bd. Leavenworth (Kans.) Mental Health Assn., 1977-81; sec. bd. trustees, Child Devel. Ctr., 2005-. Watkins scholar U. Kans., 1961-64; Grad. Fellowship award, Pi Beta Phi, 1965; recipient Hilltopper, Ten Outstanding Sr. Women, U. Kans., 1963, Greater U. Fund award, 1964, U. Kans., Eugen Kahn award, Outstanding Baylor Psychiatry Resident, 1972, 1st Disting. Svc. award, Houston-Galveston Psychoanalytic Soc., 2004; named Outstanding Woman Med. Student, AMWA, Houston Branch, 1968; named to Best Doctors in Am., 1998-. Mem. Am. Psychiat. Assn. (disting. life fellow, mem. com. quality assurance 1986-87, chair Tex. peer rev. 1984-88), Am. Coll. Psychoanalysts, Am. Psychoanalytic Assn. (cert. 1982, peer rev. com. 1985-90, prof. ins. commn. 1986-93, bd. profl. stds. 1994-2001, CME com. 1994-96, exec. coun. 1994-96, cert. com. 1995-98, preparedness and progress com. 1998-06, chair preparedness and progress com. 2000-06, coordinating com. bd. profl. stds. 2000-06, bylaws com. 2001—, fin. com. 2003—, councilor-at-large 2005—, hon. membership.com, 2005-, election oversight com., 2005—, com. on coun., 2006—), Am. Group Psychotherapy Assn., Ctr. Advanced Psychoanalytic Studies, Houston Psychiat. Soc. (v.p. 1984-85, pres.-elect 1985-86, pres. 1986-87), Houston-Galveston Psychoanalytic Soc. (sec.-treas. 1984-86, pres.-elect 1986-88, pres. 1988-90, alt. councillor 1994-96), Houston Group Psychotherapy Soc. (adv. bd. 1984-85), Mortar Bd., Phi Beta Kappa, Delta Phi Alpha, Alpha Omega Alpha, Pi Beta Phi Alumni Assn. Republican. Lutheran. Office: 2301 Westheimer Rd Houston TX 77098-1317 Office Phone: 713-590-2301. Personal E-mail: mlscharold@mindspring.com.

SCHATTSCHNEIDER, DORIS JEAN, retired mathematics professor; b. NYC, Oct. 19, 1939; d. Robert W. Jr. and Charlotte Lucile (Ingalls) Wood; m. David A. Schattschneider, June 2, 1962; 1 child, Laura E. AB, U. Rochester, 1961; MA, Yale U., 1963, PhD, 1966. Instr. in math. Northwestern U., Evanston, Ill., 1964—65; asst. prof. U. Ill., Chgo., 1965—68; prof. Moravian Coll., Bethlehem, Pa., 1968—2002, prof. emerita, 2003—. Project dir. Fund for the Improvement of Post-Secondary Edn. U.S. Dept. Edn., 1991—93, 1995—97; vis. scholar U. V.I., 2004. Author (with W. Walker): (books and models) M.C. Escher Kaleidocycles, 1977, 1987; co-author: (videos and activities) Visual Geometry Project, 1986—91; author: M.C. Escher: Visions of Symmetry, 1990, 2d edit., 2004; co-author: A Companion to Calculus, 1995, 2d edit., 2005; editor: Geometry Turned On, 1997, M.C. Escher's Legacy, 2003. Exhbn. curator Allentown Art Mus., 1979, Payne Gallery, 1987. Grantee NEH rsch. grantee, 1988—90. Mem.: Assn. for Women in Math., Am. Math. Soc., Math. Assn. Am. (editor 1980—85, gov. 1980—89, 1st v.p. 1994—96, Allendoerfer award 1979, Meritorious Svc. award 1991, Dist. Math. Tchg. award 1993), Pi Mu Epsilon (councillor 1990—96). Mem. Moravian Ch. Office: Moravian Coll Math Dept PPHAC 1200 Main St Bethlehem PA 18018-6650 E-mail: schattdo@moravian.edu.

SCHATZ, BARBARA A., law educator; b. 1948; BA, U. Pa., 1969; JD, Harvard U., 1973. Bar: N.Y. 1974. Asst. gen. counsel Health Svcs. Adminstrn., NYC, 1973-74; assoc. Rosenman, Colin, Freund, Lewis & Cohen, NYC, 1974-77; exec. dir. Coun. NY Law Assocs., NYC, 1977-85; lectr. Columbia U., NYC, 1985, clin. prof., 1986—. Bd. dirs. Spl. Advs. Mem. Lawyers Com. Human Rights, Phi Beta Kappa (vice chmn.). Office: Columbia U Sch Law 435 W 116th St New York NY 10027-7297 E-mail: bschatz@law.columbia.edu.

SCHATZ, MONA CLAIRE STRUHSAKER, social worker, educator, consultant, researcher; b. Phila., Jan. 4, 1950; d. Milton and Josephine (Kivo) S.; m. James Fredrick Struhsaker, Dec. 31, 1979 (div.); 1 child, Thain Mackenzie BA, Metro State Coll., 1976; postgrad., U. Minn., 1976; MSW, U. Denver, 1979; D Social Work/Social Welfare, U. Pa., 1986. Tchg. fellow U. Pa., 1981—82; asst. prof. S.W. Mo. State U., Springfield, 1982—85; prof. Colo. State U., Ft. Collins, 1985—2006; dir. social work divsn. Wyo. Edn. and Rsch. Inst., 2006—. Cons. Mgmt. and Behavioral Sci. Ctr., Wharton Sch. U. Pa., 1981-82; field coord. Colo. State U., 1986-88, dir. non-profit agy. adminstrn. program, 1995-97, dir. project Edn. and Rsch. Inst. Fostering Families, 1987—, dir. youth agy. adminstrn. program Am. Humanics, 1988-90; mem. coun. foster care cert. program We. Gov.'s U., 1998—; resource specialist South N.J. Health Sys. Agy., 1982; adj. faculty mem. U. Mo., Springfield, 1994; med. social worker Rehab. and Vis. Nurse Assn., 1985-90; mem. Colo. Child Welfare Adv. Com., Family Conservation Initiative; internat. cons. and trainer Inst. for Internat. Connections, Azerbaijan, Russia, Latvia, Albania, U.S., Hungary, Ukraine, Romania, 1992—; vis. prof. U. Canberra, Australia, 2006; scholar vis. prof. Mokwon U. Korea. Contbr. articles to profl. jours. including Jour. Social Work Edn., Jour. Baccalaureate Social Work, Internat. Jour. Social Work, New Social Worker, Chosen Child: Internat. Adoption Mag., others Cons., field rep. Big Bros./Big Sisters Am., Phila., 1979-83; acting dir., asst. dir. Big Sisters Colo., 1971-78; owner Polit. Cons. Colo., Denver, 1978-79; active Food Co-op, Ft. Collins, Foster Parent, Denver, Capital Hill United Neighbors, Adams County (Denver) Social Planning Coun., Colo. Justice Coun., Denver, Regional Girls Shelter, Springfield; bd. dirs. Crisis Helpline and Info. Svc Scholar Lilly Endowment, Inc., 1976, Piton Found., 1978; recipient Spl. Recognition award Big Bros./Big Sisters Am., 1983, Recognition award Am. Humanics Mgmt. Inst., 1990, Innovative Tchg. award, Ctr. for Tchg. and Learning/Colo. State U., Jack Cermak Adv. award, 2003 Mem. Inst. Internat. Connections (bd. dirs., adv. bd.), Coun. Social Work Edn., Group for Study of Generalist Social Work, Social Welfare History Group, NASW (nominating com. Springfield chpt., state bd. dirs., No. Colo. rep.), Student Social Work Assn. Colo. State U. (adv. 1986-89), Permanency Planning Coun. for Children and Youth, NOW (treas. Springfield chpt. 1984-85), Student Nuc. Awareness Group (advisor), Har Shalom (tchr. youth edn. program), Alpha Delta Mu Democrat. Avocations: cooking, travel, reading, bicycling, sewing. Office: Univ Wyoming Divsn Social Work 1000 E Univ Ave Dept 3632 Laramie WY 82071 Office Phone: 307-766-6112. Business E-Mail: mchatz@uwyo.edu.

SCHATZ, PAULINE, dietician, educator; b. Sioux City, Iowa, Sept. 25, 1923; d. Isaac and Haya (Kaplan) Epstein; m. Hyman Schatz, Sept. 2, 1951; children: Barbara, Larry. BS, UCLA, 1945, MS, 1950, MS in Pub. Health, 1963; EdD, U. So. Calif., 1984. Head dietitian VA, 1946-54; assoc. prof. L.A. City Coll., 1958-56; prof. home econs. Calif. State U., L.A., 1968-83, prof. emeritus, 1983—, dir. ctr. dietetic edn., 1979—, Northridge, 1988-90. Adv. Mid-Career Mentoring Proj., Calif. Dietetic Assn., 1999-00. Author: Manual for Clinical Dietetics, 1978, 3d edit., 1983, Developing a Dietetics Education Program, 1994; co-author: Mentoring, The Human Touch, 1994; contbr. articles to profl. jours. Grantee VA, Kellogg Found. Mem. Am. Dietetic Assn. (disting. Svc. award 1986), Calif. Dietetic Assn. (advisor mid-career mentoring project 1999-2000, Zellmer grantee 1966-69, Disting. Svc. award 1986, Excellence in Edn. 1993, Dolores Nyhus Meml. award 1997), L.A. Dietetic Assn., Kappa Omicron Nu. E-mail: paulineschatz@netscape.net.

SCHAUB, MARILYN MCNAMARA, theology studies educator; b. Chgo., Mar. 24, 1928; d. Bernard Francis and Helen Katherine (Skehan) McNamara; m. Thomas Schaub, Oct. 25, 1969; 1 child, Helen Ann. BA, Rosary Coll., 1953; PhD, U. Fribourg, Switzerland, 1957; diploma, Ecole Biblique, Jerusalem, 1967. Asst. prof. classics and Bibl. studies Rosary Coll., River Forest, Ill., 1957-69; prof. Bibl. studies Duquesne U., Pitts., 1969-70, 73-01. Participant 8 archeological excavations, Middle East; hon assoc Am Schs Oriental Research, 1966—67, trustee, 1986—89; Danforth assoc, 1972—80; admin dir expedition to the Southeast Dead Sea Plains, Jordan, 1989—. Author: (book) Friends and Friendship for St. Augustine, 1964; translator (with H Richter): Agape in the New Testament, 3 vols, 1963—65. Mem.: Am Acad Religion, Cath Biblical Asn, Soc Biblical Literature. Democrat. Home: 25 Mckelvey Ave Pittsburgh PA 15218-1452

SCHAUER, CATHARINE GUBERMAN, public affairs specialist; b. Woodbury, N.J., Sept. 24, 1945; d. Jack and Anna Ruth (Felipe) Guberman; m. Irwin Jay Schauer, July 4, 1968; children: Cheryl Anne Schauer Crabb, Marc Cawin. AB, Miami-Dade Jr. Coll., 1965; BEd, U. Miami, 1967; postgrad., Mercer U., 1968; MPA, Troy State U., 1995. Writer Miami (Fla.) News, 1962-63; tchr. Dade County Schs., Miami, 1967-68; coord. pub. info. Macon (Ga.) Jr. Coll., 1968-69; writer Atlanta Jour., 1969-72; editor Ridgerunner, newspaper, Woodbridge, Va., 1973-75; pub. info. specialist U.S.

Dept. Interior, Washington, 1980-82; writer Dept. Army, Ft. Belvoir, Va., 1982-84, chief prodn., design and editl. publs. divsn., 1984-85; head writer-editor S.E. region U.S. Naval Audit Svc., Virginia Beach, Va., 1986; pub. affairs specialist, tech. rep. for vis. ctr. ops. NASA Langley, 1986-90, project mgr., chmn. 75th anniversary yr., 1991-92; with NASA Langley Rsch. Ctr., Hampton, Va., 1987-89, acting head Office Pub. Svcs., 1989, pub. affairs officer for space, 1993—2002, interpers. govt. assignment to prof. Embry Riddle Aero U. Daytona Beach, Fla., 2001—03; prof. commn. Embry-Riddle Aeronautical U., Daytona Beach, Fla., 2003—04, prof. bus., 2005—. Columnist, writer Potomac News, Woodbridge, 1972-85; writer Gage Publs., 2004—; writer ednl. divsn. Prentice Hall Pubs, 2004-05; guest lectr. George Washington U. Grad. Sch.; apptd. mem. comm. program industry adv. bd. Embry-Riddle Aero. U., Dayton Beach, Fla., 2001—, bd. dirs. Sch. Comm. Contbr. articles to profl. jours. Historian, publicity chmn. PTO, Woodbridge, 1974; publicity chmn. Boy Scouts Am., Woodbridge, 1974-83, Girl Scouts U.S.A., Woodridge, 1974-79; bd. dirs. Congregation Ner Tamid, Woodbridge, 1984-85. Recipient Outstanding Tng. Devel. Support award U.S. Army, 1983, 1st place news writing award and 1st place for advt. design Fla. Jr. Coll. Press Assn., 1964, 1st place feature writing award, 1964, 1st place news writing award Sigma Delta Chi, 1965, 70th anniversary team NASA, 1988, Long Duration Exposure Facility Team award NASA, Combined Fed. Campaign Spl. award for Outstanding Svc. to Va. Peninsula, 1996, Discovery Team Excellence award NASA, 1998, 2d Pl. Feature Writing At-Large Comm. Contest Nat. Fedn. Press Women, 2005 Mem. Va. Press Women (1st place govt. mags. award 1991, 3d place govt. brochures award 1993, 1st place govt. media campaign award 1993, 2d place pub. svc. campaign award 1996, 1st place govt. pub. svc. campaign award 1996, 1st place pub. svc. campaign award 1997), Women in Comm., Nat. Fedn. Press Women (life, 1st place govt. mag. award 1991, 1st place govt. media campaign award 1993, 96, 1st place govt. internal comm. campaign award 1996, 3d place pub. svc. campaign award 1997, 1st pl. feature writing award 2003, 1st Place Pub. Svc. award 2003, Nat. award, 2d Pl. award feature mags.mem. at large competition, 2005, Honarable Mention award, Mktg. Campaign 2001), Fla. Press Women (2d Pl. photography 2004, 2d Pl. feature mag. 2004, 3d Pl. newspaper article 2004), Internat. Assn. Bus. Communicators (1st place mktg. campaign award 1996, 1st place award of excellence for pub. svc. campaign 1996). Democrat. Office: Embry Riddle Aero U Bus Coll Rm C 428 600 S Clyde Morris Blvd Daytona Beach FL 32114-3900 E-mail: catharine.schauer@erau.edu.

SCHAUF, VICTORIA, pediatrician, educator; b. NYC, Feb. 17, 1943; d. Maurice J. and Ruth H. (Baker) Bisson; m. Michael Delaney; 2 children. BS in Microbiology with honors, U. Chgo., 1965, MD with honors, 1969. Intern in pediat. U. Chgo. Hosp., 1969—70; resident in pediat. Sinai Hosp. of Balt., 1970—71; chief resident pediat. Children's Hosp. Nat. Med. Ctr., Washington, 1971—72; rsch. trainee NIH, Bethesda, Md., 1972; adj. asst. prof. microbiology Rush Med. Coll., Chgo., 1972—74; prof. pediat., head pediatric infectious diseases U. Ill., Chgo., 1974—84; med. officer FDA, Rockville, Md., 1984—86; chmn. dept. pediat. Nassau County Med. Ctr., East Meadow, NY, 1986—90; prof. pediat. SUNY, Stony Brook, 1987—94; pvt. practice, 1995—; chief pediatric svcs. Ridgecrest Regional Hosp., 2005—. Vis. prof. Rockefeller U., 1990-92; mem. vis. faculty Chiang Mai (Thailand) U., 1978; mem. ad hoc com. study sects. NIH, Bethesda, 1981-82; bd. dirs. Pearl Stetler Rsch. Found., Chgo., 1982-84; cons. FDA, 1987-88, 93-95, Can. Bur. Human Prescription Drugs, Ottawa, 1990-2004, Biotech. Investors, 1993-95, Calif. Children's Svcs., 2005—; course dir. pediat. infectious diseases rev. course Cornell U. Med. Coll., N.Y.C., 1994, faculty, 1995. Co-author: Pediatric Infectious Diseases: A Comprehensive Guide to the Subspecialty, 1997; prodr. radio and TV programs in field; contbr. articles to profl. jours., chpts. to books. Vol. physician Cook County Hosp., Chgo., 1974-84; mem. adv. com. Nat. Hansen's Disease Ctr., La., 1986, Nassau County Day Care Coun., N.Y., 1988-90; mem. adv. bd. Surg. Aid to Children of World, N.Y., 1986-90; commr., sec. Kern County Children and Families Commn., 1999-2002; sec., bd. dirs. Indian Wells Valley Cmty. Found., 2001-. Am. Lung Assn. grantee U. Ill., 1977; recipient contract NIH, U. Ill., 1978-81, grantee, 1979-84. Fellow Infectious Diseases Soc. Am.; mem. Pediatric Infectious Diseases Soc. (exec. bd.), Soc. Pediatric Rsch., Am. Pediatric Soc., AAAS, Am. Soc. Microbiology, Am. Acad. Pediat., Phi Beta Kappa, Alpha Omega Alpha. Avocation: walking. Office Phone: 760-371-2128. Business E-Mail: vschauf@pol.net.

SCHAUPP, JOAN POMPROWITZ, trucking executive, writer; b. Green Bay, Wis., Sept. 29, 1932; d. Joseph and Helen Elizabeth (VanderLinden) Pomprowitz; m. Robert James Schaupp, Sept. 4, 1956; children: Margaret Schaupp Siebert, Frederick, John Robert, Elizabeth Schaupp Sidles. BS cum laude, U. Wis., 1954; cert. in theology, St. Norbert Coll. Theol. Inst., 1979; MA, U. Wis., Green Bay, 1982; DMin, Grad. Theol. Found., 1996. Woman's editor Green Bay Press-Gazette, 1955-56; freelance writer Green Bay, 1957-75; sec.-treas., dir. L.C.L. Transit Co., Green Bay, 1962-70; chmn., dir. P & S Investment Co., Green Bay, 1982—, mgmt. cons., 1984-89, dir. strategic planning, 1992, vice chmn., 1994—. Pres. The Manna Co., Green Bay, 1992—; adv. com. Women's Ctr. St. Norbert Coll., 1999—; chmn. P&S Investment Co., 2004. Author: Jesus Was a Teenager, 1972, Woman Image of Holy Spirit, 1975 (Thomas More Book award), Elohim: A Search for a Symbol for Human Fulfillment, 1995. Master gardener De Pere (Wis.) Beautification Com., 1991-92; design cons. Nat. Fedn. Grden Clubs, 2004; lector St. Francis Xavier Cathedral, Green Bay, 1991-92. Recipient Ambassador award, St. Norbert Coll., 1997, Disting. Svc. award, 2004, Disting. Citizenship award, St. Norbert Coll. Alumni Assn., 2004. Mem.: Nat. Press Club, Nat. Fedn. Press Women, Am. Acad. Religion, Franciscan Internat., Secular Franciscan Order (vice min. Assumption Province 1991—92), Equestrian Order of the Holy Sepulchre Jerusalem (lady grand cross), Soc. Bibl. Lit. Avocations: gardening, walking, swimming.

SCHEALL, NORMA, writer, editor; b. Saginaw, Mich., Feb. 22, 1924; d. Frank August Leitow and Alma Lena Nickodemus-Leitow; m. Jack James Scheall, Oct. 11, 1941 (dec. May 9, 2003); 1 child, Theodore J. Grad., Famous Writers Correspondence Sch., 1970; BS, Ind. No. U., Gas City, 1972. Freelance editor Morris Harvey Coll., Charleston, W.Va., 1960—62; reporter Maysville Ledger, Ky., 1962—64; newsletter editor Blue Cross of S.W. Ohio, Cin., 1964—66; asst. dir. info. svcs. Ind. Vocat. Tech. Coll., Indpls., 1971—73; alumni editor Wichita State U., Kans., 1974—75; area rep. Dale Carnegie, Wichita, Kans., 1975—76; owner, pres. Air Purification Kans., Wichita, 1976—89; contbg. editor Thousand Trails Mag., Frisco, Tex., 1990—. Pub. Hoot Newsletter for Escapees-North Ranch, Congress, Ariz., 1998—. Author: Kepayshowink-The History of Camp Rotary, 1967, The Basham House Story, 1986, Life After Stroke, 2005. Mem.: Penwheels. Avocations: painting, RV travel, dogs, cooking, history. Home: 21250 Obsidian PO Box 39 Congress AZ 85332-0039 Office Phone: 928-685-3552.

SCHECHTER, LORI A., lawyer; BA magna cum laude, Cornell U., 1983; JD, Yale U., 1987. Bar: Calif. 1989. Law clk. U.S. Dist. Ct. Mass., 1987—88; ptnr. Morrison & Foerster LLP, San Francisco, litig. dept. coord. Spkr. in field; mem. exec. com. sect. antitrust and trade regulation State Bar Calif., 1996—99. Contbr. articles to profl. jours. Named one of Top 50 Female Litigators, Nat. Law Jour., 2001, Top 20 under 40 Calif. Lawyers, Calif. Law Bus., 2001. Office: Morrison & Foerster LLP 425 Market St San Francisco CA 94105-2482 Office Phone: 415-268-6355. Office Fax: 415-268-7522. E-mail: lschechter@mofo.com.

SCHECHTER, LYNN RENEE, psychologist; b. NYC, July 7, 1969; d. Joel David and Sandra Bauman Schechter; m. Issam E. El-Zahr, July 8, 2001; children: Leah Joy El-Zahr, Leo Harris El-Zahr. BS, Cornell U., 1991; MA, Columbia U., 1992, EdM, 1997, PhD, 2001. Lic. psychologist N.Y. Sch. psychologist Reece Sch., N.Y.C., 1997—2000; psychologist Albert Einstein Coll. Medicine, Bronx, NY, 1997—2002; neurodevelopmentalist Jacobi Med. Ctr., Bronx, 2000—02; pvt. practice Baton Rouge, 2003—. Creator, dir. tutoring and mentoring program for children with HIV Jacobi Med. Ctr., Bronx, 2001—02. Mem.: APA (divsn. 16 sch. psychology), Golden Key, Kappa Delta Pi, Omicron Nu. Avocations: reading, music, sports. Office: Bluebonnet Psychol Svc 2356 Drusilla Ln Baton Rouge LA 70809 Office Phone: 225-926-7500. E-mail: lynnschechter@aol.com.

SCHECK, ELIZABETH A., sociologist, educator; b. Davenport, Iowa, Aug. 16, 1950; d. Michael L. and Therese M. Scheck; children: Jennifer T. Guerin, Marc E. Zaleski. MS in Sociology, Ind. State U., Terre Haute, Ind., 2001. Prof. sociology Ivy Tech C.C., Terre Haute, Ind., 2000—04, Fla. C.C., Jacksonville, Fla., 2005—. Faculty co-chmn. domestic violence awareness learning cmty. project Fla. C.C. Campaign assoc. Charlie Crist for Gov., Jacksonville, 2006—06. Mem.: Alpha Kappa Delta (hon.; campus pres. 1999—2000). Republican. Roman Cath. Avocations: travel, reading, fitness, cooking. Home: 6944 Goldilocks Lane Jacksonville FL 32210 Office: Florida Community College 3939 Roosevelt Jacksonville FL 32205 Office Phone: 904-381-3436. Business E-Mail: escheck@fccj.edu.

SCHECKTER, STELLA JOSEPHINE, retired librarian; b. Phila., Nov. 30, 1926; d. Isaar Jerome and Rose (Levin) S. AB, Temple U., 1948; MLS, Drexel U., 1952. Continuations asst. acquisitions dept. Temple U. Libr., Phila., 1949-52; jr. asst. ref. libr. Hartford (Conn.) Pub. Libr., 1952-53, asst. br. libr., 1953-54; asst. lit. and lang. dept. Enoch Pratt Free Libr., Balt., 1954-56, asst. bus. and econs. dept., 1956-58; dir. ref. and loan bur. N.H. State Libr., Concord, 1958-90, ret., 1990. Vol. Concord Cmty. Concert Assn., 1975—, bd. dirs. 1977-90; selected participant Concord's Civic Profile, City of Concord, 1991; archivist Friends Concord City Auditorium. Recipient Best Set Design award New England Theatre Conf., 1968; nominated Charles McCarthy award for outstanding svc. to state govt. Coun. of State Govts., 1989. Mem. ALA (state membership com. chair 1964-69), N.H. Libr. Assn. (life, pub. rels. com. 1971-74), New England Libr. Assn. (chmn. bibliography com. 1971-72), N.H. Hist. Soc. (libr. vol. 1992—), State Employees Assn. (councillor 1991-98), Freedom to Read Found., Cmty. Players Concord (bd. dirs. 1965-67), Music Club Concord (bd. dirs. 1967-69), Hadassah (life, bd. dirs. 1989-91, 96—). Avocations: travel, photography, painting. Home: 27 Church St Concord NH 03301-6417

SCHEETZ, ALLISON PAIGE, medical educator; b. Atlanta, Nov. 19, 1963; d. Bobby Reid Scheetz and Augusta Claire (Dunn) Sherrer; m. David Edwin Mathis, Feb. 13, 1993; children: Taylor Nicole Mathis, Morgan Lindsay Mathis. BA in Psychology, BS in Biology, Mercer U., 1986, MD, 1992. Diplomate Am. Bd. Internal Medicine, Adolescent Medicine. Intern Med. Ctr. Ctrl. Ga./Mercer U. Sch. Medicine, Macon, 1992-93, resident, chief resident in internal medicine, 1993-95, instr. medicine dept. internal medicine, 1995-96, asst. prof., 1996-2001, asst. program dir., 1996-00, dir. resident edn., 1996-00, instr. dept. pediats., 1996-99, asst. prof. dept. pediats., 1999—2005, clerkship dir., 2000—, assoc. prof., 2001—; med. dir. Health South Rehab. Hosp., 2002—. Consulting physician Health South Rehab. Hosp., Macon, 1997—. Mem. ACP, AMA, Soc. Gen. Internal Medicine, So. Med. Assn., Bibb County Med. Soc., Mercer U. Sch. Medicine Alumni Assn. (bd. dirs. 1997-99), Alpha Omega Alpha. Republican. Baptist. Achievements include research on thiazolidinedione, community acquired pneumonia, and medical student attitudes. Office: Mercer Health Sys Dept Internal Medicine 707 Pine St Macon GA 31201-2106

SCHEETZ, SISTER MARY JOELLEN, English language educator; b. Lafayette, Ind., May 20, 1926; d. Joseph Albert and Ellen Isabelle (Fitzgerald) S. AB, St. Francis Coll., 1956; MA, U. Notre Dame, 1964; PhD, U. Mich., 1970. Tchr. English, Bishop Luers High Sch., Fort Wayne, Ind., 1965-67; acad. dean St. Francis Coll. (now U. St. Francis), Fort Wayne, 1967-68, pres. Ft. Wayne, Ind., 1970-93, pres. emeritus, English lang. prof. Ft. Wayne, Ind., 1993—. Mem.: Delta Epsilon Sigma. Office: U St Francis 2701 Spring St Fort Wayne IN 46808-3939 Office Phone: 260-434-3229. Business E-Mail: jscheetz@sf.edu.

SCHEFFEL, DONNA JEAN, elementary school educator; b. Balt., Sept. 20, 1953; d. G. Donald Scheffel and Mary LaVerne (Perry) Jones; 1 child, Amanda Lynne. BS, Salisbury (Md.) State Coll.; Cert., Baldwin-Wallace Coll., Berea, Ohio, 1983. Tchr. Wadsworth (Ohio) city schs., 1984-85, Parma (Ohio) city schs., 1984-85; elem. tchr. St. Leo the Great Sch., Cleve., 1985-91. 1st aux. svcs. computer sci. tchr. Bethel Christian Acad., Parma. Named one of Outstanding Young Women of Am., 1986. Mem.: ASCD, PEA, NEA, NAFE, Ohio Edn. Assn., N.E. Ohio Edn. Assn. Office: Bethel Christian Acad 12901 W Pleasant Valley Rd Parma OH 44130-5702

SCHEFFING, DIANNE ELIZABETH, special education educator; b. St. Louis, Mar. 17, 1963; d. Eugene Shibley Scheffing Jr. and Sarah Ann (Lukens) Scheffing. BS, Mo. Bapt. Univ., 1988; MA, Fontbonne U., St. Louis, 1999, A in Computer Edn., 2005; postgrad., Webster U., St. Louis, 2002. Cert. elem. edn. grades 1-8 Mo., mild/moderate cross-category grades K-12 Mo., severely developmentally delayed 2002. Kindergarden tchr. asst. Andrews Acad., St. Louis, 1989—91; sci. tchr. edn. dept. St. Louis Sci. Ctr., 1994—96; tchr. asst. multi-handicapped Kehrs Mill Elem./Rockwood Sch. Dist., St. Louis, 1996—2000; tchr. spl. edn. Gateway/Hubert Wheeler State Sch. for Severely Handicapped, St. Louis, 2000—. Mem., sec. St. Louis Young Reps. Club, 1988—94; majority mem. Bethel #44 Internat. Order of Job's Daughters, Ballwin, 1978—84. Named Woman of Yr., St. Louis Young Reps. Club, 1992, 1994. Mem.: Am. Cancer Soc. Methodist. Avocations: Olympic supporter, bowling, travel. Office: Gateway/Hubert Wheeler State Sch 100 S Garrison Saint Louis MO 63103 Personal E-mail: applecore@prodigy.net.

SCHEFSTAD, THERESA, bank executive; b. Va., Feb. 5, 1958; BSBA in Fin., Computer Sci., U. Cen. Fla., 1980. Cert. fin. planner; lic. mortgage broker. V.p. S.E. Bank, Orlando, Fla., 1976-91; exec. v.p. Coast Bank, Sarasota, Fla., 1991-93; pres., CEO Raymond James Bank, St. Petersburg, Fla., 1993—, dir. Mem. adj. faculty Coll. Fin. Planning, 1988-91. Co-editor Inner Cir. newsletter, 1990-91. Mem. adv. bd. Valencia Community Coll., Orlando, 1989-90; mem. Winter Park (Fla.) Meml. Hosp. Coun., 1988-91. Mem. Internat. Assn. Fin. Planning, Internat. Bd. Cert. Fin. Planners (registrant 1990-91), Winter Park C. of C. (v.p. 1986-91), Orlando C. of C. (exec. dir., treas. grad. leadership 1991). Office: Raymond James Bank PO Box 11628 Saint Petersburg FL 33733-1628

SCHEIB, RACHEL THERESA, psychiatrist; b. Cin., May 3, 1976; d. Paul Richard and Rose Mary Piening; m. Charles Joseph Scheib, June 5, 2004. BSc, St. Ursula Acad., Cin., Ohio, 1994; degree cum laude, Xaner U., Cin., Ohio, 1998; MD, Wright State U., Dayton, Ohio, 2004. Rsch. asst. VA Med. Ctr., Cin., 1997—98; coord. unit Dept. Surgery Bethesda North Hosp., Cin., 1997—2003; resident Mich. State U., Grand Rapids, Mich., 2004—05; resident psychiatry Wright State U., Dayton, Ohio, 2005—. Rsch. asst. Wood Hudson Cancer Rsch. Lab., Newport, Ky., 1999—2000; med. externship Kettering Med. Ctr., Dayton, Ohio, 2001. Vol. Am. Heart Assn., Dayton, 2001—02, Spl. Olympics, Dayton, 2001; vol. anatomical gift program Wright State U., Dayton, 2000—01; vol. Montgomery Free Clinic, 2000—02. Recipient Academic award, Xaner U., 1995; scholar, 1994. Mem.: Am. Med. Women's Assn., Mortor Bd., Alpha Sigma Nu, Phi Rho Sigma. Avocation: volleyball.

SCHEIBERG, SUSAN L., librarian; b. Chgo., Dec. 19, 1962; d. Steven M. Scheiberg, Margo Scheiberg. BA (hon.), Ind. U., 1984; MA, UCLA, 1986; MS in Libr. Sci., U. Ky., 1997. Grad. rsch. libr. U. So. Calif., 1997—98, team leader, serials acquisitions, 1998—2001; head acquisitions and serials, coord. outreach and cost-ctr. svcs. RAND Corp., Santa Monica, Calif., 2001—02, assoc. dir., 2002—. Editor: (book) NASIG 2001: A Serials Odyssey, 2002, Transforming Serials: The Revolution Continues, 2003; contbr. articles to profl. jours. Fellow Univ., UCLA, 1984-1987; grantee Bardin Endowment Rsch., U. So. Calif., 1998, 1999, 2000. Mem.: ALA (Tony B. Leisner grantee 1996), Reference and User Svcs. Assn., Assn. Coll. & Rsch. Librs., N.Am. Serials Interest Group (proceedings editor 2000—), Libr. Adminstrn. and Mgmt. Assn., Assn. Libr. Collections and Tech. Svcs., Spl. Librs. Assn., Beta Phi Mu, Phi Beta Kappa. Office Phone: 310-393-0411. Personal E-mail: susanls@rand.org.

SCHEID, CATHERINE MARIE, elementary school educator; d. William John and Bernardine Joan Scheid. BA in Edn., U. Ill., 1976; MA, Roosevelt U., 1984, MEd, 1985. Sci. tchr. Hickory Hill Mid. Sch., 1978—82; tchr. Sunny Hill Elem. Sch., Barrington, Ill., 1982—92; sci. tchr. Barrington Mid. Sch. Prairie Campus, 1992—2000, asst. prin., 2000—. Sec. Barrington Credit Union. Named to Profiles of Excellence, Barrington Mid. Sch.; recipient 35 Yrs. of Excellence award, Barrington Sch. Dist. Mem.: NEA, Nat. Mid. Sch. Assn., Barrington Edn. Assn., Ill. Edn. Assn. Avocation: travel. Office: BMS Prairie Campus 40 E Dundee Rd Palatine IL 60067 Office Phone: 847-304-3990.

SCHEIDT, REBECCA LYNNELL, psychologist, educator; b. Escondido, Calif., June 25, 1972; d. Charlene Johnston, James Preston Johnston; m. Billy Clayton Scheidt. MA in Psychology and Counseling, La. Bapt. U., PhD in Psychology and Counseling, 2001. Cert. sch. counselor Assn. Christina Schs. Internat. Visual merchandiser, sSales Barsa, El Centro, Calif., 1987—88; merchandiser, mgr. The Wet Seal, San Diego, 1989—93; counselor, sch. psychologist The Acad. of San Antonio, 1994—98; sch. psychologist, tchr. The Christian Academy, Shelbyville, Ky., 1998—. Counselor Charlie Home Foster Care, El Centro, 1988—90. Author: A Handbook for Parents of Teenagers, 2001. Mem.: Ky. Assn. Christian Counselors. Baptist. Avocations: orchid breeding, reading. Office: Cornerstone Christian Academy 3850 Frankfort Rd Shelbyville KY 40065-9407 Office Phone: 502-633-4070. Home Fax: 502-633-9257.

SCHEIN, VIRGINIA ELLEN, psychologist, editor; b. June 23, 1943; d. Jacob Charles and Anne Schein; m. Rupert F. Chisholm (dec. 2004); 1 child, Alexander Nikos. BA cum laude, Cornell U., 1965; PhD, NYU, 1969. Lic. psychologist, Pa. Sr. rsch. assoc. Am. Mgmt. Assn., N.Y.C., 1969-70; mgr. personnel rsch. Life Office Mgmt. Assn., N.Y.C., 1970-72; dir. personnel rsch. Met. Life Ins. Co., N.Y.C., 1972-75; assoc. prof. Sch. Mgmt. Case Western Res. U., Cleve., 1975-76; vis. assoc. prof. Sch. Orgn. and Mgmt. Yale U., New Haven, 1977-80; mgmt. cons. Va. E. Schein, PhD, P.C., 1975—; assoc. prof. psychology Bernard M. Baruch Coll. CUNY, 1982-85; prof. mgmt. and psychology Gettysburg Coll., Pa., 1986—, chair mgmt. dept., 1993-95. Co-author: Power and Organization Development, 1988; author: Working from the Margins, 1995; mem. editl. rev. bds. Women Mgmt. Rev., Acad. Mgmt. Execs.; contbr. articles to profl. jours. Bd. dirs. Family Planning Ctr., 1988-91, Pvt. Industry Coun., 1990-93, Keystone Rsch. Ctr., 1996-98, Women Cmty. Svc., 1997-2003; bd. dirs. Survivors, Inc., pres. bd. dirs., 1991-92, Adams County Children and Youth Adv. Bd., 2003-04. Mem.: APA (coun.rep. 1978—80, com. women 1980—83), Internat. Assn. Applied Psychology (divsn. orgnl. psychology chair sci. program com. 1995—98, pres.-elect 1998—2002, pres. 2002—06), Acad. Mgmt. (rep. orgn.devel. divsn. 1979—81, exec. com. women mgmt. divsn.), Met. Assn. Applied Psychology (pres. 1973—74), Psi Chi. Office: Gettysburg Coll Dept Mgmt Gettysburg PA 17325

SCHEINBERG, PHYLLIS F., federal agency administrator; BA, Simmons Coll.; MS, U. Calif. Sr. budget examiner trasp. and natural resources, office mgmt. and budget Exec. Office Pres., Washington, 1981—90; dir. transp. issues U.S. Gen. Acctg. Office, Washington; acting asst. sec. budget and programs, CFO US Dept. Transp., Washington, dep. asst. sec. budget & programs, 2001—05, asst. sec. budget & programs, CFO, 2005—. Office: US Dept Transp 400 Seventh St SW Rm 10101 Washington DC 20590 Office Phone: 202-366-9191. Office Fax: 202-366-6031.

SCHEINDLIN, SHIRA A., federal judge; b. Washington, Aug. 16, 1946; d. Boris and Miriam Joffe; m. Stanley Friedman, May 22, 1982; 2 children. BA cum laude, U. Mich., 1967; MA in Far Ea. Studies, Columbia U., 1969; JD cum laude, Cornell U., 1975. Bar: N.Y. 1976. With Stroock, Stroock & Lavan, 1975-76; gen. counsel N.Y.C. Dept. of Investigation, 1981-82; asst. U.S. atty. U.S. Dist. Ct. (ea. dist.) N.Y., 1977-81, U.S. magistrate, 1982-86; with Budd, Larner, Gross, Rosenbaum, Greenberg & Sade, Short Hills, N.J., 1986-90, ptnr., 1990, Herzfeld & Rubin, N.Y.C., 1990-94; law clk. to Hon. Charles L. Brieant, Jr. U.S. Dist. Ct. (So. Dist.), NY, 1976-77, judge NY, 1984—; endispute mem. Jud. Panel, 1992—. Adj. prof. law Bklyn. Law Sch., 1983—; mem. 2d Cir. Conf. Planning Com., So. Dist. Adv. Com., 1991-94. Recipient Spl. Achievement award Dept. of Justice, 1980. Mem. Fedn. Bar Coun. (trustee 1986-88, 90—, v.p. 1988-90), N.Y. State Bar Assn. (chair comml. and fed. litigation sect. 1991-92), N.Y. County Lawyers Assn. (bd. dirs. 1992-95, chair tort sect. 1992-94), Assn. of Bar of City of N.Y. Avocations: jogging, hiking. Office: US Courthouse 500 Pearl St Rm 1050 New York NY 10007-1316

SCHEINMAN, NANCY JANE, psychologist; b. N.Y.C., June 23, 1955; d. Norman Sinclair and Vivian Estelle (Goodwin) Tischenkel; m. Stephen Robert Scheinman, June 15, 1990; children: Cassie Leigh, William Mayer. BA, Vassar Coll., 1977; MS, U. Miami, 1986, PhD, 1988. Intern Duke Med. Ctr., Durham, N.C., 1988; pvt. practice Miami, Fla., 1991—. Founder, dir. Hosp. Based Alternative Medicine Ctr. Contbr. to books and articles to profl. jours. U. Miami fellow, 1988-90. Mem. Am. Psychol. Assn., Soc. Behavioral Medicine, Phi Beta Kappa. Independent. Jewish. Avocations: swimming, tennis. Personal E-mail: nancyscheinman@aol.com.

SCHELL, CATHERINE LOUISE, physician; b. Niskayuna, N.Y., Jan. 27, 1948; m. Richard J. Rathe, Jan. 7, 1986. BA, Ind. U., 1970, MA, 1974; MLS, Simmons Coll., 1975; MD, Am. U. Caribbean, Montserrat, 1983. Diplomate Am. Bd. Family Practice; cert. CAQ Geriatrics. Libr. Calder Med. Libr., U. Miami, Fla., 1975-78; libr., dir. Mercy Hosp., Miami, 1978-79; libr. Miami-Dade C.C., 1978-80; intern Med. Coll. Ga., Rome, 1983; resident U. Wyo., Cheyenne, 1985-87; staff physician Vets. Hosp., Cheyenne, 1986-88, Dept. of Army, U.S. Dept. Def., Ft. Devens, Mass., 1988-90, Vets. Hosp., Lake City, Fla., 1990-93, staff physician, fellow Gainesville, Fla., 1993-95; fellow in geriatrics U. Fla., 1993-95, fellow in geriatrics internal medicine, 1995, fellow geriatrics internal medicine, 1995; physician Dept. of Navy, 1995-96; pres. Med. Decisions Software, Inc., 1999—; physician Vets. Outpatient Clinic, 2004—. Tchr. ESL YMCA Internat., Taipei, Taiwan, 1970-71. Title IIB fellow Simmons Coll., 1974-75; Ford Found. grantee, Ind. U., 1969-70. Fellow Am. Acad. Family PRactice; mem. Acad. Health Sci., Med. Libr. Assn.

SCHELL-BRADY, G. JANELLE, dancer, educator; d. Gloria J. Gaslin and Claude Allen Schell; m. Jeffrey S. Brady; children: Jeffrey C. Brady, Camille Maeschell Brady, Ethan Allen Brady. Cert. Paraprofl. Tex., 2003. Choreographer U. No. Colo., Greeley, 1977—79; principle dancer Canyon Concert Ballet, Fort Collins, Colo., 1978—81; owner, instr. Janelle's Studio of Dance, Terlingua, Tex., 1981—; dance/music instr. Terlingua Common Sch. Dist., Tex., 1997—; dance/folklorico instr. Big Bend HS, Terlingua, Tex., 1997—; dance/music instr. San Vicente ISD, Big Bend National Park, Tex., 2000—; choreographer Sul Ross State U., Alpine, Tex., 2005. Creator, coord. Big Bend Regional Spring Festival for the Arts, Terlingua, Tex., 1998—. Dir.(choreographer, prodr., costume maker): (9 years performances/competitions) (Best Technique, Best Choreography, Best Overall, Best Traditional, Best Costume, Best Creative, 2004). Recipient K - 12 Dance Educator of Yr., So. Dist. Am. Alliance of Health, Phys. Edn., Recreation and Dance, 2005, K - 12 So. Dist. Dance Educator of Yr., Nat. Dance Assn., 2005. Mem.: Tex. Assn. of Health, Phys. Edn., Recreation and Dance (sec. 2003—05, chair elect 2005—06, K-12 Dance Educator of Yr. 2004). Achievements include Texas House of Representatives 79th Legislature Resolution 1592: Expression of High Regard and Congradulations on contributing to the cultural heritage of the Lone Star State. Office: Big Bend HS 2281 Roadrunner Cir Terlingua TX 79852 Office Phone: 432-371-2281. Business E-Mail: jbrady@esc18.net.

SCHELLIN, PATRICIA MARIE BIDDLE, secondary school educator; b. Columbus, Wis., Apr. 1, 1955; d. Charles Westly Sr. and Dorothy (Madigan) Biddle; m. Edwin O. Schellin, June 21, 1980; children: Jennifer, Jeremy, Jonathan. BS, U. Wis., LaCrosse, 1978. Cert. tchr., Wis. Tchr., coach Freedom (Wis.) Schs., 1978-80, Fall River (Wis.) Schs., 1983-84; tchr. St. Jerome's Sch., Columbus, 1984-86, 90—, Dickason Mid. Sch., Columbus, 1987; substitute tchr. Columbus Schs., 1980—. Swimming instr. Columbus Recreation Dept., 1979—; coach girls basketball, Columbus High Sch., 1983—, varsity girls soccer, 1993-2002; instr. CPR ARC, Columbus, 1986—, water safety chair, 1984—; aquatic dir. Columbia Area Aquatic Ctr., 2002—. Coach soccer, baseball Columbus Recreation Dept., 1988—; recreation dir. City of Columbus, 1993-2002. Mem. AAHPERD. Lutheran. Avocations: travel, sports. Office: Saint Jeromes Sch 156 W James St Columbus WI 53925-1569

SCHELLING, GLORIA ANN, art educator; b. Shenandoah, Pa., July 26, 1951; m. Andrew W. Schelling, Aug. 18, 1973; 1 child, Andrew. BS in Art Edn., Mansfield U., 1972; postgrad., Bucknell U., Pa. State U., 1984. Cert. elem. and secondary tchr., Pa. Art tchr. Loyalsock Jr. High Sch., Williamsport, Pa., 1972-74; art tchr. grades K-5 Big Spring Sch. Dist., Newville, Pa., 1974-84; art tchr. grades 7-9 Downingtown (Pa.) Jr. High Sch., 1984-86; art tchr. grades K-12 Tredyffrin Easttown Sch. Dist., Berwyn, Pa., 1986—. Mem. Mid. States Evaluation Team, Guyned/Mercy, 1988; facilitator-trainer GENDER Equity Student Achievement, Reading, 1990; instr. Collaborative Problem Solving in Learning Styles, Berwyn, 1991. Paintings entered in juried shows, Oakland Corp. Ctr., local Pa. galleries, 1980—; represented in pvt., pub. and corp. collections Pa., N.J., Del. Mem. ASCD, U.S. Soc. for Edn. Through Art, Nat. Art Edn. Assn., Pa. Art Edn. Assn. (nominated Outstanding Pa. Art Educator 1985, pub. rels. com.), Pa. Coalition for the Arts, Pa. Staff Devel. Coun., Chester County Art Assn., Women's Caucus for Art (bd. dirs.), Internat. Soc. Photographers. Home: 103 Piedmont Rd West Chester PA 19382-7257

SCHELS, MARGARETE THERESA, secondary school educator; b. Waldkirchen, Bavaria, Fed. Republic of Germany, Nov. 2, 1955; came to U.S., 1957; d. Joseph and Monika (Rodler) S. AA in Early Childhood, Oakton Community Coll., Morton Grove, Ill., 1975; BA in Elem. Edn., Northeastern Ill. U., 1977; MEd in Mid. Sch. Math., Nat. Louis U., 1990. Cert. elem. edn. tchr., Ill. Tchr. St. Peter Sch., Skokie, Ill., 1977-79, St. Athanasius Sch., Evanston, Ill., 1979—, St. John the Bapt. Cath. Sch., 1996—. Vol. Parkside Rehab. Ctr. Luth. Hosp., Park Ridge, Ill., 1980—; mem. parish ministry substance abuse referral team St. Peter Ch., Skokie, 1987—. Named Outstanding Educator, WCATY, 2005; fellow, Kohl Ednl. Found., 2003. Mem. Nat. Council Tchrs. Maths. Roman Catholic. Avocations: music, volleyball, reading, travel. Home: W9195 Blue Spruce Ln Cambridge WI 53523-8801 Office: St Athanasius Sch 2510 Ashland Ave Evanston IL 60201-2319 Office Phone: 920-674-5821. Business E-Mail: mschels@straphael.org.

SCHENCK, SUSAN JANE, special education educator; b. Providence, July 20, 1949; d. Donald Elwood and Geraldine Frances (Dansereau) S. AA, R.I. Jr. Coll., Providence, 1969; BS, R.I. Coll., 1972, MEd, 1975; cert. advanced grad. study, U. Conn., 1977, PhD, 1979. Cert. elem. and spl. edn. tchr., cert. adminstr. Tchr., title I Coventry, R.I. Pub. Schs., 1972; tchr. mentally handicapped North Kingston, R.I. Pub. Schs., 1972-76; research asst. U. Conn., Storrs, 1976-78; asst. prof. SUNY, Plattsburgh, 1978-79, Coll. of Charleston (S.C), 1979-84, assoc. prof., 1985-89, coordinator LD services, 1984-89, dir. tchr. cert. and student teaching, 1985-87; dir. clin. experiences in tchr. edn. R.I. Coll., Providence, 1989—. Curriculum cons. Bristol, Conn. schs. 1976-77; field reader U.S. Office Edn. (Spl. Edn.), Washington, 1983—. Author: Math That Pays Off, 1978; (monograph with others) IEP's: State of the Art; contbr. articles to periodicals. Bd. dirs. Ronald McDonald House, Charleston, 1985-89, ops. bd. dirs., 1989—; bd. dirs. Exch. Club Prevention of Child Abuse, Charleston, 1986-89, Friends of Children, Med. Univ. S.C., 1988-89; mem. sch. bd. Christ Our King Ch., Mt. Pleasant, S.C., 1986-87. Spl. Edn. fellow, U. Conn., 1976-78; U.S. Dept. Edn. grantee, Office Spl. Edn., 1983-86, Project Omni grantee, S.C. Office the Handicapped, 1981. Mem. Am. Edn. Research Assn. (treas. 1980-84, chmn. 1984-87, chair spl. edn. research), Council Exceptional Children, S.C. Tchr. Recruitment Ctr. (policy bd.), Council Learning Disabilities. Avocations: reading, photography, cooking, travel, golf. Office: RI Coll 600 Mt Pleasant Ave Providence RI 02908-1924

SCHENDAN, HALINE ELIZABETH, cognitive neuroscience educator; b. Schenectady, N.Y., June 29, 1965; d. David James and Edna May S.; m. Giorgio Ganis, Apr. 24, 1992 BA Neurobiology, U. Calif., Berkeley, 1980; MS Neurosci., U. Calif., San Diego, 1992, PhD Neurosci. and Cognitive Sci., 1998. Lab. asst. San Jose State U., 1989—90; rsch. lab. asst. U. Calif., Berkeley, 1989—90, tchg. asst. San Diego, 1992, rsch. asst., 1992—97; rsch. assoc. Boston U., 1997—2003, rsch. asst. prof., 1999—2003; asst. prof. dept. psychology Tufts U., Medford, Mass., 2003—. Adj. asst. prof. Boston U., 2004—; vis. scientist Martinos MGH-NMR Ctr. Harvard Med. Sch., 2004—. Contbr. articles to profl. jours. Travel grantee Affective Neurosci. Symposium, Madison, 1998, NIMH, 2002—; Grad. fellow McDonnell-Pew Cognitive Neurosci., San Diego, 1990-96, U. Calif. fellow, San Diego, 1996-97; recipient Nat. Rsch. Svc. award, 2000— Mem. Soc. Neurosci., Cognitive Neurosci. Soc., Assn. Psychol. Sci Avocation: visual art. Office: Tufts U Dept Psychology 490 Boston Ave Medford MA 02155

SCHENDEL, KELLY RYAN, literature educator, writer; b. Phila., Dec. 5, 1950; d. James and Beatrice Elizabeth (Brown) Wobensmith, Charles W. Kelly (Stepfather); m. Ronald L. Schendel, Aug. 22, 1992; 1 child, Amy J. AA English, El Camino Coll., Torrance, Calif., 1998; BA English, Calif. State U., Long Beach, Calif., 2001, MFA English, creative writing, 2003. Cert.: U. of So. Calif. Law Ctr. (Law Practice Mgmt.) 1988; Transportation Demand Mgmt. UCLA, 1994. Legal adminstr. Ball, Hunt, Hart, Brown & Baerwitz, Los Angeles, Calif., 1988—90, Arter, Hadden, Lawler, Felix & Hall, Los Angeles, Calif., 1990—92; freelance writing/editing Kelly Schendel & Associates, Manhattan Beach, Calif., 1992—; faculty, English Calif. State U., Long Beach, Calif., 2001—, Orange Coast Coll., Costa Mesa, Calif., 2002—. Human resources cons. Sitag USA, Inc., Irvine, Calif., 1994—2001, Michael Devine & Associates, Manhattan Beach, Calif., 1994—2001; freelance writer City of Torrance, Torrance, Calif., 1996—; freelance editor Stephen Decker & Associates, Culver City, Calif., 2000—; human resources cons. dTank, Inc., Los Angeles, Calif., 2002—. Author: (humor columns) Daily Breeze Newspaper; author: (magazine) (articles) Women's World; mng. editor (lit. jour.) Rip Rap. Recipient Long Beach Professional Writer's Award for Best Novel in Progress, Long Beach Professional Writer's Assn., 2001; scholar Phi Kappa Phi Scholarship, Phi Kappa Phi Honor Soc., 2001. Mem.: Phi Kappa Phi (Phi Kappa Phi Scholarship 2001), Golden Key Honor Soc. (life), Nat. Honor Soc. (life), Sigma Tau Delta, English Honor Soc. (life). D-Liberal. Avocations: travel, cooking, entertaining.

SCHENK, DEBORAH HUFFMAN, law educator; b. 1947; BA, Cornell U., 1969; JD, Columbia U., 1972; LLM in Taxation, NYU, 1976. Bar: NY 1973. Asst. prof. Bklyn. Law Sch., 1974—77, assoc. prof., 1977—80, prof., 1980—85. NYU Sch. Law, 1985—, AAA-CPA Olincey prof. law, 1995—96, Ronald and Marilyn Grossman prof. taxation, 1996—, editor-in-chief Tax Law Rev. Vis. prof. Harvard U., spring 1982, NYU, 1983-85, Yale U., 1989. Author: Federal Taxation of S Corporations, 1985, 2000; co-author: (with M. Graetz) Federal Income Taxation, Principles and Policies, 1995; (with B. Wolfman & J. Holden) Ethical Problems in Federal Tax Practice, 1995. Mem. ABA (tax sect.), Am. Law Inst., Am. Coll. Tax Counsel, NY State Bar Assn. Office: NYU Sch Law Vanderbilt Hall Rm 430H 40 Washington Sq S New York NY 10012-1099 Office Phone: 212-998-6163. E-mail: deborah.schenk@nyu.edu.

SCHENK, SUSAN KIRKPATRICK, nursing educator, consultant, small business owner; b. New Richmond, Ind., Nov. 29, 1938; d. William Marcius and Frances (Kirkpatrick) Gaither; m. Richard Dee Brown, Aug. 13, 1960 (div. Feb. 1972); children: Christopher Lee, David Michael, Lisa Catherine; m. John Francis Schenk, July 24, 1975 (widowed Apr. 1995). BSN, Ind. U., 1962; postgrad., U. Del., 1973-75. RN, PHN, BCLS; cert. community coll. tchr., Calif.; cert. vocat. edn. tchr., Calif. Staff nurse, then asst. dir. nursing Bloomington (Ind.) Hosp., 1962-66; charge nurse Newark (Del.) Manor, 1967-69; charge nurse GU Union Hosp., Terre Haute, Ind., 1971-72; clin. instr. nursing Ind. State U., Terre Haute, 1972-73; clin. instr. psychiatric nursing U. Del., Newark, 1974-75; psychiatric nursing care coord. VA Med. Ctr., Perry Point, Md., 1975-78; from nurse educator to cmty. rels. coord. Grossmont Hosp., La Mesa, Calif., 1978—91; dir. psychiat. svcs. Scripps Hosp. East County, El Cajon, Calif., 1991-97; nursing instr., adult edn. Grossmont Union H.S. Dist., La Mesa, 1996—. Tech. advisor San Diego County Bd. Supervisors, 1987; tech. cons. Remedy Home and Health Care, San Diego, 1988; expert panelist Srs. Speak Out, KPBS-TV, San Diego, 1988; guest lectr. San Diego State U., 1987. Editor: Teaching Basic Caregiver Skills, 1988; author, performer tng. videotape Basic Caregiver Skills, 1988. Mem. patient svcs. com. Nat. Multiple Sclerosis Soc., San Diego, 1986-89; bd. dirs. Assn. for Quality and Participation, 1989. Adminstrn. on Aging/DHHS grantee, 1988. Mem. Ind. U. Alumni Assn. (life), Calif. Coun. Adult Edn., Mensa, Sigma Theta Tau. Avocations: piano, gardening, reading. Home and Office: 9435D Carlton Oaks Dr Santee CA 92071-2582 Personal E-mail: susansks@aol.com.

SCHENKEL, BARBARA ANN, minister, nurse, social worker; b. Albuquerque, Mar. 17, 1951; d. Richard Henry and Mildred (Voth) S. BSN, U. N.Mex., 1972; MDiv, Iliff Sch. Theology, 1978; MSW, Ariz. State U., 1988. RN, N.Mex.; ordained to ministry Meth. Ch., 1979. Minister intern Christ Ch. U. Meth. Ch., Denver, 1975-77; parish minister Herman (Nebr.) Federated and Riverside Bapt. Ch., 1978-82, Cambridge (Nebr.) Bartley U. Meth. Ch., 1982-85; family minister Red Mountain U.M.C., Mesa, Ariz., 1988-94; nurse Ariz. Health Cost Containment Sys., Phoenix, 1994—; minister Life in the Spirit Ministry, Crossroads, Ariz., 1999—2003; prayer coord., life in spirit leader Sunrise United Meth. Ch., Phoenix, 2005—. Christ Ch. Caring Community Coordinator, Denver, 1975-77; advisor alcohol treatment program Immanuel Hosp., Washington County, Nebr., 1980-82; mem. task group to study Ministry Effectiveness in Nebr., 1981; vis. del. to World Meth. Conf., Honolulu, 1981; registrar for candidacy Bd. or Ordained Ministry, 1980-84, strategy com., 1984-85; drug and alcohol cons. Salvation Army Adult Rehab. Ctr., Phoenix, 1987-88, Adult Protective Svcs., 1988—. Chaplain Jackson-Peck Am. Legion Post, Herman, 1980—82; prayer coord., spiritual life min. Sunrise United Meth. Ch., Phoenix, 2005—. Served to 1st lt. USAF Nurse Corps, 1973—75. Mem. Nebr. Ann. Conf. United Meth. Chs., Cambridge Ministerial Assn. (pres. 1984), Tekamah-Herman Ministerial Assn. (pres. 1981), S.W. Dist. Coun. Ministries (past com. memberships). Avocations: horseback riding, bowling, crochet, needlepoint, crewel. Office: Ariz Health Cost Containment Sys 2830 W Glendale Ave Phoenix AZ 85051-8400 Home: Unit 1134 2150 E Bell Rd Phoenix AZ 85022

SCHENKEL, SUZANNE CHANCE, retired natural resource specialist; b. Phila., Mar. 12, 1940; d. Henry Martyn Chance II and Suzanne (Sharpless) Jameson; m. John Lackland Hardinge Schenkel, June 15, 1963 (div. 2002); children: John Jr., Andrew Chance. BS in Edn., Tufts U., 1962. Tchr. Roland Pk. Country Sch., Balt., 1962-65; exec. dir. Mass. Citizens' Com. for Dental Health, Springfield, 1981-83; pub., editor Women's Investment Newsletter, Longmeadow, Mass., 1985-89; pub. affairs officer USDA's Soil Conservation Svc., Amherst, Mass., 1990-93; resource conservationist conservation & ecosys. assistance divsn. USDA's Natural Resources Conservation Svc., Washington, 1993-97; ops. partnership liaison East Regional Office, Beltsville, Md., 1997—2002; ret., 2002. Staff Merchant Marine and Fisheries com. U.S. Ho. of Reps., Washington, 1993. Author Wetlands Protection and Management Act. Chmn. Longmeadow (Mass.) Conservation Commn., 1984-90; supr. Hampden County (Mass.) Conservation Dist., 1985-90; bd. dirs., v.p. League of Women Voters of Mass., Boston, 1974-85; exec. com. Water Supply Citizens' Adv. Com.; adv. bd. Water Resources Authority, Mass., 1979-90; bd. dirs. Alliance for Chesapeake Bay, 2001. Mem. Soil and Water Conservation Soc., Nat. Assn. Conservation Dists. Episcopalian. Avocations: golf, tennis, sailing. Home: 304 W Coral Trace Cl Delray Beach FL 33445

SCHEPARTZ, ALANNA, biochemist, educator; b. NYC, Jan. 9, 1962; m. Thomas E. Schrader; 1 child, Abigail BS, SUNY, Albany, 1982; PhD in Chemistry, Columbia U., 1987. NIH fellow Calif. Inst. Tech., 1988; asst. prof. Yale U., New Haven, Conn., 1988-92, assoc. prof. chemistry, 1992-94, Milton Harris assoc. prof. chemistry, 1994-95, prof., 1995—. And prof. Howard Hughes Med. Inst., 2002—. Contbr. numerous articles to profl. jours. Recipient Presdl. Young Investigator award NSF, 1991, Camille and Henry Dreyfus Teacher-Scholar award, 1993; David and Lucille Packard Found. fellow, 1991, Eli Lilly Biochemistry fellow, 1991, Alfred P. Sloan Rsch. fellow, 1994, Howard Hughes Med. Inst. grantee for chemistry, 2002. Mem. Am. Chem. Soc. (Arthur C. Cope Scholar award 1995, Eli Lilly award 1997). Achievements include rsch. in bioorganic chemistry. Office: Dept Chemistry Yale Univ PO Box 208107 New Haven CT 06520-8107 Office Phone: 203-432-5094. Office Fax: 203-432-3486.

SCHEPPELE, KIM LANE, law educator; AB, Barnard Coll., 1975; MA, U. Chgo., 1977, PhD in Sociology, 1985. Asst. prof. sociology Bucknell U., 1980—84; rsch. assoc. Ctr. for Social Scis. Columbia U., 1980; asst. prof. sociology U. Mich., 1985—86, assoc. prof. polit. sci., 1990—96, Arthur F. Thurnau assoc. prof. polit. sci. and pub. policy, 1993—96; co-dir. Program on Gender and Culture Ctrl. European U., Budapest, 1996—98; prof. law and sociology U. Pa. Law Sch., Phila., 1996—2004, John J. O'Brien prof. of comparative law and sociology, 2004—. Contbr. articles to profl. jours. Mem.: Am. Polit. Sci. Assn., Nat. Constitution Ctr., Am. Sociological Assn., Assn. Am. Law Schs., Law and Soc. Assn. Office: U Pa Law Sch 3400 Chestnut St Philadelphia PA 19104 Office Phone: 215-898-7674. Office Fax: 215-573-2025. E-mail: kimlane@law.upenn.edu.

SCHEPS, LYNN RUTH, dancer, educator; b. Passaic, N.J., Aug. 9, 1949; d. Saul Oscar Leibowitz and Phyllis Selma Eisenberg; m. Sanford Wayne Scheps, Mar. 18, 1976; children: Lori, Leigh. BA, Fairleigh Dickinson U., Madison, N.J., 1971. Dir. dance Pine Brook Country Club, NJ, 1964—65; dir. dramatics Hickory Hill Country Club, Totowa, NJ, 1965—70; tchr. dance Niki Simon Sch. of Dance, Passaic, NJ, 1965—79; dir. drama Camp Trupin, Conn., 1971; social dir. Hazlet Social Club, NJ, 1975—77; dir. dance Shadybrook Club, Livingston, NJ, 1975—77; tchr. dance Bayshore Acad. Dance, Holmdel, NJ, 1970—2006; social dir. Breakwater Club, Elko, NJ, 1995. Adj. dance prof. Brookdale Coll., Lincroft, NJ, 2005; tchr. dance Holmdel Recreation, NJ, 2001—06, Marlboro Recreation, NJ, 2005—06. Mem.: Profl. Dance Tchrs. Assn., Dance Tchrs. Assn., Dance Educators of Am. Avocations: reading, theater, beach. Office Phone: 732-739-2829.

SCHERER, BEVERLY, retired elementary school educator; b. NYC, Dec. 12, 1931; d. Fredrick Herman and Nettie Schlam; m. Charles Samuel Adler (dec.); children: Amy Scotti, Jeffrey Adler; m. Arthur Scherer; 1 stepchild, Steven. BA in Edn., Queens Coll., Flushing, NY, 1953. Buyers asst. Weisberg-Jaffee, NYC, 1953—54; prodn. asst. Julius Pollock Greeting Cards, Long Island City, NY, 1954—58; mid. sch. tchr. Solomon Schechter Sch. Queens, Flushing, NY, 1968—92; ret., 1992. Substitute tchr. All Star Acad., Delray Beach, Fla., Donna Klein Hebrew Acad., Delray Beach. Contbr. poetry to lit. publs. Rec. sec. Citizens for Social Responsibility, Delray Beach, Fla., 1999—; campaign worker South County Dem. Club, Delray Beach, 1999—; rec. sec. Sisterhood Temple Emeth, Delray Beach, 1999—. Photograph hung in Delray City Hall. Mem.: Bus. Women, Delray Photography Club. Jewish. Avocation: writing. Home: 12 Valencia Delray Beach FL 33446

SCHERER, DEANNA, principal; b. Quinter, Kans., June 10, 1963; d. John Albert and Margaret Ann Feldt; m. John Patrick Scherer, July 27, 1985; children: Jenna, Jordan, Jaclyn, Jentry. BS in Biology, Emporia State U., Kans.; MEd, Benedictine Coll., Atchison, Kans., 2002. Sci. educator Midway H.S., Denton, Kans., 1993—2004; prin. Midway Elem., Denton, 2003—, Doniphan West Middle Sch., Denton, 2004—. Mem.: Kans. Assn. Elem. Sch. Prins., Kans. Assn. Secondary Sch. Prins., United Sch. Adminstrs. Avocations: reading, gardening. Office: Midway Schs 642 Hwy 20 East Denton KS 66017

SCHERGER, NICOLE, mathematics educator; b. Dixon, Ill., Apr. 2, 1976; d. Bruce and Ellen Scherger. AS, Kishwaukee Coll., Malta, Ill., 1994—96; BS in Math., Loyola U., Chgo., 1996—98, MS in Math., 2002—03; MA in Tchg., Rockford Coll., Ill., 2000—05. Math. tchr. Bur. Valley HS, Manlius, Ill., 2000—02; asst. prof. math. Elgin CC, Ill., 2003—. Mem.: Ill. Math. Assn. Two-Yr. Colls. Office: Elgin CC 1700 Spartan Dr Elgin IL 60123 Business E-Mail: nscherger@elgin.edu.

SCHERSTEN, KATHERINE ANNE, volunteer; b. Eau Claire, Wis., Sept. 22, 1941; d. Robert John Conley and Bettie Margaret Conley (Jobs) Helis; m. H. Donald Schersten, Jan. 20, 1973. Student, Nat. U. Mex., Mexico City, 1962; BA, St. Mary's Dominican Coll., New Orleans, 1964. Cert. tchr. La., Fla. Tchr. Orleans Sch. Bd., New Orleans, 1964; tchr. 5th grade Colegio Karl Parrish, Barranquilla, Colombia, 1964-65; tchr. Academia La Castellana, Caracas, Venezuela, 1965-67; ESOL tchr. Lang. Inst., Madrid, 1967-68, ESOL tchr., owner Caracas, 1968-69; tchr. Colegio Internacional de Caracas, 1968-73. Acad. olympics moderator Edn. Found., Sarasota, 1984—; mem. appeals bd. Sarasota County Sch. Bd., 1984—85. Mem. Sarasota Civic League, 1984—; campaign mgr. Tax Collector, Sarasota, 1984, 1988, 1992; bd. dirs. Edn. Found., Sarasota, 1996—2002, chmn. bd. dirs., 2001—02; chmn. bd. govs. Sr. Friendship Ctrs., 1997—99; chmn. adv. bd. Van Wezel Performing Arts Hall, 1990; pres. Women's Resource Ctr., 1985—90. Named to Hall of Fame, Cmty. Video Archives, 2001; recipient Cert. of Recognition, County of Sarasota, 1992, 1994. Mem.: AAUW (pres. 1982—84), Hispanic Am. Assn. (pres. bd. dirs. 1986—87, Cmty. award 1985), Sr. Friendship Ctrs. Found. (trustee 1995—2000), Exxon Annuitants Club (pres. bd. dirs. 1992—94). Roman Catholic. Avocations: volunteering, reading.

SCHETLIN, ELEANOR M., retired associate dean; b. NYC, July 15, 1920; d. Henry Frank and Elsie (Chew) Schetlin. BA, Hunter Coll., 1940; MA, Tchrs. Coll., Columbia U., 1942, EdD, 1967. Playground dir. Dept. Parks, N.Y.C., 1940-42; libr. Met. Hosp. Sch. Nursing, N.Y.C., 1943-44, dir. recreation and guidance, 1945-58, historian Alumnae Assn., 2000—06; coord. student activities SUNY, Plattsburgh, 1959-63, asst. dean students, 1963-64; asst. prof., coord. student personnel svcs. CUNY, Hunter Coll., 1967-68; asst. dir. student personnel Columbia U., Coll. Pharm. Scis., N.Y.C., 1968-69, dir. student personnel, 1969-71; assoc. dean students Health Scis. Ctr. SUNY, Stony Brook, 1971-73, asst. v.p. student svcs., 1973-74, assoc. dean students, dir. student svcs., 1974-85. Founding mem. Sea Cliff unit 300 Nassau County Aux. Police; founding mem. Nassau NOW Women of Color Task Force. Author: Myths of the Student Personnel Point of View, The Peter Principle and Student Personnel Work; contbr. articles to profl. jours. Recipient NOW Alliance PAC award, 1991, 1999, Lifetime Achievement award, Nassau NOW, 1992, Task Force Women of Color award, NOW, 1994. Mem.: So. Poverty Law Ctr., Wellesley Ctrs. Rsch. Women, Nat. Women's History Project, Women's Environment and Devel. Orgn., Nat. Mus. Women in the Arts. Home: 60 Hildreth Pl East Hampton NY 11937

SCHEUBLE, KATHRYN JEAN, social worker, family therapist; b. Pitts., Sept. 4, 1951; d. Charles Joseph and Ann Mary (Powers) S. BA in Social Work, Pa. State U., 1973; MSW, Ohio State U., 1982; postgrad. cert., U. Pitts., 1997. Lic. social worker, Pa.; cert. home and sch. visitor, Pa. Foster care caseworker Family and Children's Svcs., Pitts., 1973-80; clin. instr. child psychiatry Ohio State U. Dept. Psychiatry, Columbus, 1982-86; chief social worker Western Psychiat. Inst., U. Pitts. Med. Ctr., 1986—. Vol. Carnegie Museum, Pitts., 1992-93, Columbus Ensemble Theater, 1985-86. Mem. NASW, Nat. Alliance for the Mentally Ill. Pa. Assn. Social Workers. Avocation: travel. Office: Western Psychiat Inst & Clinic 3811 Ohara St Pittsburgh PA 15213-2593

SCHEUERER, DIANE THOMPSON, home economics educator; b. Stuart, Fla., Jan. 23, 1943; d. Frances Earl Thompson and Ida Ann (Minschke) Nall; m. Daniel Thomas Scheuerer, June 11, 1966; children: Daniel "Todd", David W. BS, Barry Coll., 1965. cert. vocat. home econ. tchr., Fla. Tchr. Melbourne (Fla.) High Sch., 1965-66, Southwest Jr. High, Melbourne, 1966-67, Cen. Cath. High Sch., Melbourne, 1971-79; tchr. edn. of teenage parents Brevard County Sch. Bd., Melbourne, 1979—. Adv. bd. mem. Child Care Aide Adv. Com., South Brevard, Fla., 1990—. Active West of EauGallie Civic Assn., Melbourne, 1986—, Ascension Cath. Women's Guild, Melbourne, 1990—. Recipient Nat. Second Place award Nat. FEdn. Indep. Bus., Washington, 1990, Second Place Entrepreneurship award Fla. Coun. on Econ. Edn., Tapma, 1991, Martha Schenck Priv. Enterprise Edn. award U. Cen. Fla., Orlando, 1992, Nat. Hon. Mention award Joint Coun. on Econ. Edn., New Orleans, 1992, Burps, Bibs, Bonnets Leavey award Freedoms Found., Beverly Hills, 1992. Mem. Am. Home Econ. Assn. (local arrangements com.), Fla. Vocat. Assn., Fla. Home Econs. Assn., Cen. Fla. Home Econs. Assn. (sec. 1992—), Brevard Vocat. Assn. Roman Catholic. Avocations: gardening, sewing, club work. Office: Sch Bd Brevard County 1400 Commodore Blvd Melbourne FL 32935-4122

SCHEUNEMAN, CHRISTINE A., lawyer; b. Kansas City, Mo., Dec. 30, 1950; BA, Univ. Kansas, 1972; JD, DePaul Univ., 1981. Bar: Ill. 1981, Calif. 1984. Ptnr., chmn. Orange County Litigation group Pillsbury Winthrop Shaw Pittman, Costa Mesa, Calif. Mem. nat. panel of arbitrators Am. Arbitration Assn. Pres. bd. dir. Orange County Chamber Orch. Mem.: Order of the Barristers. Office: Pillsbury Winthrop Shaw Pittman 7th Fl 650 Town Ctr Dr Costa Mesa CA 92626 Office Phone: 714-436-6814. Office Fax: 714-436-2800. Business E-Mail: christine.scheuneman@pillsburylaw.com.

SCHEXNAYDER, CHARLOTTE TILLAR, state legislator; b. Tillar, Ark., Dec. 25, 1923; d. Jewell Stephen and Bertha (Terry) Tillar; m. Melvin John Schexnayder Sr., Aug. 18, 1946; children: M. John Jr., Sarah Holden, Stephen. BA, La. State U., 1944, postgrad., 1947-48. Asst. editor La. Agrl. Extension, Baton Rouge, 1944; editor The McGehee (Ark.) Times, 1945-46, 48-53; editor, co-publisher The Dumas (Ark.) Clarion, 1954-85, pub., 1985-99; mem. Ark. Ho. of Reps., Little Rock, 1985-99, asst. speaker pro tem, 1995—. Pres. Ark. Assn. Women, 1955, Nat. Newspaper Assn., Washington, 1991-92, Ark. Press. Assn., Little Rock, 1982, Nat. Fedn. Press Women, Blue Springs, Mo., 1977-78, Litte Rock chpt. Soc. Profl. Journalists, 1973; mem. pres.'s coun. Winrock Internat., 1990—; chmn. Dumas Area Cmty. Found., 2000-02; pres. Main Street Dumas. Editor: Images of the Past, 1991. 1st woman mem. Ark. Bd. Pardons and Parole, 1975-80; mem. Ark. Legis. Coun., 1985-92; bd. dirs. Women's Found. Ark., sec. 1999—; bd. dirs. Chicot-Desha Port Indsl. Com.; v.p. Desha County Mus., 1989—; dir. Dumas Indsl. Found., 1986—; exec. com. Ark. Ctrl. Radiation Therapy Inst., 1991-92; mem. adv. bd. Ark. Profl. Women Achievement, 1992—; vice chair Ark. Rural Devel. Commn., 1991-96, chair 1996-97; mem. Winrock Internat. Adv. Coun., 1991—; founding incorporator Ark. Waterways Commn., 1996—, bd. dirs.; bd. visitors Manship Sch. Commn., La. State U., 1998—; bd. dirs. Main Street Ark., Hist. Preservation Alliance Ark.; active Ark. Transitional Employment Coun., 1999—, Ark. Transitional Employment Assistance Bd., 2000; sec. Dumas Area Cmty. Fund, 2000—; bd. dirs. Enterprise Corp. for the Delta, 1999-2002, Dumas Main St., v.p.; bd. dirs. Historic Preservation Alliance Ark. 2000—; outstanding bd. mem. Ark. Main St., 2002; outstanding bd. chair Ark. Cmty. Found., 2003. Named Disting. Alumnus Ark. A&M Coll., 1971, Woman of Achievement Nat. Fedn. Press Women, 1970, Outstanding Arkansan C. of C., 1986; recipient Ark. Profl. Women of Distinction award No. Bank, Little Rock, 1990, Emma McKinney award Nation's Top Cmty. Newspaper Woman, 1980, Journalist award Nat. Conf. of Christians and Jews, 1989, Lifetime Achievement award Nat. Fedn. Press Women, 1992, Outstanding Svc. award Ark. Assn. Elem. Prins., Disting. Svc. award Ark. Press Assn., 1993, Disting. Svc. award Internat. Soc. Weekly Newspaper Editors, 1996, Golden Svc. award Ark. Press Assn., 1996, State Leadership award Ark. Waterways Commn., 1996, Horizon award League Women Voters Ark., 1998 Ernie Deane award U. Ark., 2005, Chilcote award

Ark. Cmty. Found., 2006; named to La. State U. Alumni Hall of Distinction, 1994, Journalism Hall of Fame La. State U., 1998; named one Top 100 Ark. Women, Ark. Bus., 1995-98; named Outstanding Bd. Mem. of Yr., Main Street Ark., 2002, Outstanding Bd. Mem., Ptnrs. of Ark. Cmty. Found., 2003, Extraordinary Svc. award Ark. Cmty. Found., 2006; honored Outstanding Svc. Women's Found. Ark., 2003. Mem.: Main St. Dumas (pres. 2005), Ark. Delta Coun. (chmn., pres. Dumas Main St., mem. Main St. Ark. adv. bd.), Pi Beta Phi (Crest award 1992). Democrat. Roman Catholic. Home: 322 Court St Dumas AR 71639-2718 Office: PO Box 160 Dumas AR 71639-0160 E-mail: cts@seark.net.

SCHIAVI, ROSEMARY FILOMENA, secondary school educator; b. Syracuse, N.Y., Feb. 20, 1947; d. Stefano and Rose (Falso) Schiavi; AA, Maria Regina Coll., 1967; BA, Brescia Coll., 1969; MS, Syracuse U., 1973, EdD U. S.C., 1989; cert. advanced studies tchr. edn. and curriculum devel., Syracuse U., 1987. Tchr., Syracuse City Sch. Dist., 1969-83, tchr. Meachem Sch., 1973-83, acting prin., 1979; adminstrv. intern Syracuse U./West Genesee Teaching Ctr., 1985-86; rsch. asst. U. S.C., 1986-89; asst. office of profl. devel. and field programs Syracuse U., 1984-85; asst. prof. edn., U. Evansville, Ind., 1989-94, assoc. prof. edn., dir. elem. middle sch. edn. U. Evansville, Ind., 1994—. adminstrv. intern West Genesee/Syracuse U. Teaching Ctr., 1985, Bus. Ednl. Exchange Com. Mem. exec. bd. Maria Regina Coll., pres. exec. alumni assn. Mem. AAUW, S.C. Assn. for Supervision and Curriculum Devel., Am. Fedn. Tchrs., N.Y. United Tchrs. Assn., Syracuse Tchrs. Assn., N.Y. State Assn. Tchr. Educators, Brescia Coll. Alumni Assn., Syracuse U. Alumni Assn., S.C. Alumni Assn., Ind. Assn. Tchr. Educators, Am. Edn. Rsch. Assn., Assn. Tchr. Educators, Assoc. Photographers Internat., NAFE, Audubon Soc., U. Evansville Women's Club, Phi Delta Kappa, Pi Lambda Theta. Home: 196 Elliott Cir Anderson SC 29621-3361 E-mail: lschiavi@andersonuniversity.edu.

SCHICK, ALICE EDITH (LISL SCHICK), civic leader; b. Vienna, Dec. 20, 1927; came to U.S., 1945; d. Paul and Charlotte Porges; m. Alfred Schick, July 17, 1949; children: Kenneth, Nancy, Robert, Kathryn. Student, Miss Porter's Sch. Bus., 1945-47, CUNY, 1947-49. Pres. Oak Grove PTA, 1968-69; v.p. Pinellas County Med. Aux., Clearwater, Fla., 1973-74; founding mem. Performing Arts Ctr. and Theater, Clearwater, 1982—, bd. dirs., 1982-88; visited with Refusnicks in Russia as part of Nat. Hadassah Fact Finding Team, 1988; leader in move to free Soviet Jewry, 1988—; v.p. Fla. Holocaust Mus., 2005—. Recipient Generation award State of Israel, 1978, cert. of Honor Temple B'nai Israel, Clearwater, 1981, Celebrity award Gulf Coast Jewish Family Svcs., 2006, To Life award Fla. Holocaust Mus., 2006. Mem. Hadassah (nat. v.p. 1987-89, bd. dirs. 1982—, pres. Clearwater chpt. 1974-76, pres. Fla. Cen. Region 1982-85, founders cert. 1984). Jewish. Avocations: tennis, bridge, creative knitting designs. Home and Office: 7791 Bent Grass Ct Largo FL 33777-4907

SCHIEFLER, KAREN ROSALIE, artist, educator; b. Tampa, Fla., Oct. 3, 1967; d. Louis Edward and Myrta Lind Giunta; m. Mark Schiefler, Apr. 15, 2000. AA, Hillsborough CC, Tampa, 1989; BFA in Art and Edn., U. Tampa, 1992. Cert. art tchr. K-12 Fla., 1992, ESE K-12 Fla., gifted K-12 Fla., guidance and counseling pre K-12 Fla. Art specialist Hillsborough County Sch. Sys., Tampa. Grantee, Arts Coun. Hillsborough County, 2003—04, Hillsborough Edn. Found., 2004—06. Mem.: NEA, Am. Fedn. Tchrs., Classroom Tchrs. Assn., Hillsborough Art Educators Assn., Omicron Delta Kappa, Kappa Delta Pi. Democrat. Christian. Avocations: painting, sculpting, exercise. Office: Hillsborough County 901 W Kennedy Blvd Tampa FL 33629 Office Phone: 813-872-5364. Personal E-mail: schieflers@hotmail.com.

SCHIELE, MICHELE M., not-for-profit fundraiser, medical association administrator; b. 1967; Grad., Boston U. Coll. Communication, 1989, Northwestern U. Sch. Communication, 1995. V.p. & assoc. dean devel. U. Chgo. Biol. Sciences Divsn./U. Chgo. Hospitals, 2003—. Active in YWCA, Chgo. Named one of 40 Under 40, Crain's Chgo. Bus., 2006. Office: U Chgo Hospitals 5841 S Maryland Ave Chicago IL 60637-1470 also: U Chgo Divsn Biol Sciences 5812 S Ellis St Chicago IL 60637 Office Phone: 773-702-4767. Office Fax: 773-702-1670. E-mail: mschiele@medmail.uchicago.edu.*

SCHIER, MARY JANE, science writer; b. Houston, Mar. 10, 1939; d. James F. and Jerry Mae (Crisp) McDonald; B.S. in Journalism, Tex. Woman's U., 1961; m. John Christian Schier, Aug. 26, 1961; children— John Christian, II, Mark Edward. Reporter, San Antonio Express and News, 1962-64; med. writer Daily Oklahoman, also Oklahoma City Times, 1965-66; reporter, med. writer Houston Post, 1966-84; sci. writer, univ. editor U. Tex. M.D. Anderson Cancer Ctr., 1984—. Recipient award Tex. Headliners Club, 1969, Tex. Med. Assn., 1972-74, 76, 78, 79, 80, 82 Tex. Hosp. Assn., 1974, 82, Tex. Public Health Assn., 1976, 77, 78, others. Mem. Houston Press Club Ednl. Found. (pres 1992—). Lutheran. Home: 9742 Tappenbeck Dr Houston TX 77055-4102 Office: 1515 Holcombe Blvd Houston TX 77030-4009

SCHIESS, BETTY BONE, priest; b. Cin., Apr. 2, 1923; d. Evan Paul and Leah (Mitchell) Bone; m. William A. Schiess, Aug. 28, 1947; children: William A. (dec.), Richard Corwine, Sarah. BA, U. Cin., 1945; MA, Syracuse U., 1947; MDiv, Rochester Ctr. for Theol. Studies, 1972. Ordained priest Episcopal Ch., 1974. Priest assoc. Grace Episc. Ch., Syracuse, NY, 1975; mem. NY Task Force on Life and Law (apptd. by gov.), 1985—; chaplain Syracuse U., 1976-78, Cornell U., Ithaca, NY, 1978-79; rector Grace Episc. Ch., Mexico, NY, 1984-89. Cons. Women's Issues Network Episc. Ch. in US, 1987—; writer, lectr., cons. religion and feminism, 1979—. Author: Take Back the Church, Indeed The Witness, 1982, Creativity and Procreativity: Some Thoughts on Eve and the Opposition and How Episcopalians Make Ethical decisions, Plumline, 1988, Send in the Clowns, Chrysalis, Journal of the Swedenborg Foundation, 1994, Cassandra in the Temple, Chrysalis, Journal of the Swedenborg Foundation, 1998, Why Me, Lord: One Woman Ordination to the Priesthood with Commentary and Complaint, 2003; contbr. forward to book, A Still Small Voice! Women Ordination and the Church, Frederick W. Schmidt Jr., 1996. Bd. dir. People for Pub. TV in NY, 1978, Religious Coalition for Abortion Rights; trustee Elizabeth Cady Stanton Found., 1979; mem. policy com. Coun. Adolescent Pregnancy; mem. NY State Task Force Life and the Law, 1983-96. Recipient Gov. award Women of Merit in Religion, 1984, Ralph E. Kharas award ACLU Ctr., NY, 1986, Goodall disting. alumna award & Hills Sch., 1988, Human Rightes award Human Rights Commn. of Syracuse and Onondaga County, NY, 1989; inducted into Nat. Women's Hall of Fame, 1994. Mem. NOW (Syracuse), Internat. Assn. Women Ministers (dir. 1978 pres. 1984-87), Na'amat US (hon. life), Mortar Bd., Theta Chi Beta. Democrat. Home and Office: 6987 Van Antwerp Dr Cicero NY 13039-9739 E-mail: wschiess@twcny.rr.com.

SCHIEWE, MISTI D., secondary school educator; d. Bill Buckley and Susie Moon; m. Reid Schiewe; 1 child, Sabrina L. BS in Math., Western Oreg. U., Monmouth, 1999; MS in Math. Edn., Oreg. State U., Corvallis, 2001. Tchr. secondary sch. SE Island Sch. Dist., Thorne Bay, Alaska, 2002—; tchr. math. Jefferson County Sch. Dist., Madras, Oreg. Mem.: Nat. Coun. Tchrs. Math. Avocations: volleyball, scrapbooks.

SCHIFF, JAN PEDERSEN, conductor, voice educator; b. Chicago, Dec. 26, 1945; d. Charles Albert and Thelma Jane Pedersen; m. Tom Schiff, Oct. 1, 1988. BA in Music Edn./Voice, Augsburg Coll., Mpls., 1968; MusM in Conducting, U. Colo., 1974. Vocal music tchr. DuSable Upper Grade Ctr., Chgo., 1968—69; music tchr., choral dir. Kelvyn Pk. H.S., Chgo., 1969—70; choral cons. Oslo Barnasangerlag, 1970—71; music tchr. Broomfield Secondary Sch. for Boys, London-Woolwich, 1971—72; choral/vocal instr. Wilkes Coll., Wilkes-Barre, Pa., 1974—76; choral condr. Somerset County Coll., Northbranch, NJ, 1976—77; vocal instr. L.A. City Coll., 1977—86; choral condr., vocal instr. Long Beach City Coll., Calif., 1978—86; founder/condr. Hollywood Chorale, Calif., 1980—86; music dir. Cmty. Congl. Ch., Tiburon, Calif., 1987—91; voice class instr. Coll. Marin, Kentfield, Calif., 1988—93; founder, artistic dir. SingersMarin, Mill Valley, Calif., 1987—. Pvt. vocal instr., Mill Valley, Calif., 1976—; guest condr. Singer: (cd of original songs) Dreamer. Mktg. com. Marin Symphony, San Rafael, Calif., 1996—2001. Recipient Bronze Halo award, So. Calif. Motion Picture Coun., 1983, Susan B. Anthony award for cultural achievement in Hollywood, Hollywood Bus. Women, 1985, Vol. of Yr. award, Mill Valley C. of C., 2001, Cert. of Commendation, Marin County Women's Commn., 2002, Milley award for contbns. to music in Mill Valley, Milley Award Com., 2003; scholar Peggy Christiansen Benson Meml. scholarship, Music Dept., Augsburg Coll., 1967. Mem.: Internat. Fedn. of Choral Music, Music Tchrs.s Assn. Calif., Conductors Guild, Chorus Am., Nat. Assn. Tchrs. of Singing (L.A. chpt. pres. 1983—84, San Francisco chpt. treas. 1989—91), Am. Choral Dirs. Assn. (life), Beta Chi Epsilon, Pi Kappa Lambda. Avocations: gardening, gourmet cooking. Home: 308 Shoreline Hwy Mill Valley CA 94941 Office: SingersMarin 1038 Redwood Hwy Bldg A Mill Valley CA 94941 Office Phone: 415-383-3712. Office Fax: 415-383-7289. Business E-Mail: sing@singersmarin.org.

SCHIFF, JANIS BOYARSKY, lawyer; b. Bridgeport, Conn., July 6, 1958; BA cum laude, Brandesi U., 1980; JD, Suffolk U. Law Sch., 1983. Bar: Md. 1983, DC 1984, US Dist. Ct. (DC and Md.) 1985. Law clerk to Hon. Alan Wilner Md. Ct. of Appeals, 1883—1984; ptnr. Holland & Knight LLP, Washington, dir. on dir. com., dep. sect. leader, real estate sect., runs Rising Star mentoring and leadership program. State dir., gov. affairs chair, state ops. chair for Md., DC, No. Va. Internat. Coun. Shopping Ctrs., 1996—99; past pres. Suburban Md. Chpt. of Comml. Real Estate Women; active mem. Women in Real Estate; mem. Nat. Network Comml. Real Estata; serves on Washington, DC Dist. Coun. of Urban Land Inst.; instr. Allan Berman Inst., John Hopkins U.; bd. dir. Georgetown U. Law Sch. Advanced Comml. Leasing Inst.; lectr. in field. Comment editor Suffolk Transnational Law Jour., 1982—83; contbr. articles to profl. jours. Named one of Top Women in Comml. Real Estate, Real Estate Forum Mag. Mem.: Women's Bar Assn., DC Bar, ABA, Md. Bar Assn., Montgomery County Bar Assn. Office: Holland & Knight LLP 2099 Pennsylvania Ave NW Ste 100 Washington DC 20006 Office Phone: 202-862-5994. Business E-Mail: jschiff@hklaw.com.

SCHIFF, JAYNE NEMEROW, underwriter; b. NYC, Aug. 8, 1945; d. Milton E. Nemerow and Shirley (Kaplan) Wachtel; m. Albert John Schiff, Mar. 7, 1971; children: Matthew Evan, Kara Anne. BS in Bus., Marymount Coll., 1981; M.Profl. Studies in Elem. and Spl. Edn., Manhattanville Coll., 1995. Corp. sec., treas. Albert J. Schiff Assocs., Inc., NYC, 1970—78; field underwriter Mut. NY Fin. Svcs., Greenwich, Conn., 1973—90; freelance employee benefit cons. Greenwich, 1990—99; sr. account exec., contr. Nylex Benefits, Stamford, Conn., 1999—2005; dir. exec. benefits The NIA Group, LLC, 2005—. Regional dir. mktg., MONY Fin. Svcs., NYC, 1978-79; tutor HELP program Manhattanville Coll., 1996-2000. Bd. dirs. NY League Bus. Profl. Women, 1976-78, Temple Sinai, Stamford, Conn., 1979-84; leader Webelos Cub Scouts, 1977-78; treas. Ann. Mothers Bd. Benefit Greenwich Acad., 1988, upper sch. acquisitions chmn., 1989, chmn. spl. acquisitions Greenwich Acad. Benefit, 1990-91, chmn. advt., 1992; ESL tutor Lit. Vols. Am., ESL tutor, trainer, 1993; co-chair U. Rochester Parents Coun., 1993-96. Named Conn.'s Outstanding Young Woman, 1979. Mem. LWV, Am. Soc. Chartered Life Underwriters, NY Ctr. Fin. Studies (bd. dirs.), NYC Life Underwriters Assn. (bd. dirs. 1977-78). Jewish. Avocations: sailing, knitting, playing piano, reading. Office: Nylex Benefits 301 Tresser Blvd Stamford CT 06901-3284 Personal E-mail: jayneschiff@earthlink.net.

SCHIFF, MOLLY JEANETTE, artist, researcher; b. Chgo., Oct. 19, 1927; d. David Nathan and Beatrice (Aisenberg) Rice; m. Haskell Schiff, June 12, 1946; children: Darryll Nat, Lesley Nan, Brad Scott, Rae Ellyce Student, U. Chgo., 1958—63, student, 1968—69; BFA, Art Inst., Chgo., 1962, MFA, 1963, MA Edn., 1969. Cert. Art tchr. Ill. Instr. art Chgo. Bd. Edn. and Park Dist., 1962—66, Jewish Cmty. Ctrs., Chgo., 1962—65; pvt. practice Chgo., 1962—; instr. art New Trier Extensions, Winnetka, Ill., 1965—78, Evanston Art Ctr., Ill., 1965, St. Tarsissus Sch., Chgo., 1968, Young Artists Studio Art Inst., Chgo., 1968—69, Ill. Visually Handicapped Inst., Chgo., 1968—73, Govs. State U., Monee, Ill., 1975—76. Cons. Markal Corp., Chgo., 1968-94; cons., presenter, regional rep. Shiva Corp., Chgo., 1984-87 Prin. works include Facades, 1971 (Honors award 1971), Drawn Paintings, 1976 (Honors award 1976), Acapulco Balcony, 1978 (Honors award 1980), Mexican Scenics, 1980 (Honors award 1980), Figures on Paper, 1988-89 (Honors award 1989), Low Seam, 1988 (Honors award), Later Impressions, 1989 (Honors award), Acapulco Nite View, 1989 (Honors award), Impressions, 1990 (Honors award), Mannequin Cut Outs, 1990 (Honors award), Mannequin Soiree 1992 (Honors award 2000), Union League, 1993 (Honors award), Jarvis Still Life, 1993 (Honors award), Blue Moon, 1997 (Honors award), Triplets, 1997 (Honors award 1998), Sunset at Pushkar, 1998 (Honors award 1999), Rain Forest, Brazil, 2003 (Honors award 2003), I'm Not Square, 2003 (Honors award 2003-2004), I Forgot My Sketch Book, 2003 (Honors award 2004), V is For Vashti, 2003 (Honors award 2003-2004), I Remember Purim-A Visual Narrative, 2006 (Honors award 2006); exhbns. include Biennale Internat., Florence, Italy, 2003 Pres. I.G.C. chpt. Am. Jewish Congress, Chgo., 1955 Recipient Cash award Foremost Corp., 1963, Ill. Dept. Energy and Natural Resources, 1988, Purchase award Rotarian Mag., 1978, Ill. State Mus., 1978, Nite View, 1989, Honors award U.S. State Dept., 1996-2000. Mem. Archives, Figurative Art League, Nat. Mus. Women in Arts, Chgo. Artists Coalition, Chgo. Soc. Artists, Am. Jewish Artists Assn. (program dir. 1970-74, 89-93, pres. 2004-2005, exhbn. com. 2006), Dutch Folk Art Assn. (cons., juror 1979), Alumni Assn. Art Inst. Chgo., Am. Jewish Artists Club, Scan Chgo. (bd. dir. 1988-91) Avocations: tour directing, travel. Office Phone: 312-274-0930. E-mail: mollyjart@msn.com.

SCHIFF, STACY, writer; b. Adams, Mass., Oct. 26, 1960; married. BA, Williams Coll. Sr. editor Simon and Schuster. Author: Saint-Exupery: A Biography, 1994 (Pulitzer prize finalist for Biography, 1995), Véra (Mrs. Vladimir Nabokov): Portrait of a Marriage, 1999 (Pulitzer prize for Biography, 2000), A Great Improvisation: Franklin, France, and the Birth of America, 2005 (George Washington Book prize, 2006); contbr. The New Yorker, The N.Y. Times Book Rev., The Times Literary Supplement, others. Fellow, Guggenheim Found., 1996, Nat. Endowment for the Humanities.*

SCHIFFER, CLAUDIA, model; b. Rheinberg, Germany, Aug. 25, 1970; m. Matthew Vaughn, May 25, 2002; 2 children. Model Guess? jeans, 1989, Revlon cosmetics, Chanel; amb., internat. spokesperson L'Oréal; co-owner Fashion Cafe restaurants. Ptnr. Fashion Cafe, N.Y.C., London, New Orleans, Barcelona, Jakarta, Manila, others; host World Music Awards with Luke Perry, Monte Carlo, 1995. Runway debut in Chanel fashion show, 1990; appeared on covers of Mademoiselle, Cosmopolitan, Vogue, and over 100 others; creator series of exercise videos (with Kathy Kaehler) Claudia Schiffer's Perfectly Fit, 1996; pub.: (pictorial book) Memories. Hon. bd. dirs. Dishes AIDS; spokesperson Nat. Breast Cancer Coalition.

SCHIFFER, LOIS JANE, lawyer; b. Washington, Feb. 22, 1945; d. Benjamin and Clara (Goldberg) S. BA, Radcliffe Coll., 1966; JD, Harvard U., 1969. Bar: Mass. 1969, D.C. 1971, U.S. Supreme Ct. 1973. Legal svcs. lawyer Boston Legal Assistance Project, 1969-70; ct. law clk. D.C. Circuit Ct., Washington, 1970-71; assoc. Leva, Hawes, Symington, Martin, Oppenheimer, Washington, 1971-74; lawyer Ctr. for Law and Social Policy, Washington, 1974-78; chief gen. litig. sect. Land and Natural Resources divsn. U.S. Dept. Justice, Washington, 1978-81, spl. litig. counsel, 1981-84; gen. counsel Nat. Pub. Radio, Washington, 1984-89; ptnr. Nussbaum & Wald, Washington, 1989-93; acting asst. atty. gen. environ. and natural resources divsn. U.S. Dept. Justice, Washington, 1993-94, asst. atty. gen. environ. and natural resources divsn., 1994-2001; sr. v.p. for pub. policy Nat. Audubon Soc., 2001—02; ptnr. Baach Robinson & Lewis, Washington, 2002—05; gen. counsel Nat. Capital Planning Commn., Washington, 2005—. Adj. prof. environ. law Georgetown U. Law Ctr., Washington, 1986—; lectr. Harvard Law Sch., 2004; bd. dirs. DC Appleseed, Keystone Ctr., Internat. Sr. Project. Bd. dirs. Women's Legal Def. Fund, 1975-86, Am. Rivers, 1989-93; bd. dirs. ACLU/NCA, 1982-93, pres., 1988-90. Fellow Am. Bar Found.; mem. ABA (del.), Am. Law Inst., Phi Beta Kappa Democrat. Jewish. Avocations: reading, movies, hiking. Home: 4640 Brandywine St NW Washington DC 20016-4449 Office Phone: 202-482-7223. Business E-Mail: lois.schiffer@ncpc.gov.

SCHIFFMAN, KAREN ASHDOWN, secondary school educator; d. Don Ashdown and Theresa Marie Hill; m. Lynn F. Schiffman, Dec. 16, 1967; children: Travis Reed, Michael Troy, KariLyn, Susan Elizabeth, Joshua Ashdown. BA, Utah State U., Logan, 1969; MEd, U. Phoenix, Ariz., 1998. Cert. educator Utah Office Edn., 2005. Dept. chairperson Manti H.S., Utah, 1990—. Adj. instr. Snow Coll., Ephraim, Utah, 1990—; selection com. for prin. Manti H.S., 1992, selection com., 2001—; sch. rep. South Sanpete Edn. Assn., Manti, 2000—01; com. mem. Inclusion Project, Manti, 2001—. City rep. Rep. Party, Ephraim, 2000; presidenct Relief Soc. LDS Ch., Ephraim, 2002—06. Mem.: Nat. Coun. Tchrs. English. Avocation: poetry. Office: Manti High School 100 W Templar Way Manti UT 84642 Office Phone: 435-835-2281. Business E-Mail: karen.schiffman@ssanpete.k12.ut.us.

SCHIFFMAN, SUSAN STOLTE, medical psychologist, educator; b. Chgo., Aug. 24, 1940; d. Paul R. and Mildred (Glicksman) Stolte; m. Harold Schiffman (div.); 1 child, Amy Lise; m. H. Troy Nagle, July 22, 1989. BA, Syracuse U., 1965; PhD, Duke U., 1970. Lic. psychologist, N.C. Postdoctoral fellow Duke U., Durham, N.C., 1970-72, asst. prof., 1972-77, assoc. prof., 1978-83, full prof., 1983—. Cons., mem. adv. bd. Nestle, Vevey, Switzerland, 1990-98, Sense of Smell Inst., N.Y.C., 1986—, and others. Author: Introduction to Multidimensional Scaling: Theory, Methods and Applications, 1981, Flavor Set-Point Weight Loss Cookbook, 1990. Nat. Inst. Aging grantee, 1972—. Mem. Assn. Chemoreception Scis., Internat. Behavioral Neurosci. Soc., Soc. for Neurosci. Office: Duke U Med Sch PO Box 3259 Durham NC 27710-3259 E-mail: sss@duke.edu.

SCHIFFNER, ADRIENNE ANITA, art historian, educator; b. Jersey City, June 7, 1947; d. Thomas B. and Anita (Grosvenor) McAndrews; m. Richard Burchett (div.); children: Anita Claussen, Arianne Burchett; m. Charles Robert Schiffner, Jan. 22, 1983. BA in Art History, Ariz. State U., 1989, MA in Art History, 2001. Cert. CC tchr. Ariz. Dir. Main Trail Galleries, Scottsdale, Ariz., 1972—73; archivist Frank Lloyd Wright Found., Scottsdale, 1977—83; v.p. Charles Schiffner Arch. Ltd., Phoenix, 1983—2000; program coord. pres. cmty. enrichment programs Ariz. State U., Tempe, 2000—03, instr. art history, 2003—04; tchr. art history Xavier Coll. Prep., Phoenix, 2002—. Lectr. in field; adj. faculty mem. Rio Salado CC, Phoenix, 2003—06. Chmn. living rm. restoration project Taleisin West, Scottsdale; mem. Phoenix Arts Commn.; mem. adv. bd. Ariz. State U. Art Mus., Tempe, 1998—2000; chmn. grants com. Phoenix Arts Commn., 1985—88; bd. dirs. Ariz. chpt. Nat. Soc. Arts and Letters, 1992—95; bd. dirs. Ballet Ariz., Phoenix, 1999—2001. Taliesin fellow, Frank Lloyd Wright Found., 1973—83. Mem.: Coll. Art Assn., Soc. Archtl. Historians, French Heritage Soc. (pres.), Ariz. State U. Coll. Fine Arts Alumni Assn. (co-pres. 2002—). Home: 5202 E Osborn Phoenix AZ 85018 Office: Xavier Coll Prep 4710 N 5th St Phoenix AZ 85012

SCHILD, NANCY LOIS, realtor, music educator; b. Hartford, Conn., May 31, 1947; d. William and Elsie Lena Brusick; m. William Adrian Schild, Mar. 19, 1947. B in Music Edn., Fla. State U., 1967; MS, Portland State U., 1976; MusM in Conducting, U. Wis., Milw., 2001. Music tchr. Orlando (Fla.) Luther H.S. and Middle Sch., 1996—99, Hales Corner (Wis.) Luth. Sch., 1996—99, choir dir., 1997—2002; music tchr. St. Joan Antida H.S., Milw., 1999—2002; accompanist, part-time organist Christ Our Redeemer Luth. Ch., Temple Terrace, Fla., 2002—; music tchr. Christ Our Redeemer Luth. Sch., Temple Terrace, 2004—; realtor Century 21, Tampa, Fla., 2004—05, Exit Realty Advisors, Tampa, 2005—. Founder, condr. Hales Corners Children's Choir, 1997—2001; singer Master Singers Milw., 1997—99, Milw. Choral Artists, 1999—2002. Mem.: Temple Terrace C. of C. (amb. 2005—), Greater Tampa Assn. Realtors, Nat. Assn. Realtors, Temple Terrace Svc. League. Republican. Lutheran. Avocations: golf, oil painting. Office: Exit Realty Advisors 11502 N 56th St Tampa FL 33617

SCHILD, SYLVIA G., retired elementary school educator, realtor; b. LA, Nov. 3, 1925; d. Harry Bernstein and Eva Chaden; widowed; 1 child, Rachelle Heartte. AA, L.A. City Coll., 1947; BA, U. Calif., Berkeley, 1950; postgrad., Sorbonne, Paris, 1952. Tchr. Berkwood Coop. Sch., Berkeley, Calif., 1957—63, Oakland (Calif.) Pub. Schs., 1963—76; ret., 1976; realtor Crump & Jones, Berkeley, 1976—82. Mem. task force Cesar Chavez Pk., Berkeley; bd. dirs. Point Isabel Dog Owners, Richmond-East Bay, 2003—05, sec., founder, pres., 1985—2003; mem. Cal Dog, Calif., 2002—03. Named Sylvia Schild Day named in her honor, City of Berkeley, 2000; named one of Outstanding Berkeley Women, Commn. Status of Women, 2002. Mem.: Calif. Ret. Tchrs. Assn. Democrat. Jewish. Avocations: travel, music. Home: 1321 Carlotta Ave Berkeley CA 94703

SCHILLER, BARBARA, retired special education educator; b. NYC, Jan. 1, 1943; d. Harry M. and Lee C. Browner; m. Charles Philip Schiller, July 16, 1967; children: Andrew Barry, Zachary Alan. BS in Edn., SUNY, Cortland, 1964; MS in Edn. of Visually Impaired, Hunter Coll., 1971. Tchr. children with limited vision NYC Bd. Edn., 1964—95. Sculpture exhbns., SUNY, Purchase, 1980—2005, sculpture in two-person show, Gallery at Marmara, N.Y.C., 2003, Cirque d'Art, N.Y., 2003, sculpture juried show, Katonah Mus., N.Y., 2003, sculpture in one-woman shows, John C. Hart Libr., Shrub Oak, N.Y., 2003, sculpture in permanent collections, Amsterdam Whitney Gallery, N.Y.C., 2004. Mem. bd. gov. Temple Beth Shalom, Mahopac, NY, 1995—2004. Named Woman of Yr., Temple Beth Shalom, Mahopac, NY, 2004; recipient NY award for sculpture, Knickerbocker Artists, multiple awards 4 first place, Quilts Along the Bay, Barnegat, NJ, 2003—04. Mem.: Katonah Mus., Nat. Women in Arts, Hadassah (life), No. N. Mex. Quilters Guild, State Quilter Guild NJ, No. Star Quilters Guild (3d pl. 2004, 2d pl. 2006, 2006). Hadassah. Avocations: reading, interior decorating, music, doll making. Home: 3600 Curry St Yorktown Heights NY 10598

SCHILLER, PAMELA ANN, physical education educator; d. Raymond and Dorothy Schiller. BS in Phys. Edn., SUNY BRockport, 1979; MA. in Phys. Edn., East Carolina U., Greenville, N.C., 1993. Cert. curriculum specialist, adminstr. N.C., 1996. Phys. edn. specialist J.W. Smith Elem. Sch., Cove City, NC, 1985—. Water safety instr. New Bern Golf and Country Club, New Bern, 1986—2003; a+ fellow U. N.C., Greensboro, 2002—. Mem.: Profl. Educators of N.C., NCAAPHERD, Craven County Humane Soc. Democrat-Npl. Catholic. Office: JW Smith Elementary School 150 Kooncetown Rd Cove City NC 28523 Office Phone: 252-514-6466. Office Fax: 252-514-6469. E-mail: pam.schiller@craven.k12.nc.us.

SCHILLER, SOPHIE, artist, graphics designer; b. Moscow, Feb. 10, 1940; came to U.S., 1974; d. Samuel and Rebecca (Lagovier) Elinson; m. Mikhail Schiller, Apr. 29, 1960; 1 child, Maria. Student, Moscow State Art Sch., 1954-58; MA, Moscow Inst., 1964; cert. in graphic and book design, Mass. Coll. Art, Boston, 1977. Graphic artist Progress Pub. House, Moscow, 1964-70, Popular Sci. mag., Moscow, 1970-74; artist, graphic designer Boston, 1974—. Freelance graphic designer Harvard Press, Boston, M.E. Sharpe Pub., N.Y., Ginn Press, Simon & Schuster, Boston, Tech. Rev., MIT, Cambridge, Mass. One person shows include Galleria del Corso, Rome, 1974, Wennigar Gallery, Boston, 1977; exhibited in group shows Taganka Exhibit, Moscow, 1962, Moscow Artists Union, 1962, Am. Painters in Paris Exhbn., 1975, Unofficial Art from Soviet Union, Washington, 1977, Mariland Gallery, St. Mary's City, 1977, Bard Coll., N.Y., 1991, Rose Art Mus., Brandeis U., Boston, 1992, Tofias Gallery, Boston, 1994, Zimmerly Art Mus., Rutgers U., N.J., 1995; group shows include The Dorland-Haight Gallery, Milton, Can., 1993; author (illustrator): The Russian Alphabet, 2004 Mem. Nat. Mus. Women in the Arts. Avocations: travel, hiking, collecting children's art. Home: 63 University Rd Brookline MA 02445-4532 Personal E-mail: sschiller@rcn.com.

SCHILLER, VIVIAN, Internet company executive; BA in Russian and Soviet Studies, Cornell U., 1983; MA in Russian, Middlebury Coll., 1984. Russian interpreter, prodn. coord. Turner Broadcasting Systems, Inc., v.p., gen. mgr. Turner Original Productions, exec. v.p. CNN productions; sr. v.p., gen. mgr. Discovery Times Channel The NY Times Co., 2002—05, sr. v.p. TV and video, 2005—06, exec. v.p., gen. mgr. Discovery Times Channel, 2005—06; sr. v.p., gen. mgr. NYTimes.com, 2006—. Recipient five Emmy awards, two Peabody awards. Office: The NY Times Co 229 W 43rd St New York NY 10036*

SCHILLING, AMY JO, private school educator; b. Aberdeen, SD, May 3, 1973; d. Gerald Curtis and Jolaine June Hegge; m. Brandon David Schilling, Dec. 30, 1995; 1 child, Gunar Jameson. BS in Psychology, No. State U., Aberdeen, 1996; MA in Orgnl. Mgmt., U. Phoenix, 1999. Trainer Marc Ctr., Mesa, Ariz., 1996—97, lead behavioral health technologist, 1997—98, human resource generalist, 1998—99; hiring coord. Am. West Airlines, Tempe, Ariz., 1999; case mgr. Maricopa County Long Term Care, Phoenix, 1999—2000; tchr. James Madison Prep. Sch., Tempe, 2000—. Office: James Madison Prep Sch 5815 S McClintock Dr Tempe AZ 85283-3227

SCHILLING, EMILY BORN, editor, professional society administrator; b. Lawton, Okla., Oct. 2, 1959; d. George Arthur and Sumiko (Nagamine) Born; m. Mark David Schilling, June 26, 1995. BS, Ball State U., 1981. Cert. coop. communicator Nat. Rural Electric Coop. Assn. Feature writer The News-Sentinel, Fort Wayne, Ind., 1981-83; wire editor The Noblesville (Ind.) Daily Ledger, 1983; staff writer Ind. Statewide Assn. Rural Electric Coops., Indpls., 1983-84, mng. editor, 1984-85, editor, 1985—. Author: Power to the People, 1985. Mem. Coop. Communicators Assn. (Michael Graznak award 1990), Internat. Assn. Bus. Communicators (award of excellence dist. 7 1985), Women's Internat. Network of Utility Profls. (pres. 1999, Mem. of Yr. 1999, Power award 1994), Nat. Electric Coops. Statewide Editors Assn. Office: Ind Statewide Assn RECs 720 N High School Rd Indianapolis IN 46214-3756

SCHILTZ, POLLY JO, special education educator; b. St. Paul, Nov. 27, 1953; d. Gareth David and Janet Ann Hiebert; m. Leon Joseph Schiltz, Aug. 8, 1981; children: Nicholas Joseph, Katherine Jo. BS, Mankato State U., 1975, MS, 1980. Spl. edn. tchr. Austin (Minn.) Pub. Sch., 1976—77, Northwood-Kensett (Iowa) Cmty. Sch., 1977—. Adj. prof. Buena Vista U., Storm Lake, Iowa, 2000—, Morningside Coll., Sioux City, Iowa, 2002—. Mem.: ASCD, NEA, Coun. Exceptional Children. Avocations: swimming, horseback riding, walking, reading, bicycling. Home: 84444 130th St Glenville MN 56036 Office: Northwood-Kensett Cmty Sch PO Box 289 704 7th St N Northwood IA 50459

SCHIMBERG, BARBARA, organizational development consultant; b. Chgo., Nov. 30, 1941; d. David and Tybe Zisook; children from previous marriage: Brian Hodes, Valery Lodato; m. A. Bruce Schimberg, Dec. 29, 1984. BS, Northwestern U., 1962. Ptnr. Just Causes, cons. not-for-profit orgns., Chgo., 1978-86. Cons. in philanthropy, community involvement, and organizational devel., 1987—; Chgo. cons. Population Resource Ctr., 1978-82. Mem. women's bd. dirs. Mus. Contemporary Art; bd. dirs., vice chmn. Med. Rsch. Inst. Coun., Michael Reese Med. Ctr.; bd. dirs., chmn. Midwest Women's Ctr.; trustee Francis W. Parker Sch.; bd. dirs. Women's Issues Network Found., 1991-98, pres., 1993-94; mem. adv. bd. Med. Rsch. Inst. Coun., Children's Meml. Hosp. Mem. ACLU (adv. com.), Women's Bd. U. Chgo. Office: 132 E Delaware Pl Apt 5002 Chicago IL 60611-4944 Personal E-mail: bschimberg@sbcglobal.net.

SCHIMEK, DIANNA RUTH REBMAN, state legislator; b. Holdrege, Nebr., Mar. 21, 1940; d. Ralph William and Elizabeth Julia (Wilmot) Rebman; m. Herbert Henry Schimek, 1963; children: Samuel Wolfgang, Saul William. AA, Colo. Women's Coll., 1960; student, U. Nebr., Lincoln, 1960-61; BA magna cum laude, U. Nebr., Kearney, 1963. Former tchr. and realtor; mem. Nebr. Legislature from 27th dist., Lincoln, 1989—; chmn. govt., mil. and vets. affairs com. Nebr. Legislature, Lincoln, 1993-94, 99—, vice chair urban affairs com., 1995-98. Dem. Nat. committeewoman, 1984-88; chmn. Nebr. Dem. Com., 1980-84; mem. exec. com. Dem. Nat. Com., 1987-88; past pres., sec. bd. dirs. Downtown Sr. Ctr. Found., 1990-96; mem. exec. bd. Midwestern Legis. Conf., 1995—, co-chair health and human svcs. com., 1995-96; exec. dir. Nebr. Civil Liberties Union, 1985; former bd. dirs. Nebr. Repertory Theater, Exon Found., 1997-2000; mem. adv. bd. Martin Luther Home, 1997-2003; chair Midwestern Legis. Conf. Coun. of State Govts., 2000-01, co-chair com. intergovtl. affairs; mem. Midwest Interstate passenger Rail Commn., 2001-05; mem. exec. bd. Coun. State Govts., 2000-05; chair NCSL Task Force on Initiative and Referendum, 2001-02; bd. dirs. Habitat Humanity, 2006—. Toll fellow, 1999; recipient Outstanding Alumni award U. Nebr., 1989, Tribute award YWCA, 1992, Friend of Psychology award N.E. Psychol. Assn., 1998, Woman of Yr. award Nova Chpt. Bus. & Profl. Women, 1999, Disting. Svc. award Nat. Guard Assn., 2000, Woman of Distinction award Soroptomists, 1999, Legis. of Yr. award N.E. Dental Hygienists Assn., 2001, Disting. Svc. award N.E. League of Municipalities, 2002, Lincoln Interfaith Leadership award, 2003, Harold Steck award ARC of N.E., 2004, Alice Paul award Lancaster Status of Women Commn., 2006, Civil Libertarian of Yr. award ACLU Nebr., 2006, others. Mem. Nat. Conf. State Legislators Women's Network (bd. dirs. 1993-96, 1st vice chmn.), PEO, Soroptomists, Delta Kappa Gamma (hon.), Mortar Bd. (cmty. advisor 1998, hon.), Rotary Internat. Democrat. Unitarian Universalist. Home: 437 Lone Tree Dr Lincoln NE 68512 Office: Dist # 27 State Capital Lincoln NE 68509 Office Phone: 402-471-2632. Business E-Mail: dschimek@unicam.state.ne.us.

SCHIMMELMAN, JANICE G., art historian; b. Helena, Ark. m. John B. Cameron. PhD, U. Mich., Ann Arbor, 1980. Prof. art history Oakland U., Rochester, Mich., 1976—. Author: (book) The Tintype in America 1856-1880 (American Philosophical Society), American Photographic Patents 1840-1880 (Mautz Publishing), Architectural Books in Early America (Oak Knoll Press), American Imprints on Art through 1865 (G.K. Hall), (monograph) Art in the Early English Magazine (American Antiquarian Society), Architectural Treatises and Building Handbooks Available in American Libraries and Bookstores Through 1800 (American Antiquarian Society), A Checklist of European Treatises on Art and Essays on Aesthetics Available in America Through 1815 (American Antiquarian Society). Fellow, Libr. Co. Phila., 1987, NEH, 1987; grantee, U.S. Dept. Interior, 1982—84, Oakland U., 1982, 1984, 1985, 1987, 1991, 1999, NEH, 1984—85. Mem.: Mich. Photographic Hist. Soc. (editor The Photogram 2003—), Daguerrian Soc. Office: Oakland University Department of Art and Art History Rochester MI 48309-4401 Office Phone: 248-370-3379.

SCHIMPF, KATHLEEN, elementary school educator; b. Passaic, NJ, Dec. 13, 1957; d. Michael Joseph and Carol Elizabeth Schimpf. BA in Phys. Edn. and Health, William Paterson U., Wayne, NJ, 1979. Tchr. phys. edn. and health St. Mary's Sch., Paterson, NJ, 1979—90; tchr. math., social studies St. Stan;s Sch./Garfield Cath. Acad., 1990—2002; tchr. phys. edn. and health Alexander Hamilton Acad., Paterson Pub. Sch., 2002—. Mem. sch. leadership coun. Alexander Hamilton Acad., 2004—06. Named Tchr. of Yr., Newark Archdiocese, 1995—96, 1998—99. Mem.: AAHPERD, Am. Alliance Health Edn., Nat. Alliance Sports and Phys. Edn., NJ Edn. Assn. Avocations: golf, tennis, gardening, travel, reading. Home: 84 Summit Ave Elmwood Park NJ 07407 Office: Alexander Hamilton Acad Paterson Pub Schs 11-27 16th Ave Paterson NJ 07501 Personal E-mail: k40sunshine@aol.com.

SCHINDEL, ALICE, social worker; b. Chgo., Sept. 26, 1936; d. Leonard Earl and Mina Hecht Andrews; m. Donald M. Schindel; children: Susan Yost, Judi Harris, Andrea Glickman. BS in Edn., U. Ill., 1958, MSW, 1977. LCSW Ill. Tchr. Chgo. Pub. Schs., 1958—62; social worker Counsel for Jewish Elderly, Chgo., 1977—82; social worker home health Highland Park (Ill.) Hosp., 1982—83; social worker Family Svc. South Lake County, Highland Park, 1985—2006. Michal Reese Hosp. fellow, 1983—85, Family Inst. Chgo. fellow, 1985—87. Mem.: NASW, Am. Assn. Marital Family Therapists (cert.). Avocations: reading, swimming, bridge. Home: 636 Rice Highland Park IL 60035 Office: 480 Elm Pl Ste 208 Highland Park IL 60035

SCHINDERLING, SANDRA, mathematics educator; BA, SD State U. Cert. tchr. Tex. Tchr. Guam Pub. Sch. Dist., Yigo, 1990—95, Tucson, Spring Ind. Sch. Dist., Houston. Algebra 2 team leader Spring Ind. Sch. Dist., Houston, tim; dept. chair FBLG Mid. Sch., Yigo; gymnastic coach Huron Pub. Sch. Dist. Office Phone: 281-586-1300.

SCHINDLER, EVELYN, medical/surgical nurse, educator; b. Bogalusa, La., June 4, 1941; d. Jewell Lavelle and Edith Evelynn (Bahm) Sumrall; m. Edmund Karl Schindler, Sept. 1, 1962; children: Mark Edmund, Cindy Maria, Stefan Karl. Diploma, Mather Sch. Nursing, New Orleans, 1962; BSN, Clayton State Coll., Morrow, Ga., 1992. Cert. enterostomal therapy nurse. Charge nurse Bapt. Hosp., New Orleans, enterostomal therapy nurse Miami; enterostomal therapy coord. So. Regional Med. Ctr., Riverdale, Ga. Mem. Nursing Wound Ostomy Continence Assn.(S.E. region sec. and newsletter editor 1983-87, S.E. region trustee 1989-92, S.E. region pres. 1992-94).

SCHINDLER, GAIL LEWIS, psychologist; b. Houston, Sept. 3, 1930; d. Abraham Boris Lewis and Mary Frances (Dorenfield) Lowry; m. William Joseph Schindler, Dec. 17, 1972; children— Steven Sean Callahan, Cynthia Gail Orman, Marc Benjamin Schindler. Student, So. Meth. U., 1947-48, Rice U., 1949-51; B.A., U. Houston, 1952, M.Ed., 1969, Ed.D., 1979. Tchr. Houston Ind. Sch. Dist., 1955-63, Spring Branch Ind. Sch. Dist., Houston, 1963-65, Houston Community Coll., 1972; tchr., staff devel. counselor, coordinator Deer Park Ind. Sch. Dist., Tex., 1967-77, cons., 1980—; research asst., teaching fellow U. Houston, 1975; sole practice psychology, Houston, 1980—; cons. Tex. Edn. Assn., Houston, 1973, Pre-Menstrual Syndrome Clinic, Houston, 1983. Mem. Southwest Civic Club, Houston; contbr. Democrats of Tex. Paige Besch grantee Baylor Coll. Medicine, 1978-79. Mem. Houston Psychol. Assn., Tex. Psychol. Assn., Am. Psychol. Assn., Soc. for Clin. and Exptl. Hypnosis, NOW. Democrat. Jewish. Avocations: reading; aerobics; bridge; theater; grandchildren. Home and Office: 3210 Hickory Brook Ln Humble TX 77345-1130 Office Phone: 281-361-3340. E-mail: drbill@ev1.net.

SCHINDLER, HOLLY SUZANNE, freelance/self-employed writer; b. Springfield, Mo., Jan. 10, 1977; d. John Whitmore and Edith Joanne (Jackson) Schindler. BA in English, S.W. Mo. State U., 1999, MA in English, 2001. Instr. S.W. Mo. State U., Springfield, 1999—2000, tutor, 2001; freelance writer Springfield, 2001—.

SCHINDLER, JO ANN, librarian, director; BA, U. Hawaii, Manoa; MLS, U. Calif., Berkeley. With San Francisco Pub. Libr. Sys., LA County Libr. Sys.; head Bus., Sci., and Tech. Sect. Hawaii State Pub. Libr. Sys., dir., state libr. Named Hawaii State Pub. Libr. Sys. Employee of Yr., 1999, MCI Cybrarian of Yr. for State of Hawaii. Mem.: ALA, Hawaii Libr. Assn. Office: Hawaii State Pub Libr Sys 235 S Beretania St Honolulu HI 96813*

SCHINDLER, JUDI(TH) (JUDITH KAY SCHINDLER), public relations executive, marketing professional, consultant; b. Chgo., Nov. 23, 1941; d. Gilbert G. and Rosalie (Karlin) Cone; m. Jack Joel Schindler, Nov. 1, 1964; 1 child, Adam Jason. BS in Journalism, U. Ill., 1964. Assoc. editor Irving Cloud Publs., Lincolnwood, Ill., 1963-64; asst. dir. publicity Israel Bond Campaign, Chgo., 1965-69; v.p. pub. relations Realty Co. of Am., Chgo., 1969-70; dir. pub. relations Pvt. Telecomm., Chgo., 1970-78; pres. Schindler Comm., Chgo., 1978—. Del. White House Conf. on Small Bus., Washington, 1980, 86; mem. adv. bd. Entrepreneurship Inst., Chgo., 1988—92. Appointee small bus. com. Ill. Devel. Bd., 1988—89. Named Nat. Women in Bus. Adv. SBA, 1986, Chgo. Woman Bus. Owner of Yr., Continential Bank and Nat. Assn. Women Bus. Owners, 1989, Ill.; named to Hall of Fame, Nat. Assn. of Women Bus. Owners, 2003. Mem. Nat. Assn. Women Bus. Owners (pres. Chgo. chpt. 1980-81, nat. v.p. membership 1988-89), Publicity Club Chgo., Alpha Epsilon Phi. Office: Schindler Comm 500 N Clark St Chicago IL 60610-4288 Office Phone: 312-464-9660. Business E-Mail: jschindler@schindlercommunications.com.

SCHINDLER, TERI, sports association executive; m. Mike Gorman, 1988. Grad. summa cum laude, U. Notre Dame, Ind., 1983. News/sports desk runner 1984 Summer Olympic Games, 1984; exec. prodr. women's basketball Conn. Pub. TV; mgr. Big East TV Network; dir. broadcasting NBA Entertainment, 1997—2004; v.p. programming, mktg. Nat. Basketball Assn. Entertainment, N.Y.C., 2004—. Freelance writer specializing in women's and environ. issues. Contbr. articles to newspapers including the Boston Globe. Nominee 8 Emmoy awards for basketball, football; recipient Emmy award (New Eng. region), 1993, Emmy award, NBC Sports, Olympics Sydney, 2000; scholar, Rotary scholar, 1983. Mem.: Phi Beta Kappa. Home: 5 Truesdale Lake Dr South Salem NY 10590-1317

SCHINZEL, SUE MADELINE, nurse; b. Oct. 16, 1938; d. Richard Bernard and Madeline (Helmer) Nalty; m. Donald Lee Schinzel, Oct. 20, 1962; children: David, Denise, Daniel. Diploma, St. Josephs Hosp., Omaha, Nebr. Cert. RN. Office RN Prairie Clin., Omaha, Nebr., 1960-64; staff RN St. Joseph's Hosp., Omaha, 1961-62; pm team leader Doctors Hosp., Omaha, 1968-72; office RN Specialist Clin., Omaha, 1972-82; health clin. RN Interim Health, Omaha, 1989—. Vol. RN ARC, Omaha, Nebr., 1980-89, Democratic Party, 1958-61, Redcross, 1988. Recipient Hon. plaque West YMCA, 1986. Avocations: sewing, tennis, basketball. Office: Interim Health 7604 Pacific St Omaha NE 68114-5421

SCHIOLDAGER, AMY LEE, investment company executive; BSc in Bus. Adminstrn., Fin., Calif. State U., Hayward, 1989. Registered rep. series 7, 63, 24, 3 NASD, 2000. Fund acct. Barclays Global Investors, Orinda, Calif., 1989—2001, mng. dir., chief investment officer, equity indexing San Francisco, 1991—. Mem. adv. bd. Russell Investment Group, Tacoma, 2002—. Author: Active Index Investing: The Unique Challenges of US Equity Index Management, Real Estate Investing: The REIT Way. Recipient award, Wall St. Jour., 1989. Mem.: Fin. Women's Assn. Office: Barclays Global Investors 45 Fremont St San Francisco CA 94105 Business E-Mail: amy.schioldager@barclaysglobal.com.

SCHIRMEISTER, PAMELA, dean, language educator; d. Charles and Barbara Schirmeister; m. Everett Seymour, June 11, 1994; children: Sara Seymour, Charles Seymour. BA, Yale U., New Haven, 1980, PhD, 1988. Reporter Time, Inc., Paris, 1981—83; prof. Middlebury Coll., Vt., 1988—89, NYU, NYC, 1989—98; assoc. dean Yale U. Grad. Sch., New Haven, 1999—; lectr. English Yale U., 1999—. Vis. prof. U. Tuebingen, Germany, 2005, U. Konstanz, 1998—99. Author: (literary criticism) The Consolations of Space: The Place of Romance in Hawthorne, Melville and James, Less Legible Meanings: Between Poetry and Philosophy in the Work of Emerson, (short stories) in The Quarterly, vols. 1, 2 and 6; editor: (edition) Representative Men, by Ralph Waldo Emerson. Recipient Excellence Tchg., NYU, 1992; fellow, Fulbright Commn., 1994; Peterson fellow, Am. Antiquarian Soc., 1994—95. Office: Yale Univ PO Box 208236 New Haven CT 06520 Office Phone: 203-432-9098. Office Fax: 203-432-7765. Business E-Mail: pamela.schirmeister@yale.edu.

SCHIRMER, HELGA, retired chiropractor; b. Stavanger, Norway, Oct. 7, 1923; came to U.S., 1927; DC, Palmer Coll., Davenport, Iowa, 1964. Lic. chiropractor, N.Y., N.J., Mass., P.R., N.H., Fla. Practiced chiropractic, N.Y.C., 1965-96. Mem. N.Y. State Chiropractic Assn., Internat. Chiropractic Assn., Garden State Chiropractic Soc., N.J. Coun. Chiropractic. Address: 2200 N Central Rd Ste 12 Fort Lee NJ 07024-7557

SCHIRMER-SMITH, SARA JANE (SALLY SCHIRMER-SMITH), director; b. Saginaw, Mich., June 5, 1963; d. Charles Albert and Jeanne Marie (Ashbaugh) Schirmer; m. Steven John Smith, June 20, 1992; children: Katherine Margaret Smith, Matthew John Schirmer Smith. BS, Ctrl. Mich. U., 1985; MEd, Springfield Coll., 1989. Dir. student activities Bay Path Coll., Longmeadow, Mass., 1989—2002, asst. dean students, 1996—2002, dir. career svcs., 2002—. Bd. mem. Children's Ministries First Ch. Christ, Longmeadow. Mem. AAUW, Zonta Internat. Avocations: tennis, golf, art, reading, travel. Home: 33 Farmlea Rd Longmeadow MA 01106-1837 Office: Bay Path Coll 588 Longmeadow St Longmeadow MA 01106-2212 E-mail: salsmith@baypath.edu.

SCHLAFF, BARBARA E., lawyer; b. Detroit, Mar. 21, 1950; BA, Brandeis U., 1971; attended, U. Mich. Law Sch.; JD, Boston Coll., 1974. Bar: D.C. 1979, Md. 1980. Ptnr., Employee Benefits, Taxation practices Venable LLP, Balt. Mem. adv. com. Univ. Balt. Law Sch. Officer Ctr. for Jewish Edn.; trustee, past v.p. Har Sinai Congregation. Mem. ABA, Md. State Bar Assn., D.C. Bar, Bar Assn. Balt. City. Office: Venable LLP 1800 Mercantile Bank & Trust Bldg 2 Hopkins Plz Baltimore MD 21201 Office Phone: 410-244-7494. Office Fax: 410-244-7742. Business E-Mail: beschlaff@venable.com.

SCHLAFLY, PHYLLIS STEWART, writer; b. St. Louis, Aug. 15, 1924; d. John Bruce and Odile (Dodge) Stewart; m. Fred Schlafly, Oct. 20, 1949; children: John F., Bruce S., Roger S., Phyllis Liza Forshaw, Andrew L., Anne V. BA, Washington U., St. Louis, 1944, JD, 1978; MA, Harvard U., 1945; LLD, Niagara U., 1976. Bar: Ill. 1979, DC 1984, Mo. 1985, U.S. Supreme Ct. 1987. Syndicated columnist Copley News Svc., 1976—. Broadcaster Spectrum, CBS Radio Network, 1973—78; commentator Matters of Opinion sta. WBBM-AM, Chgo., 1973—75, Cable TV News Network, 1980—83; pres. Eagle Forum, 1975—. Author, pub.: Phyllis Schlafly Report, 1967—; author: A Choice Not an Echo, 1964, The Gravediggers, 1964, Strike From Space, 1965, Safe Not Sorry, 1967, The Betrayers, 1968, Mindszenty The Man, 1972, Kissinger on the Couch, 1975, Ambush at Vladivostok, 1976, The Power of the Positive Woman, 1977, First Reader, 1994, Turbo Reader, 2001, Feminist Fantasies, 2003, The Supremacists: The Tyranny of Judges and How to Stop It, 2004; editor: (book) Child Abuse in the Classroom, 1984, Pornography's Victims, 1987, Equal Pay for Unequal Work, 1984, Who Will Rock the Cradle, 1989, Stronger Families or Bigger Government, 1990, Meddlesome Mandate: Rethinking Family Leave, 1991. Del. Rep. Nat. Conv., 1956, 1964, 1968, 1984, 1988, 1992, 1996, 2004, alt., 1960, 1980, 2000; 1st v.p. Nat. Fedn. Rep. Women, 1964—67; nat. chmn. Stop ERA, 1972—; mem. Ronald Reagan's Def. Policy Adv. Group, 1980, Commn. on Bicentennial of U.S. Constn., 1985—91, Adminstrv. Conf. U.S., 1983—86; pres. Ill. Fedn. Rep. Women, 1960—64; mem. Ill. Commn. on Status of Women, 1975—85. Named Woman of Achievement in Pub. Affairs, St. Louis Globe-Democrat, 1963; named one of 10 Most Admired Women in World, Good Housekeeping poll, 1977—90, 100 Most Important Women of 20th Century, Ladies Home Jour., 1998; recipient 10 Honor awards, Freedom Found., Brotherhood award, NCCJ, 1975. Mem.: DAR (nat. chmn. Am. history 1965—68, nat. chmn. bicentennial com. 1967—70, nat. chmn. nat. def. 1977—80, 1983—95), ABA, Ill. Bar Assn., Phi Beta Kappa, Pi Sigma Alpha. Office: Eagle Forum 7800 Bonhomme Ave Saint Louis MO 63105-1906 Office Phone: 314-721-1213. E-mail: phyllis@eagleforum.org.

SCHLAIN, BARBARA ELLEN, lawyer; b. NYC, May 28, 1948; d. William and Evelyn (Youdelman) S. BA, Wellesley Coll., 1969; MA, Columbia U., 1970; JD, Yale U., 1973. Bar: N.Y. 1974, U.S. Dist. Ct. (so. dist.) N.Y. 1974, U.S. Ct. Appeals (2d cir.) 1975, U.S. Dist. Ct. (ea. dist.) N.Y. 1977. Assoc. firm Donovan Leisure Newton & Irvine, N.Y.C., 1973-76, Graubard Moskovitz McGoldrick Dannett & Horowitz, N.Y.C., 1976-79; atty. McGraw-Hill, Inc., N.Y.C., 1979-80, asst. gen. counsel, 1980-86, v.p., assoc. gen. counsel, asst. sec., 1986—. Sec. proprietary rights com. Info. Industry Assn., 1982-83. Author: outlines Practicing Law Inst., 1983, 84, 85, 86, 88; contbr. numerous articles to profl. jours. Bd. dirs., v.p., sec. Dance Rsch. Found., N.Y.C., 1983-86, chmn., 1986-98. Phi Beta Kappa scholar, Durant scholar Wellesley Coll., 1967-69. Mem. ABA, Assn. Am. Pubs. (lawyers com. 1979—), Assn. Bar City N.Y. (comm. law com. 1985-88). Office: The McGraw-Hill Companies Inc 1221 Avenue Of The Americas New York NY 10020-1095

SCHLEGEL, GENA MARIE, paramedic; b. Summit, N.J., Jan. 26, 1979; d. John William Schlegel and Geraldann Peins. BS in health sci., Eastern Coll., Pa., 2001; MEd, Eastern U., Pa., 2003; PhD candidate, Capella U., Minn., 2005—. Nat. registered paramedic; cert. athletic trainer. Part time paramedic Layfette Ambulance, King of Prussia, Pa., 2002—, Plymouth Ambulance, Pa., 2002—; athletic trainer Benchmark Med., Malmore, Pa., 2003—04; paramedic Norberth Ambulance, Ardmore, Pa., 2004—; asst. athletic trainer Eastern U., St. Davids, Pa., 2004—05; part time paramedic Second Alarmers Roach Squad, Abington, Pa., 2006—. Asst. coach field hockey Eastern U., St. Davids, Pa., 2005—. Sec. Rednar Eye Co., Wayne, Pa., 2001—06, ambulance lt., 2002—03, ambulance capt., 2003—04, ambulance chairperson, 2004—06. Mem.: Nat. Athletic Trainers Assn. Republican. Home: 114 Bloomingdale Ave Apt 4 Wayne PA 19087 Office: Norberth Ambulance 101 SIbley Ave Ardmore PA 19004 Personal E-mail: schlegs11@aol.com.

SCHLEICHER, NORA ELIZABETH, bank executive, treasurer, accountant; b. Balt., Aug. 10, 1952; d. Irvin William and Eleanor Edna S.; m. Ray Leonard Settle Jr., July 27, 1985. AA cum laude, Anne Arundel Community Coll., 1972; BS summa cum laude, U. Balt., 1975. CPA, Md. Staff auditor Md. Nat. Bank, Balt., 1975-76, sr. staff auditor, 1976-77, supr. auditing dept., 1977-78; full charge acct. Wooden & Benson, CPA's, Balt., 1978-81; asst. to treas. First Fed. Savs. & Loan Assn., Annapolis, Md., 1981, asst. treas., 1982-83, v.p., 1984; v.p., treas. First Fed. Savs. & Loan Assn. (now First Annapolis Bank), 1984—. Bd. dirs., treas. Coll. Manor Community Assn. Mem. AICPA, Md. Assn. CPA's, Fin. Mgrs. Soc., Coll. Manor Community Assn. (bd. dirs., treas.). Methodist. Office: First Annapolis Savs Bank 1832 George Ave Annapolis MD 21401-4103

SCHLEINER, ANNE-MARIE, computer graphics designer; b. Providence, 1970; Attended, U. Michoacan, Mex., U. Kiel, U. Calif., Santa Cruz; MFA, San Jose State U. Asst. prof. interactive arts Tech. U., BC, Canada, 1999—2000; adj. faculty of digital art U. Calif., Irvine, 2001; fellow Akademie Schloss Solitude, 2003; asst. prof. U. Colo., Boulder, 2003—. Madame Polly Game Patch, 1998, Epilepsy Virus Patch, 1999, Cracking the Maze, 1999, mutation.fem, 2000, Luckykiss xxx, 2000, Skool, 2001, Snow Blossom House, 2001, Anime Noir, 2002, Velvet Strike, 2002, Parangari Cutiri, 1999—, PS2 Diaries, 2004—, OUT: Operation Urban Terrain, 2004—, Whitney Biennial, Whitney Mus. Am. Art, NY, 2004. Office: University Art & Art History University Colorado at Boulder 318 UCB Boulder CO 80309

SCHLESINGER, DEBORAH LEE, retired librarian; b. Cambridge, Mass., Sept. 13, 1937; d. Edward M. and Edith D. (Schneider) Hershoff; divorced; children: Suzanne, Richard. BA, U. Mass., 1961; MS, Simmons Coll., 1974; postgrad., U. Pitts., 1983. Reference librarian Bently Coll., Waltham, Mass., 1964-65; dir. Carnegie Library, Swissvale, Pa., 1973-77, South Park Twp. Library, Library, Pa., 1977-81, Monessen (Pa.) Library, 1981-82, Lewis & Clark Library, Helena, Mont., 1983—88, 1989—2004, ret., 2004; state librarian Mont. State Library, Helena, Mont., 1988-89. Vis. scholar Pitts. Regional Library Ctr., 1982-83. Editor Pa. Union List, 1982-83. Mem. exec. bd. Mont. Cultural Advocacy, 1983-2004. Mem. Mont. Libr. Assn. (chmn. legis. com. 1984-92, lobbyist 1992-2001), AAUW (exec. com. 1985-86). Clubs: Montana (Helena). Democrat. Avocations: flying, painting, reading, rafting, travel. Personal E-mail: dbooks@aol.com.

SCHLESINGER, HARRIET ROSE, retired psychiatrist; b. Pitts., Dec. 22, 1915; d. Monroe Jacob Schlesinger and Millie Romansky; m. Israel Alan Annis (dec.); children: Jonathan, Eleanor. BA, Wellesley Coll., Mass., 1937; MD, Tufts U., Boston, Mass., 1941. Lic. physician Mass. War rschr. Harvard Med. Sch., Boston, 1945—46; resident in psychiatry Gaebler Children's Ctr., Waltham, Mass., 1960—64, staff, 1965—86; ret., 1986. Recipient Outstanding Alumnus award, Girls' Latin Sch., 1989. Mem.: AMA, Mass. Med. Soc. Home: 100 Forest Pl # 310 Oak Park IL 60301

SCHLESS, PHYLLIS ROSS, investment banker; d. Lewis H. and Doris G. Ross; m. Aaron Backer Schless, July 7, 1970; 1 son, Daniel Lewis Ross. Cert., Neighborhood Playhouse Sch. of Theatre, 1962, N.Y. Sch. Interior Design, 1964; BA in Econs., Wellesley Coll., 1964; MBA, Stanford U., 1966. Cert. theater prodns. Am. League Theater Owners and Prodrs. Assoc. internat. fin. Kuhn Loeb & Co., N.Y.C., 1966—70; fin. cons., 1971—73; sr. fin. analyst Trans World Airlines, N.Y.C., 1974—75; corp. fin., mergers and acquisitions Lazard Freres & Co., 1976—79; dir. mergers and acquisitions Am. Can Co., Greenwich, Conn., 1979—82; v.p. mergers and acquisitions Bear, Stearns & Co., N.Y.C., 1982—84; sr. v.p. corp. acquisitions Integrated Resources, 1984—85; chmn., CEO Ross Fin. Svcs. Group Inc., 1986—; supervisory dir. Merrill Lynch HYTS Funds, 1991—96. Bd. dirs. Calvary Hosp. Fund Bd., 1990-2000, chair investment com., 1995-99; trustee A.R. Tinker Fund, 1993-2004, hon. trustee, 2004—; trustee Nat. Child Labor Com., 1981-95, chmn., 1992-94; trustee New World Found., 1986-92, chair fin. com., treas. 1988-92; bd. dirs. Stanford Bus. Sch. Assn., N.Y., 1994-2004; adj. asst. prof. NYU, 1996—, Columbia U. Sch. Bus., 2001—; bd. dirs. Nat. Found. Tchg. Entrepreneurship, metro. N.Y. chair, 2000-05. Pres. Greater Bridgeport Nat. Coun. Jewish Women, 1971-73, bd. dirs., 1974-75; bd. dirs. Girls Clubs Am., 1975-89, mem. exec. com., 1982-89, pres., 1984-86; bd. dirs. Pauline Koner Dance Co., 1979-81, So. Conn. Child Guidance Clinic, 1981-83, New Canaan United Way, 1981-83; treas. Wellesley Class '64, 1984-89. Mem. Univ. Club.

SCHLESSINGER, LAURA, radio talk show host; b. Bklyn., Jan. 16, 1947; d. Monroe and Yolanda Schlessinger; m. Lewis G. Bishop, 1982; 1 child, Deryk. BS in Biological Sciences, SUNY, Stonybrook; MS in Physiology, M Phil in Physiology, Columbia U., PhD in Physiology, 1974. Lic. in marriage and family therapy; cert. marriage, family and child counseling, U. So. Calif. Psychotherapist in private practice, L.A., Calif., 1980—90; nat. syndicated radio talk show host The Dr. Laura Schlessinger Program, 1990—; columnist Santa Barbara News Press, 2006—. Past mem. faculty U. So. Calif., Pepperdine U, instr. UCLA, UC Irvine; founder, pres. Dr. Laura Schlessinger Found., 1998- Author: Ten Stupid Things Women Do to Mess Up Their Lives, 1994, How Could You Do That?! The Abdication of Character, Courage and Conscience, 1996, Ten Stupid Things Men Do To Mess Up Their Lives, 1997, The Ten Commandments: The Significance of God's Law in Everyday Life, 1998, Damsels, Dragons, and Regular Guys, 2000, Parenthood by Proxy; Don't Have Them If You Won't Raise Them, 2000, Ten Stupid Things Couples Do To Mess Up Their Relationships, 2002 The Proper Care & Feeding Of Husbands, 2004, Bad Childhood Good Life: How to Blossom and Thrive in Spite of an Unhappy Childhood, 2006; (children's books) Why Do You Love Me?, 1999, But I Waaannt It!, 2000, Growing Up is Hard, 2001, I Hate My Life!, 2001, Where is God?, 2003; featured on The Oprah Winfrey Show, A&E Biography, Larry King Live, Lifetime's Intimate Portrait, 20/20, The Today Show, PBS, Hannity & Colmes, CBS This Morning, 48 Hours, Meet the Press with Tim Russert, Crier Today, Eye to Eye with Connie Chung, ABC This Week, Dateline; featured in Time, U.S. News and World Report, People, USA Today, The New York Times Magazine, The Los Angeles Times, The Wall Street Journal and others; featured spkr. Nat. Congressional Prayer Breakfast, Mus. Radio and Television, Claremont Inst., PBS, Nat. Religious Broadcasters, Country Radio Seminar. Named Woman of the Yr., State of Calif. 19th Dist., 2006; recipient Marconi Award for Network/Syndicated Personality of the Yr., 1997, Genii Award, American Women in Radio & Television, 1998, Israel 50th Anniversary Tribute award, 1998, Crystal Cathedral Academy award, 1998, Love of a Child award, Childhelp USA, 1998, Chairman's award, Nat. Religious Broadcasters, 2000, Nat. Heritage award, Nat. Council of Young Israel, 2001, Conservative Leadership award, Clare Booth Luce Inst., 2001, Woman of the Yr. award, 2002, Women Extrardinaire award, Internat. Women's Conf., 2004, Truth in Media award, Pacific Justice Inst., 2006. Mem.: AFTRA, SAG, Nat. Assn. At-Home Mothers (bd. adv.). Achievements include being broadcasted on approximately 300 stations with 12 million listeners; the second most popular talk show host in the country; show syndicated since June 1994; on air radio career for more than 25 years. Office: Premire Radio Networks 15260 Ventura Blvd Ste 300 Sherman Oaks CA 91403-5337*

SCHLETTE, SHARON ELIZABETH, utility company executive; b. Bklyn., May 25, 1945; d. Albert Valentine and Dorothy Lee (Jacobs) Kunz; m. Arthur F. Schlette, Oct. 12, 1985. Student, St. Johns U., 1978-82. With Consol. Edison Co., 1963-89; acctg. clk., 1963-67; dist. office teller, 1967-69; customer service rep. Consol. Edison Co., 1969-72, asst. supr. Manhattan customer service, 1972-78; unit mgr. Br. III-Westside, Manhattan customer service, 1978-81, Lincoln Center Br., 1981-82, Yorkville Br., 1982-87, unit mgr. final accounts/collections dept., 1987-89; adjustor bankcard svcs. Barnett Bank of Fla., Jacksonville, 1990-91; bus. prof. Pitney Bowes Corp., 1992—, dist. sales coord., 1999—. Mem. Nat. Rifle Assn. Republican. Home: 1257 Willow Oaks Dr W Jacksonville FL 32250-2640 E-mail: sharon.schlette@pb.com.

SCHLICHTING, CATHERINE FLETCHER NICHOLSON, librarian, educator; b. Huntsville, Ala., Nov. 18, 1923; d. William Parsons and Ethel Loise (Breitling) Nicholson; m. Harry Fredrick Schlichting, July 1, 1950 (dec. Aug. 1964); children: James Dean, Richard Dale, Barbara Lynn. BS, U. Ala., 1944; MLS, U. Chgo., 1950. Asst. libr. U. Ala. Edn. Libr., Tuscaloosa, summers 1944-45; libr. Sylacauga (Ala.) H.S., 1944-45, Hinsdale (Ill.) H.S., 1945-49; asst. libr. Centre for Children's Books, U. Chgo., 1950-52; instr. reference dept. libr. Ohio Wesleyan U., Delaware, 1965-69, asst. prof., 1969-79, assoc. prof., 1979-85, prof., 1985—, curator Ohio Wesleyan Hist. Collection, 1986—, student pers. libr., 1966-72. Author: Introduction to Bibliographic Research: Basic Sources, 4th edit., 1983, Checklist of Biographical Reference Sources, 1977, Audio-Visual Aids in Bibliographic Instruction, 1976, Introduction to Bibliographic Research: Slide Catalog and Script, 1980; info. cons. (documentary) Noble Achievements: The History of Ohio Wesleyan 1942-1992, 1992, 150 Years of Excellence: A Pictorial View of Ohio Wesleyan University, 1992. Mem. adminstrv. bd. Meth. Ch., 1973-81, chmn. adminstrv. bd., 1985—, mem. coun. on ministries, 1975-81, chmn., 1975-77, trustee, 1999—2003. Recipient Algernon Sidney Sullivan award U. Ala., 1944, Hon. Alumna award Ohio Wesleyan U., 1997; Ohio Wesleyan U.-Mellon Found. grantee, 1972-73, 84-85; GLCA Tchg. fellow, 1976-77. Mem. ALA, Ohio Libr. Assn., Midwest Acad. Libr. Conf., Acad. Librs. Assn. Ohio (dir. 1984-86), AAUP (chpt. sec. 1967-68), United Meth. Women (pres. Mt. Vernon dist. 1994-97, newsletter editor 1998-2002), Ohio Wesleyan Woman's Club (exec. bd. 1969-72, 77-79, 81-84, pres. 1969-70, sec. 1977-78), History Club (pres. 1971-72, v.p. 1978-79, 2003-04) Fortnightly Club (pres. 1975-76, 87-88, 2003-04), Am. Field Svc. (pres. Delaware chpt. 1975-76), Kappa Delta Pi, Alpha Lambda Delta. Democrat. Home: 57 Willow Brook Way S Delaware OH 43015 Office: Ohio Wesleyan U La Beeghly Library Delaware OH 43015

SCHLICHTING, NANCY MARGARET, hospital administrator; b. N.Y.C., Nov. 21, 1954; BA, Duke U., 1976; MBA, Cornell U., 1979. Adminstrv. resident Meml. Hosp. Cancer, N.Y.C., 1978; fellow Blue Cross-Blue Shield Assn., Chgo., 1979-80; asst. dirs. ops. Akron (Ohio) City Hosp., 1980-81, assoc. dir. planning, 1981-83, exec. v.p., 1983-88, Riverside Meth. Hosps., Columbus, Ohio, 1988-92, pres., COO, 1992-93, pres., CEO, 1993-96; pres. Ea. region Cath. Health Initiatives, Aston, Pa., 1996-97; exec. v.p., COO Summa Health Sys., Akron, Ohio, 1997—98; sr. v.p., chief adminstrv. officer Henry Ford Healthcare Sys., Detroit, 1998—99, exec. v.p., COO, 1999—2003, pres., CEO, 2003—, Henry Ford Hosp., 2001—03. Bd. dirs. Fifth Third Bank Corp., First Nat. Bank of Ohio, Mich. Health and Hosp. Assn., Greater Detroit Area Health Council, Walgreen Co., 2006—. Trustee Kresge Found. Office: Henry Ford Health Sys 1 Ford Pl Detroit MI 48202*

SCHLITZ, STEPHANIE ANN, adult education educator; b. Elmhurst, Ill. d. Don and Geraldine Schlitz; m. Garrick Shannon Bodine. PhD, U. Ga., Athens, 2003. Asst. prof. Bloomsburg U., Pa., 2005—. Fulbright scholar. Office Phone: 570-389-4974.

SCHLOSS, HADASSAH, auditor; b. Buenos Aires, Nov. 18, 1950; came to US, 1977; d. Moises Zysman and Sofia (Zack) Kuperwasser; m. Peter Gordon Schloss, Mar. 27, 1977; 1 child, Merav Karen (dec.). BBA in Acctg., U. Tex., Austin, 1993. Clk. State of Tex., Austin, 1990—93, adminstrv. tech. III, 1993, internal auditor I, 1993—94, internal auditor II, 1994—95, program adminstr. open records sect., 1995—2005, cost rules adminstr., 2005—. Co-chair Open Records Steering Com., Austin, 2005—; mem. Freedom of Info. Found. Tex.; mem. Electronic Recording Adv. Com., Austin. Recipient James Madison award Freedom Info. Found. Tex., 1996. Jewish. Avocations: reading mystery, suspense, biographies, sewing, cooking. Home: 6704 Roseborough Dr Austin TX 78747-4023 Office: Office of Attorney General 209 W 14th St Austin TX 78701 Address: PO Box 12548 Austin TX 78711-2548 Office Phone: 512-475-2497.

SCHLOSSBERG, CAROLINE BOUVIER KENNEDY (CAROLINE KENNEDY), writer, lawyer; b. NYC, Nov. 27, 1957; d. John Fitzgerald and Jacqueline Bouvier; m. Edwin A. Schlossberg, July 19, 1986; children: Rose, Tatiana, John (Jack) Bouvier Kennedy. Grad., Radcliffe Coll. (now part of Harvard), 1979; JD, Columbia Law Sch. Intern NY Daily News, 1977, Metropolitan Mus. Art, 1980; pres. John F. Kennedy Library Found.; chief exec. NYC Dept. Edn. Office Strategic Partnerships, 2002—; vice-chair Fund for Public Schools, N.Y.C. Author: In Our Defense- The Bill of Rights in Action, 1990, A Family of Poems: My Favorite Poetry for Children, 2005; co-author: The Right to Privacy, 1995. Co-founder Profiles in Courage Awards, 1989; hon. chairwoman Am. Ballet Theatre. Speaker at 2000 Dem. Nat. Conv. Office: Office of Strategic Partnerships Room 320 Fl 52 Chambers St New York NY 10007

SCHLOSSER, ANNE GRIFFIN, librarian; b. NYC, Dec. 28, 1939; d. C. Russell and Gertrude (Taylor) Griffin; m. Gary J. Schlosser, Dec. 28, 1965. BA in History, Wheaton Coll., Norton, Mass., 1962; MLS, Simmons Coll., 1964; cert. archives adminstrn., Am. U., 1970. Head UCLA Theater arts Libr., 1964-69; dir. Louis B. Mayer Libr., Am. Film Inst., L.A., 1969-88, dir. film/TV documentation workshop, 1977-87; head Cinema-TV Libr. and Archives of the Performing Arts, U. So. Calif., L.A., 1988-91; dir. Entertainment Resources Seminar, 1990; dir. rsch. libr. Warner Bros., 1991—2001; part-time libr. Nevada County Libr., 2002—. Project dir. Motion Pictures, Television, Radio: A Union Catalogue of Manuscript and Special Collections in the Wesern U.S., 1977. Recipient numerous grants for script indexing, manuscript cataloging, libr. automation. Mem. Soc. Calif. Archivists (pres. 1982-83), Theater Libr. Assn (exec. bd. 1983-86), Spl. Librs. Assn. Democrat. Episcopalian. Avocations: swimming, reading, dog training.

SCHLUB, TERESA RAE, minister; b. Oak Park, Ill., July 11, 1946; d. Robert Carl and Shirley Rae (Listhartke) Grupe. BA, Westmar Teikyo U., 1971; MDiv, Garrett Evangel. Seminary, Evanston, Ill., 1974. Ordained deacon United Meth. Ch., 1973, elder, 1978. Asst. minister First United Meth. Ch., Morris, Ill., 1974-76; minister Leaf River (Ill.) German Valley United Meth. Ch., 1976-82, East Jordan United Meth. Ch., Sterling, Ill., 1982-86, Paw Paw (Ill.) United Meth. Ch., 1986-89, Community United Meth. Ch., LaMoille, Ill., 1989-95, Capron (Ill.) United Meth. Ch., 1995—2000, North Boone Coop. Ministries, Poplar Grove, Ill., 1998—2000. Mem. alumni coun., sec. Garrett Evangel. Theol. Seminary, Evanston, 1974-76; mem. Conf. Bd. of Evangelism, 1974-76, founder, Schlub Ministries Bd. dirs. Green Hills coun. Girls Scouts U.S., Freeport, Ill., 1986-88, Lee County Red Cross, Dixon, Ill., 1986-89, Crossroads Counseling Ctr., Mendota, 1989-91; bd. dirs. Quad County Counseling Ctr., Princeton, 1991—, treas., 1993-94; mem. Ill. Home Extension Assn., Grundy, Ogle, Whiteside and Lee Counties, 1974-89; sec. DeKalb Dist. Com. Ordained Ministry; mem. Boone County Coun. Aging, 1997-2000, Boone County Planning Commn., 1998-2000; founder Schlub Ministries, Pathways to Paralegal, Kaplan U., 2005. Home: 4027 Albright Ln Rockford IL 61103

SCHLUCKEBIER, CAROL J., librarian; b. Seymour, Ind., Aug. 26, 1937; d. Ralph William and Frieda Henrietta Rebber; m. Bert Hilbert Schluckebier, June 23, 1962; children: Cynthia Carol, Philip Andrew. BS, Concordia Tchrs. Coll., 1959; MLS, U. Mich., 1971. Asst. libr. Seymour (Ind.) Pub. Libr., 1950—55; asst. children's libr. Oak Park (Ill.) Pub. Libr., 1955—59; tchr. Peace Luth. Sch., Saginaw, Mich., 1959—62; tchr., libr. St. Lorenz Luth. Sch., Frankenmuth, Mich., 1962—66; libr. Saginaw (Mich.) H.S., 1967—80; libr., tchr. Arthur Hill H.S., Saginaw, 1980—92; libr. North Mid. Sch., Saginaw, 1992—2003, ret., 2003; prin., owner Bloomin Treasures, Birch Run, Mich., 2003—. Cons. in field. Pres. St. Lorenz Luth. Ch., mem. missionary guild. Mem.: Mich. Assn. Media in Edn. (treas. 1973—2005), St. Lorenz Missionary Guild (pres. 1972—73), St. Lorenz Young Married Soc. (pres. elect 2006), U. Mich. Alumni Assn., 4-H Club (leader 1972—, scholarship 1982). Republican. Luth. Avocations: gardening, crafts, antiques. Home: 8470 WTuscola Rd Frankenmuth MI 48734 Office: Bloomin Treasures 10995 Dixie Hwy Birch Run MI 48734

SCHLUETER, JUNE MAYER, literature educator, writer; b. Passaic, N.J., Nov. 4, 1942; m. Paul Schlueter. BA in English magna cum laude, Fairleigh Dickinson U., 1970; MA in English, Hunter Coll., CCNY, 1973; PhD in English and Comparative Lit., Columbia U., 1977. Asst. prof. Lafayette Coll., Easton, Pa., 1977-84, assoc. prof., 1984-91, prof., 1991-92, Charles A. Dana prof., 1992—, head English dept., 1992-93; asst. to provost, 1986-90; acting provost., 1993-94; provost Lafayette Coll., Easton, Pa., 1994—2006. Fulbright prof. Gesamthochschule Kassel Univ., Fed. Republic Germany, 1978-79; chmn. Shakespeare Seminar Columbia U., 1989-91, 2004-06, exec. bd., 1989—; active NEH summer seminar for coll. profs., 1981, lectr. Commonwealth Partnership Summer Lit. Inst., 1985-87, dir. summer seminar for sch. tchrs., 1988, selection panel, 1989, 91, evaluator Instl. Grant Program, 1990. Author: Metafictional Characters in Modern Drama, 1979, The Plays and Novels of Peter Handke, 1981, Dramatic Closure: Reading the End, 1995; (with James K. Flanagan) Arthur Miller, 1987; (with James P. Lusardi) Reading Shakespeare in Performance: King Lear, 1990; editor: Feminist Rereadings of Modern American Drama, 1989, Modern American Drama: The Female Canon, 1990, Critical Essays: The Two Gentlemen of Verona, 1995; (with Paul Schlueter) The English Novel: Twentieth Century Criticism, Vol. 2: Twentieth Century Novelists, 1982, Modern American Literature, Supplement II, 1985, An Encyclopedia of British Women Writers, 1988, Francis A. March: Selected Writings of the First Professor of English, 2005; (with Enoch Brater) Approaches to Teaching Beckett's Waiting for Godot, 1991; (with Paul Nelsen) Acts of Criticism: Performance Matters in Shakespeare and His Contemporaries, 2006; co-editor Shakespeare Bull., 1983-2003; assoc. editor Stages, 1984-90; editl. bd. Studies in Am. Drama, 1945-Present, 1989—2000; editl. cons. Modern Drama, Theatre Jour., PMLA, Studies in Twentieth Century Lit., Shakespeare Quar., others; contbr. revs., essays to profl. jours. Bd. govs. Fairleigh Dickinson U., Rutherford, N.J., 1985-90, bd. dirs., Madison, N.J., 1997-2005; mem. adv. com. Lehigh Valley Ednl. Coop., 1988-90; selection panel German Acad. Exch. Svc., Bonn, 1979. Rsch. grantee Lafayette Coll., 1977-93, NEH summer rsch. grantee, 1990, DAAD summer rsch. grantee, 1991. Mem. MLA, Shakespeare Assn. Am., Internat. Shakespeare Assn., Coll. English Assn., Samuel Beckett Soc., AAUP, Columbia Shakespeare Seminar. Home: 123 High St Easton PA 18042-1609 Office: Lafayette Coll Lafayette College Easton PA 18042

SCHMALZ, ELIZABETH MOODY, cosmetics company executive; b. Pittsburgh, Pa., Feb. 18, 1951; d. Norman F. and Mary Edith (Husted) Moody; m. David A. Forsythe, Sept. 16, 1978 (div. 1988); m. Brian F. Schmalz, Dec. 16, 1989; children: Brian Norman, Elizabeth Mary. Studentt, Rumson Fair Haven, 1969; student, Vermont Coll., 1971, U. Arizona, 1973. Mgr. AGI Inc., N.Y.C., 1974-75; mktg. mgr. Germaine Monteil Cosmetics Inc., N.Y.C., 1976-79; product mgr. Estee Lauder Clinique Inc., N.Y.C., 1980-86; v.p. Revlon Inc., N.Y.C.; v.p. corp. product Estee Lauder, N.Y.C., 1986—2006, sr. v.p., 1986—93; prin., owner Elizabeth Forsyth Schmalz & Co., LLC, 1993—98; exec. v.p. Bath & Bodyworks, 1998—, exec. v.p. creative tech. innovations, 1998—; exec. v.p. creative tech. innovation Beauty Avenues, 2006—, exec. v.p. creative, tech., fragrance innovations N.Y.C., 2006—. Mem. Cosmitsi Exec. Women, Fashion Group. Home: 15 Downing Hill Ln Colts Neck NJ 07722-1414 Office Phone: 212-904-8030. Business E-Mail: BSchmalz@beautyavenues.com.

SCHMANDT-BESSERAT, DENISE, archaeologist, educator; b. Ay, France, Aug. 10, 1933; came to U.S., 1965, naturalized, 1970; d. Victor and Jeanne (Crabit) Besserat; m. Jurgen Schmandt, Dec. 27, 1956; children: Alexander, Christopher, Phillip. Ed., Ecole du Louvre, 1965. Rsch. fellow in Near Eastern Archaeology Peabody Mus. Harvard U., Cambridge, Mass., 1969-71; fellow Radcliffe Inst., Cambridge, 1969-71; asst. prof. Middle Eastern studies U. Tex., Austin, 1972-81, assoc. prof., 1981-88, prof., 1988—2004; acting chief curator U. Tex. Art Mus., 1978—79. Vis. assoc. prof. U. Calif., Berkeley, 1987-88; curator Legacy of the Middle East exhbn. Jeddah (Saudi Arabia) Hist. Preservation Dept. Author: Before Writing, 1992, How Writing Came About, 1996, History of Counting, 1999; adv. editor Tech. and Culture, 1978-92; editl. adv. bd. Archaeology Odyssey, 2003-06; mem. editl. bd. Written Communication, 1993-95, Visible Lang., 1985—, Explorations in Media Ecology, 2001-05, Ancient Adminstrn., 2001; mem. editl. bd. Near Eastern Archaology, 2005—; contbr. articles to profl. jours. Recipient Kayden Nat. U. Press Book award, 1992, Robert W. Hamilton Author award, 1998, Walter J. Ong award Media Ecology Assn., 2004; named in Am. Scientist, 1999; Wenner-Gren Found. grant, 1970-71, NEA grant, 1974-75, 77-78, ACLS grant, 1984, Deutscher Akademischer Austauschdienst grant, 1986, NEH grant, 1992; NEH fellow, 1979-80, U. Wis. Inst. for Rsch. in Humanities fellow, 1984-85, USIA, Am. Ctr. Oriental Rsch. fellow, 1994-95, 97, 2001, Malone fellow 1997, 99, 2005, Weeks fellow Humanities Rsch. Ctr. Stanford U., 2003—. Mem. Am. Oriental Soc., Archeol. Inst. Am. (governing bd. 1983-89), Am. Anthropol. Assn., Am. Schs. of Oriental Rsch., Centro Internat. Rsch. Archeologiche Anthropologiche e Storiche (Rome). Business E-Mail: dsb@mail.utexas.edu.

SCHMEER, ARLINE CATHERINE, research scientist; b. Rochester, N.Y., Nov. 14, 1929; d. Edward Jacob and Madeline Margaret (Haines) S. BA, Coll. St. Mary of the Springs, Columbus, Ohio, 1951; MS in Biology, Notre Dame U., 1961; PhD in Biomedicine, U. Colo., 1969; DSc (hon.), Albertus Magnus Coll., New Haven, Conn., 1974, SUNY, Potsdam, 1990. Chmn. sci. dept. Watterson High Sch./Diocese of Columbus, 1954-59, St. Vincent Ferrer High Sch./Archdiocese of N.Y., N.Y.C., 1959-62; chmn. dept. biology Ohio Dominican Coll., Columbus, 1963-72; chmn. dept. anti-cancer agents of marine origin Am. Cancer Rsch. Ctr., Denver, 1972-82; dir. Mercenene Cancer Rsch. Inst., New Haven, 1982-93; dir. Mercenene Cancer Rsch. Inst. U. Cin. Med. Sch., 1996—. Sr. prin. investigator Marine Biol. Lab., Woods Hole, Mass., 1962-72, corp. mem., mem. libr. com., 1964—; rsch. prof. Med. Sch., U. Wüzburg, Germany, 1969-70; pres., chief exec. officer Med. Rsch. Found., 1972—; participant, contbr. Internat. Cancer Congress, 1966—. Contbr. articles to biol. publs. Grantee Am. Cancer Soc., 1965; NSF fellow, 1957-62, NIH fellow, 1966-69; recipient numerous teaching awards, Ohi Acad. Scis. and others. Fellow Royal Microscopical Soc. Eng. (life); mem. N.Y. Acad. Sci. (life), Am. Soc. Cell Biology, Internat. Cancer Congresses. Roman Catholic. Avocations: photography, fishing.

SCHMEIDLER, GERTRUDE RAFFEL, psychology educator; b. Long Branch, N.J., June 15, 1912; d. Harry B. and Clare (Holzman) R.; m. Robert Schmeidler, Aug. 27, 1937; children: James, Richard, Emilie, Katherine. BA, Smith Coll., 1932; MA, Clark U., 1933; PhD, Radcliffe/Harvard U., 1935. Instr. Monmouth Coll., Long Branch, N.J., 1935-37; rsch. assoc. Harvard U., Cambridge, Mass., 1942-45; rsch. officer Am. Soc. for Psychical Rsch., N.Y.C., 1946-47; instr. to prof. emeritus CUNY, N.Y.C., 1947—. Author: ESP and Personality Patterns, 1958, Parapsychology and Psychology: Matches and Mismatches, 1988; editor: Extrasensory Perception, 1974, Parapsychology: Its Relation to Physics Psychology, 1976, Research in Parapsychology 1990, 1992. Rep. LWV, Hastings-on-Hudson, 1990. Recipient McDougall award Found. for Rsch. on the Nature of Man, 1964, Disting. Achievement in Parapsychology award So. Calif. Soc. for Psych. Rsch. Inc., 1981. Fellow AAAS, APA, Soc. for Psychol. Study of Social Issues; mem. Am. Soc. for Psychical Rsch. (pres. 1982-84), Parapsychol. Assn. (program chair conv. 1990, pres. 1959, 71, Career award 1988).

SCHMEISER, MELVA LOUISE, history educator; b. Oklahoma City, Okla., July 29, 1941; d. Rex Alvin and Beulah Myrtle (Gilley) Haskins; m. Larry West Schmeiser, June 12, 1964; children: Sarah May, David West. BA in History, Seattle Pacific U., 1963. Cert. 5th yr. Tchr. Harvard Sch. Dist., Mass., 1968—72, Edmonds Sch. Dist., 1963—68, 1972—73, Limon Pub. Schs., Colo., 1992—. Adviser Youth Heritage Orgn., Limon, Colo., 2005—. Avocations: reading, gardening. Office: Limon Pub Schs 874 F Ave Limon CO 80828

SCHMERLER, BARBARA ANN, social worker; b. Daytona Beach, Fla., Dec. 6, 1957; d. Bernie and Martha (Walsh) S. BS in Social Work summa cum laude, East Carolina U., 1978; MSW, U. Ark., Little Rock, 1982. Lic. social worker, Colo.; cert. chem. abuse counselor III, Colo. Resident crisis counselor Real Crisis Intervention Inc., Greenville, N.C., 1976-78; youth counselor Peace Corps, Palau, Western Caroline Islands, 1979-81; clin. social worker Youth Home, Little Rock, 1981-82; therapist Yellowstone Boys and Girls Ranch, Billings, Mont., 1982-85, Cen. Wash. Comprehensive Mental Health, Yakima, 1985-86, Midwestern Colo. Mental Health Ctr., Montrose, 1986—2003; family therapist Mesa County Dept. Human Svcs., 2003—. Bd. dirs. coun. for the prevention of adolescent pregnancy Planned Parenthood, Yakima, 1985-86. Mem. Sierra Club (vice chmn. Mont. chpt. 1984-85), Cascadians Club (Yakima, Wash.), Colo. Mountain Club, Phi Kapa Phi, Alpha Delta Mu. Avocations: hiking, backpacking, cross country skiing, mountain climbing. Home: 67303 Lea Ct Montrose CO 81401-7506 Office: Mesa County Dept Human Svcs 510 29 1/2 Rd Grand Junction CO 81502-5035

SCHMERTZ, MILDRED FLOYD, editor-in-chief, writer; b. Pitts., Mar. 29, 1925; d. Robert Watson and Mildred Patricia (Floyd) S B.Arch., Carnegie Mellon U., 1947; M.F.A., Yale U., 1957. Archtl. designer John Schurko, Architect, Pitts., 1947-55; assoc. editor Archtl. Record, N.Y.C., 1957-65, sr. editor, 1965-80, exec. editor, 1980-85, editor-in-chief, 1985-90. Vis. lectr. Yale Sch. Architecture, 1979— Editor, contbr.: New Life for Old Buildings; contbr. articles to profl. jours.; chpts. to books. Bd. mgrs. Jr. League, City of N.Y., 1964-65; commr. N.Y. Landmarks Preservation Commn., 1988-92 Fellow AIA; mem. Mcpl. Art Soc. N.Y., Century Assn. (N.Y.C.) Home and Office: 310 E 46th St Apt 15E New York NY 10017-3002

SCHMID, LYNETTE SUE, child and adolescent psychiatrist; b. Tecumseh, Nebr., May 28, 1958; d. Mel Vern John and Janice Wilda (Bohling) S.; m. Vijendra Sundar, June 13, 1987; children: Jesse Christopher Mikaéle, Eric Lynn Kalani, Christina Elizabeth Ululani. BS, U. Nebr., 1979; MD, U. Nebr., Omaha, 1984; postgrad., U. Mo., 1984—89. Diplomate Am. Bd. Med. Examiners, Am. Bd. Psychiatry and Neurology. Child and adolescent psychiatrist Fulton (Mo.) State Hosp., 1990-91, Mid-Mo. Mental Health Ctr., Columbia, Mo., 1991-96; owner Fairview Motel, Kemmerer, Wyo., 1996—. Clin. asst. prof. psychiatry U. Mo., Columbia, 1990-96. Contbr. articles to profl. jours. Mem. Am. Psychiat. Assn., Am. Acad. Child and Adolescent Psychiatry, Ctrl. Mo. Psychiat. Assn. (sec.-treas. 1992-93, pres.- elect 1993-94, pres. 1994-95), U. Nebr. Alumni Assn., Phi Beta Kappa, Alpha Omega Alpha. Republican. Avocations: walking, reading, studying scripture. Office Phone: 307-877-3938 ext. 0.

SCHMID, MICHELLE LOUISE, elementary school educator; b. Joliet, Ill., Mar. 14, 1983; d. John G. and Lois E. Schmid. B, Ill. State U., 2005. Dance tchr. Major Sch. of Dance, Coal City, Ill., 2000—01; student admnistr. Ill. State U., 2001—05; summer sch. tchr. Mt. Assisi Acad., Lemont, Ill., 2006; tchrs. aide WoodView Elem., Bollingbrook, Ill., 2006—. Avocations: dance, piano, exercise.

SCHMIDER, MARY ELLEN HEIAN, American studies educator, academic administrator; b. Chippewa Falls, Wis., Apr. 17, 1938; d. A. Bernard and Ellen Dagmar (Gunderson) Heian; m. Michael Heaton Leonard, June 16, 1962 (div. Oct. 1969); 1 child, William Gunerius S. Leonard; m. Carl Ludwig Schmider, June 17, 1970; 1 child, Dagmar Heian (née Schmider) Meinders. BA in English Lit. magna cum laude, St. Olaf Coll., Northfield, Minn., 1960; MA in English Lit., U. So. Calif., 1962; PhD in Am. Studies, U. Minn., 1983. Mem. founding faculty in English, Calif. Luth. Coll., Thousand Oaks, Calif., 1961-64; instr. dept. English U. Vt., Burlington, Vt., 1964-70; instr. Univ. writing program U. RI, South Kingston, RI, 1973-77; grad. asst. dept. rhetoric U. Minn., Mpls., 1975-76; dir. continuing edn./cmty. svc. Moorhead State U., Minn., 1977-86, dean grad. studies and grad. faculty Minn., 1983-95; US Fulbright lectr. Lanzhou U., China, 1997. Mem. bd. pensions Luth. Ch. in Am., Mpls., 1982—87; mem. bd. higher edn. and schs. Evang. Luth. Ch. in Am., Chgo., 1987—95; cert. coll. mgmt. Carnegie Mellon U., 1987; bd. dirs. Luth. Brotherhood, Mpls., 1988—2001; collegiate full prof. U. Md., U. Coll., Europe, Heidelberg, Germany, 2000—05; mem. Am. Speakers Program, Cultural Sect., U.S. Embassy, Austria & Italy, 1988, Japan, 93, China, 2004—, Romania, 2006; Fulbright sr. lectr. Cyril and Methodius U., Skopje, Macedonia, 2005—; resource faculty Gender Studies inst. Euro-Balkan Region, 2006. Contbg. author: Biog. Dictionary of Social Welfare, esp. Jane Addams, Dictionary of Literary Influences 1914-2000, 2004. Mem. exec. comm. Minn. Humanities Commn., St. Paul, 1983-89, chair, 1987-88. Bush Leadership fellow, 1987; Fulbright scholar, Skopje, Macedonia, 2005—. Mem. US Fulbright Assn., Am. Studies Assn., Phi Beta Kappa, Phi Kappa Phi. Lutheran. Avocations: swimming, design, music, travel, knitting. Personal E-mail: mehscls@yahoo.com.

SCHMIDT, CHRISTINE ALICE, art gallery owner; b. St. Albans, NY, Sept. 1, 1932; d. Paul Joseph and Alice Patricia (McKane) Schmidt. BA magna cum laude, Adelphi U., 1964; MA, Pratt Inst., 1968. Cert. clothing design McDowell Art Sch., 1952, edn. NY, 1964. Asst. buyer May Co., N.Y.C., NY, 1952—54; asst. and designer Finger & Rabiner, Linker, Grioni, N.Y.C., 1955—59; fashion illustrator, freelance clothing designer NYC, 1959—63; parochial sch. art tchr. St. Brigid's, St. Francis, St. Christopher, 1963—64; art tchr. Cold Spring Harbor (NY) HS, 1964—84; owner, operator Christine's Gallery, Southwest Harbor, Maine, 1972—. Etchings and watercolor paintings in numerous collections in Europe and US, 1972—. Ambulance driver Am. Red Cross, Garden City, NY, 1950—65; bd. mem. Southwest Harbor C. of C., Southwest Harbor, Maine, 1994—99. Achievements include various coat and suit designs for the covers and interior of Vogue, Harper's Bazaar, Mademoiselle. Avocations: sewing, photography, european travel. Home and Office: 19 Artists Way Lamoine ME 04605 Office Phone: 207-664-2667.

SCHMIDT, DIANE, retired elementary school educator; b. Alhambra, Calif., Oct. 12, 1945; d. William Francis and Beatrice Marie (Kielty) Schieberl; m. Charles Edwin Schmidt, Aug. 17, 1968; children: Mary Josephine Holmes, Diane Marie. BA, Cath. U. Am., 1968; MS, Fla. Atlantic U., 1978, EdD, 1991. Cert. tchr., Fla. Tchr. Riverdale Hills (Md.) Elem., 1968-70, The Blake Sch., Plantation, Fla., 1974-77, L'Academie Montessori, Margate, Fla., 1977-80; office mgr. Dr. Schmidt, Ft. Lauderdale, Fla., 1980-81; tchr. U. Sch. at Nova U., Coral Springs, Fla., 1981-84, Pine Crest Sch., Ft. Lauderdale, Fla., 1984—2005, asst. prin., 1987-95, ret., 2005. Organizer Nat. Elem. Chess Championship, 1990. Mem. NSTA (Newest award 1993), Broward County Chess Assn. (pres. 1997—), U.S. Chess Fedn. Scholastic Com., Fla. Assn. Sci. Tchrs., Kappa Delta Pi. Avocations: flower arranging, reading, tennis, travel.

SCHMIDT, DIANE JOY, photographer, writer, creative arts educator; b. Lake Forest, Ill., Oct. 10, 1953; d. John and Miriam (Friedman) S. BA in Lit., Prescott (Ariz.) Coll., 1974; BFA, RI Sch. Design, 1976; MA, U. N.Mex., 2002. Pvt. practice, Chgo., 1977—, Chgo. and Ariz., 1992—, Chgo., Ariz., N.Mex., 1998—; grad. fellow U. N.Mex., 1999, instr. English creative writing and composition, 2000—02. Adj. faculty dept. photography Columbia Coll., 1991-92; photographer Northwestern U., U. Ariz., U. Chgo., 1987-98; CEO Creative Projects Assocs., 2005. Author, photographer: Night Moves, 1984, Amen Corners: Chgo.'s Storefront Churches, 1987, Mother's Table, 1989, I Am a Jesse White Tumbler, 1990, WISE, 1996, Collected Stories of Ernestine the Bad, 2002, Darkening of the Light, 2006, co-author, photographer: Abstract Relations, 1980, The Chicago Exhibition, 1985, Where's Chimpy, 1988; photographer, designer Navajo Psychology, 1997, Diné Terminology, 2003; co-dir.: Elders Album Project, 1994; contbr. articles to profl. jours. Recipient Children's Reading Round Table award, 1988, 89, IABC Silver Quill award, 1994, PIX Photo Dist. News Digital Photo award, 1996, Arts Genesis Vol. of Yr. award, 1994, Health Edn. Sci. Comm. award, 1996; Arts Midwest fellow Nat. Endowment for Arts, 1988.

SCHMIDT, ELIZABETH SUZANNE, history professor; d. Albert John and Kathryn Jung Schmidt; 1 child, Jann Grovogui. BA in History, Oberlin Coll., Ohio, 1977; MA in African History, U. Wis., Madison, 1992, MA in Comparative World History, 1983, PhD in History, 1987. Vis. asst. prof. Macalester Coll., St. Paul, 1987—90; Fulbright prof. U. Conakry, Guinea, 1990—91; prof. Loyola Coll., Balt., 1991—, chmn. history dept., 1995—98. Mem. editl. bd. Jour. Urban History, 2002—. Author: Decoding Corporate Camouflage: U.S. Business Support for Apartheid, 1980, Peasants, Traders, and Wives: Shona Women in the History of Zimbabwe, 1870-1939, 1992 (Choice Outstanding Academic Book for 1994), Mobilizing the Masses: Gender, Ethnicity, and Class in the Nationalist Movement in Guinea, 1939-1958, 2005. Recipient Spl. Mention, Alpha Sigma Nu, 1993; Woodrow Wilson Doctoral Dissertation Rsch. grantee in Women's Studies, Woodrow Wilson Nat. Fellowship Found., 1985—86, Fulbright-Hays Doctoral Dissertation Rsch. Abroad fellow, U.S. Dept. Edn., 1985, Caroline Spurgeon Residential scholar, Brit. Fedn. U. Women, 1985, Fulbright Sr. Rsch. and Lecturing fellow, Coun. Internat. Exch. of Scholars, 1990—91, Rsch. fellow in Guinea, Senegal, and France, Am. Coun. Learned Societies/Social Sci. Rsch. Coun., 1990—92. Mem.: AAUW, Assn. Concerned Africa Scholars (bd. dirs. 2005), African Studies Assn. (bd. dirs. 2006). Democrat. Office: Loyola Coll Md 4501 N Charles St Baltimore MD 21210-2699 Office Phone: 410-617-2432. Office Fax: 410-617-2832. Business E-Mail: eschmidt@loyola.edu.

SCHMIDT, HILDRED DORIS, music educator; b. Marion County, Kans., Aug. 13, 1932; d. Rudolf B Schmidt and Susie Voth. B of Music Edn., Coll. Emporia, 1954, BA, 1954; M of music edn. with highest distinction, Ind. U., 1958. Cert. Teacher Kans. State Bd. Edn., Service Playing Certificate Am. Guild Organists. Music tchr. Mullinville Grade Sch., Kans., 1954—57, Zenda Grade and H.S., Kans., 1958—60, Inman Grade Sch., 1960—67, Lyons Jr. High, Mid. and H.S., Lyons, Kans., 1967—96; ret., 1996. Founding mem. The Silver Sounds (flute quartet); organizer music festivals Lyons Jr. High Music Dept. Mem. People to People Lifeline et al., Bob Larson Communicator Club. Recipient Master Teacher award, Discipline and Classroom Mgmt., 1984. Mem.: Kans. Assn. of Retired Sch. Personnel, Kans. Bandmasters Assn., Music Educators Nat. Conf. (50 yr. mem.), Am. Guild Organists (sub-dean, Hutchinson chpt. 1988—93, 1996—98, dean Hutchinson chpt. 1998—2001, sub-dean, Hutchinson chpt. 2001—05), Kans. Music Educators Assn. So. Ctrl. Dist. (exec. sec. 1974—2004, 50 yr. mem.), Tabor Mennonite Ch., Coll. Emporia Alumni Assn. (bd. dirs.), Mu Phi Epsilon (pres. chpt. Phi Epsilon 1952—54). Avocations: gardening, needlecrafts, travel, photography.

SCHMIDT, JEAN, congresswoman; b. Cin., Nov. 29, 1951; m. Peter W. Schmidt; 1 child, Emilie. BS in Polit. Sci., U. Cin., 1974. Tchg. cert. in secondary edn. U. Cin., 1986. Trustee, Miami, Ohio, 1989—2000; mem. Ohio State Ho. Reps. from Dist. 66, 2001—04, US Congress from 2nd Ohio dist., 2005—. Chmn. Clermont County Rep. Party, 1996—98, Taft for Gov., 1998; mem. agr. com. US Congress, mem. govt. reform com., mem. transp. and infrastructure com. Mem. Milford Miami Twp. C. of C., 1989—, Ohio Twp. Assn., 1990—, Clermont County Twp. Assn., 1990—, Clermont County 20/20 Com., 1990—, Clermont County League of Women Voters, 1990—, Clermont County Agrl. Soc., 1990—, Clermont County C. of C., 1990—, mem. econ. devel. com., 1995—2005; mem. Leukemia Soc. Team in Tng., 1994—, mentor, 1996—; bd. trustees Clermont County Libr., 1980—92, 1994—2000, 2005—; bd. mem. Clermont County Mercy Hosp. Found., 1997—, Phoenix Pl., 2005—; founder, chmn. Sauls Found. 5K Race, 1995—. Named Marriage & Family Therapy Legislator of Yr., 2003, Empowerment Coalition Legislator of Yr., 2004, Am. Liver Found. Legislator of Yr., 2004, Bioscience Legislator of Yr., 2004; recipient Clermont County Cmty. Devel. of the Greater Cin. Found. Appreciation award, 2003, Clermont County Mental Health Svc. Recognition Award, 2003, Children's Hosp. Award of Distinction, 2003, So. Ohio Agrl. and Cmty. Devel. Found. Disting. Svc. Award, 2004. Republican. Roman Catholic. Avocations: long distance running, auto racing. Office: US Ho Reps 238 Cannon Ho Office Bldg Washington DC 20515 Office Phone: 202-225-3164.*

SCHMIDT, JOAN E., educational association administrator; b. Mont. Sch. bd. Fairfield Sch. Dist. #21, Mont. Guest appearance Today Show, NBC, Washington Report, C-Span. Bd. examiners Nat. Coun. for Accreditation of Teacher Edn.; chair Nat. Music Edn. Task Force, 1999—2002. Recipient Lay Citizen of Yr., Mont. Assn. Secondary Sch. Principals. Mem.: Mont. Teacher Certification Standards and Practices (chair, adv. coun.), Mont. Sch. Bd. Assn. (pres., chair, Mont. Goals 2000 Panel), Nat. Sch. Bd. Assn. (bd. dir. 1997—, sec.-treas. 2003—04, pres.-elect 2004—05, pres. 2005—06), Delta Kappa Gamma (hon.). Office: Nat Sch Bd Assn 1680 Duke St Alexandria VA 22314

SCHMIDT, KAREN LEE, marketing professional, sales executive; b. Milw., Oct. 14, 1953; d. Walter K. and Marilyn V. Schmidt. BSBA, Colo. State U., 1975; postgrad., U. Louisville, 1978—79; MBA, Colo. State U., 2006. Fin. analyst FICB of Louisville, 1975—79; sales rep. STSC, Inc., Chgo., 1979—81; regional software sales mgr. Xerox, Chgo., 1981—85; ctrl. region mgr. Datext, Inc., Chgo., 1698—1987; regional mgr. Sys. Software Assocs., Chgo., 1987—88; dir. group Accenture, Chgo., 1988—94; nat. dir. mktg. fin. svcs. KPMG, Chgo., 1994—95; chief mktg. officer Quantra Corp., Chgo., 1995—97; ptnr. in charge mktg. and sales BDO Seidman, Chgo., 1997—2000; exec. v.p. mktg. Land America, Richmond, Va., 2001—02; pres. KLS Group, Chgo., 2002—. Bd. mem. DuPage Habitat for Humanity, 2005; deacon 1st Presbyn. Ch., Glen Ellyn, 1996—99, elder, 2005—; bd. trustees Theatre Va., 2002—04; bd. mem. Ryall YMCA, 2006—. Mem.: Beta Gamma Sigma. Home: 149 Forest Ave Glen Ellyn IL 60137

SCHMIDT, LEEANNE, artist; b. Dayton, Ky., June 13, 1940; d. Douglas Walter and Marian Brown; m. Edward Schmidt; children: Douglas, Eric. BS, U. Cin., 1962, MFA, 1992. Tchr. Gov.'s Inst. for Talented and Gifted, Miami U. Cin., 1962, MFA, 1992. Tchr. Gov.'s Inst. for Talented and Gifted, Miami U., 1997, U. Cin., 1991-92, 94, 96, 97, No. Ky. U., Highland Heights, 1992-96, Cairo Am. Coll., 1998, U. Calif., San Diego, 1999; vis. artist Art Acad. Cin., 1997, instr., 1998; vis. artist Morehead State U., 1997, U. Louisville, 1996, Thomas More Coll., Crestview Hills, Ky., 1996, U. Cin., 1996, numerous others; curator Summerfair, Inc., Cin., 1997, Images Gallery, Cin., 1995, others. One-person shows include: The Marta Hewett Gallery, Cin., 1997, Morehead State U., Ky., 1997, Gallery 292, N.Y.C., 1997, Gallery of So. Photographers, New Orleans, 1996, Miami U., Oxford, Ohio, 1996, U. Louisville, 1996, Lycoming Coll., Williamsport, Pa., 1996; groups exhbns. include Huntington Mus. Art, W.Va., 1997, Swann Galleries, N.Y.C., 1997, Wellington B. Gray Art Gallery, E. Carolina U., Greenville, 1997, Bank One Gallery, Louisville, 1997, Art Acad. Cin., 1997, Marta Hewett Gallery, Cin., 1992-96, Gallery for So. Photographers, New Orleans, 1996, U. Minn., Mpls., 1996; selected books and catalogues include: Nudes 2, 1997, Signs, 1997, Eros, 1996, Love, Flesh, and Water, 1996, Horizons, 1996, Body of Evidence, 1995, The Myth and Madness of Ophelia, 2001, Houston Grand Opera patron brochure, 2005; corp. commns. include No. Ky. U., 1993; selected pub. collections include: The Bibliotek Nationale, Paris, J.B. Speed Art Mus., Louisville, Ogden Coll., New Orleans, Dayton Art Inst., Ohio, Cin. Art Mus., Cin. Bell Corp. Collections, U. Louisville; works collected in pvt. collections; represented by Gallery 292, N.Y.C. Artist Profl. Devel. grantee Ky. Arts Coun., Frankfort, 1997, 98; recipient scholarships U. Cin., 1990-92, Kodak Educator scholarship, Palm Beach Workshops, Boca Raton, Fla., 1994, fellowships Ky. Found. for Women, Louisville, 1996, Al Smith Artist Fellowship, Frankfort, 1994, Wolfstein Travel fellowship U. Cin., 1991, others; recipient exhbn. awards that include: Inst. Nacional de Bellas Artes, San Miguel de Allende, Mexico, 1995, Hunter Mus. of Am. Art, Chattanooga, 1995, Louisville Visual Art Assn., 1993, 94, others. Address: 3646 Ashworth Dr Unit 205 Cincinnati OH 45208-1828 E-mail: clestialee@fuse.net.

SCHMIDT, LYNDA WHEELWRIGHT, psychotherapist; b. Beijing, July 29, 1931; came to the U.S., 1931; d. Joseph Balch and Jane Byers (Hollister) Wheelwright; m. Klaus Dieter, May 8, 1930; children: Karen Calley, Claudia Lewis. BA, U. Calif., Berkeley, 1965, MSW, 1968. Cert. Jungian analyst; bd. cert. diplomate Am. Bd. Examiners Clin. Social Work. Staff psychiat. social worker Pacific Med. Ctr., San Francisco, 1968-71; pvt. practice psychotherapy and Jungian analysis San Francisco, 1971-87, Brooklin, Maine, 1985—. Tng. analyst CG Jung Inst., San Francisco, 1978—; mem. certifying com. CG Jung Inst., San Francisco, 1980-84; cons. and lectr. in field. Author: Time Out of Mind: Trekking the Hindu Kush, 1978, The Long Shore, A Psychological Experience of the Wilderness, 1991; contbr. articles to profl. jours. Fellow Calif. Soc. Clin. Social Workers; mem. NASW, Acad. Cert. Social Workers, Inc., CG Jung Inst. (chair certifying com. 1980-84), Alpha Phi Sorority. Democrat. Avocations: reading, horseback riding, travel, music. Home and Office: PO Box 269 Brooklin ME 04616-0269

SCHMIDT, MARY LOUISE DONNEL, banker; b. Glendale, Calif., Mar. 1, 1957; d. Roscoe John and Esther Maria Donnel; m. Jack H. Schmidt, Apr. 21, 1984 (div.); 1 child, Alexandra Louise; m. Tracy Forrest Robbins. Cert. in Spanish, U. Guadalajara, Mex., 1977; AA, Glendale Coll., 1982; BS, LaVerne U., 1989. Cert. broker Calif. Optical engr. Aerojet Electro Systems, Azusa, Calif., 1983—91; sr. loan officer Western Cities Mortgage, Carlsbad, Calif., 1991—93; sr. loan specialist Prudential Fin., Del Mar, Calif., 1993—95; sr. loan rep. Coastal Cities Mortgage, Del Mar, Calif., 1995—2001; v.p. Keller Williams, Carlsbad, 2001, MLS Fin. Group, Carlsbad, 2001—. Spkr. in field, 1993—. Mem.: Mortgage Bankers Assn., Better Bus. Bur., Alpha Gamma Sigma. Office: MLS Financial Group 5620 Paseo del Norte # 127-434 Carlsbad CA 92008 E-mail: mdonnel@hotmail.com.

SCHMIDT, MICHELLE MOORE, music educator; b. Pottsville, Pa., Nov. 16, 1975; d. Bruce William and Jane Elizabeth Moore. MusB in Music Edn., Rider U., Princeton, N.J., 1998; postgrad. in Music Edn., Rider U., Princeton, N.J. Cert. K-12 music tchr. N.J. Tchr. music Bridgewater-Raritan Sch. Dist., NJ, 1999—2002, East Brunswick Sch. Dist., NJ, 2002—; tchr. choral readiness Westminster Conservatory of Music, Princeton, NJ, 2003—. Soloist, sect. leader, dir. children's choir Lamington Presbyn. Ch., Bedminster, NJ, 1996—2003. Office: Irwin Elem Sch 71 Race Track Rd East Brunswick NJ 08816-3742

SCHMIDT, RITA, librarian, retired media specialist; b. Tacoma, Wash., Aug. 9, 1947; d. Robert V. and Ann Regine (Minette) Westermark; m. Guy Douglas Schmidt, June 29, 1972. BA, Knox Coll., 1969; MSLS, Case Western Res. U., 1970. Cert. tchg., sch. adminstrn., Mont. Libr. cataloger Trenton Pub. Libr., 1970-71; libr. media specialist Great Falls (Mont.) Pub. Schs., 1971—2001; part-time libr. Mont. State U., Coll. Tech., Great Falls, 2002—05; ret. Part-time instr. Coll. Great Falls, 1973-76. Chair, mem. Mont. Libr. Svcs. Adv. Coun., Helena, Mont., 1983-84, 85-89; mem. Project Excellence Sch. Accreditation Stds., Helena, 1988-89. Recipient scholarship Mountain Plains Libr. Assn., 1985. Mem. ALA (coun. 1986), Mont. Edn. Assn. (bd. dirs. 1989-90), Great Falls Edn. Assn. (v.p. 1988-90, Silver Key award 1983, 84, 85, 89, 90, 94, 98), Mont. Libr. Assn. (pres. 1983-84). Democrat. Home: 3721 7th Ave N Great Falls MT 59401-2222

SCHMIDT, RUTH ANN, retired academic administrator; b. Mountain Lake, Minn., Sept. 16, 1930; d. Jacob A. and Anna A. (Ewert) S. BA, Augsburg Coll., Mpls., 1952; MA, U. Mo., 1955; PhD, U. Ill., 1962; LLD, Gordon Coll., 1987. Asst. prof. Spanish Mary Baldwin Coll., Staunton, Va., 1955-58, SUNY-Albany, 1962-67, assoc. prof., 1967-78, dean of humanities, 1971-76; prof. and provost Wheaton Coll., Norton, Mass., 1978-82; pres. Agnes Scott Coll., Decatur, Ga., 1982-94, pres. emerita, 1994—. Interim pres. Lyon Coll., 1998; chair Women's Coll. Coalition, 1986-88. Author: Ortega Munilla y sus novelas, 1973, Cartas entre dos amigos del teatro, 1969. Trustee Gordon Coll., Wenham, Mass., 1980-86, Lyon Coll., 1993-2001; bd. dirs. DeKalb C. of C., 1982-85, Atlanta Coll. Art, 1984-94; mem. exec. com. Women's Coll. Coalition, 1983-88; v.p. So. Univ. Conf., 1993. Named Disting. Alumna Augsburg Coll., 1973 Mem. Assn. Am. Colls. (dir. 1979-82, treas. 1982-83), Soc. Values in Higher Edn., Am. Coun. Edn. (commn. on women in higher edn. 1985-88), AAUW, Assn. Pvt. Colls. and Univs. Ga. (pres. 1987-89), Internat. Women's Forum, Young Women's Christian Assn. Acad. Women Achievers, Women's Action for New Directions. Democrat. Presbyterian. E-mail: ruthschmidt@mindspring.com.

SCHMIDT, SANDRA JEAN, secondary school educator; b. Limestone, Maine, Mar. 21, 1955; d. Dale Laban and Marie Audrey (Bailey) Winters; m. Lee Lloyd Schmidt, Oct. 20, 1973; children: Colby Lee, Katrina Leesa. AA summa cum laude, Anne Arundel Community Coll., 1987; BS summa cum laude, U. Balt., 1990; MAT, Johns Hopkins U., 2003. CPA, Md. Enlisted U.S. Army, 1973, traffic analyst, 1973-85, resigned, 1985; auditor Md. State Office of Legislative Audits, Balt., 1990-93; fin. analyst Md. Ins. Adminstrn., Balt., 1993-2000; tchr. math. Baltimore City Pub. Schs., 2000—. Tutor Anne Arundel County Literacy Coun., Pasadena, Md., 1990-97; mentor U. Balt., 1991; host family Am. Intercultural Student Exchange, 1992-98. Named Tchr. of Yr., Balt. City Coun. of PTAs, 2001. Mem.: Md. Coun. Tchrs. Math., Nat. Coun. Tchrs. Math., U. Balt. Alumni Assn., Phi Theta Kappa, Beta Gamma Sigma, Alpha Chi. Republican. Baptist. Home: 7716 Pinyon Rd Hanover MD 21076-1585 E-mail: beadmaniac@hotmail.com.

SCHMIDT, SARA JEAN, special education educator; b. Wheeling, Ill., Aug. 26, 1980; d. William Roy and Julie Ann Schmidt. BA Elem. Edn. and Spl. Edn., Monmouth Coll., Ill., 2002. Tchr. spl. edn. Nippersink Sch. Dist. #2, Richmond, Ill., 2002—. Mem.: Alpha Lambda Delta, Mortar Bd., Psi Chi, Kappa Delta Pi (sec. 2001—02). Home: 420 Spring Street Lake Geneva WI 53147 Office: Nippersink School District #2 10006 Main Street Richmond IL 60071

SCHMIDT, SHELLEY RAE, cosmetics executive, educator; b. Medicine Lodge, Kans., Apr. 13, 1961; d. Ernest Ray and Mary Ellen Schmidt. Cosmetology degree, Hairbenders Sch. of Hair Styling, Lawrence, Kans., 1980. Stylist Mercentile Dept. Stores, Overland Park, Kans., 1989—99; cert. color trainer TSP Aveda Inst., St. Petersburg, Fla., 2005; performing artist Redken 5th Ave., N.Y.C., 2000—; dir. of edn. Dillard's Salons and Spas, Overland Park, Kans., 1999—. Author: (book) Manual Technical, 2005. Named one of Top 20, Mercantile Dept. Stores, 1984—99. Office: Dillard's South Store 11601 W 95th St Overland Park KS 66214

SCHMIDT, SHERRIE, library director, dean; BA, Ohio State U., 1970, MLS, 1974. With Ohio State U.; cataloger U. Fla., 1974—75; head user svcs. AMIGOS Bibliographic Coun., 1975—78; assoc. dir. libr. svcs. U. Tex., Dallas, 1979—82; S.W. US sales rep. Faxon Co., 1982—84; asst. info. sys. planning U. Tex., Austin, 1984—86; asst. dir. collections and bibliographic svcs. Tex. A&M U., 1986—90; assoc. dean libr. svcs. Ariz. State U., 1990—91, dean univ. librs., 1991—. Contbr. articles to profl. jours. Sr. fellow, UCLA, 1989. Mem.: ALA (mem. Office for Info. Tech. Policy Adv. Com. 2002—04). Office: Ariz State U 113 Hayden Libr PO Box 871006 Tempe AZ 85287-1006 Office Phone: 480-965-3417. Office Fax: 480-965-9169.*

SCHMIDT, SUSAN, journalist; m. Glen Nishimura; 2 children. BA, Mary Baldwin Coll., 1975. News asst. Washington Star; reporter Herald Examiner, L.A., Patriot Ledger, Quincy, Mass.; metro desk editor to bus. news reporter Washington Post, 1983—92, nat. news desk reporter, 1992—. Co-author: Truth at Any Cost, 2000. Co-recipient Pulitzer Prize for nat. reporting, 2002; recipient Pulitzer Prize for investigative reporting, 2006, Seldon Ring award, 2006, Worth Bingham prize, 2006. Office: Washington Post Nat News Desk 1150 15th St NW Washington DC 20071-0070 Office Phone: 202-334-6157. Office Fax: 202-496-3883. Business E-Mail: schmidts@washpost.com.

SCHMIDT, SUZANNE M., music educator; m. David A. Schmidt, Aug. 16, 1975; children: Kathryn Anne Schmidt-McMurry, Timothy David. MusB, U. Mich., 1974. Kodaly Certification Westminster Choir Coll. of Rider U., 1995, Music Technology Certification TI:ME Level I Villanova U., 2002, Teaching Certificaiton Commonwealth of Pa., 1986. Music tchr. Crestwood Sch. Dist., Dearborn Heights, Mich., 1974—75, Faith Christian Acad., Hamilton, NJ, 1975—78, Mercer Christian Acad., Ewing Township, NJ, 1977—81, Pennsbury Sch. Dist., Fallsington, Pa., 1991—; pvt. piano tchr. self-employed, Yardley, Pa., 1976—93; adj. instr. Westminster Choir Coll. of Rider U., Princeton, NJ, 2004—. Faculty cons. and reader-ap music theory exam Ednl. Testing Svc., Princeton, NJ, 2002—; guest lectr. and clinician Various Organizations, Yardley, Pa., 1991—; adjudicator for piano competitions and auditions Bucks County Piano Teachers Assn., Piano Teachers Forum, Nat. Guild of Piano Teachers, Yardley, Pa., 1985—. Sponsor, facilitator CDs for Iraq Campaign, Yardley, Pa., 2003—04; ch. choir dir. First Bapt. Ch. at Grace Point, Newtown, Pa., 2000—. Mem.: Nat. Guild of Piano Teachers, Tchr. Divsn. of the Am. Coll. of Musicians, Music Educators Nat. Conf., Pa. Music Educators Assn., Bucks County Music Educators Assn. Avocations: sewing, gardening, crocheting, scrapbooks. Office: Pennsbury HS West 608 S Olds Blvd Fairless Hills PA 19030

SCHMIDTKE, SUZANNE DE FINE, retired social worker; d. Poul and Else de Fine Lassen; m. Edwin (Ned) C. Schmidtke, June 7, 1964; children: Peter Christian, Elizabeth de Fine Knudsen. MSW, U. Ill., Chgo., 1980. Cert. social worker NASW, 1982, diplomate NASW, 1988, Am. Bd. Examiners in Clin. Social Work, 1988, LCSW Ill. Dept. Profl. Regulation, 1989. Social worker Madden Mental Health Ctr., Ill. Dept. Mental Health, Hines, 1980—84, Ill. State Psychiat. Inst., Chgo., 1984—87, social worker adminstr., 1987—94; mgr., rsch. patient recruitment dep. psychiatry U. Ill., Chgo., 1994—2004; ret., 2004. Adj. instr. art therapy Sch. of Art, Inst. Chgo., Chgo., 1989—93; social work field instr. Jane Addams Coll. Social Work, U. Ill., Chgo., 1992—2004; family-to-family tchr. Nat. Alliance for Mental Illness of Calif. Bd. mem. Nat. Alliance for Mentally Ill, Chgo., 1996—2003; pres. Nat. Alliance for Mentally Ill of Ill., Springfield, 2001—03, family-to-family tchr. Recipient Vol. of the Yr., Nat. Alliance for Mentally Ill., 2000. Avocations: theater, hiking, travel, films. Personal E-mail: suzned@sbcglobal.net.

SCHMIDT-NIELSEN, BODIL MIMI (MRS. ROGER G. CHAGNON), retired physiologist, educator; b. Copenhagen, Nov. 3, 1918; came to U.S., 1946, naturalized, 1952; d. August and Marie Jorgensen Krogh; m. Knut Schmidt-Nielsen, Sept. 20, 1939 (div. Feb. 1966); children: Astrid, Bent, Bodil; m. Roger G. Chagnon, Oct. 1968 (dec. 2003). DDS, U. Copenhagen, 1941, DOdont, 1946, DPhil, 1955; DS (hon.), Bates Coll., 1983; MD (hon.), U. Aarhus, Denmark, 1997. Mem. faculty Duke U., Durham, NC, 1952-64; prof. biology Case Western Res. U., Cleve., 1964-71, chmn. dept., 1970-71, adj. prof., 1971-74; trustee Mt. Desert Island Biol. Lab., Maine, rsch. scientist Maine, 1971-86, exec. com. Maine, 1978-85, v.p. Maine, 1979-81, pres. Maine, 1981-85; prof. dept. physiology U. Fla., Gainesville, 1985—. Adj. prof. Brown U., Providence, 1971-75, dept. physiol. U. Fla., Gainesville, 1986—; mem. tng. grant com. NIGMS, 1965-71. Author: August and Marie Krogh, Lives in Science, 1995, Danish edit., 1997; editor: Urea and the Kidney, 1970; assoc. editor Am. Jour. Physiology: Regulatory, Integrative and Comparative Physiology, 1978-81. Trustee Coll. of Atlantic, Bar Harbor, Maine, 1972-92. Recipient Career award NIH, 1962-64, John Simon Guggenheim Meml. fellow, 1952-53, Bowditch lectr., 1958, Jacobaeus lectr., 1974. Fellow AAAS (del. coun. 1977-79), NY Acad. Scis., Am. Acad. Arts and Scis.; mem. Am. Physiol. Soc. (coun. 1971-77, pres. 1975-76, Ray G. Daggs award 1989, Orr Reynolds award 1994, August Knogh lectr. 1994, Berliner award 1998), Soc. Exptl. Biology and Medicine (coun. 1967-71). Achievements include research, publications on biochemistry of saliva, water metabolism of desert animals, urea excretion, peristalsis of renal pelvis and concentrating mechanism, comparative kidney physiology, comparative physiology of excretory organs. Office: U Fla Dept Physiology 2015 SW 16th Ave Gainesville FL 32605 Business E-Mail: bodil@gator.net.

SCHMITH, ROSALIE LAVERNE, special education educator; b. Wadena, Minn., May 9, 1952; d. Julius Emil Milbradt and LaVerne Joan Redetzke-Milbradt; m. William Jon Schmith, June 15, 1974; children: Travis, Brandon, Brook. BS, Bemidji State Coll., Bemidji, Minn., 1994. Cert. kindergarten, early edn., special edn. tchr. Elem. substitute tchr. Wadena Pub. Sch., Wadena, Minn., 1974—75; elem. tchr. Verndale Pub. Sch., Verndale, Minn., 1975—85, Sebeka Elem. Sch., 1985—. Parent leader Wadena County 4-H, Wadena, Minn.; Sun. sch. tchr. Grace Luth. Ch., Sebeka, Minn., 1966—85. Recipient Disabilitie Tchr. of the Yr., 1995, Tchr. of the Yr. Sebeka Pub. Sch., 1993. Mem.: NEA, Edn. Minn., Delta Kappa Gamma (master's scholarship 1990). Avocations: gardening, camping.

SCHMITT, CLAIRE KUNZ, environmentalist, writer; b. N.Y., July 11, 1928; d. Louis Cornelius and Elizabeth Freeman Kunz; m. Roland Walter Schmitt, Sept. 19, 1957; children: Lorenz, Brian, Alice, Henry. AB, Wash. Univ., St. Louis, Mo., 1950. Sec. Doubleday & Co., N.Y., 1951—55, Gen. Elec. Co., Schenectady, NY, 1957; dir. Environ. ClearingHouse, Schenectady, NY, 1972—73; adj. curator N.Y. State Mus., Albany, NY, 1980—. Author: Natural Area of Schenectady County, NY, 1981, edit., 1982, 1986, 1989, 1992, 2005, Natural Areas of Albany County, Natural Areas of Rensseiaer County, Natural Areas of Saratoga County, 1998; co-author: Environmental Tips, 1982. Chmn. Envrion. Clearinghouse, 1975, Schenectady County Environ. Adv. Coun., 1983—84; bd. mem. WMHT Pub. TV Sta., 1980—84, Schenectady Mus., 1982—85, Eastern N.Y. Chapter, Nature Conservancy, 1992—2003, Lake George Land Conservancy, 2005—. Home: PO Box 223 Rexford NY 12148

SCHMITT, DIANA LYNN, secondary school educator; b. Freeport, Ill., Sept. 29, 1953; d. Dewaine Dewey and Allene Francis (Bruning) Cox; m. John Wayne Schmitt, July 14, 1973; children: Jennifer Marie, Jessica Rae. BS, Western Ill. U., 1975; MS, No. Ill. U., 1996. Cert. tchr., Ill. Tchr. sci. Dakota (Ill.) Community Unit Dist., 1975-87; tchr. biology Byron (Ill.) Sch. Dist., 1987—. Republican. Lutheran. Avocations: volleyball, golf, swimming, reading, coach. Home: 17626 Sumner Rd Pecatonica IL 61063-9720 Office: Byron High Sch PO Box 911 Byron IL 61010-0911

SCHMITT, DIANA MAE, elementary school educator; b. Dubuque, Iowa, Jan. 19, 1950; d. Raymond J. and Marie Arlen Schmitt. BA, U. Iowa, 1972; MA, Clarke Coll., Dubuque, 1981; postgrad., U. Wyo. 6th grade tchr. Shelby County Sch. Dist., Shelby, Iowa, 1972-73; 4th and 5th grade tchr. Dist. 200, Woodstock, Ill., 1973-76; rural sch. tchr. Albany County Sch. Dist., Laramie, Wyo., 1976-83, 1st, 3d, 5th and 6th grade tchr., 1983-98; chmn. outdoor classrm. devel. Indian Paintbrush Elem., 1992—. Mem. rev. com. for excellence in sci. edn., adv. com. Western Edn. Adv. Com. for Wyo., 1989; tchr. sci. methods for elem. sch. U. Wyo., 1990-91; mem. Higher Edn. Grant Reading State Com., 1994; participant Sci. Grasp, 1990, Inst. Chemical Edn. Fundamental, 1992; presenter 1st Soviet-Am. Sci. Conv., Moscow, 1991; mem. workshop on water, Nat. Geog. Soc., 1993; presenter NSTA nat. and regional convs., state Wyo. Interdisciplinary Conf. convs., No. Iowa Beginning Reading conf. Recipient Delta award, 1993; named Dist. Exemplary Sci. Tchr., 1986-87; Wyo. Game and Fish grantee, 1993-95, Nat. Geog. Soc. grantee, 1997. Mem. NEA, Internat. Reading Assn., Nat. Sci. Tchrs. Assn., Wyo. Sci. Tchrs. Assn. (sec.), Alpha Delta Kappa (pres.). Home: 5737 Southview Rd Laramie WY 82070-6801 Office: Indian Paintbrush 1653 N 28th St Laramie WY 82072-9200 Personal E-mail: msdmschmitt@yahoo.com.

SCHMITT, JOHANNA MARIE, plant population biologist, educator; b. Phila., Mar. 12, 1953; d. William Francis and Laura Belle (Wear) S.; m. Darrell Marion West, Aug. 6, 1983. BA, Swarthmore (Pa.) Coll., 1974; PhD, Stanford U., 1981. Postdoctoral rsch. assoc. Duke U., Durham, N.C., 1981-82; asst. prof. Brown U., Providence, 1982-87, assoc. prof. biology, 1987-94, prof., 1994—. Mem. R.I. Task Force, New Eng. Plant Conservation program, 1991—; mem. regional advisory com. New Eng. Plant Conservation program, 2000-. Assoc. editor Evolution, 1990-92, Am. Naturalist, 2000-2001; contbr. articles to profl. jours. including Evolution, Ecology, Am. Naturalist, Genetics, Nature. Bd. dirs. Sojourner House, Providence, 1989-92. NSF grad. fellow, 1974, mid. career fellow, 1992-93; rsch. grantee, 1984—; recipient faculty award for women, 1991—. Mem. Soc. for Study of Evolution (coun. mem. 1990-92, exec. v.p. 1994-95, v.p. 1999), Bot. Soc. Am., Ecol. Soc. Am., Am. Soc. Naturalists (v.p. 1997, pres. 2002). Achievements include research on ecological genetics and genomics of natural plant populations: density-dependent phenomena, gene flow and population structure, inbreeding depression, the evolution of sex, maternal effects, seed ecology, natural selection, evolution of plasticity, adaptive significance of phytochrome, ecological risks of transgenic plants. Office: Brown Univ Dept Ecology & Evolution Providence RI 02912-0001

SCHMITT, MARY ELIZABETH, retired postal supervisor; b. Detroit, Sept. 16, 1948; d. Jerome Ferdinand and Margaret Ellen (Beauregard) S. BS, Ea. Mich. U., 1979. Waitress, hostess Mr. Steak, Westland, Mich., 1969-70; mgr. housewares K-Mart, Ypsilanti, Mich., 1971, asst. mgr., jewelry, 1972; postal clk. U.S. Postal Svc., Ann Arbor, Mich., 1972-88, postal supr., 1988—2005; ret., 2005. Crisis intervention counselor Ozone House, Ann Arbor, 1978; convenor Gray Panthers of Huron Valley, Ann Arbor, 1979-80; active Greenpeace. Mem. LWV, Nat. Assn. Postal Suprs., Ann Arbor Postal Fed. Credit Union (v.p. 1987—), Sierra Club, Ancestry Club. Roman Catholic. Avocations: travel, reading, hiking, canoeing, genealogy. Home: PO Box 1833 Ann Arbor MI 48106-1833

SCHMITT, NANCY CAIN, retired public and corporate relations executive, writer; b. Fayetteville, N.C., June 12, 1942; d. Carlton White and Cleo Margaret (Parnell) Cain; m. Louis Dennis Schmitt, July 13, 1974 (div.). BA, Wake Forest U., 1960-64; postgrad., U. Alaska, 1989-90. Intern Winston-Salem (N.C.) Jour.-Sentinel, 1963-64; reporter Gastonia (N.C.) Gazette, 1964-66; copy editor, reporter Twin City Sentinel, Winston-Salem, 1966-67; entertainment editor Fayetteville Observer, 1967-78; lifestyle editor Anchorage Times, 1978-83; pub. rels. specialist Multivisions Cable TV Co., Anchorage, 1983-84; editor Alaska Jour. of Commerce, Anchorage, 1984-85; sr. comms. specialist U.S. Postal Svc., 1985—2003; ret., 2003; freelancer. Author: How to Care for Your Car: A Women's Guide to Car Care in Alaska, 1978 (nat. award 1979); mem. editl. bd. Episc. Diocean of Alaska, Fairbanks, 1983-86; contbr. articles to profl. jours. and nat. publs. Mem. Advocates for (Foster) Children in Alaska. Recipient Asst. Postmaster Gen.'s award for excellence, USPS Legis. Affairs Corp. Rel. Sr. VP Opportunity award, Sr. Op-Ed Writing award, Patriotic Writing award VFW. Mem. Nat. Fedn. Press Women (nat. bd. dirs. 1990-91, 97-98), Pub. Rels. Soc. Am., Alaska Press Women (pres. 1990-91, 97-98, treas., sec., communicator of achievement, recipient numerous awards), Alaska Press Club (recipient 3 awards), Rotary Internat. (bd. dirs. 1991-92). Home: 6716 E 16th Ave Apt A Anchorage AK 99504-2513

SCHMITTMANN, BEATE, physics professor; b. 1957; Grad., U. Aachen, 1981; PhD in Physics, U. Edinburgh, 1984. Rsch. assoc. Physics Dept. U. Dusseldorf, Germany, 1984—86, rsch. asst. prof., 1991—97; vis. asst. prof. Va. Tech. U., Blacksburg, 1990—91, assoc. prof., 1991—97, prof., 1997—, chair physics dept., 2006—. Lectr. in field. Contbr. articles to profl. jours. Grantee Pro Renovanda Cultura Hungarica Fellow, Hungarian Ministry of Sci., 1995. Fellow: Am. Physical Soc. Office: Va Tech U 111 Robeson Hall Blacksburg VA 24061 Office Phone: 540-231-6518. Office Fax: 540-231-7511. E-mail: schmittm@vt.edu.*

SCHMITZ, ALICE J., secondary school educator; b. Milw., Sept. 27, 1951; d. Roy Frederick and Loraine Anna (Schmidt) Schoeni; m. Gerald Wayne Schmitz, June 30, 1984; 1 child, Tyler Gerald. BS, U. Wis., Whitewater, 1973, MS, 1983; cert. in sch. adminstrn., Northern Ill. U., 1989. Secondary sch. tchr., dept. chmn. Richland Ctr. (Wis.) H.S., 1973—80, Nicolet H.S., Glendale, Wis., 1980—84; secondary sch. tchr. Township H.S., Palatine, Ill., 1984—2001; tech. coord. Township H.S. Dist. 211, Palatine, Ill., 2001—. Mem. awards com. and staff devel. com. Hoffman Estates (Ill.) H.S., 1995-2003, lead tchr. Project Link for at-risk students, 1993-99. Webmaster Lake Zurich Cougars Travel Baseball. Named Tchr. of Month, Coca Cola N.W. Suburban Ill., 1997; recipient Those Who Excel award, Ill. State Bd. Edn., 1998, Prin.'s award of excellence, 1996, Prin.'s award in celebration of learning, 2003, Those Who Excel Team award Ill. State Bd. Edn., 2004. Mem. Nat. Bus. Edn. Assn., Ill. Bus. Edn. Assn., Ill. Computer Educators, Parent Tchr. Orgn. (sec. 1999-2002, editor newsletter 2002—), Delta Pi Epsilon (pres. 1983-85). Avocations: reading, son's sporting events, computers. Office: Hoffman Estates HS 1100 W Higgins Rd Hoffman Estates IL 60195-3098 Office Phone: 847-755-5760.

SCHMITZ, BARBARA, art preservationist; b. Cin., 1936; AM, U. Chgo., 1960; MA, PhD, NYU, 1981. Author: (illustrated catalogs of Islamic paintings) Islamic Manuscripts, N.Y. Pub. Libr., 1992, Islamic and Indian Manuscripts and Paintings, Pierpont Morgan Libr., 1996; co-author (with Z.A. Desai): Mughal and Persian Painting and Illustrated Manuscripts in the Raza Library, Rampur (U.P.), 2006; editor, contbr.: After the Great Mughals: Painting in Delhi and the Regional Courts in the 18th-19th Centuries, 2004. Fulbright grantee, 1992—93, 1997—98, Indira Gandhi Nat. Ctr. for the Arts grantee, New Delhi, 1995, Am. Inst. Indian Studies grantee, 1998—99, Browniee Grant, Mo. Hist. Soc., 2002. E-mail: barbaraschmitz65016@yahoo.com.

SCHMITZ, DOLORES JEAN, primary school educator; b. River Falls, Wis., Dec. 27, 1931; d. Otto and Helen Olive (Webster) Kreuziger; m. Karl Matthias Schmitz Jr., Aug. 18, 1956; children: Victoria Jane, Karl III. BS, U. Wis., River Falls, 1953; MS, Nat. Coll. Edn., 1982; postgrad., U. Minn., Mankato, 1969, U. Melbourne, Australia, 1989, U. Wis., Milw., 1989, Carroll Coll., 1990, Cardinal Stritch Coll., 1990. Cert. tchr., Wis. Tchr. Manitowoc (Wis.) Pub. Schs., 1953-56, West Allis (Wis.) Pub. Schs., 1956-59, Lowell Sch., Milw., 1960-63, Victory Sch., Milw., 1964, Palmer Sch., Milw., 1966-84, 86-94, unit leader, 1984-86; ret., 1994. Co-organizer Headstart Tchg. Staff Assn., Milw., 1968; insvc. organizer Headstart and Early Childhood, Milw., 1969-92; pilot tchr. for Whole Lang., Hi-Scope and Math. Their Way, 1988-93; bd. dirs. Curriculum Devel. Ctr. of Milw. Edn. Ctr., 1993-94. Author: (curriculum) Writing to Read, 1987, Cooperation and Young Children (ERIC award 1982), Kindergarten Curriculum, 1953. Former supporter Milw. Art Mus., Milw. Pub. Mus., Milw. County Zoo, Whitefish Bay Pub. Libr., Riveredge Nature Ctr.; vol. fgn. visitor program Milw. Internat. Inst., 1966-94, holiday folk fair, 1976-94, Earthwatch, 1989; lobbyist Milw. Pub. Sch. Bd. and State of Wis., 1986-93; coord. cmty. vols., 1990-94. Grantee, Greater Milw. Ednl. Trust, 1989. Mem. NEA (life), ASCD, Milw. Kindergarten Assn. (rec. sec. 1986-93), Nat. Assn. for Edn. of Young Children, Tchrs. Applying Whole Lang., Wis. Early Childhood Assn., Milw. Tchrs. Ednl. Assn. (co-chmn. com. early childhood 1984-86), Assn. for Childhood Edn. Internat. (charter pres. Manitowoc chpt. 1955-56), Milw. Educating Computer Assn., Alpha Psi Omega. Roman Catholic. Avocations: bicycling, nature, world travel. Home: 9572 Commodore Dr Seminole FL 33776 Personal E-mail: dolintv@aol.com.

SCHMOLL, EDITH MARGARET, music educator; b. Boston, Mar. 10, 1924; d. William James Pruyn, Sr. and Ida Mary Langan; m. John Arthur Pickering (div.); children: Nancy Pickering, Lois Pickering, Barry Pickering; m. Mariel Theodore Schmoll, Sr., Jan. 10, 1969 (dec. 2002). Grad., Boston Clerical, Mass., 1941; student in Piano Performance, New Eng. Conservatory, Boston, 1945—46; student in Accordian Performance, Conservatory of Music, Kaiserslautern, Germany, 1954—55. Cert. tchr. music Calif. Tchr. music, LA, 1960—; br. mgr. Int. Rectifier Fed. Credit Union, Temecula, Calif., 1991—97. Concert pianist, 1940—; church musician, 1965—2006; pres. Music Songs, Sun City, Calif., 1976—2006. Editor: (college piano books) Creative Keyboard Experience, 1970. Mem. Legacy Soc., Mt. San Jacinto Coll. Found., Calif., 2006; past. pres. Sun City Hermosa Homeowners Assn., Calif., 1995—97. Mem.: Mensa. Avocations: portrait and mural painter, writing. Office: Music Songs 28108 Gardena Dr Ste A Sun City CA 92586 Office Phone: 951-679-4201.

SCHNACKENBERG, GJERTRUD CECELIA, poet; b. Tacoma, Aug. 27, 1953; d. Walter Charles and Doris Ione Schnackenberg; m. Robert Nozick, Oct. 5, 1987. BA summa cum laude, Mount Holyoke Coll., 1975, LittD (hon.), 1985. Fellow The Bunting Inst., Radcliffe and Cambridge, Mass., 1979-80; lectr. in writing MIT, Cambridge, 1980-81; Hurst prof. poetry Washington U., St. Louis, 1987; Conkling writer in residence Smith Coll., Northampton, Mass., fall 1994. Vis. fellow St. Catherine's Coll., Oxford U., 1997, Getty Rsch. Inst., 2000. Author: numerous poems. Recipient Rome prize in lit. Am. Acad. Arts and Letters, 1983, Acad. award in lit. Am. Acad. Arts and Letters, 1998, Brandeis citation in poetry, 1989, Berlin prize, 2004; Nat. Endowment for the Arts fellow in poetry, 1986, Guggenheim fellow, 1987; Book Prize in Poetry, L.A. Times, 2000. Fellow: Am. Acad. Rome, Am. Acad. Arts and Scis., Am. Acad. in Berlin. Democrat.

SCHNALL, EDITH LEA, microbiologist, educator; b. N.Y.C., Apr. 11, 1922; d. Irving and Sadie (Raab) Spitzer; m. Herbert Schnall, Aug. 21, 1949 (dec. Feb. 17, 2005); children: Neil David, Carolyn Beth. AB, Hunter Coll., 1942; AM, Columbia U., 1947, PhD, 1967. Clin. pathologist Roosevelt Hosp., N.Y.C., 1942-44; instr. Adelphi Coll., Garden City, N.Y., 1944-46; tchg. asst. Columbia U., 1946; asst. med. mycologist Columbia Coll. Physicians and Surgeons, N.Y.C., 1946-47, 49-50; instr. Bklyn. Coll., 1947; mem. faculty Sarah Lawrence Coll., Bronxville, N.Y., 1947-48; lectr. Hunter Coll., N.Y.C., 1947-67; adj. assoc. prof. Lehman Coll., CUNY, 1968; hon. curator N.Y. Bot. Garden, 1968; asst. prof. Queensborough C.C., CUNY, 1967, assoc. prof. microbiology, 1968-75, prof., 1975—2002, adminstr. Med. Lab. Tech. program, 1985—2003, prof. emerita, 2003—. Vis. prof. Coll. Physicians and Surgeons, Columbia U., N.Y.C., 1974; advanced biology examiner U. London, 1970—. Editor: Newsletter of Med. Mycology Soc. N.Y., 1969-85; founder, editor Female Perspective newsletter of Queensborough Community Coll. Women's Club, 1971-73. Mem. Alley Restoration Com., N.Y.C., 1971—; mem. legis. adv. com. Assembly of the State of N.Y., 1972; mem. Cmty. Bd. 11, Queens, N.Y., 1974-78, 3d vice-chmn., 1987-92, 2d vice chmn., 1992-97; pub. dir. of bd. dirs. Inst. Continuing Dental Edn. Queens County, Dental Soc. N.Y. State and ADA, 1973-97. Rsch. fellow NIH, 1948-49; faculty rsch. fellow, grantee-in-aid Rsch. Found. of SUNY, 1968-70; faculty rsch. grant Rsch. Found. CUNY, 1971-74. Mem. AAAS, Internat. Soc. Human Animal Mycology, Am. Soc. Microbiology (coun., N.Y.C. br. 1981—, co-chairperson ann. meeting com. 1981-82, chair program com. 1982-83, v.p. 1984-86, pres. 1986-88), Med. Mycology Soc. N.Y. (sec.-treas. 1967-68, v.p. 1968-69, 78-79, archivist 1974—, fin. advisor 1983-97, pres. 1969-70, 79-80, 81-82, Lifetime Achievement award, 2002), Bot. Soc. Am., Med. Mycology Soc. Americas, Mycology Soc. Am., N.Y. Acad. Scis., Torrey Bot. Club (N.Y. State), Queensborough Community Coll. Women's Club (pres. 1971-73, N.Y.C.), Sigma Xi, Phi Sigma. Home: 21406 29th Ave Flushing NY 11360-2622

SCHNEEBERG, HELEN BASSEN, retired elementary school educator; b. Phila., Apr. 5, 1920; d. Carl and Minnie (Aion) Bassen; m. Norman Grahn Schneeberg, Nov. 3, 1940; children: Susan, Karen. BA, U. Pa., 1941, cert. advanced studies, 1984; MLS, Drexel U., 1966. Cert. librarian. Bacteriologist Mount Sinai Hosp., Phila., 1941—43; libr. W. Phila. H.S., 1966—67, Temple U., Phila., 1967—68; rsch. asst. Franklin Inst. Rsch. Lab., Phila., 1968—69; tchg. assoc. Temple U., 1970—71; dir. Listen-Read Project Phila. Sch. Dist., 1971—76; ret., 1976. Contbr. articles to rsch. reports. Bd. dirs. Please Touch Mus., Phila., 1979—81, Citizens Com. for Pub. Edn. in Phila., 1991—; steering com. mem. Physicians for Social Responsibility, Phila., 1982—84; area legis. coord. Women's Agenda, Phila., 1984—; mem. steering com. Sch. Age Child Care Coalition, Phila., 1988—, Ctr. City Concerned Citizens, 1994—, 2000—; mem. Millenium Club Phila. Citizens Children & Youth. Avocations: travel, reading, music, theater, sailing. Home: 2401 Pennsylvania Ave Apt 17a5 Philadelphia PA 19130-3054

SCHNEIDER, ANN IMLAH, federal agency administrator, education consultant; b. Boston, Jan. 3, 1934; d. Albert Henry and Helen (Woodbridge) Imlah; m. John Hoke Schneider, Mar. 26, 1966 (div. 1978); children: Helen May, James Christopher. BA, Swarthmore Coll., 1955; MA, Fletcher Sch., 1956; PhD, London Sch. Econs., 1963. Asst. dir. Davis House, Am. Friends Service Com., Washington, 1956-57; adminstrv. asst. Nat. Acad. Scis., Washington, 1957-60; fgn. affairs research analyst U.S. Dept. State, Washington, 1964-70; sr. program specialist U.S. Dept. Edn., Washington, 1970—95; internat. edn. cons., 1995—. Author: Britain and Switzerland 1845-60, 1966, Federal Funding for International Studies: Does It Help? Does It Matter?, 1999, Internationalizing Teacher Education: What Can Be Done?, 2003; contbr. articles. Sec. Alumni and Friends of London Sch. Econs., Washington, 1983—91, chair scholarship com., 1990—98, pres., 1999—2003. Mem.: AAAS, Soc. for Hist. in Fed. Gov., Am. Hist. Assn., Soc. Woman Geographers (asst. treas. 1987—90, treas. 1990—96, oral history com. 1996—, chair membership com. 2003—), Internat. Studies Assn. (editl bd. for Internat. Studies Perspectives 1979—2005, pres. local chpt. 1980—81, nat. exec. coun. 1981—82). Avocations: hiking, theater, concerts, gardening, needlecrafts. Home: 3319 Fessenden St NW Washington DC 20008-2034 Office Phone: 202-363-0109. Personal E-mail: aimlahs@aol.com.

SCHNEIDER, CAROL GEARY, educational association administrator; BA in History, magna cum laude, Mount Holyoke Coll.; postgrad., U. London Inst. Historical Rsch.; PhD in Early Modern History, Harvard U. Instr. Chgo. State U., DePaul U., Boston U., U. Chgo., 1978—88, dir. Midwest Faculty Seminar, founding dir. Inst. on Teaching and Learning; exec. v.p. Assn. Am. Colls. and Univs., Washington, 1988—98, pres., 1998—. Contbr. articles to profl. jours. Bd. trustees Mt. Holyoke Coll. Woodrow Wilson fellow, Harvard U., Kent fellow, Harvard Prize fellow, Mina Shaughnessy fellow, U.S. Dept. Edn., 1982. Mem.: Phi Beta Kappa. Office: Am Assn Colls and Univs 1818 R St NW Washington DC 20009

SCHNEIDER, CAROLYN ANNE, educator, director; b. New Bedford, Mass., Mar. 16, 1962; d. Americo Gilbert and Laura Souza Perry; m. Walter Thomas Schneider, Sept. 28, 1996; 1 child, Cecilia. BS, Salve Regina U., Newport, R.I., 1984; MS, Boston Coll., Chestnut Hill, Mass., 1987, PhD, 1991. Rsch. assoc. Boston Coll., Chestnut Hill, 1991—94; faculty Fisher Coll., Boston, 1995—96, Salve Regina U., Newport, 1997—, lab. coord., 2005—. Editor: My Life As a Soldier in the Fifth Army Antiaircraft Artillery, 1942-1945, 2000. Roman Catholic. Avocations: reading, travel, antiques, genealogy, history. Office: Salve Regina University 100 Ochre Point Ave Newport RI 02840 Office Phone: 401-341-3248. Office Fax: 401-341-2993. Business E-Mail: carolyn.schneider@salve.edu.

SCHNEIDER, CATHERINE CHEMIN, occupational therapist, consultant; d. Anthony Joseph Chemin and Irma Gema Bizzotto; m. Daniel Patrick Schneider, Sept. 25, 1970; children: David Patrick, Patricia Marie. BS in Occupl. Therapy, Wayne State U., 1970. Staff therapist Henry Ford Hosp., Detroit, 1971, Plymouth Ctr. for Human Devel., 1971—73, Oak Park Devel. Tng. Ctr., Mich., 1973—75; itinerant staff therapist, cons. Ingham Intermediate Sch. Dist., Mich., 1975—76; sch. therapist, cons. Birmingham (Mich.) Pub. Schs., 1978—91; cons., pres. The Positive Difference, LLC, Northville, Mich., 1992—2000; sch. therapist, cons. Bloomfield Hills (Mich.) Sch., 1992—99; presenter in field, 2003—. Author: Sensory Secrets: How to "Jump-Start" Learning in Children, 2001, 2006; co-author (with Carol Poltorak): Your Sensational Brain, 2006. Mem.: Am. Occupl. Therapy Assn. Avocations: reading, music, needlecrafts. Office Phone: 248-344-8188. E-mail: posdiff@aol.com.

SCHNEIDER, CHRISTINE LYNN, customs inspector; b. SI, NY, Feb. 3, 1960; d. Howard Thomas and Ina Elise (Beyer) S. BS, SUNY Maritime Coll., Bronx, 1984. Lic. 3d mate, U.S. Mcht. Marine; cert. U.S. customs firearms instr. Chief inspector Customs and Border Protection, San Diego, 1989—. Served to lt. comdr. USNR, 1984-87, 91—. Democrat. Lutheran. Avocations: coin collecting/numismatics, pistol shooting, golf. Home: 3505 Valley Rd Apt 3 Bonita CA 91902 Office: Customs and Border Protection 720 E San Ysidro Blvd San Ysidro CA 92173-3115 Office Phone: 619-690-8800. Personal E-mail: cschne6548@aol.com.

SCHNEIDER, CYNTHIA PERRIN, former ambassador, political science professor; b. Pa., Aug. 16, 1953; m. Thomas J. Schneider; 2 children. BA in Fine Arts magna cum laude, Harvard U., 1977, PhD in Fine Arts, 1984. Asst. curator European paintings Mus. Fine Arts, Boston, unitl 1984; asst. prof. art history Georgetown U., Washington, 1984-90, assoc. prof. art history, 1990—2004; amb. to The Netherlands Am. Embassy, The Hague, 1998-2001; dir., life sciences & society initiative Georgetown U., Washington, 2003—, disting. prof. in practice of diplomacy, Pfizer Med. Humanities Initiative scholar-in-residence. Lectr. on Rembrandt and Dutch art in US and Europe; vice-chair President's Com. on Arts and Humanities. Author: Rembrandt's Landscapes, 1990; organizer, writer (catalog) Rembrandt's Landscape Print and Drawings, Nat. Gallery Art, 1990; contbr. articles to profl. jour. Mem. steering com. Creative Am., chair fed. design subcom.; coord. arts policy Clinton-Gore Campaign, 1992; bd. dir. Nat. Mus. Women in Arts, Australian-Am. Leadership Dialogue; supervisory bd. Royal Ahold, 2001—05; adv. bd. Strawberry Frog, Inc.; bd. dir. Wesley Theological Sem., Coun. Am. Ambassadors; bd. adv. Inst. for Cultural Diplomacy; internat. bd. adv., Inst. for the Study of Europe Columbia U.; Am. bd. Anne Frank House Found. Recipient Exceptional Svc. Order, Office of US Sec. of Def., 2001. Office: Distinguished Prof in Practice of Diplomacy Georgetown Univ 3300 Whitehaven St NW Ste 500 Washington DC 20057 Office Phone: 202-687-0703. Office Fax: 301-924-8715. E-mail: schneidc@georgetown.edu.

SCHNEIDER, ELAINE CAROL, lawyer, researcher, writer; b. Mpls., Aug. 28, 1957; d. Allan William and Deborah G. Schneider; m. William Mack Olivé, Oct. 10, 1987 (div. July 1996); 1 child, Vanessa Inez Olivè; m. G.R. Smith, Jan. 2, 2002. BA, U. Minn., 1979; JD, William Mitchell Coll. Law, St. Paul, 1982. Bar: N.Mex. 1984, Minn. 1998, D.C. 1999. Assoc. Settles, Kalamarides & Assocs., Anchorage, 1982, Dickson, Evans & Esch, Anchorage, 1982; legal rschr. John Hanson, Anchorage, 1983; acct. rep. Westlaw Svcs., Inc., Albuquerque, 1984, sales rep. New Orleans, 1985-86; libr. sales rep. West Pub. Co., Spokane, Wash., 1986-87, reference atty. St. Paul, 1988-97, product mgr., 1997-2001; pvt. practice Mpls.; CEO, mem. Coeur à Coeur Fashion Beauty Products, LLC, Minn., 2004. Ethics adv. bd. N.Mex. Bar, Albuquerque, 1984-85; midwest regional conf. com. Am. Immigration Lawyers Assn., 2000. Author: Substantive Judicial Law Outline of Habeas Corpus, 1984, What They Don't Teach You in the Bar Review Course, 1991, Challenging an Incredibility Finding on Appeal, An Incredibility Paradigm, 2001; mem. law rev. staff: William Mitchell Coll. Law, 1980—81. Atty. immigration and naturalization law Minn. Advocates for Human Rights, Refugee and Immigrant Project. Recipient Vol. Pro Bono Atty. award, 15th Ann. Minn. Advocates for Human Rights, 1999. Mem. Phi Beta Kappa. Avocations: ventriloquism, skiing, swimming, travel, languages. Office: 701 4th Ave' S Ste 500 Minneapolis MN 55415-1810 Personal E-mail: avocatecs@aol.com.

SCHNEIDER, GISELA, art educator; b. Frankfurt, Germany, June 1, 1949; BA in Visual Art, Mont. State U., 1972. Cert. tchr., Mont. Instr. H.S. visual art Great Falls Sch. Dist. #1, Mont., 1972—80, Missoula County Sch. Dist., Mont., 1985—86, Colstrup Sch. Dist. #9, Mont., 1986—. Visual art workshop presenter Mont. Edn. Assn. Annual State Convs., 1988—; visual art juror and inservice presenter in field. Mem. Mont. Art Edn. Assn. (secondary art edn. com. 1972—, rep. 1989-92, Mt. Art Educator of Yr. 1993).

SCHNEIDER, GRETA, economist, writer, speaker, efficiency expert, security consultant, public administration expert; b. Bklyn. Student, Bklyn. Conservatory of Music, 1961—66; BA, MA, CUNY, 1975, MA, 1976. Writer, cons., Pitts., 1972-73; cons. Flushing, N.Y., 1973-85; sr. writer, cons. Buck Cons. Inc., N.Y.C., 1985-86; chmn., CEO Schneider Cons. Inc., N.Y.C., 1986-90; pvt. cons. Greta Schneider Cons., N.Y.C., 1991—; prin. Schneider Consulting Group, 1996—. Advisor Am. Women's Econ. Devel. Corp., 1988—; adv. bd. Women's Profl. Coun., 1998; guest mem. discussion Reuters Bus. Report, 1998; mem. Women's Econ. Round Table, 1998, Profl. Women's Adv. Bd., 1998; lectr. The Learning Annex, 1995—96, 2002, Seminar Ctr., N.Y.C., 1998—; voiceover talent Such a Voice, 2004—, Utter Words, 2004—; instr. Port Washington Continuing Edn., 2005—; counterterrorism/security cons.; spkr. in field. Author: Exploding the Bankruptcy Mystique, 1993, Holistic Bankruptcy, 1998, 2002. Active Bklyn. Conservatory Music, 1961-66, Little Theatre Group, Marathon Cmty. Ctr., Little Neck, NY, 1980-83; founder, pres. Bankruptcy Anonymous, 1996 Cambridge Biographical Inst. fellow, 1993. Mem. AFTRA, Nat. Assn. Women Bus. Owners, Nat. Assn. Bus. Communicators, Internat. Platform Assn. (spkr. 2001), Employee Assistance Profls. Assn., Soc. Human Resource Mgmt., U.S. C. of C., Writers Guild Am., Rotary. Avocations: chef, pilot, tennis, chess, speech coach.

SCHNEIDER, HILARY A., Internet company executive; BA in Econs., Brown U., 1982; MBA, Harvard Bus. Sch., 1986. Dir. devel. The Balt. Sun Co., 1992—94, v.p. new bus. devel., 1994—95, v.p. sales, 1996—97, v.p. sales and mktg., 1997—98, gen. mgr., 1998—99; v.p. corp. fin. Drexel Burnham Lambert Inc., 1986—90; dir. bus. devel. Times Mirror Corp., 1990—92; pres., CEO Times Mirror Interactive, Balt., 1999—2000; CEO Red Herring Comm., 2000—02; v.p. Knight Ridder Digital, 2002—04, pres., CEO, 2002—04; sr. v.p. Knight Ridder, 2005—06; sr. v.p. marketplaces Yahoo! Inc., Sunnyvale, Calif., 2006—. Bd. dirs. CareerBuilder.com. Office: Yahoo Inc 701 1st Ave Sunnyvale CA 94089*

SCHNEIDER, JANE HARRIS, sculptor; b. Trenton, NJ, Jan. 2, 1932; d. Leon Harris and Dorothy (Perlman) Rosenthal; m. Alfred R. Schneider, July 25, 1953; children: Lee, Jeffry, Elizabeth. BA, Wellesley Coll.; postgrad., Columbia U., Coll. New Rochelle. One-woman shows include June Kelly Gallery, 1990, 1993, 1995, 1997, 2000, 2003, 2006, Phila. Art Alliance, 1984, Alternative Mus., NYC, 1985, Nassau County Mus. Fine Art, Roslyn, NY, 1988, Atrium Gallery, St. Louis, 1993, 1996, 1997—2000, 2001, 2003, 2005, Collaborative Concepts, Cold Spring, N.Y., 1998—99, Interch. Ctr., NYC, 2001, Marist Coll. Art Gallery, Poughkeepsie, N.Y., 2001, Clark U., Worcester, Mass., 2001, L.I. U., Bklyn., 2005, exhibited in group shows at 7th Regiment Armory, NYC, 1998—2006, June Kelly Gallery, Chgo., 2001—04, Biennale Internat. Dell'Arte Contemporanea, Florence, Italy, 2003, East Ctrl. Coll., Union. Mo., 2006, Byrdcliffe Art Colony, Woodstock, NY, Hudson River Mus., Yonkers, NY, Fine Arts Mus. L.I., Hempstead, Isis Conceptual Lab., West Branch, Iowa, Sculptor Ctr., NYC, Represented in permanent collections Fine Arts Mus. L.I., Davis Mus. and Cultural Ctr., Wellesley, Mass., Paterson Mus., N.J., N.J. State Mus., Trenton, Ark. Art Ctr., Little Rock, Neuberger Mus., Purchase, N.Y., Kutztown U., Pa., Munson-Williams Proctor Inst., Utica, N.Y., U. Wis. Art Galleries, La Crosse, Phila. Art Alliance, Villa Taverna Found., Washington, N.Y. Hosp. for Joint Diseases. Avocations: swimming, gardening. Studio: 75 Grand St New York NY 10013-2235 Office Phone: 212-925-1477. Personal E-mail: jhsart@earthlink.net.

SCHNEIDER, JANET M., arts administrator, curator, painter; b. N.Y.C., June 6, 1950. d. August Arthur and Joan (Battaglia) S.; m. Michael Francis Sperendi, Sept. 21, 1985. BA summa cum laude, Queens Coll., CUNY, 1972; spl. study fine arts Boston U. Tanglewood Inst., 1971. With Queens Mus., Flushing, N.Y., 1973-89, curator, 1973-75, program dir., 1975-77, exec. dir., 1977-89. Collections arranged include: Sons and others, Women Artists See Men (author catalog), 1975, Urban Aesthetics (author catalog), 1976, Masters of the Brush, Chinese Painting and Calligraphy from the Sixteenth to the Nineteenth Century (co-author catalog), 1977, Symcho Moszkowicz: Portrait of the Artist in Postwar Europe (author catalog), 1978, Shipwrecked 1622, The Lost Treasure of Philip IV (author catalog), 1981, Michaelangelo: A Sculptor's World (author catalog), 1983, Joseph Cornell: Revisited (author catalog), 1992, Blueprint for Change: The Life and Times of Lewis H. Latimer (co-author catalog), 1995. Chmn. Cultural Instns. Group, N.Y.C., 1986-87; mem. N.Y.C. Commn. for Cultural Affairs, 1991-93; bd. dirs. N.Y.C. Partnership, 1987-88, Gallery Assn. N.Y. State 1979-81; exec. dir. Cultural Inst. Group, 1995—. Mem. Artists Choice Mus. (trustee 1979-82), Am. Assn. Mus., Phi Beta Kappa.

SCHNEIDER, JOANNE, artist; b. Lima, Ohio, Dec. 4, 1919; d. Joseph and Laura (Office) Federman; m. Norman Schneider, May 15, 1941; children—Melanie Schneider Tucker, Lois Schneider Oppenheim. BFA, Syracuse U., 1941. One-man shows John Heller Gallery, N.Y.C., 1954, 55, 57, 58, Tirca Karlis Gallery, Provincetown, Mass., 1963, Frank Rehn Gallery, N.Y.C., 1965, 66, 69, 72, 75, Elaine Benson Gallery, Bridgehamton, N.Y., 1972, 74, 79, 85, St. Mary's Coll., St. Mary's City, Md., 1978, Alonzo Gallery, N.Y.C., 1978, Discovery Art Gallery, Clifton, N.J., 1978; group shows include Whitney Mus., N.Y.C., Pa. Acad. Arts, Corcoran Galleries, Washington, Toledo Mus., U. Nebr., Everson Mus., Syracuse, N.Y.; represented in permanent collections Met. Mus. Art, N.Y.C., Colby Coll., Syracuse U., Butler Inst., St. Mary's Coll., U. Notre Dame, Guild Hall, East Hampton, N.Y. Recipient Audubon Artists Stanley Grumbacher Meml. award, 1972 Address: 35 E 75th St New York NY 10021-2761

SCHNEIDER, JULIA, library director; b. St. Joseph, Mo., Feb. 17, 1947; d. Lewis Wilber and Rosella Thompson; m. Thomas Edwin Schneider, Jan. 31, 1975; children: Jedd Christian, Jeremy Adam, Jacob Martin. AA, Mo. Western State Coll., St. Joseph, 1967; BA, NW Mo. State U., Maryville, 1969; MA, U. Mo., Columbia, 1971. Cataloger St. Joseph Pub. Libr., 1969-70; acquisitions libr. Mo. We. State U., St. Joseph, 1971-75, tech. processes libr., 1975-83, coord. tech. svcs., 1983-90, libr. dir., 1990—. Pres. Mo. Libr. Assn., 1994; bd. dirs. Mo. Libr. Network Corp., v.p., 1998—2001, pres., 2001—04; treas., pres.-elect MOBIUS Consortium, Columbia, Mo., 2006—. Mem. St. Joseph Area Literacy Coalition, 1994—; mem. fund drive steering com. Allied Arts Assn., St. Joseph, 1991—; vol. United Way, St. Joseph, 1990—. Mem.: ALA, Mo. Libr. Assn. (pres. 1994, bd. dirs. 1995), Bus. and Profl. Women (pres. 1998, 1999), The Runcie Club, Delta Kappa Gamma, Beta Phi Mu. Methodist. Avocations: antiques, music, organ. Home: 4908 NE County Line Rd Saint Joseph MO 64505-9329 Office: Mo Western State U 4525 Downs Dr Saint Joseph MO 64507-2246 Office Phone: 816-271-4369. Business E-Mail: schneide@missouriwestern.edu.

SCHNEIDER, LESLIE JEAN, elementary school educator; b. Vancouver, Wash. d. James Dwight and Georgia Julia Larsen; m. Al Kukes, Apr. 2, 1976; m. Paul Scheider, Dec. 1, 1996; children: James Alfred Kukes, Kimberly Julia Howard. BA in Edn., Ctrl. Wash. U., Ellensburg, 1973, MusM, 1996. Tchr. elem. music Yakima Sch. Dist., Wash., 1973—76, Ellensburg Sch. Dist., 1991—. Named Tchr. of Yr., Ellensburg Sch. Dist., 2005—06; recipient award, Oscar Mayer, 2002; grantee, Shopa Kids Need Found., 2005, Ellensburg Edn. Found., 2005. Mem.: Ellensburg Edn. Pres. (bldg. rep. 2002—06), Music Educator's Nat. Conf. (choir selected as part of World's Largest Concert 2006), Pi Kappa Lambda. Avocation: gardening. Home: 208 Mt Daniels Drive Ellensburg WA 98926 Office: Valley View Elementary 1508 E 3rd Ave Ellensburg WA 98926 Office Phone: 509-925-7316. E-mail: lschneider@wonders.eburg.wednet.edu.

SCHNEIDER, LYNETTE D., secondary school educator, department chairman; b. Sacramento, Calif., May 22, 1959; d. Gary A. Brown and Sharon R. Harmon; m. Steven P. Schneider, Aug. 24, 1985; children: Ariel L., Kaitlyn M. BS, Calif. Inst. Tech., Pasadena, 1981. Cert. tchr. Ind. R&D supr. Syntex Med. Devices, Palo Alto, Calif., 1983—85; sr. staff scientist product devel. Beckman Instruments, Brea, Calif., 1985—89; biology tchr., chmn. sci. dept. Harrison HS, West Lafayette, Ind., 1996—. Bd. dirs. Montessori Sch. Greater Lafayette, West Lafayette, 1994—98, Ind. Quiz Bowl Assn., 2004—06. Recipient Outstanding Employee Merit award, Beckman Instruments, 1988, Golden Apple Tchg. award, Greater Lafayette C. of C., 2006; Nat. Merit scholar, Ford Found., 1977. Mem.: Ind. Assn. Biology Tchrs., Hoosier Assn. Sci. Tchrs., Nat. Assn. Biology Tchrs., Calif. Inst. Tech. Alumni Assn. Office: Harrison HS 5701 N 50 W West Lafayette IN 47906 Office Phone: 765-463-3511. Business E-Mail: lschneider@tsc.k12.in.us.

SCHNEIDER, MARGARET PERRIN, scriptwriter; b. N.Y.C., Dec. 31, 1923; d. Sam and Peggy (Flood) Perrin; m. Paul Schneider, Apr. 10, 1950; children: Peggy Lee, Peter-Lincoln, Ann Rose. BA in Psychology and Edn., UCLA, 1949. Gen. elem. tchg. credential, Calif. Tchr. L.A. City Schs., North Hollywood, 1944-55; script writer MGM Studios, 1957-75; staff writer Universal Studios, 1957-75; head writer CBS Studios, N.Y.C., 1975-76. Participant Women in Film, L.A., 1975; chmn. Writers Craft Conf., Arrowhead, Calif., 1975. Mem. Writers Guild Am. (freelance writers com. 1985), Dems. for Action. Avocations: wild flower photography, birding, gardening, travel. Home: PO Box 65 54386 Village View Idyllwild CA 92549

SCHNEIDER, MARY ETTA, finance company executive; m. John Beardsley. Grad. cum laude, SUNY, Oswego; grad., Coll. Europe, Brugge, Belgium, Center Latin Am. Studies, Mex. City. Mng. dir., head loan syndications BankBoston, 1996—97, mng. dir., investment bank, 1997—98; exec. VP, specialized fin. Bank Boston Corp.; exec. VP, corp. banking group FleetBoston Fin. Corp., exec. VP, capital markets, 2002—. Mem. adv. bd. Metropolitan Opera; bd. dirs. Boys & Girls Club Boston.

SCHNEIDER, MARY LOUISE, retired elementary school educator; b. Waterville, Wash., Oct. 17, 1918; d. John Steve and Alice Ray (Jones) S. BA in Edn., Holy Names Coll., 1940. Cert. elem. tchr. Wash., 1940. Tchr. Mud Springs/Douglas County, Mansfield, Wash., 1941-42; elem. tchr. Mansfield Sch. dist., Douglas County, Wash., 1942-43, Waterville (Wash.) Sch. Dist., Douglas County, Wash., 1943-49, Lewis and Clark Elem. Sch., Wenatchee, Wash., 1949-60; spl. reading tchr. H.B. Ellison Jr. High, Wenatchee, 1960-62, Orchard Jr. High, Wenatchee, 1962-67; lang. arts tchr. Pioneer Jr. High, Wenatchee, 1967-77; retired, 1977. Author lang. arts learning packages for students, 1967; co-author: Name on the Schoolhouse, 1989. Vol. Am. Heart Assn., Wenatchee, 1975-90, Am. Cancer Soc., Wenatchee, 1975-88. Recipient Cert. of Recognition, Wash. State Ct. Cath. Daus. of the Ams., 1970, 72, 74. Mem.: AAUW (treas. 1973—75), PEO (pres. 1980—82, 1988—90), Chelan-Douglas County Sch. Retirees Assn. (com. chmn. 1989—90), Cath. Daus. of the Ams. (state pres. 1984—86, nat. evangelization chmn. 1986—88, local ct. pres. 1958—60, 1999—2001, author Wash. State Ct. of Cath. Daus. 1988). Avocation: sewing.

SCHNEIDER, PAM HORVITZ, lawyer; b. Cleve., Nov. 29, 1951; m. Milton S. Schneider, June 30, 1973; 1 child, Sarah Anne. BA, U. Pa., 1973; JD, Columbia U., 1976. Bar: N.Y. 1977, Pa. 1979. Assoc. White & Case, N.Y.C., 1976-78, Drinker Biddle & Reath LLP, Phila., 1978-84, ptnr., 1984-2001; founding ptnr. Gadsden Schneider & Woodward LLP, King of Prussia, Pa., 2001—. Contbr. articles to profl. jours. Fellow Am. Coll. Trust and Estate Counsel (past regent); mem. ABA (past chair, real property probate and trust law sect.), Internat. Acad. Estate and Trust Law (academician). Office: Gadsden Schneider & Woodward LLP The Merion Bldg 700 S Henderson Rd Ste 345 King Of Prussia PA 19406 E-mail: pschneider@gsw-llp.com.

SCHNEIDER, PAULINE A., lawyer; b. Bridgeton, N.J., May 25, 1943; BA, Glassboro State Coll., 1965; postgrad., Syracuse U., 1966; M Urban Studies, Howard U., 1972; JD, Yale U., 1977. Bar: DC 1978. Staff asst. White House Office Intergovtl. Affairs, 1978—81; dir. Office Intergovtl. Rels., DC Govt., 1983—85; ptnr. Hunton & Williams, Washington, 1985—. Bd. dirs. MedStar Health Inc., Potomac Elec. Power Co., Diamond Cluster Internat., MDL Capital Mgmt. Bd. dir. Nat. Partnership for Women and Families; bd. dirs. Access Group, Lab Sch. of Washington; trustee Shakespeare Theatre, U. Md. Balt. Found.; mem. Pres. Adv. Coun. Washington Coll. Named one of Women Who Shape Future, Women's Legal Def. Fund, 1994; recipient Woman Lawyer of Yr., Women's Bar Assn. DC, 1995, Pres. award, Nat. Assn. Women Lawyers, 1998, Margaret Brent Women of Achievement award, ABA Commn. on Women, 1999, Woman of Genius award, Trinity Coll., 2000, Woman of Achievement, Anti-Defamation League, 2001, Outstanding Alumni, Rowan Univ., 2001. Mem.: ABA (bd. govs. 2003—06, mem.exec. com. 2005—, ho. of dels. 1993—, chair coun. sect. on legal edn. 2004—05), Econ. Club of Washington (bd. dirs.), Nat. Bar Assn., DC Bar Assn. (bd. dirs. 1988—94, pres. 1994—95), Am. Bar Found., Am. Law Inst., Nat. Assn. Securities Professionals, Nat. Assn. Bond Lawyers. Office: Hunton & Williams LLP 1900 K St Washington DC 20006-1110 Office Phone: 202-955-1660.

SCHNEIDER, PHYLLIS LEAH, writer, editor; b. Seattle, Apr. 19, 1947; d. Edward Lee Booth and Harriet Phyllis (Ebbinghaus) Russell; m. Clifford Donald Schneider, June 14, 1969; 1 child, Pearl Brooke. BA, Pacific Luth. U., 1969; MA, U. Wash., 1972. Fiction, features editor Seventeen Mag., N.Y.C., 1975-80; mng. editor Weight Watchers Mag., N.Y.C., 1980-81; editor YM mag., N.Y.C., 1981-86. Author: Parents Book of Infant Colic, 1990, Kids Who Make a Difference, 1993, Straight Talk on Women's Health: How to Get the Health Care You Deserve, 1993, Hot Health Care Careers, 1993, What Kids Like To Do, 1993; contbr. The Parents Answer Book, 1998; The Prose Reader, 2001, 2004. Recipient Centennial Recognition award Pacific Luth. U., 1990. Democrat. Episcopalian.

SCHNEIDER, SHERRI, library clerk; b. Bloomington, Ill., Oct. 9, 1954; d. Ronald Deane and Barbara Hinton; m. Kevin Donald Schneider, oct. 29, 1977; 1 child, Rachael. BA magna cum laude, U. Wis., Platteville, 1976; MLS, Drake U., 1982. Intern to editor The Annals of Iowa, Des Moines, 1980-82; spl. collections asst. Bradley U., Peoria, Ill., 1983—. Cons. local history course, divsn. continuing edn. Bradley U., 1986; mem. steering com. Friends of Cullom-Davis Libr., Peoria, 1990; instr. Preservation Workshops at Bradley, 1991, 92. Author law firm history; rschr. Peoria history brochure. Mem., sec. Heart of Ill. Fancy Cats, Peoria, 1983-86; sec. Peoria Hist. Soc., 1986-94; libr. vol. St. Thomas Sch., Peoria Hts., Ill., 1993—; v.p. Jackson Found., Peoria, 1990—. Mem. Ill. State Hist. Soc., Peoria County Old Settlers, Peoria County Lawyers Aux., Bradley Women's Club. Avocations: travel, gardening, reading, needlecrafts, sewing.

SCHNEIDER, SUE R., music educator; b. Rochester, N.Y., Feb. 13, 1955; d. Irving M. and Barbara S. Robinson; m. Steven J. Schneider, Aug. 6, 1977; children: Scott, Jonathan, Jacquelyn. B in Music Edn., Wittenberg U., 1977; MEd, Nazareth Coll., 1983. Music educator vocal and instrumental Springfield (Ohio) Local Schs., 1977—79; music educator instrumental Greece Ctrl. Schs., Rochester, 1979—. Music dir. choir Aldersgate United Meth. Ch., Rochester, 1983—88, music dir. contemporary worship, 1992—. Mem.: Monroe County Music Assn. (exec. bd. dirs. 1999—2002). Methodist. Home: 8 Wainswright Cir Rochester NY 14626 Office: Arcadia Mid Sch Elem 130 Island Cottage Rd Rochester NY 14612 Personal E-mail: bandir@rochester.rr.com. Business E-Mail: Sue.Schneider@greece.k12.ny.us.

SCHNEIDER, URSULA WILFRIEDE, author; b. Stuttgart, Germany, June 13, 1936; came to U.S., 1966; d. Kurt and Anna Schneider; children: Kurt Mihran, Yvonne Ulrike. BA in French, CUNY, 1977, MA in French Lit., 1979, ABD in Comparative Lit., 1988, PhD in Comparative Lit., 1992. Mgr. export/import of chems. A.K. Peters Co., N.Y.C., 1967-80; asst. to sales mgr. FBA Pharms., N.Y.C., 1981; pvt. sect. to sr. ptnr., head internat. dept. Bear Stearns, N.Y.C., 1982-84; in-house translator for acquisition Siemens Capital Corp., N.Y.C., 1985-86; adj. lectr. German Hunter Coll./CUNY, 1987-90, Montclair (N.J.) State U., 1991-92. Prof. World Trade Ctr./Internat. Inst. for Langs., 1988-89, UN Internat. Sch., N.Y.C., 1979. Author: Ars amandi: The Erotic of Extremes in Thomas Mann and Marguerite Duras, 1995, The Cross-Eyed God, 1995, Velvet Cages, 2001, Vernal Amours, 2004. Helena Rubinstein Found. grantee, Bd. Higher Edn. grantee; recipient Marta Retzler award. Mem. MLA, Fgn. Lang. Educators of N.J., Northeastern MLA, Am. Coun. Tchrs. English Lang., Phi Beta Kappa. Avocations: running, skiing, swimming, skating, tennis. Home: 1201 River Reach Dr Apt 204 Fort Lauderdale FL 33315-1179 Personal E-mail: uwsftlaud@aol.com.

SCHNEIDER, VALERIE LOIS, retired speech educator; b. Chgo., Feb. 12, 1941; d. Ralph Joseph and Gertrude Blanche (Gaffron) S. BA, Carroll Coll., 1963; MA, U. Wis., 1966; PhD, U. Fla., 1969; CAS, Appalachian State U., 1981. Tchr. English and history, dir. forensics and drama Montello (Wis.) H.S., 1963-64; instr. speech U. Fla., Gainesville, 1966-68, asst. prof. speech, 1969-70, Edinboro (Pa.) State Coll., 1970-71; assoc. prof. speech East Tenn. State U., Johnson City, 1971-76, prof. speech, 1976-97. Instr. newspaper course Johnson City Press Chronicle, 1979, Elizabethton Star, Erwin Record, Mountain City Tomahawk, Jonesboro Herald and Tribune, 1980; mem. investor panel USA Today, 1991-92. Editor East Tenn. State U. evening and off-campus newsletter, 1984-91; assoc. editor Homiletic, 1974-76; columnist Video Visions, Kingsport Times-News, 1984-86; book reviewer Pulpit Digest, 1986-90; contbr. articles to profl. jours. Chmn. AAUW Mass Media Study Group Com., Johnson City, 1973-74. Recipient Creative Writing award Va. Highlands Arts Festival, 1973, award Kingsport Times News, 1984, 85, Tri-Cities Met. Advt. Fedn., 1983, 84, hon. life mem. Tenn. Presbyn. Women, 2000; named Danforth assoc., 1977; finalist Money mag. contest, 1994, Writer's Digest contest, 2000. Mem.: AAUW (v.p. chpt. 1974—75, pres. 1975—76), Tenn. Basic Skills Coun. (pres. 1975—76, exec. bd. 1979—80, v.p. 1980—81), Religious Speech Comm. Assn. (Best Article award 1976), Tenn. Speech Comm. Assn. (exec. bd. 1974—77, publs. bd. 1974—78, pres. 1977—78), So. Speech Comm. Assn., Speech Comm. Assn. (Tenn. rep. to states adv. coun. 1974—75), Mensa, Presbyn. Women (hon.; life mem.), Johnson City Book Club (pres. 2001—03), Bus. and Profl. Women's Club (chpt. exec. bd. 1972—73, v.p. 1976—77), Pi Gamma Mu, Phi Delta Kappa, Tau Kappa Alpha, Delta Sigma Rho. Presbyterian.

SCHNEIDER, WILLYS HOPE, lawyer; b. NYC, Sept. 27, 1952; d. Leon and Lillian (Friedman) S.; m. Stephen Andrew Kals, Jan. 21, 1979; children: Peter, Josefine. AB cum laude, Princeton U., 1974; JD, Columbia U., 1977. Bar: NY 1978, US Dist. Ct. (ea. and so. dists.) NY 1978, US Tax Ct. 1979. Law clk. to hon. Jack B. Weinstein US Dist. Ct. (ea. dist.) NY, Bklyn., 1977-78; assoc. Paul, Weiss, Rifkind, Wharton & Garrison, NYC, 1978-83, Kaye Scholer LLP, NYC, 1983-87, 1987—. Articles editor Columbia Law Rev., 1976—77; contbr. articles to profl. jours. Mem.: ABA, Internat. Tax Inst. (pres.), Assn. Bar City of NY, NY State Bar Assn. Home: 320 W End Ave New York NY 10023-8110 Office: Kaye Scholer LLP 425 Park Ave New York NY 10022-3506 Office Phone: 212-836-8693. E-mail: wschneider@kayescholer.com.

SCHNEIDER-CRIEZIS, SUSAN MARIE, architect; b. St. Louis, Aug. 1, 1953; d. William Alfred and Rosemary Elizabeth (Fischer) Schneider; m. Demetrios Anthony Criezis, Nov. 24, 1978; children: Anthony, John and Andrew. BArch, U. Notre Dame, 1976; MArch, MIT, 1978. Registered architect, Wis. Project designer Eichstaedt Architects, Roselle, Ill., 1978-80, Solomon, Cordwell, Buenz & Assocs., Chgo., 1980-82; project architect Gelick, Foran Assocs., Chgo., 1982-83; asst. prof. Sch. Architecture U. Ill., Chgo., 1980-86; exec. v.p. Criezis Architects, Inc., Northfield, Ill., 1986—2005; dir. cmty. devel. Village of Kenilworth, 2005—. Graham Found. grantee MIT, 1977, MIT scholar, 1976-78; Prestressed Concrete Inst. rsch. grantee, 1981. Mem. AIA, Chgo. Archtl. Club, Chgo. Women in Architecture, Am. Solar Energy Soc., NAFE, Jr. League Evanston, Evanston C. of C. Roman Catholic. Avocations: tennis, swimming. Office: 419 Richmond Rd Kenilworth IL 60043 Office Phone: 847-251-1666. E-mail: scriezis@villageofkenilworth.org.

SCHNEIDER VAULMAN, SHARON KAY, neuropsychologist, educator; b. St. Paul, Oct. 12, 1950; d. Lawrence Emil and Victoria (Roske) Mortenson; m. John Arthur Schneider Jr. (dec. 1999); children: Jennifer Anne, John Arthur III; m. Vincent Charles Vaulman, Nov. 13, 2003) BA, U. Minn., 1984; MS, Fla. Inst. Tech., Melbourne, 1986; D of Psychology, Fla. Inst. Tech., 1988. Diplomate in clin. neuropsychology Am. Bd. Profl. Psychology; lic. clin. psychologist. Dir. behavioral med. rehab. div. Mobile Infirmary, Ala., 1988-90; asst. prof. neurology U. South Ala., Mobile, 1990-95; pvt. practice Mobile, 1995—2000; dir. med. edn. Johnson & Johnson/Ortho Biotech, 2000—. Asst. dean Leadership Mobile, 1993-94; fellow Am. Stroke Coun. Recipient Rsch. award Isabel Myers Briggs Found., 1987. Mem. APA, Internat. Neuropsychol. Soc., Nat. Neuropsychol. Soc., Nat. Acad. Neuropsychologists, Mobile Assn. Psychologists (pres. 1990, 97), Sigma Xi, Psi Chi. Lutheran. Avocations: painting, stained glass design.

SCHNEIROV, ALLISON R., lawyer; b. Phila., 1966; BA magna cum laude, U. Pa., 1988; JD cum laude, NYU, 1991. Bar: N.Y. 1992. Atty. Skadden, Arps, Slate, Meagher & Flom LLP, N.Y., 1993—. Office: Skadden Arps Slate Meagher & Flom LLP Four Times Sq New York NY 10036

SCHNEKLOTH, CINDEE J., elementary school educator; d. Thelma G. and Herbert C. Johnson; m. John A. Schnekloth, Feb. 15, 1970; children: Clint A., Valerie J. Connor, Hans P. BA in Elem. Edn. with highest distinct honors, Marycrest Coll., Davenport, 1972. Cert. K-6 Elem. Classroom Tchr. State of Iowa Bd. Ednl. Examiners, 2003. Substitute tchr. North Scott Cmty. Schs., Eldridge, Iowa, 1982—86, tchr. 8th grade, 2000—; tchr. extended learning program Pleasant Valley Jr. HS, Bettendorf, Iowa, 1994—2000. Bldg. leadership team North Scott Jr. H.S., Eldridge, 2003—. Chairperson, mem. Christ's Family Daycare, Davenport, Iowa, 1995—2000; pres. Scott County Farm Bur., Eldridge, 1993—94. Named State Iowa Mother, Iowa Mothers' Assn., 2002, Iowa Master Farm Homemaker, 1993; recipient Mem. Acad. Honor Sorority, Kappa Gamma Pi, 1972. Mem.: ASCD, Iowa Talented and Gifted Orgn., Nat. Assn. Gifted Children. Mem. Reformed Church Am. Avocations: golf, skiing, hiking, scrapbooking and stamping, singing. Home: 21539 250th Street Eldridge IA 52748 Office: North Scott Jr High 502 South Fifth Street Eldridge IA 52748 Office Phone: 563-285-8272.

SCHNELL, GERTRUDE HELEN, retired elementary school educator; b. Olean, N.Y., July 29, 1934; d. Edwin J. and Grace (Mallory) S. BS in Edn., Mansfield (Pa.) State Coll., 1955; MS in Edn., St. Bonaventure (N.Y.) U., 1973. Tchr. elem. Franklinville (N.Y.) Cen. Sch., 1955-90. V.p. Ischua Valley Hist. Soc., Franklinville, 1989-92, pres., 1992-2002, v.p., 2003-2004, pres.2004-05. Mem. N.Y. State United Tchrs., Ischur Valley Hist. Soc. (pres. 2004-2005) Republican. Roman Catholic. Avocations: crafts, sewing, reading, travel, camping. Home: 25 Second Ave Franklinville NY 14737-1303

SCHNELLER, MARINA VELENTGAS, lawyer; b. Portland, Maine, Feb. 24, 1943; d. Peter Constantine and Katherine Rena (Zolotas) Velentgas; 3 children. AB, Smith Coll., 1965; MS, U. Vt., 1968; JD, Am. U., 1972. Bar: Va. 1972, D.C. 1973, U.S. Patent & Trademark Office, U.S. Ct. Appeals (DC cir.), U.S. Supreme Ct. Atty. Cushman Darby & Cushman, Washington, 1974-80; pvt. practice, 1980-82; tech. asst. Cir. Judge Nies US Ct. Appeals, Washington, 1982-84; counsel Mobil Oil Corp., Fairfax, Va., 1984-98; ptnr., Patent Prosecution, Intellectual Property Group Venable LLP, Washington, 1998—. Lectr. George Mason Univ. Sch. Law. Adv. bd. mem. BNA U.S. Patents Quarterly, Washington; contbr. articles to profl. jours. Coach Alexandria (Va.) Soccer Assn., 1986-89, 91-93. Mem. Am. Chem. Soc. (Am. Chemists Medal 1961), ABA, Am. Intellectual Property Law Assn. (patent law com. 2005-), Patent Lawyers Club, Women Patent Lawyers Club, Hellenic Lawyers Assn. (pres.), Sigma Xi. Office: Venable LLP 575 7th St NW Washington DC 20004 Office Phone: 202-344-4062. Office Fax: 202-344-8300. Business E-Mail: mvschneller@venable.com.

SCHNEPP, ANGELA J., secondary school educator; b. Bklyn., Mar. 17, 1951; d. Paul Michael Canino and Laura Ann Bruccoleri; m. Arthur George Scnnepp. June 22, 1973; children: Deanna, Audra. BA in English, SUNY, Oneonta, 1973; MA, LI U., 1980; student, Stonybrook U. English tchr.

Babylon Jr./Sr. HS, NY, 1973—. Classical pianist Various nursing homes, churches and schools, 1992—2002. Mem.: Nat. Coun. of Tchrs. of English. Avocations: piano, watercolor painting, reading. Home: 106 Hobson Ave Saint James NY 11780 Office: Babylon Jr H S 50 Railroad Ave Babylon NY 11702

SCHNITZER, IRIS TAYMORE, diversified financial services company executive, lawyer, arbitrator, mediator; b. Cambridge, Mass., Aug. 3, 1943; d. Joseph David and Edith (Cooper) Taymore; m. Stephen Mark Schnitzer, Sept. 10, 1966. BA in Econ., Boston U., 1967; JD, Mass. Sch. Law, 1996. CLU; bar: Mass. 1996; lic. real estate broker, registered rep. NASD, CFP, cert. fin. counseling advanced pension planning. Real estate broker Woods Real Estate, Braintree, Mass., 1968; real estate broker, property mgr. Village Gate Realty, Brockton, Mass., 1969; agt. Prudential Ins., Boston, 1970-73, Northwestern Mut. Life, Boston, 1973—78; fin. planning cons. Iris Taymore Schnitzer Assoc., Boston, 1973-79; supr. edn. and advanced underwriting Northwestern Mut. Life, Boston, 1976—78; trainer fin. planners Gerstenblatt Co., Newton, Mass., 1978-79; founder, CEO Fin. Forum, Inc., Boston, 1979-91; CEO TFF, Inc. at Chase Exch., NYC, 1980—83; prin. I&S Assoc., Boston, 1991—; arbitrator Nat. Assn. Securities Dealers Dispute Resolution, 1992—; v.p. Fleet Pvt. Clients Group, Boston, 1993-2000; pvt. practice Law Office of Iris Taymore Schnitzer, Boston, 2000—; mediator Mediation Works, Inc., Boston, 2002—, Boston Municipal Ct., Boston Bar Assn., Alternative Dispute Resolution Program, Boston, 2003—. Bd. dirs. Mister Tire, Inc. Contbr. articles to profl. jours. Pres. Mass. divsn. Women's Equity Action League, 1977—79; treas., bd. dirs. Festival of Light and Song, 1989—92; bd. dirs. Achievement Rewards Coll. Scientists, Boston, 1991—95; mem. steering com. Fleet Bank Mass. United Way, 1994—95; chair Girls' Bank Patriots' Trail Girl Scout Coun., 1996—98; overseer Boston Lyric Opera, 1999—2004; bd. dirs. Ledgewood, Brookline, Mass., 1967—70, LWV, Brockton, 1968—70, NOW, Boston, 1972—73; chair credit com., bd. dirs. Mass. Feminist Fed. Credit Union, Cambridge, Mass., 1975—77. Named one of Best Fin. Planners in the U.S., Money Mag., 1987; named to Mut. Funds Panel, Silvia Porter's Personal Fin. Mag., 1988, 1989. Fellow: Mass. Bar Found.; mem.: Boston Estate Planning Coun., Boston Bar Assn., Am. Assn. Individual Investors (bd. dirs. 1985—95, pres. Boston chpt. 1987—89), Navy League U.S. (life), Boston Club. Republican. Avocations: horseback riding, sailing, gardening, interior and fashion design, animals. Office: Law Office of Iris Taymore Schnitzer 65 E India Row Boston MA 02110-3308

SCHNORR, JANET KAY, psychology educator, researcher; b. Clintonville, Wis., Dec. 16, 1944; d. Arthur Albert and Louise Martha (Kreuger) S. BS, U. Wis., Oshkosh, 1967; MS, Iowa State U., 1969, PhD, 1971. Asst. prof. No. Ariz. U., Flagstaff, 1971-74, assoc. prof., 1975-85, 86—; rsch. assoc. office med. edn. U. Ariz., Tucson, 1985-86. Loaned exec. Ariz. Bd. Regents, 1991-92. Contbr. articles to profl. jours. Bd. dirs. Environ. Rsch. and Devel., Tucson, 1985—, Ariz. Solar Energy Commn., Phoenix, 1981-87; bd. dirs., v.p. Child Abuse Ctr., Flagstaff, 1982—; del. Ariz. Dem. Caucus, Phoenix, 1984. Mem. Am. Psychol. Assn., Western Psychol. Assn., Rocky Mtn. Psychol. Assn. (treas. 1989—), AAUP, Women in Higher Edn. (bd. dirs. 1987-90, vice-chair 1988-90), Sigma Xi (faculty senate, vice-chair 1990-91). Avocations: flyfishing, camping, watercolors, skiing, archaeology.

SCHOCKAERT, BARBARA ANN, marketing professional; b. Queens, N.Y., Dec. 13, 1938; d. Lawrence Henry and Eleanor Veronica (Tollner) Grob; children: Donna Ann, Don. Grad., Ocean County Coll., Toms River, N.J., 1999. Cert. notary pub. V.p. ops. Am. Vitamin Products, Inc., Freehold, N.J., 1977-89, v.p. ops. Foods Plus div., 1990-94, sales coord., 1994—2003, product devel. mgr., 1996—2003, pvt. label mgr., DSD mgr., 1998—2003; assoc. Ocean County Realty, Toms River, N.J., 1987-90, Crossroads Realty, Toms River, 1990—2000; pvt. label mgr. Accumed Inc., 2005—. Contbg. author: Greatest Poems of the Western World, 1989 (Golden Poet award). Past pres. mayor's adv. coun., past pres. of help line Town of Jackson, N.J.; past bd. dirs. Big Bros. of Ocean County; speaker community svc. orgns. Named Woman of Yr., Jaycees, 1974; recipient Capitol award Nat. Leadership Coun., 1991, Silver Bowl award for 1st pl. poetry contest, 1996. Mem. N.J. Realtors Assn., Internat. Platform Assn., Alpha Beta Gamma. Home: 977 Fairview Dr Toms River NJ 08753-3064

SCHOELEN, MARY JEANETTE, federal judge; b. Rota, Spain; BA, U. Calif. Irvine, 1990; JD, George Washington U. Law Sch., 1993. Law clk. Nat. Veterans Legal Services Project; staff atty., veteran's benefits program Vietnam Veterans of Am., 1994; intern, com. veterans' affairs US Senate, 1994, minority counsel, com. veterans' affairs, 1997—2001, minority gen. counsel, com. veterans' affairs, 2001, dep. staff dir. benefits programs and gen. counsel, com. veterans' affairs, 2001—04; judge US Ct. Appeals Veterans Claims, 2004—. Office: US Ct Appeals Veterans Claims 625 Indiana Ave NW Ste 900 Washington DC 20004 Office Phone: 202-501-5970.

SCHOEN, CAROL BRONSTON, retired English language educator; b. Plainfield, NJ, May 14, 1926; d. Harry E. and Yetta (Cohen) Bronston; m. Andrew J. Schoen, June 26, 1949 (div.); children: Douglas, Sarah. BA, Radcliffe, 1948; MA, Columbia U., 1963, PhD, 1968. Lectr. Lehman Coll. CUNY, N.Y.C., 1968-75, asst. prof., 1975-85, assoc. prof., 1986-91; ret., 1991. Author: The Writing Experience, 1978, Anzia Yezierska, 1982, Sara Teasdale, 1986, Thinking & Writing in College, 1986. E-mail: cbschoen@nyc.rr.com.

SCHOEN, JILL F., psychologist, educator; b. Aberdeen, S.D., Nov. 28, 1945; d. Fred M. and Ina D. Bruns; m. Rodney Schoen, June 12, 1965; children: Lisa DeJean, Laura Joy, Andrea Jo, Erika Jill. BS in Elem. Edn., No. State U., 1968, MS in Guidance/counseling, 1977; EdD in Ednl. Psychology/counseling, U. S.D., 1991. Lic. psychologist, profl. counselor in mental health Nat. Bd. Cert. Counselors, cert. tchr. S.D., lic. approved clin. supr. Case mgr. QMRP S.D. Devel. Ctr., Redfield, 1986—88, psychologist, 1990—93; counselor educator S.D. State U., Brookings, 1993—98, Minn. State U., Moorhead, 1998—2000, No. State U., Aberdeen, SD, 2000—03; psychologist cons. S.D. Devel. Ctr., Redfield, 2000—03, psychologist, 2003—. Editor: (jour.) The Dakota Counselor, 2003; reviewer: numerous books in field. Vol. Salvation Army, Aberdeen, 2002; mem. ministry com. St. Johns Luth. Ch., Warner, SD, 2000—. Mem.: S.D. Assn. Adulthood-Aging (pres. 2002—03), S.D. Mental Health Counselors (pres. 2003), S.D. Counseling Assn. (co-chair govt. rels. coun. 2001—03, Mary Lark Humanitarian award 1998), Aberdeen Arts Coun. Democrat. Lutheran. Avocations: reading, travel, playing piano. Home: 38745 146th St Mansfield SD 57460 Office: SD Devel Ctr Redfield SD 57469 Office Phone: 605-472-2400 4376. E-mail: jill.schoen@state.sd.us.

SCHOENBERG, COCO, sculptor; b. Paris, May 3, 1939; arrived in U.S., 1941; d. Heinz Ernst and Kathe (Gassman) Oppenheimer; m. Bernard Schoenberg, Aug. 11, 1963 (dec. Apr. 1979); children: Nara, Jonathan Alexander, Amanda; m. William G. Swartchild III, June 5, 1988. BS in Lit., Sci. and Arts, U. Mich., 1961; MA in Art, Columbia U., 1964. Tchr. handicapped children Steven Sch., N.Y.C., 1962-63; assoc. in pottery for occupational therapy Columbia Tchrs. Coll., N.Y.C., 1963; studio potter, tchr., lectr. various cities, NY, 1965—. Chmn. N.J. Designer Craftsman, New Brunswick, 1983—85; coord. Ctr. Crafts Fair-Old Ch., Demarest, NJ, 1983—84, ACC Craft Fair, Balt., 1985—98, West Springfield, 1985—94; juror Lincoln Ct. Craft Fair, N.Y.C., 1985, Art Rider Craft Fairs, N.Y.C., 1986, Sta. WBAI Craft Fair, N.Y.C., 1989, Am. Craft Exposition, 1992; commd. by Gulick Group, 1988, Harrison, Star Weiner and Beitler Advt., N.Y.C., 1989. Exhibited in group shows at Montclair (N.J.) Mus., Bergen Mus., Paramus, N.J., Morris Mus., Morristown, N.J., Noyes Mus., Oceanville, N.J., Mus. Am. Jewish History, Phila., High Mus., Atlanta, Craft and Folk Mus., L.A., Brockton (Mass.) Mus., Summit (N.J.) Art Ctr., Campbell Mus., State Mus. NY, 1996, Hamburg (Germany) Mus., 1996, Represented in permanent collections Art Inst. Chgo., Hamburg Mus. Recipient Innovative Sculpture award, Texaco, 1982, Charlotte Simons Glicksman Meml. award, 1983, Mamoroneck Artist Guild award, 1984, Juror's award, Summit Art Ctr., 1985, Purchase award, Noyes Mus., 1986, Highest award for crafts, Craft Concepts, 1986, Merit award in Ceramics, N.Y.C. Artist/Craftsmen N.Y., 1987, Most Innovative Use of Medium award, Toshiko Tokaezu, 1994; grantee N.J. State Coun. Arts, 1983—84. Avocation: horseback riding. Home: 119 Erledon Rd Tenafly NJ 07670-2503

SCHOENBRUN, LOIS, medical association administrator; Former dep. dir. Am. Med. Women's Assn., Alexandria, Va.; now exec. dir., found. dir. Am. Acad. Optometry, Rockville, Md. Fellow: Am. Acad. Optometry. Avocation: Tae Kwon Do. Office: Am Acad Optometry #506 6110 Executive Blvd Rockville MD 20852 Office Phone: 301-984-1441 ext. 3006. Office Fax: 301-984-4737. Business E-Mail: LoisS@aaoptom.org.*

SCHOENDORFF, CHRISTINE JOY, elementary school educator; b. Flint, Mich., Nov. 15, 1973; d. Barbara Lee Kaufmann; m. Paul Anthony Schoendorff, Nov. 23, 1996; 1 child, Mallory Catherine. B in Liberal Arts, Albion Coll., Mich., 1995; M in Art of Tchg., MaryGrove Coll., Detroit, 1999. Music tchr. Challenger Elem., Howell, Mich., 1996—98, SW Elem., Howell, 1996—99, Latson Elem., Howell, 1998—2001, Voyager Elem., Howell, 1998—. Union rep. Voyager Elem., Howell, 2004—06; profl. devel. com. mem. Howell Pub. Schs., 2003—05, webgrader/report card design com., 2005—06. Composer: Voices of Voyager. Recipient Edn. Excellence award, 2003, Recognition of Achievement, Howell Bd. Edn., 2006. Home: 5379 S Linden Rd Swartz Creek MI 48473 Office: Voyager Elementary 1450 Byron Rd Howell MI 48843 Office Phone: 517-552-7500. Personal E-mail: schoendc@howellschools.com.

SCHOENFELD, DIANA LINDSAY, photographer, educator; b. Knoxville, Tenn., Sept. 3, 1949; d. David Lindsay and Martha Jane (Zigler) S. Student, Fla. Presbyn. Coll., 1967-69, U. Neuchâtel, Switzerland, 1969-70; B in Visual Arts in Art and Art History, Ga. State U., 1972; MA in Studio Art, U. N.Mex., 1974, MFA in History, Practice of Photography, 1984. Instr. Rio Hondo Coll., Whittier, Calif., 1975-76, Coll. of Redwoods, Eureka, Calif., 1976-85; vis. asst. prof. U. Nebr., Lincoln, 1985, U. Mich., Ann Arbor, 1986-87; vis. asst. prof., guest curator U. Hawaii at Manoa, Honolulu, 1987, 88-89; vis. asst. prof. U. Oreg., Eugene, 1994; vis. lectr., artist in residence Ohio State U., Columbus, 1996-97; instr. art studies in Am. West Ohio Wesleyan U., Mont. State U., Bozeman, 1999; instr. mus. and gallery practices Humboldt State U., 2003, instr. photography, 1999—. Diversity cons. Calif. Arts Project, 1995-96, instr., participant summer insts. and visual arts wokshops, 1994—; rep. Calif. Arts Project Leadership Acad., 2002; presenter, exhibitor Northcoast Edn. Summit, Humbolt State U., 2003, 04, 06; exhbn. curator, co-curator Rio Hondo Coll., Clarke Mus., Coll. Redwoods, Ohio State U., U. Hawaii, Maine Photog. Workshops, Rockport, others; exhbn. dir., juror Coll. Redwoods with Eureka C. of C., 1983; lectr. U. Hawaii, Claremont Coll., Pomona, Calif., nat. conf. Soc. for Photog. Edn., New Orleans, 1990, Humboldt State U., Arcata, Calif., 1999-2000, 02, U. Calif., Berkeley, 2003; juror Humboldt Cultural Ctr., Eureka, Calif., 1999, Humboldt County Fair, Ferndale, Calif., 2002; instr., 2000; cons. Redwood Arts Project, Klamath-Trinity Schs., Calif., 2001-02; actor, Castle Rock Prodns., 2001; photographer Ferndale Repertory Theater, Calif., 2002; outreach coord. Clarke Hist. Mus., Eureka, 2006; exhbn. juror Images of Water, Morris Graves Mus. Art, Eureka, 2006, lectr., presenter, 2006; lectr., spkr., presenter in field. Author, curator exhbn. and illus. catalog with essay Symbol and Surrogate: The Picture Within, 1989-90; artist, author, Fractures and Severances: Patient as Artist, 1982-84, 84—; artist: Illusory Arrangements, 1978; exhibited photog. Albuquerque Mus. Art., Vietnam Vets' State Memls. West of Miss.; illustrated brochure Diana Schoenfeld: Landscape and Memory sponsored by Humboldt State U. and First St. Gallery, 1999; interviewed by KHSU radio, Arcata, Calif., 2000-01; exhibited in group shows at San Francisco Mus. Modern Art, 1980 (Print awards 1978, 79), 1st St. Gallery, Eureka, 1999, Alinder Gallery, Gualala, Calif., 1992-93, 95, Art Ctr., Eureka, 1992, Ink People Gallery, Eureka, 1992, Solomon-Dubnick Gallery, Sacramento, 1994, Tokyo Inst. Polytechnics, 1995, Ohio State U., 1996, B.C. Space, Laguna Beach, Calif., 1997, Internat. Ctr. Photography, NYC, 1997, Humboldt State U., Arcata, Internat. Photography Hall of Fame and Mus. Okla. City, 1999-2000, Morris Graves Mus. Art, Eureka, 2000; one-woman shows include Humboldt Bay Nat. Wildlife Refuge Welcome Ctr., Loleta, Calif., 2001-02, Travel Advantage, Eureka, 1999, Art Ctr., 1991, Orange Coast Coll., Costa Mesa, Calif., 1991, A.G. Edwards, Eureka, 1992, Ambiance, Eureka, 1993, Iris Inn, Eureka, 1994, Redwood Arts Project, Arcata, 1996, Humboldt State U., 1997-99, Players' Theatre, Ukiah, Calif., 1997, 1st St. Gallery, Eureka, 1999, Morris Graves Mus. Art, 2002, Humboldt Sr. Resource Ctr., Eureka, 2002, others; represented in permanent collections including Houston Mus. Art, Ctr. Creative Photography, Tucson, Ariz., Graham Nash Collection, Barrow Neurol. Inst., Phoenix, Avon Collection, Mus. Contemporary Photography, Chgo., LA Ctr. for Photog. Studies, Nat. Mus. Women in Art, Washington, San Francisco Mus. Modern Art, Princeton U., Laguna Beach Mus. Art, Ohio Wesleyan U., Women Photographers Internat. Archive, Yale U., Beinecke Rare Book and Manuscript Libr., Yale U., pvt. collections, others; creator CD-ROM multimedia presentation Schoolhouse Odyssey. Exploring Remote, Rural and Ghost Schools-A Photographer's Notes, 1998. Ctr. for Internat. Media Rsch., Internat. Conf. Visual Sociology, Bielfield, and others. Vol. Ferndale Repartory Theatre, Ferndlae, Calif., Clarke Mus., Eureka Calif., Humbolt Bay Nat. Wildlife Refuge, Loleta Calif. Recipient Grand Prize Northwest Eye, Morris Graves Mus. Art, 2006; selected for Gov. of Ga. Honors Program in Art, Wesleyan Coll., 1966; Marion Crowe scholar Atlanta Press Photographers Assn., 1971; Nat. Endowment for Arts Emerging Artist fellow/grantee, 1980; recipient Reva and David Logan award Boston U., 1985, Discovery award Art of Calif. Jour., 1992. Mem. Soc. for Photog. Edn. Avocations: carpentry and construction, camping, hiking, writing, gardening. Home and Office: PO Box 596 Loleta CA 95551-0596 Office Phone: 707-733-5677. Business E-Mail: dianas@northcoast.com.

SCHOENHOLT, HELENE M., elementary school educator; m. Donald N. Schoenholt, May 25, 1975; 1 child, David L. BA, Queens Coll., NY, 1972; MS, Syracuse U., 1973; cert. in reading recovery, NYU, 1990. Tchr. 3rd grade Pub. Sch. 106, 1973—75; reading clinician Dist. 25, Queens, 1975—79; remedial reading and writing tchr. Pub. Sch. 165, Queens, 1979—87; reading recovery, remedial reading tchr. E.M. Baker Sch., Great Neck, NY, 1987—94; reading resource tchr. Saddle Rock Elem., Great Neck, 1994—. Fellow, Syracuse U., 1973. Mem.: Reading Recovery Coun. N.Am., Internat. Dyslexia Assn., Internat. Reading Assn. Avocations: reading, travel, gardening. Office: Saddle Rock Sch 10 Hawthorne Ln Great Neck NY 11023

SCHOENIGER, JANE, music educator; b. Phila., Mar. 25, 1935; d. Robert Morgan and Evelyn (Beckman) Williamson; m. Whitman Cross II, July 13, 1957 (div. Jan. 1978); children: Robert Stevens, Jonathan Whitman, Elizabeth Pendleton, Mary Evelyn; m. Robert Kurt Schoeniger, June 14, 1980. BS in Elem. Edn., U. Pa., 1956; BA in Music, Chestnut Hill Coll., 1991, BA in Art History, 2000; MS in Music Edn., U. Ill., 1994. Tchr. 6th grade Erdenheim (Pa.) Elem. Sch., 1956-57; tchr. piano Phila. Area, 1980—. Active art goes to sch. Jr. League, Phila., 1962-67. Scholar U. Oslo, 1955, U. Pa., Phila., 1956, U. Ill., Champaign-Urbana, 1991-94. Mem. Nat. Guild Piano Tchrs., Music Tchrs. Nat. Assn. Republican. Episcopalian. Avocation: ice skating.

SCHOENLAUB, ELIZABETH MAE, elementary school educator; b. Newport News, Va., July 28, 1928; d. Leon Millard and Miriam Sophia (Gildner) Cornman; m. Fred Edward Schoenlaub, Aug. 16, 1952 (div. 1976); children: Jeanette Ann Schoenlaub Jackson, Susan Lynn Schoenlaub Alden, Paul Edward, Judith Leigh Schoenlaub Dewey, Deborah Mae Schoenlaub Schaaf. BS in Elem. Edn., Mo. Western State Coll., 1974; MS in Reading, Northwest Mo. State U., 1985. Cert. elem. tchr., Mo. Tchr. Buchanan County R IV Sch. Dist., Rushville, Mo., 1974-87, St. Joseph (Mo.) Sch. Dist., 1987—97; ret., 1997. Sec. ch. and ministry commn. Faith United Ch. of Christ, 1988-90, tchr., 1990-98. Mem. Internat. Reading Assn. (Northwest Mo. coun. 1987-97), Mo. Tchrs. Assn., Community Tchrs. Assn., Delta Kappa Gamma, Gamma Zeta. Avocations: reading, sewing, knitting, cooking. Home: 3606 Seneca St Saint Joseph MO 64507-2035

SCHOENRICH, EDYTH HULL, internist, preventive medicine physician; b. Cleve., Sept. 9, 1919; d. Edwin John and Maud Mabel (Kelly) Hull; m. Carlos Schoenrich, Aug. 9, 1942; children: Lola, Olaf. AB, Duke U., Durham, N.C., 1941; MD, U. Chgo., 1947; MPH, John Hopkins U., Balt., 1971. Diplomate Am. Bd. Internal Medicine, Am. Bd. Preventive Medicine. Intern John Hopkins Hosp., Balt., 1948-49, asst. resident medicine, 1949-50, fellow medicine, 1950-51, chief resident, pvt. wards, 1951-52; asst. chief, acting chief dept. chronic and cmty. medicine Balt. City Hosp., Balt., 1963-66; dir. svc. to chronically ill and aging Md. State Dept. Health, Balt., 1966-74; dir. divsn. pub. health adminstrn. Sch. Pub. Health, John Hopkins U., Balt., 1974-77, assoc. dean acad. affairs, 1977-86, dir. part time profl. programs and dep. dir. MPH program, 1986—, prof. dept. health policy and mgmt., 1974—, joint appointment medicine, 1978—. Contbr. articles to profl. jours. Trustee Friends Life Care Cmty., 1984—, Kennedy-Krieger Inst., Balt., 1985—, Vis. Nurses Assn., 1990-95, Md. Home and Cmty. Care Found., 1995—. Recipient Stebbins medal John Hopkins U., 1989, Disting. Med. Alumna award, 1997; named to Md. Women's Hall of Fame, 2005. Fellow ACP, Am. Coll. Preventive Medicine; mem. APHA, Assn. Tchrs. Preventive Medicine, Med. and Chirurg. Soc. Md., Balt. City Med. Soc., Phi Beta Kappa, Alpha Omega Alpha, Delta Omega. Avocations: gardening, music, theater, swimming. Home: 1402 Boyce Ave Baltimore MD 21204-6512 Office: Johns Hopkins Univ Sch Pub Health 615 N Wolfe St Baltimore MD 21205-2103 Office Phone: 410-825-1291. E-mail: eschoenr@jhsph.edu.

SCHOENSTADT, BARBARA LAISON, special education educator; b. Phila., Mar. 23, 1940; d. Oscar Z. and Fay (Tecker) Laison; m. Steven Ellis Schoenstadt; children: Scott, Bruce, Cori. BA in Edn., Temple U., 1962; MS in Edn., Beaver Coll., 1979. Cert. tchr., Pa. Tchr. 1st grade U.S. Army, Kaiserlautern, Germany, 1962-64; tchr. nursery sch. Temple Beth Ami, Phila., 1973-74; subs. tchr. Phila. Sch. Dist., 1974-78; tchr. 4th grade Neshaminy Sch. Dist., Langhorne, Pa., 1978-79; tchr. gifted and talented Bensalem (Pa.) Sch. Dist., 1979-82, 87—, tchr. 3rd grade, 1982-87, tchr. 2d grade, 1988—2002; ret., 2002. Coord. sci. fair Bensalem-Struble Sch., 1988—2002; adj. prof. lang. arts and reading jr. course Temple U., Phila., 2002—, student tchr. supr., 2002—; tchr. Kids on Campus Bucks County C.C., 1997—. Sisterhood bd. dirs. Congregation Shir Ami. Mem. NEA, Pa. Edn. Assn., Pa. Assn. Gifted Edn., Bensalem Edn. Assn. Democrat. Jewish. Home: 736 Hunter Dr Langhorne PA 19053-1910

SCHOEPF, VIRGINIA ANNE, retired librarian; b. Balt., Dec. 9, 1946; d. Ridgely Harry and Mildred Lorena Dorsey; m. Richard Walter Schoepf, Feb. 16, 1973. BS, Towson State Coll., 1968; MLS, U. Md., 1971. Asst. chief team leader decimal classification divsn. Libr. of Congress, Washington, 1971—2002; ret. Avocations: reading, computer games, travel. Home: 62188 E Amberwood Dr Saddlebrooke AZ 85739

SCHOETTLE, ENID C.B., federal agency administrator; m. Herbert Stuart Okun, Dec. 27, 1990. BA, Radcliffe Coll.; PhD in Polit. Sci., MIT, Cambridge, Mass. Faculty polit. sci. U. Minn., Mpls., Swarthmore Coll.; staff mem. Ford Found., 1976—91, dir. internat. affairs program, 1981—91; sr. fellow Coun. on Fgn. Rels., 1991—93; nat. intelligence officer for global and multilateral issues Nat. Intelligence Coun., 1993—96; chief advocacy and external rels. unit UN Dept. Humanitarian Affairs, 1996—97; spl. advisor Nat. Intelligence Coun., Washington, 1997—. Prof. polit. sci. Univ. Minn., Swarthmore Coll. Office: Central Intelligence Agy Nat Intelligence Coun Washington DC 20505

SCHOETTLER, GAIL SINTON, former ambassador; b. LA, Oct. 21, 1943; d. James and Norma (McLellan) Sinton; children: Lee, Thomas, James; m. Donald L. Stevens, June 23, 1990. BA in Econs., Stanford U., 1965; MA in History, U. Calif., Santa Barbara, 1969, PhD in History, 1975. Businesswoman, Denver, 1975-83; exec. dir. Colo. Dept. of Personnel, Denver, 1983-86; treas. State of Colo., Denver, 1987—95, lt. gov., 1995—99; chmn. bd. Fischer Imaging Corp. U.S. amb. World Radio Comm. Conf., Istanbul, 1999-2000; bd. dirs. AspenBio, Inc., CancerVax Corp., A4S Security, Inc. Active Douglas County Bd. Edn., Colo., 1979-87, pres., 1983-87; trustee U. No. Colo., Greeley, 1981-87; pres. Denver Children's Mus., 1975-85; bd. dirs. Gunnison Ranchland Conservation Legacy, Colo. Conservation Trust, Progress Now, Ctr. for Women's Health Rsch. Decorated chevalier French Legion of Honor; recipient Disting. Alumna award U. Calif., Santa Barbara, 1987, Trailblazer award AAUW, 1997, Childrens Advocacy award Colo. Soc. Sch. Psychologists, 1997. Mem. Internat. Women's Forum (mem. bd. dirs. 1981-89, pres. 83-85), Women Execs. in State Govt. (bd. dirs. 1981-87, chmn. 1988), Leadership Denver Assn. (bd. dirs. 1987, named Outstanding Alumna 1985), Nat. Congress Lt. Govs., Stanford Alumni Assn. Democrat.

SCHOFF, MARCIA ANNE, elementary school educator; b. Gloversville, N.Y., Apr. 30, 1951; d. Franklin J. and Gloria I. Wendell; m. Philip H. Schoff, June 9, 1973; children: Wendi, Caryn, Phil. AA, Fulton-Montgomery C. C., Johnstown, N.Y., 1972; BS, Empire State Coll., Saratoga Springs, N.Y., 1981; MEd, SUNY, Cortland, 1988. Cert. tchr. N-6, bus. edn. N.Y., Nat. Bd. Profl. Tchg. Stds. cert., 2003. Computer specialist Knolls Atomic Power Lab, Schenectady, NY, 1970—72, White Mop Wringer Co., Fultonville, NY, 1973—80; tchr. St. Johnsville (N.Y.) Ctrl. Sch., 1982—83, Oppenheim-Ephratah Ctrl. Sch., St. Johnsville, 1983—. Tchr. summer sch., Fonda and Oppenheim; colorguard dir., Oppenheim. Mem.: NEA, Am. Fedn. Tchrs., NY Soc. Univ. Tchrs., Oppenheim-Ephratah Tchrs.' Assn. (pres., v.p.). Roman Catholic. Avocations: running, gardening, reading, movies, music. Office: Oppenheim-Ephratah Ctrl Sch 6486 State Highway 29 Saint Johnsville NY 13452

SCHOFIELD, LORNA GAIL, lawyer; b. New Haven, Ind., Jan. 22, 1956; d. Donald Earl and Priscilla (Tiango) S.; 1 child, Sarah. BA, Ind. U., 1977; JD, NYU, 1981. Bar: N.Y. 1982, U.S. Dist. Ct. (so and ea. dists.) N.Y. 1982, U.S. Ct. Appeals (11th cir.) 1983, U.S. Ct. Appeals (2d cir.) 1985, U.S. Tax Ct. 1991, U.S. Dist. Ct. Fed. Claims 1992, U.S. Ct. Appeals (10th cir.) 1993, U.S. Ct. Appeals (6th cir.) 1995, U.S. Supreme Ct. 1996, U.S. Ct. Appeals (3d cir.) 1997. Assoc. Cleary, Gottlieb, Steen & Hamilton, N.Y.C., 1981-84; asst. U.S. atty. U.S. Dist. Ct. (so. dist.) N.Y., N.Y.C., 1984-88; assoc. Debevoise & Plimpton, N.Y.C., 1988-91, ptnr., 1991—. Contbr. articles to profl. jours. Mem. ABA (litig. sect., budget officer 2002-, mem. standing com. Judiciary, co-dir. divisions 2000-01, co-chair task force on discovery 1997—2000, coun. 1997—2000, co-chair class actions and derivative suits com. 1994-97, vice chair accts.' liability subcom. 1993-94, co-chair Woman Advocate Com. 1994, planning com. 1993), Am. Law Inst., Fed. Bar Coun., N.Y. Coun. Def. Lawyers, Assn. of Bar of City of N.Y. Office: Devevoise & Plimpton LLP 919 Third Ave New York NY 10022-3904 Office Phone: 212-909-6094. Business E-Mail: lgschofield@debevoise.com.

SCHOFIELD, REGINA BROWN, federal agency administrator; b. Natchez, Miss., Jan. 14, 1962; d. Elvia John and Velma Marie (Cameron) Brown; m. Stephen Gerard Schofield, Nov. 2, 1996. BSBA, Miss. Coll., 1983; MBA, Jackson (Miss.) State U., 1990. Sales rep. Philip Morris, USA, Jackson, 1983-91; spl. asst. U.S. Dept. Edn., Washington, 1991-92, White House liaison, 1992-93; mgr. environ. issues Internat. Coun. Shopping Ctrs., Alexandria, Va., 1993—98; mgr. govt. rels US Postal Svc., 1998—2002; dir., Office of Intergovernmental Affairs US Dept. HHS, 2002—05, White House liaison, 2002—05; asst. atty. gen., Office of Justice Programs US Dept. Justice, Washington, 2005—. Bd. dirs. Nat. Wetlands Coalition, 1997—99, Va. Dept. Agrl. and Consumer Svcs., Richmond, 1995—99, Va. Fedn. Rep. Women, Richmond, 1996-98, 2001-05; bd. visitors Coll. William and Mary, Williamsburg, Va., 1997—2001, The Endowment Assn. of the Coll. of William and Mary, 2004-05; mem. Commonwealth Rep. Women's Club, Alexandria, 1995, Am. Coun. Young Polit. Leaders, 1998-2005. Roman Catholic. Avocation: reading. Office: US Dept Justice 810 7th St NW Rm 6400 Washington DC 20531

SCHOLER, SUE WYANT, retired state legislator; b. Topeka, Oct. 20, 1936; d. Zint Elwin and Virginia Louise (Achenbach) Wyant; m. Charles Frey Scholer, Jan. 27, 1957; children: Elizabeth Scholer Truelove, Charles W., Virginia M. Scholer McCal. Student, Kans. State U., 1954-56. Draftsman The Farm Clinic, West Lafayette, Ind., 1978—79; assessor Wabash Twp., West Lafayette, 1979-84; commr. Tippecanoe County, Lafayette, Ind., 1984-90; state rep. Dist. 26 Ind. Statehouse, Indpls., 1990—2004, ret., 2004. Asst. minority whip, 1992-94, Rep. whip, 1994-2000, asst. Rep. leader, 2001—04; mem. Tippecanoe County Area Plan Commn., 1984-90; chmn. Midwestern legis. conf. CSG, 1998. Bd. dirs. Crisis Ctr., Lafayette, 1984-89, Tippecanoe Arts Fedn., 1990-99, United Way, Lafayette, 1990-93; mem. Lafayette Conv. and Visitors Bur., 1988-90. Recipient Salute to Women Govt. and Politics award, 1986, United Sr. Action award, Outstanding Legislator award, 1993, Small Bus. Champion award, 1995, Ind. Libr. Fedn. Legislator award, 1995, Disting. Legislator award Nat. Alliance for Mentally Ill, 1997,, 2003, West Ctrl. Ind. Advocate award, 2003, Friend of Cmty. Action award, 1999, Disting. Pub. Svc. award Am. Legion, 2004, Family Svcs. Advocacy award Family Svcs., 2004, Sagamore of the Wabash, 2004, Order of the Griffin, Purdue U., 2004. Mem. Ind. Assn. County Commrs. (treas. 1990), Assn. Ind. Counties (legis. com. 1988-90), Greater Lafayette C. of C. (ex-officio bd. 1984-90), LWV, P.E.O., Purdue Women's Club (past treas.), Kappa Kappa Kappa (past pres. Epsilon chpt.)., Delta Delta Delta (past pres. alumnae, house corp. treas.). Republican. Presbyterian. Avocations: golf, needlecrafts, reading. Home: 807 Essex St West Lafayette IN 47906-1534

SCHOLES, JANIS WOLF, science educator; b. Cin., Feb. 17, 1953; d. John Louis and Marie Enneking Wolf; children: Ben, Daniel, Micah. BA, U. Ky., Lexington, 1971; MA, Ea. Ky. U., Richmond, 1978, Ind. U. S.E., New Albany, 2005. Cert. elem. edn., gen. sci., spl. edn. Ind. Tchr. Jessamine County Schs., Nicholasville, Ky., 1975, Scott County Schs., Georgetown, Ky., 1975—78, Fayette County Schs., Lexington, 1978—85, Greater Clark County Schs., Jeffersonville, Ind., 1985—. Coord. SECME Ga. Tech., 2004—06; mem. INSIG Nat. Grant Com., Bloomington, Ind., 2003—06; presenter in field. Supporer, mem. Com. to Elect Redden Sheriff, Jeffersonville, 2005, Com. to Elect Bades Sch. Bd., Jeffersonville, 2006. Grantee, GCCS Edn. Found., 2005. Mem.: NEA, Nat. Tchrs. of Math. Assn. Office: River Valley Mid Sch Jeffersonville IN 47130

SCHOLEY, DIANN PATRICIA, accountant; b. Sacramento, Calif., July 15, 1968; d. Melvn Alvin and connie Mae Ehresman; m. Todd Alan Scholey, Sept. 3, 1994 (div. Aug. 1996); children: Robert, Alexander. AS in Bus., Yuba Coll., Woodland, Calif., 1995; BS in Acctg., U. Phoenix, Sacramento, 1999. Office adminstr. Sutter Med. Found., Woodland, 1992-95; office mgr. Ron Brown PT, Woodland, 1996-97; devel. assoc. WMH Found., Woodland, 1997-98; contr. WECA, Sacramento, 1998-99; staff acct. S.J. Gallina & Co. LLP, CPAs, Sacramento, 1999—. Named Miss Congeniality, County of Yolo, Woodland, 1986. Mem. AICPA. Avocations: exercising and fitness, horseback riding, flying. Office: S J Gallina & Co LLP 8001 Folsom Blvd Ste 211 Sacramento CA 95826-2621 E-mail: SaavyDi@aol.com.

SCHOLL, BELINDA K., librarian; b. Killeen, Tex., Oct. 26, 1957; d. Burton Thomas King and Alice Rose Coghlan-King; m. Timothy J. Scholl, May 31, 1980. MusB in Piano cum laude, Southwestern U., 1979; MusM in Piano Pedagogy, Tex. Christian U., 1987; MSLS, U. North Tex., 1992. Music dir. Rochester (N.Y.) Acad. Performing ARts, 1981-85; tchg. asst. in piano and theory Tex. Christian U., Ft. Worth, 1985-87; organist, accompanist Genesis United Meth. Ch., Ft. Worth, 1987-93; librarian, cataloger Hotho & Co., Ft. Worth, 1994-97; head librarian S.W. Christian Sch., Ft. Worth, 1997—. Mem. regional librarians' forum Ednl. Svc. Ctr., Ft. Worth, 1997—. Contbr. articles to profl. jours. V.p. Southbrook Neighborhood Assn., 1990-92; judge local and state piano contests and festivals, 1993—. Mem. ALA, Tex. Libr. Assn., Am. Coll. Musicians (judge 1997—), Nat. Guild Piano Tchrs. (co-chair Ft. Worth 1993—), Phi Kappa Lambda. Methodist. Avocations: theater, concerts, antiquing, reading, family and friends. Home: 7928 Regency Ln Fort Worth TX 76134-5017 Office: SW Christian Sch 6801 Dan Danciger Rd Fort Worth TX 76133-4903

SCHOLL, VIRGINIA MAY, retired plastic surgeon; b. Vancouver, Wash., June 6, 1925; d. Cornelius Bernard Scholl and Melanie Mary Rausch. BS, U. Oreg., Eugene; MD, U. Oreg., Portland. Intern Yale U., New Haven; resident Mayo Clinic, Rochester, Minn.; pvt. practice plastic surgery Seattle. Home: 1155 N Etheridge Pl Boise ID 83704-8478

SCHOLZ, JANE, newspaper publisher; b. St. Louis, July 31, 1948; d. Robert Louis and Mildred Virginia (Hudgins) S.; m. Jay W. Johnson, June 1979 (div. Dec. 1981); m. Douglas C. Balz, Jan. 1, 1983 BA, Mich. State U., 1970; MBA, U. Miami, 1981. Reporter Jour.-Gazette, Fort Wayne, Ind., 1970-73, The Miami Herald, Fla., 1973-77, asst. city editor Fla., 1977-80; advanced mgmt. devel. participant Knight-Ridder Inc., Miami, Fla., 1980-85; pres., pub. Post-Tribune, Gary, Ind., 1985-91; editor Knight-Ridder/Tribune News Svc., Washington. Bd. dirs. United Way of Lake county, Ind., Gary chpt. Urban League, Ind., NW Ind. Forum. Mem. Am. Newspaper Pubs. Assn., Ind. C. of C. (bd. dirs.), Inland Press Assn. (bd. dirs.), Sigma Delta Chi Office: Knight Ridder Tribune/ Info Svc Ste 1000 700 12th St NW Washington DC 20005

SCHOMMER, TRUDY MARIE, minister, religious studies educator; b. Wayzata, Minn., May 18, 1937; d. Edward and Gertrude (Mergen) S. BA, Coll. St. Catherine, St. Paul, 1966; MA, Manhattanville Coll., 1971, Pacifica Grad. Inst., 1996. Joined Order of Franciscan Sisters of Little Falls, Minn., 1955. Dir. religious edn. St. Pius X, White Bear Lake, Minn., 1971-77; campus min., theology tchr. St. Cloud (Minn.) State Univ., 1977-81; pastoral min. St. Galls, St. Elizabeth, Milw., 1981-85; dir. religious edn. St. Alexander's, Morrisonville, N.Y., 1985-90; pastoral min. of religious edn. St. Mary's, Bryantown, Md., 1990-91; diocesan dir. religious edn. Diocese of New Ulm, Minn., 1991—. Exec. bd. mem. Nat. Assembly Religious Women, Chgo., 1974-78. Author: Easiest Gospel Stories Ever, 1993; book reviewer Sister's Today, 1988-91. Mem. Network, Washington, 1978—. Mem. Nat. Cath. Edn. Assn., Nat. Parish Coords. and Dirs. Democrat. Roman Catholic. Home and Office: 113 Saint Paul St NW Apt 13 Preston MN 55965-8906 Personal E-mail: trudyschommer@yahoo.com.

SCHON, SANDRA DIANE, elementary school educator; b. Oak Park, Ill., May 17, 1961; d. Edwin and Dolores (Donald) Czubakowski; m. Donald Eugene Schon, June 25, 1994. BS in English, Reading, North Tex. State U., 1983. Cert. tchr. English, reading, Tex. Supr. acad. support svcs. So. Ill. U., Carbondale, 1984-87; acct.'s asst. Tex. Woman's U., Denton, 1987-90, memtor trainer, 1995—; tchr. Little Elm (Tex.) Ind. Sch. Dist., 1991-99, site-base team mem., 1994-99, curriculum devel. mem., 1996-99; tchr. grade 5 Lewisville Ind. Sch. Dist., 1999—. Named to Outstanding Young Women in Am., 1988; McMath Music scholar, 1979. Mem. ASCD.

SCHOOLEY, TONI ANN, gifted and talented educator; b. New Castle, Pa., Jan. 7, 1955; d. Anthony John and Nancy Estena Orelli; m. Jeffrey R. Schooley, May 1, 1982; children: Patrick Elijah, Shane Michael. BS in Spl. and Elem. Edn., Slippery Rock U., Pa., 1977. Cert. tchg. Pa. Dept. Edn., 1977. Spl. edn. tchr. Shenango Area Sch. Dist., New Castle, Pa., 1988—92; spl. edn. tchr./gifted coord. K-12 Laurel Sch. Dist., New Castle, 1995—. Student coun. advisor Laurel Jr./Sr. HS, New Castle, 1997—. Charter mem. Ind. Meth. Ch., New Castle, 1988—2005. Recipient Educator of Distinction award, Nat. Soc. HS Scholars, 2004, Outstanding Am. Tchr., Nat. Honor Roll, 2005—06. Mem.: PSEA, LEA, PASC Dist. 2 Bd. (bd. mem. 1999—2005), Nat. Assn. Student Couns., NEA (assoc.). Methodist. Avocations: swimming, travel, reading. Office: Laurel Sch District 2497 Harlansburg Rd New Castle PA 16101 Office Phone: 724-658-9056. Office Fax: 724-658-2992. Business E-Mail: tschooley@laurel.k12.pa.us.

SCHOON, DORIS VIVIEN, ophthalmologist; b. Luverne, Minn., Dec. 31, 1928; d. Jacob and Esther Viola S. BA, U. Minn., 1950, MD, 1954; MSEE, Calif. State U., 1991. Diplomate Am. Bd. Ophthalmology. Intern Kings County Hosp., Bklyn., 1954-55; physician Embudo Presbyn. Hosp., N.Mex., 1955-57; resident in clin. pathology U. Colo. Med. Ctr., Denver, 1957-58; gen. practice medicine Anaheim, Calif., 1958-61; resident in ophthalmology L.A. Eye and Ear Hosp. at Hollywood Presbyn. Hosp., 1961-64; ophthalmologist Anaheim, 1965-75; pvt. practice electrophysiology related to vision, 1997—2003; prof. clin. ophthalmology U. Calif., Irvine, 2004—. Physician Long Beach Vets. Hosp., 1998—. Fellow Am. Acad. Ophthalmology; mem. IEEE, Am. Women's Med. Assn., Internat. Soc. Clin. Electrophysiology in Vision, Soc. of Women Engrs., Order Eastern Star. Republican. Presbyterian. Achievements include research in field of using fast random stimuli to obtain electroretinograms and visually evoked potentials.

SCHOON, MARION ELSE, librarian; b. Berlin, Nov. 28, 1940; d. Kurt and Else Henriette Jacob; m. John George Schoon, Sept. 14, 1963 BA, U. Toronto, 1966; M.L.S., Columbia U., 1970. Librarian N.Y. Pub. Library, N.Y.C., 1968-72; reference librarian Harvard Coll. Library, Harvard U., Cambridge, Mass., 1972—, head div., 1979—. Avocations: sailing; photography. Office: Harvard Univ Widener Library Cambridge MA 02138

SCHOONMAKER, DORIS, mathematics professor; MA in Math., SUNY, Albany. Prof. math. Hudson Valley C.C., Troy, NY, 1978—. Office: Hudson Valley CC; Mathematics/ENS Dept 80 Vandenburgh Ave Troy NY 12180 Office Phone: 518-629-7265.

SCHOONMAKER POWELL, THELMA, film editor; b. Algeria, Jan. 3, 1940; m. Michael Powell, May 19, 1984 (dec. Feb. 19, 1990). Editor: (films) Finnegan's Wake, 1966, The Virgin President, 1968, Who's That Knocking at My Door, 1968, Woodstock, 1970 (nominee Best Film Editing Acad. award, 1970, Best Film Editing Am. Cinema Editors award, 1980), Rockshow, 1980, Raging Bull, 1980 (Best Film Editing Acad. award, 1980, Best Film Editing award Am. Cinema Editors, 1980, Best Film Editing award Brit. Acad., 1981, Best Film Editing Am. Cinema Editors award, 1980), The King of Comedy, 1983, After Hours, 1985, The Color of Money, 1986, The Last Temptation of Christ, 1988, New York Stories (Life Lessons segment), 1989, GoodFellas, 1990 (nominee Best Film Editing Acad. award, 1990, Best Dramatic Film Editing Brit. Acad. award, 1990), Cape Fear, 1992, The Age of Innocence, 1993, A Personal Journey with Martin Scorsese Through American Movies, 1995, Casino, 1995 (nominee Best Film Editing Am. Cinema Editors, 1995), Grace of My Heart, 1996, Kundun, 1997, Bringing Out the Dead, 1999, Il Mio Viaggio in Italia, 2000, Gangs of New York, 2002 (Best Dramatic Film Editing Am. Cinema Editors award, 2003, nominee Best Film Editing Acad. award, 2003), The Aviator, 2004 (Best Film Editing Acad. award, 2005, Best Dramatic Film Editing Am. Cinema Editor award, 2005), The Departed, 2006.

SCHOONOVER, BRENDA B., ambassador; BA, Morgan State U., Balt.; postgrad., Howard U. Vol. Peace Corps, Philippines, 1961, adminstr. Office Talent Search Washington, assoc. dir. Tanzania, dir. sch. partnership program Washington; affirmative action officer Govt. of Arlington County, Va.; with Fgn. Svc. U.S. Dept. State, Manila, Colombo, Sri Lanka, Tunis, Tunisia, with Bur. Near East and South Asia Washington, 1978-88, chief pers. Bur. European and Can. Affairs, 1988-91, mem. Sr. Seminar, 1996-97; adminstrv. officer, dept. dir. Office Joint Adminstrv. Svcs. Am. Embassy, Brussels, 1992-96; Capstone fellow Nat. Def. U., Washington, 1997; U.S. amb. to Togo Am. Embassy, Lome, 1998-2000; amb.-in-residence Chapel Hill, NC, 2000—01; chargé d'affaires, ad interim min. counselor Am. Embassy, Brussels, 2001—04. Bd. dirs. Am. Diplomacy On-line Mag. Mem. adv. bd. Carolina for Kibera. Recipient Order of the Mono award, The Togolese Govt., 2000, Presdl. Meritorious award, U.S., 2003, Sec. of State Career Achievement award, 2004. Mem.: LWV. Office: 108 Ironwoods Dr Chapel Hill NC 27516 E-mail: RCSchoon2@aol.com.

SCHOONOVER, JEAN WAY, public relations consultant; b. Richfield Springs, NY; AB, Cornell U., 1941. With D-A-Y Pub. Rels., Ogilvy & Mather Co., N.Y.C., 1949-91, D-A-Y Pub. Rels. Inc. and predecessor, N.Y.C., 1949—; owner, pres. Dudley-Anderson-Yutzy Pub. Rels. Inc. and predecessor, N.Y.C., 1970—, chmn., 1984-88; merger with Ogilvy & Mather, 1983; sr. v.p. Ogilvy & Mather U.S., 1984-91; vice chmn. Ogilvy Pub. Relations Group, 1986-91; ind. cons., 1992—; pres. YWCA of the City of N.Y., 1994-98. Historian, Pub. Rels. Seminar; mem. USDA Agribus. Promotion Coun., 1985-86. Trustee Cornell U., 1975-80; mem. Def. Adv. Com. on Women in Svcs., 1987-89. Named Advt. Woman of Yr. Am. Advt. Fedn., 1972, one of Outstanding Women in Bus. & Labor, Women's Equity Action League, 1985; recipient Matrix award, 1976, Nat. Headliner award, 1984, N.Y. Women in Comm., 1976, Leadership award Internat. Orgn. Women Bus. Owners, 1980, Entrepreneurial Woman award Women Bus. Owners N.Y., 1981, Women of Distinction award Soroptimists Internat. N.Y., 1995, Achievement award LWV of N.Y.C., 1997. Mem. Women Execs. in Pub. Rels. N.Y.C. (pres. 1979-80), Pub. Rels. Soc. Am., Pub. Rels. Soc. N.Y. (pres. 1979), Womens Forum, Women's City Club. Home and Office: 25 Stuyvesant St New York NY 10003-7505

SCHOONOVER, MARGARET See LEFRANC, MARGARET

SCHOONOVER, MELISSA, music educator; b. Pine Bluff, Ark., July 8, 1976; d. James Philip and Janet Schoonover. B in Music Edn., U. Ill., Champaign-Urbana, 2000. Cert. tchr. State Tchr. Certification Bd., Ill., 2005. Orch. tchr. Elmhurst Pub. Schs., Ill., 2000—01, Joliet Pub. Schs. Dist. 86, Ill., 2001—. Youth group leader Aldersgate United Meth. Ch., Wheaton, Ill., 2000—06. Recipient Star Employee award, Joliet Grade Schs., 2004. Mem.: Ill. Grade Sch. Music Assn. (dist. VI chairperson 2003—06), Am. String Tchrs. Assn., Music Educator Nat. Conf., Ill. Music Educators Assn., Kappa Delta Pi, Golden Key Nat. Honor Soc., Sigma Alpha Iota (life; v.p. for ritual 1997—98, Sword of Honor 1997). Office: Washington Jr HS 402 S Richards St Joliet IL 60433 Office Phone: 815-727-5271. Personal E-mail: mell0cell0@aol.com.

SCHOR, LAURA STRUMINGHER, historian; b. NYC, June 24, 1945; d. David Charles and Esther Rachel (Pearl) Gross; children: Eric Alain, Neil Remy; m. Joseph Martin Schor, June, 1992. BA, Queens Coll., CUNY, 1967; MA, U. Rochester, 1970, PhD, 1974. Asst. prof. SUNY, Fredonia, 1973-79; assoc. prof., dir. women's studies U. Cin., 1979-85, prof., vice provost, 1985-89; prof., provost, v.p. acad. affairs Hunter Coll., CUNY, N.Y.C., 1989-98; exec. dir. Hadassah, The Women's Zionist Orgn. of Am., Inc., N.Y.C., 1998-2000; dean CUNY Honors Coll., 2001—. Author: Women and the Making of the Working Class, 1979, What Were Little Boys and Girls Made Of?, 1984, The Odyssey of Flora Tristan, 1988, Les Jolies Femmes d'Edouard de Beaumont, 1994, The Life and Legacy of Baroness Betty de Rothschild, 2006. Mem.: Internat. Soc. for Study European Ideas, Am. Hist. Assn., French Hist. Assn., Phi Beta Kappa.

SCHOR, LYNDA, author, educator; b. Bklyn., Apr. 18, 1938; d. Louis and Julia (Schleifer) Nyfield; m. Halvard Brooks Johnson, June 1990; children: Alexandra, Timothy, Zachary. BFA, The Cooper Union, 1959. Prof. writing NYU, 1979; disting. vis. writer Western Wash. U., Bellingham, 1980-81, Fla. Internat. U., Miami, 1983-84; prof. The New Sch., N.Y.C., 1983—. Author: True Love and Real Romance, 1980, Appetites, 1976, The Body Parts Shop, Adventures in Capitalism; contbr. articles to profl. jours. Recipient Individual Artist award State of Md., 1995; City Arts grant, 1993. Fellow Macdowell Colony, Va. Ctr. for the Creative Arts; mem. PEN Am. Ctr.

SCHORER, SUKI, ballet teacher; b. Boston; d. Mark and Ruth (Page) S.; 1 child, Nicole. Studied with, George Balanchine. Dancer San Francisco Ballet, 1956-59, N.Y.C. Ballet, 1959-72; prin. dancer N.Y.C. Ballet Co., 1968-72, artistic assoc. lecture demonstration program, 1972-95; mem. faculty Sch. Am. Ballet, 1972—, Brown Found. sr. faculty chair, 1998—. Internat. guest tchr. and lectr. specializing in Balanchine tng. and technique; artist dir., tchr. on Balanchine Essays (videos). Author: Suki Schorer on Balanchine Technique, 1999 (de la Torre Bueno prize 2000), Put Your Best Foot Forward, 2005; created roles in Balanchine's Harlequinade, Don Quixote, Midsummer Night's Dream, Jewels, La Source, Raymonda Variations; repertory included prin. roles in Apollo, Serenade, Concerto Barocco, Symphony in C, La Sonnambula, Stars and Stripes, Tarantella, Valse Fantaisie, The Nutcracker, Brahams Schoenberg, La Valse, Western Symphony, Ivesiana, Divertimento # 15, Ballet Imperial, others. Recipient Disting. Tchr. in Arts award Nat. Found. Advancement in Arts, 1997, award Dance mag., 1998. Office: Sch of Am Ballet 70 Lincoln Center Plz New York NY 10023-6548 Office Phone: 212-769-6600.

SCHORI, KATHARINE JEFFERTS, bishop; b. Pensacola, Fla., Mar. 26, 1954; m. Richard M. Schori, 1979; 1 child, Katharine. BS in Marine Biology, Stanford U., 1974; MS in Oceanography, Oreg. State U., Corvallis, 1977, PhD in Oceanography, 1983; MDiv, Ch. Div. Sch. of the Pacific, Berkeley, Calif., 1994. Worked in oceanography, including at the Nat. Marine Fisheries Svc. in Seattle; ordained deacon, 1994, priest, 1994; asst. rector Episcopal Ch. of the Good Samaritan, Corvallis, Oreg., 1994—2001; consecrated bishop, 2001; bishop Episcopal Diocese of Nev., Las Vegas, 2001—; chief pastor elect Episcopal Church USA, 2006. Achievements include being first woman to lead a church in the worldwide Anglican Communion. Office: Episcopal Church Ctr Second Ave New York NY 10017 Office Phone: 702-737-9190. Office Fax: 702-737-6488.*

SCHORR, COLLIER, artist; b. NYC, 1963; BFA, Sch. Visual Arts, NYC. Exhibited in group shows at Internat. Ctr. for Photography Triennial, 2003, Whitney Biennial, Whitney Mus. Am. Art, NYC, 2002, 2006, Walker Art Ctr., Minn., The Jewish Mus., NYC, Stedelijk Mus, Amsterdam, Consorcio Salamanca, Spain, exhibitions include 303 Gallery. Office: c/o 303 Gallery 525 W 22nd St New York NY 10011*

SCHORR, LISBETH BAMBERGER, sociologist, researcher; b. Munich, Jan. 20, 1931; d. Fred S. and Lotte (Krafft) Bamberger; m. Daniel L. Schorr, Jan. 8, 1967; children: Jonathan, Lisa. BA with highest honors, U. Calif., Berkeley, 1952; LHD (hon.), Wilkes U., 1991, U. Md., 1994, Bank St. Coll. Edn., 1999, Wheelock Coll., 2000, Lewis & Clark Coll., 2001, Whittier Coll., 2003. Med. care cons. U.A.W. and Community Health Assn., Detroit, 1956—58; asst. dir. Dept. Social Security AFL-CIO, Washington, 1958—65; acting chief CAP Health Svcs., OEO, 1965—66; chief program planning Office for Health Affairs, OEO, Washington, 1967. Cons. Children's Def. Fund, Washington, 1973—79; scholar-in-residence Inst. of Medicine NAS, 1979—80; chmn. Select Panel on Promotion Child Health, 1979—80; adj. prof. maternal and child health U. N.C., Chapel Hill, 1981—85; lectr. social medicine Harvard U. Med. Sch., 1984—; dir. project on effective interventions Harvard U., 1988—; founder www.PathwaysToOutcomes.org; nat. coun. Alan Gutmacher Inst., 1974—79, 1982—85; pub. mem. Am. Bd. Pediat., 1978—84; vice chmn. Found. for Child Devel., 1978—84, bd. dirs., 1976—84, 1986—94; mem. coun. Nat. Ctr. for Children in Poverty, 1987—96; mem. children's program adv. com. Edna McConnell Clark Found., 1987—97; bd. dirs. Pub. Edn. Fund Network, 1991—93; co-chair Roundtable on Cmty. Change Aspen Inst., 1992—; mem. bd. on children and families NAS, 1993—95; mem. Nat. Commn. State and Local Pub. Svcs., 1992—94; mem. task force on young children Carnegie Corp., 1992—94; mem. sec.'s adv. com. Head Start quality and expansion, 1993—94; mem. nat. selection com. Ford Found./Kennedy Sch. Awards for Innovations in Am. Govt., 1998—. Author: Within Our Reach: Breaking the Cycle of Disadvantage, 1988, Common Purpose: Strengthening Families and Neighborhoods to Rebuild America, 1997. Co-chmn. Boundaries task force Harvard Children's Initiative, 1998—2000; mem. Brookings Children's Roundtable, 1999—2002; bd. dirs. Nat. Student Partnerships, 2001—03, Eureka Cmtys., 1995—, Civic Ventures, 1997—99. Recipient Dale Richmond Meml. award, Am. Acad. Pediat., 1977, 9th ann. Robert F. Kennedy Book award, 1989, Nelson Cruikshank award, Nat. Coun. Sr. Citizens, 1990, Porter prize, 1993, PASS award, Nat. Coun. on Crime and Delinquency, 1997, Marian F. Langer award, Am. Orthopsychiat. Assn., 1999, Empatheia award, Vols. of Am., 1999. Mem.: Nat. Acad. on Social Ins., Inst. Medicine NAS, Phi Beta Kappa. Home and Office: 3113 Woodley Rd NW Washington DC 20008-3449 Office Phone: 202-462-3071. Business E-Mail: lisbeth_schorr@hms.harvard.edu.

SCHORR-RIBERA, HILDA KEREN, psychologist; b. N.Y.C., May 2, 1942; d. Leon and Rosa Schorr-Ribera; m. Ira Eli Wessler, Aug. 6, 1971; children: Mike, Daniel. BA, Hunter Coll., 1963; MEd, U. No. Fla., 1982; PhD, U. Pitts., 1988. Lic. psychologist, Pa.; diplomate Am. Bd. Forensic Examiners; diplomate, fellow Am. Bd. Med. Psychotherapists and Psychodiagnosticians; diplomate Am. Bd. Forensic Medicine, Am. Acad. Experts in Traumatic Stress; cert. in clin. hypnosis. Psychotherapist South Hills Interfaith Ministries, Bethel Park, Pa., 1989-92, Profl. Psychol. Assn. of Greater Pitts., 1992; pvt. practice psychologist Pitts., 1993—. Child therapist Forbes Hospice, 1993—; group facilitator of adult wellness group and children's support groups Burger King Cancer Caring Ctr., Pitts., 1989—, Allegheny Hospice, Pitts., 1994—96; psychol. evaluator Washington (Pa.) County Ct., 1993—2005, Allegheny County Ct., Pitts., 1995—98; cons. psychologist to sch. dists. Allegheny and Washington Counties. Author (with others): Educating the Child With Cancer, 1993. Keynote spkr. on illness and bereavement to profl. assns., hosps., schs. and agys., Pitts., 1989—. Mem. APA, Internat. Soc. Hypnosis, Am. Soc. Clin. Hypnosis, Am. Acad. Experts in Traumatic Stress, Am. Counseling Assn., Am. Coll. Forensic Examiners, Pa. Psychol. Assn., Greater Pitts. Psychol. Assn. Avocations: music, bilingual activities, reading, walking, travel. Office: 117 Ridgeway Ct Pittsburgh PA 15228-1729 Office Phone: 412-344-0222. Personal E-mail: schorrribera@yahoo.com.

SCHOTLAND, JUDITH, education educator; b. Ponca City, Okla., Sept. 26, 1950; d. Roy Cordis and Patricia Irene Schotland. BS, Okla. State U., Stillwater, 1974; PhD, Northwestern U., Chgo., 1990; MS, Simmens Coll., Boston, 2002. Rsch. assoc. Karolinska Inst., Stockholm, 1990—92, M.I.T., Cambridge, Mass., 1993—95; assoc. prof. Boston U., 1995—. Author: (article) Nature, 1995. Recipient Nat. Rsch. Svc. award, NIH, 1987—90, Whitney R. Powers Excellence in Tchg. award, Sargent Coll., 2005; fellow, Fogarty Internat., 1991, Internat. Brain Rsch. Orgn., 1992; grantee, NSF, 1996—99. Mem.: Soc. Neurosci., Am. Assn. for Advancement of Sci., Sigma Xi. Avocations: gardening, reading, glass bead making. Office: Boston Univ Dept Health Scis 635 Commonwealth Ave Rm 472 Boston MA 02215 Office Phone: 617-353-8449. Business E-Mail: schotlnd@bu.edu.

SCHOTT, SALLY MARIA, music publisher, arts education consultant; b. San Antonio, Feb. 7, 1943; d. Valentine Felix Schott, Jr. and Doris Faye. MusB, Okla. Coll. Women, 1964; MusM Edn., North Tex. State U., 1966. Choral dir. Jackson Intermediate, Pasadena, Tex., 1965—74, South Houston H.S., 1974—2004; founding ptnr. Alliance Music Publs., Houston, 1994—. Ednl. cons. Bay Area Chorus, Houston, 2004—; supr. student tchrs. U. Houston, 2004—; text correlations writer McGraw-Hill, Woodland Hills, Calif., 2005—; minority ptnr. AMC Music, Houston, 1975—2006; pres. Quaid/Schott Media Prodns., LLC, 2005—, Schott Bradshaw Publ., LLC, 2006—. Editor: Something to Sing About, 1981, Howard Swan: Conscience of a Profession, 1987; coord. writing team Sing, 1988. Mem. adv. bd. Am. Classic Festivals, San Antonio, 2004—; ednl. adv. bd. Houston Chamber Choir, 2004—. Named to Hall Fame, U. Sci. & Arts Okla., 1996; recipient Outstanding Young Educator, Pasadena Jaycees, 1974, Tchrs. Make a Difference award, KTRK, 1988. Mem.: Tex. Choral Dirs. Assn. (state v.p. 1976—77), Am. Choral Dirs. Assn. (R&S 1994—98, pres. 2000—02, editor newsletter 2002—04), Tex. Music Educators Assn. (pres., state vocal chair 1981—86), Pasadena Area Ret. Sch. Employees, Delta Kappa Gamma, Sigma Alpha Iota (pres. 1966, Leadership award Svc. to Music in Houston 1987). Republican. Methodist. Avocations: photography, travel, sports. Home: 4403 Regal Pine Trail Houston TX 77059

SCHRADE, ROLANDE MAXWELL YOUNG, composer, pianist, educator; b. Washington, Sept. 13; d. Harry Robert and Isabelle Martha (Maxwell) Young; m. Robert Warren Schrade, Dec. 21, 1949; children: Robelyn, Rhonda

Lee, Rolisa, Randolph, Rorianne. Studied with, Harold Bauer, NYC, Vittorio Giannini; student, Manhatten Sch. Music, Juilliard Sch. Music. Debut as concert pianist Town Hall, NYC, 1953, Nat. Gallery, Washington, 1954; concert pianist Constitution Hall, Washington, 1972; founder, dir. ann. performances Sevenars Concerts, Inc., Worthington, Mass., 1968—, music dir., 1975—, also broadcasts, 1984, 85; recitalist Radio Sta. WGMS-FM, Washington; mem. music faculty Allen-Stevenson Sch., NYC, 1968-89; co-founder, v.p., treas. Sevenars Music House, Inc., NYC, 1968—. Concerts include Lincoln Ctr., Alice Tully Hall, 1980, 93, Sevenars Concerts, Inc., 1968—, Lincoln Ctr., 2000; Lifetime TV film Tour, New Zealand, 1982-84; featured NBC Today Show with Schrade family pianists, 1993; named to Steinway Piano Co. Global Artist List; appearances PM Mag., TV film, 1980-81; composer, pub., recs. of over 100 songs; albums include America 76, Original and Traditional Songs for Special Days, 1988; editor: songs of Carrie Jacobs Bond, Boston Music Co.; TV feature film with Schrade Family Pianists, 1997; performed in Schrade-James Family Concert Lincoln Ctr., NYC, 2000, Lifetime TV showing. Mem.: ASCAP, DAR (Bicentennial award 1972), Mut. Artists Mgmt. Alliance (founder, bd. dirs.). Episcopalian. Home and Office: 30 East End Ave Ste 3A New York NY 10028-7053 Office: Sevenars Concerts Ireland St S at Rte 112 Worthington MA 01098

SCHRADER, JANET E., music educator; b. Dover, Del., May 19, 1954; d. Edwin Francis and Hazel Leonore Englehart; m. Harold David Schrader, Aug. 13, 1988. B of Music Edn., U. Del., Newark, 1972—77; post-grad., Pa. State U., State College, 1978, E. Stroudsburg U., Pa., 1978—79. Music tchr. Harrisburg City Schs., Pa., 1977—2006. Prin. tympanist: Ctrl. Pa. Symphony, vocal soloist:. Soloist, choir mem. Silver Spring Presbyn. Ch., asst. choir dir. Named Tchr. of Month, Harrisburg City Schs., 2001; recipient Team Tchg. award, 1996. Mem.: Dauphin County Music Educators, Music Educator's Nat. Conf. Republican. Presbyn. Office: Harrisburg City Schs 2451 Market St Harrisburg PA 17103

SCHRADER, LUANN CAROL, art educator; b. Alexandria, Minn., Oct. 19, 1942; d. John Charles and Clara Katherine (Klimek) Bartos; m. Richard Lloyd William, July 25, 1970; children: William, Lynnae, Charles. BS, St. Cloud State U., 1965. Cert. tchr., math., art. Tchr., art and math Wells-Easton Sch. #224, Wells, Minn., 1965-72; tchr., art Our Lady of Mt. Carmel Sch., Easton, Minn., 1983—2000; tchr. art St. Casimir's Sch., Wells, Minn., 2000—. Co-editor: History of Faribault County, Minn., 1974-76; editor community calendar, Easton, 1985—. Mem. sch. bd. United South Ctr., Wells, 1990-93, 94-96; owner, mgr. Eastown Apts, Wells, Minn., Bricelyn (Minn.) Apts., 1993—; ch. organist Our Lady of Mt. Carmel, Easton, 1972—, officer numerous coms., others. Mem. Minn. Geneal. Soc., Czech. Geneal. Soc., Am. Legion Aux. (officer 1970—). Avocations: genealogy, history. Home: 8 Main St Easton MN 56025-0113 Personal E-mail: schrader@bevcomm.net.

SCHRADER, SUSAN RAE, elementary school educator; b. Tucson, Nov. 12, 1972; d. Edward Arthur and Nancy Young Schrader. BS, Nebr. Wesleyan U., Lincoln, 1994; M in Elem. Edn., No. Ariz. U., Phoenix, 2001. Cert. Ariz., 1995. Tchr. Tucson Unified Sch. Dist., 1995—96, Alhambra Sch. Dist., Phoenix, 1997—. Coach Peoria (Ariz.) Sch. Dist., 2004—06. V.p. Catalina Booster Club, Phoenix, 2002—04. Named Dist. Employee of Month, Alhambra Sch. Dist.; named to Athletic Hall of Fame, Nebr. Wesleyan U., 2005; recipient Spirit of Catalina, Catalina Ventura Elem., 2004. R-Consevative. Roman Catholic. Avocations: travel, gardening, home improvements, movies, reading. Office: Catalina Ventura 6331 N 39th Ave Phoenix AZ 85019 Office Phone: 602-841-7445. E-mail: sschrader@alhambra.k12.az.us.

SCHRAG, ADELE FRISBIE, business education educator; b. Cynthiana, Ky., May 7, 1921; d. Shirley Ledyard and Edna Kate (Ford) S.; m. William Albert Schrag, Apr. 6, 1963; 1 stepchild, Marie Carol. BS, Temple U., 1942; MA, N.Y. U., 1944, PhD, 1961. Tchr. Manor Twp. High Sch., Millersville, Pa., 1942-43, Downingtown (Pa.) Sr. High Sch., 1943-50; instr., asst. prof. Temple U. Sch. Bus. and Pub. Administrn., Phila., 1950-60; prof. bus. edn. and vocat. edn. Coll. Edn., 1960-85, sr. prof. edn., 1985-88, prof. emeritus, 1988—. Vis. lectr. N.Y. U.; cons. Phila. Community Coll., 1967-82 Editor: Business Education for the Automated Office, 1964; author: (with Estelle L. Popham and Wanda Blockhus) A Teaching-Learning System for Business Education, 1975, How to Dictate, 1981, Office Procedures Update, 1982, (with Robert Poland) A Teaching System for Business Subjects, 1988; contbr. articles to profl. jours., chpts. to books. Trustee Meth. Hosp., 1981—85, Sun Cities Symphony Assn., 1988—93, Habitat for Humanity West Valley, 1994—2005, co-pres., 1999—2001; trustee Habitat for Humanity Ariz., 1999—2003. Recipient Profl. Panhellenic award, 1963; Kensington High Sch. Alumnae award, 1972 Mem. Soc. Automation in Bus. Edn. (pres. 1969-73, dir. 1974), Nat. Assn. Bus. Tchr. Edn. (pres. 1983-84), Bus. Edn. Certification Council, Phi Gamma Nu (nat. treas. 1952-54, nat. sec. 1954-56), Delta Pi Epsilon (policy commn. for bus. and econ. edn. 1975-78, dir. research found. 1978-83, pres. research found. 1983). Home: 14515 W Granite Valley Dr # 644 Sun City West AZ 85375-6021 E-mail: as107@cox.net.

SCHRAGE, ROSE, retired academic administrator; b. Montelimar, France, Apr. 15, 1942; came to U.S., 1947; d. Abraham and Celia (Silbiger) Levine; m. Samuel Schrage, Dec. 12, 1935 (dec. 1976); children: Abraham, Leon. BRE, Beth Rivkah Tchrs. Sem., Bklyn., 1968; Paralegal, Manpower Career Devel. Agy., Bklyn., 1973; MS, L.I. U., 1975; Advanced Cert. Ednl. Adminstrn., Bklyn. Coll., 1983. Cert. sch. dist. adminstr., guidance counselor, tchr., asst. prin. Sec., N.Y.C., 1964-68; police adminstrv. aide N.Y.C. Police Dept., 1974-75; coord. state reading aid program Sch. Dist. 14, Bklyn., 1977-78, project dir. Title VII, 1978-81, asst. dir. reimbursable fed. and state programs, 1981-85, dist. bus. mgr., 1985-94, asst. prin., 1994—99, spl. edn. instrn. specialist, adminstr., 1999—; ednl. adminstr. Ctrl. Liaison Office for Impartial Hearings divsn. student support svcs. Dept. Edn., NYC, 2001—04; ret., 2004. Chmn. N.Y.C. Bd. Edn. IMPACT Com., Bklyn., 1986—. Author (poem): Never Again, 1983; contbg. editor Chai Today; contbr. articles to profl. jours. Del. Republican. Jud. Conf., 1968; founder, pres Concerned Parents, Bklyn., 1977; radio co-host Israeli War Heroes Fund-Radiothon, Bklyn.; family counselor local social agys., Bklyn.; co-founder cmty. vol. ambulance Hatzalah, 1977. Recipient Cert. of Appreciation as vol. regional coord. N.Y. State Mentoring Program N.Y. Gov. Cuomo, 1991, Proclamation, N.Y. City Coun., 2003, State of N.Y. Legis. Resolution Proclamation N.Y. State Senate, 2003, U.S. Congress Proclamation, 2003, Excellence in Fiscal Mgmt. award IMPACT. Mem. Am. Assn. Sch. Adminstrs., Assn. Orthodox Jewish Tchrs. (v.p. exec. bd., pres. 2004, Orgn. award 2003), N.Y. State Assn. Sch. Bus. Ofcls., N.Y.C. Assn. Sch. Bus. Ofcls., Coun. Suprs. and Adminstrs. Avocations: piano, reading, composing music.

SCHRAM, LAUREEN ANN, reading specialist; b. Dell Rapids, S.D., June 14, 1959; d. Lester Howard and Lillian Frieda (Hilda) Gregersen; m. Jeffrey Ray Schram; children: Karlee Renae, Krista Lenae. BA, Northwestern Coll., Orange City, Iowa, 1993; Masters, U. Sioux Falls, S.D., 2002. Reading specialist Ctrl. Lyon Cmty. Sch. Dist., Rock Rapids, Iowa, 1997—. Bd. dirs. Healthy Families, Rock Rapids, Iowa. Sgt. USAF, 1978—82. Mem.: NEA, N.W. Iowa Reading Assn. (sec. 1999—2006), Iowa Reading Assn., Alpha Xi Delta, Beta Sigma Phi (pres. 1985—2006). Reformed Ch. Of Am. Avocations: walking, reading, spending time with family and friends. Home: 1003 S Tama St Rock Rapids IA 51246 Office: Ctrl Lyon Cmty Sch Dist 1105 S Story Rock Rapids IA 51246 Office Phone: 712-472-4041. E-mail: LSchram@central-lyon.k12.ia.us.

SCHRECK-ROSEN, ELLEN ELIZABETH, special education educator; d. John Joseph Schreck and Eileen Elizabeth Hickey; m. Ira Rosen, Aug. 9, 1980. BA, Caldwell Coll., Caldwell, NJ, 1973; MA, Montclair State U., Upper Montclair, NJ, 1978. Cert. tchr. elem. edn., reading cons., handicapped, reading, sign lang. NJ., adult/child CRP and AED ARC, 2005. Student intern Caldwell/W. Caldwell Bd. of Edn., Caldwell, 1972—73; classroom tchr. Parsippany/Troy Hills Bd. of Edn., Parsippany, NJ, 1973—83, com. handicapped tchr., 1983—85; spl. edn. tchr. Red Bank Bd. of Edn., NJ, 1985—87; learning disabilities tchr. Bradley Beach Bd. of Edn., NJ, 1987—. Coord. N.J. project fair Rockaway Meadow Sch., Parsippany, NJ, 1977—82; chairperson of the bd. Entertainment On Location, Point Pleasant, NJ, 1989—; faculty liaison Bradley Beach PTA, Bradley Beach, NJ, 1990—92. Author: (children's book) P.S. There's a Spidgit Under My Bed, Penguin Paradise, 2004, (children's poem) A Holiday Alphabet. Cmty. rels. chairperson Bradley Beach Sch., 1992—97; chairperson Cirriculm Cmty., 2003—04; coach Monmouth County Tournament of Champions, Bradley Beach, 1987—91. Grantee Effective Schools grantee, Red Bank Primary Sch., 1985. Mem.: Coun. for Exceptional Children, Bradley Beach Edn. Assn. (corr. sec. 1993—96), N.J. Edn. Assn., NEA, Meridian Life Fitness. Independent. Roman Catholic. Avocations: literature, travel, water sports, arts and crafts, tennis. Office Phone: 732-775-4413.

SCHREIBER, CLARE ADEL, journalist; b. Chgo., Feb. 22, 1914; d. Otto Herman Mentz and Martha Toll; m. William I. Schreiber, June 18, 1934 (dec. Jan. 1998); children: William M., James L., Ralph W.(dec.), Stephen T. BS in Journalism, U. Ill., 1935; LHD, Coll. of Wooster, 1985. Freelance writer Fairfield Iowa Ledger, 1937, The Daily Record, Wooster, Ohio, 1956; dir. Coll. of Wooster Nursery Sch., 1956—85; family life educator Cmty. Action Wayne Medina, 1985—. Exec. bd. Wayne Assn. of the Edn. of Young Children, Wooster, Ohio, 1983—. Author, editor (book) Green Grow the Children, 1984; contbr. articles. Mem. human rights group Am. Assn. for Univ. Women, Wooster, Ohio; mem. League of Women Voters, Nat. Assn. for Edn. of Young Children, Philos. Edn. Orgn. Internat. Recipient Child Advocate of the Yr., Wayne County Children's Services, 2002; fellow Paul Harris fellow, Rotary Internat., 2004. Mem.: Theta Phi Alpha, Kappa Tau Alpha. Democrat. Presbyn. Home: 1471 Cleveland Rd Wooster OH 44691 Office: Cmty Action Wayne/Medina 2375 Benden Dr Wooster OH 44691

SCHREIBER, EILEEN SHER, artist; b. Denver, 1925; d. Michael Herschel and Sarah Deborah (Tannenbaum) Sher; m. Jonas Schreiber, Mar. 27, 1945; children: Jeffrey, Barbara, Michael. Student, U. Utah, 1942-45, NYU, 1966-68, Montclair State Coll., NJ, 1975-79; also pvt. art study. Exhibited Morris Mus. Arts and Scis., Morristown, N.J., 1965-73, N.J. State Mus., 1969, Lever House, N.Y.C., 1971, Paramus (N.J.) Mus., 1973, Newark Mus., 1978, 1991-92, Am. Water Color Soc., Audubon Artists, N.A.D. Gallery, N.Y.C., Pallazzo Vecchio Florence, Italy, Art Expo 1987, 1988, India Mus., 1994, 95, Athens (Greece) Mus., 1996, 97, Gaelin Gallery, Whippany, N.J., 2004, Solstice Gallery, Beach Haven, NJ, Municipal Bldg. of West Orange, NJ; represented in permanent collections Tex. A&M U., Telesoft Inc., Phoenix, State of N.J., Morris Mus., Seton Hall U., Bloomfield (N.J.) Coll., Barclay Bank of Eng., N.J., Somerset Coll., NYU, Morris County State Coll., Broad Nat. Bank, Newark, Ind. Cmty. Bank, Consulting Actuaries, Internat., IBM, Am. Tel. Co., RCA, Johnson & Johnson, Champion Internat. Paper Co., Sony, Mitsubishi, Celanese Co., Squibb Corp., Nabisco, Nat. Bank Phila., Data Control, Ind. Cmty. Bank, Sperry Univac, Ga. Pacific Co., Pub. Svc. Co. N.J., Diane Levine Gallery, Boston, S.W. Gallery, Long Beach Island, N.J., Solstice Gallery, Beach Haven, NJ, Town Hall Libr., West Orange, NJ, others; also pvt. collections. Recipient awards N.J. Watercolor Soc., 1969, 72, 1st award in watercolor Hunterdon Art Ctr., 1972, Best in Show award Short Hills State Show, 1976, Tri-State Purchase award Somerset Coll., 1977, Art Expo, N.Y.C., 1987, 88, numerous others. Mem. Nat. Assn. Women Artists (chmn. watercolor jury, Collage award 1983, Marian Halpren Meml. award 1995), Nat., N.Y. Artists Equity, Printmaker Coun. Visual Artists (1st award in printmaking 1996), Women Visual Artists (Fla.). Home and Office: 10 Jackson Dr Egg Harbor Township NJ 08234 Office Phone: 609-927-0440. Personal E-mail: artess25@aol.com.

SCHREIBMAN, THELMA RABINOWITZ, psychotherapist, educator; b. N.Y.C., July 29, 1945; d. Philip and Gussie (Lubowsky) Rabinowitz; divorced; children: Andrea Rudolph, Jill Schreibman. BA, Coll. of New Rochelle, 1984; MSW, Fordham U., 1989; postgrad., Riverdale Sch. Modern Psychoanalysis. Cert. social worker N.Y. Coord. Albert Einstein Hosp., Bronx, N.Y., 1977-84; adminstr. Goldwater Meml. Hosp., N.Y.C., 1984-96; pvt. practice psychotherapist Bronx and New Rochelle, N.Y., 1984—; adj. prof. Coll. of New Rochelle, N.Y., 1990—. Analyst, tng. supr. Riverdale Sch. Modern Psychotherapy, Bronx, 1985-95. Mem. NASW, N.Y. State Med. Staff Adminstrs. Avocations: photography, swimming. Home: 463 Pelham Rd New Rochelle NY 10805-2240

SCHREIER, KAREN ELIZABETH, judge; b. Sioux Falls, SD, 1956; AB, St. Louis U., 1978; JD, St. Louis U. Law Sch., 1981. Law clk. to Hon. Francis Dunn, SD Supreme Ct., 1981—82; pvt. practice Sioux Falls, SD, 1982—93; US atty. US Dept. Justice, Sioux Falls, SD, 1993-99; judge US Dist. Ct., Rapid City, SD, 1999—. Office: US Dist Ct 515 9th St Rm 318 Rapid City SD 57701-2626 Office Phone: 605-343-3744.

SCHREMP, FAITH MARYANNE, writer; b. Pickerel, Wis., May 15, 1921; d. Victor W. and E. Elizabeth (Wilkins) Iames; m. Lester V. Schremp, Sept. 19, 1942 (dec. Jan. 2, 2002); children: Mary, Gloria, Tom, Deedee. Student, U. Wis. Author: (as Faythimes) The Last Switcheroo, 1989, Smalltown Wife and Mom, 1989, Gram's Good Grub, 1992; also contbr. poetry, short stories to profl. jour., anthologies. Mem. Internat. Women's Writing Guild, Nat. Writers Club, Wis. Regional Writers, Antigo Writers Club (pres.). Roman Catholic. Avocations: swimming, crafts, reading, sewing, knitting.

SCHREUR, LYNNE ELIZABETH, advertising executive; b. Ridgewood, NJ, Oct. 21, 1980; d. Kevin M. and Deborah Lynne Schreur. BA in Comm. Studies, Montclair State U., NJ, 2003; MS in Arts Adminstrn., Drexel U., Phila., 2005. Broadway mktg. assoc. Kimmel Ctr. Inc., Phila., 2003—05; advt. coord. Disney Theatrical Prodns., NYC. Recipient Comm. Achievement award, Montclair State U., 2003, First Pl. award Dannis B. Eaton Pub. Speaking Competition, 2003; Lambda Pi Eta scholar, 2002, Deans fellow, Drexel U., 2003—05, Profl. Devel./Edn. grantee, SAI Philanthropies, Inc., 2005. Mem.: Theatre Comm. Group, Lambda Pi Eta (pres. 2002—03), Arts Adminstrn. Grad. Assn. (pres. 2004—05), Sigma Alpha Iota (life; corr. sec. NY alumnae chpt. 2006—). Office: Kimmel Ctr Inc 260 S Broad St Ste 901 Philadelphia PA 19102 Office Phone: 212-827-5507.

SCHRIBMAN, SHELLEY IRIS, database engineer, consultant; b. Weehawken, N.J., July 29, 1944; d. George and Mildred (Kamen) Shulman; m. Marshall Melvin Schribman, Aug. 26, 1979. BFA cum laude, Art Inst. Chgo., 1966; MBA, Simmon Coll. Grad. Sch. Mgmt., 1982. Asst. dir. Advanced Inst. Devel. Am. Repertory Theatre, N.Y.C., 1970—71; ptnr. Sir Charles Cleaning Co., Boston, 1982—83; owner SIS Internat., Boston, 1984—87; database developer (freelance) Boston, 1995—; sys. analyst Dept. Pub. Health, Boston, 2000—. Cons. Boston Computer Soc., 1995-96, Catchpole Corp., Wellesley, Mass., 1996-97, Ptnrs. In Home Care Inc., Missoula, Mont., 1996-97; designer, developer Shulman Bankruptcy Program, 1998-99 Pres. Orgn. for Rehab. Through Tng., Boston, 1986-88; mem. LWV, Boston (housing specialist 1989-91, pres. 1990-91, nat. credentials chairperson 1991-92). Mem. Belmont Dramatic Club, Alumni Theatre, Lexington Players. Jewish. Avocations: acting, composing music. Home: 8 Whittier Pl #23D Boston MA 02114-1402 Office: Dept Public Health 250 Washington St Fl 5 Boston MA 02108-4619 Office Phone: 617-624-5595. Personal E-mail: ShelleyISchribman@rcn.com.

SCHRICKER, ETHEL KILLINGSWORTH, retired business management consultant; b. Hagerstown, Md., July 22, 1937; d. Lloyd Granville and Ethel Mull; children: Jeanne, Lori, Jerri. BA in Mgmt., Hood Coll., 1994. Vol. Literacy Coun., Frederick, 1976-84, Dept. Social Svcs., Frederick, 1984; active Frederick County Commn. for Women, 1996, Nat. Presbyn. Ch., Washington. Named Bus. Woman of Yr., 1991, Frederick Bus. and Profl. Women. Mem. Assn. Sch. Bus. Ofcls (chairperson seminar devel. com. 1990-94, dir. emeritus 1999-2000), Frederick County Assn. Adminstrv. and Supervisory Pers. 1987-94, Frederick County C. of C., Frederick County Advt. Fedn. 1995-97, Rotary Club of Carroll Creek (pres. 1999-2000), Toastmasters Internat. (area gov. 1991-92, pub. rels. 1991-93, v.p. pub. rels. 1995-97). Avocations: photography, bicycling, watercolor. Home: PO Box 15 Frederick MD 21705-0015

SCHROCK, RUTH, elementary school educator; b. Canton, Ohio, Sept. 10, 1947; d. Roman Miller and Amanda Overholt; m. Ray Schrock; children: Maria DelValle, Jorge DelValle, Stephen. BSc, Malone Coll., Canton, Ohio, 1973. Tchr. Hartville Christian, Ohio, prin. Home: 911 Pontius Barberton OH 44203

SCHROEDER, BETH ELLAN, school counselor; BS, U. S.D., Vermillion, 1997, MA, 1999. Lic. profl. counselor S.D. Bd. Counselor Examiners, nat. cert. counselor Nat. Bd. Cert. Counselors. Activities dir. S.D. C. of C., Pierre, 2002—. Mem.: Am. Sch. Counselor Assn., Ind. Counselor Assn., Ind. Sch. Counselor Assn., S.D. Counselor Assn. (chairperson pub. rels. 2003—05, S.D. Emerging Leader 2005), S.D. Sch. Counselor Assn. (pres.-elect 2005, S.D. Elem. Sch. Counselor of Yr. 2005).

SCHROEDER, JONI LYNN, secondary school educator; b. Cheverly, Md., June 20, 1958; d. James Albert and Betty Jean Schroeder. BS, Lipscomb U., Nashville, Tenn., 1983. Cert. tchr. Tenn. Tchr. health and phys. ed. Haynes Design Ctr., Nashville, 1988—. Named Tchr. of Yr., Metro Nashville Bd. Edn., 2002. Mem.: AAHPERD (assoc.). Office: Haynes Design Ctr 510 W Trinity Ln Nashville TN 37207 Office Phone: 615-262-6688. Personal E-mail: joni.schroeder@mnps.org.

SCHROEDER, JOYCE KATHERINE, state agency administrator, research analyst; b. Moline, Ill., Apr. 1, 1951; d. Reinhold J. and Miriam May (Schroeder). BS in Math., U. Ill., Champaign-Urbana, 1973; MA in Ops. rsch., U. Ill., Springfield, 1978. Underwriter, programmer, Springfield, Ill., 1973—76; ops. rsch. analyst Ill. Dept. Transp., Springfield, 1976—78, data analyst, 1978—80, team leader, fatal accident reporting sys., 1980—83, mgr. safety project evaluation, 1983—92, mgr. accident studies and investigation, 1992—. Sys. engring. del. to China, China Assn. Sci. and Tech., 1986; mem. staff Driving While Intoxicated Adv. Coun. and Task Force, State of Ill., 1983-86, 89-92, Gov. Task Force on Occupant Protection, 1988-90; Ill. Traffic Safety Info. Sys. Coun., 1993-95; mem. safety engring. tech. adv. group Ill. Ctr. Transp., 2005—; mem. Ill. Traffic Records Coord. Com., 2004-. Vol. Animal Protective League, Springfield; leader bd., co-chair LPGA Rail Classic, Springfield, 1983-87. Named to Pres.'s Coun., U. Ill., 2004. Mem.: Ill. Traffic Safety Leaders, N. Am. Conf. Lions Found. (ann. conf. steering com. 2001—03, bd. dir., treas. 2005—), Past Dist. Gov. Assn. (sec.-treas. 1993—), Lions of Ill. Endowment Fund (trustee 1998—99, coord. meml. and endowments 1999—), Springfield Lincoln Land Lions Club (charter pres. 1988—90, treas. 1993—95, news editor 1995—, treas. 2002—), Lions Ill. Found. (amb. goodwill 1993, trustee 1995—99, treas. found. bd. 1996—97, v.p. found. bd. 1997—98, chmn. long range planning com. 1997—, pres. found. bd. 1998—99, policy ad hoc com. 1999—, chmn. policy ad hoc com. 2002—, fellow 1995, fellow laureate 2002, Disting. Svc. award 2003), Internat. Assn. Lions Clubs (dist. Gov. Ill. 1992—93, state membership coord. 1994—96, Melvin Jones fellow 1993), Kappa Delta Pi, Phi Kappa Phi. Avocations: travel, dogs, music, sports, humanitarian service. Office: Ill Dept Transp 3215 Exec Pk Dr Springfield IL 62703-4514 Personal E-mail: jksplus3@sbcglobal.net.

SCHROEDER, KATHLEEN ANNE, secondary school educator; b. Lynn, Mass., Jan. 4, 1949; d. Edmund Matthew and Angela Dorothy Maleszyk; m. John Stephen Schroeder, May 26, 1974; 1 child, Karla Elizabeth. BSAE, Syracuse U., 1970. Math/reading5, math./sci. tchr. St. Rose Sch., Murfreesboro, Tenn.; mid-day asst. Cason Lane Acad., Murfreesboro, Tenn.; algebra instr. Cason Lane Acad., Bellwood Sch., Murfreesboro, Tenn.; OSHA program mgr. Animal Care Clinic, Murfreesboro, Tenn., receptionist; clk. Daily News Jour., Murfreesboro, Tenn.; substitute tchr. Murfreesboro City Schs.; performance engr. GE, Lynn, Mass., Evendale, Ohio. Math. tutor, Murfreesboro. Bd. dirs. Mid. Tenn. Choral Soc., Murfreesboro; leader, troop chmn. Girl Scouts U.S.A., Murfreesboro. Mem. AIAA, ASME. Roman Catholic. Home: 676 Cottonfield Ln Murfreesboro TN 37128-4712

SCHROEDER, LAVERNE, medical/surgical nurse; b. Dover, Colo., Mar. 2, 1925; d. Chester Albert and Thelma May (Warren) Hutchison; m. Herman D. Schroeder, Sept. 5, 1947; children: Gloria, Rodger, Colleen, Darlene. Diploma, St. Anthony Hosp. Sch. Nursing, 1947. RN Colo., Wyo. Head nurse Poudre Valley Hosp., Ft. Collins, Colo., 1948, Longmont (Colo.) Hosp., 1950, Platte County Meml. Hosp., Wheatland, Wyo., 1957—76. Contbr. poetry to anthologies; author: A Blessed Trinity, 2003, The Queen's Secret, 2005. Pres. PTA; pres. bd. dirs. Platte County Meml. Hosp., Wheatland; Platte County del. Wyo.State Rep. Conv. Mem.: Wyo. Nurse Assn., Am. Vet. Med. Assn. Aux. (pres.).

SCHROEDER, MARVIS LYNN, accountant, artist; b. Gary, Ind., June 19, 1946; d. William Isaac and Leva Marcella (Pierce) Marlatt; m. Douglas Eugene Testerman (div.); 1 child, Tiffany Lynn Courtois; m. Charles Edward Schroeder, July 19, 1988. BS in Art Edn., Ind. U., 1969, MSBA, 1984; MA in Spl. Edn., U. Wyo., 1975. Cert. in Acctg., 1992; tchr. Wyo., Ind., Calif. Tchr. Glasgow AFB (Mont.) Jr. High, 1967—68; tchr. art and spl. edn. Cheyenne (Wyo.) Pub. Schs., 1969—71; tchr. spl. edn. NW Ind. Spl. Edn. Coop., Crown Point, 1974—80; tchr. learning disabilities Riverside (Calif.) Schs., 1980—81; tchr. art Hobart (Ind.) Schs., 1981—84; group mgr. softlines Zayre, Merrillville, Ind., 1985; fin. aid counselor Ind. U., Northwest Gary, 1986—2001; acct. Harold Sullivan CPA, Portage, Ind., 2001—03. Exhibitions include Portage Sr. Artists Exhibit, 2002, 2003, 2004, 2005, 2006, 1st United Meth. Ch., 2003, Chesterton Women's Art Ctr., Ind., 2003, 2005, 2006, Art Barn Gallery, Valparaiso, Ind., 2004, Valparaiso Art Acad. Gallery, 2005, Porter County Adminstrn. Ctr., Valparaiso, 2005, 2006. Mem.: Illiana Artists Assn., Chesterton Art Ctr. Home: 2527 Pryor Rd Portage IN 46368 Personal E-mail: user754642@aol.com.

SCHROEDER, MARY MURPHY, federal judge; b. Boulder, Colo., Dec. 4, 1940; d. Richard and Theresa (Kahn) Murphy; m. Milton R. Schroeder, Oct. 15, 1965; children: Caroline Theresa, Katherine Emily. BA, Swarthmore Coll., 1962; JD, U. Chgo., 1965. Bar: Ill. 1966, D.C. 1966, Ariz. 1970. Trial atty. Dept. Justice, Washington, 1965—69; law clk. to Hon. Jesse Udall Ariz. Supreme Ct., 1970; mem. Lewis and Roca, Phoenix, 1971—75; judge Ariz. Ct. Appeals, Phoenix, 1975—79, U.S. Ct. Appeals (9th cir.), Phoenix, 1979—2000, chief judge, 2000—. Vis. instr. Ariz. State U. Coll. Law, 1976—78. Contbr. articles to profl. jours. Recipient Disting. Achievement award, Ariz. State U. Coll. of Public Programs. Mem.: ABA (Margaret Brent award 2001), Am. Judicature Soc., Am. Law Inst. (coun. mem.), Fed. Bar Assn., Ariz. Bar Assn. (James A. Walsh Outstanding Jurist award 2004), Soroptimists. Office: US Ct Appeals 9th Cir US Courthouse Ste 610 401 W Washington St SPC-54 Phoenix AZ 85003-2156 Fax: 602-322-7320. E-mail: mary_schroeder@ca9.uscourts.gov.

SCHROEDER, PATRICIA SCOTT, trade association administrator, former congresswoman; b. Portland, Oreg., July 30, 1940; d. Lee Combs and Bernice (Lemoin) Scott; m. James White Schroeder, Aug. 18, 1962; children: Scott William, Jamie Christine. BA magna cum laude, U. Minn., 1961; JD, Harvard U., 1964. Bar: Colo. 1964. Field atty. NLRB, Denver, 1964-66; practiced in Denver, 1966-72; mem. faculty U. Denver, 1969-72, C.C. Denver, 1969-70, Regis Coll., Denver, 1970-72; hearing officer Colo. Dept. Personnel, 1971-72; mem. 93d-104th Congresses from 1st Colo. dist., Washington, 1973-96; co-chmn. Congl. Caucus for Women's Issues, 1976-96; prof. Woodrow Wilson Sch. of Pub. and Internat. Affairs Princeton U., 1997; pres., CEO Assn. Am. Pubs., Washington, 1997—. Mem. Nat. Security Com.; dean Congl. Women; chair Ho. Select Com. Children, Youth and Families, 1991—93. Author: Champion of the Great American Family, 1989, 24 Years of House Work and the Place is Still a Mess: My Life in Politics, 1998. Bd. dirs. Marguerite Casey Found. Named to Nat. Women's Hall of Fame, 1995. Congregationalist. Office: Assn Am Publishers 50 F St NW Fl 4 Washington DC 20001-1530 Office Phone: 202-347-3375. Business E-mail: pschroeder@publishers.org.

SCHROEDER, TERESA MARIE, athletic trainer; b. Bryan, Ohio, Jan. 22, 1972; d. Larry George and Janet Marie Jerger; m. Steve Owen Schroeder, Oct. 15, 1994; children: Cameron Owen, Kendra Marie. BA in Sports Medicine, U.Findlay, Ohio, 1994. Cert. athletic trainer. Lic. personal trainer Chrysalis Fitness ctr., Bowling Green, Ohio, 2002—05; athletic trainer St. Luke's Hosp., Maumee, Ohio, 2004—05, Cmty. Hosp. Williams County, Bryan, Ohio, 2005—. Home: 8446 W Rd A Edgerton OH 43517 Office: Cmty Hosp of Williams County Bryan OH 43506

SCHROEDER, TRACIE BETH, secondary school educator; b. Emporia, Kans., Oct. 15, 1974; d. Dan and Patti Nurnberg; m. Jeff Schroeder, Aug. 1, 1998; 1 child, Abbie Jo. BS, Ft. Hays State U., Hays, KS, 1997. Sci. tchr. Marion (Kans.) Mid. Sch., 1999—2001, Council Grove (Kans.) HS, 2001—. Recipient Nat. Honor Roll's Outstanding Am. Teachers, 2006. Mem.: NEA, NSTA, Nat. Coaches Assn. Home: Rt 1 Box 24 Strong City KS 66869 Office: Council Grove High Sch 129 Hockaday Council Grove KS 66846 Office Phone: 620-767-5149. Personal E-mail: tschroeder@cgrove417.org. E-mail: traciebeth@hotmail.com.

SCHROERLUCKE, LESLIE JEAN, music educator; b. Boston, Nov. 29, 1962; d. Ernest Charles and Marceline Jean Gerbasi; m. Steven Wayne Schroerlucke, Aug. 17, 1991; children: Sara Kirsten, Laura Kathryn. MusB, Eastman Sch. Music, Rochester, NY, 1984; MusM, Fla. State U., Tallahassee, 1988. Clarinetist Fla. Philharm., Ft. Lauderdale, 1985—91, Miami Opera, 1985—91; instr. clarinet Fla. Internat. U., 1990—98; lectr. Broward C.C., Davie, 1991—98; instr. clarinet New World Sch. Arts, Miami, 1994—98; elem. music specialist Walnut Valley Unified Sch. Dist., Calif., 2000—03; band dir. Chaparral Mid. Sch., Diamond Bar, 2004—. Faculty rep. Claremont Cmty. Sch. Music, Calif., 2005—, bd. dirs.; adjudicator So. Calif. Band and Orch. Assn., LA, 1999—. Musician: (recording) Florida Philharmonic, Mahler's 1st Symphony, Eastman Wind Ensemble, (world premiere) Nodus by Frederick Kaufmann, Brooklyn Bridge by Ronald Weidnaar. Vol. Hope Worldwide, Guatemala City, Guatemala, 2005—05. Recipient Margaret Fox Firman award, Eastman Sch. Music, 1984, Merit award, Nat. Fedn. Music Clubs, 1989. Mem.: Am. Fedn. Musicians, Calif. Music Educator's Assn., So. Calif. Band and Orch. Assn., Calif. Tchrs. Assn. Avocations: travel, sailing. Home: 1275 Lane Ct Claremont CA 91711 Office Phone: 909-861-6227. E-mail: lschroerlucke@walnutvalley.k12.ca.us.

SCHRONK, PATRICIA LYNN, secondary school educator; b. Hubbard, Tex., Apr. 19, 1947; d. Harvey Herman and Bessie Jo (Blackmon) Schronk. Assocs. Degree, Navarro Coll., 1972; BS, Baylor U., 1974, MS, 1979. Cert. tchr. Tex., all-level cert., reading specialist 1979. Jr. high lang. arts/reading tchr. Hubbard Ind. Sch. Dist., 1974—91, family and consumer sci. edn./home econs. tchr., 1991—, tchr. English, 2003—, instr. work program, 2005—. Advisor Family Career Cmty. Leaders, Hubbard, 1991—, Future Homemakers Am., 1991—; dist. planning com. Hubbard Ind. Sch. Dist., 2000—04. Mem.: Tex. Adult Educators Assn., Tex. Literacy Assn., Assn. Tex. Profl. Educators, Delta Kappa Gamma. Avocations: reading, crafts, farming and cattle ranching. Office: Hubbard Ind Sch Dist PO Box 218 Hubbard TX 76648

SCHROTH, JOYCE ABLE, social worker; b. Bloomington, Ill., Apr. 4, 1948; d. Raymond Daniel Able and Lois Martha Vielhak; m. Thomas H. Schroth, July 22, 1972; children: Bradley, Michael. BA, Ill. Wesleyan U., 1971. Dir. City of Westlake, Ohio, 1998—. Mem. cmty. adv. bd. Lakewood Hosp., Ohio, 1998—, St. John West Shore Hosp., Westlake, 1998—, mem. mission & values com., 1998—; pres. adv. coun. Retired Sr. Vol. Program, Brookpark, 1999—; mem. adv. bd. Brighton Gardens by Marriott, Westlake, 2000—, Westlake Healthcare Ctr., 2002—; pres. Cuyahoga County Mcpl. Offices on Aging Assn.; mem. cmty. adv. bd. Fairview Hosp., 2003—; mem. Cuyahoga County Adv. Coun. Dept. Sr. and Comty. Svc. Chmn. citizen's adv. com. Westlake City Schs., 1985—88, chair levy com., 1988; mem. Westlake Bd. Edn., 1987—90, Cuyahoga County Adv. Coun. on Sr. and Adult Svcs., 2003; bd. dirs. Univ. Settlement, 2005. Recipient Cmty. Leadership award, St. John West Shore Hosp., 2002, Cleve. State U., 2005, Luth.'s Maldonado award, 2005. Mem.: Westlake Lions Club, Sigma Kappa. Republican. Mem. Lds Ch. Avocations: travel, reading, genealogy. Home: 1800 Holdens Arbor Run Westlake OH 44145-2040 Office: City Westlake 29694 Ctr Ridge Rd Westlake OH 44145-5114 Office Phone: 440-899-3544. Business E-Mail: jschroth@cityofwestlake.org.

SCHUBART, CAREN NELSON, psychologist; b. S.I., N.Y., Sept. 26, 1945; d. Kenneth Warwick and Carey Boone Nelson; m. Richard Douglas Schubart, July 5, 1969; children: Darcy, Lindsey, Nelson. BA in Psychology, Wittenberg U., Springfield, Ohio, 1967; MEd in Rehab. Counseling, Kent State U., Ohio, 1968; postgrad., Syracuse U., N.Y., 1972—73, Boston U., 1974—88, Plymouth State U., Mass., 2001—. Lic. psychologist N.H. Bd. Mental Health Practice, nat. cert. sch. psychologist Nat. Assn. Sch. Psychologists; cert. learning disability specialist N.H. Assn. Sch. Psychologists, lic. sch. psychologist N.H. Bd. Edn., N.Y. State Edn. Dept. Rehab. counselor Ohio Bur. Vocat. Rehab., Akron, 1967—68, N.Y. Dept. Vocat. Rehab., Syracuse, 1968—73; regional dir. spl. edn. N.H. Sch. Unions 16, 19, 21, Exeter, 1973—79; sch. psychologist N.H. Supervisory Sch. Union 16, Exeter, 1979—89, 1989—. Contbr. articles to profl. jours. Vol. Rockingham County Family Planning, Exeter, bd. dirs. Recipient full scholarship, U.S. Govt. Dept. Rehab. Edn., 1967—68. Mem.: APA, N.H. Assn. Sch. Psychologists, N.H. Psychol. Assn., Nat. Assn. Sch. Psychologists. Independent. Episcopalian. Avocations: photography, genealogy, outdoor activities, travel. Home: 65 Court St Exeter NH 03833 Office: Exeter Regional Coop H S Exeter NH 03833

SCHUBERT, BARBARA SCHUELE, retired performing arts association administrator; b. Cleve., Feb. 21, 1939; d. William Edward and Mildred Marianne (Matousek) Schuele; m. John Dwan Schubert, June 15, 1963; children: William Edward, Christopher John, David Matthew. BS in Social Scis., John Carroll U, 1962, MA in English, 1967; MEd, 1980. Cert. secondary tchr., elem. remedial reading tchr., Ohio. Tchr. Sch. on Magnolia, Cleve., 1980-82, Ruffing Montessori, Cleve., 1982-83; tchr. English U. Sch., Chagrin Falls, Ohio, 1983-86; gen. mgr. Ohio Ballet, Akron, 1987-90, assoc. dir., 1990-99; ret. Bd. trustees Ohio Ballet, 1974-87, 91-99. Bd. dirs. John Carroll U., 1990—; trustee Boys Hope Girls Hope, 2001. Mem.: Cleve. Skating. Roman Catholic. Personal E-mail: BJSchubert@earthlink.net, matousek04@yahoo.com.

SCHUBERT, HELEN CELIA, public relations executive; b. Washington City, Wis. d. Paul H. and Edna (Schmidt) S. BS, U. Wis., Madison. Dir. pub. rels. United Cerebral Palsy, Chgo., 1961; adminstrv. dir. Nat. Design Ctr., Chgo., 1962-67; owner Schubert Pub. Rels., Chgo., 1967—. Bd. dirs. Fashion Group, Chgo., 1988—95; adj. prof. comm. Roosevelt U., 1992—. Mem. women's bd. Am. Cancer Soc., Chgo., 1988—, Art Resources in Tchg., Chgo., 1988-92. Recipient Comm. award Am. Soc. Interior Designers, Chgo., 1979, 83, 88, 94; named to Chgo. Women's Hall of Fame City of Chgo., 1990. Fellow Nat. Home Fashion League; mem. Women's Ad Club Chgo. (pres. 1981-83, Woman of Yr. award 1987), Women in Comm. (pres. 1969-70, Matrix award Lifetime Achievement 1996), Am. Advt. Fedn. (lt. gov. 1983-85). Lutheran. Personal E-mail: schube@mail.com.

SCHUBERT, JEANNE, artist; b. Harlan, Ky., June 2, 1932; d. Lewis Marion and Bertha Faye (Paul) Conklin; m. Robert Breckenridge Stroup, Feb. 5, 1953 (dec. May 1954); 1 child, Robert Breckenridge; m. Robert Buxton (div. 1967); 1 child, Beverly Buxton; m. Robert Kenyon Schubert, Apr. 25, 1970 Student, Cumberland Coll., Williamsburg, Ky., 1951, Rollins Coll., Winter Park, Fla., 1974, Art Students' League, N.Y.C., 1984. Mortgage clk. Orlando (Fla.) Fed. Savs., Fla., 1962—76; real estate broker Orlando; co-owner, creator Art Works Orlando, 1993—96. Mem./exhibitor Orlando Mus. Art, 1972—, Dayton Beach Mus., 1972—, Arts on Douglas, New Smyrna Beach, Fla., 1995—, Albertson-Peterson Gallery, Winter Park, 1990-99 One woman shows include Lighthouse Gallery, Tequesta, Fla., Orlando Mus Art Assocs., Valencia C.C., Orlando, LeMoyne Ctr. for Visual Arts, Tallahassee, Melvin Gallery, Lakeland, U. Ctrl. Fla., Orlando, Vero Beach (Fla.) Ctr. for the Arts, Osceola Ctr. for Arts, Kissimmee, Fla., Gallery Contemporanea, Hot Springs, Ark., Brevard Art Ctr. and Mus., Melbourne, Fla., Melvin Gallery, Fla. So. Coll., Albertson-Peterson Gallery, First Union Tower, Orlando, Arts on Douglas, New Smyrna Beach, Orlando City Hall, 2006; exhibited in group shows at Orlando Mus. Art, 1984, 87, 88, 92, Barbara Gilman Gallery, Miami, Miami-Dade Coll., 1986, North Miami Mus. Art, Salmagundi Club, N.Y., Fla. Gulf Coast Art Ctr., Belleaire, 1986, U. Ctrl. Fla., 1987, Harmon Gallery Am. Art, Sarasota, Fla., Crealde Art Ctr. Gallery, Winter Park, Mus. Arts and Sci., Daytona Beach, Daytona Beach Art Ctr., Epcot Ctr., Lake Buena Vista, 1994-2001, Soc. of Four Arts, West Palm Beach, 1997-2001; works in permanent collections at Maitland Art Ctr., Rollins Coll., Valencia C.C., Mus. Arts and Scis., Walt Disney World, Flagship Banks, Melbourne, Gen. Mills Corp., Orlando, Hyatt Regency Corp., Orlando, Orlando City Hall, Barnett Bank Fla., Jacksonville, Orange County Courthouse, Shands Hosp., Gainesville, Mayo Clinic, Jacksonville, Baker & Hostetler, Orlando, Akerman, Senterfitt & Eidson, Orlando, Holland and Knight, Orlando, City Orlando Collections, Orange County Collection, Suntrust Collection, Orlando. Bd. dirs. Maitland (Fla.) Art Ctr. Art Svcs. Coun. Art grant Mem. Fla. Watercolor Soc., Fla. Artist Group (area rep. 1985-2001) Home: 318 N Riverside Dr Edgewater FL 32132

SCHUBERT, RUTH CAROL HICKOK, artist, educator; b. Janesville, Wis., Dec. 24, 1927; d. Fay Andrew and Mildred Wilamette (Street) Hickok; m. Robert Francis Schubert, Oct. 20, 1946; children: Stephen Robert, Michelle Carol. Student, DeAnza Coll., 1972—73; AA Scholarship, Monterey Peninsula Coll., Calif., 1974; BA with honors, Calif. State U., San Jose, 1979. Owner, mgr. Casa De Artes Gallery, Monterey, Calif., 1977—86; dir. Monterey Peninsula Mus. Art Coun., 1975—76; quick-draw artist So. Oreg. Pub. TV, KSYS; leader painting workshops; demonstrator, lectr., judge in U.S., B.C. Can., New Zealand and Loreto, Baja, Mexico. One-woman shows include Aarhof Gallery, Aarau, Switzerland, 1977, Degli Agostiniani Recolletti, Rome, 1977, Wells Fargo Bank, Monterey, 1975, 1978, 1979, Seaside (Calif.) City Hall Gallery, 1979, 1989, Village Gallery, Lahaina, Hawaii, 1983, 1986, 1989, 1994, Portola Valley Gallery, 1984, 1985, Rose Rock Gallery, Carmel, 1984—86, Taupo (N.Z.) Arts Soc., 1988, Geyserland Art Mus., Rotorua, N.Z., 1988, Wanganui (N.Z.) Art Soc., 1988, Hallei Brown Ford Gallery, Roseburg, Oreg., 1991, 1995, Collection of Ann Cunningham, Carmel, 1993—95, Libr. Found., Medford, Oreg., 2005, catalog nat. group juried shows include, Sierra Nev. Mus. Art, Reno, 1980, Bard Hall Gallery, San Diego, 1980, San Diego Nat. Watercolor Show, Mid-West Nat. Watercolor Show, Rahr-West Mus., Manitowoc, Wis., 1980, Rosicrucian Mus., San Jose, 1981, 1984, Calif. State Agri-Images, Sacramento, 1984, XVII Watercolor West, Brea Civic Cultural Ctr., 1985, Watercolor West XXIII, Grand Art Galleries, Glendale, Calif., 1991, Watercolor West XXV, Riverside (Calif.) Art Mus., 1993, Nat. Pen Women at Marjorie Evans Gallery, Carmel, 1986, Monterey County Juried Expo, Monterey Peninsula Mus. Art, 1986, 1987, Am. Artists Group Exhbn., 1993, 1994, 1995, Gallery Hirose, Tsukuba, Ibaragi, Japan, Internat. Art Show and End of World Hunger, Ashland, Oreg., 1990, biann. art exhbn. Sumner Mus., Washington, D.C., 1992, State of the Art, New Eng. Fine Arts, Boston, 1993, N.W. Wildlife, Nightingale Gallery, Ea. Oreg. Coll., La Grande, 1993, N.W. Visual Arts Ctr. 19th Ann., Panama City, Fla., 1993, NW Watercolor Soc. Waterworks N.W. Julie Tolles Gallery, Mercer Island, Wash., 1994, Represented in permanent collections Rogue Valley Manor Spl. Svcs., Medford, Oreg., Monterey Calif. Peninsula Mus. Art, Nat. Biscuit Co. subs. RJR Nabisco, San Jose, Waikato Mus. Art, Hamilton, N.Z., Muscular Dystrophy Assn., San Francisco, Old Sch. Hous Mus., Qualicum Bay, Vancouver Island, B.C., USS George Washington Aircraft Carrier, Adm. Robert Sprigg, Pres. Bill Clinton, Barbara Bush, George Montgomery, Marilyn Horne, Alison Krauss, also numerous pvt. collections. Recipient 1st prize, Monterey County Fair, 1979, Jade Fon Watercolor award, Hall of Flowers, San Francisco, 1980, 1st Nat. Art Show, NY Am. Artist mag., 1980, Nat. Art Appreciation award, 1984, award, Norcal State Art Fair, 1985, Watercolor award, 25 Ann. Aqueous Media Show, Salem, Oreg., 1990, award, Calif. Watercolor Soc., 2001, Silver award, Oreg. Watercolor Soc. Portland, 2000, numerous other awards for watercolor paintings. Mem.: NW Watercolor Soc. (signature, Watercolor Transparent award, Mercer Island 1994, Waterworks, Seattle 1999), Art Du Jour Gallery (dir. Medford, Oreg.), Watercolor West (signature), Women Artists Registry N.Am., Nat. Mus. Women in Arts, Art Alumni San Jose State U., Nat. League Am. Pen Women (pres. 1983—84, 1986—87), Cen. Coast Art Assn. (pres. 1982—85), Arts Coun. So. Oreg., Watercolor Soc., Rogue Valley Art Gallery (bd. officer 2004—05), LaHaina Arts Soc., Artists Equity Assn., Nat. Watercolor Soc. (assoc. Nat. award 2005, Viva Sherman Oaks (Calif.) award), Am. Watercolor Soc. (assoc.). Achievements include Artwork selected for inclusion in profl. pubs. including "Best of Watercolor" in Rockport Publr. and "The California Art Preview" Les Krantz. Home: 3533 Southvillage Dr Medford OR 97504-9283 Office Phone: 541-772-0136. E-mail: schubert0136@msn.com.

SCHUCHAT, ANNE, health facility administrator; B in Philosophy, with minor in Biology, Swarthmore Coll., 1980; MD, Dartmouth U., 1984. Resident in internal medicine Manhattan VA Hosp.; epidemic intelligence svc. officer Centers for Disease Control, Atlanta, 1988, chief respiratory diseases br., acting dir. Nat. Ctr. Infectious Diseases, dir. Nat. Immunization Program, 2005—; clin. asst. prof. medicine Emory U. Contbr. chapters to books, articles to profl. jours. Office: Nat Immunization Program CDC Mailstop C23 1600 Clifton Rd Atlanta GA 30333 E-mail: aschuchat@cdc.gov.*

SCHUCK, JOYCE HABER, author; b. N.Y.C., Dec. 9, 1937; d. Frank F. and Florence (Smith) H.; m. Stephen Martin Schuck, June 15, 1958; children: William David, Thomas Allen, Ann Elizabeth BA Human Svcs. and Counseling, Loretto Hts. Coll., Denver, 1982. Counselor, tchr. Vision Quest, Colorado Springs, 1973—82; cons., program designer for govt. agys. Colorado Springs, 1982—85; author, 1987—. Asst. to cons. Volusia County Dept. Corrections, Daytona Beach, Fla., 1982; cons. student svcs. program Pikes Peak C.C., Colorado Springs, 1982; cons., designer Juvenile Probation of El Paso County, Colorado Springs, 1982, 4th Jud. Dist./Dist. Atty.'s Office, Colorado Springs, 1984, program design cons., 1998 Author: Political Wives, Veiled Lives, 1991 Co-founder Cmty. Transitions, Colorado Springs, 1984, Parents Challenge, 2000; coord. El. Paso County Shape Up Program, 1982; v.p. Cmty. Coun. Pikes Peak Region, Colorado Springs, 1983, Women's Found. Colo., Denver, 1987 Recipient Mayor's Civic Leadership award City of Colorado Springs, 1983 Mem. Jr. League Colorado Springs (sustaining), Salon de Femme (founding) Avocations: tennis, skiing, hiking.

SCHUCKER, VERONICA JEAN, music educator; d. Ronald James Morgan and Jean Marie Bond; children: Kelly, Sarah, Emma, Brian. MusB, SUNY, Fredonia, 1990, MusM, 1995. Cert. tchr. N.Y. Tchr. music South Lewis Jr. and Sr. H.S., Turin, NY, 1990—91, S.G. Falk Sch., Buffalo, 1992, Niagara Falls City Sch. Dist., NY, 1992—95, 1996—, East Aurora Union Free Sch. Dist., Niagara Falls, 1995—96. Mem.: Music Educators Nat. Conf., We. N.Y. Orff Schulwerk Assn. (bd. dirs. 1999—2006), Am. Orff Schulwerk Assn. (grantee 2003).

SCHUDSON, RUTH, actress; b. Milw., Aug. 23, 1926; d. Boris David and Bella Shechtman; m. Armand Pierce Schudson, Aug. 2, 1955 (dec. May 1997); children: David, Nia. BFA in Acting, Art Inst. Chgo. Goodman Theater, 1947, MFA in Directing, 1951. Actress Milw. Repertory Theater, 1956—88, Milw. Chamber Theater, 1975—, McCarter Theater, Princeton, NJ, Melody Top Theater, Milw., Madison Repertory Theater, Madison, Wis., 2001—03. Co-founder Milw. Chamber Theater, 1975—; instr. theater arts Alverno Coll., Milw., 1975—79, U. Wis., Milw., 1981—82. Actor: (films) The Hinderburg, 1975. Recipient Lifetime Achievement award, Common Coun. Milw., 2000. Avocations: reading, tennis, puzzles.

SCHUECKLER, AMY K., obstetrician, gynecologist; b. Buffalo, Mar. 7, 1958; d. John Theodore and Ethel Rita (Swierat) S.; m. Kevin peter Rosteing, May 5, 1984; children: Andre Michael, Monique Patrice. BS, BA summa cum laude, SUNY, Buffalo, 1980, MD, 1984. Diplomate Am. Bd. Ob-Gyn. Intern Sisters of Charity Hosp., 1984-85; resident in ob-gyn. SUNY-Buffalo Hosps., 1985-88; mem. group practice; mem. staff St. Vincent-Bellin Hosp., Green Bay, Wis. Mem. AMA, Christian Med. Soc., Phi Beta Kappa, Phi Eta Sigma, Alpha Epsilon Delta, Gibson Anatomical Socs. Republican. Roman Catholic. Address: 2126 William Francis Ct Green Bay WI 54311-6352

SCHUENEMAN, DIANE L., diversified financial services company executive; Account exec. instl. sales Merrill Lynch, 1971, head global ops. and infrastructure svcs., 2004—06, sr. v.p., head global infrastructure solutions grp., 2006—. Bd. mgrs. Omgeo; bd. dirs. Depository Trust and Clearing Corpn. Office: Merrill Lynch 4 World Fin Ctr 250 Vesey St New York NY 10080*

SCHUESSLER FIORENZA, ELISABETH, theology studies educator; b. Tschanad, Romania, Apr. 17, 1938; parents German citizens; d. Peter and Magdalena Schuessler; m. Francis Fiorenza, Dec. 17, 1967; 1 child, Chris. MDiv, U. Wuerzburg, Germany, 1962; Lic. Theol., U. Wuerzburg, 1963; DrTheol, U. Muenster, Germany, 1970. Asst. prof. theology U. Notre Dame, South Bend, Ind., 1970-75, assoc. prof., 1975-80, prof., 1980-84; instr. U. Muenster, 1966-67; Talbot prof. N.T., Episcopal Div. Sch., Cambridge, Mass., 1984-88; Krister Stendahl prof. Divsn. Scripture and Interpretation Harvard U., Cambridge, Mass., 1988—. Harry Emerson Fosdick vis. prof. Union Theol. Sem., N.Y.C., 1974-75; guest prof. U. Tuebingen, Federal Republic of Germany, 1987, Cath. Theol. Faculty Luzern, Switzerland, 1990; Stiftungs prof. Humboldt U., Berlin, 1997; Ernst Troeltsch prof. U. Heidelberg, Germany, 1999. Author: Der Vergessene Partner, 1964, Priester für Gott, 1972, The Apocalypse, 1976, Invitation to the Book of Revelation, 1981, In Memory of Her, 1983, Bread not Stone, 1984, Judgement or Justice, 1985, Revelation: Vision of a Just World, 1991, But She Said - Feminist Practices of Biblical Interpretation, 1992, Discipleship of Equals: A Critical Feminist Ekklesialogy of Liberation, 1993, Jesus: Miriam's Child and Sophia's Prophet, Critical Issues in Feminist Christology, 1994, Sharing Her Word, 1998, Rhetoric and Ethic The Politics of Biblical Studies, 1999, Jesus and the Politics of Interpretation, 2000, Wisdom Ways, 2001, Grenzen uberschreiten, 2004; editor: Searching the Scriptures, 2 vols, 1993, 94, The Power of Naming, 1996; founding co-editor Jour. Feminist Studies in Religion; also editor other works. Mem.: Am. Acad. Arts and Scis., Soc. Bibl. Lit. (past pres.), Am. Acad. Religion. Office: Harvard Div Sch 45 Francis Ave Cambridge MA 02138-1911 Office Phone: 617-495-5751.

SCHUETZE-COBURN, MARJE, university librarian; BA in German and History, Univ. Calif., Berkeley; MLS, UCLA, MA in History. Cataloger, Feuchtwanger Collection USC, 1989—91, Feuchtwanger Libr. and Curator, 1991—2001, dir., Spl. Libraries and Archival Collections, 2001—, also assoc. dean faculty affairs for Univ. Libraries, interim libr. head, 2006—. Office: Dir SLAC Univ So Calif Los Angeles CA 90089 Office Phone: 213-740-7119. Business E-Mail: schuetze@usc.edu.*

SCHUK, LINDA LEE, legal assistant, business educator; b. Scott Field, Ill., July 19, 1946; d. Frank A. Schuk and Jessie (Bumpass) Stearns; div.; 1 child, Earl Wade (dec.) BBA, U. Tex., El Paso, 1968. Lic. life and health ins. agt., Tex. Acct., traffic mgr. Farah Mfg. Co., El Paso, 1970—71; adminstrv. asst. Horizon Corp., El Paso, 1971—76; adminstrv. asst. in charge office ops. Foster-Scwartz Devel. Corp., El Paso, 1976—78; legal sec. Howell and Fields, El Paso, 1979—80; supr. Southland Corp., San Antonio, Waco, El Paso, 1980—83, sales mgr. San Antonio, 1983—84, dist. mgr., 1984—87; dist. supr. E-Z Mart Convenience Stores, San Antonio, 1987—89; legal asst. Brock & Brock, San Antonio, 1989—. Instr. San Antonio C.C., 1989— Mem. NAFE Democrat. Baptist. Avocation: music. Office: Brock & Brock 803 E Mistletoe Ave San Antonio TX 78212-3524 Home: 5046 Mayspring San Antonio TX 78217 E-mail: lschuk@yahoo.com.

SCHULEIT, ANNA, artist; b. Mainz, Germany, 1974; BFA, RI Sch. Design, 1998; MFA, Dartmouth Coll., Hanover, NH, 2005. Cons. Met. Transit Authority, NYC, 2005; art instr. Nightingale-Bamford Sch., NYC, 2005. Guest lectr. Dept. Sociology, Brown U., 1999, 2002, 05, Smith Coll., 2000, Conn. River Valley Hospital, Middletown, Conn., 2000, Springfield Coll., 2001, Brattleboro Mus. and Art Ctr., 2001, The Delaney House, Holyoke, Mass., 2001, RI Sch. Design, 2005; presenter Forum on Hist. Records, U. Mass. Amherst, 2001, Nat. Conv. State Art Agencies, 2001, Sch. Arch., McGill U., Montréal, 2003; vis. artist Westborough Sate Hospital, Mass., 2001—04; disting. visitor Sch. Art & Design, U. Mich., 2006. Exhibitions include A Translatlantic Project, Muhle der schoenen Kunste, Germany, 1995, Off the Wall, 16 S. Main St. Gallery, Providence, 1998, National Prize Show, Cambridge Art Assn., Mus. Fine Art, Boston, 1998, Summer Show, Harvard U., 1999, Medfield State Hospital Closing: Projections, Dept. Mental Health, Westborough, Mass., 2004, Amherst Art Show, 2004, The Matzo Files, NYC, 2004—05, one-woman shows include Nada Mason Gallery, Northfield, Mass., 2000, Northampton Ctr. for Arts, 2000, exhibited in group shows at Kaelin Gallery, Boston, 2002, Pioneers of Public, Revolving Mus., Lowell, Mass., 2002, Inch x Inch, Arlington Ctr. for Arts, 2002, CHi of Ancestry, Gallery Luna, Salem, Mass., 2004, 1939 The Missing Year, New Art Ctr., Newton, Mass., 2005, Goliath, Brooklyn, 2006, installations, Habeas Corpus, Northampton State Hospital, 2000, When At Last, Brattleboro Mus. and Art Ctr., 2001, Bloom, Mass. Mental Health Ctr., 2003. Recipient Grad. Alumni award, Dartmouth Coll., 2005, Thesis Rsch. award, 2005; fellow MacDowell Colony, 2002, 2006, Yaddo, 2005, Radcliffe Inst., Harvard U., 2006—07; Artist Grant, Elizabeth Greenshields Found., 1996, Northampton Arts Coun., 2000, Mass. Found. for Humanities, 2000, Chubb Life Am. Fellow, MacDowell Colony, 2000—01, MacArthur Fellow, John D. and Catherine T. MacArthur Found., 2006. Office: HIstoric Northampton 46 Bridge St Northampton MA 01060 Office Phone: 413-584-6011. Office Fax: 413-584-7956.*

SCHULER, DOROTHY R., education educator, consultant, retired elementary school educator; b. Tex., May 1, 1947; d. Raymond Lowell and Violet Marie Hayes; m. Robert Dale Schuler, Aug. 17, 1968; children: Christy Anne Bryant, Amy Lynne. BS in Elem. Edn., U. Tex., Austin, Tex., 1968; MS in Edn., So. Ill. U. at Edwardsville, Edswardsville, Ill., 1989. Cert. Nat. Bd. Tchr. Nat. Bd. for Profl. Tchg. Standards, 2001. Third grade tchr. Ashlawn Elem., Arlington, Va., 1968—69; fourth grade tchr. Bret Harte Elem., Cherry Hill, NJ, 1969—70; kindergarten tchr. Dow Elem. Sch., Dow, Ill., 1982—86; second grade tchr. Grafton Elem. Sch., Grafton, Ill., 1986—2004; coll. instr. and cons. Greenville Coll., Greenville, Ill., 2004—. Cons./presenter Schuler's Schoolars Consulting, Elsah, Ill., 1996—; coll. instr. So. Ill. U. at Edwardsville, Edwardsville, Ill., 1998—2000. Contbr. scientific papers to profl. jours. Recipient Tchr. of the Yr., Wal Mart, 1999. Mem.: Nat. Assn. Edn. of Young Children, Ill. Project Support Group. Methodist. Avocations: golf, writing, reading, gardening. Office: 13610 Schuler Ln Dow IL 62022-9721 Office Phone: 618-466-5345. Business E-Mail: dorothy.schuler@greenville.edu.

SCHULER, MARY CALLAGHAN, artist, educational association administrator; b. Upper Darby, Pa., Aug. 15, 1938; d. John J. Callaghan and Catherine Graham Callaghan O'Reilly; m. Richard E. Schuler, May 12, 1962; children: Richard E., Anne E., Judith M. Cert. in Oil Painting, R.I. Sch. Design, 1972; BS, Cornell U., 1979. Dir. activities Ithacare Ctr., Ithaca, NY, 1979—82; exec. staff asst. Einaudi Ctr. Internat. Studies Cornell U., Ithaca, 1983—93. Exhibitions include Logan Ridge Winery, 2002, Clinton Ho. Artspace, 2002, State of the Art Gallery, 2004—06, Upstairs Gallery, 2005, 2006. Bd. dirs. State of the Art Gallery, Ithaca, 2004—06. Mem.: Cornell Alumni Assn. and Club, Cornell Campus Club, Ithaca Garden Club, Sigma Alpha Iota. Avocations: painting, reading, walking. Home: 2 Captains Walk Ithaca NY 14850-8502 Personal E-mail: mcs@lightlink.com.

SCHULKERS, JOAN M., lawyer; Grad., William Mitchell Coll. Law, 1999. Bar: Minn. Ptnr. Borman & Schulkers, P.L.L.P., Mpls. Named a Rising Star, Minn. Super Lawyers mag., 2006. Mem.: Minn. Women Lawyers, Minn. State Bar Assn. (bd. govs. 2001—, chair new lawyers sect. 2003—04, vice chair new lawyers sect. 2002—03, sec. new lawyers sect. 2001—02), Hennepin County Bar Assn. (sec. 2001—02, bd. govs. 2001—04, mem. exec. com. 2002—03, chair new lawyers sect. 2002—03, co-chair litig. sect. 2004—06). Office: Borman & Schulkers PLLP 250 3rd Ave North Ste 530 Minneapolis MN 55401 Office Phone: 612-332-3096. E-mail: joan@bormanschulkers.com.*

SCHULLER, DIANE ETHEL, allergist, immunologist, educator; b. Bklyn., Nov. 27, 1943; d. Charles William and Dorothy Schuller. AB cum laude with honors in Biology, Bryn Mawr Coll., 1965; MD, SUNY, Bklyn., 1970. Diplomate Am. Bd. Allergy & Immunology, Am. Bd. Pediatrics, Nat. Bd. Med. Examiners. Intern, resident in pediats. Roosevelt Hosp., Bklyn., 1970-72; resident in allergy Cooke Inst. Allergy, 1972-74; assoc. in pediatrics Geisinger Med. Ctr., Danville, Pa., 1974-78, dir. dept. pediat. allergy, immunology & pediat. diseases, 1978-95; asst. clin. prof. pediats. Hershey Med. Coll. Pa. State U., 1974-79, assoc. clin. prof., 1979-88; clin. prof. Jefferson Med. Coll., Phila., 1989-95; dir. pediat. allergy, immunology, pulmonology Pa. State U./Hershey Med. Coll., 1995—, prof. pediats., 1995—. Bd. dirs. Ctrl. Pa. Lung and Health Assn.; bd. dirs., exec. com. Am. Lung Assn. Pa., sec., 1992—; chmn. Susquehanna Vly. Lung Assn., 1983—; scholarship com. Bryn Mawr Club, N.Y., 1970-75; Columbia-Montour Home Health Svcs. Adv. Group Profl. Personnel, 1975-95. Editl. bd. Annals of Allergy, Asthma and Immunology. Recipient physician's recognition award AMA, 1973-76, 74-76, 75-78, 79-82, 83-86, 87-90, 91-94, 95-98, 1999-2005. Fellow Am. Acad. Pediats. (exec. com. 1998-2004), Am. Coll. Allergy Asthma and Immunology (2d v.p. 1988, bd. regents 1989-92, exec. com. 1990-93, v.p. 1992-93, pres.-elect 1993-94, pres. 1994-95), Am. Acad. Allergy and Immunology, Am. Assn. Clin. Immunology and Allergy (regional dir., exec. com.), Joint Coun. Allergy and Immunology (bd. dirs. 1986-95, treas. joint coun. 1991-93); mem. Am. Assn. Cert. Allergists (v.p. 2002, pres.-elect 2002-03, pres. 2003-04), Pa., N.Y. State Allergy Soc., N.Y. State Med. Soc., N.Y. County Med. Soc. Office: Milton S Hershey Med Coll Pa State U Hershey PA 17033 Office Phone: 717-531-1846.

SCHULMAN, JEAN ELLEN, artist, retired educator; b. Athens, Ala., Sept. 20, 1927; d. Eugene and Evelyn Polytinsky; children: Stephen C., David Alan, Edward Stuart. BFA, Wash. U., 1948; MA, Florence State U., 1975; EdS, U. North Ala., 1981. Tchr. Muscle Shoals HS, 1961—85; adj. prof. U. North Ala., 1980. Clay-dyed batiks in collection of Smithsonian Inst. Mem.: Surface Design Assn., Nat. Art Edn. Assn. Avocations: bridge, movies, travel. Home: 310 Columbus Ave Florence AL 35630-5910

SCHULTE, JILL MARIE, elementary school educator; b. Platte, S.D., Apr. 12, 1968; d. Donavon Ray and Arlene Dorothy (Pedersen) Mason; m. Dale Mark Schulte, June 16, 1990; 2 children, Kyle Mason, Madison Jean. BS in Edn., U. S.D., 1990; MA in Edn., U. No. Iowa, 1994. Cert. elem. tchr. Tchr. elem. Hansen Elem. Sch., Cedar Falls, Iowa, 1991—. Republican. Lutheran. Avocations: aerobics, reading, dance. Office: Helen A Hansen Elem Sch 616 Holmes Dr Cedar Falls IA 50613-2099

SCHULTHEIS, ANN LUCIA, curriculum specialist; b. Kalamazoo, Mich., Aug. 22, 1946; d. Mario Salvatore Cioffari and Kathleen Loretta Mahoney; m. Patrick James Schultheis, Aug. 17, 1968 (dec.); children: Michael Patrick, Jennifer Ann O'Donoghue. BS, Western Mich. U., Kalamazoo, 1968. Tchr. elem. sch. Portage Pub. Schs., Mich., 1968—70, Allegan Pub. Schs., 1971—95; dir. arts edn. United Arts Coun., Battle Creek, 1996—98; asst. prin. Nat. Heritage Acads., Grand Rapids, 1998—2000, core knowledge curriculum specialist, 2000—05, state stds. specialist, 2005; ret., 2005. Co-owner, operator Hayloft Farm, Kalamazoo, 1971—2006, Celebration Hall, 1981—2003. Avocations: pottery, painting, poetry, history, gardening. Home: 3950 Mary Rd Bloomingdale MI 49026 Personal E-mail: hayloft@btc-bci.com.

SCHULTHEIS, PATRICIA ANN, writer, editor; b. Bridgeport, Conn., Aug. 11, 1943; d. Ralph and Clare Podufaly; m. William Christian Schultheis, Oct. 15, 1966; children: Kurt Christian, Matthew Christian. BA, Albertus Magnus Coll., 1965; MA in Liberal Arts, Johns Hopkins U., 1973. Prodn. mgr. Balt. Mag., 1976—77; rschr. Md. Pub. TV, Owings Mills, 1977—79; rsch. assoc. Changing Times Mag., DC, 1979—81; editor U. Md., Balt., 1981—85; dir. publs. CC Balt., 1985—89; copy editor The Balt. Sun, 1990; editor Skills Bank Corp., Baltimore County, 1991—95; freelance writer, 1995—; fiction editor Balt. Review, 2001—. Editor Mt. Wash. Newsletter, Balt., 1973—75, U. Md. Sch. Law Alumni Newsletter, Balt.; contbr. Bread Loaf Writer's Conf.; rschr. Ft. McHenry Nat. Monument. Co-author: Personal Mathematics, Media Materials. Sec. Charles Village Improvement Assn., Balt., 1967—69; mentor Dickey Hill Elem. Sch., Balt., 2002—. Mem.: Hamilton St. Club. Avocations: ice skating, folk art painting, embroidery. Home: 2509 Pickwick Rd Baltimore MD 21207 Personal E-mail: bpschult@yahoo.com.

SCHULTIS, GAIL ANN, library director; b. Freeport, Ill., May 12, 1951; d. Richard C. and Ida G. Schultis. BA, Cornell Coll., 1973; MLS, U. Mo., 1976; MA, U. Tex., San Antonio, 1989. Reference libr. U. Tex., San Antonio, 1976-79, El Paso, 1979-84, 89, head access svcs., 1984-88; reference libr. Park U., Parkville, Mo., 1989-96, dir. libr. sys., 1996—. Co-author: Best Self-Help & Self-Awareness Books, 1995. Mem. ALA, Am. Hist. Assn., Orgn. Am. Historians. Home: 10307 NW 57th Ter Parkville MO 64152-3396 Office: Park Univ Libr 8700 NW River Park Dr Parkville MO 64152-4358 Office Phone: 816-584-6704. Business E-Mail: ann.schultis@park.edu.

SCHULTZ, ARLENE ELAINE, literature educator; b. Houston, Tex., Mar. 9, 1948; d. Ernest H. and Irene C. Schultz. BA, Sam Houston State U., Huntsville, Tex., 1969, MA, 1976. Tchr. English Spring (Tex.) H.S., 1969—75; adj. instr. English North Harris Coll., Houston, 1976—77, prof. English, 1977—. Mem.: Nat. Conf. Tchrs. English. Republican. Luth. Avocations: travel, reading, gardening. Office: North Harris College 2700 W W Thorne Dr Houston TX 77073 Office Phone: 281-618-5561. Business E-Mail: arlene.schultz@nhmccd.edu.

SCHULTZ, BARBARA MARIE, investment advisor; b. Chgo., Sept. 9, 1943; d. Edwin and Bernice (Barstis) Legner; m. Ronald J. Schultz, Sr., May 1, 1965; 1 child, Ronald J. Student, Prairie State Coll. Fin. planner Metlife Fin. Svcs., NYC, 1981—2001; fin. advisor Morgan Stanley Dean Witter, NYC, 2001—02; agt., investment advisor rep. Country Ins. and Fin. Svcs., Hickory Hills, Ill., 2002—04; investment advisor Edward Jones Investments, Palm Harbor, Fla., 2004; mature mktg. specialist AIG/Am. Gen., Tampa, 2005—. Qualifier Met. Life Leaders Conf., 1990. Fellow: South Cook County Assn. Life Underwriters (edn. chmn. 1988—91), Life Underwriters Tng. Coun. (chmn. 1986—88), Nat. Assn. Life Underwriters (edn. chmn. 1988—91, citation 1987, nat. quality award, Robert L. Rose award 1990), Country Club (1st pl. award 2002). Roman Catholic. Avocations: boating, aerobics, golf. Office: 6800 N Dale Mabry Hwy Tampa FL 33614 Office Phone: 813-884-7553.

SCHULTZ, DODI, writer, editor; b. Lancaster, Pa., Aug. 21, 1930; m. Ed Schultz, Dec. 23, 1955. Student, Goucher Coll., 1947-50. Various positions Dell Pub., 1960-64. Speaker in field. Author (with Virginia E. Pomeranz): The Mothers' and Fathers' Medical Encyclopedia, 1977, From 1 to 2: Your Baby's Second Year, 1984, The First Five Years rev. edit., 1984, 1987; author: (with Sheldon Paul Blau) Living with Lupus: The Complete Guide rev. edit., 2004; author: (with James T. Howard Jr.) We Want to Have a Baby, 1979, 12 others; editor: Tools of the Writer's Trade, 1990, 1991, The Toddler Years, 1986, Your Child's First Year, 1986, Pregnancy and Childbirth, 1986, others, CompuServe usage/grammer sect. sysop, 1995—2003; contbr. articles, puzzles to consumer mags. Recipient Journalism awards (2) Am. Acad. Family Physicians, (2) Am. Acad. Pediatrics, Epilepsy Found. of Am. Mem.: Nat. Assn. Sci. Writers (past pres.), Authors Guild. Avocation: conchology.

SCHULTZ, EILEEN HEDY, art director, advertising executive; b. Yonkers, N.Y. d. Harry Arthur and Hedy Evelyn (Morchel) S. BFA, Sch. Visual Arts, 1955. Staff artist C.A. Parshall Studios, N.Y.C., 1955—56; editorial art dir. Paradise of the Pacific, Honolulu, 1956—58; graphic designer Adler Advt. Agy., N.Y.C., 1958-59; art dir. Good Housekeeping Mag., N.Y.C., 1959-82, creative dir. advt. and sales promotion, 1982—86; creative dir. Hearst Corp., 1986—87; pres. Design Internat., 1987—. Creative dir. The Depository Trust Co., 1987-99; prof. Sch. Visual Arts, 1974—. Art dir., editor, designer, 50th Art Directors Club Annual, 1973; columnist: Art Direction, 1969-1994. Dir. Sch. Visual Arts, N.Y.C., 1978—; trustee Sch. Art League, 1978—; advisor Fashion Inst. Tech., 1979—; adv. commn. N.Y.C. Cmty. Colls., 1979—. Named Yonkers Ambassador of Good Will to Netherlands, 1955; recipient Outstanding Achievement Sch. Visual Arts Alumni Soc., 1976, Sch. Art League Youth award, 1976. Mem. Art Dirs. Club (pres. 1975-77), Soc. Illustrators (pres. 1991-93), Joint Ethics Com. (chmn. 1978-80), Am. Inst. Graphic Arts, Soc. Publ. Designers, Type Dirs. Club. Office Phone: 212-371-0121.

SCHULTZ, ELIZABETH FRANCES, elementary school educator; b. Waukesha, Wis., Feb. 16, 1971; d. Erwin Charles and Shirley Jeanne Schilling; m. Timothy Michael Schultz, May 29, 1993; children: Carlie Elizabeth, Jacob William. Bachelor's in Edn., Alverno Coll., Milw., 1994, Master's in Edn., 2004. Cert. elem. and mid. sch. tchr. Wis., reading tchr. Wis., reading specialist Wis. Tchr. social studies Cath. East Elem., Milw., 1995—98; tchr. English St. Gregory the Gt., Milw., 1998—2000, Lake Geneva Mid. Sch., Wis., 2001—04, alternative edn. tchr., 2004—. Named Mid. Sch. Tchr. of Yr., Lake Geneva Sch. Bd., 2006. Mem.: Nat. Reading Assn., Nat. Coun. Tchrs. Sci., Nat. Coun. Tchrs. English. Roman Catholic. Avocations: travel, reading. Office Phone: 262-348-3000 3215.

SCHULTZ, JANET W., intelligence research analyst; b. Balt., Nov. 25, 1957; d. Richard W. and Minna M. (Glaser) S.; m. Jacob L. Williams Jr., Feb. 1, 1992. BA cum laude, U. Md., 1979, BS, 1986; MA, George Washington U., 1982. Crew leader U.S. Bur. of Census, Baltimore County, Md., 1980; mgmt. analyst NASA Hdqrs., Washington, 1981; tech. writer Dynatech Data Sys., Springfield, Va., 1982-85, Catalyst Rsch., Owings Mills, Md., 1985-86; intelligence rsch. analyst U.S. Dept. Def., Ft. Meade, Md., 1986—. Intern U.S. Dept. of State, Washington, 1978. Coach, umpire Arbutus Girls' Athletic Assn., Balt., 1969-80; Sunday sch. tchr. Emmanuel Luth. Ch., Balt., 1972-80; basketball coach Luth. Ch. of St. Andrews, Wheaton, Md., 1984-85; branch v.p. Aid Assn. for Lutherans Holy Nativity Lutheran Ch., Balt., 1996-98. Recipient Merit Scholastic award State of Md., 1975; Wolcott Found. fellow High Twelve Internat., 1980-82. Mem. Phi Beta Kappa, Phi Kappa Phi, Pi Sigma Alpha, Phi Alpha Theta, Alpha Lambda Delta. Democrat. E-mail: jschultz3@hotmail.com.

SCHULTZ, JANICE ELAINE, librarian; d. Alan Israelson Lindgren and Blanche Ione Harvey; m. Steven Paul Schultz, Apr. 10, 1971; children: Brian Christopher, Michael Richard. BA in Elem. Edn., Mich. State U., 1971; MLS, Mo. U., 1999. Tchr. Grand Rapids Pub. Schs., Mich., 1971; tchr./dir. Downey Duck Preschool, Independence, Mo., 1985—89; libr. asst. I Mid-Continent Pub. Libr., Independence, 1987—99, ref. libr., 1999—2000, genealogy libr., 2000—. Pres. Am. Family Records Assn., Kansas City, Mo., 2002—04; libr. Mo. State Genealogical Assn., Columbia, 2002—. Mentor Youth Friends, Independence, 2000—. Mem.: ALA (chair local history com. 2005), Noland Road Lion's Club (pres. 2003—04). Community Of Christ. Avocations: piano, organ, genealogy, reading, needlework. Office: Mid-Continent Pub Libr 317 W 24 Hwy Independence MO 64050

SCHULTZ, JUDY KAY, guidance counselor; b. McCook, Nebr., Nov. 9, 1946; d. Lenord L. and Velma M. Walker; m. Arvene A. Schultz, Apr. 9, 1966; children: Anthony A., Schultz Galik Andrea. BA in Bus. Edn., English, Kearney State Coll., Kearney, Nebr., 1968; MA in K-12 Sch. Counseling, Chadron State Coll., Nebr., 1998; MA in Mental Health Counseling, Chadron State Coll., 1998. Cert. profl. guidance counselor Nebr. Tchr. English, bus. Stratton Pub. Schs., Nebr., 1968—73; tchr. bus. edn., vocat. edn. Maywood Pub. Schs., Nebr., 1977—95, K-12 guidance counselor, 1995—. Contbr. articles to profl. jours. Mem. Frontier County #1184 Team, Frontier County, Nebr., 1998—; edn. position statement com. Nebr. Dept. Edn., 1993; bd. dirs. S.W. Nebr. Domestic Violence/Sexual Assault Svcs., S.W. Nebr. Youth Svc., McCook. Recipient Best award, Nebr. Dept. Edn., 1994. Mem.: Am. Sch. Counselor Assn., Nebr. State Bus. Edn. Assn. (exec. coun. 1992—95, Tri-Valley dist. rep. 1994—95, chair awards com. 1993—95), Am. Counseling Assn., Nebr. Counseling Assn. (bd. dirs. 1999—2002, state officer 1999—2002, treas. 1999—2002), Chi Sigma Iota. Avocation: reading. Office: Maywood Public Schools 1 Tiger Dr Box 46 Maywood NE 69038

SCHULTZ, KAREN ROSE, clinical social worker, author, publisher, speaker; b. Huntington, NY, June 16, 1958; d. Eugene Alfred and Laura Rose (Palazzolo) Squeri; m. Richard S. Schultz, Apr. 8, 1989; children: Carlos, Sarah Rose. BA with honors, SUNY, Binghamton, 1980; MA, U. Chgo., 1982. LCSW Ill. Unit dir., adminstr. Camp Algonquin, Ill., 1981; clin. social worker United Charities Chgo., 1982-86; social worker Hartgrove Hosp., Chgo., 1986-87; pvt. practice Oak Brook, Ill., 1987—. Owner, founder Inner Space pub. Co., 1993; trainer, spkr. various groups, schs. and orgns., 1988-89; group leader Optifast Program, Oak Park and Aurora, Ill., 1989-90; instr. social work Morraine Valley C.C., Palos Hills, Ill., 1989-90; instr. eating disorders Coll. of Dupage, Glen Ellyn, Ill., 1990-92, tchr. intuition and counseling, 1995—; spkr. in field. Author: The River Within, 1993, Shelter in the Forest, 1998, Flashes of Brilliance, 2002; editor, contbg. author: The River Within newsletter, 1989—2000. Mem. NASW (registered, diplomate), Acad. Cert. Social Workers. Avocations: creative writing, aerobics, yoga, personal growth. Office: 900 Jorie Blvd Ste 234 Oak Brook IL 60523-3841 Office Phone: 630-571-7010. E-mail: karenrschultz@earthlink.net.

SCHULTZ, MARIAN STARR, musician, educator; b. Buffalo, Aug. 4, 1956; d. Joseph Starr and Catherine Marian Haroney; m. Paul Howard Schultz, July 29, 1985; 1 child, Alexandra Louise. MusB, Shenandoah Conservatory, 1979, PhD in Music Arts, 2000; MusM, Cath. U. Am., 1988. Music specialist Green Acres Sch., Rockville, Md., 1983—2003, FCPS, Fairfax City, Md., 2003—. Advisory council mem. Assn. Ind. Md. Schs., 1992—94, conf. chair, 1993. Author: (book) A Study to Determine the Effect., 2005. Donor St. Louis RC Ch., Buffalo, 2004, St. Anthony's Parish, Buffalo, 2003—04. Mem.: Music Educators Nat. Conf., Sigma Alpha Iota (treas. 1986—88). Avocations: fencing, swimming, gardening, travel.

SCHULTZ, NANCY JANSSON, artist; b. Kanas City, Mo., Apr. 15, 1933; d. Carl Albert Jansson and Lora Elizabeth Wilson; m. Everett Hoyle Schultz, June 24, 1955; children: Susan, Frank, Janet, Sally. Student, Park Coll., Parkville, Mo., 1951—54. Founder Women on Paper, Augusta, Ga., 1987—; exhibit organizer Art of the Sketchbook, Ga., 2005. Exhibitions include Genema Gallery, Altanta, McCormick Arts Ctr., S.C. (Purchase award, 2004, 2005, 2006), Quinlan Arts Ctr., Gainsville, Ga., Gwinnett Fine Arts Ctr., Duluth, Ga., U. S.C., Aiken, Cotton Exch. Gallery, Augusta, 1998, Clayton St. Gallery, Athens, Ga., 1998, Emory U. Law Sch. Libr., Atlanta, 2000, Barnes & Noble Bookstore, Augusta, 2000, State Capitol Gallery, Ga. Arts Day, Atlanta, 2001, Aiken Ctr. Arts, 2001, State Bot. Gardens, Athens, 2002, Cork Gallery, Avery Fisher Hall, N.Y.C., 2002—05, Birmingham So. Coll. Durbin Gallery, 2006 (Merit award, 2006), Represented in permanent collections Bank Fla., Deloritte & Touche, Charlotte, N.C., Med. Coll. Ga., U. Hosp., Augusta, St. Joseph's Hosp., PAC 2000, N.H., Jud. Ctr., Ocala, Fla., prin. works include Carptenter's Gallery, Augusta, Ann Jacob Gallery, Highlands, NC, The Pheasants Eye, Lynchburg, Va., Suzannes Frame Design, St. Petersburg, Fla., McCormick Arts Coun., S.C.; artist (represented by) Broad Strokes Gallery, Augusta, Art on Broad. Named to Archives on Women Artists, Nat. Mus. of Women in the Arts, Washington, 1995; recipient Honorable Mention, Eyes for the Art, Augusta, 1992, Merit award, Images in Art, Ocala, 1992, First Pl., Fine Arts for Watercolor, Blue Crab Festival, N.C., 1989, Merit award, Miss. Watercolor Soc., 1989, 1st pl. Watercolor, Columbia County Renaissance Festival, 2005, Honorable Mention, Art on Main Hendersonville, N.C., 2005, Merit award, Ala. Watercolor Soc., 2006. Mem.: Gertude Herbert Inst. of Art, Nat. League of Am. Pen Women (1st pl. 1994, 3d pl. 1997, Pres. award. 1997, Marel Brown award 1999, 1st pl. in mixed media 2002, 3d pl. 2002, 2d pl. 2005, 2d pl. Watercolor Spring Juried Show 2006), Ga. Watercolor Soc. (newsletter editor 1990—92, signature mem.). Achievements include development of booklet for newcomers to Augusta area 'A Guide For Visual Artists'. Avocations: aerobics, writing, reading, making hand made books. Home and Studio: 608 Aumond Rd Augusta GA 30909

SCHULTZ, PATRICIA BOWERS, vocal music educator, conductor; b. Gomer, Ohio, Apr. 26, 1941; d. Paul Edward and Blodwen (Watkins) Bowers; m. Charles Albert Schultz; children: Todd Matthew, Vaughn Andrew, Cinnamon Paulette. BS in Edn., French & Music, Miami U., Oxford, Ohio, 1963; MEd in Counseling, U. Ill., 1964; D of Musical Arts in Vocal Performance, U. Mo-Kansas City, 1984. Performer freelance USA and Europe, 1964—; music educator, counselor Northmont Pub. Schs., Dayton, Ohio, 1964-66; French educator Bowling Green (Ohio) H.S., 1967-68; instr. music and French Dickinson (N.D.) State U., 1972-74; instr. voice Ctrl. State U., Wilberforce, Ohio, 1975-76; dir. choral activities Savannah (Mo.) H.S., 1979-80; prof. music N.W. Mo. State U., Maryville, 1981—2002. Dir. music First United Meth. Ch., Maryville, 1977—88; tour mgr. Jenny Lind Ensemble, 1978—; musical dir. N.W. MO. State U., Maryville, 1981—2002; vis. prof. Internat. Enrichment, London, 2000, 02, 06, 2004—06, 2006; adjudicator Nat. Assn. Tchrs. of Singing, Mo. H.S. Activities Assn.; co-dir. Summer in London Program Internat. Enrichment, 2006. Accomplishments in music include author, lead role in music drama Encore for Jenny Lind, 1976—(London Premiere 1992); conductor choral music Welsh Gymanfoedd Ganu, 1989— (Nat. Selection 1992, 1993, 2005); Coloratura soprano recitals and concerts throughout U.S.; soloist European tour Cin. Symphony, 1969; presentator Am. Assn. Higher Edn. Teaching Learning & Tech. Conf., 1997. Pres. Univ. Women, Maryville, 1978-79; first judge of vocal competition Nat. Glenn Miller Scholarship Competition, Clarinda, Iowa, 1992, 94, 2001; pres. Faculty Senate N.W. Mo. State U., 1993-95, Centennial Soc. 2002-; organizer, charter mem. Mo. Assn. Faculty Senates, Springfield, Mo., 1993-94. Named Faculty Fellow Mo. Coordinating Bd. Higher Edn., 1997-98, Outstanding Alumnae Conservatory of Music, U. Mo.-Kansas City, 1990; grantee Mo. State Coun. on Arts, 1991-95. Mem. AAUW, Coll. Music Soc., Nat. Assn. Tchrs. Singing (Teacher of regional state and chpt. winners in Mo., Nebr. and eight state region 1986, 88, 90, 92, 97, 98), Am. Choral Dirs. Assn., (hon.) Mortar Bd. (Outstanding advisor, 2003), Sigma Alpha Iota (patroness and advisor 1995-2002), Delta Omicron. Avocations: gardening, reading, travel. Home: 1004 W Cooper St Maryville MO 64468-2005 Office: NW Mo State Univ Dept Music 800 University Dr Maryville MO 64468-6015

SCHULTZ, SUSAN D., gifted and talented educator; d. Johnny W. Kramer and LaVerne M. Kramer/Thonsgaard; m. Phillip S. Schultz, Feb. 18, 1972; children: Heath S., Holly D. BS in Edn., U. Ark., Pine Bluff, 1989, M in Gifted Edn., 2002. Facilitator of gifted and talented Watson Chapel Pub. Schs., Pine Bluff, Ark., 1999—. Certifiied coach U.S. Chess Fedn., Pine Bluff, United States, 1995—; personal policy rep. Watson Chapel Pub. Schs., Pine Buff, United States, 2000—04; Praxis III assessor Ark. Dept. Edn., Little Rock, 2002—, state mentor, 2002—03. Author: (writer of workshop) The Internet and One C.O.W.; contbr. workshop presentor; author: (writer) There's No Place Like L.L. Owen. V.p. Watson Chapel Booster Club, Pine Bluff, 1998—2002. AGATE scholar, U. Ark., 2001. Mem.: Kappa Delta Gamma (assoc.), Kappa Delta Pi. Baptist. Office Phone: 870-879-3741.

SCHULTZ, VICTORIA L., music educator, entertainer; b. Kansas City, Mo., May 12, 1952; d. Kenneth Leroy and Russie Juanita (McIntosh) S. BMusic, U. Mo., Kansas City, 1975; M Music, Drake U., 1977. Opera coach, accompanist, prof. piano U. Ctrl. Fla., Orlando, 1977-80; prof. voice and piano Valencia C.C., Orlando, 1980-86; music dir. Pine Castle (Fla.) Ctr. of the Arts, 1983-84; pianist, harpist Hyatt Regency Grand Cypress, Orlando, 1984-96; pianist Altamonte Springs (Fla.) Hilton and Towers, 1985-89; pianist, harpist Caruso's Palace, Orlando, 1990-94; harpist Sergio's Restaurant, Orlando, 1994-95. Adj. prof. voice Rollins Coll., Winter Park, Fla., 1991-92; entertainer Walt Disney World, Orlando, 1996—; adj. prof. harp U. Ctrl. Fla., Orlando, 1998—, adj. prof. voice Valencia CC, Orlando, 2002—; pvt. tchr. and freelance entertainer, Fla., 1980—; clinician Harpcon, 2003. Composer: (music for piano and voice) Set of Songs, 1979; arranger/composer: albums Orange Blossom Tale, 1996, arranger/performer: albums Harp Dreams, 1997, Harp Favorites, 1998, Soothing Harp, 1999, Victoria Lynn-Live in Concert, 2004, composer, harpist: Harp Meditation for Chakra Attunement, 2001, Celtic Crossings with Tryskelon, 2006; author: (textbook) You CAN Play the Harp, 2002. Sponsor, Riverside Musicale Jr. Music Club, Orlando, 1991—; entertainer fund raising events for AHA, Am. Cancer Soc., Muscular Dystrophy, Am. Diabetes Assn.; artist-in-residence Fla. Hosp. Recipient Nat. 1st Place award Encore Prodns. Talent Competition, 1985, 86, State Young Artist 1st prize Fla. Fedn. Music Clubs, 1976, Silver medal Internat. Piano Rec. Competition, Am. Coll. Musicians, 1978. Mem. Ctrl. Fla. Musicians Assn. (local 389), Am. Harp Soc., Fla. Harpers and Friends (1st Place Composition award 2002, People's Choice award 2002), Ctrl. Fla. Music Tchrs. Assn. (recital chmn. 1999-2000), Orlando Music Club (founding mem.), Music Tchrs. Nat. Assn., Scottish Harp Soc. of Am. Democrat. Avocations: reading, movies, going to concerts, shopping. Home: 848 River Cove Ave Orlando FL 32825-8107 Office: Harpspun Prodns PMB 306 509 S Chickasaw Trl Orlando FL 32825-7852 Office Phone: 407-381-4440.

SCHULZ, AMANDA JEAN, real estate consultant, lawyer; b. Dallas, Tex., Sept. 22, 1975; d. Stephen Wayne and Joanna Elizabeth Tenpenny; m. Norbert Jon Schulz, Sept. 4, 1999. BA in Sociology, U. Tex., 1996; JD, St. Mary's U., 1999. Bar: Tex. 1999; lic. real estate salesperson Tex., 2000. Atty. worker's compensation Christian Hill & Assocs., Houston, 1999—2000; real estate sales cons. Keller Williams Realty, Houston, 2000—02, Re/Max, Houston, 2002—. Agt. trainer Keller Williams Realty Greater NW, Houston, 2001—02, mem. leadership coun., 2002. Chmn. com. Longwood Grounds and Maintenance Reforestation Project, Cypress, Tex., 2002. Mem.: Nat. Assn. Realtors, Tex. Assn. Realtors, Houston Assn. Realtors, Delta Gamma Alumnae Assn. (pres. Houston NW chpt. 2003—). Republican. Lutheran. Avocations: home renovation, interior decorating, antiques, writing, poetry. Office: Re/Max Professional Group 9234 FM 1960W Houston TX 77070 Office Phone: 281-894-1000.

SCHULZ, DIANA, film company executive; Grad. summa cum laude, Claremont McKenna Coll.; MBA, Stanford U. With Bain and Co., Microsoft Corp., McKinsey and Co. Consulting, L.A., 1991—97; mem. corp. devel. and strategic planning roup Vivendi Universal Entertainment, Universal City, Calif., 1997—99, head of group, 1999—2001, sr. v.p. corp. devel. and strategic planning, 2001—. Office: Vivendi Universal Entertainment 100 Universal City Plaza Universal City CA 91608-1002

SCHULZ, JILL ANN, elementary school educator; b. Quincy, Ill., Oct. 22, 1965; d. Donald Joseph and Sharon Louise Zipse; m. Christopher John Schulz, Aug. 6, 1988; children: Nicole Marie, Stephanie Lauren. BS in Edn., No. Ill. U., DeKalb, 1987; MA in Tchg., Aurora U., Ill., 1992. Type 03 tchg. cert. Ill., 1988. 8th grade lang. arts and social studies tchr. Rotolo Mid. Sch., Batavia, Ill., 1988—. Sec. Geneva Coalition For Youth, Ill., 2005; dir. Holy Cross Contemporary Ensemble Holy Cross Ch., Batavia, 1996. Recipient Award of Excellence, Ill. Math and Sci. Acad., 1997. Mem.: Batavia Edn. Assn. (sec. 2000—04). Office: Rotolo Middle School 1501 S Raddant Rd Batavia IL 60510 Office Phone: 630-879-4620. Business E-Mail: jill.schulz@bps101.net.

SCHULZ, KAREN ALICE, psychologist, medical psychotherapist, medical and vocational case manager; b. Detroit, Aug. 18, 1952; d. Donald E. and Ethel B. (Johnston) Wallinger. BA, Concordia U., 1974; MA, Wayne State U., 1991. Cert. cognitive behavioral sex therapist; cert. cognitive forensic therapist, cert. med. psychotherapist, disability analyst; lic. psychologist,

Mich. Case mgr. Comprehensive Case Mgmt. Svcs., Dearborn, Mich., 1993—; mem. faculty Davenport U., Dearborn, 1993—. Cert. rehab. counselor, addictions counselor, Am. Bd. Disability Analysts, Am. Bd. Med. Psychotherapists; lic. profl. counselor, psychologist. Mem. CMSA, ACA, Mich. Self Insurers Orgn. Office: Comprehensive Case Mgmt Svcs PO Box 871344 Canton MI 48187-6344

SCHULZ, LAURA JANET, writer, retired executive secretary; b. Alba, Tex., Aug. 12, 1931; d. Joseph Clifton and Laura Oza (Carruth) English; m. Gordon Robert Schulz, Dec. 4, 1953; children: LeAnn Clarinda Barclay, Peggy Gaynell Berry. Grad. h.s., Denison, Tex., 1948. Sec. history dept. Tex. Christian U., Ft. Worth, 1948-49; continuity editor Sta. KDSX, Denison, 1949-51; sec. Perrin AFB, Sherman, Tex., 1951-55; acctg. clk. England AFB, Alexandria, La., 1955; sec. Emile R. Jardine, CPA, Stockton, Calif., 1957-59; tchr. Little Meth. Pre-Sch., Lodi, 1968-69; sec. Heather, Sanguinetti, Caminata & Sakai, CPAs, Stockton, 1983-92; sec., feature writer, photographer Lodi (Calif.) Dist. C. of C., 1993-97. Author: Katy's Children, 1990, Little Rocky's True Adventures, 1991, Depot Days- a Cicada Summer, 2006. Hon. life mem. Wesleyan Svc. Guild Trinity Meth. Ch., Denison, 1955—, Calif. Congress of PTA, 1984—; pres. PTA Needham Sch., Lodi, 1968-70; leader Camp Fire, Lodi, 1974-82; vol. advisor, tchr. Grapevine Newspaper Vinewood Sch., Lodi, 1974-82; tchr. First United Meth. Ch., Lodi, 1961-80, circle chair. Recipient Appreciation awards, Vinewood Sch., Lodi Unified Sch. Dist., 1974—82, Lodi Dist. C. of C., 1993—97, City of Lodi, Lodi Dist. C. of C., 1996. Mem. Nat. League Am. Pen Women, Sierra Club. Democrat. Methodist. Avocations: photography, reading, nature, writing. Home: 1910 W Tokay St Lodi CA 95242-3440

SCHULZ, RENATE ADELE, German studies and second language acquisition educator; b. Lohr am Main, Germany, Feb. 24, 1940; came to U.S., 1958; 1 child, Sigrid Diane. BS, Mankato State Coll., 1962; MA, U. Colo., 1967; PhD, Ohio State U., 1974. Edn. officer U.S. Peace Corps, Ife Ezinihitte, Nigeria, 1963-65; asst. prof. Otterbein Coll., Westerville, Ohio, 1974-76, State U. Coll. N.Y., Buffalo, 1976-77; from asst. to assoc. prof. U. Ark., Fayetteville, 1977-81; from assoc. to prof. U. Ariz., Tucson, 1981—, head dept. German, 1984-90, chair PhD program in second lang. acquisition and teaching, 1994-97. Disting. vis. prof. USAF Acad., Colorado Springs, Colo., 1990-91. Recipient Creative Tchg. award, U. Ariz. Found., Tucson, 1984, Stephen A. Freeman award, N.W. Conf. Tchg. Fgn. Langs., 1984, Bundesverdienstkreuz, Fed. Govt. Germany, 1990, Anthony Papalia award for excellence in tchr. edn., Am. Coun. on the Tchg. of Fgn. Langs./N.Y. State Assn. Fgn. Lang. Tchrs., 2002, Henry and Phyllis Koffler prize for outstanding accomplishments in tchg., U. Ariz., 2005. Mem.: MLA (del. 1989—91), Nat. Fedn. Modern Lang. Tchrs. Assns. (v.p. 2004—05, pres. 2006—), Am. Assn. Applied Linguistics, Tchrs. of ESL, Am. Assn. Tchrs. German (v.p. 1988—90, pres. 1990—91), Am. Coun. on the Tchg. of Fgn. Langs. (exec. coun. 1979—81, Florence Steiner award 1993). Office: U Ariz Dept German Studies Tucson AZ 85721-0105 Office Phone: 520-621-7388. Business E-Mail: schulzr@u.arizona.edu.

SCHULZ, SALLY ANN, pastoral musician, conductor, educator; b. Red Oak, Iowa, Mar. 12, 1951; d. Robert Lionel and Mary Ellen Evans; m. Thomas Richard Schulz, Dec. 29, 1972; children: Matthew Thomas, Joanne Elizabeth. MusB, U. of Iowa, 1969—73. Indepent piano tchr. Schulz Studio, Bettendorf, Iowa, 1973—77; ind. piano & organ tchr. Freeport, Ill., 1977—88; dir. music St. Thomas Aquinas Ch., Freeport, Ill., 1984—90; elem. vocal music tchr. Freeport Cath. Sch., Freeport, Ill., 1988—90, Trinity Episcopal Day Sch., Baton Rouge, 1991—92; dir. music St. Ann's Ch., Long Grove, Iowa, 1993—95; dir. music & liturgy St. John Vianney Ch., Bettendorf, Iowa, 1995—2005. Mem. Diocesan Liturgical Commn., Davenport, Iowa, 2002—05. Mem.: Am. Guild of English Handbell Ringers, Am. Guild of Organists, Nat. Pastoral Musicians, Nat. Soc. Colonial Dames of Am., Delta Gamma. Achievements include Selected as a member of the MASTER CHORALE of the USA for the 2003 Festival Internazionale di Music e Arte Sacra in Rome; Selected by Paul Wilkes for his book Excellent Catholic Parishes published by Paulist Press. Home: 2993 Greenview Dr Bettendorf IA 52722

SCHULZ, SANDRA E., art educator; b. Dallas, July 2, 1963; d. Lionel Leigh and Ida Maria Johanna Schulz. BS in Art Edn., Tex. Woman's U., 1985, MFA in Sculpture, 1990. Cert. tchr. art all levels Tex. Clk. and advt. Bartos Inc., Dallas, 1982—90; art tchr. 7th and 8th grades Harry Stone Mid. Sch., Dallas, 1990—91; art tchr. 9-12th grades Thomas Jefferson H.S., Dallas, 1992—. Art club sponsor, robotics team sponsor Thomas Jefferson H.S., Dallas. Chair publicity and decoration Tex. Cultural Partnership, Dallas, 1994-2001; publicity chair Am. Czech Culture Soc., Dallas, 1992-2001. Named Citizen of the Week, KRLD Radio Sta., 2002; recipient Brookhaven Coll. Pyramid award for tchg., 2001, Tex. Senate Excellence award for outstanding tchrs., Outstanding H.S. Tchr. award, Dallas Rotary Club, 2001—02. Mem. Nat. Art Educators Assn., Tex. Art Educators Assn., Dallas Art Educators Assn. (publicity chair 1996-98), Sculpture Assn. (sec. 1993-95). Lutheran. Avocations: camping, fishing, gardening, music, electric trains. Home: 9218 Clear Dr Sanger TX 76266 Office: Thomas Jefferson HS 4001 Walnut Hill Ln Dallas TX 75229-6239

SCHULZ, SUSAN, magazine editor; b. 1971; Grad., Loyola Coll. Editl. asst. Good Housekeeping; sr. articles editor YM; dep. editor CosmoGIRL, 2000—02, exec. editor, 2002—03, editor-in-chief, 2003—. Office: CosmoGIRL 224 W 57th St New York NY 10019 Office Phone: 212-649-3887.

SCHULZ, SUZON LOUISE, fine artist; b. Chgo., Sept. 2, 1946; d. Carl George and Ruth Ada (Eberhardt) S.; m. Vernon Ray Adams. BFA, R.I. Sch. Design, 1968. Studio ptnr. Michael Eaton Smith, El Valle, N.Mex., 1976-79; artist-in-residence Idaho Com. on the Arts, 1980—, Wash. State Arts Com., 1980-82, Mississippi County C.C. Libr., Blytheville, Ark., 1984-85, various art couns., Oreg., 1983—; tchr. elem. art seminar Ea. Oreg. Coll. Bend Br., Bend, 1996. Owner Flying Shoes Studio, Prineville, 1982—; cartoonist, writer, illustrator NOW News, Bend, 1991-94. Painter: (series) In the Home, 1982—, The World Beyond, 1984—, Living With a Man, 1986—, Tipi Now, 1988—, Cats, 1996—, Paintings of Collages, 2002—, Synchonicity, 2002-. Mem. Nat. Mus. Women in Arts, Arts Central. Avocations: walking, hiking, reading, writing, cross country skiing. Home: 15887 SE Chippewa Rd Prineville OR 97754-8895

SCHULZE, JOAN THERESA, artist; b. Chgo., Oct. 13, 1936; d. Joseph Robert and Ann Teresa (Folta) Smith; m. James Wallace Schulze, Jr., June 27, 1959; children: Derk Gavin, Dustyne Ann, Nicole Marie, Trevor Alan. BS in Edn., U. Ill., 1958. Freelance instr. art, USA, Europe, Australia, 1974—. Mem. adv. bd. Calif. Crafts Mus., San Francisco, 1980-93; vis. artist, instr. Haystack Mountain Sch. Arts and Crafts, Deer Isle, Maine, 1983, 84; vis. artist, lectr. Crafts Coun. Australia, 1984, 89, 91; keynote spkr. San Diego Mus. Art, 1987; instr., lectr. East Bay Heritage Quilt Symposium, Mills Coll., Oakland, Calif., 1988; instr. Arrowmont Sch., Gatlinburg, Tenn., 1994; spkr. in field. Author: Leftover Traces of Yesterday, 1991; contbr.: 88 World Leaders in Quilts, 1995; quilt artist; represented in permanent collection at Renwick Gallery/Smithsonian, Washington, 1996; invited artist Art in Embassy Program, U.S. Embassy, Accra, Ghana, 1995—. Mem. LWV, Calif., 1980—. Recipient Gold Discovery award Art of Calif., 1994; represented in Northwest Poets and Artists Calendar, Bainbridge Arts Coun., 1994. Mem. Friends of Fiber, Internat., Am. Crafts Coun. Avocations: photography, poet. Home: 808 Piper Ave Sunnyvale CA 94087-1245 Office: Goodman 2 Art Ctr 1695 18th St Ste 302 San Francisco CA 94107-2383

SCHUMACHER, CYNTHIA JO, retired elementary and secondary education educator; b. Sebring, Fla., Sept. 24, 1928; d. Floyd and Espage S. BA, Fla. State U., 1950, MA, 1951; MS, Nova U., 1978; postgrad., Fla. State U., 1968-69. English tchr. Grady County Sch. System, Cairo, Ga., 1951-53; elem. tchr. Brevard County Sch. System, Melbourne, Fla., 1953-55; elem. tchr., curriculum generalist, secondary tchr. Lake County Schs., Tavares, Fla. area, 1955-85; retired, 1985. Mem. Edn. Standards Commn., Fla., Fla., 1980—85, Quality Instrn. Incentives Coun., Fla., 1983—84. Author: (poetry) Seeds from Wild Grasses, 1988, Creekstone Crossings, 1993, Soul Candles, 1998, Wellspring Legacies, 2000; (poetry and stories) Butterfly Excursions, 1996; (children's books) Colorful Character, 1998, Searching for S, 1998. Pres. League of Women Voters of Lake County, 1989-91; mem. Lake Conservation Coun., The Nature Conservancy, Habitat for Humanity of Lake County. Named Fla. Tchr. of Yr., Fla. Fedn. Women's Clubs, 1966, Lake County Tchr. of Yr., Lake County Sch. Sys., 1985, East Cen. Fla. Tchr. of Yr. finalist, State of Fla., 1986; recipient Good Egg award, Leesburg Area C. of C., 1991, Lifetime Achievement award, Fla. Edn. Assn. United, 2000. Mem. Lake County Edn. Assn. (pres. 1971-72, cons. 1985—). Democrat. Roman Catholic. Avocations: gardening, creative writing, macrobiotic cooking, environmental support activities.

SCHUMACHER, JULIE ALISON, literature and language professor; b. Wilmington, Del., Dec. 2, 1958; d. Frederick George and Winifred Jean (Temple) Schumacher; m. Lawrence Rubin Jacobs, July 9, 1983; children: Emma Lillian Jacobs, Isabella Nan Jacobs. BA, Oberlin Coll., 1981; MFA, Cornell U., 1986. Assoc. prof. U. Minn., Mpls. Author: (book) The Body is Water, 1995, An Explanation for Chaos, 1997, Grass Angel, 2004, The Chain Letter, 2005. Recipient Best Am. Short Stories award, 1983, Prize Stories: the O. Henry awards, 1990, 1996.

SCHUMACHER, MARIA, biomedical researcher, educator; Undergradate, Portland State U.; PhD in Biochemistry, 1995. Asst. prof. biochemistry and molecular biology Oregon Health and Sci. U., 2002—. Recipient Career award in Biomedical Sciences, Burroughs Wellcome Fund Ctr., 1999—. Office: U Oregon Dept Biochemistry and Molecular Biology MRB 524A 3181 SW Sam Jackson Park Rd Portland OR 97239-3098 Office Phone: 503-494-2256. Office Fax: 503-494-8393. Business E-Mail: schumacm@ohsu.edu.

SCHUMACHER, SILVIA C., performing arts educator; d. Armando R. and Estela Macias Casas; m. Michael Scott Schumacher, July 3, 1983; 1 child, Jennifer Hannah. BA in French, U. P.R., Rio Piedras, 1981; BFA in Dance, New World and Fla. Internat. U., Wolfson, 1994; MS in Ednl. Tech., Barry U., Miami Shores, Fla, 2001; post grad. in Philosophy Ednl. Leadership Ednl. Computing and Tech. Cert. profl. tchr. Fla. Dept. Edn., 1995. Tchr. Miami-Dade County Pub. Schs., Miami, Fla., 1994—. Performer: (dance) Against All Odds. Mem.: Dade Assn. Dance Educators (sec. 2000—), Nat. Dance Assn., Kappa Delta Pi (life). Office: Miami Northwestern Sr HS 1100 NW 71 St Miami FL 33150 Office Phone: 305-836-0991.

SCHUMAN, PATRICIA GLASS, publishing company executive, educator; b. NYC, Mar. 15, 1943; d. Milton and Shirley Rhoda (Goodman) Glass; m. Alan Bruce Schuman, Aug. 30, 1964 (div. 1973); m. Stanley Robert Epstein, June 14, 1997 (dec. 2005) AB, U. Cin., 1963; MS, Columbia U., 1966. Libr. trainee Bklyn. Pub. Libr., 1963-65; tchr. libr. Brandeis High Sch., N.Y.C., 1966; asst. prof. libr. N.Y. Tech. Coll., Bklyn., 1966-71; assoc. editor Sch. Libr. Jour., N.Y.C., 1970-73; sr. editor R.R. Bowker Co., N.Y.C., 1973-76; pres. Neal-Schuman Pubs., N.Y.C., 1976—. Vis. prof. St. John's U., Queens, N.Y., 1977-79, Columbia U., N.Y.C., 1981-90, Pratt Inst., 1993-2000, Syracuse U., 1997—; cons. N.Y. State Coun. on Arts, 1987, Office Tech. Assessment, U.S. Congress, 1982, 84, Coord. Coun. Lit. Mags., N.Y.C., 1987, NEH, 1980, Temple U., 1978-80; bd. visitors Sch. Libr. and Computer Studies Pratt Inst., 1987-2001; juror Best of Libr. Lit., 1980-88; mem. adv. bd. Sch. Libr. and Info. Studies, Queens Coll., 1989-91. Author: Materials for Occupational Education, 1973, 2d edit., 1983 (Best Edn. Book award 1973), Library Users and Personnel Needs, 1980, Your Right to Know: The Call to Action, 1993; editor: Social Responsibilities and Libraries, 1976; mem. editorial bd. Urban Acad. Libr., 1987-89, Multicultural Review, 1991-95; contbr. articles to profl. jours. Bd. dirs. Women's Studies Abstracts, Albany, N.Y., 1970-74, Pratt Inst. Sch. of Libr. and Info. Studies, 1993—2000, Ctr. for Publ., NYU, 1996—, Am. Libr. in Paris, 2004-; mem. Com. To Elect Major Owens to U.S. Congress, 1983, N.Y.C. Mayor's Com. for N.Y. Pub. Ctr., 1984-85; pres. Met. Reference and Resources Coun./Met. N.Y. Libr. Coun, Neal Schumen Found., Inc. Recipient Fannie Simon award Spl. Librs. Assn., 1984, Disting. Alumni award Columbia U., 1992, Disting. Alumni award U. Cin., 2006; U.S. Office Edn. fellow, 1969. Mem. ALA (councillor 1971-79, 84-88, exec. bd. 1984-88, 90-93, treas. 1984-88, chmn. legis. com. 1989-90, 94-96, chmn. internat. rels. com. 1998, 99, chmn. Libr. Advocacy NOW!, v.p., pres.-elect 1990-91, pres. 1991-92, Disting. Coun. Svc. award 1979, 88, Equality award 1993, hon. mem. Black Caucus, appreciation award 1993, Freedom to Read Found. Honor Roll 1999, Lippincott award for disting. svc. 2001), N.Y. Libr. Assn., Assn. for Libr. and Info. Sci. Edn., Spl. Librs. Assn. Office: Neal-Schuman Pubs Inc 100 William St Ste 2004 New York NY 10038 Business E-Mail: pgs@neal-schuman.com.

SCHUMANN, JANE ANNE, education educator; BA, U. Nebr., 1969; MA, Ariz. State U., 1974. Cert. social sci. tchr., guidance counselor, Tenn. Tchr. Scottsdale (Ariz.) Pub. Sch. Dist., 1969-78; counselor New Directions Ctr./Columbia (Mo.) Pub. Sch. dist., 1982-85; instr. dept. of reading and study skills Pellissippi State Tech. C.C., Knoxville, Tenn., 1987-94, asst. prof. dept. social and behavioral sci., 1994—. Presenter in field. Mem. Vision Adv. Bd., 1991-93; vol. Habitat for Humanity, 1992; mem. Knoxville Mus. of Art, 1991—, other civic activities. Recipient Outstanding Devel. Educator award Tenn. Nat. Assn. of Devel. Educators, Memphis, 1991, NISOD Excellence award NISOD Conf., Austin, Tex., 1997, others. Mem. AAUP, Nat. Assn. Devel. Educators, Tenn. Assn. for Devel. Educators, Am. Assn. for Counseling and Devel. Home: 2112 River Sound Dr Knoxville TN 37922-5663 Office: Pellissippi State Tech Cmty Coll Dept Social/Behavioral Sci 10915 Hardin Valley Rd Knoxville TN 37932-1412

SCHUMANN, JILL, religious organization administrator; b. Pitts. m. Mark W. Oldenburg. BA, Ind. U. of Pa.; MBA, Mount St. Mary's Coll. Dir. outpatient svcs. Ctr. for Addictive Illnesses, Morristown, NJ; substance abuse program developer Gettysburg Coll., Pa.; dir., v.p. Craig and Assocs., York, Pa.; exec., v.p. planning and mktg. Tressler Luth. Svcs., Mechanicsburg; exec. v.p. Kairos Health Sys.; dir. mem. svcs. Luth. Svcs. in Am., Balt., pres., CEO, 2001—. Office: Luth Svcs in Am 700 Light St Baltimore MD 21230-3850 Office Phone: 410-230-2702. Office Fax: 410-230-2710. E-mail: jschumann@lutheranservices.org.*

SCHUMANN, LAURA ELAINE, conductor; b. Mpls., May 13, 1963; d. Aubrey Paul Schumann, Elaine Anne Topka. BMus, U. Colo., 1985; MA, U. Calif., Santa Barbara, 1988; D in Musical Arts, Tex. Tech. U., 2001. Instr. violin and string methods Wake Forest U., Winston-Salem, NC, 1990—91; instr. upper strings and music theory Winston-Salem State U., NC, 1991—92; asst. condr. orch., instr. strings Murray State U., Murray, Ky., 1992—94; asst. prof. music, dir. orchestral activities, studio strings We. State Coll., Gunnison, Colo., 1994—99; asst. prof. music, music dir., condr. SE Ohio Symphony Muskingum Coll., New Concord, Ohio, 1999—. Instr. violin and string methods Salem Coll., Winston-Salem, 1990—91; asst. condr. orch. Tex. Tech. U., Lubbock, 1997—98; music dir., condr. Ovations Youth Orch. Wheeling (W.Va.) Symphony, 2000—02; freelance violinist; competitor Jordania Internat. Conducting Competition, Kharkov, Ukraine, 2003. Condr.: Nutcracker Ballet, 2001; Musical Odyssey, 2001—02; musician (violinist): Tanglewood Inst. Orch., 1980, L.A. Philharm. Inst., 1982, Santa Barbara Symphony, 1985—87, Santa Barbara Chamber Orch., 1985—87, Salisbury Symphony, 1987—92, Winston-Salem Symphony, 1987—92, 1990—92, Colo. Music Festival, 1991—97, Memphis Symphony, 1993, 1994, Grand Junction Symphony, 1996, Lubbock Symphony, 1997, 1998, River Cities Symphony, 2000, W.Va. Symphony, 2000, 2001—06, Ohio Valley Symphony, 2001; violinist, asst. concertmaster: We. Piedmont Symphony, 1989, Paducah Symphony, 1992—94, Jackson Symphony, 1992—94, Key West Symphony, 2001—05. Recipient Women of Achievement award, YMCA/YWCA, 2001, Cambridge Heritage Leadership award, 2004. Mem.: ASCAP (Adventurous Programming award 2001), Ohio Music Educators Assn., Coll. Music Soc., Music Educators Nat. Conf., Condr.'s Guild, Am. String Tchrs. Assn., Am. Fedn. Musicians, Am. Symphony Orch. League. Office: Music Dept Muskingum Coll New Concord OH 43762 Office Phone: 740-826-8314. E-mail: schumann@muskingum.edu.

SCHUMANN, PAULA M. L., writer; b. Phila., Oct. 23, 1938; d. Paschal Francis and Paula Marie Libonati; m. Walter Francis Schumann, June 17, 1967; 2 children. MT, Philadelphia County Med. Soc., 1972. Cert. med. technologist Phila. Gen. Hosp. Sch. Med. Tech., Pa.; admitted to holy profession Secular Franciscan Order, 2004. Author and pub. Renaitre Press, King of Prussia, Pa., 1998—. Author (publisher): A Chapter in the Life of a Poet (a story in verse), 1995, With His Love, Prayers and Poems, 2002; author: (poetry) Les Saisons de la Vie, 1998. Pres. Legion of Mary, King of Prussia, Pa., 2000—02., Franklin Sch. Sci. and Arts scholar, 1960—61. Mem.: Internat. Soc. Poets (disting. mem.), Phila. Writers' Conf., Poetry Soc. Am., Acad. Am. Poets. Roman Catholic. Avocations: cooking, travel, swimming, piano, dance. Office: Renaitre Press P O Box 61163 King Of Prussia PA 19406-1163 Business E-Mail: renaitrepress@yahoo.com.

SCHUMM, DARLA YZONNE, religious studies educator; b. Kitchner, Ontario, Can. d. Claire Floyd and Katie Ann Schumm; m. Jonathan Fisher Harris, Oct. 14, 2000. BA, Goshen Coll., NY, 1987; MA, Pacific Sch. Religion, 1992; PhD, Vanderbuilt U., Nashville, 2002. Case mgr. Cath. Charities, Washington, 1987—89; clin. dir. Gould Farm, Monterey, Mass., 1992—94; asst. prof. Hollins U., Roanoke, Va., 2001—. Fellow, Am. Ctr. Oriental Rsch., 2005. Mem.: Menoanite Scholars Network, Am. Acad. Religion, Delta Kappa Gamma. Avocations: knitting, reading, running. Office: Hollins Univ PO Box 9623 Roanoke VA 24020

SCHUNK, MAE GASPARAC, former state official; b. Chgo., May 21, 1934; m. William Schunk; 1 child. BS in Elem. Edn., U. Wis., Eau Claire, 1958; MA in Curriculum and Instrn., Gifted Edn., U. St. Thomas, St. Paul, 1989, lic. in adminstrv. leadership, 1992. Curriculum specialist, asst. prin., elem. tchr. various pub. schs. in Wis. and St. Paul; lt. gov. State of Minn., St. Paul, 1999—2003; instr. dept. edn. Inver Hills C.C., 2003—. Mem. Minn. Exec. Coun.; chair Capitol Area Archtl. Planning Bd.; co-chair The Minn. Alliance with Youth, the NetDay Minn. Program, Minn. Office of Citizenship and Vol. Svcs. Recipient 1st pl. state award, U. Minn. Coun. on Econ. Edn., 1984, award of commendation, Gov. Perpich, 1986, 1990, award, United Def., 1999, Hmong Am. New Yr., Inc., 1999, St. Paul Fedn. Tchrs., 1999, Mpls. Police Dept., 1999, Minn. Sch. Counselors Assn., 1999, United Vietnamese Mut. Assistance Assn., 1999, Dept. Corrections, 2000, 82d Airborne Divsn. Assn. Am.'s Guard of Honor, 2000, Forward Support Bn., 2000, Outstanding Citizen award, 2000, award, Jobs for Am. Grads., Washington, 2000, Recognition award, Gov. Jesse Ventura, 2002, Minn. State Founders award, Jobs for Minn. Grads. Bd., 2002, proclamation from Gov. Ventura, 2002. Independent. Avocations: flower and vegetable gardening, creative cooking and baking, stained glass, watercolor painting, fishing.

SCHUNKE, CRYSTAL, physical education educator; b. Buffalo, Aug. 15, 1978; d. George and Carolyn Smith; m. Edward Schunke, May 17, 2003. BS, Ctrl. Mich. U., Mount Pleasant, 1999; MS, Canisius Coll., Buffalo, NY, 2003. Cert. tchr. NY, 2003. Phys. edn. tchr. Lancaster Ctrl. Sch. Dist., NY, 2004—. Coach at field hockey summer camp Sweet Home H.S. Cmty. Edn., Amherst, NY, 1997—2006; jr. varsity field hockey coach, jr. varsity girls lacrosse coach Williamsville North H.S., East Amherst, NY, 2000—04; jr. varsity softball coach Lancaster H.S., 2005—, varsity asst. field hockey coach, 2005—. Mem.: NY State Assn. for Health, Phys. Edn., Recreation and Dance (assoc.), Nat. Assn. for Sports and Phys. Edn. (assoc.). Home: 164 Campbell Rd Cheektowaga NY 14215 Office: Lancaster CSD 1 Forton Dr Lancaster NY 14086 Office Phone: 716-686-3299.

SCHUNKE, HILDEGARD HEIDEL, accountant; b. Indpls., Nov. 24, 1948; d. Edwin Carl and Hildegard Adelheid (Baumbach) S. BA, Ball State U., Muncie, Ind., 1971, MA in German, English, 1973, MA in Acctg., 1975. CPA Ind., Calif. Exch. tchg. grad. asst. Padagogische Hochschule, Germany, 1971-72; tchg. grad. asst. in German and acctg. Ball State U., 1972, 74-75, asst. prof. acctg., 1975-78; investing rschr. Family Partnership, Muncie, 1977-83; staff acct. Am. Lawn Mower Co., Muncie, 1984-88, G&J Seiberlich, CPAs, St. Helena, Calif., 1988-89, R.A. Gullotta, MBA, CPA, Sonoma, Calif., 1989-90; plant acct. Napa (Calif.) Pipe Corp., 1990—2001; sys. engr. Napa Pipe Divsn. Oreg. Steel Mills, Napa, 2002—04; freelance acct. Fairfield, Calif., 2004—. ESOL instr. Napa County Project Upgrade, 1988-92; ticketing and refreshments com. North Bay Philharm. Orch., Napa, 1988-2004, North Bay Wind Ensemble, Napa, 1988-2004; mem. steering com. Cordelia Cmty. Park, 2005—. Mem. AICPA, Calif. Soc. CPAs (continuing edn. instr. Redwood City 1990, bd. dirs. East Bay chpt. 1998-2000), Inst. Internal Auditors. Avocations: gardening, building computers, networks and websites. Home: 1117 Devonshire Ct Fairfield CA 94534-7443 Office: HH Schunke MA CPA 1117 Devonshire Ct Fairfield CA 94534-7443 Office Phone: 707-864-2640. Personal E-mail: hsg_1@juno.com.

SCHUR KAUFMAN, SUSAN, retired public affairs consultant; b. Feb. 27, 1940; d. Norman and Jeanette (Handelman) Dorfman; m. Clayton Kaufman; children from previous marriage: Diana Elisabeth Schur, Erica M. Rydzewski. BA, Goucher Coll., 1961. Adminstr. fed. housing, fgn. aid, anti-poverty programs, 1961-67; mem. Mass. Housing Appeals Com., 1977-86; mem., v.p. Bd. of Alderman, Newton, Mass., 1974-81; mem. Mass. Ho. of Reps., 1981-94; pvt. pub. affairs cons., 1995—2000. Bd. dirs. Middlesex Bank & Trust Co. Bd. dirs. Newton Cmty. Devel. Found., 1995-99; overseer New Philharmonia Orch., 1997-99; mem. Newton Dem. City Com., 1970-99.

SCHURTZ, ORA SEARS, hypnotist, educator; b. Indpls., July 30, 1919; d. Fred Harrison Sears and Stella; widowed; children: Carl Frederick, Penelope Ann. Student, Ind. Ctrl. Bus. Coll., 1939—40, Ind. U., 1943—44, Rutgers U., 1969—70; BS, Union U., 1978; PhD in Alternative Nutrition, Donsbach U., 1980. Ordained minister Alliance of Divine Love, West Palm, Fla., 1994; cert. hypnosis Hyphodyne Found., 1990, instr. Hyphodyne Found., 1996, master hypnotherapists Hyphodyne Found., 1998. Asst. to gen. foreman tool and dye dept. Gen. Motors, Indpls., 1942—43; with Pan Am. Airways, Miami, Fla., 1944—46; mgmt. Macy's, N.Y.C., 1946—47, Mandell Bros., Chgo., 1948—49; co-owner Renor Co., Milw., 1950—53; pub. rels. Bissill Corp., NJ; pres. Food Power Naturally, Inc., 1970—77; owner Survival, Inc., 1976—80; pvt. practice, 1980—. Instr. hypnotist tng., 1996—; workshop leader. Contbr. articles to profl. jours. Mem.: Palm Beach Ctr. Living, Internat. Assn. Counselors and Therapists (nat. instr. 2000—), Nat. Guild Hypnotists. Avocation: walking. Office: Bldg 3-1D 11811 Ave of Pga Palm Beach Gardens FL 33418 Office Phone: 561-627-6988. Personal E-mail: peg2490@aol.com.

SCHUSTER, CARLOTTA LIEF, psychiatrist; b. NYC, Sept. 16, 1936; d. Victor Filler and Nina Lincoln (Rayevsky) Lief; m. David Israel Schuster, Sept. 2, 1962; 1 child, Amanda. BA, Barnard Coll., 1957; MD, NYU, 1964. Cert. Am. Bd. Psychiatry and Neurology; cert. addiction psychiatry. Intern Lenox Hill Hosp., N.Y.C., 1964-65; resident St. Luke's Hosp., N.Y.C., 1965-68; fellow Inst. Sex Edn. U. Pa., Phila., 1968-69; instr. N.Y. Med. Coll., N.Y.C., 1969-72; asst. attending Met. Hosp., N.Y.C., 1969-72; assoc. attending St. Luke's-Roosevelt Hosp. Ctr., N.Y.C., 1972-95; staff psychiatrist Silver Hill Hosp., New Canaan, Conn., 1972-95; clin. assoc. instr. Columbia U., N.Y.C., 1990-95. Chief substance abuse svc. Silver Hill Hosp., New Canaan, 1976-95; dir. Recovery Clinic Bellevue Hosp., N.Y.C., 1995-2003; mem. faculty Dept. Psychiatry Sch. Medicine NYU, 1995—. Author: Alcohol and Sexuality, 1988; co-author: Chapter in Advances in Alcohol and Substance Abuse, 1987; contbr. chpts. to books. Mem. Am. Psychiat. Assn., Am. Med. Soc. on Addictions, Am. Acad. Addiction Psychiatry. Democrat. Jewish. Avocations: cooking, attending concerts, opera, films. Home: 130 E 30th St New York NY 10016-8230 Office Phone: 212-213-2513. Personal E-mail: carlotta_schuster@msn.com.

SCHUSTER, CAROL JOYCE, special education educator, consultant; d. Samuel Saul and Ruth Edna Levine; m. George M. Schuster, Sept. 18, 1964; 1 child, Robert Churchill. BS in Edn., SUNY, Oswego, 1952; MS in Edn., Queens Coll., SUNY, 1958. Lic. heath conservation for physically handicapped NYC, 1963, tchr. orthop. handicapped NY, 1976, elem. tchr. NYC. Tchr. NYC Bd. Edn., 1953—62, tchr. physically handicapped, 1963—67, St. Francis Hosp., Roslyn; tchr. in charge Queens Gen. Hosp., Queens, NY; cons. in spl. edn. Dep. for handicapped, Huntington, NY, 1982—86; mem. adv. bd. and founding com. Dolan Family Health Ctr., Huntington, 1997—. Mem. prin. selection com. Half Hollow Hills Dist., Dix Hills, NY, 1979—80; cmty. activist Huntington, 1979—; mem. campaign com. election for US congressman Dix Hills, Huntington, LI, 1986—89; mem. Dem. campaign com. US pres. Huntington, 2003—04; youth edn. mentor AAUW; cert. instr. Literacy Vols. of Am. Recipient Lifetime award for Outstanding Achievement in Career and Cmty. Svc., SUNY, Oswego, 1997. Achievements include invention of an adjustable wheelchair desk in 1963. Avocations: reading, writing poetry and prose, painting, Sherlockian literature, travel.

SCHUSTER, ELAINE, retired civil rights professional; b. Detroit, Sept. 26, 1947; d. William Alfred and Aimee Isabelle (Cote) LeBlanc; m. James William Schuster, Sept. 6, 1969; 1 child, Cambrian James. BA, Wayne State U., 1972, postgrad., 1974-75, paralegal cert., 1991; student, Bay Mills Com. Coll., 2003—. Asst. payments Mich. Dept. Social Svcs., Detroit, 1972-73; rights rep. Mich. Dept. Civil Rights, Detroit, 1973-80, 82-87, 90, asst. dir. div., 1987-90, supr., 1993-97, dir. Svc. Ctr., 1997-99, contract coord., 1999—2002, ret., 2003; ct. adminstr. Chippewa-Ottawa Conservation Ct., Bay Mills, Mich., 1980-82; quality assurance coord. State Mental Health Facility, Southgate, Mich., 1991-93; acting interim dir. Mich. Indian Commn., Detroit, 1995; proprietor Good Things to Share, 2003—; trainer HIV/AIDS health support profls., 2004—. Author: Walking in Two Worlds, Delivering Culturally Competent Care in the American Indian Community, 2004, Critique, An Indian Tours Michilimackinac, 1981; contbr. articles and poems to mags. and profl. jours. Bd. dirs. Tri-County Native Ams., Warren, Mich., 1982-89, sec. Native Am. Sesquicentennial subcom., Mich., 1987; mem. Linking Lifetimes, mentor program for Native Am. youth, 1992-93; sec., newsletter editor various civic orgns.; also other polit. and civic activities. Native Am. fellow Mich. State U., 1989. Mem. NAACP (housing com. S. Oakland br. 2000), ACLU (bd. dirs. Union-Oakland county 1987-88, 2002-04). Democrat. Avocations: exploring local historical and natural places of interest, historical re-enactment, research, exercise. E-mail: ikwewe@comcast.net.

SCHUSTER, INGEBORG IDA, chemistry professor; b. Frankfurt, W. Ger., Oct. 30, 1937; came to U.S. 1947; d. Ludwig Karl and Mariluise (Kautetzky) S. BA, U. Pa., 1960; MS, Carnegie Inst. Tech., Pitts., 1963; PhD, Carnegie Inst. Tech., 1965. Postdoctoral fellow Bryn Mawr (Pa.) Coll., 1965-67; asst. prof. chemistry Pa. State U., Abington, 1967-73, assoc. prof. chemistry, 1973-83, prof. chemistry, 1983—. Contbr. articles to profl. jours. Huff fellow, 1966; E. Gerry fellow, 1982. Mem. Am. Chem. Soc. Republican. Roman Catholic. Avocations: skiing, violin, cartooning. Office: Pa State Univ 1600 Woodland Rd Abington PA 19001-3918 Business E-Mail: iis@psu.edu.

SCHUSTER, PEGGY LINDNER (PRAVRAJIKA BRAHMAPRANA), sister, nun; b. Seattle, Apr. 7, 1949; d. Philip Frederick Schuster and Ruth Elizabeth Robar. BA in History, Occidental Coll., Calif., 1970, U. Calif., Santa Barbara, 1973; solemn ordination (hon.), Vedanta Soc. So. Calif., 1984. Sr. monastic Vedanta Soc. So. Calif., 1973—. Convent bookstore mgr. Vedanta Soc., 1984—2004, interfaith dialog, 1984—, mem. monastic coun., 1995—2004; nun Ramakrishna Order of India; spkr. and presenter in field. Contbr. articles to religious and profl. jours.; editor: Vivekananda Swami: The Complete Works of Swami Vivekananda, 1997, of numerous works and works in progress. Interfaith seminar participant, Calcutta, India, 1977—98; lectr. Hospice, Santa Barbara, Calif., 1995—2004. Mem.: Amnesty Internat. Avocations: swimming, writing, music, cooking. Home: Vedanta Convent 2027 Vine St Hollywood CA 90068 Personal E-mail: brahmaprana@yahoo.com. Business E-Mail: peggylschuster@yahoo.com.

SCHUSTER, SYLVIA M., education educator; b. Germany, July 16, 1949; d. Morris N. and Genia Bergstein; 1 child, Maggie Noah. BA in English Lit., CUNY, 1972, MA in English Lit. and Creative Writing, 1976. Cert. English tchr. NY. Tchr. Brandeis H.S., N.Y.C., 1978—80; homebound English tutor Plainview (NY) H.S., 1984—; asst. dir. RISE program L.I. U., C.W. Post Campus, Brookville, NY, 1992—96, dir. RISE program, 1996—2000; lectr. in English BOCES Cultural Arts Ctr., Syosset, NY, 1999—2002. Adj. prof. english L.I. U., 1986—, Nassau (NY) C.C., 1994—, SUNY, Farmingdale, 2001—; owner pvt. tutoring bus., L.I., NY, 1984—. Contbr. poetry to anthologies, photographs to mags. Mem. L.I. Jr. Soccer League, 1992—; vol. Am. Cancer Assn., 1997, Am. Diabetes Found., 1999. Recipient Pres.' award, Iliad Press, 1996. Mem.: Am. Acad. Poets, Nat. Author's Registry, Nat. Coun. Tchrs. English, Nat. Soc. Poets, Internat. Soc. Poets (Outstanding Achievement award 1997—2002), Nat. Writers Club. Avocations: writing, photography, music, theater, art.

SCHUTT, CHRISTINE, writer, educator; b. May 3, 1948; MFA in Creative Writing, Columbia U.; attended, Barnard Coll. Tchr. Sarah Lawrence Coll., Bernard Coll. Assoc. editor NOON. Author: Nightwork: Stories, 1996 (Best Book, N.Y. Times Lit. Supplement, 1996, Nat. Book award nominee), Florida, 2003 (Nat. Book award finalist, 2004), A Day, A Night, Another Day, Summer, 2005. Recipient O'Henry Prize, Pushcart Prize.

SCHUTZ, ROBERTA MARIA (BOBBI SCHUTZ), social worker; b. Smithtown, N.Y., July 19, 1962; d. Robert N. S. and Janice (Sharpe) Taylor. BS, U. Utah, Salt Lake City, 1988, MSW, 1996. Lic. clin. social worker, Divsn. Occupl. and Profl. Licensing, Utah. Intern Salt Lake Rape Crisis Ctr., 1987-88, VA Med. Ctr., 1992, East Valley Mental Health, 1994-95, Obs. & Assessment. Divsn. Youth Corrections, 1995-96; behavior/employment specialist Columbus Cmty. Ctr., Salt Lake City, 1986-88; skills instr. Project TURN/Possibilities, Salt Lake City, 1987-90; indsl. unit supr. South Valley Tng. Co., Sandy, Utah, 1988-90; case mgr. Office Social Svcs./Divsn. Svcs. People with Disabilities, Midvale, Utah, 1990-91; DD/MR home & cmty.-based waiver specialist Dept. Human Svcs./Renevue Mgmt. Unit, Salt Lake City, 1991-93; case mgr. Dept. Human Svcs./Divsn. Svcs. People with Disabilities, Murray, Utah, 1993-96, social worker, 1996-97, Utah State Prison Dept. of Corrections, Draper, 1997—2003, Utah Dept. WorkForce Svc., 2003—05, Dept. Human Svcs./Adult Protective Svcs., Murray, Utah, 2005—. Mem. Nat. Health Svc. Corps Utah State Prison, 2000—02. Author of poems. Vol. Winter Olympics, Salt Lake City, 2002; gen. mgr. Salt Lake Black Diamonds Women's Ice Hockey, 2005—. Mem.: NASW (Utah PACE com. 1995—, Utah bd. dirs. 1995—2000, Salt Lake City rep. 1996—98), Am. Assn. Mental Retardation (Utah bd. dirs. 1996—98). Democrat. Avocations: ice hockey, running, stamp collecting/philately, reading, poetry. Office: Dept Human Svcs Aging and Adult Svcs 645 E 4500 S Murray UT 84107 Business E-Mail: bschutz@utah.gov.

SCHUTZIUS, LUCY JEAN, retired librarian; b. Cin., Dec. 27, 1938; d. Gregory Girard and Harriet Elsa (Wiggers) Wright; m. Paul Robert Wilson, Aug. 25, 1962 (div. 1968); 1 child, Ellen Field; m. William Carl Schutzius, Dec. 12, 1976; stepchildren: Christopher Matthew, Catharine Alexander, John Benedict, Margaret Elizabeth. BA in French, Middlebury Coll., 1960; MLS, U. Ill., 1963. Tech. libr. Chanute AFB, Rantoul, Ill., 1963-65; libr. Coll. Prep. Sch., Cin., 1969-74; pub. svcs. libr. Raymond Walters Coll., Cin., 1974-79, dir. libr., 1979-92, sr. libr., 1988—2001, sr. libr. emerita, 2001—. Access svcs. libr. U. Cin. Coll. Engring., 1992—2001. Mem.: Friends of Univ. Librarians. Home: 3444 Stettinius Ave Cincinnati OH 45208-1204 E-mail: lucy.wilson@uc.edu.

SCHUTZIUS, MARY JANE, volunteer activist; b. St. Louis, Mar. 12, 1931; d. Francis Xavier and Margaret Mary (Lavin) Krekeler; m. Robert Edward Schutzius, Dec. 11, 1969; children: Mary Jane Schutzius Horvath, Ann Marie Schutzius. AB English, Fontbonne Coll., St. Louis, 1952; MA Psychology, So. Ill. U., Edwardsville, 1979. Caseworker Mo. Divsn. Welfare, St. Louis, 1952—55; claims rep. Social Security Adminstrn., Clayton, Mo., 1955—61; lay vol. Papal Vols. for L.Am., La Paz, Bolivia, 1961—68; tng. and devel. specialist Dept. of Army, St. Louis, 1969—70; talk show host WGNU, St. Louis, 1986—95. Translator: (book) On the Holy Mountaintop, 1981; editor Diaspora quar., 1981-84; co-editor St. Louis W.I.L.P.F. Bull., 1995-97. Co-chair Women's Internat. League for Peace and Freedom, St. Louis, 1997—2001, 2003—; mem. Bolivian Soc. St. Louis, treas., 1987—2001; pres. Mo. State Ch. Women United, 1992—96, sec., 2001—04; pres. Ch. Women United, St. Louis, 1988—90, sec., 2004—, editor, quarterly, 2004—. Named Valiant Woman, Ch. Women United, 1991; named to Outstanding Young Women of Am., 1965; honoree Mo. Women's Network, 1997. Mem.: Missourians for Single Payer East (chair 1996—97, sec. 1998—99), Missourians for Single Payer (sec. 1997—99, vice-chair 2001—02, treas. 2002—), Mo. Alliance for Campaign Reform (treas. 1996—2001), Fedn. Christian Ministries (pres. 1984—88), Women's Internat. League for Peace & Freedom. Roman Catholic. Home: 3150 Newgate Dr Florissant MO 63033-6218 E-mail: mjschutz@prodigy.net.

SCHUUR, DIANE JOAN, vocalist; b. Tacoma, Dec. 10, 1953; d. David Schuur. Singer: (albums) Pilot of My Destiny, 1983, Deedles, Schuur Thing, 1986, Timeless (Grammy award for female jazz vocal, 1986), Diane Schuur and the Count Basie Orchestra (Grammy award for female jazz vocal, 1987), Talkin' 'Bout You, 1988, Pure Schuur, 1991 (#1 on Billboard contemporary jazz chart, 1991, nominated for Grammy award, 1991), In Tribute, 1992, Love Songs, 1993 (Grammy nomination, Best Traditional Vocal, Grammy nomination for The Christmas Song), Love Walked In, 1996, Blues For Schuur, 1997, The Best of Diane Schuur, 1997, Music Is My Life, 1999, Friends for Schuur, 2000; singer: (with B.B. King) Heart to Heart, 1994 (No. 1 on Billboard contemporary jazz chart); singer: (with Maynard Ferguson) 'Swingin' for Schuur, 2001, Midnight, 2003; singer: Schuur Fire, 2005, (performances) White House, Monterey Jazz Festival, Hollywood Bowl, Carnegie Hall, Moscow Symphony, (tours) Japan, Far East, Near East, South Am., Europe, South Africa. Recipient 1st Ella Fitzgerald ann. award, Montreal Jazz Festival, 1999, Helen Keller Personal Achievement award, Am. Found. Blind, 2000. Office Phone: 949-240-4400. Personal E-mail: paulcantor@cox.net.

SCHUYLER, JANE, fine arts educator; b. Flushing, N.Y., Nov. 2, 1943; d. Frank James and Helen (Oberhofer) Schuyler. BA, Queens Coll., 1965; MA, Hunter Coll., 1967; PhD, Columbia U., 1972. Asst. prof. art history Montclair State Coll., Upper Montclair, NJ, 1970; assoc. prof. C.W. Post Coll. L.I. U., Greenvale, NY, 1971—73; asst. prof., coord. fine arts York Coll. CUNY, Jamaica, 1973—87, assoc. prof., 1988—92, prof., 1993—96, prof. emerita, 1996—. Adj. assoc. prof. L.I. U., 1977—78. Author: Florentine Busts: Sculpted Portraiture in the Fifteenth Century, 1976; contbr. articles to profl. jours. Mem. internat. fine arts com. Women's Art Festival, 1974—76; pres. United Cmty. Dems., Jackson Heights, NY, 1987—89. Recipient Rsch. award, PSC-CUNY, 1990—91; summer travel and rsch. grantee, Columbia U., 1969. Mem.: Renaissance Soc. Am., Coll. Art Assn., Nat. Trust Hist. Preservation. Roman Catholic. Home: 35-37 78th St Jackson Heights NY 11372

SCHWAB, EILEEN CAULFIELD, lawyer, educator; b. NYC, Feb. 11, 1944; d. James and Mary (Fay) Caulfield; m. Terrance W. Schwab, Jan. 4, 1969 (dec. Apr. 25, 2004); children: Matthew, Catherine Welykoridko, Claire. BA, Hunter Coll., 1965; JD, Columbia U., 1971. Bar: N.Y. 1972, U.S. Dist. Ct. (so. and ea. dists.) N.Y. 1975, U.S. Ct. Appeals (2d cir.) 1975, U.S. Tax Ct. 1980, U.S. Ct. Appeals (10th cir.) 1993. Assoc. Poletti Friedin, N.Y.C., 1971-72, Hughes Hubbard & Reed, N.Y.C., 1972-75, Davis Polk & Wardwell, N.Y.C., 1975-81; dep. bur. chief Charities Bur., Atty. Gen. of N.Y., 1981-82; counsel Sidley Austin LLP, N.Y.C., 1983—, ptnr., 1984. Adj. prof. N.Y. Law Sch. Trustee, sec., exec. com. Caramoor Ctr. Music and the Arts; trustee Cath. Communal Fund; chair planned gifts, bequests and endowment com. Archdiocese of NY; mem. profl. adv. com. Mus. Modern Art, Met. Mus. Art, Cen. Park Conservancy, Calvary Hosp., Mus. Arts and Design, N.Y. Pub. Libr., Meml. Sloan-Kettering Cancer Ctr.; chmn. adv. com. Ascension Sch.; trustee Cooke Ctr. Learning and Devel. Fellow Am. Coll. Trust and Estate Counsel; mem. N.Y. State Bar Assn., Phi Beta Kappa. Democrat. Roman Catholic. Office Phone: 212-839-5300. Personal E-mail: eschwab@sidley.com.

SCHWAB, JUDITH, artist, educator, sculptor; b. Phila., Feb. 22, 1935; d. Henry Ellick and Eleanor Adelman; m. Ralph Schwab, 1956; children: Linda Deutsch, Andrea Cohen. BA cum laude, Kean Coll., N.J., 1975; postgrad., Rutgers U., Union, N.J., 1978—79; MFA in Sculpture, U. Del., Newark, 1986. Cert. art tchr. Pa. Substitute art tchr. Manalapan-Englishtown Pub. Schs., Englishtown, NJ, 1970—77, art tchr., 1978—79; artist Sterk Sch. Hearing Impaired, Newark, Del., 1981, art tchr., 1982; vis. artist, facilitator Xian Art Sch., Xian, China, 1998; substitute art tchr. Del. Pub. Schs., Wilmington, 1990—93; art tchr. Shortlidge Elem. Sch., Wilmington, 1994—98. Initiator internat. exchanges Pacem in Terris, 1998; lectr. in field. One-woman shows include No. Ariz. U. Art Gallery, Flagstaff, 1985, Thompson Park Gallery, Lincroft, N.J., 1985, West Gallery and East Gallery, 1995, U. Tenn. Art Galleries I and II, Chattanooga, 1987, Susan Isaacs Gallery, Wilmington, 1990, U. Del. Clayton Hall Conv. Ctr. Gallery, 1990, Ctrl. House of Art, Tbilisi, Ga., Russia, 1991, Del. Ctr. for Contemporary Art, 1991, Jewish Cmty. Ctr. Art Gallery, 1993, Cecil CC Cultural Art Ctr., 2005, exhibited in group shows at Del. Art Mus., 1991—92, The Lorelton Gallery, Wilmington, 1999, U. Del., 1992—94, Xian Art Sch., 1998, Artemis Gallery, Richmond, Va., 1999—2001, Synergy Gallery, West Palm Beach, Fla., 2000—01, Del. Art Mus., Wilmington, 2001—04, Grace Gallery, 2005, Cecil Cultural Arts Ctr., Cecil C.C., 2005, East of the Bay Gallery, Md., 2006, Ft. Lauderdale History Mus., 2006, Represented in permanent collections Corp. Holding Svcs., One on Fitness Ctr., Wilmington, Skadden Arps Slate Meagher and Flom, Salva Profl. Assn., The Arches, Del. History Mus. Mem. Nat. Mus. for Women in the Arts, NOW; bd. dirs. People to People Internat., 1993—2000, Jewish Family Svc., Wilmington, 1983—84. Grantee, U. Del., 1985; Emerging Artist fellowship in Sculpture, Del. Divsn. of the Arts, 1986—87, Established Artist fellow in Sculpture, 1993—94, Art fellow, Del. State Arts Coun., 1993—94, Opportunity grantee in Painting, Del. Divsn. of the Arts, 2005. Mem.: Del. Ctr. for Contemporary Art, Del. Art Mus. Avocations: dance, yoga, music, ceramics, voice. Office: 9325 Lagoon Pl 209 Davie FL 33324 Office Phone: 954-452-4615.

SCHWAB, NANCY JEAN, middle school educator; b. Washington, June 4, 1951; d. Ruthe J. Michael; m. Rudolph T Schwab, June 16, 1973; children: Brian M., David M., Jennifer L. BS in Elem. Edn., George Mason U., Fairax, Va., 1973. Tchr. Williams /James City County Schs., Williamsburg, Va., 1989—; tchr. 6th grade US history Berkeley Mid. Sch., 1989—. Home: 2895 Hidden Lake Drive Williamsburg VA 23185 Office: Berkeley Middle School 1118 Ironbound Road Williamsburg VA 23188 Office Phone: 757-229-8051. Business E-Mail: schwabn@wjcc.k12.va.us.

SCHWAB, SUSAN CARROLL, ambassador, former academic administrator; b. Washington, Mar. 23, 1955; d. Gerald and Joan Inga (Newton) Schwab. BA in Polit. Economy, Williams Coll., 1976; MA in Devel. Policy, Stanford U., 1977; PhD in Pub. Adminstrn., George Washington U., 1993. US trade negotiator Office of US Trade Rep., Washington, 1977-79; internat. economist & trade policy officer U.S. Embassy, Tokyo, 1980-81; chief economist, legis. asst. for internat. trade for Senator John C. Danforth, Washington, 1981-86, legis. dir., 1986—89; asst. sec. commerce, dir. gen. US and Fgn. Comml. Svc. US Dept. Commerce, Washington, 1989-93; dir. corp. bus. devel. Motorola, Inc., Schaumburg, Ill., 1993-95; dean U. Md. Sch. Pub. Affairs, College Park, 1995—2003; pres., CEO U. Md. Found., Adelphi, Md., 2004—05; vice chancellor U. Md. Sys., Adelphi, Md., 2004—05; dep. US Trade Rep. Exec. Office of the Pres., Washington, 2005—06, US Trade Rep., 2006—. Bd. dirs. Calpine Corp., 1997—2005. Office: US Trade Rep 600 17th St NW Rm 200 Washington DC 20508 Office Phone: 301-445-1941.*

SCHWAGER, LINDA HELEN, lawyer; b. Bronx, N.Y., Dec. 30, 1948; d. Joseph David and Rose Polonetsky; m. Steven Schwager, Aug. 15, 1971; children: Russell, Mark, Eric. BA, Queens Coll., Flushing, N.Y., 1970; MS, Bklyn. Coll., 1973; JD, CUNY, Flushing, 1995. Bar: N.J. 1996, N.Y. 1997, D.C. 1998, U.S. Supreme Ct. 1999. Tchr. Pub. Sch. 274, Bklyn., 1970-75; retail bus. owner Party Emporium, Oakland, N.J., 1985-92; pvt. practice Oakland, 1996—; councilwoman Borough of Oakland, 1991-99. Co-feature editor Bergen Barrister mag., 1998—. Chairperson Rep. party Borough of Oakland, 1980. Named Oakland Woman of Yr. Woman's Club of Oakland, 1989, Woman of Yr. Oakland C. of C., 1996; Paul Harris fellow Oakland-Franlin Lakes Rotary Club, 1999. Mem. N.J. Bar Assn., N.Y. Bar Assn., D.C. Bar Assn., Bergen County Bar Assn. (membership legal svcs. bd. 1995), Women Lawyer in Bergen County (newsletter editor 1996—). Jewish. Office: 413 Ramapo Valley Rd Oakland NJ 07436-2707 E-mail: lin822@aol.com.

SCHWALM, LAURA, school system administrator; BA, U. Calif., Riverside; MA, Calif. State U., Fullerton; PhD, U. So. Calif. Tchr. Garden Grove Unified Sch. Dist., Calif., 1973—79, prin., dir. ednl. svcs., dir. pers. svcs., supt., 1999—. Finalist Broad Prize Urban Edn., 2003. Office: Garden Grove Unified Sch Dist 10331 Stanford Ave Garden Grove CA 92840

SCHWARCZ, VERA, historian, educator, poet; d. Elmer and Katherine Savin; m. Jason Wolfe, July 31, 1983; children: Elie, Esther. BA in French Lit. and Oriental Religions, Vassar Coll., 1969; MA in East Asian Studies, Yale U., 1971; PhD in Chinese History, Stanford (Calif.) U., 1977. Instr. Stanford U., 1973; lectr. Chinese history Wesleyan U., Middletown, Conn., 1975-77, asst. prof. Chinese history, 1975-83, assoc. prof. history, 1983-87, prof. history, 1987—, chair East Asian studies, 1985-88, 94-96, Mansfield Freeman prof. East Asian Studies, 1987—; dir. Ctr. East Asian Studies, 1998—99. Dir. Mansfield Freeman for East Asian Studies, 1987-88, 94-96; exch. scholar Beijing U., 1979-80, vis. scholar, 1983, 86, 89; vis. scholar Ctr. de Documentation sur la Chine Contemporaine, Paris, 1985, DAO Assn., Cluj, Romania, 1993, Miskenot Sha'ananim, Jerusalem, 1991; vis. prof. East Asian studies Hebrew U., Jerusalem, 1996-97; presenter, referee in field Author: Long Road Home: A China Journal, 1984, Chinese Enlightenment: Intellectuals, and the Legacy of the May Fourth Movement in Modern China, 1986, Zhongguo de qimeng yundong, 1989, Time for Telling Truth is Running Out: Conversations with Zhang Shenfu, 1992, Bridge Across Broken Time: Chinese and Jewish Cultural Memory, 1998, Fresh Words for a Jaded World, 2000, A Scoop of Light: Poems, 2000, Zhonguo Oimeng Yundong, 2000, Zhang Shenfu Fangtan Lu, 2001, In the Garden of Memory, 2004, Truth is Woven, 2005; author numerous poems; co-editor: China: Inside the People's Republic, 1972; mem. editl. bd. History and Theory, 1981-84, 96-99, China Rev. Internat., 1994—; contbr. articles to profl. jours. Fellow Danforth Found., 1971-73, NDFL, 1973-74, NAS, 1979-80, Guggenheim Found. fellow, 1989-90, Great River Arts Inst. poetry fellow, 2000, Founders fellow AAUW, 1988-89, Faculty fellow Ctr. for Humanities Wesleyan U., 1988; grantee AAUW, 1974-75, Am. Philos. Soc., 1985, Am. Coun. Learned Socs., 1978, 96; finalist Nat. Jewish Book award in History, 1999; recipient Wesleyan Writers Conf. Poetry scholarship, 1999; poetry fellow Great River Arts Inst., Mex., 2000; recipient Poetry prize Taproot Lit. Rev., 2002-03. Mem. Assn. for Asian Studies (coun. on confs. 1989—, mem. Levenson prize com. 1991-92, chair 1992-93), New Eng. Assn. for Asian Studies (pres. 1988-89). Home: 42 Seneca Rd West Hartford CT 06117-2245 Office: Wesleyan U History Dept Middletown CT 06459-0001 Office Fax: 860-685-2781.

SCHWARTZ, ALLYSON Y., congresswoman; b. NYC, Oct. 3, 1948; d. Everett and Renee Perl Young; m. David Schwartz, 1970; children: Daniel, Jordan. BA in Sociology, Simmons Coll., Boston, 1970; MSW, Bryn Mawr Coll., Pa., 1972. Founder, exec. dir. Elizabeth Blackwell Health Ctr. for Women, 1975-88; acting commr., 1st dep. commr. Dept. Human Svcs., 1988-90; mem. Pa. State Senate, Harrisburg, 1990—2004, minority chmn. edn. com., 1994—2004; mem. US Congress from 13th Pa. dist., 2005—, mem. budget com., mem. transp. and infrastructure com. Mem. Pa. State Bd. Edn., Pa. Coun. Higher Edn., 2000, Pa. Hist. and Mus. Commn., Edn. Commn. States, Nat. Dem. Leadership Coun.; v.p. Women's Network; co-chair Pa. New Dem. Coalition; bd. trustees Arcadia U., Chestnut Hill Healthcare; chair Instl. Rev. Bd., Phila. Health Mgmt. Corpn.; bd. dirs. Nat. Jewish Dem. Coun.; adv. bd. Tuition Assistance (TAP) Democrat. Jewish. Office: US Ho Reps 423 Cannon Ho Office Bldg Washington DC 20515-3813 Office Phone: 202-225-6111.*

SCHWARTZ, ANA STELLA, art dealer, gallery owner; b. San Salvador, El Salvador, July 27, 1957; came to the U.S., 1976; d. José M. (dec.) and Stella Durán de Comas; m. Daniel Marc Schwartz, Apr. 12, 1980; children: Michael, Jessica. BA, Lewis and Clark Coll., 1980; M in Internat. Affairs, Columbia U., 1982. Corr. banking officer Bank of Am., Santiago, Chile, 1982-86; art dealer Schwartz & Martinez, Miami, Fla., 1997—. Com. mem. WIZO, Miami, 1998—.

SCHWARTZ, ANNA JACOBSON, economist; b. NYC, Nov. 11, 1915; married; 4 children. BA, Barnard Coll., 1934; MA, Columbia U., 1935, PhD, 1964; LittD (hon.), U. Fla., 1987, Emory U., 2000; ArtsD (hon.), Stonehill Coll., 1989; LLD (hon.), Iona Coll., 1992, Rutgers U., 1998; LHD (hon.), CUNY, 2000; LLD (hon.), Williams Coll., 2002; LHD (hon.), Loyola U., Chgo., 2003; ScD (hon.), City U., London, 2006. Rschr. USDA, 1936, Columbia U. Social Sci. Rsch. Coun., 1936-41; sr. rsch. staff Nat. Bur. Econ. Rsch. Inc., N.Y.C., 1941—. Instr. Bklyn. Coll., 1952, Baruch Coll., 1959-60; adj. prof. econs. grad. CCNY, 1967-69, grad. sch. CUNY, 1986—, NYU Grad. Sch. Arts and Sci., 1969-70; hon. vis. prof. City U. Bus. Sch., London, 1984—; hon. fellow Inst. of Econ. Affairs, London, 1998. Mem. editorial bd. Am. Econ. Rev., 1972-78, Jour. Money, Credit and Banking, 1974-75, 84—, Jour. Monetary Econs., 1975—, Jour. Fin. Svcs. Rsch., 1993—; contbr. articles to profl. jours. Disting. fellow Am. Econ. Assn., 1993; hon fellow Inst. Econ. Affairs, London. Mem. Western Econ. Assn. (pres. 1987-88). Office: Nat Bur Econ Research 365 Fifth Ave 5th Fl New York NY 10016-4309 Business E-Mail: aschwartz@gc.cuny.edu.

SCHWARTZ, ANNA R., musician, educator; b. Bklyn., Jan. 12, 1946; d. Abraham and Anna (Gross) Schwartz; m. Alan Leonard Schwartz, June 16, 1968. BS, Lebanon Valley Coll., 1968; MS, C.W. Post Coll., L.I. U., 1974. Cert. music tchr. K-12 N.J., elem. tchr. N.J. Music tchr. grades 1-6 Buena Vista Sch. Dist., Buena, NJ, 1968—72; music tchr. grades 1-8 and choral dir. Howell Twp. Sch. Dist., NJ, 1974—2000; freelance accompanist Toms River Sch. Dist., NJ, 2001—03. Mem. N.J. Symphony Orch. Master Tchr. Collaborative, Newark, 1997—98, mem. gov. com., 1999—; accompanist the chorale Georgian Ct. U., Lakewood, NJ, 1996—; music dir. Taunton Sch. PTA Drama Club, Howell, 1978—81; mem. faculty N.J. State Star Sch., 1997—98. Founder and cons. cultural arts com. Taunton Sch. PTA, Howell, 1984—2000. Mem.: NEA, Music Educators Nat. Conf. Home: 3 Bay Breeze Dr Toms River NJ 08753

SCHWARTZ, BETH MERYL, psychology professor; d. Edwin Joel and Bernice Schwartz; children: Lauren Elizabeth Kenney, Meagan Elena Kenney. BA, Colby Coll., Waterville, Maine, 1986; MA, SUNY, Buffalo, 1989, PhD, 1991. Prof. psychology Randolph-Macon Woman's Coll., Lynchburg, Va., 1991—. Mem.: APA, Soc. for the Tchg. of Psychology, Am. Psychol. Law Soc. (Tchg. & Mentoring award 2006).

SCHWARTZ, CAROL ANN, investment company executive; m. Michael D. Schwartz, Jun., 1985; children: Matthew, Allison, Elana. B in Bus. Adminstrn., U. Cin., 1983; M in Bus. Adminstrn., Finance, Xavier U., 1984; graduate, Grad. Real Estate Inst., 1992. Lic. real estate sales agent. Asst. v.p. Fifth Third Bank, 1984-91; exec. v.p. Morris Investment Co., 1991—. Spkr. in field. Group fundraiser United Appeal, 1986—89; group adv. Jr. Achievement, 1984—86; vol. neighborhood coord., solicitor March of Dimes, 1993—; lox box com. Orgn. Rehab. and Tng. Blue Chip chpt., 1993, 1995—96; bd. mem. Yavneh PTA, 1995—97, Sukkot decorating com., Rosh

Hashanah Treats co-chair, Tu'Bishvat spkr., 1997, Tu'Bishvat Seder com., 1998; v.p. fundraising Yavneh Day Sch., 2000—, bd. dirs., 1997—, Friends of Yavneh Campaign chair, 1998—2000; young women/young leaders mission to Israel Hadassah Nat., 1997, nat. conv. chat room facilitator, 1998—99, nat. young leaders adv. coun., 1999—2000, conv. attendee, 1996—99; awards dinner com. Nat. Conf. Christians and Jews, 1993; bus. and profl. group program com. Nat. Coun. Jewish Women, 1990—91, bus. and profl. group program com., chpt. legis. com., 1991—92, bus. and profl. group program com., 1992—93, pub. affairs com., computer analysis com., 1992—93, fin. analysis com., 1993—94, life mem., 1993—; mem. United Jewish Cmtys. Nat. Young Leadership Cabinet, 2000—; bd. dirs. Hadassah Cin. chpt., 1993—, donor com. publicity, pre-donor brunch chair, 1992—93, donor com. publicity, 1996—97, chair, 1993—94, donor book, 1994—96, jewels and memorials, 1995—99, budget chair, 1995—97, com., 1997—, leading gifts divsn. co-chair, 1996—97, pres., 1997—99, cons., 1999—2000; fundraising conf. coord. Hadassah Regional, 1993, regional conf. com., 1997—98, bd. dirs., 1995—2000; Nat. Young Leaders adv. coun. rep. Hadassah Regional, 1999—; fundraising conf. attendee Hadassah Midwest Area Coop., 1993, pres. tng. attendee, 1997, young women's co-chair, 1999—2000; bd. dirs. Hillel, 1998—, alumni com., 1998—2000, auction com., 1998—2000; leadership coun. Jewish Fedn. of Cin., 1987—92, solicitor, 1991—92, lect. series com., 1989, kickoff party com., 1990, women's divsn. group, 1992—, campaign co-chair, 1996—97, bus. and profl. women co-chair, 1998—99, Israel programs cabinet, 1998—99, chair, 1999—2000, campaign cabinet program co-chair, 1999—2000, bd. dir., 1999—; hostess liquid assets luncheon Jewish Nat. Fund, 1993, bd. dirs., 1995—, v.p. edn., 1996—99, tchrs. edn. day chair, 1997—99, four star dining com., 1998—2000, trade and industry dinner com., 1997—98, Green Sunday com., 1996—, Walk for Water com., 1998—; life mem. Jewish Women's Auxilliary, 1995—; v.p. Adath Israel Synagogue, 2001—, bd. dirs., 1992—. Recipient State Member of Yr. Fin. Women Internat., 1987, Cin. chpt. Mem. of Yr., 1988, Nat. Leadership award Cin. chpt. Hadassah Ya'al Group, 1994, Clara Geller Young Leadership award Jewish Fedn. Cin.; named among Outstanding Women of Am., 1985, The Cincinnati Business Courier's Who's Who Among Women in Bus. in Cin., 1992, Top 40 Women in Bus., 1993. Mem. AAUW, Cin. Bd. of Realtors (mem. svcs. com. 1992-93), Ohio Assn. Relators (conv. attendee), Nat. Assn. Realtors (conv. attendee), Comm. Indsl. Real Estate Industry (CCIM designate), Cin. Art Mus., Cin., Historical Soc., Cin. Playhouse in the Park, Contemporary Arts Ctr., Nat. Assn. Female Execs., Nat. History Mus., U. Cin. Alumni Assn. (life mem. 1986—), Women's City Club, World Jewish Cong., Xavier U. Alumni Assn. (life).

SCHWARTZ, CAROL LEVITT, government official; b. Greenville, Miss., Jan. 20, 1944; d. Stanley and Hilda (Simmons) Levitt; m. David H. Schwartz (dec.); children: Stephanie, Hilary, Douglas. BS in Spl. and Elem. Edn., U. Tex., 1965. Mem. transiton team Office of Pres. Elect, 1980-81; con. office presdl. personnel The White House, Washington, 1981; cons. U.S. Dept. Edn., Washington, 1982; pres. sec. U.S. Ho. Reps., Washington, 1982-83; mem.-at-large Coun. of D.C., Washington, 1985-89, 97—; candidate for mayor, Washington, 1986, 1994, 1998, 2002. Vice chmn. Nat. Edn. Commn. on Time and Learning, 1992-94, Nat. Adv. Coun. on Disadvantaged Children, 1974-79; lectr. in field; radio commentator, 1990-91; chair transp., vice-chair planning bd. Coun. Govts. Regional columnist Washington Jewish Week, 1995-97. Mem. D.C. Bd. Edn., 1974-82, v.p., 1977-80; bd. dirs. Met. Police Boys and Girls Club, 1st v.p., 1989-93, pres., 1994-96, chmn. membership com., 1984-93; mem. adv. com. Am. Coun. Young Polit. Leaders, 1982-90; mem. Nat. Coun. Friends Kennedy Ctr., 1984-91; bd. dirs. Whitman-Walker Clinic, 1988-2006, v.p., 1995-96; bd. dirs. St. John's Child Devel. Ctr., 1989-91, Hattie M. Strong Found., 1995—; trustee Kennedy Ctr. Cmty. and Friends Bd., 1991—, chmn. ednl. task force, 1993—; trustee Jewish Coun. on Aging, 1991-93; v.p. adv. bd. Am. Automobile Assn., 1988-06; bd. dirs. Washington Hebrew Congregation, 1995-98. Mem. Cosmos Club. Republican. Jewish.

SCHWARTZ, CAROL VIVIAN, lawyer; b. Newark, Apr. 5, 1952; d. A. Harold and Helen (Schwartz) S.; m. Robert L. Sills, June 9, 1985. BA, Tufts U., 1974; JD, Columbia U., 1977. Law clk. to presiding justice U.S. Dist. Ct. N.Y, N.Y.C., 1978-79; assoc. DeLevoise & Plimpton, N.Y.C., 1979-81; assoc. counsel Am. Express Co., N.Y.C., sr. counsel, now group counsel, 1981—. Mem. ABA. Avocation: sailing. Office: Am Express Co Am Express Tower 200 Vesey St New York NY 10285-1000

SCHWARTZ, ELEANOR BRANTLEY, academic administrator; b. Kite, Ga., Jan. 1, 1937; d. Jesse Melvin and Hazel (Hill) Brantley; children: John, Cynthia. Student, U. Va., 1955, Ga. Southern Coll., 1956-57; BBA, Ga. State U., 1962, MBA, 11963, DBA, 1969. Adminstrv. asst. Fin. Agy., 1954, Fed. Govt., Va., Pa., Ga., 1956-59; asst. dean admissions Ga. State U., Atlanta, 1961-66, asst. prof., 1966-70; assoc. prof. Cleve. State U., 1970-75, prof. and assoc. dean, 1975-80; dean, Harzfeld prof. U. Mo., Kansas City, 1980-87, vice chancellor acad. affairs, 1987-91, interim chancellor, 1991-92, chancellor, 1992-99; prof. mgmt. U. Mo. Block Sch., Kansas City, 1999—2003, prof. emeritus, 2003—. Disting. vis. prof. Berry Coll., Rome, N.Y. State U. Coll., Fredonia, Mons U., Belgium; cons. pvt. industry U.S., Europe, Can.; bd. dirs. Rsch. Med. Ctr., Waddell & Reed Funds, Inc., Toy and Miniature Mus., Menorah Med. Ctr. Found., NCAA, NCCJ, Econ. Devel. Corp. of Kansas City, Silicon Prairie Tech. Assn. Author: Sex Barriers in Business, 1971, Contemporary Readings in Marketing, 1974; (with Muczyk and Smith) Principles of Supervision, 1984. Chmn., Mayor's Task Force in Govt. Efficiency, Kansas City, Mo., 1984; mem. comm. unity planning and rsch. coun. United Way Kansas City, 1983-85; bd. dirs. Jr. Achievement, 1982-86. Named Jones Store Career Woman of Yr., Kansas City, Mo., 1989, Ctrl. Exch. Woman of Yr., 1995; named one of 60 Women of Achievement, Girl Scouts Coun. Mid Continent, 1983; recipient Disting. Faculty award, Cleve. State U., 1974, Disting. Svc. award, Kans. State U., 1992, YWCA Hearts of Gold award, 2002. Mem.: Alpha Iota Delta, Golden Key, Phi Kappa Phi. Office Phone: 816-942-1840.

SCHWARTZ, ESTAR ALMA, lawyer; b. Bklyn., June 29, 1950; d. Henry Israel and Elaine Florence (Scheiner) Sutel; m. Lawrence Gerald Schwartz, June 28, 1976 (div. Dec. 1977); 1 child, Joshua (dec.); m. James Frances Edward Stuart, Sept. 25, 1999 (div. Aug. 2001). JD, NYU, 1980. Mgr., ptnr. Scheiner, Scheiner, DeVito & Wytte, N.Y.C., 1966-81; social security fraud specialist U.S. Govt., 1982—83; pensions Todtman, Epstein, et al, 1983—85; office mgr., sec. Sills, Beck, Cummis, 1985—86; office mgr., bookkeeper Philip, Birnbaum & Assoc., 1986—87; office mgr., sec. Stanley Posses, Esq., Queens, 1989—90. Owner Estaris Paralegal Svc., Flushing, N.Y., 1992—, Sutel Creative Mgmt. Agy., Flushing, 1999—. Democrat. Jewish. Avocations: needlepoint, horseback riding, tennis, bowling, writing books and cookbooks. Home and Office: 67-20 Parsons Blvd Apt 2A Flushing NY 11365-2960 Office Phone: 718-820-0432. Personal E-mail: sutelmmgmt12345@msn.com. Business E-Mail: sutel@email.com, estaris@email.com.

SCHWARTZ, HEIDI K., science educator; d. Russell and Joyce Sandstrom; m. Shannon D. Schwartz, Sept. 2, 1989; children: Shandi, Wyatt. BA, Idaho State U., Pocatello, 1988; M in Learning and Tech., Western Govs. U., Salt Lake City, 2006. Cert. secondary edn.Level 2 Utah. Sci. tchr. Centerville Jr. High, Utah, 1990—. Sci. dept. chair Centerville Jr. High, 1998—2002. SB 61 Ednl. scholar, Utah State Senate, 2002. Mem.: NEA, Nat. Sci. Tchrs. Assn., Davis Edn. Assn. Office: Centerville Jr High 625 S Main Centerville UT 84014 Office Phone: 801-402-6100. Office Fax: 801-402-6101.

SCHWARTZ, ILENE, psychotherapist; b. Phila., June 19, 1942; d. Israel Gerson and Jean Schiffman. BS, Temple U., 1970; MEd, Antioch U., 1990. Crisis counselor, Phila., 1972-82; pvt. practice counseling, 1972-84; writer, 1979—. Cons., crisis counselor in field; instr. psychology and edn., 1974-79; designer, writer, crafts coord. for children. Mem. ACA, AAUW, Freud Friends.

SCHWARTZ, JUDY ELLEN, thoracic surgeon; b. Mason City, Iowa, Oct. 5, 1946; d. Walter Carl and Alice Nevada (Moore) Schwartz. BS, U. Iowa, 1968, MD, 1971; M.P.H., Johns Hopkins U., 1996. Diplomate Am. Bd. Surgery, Am. Bd. Thoracic Surgery, Am. Bd. Med. Mgmt., cert. physician exec. Cert. Commn. Med. Mgt. Intern Nat. Naval Med. Ctr., Bethesda, Md., 1971-72, gen. surgery resident, 1972-76, thoracic surgery resident, 1976-78, staff cardiothoracic surgeon, 1979-82, chief cardiothoracic surgeon, 1982-83; chmn. cardiothoracic surg. dept. Naval Hosp., San Diego, 1983-85, quality assurance program dir., 1985-88. Exec. office Rapidly Deployable Med. Facility Four, 1986—88; asst. prof. surgery Uniformed Svcs. U. Health Sci., Bethesda, 1983—99; sr. policy analyst quality assurance Profl. Affairs and Quality Assurance, 1988—90, drp. dir. quality assurance, 1990; dir. clin. policy Health Svcs. Ops., Washington, 1990—94; head performance evaluation and improvement Nat. Naval Med. Ctr., 1994—99; cardiothoracic splty. cons. to naval med. command USN, Washington, 1983—84; Dept. Def. rep. to task force info. mgmt. Joint Commn. Accreditation Health Care Orgn., 1990—93, chmn., 1991—93, mem. task force IMS Tech., 1993—94; chmn. info. mgmt. workshop Fed. Health Care Study Commn.'s Coord. Fed. Health Care, 1993; corp. med. dir. Medcenter One Health Sys., 1999—2002, trustee, 1999—2003; corp. med. dir. ND Dept. Corrections & Rehab., 1990—2002; v.p. med. affairs Medcenter One, 2002; v.p. Surg. Svc. and Electronic Med. Records Informatics, 2003—05, Surg. Svc., 2005—; bd. dirs. SCCI; mem. adv. com. Blue Cross Blue Shield Care Mgmt., 1999—2002, v.p. med. affairs, 2002; chmn. rsch. and bioethics com. Instnl. Rev. Bd., 2000—; mem. exec. adv. bd. Surg. Info. Sys., 2005—. Contbr. articles to various publs. Mem. nat. physician's leadership coun. VHA, 2000—02; trustee St. Vincent's Nursing Home, 2001—05. Capt. USN, 1969—99, ret. USN, 1999. Decorated Legion of Merit, Commendation Medal Navy and Marine Corps, Meritorious Unit Commendation; recipient Baldrige award, Examiner, 2006. Fellow: ACS (mem. com. allied health pers. 1985—91, mem. exec. com. 1987—91, mem. accreditation rev. com. edn. physician asst. 1988—94, treas. accreditation rev. com. 1991—93, sr. mem. com. allied health pers. 1991—94), Am. Coll. Cardiology; mem.: AMA, Am. Coll. Physician Execs., Am. Mgmt. Assn., Am. Med. Women's Assn., Am. Thoracic Soc. Office: Medcenter One Health Systems PO Box 5525 300 N 7th St Bismarck ND 58506-5525 Business E-Mail: jschwartz@mohs.org.

SCHWARTZ, LILLIAN FELDMAN, artist, filmmaker, critic, nurse, writer; b. Cin., July 13, 1927; d. Jacob and Katie (Green) Feldman; m. Jack James Schwartz, Dec. 22, 1946; children: Jeffrey Hugh, Laurens Robert. BSE, U. Cin., 1947; Dr. honoris causa, Kean Coll., 1988. Nurse Cin. Gen. Hosp., 1947; head supr. premature nursery St. Louis Maternity Hosp., 1947-48; cons. AT&T Bell Labs., Murray Hill, NJ, 1968-97; pres. Computer Creations Corp., Watchung, NJ, 1989—2004; cons. Bell Communications Research, Morristown, NJ, 1984-92, Lucent Technologies/Bell Labs. Innovations, 1996—2001. Artist-in-residence Sta. WNET, N.Y.C., 1972-74; cons. T.J. Watson Rsch. Lab. IBM Corp., Yorktown, N.Y., 1975, 82-84; vis. mem. computer sci. dept. U. Md., College Park, 1974-80; adj. prof. fine arts Kean Coll., Union, N.J., 1980-82, Rutgers U., New Brunswick, N.J., 1982-83; adj. prof. dept. psychology NYU, N.Y.C., 1985-86, assoc. prof. computer sci.; guest lectr. Princeton U., Columbia U., Yale U., Rockefeller U.; mem. grad. faculty Sch. Visual Arts, N.Y.C., 1990-91; dir. team from Rutgers U. to create world's first computer-generated 3-D model of Leaning Tower of Pisa to test structures, 1999; invited com. mem. info. tech. and creativity NAS, 2000-03; invited juror L'Oreal/Color/Internat., 2000-01; film retrospective Leeds, Eng. Lumen-Evolution, 2002, 2003-04. Co-author: Information Technology and Creativity, 2001, The Computer Artist's Handbook; contbd. articles to profl. jours including Scientific Am., 1995; contbr. chpts. to books, also Trans. Am. Philos. Soc., vol. 75, Part 6, 1985; one-woman shows of sculpture and paintings include Columbia U., 1967, 68, Rabin and Krueger Gallery, Newark, 1968, Computer Animation, Amsterdam, 2006, Florence, Italy, 2006, Pacific Film Archive, 20056 films shown at Met. Mus., N.Y.C., Franklin Inst., Phila., 1972, U. Toronto, 1972, am. Embassy, London, 1972, L.A. County Mus., Corcoran Gallery, Washington, 1972, Whitney Mus., N.Y.C., 1973, Grand Palais, Paris, Musee Nat. d'Art Moderne, Paris, IBM, (digital print show) Bklyn. Mus. Art, 2001, Chelsea Mus. Art, N.Y.C., 2004, Computer Animation Retrospective, U.K., U.S., 2005, Holland, Italy, U.S., 2006, others; dir.: Save the Leaning Tower. Recipient numerous art and film awards, Emmy award Mus. Modern Art, 1984, Computer Graphics World Smithsonian awards for virtual reality, art analysis, inventing computer medium for art and animation, 1993; named Outstanding Alumnus, U. Cin., 1987; grantee Nat. Endowment for Arts, 1977, 81, Corp. Pub. Broadcasting, 1979, Nat. Endowment Composers and Librettists, 1981, Arts Coun. Eng., 2003. Fellow World Acad. of Art and Sci.; mem. NATAS, Am. Film Inst., Info. Film Prodrs. Am., Soc. Motion Picture and TV Engrs., Internat. Sculptors Assn., Centro Studi Pierfrancescani (Sansepolcro, Italy, founding mem.). Achievements include discovery of morphing algorithms to determine Leonardo's creative decision-making steps in transforming the Duchess of Aragon into the Mona Lisa using his own features to segue; reason for position of Christ's right hand and Judas's left hand in Leonardo da Vinci's Last Supper. Personal E-mail: lillianschwartz@lillian.com.

SCHWARTZ, LISA M. (LISA SHEPARD), research and development chemist; b. Cherry Point, N.C. d. Luverne M. and Janet M. Shepard; m. Alan J. Schwartz. BS in Chemistry/Geology, S.W. Mo. State U.; MS in Analytical Chemistry, Ind. U. Assoc. instr. Ind. U., Bloomington, rsch. assoc.; rsch. and devel. chemist Applied Labs., Columbus, Ind. Contbr. articles to profl. jours. Recipient 1st place geology presentation, Mo. Acad. Scis., Outstanding Pres. award, Mo. ARK Cir. K. Internat.; scholar Presidential and Nat. Merit, SMSU, Springfield, Mo. Mem. Am. Chemical Soc. Avocations: music, cooking, crafts, reading, travel.

SCHWARTZ, LOUISE MARGUERITE, physical education educator; b. Toledo, July 9, 1951; d. Ernest John and Bernice Caroline Matilda Warns; m. James Allen Schwartz; children: Chad Allen, Cortny Renee. Grad., Bowling Green State U., Ohio, 1974, postgrad. Tchr. Toledo Pub. Schs., 1976—77, Woodmore Local Schs., Woodville, Ohio, 1978—83, Oregon City Schs., Ohio, 1984—. Coach track and volleyball Woodmore and Oregon City Schs., 1979—92; youth to youth advisor Oregon City Schs. Recipient Good Neighbor award, News Messenger, Fremont, Ohio, 1984. Mem.: Toledo Area Volleyball Assn. (ofcl. 1980—2006), Greater Toledo Volleyball Assn. (exec. bd. 1994—95, ofcl., 25 Yr. award 2005), Am.'s Pride, Kappa Delta Pi. Achievements include Grand Marshall of Oak Harbor Apple Parade, 1997. Avocations: swimming, gardening, tennis. Home: 9287 Oak Harbor SE Rd Oak Harbor OH 43449 Office: Oregon City Schs Seaman Oregon OH 43618 Office Phone: 419-693-0661. E-mail: bdrifter@cros.net.

SCHWARTZ, LYNNE SHARON, freelance/self-employed writer; b. NYC, Mar. 19, 1939; d. Jacob M. and Sarah (Slatus) Sharon; m. Harry Schwartz, Dec. 22, 1957; children: Rachel Eve, Miranda Ruth. BA, Barnard Coll., 1959, MA; Woodrow Wilson Nat. fellow, Bryn Mawr Coll., 1961; postgrad., NYU, 1967-72. Asso. editor The Writer mag., Boston, 1961-63; editorial dir. Calliope Records, spoken records, Boston, 1962-64; pub. relations writer Operation Open City, N.Y. Urban League, N.Y.C., 1965-67. Adj. lectr. English Hunter Coll., 1971-77; vis. lectr. U. Iowa Writers' Workshop, 1982-83, Columbia U., 1983, Boston U., 1984, 87, Rice U., 1987. Author: (novel) Rough Strife, 1980, Balancing Acts, 1981, Disturbances in the Field, 1983, Acquainted with the Night, 1984, The Fatigue Artist, 1995, Ruined by Reading, A Life in Books, 1996, In the Family Way, 1999, Face to Face, 2000, The Writing on the Wall, 2005, In Solitary, 2002, (stories) We are Talking about Homes, 1985, The Melting Pot and Other Subversive Stories, 1987, Leaving Brooklyn, 1989, Referred Pain, 2004, (transl.) Smoke Over Birkenau by Liana Millu, 1991, A Place to Live by Natalia Ginzburg, 2002; author short stories, numerous poems; contbr. articles to popular mags. Recipient James Henle award for prose Vanguard Press, 1974-75, Lawrence Found. award for fiction in Mich. Quar. and Prarie Schooner, 1987, N.Y. State Found. for the Arts award, 1988, 2002, Renato Poggioli award PEN, 1991; grantee Guggenheim Found., 1984, Nat. Endowment for the Arts, 1985, 2002; fiction selected for inclusion The Pushcart Prize III: Best of the Small Presses, The Best American Short Stories, 1978, 1979, 1996, 1998, 2005, O. Henry Prize Stories, 1979.

SCHWARTZ, MARIE JENKINS, historian, professor; PhD, U. Md., College Park, 1994. Vis. prof. history Anne Arundel CC, Arnold, Md., 1994—95; prof. of history U. RI, Kingston, 1995—. Author: Born in Bondage: Growing Up Enslaved in the Antebellum South (Julia Cherry Spruill Prize for Best Book in So. Women's History, So. Assn. of Women Historians, 2000), Birthing a Slave: Motherhood and Medicine in the Antebellum South. Mem. RI Coun. for Humanities, Providence, 2005—06. Fellow, NEH, 1993, 1996. Mem.: So. Hist. Assn., So. Assn. Women Historians (editor h-net listserv 2004—06), Orgn. Am. Historians (chmn. com. on status of women in hist. profession 2003—04). Office: U RI History Dept 80 Upper College Road Kingston RI 02879 Office Phone: 401-874-4090.

SCHWARTZ, NAOMI J., education educator; b. N.Y.C., Dec. 30, 1950; d. Richard Kittay and Selma Schwartz; m. Jack Marshall, Dec. 28, 1988. BA, San Francisco State U., 1975; MA in creative writing, U. Calif., Davis, 1985, PhD student, 1989—92. Cert. tchr. Calif., 1975. Composition and literature tchr. Galileo HS, San Francisco, 1976—78; instr. composition St. Mary's Coll., Moraga, Calif., 1985—; English instr. U. Calif., Davis, 1984—85, English instr. 3, 1990—91; English instr. grad. program John F. Kennedy U., 1988—90; owner antiques Born Yesterday, 1992—2006; adminstr. visiting writers program, creative writing tchr. St. Mary's, 1994—95. Author: (review) San Francisco Chronicle, 1984, 1985, 1986, 1988, (poem in anthology) I Never told Anyone, 1983, (book) The Happy World, 2000. Home: 845 Everett St El Cerrito CA 94530 Office: St Mary's Coll Moraga CA 94575 Personal E-mail: dollycat@sbcglobal.net.

SCHWARTZ, NEENA BETTY, endocrinologist, educator; b. Balt., Dec. 10, 1926; d. Paul Howard and Pauline (Shulman) S. AB, Goucher Coll., 1948, DSc (hon.), 1982; MS, Northwestern U., 1950, PhD, 1953. From instr. to prof. U. Ill. Coll. Medicine, Chgo., 1953-72, asst. dean for faculty, 1968-70; prof. physiology Northwestern U. Med. Sch., Chgo., 1973-74; Deering prof. Northwestern U., Evanston, Ill., 1974—99, chmn. dept. biol. scis., 1974-78, acting dean, Coll. Arts and Scis., 1996-97, prof. emeritus, 2000—. Contbr. articles to profl. jours., chapters to books. NIH rsch. grantee, 1955—. Fellow: AAAS (exec. bd. 1998—2002, Lifetime Mentor award 2003); mem.: Soc. for Neurosci., Am. Physiol. Soc., Soc. for Study of Reproduction (dir. 1975—77, exec. v.p. 1976—77, pres. 1977—78, Carl Hartman award 1992), Endocrine Soc. (v.p. 1970—71, mem. coun. 1979—83, pres. 1982—83, Williams award 1985, Disting. Educator award 1998), Am. Acad. Arts and Scis. Home: 1511 Lincoln St Evanston IL 60201-2338 Office Phone: 847-491-5529. Business E-Mail: n-schwartz@northwestern.edu.

SCHWARTZ, PEPPER JUDITH, sociologist, educator; b. Chgo., May 11, 1945; d. Julius J. and Gertrude (Puris) Schwartz; m. John A. Strait, June 19, 1971; m. Arthur M. Skolnick, Jan. 9, 1982 (div. 2001); children: Cooper, Ryder. BA, Washington U., St. Louis, 1968, MA, 1970; M in Philosophy, Yale U., 1972, PhD, 1974. Assoc. prof. sociology, adj. assoc. prof., 1972—88; prof. psychiatry and behavioral sci. U. Wash., Seattle, 1988—. Chmn. rev. com. NIMH; bd. dirs. Women's Rsch. Ctr.; frequent guest and host local and network TV shows; appt. to Pres. Reagan's ad hoc adv. roundtable on the family, 1984; expert appearance in NBC Sacred Sexless, 1987, Some Thoughts on Being Single, 1984, ABC After The Sexual Revolution, 1986; relationship expert LifetimeTV.com, 1998—, PerfectMatch.com, 2003—. Author: Women at Yale, 1976; author: (with Judith Laws et al) Sexual Scripts, 1977; author: (with P. Blumstein) American Couples, 1983; author: (with V. Rutter) The Gender of Sexuality, 1995; author: (with D. Cappello) Ten Talks Parents Must Have with their Children About Sex and Character, 2002; author: Everything You Know About Love & Sex is Wrong, 2002, Lifetime Book of Love & Sex Quizzes, 2003, Finding Your Perfect Match, 2006; contbr. numerous articles to mags. and jours.; profiles in Savvy, Ladies Home Jour., Playboy, Cosmopolitan, NY Times, Newsweek, others, articles on work in Time, Redbook, New West, American Baby Mag., others; co-author, editor: A Student's Guide to Sex on Campus, 1971. Guardian Ad-Litem Program; bd. dirs. Empty Space Theater, Seattle, pres., 1980; past mem. Gov.'s Commn. Venereal Disease; mem. Presdl. Adv. Rountable on Family, 1984; bd. dirs. Nat. Abortion Rights Action League, Anti-Defamation League, ACLU; nat. bd. dirs. YWCA, Jewish Family Svc. Named Oustanding Young Woman of the Future, Time-Life mag., 1978; named one of Most Powerful People of the 1980s, Next mag., 1981. Fellow: Internat. Acad. Sex Rsch.; mem.: Lluminari Women's Expert Health Network, Nat. Conf. Family Relations, Am. Sociol. Assn. (chairperson com. on coms., Outstanding Contbn. Pub. Understanding Sociology 2005), Soc. for Sci. Study of Sexuality (pres. 1998—), Pacific Sociol. Assn. (mem. coun., pres. 2004—), Yale Club (N.Y.C.), The Diet Club. Office: Dept Sociology Dk 40 U Seattle WA 98195-0001 Office Phone: 206-543-4036. E-mail: pepperschwartz@hotmail.com.

SCHWARTZ, RENEE GERSTLER, lawyer; b. Bklyn., June 18, 1933; d. Samuel and Lillian (Neulander) Gerstler; m. Alfred L. Schwartz, July 30, 1955; children: Carolyn Susan, Deborah Jane. AB, Bklyn. Coll., 1953; LLB, Columbia U., 1955. Bar: N.Y. 1956, U.S. Dist. Ct. (so. and ea. dists.) N.Y. 1956, U.S. Ct. Appeals (2d cir.) 1956, U.S. Dist. Ct. D.C. 1983, U.S. Supreme Ct. 1986. Assoc. Botein, Hays & Sklar, N.Y.C., 1955-64, ptnr., 1965-89, Cooley Godward Kronish (formerly Kronish, Lieb, Weiner & Hellman), N.Y.C., 1990—. Bd. dirs. New Land Found., N.Y.C., 1965—. Mem. Bar Assn. City of N.Y. Home: 115 Central Park W New York NY 10023-4153 Office: Cooley Godward Kronish 1114 Avenue Of The Americas New York NY 10036-7703 Office Phone: 212-479-6040. Business E-Mail: rschwartz@cooley.com.

SCHWARTZ, RHONDA ALENE, learning disabilities specialist; b. L.A., Feb. 12, 1954; D. Raymond A. and Harriett Frances (Pollak) S. BA, U. Calif., Berkeley, 1975; MA, Calif. State U., L.A., 1982. Lic. childrens insts. tchr.; cert. learning handicapped tchr., cert. resource specialist; cert. in ednl. tech. Learning disabilities grouping tchr. Westside Union Sch. Dist., Lancaster, Calif., 1977-79; learning handicapped resource specialist San Diego Unified Sch. Dist., 1979—. Mem. Vocat. Edn. Adv. Com., San Diego, 1980-82, Spl. Edn. Computer Com., 1984-86, Learning Handicapped/Resource Specialist Handbook Com., 1983-86. Contbr. articles to profl. jours. Mem. Coun. for Exceptional Children (mem. Div. on Career and Vocat. Edn. 1977-81, pres. 1980-82, co-chmn. local arrangement com. 1980-81), Calif. Resource Specialists, San Diego Tchrs. Assn., Computer Using Educators, Phi Delta Kappa (officer 1990—), Alpha Delta Pi (past ways and means chmn., chmn. Founder's Day luncheon 1988). Democrat. Jewish. Avocations: theater, symphony, ballet, visual arts, baking. Office: San Diego City Schs 4100 Normal St San Diego CA 92103-2653

SCHWARTZ, ROSALYE ANN, retired education educator; b. Detroit, Mar. 9, 1936; d. Oscar and Goldie (Rubin) Klaper; m. Sy E. Schwartz (div. Jan. 1976); children: Todd, Loren. BS, Wayne State U., 1967; MS, Western Wash. U., 1975. Tchr. Thurston High Sch., Detroit, 1957-62; instr. edn. R.I. Coll., Providence, 1965, Cen. Wash. U., Ellensburg, 1966, Whatcom Community Coll., Bellingham, Wash., 1975-84, Western Wash. U., Bellingham, 1984—, supr. student teaching edn. dept., 1987—; disciplinary hearing officer Seattle Pub. Schs., 1988-90; curriculum devel. tng. specialist, 1984—96. Bd. dirs. Planned Parenthood, Bellingham, 1982-86; mem. Wash. Women United, Olympia, 1985—; vol. Seattle Insight Meditation Soc., vol. Millionaire's Club, Children's Theatre. Am. Soc. for Tng. and Devel. Avocations: walking, swimming. Home: 1066 NE 106th St Seattle WA 98125-7533

SCHWARTZ, SHIRLEY E., retired chemist, researcher; b. Detroit, Aug. 26, 1935; d. Emil Victor and Jessie Grace (Galbraith) Eckwall; m. Ronald Elmer Schwartz, Aug. 25, 1957; children: Steven Dennis, Bradley Allen, George Byron. BS, U. Mich., 1957, Detroit Inst. Tech., 1978; MS, Wayne State U.,

1962, PhD, 1970. Asst. prof. Detroit Inst. Tech., 1973—78, head divsn. math. sci., 1976—78; mem. rsch. staff BASF Wyandotte Corp., Mich., 1978—81, head sect. functional fluids, 1981; sr. staff rsch. scientist GM Rsch., Warren, Mich., 1981—99; materials engr. GM Powertrain, 1999—2003; ret., 2003. Contbr. articles to profl. jours.; patentee in field. Recipient Gold award Engring. Soc. Detroit, 1989 Fellow Soc. Automotive Engrs. (Excellence in Oral Presentation award 1986, 91, 94, Arch T. Colwell Merit award 1991, Lloyd L. Withrow Disting. Spkr. award 1995), Soc. Tribologists and Lubrication Engrs. (treas. Detroit sect. 1981, vice chmn. 1982, chmn. 1982-83, chmn. wear tech. com. 1987-88, bd. dirs. 1985-91, assoc. editor 1989-90, contbg. editor 1989—2003, Wilbur Deutsch award 1987, P.M. Ku award 1994); mem. Am. Chem. Soc., Soc. In Vitro Biology, Soc. Women Engrs. Life Achievement award 1989), Mich. Women's Hall of Fame (lifetime achievement award 1996), Women of Wayne (headliners award 2000), U.S. Nat. Acad. Engring., Mensa, Classic Guitar Soc. Mich., U.S. Power Squadrons, Detroit Navigators, Sigma Xi. Lutheran.

SCHWARTZ, SUSAN EVALYN, psychologist; d. Louis M. and Bess Beverly Schwartz; m. John Frederic Wallace, Mar. 7, 1982. Student, Wash. U., St. Louis, Mo., 1964—65; BA magna cum laude, U. Minn., 1968; MSW, Boston U., 1970; diplomate in Jungian analytical psychology, C.G. Jung Inst., Zurich, Switzerland, 1986; PhD in Clin. Psychology, Union Inst., Cin., 1991. Lic. clin. psychologist Bd. of Psychology Examiners, Ariz., clin. counselor N.Mex. Jungian analyst, Phoenix, 1986—; lectr. Jung Inst., England, Canada, South Africa, Denmark, Poland; tchr. CG Jung Inst., Santa Fe, 1987—. Contbr. counseling textbook, articles to profl. jours. Recipient undergrad. and grad. studies scholarship, Sigma Delta Tau, 1964—65, 1968—69; freshman studies scholar, Wash. U., St. Louis, 1964—65, grad. studies scholar, C.G. Jung Inst., 1984—86, Jewish Fedn. Mem.: APA, Phoenix Friends of Jung (bd. mem. 1987—90), Internat. Assn. Analytical Psychology (lectr. at various Jung Inst. worldwide), Nat. Assn. for Advancement of Psychoanalysis (bd. mem. 2002—05), N.Mex Soc. Jungian Analysts (sec. 1995—2001, tchr.). Avocation: marathon runner. Personal E-mail: sesphd@cox.net.

SCHWARTZBERG, JOANNE GILBERT, physician; b. Boston, Nov. 30, 1933; d. Richard Vincent and Emma (Cohen) Gilbert; m. Hugh Joel Schwartzberg, July 7, 1956; children: Steven Jonathan, Susan Jennifer. BA magna cum laude, Radcliffe Coll., 1955; MD, Northwestern U., 1960. Diplomate Am. Bd. Quality Assurance and Utilization Rev. Physicians. Founder, med. dir. Chgo. Home Health Svc., 1972—95; founder, v.p., med. dir. Suburban Home Health Svc., Chgo. area, 1975—87; clin. asst. prof. preventive medicine and cmty. health U. Ill. Coll. Medicine, 1985—. Dir. Aging and Cmty. Health AMA, 1990—; pres. Inst. Medicine of Chgo., 1994—95, bd. dirs., 1990—2000; co-chair Ill. Health and Social Svc. Caucus to the White House Conf. on Aging, 1995; presdl. appointee to adv. com. White Ho. Conf. on Aging, 2005. Contbr. articles to profl. jours. Pres. Near North Montessori Sch., Chgo., 1972—75, bd. dirs., 1970—83. Recipient Mayor's citation, City of Chgo., 1963, Physician of Year award, Nat. Assn. Home Care, 1988, Henry P. Russe Exemplary Compassion in Medicine citation, Inst. Medicine Chgo. & The Rush Presbyn. St. Luke's Med. Ctr., 2001. Mem.: Alexander Graham Bell Assn. for Deaf (bd. dirs. 1984—90, gen. chmn. internat. conv. 1986, chmn. internat. parents orgn. 1988—90), Am. Geriat. Soc, Chgo. Med. Soc., Ill. Med. Soc., Ill. Geriat. Soc. (pres. 1990—92), Am. Coll. Med. Quality, Am. Acad. of Home Care Physicians (founding bd. dirs. 1987—, pres. 1992—94, Physician of Yr. 1994). Jewish. Home: 853 W Fullerton Ave Chicago IL 60614-2412 Office: 515 N State St Chicago IL 60610-4325

SCHWARTZBERG, NEALA SPIEGEL, psychologist, writer; b. N.Y.C., Oct. 16, 1947; d. Nathan and Frances (Gitlin) Spiegel; m. Steven Schwartzberg, June 9, 1968; 1 child, Flynn. BA, Queens Coll., 1968, MA, 1972; PhD, SUNY, Stony Brook, 1982. Adj. prof. psychology L.I. U., Greenvale, 1984-89; dep. dir. edn. and tng. Creedmoor Psychiat. Ctr., Queens, 1989-91; rsch. corod. North Shore Child and Family Guidance Ctr., Nassau, 1994—. Writer Syosset, N.Y., 1986—. Creator, author: (series parenting audiotapes) Talking About Children; editor: (newsletter) Parent & Preschooler; contbr. chpt. in book and articles to profl. jours. Mem.: North Am. Travel Jounalists Assn. (NATJA). Avocations: travel, reading, computers. Office: North Shore Child and Family Guidance Ctr 480 Old Westbury Rd Roslyn Heights NY 11577-2215

SCHWARTZ-GIBLIN, SUSAN TOBY, neuroscientist, educator, dean; b. N.Y.C., Dec. 27, 1938; d. David Jack and Anne Lila (Garfinkle) S.; m. Denis Richard Giblin, Sept. 9, 1966 (dec.); children: Vanessa Elizabeth Giblin, Timothy Norris Giblin. BA in Zoology, Columbia U., 1959; PhD in Physiology, Albert Einstein Coll. Medicine, 1965. NATO postdoctoral fellow McGill U., Montreal, Can., 1965-66; instr. exptl. psychiatry NYU Med. Ctr., N.Y.C., 1966-75, head neurophysiology lab., 1966-72; adj. asst. prof. CUNY, 1975-78; guest investigator Rockefeller U., N.Y.C., 1978-81, asst. prof. neurobiology and behavior, 1981-87, assoc. prof. neurobiology and behavior, 1987-93; prof. physiology, dean grad. sch. Med. Coll. Pa., Hahnemann U. (now Drexel U. Med. Sch.), Phila., 1993—97; dean, sch. grad. studies, prof. neurology SUNY Downstate Med. Ctr., 1997—; developer joint PhD biomedical engring. program SUNY Downstate Med. Ctr., Polytechnic U., 2004—. Lectr. in field. Reviewer jours.; contbr. numerous articles to peer-reviewed profl. jours. Recipient: Citation Classic Current Contents Jour., 1981; Mark Cohen fellow, 1982-85, Philip Femano fellow, 1982-86, Sandra Cottingham fellow, 1983-86, Ann Robbins fellow, 1986-90, Margaret McCarthy fellow, 1989-92, David Holtzman fellow, 1990-92; grantee USPHS, 1968-71, 81-87, 91-95, Whitehall Found., 1990-92. Mem. AAAS, Internat. Brain Rsch. Orgn., Soc. Neurosci., Sigma Xi. Office: SUNY Downstate Medical Ctr Sch Graduate Studies 450 Clarkson Ave Box 41 Brooklyn NY 11203 Office Phone: 718-270-2740. Office Fax: 718-270-3378. Business E-Mail: susan.schwartz-giblin@downstate.edu.

SCHWARZ, BARBARA RUTH BALLOU, elementary school educator; b. East Orange, N.J., Aug. 8, 1930; d. Robert Ingram Ballou and Ruth Edna Sweeney; m. Eugene A. Schwarz, Jr., Dec. 24, 1954 (div. 1977); children: Ruth Ellen, Eugene A. III. BS, Trenton State Coll., 1952. Tchr. West Orange N.J. Schs., 1952-54, Franklin Sch., Ft. Wayne, Ind., 1955-56, Parliament Place Sch., North Babylon, N.Y., 1965-91. Trustee welfare trust fund North Babylon Tchrs. Orgn., N.Y., 1988-91. Vol. Safe Home, Suffolk County Coalition Against Domestic Violence, Bayshore, NY, 1979—90; sec. Victims Info. Bur., Suffolk, 1987—88, v.p., 1989—90, pres. bd. dirs., 1990—94, rep. to Women's Equal Rights Coalition, Suffolk County Human Rights Commn., 1989—94; mem. adv. bd. Suffolk County Women's Svcs., 1990—96, vice-chair, 1991—93; rep. LD 14 Suffolk County Women's Adv. Commn., 2001—06; bd. dirs. Suffolk Abortion Rights Coun., 1992—96; mem. Suffolk-Nassau Abortion Def., 1991—94; pub. affairs com. Planned Parenthood Suffolk County, 1990—92; mem. Long Islanders for Fairness and Equality, 1994—97; mem. subcom. Islip Presbyn. Ch. on Legis. Com. of N.Y. State Coalition Against Domestic Violence, 1999—2001; steering com. Save Our Svcs., Long Island, 1998—2001; mem. coun. on women L.I. Presbytery, 2002—; sec. sr. lunch program Presbyn. Ch. of Islip. Women's History Month Community Svc. honoree Town of Babylon, 1997. Mem. AAUW (mem. v.p. Islip area br. 1982-84, pres. 1984-88, legis. chair 1988-93, mem. com. promoting individual liberties Nassau-Suffolk dist. VI 1989-91, pro-choice coord. N.Y. state 1990-92, rep. to women on job task force 1986-98, chair dist. VI inter-br. 1991-92, chair N.Y. state pub. policy 1992-96, rep. on L.I. and N.Y. State Pro-Choice Coalitions, chair N.Y. state voter edn. campaign, 1995-98, assoc. pub. policy com. 1996-98, L.I. Achievement award 1996), N.Y. State Ret. Tchrs. Assn., Western Suffolk Ret. Tchrs. Assn., Coalition Ret. Tchrs. L.I., North Babylon Tchrs. Orgn. (retirees chpt.). Republican. Avocations: lobbying, reading, handcrafts, gourmet cooking, volunteer activities. Home: 23 Wyandanch Ave Babylon NY 11702-1920 E-mail: bbschwarz@optonline.net.

SCHWARZ, CHERYL MARITA, special education educator; b. Waukegan, Ill., Aug. 25, 1956; d. Walter George and Catherine Mary Nieds; children: Lindsay, Sarah. BS in Edn., Western Ill. U., 1978; MA in Edn., Northeastern Ill. U., 1992; MS in Edn., No. Ill. U., 2004. Learning disabilities tchr. Golf Jr. HS, Morton Grove, Ill., 1978—81; learning disabilities tchr., coord. Dept. Spl. Edn. Wauconda (Ill.) HS, 1986—, spl. svcs. dist. coord., 2004. Recipient Citizenship Edn. award, Dept. Ill. VFW, 1999—2000. Avocations: tennis, golf, reading, walking, running, pilates. Home: 1189 Hunters Ln Lake Zurich IL 60047-2249 Office Phone: 847-526-7950 ext. 133.

SCHWARZ, ROSE OBERMAN, artist; b. Jan. 24, 1910; d. William and Florence Oberman; m. Sidney Schwarz, July 31, 1929 (dec. Mar. 1984); children: Lillian, Elaine. Student, South Fla. Art Inst., 1977—99. Ins. salesperson. Exhibitions include Bacardi Gallery, Miami, Fla., 1979, Miami Beach City Hall, Fla., 1981—82, Viscaya, 1981, Met. Mus., Coral Gables, Fla., 1985, Bay Harbor Gallery, Fla., 1985—. Recipient Rex Art award, Hollywood Cultural Ctr., 1981, hon. mention, Pioneer Mus., 1982, Best in Show award, Hollywood Art Guild, 1983, hon. mention, Pioneer Mus., 1983, Best in show, Hollywood Cultural Ctr., 1984, Best in Show, 1985. Avocations: dress making, piano.

SCHWARZENBART, AMY JO, psychiatric nurse, case manager; b. Green Bay, Wis., Dec. 20, 1958; d. Donald Louis and Nancy Lou Kust; m. John Frank Schwarzenbart, Mar. 30, 1992; children: Reggie Louis, Riley Cledwyn. BFA, Drake U., 1981, MS, 1985; AS in Nursing, Lakeshore Tech. Coll., 1993. RN; cert. social worker, ANCC Psychiatric and Mental Health nurse. Program dir., social worker Manitowoc County Health Care Ctr., Manitowoc, Wis., 1985-92; case mngr. human svcs. dept. Manitowoc County, manitowoc, 1992-94; RN Holy Family Meml. Med. Ctr., Manitowoc, 1994-95; mental health profl., owner Kust's Assessments, Two Rivers, Wis., 1994-95; svc. coord. New Beginnings Inc., Manitowoc, 1995—. Bd. suprs. Manitowoc County, wards 5 and 6, Manitowoc, 1994-96; vol. mem. Two Rivers Block Grant Housing and Development, 1997—. Mem. Alliance for Psychosocial Nursing, Wis. Nurses Assn. (sec. 1993-95, 96-98, v.p. 1998—). Avocations: reading, cross-stitch, swimming. Office: New Beginnings Inc 1526 S 37th St Manitowoc WI 54220-5811 E-mail: jsbart1@juno.com.

SCHWARZKOPF, GLORIA A., psychotherapist, educator; b. Chgo., Apr. 20, 1926; m. Alfred E. Grossenbacher. BE, Chgo. State U., 1949, ME in Libr. Sci., 1956. Cert. nat. recovery specialist, reality therapist; libr. sci. endorsement; cert. hypnotherapist; cert. nat. forensic counselor; nat. cert. domestic violence counselor. Tchr. Chgo. Bd. Edn., 1949-91, inservice trainer in substance abuse, 1990—98, libr. aide, 2001—05, mentor in sci. instrn., 2006; co-therapist ATC outpatient unit Ingalls Meml. Hosp., Chgo., 1981-86; recovery specialist Interaction Inst., Evergreen Park, Ill., 1993-95; ct. watcher Cook County, Chgo., 1994—2003; quality assurance evaluation Ill. State Bd. Edn., 1997-2000. Instr. Govs. State U., University Park, Ill., 1987, South Suburban Coll., South Holland, Ill., 1991, Prairie State Coll., Chicago Heights, Ill., 1993, Chicago Heights, 96; with CP5 Project Assist Program, 2000—03; presenter in field; co-facilitator CPS Summer Sci. Camp Intervention project, 2000, 03, 04, Ford Grant Camp Invention Summer '01, '03 & '04. Columnist Peoples Choice Weekly, 1991-93. Del. to Russia and Czechoslovakia Citizens Amb. Program; vol. libr. aide Chgo. Pub. Schs., Chgo., 2005; vol. Children's Tale Bearer Calumet City Schs., 2006—; vol. My Sisters Keepers, 2006. Recipient Sci. Tchr. of Yr. award, 1976, Svc. Recognition award, 1985, IMSA Recognition award, 1988; grantee Chgo. Pub. Sch., 1981. Mem.: NEA, Am. Assn. Behavioral Therapists, Am. Assn. Hypnotherapists, Nat. Alcoholism Coun., Ill. Alcoholism Counselors Alliance, Sci. Tchrs. Assn., Nat. Assn. Forensic Counselors.

SCHWARZSCHILD, JANE L., lawyer; b. Richmond, Va., 1949; BA, Smith Coll., 1971; JD, Univ. Va., 1974. Bar: Va. 1974. Ptnr. practice group leader trusts and estates Troutman Sanders LLP, Richmond, Va. Named one of Best Lawyers in Am. Trusts and Estates, 1993—2006; named to Legal Elite in Taxes, Estates, and Trusts, Va. Bus. Mag., 2000—06; recipient Spl. Achievements and Contributions award, Va. Women Attys. Assn., 1986. Mem.: Am. Coll. Trusts and Estate Counsel, Richmond Estate Planning Coun., Va. State Bar, Va. Bar Assn. Home and Office: Troutman Sanders LLP PO Box 1122 Richmond VA 23218 Office Phone: 804-697-1382. Office Fax: 804-698-5183. Business E-Mail: jane.schwarzschild@troutmansanders.com.

SCHWEBEL, RENATA MANASSE, sculptor; b. Zwickau, Germany, Mar. 6, 1930; came to U.S., 1940, naturalized, 1946; d. George and Anne Marie (Simon) Manasse; m. Jack P. Schwebel, May 10, 1955; children; Judith, Barbara, Diane. BA, Antioch Coll., 1953; MFA, Columbia U., 1961; student, Arts Students League, 1967-69. Cartographer Ecostate Inc., Ridgewood, NJ, 1949; display artist Silvestri Inc., Chgo., 1950-51; asst. Mazzolini Art Foundry, Yellow Springs, Ohio, 1952. One-woman shows include Columbia U., 1961, Greenwich Art Barn, Conn., 1975, Sculpture Ctr., N.Y.C., 1979, Pelham Art Ctr., N.Y., 1981, New Rochelle Libr. Gallery, 1980, Outdoor Installations Katonah Gallery, 1986, 1989, Berman/Daferner Gallery, N.Y.C., 1992—93; artist (group shows) Stamford Mus., Conn., 1967, 1996, Hudson River Mus., Yonkers, N.Y., 1972, 1974, Wadsworth Atheneum, Hartford, 1974, Silvermine Art of the Northwest U.S.A. Anns., 1972, 1976, 1980, 1995, 1998, Silvermine Gallery, 1986, 1991, 2000, 2001, 2002, 2003, New Britain Mus. Am. Art, Conn., 1974, Imprimatur Gallery, St. Paul, 1985, 1986, Bergen County Mus., N.J., 1983, Sculpture Ctr., 1978—88, Katonah Gallery, N.Y., 1986—90, Cast Iron Gallery, N.Y.C., 1991, 1993, Kyoto (Japan) Gallery, 1993; exhibitions include Sculptors Guild Anns., 1974—, traveling show exhibitions, in Am. cultural ctrs. in Egypt and Israel, 1981, 3 Rivers Art Festival, Pitts., 1994, FFS Gallery, N.Y.C., 1994, 1995, Russian Consulate, 1998, Long Beach Island Assn. Arts and Scis., N.J., 1999, Grounds for Sculpture, Hamilton, N.J., 1999, Chesterwood Mus., Stockbridge, Mass., 2000, Troy Arts Ctr., N.Y., 2000—01, Rockland Ctr. for Arts, 2001—02, No. Westchester Arts Coun., 2002, 2003, Westport Arts Ctr., 2003, Ednl. Alliance Gallery, N.Y.C., 2003, Carriage Barn Arts Ctr., New Canaan, Conn., 2005, Pleiades Gallery, N.Y.C., 2006, Represented in permanent collections S.W. Bell, Columbia U., Colt Industries, Am. Airlines, Comcraft Industries, Nairobi, Gruber Haus, Berlin, Mus. Fgn. Art, Sofia, Bulgaria, Housatonic Mus., Jule Collins Smith Mus. Fine Art, Auburn, Ala. Bd. dirs. Fine Arts Fedn., N.Y., 1985-87; trustee Sculpture Ctr., 1980-88, chmn. exhbn. com., 1986-88; adv. bd. Pelham Art Ctr., 1982. Mem.: N.Y. Artists Equity, Silvermine Guild, Conn. N.Y. Soc. Women Artists, Conn. Acad. Fine Arts, Audubon Artists (Chaim Gross award 1980, Medal of Honor 1982, Rennick award 1986, 1990, 1992, 1995), Nat. Assn. Women Artists (Willis Meml. prize 1974, Medal of Honor 1981, Paley Meml. award 1979), Sculptors Guild (bd. dirs. 1975—94, pres. 1980—83, bd. dirs. 1995—2004), Katonah Gallery (artist mem. 1986—90), Ams. for Peace Now (bd. dirs. 1991—2001), Antioch Coll. Assn. (bd. dirs. 1971—77). Home: 10 Dogwood Hills Pound Ridge NY 10576-1508 Personal E-mail: RENATA99M@aol.com.

SCHWEDT, RACHEL ELAINE, librarian; b. Lockport, N.Y., Dec. 2, 1944; d. Richard Thomas and Una May Traver; m. Ronald Anthony Schwedt, Feb. 3, 1967; children: Julie Lynn, Alan Ernest. BA, Roberts Wesleyan Coll., 1967; MLS, SUNY, Geneseo, 1979. Libr. Frewsburg (N.Y.) Ctrl. Sch., 1969-85; adminstrv. asst. Regent U., Virginia Beach, Va., 1986-88; libr. Lynchburg (Va.) Christian Acad., 1989-92, Liberty U., Lynchburg, 1992—. Spkr. various tchr. convs. Author: Core Collection for Small Libraries, 1997, Contemporary Christian Authors, 2000, A Guide to Poetry for Adolescents, 2001; author (newsletter) Libr. News, 1992-97. Tchr. various chs.; singer various choral groups. Mem. Assn. Christian Schs. Internat. (accreditation teams 1994-98), Assn. Christian Librarians. Avocations: reading, antiques, music, interior design, gardening. Home: 4052 Fort Ave Lynchburg VA 24502 Office: Libr Univ 1971 University Blvd Lynchburg VA 24502 Office Phone: 434-592-3357. E-mail: reschwed@liberty.edu.

SCHWEGLER, NANCY ANN, librarian, writer; b. Bklyn., Jan. 22, 1946; d. Richard Donald Newman and Beatrice Ella Stirba; m. Robert Andrew Schwegler, Apr. 6, 1968; children: Brian Alexander, Christopher Robert, Ashley Marie. BA, Hope Coll., Holland, Mich., 1967; MLIS, U. R.I., 1991. Libr. asst. Art Libr., U. of Chgo., Chgo., 1968—71; children's libr. Watertown (Mass.) Pub. Libr., 1971—72; cataloguer Astronomy Libr., U. Cin., 1972—73; children's libr. East Greenwich (R.I.) Free Libr., 1984—89, Bradley Hosp., Riverside, RI, 1988—. Author: (bibliography) Rhode Island Parents' Paper, Writing in Depth, 2004, Choices: Voices Values and Writing Strategies, 2006; contbr. articles to newspapers and jours. Mem.: ALA, Delta Phi Delta, Beta Phi Mu, Phi Kappa Phi. Reformed Church Of America. Avocations: lighthouse preservation advocacy, international adoption advocacy, watercolour painting. Home: 83 Darling St Warwick RI 02886 Office: Bradley Hospital 1011 Veterans Meml Pkwy Riverside RI 02915 Personal E-mail: nnschweg@aol.com. E-mail: nschwegler@lifespan.org.

SCHWEICHLER, MARY ELLEN, childhood education educator, consultant; b. Buffalo, Oct. 19, 1931; d. Joseph John and Teresa Mary (McVey) Carter; divorced; children: Michele, Richard, Maria Regina, Beth, David. Cert. Indsl. and Labor Rels., Cornell U., 1983; BS magna cum laude, SUNY, Buffalo, 1986, postgrad., 1986—. Cert. early childhood edn. Postulant and tchr. Missionary Servants Blessed Trinity Pre-Sch., Phila., 1950-51; tchr., adminstr., founder Southtowns Pre-Sch. Devel., Blasdell, N.Y., 1975-82; asst. coord. dept. surgery 3d yr. student program dept. surgery SUNY, Buffalo, 1982-84, asst. to chair health and behavioral scis., 1984-88. Lectr. early childhood edn. Orchard Pk. (N.Y.) Sch. Dist., 1975-82, SUNY Buffalo, 1975-82; cons. early childhood edn. Day Care Assn. Resource Ctr., Buffalo, 1987—. Contbr. articles profl. publs.; author numerous poems. Vol. Head Start, Lackawanna, N.Y., 1970-75, P.R. Teen Ctr., Lackawanna, 1970-72; mem. Orchard Pk. Enrollment and Bldg. Utilization Com., 1982, Orchard Pk. Edn. Adv. Bd., 1988, Nat. Multiple Sclerosis Soc., 1990—, Found. Internat. Cooperation, 1965-69, Christian Family Movement, 1962-70, U-U Task Force on Domestic Violence, 1993—; founding mem. West N.Y. chpt. Reyes Syndrome Found., 1979-83; ombudsman ARC, Buffalo, 1989—; workshop leader Career Devel. Ctr. Women in Govt., Albany, N.Y., 1982-84; trainer Smoking Cessation Am. Lung Assn., Buffalo, 1984-86; mem. elderly and disabled adv. coun. Jefferson County, 2003; vol., Ky. Assn. Sr. Svcs. Corps Program, Srs. Saving Medicare. Named to Nat. Leadership Cir., Nat. MS Soc., 2005—06; recipient appreciation award, Orchard Park Sch. Bd., 1988. Mem. AAUW, Women's Aux. Am. Phys. Therapy Assn. (founder, pres. 1965-72), Nardin Acad. Alumni (bd. dir. 1965-70), Alpha Sigma Lambda (sec. 1987—). Unitarian Universalist. Avocation: reading. Home: Masonic Home Village 200 Masonic Home Dr Apt 105 Masonic Home KY 40041-9011

SCHWEIKERT, MARY LOU, elementary school educator; b. Bklyn., Aug. 6, 1938; d. Frank Salvatore Como and Angela Licciardi-Como; m. Edgar O. Schweikert, Apr. 7, 1969; 1 child, Marisa. Ba in Journalism, L.I. U., 1962; MSc in Edn., Wagner Coll., 1978. Lic. tchr. N.Y.C., 1965, N.Y., 1965. Tchr. N.Y.C. Bd. Edn., Bklyn., 1962—65, Dept. Def., 1965—72; mgr. dental office Dr. Edgar Schweikert, Bklyn., 1973—. Editor: Multiple Cantilevers in Fixed Prosthesis, 1988, Jour. Prosthetic Dentistry, 1984, Dentistry Today, 1994, 1995, 1999. Mem.: Nat. Assn. Women. Democrat. Roman Catholic. Avocations: tennis, gardening, stock market, travel. Home and Office: Dr Edgar Schweikert Dentistry 429 77th St Brooklyn NY 11209 Office Phone: 718-680-4717. Personal E-mail: mschweik@earthlink.net.

SCHWEINHAUT, MARGARET COLLINS, state senator; b. Washington; Student, George Washington U., Nat. U.; LLD, St. Joseph Coll. Mem. Md. Ho. of Dels., 1955—61, Md. Senate, 1961—63, 1967—. Chmn. Md. Commn. on Aging, Md., 1959—82. Bd. dirs. Nat. Coun. Aging. Named Margaret Schweinhaut Sr. Ctr. in her honor, 1982; recipient Cert. of Merit, Nat. Coun. Sr. Citizens. Mem.: Montgomery Retarded Children's Assn., Internat. Gerontological Soc.

SCHWEITZER, CAREN S., social worker; b. N.Y.C., Aug. 1, 1931; d. Robert David and Margaret Lane Steefel; m. Ulrich Schweitzer, Jan. 27, 1984; m. Austin K. Haldenstein, Nov. 26, 1953 (div. June 1970); children: Susan Federspiel, Kenneth Haldenstein. BA, Wellesley Coll., Mass., 1953; MSW, Hunter Sch. Social Work, NYC, 1974. LCSW Acad. Cert. Social Workers, N.Y. Job placement for people with disabilities Just One Break, N.Y.C., 1953—56; job placement Cmty. Action Program, Mamaroneck, NY, 1965—70; asst. to psychologist, 1970—72; program dir. West Assn. for Retarded Citizens, White Plains, NY, 1974—80; supr. group homes Westchester Jewish Cmty. Svcs., White Plains, NY, 1980—85; program coord., Tel. support networks Westchester Self-Help Clearinghouse, Hartsdale, NY, 1985—. Author: (column) Westchester Women's News, 1990—99. Campaign mgr. several Dem. party candidates, Westchester, NY, 1960—69. Phi Beta Kappa, Wellesley Coll., Mass., 1953. Democrat. Jewish. Avocations: tennis, bridge, singing. Home: 214 Dogwood Ln Hartsdale NY 10530 Office Phone: 914-761-0600 314. E-mail: ulcare@aol.com.

SCHWEITZER-MORRIS, NANCY N., retired science educator, writer; b. La Place, La., Dec. 2, 1937; d. Gustave Joseph and Georgie Marie (Talbot) Naquin; m. James P. Schweitzer (dec.), June 8, 1975; children: Merlin James, Ricky John, m. John C. Morris, May 27, 2000. BS, Dominican Coll., 1963; MEd, La. State U., 1978. Sci. tchr. Orleans Parish, New Orleans, 1963-70, Jefferson Parish Pub. Sch. Sys., Harvey, La., 1970-75, E. Baton Rouge Parish, 1975-92; sci. tchr. Sch. Nursing So. U., Baton Rouge, 1991, 92; ret., 1992. Coord. marine sci. E. Baton Rouge Sch. Sys., 1981-82, phys. sci., 1991-92; chair sci. dept. Baton Rouge Magnet H.S., 1986-88, Scottondville Magnet H.S., Baton Rouge, 1989-92. Contbr. articles to profl. jours. Mem. N.W. Fla. Symphony Chorus, 1998—. Named La. State Outstanding Biology Tchr. Nat. Assn. Biology Tchrs., 1974, Disting. Sci. Tchr. La. Acad. Sci., 1987. Mem. AAUW (pres. Niceville/Valparaiso br. 1997-2000), Delta Kappa Gamma. Roman Catholic. Avocations: coaching soccer, painting.

SCHWENDINGER, JULIA ROSALIND SIEGEL, sociology researcher; b. Rockaway Beach, N.Y., Sept. 3, 1926; d. Jacob and Lena (Pliskin) Siegel; m. Herman Schwendinger, Nov. 26, 1946; children: Jane Leni, Joseph Tom. BA, Queens Coll., 1947; MSW, Columbia U., 1950; D Criminology, U. Calif., Berkeley, 1975. Cert. tchr., Calif. Project dir. Adolescent Cmty. Survey U. Calif., Berkeley, 1963-67; dir. Women's Resource Ctr., San Francisco Sheriff's Office, 1975-76; dep. parole commr. San Francisco Bd. Parole, 1976; asst. prof. U. Nev., Las Vegas, 1976-77; vis. scholar Humboldt U., Berlin, summer 1979; adj. prof., lectr. SUNY, New Paltz, 1978-88; rsch. assoc. Inst. for Study of Social Change, Berkeley, 1986—. Vis. prof. Vassar Coll., Poughkeepsie, N.Y., spring 1980, 82; vis. scholar Moscow State U., fall 1988; cons. criminologist, Berkeley, 1988; cons. Women's Crisis Ctr., SUNY, New Paltz, 1983-86, Nat. Inst. for Juvenile Justice and Delinquency Prevention, Washington, 1981-84; criminal justice planning cons. San Francisco Sheriff's Dept., 1974. Co-author: The Sociologists of the Chair, 1974, Rape and Inequality, 1983, Delinquency and Adolescent Subcultures, 1985. Recipient Outstanding Scholarship award Soc. Study of Social Problems, 1986, Career award Women's divsn. Am. Soc. Criminology, 1994. Mem. Am. Sociol. Assn. (Disting. Scholar award 1987), Western Soc. Criminology (Paul Tappan award for Most Original and Seminal Contbn. to Criminology, 1984). Avocations: pottery, piano, singing in chorale, folk dance, gardening.

SCHWENN, KIM ELIZABETH, language educator; b. Milwaukee, Wis., Nov. 15, 1958; d. James E. and Janet L. Thiel; m. Mark William Schwenn, Apr. 3, 1996; children: A.J. Robitschek, Nate B. Robitschek, Tyler S. Robitschek. BS in Edn., U. Wis., Eau Claire, 1980; MSc in Ednl. Adminstrn., Nat. U., Palm Springs, Calif., 1986. Cert. tchr. elem., spl. edn. U. Wis., Eau Claire, 1980, adminstrn. K-12 Nat. U., Calif., 1986. Spl. edn. tchr. Desert Sands Sch. Dist., Indio, 1982—87; tchr. English Savanna Oaks Mid. Sch., Fitchburg, Wis., 1987—. Home: 301 Birchwood Lane Verona WI 53593 Office: Savanna Oaks Mid Sch 5890 Lacy Rd Fitchburg WI 53711 Office Phone: 608-845-4086. Business E-Mail: schwennk@verona.k12.wi.us.

SCHWENNESEN, CAROL ANN, artist, educator; b. Orange, Calif., Aug. 28, 1945; d. Jarvis Larson and Marie Theresa (Riedel) S.; children: Aaron, Molly, Leslie. BA in Art History magna cum laude, Western Wash. U., Bellingham, 1984, BFA, 1984; MFA, Claremont (Calif.) Grad. U., 1987. Cert. tchr., Calif. Lectr. art Cypress (Calif.) Coll., 1987, Mt. San Antonio Coll., Walnut, Calif., 1987-89, Chaffey Coll., Alta Loma, Calif., 1988-90; asst. prof.

Scripps Coll., Claremont, Calif., 1988-90; instr. Blue Heron Art Ctr., Vashon Island, Wash., 1990-96; adj. faculty Crafton Hills Coll., Yucaipa, Calif., 1997—2001; artist in residence Vashon (Wash.) H.S., McMurry Middle Sch., Vashon. Cons. ABC-TV, N.Y., Calif., 1990, Fortune 500, Washington, 1996; juror Art in Pub. Places, King County/Metro Seattle, 1993, King County Work-Study Acad. Tng. Program, Vashon H.S., Seattle, Tacoma, Vashon Island, Wash., 1994-97. Artist paintings, drawings in Beetlejuice, 1988; group shows include Silverwood Gallery, Vashon Island, Wash., Art Works Gallery, Riverside, Calif, Gallery Oresti Marchesi, Copparo, Italy, Blue Heron Art Ctr., 2005, Burien City Hall, Wash., 2006. Recipient merit scholarship Swedish Club L.A., 1985, travel grant Coll. Art Assn., N.Y., 1994; UCross Found. resident, 2006. Avocations: physics, psychoneuroimmunology, systems of teaching/learning. Home and Studio: PO Box 2282 Vashon WA 98070-2282

SCHWERDT, LISA MARY, language educator; b. Coral Gables, Fla., Feb. 7, 1953; d. Henry G. and Dilys Doris (Bandurske) S. BS, Fla. Internat. U., 1973, BA, 1977; MA, Purdue U., 1979, PhD, 1984. Cert. secondary educator English, spl. edn., Fla. Tchr. English, Green Sch. English, Tokyo, 1973-75; tchr. spl. edn. Carol City (Fla.) Elem. Sch., 1975-77; grad. instr. Purdue U., West Lafayette, Ind., 1977-85; asst. prof. U. North Ala., Florence, 1985-89; adj. lectr. U. Ctrl. Fla., Orlando, 1989-90, Rollins Coll., Winter Park, Fla., 1989-90; prof. English, California U. Pa., 1990—, interim assoc. dean, 1995-98. Author: Isherwood's Fiction, 1989; contbr. articles and book revs. to profl. jours. Grantee Purdue Found., 1982; recipient Excellence in Teaching award Purdue U., 1979, 81. Mem. MLA, Coll. English Assn., Nat. Assn. Scholars, Nat. Coun. Tchrs. English, N.E. MLA, Pa. Coll. English Assn., Soc. for the Study of Narrative Lit. Unitarian Universalist. Home: 5337 California Ave Bethel Park PA 15102-3821 Office: California U of Pa Dept English 250 University Ave California PA 15419 E-mail: schwerdt@cup.edu.

SCHWIEBERT, VALERIE L., counselor; b. Brunswick, Maine; d. Richard L. Babb; m. Ryan Schwiebert; children: Kristi, Alexis, Bryanna. PhD, U. Fla., Gainesville, 1991. Cert. Counselor NC. Prof. in counseling Western Carolina U., Cullowhee, NC; counselor Pvt. Practice, Cullowhee, NC. Contbr. articles to profl. jours. Pres. Assn. for Assessment in Counseling and Edn., Alexandria, Va., 2006—. Recipient Outstanding Rsch. award, Assn. for Adult Develop. and Aging, 1993. Mem.: Chi Sigma Iota Internat. (life; sec. 1987—2006, Award for Outstanding Rsch. 1992). Office: Western Carolina Univ 213 Killian Dept of Human Svcs Cullowhee NC 28723 Office Phone: 828-227-3281.

SCHWIER, PATRICIA BRANSCOME, science educator, department chairman; b. New Castle, Pa., Dec. 3, 1946; d. William Clyde and Opal Bolt Branscome; m. Robert Schwier, Dec. 17, 1988; 1 child, Melanie Dawn Osterhouse. BS, Va Tech. U., Blacksburg, 1968, MA, 1977. Cert. advanced profl. Md. Bd. of Edn., 2006. Chair sci. dept. Thomas Stone H.S., Waldorf, Md., 1979—. Sec. Trinish Parish Vestry, Hughesville, Md., 2001—. Mem.: NEA (assoc.). Avocations: travel, reading. Office: Thomas Stone HS 3785 Leonardtown Rd Waldorf MD 20601 Office Phone: 301-645-2601.

SCHWINDT, MARY E., retired secondary school educator; b. Wilburton, Okla., Jan. 10, 1940; d. Wayne G. and Marie H. Boone; m. Gail M. Schwindt, Nov. 28, 1963; children: Jeffrey, Elizabeth. AA, Ea. Okla. A&M, 1959; BS in Edn., Southeastern State U., 1961; MS in English, Ft. Hays State U., 1968; postgrad., Kans. State U., 1992, postgrad., 1996. Cert. tchr. Okla. Ariz., Kans. Tchr. English, journalism Velma (Okla.)-Alma Sch., 1961—62; English tchr. Dodge City (Kans.) High, 1962—64, Chinle (Ariz.) Pub., 1966—68; English tchr. HS equivalency program for migrants Ft. Hays State U., 1985—87; tchr. English journalism Pawnee Hts. HS, Rozel, Kans., 1987—2003; ret., 2003. Adj. English instr. Barton County C.C., Great Bend, Kans., 1977—79, 1993—2004; chmn. prof. devel. coun. Unified Sch. Dist. 496, Rozel, 2001—03, sch. improvement com., 1992—2003. Vestry St. Michael's Episc., Hays, Kans., 2004, 2006—; bd. dirs. United Way Rush County, LaCrosse, Kans., 2003—. Episc. Avocations: reading, sewing, cooking, travel, volunteer work. Home: RR2 Box 8253 Timken KS 67575-9052 Personal E-mail: gailmax@gbta.net.

SCHWINGHAMER, MARY DENISE, veterinarian; b. Jasper, Ind., Aug. 25, 1953; DVM, Auburn U., 1978. Preceptor Brentwood Vet. Clinic, Tenn., 1978—79; staff veterinarian Birmingham Humane Soc., Ala., 1980—81; emergency animal clinician Emergency Animal Clinic, Birmingham, 1980—83; small animal clinic propr. Companion Animal Clinic, Irondale, Ala., 1981—94; tech. writer, 1994—. Contbr. articles to profl. jours. Roman Catholic. Achievements include invention of; research in treatment for canine parvovirus enteritis; treatment for HIV-AIDS and Systemic Viremias in human population with companion animals as in vivo models. Avocations: swimming, dog and horse care and breeding. Home: 78 Cromer St Talladega AL 35160 Office Phone: 256-362-1664.

SCHYVINCK, CHRISTINE, electronics executive; b. Minn., 1967; BS in mech. engring., U. Wis.; MS in engring. mgmt., Northwestern U. Engr., corp. quality divsn. Shure Inc., Niles, Ill., 1989—97, mgr., process engring. dept., 1997—98, v.p. corp. quality, 1998—2000, v.p. ops., 2000—04, exec. v.p. ops., 2004—06, exec. v.p. global mktg. & sales, 2006—. Named one of 40 Under 40, Crain's Chgo. Bus., 2006. Office: Shure Inc 5800 W Touhy Ave Niles IL 60714-4608 Office Phone: 847-600-2000. Office Fax: 847-600-1212. E-mail: info@shure.com.*

SCIACCHETANO, GAIL MARY, lawyer; b. Jersey City, N.J., June 10, 1952; d. John Vincent and Anna Veronica (Ciani) Sciacchetano; m. Kevin Casey Dopf, Nov. 2, 1975 (div. Mar. 27, 1998); 1 child, Adrienne Gail. BA cum laude, Seton Hall U., 1974; MA, Villanova U., 1975; JD, U. Louisville, 1982. Bar: Ky. 1989, Kans. 1993, Mo. 2001, diplomate: Am. Coll. Healthcare Execs. Staff counsel Ky. Hosp. Assn., Louisville, 1982—84; dir. cmty. rels. Good Samaritan Hosp., Suffern, NY, 1984—87; dir. quality care mgmt. Phelps County Med. Ctr., Rolla, Mo., 1989—91; risk mgr. Mid-Am. Rehab. Hosp., Overland Pk., Kans., 1992—96; spl. projects dir. Carondelet Health, Kans. City, Mo., 1996—2000; assoc. counsel Cath. Health Initiatives, Seattle, 2000; gen. counsel U. Physician Assocs., Kans. City, 2000—04, dep. gen. counsel, 2005—. Scholar, Villanova U., 1974—75. Mem.: ABA, Mo. Bar Assn., Ky. Bar Assn., Kans. City Metro Bar Assn., Kans. Bar Assn., Delta Theta Phi. Roman Cath. Avocations: music, photography, reading.

SCIALABBA, ELMERINDA CACCAVO, retired pediatrician; b. Bklyn., July 12, 1933; d. Nicholas James and Gilda (DeMare) Caccavo; m. Dominick Anthony Scialabba, Apr. 29, 1961; children: Fred Anthony, Damian Angelo, Marion Alexia Scialabba Brown. BS in Chemistry, St. John's U. Coll., Bklyn., 1955; MD, Woman's Med. Coll., Phila., 1959. Internship Kings County Hosp. Ctr., Bklyn., 1959—60; resident, chief resident L.I. Coll. Hosp., 1960—61; chief resident Coney Island Hosp., 1962—63; pediatrician pvt. practice, 1963—64, Plainfield, NJ, 1964—65; staff physician Woodbridge State Sch., 1965—66, med. dir., 1966; pvt. practice and counseling in child devel. and child neurology, 1966—94; ret., 1994. Fellow: Am. Acad. Pediatrics; mem.: NJ Med. Soc., Union County Med. Soc. Roman Catholic. Avocation: gardening.

SCIALDO, MARY ANN, musician, educator; b. Westchester, NY, Sept. 21, 1942; d. Camille George Scialdo. MusB, Seton Hill Coll., 1963; MusM, Pius XII Inst. Fine Arts, Florence, Italy, 1964; prof. diploma, Manhattan Sch. Music, 1978; postgrad., Peabody Cons. Cert. tchr. NY, Fla. Supr. music Great Barrington (Mass.) Sch. Sys., 1967—68; music, theater prof. Simons Rock Coll., Great Barrington, 1968—70, Cath. U. PR, Ponce, 1971; performing arts instr. Briarcliff Sch. Dist., 1981, Ossining (NY) Sch. Dist., 1982, Albert Leonard Jr. H.S., 1983, Pleasantville (NY) Sch. Dist., 1984; theater and music tchr. Briarcliff Manor Schs., 1984—98; music tchr. Hillsborough County Schs., Tampa, Fla., 1999—. Dir., prodr., mus. and vocal dir., set and costume numerous student prodns. Debut concert: Merkin Hall, N.Y.C., internat. debut concert: Glinka Mus.; performer: (fund raising concert) Chopin Found. NY, (Giannini retrospective) WQXR, WNCN, (CD) Scriabin 24 Preludes, Opus 11, 1998—99. Recipient Outstanding Drama Tchr. award, Emerson Coll., 1st place award, Young Artist Nat. Competition, Nat. Fedn. Music Clubs competition, Disting. Alumna Leadership award, Seton Hill U. Mem.: Sigma Alpha Iota (life). Democrat. Roman Catholic. Office: Webb Middle Sch 6035 Hanley Rd Tampa FL 33634-4913

SCINTO, CAROL MURDOCK, writer, editor, social worker; b. South Bend, Wash., Dec. 16, 1925; d. Glen and Florence Blythe Murdock; m. Joseph Francis Scinto, Aug. 22, 1959; children: Catherine Blythe, Blaise Andrea, Maria Francesca, Tania McClain. BJ, Univ. Wash., Seattle, Wash., 1948. Womens editor Hoquiam Daily Wash., Hoquiam, 1948; pub. rels. dir. Seattle YWCA, Seattle, 1948—50; youth club leader Main Club YWCA, Croydon, England, 1951—52; svc. club dir. USAF, Shepherds Grove, England, 1952—53; editor employee pub. Sea First Bank, Seattle, 1953—56; pub. rels. asst. Campfire Girls Nat. Office, N.Y., 1957; editor employee mag. Mfgrs. Trust Bank, N.Y., 1958; sr. editor U.S. Radio Mag., N.Y., 1959; cowriter/editor Greater Southeast Cmty. Hosp., Wash., DC, 1974—82, ret., 1982. Treas. Internat. Coun. of Inds. Editors, Seattle, 1954—56; pub. rel. bd. dir. YWCA, Albany, NY, 1969—70; chair Theta Sigma Phi, Matrix Table, Seattle, 1956. Contbr. hosp. materials to various orgn. Editor PTA Newsletter, Elsmere, NY, 1968—70, Rockville, Md., 1971—82; v.p. Elsmere PTA, 1970; vol. editor Womens Alliance for Theology, Ethics & Ritual, supporter; activist ERA, 1984—2000. Avocations: travel, reading, writing. Home: 807 W Edmonston Dr Rockville MD 20852

SCIOLINO, ELAINE, reporter; m. Andrew Plump; children: Alessandra, Gabriela. M of History, NYU, 1971; D (hon.), Syracuse U., Canusius Coll., Dowling Coll. Vaious positions Newsweek, 1970—84, foreign corr. Paris, 1978—80, bur. chief Rome, 1980—82, internat. corr. NYC, 1983—84; metropolitan reporter UN Newspapers, 1984, bur. chief, 1985-87; diplomatic corr. The NY Times, 1987-91, covered intelligence beat, 1991-92, chief diplomatic corr., 1992-96, sr. writer, Washington bur.; sr. fellow U.S. Inst. Peace, Washington, 1998. Edward R. Murrow Press Fellow Coun. on Foreign Rels., 1982—83. Author: The Outlaw State: Saddam Hussein's Quest for Power and the Gulf Crisis, 1991, Persian Mirrors: The Elusive Face of Iran, 2000. Recipient Page One Award, 1978, Nat. Headliners Award, 1981, Overseas Press Club citation, 1983, Helen Bernstein Book Award for Excellence in Journalism, NY Public Library, 2001.

SCIORRA, ANNABELLA, actress; b. Wethersfield, Mar. 24, 1964; Appeared in films, including True Love, 1989, Internal Affairs, 1990, Cadillac Man, 1990, Reversal of Fortune, 1990, The Hard Way, 1991, Jungle Fever, 1991, The Hand That Rocks the Cradle, 1992, Whispers in the Dark, 1992, The Night We Never Met, 1993, Romeo is Bleeding, 1994, The Cure, 1995, The Addiction, 1995, The Funeral, 1996, Underworld, 1996, Copland, 1997, Mr. Jealousy, 1997, Highball, 1997, Underworld, 1997, Destination Anywhere, 1997, What Dreams May Come, 1998, New Rose Hotel, 1998, Little City, 1998, Sam the Man, 1999, King of the Jungle, 1999, American Crime, 2003, Chasing Liberty, 2004; (TV series) The Sopranos, 1999, 2001, 2002, Queens Supreme, 2003; (TV miniseries) Asteroid, 1997

SCITES, JAN, business consulting services company executive; BGS summa cum laude, Ohio U., Athens, 1971; JD, U. Conn.Law School, 1977. Registered principal (Series 24), rep. (Series 7), chartered financial cons. 1986, chartered life underwriter 1980. Systems and cost analyst, youth commn. and mgr., statistics divsn. Ohio Govt., Columbus, Ohio, 1971—74; paralegal and trust adminstrn. mgr., trust dept. Conn. Bank and Trust Co., Hartford, Conn., 1974—77; asst. counsel, dir. law dept. Phoenix Mutual Life Ins. Co., 1977—80, dir., group product develop. and group compensation unit, 1980—83, dir., corp. planning, 1983—84, pres., equity planning corp., 1984—90; chief adminstrv. officer, individual life ins. line Conn. Mutual Life Ins. Co., 1990—92, sr. v.p., individual life ins. line, 1992—93, pres., customer svc. group, 1993—95; v.p., bus. customer care AT&T, 1995—96, v.p., value-added svcs., 1996—97, v.p., broadband and corp. strategy, 1997—2001; pres. Scites Assocs., Inc., Basking Ridge, NJ, 2001—. Bd. dr. Ctrl. Vermont Pub. Svc. Corp., 1998—, mem. compensation com., 1999—2003, mem. audit com., 2003—; bd. dir. Venturi Partners (formerly Personnel Group of Am.), 1999—2004, mem. audit com., 1999—2004, mem. compensation com., 2003—04, chair, mem. governance com., 2003—04; bd. dir. Home Svc. Solutions, 2000—; bd. advisor RxCentric.com, 2000—03, Strategic Light, Inc., 2000, CyberTel, inc., 2000—01, Guideware (formerly Centrica Software), 2001—03, edocs, 2002—, Electronic Document Sys. Found., 2000—, Pendergast Partners, 2002—, Glasshouse Technologies, 2003—, ERI, 2004—, Cerylion, 2004—; mem. IT advisory coun. Business Week, 1996; prog. co-chair NJ Inst. of Mgmt. Consultants, 2003—04; extensive spkr. in field, 1991—2004. Guest columnist Best's Review, 1994—95, by-lined articles in various magazines, 1992—2004. Assembled and lead vol. adv. bd. World Food Program, 2001; bd. dir. Salvation Army, Hartford, Conn., 1994—97; chairperson United Way-Phoenix Mutual Fall 1987 Campaign and Greater Hartford Arts Campaign Phoenix Mutual Spring 1987 Campaign; bd. dir., mem. exec. com. Am. Lung Assn., 1983—91, chairwomen personnel practices com., 1983—85, treas., 1985—87, first v.p., 1987—89, pres., 1989—91; chairwomen, mem. exec. com. Phoenix Fed. Credit Union, 1985—90. Named one of Top 100 Women in Computing, 1996; recipient Gold Winner, achievement in mng. information tech., Am. Mgmt. Sys. and Carnegie Mellon Univ. Mem.: Venture Assn. NJ, NJ Soc. for Information Mgmt., NJ Bar Assn. (probate and eldercare law sect.), Conn. Bar Assn. (pub. utilities sect.), Hartford Bar Assn., ABA, LOMA (bd. dir. 1993—96). Office: Scites Assoc 11 North Stone Hedge Drive Basking Ridge NJ 07920 Office Phone: 908-903-1102. Office Fax: 908-903-1105.

SCITOVSKY, ANNE AICKELIN, economist, researcher; b. Ludwigshafen, Germany, Apr. 17, 1915; arrived in U.S., 1931, naturalized, 1938; d. Hans W. and Gertrude Margarete Aickelin; 1 child, Catherine Margaret. Student, Smith Coll., 1933—35; BA, Barnard Coll., 1937; postgrad., London Sch. Econs., 1937—39; MA in Econs., Columbia U., 1941. Mem. staff legis. reference svc. Libr. of Congress, 1941—44; mem. staff Social Security Bd., 1944—46; with Palo Alto (Calif.) Med. Found./Rsch. Inst., 1963—, chief health econs. div., 1973—94, sr. staff scientist, 1994—. Lectr. Inst. Health Policy Studies, U. Calif., San Francisco, 1975—94; mem. Inst. Medicine of NAS, Nat. Acad. Social Ins., Pres.'s Commn. for Study of Ethical Problems in Medicine and Biomed. and Behavioral Rsch., 1979—82, U.S. Nat. Com. on Vital and Health Stats., 1975—78, Health Resources and Svcs. Adminstrn., AIDS adv. com., 1990—94; cons. HHS, Inst. Medicine Coun. on Health Care Tech. Assessment, 1986—90. Home: 161 Erica Way Portola Valley CA 94028-7439 Office: Palo Alto Med Found Rsch Inst Ames Bldg 795 El Camino Real Palo Alto CA 94301-2302 Personal E-mail: ascitovsky@aol.com.

SCIUVA, MARGARET W., counselor; b. Cleve., Dec. 22, 1962; d. Joseph Aloysius and Katharine Elizabeth Williams; m. James Salvatore Sciuva, May 23, 1987; children: James Jr., Anthony, Richelle. BA in Comm. and Psychology, John Carol U.; postgrad. in counseling, John Carroll U.; MA in Counseling, Webster U. Rape crisis counselor Safe Homes Rape Crisis Ctr., Lauren, SC; family preservation therapist Spartanburg Mental Health, HSA, Cayce, SC; founder, exec. dir. SC Mental Health Counselors Assn. Treas. Polk County Mid. Sch. PTA, Tryon, NC, 2000; active Polk County Hist. Soc., Tryon, 2003. Mem.: SC Lic. Profl. Counselors, Nat. Bd. Cert. Counselors, NC Lic. Profl. Counselors. Avocations: reading, travel, gardening. Personal E-mail: mwsciuv@attglobal.net.

SCLAFANI, SUSAN K., educational consultant, former federal agency administrator; b. Albany, NY, Sept. 22, 1944; AB in German and Math., Vassar Coll., 1966; MA in German Lang. and Lit., U. Chgo., 1967; ME in Ednl. Adminstrn., U. Tex., Austin, 1985, PhD, 1987. Cert. Tchr.Math. Ill., N.Y., Lifetime Tchr. Math. and German 6-12 Tex., Adminstr., Supt., Supr., Midmgr. Tex. Tchr. Ctrl. YMCA H.S., Chgo., 1971—72, Woodson Jr. H.S. Houston Ind. Sch. Dist., Tex., 1972—74, H.S. for Engring. Professions, Houston Ind. Sch. Dist., Tex., 1975—78; coord. magnet sch. Washington H.S. Houston Ind. Sch. Dist., 1978—83; ctrl. office coord. instrnl. tech. Houston Ind. Sch. Dist., Tex., 1983—84, exec. dir. curriculum devel., 1987—89, asst. supt. constrn. mgmt. and program planning, 1989—92, assoc. supt. dist. adminstrn., 1992—94, chief of staff, 1994—96, chief of staff ednl. svcs., 1996—2001; counselor to sec. US Dept. Edn., Washington, 2001—06, acting sec., vocational & adult edn., 2003—04, asst. sec., vocational & adult edn., 2004—06; mng. dir. Chartwell Education Group LLC, NYC, 2006—. V.p. and gen. mgr. Quantum Access, Inc., 1986—87; adj. prof. dept. curriculum and instrn. U. Houston, Tex., 1988—94, adj prof. dept. ednl. leadership, 1999—2001; presenter to numerous ednl. groups. Co-author (with R. Paige): (Book) Strategies for Reforming Houston's Schools; School Choice or Best Systems, What Improves Education, 2001; contbr. articles to profl. jours. Vol. Star of Hope Women and Family Shelter, Houston, 1988—90; mem. com. Tex. Alliance for Minorities in Engring., Houston, 1975—85; activity vol., conf. spkr. Coun. for Exceptional Children, Houston, 1989—91; com. mem. Tex. Task Force for the Homeless, 1990—92; mem. Hispanic Youth Leadership Forum Steering Com., Houston, 1990—, Pub. Policy, Comty. and Agy. Support, Success by Six Coms., United Way, Houston, 1987—2001; chair Children's Policy Com. United Way, Houston, 1987—2001. Office: Chartwell Education Group LLC Empire State Bldg Ste 7506 New York NY 10118 E-mail: sclafani@chartwelleducation.com.*

SCOBEY, MARGARET, ambassador; b. Memphis; d. James and Delores Scobey. B in History, U. Tenn., 1971, M in History, 1973. Consular, Lima, 1981—83; polit. officer Peshawar, 1983—86; chief polit. sect. Jerusalem, 1990—91; polit. counselor U.S. Embassy, Kuwait, 1994—96; dep. chief of mission Sanaa, Yemen, 1996—99; dir. Office of Arabian Peninsula at Dept. of State, 2000—01; dep. chief of mission Am. Embassy, Riyadh, Saudi Arabia, 2001—03; U.S. Amb. to Syrai, 2003—. Staff asst. to asst. sec. Near East and South Asian Affairs; watch officer Operation Ctr.; polit. mil. officer Office of Israeli and Arab-Israeli Affairs, dep. dir. of sec. staff. Office: Embassy of USA Abou Roumaneh 2 Al Mansour St PO Box 29 Damascus Syria also: Embassy of USA Damascus Syria Dept State Washington DC 20521-6110

SCOFIELD, NADINE RENÉE, special education educator; b. St. Louis, July 20, 1956; d. Ralph and Eugenia Ruhland; m. Donald Lee Scofield, July 15, 1978; children: Eric, Christopher, Alexander. BE, NE Mo. State U., Kirksville, 1978, MA in Learning Disabilites, 1982; MEd in Edn. Adminstrn., U. Mo., St. Louis, 1987. Learning disability, behavior disability tchr., diagnostician R-III Sch. dist., Milton, Iowa, 1979—81; behavior disability tchr. Jefferson County Co-op, Festus, Mo., 1981—83; head edn. dept. Weldon Springs Psychiat. Hosp., St. Charles, Mo., 1983—85; learning disability, behavior disability tchr., diagnostician Henderson Jr. High, St. Charles, 1985—86; dept. chair, learning disability tchr., diagnostician Francis Howell North HS, St. Charles, 1986—91; learning disability tchr., diagnostician Harvest Ridge Elem., St. Charles, 1991—2000, Francis Howell Ctrl. HS, St. Charles, 2001—. Mem. Profl. Learning Cmty.-Am. Lit., St. Charles, 2004—06. Com. mem. Disabled Am. Vets., 2002—. Recipient Svc. award, Francis Howell Sch. Dist. St. Charles, 2005. Avocations: reading, travel, swimming, gardening. Office: Francis Howell Cen High Sch 5199 Hwy N Saint Charles MO 63304

SCOGNO, STACIE JOY, financial services company executive; b. Camden, N.J., Dec. 5, 1957; d. Albert Joseph Scogno and Josephine Geovanni Fiorello. AAS, Bay State Coll., Boston, 1978; BS in mgmt., Boston Coll., 1986; cert. of mgmt. and spl. scis., Harvard Ext. Sch., 1994. Software sys. cons., owner North Shore Svcs., Boston, 1984-88; tech. cons. Lotus Devel. Corp., Boston, 1988-90; mgr. MIS Blackwell Sci. Publs., Boston, 1990-93; product design analyst Thomson Fin. Corp., Boston, 1993-95; sr. cons. The Hunters Group, Boston, 1995-96; N.E. regional mgr. nat. fin. systems Coopers & Lybrand, Boston, 1997—, co-dir. Natl. PeopleSoft Ctr. of Excellence, 1996—, dir. east region, 1998-99, dir. global programme office, 1999-2001; v.p. profl. svcs. Paradigm Tech., 2001—; Peoplesoft ERP practice leader Atos Origin, 2003—. Notary pub. Commonwealth of Mass., 1980—. Trustee Action Dance Theater, treas., 1980-91; bd. dirs. Friends of City Sq., Charlestown, Mass., 1996—. Avocations: triathlons, body building. Office: 5000 S Bowden Rd Arlington TX 76017

SCOLES, MARIE Y., elementary school educator; d. Richard and Doris Scheg; m. Thomas E. Scheg, Oct. 26, 1991; children: Ian, Courtney. BS in Secondary Edn. Math., SUNY, 1985, MS in Secondary Edn. in Math., 1991. Cert. secondary education mathematics educator N.Y., 1985. Mid. sch. math. tchr. South Seneca H.S., Ovid, NY, 1985—2003, math. tchr., 1985—. Adivsor Jr. Nat. Honor Soc., Ovid, 1997—98. Mem.: Assn. of N.Y. State Math. Tchrs. (assoc.). Office: South Seneca High School 7263 Main St Ovid NY 14521 Office Phone: 607-869-9636. Personal E-mail: courian@aol.com. E-mail: mscoles@southseneca.k12.ny.us.

SCOLL, EULALIE ELIZABETH, writer, researcher; b. Vancouver, Wash., Mar. 6, 1920; d. Frederick and Elizabeth (Williamson) Laws; m. James Leslie Hildebrand; children; James, Frederick. BS, Women's U. Tex., 1941; MS, Salve Regina U., 1989, PhD, 1996. Engring. draftsman for Dr. Urey Manhattan Project, N.Y.C.; high fashion designer N.Y.C. Interior decorator. Author: The Role and Abuse of Women as Portrayed in Three Dostoevsky's Major Novels, 1989, Nietzsche Journal of Antichrist Tibetan Buddhism Versus Christianity, 1991, Dostoevsky's Sonya and Martha: Fiction and Reality, 1996. Mem. AAUW, Am. Assn. Advancement Slavic Studies, Nat. Trust for Historic Preservation, Nat. Mus. Women in the Arts, Am. Soc. Phys. Rsch., Inc., The Authors Guild, Inc., Newport Preservation Soc., Newport Hist. Soc., Asian Soc., Naval War Found., Internat. Dostoevsky Soc., Bailey's Beach Oldest Beach Club Am. Achievements include a great contribution to both world literature and specifically Russian literature; research in top Dostoyevsky scholars, who the prototype for the prostitute Sonya in Crime and Punishment was in real life.

SCORNAIENCHI, JOAN WEBB, supervisor, consultant; b. Johnstown, Pa. d. Calvin John and Amelia Maystrovich Webb; m. John Joseph Scornaienchi, Apr. 19, 1997. BSc, Ind. U. Pa., 1981, MA, 1982. Specialist drug and alcohol prevention Highland Ctr. of Mercy Hosp., Johnstown, Pa., 1982—83; adminstr. Kent State U., Ohio, 1983—94; bus. and industry liaison officer Cambria County C.C., Johnstown, 1995—96; customer svc. rep. Caterpillar Fin. Svcs., Columbia, Md., 1997—2000; edn. program specialist Md. State Dept. Edn., Balt., 2001—; co-founder, etiquette and protocol cons. Ambassador Protocol, Columbia, 2005—. Trainer presentation Bus. Etiquette, 2006, Modern Manners, 2006. Co-author: (article) The Residence Hall Experience, 1985. Mem. Balt./Wash. C. of C., 2005—; vol. Balt. City Teen Ct., 2003—, mem. adv. com., 2003—. Recipient Diversity award, Kent State U., 1991, Orientation Week Creative Program award, 1992, citation, City of Balt. Mayor's Office, 2004, Emerging Leader award, South Atlantic Region Soroptimist Internat., 2006. Mem.: Soroptimist Internat. Howard County (treas. 2004—06, com. chair 2004—06, pres. 2006—), Nat. Assn. Multicultural Edn., Nat. Grants Mgmt. Assn. Avocations: travel, reading, writing, etiquette training, bicycling. Home: 6209 Bird Race Columbia MD 21045 E-mail: joanwebbs@comcast.net.

SCOTLAND, SUSAN JANE, artist, educator; b. Oakland, Calif., Feb. 01; d. Marie M. Sutton; 1 child, Spencer Joseph. BA, U. Tex., 1992; studied painting with Neal Wilson and Jill Penke, Tex. State U. Cert. tchg. State of Tex. Tchr. Waco (Tex.) Sch. Dist., 1993—. Author various poetry; exhibitions include Amsterdam Whitney Gallery, N.Y.C., Montserrat Gallery, Gallerie Gora, Montreal, Can., 2005. Mem.: Art Ctr. Waco, Mus. of Art, Austin Tex., Mexic Arte Mus., Art House at Jones Ctr., Women and Their Work. Independent. Avocations: theater, tennis, travel, painting, golf. Office Phone: 251-715-1326. Personal E-mail: sscotland_88@hotmail.com.

SCOTT, ADRIENNE, social worker, psychotherapist; b. N.Y.C. BA, Finch Coll., 1957; MA in English, NYU, 1958, postgrad., 1958-62, NY Psychoanalytic Inst., 1998—2000; MSW, Adelphi U., Garden City, N.Y., 1988. Mem. English faculty Fordham U., N.Y.C., 1966-68; editor-in-chief Blueboy Mag., Miami, Fla., 1974; editor "M" Mag., N.Y.C., 1976; mem. English faculty NYU, 1958-65; pres. Googolplex Video, N.Y.C., 1981-86; clin. social worker

Mt. Sinai Hosp., N.Y.C., 1988-93, Stuyvesant Polyclinic, N.Y.C., 1993-95. Presenter Nat. Methadone Conf., 1992. Author: Film as Film, 1970; contbg. editor Menstyle Mag., 1995; contbr. articles to numerous mags., including Vogue, Interview, N.Y. mag.; pioneer in fashion video; videographer documentaries; performance artist in Robert Wilson's King of Spain, 1973. Mem. exec. com. Adopt-An-AIDS Rschr. Program Rockefeller U.; nat. co-chairperson Gay Rights Nat. Lobby, 1976. Mem. NASW (cert.), AAUW, Assn. for Psychoanalytic Self Psychology, Am. Psychoanalytic Assn. (assoc.). Office: 165 E 66th St New York NY 10021-6132 Business E-Mail: freudnut@nyc.rr.com.

SCOTT, ANN MARIE, medical/surgical nurse; b. Memphis, July 6, 1956; d. Calvin G. and Peggy Ann (Graham) Youngblood; m. Ronnie W. Scott, Nov. 9, 1974 (div. 2000); children: Kelly Marie, Tyler Andrew. BSN, U. Tenn., Memphis, 1985. Staff nurse ENT/thoracic VA Med. Ctr., Memphis, 1985-88; staff nurse Plus team Meth. Hosp., Memphis, 1990-92; staff nurse registry Ft. Sanders Park West Hosp., Knoxville, Tenn., 1992-95; substitute nurse Sch. Health Clinic Fayette County Sch. Sys., Ga., 2001—; night shift charge nurse LaFayette Nursing and Rehab., Fayetteville, Ga., 2004—. Home: 610 Grecken Grn Peachtree City GA 30269-2728 Personal E-mail: anngsofptc1@juno.com.

SCOTT, ANNE BYRD FIROR, history professor; b. Montezuma, Ga., Apr. 24, 1921; d. John William and Mary Valentine (Moss) Firor; m. Andrew Mackay Scott, June 2, 1947; children: Rebecca, David MacKay, Donald MacKay. AB, U. Ga., 1941; MA, Northwestern U., 1944; PhD, Radcliffe Coll., 1958; LHD (hon.), Lindenwood Coll., 1968, Queens Coll., 1985, Northwestern U., 1989, Radcliffe Coll., 1990, U. of the South, 1990, Cornell Coll., 1991. Congressional rep., editor LWV of U.S., 1944-53; lectr. history Haverford Coll., 1957-58, U. N.C., Chapel Hill, 1959-60; asst. prof. history Duke U., Durham, N.C., 1961-67, assoc. prof., 1968-70, prof., 1971-80, W.K. Boyd prof., 1980-91, W.K. Boyd prof. emerita, 1992—, chmn. dept., 1981-85; Gastprofessor Universität, Bonn, Germany, 1992-93. Vis. prof. Johns Hopkins U., 1972-73, Stanford U., 1974, Harvard U., 1984, Cornell Coll., 1993, Williams Coll., 1994, U. Miss., 2000; Times-Mirror scholar Huntington Libr., 1995; vice chmn. Nat. Humanities Ctr., 1991-98; mem. adv. com. Schlesinger Libr.; lectr. in field. Author: The Southern Lady, 1970, 25th anniversary edit., 1995, (with Andrew MacKay Scott) One Half the People, 1974, Making the Invisible Woman Visible, 1984, Natural Allies, 1991; editor: Jane Addams, Democracy and Social Ethics, 1964, The American woman, 1970, Women in American Life, 1970, Women and Men in American Life, 1976, Unheard Voices, 1993; mem. editl. bd. Revs. in Am. History, 1976-81, Am. Quar., 1974-78, Jour. So. History, 1978-84; contbr. articles to profl. jours. Chmn. Gov.'s Commn. on Status of Women, 1963-64; mem. Citizens Adv. Council on Status of Women U.S., 1964-68; trustee Carnegie Corp., 1977-85, W.W. Ctr. for Scholars, 1977-84; chmn. bd. dirs. Nat. Cmty. Investment Fund, 1996—2002. AAUW fellow, 1956-57; grantee NEH, 1967-68, 76-77, Nat. Humanities Ctr., 1980-81; grad. medal Radcliffe Coll., 1986, Duke U. medal, 1991, John Caldwell medal N.C. Humanities Coun., 1994; fellow Ctrl. Advanced Study in Behavioral Sci., 1986-87; Fulbright scholar, 1984, 92-93. Fellow Am. Acad. Arts & Sci; mem. Am. Antiquarian Soc., Orgn. Am. Historians (exec. bd. 1973-76, pres. 1983, Disting. Pub. Svc. award 2002), So. Hist. Assn. (exec. bd. 1976-79, pres. 1989), Soc. Am. Historians, Phi Beta Kappa. Democrat. E-mail: ascott2@email.unc.edu, ascott@duke.edu.

SCOTT, ARISTA V., secondary school educator; b. Sylacauga, Ala., Feb. 19, 1957; d. Johnny G. and Mary E. Varner; m. James K. Scott, May 13, 1978; children: Caleb Raleigh, John Lucas. BS in Environ. Health, Auburn U., Ala., 1977; MEd in Secondary Sci., U. Montevallo, Ala., 1988, EdS Tchr. Leader, 2005. Nat. Bd. Cert. Tchr., Chemistry 2005. Tchr. Childersburg HS, Ala., 1988—92, Sylacauga HS, 1992—. Mem.: Phi Kappa Phi. Avocations: gardening, reading. Office: Sylcauga HS 701 N Broadway Sylacauga AL 35150

SCOTT, BERNICE G., county official; b. Nov. 16, 1944; d. Alexander and Adeline Finch Green; m. Thomas Edward Gilmore, Feb. 25, 1987; children: Valerie La-Mon Scott Washington, Kent Orlando. AA (with honors), Midlands Tech. Coll., 1976. Tax collector Richland County Treasurer's Ofc., Columbia, S.C., 1979-85; asst. clerk of coun. Richland County Council, Columbia, 1984-85; ombudsman Richland County Adminstrn., Columbia, 1985-87; courtroom asst., court adminstrn. Richland County Court Adminstrn., Columbia, 1987-88; paralegal Lewis, Rogers & Lark P.A., Columbia, 1993—. Coun. mem. Richland County, Columbia, S.C., 1988—; mem. Mt. Nebo Bapt. Ch. (sr. choir pres., young adult sch. tchr., usher bd., deacon bd. mem.); appointed mem. transition team Gov.-elect James Hodges, S.C., 1998; chairperson Richland County Devel. and Svcs. com., 1996; mem. Lower Richland Devel. Coun.; chairperson of bd. Lower Richland Cmty. Health Care Assn. Mem. Nat. Assn. of Counties, Nat. Assn. of Black County Officials. Office: Office County Council PO Box 192 Columbia SC 29202-0192

SCOTT, BRENDA D., writer; b. Tampa-Sneads, Fla. d. Alonzie III and Felicia (Lopez) Scott. Diploma in child guidance, Lively Vocat. Tech. Ctr., Tallahassee, 1987; AA in Sci. Edn., Tallahassee C.C., 1993; BS in Reading Edn., Fla. State U., 1995; AA in Criminal Justice, Tallahassee CC, 2000. Contbr. poetry to mags., other publs including Internat. Women's Writing Guild; author: (screenplay) Surprise (Guild Membership movie), 1998, Mrs. Jellie Mae's Store, 1999, poetry book, Down-Home-News, 2000. Mem. West Fla. Literary Assn., Am. Black Book Writers Assn., Acad. Am. Poets, Internat. Soc. Poets, Women Ministering Biblically. Democrat. African Meth. Episcopalian. Avocations: reading, writing, movies, church activities, sports. Home and Office: PO Box 171 Sneads FL 32460-0171

SCOTT, BRENDA SUE, elementary school educator; b. Booneville, Miss., July 18, 1945; d. Rupert E. and Christine (Gooch) Pike; m. Derryl Anthony Scott, Oct. 29, 1965; children: Kelley Scott Baldwin, Sabrina Svetlana. BA in Elem. Edn., U. Miss., 1985, MEd in Elem. Edn., 1989. Kingergarten tchr. Goodwin Presch., Booneville, 1972-83; tchr. Booneville Sch. Dist., 1985—. Recipient Presdl. award for excellence in edn. Pres. Clinton, 1993, Tchr. of Yr. award Booneville Rotary, 1995. Mem. NSTA, Miss. Sci. Tchrs. Assn. (State Presdl. award 1993, Outstanding Miss. Sci. Tchr. award 1993), Kappa Kappa Iota (pres.-elect 1995). Avocations: gardening, hunting, fishing, cooking, crafts. Home: RR 1 Box 71A Booneville MS 38829-9801 Office: Booneville Mid Sch 300A W George Allen Dr Booneville MS 38829

SCOTT, CARLA ANNE, musician, educator; b. Elmhurst, Ill., Feb. 6, 1951; d. William Frederick and Clara Lou Sommer; m. Kinney Duane Scott, Dec. 22, 1984; 1 child, Joelle Lynn Jewell. BA, Adams State Coll., Alamosa, Colo., 1973; Kodaly level 1, Colo. Coll., 1998; Kodaly Level 2, U. Colo., Boulder, 1999. Asst. libr., music instr. Lamar C.C., Colo., 1974—75; tchr. elem. band and gen. music Harrison Sch. Dist. 2, Colorado Springs, 1975—. Prin. oboist Pueblo Symphony Orch., Pikes Peak Philharm.; 2d oboe and English horn Chamber Orch. of the Springs; free lance musician, Colo.; presenter in field. Pres. Pikes Peak Philharm., Colorado Springs, 2002—; orch. rep. Pueblo Symphony Orch., Colo. Recipient 25 Yr. award, Colo. Music Educators Assn., 2004. Home: 3267 Teardrop Cir Colorado Springs CO 80917-3319 Office: Ivywild Elem Sch 1604 S Cascade Colorado Springs CO 80906 Office Phone: 719-328-4349. E-mail: casoboe@pcisys.net.

SCOTT, CAROL LEE, child care educator; b. Monte Vista, Colo., Jan. 10, 1944; d. Robert A. and Thelma G. (Allen) Jay; m. Bates E. Shaw, June 4, 1966 (dec. Feb. 1976); children: Crystal A., Sharon L.; m. James W. Scott, July 23, 1977. BA in Home Econs., Friends U., 1965; MS, Okla. State U., 1973. Cert. in family and consumer scis., child and parenting specialist; lic. profl. counselor. Receptionist Cen. Assembly of God Ch., Wichita, Kans., summer 1965; office worker Henry's Inc., Wichita, 1965-66; tchr. home econs. Wichita High Sch. South, 1966, Cir. High Sch., Towanda, Kans., 1966-68, Fairfax (Okla.) High Sch., 1968-74; tchr. vocat. home econs. Derby (Kans.) High Sch., 1974-75; child devel. specialist Bi-State Mental Health Found., Ponca City, Okla., 1975-87; instr. child care Pioneer Tech. Ctr., Ponca City, 1987-98, dir., 1987-89, 93-98; training, curriculum splst. Tinker AFB, Ponca City, Okla., 1998—2001; dir. CDC East Tinker AFB, Okla., 2001—05, CDC West Tinker AFB, 2005—. Cons. Phil Fitzgerald Assocs. Archs., Ponca City, 1980, Head Start Okla., 1981-86; trainer, paraprofl. Child Care Careers, 1980—; validator Early Childhood programs, Nat. Assn. Edn. Young Children 1992—; adj. faculty Rose State Coll., Midwest City, Okla., 2002-. Contbg. author Child Abuse Prevention Mini Curriculum. Mem. sch. bd. Ponca City Schs., 1982-85, title IV-A parent com., 1985-89; area chmn. Heart Fund, 1985; chmn. edn. com. Dist. XVII Child Abuse Prevention Task Force, Okla., 1985-98, treas., 1989-98; mem. cultural affairs com. Ponca City Adv. Bd., 1986-89; co-chair Week of the Young Child Com. for Kay County, 1991-98; mem. curriculum adv. com. Ctr. Early Childhood Profl. Devel., Univ. Okla., 1998-. Mem. Am. Assn. Family and Consumer Scis., Okla. Assn. Family and Consumer Scis., Early Childhood Assn. Okla., (sec. 1999-2000), So. Early Childhood Assn., No. Okla. Early Childhood Assn. (chmn. 1992-93, 93-94, exec. com. at-large 1994-98), Mid Del. Early Childhood Assn. (pres. 2002, sec. 2005, 06), Nat. Assn. for Edn. Young Children, Am. Assn. U. Women. Republican. Methodist. Home: 205 Wimbledon Rd Midwest City OK 73130-4917 Office: 72MSG/SVYW 6120 Arnold St Tinker Afb OK 73145-8106

SCOTT, CATHERINE DOROTHY, librarian, library and information scientist, consultant; b. June 21, 1927; d. Leroy Stearns Scott and Agnes Frances (Meade) Scott Schellenberg. AB in English, Cath. U. Am., 1950, MS in Libr. Sci., 1955. Asst. libr. Export-Import Bank USA, Washington, 1951-55, Nat. Assn. Home Builders, 1955-62, reference libr., 1956-62; founder, chief tech. libr. Bellcomm, Inc., subs. AT&T, 1962-72; chief libr. Nat. Air, Space Mus. Smithsonian Instn., 1972-82, chief libr. Mus. Reference Ctr., 1982-88, sr. reference libr., 1989-95; info. cons., 1995—. Presdl. appointee, mem. Nat. Commn. Librs., Info. Sci., 1971—76; bd. visitors Cath. U. Am. Libr. Sci. Sch., Librs., 1984—93. Editor: International Handbook of Aerospace Awards and Trophies, 1980, 81; guest editor: Aeronautics and Space Flight Collections, 1985, in Spl. Collections, 1984. Vice chmn. DC Rep. Com., Washington, 1960—68; del. Rep. Nat. Conv., San Francisco, 1964; mem. platform com. Rep. Nat. Com., 1968, sec., 1964; del. Rep. Nat. Conv., Miami, Fla., 1968, mem. Inaugural Com., 1969, 1972. Named to Hon. Order Ky. Cols., 1968; recipient Sec.'s Disting. Svc. award Smithsonian Instn., 1976, Alumni Achievement award Cath. U. Am., 1977, Century Circle, 1998—, Disting. Fed. Svc. Nat. Commn. Libr. and Info. Sci. medal, 1985. Mem.: Cath. U. Am. Saint Thomas Aquinas Soc., Spl. Librs. Assn. (cons. com. 1976—91, bd. dirs. 1987—94, award com. 1990—91, pres.-elect 1991—92, bd. dirs. 1991—94, immediate past pres. 1993—94, chpt. cons. com. 1994—98, conf. program facilitator 1998—2006), Am. Soc. Info. Sci, League Rep. Women DC (bd. dirs. 1995—97, nominating com. 1996—97, contbg. 1999—), Nat. Fedn. Rep. Women, Cath. U. Am. Devel. Com., Friends of Cath. U. Librs. (founder, pres. 1984—88, exec. coun. 1984—96, sustaining 1998—), Internat. Fedn. Libr. Assns. (del. 1976, 1983, 1985, 1988—89), Nat. Mus. Women in Arts, Am. Soc. Assn. Execs., Spl. Librs. Assn. (Washington chpt. pres. 1973—74, chair aerospace divsn. 1974—75, pres. 1992—93, past pres. 1993—94, chair assn. awards and honors 1994—95, conf. planner 1996—2006, convenor ret. caucus 1997—99, assn. dir. 1987—90, Hall of Fame 1996), Cath. U. Century Club, Spl. Librs. Assn. Legacy Club, Capital Yacht Club. Fax: 202-488-9223. Office Phone: 202-554-3928.

SCOTT, CHARNETA CLAUDETTA, psychologist, educator; b. Jacksonville, Fla., May 3, 1963; d. Charles Alexander Scott and Venetia Lemar McLemoure. BS, U. of Fla., 1981—85; MA, Ea. N.Mex U., 1985—86; PhD, Howard U., 1992—2003. Lic. Professional Counselor D.C. Dept. of Health Health and Licensing, 2004. Clin. psychologist D.C. Dept. of Mental Health, 1996—; coord. of ct. services, therapist Francis and Associates, P.C., Washington, 2001—; adj. faculty Trinity U., Washington, 2000—. Assoc. dir. for conf. adminstrn. WBC Learning Conf., Washington, 2005—. Team mem. Capitol Area Crisis Response Team, Washington, 2004. Recipient Dedication to Work with Children, Francis and Associates, 2004, U. of Fla. Hall of Fame, 1984—85; Walter and Theodora Daniel Endowed Ednl. Rsch. Grant, Walter and Theodora Daniel Ednl. Rsch. Fund, 1998. Mem.: APA, Assn. for Play Therapy, Inc., The Am. Acad. of Experts in Traumatic Stress. D-Liberal. Roman Cath. Avocation: dance. Home: 520 U St NW Washington DC 20001 Office Phone: 202-409-7100. Personal E-mail: charneta@aol.com.

SCOTT, CHERYL M., foundation administrator, healthcare educator; BA, U. Wash., 1975, MA in Health Adminstrn., 1977. Joined Group Health Coop., Seattle, 1979, regional v.p., exec. v.p., COO, pres., CEO, 1997—2004, pres. emerita, 2004—; COO Bill and Melinda Gates Found., Seattle, 2006—. Clin. assoc. prof. Dept. Health Svcs. U. Wash. Sch. Pub. Health and Cmty. Medicine, 2004—; past bd. mem. Am.'s Health Insurance Plans; past chair Alliance of Cmty. Health Plans and Healthcare Forum; bd. chair Health Tech. Ctr.; mem. Com. on Redesigning Health Insurance Benefits, Payment and Performance Improvement Programs Inst. Medicine. Past chair Alliance for Edn. U. Wash. Health Adminstrn. Program, chair External Adv. Com.; chair King County's Blue Ribbon Com. on Election Reform; trustee Wash. State Life Scis. Discovery Fund. Office: Bill and Melinda Gates Found 1551 Eastlake Ave E Seattle WA 98101 Office Phone: 206-448-6755. Office Fax: 206-448-6464. E-mail: scott.cm@ghc.org.*

SCOTT, CONCETTA CIOTTI, artist, educator; b. Phila., Jan. 17, 1927; d. Giulio J. Ciotti and Adelina D'Andrea; m. Pierre Brutsche Scott, Apr. 20, 1963; children: Elizabeth Ann, Christopher John. Assocs. Degree, Moore Coll. Art and Design, 1951; student, Embroiders Guild Am., Inc., 1967—78, No. Va. C.C., Woodbridge, Va., 1988. Graphics designer, illustrator, freelance artist various advt. agys. and dept. stores, Phila., 1946—54; tchr. art grades 1-12 Melrose Acad., Melrose Park, Pa., 1951—54; designer ads and direct mail The Hecht Co., Washington, 1954—56; designer, dir. art Woodward and Lothrop Stores, Washington, 1956—63; freelance artist Alexandria, McLean, Va., 1963—66; tchr. art St. Luke's Sch., McLean, Va., 1974—75; tchr. art, cons. Montessori Sch. McLean, 1975—98. McLean rep. Fairfax County Coun. Arts, Annandale, Va., 1988—93. Splash 6 Book 4, 2000, Elan Mag., Sept., 2000, cover-illustrations, Roster Nat. League Am. Pen Women, 1982, 1984, rhyme and play book, Move Over Mother Goose, 1987, one-woman shows include Atrium Gallery, Falls Ch., Va., 2003, McLean Art Juried Show, 2003, Arlington Free Clinic, 2003, Brookside Gardens Gallery, Wheaton, Md., 1989, The Charles Sumner Sch. Mus., Washington, 1990, The Manor House Gallery, Green Spring, Alexandria, 1991, Alexandria, Va., 2001, NIH Galleries, Bethesda, Md., 1992, GTE Govt. Sys. Corp., Chantilly, Va., 1993, Barry Gallery, Marymount U., Arlington, Va., 1994, The Asman Gallery, NBC-TV Studios, Washington, 1995, 2000, Clin. Ctr. Galleries, NIH, Bethesda, 1996, La Vignette, Dinan, Brittany, France, 1999, Gallery West, Goodwin House West, Falls Church, 1999, Gallery Walk, Goodwin House, East, Alexandria, 2000, Atrium Gallery, Fairfax, 2003, LMI Corp., McLean, 2005, Quiet Waters, Md., 2006, Brookside Gardens, 2006, two-persons shows, The XXth Century Gallery, Williamsburg, Va., 1991, The Sporting Club Gallery, McLean, 1992, Georgetown Med. Ctr. Gallery, Washington, 1996, Am. Hort. Soc., River Farm, Alexandria, 1997, U.S. Geol. Survey Gallery, Reston, Va., 2001, exhibitions include Miniature Painters, Sculptors and Gravers Washington, 1993, internat. exhbn., 1997—2004, exhibitions include Nat. League Am. Pen Women, Roanoke, Va., 1985, Furman U., S.C., 1987, Fells Point Gallery, Balt., 1994, 1997, 1998, 1999, Miniature Arts Soc. Fla., Dunedin, 2000, 2001, Seaside Gallery Miniature Paintings Show, Nags Head, N.C., 2001, Paper Mill Gallery Miniatures, 2004, World Fedn. Miniatures, Smithsonian Instn., Washington, 2004, numerous group shows including, Nat. League Am. Pen Women, George Mason U., 2000, exhibited in group shows at Va. Watercolor Soc., Martinsville, Va., 2000, Phila. Watercolor Soc., Atlantic City, 2000, McLean Art Club, Emerson Gallery, 2000, 2004, Arts Coun. Fairfax, Annandale, Va., 2000, Balt. Watercolor Soc., Bethesda, Md., 2001, Va. Watercolor Soc., Richmond, 2001, Washington Water Color Assn., Bethesda, 2001, Ctrl. Va. Watercolor Guild, Charlottesville, 2001, Berryville-Clarke County Coun., Millwood, Va., 2001, Art League/Torpedo Factory, Alexandria, 2001, Phila. Watercolor Soc., The Am. Coll., Bryn Mawr, Pa., 2001, Atlantic City, 2002, Art League, 2002, Internat. Miniature Shows, 2002, Art League, 2003, Internet Miniature Shows, 2003, Left Bank Cafe, 2003, Sumner Mus., Washington, D.C., 2004, Art League, 2004, 2005, Paper Mill Gallery, NJ, 2005, Strathmore Hall, Md., 2005, Moore College Alumni Juried Show, 2006. Vol. art tchr. grades 1-3 Churchill Rd. Sch., McLean, 1972; aide 4H Club, McLean, Great Falls, 1973—75; vol. mail and phones Dem. Party, Washington, 1960. Recipient Distinctive Merit award, Art Dirs. Club Washington, 1961, 1962, 1963, grant, artist residency, Les Amis de La Grande Vigne, 1999; fellow P.P. Morris Grad. fellow, Moore Coll. Art and Design, Phila., 1951. Mem.: Nat. League Am. Pen Women (art editor 1980—82, biennial conv. chmn. 1983—84, lectr. history miniature art 2005), Vienna Arts Soc. (lectr. miniature painting 2004), Fairfax Art League (workship instr. miniature painting 2003, group shows 2003), Art League, Miniature Arts Soc. Fla., Miniature Painters, Sculptors and Gravers Soc. Washington, McLean Art Club (show chmn. 1977, program chair 2003—05, lectr. 2004, chmn. registration 2004, program chmn. 2004—06, bd. dirs., v.p. 2006—), Potomac Valley Watercolorists (publicity/telephone 1996—98), Washington Water Color Assn. (show chmn. 1996—2001, show co-chmn. 2002—), Balt. Watercolor Soc. (signature), Phila. Water Color Soc. (signature), Va. Watercolor Soc. (art bd. 1993, shows 2004, signature, awards com.). Roman Catholic. Avocations: photography, reading, music, opera. Home: 1111 Dead Run Dr Mc Lean VA 22101 Office Phone: 703-356-5053.

SCOTT, DANELLE KAY, secondary school educator; b. Greenville, Mich., Aug. 29, 1978; d. Darcia June Kelley; m. Jamie Allen Scott, Dec. 3, 1975; 1 child, Aidan Ezra. BA, Spring Arbor U., Mich., 2000; MA, Spring Arbor U., 2006. Secondary educator Mich., 2000, cert. sch. counselor Mich., 2006. Social studies tchr. Tri County H.S., Howard City, Mich., 2001—. Varsity soccer coach Tri County H.S., 2004—06. Office Phone: 231-937-4338.

SCOTT, DEBORAH EMONT, curator; b. Passaic, N.J. d. Harold and Rhoda (Baumgarten) Emont; m. George Andrew Scott, June 4, 1983; children: Meredith Suzanne, Diana Faith. BA, Rutgers U., 1973, Livingston Coll.; MA, Oberlin Coll., 1979. Asst. curator Allen Meml. Art Mus., Oberlin, Ohio, 1977-79; curator collections Memphis Brooks Mus. Art, 1979-83; curator The Nelson-Atkins Mus. Art, Kansas City, 1983—, chief curator, 1998—. Project dir. Kansas City Sculpture Pk., 1986-01. Author: (catalogue) Alan Shields, 1983, (essay) Jonathan Borofsky, 1988, (essay) Judith Shea, 1989, (interview) John Ahearn, 1990, (essay) Gerhard Richter, 1990, (essay) Kathy Muehlemann, 1991, (essay) Nate Fors, 1991, (essay) Julian Schnabel, 1991, (essay) Louise Bourgeois, 1994, (essay) Joel Shapiro, 1995, (essay) Lewis deSoto, 1996, (catalogue) Ursula von Rydingsvard, 1997; contbr.: Celebrating Moore: Works from the Collection of the Henry Moore Foundation, Selected by David Mitchinson, 1998, Modern Sculpture at The Nelson-Atkins Museum of Art: An Anniversary Celebration, 1999, (CD ROM) Masterworks for Learning: A College Collection Catalogue, Allen Memorial Art Museum, Oberlin College, 1998. Office: Nelson-Atkins Mus Art 4525 Oak St Kansas City MO 64111-1873

SCOTT, DEBORAH KATHLEEN, private investigator; b. Lakewood, NJ, Dec. 2, 1949; d. Joseph Paul and Emaret Dorothy Jackson; divorced; children: Brian, Emaret, Carmin. GED, 1988. Cert. clerk typist, office procedures 1988, prvt. investigator 2000. Part-time driver limo and taxi svc., 1985—91; bartender, 1981—2000; pvt. investigator Krayer Investigators, 2000—02, Aunley/Foss Investigators, 2002—03; elected constable Warrior Run, 2002—04; pvt. investigator, supr. U.S. Security, 2003—05. Author: Are We Living in a Third World Country?, 1996, Creation of the World who Children ask and How Would God Answer., 2005. Mem. baseball league, Warrior Run, Sugar Notch, Pa., 1984—88; mem. Hanover Football League, 1982—88; advisor, pub. rels., pres., coord. Blue Knights Drum and Bugle Corp., bd. dirs., 1982—87. Recipient Luzerne Dist. Atty. Office, Wilkes-Barre, 2001, 2002. Mem.: DAR, Ea. Del. Nation, Daus. Am. Republican. Avocations: swimming, dance, boating, baseball, rollerskating. Office: 395 Hanover St Warrior Run PA 18706 Office Phone: 570-239-7717. Personal E-mail: lazydks@aol.com.

SCOTT, DEBRA A., special education educator; b. Heidelberg, Germany, Aug. 21, 1958; arrived in U.S., 1963; d. John Thomas Sr. and Ada Mae (Lavoine) Johnston; 1 child from previous marriage, David Adam. AA, Edison C.C., Piqua, Ohio, 1996; BS in Edn. magna cum laude, U. Dayton, Ohio, 1999, MS in Edn., 2004. Tchr. multi-handicapped Miami County Ednl. Svc. Ctr., Troy, Ohio, 1999—2001; resource room tchr. Sidney City Schs., 2001—05, tchr. multi-disabilities, 2005—. Yearbook advisor Sidney Mid. Sch., 2005—; data specialist cadre Ohio Edn. Assn, Columbus, Ohio, 2005; mem. profl. rights and responsibilities com. We. Ohio Edn. Assn., 2005—. With USN, 1981—88. Mem.: Golden Key. Democrat. Roman Catholic. Avocations: poetry, drawing. Home: 9130 Brush Creek Dr Piqua OH 45356-9384 Office: Sidney Mid Sch 980 Fair Rd Sidney OH 45365

SCOTT, ELIZABETH S., law educator; b. Washington, 1945; BA, Coll. William and Mary, 1967; JD, U. Va., 1977. Bar: Va. 1977. Atty. Michie, Hamlett, Donato & Lowry, Charlottesville, Va., 1977—78; legal dir. Forensic Psychiatry Clinic of Inst. Law, Psychiatry, and Pub. Policy U. Va., 1979—87, Univ. prof., 1992—, Robert C. Taylor rsch. prof., 1997—2001, Joseph C. Carter, Jr. rsch. prof., 2003—, now Class of 1962 prof. law, also founder & co-dir. Ctr. for Children, Families and the Law. Vis. prof. Columbia U. Sch. Law, 1987—88, 2001—02. Co-author: Children in the Legal System, 1997, Family Law: Cases, Text, Problems, 1998. Mem. rsch. ethics com. U. Va. Med. Sch.; bd. dirs. Children, Youth and Family Services, Charlottesville. Mem.: John D. and Catherine T. MacArthur Found. Rsch. Network on Adolescent Devel. and Juvenile Justice. Office: U Va Sch Law 580 Massie Rd Charlottesville VA 22903-1789 Office Phone: 434-924-3217. E-mail: es@virginia.edu.

SCOTT, EUGENIE CAROL, science foundation director, anthropologist; b. LaCrosse, Wis., Oct. 24, 1945; d. Allen K. and Virginia Meliss (Derr) S.; m. Robert Abner Black, Oct. 18, 1965 (div. 1970); m. Thomas Charles Sager, Dec. 30, 1971; 1 child, Carrie Ellen Sager. BS, U. Wis., Milw., 1967, MS, 1968; PhD, U. Mo., 1974; DSc (hon.), McGill U., 2003, Ohio State U., 2005, Mt. Holyoke Coll., 2006. Asst. prof. anthropology U. Ky., Lexington, 1974-82; postdoctoral fellow U. Calif., San Francisco, 1983-84; asst. prof. U. Colo., Boulder, 1984-86; exec. dir., pub. newsletter NCSE Reports, Nat. Ctr. Sci. Edn., Oakland, Calif., 1987—. Vis. prof., U. Kans., 1976; bd. dirs. Biol. Scis. Curriculum Study, Colorado Springs, Colo., 1993-99; pub. Bookwatch Revs., 1988-92. Author, editor: Biology Textbooks, The New Generation, 1990, Evolution and Creationism: An Introduction, 2004; co-author: Teaching About Evolution and the Nature of Science, 1998; prodr. videotape series How Scientists Know About.; featured guest as sci. authority on creationism and/or pseudosci. Mem. nat. adv. bd. Ams. United for Separation of Ch. and State, Washington, 1995—. Recipient Disting. Alumnus award U. Mo. Arts and Scis., 1993, Isaac Asimov Sci. award Am. Humanist Assn., 1998, James Randi Skeptic of Yr. award Skeptic Soc., 1999, Bruce Alberts award Am. Soc. Cell Biology, 1999, 1st Amendment award Playboy Found., 1999, Nat. Sci. Bd. Pub. Svc. award, 2003, Geol. Soc. Am. Pub. Svc. award, Calif. Sci. Tchr. Margaret Nicholson Dist. Svc. award, Ctr. for Inquiry Def. Sci. award. Fellow Com. for Sci. Investigation Claims of Paranormal (Sci. and Edn. award 1991), Calif. Acad. Scis. (elected 1994); mem. AAAS, Am. Assn. Phys. Anthropology (bd. dirs., exec. com. 1988-93, sec.-treas. 1993-97, pres. 2001-2003), Am. Anthropol. Assn. Office: Nat Ctr Sci Edn PO Box 9477 Berkeley CA 94709-0477 also: Nat Ctr Sci Edn 420 40th St Ste 2 Oakland CA 94609-2509 Office Phone: 510-601-7203. E-mail: scott@ncseweb.org.

SCOTT, FELICITY DALE ELLISTON, architecture educator, editor; d. Malcolm Elliston and Ruth Scott; m. Branden Wayne Joseph, May 3, 1996. BArch with honors, RMIT, Melbourne, 1990; BSc in History and Philosophy of Sci., U. Melbourne, 1991; MAUD, Harvard U., Cambridge, Mass., 1994; PhD, Princeton U., NJ, 2001. Asst. prof. art history and visual studies U. Calif., Irvine, 2003—06; asst. prof. architecture Columbia U., NYC, 2006—. Editor Grey Rm. jour., NYC, 1997—. Author: Architecture or Techno-Utopia: Politics After Modernism. ACLS/Henry Luce Dissertation fellow, Am. Coun.

Learned Societies, 1998—99, J. Paul Getty Postdoctoral fellow in Arts and Humanities, Getty Trust, 2002—03. Office: Columbia U GSAPP 1172 Amsterdam Ave New York NY 10027

SCOTT, GLORIA RANDLE, former college president; b. Apr. 14, 1938; d. Freeman and Juanita (Bell) Randle; m. Will Braxton Scott. AB, Ind. U., 1959, MA, 1960, PhD, 1965, LLD, 1977; DHL, Fairleigh Dickinson U., 1978, Westfield State Coll., 1992, Wilson Coll., 1992, Mt. Vernon Coll., Marian Coll., 1999. Rsch. assoc. in genetics Inst. Psychiat. Rsch. Ind. U. Med. Ctr., Indpls., 1961-63; instr. biology Marian Coll., Indpls., 1961-65; dean students Knoxville Coll., Tenn., 1965-67; asst. to pres. N.C. Agrl. and Tech. State U., 1967-68, prof., 1967-76, dir. planning Inst. Rsch., 1973-76; prof. Tex. So. U., 1976-78; v.p., prof. Clark Coll., 1978-86; prof. Grambling State U., 1987; pres. Bennett Coll., Greensboro, NC, 1987-2001, founder Women's Leadership Inst., 1989; owner Scott's Bay Enterprises on Baffin Bay, Riviera, Tex., 1973—. Founding sec. bd. dirs. Africa U., Mutare, Zimbabwe, 1988-97; bd. dirs. Loew Corp.; vice chair Women's Coll. Coalition, 1990-94; bd. dirs. Nat. Assn. Ind. Colls. and Univs., 1992-96, Nat. Assn. Schs. and Colls. of the United Meth. Ch., 1993-95. Del. UN Decade for Women Internat. Forum, Nairobi, Kenya, 1985; chmn. del. UN Decade for Women Conf., Beijing, 1995; chmn. bd. Nat. Scholarship Fund for Negro Students, 1984-85; 1st v.p. Girl Scouts U.S., 1972-75, pres., 1975-78; bd. dirs. Wilson Coll., 1978-83, Nat. Urban League, 1976-85, Neal Marshall Club, Indian U. Alumni; mem bd. visitors Ind. U. Sch. Edn., Bloomington, 1988-94; bd. dirs. United Negro Coll. Fund, 1993-95, chair golden anniversary com., 1992-95; chair edn. adv. com. Delta Sigma Theta, 1989—; mem. adv. bd. James McGregor Leadership Acad., Md., 2000-05; mem. divsn. III pres.'s coun. NCAA, 1998-2001; founder Nat. African Am. Women's Leadership Inst., 1999; mentor Leadership Inst., 1997-98; mem. Internat. Women's Forum; chmn. Coun. Presidents Black Coll. Fund, UMC, 1997-99. Recipient Drum Major for Justice award, 1993, N.C. Gov's. award for Outstanding N.C. Women, 1991, Achievement award Delta Sigma Theta, 1994. Mem. Rotary (organizing founder East Greensboro 2000-01). E-mail: randle@rivnet.com.

SCOTT, GWENDOLYN LUTZ, internist; b. Akron, Ohio, May 25, 1924; d. Alfred C. and Charlotte Armstrong Lutz; m. Glen Turner Scott, Sept. 28, 1968; m. Joseph V. Morris (div.). BS, Ohio State U., Columbus, 1946; MD, U. Cin., 1950. Intern Grant Hosp., Chgo., 1950—51; resident U. Chgo., 1951—53; instr. medicine, cardiac clinician U. Cin. Med. Sch., 1953—67; physician pvt. practice, 1955—67; resident Rollman Psychiatric Inst., 1967—69, chief resident, 1969—70, dir. outpatient dept., cmty. svc. unit, 1970—71; staff psychiatrist Anclote Manor Hosp., Tarpon Springs, Fla., 1971—84, dir. tng. and edn., 1976—84; clin. assoc. prof. psychiatry U. Fla., Gainesville, 1977—84. Med. advisor, mem. adv. bd. Hospice Macon County, Highland, NC, 1981—93. Contbr. articles to profl. jours. Cardiology fellow, U. Cin., 1953—55. Mem.: APA, AMA (50 Yr. award), Fla. Psychiat. Soc., Fla. Med. Soc. (Physician Who Cares award 2004), Pinellas Psychiat. Assn., Pinellas Med. Soc., Mease Manor Residents Assn. (bd. dirs.), Dunedin Country Club, Sigma Xi, Chi Delta Phi, Alpha Epsilon Delta, Kappa Kappa Gamma. Presbyterian. Avocations: bridge, golf, organ, painting. Home: 700 Mease Plz Apt 802 Dunedin FL 34698

SCOTT, HELEN S., law educator; b. 1949; BA, Barnard Coll., 1970; JD, Columbia U., 1977. Bar: NY 1978, DC 1978. Atty., adviser Office of Chmn. FTC, Washington, 1977-78, atty., adviser Office of Commr., 1978-79; assoc. Shearman & Sterling, NYC, 1980-82; asst. prof. law NYU Sch. Law, NYC, 1983—85, assoc. prof., 1985—88, prof., 1988—. Co-chair Listing and Hearing Rev. Coun. NASDAQ. Recipient Legal Adv. of Yr. Award, US Small Bus. Adminstrn. Office: NYU Sch Law Vanderbilt Hall Rm 338 40 Washington Sq S New York NY 10012-1099 Office Phone: 212-998-6206. E-mail: helen.scott@nyu.edu.

SCOTT, JANE VICROY, microbiologist; b. Selma, Ala. d. C.E. and Eileen (Yeager) Vicroy; m. Jeffrey Glassberg, Jan. 9, 1977; 1 child, Matthew Scott. Student, Judson Coll., 1962-64; BA, Tex. Christian U., 1966, MS, 1968; PhD in Microbiology in Immunology, Baylor Coll. of Medicine, 1976. Postdoctoral fellow U. Calif., San Francisco, 1976-79; rsch. assoc. Rockefeller U., N.Y.C., 1979-82; rsch. microbiologist Lederle Labs., Pearl River, N.Y., 1982-84, group leader, 1985, dept. head vaccines R & D, 1986-89, sect. head, 1989-90, dir. bus. devel., 1991-95; dir. indsl. liaison NYU Med. Ctr., N.Y.C., 1996-2000; dir. bus. devel. PLIVA, Inc., Livingston, NJ, 2000—05; prin. HVA, Inc., Livingston, 2005—. Adj. faculty Rockefeller U., N.Y.C., 1982-84. Campaign mgr. for Town Supr., 1990; dist. leader Dem. Com., New Castle, N.Y., 1988-94. Mem. Am. Soc. for Microbiology, Assn. U. Tech. Mgrs., N.Am. Butterfly Assn. (sec.-treas. 1997—), Licensing Execs. Soc., Sigma Xi. Achievements include identification of lymphocytes as carrier of virus; antigenic variation in visna; development of acellular pertussis vaccine for U.S.; patent for purification of acellular pertussis vaccine; research in various drugs and delivery technology, licensing transactions. Office: HVA Inc 23 Fawn Dr Ste B Livingston NJ 07039 Office Phone: 973-597-0080.

SCOTT, JEAN A., university president; b. 1946; B in History, U. Richmond, 1968; M in History, Harvard U., 1969, PhD in History, 1974. Asst. prof. history Duke U., dir. admission; dean undergrad. admission Case We. Res. U., Ohio; assoc. provost acad. adminstrn., dean admissions Coll. William and Mary, Williamsburg, Va., 1989-94; v.p. enrollment and student svcs. SUNY, Potsdam, 1994—. Office: Potsdam Coll Pierrepont Ave Potsdam NY 13676-2294

SCOTT, JENNIFER MARIE, special education educator; b. Royal Oak, Mich., Dec. 10, 1973; d. Bruce Craven and Mary Helen Best Scott. BA in sci. and Psychology, Purdue U., 1996; MS in Edn., Ind. U., 1998, postgrad., 2003—. Cert. tchr. learning disabled/mentally handicapped Ind., dist. adminstr. Ind. Paraprofessional spl. edn. Paoli (Ind.) Jr. Sr. H.S., 1996—97; ADL supr., instr. Orange County Devel. and Rehab. Ctr./First Chance Ctr., Paoli, 1997—98; spl. edn. tchr. K-12 Medora (Ind.) Cmty. Schs., 1999; spl. edn. tchr. K-6 New Albany-Floyd County Schs., Georgetown, Ind., 1999—2002; assoc. instr., field experience supr. Ind. U., Bloomington, 2002—03; spl. edn. tchr. 9-12 Westfield (Ind.) Washington Schs., 2003—04; spl. edn. adminstr., program coord. N.W. Ind. Spl. Edn. Coop., Crown Point, 2005—05; spl. edn. adminstr., asst. dir. R.I.S.E. Spl. Svcs., Indpls., 2005—. Corp. joint spl. edn. adv. com. New Albany/Floyd County Sch. Corp., 2001—02; mem. leadership team com. Georgetown Elem. Sch., 2001—02, PTA sci. fair chmn., 1999—2001. RCIA sponsor St.Paul's Cath. Ch., Bloomington, 2002—03. Mem.: Ind. U. Sch. Adminstrs. Assn., Assn. Supervision and Curriculum, Coun. for Exceptional Children (polit. action com. 2003), Nat. Alliance for Mentally Ill, Pi Lambda Theta, Phi Delta Kappa. Democrat. Roman Catholic. Avocations: skiing, running, travel, reading.

SCOTT, JOAN WALLACH, historian, educator; b. Bklyn., Dec. 18, 1941; d. Samuel and Lottie (Tanenbaum) Wallach; m. Donald M. Scott, Jan. 30, 1965; children: Anthony Oliver, Elizabeth Rose. BA, Brandeis U., 1962; MA, U. Wis., 1964, PhD, 1969; LittD (hon.), SUNY, Stony Brook, 1989, Brown U., 1992; D honoris causa (hon.), U. Bergen, Norway, 2004. Asst. prof. history U. Ill., Chgo., 1970—72; asst. prof. Northwestern U., 1972—74; assoc. prof. U. NC, Chapel Hill, 1974—77, prof., 1977—80; Nancy Duke Lewis prof. history Brown U., Providence, 1980—85; Harold F. Linder prof. Sch. Social Sci., Inst. for Advanced Study, Princeton, NJ, 1985—. Dir. Pembroke Ctr. for Tchg. and Rsch. on Women, 1981—85, NEH Seminar for Coll. Tchrs., 1977, 1980—81; mem. Inst. for Advanced Study, Princeton, 1978—79; mem. editl. bd. Jour. Modern History, 1980—83; chair adv. com. Princeton U. Women's Studies Program, 1985—97; adv. com. Stanford Humanities Ctr., 1987; bd. govs. U. Calif. Humanities Rsch. Inst., 1998—2000. Author: The Glassworkers of Carmaux, 1974; author: (with Louise Tilly) Women Work and Family, 1978, rev. edit., 1987, Gender and the Politics of History, 1988; author: Only Paradoxes to Offer: French Feminists and the Rights of Man, 1996; editor (with Brian Tierney): Western Societies: A Documentary History, 1984; editor: (with Jill Conway and Susan Bourque) Learning About Women: Gender, Power and Politics, 1987; editor: (with James Gilbert) The Myth Making Frame of Mind: Social Imaginations of American Culture, 1992; editor: (with Judith Butler) Feminists Theorize the Political, 1992, Love and Politics in Wartime: Letters to My Wife, 1943-45, 1992 (Benedict S. Alper); editor: (with Cora Kaplan and Debra Keates) Transitions, Environments, Translations: Feminisms in International Politics; editor: (with Debra Keaates) Schools of Thought: Twenty-five Years of Interpretive Social Science, 2001; contbr. articles to profl. jours. Fellow NEH, 1975—76; grantee, Am. Coun. Learned Socs., 1978; Rsch. Tng. fellow, Social Sci. Rsch. Coun., 1966—68. Fellow: Sch. Criticism and Theory (sr.); mem.: AAUP (mem. Com. A (Acad. Freedom) 1993—, chmn. Com. A 1999—), Soc. French Hist. Studies, Berkshire Conf. Women Historians, Am. Hist. Assn. (chair com. on women historians 1978—80, Joan Kelly prize com. 1987—88, sec. Mod. European Sect. 1988—89, Joan Kelly prize 1989). Office: Inst for Advanced Study Einstein Dr Princeton NJ 08540-1914

SCOTT, JOY MARIE, elementary school educator, educator; b. Unionville, Mo., Sept. 19, 1953; m. Gerald Vincent Scott, Feb. 24, 1979. AA, Trenton Jr. Coll., 1973; BS, Northwest Mo. State U., Maryville, 1975; MS, Sul Ross State U., Alpine, Tex., 1980; teaching cert., 1990. Cert. English as a second lang., elem. reading. Form mgr. Byland's Double B Farms, Maryville, Mo., 1976-78; profl. farrier pvt. practice, Alpine, Tex., 1981-87; horseback riding dir. Permian Basin Girl Scout Coun., Odessa, Tex., 1988-90; tchr. 6th grade Culberson County ISD, Van Horn, Tex., 1990-91, chpt. I tchr., 1991—. Horseshow judge 4-H, Van Horn, Alpine, Tex., 1986, 87; owner Los Nopales. Contbr. articles to profl. jours. Steering com. Big Bend Food Coop., Alpine, Tex., 1986-89; bd. dirs. Culberson County Mus., Van Horn, Tex., 1994. Named Hardest Working Upper Classman Agriculture Club, Northwest Mo. State U., 1976. Mem. Internat. Reading Assn., Tex. State Reading Assn., Nat. Coun. Tchrs. Math. Mem. Soc. Of Friends. Avocations: gardening, reading, collecting antiques, upholstery, refinishing antiques. Home: PO Box 1046 Van Horn TX 79855-1046 Office: Eagle Elementary PO Box 899 Van Horn TX 79855-0899

SCOTT, JOYCE, writer; d. Charles William and Emma Reardon; m. Edward Dale Scott, Sept. 13, 1971; 1 child, Tonia Louise. Student, Inst. Children's Lit., 1984, student, 1993, Long Ridge Writers Group, 1994. Mem.: The Internat. Women's Writing Guild, Soc. Children's Book Writers and Illustrators.

SCOTT, JOYCE ALAINE, academic administrator; b. Long Beach, Calif., May 21, 1943; d. Emmett Emery Scott and Grace (Evans) Wedum. BA, U. Conn., 1964; MA, U. Va., 1966; PhD, Duke U., 1973. From instr. to assoc. prof. U. Wyo., Laramie, 1971-74, asst. dean, 1974-78, asst. v.p. acad. affairs, 1976-81, assoc. v.p. acad. affairs, 1981-84; provost, v.p. SUNY-Potsdam, 1984-86; exec. v.p. Wichita (Kans.) State U., 1986-90, v.p. on spl. assignment, 1990-91; sr. cons. Am. Assn. State Colls. and Univs., 1991-92, v.p. acad. and internat. programs, 1992-97; dep. commr. Mont. U. Sys., Helena, 1998—2003; provost, v.p. acad. and student affairs Tex. A&M U., Commerce, 2003—06, assoc. prof., dept. ednl. leadership, 2004—06, assoc. prof. ednl. leadership, 2005—. Mem. Commn. on Ednl. Credit and Credentials of Am. Coun. on Edn., Washington, 1982-87; cons. faculty Am. Open U., Lincoln, Nebr., 1981-82. Contbr. articles to profl. jours. Trustee Jones Internat. U. Mem. MLA, Am. Assn. Tchrs. French, Phi Beta Kappa, Phi Kappa Phi, Phi Sigma Iota. Republican. Presbyterian. Office: Dept Educational Leadership PO Box 3011 Commerce TX 75429-3011 Office Phone: 903-886-5503. Business E-Mail: Joyce_Scott@tamu-commerce.edu.

SCOTT, JUANITA, elementary school educator; b. Dallas, Nov. 21, 1974; d. Benjamin and Tessie Berlene Scott. BS, Tex. A&M U., Commerce, 1998; MS in Counseling, Prairie A&M Grad. Sch., Tex., 2006. Cert. tchr. Tex. Dept. Edn., 1998, counselor Tex. Dept. Edn., 2006. Master tchr. Seagoville Elem. Sch., Tex., 2006—. Mentor chairperson Seagoville Elem. Sch., 2004—05. Founder, chairperson Unified Praise Steppers Vision of Faith, 2003. Recipient Cmty. Activist award, A. Maceo Smith HS, Dallas, 2004. Mem.: Delta Sigma Theta. Democrat. Avocations: art, singing, reading.

SCOTT, KAMELA KOON, psychologist, educator; b. Carson City, Nev., July 28, 1964; d. Ray Harold and Bert Gardner Koon; m. David Keitt Scott, Feb. 13, 1993; children: Nicolas Keitt, Isaac David. BA, Baylor U., Waco, Tex., 1986; PhD, U. No. Tex., Denton, 1992. Lic. Clin. Psychologist Divsn. Med. Quality Assurance, Fla., 1994. Psychology intern U. Tex. Med. Br. and Shriner's Burns Inst., Galveston, Tex., 1991—92; instr. dept. psychiatry Emory U. Sch. Medicine, Atlanta, 1992—93; asst. prof. dept. of Pediat. U. Fla. Coll. Medicine, Jacksonville, Fla., 1993—96, asst. prof., 1996—2002, assoc. prof. dept. surgery, 2002—. Program dir., psychol. svcs. U. Fla., Dept. Pediat., Dist. Hematology/Sickle Cell Program, Jacksonville, 1993—96, U. Fla. Regional Trauma Sys., Jacksonville, 2001—; chmn. Sexual Harassment Com. U. Fla., Jacksonville, 1997—; mem. Jacksonville Pediat. Injury Control Sys., 1996—; bd. mem. Shands Jacksonville Ethics Com., 1996—. Shands Jacksonville Emergency Preparedness Com., 1998—; adv. bd. mem. Shands Jacksonville Clin. Pastoral Edn. Adv. Bd., 1998—2004; supervising psychologist Shands Jacksonville Trauma Psychology Post-Doctoral Fellowship, 1998—; site reviewer Fla. Brain and Spinal Cord Injury Program, Tallahassee, 1998—; lectr. U. Fla. Risk Mgmt. Ednl. Series, Gainesville, 2002—. Author: (book chapter) Surg. Clinics of North Am., (book chapters (2) Behavioral Aspects of Pediatric Burn Injuries, (jour. article) Current Surgery, Jour. of Trauma, Jacksonville Medicine. Adv. bd. mem. Partnerships for Preventing Violence, Jacksonville, 1998—2003, Serving Child Victims of Traumatic Abuse, Jacksonville, 2002—03; active mem. Compassionate Families, Inc., Jacksonville, 1998—2003. Named Outstanding Alumnae of Yr., U. North Tex., 2005; grantee, City of Jacksonville, Fla., 2001—05, State of Fla. Byrne Grant, 2001-2002, The Blue Found. for a Healthy Fla., 2001—05, The Jacksonville Jaguars Found., 1999-2001, U. of Fla. Dean's Fund, 1997-1998; scholar, Pres. U.S., Washington, D.C., 1982. Mem.: APA. Republican. Baptist. Avocations: scuba diving, skiing, deep sea fishing, camping. Office: U Fla Surgery 655 West 8th St Jacksonville FL 32209 Office Phone: 904-244-3352. Business E-Mail: kamela.scott@jax.ufl.edu.

SCOTT, KAREN BONDURANT, consumer catalog company executive; b. East Orange, NJ, June 4, 1946; d. Walter James and Wanda (French) Schmidt; m. Ian James Anderson, May 12, 1982; children: Steven, Michael. BS, U. Mass., 1968; MBA, Northwestern U., 1977. Bus. analyst Dun & Bradstreet, N.Y.C., 1968-69; asst. mgr. Shay Med. Employment, Chgo., 1970-72; mgr. recruitment Michael Reese Med. Ctr., Chgo., 1972-76; brand mgmt., new bus. devel., dir. mergers & acquisitions Kraft Foods, Inc., Glenview, Ill., 1977-95; pres. Chelsea & Scott dba One Step Ahead, Lake Bluff, Ill., 1987—. Sec.-treas. adv. bd. Lincolnshire (Ill.) Nursery Sch., 1987-89; co-leader Boy Scouts Am., Lincolnshire, 1991. Mem. Juvenile Product Mfrs. Assn. (new product judge 1992-99, speaker nat. catalog conf.), Nat. Assn. Women Bus. Owners (mem. Lake Forest cmty. task force). Office: Chelsea & Scott Ltd 75 Albrecht Dr Lake Bluff IL 60044-2226

SCOTT, KAREN MICHELE, television producer; b. Saratoga Springs, NY, July 3, 1949; d. Alfred and Rosalie (Martin) Silberman; m. Guy B. Scott III, Aug. 20, 1973 (div. Nov. 1982). BA in Journalism, Ohio State U., 1971. Reporter Radio Sta. WRFD-WNCI, Columbus, Ohio, 1971—73; assoc. prodr. Sta. WKBD-TV, Detroit, 1975—76; prodr., news writer Sta. WXYZ-TV, Detroit, 1976—78; prodr., exec. prodr. spl. projects Sta. WFSB-TV, Hartford, Conn., 1979—83; prodr. Sta. WNBC-TV, NYC, 1983—. Mem.: Women in Comm., Nat. Acad. TV Arts and Scis., Radio-TV News Dirs. Assn. Jewish. Office: Sta WNBC-TV 30 Rockefeller Plz New York NY 10112-0002

SCOTT, LINDA KAY See GRANT, LINDA

SCOTT, LINDA PRESTON, psychologist, educator; b. Boones Camp, Ky., Feb. 20, 1941; d. E. Jay and Grayce Jean (Mollette) Preston; m. Brett Dorse Scott, Aug. 7, 1960(div.); 1 child, Brett Preston Scott; m. Arthur Henry DeRosier, Jr., Dec. 26, 1979; children: Deborah DeRosier, Marsha DeRosier, Melissa DeRosier. BA, Pikeville Coll., 1962; MA, Ea. Ky. U., 1968; PhD, U. Ky., 1972; EdM, Harvard U., 1995. Claims rep. Social Security Adminstrn., 1962-67; prof. Psychology Rocky Mountain Coll., Billings, Mont., 1988—; teaching asst. Ea. Ky. U., Richmond, 1967-68; instr. U. Ky., Lexington, 1968-72; asst. prof. psychology Ky. State U., Frankfort, 1972-74, 74-78, U. Louisville, 1972-74; prof. psychology, dir. rsch. ctr. Ky. State U., 1974-78; dir. Appalachian Inst. E. Tenn. State U., Johnson City, 1978-79, prof. psychology, 1978-80, Coll. of Idaho, Caldwell, 1980-88; pvt. prac., 1995—. Pres. Appalwest, Inc., Caldwell, Idaho, Billings, Mont., 1986—. Author: Creeker, 1999, Songs of Life & Grace, 2003, (textbook) Understanding Psychology, 2004, Study Guide for Understanding Psychology, 2005. Bd. dirs. Billings Symphony, Rimrock Found., Billings, 1989—. Mem. Am. Psychol. Soc., Mensa. Presbyterian. Home: 1809 Mulberry Dr Billings MT 59102-0601 Office: Rocky Mountain Coll Psychology Dept 1511 Poly Dr Billings MT 59102-1739

SCOTT, LORRY ANN, elementary school music specialist; b. Bridgeport, Conn., Aug. 4, 1961; d. Walter and Eleanor Louise (Barrett) S. BS in Mus. Edn., Concordia Coll., Bronxville, N.Y., 1983; MA in Sch. Adminstrn., Fairfield U., 1992. Lic. tchr. grades kindergarten through 12, Conn. Organist St. Raphael's Roman Cath. Ch., Bridgeport, 1976-79, Holy Cross Roman Cath. Ch., Fairfield, Conn., 1976-87; music specialist grades kindergarten through 8 Assumption Sch., Westport, Conn., 1983-84; elem. music specialist Bridgeport Bd. Edn., 1983-84, Stratford (Conn.) Bd. Edn., 1984—. Drama dir. Fairfield Summer Sch., 1984—; choir dir. Lorry Scott Singers, Fairfield, 1985-2004; musical dir. Gaelic-Am. Glee Club, 2006—. Founder, dir., mus. dir. non-profit fundraising orgn. Lorry A. Scott & Co., Fairfield, 1981—. Runner-up Woman of Yr. award Conn. Post newspaper, Bridgeport, 1993. Mem. Strafford Edn. Assn. (Human Rels. award 1993). Democrat. Avocations: musical theater, history. Home: 9 Greenbrier Cir Fairfield CT 06824-3407 Office: Stratford Bd Edn 1000 E Broadway Stratford CT 06615-5911

SCOTT, LYNN THOMSON, Spanish language and literature educator; b. Mineola, N.Y., Oct. 2, 1942; d. George Campbell and Helen (Gordon) Thomson; m. John Fredrik Scott, July 25, 1964; children: Erik Anderson, Elizabeth Cameron. BA, Vassar Coll., 1964; MA, U. Fla., 1990, PhD, 1999. Editl. asst. McGraw-Hill Pub., N.Y.C., 1964-66; Spanish tchr. St. Thomas More Sch., Houston, 1978-81, Buchholz H.S., Gainesville, Fla., 1983-84; tchg. asst. U. Fla., Gainesville, 1988—. Guest lectr. U. Andes, Bogota, Colombia, 1996. Contbr. articles to profl. jours. Active Christian unity & inter-religious concerns Trinity United Meth. Ch., Gainesville, 1993-95, Project Graduation The Corner Drugstore, Gainesville, 1989. Travel grantee Tinker Found., 1996, rsch. grantee Program Cooperation Spanish Ministry Culture, Madrid, 1996; dissertation fellow U. Fla. Coll. Liberal Arts, 1996; Tybel Spivack award, U. Fla., 1993. Mem. MLA, AAUW, South Atlantic Modern Lang. Assn., PEO, SSSAS, Sigma Delta Pi, Phi Sigma Iota, Phi Kappa Phi. Avocations: cooking, swimming, bird watching, travel. Office: U Fla Dept Romance Langs & Lit Gainesville FL 32611

SCOTT, MARIAN ALEXIS, journalist; b. Atlanta, Feb. 4, 1949; d. William Alexander and Marian (Willis) Scott; m. Marc Anthony Lewis, Sept. 14, 1968 (div. 1973); m. David Leslie Reeves, Mar. 16, 1974 (div. 1998); children: Cinque Scott, David Leslie Jr. Student, Barnard Coll., 1966-68, Spelman Coll., 1989-90, Regional Leadership Inst., 1992; LHD, Argosy U., 2003. Reporter, asst. city editor, cable TV editor, mgr., video, v.p. cmty. affairs Atlanta Jour. and Constn., 1974-93; dir. diversity Cox Enterprises Inc., 1993-97; pub. Atlanta Daily World, 1997—. Bd. dirs. Atlanta Life Ins. Co.; vis. instr. summer program for minority journalists, Berkeley, Calif., 1980, 81, 84, 85, 87 Grady High Sch., Atlanta, 1982-83; journalist-in-residence Clark Coll., Atlanta, 1983. Rschr., writer: The history of Atlanta NAACP, 1983 (NAACP award 1984). Moderator First Congl. Ch., 1982-92. Named one of 100 Top Black Bus. and Profl. Women, 1986, 20 Women Making a Mark in Atlanta, Atlanta Mag., 1998, Top 25 Women in Bus., The Network Jour., 2004; recipient Disting. Urban Journalism award, Nat. Urban Coalition, 1980, Acad. Achievement award, YWCA, 1989, Media of Yr. award, Ga. Legisl. Black Caucus, 2001, Citizen of Yr. award, Southwest Hosp., 2001, 1st Place Column Writing award, Ga. Press Assn., 2004, Millennium Pacesetter award, Atlanta Bus. League, 2005; Michele Clark fellow, Columbia U. Sch. Journalism, 1974, Grimes fellow, Cox Family Enterprise Ctr., Kennesaw State U. Mem.: Nat. Assn. Black Journalists, Atlanta Assn. Black Journalists (Commentary Print award 1983, Pioneer Black Journalist award 1998), Nat. Assn. Media Women (pres Atlanta chpt. 1985—87, Media Woman of Yr. award 1983, Media Woman of Yr. nat. award 1993), Atlanta Press Club (pres. 2000), Sigma Delta Chi (bd. dirs. 1980—84, treas. 1985—88). Office: Atlanta Daily World 145 Auburn Ave NE Atlanta GA 30303-2503

SCOTT, MARIANNE FLORENCE, retired librarian, educator; b. Toronto, Dec. 4, 1928; d. Merle Redvers and Florence Ethel (Hutton) Scott. BA, McGill U., Montreal, Que., Can., 1949, BLS, 1952; LLD (hon.), York U., 1985, Dalhousie U., 1989; DLitt (hon.), Laurentian U., 1990. Asst. librarian Bank of Montreal, 1952-55; law librarian McGill U., 1955-73, law area librarian, 1973-75, dir. libraries, 1975-84, lectr. legal bibliography faculty of law, 1964-75; nat. librarian Nat. Library of Can., Ottawa, Ont., 1984-99, ret., 1999. Co-founder, editor: Index to Can. Legal Periodical Lit, 1963—; contbr. articles to profl. jours. Decorated officer Order of Can.; recipient Queen Elizabeth II Silver Jubilee medal, 1977, IFLA medal, 1996, Queen Elizabeth II Golden Jubilee medal, 2002. Mem. Internat. Assn. Law Libraries (dir. 1974-77), Am. Assn. Law Libraries, Can. Assn. Law Libraries (pres. 1963-69, exec. bd. 1973-75, honored mem. 1980—), Can. Library Assn. (coun. and dir. 1980-82, 1st v.p. 1980-81, pres. 1981-82), Corp. Profl. Librarians of Que. (v.p. 1975-76), Can. Assn. Rsch. Librs. (pres. 1978-79, past pres. 1979-80, exec. com. 1980-81, sec.-treas. 1983-84), Can. Writers Found. (bd. dirs. 1999—, treas. 2003—), Ctr. for Research Libraries (dir. 1980-83), Internat. Fedn. Library Assns. (honor com. for 1982 conf. 1979-82, chair com. on copyright and other legal matters 1998-2003, hon. fellow 2003), Conf. of Dirs. of Nat. Libraries (chmn. 1988-92). Home: 119 Dorothea Dr Ottawa ON Canada K1V 7C6 E-mail: mfscott@rogers.com.

SCOTT, MARIE CLAUDINE, ceramic artist, writer; b. Pitts., Aug. 9, 1953; d. Walter Phelps and Janine Baptistine (Decruck) Scott; m. David Lovattsmith, Feb. 24, 1984 (div. 1985); m. Jeffrey Lloyd White, Dec. 31, 1990 (div. 1993); children: Jeffrey Lloyd II, Trayton. Student in interior design, E.S.A.M., Paris, 1975. Self-employed interior decorator, Paris, 1975-76; lyric writer for popular songs E.P.O.C.C., Paris, 1976-77; pub. rels. cons. Theo Cowan, Ltd., London, 1977-91; art buyer McCann-Erickson, Paris, 1980-89. Student animator NYFA Harvard. Contbr. articles to mags. including Lady's Circle, Woman's Circle, South Florida. Mem. Ponte Vedra Inn and Club. Avocations: travel, art history, swimming, ceramics handpainting. Home: 312 Ponte Vedra Blvd Ponte Vedra Beach FL 32082-1812 Personal E-mail: marieclaudinescott@mac.xom.

SCOTT, MARIETTE A., marketing executive; b. Darien, Conn., July 18, 1953; d. Vincent Charles Arguimbau and Carmen Perez de Guzman de Arguimbau; m. Edward Barton Scott, Sept. 6, 1986. BA cum laude, Skidmore Coll., 1976; MA, Johns Hopkins U., 1980; PhD, NYU, 1985. Instr. Goucher Coll., Towson, Md., 1977, Johns Hopkins U., Balt., 1978—80, NYU, NYC, 1981—83, Princeton U., NJ, 1984—85; dir. Latin Am. Cultural Ctr., NYC, 1980—84; mng. dir. Tucker Capital Corp., Princeton, 1984—85; mktg. mgr. Univision Inc., NYC, 1985—89; pres. Silk Serum Enterprizes, Greenwich, Conn., 1986—; ptnr. Argoimbau Co., Greenwich, 1989—. Dir. US-Spain C. of C., NYC, 2002—; trustee Hispanic Soc. Am., NYC, 2000—. Fulbright scholar, 1976. Mem.: Wee Burn Country Club. Republican. Roman Catholic. Avocations: calligraphy, clothing design, sewing, tennis, skiing. Home: 444 E 57th St New York NY 10022 Office: Argoimbau Co 4 Davenport Ave Greenwich CT 06830

SCOTT, MARTHA ANN, clinical social worker; b. Cin., July 19, 1952; d. Richard Arthur and Dorothy (Hewitt) S.; m. Douglas Stephenson Magee, May 3, 1975. BA in Sociology, Denison U., 1973; MSW, Ohio State U., 1977; postgrad., U.Cin., 1981-82. Lic. ind. social worker, Ohio; cert. Nat. Bd. Examiners in Clin. Social Work; cert. fellow in managed care. Med. social worker Bethesda North Hosp., Cin., 1977-78; clin. social worker Cancer Family Care, Cin., 1978-85, casework supr., 1985-91, interim dir., 1988, 90;

clin. social worker Edward J. Fisher, Jr., MD Inc., Cin., 1991-97, Bethesda Counseling, 1997-99, Integrated Behavioral Svcs., Cin., 1988—95. Mem. NASW, Acad. Cert. Social Workers, Nat Assn. Oncology Social Workers (chmn. registration com. nat. conf. 1988), Ohio Soc. for Clin. Social Workers, Social Work Oncology Group Greater Cin. (v.p. 1987, pres. 1988-90). Office: Integrated Behavioral Svc 7124 Miami Ave Cincinnati OH 45243-2675 Office Phone: 513-792-3482 219. Personal E-mail: shrewd@iglou.com.

SCOTT, MARY CELINE, pharmacologist; b. L.A., July 14, 1957; d. Walter Edward and Shirley Jean (Elvin) S. BS in Biol. Sci., U. Calif., Irvine, 1978; MS in Biology, Calif. State U., Long Beach, 1980; PhD in Pharmacology, Purdue U., 1985; MBA in Pharm.-Chem. Studies, Fairleigh Dickinson U., 1995. Tchg. asst. Calif. State U., Long Beach, 1979-80, Purdue U., West Lafayette, Ind., 1980-82, grad. instr., 1982-83, rsch. fellow, 1983-85, 1988-89, Mayo Found., Rochester, Minn., 1985-87; sr. scientist Schering-Plough, Bloomfield, NJ, 1989-92; assoc. prin. scientist Schering-Plough Rsch. Inst., Kenilworth, NJ, 1993-98, prin. scientist, 1998-2000, mgr. U.S. regulatory affairs, 2000—02, mgr. global regulatory affairs, 2002—04; sr. mgr. U.S. regulatory affairs Amgen, Thousand Oaks, Calif., 2004—. Contbr. articles to profl. jours. Mem.: AAAS, Soc. Neurosci., Internat. Soc. for Study Xenobiotics, Am. Soc. Pharm. and Exptl. Therapeutics, Am. Chem. Soc. Democrat. Office: Amgen One Amgen Center Dr Thousand Oaks CA 91320-1799 Office Phone: 805-447-3741. Business E-Mail: mascott@amgen.com.

SCOTT, MARY EDITH, special education educator; b. Plantersville, Tex., Nov. 10, 1930; d. Charles Martin Nelson and Kathryn Agnes (McNeir) Stuart; m. Floyd Wayne Scott, Sept. 24, 1950; 1 child, Pamela Kathleen. BS in Elem. Edn., Tex. Arts and Industries U., 1956; MEd, U. Tex., 1962. Tchr. Petronila Ind. Sch. Dist., Robstown, Tex., 1951-52, 56; elem. tchr., then spl. edn. tchr. Uvalde (Tex.) Ind. Sch. Dist., 1956-57, 59-61; spl. edn. tchr. Austin (Tex.) Ind. Sch. Dist., 1961-67, Borger (Tex.) Ind. Sch. Dist., 1967-69; assoc. prof. Sam Houston State U., Huntsville, Tex., 1969-71; ednl. diagnostician, spl. edn. supr. Dayton (Tex.) Ind. Sch. Dist. Coop., 1971-72, Channelview (Tex.) Ind. Sch. Dist., 1972-92, part-time diagnostician, 1992-98. Demonstration tchr. Cerebral Palsy Ctr., Austin, 1964. Contbr. articles to profl. publs. Mem. Coun. Exceptional Children, Coun. Edn. Diagnostic Svcs., Tex. Ednl. Diagnosticians Assn. (pres. 1981-82, exam. coord. Houston Met. chpt. 1980), Tex. State Tchrs. Assn., DAR, Chieftains Mus., Smithsonian Instn., Nat. Mus. Am. Indian, Sons of Norway. Episcopalian. Avocations: swimming, sewing, travel, reading. Home: 1030 Wilkes Cir Smithville TX 78957-1138

SCOTT, MELLOUISE JACQUELINE, retired media specialist; b. Sanford, Fla., Mar. 1, 1943; d. Herbert and Mattye (Williams) Cherry; m. Robert Edward Scott, Jr., July 1, 1972; 1 child, Nolan Edward. BA, Talladega Coll., 1965; MLS, Rutgers U., 1974, EdM, 1976, EdS, 1982. Media specialist Seminole County Bd. Edn., Sanford, 1965-72, Edison (N.J.), 1972-98; ret. Edison (N.J.) Bd. Edn., 1999. Mem. ALA, N.J. Ret. Educators Assn., NEA. Baptist. Home: PO Box 1771 Sanford FL 32772-1771

SCOTT, MIMI KOBLENZ, psychotherapist, actress, journalist, playwright; b. Albany, NY, Dec. 15, 1940; d. Edmund Akiba and Tillie (Paul) Koblenz; m. Barry Stuart Scott, Aug. 13, 1961 (dec. Nov. 1991); children: Karen Scott Zantay, Jeffrey B. BA in Speech and English Edn., Russell Sage Coll., 1962; MA in Speech Edn., SUNY, Albany, 1968; M in Social Welfare, SUNY, 1985; PhD in Psychology, Pacific Western U., Encino, Calif., 1985. Cert. tchr., social worker. Tchr. English, speech Albany Pub. Schs., 1961-63; hostess, producer talkshow Sta. WAST-TV 13, Albany, 1973-75; freelance actress N.Y.C., 1975-77; producer, actress Four Seasons Dinner Theater, Albany, 1978-82; instr. of theatre Albany Jr. Coll., 1981-83; pvt. practice psychotherapy Albany, NY, 1985-92, N.Y.C., 1992—; exec. producer City of Albany Park Playhouse, 1989-92; actor self-employed N.Y.C., 1992—; actor Off Broadway show Grandma Sylvia's Funeral, 1996-98, Split Ends, 2004. Guest psychotherapist Sally Jessy Raphael Show, 1992, 93, Jane Whitney Show, 1994, A Current Affair, 1995, News Talk TV, 1995; founder Manhattan Playwrights Inc., 2001—, producing artistic dir., 2001—06. Scriptwriter, dir., actor (TV films) To Liberty and Justice for All, 1985, featured writer Backstage, 1995—96, featured in ind. film Mr. Vincent, Sundance, 1997, book and lyricist (musical) Dressing Room, Soho Playhouse, N.Y.C., 2000; author: Mind Tricks, 2003; dir.: Mind Tricks, 2003; featured on NBC Dateline, 2005, VH1's So Jewtastic, 2006. Event organizer AmFar, 1985; co-chmn. March of Dimes Telethon, 1985-86; fundraiser Leukemia Found., 1987, AIDS Benefit, North Miami Beach, Fla., 1988; elected to SUNY Albany U. Found., 1990. Recipient FDR Nat. Achievement award March of Dimes, 1985, Recognition Cert. Capital Dist. Psychiat. Ctr., 1983-85; named Woman of Yr. YWCA, 1986, Commr. Albany Tricentennial Celebration, 1986; named Mimi Scott Day in her honor Mayor of Albany, 1989. Mem.: NASW, AFTRA, SAG, AEA, Drama League of N.Y., N.Y. League Profl. Theatre Women. Jewish. Avocations: boating, golf, tennis. Home and Office: 155 W 70th St PH2A New York NY 10023-3767 Office Phone: 212-721-2979. Personal E-mail: mscott13@aol.com.

SCOTT, NANCY ELLEN, psychologist; b. El Paso, Tex., Nov. 1, 1960; d. Robert Churchill and Annie Jo (Schmidt) S. BS, U. Tex., El Paso, 1982; MS, Springfield Coll., 1985; MA, Columbia U., 1987, EdM, 1989; PhD, Fordham U., 1996. Cert. tchr., Tex., cert. clin. hypnotherapy; lic. psychologist, N.Y. Assoc. Occupl. Health Consulting Inc., West Nyack, N.Y., 1985-88; psychiat. rehab. counselor Met. Hosp., N.Y.C., 1988-91; psychotherapist Met. Ctr. for Mental Health, N.Y.C., 1991-96; psychology intern Albert Einstein Coll. of Medicine, Bronx, N.Y., 1991-92; psychologist Albert Einstein Coll. Medicine, Bronx, N.Y., 1992-94, Bronx Psychiat. Ctr., Bronx, N.Y., 1994-95; assessor Assessment Sys., Inc., N.Y.C., 1995; pvt. practice N.Y.C., 1995—; neuropsychologist Burke Med. Rsch. Inst., White Plains, NY, 1996-99, dir. neuropsychol. assessment program, 1999—2001. Contbr. articles to profl. jours. Office: Ste 823 156 Fifth Ave New York NY 10010 Office Fax: 212-304-9758. Business E-Mail: Nscottphd5ave@cs.com.

SCOTT, NANCY L., information technology manager, health facility administrator, consultant; b. Berwyn, Ill., Sept. 11, 1962; d. Kenneth N. and Lolita L. Unger; m. Paul A. Scott, Dec. 29, 1990 (div. Sept. 1995). BS, Univ. of Ill., 1983; MBA with hons., U. of Chgo., 1991. Cert. CHE Am. Coll. of Healthcare Execs., Chgo., 2000. Various positions including implementation specialist to fin. product mgr. Enterprise Systems, Inc., Wheeling, Ill., 1993—96; cytogenetics technologist Univ. of Chgo., 1986—88; supr. Reproductive Genetics Inst., Chgo., 1988—90; dist. agt. The Prudential, Des Plaines, Ill., 1992; mgr., sr. cons. Cap Gemini Ernst & Young U.S., Chgo., 1996—2003; acct. exec. AHA Fin. Solutions, Inc., Chgo., 2003—04; payroll project mgr. Hewitt Assocs. LLC, Chgo., 2005—. Home: 3238 Elm Ave Brookfield IL 60513 Office: Hewitt Assocs LLC 120 S Riverside Plz Chicago IL 60606 Office Phone: 312-279-6643. Personal E-mail: NLScott@aol.com.

SCOTT, PAMELA MOYERS, physician assistant; b. Clarksburg, W.Va., Jan. 5, 1961; d. James Edward and Norma Lee (Holbert) Moyers; m. Troy Allen Scott, July 19, 1986. BS summa cum laude, Alderson-Broaddus Coll., 1983; M Physician Asst. Studies, U. Nebr., 1999. Cert. physician asst. Physician asst. Weston (W.Va.) State Hosp., 1983-84, Rainelle (W.Va.) Med. Ctr., 1984-2000, Brierwood Med. Ctr., 2000—01; pvt. practice Williamsburg, W.Va., 2001—. Adj. faculty Mountain State U., Beckley, W.Va., 2003; support faculty physician asst. program Coll. W.Va., 1994-99, mem. physician asst. adv. coun. 1993-94, physician asst. program admission selection com., 1994-99; keynote spkr. Alderson-Broaddus Coll. Ann. Physician Assn. Banquet, 1992, 2001, 1st Physician Asst. Convocation Ceremony, 1998; spkr., presenter in field; guest Lifetime TV med. program Physician Jour. Update, 1993; adv. coun. W.Va. Rural Health Networking, 1994-95, W.Va. Rural Networking Managed Care Policy Group, 1996, W.Va. Coalition for Managed Care Options, 1997; mem. coalition W.Va. Comprehensive Cancer Ctr., 2004-06; people to people physician asst. del. China, 1992, 04, Brazil, 2003, del. leader 2003, 2004. Mem. editl. bd. Jour. Am. Acad. Physician Assts., 1995-98, 04-05, manuscript reviewer, 1995—; dept. editor Procedures in Family Practice Dept., 1996-04, When the Patient Asks, 2005—; author, illustrator Mikie Meets the Physician Assistant, 2005; contbr. articles to profl. jours., chpts. to textbook. Mem. W.Va. State Task Force on Adolescent Pregnancy and Parenting, 1992-2000, sec., 1996-98; mem. W.Va. Rural Networking Managed Care Study Group, 1995, W.Va. Rural Networking Managed Care Policy Group, 1996; mem. adv. com. W.Va. State Bur. Pub. Health Family Planning, 1997-2000; mem. Greenbrier County P.A.T.C.H. Spkr.'s Bur., 1996-2003; mem. Meadow Bridge Cmty. Adv. Group, 1997-2000, Meadow Bridge Domestic Violence Prevention Task Force, 1998-2000; mem. heart profl. edn. adv. panel Nat. Heart, Lung & Blood Inst., 2003-2005; mem. N.H.L.B.I. profl. edn. dissemination adv. panel, 2005; bd. trustees Physician Asst. Found., 2002-03; mem. physician asst. alumni subcom. for renewing the promise campaign Alderson-Broadus Coll., 2004-2005; mem. Am. Heart Assn. Childhood Obesity Healthcare Expert Panel, 2005—, liaison Am. Acad. Pa., Heart Truth Profl. Edn. Dissemination Campaign Adv. Panel, Nat. Heart, Lungs & Blood Inst., 2005-06, Heart Truth Profl. Edn. Devel. Panel, 2004-05. Named Young Career Woman of Yr. Rainelle chpt. and Dist. V of W. Va., Citation of Honor at State Level of Competition, Bus. and Profl. Women's Club, 1986, W.Va. Women's Commn. Celebrate Women award, Mountaineer Spirit, 2005; recipient W.Va. Gov.'s award for Outstanding Rural Health Practitioner, 1997, Alderson Broaddus Coll.'s Alumni Achievement award, 1995, Harry Bennington Meml. award, 2001, Hu C. Avanelle Myers award, 2004. Fellow: Assn. Family Practice Physician Assts. (newsletter editor 2001—02, Appreciation award 2002, 2004), W.Va. Assn. Physician Assts. (chmn. membership com. 1989—91, nominations and elections com. 1990—91, pres. 1991—94, chair ann. med. Jeopardy tournament 1997—2001, student activities com. 1999—2000, chmn. mentoring program 1999—2000, ann.scholarhsip named in honor 2005, Outstanding Physician Asst. of Yr. 2003), Am. Acad. Physician Assts. (mem. rural health caucus 1991—98, W.Va. chief del. Ho. of Dels. Nat. Conv. 1992, W.Va. del. 1992—98, mem. pub. edn. com. 1992—98, W.Va. chief del. Ho. of Dels. Nat. Conv. 1994—98, chair pub. edn. com. 1996—98, bd. advisor elections com. 1998—99, dir.-at-large 1998—2002, bd. on fin. 1998—2005, alt. del. 1999—2000, chmn. bd. commn. on external affairs 1999—2001, bd. advisor pub. rels. com. 2000—01, chair bd. commn. internal affairs 2001—02, bd. advisor clin. affairs coun. 2001—02, chmn. bd. on appts. 2002—03, chmn. bd. commn. on external affairs 2002—03, mem. coord com. 2002—03, pres.-elect 2002—03, bd. advisor to constituent rels. com. 2002—03, co-chair ad hoc work group on governance 2002—03, bd. on budget 2002—05, mem. exec. com. 2002—05, clin. and sci. affairs coun. 2002—05, edn. coun. 2002—05, mem. found. bd. trustees 2002—05, profession practice coun. 2002—05, bd. advisor leadership adv. commn. 2002—05, pres. 2003—04, chair exec. com. 2003—04, alt. del. 2003—05, bd. rep. nominating com. 2005—06, Outstanding Physician Asst. of Yr. 1991); mem.: Soc. Preservation Pa. History (founding mem., bd. dirs. 2004—, chair publicity com., newsletter editor 2004—06, pres. 2006—, pres. elect 2005—06). Republican. Baptist. Avocations: reading, handicrafts, shopping. Home and Office: PO Box 43 Williamsburg WV 24991-0043 E-mail: pamscottpa@citlink.net.

SCOTT, PHYLLIS WRIGHT, coach, music educator; b. Lancaster, Pa., Nov. 9, 1925; d. George Bronson and Edythe Heckroth Wright; m. Edgar Lee Arthur Mixon, Oct. 12, 1946 (div. Nov. 1954); children: Thomas Lee, Raymond Dean, Michael George; m. Gilbert Henry Scott, June 23, 1976 (dec. May 1995). Grad., H.S., 1963; studied music, studied skating. Skating tchr. Health Ctr., Norfolk, Va., 1947, Ringing Rocks Park, Pottstown, Pa., 1945, Gt. Leopard Roller Rink, Chester, Pa., 1946—47, Ringing Rocks Park Roller Rink, Lancaster, Pa., 1948—49, Playland Roller Rink, York, Pa., 1950—51, Skateland Roller Rink, Camden, NJ, 1952—55, Exton (Pa.) Roller Rink, 1956—57; music tchr. Holiday Music, Pennsauken, NJ, 1962—64; pvt. practice Bellmawr, NJ, 1965—98; tchr. organ, piano and keyboard Keyboard Am., Lewes, Del., 1998—. Prodr.: (skating shows), 1944—62. Den mother Cub Scouts of Am., Bellmawr, NJ, 1950—54. Recipient Silver-Bronze Dance medal, Roller Skating Rinks Operator Assn., 1943, Bronze Figures award, 1944. Mem.: Order of Eastern Star. Republican. Baptist. Avocations: needlepoint, playing keyboard instruments. Home: 29261 White Pine Rd Milton DE 19968 Personal E-mail: phylliswscott@msn.com.

SCOTT, PORTIA ADELE, paralegal; b. Port Chester, N.Y., Nov. 1, 1946; d. Frank Thomas, Jr. and Hattie N. Thomas; 1 child, Nicole L. BS, U. Md., 2005. Cert. paralegal Md., 2003. Mgr. adminstrn. YMCA of the USA, Washington, 1990—91; office mgr. Thatcher Proffitt & Wood, Washington, 1991—96; paralegal Wilmer Cutler & Pickering, Hale and Dorr, Washington, 1996—. Mem. adv. bd. Legal Studies Dept. U. Md., Adelphi, Md.; bd. dir. Seed, Inc., Riverdale, Md. Author: At Twilight, 2001 (Editor's award, 2003). Mem.: NAFE, Nat. Fedn. of Paralegal Assn. Avocations: writing, singing, poetry. Office: Wilmer Cutler Pickering Hale and Dorr LLP 2445 M St NW Washington DC 20037 Business E-Mail: portia.scott@wilmer.com.

SCOTT, REBECCA J., law educator; AB, Radcliffe Coll.; MPhil in econ. history, London Sch. Econs.; PhD, Princeton U. Charles Gibson Disting. Univ. Prof. of History, prof. law U. Mich. Law Sch., Ann Arbor. Author: Degrees of Freedom: Louisiana and Cuba after Slavery, 2005; contbr. articles to profl. jours. Grantee Guggenheim fellowship, 2004. Mem.: Am. Acad. Arts and Scis. Office: Mich U Law Sch 969 Hutchins Hall 625 S State St Ann Arbor MI 48109-1215 Office Phone: 734-615-2082. Office Fax: 734-764-8309. E-mail: rjscott@umich.edu.

SCOTT, ROSA MAE, art educator, artist; b. East Hampton, NY, Apr. 12, 1937; d. James Alexander and Victoria (Square) Nicholson; m. Frank Albert Hanna, Apr. 1, 1957 (div. Mar. 1985); 1 child, Frank Albert Hanna III; m. Warner Bruce Scott, Aug. 3, 1985 (dec. Oct. 2002); children: Bernadine, John, Patricia, Charlene, Lawrence. AA, Dabney Lancaster, 1989; BA, Mary Baldwin, 1992. Cosmetologist Rosa's Beauty Shop, East Hampton, 1962-68; sec. Frank Hanna's Cleaning Co., East Hampton, 1962-77; cashier, clk. Brook's Pharmacy, East Hampton, 1992; lead tchr. East Hampton Day Care, 1992-94, 97-98; substitute tchr. Lexington (Va.) Schs., 1994—; lead tchr. Suffolk C.C. Child Care Ctr., River Head, N.Y., 1999; substitute tchr. East Hampton Sch., 2000—03; lead tchr. after sch. program Springs Sch., 2000—02, 2004—05, substitute tchr., 2000—03. Substitute tchr. East Hampton Sch., 1996-97, 2000-04; sec. Lylburn Downing Cmty. Ctr., Inc., Lexington, 1985-92; arts and crafts tutor, supr. East Hampton Town Youth After Sch. Program, 1996—. Pres. Rockbridge Garden Club, Lexington, 1996; co-organizer Va. Co-op. Ex. Garden Clubs, Lexington, 1995; bd. dirs. Rockbridge Area Pres. Homes, 1996, Fine Arts of Rockbridge, 1985-92, Friends of Lime Kiln, Lexington, 1985-92. Mem.: Guild Hall, East End Arts, Montauk Artists Assn. (receptionist 2003—05), Artist Alliance East Hampton, L.I. Black Artists (v.p. 2000—05), Rockbridge Arts Guild (pres. LI Black Artists 2006—). Avocations: collecting emmett kelly clowns, art, reading, theater, tennis. Home: PO Box 1265 East Hampton NY 11937-0708 Personal E-mail: rosahannascott@aol.com.

SCOTT, RUTH ELLEN, music educator; b. Nome, Alaska, July 8, 1956; d. Robert Emmitt and Helen Faye Thompson; m. Henry Virgil Scott, Dec. 24, 1975 (dec.). BA in Broad Area Music Edn., Ctrl. Wash. U., Ellensburg, 1978. Cert. music tchr. Wash., 1978. Tchr. band/choir/orch. Yakima Sch. Dist. 7, Wash., 1978—79, tchr. band/choir, 1991—; tchr. band grades 5-12 Wapato Sch. Dist., Wash., 1979—81; H.S. tchr. band/choir Grandview Sch. Dist., Wash., 1981—83; tchr. band/choir Toppenish Sch. Dist., Wash., 1983—91. Marksmanship rifle team USAR, St. Louis, 1993—98, trumpet player 104th div. band, Vancouver, Wash., 1999—. Mem. Yakima Cmty. Band, 2002—06. Decorated Pres. 100 Gold Marksmanship badge U.S. Army. Mem.: Music Educator's Nat. Conf. Conservative. Wash. Avocations: golf, marksmanship, reading, trumpet, weightlifting. Home: 1491 Selah Loop Rd Selah WA 98942 Office: Washington Middle School 510 South 9th St Yakima WA 98901 Office Phone: 509-573-2335. Personal E-mail: brassigloo@aol.com. E-mail: scott.ruth@ysd.wednet.edu.

SCOTT, SHARON ANN, retired librarian, archivist; b. Wyandotte, Mich., Apr. 15, 1938; d. Jack Leroy Hessler, Anne Margaret (Zellner) Stone; m. Martin Loren Scott, Aug. 20, 1960; children: Laura, Arthur, Sheila Weber. BS, Ea. Mich. U., 1960; MLS, U. Mich., 1985. Cert. media specialist State of Mich. Cataloger reference libr. Toledo Mus. Art, Toledo, 1987—93; bindery clk. law libr. U. Mich., Ann Arbor, Mich., 1993—94; media specialist Dundee Cmty. Schs., Dundee, Mich., 1995—2000. V.p., bookkeeper Scott Equipment and Fabricating, Toledo, 1976—92; archivist Hist. Soc. Clinton, Clinton, Mich., 1974—. Author: School Library Media Annual, 1995, Robinson's 1988-Villages of Lenawee County, 1988, Village of Clinton, Michigan: a History, 1981; co-editor, dir. exhbn.: Wirt C. Rowland Exhbn., 2004; editor: Early History of Clintonites, 2006. Pres. Clinton Township Libr. Bd., Clinton, Mich., 1985—92; sec. Planning Commn. Village of Clinton, 1983—92; chmn. US 12 Heritage Hwy. Com., Clinton, 1999—; rep. Lenawee County coun. US 12 Heritage Trail, Adrian, Mich., 2001—. Mem.: Mich. Archives Assn., Midwest Archives Assn., Friends of the Archives (sec.-treas. Detroit conf. 1984—), Dexter Cmty. Band. Methodist. Avocations: singing, playing tuba, collecting children's books and fine art. Home: 214 E Michigan Ave Clinton MI 49236

SCOTT, SHERIE RENÉ, actress; m. Kurt Deutsch. Grad., Neighborhood Playhouse Sch. of Theatre. Actress (Broadway plays) The Who's Tommy, 1993, Grease, 1994, Rent, 1996, Aida, 2000, Dirty Rotten Scoundrels, 2005, 2006, (off-Broadway plays) The Last Five Years (Drama League award), Debbie Does Dallas, Landscape of the Body, 2005 (OBIE award, Village Voice, 2006), (regional plays) Over and Over, Faust, (films) Marci X, (TV films) Vault of Love, My Guys; singer: (albums) Men I've Had.*

SCOTT, SHIRLEY CLAY, dean; PhD, Kent State U., 1973. Dean Grad. Coll. Western Mich. U.; dean Coll. Liberal Arts Southern Ill. U., 1999—, prof. Office: Office of the Dean Coll Liberal Arts So Illinios U Mailcode 4522 Carbondale IL 62901 Office Phone: 618-453-2466. E-mail: scotts@siu.edu.

SCOTT, SUE A., music educator; b. Brenham, Tex., Oct. 12, 1937; d. Oscar Lee and Ruby Faye Jameson; m. Calvin John Scott, June 16, 1962; children: Cedric John, Kalva Sue BA, Prairie View A&M U., 1959, MA, 1969. Dir. H.S. choir Marlin Ind. Sch. Dist., Tex., 1959—64; sch. sec. Garland Ind. Sch. Dist., Tex., 1964—65; clk., proofreader White Hall Lab., Dallas, 1965—67; dir. H.S. choir Wilmer Hutchins Ind. Sch. Dist., Tex., 1967—72; tchr. instrumental ensemble Dallas Pub. Schs., 1972—99. Chmn. music dept. Wilmer Hutchins H.S., 1967-72, Boude Storey Mid. Sch., Dallas, 1980-99 Fellow Nat. Assn. Negro Musicians; mem. NEA, Tex. Music Tchrs. Assn., Prairie View A&M U. Music Club (pres. 1958-59, cert. 1959), Mu Alfa Sigma (pres. 1957-59, cert. 1959) Democrat. Baptist.

SCOTT, SUSAN CRAIG, plastic surgeon; b. NYC, 1948; MD, Columbia U., 1974. Diplomate Am. Bd. Plastic Surgery with subspecialty in hand surgery. Intern Roosevelt Hosp., N.Y.C., NY, 1974—75, resident in gen. surgery, 1975—79; resident in plastic surgery NYU Med. Ctr., 1979—81; fellow in hand surgery Roosevelt Hosp., 1981—82; pvt. practice plastic surgery N.Y.C., 1987—. Office: 150 E 77TH St New York NY 10021-1922 Office Phone: 212-288-9922. Personal E-mail: smcscott@verizon.net.

SCOTT, TAMMY CHARLENE, secondary school educator; b. Pennington Gap, Va., Oct. 3, 1961; d. Herbert Hoover and Margaret Ella (Gregg) S. BS, Radford (Va.) U., 1984; MS in Edn., cert. supervision and edn., Lincoln Meml. U., 1999. Cert. in secondary social studies and math., Va. Tchr. social studies Dryden H.S., Jonesville, Va., 1984-89, Lee H.S., Jonesville, 1989—. Mem. NEA, DAR (Ba. Lovelady chpt.), Va. Edn. Assn., Lee County Edn. Assn. (sec. 1986-88, pres. 1988-89), Va. Coun. Social Studies Tchrs., Delta Kappa Gamma. Methodist. Avocations: reading, piano, walking. Office: Lee HS RR 2 Box 3145 Jonesville VA 24263-9417

SCOTT, TIFFANY, ice skater; b. Weymouth, Mass., May 1, 1977; Student, Del. Tech. U., 1999. Pairs ice skater with Philip Dulebohn. Recipient Bronze medal, U.S. Jr. Championships, 1997. Avocations: sewing, bicycling, camping, collecting stamps, postcards. Office: US Figure Skating Headquarters 20 First St Colorado Springs CO 80906

SCOTT, VANESSA KATHLEEN, writer; b. Flushing, N.Y., Aug. 28, 1963; d. John Crennan and Sonia (Rossi) Scott. BA, Hunter Coll., 1990; MA, NYU, 1993. Instr. New Sch. U., NYC. Author: Modern Words 7, 1999; contbg. author: Best Lesbian Erotica, 1996; contbr. online jour. SpoonFedAmerika-.com, online jour. Velvetmafia.com, 2001. Recipient Honorary Mention Creative Writing Silver Quill Writing Contests, 1993; nominee Pushcart prize, 2006. Avocations: bicycling, films, painting, modeling, art collecting. Home: 94-32 133rd Ave Ozone Park NY 11417-2022

SCOTT-BATTLE, GLADYS NATALIE, retired social worker; b. Cambridge, Mass., Sept. 16, 1933; d. Dudley Fairfax and Bessie Mae (Mitchell) Scott; m. James Henry Battle, Jr., Oct. 18, 1953 (div. 1975); children: Gregory, James, Jameel. BA, Fordham U., 1975; MSW, Columbia U., 1978. Lic. psychiat. social worker; cert. social worker, tchr., NY. Program dir. Cmty. Svc. Soc., N.Y.C., 1978—79; corp. liaison cities and schs., N.Y.C., 1979—80; psychotherapist Harlem Interfaith Counseling, N.Y.C., 1980—82; psychiat. social worker Met. Hosp., N.Y.C., 1982—93; psychiat. social worker Bronx clin. divsn. N.Y.C. Bd. Edn., 1982—92; ret., 1992. Cons. NY State Disability Determinations, 1982—, NYC Family Ct., 1987-92, family and criminal ct.-selected cases. V.p. Women Who Help Other People, NYC, 1985; bd. dirs. Morningside Gardens Coop., NYC, 1986-88; vol. Met. Mus. Art. Mem. NASW, Nat. Assn. Black Social Workers, United Fedn. Tchrs., Internat. Assn. Social Workers, Bus. and Profl. Women's Club. Democrat. Avocations: visiting museums and art galleries, painting, theater, travel, exploring Hudson Valley landmarks and museums. Home: 119 Nyack PLZ Nyack NY 10960-3851

SCOTT-FINAN, NANCY ISABELLA, government administrator; b. Canton, Ohio, June 13, 1949; d. Milton Kenneth and Gertrude (Baker) Scott; m. Robert James Finan II, Aug. 23, 1986. Student, Malone Coll., 1970-73; BA magna cum laude, U. Akron, 1976, postgrad., 1976, Kent State U., 1977; MA in Internat. Transactions, George Mason U., 1995. Legal sec. Krugliak, Wilkins, Griffiths & Dougherty, Canton, 1969, Amerman, Burt & Jones, Canton, 1970-77; legal sec., paralegal Black, McCuskey, Souers & Arbaugh, Canton, Ohio, 1977-81; adminstrv. staff mem. com. on judiciary U.S. Senate, Washington, 1981-86; adminstrv. asst. to counsel to Pres., The White House, Washington, 1986-89; adminstrv. asst. to former counsel to pres. O'Melveny & Myers, Washington, 1989; asst. dir. congl. rels. Office Legis. Affairs U.S. Dept. Justice, Washington, 1989-91; spl. asst. to asst. atty. gen. U.S. Dept. of Justice, Washington, 1991—. Substitute tchr. North Canton City Sch. System, 1979-80; residential tutor Canton City Sch. System, 1980-81, Fairfax (Va.) County Sch. System, 1983; instr. dance and exercise Siffrin Home for Developmentally Disabled, Canton, 1980. East coast regional v.p. for spl. projects Childhelp U.S.A., Washington, 1988-90; mem. Rep. Women of Capitol Hill, Washington, 1984-95; bd. mem. Have a Heart Homes for Abused Children, Washington, 1990-91. Mem. AAUW, Women of Washington, Corcoran Gallery Art, Nat. Mus. Women Arts. Presbyterian. Office: US Dept Justice 950 Pennsylvania Ave NW Washington DC 20530-0001 Business E-Mail: nancy.scott-finan@usdoj.gov.

SCOTTI, R. A., writer; b. Providence, Dec. 25, 1947; d. Ciro Ottorino and Rita Ward (Dwyer) S.; children: Francesca, Ciro. Student, U. Rome, 1964—65, Loyola U., Chgo., 1965—67. Author: Kiss of Judas, 1984, The Devil's Own, 1985, The Hammer's Eye, 1987, Cradle Song, 1987, (as Angelica Scott) For Love of Sarah, 1995, Sudden Sea, 2003, Basilica: The Splendor and the Scandal-Building St. Peter's, 2006. Roman Catholic. Home: 224 E 18th St Apt 3A New York NY 10003-3632 Office Phone: 212-677-9070. Personal E-mail: chapverseink@aol.com.

SCOTTO, RENATA, soprano; b. Savona, Italy, Feb. 24, 1935; m. Lorenzo Anselmi. Studied under, Ghirardini, Merlino and Mercedes Llopart, Accademia Musicale Savonese, Conservatory Giuseppe Verdi, Milan. Opera singer Robert Lombardo Assocs., 1979—. Presenter master classes Juilliard Sch., N.Y.C., Curtis Inst., Phila., Yale U., Russian Opera Ctr., Moscow, Tokyo U., young artist program La Scale, Milan, N.Y. Met. Opera; opened Renata Scotto

Opera Acad., Albisola Marina, Italy, 1997—, Music Conservatory of Westchester, White Plains, NY, 2003—; dir. young artist program Verdi Festival, Parma, Italy, 2000 Roles include Feldmarschallin in Der Rosenkavalier (Franco Abiati and Frankfurter Allgemeine awards), 1992, performs Les Nuits d'Ete (Berlioz), Strauss and Mahler songs, Erwartung (Schoenberg), Santa Cecilia Acad. Orch., Rome, 1994, staged Il Parata (Bellini), Festival Belliniano, Catania, Italy, 1993, staged new prodn. La Sonnambula, 1994; dir. new prodn. La Traviata, N.Y.C. Opera, 1995.Kundry in Parsifal, German Schweing Fewtival, 1995, La Voix Humaine, Maggio Musicale Fiorentino, also in Barcelona, Spain, Amsterdam, The Netherlands, Klytemnestra in Elektra, Balt., 2000; dir. Tosca, Grand Opera Miami, 2001; performs with leading orchs. of world, giving concerts and master classes Bd. dirs. Santa Cecilia Acad., Rome Recipient Emmy award for Best Live Mus. Event in TV for Live from Lincoln Ctr., 1995. Office: 5 Stone Hollow Way Armonk NY 10504 Also: care Theatre of La Scala via Filodrammatici 2 Milan Italy

SCOTTO, ROSANNA, newscaster; b. Bklyn. BA in Fine Arts, Catholic U. Reporter, assoc. prodr. WTBS, Atlanta; reporter WABC-TV NY, reporter Eyewitness News N.Y.C.; corr., anchor FOX 5/WNYW News, N.Y.C., 1986—. Co-owner Fresco by Scotto, 1993—. Co-author: Fresco: Modern Tuscan Cooking for All Seasons, 1997; actor: (films) Miracle on 34th Street, 1994, Ransom, 1996, The Object of My Affection, 1998, Famous, 2000. Nominee Emmy award, 1990, 1995; recipient First Place award for indiv. reporting, NY St. Associated Press Assoc., 1995. Office: WNYW-TV/Fox Broadcasting Co 205 E 67th St New York NY 10021-6050

SCOTT-THOMAS, KRISTIN, actress; b. Redruth, Cornwall, England, United Kingdom, May 24, 1960; m. Francois Olivennes, 3 children, Hannah, Joseph, George. Student, Cen. Sch. Speech and Drama, Ecole Nat. des Arts. Stage debut in Schnitzler's La Lune Déclinante Sur 4 ou 5 Personnes Qui Danse; stage appearances include La Terre Etrangère, Naive Hirondelles, Yes Peut-Etre, Bérénice, 2001, Three Sisters, 2003, As You Desire Me, 2005; appearances on French, German, Australian, U.S. and Brit. TV include L'Ami d'Enfance de Maigret, Blockhaus, Cameleon La Tricheuse, Sentimental Journey, The Tenth Man, Endless Game, Framed, Titmuss Regained, Look at it this Way, Body and Soul; film appearances include Djamel et Juliette, L'Agent Troubé, La Méridienne, Under the Cherry Moon, A Handful of Dust, Force Majeure, Bille en Tete, The Bacheloir, Bitter Moon, Four Weddings and a Funeral (B.A.F.T.A. award), Angels and Insects (Evening Standard Film award), Richard III, 1995, Angels & Insects, 1996, Somebody to Love, 1996, The Pompatus of Love, 1996, Mission: Impossible, 1996, The English Patient, 1996, Amour et confusions, 1997, Souvenir, 1998, The Revenger's Comedies, 1998, The Horse Whisperer, 1998, Up at the Villa, 1999, Random Hearts, 1999, Life as a House, 2001, Gosford Park, 2001. Office: c/o Kevin Huvane & Bryan Lourd Creative Artists Agy 9830 Wilshire Blvd Beverly Hills CA 90212*

SCOTT-WILLIAMS, MILDRED P., food service specialist; b. Americus, Ga., Mar. 21, 1928; d. Bouie Lee and Mary (Jackson) Paschal; m. Mar. 10, 1986 (div.); 1 child, Alan Meadows. BS, Fort Valley State Coll., 1949; MA, Antioch U., 1980. Tchr. elem. schs., Ga., 1949-54; asst. dietitian Met. Hosp., Phila., 1954-57, head dietitian, 1957-67; tchr. home econs. Phila. Bd. Edn., 1967-68, food svc. mgr., 1969-71; dietitian Germantown Hosp., Phila., summer 1968; supr. tng. H.E.A.R.T. (Household Employment Assn. Reevaluation Tng.), Phila., 1968-69; tchr. food svc. Camden (N.J.) Bd. Edn., 1971-73, adminstrv. asst., 1973-81, food svc. supr., 1981-99; ret., 1999. Author: Metropolitan Diet Manual, 1965. Cub mother Boy Socuts Am., Phila., 1970-71; block chairperson 5900 Neighborhood Assn., Phila., 1980-89; Dem. committeewoman 17 Ward 28th Divsn.; mem. Phila. Dist. Atty. Panel for Youth. Recipient award The Chapel of Four Chaplains, Phila., 1977, Disting. Svc. Key award LKM Sorority, 2000, Cert. of Appreciation, USDA, 2000, Recognition of Svc. award Camden City Fedn. Sch. Adminstrs., 2000. Mem. Am. Fedn. Sch. Adminstrs. (merit award 1987), Am. Sch. Food Svc. Assn. (cert., Star Club cert. 1999), N.J. Food Svc. Assn. (sec. 1980-82, appreciation award Elizabeth 1987, President's award New Brunswick 1989), Order Ea. Star (sec. 1979-84). Home: 5956 N 21st St Philadelphia PA 19138-2922 Personal E-mail: mscott9837@aol.com.

SCOTT-WILLIAMS, WENDY LEE, library and information scientist; b. Buffalo, Jan. 22; d. Arthur Raymond and June Amelia Schutt; m. Nigel Simon Scott-Williams, Feb. 29, 1980. BA cum laude, SUNY, Buffalo, 1975; MA with honors, Cambridge U., 1979; MLIS with honors, CUNY-Queens Coll., 1987. Applications rep. Barrister, N.Y.C., 1982-83; coord. computer systems Stroock & Stroock & Lavan, N.Y.C., 1983-87; tech. svcs. mgr. Batten, Barton, Durstein & Osborn (BBDO) Worldwide, N.Y.C., 1987-92; adminstr., mgr. info. resources Fairchild Publs., N.Y.C., 1992-96; info. resource mgr. March of Dimes Birth Defects Found., White Plains, NY, 1996—. Active N.Y. Zool. Soc. Mem. Spl. Librs. Assn., Cambridge Union Soc., Oxford-Cambridge Soc., Nature Conservancy, Greenpeace. Presbyterian. Avocations: travel, gardening. Office: March of Dimes Birth Defects Found Nat Hdqs 1275 Mamaroneck Ave White Plains NY 10605-5298

SCOVEL, MARY ALICE, retired music therapy educator; b. Grand Rapids, Mich., Jan. 28, 1936; d. Carl Edward and Alice Bertha (Bieri) Sennema; m. Ward Norman Scovel, July 7, 1956; children: Marcia, Katherine, Steven (dec.), Carl (dec.). MusB, Western Mich. U., 1969; MusM, Mich. State U., 1975. Registered music therapist; bd. cert. Asst. prof. music Grand Valley State U., Allendale, Mich., 1969-75; instr. U. Dayton (Ohio), 1975-78, Muskegon (Mich.) Community Coll., 1978-80; intern dir. Battle Creek (Mich.) Adventist Hosp., 1980-84; prof. music therapy Western Mich. U., Kalamazoo, 1984-95; ret., 1995; owner, pvt. practice Health Harmonics, Honolulu, 1997-98; ret., 1998. Cons. Pre-sch. Physically Handicapped, Wyo., Mich., 1974, Doris Klausen Devel. Ctr., Battle Creek, 1985-86; music therapist, sound practitioner and trainer, Tahlequah, Okla., 1995-97; pvt. practice health harmonics, 1997—; chmn. Multi-clinic, Kalamazoo, 1988-89. Author: Music Therapy in Treatment of Adults, 1990, Surviving Suicide: My Journey to the Light Within, 2003; co-editor Music Therapy Perspectives; cited in The Mozart Effect by Don Campbell, 1997; contbr. articles to profl. jours. Lay del. United Meth. Ch., Albion, Mich., 1991; vol. coord. United Hospice Beaufort, S.C., 2005—, dir. choir chimes PEP/Programs for Exceptional People, 2005—. Mem. Am. Music Therapy Assn. (del.), Nat. Assn. Mental Illness, Great Lakes Region Music Therapy (past pres.), Mich. Music Therapists, AAUW, Pi Delta Alpha, Pi Kappa Lambda. Avocations: reading, cross country skiing, singing, swimming, quilting. Home: 112 Doncaster Ln Bluffton SC 29909 Personal E-mail: mwscovel@davtv.com.

SCRANTON, MEGAN JENNIFER, speech therapist, educator; b. Warminster, Pa., Sept. 25, 1972; d. H. Chadwick and Judith Ann Idell; m. David Bruce Scranton, Oct. 23, 1999; children: Jacob Davis, Kara Mackenzie. BA, Bucknell U., Lewisburg, Pa., 1995; MS, Boston U., 1997; student in Sch. Adminstrn., Widener U., Pa., 2006—. Cert. tchr. speech and lang. impaired, instr. II, reading specialist Millersville U., Pa, 2002. Speech and lang. therapist Carlisle Pub. Schs., Mass., 1997—99, Lancaster -Lebanon IU 13, Pa., 1999—2001, SpeechCare, Inc., Lancaster, 2004—; literacy coach, reading specialist Lafayette Elem. Sch., Lancaster, 2001—, facilitator, supr., 2002—. Named RA of Yr., Bucknell U., 1994; recipient Varsity Cross Country Track and Field letter, 1991—95. Mem.: NEA, ASCD, Lancaster Edn. Assn., Pa. State Edn. Assn., Am. Speech-Lang.-Hearing Assn. Avocations: running, reading, scrapbooks, photography. Home: 118 Chelsea Loop Lancaster PA 17602

SCREEN, ROBIN MARIE, secondary school educator; b. Blue Island, Ill., Apr. 18, 1965; d. Donald Albert Anderson and Rosemary (Campbell) King; married. BA in English, No. Ill. U., DeKalb, 1988; MEd, U. North Tex., Denton, 1997. Cert. tchr. secondary edn., English, reading, Tex.; cert. libr., Tex. Tchr. English North Garland (Tex.) H.S., 1990-92, Lakeview Centennial H.S., Garland, 1992-93; tchr. reading Nimitz H.S., Irving, Tex., 1993-99; 8th grade reading tchr. Bowman Middle Sch., Plano, Tex., 1999—2002; libr. media specialist Ford Middle Sch., Allen, Tex., 2002—. Attendance policy violators com., student vol. svc. hour com. Nimitz H.S.; prin.'s coun. Bowman Mid. Sch., Allen, Tex., safety coun. Chmn. adv. bd. Irving C.A.R.E.S., 1995; sponsor Cultural Awareness Soc., Irving, 1995-96, Jr. Historians, Irving, 1994-1999; co-sponsor Bowman Raiders Are Great (BRAG); mem. Safety Coun., Bowman; mem. Bowman Reads Com. Recipient High Spirited Citizen award Irving Conv. and Visitors Bur., 1996. Mem. ASCD, Internat. Reading Assn., Assn. Tex. Profl. Educators, Tex. Assn. for Improvement of Reading (conf. spkr. 1995), Discovery Educator Network. Avocations: reading, music, environmental issues, aerobics, movies. Office: Ford Middle Sch 630 Park Pl Dr Allen TX 75002 Office Phone: 972-727-0590 x. 1710.

SCRIBNER, PRINCESS ROSE-MARIE, not-for-profit developer; b. Gardiner, Maine; d. Harvey Clinton and Harriet Gertrude Mason; m. Henry Elden Scribner, Jan. 18, 1958; children: Randall, Dawn, Debra, Shawn, Todd. BS, U. Ea. Conn., 1971; degree (hon.), U. Maine, 2002. Pres., founder White Cloud Indians for Devel., Norwich, Conn., 1970—86; adminstr. Indian Health Clinic, Pequot Nation, Ledyard, Conn., 1977—86. Founder, pres. Indian Women's Non-Profit Orgn., Indian Island, Maine. Active mem. Women's Polit. Caucus, Hartford, Conn., 1970, Nat. Women's Polit. Orgn., Washington, 1971. Recipient Volunteering Recognition award, Pres. Reagan. Democrat. Roman Catholic. Avocations: dance, decorating, puzzle-making, gardening, writing. Home: 65 West St II Old Town ME 04468

SCRIMSHAW, SUSAN CROSBY, academic administrator; b. Nov. 12, 1945; m. Allan Stern; 1 child from previous marriage, Mary Corey March. AB, Barnard Coll., 1967; MA, Columbia U., 1969, PhD in Anthropology, 1974. Rsch. assoc. Internat. Inst. for Study of Human Reporduction, 1969—75; asst. prof. health adminstrn. Columbia U., 1975; asst. prof. pub. health Div. Population, Family and Internat. Health, Sch. Pub. Health UCLA, 1975—80, assoc. prof. Div. Population and Family Health, 1980—85, assoc. dir. Latin Am. Ctr., 1984—88, prof. pub. health and anthropology, 1985—96, acting chair Dept. Pub. Health, 1988—89, assoc. dean Academic Programs, 1988—94, acting dean, 1991—92, 1992—93; dean, prof. cmty. heath scis. and anthropology U. Ill. Sch. Pub. Health, Chgo., 1995—2006; pres. Simmons Coll., Boston, 2006—. Co-editor: The Handbook of Social Studies in Health & Med. Recipient Margaret Mead award, 1985. Fellow: AAAS; mem.: Nat. Soc. Med. Anthropology (pres. 1985), Soc. Applied Anthropology, Am. Anthropology Assn., Inst. Medicine NAS. Office: Simmons Coll Office of Pres 300 The Fenway Boston MA 02115*

SCRIPTURE, LOIS JEAN, retired social services director; b. Pine Island, Minn., July 6, 1943; d. Henry and Erma Mae Yennie; m. Jim Wesley Scripture, Jan. 31, 1970; children: David James, Anne Marie. BA, San Jose State Coll., San Jose, Calif., 1964; MSW, U. Minn., Mpls., Minn., 1966. LISW Minn. Bd. of Social Work, 1991. Psychiat. social worker Rochester State Hosp., 1966—70; social svcs. dir. Rochester Health Care Ctr., Rochester, 1977—91, Samaritan Bethany Home on Eighth, Rochester, 1991—94, Pine Haven Care Ctr., Pine Island, Minn., 1994—2004. Vice chair of bd. Pine Island Area Home Svcs., Pine Island, Minn., 2002—. Contbr. articles pub. to profl. jour. Spkr. on living wills Cmty. Edn., Pine Island, Minn., 2004—05; co-facilitator for adult day care Pine Island Area Home Svcs., Pine Island, Minn., 2004—05. R-Consevative. Protestant. Achievements include Polio at age 3, resulting in paralysis of both legs Attended Luther Coll. 1960-61 and was in the honor soc. and the Luther College Concert Band, giving concerts in Europe 1961. Avocations: writing, travel, gardening.

SCRIVNER, B(ARBARA) E., piano educator; b. Medford, Oreg., May 25, 1931; 4 children. Student (piano student Lawrence Morton), Bob Jones U., 1962-66; corr. student, Inst. Children's Lit., Redding Ridge, Conn., 1974-76. Part time sec., Oreg., 1948-50, 60-62, SC, 1974-76, 80-86, Census Bur., SC, 1980-82; piano tchr. Greenville, SC, 1963—2003. Contbr. column A Life Within, also by-line columns-opinion to Times Examiner, Greenville, 1995-97; writer for monthly newsletter From Whence We Came, 1997—; contbr. articles to local newspapers. Mem. Nat. Presdl. Task Force; active Rep. Nat. Com., S.C. Rep. Party; mem. Nat. Rep. Congl. Com.; coord. hdqs. Greenville County Rep. Party, 1993—94.

SCRIVNER, ELLEN M., psychologist; d. John P. O'Shea and Dorothy Mary O'Shea-Hanley; m. Peter C. Scrivner, Aug. 25, 1962; children: Anne Collins (Scrivner) Kuban, Thomas C. BS, St. Louis U., 1961, MS, 1963; PhD in Psychology, Cath. U. Am., 1986. Lic. psychologist Bd. of Examiners, Md. Police psychologist, Fairfax County, Va., Prince Georges County, Md.; dep. dir. COPS Office, U.S. Dept. of Justice, Washington, 2000—02; sr. advisor FBI Office Law Enforcement Coords., 2002—04; dep. supt. bur. of adminstrv. svcs. Chgo. Police Dept., 2004—. Pres. Pub. Safety Innovations, Washington, 2003—04; vis. fellow Nat. Inst. Justice, U.S. Dept. Justice. Author: Law Enforcement Families: Issues and Answers, 1994, Police Psychology Into The 21st Century, 1995. Mem. adv. bd. Local Initiatives Support Corp., N.Y.C., 2003—05. Recipient Women of Courage and Vision award, U.S. Dept. of Justice, 2001, Lifetime Achievement award, 2000. Mem.: APA (life; divsn. pres. 1991—92, Disting. Svc. award 1990). Achievements include research in excessive force/violence, community policing, police psychology. Home: 700 New Hampshire Ave NW Washington DC 20037 Office Phone: 312-745-6288. Personal E-mail: ellenscrivner284@msn.com. E-mail: ellen.scrivner@chicagopolice.org.

SCROGGINS, M. SUZANNE PAONESSA, budget analyst; b. Albany, N.Y., May 1, 1974; d. Thomas and Mary Laura (Maresca) Paonessa; m. Josh Scroggins. BS in Fin., Siena Coll., 1996. Fin. mgmt. specialist U.S. Dept. Energy, Schenectady (N.Y.) Naval Reactors Office, 1996-99; assoc. dir. fin. aid Siena Coll., 1999-2001; assoc. dir. budget and bus. svcs. U. Maine, Orono, 2001—, instr., Profl. Employees Adv. Coun. (PEAC), mem. athletic adv. bd., co-chair, site coord. wellness program. Treas. Schenectady Naval Reactors Office Employee Assn., 1997—98. Vol. YMCA; ch. lector, greeter; co-dir. Siena Coll. Friendly's Fanfest, 1997—98; mem. Siena Coll. Career Adv. Network. Mem.: Nat. Youth Sports Coaches Assn., DOE Women's Golf League (treas. 1998—, named Most Improved Player 1998), Fin. Mgmt. Assn., 21st Century Leaders Soc., Kensho-Do Karate Club (asst. instr. 1998—2000, brown belt), Sigma Beta Delta, Delta Epsilon Sigma, Alpha Kappa Alpha. Roman Catholic. Avocations: golf, softball, dancing. Home: 398 Old County Rd Apt 9 Hampden ME 04444-1936 Personal E-mail: sqboo@yahoo.com.

SCRUGGS, ELAINE M., mayor; m. Larry Scruggs; 1 child, Jennifer. Former mgmt. specialist; elected mem. Glendale (Ariz.) City Coun., 1990-93; mayor City of Glendale, 1994—. Past chmn. Maricopa (Ariz.) Assn. Govts., chair youth policy adv., chmn. Regional Pub. Transp. Authority, chmn. Ariz. Mcpl. Water Users Assn., chair Maricopa Assn. Govt. Regional Aviation Systems policy com.; chair Ariz. Mcpl. Tax Code Commn. Dir. Glendale Leadership Program, 1984-89; mem. Ariz. Coalition for Tomorrow, Ariz. Women in Mcpl. Govt.; mem. youth adv. commn., Mayor's Alliance Against Drugs and Gangs. Mem. Glendale C. of C. Office: Office Mayor 5850 W Glendale Ave Glendale AZ 85301-2563

SCRUGGS, SANDRA NELL, writer, former school teacher; b. Tupelo, Miss., Mar. 17, 1948; d. Luther Herman and Gladys Lavelle Scruggs; 1 child, Tara Leigh Turner. BS in Edn., Miss. State U., 1970; degree in gifted and talented edn., Delta State U., 1979. Tchr. pub. schs., Miss., 1970-72, 78-89, Bremerhaven (German) Mil. Sch., 1973-75, Anniston (Ala.) Pub. Schs., 1976-77; writer New Orleans, 1989—. Writer Poetry Forum, New Orleans, 1999. Recipient Woman of Yr. award Nat. Club, 1979. Avocations: recording, songwriting, writing children's books, birdwatching, camping.

SCRUGGS, TERESA EILEEN, science educator; d. Wesley Martin and Sarah Clark Scruggs. BS in Edn., Delta State U., Cleveland, Miss., 1996. Lic. tchr. Miss. Pvt. Sch. Assn. Dept. Instrn., 1997. Preschool tchr. Freeman's Little People's Pl., Grenada, Miss., 1994—97; tchr., coach Strider Acad., Charleston, Miss., 1997—2002, Humphreys Acad., Belzoni, 2002—. Sponsor Fellowship Christian Athletes, Belzoni, 2002—; mem. Student Month Com., 2004—; sec., treas. Dist. III - A Coaches, 2006—. Recipient Tchr. Yr., Strider Acad., 1996—99, Dist. Basketball Coach Yr., Dist. II - A Basketball Coaches, 2006, Tchr. of Yr., Strider Acad., 1999—2000. Mem.: Miss. Pvt. Sch. Coaches Assn., Miss. Pvt. Sch. Edn. Assn. Methodist. Avocations: softball, basketball, fishing, attending church, movies.

SCUDIERE, DEBRA HODGES, lawyer; b. Columbus, Ohio, Sept. 18, 1954; d. L.L. and Anita Lillian (Campbell) Hodges; m. William A. Scudiere, July 16, 1988; 1 child, Rachel Giovanna. BA magna cum laude, W.Va. U., 1976, JD, 1982. Bar: W.Va. 1982, U.S. Dist. Ct. (no. and so. dists.) W.Va. 1982, U.S. Supreme Ct. 1989. With Furbee, Amos, Webb & Critchfield, Morgantown, W.Va., 1982—2001; atty. Kay Casto & Chaney, PLLC, Morgantown, W.Va., 2001—. Mem. W.Va. Law Rev., 1981-82; adj. lectr. trial advocacy W.Va. U., Morgantown, 1991—. Staff mem. W.Va. Law Rev., 1981-82; rsch. editor Jour. Coll. and Univ. Law, 1981-82. Pres., chmn. bd. dirs. North Cen. W.Va. Legal Aid Soc., Morgantown, 1989-95; bd. dirs. W.Va. Sr. Legal Aid, Inc., 1999—. Mem. Def. Rsch. Inst., Def. Trial Counsel W.Va., Marion County Bar Assn., Monongalia County Bar Assn., W.Va. Bar Assn., W.Va. State Bar (mem. bd. govts., v.p., pres.-elect 2004-05, pres. 2005—), So. Conf. Bar Pres. (pres. 2005—), Nat. Conf. Bar Pres., Order of Barrister, Pi Delta Phi, Phi Delta Phi. Mem. Lds Ch. Office: 50 Clay St Morgantown WV 26501 Office Phone: 304-296-1100. Business E-Mail: debras@kaycasto.com.

SCULLION, ANNETTE MURPHY, lawyer, educator; b. Chgo., Apr. 6, 1926; d. Edmund Patrick and Anna (Nugent) Murphy; 1 child, Kevin. BEd, Chgo. Tchrs. Coll., 1960; JD, DePaul U., 1964, MEd, 1966, Loyola U., Chgo., 1970; EdD, No. Ill. U., 1974. Bar: Ill. 1964, U.S. Dist. Ct. (no. dist.) Ill. 1965, U.S. Ct. Appeals (D.C. cir.) 1978. Lectr. Chgo. C.C., 1964-68; pvt. practice Chgo., 1964—; from asst. prof. bus. edn. to prof. Chgo. State U., 1966-98. Founder, adviser Bus. Edn. Students Assn., Chgo. State U., 1976—; sch. law workshop coord. Ill. Divsn. Vocat. and Tech. Edn., 1981, coord. edn. workshops, 1990—. Mem. ABA, Nat. Bus. Edn. Assn., Womens Bar Assn. Ill., Am. Tchr. Edn., Beta Gamma Sigma. Home: 386 Muskegon Ave Calumet City IL 60409-2347

SCULLY, SUSAN, artist; b. Phila., Aug. 3, 1950; d. Francis J. and Eileen (O'Connor) S. BA in English, Chestnut Hill Coll., 1972. Designer of life-like masks, costumes, art work. Personal E-mail: emeraldlion@comcast.net.

SCUPHAM, CAROLE JEAN, elementary school educator; b. Cedar Rapids, Iowa, Nov. 3, 1947; d. William and Jean (Duncalf) Lynch; m. Garry Francis Rudish, June 21, 1969 (div.); 1 child, Stephanie; m. George William Scupham II, Nov. 25, 1988; children: Amanda, Christopher. BA, Mt. Mercy Coll., 1969. 2d grade tchr. Linn Mar Sch., Marion, Iowa, 1969-74; Vietnamese student instr. Cedar Rapids Sch. Sys., 1974-75; substitute tchr. Davenport Schs., Iowa, 1975-85, 4th & 5th grade tchr., 1985—2004, first grade tchr., 2004—. Vol. St. Luke's Hosp., Davenport. Mem. NEA, AAUW, Iowa State Edn. Assn. Roman Catholic. Avocations: reading, boating, swimming, needlepoint, travel. Home: 4420 Stone Haven Dr Bettendorf IA 52722-2017

SCURLOCK, JOY SHELTON, elementary school educator; b. Birmingham, Mar. 13, 1958; d. Roy Wesley and Charlotte Marie Shelton; m. Don Edward Scurlock, Aug. 14, 1976; children: Blake, Dustin. BS, U. Montevallo, Ala., 1979, MS, 1983. Tchr. Valley Elem. Sch., Pelham, Ala., 1980—83, Inverness Elem. Sch., 1983—89, Helena Elem. Sch., 1989—92, Grassland Elem. Sch., Brentwood, Tenn., 1992—2005, Scales Elem. Sch., 2003—. Author: The Ease of Questioning, 2004. Mem.: Internat. Reading Assn., Nat. Coun. Tchrs. English. Home: 2034 Hunterwood Dr Brentwood TN 37027 Office: Scales Elem Sch 6480 Nurray n Brentwood TN 37027

SCURRY, BRIANA COLLETTE, professional soccer player; b. Mpls., Sept. 7, 1971; BS in Polit. Sci., U. Mass., 1995. Goalkeeper U.S. Women's Nat. Soccer Team, Chgo., 1994—99, 2002—; profl. soccer player Atlanta Beat (WUSA), 2001—03. Mem. U.S. Olympic Soccer Team, Athens, 2004. Named Goalkeeper of Yr., Mo. Athletic Club Sports Found., 1993; recipient Gold medal, Atlanta Olympics, 1996, Athens Olympic games, 2004, World Cup champion, 1999, Silver medal, Sydney Olympic Games, 2000. Office: US Soccer Fedn US Soccer House 1801 S Prairie Ave Chicago IL 60616-1319

SEACAT, MARIAN LOUISE, music educator; b. Washington, Kans., Nov. 7, 1964; d. Duane William and Patricia Josephine Klozenbucher; m. Dwann Alan Seacat, June 2, 1990; children: Brian Lane, Colin Reed. MusB Edn., Kans. State U., Manhattan, 1988. Computer endorsement Ft. Hays State U., Kans., 1989, cert. ESL Ft. Hays State U., Kans., 2003. Band and music tchr. Mullinville Sch. Dist., Kans., 1988; music and band tchr. Unified Sch. Dist. 225 Fowler Sch. Dist., Kans., 1989—. Grade sch. chair 6 trait writing com. Unified Sch. Dist. 225, Fowler, 2005—. Flutist: Dodge City Cowboy Band. Mem.: Fowler Tchrs. Assn. (pres. 1996—99). Avocations: reading, gardening. Office Phone: 620-646-5234. Personal E-mail: seacat2@rurallink.net.

SEACHRIST, DENISE, music educator; b. Youngstown, Ohio, Feb. 2, 1960; d. Glen Wilbert and Eloise Rapp Seachrist. MusB, Heidelberg Coll., 1982; MusM, Youngstown State U., 1985; PhD, Kent State U., 1993. Assoc. prof. Kent State U., Warren, Ohio, 1994—. Dir. Kent Trumbull Choir, Warren, 1996—; bd. mem. Warren Philharm., 1998—; guest dir. Symphony Women's Chorus, Youngstown, 1998; spkr. in field. Author: Musical World of Halim El-Dabh, 2003; contbr. chapters to books, entries to dictionaries. Mem.: Soc. for Ethnomusicology (sec. Niagara chpt. 1997—98), Am. Musicological Soc., Soc. for Am. Music, Coll. Music Soc., Internat. Alliance for Women in Music. Democrat. Mem. United Church of Christ. Avocations: reading, swimming, music, golf, photography. Home: 1443 Stafford Ave NE Warren OH 44483-4339 Office: Kent State Univ 4314 Mahoning Ave NW Warren OH 44483-1998 E-mail: dseachri@kent.edu.

SEAGRAVES, HELEN LEONARD, librarian; b. Havre, Mont., Dec. 28, 1929; d. Robert Walter and Helen Louise (Henderson) Leonard; children: Ben, Hal, Jan, Roxanne, Louisa. AB, Reed Coll., 1951; MLS, U. N.C., 1971. Cert. social studies tchr., librarian, N.C., Oreg. Libr. media specialist Wake County Schs., Raleigh, N.C., 1971-79; libr. Estacada (Oreg.) Schs., 1980-81, Sch. Dist. #12, The Dalles, Oreg., 1981-87, Hood River (Oreg.) County Schs., 1987—94. Cons. Colegio Roosevelt Libr., Lima, Peru, 1976. Contbr. articles, photographs to profl. publs. Mem. NEA, ALA, Oreg. Hist. Soc., Am. Assn. Sch. Librs., Oreg. Ednl. Media Assn., Internat. Coun. for Computers in Edn., Spotted Chicken Soc. Avocations: photography, travel, writing, hiking.

SEAGRAVES, KAREN DENISE, elementary school educator; b. Fulton Cty., Ga., July 15, 1965; d. Robert Harold and Martha Elizabeth Seagraves. Med, Ga. State U., Atlanta, 1988—90. Tchr. Stockbridge Mid. Sch., 2001—; 7th grade sci. tchr. Henry County HS, McDonough, Ga. Recipient Tchr. of Yr., Clayton County Bd. Edn., 1998, Henry County Bd. Edn., 2003. Home: 100 Goldfinch Dr Monticello GA 31064 Office: Stockbridge Mid Sch 553 Old Conyers Rd Stockbridge GA 30281 Office Phone: 770-474-5710. Office Fax: 770-507-8406. Business E-Mail: kdseagraves@henry.k12.ga.us.

SEAGREN, ALICE, school system administrator, former state legislator; b. 1947; m. Fred Seagren; 2 children. BS, SE Mo. State U. Mem. Minn. Ho. of Reps., 1993—2004, chmn. edn. fin., 1999—2004; commr. of edn. State of Minn., 2004—. Active Bloomington (Minn.) Sch. Bd., 1989-92. Mem. Bloomington C. of C. (bd. dirs. 1990-92), Phi Gamma Nu, Alpha Chi Omega. Republican. Home: 9730 Palmer Cir Bloomington MN 55437-2017 Office: Minn Dept Children, Famlies, Learning 1500 Highway 36 W Roseville MN 55113-4035 Office Phone: 651-582-8204. E-mail: mde.commissioner@state.mn.us.

SEAGROVES, JEAN FRANZEN, secondary school educator; b. Glens Falls, N.Y., Oct. 25, 1934; d. Werner Gustav and Ethel Edith (Salstrom) Franzen; m. Monroe O. Seagroves, Nov. 24, 1965 (dec. 1987); 1 child, Bonnie Jean. BA, SUNY, 1961; MA, U. N.Mex., 1984. Tchr. English, Tuba City (Ariz.) H.S., 1984—2000; examiner-at-large G.E.D., Tucson, 2001—. G.E.D.

adminstr. State of Ariz., Tuba City, 1990-96. Avocations: family, reading, travel, music. Home and Office: 7237 S Camino Del Arco Iris Tucson AZ 85746-8234 E-mail: sylvergene@aol.com.

SEALS, KRISTI DAWN, elementary school educator; b. Huntington, W.Va. m. Billy Seals. BA, Liberty U., Lynchburg, Va., 2000; MEd, Lincoln Meml. U. Child devel. specialist Cherokee Health Systems, Morristown, Tenn., 2002—04; tchr. East Ridge Middle Sch., Whitesburg, Tenn. Home: 5730 Charlene Dr Russellville TN 37860 Office: East Ridge Middle School Whitesburg TN

SEALS, MARGARET LOUISE CRUMRINE, managing editor; b. Buckhannon, W.Va., Oct. 27, 1944; d. James Richard and Helen Margaret (Brown) Crumrine; m. Harry Eugene Seals, Jan. 10, 1975. BS in journalism, W. Va. U., 1966; MS in mass. comm., Va. Commonwealth U., 1983. Reporter, copy editor Democrat & Chronicle, Rochester, NY, 1966-67, Dayton (Ohio) Daily News, 1967-68; copy editor Richmond (Va.) Times-Dispatch, 1968-75, copy desk slot editor, 1975-81, exec. news editor, 1981, asst. mng. editor, 1982-92, dep. mng. editor, 1992-93, mng. editor, 1994—. Mem. Leadership Metro Richmond, 1986, mem. alumni adv. bd. sch. mass. comm. Va. Commonwealth U., 1988-93, 04-; mem. vis. com. Sch. Journalism, W.Va. U., 1999—. Named Outstanding Woman in Comms. YWCA Met. Richmond, 1989; recipient Perley Isaac Reed award W.Va. U. Journalism Sch. Alumni Assn., 1996; inducted into Va. Comm. Hall of Fame, 2003. Mem.: Va. Press Assn. (dir. 2001—03, treas. 2003—04, sec. 2004—05, v.p. 2005—), AP Mng. Editors (editor APME News 1993—94, dir. 1993—95, treas. 1996—97, dir. 1998—2001, Disting. Svc. award 2002), Va. Press Women (treas. 1986—88, 2d v.p. 1988—90, pres. 1990—92, Press Woman of Yr. 1986, Communicator of Achievement award 1997), Soc. Profl. Journalists (bd. dirs. Va. profl. chpt. 1998—2003, pres. Va. profl. chpt. 2000—02), Nat. Fedn. Press Women (bd. dirs. 1990—92, Communicator of Achievement award 1997), Phi Kappa Phi. Avocations: history, historical fiction, jazz. Office: Richmond-Times Dispatch PO Box 85333 Richmond VA 23293-5333 E-mail: lseals@timesdispatch.com.

SEAMAN, BARBARA (ANN ROSNER), author; b. NYC, Sept. 11, 1935; d. Henry Jerome and Sophie Blanche (Kimels) Rosner; m. Gideon Seaman, Jan. 13, 1957 (div.); children: Noah Samuel, Elana Felicia, Shira Jean. BA (Ford Found. scholar), Oberlin Coll., 1956, LHD (hon.), 1978; cert. in advanced sci. writing (Sloan-Rockefeller fellow), Columbia U., 1968. Columnist Brides Mag., NYC, 1964-68; columnist, contbg. editor Ladies' Home Jour., NYC, 1965-69; editor child care and edn. Family Cir., NYC, 1970-73; contbg. editor Omni mag., 1978; cons. FYI, ABC-TV, 1979-80; v.p. for devel. David Brooks Prodn., 1990-94; contbg. editor MS Mag., 1993—; columnist Hadassah Mag., 2000—03. Cons. US Senate subcom. on monopoly: Nelson pill hearings, 1970; presented testimony to Senate and Congl. coms., 1970—; lectr. in field; participant TV discussion shows; tchr. Coll. New Rochelle, 1975, Sagaris Inst., 1975, CUNY, 1993; founding mem. NY Women's Forum, 1973-99; co-founder Nat. Women's Health Network, 1975—, Comm. Consultants for Choice, 1985-86, Nat. Task Force Sexual Malpractice, 1985-86, Families Against Sexually Abusive Therapists and Other Profl., 1992—; v.p. Women's Med. Ctr., NYC, 1971-73; mem. ERA Emergency Task Force, 1979; adv. coun. Feminist Press, Old Westbury, NY, 1975; adv. bd. Feminist Ctr. for Human Growth and Devel., 1979, Women's History Libr., Berkeley, Calif., 1973-75; steering com. Women's Forum, 1974; adv. bd. NOW, NY, 1973, Women's Guide to Books, 1974, Jewish Women for Affirmative Action, Evanston, Ill., 1973—, Jour. Women and Health, 1975, Jewish Feminist Orgn., NYC, 1975; chair com. domestic violence Nat. Coun. Women's Health, 1993-98; judge for various journalism awards. Author: The Doctors' Case Against the Pill, 1969, rev. edit., 1980, 25th anniversary edit., 1995, Free and Female, 1972; (with G. Seaman) Women and the Crisis in Sex Hormones, 1977, Lovely Me: The Life of Jacqueline Susann, 1987, anniversary edit., 1996; (with Gary Null) For Women Only: Your Guide to Health Empowerment, 2000; The Greatest Experiment ever Performed on Women: exploding the Estrogen Myth, 2003; contbg. author: foreword to Lunaception, 1975; The Bisexuals, 1974, Career and Motherhood, 1979, The Menopause Industry, 1994; author (play) I Am a Woman, 1972; (movie) Scandalous Me: The Jackie Susann Story, 1998; contbr. (anthologies) Rooms with No View, 1974, Women and Men, 1975, Seizing Our Bodies, 1978, Women's Health Care: A Guide to Alternatives, 1984; Encyclopaedia of Childbirth, 1992, Lawyers Manual on Domestic Violence: Representing the Victim, 1995, The Conversation Begins, 1996, Real Majority Media Minority, 1997, The Reader's Companion to US Women's History, 1997, Jewish Women in America: An Historical Encyclopedia, 1997, Textbook of Women's Health, 1997, Women's Health, 1999, Routledge International Encyclopedia of Women,2001; George Mag., 250 ways to make Am. Better, 1999; Hands On! 33 More Things Every Girl Should Know, 2001, Sexual Revolution, 2003, Controversies in Science and Technology, 2005, Jewish Women's Archive: Femenism and Jewish Women Web Exhibit; cons. (film) The Pill, 1999; PBS Am. Experience the Pill, 2003; narrator (film) Taking Our Bodies Back, 1974; contbr. articles to newspapers, popular mags.; books and articles translated into Spanish, German, Dutch, Turkish, Japanese, Hebrew, French, Italian. Alumni cons. women's studies program Oberlin Coll., 1975; motivation com. Am. Cancer Soc., 1973; adv. com. Older Women's Health Project, NYU Med. Ctr., 1980; bd. dir. Safe Transp. of People, NYC, 1975, Women's Health Newsletter, 1983; adv. bd. DES Action, 1977, 7 Stories Press, 1997-; cons. Nat. Task Force on DES, 1978; contraceptive rsch. br. HEW, 1980; v.p., bd. dir. ARM (Abortion Rights Moblzn.), 1981—; hon. bd. dir. Carcinogen Info. Program, St. Louis, 1981, Am. Friends of Rabin Med. Ctr., 1998—;; trustee Nat. Coun. on Women in Medicine, 1989-1991, Nat. Coun. on Women's Health, 1992-2000; chmn. adv. bd. Coalition for Family Justice, 1991—; co-chair Domestic Violence com. NY Women's Agenda, 1992-93, del. Can.-USA Women's Health Forum, 1996; host com. Womens Health Day, Beijing, Plus-Five UN Reunion, 2000; cons. FDA Patient Labels on Oral Contraceptives, 2000-01; nat. judge Project Censored Award, 1997-. Recipient citation for books as first to raise issue of sexism in health care as world-wide issue Libr. of Congress, 1973, citation as author responsible for patient package inserts on prescriptions HEW, 1970, Matrix award, 1978, Pioneer Woman award Resources Divsn. of Am. Assn. Retired Persons, 1986, Athena award Nat. Coun. Women's Health, 1992, Health Advocacy award Health Policy Adv. Ctr., APHA, 1994, Project Censored award, 1996, Postal Service Women's Rights Movement stamp, 2000; Poynter Journalism Fellow, Yale U., 2003; inviting com. Am. Writers Congress. Mem. PEN, Authors Guild, Nat. Assn. Sci. Writers. Address: 110 W End Ave Apt 5D New York NY 10023-6348

SEAMAN, DONNA JEAN, editor, writer; b. Seattle, July 5, 1955; d. Harold A. and Elayne S. BFA, Kansas City Art Inst.; MA in English Lit., DePaul U. Assoc. editor, reviewer Booklist, Am. Libr. Assn., Chgo.; host, radio show, Open Books WLUW, Chgo., NW U., Chgo., Columbia Coll., Chgo. Vis. faculty Gloucher Coll., Balt., Sch of the Art Inst. of Chgo.; dir., judge Claudia Ann Seaman Poetry award, 1984—; judge Carl Sandburg Lit. Arts Coun., 1997. Author: In Our Nature, 2000, Writers on the Air, 2005, contbr. essays and revs. to Chgo. Tribune, 1996—; author, host, prodr.: (radio program) Open Books (Ill. Arts Coun. award 1997). Recipient James Friend Meml. award for lit. criticism, Writers Who Make a Difference award, The Writer's Mag. Mem. Nat. Book Critics Cir. Address: Booklist Am Libr Assn 50 E Huron St Chicago IL 60611-5295 Business E-Mail: dseaman@ala.org.

SEAMAN, TANYA, urban planner; B in Environ. Design, U. Calif., Davis; M in City and Regional Planning, U. Pa. Co-founder, exec. dir. PhillyCarShare, 2002—. Named one of 40 Under 40, Phila. Bus. Jour., 2006. Office: PhillyCarShare 701 S 50th St Philadelphia PA 19143 Office Phone: 215-730-0988. Office Fax: 215-730-0650.*

SEAPKER, JANET KAY, museum administrator, historic site director, consultant; b. Pitts., Nov. 2, 1947; d. Charles Henry and Kathryn Elizabeth (Dany) Seapker; m. Edward F. Turberg, May 24, 1975. BA, U. Pitts., 1969; MA, SUNY, Cooperstown, 1975. Park ranger Nat. Park Svc., summers 1967-69; archtl. historian N.C. Archives and History, Raleigh, 1971—76, hist. preservation adminstr., 1976—77, grant-in-aid adminstr., 1977—78; dir. Cape Fear Mus. (formerly New Hanover County Mus.), Wilmington, NC, 1978—2000, ret.; archtl. historian-preservation/mus. cons.; curator U. N.C. Wilmington's Kenan House, 2003—04. Bd. dirs. Bellamy Mansion Found., Wilmington, 1986-89, 91-97, Lower Cape Fear Hist. Soc., Wilmington, 1985-88; N.C. rep. S.E. Mus. Conf., 1986-90; bd. dirs. Cape Fear Coast Conv. and Vis. Bur., 1997-2001, sec., 2001, Wrightsville Beach Mus., 2004-05; field reviewer Inst. Mus. Svcs., 1982-2001 Contbr. articles to profl. jours. Bd. dirs. Downtown Area Revitalization Effort, Wilmington, 1979-81, Thalian Hall Ctr. for Performing Arts, 1996-98; bd. dirs. Hist. Wilmington Found., 1979-84, pres., 1980-81; mem. Cmty. Appearance Commn., Wilmington, 1984-88, 250th Anniversary Commn., Wilmington, 1986-90; mem. Wilmington Historic Preservation Commn., 2005-; pres. Friends of Oakdale Cemetery, Inc., 2004-. Grad. program fellow SUNY, Cooperstown, 1969-70; recipient Profl. Svc. award N.C. Mus. Coun., 1982, Woman of Achievement award YWCA, 1994. Mem. Am. Assn. Mus. (accreditation vis. com. 1983-2001, reviewer mus. assessment program 1982-2002), Nat. Trust Hist. Preservation, Southeastern Mus. Conf. (N.C. state rep. 1986-90), N.C. Mus. Coun. (sec.-treas. 1978-84, pres. 1984-86; recipient William T. Anderson award 2004), Hist. Preservation Found N.C. (sec. 1976-78). Presbyterian. Home and Office: 307 N 15th St Wilmington NC 28401-3813 Office Phone: 910-762-6301. Personal E-mail: jseapker@ec.rr.com.

SEARLES, EDNA LOWE, artist, illustrator, composer, poet; b. Minden, La., Sept. 10, 1936; m. Thomas D. Searles. AA, Mont. Coll., 1975; BA in Edn., La. Poly., 1958. Tchr. pub. sch., 1958—65. Guest curator Delaplaine Visual Arts Ctr., Frederick, Md., 1995, East Meets West. Illustrator Soy for the 21st Century, 1984, ABC Coloring Book, 1994, Mind Children, 1995, Mind Travel, 1998, About You, 1998, Choose Life, 2002, Animal Alphabet Coloring Book, 2003, Creator and Creativity, 2004; illustrator: Music ABC Book, 2006; illustrator Musical Alphabet Coloring Book, 2006; one-woman shows include Arnot Art Mus., Elmira, N.Y., 1988, Va. Tech State U. Grad. Ctr., 1989, Gwinnett County Art Gallery, Ga., 1990, VA Honorarium, 1990, Other: Affiliation and Exhibits, Janice Aldridge Gallery (Cat Series), Washington, 1996, Sculpture on the Ground, Md., 1994, 1999, The Artist's Gallery, Frederick, Md., 1997—2002, The Garden Gallery, Carlisle, Pa., 1999—, Nancy Stamm's Galleria, 1999—, Gallery of New Masters, Sandy Spring, Md., 2000—01, Millinneum Exhibit Music for the Eyes, 1999—2000, Musicians and All that Jazz, Frederick, Md., 2000, Gallery of New Masters, Olney, Md., 2000—01, others, exhibited in group shows at Boarman Art Ctr., Martinsburg, W.Va., 2001, Nat. League Am. Pen Women, 2003, Summer Sch. Mus., Washington, 2004, Sandy Spring Mus., Md., 2004, Friendship Gallery, Chevy Chase, 2004, Ratner Mus., 2005, murals, Ambrosia Restaurant, 1991, Still Lake Greenhouse and Florist, 1999, Damascus United Meth. Ch., 2000, The Original Ambrosia Greek Restaurant, 2004, Baronessa Italian Restaurant, 2005, jazz poster for, Mel Brown and Western Oreg. U., 2001. Past pres. Clarksburg (Md.) Cmty. Assn. Recipient Juror's award for painting Montgomery County Art, 1993, Internat. Gold medal for painting Accademia Italia, 1973, 4 grants Crabtown Fund of Balt. Cmty. Found., 2005, others; named Wilson Wims Citizen of Yr., Clarksburg Comm. Assn., 1974. Mem.: DAR (vice regent Pleasant Plains of Damascus chpt. 2001—02), Nat. League Am. Pen Women (pres. Chevy Chase br. 1980—82, 2002—04, Md. state pres. 2004—05, 3d v.p. Chevy Chase br. 2004—, 2005, Poetry award). Methodist. Achievements include invention of music system for the deaf to "see" music as art "Music for the Eyes". Avocations: hammered dulcimer, music, folk singer, harp, piano.

SEARLS, EILEEN HAUGHEY, retired lawyer, law librarian, educator; b. Madison, Wis., Apr. 27, 1925; d. Edward M. and Anna Mary (Haughey) S. BA, U. Wis., 1948, JD, 1950, MS in LS, 1951. Bar: Wis. 1950. Cataloger Yale U., 1951-52; instr. law St. Louis U., 1952-53, asst. prof., 1953-56, assoc. prof., 1956-64, prof., 1964-2000, law libr., 1952-2000. Chmn. Coun. Law Libr. Consortia, 1984-90; sec. Bd. of Concilaiton and Arbitration, Archdiocese of St. Louis, 1986-98. Named Woman of Yr. Women's Commn., St. Louis U., 1986. Mem. ABA, ALA, Wis. Bar Assn., Bar Assn. Met. St. Louis, Am. Assn. Law Librs. (Marian Gould Gallagher Disting. Svc. award 1999), Mid Am. Assn. Law Librs. (pres. 1984-86), Mid Am. Law Sch. Libr. Consortium (chmn. 1980-84), Southwestern Assn. Law Librs., Altrusa Club. Office: 3700 Lindell Blvd Saint Louis MO 63108-3412 Business E-Mail: searlseh@slu.edu.

SEARS, JOANNE CAROL, secondary school educator; b. Eugene, Oreg., Aug. 14, 1948; d. Lester O. and Kathryn H. (Hansen) Goddard; m. Daniel Ray Sears, June 7, 1969; children: Timothy Alan, Ryan David. BA, U. Redlands, 1970. Cert. secondary tchr., Colo. Substitute tchr., Colo., 1985-89; tchr. English Hi-Plains Sch. Dist., Seibert, Colo., 1989—. Pres. Liberty Sch. Action Com., Joes, Colo., 1988—89; speech team advisor Hi-Plains Sch. Dist., Siebert, Colo., 1989—, HS theatre dir., 1989—, Knowledge Bowl coach, 1989—99, Siebert, 2002—. V.p. Kirk (Colo.) Lions, 1988; pres. Yuma County (Colo.) Cattlewomen, 1980. Mem. Nat. Coun. Tchrs. English. Democrat. Episcopalian. Avocations: clay sculpture, acting in and directing plays, fine arts. Office: Hi-Plains Jr/Sr High Sch PO Box 238 Seibert CO 80834 Home: 816 S Albany St Yuma CO 80759-2806

SEARS, LEAH WARD, state supreme court chief justice; b. June 13, 1955; d. Thomas E. and Onnye J. Sears; married; children: Addison, Brennan. BA, Cornell U., 1976; JD, Emory U., 1980; M in Apellate Jud. Process, U. Va.; JD (hon.), Morehouse Coll., 1993. Judge City Ct. Atlanta; atty. Alston & Bird, Atlanta; trial judge Superior Ct. Fulton County, Atlanta; justice Ga. Supreme Ct., Atlanta, 1992—, former presiding justice, chief justice, 2005—. Contbr. articles to profl. jours. Bd. dirs. Sadie G. Mays Nursing Home, Ga. chpt. Nat. Coun. Christians & Jews; mem. adv. bd. United Way Drug Abuse Action Ctr., Outdoor Activity Nature Ctr.; mem. Cornell U. Women's Coun.; mem. steering com. Ga. Women's History Month, Children's Def. Fund Black Cmty. Crusade Children; founder Battered Women's Project, Columbus, Ga. Recipient Outstanding Young Alumna award Emory U., One of 100 Most Influential Georgians Ga. Trend mag., Excellence in Pub. Svc. award Ga. Coalition Black Women, 1992, Outstanding Woman of Achievement YWCA Greater Atlanta, One of Under Forty & On the Fast Track, 1993. Mem. ABA (chair bd. elections), Nat. Assn. Women Judges, Ga. Bar Assn., Women's Forum Ga., Gate City Bar Assn., Atlanta Bar Assn. (past chair jud. sect.), Ga. Assn. Black Women Attys. (founder, pres.), Fourth Tuesday Group, Jack & Jill Am. (Atlanta chpt.), Links Inc. (Atlanta chpt.), Alpha Kappa Alpha. Office: Ga Supreme Ct 244 Washington Street Atlanta GA 30334-9007*

SEARS, MARY HELEN, lawyer; b. Syracuse, N.Y. d. James Louis and Helen Mary (Fitzgerald) Sears. AB, Cornell U., 1950; JD with honors, George Washington U., 1960. Bar: Va. 1960, D.C. 1961, U.S. Supreme Ct. 1963. Chemist Allied Chem. and Dye Corp., Syracuse, 1950-52, Hercules Powder Co., Wilmington, Del., 1952-55; patent examiner U.S. Patent Office, Washington, 1955-60; pvt. practice Washington, 1960-61; assoc. Irons, Birch, Swindler & McKie, Washington, 1961-69; mem. firm Irons and Sears, Washington, 1969-84; chmn. trade regulation practice dept. Memel, Jacobs, Pierno, Gersh & Ellsworth, Washington, 1984-87; ptnr., chmn. intellectual property and unfair competition practice dept. Ginsburg, Feldman & Bress, Washington, 1987-91; ptnr., chmn. intellectual property and telecomm. practice group Reid & Priest, Washington, 1991-94; founder, chmn. M. H. Sears Law Firm, 1994—. Mem. adv. bd. Boardroom Reports, Inc., N.Y.C., 1980-85; mem. Cornell U. Coun., 1981-87, 89-93, life mem., 1995—, mem. adminstrv. bd., 1984-86. Contbr. articles to various publs. Named to Guide to the World's Leading Patent Law Experts Euromoney Publs., PLC, 1995, 1997, 2005; recipient Outstanding Performance award, U.S. Dept. Commerce, 1957. Mem.: ABA (co-chmn. appellate practice com., litigation sect. 1989—92), D.C. Bar Assn., Va. State Bar Assn., Internat. Trademark Assn., Am. Soc. Internat. Law, Am. Intellectual Property Law Assn., George Washington U. Law Alumnae Assn. (bd. dirs. 1995—2001), Order of Coif, Phi Alpha Delta. Republican. Office: MH Sears Law Firm Chartered NW Ste 800 910 17th St Washington DC 20006-2601 Office Phone: 202-463-3892. Business E-Mail: mhsears@mhsears.com.

SEARS, PATRICIA MARIE, elementary school educator, consultant; b. Portsmouth, Va., Aug. 19, 1952; d. Peter Paul and Esther Marie Vispo; 1 child, Stephanie Marie. BS magna cum laude in Elem. Edn., Old Dominion U., 1974; MEd, Campbell Coll., 1979. Cert. early edn. Va., gifted edn. Va., elem. sch. prin. Va., elem. sch. supr. Va. Tchr. Norfolk (Va.) Pub. Sch., 1974—75, 1979—80, Wake County Pub. Sch., Raleigh, NC, 1975—79; gifted tchr. Virginia Beach City Pub. Sch., 1980—87, gifted resource tchr., 1987—89, early childhood coord., 1989—2003, lang. arts. coord., 2003—05; cons. Person Learning Group, Parsippany, NJ, 2005—. Assoc. prof. Tidewater C.C., 1994—95; pres. Reel Connections, Ltd., 1997; reviewer Pearson Learning Group, Parsippany, NJ, 1999—; presenter in field. Author: Language Arts Birth-5, 1998. V.p. Princess Anne Rep. Women's Club, Virginia Beach, 2002—03; mem. Friends of Libr., Virginia Beach, 2000—. Mem.: Nat. Assn. Gifted Children, Delta Kappa Gamma. Roman Catholic. Avocations: reading, travel. Home: 4768 Red Coat Rd Virginia Beach VA 23455

SEASE, SUSAN G., social worker; b. Columbia, S.C., Sept. 8, 1955; d. David Lloyd and Betty Lou Gore; m. George Andrew Sease Jr., Apr. 28, 1978; children: Ruth Aurelia, Mary Lebannon. AD, Florence Darlington Tech Coll., Florence, S.C., 1977; BA, Coker Coll., Hartsville, S.C., 1978, MAT in Learning Disablities, 2005. Lic. social worker; cert. criminal justice specialist. Rsch. and planning technician Florence Police Dept., 1978-79; juvenile police officer Darlington Police Dept., 1979-80; cmty. specialist Dept. Juvenile Justice, Marion, S.C., 1980-88; social worker, svc. coord. Continuum of Care for Emotionally Disturbed Children, Florence, 1989—2001; tchr. autistic resource Lester Elem. Sch., 2001—. Sec. Pee Dee Criminal Intelligence Coun., Florence, 1978-80; resource person Gov.'s Subcom. on Mentally Retarded Offender, Columbia, S.C., 1981. Bd. dirs. Big Sisters of S.C. Florence, 1984-87; chair St. Jude Bike a Thon, Quinby, S.C., 1983, 84, 88. Mem. N.Am. Assn. Christians in Social Work, Nat. Assn. Forensic Councelors, United Meth. Women (v.p. Florence dist. 1994-98, chair social concerns 1999—), Order Eastern Star. Republican. Methodist. Avocations: directing children and youth choir at church, poetry, reading. Home: 203 Wildwood Dr Quinby SC 29506-7220 Office: Johnakin Mid Sch Marion SC

SEASHORE, MARGRETTA REED, physician, educator; b. Red Bank, NJ, June 20, 1939; d. Robert Clark and Lillie Ann (Heaviland) Reed; m. John Seashore, Dec. 26, 1964; children: Robert H., Carl J., Carolyn L. BA, Swarthmore Coll., 1961; MD, Yale U., 1965. Diplomate Am. Bd. Pediatrics, Am. Bd. Med. Genetics, Nat. Bd. Med. Examiners. Intern in pediat. Yale U. Sch. Medicine, New Haven, 1965-66, asst. resident in pediat., 1966-68, postdoctoral fellow in genetics and metabolism, depts. pediat. and medicine, 1968-70, asst. clin. prof. human genetics and pediat., 1974-78, from asst. prof. to assoc. prof., 1978-90, prof. genetics and pediatrics, 1990—; clin. asst. prof. pediat. U. Fla. Coll. Medicine, Gainesville, 1970-71, asst. prof., 1971-73; attending physician Duvall Med. Ctr., U. Hosp. Jacksonville, 1970-73, asst. prof., 1970-71; attending physician Hope Haven Children's Hosp., Jacksonville, Fla., 1970-73, Shands Tchg. Hosp., Gainesville, 1971-73, Danbury (Conn.) Hosp., 1977—, Yale-New Haven Hosp., 1974—, dir. Genetic Consultation Svc., 1977-86, 1989—; cons. physician Bridgeport (Conn.) Hosp., 1974—, Lawrence and Meml. Hosp., New London, Conn., 1979—, Norwalk (Conn.) Hosp., 1981—. Contbr. chapters to books. Fellow: Am. Coll. Med. Genetics (founding fellow), Am. Acad. Pediat. (mem. screening com. Conn. chpt. 1977—, mem. genetics com. 1989—94, chair com. genetics 1990—94); mem.: AAAS, AMA, New Eng. Genetics Group (chmn. outreach com. 1979—89, mem. steering com. 1979—98, chmn. screening com. 1989—93, co-dir. 1992—95), Soc. Study Inborn Errors of Metabolism, Am. Bd. Med. Genetics (bd. dirs. 2004—), Soc. Inherited Metabolic Disorders (bd. dirs. 1989—, sec. 1991—96, pres. 1997), Am. Soc. Human Genetics (mem. genetic svcs. com. 1986—91). Avocations: music, gardening, sewing, computers. Office: Yale U Sch Med Dept Genetics 333 Cedar St New Haven CT 06510-3289 Office Phone: 203-785-4938. Business E-Mail: margretta.seashore@yale.edu.

SEASTREAM, DORIS, science educator; b. Lowell, Mass., Sept. 25, 1961; d. Franklin B. and Dorothy T. Fillmore; m. Robert Seastream, July 27, 2002; 1 child, Jessica L. Fillmore. MEd, Plymouth State U., N.H., 2001. Cert. experienced educator N.H., 1985. Tchr. Goffstown H.S., NH, 1985—. Leader Upreach Therapeutic Riding Ctr., Goffstown, NH, 2005—06. Sgt. U.S. Army, 1981—83. Mem.: VFW (life), Nat. Sci. Tchr. Assn. Independent. Avocations: sailing, reading, gardening. Office: Goffstown High School 27 Wallace Rd Goffstown NH 03045 Office Phone: 603-497-4841. Personal E-mail: dseastream@goffstown.k12.nh.us.

SEATON, ALBERTA JONES, biologist, educator, consultant; b. Houston, Dec. 31, 1924; d. Charles Alexander and Elizabeth (Polk) Jones; m. Earle Edward Seaton, Dec. 24, 1947 (dec. Aug. 1992); children: Elizabeth Wamboi, Dudley Charles. BS in Zoology and Chemistry, Howard U., 1946, MS in Zoology, 1947; ScD in Zoology, U. Brussels, 1949. Asst. prof. Spelman Coll., Atlanta, 1953-54; assoc. prof. biology Tex. So. U., Houston, 1954-60, prof. biology, 1960-72, 91-95; adminstr. Ministry Edn., Bermuda, 1973-76; lectr. biology Bermuda Coll., Devonshire, 1976-78; prof. anatomy Sch. Allied Health U. Tex. Health Ctr., Houston, 1979-80; cons. sci. sect. Nat. Inst. Pedagogy Ministry of Edn. Sci., Victoria, Seychelles, 1980-89. Head dept. biology Wiley Coll., Marshall, Tex., 1950-51; dir. NSF Summer Sci. Inst. Tex. So. U., 1957-59, gen. studies program, 1970-72, undergrad. and grad. rsch. in biology, 1954-72; honors program com. Tex. So. U., 1960-70; chair self-study com., Tex. So. U., 1969-71, ednl. policies com., 1968-72; lectr. biology U. Md., USN Air Sta., Bermuda, 1972-78; supr. adminstrn. and budget Office of Ministry Edn., Bermuda, 1973-76; lectr. in field. Author, editor: Conserving the Environment, Part 1, 1984; editor: Reprints of Agrinews, 1982; co-author, co-editor: Conserving the Environment, Part 2, The Seychelles, 1986, Conserving the Environment, Part 3, Focus on Aldabra, 1991; contbr. articles to profl. jours. Evaluator grant proposals NSF, 1957-72; active regional meetings Com. on Undergrad. Edn. in Biol. Sci., 1967-72, AAC-AAUP confs. on curriculum improvement, 1970-72; chair nurses licensing bd., Hamilton, Bermuda, 1973-75; mem. Endangered Species Com., Hamilton, 1974-77. Postdoctoral fellow Calif. Inst. Tech., Pasadena, 1959-60, NSF postdoctoral fellow Roscoe B. Jackson Lab., Bar Harbor, Maine, 1959, U. Brussels, 1965-66. Mem. AAAS, AAUP (apptd. to ad hoc coms. 1968-71, sec.-treas. Tex. State Conf. 1968-70), AAUW, Am. Assn. Zoologists, Assn. des Anatomistes, Assn. Women in Sci., Tex. Acad. Sci., Beta Kappa Chi, Beta Beta Beta. Episcopalian. Home and Office: 3821 Gertin St Houston TX 77004-6503 Personal E-mail: seatonstar@aol.com.

SEATON, JEAN ROBARTS, psychology educator; b. Atlanta, Apr. 1, 1931; d. Faye Huntington and Helen (Hooker) Robarts; m. Robert Finlayson Seaton, Apr. 18, 1954; children: Scott Ward, Sandra Jean. BA, Agnes Scott Coll., 1952; MEd, U. Cin., 1968; PhD, Case Western Res. U., 1982. Pers. dir. Macy's Calif., San Mateo, 1954-59; instr. U. Cin., 1968-72; prof. psychology Ursuline Coll., Cleve., 1973-96, head psychology dept., 1973-96, chair div. natural and social scis., 1984-92. Trustee St. Luke's Med. Ctr., Cleve., 1981-95; com. mem. Garfield Ch., Pepper Pike, Ohio, 1073-; mem. coun. City of Pepper Pike, 1981-97. Lt. WAVES USNR, 1952-54. Recipient Outstanding Teaching award Ursuline Coll., 1990. Republican. Methodist. Avocation: travel. Home: 16 Pepper Creek Dr Pepper Pike OH 44124-5248

SEATON, JOYAH A., nursing assistant; b. Chgo., Sept. 2, 1968; d. Sherman and Bettye Sue (Payton) Rivers; m. Milton Seaton, Jr., Apr. 8, 1994; 1 child, Christopher Allen Rivers-Collins, Devin Eugene Seaton. Nurse asst., Olive-Harvey, Chgo., 1991, student in phlebotomy, 1996—. Receptionist Braun, Lynch, Strobel & Smith, Chgo., 1995-96; nurse asst. U. Chgo. Hosp., 1995—. Mem. OES/PHA. Baptist. Avocations: remodeling, reading, exercise, praying, helping others.

SEATON, SHIRLEY SMITH, academic administrator, consultant; b. Cleve. d. Kibble Smith and Cecil Wright; m. J. Lawrence Seaton, Oct. 2, 1965; 1 child, Eric Dean BA, MA History, Howard U., 1949; MEd, Case We. Res. U., 1956; EdD, U. Akron, 1981; cert. Chinese history and culture, Beijing Normal U. Tchr. Cleve. Dist., 1950—59, dir. social studies, 1976—87; prin. Lafayette,

Dike, Cleve., 1959—63, 1965—78; with Stas. WEWS-TV, WVIZ-TV, Cleve., 1963—67; adj. prof. Cleve. State U., 1988—90; adminstr. John Carroll U., University Heights, Ohio, 1990—. Program dir. OEO, Cleve., 1965; peer rev. Ohio Proficiency Test, 1986—2005; cons. Basics and Beyond, Cleve., 1990— Coord. Ctr. Civic Edn., 11th Congress Dist., 1987—; peer interview chair Fulbright tchr. exch. U.S. Dept. State, 1994-99, 2001-05; trustee We. Res. Hist. Soc., Cleve., 1996—, Ret. Vol. Program, Cleve., 1997-2003; commr. City of Cleveland Heights, 1997— Recipient Ohio Humanitarian award Govt. of Ohio, 1992; Fulbright grantee USIA, 1959, 82 Mem. AAUW, Fulbright Assn., Nat. Alliance Black Edn., Coalition 100 Black Women, Phi Delta Kappa, Alpha Kappa Alpha, Phi Beta Delta, Alpha Sigma Nu Episcopalian. Avocation: bridge. Home: 3680 Bendemeer Rd Cleveland Heights OH 44118 Office: John Carroll U 20700 North Pk Blvd University Heights OH 44118 Office Phone: 216-397-1604. Personal E-mail: sseaton664@aol.com. Business E-Mail: sseaton@jcu.edu.

SEATS, PEGGY CHISOLM, public affairs executive; b. Lisman, Ala., Oct. 12, 1951; d. William H. and Bernice (Berry) Chisolm; m. Melvin Seats (dec.). BA in Communications cum laude, Lewis U., 1974; grad. cert. in event mgmt., George Washington U., 1995; MA in Pub. Comm., Am. U., 1997; grad. cert. in intercultural comm., Vaxjo (Sweden) U., 1997; Master's cert. in Pub. Affairs & Exec. Non-profit mgmt., Georgetown U., 2005. Account exec. Globe Broadcasting, Chgo., 1976-78, Merrill Lynch, Chgo., 1978-79, Transp. Displays, Inc., Chgo., 1979-81; with Reverie, Inc., 1981—; nat. accounts mgr. Soft Sheen Products Co., Chgo., 1981-83; mktg. cons. Reverie, Inc., Chgo., 1983-85; pub. rels., mktg. mgr. Proctor & Gardner Advt., Chgo., 1985-86; dir. pub. rels., mktg. Morris Brown Coll., Atlanta, 1986-87; mgr. mktg. Howard U. Press, Washington, 1989-90; cons. White House Initiative on Historically Black Colls., Univs., 1990-92. State advisor U.S. Congl. Adv. Bd., Ill., 1982. Contbr. numerous articles to newspapers and mags. Founder Benjamin Banneker Meml. Found., Washington, 1996; organizer S.W. Waterfront Initiative, 2000—; facilitator L'Enfant Plaza Revitalization Project, 1997—; bd. dir. Congl. Award Found. Recipient Kizzie award Black Women Hall of Fame, Chgo., 1981, Svc. award Nat. Assn. Women in Media, Chgo., 1982. Mem. Internat. Platform Assn., Internat. Assn. Bus. Communicators, Internat. Spl. Events Soc., Pub. Rels. Soc. Am., Black Pub. Rels. Soc. (founder Atlanta chpt.), Nat. Assn. Market Developers, World Affairs Coun., Comittee of 100, Lewis U. Alumni Assn. (bd. dirs. Ill. 1979), Washington Interdependence Coun. (founder, CEO 1996), Benjamin Banneker Inst. Math. and Sci. (founder). Unitarian Universalist. Avocations: music, art collecting, reading. Home: 2020 Pennsylvania Ave NW Washington DC 20006-1811 Office Phone: 202-387-3380. Business E-Mail: info@bannekermemorial.org.

SEAVER, ELIZABETH MARY, music educator; d. Lewis Joseph and Annie Eva Novak; m. Robert Nicolson Seaver, Mar. 22, 1975 (dec.); children: Shelly Ann, Shawn Keith. MusB, Diverna Coll., Milw., 1967; M in Music Edn., U. Mich., 1969. Cert. music Iowa, music tchr. Fla. Music tchr. Chgo. Cath. Diocese Schs., Colenview, Ill., 1959—64, Idaho, 1964—68; adj. tchr. Luther Coll., Decorah, Iowa, 1969—70; music tchr. N. Winneshiet Cmty. Sch., Decorah, Iowa, 1969—70, Tama Cmty. Schs., Iowa, 1970—72; adj. tchr. Brevard CC, Cocoa, Fla., 1972—74; music tchr. Orange Co. Schs., Orlando, 1974—2000. Accompanist, supr. Chgo. Cath. Tchrs. Group, 1965—67; supr. music edn. Chgo. Cath. Schs., 1967—68; accompanist Brevard Cmty. Chorale, Cocoa, Fla., 1970—72. Compiler (music works) PTA sch. programs, 1983—2000. Grantee Adminstrn. and Supervision Grant, U. Mich., 1968—69. Mem.: Pulashek Mus., Spl. Olympics (vol. supporter 1990—2006), Down Syndrome Orgn., Ret. Tchrs. Assn. Home: 1206 Winterberry Ln Ferry Park FL 32730 Personal E-mail: lizseaver@netzero.net.

SEAY-BELL, MARGARETTA, pastoral counselor; b. Bklyn., Jan. 26, 1928; d. William McKinley and Lucy Rose (Puryear) Pankey; adopted children: Ronald K. Bell, Mark David Bell. BS, Longwood Coll., Farmville, Va., 1982; MDiv, Va. Union U., 1992; MA, Presbyn. Grad. Sch. Christian Edn., Richmond, Va., 1993; D in Ministry, Howard U., 1995; D in Ministry (hon.), Ea. Theol. Sem./Md. Theol. Sem., Lynchburg, Va., 2000. Cert. Ctr. Bibl. Counseling, Forest, Va., 2000. 25 years in positions of increasing scope and responsibility, including 6 yrs. with U.S. State Dept. in Japan and Republic of Korea; with U.S. Dept. Labor, regional office, Phila., 1971—73; ret., 1974. Mem. Amherst County Violence Prevention Team, Amherst County Commn. on Youth Svcs., Amherst County Healthy Beginnings Program; parent rep. Amherst County Family Assessment Program; mem. Amherst County Commn. against Domestic Violence; ct. advocate Women Victims of Domestic Violence; tchr. Parent Nurturing Program, Child Abuse Prevention, Lynchburg, Va.; mem. state governing bd., 1st sect. Va. Organizing Project, Charlottesville, 1997—99; assoc. min. Deliverance Ch. of Christ, Gladstone, Va., 1986—89; elder, adminstr. The Way of the Cross Full Gospel Bapt. Ch., Lynchburg, Va., 1996—98; asst. pastor, pastoral counselor NIA Cmty. Fellowship, Charlotte, NC, 1998—99; guest min. Springfield Bapt. Ch., Appomattox, Va., 2001; vacation bible sch. tchr. Union Hill Bapt. Ch., Buckingham, Va., 2001—02; adminstr., pastoral counselor Spirit and Truth Ministries, Oak Hill, W.Va., 2000—01; vol. tchr. bible study Hidden Valley Nursing Home, Oak Hill, W.Va.; bd. dirs. YMCA, Phila., 1972. Recipient Achievement award, Commonwealth of Va., Welfare Reform Initiative, 1996. Mem.: Am. Assn. Christian Counselors, Assn. Clin. Pastoral Edn., Inc., Zeta Phi Beta (Alpha Phi Zeta chpt.). Democrat. Avocations: golf, writing, travel. Home: Rte 1 Box 1110 Fayetteville WV 25840-9731

SEBALD, CAROL JUNE, retired secondary school educator; b. Massillon, Ohio, Oct. 11, 1939; d. Alfred La Verne and Catherine Margaret (Seward) Dessecker; m. Robert Vernon Sebald, Dec. 10, 1960 (div. Jan. 1975); children: Michael Kevin, Teresa Kay. BS, Kent State U., 1964; MS, Coll. of Mt. St. Joseph (Ohio), 1987. Tchr. Jackson Schs., Massilon, 1959-61, 68-69, Corona (Ind.) Schs., 1962, Perry Schs., Massillon, 1963-64, Angola (Ind.) Schs., 1964-66, North Canton (Ohio) City Schs., 1969—97; ret., 1997. Martha Jennings scholar North Canton City Schs., 1988. Mem. NEA, Ohio Edn. Assn., North Canton Jr. Women's Club, Coll. Club of Canton, Stark County Ret. Tchrs. Republican. Home: 919 Oakwood St SE North Canton OH 44720

SEBALD, JAMA LYNN, academic administrator; b. Dayton, Ohio, Jan. 16, 1949; d. James Arthur and Betty Jean Sebald. BA, Ohio U., 1971; MA, U. No. Colo., 1973, ednl. specialist cert., 1975. Grad. asst., fin. aid counselor U. No. Colo., Greeley, 1974—75; asst. dir. fin. aid Med. Coll. Ga., Augusta, 1975—76; student fin. aid advisor U. Idaho, Moscow, 1976—. Recipient Outstanding Young Woman of Am. award, 1978. Mem.: AAUW (Moscow br. treas. 1982—84, Moscow br. corr. sec. 1984—86, Moscow br. pres. 1987—88, Idaho divsn. bd. dirs. 1987—88, 1992—93, Moscow br. pres. 1992—93, Moscow br. co-pres. 1998—99, Moscow br. pres. 1999—2000, Ednl. Found. Name Gift award 1991, 1995), U. Idaho Women's Caucus, Idaho Student Fin. Aid Adminstrs. (pres. 1989—90), Western Assn. Student Fin. Aid Adminstrs. (mem. exec. coun. 1989—90), Nat. Assn. Student Fin. Aid Adminstrs., Moscow Pregnancy Counseling Svc. (bd. dirs. 1984—86), Athena. Home: 615 N Washington Moscow ID 83843-2626 Office: U Idaho Student Fin Aid Svcs Moscow ID 83844-4291 Office Phone: 208-885-6312. Business E-Mail: jama@uidaho.edu.

SEBASTIAN, PHYLIS SUE (INGRAM), real estate broker, appraiser, antique appraiser; b. Childersburg, Ala., Jan. 24, 1945; d. Albert Freeman and Era Mae (McGowin) Ingram; m. Robert Emmett Martin, March 31, 1965 (div. Sept. 1976); children: Connie, Michael, Toni, Steve; m. Thomas Haskell Sebastian III, June 26, 1985; stepchildren: Shellie, Tabatha, Cherie, Thomas IV. Ordained minister Progressive Universal Life Ch., 2002; lic. real estate broker Mo., real estate appraiser Tenn., Mo., PREA, CIMA. Owner, broker Phylis Sebastian Real Estate, Farmington, Mo., 1989—, U.S. Auto Sales, Park Hills, Mo., 1993—96; owner Bus. Legal Svs., Park Hills, Mo., 1993—; ptnr. La Femme Fine Antique Auction Svc., Ironton, Mo., 1997—. Owner Astrology Cons., 1970—; numerous appearances St. Louis TV; hostess radio show, St. Louis. Contbr. articles to newspapers; author: Marriages in Madison County Missouri for 1848-1868, 1998, 1910 Census for Madison County Missouri, 1998, numerous poems. Co-founder Astrological Assn., St. Louis, 1976-77, Mo. Mental Health Consumer Network, 1989-93, Mineral Area chpt. 1989-93. Mem. Nat. Gardening Club, Libr. Congress, Smithsonian, Nat. Hist. soc., Geneal. Assn. Madison County, Mo. (founder, sec., treas., genealogist). Mem. Lds Ch. Avocations: reading, walking, gardening, piano, guitar. Home: 5231 West 72 Highway Fredericktown MO 63645 Office: Arcadia Valley Auction Company Inc and Real Estate 315A W Russell St Ironton MO 63650-1316 Office Phone: 573-546-3900, 573-546-7440. Personal E-mail: phylis@phylissebastian.com. E-mail: avac@myway.com.

SEBASTIAN, SUZIE, television producer; b. Redding, Calif., Aug. 2, 1962; d. Richard Werner and Hildegard (Goettel) Guenther; m. Ted Sebastian, June 6, 1984 (div. July 1990). AA, Shasta Coll., 1985. Freelance tv prodr., prodn. mgr. commls., 1985-91; freelance underwater model, stunt woman; expedition leader, hostess Adventures on Scuba Dive Travel, Santa Barbara, Calif., 1991—; documentary TV prodr. Discovery Channel, 1998-2000. Asst. instr. Filming Sharks in the Wild, Nassau, Bahamas, 1996—. Prodr.: documentaries, ednl. videos; picture editor, underwater model: Tom Campbell's Film and Video Prodns., 1991—; prodr.: Navy Seals: In Harms Way; (films) How to Survive Hellweek, FBI: Critical Incident Class 234, Breathe, 2006. Mem.: Internat. Documentary Assn., Divers Alert Network, Aquatic Bodyworks. Avocations: skiing, triathlon. Home: 919 Veronica Springs Rd Santa Barbara CA 93105-4500 Office: Adventures on Scuba 238 Las Alturas Rd Santa Barbara CA 93103-2170 E-mail: suzies@silcom.com.

SEBELIUS, KATHLEEN GILLIGAN, governor; b. Cin., May 15, 1948; d. John J. and Mary K. (Dixon) Gilligan; m. Keith Gary Sebelius, 1974; children: Edward Keith, John McCall. BA, Trinity Coll., 1970; MA in Pub. Adminstrn., U. Kans., 1977. Exec. dir. Kans. Trial Lawyers Assn., 1978—86; mem. Kans. Ho. of Reps., 1987-95; ins. commr. State of Kans., 1995—2002, gov., 2003—. Founder Women's Polit. Caucus; precinct committeewoman, 1980-86; mayor, Potwin, 1985-87; appointed Presdl. adv. commn. consumer protection and quality in Health Care, 1997. Mem. Common Cause (state bd., nat. gov. bd. 1975-81), Nat. Assn. Ins. Commrs. (chair). Democrat. Roman Catholic. Office: Office of the Gov State Capitol 2nd Fl Topeka KS 66612-1590 Office Fax: 785-296-7973.*

SEBERT, MICHELLE ANN, school system network administrator; b. Pt. Pleasant, N.J., Feb. 8, 1970; d. Michael Patrick and Lynn Ann McKnight; m. Herman Arthur Sebert Jr., July 24, 1994; 1 child, Herman Arthur III. BA in English, Rutgers U., 1992; MA in Edn., Chapman U., Tucson, Ariz., 1995. Cert. elem., secondary and adult educator, Ariz. Title I reading and phys. edn. tchr. Elgin (Ariz.) Sch., 1994-95, tchr. 3d grade, then 6th grade, 1995-97, tchr. computer skills, 1997—, tech. coord., 1997—, network adminstr., 1998—. Mem. site-based coun., Elgin Sch., also facility planning com. Mem. NEA, Assn. for the Advancement of Computing in Edn., Ariz. Edn. Assn., Sonoita Edn. Assn., Nat. Assn. Elem. Sch. Prins. Republican. Roman Catholic. Avocations: reading, scrapbooking. Home: PO Box 583 Sonoita AZ 85637-0583 E-mail: michelle@server1.sonoita.k12.az.us.

SEBOLD, ALICE, writer; b. Madison, Wis., 1963; d. Jane and Russell Sebold; m. Glen David Gold, 2001. BA, Syracuse U., 1984; studied poetry, U. Houston, 1984—85; MFA in fiction, U. Calif., Irvine, 1998. Author: (memoir) Lucky, 1999, (novels) The Lovely Bones, 2002. Office: c/o Steven Barclay Agy 12 Western Ave Petaluma CA 94952

SEBRIGHT, MELISSA MARIE, special education educator; b. York, Pa., Dec. 15, 1971; d. James Richard and Mary Penny Sebright. BS, Millersville U. Pa., 1993; MS, Western Md. Coll., 1999. Learning support tchr. Ctrl. York HS, York, 1999—. Mem. Veteran's Polit. Assn., York. Mem.: Am. Counseling Assn., Pa. State Edn. Assn., Coun. Exceptional Children, Loyal Order Moose. Avocations: kickboxing, education. Home: 1883 Idylwyld Rd York PA 17402 Office: Ctrl York HS 601 Mundis Mill Rd York PA 17402 Office Phone: 717-846-6789. Personal E-mail: msebright123@suscom.net. Business E-Mail: msebright@cysd.k12.pa.us.

SEBRING, MARJORIE MARIE ALLISON, former home furnishings company executive; b. Burnsville, N.C., 1926; d. James William and Mary Will (Ramsey) Allison Shockey; 1 child, Patricia Louise Banner Krohn (dec.). Student, Mars Hill Coll., 1943, Home Decorators Sch. Design, N.Y.C., 1948, Wayne State U., 1953; cert. home furnishings rep., U. Va., 1982. Dir. decorating divsn. Robinson Furniture, Detroit, 1949—57; head buyer Tyner Hi-Way House, Ypsilanti, Mich., 1957—63, Town and Country, Dearborn, Mich., 1963—66; instr. Nat. Carpet Inst., 1963—71; owner Adams House, Inc., Plymouth, Mich., 1966—72; exec. v.p. mktg. and sales, regional sales mgr. mktg. mgr. Triangle Industries, L.A., 1972—89; co-owner Markham-Sebring, Inc., St. Petersburg, Fla., 1983—89. Co-owner Accessories, Etc., 1985-89, Talamanca Pipeline Ltd., Costa Rica, dir.; chmn. bd. U.S. Homed, Heritage Lakes, 2002-04, bd. dirs. Vol. coord. Pasco County Clk. Ct., Suncoast Theatre; adv. bd. Webster Coll.; charter mem. Presdl. Task Force; pres. Presbyn. Ch. Seven Springs; bd. dirs. Fla. Presbyn. Homes, Gills Trinity YMCA, 2001—; mem. Tampa Bay Presbytery Rev. and Evaluation; bd. dirs. James P. Gills Suncoast YMCA, 2001-05; citizens adv. com. Pasco County, 2001-06. Recipient recognition for work with youth and aged; named to Fla. Finest List, Gov. of Fla., 1994. Mem. Internat. Home Furnishings Assn., Fla. Home Furnishings Rep. Assn. (officer), Am. Security Coun. (coun.), Williamsburg Found., USCG Aux., Nat. Audubon Soc., Internat. Platform Assn. (jouvenile justice coun. 2003-05), Pasco County Planning Com., Heritage Lake Assn. (bd. dir. 2002-06, chmn.), II Westminster Assn.(chmn. bd. 1992-95, 2001-05, pres. 2002-06), Pasco Rep. Club. Republican. Achievements include contbr. creative display to Better Homes & Gardens, 1957-64. Home: 4902 Cathedral Ct New Port Richey FL 34655-1486 Office Phone: 727-808-7992. Home Fax: 727-376-9533.

SECKEL, CAROL ANN, Methodist minister; b. Bklyn., Oct. 28, 1949; d. Leonard Immanuel and Anna Beth (Eggleston) Klotz; m. Richard Kevin Seckel, June 27, 1970; children: Joshua Allen, Jason Andrew, Jeremy Jacob. B in Edn., U. Toledo, 1971; MDiv, MA in Christian Edn, Meth. Theol. Sch. Ohio, 1978. With Stouffer's Restaurant, Toledo, 1971-72; pre-sch. tchr. Liberty Community Ctr., Delaware, Ohio, 1972-73; co-dir. work study program Early Childhood Ctr., Methesco, Delaware, 1977-78; co-pastor numerous chs., Middleburg, Ohio, 1975-78, Chiloquin, Oreg., 1978-82; pastor Sitka (Alaska) United Meth. Ch., 1982-86; dist. supt. Oreg. Idaho Conf. United Meth. Ch., Salem, Oreg., 1986-88; conf. supt. Alaska Missionary Conf. United Meth. ch., Anchorage, 1988-94; sr. pastor First United Meth. Ch., Anchorage, 1994-95; co-spiritual life dir. Alaska Children's Svcs., Anchorage, 1996—. Co-presenter United Meth. Bishops Com. on Faithful Disciples-Vital Congregation, Nashville, 1987. Mem., pres. bd. dirs. Klamath County Women's Crisis Ctr., Klamath Falls, Oreg., 1979-82, Sitkans Against Family Violence, Sitka, 1983-86, Planned Parenthood Alaska, 1997-99; trustee Willamette U., Salem, 1986-88, Alaska Pacific U., Anchorage, 1988-98; mem. Community Choir, Sitka, 1983-85; v.p. Tongass coun. Girl Scouts U.S., 1984-86; bd. dirs. Planned Parenthood Alaska, 1996-99, pres., 1997-99. Fellowship United Meths. in Worship, Music and Other Arts. Democrat. Avocations: hiking, music, cross country skiing, cross-stitching.

SECOR, MARGARET J., science educator; m. Garry P. Secor; children: Zachary S., William G. BS, Va. Tech, Blacksburg, 1982. Cert. tchr. Va., 1983. Tchr. City of Salem Schs., Va., 1983—, sci. coord., 1993—. Office: City of Salem Schools 510 S College Ave Salem VA 24153 Office Phone: 540-389-0130.

SECREAST, PATRICIA LINEBERGER, elementary school educator; b. Salisbury, N.C., Mar. 28, 1949; d. William Gilmer and Frances (Bruce) Lineberger; m. Roger Ervin Secreast, June 14, 1970; children: Melissa, Molly. BA in History, Western Carolina U., 1970; MEd in Curriculum and Instrn., U. N.C., Carhlotte, 1976. Cert. 6-12 social studies tchr., N.C., cert. 6-9 English lit. tchr., cert. 6-9 math. tchr., cert. 6-9 sci. tchr. Tchr. social studies North Rowan Mid. Sch., Spencer, NC, 1974—. Summer sch. tchr. CETA, Salisbury-Rowan Community Svc. Coun., 1976-82; presenter in field; instr. adult basic edn. Rowan-Cabarrus C.C., 1986-93; mem. accreditation team Jamestown Mid. Sch., 1987, East Union Mid. Sch., 1988. Elder, mem. choir, Sunday sch. tchr., leader Bible study, officer Women of Ch., Spencer Presbyn. Ch.; past mem. Spencer Recreation and Parks Com., Jr. League, Mooresville, N.C.; mem. Neighborhood Improvement Team, Spencer; historian Rowan-Salisbury PTA Coun., 1989-90; mem. Spencer Hist. Commn. Recipient Outstanding Young Educator award Spencer Jaycees, 1978, Gov.'s Excellence award State of N.C., 1992; named Outstanding Educator, Spencer Jaycees, 2005;; James Iredell fellow, 1989. Mem. NEA, N.C. Assn. Educators, Kappa Delta Pi (Rowan County Tchr. of Yr. 1997-98). Democrat. Avocations: reading, dance, music, sporting events, animals. Home: 225 N Rowan Ave Spencer NC 28159-2425 Office: North Rowan Mid Sch 512 Charles St Spencer NC 28189

SEDARIS, AMY, writer, actress; b. Endicott, NY, Mar. 19, 1961; d. Lou Sedaris. Performer: (TV series) Exit 57, 1995—96; co-writer (TV series) Exit 57, 1995—96, co-creator, 1995—96; performer: (TV series) Strangers With Candy, 1999—2000; co-writer (TV series) Strangers With Candy, 1999—2000, co-creator, 1999—2000; actor(guest appearances): (TV series) Just Shoot Me, Monk, Sex and the City, Ed, Cracking Up,; (films) Commandments, 1997, Bad Bosses Go to Hell, 1997, Six Days Seven Nights, 1998, Jump Tomorrow, 2001, Maid in Manhattan, 2002, The School of Rock, 2003, Elf, 2003, My Baby's Daddy, 2004, Strangers with Candy, 2005, Stay, 2005, Bewitched, 2005, Romance and Cigarettes, 2005, (voice) Chicken Little, 2005, Full Grown Men, 2006; (TV films) Untitled New York Pilot, 2003; (plays) Jamboree, 1993; co-author (with brother David Sedaris): (plays) Jamboree, 1993; actor: (plays) Stump the Host, 1993; co-author (with brother David Sedaris): (plays) Stump the Host, 1993; actor: (plays) One Woman Shoes, 1995; co-author (with brother David Sedaris): (plays) One Woman Shoes, 1995 (Obie award, 1995); actor: (plays) Froggy, The Country Club, 1998—99 (nominated Drama Desk award, 1999), The Most Fabulous Story Ever Told, 1998—99, The Little Freida Mysteries, 1999; co-author (with brother David Sedaris): (plays) The Little Freida Mysteries, 1997; actor: (plays) The Book of Liz; co-author (with brother David Sedaris): (plays) The Book of Liz, 2001; co-author: (book), 2002; actor: (plays) Drama Department, 2001, Wonder of the World, 2001—02 (Lucille Lortel award for outstanding featured actress League of Off-Broadway Theatres and Prodrs., 2002), (short film) Wheels of Fury, 1998; co-writer (short film) Wheels of Fury, 1998; co-author (with brother David Sedaris): (plays) Stitches, Incident at Cobbler's Knob; co-author: (books) Wigfield: The Can-Do Town That Just May Not, 2003; author: I Like You, 2006. Office: c/o Jonathan Bluman Paradigm 10100 Santa Monica Blvd 25th Fl Los Angeles CA 90067*

SEDDON, JOHANNA MARGARET, ophthalmologist, epidemiologist; b. Pitts. BS, U. Pitts., 1970, MD, 1974; MS in Epidemiology, Harvard U., 1976. Intern Framingham (Mass.) Union Hosp., 1974-75; resident Tufts New Eng. Med. Ctr., Boston, 1976-80; fellow ophthalmic pathology Mass. Eye and Ear Infirmary, Boston, 1980-81, clin. fellow vitreoretinal Retina Svc., 1981-82; instr. clin. ophthalmology Harvard Med. Sch., Boston, 1982-84, asst. prof., asst. surgeon ophthalmolgy, 1984, assoc. prof., 1989—; assoc. surgeon, dir. ultrasound svc. Mass. Eye and Ear Infirmary, Boston, 1989—, founder epidemiology rsch. unit, 1984-85, dir. epidemiology unit, 1985—, surgeon in ophthalmology, 1992—; assoc. prof. faculty dept. epidemiology Harvard Sch. Pub. Health, Boston, 1992—. Mem. com. vision Commn. Behavioral and Social Scis. and Edn., NRC, NAS, Washington, 1984; mem. divsn. rsch. grants NIH, 1987-89, 94—; mem. sci. adv. bd. Found. for Fighting Blindness, 1994—. Macular Degeneration Internat., 1994—, adv. panel, Age-Related Macular Degeneration Alliance Internat.; spkr. in field; lectr. in field. Author books and articles in field, especially in field of ocular tumors and macular degeneration; mem. editl. staff ophthalmic jours. Recipient NIH Nat. Svc. Rsch. awards, 1975, 80-81, Lewis R. Wasserman Merit award Rsch. to Prevent Blindness for contbns. to ophthalmic rsch., 1996, 1st Maurice Rabb, Jr. award Prevent Blindness Am. Orgn., 2005; grantee, prin. investigator Nat. Eye Inst., 1984—, Nat. Cancer Inst., 1986; med. sch. scholar, 1970-74, Henry H. Clark Med. Edn. Found. scholar, 1973, voted one of Am.'s top ophthalmologists, Consumer Rsch. Coun. Am., 2004. Mem. AMA (Sr. Honor award 2003), APHA, Am. Acad. Ophthalmology (Honor award 1990, Sr. Honor award 2003), Am. Med. Women's Assn., Assn. Rsch. in Vision and Ophthalmology (elected, chair epidemiology sect. 1990, trustee clin. vision epidemiology sect. 1992-97, v.p. 1996-97, Spl. Recognition award 1997), Soc. Epidemiologic Rsch., New Eng. Ophthal. Soc., Am. Coll. Epidemiology, Retina Soc., Macula Soc. (mem. com. 2006—), Mass. Soc. Eye Physicians and Surgeons (v.p. 2000-02, mem. com. 2006—), Am. Epidemiol. Soc., Am. Soc. Ret. Surgeons (Hon. award 2005). Achievements include being first to evaluate association between nutrition, dietary antioxidants, and inflammatory biomarkers and age-related macular degeneration. Home: 4 Louisburg Sq Boston MA 02108-1203 E-mail: jseddon@earthlink.net.

SEDDON, MARGARET RHEA, retired astronaut, physician, researcher; b. Murfreesboro, Tenn., Nov. 8, 1947; d. Edward C. and Clayton Dann Seddon; m. Robert L. Gibson; three children. BA in Physiology, U. Calif., Berkeley, 1970; MD, U. Tenn., 1973. Intern, resident, Memphis; astronaut NASA Lyndon B. Johnson Space Ctr., Houston, 1979—97; mission specialist shuttle flight STS-51D, 1985; mission specialist shuttle flight STS-40, 1991; payload comdr. shuttle flight STS-58, 1993; asst. chief med. officer Vanderbilt Med. Group, Nashville, 1997—. Mem. Am. Coll. Emergency Physicians, Am. Med. Women's Assn., Tex. Med. Assn., Harris County Med. Soc., 99's. Office: Vanderbilt Med Ctr 3601 TVC Nashville TN 37232-5100

SEDDON, PRISCILLA TINGEY, painter; b. Boston, Apr. 1, 1938; d. Richard Hume and Mildred Gurina (Lundgren) Tingey; m. James Alexander Seddon, Jr., Nov. 28, 1959; children: Amy, Sarah, Carroll, Alice. BFA, Tufts U., 1989; Cert., Sch. of the Mus. of Fine Arts, Boston, 1990, Postgrad. 5th Yr., 1991. Associated with Imagining Angels: World AIDS Day Show, Howard Yezersky Gallery, Boston, 1995, others. Exhbns. include: U. Bridgeport, Conn., 1997, Gallery 84, N.Y.C., 1996, Erector Square Gallery, New Haven, Conn., 1996, Harvard U., Cambridge, Mass., 1996, ArtsWorcester Gallery, Worcester, Mass., 1995, Wellesley Coll., Mass., 1994, Grove Street Gallery, Worcester, 1993, Carvajal Sculpture Gallery, Boston, 1992; works include metal work, paintings and sculptures. Grantee MIT Coun. for Arts, Cambridge, 1988, Firstnight, Inc., Boston, 1991, Hingham Edn. Found., Mass., 1993. Mem. Womens Caucus for Art, Visual AIDS. Avocation: watercolour.

SEDEI RODDEN, PAMELA JEAN, psychologist, director; b. Johnstown, Pa., Jan. 31, 1956; d. Joseph and Betty Ruth (Watkins) Sedei; m. William Eugene Rodden, Dec. 4, 1982; 1 child, Gretchen Jean Rodden. BA, Southwestern Coll., Winfield, Kans., 1977; MS, Pittsburg (Kans.) State U., 1979; PhD, Western Colo. U., 1983. Lic. profl. counselor Colo., diplomate in psychotherapy, cert. cognitive behavior therapist, nat. cert. counselor, domestic violence counselor, criminal justice specialist. Staff psychologist Autumn Manors Inc., Florence, Kans., 1982-83; clin. psychologist Richmond (Tex.) State Hosp., 1984-86; unit psychologist Wheat Ridge (Colo.) Regional Ctr., 1986-89, acting unit dir., 1989; dir. behavioral svcs. Colo. State Divsn. Devel. Disabilities, Denver, 1989-97; dir. Forensic Mental Health Svcs., Boulder, Colo., 1997—2001, Pamela JS Rodden & Assocs., Fort Collins, Colo., 2001—. Dir. Rodden Consultants, Longmont, Colo., 1986—90, Rodden Assocs., 2001—. Co-author: A Model For Interdisciplinary On Site Evaluation of People Who Have Dual Diagnosis, 1991. Fellow: Am. Coll. Forensic Examiners; mem.: ACA, Assn. Treatment of Sexual Abusers (clin. mem.). Republican. Roman Catholic. also: 315 W Oak St Ste 204 Fort Collins CO 80521-2724 Office Phone: 970-482-8553. E-mail: Pjsrodden@juno.com.

SEDGWICK, KYRA, actress; b. NYC, Aug. 19, 1965; m. Kevin Bacon, Sept. 4, 1988; children: Travis, Sosie. Appeared in off-Broadway prodns. Time Was, 1981, Dakota's Belly Wyoming, 1989; stage appearances in Ah Wilderness!, 1988 (Theatre World award), Maids of Honor, 1990, Oleanna, 1994; Actress (films) War and Love, 1985, Tai-Pan, 1986, Kansas, 1988, Born on the Fourth of July, 1989, Mr. and Mrs. Bridge, 1990, Pyrates, 1991, Singles, 1992, Heart and Souls, 1993, Murder in the First, 1995, Something to Talk About, 1995, Losing Chase, 1996, Phenomenon, 1996, Montana, 1997, Critical Care, 1997, Twelfth Night, 1998, The Red Door, 1999, Labor

Pains, 1999, What's Cooking, 2000, Just a Kiss, 2002, Behind the Red Door, 2002, Secondhand Lions, 2003, The Woodsman, 2004, Loverboy, 2005; (TV movies) The Man Who Broke 1,000 Chains, 1987, Women & Men II, 1991, Hallmark Hall of Fame, 1992 (Golden Globe award nomination 1993), The Wide Net, 1997, Door to Door, 2002, Cavedweller, 2004, Something the Lord Made, 2004, (TV series) Another World, 1982-83, Talk to Me, 2000, The Closer, 2005-; (mini-series) Family Pictures, 1983; (TV appearances) ABC Afternoon Spls., 1985, Am. Playhouse, 1987, 88, Miami Vice, 1985, Amazing Stories, 1986, Ally McBeal, 2002, Queens Supreme, 2003 Address: WMA 151 S El Camino Dr Beverly Hills CA 90212-2704

SEDGWICK, SHANNELL ANGELA, elementary school educator, advocate; b. St Louis, Oct. 19, 1972; d. David Shaun Sedgwick and Charlotte Baxter, Beverly Sedgwick (Stepmother). AA, Saddleback Coll., Mission Viejo, Calif., 1993; BA in Anthropology, Colo. State U., Ft. Collins, 1997. Caregiver Ziggurat Child Devel. Ctr., Laguna Niguel, Calif., 1990—93; tchr.'s asst. Braille Inst., LA, 1992—93, Mardan Ctr. for Edn. Therapy, Irvine, Calif., 1997—98; tchr. Orange Unified Sch. Dist., Calif., 1998—2000, Tustin Unified Sch. Dist., Calif., 2000—. Mem. negotiations team Tustin Educators Assn., 2002—04, chief negotiator, 2004—06; rep. assembly attendee NEA, Calif., 2003—05; internat. human rights conf. attendee Internat. Students Festival, Trondheim, Norway, 2003; project coord. Beswick Sch. and Shadetree Cmty. Project, Tustin, 2006. Mem., vol. Surfrider Found., Dana Point, Calif., 2003—06; vol. Habitat for Humanity, 2003—05, Boarding for Breast Cancer, Amnesty Internat., 2003—06; vol., participant Planned Parenthood, Santa Ana, Calif., 2003—06. Nominee Sch. Tchr. of Yr., Beswick Elem. Sch., 2005—06; named Gift Honoree, Ednl. Found. of AAUW, 2005—06; recipient commendation for excellent svc. as chief negotiator, Tustin Educators Assn., 2005—06; Opera scholar, Colo. State U., 1993—96. Mem.: AAUW (assoc.; state pub. policy com. 2003—06, pres. Tustin br. 2005—06), Orange County Assn. for Edn. of Young Children (assoc.). Democrat. Avocations: travel, languages, singing.

SEDLAK, VALERIE FRANCES, retired English language and literature educator, academic administrator; b. Balt., Mar. 11, 1934; d. Julian Joseph and Eleanor Eva (Pilot) Sedlak; 1 child, Barry. AB in English, Coll. Notre Dame of Md., 1955; MA, U. Hawaii, 1962; PhD, U. Pa., 1992. Grad. tchg. fellow East-West Cultural Ctr. U. Hawaii, 1959-60; adminstrv. asst. Korean Consul Gen., 1959-60; tchr. Boyertown (Pa.) Sr. H.S., 1961-63; asst. prof. English U. Balt., 1963-69; assoc. prof. Morgan State U., Balt., 1970-2000, assoc. prof. English emerita, 2001—, asst. dean Coll. Liberal Arts, 1995-2000, sec. to faculty, 1981-83, faculty rsch. scholar, 1982-83, 92-93, comm. officer, 1989-90, dir. writing for TV program, 1990-97; exec. dir. Renaissance Inst. Coll. of Notre Dame of Md., 2000—03, ret., 2003—. Cons. scholar Md. Humanities Coun., 1992—; adj. prof. York (Pa.) Coll., 2004-. Author numerous poems and lit. criticism; editor Liberal Arts Rev., 1996-2000; assoc. editor Md. English Jour., 1994-2000; assoc. editor Morgan Jour. Rsch., 1995-2000, CEA mag., 2002—; mem. editl. bd. CEA Critic, 2003—; contbr. articles to lit. jours. Coord. Young Reps., Berks County, Pa., 1962-63; chmn. Md. Young Reps., 1964; election judge Baltimore County, Md., 1964-66; regional capt. Am. Cancer Soc., 1978-79; mem. adv. bd. Md. Our Md. Anniversary, 1984, The Living Constitution: Bicentennial of the Fed. Constitution, 1987. Morgan-Penn Faculty fellow, 1977-79, NEH fellow, 1984; named Outstanding Tchg. prof., U. Balt. Coll. Liberal Arts, 1965, Outstanding Tchg. Prof. in English Dept., Morgan State U., 1987. Mem. MLA, South Atlantic MLA, Coll. Lang. Assn., Coll. English Assn. (Mid-Atlantic Group v.p. 1987-90, pres. 1990-92, exec. bd. 1992-2005, nat. bd. dir. 2001-04, nat. liaison officer 1993-2004), Women's Caucus for Modern Langs., Md. Coun. Tchrs. English, Md. Poetry and Lit. Soc., Md. Assn. Depts. English (bd. dir. 1992—), Mid. Atlantic Writers' Assn. (founding 1981, exec. assoc. editor Mid. Atlantic Writers' Assn. Rev. 1989-2000), Delta Epsilon Sigma (v.p. 1992-94, pres. 1994-96), Pi Kappa Delta Roman Catholic. Home: 17049 Keeney Mill Rd New Freedom PA 17349 Personal E-mail: vfsedlak@aol.com.

SEDLER, ROZANNE FRIEDLANDER, social worker, educator; b. Greensburg, Pa., June 16, 1938; d. Ernest and Belle (Marchel) Friedlander; m. Robert Allen Sedler, Jan. 24, 1960; children: Eric Mark, Beth Ellen. BA, U. Pitts., 1960; MSW, St. Louis U., 1962. Social worker Family & Children's Svc., St. Louis, 1962—63; lectr. Sch. of Social Work Haile Selassie U., Addis Ababa, Ethiopia, 1963—66; social worker U. Ky. Med. Ctr., Lexington, 1966—68, Renaissance Home Health Care, Detroit, 1984—86; geriatric social worker Jewish Family Svc., Southfield, Mich., 1986—. Mem.: AFSME (chair Jewish Family Svcs. bargaining unit 1998—2006, bd. dir. 2000—06, exec. bd. local 1640 2000—06), ACLU Mich. (chpt. pres. 2001—04, chmn. bd. dir. Oakland County, Mich.). Democrat. Jewish. Home: 18851 Capitol Dr Southfield MI 48075-2680 Office: Jewish Family Svc 24123 Greenfield Rd Southfield MI 48075-3116 Office Phone: 248-592-2348. Personal E-mail: rozsedler@aol.com.

SEDWAY, LYNN MASSEL, real estate economist; b. Washington, Nov. 26, 1941; d. Mark S. and Jean M. (Magnus) Massel; m. Paul H. Sedway, June 12, 1966; children: Mark, Carolyn, Jan. BA in Econs., U. Mich., 1963; MBA, U. Calif., Berkeley, 1976. Economist San Rafael (Calif.) Redevel. Agy., 1976-78; prin. Sedway Group, San Francisco, 1978—99; exec. mng. dir. CB Richard Ellis, San Francisco, 1999—. Instr. Appraisal Bus. Sch. U. Calif., Berkeley; corporate bd. mem. Hunting Gate Capital, Swig Co., AMB Alliance Fund III Bride Housing. Bridge housing bd., exec. com. trust Public Land Real Estate Coun. 1984-86, Internat. Coun. of Shopping Ctrs.; chmn San Rafael Downtown Retail Com., 1985; former trustee Urban Land Inst., former chmn. retail comml. coun., San Francisco District Council. Fellow, Homer Hoyt. Mem. Counselors of Real Estate, San Francisco Chamber of Commerce (former bd. of dirs.), City Club, Intl. House, Lambda Alpha (past pres., bd. dirs.), Internat. Land Econs. Soc., San Francisco Mayors Mcpl. Fiscal Advisory Com. Avocation: tennis. Home: 765 Market St Apt 26G San Francisco CA 94103-2038 Office Phone: 415-733-5321. Personal E-mail: lynn.sedway@cbre.com.

SEE, CAROLYN, English language educator, writer, book critic; b. Pasadena, Calif., Jan. 13, 1934; d. George Newton Laws and Kate Louise (Sullivan) Daly; m. Richard Edward See, Feb. 18, 1955 (div. June 1959); 1 child, Lisa Lenine; m. Tom Sturak, June 11, 1959; 1 child, Clara Elizabeth Marya. BA, Calif. State U., L.A., 1958; PhD, UCLA, 1963. Prof. English Loyola Marymount Coll., L.A., 1970-85, UCLA, 1985—; book critic L.A. Times, 1981-93, Washington Post, 1993—. Author: Rhine Maidens, 1980, Golden Days, 1986, Making History, 1991, Dreaming: Hard Luck and Good Times In America, 1995, The Handyman, 1999, Making a Literary Life, 2002, There Will Never Be Another You, 2006 Bd. dirs. Calif. Arts Coun., L.A., 1987-91, Day Break, for homeless, Santa Monica, Calif., 1989—, Friends of English, UCLA, 1990—; buddy for life AIDS Project L.A., AIDS relief, L.A., 1990—. Recipient award Sidney Hillman Found., 1972, Robert Kirsch award L.A. Times, 1994; PEN Ctr. USA West Lifetime Achievement award 1998; grantee Nat. Endowment for Arts, 1980, Guggenheim fellow, 1990-91. Mem. Writers Guild Am., Libr. Found. Calif., PEN Ctr. USA West (pres. 1990-91), Nat. Book Critics Cir. (bd. dirs. 1986-90). Democrat. Avocations: gardening, sailing, dance, brush clearing. Home: 17339 Tramonto Dr Pacific Palisades CA 90272-3124 Office: UCLA Dept English 405 Hilgard Ave Los Angeles CA 90095-9000 Office Phone: 310-454-7724. Business E-Mail: csee@ucla.edu.

SEE, PATTI K., humanities educator; d. Joseph and Virgiline See; 1 child, Alexander Thornton. MA, U. Wis., Eau Claire, 1994. Sr. student svcs. coord. Ednl. Support Svcs. U. Wis., Eau Claire, 1994—, sr. lectr. Women's Studies Program, 2001—, sr. student svcs. coord. Cons. Upward Bound, Eau Claire, 1999—2001, Drexel U., Phila., 2000; advisor Coll. Feminists U. Wis., 2002—; invited spkr. various local and nat. confs. Editor: (anthology) Higher Learning: Reading and Writing About College, 2d edit., 2005 (Sys. Regents award for excellence, U. Wis., 2006); author: (poetry collection) Love's Bluff, 2006, (book) Family Story (Vol. One Fiction contest, 2005); contbr. over 50 poems, stories and essays in mags. and athologies. Team leader Cmty. Table, Eau Claire, 1998—2006; creative writing instr. L.E. Phillips Meml. Pub. Libr., Eau Claire, 1997—98. Recipient Disting. Svc. award, U. Wis., 1997, Academic Staff Excellence in Performance award, 2004; grantee Academic Strategies Project, West Ctrl. Wis. Consortium, 1997—99; Rsch. grant, Office of Rsch. & Sponsored Programs, 1997—2005, U. Wis. Sys. Inst. on Race and Ethnicity, 1998. Mem.: AAUW (assoc.). Office: Univ Wis Old Library 2112 Eau Claire WI 54702 Office Phone: 715-836-4826. Business E-Mail: seepk@uwec.edu.

SEEBACH, ELIZABETH EMILY, psychologist, educator; b. Springfield, Mass., Dec. 28, 1960; d. Willard Ervin and Suzanne Roberta (Bowman) Jones; m. Bradley Scott Seebach, Aug. 8, 1987; 1 child, Rachel Emily. AB cum laude, Washington U., St. Louis, 1982; MS in Psychology, Vanderbilt U., 1985, PhD in Clin. Psychology, 1988. Lic. psychologist. Psychol. examiner Columbia (Tenn.) Comprehensive Mental Health, 1984-85, Psychiat. Cons., Nashville, 1985-86; intern in psychology Brown U., Providence, 1986-87, postdoctoral fellow Med. Sch., 1987-89; asst. prof. Lawrence U., Appleton, Wis., 1989-91; psychologist Psychology Ctr., Madison, Wis., 1991-94, Cath. Learning Ctr., N.Y.C., 1994-95, Brick Kiln, Bohemia, NY, 1995—98; lectr. Vilerbo U., 1998—99; asst. prof. U. Wis., La Crosse, 1999—. Adv. Psychology Student Assn., Appleton, 1990-92; lectr. U. Wis., Madison. Contbr. numerous articles to profl. jours. Member steering com. Sabin Alliance, Lawrence U., 1989-91; girl scout leader, 2001—; mem. La Crosse Area Health Initiative, 2004—; mem. Coulee Region Brain Team, 2000-2004. Mem. APA (teaching psychology div. 2. clin. psychology div. 12, neuropsychology div. 40), Fox Valley Psychol. Assn. Home: W7786 Meadow Way Holmen WI 54636-9432 Office: U Wis 341D Graff Main Hall La Crosse WI 54601

SEEBACH, LYDIA MARIE, physician; b. Red Wing, Minn., Nov. 9, 1920; d. John Henry and Marie (Gleusen) S.; m. Keith Edward Wentz, Oct. 16, 1959; children: Brooke Marie, Scott. BS, U. Minn., 1942, MB, 1943, MD, 1944, MS in Medicine, 1951. Diplomate Am. Bd. Internal Medicine. Intern Kings County Hosp., Bklyn., 1944; fellow Mayo Found., Rochester, Minn., 1945-51; pvt. practice Oakland, Calif., 1952-60, San Francisco, 1961—. Asst. clin. prof. U. Calif., San Francisco, 1981—; mem., vice chmn. Arthritis Clinic, Presbyn. Hosp., San Francisco, 1961-88, pharmacy com., 1963-78; chief St. Mary's Hosp. Arthritis Clinic, San Francisco, 1968-72; exec. bd. Pacific Med. Ctr., San Francisco, 1974-76. Contbr. articles to med. jours. Fellow ACP; mem. AMA, Am. Med. Womens Assn. (pres. Calif. chpt. 1968-70), Am. Rheumatism Assn., Am. Soc. Internal Medicine, Pan Am. Med. Womens Assn. (treas.), Calif. Acad. Medicine, Calif. Soc. Internal Medicine, Calif. Med. Assn., San Francisco Med. Soc., San Francisco Med. Assn., San Francisco Soc. Internal Medicine, No. Calif. Rheumatism Assn., Internat. Med. Women's Assn., Mayo Alumni (bd. dirs. 1983-89), Iota Sigma Pi. Republican. Lutheran. Avocations: music, cooking, gardening, needlepoint. Office: 490 Post St Ste 939 San Francisco CA 94102-1414 Office Phone: 415-397-9571. Personal E-mail: lseebach@sbcglobal.net.

SEEBERT, KATHLEEN ANNE, international sales and marketing executive; d. Harold Earl and Marie Anne (Lowery) S. MM, MA, Northwestern U., 1983. Dir. mktg. MidAm. Commodity Exch., 1982—85; internat. trade cons. to Govt. of Ont. Canada, 1985—90; dir. mktg. and program devel. Internat. Orientation Resources, 1990—94; v.p. Am. Internat. Group, 1995—97; dir. KPMG Peat Marwick LLP, 1997—98; cons. Watson Wyatt & Co., 1999—2005, Marshall Goldsmith Ptnrs. LLC, 2006—. Guest lectr. U. Dayton, U. Notre Dame, Northwestern U., Kellogg Alumni Chgo., French-Am. C. of C., Internat. Employee Relocation Coun., Soc. Intercultural Educators, Trainers and Rschrs., ASTD, Ill. CPA Soc., SBA, KPMG Peat Marwick, Pricewaterhousecoopers, Ernst & Young, Nat. Fgn. Trade Coun., William M. Mercer, Inc. Nat. bd. dirs. U. Dayton. Mem. Futures Industry Assn. Am. (treas.), Notre Dame Club Chgo., Kellogg Mgmt. Club Chgo. Republican. Roman Catholic. Office: 191 N Wacker Dr Ste 2100 Chicago IL 60611

SEEDS, SHARON LYNN, bank processor; d. Don A. and Marguerite Morairty Seeds. BA in Edn., Ariz. State U., 1972. Tchr. gen. and vocal music edn. Paradise Valley Unified Sch. Dist. # 69, Phoenix, 1973—76; advt. coord. Greater Phoenix Jewish News, 1976—83; disbursements/loan rev. processor Merabank, Phoenix, 1984—88; loan processor II Citibank, Scottsdale and Mesa, Ariz., 1989—91; acctg. specialist, ops. processor I and II, store acctg. support, mortgage lending home equity Internet divsn. Wells Fargo & Co., Phoenix, 1992—. Festival adjudicator Ariz. Solo and Ensemble Festival, Phoenix, 1973—; jr. choir dir. Christ Ch. of the Ascension, Paradise Valley, 1983—87; soloist and sect. leader Congregation Ch., Tempe, Presbyn. Ch., Phoenix, Ch. of Divine Sci., Trinity Episcopal Cathedral, St. Barnabas-on-the Desert, 1976—2002. Contr.ghost editor: textbook Arizona Construction Lending and the Law, 1988. Vol. libr. catalog and music areas Lillian Valley Sch., Blackfoot, Idaho, 2002, 2004; neighborhood activist on hist. preservation com. Sunview Estates II, Phoenix, 2002—; vol. press release area Episcopal Ch. Gen. Conv., Phoenix, 1991. Mem.: Am. Choral Dirs. Assn., Music Educators Nat. Conf., Phi Kappa Phi, Kappa Delta Pi, Pi Lambda Theta, Sigma Alpha Iota (local chair/co-chair for nat. bazaar at triennial conv. 1987—, nat. elections chair triennial conv. 2003, Sword of Honor 1972, Rose of Honor 1995, Rose of Dedication 2003). Episcopalian. Avocations: music theater/liturgical drama, needlecrafts, reading. Personal E-mail: seedssl@hotmail.com.

SEEFELT, NANCY E., academic administrator, educator; d. Robert J. and Sylviann Seefelt; m. Jeffrey A. Scofield, Oct. 12, 1996. BS, Ctrl. Mich. U., Mt. Pleasant, Mich., 1993, MS, 1997; PhD, Mich. State U., Lansing, Mich., 2005. Instr. biology Ctrl. Mich. U., Mt. Pleasant, Mich., 1997—2005, academic dir. Sci. and Tech. Residential Coll., 2004—, asst. prof. biology, 2005—. Sec. mus. studies coun. Ctrl. Mich. U., 1999—2006, mem. first yr. experience coun., 2004—; piping plover patrol Gt. Lakes Population U.S. Fish and Wildlife Svc., Mich., 2000—. Author: (book chapter) The State of Lake Michigan, 2005; contbr. articles to profl. jours. Recipient Wallace award, Mich. State U., 2004. Mem.: Natural Resource Def. Coun., Soc. Preservation of Natural History Collections, Am. Ornithologist's Union, Waterbirds Soc., Internat. Assn. of Gt. Lakes Rsch., Defenders Wildlife, World Wildlife Fund, Friends Beaver Island. Office: Biology Dept Brooks 217 Central Michigan Univ Mount Pleasant MI 48859 Office Phone: 989-774-3227. Business E-Mail: seefe1ne@cmich.edu.

SEEGER, LAUREEN E., health products executive; BBA, U. Wis., Eau Claire, 1983; JD, U. Wis., Madison, 1986. Atty. Jones, Day, Reavis & Pogue, 1986—92; ptnr.-in-charge tech. litigation sect. Morris, Manning & Martin, LLP, 1992—2000; v.p., gen. coun. McKesson Provider Technologies, 2000—06; exec. v.p., gen. counsel, sec. McKesson Corp., San Francisco, 2006—. Office: McKesson Corpn 1 Post St San Francisco CA 94104

SEEGER, MELINDA WAYNE, realtor; m. Robert Charles Seeger; 1 child, Jeffrey Wayne. Chief occupl. therapy Rehab. Inst. Oreg., Portland, 1964-66; supr. phys. disabilities and gen. medicine and surgery occupl. therapy Mpls. VA Hosp., 1966-68; supr. phys. disabilities occupl. therapy Nat. Naval Med. Ctr., Bethesda, Md., 1968-71; assoc. chief rehab. svcs., dir. occupl. therapy UCLA Med. Ctr., 1974-85, cons., prin. investigator rheumatology divsn. dept. medicine, 1985-86; realtor Merrill Lynch Realty, L.A., 1987-95, Re/Max Estate Properties, Beverly Hills, Calif., 1995-96, Nelson Shelton & Assocs., Beverly Hills, 1996—. Author, editor articles in field. Mem. utilization rev. com. Vis. Nurse Assn. L.A., 1975-85, mem. profl. adv. com., 1979-80; mem. exec. com. Allied Health Professions sect. Arthritis Found., 1980-85, chmn. edn. com., 1982-85, mem. profl. edn. com.; bd. dirs. Calif. Occupl. Therapy Found., 1984-85, Westwood-Holmby Hills Homeowners Assn.; mem. adv. bd. Save Westwood Village L.A. Recipient Spl. Achievement award Nat. Naval Med. Ctr., 1971, Outstanding Performance award, 1971, Spl. Performance award UCLA, 1980, 84, Addie Thomas Svc. award for outstanding svc. to rheumatology cmty. Arthritis Found., 1986, Cert. of Appreciation award, 1989; mem. Million Dollar Club. Mem. Am. Occupl. Therapy Assn., Occupl. Therapy Assn. Calif., Allied Health Professions Assn. (chmn. edn. com. 1982—), L.A. Bd. Realtors, San Fernando Valley Bd. Realtors, West L.A. C. of C., Million Dollar Club, Blue Diamond Club. Office: 355 N Canon Dr Beverly Hills CA 90210-4704

SEEGER, VIRGINIA VINCENT, painter; b. San Francisco, May 29, 1923; Student, Cornish Sch. Art, Seattle, U. Wash. Portrait painter, 1948—. Creative works include cartoons for various orgns. Mem. Pacific Art League. Home: PO Box 3291 Sunriver OR 97707-0291 also: PO Box 3291 Bend OR 97707-0291

SEEGERS, LORI C., lawyer; b. Miami Beach, Fla., June 17, 1955; BA cum laude, U. Pa., 1977; JD, Fordham U., 1982. Bar: N.Y. 1983, Ill. 2002, U.S. Dist. Ct. (so. dist.) N.Y. 1983. Ptnr. Anderson, Kill & Olick, P.C., N.Y.C.; gen. counsel PPM Am., Inc. Contbr. articles to profl. jours. Mem. ABA, N.Y. State Bar Assn. (sect. banking, corp. and bus. law), Assn. of Bar of City of N.Y. Office: PPM Am Inc Ste 1200 225 W Wacker Dr Chicago IL 60606-1276 E-mail: lori.seegers@ppmamerica.com.

SEEKLANDER, MARLENE KAY, educational association administrator; b. Brookings, S.D., Aug. 31, 1962; d. Harold T. and Margaret E. Seeklander. Diploma, Canby Vo-Tech, 1981; BBA, Dakota State U., 1989; MEd, S.D. State U., 1992. Asst. dir. fin. aid S.D. State U., Brookings, 1994—97; mgr. rsch. & spl. projects Edn. Assistance Corp., Aberdeen, 1997—. Vol. Aberdeen Cmty. Theatre, 2003—06; vol., walker Mar. Dimes WalkAmerica, 1998—2006. Mem.: Nat. Assn. Student Fin. Aid Adminstrs., Rocky Mountain Assn. Student Fin. Aid Arminstrs., S.D. Assn. Student Fin. Aid Adminstrs. (Douglas Steckler Profl. Devel. award 2004), Mapping Your Future (Mapping Your Future Excellence award 2001), Nat. Coun. Higher Edn. Loan Programs. Lutheran. Avocations: antiques, travel, reading, writing. Home: 221 North Dakota St Aberdeen SD 57401 Office: Education Assistance Corp 115 First Ave SW Aberdeen SD 57401 Office Phone: 605-622-4318. Office Fax: 1-800-354-7070. Personal E-mail: sdantiquer@iw.net. E-mail: marlene.seeklander@eac-easci.org.

SEELBACH, ANNE ELIZABETH, artist; b. Detroit, July 27, 1944; BA, NYU, 1967; MFA, CUNY, 1985. Curator Monhegan (Maine) Mus., 1992—95; art instr. The Victor d'Amico Inst. of Art, Napeague, N.Y., 1994—, Arts Pro Tem, Hancock, NH, 1991—95. One-woman shows include Tower Gallery, Southampton, N.Y., 1981, Newark (N.J.) Mus., 1984, Tower Gallery, N.Y.C., 1985, The Conn. Gallery, Marlborough, 1989, Radcliffe Inst. Advanced Studies, Cambridge, Mass., 1990, Frick Gallery, Belfast, Maine, 1991, Simmons Coll., Boston, 1991, The Painting Ctr., N.Y.C., 1994, Kouros Gallery, 1996, Alva Gallery, New London, Conn., 2002, Wheaton Coll., Norton, Mass., 2004, numerous group shows including most recently, —, exhibited in group shows at Fed. Res. Bank, Boston, 1995, Kouros Gallery, N.Y.C., 1995—96, Attleboro Mus., Mass., 1996, Alva Gallery, New London, Conn., 2000, Norwalk Mus., Conn., 2002, Wheaton Coll., Norton, Mass., 2004, Smolyan Art Mus., Bulgaria, 2006, Represented in permanent collections Newark Mus., Frauenmuseum, Bonn, Germany, Centrum Frans Masereel, Kasterlee, Belgium, Lyman Allyn Mus., New London, Conn., Radcliffe Inst. Advanced Studies, Prudential Ins. Co., Newark, Continental Grain Corp., N.Y.C., Phoenix Mut. Life Ins. Co., Hartford, Conn., The Hillier Group, Princeton, N.J. Recipient painting fellowship Radcliffe Inst. Advanced Studies, 1989-90, artist fellowship Triangle Artists' Workshop, Pine Plains, N.Y., 1988, MacDowell Colony, Peterborough, N.H., 1987; artist-in-residence I-Park, East Haddam, Conn., 2003. Mem.: Soc. Bunting Fellows. Address: PO Box 0812 Amagansett NY 11930

SEELE, PERNESSA C., immunologist, health science association administrator; b. Lincolnville, SC, 1954; MS, Clark Atlanta Univ. Rschr. Rockefeller Univ., NYC; immunologist Harlem Hosp.; founder, CEO Balm In Gilead non-profit AIDS edn. program, NYC, 1989—. Organizer Week of Prayer for the Healing of AIDS, Harlem, 1989—. Named one of 35 Most Beautiful Women, Essence mag., 2005, 100 Most Influential People, Time mag., 2006. Office: The Balm In Gilead Inc Ste 450 130 W 42nd St New York NY 10036 Office Phone: 212-730-7381. Office Fax: 212-730-2551. Business E-Mail: pseele@balmingilead.org.

SEELER, RUTH ANDREA, pediatrician, educator; b. NYC, June 13, 1936; d. Thomas and Olivia Seeler. BA cum laude, U. Vt., 1959, MD, 1962. Diplomate Am. Bd. Pediat., Am. Bd. Pediatric Hematology/Oncology. Intern Bronx (N.Y.) Mcpl. Hosp., 1962—65; pediats. hematology/oncology fellow U. Ill., 1965—67; dir. pediatric hematology/oncology Cook County Hosp., 1967—84; prof. pediatrics and pediatric edn. Coll. Medicine U. Ill., Chgo., 1984—; assoc. chief pediatrics Michael Reese Hosp., Chgo., 1990—97, acting chief pediatrics, 1997—99; pediatrician St. Anthony's Hosp./U. Ill. Coll. Medicine, 1999—2001. Course coord. pediatrics Nat. Coll. Advanced Med. Edn., Chgo., 1987-96; mem. subboard Pediatric Hematology/Oncology, Chapel Hill, 1990-95; chief Midwest Am. Bd. Pediat., 1990-, Mem. editl. bd. Am. Jour. Pediat. Hematology/Oncology, 1985-95. Founder med. dir. camp for hemophiliacs Ill. Hemophilia Found., 1973—2000, pres. Ill., 1981—85; sec. exec. com. U. Vt. Med. Sch. Alumna Assn.; jr. and sr. warden, treas. Ch. Our Saviour, Chgo., 1970—92. Mem.: U. Vt. Med. Sch. Alumna Assn. (pres.-elect), Phi Beta Kappa, Gamma Phi Beta Found. (trustee 1994—2000, 2002—). Avocations: triathalons, biking, swimming. Office: U Ill Coll Medicine Pediats M/C 856 840 S Wood St Chicago IL 60612-7317 Office Phone: 312-355-1021. Business E-Mail: seeler@uic.edu.

SEELIG, JILL, publishing executive; MBA, Fordham U., NY. With fin. svcs. ind., 1984—89; sales rep. NY Mag.; advt. sales rep. Self Mag., 1993—94, beauty dir., 1994—95; nat. sales mgr. Self Mag., 1996—99; advt. dir. Vanity Fair, 1998—99, O, The Oprah Mag., 1999—2000, pub., 2000—. Office: O, The Oprah Magazine 1700 Broadway New York NY 10019*

SEELY, MARIBETH WALSH, elementary school educator; d. William F. and Agnes C. Walsh; m. Thomas P. Seely; children: Timothy Patrick Francis, Keribeth Francis. BS in Elem. Edn., Lowell U., 1966. Cert. reading specialist Mass. Tchr. Town of Methuen, Mass., 1966—71, City of Lawrence, Mass., Sandyston-Walpack Sch., Layton, NJ. Testified to Ho. Reps. Am. Legion and Citizens Flag Alliance, Washington, 1997; testified for Am. flag Senate Judiciary Com., Washington, 1999. Nominee Gov.'s Tchr. Recognition award, State N.J., 1994; named Woman of Distinction, Lenni-Lenape Girl Scouts, 1995, Woman of the 90's, N.J. Herald Newspaper, 1995; recipient Inspiring Tchr. award, Sussex County C.C., 2005, Cert. Appreciations, Vietnam Vets. Am., 2005. Mem.: Sierra Club (assoc.). Roman Catholic. Avocations: hiking, art museums, travel, baseball. Home: 19 Summit Dr Branchville NJ 07826 Office: Sandyston-Walpack School PO Box 128 Layton NJ 07851

SEELY, MEGAN, activist, educator; b. San Jose; BA, Calif. State U., Chico, 1995; MA, Calif. State U., Sacramento, 1998. Pres. Calif. NOW, Sacramento, 2001—05; prof. Sierra Coll., Rocklin, Calif., 2005—. Author: (non fiction) Fight Like a Girl: How to be a Fearless Feminist. Bd. dirs. Women's Health Specialists, Calif.

SEEM, EVELYN ASHCRAFT, music educator; b. Sedgwick, Kans., July 10, 1915; d. Frank T. and Esther Hege Ashcraft; m. Herbert A. Seem, June 19, 1938 (dec. Mar. 1994); children: Herbert A. Jr., Quinda Marie Seem-Hatfield. Diploma, Sherwood Music Sch., 1936; B in Piano, Phillips U., 1936, postgrad. Tchr. Phillips U., Enid, Okla., 1960—80; pvt. piano tchr. Enid, 1980—. Mem. Nat. Music Tchrs. Assn., Okla. Music Tchrs. Assn. Presbyterian. Home: 722 W Illinois Ave Enid OK 73701-7302 Office Phone: 580-234-4967.

SEEP, DOROTHY M., music educator; d. Frederick Henry and Estelle May Muller; m. Ralph Vincent Seep, Nov. 11, 1978; children: Jessica, Jeremy. MusB, Eastman Sch. Music, 1969, MusM, 1972. Music tchr. Taft Elem. Sch., Washingtonville, NY, 1969—71, Wayne Ctrl. Sch., Ontario, NY, 1972—81, Rochester Christian Sch., Penfield, NY, 1987—92; sr. choir dir. Rochester

Christian Reformed Ch., Penfield, NY, 1988—91; music tchr. Annapolis Area Christian Sch., 1998—. Founder and dir. children's chorale Annapolis Area Christian Sch., Md., 1998—; founder and dir. adult cmty. choir and orch., 2003. Mem. choir Nat. Presbyn. Ch., Washington, 2004—; music dir. Safe Harbor Presbyn. Ch., 2000—03. Mem.: Music Educators Nat. Conf., Am. Choral Dir. Assn., Phi Kappa Lambda, Sigma Alpha Iota. Presbyterian. Avocations: sewing, gardening, reading, cooking. Office: Annapolis Area Christian Sch 710 Ridgely Ave Annapolis MD 21401 Office Phone: 410-266-8255.

SEFTEL, DONNA SELENE, architect; b. N.Y.C., Apr. 26, 1956; d. Lawrence and Roslyn (Kaufman) S.; 1 child, Morgan Luc. Student, 1st Berlin Summer Acad., 1977, Royal Danish Acad. Fine Arts, 1978, Columbia U., 1978; BArch, Cornell U., 1980; postgrad., New Sch. for Social Rsch., 1997. Registered arch., N.Y., N.J. Arch. Steven Holl Archs., N.Y.C., 1985—86; prin. Donna Selene Seftel Archs., N.Y.C., 1986—; lectr. RISD, 1993, Queensland U., Australia, 1999; critic Royal Swedish Inst. Tech., Stockholm, 1991, Cornell U., 1991, Columbia U., 1992, 1995, Parsons Sch. Design, 1992—95, Fla. Internat. U., 2005. Artist-in-residence Mott Hall, N.Y.C., 1987—88; lectr. Archtl. League N.Y., 1987, Acad. Art and Design, Linz, Austria, 1988, Cooper-Hewitt Nat. Mus. Design, 1988, CCNY, 1990, 92, Cornell U., 1991, Pa. State U., 1994, Columbia U., 1992, 95. Projects include Rapid Indsl. Plastics, 1985, Vacant Lots, 1987, Calif. Life Guard Tower, 1988, Theatricus Formicus, Gordon Lighting and Lightscreen, 1989, Recycling Industry, 1990, Nara Conv. Ctr. Competition, 1991, Lego: Gate of Gates, Culebra House, P.R., 1992, Kulturzeile, Vienna, Austria, 1993, Interactive Playhouse, Greene Loft, N.Y.C., 1996, S-network offices, 1994-97, Wild Pitch Records, Filiberti House, 1994, Tribeca Loft, 1995; prodn. designer ind. feature film Burn, 1997, Holey Landscape: World Trade Ctr. Meml. Competition, 2003; one-woman show Atelier Lorenz Mandl Gasse, Vienna, 1993; exhibited in group shows, including Urban Ctr., N.Y.C., Archtl. League N.Y., 1987, Kirsten Kiser Gallery for Arch., L.A., 1988, Grand Ctrl. Sta., 1989, Downtown Whitney Mus., N.Y.C., Gallery 91, N.Y.C., 1989, Storefront for Art & Arch., Nat. Inst. Archtl. Edn., N.Y.C., Cooper-Hewitt Nat. Mus. Design, N.Y.C., 1990, Moderna Museet, Kulturhuset, Stockholm, 1991, Deutsches Architektur Mus., Frankfurt am Main, 1992, Gammel Dok Ctr. for Danish Architecture, Copenhagen, Kasteel d'Erp, Baarlo, Belgium, Kunsthal, Rotterdam, Cornell U., Ithaca, N.Y., 1993, City Art Ctr., Edinburgh, Mus. Finnish Architecture, Helsinki, Mus. fur Gestaltung, Zurich, Katonah Mus. of Art, Haus der Arch., Graz, 1994, Grande Arche in La Defense, Paris, Norton Mus. Art, Palm Beach, 1995, Mus. Decorative Arts, Lausanne, 1996, Gemeente Mus., Helmond, Netherlands, Mus. de Civilisation, Quebec City, Arch. Ctr., Berlin, 1997; pub. in various publs. including N.Y. Times, DOMUS, Metropolis, Architecture Record, AIA N.Y. Architecture, World Architecture, Shelter & Dreams-Katonah Mus. Catalogue, Unpvt. House-MOMA Catalogue, Mama 27, Gate of The Present-LEGO Catalogue, Ideas for New Social Bldgs., Vacant Lots, New Schs. for N.Y., Showrooms, Front 3, Archtl. Edn. for Children at Mott Hall-Dist. 6, N.Y.C. Recipient award Young Archs. Forum 6, Archtl. League N.Y., 1987, project award N.Y. chpt. AIA, 1989; architecture fellow N.Y. Found. for Arts, 1988; Pritzger fellow Djerassi Resident Artists Program, Woodside, Calif., 1995, in collections of Lego, Denmark and Yamagiwa, Japan. Democrat. Jewish. Address: 95 Drake Ln Manhasset NY 11030-1227 Office Phone: 516-627-6906. Personal E-mail: dseftel@earthlink.net.

SEGAL, JACQUELINE GALE, lawyer; b. Bryn Mawr, Pa., Aug. 11, 1959; d. David and Harriet Segal; m. Douglas R. Widin, June 1, 1988. B in Music Edn., Temple U., Phila., 1981, JD, 1990. Bar: Pa. Supreme Ct. 1990, U.S. Dist. Ct. (ea. dist.) Pa. 1991, U.S. Supreme Ct. 2005. Legal intern Pa. Superior Ct., Phila., 1988—89; law clk. Phila. Ct. Common Pleas, 1990—93; with Astor Weiss Kaplan & Rosenbloom, Bala Cynwyd, 1993—95, Bennett & Assoc., 1995—97, Wolf, Block, Schorr and Solis-Cohen LLP, Phila., 1997—2005, Fox Rothschild LLP, 2005—. Spkr. in field. Mem. Brandywine Conservancy, Chadds Ford, Pa., 1997—. Recipient Kranzel award, Temple U. Sch. Law, 1990. Mem.: ABA, Montgomery Bar Assn., Phila. Bar Assn. (exec. com. 1997—, family law sect. sec. 2003, family law sect. treas. 2004, family law sect. chair-elect 2005, family law sect. chair 2006, chair exec. com. 2006, com. jud. selection and retention, chancellor's ad hoc com. pandemic, disaster planning, chair, child support legis. com., former chair, divorce and equitable distribution com., domestic violence com.), Pa. Bar Assn., Am. Inns of Ct. (Don's Jonas Freed chpt., U. Pa. Law Sch. chpt.). Avocations: gardening, music, bicycling, kayaking, tennis. Office: Fox Rothschild LLP Eagleview Corp Ctr Ste 100 747 Constitution Dr Box 673 Exton PA 19341-0673 Office Phone: 610-458-3110. Office Fax: 610-458-7337. Business E-Mail: jsegal@foxrothschild.com.

SEGAL, JOAN SMYTH, library consultant, small business owner; b. Bklyn., Sept. 14, 1930; d. John Patrick and Anna Catherine (Green) Smyth; m. William Segal, June 25, 1955; children: Harold M., Nora A. BA, Rutgers U., 1951; MS in LS, Columbia U., 1955; PhD, U. Colo., 1978. Cert. assn. exec. Libr. Math. Inst., NYU, N.Y.C., 1955-58; libr. Western Interstate Commn. for Higher Edn., Boulder, Colo., 1970-76; libr. cons., Boulder, 1976-78; mgr. resource sharing program Bibliog. Ctr. for Rsch., Denver, 1978-80, exec. dir., 1980-84, Assn. Coll. and Rsch. Librs., ALA, Chgo., 1984-90; assoc. exec. dir. programs ALA, 1990-93; owner Vintage Ventures, Boulder, 1993—. Trainer libr. automation, group devel., resource sharing; cons. in field. Contbr. articles to profl. publs. Mem. bd. dir., Boulder Cmty. Network, 2005-; pres., Boulder Chorale Group, 2005-, Named Colo. Libr. of Yr., Colo. Libr. Assn., 1984. Mem. ALA, Spl. Librs. Assn. (chmn. edn. divsn. 1981-82, pres. Rocky Mountain cpt. 1981-82, 94-95, bd. dirs. 1983-86, chmn. mus., arts and humanities divsn. 1998-99), OCLC Network Dirs. (chmn. 1983), Mountain Plains Libr. Assn., Douglass Soc. (hon.).

SEGAL, LINDA GALE, retired insurance company executive; b. Panama City, Fla., Dec. 14, 1947; d. Homer Ford Jr. and Mary Virginia (Phillmon) F. m. Howard Arthur Segal, Dec. 29, 1970; 1 child, David Samuel. Student, Orlando Jr. Coll., Fla., 1966-69, Rollins Coll., 1972. Sales asst. Sta. WESH-TV, Orlando, Fla., 1973-76; mktg. coordinator Sta. WFBC-TV, Grenneville, S.C., 1976-77; traffic mgr. STa. WRDW-TV, Augusta, Ga., 1978-80; field underwriter Liberty Life Ins. Co., Greenville, 1980-81; agt. benefits dept. J. Rolfe Davis Ins. Agy., Orlando, 1981-84; sr. market sales rep. Humana, Inc., Orlando, 1984-86; dir. mktg. Nat. Med. Mgmt., Orlando, 1986-87; sr. account exec. Physicians Health Plan Fla., Inc., Tampa, 1987-88, N.E. Fin. Services, Orlando, 1988-89; mktg. mgr. Ins. Mgmt. Svcs., Inc., Greenville, S.C., 1989-90; regional mktg. dir. Horizons Internat. Inc., St. Augustine, Fla., 1991-92; dir. bus. devel. ResCare Home Health, Inc., Jacksonville, Fla., 1992—. Pvt. practice ins. cons., Tampa and Orlando, Fla., 1986-89. Mem. Am. Bus. Women's Assn., Nat. Assn. Profl. Saleswomen, Nat. Assn. Health Underwriters, Assn. Life Underwriters, Women Life Underwriters Confedn., Nat. Assn. Securities Dealers (registered rep.). Republican. E-mail: lgs@itilink.com.

SEGAL, LORE, writer; b. Vienna, Mar. 8, 1928; came to U.S., 1951, naturalized, 1956; d. Ignatz and Franzi (Stern) Groszmann; m. David I. Segal, Nov. 3, 1960 (dec.); children: Beatrice Ann, Jacob Paul. BA in English, Bedford Coll., U. London, Eng., 1948. Prof. writing div. Sch. Arts, Columbia U., also Princeton U., Sarah Lawrence Coll., Bennington Coll.; prof. English U. Ill., Chgo., 1978-92, Ohio State U., 1992-97. Author: Other People's Houses, 1964; Lucinella, 1976, Her First American, 1985; (children's book) Tell Me A Mitzi, 1970, All the Way Home, 1973, Tell Me a Trudy, 1977; The Story of Mrs. Brubeck and How She Looked for Trouble and Where She Found Him, 1981, The Story of Mrs. Lovewright and Purrless Her Cat, 1985, Morris the Artist, 2003, Why Mole Shouted and Other Stories, 2004, More Mole Stories and Little Gopher Too, 2005; translator: (with W.D. Snodgrass) Gallows Songs, 1968, The Juniper Tree and Other Tales from Grimm, 1973, The Book of Adam to Moses, 1987, The Story of King Saul and King David, 1991; contbr. short stories, articles to N.Y. Times Book Rev., Partisan Rev., New Republic, The New Yorker, others5 Guggenheim fellow, 1965-66; Council Arts and Humanities grantee, 1968-69; Artists Public Service grantee, 1970-71; CAPS grantee, 1975; Nat. Endowment Arts grantee, spring 1982, 1987; NEH grantee, 1983; Acad. Arts and Letters award, 1986. Fellow: Acad. Arts & Scis. Address: 280 Riverside Dr New York NY 10025-9010 Office Phone: 212-663-1524. E-mail: Lore@usa.net.

SEGAL, MARILYN MAILMAN, psychologist, educator; b. Utica, N.Y., Aug. 9, 1927; d. Abraham and Alice (Lyons) Mailman; children— Betty, Wendy, Richard, Patti, Debbie. BA, Wellesley Coll., 1948; BS, McGill U., 1949; PhD, Nova U., 1970. Social worker Floating Hosp., Boston, 1950-51; dir. Preschool of Hollywood, Fla., 1955-60, U. Sch., Fort Lauderdale, Fla., 1960-62; prof. devel. psychology Nova U., Fort Lauderdale, 1970-72; dir. Nova U. Family Ctr., Fort Lauderdale, 1972-91, dean Family & Sch. Ctr., 1990—; bd. dir. Nat. Ctr. for Clin. Infant Studies, 1991—; trustee U. Miami, Fla., 1970—; chmn. A.L. Mailman Family Found. Author: Run Away Little Girl, 1975; Social Competence, 1977; Play and Learn, 1978; Just Pretending, 1981; Making Friends, 1982; All About Child Care, 1983; Your Child at Play: Birth to One, One to Two, Two to Three, 1985, Three to Five, In Time and With Love; Play Together, Grow Together, 1985, Creative Beginings, 1994, Poems To Learn By, Building Literacy With Love, 2003. Chmn. nat. vis. com. Sch. Nursing, U. Miami, 1982—. Recipient Chief award Ind. Colls. and Univs., 1982-83, Kathleen Wright award, 1990; named Woman of Yr., Fort Lauderdale Bus. and Profl. Women's Club, 1981-82; Woman of Yr., Brandeis U. Nat. Woman's Commn., 1982; Citizen of Yr., Hollywood Civitan Club, 1978; recipient Silver Medallion Brotherhood award Nat. Conf. Christians and Jews, 1994. Mem. Am. Psychol. Assn., Soc. Research in Child Devel., Delta Kappa Gamma. Democrat. Jewish. Home: 919 S South Lake Dr Hollywood FL 33019-1929 Office: Nova U Family Ctr 3301 College Ave Fort Lauderdale FL 33314-7721 Office Phone: 954-262-6925. Personal E-mail: segal78@bellsouth.com.

SEGAL, NANCY LEE, psychology professor, researcher; b. Boston, Mar. 2, 1951; d. Alfred Maurice and Esther (Rubenstein) S. BA in Psychology and English, Boston U., 1973; MA in Social Sci., U. Chgo., 1974, PhD in Human Devel., 1982. Asst. dir., rsch. assoc. Minn. Ctr. for Twin and Adoption Rsch., Mpls., 1985-91; prof. dept. psychology Calif. State U., Fullerton, 1991—. Cons. on twin loss, Mpls., 1984, 87. Author: Entwined Lives: Twins and What They Tell Us About Human Behavior, 1999, Indivisible by Two: Lives of Extraordinary Twins, 2005. Co-editor: Uniting Psychology and Biology: Integrative Perspectives on Human Development, 1997; contbg. editor Twins Mag., 1984—, mem. editorial bd., 1985—; contbr. articles to profl. jours. Recipient Disting. Alumni award Boston U., 1990. Fellow Am. Psychol. Soc., APA (divsn. 7); mem. Twins Found., Internat. Soc. for Twin Studies, Internat. Soc. for Human Ethology (membership chair), N.Y. Road Runners Club, Sigma Delta Epsilon (rsch. award 1989), Sigma Xi. Avocation: running. Office: Calif State U Dept Psychology H-426C 800 N State College Blvd Fullerton CA 92831-3547 Office Fax: 714-278-4843. Business E-Mail: nsegal@fullerton.edu.

SEGAL, PHYLLIS NICHAMOFF, mediator; b. Apr. 18, 1945; d. Sidney and Theresa Helen (Uroff) Nichamoff; m. Eli J. Segal, June 13, 1965; children: Jonathan, Mora. Student, Brandeis U., 1962-65; BA, U. Mich., 1966; JD, Georgetown U., 1973. Bar: N.Y. 1974, U.S. Dist. Ct. (so. and ea. dists.) N.Y. 1975, Mass. 1983, U.S. Supreme Ct. 1979. Deputy atty. gen. Commonwealth Mass., 1986—88; assoc. Weil, Gotshal and Manges, N.Y.C., 1973-77; legal dir. NOW Legal Def. and Edn. Fund., N.Y.C., 1977-82, gen. counsel, 1986—94; mediator ADR Assoc., L.L.C., Boston, 2001—. Chmn. Fed. Labor Rels. Auth., Washington, 1994-2000; gen. counsel Exec. office Transp. and Constrn., Commonwealth of Mass., 1984-86; adj. asst. prof. law NYU, 1980-82; fellow Bunting Inst. Radcliffe Coll., 1982-83; cons. U.S. Commn. Civil Rights. Contbr. articles to profl. jours. Mem. Commn. on Party Reform Nat. Dem. Party, 1972-73, mem. Compliance Rev. Commn., 1974-76; mem. adv. bd. Mass. Commn. Against Discrimination, 1983—; bd. chmn. Handgun Control Inc./Ctr. to Prevent Handgun Violence; former chairwoman Nat. Labor Rels. Authority. Mem. ABA, Fedn. Women Lawyers Jud. Screening Panel, Mass. Bar Assn.

SEGAL, RENA BETH, artist; b. New Brunswick, N.J., May 27, 1953; d. George and Helen (Steinberg) S BFA, Montclair State Coll., 1975; MFA, Rutgers U., 1977. One person shows include Ocean County Coll., Toms River, N.J., 1978, Piscataway (N.J.) Mcpl. Bldg., 1983, Johnson and Johnson, New Brunswick, 1985, N.J. State Mus., Trenton, 1989, Mystic Knight Gallery, New Brunswick, 1990, Advocate Bldg., Stamford, Conn., 1991, Gratz Gallery, New Hope, Pa., 2001, Rutgers U. Art Libr., New Brunswick, 2004, Princeton U., 2004, CAS Gallery Kean U., Union, N.J, 2005.; exhibited in group shows Dumont Landis Gallery, New Brunswick, 1981, Sidney Janis Gallery, N.Y.C., 1984, Laforet Mus. Harajunku, Tokyo, 1986, Morris Mus., Morristown, N.J., 1987, Hunterdon Art Ctr., Clinton, N.J., 1990, Phoenix Group, Metuchen, N.J., 1993, Sound Shore Gallery, Stamford, 1994, 95, 96, The Gallery at Bristol-Meyer Squibb, Princeton, 1995, 98, Collectors Edge Summit, N.J., 1999, N.J. Ctr. Arts, Summit, 1999, Marsh Ins. Co., Morristown, 2000, Rutgers U. Art Libr., New Brunswick, 2003, Gallery at StageWorks Hudson, N.Y., 2005, others; represented in permanent collections Pub. Svc. and Electric, Newark, Pepsico, Purchase, N.Y., Bristol-Meyers Squibb, Lawrenceville, N.J., Johnson & Johnson, New Brunswick, Chase Manhattan Bank, N.Y., Marsh Ins. Co., Morristown, Frederick R. Weisman Found., L.A. N.J. State Coun. on Arts fellow, 1985

SEGAL, SABRA LEE, artist, graphics designer, illustrator, actress; b. Boston; Student, Elmira Coll., N.Y., 1955-57; BFA, Boston U., 1963; MA in Art Edn., U. Wis., Madison, 1968, MFA, 1969. Narrator, recorder Acad. Resource Ctr. Vassar Coll., Poughkeepsie, NY, 1996—98; actor Pharaoh Audiobooks, Sedona, Ariz., 1994—96, 1999. Author: (poetry) To All Things Alive, 1968, An Artist's Life: Dreams, Letters and Real Things, 2000; one-woman shows include Schenectady (NY) Mus., 1985, Watermark/Cargo Gallery, Kingston, NY, 1991, Woodstock (NY) Artists Assn., Inc., 1992; exhibited in group shows at Smithsonian Inst., 1981, Albany (NY) Inst. History and Art, 1984, Donskoj & Co., Kingston, 1994, Rice Gallery, Albany, 1990, Barnes and Noble, 1997, Syracuse Cultural Workers Women Artist's Calendar, Syracuse, NY, 1999-2000, Living Rm. Gallery, Kingston, NY, 2003, Woodstock Watercolors Gallery, 2003, Richard Sena Gallery, Hudson, NY, 2003, Art Upstairs, Phoenicia, NY, 2005, Selected Works Artist's Gallery, Howard Gallery Bldg., Pittsfield, Mass., 2005, Varga Gallery, Woodstock, NY, 2006, Pittsfield Art Show, 2006; contbr. Women Artists' Calendar, Syracuse, NY, 1999-2000; actor War of the Worlds Audiobook, 1994-96, (film) The Road to Wellville, 1993. Lady exercisor, vis. guest Perfo Prodns. NC, 1993. Home: PO Box 821 Woodstock NY 12498-0821 Office Phone: 845-679-7230. Personal E-mail: sabra_segal@yahoo.com.

SEGALE, ALTHEA FRANCES, music educator; b. Huntington, N.Y., May 2, 1951; d. Joseph Thomas and Amalia Mary Hansen; m. Andrew William Segale, Mar. 23, 2002; 1 stepchild, Amanda Michelle; children: Amalia Anna Hansen Wendell, Chloe June Wendell. BA, SUNY, Oneonta, 1973; MA, SUNY, Stony Brook, 1986. Tchr. band Farmingdale Pub. Schs., NY, 1983—. Asst. condr. Bay Shore Cmty. Band, NY, 1996—99; v.p. Farmingdale Fedn. of Tchrs., 1986—91; asst. dir. marching band, dir. symphonic band Farmingdale H.S., 1996—. 1st basson Northport Cmty. Band, 1969—99; dir. youth choir Northport Presbyn. Ch., NY, 1985—96; elder First Presbyn. Ch., Greenlawn, NY, 2005—. Recipient U.S. Congl. Achievement citation, 1998. Mem.: Nassau County Music Educators Assn. (publicity exec. bd. 1987), Music Educators Nat. Conf., Neptune Power Squad (1st lt. 2001—02). Democrat. Avocation: boating. Home: 606 6th St East Northport NY 11731 Office: Farmingdale High Sch 150 Lincoln St Farmingdale NY 11735 Office Phone: 516-752-6761 391. E-mail: reedldy@optonline.net.

SEGALL, SARAH OSTROVSKY, psychoanalyst; b. Montreal, Que., Can., Nov. 22, 1930; d. Samuel Benjamin Ostrovsky and Nina Litvack; m. Maurice Segall, Nov. 25, 1951; children: Elizabeth, Eric, Peter. BS, McGill U., Montreal, 1951; MLS, Columbia U., 1967; grad. psychoanalyst, Boston Ctr. for Modern, Psychoanalysis, 1981. Lab. asst. and demonstrator dept. genetics McGill U., 1950-51; rsch. asst. Nat. Rsch. Coun., Ottawa, Can., 1951-55; bibliographic asst. Parkinson's Info. Ctr./Columbia U., N.Y.C., 1966-67; reference libr. Manhasset (N.Y.) Pub. Lib., 1968-71, Port Washington (N.Y.) Pub. Libr., 1968-71; psychoanalyst Boston Ctr. for Modern Psychoanalytic Studies, 1985—. Fiscal officer Boston Ctr. for Modern Psychoanalytic Studies, 1985—; rsch. cons. Preterm, Boston, 1980-84; spl. asst. to dir. Port Washington Pub. Libr., 1977-79. Bd. dirs., treas. UNA/USA, North Shore Chpt., 1970-79; co-founder, treas., bd. dirs. Creative Arts Workshop of Port Washington, 1970-79; steering com./film com. Mus. of Fine Arts, Boston. Mem. Nat. Assn. of Psychoanalysts, Assn. Modern Psychoanalysts, Soc. Modern Psychoanalysts. Avocations: photography, films.

SEGALLA, MARY LOUISE, elementary school educator; b. Buffalo, Jan. 17, 1943; d. Ignatius George and Eileen Dorothy (Chatwin) Privateer; m. Thomas Francis Segalla, Aug. 15, 1967. BFA, SUNY, Buffalo, 1966, MEd cum laude, 1971. Cert. elem. tchr., N.Y. Art tchr. Lancaster (N.Y.) Schs., 1966-67; art tchr. Southington (Conn.) Schs., 1967-68, Maryvale Schs., Cheektowaga, N.Y., 1968-82, Clarence (N.Y.) Schs., 1984—2003; chair art dept., 1993-95. Mem. Albright-Knox Art Gallery, Buffalo, 1965—, Burchfield-Penny Art Ctr., Buffalo, 1990—. Bd. dirs. Spotlight Com. for The Shea's Performing Arts Ctr., Buffalo, 1985—. Mem. Nat. Art Edn. Assn., N.Y. Art Tchrs. Assn., Clarence Tchrs. Assn., Alpha Delta Kappa. Roman Catholic. Avocations: collecting antiques, golf, travel, gardening. Home: 25 Westfield Rd Eggertsville NY 14226-3492

SEGER, LINDA SUE, script consultant, lecturer, writer; b. Peshtigo, Wisc., Aug. 27, 1945; d. Linus Vauld and Agnes Katherine Seger; m. Theodore Newton Youngblood, Jr., Aug. 28, 1968 (div. Jan. 1970); m. Peter Hazen LeVar, April 12, 1987. BA in English, Colo. Coll., Colorado Springs, 1967; MA in theatre arts, Northwestern U., Evanston, 1968; MA in religion and arts, Pacific Sch. of Religion, Berkeley, 1973; ThD in drama and theology, Graduate Theological U., Berkeley, 1976; MA in Feminist Spirituality, Immaculate Heart Coll. Ctr., L.A., 2000. Instr. drama Grand Canyon Coll., Phoenix, 1969-71; instr. drama and theology McPherson (Kans.) Coll., 1976-77; instr. drama and humanities LaVerne (Calif.) U., 1977-79; asst. Provisional Theatre, L.A., 1979-80, Tandem/TAT, L.A., 1980-81; story analyst EMI Films, L.A., 1982-83; pvt. practice script cons. L.A., 1981—; pvt. practice lectr., author, 1984—. Guest prof. The Colo. Coll., 1993—. Author: Making a Good Script Great, 1988, Creating Unforgettable Characters, 1990, The Art of Adaptation, 1992, When Women Call the Shots, 1996, Making a Good Writer Great, 1999, Webthinking: Connecting Not Competing for Success, 2002, Advanced Screenwriting: Raising your Script to the Academy Award Level, 2003, Jesus Rode a Donkey, 2006; co-author: From Script to Screen, 1994. Democrat. Mem. Soc. Of Friends. Avocations: horseback riding, piano, travel. Home and Office: 4705 Hagerman Ave Cascade CO 80809 Office Phone: 719-684-0405. Business E-mail: lsseger@aol.com.

SEGIL, LAURA CHIPMAN, art dealer, consultant; b. Honolulu, Jan. 6, 1968; d. Gordon Ernest and Mary Ann Dickie; m. William Segil, Apr. 15, 2000. BA in Art History, U. Colo., 1992; fine arts cert., Christie's Edn., London, 1993. Intern Christie's Auction House, San Francisco, 1994—95; ind. interior designer Aspen and Denver, 1995—2000; owner, dir. Segil Fine Art Gallery, Monrovia, Calif. Bd. mem. Assistance League So. Calif., 2003—; prodn. chair Nine O'Clock Players, 3rd vice chair, 2003—. Mem.: Calif. Ind. Art Rep. Assn. (co-founder 2003). Office Phone: 626-358-5563. Personal E-mail: laurachipman@cs.com.

SEGRETO, LINDA MARY JANECZEK, special education educator; b. Troy, N.Y., July 2, 1948; d. Walter John and Margaret Angela (Catallozzi) Janeczek; m. Anthony Joseph Segreto; children: Anthony Walter, Amanda Margaret. AAS, Maria Coll., 1968; BS in Bus. Edn., SUNY, Albany, 1970, M in Libr. Sci., 1976; spl. edn. credentials, Calif. State U., Long Beach, 1999. Tchr. Calif., C.C. tchr. Calif., tchr. N.Y. Bus. tchr. Lansingburgh Ctrl. Sch. Dist., Troy, NY, 1970—78; bus. adminstr. TRW Def. and Space Sys., Redondo Beach, Calif., 1978—87; bus. instr. Cypress (Calif.) Coll., 1980—82; spl. edn. tchr./transition specialist Manhattan Beach (Calif.) Unified Sch. Dist., 1997—. Sch. host, coord., vol. Best Buddies Calif., L.A., 1999—. Active PTA, Palos Verdes, Calif., 1990—, Friends of the Libr., Palos Verdes, 1990—; mem., vol. L.A. Mission, 2000—. Mem.: Calif. Tchrs. Assn., Coun. for Exceptional Children, Pi Lambda Theta. Avocations: travel, music, dramatics, yoga, golf.

SEHRING, HOPE HUTCHISON, library science educator; b. Akron, Ohio; d. Wesley Harold and Jane (Brown) H.; m. Frederick Albert Sehring, July 15, 1978. BS, Slippery Rock U., Pa., 1968; MEd, U. Pitts., Pa., 1973; MLS, Seton Hill U., Greensburg, Pa., 2002. Cert. instructional media specialist. Reference libr.-intern Carnegie Mellon U., Pitts., 1981; libr. media specialist Gateway Sch. Dist., Monroeville, Pa., 1968—2003; dir. Jeannette Pub. Libr., 2006—. Assoc. Wal-Mart, Delmont, Pa., 2006—. Contbr. articles to profl. jours. Active Pa. Citizens for Better Libraries, Friends of Monroeville Pub. Libr. Recipient Gift of Time Tribute Am. Family Inst., 1992, 96; Henry Clay Frick Found. U. of London scholar, 1969, 73. Sch. Librs. Assn. (treas. 1982-84), Pa. State Edn. Assn., Pa. Citizens for Better Librs., Gateway Edn. Assn., Alpha Xi Delta. Avocation: culinary arts. Home: 265 Fenneltown Rd New Alexandria PA 15670 Office Phone: 724-523-5702. Personal E-mail: gg7495@yahoo.com.

SEIBERT, BARBARA, science educator; b. Hammond, Ind. BS, We. Ill. U., Macomb, 1975; MS, U. Ill. Chgo., 1988. Tchr. sci. Dobson H.S., Mesa, Ariz., 1988—. Instr. sci. Rio Salado Coll., Tempe, Ariz., 1996—. Mem.: Mesa Profl. Educators. Achievements include discovery of DNA sequence of a bacterial gene. Avocations: horseback riding, travel. Office: Dobson High School 1501 W Guadalupe Rd Mesa AZ 85202 Office Fax: 480-472-3075.

SEIBERT, LESA MARIE, education educator; b. York, Pa., Sept. 4, 1960; d. Lee Allen and Frances Marie Seibert. BS in English Edn., Bob Jones U., Greenville, S.C., 1982, MEd in English Edn., 1988, EdS in Spl. Edn., 2001, EdD in Curriculum and Instrn., 2006. Cert. tchr. English edn. Pa., tchr. English edn. and spl. edn. S.C. HS English tchr. Mt. Calvary Christian Sch., Elizabethtown, Pa., 1982—86, Sumter (S.C.) Christian Sch., 1986—87, Mountain View Christian Sch., Hummelstown, Pa., 1989—94, Bob Jones Acad., Greenville, SC, 1994—2001, HS spl. edn. tchr. and distance edn. tchr., 2001—04, prof. English edn., 2004—. Spkr. in field. Contbr. articles to profl. jours. Named Tchr. of Yr., Keystone Christian Tchrs. Assn., 1990—91. Republican. Baptist. Avocations: reading, cross stitch, writing, singing, speaking. Office: Bob Jones Univ 1700 Wade Hampton Blvd Greenville SC 29614

SEIDE, JANET H., psychologist; d. Bernard Gordon and Rhoda Seide. PhD, Boston Coll., Chestnut Hill, Mass., 1983. Lic. psychologist Mass., 1985. Intern Children's Hosp., Boston, 1979—80; pvt. practice Lexington, Mass., 1983—; consulting psychologist Arbour Sr. Care, Rockland, Mass., 2004—. Mem.: APA. Office: Dept Psychology Bridgewater State Coll Bridgewater MA 02325 E-mail: jseide@bridgew.edu.

SEIDEL, JOAN BROUDE, securities dealer, investment advisor; b. Chgo., Aug. 16, 1933; d. Ned and Betty (Treiger) Broude; m. Arnold Seidel, Aug. 18, 1957; children: David, Craig. BA, UCLA, 1954; postgrad., N.Y. Inst. Fin. Registered prin., investment advisor Morton Seidel & Co. Inc., L.A., 1970-74, v.p., 1974-93; pres., 1993—; also bd. dirs. Morton Seidel & Co. Inc., L.A. Instr. UCLA Extension, 1979—84; bd. overseers Hebrew Union Coll. Treas. City of Beverly Hills, Calif., 1990-2001, chmn. rent adjustment bd., 1989-90, mem., 1983-89; investment com. YWCA of greater LA, 1987-2002, treas. 1992-95; bd. dirs. Discovery Fund for Eye Rsch., LA, 1987—, treas., 1999—; corp. bd. dirs. Queen's Care, 1999-2005, fin. com., 1999-2005, audit com., 2004-05; bd. dirs. LA Opera, 2002—; CFO Maple Couns. Ctr., 2002-04; bd. govs. Cedars Sinai Med. Ctr. Named Citizen of Yr. Beverly Hills C. of C., 1993. Fellow Assn. for Investment Mgmt. and Rsch., Israel Inst. Tech. (hon.); mem. Am. Technion Soc. (v.p. 1998-2002, pres. So. Calif. chpt. 2001-04, nat. bd. dirs. 2002—, internat. bd. 2003—, nat. pres.

2006—), Nat. Assn. Security Dealers (dist. bus. conduct com. 2S 1993-95, 98-2000, small firm adv. bd. 1998-2000, chair dist. 2 1999-2000), L.A. Soc. Fin. Analysts, Orgn. Women Execs., Rotary, Phi Sigma Alpha. Avocations: reading, travel. Office: Morton Seidel & Co Inc 8730 Wilshire Blvd Ste 530 Beverly Hills CA 90211-2792 Office Phone: 310-360-7541. Personal E-mail: seidel350@aol.com.

SEIDENBERG, RITA NAGLER, education educator; b. N.Y.C., Mar. 24, 1928; d. Jack and Anna (Weiss) Nagler; m. Irving Seidenberg, Apr. 10, 1949; children: Jack, Melissa Kolodkin. BA, Hunter Coll., 1948; MS, CCNY, 1968; PhD, Fordham U., 1985. Cert. reading tchr., specialist, N.Y. Reading tchr. East Ramapo (N.Y.) Sch. Dist., 1967-68, clinician reading ctr., 1968-83, reading diagnostician, 1983-85, student support specialist, 1985-94. Instr. N.Y. State Dept. Edn., 1978; presenter Northeastern Rsch. Assn., 1978, 85, N.Y. State Reading Assn., 1986-94, 96, 97, Parents and Reading: IRA, 2000; adj. asst. prof. Fordham U. Grad. Sch. Edn., 1986-89, adj. assoc. prof., 1989—. Mem. Internat. Reading Assn., N.Y. State Reading Assn. (presenter 1997, 2000), Phi Delta Kappa, Kappa Delta Pi. Avocations: reading, opera, travel, art museums. Office: Fordham U Grad Sch Edn 113 W 60th St New York NY 10023-7484

SEIDLER, DORIS, artist; b. London, Nov. 26, 1912; m. Bernard Seidler, Sept. 5, 1935; 1 child, David. Exhibited in group shows at Bklyn. Mus. Bi-Ann., Vancouver Internat., Honolulu Acad. Arts, Pa. Acad. Fine Arts, Phila., Soc. Am. Graphic Artists, Assoc. Am. Artists Gallery, Jewish Mus., N.Y.C., Albright-Knox Mus., 1994, Brit. Mus. Recent Acquisitions, 1997, Whitworth Gallery, Manchester, Eng., 2003, Represented in permanent collections Libr. of Congress, Smithsonian Instn., Washington, Phila. Mus. Art, Bklyn. Mus., Seattle Mus. Art, Whitney Mus., Nat. Gallery Art, Nassau County (N.Y.) Mus. Fine Arts, Brit. Mus., London, Victoria and Albert Mus. London, Pallant House Coll., Eng., Portland Mus. Art, Oreg., Birmingham Mus., Eng. Address: 14 Stoner Ave Great Neck NY 11021-2101

SEIDMAN, CHRISTINE E., medical educator; BA, Harvard U.; MD, George Washington U., 1978. Resident in internal medicine Johns Hopkins U., Balt.; resident in cardiology Mass. Gen. Hosp., Boston; staff Brigham and Women's Hosp. Harvard U., Boston, 1987, dir. cardiovasc. genetics svc., prof. Dept. Medicine and Dept. Genetics; assoc. investigator Howard Hughes Med. Inst., 1994, investigator. Recipient Bristol-Myers Squibb award, 2002. Mem.: NAS, Inst. Medicine. Office: Harvard U Med Sch Genetics NRB 256 77 Avenue Louis Pasteur Boston MA 02115 Business E-Mail: cseidman@genetics.med.harvard.edu.*

SEIDMAN, ELLEN SHAPIRO, lawyer, government official; b. NYC, Mar. 12, 1948; d. Benjamin Harry Shapiro and Edna (Eysen) Stern; m. Walter Becker Slocombe, June 14, 1981; 1 child, Benjamin William. AB, Radcliffe Coll., 1969; JD, Georgetown U., 1974; MBA, George Washington U., 1988. Bar: D.C., 1975. Law clk. US Ct. of Claims, Washington, 1974-75; assoc. Caplin & Drysdale, Washington, 1975-78; atty., advisor US Dept. Transp., Washington, 1978-79, dep. asst. gen. counsel, 1979-81; assoc. gen. counsel Chrysler Corp Loan Guaranty Bd., Washington, 1981-84; atty., advisor US Dept. of Treasury, Washington, 1981-86, spl. asst. to the Under Sec. Fin., 1986-87; dir. strategic planning Fed. Nat. Mortgage Assn., Washington, 1987-88, v.p., asst. to chmn., 1988-91, sr. v.p. regulation rsch. and econs., 1991-93; spl. asst. to the pres. for econ. policy The White House, Washington, 1993-97; dir. Office Thrift Supervision US Dept. Treasury, Washington, 1997—2001; sr. counsel, Minority Staff, fin. svcs. com. US Ho. of Reps., Washington, 2002; sr. mng. dir. nat. practice Shorebank Adv. Svcs., 2002—05; exec. v.p. Shorebank Corp., 2006—. Office Phone: 202-822-9146. Business E-Mail: ellen_seidman@sbk.com.

SEIFERLE, REBECCA ANN, poet, editor, publisher; b. Denver; d. Arthur Mase and Mary Kathryn S.; m. Phillip Joseph Valencia, Aug. 11, 1978 (div. 2003); children: Ann Seiferle-Valencia, Maria Seiferle-Valencia, Jacob Seiferle-Valencia. BA in English and History, U. State N.Y., 1984; MFA, Warren Wilson Coll., 1989. Poet Tumblewords: N.Mex. Arts Program, Santa Fe, 1986—; creative writing instr. San Juan Coll., Farmington, N.Mex., 1990—. Editor, pub. (online mag.) The Drunken Boat, 2000—. Author: (poetry collections) The Ripped Out Seam, 1994 (Bogin award Poetry Soc. Am. 1991), The Music We Dance To, 1999 (Cecil Hemley award Poetry Soc. Am. 1998), Bitters, 2001 (We. States Book award, Pushcart prize 2002); contbr. (anthology) New Mexico Poetry Renaissance, 1994, Saludos: Poemas de Nuevo Mexico, 1995, Best American Poetry 2000, The Poet's Child, 2002, The Extraordinary Tide: New Poetry by American Women, 2001; translator Spanish of Cesar Vallejo, Trilce, 1992, Spanish of Alfonso d'Aquino and Ernesto Lumbreras, Reversible Monuments, 2002, The Black Heralds, 2003. Active letter writing campaigns Amnesty Internat., 1984-2001. Recipient prize Nat. Writer's Union, 1986, award Embers Poetry Contest, 1985. Mem. PenWest, Poets and Writers (Writers Exch. award 1990). Home: 134 Clark St Waltham MA 02453-6577 E-mail: editor@thedrunkenboat.com.

SEIFERT, CAROLINE HAMILTON, community health nurse; b. Warren, Ohio, May 28, 1937; d. Oliver L. and Martha (Moran) Hamilton; m. Dale E. Seifert, Sept. 5, 1959; children: Brian Dale, Joan Kimberly. Diploma, Youngstown (Ohio) Hosp. Assn., 1959; BSN, U. Cin., 1964, MEd, 1979. Cert. sch. nurse, health educator, spl. edn. educator. Caseworker Children's Svcs. div. Dept. Health and Human Svcs., Batavia, Ohio, 1966-68; dir. Happy Days Nursery Sch. Bethel (Ohio) United Meth. Ch., 1970-73; social worker Clermont County Bd. Mental Retardation/Devel. Disabilities, Batavia, 1973-97; sch. nurse, health educator Thomas A. Wildey Sch., Owensville, Ohio, 1973-97; retired, 1997. Instr. Sch. Health Svcs. U. Cin., 1976, preceptor nursing students, 1992-97. Mem. Hamilton/Clermont Sch. Nurses Orgn. (v.p.), S.W. Ohio Sch. Nurses Assn. (program chmn.), Profl. Assn. for Retardation (v.p. nursing div., Nurse of Yr.). Home: 2631 Oldforge Ln Cincinnati OH 45244-2831 Office: Thomas A Wildey Sch PO Box 8 Owensville OH 45160-0008

SEIFERT, PATRICIA CLARK, cardiac surgery nurse, educator, consultant; b. Springfield, Mass., Apr. 4, 1945; d. Thomas W. and Kathleen E. (O'Malley) Clark; m. Gary F. Seifert, Sept. 10, 1966; children: Kristina S. Glenn, Philip A. BA in History, Trinity Coll., 1967; ADN, No. Va. Community Coll., 1976; MS in Nursing, Cath. U. Am., 1988. RN, Va., D.C.; cert. oper. rm. nurse, first asst. nurse. Head nurse cardiac surgery Fairfax Hosp., Falls Church, Va., 1976-88; adminstrv. dir. Washington Hosp. Ctr., 1988-89; oper. room coord. cardiac surgery Arlington (Va.) Hosp., 1989-97, Alexandria (Va.) Hosp., 1995—97; mgr. open heart surgery Halifax Med. Ctr., Daytona Beach, Fla., 1997—98; coord. cardiovasc. svcs. Arlington (Va.) Hosp., 2000—02; innovations liaison Sandel Med. Industries, Chatsworth, Calif., 2002—02; perioperative cardiac care coord. Inova Fairfax Hosp., Inova Heart and Vascular Inst., Falls Church, Va., 2002. Mem. adv. bd. Surg. Info. Sys., Ethicon Endo-surgery Nursing; lead coord. Nursing Orgns. Alliance, 2001—03; lectr., cons. in field. Author: (books) Clinical Assessment Tools for Use with Nursing Diagnosis, 1989, Cardiac Surgery, 1994, 2002; co-author: Tea & Toast for the Perioperative Nursing Spirit, 2006; contbr. chpts. in Alexander's Care of the Patient in Surgery, 13th rev. edit., 2006, Cardiovascular Nursing, 7th rev. edit., 1991, Perioperative Care Planning, 2d rev. edit., 1996, The RN First Assistant: An Expanded Perioperative Role, 3d rev. edit., 1999, Core Curriculum for the RN First Assistant, 4th rev. edit., 2005, CNOR Study Guide, rev. edit., 1999; co-author Tea and Toast for the Perioperative Nursing Spirit, 2006, contbr. numerous articles to profl. jours. Fellow: Am. Acad. Nursing; mem.: Va. Nurses's Assn. (dist. 8 bd. dirs. 1987—91, Nurse of Year award 1984), Assn. Perioperative RN's (nat. nominating com. 1991—93, pres. No. Va. chpt. 1994—95, nat. bd. dir. 1994—98, nat. pres.-elect 1998—99, nat. pres. 1999—2000, RN 1st asst., award for excellence 2004), Am. Heart Assn. (coun. on cardiovasc. nursing), Assn. Perioperative RN's Found. (sec. 1999—2001), Am. Assn. for History of Nursing, Sigma Theta Tau (pres. Eta Alpha chpt. 1990—92, Virginia Henderson fellow). Home: 6502 Overbrook St Falls Church VA 22043-1942 Office Fax: 703-237-1259. Personal E-mail: seifertpc@aol.com.

SEIFERT, RACHEL A., lawyer; b. New Brunswick, NJ, 1959; BA, U. Md., 1981, JD, 1985. Bar: Md. 1985. Atty. priv. practice, Dallas, 1985—92; v.p., assoc. gen. counsel Columbia/HCA, 1992—98; sr. v.p., sec., gen. counsel Community Health Systems Inc., Brentwood, Tenn., 1998—. Bd. mem. Women Bus. Leaders of U.S. Health Care Industry Found. Mem.: ABA, Federation of Am. Hospitals, Am. Health Lawyers Assn. Office: Community Health Systems Inc 155 Franklin Rd Ste 400 Brentwood TN 37027

SEIFERT, SHELLEY JANE, bank executive, human resources specialist; b. Aug. 12, 1954; BS in Consumer Econs. and Journalism, U. Mo., 1976; MBA in Fin. with honors, U. Louisville, 1980. Fin. analyst Nat. City Bank, Ky., 1979-81, compensation analyst, 1981-85, mgr. compensation, 1985-86, mgr. compensation, recruiting and tng., 1986-91; mgr. compensation and devel. Nat. City Corp., Cleve., 1988-91, human resource dir., 1991-94, sr. v.p., 1994—2000, corp. human resource dir., 1994—2004, exec. v.p., 2000—. Spkr. in field.; bd. dirs., Blair Corp., 2006- Grad. Leadership Cleve.; vice chair bd. dirs. Bus. Vols. Unlimited, Vis. Nurse Assn. Greater Cleve.; bd. dirs. Arthritis Found.; mem. Cleve. Commn. on Econ. Partnership and Inclusion. Recipient Woman of Distinction award YMCA. Mem. Urban League (bd. dirs., chair employment com., Ohio labor adv. com.). Office: Nat City Corp Nat City Ctr 1900 E 9th St Cleveland OH 44114-3401*

SEIFERT, SUZANNE MARIE, physical education educator; b. Glens Falls, NY, Sept. 22, 1970; d. Russell James and Clarita Yvonne LaMere; m. Donald E. Seifert, Aug. 20, 1999; 1 child, Maya LaMere. BE, Valparaiso U., Ind., 1993; M in Ednl. Adminstrn., Governors State U., Ill., 2000. Edn. Adminstrn.-Type75 Ill., 2000. Phys. edn. tchr. Sch. City of East Chgo., Ind., 1993—94; health tchr., coach Sch. Town of Highland, Ind., 1994—97; conflict resolution tchr., pe tchr., coach Dolton Sch. Dist. 149, Calumet City, Ill., 1997—. Sch. adminstr. Peer Mediation program, Calumet City, Ill., 1998. Gang awareness program, Calumet City, Ill., 1998—99; leadership coun. So. Poverty Law Ctr., Montgomery, Ala., 2004—. Recipient NCAA Scholar Athlete award, NCAA, 2003, Wall Of Tolerance Honoree, So. Poverty Law Ctr., 2004. Mem.: NEA, So. Poverty Law Ctr. (leadership coun. 2004—05). Avocations: travel, exercise. Home: 222 Skyline Dr Valparaiso IN 46385 Office: Dolton Sch Dist 149 292 Torrence Ave Calumet City IL 60409 Office Phone: 708-868-7593. Personal E-mail: seiferts@schooldistrict149.org.

SEIFF, GLORIA LOUISE, volunteer; b. Denver, Apr. 3, 1929; d. Edward Hyatt and Lilliian Pearl (Blend) Holtzman; m. Stephen S. Seiff, Apr. 16, 1950; children: Stuart R., Sherri P. Seiff Sloane, Karen E. Seiff Sacks. Student, Washington U., 1947-48. Commr. Pub. Works Commn., Beverly Hills, Calif., 1990-98, bd. pres. 1993, 96; pres. Beverly Vista Elem. Sch. PTA, Beverly Hills, lif.,968-69, PTA Coun., Beverly Hills, 1972-73; bd. dirs. Beverly Hills S.W. Homeowners Assn., 1985—, Braille Inst. Aux., L.A., 1998—; founding mem., bd. dirs., trustee Beverly Hills Edn. Found., 1975-79; v.p. devel. Assistance League So. Calif., L.A., 1994-98, bd. dirs., 1994—; trustee L.A. County Mosquito Abatement Dist., 1984-92, bd. pres. 1988; pres. LWV, Beverly Hills, 1985-87; mem. long range planning com. Assistance League So. Calif., 1997-98, 2005—, mem. endowment com., 1995—, v.p. pub. rels., 1999-2002; chmn. Beverly Hills Groundwater Tech. Adv. Com., 1999—; commr. Beverly Hills Traffic and Parking Commn., 2000—, vice chmn., 2002, chair, 2002-2003; mem. City of Beverly Hills Gen. Plan Topics Com./Residential, 2002-04. Recipient Hon. Svc. award PTA, Beverly Hills, 1972, Outstanding Cmty. Svc. award, Beverly Hills City Coun., 1986-87, Resolution Cmty. Svc. award Beverly Bd. Edn., 1986. Mem. Calif. Yacht Club, Las Doñas UCLA Alumni Assn., Beverly Hills Unified Sch. Dist. Citizens Oversight Com. "Measure K". Avocation: sailing.

SEIGER, MARILYN SANDRA, public relations executive; b. Washington, Jan. 20, 1945; d. Harry R. and Claire D. Seiger; m. Stan Amatucci, June 15, 1979. BS, Ohio State U., 1966; MA, U. Pitts., 1967; MBA, Baruch Coll., 1986. Lic. tchr. NY, Pa. Editor Holt, Rinehart & Winston, Inc., NYC, 1969—73; editor, writer Redbook mag., NYC, 1973—77; mng. editor 1,001 Decorating Ideas, NYC, 1978—79; dir. public rels., promotion, advt. Brit. Consulate, NYC, 1979—80; acct. supr. Peter Martin Assocs., NYC, 1980—82; pub. rels. mgr. Marriott Hotels, NYC, 1982—85; dir. pub. rels. and promotion CARE, NYC, 1985—. Cons., writer Singer Co., Reader's Digest, Formica, Martex. Mem.: Women Execs. in Pub. Rels., Pub. Rels. Soc. Am. (chair pub. rels. workshops 1983, dir. NY chpt. 1984—).

SEIGLER, ELIZABETH MIDDLETON, retired counseling administrator; b. Athens, Ga., Aug. 18, 1928; d. Robert Meriwether and Marie (Davis) Middleton; m. Charles Judson, Aug. 24, 1955; children: Mary Seigler Peacock, Charles Middleton. BSEd, U. Ga., 1949, MEd, 1955; EdS, Ga. State U., 1976. Tchr., coach Talbot County H.S., Talbotton, Ga., 1949-50; tchr. Atlanta Public Schs., 1950-60, counselor, 1960-85. Mem. S.C. Geneal. Soc. (Old Edgefield dist. archives chpt., Anderson County chpt.), The Meriwether Soc., Inc., Ga. Ret. Educators Assn., Atlanta Ret. Tchrs. Assn., Am. Assn. Ret. Persons, Delta Kappa Gamma, Alpha Lambda Delta, Kappa Delta Pi. Baptist. Avocations: gardening, genealogy.

SEIGLER, RUTH QUEEN, college nursing administrator, educator, consultant, nurse; b. Conway, S.C., July 31, 1942; d. Charles Isaac and Berneta Mae (Weaks) Queen; m. Rallie Marshall Seigler, Sept. 1, 1963; children: Rallie Marshall Jr., Scot Monroe. ADN, Lander Coll., 1962; BSN, U. S.C., 1964, M of Nursing, 1980. Pub. health nurse Richland County Health Dept., Columbia, SC, 1964—66; dir. nurses Columbia Area Mental Health Ctr., 1966—69; program nurse specialist Midlands Health Dist., 1969—72; discharge planner Richland Meml. Hosp., 1972—73, clin. dir., 1973—75; exec. dir. S.C. State Bd. Nursing, 1976—83; v.p. nursing dept. Self Meml. Hosp., Greenwood, SC, 1983—86; exec. dir. S.C. Commn. on Aging, Columbia, 1986—95; asst. dean Coll. Nursing U. S.C., Columbia, 1995—96, assoc. clin. prof., 1996—. Cons. intergenerational family studies, 1999—; dir. Cockcroft Leadership Program for Nurse Execs., 2002—, Ctr. for Nursing Leadership, 2004-05, sr. cons., 2005—; bd. dirs. Queen Gas Co., Barnwell, S.C.; nurse cons. Creative Nursing Mgmt., Mpls., 1984—. Advisor: The Role of Cmty. Mental Health Nurse, 1971. Moderator Trinity Presbytery, 2003—. Recipient Disting. Alumni award Lander Coll., 1978, Career Woman Recognition award Columbia YWCA, 1980, William S. Hall award S.C. Assn. Residential Care Homes, 1988, U. S.C. Coll. Nursing Disting. Alumni award, 1993, award for excellence S.C. League for Nursing, 1995, Svc. Recognition award S.C. AARP, 1995; named one of Ten Women of Achievement, S.C. March of Dimes, 1987, hon. fellow AVC Leadership, 2002, Excellence in Leadership award, 2004, Ordie P. Taylor Humanitarian award, 2005, Palmetto Gold award Top 100 Nurses in S.C., 2006. Mem. ANA, APHA, S.C. Nurses Assn. (sec. 1965-68, bd. dirs. 1986-88, Excellence award 1984, Recognition award 1984), S.C. Hosp. Assn., S.C. Gerontol. Soc., S.C. Nurses Found., S.C. Healthy People 2000 (vice chair), Partnership for Older South Carolinians (founder, chair bd. dirs.), Columbia Luncheon Club (pres. 1997-98), S.C. Fedn. Older Ams., Evening Mission Action Group, Bd. Nursing Home Examiners, Pilot Club, Inc. (pres. 1988-89, 97-98), Vols. of Am.-Carolinas (bd. dirs., chair, 1998-00, elder, 1999-01), Rotary Internat., Sigma Theta Tau, Beta Sigma Phi (pres. chpt. 1997-98). Presbyterian. Avocations: gardening, travel. Home: 6 Beaver Dam Ct Columbia SC 29223-3100 Office: U SC Coll Nursing Ctr Nursing Leadership Columbia SC 29208-0001

SEILER, BONNIE, academic administrator; d. Edward and Rita Brown; m. Michael Seiler. BFA, BS, Syracuse U., 1975; MA, C.W. Post Coll., 1978, MS, 1981, PhD, 1984. Cert. adminstr., spl. edn., elem., art tchr., sch. psychologist NY. Edn. adminstr. NYC Dept. Edn. Mag. covers, Taxi Mag. Recipient cert. of appreciation, Mayor of N.Y.C., 1996. Mem.: Internat. Dyslexia Assn., Nat. Assn. Sch. Psychologists, Salmagundi Club.

SEILER, CHARLOTTE WOODY, retired elementary school educator, language educator; b. Thorntown, Ind., Jan. 20, 1915; d. Clark and Lois Merle (Long) Woody; m. Wallace Urban Seiler, Oct. 10, 1942 (dec. Aug. 2002); children: Patricia Anne Seiler, Janet Alice Seiler Sawyer. AA, Ind. State U., 1933; AB, U. Mich., 1941; MA, Ctrl. Mich. U., 1968. Tchr. elem. schs., Whitestown, Ind., 1933-34, Thorntown, 1934-37, Kokomo, Ind., 1937-40, Ann Arbor, Mich., 1941-44, Willow Run, Mich., 1944-46; instr. English divsn. Delta Coll., University Center, Mich., 1964-69, asst. prof., 1969-77; ret., 1977. Organizer, dir. Delta Coll. Puppeteers, 1972—77. Mem. Friends of Grace A. Dow Meml. Libr., 1974-2000, treas., 1974-75, 77-79, corr. sec., 1975-77; leader Sr. Ctr. Humanities program Midland (Mich.) Sr. Ctr., 1977-94; vol. Quality Health Care, North Port, Fla., 2001—; leader Bridge Refresher Harbor Cove, North Port, 2002—. Fellow AAUW; mem. Mich. Libr. Assn., Harbor Cove Civic Assn., Pi Lambda Theta, Chi Omega. Presbyterian. Home: 652 Blackburn Blvd North Port FL 34287

SEILER, KAREN PEAKE, organizational psychologist; b. Seattle, Jan. 31, 1952; d. Louis Joseph and Donna Mae (Waters) Tomaso; m. Arthur J. Seiler; children from previous marriage: Jeremy S. Peake, Anthony K. Peake. BA/BSW magna cum laude, Carroll Coll., 1987; postgrad., MIT, 1994. Cert. strategic planning Pacific Inst.; cert. orgnl. cons. Covey Learning Ctr., 1993. Admissions counselor Shodair Children's Hosp., Helena, Mont., 1984-86; asst. dir., counselor Career Tng. Inst., Helena, 1986-90; pres. Corp. Cons., Helena, 1990—. Apptd. amb. Mont. Ambs., 1990—; active Gov.'s Task Force on Econ. Devel., 1991-94; chairperson Mont. Dist. Export Coun./U.S. Dept. Commerce, 1992-96; exec. com. mem. Mont. World Trade Ctr., Missoula, 1995—, chmn. 1996—; pres. Coun. Carroll Coll., 1997—. Mem. YWCA, 1986-90, pres., 1989; mem. Bus. and Profl. Women's Orgn., 1987-93, sec., 1990; pres. Helena Area Econ. Devel. Coun., 1989-92; exec. com. Leadership Helena, 1990-91; monitoring chair Concentrated Employment Program Pvt. Industry Coun., Mont., 1990—; bd. dirs., exec. com. Mont. Women's Capital Fund, 1990-95; exec. com. Mont. Race for the Cure, 1994—. Mem. NAFE, Partnership for Employment and Tng., Delta Epsilon Sigma (Outstanding Citizen award). Roman Catholic. Avocations: sailing, world travel. Home and Office: 6970 Viscaya Ln Helena MT 59602-6445

SEILING, SHARON LEE, family economics educator; b. Okmulgee, Okla., Aug. 25, 1946; d. Dent and Ruth Burgess; m. John Seiling; 1 child, Clark. BS, Okla. State U., 1968, MS, 1971; PhD, Cornell U., 1980. Tchr. Pauls Valley (Okla.) H.S., 1968-71; grad. asst. Okla. State U., Stillwater, 1971-73; lectr. Calif. Polytechnic State U., San Luis Obispo, 1973-75; grad. asst. Cornell U., Ithaca, N.Y., 1975-78; asst. prof. Fla. State U., Tallahassee, 1978-85, Ohio State U., Columbus, 1985-91, assoc. prof., 1991—. Grad. faculty lectr. Ohio State U., 1995. Assoc. editor Family and Consumer Scis. Rsch. Jour., 1996—2002; contbr. articles to profl. jours. Bd. govs. Ohio Coun. Against Health Fraud, 1989-93; mem. Gov.'s Task Force on Housing and Cmty. Devel., Tallahassee, 1979; mem. housing adv. com. Columbus Urban League, 1994-95; bd. dirs. Creative Play Ctr., 1998-99; mem. Ohio Indoor Air Quality Coalition, 1998-2004. Mem. LWV (pres. 1983-84), Am. Assn. Housing Educators (v.p. 1988-89), Am. Assn. Family and Consumer Scis. (sec.-treas. family econs./resource mgmt. divsn. 1996-98), Ohio Assn. Family and Consumer Scis. (bd. dirs. 1995-97, chmn. North Ctrl. Regional Rsch. Team 2001-). Democrat. Methodist. Office: 265 Campbell Hall 1787 Neil Ave Columbus OH 43210-1295

SEITZ, CAROLE JANE, composer, educator; d. Charles N. Hicks and Ermagene Virginia Hicks, nee Riley; m. Richard John Seitz, Aug. 10, 1991; children: Kimberly Ann Santora, Jeffrey Ward Bean. MusM Edn., MusB Edn., Wichita State U., Wichita, Kansas, 1956—61. Assoc. chair of performing arts Creighton U., Omaha, Nebr., 1976—, assoc. prof. of music. Asst. condr., chorus master Opera Omaha, 1976—89; violinist Omaha Symphony, 1961—75; musical dir. Coun. Bluffs Cmty. Chorus, Council Bluffs, Iowa, 1969—73, Chanticleer Theatre, Council Bluffs; violinist Wichita Symphony, 1958—60, Lincoln Symphony, Nebr., 1972—79, Des Moines Symphony, 1972—79; dir. of music St. John's Luth. Ch., Council Bluffs; jr. choir dir., soprano soloist St. Andrews Episc. Ch., Omaha, 1980—89. Composer: (play) The Devils, (choral compositions) Midwinter Carol Two Wee Girls Christmas Eve Prayer Alleluia He is Risen, (music for indiv. ballet practice, dance compositions) Dances for the Young Ballerina, (dance compositions) Music for Individual Practice, (string orchestra) Little Fugue, (ballet music) Requiem inspired by poem by Desmond Egan. Founder and pres. Coun. Bluffs Arts Coun., 1970—73. Recipient Citizenship award, AAUW. Mem.: Am. Choral Dirs. Assn. (life; iowa bd. mem. 1968—69), Mortar Bd., Mu Phi Epsilon. Episcopalian. Avocations: horseback riding, travel, reading, knitting. Home: 1705 Laguna Drive Fremont NE 68025 Office: Creighton University 2500 California Plaza Omaha NE 68178 Office Phone: 402-280-2766. Office Fax: 402-280-2320. Business E-Mail: cseitz@creighton.edu.

SEITZ, MARY LEE, mathematics professor; BS in Edn. summa cum laude, SUNY, Buffalo, 1977, MS in Edn., 1982. Cert. secondary tchr., N.Y. Prof. math. Erie C.C.-City Campus, Buffalo, 1982—. Reviewer profl. jours. and coll. textbooks. Vol. Buffalo (N.Y.) Philharmonic Orch. Mem. NY Maths. Assn. Two Yr. Colls., Assn. Maths. Tchrs. NY, NY Assn. Two Yr. Colls., Inc., Buffalo (N.Y.) Philharmonic Orch. Soc., Commerative AF, Pi Mu Epsilon. Avocations: gardening, photography, bird watching. Office: Erie C C-City Campus 121 Ellicott St Buffalo NY 14203-2601 E-mail: seitzm@ecc.edu.

SEITZ, PATRICIA ANN, judge; b. Washington, Sept. 2, 1946; d. Richard J. and Bettie Seitz; m. Alan Graham Greer, Aug. 14, 1981. BA in History cum laude, Kans. State U., 1968; JD, Georgetown U., 1973. Bar: Fla. 1973, D.C. 1975, U.S. Dist. Ct. (no., mid., so. dists., trial bar) Fla., U.S. Ct. Appeals (5th and 11th cirs.), U.S. Supreme Ct. Reporter Dallas Times Herald, Washington, 1970-73; law clk. to Hon. Charles R. Richey U.S. Dist. Ct., Washington, 1973-74; assoc. Steel, Hector & Davis, Miami, Fla., 1974-79, ptnr., 1980-96; dir. office legal counsel Office of Nat. Drug Control Policy, Exec. Office of Pres., Washington, 1996-97; judge U.S. Dist. Ct. (so. dist.) Fla., 1998—. Adj. faculty U. Miami Law Sch., Coral Gables, Fla., 1984-88; faculty Nat. Inst. Trial Advocacy, Boulder, Colo., 1982, 83, 95, Chapel Hill, N.C., 1984, 87, Fla. region, 1989; lectr. in field. Contbr. numerous articles to law jours. Mem. Dade Munroe Mental Health Bd., Miami, 1982-84, United Way of Greater Miami comty. devel. com., 1984-87; chmn. family abuse task force United Way of Greater Miami, 1986; chmn. devel. com. Miami City Ballet, 1986-87, bd. dirs., 1986-90. Fellow Am. Bar Found., Am. Bd. Trial Advocacy, Internat. Soc. Barristers; mem. ABA (chmn. various coms. 1979-85, Ho. Dels. 1992-96), Am. Arbitration Assn. (nat. bd. dirs. 1995-97, complex case panel arbitrator), The Fla. Bar (bd. govs. young lawyer divsn. 1981-82, bd. govs. 1986-92, pres. 1993-94, bd. cert. civil trial), Fla. Assn. Women Lawyers, Dade County Bar Assn. (pub. interest law bank). Roman Catholic. Avocations: travel, art. Office: Fed Courthouse Square 301 N Miami Ave Fl 5 Miami FL 33128-7702

SEIVERS, LANA C., school system administrator; b. Clinton, Tenn, 1951; BEd, Middle Tenn. State U.; MA in Ednl. Adminstrn., U. Tenn., D in Ednl. Leadership. Speech pathologist Spl Edn. Oak Ridge Sch. System, Tenn.; adminstr. early childhood and edn programs Oak Ridge Sch. System, prin. Linden Elem. Sch.; supt. Clinton City Schs., Tenn., 1989—2003; commr. Tenn. Dept. Edn., Nashville, 2003—. Design cons. Inst. Sch. Leaders; mem. adv. coun. Edn of Childen with Disabilities. Mem.: Assn. Ind. and Mcpl. Schs. (bd. dirs.), Tenn. Orgn. Sch. Supts. (treas.), E. Tenn. Supts. Stidy Coun. (chair), So. Assn. Colls. and Schs. (chair). Office: Tenn Dept Edn 6th Fl Andrew Johnson Twr 710 James Robertson Pkwy Nashville TN 37243*

SEIZER, FERN VICTOR, retired mental health services administrator; b. N.Y.C., Oct. 29, 1934; d. David L. and Florence Maisel Victor; m. Robert J. Seizer, Aug. 28, 1955; children: Steven P., Susan A. BA, UCLA, 1956. Dir. pub. affairs and edn. Nat. Coun. Jewish Women, LA, 1968—80; exec. dir. Fair Housing Coun. San Fernando Valley, LA, 1980—82, Venice Family Clinic, LA, 1982—94, exec. advisor, 1994; dir. cmty. rels. Didi Hirsch Cmty. Mental Health Ctr., Culver City, Calif., 1994—2000; ret., 2000. Mng. editor, city editor UCLA Daily Bruin, 1953—54; mem. corp. coun. execs. United Way of Greater L.A., 1991—93; mem. Adminstrs. Forum and Cmty. Outreach Task Force UCLA Sch. Medicine, 1990—93. Adv. com. on primary care Calif. State Dept. Health Svcs., Sacramento, 1990—93; mem. managed care planning coun. L.A. County, 1989—90; mem. social svcs. commn. City of Santa Monica, 1998—99; bd. dirs. Nat. Multiple Sclerosis Soc., L.A.,

1995—, St. John's Hosp. and Health Ctr., Santa Monica, Calif., 1994—2000, Venice Family Clinic, 1996—. Recipient Alumni Award for excellence in Profl. Achievement, UCLA, 1995, Unsung Hero award, Calif. Cmty. Found., 2000, Most Valuable Trustee award, Nat. Multiple Sclerosis Soc., 1999, Outstanding Contbn. to the Cmty. award, L.A. City and County, 2000. Mem.: Phi Beta Kappa. Avocations: movies, theater, travel, bridge. Home: 257 S Rodeo Dr Beverly Hills CA 90212

SEKOWSKI, CYNTHIA JEAN, health products executive, medical consultant, contact lens specialist; b. Chgo., Feb. 14, 1953; d. John L. and Celia L. (Matusiak) S. PhD in Health Svcs. Adminstrn., Columbia Pacific U., 1984, PhD in Health Scis., 1984; grad., Realtor Inst., 1998. Chief contact lens dept. Lieberman & Kraff, Chgo., 1974—87; pres., CEO Seko Eye Care, Inc., Chgo., 1988—; realtor Country Club Realty Group, Naples, Fla., 1995—2002, John R. Wood, Inc. Realtors, 2002—. Rschr., technologist U. Ill., Chgo., 1976-78. Active Chgo. Zool. Soc., 1984—, Little City Inner Circle, 1991—, Aurora Lakeland Med. Ctr. Found.; sponsor Save the Children Orgn., 1983—; asst. to campaign mgr. Rep. state senatorial candidate, Chgo., 1972; pres. Compass Point Condo Assn., Naples, Fla., 1996-99; budget com. Windstar Country Club Master Homeowner's Assn., Naples, 1996-99; ptnrs. cir. Habitat for Humanity. Fellow: Contact Lens Soc. Am.; mem.: Women's Coun. Realtors, Naples Area Bd. Realtors, Nat. Assn. Realtors, Fla. Assn. Realtors, Nat. Contact Lens Examiners, Better Vision Inst., Opticians Assn. Am., Ill. Soc. Opticianry, Wis. Hist. Soc., Geneva Lakes Conservancy, Soc. of the Little Flower, Nat. Wildlife Fedn., S.W. Fla. Conservancy, Nat. Geog. Soc., U.S. Golf Assn., Columbia Pacific U. Alumnae Assn., The Phoenix Soc. (med. profl.), Bear's Paw Country Club (mktg. com. 2002—), Vanderbilt Country Club (residents adv. bd. 1999—2001, vice-chmn. adminstrn. com. 2001—03). Roman Catholic. Avocations: gardening, reading, photography, poetry, golf. Office: John R Wood Inc Realtors 3255 Tamiami Trl N Naples FL 34103 Office Phone: 239-269-5000. E-mail: luvfla@mindspring.com.

SELBE, LISA HANCOCK, medical/surgical nurse; b. Niagara Falls, N.Y., June 24, 1957; d. Benjamin Wesley and Mary Frances (Campbell) Hancock; m. James Edward Selbe, Aug. 5, 1978; children: James Wesley, Benjamin Louis. AS, Freed-Hardeman U., 1977, BS, 1978; postgrad., Memphis State U., 1981-82; ASN, Union U., 1986, BSN, 1994. Cert. diabetes educator: cert. ACLS instr., PALS instr., BLS instr. Staff nurse intermediate care unit Jackson-Madison County Gen. Hosp., Jackson, Tenn., 1986-88, staff nurse med. ICU, 1988-89, staff nurse emergency dept., 1989-97, educator in nurse devel., 1998—. Clin. instr. Union U., 1994—97; instr. Jackson State C.C., 2001—03; staff nurse emergency dept. Western Bapt. Hosp., Paducah, Ky., 2005—. Vol. ARC, Henderson, Tenn., 1984-90; bd. dirs. Am. Heart Assn., Chester County, Tenn., 1986-87; Bible class tchr. Bethel Springs (Tenn.) Ch. of Christ, 1987—2004. Mem. Am. Diabetes Assn., Am. Assn. Diabetes Educators, Freed-Hardeman U. Honors Alumni Assn., Alpha Chi Omega, Sigma Theta Tau. Home: 15 Margaret Ct Paducah KY 42001-5407 Office: Western Bapt Hosp Emergency Dept Kentucky Ave Paducah KY 42003 E-mail: lselbe@comcast.net.

SELBEE, MAXINE BUTCHER, county clerk; b. Chapmanville, W.Va., June 1, 1930; d. John Sweet Butcher and Bessie Farley; m. William Arthur Selbee, Feb. 8, 1953 (dec. July 1995). AS, Marshall U., 1951. Ins. agt. C.W. Bennett Ins. Agy., Ashland, Ky., 1954-85; chief dep. clk. County Clk.'s Office, Catlettsburg, Ky., 1986-93, county clk. county elective office, 1994—. Transportation com. mem. County Clerk's Assn., Frankfort, 1996. Mem. Ky. Dem. Women's Club, Ashland, 1986-99. Mem. Order Ea. Star (officer). Democrat. Baptist. Avocations: gardening, sewing, sports, swimming, sunday school teaching. Office: Courthouse PO Box 523 Catlettsburg KY 41129-0523 Home: PO Box 807 Ashland KY 41105-0807 E-mail: maxineselbee@hotmail.com.

SELBER, KIMBERLY ANN, communications educator, consultant; b. Fullerton, Calif., Aug. 29, 1965; d. Frank A. Paul and Genevieve R. Emry, Diane Paul (Stepmother) and Robert A. Emry (Stepfather); m. Gregory M. Selber, Aug. 3, 2002; 1 child, Danya M. BS, Calif. State U., Fullerton, 1983—94; MA, U. Ill., Urbana-Champaign, 1994—96; PhD, U. Tex., Austin, 1996—2001. Asst. prof. U. Tex., Austin, 2001—03, U. Texas-Pan Am., Edinburg, 2003—. Art director & copywriter (direct mail) Ideas too big for postage (PRINT Magazine's Regional Design Ann., 2002). Adv. bd. mem. Ctr. for Children Who Stutter, Fullerton, Calif., 2004—06. Recipient Luckman Outstanding Undergraduate Tchg. Asst., U. Ill.-Urbana-Champaign, 1996. Office: Univ Tex—Pan American Dept Comm Edinburg TX 78539 Office Phone: 956-381-3583. Home Fax: 956-316-7122; Office Fax: 956-316-7122. Business E-Mail: kp_selber@utpa.edu.

SELBY, CECILY CANNAN, dean, science educator; b. London, Feb. 4, 1927; d. Keith and Catherine Anne Cannan; m. Henry M. Selby, Aug. 11, 1951 (div. 1978); children: Norman, William, Russell; m. James Stacy Coles, Feb. 21, 1981. AB cum laude, Radcliffe Coll., 1946; PhD in Phys. Biology, MIT, 1950. Teaching asst. in biology MIT, 1948-49; adminstrv. head virus study sect. Sloan-Kettering Inst., N.Y.C., 1949-50, asst. mem. instr., 1950-55; instr. microscopic anatomy Cornell U. Med. Coll., 1955-57; tchr. sci. Lenox Sch., N.Y.C., 1957-58, headmistress, 1959-72; nat. exec. dir. Girl Scouts U.S.A., N.Y.C., 1972-75; adv. com. Simmons Coll. Grad. Mgmt. Program, 1977-78; mem. Com. Corp. Support of Pvt. Univs., 1977-83; spl. asst. acad. planning N.C. Sch. Sci. and Math., 1979-80, dean acad. affairs, 1980-81, chmn. bd. advisors, 1981-84. Cons. U.S. Dept. Commerce, 1976-77; dir. Avon Products Inc., RCA, NBC, Loehmanns Inc., Nat. Edn. Corp. pres. Am. Energy Ind., 1976; co-chmn. commn. pre-coll. math. and sci. Nat. Sci. Bd., 1982-83; adj. prof. NYU, 1984-86, prof. sci. edn., 1986-94; mem. policy steering com. Gov. Cuomo's Conf. on Sci. and Engring., 1989-90; affil. scholar Radcliffe Pub. Policy Ctr. of Harvard U., 2000-2001. Contbr. articles to profl. jours., chapters to books. Founder, chmn. N.Y. Ind. Schs. Opportunity Project, 1968-72; mem. invitational workshops Aspen Inst., 1973, 75, 77, 79; trustee MIT, Bklyn. Law Sch., Radcliffe Coll., Woods Hole Oceanographic Instn., Women's Forum N.Y., N.Y. Hall of Sci., 1982—, vice chmn., 1989—, trustee Girls Inc., 1992—, Nat. Coun. Women in Medicine, 1990-94; mem. Yale U. Peabody Mus. Adv. Coun., 1981-89; co-chair program in sci., soc. and gender Radcliffe Inst. of Harvard U., 1999-2001. Named affiliated scholar, Harvard U., 2001; recipient Woman Scientist of Yr. award, N.Y. chpt. Am. Women in Sci., 1992, Alumnae Achievement award, Radcliffe Coll., 2001. Fellow: Am. Women Sci., N.Y. Acad Scis.; mem.: Century Assn. Club, Woods Hole Golf Club, The Explorers Club, Cosmopolitan Club, Sigma Xi, Phi Delta Kappa. Home and Office: 1 E 66th St New York NY 10021-5854 also: 100 Ransom Rd Falmouth MA 02540-1652 E-mail: selbyc@aol.com.

SELBY, DIANE RAY MILLER, fraternal organization administrator; b. Lorain, Ohio, Oct. 11, 1940; d. Dale Edward and Mildred (Ray) Miller; m. David Baxter Selby, Apr. 14, 1962; children: Elizabeth, Susan, Sarah. BS in Edn., Ohio State U., 1962. Sec. Kappa Kappa Gamma Frat., Columbus, Ohio, 1962-63, editor, 1972-86; tchr. Hilliard (Ohio) High Sch., 1963-65; exec. dir. Mortar Bd., Inc. Nat. Office, Columbus, Ohio, 1986—. Editor The Key of Kappa Kappa Gamma Frat, 1972-86 (Student Life award, 1983, 84, 85). Founding officer Community Coordinating Bd., Worthington, Ohio, 1983; pres. PTA Coun., Worthington, 1984, Worthington Band Boosters, 1985; sec., treas. Sports and Recreation Facilities Bd., Worthington, 1986-90; mem. sustaining com. Jr. League Columbus, 1991-93, docent Kelton House, 1979—. Mem.: Assn. Coll. Honor Soc. (exec. com. 1999—2001, 2003—04, 2004—, chmn. bylaws com., trustee 2004—, v.p. 2005—06, pres. 2006—), Mortar Bd., Inc., Ladybugs and Buckeyes, Twig 53 Children's Hosp. (assoc.), Kappa Kappa Gamma (House Bd. v.p. 1997—2000). Republican. Lutheran. Home: 6750 Merwin Pl Columbus OH 43235-2838 Office: Mortar Bd Inc 1200 Chambers Rd Ste 201 Columbus OH 43212-1754 Business E-Mail: selby.1@osu.edu.

SELDEN, ANNIE, mathematics professor; b. Torrington, Conn., Feb. 1, 1938; d. Adolf Laurer and Annie (Wopperer) Anderson; m. Herbert Lloyd Alexander Jr., Oct. 7, 1961 (div. July 1970); children: Neil Brooks, Kim Anne; m. John Selden, May 24, 1974. BA, Oberlin Coll., 1959; MA, Yale U., 1962; PhD, Clarkson U., 1974. Instr. SUNY, Potsdam, 1969-71; sr. lectr. Bayero U., Kano, Nigeria, 1978-85; asst. prof. Hampden Sydney (Va.) Coll., 1973-74, Bosphorus U., Istanbul, Turkey, 1974-78, Tenn. Technol. U., Cookeville, 1985-90, assoc. prof., 1990—95, prof., 1995—2003, emerita, 2003—. Vis. scholar edn. in math., sci. and tech. U. Calif., Berkeley, 1993; sec.-treas. Math. Edn. Resources Co., 1994—; external examiner Fed. Advanced Tchrs. Coll., Katsina, Nigeria, 1979-82, Gumel, Nigeria, 1981-82; reader advanced placement calculus exams., 1990-92; vis. scholar Ctr. for Rsch. in Math. and Sci. Edn., San Diego State U., 1995-96; vis. prof. Ariz. State U., 1999-2000; adj. prof. N.Mex. State U., 2003—. Dept. editor: UME Trends: News and Reports on Undergrad. Math. Edn., 1989—96, MAA Online's Tchg. and Learning Sect., 1996—; mem. editl. bd. Jour. Computers in Math. and Sci. Teaching, 1992—96, Jour. for Rsch. in Math. Edn., 1997-2000; assoc. editor for tchg. and learning MAA Online, 1997—; assoc. editor Media Highlights sect. Coll. Math. Jour., 1994—; contbr. articles to profl. jours. Fulbright scholar, 1959—60, Woodrow Wilson fellow, 1960—61, NSF grad. trainee Clarkson U., 1972—73, NSF grantee, 1971, 1994—96. Fellow AAAS; mem. AAUP (Tenn. Tech. chpt. sec. 1991-92, v.p. 1992-93, pres. 1994—95), Am. Math. Soc., Math. Assn. Am. (dept. rep. 1986—2000, coord.-elect spl. interest group on rsch. in undergrad. math. edn. 1999-2000, coord. 2000-02, past coord. 2002-03), Assn. Women in Math. (Louise Hay award for contbns. to math. edn. 2002), Nat. Assn. Math., Am. Math. Assn. Two-Yr. Colls., Benjamin Banneker Assn., Nigerian Math. Soc. (organizer 5th ann. conf. 1984), Internat. Group for Psychology Math. Edn., Am. Edni. Rsch. Assn., Nat. Coun. Tchrs. Math., Rsch. Coun. for Math. Learning, Tenn. Acad. Sci., Women in Higher Edn. Tenn. (Tenn. Tech. chpt. pres. 1990-92, state 1st v.p. 1991-92, state pres. 1992-93), Women Organizing Women (treas. 1992-93), Am. Coun. Edn. (nat. indentification program for women com. 1992-93), Assn. for Sci. Study of Consciousness, Phi Beta Kappa, Sigma Xi, Pi Mu Epsilon, Kappa Mu Epsilon. Office: NMex State U Dept Mathematical Scis PO Box 30001 Las Cruces NM 88003-0001 Business E-Mail: aselden@emmy.nmsu.edu.

SELDEN, MARGERY JULIET STOMNE, music educator; b. Chgo., Sept. 05; d. Edwin and Nellie Juliet (Sorlie) Stomne; m. Paul Hubert Selden Jr., Dec. 30, 1950 (dec. July 28, 1973); children: Paul H. III, Margery Selden Johnson, Harold Frederick II, Charles B. II; m. Clem C. Williams Jr., July 22, 1989 (dec. Nov. 9, 1992). AB, Vassar Coll., 1946; MA, Yale U., 1948, PhD, 1951. Cert. vis. health aide, N.J.; lic. water safety instr. ARC, Nat. Cert. Music Tchrs. Nat. Assn. From instr. to asst. prof. to assoc. prof. Wayne State U., Detroit, 1950-65; assoc. prof. North Cen. Coll., Naperville, Ill., 1964-68; from assoc. prof. to prof. Coll. of St. Elizabeth, Convent Station, NJ, 1968—89; pvt. piano tchr., 1973—89; adj. prof. Passaic County Coll., Paterson, N.J., 1980-89, Kalamazoo Valley Coll., 1994—2002. Tchr. reviewer Willis Music Co., 2003—04. Composer anthems; contbr. numerous articles to profl. publs. Vol. Upjohn Nursing Home. Winner Patriotic Song Contest, Mil. Order of World Wars, 1976, Composition winner N.J. Chorale, 1988; recipient Cert. of Merit, Hoboken, N.J., 1981, Composer award Fisher Found., 1996. Mem.: Am. Guild Organists, Am. Musicol. Soc., Nat. Assn. Composers USA, Nat. Guild Piano Tchrs., Music Tchrs. Nat. Assn., Sons of Norway (lodge pianist), Phi Beta Kappa, Sigma Alpha Iota. Republican. Lutheran. Avocations: swimming, square dancing. Home: 6710 Evergreen St Portage MI 49024-3220 Office Phone: 269-327-9859.

SELDERS, JEAN E., retired psychology professor; b. La Junta, Colo., Nov. 6, 1942; d. Samuel Allen and Dorothy Jean Selders; m. Paul J. Fraker (div.); m. James R. Powell (div.). BA, U. No. Colo., 1964, MA, 1967; PhD, U. Denver, 1980. Cert. Colo. Dept. Edn., Colo. Soc. Sch. Psychologists, Nat. Assn. Sch. Psychologists, Nat. Cert. Sch. Psychologist. Spl. edn. tchr. Jefferson Co. Pub. Schs., Lakewood, Colo., 1964—65; elem. tchr. Mt. Calm Pub. Schs., Tex., 1965—66; spl. edn. tchr. Dept. Def. Overseas Schs., Tokyo, 1967—70, Cumberland County Schs., Fayetteville, NC, 1970—72; Ednl. diagnostician NC Dept. Pub. Health, 1972—78; sch. psychologist Littleton Pub. Schs., Littleton, Colo., 1980—2004; coll. instr. Arapahoe CC, 1990—2004; ret., 2005. Bd. dirs. Nat. Fragile X Found., Denver, 1988—92; pres., bd. dirs. Arapahoe Assn. Retarded Citizens, Littleton, 1980—88; state sec., bd. Colo. Soc. Sch. Psychologists, 1984—89. Vol. Opera Corado, Denver, 1980—, Central City Opera, Central City, 1980—. Recipient State Champion-Toastmistress, NC, 1976, Colo. Sch. Psychologist Yr., Colo. Soc. Sch. Psychologists, 1985. Mem.: APA, Arapahoe/Douglas Mental Health Assn., Colo. Soc. Sch. Psychologists (state bd. sec. 1980—85), Alpha Gamma Delta (rec. sec. 1963—64, panhellenic del. 1982—84). Republican. Lutheran. Avocations: travel, reading, theater, opera.

SELDES, MARIAN, actress; b. NYC; d. Gilbert and Alice (Hall) S.; m. Julian Claman, Nov. 3, 1953 (div.); 1 child, Katharine; m. Garson Kanin, June 19, 1990 (dec. Mar. 1999). Grad., The Dalton Sch., N.Y.C., 1945, Neighborhood Playhouse, 1947; DHL, Emerson Coll., 1979; DFA (hon.), Julliard Sch., 2003. Faculty drama and dance divsn. Juilliard Sch. Lincoln Ctr., NYC, 1969-91; faculty drama dept. Fordham U., 2003, 2005. Appeared with Cambridge (Mass.) Summer Theatre, 1945, Boston Summer Theatre, 1946, St. Michael's Playhouse, Winooski, Vt., 1947-48, Bermudiana Theatre, Hamilton, Bermuda, 1951, Elitch Gardens Theatre, Denver, 1953, The Cretan Woman, Lysistrata, 1955 (actress/artist-in residence Stanford U.), The Flowering Peach, L.A., 1956, Witness for the Prosecution, The Players' Ring, L.A., 1957; Broadway appearances include Medea, 1947, Crime and Punishment, 1948, That Lady, 1949, Tower Beyond Tragedy, 1950, The High Ground, 1951, Come of Age, 1952, Ondine, 1954, The Chalk Garden, 1955, The Wall, 1960, A Gift of Time, 1962, The Milk Train Doesn't Stop Here Any More, 1964, Tiny Alice, 1965, A Delicate Balance, 1967 (Tony award for best supporting actress), Before You Go, 1968, Father's Day, 1971 (Drama Desk award, Tony nomination), Mendicants of Evening (Martha Graham Co.), 1973, Equus, 1974-77, The Merchant, 1977, Deathtrap, 1978 (Tony nomination), Ivanov (Drama Desk nomination), 1997, Ring Round the Moon, 1999 (Tony nomination), 45 Seconds from Broadway, 2001 Dinner At Eight, 2003 (Tony nomination); off-Broadway appearances include Diff'rent, 1961, The Ginger Man, 1963 (Obie award), All Women Are One, 1964, Juana LaLoca, 1965, Three Sisters, 1969, Am. Shakespeare Festival, Stratford, Conn., Mercy Street at Am. Place Theater, N.Y.C., 1969, Isadora Duncan, 1976 (Obie award), Painting Churches, 1983, 84 (Outer Critics Circle award 1984), Other People, Berkshire Theatre Festival, 1969, The Celebration, Hedgerow Theater, Pa., 1971, Richard III, N.Y. Shakespeare Festival, 1983, Remember Me, Lakewood Theatre, Skowhegan, Maine, Gertrude Stein and a Companion, White Barn Theatre, Westport, Conn., 1985, Lucile Lortel Theatre, N.Y.C., 1986, Richard II, N.Y. Shakespeare Festival, 1987, The Milk Train Doesn't Stop Here Anymore, WPA Theatre, N.Y.C., 1987, Happy Ending, Bristol (Pa.) Riverside Theatre, 1988, Annie 2 John F. Kennedy Ctr., Washington, 1989-90, Goodspeed Opera House, Chester, Conn., 1990, A Bright Room Called Day, N.Y. Shakespeare Festival, 1991, Three Tall Women, River Arts, Woodstock, N.Y., 1994, Another Time, Am. Jewish Theatre, 1993, Breaking the Code, Berkshire Theatre Festival, 1993, Three Tall Women, Vineyard Theatre, N.Y.C., 1994, Promenade Theatre, 1994-95, nat. tour, 1995-96, Boys From Syracuse, City Ctr., N.Y.C., 1997, Dead End: Williamstown, 1997, Dear Liar, Irish Repertory Theater, 1999, The Matchmaker: Williamstown, 1998, Tongue of a Bird, Mark Taper Forum, 1998, Sail Away, Carnegie Hall, 1999, Mad About The Boy, Carnegie Hall, 1999, The Torch-Bearers, 2000, Ancestral Voices, 2000, The Skin of our Teeth, 2000, Williamstown, The Play About the Baby, Alley Theatre, Houston, 2000, The Butterfly Collection, Playwrights Horizon, NY, 2000, The Play About the Baby, Helen, NY Shakespeare Festival, 2001, Play Yourself, N.Y. Theater Workshop, 2002, Beckett/Albee, Century Ctr. Theatre, N.Y.C., 2003, The Royal Family Ahmanson Theatre, L.A., 2004, Dedication or the Stuff of Dreams, 2005; nat. tour Three Tall Women, 1995-96; film appearances include The Greatest Story Ever Told, Gertrude Stein and a Companion, 1988, In a Pig's Eye, 1988, The Gun in Betty Lou's Handbag, 1992, Tom and Huck, 1995, Digging to China, 1997, Home Alone 3, 1997, Affliction, 1997, Celebrity, 1998, The Haunting, 1999, Town and Country, 1999, Duets, 1999, Hollywood Ending, 2002, Mona Lisa Smile, 2003, (documentary) Golden Age of Broadway, 2005, (narrator documentary) Ballet Russes, 2005, August Rush, 2006; (TV series) Good and Evil, 1991, Murphy Brown, 1992, Truman, 1995, Cosby, 1996, 98, Trinity, 1998, Remember WENN, 1999, The Others, 2000, If These Walls Could Talk 2, 2000, Nero Wolfe, 2001 (A&E), The Education of Max Bickford, 2002, American Masters PBS "Juillard Documentary, 2003", Hallmark Hall of Fame, 2004, Frasier, 2004, TV: The Book of Daniel, 2005; also appeared on radio CBS Mystery Theater, 1976-81, Theatre Guild on The Air; author: The Bright Lights, 1978, Time Together, 1981; appeared in soap opera One Life to Live, 1998. Bd. dirs. Neighborhood Playhouse, The Acting Co., Nat. Repertory Theatre, Theatre Hall of Fame, 1996; bd. trustees Broadway Cares/Equity Fights Aids. Winner Ovation award Theater L.A. for Three Tall Women, 1996, Conn. Critics award for Three Tall Women, 1996; recipient Madge Kennedy/Sidney Kingsley award Dramatists Guild Fund, 2000, Obie award for sustained achievement, Lucille Lortel award for Sustained Achievement, 2003, Edwin Booth award, Players Club, 2003, Lifetime Mem. award Theatre Libr. Assn., 2003, Breukelein Inst. Gaudium award, 2003, Julliard Sch. medal svc. to arts, 2005, Drama League award sustained achievement, 2006, Dutch Treat Gold medal award, 2006, Rebekah Koht award Nat. Coun. Jewish Women, 2006. Mem. Players Club, Century Assn. Home: 210 Central Park S Apt 19D New York NY 10019-1426

SELDNER, BETTY JANE, environmental engineer, consultant, aerospace transportation executive; b. Balt., Dec. 11, 1923; d. David D. and Miriam M. (Mendes) Miller; m. Warren E. Gray, June 20, 1945 (div. 1965); children: Patricia, Deborah; m. Alvin Seldner, Nov. 15, 1965; children: Jack, Barbara. BA in Journalism, Calif. State U., Northridge, 1975, MA in Communications, 1977. Dir. pub. info. United Way, Van Nuys, Calif., 1958-63, dir. edn. Los Angeles, 1963-68; dir. pub. relations, fin. San Fernando Valley Girl Scout Council, Reseda, Calif., 1968-73; asst. dir. pub. info. Calif. State U., Northridge, 1973-75; dir. environ. mgmt. HR Textron Corp., Valencia, Calif., 1975-87; environ. engr. Northrop Aircraft, Hawthorne, Calif., 1987-88, EMCON Assocs., Burbank, Calif., 1988-92, Atkins Environ., 1992-93, Seldner Environ., Valencia, Calif., 1993—; pres. Seldner Environ. Svcs., 1993—. Author non-fiction. Named Woman of Yr., Santa City C. of C. and vol. orgns., 2000. Mem. Santa Clarita Valley Environ. Mgrs. Soc. (chmn. bd. dirs. 1984), San Fernando Valley Round Table (pres. 1971-72), Hazardous Materials Mgrs.' Assn., Zonta Internat., Valencia Indsl. Assn. (environ. chair). Republican. Jewish. Avocation: sailing. Office Phone: 661-255-6427. Personal E-mail: Betty13ix@comcast.net.

SELECKY, MARY C., state agency administrator; BA, Univ. Pa. Adminstr. NE Tri-County Health District, Colville, Wash., 1979—99; sec. Wash. Dept. Health, Olympia, 1999—. Mem.: Assn. State & Territorial Health Officials (past pres., McCormack award 2004), Nat. Assn. City & County Health Officials (bd. dir.), Wash. State Assn. Local Public Health Officials (past pres.). Office: Dept Health 101 Israel Rd SE Olympia WA 98501*

SELES, MONICA, professional tennis player; b. Novi Sad, Yugoslavia, Dec. 2, 1973; arrived in US, 1996; d. Karolj and Esther Seles. Profl. tennis player, 1989—. Mem. U.S. Fed Cup Team, 1996, 99, 2000, WTA Tour Players' Coun., 1998—99. Author: (novels) From Fear to Victory, 1996. Active Spl. Olympics. Named Sportswoman of Yr., Yugoslavia, 1985, Female Rookie of Yr., TENNIS Mag./Rolex Watch, 1989, Most Improved Player, WTA Tour, 1990, Player of Yr., 1991, Female Athlete of Yr., AP, 1991, 1992, Comeback Player of Yr., TENNIS Mag., 1995, Female Pro Athlete of Yr., Fla. Sports Hall of Fame, 1998, Player Who Makes a Difference, Family Circle Cup, 1999; recipient Ted Tinling Diamond Award, 1990, Rado Topspin Award, 1990, Comeback Player of Yr. Award, WTA Tour, 1995, 1998, Committment to Cmty. Award, Fla. Times-Union, 1999, Flo Hyman Meml. Award, Women's Sports Found., 2000, Sanex Hero of Yr. Award, WTA Tour, 2002. Achievements include 3rd player in the Open-era to capture the Australian and Roland Garros in same calendar year; World #1 ranked player, 1991, 92, 95; youngest #1 ranked player in tennis history for women and men at 17 years, 3 months, 9 days; Winner Grand Slam titles: Roland Garros, 1990, 91, 92, French Open, 1990, 91, 92, U.S. Open, 1991, 92, Australian Open, 1991, 92, 93, 96; Winner 53 Career Singles Titles and 6 Career Doubles Titles, WTA Tour. Office: c/o Internat Mgmt Group 1 Erieview Plz Cleveland OH 44114-1715

SELIG, PHYLLIS SIMS, retired architect; b. Topeka, Nov. 16, 1931; d. Willis Nolan and Victoria Clarinda (Oakley) Sims; m. James Richard Selig, Mar. 31, 1957; children: Lin Ann, Susan Nan, Sarah Jo. BS in Architecture, U. Kans., 1956. Realtor Assoc. Realty, Lawrence, Kans., 1965-70; v.p. finance and housing Alpha Phi Internat. Fraternity, Inc., Evanston, Ill., 1968-74, chief exec. officer, internat. pres., 1974-78, trustee, 1978-80; sr. engr. tech. Nebr. Pub. Power, Columbus, 1980-86, staff architect, 1986-89, archtl. supr., 1989-96; retired, 1996. Republican. Lutheran. Avocations: wood working, painting. E-mail: psselig@cs.com.

SELIGMAN, NICOLE K., broadcast executive, lawyer; BA magna cum laude, Harvard Coll., Radcliffe, 1978; JD magna cum laude, Harvard Law Sch., 1983. Assoc. editl. page editor The Asian Wall St. Jour., Hong Kong, 1978—80; law clk. to Judge Harry T. Edwards U.S. Ct. of Appeals, Wash., DC, 1983—84; law clk. to Justice Thurgood Marshall U.S. Supreme Ct., 1984—85; ptnr., litig. Williams & Connolly LLP, Wash., DC; exec. v.p., gen. counsel Sony Corp. of Am., 2001—; corp. exec. Sony Corp., Tokyo, 2003—, group deputy gen. counsel, 2003—.

SELIGSON, JUDITH, artist; b. Phila., July 8, 1950; d. David and Harriet Tutelman Seligson; m. Allan M. Greenberg, Sept. 7, 1938; 1 child, Hannah Leah. BA cum laude, Harvard U., 1973. One-woman shows include Jane Haslem Gallery, Washington, 1992, Anita Friedman Fine Art, N.Y.C., 1997, Schlesinger Libr., Radcliffe Coll., Cambridge, Mass., 1997, exhibited in group shows at Gary Snyder Fine Art, N.Y.C., 1998, 2002, Signal 66, Washington, 2001, Exit Art, N.Y.C., 2002, Amram Sunday Scholars Series, Washington, 2000; contbr. articles to profl. jours. and pubs.

SELIN, LISA K., physician; b. Helsinki, Finland, Apr. 8, 1952; d. Lauri Oscar and Hilma K Selin. BSc, Dalhousie Univ, 1970—74; MD, Dalhousie U., 1974—79, FRCP, 1980—84; PhD, Univ. Man., 1986—93. Med. intern Dalhousie U., Halifax, Canada, 1979—80, resident in internal medicine, 1980—84; fellow in infectious diseases Univ. of Man., Winnipeg, Canada, 1984—86; doctoral student Univ of Man., 1986—91; postdoctoral fellow Univ. Mass. Med. Sch., 1992—95, instr., 1995—96; asst. prof. Univ. Mass. Med Sch., 1996—2001; assoc. prof. Univ. Mass. Med. Sch., 2001—. Contbr. articles to profl. jours. Med. Coun. of Can. Student fellowship, Med. Coun. of Can., 1986—91, Dalhousie Entrance schoarship, Dalhousie Univ, 1970, Izaak Walton Killam scholarship, Izaak Walton Killam Found., 1984—86, Clin. Investigator award, Nat. Inst. of Health, 1996—99, Rsch. grant, NIH- NIAID, 2000—, NIH-NIAID, 2001—, 1999—2003. Mem.: Can. Infectious Disease Soc., Am. Assn. of Immunologists. Achievements include research in T cell-mediated heterologous immunity in viral infections. Avocations: painting, cross country skiing, swimming, gardening, travel. Office: Univ Mass Med Sch 55 Lake Ave North Worcester MA 01655 E-mail: liisa.selin@umassmed.edu.

SELINGER, PATRICIA GRIFFITHS, computer science professional; b. Cleve., Oct. 15, 1949; d. Fred Robert and Olive Mae (Brewster) Priest; m. James Alan Griffiths, Aug. 29, 1970 (div. 1973); m. Robert David Selinger, July 22, 1978; children: David Robert, Thomas Robert. AB, Harvard U., 1971, MS, 1972, PhD, 1975. Rsch. staff IBM Rsch. Lab, San Jose, Calif., 1975-78, mgr., 1978-83, mgr. computer sci., 1983-86, program dir. Database Technology Inst., 1986, with devel. team, 1997, v.p. Rsch. Area Strategy, Info. and Interaction. Patentee in field; co-author numerous tech. papers. IBM fellow, 1994; recipient YWCA Tribute to Women in Industry award, 1989; named to Hall of Fame, Women in Tech. Internat., 2004. Mem. NAE, Assn. for Computing Machinery (System Software award 1989, former vice-chmn. spl. interest group for mgmt. data). Avocations: cooking, reading. Office: IBM Almaden Rsch Ctr 650 Harry Rd San Jose CA 95120-6099

SELINGER, SHARON EVE, endocrinologist; d. Mark and Guta Selinger; m. Dennis Alan Lowenthal, May 20, 1984; 1 child, Jonathan M. Lowenthal. BA, Cornell U., Ithaca, NY, 1977; MD, Cornell U., NYC, 1981. Internship Montefiore Hosp. and Med. Ctr., Bronx, NY, 1981—82, resident in internal medicine, 1982—84; fellow in endocrinology NYY Med. Coll., NYC, 1984—87; assoc., ptnr. Endocrine Metabolic Assocs., Westfield, NJ, 1987—96; pres. Sharon E. Selinger MD, PA, Summit, NJ, 1996—. Sect. chief endocrine divsn. Overlook Hosp., Summit, 2006. Fellow: ACP, Am. Coll. Endocrinologists; mem.: Am. Assn. Clin. Endocrinologists (pres. NJ chpt. 2000—06). Office: 1 Springfield Ave Ste 1A Summit NJ 07901 Office Phone: 908-273-8300.

SELKOW, PAULA, psychologist; b. N.Y. m. Maurice Jay Rosenstraus, May 22, 1977. BA, SUNY, New Paltz, 1967; MEd, Boston U., 1969; PhD, Fordham U., 1978. Lic. psychologist, N.J., N.Y. Tchr. N.Y.C. Bd. Edn., 1967-68, 69-70; employment counselor N.Y. State Employment Svc., N.Y.C., 1970-71; sch. psychologist Bur. Child Guidance, N.Y.C., 1971-76, Princeton (N.J.) Regional Schs., 1977-78; asst. prof. William Paterson Coll., Wayne, N.J., 1979-84; pvt. practice, Somerset, N.J., 1981—. Adj. instr. Trenton (N.J.) State Coll., 1977-79; cons. psychologist Laurie Neurodevel. Inst., New Brunswick, N.J., 1981-87. Author: Assessing Sex Bias in Testing, 1984; also articles. Grantee HEW, 1979. Mem. APA, N.J. Psychol. Assn., Am. Soc. Clin. Hypnosis, Cen. N.J. Women's Profl. Network (founder). Home: 266 Longwood Ln Somerset NJ 08873-6057

SELL, ELLEN JEAN, secondary school educator; b. McPherson, Kans., Aug. 30, 1943; d. Clifford Edwin and Rosalie Elizabeth (Lindstrom) Sell. BA History, McPherson Coll., Kans., 1965; postgrad., Wis. Conservatory Music, Milw., 1965—72, U. Calif., Santa Barbara, 1972, Music Acad. of the West, 1971—75, U. So. Calif., 1976—78, British Acad. Dramatic Arts, Oxford, Eng., 1987; MA Theater, Calif. State U., LA, 1992. Cert. Tchr.music, theater Calif. Intern U.S. Senate, Washington, 1965; tchr. English, theater Milw. Sch. Dist., 1965—72; chorister, soloist Florentine Opera Co., Milw., 1966—72, LA Camerata, 1978—80; vocal instr. City of Covina, Calif., 1999—2001; soloist Angelica Luth. Ch., LA, 1975—2003; tchr. theatre, choral, English LA Unified Sch. Dist., 1975—. Soloist West L.A. Chamber Orch., 1981—85. Mem. ch. coun. Angelica Luth. Ch., LA, 1977—96. Nominee Bravo award, LA Music Ctr., 2005; recipient Outstanding Tchr. award, Calif. Scholarship Fedn., Garfield H.S., LA, 1989. Mem.: Drama Tchrs. So. Calif. (exec. sec. 1995—2002), Calif. Ednl. Theatre Assn. (bd. mem., exec. sec. 1993—99, chmn. conf. com. 2001, pres. South 2001—04, mem. conf. com. 1993, chmn. conf. com. 2005, mem. conf. com. 1995, 1999, Multicultural award 2002), Alpha Psi Omega, Phi Alpha Theta, Phi Kappa Phi. Avocations: cooking, music, reading, travel. Office: Garfield HS 5101 E Sixth St Los Angeles CA 90022 Office Phone: 323-268-9361. E-mail: ellensell@sbcglobal.net.

SELL, JOAN ISOBEL, mobile home company owner; b. Johnson City, Tenn., May 5, 1936; d. Earl Walter and Jeanne Mason (Lyle) S.; m. Dale L. Moss, Jan. 15, 1956 (div. Nov. 1977); children: Carol Anne, John D. BS, East Tenn. State U., Johnson City, 1961. Cert. tchr., Tenn., Ga. Tchr. Asbury Sch., Johnson City, 1961-62, Richard Arnold High Sch., Savannah, Ga., 1964-66, Windsor Forest High Sch., Savannah, 1966-67, Boones Creek High Sch., Jonesborough, Tenn., 1967-77; co-owner Moss-Sell Mobile Homes, Johnson City, 1978-88, Biddix Budget Homes, Inc. (formerly Budget Mobile Homes), Johnson City, 1978-87, v.p., sec., 1987—; pres., treas. Budget Homes, Inc. (formerly Biddix Budget Homes), Johnson City, 1988-92; owner McKinley Park, Johnson City, 1970—; sec. Piedmont Fin. Svcs. Inc., 1999—2001; pres. Sell Properties, Inc., Johnson City, 1997—. Pres. Sell Properties, Inc., 1997—. Bd. dirs. Ashley Acad., Johnson City, 1997-2000. Mem. Tenn. Manufactured Housing Assn. (state bd. dirs. 1993-95), N.E. Tenn. Manufactured Housing Assn. (pres.), DAR, UDC, Order Ea. Star. Mem. Brethren Ch. Home: 3 Caitlin Ct Johnson City TN 37604-1147 Office: PO Box 5189 Johnson City TN 37602-5189 Office Phone: 423-928-4297.

SELL, LEELOU, retired elementary school educator; d. Werner William and Lydia Veryl Sell. BA, Long Beach State Coll., Calif., 1960; postgrad., Pepperdine U., Calif. State U., Fullerton, U. Calif., Irvine. Cert. tchr. Calif. Tchr. Anaheim City Sch. Dist., Calif., 1960, 1961—97; chpt. counselor Zeta Tau Alpha, 1960—61; ret., 1997—. Co-author: Math for Kindergartners, 1970. Vol. Braille Inst., Anaheim, 1997—; vol., bd. dirs., mem. com. Pacific Symphony, Orange County, Calif., 1997—; bd. dirs., mem. com. Am. Heart Assn., Orange County, 1998—2001. Named Hon. Life Mem., Jefferson PTA, Anaheim, 1970, Price PTA, Anaheim, 1986. Mem.: AAUW, Calif. Ret. Tchrs. Assn., Zeta Tau Alpha (pres., v.p., sec. membership 1955—60), Delta Kappa Gamma (2d v.p., sec. rec. sec., chmn. various coms. 1985—). Avocations: reading, theater, needlecrafts, herb gardening, travel.

SELLARS, CHRISTI VON LEHE, music educator; b. Charleston, S.C., July 30, 1954; d. Diedreich Peterman and Fay Johnson von Lehe; m. Robert Marion Sellars, Mar. 21, 1981; children: Katharine Elizabeth, Patrick Grayson. MusB in Edn., Converse Coll., 1976, MusM in Edn., 1986. Choral dir. Spartanburg (S.C.) HS, 1977—82; music instr. Spartanburg (S.C.) Day Sch., 1992—2001; prof. music Wofford Coll., Spartanburg, 1993—. Choir dir. Cannon's Meth. Ch., Spartanburg, 1998—; asst. pianist Spartanburg (S.C.) Little Theatre, 1992—98; founder Spartanburg (S.C.) Day Sch. Singers, 1994, STARTS- Wofford Students in the Arts, 2003. Performer Spartanburg (S.C.) Repertory Co., 1989—92; pres. Spartanburg (S.C.) Little Theatre, 1992—98, Spartanburg (S.C.) Philharm., 1985—87; bd. dir. Spartanburg (S.C.) Little Theatre, 1992—98, Music Found., Spartanburg, 1991—95. Named Spartanburg (S.C.) City Young Career Woman, Bus. and Profl. Women, 1980. Mem.: Am. Choral Dirs. Assn., S.C. Music Educators Assn. Meth. Avocations: reading, composing. Home: 3213 Hwy 56 PO Box 132 Pauline SC 29374 Office: Wofford College Box H 429 N Church St Spartanburg SC 29303 E-mail: sellarscv@wofford.edu.

SELLECCA, CONNIE, actress; b. Bronx, N.Y., May 25, 1955; d. Primo and Ann; m. Gil Gerard, 1979 (div. 1987); 1 child, Gilbert Vincent Gerard; m. John Tesh, Apr. 4, 1992; 1 child, Prima Sellechia Tesh. Attended, Boston Coll. Appeared in The Bermuda Depths, TV films include Somebody's Killing the World's Greatest Models, Captain America, The Last Fling, Flying High, 1978, Captain America II, 1979, Circus of the Stars #5, 1980, Hotel, 1982, International Airport, 1985, Downpayment on Murder, 1987, Brotherhood of the Rose, 1989, Turn Back the Clock, 1989, Miracle Landing, 1990, People Like Us, 1990, P.S.I. Luv U, 1991, House of Secrets and Lies, 1992, Passport to Murder, 1993, She Led Two Lives, 1994, The Surrogate, 1995, Holiday to Remember, 1995, A Dangerous Affair, 1995, While My Pretty One Sleeps, 1997, Something Borrowed, Something Blue, 1997, Domesday Rock, 1997, Dangerous Waters, 1999, Anna's Dream, 2002; TV series include Beyond Westworld, Flying High, The Greatest American Hero, Arthur Hailey's Hotel, PS I Luv U; films I Saw Mommy Kissing Santa Claus, 2002. Address: William Morris Agy 151 El Camino Dr Beverly Hills CA 90212 also: Richard Grant and Assocs 8489 W Third St Los Angeles CA 90048

SELLERS, ANGELA, mathematics educator; BA Math. and Spanish, U. So. Ind., Evansville, 2002; MA Math., Ball State U., Muncie, Ind., 2005. Tchr. math. Highland H.S., Anderson, Ind., 2002—. Mem.: ASCD, Nat. Coun. Tchrs. Math. Home: 325 Crestview Ct Chesterfield IN 46017 Personal E-mail: asellers@acsc.net.

SELLERS, BARBARA JACKSON, federal judge; b. Richmond, Va., Oct. 3, 1940; m. Richard F. Sellers; children: Elizabeth M., Anne W., Catherine A. Attended, Baldwin-Wallace Coll., 1958-60; BA cum laude, Ohio State U., 1962; JD magna cum laude, Capital U. Law Sch., Columbus, Ohio, 1979. Bar: Ohio 1979, U.S. Dist. Ct. (so. dist.) Ohio 1981, U.S. Ct. Appeals (6th cir.), 1986. Jud. law clk. Hon. Robert J. Sidman, U.S. Bankruptcy Judge, Columbus, Ohio, 1979-81; assoc. Lasky & Semons, Columbus, 1981-82; jud. law clk. to Hon. Thomas M. Herbert, U.S. Bankruptcy Ct., Columbus, 1982-84; assoc. Baker & Hostetler, Columbus, 1984-86; U.S. bankruptcy judge So. Dist. Ohio, Columbus, 1986—. Lectr. on bankruptcy univs., insts., assns. Recipient Am. Jurisprudence prize contracts and criminal law, 1975-76, evidence and property, 1976-77, Corpus Juris Secundum awards, 1975-76, 76-77. Mem. Columbus Bar Assn., Am. Bankruptcy Inst., Nat. Conf. Bankruptcy Judges, Order of Curia, Phi Beta Kappa. Office: US Bankruptcy Ct 170 N High St Columbus OH 43215-2403 Office Phone: 614-469-6638 ext. 250. Business E-Mail: barbara_sellers@ohsb.uscourts.gov.

SELLERS, DONNA NORTHCUTT, science educator; b. McMinnville, Tenn., Apr. 18, 1952; d. Lyte Wilson and Myra Harris Northcutt; m. Robert Randall Sellers, Feb. 23, 1973; children: Laura, Justin. AA, Freed-Hardeman U., 1971; BA, Harding U., 1973; MEd, Cumberland U., 2002. Cert. tchr. Tenn. Lab. technician Houston Allergy Clinic, 1973—74; nuc. med. technologist VA Hosp., Houston, 1974—77; med. asst. Office of Dr. S.K. Ajmani, Internal Medicine, Houston, 1977—78; 8th grade tchr. North Elem. Sch., Altamont, Tenn., 1981—83; 4th, 6th and 7th grade tchr. Knoxville Christian Sch., Farragut, Tenn., 1988—92; sci. tchr. Chattanooga Ctrl. H.S., Harrison, Tenn., 1993—, lead tchr. Math., Tech., Sci. Acad., 2004—. Named Outstanding Educator, Chattanooga Rotary Club, 2004, Most Inspirational Tchr., Chattanooga Ctrl. H.S. Class of 2005, Margaret Hammock Outstanding Tchr., Chattanooga Ctrl. H.S., 2004; recipient Class Dedication, Chattanooga Ctrl. H.S. Class of 2004. Mem.: NEA, Hamilton County Edn. Assn., Tenn. Edn. Assn. Republican. Mem. Ch. Of Christ. Avocations: gardening, reading, singing, hiking. Office: Chattanooga Ctrl HS 5728 Hwy 58 Harrison TN 37341 Office Phone: 423-344-1447 ext. 466. E-mail: sellers_d@hcde.org.

SELLERS, ELIZABETH ELLISON, special education educator; b. Greenville, S.C., July 14, 1965; d. Larry Milton and Linda (Nash) Ellison; m. Rodney Lee Sellers, Jan. 31, 1987; children: Hogan Lee, William Andrew. BA in Edn., U. N.C., Charlotte, 1987, MEd, 1989. Cert. tchr., N.C. B/EH tchr. asst. Kings Mountain (N.C.) Dist. Schs., 1987, resource tchr., 1987—, mem. IEP adv. team, 1992—. Sales chair Cleve. County Schs., NC, 1992—2002. Sales chair Bethlehem Fire Dept. Ladies Aux., Kings Mountain, 1991—. Republican. Baptist. Avocations: golf, reading, swimming, travel, teaching sunday school. Home: 109 Chadwick Dr Kings Mountain NC 28086-9228 Office: North Elem Sch 900 Ramseur St Kings Mountain NC 28086-2052

SELLERS, LAURIE JEAN, elementary school educator; d. Stan and Carol Klekotka; m. Justin Sellers; 1 child, Joel. Masters, U. N.C., Charlotte. Cert. reading tchr. grades K-12 N.C. Tchr. Gaston County Schs., Bessemer City, NC, 1999—. Home: 1162 Lyndsey Brooke Ct Lincolnton NC 28092 Office: Tryon Elementary 2620 Tryon Courthouse Rd Bessemer City NC 28016 Office Phone: 704-629-2942. Business E-Mail: lauriesellers@gaston.k12.nc.us.

SELLERS, MARJORIE STEVENSON, retired principal; b. New Orleans, July 10, 1931; d. Samuel Sr. and Lillie Neldare Brown; m. Melvin Stevenson, Feb. 27, 1950 (dec.); children: Melvin Jr. (dec.), Carl F. Anthony (dec.).; m. Lloyd Sellers, Jan. 27, 1974 (dec.). BA in Elem. Edn., Southern U., 1964, MEd in Elem. Edn., 1967; MS in Adminstrn. and Supervision, Alcorn State U., 1982; postgrad., Grambling State U. Dir., tchr. daycare and kindergarten Immaculate Conception Ch., Baton Rouge, 1964-66; tchr. grade 2nd, 6th Carver Elem., De Ridder, La., 1966-68; tchr. math, social studies, reading grades 6,7,8 Walker (La.) Jr. High Sch., 1968-69; acting corr. title I Dept. Corrections, Baton Rouge, 1969-72; instr. reading Alcorn State U., Lorman, Miss., 1972-95; coord. tutor program E.B.R. Recreation/Parks, Baton Rouge, 1995-98; program dir. summer camp, 1995-96; prevention counselor, 1997-98; prin. St. Francis Xavier Sch., Baton Rouge, 1998—; substitute tchr./counselor East Baton Rouge Parish. Adj. faculty U. So. Miss., Natchez, 1975, Sch. Nursing Alcorn State U., Natchez, 1981-82, 90; high stakes test tutor East Baton Rouge, 2004. Stay-In-School challenge grantee Entergy Corp., 1996, Drug Prevention/Edn. program grantee Baton Rouge Found., 1997; Am. coll. scholar U.S. Achieve Acad., 1990, Grant Knights of Peter Claver, 2006. Mem. AARP, AAUW, Nat. Assn. Devel. Edn., Internat. Reading Assn., La. Recreation/Parks, Phi Delta Kappa (sec., pres. 1980), Knights of St. Peter Claver Ladies Aux. (rec. sec.). Democrat. Roman Catholic. Avocations: reading, sewing, church activities, ball games, shopping. Home Fax: 225-774-6113.

SELLERS, MARLENE, artist, educator; b. Phila., Aug. 8, 1933; d. Frank and Rose (Goldberg) S. BS, Temple U., 1955; MFA, U. Pa., 1965; MEd, Temple U., 1971. Tchr. art Sch. Dist. City of Phila., 1966—99. Out-of-Town scholar Art Students League N.Y., 1958. Fellow MacDowell Colony, "Yaddo" Artists Colony; mem. Pa. Acad. Fine Arts (fellowship), Abington Art Ctr. Home: 101 Washington Ln # 803 Jenkintown PA 19046-3505

SELLERS-EVANS, CYNTHIA, literature and language educator; b. Tacoma, Wash., Feb. 3, 1957; d. Pat Draper; m. Jay Evans; children: Kelly Waldron, Lance Evans. MEd, Nat. Lewis U., Evanston, Ill., 1999. Cert. in gen. adminstrn. Ill. Tchr. English Bismarck-Henning H.S., Bismarck, Ill., 1985—. Scholastic bowl sponsor Bismarck-Henning H.S., 1998—. Missions chairperson Rossville (Ill.) United Meth. Ch., 2001—06; relay for life team capt. Am. Cancer Soc., Danville, Ill., 2004—06. Recipient Tchr. of Yr. award, Bismarck-Henning H.S., 2001—02. Office: Bismarck-Henning HS PO Box 350 Bismarck IL 61814 Office Phone: 217-759-7291. E-mail: sellersc@bismarck.k12.il.us.

SELLINGSLOH, HULDA KNIPLING, retired artist; b. Port Lavaca, Tex., Nov. 29, 1912; d. Henry John and Hulda (Rasch) Knipling; m. August Sellingsloh, May 1, 1943 (dec. Apr. 1998); children: Susan Louise, Marian Kay, Ellen Agnes, John August. LLB, Houston Law Sch., 1939. Bar: Tex. 1940. Sec. draftsman Calhoun County Abstract Co., Port Lauaca, 1933—34; sec. to pres. Tex. Luth. Coll., Seguin, 1935—36; legal sec., draftsman Fohs Oil Co., Houston, 1936—43; draftsman, asst. engr. U.S. Coast & Gendetic Survey, Balt., 1943—45; civic leader various civic and religious orgns., Beacon and Fishkill, NY, 1945—72; profl. visual artist N.Y., N.Mex., Tex., 1973—99. Leader, pres. various chs., clubs, Beacon and Fishkill, 1950—72; artist Eastside Creative Art Club, 1960—72; pres. Santa Fe chpt. Artists Equity, N.Mex., 1973—78. Author: (life history) Top Crop, 1999—2000. Pres. Houston Women Lawyers, 1943, Santa Fe Artists Assn., 1974—76, St. John's Women's Club, Beacon, 1959—60, 1966—69; pres., leading minister St. Clare Secular Franciscan Fraternity, Crowley, Tex. Recipient numerous awards, various regional art assns., 1960—, Best of Show awards, Santa Fe, N.Y., Tex., 1960—, Editors Choice award, Nat. Libr. Poets, 1998. Mem.: Tex. Bar Assn., Pastel Soc. Am. (juried assoc.), Tarrant County Women's Section, Internat. Soc. Poets. Democrat. Roman Catholic. Home: 5 Oak Dr Hopewell Junction NY 12533

SELTZER, VICKI LYNN, obstetrician, gynecologist; b. June 2, 1949; d. Herbert Melvin and Marian Elaine (Willinger) Seltzer; m. Richard Stephen Brach, Sept. 2, 1973; children: Jessica Lillian Brach, Eric Robert Brach. BS, Rensselaer Poly. Inst., 1969; MD, NYU, 1973. Diplomate Am. Bd. Ob-Gyn. (examiner 1988-2001). Intern Bellevue Hosp., N.Y.C., 1973—74, resident ob-gyn., 1974—77; fellow gynecol. cancer Am. Cancer Soc., N.Y.C., 1977—78, Meml. Sloan Kettering Cancer Ctr., N.Y.C., 1975—79; assoc. dir. gynecol. cancer Albert Einstein Coll. Medicine, N.Y.C., 1979—83, prof. ob-gyn., 1989—. Assoc. prof. ob-gyn SUNY, Stony Brook, 1983—89; Edie and Marvin H. Shur prof. ob-gyn and women's health Albert Einstein Coll. Medicine, N.Y.C., 2003—; dir. ob-gyn. Queens Hosp. Ctr., Jamaica, NY, 1983—93, pres. med. bd., 1986—89; chair ob-gyn L.I. Jewish Med. Ctr., 1993—; v.p. women's health svcs. North Shore-L.I. Jewish Health Sys., 1999—; chair ob-gyn North Shore U. Hosp., 1999—, chair med. bd., 2001—; mem. steering com. N.Y. State Coun. Grad. Med. Edn., 2005—, chair subcom. primary care; mem. U.S. Coun. Grad. Med. Edn., 2006—. Author: Every Woman's Guide to Breast Cancer, 1987; editor: Women's Primary Health Care, 1995, 2000; editor-in-chief: Primary Care Update for the Ob-Gyn, 1993—; mem. editl. bd. Women's Life mag., 1980—82, Jour. Jacobs Inst. Women's Health, 1990—95, Ob-Gyn. Survey, 2005—, Jour. Reproductive Medicine, 2005—, mem. internat. editl. bd. Jour. Soc. Obstreticians and Gynecologists Can., 2000—; contbr. articles to profl. jours.; host (TV series) Weekly Ob-Gyn. program, Lifetime Med. TV. Mem. Mayor Beame's Task Force on Rape, N.Y.C., 1974—76; chair health com. Nat. Coun. Women, N.Y.C., 1979—84; bd. govs. Nat. Coun. Women's Health, 1985—94; chair Coun. Resident Edn. Ob-Gyn., 1987—93. Recipient citation, Nat. Safety Coun., 1978, Achiever award, L.I. Ctr. Bus. and Profl. Women, 1987; Galloway Fund fellow, 1975. Fellow: ACOG (gynecol. practice com. 1981, v.p. 1993—94, pres.-elect 1996—97, pres. 1997—98), N.Y. Obstet. Soc. (pres. 1999—2000); mem.: Am. Hosp. Assn. (governing coun. maternal and child health 2004—), N.Y. Cancer Soc., Am. Med. Women's Assn. (com. chair 1975—79, editl. bd. jour. 1986—2002, citation 1973), Internat. Fedn. Gynecology and Obstetrics (internat. steering com. to reduce maternal mortality 2000—02), Women's Med. Assn. (v.p. N.Y. 1974—79, resident rev. com. ob-gyn 1993—98, Lila Wallis Lifetime Achievement award 2002), NYU Sch. Med. Alumni Assn. (bd. govs. 1979—, v.p. 1987—91, pres. 1992—93), Alpha Omega Alpha. Office: LI Jewish Med Ctr New Hyde Park NY 11040 Office Phone: 718-470-7660. Business E-Mail: vseltzer@lij.edu.

SELTZER, VIVIAN CENTER, psychologist, educator; b. Mpls., May 27, 1931; d. Aaron M. and Hannah (Chazanow) Center; m. William Seltzer; children: Jonathan, Francesca S. Rothseid, Aeryn S. Fenton. BA summa cum laude, U. Minn., 1951; MSW, U. Pa., 1953; PhD, Bryn Mawr Coll., 1976. Lic. psychologist, cert. sch. psychologist, marriage and family therapist; lic. social worker Pa. Family counselor, Phila., Miami, Fla., 1953-60; pvt. practice Phila., 1965—; prof. human devel. and behavior U. Pa., Phila., 1976—. Exch. prof. U. Edinburgh, Scotland, 1979—80; vis. prof. Hebrew U., Jerusalem, 1984—85; chair internat. com. U. Pa., Phila., mem. various coms., chair faculty senate; cons. Org. Resolving Orgnl. Conflict, 2000—, Singapore Mgmt. U., 2002—; cons., invited guest lectr. Singamore Mgmt. U. Sch. Econs. and Social Scis., 2004, 06. Author: (book) Adolescent Social Development: Dynamic Functional Interaction, 1982, The Psychosocial Worlds of the Adolescent, 1989; contbr. articles to profl. jours. Mem. bd. regents Gratz Coll., Phila., 1965—, chair acad. affairs com., 1980—, v.p., 1989—97. Mem.: APA, Center City Resident's Assn. Phila. (exec. v.p.), Internat. Coun. Psychologists, Phila. Soc. Clin. Psychologists (bd. dirs. 1975—86, program chair 1980—86, bd. dirs. 1999—, program chair 2001—), Pa. Psychol. Assn., Phi Beta Kappa. Office Phone: 215-898-5538. E-mail: seltzer@sp2.upenn.edu.

SELVY, BARBARA, dance instructor; b. Little Rock, Jan. 20, 1938; d. James Oliver and Irene Balmat Banks; m. Franklin Delano Selvy, Apr. 15, 1959; children: Lisa Selvy Yeargin, Valerie Selvy Miros, Lauren Kroll, Franklin Michael, Madison Banks Selvy. Student, U. Ctrl. Ark., 1955—57. Founder, dir. Carolina Ballet Theater, Greenville, SC, 1973—; pres. Dance Arts Inc. and Incentives, Inc. Mem. adv. bd. dirs. Met. Arts Coun., and S.C. Govs. Sch., St. Marys Cath. Sch. Appeared in numerous TV commls., on Goodson-Toddman game show Play Your Hunch, 1958-59; toured Far East with TV show Hit Parade, 1958; named Miss Ark., 1956, Mrs. S.C., 1981; dir. and staged Mrs. Va., Mrs. N.C., Mrs. S.C. pageants; choreographed Little Theater prodns., Furman U. Opera. Mem. Nat. Rep. Congl. Com., 2003, Pres. Bush Small Bus. Adv. Coun., 2003. Mem. So. Assn. Dance Masters (ballet adviser, regional dir.), Dance Educators Am., Dance Masters of Am., Profl. Dance Tchrs. Home: 18 Oglethorpe Lane Hilton Head Island SC 29926

SEMAYA, FRANCINE LEVITT, lawyer; b. NYC, Mar. 26, 1951; d. Julie and Ann (Tannenbaum) Levitt; m. Richard Semaya, Aug. 3, 1975; children: Stefanie Rachel, David Steven, Scott Brian. BA magna cum laude, Bklyn. Coll., 1973, MS magna cum laude, 1975; JD cum laude, N.Y. Law Sch., 1982. Bar: N.Y. 1983, U.S. Dist. Ct. (ea. and so. dists.) N.Y. 1983, U.S. Supreme Ct. 2000. Sr. legal analyst, atty. Am. Internat. Group, Inc., N.Y.C., 1977-83; assoc. counsel, asst. v.p. Beneficial Ins. Group, Inc. (formerly Benico, Inc.), Peapack, NJ, 1983-87; v.p., counsel Am. Centennial Ins. Co., Peapack, 1985-87; legal, reins. cons. Peapack, 1987; counsel reins. Integrity Ins. Co. in Liquidation, Paramus, NJ, 1988-91; ptnr. Werner & Kennedy, N.Y.C., 1991-99; mem. chair ins. corp., regulatory practice group Cozen O'Connor, N.Y.C., 1999—. Spkr. in field. Author: Insurance Insolvency--A New Generation, 2001, Insurance Insolvencies 2002-2003: Is the Industry Prepared?, 2002, Insurance Insolvencies, Has the Cycle Peaked?, 2003, Insurance Insolvencies, The Day After Tomorrow, 2004, Insurance Insolvencies, The Changing Tide, 2005; editor: Law and Practice of Insurance Insolvency Revisited, 1999, State of Insurance Regulation: Today and Tomorrow, 1991; contbg. editor: Reference Handbook Ins. Co. Insolvency, 4th edit., 1999; co-editor: State Regulations Ins., 1991; contbr. articles to profl. jours. Mem.: AIDA, ABA (chmn. pub. regulation of ins. law com. tort trial and ins. practice se 1990—91, chair pub. rels. com. 1993—94, sect. coun. 1994—97, chmn. task force on ins. insolvency 1995—2000, chmn. professionalism com. 1997—98, sect. del. to ho. dels. 1998—2004, chmn. task force on state implementation ins. insolvency 2003—04, chmn. fed. involvement in ins. regulation modernization 2004—), Internat. Assn. Ins. Receivers (bd. dirs. 2003—), N.Y. State Bar Assn., Practicing Law Inst. (ins. law adv. com. 1995—), Assn. Bar City N.Y. (ins. law. com.), Fedn. Regulatory Counsel, Phi Beta Kappa. Avocations: reading, travel. Office: Cozen O'Connor 16 Fl 45 Broadway Atrium New York NY 10006-3007 Office Phone: 212-509-9400. Business E-Mail: fsemaya@cozen.com.

SEMCKEN, NANCY, elementary school educator, singer; d. Frederick Adam and Bernice Mae Fink; m. Kenneth Semcken, Oct. 3, 1970; children: Adam Frederick, Amy Brook Doering, Kenneth Jr. BS, Temple U., Phila., 1962; MS, Western Conn. U., Danbury, 1995; B Ministry, Internat. Coll. Bible Theology, Sikeston, Mich., 2006. Cert. dietary cons. Internat. Inst. Natural Health Scis., 1984. Spkr. in field; presenter in field. Performer: (Broadway plays) La Belle Helene, Milk & Honey, The Beast in Me: A Murder Among Us, George M!, The Education of Hyman Kaplan, Pickwick, more than 30 regional and stock cos.; singer: (CD) Brand New World!, 2002; singer, soloist, spkr.: (numerous orgns.); writer, dir.: The Greatest Gift of All; featured artist internet radio program, Abundant Life Inspirational Radio. Drama dir., Ukraine, 2003, 2004; seminar instr. Prison Fellowship Orgtn.; music dir. summer vacation Bible sch. Wantagh Bapt. Ch., L.I., NY; music dir. Scrub Oak Meth. Ch. Mem.: NY State United Tchrs., Am. Orff-Schulwerk Assn., Music Educators Nat. Conf. Avocations: quilting, writing, exercise, singing, sewing. Office: Lakeland Ctrl Sch Dist 1086 E Main St Shrub Oak NY 10588

SEMINARA, LYNDA ANNE, editor; b. Needham, Mass., Jan. 17, 1961; d. Donald Cecil Garaventi and Lois Ann Pichulo Garaventi; children: Daniel Joseph, Robert James. BA cum laude, U. Pa., 1985. Writer, editor, tour coord. Cultural Heritage Alliance, Phila., 1985—88; from prodn. editor to sr. ops. mgr. W.B. Saunders Co., Phila., 1988—93; self-employed editor and writer, 1993—; pres. and owner The WordShop, Cherry Hill, NJ, 1993—; sr. editor OCC N.Am., N.Y.C., 2003—. Game creator Senior Sez trivia games, 2002—. Vol. sr. citizens and children, 1996—2001; sponsor Children Internat., 2003—; music ministry, 1974—. Mem.: Internat. Scleroderma Network (sr. editor 2004—), Soc. Children's Book Writers and Illustrators. Roman Catholic. Avocations: volunteer work, writing, guitar, languages.

SEMKE-FOX, SUZANNE MARIE, elementary school educator; d. Leon and Pearl Semke; m. Dickson David Fox, July 24, 1976; 1 child, Christopher Fox. BA, U. Wash., Seattle, 1960—64. Cert. Tchr. K-12 Wash. Dept. Edn., 1964. Elem. educator Tigard Sch. Dist., Oreg., 1964—66, Burlington Sch. Dist., Ont., Canada, 1966—67, Tigard Sch. Dist., 1967—68; elem./secondary educator Washougal Sch. Dist., Wash., 1968—. Pres. Washougal Assn. Educators, 1984—88; bldg. rep. District-Wide Writing Comm., Washougal, 2003—04; charter mem. Wash. Assn. Mid.-Level Educators, Washougal. Founder Karen Jundt Found., Washougal, 2004—05. Recipient Poetic Achievement - Student Lit. Mag., Creative Comm., 2003—06; grantee, Washougal Schools Found., 2002—03, Dr. Seuss Lit. Grant, Wash. Assn. Educators. Mem.: Internat. Reading Assoc. (assoc.), Washougal Assn. Educators (assoc.; pres. 1984—88), ASCD (assoc.), NMSA (assoc.). Avocations: gardening, reading, poetry, travel. Home: PO Box 205 Washougal WA 98671 Office: Jemtegaard Mid Sch 35300 E Evergreen Blvd Washougal WA 98671 Office Phone: 360-954-3400. Personal E-mail: chrisfox10@aol.com.

SEMLIES, LORI R., lawyer; b. LI, NY, 1969; BA, SUNY, Albany, 1991; JD magna cum laude, Touro Coll., 1994. Bar: NY 1995, NJ 1995, US Dist. Ct. Ea. Dist. NY, US Dist. Ct. So. Dist. NY. Ptnr. Wilson, Elser, Moskowitz, Edelman & Dicker LLP, NYC. Mem.: NY State Bar Assn. Office: Wilson Elser Moskowitz Edelman & Dicker LLP 150 E 42nd St 23rd Fl New York NY 10027-5639 Office Phone: 212-490-3000 ext. 2390. Office Fax: 212-490-3038. Business E-Mail: semliesl@wemed.com.

SEMPLE, JANE FRANCES, health facility director; b. Lakewood, Ohio, Feb. 14, 1951; d. Frank Joseph and Margaret Eleanor (Carpenter) Semple; m. Nick N. Morana, June 24, 1977 (div. Sept. 1981). AAB, Cuyahoga CC, Cleve., 1977; BA, Baldwin-Wallace Coll., 1980; MBA, Case Western Res. U., 1984; ND, Trinity Coll. Natural Health, 1999. Diplomate Am. Bd. Naturopaths. Adminstrv. asst. DeVilbiss Co., Cleve., 1969—77; project dir. Nat. Survey Rsch. Ctr., Cleve., 1977—80; market rsch. mgr. Sherwin-Williams Co., Cleve., 1980—85; instr. Cuyahoga CC, Cleve., 1986—92, Baldwin-Wallace Coll., Berea, Ohio, 1992—93; dir. Alternative Healing Inst., 1989—. Author: Influenza, 2006, Parkinson Disease, 2006, HPV and Cervical Displasia, 2006, Fertility, 2006. Mem. S. B. Anthony Soc. Womenspace, Cleve., 1980—88. Mem.: Coalition for Natural Health, Am. Botanic Coun., Am. Assn. Nutritional Cons., Am. Naturopathic Med. Assn. Democrat. Home: 26969 Greenbrooke Dr Olmsted Falls OH 44138 Office: Alternative Healing Inst 4965 Doven Ctr Rd North Olmsted OH 44070 Office Phone: 440-777-2665. Personal E-mail: drjane@bright.net.

SENDALL, PAULA, secondary school educator; d. Garry E. and Carol S. Ryan; m. Kevin Sendall; 1 child, Alexis. A, St. Gregory's Coll., Shawnee, Okla., 1988; BS in Biology Edn., Ctrl. State U., Edmond, Okla., 1991; MS in Applied Immunology, Brunel U., Uxbridge, England, 1992. Tchr. sci. Choctaw -Nicoma Pk. Pub. Schs., Okla., 1993—. Rep. a.c.t. bldg., negotiations Choctaw-Nicoma Pk. Assn. Classroom Tchrs. Constrn. Habitat Humanity; missions United Meth. Women, Choctaw, 1995—2006. Recipient Golden Apple Tchg. award, Rose State Coll., 2003, Outstanding Influencer, Northwood U., 2006; scholar, Rotary Internat., 1991. Mem.: NEA, Okla. Coaches Assn., Okla. Sci. Tchrs. Assn., Nat. Sci. Tchrs. Assn., Okla. Edn. Assoc., Assn. Classroom Tchrs. (v.p., bldg. rep, negotiations rep 1999—2006), Kappa Delta Pi. Office: Choctaw High School 14300 NE 10th St Choctaw OK 73020 Office Phone: 405-390-8899. Office Fax: 405-390-2275. E-mail: psendall@cnpschools.org.

SENDER, MARYANN, director; b. Fairview, Ohio, Aug. 6, 1956; d. Edward John and Annamay Knecht; m. Emil Robert Syarto, Sept. 9, 1978 (div. Nov. 1991); 1 child, Shannon Syarto; m. John Peter Sender, July 20, 2001. B in Edn./Therapy, Ohio State U., 1978; M in Counseling/Art Psychology, Ursuline Coll., 1989. Cert. rehab. counselor. HPER and program dir. Lakewood (Ohio) YWCA, 1978—80; activity therapy dir. Northside Hosp., Youngstown, Ohio, 1980—87; instr. art therapy Cleve. State U., 1989—93; acad. counselor Cuyahoga C.C., Cleve., 1989—91, ACCESS dir., 1991—. NOCSD chair No. Ohio Consortium, 1993—; spkr. in field. Chair Nat. Disability Awareness Day, Cleve., 1990—; com. mem., BAC/Global Issues, Cleve. and Atlanta, 1998, 1999, 2001; creator Ed Sparre Scholarship Cuyahoga C.C., 1999—; hon. mem. adv. bd. Cleve. Rapid Transit Authority, 1995—98. Mem.: Advocates for Disabled Ohioans, Assn. for Learning Disabilities, Assn. for Higher Edn., Transition and Comm. Consortium on Learning Disabilities, Dir. of Activities Assn., Profl. Activities Therapy Assn., Assn. Higher Edn. and Disability, Mental Health Assn., Am. Heart Assn., Ams. with Disability Act (coll. chairperson 1991—), Dance Exercise Assn., Am. Dance Assn. Avocations: swimming, dance, art, reading, hiking. Home: 5874 Hickory Trl North Ridgeville OH 44039 Office: Cuyahoga C C 4250 Richmond Rd Highland Hills OH 44122 E-mail: maryann.sender@tri-c.cc.edu.

SENECAH, SUSAN LOUISE, environmental scientist, educator, state government policy analyst; b. Mpls., Sept. 2, 1950; d. Roy Edwin and June Alice Thompson; m. Van William Calhoun, Oct. 6, 2003. BS, Bemidji (Minn.) State Coll., 1972; MA, U. Minn., Mpls., 1987; PhD, U. Minn., 1992. Cert. secondary edn.English/speech Minn. English tchr. Duluth East HS, Minn., 1972—73; vol. English tchr. Peace Corps, Western Samoa, 1973—76; English tchr. Hastings Sr. HS, Minn., 1978—91; vis. asst. prof. SUNY, Albany, 1991—92; environ. policy spl. asst. NY State Senate, Albany, 1992—; assoc. prof. SUNY Coll. Environ. Sci. and Forestry, Syracuse, 1993—. Cons., Chatham, NY, 1992—. Contbg. author: Earthtalk: Communication Empowerment for Environmental Action; editor: Environ. Comm. Yearbook, (series) The Future of Environmental Dispute Resolution: Assessing the Past and Present to Guide the Future, (conference proceedings) Proceedings of the 1997 Conference on Communication and Environment, MacMillan Ency. of Pollution. Mem. Chatham Comprehensive Planning Steering Com., 2004—05. Recipient Pres.'s award for disting. pub. svc., SUNY Coll. Environ. Sci. and Forestry, 1999, 2005; fellow, Mott Found., 2003. Mem.: Nat. Comm. Assn. (pres. 1996—98, Founders award Environ. Comm. Divsn. 2002), Assn. for Conflict Resolution (assoc.), Phi Beta Kappa (assoc.). Office: SUNY 1 Forestry Dr Syracuse NY 13210 Office Phone: 315-470-6570. Office Fax: 315-470-6915. E-mail: ssenecah@esf.edu.

SENECHAL, ALICE R., federal magistrate judge, lawyer; b. Rugby, N.D., June 25, 1955; d. Marvin William and Dora Emma (Erdman) S. BS, N.D. State U., 1977; JD, U. Minn., 1984. Bar: Minn. 1984, U.S. Dist. Ct. Minn. 1984, N.D. 1986, U.S. Ct. Appeals (8th cir.) 1987. Law clk. U.S. Dist. Judge Bruce M. Van Sickle, Bismarck, ND, 1984-86; with Robert Vogel Law Office, Grand Forks, ND, 1986—. U.S. magistrate judge, 1990—.

SENERCHIA, DOROTHY SYLVIA, writer, urban planner; b. Warwick, R.I. d. Vincenzo Ralph and Theresa Felicia (Petrarca) S. BA, Pembroke Coll., Brown U., 1955; Cert., U. Florence, Italy, 1956. Cert. urban planner, N.Y.C. Tchr. Berlitz Sch. Langs., Florence, 1955-56; adminstrv. asst. Sheraton Corp. Am., N.Y.C., 1956-57, Inter-Am. Coun., N.Y.C., 1958-59, Roger Stevens Devel. Corp., N.Y.C., 1960-61; urban planner N.Y.C. Dept. City Planning, 1962-96. Author: Silent Menace, 1990; co-producer, co-star film The Funeral, 1980; solo concert violinist, 1945-62; co-founder singing group The Chattertocks of Brown U., 1952. One of the pioneers in cmty organization in the urban planning process, N.Y.C., 1962-68; one of the early pioneers in women's movement, N.Y.C., 1969; mem. planning com. 1970 Women's March, N.Y.C., 1970; counselor Big Sisters Orgn., N.Y.C., 1969-82. Mem.: Vet. Feminists Am. (co-founder), The East River Round Table (founder), Nat. Arts Club. Avocations: foreign languages, music, travel, floral design.

SENESE, SUZANNE MARIE, art and music educator, performance artist; b. Chgo., Dec. 6, 1950; d. Louis Michael and Angeline Mary Olivo Senese. Student, Quincy Coll., Ill., 1968—70; BS in Music Edn. and Vocal, No. Ill. U., DeKalb, 1972; MA in Interdisiplinary Arts, Columbia Coll., 2003. Music educator St. John Vianney Sch., Northlake, Ill., 1973—76, St. Pius X Elem. Sch., Lombard, Ill., 1976—85; choir/orch. dir. Seton H.S., South Holland, Ill., 1985—87; choir, orch., music and theatre educator Regina Dominican H.S., Wilmette, Ill., 1984—99; fine arts and choir educator Fenwick H.S., Oak Park, Ill., 1999—. Student tchr. supr. Columbia Coll. Chgo. MAT Program. Vol. St. Leonard's House; mem. Park Ridge Civic Orch. Chorus, Northwestern U. Summer Chorus; music dir., cantor, organist Santa Lucia Ch., Chgo., 1983—91. Recipient Heart of Sch. Arts award, Archdiocese of Chgo., 2001. Mem.: Nat. Assn. Art Edn., Nat. Assn. Pastoral Musicians, Nat. Cath. Edn. Assn., Ill. Arts Edn. Assn., Am. Choral Dir. Assn., Music Educators Nat. Conf. Roman Catholic. Avocations: theater, reading, crossword puzzles, baseball. Office: Fenwick High Sch 505 Washington Blvd Oak Park IL 60302 Office Phone: 708-386-0127 198. Personal E-mail: ssenese@msn.com.

SENESHEN, SUSAN, music educator; b. Edmonton, Alberta, Can., May 13, 1956; d. Gordon Kay and Lucy Genevieve Greene; 1 child, Daniel Secor. BS Biology, U. Western Ontario, London, 1979; BA Music Therapy, Colo.State U., Fort Collins, 1990. Piano tchr. private studio, Fort Collins., 1985—2004; massage therapist, instr. Colo. State U., pvt. practice, Fort Collins, Colo., 1987—2003; Yoga instr. Fort Collins Club, others, Colo., 1989—; music specialist Weld County Sch. Dist., Evans, Colo., 2004—05, Poudre Sch. Dist., Ft. Collins, 2005—. Composer: (Children's Musical) Kwanza Celebration, 2003, The Magic Recorder (based on Mozart's opera The Magic Flute), 2006. Trustee and pub. Students of Yoga, Fort Collins, Colo., 1987—2001. Avocations: cooking, gardening, swimming, singing, movies.

SENF, CAROL ANN, literature educator; b. Gallipolis, Ohio, Nov. 11, 1947; d. Marlie Ann and Harold Edgar Senf; m. James Alan Farlow, Jan. 21, 1977; children: Jeremy Alan Farlow, James Andrew Farlow. BS, Miami U., Oxford, Ohio, 1965—68, MA, 1969—72; PhD, SUNY, Buffalo, 1972—79. Asst. prof., English dept. Furman U., Greenville, SC, 1980—81, Ga. Tech, Atlanta, 1981—87; assoc. prof. Sch. of LCC/Ga. Tech, Atlanta, 1987—2001, faculty advisor, 2001—05, assoc. chair & prof., 2005—. Author: (critical study) The Vampire in Nineteenth-Century English Fiction, (introduction) The Heavenly Twins by Sarah Grand, (critical study) Dracula: Between Tradition and Modernism (Lord Ruthven award, 1992), Science and Social Science in Bram Stoker's Fiction. Home: 1895 Windham Pk Atlanta GA 30324 Office: Literature Communication & Culture Georgia Inst Tech Atlanta GA 30332-0165 Office Phone: 404-894-7003. Business E-Mail: carol.senf@lcc.gatech.edu.

SENG, COLEEN JOY, mayor; b. Council Bluffs, Iowa, Feb. 8, 1936; d. Otis A. and Helen V. (Anderson) McElwain; m. Darrel E. Seng, Oct. 22, 1960 (dec. 1993); children: Marcee Lee, Christopher Charles, Phillip Scott. BA, Nebr. Wesleyan U., 1958. Dist. dir. Girl Scouts U.S.A., Saginaw, Mich., 1958-60, Lincoln, Nebr., 1960-62; cmty. ministry 1st United Meth. Ch., Lincoln, 1977-97; mem. Lincoln City Coun., 1987—2003; mayor City of Lincoln, 2003—. Mem. Mayor's first multi-cultural task force, co-chair of Gov. Nelson's urban adv. team, chmn. railroad transp. safety dist. Lincoln/Lancaster county joint budget com., mem. Lincoln/Lancaster county homeless coalition; active U. Place Cmty. Orgn. N.E. Family Resource Ctr.; past chair Lincoln/Lancaster county family resource ctr. bd.; past pres. Lincoln Fellowship of Chs.; mem. Lincoln Interfaith Coun.; mem Lincoln Urban Ministries com.; past pres. Homestead Girl Scouts Coun. Democrat. United Methodist. Avocations: reading, movies, gardening. Home: 6101 Walker Ave Lincoln NE 68507-2467 Office: County City Bldg 555 S 10th St Lincoln NE 68508-2810 Office Phone: 402-441-7511.

SENGERS, JOHANNA M. H. LEVELT, physicist; b. Amsterdam, The Netherlands, Mar. 4, 1929; married, 1963; 4 children. Drs, U. Amsterdam, 1954, PhD in Physics, 1958; PhD (hon.), Delft U. Tech., 1992. Rsch. assoc. U. Amsterdam, Van der Waals Lab, 1954-58, 59-63, U. Wis., Inst. Theoretical Chemistry, Madison, 1958-59; physicist heat divsn. Inst. Basic Stds., Nat. Bur. Stds., Gaithersburg, Md., 1963-78; group leader thermophysics divsn. Nat. Engrng. Lab., 1978-87; sr. fellow thermophysics divsn. Nat. Inst. Standards and Tech., 1983-95, fellow emeritus, 1995—. Lectr Cath. U., Louvain, Belgium, 1971; rsch. assoc. Inst. Theoretical Physics, U. Amsterdam, 1974—75; regent's prof. chemistry U. Calif., LA, 1982. Chair working group A Internat. Assn. Properties Steam, 1985-90; pres. Internat. Assn. Properties Water and Steam, 1991-92. Recipient Silver medal U.S. Dept. Commerce, 1972, Gold medal, 1978, Wise award Interagy. Com. Women in Sci. and Engring., 1985, Alexander von Humboldt Rsch. award Alexander von Humboldt-Stiftung, Bonn, Germany, 1991, L'Oreal-UNESCO Women in Sci. award, 2003. Fellow: AAAS, ASME (Yeram S. Touloukian award 2006), Am. Phys. Soc., Internat. Assn. Properties Water and Steam (hon.); mem.: AIChE, Assn. Women in Sci., Royal Holland Soc. of Scis. and Humanities, Dutch Phys. Soc., Netherlands Royal Acad. Arts and Sci. (corr.), European Phys. Soc., Nat. Acad. Engring., Nat. Acad. Sci., Cosmos Club. Office: Phys & Chem Properties Div Nat Inst Stds & Tech 100 Bureau Dr Stop 8380 Gaithersburg MD 20899-8380 Office Phone: 301-975-2463. Business E-Mail: johanna.sengers@nist.gov.

SENGUPTA, CHAITALI, computer engineer; BS in Tech., Indian Inst. Tech., Kharagpur, 1992; MS in Elec. and Computer Engrng., Rice U., 1995, PhD in Elec. and Computer Engring., 1999. Sr. mem. tech. staff Texas Instruments, Inc. Contbr. articles to profl. jours. Named one of Top 100 Young Innovators, MIT Tech. Review, 2004. Office: Texas Instuments Inc MS8723 12500 Texas Instruments Blvd Dallas TX 75243-4136

SENIOR MORANDI, GRACE ESTHER, mechanical engineer; b. Barranquilla, Colombia, S.Am., Nov. 9, 1940; arrived in U.S., 1966; d. Jose Manuel Senior and Mercedes Alicia Simmonds de Senior; m. Edward Raphael Morandi; children: Joseph Morandi, Alexander Morandi. Grad. in Mech. Engring., Archtl. Design, Antioquia U. Engr. Road and City Planning Dept., Barranquilla, Colombia, UNIAL Co., FMC Corp., Calif., Link Belt, Chgo., G.S. Blakeslee, Chgo., Smith and Assocs. Engrng. Co., Miami, Fla., 1972, Allied Leisure, Miami, Fla., Marshal Novak, Tampa, Fla., 1976; owner, adminstr. Disting. World, 1980—82; bridal cons. Main Even Bridal and Formalwear Salon; vendor coord. Hobard Kitchen Equip.; cosmetic cons. Dillard Stores; sales cons. Hispanic Yellow Pages, Tampa and Orlando, Fla. Exhibitions include include Colombia, Calif., Ill., Ga. and Fla., Represented in permanent collections U.S., Australia, Can., Colombia, Spain, Greece and India. Recipient numerous art awards. Republican. Avocations: piano, violin, tennis, golf, visual artist. Home Fax: 352-732-0170. E-mail: grete2214@aol.com.

SENIORS, PAULA MARIE, history professor, researcher; b. Cleve., Mar. 29, 1963; d. Audrey Proctor and Clarence Henry Seniors. BFA Dance, CCNY, 1985; MA Music, NYU, 1996; MA, PhD Ethnic Studies, U. Calif., San Diego, 2003. Tchg. asst. U. Calif., San Diego, 1998—2003; asst. prof. African Am. studies Coll. NJ, 2005—. Bd. mem. African and African-Am. Studies Rsch. project, San Diego; mem. book award com. Assn. Black Women Historians, Lansing, Mich., 2004—; rschr. Bldg. Curriculum Focused on S.Am. and the Caribbean: United Negro Coll. Fund Spl. Programs, Fla. Meml. Coll., Washington, 2004—; com. mem., rschr. creation history maj. Fla. Meml. Coll., Miami, 2004—; rschr. San Diego Urban League; presenter at confs. Contbr. book manuscripts for profl. seminars. Facilitator, organizer Themes in African Am., U.S. History, and Contemporary Soc. Student Conf. Fla. Meml. Coll., Miami, 2003—. Thelma Hill Meml. Dance scholar, CCNY, 1982, fellow, Dept. Ethnic Studies, U. Calif. San Diego, 1998—2002. Mem.: Nat. Coun. for Black Studies, Am. Studies Assn., Assn. Black Women Historians (book award com. 2004—), Assn. Study African Am. Life, Am. Hist. Assn. Avocation: rollerblading. Personal E-mail: pseniors@comcast.net. E-mail: seniors@tcnj.edu.

SENNA, DOBORAH JEAN, psychology professor; b. Sacramento, Feb. 11, 1950; d. Gloria Marquette-Senna. MS in Counseling, Calif. State U., Sacramento, 1990. Exec. dir. Transitional Living & Cmty. Support, Sacramento, 1987—90; prof. psychology Am. River Coll., 1990—. Tv host Sacramento City Unified Sch. Dist., 1984—88; radio host KGNR AM Radio; commr. Human Rights and Fair Housing Commn., 1990—92; mem land use com. Sacramento City Coun., 1991—. Recipient Instr. Yr., Am. River Coll., 1995, Patrons Chair award, Patrons Am. River Coll., 2000. Mem.: Am. Fedn. Tchrs., ACA, Nat. Assn. Alcoholism and Drug Abuse Counselors, Calif. Assn. Drug and Alcohol Counselors. Avocations: travel, cooking, collecting fine wines, bicycling. Office: American River College 4700 College Oak Drive Sacramento CA 95841 Office Phone: 916-484-8119. Office Fax: 916-484-8519. Business E-Mail: sennad@arc.losrios.edu.

SENNETT, NANCY J., lawyer; b. Milw., Nov. 26, 1951; BS in English & comm. arts with honors, U. Wis., 1973; JD cum laude, Northwestern U., 1979. Bar: Wis. 1979. With Foley & Lardner LLP, Milw., 1979—, chair securities litig. practice group, mng. ptnr. Milw. office. Chair merit selection com. reappointment magistrate judges Ea. Dist. Wis. Notes and comments editor Northwestern U. Law Rev., 1978-79. Active Jr. Achievement. Mem.: ABA (securities litig. com.), Securities Industry Assn. (compliance & legal divsn.), State Wis. Bar Assn., Milw. Bar Assn. (Lawyer Year 2003), ABCD, Inc. (bd. dirs.), Betty Brinn Children's Mus. (founding bd. dirs.), Greater Milw. Com., Tempo & Rotary, U. Wis. Alumni Assn. (bd. dirs., Distinguished Alumni Award 2003). Office: Foley & Lardner LLP US Bank Ctr 777 E Wisconsin Ave Milwaukee WI 53202-5367 Office Phone: 414-297-5522. Business E-Mail: nsennett@foley.com.

SENNETT, PATRICIA M., artist, educator; b. Pitts., May 1, 1934; d. Nikola L. and Mary C. (Stefanac) Knezevich; m. Arthur Hugh Sennett; children: Michael Sean, Susan Hope Sennett Paperno, Peter Hugh. Student, Carnegie-Mellon U.; BS in Art Edn., Edinboro U., 1956; postgrad., SUNY, Potsdam; MFA, Rochester Inst. Tech., 1970. Art tchr. Moorestown (N.J.) Pub. Schs., 1956—57, Hammondsport (N.Y.) C.S., 1958—59, Haverling Cen. Sch., Bath, NY, 1959—60, Campus Sch., State U. Coll., Potsdam, NY, 1963—64; faculty art dept. St. Lawrence C.S., Brasher Falls, NY, 1964—95; adj. instr. SUC, Potsdam, 1995—96; instr. winter classes Jekyll Island, Ga. Art Assn., 1997—2006; instr. summer classes Handweaving Mus. and Arts Ctr., Clayton, NY, 2001—05. Condr. workshops in field. Represented in permanent collections Carnegie-Mellon U., Pitts., St. Lawrence U., Canton, N.Y., SUNY, Potsdam, Clarkson Coll., Rochester Inst. Tech., St. Lawrence Nat. Bank, Potsdam, Canton, N.Y., Kraft, Inc., North Lawrence, N.Y., one-woman shows include Warren Meml. Libr., Friends Gibson Gallery, 1990, Friends Gibson Gallery, SUNY, 1993, two-person show, Fox-Richmond Gallery, Moulinette Gallery, exhibitions include Massena Artists' Assn., 1990, 1991, 1992, 1992, 1995, North Country Regional, 1990, 1991, Lake Placid Ctr. for the Arts, exhibited in group shows at Friends Gibson Gallery, 1990, 1991, Massena Artists' Assn., 1994, Canton Gallery, 1994, exhibitions include North Country Regional, 1995, 1996, 1997, 1998, 2000, 2001, 2002, 2005, 2003, 2006, Goodyear GAllery, Creative Spirit Gallery, Potsdam, NY. Recipient Disting Alumna award, Edinboro U., Excellence in Tchg. award, St. Lawrence C.S., Brasher Falls. Mem.: Friends Hist. Jekyll Island, Jekyll Island Arts Assn., Inc., Friends Gibson Gallery (past pres., v.p., bd. dirs.). Home (Winter): 554 Old Plantation Rd Jekyll Island GA 31527

SENSENICH, ILA JEANNE, judge; b. Pitts., Mar. 6, 1939; d. Louis E. and Evelyn Margaret S. BA, Westminster Coll., 1961; JD, Dickinson Sch. Law, 1964, JD (hon.), 1994. Bar: Pa. 1964. Assoc. Stewart, Belden, Sensenich and Harrington, Greensburg, Pa., 1964-70; asst. pub. defender Westmoreland (Pa.) County, 1970-71; U.S. magistrate judge We. Dist. Pa., Pitts., 1971—. Adj. prof. law Duquesne U., 1982-87. Author: Compendium of the Law of Prisoner's Rights, 1979; contbr. articles to profl. jour. Vis. fellow Daniel & Florence Guggenheim program in criminal justice Yale Law Sch., 1976-77. Mem. ABA, Fed. Magistrate Judges Assn. (sec. 1979-81, 88-89, treas. 1989-90, 2d v.p. 1990-91, pres.-elect 1992-93, pres. 1993-94), Pa. Bar Assn. (commn. on women in the profession 1998—), Nat. Assn. Women Judges, Westmoreland County Bar Assn., Allegheny County Bar Assn. (fed. ct. sect., com. women in law), Womens Bar Assn. We. Pa., Am. Judicature Soc. Democrat. Presbyterian. Avocations: skiing, sailing, bicycling, classical music, cooking. Office: US PO and Courthouse 3d Fl Pittsburgh PA 15219 Office Phone: 412-208-7480.

SENTENNE, JUSTINE, corporate ombudsman consultant; b. Montreal, Que., Can. d. Paul Emile and Irene Genevieve (Laliberte) Sentenne. MBA, U. Que., Montreal, 1993; postgrad., McGill U., Ecole Nat. d'Adminstrn. Publique, 1989—91. Fin. analyst, assoc. mgr. portfolio Bush Assocs., Montreal, 1970-82; city councillor, mem. exec. com. City of Montreal and Montreal Urban Com., 1978-82; adminstrv. asst. Montreal Conv. Ctr., 1983; dir. sponsorship Ctrl. Com. for Montreal Papal Visit, 1984; dir. pub. rels. Coopers & Lybrand, Montreal, 1985-87; exec. dir. Que. Heart Found., 1987-89; corp. ombudsman Hydro-Que, Montreal, 1991—. Tchr. DSA program Concordia U.; mem. jury John Labatt Ltd., London, 1982—86. V.p., bd. dirs. Armand Frappier Found., Canada, Chateau Dufresne Mus. Decorative Arts, Montreal, 1985—90; chmn. bd. dirs. Wilfrid Pelletier Found., Montreal, 1986—91; bd. govs. Youth and Music Can., Montreal, 1981—86; chmn. bd. dirs. Women's Ctr., Montreal, 1986—88, Vol. Bur. Montreal, 1986—87; bd. dirs. Palais des Congres de Montreal, 1981—89, Port of Montreal, 1983—84, Can. Ctr. Eucumenism, Montreal, 1968—85, 2006—, Montreal Diet Dispensary, 1989—2001, treas., 1996; bd. mgmt. Saidye Bronfman Ctr. Arts, 1994—99; Notre Dame de Grace v.p. riding assn. Liberal Party of Can., chairperson women's commn., 2000—; mem. exec. com. Ville Marie Liberl Party of Can.; bd. dirs. Pathways to Faith, 1990—2000. Named Career Woman of the Yr., Sullivan Bus. Coll., 1979; recipient Silver medal, ville de Paris, 1981, Women's Kansas City Assn. Internat. Rels. and Trade medal, 1982. Fellow: Montreal Soc. Investment Analysts, Inst. Fin. Analysts, Fin. Analysts Fedn. N.Y.; mem.: Health and Welfare Svcs. Ctr. (Cr. Santé Svcs. Sociaux) Cavendish (chair, bd. dirs. 2004—, chair bd. dirs. 2004—06), Internat. Ombudsman Assn. (bd. dirs. 1996—99, 2000—03, founding mem. Forum of Can. Ombudsmen, bd. dirs. 2001—, sec.). Roman Catholic.

SENTER, MERILYN P(ATRICIA), former state legislator, freelance/self-employed reporter; b. Haverhill, Mass., Mar. 17, 1935; d. Paul Barton and Mary Etta (Herrin) Staples; m. Donald Neil Senter, Apr. 23, 1960; children: Karen Anne Senter, Brian Neil. Grad., McIntosh Bus. Coll., 1955. Sec. F.S. Hamlin Ins. Agy., Haverhill, Mass., 1955-60; free lance reporter Plaistow-Hampstead News, Rockingham county newspapers, Exeter and Stratham, N.H., 1970-89; mem. N.H. Gen. Ct., 1988-96. Mem. Hwy. Safety Com., Plaistow, N.H., 1976-2005; bd. dirs. Region 10 Commn. Support Svcs. Inc., Atkinson, N.H., 1982-88, 2003-; chmn. Plaistow Area Transit Adv. Com., 1990-93, mem., 1994-; active Devel. Disabilities Coun., 1993-99; mem. Plaistow Bd. Selectmen, 1996-2005, chmn. 2001, 04; mem. Rockingham Planning Commn., 1994-; chmn., 2000-01; bd. dirs. Greater Salem/Derry Regional Transp. Coun., 2000—, chmn. bd., 2006. Named Woman of Yr., N.H. Bus. and Profl. Women, 1983, Nat. Grange Citizen of Yr., 1992. Republican. Avocation: nature. Home and Office: 11 Maple Ave Plaistow NH 03865-2221 E-mail: mse1056673@aol.com.

SEPCIE, CHRISTINE, secondary school educator; b. SI, NY, Apr. 19, 1978; d. Santanella Sepcie; m. Jereme Conti, Apr. 24, 2004. BA in History, Montclair State U., Upper Montclair, N.J., 2000; MA of Tchg. in History, Rutgers U., Newark, N.J., 2005. Tchr. Verona H.S., NJ, 2000—. Academic bowl adviser Verona H.S., NJ, 2002—, varsity girls volleyball coach, 2004—. Team capt. Relay Life Am. Cancer Soc., West Orange, NJ, 2006. Mem.: Nat. Coun. Social Studies. Roman Catholic. Avocations: travel, skiing. Office: Verona HS 151 Fairview Ave Verona NJ 07044 Office Phone: 973-239-3300. E-mail: sepcie97@hotmail.com.

SEPLOWIN, JUDITH, cantor; d. Benjamin and Marian Seplowin; m. Mark H. Kalish, Oct. 27, 1996; 1 child, Jessica L. Kalish. M Sacred Music, Hebrew Union College-Jewish Inst. of Religion Sch. of Sacred Music, NYC, 1995. Cantorial investiture Hebrew Union Coll. - Jewish Inst. of Religion, 1995. Cantor Temple - Congregation Shomer Emunim, Sylvania, Ohio, 1995—2000, Temple Beth-El, Providence, 2000—. Mem.: Am. Conf. Cantors. Jewish. Avocations: music, travel, theater. Office Phone: 401-331-6070.

SEPULVEDA, SONJA MARIAN ATKINSON, choral director, accompanist; b. Lancaster, S.C., May 15, 1952; d. Leo Laten and Mary Lou Hatfield Atkinson; m. Juan Pablo Sepulveda, June 10, 1972; children: Dru Adrian, Brys Kristofer. MusB in Edn., Winthrop U., Rock Hill, S.C., 1974; MusM in Choral Conducting, Winthrop U., 1975; D in Mus. Arts, U. S.C. Cert. tchr. music edn., choral edn. S.C., 1975. Choral dir. Wilder Fine Arts and Elem. Sch., Sumter, SC, 1975—81, Sumter H.S., SC, 1981—99, Clarendon Sch. Dist. 1, Summerton, SC, 2000—02, DuBose Mid. Sch., Summerville, SC, 2002—; condr. Carolina Alive and Renaissance Singers of U. S.C., 2005—. Choral dir. Palmetto Choirs, Sumter, 2000—; choral dir. and organist St. John Meth. Ch., Sumter, 2002—; dance tchr. Freed Spirits Dance Co., Sumter, 1979—89; piano tchr., Sumter, 1975—81; music edn. tchr. U. S.C., Sumter, 1979—83; choral dir. First Presbyn. Ch., Sumter, 1985—2001, Shaw Heights Bapt. Ch., Sumter, SC, 1978—81, Crosswell Bapt. Ch., Sumter, 1965—78. Composer: (musical) Robin Hood. Named SC. Outstanding Educator of the Yr., Jaycees, 1987, Tchr. of the Yr., Wilder Elem. Sch., 1981; recipient Ivey Reuben Edn. award, NAACP, 1990, Paul Harris fellow, Rotary Internat., 1992. Mem.: PTA (life), Music Educators Nat. Conf. (chmn. S.C. all state com. 1994—98), Am. Choral Dirs. Assn. (jazz choir chmn. S.C. 1995—96), Delta Kappa Gamma (music chmn. 1991—2002). R-Conservative. Presbyterian. Achievements include Choral Director for mini seriesNorth and South; Singer in the Robert Shaw Festival Chorus, 1991-1997; Solo performance at the Lincoln Center; Montreat Chamber Singer, 1988-2001; Singer in the National American Choral Directors Multicultural Choir, 2001; Solo performance for the National Television in Mexico. Avocations: travel, bicycling. Home: 618 Antlers Dr Sumter SC 29150 Office: U SC Sch Music Columbia SC 29208 Personal E-mail: sonjasepulveda@hotmail.com.

SEREBRENNIKOVA, EMILIYA, musician, educator; b. Kharkov, Ukraine, Sept. 27, 1944; came to the U.S., 1992; m. Vladimir Resnikovsky, Oct. 11, 1980 (div. Nov. 1994); m. Boris Zatulovsky, July 27, 1996. MA, St. Petersburg Conservatory, 1968, PhD, 1973. Cert. artist, prof. Concert pianist, piano tchr., San Francisco, 1992—. Mem. Nat. Assn. Profl. Music Tchrs., No. Calif. Fortnightly Music Club, Calif. Music Tchrs. Assn. Home: 255 S Rengstorff Ave Apt 67 Mountain View CA 94040-1738

SERENA, MONIQUE, apparel executive; Former exec. v.p. Rocawear Juniors; former v.p. JLO by Jennifer Lopez; former v.p. sales, missy div. Gloria Vanderbilt; pres. ABS Jeans, 2005—. Office: ABS 1231 Long Beach Ave Los Angeles CA 90021

SERENSON, LYNN ANN, mathematics educator; d. Roy William and Marie Elizabeth Eden; m. Peter Martin Serenson, Aug. 3, 1975; children: Traci Lynn, Heather Lisa. BSc, Ctrl. Mich. U., Mt. Pleasant, 1974; M in Curriculum Edn., Oakland U., Rochester, Mich., 1979. Tchr. math. Novi Cmty. Schs., Mich., 1974—. Recipient Edith Slyth award, Am. Math. Coun., 2006. Mem.: Mich. Assn. Mid. Sch. Educations, Detroit Area Coun. Tchrs. Math. (v.p. 1992—94), Mich. Coun. Tchrs. Math. (h.s. proficiency test bd.), Nat. Coun. Tchrs. Math. Catholic. Avocations: reading, travel, swimming, racquetball, jet ski. Home: 3572 Loon Lake Rd Wixom MI 48393 Office: Novi Middle Sch 49000 11 Mile Novi MI 48374 Office Phone: 248-449-1600.

SERGESKETTER, SARAH KAY KUNTZ, elementary school educator; d. George Lester and Kathryn Shearer Kuntz; m. Dan Lee Sergesketter, Feb. 22, 1954. BS in Music Edn., Lebanon Valley Coll., Annville, Pa., 1974; M in Music Edn., Ind. U., Bloomington, 1978. Music tchr. grades 5-8 Pine Grove Middle Sch., Pa., 1974—79; elem. vocal music tchr. grades K-6 North Spencer County Schs., 1979—, Lincoln Trail, Lamar, Ind., Chrisney Elem., Ind. Organist, choir dir. Trinity United Ch. of Christ, Jasper, Ind., 1982—. Mem.: Ind. Choral Dirs. Assn. (area 7 rep.), Ind. Music Educators Assn., Ind. State Tchrs. Assn., Philharmonic Club (libr., sec.), Alpha Delta Kappa (Beta Gamma chpt.).

SERIDO, JOYCE, psychologist, researcher; b. Plainfield, N.J., May 13, 1953; d. Mary Ann Gibriano and John Carmen Serido; m. Barry Edward Runyon, Jan. 1, 1985; 1 child, Evan Tyler Runyon. BA, Rutgers U., 1971—75; MBA, Seton Hall U., 1976—81; MS, U. Ariz., 1999—2001, PhD, 2001—03. Programmer First Nat. State Bank, Newark, 1975—76; programmer/analyst A T & T, Piscataway, NJ, 1976—83; sr. ptnr. CSC Cons., Roseland, 1983—91; mng. ptnr. Egal Inc., Milford, 1991—94; pres. Methods & Solutions, Tucson, Ariz., 1994—98; project mgr. Sunquest Info. Sys., Tucson, 1998—2000; post-doctoral assoc. Cornell U., Ithaca, NY, 2004—05; rsch. scientist U. Ariz., 2005—. Author: (jour. article) Chronic Stressors and Daily Hassles: Unique and Interactive Relationships with Psychological Distress. Recipient Tribute to Women and Industry, YWCA, 1990; grantee Paolucci Rsch. grant, Kappa Omicron Nu / W. K. Kellogg Found., 2002; scholar Travel scholarship, APA, 2001, Ruth R. Cowden scholarship, U. Ariz., 2003. Mem.: AAUW (assoc.), Gerontol. Soc. Am. (assoc.), Am. Psychol. Assn. (assoc.), Nat. Coun. Family Rels. (assoc.). Avocations: hiking, travel, dance. Office: Univ Arizona PO Box 210033 Tucson AZ 85712-0033 Office Phone: 520-621-7127. Office Fax: 520-621-3401. Personal E-mail: jserido@email.arizona.edu, joyceserido@hotmail.com.

SERLIN, MARSHA, waste management service administrator; CEO/pres. Ill. United Scrap Metal, Cicero, 1978—. Recipient Nat. Small Bus. Subcontractor Yr. award, U.S. Small Bus. Adminstrn., 1996, Mass. Mut.-Nat. Family Bus. of Yr. award, Ernst and Young's Entrepreneur of Yr. award, Outstanding Recycling Bus. award Ill. Recycling Assn.; named Grant Thorton Exec. Woman of Yr.; inductee Jr. Achievement Chgo. Bus. Hall of Fame. Office: United Scrap Metal Inc 1545 S Cicero Ave Chicago IL 60804-1529

SERNA, JAYNE ELIZABETH, history educator; d. James Lynn and Cindy Lou Sours; m. Gabriel Paul Serna, Aug. 1, 1987. BA, Angelo State U., San Angelo, Tex., 1989; MA, Tex. State U., San Marcos, 2003. Cert. tchr. Tex. Edn. Agy., 1989. English instr. Austin ISD, Tex., 1990—93; AP history instr. Cedar Pk. High Sch./Leander ISD, Tex., 1993—; adj. assoc. prof. of history Austin C.C., Tex., 2003—. Coll. bd./AP U.S. history exam grader Ednl. Testing Svc./Coll. Bd., Princeton, NJ, 1999—. Sec. Leander Parks and Recreation Adv. Bd., Tex., 1999—2006; founder and pres. Leander Youth Soccer Assn., 2003—06. Named Educator of Distinction, Nat. Soc. of H.S. Scholars, 2005—06; fellow James Madison Meml. fellow, James Madison Meml. Fellowship Found., 1999; scholar Profl. Devel. scholar, ATPE Region 13, 2002, NEH, 2005. Mem.: Leander Assn. Profl. Educators (pres. 1995—2006), Assn. of Tex. Profl. Educators (region 13 treas. 2003—06, region treas., local pres., Profl. Educator of the Yr. 2005—06). Office: Cedar Park High School 2150 Cypress Creek Rd Cedar Park TX 78613 Office Phone: 512-435-8538. E-mail: jayne.serna@leanderisd.org.

SEROOGY, LOUISE AMY, medical/surgical nurse; b. Campbellsport, Wis., Dec. 30, 1957; d. Joseph and Ella (Metzler) Koch; m. Richard J. Seroogy, July 31, 1993. BSN, Marian Coll., 1981. Staff and charge nurse St. Vincent Hosp., Green Bay, Wis., 1981-86, asst. dir. orthopedic/urology unit, 1986—97, team leader orthop., neurology unit, 1998—2002, staff and charge nurse orthop., neurology unit, 2002—. Mem. Nat. Assn. Orthopaedic Nurses (cert., v.p. Green Bay chpt. 1985, pres. 1986, 87).

SEROTA, SUSAN PERLSTADT, lawyer, educator; b. Chgo., Sept. 10, 1945; d. Sidney Morris and Mildred (Penn) Perlstadt; m. James Ian Serota, May 7, 1972; children: Daniel Louis, Jonathan Mark. AB, U. Mich., 1967; JD, NYU, 1971. Bar: Ill. 1971, DC 1972, NY 1981, US Dist. Ct. (no. dist.) Ill. 1971, US Dist. Ct. (so. dist.) NY 1981, US Dist. Ct. (ea. dist.) NY 1985, US Ct. Claims 1972, US Tax Ct. 1972, US Ct. Appeals (DC cir.) 1972. Ptnr. Pillsbury Winthrop Shaw Pittman LLP, NYC, 1982—, ptnr., chmn. Exec. Compensation & Benefits practice, 2001—. Adj. prof. Sch. Law, Georgetown U., Washington, 1974-75; mem. faculty Practicing Law Inst., NYC, 1983—. Editor: ERISA Fiduciary Law, 1995, Supplement, 2003; assoc. editor Exec. Compensation Jour., 1973—75, dep. editor Tax Mgmt., Estate and Gift Taxation and Exec. Compensation, 1973—75, mem. editl. adv. bd. Benefits Law Jour., 1973—, Tax Mgmt. Compensation Jour., 1993—, mem. bd. editors ERISA and Benefits Law Jour., 1992—; contbr. articles to profl. jours. Fellow: Am. Coll. of Employee Benefits Counsel (pres. 2004—05, dir., charter fellow), Am. Coll. Tax Counsel (regent 1999—2005); mem.: ABA (chmn. joint com. employee benefits 1987—88, chmn. com. employee benefits 1991—92, vice-chair taxation sect. 1999—2001, chair taxation sect. 2006—), Am. Bar Retirement Assn. (dir. 1994—2004, pres. 1999—2000), NY State Bar Assn. (exec. com. tax sect. 1988—92), Internat. Pension and Employee Benefit Lawyers Assn. (co-chair 1993—95). Democrat. Office: Pillsbury Winthrop Shaw Pittman 1540 Broadway New York NY 10036 Office Fax: 212-858-1500. Business E-Mail: susan.serota@pillsburylaw.com.

SERRAO, SUSAN, social studies educator; children: Jeffrey, Bryan, Graigory. BA, Trenton State Coll., NJ, 1973. Tchr. Intermediate West, Toms River, NJ, 1991—2003, Toms River H.S. North, 2003—. Pres. Laurel Twig - Hosp. Aux., Toms River, 1985—91; founder, pres. Open Arms-Charity Abused Children, 1986—93. Mem.: NJ Edn. Assn., Toms River Investment Ptnrs. (pres. 2001—03). Home: 1245 Old Freehold Rd Toms River NJ 08753 Office: Toms River High School North Old Freehold Road Toms River NJ 08753 Office Phone: 732-505-5705.

SERSTOCK, DORIS SHAY, retired microbiologist, civic worker, educator; b. Mitchell, SD, June 13, 1926; d. Elmer Howard and Hattie (Christopher) Shay; m. Ellsworth I. Serstock, Aug. 30, 1952; children: Barbara Anne, Robert Ellsworth, Mark Douglas. BA, Augustana Coll., 1947; postgrad., U. Minn., 1966-67, Duke U., summer 1969, Communicable Disease Ctr., Atlanta, 1972. Bacteriologist Civil Svc., S.D., Colo., Mo., 1947-52; rsch. bacteriologist U. Minn., 1952-53; clin. bacteriologist Dr. Lufkin's Lab., 1954-55; chief technologist St. Paul Blood Bank of ARC, 1959-65; microbiologist in charge mycology lab. VA Hosp., Mpls., 1968-93; ret. Instr. Coll. Med. Scis., U. Minn., 1970-79, asst. prof. Coll. Lab. Medicine and Pathology, 1979-93. Contbr. articles to profl. jours. Mem. Richfield Planning Commn., 1965-71, sec., 1968-71; extended ministries commn. Wood Lake Luth. Ch., Richfield, 1993-94; rep. religious coun. Mall Am., Bloomington, Minn., 1993-94; chief nursery caregiver Christ the King Luth. Ch., Bloomington, 1994-99, Hope Presbyn. Ch., Richfield, Minn., 1994-2003; mem. Rep. Presdl. Task Force, Nat. Rep. Senatorial Com., 1997. Fellow Augusta Coll.; named to Exec. and Profl. Hall of Fame; recipient Alumni Achievement award Augustana Coll., 1977, Superior Performance award VA Hosp., 1978, 82, Cert. of Recognition, 1988, Golden Spore awards Mycology Observer, 1985, 87, Congl. Order of Merit Nat. Rep. Congl. Com., 2003; name engraved on founders' wall Ronald Reagan Rep. Ctr., 2000; named Minn. Rep. of Yr. Nat. Rep. Congl. Com., 2003; recipient Congl. Order Merit, NRCC, 2005. Mem. Richfield Women's Garden Club (pres. 1959), Wild Flower Garden (chmn. 1961). Republican. Home: 7201 Portland Ave Minneapolis MN 55423-3218

SERVANTEZ, MELINDA, elementary school educator; d. Sixto Ojeda and Bertha Bond. BS in Interdisciplinary Studies, SW Tex. State U., 1995. Elem., ESL, spl. edn., early childhood tchr. Tex. Kindergarten tchr. Del Valle Ind. Sch. Dist., Austin, 1996—, reading intervention tchr., 2000—03, first grade tchr., 2003—04, fifth grade tchr., 2004—05. Kindergarten cons. Allison Elem. Sch., Austin Ind. Sch. Dist., 2000; fellowship tchr. U. Tex., Austin. Office: Del Valle Ind Sch Dist 6910 East William Cannon Austin TX 78747 Office Phone: 512-386-3550. Personal E-mail: m_servantez@hotmail.com.

SERVEDIO, MARIA R., science educator; b. Nova Scotia, Canada; d. Frank J. and Margaret M. Servedio. BA, Harvard U., 1993; PhD, U. Tex., Austin, 1998. Lectr. Cornell U., Ithaca, NY, 1998—99; postdoctoral scholar U. Calif., Davis, 1999—2001, San Diego, 2001—02; asst. prof. U. NC, Chapel Hill, 2002—. Contbr. articles various profl. jours. Recipient Young Investigators award, Am. Soc. Naturaslists, 2000; Rsch. grant, NSF, 2001-2005. Mem.: Soc. Study Evolution. Office Phone: 919-843-2692.

SERVIDIO, BARBARA J., mathematics educator, science educator; b. Cleve., Apr. 10, 1950; d. Anthony G. and Angela B. Laurenzi; m. Carmine F. Servidio, July 1, 1978 (dec. May 1998); children: Carmine R., John A. BA in Math. and Physics, Kent State U., 1972; MS in Physics, Fairleigh Dickinson U., 1975. Math tchr. Caldwell (NJ) Bd. Edn., 1972—79; math and sci. tchr. Stuart Country Day Sch., Princeton, 1988—90, Montgomery Bd. Edn., Skillman, 1990—, math supr. Trainer assessors for nat. bd. cert. of tchrs. Ednl. Testing Svc., Princeton, 1995—. Mem.: NEA, Assn. Math. Tchrs. NJ, NJ Edn. Assn., Delta Kappa Gamma (treas. 1996—97).

SESIN, MARIA CARMEN, psychologist, researcher; b. Havana, Cuba, June 14, 1954; d. Cecilio Sesin and Balbina Vazquez; 1 child, Martin Manzanares-Sesin. BS, CUNY, 1979; MA, Columbia U., N.Y.C., 1981; PhD, Yeshiva U., N.Y.C., 1998. Tchr. gifted and talented Grants Mcpl. Sch., Grants, N.Mex., 1981—82; elem. tchr. N.Y.C. Bd. Edn., 1982—85; psychologist Luth. Med. Ctr., N.Y.C., 1988—. Psychologist Behavioral Medicine Assocs., N.Y.C., 2004—; sole proprietor The Healing Arts, N.Y.C., 2004—; presenter workshops on group therapy. Contbr. articles to profl. jours. Mem.: APA. Avocations: piano, poetry. Office: Lutheran Medical Ctr Sunset Park Mental Health Ctr 514 49th St Brooklyn NY 11220 Office Phone: 718-437-5229.

SESLAR, TANYA L., music educator; Tchr. Kenton Elem., Aurora, Colo., 1995—. Violin outreach tchr. Colo. Youth Symphony, Aurora, 2000—. Office: Kenton Elem 1255 Kenton Aurora CO 80010 Office Phone: 303-364-0947.

SESSIONS, BARBARA C., lawyer; b. St. Johns, Mich., Jan. 23, 1961; d. John C. and Patricia H. (England) Cary; m. Rex L. Sessions, Oct. 10, 1989; 1 child, Isabel P. BA in English, U. Mich., 1983; JD, DePaul U., 1986. Bar: Ill. Comml. litigator Hinshaw & Culbertson, Chgo., 1986-90; sr. acct. exec. Edelman Pub. Rels. Worldwide, N.Y.C., 1990-91; mgr. mktg. and comms. Skadden, Arps, Slate, Meagher & Flom, N.Y.C., 1991-94; ptnr., dir. bus. devel. mktg. and planning Winston & Strawn LLP, Chgo., 1994—. Mem. Jr. League, N.Y.C, 1990-94, Chgo., 1989-99. Mem. Law Mktg. Assn. (pres., pres-elect 1998, bd. dirs. 1996—), Info. Innovators (editl. bd.). Office: Winston & Strawn LLP 35 W Wacker Dr Chicago IL 60601-9703 Fax: 312-558-5700. Office Phone: 312-558-5834. E-mail: bsessions@winston.com.

SESSIONS, BETTYE JEAN, humanities educator; b. Jacksonville, FL, Jan. 29, 1934; d. John Henry and Willene Porter Hayes; m. Malcolm G.A. Sessions, July 7, 1956; children: Sabrina F., Malcolm G.A. II, Byron Craig. BA, Fla. A&M U., 1956; MAT, Jacksonville U., 1967. Tchr. English, humanities Duval County Pub. Schs., Jacksonville, Fla., 1957—72; prof. humanities Fla. C.C., Jacksonville, Fla., 1972—90; news corr. Fla. Times - Jacksonville Jour., 1981—86; profl. writer, author and poet Jean-Aubrey Ideas, Inc., Jacksonville, 1985—2001.

SESSIONS, JOAN T., director, educator; d. David Pyper and Rose Smith Thomas; children: Linda Ann Hadley, Gina Louise. BS in Edn., Kent State U., 1962; postgrad., U. Akron, 1970; MA in Edn. with honors, Ohio State U., 1966; PhD in Edn., Kent State U., 1975; postgrad., U. Chgo., 1996, St. Michael's Coll., Burlington, Vt., 1998. Elementary Principal's Provisional State of Ohio, 1966, cert. elem. tchr., elem. prin. Ohio. Rsch. asst. Ohio State U., 1965—66; tchr. pub. schs., Wooster, Ohio, 1962—64, Elyria City Schs., 1966—67; dir. of info. systems, planning quality assurance Ctr. for Human Services, Cleve., 1974—91; program specialist UN Volunteers, Beijing, 1991—96; tutoring program dir. U. of Chgo., 1998—; Headstart dir. Elyria City Schools, 1967—70, elem. prin. Ohio, 1970—72; tchg. fellow Kans. State U., 1972—73; rsch. assoc. Bur. Ednl. Rsch., 1973—74; rsch. assoc. to dir. evaluation Ctr. for Human Svcs., Cleve., 1974—91; instr. John Carroll U., 1985—90; vol. UN, Beijing; lang. evaluation cons. Beijing Diplomatic Svc. Grad. sch. lectr. John Carroll U., Cleve., 1987—89; grad. tchg. fellow Kent State U., 1972—74; cons. and lectr. in field; tutor program dir., mgr. VISTA and AmeriCorps, 1999—2005; primary literacy tutoring cons. City Yr. Chgo., 2001—05; USI primary literacy tutor program tng. materials evaluation methodology dir. Dept. Neighborhood Schs., U. Chgo., 2006—. Pres. Ohio City Redevelopment Assn., Cleve., 1986—91; treas., pres., deacon, trustee and elder Fairmont Presbyn. Ch.; bd. dirs. 5000 S Cornell Condominium Assn., 2001—, Literacy Vols. of Ill. Recipient Descone award, Fairmond Frost Clare Ho., 1984, award, Luth. Med. Ctr. Women's Bd., 1988, Cmty. Svc. award, Mayor George Voinovich, City of Cleve., 1991, Moccasin award for cmty. svc., City Yr. Chgo., 2004; grantee, Cleve. Found., United Way of Cuyahoga County, Gund Found., Luth. Med. Ctr. Found., 1989, BP Am. Found., numerous others. Mem.: Wooster Edn. Assn., Ohio Fedn. Women, Wooster Jr. Women's Club. Avocations: collecting art, studying Chinese language and culture. Home: 5000 S Cornell #3A Chicago IL 60615 Office Phone: 773-834-3286. Office Fax: 773-702-2010. Personal E-mail: joansessions@comcast.net.

SESSIONS, JUDITH ANN, librarian, university library dean; b. Lubbock, Tex., Dec. 16, 1947; d. Earl Alva and Anna (Mayer) S. BA cum laude, Cen. Fla. U., 1970; MLS, Fla. State U., 1971; postgrad., Am. U., 1980, George Washington U., 1983. Head libr. U. S.C., Salkehatchie, 1974-77; dir. Libr. and Learing Resources Ctr. Mt. Vernon Coll., Washington, 1977-82; planning and systems libr. George Washington U., Washington, 1981-82, asst. univ. libr. for adminstrn. svcs., acting head tech. svcs., 1982-84; univ. libr. Calif. State U., Chico, 1984-88; univ. libr., dean of libr. Miami U., Oxford, Ohio, 1988—. Cons. Space Planning, SC, 1976, DataPhase Implementation, Bowling Green U., 1982, TV News Study Ctr., George Washington U., 1981; asst. prof. dept. child devel. Mt. Vernon Coll., 1978—81; mem., lectr. U.S.-China Libr. Exch. Del., 1986, 91; lectr., presenter in field; mem. coord. com. OhioLink Adv. Coun., 1995—2003, v.p., 1996—97, chair, 1998—2000; mem. gov. bd. OhioLink, exec. com., 1998—2001; mem. OCLC Users Coun., 1998—2001; convenor Pub. Acad. Libr. Group, 1999—2000; mem. OCLC Preservation Resources Interest Group, 1999—2001, chmn., 2001. Contbr. articles, book revs. to profl. jours. Trustee Christ Hosp., Cin., 1990-94, Deaconess Gamble Rsch. Ctr., Cin., 1990-94, OhioNet, 1990-94, treas. 1993; bd. dirs. Hamilton (Ohio) YWCA, 1994-98, pres., 1995-96, v.p., 1996-97, 97-98; mem. OCLC user's coun., 1998—; mem. steering com. Tri City Reading Initiative, 2002-03. Recipient award for outstanding contbn. D.C. Libr. Assn., 1979; rsch. grantee Mt. Vernon Coll., 1980; recipient Fulbright-Hayes Summer Travel fellowship to Czechoslovakia, 1991. Mem. ALA (Olofson award 1978, councillor-at-large policy making group 1981-94, coun. com. on coms. 1983-84, intellectual freedom com. 1984-88, directions and program rev. com. 1989-91, fin. and audit subcom. 1989-90, mem. exec. bd. 1989-94, mem. del. to Zimbabwe Internat. Book Fair 1997), Assn. Coll. and Rsch. Librs. (editorial bd. Coll. and Rsch. Librs. jour. 1979-84, nominations and appointments com. 1983-85, faculty status com. 1984-86), Libr. and Info. Tech. Assn. (chair legis. and regulation com. 1980-81), Libr. Adminstrn. and Mgmt. Assn. (bd. dirs. libr. orgn. and mgmt. sect. 1985-87), Calif. Inst. Librs. (v.p., pres. elect 1987-88), Mid-Atlantic Regional Libr. Fedn. (mem. exec. bd. 1982-84), Jr. Mems. Round Table (pres. 1981-82), Intellectual Freedom Round Table (sec. 1984-85), Freedom to Read Found. (trustee 1984-88, v.p. 1985-86, treas. 1986-87, pres. 1987-88), Rotary, Beta Phi Mu. Home: 45 Waters Way Hamilton OH 45013-6324 Office: Miami U Edgar W King Oxford OH 45056

SESTANOVICH, MOLLY BROWN, writer; b. Denver, Nov. 30, 1921; d. Ben Miller and Mary (McCord) Brown; m. Stephen Nicholas Sestanovich, July 9, 1949; children: Stephen, Mary, Robert Benjamin. Student, Fairmont Jr. Coll., 1939-41. Radio comml. writer Young & Rubicam Advt., N.Y.C. and Hollywood, Calif., 1941-47; radio scriptwriter Korean Broadcasting Co., Seoul, 1947-48; substitute tchr. County Sch. Bd., Montgomery County, Md., 1956-58; syndicated polit. columnist Lesher Newspapers, various locations, 1971-91; freelance polit. writer Moraga, Calif., 1991—. Active internat. women's orgns., Italy, Thailand, Singapore, Finland, Venezuela, 1949-70. Writer LWV, Diablo Valley, Calif., 1970, 91. Recipient prize for contbn. to cause of peace and justice Mt. Diablo Peace Ctr., 1989. Mem. Am. Fgn. Svc. Assn., Lamorinda Dem. Club (program chmn. 1985). Unitarian Universalist. Avocations: genealogy, gardening. Home: 15 Idlewood Ct Moraga CA 94556-1107 Personal E-mail: mollynsteve@cs.com.

SETASH, KATHLEEN DOUGLAS, music educator; b. Cleve., Apr. 28, 1957; d. James Nicholas and Mary Valeria Douglas; m. Mark Allen Setash, Apr. 8, 1989; children: Michael Andrew, Casey Marie. MusB Edn., Bowling Green State U., Ohio, 1979; MusM, Cath. U. Am., Washington, 1984. Kodaly cert. Cath. U., Washington, 1985, Orff cert. George Mason U., Va., 1998. Vocal music tchr. Toledo Public Schs., 1979—83, Alexandria City Pub. Schs., Va., 1984—99, Pennsbury Pub. Schs., Fallsington, Pa., 1999—. Nominee Tchr. of Yr., Douglas MacArthur Faculty, 1997. Mem.: Ctrl. NJ Am. Orff Assn. (v.p. 2006—). Avocation: running. Home: 1311 Chase Rd Newtown PA 18940 Office: Quarry Hill Elementary School 1625 Quarry Rd Yardley PA 19067 Office Phone: 215-321-2400. Personal E-mail: musiktchr@aol.com. Business E-Mail: ksetash@pennsbury.k12.pa.us.

SETHI, CHANDER MOHINI, gynecologist, obstetrician, consultant; b. Punjab, India, May 11, 1942; arrived in U.S., 1976; d. Bansi Lal and Shanti Kumari Sahni; m. Brahm D. Sethi, July 31, 1971; children: Rajiv, Manish. MBBS, Lady Harding U., Delhi, India, 1969; MD, Faculty Cook County Hosp., Chgo., 1980—83; physician ob-gyn. Harten Hosp., Tullanoma, Tenn., 1983—2005. Clin. instr. Harvard U., Brigham U., and Women's Hosp., Boston, 2006. Fellow: Royal Coll. Ob-gyns., Am. Coll. Ob-gyns. Home: Apt 501A 44 Washington St Brookline MA 02445-7104

SETLOW, JANE KELLOCK, biophysicist; b. NYC, Dec. 17, 1919; d. Harold A. and Alberta (Thompson) Kellock; m. Richard Setlow, June 6, 1941; children: Peter, Michael, Katherine, Charles. BA, Swarthmore Coll., 1940; PhD in Biophysics, Yale U., 1959. With dept. radiology Yale U., 1959-60; with biology div. Oak Ridge Nat. Lab., 1960-74; biophysicist Brookhaven Nat. Lab., Upton, N.Y., 1974—. Mem. recombinant DNA molecule program adv. com. NIH, chmn., 1978-2005. Editor: Genetic Engineering, Principles and Methods; mem. editl. bd. various jours.:; contbr. articles to profl. jours. Predoctoral fellow USPHS, 1957-59; postdoctoral fellow, 1960-62 Mem. Biophys. Soc. (pres. 1977-78), Am. Soc. Microbiology. Democrat. Home: 57 Valentine Rd Shoreham NY 11786-1243 Office: Biology Dept Brookhaven Nat Lab Upton NY 11973

SETLOW, NEVA DELIHAS, artist, research biologist; b. New Haven, Dec. 29, 1940; m. Richard Burton Setlow; children: Nicholas Delihas, Marcia Hermus, Cynthia DiGiacomo. BA, Empire State Coll., 1975. Rschr. Brookhaven Nat. Lab., Upton, NY, 1976—96, guest rschr., 2005—06. Exhibited in group shows at Guild Hall, East Hampton, 1985—2002, 2005—06, Ward Nasse Gallery, N.Y.C., 1993—97, Islip Art Mus., 1993, 1996—2000, Planetary Art Soc., Pasadena, Calif., 1997, Salon des Femmes, Southampton, 1997, Faber Biren Color Award Show, Stamford, Conn., 1997, 2001, Smithtown Arts Coun., 1998, Elaine Benson Gallery, Bridgehampton, N.Y., 1999, Broome St. Gallery, N.Y.C., 1999—2005, Islip Art Mus., 2000, Shelter Rock Art Gallery, Manhasset, N.Y., 2000, Gallery at Edison, Piqua, Ohio, 2001, Huntington Arts Coun., Melville, N.Y., 2001, Grounds for Sculpture, N.J., 2001, Binney and Smith Gallery, Bethlehem, Pa., 2002, East End Arts Coun. (Contact!), Riverhead, N.Y., 2003, Tex. A&M Coll., Station, Tex., 2004, J. Wayne Stark Galleries, Tex., 2004, Rosetta Stone Gallery, Juno, Fla., 2004, Silvermine Guild of Artists, New Canaan, Conn., 2005. Recipient Purchase prize, Berkshire Art Assn., Pittsfield, Mass., 1972, 25th Anniversary award, Silvermine Art Guild, New Canaan, Conn., 1972, Sculpture award, Huntington Twp. Art League, 1974, 1976, Painting award, North Shore Art Guild, 1996, Am. Icon - Outer Space award, Nat. Assoc. of Women Artists, 2001, Cleo Hartwig award, 2003, The Gretchen Richardson Meml. award, 2004, Kreindler Meml. award, 2005. Mem.: East End Arts Coun. (Honorable Mention 2005), Am. Soc. Contemporary Artists, Nat. Assn. Women Artists, Internat. Sculpture Ctr. Home and Office: 4 Beachland Ave East Quogue NY 11942-4941 Personal E-mail: setlow@optonline.net.

SETSER, CAROLE SUE, food scientist, educator; b. Warrenton, Mo., Aug. 26, 1940; d. Wesley August and Mary Elizabeth (Meine) Schulze; m. Donald Wayne Setser, June 2, 1969; children: Bradley Wayne, Kirk Wesley, Brett Donald. BS, U. Mo., 1962; MS, Cornell U., 1964; PhD, Kans. State U., 1971. Grad. asst. Cornell U., Ithaca, NY, 1962-64; instr. Kans. State U., Manhattan, 1964-72, asst. prof., 1974-81, assoc. prof., 1981-86, prof., 1986-2001, prof. emeritus, 2001—. Vis. prof. Bogazici U., Istanbul, Turkey, 2000—01. Recipient Rsch. Excellence award, Coll. of Human Ecology, Manhattan, 1990. Mem.: Inst. Food Techs. (chmn. sensory evaluation divsn. edn. com. 1989—92, continuing edn. com. 1992—95, sec. product devel. divsn. 1997—99, also other offices), Am. Assn. Cereal Chemists (assoc. editor 1989—93), Kappa Omicron Nu (Excellence for Rsch. award 1987), Sigma Xi, Phi Tau Sigma (Outstanding Food Scientist 1998), Gamma Sigma Delta, Phi Upsilon Omicron, Phi Kappa Phi (Scholar award 1998). Business E-Mail: setser@ksu.edu.

SETSER, PATRICIA A., music educator; b. Kansas City, Mo., June 29, 1951; d. Flo Daulton and George Sterling Waugh; m. Michael W. Setser, Sept. 9, 1972. MusB Edn., Ctrl. Mo. State U., 1973, MA in Music Edn., 1978. Cert.

tchr., life - music coord. K-12, history K-8 Mo., 1973. Coord. music North Kansas City Sch. Dist., 1996—; band dir. Winnetonka HS, Kansas City, 1983—. Guest condr., adjudicator Heart of Am. Wind Symphony, Mo., 1978—, musician, Mo., 2001—; musician, guest conductor Kansas City Wind Symphony, Shawnee Mission, Kans., 2002—. Condr. (music contest) St. Louis Music Festival (Grand Champions, 2001, 2005), Nat. Adjudicators Nat. Festival, Va. (Grand Champions, 2002), Chgo. Music Festival (Grand Champions, 2000); instr. (tchg.) Tchg. (Excellence in Tchg. Award, 1994); condr. (orch. condr.) State Contest (First Pl. Ratings), band condr. (conducting) State Music Contests (First Pl. Ratings - all years); composer: (entry level jazz for young band students) Musical composition. Bd. mem. Warrensburg Cmty. Band, Mo., 2001—. Named Disting. Music Alumnus, Ctrl. Mo. State U., 2005—06. Mem.: Mo. Music Educators Assn. (assoc.), Music Educators Nat. Conf. (assoc.), Am. Quarter Horse Assn. (assoc.), Epsilon Omega - Sigma Alpha Iota (assoc.; pres., v.p, sec. 1970—73, Sword of Honor - Leadership 1974). Avocations: antique automobiles, gardening, genealogy. Office: North Kansas City Sch Dist 1950 NE 46th St Kansas City MO 64116 E-mail: psetser@nkcsd.k12.mo.us.

SETTERLUND, TINA A.M., music educator; b. Belleville, Ill., Mar. 3, 1955; d. William L. and Elizabeth A. Marietta; m. D. Phillip Setterlund, Dec. 29, 1973 (div.); children: Reid, Lauren; m. Grady A. White, Dec. 21, 1992. AA, Belleville Area Coll., 1987; B in Music Edn., So. Ill. U., 1989. Music dir. St. John U. C.C., Mascoutah, Ill., 1971—; tchr. High Mt. Sch., Swansea, Ill., 1989—95; dir. vocal music Belleville (Ill.) East H.S., 1995—2005; pvt. practice vocal coach Belleville, 2005—. Dir. Belleville Philharm. Chorale, 1983—91; asst. dir., accompanist Masterworks Children's Chorale, Belleville, 1990—95; dir. Metro-East Cmty. Chorale, Belleville, 1991—94, Coca-Cola Choir, St. Louis, Olympic Torch Relay Festivities; music dir. St. John's U. Cmty. Coll., 1971—. Recipient Excellence in Tchg. award, So. Ill. Univ., 2003. Mem.: St. Clair County Music Dirs. Assn. (treas. 2004—05, v.p. 2005—), Music Educators Nat. Conf., Ill. Music Educators Assn., Pi Kappa Lambda. Avocations: interior decorating, reading, gardening, harp. Home: 57 W State Mascoutah IL 62258 Personal E-mail: tamsetterlund@yahoo.com.

SETTLES, JEANNE DOBSON, retired librarian; b. Covington, Tenn., Nov. 21, 1928; d. Garrett Edward and Lula Mai (Birmingham) Dobson; m. Andrew Settles, Dec. 26, 1948; children: Thomas E., Anthony Dobson. BS, Memphis State U., 1966, MEd, 1977. Cert. tchr., Tenn. Libr. Memphis City Schs., 1966—72, 1977—91; ret., 1991. Mem. Delta Kappa Gamma (treas.). Avocations: painting, writing, sewing, travel.

SETZER, ARLENE J., state representative, retired secondary school educator; b. Dayton, Ohio, Mar. 2, 1944; BS in Bus. Adminstrn., U. Dayton, 1966; MEd, Wright State U., 1973, postgrad. Tchr. bus. and computer applications Vandalia-Butler HS, 1967—2000; rep. Ohio State Ho. Reps., Columbus, 2000—. Mem. agr. and natural resources com. Ohio State Ho. Reps., chmn. edn. com., mem. ins. com. Mem. ins. rev. com. and state govt. com. City of Vandalia, 1998—2000; chair Vandalia-Butler Food Pantry Bldg. Fund; pres. Pres.'s Club of Vandalia, 1997—99; mem. Ednl. Trust Project, Advocates for People with Devel. Disabilities, Montgomery County Ednl. Advancement Dialogue; precinct capt. Montgomery County Rep. Party, mem. ctrl. com., exec. com.; mem. Vandalia City Coun., 1982—2000, vice-mayor, 1986—88, 1995—2000. Named Rep. Woman of Yr., 1997, 2001, 2003; recipient Clara Weisenborn award, 1999, Horace M. Huffman Jr. Svc. to Bicyclists award, Ohio Bicycle Fedn., 2001, Appreciation award, S.W. Ohio Hemophilia Found. and W. Ctrl. Ohio Hemophilia Ctr., 2002, Rep. of Yr. award, Ohio Coll. Rep. Fedn., 2003; Martha Holden Jennings scholar, 1983—84. Mem.: Sister Cities of Vadalia, Montgomery County Farm Bur., Inc., Montgomery County Cattlemen's Assn., Montgomery Agrl. Soc., Sr. Citizens of Vandalia-Butler, Miami Valley Mil. Affairs Assn., Vandalia-Butler (Ohio) Hist. Soc. (v.p. 2000), Rotary (hon.; Dist. 6670 dir. 1992—96, pres. 1994—95, Dist. 6670 scholarship com. 1997, Dist. 6670 bd. dirs., asst. dist. gov. 1998—2000, named to Hall of Fame). Republican. Office: Ohio State Ho of Reps 77 S High St 13th Fl Columbus OH 43215-6111

SEUBERT, LORI A., elementary school educator; d. Harry Marx Seubert Jr. and Ruth Janice Seubert. BA in English and Elem. Edn. cum laude, U. Toledo, 1981, MEd in Sci. and Early Childhood cum laude, 1990. Tchr. Franklin Sch., Toledo, 1985—90; NSF-funded Toledo Area Partnership in Edn: Support Tchrs. as Resources to Improve Elem. Sci. sci. support tchr. Toledo City Schs., U. Toledo, Bowling Green State U., 1998—2002; TAPESTRIES summer inst. educator Bowling Green State U., Ohio, 2000, U. Toledo, 1999—2002; tchr. Toledo City Schs., 2002—04; tchr., grade 5 Reynolds Sch., Toledo, 1990—. Young exptl. scientist tchr. intern Columbus's Ctr. Sci. and Industry, Ohio Coun. for Elem. Sch. Sci., 1989, workshop coord., 1990—93; edn. cons., Toledo, 1996—; Full Option Sci. Sys. cons. Delta Edn., Nashua, NH, 1999—. Author: (book) A Unit on Physics of Flight for Third Graders, 1990; co-author, editor: guide TAPESTRIES's K-6 Science Curriculum Alignment to Ohio Outcomes for Toledo City Schools, 2001. Recipient Outstanding K-3 Tchr. award, Toledo Assn. for Edn. of Young Children, 2004, Impact II award, Ameritech Ohio Dept. Edn., 1995, 1996, Bd. Trustees award, U. Toledo, 1989—91; Award grant, Ohio Space Grant Consortium, 2000, 2 Ohio's BEST Practice Award grants, NSF-funded TAPESTRIES, 2002. Mem.: DAR, NSTA, Ohio Coun. Elem. Sch. Sci. (bd. dirs. 1992—95, pres.-elect to pres. 1994—96), Nat. Assn. for Edn. of Young Children, Assn. Supervision and Curriculum Devel., Kappa Delta Pi, Delta Delta Delta. Avocations: photography, hiking, reading, art and antique collecting, travel. Office: Toledo City Schs 420 E Manhattan Blvd Toledo OH 43608 Business E-Mail: lori.seubert@tps.org.

SEURKAMP, MARY PAT, college president; b. Pitts., Sept. 6, 1946; d. Frank H. and Loretta (Husic) Reuwer; m. Robert W. Seurkamp, Aug. 6, 1983; children: Kris, Robert, Brooke. BA, Webster U., 1968; MA, Washington U., 1969; PhD, SUNY, Buffalo. Counselor to dir. student living Gannon U., Erie, Pa., 1969-76; assoc. v.p. St. John Fisher Coll., Rochester, N.Y., 1976-92, adj. asst. prof. dept. psychology, 1992—, acting v.p. academic affairs, dean, 1992-98; pres. Coll. of Notre Dame of Md., Balt., 1998—. Mem. planning team Monroe County Ednl. Outcomes Conf.; bd. dirs. Bishop Kennedy High Sch.; cons. Women's Career Ctr., Rochester, N.Y., 1987—. Com. mem. various parish coms., Pittsford, N.Y., 1983—, Diocesan Com. Devel. of Mins. and Employees, Rochester, 1986-89, Internat. Alliance Leadership Conf., 1991; mentor Career Beginnings Program; vol. Career Connections Mentoring Program, 1988-90. Mem. AAUP, Am. Assn. High Edn., Nat. U. Continuing Edn. Assn., Rochester Women's Network. Republican. Roman Catholic. Home: 5502 Lombardy Pl Baltimore MD 21210-1420 Office: Office of the President Coll Notre Dame Md 4701 N Charles St Baltimore MD 21210-2404

SEVEL, FRANCINE, advocate, researcher; d. Morris and Harriet Sevel; 1 child, Drew. BA, Miami U., Oxford, Ohio, 1976; MA, Ohio State U., 1977, PhD, 1981. Asst. prof. Ohio State U., Columbus, 1984—91; publs. editor Nat. Regulatory Rsch. Inst., Columbus, 1992—96, rsch. assoc., 1996—99, sr. rsch. assoc., 1999—2001, consumer affairs program manger, 2001—. Editor: (journal) NRRI Quar. Bull., author public policy reports: consumer issues. Grad. Leadership Columbus, Columbus, Ohio, 2000—01; bd. mem. Nat. Low-Income Energy Consortium, Washington, 2003—; com. mem. Nat. Assn. of Regulatory Utility Commissioners Staff Subcom. on Consumer Affairs, Washington, 1996—2003; pub. policy panel chair Commn. on Interprofl. Edn. and Practice, Columbus, Ohio, 1988—92. Rsch. grantee, US Dept. HHS, 1988—91, Tandy Corp., 1984. Mem.: Hadassah (co-v.p. membership, Columbus chpt. 2003). Jewish. Achievements include research in consumer affairs issues within the field of public utility regulation; regarding problems of high energy bills and low-income consumers; Regarding Health Promotion And Disease Prevention; Regarding Prevention Of Family Violence. Avocations: crafts, cooking, travel, graphic arts, Judaism. Office: Nat Regulatory Rsch Inst 1080 Carmack Rd Columbus OH 43210 Business E-Mail: sevel.1@osu.edu.

SEVELY, MARIA, architect; b. Ankara, Turkey, Sept. 28, 1957; d. Marvin and Josephine (Lowndes) S. BArch, Tulane U., 1978; vis. scholar, Harvard U., 1980—82; student, Wellesley Coll., R.I. Sch. Design. Designer with August Perez & Assocs., New Orleans, 1977, Curtis & Davis/Daniel Mann Johnson & Mendenhall, New Orleans, 1978-80; with Richard Meier & Ptnrs., N.Y.C., 1981-82, Bruner/Cott & Assocs., Cambridge, Mass., 1985; project designer Sasaki Assocs., Boston, 1985—91; project designer, assoc. Akira Yamashita & Assocs., Boston, 1992-95; sr. arch., designer Pei Cobb Freed & Ptnrs., NYC, 1996-98; project arch. Philip Johnson/Alan Ritchie Archs., NYC, 1999—, FORM Archs., NYC, 2005. Archtl. projects include Piazza d'Italia, New Orleans, 1977, One Magazine Square (AIA Honor award 1979), New Orleans, La Regie Renault, Paris, 1981, Windsor Place, Boston, 1985, Holyoke (Mass.) C.C., 1985, Sage Labs., Natick, Mass., 1986, Corp. Ctr., Boston, 1986, Resort at Ocean Edge (AIA/Boston Soc. Archs. PRISM Gold award 1987, Builders' Choice award 1987), Cape Cod, Dartmouth Park housing, Marborough, Mass., 1987, U.S. Holocaust Meml. Mus., Washington, Cathedral of Hope, Dallas. Mem. AIA (assoc., N.Y. chpt. dialogue com. 1996—, vice chair 2000—), The Copley Soc. (fresh paint artists 1993, 94). Office: FORM Archs 38 E 29th St 5 Fl Severud New York NY 10016 Office Phone: 212-986-3700 ext. 476. Office Fax: 212-689-5440. Personal E-mail: mlsline@gmail.com. E-mail: msevely@ureach.com.

SEVERANCE, JERI-LYNNE WHITE, elementary school educator; b. El Paso, Tex., Nov. 30, 1965; d. James Claude and Carol Ann (Magee) White; m. Scot Clark Severance, Dec. 30, 1989; children: Jacie, Jared. BA in Music Edn., Eckerd Coll., 1987; M in Music Edn., U. Tex., Austin, 1989; degree in Ednl. Leadership, Nat. Louis U., 2006. Cert. music tchr. K-12 Fla., English spkrs. of other langs.(ESOL) K-12, exceptional student edn. K-12. Music tchr. Dunnellon (Fla.) H.S., 1989—90, Gateway H.S., Kissimmee, Fla., 1990—91, Grover C. Fields Middle Sch., New Bern, NC, 1991—92; pres-sch. tchr. 1st Alliance Ch., Orlando, Fla., 1992—93; fine arts tchr. Vanguard Sch., Lake Wales, Fla., 1993—94; music tchr. Midway Elem., Sanford, Fla., 1994—95; instr. Barry U., Orlando, Fla., 1995—97; music tchr. Pleasant Hill Elem., Kissimmee, 1995—98, tchr. exceptional student edn., 1998—. Co-founder, co-chair Pleasant Hills Elem. Festival of Arts, Kissimmee; sch. rep. Osceola County Edn. in Park, Kissimmee; exceptional student edn. rep. child study com., Kissimmee. Chamber singers choir dir. First United Meth. Ch., Kissimmee. Mem.: AAUW (sec., com. chair 1995—2001), Coun. for Exceptional Children (com. chair 2000—02), Phi Delta Kappa (com. chair 2003—04, exec. bd. 2003—), Alpha Delta Kappa (chaplain, pres.-elect 1996—2002, pres. 2003—04). Democrat. Methodist. Avocations: reading, sewing, dancing. Office: Pleasant Hill Elem Sch 1253 Pleasant Hill Rd Kissimmee FL 34741 Office Phone: 407-935-3700. Business E-Mail: severancej@osceola.k12.fl.us.

SEVERIN, CHRISTINA, public health service officer; BS in Polit. Econ., Univ. Mass. Amherst; MS in Publ. Health Svcs., Boston Univ. Sch. Publ. Health. Dir. community health ctr. svcs. Boston Univ. Hospital; dir., managed care, practice mgmt. Health Svcs. Partnership, Boston; practice mgr. Codman Sq. Health Care, Dorchester, Mass.; dir. quality Network Health, COO, v.p., mng. dir., now exec. dir. Instr., health care admin. Tufts Health Care Inst. Office: Network Health Ste 23 432 Columbia St Cambridge MA 02141*

SEVERINO, SALLY K., retired psychiatrist; b. McPherson, Kans., June 26, 1937; d. Vernon Lee Kasparek and Edna Alice Maxine Johnson; children: Andrew Lawrence, Michael John. BA magna cum laude, Wichita U., Kans., 1961; MA, Columbia U., N.Y.C., N.Y., 1965; MD, Columbia Coll. Physicians and Surgeon, N.Y.C., N.Y., 1970. Cert. psychoanalyst. Tchr. English, Walton Wittaya Acad. for Girls, Bangkok, 1958—80; asst. prof. psychiatry Cornell U. Med. Coll., N.Y.C., 1983—88, assoc. prof. psychiatry, 1988—95; prof. psychiatry U. N.Mex. Sch. Medicine, Albuquerque, 1995—2000, prof. emeritus psychiatry, 2000—. Mem.: Alpha Omega Alpha (hon. faculty mem.). Home: 1050 Joshua Dr SE Rio Rancho NM 87124-1258

SEVERNS, KAREN S., family court services administrator; d. Dan Vassar and Susan Darlene Peckham; m. Michael Martin Karen Vassar, Apr. 7, 1986; children: Camilla, Hannah, Joshua Michael. AA, U. Alaska, 1995; BS, Wayland Bapt. U., Alaska, 1998; MSW, Boston Coll., 2003. Asst. prof., Title IV-E coord. Lewis & Clark State Coll., Lewiston, Idaho, 2004—; family ct. svcs. coord. 2d Jud. Dist. Nez Perce, Lewiston, 2005—. Psycho-social rehab. social worker Child and Family Enrichment Ctr., Moscow, 2004—. Mental health profl. Red Cross, Lewiston, Idaho, 1981—2006. Recipient Nat. Mil. Important Patriot: donned frosted flakes cereal box, Nat. Mil. Family Assn., 1998-1999. Mem.: NASW (life). Avocations: international travel, Native American art, swimming, singing karoke, dancing. Home: PO Box 3 Princeton ID 83857 Office: Family Ct Svcs 2nd Jud Dist PO Box 3 Princeton ID 83857 Office Phone: 208-301-0299. Personal E-mail: karenseverns@yahoo.com.

SEVIC, SYBIL GIBSON, elementary school educator; b. Columbia, S.C., Oct. 10, 1946; d. John Thomas Jr. and Sybil (Sutherland) Gibson; m. Jimmy J. Sevic, Nov. 6, 1966; children: Joanna Lyn Sevic Joyce, James Andrew. BA in English, U. N.C., 1971, MEd, 1976. 6th and 8th grades tchr. North Belmont Elem. Sch., Belmont, N.C., 1971-73; English tchr. Walhalla (S.C.) H.S., 1973-76; 3d grade tchr. Ravenel Elem. Sch., Seneca, S.C., 1977—. Presenter in field. Contbr. articles to profl. jours. Various positions St. Mark United Meth. Ch., Seneca, 1973—; bd. dirs. Oconee Cmty. Theatre, Seneca, 1992—. Recipient Presdl. Excellence in Math award NSF, 1994. Mem. Nat. Coun. Tchrs. Math, S.C. Tchrs. Math, Alpha Delta Kappa (v.p., S.E. Regional Scholarship winner 1994), Phi Delta Kappa. Avocations: interior decorating, walking. Office: Ravenel Elem Sch 150 Ravenel School Rd Seneca SC 29678-1259 Home: 147 Cane Creek Harbor Rd Seneca SC 29672-6811

SEVICK, SUZANNE, secondary school educator; b. Wichita, Kans., Jan. 16, 1971; d. Dale and Elizabeth Gordon; m. George Sevick, Feb. 13, 1971; children: George Noah, Connor Gordon. BS in Secondary Edn., U. Kans., Lawrence, 1994; M in Curriculum and Instrn., Baker U., Ottawa, Kans., 2001. Cert. secondary lang. arts Kans. Secondary lang. arts tchr. USD 260, Derby, Kans., 1994—. Mem.: NEA.

SEVILLA, EMERITA NEPOMUCENO, writer; b. Manila, Philippines, Dec. 7, 1926; arrived in U.S., 1979; d. Perfecto Jardiniano and Dolores Mapa (Alvarez) Nepomuceno; m. Victor Jocson Sevilla, Dec. 10, 1949 (dec. May 20, 1993); children: Mary Therese Victoria, Victor, Mary Enid, Vincent, Vidal, Virgil, Valentin, Vinci, Mary Elaine. BJ, U. Santo Tomas, Manila, 1949. Writer, rschr. Red Cross Philippines, Manila, 1947—48; reporter Evening News, Manila, 1948—49; sec. to dept. head Dept. Commerce and Industry, Manila, 1949—51; owner, co-founder, treas. Sevilla Bookshop, Davao City, Philippines, 1951—67; mgr. Ency. Britannica, Manila, 1968—71; cons. Philamlife Ins. Co., Manila, 1972—92. Author: (poetry) Springs of Joy, 1992, Silver and Gold, 1995, (prayerbook) Treasures from Heaven, 1997. Mem.: DAV, Rancho Cucamonga Pub. Libr., Help Hospitalized Vets. (Donor of Yr. 2004), Trinitarians, Perpetual Rosary Assn. (life; Regina Coeli divsn.), Priests Sacred Heart, Rancho Cucamonga Sr. Citizen Club. Roman Catholic. Avocations: reading, collecting books and mugs.

SEVILLA-SACASA, FRANCES ALDRICH, bank executive; BA in Langs., U. Miami, 1977; MA in Internat. Mgmt., Am. Grad. Sch. Internat. Mgmt., 1978. Joined Bankers Trust, 1983; mng. dir. L.Am. pvt. banking Bankers Trust Internat. Pvt. Banking Group, Miami, Fla.; sr. v.p. pvt. client svcs. Lehman Bros., Miami, 1997—98; mng. dir. L.Am. pvt. bank divsn. Deutsche Bank; pres. Bankers Trust Internat. Pvt. Banking Corp., 1998—2000; mng. dir., S.E. region head Citibank Pvt. Bank, 2000—01; mng. dir., head L.Am. Citigroup, NYC, 2001—05, head Europe Citigroup Pvt. Bank, 2003—04, CEO Latin Am. Citigroup Private Bank, 2004—05; pres. US Trust Corp. Charles Schwab Corp., NYC, 2005—, exec. v.p. Office: US Trust Corp 114 W 47th St New York NY 10036 Office Phone: 415-627-7000. Office Fax: 212-852-1140.*

SEWARD, TROILEN GAINEY, retired psychologist; b. Petersburg, Va., Nov. 26, 1941; d. Troy L. and Mary (Nester) Gainey; m. William E. Seward III, June 29, 1963; children: Susan Blair, William E. IV. BA, Coll. William and Mary, 1963, MEd, EdS, Coll. William and Mary, 1980; MEd, Va. Commonwealth U., 1977. Tchr. elem., Petersburg, 1963—67; tchr. secondary Surry Acad., Va., 1967—76, guidance counselor, 1976—77; headmistress Tidewater Acad., Wakefield, Va., 1977—79; psychologist Peninsula Child Devel. Clinic, Newport News, Va., 1980—82; sch. psychologist Dinwiddie Pub. Sch., Va., 1982—89, dir. pupil pers. svcs., spl. edn., 1990—93, dir. student svcs., 1993—95, supt., 1996—2001; ret., 2002. Mem. human rights com. Southside Tng. Ctr., Petersburg, 1986—. Trustee Ritchie Meml. ch., Claremont, Va., 1971—; mem. Town Coun., Claremont, 1984-90, mem. fin. com., 1984-90. Mem. Nat. Assn. Sch. Psychologists (del. 1992-94), Va. Assn. Sch. Psychologists (chair cert. and licensure com. 1985-87, legis. chair 1987—, pres. 1989-91), Delta Kappa Gamma, Phi Kappa Phi. Episcopalian. Home: PO Box 266 Claremont VA 23899-0266

SEWELL, AMY J., elementary school educator; d. Joe N. and Joyce M. Sewell. BEd, Fla. State U., Panama City, 1995. Elem. sch. tchr. West Bay Elem., Panama City Beach, 1996—. Vol. Bay Arts Alliance, Panama City, 2000—. Recipient Tchr. of Yr. award, West Bay Elem., 2006, Wal-Mart, 2006. Mem.: Fla. State U. Alumni Club (pres. 2004—), Alpha Delta Kappa (assoc.; pres. 2006—). Baptist. Avocations: reading, volunteering.

SEWELL, GLORIANA, music educator; b. Huntington, NY, June 6, 1948; d. Reavis Staggs and Evelyn (Vilches) Kurlowich; m. C. Eugene Sewell, Aug. 8, 1969; children: Keren Ligowski, Daniel Sewell. BA in Piano, Bob Jones U., 1970. Piano tchr. in pvt. practice, Santa Barbara, Calif., 1970-71, Sodus, N.Y., 1971-78; Suzuki piano tchr. in pvt. practice Quakertown, Pa., 1979-86, Milford Square, Pa., 1986—; Kindermusik tchr. Milford Square Music Studio, 1996—. Piano accompanist ch. choir Assembly of the Word, Milford Square, 1993—. Recipient Tchr. award for 1st Pl. Winner, Baldwin Jr. Keyboard Competition, 1985, 1992, 2000, Tchr. of Yr. award, 1989, award, Music Tchrs. Nat. Assn. Student Composition Competition, 1993, 1994, 2001, Tchr. award 1st Pl., Yamaha H.S. Keyboard Competition, 2002. Mem.: Dalcroze Soc. Am., Nat. Guild Piano Tchrs., Am. Orff-Schulwerk Assn., Kindermusik Educations Assn., Suzuki Assn. of Ams., Pa. Music Tchrs. Assn. (pres. Lehigh Valley chpt. 1991—92, co-dir. spring music festival 1997, v.p. 1999—2001, pres. 2001—03, immediate past pres. 2003—), Music Tchrs. Nat. Assn. (Disting. Svc. award 2003). Avocation: gardening. Home and Office: Milford Square Music Studio PO Box 199 2244 Milford Square Pike Milford Square PA 18935 Office Phone: 215-536-8142. Personal E-mail: gloriana.s@comcast.net.

SEWELL, LAURA J. POLLOCK, social worker; b. Zolfo Springs, Fla., May 9, 1962; d. Abraham and Catherine Rollins Pollock; m. Clinton James Sewell, May 18, 1991; children: Nkiru Amanda, Imani Katherine. BSW, Tuskegee U., 1987; MSW, Fordham U., 1992. Cert. social worker SUNY, Westbury, 1992; sch. social worker The State Edn. Dept., Westbury, 1995; acad. cert. social workers SUNY, N.Y.C., 1998. Counselor Alliance Counseling Ctr., Hempstead, N.Y., 1987-88; caseworker Harlem Hosp. Ctr., N.Y.C., 1988-90; social worker Louise Wise Svcs., N.Y.C., 1990-94, Queens Hosp. Ctr., Jamaica, N.Y., 1995-96. Rec. sec. Jericho Gardens Civic Assn., Westbury, 1997-99. Democrat. Mem. Church of Christ. Avocations: cooking, reading, gardening, shopping, helping others. Home: 2 Brook Ln Glen Head NY 11545-3136

SEWELL, PHYLLIS SHAPIRO, retail chain executive; b. Cin., Dec. 26, 1930; d. Louis and Mollye (Mark) Shapiro; m. Martin Sewell, Apr. 5, 1959; 1 child, Charles Steven. BS in Econs. with honors, Wellesley Coll., 1952. With Federated Dept. Stores, Inc., Cin., 1952-88, research dir. store ops., 1961-65, sr. research dir., 1965-70, operating v.p., research, 1970-75, corp. v.p., 1975-79, sr. v.p., research and planning, 1979-88. Bd. dirs. Lee Enterprises, Inc., Davenport, Iowa, Pitney Bowes, Inc., SYSCO Corp. Chmn. divsn. United Appeals, Cin., 1982; trustee Cin. Cmty. Chest, 1984—94, Jewish Fedn., 1990—92, 2001—, Jewish Hosp., 1990—; bd. dirs. Nat. Cystic Fibrosis Found., Cin., 1963—; mem. bus. adv. coun. Sch. Bus. Adminstrn., Miami U., Oxford, Ohio, 1982—84; mem. bus. leadership coun. Wellesley Coll., 1990—, Fordham U. Grad. Sch. Bus., 1988—89. Named Career Woman of Achievement, YWCA, 1983, Great Living Cincinnatian, 2003; named one of 100 Top Corp. Women, Bus. Week mag., 1976; named to Ohio Women's Hall of Fame, 1982; recipient Alumnae Achievement award, Wellesley Coll., 1979, Disting. Cin. Bus. and Profl. Woman award, 1981, Dirs.' Choice award, Nat. Women's Econ. Alliance, 1995. Home and Office: Apt 807 2444 Madison Rd Cincinnati OH 45208-1264 Personal E-mail: phyllisssewell@aol.com.

SEXAUER, ROXANNE DENISE, artist, educator; b. N.Y.C., Nov. 24, 1952; d. Roland Dietrich and Ann Margaret (Pacsuta) S.; m. David Robert Joseph, Nov. 24, 1982. BFA, U. Iowa, 1979; MFA, SUNY, Purchase, 1989. Instr. City of Iowa City, 1976-86, Iowa Arts Coun., Washington & Williamsburg, 1978; lectr. SUNY-Purchase, 1989, Calif. State U., Long Beach, 1989-90, asst. prof., 1990—2000, full prof., 2000—. Ind. artist, 1974—; guest curator Neuberger Mus., Purchase, 1988-89; resident Dorland Mountain Arts Colony, Temecula, Calif., 1996, Plains Art Mus., Hannaher's Print Studie, Fargo, N.D., 2002 Illustrator (books) Charles Olson: Early Poems, 1978, Robert the Devil, 1981, Blood Harvest, 1986; one-woman shows include Hiram (Ohio) Coll., 1989, MiraCosta Coll., Oceanside, Calif., 1992; numerous other solo, group exhbns. Artist dialogue South Bay Contemporary Mus. Art, Torrance, Calif., 1992; panel mem. Mus. of Art Calif. State U.-Long Beach, 1990. Resident The Hambidge Ctr., Rabun Gap, Ga., 1992, Palenville (N.Y.) InterArts, 1991; recipient touring citation Mid-Am. Arts Alliance, 1990. Mem. Calif. Women in Higher Edn., Coll. Art Assn., L.A. Printmaking Soc., Phila. Print Club, U. Iowa Alumni Assn., Women's Caucus for Arts. Democrat. Home: 4139 Marwick Ave Lakewood CA 90713-3035 Office: Art Dept Calif State U Long Beach 1250 N Bellflower Blvd Long Beach CA 90840-0006

SEXTON, BRENDA, film agency director; b. N.Y.C., Aug. 1, 1954; d. Daniel Francis and Eve (Lucas) Sexton; m. James Daniel Ryndak, July 7, 1984 (div. Sept. 1990); 1 child, Christine Ryndak; m. M Blair Hull, Nov. 30, 1995 (div.). BA, U. Denver, 1977; M of Internat. Mgmt., Am. Grad. Sch. Internat. Mgmt., Phoenix, 1980. Account exec. Ogilvy & Mather, N.Y.C., 1980-81, J. Walter Thompson, Chgo., 1981-82; sr. v.p. Irvine Assocs., Chgo., 1982-86; sr. mng. dir. Julien J. Studley, Chgo., 1987-93; pres. corp. svcs. The Galbreath Co., Chgo., 1993-97; sr. mng. dir. The Williams Co., Chgo., 1997—2003; mng. dir. Ill. Film Office, Chgo., 2003—. Editl. bd.: Bldg. and Owners Management Organization, Chgo., 1995-96. Chmn. State Street Revitalization Task Force, Chgo., 1996-97, The Latin Sch./Silent Auction Restaurant Com., Chgo., 1996-97, Major Fundraising Com./Old Saint Patrick's Sch., Chgo., 1993-94; officer Chgo. Film Critics' Assn.; mem. women's bd. Goodman Theatre; v.p. exec. bd. PAWS (Pets Are Worth Saving), Chgo. Named to Top 40 Under 40 Crain's Chgo. Bus., 1994, Top Comml. Broker in Chgo., Sun Times, 1991, 95, Top Broker in U.S., Julien J. Studley, 1995, Hot Broker, Comml. Property News, 1994, one of Chgos. 100 Most Influential Women, Crain's Chgo. Bus., 2004. Mem. Econ. Club of Chgo., The Exec. Club, The Glen View Club. Office: Ill Film Office Ste 3-400 100 W Randolph Chicago IL 60601

SEXTON, CAROL BURKE, finance company executive, consultant; b. Chgo., Apr. 20, 1939; d. William Patrick and Katharine Marie (Nolan) Burke; m. Thomas W. Sexton Jr., June 30, 1962 (div. June 1976); children: Thomas W., J. Patrick, M. Elizabeth. BA, Barat Coll., 1961; cert. legal, Mallinckrodt Coll., 1974. Tchr. Roosevelt High Sch., Chgo., 1961-63, St. Joseph's Sch., Wilmette, Ill., 1975-80; dir. Jane Byrne Polit. Com., Chgo., 1980-81; mgr. Chgo. Merc. Exch., 1981-84, sr. dir. govt. and civic affairs, 1984-87, v.p. pub. affairs, 1987-94, exec. v.p. corp. rels., 1995-2001. Mem. internat. trade an investment subcom. Chgo. Econ. Devel. Commn., 1989, 90. Bd. dirs. Chgo. Sister Cities, 1992—2000, Ill. Ambs., 1991—98, pres., 1994—98; bd. dirs., sec. Internat. Press Ctr., 1992—97, chmn. bd., 1994. Mem. Chgo. Conv. and Tourism Bur. (sec. 1989-90, exec. com. 1987-2000, chmn.-elect 1990, chmn. 1991-92). Roman Catholic. Avocations: books, gardening, travel.

SEXTON, CHARLENE ANN, education consultant; b. Mobile, Ala., Sept. 13, 1946; d. J.D. and Melvina Grace (Kisner) S.; m. Joseph Michael Hesse, May 26, 1978; 1 child, Caroline Aimee Sexton Hesse. BA, St. Mary Coll., 1968; MA, U. Mich., 1969-70; postgrad., U. Wis., 1977-85. Clin. social worker Topeka State Hosp., 1970-72; ESL tchr. Peace Corps, U.S., Korea, Japan, 1974-76; instr. Troy State U., Berlin, 1985-87; asst. prof. edn. Kans. State U., Manhattan, 1988-89, U. Nebr., Lincoln, 1989-90; assoc. dir. The Internat. Ctr. St. Norbert Coll., DePere, Wis., 1990-95. Adv. bd. Global Studies Resource Ctr. for K-12 Tchrs., DePere, 1992—. Contbg. editor Adult Edn. Quarterly, 1993—; cons. editor Global Awareness Publ. Co., Madison, Wis. 1992-; author, editor The Geography of the Geart, 2001 (finalist Minn. Book award, 2002). Bd. dirs. Wis.-Chiba, Inc., 2000-03; program dir. Japan-Wis. Edn. Connection, 1996-2002; social worker VA Hospice/Pall. Care, 2006-. Fellow Nat. Acad. Advisors Assn. (book reviewer 1991), Poetry and Spirituality Soc. (founder). Avocations: hiking, singing. Home: 128 N Peterson Ave 9 Louisville KY 40206

SEXTON, CHARLINE, secondary school educator; b. Kennett, Mo., Dec. 01; d. Charles Jerome and Dora Myrtle (Wilburn) Lemonds; m. Marcus L. Sexton, Mar. 3, 1939; children: Charolyn Linch, Dan Sexton, Marc Sexton, Elizabeth Morrison. BA with honors, U. Tex Arlington, 1969, MA, 1976. Tchr. English Ft. Worth I.S.D., 1969-83. Author: (mag.) Arlington Review, 1966. Lectr. various churches, Tex., Ark., Tenn., 1963-98. Mem. Ex Libris Book Review Club. Avocation: reading.

SEXTON, CHERYL BOOTH, secondary school educator; b. Wilmington, N.C., June 11, 1949; d. Walter Scott and Annie Elizabeth (Chamblee) Booth; m. Walter Daniel Sexton (div. Jan. 1982); 1 child, Jonathan David. BSE, Appalachian State U., Boone, N.C., 1971. Tchr. Catawba County, Newton, 1971—89, Zebulon Mid. Sch., 1990—95, S. Caldwell HS, Hudson, 1995—2006; tchr., basic skills Caldwell CC, Hudson, 1996—2000; cvcc tchr. CC, Hickory, 2003—. Mem.: Alpha Nu (World scholarship 2004—06). Roman Catholic. Avocation: reading.

SEXTON, JACQUELINE MADELINE, lawyer; b. Bethpage, NY, Aug. 14, 1974; d. Edward Gerard and Dorothy Lorraine Barber; m. Charles E. Sexton, June 8, 1996; children: Katelynn Rose, Chase Edward. BA in Polit. Sci. and Sociology, U. Kans., Lawrence, 1996, JD, 2000. Bar: Kans. 2000, Mo. 2001. Assoc. Sloan, Listrom, Eisenbarth, Sloan Glassman, Overland Park, Kans., 2000—01, Roland, Wickens, Eisfelder, Roper & Hofer, PC, Kansas City, Mo., 2001—. Mem.: ABA, ATLA, Mo. Orgn. Def. Lawyers, Def. Rsch. Inst. Address: 911 Main St Ste 300 Kansas City MO 64105-5300

SEXTON, JEAN ELIZABETH, librarian; b. Boone, NC, June 24, 1959; d. Warren G. and Carol Jean (Smith) S. AA, Chowan Coll., Murfreesboro, N.C., 1979; AB, U. N.C., 1981, MLS, 1983. Cataloging libr. U. N.C. (formerly Pembroke State U.), 1983—89, coord. tech. svcs., 1989—92, asst. dir., coord. tech. svcs., 1992—2003, assoc. libr., coord. tech. svcs., 2003—. Cons. Whitaker Libr. Chowan Coll., 1989—2001. Editor Libr. Lines, 1992, 1998-; contbr. articles to profl. jours. Order of Silver Feather. Mem. NC Libr. Assn., Southeastern Libr. Assn., Am. Hemerocallis Soc., NC Zool. Soc., NC Aquarium Soc., Nat. Trust for Historic Preservation, Sandhills Daylily Club (sec.). Democrat. Baptist. Avocations: growing/breeding daylilies, collecting estate jewelry, needlecrafts. Home: 8662 NC Highway 211 W Red Springs NC 28377-6036 Office: U NC Pembroke Sampson-Livermore Libr Pembroke NC 28372 E-mail: jean.sexton@uncp.edu.

SEXTON, KAREN KAY, music educator, actress; b. Knoxville, Iowa, Jan. 28, 1943; d. Eugene Hufford and Stella Arloise (Smith) Dodds; m. Loren Lee Splittgerber, June 10, 1962 (div. July 1970); 1 child, Brek Loren; m. Charles Benny Sexton, Sept. 6, 1970. Student, U. Oreg., Eugene, 1960-61, U. Colo., 1961-62. Cert. Master's Tchr., 1975. Singer Houston Pops Orch., 1980-82; actress, Dallas, 1988—; ind. piano tchr. Sexton Piano Studio, Mission Viejo, Calif., 1972-77, Houston, 1977-82, Plano, Tex., 1982—. Adjudicator in numerous states, 1979—; singer Dallas Symphony Chorus, 1995—; speaker and panel mem. numerous local, regional and state confs. Author articles; appeared in comml. and indsl. films. Vol. Rep. Party, Mission Viejo, 1974, Am. Heart Assn., Plano, 1995—. Mem. Nat. Guild Piano Tchrs. (adjudicator), Houston Piano Tchrs. Forum (pres. 1978-82), Houston Music Tchrs. Assn., Music Tchrs. Nat. Assn. Tex. Music Tchrs. Assn. (dist. chmn.), Dallas Music Tchrs. Assn. (pres. 1990-92). Republican. Baptist. Avocations: tennis, handiwork, reading. Home and Office: 9141 Rio Blanco Frisco TX 75034 Office Phone: 972-712-8531. Personal E-mail: mozart6800@yahoo.com.

SEXTON, TONI T, school system administrator, educator; b. Phila., Pa., Feb. 21, 1966; d. Frank F and Beatrice V Faranca; m. Michael G Sexton, Apr. 10, 1999; children: Gabrielle Michael, Danielle Grace. AA in commn., Bucks County C.C., Pa., 1986; BA in psychology, West Chester U., Pa., 1990, MEd in counseling, 1994. Cert. School Counselor State of Mont. Dir. counseling Seeley Lake Elem. Sch., 1994—; dir. counseling, sch. counselor Seeley-Swan H.S., 2001—. Adv. peer mediators Seeley Lake Sch., 1999—; adv. dir. adv. placement classes Seeley Swan H.S., 2001—; supr. crisis team Seeley Lake Sch., 2004—. Mem.: Am. Counseling Assn. Christian. Avocations: horseback riding, hunting. Home: Box 1171 Seeley Lake MT 59868 Office: Seeley Lake Sch H S Box 416 Elem Box 840 Seeley Lake MT 59868

SEYBERT, JANET ROSE, lawyer, military officer; b. Cin., Feb. 7, 1944; d. Peter Robert and Helen Rose (Young) S. BA in Classics, BS in Edn., U. Cin., 1966; MA in Classics, U. Iowa, Iowa City, 1968; JD, Chase Coll. Law, Cin., 1975; ML, Army JAG Sch., 1984. Bar: Ohio 1975, U.S. Ct. Mil. Appeals 1975, Colo. 1981, U.S. Ct. Claims 1985; cert. mortgage investor; cert. profl. clown. Instr. Latin, ancient history Salem Coll., Winston-Salem, N.C., 1968-70; instr. N.C. Gov.'s Sch., Winston-Salem, N.C., 1969; instr. phys. edn., Latin Kemper Hall, Kenosha, Wis., 1970-71; instr. in Latin Carthage Coll., Kenosha, Wis., 1970-71; commd. 2d lt. USMC, 1972; completed interservice transfer to USAF, 1978, advanced through grades to maj., 1982, lawyer USAF Acad. Colorado Springs, Colo., 1978-81; chief civil law Sheppard AFB, Tex., 1981-84; dep. staff judge adv., chief mil. justice Homestead AFB, Fla., 1984-88; chief civil law Lowry AFB, Colo., 1988-91; pvt. practice, 1991—; owner, pres. The Seybert Funding Cos., 1991—. Atty. The Seybert Funding Cos.; legal advisor Armed Forces Disciplinary Control Bd., Child and Family Advocacy Coun. USAF, Homestead AFB, 1984-88; designer handicapped accessible houses, 2000—. Vol. Muscular Dystrophy Assn., Colorado Springs, 1978-81; contbr. Ellis Island Resoration Program, Homestead AFB, 1985-88; active Nat. Mus. Women in Arts, Nat. Air and Space Mus.; officer in charge Lowry Silver and Blue Choir; charter mem. Women in Military Svc. to Am. Meml. Mem. ABA, Judge Adv. Assn., Edn. Profl. Assn., Ohio Bar Assn., Fed. Bar Assn., Colo. Bar Assn., Colo. Women's Bar Assn., Am. Bus. Women's Assn. (chmn. audit com. Homestead charter chpt., hist. com. 1987, pres. Visions charter chpt. 1990-91, 91-92, Top 10 Bus. Women 1987, Woman of Yr. 1987), Am. Legion, Ret. Officers Assn., Colo. Clowns, Phi Beta Kappa, Kappa Delta Pi. Avocations: photography, woodcarving, knitting, drawing, crocheting. Home and Office: 1175 S Lima St Aurora CO 80012-4111 Office Phone: 303-368-9405.

SEYBERT, JOANNA, federal judge; b. Bklyn., Sept. 18, 1946; BA, U. Cin., 1967; JD, St. John's U., 1971. Bar: N.Y. 1972, U.S. Dist. Ct. (ea. and so. dists.) N.Y. 1973. Trial staff atty. Legal Aid Soc., N.Y.C., 1971-73, sr. staff atty. Mineola, N.Y., 1976-80; sr. trial atty. Fed. Defender Svc., Bklyn., 1973-75; bur. chief Nassau County Atty's Office, Mineola, 1980-87; judge Nassau County Dist. Ct., Hempstead, N.Y., 1987-92, Nassau County Ct., Mineola, 1992-94, U.S. Dist. Ct. (ea. dist.) N.Y., Uniondale, 1994—. Mem.: Nassau Lawyers Assn. (past pres.), Fed. Judges Assn. (v.p.), Theodore Roosevelt A. Inns of Ct. (past pres.), Suffolk County Bar Assn., Internat. Assn. Judges (del.). Office: 100 Fedl Plz Central Islip NY 11722

SEYLER, DOROTHY U., literature and language professor, writer; d. Joseph and Kathryn Foltz Upton; 1 child, Ruth Elizabeth. BA, Coll. William Mary, Williamsburg, Va., 1959; MA, Columbia U., NYC, 1960; PhD, SUNY, Albany, 1972. Prof. English No. Va. C.C., Annandale, 1972—. Editor-in-chief No. Va. Rev., Annandale, 1999—. Author: (textbook) Read, Reason, Write, 8th edition, Doing Research, 2nd ed., Patterns of Reflection, 6th ed., The Reading Context, 3rd. ed., Steps to College Reading. Bd. mem., v.p. Porto Vecchio Unit Owners Assn., Alexandria, Va., 2000—06. Grantee, No. Va. C.C., 2006. Mem.: Nat. Press Club (assoc.). Achievements include design of A college textbook that focuses on critical thinking as essential to reading, writing, and creating effective arguments. Avocations: golf, tennis, travel. Home: 1250 S WashingtonSt Alexandria VA 22314 Office: Northern Virginia Community College 8333 Little River Turnpike Annandale VA 22003 Office Phone: 703-323-3464. Personal E-mail: duseyler@earthlink.net. E-mail: dseyler@nvcc.edu.

SEYMOUR, B(ARBARA) J(EAN), social worker; b. Chgo., Feb. 7, 1930; d. Louis C. and Amelia (Potasch) Jacobson; m. Douglas Seymour, Sept. 15, 1963 (div. 1984); children: Colin, Leif. PhB, U. Chgo., 1948, MA in Social Service Adminstrn. with honors, 1962; MA in English, Portland State U., 1982; PhD in English, U. Oreg., 1985. Caseworker Oreg. Pub. Welfare Commn., Portland, 1950-51, 54-60, asst. to adminstr. Salem, 1963-71; info. dir. Oreg. Dept. Environ. Quality, Portland, 1971-74; lobbyist Tri-Met Transit Dist., Portland, 1974-76, Oreg. Environ. Council, Portland, 1977; dir. social services Pacific U. Optometry Clinics, Portland, 1978-86; pvt. practice psychotherapy Portland, 1976—; pvt. practice in gender identity, 1987—; asst. prof. social work, English Pacific U., Forest Grove, Oreg., 1986—90. Lectr. social work Portland State U., 1972, 76; adj. prof. Pacific U., Forest Grove, Oreg., 1986; cons. in field. Bd. dirs. Columbia-Willamette Planned Parenthood, Portland, 1975-81, 1st v.p., 1978, Downtown Neighborhood Assn., Portland, 1988-94, 2000-06, v.p. 2005-06. Grantee Met. Arts Commn., 1978. Mem. Nat. Assn. Social Workers (cert., chmn. local chpt. 1978-79), Am. Pub. Welfare Assn. (bd. dirs. 1969-70), Harry Benjamin Internat. Gender Dysphoria Assn., Mensa (Oreg. local sec. 1990-93), U. Chgo. Alumni Assn. (local pres. 1983-86, v.p. programs 1986-94). City Club Portland (rsch. bd. 1993-96, 2003-06). Avocations: theater, poetry, literature. Home and Office: Apt 34 1405 SW Park Ave Portland OR 97201-3455 Office Phone: 503-228-2472.

SEYMOUR, CHARLENA, academic administrator; m. Harry Seymour. BA, Howard U., 1965; MA, Ohio State U., 1967, PhD in Speech and Hearing Sci., 1981. Asst. prof. U. Mass., Amherst, 1971—78, assoc. prof., 1978—89, chair dept. comm. disorders, 1984—92, dean Grad. Sch., 1994—2001, provost, 2001—. Chair Coun. Grad. Schs. Adv. Com. on Minorities in Grad. Edn. Creative editor: Communication Disorders Textbook Series. Recipient Disting. Alumni award, Sch. Intercultural and Race Rels., Harvard Found., Harvard U., 1997. Fellow: Am. Speech-Lang. Hearing Assn.; mem.: N.E. Assn. Grad. Schs. (pres.-elect). Office: U Mass Office of The Provost 362 Whitmore Bldg 181 Presidents Dr Amherst MA 01003

SEYMOUR, JANE, actress; b. Hillingdon, Middlesex, Eng., Feb. 15, 1951; came to U.S., 1976; d. John Benjamin and Mieke Frankenberg; m. David Flynn, July 18, 1981 (div. 1991); 2 children; m. James Keach, May 15, 1993; 2 children (twins). Student, Arts Ednl. Sch., London. Appeared in films Oh What A Lovely War, 1968, The Only Way, 1968, Young Winston, 1969, Live and Let Die, 1971, Sinbad and the Eye of the Tiger, 1973, Somewhere in Time, 1979, Oh Heavenly Dog, 1979, Lassiter, 1984, Head Office, Scarlet Pimpernel, Haunting Passion, Dark Mirror, Obsessed with a Married Woman, Killer on Board, The Tunnel, 1988, The French Revolution, Tochiny Wild Horses, 2002; TV films include Frankenstein, The True Story, 1972, Captains and The Kings, 1976 (Emmy nomination), 7th Avenue, 1976, The Awakening Land, 1977, The Four Feathers, 1977, Battlestar Galactica, Dallas Cowboy Cheerleaders, 1979, Our Mutual Friend, PBS, Eng., 1975, Jamaica Inn, 1982, Sun Also Rises, 1984, Crossings, 1986, Keys to Freedom, Angel of Death, 1990, Praying Mantis, 1993; A Passion for Justice: The Hazel Brannon Smith Story, 1994; Broadway appearances include Amadeus, 1980-81, I Remember You, 1992, Matters of the Heart, 1991, Sunstroke, 1992, Praying Mantis, 1993, Heidi, 1993; TV mini-series include East of Eden, 1980, The Richest Man in the World, 1988 (Emmy award), The Woman He Loved, 1988, Jack the Ripper, 1988, War and Remembrance, 1988, 89; host PBS documentary, Japan, 1988; TV series: Dr. Quinn: Medicine Woman, 1993-98 (Emmy nomination, Lead Actress - Drama, 1994, 98, Golden Globe award 1996), A Marriage of Convenience, CBS, 1998, A Memory in My Heart, CBS, 1999, Murder in the Mirror, CBS, 2000, Enslavement: The True Life Story of Fanny Kemble, Showtime, 2000, Blackout, CBS, 2000, Yesterday's Children, CBS, Dr. Quinn Winters Heart, 2001, Heart of a Stranger, 2002; author: Jane Seymour's Guide to Romantic Living, 1986, Two at a Time, 2001; co-author: Yum, Splat, 1998, Boing, 1999. Decorated Order Brit. Empire; recipient OBE award, 2000; named Hon. Citizen of Ill., Gov. Thompson, 1977. Mem. Screen Actors Guild, AFTRA, Actors Equity, Brit. Equity. Office: Guttman Assocs 118 S Beverly Dr Ste 201 Beverly Hills CA 90212-3016

SEYMOUR, KAREN PATTON, lawyer, former prosecutor; b. Big Springs, Tex. m. Samuel Seymour; 2 children. BA, So. Methodist U., 1983; JD, U. Tex., 1986; LLM, U. London, 1987. Bar: NY 1988. Fed. prosecutor US Attys. Office, So. Dist. NY, 1990—96, Asst. US Atty., Criminal Div. Chief, 2002—04; ptnr. Sullivan & Cromwell, New York, NY, 1996—2002, 2004—. Office: Sullivan & Cromwell 125 Broad St New York NY 10004-2498

SEYMOUR, PEARL M., retired psychologist; b. St. Louis, Oct. 22, 1929; d. Carl S. and Leland Pearl (Disbrow) S. AB, Hunter Coll., 1969; MS, George Williams Coll., 1972. Psychologist III Elgin Mental Health Ctr., Elgin, Ill., 1971-89; ret., 1989. Mem.: Instl. Animal Care and Use Com. Episcopalian. Personal E-mail: seymour@sbcglobal.net.

SEYMOUR, STEPHANIE, model; b. San Diego, July 23, 1968; children: Dylan, Peter Jr., Harry. Appeared on the covers of Vogue, Elle, Cosmopolitan, Allure, Marie Claire; featured in comml. Diet Coke, Victoria's Secret, L'Oreal; worked with Helmut Newton, Herb Ritts, Francesco Scavullo, Irving Penn, Albert Watson, Arthur Elgort, Richard Avedon. Office: IMG Models 304 Park Ave S Ph N New York NY 10010-5339

SEYMOUR, STEPHANIE KULP, federal judge; b. Battle Creek, Mich., Oct. 16, 1940; d. Francis Bruce and Frances Cecelia (Bria) Kulp; m. R. Thomas Seymour, June 10, 1972; children: Bart, Bria, Sara, Anna. BA magna cum laude, Smith Coll., 1962; JD, Harvard U., 1965. Bar: Okla. 1965. Practice, Boston, 1965—66, Tulsa, 1966—67, Houston, 1968—69; assoc. Doerner, Stuart, Saunders, Daniel & Anderson, Tulsa, 1971—75, ptnr., 1975—79; judge US Ct. Appeals (10th Cir.), Tulsa, Okla., 1979—, chief judge, 1994—2000, sr. judge, 2006—. Mem. U.S. Jud. Conf., 1994—, com. defender svcs., 1985—90, chmn., 1987—90, com. to review cir. council conduct and disability, 1996—; joint fed. tribal rels. com. 9th and 10th cirs., 1993—; mem. Okla. State Fed. Tribal Judicial Coun., 1993—94. Task force Tulsa Human Rights Commn., 1972—76; legal adv. panel Tulsa Task Force Battered Women, 1971—77; trustee Tulsa County Law Libr., 1977—78. Mem.: ABA, Am. Inns of Ct. (Council Oak chpt.), Nat. Assn. Women Judges, Fed. Judges Assn., Tulsa County Bar Assn., Okla. Bar Assn. (assoc. bar examiner 1973—79), Phi Beta Kappa. Office: US Courthouse 333 W 4th St Ste 4-562 Tulsa OK 74103-3819*

SFIROUDIS, GLORIA TIDES, library and information scientist, educator; d. George and Mary Despotides; m. Harry Sfiroudis, June 30, 1957; children: Steven, Christina. BA in Geography and Geology, Hunter Coll., 1954, MS in Edn., 1957; Profl. Diploma in Adminstrn. and Supervision, Queens Coll., 1981. Cert. tchr. effectiveness instrn. N.Y. Tchr. North Babylon Sch., L.I., NY, 1954—55, P.S. 123, Bklyn., 1955—61; tchr. 2nd and 3rd grade P.S. 229, Queens, NY, 1970—72, tchr., libr., 1972—74, corrective reading tchr., 1974—82, talented and gifted tchr., 1982—89, acting asst. prin., 1989—90, ednl. enrichment specialist, 1991—2000, tchrs. coll. literacy coach, 2000—04, libr./rsch. tchr., 2004—. Chairperson sch. bd. William Spyropolous Sch. of St. Nicholas, Flushing, NY, 1982—2000; mem., participant Law in a Free Soc., Albany, NY, 1985—89. Co-author: (handbook) The Opera, 1990. Vol. Hosp. Audiences, Inc., N.Y.C., 1975—; active fundraiser Reading Olympics, March of Dimes, UNICEF, Am. Cancer Soc.; mem. exec. bd. St. Nicholas Shrine Ch., Flushing, 1995—. Recipient Vol. Cmty. Action award, Hosp. Audiences, Inc., award, Audubon Soc., 1995; CVS Innovations Charitable Trust Inc. grant, TPI Philanthropic Initiative, 2002—05, Greenwich Conn. fellow, Korean Summer Inst. Yale U. fellow, 1997. Mem.: St. Nicholas Ladies Philoptochos Soc. (sec. 1999—, Pastor's award 2002). Avocations: piano, swimming. Office: Emanuel Kaplan Sch PS 229 67-25 51st Rd Woodside Woodside NY 11377 Office Phone: 718-446-2120.

SGRO, BEVERLY HUSTON, principal, elementary school educator, state official; b. Ft. Worth, Jan. 12, 1941; d. James Carl and Dorothy Louise (Foster) Huston; m. Joseph Anthony Sgro, Feb. 1, 1964; children: Anthony, Jennifer. BS, Tex. Woman's U., 1963; MS, Va. Poly. Inst. and State U., 1974, PhD, 1990. Cert. tennis teaching profl. Instr. of deaf Midland (Tex.) Ind. Sch. System, 1963-64; speech pathologist Arlington (Tex.) Pub. Sch. System, 1964; rsch. asst. Tex. Christian U., 1964-65; tennis profl. Blacksburg (Va.) Country Club, 1977-81; from coord. for Greek affairs to exec. asst. to v.p. student affairs Va. Poly. Inst. and State U., Blacksburg, 1981-89, dean of students, 1989-93; sec. of edn. Commonwealth of Va., Richmond, 1994-98; interim head Collegiate Sch., Richmond, 1998-99; head Carolina Day Sch., Asheville, N.C., 1999—. Adj. faculty Coll. Edn., Va. Poly. Inst. and State U.; lectr., presented papers at numerous symposia and convs., 1983—. Trustee Foxcroft Sch., Middleburg, Va., 1989-98, pres. bd. trustees, 1993-96; bd. dirs. Habitat Humanity. Mem. AACD, Nat. Assn. Student Pers. Adminstrs., Am. Coll. Pers. Assn. (sec., com. mem. 1986-88), Omicron Delta Kappa, Phi Kappa Phi, Phi Upsilon Omicron, Pi Lambda Theta, Sigma Alpha Eta, Zeta Phi Eta. Avocations: reading, travel, theater. Home: 22 Hilltop Rd Asheville NC 28803-3030 Office: Carolina Day Sch 1345 Hendersonville Rd Asheville NC 28803-1923 Office Phone: 828-274-0757. Business E-Mail: bsgro@cdschool.org.

SHABAZZ, FRANCES, lawyer; b. Louisville, Dec. 8, 1962; d. William Norris Thornton Jr. and Martha Anna (Manuel) Morris. AA, U. Louisville, 1991, BA, 1994; JD, NC Ctrl. U., Durham, 1998. Bar: SD 2004. Pub., co-founder, writer Louisville Communicator, 1987—94; pub., co-founder Big Drum Press, Chapel Hill, NC, 1998—2004; in-house counsel Mark Properties, Durham, 1998—2001; paraprofl. NC Dept. Justice, Raleigh, 2001—05; mng. atty. Dakota Plains Legal Svcs., Mission, SD, 2005—. Adj. faculty mem. Shaw U., Raleigh, 1999—2001, Durham Tech. CC, 1999—2000; mem. NC Coalition to Abolish Slaver of Human Trafficing, Raleigh, 2004. Exhibited in group shows at Bernheim Gallery, Louisville. Sec. UN Assn., Chapel Hill, 1994—96. Recipient award for outstanding contbn. to human rels., NCCJ; scholar, Ill. Jud. Coun., 1994; M.E. Glass scholar, NC, 1994. Mem.: ABA, ATLA, SD Bar Assn. Avocations: cross training, reading, music, travel, horses. Office: Dakota Plains Legal Svcs PO Box 727 Mission SD 57555

SHACKELFORD, LOTTIE HOLT, civic worker, former mayor; b. Pulaski County, Ark., Apr. 30, 1941; d. Curtis and Bernice Linzy Holt; m. Calvin H. Shackelford Jr. (div.); children: Russell, Karla, Karen. BS, Philander Smith Coll., 1979, LHD (hon.), 1988; student, Harvard U., 1983, U. Ark., Little Rock; LHD (hon.), Shorter Coll., 1987. City dir. City of Little Rock, 1978—, mayor, 1987—91; dir. Overseas Private Investment Corp., 1993—2002; vice chmn. DNC, 1989—. Del. Italian Econ. Trade Mission, 1987, U.S.-Soviet Women's Wilderness Dialogue, USSR, 1987; panelist Harvard U. Inst. Polits. Pub. Affairs Forum, 1987; bd. dirs. Little Rock Advt. and Promotion, Econ. Opportunity Agy., Little Rock Job Corps, Elizabeth Mitchell's Children Ctr., Links, Inc.; adv. com. Ark. Vocat. and Tech. Edn., Sta. KARK-TV; speaker in field. Del., mem. platform com. Dem. Nat. Conv., 1984; vice chmn. Dem. Nat. Com.; mem. Dem. Policy Commn.; bd. dirs. Nat. League Cities, Ark. Mcpl. League, Ark. Women's Polit. Coun., Urban League, ARC, Ark. PTA, YWCA; bd. dirs. So. Regional Coun., pres., 1988-90; regional bd. dirs. Nat. Black Caucus Local Elected Ofcls., 1979-92; youth dir. St. Peter's Bapt. Ch., 1969-73; pres. Little Rock PTA Coun., 1973; coord. human and civil rights workshops, 1975-77, others. Recipient Women of Style award Pulaski County Council, 1987. Mem. Nat. Assn. State Dem. Chairmen (sec.), Links, Delta Sigma Theta, Gamma Phi Delta, Alpha Kappa Mu.

SHACKELFORD, NANCY KAY, retail executive; b. Wrightsville Beach, N.C., Dec. 28, 1974; d. Rudolph Calder Shackelford, Jr. and Kay (Mathews) Shackelford. BA in Criminal Justice, U. N.C., 1997, BA in Psychology, 1997. Mem. exec. team Lead Assets Protection Target Corp., Raleigh, NC, 1998—. Mem.: NAFE. Avocations: reading, gardening, movies, concerts.

SHACKELFORD, RENAE N., literature educator, writer; d. Raymond Nathaniel and Yvonne Washington Shackelford; m. James Robert Saunders, July 6, 1982; 1 child, Monica Saunders. BA in English, U. Toledo, Ohio, 1990, MA in African-Am. Lit., 1995. Cert. tchr., adminstr. Ohio. Coord. student employment U. Mich., Ann Arbor, 1982—84, U. Toledo, 1989; tchr. 3d grade 1st Ch. of God Christian Sch., 1990—92; writing specialist U. Toledo, 1995, lectr., 1995—97, Purdue U., West Lafayette, Ind., 1997—99, continuing lectr., 1999—. Cons. urban renewal U. Va., Charlottesville, 2003, vis. prof., 2004—05; mentor grad. tchg. assts. Purdue U., West Lafayette, Ind., 2005; founder, dir. Black Am. Student Experiencees, Purdue U., West Lafayette, Ind., 2005. Co-author: Urban Renewal and the End of Black Culture, 1998; co-editor: The Dorothy West Martha's Vineyard, 2001. Vol. Boys and Girls Club, Lafayette, Ind., 2000, Prospect Housing Project, Charlottesville, Va., 2004; founder children's ch. Bethel AME Ch., Lafayette, Ind., 2002—03. Recipient Acad. scholarship, NAACP, 1973, Alva Gordon Sink scholarship, U. Mich., 1984. Avocations: travel, gardening, playing clarinet. Home: PO Box 2624 West Lafayette IN 47996 Office: Purdue Univ 500 Oval Dr West Lafayette IN 47907 Office Phone: 765-494-3740. Office Fax: 765-494-3780. Business E-Mail: rshackelford@sla.purdue.edu.

SHACKLETON, JEAN L., music educator; b. Clare, Mich., Jan. 18, 1948; d. Paul Estel and Martha Ardeth (Cleveland) Helbling; m. Martin Lynn Shackleton, July 11, 1969; children: Aaron, Jeana, Joann. BA, Azusa Pacific U., 1970; MusM in Piano Performance, U. So. Calif., L.A., 1972. Jr. coll. cert. tchg. credential, Calif. Organist Bixby Knolls Christian Ch., Long Beach, Calif., 1966-67; diet aid Long Beach Hosp., 1966-67; self-employed piano and organ tchr. Calif. and Okla., 1968—; instr. Azusa (Calif.) Pacific U., 1972-73; staff accompanist jr. colls. and univs. Stockton, Calif., 1973-91; instr. Mid. Am. Bible Coll., Oklahoma City, 1991—; profl. accompanist Canterbury Choral Soc., Oklahoma City, 1999. Adj. faculty accompanist Oklahoma City U., 1991—; accompanist Crossings Cmty. Ch., Oklahoma City, 1991—. Arranger: (voice book) Basics of Singing, 1989, 97 Mem. Music Tchrs. Nat. Assn. (bd. dirs. 1973—), Music Tchrs. Assn. Calif. (bd. dirs. 1973—), MTAC (bd. dirs. 1973—, adjudicator 1988-89). Republican. Mem. Ch. of God. Avocation: traveling with musical groups. Home: 12117 S Wentworth Pl Oklahoma City OK 73170-4822 Office: Mid Am Bible Coll 3500 SW 119th St Oklahoma City OK 73170-4500 E-mail: jlshackle@aol.com.

SHACKLETON, MARY JANE, small business owner; b. Colorado Springs, Colo., Oct. 20, 1934; d. James Emrie and Thelma Isabella (Vittetoe) Mc Carty; m. William H. Shackleton, Apr. 25, 1953; children: Denise, Dennis, Danette, Donna, Donald. Grad. high sch., Montebello, Calif. Owner Chi Town/Radio Shack, Oscoda, Mich., 1978—, East Tawas, Mich., 1983-97. Bd. dirs. Oscoda Downtown Devel. Authority; founder Oscoda/Ausable Snowbox Derby, 1991—. Named Woman of Distinction Mitten Bay Girl Scout Coun., 1999. Mem. Toastmasters (competent, sec. Lake Huron chpt. 1988-89, sec.-treas. 1991-92), Oscoda C. of C. (bd. dirs. 1985-90), Oscoda Mchts. Assn. (sec.-treas.), Quota Club Iosco (bd. dirs. 1990-91). Republican. Roman Catholic. Avocations: bicycling, golf. Home: 3852 N Huron Rd Oscoda MI 48750-8806 Office Phone: 989-739-4471. Personal E-mail: chitownoscoda@hotmail.com.

SHADE, MARSHA J., elementary school educator; b. Clovis, N.Mex., Oct. 1, 1949; d. Maurice T. and Lula Maye Sims; m. Gerald L. Shade, May 24, 1991; m. Brian T. Miller, June 20, 1970 (div. May 28, 1989); children: Chad T. Miller, Alisa R. Miller. BS in Elem. Music Edn., Ea. N.Mex U., 1977, MEd, 1981. Cert. tchr. Dept. of Edn., N.Mex., 1977. From music specialist to reading recovery specialist Clovis (N.Mex.) Mcpl. Schs., 1978—2003, reading recovery specialist Ranchvale Elem. Sch., 2003—. Presenter in field. Lay dir. S.E. secretariat Cursillo-Episcopal Diocese of Rio Grande, Albuquerque, 1998—2000; diocesan youth advisor Episcopal Diocese of Rio Grande, Albuquerque, 1991—94. Mem.: Christian Educators Assn. Internat., Order of the Ea. Star (worthy matron 1983—84, grand organist 1985—86), Daughters of the Nile (pres. 2000—03). Republican. Episc. Avocations: praise music teams, working with the alpha program. Home: 1516 Hickory St Clovis NM 88101-4931 Office: Clovis Municipal Schools P O Box 19000 Clovis NM 88102-9000 Personal E-mail: marshade@3lefties.com. E-mail: mshade@3clovis-schools.org.

SHADEROWFSKY, EVA MARIA, photographer, writer, computer communications specialist; b. Prague, Czechoslovakia, May 20, 1938; arrived in U.S., 1940; d. Felix Resek and Gertrude (Telatko) Frank; children: Tom, Paul. Student, Oberlin Coll., 1955—56; BA, Barnard Coll., 1960. One-woman shows include Esta Robinson Gallery, 1982, Fairleigh Dickinson U., 1983, Donnell Libr., N.Y.C., 1985, Piermont (N.Y.) Libr., 1987, The Turning Point, Piermont, 1988, Hopper House, Nyack, N.Y., 1989, Puchong Gallery, N.Y., 1991, Rockland Ctr. for Arts, 1992, Valley Cottage Libr., 2005, exhibited in group shows at Soho Photo Gallery, N.Y., 1974, Fashion Inst. Tech., N.Y.C., 1975, Portland (Maine) Mus. Art, 1977, Maine Photog. Workshop, Rockport, 1978, Marcuse Pfeifer, N.Y., 1977, 1978, Foto, 1982, Barnard Coll., N.Y.C., 1983, Rockland Ctr. for Arts, 1978, 1987, 1989, 1996, 1998, Print Club, Phila., 1988, Burd House, Nyack, N.Y., 2003, 2005, Represented in permanent collections Bklyn. Mus., Portland Mus. Art, Met. Mus. Art, N.Y.C., Chrysler Mus. Art, Va., Ilford Collection, N.J.; author, photographer: Suburban Portraits, 1977; photographer Women in Transition, 1975, Earth Tones, 1993, The Womansource Catalog and Review: Tools for Connecting the Community of Women, 1996, poetry critic/essayist Contact II, 1980—93, contbr. story to anthology, 1980—93, Moondance Mag., 1999, Touching Fire, 1989, Sexual Harassment: Women Speak Out, 1992, Lovers, 1992, The Time of Our Lives, 1993, photography to Camera 35 mag., Shots mag., Shutterbug. Recipient Photography award Rockland Ctr. for Arts, 1978, Gt. Am. Photo Contest, 1981, Demarais Press, 1982, Harrison Art Coun., SUNY-Purchase, 1982, The Cape Codder, 1976, 79-82. Personal E-mail: evas@aol.com.

SHADRACH, JEAN HAWKINS (MARTHA SHADRACH), artist; b. La Junta, Colo., Nov. 7, 1926; d. Lloyd Marion Hawkins and Martha May (Hawkins) Sudan; widowed, 1987; children: John M., Karolyn Sue Shadrach Green. BA, U. Colo., 1948. Owner Artique, Ltd. Gallery, Anchorage, 1971-87; dir. Shadrach Arts Workshops, 1998—. Instr. Foothills Art Ctr., Golden, 1988-89, Prince William Sound C.C., Cordova, Alaska, 1993, Kachemak Bay C.C., Homer, Alaska, 1994, 97, UAA, 1996, 97, 98, 99; facilitator mktg. art seminars; guest lectr. Cunard Cruise Lines, 1988-90, 95, 97; dir. workshops Shadrach Arts, 1997—. Bd. dirs. Bird Treatment and Learning Ctr., Anchorage, 1994, 97, Anchorage Art Selection Com., 1984. Recipient gov.'s award for excellence in art, Anchorage, 1970, drawing award All Alaska Juried Show, 1970, 1st prize Fairbanks Watercolor Soc., 1987, Paul Schwartz Meml. award Sumi-e Soc. Am., 1993. Mem. Alaska Watercolor Soc. (v.p. 1994-95, award 1988). Home: 3530 Fordham Dr Anchorage AK 99508-4558 Office Phone: 907-279-5965. Personal E-mail: jeanshadrach@gci.net.

SHAEFFER, THELMA JEAN, primary school educator; b. Ft. Collins, Colo., Feb. 1, 1949; d. Harold H. and Gladys June (Ruff) Pfeif; m. Charles F. Shaeffer, June 12, 1971; 1 child, Shannon Emily. BA, Regis U., Denver, 1970; MA, U. No. Colo., 1972. Cert. profl. tchr., type B, Colo. Primary tchr. Adams County Dist 12 Five Star Schs., Northglenn, Colo., 1970—2006, Title I lang. arts tchr., 1984—2006, Title I reading tchr., 1992—2006; tchr. McElwain Elem. Sch., Denver, 1999—2006, Title I resource coach for staff, 2003—04, Title I interventionist, 2004—, mem. leadership team, 2005—06. Mem. policy coun. Adams County Dist. # 12 Five Star Schs., Northglenn, 1975-79, dist. sch. improvement team, 1987-89; presenter Nat. Coun. Tchrs. of English, 1990; assessor Nat. Bd. Tchrs., 2000. Vol. 1992 election, Denver, alumni advisor for Career Connections U. No. Colo., 1993-97; mem. supervisory bd. Sch. Dist. 12 Credit Union. Mem. Colo. Tchrs. Assn. (del. 1992), Dist. Tchrs. Edn. Assn. (exec. bd. mem. 1991-93), Internat. Reading Assn. (pres. Colo. coun. 1988), Internat. Order of Job's Daus. (coun.), Order Ea. Star, Delta Omicron. Episcopalian. Home: 2575 Urban St Lakewood CO 80215-1130 Office: Rocky Mountain Elem Sch 3350 W 99th Ave Westminster CO 80030-3260 Office Phone: 720-972-3501.

SHAFER, BEATRICE R., medical/surgical nurse, researcher; b. New Market, Va., June 24, 1934; d. Virgil Newman and Mary Hester (Greenup) Richardson; m. William Henry Shafer III, May 6, 1966 (dec.). BSN, Columbia Union Coll., 1956. RN Ky., Ga., Tenn. Assoc. head nurse Oneida Mountain Hosp., Ky., 1956—58; supr. Wildwood (Ga.) Sanitarium and Hosp., 1958—61; head nurse Chestnut Hill Nursing Home, Portland, Tenn., 1961—84; home care nurse Portland and Gallatin, Tenn., 1991—2003; ret., 2003.

SHAFER, SUSAN WRIGHT, retired elementary school educator; b. Ft. Wayne, Dec. 6, 1941; d. George Wesley and Bernece (Spray) Wright; 1 child, Michael R. BS, St. Francis Coll., Ft. Wayne, 1967, MS in Edn., 1969. Tchr. Ft. Wayne Community Schs., 1967-69, Amphitheatre Pub. Schs., Tucson, 1970-96; ret., 1996. Odyssey of the Mind coord. Prince Elem. Sch., Tucson, 1989-91, Future Problem Solving, 1991-95. Tchr. Green Valley (Ariz.) Cmty. Ch., Vacation Bible Sch., 1987-89, dir. vacation bible sch., 1989-93. Mem.: PEO (pres. chpt. 2001—02), AAUW, NEA (life), Phi Delta Kappa, Alpha Delta Kappa (historian Epsilon chpt. 1990—96), Delta Kappa Gamma (pres. Alpha Rho chpt.). Republican. Methodist. Avocations: reading, travel, walking. Home: 603 W Placita Nueva Green Valley AZ 85614-2827

SHAFER-KENNEY, JOLIE E., writer, columnist; b. Roswell, N.Mex., Oct. 26, 1953; d. Jack Ernest and Betty Marie (Halstead) Shafer; m. David A. Kenney (div.); children: Matthew Alan, Jack Andrew. Grad., Parks Sch. Bus., 1972; student, Colo. State U., 1971, 74, U. Pitts., 1995-96. Dept. mgr. Joslins Dept. Store, Aurora, Colo., 1972-73; flight attendent United Airlines, 1974-84, publicity rep. com., 1980-84; v.p. Surg. Assocs., Inc., Latrobe, Pa., 1991-98; asst. Women and Talent Gifted Women Forum, Am. Online, 1997-98; ind. contractor AOL, Inc., 1997-99; staff Online Psychol. Svcs., Inc. AOL, 1995-97, seminar host, 1995-97; with prodn. staff AOL's Comty. Matters, 1997-98, AOL's Alt. Health and Healing, 1997-98. Editl. dir. CelebrityStores.com., 1999—; editor-in-chief Winetree Pub. and The Wine Mag., 1999-2000. Feature/content writer Entertainment Asylum, 1997-99, Electra, 1997-98; editl. dir. Celebritystores.com, 1999—; editor-in-chief Winetree Pub., 1999-2000, www.thewineadvisor.com, www.thewinemagazine.com, www.winetreepublishing.com, 1999-2000; featured columnist ShoutingOut.com; contracted feature writer Gaiam, Inc., 2000—; nat. content writer digitalcity.com, 2000—; author: ASK JES, 1999 (pub. in Chicken Soup for the Soul 1999); contbr. 6th Bowl of Chicken Soup for the Soul, 1999; journalist: AOL's Internat. News, 1997-98, AOL TW's Digital City, Inc. (www.digitalcity.com, cbsswitchboard.com, AOL KW: Pitts.), 1999—; lic. syndicated columnist, ASK JES tm and TEENS ASK JEStm; content provider: iSyndicate.com, 1999—; mng. editor: Feedbackforthought.com, 2001—; contbr. articles to online jours. and newspapers; patent pending in field. Mem. AAUW, Nat. Mus. of Women in Arts, Inst. Noetic Scis., Sea Shepherd Conservation Soc., Ctr. for Marine Conservation, Sierra Club, MADD. Avocations: french language and culture, philosophy, gun control, patient's rights, spirituality.

SHAFF, KAREN E., lawyer, insurance company executive; BA, Northwestern U., Evanston, Ill.; JD, Drake U., Des Moines. Atty. Austin and Gaudineer, Des Moines, 1979—82, Principal Fin. Group, 1982—83, asst. counsel, 1983—86, assoc. counsel, 1986—90, sr. v.p., gen. counsel, 1999—2004, exec. v.p., 2004—, gen. counsel, 2004—. Bd. mem. Hospice of Ctrl. Iowa Found., Sci. Ctr. of Iowa. Mem.: ABA, Am. Life Ins. Coun., Am. Corp. Counsel Assn., Polk County Bar Assn., Iowa Bar Assn., Am. Coun. Life Ins. Office: Principal Fin Group 711 High St Des Moines IA 50392

SHAFFER, BRENDA JOYCE, minister; b. Somerset, Pa., Oct. 29, 1944; d. James Howard and Eva Lorene (Olsen) Folk; m. Thomas Neil Shaffer, June 11, 1966; children: Michael Alan, Christopher James. BS Elem. Edn., Indiana U. Pa., 1966, MS Ednl. Psychology, 1974, postgrad., 1992, Duke U., 2003—06. Cert. elem. prin. Tchr. Prince George's County Sch., North Forestville Elem., Lanham Elem., Md., 1966—69; tchr. elem. schs. Anne Arundel County Schs., Md., 1969—70, Shade-Ctrl. Sch. Dist., Cairnbrook, Pa., 1971—91, tchr. instrnl. support, 1991—98; min. Beulah United Meth. Ch., Friedens, Pa., 2003—. Computer assoc. U. Pitts., 1987—; presenter computer workshops Sunday sch. tchr., chair edn. com. Otterbein United Meth. Ch., Wilbur, Pa., 1990—; mem. Central City (Pa.) Choir, 1991, Somerset (Pa.) Cmty. Choir, 1992, Johnston (Pa.) Choraleers, 1993, Johnstown Symphony Chorus, 1994-95; com. Red Ribbon Campaign, Somerset, 1991, We. Pa. Minister's Chorus, 2002-, Duke U. Course of Study Choir, 2003-04; mem. western Pa. supportive ministries team, children's ministry team United Meth. Ch. Mem. ASCD, NEA, Pa. ASCD, Pa. State Edn. Assn., Shade Edn. Assn. (v.p. 1980-81), Nat. Coun. Tchrs. Math., Kappa Delta Pi Avocations: reading, walking, choir. Home: 3023 Whistler Rd Stoystown PA 15563-9802 Office: Beulah United Meth Ch 433 Bicycle Rd Friedens PA 15541

SHAFFER, DOROTHY BROWNE, retired mathematician, educator; b. Feb. 12, 1923; arrived U.S., 1940; d. Hermann and Steffy (Hermann) Browne; m. Lloyd Hamilton Shaffer, July 25, 1943 (dec. 1978); children: Deborah Lee, Diana Louise, Dorothy Leslie. AB, Bryn Mawr Coll., 1943; MA, Harvard U., 1945, PhD, 1962. Mathematician MIT, Cambridge, 1947-48; assoc. mathematician Cornell Aero. Lab., Buffalo, 1952-56; mathematician Dunlap & Assocs., Stamford, Conn., 1958-60; lectr. grad. engring. U. Conn., Stamford, 1962; prof. math. Fairfield (Conn.) U., 1963-92, prof. emeritus, 1992—. Vis. prof. Imperial Coll. Sci. and Tech., London, fall 1978, U. Md., College Park, spring 1981; vis. prof. U. Calif.-San Diego, summer 1981; vis. scholar, 1986; NSF faculty fellow IBM-T.J. Watson Research Center, Yorktown Heights, N.Y., 1979. Contbr. numerous papers in math. analysis. Mem. Am. Math. Soc., Math. Assn. Am., Assn. Women in Math., London Math. Soc. Achievements include patent in Viscosity Stabilized Solar Pond. Home: Apt 3119 122 Palmers Hill Rd Stamford CT 06902 Office: Fairfield U Dept Math & Computer Sci Fairfield CT 06430 Personal E-mail: dbshaffer507@msn.com. E-mail: dbshaffer@fair1.fairfield.edu.

SHAFFER, DOROTHY TIEN, clinical psychologist; b. Buffalo, Oct. 11, 1956; d. Lloyd Hamilton and Dorothy Angela (Browne) S.; m. Stephen Slade Tien, Oct. 17, 1987; children, Nicholas Lloyd Tien, James Shaffer Tien. AB in Comparative Lit., Princeton U., 1978; MA in Psychology, Yeshiva U., 1985, PsyD in Clin. Psychology, 1988. Lic. psychologist, N.Y., 1989. Psychology extern mental health program Children's Aid Soc., N.Y.C., 1984-86; psychology extern Bellevue Hosp. Ctr., N.Y.C., 1985-86; training psychotherapist Ferkauf Grad. Sch. of Psychology, Bronx, N.Y., 1985-87; clin. asst. instr. psychiatry dept. SUNY-Downstate Med. Ctr., Bklyn., 1987-88; psychology intern King's County Hosp. Ctr., Bklyn., 1987-88; asst. psychologist Stony Lodge Hosp., Briarcliff Manor, N.Y., 1988-89; lic. psychologist Rockland Children's Psychiat. Ctr., Orangeburg, NY, 1989-91, Rockland County B.O.C.E.S., West Nyack, NY, 1991-93; sr. psychologist Graham-Windham Svcs. for Children, Hastings-on-Hudson, NY, 1993—94; supervising psychologist Tompkins County Mental Health, Ithaca, NY, 1994—95; pvt. practice Ithaca, NY, 1994—; counselor, psychologist Wells Coll., Aurora, NY, 2002—. In-house and field researcher, writer Heron House Assocs., London, 1978-79; subsidiary and foreign rights assoc. Springer Pub. Co., N.Y.C., 1980-81. Freelance copywriter Behavioral Sci. Book Svc., Macmillan Book Clubs, N.Y.C., 1984-87. Mem.: APA, Ithaca Therapists' Group, NY State Psychol. Assn. Avocations: international folk dancing, swimming, reading. Office Phone: 607-257-5008. Business E-Mail: dtshaffer1@msn.com.

SHAFFER, ETHEL ARMSTRONG, volunteer speaker; b. Gloversville, N.Y., Feb. 12, 1914; d. Clarence Edwin and Edith May (Collins) Armstrong; m. Rollin Gregory Shaffer, May 31, 1941; children: Nancy Elizabeth, Gregory John. BS in Edn., Syracuse U., 1935, MS in Edn., 1938. Exec. sec. Syracuse-in-China, Syracuse, N.Y., 1935-42; women's chapel counselor Syracuse U., 1938-42, chapel adviser oriental students, social svc. coms., 1938-42; vol. speaker Luth. World Fedn., 1952—. Contbr. book revs., daily devotionals to ch. publs. Vice pres. Nutley (N.J.) Bd. Edn., 1959-68; bd. dirs. ARC, Nutley, 1968-84, pres., 1981-84; bd. dirs. social missions Luth. Synod, N.J., 1954-60, campus ministry, 1962-65; del. Nat. Luth. Ch. Conv., 1964-66; treas. residents coun. S.W. Fla. Retirement Ctr., 1990—. Mem. AAUW (pres. Nutley chpt. 1955-57, hon. life mem., fellowship named in her honor 1973), Friday Afternoon Club (pres. 1967-69), P.E.O. Democrat. Avocations: reading, travel, world affairs. Home: 900 Tamiami Trl S Apt 514 Venice FL 34285-3627

SHAFFER, JOANNE TYLER, music educator; b. Wabash, Ind., Oct. 13, 1951; d. James W. and O. Faye Tyler; m. Michael L. Shaffer, Nov. 24, 1972; children: Marijke A., Monika L. B of Music Edn., Wright State U., 1974, M of Edn., 1989. Tchr. music Tipp City Exempted Village, Ohio, 1974—78, Huber Heights City Schs., Ohio, 1978—, orch. dist. supr., 1996—. String bass player Middletown Symphony Orch., Ohio, 1979—, Lima Symphony Orch., Ohio, 1997—. Orch. musician Salem Ch. of God, Clayton, Ohio, 1980—. Mem.: Music Educator's Nat. Conf. (sec. 1973—74), Sigma Alpha Iota. Republican. Avocation: umpiring college and adult baseball. Home: 7758 Leatherback Ct Dayton OH 45414

SHAFFER, JUDY ANN, retired data processing professional, educator; d. Vernon Sherwood and Josephine (Bean) Peterson; m. James Nelson Shaffer Jr., Feb. 28, 1970. BS, Morningside Coll., 1965; MS, Iowa State U., 1969. Tchr. math. Plaza Jr. H.S., Virginia Beach, Va., 1971; instr. Ivy Ind. Vocat. Tech. Coll., Ft. Wayne, Ind., 1973—74, Ind. Purdue U., Ft. Wayne, 1974—76; programmer Bowmar, Ft. Wayne, 1976—77; programmer analyst GTE Data Svc., Ft. Wayne, 1977—79, Experior Corp., Ft. Wayne, Ind., 1979—87, 1990; instr. dept. math. scis. Ind. Purdue U., Ft. Wayne, 1987—89; edn. specialist Misys Health Care Sys., 1993—2002; ret., 2002. Instr. Star II Purdue U., Lafayette, Ind.; mem. assoc. faculty Ind. Purdue U., Ft. Wayne, 1984—85. Charter mem. Ft. Wayne Area Cmty. Band, 1979—90; mem. Raleigh Concert Band, 1990—2002, Kingdom of the Sun Concert Band, 2002—. Mem.: PEO, Kappa Mu Epsilon. Avocations: music, rail fan, golf.

SHAFFER, PEGGY S., music educator; b. South Bend, Ind., Dec. 25, 1951; d. Phyllis L. White. MusM, Ind. State U., 1970—76; M in Guidance, Purdue U.-Calumet, 1994—97. Music Ind. Dept. Edn., 1976. Tchr. Crown Point Schs., Ind., 1977—. Musician: (free-lance performer) drummer. Bd. mem. Ind. Music Educator's Assn., Crown Point, 1986—88. Mem.: Music Educators Nat. Conf., Nat. Band Assn., Ind. Bandmasters Assn., Ind. State Teachers Assn. Home: 702 W Sigler Hebron IN 46341 Office: Crown Point HS 1500 S Main St Crown Point IN 46307 Office Phone: 219-663-4885. Office Fax: 219-662-5661. Personal E-mail: pshaffer@cps.k12.in.us.

SHAFFER, SHIRLEY POLLACK, secondary school educator, sales executive; b. Bklyn., Dec. 5, 1921; d. Harry Lionel and Sylvia Ruth (Smith) Pollack; m. Alfred Shaffer, Feb. 14, 1943 (dec. July 1995); children: Robert Stuart, Steven Michael. BA magna cum laude, Bklyn. Coll., 1955; MA, Calif. State U., L.A., 1967. Life certificates in elem. and secondary edn., Calif. Sec. Am. Foreign Credit, N.Y.C., 1939-41, Victor M. Calderon Co., N.Y.C., 1941-43, sales, 1943-46; tchr. Bklyn. Pub. Sch., 1955-56, West Covina (Calif.) S.D., 1957-83; retired, 1983; mem. Calif. Sr. Legis. Assembly, 1985-95. Mem. NEA, Calif. Tchrs. Assn. (local sec. 1983), Calif. Retired Tchrs. Assn. (legis. chair), Brandeis U. Women's Aux. Com., Phi Beta Kappa, Kappa Delta Pi, Sigma Delta Pi. Avocations: writing, reading, poetry, lecturing, local civic participation.

SHAFFER-SHRIVER, JULIE RENÉE, science educator; b. Washington, Pa., June 10, 1975; d. James Charles and Karen Louise Shaffer; m. Jeffrey Wade Shriver, Sept. 1, 1995; 1 child, Audrina Renée Shriver. BS in Chemistry, Waynesburg Coll., 1996; MEd magna cum laude, Kutztown U., 2002. Lab. asst., tutor Waynesburg (Pa.) Coll., 1993—96, analytical rsch. chemist, 1996; tchr. sci. DaVinci Discovery Ctr. Sci. and Tech., Bethlehem, 2003—. Coord. summer camp DaVinci Discovery Ctr. Sci. and Tech., 2003—. Mathcounts com., vol. Pa. Soc. Profl. Engrs.; Sunday sch. tchr. St. Paul's Cmty. Ch., Trexlertown, Pa., 1995—2003, event organizer, 2002—03; Sunday sch. tchr., event organizer Wellspring Cmty. Ch., Wescosville, Pa., 2004. Republican. Avocations: antiques, reading, walking. Office: DaVinci Discovery Ctr Sci and Tech 3145 Hamilton Blvd Bypass Allentown PA 18103 Home: 132 S Home Ave Topton PA 19562 Office Phone: 484-664-1002. Office Fax: 484-664-1002. Business E-Mail: jshriver@davinci-center.org.

SHAFRAN, FAITH, artist; b. Oct. 5, 1948; Student, Boston U., 1966-67, Queens Coll., 1968-69, Art Student's League, 1980-81. Exhbns. include Waters Gallery, N.Y.C., 1992, Hoboken (N.J.) Open Studio Tour, 1993, 14th Street Painters Atelier, N.Y.C., 1994, Centennial Art Ctr., Nashville, 1997, 98, Tenn. State Mus., Nashville, 1998-99, Parthenon, Nashville, 2002; Pollock-Krasner Support grant, 2003.

SHAFRIR, DOREE, editor, journalist; b. 1977; BA, U. Pa., Phila., 1999; MA, Columbia U. Grad. Sch. Journalism, 2006. Intern Slate mag.; editor Go mag., Phila., CampusPhilly.org, Phila.; arts & entertainment editor Phila. Weekly, 2003—05; co-founder & editor Crier lit. mag., Bklyn., 2005—; assoc. editor Gawker.com, NYC, 2006—. Office: Gawker Media 76 Crosby New York NY 10012 Office Phone: 212-655-9524.*

SHAH, MUNIZA, psychiatrist; b. Karachi, Sind, Pakistan, Aug. 22, 1967; arrived in U.S., 1994; d. S.G.M. and Farzana Shah; m. Azmat S. Hussain, Jan. 24, 2000; 1 child, Mehreet T. Hussain. MBBS, Sind Med. Coll., 1991; MD, ESFMG, 1995. Cert. ABPN, ACCAP. Psychiatrist U. Physicians, South Dakota, Ind., 2000—02; staff psychiatrist Four County Counseling Ctr., Logansport, Ind., 2002—06. Author: Koocha Koocha Phercy. Mem.: Ind. State Med. Soc., Am. Psychiatric Assn. Avocation: writing. Office Phone: 574-722-5151 ext. 227. E-mail: munizashah@hotmail.com.

SHAHEEN, C. JEANNE, political organization administrator, former governor; b. St. Charles, Mo., Jan. 28, 1947; m. William H. Shaheen; 3 children. BA, Shippensburg U., 1969; M of Social Sci. in Polit. Sci., U. Miss., 1973. Campaign mgr. Pres. Jimmy Carter, 1980, Gary Hart, 1984, Gov. Paul McEachon, 1986, 1988; mem. N.H. Senate, 1991-96; gov N.H., 1997—2003; vice chair Democratic Nat. Convention Com., 2004; nat. chair John Kerry Presidl. Campaign, 2004; dir. Inst. Politics Harvard Univ., 2005—. Democrat. Protestant. Office: Inst of Politics Harvard Univ 75 JFK St Cambridge MA 02138 Office Phone: 617-495-1363.

SHAHON, LAURIE MERYL, investment company executive; b. Boston, Jan. 28, 1952; m. Kenneth Meister. AB, Wellesley Coll., 1974; MBA, Columbia U., 1976. Assoc. Morgan Stanley and Co. Inc., N.Y.C., 1976-80; dir. retailing and consumer products group Salomon Bros., N.Y.C., 1980-88; mng. dir. '21' Internat. Holdings Inc., N.Y.C., 1988-93; founder, pres. Wilton Capital Group, N.Y.C., 1994—. Bd. dirs. Knight Capital Group, Inc., 2006—, The Bombay Company, Inc., Eddie Bauer Holdings, Inc., Kitty Hawk, Inc. Office: Wilton Capital Group 181 Berkeley Pl Brooklyn NY 11217-3801*

SHAINWALD, SYBIL, lawyer; b. N.Y.C., Apr. 27, 1928; d. Samuel and Anne; m. Sidney Shainwald; children: Robert, Louise, Laurie, Marsha. BA, Coll. William and Mary, 1948; MA, Columbia U., 1972; JD, N.Y. Law Sch., 1976, LLD (hon.), 2000. Bar: N.Y. 1976. Pvt. practice, NYC, 2005—. Legal advisor Am. Found. for Maternal Child and Health; adj. prof. dept. law Baruch Coll., 1981—82. Co-editor: Jour. Women and Health; contbr. articles to profl. jours. Active Abortion Rights Action; co-founder, bd. mem. Trial Lawyers for Pub. Justice, 1982—88; bd. mem. Hysterectomy Edn. Resources and Svcs., 1985—, Dalkon Shield INfo. Network, Nat. Network to Prevent Birth Defects, No. Ariz. Sch. Midwifery, 1989—; bd. advisors Med. Legal Aspects of Breast Implants; bd. dirs. Consumer Interest Rsch. Inst.; fellow Roscoe Pound Inst., Morgan Libr.; trustee Civil Justice Found., 1998—99; bd. dirs. Am. Friends of Tel Aviv Mus., 2000, Friends of Tel Aviv Mus., 2000-; trustee N.Y. Law Sch., 2000—; adv. bd. Southampton The Hamptons Shakespeare Festival, 2000—; co-chair Take Home a Nude N.Y. Acad. Art, 2001; active Sybil Shainwald Charitable Found., N.Y.C. Comptrs. Health Task Force. Recipient Susan B. Anthony award, NOW; grantee, Nat. Endowment for the Humanities, Rockefeller Found., Gov. W. Averell Harriman; scholar Pres. Bryan scholar, Coll. of William and Mary, Edward Coles scholar. Mem.: ATLA (chair environ. and toxic tort sect. 1988—89, co-chair breast implant litigation group 1992—2000, mem. Dalkon shield litigation group 1995, mem. contraceptive implant litigation group 1995, co-chair DES litigation group, environ. law adv. com.), N.Y. State Trial Lawyers (bd. govs.), Assn. of the Bar of the City of N.Y. (judge nat. moot ct. competition 1988—2003), Soc. Med. Jurisprudence, Health Action Internat.-U.S. (co-founder, mem. steering com.), Lawyers Com. for Human Rights, Am. Soc. Law, Medicine and Ethics, Nat. Women's Health Alliance (pres.), Nat. Women's Health Network (bd. mem. 1980—86, chair litigation svc. 1980—86, chair health law and regulation 1981—88, chmn. bd. dirs. 1982—86, chair N.Y. state affiliate), Phi Beta Kappa. Avocations: art, music. Home: 955 5th Ave 15B New York NY 10021 Office: Law Offices of Sybil Shainwald 111 Broadway 4th Fl New York NY 10006 Business E-Mail: shainwaldlaw@aol.com.

SHAKLEY, HEATHER, physical education educator; b. State College, Pa., Nov. 25, 1976; d. Conrad Dale and Linda Lucille Shakley. BS in Kinesiology, Pa. State U., State College, 1999, tchg. cert. K-12 in health and phys. edn., 2000. Cert. aquatic facility oper. Pa., tchr. adapted aquatics Pa. Aquatic paraprofl. State College Area Sch. Dist., 2000—01, tchr. aquatic phys. edn., 2001—04, dir. aquatics, 2004. Dist. rep., track and field coach State College Area Sch. Dist., 2003—; mem. pool renewal project com. Ctr. Region Parks and Recreation, State College, 2006. Lifeguard instr. ARC, State College, 2002—, water safety instr., 2002—, water safety instr. trainer, 2006. Grantee, Future Fisherman Found. Mem.: AAPHERD, Am. Assn. for Phys. Activity and Recreation, Trout Unltd. Avocations: fly fishing, kayaking, antiques, gardening. Office: State College Area Sch Dist 653 Westerly Pkwy State College PA 16801

SHALALA, DONNA EDNA, academic administrator, former secretary of health and human services; b. Cleve., Feb. 14, 1941; d. James Abraham and Edna (Smith) S. AB, Western Coll., 1962; MSSC, Syracuse U., 1968, PhD, 1970; 39 hon. degrees, 1981-91. Vol. Peace Corps, Iran, 1962-64; asst. prof. polit. sci. CUNY, 1970-72; assoc. prof. politics and edn. Tchrs. Coll. Columbia U., 1972-79; asst. sec. for policy devel. and research HUD, Washington, 1977-80; prof. polit. sci., pres. Hunter Coll., CUNY, 1980-87; prof. polit. sci., chancellor U. Wis., Madison, 1987-93; sec. US Dept. Health & Human Services, Washington, 1993-2001; pres. U. Miami, 2001—. Dir., treas. Mcpl. Assistance Corp. for the City of N.Y., 1975—77. Author: Neighborhood Governance, 1971, The City and the Constitution, 1972, The Property Tax and the Voters, 1973, The Decentralization Approach, 1974. Mem. Trilateral Commn., 1988—92, Knight Commn. on Intercollegiate Sports, 1989—91; bd. govs. Am. Stock Exch., 1981—87; trustee TIAA, 1985—89, Com. Econ. Devel., 1982—92, Brookings Inst., 1989—92; bd. dirs. Children's Def. Fund, 1980—93, Am. Ditchley Found., 1981—93, Spencer Found., 1988—92, M&I Bank of Madison, 1991—92, NCAA Found., 1991, Inst. Internat. Econs., 1981—, Gannett Co., Inc., McLean, Va., United Health Group, Mpls., Lennar Corp., Miami; trustee emeritus Kennedy

Ctr. Bd. of Trustees, Washington. Ohio Newspaper Women's scholar, 1958, Western Coll. Trustee scholar, 1958-62; Carnegie fellow, 1966-68; Guggenheim fellow, 1975-76; recipient Disting. Svc. medal Columbia U. Tchrs. Coll., 1989. Mem. ASPA, Am. Polit. Sci. Assn., Nat. Acad. Arts and Scis., Nat. Acad. Pub. Adminstrn., Coun. Fgn. Rels., Nat. Acad. Edn. (Spencer fellow 1972-73). Office: U Miami Office Pres 230 Ashe Bldg Coral Gables FL 33146

SHALLCROSS, DEANNE J., finance company executive; Mktg. exec. TIAA-CREF, N.Y.C., 1996—. Office: TIAA-CREF 730 3d Ave New York NY 10017 E-mail: dshallcross@tiaa-cref.org.

SHALOM, GALIT, psychologist; b. Béer-Sheva, Israel, Dec. 26, 1969; arrived in US, 1992; d. Emil and Nourit Assor; m. Moshe Shalom, July 7, 1996; children: Nathan, Brit. BA in Edn. & Behavioral Scis., Ben-Gurion U. Negev, 1995; MA in Clinical Psychology, Forest Inst. Profl. Psychology, 1998, PsyD in Clinical Psychology, 2000. Lic. psychologist Fla., 2002. Evening news anchor ICS, Beer-Sheva, 1991—92; psychologist-in-tng. Forest Human Svcs. Ctr., Springfield, Mo., 1997—99, Neuropsychological & Assocs. SW Mo., 1999; intern Forest Inst. Profl. Psychology, Springfield, Mo., 1999—2000, tchg. asst., 1999—2000, clinical supr., 1999—2000; clinical psychologist Greene County Jail, Springfield, 2000; adj. prof. psychology Fla. Internat. U., Miami, 2001—02, post-doctorate residence, 2001—02; postdoctoral resident Fla. Internat. U. Counseling and Psychol. Svcs. Ctr., Miami, 2001—02; licensed clinical psychologist S. Fla. State Hosp., Atlantic Shores Healthcare, Inc., Pembroke Pines, Fla., 2003, pvt. practice, Boca Raton, Fla., 2003—, Jewish Family Svc., Inc. Broward County, Plantation, Fla., 2004—. Guest spkr. various seminars & presentations, 1999—2001. With Israeli mil., comdr. naval divsn. Israeli Defence Force, 1988—90. Recipient Outstanding Psychological Trainee of Month, The Resident Com., Forest Human Svcs. Ctr., 1998. Mem.: APA, Soc. for Psychology of Women. Jewish. Avocation: reading. Office: 370 W Camino Gardens Blvd Ste 204 Boca Raton FL 33432 E-mail: drshalom@bellsouth.net.

SHAMBAN, AVA T., dermatologist; BS, Harvard U., 1977; MD, Case Western Res. U. Pvt. practice dermatology, Santa Monica, Calif.; asst. clin. prof. dermatology UCLA. Cons. ABC's Extreme Makeover; investigator Nat. Acne Rsch. Project; featured regarding cosmetic dermatology Discovery Channel. Bd. dirs. Santa Monica Coll. Found. Fellow: Am. Acad. Dermatology. Office: Laser Inst for Dermatology 2021 Santa Monica Blvd #600E Santa Monica CA 90404

SHAMBERG, BARBARA A(NN), psychologist; b. Atlantic City, July 22, 1953; d. Martin and Margaret (Fox) S.; m. Allan Weisberg, Aug. 29, 1987; children: Lauren Margaret, Alana Miriam. BA, New Coll., 1975; MA, Hofstra U., 1979, PhD, 1984. Lic. psychologist NY, bd. cert. forensic examiner, bd. cert. in forensic medicine. Mem. faculty Fairleigh Dickinson U., Madison, NY, 1977; psychologist Hofstra U., Hempstead, NY, 1978-84, SUNY, Farmingdale, 1981-82, Bd. of Coop. Ednl. Svcs., Yorktown, NY, 1982-83, NYC Bd. Edn., 1983-88; supervising psychologist Childrens' Village, Dobbs Ferry, NY, 1989-91; pvt. practice clin. psychology NYC, White Plains and Scarsdale, NY, 1984—; dir. psychol. svcs. Midtown Med. and Health Svcs., NYC, 1994—. Sr. clin. cons. psychologist Ctr. for Behavior Therapy, Scarsdale, 1989—; lectr., workshop leader in field; expert interviewee ABC News, NYC, Sta. WMID, Atlantic City. Author: Wives' Marital Satisfaction, 1984. Bd. dirs. 218 E. 29th St. Owners' Corp., 1984-89. Mem. Am. Psychol. Assn., NY State Psychol. Assn., Westchester County Psychol. Assn., Manhattan Psychol. Assn., Am. Assn. Behavioral Therapists, Am. Coll. Forensic Examiners. Office: Midtown Med Corp 235 E 49th St New York NY 10017-1501 Office Phone: 212-688-2900. Business E-Mail: drbsw@aol.com.

SHANAHAN, BETTY, professional society administrator; BSEE, Mich. State. U.; M of Software Engring., Wang Inst. of Grad. Studies; MBA in Strategic Mgmt., U. Chgo. Grad. Sch. of Bus. Various positions in devel., engring. mgmt. and mktg. Data Gen., Alliant Computer Sys., 1978—90; mktg. mgmt., including v.p., prod. mgmt. and mktg., software components divsn. Stellent, Inc., 1990—2002; exec. dir. Soc. of Women Engr., Chgo., 2002—. Bd. dir. Women in Engring. Programs and Adv. Network. Fellow: Soc. Women Engr. (life); mem.: IEEE, Am. Soc. of Assn. Execs., Assn. for Computing Machinery. Office: Exec Dir Soc of Women Engr 230 E Ohio St Chicago IL 60611*

SHANAHAN, EILEEN FRANCES, retired secondary school educator; b. Bethlehem, Pa., Sept. 10, 1949; d. Edward Vincent and Geraldine Mary (Gilligan) S. BA, Moravian Coll., 1971. Cert. secondary tchr. in Spanish, English, NJ. Tchr. Kingsway Regional HS Dist., Swedesboro, NJ, 1971—2006; ret., 2006. Trustee Gloucester Co. Historical. Mem. NEA, NJ Edn. Assn., Gloucester County Edn. Assn., Fgn. Lang. Educators NJ, Kingsway Edn. Assn. (sec. membership), Archaeol. Soc. NJ, Hellertown Hist. Soc., Gloucester County Hist. Soc. (trustee). Democrat. Roman Catholic. Avocations: archaeology, historical research, genealogy.

SHANAHAN, ELIZABETH ANNE, art educator; b. High Point, NC, Apr. 5, 1950; d. Joe Thomas and Nancy Elizabeth (Moran) Gibson; m. Robert James Shanahan, Aug. 31, 1969 (div. Mar. 1987); children: Kimberly Marie Shanahan Conlon, Brigette Susanne Shanahan Foshee. Student, Forsyth Tech. Coll., 1974-83, Tri-County Tech. Coll., 1989, Inst. of Children's Lit., 1989. Owner cleaning bus., Winston-Salem, NC, 1985-86, 87; instr. Anderson (S.C.) Arts Coun., 1987—, Tri-County Tech. Coll., Pendleton, SC, 1987-98. Exhibited in group shows at Wild Geese, 1985 (Best in Show), exhibitions include Triad Art Assn. Gallery, Kernersville, N.C., 1985 (Best in Show, 1985). Active Libr. of Congress, 1994. Mem. Anderson Art Assn. (con. 1987—), Met. Arts Coun. (Upstate Visual Arts divsn.), Triad Art Assn. (pres. Kernersville, N.C. chpt. 1984-85), Nat. Mus. Women in Arts (charter), Libr. of Congress (charter). Avocations: writing, sewing, travel, decorating. Home: 2519 Mountain View Church Rd King NC 27021-7645

SHANAHAN, LAURI M., lawyer; b. 1962; BS, U. Colo., Boulder; JD, UCLA. Bar: Calif. 1987. Assoc. Thelen Reid & Priest, San Francisco, 1987—92; dir. legal dept. Gap Inc., San Francisco, 1992—98, sr. v.p., gen. counsel, 1998—2004, corp. sec., 2000—04, chief compliance officer, 2001—04, exec. v.p., chief compliance officer, gen. counsel, corp. sec., 2004—. Co-chmn. Lawyers Com. for Civil Rights. Office: Gap Inc 2 Folsom St San Francisco CA 94105 Office Phone: 415-427-7694. Office Fax: 415-427-2670.

SHANAHAN, REBECCA M., lawyer; b. 1953; BA, Ind. U., 1974, JD cum laude, 1977. Bar: Ind. 1977, Ill. 1997, Fla. 2003. Of counsel RCA Consumer Electronics, 1980—86; v.p., gen. counsel Cmty. Hosps. Ind., Inc., 1986—91; sr. v.p. Methodist Health Group, 1991—96; v.p. managed care and bus. devel. U. Chgo. Hosps. and Health Systems, 1997—2002; exec. v.p. adminstrn., gen. counsel, sec. Priority Healthcare Corp., Lake Mary, Fla., 2002—. Cons. The Shanahan Group, 1996—97; bd. dirs. SinusPharma. Office: Priority Healthcare Corp 250 Technology Pk Ste 124 Lake Mary FL 32746 Office Phone: 407-804-6700. Office Fax: 407-804-5675. E-mail: rebecca.shanahan@priorityhealthcare.com.

SHANAHAN, SHEILA ANN, pediatrician, educator; m. Justin Laurence Cashman Jr., Sept. 14, 1968; children: Justin III, Gillis. BA, Trinity Coll., 1963; MD cum laude, Med. Coll. Pa., 1969. Diplomate Nat. Bd. Med. Examiners, Am. Bd. Pediats. Intern Presbyn. Hosp., N.Y.C., 1969-70, resident in pediats., 1970-72, asst. in clin. pediats., 1972-75, assoc. clin. pediats., 1975-78; pvt. practice specializing in pediats. Greenwich, Conn., 1972-78; asst. attending Greenwich Hosp., 1972-73, assoc. attending, 1973-78; from instr. to assoc. Columbia Coll. Physicians and Surgeons, N.Y.C., 1972-78; asst. prof. pediats. George Washington U. Sch. Medicine, Washington, 1980—, Georgetown U. Sch. Medicine, Washington, 1984—; pvt. practice specializing in pediats. Washington, 1984—. Attending dept. ambulatory medicine Children's Hosp. Nat. Med. Ctr., Washington, 1980—84; courtesy staff Georgetown U. Hosp., Washington, 1984—, Sibley Meml. Hosp., Washington, 1984—, Columbia Hosp. for Women, 1984—2002, Children's Hosp. Nat. Med. Ctr., 1984—. Fellow Am. Acad. Pediats.; mem. Am. Women's Med. Assn. Office: 4900 Massachusetts Ave NW Washington DC 20016-4358

SHAND, KIMBERLY, information technology consultant company executive; Co-founder, CEO, pres. Vega Consulting Solutions, Inc., Moutain Lakes, NJ, 1993—. Guest spkr. on issues regarding women in the workplace, gender and technology, and high tech edn. initiatives. Mem. Women's Polit. Caucus of NJ; co-chair NJ Technology Workforce Com.; mem. adv. bd. NJ Women in Technology; bd. dor. Ctr. For Great Expectations. Office: Vega Consulting Solutions Inc 3 Romaine Rd Mountain Lakes NJ 07046 Office Phone: 973-335-7800, 800-810-8342. Office Fax: 973-335-1677.

SHANDS, GAIL MAXINE, environmental scientist; b. Bklyn., Apr. 10, 1952; d. Leon and Mitzi (Edelman) Shands; m. Miles B. Kessler, Dec. 30, 1973; children: Marc Philip, Jeff Eric. BS, Cornell U., 1973; MS, Purdue U., 1975; MPA, NYU, 1985. Soil scientist USDA-NRCS, Colo., 1976, soil conservationist Colo., 1977; project mgr. U.S. AID, Washington, 1978-82; owner/mgr. Coll. Scholarship Network, Colo., 1988-90; dir. urban edn. project Denver Audubon Soc., 1993-97; owner Gail Shands Assocs., Inc., 1998—. Cons. natural resources, environ. scis., NEPA compliance; reservist Fed. Emergency Mgmt. Agy., 1999—. Reviewer state environ. edn. master plan Colo. Alliance for Environ. Edn.; vol. Denver Russian Resettlement Program, 1992-94, Women's Am. Orgn. for Rehab. and Tng., Denver, 1993—, Hadassah, Denver, 1990—. NYU Acad. scholar, 1982-85. Mem. Am. Soc. Pub. Adminstrn., Am. Soc. Agronomy, Am. Planning Assn. (task force on pub. lands policy 1985). Achievements include participation in initial evaluation of the Senegal River basin development.

SHANE, DORIS JEAN, respiratory therapist, administrator; b. Granite City, Ill., June 30, 1949; d. Elbert Paul and Arline Marie (Zitt) S. AS with clin. honors in respiratory therapy, Presbyn.-St. Luke's Hosp., Chgo., 1973. Registered respiratory therapist; cert. asthma educator. Chief therapist Michael Reese Med. Ctr., Chgo., 1973-78; dir. respiratory therapy Edgewater Hosp., Chgo., 1978-81; dir. respiratory care svcs. Mt. Sinai Med. Ctr., Miami Beach, Fla., 1981-87; chmn. adv. coun. Respiratory Therapy Miami-Dade Cmty., 1984-87. Healthcare cons. Shane and Assoc., 1987—; coord. rep. Care-Green Briar Nursing Ctr., South Miami Hosp., 1987-88; adminstrv. program dir. of vent and TBI programs West Gables Rehab. Hosp., 1988-89, v.p. health care planning and devel. Intergrated Health Svcs., 1989-97; pres. Shane Assocs., 1997-98; dir. profl. svcs. Home Med. of Am., Inc., 1997-2000; v.p. Profl. Bus. Svcs.: Life Care Solutions, 2000-06; br. dir. Gentiva Health Svcs., Ft. Lauderdale, 2006—. Bd. dirs. Sunny Shores Sea Camp, Miami, 1983-87, Frank M. Rodde Cmty. Ctr., Chgo., 1980; chmn. credit com. Mt. Sinai Fed. Credit Union, 1986. Mem. NAFE, Dade-Monroe Am. Lung Assn. (bd. dirs. 1982-90), Fla. Soc. Respiratory Care (v.p. 1984-85), Am. Assn. Respiratory Care, Am. Assn. Cardiovasc. Pulmonary Rehab., Internat. Assn. Quality Circles, Am. for Respiratory Care Adminstrs., Am. Bus. Women Assn., Fla. Coun. Aging. Democrat. Avocations: tennis, biking. Home and Office: 1085 Scarlet Oak St Hollywood FL 33019-4810 Office Phone: 954-485-5500. E-mail: doris.shane@gentiva.com.

SHANE, PENNY, lawyer; b. NYC, 1963; BA, Barnard Coll., 1985; JD, NYU, 1988. Bar: NY 1989, US Ct. of Appeal (2nd cir.) and (DC cir.), US Dist. Courts (so., ea., we. districts) NY, NY State Courts. Law clk. Judge Richard Owen US Dist. Ct. (so. dist.) NY, 1988—90; ptnr. and mem. litig. group, fin. institutions group, criminal def. and investigations group Sullivan & Cromwell, NYC. Office: Sullivan & Cromwell 125 Broad St New York NY 10004-2498 Office Phone: 212-558-4000. Office Fax: 212-558-3588. Business E-Mail: shanep@sullcrom.com.

SHANE, RITA, opera singer, educator; b. NYC; d. Julius J. and Rebekah (Milner) S.; m. Daniel F. Tritter, June 22, 1958; 1 child, Michael Shane. BA, Barnard Coll., 1958; postgrad., Santa Fe Opera Apprentice Program, 1962-63, Hunter Opera Assn., 1962-64; pvt. study with, Beverly Peck Johnson. Adj. prof. voice Manhattan Sch. of Music, 1993-95. Prof. voice Eastman Sch. Music Rochester U., 1989—, Aspen Music Sch., 1999, Hamamatsu, Japan, 2000—02; pvt. tchr., N.Y.C., 1978—; judge Richard Tucker Music Found., Met. Opera Regional Auditions, Licia Albanese Puccini Found. Performer with numerous opera cos., including profl. debut, Chattanooga Opera, 1964, Met. Opera, San Diego Opera, Santa Fe Opera, Teatro alla Scala, Milan, Italy, Bavarian State Opera, Netherlands Nat. Opera, Geneva Opera, Vienna State Opera, Phila., New Orleans, Balt. Opera, Opera du Rhin, Strasbourg, Scottish Opera, Teatro Reggio, Turin, Opera Metropolitana, Caracas, Portland Opera, Minn. Opera, also others; world premiere Miss Havisham's Fire, Argento; Am. premieres include Reimann-Lear, Schat-Houdini, Henze-Elegy for Young Lovers; participant festivals, including Mozart Festival, Lincoln Center, N.Y.C., Munich Festival, Aspen Festival, Handel Soc., Vienna Festival, Salzburg Festival, Munich Festival, Perugia Festival, Festival Canada, Glyndebourne Festival, performed with orchs. including Santa Cecilia, Rome, Austrian Radio, London Philharmn., Louisville, Cin., Cleve., Phila., RAI, Naples, Denver, Milw., Israel Philharm., rec. artist, RCA, Columbia, Louisville, Turnabout, Myto labels, also radio and TV. Recipient Martha Baird Rockefeller award, William Matheus Sullivan award. Mem. Am. Guild Mus. Artists, Screen Actors Guild, Nat. Assn. Tchrs. Singing.

SHANE, SANDRA KULI, postal service administrator; b. Akron, Ohio, Dec. 12, 1939; d. Amiel M. and Margaret E. (Brady) Kuli; m. Fred Shane, May 30, 1962 (div. 1972); 1 child, Mark Richard; m. Byrl William Campbell, Apr. 26, 1981 (dec. 1984). BA, U. Akron, 1987, postgrad., 1988-90. Scheduler motor vehicle bur. Akron Police Dept., 1959-62; flight and ops. control staff Escort Air, Inc., Akron and Cleve., 1972-78; asst. traffic mgr. Keen Transport, Inc., Hudson, Ohio, 1978-83; mem. ops. and mktg. staff Shawnee Airways and Essco, Akron, 1983-86; in distbn. U.S. Postal Svc., Akron, 1986—. Rec. sec. Affirmative Action Coun., Akron, 1988-90. Asst. art tchr. Akron Art Mus., 1979; counselor Support, Inc., Akron, 1983-84; com. chmn. Explorer post Boy Scouts Am., Akron, 1984-85. Mem. Bus. and Profl. Women's Assn. (pres.), Delta Nu Alpha. Democrat. Roman Catholic. Avocations: painting, sculpting, fabric design. Home: 745 Hampton Ridge Dr Akron OH 44313

SHANE, VIRGINIA, tribal court judge, lawyer; b. Norwalk, Conn., Nov. 26, 1935; d. David Hoyt Rogers and Carolyn Elizabeth Mitchell; 1 child, Christopher M. JD, U. Pacific, Sacramento, 1980. Bar: Nev. 1980, US Dist. Ct. Nev. 82. Ticket office mgr. Air New Zealand, Honolulu, 1966—70; sales rep., sales mgr. Hughes Airwest, San Francisco and Reno, Nev., 1970—73; dep. dir. econ. devel. State of Nev., Carson City, 1973—76; pub. defender Nev. State Pub. Defender Office, Winnemucca, 1980—82; dist. atty. Humboldt County, Winnemucca, 1983—86; pvt. practice Winnemucca, 1987—; chief judge Shoshone-Pauite Trives, Owyhee, Nev., 2004—. Address: Po Box 249 Owyhee NV 89832-0249

SHANEYFELT, PATRICIA THARIN, elementary school educator; b. Dunedin, Fla., Apr. 12, 1954; d. Robert M. and Ruth (Black) Tharin; m. James L. Shanyfelt, Dec. 28. 1973 (div. 1983); children: Daniel J., Randall D. AA with honors, St. Petersburg Jr. Coll., 1974; BA, U. South Fla., 1986. Second and third grade tchr. Cross Bayou Elem. & Deaf Edn., Pinellas Park, Fla., 1986-90; second and fourth grade tchr. Garrison Jones Elem. Sch., Dunedin, Fla., 1990—. Author: Heart Connections, The Character Factory. Recipient Fla. State Teaching Econs. award, 1989, 91, 2nd Place award Pinellas County Econs. Fair, 1989, 1st Place award Nat. Awards Program Teaching Econs., 1990, 92; named Cross Bayou's Tchr. of Yr., 1990, Garrison Jones Tchr. of Yr., 1992. Democrat. Episcopalian. Avocations: swimming, boating, camping. Home: 238 Garden Cir S Dunedin FL 34698-7544

SHANKLIN, CAROL W., dietician, educator; BS in Home Econs. Edn., U. Tenn., Martin, 1973; MS in Food Sys. Adminstrn., U. Tenn., Knoxville, 1974, PhD in Food Sys. Adminstrn., 1976. Asst. prof. foods and nutrition Tex. Tech. U., 1977—78; asst. food svc. dir. Highland Hosp., Lubbock, Tex., 1978; asst. prof. food sys. mgmt. Tex. Women's U., 1978—82, assoc. prof. food sys. mgmt., 1982—88, assoc. prof., chair Dept. Nutrition and Food Scis., 1985—87, prof., chair Dept. Nutrition and Food Scis., 1987—90; tech. advisor, cons. Miss. Inst. Higher Learning, 1988—89; grad. program dir., prof. dept. hotel, restaurant, instn. mgmt. and dietetics Kans. State U., Manhattan, 1990—2001, asst. dean. Grad. Sch., prof. dept. hotel, restaurant, instn. mgmt. and dietetics, 2001—04, assoc. dean. Grad. Sch., prof. dept. hotel, restaurant, instn. mgmt. and dietetics, 2004—. Contbr. articles to profl. jours. Recipient Michael Olsen Rsch. Achievement award, U. Del. Mem.: Am. Dietetic Assn. (Medallion award 2001). Achievements include research in on environmental issues in the foodservice and hospitality industry; dietetics and hospitality education; quality service in foodservice operations; and foodservice management, food safety and nutrition in foodservice operations. Office: Kansas State U Graduate Sch 103 Fairchild Manhattan KS 66502-1404 Office Phone: 785-532-7927. Business E-Mail: shanklin@k-state.edu.

SHANKLIN, ELIZABETH E., secondary school educator; b. Nashville, July 23, 1934; d. J. Gordon and Emily (Shacklett) S. BS, Columbia U., 1956; MA, Sarah Lawrence Coll., 1990. Tchr. N.Y.C. Bd. of Edn., 1968—. Author: The Answer is Matriarchy, 1978, Toward Matriarchy: The Radical Struggle of Women in the United States to Reconstruct Motherhood 1785-1925, 1990, Authorizing Mothers, 1824-1833, 2004. Mem. AAUW, AFT, Am. Hist. Assn., Orgn. Am. Historians, The Feminists. Green Party. Home: 2600 Netherland Ave Bronx NY 10463-4801 Personal E-mail: eshanklin@optonline.net.

SHANKS, ANN ZANE, filmmaker, film producer, director, photographer, writer; b. NYC; d. Louis and Sadye (Rosenthal) Kushner; m. Ira Zane (dec.); children— Jennifer, Anthony; m. Robert Horton Shanks, Sept. 25, 1959; 1 child, John. Student, Carnegie-Mellon U., Columbia U., 1949. Tchr., moderator spl. symposiums Mus. Modern Art, N.Y.C.; tchr. New Sch. U. Photographer, writer: for numerous mags. and newspapers; prodr., dir. (films) Ctrl. Pk., 1969 (U.S. entry Edinburgh Film Festival, Cine Golden Eagle award, Cambodia Film Festival award), Denmark.A Loving Embrace (Cine Golden Eagle award, 1973), Tivoli, 1972—79 (San Francisco Film Festival award, Am. Film Festival award), (TV series) Am. Life Style (Silver award, 5 Gold medal awards Internat. TV and Film Festival N.Y., 2 Cine Golden Eagle awards), He's Fired, She's Hired; prodr.: Drop-Out Mother; prodr., dir., writer (TV) Mousie Baby; dir.: (TV films) Drop-Out Father; prodr.: (plays, video spl.) The Avante-Garde in Russia 1910-1930 (Emmy award nomination); prodr., dir. (TV spl.) A Day in the Country, PBS, (plays) S.J. Perelman in Person; prodr.: (Broadway plays) Lillian; prodr., dir.: Gore Vidal's Am. Pres.; exhibitions include Mus. Modern Art, Mus. City NY, Transit Mus., Bklyn. Heights, NY, Met. Mus. Art, Jewish Mus., Howard Greenberg Gallery, NYC, 1999, one-woman shows include NY Hist. Soc., 2003—04, NY State Mus., Albany, 2005—06, Represented in permanent collections Merv Griffin, NY Pub. Libr., Mus. of City of NY, Met. Mus., NY, others, catalog, Ann Zane Shanks Behind the Lens, 2003; author (photographer, author): Old is What You Get, Busted Lives.Dialogues with Kids in Jail, 1983, Garbage and Stuff. Recipient awards from internat. photography competitions. Mem. Am. Soc. Mag. Photographers (bd. govs.), Women in Film (v.p.), Dirs. Guild Am.; trustee Overseas Press Club. Office Phone: 413-229-0444.

SHANKS, KATHRYN MARY, health facility administrator; b. Glens Falls, NY, Aug. 4, 1950; d. John Anthony and Lenita (Combs) S. BS summa cum laude, Spring Hill Coll., 1972; MPA, Auburn U., 1976. Program evaluator Mobile (Ala.) Mental Health, 1972-73; dir. spl. projects Ala. Dept. Mental Health, Montgomery, 1973-76; dir. adminstrn. S.W. Ala. Mental Health/Mental Retardation, Andalusia, 1976-78; adminstr. Mobile County Health Dept., 1978-82; exec. dir. Coastal Family Health Ctr., Biloxi, Miss., 1982-95; cons. med. group practice, 1995—; ptnr. Shanks & Allen, Mobile, 1979—; healthcare consulting pvt. practice, 1995—; practice dir. USA Health Svcs. Found., 1999—2001; practice mgr. Humana Mil. Healthcare Svcs., 2002—06; bus. mgr. Lynn Meadows Discovery Ctr., 2006—. Cons. S.W. Health Agy., Tylertown, Miss., 1984-86; instr., mgr. dept. pediats. U. South Ala., 1997-99; preceptor Sch. Nursing, U. So. Miss., Hattiesburg, 1983, 84; advisor Headstart Program, Gulfport, Miss., 1984-95; LPN Program, Gulf Coast C.C., 1984-95; lectr. Auburn U., Montgomery, 1977-78. Bd. dirs. Mobile Cmty. Action Agy., 1979-81, Moore Cmty. House; mem. S.W. Ala. Regional Goals Forum, Mobile, 1971-72, Cardiac Rehab. Study Com., Biloxi, Miss., 1983-84, Mothers and Babies Coalition, Jackson, Miss., 1983-95, Gulf Coast Coalition Human Svcs., Biloxi, 1983-95; exec. dir. Year for Miss., 1993-94. Pres.'s scholar, Spring Hill Coll., 1972. Mem. ACLU, Miss. Primary Health Care Assn. (pres.), Med. Group Mgmt. Assn., Soc. for Advancement of Ambulatory Care, Spring Hills Alumni Assn. Avocations: tennis, home restoration, golf.

SHANKS, PATRICIA L., lawyer; b. Salt Lake City, Apr. 3, 1940; BA in Microbiology with honors, Stanford U., 1962; JD, U. Colo., 1978. Bar: Calif. 1978. Mng. ptnr. McCutchen, Doyle, Brown & Enersen, L.A., 1990-94, ptnr., 1985—. Trustee L.A. County Bar Found., 2001-04. Recipient West Publishing award; Stork scholar. Mem. Order of the Coif, Practice in Environ. Law. Office: Bingham McCutchen 355 S Grand Ave Ste 4400 Los Angeles CA 90071-3106

SHANLEY, PATRICIA CAROLIN, retired school media specialist; b. Syracuse, N.Y., Aug. 3, 1940; d. Edward Anthony Carolin and Anne Marie Degan; m. Brian James Shanley, June 28, 1975. BS in Humanities, Le Moyne Coll., Syracuse, 1962; MLS, Syracuse U., 1967. Cert. libr. media specialist N.Y., 1971. Libr. media specialist Jefferson County Bd. Coop. Ednl. Svcs., Watertown, NY, 1962—64, Indian River Ctrl. Sch. Dist., Philadelphia, NY, 1964—65, Clinton Ctrl. Sch. Dist., NY, 1965—66, Pearl River Union Free Sch. Dist, NY, 1966—99; ret., 1999. Trustee Monroe Free Libr., NY, 2005—. Mem.: N.Y. State Acad. for Tchg. and Learning, N.Y. Libr. Assn. (regional coord. sch. libr. media sect. 1995—99, pres. sch. libr. media sect. 2005—06, v.p. confs. sch. libr. media sect. 1999—2003, v.p./pres.-elect sch. libr. media sect. 2004—05), Sch. Libr. Media Specialists Southeastern N.Y. (pres. 1993—95), Delta Kappa Gamma. Democrat. Roman Catholic. Avocations: reading, gardening, travel, tai chi. Home: 123 Cromwell Hill Rd Monroe NY 10950 Personal E-mail: pshanley@frontiernet.net.

SHANNON, BARBARA HELEN, secondary school educator; b. San Francisco, Jan. 22, 1942; d. Meyer and Anny Levin; m. Ron Shannon, Sept. 29, 1965; children: Brent, Jeannine. BA, Calif. State U., San Jose, 1963. Cert. secondary sch. tchr. Calif. Tchr. Camarillo HS, Calif., 1964—65, Oxnard Union Adult Sch., Camarillo, 1964—74, Thousand Oaks HS, Calif., 1965—70, Conejo Valley Ind. Study, Thousand Oaks, 1986—2005, Conejo Valley Adult Sch., Thousand Oaks, 1985—. Home: 644 Briar Cliff Rd Thousand Oaks CA 91360-5101

SHANNON, DONNA LYNNE, physical education educator, real estate broker; b. Martins Ferry, Ohio, Mar. 19, 1951; d. Donto and Norma Dolfi Spong; m. David Shannon, Aug. 25, 1973 (div. Oct. 10, 1993); children: Mathew, Lauren Ferency. BS in Edn., Ohio U., Athens, 1973; MLIS, Wayne State U., Detroit, 1997. Cert. tchr. Mich., 1993. Tchr. phys. edn., lifetime fitness, dance instr. Hillside Mid. Sch., Northville, Mich., 2000—; CEO, owner MD Properties of Mich., Brighton, 2003—. Mem. adv. bd. Northville Health Initiative, 2004—05. Mem. devel. com. No Stopping Northville Health Initiative, 2004—05; dir. edn. Licking County Mar. of Dimes, Newark, Ohio, 1975—78; conf. presenter Mich. Assn. Health Phys. Edn. Recreation, Traverse City, 1998—2004. Recipient Outstanding Tchr. award, Wayne County Regional Ednl. Svcs., 2004, 2005, Excellence in Tchg. award, Ford Motor Co.; grantee Keep Mich. Moving, Mich., 2001, Northville Mothers Club, 2001, 2002, 2003, 2004, Coca-Cola, 2006. Mem.: Mich. Assn. Health, Phys. Edn. and Recreation (assoc.), Am. Assn. Health, Phys. Edn., Recreation (assoc.). Office Phone: 810-923-5511.

SHANNON, IRIS REED, health facility administrator, consultant; b. Chgo. d. Ira Paul and Iola Sophia Reed. BS in Nursing, Fisk U.-Meharry Med. Coll., 1948; MA, U. Chgo., 1954; PhD, U. Ill., Chgo., 1987; D in Pub. Svc. (hon.), Elmhurst Coll., 1993. Staff nurse Chgo. Bd. Health, 1948-50; instr. pub. health nursing Meharry Med. Coll., Nashville, 1951-56; tchr.-nurse, health coordinator child devel. Head Start, Chgo. Bd. Edn., 1957-66; dir. community nursing Mile Sq. Neighborhood Health Center, Presbyn.-St. Luke's Hosp., Chgo., 1966-69; co-dir. nurse assoc. programs Rush Presbyn.-St. Luke's Hosp., 1971-76; chairperson community nursing Rush U., Chgo., 1972-77, acting chairperson, 1988-90; asst. prof. pub. health nursing U. Ill., 1971-74; assoc. prof. cmty. nursing Rush U., 1974-97, health sys. mgr., 1988—, health cons., 1974—. Adj. faculty Sch. Pub. Health, U. N.C., 1977—85; mem. profl. adv. bd. Vis. Nurse Assn. Chgo., 1973—75; cons. Video Nursing, Inc.; mem. profl. adv. com. Mile Sq. Home Health Unit, Chgo., 1975—77; mem. nat. adv. coun. on nurse tng. HEW, 1978—81; mem. Nat. Task Force on Credentialing in Nursing, 1979—82; mem. Chgo. regional com. Ill. White House Conf. on Children, 1979—80; v.p. Chgo. Bd. Health, 1989—99. Named Prin. for a Day, Brownell Elem. Sch., Mayor's Office, City of Chgo., 1998—99, Englewood Tech. Prep. Acad., 2000—01; recipient award of merit, Ill. Pub. Health Assn., 1979, 1989—2000, Outstanding Achievement award, YWCA of Met. Chgo., 1988, Disting. Svc. award, Chgo. chpt. Meharry Alumni, 1989, Lowenberg Chair of Excellence in Nursing, Memphis State U., 1993, Bd. Trustees' Svc. medal, Rush-Presby. St. Luke's Med. Ctr., 1996, Lifeline award, Cmty. Mental Health Coun., 2002. Fellow: APHA (chmn. pub. health nursing sect. 1977—79, governing coun. 1980—82, exec. bd. 1985—87, pres. 1988—89, governing coun. 1989—99), Am. Acad. Nursing, Royal Soc. Health (hon. 1989); mem.: ANA (Pearl McIver Pub. Health Nurse award 1998), Inst. of Medicine of NAS, Delta Sigma Theta, Sigma Theta Tau. Home: 3100 S King Dr Chicago IL 60616-3634 Office Phone: 312-842-6164. E-mail: irisshannon@aol.com.

SHANNON, JONNIE LYNN, nursing administrator; b. Richland Ctr., Wis., Aug. 28, 1959; d. John L. and Glenda Jean (Dyer) Laue; m. Michael Robert Shannon, Sept. 15, 1979; Ryan John, Sean Michael. Nursing diploma, Moline (Ill.) Sch. Nursing, 1980. Staff nurse Moline Pub. Hosp., 1980-83, Mercy Hosp., Davenport, Iowa, 1987-88, United Med. Ctr., Moline, Ill., 1988-91; dir. nursing East Moline Garden Pla., East Moline, Ill., 1991—. Asst. DON Manor Care, 1991-92; instr. med. assisting program, co-author curriculum Hamilton Tech. Coll., 1992-95; med. case mgr. Concentra Managed Care, 1995—; mem. adv. bd. Hamilton Tech. Coll. Mem. AACN (chair person merit program Twin River Valley chpt., newsletter editor). Avocation: reading.

SHANNON, JULIE (JULIE GELLER), musician, educator, composer, lyricist; b. Springfield, Ohio, Mar. 15, 1941; d. LeRoy Stewart and Marie Arment; m. William Alan Geller, Oct. 1, 1978. MusB, U. Mich., 1963, MusM, 1964. Tchr. vocal music Deerfield (Ill.) Pub. Schs., 1964—83; artist-in-residence Ill. Arts Coun., Chgo., 1985—2000, North Shore Country Day Sch., Winnetka, Ill., 1991—, numerous other pub. & pvt. schs., Ill., 1990—. Composer, lyricist: songs Chicago - It's the People, 1979, One Breath, 1989 (selected for choral arrangement by Kirby Shaw, 2003), plays The Christmas Schooner, 1993 (After Dark Outstanding New Work award, Chgo., 1996), Stones, 1989 (Best Musical award, Phoenix, 1994, Black Theatre Alliance award, 2000), Let the Eagle Fly: The Story of Cesar Chavez & the Farm Workers, 2003 (Am. Music Ctr. Copying Assistance Ctr. award, 2003, Yip Harburg Found. Devel. award, 2003), albums Let's Fill Up the House with Stories & Songs, 1999 (Parents Choice Approved award, 2000), We All Have Songs, We All Have Stories, 1995, films Baby, You're OK, 1983 (Excalibur award for best pub. film from Pub. Rels. Assn., 1984), Soxfest, 1989 (Top Mktg. award Baseball Promotion Corp., 1983), intergenerational church svc. We All Have Stories (Unitarian Churches of Am. award for most outstanding intergenerational worship svc., 1998); composer: (TV series) Beyond the Magic Door (Emmy award, Chgo., 1983). Fellow, Ill. Arts Coun., 1984; grantee Chmn.'s Grant, 1986. Mem.: ASCAP (Popular Music award 1986—2003), Am. Fedn. Musicians, Dramatists Guild. Home: 2116 Thornwood Ave Wilmette IL 60091-1452

SHANNON, MARGARET ANNE, lawyer; b. Detroit, July 6, 1945; d. Johannes Jacob and Vera Marie (Spade) Van De Graaf; m. Robert Selby Shannon, Feb. 4, 1967. Student, Brown U., 1963-65; BA in History, Wayne State U., 1966, JD, 1973. Bar: Mich. 1973. Housing aide City of Detroit, 1967-68; employment supr. Sinai Hosp., Detroit, 1968-69; assoc. gen. counsel regulatory affairs Blue Cross Blue Shield Mich., Detroit, 1969-80; ptnr. Honigman Miller Schwartz and Cohn, Detroit, 1980-95, of counsel, 1996—. Nat. Merit scholar, 1963-66. Mem. Mich. State Bar (chmn. health care com. 1991, 92, co-chmn. payor subcom. health law sect.). Home: 1111 Orinoco Way Palm Beach Gardens FL 33410 Office: Honigman Miller Schwartz and Cohn 2290 First National Bldg Detroit MI 48226-3583 Office Phone: 313-465-7552. E-mail: mshannon@honigman.com.

SHANNON, MARGARET BARRETT, lawyer; b. 1949; BA, Baylor U., 1971; JD, Southern Methodist U., 1976. Bar: 1976. Ptnr. Andrews Kurth LLP, 1984—94; v.p., gen. counsel BJ Services Co., 1994—. Mem. United Way Women's Initiative of Alexis de Tocqueville Soc., 2003—04; mem. bd. dirs. St. Luke's Episcopal Health Charities, Houston. Mem.: ABA. Office: BJ Services Co 5500 NW Central Dr Houston TX 77092

SHANNON, MARGARET RITA, retired education educator, retired college dean; b. Cambridge, Mass. d. James J. and Catherine M. (McDonough) S. BS, U. Mass., Lowell, 1936; MEd, Harvard U., 1947, Ed.D., 1959. Tchr. pub. schs., Cambridge, 1936-51; from asst. prof. to prof. Univ. Mass., Lowell, 1951-79, chmn. dept. edn., 1969-74, dean Coll. Edn., 1974-79, prof. emeritus, dean emeritus, 1979—. Lectr. in field. Author textbooks; contbr. articles to profl. jours. Mem. Internat. Reading Assn. (cons. nat. conf.), Am. Ednl. Research Assn., Nat. Council Tchrs. English (com. on linguistics and reading), Delta Kappa Gamma, Pi Lambda Theta (chpt. pres. 1958-61) Home: 6 Kent Rd Needham MA 02492-1849

SHANNON, MARILYN MCCUSKER, biologist, educator; b. McKeesport, Pa., June 16, 1952; d. David Edward and Margaret Ellen McCusker; m. Ronald Ellis Shannon, Jan. 8, 1977; children: John, Rosemary Shannon Imrick, Stephen, Gregory, Regina, Ellen, Vahn, Monica, Lucia. BA, U. Pitts., 1974; MA, Ind. U., Bloomington, 1979. Instr. biology Alverno Coll., Milw., 1979—80, Ind. U.-Purdue U., Ft. Wayne, Ind., 1983—. Vol. tchr. Couple to Couple Legue, Cin., 1982—, faculty Ann. Physician's Conf., 1998—; spkr. in field. Author: Fertility, Cycles and Nutrition, 1990, 3d edit., 2001, (booklet) Managing Morning Sickness, 1996; co-author (with Jay Wile and Marilyn Shannon): (textbook) The Human Body, 2002. Key leader Allen County 4-H Clubs, Ft. Wayne, Ind., 2001—, bd. dirs., 2006—; parish coun. Sacred Heart Cath. Ch., Ft. Wayne, Ind., 2005—. Recipient Edward M. Keefe award, Couple to Couple League, Cin., 1992. Roman Catholic. Avocations: gardening, dairy goat breeding and care, hiking, cooking, writing. E-mail: shannon@ipfw.edu.

SHANTZ, DEBRA MALLONEE, lawyer; b. Springfield, Mo., Aug. 12, 1963; d. Arnold Wayne and Jean Marie (Pyle) Mallonee; m. Joseph Benjamin Shantz, Dec. 26, 1987; children: Benjamin, Riley. BS, S.W. Mo. State U., 1984; JD, U. Mo., 1988. Ptnr. Farrington & Curtis, P.C., Springfield, Mo., 1988-95; corp. counsel John Q. Hammons Hotels, Springfield, Mo., 1995—2003, sr. v.p., gen. counsel, 2003—. Bd. mem. Springfield City Utilities; Discovery Ctr.; Jordan Valley Park Cmty. Improvement Dist. Mem.: ABA, State Bar Mo., Springfield Met. Bar Assn. Home: 1635 E Delmar St Springfield MO 65804-0207 Office: John Q Hammons Hotels Ste 900 300 John Q Hammons Pkwy Springfield MO 65806 E-mail: debbie.shantz@jqh.com.

SHAO COLLINS, JEANNINE, magazine publisher; married; 1 child. BA in Econs., U. Rochester. Various advt. sales mgmt. positions Woman's Day, N.Y.C., Prevention mag.; N.Y. advt. mgr. Ladies' Home Jour., Meredith Corp., N.Y.C., 1993-95, advt. dir. Better Homes and Gardens, Des Moines, 1995-98, assoc. pub., 1998-99, pub., 1999—2002, v.p., 2000—02, v.p., group pub. N.Y.C., 2002—.

SHAPIRO, ABRA BLAIR, real estate company executive; b. Akron, Ohio, Aug. 15, 1956; d. Norman Nathan and Merrill Barron Shapiro; m. Sanford Robert Epstein, Aug. 29, 1982 (div. July 1986). AA, Dekalb C.C., 1976; BA, Ga. State, 1978; CPM, Inst. Real Estate Mgmt., 1987. Lic. realtor Minn. Bd. Realtors, Ga. Bd. Realtors. V.p. Sidney's Mgmt. Co., Chaska, Minn., 1982—2002; ops. dir. Jon Shapiro, Atlanta, 2002—. Adv. bd. Barbers Hairstyling Inc., Mpls., 1986—88; cons. in field. Mem. Designers in Fight for AIDS, Mpls., 1996. Named Restaurator of Yr., Mpls. St. Paul Mag., 1995; recipient Hometown Hero award, WCCO, 2001, honor, Dayton Hudson Found., 1997. Home: 1008 Saddle Hl Marietta GA 30068-4916

SHAPIRO, ANN R., English educator; b. Bklyn., Feb. 28, 1937; d. Murray and Jeanette Rabinowitz; children: Rona Gail, Wendy Lynn, Edward Ira. AB cum laude, Radcliff Coll., 1958; MA in Teaching, Harvard U., 1960; PhD, NYU, 1985. Instr. English Rider Coll., 1962-65, Suffolk County (N.Y.) Community Coll., 1966-67; prof. SUNY, Farmingdale, 1974—. Adv. bd. Greenwood Ency. Multiethnic Am. Lit.; speaker in field. Author: Unlikely Heroines: Nineteenth-Century American Women Writers and the Woman Question; Introduction (with Joy Gould Boyum), A Country Doctor (Sarah Orne Jewett); editor: Jewish American Women Writers: A Bio-Bibliographical and Critical Sourcebook, 2006; contbg. author: Smashing the Idols; contbr. articles to profl. jours. Fellow Nat. Inst. Leadership Devel., 1987, Salzburg, 1988, NEH, 1990, 94. Mem. MLA (mem. exec. com. discussion group). Home: 1148 5th Ave New York NY 10128-0807 Office: SUNY Dept English Farmingdale NY 11735

SHAPIRO, ANNA, microbiologist, researcher; b. N.Y.C., Jan. 11, 1910; d. Samuel and Esther (Cohen) Lewis; m. Joseph Shapiro, Feb. 7, 1933 (dec. 1985); children: Joan Elisabeth Brandston (dec.), Joel Elias. BS in Biology and Chemistry, NYU, 1931, MS in Bacteriology, 1934, PhD in Microbiology, 1971. Lab. asst. Bellevue Med. Sch., NYU, 1931-33, instr., 1933-36; lectr. Hofstra U., L.I., 1963, Queensborough U., CUNY, Queens, 1964; rsch. asst. Haskins Lab. of Pace Univ., N.Y.C., 1971-80, rsch. assoc., 1980-83. Author: Methods of Enzymology, 1980, The In Vitro Cultivation of Pathogens of Tropical Diseases, 1980; contbr. articles to profl. jours. Mem. AAAS, N.Y. Acad. Sci. (Disting. Svc. award 1992), Sigma Xi. Achievements include rsch. in the conversion of Nitrobacter agilis from a strict autotroph to a heterotroph by using replica plating techniques which can be considered an adaptive mutation; blockade of respiratory systems of parasites by using iron chelators--this work led to further research in pathogenic African trypanosomes. Home: 130 E 67TH St New York NY 10021-6136

SHAPIRO, BETH JANET, librarian; b. Newton, Mass., July 18, 1946; d. Harold H. and Marilyn Ann (Katz) S.; m. Russell Carl Barnes, May 15, 1987; children: Gabrielle Alexandra Barnes. BS in Sociology, Mich. State U., 1968, MA in Sociology, 1971; MLS, Western Mich. U., 1974; PhD in Sociology, Mich. State U., 1981. Urban affairs bibliographer Mich. State U. Librs., East Lansing, 1972-76, urban policy and planning librarian, 1976-79, social sci. coord., 1979-81, asst. dir., 1981-85, assoc. dir., 1985-87, deputy dir., 1987-90; univ. libr. Rice U., Houston, 1991—. Mem. rsch. librs. adv. com. Online Coll. Libr. Ctr., Inc., 1992—; bd. dirs. Ctr. for Rsch. Librs., 1994—. Editor: Selection of Library Materials in the Humanities, Social Sciences. and Sciences., 1985, Selection of Library Materials in Applied and Interdisciplinary Fields, 1987. Mem. Ingham County Equal Opportunity Com., Mason, Mich., 1974-75, Lansing Com. on Affirmative Action, 1976-78, Capital City Revitalization Task Force, Lansing, 1986; mem. Mich. Consumers Coun., Lansing, 1982-88, chmn., 1987-88; bd. dirs. Interracial Family Alliance of Houston, 1993—. Grantee Coun. on Libr. Resources, 1978, 83, 93. Mem. ALA (councilor 1991-95), N.Am. Soc. for Sociology Sport. Office: Rice University Fondren Library MS44 6100 Main St Houston TX 77005-1892

SHAPIRO, ELLEN M., graphics designer, writer; b. L.A., June 26, 1948; d. Leon E. and Elizabeth (Nussbaum) S.; 1 child, Alex Miller; m. Julius Rabinowitz, Sept. 6, 1992. BA, UCLA, 1970. Art dir. UCLA, 1970-72; sr. designer Lubalin Smith Carnase, Inc., N.Y.C., 1972-74; art dir. Barton-Gillet Co., N.Y.C., 1974-76; ptnr. Design Concern, N.Y.C., 1976-78; pres. Shapiro Design Assocs. Inc., Irvington, NY, 1978—, Alphagram Learning Materials, 1997—. Adj. faculty Purchase Coll., SUNY, Sch. Visual Arts, Parsons Sch. Design, Pratt Inst.; judge design and advt. shows, U.S. and Can. Art dir., Upper & Lower Case, 1988; author: Clients and Designers, 1989, Ready, Set, Read! Skills and Activities That Help Build Confident Readers, 1999, The Graphic Designer's Guide to Clients, 2004; contbr. over 100 articles to mags. and profl. jours.; patentee in field of phonics and spelling; developer manipulative tools and visual aids for tchg. reading. Recipient over 60 awards from profl. orgns. Mem. Am. Inst. Graphic Arts (v.p. N.Y. chpt. 1987-89), N.Y. Art Dirs. Club (Gold and Silver awards), N.Y. Type Dirs. Club. Avocations: cooking, gardening, yoga, swimming, hand drumming. Mailing: Shapiro Design Assocs Inc 25 Whitetail Rd Irvington NY 10533-1037 Office Phone: 914-693-7799. E-mail: ellen@visualanguage.net.

SHAPIRO, FLORENCE, state legislator, advertising executive, public relations executive; b. NYC, May 2, 1948; d. Martin Nmi and Ann (Spiesman) D.; m. Howard Nmi Shapiro, Dec. 28, 1969; children: Lisa, Todd, Staci. BS, U. Tex., 1970. Tchr. Richardson High Sch., Tex., 1970-72; advt., pub. rels. Shapiro & Co., Plano, Tex., 1982—; formerly mayor and mem. city coun. City of Plano, Tex.; now mem. Tex. Senate, 1992—, chmn. edn. com., mem. fin. com., adminstrn. com. and transp. and homelend security coms. Bd. dirs. Plano C. of C., Presbyn. and Children's Healthcare Ctr., Plano Econ. Devel. Bd., U. Tex. at Dallas Adv. Coun., The North Tex. Commn., The Dallas Regional Mobility Coalition; mem. nat. bd. dirs. Susan B. Komen Breast Cancer Found.; mem. adv. bd. Children's Edn. Fund Dallas, Dallas County Domestic Violence Task Force, Family Violence Prevention Coun. Injury Prevention Ctr. Greater Dallas. Recipient Plano Vol. of Yr. award, 1983, Plano Citizen of Yr. award, 1985, Athena award Plano C. of C. for Businesswoman of Yr., 1990, Child Advocate award Dallas Children's Advocacy Ctr., 1995, Legislator of Yr. award Tex. Mcpl. League, 1995, 97, Nat. Rep. Legislators Assn., 1997, Tex. Ct. Apptd. Spl. Advs., 1997; Outstanding Legislator of Yr. award Tex. Police Chiefs Assn., 1995, Legislator of Yr. award, 1997, Friend of the Taxpayer award Citizens for a Sound Economy, 1999, Centennial Hero award Plano Ind. Sch. Dist., 1999, Voice of Children award, Ct. Apptd. Spl. Advs. of Collin County, 2001, others; Outstanding Legislator award Tex. Assn. Dist. and County Attys., 1997, Leader of Excellence award Free Market Com., 1997, Senate Statesman award Lonestar Found., 1997, Polit. Courage award John Ben Sheppard Pub. Leadership Forum, 1997; named One of 10 Best Legislators family law session State Bar Tex., 1997, One of 3 State Senators on YCT Honor Roll, 1997, Legis. Star, Tex. Classroom Tchrs. Assn., 1997, Guardian of Free Enterprise, Nat. Fedn. Ind. Bus., 1999, Woman of Yr., Les Femmes du Monde, 2002, Woman of Yr., Women's Transp. Seminar Dallas-Ft. Worth, 2002, others; honored by Texans for Lawsuit Reform, 1997, Assn. Ob-Gyn. and Southwestern Med. Sch., 1997. Mem. Rotary (Paul Harris fellow 1990), Alpha Epsilon Phi (Nat. Outstanding Young Alumnae award). Republican. Jewish. Office: Tex Senate PO Box 12068 Austin TX 78711-2068 Home: 1500 Eastwick Ln Plano TX 75093-2443

SHAPIRO, JOAN ISABELLE, lab administrator, medical/surgical nurse; b. Aug. 26, 1943; d. Macy James and Frieda Lockhart; m. Ivan Lee Shapiro, Dec. 28, 1968; children: Audrey, Michael. Diploma, Peoria Meth. Sch. Nursing, 1964. RN. Nurse Nurse Grant Hosp., Columbus, Ohio, 1975—76, Cardiac Thoracic and Vascular Surgeons Ltd., Geneva, Ill., 1977—, mgr. non-invasive lab., 1979—. Owner operator Shapiro's Mastiff's 1976-82; sec.-treas. Sounds Svcs., 1976—, Mainstream Sounds Inc., 1980-84; co-founder Cardio-Phone Inc., 1982-99, Edgewater Vascular Inst., 1987-89, Associated Profls., 1989-92; v.p. Computer Specialists Inc., 1986-89; founder, pres. Vein Ctr., Edema Ctr. Ltd. Mem. DAR (sec. Katahdin Valley-Lydia Putman chpt. 2004—), Soc. Non-invasive Technologists, Soc. Peripheral Vascular Nursing (cmty. awareness com. 1984-2004), Kane County Med. Soc. Aux. (pres. 1983-84, adviser, 1984-85), Katahdin Valley Putnam Cpt. of DAR (sec. 2004-). Lutheran. Home: Cardiac Thoracic/Vas Surg PO Box 325 Fort Fairfield ME 04742-0325 Business E-Mail: joan@ivanshapiro.com.

SHAPIRO, JUDITH R., academic administrator, anthropology educator; b. NYC, Jan. 24, 1942; Student, Ecole des Haute Etudes Inst. d'Etudes Politiques, Paris, 1961—62; BA, Brandeis U., 1963; PhD, Columbia U., 1972. Asst. prof. U. Chgo., 1970—75; fellow U. Calif., Berkeley, 1974—75; Rosalyn R. Schwartz lectr., asst. prof. anthropology Bryn Mawr Coll., Pa., 1975—78, assoc. prof. Pa., 1978—85, prof. Pa., 1985—94; pres. Barnard Coll., 1994—. Chmn. dept. Bryn Mawr Coll., 1982—85, acting dean undergrad coll., 1985—86, provost, 1986—94; bd. dir. Fund for City of NY; ptnr. NYC Partnership and C. of C.; exec. com. NY Bldg. Congress. Contbr. articles to profl. jours. Nat. adv. com. Woodrow Wilson Nat. Fellowship Found.; chair bd. dirs. Consortium on Financing Higher Edn.; bd. dirs. Fund for the City of N.Y.; chair bd. dirs. Women's Coll. Coalition. Recipient Gold Medal, Nat. Inst. of Social Sciences, 2002; fellow, Woodrow Wilson Found., 1963—64, Columbia U., 1964—65, Younger Humanist fellow, NEH, 1974—75, Am. Coun. Learned Socs., 1981—82, Ctr. for Advanced Study in the Behavioral Scis., 1989; grantee Summer Field Tng. grant, NSF, 1965, Ford Found., 1966, NIMH, 1974—75, Social Sci. Rsch. Coun., 1974—75. Mem.: NY State Leadership Coun. (devel. of World's Mus., NYC), Am. Philos. Soc., Social Sci. Rsch. Coun. (com. social sci personnel 1977—80), Am. Anthrop. Assn. (ethics com. 1976—79, bd. dirs. 1984—86, exec. com. 1985—86), Am. Ethnol. Soc. (nominations com. 1983—84, pres. elect 1984—85, pres. 1985—86), Phila. Anthrop. Soc. (pres. 1983), Morningside Area Alliance (pres. 2003—04), adv. com. Save the Children, Women's Forum, Sigma Xi, Phi Beta Kappa. Office: Barnard Coll Office of Pres 109 Milbank Hall New York NY 10027 Office Phone: 212-854-2021.*

SHAPIRO, LARA RUTH, lawyer; d. Jonathan Shapiro and Barbara Ann Milman. LVN, Sacramento City Coll., 1988; BA in Philosophy, Calif. State U., Chico, 2000; JD, McGeorge Sch. Law, Sacramento, 2003. Bar: Calif. 2003. Assoc. Clement & Assoc., Sacramento, 2003—05, Gwire Law Offices, San Francisco, 2006—; pvt. practice law Sacramento, 2005—06. Home: 2807 H St Apt 10 Sacramento CA 95816-4346

SHAPIRO, LUCY, molecular biology educator; b. NYC, July 16, 1940; d. Philip and Yetta (Stein) Cohen; m. Roy Shapiro, Jan. 23, 1960 (div. 1977); 1 child, Peter; m. Harley H. McAdams, July 28, 1978; stepchildren: Paul, Heather. BA, Bklyn. Coll., 1962; PhD, Albert Einstein Coll. Medicine, 1966. Asst. prof. Albert Einstein Coll. Medicine, N.Y.C., 1967-72, assoc. prof., 1972-77, Kramer prof., chmn. dept. molecular biology, 1977-86, dir. biol. scis. divsn., 1981-86; Eugene Higgins prof., chmn. dept. microbiology, Coll. Physicians and Surgeons Columbia U., N.Y.C., 1986-89; Joseph D. Grant prof. devel. biology Stanford (Calif.) U. Sch. Medicine, 1989-97, chmn. dept. devel. biology, 1989-97, Virginia and D.K. Ludwig prof. cancer rsch., dept. devel. biology, 1998—; dir. Beckman Ctr. Molecular and Genetic Medicine, Stanford U., 2001—. Mem. bd. sci. counselors NIH, Washington, 1980—84; mem. bd. sci. advisors G.D. Searle Co., Skokie, Ill., 1984—86; trustee Scientists Inst. for Pub. Info., 1990—94; mem. sci. adv. bd. SmithKline Beecham, 1993—2000, Anacor Pharms., Inc., 2001—, PathoGenesis, 1995—2000, Ludwig Found., 2000—, Glaxo Smith Kline, 2001—; mem. adv. bd. Biodesign Inst., Ariz. State U., 2006—, Singapore Inst. Molecular and Cell Biology, 2006—, Lawrence Berkeley Nat. Labs., 2006—; bd. dirs. Anacor Pharms. Inc., 2001—. Editor: Microbiol. Devel., 1984; mem. editl. bd. Jour. Bacteriology, 1978-86, Trends in Genetics, 1987—, Genes and Development, 1987-91, Cell Regulation, 1990-92, Molecular Biology of the Cell, 1992-98, Molecular Microbiology, 1991-96, Current Opinion on Genetics and Devel., 1991—; contbr. articles to profl. jours. Mem. sci. bd. Helen Hay Witney Found., N.Y.C., 1986-94, Biozentrum, Basel, 1999-2001, Hutchinson Cancer Ctr., Seattle, 1999; mem. grants adv. bd. Beckman Found., 1999—; co-chmn. adv. bd. NSF Biology Directorate, 1988-89; vis. com., bd. overseers Harvard U., Cambridge, Mass., 1987-90, 2003—; mem. sci. bd. Whitehead Inst., MIT, Boston, 1988-93; mem. sci. rev. bd. Howard Hughes Med. Inst., 1990-94, Cancer Ctr. of Mass. Gen. Hosp., Boston, 1994; mem. Presidio Coun. City of San Francisco, 1991-94; mem. pres. coun. U. Calif., 1991-97. Recipient Hirschl Career Scientist award, 1976, Spirit of Achievement award, 1978, Alumna award of honor Bklyn. Coll., 1983, Excellence in Sci. award Fedn. Am. Soc. Exptl. Biology, 1994; Jane Coffin Child fellow, 1966; resident scholar Rockefeller Found., Bellagio, Italy, 1996. Fellow AAAS, Am. Acad. Arts and Scis., Am. Acad. Microbiology, Calif. Coun. on Sci. and Tech.; mem. NAS (Selman A. Waksman award 2005), Inst. Medicine of NAS, Am. Philos. Soc., Am. Soc. Biochemistry and Molecular Biology (nominating com. 1982, 87, coun. 1990-93), Am. Heart Assn. (sci. adv. bd. 1984-87). Avocation: watercolor painting. Office: Stanford U Sch Medicine Beckman Ctr Dept Devel Biology Stanford CA 94305 Office Phone: 650-725-7678.

SHAPIRO, MARIAN KAPLUN, psychologist; b. N.Y., July 13, 1939; d. David and Bertha (Pearlman) Kaplun; m. Irwin Ira Shapiro, Dec. 20, 1959; children: Steven, Nancy. BA, Queens Coll., 1959; MA in Tchg., Harvard U., 1961, EdD, 1978. Cert. psychologist. Tchr. North Quincy (Mass.) HS, 1962-64; instr. Carnegie Inst., Boston, 1968-74; staff psychologist South Shore Counselling Assn., Hanover, Mass., 1978-80; pvt. practice Lexington, Mass., 1980—. Adj. instr. Mass. Sch. Profl. Psychology, Dedham, 1985—. Author: (book) 2nd Childhood: Hypnoplay Therapy with Age--Regressed Adults, 1989; contbr. articles to profl. jours., poetry to lit. jours. Fellow: Am. Orthopsychiatric Assn.; mem.: APA, New Eng. Soc. Clin. Hypnosis, Internat. Soc. Study Dissociation, New Eng. Soc. Treatment Trauma and Dissociation, Am. Soc. Clin. Hypnosis (cert. cons.), Am. Soc. Group Psychotherapy (clin.), N.E. Soc. Group Psychotherapy, Mass. Psychol. Assn., Pi Lambda Theta, Sigma Alpha. Avocations: music, singing, piano, violin, poetry. Home and Office: 17 Lantern Ln Lexington MA 02421-6029 Office Phone: 781-862-3728.

SHAPIRO, MARJORIE D., physics professor; PhD, U. Calif., Berkeley, 1984. Postdoctoral fell. Harvard Univ., Cambridge, Mass., 1984—86, asst. prof., Dept. Physics, 1986—90; prof., Dept. Physics Univ. Calif., Berkeley, Calif., 1990—, now chmn. Dept. Physics. Rschr. Fermilab (CDF), Atlas experiment at CERN, Lawrence Berkeley Labs; spkr. in field. Contbr. articles to numerous profl. jours. Fellow: Am. Physical Soc. Office: UC Berkeley Dept Physics 366 Leconte Berkeley CA 94720-7300 Office Phone: 510-642-3316. Office Fax: 510-643-8497. E-mail: mdshapiro@lbl.gov.*

SHAPIRO, MARSHA N., social worker; b. Phila., July 19, 1954; MSW, U. Pa., 1981. LCSW N.J. Lic. clin. social worker Jewish Family Svc., Harrisburg, Pa., 1981—83, Asbury Park, NJ, 1984—90, Advanced Psychol. Assessments, Freehold, NJ, 1990—94; pvt. practice clin. social work North Brunswick and Toms River, NJ, 1994—. Avocations: dance, hiking, photography, guitar, swimming. Office: 1626 Rt 130 Ste K North Brunswick NJ 08902-1344 Office Phone: 732-422-9400.

SHAPIRO, MARY JO FARLEY, elementary school educator; b. Milw., May 9, 1957; d. Clyde Leroy and Doris Mary Farley; m. Larry Fred Shapiro; children: Matthew Jacob, Luke Joseph, Leah Mary. BBA, U. Wis., Milw., 1979; MEd Interdisciplinary Studies in Curriculum and Instruct. in Interdisciplinary Studies in Curriculum, Nat.-Louis U., Wheeling, Ill., 2002. Cert. adult educator Wis., 1985, tchr. Cardinal Stritch U., Wis., 1993, National Bd. Profl. Tchg. Stds., 2004, instr. Fitness Firm. Fitness instr. Fitness Firm, Brookfield, Wis., 1981—2002; adult edn. instr. Milw. Area Tech. Coll., Milw., 1984—88; tchr. Hartford Ave. U. Sch., Milw., 1993—94, St. Rose Cath. Urban Acad., Milw., 1994—95, Kosciuszko Mid. Sch., Milw., 1995—96, Bayside Mid. Sch., Milw., 1996—. Summer sch. tchr. Bayside Mid. Sch., 2003—. Parent involvement coord. Pilgrim Pk. Mid. Sch., Elm Grove, Wis., 1998—99; co-facilitator tsunami relief fund Bayside Mid., Milw.; polit.

campaign worker Dem. Party, Brookfield; catechist St. Dominic Cath. Ch., Brookfield, 1998; singer Salvator, Christian contemporary musical group, Milw., 1996; choir mem. St. Dominic Adult Ensemble, Brookfield, 2004; catechist Mother of Good Counsel Ch., Milw., 1998—99. Named Bayside Tchr. of Yr., Fox Point - Bayside Tchr. Assn., 2005—06; Kohl fellow, Herb Kohl Ednl. Found., 2006. Mem.: Fox Point - Bayside PTO (assoc.), Wis. Nat. Bd. Cert. Tchrs. Network (assoc.), Wis. Edn. Assn. Coun. (assoc.), Brookfield East H.S. PTO (assoc.). Democrat. Roman Catholic. Avocations: aerobic exercise, singing, hockey. Home: 14665 Cameron Dr Lower Brookfield WI 53005 Office: Bayside Mid Sch 601 E Ellsworth Ln Milwaukee WI 53217 Office Phone: 414-351-7486. Personal E-mail: mjfsteach@aol.com. Business E-Mail: mshapiro@foxbay.k12.wi.us.

SHAPIRO, MYRA STEIN, poet; b. Bronx, N.Y., May 21, 1932; d. David M. and Ida Betty (Leader) Stein; m. Harold M. Shapiro, Feb. 15, 1953; children: Karen S., Judith M. BA, U. Tenn., 1968; MA in English, Middlebury Coll., 1973; MFA, Vt. Coll., 1993. Reader, Internat. Women's Day, Jefferson Market Libr., N.Y.C., 1989, Notre Dame U., 1997, Butler U., 1997, NYU, 1997, Libr. of Congress, 1998; leading performance Midday Muse Series, Folger Shakespeare Libr., Washington, 1983, NEA Hunter Mus., Chattanooga, 1985, Bower's Mus., Santa Ana, Calif., 1986, 88. Author: (poetry) The Ohio Review, 1989, Education for Peace, 1988, Kalliope, 1988, Ploughshares, 1990-91, The Harvard Review, 1994, (book of poems) I'll See You Thursday, 1996, The Best American Poetry, 1999, 2d edit., 2003 Recipient Dylan Thomas Poetry award The New Sch., N.Y.C., 1981; fellow, The MacDowell Colony, Peterborough, N.H., 1985, 87; finalist Allen Ginsburg Poetry award The Poetry Canter, Passaic County C.C., 1994. Mem. Poetry Soc. Am. (finalist Robert H. Winner award 2005), Poets House (bd. dirs.). Internat. Women's Writing Guild. Office: 111 4th Ave Apt 12I New York NY 10003-5243

SHAPIRO, NELLA IRENE, surgeon, educator; b. NYC, Nov. 13, 1947; d. Eugene and Ethel (Pearl) Shapiro; m. Jack Schwartz, Oct. 16, 1977; children: Max Schwartz, Molly Schwartz. BA, Barnard Coll., 1968; MD, Albert Einstein Coll., 1972. Resident in gen. surgery Montefiore Hosp., NYC, 1972-76; mem. staff N. Ctrl. Hosp., Bronx, NY, 1976-77, Bronx Mcpl. Hosp., 1977-87, chief gen. surgery, 1983-87; mem. staff gen. surgery Albert Einstein Coll. Hosp., Bronx, 1977-93, chief gen. surgery, 1991-93; atty. Lear Surg. Assocs., 1993-94; pvt. practice Bronx, 1994—; dir. breast surgery Eastchester Ctr. Cancer Care, Bronx, 2004—. Asst. prof. surgery Albert Einstein Coll., Bronx, 1980—; assoc. dir. gen. surgery Weller Hosp., Bronx, 1991—93; co-founder Whaecom Breast Ctr., Bronx, 1991—. Fellow: ACS. Avocations: travel, opera. Office: Eastchester Ctr Cancer Care 2330 Eastchester Rd Bronx NY 10469 Office Phone: 718-405-0400, 718-732-4000.

SHAPIRO, NORMA SONDRA LEVY, federal judge; b. Phila., July 27, 1928; d. Bert and Jane (Kotkin) Levy; m. Bernard Shapiro, Aug. 21, 1949; children: Finley, Neil, Aaron. BA in Polit. Theory with honors, U. Mich., 1948; JD magna cum laude, U. Pa., 1951. Bar: Pa. 1952, U.S. Supreme Ct. 1978. Law clk. to presiding justice Pa. Supreme Ct., 1951-52; instr. U. Pa. Law Sch., 1951-52, 55-56; assoc. Dechert Price & Rhoads, Phila., 1956-58, 67-73, ptnr., 1973-78; judge U.S. Dist. Ct. 3rd circuit (ea. dist.) Pa., 1978—. Assoc. trustee U. Pa. Law Sch., 1978-93; former trustee Women's Law Project, Albert Einstein Med. Ctr.; v.p. Jewish Pub. Soc.; trustee Fedn. Jewish Agys., 1980-83; mem. lawyers adv. panel Pa. Gov.'s Commn. on Status of Women, 1974; legal adv. regional Coun. Child Psychiatry, bd. dirs. Women Judges' Fund for Justice. Guest editor: Shingle, 1972. Mem. Lower Merion County (Pa.) Bd. Sch. Dirs., 1968-77, pres., 1977, v.p., 1976; v.p. Jewish Community Relations Council of Greater Phila., 1975-77; chmn. legal affairs com., 1978; pres. Belmont Hills Home and Sch. Assn., Lower Merion Twp.; legis. chmn. Lower Merion Sch. Dist. Intersch. Council; mem. Task Force on Mental Health of Children and Youth of Pa.; treas., chmn. edn. com. Human Relations Council, Lower Merion; v.p., parliamentarian Nes Ami Penn Valley Congregation, Lower Merion Twp. Named Woman of Yr., Oxford Circle Jewish Community Center, 1979, Woman of Distinction, Golden Slipper Club, 1979; Gowen fellow, 1954-55; recipient Hannah G. Solomon award Nat. Coun. Jewish Women, 1992; Disting. Daughter of Pa.; Liberty Bell award, Berks County Bar Assn. Mem. Am. Law Inst., Am. Bar Found., ABA (ho. dels. 1990-96, coun./chmn. conf. fed. judges 1986-87, chmn. jud. divsn. 1996-97, Margaret Brent Women Lawyers Achievement award 1999, bd. gov. 2003-), Pa. Bar Assn. (ho. of dels. 1979-81), Phila. Bar Assn. (chmn. com. women's rights 1972, 74-75, chmn. bd. govs. 1977-78, chmn. pub. rels. com. 1978, Sandra Day O'Connor award), Fed. Bar Assn. (Bill of Rights award 1991), Nat. Assn. Women Lawyers, Phila. Trial Lawyers Assn., Am. Judicature Soc., Phila., Nat. Assn. Women Judges (exec. comm. bd. dir.), Fellowship Commn., Order of Coif (chpt. pres. 1973-75), Tau Epsilon Rho. Office: US Dist Courthouse Independence Mall West 601 Market St Rm 10614 Philadelphia PA 19106-1714

SHAPIRO, PAULA, retired maternal/women's health nurse; b. Pitts., Nov. 16, 1927; d. Ben and Esther (Halpert) Cohn; m. Bernard Shapiro, July 17, 1982; children: Eugene Hershorin, Abby Hershorin, Marc Hershorin, Jay Hershorin, Ellen Fenerty, Kenneth, Fred, Stacy Pierce. RN, Montefiore Hosp. Sch. Nursing, 1948; BS, Phila. U., 1987. RN, Pa. Nursing care coord. Thomas Jefferson U. Hosp., Phila.; asst. supr. operating rm. Wakefield (R.I.) Gen. Hosp.; staff RN operating rm. Jefferson Hosp., Phila., ret., 1993. Contbr. articles to profl. jours. Vol. Thomas Jefferson U. Hosp., gift shop Nat. Mus. Am. Jewish History; vol. o.r. nurse Tel Aviv, Israel, 1977; election judge. Home: 1500 Locust St Apt 2216 Philadelphia PA 19102-4317 E-mail: paulashapiro@hotmail.com.

SHAPIRO, ROBERTA, secondary school educator; b. Poughkeepsie, NY, July 12, 1970; d. Robert M. and June L. Roach; m. Jason Shapiro; children: Matthew, Molly. B, Swarthmore Coll., Pa., 1992. Social studies tchr. Strath Haven H.S., Wallingford, Pa., 1993—. Fellow, Nat. Humanities Ctr., 1995. Office: Strath Haven HS 205 South Providence Rd Wallingford PA 19086 Office Phone: 610-892-3400. Personal E-mail: robertashapiro@gmail.com. E-mail: rshapiro@w-ssd.org.

SHAPIRO, ROBYN SUE, lawyer, educator; b. Mpls., July 19, 1952; d. Walter David and Judith Rae (Sweet) S.; m. Charles Howard Barr, June 27, 1976; children: Tania Shapiro-Barr, Jeremy Shapiro-Barr, Michael Shapiro-Barr. BA summa cum laude, U. Mich., 1974; JD, Harvard U., 1977. Bar: D.C. 1977, Wis. 1979, U.S. Supreme Ct. 1990. Assoc. Foley & Lardner, Washington, 1977-79; ptnr. Barr & Shapiro, Menomonee Falls, Wis., 1980-87; assoc. Quarles & Brady, Milw., 1987-92; ptnr. Michael Best & Friedrich, Milw., 1992—2005, chair health law practice, 2003—05; ptnr. Gardner Carton & Douglas LLP, Milw., 2005—. Adj. asst. prof. law Marquette U., Milw., 1979-83; assoc. dir. bioethics ctr. Med. Coll. Wis., Milw., 1982-85, dir., 1985—; asst. prof. bioethics Med. Coll. Wis., 1984-89, assoc. prof. bioethics, 1989-97, prof. bioethics, 1997—, Ursula Von der Ruhr prof. bioethics, 2000—; dir. Wis. Ethics Com. Network, 1987-98, Midwest Ethics Com. Network, 1998-2004, Med. Ethics Com. Network, 2004—; bd. dirs. Wis. Health Decisions, 1990-93; drug safety and risk mgmt. adv. com. FDA, 2003—; mem. data and safety monitoring bd. Med. Coll. Wis., 2003—; mem. recombinant DNA adv. com. NIH, 2005—. Mem. editl. bd. Cambridge Quar., 1991—, HEC Forum, 1988—91, Human Rights, 1998—; contbr. articles to profl. jours. Mem. ethics com. St. Luke's Med. Ctr., Milw., 1983—, Elmbrook Meml. Hosp., Milw., 1983-86, Cmty. Meml. Hosp., Menomonee Falls, 1984—, Aurora Sinai Med.Ctr., Milw., 1986—, Milw. County Mental Health Complex, 1984—, Froedtert Meml. Luth. Hosp., 1985—; mem. subcom. organ transplantation Wis. Health Policy Coun., Madison, 1984, bioethics com., 1986-89; mem. com. study on bioethics Wis. Legis. Coun., Madison, 1984-85; bd. dirs. Jewish Home and Care Ctr., 1994—, chair ethics com., 1994—; chair Bayside Ethics Bd., 1994—; bd. dirs. Milw. area chpt. Girl Scouts U.S., Am. Bioethics Assn., 1995-97, Wis. Perinatal Found., 1996-99, Am. Soc. Bioethics and Humanities, 1997-00, Manor Park Found., 2002—; mem. sec.'s adv. com. on xenotransplantation U.S. Dept. Health and Human Svcs., 2001-05; mem. sci. adv. com. Alzheimer's Assn. Southeastern Wis., 1997—; mem. data and safety monitoring bd. GlaxoWellcome, 1995-03; mem. med. and cmty. adv. bd. After Breast Cancer Diagnosis, 1999—. James B. Angell scholar, 1971—72. Mem. ABA (health law sec., coordinating com. on bioethics and law 1993—, individual rights and responsibilities sect., health rights com. chair 1994-99, vice chair clin. ethics group 1998-01, coun. 1999—, mem. working group on health info. privacy 2000-02, adv. nat. conf. of commrs. on uniform state laws, misuse of genetic info. study group 2002—, sec. 2004-05, vice chair 2005-06, chair-elect 2006—, AIDS coordinating com. 2003—), Am. Health Lawyers Assn., Am. Hosp. Assn. (bioethics tech. panel 1991-94, spl. com. HIV practitioners 1991-93), Wis. Bar Assn. (chair Wis. health law sect. 1988-89, individual rights sect. coun. 1987-90), Assn. Women Lawyers, ACLU, Wis. Found. (Atty. of Yr. 1988), Assn. Post-Doctoral Programs in Clin. Neurophysiology (bd. dirs.), Am. Soc. Law, Medicine, and Ethics, Milw. Acad. Medicine (coun. 1992-98, chair bioethics com. 1992-98), Milw. AIDS Coalition (steering com. 1988-91), Am. Soc. Transplant Surgeons (ethics com. 1999—), Internat. Bioethics Assn. (chair task force on ethics coms.), Profl. Dimensions (Golden Compass award 1994), Phi Beta Kappa (Wis. chpt. scholarship com. chair 1990-93), Susan G. Komen Breast Cancer Found., others. Home: 9474 N Broadmoor Rd Milwaukee WI 53217-1309 Office: Med Coll Wis Bioethics Ctr 8701 Watertown Plank Rd Milwaukee WI 53226-3548 Office Phone: 414-221-6040. Business E-Mail: rshapiro@mcw.edu, rshapiro@gcd.com.

SHAPIRO, SANDRA, lawyer; b. Providence, Oct. 17, 1944; d. Emil and Sarah (Cohen) S. AB magna cum laude, Bryn Mawr Coll., Pa., 1966; LLB magna cum laude, U. Pa., 1969. Bar: Mass. 1970, U.S. Dist. Ct. Mass. 1971, U.S. Ct. Appeals (1st cir.) 1972, U.S. Supreme Ct. 1980. Law clk. U.S. Ct. Appeals (1st cir.), Boston, 1969-70; assoc. Foley, Hoag & Eliot LLP, Boston, 1970-75, ptnr., 1976—. Mem. bd. bar overseers Mass. Supreme Judicial Ct., 1988-92, mem. gender bias study com., 1986-89; dir. Mass. Govt. Land Bank, 1994-96; dir. Lex Mundi, 2004—. Contbr. articles to profl. jours. Bd. dirs. Patriots' Trail coun. Girl Scouts U.S., 1994—97; mem. bd. overseers Boston Lyric Opera, 1993—99, New Eng. Conservatory of Music, 1995—2001, Celebrity Series of Boston, 1997—, chair, 2003—. Woodrow Wilson fellow, 1966. Mem.: ABA (ethics, profl. and pub. edn. com. 1994—), U. Pa. Law Sch. Alumni Assn. (bd. mgrs. 1990—94), Boston Bar Assn. (mem. coun.), Mass. Bar Assn. (chmn. real property sect. coun., com. on profl. ethics), Nat. Women's Law Ctr. Network, New Eng. Women in Real Estate, Women's Bar Assn. Mass. (pres. 1985—86), Boston Club, Order of Coif. Office: Foley Hoag LLP 155 Seaport Blvd Boston MA 02210-2600 Office Phone: 617-832-1156. Business E-Mail: sshapiro@foleyhoag.com.

SHAPIRO, SANDRA M., psychologist, psychoanalyst, educator; b. N.Y.C., May 23, 1938; d. Jacob and Vera (Gordon) Milstein; m. Robert Shapiro, Apr. 12, 1964; 1 child, Michael. BA, Hunter Coll., 1957; MA, Bryn Mawr Coll., 1960, PhD, 1964. Lic. psychologist, N.Y. Instr. Queens Coll., CUNY, 1965-67, asst. prof., 1967-75, assoc. prof., 1975-95, assoc. prof. emeritus, 1999—. Bd. dirs. Nat. Inst. Psychotherapies, N.Y.C. Contbr. articles to profl. jours. Recipient Coop. Grad. fellowship NSF, 1960-62. Mem. APA, Am. Psychol. Soc. Office: Nat Inst for the Psychotherapies 250 W 57 St Ste 501 New York NY 10019

SHAPIRO, SUSAN JANINE, social worker, educator, consultant; b. Chgo., Apr. 27, 1951; d. Wilbur and Bernice (Pervin) S.; m. Steven Sable, Mar. 15, 1980; children: Aimee, Rebecca. BA, U. Mich., 1972, MSW, 1974. Lic.social worker, Mich.; lic. marriage counselor, Mich.; lic. clin. social worker, Fla.; bd. cert. diplomate in clin. social work. Social worker St. Joseph Mercy Hosp., Pontiac, Mich., 1974-75; supr., social worker Problems of Daily Living Clinic, Detroit, 1975-78; clin. social worker Inst. for Neuropsychiat. Rehab., Southfield, Mich., 1978-80; exec. dir. Southfield Psychotherapy, Inc., 1980-91, Susan J. Shapiro, A.C.S.W., P.A., Orlando, Fla., 1991—; supr. Jewish Family Svc. of Orlando, 1995—99. Coord. sex edn. and staff devel. Ann Arbor (Mich.) Free People's Clinic, 1970-72; co-dir. Oakland Crisis Ctr. for Rape and Sexual Abuse, Pontiac, Mich., 1974-77; dir., founder Oakland County Suspected Child Abuse and Neglect, Pontiac, 1974-76; cons., lectr. Wayne State U., Detroit, 1976-91; lectr. Mayor's Coun. on Child Abuse and Neglect, 1987-91. Contbr. articles to profl. jours. Coach Odyssey of the Mind, Farmington, Mich., 1986-88; troop leader Girl Scouts U.S., Farmington, 1987-89; pres. Kingswood Pl. Condo. Assn., Southfield, 1978-81; pres., founder Highmeadow PTA, Farmington, 1988-90; v.p. Farmington PTA Coun., 1989-90, pres., 1990-91; bd. dirs. Jewish Cmty. Ctr. of Greater Orlando, 199-98, v.p. youth dept., 1995-96, chair cultural series, 1995-2000; mem. human resource and devel. com. Jewish Fedn. of Greater Orlando, 1991-93; mem. steering com. Maimonedes' Soc., Hands of Destiny, 1991-93, Lions of Judah, 1993-2001; charter mem. Sabra Hadassah; v.p. Temple Isreal, 1998-99, bd. dirs 1997-99. Mem. NASW, Am. Assn. for Marriage and Family Therapy, Acad. Cert. Social Workers, Fla. Soc. for Clin. Social Workers. Avocations: swimming, gardening, sewing, shopping, reading. Home: 499 E Central Pkwy Ste 150 Altamonte Springs FL 32701-3409 Office Phone: 407-260-1001.

SHAPIRO, SUSAN STOBBART, lawyer; b. Stone Harbor, NJ, July 19, 1969; BA, Washington Coll., 1991; JD, Villanova U., 1994. Bar: Pa. 1994, Md. 1995, NJ 1995, U.S. Dist. Ct. (Md. dist.) 1998, DC 2000, U.S. Dist. Ct. (DC dist.) 2002, U.S. Ct. Appeals (fourth cir.) 2003. Dir. law firm of coun. Council, Baradel, Kosmerl & Nolan, P.A. Pres. alumni coun. Washington Coll., 2000—02; bd. dirs. Marine Trades Assn. Md., 2000—02; mem. Annapolis & An Arundel County C. of C.; spkr. in field. Mem. editl. adv. bd.: The Daily Record, 2004—; contbr. articles to profl. jours. Named one of Top Lawyers, Balt. Mag., 2003. Mem.: ABA, Anne Arundel County Bar Assn., Md. State Bar Assn. Office: CouncilBaradel Kosmerl & Nolan PA 125 West St 4th Fl PO Box 2289 Annapolis MD 21404-2289 Office Phone: 410-268-6600 ext. 114. Business E-Mail: shapiro@cbknlaw.com.

SHAPIRO, SYLVIA, psychotherapist; b. Bklyn., Aug. 16, 1938; d. Benjamin B. and Rose (Friedman) Bluming; m. Jay Citron, Oct. 25, 1962 (div. May 1976); children: Doni, Yosi, Eli, Yoav, Ilana. DSW, Yeshiva U., 1988. Cert. social worker; lic. social worker, N.Y.; cert. marriage and family therapist. Pvt. practice psychotherapy, Hackensack, N.J., 1989—. Home and Office: 240 Prospect Ave Apt 694 Hackensack NJ 07601-7700 Office Phone: 201-968-1567. Personal E-mail: sdiyya@aol.com.

SHAPIRO-MATHES, ANGELA, broadcast executive; BA, St. Peter's Coll. Co-owner Brookville Mktg/Greybark Advt.; owner, oper. several businesses; co-founder, pub. Soap Opera Digest, 1975, Soap Opera Update, 1988; co-prodr. Soap Opera Awards; sr. v.p. mkg. and promotion ABC Daytime, 1995, pres., 1998, Buena Vista Prodns., 2000; pres. ABC Family Channel Walt Disney Co., Burbank, Calif., 2002—03; pres. Fox TV Studios, 2004—. Office: Fox Television Studios Po Box 900 Beverly Hills CA 90213*

SHAPO, HELENE S., law educator; b. NYC, June 5, 1938; d. Benjamin Martin and Gertrude (Kahaner) Seidner; m. Marshall S. Shapo, June 21, 1959; children: Benjamin Mitchell, Nathaniel Saul. BA, Smith Coll., 1959; MA in Teaching, Harvard U., 1960; JD, U. Va., 1976. Bar: Va. 1976, U.S. Dist. Ct. (we. dist.) Va. 1977, Ill. 1993. Tchr. Dade County, Miami, Fla., 1960-64; assoc. Robert Musselman & Assocs., Charlottesville, Va., 1976-77; law clk. to presiding justice U.S. Dist. Ct. Va., Charlottesville, 1977-78; asst. prof. law Northwestern U., Chgo., 1978-81, assoc. prof. law, 1981-83, prof. law, 1983—, Perkins-Bauer prof., 1987. Instr. Sweet Briar Coll., Va., 1976-77, U. Va., Charlottesville, 1976-78; vis. fellow Wolfson Coll., Cambridge U., 2001, vis. scholar, 1992; mem. com. law sch. admissions coun./testing and devel., 1983—; cons. in field. Author (with Walter and Fajans): Writing and Analysis in the Law, 1989, 4th edit., 2003; author: (with Marshall Shapo) Law School Without Fear, 1996, 2d edit., 2003; author: Writing for Law Practice, 2004; contbr. articles to legal jours. Recipient award, sect. on legal writing, Assn. Am. Law Schs., 2002, award for disting. achievement, Assn. Legal Writing Dirs., 2005. Mem. ABA, Va. Bar Assn., Assn. of Am. Law Schs. (sect. chairperson 1985—), Women's Bar Assn. Chgo. Office: Northwestern U Sch Law 357 E Chicago Ave Chicago IL 60611-3059 E-mail: h-shapo@law.northwestern.edu.

SHAPPERT, GRETCHEN C. F. (GRETCHEN CECILIA FRANCES SHAPPERT), prosecutor, lawyer; b. 1956; AB, Duke U.; JD, Washington & Lee U. Bar: 1980. Assoc. Maupin, Taylor, & Ellis, P.A., Raleigh, 1980—81, Tucker, Hicks, Sentelle, Moon, & Hodge, P.A., Charlotte, 1981—83; asst. pub. defender Mecklenburg County, NC, 1983—88, asst. dist. atty., 1988—90; asst. US atty. (we. dist.) NC US Dept. Justice, 1990—2004, acting US atty., 2004—05, US atty. (we. dist.) NC, 2005—. Republican. Office: US Attys Office 227 West Trade St Ste 1650 Charlotte NC 28202 Office Phone: 704-344-6222.*

SHARAPOVA, MARIA, professional tennis player; b. Nyagan, Russia, Apr. 19, 1987; d. Yuri and Yelena Sharapova. Trained, Bollettieri's Acad., 1996. Prof. tennis player WTA Tour, 2001—; model IMG Modeling Agy., 2003—; winner Wimbledon, 2004. Nominee Laureus World Newcomer Yr., 2004; named Sports-Choice Athlete (Female), Teen Choice Awards, 2006. Achievements include 14 career singles WTA championships; 3 career doubles championships; 4 career ITF Women's Circuit singles titles; first Russian woman to win at Wimbledon, 2004; signed endorsement deals with Parlux Fragrances Inc and Motorola. Avocations: singing, reading, stamp collecting/philately, fashion, music. Mailing: WTA Tour One Progress Plz Ste 1500 Saint Petersburg FL 33701*

SHARBAUGH, KATHRYN KENNEDY, artist; d. Theodore and Mary (Waters) Kennedy; m. Charles Carroll Sharbaugh, June 21, 1975 BFA, Kans. City Art Inst., 1971; MFA, Cranbrook Acad. Art, Bloomfield Hills, Mich., 1974. Freelance pattern designer Corning Glass Works, NY, 1974, Mikasa, 1975, Lauffer, 1975; instr. Flint Inst. Arts, Mich. Dir. devel. Flint Inst. Arts. Maker: dinnerware, teapots, columbarin; exhibited in pub. collections including Cranbrook Mus. Art, Flint Inst. Arts, Mus. R.I. Sch. Design, Renwick Gallery, Cooper-Hewitt Decorative Arts Mus. of Smithsonian Inst., Slater Mus., Mus. Het Kruithuis/Netherlands Mem. citizens adv. bd. U. Mich. Flint. Fellow, Nat. Endowment of Arts, 1980, 1993, Mich. Coun. of Arts, 1985, 1994. Mem.: Detroit Inst. Arts, Women's Forum, Audubon Soc., Pewabic Soc. Avocation: birdwatching. Office: Flint Inst of Arts E Kearsley Flint MI 48503 Office Phone: 810-234-1695.

SHARBEL, JEAN M., editor; b. Lansford, Pa. d. Joseph and Star S. BA in Journalism, Hunter Coll. Editl. dir., v.p. Dauntless Books, N.Y.C., 1962-75; editor romance mags., True Confessions mag. Macfadden Holdings, Inc., N.Y.C., 1976-92; freelance editor fiction and non-fiction books, N.Y.C., 1989—. Home: 165 E 66th St New York NY 10021-6132

SHARE, ELLEN, librarian; b. Washington, June 6, 1946; d. Ernest M. and Doris Esther (Frankel) Levin; m. Stewart Share, May 17, 1970; children: Elliot, Deborah. BA, U. Md., 1969, MLS, 1983. Libr. Prince George's County-Laurel (Md.) Br., 1984-86, Washington Hebrew Congregation, 1986—. Speaker in field. Book reviewer: AJL Newsletter. Mem. Assn. Jewish Librs. (v.p. Capital area chpt. 1991-93), Hadassah, Women's Am. Orgn. Rehab. through Tng., Coalition for Advancement of Jewish Edn. Office: Washington Hebrew Congregation 3935 Macomb St NW Washington DC 20016-3741 Office Phone: 301-354-3212. Business E-Mail: eshare@whctemple.org.

SHARKE, INGRID, librarian; b. Troy, N.Y., July 21, 1951; d. Karl G.E. and Ann (Swensson) Sharke. BA, We. Coll., Oxford, Ohio, 1973; MLS, SUNY Genesso, 1974. Libr. Samaritan Hosp. Sch. Nursing, Troy, 1975; asst. libr. Times Record and Sun. Record, Troy, 1977—80, libr., 1980—87; libr., adminstrv. asst. Bruno Machinery Corp., Troy, 1987—2005; corp. sales rep. customer svc. Arcadia Supply, Inc., Albany, NY, 2006—. Republican. Mem. United Ch. Christ. Office: Arcadia Supply Inc 67 Erie Blvd Albany NY 12204

SHARKEY, CATHERINE MOIRA, law educator; b. Balt., May 1, 1970; BA in Economics, summa cum laude, Yale U., 1992; JD, Yale U., 1997; MS in Economics for Devel., Oxford U., 1994. Bar: Md. 1998, DC 2000, NY 2000. Jud. clk. to Hon. Guido Calabresi US Ct. Appeals 2nd Cir., New Haven, 1997—98; jud. clk. to Hon. David H. Souter US Supreme Ct., Washington, 1998—99; Supreme Ct. & appellate litig. assoc. Mayer, Brown Rowe & Maw, NYC, 2000—02, cons., 2002; assoc. prof. law Columbia U., NYC, 2003—. Rhodes Scholar, 1992—94. Office: Columbia U Sch Law 435 W 116th St New York NY 10027 Office Fax: 212-854-0739, 212-854-7946. Business E-Mail: csharl@law.columbia.edu.

SHARKEY, VIRGINIA GRACE, artist; b. Grosse Pointe Farms, Mich., Mar. 6, 1945; d. Harold Arnold Sharkey and Antoinette Dorothy Andrews; m. Samuel Pitts Edwards (div.). BA, Vassar Coll., 1967. Instr. Coll. of the Redwoods, Ft. Bragg, Calif., 1990—92; violin tchr. Ukiah Sch. of Music, 1995—, Mendocino Waldorf Sch., Calpella, Calif., 1991—94. Violinist Peregrine String Quartet, Santa Rosa, Calif., 1995-96. Exhibns. in galleries and mus., U.S., Germany, 1974—. Co-dir. Albion River Watershed Protection Assn., Little River, Calif., 1989. Fellow Corp. of Yaddo, 1981. Mem. Symphony of the Redwoods (violinist 1987—), Mendocine Music Festival (violinist 1987—). Avocations: hiking, reading, canoeing. Office: PO Box 20 Mendocino CA 95460-0020

SHARMA, JEANNE ALEXANDRA, artist, educator; b. Norfolk, Va., Sept. 27, 1943; d. John Cranston Heintzelman and Elizabeth Townshend Howlett; m. Shashi Nath Sharma, Aug. 2, 1965; children: Ravi Ivan, Sonya Heintzelman Sharma-Scott. BFA, Kans. State U., Manhattan, 1966; MFA, Pacific Western U., 2004. Painting instr. North York (Ont., Can.) Bd. of Edn., 1975—94; prof. fine arts Seneca Coll., Toronto, 1983—85; founder, instr. Northview Group of Artists, Toronto, 1992—98; adj. asst. prof. U. S.C. Beaufort, Hilton Head Island, 1999—; art instr. Beaufort Parks and Leisure Svcs., Hilton Head Island, SC, 2000—; instr. U. S.C. Beaufort Continuing Edn., 2000—, Hilton Head Art League, Hilton Head Island, SC, 2003—. Chmn. edn. com. Hilton Head Art League, Hilton Head Island, 2004—; juror Oakville Art Assn., Canada, 2000, Hilton Head Plantation Artists, 2006; instr. and artist-in-residence Aspotogan Painting Workshop, Northwest Cove, N.S., Canada, 2004, Culpeper, Va., 05; invited artist Charles St. Gallery, Beaufort, 2003, 04, 05, 06; artist in residence Windmore Group of Artists, Culpepper, Va., 2005—. Exhibitions include Four images of Native American Chieftans, 1999, Island Treasures Revealed, As We See it, 2006, one-woman shows include Oil and Water, 2004, Oil and Water II, 2004, Water-Color-Ink, Island Perspectives, 2005, East Meets West, 2006. Recipient 1st in class for woodcarving in the round, Internat. Woodcarver's Exhbn., 1978, 2d pl. award sculpture in the round, 1977, 3d pl. award sculpture in the round, 1976. Mem.: Apple Pie Painters, Beaufort Art Assn., Hilton Head Art League, Sertoma Club, Delta Phi Delta (life). Achievements include design of corporate logos for seven independent businesses.

SHARMA, MARTHA BRIDGES, geography educator; b. Balt., Feb. 2, 1945; d. Gail and S. Evelyn Bridges; m. Narendra P. Sharma, Aug. 16, 1968; 1 child, Stephanie. BA in Geography, Internat. Studies, U. N.C., 1967; postgrad., U. Hawaii, 1967—68, George Washington U., 1986. Tchr. geography Washingtom Internat. Sch., 1976—80; dir. records/accounts Washington Internat. Sch., 1981—82, adminstrv. dean, 1983—84; tchr. geography Nat. Cathedral Sch., Washington, 1984—2004. Mem. AP Human Geography Test Devel. Com., 1996—2005; geography cons.; lectr. in field. Joint author: 7-12 Geography: Themes, Key Ideas, and Learning Opportunities, 1989; co-author: The National Council for Geographic Education: The First Seventy-Five Years and Beyond, 1990, Using Internet Primary Sources to Teach Critical Thinking Skills in Geography, 2000; contbg. author: Revisiting the Americas: Teaching and Learning the Geography of the Western Hemisphere, 1992; author: (online) Making Population Real, 2005; contbr. articles to profl. jours. Mem. Nat. Coun. Geographic Edn. (Region VIII awards com. 1988-90, dir. spl. pub.s 1989-92, gender/ethnicity project task force 1991-92, v.p. curriculum and instrn. 2002-04, pres. 2005), Assn. Am. Geographers, Soc. Woman Geographers. Avocations: reading, music, needlecrafts, travel. E-mail: geogsharma@yahoo.com.

SHARMA, SANTOSH DEVRAJ, obstetrician, gynecologist, educator; b. Kenya, Feb. 24, 1934; arrived in US, 1972; d. Devraj Chananram and Lakshmi (Devi) S. BS, MB, B.J. Medical Sch., Pune, India, 1960. House surgeon Sasson Hosp., Poona, India, 1960-61; resident in ob-gyn. various hosps., England, 1961-67; house officer Maelor Gen. Hosp., Wrexham, U.K., 1961-62; asst. prof. ob-gyn. Howard U. Med. Sch., Washington, 1972-74; assoc. prof. John A. Burns Sch. Med., Honolulu, 1974-78, prof., 1978—. Fellow Royal Coll. Ob-Gyn., Am. Coll. Ob-Gyn. Avocations: travel, photography, environmental protection. Office: 1319 Punahou St Rm 824 Honolulu HI 96826-1032 Business E-Mail: santosh@hawaii.edu.

SHARMA, TINA, lawyer; b. New Delhi, Sept. 25, 1968; BS, Georgetown U., 1990; JD, Fordham U., 1993. Bar: NY 1994, NJ 1994, Md. 1996, US Dist. Ct. Dist. Md. 1996, US Ct. Appeals 4th Cir. 1996, DC 2005. Shareholder, immigration practice group Jenkens & Gilchrist, P.C., Washington, mng. shareholder Washington DC office. Mem.: ABA, Assn. Am. Lawyers from the Indian Subcontinent, NY State Bar Assn., Md. State Bar Assn., Network of Indian Professionals, Am. Immigration Lawyers Assn. Office: Jenkens & Gilchrist PC Ste 900 901 15th St NW Washington DC 20005-2301 Office Phone: 202-326-1516. Office Fax: 202-326-1555. Business E-Mail: tsharma@jenkens.com.

SHARMAN, DIANE LEE, mathematics professor; b. Harvey, Ill., May 12, 1948; d. Eric Melvin and Josephine A. (Kut) Van Patten; m. Richard Lee Sharman, Nov. 3, 1973; children: Daria Lee, Deedra Lee. BS, Purdue U., 1970; MBA, U. Chgo., 1973. Cert. secondary sch. math. tchr., Tex. Computers sales rep. GE, Chgo., 1970-73; mgr. sold equipment Xerox Corp., Rochester, NY, 1973-81, mgr. fin. ops. analysis worldwide Stamford, NY, 1981-84; math. tchr. Conroe (Tex.) Ind. Sch. Dist., 1993—2004, Montgomery Coll., Conroe, 2005—. Mem. DAR, Purdue Alumni Assn. (life), Nat. Charity League, U. Chgo. Alumni Assn., Chi Omega. Avocations: golf, horseback riding. Home: 26 Fernglen Dr The Woodlands TX 77380-3955 Office: Montgomery Coll 3200 Coll Pk Dr Conroe TX 77384-4500 Office Phone: 936-273-7301. Personal E-mail: fernglendr@aol.com. Business E-Mail: diane.l.sharman@nhmccd.edu.

SHARON, MOMANY, retired elementary school and music educator; b. Gary, Ind., Aug. 9, 1936; d. Peter Garhardt Miller and Leona Trump; m. Frank Momany, Jan. 23, 1960 (div. Jan. 1990); children: Cory, Shelley. BM, DePauw U., 1958; MM, Memphis State U., 1984, D in Mus. Arts, 1990; postgrad., Ind. U., 1060-61. Cert. tchr., Tenn. Pvt. piano tchr., 1964-97; class piano asst. Cont. Edn. Memphis State U., 1981-87; staff accompanist Lambuth U., Jackson, Tenn., 1987-88; organist St. Paul the Apostle, Humboldt, Tenn., 1990-94; tchr. Bethel Coll., 1990-94; tchr. Capa keyboard Colonial Middle Sch., Memphis, 1997—2006; ret., 2006. Adj. faculty various colls., 1987-96; accompanist dance, opera, chamber groups. Contbr. articles to profl. jours. Pres. Germantown Symphony Orch., Tenn., 1980, pres.-elect, 2005-2006, pres., 2006-; v.p. Germantown Arts Coun., 1980; coord. Cornell Performers Group, Ithaca, N.Y., 1968. Grantee various orgns. including Rotary Club, Tenn. Arts Coun. Mem. Music Educators Nat. Conf., Nat. Middle Sch. Assn., Tenn. Music Tchrs. Assn., Pi Kappa Lambda, Mu Phi Epsilon. Episcopalian. Avocations: reading, baseball, football, arts and crafts. Home: 1155 Dearing Rd Memphis TN 38117-6147 Personal E-mail: drmomis@hotmail.com.

SHARP, ANGELA CHRISTINE, dance educator; d. Lahonda S. and Keith W. Sharp. BS in Kinesiology and Dance Edn., U. Houston, 1995. Cert. tchr. Tex., 1995. Dance tchr., drill team dir. Clear Brook H.S., Friendswood, Tex., 1998—99, Northbrook H.S., Houston, 1999—. Mem.: Tex. Dance Educators Assn. (assoc.). Office Phone: 713-365-4430.

SHARP, ANNE CATHERINE, artist, educator; b. Red Bank, NJ, Nov. 1, 1943; d. Elmer Eugene and Ethel Violet (Hunter) S. BFA, Pratt Inst., 1965; MFA, Bklyn. Coll., CUNY, 1973. Tchr. art Sch. Visual Arts, 1978-89, NYU, 1978, SUNY, Purchase, 1983, Pratt Manhattan Ctr., N.Y.C., 1982-84, Parsons Sch. Design, N.Y.C., 1984-90, Visual Arts Ctr. of Alaska, Anchorage, 1991, Anchorage Mus. Hist. and Art, 1991, 93, 94, 95, U. Alaska, Anchorage, 1994-96, Fashion Inst. Tech., SUNY, 1997-98; lectr. AAAS, The 46th Arctic Divsn. Sci. Conf., U. Alaska, Fairbanks, 1995, Cmty. Ch., Ho-Ho-Ku, N.J., 2005. One-person shows Pace Editions, N.Y.C., Ten/Downtown, N.Y.C., Katonah (N.Y.) Gallery, 1974, Contemporary Gallery, Dallas, 1975, Art in a Public Space, N.Y.C., 1979, Eatontown Hist. Mus., N.J., 1980, N.Y. Pub. Library Epiphany Br., 1988, Books and Co., N.Y., 1989, The Kendall Gallery, N.Y.C., 1990, Alaska Pacific U., Carr-Gottstein Gallery, Anchorage, 1993, Internat. Gallery Contemporary Art, Anchorage, 1993, Art Think Tank Gallery, N.Y.C., 1994, U.S. Geol. Survey, Reston, Va., 1994, Stonington Gallery, Anchorage, 1994, on TV Ltd. Benefit, N.Y.C., 1998-2000; group shows include Arnot Art Mus., Elmira, N.Y., 1975, Bronx Mus., 1975, Mus. Modern Art, N.Y.C., 1975-76, Nat. Arts Club, N.Y.C., 1979, Calif. Mus. Photography, Riverside, 1983-92, Jack Tilton Gallery, N.Y.C., 1983, Lincoln Ctr., N.Y.C., 1983, Cabo Frio Print Biennale, Brazil, 1983, Pratt Graphic Ctr., N.Y.C., 1984, State Mus. N.Y., Albany, 1984, Kenkeleba Gallery, N.Y.C., 1985, Hempstead Harbor Art Assn., Glen Cove, N.Y., 1985, Mus. Mod. Art, Weddel, Fed. Republic of Germany, 1985, Kenkeleba Gallery, N.Y.C., 1985, Paper Art Exhbn. Internat. Mus. Contemporary Art, Bahia, Brazil, 1986, Mus. Salon-de-Provence, France, 1987, Mus. Contemporary Art, Sao Paulo, Brazil, 1985-86, Salon de Provence, France, 1987, Adirondack Lakes Ctr. for Arts, Blue Mountain Lake, N.Y., 1987, Kendall Gallery, N.Y.C., 1988, Exhibition Ctr. Parsons Sch. Design, N.Y.C., 1989, F.M.K. Gallery, Budapest, Hungary, 1989, Galerie des Kulturbundes Schwarzenberg, German Dem. Republic, Q Sen Do Gallery, Kobe, Japan, 1989, Anchorage Mus. History and Art, 1990-91, 94, U. Alaska, Anchorage, 1990, 91, Coos Art Mus., Coos Bay, Oreg., 1990, Spaceship Earth, Mus. Internat. de Neu Art, Vancouver, Can., 1990, Councourse Gallery, Emily Carr Coll. Art and Design, 1990, Nat. Mus. Women in the Arts, Washington, 1991, Visual Arts Ctr. Alaska, 1991, 92, Nomad Mus., Lisbon, Portugal, 1991, Mus. Ostdeutsche Gallery, Regensberg, Germany, 1991, Mcpl. Mus. Cesley Krumlov (So. Bohemia) CSFK, Czechoslovakia, 1991, Böltmiche Dörter Exhbn. Hochstrass 8, Munich, 1992, BBC-TV, Great Britain, U.K., Sta. WXXI-TV, Rochester, N.Y., 1992-93, Site 250 Gallery Contemporary Art., Fairbanks, 1993, Santa Barbara (Calif.) Mus. Art, 1993, The Rochester (N.Y.) Mus. and Sci. Ctr., 1990-94, Space Arc: The Archives of Mankind, Time Capsule in Earth Orbit, Hughes Comm., Divec TV Satellite Launch, 1994, Stonington Gallery, Anchorage, 1994, 95, UAA Art Galley U. Alaska, 1995, Arctic Trading Post, Nome, Alaska, 1995, Allan P. Kikbuarts Ctr. Gallery at the Lawrenceville (N.J.) Sch., 1996, Blue Mountain Gallery, N.Y., 1998, The Book Room, Jersey City, 2000, 01, A.I.R. Gallery, 2002, 03, 04, 05, 06-, others; represented in permanent collections Smithsonian Instn., Nat. Air and Space Mus., Washington, Albright Knox Gallery, Buffalo, St. Vincent's Hosp, N.Y.C., N.Y. Pub. Libr., N.Y.C., U.S. Geol. Survey, Reston, Va., White House (Reagan, Bush adminstrns.), Site 250 Gallery Contemporary Art, Fairbanks, Alaska, Anchorage Mus. History and Art, others; Moon Shot series to commemorate moon landing, 1970-76, Cloud Structures of the Universe Painting series, 1980-86, Am. Landscape series, 1987-89, Thoughtlines, fall 1986, Swimming in the Mainstream with Her, U. Va., Charlottesville; author: Artist's Book - Travel Dreams U.S.A., 1989, Artworld-Welt Der Kunst, Synchronicity, 1989—, Art Think Tank: Projects in Art and Ecology, 1990—, The Alaska Series, 1990—, Portraits in the Wilderness, 1990—, Family History Project J. Lindemann, 2004—; columnist: Anchorage Press, 1995. Sponsor Iditorod Trail Com., Libby Riddles. Tchg. fellow Bklyn. Coll., 1972; Artist-in-residence grantee Va. Ctr. for Creative Arts, 1974, Artpark, Lewiston, N.Y., 1980, Vt. Studio Colony, 1989; recipient Pippin award Our Town, N.Y.C., 1984, certificate of Appreciation Art in Embassy program U.S. Dept. State, 1996. Mem. Mus. Women in Arts, Pratt Inst. Alumni Assn., Internat. Assn. Near-Death Studies.

SHARP, BRIDGET MARIE, science educator; b. Dubuque, Iowa, Dec. 21, 1960; d. John Edward and Nancy Lee Clifford; m. Bradley Lane Sharp, Nov. 28, 1992. BS in Med. Tech., Incarnate Word Coll., San Antonio, Tex., 1985; postgrad., U. St. Thomas, Houston, 1993, U. Houston, 1995—96. Med. tech. Meth. Hosp., San Antonio, 1985—92; clin. faculty med. tech. Meth. Hosp. and U. Tex., 1986—92; tchr. sci. St. Francis de Sales Sch., Houston, 1993—99, Our Lady Perpetual Help, Selma, 1999—. Chair sci. dept. Our Lady Perpetual Help Sch., 2001—; coord. sci. fair Archdioceses San Antonio, 2003—; com. mem. devel. sci. curriculm guide Diocese Galveston, Houston, 1997—98; sponsor OLPH and Nat. Beta Club, Selma, 2002—, Our Lady Perpetual Help Sch., 2004—. Recipient Pres. Vol. Svc. award, 2004. Mem.: NCEA, Alpha Phi Sorority (alumni pres. and v.p. 1986-1988). Home: 19903 Horizon Bluff San Antonio TX 78258 Office: Our Lady of Perpetual Help School 16075 N Evans Rd Selma TX 78154 Office Phone: 210-651-6811. Personal E-mail: bradandbridget@prodigy.net. E-mail: sharpb@olphselma.org.

SHARP, CHRISTINA KRIEGER, retired nursing educator; b. Ft. Montgomery, N.Y., Aug. 4, 1928; d. Joseph Lewis and Mary Agnes Krieger; m. Andrew Asa Sharp, Jr., Feb. 3, 1957 (dec. Jan. 31, 1969); children: Shawn Patrick, Sharon Paula Zegers. RN, cadet nurse, St. Lukes Hosp., Newburgh, N.Y., 1948; BS, Coll. William and Mary, 1955; MA, NYU, 1974. RN N.Y. Staff nurse Vets. Hosp., Richmond, Va., 1948—53, Army Hosp., West Point, NY, 1954—56; instr. nursing Orange County CC, Middletown, NY, 1956—57, Santa Rosa (Calif.) Jr. Coll., 1961—62; supr. nursing Vocat. Edn. and Extension Bd., New City, NY, 1957—60; coord. practical nursing program Newburgh Sch. Dist., 1963—83. Cons. N.Y. State Edn. Dept. Nursing, Albany, 1983—84. Mem.: VFW, AFL-CIO, AAUW (sec. 1999—2001), Fla. Educators Assn., N.Y. State United Tchrs. (Cmty. Svc. award 1998), Fla. Alliance Ret. Ams. (bd. mem. 2002—, sec. ctrl. Fla. chpt. 2004—), Fla. Soc. RNs Ret., Inc. (Orlando dist. pres. 1994—97, editor yearbooks 1997—, state pres. 1998—2002, Fla. state coun. 43 pres. 2001—), Widow and Widowers Soc. Ctrl. Fla. (pres. 1999—2002), Orange County Ret. Educators Assn., Tchr. Retirees Fla., Golden Rod Civic Club (bd. dirs. 2001—), Am. Legion Aux. Avocations: travel, opera, ballet, Broadway shows, ice shows. Home: 2735 Mystic Cove Dr Orlando FL 32812-5344 E-mail: tisharp@aol.com.

SHARP, JANE PRICE, retired editor; b. Marlinton, W.Va., Oct. 14, 1919; d. Calvin W and Mabel Elizabeth (Milligan) Price; m. Basil Clair Sharp (dec.); children: Basil P.(dec.), John C., Jane Jessee. Student, Davis Elkins Coll., 1936-37. Legal sec. Prosecution atty. office, Marlinton, 1937-1939; acct. Pocahontas Prodrs., Marlinton, 1945-57; acct., reporter Pocahontas Times, Marlinton, 1937-57, editor, owner, 1957-82, editor emeritus, 1982—. Chmn. Planning Commn. Pocahontas County, 1970, Town Coun. Marlinton; legis. W.Va., 1989-90; former chmn. Pocahontas County Dem. Exec. Com.; elder, sunday sch. tchr. Marlinton Presbyn. Ch.; sec. Pioneer Days. Mem. W.Va. Press Assn. (life; pres. 1978, Adam Kelley award 1996), Pocahontas County Hist Soc. (dir. 1963—, pres. 1970-71, sec. 1994-2005), Marlinton Woman's Club (sec., past pres., Woman of Yr. 1996—). Presbyterian. Avocations: gardening, genealogy. Home: 1118 2nd Ave Marlinton WV 24954-1012 Office: Pocahontas Times 810 2nd Ave Marlinton WV 24954-1091

SHARP, KAY FRANCES, psychologist; b. Long Beach, Calif., Dec. 26, 1945; d. Carl Eugene and Phyllis Jean (Sorensen) Colby; m. James Richard Sharp, Aug. 13, 1977; 1 child from previous marriage, Julie Ann Caustin. BA, Wayne State U., 1972, MA, 1977, PhD, 1978. Lic. psychologist, N.Y. Rsch. asst., then teaching asst. Wayne State U., Detroit, 1973-77; rsch. technician Ctr. for Urban Studies, Detroit, 1976-77; asst. coord. presch. mental health project Detroit Pub. Schs., 1976-78; instr. Ithaca (N.Y.) Coll., 1978-79, asst. prof., 1979-83, Miami U., Oxford, Ohio, 1983-84; program evaluation specialist Willard (N.Y.) Psychiat. Ctr., 1984-86, coord. for quality assurance, 1986-87, dir. program evaluation, 1987-93, assoc. psychologist, 1993—95; supr. psychologist Tioga County Mental Health Dept., 1995—99, Tompkins County Mental Health Dept., 1999—. Cons. Head Start, Wayne, Mich., 1976; counselor Oxford Crisis and Referral Ctr., 1984; trainee Adminstrn. on Aging, 1974-75, NIMH, 1977-78. Contbr. articles to profl. jours. Bd. dirs. Tompkins County Mental Health Svcs. Bd., Ithaca, 1988-91, Elizabeth Cady Stanton Child Care Ctr., Willard, 1992-94; bd. dirs. Suicide Prevention and Crisis Intervention Svcs. Bd., Ithaca, 1999-2003. NSF grantee, 1981-82. Mem. APA. Avocations: gardening, quilting.

SHARP, MARSHA, basketball coach; b. Wash. B, Wayland Bapt. U., 1974; M, West Tex. State U., 1976. Grad. asst. basketball coach The Flying Queens Wayland Bapt. U., 1974-75; asst. basketball coach Lockney U., 1976-82; head coach Lady Raiders basketball Tex. Tech. U., Lubbock, 1982—. Led Lady Raiders basketball to NCAA Championship, 1993, 5 S.W. Conf. titles, 3 post-season crowns; named Nat. Coach of Yr. Women's Basketball News Svc., Ohio Touchdown Club, 1993, Nat. Coach of Yr. Women's Basketball Coaches Assn., 1994. Office: Tex Tech/United Spirit Arena Jones Stadium North 18th & Indiana Ave Lubbock TX 79409

SHARP, NANCY WEATHERLY, communications educator, dean; b. Evanston, Ill., Oct. 24, 1936; d. Edward Howell and Anne (Ferring) Weatherly; m. James Roger Sharp, Dec. 18, 1957; children: Sandra Lynn, Matthew Edward. BJ, U. Mo., 1958; MSSc, Syracuse U., 1982. Reporter Columbia (Mo.) Tribune, 1958-59; researcher, writer Mo. Hist. Rev., Columbia, 1959-60; reporter, feature writer, editor Hayward (Calif.) Daily Rev., 1960-63; reporter, feature writer Oakland (Calif.) Tribune, 1963-66, Syracuse (N.Y.) Herald-Jour., 1966-70; adj. prof. Syracuse U., 1976-82, asst. prof., 1982-87, assoc. prof., 1987-94, asst. dean communications, 1991—, prof., 1994—. Book reviewer San Francisco Chronicle, 1960-63; writer Syracuse U. Alumni News, 1972-80; author/editor: Communications Research, 1988, Informing America, 1985; author/editor published study: Faculty Women in Mass Communications, 1985. Recipient Na. Teaching award Poynter Inst., 1985; Gannett Found. fellow, 1983. Mem. Assn. for Edn. in Journalism and Mass Communications. Avocations: travel, swimming, sailing, skiing, hiking. Home: 4846 Briarwood Ln Manlius NY 13104-1306 Office: Syracuse U 305 Newhouse Ln Syracuse NY 13244-0001

SHARP, STACY LYNN, media specialist; b. West End, N.J., Aug. 19, 1977; d. Leon M. and Susan Sharp. BA in History and Psychology, Georgian Ct. Coll., Lakewood, N.J., 2000; MA of Edn., Georgian Ct. U., Lakewood, N.J., 2004, credit program in cert. in media studies, 2005. Cert. tchr. N.J., media specialist N.J. Media specialist Long Branch Bd. Edn., 2000—.

SHARPE, KAREN L., science association director; b. Warrenton, Va., Nov. 10, 1963; d. Glenwood Ford Lassiter, Jr. and Charlotte Louise Digges; children: Stephanie N., Johnathan D., Chrystal A. Blowe. BS in Elem. Edn. summa cum laude, E. Carolina U., 1998; AA, R.C. CC, 1996. Tchr. Bertie County Schs., Windsor, NC, 1998—2003; sci. facilitator U. NC, NC PIMS, Chapel Hill, 2005—. Instr. desktop publishing Martin CC, Windsor, 2003. EMT-B Aulander Rescue Squad, NC, 2005—. Recipient First Class Tchrs. award, Sallie Mae, 1999, Outstanding Support award, PESA/NSF, 2000, Tchr. of Yr., Bertie County Schs., 2001—02. Mem.: Bertie County Arts Coun., NCAE, Nat. Sci. Tchrs. Assn., BYTES Computer Club (dir. 1999—). Republican. Baptist. Avocations: motorcycling, swimming. Office: U NC-GA PO Box 2688 Chapel Hill NC 27515

SHARPE, KATHLEEN T., secondary school educator; b. New Haven; BA in Econs., Albertus Magnus Coll., New Haven, 1972; MALS in Social Studies, Wesleyan U., Middletown, Conn., 1980; postgrad., So. Conn. State U., 1990. Cert. tchr., adminstrn., supervision, Conn. Tchr. social studies Guilford (Conn.) High Sch., 1972—, program chmn., 1991—. Mem. ASCD, Nat. Coun. for Social Studies, Conn. Coun. for Social Studies, Delta Kappa Gamma. Home: Indian Cove 61 Highland Ave Guilford CT 06437-3380 Office: Guilford High Sch 605 New England Rd Guilford CT 06437-1834

SHARPLES, RUTH LISSAK, communications executive; b. N.Y.C., Feb. 3, 1952; d. Saul and Nettie (Field) Lissak; m. Winston Sharples, June 26, 1981; stepchildren: Hadley, John, Gillian. BA, CUNY, 1973; MFA, Columbia U., 1975. Rschr. Am. Film Inst./Motion Picture Divsn. of Libr. of Congress, Washington, 1977-79; mgr. audio-visual programs Am. Soc. Microbiology, Washington, 1979-82; mgr. video tech. Am. Gas Assn., Arlington, Va., 1982-96; dir. comm. Am. Gas Cooling Ctr., 1996—; exec. asst., gen. counsel Quaker Fabric Corp., Fall River, Mass., 2005—06; exec. office dir. chancellor U. Mass., Dartmouth, 2006—. V.p., corp. sec. Cantab Motors, Ltd., Purcellville, Va., 1988—; corp. sec. Am. Gas Cooling Ctr., Arlington, 1996—. Editor Cool Times Newsletter, 1996-98. Mem. Nat. Trust Historic Preservation, Nature Conservancy, Mass. Audubon Soc., English Heritage, Nat. Trust, Internat. TV Assn. Avocations: hiking, archaeology.

SHARPLESS, MATTIE R., ambassador; b. Hampstead, N.C., July 1943; BA in Bus. Edn., N.C. Coll.; MBA, N.C. Cen. Univ. Former acting adminstr. USDA/Fgn. Agr. Svc.; various positions with Fgn. Agr. Svc., 1965—2001; spl. envoy to emerging economies USDA, 1999—2001; U.S. Amb. to Cen. African Rep., 2001—. Named to USDA's Yearbook of Outstanding Employees, 1990; recipient Presdl. Meritorious Svc. award. Office: DOS Amb 2060 Bangui Pl Washington DC 20521

SHARPNACK, RAYONA, management consultant; b. 1952; 1 child, Chelsea. Grad., U. Nev., Reno. Founder, pres. Inst. Women's Leadership, Redwood City, Calif., 1992—. Faculty Mills Coll., Women in Mgmt. program, 1994; bd. dirs. Profl. Bus. Women Calif. Conf., 1994—99; co-chair State of World Forum, Investing in Women Initiative, 1998—99; pres. Prof. Bus. Women in Calif., 1999; adv. coun. mem. Internat. Mus. Women, 1999—2001; player, mgr. Internat. Women's Profl. Softball League, 1979; shortstop Calif. Express. Office: Inst Women's Leadership PO Box 58 Redwood City CA 94064-0058

SHARROCK (WRENTMORE), ANITA KAY, information technology specialist; b. Logan, Ohio, Dec. 3, 1955; d. Lloyd Earl and Gayle Irene (Daubenmier) W. BS, Ohio U., Lancaster, 1978; MS, Ohio U., Athens, 1979; postgrad., Ohio State U., 1985, Cen. Ohio Tech. Coll., 1987. Cert. tchr. Vis. lectr. Denison U., Granville, Ohio, 1980; lectr. Ohio State U., Newark, 1980-83; instr. Cen. Ohio Tech. Coll., Newark, 1983-86; substitute tchr. Newark City Schs., 1986-87, Northfork Sch. Dist., Utica, Ohio, 1987, Lakewood Sch. Dist., Hebron, Ohio, 1987; with Kelly Services, Reynoldsburg, Ohio, 1986-87; computer specialist Def. Constrn. Supply Ctr., Columbus, Ohio, 1987—92, DLA Sys. Automation Ctr., 1992—2000, DLA Sys. Integration Office, 2000—04, DLA Info. Ops., Columbus, 2004—. Mem. exec. bd. Newark-Licking County Coun. Tchrs. Math., Newark, 1985-88. Mem. Nat. Coun. Tchrs. Math., Ohio Coun. Tchrs. Math., Am. Math. Soc., Assn. for Computing Machinery, Phi Kappa Phi, Kappa Delta Pi. Independent. Methodist. Avocations: swimming, dance, hiking, tv, reading. Home: 103 Ramona Ave Newark OH 43055-1334 Office Phone: 614-692-8347. Business E-Mail: anita.sharrock@dla.mil.

SHARROW, MARILYN JANE, library administrator; b. Oakland, Calif. d. Charles L. and H.Evelyn Sharrow; m. Larry J. Davis. BS in Design, U. Mich., 1967, MALS, 1969. Libr. Detroit Pub. Libr., 1968-70; head fine arts dept. Syracuse U. Librs., NY, 1970-73; dir. libr. Roseville Pub. Libr., Mich., 1973-75; asst. dir. librs. U. Wash., Seattle, 1975-77, assoc. dir. librs., 1978-79; dir. librs. U. Man., Winnipeg, Canada, 1979-82; chief libr. U. Toronto, Canada, 1982-85; univ. libr. U. Calif., Davis, 1985—. Chair bd. North Regional Libr. Facility, 1999—2001; bd. dirs. press U. Calif., 2005—. Recipient Woman of Yr. in Mgmt. award Winnipeg YWCA, 1982; named Woman of Distinction, U. Calif. Faculty Women's Rsch. Group, 1985. Mem. ALA, Assn. Rsch. Librs. (bd. dirs., v.p., pres.-elect 1989-90, pres. 1990-91, chair sci. tech. work group 1994-98, rsch. collections com. 1993-95, 2000-2002, preservation com. 1997-99, 2003-05, ARL leadership devel. task force 2006—), OCLC-Rsch. Librs. Adv. Com. (vice-chair 1992-93, chair 1993-94), Calif. State Network Resources Libr. Com., Can. Assn. Rsch. Libr. (pres. 1984-85). Office: U Calif Shields Libr 100 NW Quad Davis CA 95616-5292 Office Phone: 530-752-2110. E-mail: mjsharrow@ucdavis.edu.

SHARROW, SHEBA GROSSMAN, artist; b. Bklyn., Apr. 28, 1926; children: Mayda, David. BFA, Art Inst. Chgo.; MFA, Temple U. Speaker in field. Exhibited prin. works in numerous one-woman and group shows including Hunterdon Art Ctr., Clinton, N.J., 1994, N.J. Arts Ann., Trenton, 1994, Moravian Coll., Bethlehem, Pa., 1994, Payne Gallery, 1992, Tremellen Gallery, 1992, 91, 90, Pace Setters, Camden County, N.J., 1992, Cheltenham Art Ctr., 1992, Images of Courage & Compassion Millersville U. Pa., 1991, Noyes Mus. Art; works represented in pub. collections including Steelcase Corp., Armstrong World Industries, Citibank N.J., Jersey City Mus. Fellow Blue Mountain Art Ctr., 1987, Mishkenot Sha'ananim, 1990, Va. Ctr. for Creative Arts, 1978-79, 81, 83-93; grantee Pa. Coun. on Arts, 1983, N.J. State Coun. Arts, 1997, 2002, Pollock-Krasner Found., 2000.

SHARRY, JANICE VYN, lawyer; b. Toledo, Aug. 1, 1951; d. John Cameron and Patricia Mae (Hammontree) Vyn; m. Michael Sharry, Aug. 14, 1976; children: Jessica, Greg, Melanie. Grad. cum laude, Knox Coll., 1973; JD magna cum laude, So. Meth. U., 1977. Atty. Haynes & Boone, L.L.P., Dallas, 1977—, head corp. fin. sect., 1989—, ptnr., corp. fin., bd. dir. Rsch. editor Southwester Law Jour. Bd. dirs. Dallas Children's Theatre, 1989-93; edn. com. Greenhill Sch., Dallas, 1990; active Dallas Summer Mus. Guild, 1989—, Dallas Dem. Forum, 1993. Named a Texas Super Lawyer, Tex. Monthly Mag., 2003; named one of Best Lawyers in Dallas, D Magazine, 2003. Mem. ABA (mem. ad hoc com. on form of model simplified indenture, bus. law sect., com. on devels. in bus. fin. 1991—), Tex. Bar Assn.(bus. law sect.), Tex. Bus. Law Found. (bd. trustees 1990—), Dallas Bar Assn., Dallas C. of C. (chair, Executive Women's Roundtable), Phi Beta Kappa, Order of Coif. Presbyterian. Avocations: reading, sports, politics. Office: Haynes and Boone LLP 901 Main St Ste 3100 Dallas TX 75202-3789 Office Phone: 214-651-5562. Office Fax: 214-200-0620. Business E-Mail: janice.sharry@haynesboone.com.

SHATIN, JUDITH, composer, educator; b. Boston, Nov. 11, 1949; d. Leo and Harriet Evelyn (Sommer) S.; m. Michael Kubovy, June 28, 1992. AB, Douglass Coll., 1971; MM, Julliard Sch., 1974; PhD, Princeton U., 1979. Asst. prof. U. Va., Charlottesville, 1979-85, assoc. prof., 1985-92, prof., 1992—, chmn. McIntire dept. music, 1995—2002, William R. Kenan, Jr. prof., 1999—. Dir. Va. Ctr. Computer Music, 1988—. Composer: (orch.) Aura, 1981, (piano concerto) Passion of St. Cecilia, 1985, (flute concerto) Ruah, 1985, (piano trio) View from Mt. Nebo (commd. by Garth Newel Chamber Players), 1985, (piano trio) Ignoto Numine (commd. Monticello Trio), 1986, (flute, clarinet, violin, cello) Secret Ground (commd. by Roxbury Chamber Players), 1990, (soprano and tape) Three Summers Heat, 1989 (Barlow Found. Commn.), (orch.) Piping the Earth (commd. by Women's Philharm.), 1990, (flute and piano) Gabriel's Wing (commd. by Julia Bogorad and the Upper Midwest Flute Assn.), 1990, (flute and electronics) Kairos (Commd. Va. Commn. for the Arts), 1991, (chorus, brass quintet, tympani) We Hold These Truths (commd. U. Va., for Thomas Jefferson's 250th birthday), 1992, (string orch.) Stringing the Bow (commd. Va. Chamber Orch.), 1992, COAL (commd. as part of 2-yr. retrospective of work, sponsored by Lila Wallace- Readers Digest Arts Ptnrs. Program), 1994, (piano and percussion) 1492 (commd. Arioso Ensemble), 1992, (piano) Chai Variations on Eliahu HaNavi, 1995, (flute and guitar) Dreamtigers (commd. Ekko!), 1996, (chorus) Adonai Roi, 1995, (string quartet) Janus Quartet (commd. for the Arcata Quartet), 1994, (string quartet and electronic playback) Elijah's Chariot (commd. Kronos Quartet), 1995, (amplified clarinet with PVC extensions effects processor, foot pedals and playback sys.) Sea of Reeds (commd. F. Gerard Errante), 1997, (chorus and piano) Songs of War and Peace, 1998, (brass quintet) Fantasia sobre el Flamenco, 1998, (piano, cello, percussion) Houdini: Memories of a Conjurer, 1999 (commd. Core Ensemble), (wind quintet and piano) Ockeghem Variations (commd. Hexagon Ensemble), 2000, Run (piano quartet) (commd. Currents) 2001, (SATB chorus) Allelulia, 2001, Singing the Blue Ridge (commd. Wintergreen Performing Arts through Ams. for the Arts), 2002, Tree Music (commd. U. Va. Art Mus., interactive electronics), 2003, Penelope's Song (viola and electronics), 2003, Amulet (commd. N.Y. Treble Singers, SSA Chorus), 2005, Civil War Memories (commd. Jane Franklin Dance, electronics), 2005, Clave (commd. New Ear, flute, clarinet, saxophone, violin, viola, piano, percussion), 2006, Jabberwocky, 2006 (commd. Va. Glee Club0, (amplified cello and electronics) For the Birds, 2006. Nat. Endowment for Arts Composer fellow, 1980, 85, 89, 92; recipient award Va. Commn. for the Arts, 1989, 02. Mem. Am. Music Ctr., Am. Women Composers (pres. 1989-93), Am. Composers Alliance (bd. dirs. 1993-98), Internat. Alliance for Women in Music (chair nominating com. 1996-98, adv. bd. 1999-). Business E-Mail: shatin@virginia.edu, asst@judithshatin.com.

SHATTER, SUSAN LOUISE, artist; b. NYC, Jan. 17, 1943; d. Aubrey and Florence (Breines) S.; m. Paul Brown (div. June 1975); 1 child, Scott Brown. Student, Skowhegan Sch. Sculpture, Maine, 1964; BFA, Pratt Inst., 1965; MFA, Boston U., 1972. Artist in residence Skowhegan (Maine) Sch Painting and Sculpture, 1977, 79; art instr. Sch. Visual Arts, NYC, 1980-84, Tyler Sch. of Art, Phila., 1985, San Francisco Art Inst., 1989, Vt. Studio Ctr., Johnson, 1989, Bklyn. Coll., 1991-95. Vis. critic, U. Pa., 1974-85, acting co-chair, 1983-84; bd. govs. Skowhegan Sch. Painting and Sculpture, 1979—, chair, 1988-91. One-woman shows include Catalogue by D. Kuspit, SUNY Fine Arts Ctr., 2003, Fischbach Gallery, N.Y.C., 1973-97, Harcus Gallery, Boston, 1975-87, Mattingly Baker Gallery, Dallas, 1981, John Berggruen Gallery, San Francisco, 1986, Heath Gallery, Atlanta, 1987, SECCA, Winston-Salem, NC, 2001, Lyons Wier Gallery, N.Y.C., 2002, Staller Ctr. Arts, 2003, Lyonswier Gallery, 2005, Ancocisco Gallery, Portland, Maine, 2006; works reproduced in America '76: A Bicentennial Exhibition, 1976, Boston Watercolor Today, 1976, Realist Drawings and Watercolors: Contemporary Works on Paper, 1980, Contemporary Realism Since 1960, 1981, Perspectives on Contemporary American Realism: Works of Art on Paper from the Collection of Jalane and Richard Davidson, 1983, Eireland, McMullen Mus. of Art, Boston Coll., 2003, New Vistas: Contemporary American Landscapes, 1984, American Realism: Twentieth Century Drawings and Watercolors from the Glenn C. Janss Collection, 1984, A Graphic Muse: Prints by American Women, 1987, Spirit of Place: Contemporary Landscape Painting & the American Tradition, 1989, Twentieth Century Watercolors, 1990, American Realism and Figurative Art: 1952-1991, 1991, (catalogue) Meridian Shift, 12 yrs. of paintings by Susan Shatter, U. Tex., San Antonio, 1998; represented in permanent collections Art Inst. Chgo., Mus. Fine Arts, Boston, MIT, Cambridge, Currier Gallery of Art, Manchester, N.H., Hood Art Mus., Dartmouth Coll., Hanover, N.H., Phila. Mus. Art, Utah Mus. Fine Art, Salt Lake City, Farnesworth Mus., Maine, Buffalo Bill Hist. Soc., Cody, Wyo., U. Tex., San Antonio, Nat. Mus. Am. Art, Washington, Yale U. Art Gallery, Boise (Idaho) Mus. Recipient grants Mass. Creative Artists Humanities, Radcliff Inst., Ingram-Merrill Found., NEA, N.Y. State Found. for the Arts, Yaddo Corp., Ballinglen Artists Fellowship, Ireland, 1999, Pollock-Krasner Found, 2004-05; Brittany fellow Rochefort-en-Terre, 2002; recipient Childe Hassam Purchase award, Am. Acad. Arts and Letters, 2003; Yaddo resident, Saratoga Springs, NY, 2001, 02. Mem. NAD (W. Paten Prize 2003, treas. 1998-05, pres. 2005-), The Century Club. Office: DFN Gallery 176 Franklin St New York NY 10013-2806 E-mail: sshatter@mindspring.com.

SHATTUCK, CATHIE ANN, lawyer, former government official; b. Salt Lake City, July 18, 1945; d. Robert Ashley S. and Lillian Culp (Shattuck). BA, U. Nebr., 1967, JD, 1970. Bar: Nebr. 1970, U.S. Dist. Ct. Nebr. 1970, Colo. 1971, U.S. Dist. Ct. Colo. 1971, U.S. Supreme Ct. 1974, U.S. Ct. Appeals (10th cir.) 1977, U.S. Dist. Ct. D.C. 1984, U.S. Ct. Appeals (D.C. cir.) 1984. V.p., gen. mgr. Shattuck Farms, Hastings, Nebr., 1967-70; asst. project dir. atty. Colo. Civil Rights Commn., Denver, 1970-72; trial atty. EEOC, Denver, 1973-77, vice chmn. Washington, 1982-84; pvt. practice law Denver, 1977-81; mem. Fgn. Svc. Bd., Washington, 1982-84, Presdl. Pers. Task Force, Washington, 1982-84; ptnr. Epstein, Becker & Green, L.A. and Washington, 1984—. Lectr. Colo. Continuing Legal Edn. Author: Employer's Guide to Controlling Sexual Harrassment, 1992; co-editor Nat. Employment Law Insider, 2004-; mem. editl. bd. The Practical Litigator, 1988-2003. Bd. dirs. KGNU Pub. Radio, Boulder, Colo., 1979, Denver Exch., 1980-81, YWCA Met. Denver, 1979-81. Named Nebr. Young Career Woman, Bus. and Profl. Women, 1967, Outstanding Nebraskan, Daily Nebraskan, Lincoln, 1967. Fellow Am. Coll. of Labor and Employment Lawyers; mem. ABA (mgmt. chair labor and employment law sect. com. on immigration law 1988-90, mgmt. chair com. on legis. devels. 1990-93), Nebr. Bar Assn., Colo. Bar Assn., Colo. Women's Bar Assn., D.C. Bar Assn., Nat. Women's Coalition, Delta Sigma Rho, Tau Kappa Alpha, Pi Sigma Alpha, Alpha Xi Delta, Denver Club. Office Phone: 202-861-0900. Business E-Mail: cshattuck@ebglaw.com.

SHATZ, CARLA J., biology professor; b. NYC; BA in Chemistry, Radcliffe Coll., 1969; MPhil, Univ. Coll., London, 1971; PhD, Harvard U., 1976, postdoc., 1976—78. Assoc. prof. neurobiology Sch. Medicine Stanford U., Palo Alto, Calif., 1985—89, prof. neurobiology, 1989—92; investigator Howard Hughes Med. Inst., 1994—2000; Class of 1943 prof. neurobiology U. Calif., Berkeley, 1992—2000; prof., chair dept. neurobiology Harvard Med. Sch., Boston, 2000—. Mem. commn. on life scis. NRC, 1990—96; nat. adv. NIH, 1996—99; mem. coun. NAS, 1998—2001. Fellow: Inst. Medicine, Am. Philos. Soc., NAS, AAAS. Office: Harvard Med Sch Dept Neurobiology 220 Longwood Ave Boston MA 02115-5701

SHATZ, JAYNE EILEEN, artist, educator; b. Bklyn., Mar. 24, 1950; d. George Benton and Ann Ruth (Winick) Shatz; m. Mark Brayden Goor, May 16, 1971 (div. May 1976); m. Ronald Michael Allen, June 26, 1994. BA, SUNY, Albany, 1972; MA, Goddard Coll., Plainfield, Vt., 1979; PhD, Union Inst., Cin., 1992. Cert. tchr. in art, N.Y. Tchr. art Niskayuna (N.Y.) Ctrl. Sch., 1971-72; artist potter Kilnhaus Potters, Slingerlands, N.Y., 1972-76; dir. ceramics Coll. Continuing Studies SUNY, Albany, 1979-82; tchr. art Richmondville (N.Y.) Ctrl. Sch., 1984-87; dir. ceramics Hudson Valley C.C./Rensselaer County Coun. for the Arts, Troy, N.Y., 1982-94; tchr. art Shenandehowa Ctrl. Sch., Clifton Park, NY, 1987—2005; artist potter Jayne Shatz Pottery, Schenectady, 1976—2006, Arnold, Md., 2006—. Founder, gallery dir. Albany Ceramic Inst., 1982; founder, bd. v.p. Hudson River Clay Factory Coop, Troy, 1990-94; tutor/evaluator Empire State Coll., Albany, 1985-86; artist-in-residence N.Y. Found. for the Arts, 1985-87. Contbr. articles to profl. jours.; ceramic exhbns. include Arts Ctr., Old Forge, N.Y., 1980, Lynn Kottler's Gallery, N.Y.C., 1980, Peter's Valley Craft Gallery, N.J., 1983, Farmington Valley Arts Ctr., Conn., 1984, Albany Inst. History and Art, 1985, Brookfield (Conn.) Craft Ctr., 1985, Home Gallery, 1976-95, Ctr. Galleries, Albany, 1995, SUNY-Albany, 1996. Vol. artist N.E. Assn. for Blind, Albany, 1983, VA Hosp. Day Ctr., Albany, 1979; fundraising vol. art auction WHMT-Pub. TV, Capital Dist., N.Y., 1985; tchr. U.S. Holocaust Mus., 1994. Recipient Nat. Award Excellence in Ceramic Edn. Studio Potter Found., N.H., 1989; grantee N.Y. State Coun. on the Arts, 1984, N.Y. State Dept. Edn., 1995. Mem. N.Y. State Union for Tchrs., SUNY-Albany Alumni Assn. Democrat. Jewish. Avocations: computers, sewing, cooking, films, reading. Home and Office: Jayne Shatz Pottery 452 Laurel Valley Ct Arnold MD 21012-2378

SHATZ, MARILYN JOYCE, psychologist, educator; b. N.Y.C., Mar. 4, 1939; d. Morris and Freida Reva (Levinthal) Karpman; m. Stephen Sidney Shatz, Dec. 21, 1958 (div. July 1977); children: Geoffrey Ian, Adria Beth; m. Richard Feingold, Jan. 1, 1995. BA, U. Pa., 1971, MA, 1973, PhD, 1975. Asst. prof. Grad. Ctr. NYU, 1975-77; asst. prof. to prof. U. Mich., Ann Arbor, 1977—, dir. linguistics program, 1995—2001. Assoc. editor Lang. Jour. Linguistic Soc. Am., Washington, 1991-93; vis. scholar Inst. Human Devel., Berkeley, Calif., 1991-92. Author: A Toddler's Life: Becoming a Person, 1994; co-editor: Handbook of Language Development, 2006; contbr. articles to profl. jours. Fellow Guggenheim, Harvard U., 1980, Nat. Inst. Edn., U. Wis., 1981; Fulbright scholar Cambridge U., 1985; named First Alternate James McKean Cattell, 1991. Home: 2730 Maitland Dr Ann Arbor MI 48105-1565 Office: 530 ChurchSt Ann Arbor MI 48109 Office Phone: 734-647-3712.

SHAUERS, MARGARET ANN, author; b. Hoisington, Kans., Nov. 20, 1943; d. John Felix and Leona Ann (Stegman) Krmela; m. Gerald D. Crotinger, Apr. 14, 1959 (div. Oct. 1961); 1 child, James Allen; m. Delbert M. Shauers, Dec. 27, 1962 (dec. Sept. 1995); children: Rochelle, Debra. Student, Barton County C.C., Great Bend, Kans., Ft. Hays U. Author: (novels) Girl of the Prairie, 1975, Dark Knight, 1976, (play and activity) Birth and Childhood of Jesus, 1997, File Folder Games for the Christian Classroom, 1998, puzzle book, 2000; contbr. more than 1,000 short stories, articles to jours. Vol. Crisis Mgmt. Team, Great Bend. Mem. Authors Guild, Great Plains Writers Assn. (v.p. 1996-98), Kans. Authors Club (past dist. pres., Outstanding Journalistic Achievement award 1984). Presbyterian. Avocations: reading, grandchildren. E-mail: mshauers@mac.com.

SHAUGHNESSY, LAUREN MARGARET, music educator; b. Paterson, N.J., June 25, 1948; d. Thomas Napier and Frances Josephine McFadyen; m. John Nicholas Shaughnessy, July 24, 1972; children: Lauren Margaret, Peter Brendan, Mary Frances, Elizabeth Anna Rose, Susan Lillian. MusB, Marywood Coll., Scranton, Pa., 1970. Chorus dir. Spotswood (N.J.) H.S., Spotswood, NJ, 1989—96; music tchr., band dir. Meml. Mid. Sch., Spotswood, 1996—. Exec. bd. mem. Ctrl. Jersey YWCA, 1979—85; choir mem. Ch. of Immaculate Conception, Spotswood, 1975—; lector Ch. of the Immaculate Conception, Spotswood, NJ, 1999. Mem.: N.J. Music Educator's Assn., Music Educators Nat. Conf. Roman Catholic. Avocations: gardening, reading, knitting, sewing. Home: 330 Adirondack Av Spotswood NJ 08884 Office: Memorial Sch 115 Summerhill Rd Spotswood NJ 08884 Office Phone: 732-723-2227. Personal E-mail: lmsmom625@aol.com.

SHAUGHNESSY, LESLIE RESTAINO, secondary educator; b. N.Y.C., Nov. 19, 1945; d. Anthony A. and Libera (Zarro) Restaino; m. David John Shaughnessy, July 14, 1968; children: David Anthony, Alicia Marie, Steven James. BA, St. John's U., 1967. Cert. tchr., Va. Tchr. Massapequa (N.Y.) High Sch., 1967-68, Peninsula Cath. High Sch., Newport News, Va., 1985-90; high sch. tchr. Hampton (Va.) City Schs., 1990—2006; ret., 2006. Contbr. book revs. to local newspapers, 1985-87. Named Hon. Thespian, Internat. Thespian Soc. Troupe 290, 1991-92. Mem. Nat. Coun. Tchrs. of English, Va. Assn. Tchrs. of English. Roman Catholic. Avocations: reading, theater, bike riding. Home: 702 Essex Park Dr Hampton VA 23669-1323

SHAUGHNESSY, MARIE KANEKO, artist; b. Detroit, Sept. 14, 1924; d. Eishiro and Kiyo (Yoshida) Kaneko; m. John Thomas Shaughnessy, Sept. 23, 1959. Assocs. in Liberal Arts, Keisen U., Tokyo, 1944. Ops. mgr. Webco Alaska, Inc., Anchorage, 1970-88; ptnr. Webco Partnership, Anchorage, 1983-98, also bd. dirs. Faculty Art League Sch., Alexandria, Va., Fairfax County Pub. Sch. Adult Continuing and Cmty. Edn. Paintings, Lilacs, 1984, Blooms, 1985, The Fence, 1986 (Purchase award, 1986). Bd. dirs. Alaska Artists Guild, 1971—87; commr. Mcpl. Anchorage Fine Arts Commn., 1983—87; organizing com. Japanese Soc. Alaska, 1987. Recipient Art Affiliate award, Anchorage C. of C., 1975, 1978, 1984, Univ. Artists award, Alaska Pacific U., 1986, Am. Juror's Choice award, Sumi-E Soc. Am., 1994, Ikebana Internat. award, 1994, Dorothy Klein Meml. award, 1995, Yasutomo Calligraphy award, 1997, 1998, Oriental Calligraphy award, 1997, 1998, Sarasota Chpt Painting award, 1999, Paul Schwartz Meml. award, 2001, Sm. Works Exhibit 1st Pl. award, Wash. Watercolor Assn., 2001, Wang Chi Yuan award, 2000. Mem.: Washington Water Color Assn. (1st place award Strathmore Mansion summer exhbn. 2005), Nat. League Am. Penwomen (Grumbacher Gold medal award excellence 1993), Vienna Art Soc. (bd. dir. 1995—96), Sumi-E Soc. Am. (past pres. 1992—94, bd. dir., Nat. Capital Area chpt. past pres. awards 1990, Nat. Capital Area chpt. award 1990—92, Purchase award 1993, Nat. Capital Area chpt. award 1994), Va. Watercolor Soc. (pres. 1993, co-chmn. 2004 All State Juried Show), Potomac Valley Watercolorists (exhibits chair 1989—93, bd. dir. 1989—99, newsletter editor 1993—96, v.p., workshop chair 1996—2001, historian 2003, awards 1989, 1991, Spl. award 1995), Alaska Watercolor Soc. (life; charter, Grumbacher Silver medal 1989), McLean Art Soc. (pres. 2006—, 1st pl. award 1991). Republican. Roman Catholic. Personal E-mail: markaneko@aol.com.

SHAUGHNESSY, MARY ELLEN, educator; b. Buffalo, Oct. 21, 1938; BA in English and Edn., Medaille Coll., 1964; MA in English, Niagara U., 1967; PhD in Lit. and Psychology, SUNY, Buffalo, 1977. Adminstr., instr. Trocaire Coll., 1970-72; instr., program coord. SUNY, Buffalo, 1972-81; pers. mgr., tng. coord. Del. North Cos., 1981-85; allocations mgr., dir. cmty. problem solving United Way of Buffalo and Erie County, Buffalo, 1985-87; assoc. prof., advisor Capital U., Columbus, Ohio, 1988-92; assoc. prof., mentor, writing tutor Empire State Coll., Buffalo, 1992—. Mem. adv. coun. dept. bus. studies Buffalo State Coll.; mem. adj. faculty bus. writing and career planning Cornell U.; bd. dirs., coord. Bus. Profl. Women, Amherst, Buffalo, 1992—; cons. conflict mgmt., comm., and effective writing. Bd. dirs. Ctr. for Women in Mgmt., 1981-88; assoc. dir. leadership tng. family life dept. Diocese of Buffalo; vol. mediator Better Bus. Bur. Mem. AAUW (bd. dirs., dir. publicity), Mid. States Assn. (mem. accrediting team), Buffalo Investors Group (bd. dirs.). Avocations: reading, theater, bicycling, gardening, travel. Office: Empire State Coll 9 Ontario St Lockport NY 14094

SHAUGHNESSY, MEGHANN, professional tennis player; b. Richmond, Apr. 13, 1979; d. Bill and Joy. Profl. tennis player, 1996—. Recipient WTA Tour Doubles Title, Quebec City, 2000, German Open, 2001, Gold Coast, 2002, Moscow, 2003, WTA Tour Singles Title, Shanghai, 2000, Quebec City, 2001, Canberra, 2003, Grand Prix SAR, 2006, Forest Hills Women's Tennis Classic, 2006, Ranked #17, WTA, Ranked #6 Among U.S. Players, Highest Season Ending Single's Ranking #12, 2001, Resident Pro, Scottsdale Hyatt Gainey Ranch Resort, 6 Internat. Women's Circuit Singles Titles. Mem.: U.S. Fedn. Cup Team. Office: WTA Tour Corporate Headquarters One Progress Plz Ste 1500 Saint Petersburg FL 33701*

SHAVENDER, MARILYN FAYE, retired elementary school educator; b. Washington, Feb. 22, 1938; d. Redden Hudnell and Alice Gray Shavender; 1 child, Annette Byrd (dec.). BS in Elem. Edn., East Carolina U., 1959. 2d grade tchr. Virginia Beach Sch. Sys., Va., 1959—, lang. arts com., 1988—2003; ret., 2003. Author: (book) Poetry by Grammy, 2000, Marsh Winds.A Sentimental Journey. Mem.: DAR, Virginia Beach Edn. Assn. Republican. Mem. Church Of Christ. Avocations: piano, writing, antiques, gardening. E-mail: Twingrand@aol.com.

SHAVERS, CHERYL L., technology and business consultant; married; 3 children. BS in Chemistry, Ariz. State U., PhD in Solid State Chemistry; degree in engring. mgmt. (hon.), Calif. Poly. State U., 1996. Practicing registered patent agent Patent and Trademark Office of Dept. of Commerce. Prod. engr. Motorola; process devel. engr. Hewlett-Packard, patent agent, tech. legal dept.; microelectronics sect. mgr. Wiltron Co.; engring. mgr., thin films devel. lab. Varian Associates; sector mgr. microprocessor div., corp. bus. devel. div. Intel Corp.; under sec. commerce for tech. U.S. Dept Commerce, 1999—2001; chmn., CEO Global Smarts, Inc., Santa Clara, Calif., 2001—. Spkr., workshop leader in field; non-exec. chmn. BitArts Ltd., 2001—03; bd. dirs. Rockwell Collins, Inc., 2002—. Weekly columnist San Jose Mercury News Bus. Sect.; contbr. articles to profl. publs.; featured in articles, books and Web sites; TV appearances include documentary Wizards and Alchemists, 1995, Real Science Program, Sta. KTEH-TV, NBC New Media News, Women in Technology, 1997 Active numerous outreach programs, including Real Sci., Wizards and Alchemists, KTEH Silicon Valley Report, KRON New Media News programs; bd. dirs. San Jose Tech Mus. of Innovation, 1996—; former bd. dirs. Internat. Network Women in Tech., 1995-96, ARC, 1995-96. Recipient Janet Gray Hayes award, award Phi Lambda Upsilon, Outstanding Presenter of Yr., San Francisco Bay Area chpt. Nat. Assn. of Black MBAs, 1998; Henry Crown fellow Aspen Inst.'s Crown Fellowship Program; inductee Internat. Women in Tech. Hall of Fame, Coll. Liberal Arts and Scis. Hall of Fame, Ariz. State U., 1997, Internat. Network of Women in Tech. Hall of Fame, 1996. Mem. Libr. of Congress (assoc.). Office: Global Smarts Inc 3333 Bowers Ave Ste 130 Santa Clara CA 95050

SHAVIN, HELENE B., venture capital company executive; b. 1954; BA, Queens Coll.; MBA, Baruch Coll. Sr. acct. KPMG Peat Marwick, Hawaii; CPA Citicorp Venture Capital Ltd., NY, 1986—2000, v.p. NY, 1999—2000; v.p., controller Harris & Harris Group, Inc., NY, 2001—. Office: Harris & Harris Group Inc 111 W 57th St Ste 1100 New York NY 10019 also: Harris & Harris Group Inc 11150 Santa Monica Blvd Ste 1200 Los Angeles CA 90025 Office Phone: 212-582-0900, 310-479-2595. Office Fax: 212-582-9563, 310-312-1868. Business E-Mail: admin@tinytechvc.com.

SHAW, ANNITA LOUISE, art educator; b. Scottsbluff, Nebr., Feb. 13, 1941; d. Harold Kenneth and Velma Loraine Shaw; m. Max Le Roy Shaw, June 29, 1968; 1 child, Justin Owen. BS in Elem. Edn., Chadron State Coll., Nebr., 1963; MA in Art Supervision and Direction, NYU, 1969. Tchr. 2d grade Bridgeport Sch. Dist., Nebr., 1961—64; tchr. 3rd grade Geneva Sch. Dist., Nebr., 1964—66; elem. art specialist Omaha Sch. Dist., 1966—68; tchr. jr. high sci. New London Sch. Dist., Conn., 1968—70; tchr. jr. and sr. high visual arts and visual arts curriculum specialist Ctrl. Kitsap Sch. Dist., Silverdale, Wash., 1974—2003; owner A.Shaw Originals. Mem. adv. com. Wash. State Commn. on Student Learning, Olympia, 1993—95; mem. assessment cert. team Nat. Bd. Profl. Tchg. Stds., San Francisco, 1996; mem. People to People Art Edn. Delegation to Russia, 2006; presenter in field. Prodr.: (video) Whistle Wisdom, 1993, Perspective: More than Converging Line, 1999, Roll, Pinch, Shake and Rattle, 2001; contbr. articles to mags. and profl. jours. Mem.: Nat. Art Edn. Assn. (mem. dels. assembly 1994, historian Wash. chpt. 1994, pres. Wash. chpt., treas. Wash. chpt., Pacific Region Elem. Art Educator 1988, Christa McAuliffe Excellence in Edn. 1990, Pacific Region Mid. Level Art Educator 2001, Wash. Art Educator of Yr. 2000, Nat. Mid. Level Art Educator of the Yr. 2002), Women in the Arts (charter mem. 2006). Avocations: sculpting, designing pins and medallions, writing. Home: PO Box 737 Silverdale WA 98383-0737 Personal E-mail: mashaw@mindspring.com.

SHAW, BETTY JANE, medical/surgical nurse; b. Elvins, Mo., Jan. 13, 1943; d. Melvin Dewey Short and Catherine Marie (Steiger) Spurgeon; m. James J. Shaw, June 22, 1996; children: Martin Dale Beck, Patti Sue Beck Johnson. ADN, Mineral Area Jr. Coll., 1973. RNC; med-surg cert. Staff nurse post-op. and med.-pediats. divsn., infection control liaison Parkland Health Ctr., Farmington, Mo., 1973—; nurse Elder Helpers, Inc., Farmington, Mo. Mem. IV performance team Barnes-Jewish-Christian, St. Louis, 1994, wound/skin care/ostomy performance team, 1994. Active mem. bd. adjustment, chmn. City of Farmington, 1993—. Mem. Am. Heart Assn. (St. Francois County chpt.), Acad. Med.- Surg. Nurses, Order of Eastern Star. Democrat. Baptist. Avocations: needlecrafts, fishing, dance, camping, walking. Home: 440 Squaw Valley Dr Farmington MO 63640-2152 Office: Elder Helpers Inc 301 N Washington Farmington MO 63640

SHAW, CAROLE, editor, publisher; b. Bklyn., Jan. 22, 1936; d. Sam and Betty (Neckin) Bergenthal; m. Ray Shaw, Dec. 27, 1957; children: Lori Eve Cohen, Victoria Shaw Locknar. BA, Hunter Coll., 1962. Singer Capitol Records, Hilton Records, Rama Records, Verve Records, 1952-65; TV appearances Ed Sullivan, Steve Allen, Jack Paar, George Gobel Show, 1957; owner The People's Choice, L.A., 1975-79; founder, editor-in-chief Big Beautiful Woman mag., Beverly Hills, Calif., 1979—. Creator Carole Shaw and BBW label clothing line for large-size women. Author: Come Out, Come Out Wherever You Are, 1982. Avocations: piano, painting, swimming, travel. Office: BBW Mag 6666 Brookmont Ter Ste 412 Nashville TN 37205-4622 Personal E-mail: bibewa@comcast.net.

SHAW, CECELIA, retired chef; b. Mankato, Minn., Feb. 18, 1959; d. Maxine Adele and Robert Cyril Shaw; m. Steve Schept, Sept. 15, 1990. Degree in Culinary Arts, Mankato Tech. Coll., Minn., 1984. Owner, head chef Soupstone, Mankato, 1980—81; pvt. practice Mankato, 1981—83; salad and prep cook Maggies Cafe, Mankato, 1983; asst. kitchen mgr. Phoenix Restaurant, Mankato, 1983—84; 1st commis chaud Hotel Sofitel, Bloomington, Minn., 1984—86; supr., chef Ebenezer Soc., Mpls., 1986—87; dietary mgr. Mar. Ho., Mpls., 1987—90; kitchen mgr. Table of Contents, St. Paul, 1990—91; line chef Azur Restaurant, Mpls., 1991—92; sous chef Blue Point Restaurant, Wayzata, Minn., 1992—94; prep chef D'Amico Cucina, Mpls., 1994—96; ret., 1996. Vol. Hope Now, Arlington Heights, Ill., 2002—04. Avocations: languages, travel, gardening, cooking. Personal E-mail: ceceliasrd2@earthlink.net.

SHAW, ELEANOR JANE, newspaper editor; b. Columbus, Ohio, Mar. 23, 1949; d. Joseph Cannon and Wanda Jane (Campbell) S. BA, U. Del., 1971. With News-Jour. newspapers, Wilmington, Del., 1970-82, editor HEW desk, asst. met. editor, 1977-80, bus. editor, 1980-82; topics editor USA Today, 1982-83; asst. city editor The Miami Herald, 1983-85; projects editor The Sacramento Bee, 1985-87, news editor, 1987-91, exec. bus. editor, 1991-93, editor capitol bur. news, 1993-95, state editor, 1995-99; mgr. employee comm. The McClatchy Co., Sacramento, 1999—2004; associate HartMedia, 2004—. Bd. dirs. Del. 4-H Found., 1978-83; bd. dirs. Safety Ctr., Inc., Sacramento, 2003—, sec., 2005—. Mem. Calif. Soc. Newspaper Editors (bd. dirs. 1990-96), No. Calif. Wine Soc. (v.p. 1987-93, pres. 1993-2002). Office: 11682 Gold Country Blvd Gold River CA 95670 Office Phone: 800-732-1722. Personal E-mail: ellieshaw@sbcglobal.net. E-mail: ellie@hartmedia.com.

SHAW, GLORIA DORIS, art educator; b. Huntington, W.Va., Nov. 10, 1928; d. Charles Bert and Theodosia Doris (Shimer) Haley; m. Arthur Shaw, July 13, 1954 (dec. Aug. 1985); children: Deirdra Elizabeth, Stewart N. Student, SUNY, 1969-70, Art Students League, N.Y.C., 1969-70, 74; BA, SUNY, N.Y.C., 1980; postgrad., U. Tenn., 1982, Nat Kaz, Pietrasanta, Italy, 1992. Sculptor replicator Am. Mus. Natural History, N.Y.C., 1976-77; adj. prof. sculpture Fla. Keys C.C., Key West, 1983—2005; ret., 2005. Prof. TV art history Fla. Keys C.C., 1989—; host moderator Channel 5 TV, Fla. Keys, 1982—; presenter Humanities Studies and Art History Channel 19 TV, 1995—, TV Jour. Channel 16, 1997—. Sculptor (portrait) Jimmy Carter, Carter Meml. Libr., 1976, Tennessee Williams, Tennessee Williams Fine Arts Ctr., 1982, UNICEF, 1978-79, (series) Fla. Panther and Audubon Wall Relief, 1985, (bust) AIDS Meml., 1990; one woman shows include Bank Street Coll., 1979, Hollywood Mus. of Art, 1985, Islander Gallery, 1983, Martello Mus., 1984, Greenpeace, 1987, FKCC Gallery, 2003; exhibited in group shows at Montoya, West Palm Beach, Fla., 1989, N.Y.C. Bd. of Edn. Tour of Schs., 1979, Earthworks East, N.Y., 1987, Man and Sci., 1978, Cuban Club, Key West, Fla., 1991, Leda Bruce Gallery, Big Pine, 1992, Kaz, Pietrasanta, Italy, 1992, Fla. Keys C.C. Gallery, 1993, Tennessee Williams Fine Arts Ctr., Key West, 1993, Internat. Woman's Show, Fla. Keys, 1994, Joy Gallery, 1994, 95, 96, Baron Gallery, Girls of Mauritania to UNICEF, 1996; designer Windows at Greenpeace Bldg., Key West, 1985-88, Pieta at St. Paul's Key West, 1997, Ceramic bird murals, FKCC, 1997; curator Women's Art, Key West, 1999, murals, Tennessee Williams Fine Arts Ctr., 1999, relief nudes Fine Arts Bldg., 1999, St. Francis sculpture and seated figures Garden Club, 2001, FKCC Gallery, 2003; retrospective: Gallery Florida Keys, 2003, Arts of Key West Lazy Lane Gallery, 2004. Recipient Children and Other Endangered Species award Thomas Cultural Ctr., 1980, Purchase award Cuban C. of C., 1982, Sierra Club, 1983, Blue Ribbon, Martello Towers Art and Hist. Soc., 1985, Red Ribbon, South Fla. Sculptors, 1986, Endangered Species award Greenpeace, 1986. Mem.: Nat. Sculpture Soc. NYC, Internat. Sculpture Ctr., Art and Hist. Soc., Art Students League NYC (life). Democrat. Avocation: naturalist.

SHAW, HELEN LESTER ANDERSON, nutrition educator, researcher, retired dean; b. Lexington, Ky., Oct. 18, 1936; d. Walter Southall and Elizabeth (Guyn) Anderson; m. Charles Van Shaw, Mar. 14, 1988. BS, U. Ky., Lexington, 1958; MS, U. Wis., Madison, 1965, PhD, 1969. Registered dietitian. Dietitian Roanoke (Va.) Meml. Hosp., 1959-60, Santa Barbara (Calif.) Cottage Hosp., 1960-61; dietitian, unit mgr. U. Calif., Santa Barbara, 1961-63; rsch. asst., NIH fellow U. Wis., Madison, 1963-68; from asst. prof. to prof. U. Mo., Columbia, 1969-88, assoc. dean, prof., 1977-84; prof., chair dept. food and nutrition U. N.C., Greensboro, 1989-94, dean Sch. Human Environ. Scis., 1994-2000; ret., 2000. Cluster leader Food for 21st Century rsch. program U. Mo., 1985-88. Contbr. articles to rsch. publs. Elder First Presbyn. Ch., Columbia, Mo., 1974—89, Greensboro, NC, 1992—. Recipient Teaching award Home Econ. Alumni Assn., 1981, Gamma Sigma Delta, 1984; rsch. grantee Nutrition Found., 1971-73, NIH, 1972-75, NSF, 1980-83.

Mem. Am. Soc. for Nutrition, Am. Bd. Nutrition, Am. Soc. for Clin. Nutrition, Am. Dietetic Assn., Sigma Xi, Phi Upsilon Omicron, Kappa Omicron Nu. Democrat. Avocations: tennis, singing, volunteering, watercolor painting. E-mail: shaw713helen@aol.com.

SHAW, JUDY BROWDER, engineer; BS in Chemistry, Harding Coll.; postgrad, Texas Tech U. Process devel. engr. then process engr. mgr. Texas Instruments, 1978—2000, mgr. Silicon Tech. Devel. Process Engring. teams, 2000—. Co-founder SiTD Women's Network, 2002; mem. SiTD Business Diversity Team, Leadership Tex., 2004. Named to Hall of Fame, WITI, 2004.

SHAW, LINDA DARE OWENS, county commissioner; b. High Point, N.C., May 30, 1940; d. Elborn James Elijah and Cassandra Myrtle (Hutchens) Owens; m. Roger Bruce Chilton, July 18, 1958 (div. Aug. 1976); children: Joni Lynn Chilton Moffitt, Roger Kyle Chilton; m. Robert Gilbert Shaw, Mar. 27, 1981. Grad. h.s. County commr., Guilford County, N.C., 1999—. Trustee N.C. Mus. Art, Raleigh, 1984-90; bd. dirs. Greensboro Conv. and Visitors Bur., 1990-96; sec. Rep. Nat. Com., 1996—, nat. committeewoman, N.C., 1992-96; sec. Rep. Nat. Conv., Phila., 2000; bd. dirs. ARC, YMCA, 2002—, Guilford County Bd. Health, 1999—; sec. com. on arrangements Rep. Nat. Conv., N.Y.C., 2004, ex-officio, mem. site com., 2004; mem. Greensboro Libr. Bd., 2004—; mem. Guilford County Bd. Health, 1999-2001; mem. Greensboro Econ. Devel. Partnership, 2004—; mem. Hearth of Triad Econ., 2006—. Office: Bd County Commrs PO Box 3427 Greensboro NC 27402-3427 Home: 5105 Bennington Dr Greensboro NC 27410-3414 Mailing: O Box 8618 Greensboro NC 27419 E-mail: imlshaw@aol.com.

SHAW, LISA MARIE, secondary school educator; b. Wichita, Kans., Sept. 29, 1977; d. William Martin and Rose Ann Rhodes; m. Matthew Clayton Shaw, Jan. 1, 2001; children: Colten Matthew, Haley Ann, Madison Marie. AA, Cowley County C.C., Arkansas City, Kans., 1998; BS, Newman U., Wichita, Kans., 2000. Tchr. USD 261, Wichita, 2000—. Volleyball coach USD 261, Wichita, 2001—04. Office Phone: 316-554-2236.

SHAW, MARY JOE, nurse; d. Jimmie Earl and Mary Lee Shaw; 1 child, Andrea Ladonna. BSN, U. Phoenix, Southfield, 1997—99. RN Mich., 1984. Nurse Oakland Gen. Hosp., Madison Hts., Mich., 1989—; with Wayne County CC, Detroit, 2002—, Thompson Mid. Sch., Centerline, 2002—; nurse Nursing Poole, East Pointe, Mich., 2005; clin. coord. Davenport U., Warren, Mich., 2006—. Thompson prometric State Licensure Nursing Assts., Westland, Mich., 2001—; with Tng. For CNA, Detroit, 2001—. Adv. Greater Grace Temple, Detroit, 2002. Recipient Employee of Yr., 2000. Office: Davenport Univ 27650 Dequindre Warren MI 48092 Business E-Mail: mary.shaw@davenport.edu.

SHAW, MARY M., computer scientist, educator; b. Washington, Sept. 30, 1943; d. Eldon Earl and Mary Lewis (Holman) Shaw; m. Roy R. Weil, Feb. 15, 1973. BA cum laude, Rice U., 1965; PhD, Carnegie Mellon U., Pitts., 1972. Asst. prof. to prof. computer sci. Carnegie Mellon U., Pitts., 1972—, assoc. dean computer sci. for profl. programs, 1992-99, Alan J. Perlis chair computer sci.; co-dir. Sloan Software Industry Ctr., Pitts., 2001—. Chief scientist Software Engring. Inst., Carnegie Mellon U., Pitts., 1984-88; mem. Computer Sci. and Telecommunications Bd., NRC, Washington, 1986-93. Author: (with W. Wulf, P. Hilfinger, L. Flon) Fundamental Structures of Computer Science, 1981, The Carnegie Mellon Curriculum for Undergraduate Computer Science, 1985, (with David Garlan) Software Architecture: Perspectives on an Emerging Discipline, 1996, (with Roy Weil) Free Wheeling Easy in Western Pennsylvania, 1995, 1996, 1999; contbr. articles to profl. jours. Recipient Warnier prize, 1993, (with Roy Weil) Recreation and Outdoor Stewardship award, 2003, REI Stewards of Environment award, 2004, Stevns award, 2005; named Woman of Achievement, YWCA of Greater Pitts., 1973. Fellow AAAS, IEEE (disting. lectr.), Assn. for Computing Machinery (SIGPLAN exec. com. 1979-83, Recognition of Svc. award 1985, 90); mem. Sigma Xi. Office: Carnegie Mellon U Dept Computer Sci Pittsburgh PA 15213

SHAW, NANCY RIVARD, museum curator, art historian, consultant; b. Saginaw, Mich. d. Joseph and Jean Marcotte; m. Danny W. Shaw, Feb. 29, 1980; 1 stepchild, Christina Marie. BA magna cum laude, Oakland U., 1969; MA, Wayne State U., 1973. Asst. curator Am. art Detroit Inst. Arts, 1972-75, curator, 1975-98, curator emeritus, 1998—. Adj. prof. art and art history Wayne State U., Detroit, 1991-98; lectr. in field.; organizer exhibns. Contbg. author: American Art in the Detroit Institute of Arts, Vol. I, 1991, Vol. II, 1997, Vol. III, 2005; contbr. articles to exhbn. catalogues and profl. jours. Mem. Wayne State U. Alumni Assn. Avocations: knitting, painting, golf. Personal E-mail: nrivardshaw@yahoo.com.

SHAW, NINA L., lawyer; b. NYC; BA, Barnard Coll., 1976; JD, Columbia U., 1979. Bar: Calif. 1981. Founding ptnr., entertainment law Del, Shaw, Moonves, Tanaka & Finkelstein, Santa Monica, Calif. Bd. dirs. The Montel Williams MS Found.; mem. Barbara A. Black Professorship Com. Named one of 100 Most Powerful Women in Entertainment, Hollywood Reporter, 2003, 2004, 100 Most Influential Blacks in America; recipient Disting. Alumna/us Award, Columbia Black Law Students Assn., 2002, Women in Film Crystal award, 2005. Mem.: State Bar Calif., LA County Bar Assn., Kernochan Ctr. Law, Media and Arts (West Coast adv. bd.), Black Women Lawyers Assn.*

SHAW, PRISCILLA, music educator, coach; d. Lee and Freddie Shaw. MusB, Tex. Christian U., Ft. Worth, Tex., 1991—94. Cert. National Board Certification Nat. Bd. for Profl. Tchg. Standards, 2002. Dir. of vocal music George Wash. H.S., Denver, 1997—; tennis coach US Profl. Tennis Assn., Denver, 1999—. Tennis coach US Profl. Tennis Assn., Denver, 1999—. Bd. mem. Colo. Fund for Children and Pub. Edn., Denver, Colo., 2001—. Recipient Althea Gibson Vol. Award, Intermountain Tennis Assn., 2002, Tchr. of the Yr., Believe Productions, 2001, Harmony Award, Denver Mountainaires, 2001, Alumni Appreciation award, Tex. Christian U., 2005; grantee Nat. Coaches Conv., Intermountain Tennis Assn., 2000. Mem.: US Profl. Tennis Assn. (multicultural com. chair, lessons for life, chair 2001—03), USTA (assoc.). R-Liberal. Avocations: tennis, travel. Office: George Washington High School 655 S Monaco Parkway Denver CO 80224 Personal E-mail: tennisgalp@hotmail.com.

SHAW, RENEE S., elementary school educator; d. John Elias and Olga Joseph Salloum; m. Frank David Shaw, July 3, 1977; children: Christina Lynne, Jamie Lynne. MA, California U. of Pa., California, 1985. Cert. Title I reading specialist Pa., 1985. Title I reading specialist McKeesport Area Sch. Dist., McKeesport, Pa., 1976—. Mem.: Pa. PTA (life; sec. 2000—01). Office: McKeesport Area School District 500 Longvue Dr White Oak PA 15131 Office Phone: 412-664-3740. Office Fax: 412-664-3747. E-mail: rshaw@mckasd.net.

SHAW, ROSLYN LEE, small business owner, retired elementary school educator; b. Bklyn., Oct. 1, 1942; d. Benjamin Biltmore and Bessie (Banilower) Deretchin; m. Stephen Allan Shaw, Feb. 1, 1964; children: Laurence, Victoria, Michael. BA, Bklyn. Coll., 1964; MS, SUNY, New Paltz, 1977, cert. advanced study, 1987; cert. gifted edn., Coll. New Rochelle, 1986. Cert. sch. adminstr., supr., sch. dist. adminstr., reading tchr., tchr. N-6. Tchr. Hillel Hebrew Acad., Beverly Hills, Calif., 1965-66, P.S. 177, 77, Bklyn., 1964-65, 66-67, Middletown (N.Y.) Sch. Dist., 1974-77, reading specialist, 1977-99, compensatory edn. reading tchr., 1977-99, tchr. gifted children, 1984-87, asst. project coord. pre-K, 1988-89, instrnl. leader, 1989-93; ret., 1999; pres. Maxwell Enterprises Ltd. Adj. assoc. prof. SUNY, Coll. at New Paltz, 1997-98; newspaper in edn. coord. The Times Herald Record, 1999-2001, ednl. cons., 2001-; pres. Rotary Club of New Brunswick, 2005- Pres. Middletown H.S. Parents' Club, 1983-86; bd. dirs. Mental Health Assn., Goshen, N.Y., 1980-81; mem. Middletown Interfaith Coun., 1983-85. Mem. Amy Bull Crist Reading Coun. (pres. 1989-91, 93-95, 2001), N.Y. State Reading Assn. (Coun. Svc. award 1990, regional dir. 1991-94, bd. dirs. 1991—, chair reading tchrs. spl. interest group 1993-94, pres.-elect 1999—, pres. 2000-01, past pres. 2001, regional dir. 2001, newsletter editor The Empire State Reading Scene), Internat. Reading Assn., Univ. Women's Club, Delta Kappa Gamma. Avocations: photography, walking, reading. Home: 21 Thatchwood Ct North Brunswick NJ 08902 E-mail: iconsult@optonline.net.

SHAW, RUTH G., energy company executive; m. Colin Stuart Shaw; 2 children. BA in English magna cum laude, East Carolina U.; PhD, U. Tex. Pres. Central Piedmont Cmty. Coll., 1986—92; v.p. corp. comms. Duke Energy Corp., Charlotte, NC, 1992-94, sr. v.p. corp. resources, 1994-97, exec. v.p., chief adminstrv. officer, 1997—2002, pres., 2003—, El Centro Coll., Dallas. Dir. Wachovia Corp., MedCath Corp.; mem. bd. dirs. Edison Electric Inst., Nuclear Energy Inst., S. E. Electric Exchange; chair Charlotte Rsch. Inst.; mem. Palmetto Bus. Forum. Mem. Order of the Long Leaf Pine; trustee U. N.C., Charlotte; bd. dirs. Rsch. Triangle Found. of N.C.; mem. Conf. Bd. Chief Adminstrv. Officer's Coun.; chmn. Found. for the Carolinas; elder 1st Presbyn. Ch., Charlotte; active United Way, Arts and Scis. Coun., YMCA, Boy Scouts Am. Named Outstanding Alumni, East Carolina U., disting. grad. U. Tex., Charlotte Woman of Yr., 1992, Businesswoman of Yr., 1995; recipient award for comms. excellence, 1997. Office: Duke Energy Corp 526 S Church St Charlotte NC 28202-1802

SHAW, SONYA KING, literature and language educator; b. Enterprise, Ala., Sept. 21, 1964; d. Charles B. and Carolyn Martin King; m. John B. Shaw, May 30, 1987; 1 child, Erin Nadia. BSc, Troy State U., Ala., 1986; MSc, Troy State U., 1991. Cert. edn. specialist Troy State U., 1997. English tchr. Greenville Acad., Ala., 1987—88; sec. english tchr. Coffee County Bd. Edn., Elba, Ala., 1988—. Curriculum com. chair Coffee County Bd. of Edn., 2004—; reading initiative for soc. coach Ala. State Dept. Edn., 2006. Recipient Outstanding English Grad. Student awrd, Troy State U., 1991. Mem.: Ala. Edn. Assn., Nat. Coun. for Tchrs. of English, Sigma Tau Delta, Pi Kappa Phi. Bapt. Avocations: reading, writing. Home: 232 Martin Rd Kinston AL 36453 Office: Kinston H S 201 College St Kinston AL 36453

SHAW, SUE ANN, medical transcriptionist; b. Van Nuys, Calif., Oct. 7, 1938; d. Harry Herbert and Elizabeth (Allison) Nesbit; m. Gerald Cargile Shaw (dec.); children: Deanna Christine Rushing, Jody Ray Rushing(dec.), John Paul Rushing. Cert. med. transcriptionist Am. Assn. Med. Transcription. Med. transcriptionist Meth. Hosps. of Dallas, 1975—2005. Vol. Meals on Wheels, Waxahachie, Tex., 2003, Charlton Meth. Hosp., Dallas, 2005—. Mem.: Am. Assn. Med. Transcription (founding officer, corr. sec. Greater Dallas chpt. 1979—82, com. mem. 1989—92). Republican. Baptist. Avocations: embroidery, stained glass, quilting, painting, gardening. Home: 110 Sunglow Loop Red Oak TX 75154

SHAW, THERESA S. (TERRI SHAW), federal official; married; 2 children. BS, George Mason U., 1960; Grad. Exec. Devel. Program, George Washington U., 1991. From staff to sr. v.p. and chief info. officer SLM Corp., Reston, Va., 1988—99; exec. v.p., COO eNumerate Solutions, Inc, McLean, Va., 2000—02; COO Fed. Student Aid US Dept. Edn., Washington, 2002—. Office: Office of Federal Student Aid US Dept Edn 830 First St NE Rm 112G1 Washington DC 20202 Office Phone: 202-377-3003. E-mail: terri.shaw@ed.gov.

SHAW-SODERSTROM, KATHERINE S., retired anesthesiologist; b. Cuyapo, Philippines, Jan. 20, 1942; arrived in U.S., 1965; d. David and Josefa Shaw; m. Bjarne Gustav Soderstrom (dec.). MD, U. Santo Tomas, Manila, Philippines, 1965. Diplomate Am. Soc. Anethesiologists. Clin. instr. Harvard Med. Sch./Mass. Gen. Hosp., Boston, 1969—75; attending anethesiologist Mass. Gen. Hosp., Boston, 1969—75; dir. anethesia Greenwich Hosp., Conn., 1980—98. Recipient Horace Wells award for Outstanding Achievement, 1992. Fellow: Coll. Am. Anesthesiologists. E-mail: katesoderstrom@comcast.net.

SHAY-BYRNE, OLIVIA, lawyer; b. Trenton, N.J., Aug. 14, 1957; d. Stewart and Elizabeth (Sherrill) B. Student, Vanderbilt U., 1975-76; BA, Bowdoin Coll., 1979; JD, U. Toledo, 1982; LLM in Taxation, Georgetown U., 1987. Bar: Tex. 1982, Ohio 1984, Md. 1985. Assoc. Whiteford, Taylor & Preston, Balt., 1984-87, Linowes & Blocher, Silver Spring, Md., 1987-90; ptnr. Sutherland Asbill & Brenna LLP, Washington, 1996—2000, ReedSmith LLP, Washington, 2000—. Bd. dir. D.C. Mktg. Ctr., mem. exec. com., 2004. Author: The At-Risk Rules Under the Tax Reform Act of 1986, The Door Closes on Tax Motivated Investments, IRS Issues New Guidelines for Management Contracts Used for Facilities Financed with Tax Exempt Bonds, 1993, RRA '93 Loosens Real Estate Rules for Exempt Organizations, 1993; editor Nat. Mcpl. Fin. Jour.; contbr. articles to profl. jours. Mem. Tax Coun. for State of Md., Leadership Montgomery, 1996; bd. dirs. Bethesda Acad. Performing Arts, Inc.; chair GULC Nat. Tax Exempt Bond Conf., 1997. Mem. ABA (exempt orgn. com. sect. 1991—), Md. Bar Assn. (coun. taxation sect.), Balt. City Bar Assn. (chmn. speakers bur. young lawyers sect.), Lawyers for Arts Washington, Comml. Real Estate Woman (bd. dirs., pres.), Profls. for Strathmore Hall (co-chmn.), D.C. Bowdoin Coll. Alumni Assn. (pres. 1992—), Howard County C. of C. (legis. com. 1989), Rotary. Home: 1083 Mill Field Ct Great Falls VA 22066

SHCHERBAKOVA, ESTELLA, chemist, mathematician, educator; b. Dnepropetrovsk, Ukraine, Oct. 15, 1938; arrived in Russia, 1951, arrived in U.S., 1994; d. Stepan and Fira (Poltorak) Masko; m. Stanislav Shcherbakov; 1 child, Yuriy Shcherbakov. MA math and drawing, State Pedagogical Inst., Moscow, Russia, 1956—61; PhD chem. sci., Post grad. Sch. of L. Karpov Rsch. Physical Chem. Inst., Moscow, Russia, 1968—74. Math tchr. HS #79, Moscow, 1961—62; engr. State Inst. of Caouchouc, Moscow, 1962—64; sci. worker from jr. to maj. L. Karpov Rsch. Phys. Chem. Inst., Moscow, 1964—94. Cons. and joint rsch. Inst. of Thin Chem. Tech., Moscow, 1971—89, State External Polytech. Inst., Moscow, 1978—90. Co-author: 113 articles, SU Jour. Miscellaneous reports, 1961—91, (book, monograph) Math Matters of Investigation of Chem. Equilib., 1978, (3 inventions) SU Bull. of Inventions, 1985, 1992—93. Recipient Semicentennial, L. Karpov Inst./ Moscow, Russia, 1988. Finding common math technology for investigation of the multiple equilibriums in solutions and applying it to various chemical systems, including solutions of bromine and iodine that brought to inventions of industrial modus of their deriving from a leach. Finding the method for nonlinear optimizations, as to apply non-equilibrium thermodynamics to processes of polymerizations. Home: 2820 W 32nd St Apt 3E Brooklyn NY 11224 E-mail: shchest@aol.com.

SHE, MANJUAN, chemical engineer, food research scientist; BS in Applied Chemistry, South China U. Tech., 1999; PhD, U. Cin., Ohio, 2000—05. Rsch. asst. U. Cin., Cin., 2000—05, tchg. asst., 2000—05; scientist, product tech. ctr. Nestlé Purina Global Resources, St. Louis, Mo., 2005—. Rsch. rep., coord. NSF Industry/U. Coop. Rsch. Ctr. for Membrane Applied Sci. & Tech., U. Cin., 2001—04. Contbr. over 20 papers to profl. jours. and pubs. Recipient 1st Pl. award, Tech. Papers Competition, 2003; grantee Dow Chemistry scholarship, South China U. Tech., 1996—97, DuPont Chemistry scholarship, 1999, Grad. Rsch. scholarship, U. Cin., 2000, scholarship, EPA, 2003, Grad. Travel awards, U. Cin., 2004. Mem.: North Am. Membrane Soc., AIChE, Inst. Food Technologists, Sigma Xi. Achievements include development of a theoretical model with concentration polarization for flavor recovery by pervaporation and a modified Arhenius equation for the prediction of thermal effects on pervaporation; novel application of membrane separation process on the concentration of flavor organics; design of an engineering model for a pervaporation membrane system on wastewater treatment; research in concentration polarization and heat & mass transfer processes during pervaporation; discovery of pervaporation membrane characterization method. Office: Nestle Purina Product Tech Ctr Checkerboard Sq-4RS Saint Louis MO 63164-0001 Office Phone: 314-982-3793.

SHEA, JUDITH, artist; b. Phila. AA, Parsons Sch. Design, 1969, BFA, 1975. Sculptor, sr. critic Univ. Pa. Sch. Design. One-person shows include Willard Gallery, N.Y.C., 1980, 83, 84, 86, Acad. Fine Arts, Phila., 1986, La Jolla Mus. Contemporary Art, 1988, Nat. Mus. Women in the Arts, Washington, 1990, Laumeier Sculpture Park, St. Louis, 1992, Max Protetch Gallery, N.Y.C., 1993, St.-Gaudens Nat. Historic Site, Cornish, N.H., 1994; exhibited in group shows at SUNY, Purchase, Palazzo Farnese, Cortona, Italy, Indpls. Mus. Art, Va. Mus. Fine Arts, Richmond, Hirshhorn Mus. and Sculpture Garden, Washington, Whitney Mus. of Stamford, Conn., Albright-Knox Gallery, Buffalo, Walker Art Ctr., Mpls., New Orleans Mus. Art, U. Hawaii at Manoa Art Gallery, Columbus (Ohio) Mus. Art, Albuquerque Mus., Whitney Mus. Am. Art, N.Y.C., others; represented in collections at Bklyn. Mus., Dallas Mus. Fine Arts, Gen. Mills, Mpls., Laumeier Sculpture Park, Prudential Ins. Co., N.Y.C.; designer of clothing for dance and theater, including Trisha Brown Dance Co., Soho Baroque Opera Co.; subject of numerous articles. Recipient Rome Prize fellowship Am. Acad. in Rome, 1994, Lila Wallace-Reader's Digest Internat. Artists award, Mex., 1994; Nat. Endowment for Arts grantee, 1984, 86; Solomon R. Guggenheim sculptor-in-residence, Chesterwood, Mass., 1989; St.-Gaudens Meml. fellow, 1993, Rockefeller Found. fellow Bellagio (Italy) Study and Conf. Ctr., 1993. Office: Univ Pa Sch Design 102 Meyerson Hall 210 S 34th St Philadelphia PA 19104-6311 Office Phone: 215-898-3425.

SHEA, M., psychology professor; b. Chicago, Ill., Mar. 13, 1949; PhD, U. Kans., 1975. Rsch. assoc. Cornell U., Ithaca, NY, 1974—76; prof. psychology U. Maine, Farmington, 1976—. Office Phone: 207-778-7000.

SHEA, MARY ELIZABETH CRAIG, psychologist, educator; b. Gainesville, Fla., May 16, 1962; d. Charles Poe and Dolores Jean (Osborn) Craig; m. Steven John Shea, Sept. 1, 1991. BA, Ohio Wesleyan U., Delaware, 1980; MA, Columbia U., N.Y.C., 1986; PhD, U. S.C., Columbia, 1990. Lic. clin. psychologist. Med./geriatric psychologist VA Med. Ctr., Columbia, S.C., 1990-98; sex trauma coordinator Veterans Readjustment Counseling Ctr., Columbia, 1998—. Assoc. prof. U. S.C. Sch. Medicine, Columbia, 1991—; pvt. practice, Chapin, S.C., 1991—. Contbr. articles to Archives Sexual Behavior, Clin. Psychology Rev., Jour. Sex Rsch., Jour. Social and Clin. Psychology, others. Mem. Am. Psychol. Assn., Southeastern Psychol. Assn., Natural Resources Def. Coun., Save the Manatee Club, Psi Chi. Methodist. Office: Vet Ctr 1513 Pickens St Columbia SC 29201-3448 E-mail: mary.shea@va.gov.

SHEA, MELISSA GORDON, biology educator; d. James and Linda Gordon; m. Dan Shea, July 31, 2004. MA in Liberal Studies, SUNY, Stony Brook, 2004. Cert. tchr. biology and gen. sci. 7-12 N.Y., 2005. Biology tchr. Bay Shore H.S., NY, 2000—. Mem.: Nat. Sci. Tchrs. Assn., Nat. Assn. Biology Tchrs., STANYS. Independent. Office: Bay Shore High School 155 Third Ave Bay Shore NY 11706 Office Phone: 631-968-1198. E-mail: mshea@bayshore.k12.ny.us.

SHEA, ROSANNE MARY, artist, educator; b. Waterbury, Conn., Oct. 29, 1957; d. John Patrick and Helen Gertude (Goodridge) S.; children: Matthew Shea, Wyatt Shea-Levandoski BFA, U. Conn., Storrs, 1980; MFA, Vt. Coll., Montpelier, 1996. Freelance artist, Waterbury, 1980—90; tchr. art Creative Summer program Mead Sch., Greenwich, Conn., 1991, tchr. art Creative Summer Program, 1992, 1993, 1994; tchr. art W. Conn. State U., Danbury, 1994, Sacred Heart/St. Peter's Sch., New Haven, 1995—, Holy Cross H.S., Waterbury, 1996—. Dir. arts and crafts program Futures Initiative Program, Bridgeport, Conn., 1989; adj. tchr. art Naugatuck Valley Coll., Waterbury, 1991—; v.p. Bank St. Artists, Waterbury, 1993-94 Appeared as lead character in play Tropical Blues, 1996; one-woman exhbns. include Mattatuck C.C., Waterbury, 1992, A Frame Come True Gallery, Torrington, Conn., 1992, Discovery Mus., 1999, Mattatuck Mus., 2000; group exhbns. include Waterbury Arts Resource Coun., 1992 (mem.), Bank St. Artists Gallery, Waterbury, 1994 (mem.), Northampton Coll., Bethlehem, Pa., 1995, Talk of the Town Coffee House, Torrington, 1996, Sacred Ground Coffee House, Watertown, Conn., 1996, Wood Gallery, Montpelier, Vt., 1996, Women Only, Waterbury, 1996, John Slade Ely House, 2001, Conn. Forest Exhbn., 2004-05, Artistic License Gallery, 2005. Leader Boy Scouts Am., Waterbury, 1990-94; mgr. state visitation Conn. chpt. Nat. Holiday Project, 1986-87; course vol., mem. bd. Bridgeport Youth at Risk, 1986-88, ropes course leader, vol. enrollment mgr., 1987-99 Scholar AAUW, 1993, Philanthropic Ednl. Orgn., 1993; Inner City Cultural Devel. Program grantee Conn. Commn. Arts, 1997-99. Avocations: scuba diving, rock climbing, philosophy, health, camping. Office Phone: 860-573-5727. Personal E-mail: rosanneshea@sbcglobal.net. E-mail: r_shea@hotmail.com.

SHEAD, MARY AIRTHRLODIOS, elementary school educator; b. Holly Springs, Miss., Mar. 16, 1948; d. Willie Adolphus and Elerine Walker; widowed; children: Gail, Amy, Anthony, Gennifer. AS, Shelby State Coll., 1984; BS, U. Memphis, 1993. Ednl. asst. Memphis City Schs., 1985-93, tchr., 1993—.

SHEAFFER, KAREN, county official, treasurer; b. Lewistown, Pa., Sept. 8, 1949; d. Clyde William and Betty Beatrice Krepps; m. James G. Sheaffer, Oct. 25, 1969; children: Jeremy James, Jarrod James. Adminstrv. asst. Kyburz Constrn., Edwards, Colo., 1982-86; bookkeeper Eagle (Colo.) County Treas., 1986-89, dep. treas., dep. pub. trustee, 1989-96, county treas., pub. trustee, 1996—. Bd. dirs. Colotrust. Mem.: Internat. Assn. Clks., Recorders, Election Ofcls. and Treas., Colo. County Pub. Trustees Assn., Colo. County Treas. Assn. (cert. county treas., Outstanding Treas. of Yr. 1998, 2000). Republican. Methodist. Office: Eagle County Govt 500 Broadway Eagle CO 81631

SHEAFFER, SUZANNE FRANCES, geriatrics nurse; b. Harrisburg, Pa., Feb. 8, 1963; d. Walter Richard and Catherine Frances (Mourawski) Markham; children: William Chester, Sarah Suzanne, Katye Iona; m. Paul L. Sheaffer Jr. ADN, Harrisburg (Pa.) Area C.C., 1984; BSN, York (Pa.) Coll., 1997; B Criminal Justice Adminstrn., Ctrl. Pa. Coll., 2005; postgrad. in Criminal Justice, St. Leo U., 2005—. RN; lic. nursing home adminstr., Pa. Nurse ICU and critical care unit Meml. Hosp., York, Pa., 1987-88; staff nurse emergency dept. Polyclinic Med. Ctr., Harrisburg, 1988-91; assoc. prof. Nat. Edn. Ctr.-Jr. Coll., Harrisburg, 1991; dir. nursing Camp Hill (Pa.) Care Ctr., 1991-92; resident assessment supr. Susquehanna Ctr., Harrisburg, 1992-94; dir. nursing Susquehanna Luth. Village, Millersburg, Pa., 1994-95; asst. adminstr. Dauphin Manor, Harrisburg, 1995—; mgr. clin. svcs. ea. divsn. HCR Manor Care; med. analyst Medicaid Fraud Control Unit Pa. Atty. Gen. Office, 2003—. ACLS, CPR instr. Am. Heart Assn., Harrisburg, 1989—; BCLS, CPR instr. ARC, Harrisburg, 1992—; RN, paramedic Lebanon (Pa.) County First Aide and Safety Patrol, 1992—. Sec. Little People PTA, Harrisburg, 1991-92; pres. Student Human Resource Mgmt. Club, York (Pa.) Coll., 1992—; v.p. Prince of Peace PTO, 1997-98; cheerleading coach, Midget Football Assoc., 2002—; cheerleading coord. Susquehanna Twp. Midget Football Assn., 2003, HNJ, 2006-; acad. adviser Eta Sigma Alpha Chi Beta chpt., 2003-05; home room parent Holy Name Jesus Sch., 2002-. Recipient Nurse of Hope award Am. Cancer Soc., Dauphin County, Harrisburg, 1983-84. Mem. AACN, Pa. Nurses Assn., Pa. Dir. Nursing Assn. for Long Term Care, PANPHA (advocate), York Coll. Alumni Assn. (bd. dirs. Susquehanna Valley), Pa. Homesch. Assn., Ctrl. Pa. Alumni Assn. Roman Catholic. Avocations: ceramics, ballet, flute.

SHEAR, NATALIE PICKUS, conference and event management executive; b. N.Y.C., Oct. 18, 1940; d. Sam and Mildred (Shulman) Pickus; m. Daniel H. Shear, Dec. 14, 1968 (dec. Apr. 1989); children: Adam Brian, Tamara Beth; m. Henry D. Lewis, Jan. 10, 1999. BA in Journalism, Fairleigh Dickinson U., 1962. Editl. asst. Show Bus. Newspaper, N.Y.C., 1962-64, Jewish News, Newark, 1964-66; dir. Manhattan women's divsn., program asst. Am. Jewish Congress, N.Y.C., 1966-68; mng. editor Jewish Week, Washington, 1968-71; dir. pub. rels. United Jewish Appeal, Washington, 1973-74; pub. affairs dir. Leadership Conf. Civil Rights, Washington, 1977-83; pres. Natalie P. Shear Assocs., Inc., Washington, 1983—. Editor: (newspaper) Books Alive, 1973—74; editor, pub.: newsletter Trends, Inc., 1989—94. V.p. Nat. Child Rsch. Ctr., Washington, 1974—76; bd. dirs. Urban Philharm. Soc., 1998—99; vol., bd. dirs. Nat. Jewish Dem. Coun., Washington, 1996—; vol. nat. bd.

Ams. Dem. Action, 2001—; pres. Ohr Kodesh Sisterhood, Chevy Chase, Md., 1980—82; chairperson women's task force Am. Jewish Congress, Washington, 1984—86. Mem.: Nat. Press Club. Avocation: needlecrafts. Home: 4701 Willard Ave Chevy Chase MD 20815-4643 Office: 1730 M St NW Ste 801 Washington DC 20036 Office Phone: 202-833-4456. Business E-Mail: natalie@natalieshear.com.

SHEARER, LINDA, museum director; b. Long Island, NY, Feb. 13, 1946; BA, Sarah Lawrence Coll., 1968. Assoc. curator Solomon R. Guggenheim Mus., NYC; exec. dir. Artists Space, NYC; curator painting and sculpture Mus. of Modern Art, NYC; dir. Williams Coll. Mus. Art, Mass., 1989; Alice & Harris Weston dir. Contemporary Arts Ctr., Cin. Tchr. contemporary art Williams Coll., Sch. Visual Arts, NYC. Bd. trustees Am. Fedn. of Arts; adv. com. Skowhegan Sch. of Painting and Sculpture; chair Phila. Exhibition Initiative, 2003. Office: Contemporary Arts Ctr 44 E Sixth St Cincinnati OH 45202 Office Phone: 513-345-8412.

SHEARER, LINDA RAE, English educator; b. Connellsville, Pa., Aug. 3, 1954; d. Randall Wilbur and Gertrude Elizabeth Shearer. BA, Alderson-Broaddus Coll., Philippi, WV, 1976; MEd, Calif. U., California, Pa., 1980. Tchr. Connellsville Area Sch. Dist., Pa., 1978—. Advisor Nat. Honor Soc. Connellsville Area H.S., 1988—98; activities dir. Connellsville Area Sr. H.S., 1988—98, founder and sponsor Patriots, 2003—. Decorated Army Commendation Medal; named Fayette County Tchr. of the Yr., Fayette County C. of C., 1998; recipient Elks Disting. Citizen award, Connellsville Elks # 503, 2006, Individual Award for Vol. Svc., Connellsville C. of C., 2006, Citation from Senate of Pa.for svc. to deployed servicemen/women, Senators Jane Orie and Richard Kasunic, 2003, Disting. Alumni award, Alderson Broaddus Coll., 2005. Mem.: NEA, Connellsville Area Edn. Assn., Pa. State Edn. Assn. Baptist. Home: 304 Stadium Rd Connellsville PA 15425-1964 Office: Connellsville Area Senior High School 201 Falcon Dr Connellsville PA 15425 Office Phone: 724-628-1350. Personal E-mail: teddy@cvzoom.net. E-mail: lshearer@casdfalcons.org.

SHEARER-CREMEAN, CHRISTINE LOUISE, literature educator; b. Rochester, N.Y., Apr. 10, 1964; d. Robert and Constance Shearer; m. David Neal Cremean, May 14, 1994. BA in English, U. Dayton, Dayton, Ohio, 1989, MA in English, 1991; PhD in Rhetoric and Writing, Bowling Green State U., Ohio, 1997. Asst. prof. English St. Francis U., Loretto, Pa., 1998—2000; assoc. prof. English and humanities Black Hills State U., Spearfish, SD, 2000—. Author (with Carol Winkelmann): Survivor Rhetoric: Negotiation and Narrativity in Abused Women's Language; contbr. articles to profl. jours. Mem. svc. com. Nat. Friends, Rapid City, SD, 2000—06. Mem.: Coun. Higher Edn., Nat. Coun. Tchrs. English, We. Lit. Assn. Office: Black Hills State University 1200 University Street Spearfish SD 57799 Office Phone: 605-642-6248.

SHEARING, MIRIAM, retired state supreme court chief justice; b. Waverly, NY, Feb. 24, 1935; BA, Cornell U., 1956; JD, Boston Coll., 1964. Bar: Calif. 1965, Nev. 1969. Justice of peace Las Vegas Justice Ct., 1977-81; judge Nev. Dist. Ct., 1983-92, chief judge, 1986; justice Nevada Supreme Ct., Carson City, 1993—2005, chief justice, 1997, 2004, sr. justice, 2005—. Mem. ABA, Am. Judicature Soc. (chair 2001-03), Nev. Judges Assn. (sec. 1978), Nev. Dist. Ct. Judges Assn. (sec. 1984-85, pres. 1986-87), State Bar Nev., State Bar Calif., Clark County Bar Assn. Democrat. Office Phone: 775-831-9158. E-mail: shearing@nvcourts.state.nv.us.

SHEARMUR, ALLI, broadcast executive; married. V.p. prodn. Walt Disney Co., 1994—97; exec. v.p. prodn. Universal Pictures, Paramount Pictures, co-pres. prodn., 2005—. Office: Paramount Pictures 5555 Melrose Hwy West Hollywood CA 90038 Office Phone: 323-956-5000.*

SHEA-STONUM, MARILYN, federal bankruptcy judge; b. 1947; AB, U. Calif., Santa Cruz, 1969; JD, Case Western Res. U., 1975. Law clk. to Hon. Frank J. Battisti, Cleve., 1975-76; ptnr. Jones, Day, Reavis & Pogue, Cleve., 1984—94; bankruptcy judge U.S. Dist. Ct. (no. dist.) Ohio, Akron, 1994—. Editor-in-chief Am. Bankruptcy Law Jour., Nat. Conf. Bankruptcy Judges. Mem. Order of Coif. Office: US Bankruptcy Ct No Dist Ohio 240 Fed Bldg 2 S Main St Akron OH 44308-1813 Office Phone: 330-252-6130.

SHEBAN, LYNNE ROSENZWEIG, psychologist; b. Hicksville, N.Y., Jan. 7, 1958; d. Louis and Gloria Rosenzweig; m. Christopher Sheban. BA, U. Rochester, 1979; MA, U. Ill., Chgo., 1982, PhD, 1984. Lic. clin. psychologist. Staff psychologist Inst. for Juvenile Rsch., Chgo., 1985-91; pvt. practice clin. psychology, Skokie, Ill., 1986—2004. Clin. instr. U. Ill., Chgo., 1986—; cons. psychologist Value Options, 1994—. Mem. APA, Phi Beta Kappa, Sigma Xi, Phi Kappa Phi. Avocations: dance, kickboxing. Office: 4711 Golf Rd Skokie IL 60076-1224

SHECHTER, LAURA JUDITH, artist; b. Bklyn., Aug. 26, 1944; d. Philip and Jeannette (Newmark) Goldstein; m. Ben-Zion Shechter, Feb. 26, 1969; 1 son, Adam. BA with honors in Art, Bklyn. Coll., 1965. Case worker Dept. Social Service, N.Y.C., 1965-73; artist N.Y.C., 1965—; lectr., 1978—; curator Forum Gallery, N.Y.C., 1978; tchr. Parson Sch. Design, N.Y.C., 1984, Nat. Acad. Design, N.Y.C., 1985-88, 94-98. Exhibited one-woman shows Forum Gallery, N.Y.C., 1976, 80, 83, Greenville County Mus. Art, 1982, Wustum Mus., Racine, Wis., 1982, Schoelkopf Gallery, N.Y.C., 1985, Staemphli Gallery, N.Y.C., 1987, 88, Rahr West Mus., Manitowoc, Wis., U. Richmond, 1991, Perlow Gallery, N.Y.C., 1992, 94, Pucker Gallery, Boston, 1984, 96, 98; group shows include Akron Art Inst., 1974, Minn. Mus. Art, St. Paul, 1981, Pa. Acad. Art, Phila., 1982, Boston Mus., 1982, Bklyn. Mus., 1980, 84, Nat. Mus. Am. Art, Washington, 1985, San Francisco Mus. Modern Art, 1985, Huntsville Mus., Ala., 1987, Butler Inst., Youngstown, Ohio, 1987, 88, Ind. U. Art Mus., Joplin, Mo., 1991, Ark. Art Ctr., 1992; represented in pub. collections including Boston Mus. Fine Art, Bklyn. Mus., Carnegie Inst., Indpls. Mus., Israel Mus., NAD, Nat. Mus. of Women in Arts, Jewish Mus., NY Public Libr., 3M Corp., Bryn Mawr Coll., others. Recipient Creative Artist Pub. Service award N.Y. State, 1982 Mem. Artists Equity, Nat. Acad. Design. Home: 429 4th St Brooklyn NY 11215-2901 E-mail: laurart3@aol.com.

SHECKLER, MINDY SUE, elementary school educator; b. Topeka, Aug. 22, 1955; m. Bill Sheckler, July 1, 1980; children: Aimee Renee Crosby, Brian William, Chris Loren. Bachelors, U. Wyo., Laramie, 1977. Cert. tchr. Wyo., 1977. Tchr. East Jr. High, Rock Springs, Wyo., 1994—. Methodist. Home: 2910 Campbell Ln Rock Springs WY 82901 Office: Sweetwater School District #1 PO Box 1089 Rock Springs WY 82901 Office Phone: 307-352-3474.

SHECKTER, BONNIE, artist; m. Russell Hartenberger; children: Laura, Carla. BFA, U. Alberta, 1973, MA in Visual Arts, Printmaking, 1976. Prof. U. Calgary, U. Alberta; dir. Lithography Open Studio, 1982. Exhibitions include Burnaby Biennale, 1977, Canadian Biennale, 1977, 1980, 1983, Canadian Exhbn., World Print Coun., 1980, Ljubljiana Biennale, 1981, 1983, Internat. Impact Art Festival, Kyoto, Japan, 1984, 10th Ann. Colored Pencil Soc. Am. Exhbn., Dallas, Tex., 2002, 11th Ann. Colored Pencil Soc. Am. Exhbn., Brea, Calif., 2003, exhibited in group shows at Canadian Contemporary Printmakers, The Bronx Mus., NY, 1982, FACE, Harbourfront Exhbn., 1995, Master Class, Sightlines Symposium, Fine Arts Bldg Gallery, 1997, one-woman shows include Gallery Moos, Calgary, Alberta, 1980, Gallery Pascal, Toronto, ON, Can., 1982. E-mail: bonniesheckter@sympatico.ca.

SHEDDEN-COINGILL, EDYTHE B., artist; b. Dumont, N.J., Dec. 17, 1921; d. Milton and Vera Gladys (Meister) Bauer; m. Peter J. Shedden, Apr. 26, 1944 (div. June 1987); children: Darryl E., Peter Scott; m. William Parker Cowgill, Aug. 25, 1987. BA, Rutgers U., 1943; studied with, Adja Yunkers, Stuart Davis, Meyer Shapiro, Edythe Bauer Shedden Cowgill. Artist apprentice Abraham & Strause, Bklyn., 1943-44; artist/model Apfel Studios, N.Y.C., 1944-45, 46; tchr. art Allofus Workshop, Rochester, N.Y., 1970-75, Meml. Art Gallery, Rochester, 1970-80, Monroe County Penitentary, Rochester, 1965-75; owner/dir. Oxford Gallery, Rochester, 1971-85. Exhibits include Meml. Art Gallery, Rochester, Albright-Knox, Buffalo, Everson, Syracuse, Alfred U., Nazareth Coll., Rocheste, Reloz 46, Rochester Contemporary Artisan Works, Print Click, Arena Group, Oxford Gallery; pvt. collections include SUNY, Oswego, Alfred U., Rochester Telephone Corp., Gannett Corp., Young & Rubicam, Rochester, Amalgamated Clothing Workers, Rochester, Charles Rand Penney Collection; one man shows: Gallery 696, N.Y., Meml. Art Gallery, Kendall Gallery, Mass, Oxford Gallery, NY, Pisces Gallery, Nantucket, Sibley Gallery, Nantucket, Mass., Rochester Pub. Libr., AAUW, La Casa Verde, Mexico, Elizabeth Collection, NY. Mem. coun. Meml. Art Gallery, Rochester, 1967—; bd. dirs. Broadway Theatre League, Rochester, 1962-70, Monroe County Arts Resources Ctr., 1970-75; committeeperson Dem. Party, Rochester, 1968, 75. Unitarian Universalist. Home: 5 Elmwood Hill Ln Rochester NY 14610-3445

SHEDRICK, ALBERTA LORETTA, elementary school educator; b. Morgan, Ga., Mar. 10, 1936; d. Rowe and Beulah Mae (Sapp) Taylor; m. David Shedrick, Nov. 5, 1960; children: Bernard, Nathaniel, David Dwane. BA, Albany (Ga.) State U., 1966; MA, U. Tampa, 1976. Tchr. Wilbanks Juv. Detention Sch., 1967-73, Gibsonton (Fla.) Elem., 1974-94; ret., 1994. Mem. Progress Village Civic Coun., Tampa, 1980—; v.p. Progress Village Little League; sec. Progress Village Found., 1992; mem. Shepard of Triumph the Ch. and Kingdom of God in Christ, St. Petersbug, Fla., past fin. sec. Mem. Alpha Kappa Alpha (Gamma Theta Omega), Phi Delta Kappa. Democrat. Avocations: reading, sports, writing, crafts, baking. Home: 4910 S 84th St Tampa FL 33619-7110

SHEEDY, ALLY (ALEXANDRA ELIZABETH SHEEDY), actress; b. NYC, June 13, 1962; d. John and Charlotte (Baum) S.; m. David Lansbury, Oct. 10, 1992; 1 child, Rebecca. Student, U. So. Calif. Past ballet dancer. Film debut in Bad Boys, 1983; other films include Wargames, 1983, Oxford Blues, 1984, The Breakfast Club, 1985, St. Elmo's Fire, 1985, Twice in a Lifetime, 1985, Short Circuit, 1986, Blue City, 1986, Maid to Order, 1987, Heart of Dixie, 1989, Betsy's Wedding, 1990, Only the Lonely, 1991, Home Alone II: Lost in New York, 1992, The Pickle, 1992, Man's Best Friend, 1993, Tattle Tale, 1993, One Night Stand, 1995, Groupies, 1997, Highball, 1997, Crossroads of Destiny, 1997, Country Justice, 1997, Amnesia, 1997, High Art, 1998 (Best Actress award Nat. Soc. Film Critics 1998, Ind. Spirit award for best female lead 1999), Autumn Heart, 1998, I'll Take You There, 1999, Advice From a Caterpillar, 1999, Just a Dream, 2002, Happy Here and Now, 2002, A Good Night to Die, 2003, Shelter Island, 2003, Noise, 2004, Shooting Livien, 2005; TV films include The Best Little Girl in the World, 1981, The Day the Loving Stopped, 1981, The Violation of Sarah McDavid, 1981, Splendor in the Grass, 1981, Dead Lessons, 1983, We Are the Children, 1987, Fear, 1990, The Lost Capone, 1990, Lethal Exposure, 1993, Chantilly Lace, 1993, The Hauting of Sea Cliff Inn, 1994, Ultimate Betrayal, 1994, Parallel Lives, 1994, Tin Soldier, 1995, Hijacked: Flight 285, 1996, Sleeping With the Devil, 1997, Buried Alive 2, 1997, Amnesia, 1997, Myth America, 1998, High Art, 1998, (TV) The Fury Within, 1998, Sugar Town, 1999, Autumn Hart, 1999, (TV) Our Guys, 1999, The Warden, 2001, The Interrogation of Michael Crowe, 2002, Life On the Line, 2003, (TV guest appearances) The Dead Zone, 2002; author (children's book) She Was Nice to Mice, 1975, (poetry) Yesterday I Saw the Sun, 1991. Address: Don Buchwald & Assocs Ste 2200 6500 Wilshire Blvd Los Angeles CA 90048 also: PO Box 523 Topanga CA 90290-0523 also: 11766 Wilshire Blvd #1610 Los Angeles CA 90025-6555

SHEEHAN, CINDY, anti war activist; b. LA, July 10, 1957; d. Shirley Miller; m. Patrick Sheehan (separated); children: Casey Austin(dec.), Andy, Carly, Jane. Youth minister St. Mary's Church, Vacaville, Calif. Travelled to President George W. Bush's Prairie Chapel Ranch near Crawford, Tex. during his 5 week vacation there; demanded meeting with pres.; created Camp Casey along side of road, where she held vigil while awaiting a meeting; a meeting was never granted. Co-founder Gold Star Families for Peace, 2005. Democrat. Roman Catholic.

SHEEHAN, DENISE LUCILLE, alcohol/drug abuse services professional, writer; b. Arlington Heights, Ill., Aug. 20, 1962; d. John Phillip Sheehan and Judith Ann Bowers; 1 child. BA English Lit., U. Nev., Reno, Nev., 1990. Cert. Prevention Specialist Internat. Cert. and Reciprocity Consortium, Oreg., 2001. Program asst. U. Nev., Reno, 1988—2000; coord. U. Nev. - Western Ctr. for the Application of Prevention Technologies, Reno, 2000—. Coauthor: Substance Abuse Prevention: The Intersection of Science and Practice, 2003. Mem.: ACLU, Sierra Club, Golden Key Nat. Honor Soc., Phi Kappa Phi. Office: Univ Nev Mail Stop 279 Reno NV 89557-0258 Office Phone: 888-734-7476. Business E-Mail: denise@unr.edu.

SHEEHAN, DONNA MARIE, reading educator; d. Donald Joseph and Regina Marie Schumacher; children: Sean Patrick, David Thomas. BS, So. Ill. U., Carbondale, 1973; MEd, Ill. Nat. U., Normal, 1989. Cert. pharmacy technician Washington, tchr. reading, gen. edn. grades K-9, learning behavior specialist Ill. Transitional first grade tchr. Streator Dist. 42, Ill., 1972—73; primary resource tchr. Tazewell Mason County Spl. Edn. Coop., Pekin, Ill., 1973—77; early childhood spl. edn. tchr. Washington Dist. 52, Ill., 1982—83; intermediate spl. edn. tchr. Tremont Unit Dist. 702, Ill., 1983—88, reading specialist, 1988—. Ednl. cons. Regional Office Edn. 53, Pekin, 2000—03. Mem.: Ill. Valley Reading Coun., Ill. Reading Coun., Internat. Reading Assn. Roman Catholic. Avocations: cross country skiing, hiking, gardening. Office: Tremont Cmty Unit Dist 702 200 S James St Tremont IL 61568

SHEEHAN, PATTY, professional golfer; b. Middlebury, Vt., Oct. 27, 1956; 4th ranked woman LPGA Tour, 1992; winner U.S. Women's Open, 1992, 94, McDonald's LPGA Championship, 1983-84, 93. Inductee LPGA Hall of Fame, 1993, Sports Illustrated Sportsman of the Yr., 1987. Achievements include being the winner for 31 LPGA Tournaments including Mazda Japan Classic, 1981, 88, Inamori Classic, 1982-83, 86, Orlando Lady Classic, 1982, Safeco Classic, 1982, 90, 95, LPGA Corning Classic, 1983, LPGA Championship, 1983-84, 93, Henredon Classic, 1983-84, Elizabeth Arden Classic, 1984, McDonald's Kids Classic, 1984, 90, Sarasota Classic, 1985-86, 88, J&B Scotch Pro AM, 1985, Konica San Jose Classic, 1986, Rochester Internat., 1989-90, 92, 95, Jamaica Classic, 1990, Ping-Cellular One Championship, 1990, Orix Hawaiian Ladies Open, 1991, Jamie Farr Toledo Classic, 1992, Weetabix Women's Brit. Open, 1992, U.S. Women's Open, 1992, 94, Mazda LPGA Championship, 1993, The Nabisco Championship, 1996; in 17 tournaments earning $179,453, 1997, 16 tounaments earning $342,391, 1996, 35th victory, Nabisco Dinah Shore earning 6th major champ. title, crossed $5 million mark in career earnings, 1996, winner Michelob Light Front Runner Awd. for leading most rounds in season, 1996. Office: LPGA 100 International Golf Dr Daytona Beach FL 32124-1092

SHEEHAN, SAMANTHA, gymnast; b. Cin., May 20, 1986; d. Kevin and Cindy Sheehan. Gymnast Cincinnati Gymnastics/U.S. Natl. Team, 2002—. Achievements include Level 10 National Bar Champion; Level 10 State Champion; Qualified to 2001, 02 U.S. Gymnastics Championships, World Championships, 2002; Bronze Medal Floor Exercise, World Championships, 2002; 1st place All Around, USA-Belgium dual competition, 2003. Office: 3635 Woodbridge Blvd Fairfield OH 45014

SHEEHAN, SOPHIA ANN, marriage and family therapist, director; b. San Gabriel, Calif., May 13, 1972; d. Mary Angela and Henry C. Gonzalez; m. Joseph Scott Sheehan, Apr. 13, 1996. BA, U. of So. Calif., 1990—94; M, Peperdine U., 1994—96. Lic. Marriage and Family Therapist Bd. of Behavioral Sci., Calif., 2000. Marriage and family therapist trainee Family Assessment Counseling and Ednl. Services, Fullerton, Calif., 1996—97; marriage and family therapist intern Mid Valley Learning Ctr., Baldwin Park, Calif., 1997—99; clin. social worker Canyon Acres Children's Services, Anaheim Hills, Calif., 1999—2002; clin. program supr. Canal St. Elm. Sch. (TEC/Olive Crest), Orange, Calif., 2002—04; site dir. Therapetic Edn. Ctr., Bellflower, Calif., 2004—. Mem.: Am. Assn. of Marriage and Family Therapists. Catholic. Avocations: crocheting, dance, travel.

SHEEHAN, SUSAN, writer; b. Vienna, Aug. 24, 1937; arrived in U.S., 1941, naturalized, 1946; d. Charles and Kitty C. (Herrmann) Sachsel; m. Neil Sheehan, Mar. 30, 1965; children: Maria Gregory, Catherine Fair. BA, Wellesley Coll., 1958; DHL (hon.), U. Lowell, 1991. Editl. rschr. Esquire-Coronet, N.Y.C., 1959-60; freelance writer N.Y.C., 1960-61; staff writer New Yorker mag., N.Y.C., 1961—; contbg. writer Archtl. Digest, 1997—. Writer-in-residence, lectr. Georgetown U., 1999. Author: Ten Vietnamese, 1967, A Welfare Mother, 1976, A Prison and a Prisoner, 1978, Is There No Place on Earth for Me?, 1982, Kate Quinton's Days, 1984, A Missing Plane, 1986, Life For Me Ain't Been No Crystal Stair, 1993, The Banana Sculptor, the Purple Lady, and the All-Night Swimmer, 2002; contbr. articles to various mags., including N.Y. Times Sunday Mag., Washington Post Sunday Mag., Harper's, Atlantic, New Republic, McCall's, Holiday, Boston Globe Sunday Mag., Life. Judge Robert F. Kennedy Journalism awards, 1980, 84; mem. lit. panel D.C. Commn. on Arts and Humanities, 1979-84; mem. pub. info. and edn. com. Nat. Mental Health Assn., 1982-83; mem. adv. com. on employment and crime Vera Inst. Justice, 1978-86; chair Pulitzer Prize nominating jury in gen. non-fiction for 1988, 1994, mem., 1991. Recipient Sidney Hillman Found. award, 1976, Gavel award ABA, 1978, Individual Reporting award Nat. Mental Health Assn., 1981, Pulitzer prize for gen. non-fiction, 1983, Feature Writing award N.Y. Press Club, 1984, Alumnae Assn. Achievement award Wellesley Coll., 1984, Carroll Kowal Journalism award NASW, 1993, Disting. Grad. award Hunter Coll. H.S., 1995, Pub. Awareness award Nat. Alliance for Mentally Ill, 1995, Casey medal for meritorious journalism, 1997; Durant scholar Wellesley Coll., 1958; fellow Guggenheim Found., 1975-76, Woodrow Wilson Internat. Ctr. for Scholars, 1981, Open Soc. Inst., 1998-99. Mem.: Soc. Am. Historians, Authors Guild, Lansdowne Club (London), Phi Beta Kappa. Home: 4505 Klingle St NW Washington DC 20016-3580 Office: New Yorker Mag 4 Times Sq New York NY 10036-7441

SHEEHEY, PATRICIA ANN, secondary school educator; b. Des Moines, Sept. 25, 1946; d. James Michael Sheehey and Elizabeth Ann Markunas; m. William Elwin McConnell, June 24, 1978 (dec. Aug. 1999). BA English, Marycrest Coll., Davenport, Iowa, 1968; MA English, We. Ill. U., 1970; postgrad., U. Iowa, 1971—2000, U. London, 1971. Instr. West H.S., Davenport, 1969—, head dept. lang. arts, 1998—. Mem. alumni bd. Marycrest Coll., Davenport, 1980—84. Recipient Golden Apple Outstanding Tchr. award, Scott County, 1980. Mem.: NEA, Iowa State Edn. Assn., Davenport Edn. Assn., Nat. Coun. Tchrs. English (regional judge), Alpha Delta Kappa (sec., treas., pres. 1978—82, scholarship chair 1983—86, state bylaws chair 2004—, internat. bylaws com. 2006—). Roman Catholic. Avocations: writing, antiques, reading. Home: 5 Birchwood Dr Blue Grass IA 52726 Office: West High Sch 3505 W Locust Davenport IA 52804 Office Phone: 563-386-5500. Personal E-mail: sheeheyp@aol.com.

SHEEHY, BETTY JO, real estate company executive, investment advisor; b. Baileysville, W.Va., Oct. 1, 1936; d. Virgil and Virginia Graham Lester; m. John D. Sheehy, Sept. 21, 1963 (div. 1976); children: John, Peter, Barbara. Student, Marshall U., 1956; lic. in real estate, Southampton Coll., 2002. Fin. cons. Merrill Lynchnnnnn, Short Hills, NJ, 1984—90; fin. adv., assoc. v.p. Morgan Stanley, Southampton, NY, 1991—2002; owner, broker Betty Jo Sheehy Real Estate, Southampton, 2002—. Chpt. pres. NJ Symphony Women League, Short Hills, 1977—81; vol. Red Cross of the Oranges, NJ, 1970; benefactor Parish Art Mus., Southampton, 1999—. Named Bus. Woman of Yr., Nat. Congressional Com., 2006; recipient Leadership Devel. award, Merrill Lynch, 1985—86. Avocations: golf, music, reading, running. Home and Office: PO Box 2363 Southampton NY 11969 Office Phone: 516-318-5647.

SHEEHY, CAROLYN ARANKA, curator; b. Elizabeth, N.J., Dec. 20, 1942; d. Allen Albert and Aranka (Dorsjak) G.; m. Harry L. Sheehy, Nov. 16, 1974. BA in History, Scripps Coll., 1964; MA in Dance, Mills Coll., 1973; MA in Library and Info. Sci., No. Ill. U., 1987. Cert. elem. and jr. coll. tchr., Calif. Asst. to law library cataloger Heafey Law Library U. Santa Clara, Calif., 1975-77; rare book, modern manuscript asst. Newberry Library, Chgo., 1977-86; adminstr. Midwest Dance Collection The Newberry Library, Chgo., 1983-86, adminstrv. curator spl. collections (Chgo. Dance Collection)., 1986—. Mem. editorial bd. Horns of Plenty: Malcolm Cowley and his generation; contbr. articles to scholarly jours. Bd. dirs. Chgo. Dance Arts Coalition, 1986—; initiator, promoter renaming Street in honor of Ruth Page; mem. adv. bd. Jane Austen Soc. N. Am., Ill. region, 1986—, lector Holy Name Cathedral, Chgo., 1984. Mills Coll. scholar. Mem. ALA, Chgo. Area Archivists, Midwest Archives Conf. (local arrangements com., 1986—), Jane Austen Soc. N. Am. (adv. bd. Ill. region 1986). Office: The Newberry Library 60 W Walton St Chicago IL 60610-3380

SHEEN, PORTIA YUNN-LING, retired physician; b. Republic of China, Jan. 13, 1919; came to U.S., 1988; d. Y. C. and A. Y. (Chow) Sheen; m. Kuo, 1944 (dec. 1970); children: William, Ida, Alexander, David, Mimi. MD, Nat. Med. Coll. Shanghai, 1943. Intern, then resident Cen. Hosp., Chungking, Szechuan, China, 1943; with Hong Kong Govt. Med. and Health Dept., 1948-76; med. supt. Kowloon (Hong Kong) Hosp., 1948-63, Queen Elizabeth Hosp., Kowloon, 1963-73, Med. and Health Hdqrs. and Health Ctr., Kowloon, 1973-76, Yan Chai Hosp., New Territories, Hong Kong, 1976-87; ret., 1987. Fellow Hong Kong Coll. Family Physicians; mem. AAAS, British Med. Assn., Hong Kong Med. Assn., Hong Kong Pediatric Soc., N.Y. Acad. Sci. Methodist. Avocations: reading, music. Home: 1408 Golden Rain Rd Apt 7 Entry 1 Roosmoor Walnut Creek CA 94595-2442

SHEERIN, MARGARET M., elementary school educator; d. Cosmos Charles and Margaret Buckley Tacito; m. Philip E. Sheerin, June 29, 1975; children: Daniel P., Elizabeth A. EdB, U. Mass., Amherst, 1973; EdM in Reading, Salem. State U., Mass., 1976. Cert. prin., reading cons. Elem. tchr. City of Melrose, Mass., 1973—; head tchr. grade 1 Hoover Sch., Melrose. Pres. Stellar Investment Club, Melrose Band Aiders. Recipient Excellence in Edn. award, 2004. Mem.: LWV, AAUW, Mass. Tchrs. Union, Reading Tchrs. Assn. Republican. Roman Catholic. Home: 8 Leah St Melrose MA 02176

SHEESLEY, MARY FRANK, art educator; b. Redwood Falls, Minn., Aug. 1, 1947; d. Wencel and Lois (Dooner) Frank; m. Gary James Sheesley, Apr. 30, 1966 (div. Mar. 25, 1985); children: Jason, John. AA summa cum laude, Chipola Jr. Coll., 1984; BS magna cum laude, Troy State U., 1986; MS, Fla. State U., Panama City, 1991; PhD, Fla. State U., 2000. Child devel. assoc. credential Washington, 1976. Co-owner Qurly-Q Pork Farm, Buffalo Lake, Minn., 1969—79, Bonifay, Fla., 1979—84; editor Nat. Drillers Buyers Guide, Bonifay, Fla., 1982; art educator Bay Dist. Schs., Panama City, 1986—2003, 2005—, 2005—; tchg. asst. Fla. State U., Tallahassee, 1991—92; adj. prof. U. West Fla., Ft. Walton Beach, 1992; art educator Frankfurt Internat. Sch., Oberursel, Germany, 1995—96; adj. prof. Gulf Coast C.C., Panama City, 2002; asst. prof. U. West Ga., Carrollton, 2003—05. Mem. adv. bd. Region 6E Head Start, Willmar, Minn., 1975—79; chairperson Fla. State Art Textbook Adoption Com., Tallahassee, 1993—94; founder Global Art Exch. Program, 1994—; mem. tchr. edn. adv. coun. com. U. West Ga., 2003—05, mem. tchr. edn. field experience evaluation com., 2003—05, mem. assessment adv. com., 2003—05. V.p. Minn. Porkettes, 1978—79; treas. V.F.W. Auxiliary, Hutchinson, Minn., 1973—78; sch. restructuring task force com. Bay Dist. Sch. Sys., Panama City, Fla., 1989—91; lector, mem. ch. coun. St. John's Cath. Ch.; chairperson Cath. Charities, Hector, Minn., 1977—79; mem. ch. coun., lector Blessed Trinity Cath. Ch., Bonifay, 1982—84; euchristic minister Our Lady of Perpetual Help, Carrollton, Ga., 2005; mem. sch. bd. St. John's Cath. Sch., Panama City, 2002—03; bd. dirs. Panhandle Alcoholism Coun., Panama City. Recipient Arrowmont Scholarship, 1987; grantee Fulbright Meml. Tchr. Scholarship, Tokyo, 1997, Truth About Tobacco Ednl. Settlement, 1997; Art scholar, Chipola Jr. Coll., 1982, Returning Woman scholar, Marianna Jr. Women's Club, 1981, Acad. scholar, Troy State U., 1984—86. Mem.: Fla. Art Edn. Assn., Fla. League Art Tchrs. (charter mem.), Bay County Art Tchrs.

Assn. (pres. 1996—2001), Ga. Art Edn. Assn., Nat. Art Edn. Assn., Internat. Soc. for Edn. through Art, Garnet Key Honor Soc., Gamma Beta Phi, Phi Theta Kappa. Independent. Roman Catholic. Avocations: travel, painting, reading, gardening, scuba diving. Home: 1014 New York Ave Lynn Haven FL 32444 Office Phone: 850-872-7540. Business E-Mail: sheesmf@bay.k12.fl.us.

SHEFFEY, RUTHE T., language educator; m. Vernon R. Sheffey, Dec. 29, 1950; children: Illona Sheffey Rawlings, Renata Sheffey Strong. BA, Morgan State U., Balt., 1947; MA, Howard U., 1949; PhD, U. Pa., 1959. Prof. English Morgan State U., Balt., 1949—, chair dept. English, 1970-76. Author: Impressions in Asphalt, 1969, Trajectory (My Collected Essays), 1989; editor Zora Neale Hurston Forum, 1986—. Named Md. Outstanding Faculty Mem. of Yr., 1994, Disting. Scholar in African-Am. Studies for Yr., Towson State U., 2002, Sheroe as Honor, Women for Responsive Govt., Inc., 2003; named to Morgan State U. Hall of Fame, 2000. Mem. Nat. Coun. Tchrs. English (past mem. coll. bd.), Coll. English Assn. (past pres. Mid. Atlantic Group), Zora Neale Hurston Soc. (founder, 1984, pres.), Langston Hughes Soc. (past pres.), other lit. socs., Alpha Kappa Alpha (Golden mem.). Mem. United Ch. of Christ. Avocations: reading, theatre-going, dance. E-mail: rsheffey@moac.morgan.edu.

SHEFFIELD, ELIZABETH RASH, elementary school educator; b. Petersburg, Va., Sept. 23, 1954; d. Avery Adolphus and Ann Hudson Rash; m. Ralph Clifford Sheffield Jr., May 4, 1974; children: Anna Sheffield Leavitt, Ralph Clifford III, Katherine Beryl. BS in Edn., Longwood U., Farmville, Va., 1977, MS in Edn. Elem. tchr. Prince Edward County Pub. Schs., Farmville, 1977—79, Totaro Elem. Sch., Lawrenceville, Va., 1979—97, Victoria Elem. Sch., Va., 1997—2005, reading specialist, 2005—. Dir. vol. tutoring program Victoria Elem. Sch., 2004—, dir. lunch buddy program, 2005—. Chmn., mem. various coms. PTA, Lawrenceville, 1979—97; pianist, choir dir. Victoria Christian Ch., 1997—, Sunday sch. supt., 2006. Mem.: Delta Kappa Gamma (chmn., mem. various coms. 1996—). Avocations: reading, counted cross stitch. Home: 1908 Poorhouse Rd Victoria VA 23974 Office: Victoria Elem Sch 1521 8th St Victoria VA 23974

SHEFFIELD, NANCY, city agency administrator; b. Mpls. BA in Sociology and Psychology, U. Minn., 1969; postgrad., U. Wis., 1992. Participant City of Aurora (Colo.) Supervisory Cert. Series Program, 1988-90. Social worker LeSueur County Human Svcs., Le Centre, Minn., 1969-71; quality control reviewer Minn. Dept. Human Svcs., St. Paul, 1971-74, quality control supr., 1974-75; neighborhood planner City of Aurora, 1987, neighborhood support supr., 1987-94, acting mgr. Original Aurora Renewal, 1994-95, acting mgr. neighborhood support divsn., 1995, dir. neighborhood svcs., 1996—. Mem. PTO, vol. elem. sch. media ctr., 1980-86. Office: City Aurora Dept Neighborhood Svcs 15151 E Alameda Pkwy Aurora CO 80012 Office Phone: 303-739-7280. E-mail: nsheffie@auroragov.org.

SHEFFIELD, STEPHANIE S., portfolio and marketing management consultant; b. Richmond, Va., Aug. 2, 1970; d. Frank Budd Jr. and Carolyn Jean (Parker) Sheffield. BA, Coll. of Charleston, S.C., 1993; MBA, U. Tenn., Knoxville, 1998. Cert. Series 65; cert. intermodal transp. profl. tng. EPA grant videotape prodr. Office of Gov. of S.C., Coll. of Charleston, 1993; analyst State of Tenn., Nashville, 1994-95; portfolio asst. AmeriStar Investment Counsel, Nashville, 1995-96; portfolio mgr. Davidson Ptnrs. Investment Counsel, Nashville, 1998-99; cons. Fin. Perspectives, Nashville, 1999; pres., founder Indextron Inc., 1999—. Pres., portfolio mgr. The Clayton Torch Fund, Knoxville, 1997-98; mktg. cons. Sea Ray Boats, Knoxville, 1997-98; mem. adv. bd. The Tenn. Newspaper, A Gannett Co., 2000—. Creator, editor newsletter The Container, 1992-93; asst. editor newsletter/mag. The Gazette, 1999. Mem., coun. rep. Jr. League of Nashvlle, 1998—. Albergotti scholar, 1993. Mem. Nashville Fin. Analyst Soc., Assn. for Investment Mgmt. and Rsch., Tenn. Assn. MBAs, Tri Delta Alumni Assn. (sec. 1995-96). Republican. Episcopalian. Avocations: golf, cooking, U. Tenn. football games, walking, sailing. Home: P O Box 58051 Nashville TN 37205-8051 E-mail: stephsheff@mindspring.com.

SHEHAN, GERALDEAN HARRISON, ESL educator; b. Dallas, Sept. 4, 1950; d. Jerrold Harrison and Violet Elizabeth Herndon; m. Thomas Nelson Shehan, Dec. 13, 1986; children: David Harrison Hardy, Daniel Patrict Hardy. BS in edn., Stephen F. Austin State U., 1973; MEd, North Tex. State U., 1984. Cert. Elem. Tchr. Self Contained grades 1-8 Tex. Edn. Agy., 1973, ESL grades 1-8 Tex. Edn. Agy., 1996, Reading Recovery Tex. Woman's U., 1998. Educator reading and ESL specialist Irving Ind. Sch. Dist., Tex., 1973—2003; testing diagnostician Knowledge Point Tutoring, Colleyville, Tex., 2004—; educator reading specialist NW Ind. Sch. Dist., Fort Worth, Tex., 2005—. Chairperson Elliott Campus Improvement Com., Irving, Tex., 1997—2002; adv. mem. IISD Dist. Improvement Com., Irving, Tex., 1999—2003; pres. elect Alpha Delta Kappa Tex. Beta Omicron Chpt., Irving, Tex., 1998—; mentor and grade level chair Irving ISD, Tex., 1990—2003. Mem. PTA; tchr. First United Meth. Ch., Irving, Tex., 1984—98. Recipient Irving Dist. Elem. Tchr. of the Yr., Irving Ind. Sch. Dist., 1999—2000, Outstanding Grad., 1990; grant, Irving Schools Found., 1988, 1988, 1995, 1997. Mem.: Internat. Reading Assn., Tex. Teachers of English to Speakers of Other Languages, Reading Recovery Coun. of N.Am., Parent Tchr. Assn. (life; bd. mem. 1990—2000), Kappa Delta Pi, Alpha Chi, Tex. Beta Omicron Chpt. of Alpha Delta Kappa (pres. elect 2004—). R-Conservative. Methodist. Avocations: outdoor activities, reading, travel, farming. Home: 1812 Krokus Dr Keller TX 76248 Office: Northwest Ind Sch Dist PO Box 77070 Fort Worth TX 76177-0070 Personal E-mail: gerishehan@verizon.net.

SHEILD, CAROLYN JEAN, science educator; b. Redfield, SD, Oct. 19, 1961; d. John Morgan and Jean Jordan (Powers) Sheild. BS summa cum laude, U. Wis., Eau Claire, 1984; MS, Northeastern U., 1990. Cert. tchr. Salem State Coll., 1990. Lab & field asst. Ctr. Limnology, Madison, Wis., 1985; natural resource specialist Dept. Natural Resources, Madison, 1985—86; tchr. oceanography Acadia Inst. Oceanography, Seal Harbor, Maine, 1992; tchr. biology Souhegan HS, Amherst, NH, 1992—93; tchr. sci. Clarke Mid. Sch., Lexington, Mass., 1994—. Presenter Benthic Ecology Meeting, Mobile, Ala., 1988, 90, Mass. Libr. Assn., Worcester, 1996, Woods Hole Oceanographic Instn., 2001, Boston Harbor Educators Conf., 2003; faculty rep. Jonas Clarke Sch. Assn., Lexington, 1996—2001; pilot tchr. Ridge 2000 Office, University Park, Pa., 2003—. Contbr. articles to profl. jours. Asst. sci. Sea Edn. Assn., Woods Hole, 1989, 1992—94, alumni coun. chair, 1997—2001, bd. trustees, 2004—; harvester Food Project, Acton, Mass., 2003; Sunday sch. tchr. Wellesley Hills Congl. Ch., Mass., 1997—2000, music com., 2001—03. Named to Hall of Fame, U. Wis., Eau Claire, 1988; recipient Cmty. Svc. award, Rotary Club, Madison, 1980, Acad. All Am. award, Nat. Assn. Intercollegiate Athletics, 1981—83, Track & Field Scholar Athlete award, Wis. Women's Intercollegiate Athletic Conf., 1983—84; grantee Grant-in-aid Rsch., Sigma Xi Rsch. Soc., Boston, 1988. Mem.: NSTA (presenter 1999, 2003, 2004), Nat. Assn. Intercollegiate Athletics (Dist. 14 Hall of Fame 1994), Madison Sports Hall of Fame Club (Hall of Fame 2005). Protestant. Avocations: flying trapeze, scuba diving, photography.

SHEINDLIN, JUDITH (JUDGE JUDY), television personality, judge; b. Bklyn., Oct. 21, 1942; d. Murray and Ethel Blum; m. Ronald Levy, 1964 (div. 1976); children: Jamie, Adam; m. Gerald Sheindlin, 1977 (div. 1990); stepchildren: Greg, Jonathan, Nicole; m. Gerald Sheindlin, 1991. BA, Am. U., Wash., DC, 1963; JD, NY Law Sch., 1965; LLD (hon.), Elizabethtown Coll. Pros. atty. Family Ct., NYC, 1978—82, judge Bronx, 1982—86; supervising judge Manhattan, NYC, 1986—96. Appeared as herself (TV films) ChiPs '99, 1998, (TV series) Judge Judy, 1996— (nominee Daytime Emmy for outstanding special class series, 1999, 2000, 2001, 2002, 2003); author: Don't Pee on My Leg and Tell Me It's Raining: America's Toughest Family Court Judge Speaks Out, 1996, Beauty Fades, Dumb is Forever: The Making of a Happy Woman, 1999, Keep It Simple, Stupid: You're Smarter Than You Look: Uncomplicating Families in Complicated Times, 2000, Judge Judy Sheindlin's Win or Lose by How You Choose, 2000, You're Smarter Than You Look: Uncomplicating Relationships in Complicated Times, 2001, Judge Judy Sheindlin's You Can't Judge a Book By Its Cover: Cool Rules for School, 2001.

SHEININ, ROSE, biochemist, educator; b. Toronto, Ont., May 18, 1930; d. Harry and Anne (Szyber) Shuber; m. Joseph Sheinin, July 15, 1951; children: David Matthew Khazanov, Lisa Basya Judith, Rachel Sarah Rebecca. BA, U. Toronto, 1951, MA (scholar), 1953, PhD in Biochemistry, 1956, LHD, 1985; DHL (hon.), Mt. St. Vincent U., 1985; DSc (hon.), Acadia U., 1987, U. Guelph, 1991. Demonstrator in biochemistry U. Toronto, Ont., Canada, 1951-53, asst. prof. microbiology Ont., 1964-75, asst. prof. med. biophysics Ont., 1967-75, prof. microbiology Ont., 1975-90, assoc. prof. med. biophysics Ont., 1975-78, prof. med. biophysics Ont., 1978-90, chmn. microbiology and parasitology Ont., 1975-82, vice dean Sch. Grad. Studies Ont., 1984-89; vice-rector acad. Concordia U., Montreal, Que., Canada, 1989-94, prof. dept. biology, 1989-2000. Mem. Health Scis. Com.; vis. rsch. assoc. chem. microbiology Cambridge U., 1956-57, Nat. Inst. Med. Rsch., London, 1975-58; rsch. assoc. fellow divsn. biol. rsch. Ont. Caner Inst., 1958-67; sci. officer cancer grants panel Med. Rsch. Coun. Can.; mem. Can. Sci. Del. to People's Republic of China, 1973; mem. adv. com. Provincial Lottery Health Rsch. Awards; mem. adv. com. on biotech. NRC Can., 1984-87; mem. Sci. Coun. Can., 1984-87; adv. com. on sci. and tech. CBC, 1980-85; mem. bd. dirs. Can. Bacterial Disease Network, 1989-94; vis. prof. biochemistry U. Alta., 1971. Assoc. editor Can. Jour. Biochemistry, 1968-71, Virology, 1969-72, Intervirology, 1974-85; editl. bd. Microbiol. Revs., 1977-80; author, co-author various publs. Nat. Cancer Inst. Can. fellow, 1953-56, 58-61; Brit. Empire Cancer Campaign fellow, 1956-58; recipient Queen's Silver Jubilee medal, 1978, Woman of Distinction award Health and Edn., YWCA, 1988, Josiah Macy Jr. faculty scholar, 1981-82; fellow Ligue Contre le Cancer, France, 1981-82, Massey Coll., U. Toronto, 1981—, continuing sr. fellow, 1994—; hon. fellow Ryerson Polytech. U., 1993. Fellow Am. Acad. Microbiology, Royal Soc. Can. (chair women in scholarship com. 1990-93); mem. Can. Biochem. Soc. (pres. 1974-75), Can. Soc. Cell Biology (pres. 1975-76), Am. Soc. Virology, Am. Soc. Microbiologists, Can. Assn. Women in Sci., Internat. Assn. Women Bioscientists, Sigma Xi Rsch. Soc., Scitech. Soc. Complex Carbohydrates, Toronto Biochem. and Biophys. Soc. (pres. 1960-70, coun. 1970-74). E-mail: rosesheinin@sympatico.ca.

SHEIVE, DOREEN LAUREL, fiscal administrator; b. Waterville, Maine, Jan. 30, 1947; d. Albert Sheive and June Marguerite Brown; 1 child, Alexander Richard. Student, Am. U., Washington, 1968-69, Thomas Coll., Waterville, Maine, 1984-86. Spl. asst. to Senator Edmund S. Muskie, Washington, 1969-71; asst. scheduler Edmund S. Muskie for Pres. Com., Washington, 1971-72, Henry "Scoop" Jackson for Pres. Com., Washington, 1973-75; chief scheduler Senator Daniel Patrick Moynihan, Washington, 1976-79; spl. asst. to Gov. Joseph E. Brennan Augusta, Maine, 1980-84; dir. compliance Dept. Fin. and Adminstrn. State of Maine, Augusta, 1984-87, dir. planning and tng. Dept. Audit, 1987-93, fiscal adminstr. unorganized territory, 1993—. Chair Maine Comm. Mcpl. Deorganization, Augusta, 1993—; vice chair, bd. dirs. Maine Credit Union, Augusta, 2001—. Author: Sheive Family History, 1999. Mem. Inst. Internal Auditors, 21 Year Membership. Democrat. Office: State Maine Dept Audit 66 State House Sta Augusta ME 04333-0066 Personal E-mail: dlaurels@adelphia.net.

SHEK, EUGENIE VICTORIA, artist; b. Chatanooga, Feb. 4, 1953; d. John Leonard and Patricia Shek. BA in Hispanic Studies, Vassar Coll., Poughkeepsie, NY, 1975; MA in Am. Culture, U. Mich., Flint, 1993. Cert. Gemological Inst. Am. Gemologist Dayton Corp., Saginaw, Mich., 1988—93; instr. Spanish Mosaica Acad., 1993—2001; instr. gemology Delta Coll. Jewelry designer Each By Eugenie, 1976—. Permanent collection, Saginaw Art Mus. Vol. Reading for Blind, Talking Newspaper, Saginaw, 1989—2006. Recipient Art award, Studio 23, Bay City, Mich., 1983. Mem.: Nat. Mus. Women in Arts, Saginaw Blues Soc. Methodist. Avocation: music. Home: 1944 Allegan Saginaw MI 48602

SHELBURNE, MERRY CLARE, public information officer, educator; b. L.A., Oct. 29, 1945; d. John Bartholomew and Geneva (Hedges) Delbridge; m. David Michael Shelburne, July 20, 1968. BA, Calif. State U., L.A., 1968; MA, Calif. State U., Northridge, 1993. Editl. asst. pub. affairs Calif. State U., L.A., 1968-71; publs. supr. Papercraft Specialty Co., L.A., 1973-74; creative dir. Family Record Plan, L.A., 1975-76; pub. info. asst. Glendale (Calif.) C.C., 1977-81, pub. info. officer, asst. prof. mass. comms., 1981—. Journalism advisor CourseWise, Atomic Dog, Internet, 1997—. Author: Walking the HighWire: Effective Public Relations, 1998, Effective Public Relations: A Practical Approach, 2001; songwriter Slow Dancin', If It Feels Good, 1990. Publicist Tim Richards Found. Annual Fundraiser Cmty. Faire, La Crescenta, 1980s. Mem. Calif. C.C. Pub. Rels. Orgn. (Radio Advt. 1st pl. award, Sports Publs. 1st pl. award). Avocations: songwriting, gardening, golf, dried flower decorations, golden retrievers. Office: Glendale CC 1500 N Verdugo Rd Glendale CA 91208-2809 E-mail: mshelbur@glendale.cc.ca.us.

SHELBY, NINA CLAIRE, special education educator; b. Weatherford, Tex., Oct. 23, 1949; d. Bill Hudson and Roselle (Price) S.; m. Richard Dean Powell, May 29, 1971 (div. 1973); 1 child, Stoney Hudson. BA in English, Sul Ross State U., 1974, MEd, 1984; MA in English, U. Tex., 1995. Jr. high lang. arts educator Liberty Hill, Tex., 1974-75; H.S. resource educator Georgetown (Tex.) I. S. D., 1976-77; intermediate resource educator Raymondille (Tex.) I. S. D., 1977-81; educator of severe profound Napper Elem. Pharr (Tex.) San Juan Alamo Ind. Sch. Dist., 1981-90; H. S. life skills educator Pharr (Tex.) San Juan Alamo ISD North H.S., 1990-93; intermediate inclusion educator Carman Elem. Pharr (Tex.) San Juan Alamo Ind. Sch. Dist., 1993—2000, chair dept. spl. edn. Carman Elem., 1998—2000; primary resource/inclusion educator Elgin (Tex.) Elem. Sch., 2000—, chair dept. spl. edn., 2002—. Coach asst. Tex. Spl. Olympics, Pharr, 1981-2000, sponsor vocat. adj. club, 1990-93, adaptive asst. device team, Edinburg, Tex., 1993-95; spl. edn. rep. to Elgin Primary Campus Performance Adv. Coun., 2000—. Asst. cub scout leader Boy Scouts Am., 1994-95, sec. parental com. bd. rev., 1997—; parent vol. boy's and girl's Club McAllen, 1992-96. Mem. DAR, Daus. Republic of Tex., Assn. Tex. Profl. Educators, Alpha Delta Kappa. Democrat. Mem. Ch. Of Christ. Avocations: reading, horticulture, piano, opera. Home: PO Box 426 Elgin TX 78621-0426 Office: Elgin Elem Sch Elgin ISD 1001 W 2d St Elgin TX 78621 Office Phone: 512-281-3457. Business E-Mail: nshelby@elginisd.net.

SHELBY, ROSELLE PRICE, writer, retired special education educator; b. Granbury, Tex., Sept. 6, 1929; d. Ernest Blanton and Alice Parthenia (Merrill) Price; m. Billy Hudson Shelby, May 5, 1948; 1 child, Nina Claire. AA, Weatherford Coll., 1948; BA, Tex. Wesleyan U., Ft. Worth, 1960; NDEA diploma, U. Minn., 1963; MEd, Sul Ross State U., Alpine, Tex., 1974. Cert. tchr., Tex. Tchr. Waka Ind. Sch., Tex., 1956-57, 60-65, 69-72, Hart Ind. Sch., Tex., 1957-60, Eagar Ind. Sch., Ariz., 1966-67, New Waverly Ind. Sch., Tex., 1967-68, Willis Ind. Sch., Tex., 1968-69, Georgetown Ind. Sch., Tex., 1972-87. Author: Frogs in the Milk, 1967; editor: Quick and Easy Way to Riches, 1980. Active local Democratic Party, 1968—, precinct chair, Georgetown, 1980-90, election judge, 1991-2000; mem. sch. bd., Alpine, Ariz. Fulbright scholar U. Costa Rica, 1964; Reynolds fellow U. NC, 1971. Mem. AAUW (br. pres. Perryton 1971-72, state bd. dirs. 1971-73, 75-77, br. pres. Georgetown 1975-77), DAR, Daughters of Republic of Tex. (charter mem. Brazos River Chpt.), Am. Assn. Ret. Persons, Beta Sigma Phi, Delta Kappa Gamma (v.p. 1979-81). Mem. Ch. of Christ. Avocations: bible study, reading, cooking, travel. Home: 2006 Terry Ln Georgetown TX 78628-3338

SHELDON, BETH ANN, music educator; b. Maquoketa, Iowa, May 10, 1978; d. Kathryn Louise Gunderson and Allen Blake Sheldon. BS in Music Edn., Coe Coll., Cedar Rapids, Iowa, 2000. Lic. tchr. Iowa, 2000. Mid. sch. band tchr. West Mid. Sch., Anamosa, Iowa, 2001—04, Franklin Mid. Sch., Cedar Rapids, Iowa, 2004—06. Mem. Cedar Rapids Mcpl. Band, Iowa, 1999—. Mem.: Iowa Band Masters Assn., Mortar Bd. (life), Tri-M (life; historian 1995—96). Office Phone: 319-558-4126.

SHELDON, BROOKE EARLE, librarian, educator; b. Lawrence, Mass., Aug. 29, 1931; d. Leonard Hadley and Elsie Ann (Southerl) Earle; m. George Duffield Sheldon, Mar. 28, 1955 (dec.); children: L. Scott, G. Stephen. BA, Acadia U., 1952, D.C.L. (hon.), 1985; M.L.S., Simmons Coll., 1954; PhD, U. Pitts., 1977. Base librarian, Ent AFB, Colorado Springs, Colo., 1955-57, U.S. Army, Germany, 1956-57; br. librarian Albuquerque Public Library, 1959-61; coordinator adult services Santa Fe Public Library, 1965-67; head library devel. N.Mex. State Library, Santa Fe, 1967-72; asst. dir. leadership tng. inst. U.S. Office Edn., Washington, 1971-73; head tech. svcs. and tng. Alaska State Library, Juneau, 1973-75; dean Sch. Library Info. Studies Tex. Woman's U., Denton, 1977-90; acting provost Library Info. Studies, Tex. Woman's U., Denton, 1979-80; dean Grad. Sch. Libr. Info. Sci. U. Tex., Austin, 1991—. Author: Leaders in Libraries: Styles and Strategies for Success, 1991; editor: Library and Information Science Education in the United States, 1996; contbr. articles to profl. jours. Bd. dirs. Am. Libr. in Paris, 1992—. Recipient Alumni Achievement award Simmons Coll., 1983; Disting. Alumni award Sch. Library Info. Sci., U. Pitts., 1986 Mem. ALA (pres. 1983-84, chmn. com. on accreditation 1995-96), Tex. Libr. Assn., Rotary Internat., Beta Phi Mu. Democrat. Episcopalian.

SHELDON, EDITH LOUISE THACH, writer; b. Walsenburg, CO, Nov. 28, 1941; d. William Mason Thach and Jeannette Violet Faris-Thach; m. John Michael Sheldon, June 27, 1964; children: Michael Mason, William David. Student, Pueblo Jr. Coll., Colo. State Coll., Adam's State Coll., Colo., 1959—74. Assoc. pub. Valley Courier Newspaper, Alamosa, Colo., 1974—81; adminstrv. mgr. Colo. Press Assn., Denver, 1981—83; office mgr. The Villager Newspaper, Englewood, Colo., 1983—85; assoc. pub. The Littleton Times, Littleton, Colo., 1986—87; ad exec. The Denver Parent Newspaper, Denver, 1988—94; editor, pub. Denver Parent News Mag., Denver, 1994—. Pres. Parenting Pub. of Am., San Antonio, 1989—91; mem. Gov.'s Coun. on Edn. of Young Children, 1991—94; pres. Huerfano County Hist. Soc., 1995—97; active numerous orgns. and polit. campaigns; mayor City Walsenburg, 2005—; v.p., bd. trustees Huerfano County Hosp. Dist., 2002—05.

SHELDON, ELEANOR HARRIET BERNERT, sociologist, writer; b. Hartford, Conn., Mar. 19, 1920; d. M.G. and Fannie (Myers) Bernert; m. James Sheldon, Mar. 19, 1950 (div. 1960); children: James, John Anthony. AA, Colby Jr. Coll., 1940; AB, U. N.C., 1942; PhD, U. Chgo., 1949. Asst. demographer Office Population Rsch., Washington, 1942-43; social scientist USDA, Washington, 1943-45; assoc. dir. Chgo. Community Inventory, U. Chgo., 1947-50; social scientist Social Sci. Rsch. Coun., N.Y.C., 1950-51, rsch. grantee, 1953-55, pres., 1972-79; rsch. assoc. Bur. Applied Social Rsch. Columbia U., 1950-51, lectr. sociology, 1951-52, vis. prof., 1969-71; social scientist UN, N.Y.C., 1951-52; rsch. assoc., lectr. sociology UCLA, 1955-61; assoc. rsch. sociologist, lectr. Sch. Nursing U. Calif., 1957-61; sociologist, exec. assoc. Russell Sage Found., N.Y.C., 1961-72; vis. prof. U. Calif., Santa Barbara, 1971. Author: (with L. Wirth) Chicago Community Fact Book, 1949, America's Children, 1958, (with R.A. Glazier) Pupils and Schools in N.Y.C., 1965; editor: (with W.E. Moore) Indicators of Social Change, Concepts and Measurements, 1968, Family Economic Behavior, 1973; contbr. articles to profl. jours. Bd. dirs. Colby-Sawyer Coll., 1979-85, UN Rsch. Inst. for Social Devel., 1973-79; trustee Rockefeller Found., 1978-85, Nat. Opinion Rsch. Ctr., 1980-87, Inst. East-West Security Studies, 1984-88, Am. assembly, 1976-95. William Rainey Harper fellow, U. Chgo., 1945—47. Fellow AAAS, Am. Acad. Arts and Scis., Am. Sociol. Assn., Am. Statis. Assn.; mem. U. Chgo. Alumni Assn. (Profl. Achievement award), Sociol. Rsch. Assn. (pres. 1971-72), Coun. on Fgn. Rels., Am. Assn. Pub. Opinion Rsch., Ea. Sociol. Soc., Internat. Sociol. Assn., Internat. Union Sci. Study of Population, Population Assn. Am. (2d v.p. 1970-71), Inst. of Medicine (chmn. program com. 1976-77), Cosmopolitan Club. Home and Office: 630 Park Ave New York NY 10021-6544 E-mail: ehbsheldon@aol.com.

SHELDON, INGRID KRISTINA, retired mayor, controller; b. Ann Arbor, Mich., Jan. 30, 1945; d. Henry Ragnvald and Virginia Schmidt Blom; m. Clifford George Sheldon, June 18, 1966; children: Amy Elizabeth, William David. BS, Eastern Mich. U., 1966; MA, U. Mich., 1970; doctorate (hon.), Cleary U., 2001. Cert. tchr., Mich. Tchr. Livonia (Mich.) Pub. Schs., 1966-67, Ann Arbor Pub. Schs., 1967-68; bookkeeper Huron Valley Tennis Club, Ann Arbor, 1978—; acct. F.A. Black Co., Ann Arbor, 1984-88; coun. mem. Ward II City of Ann Arbor, 1988-92, mayor, 1993-2000. Commr. Housing Bd. Appeals, Ann Arbor, 1988—91; vice chmn. fin. and budget com. S.E. Mich. Coun.Govts.; treas. Huron Valley Child Guidance Clinic, Ann Arbor, 1984—, Ann Arbor Hist. Found., 1985—, Parks Adv. Commn., 1987—92, Ann Arbor Planning Commn., 1988—89; excellence com. Ann Arbor Pub. Schs. reorgn., 1985; treas. SOS Cmty. Crisis Ctr., Ypsilanti, Mich., 1987—93; chair United Meth. Retirement Cmty., Ann Arbor, 2003—06; trustee Cmty. Found., 2001—05; chair Ann Arbor Summer Festival, 2005. Recipient Cmty. Svc. award Ann Arbor Jaycees, 1980, DAR Cmty. Svc. award, 1997; AAUW fellow, 1982. Mem.: Mich. Mcpl. League (life; del. 1989—97, hon. life mem. 1994, trustee 1997—2000, pres. 1999—2000), Ann Arbor Rotary (pres.-elect 2005), Ann Arbor Women's City Club (fin. com. 1987—90, chair endowment com. 1989—90, treas. 2003), Alpha Omicron Pi, Kappa Delta Pi. Republican. Methodist. Avocation: musical theatre. Home: 1416 Folkstone Ct Ann Arbor MI 48105-2848 Personal E-mail: aasheldon@aol.com.

SHELDON, LOUISE ROBERTS, writer; b. Narragansett, R.I., Aug. 30, 1926; d. James Rhodes and Marjorie Starkweather (Chase) Sheldon; m. John Lucien Smith, June 9, 1962 (dec. June 1972); 1 child, Randolph Betts; m. Robert Edward MacDonald, Dec. 23, 1974. BA in German Lit. cum laude, Bryn Mawr Coll., 1948; MA in French Lit., Calif. State U., Northridge, 1972. Accredited fgn. corr. With MD Publs., N.Y., 1949-52; asst. editor LIFE Time Inc., N.Y.C., 1952-64; assoc. editor Smithsonian, Washington, 1972-74; editor Am. C. of C., Casablanca, 1975-80. Sec. Internat. Coun. of Women, Zurich, 1948-49; chmn. lang. dept. Westlake Sch., L.A., 1963-68; fgn. corr. UPI, Paris, 1977-81, Christian Sci. Monitor, Boston, 1977-81, Middle East mag., London, 1977-81; contbg. writer World and I, Washington, 1984-89, Mus. and Arts Washington, 1984-89. Author: (short stories) Casablanca Notebook, 1998, 2002, (novel) Wind in the Sahara, 2002. Docent Balt. Mus. Art, 1990-2003. Mem. Dunes Club, Cross Keys Tennis Club, Alpha Mu Gamma. Democrat. Episcopalian. Avocations: foreign languages, travel, reading, painting.

SHELDON-MORRIS, TIFFINI ANNE, clinical psychologist, consultative examiner; b. Berkeley, Calif., Apr. 20, 1976; d. Terry E. and Jan L. Sheldon; m. John Christopher Morris, Aug. 6, 2000. BS in Psychology, Abilene Christian U., 1997; MS in Psychology, Fla. Inst. Tech., 2001, D of Psychology, 2001. Licensed Clinical Psychologist Tex., 2004. Postdoctoral fellow Houston Veterans Affairs Med. Ctr., Houston, 2001—02; team leader and counselor Sr. Connections, Houston, 2003—04; clin. psychologist VeriCare, 2004—. Consultative examiner Dept. of Assistive and Rehabilitative Svcs., Austin, Tex., 2004—. Active mem. Monterey Ch. Christ, Lubbock, Tex., 2004—. Scholar Grad. Student Tchg. Assistantship, Fla. Inst. of Tech., 1998-2000. Mem.: APA, Alpha Kappa Delta Internat. Hon. Soc., Alpha Chi Nat. Honor Soc., Girls Aiming Toward Achievement. Avocations: travel, reading, swimming, music, theater. Home: 6508 89th St Lubbock TX 79424 Office: VeriCare 4715 Viewridge Ave St 230 San Diego CA 92123 Office Phone: 806-577-3050. Home Fax: 806-698-8994; Office Fax: 800-819-1655. Personal E-mail: drtiffini@yahoo.com.

SHELDRICK, BARBARA ENGLAND, music educator, consultant; d. James E. and Mary F. England; m. Robert S. Sheldrick, Jr., July 30, 1994; children: Shannon Elaine, Andrew James. B.Mus.Edn., Adrian Coll., Mich., 1979; MusM in Edn., Wayne State U., Detroit, 1995. Cert. music tchr. Music Educators Nat. Conf., 1994. Dir. of elem. bands Lake Orion Cmty. Schs., Lake Orion, 1979—81; music tchr. Kensington Acad., Bloomfield Hills, Mich., 1982—86, Anchor Bay Pub. Schs., New Baltimore, Mich., 1986—. Handbell dir. Lake Orion United Meth. Ch., 1980—84; presenter Mich. Acad. Arts, Sci., and Letters, 1995; youth choral dir. First Congl. Ch., United Ch. Christ, Rochester, Mich., 1999—2003. Mem.: Choristers Guild, Am. Choral

Dirs. Assn., Music Educators Nat. Conf. Republican. Roman Catholic. Avocations: photography, swimming, ceremony of tea, flute, preserving family history. Office: Great Oaks Elem Sch 32900 24 Mile Rd New Baltimore MI 48047 E-mail: bsheldrick@abs.misd.net.

SHELEMAY, KAY KAUFMAN, music educator; b. Houston, Mar. 26, 1948; d. Raymond R. and Lillian (Ablon) Kaufman; m. Jack S. Shelemay, Feb. 4, 1974. Student, Northwestern U., 1966-68; MusB with high distinction, U. Mich., 1970, MA in Music, 1972, PhD in Musicology, 1977. Asst. prof. music Columbia U., N.Y.C., 1977-82; assoc. prof. music NYU, N.Y.C., 1982-90; prof. music Wesleyan U., Middletown, Conn., 1990-92, Harvard U., Cambridge, Mass., 1992—. Vis. rsch. scholar Hebrew U., Jerusalem, 1972-73, Inst. Ethiopian Studies, Addis Ababa, 1973-75; guest curator Jewish Mus. Exhbn., 1986-87; faculty-in-residence CBS Records Divsn., 1986; adj. asst. prof. music Hunter Coll. CUNY, 1980; vis. prof. music Harvard U., 1991; chair dept. music Harvard U., 1994-99; chair Fromm Music Found., Harvard U., 1994-99; lectr. in field. Author: A Song of Longing, An Ethiopian Journey, 1991, (with Peter Jeffery) Ethiopian Christian Liturgical Chant. An Anthology, Vol. 1, 1993, Vols. 2-3, 1994; editor: The Garland Library of Readings in Ethnomusicology, 1990, (monograph) Music, Ritual, and Falasha History, 1986, 89 (Nat. Found. Jewish Culture Post-doctoral Pub. award, 1986), Deems Taylor award ASCAP 1987, Internat. Musicol. Soc. prize, 1988), (rec. with Sarah Weiss and Geoffrey Goldberg) Pizmon, Syrian-Jewish Religious and Social Song, 1985; mem. editorial bd. Chgo Series in Ethnomusicology, U. Chgo. Press, 1989—, Series in Music, U. Rochester Press, 1992-95, Jour. Ethiopian Studies, 1994—; mem. editorial bd., adv. Garland Pub. Inc., 1996—; also articles to profl. jours., revs. in books. Woodrow Wilson fellow, 1970-71, fellow Am. Coun. Learned Socs., 1981-82, NYU Presdl. fellow, 1986, fellow NEH, 1986-88, 92-93, Meml. Found. for Jewish Culture, 1992-93; grantee Republic N.Y. Corp., 1988-90. Mem. Nat. Endowment for Arts (site review 1997), Nat. Endowment for Humanities (panelist), Lib. Congress (panelist), Am. Musicological Soc. (com. status of women 1985-88, coun. 1987-89, 1996—, fellowship com.), Soc. for Ethnomusicology (pres.-elect 1997), Soc. Asian Music (bd. dirs. 1983-91), Jewish Music Coun. (exec. bd. 1982—), various others. Office: Harvard U Music Bldg Dept Music Cambridge MA 02138 also: Ind U Soc for Ethnomusicology Inc Morrison Hall 005 Bloomington IN 47405-2501

SHELL, (PETERSON) JUANITA, psychologist, educator; b. Winston-Salem, N.C., Apr. 21, 1940; d. Douglas James and Sallie (Saunders) Shell; m. Alonza Peterson, Dec. 24, 1961; children: Lisa Peterson, Jason Peterson. BA, CCNY, 1971; PhD, CUNY, 1977; postgrad., NYU, 1980—91. Libr. asst. Bklyn. Pub. Libr., 1959-64; sec. Haryou-Act, N.Y.C., 1965-67; psychotherapist Psychol. Ctr., N.Y.C., 1971-74; cons.-therapist Hale House, N.Y.C., 1974-77; psychology intern NYU-Bellevue Med. Ctr., N.Y.C., 1974-75; staff psychologist Bellevue Psychiat. Hosp., 1978—. Clin. instr. dept. psychiatry NYU Sch. Medicine, 1978—85, asst. clin. prof. Dept. Psychiatry Sch. Medicine NYU, 1985—; mem. faculty Bklyn. Coll., 1976-78; cons. Bklyn. Cmty. Counseling Ctr., 1976—86; mem. N.Y.C. Mayor's Adv. Subcom. on Mental Retardation and Devel. Disabilities, 1978-1982; cons. in field. Contbr. articles to profl. jours. Chairperson health com. N.Y.C. Cmty. Bd. 4, 1979-81. Black Analysis Inc. fellow 1975-76; NIMH grantee, 1971-74. Mem. APA, Metro. Jack and Jill Am. (v.p. Met. chpt. 1984-85, pres. Met. chpt. 1989), Woman's Aux. of North Gen. Hosp., NYU Bellevue Soc., NYU Psychoanalytic Soc., N.Y. State Divsn. Women, Harlem Toastmasters (founding mem., 2002—). Democrat. Episcopalian. Office: Dept Psychiatry NYU-Bellevue Med Ctr 462 First Ave at 27th St New York NY 10016 Office Phone: 212-562-4509. Personal E-mail: Juanita.Shell@att.net.

SHELLEY, CAROLE, actress; b. London, Aug. 16, 1939; arrived in U.S., 1964; d. Curtis and Deborah (Bloomstein) Shelley; m. Albert G. Woods, July 26, 1967 (dec.). Student, Arts Ednl. Sch., 1943-56, Prepatory Acad. Royal Acad. Dramatic Art, 1956-57; studies with Iris Warren and Eileen Thorndike. Trustee Am. Shakespeare Theatre, 1974—82. Actor: (plays) The Odd Couple, 1965, Absurd Person Singular, 1973, The Norman Conquests (L.A. Drama Critics Cir. award, 1975), As You Like It, King Lear, She Stoops to Conquer, 1972, The Country Wife, 1973, A Doll's House, Man and Superman, 1977, Misalliance, 1980, Grand Hunt, 1980, The Play's the Thing, 1978, Lion in Winter, 1987, The Elephant Man (Outer Critics Cir. award, 1979, Tony award for Best Actress, 1979), What the Butler Saw, 1989, Broadway Bound, 1987—88, Lettice and Lovage, 1989—90, The Miser, 1990, Cabaret Verboten, 1991, The Destiny of Me, 1992—93, Later Life, 1993 (Outer Critics nominee), Richard II, 1994, London Suite, 1995, Show Boat, 1995—96, The Film Society, 1997, The Last Night of Ballyhoo, 1997—98, Cabaret, 1999—2002, Wicked, 2002—04, 2005—, The Importance of Being Earnest, 2005—, Ring Round the Moon, 2006; (films) The Boston Strangler, The Odd Couple, 1968, The Super, 1990, Devlin, 1991, Quiz Show, 1993, The Road to Wellville, 1993, Bewitched, 2005, others; (TV series) The Odd Couple, Robin Phillips Grand Theatre Co., 1983—84, Nat. Co. The Royal Family (L.A. Drama Critics Cir. award, 1977); (Broadway plays) Noises Off, 1985, Stepping Out, 1986 (Tony nominee, 1986), Waltz of the Toreadors, 1986, Oh Coward, 1986—87, Broadway Bound, 1987—88; voice actor: (films) Robin Hood; The Aristocats; Hercules. Recipient Obie award for Twelve Dreams, N.Y. Shakespeare Festival, 1982. Jewish. Office: Robert Duva 277 W 10th St New York NY 10014 Office Phone: 212-243-7845.

SHELLHORN, RUTH PATRICIA, landscape architect; b. LA, Sept. 21, 1909; d. Arthur Lemon and Lodema (Gould) S.; m. Harry Alexander Kueser, Nov. 21, 1940. Student dept. landscape architecture, Oreg. State Coll., 1927—30; BA in Landscape Arch., Cornell U., 2005, BArch, 2005. Pvt. practice landscape architecture, various cities, Calif., 1933—; exec. cons. landscape arch. Bullocks Stores, Calif., 1945-78, Fashion Sqs. Shopping Ctrs., Calif., 1958-78, Marlborough Sch., L.A., 1968-93, El Camino Coll., Torrance, Calif., 1970-78, Harvard Sch., North Hollywood, Calif., 1974-90. Cons. landscape arch., site planner Disneyland, Anaheim, Calif., 1955, U. Calif., Riverside Campus, 1956-64, numerous others, also numerous gardens and estates; landscape arch. Torrance (Calif.) City Goals Com., 1969-70; cons. landscape arch. City of Rolling Hills (Calif.) Cmty. Assn., 1973-93. Contbr. articles to garden and profl. publs.; subject of Oct. 1967 issue Landscape Design & Constrn. mag. Named Woman of Year, L.A. Times, 1955, Woman of Year, South Pasadena-San Marino (Calif.) Bus. Profl. Women, 1955; recipient Charles Goodwin Sands medal, 1930-33, Landscape Architecture award of merit Calif. State Garden Clubs, 1984, 86, Horticulturist of the Yr. award So. Calif. Hort. Inst., numerous nat., state, local awards for excellence. Fellow Am. Soc. Landscape Archs. (past pres. So. Calif. chpt., Lifetime Achievement award, 2005), Phi Kappa Phi, Kappa Kappa Gamma (Alumni Achievement award 1960, 2006), Garden Club Am. (Civic Improvement award 2006). Achievements include oral history and biography published by Pasadena Heritage, 2002. Home and Office: 362 Camino De Las Colinas Redondo Beach CA 90277-6435

SHELLMAN-LUCAS, ELIZABETH C., special education educator, researcher; b. Thomas County, Ga., Feb. 5, 1937; d. Herbert and Juanita (Coleman) Smith; m. John Lee Lucas, Jr. (div.); 1 child, Sandie Juanita Lucas Boyce; m. Eddie Joseph Shellman; 1 child, Eddie Joseph Shellman, Jr. MS in Edn., CUNY, 1990. Cert. tchr. NY. Pvt. practice cosmetologist, N.Y.C., 1959—; tchr. N.Y.C. Bd. of Edn. High Sch. Dist., 1984—. Vol. various cmty. orgns.; citizen amb. del. People to People Internat., 1994; ch. sch. tchr., supt. Canaan Bapt. Ch., Harlem, 1990-2002. Mem. Coun. for Exceptional Children. Avocations: reading, music, dance, jogging, languages.

SHELOR, VICKIE POFF, choir director; b. Christiansburg, Va., Aug. 24, 1956; d. Sherrell Mason and Phyllis Akers Poff. BS, Radford U., Va., 1978, MA, 1979. Organist, choir dir. St. Mark Luth. Ch., Willis, Va., 1985—, Zion Luth. Ch., Floyd, Va., 1986—; music tchr. Roanoke (Va.) County Pub. Schs., 1991—95; choral dir. Carroll County H.S., Hillsville, Va., 1995—. Mem.: Am. Choral Dirs. Assn., Music Educators Nat. Conf., Am. Guild of Organists. Home: 1470 Union School Rd Floyd VA 24091 Office: Carroll County H S 100 Cavs Ln Hillsville VA 24343-1669 Office Phone: 276-728-2125.

SHELTON, CAROLYN JOHNSON, professional society administrator; d. Ernest Gustav Johnson and Anne Mabel Nemergut; m. Philo Sherwood Shelton, June 27, 1962; children: Philo Sherwood, Anne F. Mele. AS (hon.), U. Bridgeport, 1962. Dir. membership Conn. Audubon Soc., Fairfield, 1984—. V.p. Fairfield Women's Club, Conn., 1980—82. Recipient 10 Yr. Award for Volunteerism on the Four Seasons Ball Com. to raise money for the mentally challenged, The Kenndey Ctr., 10. Mem.: Greenfield Hill Garden Club. R-Consevative. Catholic. Achievements include design of Designed the pussy willow stencils and applied the stencils for a suite in a National Historic Restoration inn called the Inn at National Hall located in Westport, Conn. Home and Office: Conn Audubon Soc 2325 Burr St Fairfield CT 06824 Business E-Mail: cshelton@ctaudubon.org.

SHELTON, DARLENE, psychologist, consultant; d. Harvey Clinton and Opal Lyles Shelton; m. David Weinberg, Oct. 10, 2003. BA in Psychology, So. Ill. U., 1979, MA in Psychology, 1986, PhD in Behavioral Medicine and Psychology, 1990. Lic. clin. psychologist State of Ky., State of Conn. Dir., coord. psychol. svcs. Econ. Opportunity Family Health Ctr., Miami, 1991—94; rsch. asst. prof. dept. psychiatry U. Miami Sch. Medicine, 1993—94; assoc. prof., dir. diversity and minority affairs Spalding U. Sch. Profl. Psychology, Louisville, 1995—2003; assoc. rsch. scientist dept. psychiatry Yale U. Sch. of Medicine, New Haven, 2003—04; CEO Ctr. for Humanitarian Initiatives, Guilford, Conn., 2004—; sr. fellow Garrison Inst., NY, 2005—; assoc. of the Chaplain's Office, Yale U., New Haven, 2006—. Rsch. cons. U.S. HHS, Pub. Health Svc., Health Resources and Svcs. Adminstrn., Bur. Health Resources Devel., Washington, 1991—93; forensic psychology cons. Thematix Group, Guilford, Conn., 2001—; program cons. Garrison Inst., Garrison, 2004—; rsch. cons. Ctr. for Women Policy Studies, Washington, 1993; mem. adv. com. Pediat. AIDS Health Care Demonstration Project of U. Miami/Jackson Meml. Hosp., 1992—94; grant reviewer Women's Initiative for HIV Care and Reduction of Perinatal HIV Transmission, Maternal and Child Health Bur., Health Resources and Svcs. Adminstrn., Rockville, Md., 1995; mem. Ky. HIV Prevention Cmty. Planning Group, State of Ky. Dept. of HIV Prevention, Frankfort, 1996—98; mem. African-Am. adv. com. Ky. HIV Prevention Cmty. Planning Group, State of Ky., Dept. HIV Prevention, Frankfort, 1996—98, advisor, 1998—99; psychol. cons. State of Fla. Dept. Juvenile Justice Dist. XI, Miami, 1994—95; rsch. cons. R.E.A.C.H., Louisville, 1995—96, Coun. on Prevention and Edn.: Substances, Inc. (COPES) Family Connection Demonstration Project, Louisville, 1996—2000; psychologist U. Louisville Sch. Medicine WINGS (HIV/AIDS) Clinic Aux. Support Team, Louisville, 1996—2000; co-process evaluator Ky. Incentives for Prevention, Louisville, 1997—2000; psychologist site supr. Americana Cmty. Ctr., Louisville, 1999—2003; adj. asst. prof. dept. psychology Barry U., Miami Shores, Fla., 1995; presenter, lectr., spkr. in field. Author: (nonfiction book) Babies Mamas, (booklet) Health Care Utilization and Medical Adherence Issues Among Prenatal HIV Seropositive African American Women in Miami: The Role of The Family and The Extended Kinship Networks.; panelist (television program) KENTUCKY TONIGHT: Coping Emotionally with the Aftermath of September 11th; author: (public service television script) Make Your Next Move Count, (public service TV script) Child Abuse: Sticks and Stones and Words Can Hurt; contbr. articles to scholarly jours. Mem. planning com. Ann. Nat. Conf. on the Black Family in Am., Louisville, 2001—03; judge panelist ABA Regional Client Counseling Competition, Louisville, 2002; facilitator One Louisville, 2001—02; bd. dirs. Ctr. for Haitian Studies, Miami, 1993—95. Named Outstanding Leader and Mentor, Spalding U. Black Student Assn., 1997, Nat. Inst. of Drug Abuse Sponsored Jr. Minority Investigator, APHA, 1992; recipient White Ho. Briefing Honoring World AIDS Day invitation, 2005, NIMH Postdoctoral fellowship in psychoimmunology, Ctr. for the Biopsychosocial Study of AIDS, Dept. Psychiatry, U. Miami Sch. of Medicine, 1990—91, Cert. Appreciation for Contbns. in Devel. of Creative AIDS Edn. Programs, U.S. Dept. VA, 1990, Ill. Minority Grad. Incentive Program fellowship, State of Ill., 1986—90, So. Ill. U. Grad. Dean's fellowship, 1984—85, Cert. of Appreciation, Omega Psi Phi, 1997, 1998, 1999, 2000; grantee Ongoing Program of Stress Mgmt. for Spl. Immunology Unit Staff., U.S. Dept. VA, Office Acad. Affairs, and Regional Med. Edn. Ctr., 1989, Five-year Plan for Ethnic Minority Recruitment, Retention and Tng. in Psychology, APA, 2002, Qualitative studies addressing the sexual behaviors and biopsychosocial issues of patients in the Women's HIV/AIDS Clinic at the U. of Miami, U. Miami Sch. of Medicine Ctr. for Comprehensive Study of HIV/AIDS, 1990—92; scholar Non-Traditional Student Scholarship award, Delta Sigma Theta, Carbondale Alumnae Chpt., 1989. Mem.: APA, Inst. Noetic Scis., Kentuckiana Assn. of Black Psychologists (pres. 2002—03), Ky. Psychol. Assn., Conn. Psychol. Assn. (ethnic diversity task force 2004, co-chair 2005—), Nature Conservancy. Achievements include research in Ethnographic Study of Miami-area HIV Positive Expectant Mothers with Previous Children. Office: Ctr for Humanitarian Initiatives Deep River Center 3 Taliar Ridge Rd Guilford CT 06437 Office Phone: 203-458-3244. E-mail: darlene.shelton@chiglobal.org.

SHELTON, ELIZABETH COLLEY, social worker; b. Atlanta, Ga., Mar. 26, 1920; d. John Edmonds and Bess (Hollowell) Colley; m. Charles Bascom Shelton Jr., Oct. 22, 1940 (dec. Febr. 1990); children: Charles III, Elizabeth Colley Case, Rosser Edmonds. Attended, Sweet Briar (Va.) Coll., 1937-40; BA in Sociology, U. Tenn., Chattanooga, 1963; postgrad., U. of the South, Sewanee, Tenn., 1990-98. Caseworker Hamilton County Family Svcs., Chattanooga, 1970-72; caseworker prin. Fulton County Dept. of Family and Children Svcs., Atlanta, Ga., 1973-97. Bd. dirs. Midtown Assistance Ctr., Atlanta, 1988-97. Sustainer Jr. League of Atlanta, 1946—. Mem. Ga. Conf. on Social Welfare (bd. dirs. 1993-96), Ga. County Welfare Assn., Daus. of the King, Svc. and Prayer Group, Soc. Companions of Holy Cross, Symphony and Alliance Theater. Republican. Episcopalian. Home: Apt 821 3750 Peachtree Rd NE Atlanta GA 30319-1322

SHELTON, MARGARET, counselor; d. Henry and Lucille Dennis; m. Michael Wayne Shelton, May 21, 1988; children: Chelci Arnold, Michael, Christopher. BS Sociology, U. West Ga., Carrollton, Ga.;, 1978; MEd, U. West Ga., Carrollton, Ga., 1985. Lic. Profl. Counselor Tex., 1993, cert. Tex. Sch. Counselor Tex., 1992, Tex. Tchng. Tex., 1992, Mid-Mgmt. Adminstr. Tex., 1999. Unit therapist Murphy-Harpst Home, Cedartown, Ga., 1986—87; tchr. Harris County Dept. of Edn., Houston, 1988—94, sch. counselor, 1991—97, asst. prin., 1997—2001; sch. counselor Windham Sch. Dist., Humble, Tex., 2001—. Counseling,cons. Harris County Juvenile Justice Dept., Houston, 1999—2001. Worthy matron Ea. Stars, Houston, 1993—2001; mem. Phi Delta Kappa, Houston, 1996—2003, Civitan, Carrollton, Ga., 1986—86, Tex. Counseling Assn., Austin, Tex., 1999—2003, Nat. Dem. Party, Washington, 2003. Sgt. U S. Army, 1990—91, Fort Hood, Tex. Decorated Nat. Def. Svc. Medal (Operation Desert Storm) U. S. Army; recipient Dean's List, West Ga., 1977, Letter of Commendation, Ga. State Licensure Bd., 1987, Spl. Award, Order of Ea. Star, 2001. Mem.: Tex. Counseling Assn. Democrat-Npl. Baptist. Avocations: reading, travel, exercising.

SHELTON, ROSE E., minister, retired tax specialist; b. Nevisdale, Ky., Nov. 26, 1951; d. Nesbit Abraham Shelton and Oneda Neoma Smith-Shelton; children: Belinda Lou Wilson-Gerrald, Holly Haines. DD, U. Calif. Ordained min. With IRS, Dayton and Cin., Ohio; ombudsman Nat. Cash Register Co., Dayton and Corbin, Ky.; self-employed min. Contbr. articles to profl. jours. Leader Girl Scouts Am., 2000—, cons., co-team leader Phoenix. Sp5 U.S. Army, 1970—72. Recipient Internat. Sales Woman of Yr., Fed. Gun Sales, 1994. Mem.: DAV (life), Continental Kennel Club, Am. Kennel Club. Republican. Avocations: bow hunting, guns, reading, writing, animals. Home: 6618 W Red Fox Rd Phoenix AZ 85085

SHELTON, SAMANTHA, psychologist; b. Chgo., Ill., July 16, 1974; d. Emmett and Marie Shelton. BS, Xavier U. La., New Orleans, La., 1996; Clin. Psychology, Forest Inst. of Profl. Psychology, Springfield, Mo., 2000. Mental health provider Sinai-Mile Sq. Mental Health Clinic, Chicago, Ill., 2000—01; clin. psychologist Fed. Bur. of Prisons, Beaumont, Tex., 2001—03, drug abuse program coord. Las Vegas, Nev., 2003—. Treas. Fed. Bur. of Prisons Non Profit Orgn., Las Vegas, Nev., 2003—04. Contbr. scientific papers. Mem.: APA, Black Psychologist Assn. Office: Fed Bureau of Prisons - Nellis PO Box 9910 Las Vegas NV 89191 Office Phone: 702-644-5001. Office Fax: 702-644-7253. Business E-Mail: sshelton@bop.gov.

SHELTON, STEPHANI, broadcast journalist, consultant; b. Boston; d. Phil and Babette (Belloff) Saltman; m. Frank Herold. BS, Boston U. Corr. CBS News, N.Y.C., 1973—84; news corr. WWOR-TV, N.Y.C., 1984—88; corr., anchor Fin. News Network, N.Y.C., 1989—91. Freelance reporter Sta. WPIX-TV, 1991-95, Sta. WNBC-TV, 1993-96, WWOR-TV, 1999-02; writer, prodr., radio anchor CNBC, 2003—; cons. trainer Ctrl. and Eastern Europe broadcast journalists, 1998—; med. health prodr.-reporter PBS, The Learning Channel, 1997-99; owner The Fred Group Ltd., video/internet prodn. co., 1998—; freelance radio documentary writer Westinghouse Group W Broadcasting, NYC, 1970-73. Recipient Peabody award, 1972, N.J. Best Spot News award AP, 1987, 88, N.J. Working Press award, 1993-94; Emmy nominee, 1995, 96, 99, 2000. Mem. Soc. Profl. Journalists (award 1999), Radio and TV News Dirs. Assn., N.Y.C. Press Club, Investigative Reporters and Editors, Com. to Protect Journalists. E-mail: backbay38@aol.com, fred@fredgroupltd.com.

SHELTON, SYLVIA LAWSON, science educator; d. Jacob H. and Edna (Tootsie) Lawson; m. M. Dwight Shelton, Jr., Oct. 30, 1971; children: Christopher D., Jeffrey S. BA in Edn., Va. Tech., Blacksburg, 1990, MA in Edn., 2001. Cert. tchr. Va. Tchr. grades 6-8 Christiansburg Mid. Sch., Va., 1990—. Chair sci. dept. Christiansburg Mid. Sch., 1995—. Contbr. photographs to newspapers, 1980—. Mem.: Phi Kappa Phi, Phi Delta Kappa, Alpha Delta Kappa (sec. 2004—06, pres.-elect 2006—). United Methodist. Avocations: walking, needlecrafts, puzzles. Home: 4010 Tall Oaks Dr Blacksburg VA 24060 Office: Christiansburg Mid Sch 1205 Buffalo Dr Christiansburg VA 24073

SHEN, HUA-QIONG (JOAN), clinical research director; d. Zhongzao Shen and Deli Wen; m. Yonggang Wu, Sept. 28, 1987; children: Johnna Nan Wu, Shana Wu. MD, Nanjing Rlwy. Med. Coll., 1983; MS, West China Univ. Med. Scis., 1989; PhD, Ind. U. Sch. Medicine, 1996. Cert. Am. Bd. Neurology & Psychiatry, 2003. Surgeon Chengdu Second Hosp., Sichuan, China, 1989—91; staff psychiatrist Wabash Valley Hosp., West Lafeyette, Ind., 2001—; staff psychiatrist Mental Health Ctr. Wishard Meml. Hosp., Indpls., 2002—03; clin. rsch. physician Eli Lilly & Co., Indpls., 2003—05; dir. neuroscience clin. R & D Wyeth Pharm., Collegeville, Pa., 2005—. Professorship The Learning Disabilities Rsch. Assn. China, Beijing, 2003—. Editor: (physiology jour.) Selective Reviewer; contbr. articles to profl. jours. Bd. mem. Lilly Chinese Culture Network Eli Lilly & Co., 2003; coun. mem. Ind. Assn. Chinese Am. Inc., Indpls. Recipient Exemplary Young Physician award, Ziyiang Rlwy. Factory Hosp., 1985, APA Travel Fellowship award, Wyeth Pharm. Co., 2002. Mem.: Ind. Chinese Med. Assn. (chair), Am. Endocrine Soc., Am. Psychiat. Assn. (assoc.). Achievements include design of clinical trials for drugs pre- and post-marketing. Office: Wyeth Pharm 500 Arcola Rd Collegeville PA 19426 Home: 1550 Knobb Hill Ln Paoli PA 19301 Business E-Mail: shenj1@uyeth.com.

SHEN, RONGER, artist, educator; b. Shanghai, Nov. 11, 1942; came to U.S., 1984; d. Jianping and Huijun (Peng) S.; m. Yi Wu, Dec. 31, 1965; 1 child, Yan Wu. BA, Nat. Nanjing Acad. Arts, 1965. Dir. arts and crafts dept. Jiangsu Light Industry Bur., Nanjing, 1965-79; dir. Jiangsu Acad. Arts and Crafts, 1982—. Profl. painter Jiangsu Acad. Traditional Chinese Painting, 1979—; pres. Qigong Ctr., Inc., N.Y., 1989—; Qigong cons. to dept. orthopedics Mt. Sinai Sch. Medicine, N.Y.C., 1991—, N.J. Med. Ctr. Pain Mgmt. Ctr., Newark, 1991; NIH approved rsch. project on Life Info. Pictures, Life Info. Rhythm and Qigong, 1993; dir. Assn. Modern Chinese Arts Inc., 1994—. Mem. Artists Assn. China (Jiangsu br.), Acad. Arts and Crafts China, Eastern Am. Qigong U.S. (chmn. 1991—). Home: 32-05 146th St Flushing NY 11354-3151

SHEN, VIRGINIA SHIANG-LAN, Spanish and Chinese language educator; b. Kaohsiung, Taiwan, July 30, 1955; arrived in U.S., 1983; d. Mu-hsing and Ah-hsin (Huang) Li; m. Eric Yao-chu Shen, May 15, 1983; children: Andrew David, Alan Michael. BA in Spanish, Fu-Jen Cath. U., 1977; MA in Latin Am. Lit., Inst. Caro y Cuervo, 1983; PhD in Spanish, Ariz. State U., 1988. Instr. Wen Tzao Jr. Coll., Kaohsiung, 1982-83; tchg. assoc. Ariz. State U., Tempe, Ariz., 1983-87; asst. prof. N.Mex. State U., Las Cruces, N.Mex., 1987-88, La. State U., Shreveport, La., 1988-91, Chgo. State U. Ill., 1991-94, assoc. prof. Ill., 1994-99, prof. Ill., 1999—. Author: Encyclopedia of World Literature in the Twentieth Century, 3rd. edit., 1999, El Teatro Español del siglo XX y su contexto, 1994, Critical Perspectives of the Works of Enrique Jaramillo-Levi, 1996, Literatura y cultura Narrativa Colombiana del siglo XX, 2000; contbr. articles to profl. jours. Mem. Am. Coun. on Tchg. of Fgn. Langs., Ill. Coun. Tchg. of Fgn. Langs. Office: Chgo State U 9501 S King Dr Chicago IL 60628-1598 Office Phone: 773-995-2058. Business E-Mail: vshen@csu.edu.

SHENASSA, CHERYL RENÉE, psychologist, mediator; b. Odessa, Tex., Jan. 11, 1957; 1 child, Samantha Adams. PhD Social Psychology, Union Inst. and U., Cin., Ohio, 2001. Pres. Conciliaré, LLC, Las Vegas, Nev., 2002—. Bd. mem. Mediators of So. Nev., Las Vegas, 2003. Mem.: ACR, AFCC, ABA, APA, U.S. Com. For Unicef. Independent. Home: P O Box 371064 Las Vegas NV 89137-1064 Office: Conciliaré LLC 7945 W Sahara Ave Ste 104 Las Vegas NV 89117 Office Phone: 702-821-0800. Home Fax: 702-869-5423; Office Fax: 702-869-5423. Personal E-mail: dr_shenassa@lvcoxmail.com. Business E-Mail: conciliare@lvcoxmail.com.

SHENK, LOIS ELAINE LANDIS, writer; b. Ephrata, Pa., May 30, 1944; BA in English, Eastern Mennonite Coll., 1966; MSc in Edn., Temple U., 1984. English mistress Githumu Secondary Sch., Thika, Kenya, 1966-68; English tchr. Kraybill's Jr. High, Mount Joy, Pa., 1976-77; freelance writer, 1978—; religious news corr. Gospel Herald, Scottdale, Pa., 1978-82. Observer, corr. The U.S. Senate, Washington, 1987-2001. Author: Out of Mighty Waters, 1982 (R.I.M. excellence award 1983), The Story of Ephrata Mennonite School, 1996; (one act play) A House for David in (anthology) Swords into Plowshares, 1983; (study guide for Christian edn.) Hebrews, 1988; contbr. poems, stories & features to jours.; editl. work Mennonite Ctrl. Com., Akron, Pa., 1977. Cmty. living advisor Friendship Cmty., Lititz, Pa., 1997-99; Sunday sch. tchr. Ephrata Mennonite Ch., 1997-99; tutor English as a Second Lang., 2004. Recipient Rep. Senatorial Medal of Freedom, many other honors and awards. Avocations: reading, cooking, music. Home and Office: 444 W Marion St Lancaster PA 17603 Personal E-mail: lshenk@verizon.net.

SHEON, AMY RUTH, biomedical researcher; b. Cleve., Sept. 15, 1960; d. Robert Phillip and Irma Shainberg Sheon; m. Marvin Krislov, Aug. 25, 1991; children: Zachary Jacob, Jesse Harris, Eve Rose. BA with honors, Cornell U., 1983; MPH, U. Mich., 1984; PhD in Health Policy and Mgmt., Johns Hopkins U., 1996. Rsch. cons. com. on population NRC, Washington, 1985; country monitor Demographic and Health Surveys Program, Columbia, Md., 1985-89; sr. prevention scientist, health specialist NIH, Rockville, Md., 1989-97; sr. study dir. Westat, Inc., Rockville, 1997-98; dir. for programs Ctr. for Clin. Investigation and Therapeutics U. Mich., 1999—2000, assoc. dir. life scis. values and soc. program Ann Arbor, 2000—04, assoc. dir. Ctr. Advancing Rsch. & Solutions Soc., 2004—. Contbr. articles to profl. jours. Office: U Mich Ctr Advancing Rsch & Solutions for Soc 330 Packard Ann Arbor MI 48104-2910 E-mail: asheon@umich.edu.

SHEPARD, BRANDI R., architecture educator; b. Balt., Feb. 22, 1974; d. James M. Ogle and Patricia A. Moog, Dennis M. Moog (Stepfather) and Sharon K. Ogle (Stepmother); m. Kurt C. Shepard, Apr. 11, 1997; children: Kaylyn Danielle, Natalie Paige. AA in Arch., Anne Arundel C.C., Arnold, Md., 1994; BS in Arch., Cath. U. of Am., Washington, 1996. Chief procurement officer Sun Control Sys., Bethesda, Md., 1996—98; project mgr. Direct Path Corp., Alexandria, Va., 1998—2001; coll. prof. Anne Arundel

C.C., Arnold, 2000—. Owner, prin. Shepard Home Studios, Pasadena, Md., 2001—. Mem.: AIA (assoc.), Am. Coun. for Constrn. Edn. (assoc.), Nat. Assn. for Woman in Constrn. (assoc.), Constrn. Specifications Inst. (assoc.). Office: Anne Arundel C C 101 College Pkwy Arnold MD 21012 Office Phone: 410-777-2120. Business E-Mail: brshepard@aacc.edu.

SHEPARD, CHRISTY J., special education educator; d. William E. and Shirley M. Shepard. BS in Spl. Edn., U. Houston, 1974, MS in Occupl. Edn., 1989. Salesperson/customer svc. Sears, Roebuck & Co., Houston, 1968—93; sec. Preston Exterminating Co., Houston, 1971—74; tchr. Aldine Ind. Sch. Dist., Houston, 1974—76; tchr. of students with visual impairments Cypress-Fairbanks Ind. Sch. Dist., Houston, 1976—. Facilitator Region IV Edn. Svc. Ctr., Houston, 1999—. Asst. sec./treas. Harris County MUD #23, Houston, 1989—. Mem.: Assn. of Tex. Profl. Educators, Assn. for Edn. and Rehab. of the Blind and Visually Impaired (treas. 2000—). Avocations: reading, travel, cross stitch. Office Phone: 281-897-6490.

SHEPARD, COLLEEN, elementary school educator; b. Chardon, Ohio, Mar. 28, 1966; d. Charles Irvin and Shirley Ann (Weinstein) Hewins; m. Clifford Stephan Shepard, June 31, 1989; 1 child, Christopher. BFA, Fla. Atlantic U., 1989. Art tchr. Logger's Run Mid. Sch., Boca Raton, Fla., 1989-91, Omni Mid. Sch., Boca Raton, Fla., 1991-94, J.C. Mitchell Elem. Sch., Boca Raton, Fla., 1994—, sponsor Art Club, sch. wide art show coord., 1996—. Site coord. Project Leap, West Palm Beach, 1996-98. Artist numerous shows. Nominee William Dwyer award, 1997. Mem. Nat Art Edn. Assn., Fla. Art Edn. Assn., FAU Potter's Guild (pres. 1989-91). Roman Catholic. Avocations: painting, sculpting, gardening, breeding birds, cooking. Office: Jc Mitchell Elementary School 2470 NW 5th Ave Boca Raton FL 33431-8205

SHEPARD, EMMA LUSTER, elementary school educator; b. Shreveport, La. d. Brady Luster and Jennie Virginia Collins; m. Eddie Shepard (div.); children: Warren Craig, Kevin, Gary Edwardo. BS, La. State U., Shreveport, 1985, MS, 1993; Edn. Specialist, La. State U., Shreveport. Intake officer, sec. Ark-Tex. Coun. of Govt., Texarkana, Tex., 1980—83; kindergarten tchr. Caddo Parish Sch. Bd., Shreveport, 1986—93, recovery tchr., 1993—98, master tchr., 1998—2004, reading content coach, 2004—. Counselor YWCA Family Violence Ctr., Shreveport, 1987—98; adv. bd. Shreveport Women's Commn., 1999—2003; mem. Shreveport Dem. Women, 1998—; bd. dirs. YWCA, Shreveport, 2000—02. Named Elem. Tchr. of the Yr., Caddo Assn. Educators, 1995. Mem.: NEA (bd. dirs. 2002—05), La. Assn. of Educators (bd. dirs. 1996—2005), Phi Delta Kappa (historian 2003—05, Joseph Garner award 2003). Democrat. Baptist. Avocations: reading, aerobics, running. Home: 10305 Loma Vista Dr Shreveport LA 71115

SHEPARD, JEAN HECK, retired publishing consultant; b. NYC, Feb. 2, 1930; d. Chester Reed and Anna S. (Charig) Heck; m. Lawrence Vaeth Hastings, Mar. 29, 1950 (div. 1953); 1 child, Lance Clifford Hastings; m. Daniel A. Shepard, July 26, 1954 (div. 1981); 1 child, Bradley Reed. BA, Barnard Coll., 1950; postgrad., Columbia U., 1952. Mem. sch. and libr. svc. Viking Press, N.Y.C., 1956-57; asst. dir. sch. and libr. promotion E.P. Dutton, N.Y.C., 1957-58; dir. advt. publicity and promotion Thomas Y. Crowell Co., N.Y.C., 1958-62; dir. advt. and promotion Charles Scribner's Sons, N.Y.C., 1962-67; cons. Stephen Greene Press, Brattleboro, Vt., 1970-73; mktg. mgr. A&W Publishers, N.Y.C., 1979-80, Franklin Watts Publ., N.Y.C., 1980-82; pub. 2 mags., divsn. advt. & promotion mgr. McGraw Hill Book Co., N.Y.C., 1983-85; cons. Monitor Publ. Co., N.Y.C., 1988-2000. Author: Simple Family Favorites, 1971, Herb and Spice Sampler, 1972, Cook With Wine!, 1973, Earth Watch: Notes on a Restless Planet, 1973, Harvest Home Steak Cookbook, 1974, Fresh Fruits and Vegetables, 1974, Yankee Magazine, 1972, Let Them be Sea Captains. Mem.: Authors Guild, Am. Libr. Assn., Women's Nat. Book Assn., Pub. Ad Club. Methodist. Avocations: reading, writing, travel, music, dance. Home: 73 Kingswood Dr Bethel CT 06801-1834 Office Fax: 203-798-2924. E-mail: shepardagcy@mindspring.com.

SHEPARD, JEAN M., city health department administrator; b. San Diego; BA in Sociology, San Diego U. Employee San Diego County, 1976—, adminstrv. dept. Auditor, Contr., 1978—85, asst. chief adminstrv. officer, 1985—89, various positions Dept. Social Services, 1989—95, asst. dir. health, 1995—98, COO health and human services agy., 1998; dir. County of San Diego Health and Human Services Agy. Office: Health and Human Services Agy 1700 Pacific Hwy Rm 207 San Diego CA 92101*

SHEPARD, KATHERINE, science educator, consultant; d. Johnnie B. (Stepfather) and Jessie Beatrice Wright; m. Franklin Delano McKinney, Apr. 10, 1971 (div. Oct. 1985). BA, Goshen Coll., Ind., 1964; MA, Atlanta U., Ga., 1971; post grad., Case Western Res. U., Cleve., 1971—, Kent State U., Ohio, Hiram Coll., Suffolk U., Boston, Miami U., Oxford, Ohio. Cert. scuba diver. Summer recruiter Goshen Coll., 1967; tchr. HS physical edn. Cleve. Mcpl. Sch. Dist., 1964—65, tchr. HS health, 1993—94, tchr. HS sci., 1964—95, cons. and mentor to entry level tchrs., 1997—. Grant com. mem. Cleve. Pub. Schs. and NSF, 1993; mem. tchr. adv. com. Cleve. Pub. Schs. and Sci. Mus., 1994; mem. sch. governance com. Cleve. Pub. Schs., 1996; founder and dir. George E. Mills Gallery of Excellence, 1994; faculty adv. student coun.; faculty adv. Youth Coun. on Human Rels.; faculty adv. extracurricular clubs. Photographer (talent, fashion shows and Hall of Fame). Vol. Exec. Bd. Alumni Goshen Coll., 1981—84; newsletter publ. Shakerwood Assn., Warrensville Heights, Ohio, 1972—75, 2000—03; trustee Lee Heights Cmty. Ch., Cleve., 1986—89. Named to Gradsnet Found. Hall of Fame, 2001; recipient Inspirational Tchr. award, BP Am., 1996, Lifetime Achievement award, Harvard - Lee Times, 1996; scholar, Martha Holden Jennings Found., 1974—75. Mem.: Com. Political Edn., Assn. Supervision and Curriculum Devel., Cleve. Tchrs. Union. Avocations: photography, gardening, travel, sports, puzzles.

SHEPARD, LAURA ANN, microbiologist, researcher; b. Ft. Worth, Tex., Dec. 30, 1962; d. Larry and Montie Hopkins; m. Brett David Shepard, May 2, 1998; m. Dale Alan Utt, Jr., May 27, 1984 (div. Apr. 12, 1996); children: Dale Alan Utt, III, Amanda Leigh Utt. Student, Coll. of William and Mary, 1984; BHS summa cum laude, U. Mo., 1986; PhD, U. Okla., Oklahoma City, 1999. Cert. med. technologist Am. Soc. for Clin. Pathology, 1986. Med. technologist Boone Hosp. Ctr., Columbia, Mo., 1986—89; adj. faculty Okla. Bapt. U., Shawnee, Okla., 1991—94; postdoctoral rsch. fellow U. Okla., Oklahoma City and Norman, Okla., 2000—03; rschr. Mayo Clinic, Rochester, Minn., 2004—. Contbr. articles to profl. jours. Grad. fellow, NSF, 1995—98. Mem.: Assn. for Rsch. in Vision and Ophthalmology, Am. Soc. for Microbiology, Am. Soc. for Clin. Pathology, Lambda Tau, Golden Key, Alpha Eta, Alpha Epsilon Lambda, Phi Kappa Phi. Home: 1710 11th Ave NE Rochester MN 55906

SHEPARD, SARAH, public relations company executive; b. N.Y.C., Apr. 24; BFA, C.W. Post Coll., L.I. U., Brookville, N.Y., 1992. Mng. dir. KCSA Pub. Rels. Worldwide, N.Y.C., 1993—. Mem. Nat. Investor Rels. Inst. (profl. devel. com. 1997—). Office: KCSA Pub Rels Worldwide 800 2nd Ave Fl Dave5 New York NY 10017-4709 E-mail: sshepard@kcsa.com.

SHEPARD, SUZANNE V., language educator; b. Montour Falls, N.Y., Mar. 4, 1958; d. William Henry III and A. Louisa (Stenberg) S.; m. Tredwell Burch Jr., May 29, 1982. BA in Music and Lit., Eisenhower Coll., Seneca Falls, N.Y., 1980; MA in English, Binghamton U., 1983, PhD in English, 1995. Tchg. asst. Binghamton U., N.Y., 1981-87, adj. prof., 1987; from adj. prof. to prof. Broome C.C., Binghamton, 1991—2003, prof., 2003—, dept. chair, 2005—. Author: The Patchwork Quilt: Ideas of Community in Nineteenth Century American Women's Fiction, 2001. Elder Presbyn. Ch., Binghamton, 1988—, lay preacher, 1993—; mem. Multicultural Reading Group, Binghamton, 1995—. Mem. MLA, Nat. Coun. Tchrs. English, Phi Kappa Phi. Presbyterian. Business E-Mail: shepard_s@sunybroome.edu.

SHEPHERD, CYBILL LYNNE, actress, singer; b. Memphis, Feb. 18, 1950; d. William Jennings and Patty Shobe (Micci) S.; m. David Ford, Nov. 19, 1978 (div., 1982); 1 child, Clementine; m. Bruce Oppenheim, March 1, 1987 (div., 1990); children: Molly Ariel and Cyrus Zachariah (twins) Student, Hunter Coll., 1969, Coll. of New Rochelle, 1970, Washington Sq. Coll., NYU, 1971, U. So. Calif., 1972, NYU, 1973. Appeared in motion pictures Last Picture Show, 1971, The Heartbreak Kid, 1973, Daisy Miller, 1974, At Long Last Love, 1975, Taxi Driver, 1976, Special Delivery, 1976, Silver Bears, 1977, The Lady Vanishes, 1978, Earthright, 1980, The Return, 1986, Chances Are, 1988, Texasville, 1990, Alice, 1990, Once Upon a Crime, 1992, Married to It, 1993; star TV series The Yellow Rose, 1983-84, Moonlighting, 1985-89, Cybill, 1994-98 (also prodr.); TV films include A Guide for the Married Woman, 1978, Secrets of a Married Man, 1984, Seduced, 1985, The Long Hot Summer, 1985, Which Way Home, 1991, Memphis, 1992 (also co-writer, co-exec. prodr.), Stormy Weathers, 1992, Telling Secrets, 1993, There Was a Little Boy, 1993, Journey of the Heart, 1997, Due East, 2002, Martha, Inc.: The Story of Martha Stewart, 2003, Martha Behind Bars, 2005; record albums include Cybill Does It To Cole Porter, 1974, Cybill and Stan Getz, 1977, Vanilla with Phineas Newborn, Jr, 1978; appeared in stage plays A Shot in the Dark, 1977, Picnic, 1980, Vanities, 1981, The Muse, 1999, Marine Life, 2000; co-author Cybill Disobedience, 2000.

SHEPHERD, DEBORAH GULICK, elementary school educator; b. Edenton, N.C., Oct. 21, 1953; d. Lyman Mark and Rena (Bakker) Gulick; m. Ronald W. Shepherd. AA, Centenary Coll., Hackettstown, N.J., 1974; BA, Oral Roberts U., 1976; MA, Fairleigh Dickinson U., 1981. Cert. elem. and mid. sch. tchr., K-12 supr. N.J. Tchr. Mt. Olive Twp. Bd. Edn., Budd Lake, NJ, 1976—. Editor: (newsletter) Mountain View News, 1986—97, Light from the Steeple, 1998—. Mem. Chancel Choir, United Presbyn. Ch., Flanders, NJ, 1988—92; mem. sr. choir First Presbyn. Ch., Hackettstown, NJ, 1993—, Sunday sch. treas., 1996—2000; bd. dirs. Heaven Sent Nursery Sch., 1997—99. Recipient Gov.'s Tchr. Recognition award, State of N.J., 1991. Mem.: Edn. Assn. Mt. Olive (rep. 1987—93). Avocations: cross-stitching, sewing, knitting, reading, singing. Home: 663 Rockport Rd Hackettstown NJ 07840-5222 Office: CMS Elem Sch 99 Sunset Dr Budd Lake NJ 07828

SHEPHERD, DONNA LOU, interior designer; b. Uvalde, Tex., Sept. 25, 1948; d. Herbert Quarrels Jr. and Wanna Lou (Ray) Haile; m. Richard Ray Shepherd, June 2003; children from previous marriage: Laura Anne Howell, Christopher J. Huffman. BS, U. Houston, 1969, MEd, 1973. Owner Rainbow Design LLC, Greenwood Village, Colo., 1975—. Ptnr. Health By Design; spkr. in field. Designer Parade of Homes, 1989, Jr. Symphony Guild Showhome, 1996, designs featured in Colo. Homes and Lifestyles, Denver Post. Founder, pres. Prime Time Today, Littleton. Republican. Baptist. Avocations: water fitness, fly fishing, white-water rafting. Office: PO Box 3285 Littleton CO 80161-3285

SHEPHERD, JEAN MARIE, English educator; b. Des Moines, Aug. 8, 1950; d. Walter William and Lois Jean (DeBoest) Heimberger; m. Kenneth Brian Shepherd, Aug. 14, 1972; children: Jason B., Abbey M., Betsy K. BFA in Theatre Arts Edn., Drake U., 1972. Cert. tchr., Iowa. Lang. arts tchr. Dexfield H.S., Redfield, Iowa, 1972-76, Dallas-Center Grimes H.S., Dallas Center, Iowa, 1987—. Choir dir. 1st Presbyn. Ch., Dallas Ctr., 1991—. Named Iowa Tchr. of Yr., Masons, 2005. Mem. Beta Sigma Phi (com. mem., pres., 1997—, named Girl of Yr. 1978, 82). Presbyterian. Office: Grimes HS PO Box 512 Dallas Center IA 50063-0512

SHEPHERD, KAREN, retired congresswoman; b. Silver City, N.Mex., July 5, 1940; m. Vincent P. Shepherd. BA, U. Utah, 1962; MA, Brigham Young U., 1963. Former instr. Brigham Young U., Am. U., Cairo; former pres. Webster Pub. Co.; former adminstr. David Eccles Sch. Bus., U. Utah; former dir. Salt Lake County Social Svcs., Utah; former dir. continuing edn. Westminster Coll.; former mem. Utah Senate; mem. 103d Congress from 2d Utah dist., Washington, 1993—94; exec. dir., U.S. rep. European Bank for Reconstruction Devel., London, 1996—2002; mem. exec. com., chair East West Trade and Investment Forum Am. C. of C., England, 1998—2002; dir. EMILY's List, 2002. Mem. nat. governing bd. Common Cause, Washington, 1995-96, Internat. Delegation to Monitor Elections in West Bank and Gaza, Israel, Nat. Planned Parenthood Action Fund, 2004—; founder Karen Shepherd Fund; founding mem. Utah Women's Polit. Caucus, Project 2000; mem. trustee KeyBank Victory Funds; bd. dirs. UBS Bank, USA., O.C. Tanner. Former mem. United Way, Pvt. Industry Coun.; former mem. adv. bd. U.S. West Grad. Sch. Social Work; trustee Westminster Coll.; bd. dirs. Utah Red Cross, 2003—; chair Grad. Sch. Social Work, U. Utah, 2002—. Recipient Women in Bus. award U.S. Small Bus. Assn., Woman of Achievement award, Pathfinder award, YWCA Leadership award, 1st place award Nat. Assn. Journalists, Disting. Alumni award U. Utah Coll. Humanities, Eleanor Roosevelt award Utah Dem. Party, 2002, Merit of Honor award U. Utah, 2004. Fellow Inst. Politics Kennedy Sch. Govt., Internat. Women's Forum, Salt Lake Area C. of C. (pub. rels. com.)., Coun. on Fgn. Rels. Home: PO Box 1049 Salt Lake City UT 84110-1049

SHEPPARD, GAYLE TERESA, software executive; m. Michael T. Sheppard. Grad., U. South Fla., Tampa. V.p., sales and mktg. J.D. Edwards Asia Pacific Ltd.; pres. J.D. Edwards Japan KK; v.p., worldwide sales J.D. Edwards and Co.; pres., CEO Ketera Technologies; v.p., mng. dir., Western USA PeopleSoft, v.p., BPO Strategy. Bd. dir. NetCustomer, Inc., 2005—, Saffron Tech., NC, 2006—; mem. adv. bd. KeyMedia, Inc.; industry fellow Kenan Inst. of Private Enterprise, U. NC Kenan Flagler Bus. Sch.*

SHEPPARD, JENNIFER MODLIN, genealogist; d. Herbert Raleigh Sheppard and Cleo Virginia Price. Grad. H.S., Newport News, Va. Cert. genealogy, profl. option Brigham Young U., Provo, Utah, 1996. Property record clk. (GS-5) Naval Air Systems Command, Naval Plant Rep. Office, Burbank, Calif., 1973—75, indsl. property clearance specialist, 1975—76, indsl. property clearance specialist, (GS-9), 1976—78, indsl. property clearance specialist, (GS-11), 1978—80, Strategic Systems Project Office, Naval Plant Rep. Office, Sunnyvale, Calif., 1980—81; indsl. property mgt specialist (GS-12) Naval Air Systems Command, Arlington, 1981—85; indsl. property mgt specialist Def. Logistics Agy. (GS-13), Alexandria, Va., 1985—88. Fed. women's program coord. (EEO) Naval Air Systems Command, Naval Plant Rep. Office, Burbank, Calif., 1974—80. Author: (books) Price Family (History Book award from NC Soc. Historians, Many); contbr. articles to newspapers and profl. publs. Recipient Hist. Article award, NC Soc. Historians, 1994, Family History Book award, 1995, Robert Bruce Cooke Family History Book award, 1997, Joe M. McLauren Newsletter award, 1997, D. T. Smithwick Newspaper & Mag. Article award, 1997, D. T. Smithwick Newpaper/Mag. Article award, 2004, D. T. Smithwick Newspaper/Mag. Article award, 2005, 2005, 2006, Robert Bruce Cooke Family History Book award, 1998, Willie Parker Peace History Book award, 1999, Paul Green Multimedia award, 2000. Mem.: Friends of Oll Martin County Courthouse (life; grant writer 2004—05), Lost Colony Ctr. for Sci. and Rsch. (bd. mem. 2006, sr. advisor, geneal. rsch. 2006), UDC, Manassas Va. #175 (life; treas. 1987—88), Martin County Geneal. Soc. (life; v.p. 1993—95, pres. 1995—97, newsletter editor 1995—97, exec. com. mem. 1997), UDC, Theodore Hassell Chpt. #437 (life; pres. 1996—2000, registrar 1997—2000), Martin County Hist. Soc. (life). Office Phone: 252-792-3440. Business E-Mail: shepjr@coastalnet.com.

SHEPPARD, LENORA GERTRUDE, mathematics professor; d. Lenora Bobic Sheppard. MS, Rutgers U., Camden, NJ, 1998. Adminstrv. asst. Mt. Laurel MUA, NJ, 1985—2000; asst. prof. Atlantic Cape C.C., Mays Landing, NJ, 2000—. Mem.: Am. Math. Assn. (assoc.). Republican. Office Phone: 609-343-4959.

SHER, ELIZABETH, artist, educator, filmmaker; d. Robert Edward and Pearl Wolpert; m. Philip Allen Schnayerson; children: Crystal Brown, Ben Schnayerson. At, Smith Coll., Northampton, Mass., 1960—62; BA, U. Calif., Berkeley, 1964, MA in Fine Arts, 1967. Prof. Calif. Coll. of Arts, Oakland and San Francisco, 1977—; dir. I.V. Studios, Berkeley, Calif., 1982—. Mem. Canyon Cinema, 1983—, Bay Area Video Co., 1982—, San Francisco Cinematheque, 1983—. Ind. Feature Project, 1986—; distributed and represented by Toomey-Tourell Fine Art, San Francisco, Chip Taylor Prodns., NH, CS Assoc., Mill Valley, Calif., Fanlight Media, Inc., Boston, Harris Comms., Eden Prairie, Minn., Facets Multimedia, Chgo., Canyon Cinema, San Francisco, Microcinema. Books, India and Back, 2000, The Book of Ruth, 2002, illustrations, A Child's Library of Dreams, 1978, cover art, The Knot, by Alice Jones, 1992, I.V. Magazine vols. 1-3, 1984—86, exhibitions include San Francisco Arts Festival Exhbn., 1980 (spl. jury award, 1980), 7th Nev. Annual Exhbn., 1980 (purchase award, 1980); prodr.: (films) The Training, 1979, Wash It, 1980, Beat It, 1980, Juggling, 1981, Just Another Weekend, 1989, Celluloid Seduction, 1991, Fight the Bull, 1992 (first prize East Bay Media Festival, 1992), Chimera House, 1996, Younger, Thinner, Smoother, 2000, Lia Cook: Presence/Absence, 2000; (documentaries) The Library Series (4 programs), 1984—94 (first place Intercom Film Festival, Chgo., 1995, Chris award Performing Arts East Bay Media Fest, 1995, first place Instrnl. Super Fest, 1995, hon. mention Instrnl.Super Fest., 1995), Approaching the 14th Moon, 1993 (documentary award Calif. Works State Exposition and Fair, 1993, merit award N.C. Film Festival, 1993, silver apple award Nat. Film/Video Festival, 1994, nat. jury finalist USA Film Festival, Dallas, 1995), Three Women Artists at Mid-Career, 1994, Fingers That Tickle and Delight, 1994, The Master-Mentor Series, 3 parts, 1995, Homenaje a Tenochtitlan, 1996, When Women Go Through Menopause, Where Do Men Go?, 1996 (gold award Worldfest Charleston, 1996, documentary award Windy City Documentary Festival, 1997), Men are from Moon, 1998 (trophy award Internat. Mus. Photograpy George Eastman House, 1998, competition finalist Ariz. Film Festival, 1998), The Rejuvenation of Big Daddy's, 2002, (with Mal and Sandra Sharpe) Alma's Jazzy Marriage, 2004, (with Maggie Simpson) Stalls, 2004; Represented in permanent collections USIA, Washington, Achenbach Found. Graphic Arts Fine Arts Mus., San Francisco, Hunt Inst. Botanical Documentation Carnegie-Mellon U., Pitts., Oakland Mus., Calif., DeAnza Coll., Sierra Nev. Mus. Art, Hechinger Collection, Washington, Gertier Collection, L.A., Austin Mus. Art, Tex., Smith Coll. Mus. Art. Bd. mem. PAAC Alameda County Arts Commn., 2004—. Recipient Most Humorous Video, Hollywood Erotic Film and Video Festival, 1984, Exptl. Video award, Tucson Women's Cable Consortium Festival, 1986; grantee, Union Ind. Colls. Art, 1983, Jewish Cmty. Ctrs. Bay Area, 1986, Calif. Coll. Arts and Crafts, 1990, 1993, Pioneer Fund, 1993, The Harris Found., 1996, Anheuser-Busch Found., 1996, Trillium Summer Inst., Calif. Coll. Arts, 2002; We. Regional Media Arts fellow, Nat. Endowment Arts, Am. Film Inst. and Calif. Arts Coun., 1984. Mem.: New Am. Makers, Ind. Documentary Assn., Film Arts Found. Studio: IV Studios 985 Regal Rd Berkeley CA 94708-1427 Office Phone: 510-528-8004. Office Fax: 510-527-1031. Business E-Mail: liziv@ivstudios.com.

SHER, SUSAN, lawyer; b. 1948; children: Graham, Evan. BA, George Wash. U.; JD, Loyola U. Bar: Ill. 1974. With Mayer, Brown & Platt; former dir. labor and litigation U. Chgo.; asst. corp. counsel City of Chgo., 1989—93, corp. counsel, 1993—97; v.p., gen. counsel U. Chgo. Hosps., 1997—, v.p. legal and govt. affairs, 2001—. Mem. steering com. Ill. Hosp. Assn., 2004; spkr. in field. Office: Univ Chgo Hosps 5841 S Maryland Ave MC 1114 Chicago IL 60637 Office Phone: 773-702-1000.

SHERBELL-NA, RHODA, artist, sculptor; b. Bklyn. d. Alexander and Syd (Steinberg) S.; m. Mervin Honig, Apr. 28, 1956 (dec.); 1 child, Susan Honig. Student, Art Students League, 1950—53, Bklyn. Mus. Art Sch., 1959—61; pvt. study art, Italy, France, Eng., 1956. Cons., coun. mem. Emily Lowe Gallery, Hofstra U., Hempstead, N.Y., 1978, pres., 1989-81, instr., 1991—, life mem. bd. friends, pres. bd. trustees; tchr. instr. Mus. Modern Art, N.Y.C., 1959, NAD Art Sch., N.Y.C., 1985—, Art Students League, N.Y.C., 1980—; Nat. Portrait Gallery Mus. rep. to 150th anniversary Smithsonian Instn., Washington, 1996lectr. Nat. Arts Club, N.Y.C. One-woman shows include Huntington Township Art League, Embassy of U.S., Prague, 2002-03, Country Art Gallery, Locust Valley, N.Y., Bklyn. Mus. Art Sch., 1961, Adelphi Coll., A.C.A. Galleries, N.Y.C., 1960, Capricorn Galleries, Rehn Gallery, Washington, 1968, Huntington Hartford Mus., N.Y.C., 1969, N.Y. Cultural Ctr., 1970, Smithsonian Am. Art Mus., Smithsonian Instn., Washington (formerly Nat. Arts Collection), 1970, Montclair Mus. of Art, 1976, Nat. Art Mus. Sport, 1977, Jewish Mus. N.Y.C., 1980, Morris (N.J.) Mus. Arts and Scis., 1980, Black History Mus., 1981, Queens Mus., 1981-82, Nat. Portrait Gallery, Smithsonian Inst., Washington, 1981-82, Bergen Mus. Arts and Scis., N.J., 1984, William Benton Mus., Conn., 1985, Palace Theatre of the Arts, Stamford, Conn., Bronx Mus. Arts, 1986, Hofstra Mus. Art, L.I., N.Y., 1989-90, 97-98, County Art Gallery, N.Y.C., 1990, Heckscher Mus., L.I., 2000, Bronx Mus., N.Y., Bklyn. Mus., Mus. Modern Art, N.Y.C., Country Art Gallery, 1990, Port Washington Libr., Nat. Mus. Am. Art, Smithsonian Instn., 1982, NAD, N.Y.C., 1984, 89, Castle Gallery Mus., N.Y.C., 1987, Emily Lowe Mus., N.Y.C., 1987, Heckshire Mus., N.Y.C., 1989, Islip Art Mus., N.Y.C., 1989, Gallery Emanuel, N.Y.C., 1993, Sundance Gallery, Bridgehampton, N.Y., 1995, Artist Equity Exhbn., SoHo, 1995, NAD Exhbn., 1995, Main St. Petile Gallery, 2003, Huntington Arts Coun., 2003, 04, Huntington Twp. Art League, 2002-03, The Art Students League Instructors Exhbn., Salandes O'Reilly Gallery, N.Y.C., 2003; 2 person exhbn. Works on Paper, Hofstra Mus., Hofstra U., 1997-98, pastel exhbn., 2006; exhibited in numerous group shows including Portrait in bronze of Senator Norman J. Levy for Merrick Train Station, 2000, Aaron Copland's America, Heckscher Mus. Art, 2000, Nat. Art Mus., 2002-, Huntington Arts Coun. Inc., 2003, Petite Gallery, Baseball Hall of Fame & Mus., Cooperstown, N.Y., 2004, Queens Mus., N.Y., 2004, Allied Arts of Am., 2003-04 (New Foundry award, 2004), Nat. TiesClub Show, 2004, Nat. Burlington Soc. Art Exhibn., 2004, Salamander OReily Gallery, N.Y., The Art Students League, 2004, Nat. Acad. Design Exhibitors, 2005, Nat. Portrait Gallery, 2005, 06; represented permanent collections, Stony Brook Hall of Fame, William Benton Mus. Art, Colby Coll. Mus., Oklahoma City Mus., Montclair (N.J.) Mus., Schonberg Libr. Black Studies, N.Y.C., Albany State Mus., Hofstra U., Bklyn. Mus., Colby Coll. Mus., Nat. Arts Collection, Nat. Portrait Gallery, Smithsonian Instn., Baseball Hall of Fame Cooperstown, N.Y., Nassau C.C., Hofstra U. Emily Lowe Gallery, Art Students League, Jewish Mus., "The Subway Series: The New York Mets Our National Pastime," Queens Mus., Black History Mus., Nassau County Mus., Stamford Mus. Art and Nature Ctr., Jericho Pub. Libr., N.Y., African-Am. Mus., Hempstead, N.Y., Stamford (Conn.) Mus. Art and Scis., (Monument Work) The Am. Baseball Family Story, The Sea Dogs, MTA, Pub. Monument for Senator Norman J. Levy Merrik R.R. Sta., N.Y., Yogi Berra Portrait, Nat. Gallery Smithsonian Inst., Mose Soyer painting, Smithsonian Am. Art Mus., Raphare Soyer Portrait, Dept. State, The Embassy Program, Prague, Czech Republic, 2002-04, Nat. Acad., 2005-06, Nat. Art Club, 2005-06, Nat. Portrait Gallery, 2006; also pvt. collections, TV shows, ABC, 1968, 81; edni. TV spl. Rhoda Sherbell-Woman in Bronze, 1977; works include Seated Ballerina, portraits of Aaron Copland (Bruce Stevenson Meml. Best Portrait award Nat. Arts Club 1989), Eleanor Roosevelt, Variations on a Theme (36 works of collaged sculpture), 1982-86; appeared several TV shows; guest various radio programs; contbr. articles to newspapers, popular mags. and art jours.; mem. Conservation Art Group Coun. City of N.Y., 1994-97; exhbns. include: Petite Gallery, Huntington, N.Y., 2003, The Nat. Acad. Mus., 2003-04, Disegno Exhbn., NAD, 2005—, Nat. Sculpture Soc., 2005—, Nat. Art Club, 2005—, Brookgreen Gardens, 2005-06, Nat. Portrait Gallery, Smithsonian Inst., 2006. Trustee Nat. Art Mus. of Sport, 1959-; coun. mem. Nassau County Mus., 1978, trustee, 1st v.p. coun.; cons., cmty. liaison WNET Channel 13, cultural coord., 1975-83; host radio show Not for Artists Only, 1978-79; commr. Women's Boxing Fedn., 1978; mem. The Art Commn. The City of NY, 1993; chmn. bd. Hofstra Mus., 1978-89. Recipient Gold medal Allied Artists Am., 1989, Alfred G. B. Steel Meml. award Pa. Acad. Fine Arts, 1963-64; Jersey City Mus. prize for sculpture, 1961, 1st prize sculpture Locust Valley Art Show, 1966, 67, Ann. Sculpture prize Jersey City Mus., Bank for Savs. 1st prize in sculpture, 1950, Ford Found. purchase award, 1964, 2 top sculpture awards Mainstreams 77, Cert. of Merit Salmagundi Club, 1978, prize for sculpture, 1980, 81, award for sculpture Knickerbocker Artists, 1980, 81, top prize for sculpture Hudson Valley Art Assn., 1981, Sawyer award NAD, 1985, Gold medal of honor Audubon Artists, 1985, Silvermine Exhbn. award, Gold medal Allied Artists Am., 1990, medal of honor for Bronze Queen Catherine, Nat. Arts Club, 2004, Pres.' award Nat Arts Club N.Y.C.; MacDowell Colony fellow, 1976, AAAL and Nat. Arts and Letters grantee, 1960, Louis Comfort Tiffany Found. grantee, 1962, Ford Found. grantee, 1964, 67, also award, New Foundry award, Allied Artists Am., 2004; named one of top 5 finalist to do Monument of Queen Catherine of England, 1991; named to represent Nat. Portrait Gallery at Smithsonian Mus., 1996, sculpture selected to represent Nat. Portrait Gallery Mus., 1997; guest at Dept. of State Embassy Program, Prague, Czech Republic, 2003-04; Queen Catherine Bronze, Hofstra Mus. Sculpture Gardens, 2005. Fellow Nat. Sculpture Soc.; mem. NAD (Helen F. Barnett prize 1965, Leila Gordon Sawyer prize 1989, The Dessle Green prize 1993, Charlotte Deenevidde award 2003, award for Am. baseball founding group, 2003, award 2003), Sculpture Guild (dir.), Nat. Assn. Women Artists (Jeffery Childs Willis Meml. prize 1978), Allied Artists Soc. (dir., Gold medal 1990, The Pietro and Alfrieda Montana Meml. award 2000, award 2001), Audubon Artists (dir., Greta Kempton Walker prize 1965, Chaim Gross award, award for disting. contbr. to orgn. 1979, 80, Louis Weskeem award), Woman's Caucus for Art, Coll. Art Assn., Am. Inst. Conservation Hist. and Artistic Works, N.Y. Soc. Women Artists, Artists Equity Assn. N.Y., Nat. Sculpture Soc. (E.N. Richard Meml. prize 1989), Internat. Platform Assn., Profl. Artists Guild L.I., Painters and Sculptors Soc. N.J. (Bertrum R. Hulmes Meml. award), Am. Watercolor Soc. (award for disting. contbn. to orgn.), Catharine Lorillard Wolfe Club (hon. mention 1968), Nat. Arts Club (N.Y.C., Stevenson Meml. award 1989, Pres. award 1992, Robert Sayford award 2000, Bruce Stevenson Meml. award for Portrait 2000, Siegfort award 2000, award for sculpture 2004, award 2005).

SHERBERT, SHARON DEBRA, financial services executive; b. Bklyn., Aug. 18, 1953; d. Joseph George and Leah (Katzman) Goldstein; m. Robert Fisher, Oct. 20, 1973 (div. Nov. 1981); 1 child, Meredith Audra Fisher; m. Michael Sherbert, Apr. 4, 1982; 1 child, Jared Alan. Grad. high sch., Bklyn. Cert. fin. planner; registered fin. cons. Real estate agent Century 21 R.E., Sepulveda, Calif., 1976-80; life ins. agt. Prudential Life Ins., North Hollywood, Calif., 1980-82; sr. v.p. Profl. Planning, Encino, Calif., 1982-90; exec. v.p. Comprehensive Fin. Svcs., Burbank, Calif., 1992—. Columnist on Internet Web site Women in Tech., Inc., Van Nuys, Calif., 1996—. Co-host: (TV show) You and Your Money, 1993—. Mem. NAFE, Nat. Assn. Women Bus. Owners, Internat. Assn. for Fin. Planners, Inst. Cert. Fin. Planners, Zonta Club of Santa Clarita Valley (sunshine sec. 1992-93). Office: Comprehensive Fin Svcs 3811 W Burbank Blvd Burbank CA 91505-2116

SHERBY, KATHLEEN REILLY, lawyer; b. St. Louis, Apr. 5, 1947; d. John Victor and Florian Sylvia (Frederick) Reilly; m. James Wilson Sherby, May 17, 1975; children: Michael R.R., William J.R., David J.R. AB magna cum laude, St. Louis U., 1969, JD magna cum laude, 1976. Bar: Mo. 1976. Assoc. Bryan Cave, St. Louis, 1976-85; ptnr. Bryan Cave LLP, St. Louis, 1985—. Contbr. articles to profl. jours. Bd. dirs Jr. League, St. Louis, 1989-90, St. Louis Forum, 1992-99, pres., 1995-97; chmn. Bequest and Gift Coun. of St. Louis U., 1997-99; jr. warden Ch. of St. Michael and St. George, 1998-2000; bd. dirs. Bistate chpt. ARC, 2000—, v.p. fin.; bd. trustees St. Louis Sci. Ctr., 2000—; officer Clayton Edn. Found., 2003—. Fellow Am. Coll. Trust and Estate Coun. (regent 1997-2004), Estate Planning Coun. of St. Louis (pres. 1986-87), Bar Assn. Met. St. Louis (chmn. probate sect. 1986-87), Mo. Bar Assn. (chmn. probate and trust com. 1996-98, chmn. probate law revision subcom. 1988-96); Phi Beta Kappa. Episcopalian. Home: 47 Crestwood Dr Saint Louis MO 63105-3032 Office: Bryan Cave LLP 1 Metropolitan Sq Ste 3600 Saint Louis MO 63102-2733 Office Phone: 314-259-2224. Business E-Mail: krsherby@bryancave.com.

SHERER, WANDA C., secondary school educator; d. Joseph Grady and Joyce Abston Campbell; m. John N. Sherer, Jr., Aug. 24, 1975; children: Tori, Kendra. BS, U. West Ala., Livingston, 1977, MEd, 1984. Cert. tchr. La. Tchr. Patrician Acad., Butler, Ala., 1976—81, So. Chectaw HS, Silas, Ala., 1981—92, Remington Coll., Lafayette, La., 1992—94, Acadiana HS, Lafayette, 1994—. Pres. First Bapt. Choir, 1995—96. Mem.: Delta Kappa Gamma (sec., 2d v.p.). Baptist. Office: Acadiana High Sch 315 Rue De Belier Lafayette LA 70506

SHERFINSKI, KRISTINA LEIGH, performing arts educator; b. North Augusta, Ga., Sept. 25, 1977; d. Samuel Grady and Jan Stafford Walling; m. Scott Paul Sherfinski, Apr. 3, 2004. BA in Mass Comm. and Theatre, Lander U., Greenwood, SC, 1999. Instr., dir Shakespeare camp Greenroom Theatre, Newton, NC, 2005—05; yearbook staff Tuttle Mid. Sch., 2004—; coach dance team Tuttle Dancers, 2003—; head drama club Tuttle Mid. Sch. Drama Club, 2003—; tchr. playworks Catawba County Schs., 2005—06. Dir.: (dinner theatre) Tuttle's 1st Annual Dinner Theatre/Go For The Gold/The Wizard of Oz, (red cross benefit for hurricane katrina) Listen To Your Heart, short play Going Home. Mem.: NCTAE. Liberal. Avocations: photography, videography, dance, travel, writing. Office Phone: 828-428-3080. Personal E-mail: ksherfinski@peoplepc.com.

SHERIDAN, DIANE FRANCES, public policy facilitator; b. Wilmington, Del., Mar. 12, 1945; d. Robert Kooch and Eileen Elizabeth (Forrest) Bupp; m. Mark MacDonald Sheridan III, Dec. 7, 1968; 1 child, Elizabeth Anne. BA in English, U. Del., 1967. Tchr. English Newark (Del.) Sch. Dist., 1967-68, Lumberton (Tex.) Ind. Sch. Dist., 1969-71, Crown Point (Ind.) Sch. Dist., 1972-75; sr. assoc. The Keystone (Colo.) Ctr., 1986-98; facilitator cmty. adv. panels to chem. plants and refineries Taylor Lake Village, Tex., 1986—. Facilitator cmty. adv. panels to chem. plants and refineries, Tex., Kans.; chair Keystone Siting Process Local Rev. Com.; mem. pub. adv. panel Chem. Mfrs. Assn. Responsible Care, 1989-97. 1st v.p. LWV, Washington, 1992-94, sec. treas. voters edn. fund, sec. treas. Nat. LWV, 1994-96, bd. dirs. 1996-98; pres. LWV of Tex., 1987-91, chair edn. fund, 1987-91, bd. dirs., 1983-87; pres. LWV of the Bay Area, 1981-83, bd. dirs., 2001—; mem. adv. com. Ctr. for Global Studies of Houston Advanced Rsch. Ctr. The Woodlands, Tex., 1991-97, Ctr. for Conflict Analysis and Mgmt., bd. advisors Environ. Inst.; mem. U. Houston-Clear Lake Devel. Adv. Coun., 1989-95; mem. Bay Area Cmty. Awareness and Emergency Response Local Emergency Planning Com., 1988-92; active Tex. House-Senate Select Com. on Urban Affairs Regional Flooding Task Force, 1979-80, Congressman Mike Andrews Environ. Task Force, 1983-85, Gov.'s Task Force on Hazardous Waste Mgmt., 1984-85; dir. local PTAs, 1981-91; coord. Tex. Roundtable on Hazardous Waste, 1982-87; sec., v.p. Tex. Environ. Coalition, 1983-85; co-chair Tex. Risk Commn. Project, 1986-89; mem. Leadership Tex., Class of 1988; mem. cmty. adv. bd. U. Tex. Med. Br. Ctr. Nat. Inst. Environ. Health Studies, 1998. Mem. LWV (nat. bd. dirs. 1992-98, trustee nat. edn. fund 1992-98), Assn. for Conflict Resolution, Internat. Assn. for Pub. Participation, Mortar Board, East Harris County Mfrs. Assn. (risk mgmt. comm. com. 1994-99, cmty. emergency comm. com., 2003—), Pi Sigma Alpha, Kappa Delta Pi. Office Phone: 281-326-5253. Personal E-mail: dbsheridan@aol.com.

SHERIDAN, EILEEN, librarian; b. N.Y.C., Jan. 11, 1949; d. Edward John and Florence Veronica (Glennon) S. BA in English, U. Bridgeport, Conn., 1972; MLS, So. Conn. State U., 1974. Children's libr. I, Bridgeport Pub. Libr., 1974-80, children's libr. II, 1980-82, coord. youth svcs., 1982—. Pres. Sch. Vol. Assn., Bridgeport, 1987-89; bd. dirs. Action for Bridgeport Cmty. Devel., 1989-90; pres. Conn. Zool. Soc., 1989-91, v.p., 1991-98, bd. dirs. 1989—. Recipient vol. award for contbn. to children Mt. Aery Bapt. Ch., 1988, Champion of Children award South End Cmty. Ctr., 1992. Mem. LWV, Am. Soc. of Zoos and Aquariums, Soc. of Chldns. Bookwriters and Illustrators. Avocations: writing, travel, reading. Home: 3300 Park Ave Unit 11 Bridgeport CT 06604-1100 Office: Bridgeport Pub Libr 925 Broad St Bridgeport CT 06604-4871

SHERIDAN, MARY STOEBE, social worker; b. Pasadena, Calif., Aug. 5, 1948; d. Jacob G. and Virginia Elizabeth (Gould) S.; m. Harold C. Sheridan, Aug. 23, 1969 (dec. Aug. 1997). BA, Northwestern U., 1969; MSW, U. Ill., Chgo., 1972; PhD, U. Hawaii, 1985. Caseworker Cook County Pub. Aid, Chgo., 1969-70; instr., asst. prof. social work U. Ill. Hosp., Chgo., 1972-77; social worker Hawaii Dept. Edn., Waipahu, 1978-80; social work edn. coordinator Kapiolani Med. Ctr. for Women and Children, Honolulu, 1980-82; home monitor coordinator Kapiolani Hosp. Med. Ctr. for Women & Children, Honolulu, 1982-88; instr. human services Hawaii Pacific Coll., Honolulu, 1987-91; instr., assoc. prof., prof., social work Hawaii Pacific U., Honolulu, 1995—; dir. social svcs. Pali Momi Med. Ctr., Aiea, Hawaii, 1989-93; rsch. coord. Straub Found., 1993-95. Adj. instr. Hawaii Pacific Coll., Honolulu, 1978-79; instr./lectr. U. Hawaii, Honolulu, 1982-85, adj. instr. Hawaii Pacific U., 1989-93. Author: (novel) To Michael with Love, 1977, Pain in America, 1992; editor: The NAAP Handbook of Infant Apnea and Home Monitoring, Vol. 1, 1992, Vol. 2, 1996;co-author: (with Lousia Lasher) Munchausher by Proxy: Identification, Evaluation, & Case Management; co-editor: (with Alex Levin) Munchausen Syndrome by Proxy, 1995; contbr. articles to profl. jours. Mem. Bd. Cath. Edn., 1999—2005, chair, 2005—06. Recipient Cert. Merit Council of Nephrology Social Workers, 1977, Continuing Edn. award March of Dimes, Honolulu, 1985, Tchr. of the Yr., Hawaii Pacific U., 2003. Mem. Nat. Assn. Social Workers (sec. Honolulu chpt. 1984-85, cert.), Nat. Assn. Apnea Profls. (pres., co-founder 1987-88, Hawaii bus. dir. 1989-99), Hawaii Soc. Social Work Adminstrs. in Health Care (sec. 1991-93, 95-97), Orgn. Women Leaders (Woman of the Yr.-pvt. sector 2003). Democrat. Roman Catholic. Office: Hawaii Pacific U 1188 Fort St Mall Honolulu HI 96813-2713 Office Phone: 808-566-2489.

SHERIDAN, NICOLETTE, actress; b. Worthing, Sussex, Eng., Nov. 21, 1963; d. Sally Sheridan; m. Harry Hamlin, Sept. 7, 1991 (div. 1993). Actor: (films) The Sure Thing, 1985, Noises Off, 1992, Spy Hard, 1996, Beverly Hills Ninja, 1997, .com for Murder, 2002, Lost Treasure, 2003; (TV series) Knots Landing, 1986—93 (Soap Opera Digest award, 1990, 1991), Paper Dolls, 1984, Desperate Housewives, 2004— (co-recipient, Outstanding Performance by an Ensemble in a Comedy Series, Screen Actors Guild award, 2005, 2006); (TV films) Dead Man's Folly, 1986, Deceptions, 1990, Somebody's Daughter, 1992, A Time to Heal, 1994, Indictment: The McMartin Trial, 1995, Silver Strand, 1995, The People Next Door, 1996, Murder in My Mind, 1997, Dead Husbands, 1998, The Spiral Staircase, 2000, Haven't We Met Before?, 2002, Deadly Betrayal, 2003, Deadly Visions, 2004; (TV miniseries) Lucky/Chances, 1990, Knots Landing: Back to the Cul-de-Sac, 1997; TV appearances include Paradise, 1991, Will & Grace, 2003, Becker, 2003. Office: Desperate Housewives Touchtone Television 100 Universal City Plaza Bldg 212B Ste G Universal City CA 91608

SHERIDAN, SONIA LANDY, artist, retired art educator; b. Newark, Ohio, Apr. 10, 1925; d. Avrom Mendel and Goldie Cornelia (Hanon) Landy; m. James Edward Sheridan, Sept. 27, 1947; 1 child, Jamy. AB, Hunter Coll., 1945; postgrad., Columbia U., 1946-48; MFA with high honors, Calif. Coll. Arts and Crafts, 1961. Tchr. art public high schs., Calif., 1951-57; chmn. dept. art Taipei (Taiwan) Am. Sch., 1957-59; instr. Calif. Coll. Arts and Crafts, 1960-61; asst. prof. art Sch. Art Inst. Chgo., 1961-67, assoc. prof., 1968-75, prof., 1976-80, prof. emeritus, 1980—, founder, head generative sys. program, 1970-80. Artist-in-residence 3M Corp., 1970, 76, Xerox Corp., 1981; cons. French Ministry of Culture, 1986; lectr. univs., mus., art schs., workshops, Hungarian Acad. Scis. Symposium Collected Essays & Exhbn., Budapest, 1989, Internat. Soc. Electronic Arts, Liverpool, England; presenter in field. One-woman shows include Rosenberg Gallery, Chgo., 1966, Visual Studies Workshop, Rochester, N.Y., 1973, Iowa Mus. Art, Iowa City, 1976, Mus. Sci. Industry, Chgo., 1978, exhibited in group shows at Print Ann., Boston Mus., 1963, Software, Jewish Mus., N.Y.C., 1969—70, Photography into Art, London, 1972—73, Photokino, Cologne, Germany, 1974, Mus. Modern Art, N.Y.C., 1974, San Francisco Mus. Modern Art, 1975, 2006, U. Mich. Mus. Art, 1978, Toledo Mus. Art, 1982—83, Mus. Modern Art, Paris, 1983, Siggraph, 1982, 1983, Reina Sofia Mus., Madrid, 1986, Smithsonian Instn., 1990, Tokyo Met. Mus. Photography, 1991, Madrid City Cultural Ctr., 1992, Karl Ernst Osthaus Mus., Hagen, Germany, 1992, Circulo des Belles Artes, Madrid, 1992, Yale U. Art Gallery, 1995, Tokyo Intercom. Ctr., 1995, U. Montreal, 1995, Internat. Soc. Electronic Arts, Liverpool, 1996, Hungarian Art Mus., 1996, Scirpton Mus., The Netherlands, 1997, Video Gallery, Hungary, 2000—02, Mus. Kommunikation, Frankfurt, Germany, 2001, 2d Biennial Museo Nacional de Belles Artes, Buenos Aires, 2002, Represented in permanent collections Hood Mus. Art, Dartmouth, Langlois Found., Montreal, Art Inst. Chgo., San Francisco Mus. Art, Mus. Sci. and Industry, Chgo., U. Iowa Mus. Art, Nat. Gallery Art, Ottawa, Can., Visual Studios Workshop, Rochester, Tokyo Met. Mus. Photography, Fundacion Arte y Technologia, Madrid, Tweed Mus., U. Minn., Scrypton Mus., Tilburg, The Netherlands; author: Energized Artscience: Sonia Landy Sheridan, 1978; co-editor: Leonardo jour.; hon. editor:, 2000; contbr. articles, essays to profl. jours. Recipient citation, Nat. Assn. Schs. Art and Design, 2006; Guggenheim fellow, 1973, Workshop grantee, Nat. Endowment Arts, 1974, Pub. Media grantee, 1976, Artist grantee, 1981, Union Ind. Colls. Art grantee, 1975. Mem.: Internat. Soc. Electronic Arts, Internat. Soc. Interdisciplinary Study Symmetry, Coll. Art Assn. Personal E-mail: sonia.sheridan@valley.net.

SHERIDAN, VIRGINIA, public relations executive; Pres. M. Silver Associates, Inc., N.Y.C. Office: M Silver Associates Inc 747 3rd Ave New York NY 10017-2803

SHERIDAN LABARGE, JOAN RUTH, publishing executive; b. Forest Hills, NY, July 3, 1956; d. Thomas Patrick and Ruth B. (Stalzer) S.; 1 daughter. BS magna cum laude in Communication Arts, St. John's U., Jamaica, N.Y., 1978. Media planner BBDO, NYC, 1978-81; media supr. Ted Bates & Co., NYC, 1982-84; v.p., assoc. media dir. FCB Leber Katz Ptnrs., NYC, 1985-87; v.p., assoc. pub., Woman's Day Hachette Filipacchi Mags., NYC, 1987—95, v.p., pub. Family Life Mag., 1995—99; exec. v.p., group pub. dir. Weider Pub., 1999—2000; corp. pub., new bus. devel. G + J USA Publishing, 2001—, pub. Rosie, 2001—02, pub. YM Mag., 2003—04; pres. & pub. Working Mother mag., 2005—. Named Top Media Sales Rep, Mediaweek, 1992. Office: Working Mother 60 East 42nd St New York NY 10165 Office Phone: 212-351-6400. Office Fax: 212-351-6487. E-mail: joan.sheridan@workingmother.com.

SHERIN, ROBIN, artist; b. Bklyn., May 22, 1955; d. Leonard and Shirley (Smookler) S. BS, NYU, 1976. One-woman shows include Washington Place Artists' Gallery, NYC, 1981; group exhbns. include SUNY, Potsdam, 1982, U. ND, Grand Forks, 1982, Atlantic Gallery, NYC, 1983, Clemson (SC) U., 1983, 85, Emerging Collector, NYC, 1986, U. Mo., Columbia, 1986, 50 West Gallery, NYC, 1986, Somerstown Gallery, Somers, NY, 1990, Eleven East Ashland Gallery, Phoenix, 1990, Chattahoochie Valley Art Assn., La Grange, Ga., 1990, Fine Arts Inst., San Bernadino Cty. Mus., Redlands, Calif., 1991, West Nebr. Arts Ctr., Scottsbluff, 1991, Hill Country Arts Found., Ingram, Tex., 1991, Galesburg (Ill.) Civic Art Ctr., 1991, Boston Printmakers, Decordova Mus., Lincoln, Mass., 1991, d'Art Ctr., Norfolk, Va., 1992, Haggin Mus., Stockton, Calif., 1992, Mus. Without Walls, Bemus Point, NY, 1992, Trenton State Coll., 1992, Acad. Arts, Easton, Md., 1992, Pleiades Gallery, NYC, 1992, Amos Eno Gallery, NYC, 1992, Art Assn. Harrisburg, Pa., 1992, Cmty. Coun. for Arts, Kinston, NC, 1993, Warren St. Gallery, Hudson, NY, 1993, Allentown (Pa.) Mus., 1994, Main Line Art Ctr., Haverford, Pa., 1994, Harper Coll., Palatine, Ill., 1994, Chattahoochee Valley Art Mus., LaGrange, Ga., 1994, Womens Caucus for Art, Owen Patrick Gallery, Phila., 1994, Hill Country Arts Found., Ingram, Tex., 1994, Fine Arts Inst., San Bernardino County Mus., Redlands, Calif., 1994, Erector Square Gallery, New Haven, 1994, Chautauquea (NY) Galleries, 1995, Ottawa Gallery, Sylvania, Ohio, 1995, Wenatchee (Wash.) Valley Coll., 1995, Art Assn. Harrisburg, Pa., 1995, Women's Found. Genesee Valley, Shoestring Gallery, Rochester, NY, 1995, Galesburg (Ill.) Civic Art Ctr., 1995, Austin Peay State U., Trahern Gallery, Clarksville, Tenn., 1995, Carnegie Art Ctr., North Tonawanda, NY, 1996, 1708 Gallery, Richmond, Va., 1996, Mable Cultural Ctr., Mableton, Ga., 1996, Cooperstown (NY) Art Assn., 1996, Artlink, Fort Wayne, Ind., 1996, Pa. State U., University Park, 1996, Nat. Art League, Douglaston, NY, 1996, QCC Art Gallery, Queensborough C.C., CUNY, Bayside, NY, 1996, Cedar City Art Com., Braithwaite Fine Arts Gallery, So. Utah U., Cedar City, 1996, Artist Coun., Palm Springs (Calif.) Desert Mus., 1996, Muscarelle Mus. Art, Coll. William & Mary, Williamsburg, Va., 1996, Del Mar Coll., Corpus Christi, Tex., 1996, Nightingale Gallery, Eastern Oreg. State Coll., La Grande, 1996, Carrie Haddad Gallery, Hudson, NY, 1997, University Gallery, St. John's U., Jamaica, NY, 1997, Calif. Soc. Printmakers, Richmond (Calif.) Art Ctr., 1997, Bank of Am. World Hdqs., San Francisco, 1997, Michael Ingbar Gallery, NYC, 1998, Saddleback Coll. Art Gallery, Mission Viejo, Calif., 1999, Coll. of NJ, Ewing, 1999, 2 person exhibit, Cleary, Gottlieb, Steen & Hamilton, NY, NY, 2000; Lowe Gallery at hudson Guild, NY, NY, 2001; Hunterson Mus. of Art, Clinton, NJ, 2001; Loyola U. Chgo. Crown Ctr. Gallery, 2002, others. Studio: 214 W 29th St Rm 606 New York NY 10001 Office Phone: 212-604-0151. E-mail: rsherin@verizon.net.

SHERLOCK, JO ANNE C., librarian; b. Cedar Rapids, Iowa, Jan. 26, 1952; d. Claude Herbert Cypra and Leatrice Anne Meade Cypra; d. Jane Hightower Cypra; m. Stephen L. Sherlock, Sept. 30, 1978 (dec. June 1986); children: Stacey N. Sherlock Farmer, Samantha M. BA in French, Calif. State U., Fresno, 1974; M in Libr. and Info. Studies, U. Calif., Berkeley, 1987. Cert. vol. adminstr. Adminstrv. asst. Chevron Overseas Petroleum, San Francisco, 1974-78; children's libr. Irving (Tex.) Pub. Libr., 1987-94, cmty. rels. libr., 1994—2004; supr. Irving Cmty. Oafr., 2004—. Bd. mem. Cultural Affairs Coun. Named High Spirited Citizen, City Coun., Irving, 1992. Mem.: YWCA (bd. dirs. 2002—), LWV (v.p. publicity Irving 1994—96), AAUW (bd.dirs. 1984—86), ALA (mem. various coms.), Greater Irving Las Colinas C. of C. (bd. women's divsn. 1990—2002), Assn. Vol. Adminstrs. Avocations: needlepoint, travel, reading, cooking, pets. Office: Irving Pub Libr 801 W Irving Blvd Irving TX 75060-2845 E-mail: jsherloc@irvinglibrary.org.

SHERLOCK, PHYLLIS KRAFFT, psychologist; b. Chgo., Dec. 22, 1936; d. Lee M. and Beatrice Elliott Krafft; m. Hugh Paul Sherlock, June 4, 1960 (dec. Oct. 1991); children: William, John, James BA in Philosophy and Religious Studies, U. N.C., 1958; postgrad., Boston U., 1959—60; PhD in Clin. Psychology, Pacific Grad. Sch. Psychology, 1980. Lic. Psychologist, Marriage, Family and Child Counselor. Social work trainee ARC, Chgo., 1959—60; child welfare worker Santa Clara County Social Svcs., San Jose, Calif., 1961—62; counselor Diabesis, San Francisco, 1973—75; counselor chaplaincy svc. Stanford U. Med. Ctr., Calif., 1977—79; intern North County Cmty. Mental Health Clinic, Palo Alto, Calif., 1977—78; postdoctoral intern counseling and psychol. svcs. Cowell Health Svcs., Stanford U., 1980—81; faculty Pacific Grad. Sch. Psychology, 1989—92; pvt. practice, 1979—; supr., clin. dir. The Transitional Program, 1990—2001. Co-founder Pacific Grad. Sch. Psychology, Palo Alto, 1975-76; group facilitator Grad. Sch. Bus., Stanford U., 1980-82; supr. psychol. assts., 1988-2005, clin. dir. The Transitional Program, 1995-2002; adj. clin. faculty Sch. Edn., U. San Francisco, 1990-97 Author: The Feminine Q Set - Research on Wolf's Feminine Image and Theories, 1980; contbr. articles to profl. jours. Vol. Agnew State Hosp., 1971. Mem. Assn. Psychol. Type, Santa Clara County Psychol. Assn. Democrat. Avocations: reading, gardening, art, travel. Office: 1275 Dana Ave Palo Alto CA 94301-3112 Personal E-mail: phyllisdec22@earthlink.net.

SHERMAN, BETH MARIE, psychologist; b. Park Ridge, Ill., May 3, 1964; BS, U. Iowa, 1986; Masters, Adler Sch. Profl. Psychology, Chgo., 1996, D in Psychology, 1999. Cert. cognitive behavioral therapy. Buyer Shore Electronics, Wheeling, Ill., 1990—91; port lectr. IVM, St. Thomas, VI, 1991—92; psychol. tech., output supr. Forest Health Sys., Des Plaines, Ill., 1992—97; intern PSC, Chgo., 1998—99, resident, 1999—2000; clin. psychologist BCCP, Barrington, Ill., 2001—03; pvt. practice Arlington Heights, Ill., 2003—. Mem.: Ill. Psychol. Assn. Home: 255 N Valley Rd Barrington IL 60010-3433

SHERMAN, CINDY, artist; b. Glen Ridge, N.J., 1954; Student, State Univ. Coll. Buffalo, 1972-76. One-woman exhbns. include Hallwalls Gallery, Buffalo, 1976, 77, Contemporary Arts Mus., Houston, 1980, The Kitchen, N.Y., 1980, Metro Pictures, N.Y., 1980, 83, Saman Gallery, Genoa, 1981, Young/Hoffman Gallery, Chgo., 1981, Chantal Crousel Gallery, Paris, 1982, Stedelijk Mus., Amsterdam, 1982, St. Louis Art Mus., 1983, Fine Arts Ctr. Gallery, SUNY-Stony Brook, 1983, Rhona Hoffman Gallery, Chgo., 1983, Douglas Drake Gallery, Kansas City, 1983, 84, Seibu Gallery Contemporary Art, Tokyo, 1984, Akron Art Mus., 1984, Linda Cathcart Gallery, Santa Monica, Calif., 1992, Museo de Monterrey, Mex., 1992; group exhbns. include Albright-Knox Art Gallery, Buffalo, 1975, Artists Space, N.Y., 1978, Max Protetch Gallery, N.Y., 1979, Castelli Graphics, N.Y., 1980, Lisson Gallery, London, 1980, Centre Pompidou, Paris, 1981; NIT, 1981, Renaissance Soc. U. Chgo., 1982, Metro Pictures, N.Y., 1982, La Ciennale de Venezia, Venice, Italy, 1982, Documenta 7, Kassel, West Germany, 1982, Chantall Crousel Gallery, Paris, 1982, San Francisco Mus. Modern Art, 1982, Inst. Contemporary Art, London, 1982, Grey Art Gallery, N.Y., 1982, Inst. Contemporary Art, Phila., 1982, Young Hoffman Gallery, Chgo., 1983, Hirshhorn Gallery, Washington, 1983, 1983, Whitney Mus. Am. Art, N.Y., 1983, 85, 91; represented in permanent collections Mus. Fine Arts, Houston, Albright/Knox Art Gallery, Buffalo, Dallas Mus. Fine Arts, Mus. Boymans-van Beuningen, Rotterdam, Akron Art Mus., Ohio, Mus. Modern Art, N.Y.C., Walker Art Ctr., Mpls., Tate Gallery, London, Rose Art Mus., Brandeis U., Centre Pompidou, Paris, Stedelijk Mus., Amsterdam, Met. Mus. Art, N.Y., St. Louis Art Mus., San Francisco Mus. Modern Art. Mem.: AAAL. Address: METRO PICTURES 519 W 24th St New York NY 10011-1104

SHERMAN, FRIEDA FRANCES, writer; b. NYC, Oct. 21, 1929; d. Benjamin and Anna (Brown) Jeffe; m. Alan Morton Sherman, Feb. 21, 1952; children: Steven, Daniel, Elizabeth, Richard. BA, Hunter Coll., 1951. Market researcher Am. Broadcasting Co., N.Y.C., 1953-55, Am. Inst. Mgmt., N.Y.C., 1955-56; tchr. dance Palo Alto (Calif.), 1960-70; co-founder Workshop Unltd., Palo Alto, 1970-74; dir. client support Prognostics, Palo Alto, 1982-85; dance therapist pvt. practice, Palo Alto, 1975-90. Cons. Market Intelligence Rsch., Palo Alto, 1985. Author of poems and short stories; sr. rschr., editor: The Workshop Unlimited, Non-Profit Innovation in the 21st Century, 1998-2002. Coord. cmty. outreach Lively Arts Stanford (Calif.) U., 1990-92; bd. dirs. SPCA, Santa Cruz, Calif., 1994; judge Nat. Poetry Contest, Santa Cruz, 1994. Mem. Nat. Writers Union, Phi Beta Kappa. Avocations: dance, hiking, music. Home: 900 Glen Canyon Rd Santa Cruz CA 95060-1619 Personal E-mail: friedasherman@sbcglobal.net.

SHERMAN, JENNIFER L., lawyer; BBA, U. Mich., 1986, JD, 1989. Bar: Ill. 1989. Assoc. Barack Ferrazzano Kirschbaum Perlman & Nagelberg LLC, 1989—93; corp. counsel Hook-SupeRx, Inc./Revco Drug Stores, 1993—94; dep. gen. counsel, asst. sec. Fed. Signal Corp., Oak Brook, Ill., 1994—2004, v.p., gen. counsel, sec., 2004—. Office: Fed Signal Corp 1415 W 22nd St Oak Brook IL 60521 Office Phone: 630-954-2000.

SHERMAN, JUDITH DOROTHY, theater producer, engineer, recording industry executive; b. Cleve., Nov. 12, 1942; d. William Paul and Laverne (Spoerke) Luekens; m. Kenneth Sherman, Aug. 1, 1964 Idiv. Aug. 1972); m. Max Wilcox, Jan. 1, 1981 (div. Jan. 1988); m. Curtis Macomber, Apr. 29, 1988. BA, Valparaiso U., 1964; MFA, SUNY, Buffalo, 1971. Rec. engr. Edward at the Moog, N.Y.C., 1971-72; producer-music dir. WBAI-FM, N.Y.C., 1972-76; owner-producer Judith Sherman Prodns., N.Y.C., 1976—. Rec. engr. Marlboro (Vt.) Music Festival, 1976-94; adminstrv. dir. La Musica di Asolo, Sarasota, Fla., 1986-88; vocalist Steve Reich and Musicians, 1971-72. Recipient Corp. Pub. Broadcasting award, 1976, two Grammy award nominations, 1991, Grammy award, Classical Prodr. of Yr., 1993, Grammy award nominations, 1994, 95, 97, 98. Mem. NAFE, Chamber Music Am. (bd. dirs. 2000—), NARAS. Democrat. Home and Office: 645 W 239th St Apt 2A Bronx NY 10463-1236

SHERMAN, JULIA ANN, psychologist; b. Akron, Mar. 25, 1934; d. Roy V. and Edna Helen (Schultz) S.; m. Stanley George Payne, June 16, 1961 (div. Nov. 1995); 1 child, Michael George Sherman. BA, Case Western Res. U., 1954; PhD, U. Iowa, 1957. Diplomate Am. Bd. Psychology. Postdoctoral fellow U. Iowa, Iowa City, 1957-58; with VA Hosp., Mpls., 1958-60, Clinic of Psychiatry and Neurology, Madison, 1960-62; dir. Women Rsch. Inst. Wis.,

Madison, 1974-79; assoc. clin. cons. psychology dept. U. Wis., 1980-90; psychologist Madison Psychiatric Assn., 1980-87, Mental Health Assn., Madison, 1987-90. Part-time tchr. U. Minn., 1959; various part-time clin., writing, rsch. and teaching positions U. Wis., 1962-79; clin. work at Luth. Social Svcs. and Cen. State Hosp. Author: Psychology of Women, 1971, Sex Related Cognitive Differences, 1978, Evolutionary Origin of Bipolar Disorder, 2001; editor: Prism of Sex, 1979, Psychology of Women, 1978; also articles. Rockefeller grantee NSF, NIE, 1972-79. Fellow Am. Psychol. Assn. (chmn. fellowship commn. div. 35 1979-81, pres. sect. IV clin. div. 1986); mem. Wis. Psychol. Assn., Wis. Women in Psychology (pres. 1984). Home: 6302 Mineral Point Rd Apt 303 Madison WI 53705-4364

SHERMAN, LOUISE RINKOB, special education educator; b. Baraboo, Wis., Aug. 4, 1937; d. Severn Paul and Catherine (Wood) Rinkob; m. Jack E. Sherman, Aug. 24, 1957; children: Timothy, Pamela, Steven. BS, U. Wis., 1958; MA in Spl. Edn., U. Colo., 1981. Cert. elem. educator, spl. edn. educator, Colo., Wis. Tchr. Madison (Wis.) Pub. Schs., 1958-62, Tots Learning Ctr., USAFA Presch., Colorado Springs, Colo., 1969-81; spl. edn. resource tchr. Acad. Dist. 20, Colorado Springs, Colo., 1981—, tchr. extended sch. yr., 1990—96, tchr. reading success, 1991—; instr. spl. edn. U. Colo., Colorado Springs, Colo., 1992—2000. Tchr. rep. Acad. Dist. 20 Performance Evaluation Coun., Colorado Springs, 1985-; cadre mem. Explorer Elem., Colorado Springs, 1989. Named Outstanding Elem. Educator of Yr. Acad. Dist. 20, Colorado Springs, 1984, Elem. Spl. Edn. Resource Tchr. Leader Communicator, 1994; Tandy Computer Corp. grantee, 1988, Colo. Coun. for Learning Disabilities rsch. grantee, 1993. Mem. Nat. Coun. for Learning Disabilities, Colo. Coun. for Learning Disabilities, Assn. Tchr. Educators, Colo. Coun. Internat. Reading Assn., Reading Recovery Coun. N.Am., Explorer Parent Tchr. Orgn. Democrat. Methodist. Avocations: music, needlecrafts. Home: 1655 Collins Rd Colorado Springs CO 80920-3330 Office: Acad Dist Twenty Explorer Elem Sch 4190 Bardot Dr Colorado Springs CO 80920-7507

SHERMAN, MARY ANGUS, public library administrator; b. Lawton, Okla., Jan. 3, 1937; d. Donald Adelbert and Mabel (Felkner) Angus; m. Donald Neil Sherman, Feb. 8, 1958; children: Elizabeth, Donald Neil II. BS in Home Econs., U. Okla., 1958, MLS, 1969. Br. head Pioneer Libr. System, Purcell, Okla., 1966-76, regional libr. Norman, Okla., 1976-78, asst. dir., 1978—87, dir., 1987—. Bd. dirs. McClain Bank, chair audit com., 1997—. Mem. bd. visitors Coll. Arts and Scis. U. Okla., 1998—2005, mem. internat. programs bd. visitors, 2003—; bd. dirs. U. Okla. Found., 2004—, Women's Resource Ctr., Norman, 1998—2003, pres., 2002. Named one of Disting. Alumni, Sch. Home Econs. U. Okla., 1980; recipient award of merit, U. Okla. Sch. Libr. and Info. Sci., 2000. Mem.: AAUW (pres. Okla. chpt. 1975—77, SW Ctrl. region dir. 1983—85, nat. bd. dirs. 1983—87, v.p. nat. membership 1985—87, Woman of Yr. Purcell chpt. 1982), ALA (councilor 1988—96, internat. rels. round table 1989—, planning and budget assembly 1990—91, internat. rels. com. 1992—96, orientation com. 1998—99, membership com. 1999—2000, chair sister libr. com. 2000—02, exec. bd. 2000—02, internat. rels. com. 2001—05), Okla. Libr. Assn. (pres. 1982—83, interlibr. cooperation com. 1993—95, chair 1994—95, legis. com. 1998—, Disting. Svc. award 1986), Internat. Fedn. Libr. Assns. (standing com. on pub. librs. 1999—), Tech. in Pub. Librs. Com., Pub. Libr. Assn. (divsn. of ALA, pres. pub. policy for pub. librs. sect. 1995—96, chmn. internat. rels. com. 2002—04), Norman Sister City Com., Norman C. of C. (bd. dirs. 1988—96, pres. 1994—95), Norman Soc. Internat. Affairs (v.p. 1998—99, pres. 1999—2001), Norman Assistance League Club (cmty. assoc.), Rotary (program chair 1991—92, bd. dirs. 1993—97, pres. 1995—96, group study exch. leader to Iceland 1996, dist. literacy chair 1998—2000, dist. group study exch. chair 2001—06, dist. gov. nominee 2005—06, dist. gov.-elect 2006—, Paul Harris fellow), Phi Beta Kappa, Beta Phi Mu, Kappa Alpha Theta (pres. Alpha Omicron House Corp. 1984—87, nat. dir. ho. corps. 1987—88), Delta Gamma Mothers (pres. 1978—79). Democrat. Methodist. Office: Pioneer Libr System 225 N Webster Ave Norman OK 73069-7133 Office Phone: 405-701-2642. Business E-Mail: mary@pls.lib.ok.us.

SHERMAN, MILDRED MOZELLE, music educator, vocalist, actress, opera director; b. Mt. Grove, Mo., Nov. 21, 1932; d. William Husley and Jessie Claire (Faulkner) Clark; m. Louis Leroy Sherman, Aug. 14, 1954; children: Clark Michael, Gayla Dawn. MusB, Bethany Coll., 1953; MusM, Ind. U., 1955; PhD, U. Wis., 1971; postgrad., U. Wis., Stevens Point, Kans. U., Baylor U. Instr. music Kans. State U., Manhattan, 1962—66; prof. music Howard Payne U., Brownwood, Tex., 1973—80, Grand Canyon U., Phoenix, 1980—84; prof. ch. music, dir. ch. music, drama, theatre So. Bapt. Theol. Sem., Louisville, 1984—2001, founding dir. Ch. Music Drama Theatre, sr. prof. ch. music, 2001—. Instr., rep. Inst. Pan Americano, Panama City, 1955-56; vis. prof. Belem and Rio Bapt. Sems., Brazil; owner Sherman Svcs., 2000—, Ky. Opera Roster, 2001—; vis. lectr. Staley, Cambridge, Union, Furman, Stetson, and Fla. Bapt. univs., 1990-99. Performer, dir. over 1000 operas, musicals, and plays including Women of the Bible, 1986—; author: The Vocal Technician, 1991, also short stories; author: (with P. Landgrave) The Light!dramatic musical, 2006; translator Mozarts Obligation of the 1st Commandment, 1986, Debussy's Prodigal Son, 1987, Massenet's Herodiade, 1997, Two from Galilee prodn. kit, 1996, (with Ted Nichols) opera Word of Honor, 2005, The Light, 2006; also monologues; contbg. author: New Dictionary of Religious Arts, 2001 Recipient Orpheus award Phi Mu Alpha Sinfonia, 1978; Lily Found. grantee, 1988-90; Baylor Univ. fellow, 1990-91. Mem. Nat. Opera Assn., Nat. Assn. Tchrs. Singing, Met. Opera Guild, Ch. Music Conf., DAR, Ea. Star, Christian Opera Assn. Bd., Sigma Alpha Iota. Baptist. Avocations: genealogy, handwork, animals, travel. Home: 3602 Coronado Dr Louisville KY 40241-2611 Office: So Bapt Theol Sem 2825 Lexington Rd Louisville KY 40280-0001 Business E-Mail: msherman@sbts.edu.

SHERMAN, NANCY KAY JACKEL, elementary school educator; b. Oct. 12, 1950; d. R. Wayne and Mary Jo Jackel; m. Kim L. Sherman, 1973; 1 child, Rebecca Mae. BA, Graceland Coll., 1972; MS in Elem. Edn., Pitts. State U., 1991. Elem. tchr., 1972—; lead tchr. Thayer Consol. Unified Sch. Dist., Kans., 1995-99. Mem. site coun. Thayer Consol. Unified Sch. Dist., 1995—99, 2002—; chess coach Thayer and Galesburg, 2005—06. Treas., mem. charter bd. Reorganized Ch. of Jesus Christ of Latter-day Saints. Mem. Kans. Profl. Tchrs./Educators Assn., Intern Reading Assn. Home: 10565 Lyon Rd Erie KS 66733-5114

SHERMAN, PATSY O'CONNELL, retired manufacturing executive, chemist; b. Mpls., Sept. 15, 1930; d. James Patrick and Edna Fern (Stitzel) O'Connell m. Hubert Townsend Sherman, Aug. 15, 1953; children: Sharilyn Kay Sherman Loushin, Wendy Jane Sherman Heil. BA, Gustavus Adolphus Coll., 1952. Chemist 3M, St. Paul, 1952-67, rsch. specialist, 1967-73, tech. mgr., 1973-82, mgr. tech. devel., 1982—92; ret., 1992. Trustee GMI Engring. and Mgmt. Inst., Flint, Mich., 1986-92; bd. dirs., owner Advanced Optics Inc., Mpls.; dir. Nat. Inventors Hall of Fame Found., 1996-99, 2002—. Contbr. numerous articles to profl. jours.; patentee in field. Trustee Gustavus Adolphus Coll., 1989-92. Recipient Disting. Alumni award Gustavus Adolphus Coll., 1975, Spurgeon award Boy Scouts Am., 1980; named to Minn. Inventors Hall of Fame, 1989, Nat. Inventors Hall of Fame, 2001. Mem. Am. Chem. Soc., Am. Soc. Tng. and Devel., Am. Soc. Engring. Edn. (dir. continuing profl. devel. div. 1986-89, chair 1989-90). Achievements include invention of Scotchgard (with Samuel Smith) in 1956. Personal E-mail: patsherman@aol.com.

SHERMAN, RUTH TODD, counseling administrator, educator; b. Memphis, July 3, 1924; d. Robbie M. and Lillie M. (Shreve) Todd. BS, Memphis State U., 1972, MEd, 1975; MA, Western Mich. U., 1986; PhD, Ohio State U., 2001. Cert. tchr., counselor. Youth leader Assembly of God Ch., Memphis, 1962-64, youth dir., 1964-66; counselor Teen Challenge, Memphis, 1973-74; marriage and family therapist Memphis, 1976-77; govt. tng. advisor Def. Logistics Agy., Battle Creek, Mich., 1982-87, advisor Alexandria, Va., 1987-94, ret., 1994; tchr. computer graphics Ohio State U., Columbus, 1998—2001; instrnl. devel. specialist Global U., Springfield, Mo., 2004—. Agy. to Mil. Svc. cons. Def. Logistics Agy., Oklahoma City, 1990-94. Author: Federal Catalog Training Books/Videos, 1987 (Sustained Superior Performance award 1987). Mem. Internat. Assn. Marriage and Family Counselors, Nat. Employment Counseling Assn., Am. Mental Health Counseling Assn. Avocations: drawing, creating computer animations, photography. Home: Apt 217B 1644 Marion Springfield MO 65807

SHERMAN, SANDRA BROWN, lawyer; b. Galesburg, Ill., May 14, 1953; d. Charles Lewis and Lois Maria (Nelson) Brown; m. Robert Sherman, June 10, 1979; children: Michael Wesley, Stephen Averill, Alexander Joseph. B of Music Edn., Ind. U., 1975; JD, U. Ill., 1979, LLM, 1981. Bar: Ill. 1979, Tex. 1982, N.J. 1984, U.S. Tax Ct. 1988, N.Y. 1997. Instr. law U. Ill., Champaign, 1979-81; assoc. Law Offices of William E. Remy, San Antonio, 1984, Gutkin Miller Shapiro & Selesner, Millburn, NJ, 1985-88, ptnr., 1989-91; counsel Riker Danzig Scherer Hyland & Perretti LLP, Morristown, NJ, 1991-95; ptnr. Riker Danzig Scherer Hyland & Perretti, LLP, Morristown, NJ, 1996—. Contbr. articles to profl. jours. Trustee, sec. Found. U. Medicine and Dentistry N.J., 1998—. Scholar Ind. U., 1971-75, U. Ill., 1977-79. Mem. ABA (probate and trust law divsn.), N.J. Bar Assn., Estate Planning Coun. No. N.J., Estate Planning Coun. N.Y.C., Park Ave. Club. Avocation: music. Office: Riker Danzig Scherer Hyland & Perretti LLP Headquarters Plz 1 Speedwell Ave Morristown NJ 07961-1981 Office Phone: 973-538-0800. Business E-Mail: ssherman@riker.com.

SHERMAN, SHERRY WIGGINS, science educator; d. Donald Fowler and Rosalyn Terry Wiggins; m. Frederick Wise Sherman, Jr., Aug. 16, 1980; children: Taylor, Amy. BS in Chemistry, Longwood Coll., Farmville, Va., 1981; MA in New Profl. Studies Tchg., George Mason U., Prince William, Va., 2001. Tchr. 8th grade sci. Prospect Heights Mid. Sch., Orange, Va., 1982—84; tchr. 6th grade math. Grymes Meml. Sch., Orange, 1989—90; tchr. chemistry Louisa County HS, Mineral, Va., 1990—2001, Orange County HS, Orange, 2001—06; tchr. McLean HS, Va., 2006—. Mem.: NEA, Nat. Sci. Tchrs. Assn., Am. Chem. Soc. Office Phone: 703-714-5700.

SHERMAN, SIGNE LIDFELDT, portfolio manager, former research chemist; b. Rochester, NY, Nov. 11, 1913; d. Carl Leonard Broström and Herta Elvira Maria (Tern) Lidfeldt; m. Joseph V. Sherman, Nov. 18, 1944 (dec. Oct. 1984). BA, U. Rochester, 1935, MS, 1937. Chief chemist Lab. Indsl. Medicine and Toxicology Eastman Kodak Co., Rochester, 1937-43; chief rsch. chemist Chesebrough-Pond's Inc., Clinton, Conn., 1943-44; ptnr. Joseph V. Sherman Cons., N.Y.C., 1944-84; portfolio strategist Sherman Holdings, Troy, Mont., 1984—. Author: The New Fibers, 1946. Fellow Am. Inst. Chemists; mem. AAAS, AAUW (life), Am. Chem. Soc., Am. Econ. Assn., Am. Assn. Ind. Investors (life), Fedn. Am. Scientists (life), Union Concerned Scientists (life), Earthquake Engring. Rsch. Inst., Nat. Ctr. for Earthquake Engring. Rsch., N.Y. Acad. Scis. (life), Cabinet View Country Club. Office: Sherman Holdings Angel Island 648 Halo Dr Troy MT 59935-9415 E-mail: creative@libby.org.

SHERN, STEPHANIE MARIE, investment company executive, accountant; b. Taylor, Pa., Jan. 7, 1948; d. Joseph and Stephanie (Malodovitch) Andrews; m. George Emil Shern, Sept. 25, 1971. AA, Keystone Jr. Coll., 1967; BS, Pa. State U., 1969. CPA, N.Y. Staff acct. to ptnr., nat. dir. consumer products industry Ernst & Young, N.Y.C., 1969—, ptnr., vice chmn., global and U.S. dir. R&CP markets. Dir. Met. Retail Fin. Execs., N.Y.C. Contbr. articles to profl. jours. Named Keystonian of Yr., Keystone Jr. Coll., 1984. Mem. AICPA, N.Y. State Soc. CPAs (bd. dirs. 1985—), Women's Econ. Round Table, Panther Valley Golf (Allamuch, N.J.), Beta Alpha Psi (mem. adv. forum 1984—). Republican. Ukrainian Orthodox. Home: 11 Green Briar Ct Little Falls NJ 07424-2307

SHERONY, CHERYL ANNE, dietician; b. Lincoln, Nebr., Dec. 5, 1948; d. John Eugene and Hazel Ethel (Stites) Howe; m. Bruce Carl Sherony, Aug. 11, 1973; children: Thomas Carl, Michael Bruce. BS in Dietetics, U. Wis., Stevens Point, 1971, MS, 1979. Registered dietitian. Dietitian Marquette (Mich.) Gen. Hosp., 1979-80, self employed, 1980-85, 89-90, Alger Marquette C.C., Marquette, 1982-87, Upper Peninsula Home Nursing, Marquette, 1989-93; dietititian self employed, Marquette, 1989-93; dietitian, owner Superior Dietetic Svcs. of the Upper Peninsula Inc., Marquette, 1996-99; pvt. practice dietitian dietitian, Marquette, 1999—. Citizen amb. to China, People to People Program, 1995. Sect. reviewer Pediat. Manual of Clin. Dietetics, 1998. Capt. USAF, 1972-90. Mem. Am. Dietetic Assn., Mich. Dietetic Assn., Upper Peninsula Dietetic Assn. Roman Catholic. Avocations: reading, waterskiing, cross country skiing. Home and Office: 1781 M-28 East Marquette MI 49855

SHERPA, FRAN MAGRUDER, geography educator; b. Midland, Tex., Aug. 20, 1952; d. Edwin Howard Magruder and Barbara June Cowden; m. Ang Kazi Sherpa; children: Sarah, Susie, Sonia, Tsowang. BS in Geography, Tex. State U., San Marcos, 1995, M in Applied Geography, 1998. Registered massage therapist. Owner, operator Himalayan Excursions, Kathmandu, Nepal, 1983—85; investor, mgr. office Nepal Internat. Clinic, Kathmandu, Nepal, 1989—91; adj. prof. geography U. Tex. Permian Basin, Odessa, Tex., 2000—. Mem.: Am. Assn. Geographers. Avocations: photography, travel. Home: 2201 Neely Midland TX 79705 E-mail: fransherpa@cox.net.

SHERR, SYLVIA, artist, educator; b. Zamosc, Poland, Jan. 1, 1931; arrived in U.S.A., 1938. d. Isadore and Edna (Rifer) Feldstein; m. Allan E. Sherr, Sept. 11, 1955; children: Susan Matalon, Carol Cunn, Evan Sherr. BS, U. Wis., 1953; MA, Kean Coll., 1977. Cert. tchr., Conn. and N.J. Tchr. Wilton Bd. Edn., Conn., 1958-59, Bound Brook Bd. Edn., NJ, 1975-90, chairperson gifted and talented com. NJ, 1980-85. One-woman shows include N.J. Ctr. Visual Art, 1998, Johnson and Johnson World Hdqs., New Brunswick, N.J., 2002, exhibitions include Polo Gallery, Edgewater, N.J., 1994—99, The Collector, Merrick, LI, 1995—99, Lincoln Ctr., N.Y.C., 1995, Gallery 402, 1999, Belles Artes, San Miguel de Allande, Mex., 2000—01, Gallery Atenea, 2003. Fellow Geraldine Dodge Found., Vt. Studio Ctr., 1998; Vt. Studio Ctr. grant, 2005. Mem. Orgn. Ind. Artists, 1998. E-mail: ssherr@nj.rr.com.

SHERRARD, HARRIETT, science educator; d. Harry Maurice and Aleene Pollock (Stepmother); m. Cody Sherrard, June 4, 1965; children: Kelley, Christopher. BS, Tex. A & M, Commerce, 1972, EdM, 1977. Cert. tchr. Tex. Edn. Agy., 1972. Tchr. Terrell Ind. Sch. Dist., Tex., 1972—76, Wills Point Ind. Sch. Dist., 1976—. Sponsor Drug Free Youth in Tex., Wills Point, 1992—. Tchr. and choir officer Calvary Bapt. Ch., Wills Point, Tex., 2000—06. Named Tchr. of Yr., Wills Point Ind. Sch. Dist., 1982, 1990; recipient, 2006. Mem.: Assn. Tex. Profl. Educators, Sci. Tchrs. Assn. Tex. Baptist. Avocations: horses, reading, golf, sports, music. Office: Wills Point Jr High 200 Tiger Dr Wills Point TX 75169 Office Phone: 903-873-4946.

SHERRARD, JESSICA E., mathematics educator; b. Oceanside, NY, May 26, 1981; d. James Arthur and Dianne Marie (Reichardt) Sherrard. BA in Math., State U. of NY Coll. at Geneseo, 2003; MA in Liberal Studies, State U. of NY at Stony Brook, 2005. Math tchr. Lindenhurst Sch. Dist., NY, 2003—. Learning Tchr. grant, Bd. Coop. Edn. Svcs., 2006. Mem.: Coun. for Exceptional Children, Am. Edn., Assn. Math. Tchrs. NY State, Nat. Coun. Tchrs. of Math. Home: 20 Fairfield Way Apt 2 Commack NY 11725 Office: Lindenhurst Sch Dist 350 S Wellwood Ave Lindenhurst NY 11757

SHERRATT, HOLLY, art appraiser; BA in Art History, UCLA; MA in Visual Studies, U. Calif., Irvine. Trainee Laguna Art Mus., Laguna Beach, Calif.; intern Nat. Mus. Am. Art., Smithsonian Inst., Washington; curatorial staff Huntington Beach Fine Art Ctr., Calif.; modern, contemporary and Latin Am. art specialist Bonhams & Butterfields, San Francisco, 2000—, and cataloguer, prints and photographs dept. Exec. bd. San Francisco Mus. Modern Art contemporary ext. Lectr. in field. Mem.: Phi Beta Kappa. Office: Bonhams & Butterfields 220 San Bruno Ave San Francisco CA 94103 Office Phone: 415-503-3311. Office Fax: 415-503-3274. Business E-Mail: holly.sherratt@bonhams.com.

SHERREN, ANNE TERRY, chemistry professor; b. Atlanta, July 1, 1936; d. Edward Allison and Annie Ayres (Lewis) Terry; m. William Samuel Sherren, Aug. 13, 1966. BA, Agnes Scott Coll., 1957; PhD, U. Fla., Gainesville, 1961. Grad. tchg. asst. U. Fla., Gainesville, 1957-61; from instr. to asst. prof. Tex. Womans U., Denton, 1961-66; rsch. participant Argonne Nat. Lab., 1973-80, 93-94; assoc. prof. chemistry North Cen. Coll., Naperville, Ill., 1966-76, prof., 1976-2001, prof. emeritus, 2001—. Contbr. articles to profl. jours. Ruling elder Knox Presbyn. Ch., 1971—, clk. of session, 1976-94. Mem. Am. Chem. Soc., Am. Inst. Chemists, Sigma Xi, Delta Kappa Gamma (chpt. pres. 2002-2004), Iota Sigma Pi (nat. pres. 1978-81, nat. dir. 1972-78, nat. historian 1989—). Presbyterian. Office: North Ctrl Coll Dept Chemistry Naperville IL 60566 Business E-Mail: atsherren@noctrl.edu.

SHERRICK, REBECCA LOUISE, academic administrator; b. Carthage, Ill., May 28, 1953; d. Otho Downing and Elizabeth (Potter) S. BA, Ill. Wesleyan U., Bloomington, 1975; doctorate (hon.), Ill. Wesleyan U., 2001; PhD, Northwestern U., 1980. Asst. prof. Carroll Coll., Waukesha, Wis., 1980-85, assoc. prof., 1987—, v.p. planning, 1990-91, v.p. enrollment and planning, 1991-92, v.p. enrollment and student svcs., 1992-93, v.p. adminstrn., 1993—, provost, 1998—2000; pres. Aurora U., Ill., 2000—. Recipient Woman of Distinction award Waukesha YWCA, 1991; Lincoln Acad. of Scholars awardee State of Ill., 1975; William Randolph Hearst fellow, 1976, 77. Mem. Alpha Lambda Delta, Phi Alpha Theta, Kappa Delta Pi, Phi Kappa Phi. Methodist. Avocations: swimming, gardening. Office Phone: 630-844-5476. Business E-Mail: sherrick@aurora.edu.

SHERRILL, BETTY PEARSON, retired elementary school educator; b. Morganton, N.C., June 29, 1928; d. Robert Augustus and Cleet Cornelia (Moore) Pearson; m. Frank Junie Sherrill, Oct. 17, 1947; children: Steve, June Sherrill McKay, Scott. AB, Lenoir-Rhyne Coll., 1962, MA, 1989. Cert. elem. tchr., N.C. Tchr. 1st grade Hickory (N.C.) Pub. Schs., 1962-92, tchr. Lenoir-Rhyne summer enrichment program, 1980-92, coord. Lenoir-Rhyne summer enrichment program, 1993—2001. Mem. edn. com. Hickory Mus. Art, 1990-91. Mem. AAUW, Hickory Landmarks Soc. (docent guild chmn. 1994-2001, bd. dirs. 1997-2003, 2004—), Delta Kappa Gamma (pres. Nu chpt. 1990-92). Lutheran. Avocations: reading, gardening, sewing, hiking. Home: 630 4th St NE Hickory NC 28601-3808 Personal E-mail: bettysherrill@earthlink.net.

SHERRILL, HELEN WHITE, elementary school educator; b. Ft. Worth, Apr. 1, 1953; d. Philip Alexander and Armarilla Cordelia (Carpenter) White; m. Dheryl Mac, June 12, 1976; children: Angela, Brian. BS in Edn., Tex. Tech. U., 1976. Cert. elem. tchr., cert. spl. edn. Tchr. Mineral Wells (Tex.) Ind. Sch. Dist., 1988—. Com. mem. long range planning Mineral Wells Ind. Sch. dist., 1994. Mem. Delta Kappa Gamma/Alpha Omicron (treas.). Mem. Ch. of Christ. Avocations: reading, sewing, cross stitch. Office: Houston Elem 300 SW 13th St Mineral Wells TX 76067-5565

SHERRY, KRYSTAL A., real estate broker; b. Bayonne, N.J., July 26, 1975; d. Joseph James and Elaine M. Sherry. Grad. h.s., West Covina, Calif. Lic. real estate Nev. Realtor, Nev., 1993—2001; broker, owner Realty Success Sys., Ltd., Las Vegas, 2002—. Mem.: Nat. Assn. Realtors. Office: Realty Success Sys Ltd # 100 8064 W Sahara Las Vegas NV 89117 Office Phone: 702-968-6400.

SHERRY, MARILYN MORIN, psychiatric social worker; b. Worcester, Mass., Mar. 25, 1935; d. Jacob and Gertrude (Greenberg) Morin; A.B., Clark U., 1956; M.S., Simmons Coll., 1958; m. Gerald B. Sherry, Jan. 3, 1960; children: Samuel, Trudy. Cert. clin. social work. Social worker Child and Family Svcs. of Conn., Manchester, 1958-61, Hartford, Conn., 1966-71, Dept. Human Svcs., New Britain, Conn., 1977-79, social worker palliative care and geriatrics Mt. Sinai Hosp., Hartford, 1979-81; psychiat. social worker U. Conn. Health Ctr., Farmington, 1981-86,89; pvt. practice social work, 1981—; instr. Ea. Conn. State Coll., 1986-87; social work fellow McClean Hosp., Belmont, Mass., 1987-88; psychiatric social worker Blue Hills Hosp., 1989—; adv. bd. Encore, YWCA Post-mastectomy Program, 1980-81. Mem. Registry of Clin. Social Workers, Acad. Cert. Social Workers, Conn. Soc. Clin. Social Workers, Nat. Assn. Social Workers (com. on inquiry), Coalition Social Work Orgns. Conn. (founding mem., sec.-treas. 1981-85), Am. Group Psychotherapy Assn., Am. Assn. for Marriage and Family Therapy.

SHERTER, SELMA, retired elementary school educator; b. Boston, May 10, 1937; d. Samuel Isaac Tattelbaum and Pauline Blaustein; m. Sidney Robert Sherter, June 26, 1960; children: Bonnie Lyn, Douglas Noah, Meredith Lea. AB in Liberal Arts, Boston U., 1959, MS in Edn., 1960; MS in Spl. Edn., LI U., Southampton, NY, 1978. Cert. reading specialist NY. 1st grade tchr. Boston Pub. Schs., 1959—60, Cohasset Pub. Schs., Mass., 1960—63; Title I remedial tchr. Hampton Bays Pub. Schs., NY, 1972—78; reading specialist, spl. edn. tchr. Hampton Beach Pub. Schs., NY, 1978—99; ret., 1999. Home: 6 Pine Ct Hampton Bays NY 11946

SHERWIN, SUSAN J., retired language arts educator; m. Mark Sherwin, June 27, 1971; children: Brian, Loni. BA in Speech Arts and Speech Therapy, Montclair State U., Upper Montclair, NJ, 1970; MA, Montclair State U., Upper Montclair, N.J., 1975. Cert. reading specialist N.J., 1975. Tchr. lang. arts Mt. Olive HS, Flanders, NJ, 1995—2006; elem. tchr., 1996; tchr. handicapped St. Elizabeth Coll., NJ, 1997. Adj. instr. dept. English County Coll. Morris, Randolph, NJ, 1985—95. Mem.: Internat. Reading Assn. Personal E-mail: sk8nski18@yahoo.com.

SHERWOOD, BARBARA JEAN, art educator; b. Elmhurst, Ill., Dec. 4, 1950; d. Albert John and Elizabeth M. Krieter; m. Phillip Dale Sherwood, May 3, 1975; children: Kristin, Amy, Brian. BS Edn., No. Ill. U., DeKalb, 1973; postgrad., Concordia U., River Forest, Ill. Tchr. 4th grade St. Charles Borromeo Sch., Bensenville, Ill., 1973—82; substitute tchr. Dist. #54, Schaumburg, Ill., 1993—95; tchr. Fine Arts Byrd Sch. Dist. #59, Elk Grove Village, Ill., 1996—. Dir. children's choir St. Marcelline Cath. Ch., Schaumburg, 1985—2002; cantor weddings and funerals St. Marcelline and St. Charles Borromeo, 1973—; dir. vocal Archdiocese Chgo., 1985—88; singer St. Marcelline and KC, 2001—. Vol. Breast Cancer Awareness Fundraiser, Chgo., 2002—. Mem.: Am. Orff Schulwerk Assn., PTA (tchr. rep. Byrd Sch. 2003—, chmn. Ways and Means Com. 1986—2000). Roman Catholic. Avocations: reading, painting, crafts. Home: 702 Valley View Dr Schaumburg IL 60193 Office: Admiral Byrd Sch 265 Wellington Ave Elk Grove Village IL 60007

SHERWOOD, KATHERINE D., artist, educator; b. New Orleans, Oct. 17, 1952; m. Jeff Adams; 1 child, Odette. BA, U. Calif., Davis, 1975; MFA, San Francisco Art Inst., 1979. Asst. prof. U. Calif., Berkeley, 1989—. Adj. instr. NYU, 1983-89. One-woman shows include Anna Gardner Gallery, Stinson Beach, Calif., 1977, Nelson Gallery, Davis, Calif., 1981, ARC Gallery, Sacramento, 1982, Gallery Paule Anglim, San Francisco, 1982, M.O. David Gallery, N.Y.C., 1984, 8 B.C., N.Y.C., 1985, D.P. Fong Gallery, San Jose, 1994, others; group shows include Concord Gallery, N.Y.C., 1981, Eaton-Schoen Gallery, San Francisco, 1982, Protetch-McNeil Gallery, N.Y.C., 1983, Phila. Coll. Art, 1984, Avenue B. Gallery, N.Y.C., 1985, U. Santa Clara (Calif.), 1986, Washington Square Gallery, N.Y.C., 1987, Bruno Facchetto Gallery, N.Y.C., 1988, Worth Ryder Gallery, Berkeley, 1989, Otaru Mcpl. Mus., Hokkaido, Japan, 1991, San Francisco Art Commn. Gallery, 1992, Alexandria Mus. of Art, 1993 (Juror's Merit award 1993), Palm Springs (Calif.) Desert Mus., 1994 (Best of Show 1994), Microsoft Gallery, Beaverton, Oreg., 1995, others. U. Calif. Priorities in Edn. grantee, 1990, Faculty Mentor grantee, 1991, 93, Jr. Faculty Devel. Program grantee, 1991, Humanities Rsch. grantee, 1992; NEA Visual Artists fellow, 1989, MacDowell Colony fellow, 1984. Office: U Calif 238 Kroeber Hall Berkeley CA 94720-3750

SHERWOOD, KEHELA (KAREN KEHELA SHERWOOD), broadcast executive; Grad., UCLA. Asst. prodr. to Brian Grazer Imagine Entertainment, 1986—87, story editor, 1987, dir. devel., v.p., sr. v.p., pres. prodn., co-chair Imagine Films, 1997—. Mailing: Imagine Entertainment 7th Floor 9465 Wilshire Blvd Beverly Hills CA 90212*

SHERWOOD, LOUISE KAY, literature and language educator; b. Fortuna, Mo., Mar. 4, 1945; d. William Dorsey and Janet Louise Holst; m. James Sherwood, Aug. 2, 1974. BA, Sch. of the Ozarks, Point Lookout, Mo., 1967; MA, U. Mo., St. Louis, 1972. Cert. secondary edn. tchr. Mo., 1967, Colo., 1969. English tchr. Belle H.S., Mo., 1967—68, Hazelwood Jr. High, Mo., 1968—69, Holly H.S., Colo., 1969—. Mem. Grace Luth. Ch., Lamar, Colo., 1969—2006. Named Wal-Mart Tchr. of Yr., 2005; grantee Writing about Lit. grahtee, Nat. Endowment for the Arts, 1986. R-Consevative. Lutheran. Avocations: bicycling, hiking, reading, gardening. Home: 30325 Road LL Holly CO 81047 Office: Holly High School Box 608 Holly CO 81047 Office Phone: 719-535-6512. Personal E-mail: sherwoodk@cminet.net. E-mail: kay.sherwood@holly.k12.co.us.

SHERWOOD, MIDGE, author; b. Ironton, Ohio; d. Roy and Addie (Brace) Winters; m. Jack E. Sherwood, Jan. 19, 1946; children: Margaret Sherwood Simms, Melanie Sherwood. BJ, U. Mo., 1938. Women's editor Ironton Daily Tribune, 1933-38; city editor Ironton Daily News, 1938-40; asst. mgr. West coast news bur. TWA, Los Angeles, 1940-42; pub. relations dir. Western Air Lines, 1942-45; aviation columnist, corr. Skyways, So. Flight, 1945-48; owner, operator Midge Winters Agy., 1945-48; assoc. editor Matrix Mag., Women in Communications, 1950-55; book reviewer LA Times, 1963, Western Hist. Quarterly; free-lance writer, 1958—; columnist Pasadena Star-News, Calif., 1987; lectr. on Gen. George Smith Patton and pioneers of Western frontier. Author: And How it Grew, 1965; San Marino Ranch to City, 1977; Days of Vintage, Years of Vision, Vol. 1, 1982, Vol. II, 1987, Fremont: Eagle of the West, 2002, Days of Vintage, Years of Vision, vol. III, 2006, Western Journal Collection (1900-1995), Western Journal Collection (1995-2000); author (plays): Peace at Last; editor Western Jour.; contbr. columns newspapers. Chmn. Hertrich Meml., 1967; Paul Harris fellow Rotary; recipient Commendation award Gov. Pete Wilson, Calif., 1996. Mem. Soc. Fellows of Huntington Library, 1967; founder, archivist San Marino Hist. Soc. Recipient double award Conf. Calif. Hist. Socs., 1987; named Outstanding Citizen of San Marino, 1988. chmn. Annual Fremont's Day, 2005. Mem. Huntington Westerners (founder), Live Poet's Soc. Huntington Libr. (founder), Westerners Internat. (bd. dirs.), Phi Mu. Home: PO Box 80241 San Marino CA 91118

SHERWOOD, PATRICIA WARING, artist, educator; b. Columbia, SC, Dec. 19, 1933; d. Clark du Val and Florence (Yarbrough) Waring; widowed; children: Cheryl Sherwood Kraft, Jana Sherwood Kern, Marikay Sherwood Taitt. BFA magna cum laude, Calif. State U., Hayward, 1970; MFA, Mills Coll., Oakland, Calif., 1974; postgrad., San Jose State U., Calif., 1980-86. Cert. tchr., Calif. Tchr. De Anza Jr. Coll., Cupertino, Calif., 1970-78, Foothill Jr. Coll., Los Altos, Calif., 1972-78, West Valley Jr. Coll., Saratoga, Calif., 1978—. Artist-in-residence Centrum Frans Masereel, Kasterlee, Belgium, 1989. One-woman shows include Triton Mus., Santa Clara, Calif., 1968, 2002, RayChem Corp., Sunnyville, Calif., 1969, Palo Alto (Calif.) Cultural Ctr., 1977, Los Gatos (Calif.) Mus., 1992, Stanford U. faculty club, Palo Alto, 1993, d.p. Fong Gallery, San Jose, Calif., 1995, 97, Heritage Bank, San Jose, 1997, City Jr. Coll., City Coll., San Jose, Calif., 1997, West Valley Coll., Saratoga, Calif., 1998, Mus. West, Palo Alto, 2000-2001, Triton Mus., Santa Clara, 2001; exhibited in group shows at Tressider Union Stanford U., 1969, Oakland (Calif.) Mus. Kaiser Ctr., 1969, Sonoma (Calif.) State Coll., 1969, Bank Am., San Francisco, 1969, Alrich Gallery, San Francisco, U. Calif. Santa Clara, 1967, Charles and Emma Frye Mus., Seattle, 1968, Eufrat Gallery DeAnza Coll., Cupertino, 1975, San Jose Mus. Art, 1976, Lytton Ctr., Palo Alto, 1968 (1st award), Zellerbach Ctr., San Francisco, 1970, Works Gallery, San Jose, 1994, Inst. Contemporary Art, San Jose, 1997, Triton Mus. Art, Santa Clara, Calif., 1997, 98, San Jose Inst. Contemporary Art, 1998, San Jose City Coll. Artists Forum, 1998, Calvin Charles Gallery, Scottsdale, Ariz.; represented in permanent collections Mills Coll., Bank Am., San Francisco, Heritage Bank, San Jose, Stanford U., Palo Alto, Calif., San Jose U., Smithsonian Inst. Nat. Mus. Am. Art, Washington, Calrin Charles Gallery, Scottsdale, Ariz. Art judge student show Stanford U., Palo Alto, 1977; mem. d.p. Fong Gallery, San Jose, Calif., 1994, J.J. Brooking Gallery, San Francisco, Mus. West Gallery, Palo Alto, Calif., Gallery Ocean Avenue, Carmel, Calif., 2002, Bryant Street Gallery, Palo Alto, 2003, Calvin Charles Gallery, Scottsdale, Ariz., 1212 Gallery, Burlingame, Calif., Art Resources Galleria, Edina, Minn., Linda Durnell Gallery, Los Gatos, Calif., 2005, The Studio Gallery, Burlingame, Chelsea Art Gallery, Palo Alto, Calif., 2006. Nat. Endowment for Arts/We. States Art Fedn. fellow, 1994. Mem. NEA, Calif. Print Soc., Womens Caucus for Arts, Internat. Platform Assn., Smithsonian Instn., Nat. Mus. Am. Art. Home: 1500 Arriba Ct Los Altos CA 94024-5956

SHERWOOD-FABRE, LIESE ANNE, public health service officer; d. Charles Laverne, Jr. and Nova Anne Sherwood; m. Luis Raul Fabre, May 17, 1981; children: Luis Raul Fabre III, Carlos Roberto Fabre, Fernanda Andrea Fabre. BA, Tex. Christian U., Fort Worth, 1978; MA, Ind. U., 1981, PhD, 1984. Policy rsch. analyst U.S. HHS, Washington, 1983—85, program analyst, 1988—89, pub. health advisor Dallas, 2000—; survey statistician U.S. Bur. of Census, Washington, 1985—88; cons. U.S. AID, Tegucigalpa, Honduras, 1989—90, project mgr. Mexico City, 1990—94, Moscow, 1994—99; cons. Acad. Ednl. Devel., Va., 1999—2000; pub. health advisor U.S. Dept. Health and Human Svcs., 2000—. Co-author: Performance and Credibility: Developing Excellence in Public and Nonprofit Organizations, 1986, Drug Lessons and Education Programs in Developing Countries, 1995; author: short stories; contbr. articles to profl. jours. Recipient Meritorious Honor award, U.S. AID/Moscow, 1999, Regional Dir.'s Leadership award, U.S. Dept. HHS, 2003, 2004, 1st prize, Briarcliff Rev., 2005, Inland Empire Calif. Writers Club, 2005; grantee, Nat. Inst. Justice, U.S. Dept. Justice, 1981—82; Fulbright tchg. fellow, 1990. Mem.: Phi Sigma Iota (life; treas. 1977—78), Phi Beta Kappa (life).

SHESKEY, SUSAN E., computer company executive; b. Oct. 13, 1947; Grad., Miami U., Oxford, Ohio. With Ameritech, Ohio Bell, Dell, Inc., Round Rock, Tex., 1993—, v.p. for global sales, svcs., mfg. and fulfillment IT, interim chief info. officer, 2005, v.p., chief info. officer, 2005—. Office: Dell Inc One Dell Way Round Rock TX 78682*

SHIBA, WENDY C., lawyer; BA, Mich. State U., 1973; JD cum laude, Temple U. Sch. of Law, 1979. Atty. corp. and securities law O'Melveny & Myers, Los Angeles & NYC; corp. chair Phila. Law Dept., Phila.; v.p., sec., asst. gen. counsel Bowater, Inc., Greenville, SC, 1993—2000; gen. counsel PolyOne Corp., Avon Lake, Ohio, 2000—01, v.p., chief legal officer, sec., 2001—. Former bd. mem. Legal Services Agency of Western Carolina, S.C. Bd. of Accountancy, Greenville Little Theater, Palmetto Soc. of United Way of Greenville County; former mem. United Way of Greenville County Campaign Cabinet, Palmetto Soc. Women's Leadership Council, Greenville Professional Women's Forum. Office: PolyOne Corp 33587 Walker Rd Avon Lake OH 44012

SHIELD, JULIE MARIE KARST, artist, educator; b. St. Louis, Mar. 28, 1933; d. Lansing Peter and Margaret Mary Shield. A, Briarcliff Jr. Coll., NY, 1953; studied at, Nat. Acad. Design, N.Y.C., Art Students League. Oil painting art tchr. Buckingham Coun. Arts, Va., 1995—96, Va., 1999; owner and dir. Wooden Boat Art Gallery, River John, Canada, 1997—99; oil and still life art tchr. Longwood Ctr. for the Visual Arts, 1997-1998, 2000—01; oil and still life art tchr. Julie Shield Workshop, Farmville, Va., 1998—99, oil painting, landscape and still life art tchr., 2000—02; multi-media art tchr. Holly Manor Nursing Home, Farmville, 2001—04. Mem. coun. Longwood Ctr. for Visual Arts, Farmville, Va., 2001—. Set design, Ring Around the Moon, 1981, brush and ink drawings on wall panels, ARC, Palm Beach County Chpt., 1982, 11 oil paintings for movie set design, Illegally Yours, 1987, one-woman shows include First Nat. Bank of Palm Beach, Fla., 1984—85, Buckingham Coun. Arts, 1996, 1998, Cumberland Court House, Va., 1999, Cheese & Co., Farmville, Va., 2000, Cafe Zelia, 2002—05, Va. Southside C.C., 2002, exhibited in group shows at Va. Mus. Fine Arts, Warrenton, 1988, Hampden Sydney Music Festival, 1998—2006, Longwood Ctr. for Visual Arts, Farmville, Va., juried exhbn., Best of Show, Buckingham Arts Coun., 1995—2006. V.p. ctrl. Va. arts affiliate Va. Mus. Fine Arts, Richmond, 2004—05, pres., 2006—. Mem.: DAR (bd. mem., corr. sec. 1971—75), Buckingham Artists Guild (planning com. 1995—), Curdsville Cmty. Ctr. (sec. 2006—), English Speaking Union, Friends of the Libr., Hist. Buckingham Inc., Audubon Artists Inc. (assoc.), Art Students League N.Y.C. (life; corr. sec.), Buckingham-Dillwyn Garden Club (sec. 1996—). Episcopalian. Avocations: museums, gardening, miniature horse. Home: 843 Simpson Rd Prospect VA 23960

SHIELDS, BROOKE CHRISTA CAMILLE, actress, model; m. Andre Agassi, Apr. 19, 1997 (annulled 1999); m. Chris Henchy, Apr. 4, 2001; children: Rowan Francis Henchy, Grier Hammond Henchy. BA, Princeton U., 1987. Model for Ivory Soap commls. starting in 1966, later for Calvin Klein jeans and Colgate toothpaste commls.; Actor (films) Alice, Sweet Alice, 1975, Pretty Baby, 1977, King of the Gypsies, 1978, Wanda Nevada, 1978, Just You and Me Kid, 1978, Blue Lagoon, 1979, Endless Love, 1980, Sahara, 1983, Backstreet Strays, 1989, Brenda Starr, 1992, Seventh Floor, 1993, Running Wild, 1993, Freaked, 1993, Freeway, 1996, The Misadventures of Margaret, 1998, The Weekend, 1999, The Bachelor, 1999, Black & White, 1999, After Sex, 2000, Rent-A-Husband, 2004; (TV movies) The Prince of Central Park, 1977, After the Fall, Wet Gold, I Can Make You Love Me: The Stalking of Laura Black, 1993, Nothing Lasts Forever, 1995, What Makes a Family, 2001, Miss Spider's Sunny Patch Kids, 2003; (TV mini-series) Widows, 2002; (TV series) Suddenly Susan, 1996-99 (People's Choice award Favorite Female in New Series 1997); TV Films Bob the Butler, 2005; TV appearances include: The Tonight Show, Bob Hope spls., The Diamond Trap, 1988, Friends, 1996, Just Shoot Me, 1997, I'm With Her, 2004, That 70's Show, 2004, Niptuck 2006-; appeared on Broadway in Grease, 1994-95 (Theatre World award 1995), Wonderful Town, 2004, Chicago, 2005; Author: Down Came the Rain: My Journey Through Postpartum Depression, 2005 (NY Times Bestseller list, 2005). Named Time Mag. Face of the '80s; recipient People's Choice award Favorite Young Picture Performer, 1981—84.

SHIELDS, JULIE SELIGSON, psychologist, entrepreneur; b. Huntington, NY, Sept. 12, 1977; d. David Myer and Susan Lois Seligson; m. Joel Scott Shields, Aug. 20, 2005. BA in Psychology, Women's Studies, magna cum laude, U. Ariz., 1999; PhD in Sch. Psychology, U. SC, Columbia, 2004. Cert. sch. psychologist Md., 2005. Rsch. asst. U. Ariz., Tuscon, 1997—98, instr. for honors humanities class, 1998—99; grad. asst. for undergrad. psychology advising office, stats. lab instr., rsch. methods lab instr., rsch. lab mem. U. SC, Columbia, 1999; sch. psychologist Montgomery County Pub. Schs., Rockville, Md., 2004—. Grant asst. Safe Schs., Healthy Students, Columbia, 2001—02. Contbr. articles to profl. jours. Vol. Casa De Los Ninos, Tucson, 1998—99, Hosp. in SC, Columbia, 2002—03. Mem.: NASP (grant 2004, 2005), Phi Beta Kappa, Alpha Delta Pi (historian 1998—99, Ruth Lee Kennedy scholarship 1999, Virginia Cooney Nat. Grad. scholarship 2002). Achievements include research in 4 presentations at the National Association of School Psychologists; 1 presentation at the International Society for Quality of Life Studies; 1 presentation at the South Carolina Association for School Psychologists; 1 presentation at the South Carolina Psychological Association; 1 presentation at the University of Arizona Honors Research Forum; 1 presentation at the University of South Carolina Research Forum. Home: 9913 Tambay Ct Montgomery Village MD 20886 Office: 850 Hungerford Dr Rockville MD 20850 Office Phone: 240-485-8275. Personal E-mail: shields.julie@gmail.com.

SHIELDS, MARTHA BUCKLEY, elementary school educator; b. Ridley Park, Pa., Mar. 4, 1942; d. John Edward and Anne Josephine (Hayes) Buckley; m. James F. Shields, Aug. 22, 1964; children: James F., Martha S. Runzer, Katherine Anne Landaiche, John Edward. BA, Wheeling Jesuit U., 1964; postgrad., Widener U., 1975—76. Cert.: (paralegal). Exec. asst. Economy Engring. and Machine Works, Chester, Pa., 1970—77; tchr. gifted program RoseTree-Media Sch. Dist., Pa., 1979—80; tchr. grade 5 St. Kevin Sch., Springfield, Pa., 1980—85; tchr. honors math. grades 4-8 St. Thomas the Apostle Sch., Glen Mills, Pa., 1985—97, tchr. 7th and 8th grades, 1997—; athletic dir. St. Thomas CYO, Glen Mills, 1995—. Bd. dirs. Chester County Voices Abroad, 1994—2003. Sec. vice-chair adv. com. Children and Youth Svcs. Delaware County, Media, 1979—81, chmn. adv. com., 1999—2001, vice chair, 2003—05; volleyball and track coach St. Thomas the Apostle CYO, Glen Mills, 1977—, bd. dirs., 1977—; mem. alumni bd. Wheeling Jesuit U., 1996—, pres., 2003—05. Named Educator-Vol. of the Yr., Leadership Delaware County Alumni Assn., 1992; named to Harry Watson Track Hall of Fame, KC, 1996; recipient Clifford M. Lewis Alumnus award, Wheeling Jesuit U., 1976, Coaches award for christian leadership, Archdiocese Phila.-Cath. Youth Orgn., 1989, Julia Forst award, Archdiocese Phila., 1999, Father Francis Griffin award, St. Thomas the Apostle Parish, 1999. Roman Catholic. Avocations: travel, sewing, reading. Home: 190 Andrien Rd Glen Mills PA 19342-1168 Office: St Thomas the Apostle Sch 430 Valleybrook Rd Glen Mills PA 19342-9440 E-mail: mopsys@comcast.net.

SHIELDS, PATRICIA ALLENE, retail executive; b. Westminster, Md., June 29, 1968; d. Richard Dean and Joan Elizabeth Munroe Schnably; m. Aidan Hugh Shields, Mar. 20, 2004. BA, Wake Forest U., Winston Salem, NC, 1990. Mgr. divisional mdse. Gap, San Francisco, 2001—05; exec. v.p. Charlotte Russe, San Diego, 2005—. Alumni admissions vol. Wake Forest U., San Diego, 2001—06. Mem.: Delta Delta Delta (life; collegiate dist. officer 2003—06). Office: Charlotte Russe 4645 Morena Blvd San Diego CA 92117 Office Phone: 858-490-5912. Personal E-mail: pshields@san.rr.com.

SHIELDS, PATRICIA LYNN, educational broker, consultant; b. Bklyn. BS in Biology, Bucknell U., 1984; BA in Biology, Rutgers U., 2002; MAT in Biol. Scis., Fairleigh Dickinson U., 2002. Pres., CEO Buttercup's Internat., Inc., Middletown, N.J., 1988—. Office: Buttercup's Internat Inc PO Box 148 Middletown NJ 07748-0148

SHIELDS, PORTIA HOLMES, academic administrator; m. William H. Lewis. BS in Edn., D.C. Tchrs. Coll.; MA in Edn., George Washington U.; PhD in Early Childhood and Elem. Edn., U. Md. Various tchg. positions primary and secondary edn.; dir. med. and biomed. comm. Howard U. Coll. Medicine, Washington, 1989-93, dean Sch. of Edn., 1993-96; pres. Albany (Ga.) State U., 1996—. Presenter and cons. in field. Active Albany Mus. Art, Albany Tomorrow, Inc., Albany/Dougherty Cmty. Partnership for Edn. and Dougherty, 2000; chair steering com. Am. Reads Program; mem. bd. regents U. Sys. Ga., 1997; bd. dirs. Cmtys. in Schs. Mem.: Albany C. of C. (bd. dirs.), Nat. Coun. for Accreditation Tchr. Edn. (bd. dirs.), Am. Coun. on Edn. (bd. dirs., mem. appeals com.), Orgn. Instnl. Affiliates (bd. dirs.), Am. Assn. Colls. for Tchr. Edn. (bd. dirs.), Am. Assn. State Colls. and Univs. (com. on cultural diversity and social change). Office: Albany State U 504 College Dr Albany GA 31705 E-mail: pshields@asurams.edu.

SHIENTAG, FLORENCE PERLOW, lawyer; b. NYC; d. David and Ester (Germane) Perlow; m. Bernard L. Shientag, June 8, 1938. BS, NYU, 1940, LLB, 1933, JD, 1940. Bar: Fla. 1976, N.Y. Law aide Thomas E. Dewey, 1937; law sec. Mayor La Guardia, 1939-42; justice Domestic Relations Ct., 1941-42; mem. Tchrs. Retirement Bd., N.Y.C., 1942-46; asst. U.S. atty. So. dist. N.Y., 1943-53; cir. ct. mediator Fla. Supreme Ct., 1992; pvt. practice N.Y.C., 1960—, Palm Beach, Fla., 1976—. Lectr. on internat. divorce; mem. Nat. Commn. on Wiretapping and Electronic Surveillance, 1973—, Task Force on Women in Cts., 1985-86. Contbr. articles to profl. jours. Candidate N.Y. State Senate, 1954; bd. dirs. UN Devel. Corp., 1972-95, Franklin and Eleanor Roosevelt Inst., 1985—; bd. dirs., assoc. treas. YM and YWHA; hon. commr. commerce, N.Y.C. Mem. ABA, Fed. Bar Assn. (exec. com.), Internat. Bar Assn., N.Y. Women's Bar Assn. (pres., dir., Life Time Achievement award 1994, special award 2002), N.Y. State Bar Assn., N.Y.C. Bar Assn. (chmn. law and art sect.), N.Y. County Lawyers Assn. (dir.), Nat. Assn. Women LAwyers (sec.). Home: 737 Park Ave New York NY 10021-4256 Address: 44 Cocoanut Row Palm Beach FL 33480 Office Phone: 212-861-8800.

SHIER, ELIZABETH M., music educator; b. Woodbury, N.J., Apr. 29, 1963; d. Nick T. and Virginia (Vance) Macchiarolo; m. Wes Shier; children: Brittany, Erin, Jonathan, Nicolas. MusB in Edn. and Music Therapy, Henderson State U., 1985; MEd in Elem. Edn., U. North Tex., 1996. Cert. music tchr. preK-12 Tex., gen. elem. tchr. grades 1-8 Tex. Elem. music specialist North Little Rock (Ark.) Sch. Dist., 1986—87, Grapevine-Colleyville Ind. Sch. Dist., Euless, Tex., 1987—97, Birdville Ind. Sch. Dist., North Richland Hills, Tex., 1997—. Staff devel. trainer Birdville Ind. Sch. Dist., North Richland Hills, Tex., 2002—; cons./trainer Ctr. for Educator Devel. in Fine Arts, San Antonio, 2001—; workshop presenter Tex. Music Educators Assn., San Antonio, 1997—2003. Author: (musical play) The Wacky Wound-Up Watch; contbr. articles to ednl. jours. Vol. usher Bass Performance Hall, Fort Worth, Tex., 1998—99; team in tng. mentor Leukemia/Lymphoma Soc., Dallas, 2001—03; exec. bd. mem. Bear Creek and ACFT PTA's, Euless and North Richland Hills, Tex., 1991—2003. Mem.: Ctr. for Educator Devel. in Fine Arts, Music Educators Nat. Conf., Assn. of Tex. Profl. Educators, Tex. Music Educators Assn. (workshop presenter 1997—), Delta Omicron (life). Avocations: marathon running, triathlons and duathlons, travel, tap dancing. Office: Acad at Carrie F Thomas Elem 8200 O'Brian Way North Richland Hills TX 76180 Personal E-mail: macch1@sbcglobal.net.

SHIER, GLORIA BULAN, mathematics professor; b. The Philippines; came to U.S., 1966. d. Melecio Cauilan and Florentina (Cumagun) Bulan; m. Wayne Thomas Shier; children: John Thomas, Marie Teresita, Anna Christina. BS, U. Santo Tomas; MA, U. Ill., 1968; PhD, U. Minn., 1986. Tchr. Cagayan Valley Coll., Cagayan, Philippines, St. Paul Coll., Manila, Manila Div. City Schs.; asst. prof. U. of East, Manila; rsch. asst. U. Ill., Urbana, 1968—69; instr. Miramar C.C., San Diego, 1974—75, Mesa C.C., San Diego, 1975—80, Lakewood C.C., St. Paul, 1984, U. Minn., Mpls., 1986—87, North Hennepin C.C., Brooklyn Park, Minn., 1987—. Cons. PWS Kent Pub. Co., Boston, 1989—. Chairperson Filipino Am. Edn. Assn., San Diego, 1978-79. Fulbright scholar U.S. State Dept., U. Ill., 1966-70; fellow Nat. Sci. Found., Oberlin Coll., 1967; recipient Excellence in Teaching award UN Ednl. Scientific Cultural Organ., U. Philippines, Cert. Commendation award The Gov. of Minn., 1990, Outstanding Filipino in the Midwest Edn. Cat. award 1992, Cavite Assn., 1998, Gintong Pamana Found.; Outstanding Filipino-Am. in Edn. Mem.: Am. Statis. Assn., Minn. Math. Assn. of Two Yr. Colls., Minn. Coun. Tchrs. Math., Internat. Group for Psychology of Math. Edn., Am. Math. Assn. for Two Yr. Colls., Nat. Coun. Tchrs. Math., Philippine-Am. Acad. Sci. and Engring., Math. Assn. Am., Am. Math. Soc., Fil-Minnesotan Assn. (bd. dirs. 1991—2004, v.p. 2004—), Cultural Soc. Filipino-Ams. (pres. 2001—), Sigma Xi, Phi Kappa Phi. Roman Catholic. Avocation: piano. Office Phone: 763-424-0834. Business E-Mail: gshier@nhcc.edu.

SHIER, JULIET MARIE, social studies educator; b. Seattle, Jan. 23, 1967; d. James E. and Martha L. Hall; m. Peter M. Shier, Nov. 29, 1991; children: Katherine L., Emily A., Mary E. MS in Edn., Western Oreg. U., Monmouth, 2000. Cert. tchr. K-8 Alaska, 1991. Tchr. 2d and 6th Cath. Schs. of Fairbanks, Alaska, 1991—95; reading tchr. Hunter Elem., Fairnbanks, 1996—97; kindergarten tchr. Anderson Elem., Eielson AFB, Alaska, 1997—99; tchr. 2d grade Pearl Creek Elem., Fairbanks, 1999; tchr. English and lit. North Pole Mid. Sch., Fairbanks, 2000—03; tchr. English and social studies Tanana Mid. Sch., Fairbanks, 2003—. Mentor tchr. U. Alaska, Fairbanks, 2004—. Religious edn. and youth group Cath. D. of Fairbanks, 2002—06. Mem.: NEA (assoc.). Catholic. Avocations: travel, reading, kayaking, theater, skiing. Home: P O Box 84615 Fairbanks AK 99708 Office: Fairbanks North Star Borough School Dist 520 5th Ave Fairbanks AK 99701 Office Phone: 907-452-8145 9166. Business E-Mail: jshier@northstar.k12.ak.us.

SHIER, SHELLEY M., production company executive; b. Toronto, Mar. 15, 1957; d. Harry Shier and Rosaline (Cutler) Sonshine; m. Hank O'Neal, May 14, 1985. Student, H.B. Studio, NYC, 1975—76, Stella Adler Conservatory, 1976—80. Company mem., actor Soho Artists Theater, NYC, 1976-81; casting dir. Lawrence Price Prodns., NYC, 1981-82; pres. Hoss, Inc., NYC, 1983—; v.p. Chiaroscuro Records, NYC, 1987—; pres. Broadway Bound, Inc., NYC, 1998—. Cons. Peter Martin Assocs., NYC, 1983, Norwegian Cruise Line, Miami, Fla., 1983-98, Floating Jazz Festival, 1983—,Oslo (Norway) Jazz Festival, 1986—, New Sch. Social Rsch., NYC, 1989—, Big Bands Sea, Rhythm & Blues Cruise, Dixieland Sea, 1991—, Blues Cruise, 1991—, Beacons Jazz Awards Ceremony, Tribute Music Bob Wills Texas Playboys, Mardi Gras Sea. Talent acquisition agt. Save Children, NYC, 1986, Tomorrow's Children, NYC, 1990, Barcelona Olympics, NBC, 1992, Royal Caribbean Internat., Miami, 1994-96, Ultimate Caribbean Jazz Spectacular, Country Music Festival Caribbean, CUNARD NYC, 1994—, Broadway Sea, 1996, Millennium Sea, 1999—, Broadway Bound, 1999—, others. Avocations: Karate, photography, riding, fishing, weightlifting. Office: HOSS Inc 830 Broadway New York NY 10003-4827 Office Phone: 212-674-8631, 212-674-8631. Personal E-mail: shelleymshier@aol.com. Business E-Mail: broadwayboundinc@aol.com.

SHIER, SUSAN LYNNE, music educator; d. Elmer C. and Clara M. Werning; m. Robert L. Shier, June 4, 1982; children: Robert Matthew, Blake M. MusB in Edn., Ctrl. Mo. State U., Warrensburg, 1977, MA in Edn., 1985. Cert. instrumental and vocal music tchr. K-12 Mo., 1977. Band and vocal tchr. King City Sch. Dist., Mo., 1977—81, Platte County R-III Sch. Dist., Platte City, 1981—. V.p. North Ctrl. Mo. Bandmasters, Chillicothe, Mo., 1988—89; bldg. planning com. Platte County R-III Sch. Dist., Platte City, 1988—89, 2004—, new tchr. mentor, 1992—; corr. sec. Platte County Educator Assn., 2005—. Mem. Pk. Hill South Band Parents, Riverside, Mo., PTA, Kansas City, 1981—2005; vol. local recycling ctr.; den mother Cub Scouts, Parkville, 1994—96. Nominee Excellence in Edn., Northland C. of C., 2006. Mem.: NEA, Mo. Music Educators, Mo. Bandmasters Assn., Platte County Edn. Assn. (corr. sec. 2005—06), Mo. Edn. Assn., Kappa Delta Pi, Pi Kappa Lambda, Sigma Alpha Iota (v.p. 1979—80). Democrat. Achievements include directing high school band selected to perform at Missouri Music Educators Conference; directing bands earning I ratings at District and State festivals; directing band selected to play for U.S. president during visit to Kansas City. Avocations: gardening, reading, travel. Office: Platte County R III Sch Dist PO Box 1400 Platte City MO 64079 Office Phone: 816-436-9623. Business E-Mail: shiers@periii.k12.mo.us.

SHIERSHKE, NANCY FAY, artist, educator, real estate manager; b. St. Helens, Oreg., May 10, 1935; d. David Cline and Matilda Ruth (Pearce) Morrison; m. H. McNeal Kavanagh, Sept. 4. 1955 (dec. Dec. 1978); children: Marjorie L. Wood, David M. Kavanagh, Katherine F. Fiske; m. Richard M. Shiershke, Nov. 29, 1980. AA, Pasadena City Coll., Calif., 1956; BA, UCLA, 1965. Substitute elem. sch. tchr., Buena Park, Calif., 1967-69; property mgr. Pky. Cts., Arcadia, Calif., 1977—; libr. Reading Rm., Arcadia, 1979-87; freelance artist Kavanagh-Shiershke Art St., Arcadia, Calif., 1985—; art gallery hostess Descanso Gardens, La Canada, Flintridge, Calif., 1990—; display and sales person Village Fine Arts Gallery, Arcadia, 1991-92; art instr. Tri Cmty. Adult Edn., Covina, Calif., 1994—. Art instr. Claremont (Calif.) Adult Edn. Group shows include Pasadena Presbyn. Ch., 1985—, Hillcrest Ch., 1992—, Descanso Gardens, 1994—, San Gabriel Fine Arts, 1994—. Named Artist of the Yr. Mid Valley art League, 1990; Recipient Best of Show San Gabriel Fine Arts, 1991, Hulsebus award Pasadena Prebyn. Ch., 1996, Best of Show Eagle Rock Rennaisance Plein Air, 2002. Mem. Nat. Watercolor Soc., San Gabriel Fine Arts, Mid Valley Arts League (Artist of Yr. 1998), East Valley Art Assn., Valley Watercolor Soc., Foothill Creative Arts Group, Water Color West, Calif. Art Club, So. Calif. Plein Air Painters Assn.

SHIFFER, CANDICE CAPUTO, retired special education educator, consultant; b. Scranton, Pa., Apr. 25, 1949; d. Carmen L. and Irene (Roche) Caputo; m. Donald P. Shiffer, Jr., July 3, 1971; children: Donald Paul III,

Mark Christopher, Kristen Rene. BA in Elem. and Spl. Edn., Marywood U., 1971, MS in Spl. Edn., 1974. Cert. spl. edn. tchr. Pa., elem. tchr. Pa. Spl. edn. tchr. Northeastern Ednl. Intermediate Unit 19, Mayfield, Pa., 1971-92, Abington Heights Sch., Clarks Summit, Pa., 1992—2006; ret., 2006. Mem. adv. bd. Educators Pub. Svc., Cambridge, Mass., 1999—; pvt. tutor; supr. student tchrs., 2006; supr. field experience Marywood U., Scranton, Pa., adj. prof., 2006. Mem. Clark's Summit Elem. PTA, 1998; vol. Pa. State Spl. Olympics; pvt. tutor; mem. So. Poverty Law Ctr., 2005—06; mem. vol. United Cerebral Palsy Assn., 1998—; vol. Am. Heart Assn., Lackawanna County, 1990—; fund vol. Marywood U., Scanton, Pa., 1998—, chairperson parent divsn., co-chmn. cmty. campaign. Mem.: Coun. Exceptional Children, Pa. State Edn. Assn., Marywood Alumni Assn. (adv. bd. 1999—). Achievements include having name engraved on Freedom Wall in Washington, DC. Avocations: reading, gardening, playing piano, cooking. Home: 1142 Amherst St Scranton PA 18504-3003 Personal E-mail: cccsspeciaed@aol.com.

SHIFFER, LORENA ANNETTE, secondary school educator, artist; d. Fred Joseph Shiffer and Harriett Alice Joyce; 1 child, Jason David Feilen. BA in Indsl. Arts, San Diego State U., 1974. Cert. tchr. Calif., 1974. Tchr. photography Prescott (Ariz.) H.S., 1995—. Numerous art shows. Office Phone: 928-445-2322. Business E-Mail: lorena.shiffer@prescottschools.com.

SHIFFLET, NICOLE R., secondary school educator; b. Kankakee, Ill., Mar. 7, 1974; d. Louis F. and Rachael A. Bishop; m. Michael P. Shifflet, June 26, 2003; children: Haley G Maland, Kamryn N. AA, Joliet Jr. Coll., Ill., 1994; BS, Olivet Nazarene U., 1998, MA in Edn., 2003. Cert. tchr. Ill. Tchr. Certification Bd., 1997. Tchr. art Streator (Ill.) Twp. H.S., La-Salle-Peru (Ill.) H.S., 1997—98, Clifton (Ill.) Ctrl. H.S., 1998—, Nash M.S., Clifton, 1998—. Mem.: Ill. Edn. Tchrs. (mem. social and scholarship com. 2003—). Luth. Home: 407 Chester Cabery IL 60919 Office: Community Unit School District #4 1134 E 3100 N Rd Clifton IL 60919 Office Phone: 815-694-2321. Personal E-mail: nikkim1@prodigy.net.

SHIFFMAN, LESLIE BROWN, retired apparel executive; b. Fresno, Calif., Dec. 9, 1936; d. Albert Brown and Marion Jean (Riese) Brown; married, Jan. 20, 1957 (div. 1972); m. Sydney Shiffman, July 4, 1993; children: Susan, Steven, David, Thomas. BS, U. So. Calif., 1958. Office mgr. pvt. practice physician, Long Beach, Calif., 1971-73; cost acct. Panavision, Inc., Tarzana, Calif., 1974-76; exec. sec. Hartman Galleries, Beverly Hills, Calif., 1976-78; adminstrv. exec., corp. treas. Galanos Originals, L.A., 1978-98; adminstrv. asst., rabbinic asst., dir. adult edn. Sinai Temple, L.A., 1998—2002; ret., 2002. Alt. del. Nat. Panhellenic Conf., 2003—05. Mem. LA Alumnae Panhellenic, Woman of Yr. 2000), Alpha Epsilon Phi (nat. pres. 1985-89, 99-2003, trustee 1985-2003, sec. Found. Inc. 1990-91, pres. 1991-95, treas. 1996-98, v.p., 2005, Woman of Distinction award 1993), Order of Omega, L.A. Alumnae Panhellenic Assn. (v.p. 2003-04, pres. 2004-05), Carmel Hadassah (v.p. programs, 2006—), NCJW (bd. mem. 2006-). Democrat. Jewish. Avocation: knitting. Home: 3450 Claremore Ave Long Beach CA 90808 Personal E-mail: lbshiffman@aol.com.

SHIFFRIN, NANCY, writer, educator; d. Martin and Minna Shiffrin. BA, Calif. State U., 1972; PhD, Union Inst., 1994. Adj. prof. LA Cmty. Coll. Dist., 1990—. Author: What She Could Not Name, 1987, The Holy Letters, 2000, My Jewish Name, 2002. Recipient 1st prize, Acad. Am. Poets Coll. Competition, 1972. Jewish. Avocations: yoga, hiking, Jewish culture. Office: PO Box 1506 Santa Monica CA 90406-1506 Personal E-mail: nshiffrin@earthlink.net.

SHIGEKUNI, JULIE YURIKO, language educator, writer; d. Phillip Masanori and Marion Shigekuni; m. Jonathan Daniel Wilks, Dec. 29, 1991; children: Issa Sarah Wilks children: Kiyomi Adin Wilks, Emiko Alizah Wilks. MFA, Sarah Lawrence Coll., Bronxville, NY, 1991. Prof. creative writing Inst. Am. Indian Arts, Santa Fe, 1993—97; vis. writer Mills Coll., Oakland, Calif., 1997—98; assoc. prof. U. N.Mex, Albuquerque, 1998—. Author: (novel) A Bridge Between Us, 1995 (PEN Oakland Josephine Miles award excellence in lit., 1997), paperback edit., 1996, (novel) Invisible Gardens, 2003. Office: U NMex MSC03-2170 Humanities 374 Albuquerque NM 87131-0001 Office Phone: 505-277-4377. Home Fax: 505-277-0021. Business E-Mail: jshig@unm.edu.

SHIGEMASA, TERESA, mental health services professional, educator; d. Kermin Joseph Guidry and Melva Gene Bell; m. Greg Uichi Shigemasa, June 29, 1996; children: Emily Guidry-Nguyen, Skye. BFA, So. Meth. U., Dallas, 1977; MSCP, Chaminade U., Honolulu, 2000. Cert. LMHC #1, DCCA Hawaii, 2005, RPT-S, S-874 Assn. Play Therapy, 2006, registered play therapist, supr. play therapist candidates Assn. Play Therapy, 2006. Instr. domestic violence Child & Family Svc., Honolulu, 1998—2001; behavioral specialist Dept. Edn.-Sunset Beach Elem. Sch., Haleiwa, Hawaii, 2001—. Dancer, singer, actress profl. summer stock prodns., Dallas, Brunswick, Maine. Vol. local schs. various musical prodns. Mem.: Hawaii Assn. Play Therapy (pub. rels. 2005—06), Assn. Play Therapy, Hawaii Counseling Assn., Psi Chi Honor Soc., Alpha Lambda Delta. Avocations: dance, music. Office: Dept Edn Sunset Beach Elem Sch 59-360 Kamehameha Hwy Haleiwa HI 96712 Personal E-mail: tshigema21@yahoo.com.

SHIGEMOTO, APRIL FUMIE, language educator; b. Lihue, Hawaii, Apr. 22, 1948; d. Warren Itaru and Edith Yuriko (Yoshimura) Tanaka; m. Tom Hideo Shigemoto, July 21, 1973; children: Taylor, Tyron, Tryson, Thomas-Jay. BA in English, U. Hawaii Manoa, 1970, profl. diploma secondary, 1971. English tchr. Kapaa (Hawaii) H.S. and Intermediate Sch., 1971-81, Kauai H.S. and Intermediate Sch., Lihue, Hawaii, 1981-90, core curriculum coord., 1990—, comprehensive student support svc. dist. resource tchr., 2001, sch. assessment liaison dist. resource tchr., 2002—. Leader Boy Scouts of Am., Lihue, Hawaii, 1982—. Recipient one of seven Status of Women awards, Kauai, Lihue, Hawaii, 1988, Den Leader of the Yr. award Boy Scouts of Am., 1988, Milken Educator's award, Milken Found., L.A., 1992; named Outstanding Working Mother, Garden Island Newspaper, Lihue, Hawaii, 1989, Kauai Dist. Tchr. of Yr., State Dept. Edn., Hawaii, 1990, State Tchr. of Yr., Scottish Rite Order of Free Masons, Honolulu, 1991, one of Kauai's Outstanding Families, Garden Island Newspaper, Hawaii, 1992. Mem. Nat. Coun. Tchrs. of English, Assn. for Supervision and Curriculum Devel., Phi Delta Kappa, Delta Kappa Gamma. Democrat. Avocations: travel, reading, golf. Office: Kauai Dist Office 3060 Eiwa St Lihue HI 96766

SHIH, J. CHUNG-WEN, Chinese language educator; b. Nanking, China; came to U.S., 1948, naturalized, 1960; d. Cho-kiang and Chia-pu (Fang) S. BA, St. John's U., Shanghai, 1945; MA, Duke U., 1949, PhD, 1955. Asst. prof. English Kings Coll. N.Y., 1955-56; asst. prof. U. Bridgeport, Conn., 1956-60; postdoctoral fellow East Asian Studies Harvard, 1960-61; asst. prof. Chinese Stanford, 1961-64; asso. prof. Chinese Pomona Coll., 1965-66; asso. prof. George Washington U., Washington, 1966-71, prof., chmn. dept. East Asian langs. and lit., 1971-93, prof. emeritus, 1993—, rsch. prof., 1994—. Author: Injustice to Tou O, 1972, the Golden Age of Chinese Drama: Yuan Tsa-chu, 1976, Return from Silence: China's Writers of the May Fourth Tradition, 1983, (interactive CD and book) Learn Chinese from Modern Writers, 2002. Bd. dirs. Sino-Am. Cultural Soc., Washington, 1971-80, 95—. AAUW fellow, 1964-65; Social Sci. Rsch. Coun. fellow, 1976-77; grantee NEH, 1979-80, 89-91, 95-97, Annenberg/CPB Project, 1989-92; Sr. scholars exchange program NAS, China, 1980. Mem. Assn. Asian Studies, Am. Council Fgn. Lang. Tchrs., Chinese Lang. Tchrs. Assn. (chmn. exec. bd. 1976-78) Home: 2500 Virginia Ave NW Washington DC 20037-1901 Office: George Washington U Dept East Asian Langs Washington DC 20052-0001 Business E-Mail: cwshih@gwu.edu.

SHIKASHIO, HIROKO, artist, interpreter, educator; b. Japan; d. Koichi and Kaoru Ogihara; m. Tommy Kiyoshi Shikashio, July 26, 1969; children: Christopher, Michael. BD, Japan Christian Coll., Tokyo, 1965; BFA, Calif. State Coll., L.A., 1969. Coord. internat. art exch. R.I. Watercolor Soc., Pawtucket, 1984—86; coord. internat. art exhibit 19 On Paper, Providence, 1995—97; coord. cultural tour and workshop Japan Cultural Tour and Workshop, 2002—. Mag. cover, Lit. Mag. of Bryant Coll. Surge, 1996, New Art Internat., 2001, R.I. Medicine Health, 2003, book cover, Creation Regained, 1989, one-woman shows include Newport (R.I.) Art Mus., 2002. Recipient Gold prize, New Haven Paints and Clay Club, 1988, award, R.I. Watercolor Soc., 1992, Theilen Meml. award, Watercolor USA, Springfield, Mo., 1995, Jurors award, Wash. & Jefferson Coll., 1996, First Pl. award, Glastonbury (Conn.) Art Show, 1997, Newport Art Mus. award, Newport Artist Guild, 2001, First Pl. in Mixed Media, Narragansett (R.I.) Art Show, 2002, Best in Show, Old Saybrook (Conn.) Art Show, 2002. Mem.: Art League R.I. (licentiate), Watercolor USA Honor Soc. (licentiate), 19 On Paper (licentiate), New Haven Paints and Clay Club (licentiate), Pa. Watercolor Soc. (licentiate), R.I. Watercolor Soc. (licentiate). Office Phone: 401-827-0645.

SHILEPSKY, NANCY SUE, lawyer; b. Westport, Conn., Apr. 25, 1952; d. Morris Jacob and Rose (Pfeffer) S. BA magna cum laude, Tufts U., 1974; JD, Boston U., 1978. Bar: Mass. 1978, U.S. Dist. Ct. Mass. 1978. Dir. Legal Info. Ctr. Bklyn. Coll., 1978-79; staff atty. Western Mass. Legal Svcs., Springfield, 1980-81; ptnr. Northampton (Mass.) Law Collective, 1982-84; assoc. Schreiber & Assocs., Boston, 1984-87, McDonald, Noonan & Kaplan, Newton, Mass., 1987-88; ptnr. Rudavsky & Shilepsky, Boston, 1988, Shilepsky, Messing & Rudavsky, Boston, 1988—2005, Perkins Smith& Cohen, Boston, Shilepsky O'Connell, Boston, 2005—. Speaker Mass. Continuing Legal Edn., Inc., Boston, 1988—. Named one of top Boston lawyers, Boston Mag., 2004. Mem.: Boston Bar Assn. (treas. 2004—05), Mass. Bar Assn.-Labor & Employment Law Sect. (chmn. employee rights & responsibilities com. 1990—91, 1993—94, sect. coun. 1993—96), Boston Bar Assn.-Labor & Employment Law Sect. (co-chmn. 1996—99, sect. coun. 1996—). Office: Shilepsky O'Connell 225 Franklin St Boston MA 02110 Office Phone: 617-854-4275, 617-447-2806. Office Fax: 617-854-4040. Business E-Mail: nshilepsky@sholaw.com.

SHILLINGFORD, PAMELA LYNN, mathematics educator; b. Shamokin, Pa., June 12, 1978; d. Andrea Marie Shillingford. BA, Bloomsburg U., Pa., 2001; MA, Lehigh U., Bethlehem, Pa., 2004. Math tchr. Northwestern Lehigh HS, New Tripoli, Pa., 2002—03, Phillipsburg HS, Phillipsburg, NJ, 2004, Our Lady of Perpetual Help Sch., Bethlehem, Pa., 2004—. Personal E-mail: plshillingford@hotmail.com.

SHILLINGLAW, REGINA D., psychologist; b. Lancaster, S.C., Aug. 14, 1967; d. Rex Howland Dillingham II and Ruth Lambert Dillingham Palmer; m. Mark Andrew Shillinglaw, Oct. 24, 1992. BA, U. S.C., 1989, PhD, 1998. Lic. in Psychology NC. Psychology resident USAF, Wright Patterson AFB, Calif., 1997—98, chief psychol. svc. Robins AFB, Ga., 1998—. Team chief critical incident stress mgmt. 78th Med. Group, Robins AFB, 1999—, program dir. pet therapy program, 1999—. Contbr. articles to profl. jours. Mem. Jr. League High Point, Perry United Meth. Ch., Ga., 2000—, Wesley Meml. United Meth. Ch., High Point, NC, 2002—. Capt. USAF, 1997—2001. Decorated Achievement Medal USAF, Commendation Medal. Mem.: APA, NC Psychol. Assn., Guilford County Psychol. Assn., Ga. Psychol. Assn. Avocations: jogging, camping.

SHILLINGSBURG, CYNTHIA LYNN, medical technician, educator; b. Reading, Pa., Aug. 20, 1956; d. Louis Fudeman and Eleanor Ruth Knowles-Fudeman; m. Richard Charles Shillingsburg, June 30, 1979; children: Ashley, Britta. BA, Alvernia Coll., Reading, PA, 1977—79. Faculty Thomas Jefferson U., Philadelphia, Pa., 1999—; icavl vascular lab. dir. The Glover Clinic, Drexel Hill, Pa., 1982—2001; assoc. degree instr. Ea. Coll., St. Davids, Pa., 1994—97; vascular technologist/cardiac sonographer Christiana Care Health Ctr., Newark, Del., 1999—2000. Chair Del. Valley Regional Vascular Curriculum Com. Adv. Bd., Bryn Mawr, Pa., 1994—97. Contbr. national institute of health grant Identification of Needs of Novice Allied Health Researchers, 2001. Girl scout leader Freedom Valley Girl Scout Coun., Valley Forge, Pa., 1991—2001; judge Pa. Jr. Acad. of Sci., Pa., 1997—2002. Mem.: Americal Soc. of Echocardiography, Soc. of Diagnostic Med. Sonographers, Soc. of Vascular Tech. (continuing edn. com. 2001—02). R-Liberal. United Methodist. Avocation: swimming, scuba diving, travel, camping, hiking, reading, parenting, cardiovascular training, musicals. Office: Thomas Jefferson University 130 South 9th Street Suite 1007 Philadelphia PA 19107-5233 Home: 2017 Harbour Gates Dr Apt# 203 Annapolis MD 21401-5377 Office Phone: 215-503-2507. Personal E-mail: lfclf@aol.com. Business E-Mail: cynthia.shillingsburg@jefferson.edu.

SHILLINGSBURG, MIRIAM JONES, literature educator, academic administrator; b. Balt., Oct. 5, 1943; d. W. Elvin and Miriam R. Jones; m. Peter L. Shillingsburg, Nov. 21, 1967; children: Robert, George, John, Alice, Anne Carol. BA, Mars Hill Coll., 1964; MA, U. S.C., 1966, PhD, 1969; BGS, Miss. State U., 1994. Asst. prof. Limestone Coll., Gaffney, SC, 1969, Miss. State U., 1970—75, assoc. prof., 1975—80, prof. English, 1980—96, assoc. v.p. for acad. affairs, 1988—96, dir. summer sch., 1990—96, dir. undergrad. studies, 1994—96; dean arts and scis. Lamar U., Tex., 1996—99; dean liberal arts and scis. Ind. U., South Bend, 2000—04, dean sch. edn., 2005—06. Disting. acad. visitor Mark Twain Ctr., 1993, 2001; Simms rsch. prof. U. S.C., 1998; vis. fellow Australian Def. Force Acad., 1989; Fulbright lectr. U. New South Wales, Duntroon, Australia, 1984-85. NEH fellow in residence, Columbia U., 1976-77. Author: Mark Twain in Australasia, 1988; editor: Conquest of Granada, 1988, The Cub of the Panther, 1997, Confession, 2005; mem. editl. bd. Works of W.M. Thackeray, Miss. Quar., So. Quar.; contbr. articles to profl. jours. and mags. Mem. South Ctrl. 18th Century Soc., Am. Lit. Assn., Pop Culture Assn., Sigma Tau Delta, Phi Kappa Phi, Simms Soc. (pres. 1996-97). Business E-Mail: mshillin@iusb.edu.

SHIMABUKURO, GRACE KUO, mathematics educator; b. Taipei, Taiwan, Nov. 22, 1949; d. Chin Nian and Api Lin Kuo; m. Donald T. Shimabukuro, June 22, 1969; 1 child, Kendall. BS in Edn., N.E. Mo. State Tchrs. Coll., Kirksville, 1967. Cert. tchr., secondary math. Hawaii Dept. Edn. Math tchr. Scotland County Rural-I, Memphis, Mo., 1967—69, Paia Sch., Hawaii, 1970, Puunene Sch., 1971—72, Iao Intermediate Sch., Wailuku, 1970—77, 1972—. Sch. campaign coord. Maui United Way, Wailuku, 1996—. Recipient Tchr. of Yr. award, Iao Renaissance Ke alo hou Edn. Found., 1998—99. Mem. Christian Ch. Avocations: reading, music, piano. Office: Iao Intermediate Sch 260 S Market St Wailuku HI 96793 Office Phone: 808-984-5610.

SHIMCHICK, MARIE, music educator; d. John George and Mary Shimchick. MusB magna cum laude, Ithaca Coll., 1981—85; M in reading, U. of Hartford, 1989—90. Teaching Cert., Music K-12 Conn., Teaching Cert., Reading Cons. K-12 CT, Coaching Cert. Conn., Conn. Writing Project Conn., 1996. Music tchr. New Lebanon Elem. Sch., Byram, Conn., 1985—89, Western and Ctrl. Jr. High Schools, Greenwich, Conn., 1985—87, Ea. Mid. Sch., Riverside, Conn., 1987—2003, Greenwich H.S., Conn., 2003—. Softball coach Western Jr. H.S., Greenwich, Conn., 1986—87, Ea. Jr. H.S., Riverside, Conn., 1988—89; asst. varsity softball coach Greenwich HS, 1992—94, varsity girls' golf coach, 2005—; softball coach Ea. Mid. Sch., Riverside, Conn., 1997—2004. Conductor, artistic director (choral) Eastmen; singer: Greenwich Choral Soc. Recipient Tchr. of the Yr., Phi Delta Kappa, 1999. Mem.: Internat. Reading Assn., Orgn. of Am. Kodaly Educators, Am. Orff-Schulwerk Assn., Nat. Assn. of Teachers of English, Music Educators Nat. Conf., Am. Choral Directors Assn. (life), U.S. Golf Tchrs. Fed. (level II instr.), Phi Delta Kappa, Sigma Alpha Iota (v.p. 1983—85, Scholastic Honor award 1985). Liberal. Eastern Orthodox Christian. Avocations: skiing, racquet sports, fine dining and wines, golf. Office: Greenwich H S 10 Hillside Rd Greenwich CT 06830 Personal E-mail: riechick@hotmail.com. Business E-Mail: marie_shimchick@greenwich.k12.ct.us.

SHIMEK, ROSEMARY GERALYN, medical/surgical nurse; b. Manitowoc, Wis., Oct. 12, 1952; d. Raymond James and Margaret Rita (Zinkel) Trainor; m. Richard Joseph Shimek, May 23, 1987. Diploma, Lakeshore Tech. Inst., Sheboygan, Wis., 1972; ADN, Lakeshore Tech. Coll., Cleveland, Wis., 1989; BSN, Marian Coll., 1998. RN Wis., cert. in med-surg. nursing, ANCC, LPN. Nurse Holy Family Meml. Med. Ctr., Manitowoc, 1972-89, student nurse intern, 1988-89, unit clk., 1988-89, charge nurse med. fl., 1989—2004, RN Pain Clinic, 2004—, RN Heart Ctr., 2004—. Scholar Charles E. Wall, Lakeshore Tech. Coll., 1989, Karen Deehr, Holy Family Meml. Med. Ctr., 1997. Home: 925 N 24th St Manitowoc WI 54220-2448

SHIMELMAN, SUSAN FROMM, state agency administrator; b. NYC, May 5, 1942; BA, McGill U., Montreal, 1964; MS, Columbia U., 1970. Fellow Harvard U., Cambridge, Mass., 1964-65; Can. coun. fellow McGill U., Montreal, 1965-68; asst. dir. Yale-New Haven Hosp., 1970-80; exec. dir. New Haven Jewish Fedn., 1980-90; undersec. Office Policy and Mgmt., State of Conn., Hartford, 1991-94, sec., 1994—95, dir. presdl. debates, 1995; dir. spl. cts. jud. br. State of Conn., 1995—2001; dir. Office Fiscal Analysis, 2001—. Chair Prison and Jail Overcrowding Commn., Hartford, 1990—, Health Care State Conn., Hartford, 1992—, Exec. Com. Info. and Tech., Hartford, 1994; vice chair Cmty. Econ. Devel. Found., Hartford, 1994. Bd. dirs. Fedn. United Way, New Haven, 1970-94; alt. N.E. Regional Compact, N.J. and Conn., 1991-94; active A Conn. Party, Hartford, 1990-94. Recipient Pres. award New Haven Jewish Fedn., 1990; named Powerful Woman of Vision, YWCA, 1988. Democrat. Home: 4 Kensington Park Bloomfield CT 06002-2146 Office Phone: 860-240-0211. Personal E-mail: sueshimelman@msn.com.

SHIMMIN, MARGARET ANN, women's health nurse; b. Forbes, ND, Oct. 26, 1941; d. George and Reba S. Diploma in Nursing, St. Luke's Hosp. Sch. Nursing, Fargo, N.D., 1962; BSW, U. West Fla., 1978; cert. ob-gyn nurse practitioner, U. Ala., Birmingham, 1983, MPH, 1986. Lic. nurse, Fla., N.D., Ala. Head nurse, emergency room St. Luke's Hosps., Fargo, 1962-67; charge nurse, labor and delivery, perinatal nurse educator Sacred Heart Hosp., Pensacola, Fla., 1970-82; ARNP Escambia County Pub. Health Unit, Pensacola, 1983-89; cmty. health nursing cons. Dist. 1 Health and Rehab. Svcs., Pensacola, 1989-96; sr. cmty. health nursing supr. Escambia County Health Dept., Pensacola, 1996—, nurse program specialist OSHA staff tng. and quality assurance, 2002—05, nurse program specialist diabetes intervention program, 2005—. Capt. nurse corps U.S. Army, 1967-70, Japan. Mem. NAACOG (cert. maternal-gynecol.-neonatal nursing, ob-gyn nurse practitioner), Fla. Nurses' Assn., ANA, N.W. Fla. ARNP (past sec./treas.), Fla. Perinatal Assn., Nat. Perinatal Assn., Healthy Mothers/Healthy Babies Coalition, Fla. Pub. Health Assn., U. West Fla. Alumni Assn., U. Ala. at Birmingham Sch. of Public Health Alumni Assn., Phi Alpha Republican. Presbyterian. Avocations: cooking, music, travel, photography, reading. Home: 8570 Olympia Rd Pensacola FL 32514-8029 Office: Escambia County Health Dept 1295 W Fairfield Dr Pensacola FL 32501-1107 Office Phone: 850-595-6048.

SHIMOKUBO, JANICE TERUKO, marketing professional; b. Chgo. d. Paul Kazuso and Tsugiye Jane (Fujii) Shimokubo; m. Ronald Theodore Spreigl, Jan. 3, 1982; 1 child, Elizabeth Shimokubo Spreigl. BA, U. Ill., 1973; MBA, Loyola U., Chgo., 1976. Sales rep. 3M Co., Rockford, Ill., 1976-79, mktg. coord. St. Paul, 1979-81, mktg. supr., 1981-83, mktg. mgr., 1983-88, sales and mktg. mgr., 1988-90; mktg. dir. U S WEST Comms., Inc., Phoenix, 1990-95, exec. dir. Denver, 1995—. Advisor Jr. Achievement, St. Paul, 1980-82; mem. 3M Women's Adv. Coun., St. paul, 1984-87. Commr. Colo. Civil Rights commn., Denver, 1997—; bd. dirs. Ariz. Kidney Found., Phoenix, 1994-95, Phoenix Fire Pals, 1990-92, Melpomene Women's Health, St. Paul., 1986, YWCA USA, 1998—. Recipient Unity award KWGN-TV, 1997; Asian Pacific Am. Women's Leadership Inst. fellow, 1996. Fellow Internat. Women's Forum, 1998-99; mem. Am. Mktg. Assn. (nat. bd. dirs. 1999—), Women in Cable and Telecomms., Japanese Am. Citizens League, U. Ill. Alumni Assn., Alpha Omicron Pi. Avocations: golf, yoga, travel, needlecrafts.

SHIN, ROSE YUKINO, elementary school educator; b. Honolulu, Sept. 5, 1950; d. Edward Masami and Ellen Chiyo (Takaki) Tokushige; m. Malcolm Blevin Shin, May 18, 1974; children: Kevin E.M., Michelle S.H. BE, U. Hawaii, 1972, profl. diploma, 1973. Cert. tchr., Hawaii. Tchr. Leihoku Elem. Sch., Waianae, Hawaii, 1987-88, Nanakuli (Hawaii) Elem. Sch., 1988-91, Mauka Lani Elem. Sch., Makakilo, Hawaii, 1991—. Sec. Palehua Vista Community Assn., Makakilo, 1988-91. Mem. Hawaii State Tchrs. Assn. (Leeward editor 1989-93, leeward webmaster, 1998—), Pi Lambda Theta (Beta Zeta chpt. sec., 2000-03), Phi Kappa Phi.

SHINDE, PATRICIA SUZANN, special education services professional, educator; b. Ashtabula, Ohio, Nov. 27, 1967; d. Charles Richard Reddig and Susan Lynn (Lounsbury) Haytcher; m. Sanjeev Shinde, Jan. 9, 1991; children: Robert Alexander, Joshua Zachary. BS in Spl. Edn., Ohio State U., 1991. Cert. in spl. edn. in severely behavioral handicaps, Ohio, Fla. Tchr. spl. edn. severely behavioral handicapped Fairfax County Pub. Schs., Springfield, Va., 1991-92; tchr. spl. edn. varying exceptionalities Escambia County Pub. Schs., Pensacola, Fla., 1993-94; tchr. spl. edn. autistic Onslow County Pub. Schs., Jacksonville, N.C., 1995-97; habilitation specialist III Onslow Behavioral Health Svcs., Jacksonville, 1997—. Asst. team mem. Onslow County Pub. Schs., Jacksonville, 1996-97. Mem. CEC, Austistic Soc. Avocations: walking, gardening, playing with children.

SHINDELMAN, MARNI, artist, educator; d. Lester and Barbara Shindelman. PhB, Miami U., Oxford, Ohio, 1999; MFA, U. Fla., 2002. Asst. prof. art U. Rochester, NY, 2002—. Artist-in-residence Shands Hosp., Gainesville, Fla., 2000—02. Mem.: Soc. Photographic Edn. Jewish. Office: U Rochester 424 Morey Hall Rochester NY 14627 Office Phone: 585-274-9249.

SHINE, KATINA LYNNIECE WILBON, neuropsychologist, consultant; d. Alma Armstead. Diploma in practical nursing, Bapt. Sch. Nursing, Little Rock, 1991; ASN, AA, U. Ark., Little Rock, 1996; BS in Liberal Arts, SUNY, Albany, 1998; MS in Counseling Psychology, U. Ctl. Tex., 1999; PhD in Psychology, U. Louisville, 2002. RN Mo.; lic. psychologist Mo. Staff nurse Ark. Easter Seal Soc., Little Rock, 1993—96; primary care nurse, mgr. Hospice of Ctrl. Ark., North Little Rock, 1996—97; intake coord., psychiat. nurse Metroplex Health Sys., Killeen, Tex., 1997—99; grad. asst., neuropsychology trainee U. Louisville, 2000—01; psychology intern St. Louis VA Med. Ctr., 2001—02, clin. psychologist, neuropsychology clin. mgr., 2002—. Rschr., lectr. in field. Contbr. articles to profl. jours. Vol. ARC Disaster Mental Health Team, St. Louis, 2004, Mental Health Assn. of St. Louis, 2004. Recipient Grad. Dean's citation, U. Louisville, 2002; fellow Acad. fellow, 1999—2001; scholar Edn. Alumni Assn. scholar, 1999—2000, Marie Erma Fust Fund scholar, Truman L. Scott scholar, U. Ark.-Little Rock, 1995, L.A. Horn Meml. scholar, 1995. Mem.: APA (divsn. clin. neuropsychology, divsn. of psychologists in pub. svc.), Nat. Register of Health Svc. Providers, Mo. Psychol. Assn. Office: #1 Jefferson Barracks Dr 116A/JB Saint Louis MO 63026

SHINER, JOSETTE SHEERAN, federal agency administrator; b. Orange, N.J., June 12, 1954; d. James Joseph and Sarah Ann (Gallagher) Sheeran; children: Nicole Munier, Daniel John, Gabrielle. BA, U. Colo., 1976. Nat. desk editor N.Y. News World, 1976-77, Washington bur. chief, 1977-80; corr. The White House, 1980-82; Capital Life and mag. editor Washington Times, 1982-84, asst. mng. editor, 1984-85, dep. mng. editor, 1985-92, mng. editor, 1992-97; pres., CEO Empower Am., 1997-2000; mng. dir. Starpoint Solutions, Reston, Va., 2000—01; assoc. U.S. Trade Rep. The White House, Washington, 2001—03, dep. U.S. Trade Repr., 2003—05; under sec. for econ. bus. & agrl. affairs US Dept. State, Washington, 2005—, US alt. gov. to The World Bank, Inter-Am. Bank, African Devel. Bank, Asian Devel. Bank, European Bank for Reconstruction & Devel., 2005—. Mem. Leadership Washington Alumni Assn., 1987-88, v.p., 1988-89, alumni chmn., 1989-90. Recipient Atrium award U. Ga., 1984, 100 Most Powerful Women in Washington award Washington Mag., 1998. Mem. White House Corrs. Assn., Am. News Womens Club, Nat. Press Club (newsmaker chmn. 1980-82,

Meritorious Svc. award 1981, Vivian award 1981), Am. Soc. Newspaper Editors, Coun. Fgn. Rels. (Washington adv. bd. 1999-2001), Sigma Delta Chi. Office: US Dept State 2201 C St NW Rm 7256 Washington DC 20520

SHINOLT, EILEEN THELMA, artist; b. Washington, May 18, 1919; d. Edward Lee and Blanche Addie (Marsh) Bennett; m. John Francis Shinolt, June 14, 1956 (dec. Aug. 1969). Student, Hans Hoffman Sch Art, 1949, Pa. Acad. Arts, 1950, Corcoran Sch. Art, 1945-51, Am. U., 1973-77. Sect. chief Dept. Army, Washington, 1940-73, retired, 1973. One-woman shows include various locations, 1982, 83, 85, 90, 94, 96; group shows include Perlmutter & Co., 1981, Fitch Fox and Brown, 1986, Foundry Gallery, 1987, Ann. Add Arts, 1986, Westminster Gallery, London, 1995; represented in permanent collections Women's Nat. Mus., Washington, Cameo Gallery, Columbia, S.C., Strathmore Hall Arts Ctr., North Bethesda, Md., 1997, 98, 99, 2000, 01, 02, 03, 04. Mem. Woman's Nat. Dem. Club, Washington, 1980—. Mem. Am. Art League (editor newsletter 1985-86, 1st pl. 1987, 2d pl. 1986), Arts Club Washington (exhbn. com. 1985—, admissions com. 1987-88), Miniature Painters, Sculptors & Gravers Soc. (historian 1989-2003, editor newsletter 1986-89), Fine Arts in Miniature. Roman Catholic. Avocations: reading, studying art periodicals, art galleries. Home: 5821 Queens Chapel Rd 232 Hyattsville MD 20782-3867

SHIPLEY, HOLLY RENE, special education educator; b. Coldwater, Ohio, July 29, 1973; d. Henry C. Seibert and Karen A. Porter; m. Anthony J. Shipley, July 3, 1999. BA, Lenoir-Rhyne Coll., 1995; M Spl. Edn., U. N.C., Charlotte, 1998. Spl. edn. tchr. St. Stephens HS, Hickory, NC, 1996—2001, dept. chair, 1999—, Wakefield HS, Raleigh, NC, 2001—02, Lancaster HS, Lancaster, Ohio, 2002—. Mem.: NEA, Team in Tng. Leukemia and Lympoma Soc. (mentor). Lutheran. Avocations: coaching cross-country and track, running marathons and half marathons, sewing. Home: PO Box 33 Somerset OH 43783-0033 Office: 1312 Granville Pike Lancaster OH 43130 Office Phone: 740-681-7500.

SHIPP, THETA WANZA, social service organization administrator, educator, consultant, minister; b. Miami, Fla., June 19, 1948; d. James Willie and Fredericka Wanza; m. Robert Glenn Shipp, June 28, 1970 (div. Aug. 1975); children: Tammi LaTrice, Eloria April Michelle. BA, Fisk U., 1970; MS, So. Ill. U., 1977; postgrad., Howard U. Ordained to ministry Christian Faith Ctrs., 1998. Asst. program dir. U. South Fla., Tampa, 1971-72; adminstr. City of Tampa, 1972-74; adminstrv. supr. Juvenile Svcs. Program, St. Petersburg, Fla., 1974-76; staff asst. City of Carbondale, Ill., 1976-77; tchg./rsch. asst., editl. asst. So. Ill. U., Carbondale, 1977-78; staff asst. U.S. Rep. Claude Pepper, Washington, 1978-82; legis./spl. asst. U.S. Rep. Mervyn M. Dymally, Washington, 1982-87; chief of staff U.S. Rep. Major R. Owens, Washington, 1987-88, U.S. Rep. Earl F. Hilliard, Washington, 1993-95; project dir. Nat. Assn. for Equal Opportunity in Higher Edn., Washington, 1998-99; asst. to v.p. for pub. policy Planned Parenthood Fedn. of Am., Washington, 2000—01; instr. D.C. Pub. Schs., 2001—. Ind. cons., 1989-03; part-time instr. dept. sociology Howard U., 1978-82. Campaign worker various congl. campaigns, 1976-2000, campaign fundraiser, 1978-97; mem. ministerial staff Michigan Park Christian Ch., Washington, 2000—; vol. Black Ch. Initiative, Religious Coalition for Reproductive Choice, Washington, 2000; ministerial cons. Soul Saving Sta., Miami, 1990—; campaign coord. Dem. Nat. Com. Office of African Am. Religious Outreach, Washington, 2000. Named one of Outstanding Young Women in Am.; recipient recognition United Negro Coll. Fund, Assn. Urban Univs., Southeastern Coun. on Ednl. Opportunity Assn., Internat. Bus. and Exec. Women, Women's Dept. Ministry of Help. Mem. NAACP, Nat. Urban League, Am. Sociol. Assn., Nat. Black Women's Agenda, Nat. Coalition on Black Civic Participation, Nat. Coalition for Black Voter Participation, Friends of Africa, Delta Sigma Theta, Alpha Kappa Delta, Phi Delta Lambda. Democrat. Avocations: reading, witnessing, movies, swimming, gardening. Home: 1441 N W 168th Terr Miami FL 33169

SHIPPEY, SANDRA LEE, lawyer; b. Casper, Wyo., June 24, 1957; d. Virgil Carr and Doris Louise (Conklin) McClintock; m. Ojars Herberts Ozols, Sept. 2, 1978 (div.); children: Michael Ojars, Sara Ann, Brian Christopher; m. James Robert Shippey, Jan. 13, 1991; 1 child, Matthew James. BA with distinction, U. Colo., 1978; JD magna cum laude, Boston U., 1982. Bar: Colo. 1982, U.S. Dist. Ct. Colo. 1985. Assoc. Cohen, Brame & Smith, Denver, 1983-84, Parcel, Meyer, Schwartz, Ruttum & Mauro, Denver, 1984-85, Mayer, Brown & Platt, Denver, 1985-87; counsel western ops. GE Capital Corp., San Diego, 1987-94; assoc. Page, Polin, Busch & Boatwright, San Diego, 1994-95; v.p., gen. counsel First Comml. Corp., San Diego, 1995-96; legal counsel NextWave Telecom Inc., San Diego, 1996-98; ptnr. Procopio, Cory, Hargreaves and Savitch, LLP, 1998—. Spkr. in field. Contbr. articles to profl. jours. Active Pop Warner football and cheerleading; bd. dirs. Southwestern Christian Schs., Inc., 2002—, San Diego Christian Found., 2001—05. Mem. Calif. State Bar (co-chair uniform comml. code com.), Phi Beta Kappa, Phi Delta Phi. Republican. Mem. Ch. of Christ. Avocations: tennis, golf, photography. Home: 15839 Big Springs Way San Diego CA 92127-2034 Office: Procopio Cory Et Al 530 B St Ste 2100 San Diego CA 92101-4496 Office Phone: 619-515-3226. Business E-Mail: sls@procopio.com.

SHIRE, TALIA ROSE (TALIA ROSE COPPOLA), actress; b. Jamaica, N.Y., Apr. 25, 1946; d. Carmine and Italia (Pennino) Coppola; m. David Lee Shire, Mar. 29, 1970 (div.); 1 son, Matthew Orlando; m. Jack Schwartzman, Aug. 23, 1979; children: Jason Francesco, Robert Carmine Coppola. Films include The Wild Racers, 1968, The Dunwich Horrors, 1970, Gas-s-s-s, 1971, The Christian Licorice State, 1971, Godfather, 1972, The Outside Man, 1972, Godfather II, 1974 (Oscar nominee for Best Supporting Actress), Rocky, 1976 (Oscar nominee for best actress, N.Y. Film Critics award for Best Supporting Actress), Old Boyfriends, 1979, Rocky II, 1979, Prophecy, 1979, Windows, 1980, Rocky III, 1982, Rocky IV, 1985, Rad, 1986, New York Stories, 1989, Cold Heaven, 1991, Godfather Part III, 1990, Rocky V, 1990, Bed and Breakfast, 1992, Deadfall, 1993, (Disney channel movie) Mark Twain, 1990, (HBO movie) Getting There, 1991, A River Made to Drown In, 1997, Divorce: A Contemporary Western, 1998, Can I Play?, 1998, Palmer's Pick Up, 1999, Caminho dos Sonhos, 1999, Lured Innocence, 1999, The Visit, 2000, The Whole Shebang, 2001, Kiss the Bride, 2002, Family Tree, 2003, Dunsmore, 2003, I Heart Huckabees, 2004, Pomegranate, 2005, Homo Erectus, 2006; TV appearances include Foster & Laurie, 1975, (TV mini series) Rich Man, Poor Man, 1976, Kill Me If You Can, 1977, Daddy, I Don't Like It Like This, 1978, Blood Vows: The Story of a Mafia Wife, 1987, Murderer's Keep, 1988, Mark Twain and Me, 1991, For Richer, For Poorer, 1992, Please, God, I'm Only Seventeen, 1992, Chatilly Lace, 1993, Born into Exile, 1997; prodr. Hyper Sapien: People from Another Star, 1986, Lionheart, 1987; assoc. prodr.: The Landlady, 1998; dir. One Night Stand, 1995.*

SHIRIKIAN-HESSELTON, JOAN LEE, safety engineer; b. Schenectady, N.Y. d. Cecilia Fava Shirikian; m. Clair Russell Hesselton, Mar. 26, 1993. BA in Chemistry, Coll. St. Rose, Albany, N.Y., 1974; MBA, Union Coll., 1986; postgrad., Columbia So. U. Forensic scientist N.Y. State Police, Albany, 1973-86; chair statewide labor mgmt. safety and health com. Pub. Employees Fedn., Albany, 1986-90; agy. safety dir. 2 N.Y. State Office Gen. Svcs., Albany, 1990-96, N.Y. State Workers Compensation Bd., Albany, 1996-99; N.E. regional safety dir. Oldcastel Precast, Inc., S. Bethlehem, N.Y., 1999—. Mem. Am. Soc. Safety Engrs., Am. Indsl. Hygiene Assn., Am. Soc. Pub. Health. Avocations: veterans benefits, fibers, spinning, wild animal care. Home: 428 Settles Hill Rd Altamont NY 12009-5712 Office: Oldcastle Precast Inc 100 County Rte 101 PO Box 155 South Bethlehem NY 12161-0155

SHIRK, MARIANNE EILEEN, veterinarian; b. Detroit, Aug. 11, 1944; d. Wesley Emerson and Eleanor Jane (Grossman) Lickfeldt. Student, U. Mich., 1962—64; DVM, Mich. State U., 1968, MS in Vet. Pathology, 1969. Diplomate Am. Bd. Vet. Practitioners. Grad. asst. Mich. State U., East Lansing, 1968—69; veterinarian Dandy Acres Vet. Clinic, Hartland, Mich., 1969—71, Quartz Mountain Animal Hosp., Scottsdale, Ariz., 1972—. Owner, operator Sundown Animal Clinic, Scottsdale; host call-in talk show Pet-Vet Sta. KTAR, Phoenix, 1982—; spkr. in field. Recipient Disting. Alumnus award, Mich. State U., 1985. Mem.: AVMA, Am. Assn. Equine Practitioners, Ariz. Acad. Vet. Practice (Outstanding Continuing Edn. Record 1983), Central Ariz. Vet. Med. Assn. (pres.-elect 1980—81, pres. 1981—82, bd. dirs. 1978—80), Ariz. Vet. Med. Assn. (pres.-elect 1982—83, pres. 1983—84, chair ann. state meeting 1979—, bd. dirs. 1980—81), Am. Animal Hosp. Assn., Am. Acad. Vet. Dermatology. Republican. Home: 6900 E Gold Dust Ave Scottsdale AZ 85253-1461 Office: Sundown Animal Clinic 10616 N 71st Pl Scottsdale AZ 85254-5202

SHIRLEY, COURTNEY DYMALLY, nurse; b. Trinidad, July 17; came to U.S., 1960; d. Andrew Hamid Dymally; m. Adolph Shirley, Apr. 8, 1960; children: Ingrid, Robyne, Andrea, Kirk, Sandra. Cert. mgmt./adminstrn. health facilities, UCLA, 1978; BBA, Calif. Coast U., 1980, MBA, 1983. Cert. critical care nurse, advanced critical care nurse, nursing home adminstr., legal nurse cons. Head nurse med. unit Prince of Wales Gen. Hosp., London, 1959-60; asst. head nurse, CCU staff nurse Cedars-Sinai Hosp., L.A., 1962-73; asst. dir. nursing, dir. in-svc. edn., staff nurse Beverly Glen Hosp., 1973-75; supr. ICU/CCU/house Imperial Hosp., 1975-76; house supr. Med. Ctr. of North Hollywood, 1976-77; dir. nursing Crenshaw Ctr. Hosp., 1977-78, Mid-Wilshire Convalescent, 1978-79; supr. ICU/CCU, coord. utilization rev. Temple U., 1979-80; house supr. East L.A. Doctors' Hosp., 1980-81; pvt. nurse various hosps. and homes, 1981-86; utilization rev. coord. Managed Care Resources, L.A., 1986-88; prof. rev. sys. utilization rev. coord., case mgr. Nat. Med. Enterprises, Santa Monica, Calif., 1988—, case mgr., 1993-97; adminstr. Tri-Med Home Care, Inc., Thousand Oaks, Calif., 1997—. Mem. AACN, Internat. Case Mgmt. Assn., Sci. of Mind, Toastmasters (sgt. at arms 1990). Avocations: reading, Scrabble, dominoes, entertaining, blackjack. Office: Tri-Med Home Care Inc 299 W Hillcrest Dr Thousand Oaks CA 91360-4264

SHIRSAT, RAAKHEE NAGESH, pharmacist; b. Bombay, Jan. 12, 1976; came to U.S., 1977; d. Nagesh K. and Kanchan Shirsat. BS in Pharmacy, Arnold & Marie Schwartz Coll., 1997. Pharmacy intern Selden (N.Y.) Pharmacy & Surg. Supplies, 1995-97; pharmacy intern to intern Saint Charles Hosp., Port Jefferson, N.Y., 1997—; pharmacy intern to pharmacist Genovese Pharmacy, Islandia, N.Y., 1997—; per diem pharmacist St. Charles Hosp. and Rehab. Ctr., Port Jefferson, N.Y. Scholarship L.I. U., 1993-97, Alumni scholarship, 1994-97; Merit fellowship and scholarship C.W. Post Honors Program, 1993-94. Mem. Am. Pharm. Assn., Pharmacist's Soc. of the State of N.Y., Phi Eta Sigma. Democrat. Hindu. Avocations: studying literature, tutoring high school students. E-mail: rnshirsat@webtv.net.

SHIVELY, BONNIE LEE, pastor; b. Dover, Del., Feb. 13, 1961; d. Donald Hudson and Nancy (Durham) Shively. BS, Salisbury U., Md., 1984; MDiv, Wesley Theol. Sem., Washington, 1997. Ordained deacon Meth. Ch., 1995, ordained elder Meth. Ch., 2000. Pastor Church Creek United Meth. Ch., 1993—97, Bethel United Meth. Ch., Dagsboro, Del., 1997—2003, Hurlock-Wesley United Meth. Ch., Md., 2006—; pastor of caring ministries Kent Island United Meth. Ch., Chester, Md., 2003—06. Vol. Cmty. Food Pantry, Selbyville, Del., 1997—2003; mem. Friends of Prince George's Chapel, Dagsboro, 1998—2003, Dover Dist. Hispanic Ministries Com., 1999—2002, Peninsula Del. Conf. Disaster Relief Task Force, 2003—06; mem. adv. bd. Interfaith Vol. Caregivers, Frankford, Del., 1999—2002; bd. dirs. Queen Annes County Cmty. Partnership for Children, 2003—06; chaplain Church Creek Vol. Fire Co., 1993—97; bd. dirs. Del. Ecumenical Coun., Wilmington, 2000—03. Mem.: Commn. on Archives and History (sec. 1998—2004), Dagsboro Century Club. Avocations: genealogy, local history, needlecrafts. Office: Hurlock-Wesley United Meth Church PO Box 298 Hurlock MD 21643 Office Phone: 410-943-3222. Personal E-mail: blshively@intercom.net.

SHIVELY, JUDITH CAROLYN (JUDY SHIVELY), administrative assistant; b. Wilkinsburg, Pa., Jan. 30, 1962; d. John Allen and Edith (Crowell) S. BA in English, U. Nev., Las Vegas, 1984. Circulation aide Charleston Heights Libr., Las Vegas, 1979—86; asst. food editor Las Vegas Sun Newspaper, 1985—88, asst. horse racing editor, 1985—90, features writer, page editor, 1988—89, editor youth activities sect., 1989—90; racebook ticket writer, cashier Palace Sta. Hotel Racebook, Las Vegas, 1989—92; contract adminstr. nat. accts. Loomis, Fargo & Co., Las Vegas, 1992—2000; propr. Creative Computing, Las Vegas, 1996—; content prodn. Preference Techs., Inc., Las Vegas, 2000; data rsch. and processing PurchasePro.com, Las Vegas, 2000; adminstrv. asst. Uinta Bus. Systems, Las Vegas, 2001—02, Law Office of Frank Sorrentino, Las Vegas, 2003—; legal asst. Lee A. Drizin, 2006, Crosby & Assocs., 2006—. Horse racing historian, rschr., Las Vegas, 1985—; vol. rsch. asst. Dictionary of Gambling and Gaming, 1982-84; clk. Hometown News, Las Vegas, 1994-96. Staff writer horse race handicaps, columns, articles, feature stories Las Vegas Sun Newspaper, 1985-90; freelance writer for monthly horse racing publ. Inside Track, 1992-94. Mem. Phi Beta Kappa. Republican. Avocations: collecting horse racing books, clippings, materials for personal library of horse racing, computers. Home: PO Box 26426 Las Vegas NV 89126-0426 Personal E-mail: racehors1@aol.com.

SHIVELY, SARAH ELIZABETH, actress; b. Iowa City, Jan. 23, 1970; d. Philip Lee and Nancy Kay Shively; life ptnr. Marilys Ernst, July 11, 2003. B in Arts and Scis., Oberlin Coll., 1992; MFA, U. N.C., 1998. Tchr. Baruch Coll., N.Y.C., 1999—2000; actress Pa. Renaissance Faire, Lebanon, Pa., 2001—02; writer, prodr., actress Contemplating Emily, S.I., NY, 2003—05; tchr. Hunter Coll., NYC, 2005—. Fellow, MacDowell Colony, 2005. Mem.: SAG, Actors Equity Assn. Avocations: running, tap dancing, travel, reading, yoga. Home: 222 Castleton Ave Staten Island NY 10301 E-mail: saraheshively@verizon.net.

SHIVES, PAULA J., lawyer; b. Monongahela, Pa., Sept. 28, 1950; m. William Sutton. BA, Western Ky. U., 1973; JD, U. Ky., 1979. Bar: Ky. 1979. Assoc. gen. counsel Long John Silver Restaurants, Inc., Lexington, Ky., 1985—95, sr. v.p., gen. counsel, sec., 1995—99, Darden Restaurants, Inc., Orlando, Fla., 1999—. Mem.: ABA, Ky. Bar Assn., Fayette County Bar Assn. Office: 5900 Lake Ellenor Dr Orlando FL 32809 Home: 2011 Via Tuscany Winter Park FL 32789-1557 Office Phone: 407-245-6566.

SHMIDOV, ANNA, music educator; b. Minsk, Belarus, Nov. 16, 1947; came to U.S., 1980; d. Fayba and Sheyna-Miriam Pikus; m. Semyon Shmidov, Nov. 25, 1967; children: Julia Shmidov-Latz, Valentin. BA in Piano and Music Edn., Music Tech. Coll., Minsk, 1962; M in Piano and Music Edn., State Conservatory Music, Minsk, 1967. Tchr. music Music Sch. for Children and Adults, Minsk, 1964—67; dir. piano dept. in a music sch., Minsk, 1967—80; owner piano studio, tchr. piano Mpls., 1980—; dir. music program in 5 northwestern cities, Maple Grove, Minn., 1990. Bd. dirs. Upper Midwest Music Festival, Mpls./St. Paul, 1985—96, exec. dir., 1996—. Mem. Minn. Music Tchrs. Assn., Music Nat. Tchrs. Assn. Avocations: theater, travel, reading, concerts, art shows. Home and Office: Music for Everyone 8045 Narcissus Ln N Maple Grove MN 55311-1870 Office Phone: 763-531-5198. Personal E-mail: sshmidov@comcast.net.

SHO, JENNIFER YU-FEI, musician, educator; b. Taipei, Taiwan, Oct. 2, 1976; d. Tung-Chiao Sho and Hsiu-Ching Chen; m. Steven Robert Ceprano, June 28, 2003. B in Piano Performance (hon.), San Francisco Conservatory of Music, 1993—97; M in Piano Performance, New Eng. Conservatory of Music, 1997—99, D in Musical Arts, 2006. Pvt. piano tchr. Home Studio, Foster City, 1993—97, piano tchr. Boston, 1998—2002; pvt. piano instr. Edgewood Elem. Sch., Stoneham, 1998—2003; piano faculty The Ip Piano Sch., Boston, 1999—2002, Dana Hall Sch. of Music, Wellesley, Mass., 2002—06; pvt. piano tchr. Home Studio, Melrose, 2002—03; tchr., coach piano Gordon Coll., 2005—; pvt. music tchr. Brookline, Mass., 2004—. Soloist Grand Piano Cable TV Program, Los Altos, Calif., 1989—92, Palo Alto Chamber Orch., Calif., 1990—92, The Twilight Outdoor Concert Series, United States, 1990, Santa Rosa Chamber Music Series, United States, 1992; guest soloist A Tribute to Adolph Baller- Stanford U. Honors Concert, United States, 1992; soloist Music in The Redwoods, Portolla Valley, Calif., United States, 1992—94, Stanford U. Alumni Music Series, United States, 1993—95; pianist San Francisco Conservatory Chamber Music Honors Concerts, 1994—96; soloist Chopin Found., San Francisco, 1995, Classical Philharm. Orch., Castro Valley, Calif., 1997; pianist New Eng. Conservatory-Chamber Music Gela, Boston, 1999; soloist New Eng. Conservatory Piano Dept. Festival, Boston, 1999, Sun-Ling Hall, Taichung, Taiwan, 2001, Philips Hall, Wenham, Mass., 2005—06, Beveridge Hall, Wellesley, Mass., 2004—06; pianist Taipei Performing Arts Ctr., Taiwan, 2002, Nang Tu Performing Arts Ctr., Nang Tu, Taiwan, 2002, Taichung Performing Arts Ctr., Taiwan, 2002; guest artist, master class Longy Sch. of Music Prep. divsn., Cambridge, Mass., 2002; judge Bay State Contest of MMTA, 2003, Bay State Contest MMTA, 2005, MMTA Non-Competitive Evaluations, 2004. Mem.: New Eng. Piano Tchrs.' Assn. Inc., Music Teachers Nat. Assn., Associated Bd. of Royal Schools of Music. Home: 26A Alton Pl Brookline MA 02446 Personal E-mail: shojennifer@yahoo.com.

SHOCKLEY, CAROL FRANCES, psychologist, psychotherapist; b. Atlanta, Nov. 24, 1948; d. Robert Thomas and Frances Lavada (Scrivner) Shockley. BA, Ga. State U., Atlanta, 1974, MEd, 1976; PhD, U. Ga., Athens, 1990. Cert. in gerontology, diplomate Am. Bd. Forensic Examiners. Counselor Rape Crisis Ctr., Atlanta, 1979-80; emergency mental health clinician Gwinnett Med. Ctr., Lawrenceville, Ga., 1980-86; psychotherapist Fla. Mental Health Inst., Tampa, 1987-89, Tampa Bay Acad., Riverview, Fla., 1990-91; sr. psychologist State of Fla. Dept. of Corrections, Bushnell, 1991-92; pvt. practice psychologist Brunswick, Ga., 1992—2000, Griffin, Ga., 2002—. Mem. adv. bd. Mental Health/Mental Retardation, 1992—94. Author (with others): (book) Relapse Prevention with Sex Offenders, 1989. Vol. Ga. Mental Health Inst., Atlanta, 1972; leader Alzheimer's Disease Support Group, Athens, Ga., 1984; vol. therapist Reminiscence Group Elderly, Athens, 1984—85. Recipient Meritorious Svc. award, Beta Gamma Sigma, 1975. Mem.: APA, Ga. Psychol. Assn., Psi Chi, Sigma Phi Omega. Avocations: astronomy, archaeology, music, travel. Office: 231B S 10th St Ste B Griffin GA 30223

SHOCKLEY, PENNY MICHELLE, science educator; b. Scottsville, Ky., Mar. 5, 1974; d. James Russell and Betty Jean Risinger; m. Grady Myron Shockley, June 5, 1999 (div. Feb. 22, 2004); children: Jakob Ryan, Kataen Elizabeth. BS, Mid. Tenn. State U., 1998; MA, Tenn. Tech U., 2002, Ednl. Specialist, 2003. Sci. tchr. Warren County HS, McMinnville, Tenn., 1998—, dance coach Pioneerettes, 1996—. R-Liberal. Baptist. Home: 96 Dorey Ave Mc Minnville TN 37110 Office: Warren County HS 199 Pioneer Lane Mc Minnville TN 37110 Office Phone: 931-668-5858 267. Office Fax: 931-668-5801. Personal E-mail: ettescoach@yahoo.com. Business E-Mail: shockleyp@k12tn.net.

SHOCKLEY, THERESA SCHISLER, medical/surgical nurse; b. Salisbury, Md., Apr. 27, 1962; d. Philip Paul and Etta Lou (Hopkins) Schisler; m. Michael Edwin Shockley, Aug. 18, 1990. BSN, Salisbury State U., 1984, MSN, 1994. RN, Md. Staff nurse Peninsula Regional Med. Ctr., Salisbury, 1984—. Adj. nursing faculty Salisbury State U., 1994-95. Mem. ANA, Md. Nurses Assn., Sigma Theta Tau (edn. com. 1992). Roman Catholic. Avocations: reading, crocheting, swimming, writing poetry. Office: Peninsula Regional Med Ctr 100 E Carroll St Salisbury MD 21801-5422

SHOCKLEY-ZALABAK, PAMELA SUE, academic administrator; b. May 25, 1944; d. James William and Leatha Pearl (Cartwright) Shockley; m. Charles Zalabak, Dec. 30, 1975. BA in Comm., Okla. State U., 1965, MA in Comm., 1972; PhD in Orgnl. Comm., U. Colo., 1980. Instr. comm. Coll. Letters, Arts and Scis. U. Colo., 1976, from asst. to full prof., 1992, prof. comm. Colorado Springs, 1992—, dir., net and media ctr., 1992, spl. asst. to chancellor, 1994, vice chancellor for student success Colorado Springs, 1998—2001, interim chancellor, 2001—02, chancellor, 2002—. Cons. in field. Author six books; prodr.: (six video documentaries); contbr. articles to profl. jours. Recipient Disting. Svc. award, Colo. Speech Comm. Assn., Telly award; Lew Wentz Tri Delt scholar, 1961—65. Mem.: Internat. Comm. Assn., Speech Comm. Assn., Phi Kappa Phi. Democrat. Avocations: skiing, hiking, fly fishing. Office: Univ Colorado Chancellor's Office 1420 Austin Bluffs Pkwy Colorado Springs CO 80918

SHODEAN, LISA DIANE, military officer; b. Willmar, Minn., Jan. 24, 1964; d. David Allen and Dione Lavonne Shodean. BS in Bus. Fin., Calif. State U., Fresno, 1989; MA in Pub. Adminstrn., Hamline U., 1997. Commd. 2d. lt. U.S. Army, 1988, advanced through grades to maj., 2002—. Mil. affairs. com. C. of C., Starkville, Miss., 1999—2001. Mem.: Adj. Gen. Regimental Assn., Res. Officer Assn. (treas. Minn. 1990—99, Outstanding Jr. Officer award 1999). Lutheran. Avocations: stamp collecting/philately, skiing, bicycling, kayaking, camping. Office: Human Resources Command ARADMD-ARO (MAJ SHODEAN) 1 Reserve Way Saint Louis MO 63132 Home: 3110 23rd Ave Se Rio Rancho NM 87124-1689 E-mail: shodean@aol.com.

SHOEBRIDGE, SYLVIA B., retired historian, educator; b. Pompey, NY, Mar. 2, 1923; d. Mason William Berry and Mabel Frances ELlis; m. Harold Jack Shoebridge, Dec. 18, 1948 (dec.); children: Cedric, Heather(dec.), Tamara. BS, Drexel U., Phila., 1945; MA, Syracuse U., NY, 1967. Instr. Syracuse U., NY, 1948—50; tchr. Syracuse Schs., 1955—60, Georgetown Ctrl. Sch., 1963—68, Syracuse Pub. Schs., 1968—69, BOCES, Whitesboro, 1969—77; historian Town of Pompey, NY, 1988—2005; ret. Organist Pompey United Ch., 1963—78. Recipient Merit award, Regional Coun. Hist. Agys., NY, 1998. Mem.: Pompey Hist. Soc., Assn. Pub. Historians NY State.

SHOEMAKER, ANNE CUNNINGHAM, retired mathematics educator; b. Milton, Mass., Aug. 26, 1922; d. George Clarendon Cunningham and Anne Bryan Parker; m. Reed Shoemaker, Aug. 25, 1951 (dec. Feb. 1, 2003); children: Edwin Reed (dec.), George Edwin, William Reed. AB in Math., Boston U., 1946; postgrad., Harvard U., U. Mass., Villanova U. Co-dir. Green Mountain Camp for Girls, Brattleboro, Vt., 1941; cartographer Inst. Geog. Exploration Harvard U., Cambridge, Mass., 1942; biometrician R&D divsn. Distiller's Co. Ltd., London, 1946-48; rsch. statistician Smith Kline & French Labs., Phila., 1948-52; math. tchr. Baldwin Sch., Bryn Mawr, Pa., 1962-72, head math. dept., 1964-70, head of sch., 1970-80; ednl. cons. com. for accreditation of elem. schs. Assn. of Ind. Md. Schs., 1980-85. Mem. scholarship selection com. Penwalt Corp., Phila., 1971-86 Bd. trustees, chair Gunston Sch., Centreville, Md., 1973-93, 95-97, sec. bd., 1974-80, v.p., chair oper. com., 1980-85, pres. bd., 1985-90, emeritus, 1999—; bd. trustess Country Sch., Easton, Md., 1981-85; bd. dirs. Coun. for Religion in Ind. Schs., 1976-86, pres., 1983-86; treas., vestryperson, Eucharistic min. St. Luke's Parish, Church Hill, Md., 1989—; judge pub. speaking competition 4-H Pony Club, Centreville, 1991-94; mem. CAPE secretariat screening panel Nat. Elem. Sch. Recogniton Program of US Dept. Edn., 1986-88; chair devel. com. Queen Anne's County Hospice, 2001-02, bd. dirs. 2004-, bd. trustees 2000-01, 03—. Elected to Coll. Disting. Alumni, Coll. Liberal Arts, Boston U., 1981. Mem. Nat. Assn. Ind. Schs. (admissions com. 1972-74, staff mem. workshop for new heads of schs. 1976-80, trustee rep., bd. dirs. 1982-86), Nat. Assn. Prins. of Schs. for Girls (chmn. sch. sect. of sch. and jr. coll. com. 1973-74, v.p. Cen. Atlantic area 1976-78), Assn. Headmistresses of the East (sec. to bd. dirs. 1973-75, chmn. nominating com. 1976-77), Pa. Assn. Pvt. Acad. Schs. (exec. com. 1970-79, sec. 1974-76, pres., bd. dirs. 1976-79), Pa. Assn. Ind. Schs. (exec. com. 1972-79, v.p. 1973-74), Mass. Women's Def. Corps of Mass. State Guard (capt. motor transport divsn. 1941-42), Miles River Sail & Power Squadron (comdr. 1992-93), St. Andrews Soc. Ea. Shore. Republican. Episcopalian. Avocations: gardening, music, genealogy. Home: PO Box 328 Centreville MD 21617-0328 E-mail: acshoe@intercom.net.

SHOEMAKER, CAROLYN SPELLMAN, planetary astronomer; b. Gallup, N.Mex., June 24, 1929; d. Leonard Robert and Hazel Adele (Arthur) Spellmann; m. Eugene Merle Shoemaker, Aug. 18, 1951 (dec. July 1997); children: Christine Shoemaker Abanto, Patrick Gene, Linda Shoemaker

Salazar. BA cum laude, Chico State Coll., 1949, MA, 1950; ScD, No. Ariz. U., 1990, St. Mary's U., N.S., Can., 2003. Vis. scientist Br. astrogeology U.S. Geol. Survey, Flagstaff, Ariz., 1980—; rsch. asst. Calif. Inst. Tech., Pasadena, 1981-85; rsch. prof. astronomy No. Ariz. U., Flagstaff, 1989—; mem. staff Lowell Obs., Flagstaff, 1993—. Guest observer Palomar Obs., Palomar Mountain, Calif., 1982-94; Ruth Northcott Meml. lectr. R.A.S.C., 1995; co-McGovern lectr. Cosmos Club Found., 1995. Co-recipient Rittenhouse medal Rittenhouse Astron. Soc., 1988, Scientist of Yr. award ARCS Found., 1995, James C. Watson medal NAS, 1998; recipient Woman of Distinction award Soroptimists, 1994, 20th Anniversary Internat. Women's Yr. award Zonta and 99s, 1995, NASA Exceptional Scientific Achievement medal, 1996, Woman of Distinction award Nat. Assn. Women in Edn., 1996, Shoemaker award Am. Inst. Profl. Geologists, 1997, plaque Internat. Forest Friendship, Atchison, Kans., 1997, Robert Burnham Jr. award Western Regional Astron. League, 2000, Ariz. Woman of Distinction award Alpha Delta Kappa, 2004; named Disting. Alumna of the Calif. State U., Chico, 1996. Fellow AAAS, Am. Acad. Arts and Scis.; mem. Am. Geophys. Union, Meteoritical Soc., Sigma Xi. Achievements include discovery of 32 comets including Periodic Comet Shoemaker-Levy 9 which impacted Jupiter in July 1994, more than 500 asteroids including 44 Earth approachers and approximately 68 Mars crossers, meteorites at Veevers Crater, Australia and impactites at Wolfe Creek Crater, Australia. Home: 5231 Hidden Hollow Rd Flagstaff AZ 86001-3821 Office: Lowell Obs 1400 W Mars Hill Rd Flagstaff AZ 86001-4499 E-mail: cshoemaker@usgs.gov.

SHOEMAKER, CLARA BRINK, retired chemistry professor, researcher; b. Rolde, Drenthe, The Netherlands, June 20, 1921; came to U.S., 1953; d. Hendrik Gerard and Hendrikje (Smilde) Brink; m. David Powell Shoemaker, Aug. 5. 1955; 1 child, Robert Brink. PhD, Leiden U., 1950. Instr. inorganic chemistry Leiden U., 1946—50, 1951—53; postdoctoral fellow Oxford U., England, 1950—51; rsch. assoc. dept. chemistry MIT, Cambridge, 1953—55, 1958—70; rsch. assoc. biochemistry Harvard Med. Sch., Boston, 1955—56; project supr. Boston U., 1963—64; rsch. assoc. dept. chemistry Oreg. State U, Corvallis, 1970—75, rsch. assoc. prof. dept. chemistry, 1975—82, sr. rsch. prof. dept. chemistry, 1982—84, prof. emerita, 1984—. Sect. editor: Structure Reports of International Union of Crystallography, 1967-69; contbr. chpts. to books, articles to profl. jours. Bd. dirs. LWV, Corvallis, 1980-82, bd. dirs., sec., Oreg., 1985-87. Fellow, Internat. Fedn. Univ. Women, Oxford U., 1950—51. Mem. Metall. Soc. (com. on alloy phases 1969-79), Internat. Union of Crystallography (commn. on structure reports 1970-90), Am. Crystallographic Assn. (crystallographic data com. 1975-78, Fankuchen award com. 1976), Sigma Xi, Iota Sigma Pi (faculty adv. Oreg. State U. chpt. 1975-84), Phi Lambda Upsilon. Avocation: outdoor activities. Office: Dept Chemistry Oreg State U Corvallis OR 97331

SHOEMAKER, CYNTHIA LOUISE, music educator; b. Huntington, W.Va., Feb. 19, 1954; d. Clyde Richard and Alice Mae Sperry; m. William Jerald Shoemaker, Sept. 16, 1951; children: Bethany Lea Hendricks, William Jeremy. BA, Marshall U., Huntington, W. Va., 1972—76, MA, 1981—85. Cert. Tchr. W. Va., 1976, Ohio, 1998. Music tchr. Wayne County Schs., Wayne, W.Va., 1976—98; music tchr. grades 608 McComb Local Schs., Ohio, 1998—. Curriculum goals com. mem. W.Va. State Dept. Edn., Charleston, 1994—96. Vol. Republician Campaign Hdqs., Findlay, Ohio, 2004; musician Grace Gospel Ch., Huntington, W.Va., 1983—98, Cornerstone Bapt. Ch., Findlay, Ohio, 2001—06. Recipient Student Tchr. of Yr., Marshall U., 1976, Tchr. of Yr., Wayne County Schs., 1994, Golden Apple award finalist, Findlay Rotary Club, 2005, 2006. Mem.: Nat. Educator Assn., Ohio Educators Assn., Ohio Music Educators Assn. Republican. Baptist. Avocation: perennial gardening. Office: McComb MidSch 20221 West Church St Hoytville OH 43529 Office Phone: 419-278-8194. Office Fax: 419-278-7166. Business E-Mail: shoemakc@mb.noacsc.org.

SHOEMAKER, DEIRDRE MARIE, physics professor; d. Harry and Anne Shoemaker; m. Pablo Laguna. PhD, U. Tex., Austin, 1999. Rsch. assoc. Cornell U., Ithaca, NY, 2002—04; asst. prof. Pa. State U., U. Park, 2004—. Office Phone: 814-863-9595.

SHOEMAKER, INNIS HOWE, art museum curator; b. Reading, Pa. d. William Erety and Jean (Miller) S. AB, Vassar Coll., 1964; MA, Columbia U., 1968, PhD, 1975. Curator Vassar Coll. Art. Gallery, Poughkeepsie, NY, 1965-68, 73-76; asst. dir. Ackland Art Mus., U. N.C., Chapel Hill, 1976-82, dir., 1983-86; Audrey and William H. Helfand sr. curator prints, drawings and photographs Phila. Mus. Art, 1986—; adj. prof. U. Pa., 2001—. Fellow in art history Am. Acad. in Rome, 1971-73; adj. prof. U. N.C., Chapel Hill, 1983-86. Author: Mad for Modernism: Earl Horter and His Collection, 1999, Jacques Villon and his Cubist Prints, 2001; co-author: The Engravings of Marcantonio Raimondi, 1981, Paul Cézanne: Two Sketchbooks, 1989, Mexico and Modern Printmaking: A Revolution in the Graphic Arts, 2006. Mem. vis. com. Lehman Loeb Art Ctr., Vassar Coll., 1993-. Mem. Coll. Art Assn. Am., Am. Assn. Mus., Print Coun. Am. (bd. dirs. 1986-89). Office: Phila Mus Art PO Box 7646 Philadelphia PA 19101-7646

SHOHEN, SAUNDRA ANNE, health facility administrator, public relations executive; b. Washington, Aug. 22, 1934; d. Aaron Kohn and Malvina (Kleiman) Kohn Blinder; children: Susan, Brian. BS, Columbia Pacific U., 1979, MS in Health Svcs. Adminstrn., 1981. Adminstr. social work dept. Roosevelt Hosp., N.Y.C., 1978-79; adminstr. emergency dept. St. Luke's-Roosevelt Hosp. Ctr., N.Y.C., 1979-83, assoc. dir. pub. rels., 1983-87; pres. Saundra Shohen Assocs., Ltd., N.Y.C., 1987-92; v.p. Prism Internat., N.Y.C., 1988-91; bd. dirs. Tureck Bach Inst., N.Y.C., 1985—. Panelist ann. Emmy awards NATAS, N.Y.C., 1983, 84; tchr. healthcare mktg. Baruch Coll., N.Y.C., 1994. Author: Health Scripts for Radio, 1983, Voice of America, 1983 (Presdl. Recognition award, 1984); author: (with others) AIDS: A Health Care Management Response, 1987; author: EMERGENCY!, 1989. Mem. NATAS, Internat. Hosp. Fedn., Am. Soc. Hosp. Mktg. and Pub. Rels., Vols. in Tech. Assistance. Democrat. Jewish. Home: 240 Central Park S New York NY 10019-1413

SHOJI, JUNE MIDORI, import and export trading executive; b. Long Beach, Calif., June 21, 1957; d. Sam Masatsugu and Tomiyo (Kinoshita) S. BA in Psychology and Econs., UCLA, 1975-79; cert. Japanese, Waseda U., Tokyo, 1980-82; Grad. Gemologist, Gemol. Inst., Santa Monica, Calif., 1984. Mktg. rep. IBM Corp., L.A., 1982-84, Xerox Corp., El Monte, Calif., 1984-86; adminstrv. drilling analyst Arco Internat. Oil & Gas, L.A., 1986-89, logistics analyst, 1989—91; precious metals buyer Honda Trading Am. Corp., Torrance, Calif., 1992—95, sr. asst. mgr., 1996—, v.p. ops., 2006—. Home: 5959 E Naples Plz Long Beach CA 90803-5064 Office Phone: 310-787-5065. Business E-Mail: jmshoji@hta.honda.com.

SHOLARS, JOAN DIANNE, mathematics professor; d. Frances Dawson; m. Javier Gomez, May 30, 2000; children: Sheila Marie Griffin, Karry James Buckanis, Kristal Alegria Mathis, Tanya Karin Gomez. MS, Calif. State U., Fullerton, 1991. Prof. Mt. San Antonio Coll., Walnut, Calif., 1991—. Mem.: C.C. Assn. (dir. 2000—), Calif. Tchrs. Assn. (state coun. del. 2004—), Calif. Math. Coun. C.C. (conf. chair 1992—2006). Liberal. Home: 2052 Valor Dr Corona CA 92882 Office: Mt San Antonio College 1100 N Grand Ave Walnut CA 91789 Office Phone: 909-594-5611. Business E-Mail: jsholars@mtsac.edu.

SHOMAKER, ANDREA KAY, secondary school educator; d. Leon A. and Diane D. Strickland; m. Paul Clay Shomaker, Aug. 17, 1971; children: Emma Catherine, Paul Carson, Ava Elizabeth. AA in Psychology, Macon State Coll., Ga., 1996; BA in French and Politcal Sci., Ga. Coll. and State U., Milledgeville, 1995; MAT Fgn. Lang. Edn., Ga. Coll. and State U., Macon, 1996, EdS in Social Sci. Edn., 2001; PhD in Ednl. Policy Studies, Ga. State U., Atlanta, 2003. Sales assoc. Belk Matthews, Macon, Ga., 1992—94; resident adviser, sr. resident adviser Ga. Coll. and State U., Milledgeville, 1993—95, distance learning site coord. Macon, 1995—96; instr., head fgn. lang. dept. Bibb County Pub. Schs., 1996—2001; sales assoc. Carlyle & Co. Jewelers, 1997—97; tchr., French, Spanish, social studies Monroe County Bd. Edn., Forsyth, 2001—04; instr., head fgn. lang. dept. First Presbyn. Day Sch., Macon, 2004—. Lang. cons. Evans Clay Kaolin, McIntyre, Ga., 1997—97; editl. cons. Carlyle & Co. Jewelers, Macon, 1997—97; ednl. and rsch. cons. pvt. practice, 1996; polit. campaign cons. Cecil Staton, 2002—02; standardized patient pilot program assessment participant Mercer U., Nat. Bd. Med. Examiners, 1999—2000; instr. continuing edn. Macon State Coll., 1995—97; adj. prof. French Mercer U, Macon, 2004. Coord. blood donor ARC, 2004; mem. Jr. League, Macon, Ga., 2005; sponsor FPD Spanish Club Cmty. Outreach, Macon, 2004, various youth orgns., 1995; artist donating works benefit Macon-Bibb County Citizens Advocacy, 2006; vol. translator Macon-Bibb County Conv. and Visitor's Bur., 1996—97; mem., sponsor Macon Hist. Found., 2005, Mus. Arts and Sciences, 2004; web designer Bibb County Young Reps., Macon, 2002—03; mem. Bibb County Rep. Party Exec. Com., 2002—04; sec. Children's Coun. Mulberry United Meth. Ch., 2005; mem., former treas., current leader Deborah Cir. Mulberry United Meth. Ch., 2003; mem. Meth. Home Aux., 2005; social chair, corr. sec., web site designer Mustard Seed Class Mulberry United Meth. Ch., 2002—04; 2k and 3k sunday sch. tchr. Mulberry United Meth. Ch., 2003, vacation bible sch. tchr., 2004; mem., chair young alumnae com. St. Timothy's Sch., Stevenson, Md., 2003, reunion chair 1991, 2001; site sponsor EF Ednl. Tours Abroad, 2000; organizer, dir., and com. chair pub. rels. Internat. Dinner Festival of Westside H.S., 1997—99. Mem.: Ga. Educators Assn. (assoc.), Tchrs. English as Second Lang. (assoc.), Fgn. Lang. Assn. Ga. (assoc.), Am. Ednl. Rsch. Assn. (assoc.), United Meth. Women (sec. children's coun. 2005), Nat. Soc. DAR (life; chair jr. membership 1995—97), Healy Point Country Club (assoc.), Mensa. Avocations: travel, study of languages and linguistics, distance education and web design. Office: First Presbyterian Day School 5671 Calvin Drive Macon GA 31210 Office Phone: 478-477-6505.

SHOMIN, JANET L., paralegal; d. Walter Frederick and Betty Darlene Redsted; 1 child from previous marriage, Matthew James. Student, Rockhurst U., Kansas City, Mo., 2006—. Legal sec. Shughart, Thomson & Kilroy, Kansas City, 1975—87; paralegal Cochran Oswald & Room, Blue Springs, Mo., 1987—2004, Dodig, Arbuckle & Carey, Lee's Summit, Mo., 2004—05, Thompson Law Office, Kansas City, 2005—06, Wagstaff & Cartmell, Kansas City, 2006—. Active Raytown Cmty. Svcs., Raytown, Mo., 2003—04, Grain Valley Cmty. Svcs., Mo., 2004; neighborhood coord. Night Out Against Crime, Blue Springs, 1990; mem. Celebrate Am. benefit, 2000, 2003, 2004; bd. dirs. First United Meth., Blue Springs, 2000. Mem.: Assn. Trial Lawyers Am. Avocations: singing, volleyball. Home: 609 NE Sunnybrook Dr Blue Springs MO 64014 Office: Wagstaff & Cartmell 4740 Grand Ave Ste 300 Kansas City MO 64112

SHOPTAW, SHAUNA LYNN, middle school educator; b. Hayward, Calif., Oct. 23, 1966; d. Larken Clarence III and Loranne Jean (Long) S. BA in English Lit., Calif. State U., Hayward, 1987. Summer sch. tchr. San Lorenzo (Calif.) HS, 1988, Castro Valley (Calif.) Unified Sch. Dist., 1989—; tchr. 8th grade English and drama leadership Canyon Mid. Sch., Castro Valley, 1988—. Summer youth concert condr. Jenny Lin Found., Castro Valley, 1995-200; workshop leader Kids Turn, East Bay San Francisco, 1992-97; choir mem., soloist Calif. Singing Churchwomen, East Bay Area, Calif., 1989—99; youth leader First So. Bapt. Ch., San Lorenzo, 1988-98, music dir., 1997—. Mem. Nat. Educator's Assn., Calif. Tchrs. Assn., Castro Valley Tchrs. Assn., Calif. Assn. Dirs. of Activities. Democrat. Southern Baptist. Avocations: music, reading, computers. Office: Canyon Mid Sch 19600 Cull Canyon Rd Castro Valley CA 94552-3715 Business E-Mail: sshoptaw@mail.cv.k12.ca.us.

SHORE, ELEANOR GOSSARD, retired medical school dean; b. Ottawa, Ill., Aug. 11, 1930; d. Arthur Paul and Mary Catherine (Lineberger) Gossard; m. Miles Frederick Shore, July 4, 1953; children: Miles Paul, Rebecca Shore Lewin, Susanna Shore LeBoutillier. BA magna cum laude, Radcliffe Coll., 1951; MD, Harvard U., 1955, MPH, 1970. Diplomate Am. Bd. Preventive Medicine. Med. intern New Eng. Med. Ctr. Hosp., Boston, 1955-56; resident in occup. medicine Harvard U. Health Svcs., Cambridge, Mass., 1966-68; Macy scholar Radcliffe Inst., Radcliffe Coll., Cambridge, 1966-68; resident in preventive medicine Harvard Sch. Pub. Health, Boston, 1970-71; asst. physician Radcliffe Coll., 1959-61, Harvard U. Health Svcs., 1961-73; rsch. assoc. dept. microbiology Harvard U. Sch. Pub. Health, 1971-76; asst. to pres. Harvard U., 1972-81; assoc. dean for faculty affairs Harvard Med. Sch., 1978-89, mem. faculty, 1978—2004, dean for faculty affairs, 1989—2004, sr. cons. to office acad. and clin. programs, 2005—. Mem. editl. bd. Harvard Med. Alumni Bull., 1976—. Bd. dirs. Mass.-Ukraine Citizens Bridge, Brockton, Mass., 1989-94, pres., 1991-92; bd. dirs. Needham (Mass.) Found. for Pub. Sch. Edn., 1990-94; bd. dirs. Mass. Health Rsch. Inst., Inc., 1990-99, sec., 1995-99; overseer Boston Mus. Sci., 1981—; trustee Schepens Eye Rsch. Inst., Boston, 1993—; mem. acad. coun. Real Colegio Complutense, Harvard U., 1995—; dep. dir. Harvard Med. Sch. Ctr. for Excellence in Women's Health, 1998-2004. Recipient Pres.'s Recognition award Am. Med. Women's Assn., 1996. Fellow Am. Acad. Preventive Medicine; mem. AAAS, APHA, Mass. Pub. Health Assn., Assn. Am. Med. Colls., Mass. Med. Soc., Aesculapian Club (treas. 1986-89, pres. 1990-91), E-mail: eleanor_shore@hms.harvard.edu.

SHORENSTEIN, ROSALIND GREENBERG, internist; b. NYC, Jan. 14, 1947; d. Albert Samuel and Natalie Miriam (Sherman) Greenberg; m. Michael Lewis Shorenstein, June 18, 1967; children: Anna Irene, Claire Beth. BA in Chemistry, Wellesley Coll., 1968; MA in Biochemistry and Molecular Biology, Harvard U., 1970, PhD in Biochemistry and Molecular Biology, 1973; MD, Stanford U., 1976. Diplomate Am. Bd. Internal Medicine. Resident in internal medicine UCLA Med. Ctr., 1976-79; pvt. practice internal medicine Santa Cruz, Calif., 1979—. Mem. dept. internal medicine Dominican Hosp., Santa Cruz, 1979—; co-dir. med. svcs. Health Enhancement & Lifestyle Planning Systems, Santa Cruz, 1983—. Contbr. articles to profl. journals. Dir. Santa Cruz Chamber Players, 1993-94, pres., bd. dirs., 1994—. Recipient Charlie Parkhurst award Santa Cruz Women's Commn., 1989; NSF fellow, 1968-72, Sarah Perry Wood Med. fellow Wellesley Coll., 1972-76. Mem. Am. Soc. Internal Medicine (del. 1994, 95), Calif. Soc. Internal Medicine (trustee 1994—, sec.-treas. 1996-2000), Am. Med. Women's Assn. (Outstanding Svc. award 1987, br. #59 pres. 1986—), Calif. Med. Assn. (com. on women 1987-93), Santa Cruz County Med. Soc. (mem. bd. govs. 1993—, sec. 1997-99, pres. 2000-01, sec. 2002-), Phi Beta Kappa, Sigma Xi. Jewish. Office: 700 Frederick St Ste 103 Santa Cruz CA 95062-2239 Office Phone: 831-458-1002.

SHORENSTEIN HAYS, CAROLE, theater producer; m. Jeffrey Hays; 2 children. Co-owner Curran Theatre, Golden Gate Theatre, Orpheum Theatre, San Francisco. Prodr.: (Broadway plays) Can-Can, 1981, Woman of the Year, 1981—83 (Tony nom. best musical, 1981), Oliver!, 1984, Fences, 1987 (Tony award best play, 1987), A Midsummer Night's Dream, 1996 (Tony nom. best revival of a play, 1996), The Old Neighborhood, 1997—98, The Chairs, 1998 (Tony nom. best revival of a play, 1996), Not About Nightingales, 1999 (Tony nom. best play, 1999), Closer, 1999 (Tony nom. best play, 1999), The Tale of the Allergist's Wife, 2000—02 (Tony nom. best play, 2001), Proof, 2000—03 (Tony award best play, 2001), The Goat, or Who Is Sylvia?, 2002 (Tony award best play, 2002), Topdog / Underdog, 2002 (Tony nom. best play, 2002), Take Me Out, 2003—04 (Tony award best play, 2003), Caroline, or Change, 2004— (Tony nom. best musical, 2004). Office: Curran Theatre 445 Geary St San Francisco CA 94102 also: Golden Gate Theatre P O Box 7110 San Francisco CA 94102

SHORES, PEARL MARIE, health care company executive; b. Warsaw, N.Y., Aug. 29, 1946; d. Lawrence Dean and Mary Ellen (Sly) Arnold; m. Bruce Reid Dedrick, May 9, 1964 (div. 1966); 1 child, Dawn Aileen; m. James Lee Shores, Sept. 13, 1981. BBA cum laude, Nat. U., San Diego, 1979; MBA, Nat. U., 1981. Chief lab. technician Schoenfeld Clin. Lab., Albuquerque, 1970-76, Allergy Med. Group, San Diego, 1976-78; chemstrip specialist BioDynamics/BMC, San Diego, 1978-80; sr. ter. mgr. Hollister, Inc., San Diego, 1980-84, dist. mgr. New Eng. dist., 1984-86; sales rep. E.R. Squibb/CONVATEC, San Diego, 1986-87; br. mgr. HOMEDCO, San Diego, 1987-89; dir. infusion therapy Spl. Solutions, 1989-90; territory mgt. Sween Corp., 1990-93; dir. Mercy Infusion Therapy, Escondido, Calif., 1993-96; regional sales cons. Dezinc Healthcare Solutions, 1996—; infusion therapy cons., accounts receivable mgr. Shores Enterprises, 1997—. Avocation: tennis. Fax: (760) 432-6618.

SHORR, HARRIET, artist; b. NYC, May 14, 1939; BA, Swarthmore, 1960; BFA, Yale Sch. Art and Arch., 1962. One-woman shows include Gross McCleaf Gallery, Phila., 1970, Green Mountain Gallery, NYC, 1972, 1973, 1975, Fischbach Gallery, 1979, 1980, 1983, 1984, J. Rosenthal Fine Arts, Chgo., 1988, Galveston Art Ctr., Tex., 1989, Rahr West Mus., Manitowac, Wis., 1991, Neuberger Mus., Purchase, NY, 1992, Gallery Camino Real, Boca Raton, Fla., 1994, Cheryl Pelavin Fine Art, NYC, 2001, 2002, exhibited in group shows at Am. Fedn. of Arts, 1971, Hobart Coll., Geneva, NY, 1975, at Goddard Riverside Arts Ctr., NYC, 1980, at Marion Koogler McNay Art Mus., San Antonio, Tex., 1981, Mus. of Art, Carnegie Inst., Pitts., 1986, Am. Acad. Arts and Letters, NYC, 1990, Levinson-Kane Gallery, Boston, 1992, NY Studio Sch., NYC, 1996, Fischbach Gallery, 1997, Del. Ctr. Contemporary Arts, Wilmington, 2002, others, Represented in permanent collections Chgo. Art Inst., Bklyn. Mus., Chemical Bank, NYC, Milbank, Tweed, Hadley and McCloy, Lehman Bros., Estee Lauder Corp., Champion Internat., Stamford, Conn., one-woman shows include Clarion (Pa.) Coll., 2005, Cheryl Pelavin, N.Y.C., exhibited in group shows at Armory Arts Ctr., West Palm Beach, Fla., 2004, 2005. Recipient Nat. Endowment of Arts award, 1980, Am. Artist Achievement award, 1994, Purchase award, Am. Acad. Arts & Letters, 1999, Pollock-Krasner award, 2000. Mem.: NAD (academician 1994—).

SHORT, BETSY ANN, elementary school educator; b. Macon, Ga., Mar. 18, 1958; d. Garland Brooks Jr. and Mary Eleanor (Jordan) Turner; m. Lynn Robin Short, July 21, 1984 BS Early Childhood Edn., Ga. Coll., Milledgeville, 1981, M Early Childhood Edn., 1993, EdS Early Childhood Edn., 1995; EdS Reading, U. West Ga., 2001, cert. specialist in reading, 2001; intech cert., Macon State Coll., 2001; degree Adminstrn. and Supervision, Ga. Coll. and State U., 2002; EdD ednl. leadership, Argosy U., 2004. Cert. elem. tchr. and tchr. support specialist, Ga., early childhood generalist, Nat. Bd. Early Childhood Generalist, 2003. Tchr. 3d grade Stockbridge Elem. Sch., Ga., 1983—84, tchr. kindergarten, 1984—93; tchr. augmented spl. instrnl. assistance Locust Grove Elem. Sch., Ga., 1993—97, tchr. kindergarten, 1997—99, tchr. first grade, 1999—2000, tchr. early intervention reading, 2000—02; student support specialist Unity Grove Elem. and Ola Elem., 2002—03; asst. prin. Morgan County Primary Sch., Madison, Ga., 2003—. Cons. Saxon Pub. Co.; specialist in Reading, U. West Ga., Carrollton, 2001 Author: Spinning Yarns, 1995; mem. editl. adv. bd. Ga. Jour. Reading; contbr. articles to profl. jours.; artist oil painting/pen and ink drawing Recipient Outstanding Educator award, Morgan County Chpt. Retired Educators of Ga., 2004. Mem. Profl. Assn. Ga. Educators, Ga. Coun. Tchrs. Maths., Ga. Coun. Internat. Reading Assn., Ga. Coun. Social Studies, Ga. Sci. Tchrs. Assn., Henry Heritage Reading Coun. (v.p. 1999-2001), Phi Delta Gamma Baptist. Avocations: painting, cross-stiching, writing short stories, story telling. Office: Morgan County Primary Sch 993 East Ave Madison GA 30650 Office Phone: 706-342-3475. Business E-Mail: betsy.short@morgan.k12.ga.us.

SHORT, ELIZABETH M., internist, educator, retired federal agency administrator; b. Boston, June 2, 1942; d. James Edward and Arlene Elizabeth (Mitchell) Meehan; m. Michael Allen Friedman, June 21, 1976; children: Lia Gabrielle, Hannah Ariel, Eleanor Elana. BA in Philosophy magna cum laude, Mt. Holyoke Coll., 1963; MD cum laude, Yale U., 1968. Diplomate Am. Bd. Internal Medicine, Am. Bd. Med. Genetics. Resident in internal medicine Yale New Haven Hosp., 1968-70; postdoctoral fellow in human genetics Yale Med. Sch., 1970-72; resident U. Calif., San Francisco, 1972-73; sr. chief resident Stanford (Calif.) Med. Sch., 1973-75, asst. prof. medicine, 1975-83, assoc. dean student affairs, med. edn., 1978-83; dep. dir. acad. affairs, dir. biomed. rsch. Assn. Am. Med. Colls., Washington, 1983-88; dep. assoc. chief med. dir. for acad. affairs VA, Washington, 1988-92, assoc. chief med. dir. for acad. affairs, 1992-96; health policy cons. HHS, 1996—2001; ret., 2001. Vis. prof. human biology Stanford U., 1983-86; mem. Accreditation Coun. Grad. Med. Edn., 1988-97; mem. White House Task Force on Health Care Reform, 1993. Assoc. editor Clin. Rsch. Jour., 1976-79, editor 1980-84; contbr. articles to profl. jours. Mem. Nat. Child Health Adv. Coun., NIH, 1991-97; com. edn. and tng. Office Sci. and Tech. Policy, White House, Washington, 1991-96, bd. dirs., treas. Calif. Philharm., 2003—; exec. com. bd. dirs. Hillsides Home for Children, 2003. Recipient Maclean Zoology award; Munger scholar, Markle scholar, Sara Williston scholar Mt. Holyoke Coll., 1959-63, Yale Men in Medicine scholar, 1964-68; Bardwell Meml. Med. fellow, 1963. Mem. AAAS, Am. Soc. Human Genetics (pub. policy com. 1984-95, chmn. 1986-94), Am. Fedn. Clin. Rsch. (bd. dirs. 1973-83, co-chmn. com. status women 1975-77, editor Clin. Rsch. Jour., 1978-83, nat. coun., exec. com., pub. policy com. 1977-87), Western Soc. Clin. Investigation, Calif. Acad. Medicine, Phi Beta Kappa, Alpha Omega Alpha. Home and Office: 3535 Ranch Top Rd Pasadena CA 91107 Personal E-mail: elizshort@aol.com.

SHORT, JUDITH ARDUINO, media specialist, educator; b. Rockford, Ill., Sept. 26, 1940; d. Vincent Joseph and Lois Vivian (Molson) Arduino; m. Burdette Lee Short, July 24, 1960; children: Melinda Jo Scott, Amy Lynn Watts. Student, No. Ill. U., 1958—60; BS, Towson State U., 1980; MA, Johns Hopkins U., 1985; postgrad., Western Md. U., 1990—99. Libr. technician Aberdeen (Md.) HS, 1976—80; libr. media specialist Joppatowne HS, Joppa, Md., 1980—. Mem. Gen. Curriculum Com., Harford County, Md., 2000—02; coach HS tennis and golf. Author curriculum materials, policies and procedures manual. Pres. Newcomer's Club, Bel Air, Md., 1971. Mem.: Harford County Media Assn. (pres. 1982—83), Md. Ednl. Media Orgn. (bd. dirs. 1985—91), Kappa Delta Alumni Assn. (pres.). Home: 2419 Munford Dr Fallston MD 21047 Office: Joppatowne HS 555 Joppa Farm Rd Joppa MD 21085

SHORT, MARIANNE DOLORES, lawyer; b. Mpls., Mar. 12, 1951; d. Robert Earl and Marion (McCann) S.; m. Raymond Louis Skowyra Jr., Nov. 1, 1980; 2 children, R. Louis Skowyra III & Nicholas Skowyra. BA in Philosophy and Polit. Sci., Newton Coll. of Sacred Heart, 1973; JD, Boston Coll., 1976. Bar: Minn. 1976, Mass. 1977, U.S. Dist. Ct. Minn. 1976, U.S. Dist. Ct. Mass. 1980, U.S. Dis. Ct. ND 2000, U.S. Ct. Appeals (8th cir.) 1980, U.S. Supreme Ct. 1988; civil trial specialist, Minn. State Bar Assn. Spl. asst. atty. gen., St. Paul, 1976-77; assoc. Dorsey & Whitney LLP, Mpls., 1977-82, ptnr., litig. practice, 1983—88, mem. policy com., 1987—88, 2000—; judge Minn. Ct. Appeals, 1988—2000. Chmn. recruiting com. Dorsey & Whitney, Mpls., 1985-87. Trustee Boston Coll., 1985—, Visitation Convent, St. Paul, 1985-91, St. Thomas Acad., 2000—; bd. overseers Boston Coll. Law Sch., 1998—, U. Minn. Law Sch., 2001—. Named Minn. Super Lawyer, Minn. Law & Politics Mag., 2000—06, Women to Watch, Bus. Jour., 2005, Atty. of Yr., Minn. Lawyer, 2005; named one of 15 Top Attys. in Minn., Minn. Lawyers, 2005; recipient Corp. Woman of Achievement award, Nat. Assn. Women Bus. Owners, 2004. Mem. ABA, Mass. Bar Assn., Minn. Bar Assn., Hennepin County Bar Assn. (ethics com.), Ramsey County Bar Assn., Am. Arbitration Assn. (arbitrator). Club: Town and Country (St. paul), Mpls. Club (bd. govs.) Avocations: running, skiing. Office: Dorsey & Whitney LLP Ste 1500 50 S Sixth St Minneapolis MN 55402-1498 Office Phone: 612-340-2833. Office Fax: 612-340-2807. Business E-Mail: short.marianne@dorsey.com.

SHORT, MARION PRISCILLA, neurogenetics educator; b. Milford, Del., June 12, 1951; d. Raymond Calistus and Barbara Anne (Ferguson) S.; m. Michael Peter Klein; 1 child, Asher Calistus Klein. BA, Bryn Mawr Coll., 1973; diploma, U. Edinburgh, Scotland, 1975; MD, Med. Coll. Pa., 1978. Diplomate Am. Bd. Psychiatry and Neurology, Am. Bd. Internal Medicine. Intern in internal medicine Hahnemann Med. Coll. Hosp., Phila., 1978-79; med. resident in internal medicine St. Lukes-Roosevelt Hosp., N.Y.C., 1979-81; neurology resident U. Pitts. Health Ctr., 1981-84; fellow in med. genetics Mt. Sinai Med. Ctr., N.Y.C., 1984-86; fellow in neurology Mass. Gen. Hosp., Boston, 1986-90, asst. neurologist, 1990-95; asst. prof. dept.

neurology Harvard Med. Sch., Boston, 1990-95; asst. prof. dept. neurology, pediat. and pathology U. Chgo., 1995—2000, clin. assoc. pediat. neurosurgery, 2000—, fellow McLean Ctr. for Clin. Med. Ethics, 2002—03, sr. fellow McLean Ctr. for Clin. Med. Ethics, 2003—04; program dir. genetics, transplantation and clin. rsch. AMA, Chgo., 1997—2002. Recipient Clin. Investigator Devel. award, NIH, 1988—93; fellow, Inst. Medicine, Chgo., 1999. Mem. AMA, Am. Acad. Neurology, Am. Soc. for Human Genetics, Am. Coll. Med. Genetics. Office: Pediat Neurosurgery U Chgo MC 4066 5481 S Maryland Ave Chicago IL 60637-4325 Office Phone: 773-702-2475. Business E-Mail: mpshort@surgery.bsd.uchicago.edu.

SHORT, SALLIE LEE, physical plant service worker; b. Knoxville, Tenn., Feb. 17, 1932; d. John J. and Louise Maude (Robertson) Bassett; children: Jacqueline, Carita, Paulette, Shelia, Marilyn, Regina, Panthea, Greta, Michael (dec.). Legal sec. Earl Rossin, Atty., Cleve., 1952-53; nursing technician Meharry Med. Hosp., Nashville, 1958-64; inspector May Hosiery Mill Corp., Nashville, 1964-81; trustee sick leave bank Nashville State Tech. Inst., 1993—. Author poems; guest appearence Cable TV Channel 19 Read Poetry. Campaign worker Dem. Party, Nashville, 1975-80; mem. Com. on Svc. to Persons with Disabilities and Ams. with Disabilities Act. Recipient Poet of Merit award Internat. Soc. Poets, 1997; elected to Internat. Poetry Hall of Fame, 1998. Roman Catholic. Avocations: writing, hiking, reading, travel. Home: 4113 Meadow Hill Dr Nashville TN 37218-1730 Office: Nashville State Tech Inst 120 White Bridge Rd Nashville TN 37209-4515

SHORT, SHARON HOLEFELDER, music educator; b. Wellington, Kans., Aug. 26, 1954; m. William D Short, July 21, 1979; children: William Donald III, Andrew Charles, Samuel Brady. MusB in edn., U. of Kans., 1972—77. Kansas State Dept. of Education Teaching Certificate Kans. Dept. of Edn., 1977. Tchr. St. Matthews Cath. Sch., Topeka, 1977—79; elem. music tchr. Usd 353, Wellington, Kans., 1979—80, Oxford Elem. USD 358, Kans., 1989—. Adult choir dir., children's choir dir. St. Anthony Cath. Ch., Wellington, Kans., 1979—91; working bd. mem. Winfield Cmty. Entertainment Group, Kans., 2004—; fund-raising CASA (Ct. Apptd. Services Adv.), Wellington, Kans., 1984—87; bd. mem. Oxford Libr. Bd., Kans., 1982—89. Mem.: Kans. Music Educators Assn., Music Educators Nat. Conf., Kappa Alpha Theta (life; pres. 1974—75). Avocations: music, travel, doll collecting. Personal E-mail: sfshort@hotmail.com. Business E-Mail: sharon.short@usd358.com. E-mail: sshort@usd358.com.

SHORTER, MICHELLE ANNE, secondary educator; b. Detroit, Aug. 18, 1963; d. Sidney E. and Anna N. (Cotton) S. BA in Polit. Sci., Spelman Coll., 1985; MPA, Ea. Mich. U., 1996; MEd, U. Mich., 1997. Tchr. Detroit Pub. Schs., 1987—. Vol. United Negro Coll. Fund, Detroit, 1985-98. Office: 14634 Abington Ave Detroit MI 48227-1410

SHORT-MAYFIELD, PATRICIA AHLENE, business owner; b. Ft. Benning, Ga., Oct. 12, 1955; d. William Pressley and Ilse Marie (Hofmann) Short; m. Thomas Hicks Fort, June 2, 1973 (div. Jan. 1981); m. Michael Patrick Mayfield, Aug. 11, 1984; 1 child, William Zachary. Grad. HS, Butler, Ga. Notary pub., Ga. Staff mem. Fairyland Day Care, Canton, Ga., 1973-74, Small World Child Care, Thomaston, Ga., 1974-77; nurses aide Kenneston Hosp., Marietta, Ga., 1978-80; staff worker Mental Health Ctr., Smyrna, Ga., 1980-81; dir. Kiddie Kollege, Marietta, 1981-85; bus. owner, mgr. Spiffy Clean by Mayfield, Marietta, 1985—95; lead cashier Petsmart, Kennesaw, Ga., 1994—. Choir staff Eastside Bapt. Ch., Marietta, 1988-89; vol. East Valley Elem. Sch., 1989-95, chorus vol., 1994-95; vol. East Cobb Middle Sch., 1995-98; active Nat. Congress Parents and Tchrs., Cobb County Humane Soc., 1991—. Mem. NAFE, Cobb County C. of C., Atlanta High Mus. Art, Dog Lovers Am. Republican. Baptist. Avocations: reading, walking, symphony, art, bicycling. Office: Spiffy Clean By Mayfield 2791 Georgian Ter Marietta GA 30068-3625 Office Phone: 770-424-5226. Personal E-mail: pshortm7@comcast.net.

SHORT-THOMPSON, CADY W., educator, director; b. Cin., Apr. 22, 1968; d. Alexander Walker and Kay Sears Short; m. Steven D. Thompson, Sept. 8, 1965; children: Alexander Martin Thompson, Skye Yoon Thompson, Seth Walker Thompson. BA, U. Cin., 1991, MA, 1992, PhD, 1997. Assoc. prof. No. Ky. U., Highland Heights, 1996—, dir. grad. program, 2005—. Author (researcher): (textbook) See Jane Run: Women's Political Campaign Communication. Youth group dir. Friendship United Meth. Ch. Sr. High Youth Group, 1994—2006; founding mem. No. Ky. U. Rsch. Found. Bd., 2005—; mem. Wyo. Youth Services Bur. Bd., Ohio, 2002—06. Recipient Spark award, NKU Presdl. Ambassadors, 2001, Strongest Influence award, NKU Alumni Assn., 2004. Mem.: Ctrl. States Comm. Assn. (assoc.), Ea. Comm. Assn. (assoc.), Nat. Comm. Assn. (life). Office: Northern Kentucky University 129 Landrum Highland Heights KY 41099 Office Phone: 859-572-6614. Office Fax: 859-572-6187. Business E-Mail: shortthomp@nku.edu.

SHOSS, CYNTHIA RENÉE, lawyer; b. Cape Girardeau, Mo., Nov. 29, 1950; d. Milton and Carol Jane (Duncan) S.; m. David Goodwin Watson, Apr. 13, 1986; 1 child, Lucy J. Watson. BA cum laude, Newcomb Coll., 1971; JD, Tulane U., 1974; LLM in Taxation, NYU, 1980. Bar: La. 1974, Mo. 1977, Ill. 1978, N.Y. 1990. Law clk. to assoc. and chief justices La. Supreme Ct., New Orleans, 1974-76; assoc. Stone, Pigman et al, New Orleans, 1976-77, Lewis & Rice, St. Louis, 1977-79, Curtis, Mallet-Prevost, et al, N.Y.C., 1980-82; ptnr. LeBoeuf, Lamb, Greene & MacRae, L.L.P., N.Y.C., 1982—; mng. ptnr. London office LeBoeuf, Lamb, Leiby & MacRae, 1987-89. Assoc. editor Tulane Law Rev., 1972-74; frequent speaker before profl. orgns. and assns. Contbr. articles to profl. jours. Mem. bd. overseers Sch. Risk Mgmt., Ins. and Actuarial Sci., St. John's U. Mem.: ABA, The Risk Found., Assn. Life Ins. Counsel (bd. govs.). Office: LeBoeuf Lamb Greene Et Al 125 W 55th St New York NY 10019-5369 Office Phone: 212-424-8129. Business E-Mail: cshoss@llgm.com.

SHOSS, DEANNA, theatre executive; m. Eugenio Shoss; children: Andre, Lucca. BA in Comparative Lit., Indiana U., 1985; MA, DePaul U., 2003. Exec. dir. Newbury Street League, Boston, 1986—93; account exec. Arnold Pub. Relations, Boston, 1994; marketing and communications mgr. Lakefront Region, Chgo. Pk. Dist.; dir. promotions Chgo. Dept. Aviation, 1997—2005; pres. & CEO League of Chgo. Theatres, 2005—. Fluent in Portuguese, Spanish and French. Office: Chgo League Theatres 228 S Wabash Ave Ste 900 Chicago IL 60604

SHOTWELL, COLLEEN AARON, personal trainer, educator; b. Scranton, Pa., Apr. 10, 1975; d. Patrick John and Deborah Lynn Shotwell. BS, U. Pitts., 1997, MS, 2000. Cert. first aid and CPR ARC, 2006, first aid and CPR instr. ARC, 2006. Asst. athletic trainer Albright Coll. Reading Berks Phys. Therapy, Pa., 2000; athletic trainer Pittston Area H.S. Phys. Therapy Assocs. Northeastern Pa., Old Forge, 2000—01; athletic trainer, instr. East Stroudsburg U., Pa., 2002—. Mem. safety com. East Stroudsburg U. Mem.: Pa. Athletic Trainers Soc., Nat. Athletic Trainers Assoc (cert. athletic trainer). Office: East Stroudsburg University Koehler Fieldhouse East Stroudsburg PA 18301 Office Phone: 570-422-3165. Office Fax: 570-422-3665. Business E-Mail: cshotwell@po-box.esu.edu.

SHOU, SHARON LOUISE WIKOFF, vocational rehabilitation counselor; b. Mpls., Oct. 23, 1946; d. Wallace S. and Phyllis Wikoff; m. James Kouping Shou, Dec. 27, 1969 (dec. June 4, 1989); children: Michelle, Darren. Student, U. Colo., 1971-72, Chinese U. Hong Kong, 1966-67; BA, Macalester Coll., 1968; MA, U. Denver, 1975. Cert. vocat. rehab. counselor, case manager, employment counselor; lic. clin. profl. counselor. Employment counselor Colo. Dept. of Employment, Denver, 1971-74; acad. advisor U. Ky., Lexington, 1978-81; employment advisor DeVry Inst. Tech., Lombard, Ill., 1985-86; trainee asst. specialist County of DuPage, Wheaton, Ill., 1987; sr. rehab. case mgr. CRA Managed Care (Comprehensive Rehab. Assoc.), Boston, 1987-97; rehab. specialist EVR, Batavia, Ill., 1997—2000; sr. vocat. rehab. counselor Unum Provident, 2000—. Vocat. rehab. expert witness. Fellow: Am. Bd. Vocat. Experts; mem. AAUW (internat. rels. com. 1983), Naperville (Ill.) Chinese Assn. (adminstrv. com. 1984), Internat. Assn. Rehab. Profls. in the Pvt. Sector. Office: Unum Provident 655 North Central Ave Ste 900 Glendale CA 91203

SHOUN, ELLEN LLEWELLYN, retired secondary school educator; b. Germantown, Pa., Sept. 8, 1925; d. William Thomas and Ella (Hall) Llewellyn; m. Glenn Harte Shoun, June 25, 1949; children: Mary Deborah, Paul L., Eleanor C., Peter G., Elizabeth A. AB in Chemistry, Oberlin Coll., 1947; MA in Sci. Edn., Western Mich. U., 1972. Cert. libr. (ltd. profl.) Mich., secondary sch. tchr. Mich. Jr. chemist Am. Cyanamid, Stamford, Conn., 1947-49; Charles M. Hall Chem. instr. Oberlin (Ohio) Coll., 1949-51; br. libr. Bronson (Mich.) Pub. Libr., 1966-67; math. and sci. tchr. Bronson H.S., 1967-79; crew leader 1980 U.S. Census, Branch County, Mich., 1980; bus. mgr. Dr. C.F. Cole's Dental Office, Sturgis, Mich., 1982; reference aide Br. Dist. Libr., Coldwater, Mich., 1982-99; ret., 1999. Co-founder Bronson HS Cmty. Recycling Group, 1972—79. Trustee Bronson Pub. Libr., 1968—82, Housing Commn., 1975—, Bronson Cmty. Found., 2003—; instr. CPR Cmty. health Ctr., Coldwater, Mich., 1978—80; cmty. chorus Cmty. Found., 1987—; chair refugee family com. Bronson United Meth. Ch., 1974—82, ch. choir, 1967—, sec. adminstrv. bd., 1987—, chair adminstrv. bd., 1984—86; bd. dirs., treas., mgr. Food Pantry, 5 Ch. Coop., Bronson, 1993—. Named Hon. Grand Marshal, Polish Festival Parade, Bronson, 2002; recipient Cmty. Vol. of Yr. award, Gleaner Life Ins. Soc., 2001. Mem.: Phi Beta Kappa. Democrat. Avocations: photography, knitting, Scrabble.

SHOWALTER, DEANNA JO, secondary school educator; b. Memphis, Oct. 20, 1963; d. David Jerome and Iris (Neher) Showalter; 1 child, Victoria Deanna. BEd, U. North Tex., Denton, 1987; MSc in Biology, U. Tex., Arlington, 2001. Tchr. Krum H.S., Tex., 1987—89, Draughn's Coll. Bus., Ft. Worth, 1989—90, Grapevine H.S., Tex., 1990—. Nominee Disney Tchr. of Yr., 2006. Mem.: Nat. Sci. Tchr. Assn., Team Bicycles Inc. (pres. 1996—2000). Achievements include ranked 11th in nation in bicycle stage racing; state champion Tex. in bicycle road racing and time trials, 1998, bicycle time trial and criterium racing, 2000. Avocations: bicycle racing, ferret rescue, house remodeling, crafts. Business E-Mail: deanna.showalter@gcisd.net.

SHOWALTER, ELAINE, humanities educator; b. Cambridge, Mass., Jan. 21, 1941; d. Paul and Violet (Rottenberg) Cottler; m. English Showalter, June 8, 1963; children: Vinca, Michael. BA, Bryn Mawr Coll., 1962; MA, Brandeis U., 1964; PhD in English, U. Calif., Davis, 1970; LittD (hon.), Rutgers U., 2001. Teaching asst. English U. Calif., 1964-66, from instr. to assoc. prof., 1967-78; prof. English Rutgers U., from 1978, Princeton (N.J.) U., 1984—2003; Avalon Found. prof. humanities Princeton (N.J.) U., 1987—, prof. emeritus, 2003—. Vis. prof. English and women's studies U. Del., 1976-77; vis. prof. Sch. Criticism and Theory, Dartmouth Coll., 1986; prof. Salzburg (Austria) Seminars, 1988; Clarendon lectr. Oxford (Eng.) U., 1989; vis. scholar Phi Beta Kappa, 1993-94; numerous radio and TV appearances. Author: A Literature of Their Own, 1977, The Female Malady, 1985, Sexual Anarchy, 1990, Sister's Choice, 1991, Hystories, 1997, Inventing Herself, 2001, Teaching LIterature, 2002; co-author: Hysteria Beyond Freud, 1993; editor: These Modern Women, 1978, The New Feminist Criticism, 1985, Alternative Alcott, 1987, Speaking of Gender, 1989, Modern American Women Writers, 1991, Daughters of Decadence, 1993, Scribbling Women, 1997; also articles and revs. Recipient Howard Behrman humanities award Princeton U., 1989; faculty rsch. coun. fellow Rutgers U., 1972-73, Guggenheim fellow, 1977-78, Rockefeller humanities fellow, 1981-82, fellow NEH, 1988-89; Cotsen fellow Princeton U., 1998-2001; Mellon fellow, 2003—; Huntington fellow, 2004—. Mem. MLA (v.p. 1996-97, pres. 1998). Office: Princeton U Dept Of English Princeton NJ 08544-0001

SHOWALTER, MARILYN GRACE, trade association administrator, director; AB, Harvard U., 1972, JD, 1975. Bar: Wash. 1975. Dep. pros. atty. King County, Wash., 1975—81, counsel to gov., 1981—83; pvt. practice, 1985—89; counsel house appropriations com. Wash. State House of Reps., 1989—92, dep. chief clk., house counsel, 1992—93, chief clk., 1994—95; advisor to Gov. Gary Locke, 1997—99; chair Utilities and Transp. Com., Portland, Oreg., 1999—2005, exec. dir., 2005—. Office: Pub Power Coun 1500 NE Irving Ste 200 Portland OR 97232 Business E-Mail: mshowalter@ppcpdx.org.

SHOWALTER, SHIRLEY H., academic administrator; b. July 30, 1948; BA cum laude in English, Ea. Mennonite U., Harrisonburg, Va., 1970; MA in Am. civilization, U. Tex., Austin, 1974, PhD in Am. civilization, 1981. Tchr. English Harrisonburg (Va.) H.S, 1970—72; tchg. asst. English and Am. Studies depts. U. Tex., Austin, 1973—75, asst. instr. Am. Studies dept., 1976; dir. continuing edn. Goshen Coll., Ind., 1979—82, project dir. Title II tech. and liberal arts devel. grant, 1982—85, project dir. Consortium Advancemet of Pvt. Higher Edn. grant, 1985—86, asst. to prof. English, 1967—, pres., 1997—. Coord. Humanities program Harrisonburg (Va.) H.S., 1970—72; co-dir. Study-Svc. Term in Haiti Goshen Coll., 1981—82; rsch. asst. Consortium Advancement of Pvt. Higher Edn., Washington, 1986—87, interim v.p., 1987; chair English dept. Goshen Coll., 1990—93; sr. fellow Lilly Fellows program in Humanities and Arts Valparaiso U., Ind., 1993—94; co-dir. Study-Svc. Term in Ivory Coast Goshen Coll., 1993; lectr. and spkr. in humanities. Contbr. chapters to books, articles to profl. jours. Bd. mem. South Bend Symphony Assn.; mem. blue ribbon adv. group Boys and Girls Club; vice chair and mem. Hist. Com. of Mennonite Ch., 1984—88; co-sponsor Kid's Club No. Va. Mennonite Ch., 1987—88; chair curriculum com. Sojourner's Sunday Sch. class Coll. Mennonite Ch., 1987—88, mem. constn. revision com., 1988—92, tchr. H.S. age class, 1988—91, mem. worship commn., 1994—96; bd. mem. Coun. Christian Coll. and U., 2000—, Ind. Colls. of Ind., 1999—, Lantz Ctr. Christian Vocations, Indpls., 1998—; dir. Coun. Ind. Colls., 1999—; bd. dir. Mennonite Mutual Aid Trust; dir. Elkhart County Cmty. Found. Recipient Tchg. Excellence and Campus Leadership award, Sears Roebuck Found., 1990, Faculty Rsch., Goshen Coll., 1990, Knight Presdl. Leadership award, John S. and James L. Knight Found., 1999, 1999; fellow, George H. Gallup Rsch. Inst., 1999—2000, Coolidge Fellow, Yale U., Assn. Religion in Intellectual Life, 1996; grantee Faculty Rsch., Goshen Coll., 1977, 1982, Summer Stipend, Lilly Endowment, 1991. Mem.: AAUW, Am. Studies Assn., Am. Assn. Higher Edn. (Goshen Coll. rep. Forum on Exemplary Tchg. 1992, bd. dir. 1992—96), No. Ind. Partnership for the Arts, Willa Cather Pioneer Mem., Ind. Hist. Soc., Ellen Glasgow Soc., Blue Sky Assoc. Office: VP Programs Fetzer Inst 9292 West KL Ave Kalamazoo MI 49004-9398

SHOWELL, ANN LOCKHART, small business owner; b. Wadesboro, North Carolina, Nov. 4, 1924; d. Adam and Elizabeth Hardison Lockhart; m. John Dale Showell, III, Mar. 22, 1947 (dec.); children: John Dale IV, Ann S. Mariner, Sarah Elizabeth, Adam Lockhart. BA, Duke U., Durham, N.C., 1946. Comptroller, v.p. Castle-in the Sand, Inc., Ocean City, Md., 1958. Dir. Atlantic Nat. Bank, Ocean City, 1976, Ocean City, 84. Founding dir. Atlantic Gen. Hosp., Berlin, Md., 1982. Recipient Parent of Yr., Ocean City Elem. Sch. Mem.: DAR, Nat. Soc. Colonial Dames Am. Democrat. Episc. Avocations: bridge, reading, handwork, computer research. Home: 12737 Center Dr Ocean City MD 21842

SHOWERS JOHNSON, VIOLET MARY-ANN IYABO, history professor; b. Lagos, Nigeria; arrived in US, 1985, naturalized, 2002; d. Samuel Dandeson and Edna Taiwo Showers; m. Percy Ayomi Johnson; 1 child, Percy Ayomi Johnson, Jr. BA in History with honors, U. Sierra Leone, Freetown, 1979; MA, U. NB, Fredericton, NB, Canada, 1983; PhD, Boston Coll., Chestnut Hill, Mass., 1992. Lectr. dept. modern history Fourah Bay Coll., U. Sierra Leone, Freetown, 1983—85; history prof. Agnes Scott Coll., Decatur, Ga., 1992—, chair dept. history, 2001—, dir. African studies, 1995—2002. Proposals reviewer NEH Summer Seminars and Insts., 2000; grant screener Am. Coun. Learned Scholars, 2000—01; mem. scholars working group Atlanta Regional Consortium for Higher Edn. Civil Rights Virtual Libr. Project, 2001—03; external reviewer dept. history Spelman Coll., 2003. Author: The Other Black Bostonians: West Indians in Boston, 1900-1950, 2006; mem. editl. bd.: Jour. Am. Ethnic History; contbr. articles to profl. jours. Mem. African Am. initiatives bd. Atlanta History Ctr., 2001—05; applications reviewer, scholarship com. Atlanta Caribbean Assn., 2004; spkr. various events Auburn Ave. Rsch. Libr. on African-American Culture and History, Atlanta. Recipient Durham prize for the best result in the Faculty of Arts, Fourah Bay Coll., U. Sierra Leone, 1979, Vulcan Tchg. Excellence award, Vulcan Materials Co., 2002, Outstanding Woman award, Women Multi-Ethnicity and Nationality, 2004, Joseph R. Gladden Pub. Lecture award for noteworthy scholarship, Bd. Trustees, Agnes Scott Coll., 2005; grantee, NEH, 1998; Jr. Fulbright fellow, Fulbright Found., 1985—92. Mem.: Soc. for Multi-Ethnic Studies: Europe and the Americas, Forum for European Contbns. in African Am. Studies (mem. editl. bd.), Am. Hist. Assn., Assn. for the Study of African Am. Life and History, Immigration and Ethnic History Soc., Collegium African Am. Rsch. (exec. bd. mem.). Office: Agnes Scott College 141 East College Ave Decatur GA 30030 Office Phone: 404-471-6191. Home Fax: 404-471-6369; Office Fax: 404-471-6369. Business E-Mail: vjohnson@agnesscott.edu.

SHOWS, WINNIE M., speaker, consultant, writer; b. LA, Apr. 2, 1947; d. William Marion Arvin and Joan Catherine (Sperry) Wilson; m. George Albert Shows, Mar. 18, 1967 (div. May 1980); 1 child, Sallie; m. Michael P. Florio, Jan. 1, 1990 (div.). BA in English, UCLA, 1969; MEd, Calif. State U., Long Beach, 1976. Tchr. St. Joseph High Sch., Lakewood, Calif., 1969-71; tchr. high sch. Irvine (Calif) Unified Sch. Dist., 1972-79; freelance writer, 1979-80; mgr. pub. rels. Forth, Inc., Hermosa Beach, Calif., 1980-81; account mgr., account supr., dir. mktg. Franson & Assoc., San Jose, Calif., 1981-84; v.p., pres. Smith & Shows, Menlo Park, Calif., 1984-96; spkr., author, cons. in field; co-founder Spkrs. in the Mountains. Presenter seminar in field. Author: (newsletter) Smith & Shows Letter, 1989—94, Hairball and Other Poems of Trans Formation, 2000. Vol. Unity Palo Alto (Calif.) Cmty. Ch., 1989-99, Newcomers, Menlo Park, 1990-93, Kara, Palo Alto, 1991-98, Menlo Park Sch. Dist., 1993-95, Asistencia Para Latinos, 2000. Named Woman of Vision, Career Action Ctr., 1994; named one of Colorado Springs Most Dynamic Women, CS Bus. Jour., 2001. Mem.: Colorado Springs Women and Tech., Nat. Spkrs. Assn., Colorado Spring Women and Tech. (pres. 2001—02, founder, co-founder, pres. 2001—02), Nat. Spkrs. Assn. (treas.,. Mem. of Yr. No. Calif. chpt. 1999, Mem. of Yr. 1999, Mem. of Yr. No. Calif. chpt. 1999, Mem. of Yr. 1999, SRI Organon Toastmaster of Yr. 1995, Karl Lind award 1996). E-mail: winnie@wshows.com.

SHRADER-FRECHETTE, KRISTIN, science educator; m. Maurice Frechette; 2 children. B in Math. summa cum laude, Xavier U., 1967; PhD in Philosophy, U. Notre Dame, 1972. O'Neill Family prof. philosophy, concurrent prof. biol. sci. U. Notre Dame. Mem. exec. com. sci. adv. bd. EPA, chair com. bioethics; prin. investigator grants NSF, Nat. Endowment for the Humanities, Coun. Philosophical Studies, U.S. Dept. Energy. Author: (books) Nuclear Power and Public Policy, 1983, Environmental Ethics, 1991, Four Methodological Assumptions in Cost Benefit Analysis, 1983, Science, Policy, Ethics, and Economic Methodology, 1984, Risk Analysis and Scientific Method, 1985, Nuclear Energy and Ethics, 1991, Risk and Rationality, 1991, Policy for Land: Law and Ethics, 1992, Burying Uncertainty: Risk and the Case Against Geological Disposal of Nuclear Waste, 1993, Method in Ecology, 1993, The Ethics of Scientific Research, 1994, Technology and Human Values, 1996, Environmental Justice: Creating Equality, Reclaiming Democracy, 2002; assoc. editor: Bioscience, editor-in-chief: Oxford U. Press monograph series Environ. Ethics and Sci. Policy, mem. editl. bd.: 18 profl. jours.; contbr. over 300 articles to profl jours. including Ethics, Jour. Philosophy, Philosophy of Sci., Synthese, Trends in Ecology Revolution, others. Fellow, Woodrow Wilson Found., NSF, Carnegie Found. Mem.: NAS (bd. dirs. environ. studies and toxicology, com. risk characterization, com. zinc-cadmium-sulfide dispersions), Internat. Soc. Environ. Ethics (past pres.), Risk Assessment and Policy Assn. (past pres.), Soc. Philosophy and Tech. (past pres.), Philosophy Sci. Assn., Am. Philosophical Assn. Office: Dept Philosophy and Dept Biol Scis 100 Malloy Hall Univ Notre Dame Notre Dame IN 46556 Business E-Mail: kristin.shrader-frechette.1@nd.edu.

SHRAMEK, ERIN ELIZABETH, language educator; b. Downers Grove, Ill., Feb. 12, 1977; d. John Mason and Susan Beth Satterthwaite; m. Timothy Charles Shramek, July 22, 2000; children: Sofia Elizabeth, John Kenneth. BS in English Secondary Edn., U. Wis., Whitewater, 2000; MEd, U. Wis., LaCrosse, 2003. Tchr. H.S. English, Dodgeland Sch. Dist., Juneau, 2000—. Forensics coach Dodgeland H.S., Juneau, Wis., 2000—, debate coach, 2000—03, nat. honor soc. advisor, 2003—06. Mem.: Wis. State Reading Assn. Office: Dodgeland Sch Dist 401S Western Ave Juneau WI 53039 Office Phone: 920-386-4404. E-mail: shramek@dodgeland.k12.wi.us.

SHRAUNER, BARBARA WAYNE ABRAHAM, electrical engineer, educator; b. Morristown, N.J., June 21, 1934; d. Leonard Gladstone and Ruth Elizabeth (Thrasher) Abraham; m. James Ely Shrauner, 1965; children: Elizabeth Ann, Jay Arthur. BA cum laude, U. Colo., 1956; AM, Harvard U., 1957, PhD, 1962. Postdoc. mrschr. Free U. Brussels, 1962-64, NASA-Ames Rsch. Ctr., Moffett Field, Calif., 1964-65; asst. prof. Washington U., St. Louis, 1966-69, assoc. prof., 1969-77, prof., 1977—2003, sr. prof., 2003—. Sabbatical Los Alamos (N.Mex.) Sci. Lab., 1975-76, Lawrence Berkeley Lab., Berkeley, Calif., 1985-86; cons. Los Alamos Nat. Lab., 1979, 84, NASA, Washington, 1980, Naval Surface Weapons Lab., Silver Spring, Md., 1984. Contbr. articles on transport in semiconductors, hidden symmetries of differential equations, plasma physics to profl. jours. Fellow Am. Phys. Soc. (sr. divsn. plasma physics, exec. com. 1980-82, 96-98); mem. IEEE (sr.; sr. exec. com. of standing tech. com. on plasma sci. and applications 1996-98), AAUP (local sec.-treas. 1980-82), Am. Geophys. Union, Phi Beta Kappa, Sigma Xi, Eta Kappa Nu, Sigma Pi Sigma. Home: 7452 Stratford Ave Saint Louis MO 63130-4044 Office: Washington U Dept Elec and Systems Engring 1 Brookings Dr Saint Louis MO 63130-4899 Office Phone: 314-935-6134. Business E-Mail: bas@wustl.edu.

SHREEVE, JEAN'NE MARIE, chemist, educator; b. Deer Lodge, Mont., July 2, 1933; d. Charles William and Maryfrances (Briggeman) Shreeve. BA in Chemistry, U. Mont., 1953, DSc (hon.), 1982; MS in Analytical Chemistry, U. Minn., 1956; PhD in Inorganic Chemistry, U. Wash., 1961. From asst. prof. to assoc. prof. chemistry U. Idaho, Moscow, 1961—67, prof., 1967-73, 2000—, acting chmn. dept. chemistry, 1969-70, 1973, head dept. and prof., 1973-87, v.p. rsch. and grad. studies, prof. chemistry, 1987-99, Jean'ne M. Shreeve chemistry prof., 2004—. Mem. nat. com. Stds. Higher Edn., 1965—67, 1969—73; Lucy W. Pickett lectr. Mt. Holyoke Coll., 1976; George H. Cady lectr. U. Wash., 1993; chmn. con. nat. medal sci. Pres. U.S., 2003—. Mem. editl. bd. Jour. Fluorine Chemistry, 1970—, Jour. Heteroatom Chemistry, 1988—95, Accounts Chem. Rsch., 1973—75, Inorganic Synthesis, 1976—; contbr. articles to sci. jours. Mem. bd. govs. Argonne (Ill.) Nat. Lab., 1992—98. Named Hon. Alumnus, U. Idaho, 1972; named to Idaho Hall of Fame, 2001; recipient Disting. Alumni award, U. Mont., 1970, Outstanding Achievement award, U. Minn., 1975, Sr. U.S. Scientist award, Alexander Von Humboldt Found., 1978, Excellence in Tchg. award, Chem. Mfrs. Assn., 1980; NSF Postdoctoral fellow, U. Cambridge, Eng., 1967—68, U.S. Hon. Ramsay fellow, 1967—68, Alfred P. Sloan fellow, 1970—72. Mem.: AAUW (officer Moscow chpt. 1962—69), AAAS (bd. dirs. 1991—95), Idaho Acad. Sci. (Disting. Scientist 2001), Am. Chem. Soc. (bd. dirs. 1985—93, chmn. fluorine divsn. 1979—81, mem. adv. bd. Petroleum Rsch. Fund 1975—77, mem. women chemists com. 1972—77, Harry and Carol Mosher award Santa Clara Valley sect. 1992, Shirley B. Radding award Santa Clara Valley sect. 2003, Garvan medal 1972, award for creative work in fluorine chemistry 1978), Göttingen (Germany) Acad. Scis. (corr.), Phi Beta Kappa. Avocations: fishing, gardening. Office: U Idaho Dept Chemistry Moscow ID 83844-2343 Fax: 208-885-9146. Office Phone: 208-885-6215. Business E-Mail: jshreeve@uidaho.edu.

SHREVE, ANITA, writer; b. Boston, Oct. 7, 1946; d. Richard H. and Bibiona (Kennedy) S.; children: Katherine, Christopher. BA in English, Tufts U., 1968. Tchr. high sch. Author: (non-fiction) Remaking Motherhood, 1987,

Women Together, Women Alone, 1989, (novels) Eden Close, 1989, Strange Fits of Passion, 1991, All He Ever Wanted, 1991, Where or When, 1993, Resistance, 1995, The Weight of Water, 1997, Fortune's Rocks, 1999, The Pilot's Wife, 1998 (Oprah Book Club Selection), The Last Time They Met, 2001, Sea Glass, 2002, Light on Snow, 2004, A Wedding in December, 2005; (short stories) Past the Island, Drifting (O. Henry prize, 1975). Recipient Page One award Newspaper Guild, NYC, 1984, PEN/LL Winship award, 1998, New England Book award for fiction, 1998. Mem. PEN, Authors's Guild. Office: Little Brown and Co 1271 Avenue Of The Americas New York NY 10020-1300

SHREVE, ELIZABETH STEWARD, public relations executive, former publishing executive; b. Charlottesville, Va., Feb. 19, 1970; d. Porter Gaylord Shreve Jr. and Susan Richards Shreve; m. Russell David Greiff; 2 children. BA, Kenyon Coll. Spl. asst. Corp. for Nat. Svc., Wash., DC, 1993—94; sr. pub., editor Counterpoint Books, Wash., 1995—96; publicity mgr. Dutton Publ., NYC, 1996—97, Vintage Books, NYC, 1997; v.p., dir. publicity Henry Holt & Co., NYC, 1997—2005; with Discovery Comm. Inc., Silver Spring, Md., 2005; pres. Elizabeth Shreve Pub. Rels., Washington, 2006—. Bd. dir. Publishers Publicity Assn., N.Y.C., 1998—2003, Am. Voices, Wash., 1995—. Mem.: Women's Media Group. Democrat. Avocations: cooking, singing. Office: Elizabeth Shreve Pub Rels 6208 32nd Pl NW Washington DC 20015 Office Phone: 202-362-0770.*

SHREVE, SUE ANN GARDNER, retired health products company administrator; b. Bklyn., Jan. 26, 1932; d. Homer Frank and Grace Emily (Kohlhagen) Gardner; m. Eugene Sheldon Shreve II, Nov. 20, 1954; children: Pamela Ann, Cynthia Ann Shreve Richard. BBA, Hofstra U., 1955. Co. rep. N.Y. Tel. Co., Bay Shore, 1954-55; engr. Republic Aviation, Farmingdale, N.Y., 1955-58; substitute tchr. East Islip (N.Y.) Sch. Dist., 1966-71; mgr. Patchogue Surg. and Athletic Supplies, Sayville, N.Y., 1971-81, ret., 1981. Invited guest writer Nat. Geneal. Soc. newsletter, 1996, 99, 2004; lectr. in genealogy, 1997—; condr. genealogy workshops, 1996—. Author, editor, pub.: The Kohlhagen Family Genealogy, 1994, The Shreve Family Genealogy, an update from 1641, 1997, Hendrickson Genealogy England to Illinois before 1840, 1999, Piscitelli Genealogy Italy to NYC before 1912, 2000; compiler, editor newsletter Gardner/Gardiner Rschrs., 1993—, Amos F.F. Gardner His Maternal Ancestors—Kirkpatrick & Barkley & Descendants, 2001, The Coates Family Genealogy, 2002, The Ridgeway Family Genealogy, 2003, The Mendenhall Family Genealogy, 2003, The Stockton Family Genealogy, 2003, The Becker Family Genealogy Germany to St. Clair County Ill. and Madison County Ill. in 1846-2005; issue reviewer Geneal. Helper Mag., 1995. Life mem. N.Y. State Congress of Parents and Tchrs., 1963—, past pres.; mem. Penataquit Aux. Southside Hosp., 1985—; mem., fundraiser Hospice of South Shore, 1983—; mem. Bay Shore N.Y. Hist. Soc., 1997—; rec. sec. Bay Shore Beautification Soc., 2000—, Bradish Ln. Homeowners Assn., 1997—2001, treas., 2002—; mem. Sagtikos Manor Hist. Soc., 2003—; maj. sponsor Bay Shore Arts Festival, 2001—06. Recipient Ofcl. proclamation Village of Frankfort, Ill., 1996; named one of Outstanding Young Women of Am., 1967. Mem.: DAR/Nat. Soc. DAR (vice regent 2001—05, regent 2005—), AAUW (charter, past pres., past treas. Islip area br., rsch. and project grantee 1989), Nat. Soc. Sons of the Am. Revolution (Medal of Appreciation 2005), Bay Shore C. of C., 1st Families of Ohio, Daus. Union Vets. of Civil War (rec. sec. 2004—), German Genealogy Group of L.I. (rec. sec. 2003—), Bay Shore Garden Club (past pres., treas., dir., 2d v.p. 2000—, Woman of Yr. 1997, 2003). Republican. Methodist. Avocations: tennis, gourmet cooking, gardening, needlecrafts, international travel. Home: 5 Anderson Ct Bay Shore NY 11706-7701 Personal E-mail: sue12632@aol.com.

SHREVE, SUSAN RICHARDS, writer, educator; b. Toledo, May 2, 1939; d. Robert Kenneth and Helen (Greene) Richards; children— Porter, Elizabeth, Caleb, Kate. BA, U. Pa., 1961; MA, U. Va., 1969. Prof. English lit. George Mason U., Fairfax, Va., 1976—. Vis. prof. Columbia U., NYC, 1982—, Princeton U., 1991-93 Author: (novels) A Fortunate Madness, 1974, A Woman Like That, 1977, Children of Power, 1979, Miracle Play, 1981, Dreaming of Heroes, 1984, Queen of Hearts, 1986, A Country of Strangers, 1989, Daughters of the New World, 1992, The Train Home, 1993, Skin Deep: Women & Race, 1995, The Visiting Physician, 1995; (pseudonym Annie Waters) Glimmer, 1997, Plum & Jaggers, 2000, A Student of Living Things, 2006; (children's books) The Nightmares of Geranium Street, 1977, Family Secrets, 1979, Loveletters, 1979, The Masquerade, 1980, The Bad Dreams of a Good Girl, 1981, The Revolution of Mary Leary, 1982, The Flunking of Joshua T. Bates, 1984, How I Saved the World on Purpose, 1985, Lucy Forever and Miss Rosetree, Shrinks, Inc., 1985, Joshua T. Bates In Charge, 1992, The Gift of the Girl Who Couldn't Hear, 1991, Wait for Me, 1992, Amy Dunn Quits School, 1993, Lucy Forever & the Stolen Baby, 1994, The Formerly Great Alexander Family, 1995, Zoe and Columbo, 1995, Warts, 1996, A Goalie, 1996, Joshua Bates in Trouble Again, 1997, Jonah, The Whale, 1997, Ghost Cats, 1999, The End of Amanda, The Good, 2000, Blister, 2002, Trout & Me, 2003, Under the Watson's Porch, 2004; editor: Dream Me Home Safely, 2003; co-editor: How We Want to Live: Narratives on Progress, 1996, (with Porter Shreve) Outside the Law: Narratives on Justice, 1997, How We Want to Live: Narratives on Progress, 1998, Tales Out of School: Narratives on Education, 1999, Blister, 2001, Trout & Me, 2002, Under the Watson's Porch, 2003, Kiss Me Tomorrow, 2006. Recipient Jenny Moore award George Washington U., 1978; John Simon Guggenheim award in fiction, 1980, Nat. Endowment Arts fiction award, 1982 Mem. PEN/Faulkner Found. (pres.), Phi Beta Kappa. Office Phone: 703-993-1338. Personal E-mail: srshreve@aol.com.

SHREVES, JUDY RAE, director; b. St. Louis, Sept. 27, 1960; d. George Vincent and Kathleen O'Neill Schwartz; m. Michael Shreves, Aug. 7, 1999. BS in Theatre and Pub. Speaking, N.E. Mo. State U., Kirksville, Mo., 1983; MA in English and ESOL, S.E. Mo. State U., Cape Girardeau, Mo., 2000; postgrad. in Elem. and Secondary Edn., Lindenwood U., St. Charles, Mo., 2005—. Tchr. H.S. Dunklin County Sch. Dist., Herculaneum, Mo., 1983—85; tchr. speech, drama Ritenour Sch. Dist., St. Louis, 1985—86; from tchr. ESOL to coord. Hazelwood Sch. Dist., Florissant, Mo., 1994—2003, coord. ESOL, 2003—05, Warren County R III. Home: 610 Florland Dr Florissant MO 63031 E-mail: judyshreves@sbcglobal.net.

SHRIER, DIANE KESLER, psychiatrist, educator; b. Mar. 23, 1941; d. Benjamin Arthur and Mollie (Wortman) Kesler; m. Adam Louis Shrier, June 10, 1961; children: Jonathan Laurence, Lydia Anne, Catherine Jane, David Leopold. BS in Chemistry/Biology magna cum laude, Queen's Coll., CUNY, 1961; postgrad., Washington U. Sch. Medicine, St. Louis, 1960-61; MD, Yale U., 1964. Diplomate Am. Bd. Psychiatry and Neurology. Pediat. intern Bellevue Hosp., N.Y.C., 1964-65; psychiat. resident Albert Einstein Coll. Medicine-Bronx Mcpl. Hosp. Ctr., 1966-68, child psychiatry fellow, 1968-70; staff cons. Family Svc. and Child Guidance Ctr. of the Oranges, Maplewood, Milburn-Orange, N.J., 1970-73, cons., 1973-79; pvt. practice Montclair, N.J., 1970-92, Washington, 1994—. Cons. Cmty. Day Nursery, East Orange, NJ, 1970—79, Montclair State Coll., 1976—78; psychiat. cons. Bloomfield (N.J.) pub. schs., 1974—75; clin. instr. Albert Einstein Coll. Medicine, 1970—73; clin. asst. prof. psychiatry U. Medicine and Dentistry N.J., 1978—82, clin. assoc. prof., 1982—89, prof. clin. psychiatry, 1989—92; vice-chmn., dir. clin. psychiat. svcs. dept. psychiatry Children's Nat. Med. Ctr., 1992—94, attending staff, 1994—; prof. psychiatry and pediats. George Washington U. Med. Ctr., 1992—94, clin. prof. psychiatry, behavioral scis. and pediat., 1994—; cons. Walter Reed Med. Ctr., 1994—. Contbr. articles to med. jours. Trustee Montessori Learning Ctr., Montclair, 1973-75. Regents scholar Queen's Coll., 1961. Fellow Am. Psychiat. Assn., Acad. Child Psychiatry; mem. Tri-County Psychiat. Assn. (exec. com., rec. sec. 1977-78, 2d v.p. 1978-79, 1st v.p. 1979-80, pres. 1977-81), N.J. Psychiat. Assn. (councillor 1981-84), Am. Acad. Child and Adolescent Psychiatry (councillor at large 1992-95), Phi Beta Kappa. Home: 4000 Cathedral Ave NW Apt 317B Washington DC 20016-5267 Office: Ste 104 1616 18th St NW Washington DC 20009-2521 Office Phone: 202-667-9005. Business E-Mail: diane.shrier.med.64@aya.yale.edu. E-mail: dianeshrier@rcn.com.

SHRINER, DARLENE KAY, professional athletics coach; b. Coeur d' Alene, Idaho, June 6, 1951; d. Rodney Leroy and Evelyn Mae Shriner. AS, North Idaho Jr. Coll., 1971; BS, U. Idaho, 1973. Cert. edn.-biol. scis., phys. edn. Tchr., coach Asotin Sch. Dist., Wash., 1973—74, Coeur d'Alene Sch. Dist., Idaho, 1974—. DNA vector workshop Cold Spring Harbor, Moscow, 1994—95; cert. track coach Level I and II U.S. Track and Field, Seattle, 1999, coach U.S. Olympic Trials Track and Field qualifier 1992, New Orleans; coach many state champions and placers; coach nat. H.S. indoor and outdoor high jump champion, 1991—92. Mem.: NSTA, NEA, Phi Kappa Phi. Avocations: hiking, gardening, bicycling, jogging. Office: Lake City HS 6101 Ramsey Rd Coeur D' Alene ID 83815 Office Fax: 208-769-2944. Business E-Mail: dshriner@SD271.K12.ID.US.

SHRINER, JOAN WARD, secondary school educator; b. Bemidji, Minn., Mar. 15, 1938; d. Robert Francis and Ruby Mae (Hagelberg) Ward; m. Larry J. Shriner; 1 child, Natasha. BS, Bemidji State U., 1960; MS, Nova U., 1987. Tchr. Franklin Jr. H.S., Brainerd, Minn., 1960-61, Evanston (Wyo.) H.S., 1963-65, Western H.S., Las Vegas, Nev., 1965-66, Rancho H.S., Las Vegas, 1966-91; chair English dept., 1980-91; tchr. Cheyenne H.S., Las Vegas, 1991—; chair English dept., 1991—. Table leader Proficiency Testing, Nev., 1986-2001, Analytical Trait Assessment, Nev., 1992-2001; head reader Nev. H.S. Proficience Exam, Nev. State Writing Proficiency, 1998—; mem. curriculum com. Clark County, 1980-2001, mem. adv. team N.E. Tchrs., 2001—, Clark County Dist. N.E. Area; mem. Nev. Curriculum Framework Com., 1995, state stds. com., 1999. Mem. NEA, ASCD, Nat. Coun. Tchrs. English, Nev. State Edn. Assn., Nev. English Lang. Arts Network, Clark County Edn. Assn., Clark County English/Lang. Arts Bd. Democrat. Avocations: reading, arts and crafts, aviculture, swimming. Home: 2825 Michael Way Las Vegas NV 89108-4171 E-mail: jmshriner@aol.com.

SHRIVASTAVA, SUNITA, secondary school educator; b. Jabalpur, India, Aug. 25, 1958; d. Mohan Kumar and Shanti Devi Nigam; m. Kirti Shankar Shrivastava, June 2, 1986; children: Siddharth, Shreya. BS, MLC Coll., Khandwa, India, 1977; MS of Chemistry, S.N. Coll., Khandwa, 1979; BE, Regional Coll. of Edn., Bhopal, 1981. Tchr., HS sci. Kendriya Vidyalaya, Nepanagar, India, 1982—99, Cleve. Mcpl. Sch. Dist., Ohio, 2001—. Recipient Best Tchr. award, Ohio's Greatest Tchr. award, 2006; grantee Mini grant, Ohio Space Grant Consortium, NASA, Ohio, 2003, Cleve. Leadership in Sci., Woodrow Wilson Nat. Fellowship Found., 2004, Jennings Scholar award, Martha Holden Jennings Found., 2006. Mem.: NSTA. Avocations: reading, travel, tennis, nature walking. Home: 1693 Roselawn Rd Mayfield Heights OH 44124 Office: Glenville HS 650 E 113th St Cleveland OH 44108

SHRIVER, EUNICE MARY KENNEDY (MRS. ROBERT SARGENT SHRIVER JR.), foundation administrator, volunteer, social worker; b. Brookline, Mass., July 10, 1920; d. Joseph P. and Rose (Fitzgerald) Kennedy; m. Robert Sargent Shriver, Jr., May 23, 1953; children: Robert Sargent III, Maria Owings Shriver Schwarzenegger, Timothy Perry, Mark Kennedy, Anthony Paul Kennedy. BS in Sociology, Stanford U., Palo Alto, Calif., 1943; student, Manhattanville Coll. of Sacred Heart, LHD (hon.), 1963, D'Youville Coll., 1962, Regis Coll., 1963, Newton Coll., 1973, Brescia Coll., 1974, Holy Cross Coll., 1979, Princeton U., 1979, Boston Coll., 1990; LittD (hon.), U. Santa Clara, 1962, Yale U., 1996, Cardinal Strich U., 2002. With spl. war problems div. State Dept. Washington, 1943—46; sec. Nat. Conf. on Prevention and Control juvenile Delinquency, Dept. of Justice, Washington, 1947-48; social worker Fed. Penitentiary for Women, Alderson, W.Va., 1950, House of Good Shepherd & Juvenile Court, Chgo., 1951-54; exec. v.p. Joseph P. Kennedy, Jr. Found., 1956—; regional chmn. women's div. Community Fund-Red Cross Joint Appeal, Chgo., 1958; founder, CEO Spl. Olympics, 1968—90, founder, hon. chmn., 1990—. Cons. to Pres. John F. Kennedy's Panel on Mental Retardation, 1961; founder Community & Caring, Inc., 1981; mem. Chgo. Commn. on Youth Welfare, 1959-62; mem. bd. Special Olympics Internat. Editor: A Community of Caring, 1982, 85, Growing Up Caring, 1990. Co-chmn. women's com. Dem. Nat. Conv., Chgo., 1956. Decorated Legion of Honor; recipient Albert Lasker Pub. Svc. award, Lasker Found., 1966, Philip Murray-William Green award (with Sargent Shriver), AFL-CIO, 1966, Humanitarian award A.A.M.D., 1973, Nat. Vol. Service award, 1973, Phila. Civic Ballet award, 1973, Prix de la Couronne Française, 1974, Presdl. Medal of Freedom, 1984, Freedom From Want medal, Roosevelt Inst., 1993, Jewish Sports Hall of Fame Humanitarium award, 2000, Champion of Children award, Phoenix Found. for Children, 2000, Aetna Voice of Conscience award, 2002, Juanita Kreps award, 2002, Life award, Noel Found., 2002, Theodore Roosevelt award, NCAA, 2002; inducted into Nat. Women's Hall of Fame, 2002; appeared on Special Olympics World Summer Games silver commemorative coin, 1995.

SHRIVER, LIONEL (MARGARET ANN SHRIVER), writer; b. Gastonia, NC, May 18, 1957; married. BA, Barnard Coll., 1978; MFA in Fiction Writing, Columbia Univ., 1982. Author: (novels) The Female of the Species, 1987, Checker & the Derailleurs, 1988, The Bleeding Heart, 1990, Game Control, 1995, A Perfectly Good Family, 1996, Double Fault, 1997, We Need to Talk about Kevin, 2003 (Orange Prize for fiction, Great Britain, 2005); contbr. articles Wall St. Jour., Economist, Phila. Enquirer. Mailing: c/o Author Mail Counterpoint Press 387 Park Ave S New York NY 10016*

SHRIVER, MARIA OWINGS, news correspondent; b. Chgo., Nov. 6, 1955; d. Robert Sargent and Eunice Mary (Kennedy) S.; m. Arnold Schwarzenegger, Apr. 26, 1986; children: Katherine, Christina, Patrick & Christopher. BA, Georgetown U. Coll. Am. Studies, Washington, 1977. News producer Sta. KYW-TV, 1977-78; producer Sta. WJZ-TV, 1978-80; nat. reporter PM Mag., 1981-83; news reporter CBS News, Los Angeles, 1983-85; news correspondent, co-anchor CBS Morning News, N.Y.C., 1985-86; co-host Sunday Today, NBC, 1987-90; anchor Main Street, NBC, 1987; co-anchor Yesterday, Today, and Tomorrow, NBC, 1989; anchor NBC Nightly News Weekend Edition, 1989-90, Cutting Edge with Maria Shriver, NBC, 1990, First Person with Maria Shriver, NBC, 1990—2004; First Lady of Calif., 2003—. Co-anchor summer olympics, Seoul, Korea, 1988; substitute anchor NBC News at Sunrise, Today, NBC Nightly News with Tom Brokaw; contbg. anchor Dateline, NBC, 1995-2004. Appeared in Last Action Hero, 1993; correspondent TV series The American Parade, 1984; prodr. (TV Series) Portrait of a Legend, 1981; author What's Heaven, 1999, Ten Things I Wish I'd Known Before I Went Into the Real World, 2000, What's Wrong With Timmy, 2001, What's Happening to Grandpa?, 2003, And One More Thing Before You Go., 2005 (Publishers Weekly bestseller list). Recipient Christopher award for "Fatal Addictions", 1990, Exceptional Merit Media award Nat. Women's Political Caucus, first-place Commendation award Am. Women in Radio and TV, 1991, Emmy nomination, George Peabody Award, 1998. Democrat. Roman Catholic. Office: First Lady Maria Shriver State Capitol Bldg Sacramento CA 95814-4906

SHROUDER, HORTENSE EAILEEN, dietitian; b. Bath, Jamaica, Jan. 9, 1953; came to U.S., 1971; d. Lincoln S. and Christiana (Bryce) Darlington. AAS, N.Y.C. Coll., 1977; BS, Hunter Coll., 1982; MS, NYU, 1989. Cert. dietitian-nutritionist, N.Y. Dietitian tech. Bronx Psychiat. Ctr., 1982-84; sch. lunch mgr. Bklyn. Bd. Edn., 1984-85; dietitian II Manhattan Psychiat. Ctr., N.Y.C., 1985—. Mem. Am. Dietetic Assn., N.Y. Dietetic Assn., Am. Diabetes Assn., Food & Nutrition Coun., The Dairy Coun., Am. Heart Assn. Democrat. Mem. Grace Faith Assembly. Avocations: alto singing in choir, church activities, cooking, sports, walking, swimming. Office: Manhattan Psychiat Ctr Nutrition Svcs Wards Island New York NY 10035

SHUART, CAREY CHENOWETH, farmer, volunteer; b. Houston, June 1, 1944; d. Robert Carey Chenoweth and Elizabeth Dorothy Smith; m. Willard Warren Shuart, Apr. 17, 1965 (dec. Mar. 1996); children: Nora Wellington Shuart-Faris, Sarah Espy Shuart Szymanski. Student, Tex. U., 1962—66, U. Houston, 1991—93, Glassell Sch. Mus. of Fine Arts, Houston, 1990—2005. Owner, cons. Bien Trouvé Art Gallery, Houston, 1979—85; rice farmer Shuart Farms, Houston. Mem. adv. bd. Blaffer Gallery U. Houston, 2002—. Editor: (newsletter) U Friends, 1992—98. Mem. alumni bd. St. John's Sch., Houston, 1973—75; sustainer Jr. League of Houston, 1975—2004; founder, pres. Pink Ladies-Eagle Lake Cmty. Hosp., 1967—72, Civic Garden Club, Eagle Lake, Tex., 1983—85; chmn. adv. bd. Friends of Women's Studies U. Houston, 2001—; founder, patron Women's Archive and Rsch. Ctr. U. Houston; mem. photo subcom. Mus. Fine Arts, Houston, 2000—; bd. dirs. Friends of Women's Studies U. Houston, 1992—2004, Honors Coll., U. Houston, 1992—95. Named Vol. of Yr., U. Houston U. Rels. Divsn., 1992, 1995, U. Houston, 1995, 1996; recipient Nat. CASE award, St. Johns Sch., Houston, 1982, Outstanding Alumni award, 1991. Mem.: Nat. Soc. Colonial Dames in State of Tex. (chmn. 1982—86, 2003—05). Episcopalian. Avocations: photography, golf, social work. Office: Shuart Farms 2121 San Felipe #118 Houston TX 77019

SHUBERT, ABBY NOONAN, language educator; BS in Secondary Edn., Pa. State U., University Park, 2003; MEd in Curriculum and Instrn., U. Del., Newark, 2006. Tchr. English State of Del., Middletown, 2003—. Mem.: Pa. State Alumni Assn. (life), Pi Lambda Theta, Mensa, Phi Sigma Pi.

SHUBIN, JOANNA, science educator; b. LI City, NY, June 24, 1945; d. Vincent and Theresa Spampanato; m. Jonathan Simon Shubin, Mar. 30, 1980; 1 child, David Jonathan. BA, Queens Coll., 1967, MS, 1972. Cert. Teacher N-6 1973, Social Studies Teacher 1972, Biological Science Teacher 1991, Teacher Nat. Sci. Tchrs. Assn., 1987. Sci. tchr. St. Stanislaus Sch., Bklyn., 1969—71, Most Precious Blood Sch., LI City, 1971—81, Garden Sch., Jackson Heights, NY, 1981—85, Sci. Mus. LI, Manhasset, NY, 1985—86, Garden Sch., 1986—90, Great Neck South Mid. Sch., NY, 1992, Roslyn Mid. Sch., Roslyn, NY, 1992—. Contbr. articles to jours. Sci. tchr. Schneider Children's Hosp., Queens. Recipient Educator of Month, Hofstra U. and News 12, 2001, Excellence in Tchg., Sci. Tchrs. Assn. of NY State, 2002. Mem.: LI Sci. Edn. Leadership Assn. Inc., Astronomical Soc. of the Pacific, Sci. Tchrs. Assn. NY State, Nat. Sci. Tchrs. Assn. Avocations: astronomy, travel, reading. Home: 427 Bellmore Rd East Meadow NY 11554 Office: Roslyn Mid Sch Locust Lane Roslyn NY 11576

SHUE, ELISABETH, actress; b. Wilmington, Del., Oct. 6, 1963; m. Davis Guggenheim, 1994; children: William, Stella Street, Agnes Charles Student, Wellesley Coll.; BA in Govt., Harvard U., 2000; studied with Sylvie Leigh, Showcase Theater. Appeared in Broadway plays including Some Americans Abroad, Birth and After Birth; Actor (films) The Karate Kid, 1984 (Young Artist award 1984), Link, 1986, Adventures in Babysitting, 1987, Cocktail, 1988, Body Wars, 1989, Back to the Future Part II, 1989, Back to the Future Part III, 1990, Soapdish, 1991, The Marrying Man, 1991, Twenty Bucks, 1993, Heart and Souls, 1993, Radio Inside, 1994, Blind Justice, 1994, The Underneath, 1995, Leaving Las Vegas, 1995 (Oscar nominee for Best Actress), The Trigger Effect, 1996, The Saint, 1996, Palmetto, 1997, Deconstructing Harry, 1997, Cousin Bette, 1997, Molly, 1998, Hollow Man, 2000, Tuck Everlasting, 2002, Leo, 2002, Mysterious Skin, 2004, Hide and Seek, 2005, Dreamer: Inspired by a True Story, 2005; (TV movies) Charles and Diana, Double Switch, 1987, Hale the Hero, 1992, Blind Justice; (TV series) Call to Glory, 1984, Amy & Isabelle, 2001. Office: Creative Arts Agy 9830 Wilshire Blvd Beverly Hills CA 90212-1804*

SHUGART, ANITA CAROL, research and development cosmetologist; b. Memphis, July 2, 1943; d. Thomas Edwin and Lula P. (Shults) Brumbelow; m. Cecil Glen Shugart, Dec. 14, 1985; m. Robert E. Henry (div. Jan. 1985); children: Robert Eugene Henry Jr., Lisa Carol Henry Brown. BA, Memphis State U., 1989, postgrad., 1990-91. Cert. cosmetologist, aesthetician. Cosmetologist, Memphis, 1981-86; aesthetician mgr. Adian Arpel Cosmetics, 1991-92; cosmetologist Maybelline R & D, Memphis, 1992—. Mem. NAFE, Soc. Cosmetic Chemists, Adult Student Assn. (pres. 1987-89), Sigma Tau Delta (sec. 1987-89), Omicron Delta Kappa. Avocations: tennis, dance, reading, travel, the beach.

SHUGART, JILL, academic administrator; b. Dallas, July 15, 1940; d. Claude Ernest and Allie Merle (Hamilton) S. BA, Baylor U., 1962; MA, Tex. Woman's U., 1972, PhD, 1980. Middle sch. English tchr. Garland (Tex.) Ind. Sch. Dist., 1962-63, high sch. social studies tchr., 1963-76, high sch. asst. prin., 1976-79, dir. communications, 1979-82, asst. supt., 1982-85, supt., 1985—99, ret., 1999—; exec. dir. Region X Edn. Svc. Ctr., 2004—. Mem. legis. coun. U. Interscholastic League, Tex., 1989-99; chmn. Dist. III music com., Tex., 1989-99; adj. prof. Tex. Women's U., Denton, 1983; chmn. Region X ESC Adv. Coun., rep. to commr.'s supt.'s com., 1993-95; cons. Richardson and Carrollton-Farmers Br. Sch. Dists., 2000-04; coord. Region 10 ESC Supr.'s Acad., 2004-04. Gen. chmn. Boy Scouts Am. Scouting Night, Dallas, 1988-89; chmn. City of Garland Comty. Action Com., 1995-99; sec. Tex. Sch. Alliance, 1995-96, chmn., 1998-99; life mem. Tex. and nat. PTA; pres. Garland br. Am. Heart Assn., 1990-91; co-chmn. sustaining dr. Garland YMCA, 1995-96; mem. Adv. Com. to Gov. and State Legisture, 1998; mem. steering com. Garland Econ. Devel. Partnership, 1994-99, Tex. Fast Growth Sch. Coalition; chair Tex. Sch. Alliance, 1998—. Recipient Lamar award for excellence Masons, Award of Distinction, Tex. Ret. Tchrs. Assn.; named Top 100 Educators to Watch, Executive Educator mag., 1985, Finalist as Outstanding Tex. Sch. Supt., 1990, Woman of Distinction, Soroptomist Club, Disting. Alumnus, Garland H.S., 2005; Paul Harris fellow. Mem. Quality Tex. Bd. Examiners, Garland Edn. Found. (bd. dirs. 1999-2006), Baylor Med. Ctr. Garland (bd. dirs. 2001-2006). Baptist. Avocations: travel, lake activities. Business E-Mail: jill.shugart@region10.org.

SHUHLER, PHYLLIS MARIE, physician; b. Sellersville, Pa., Sept. 25, 1947; d. Raymond Harold and Catherine Cecilia (Virus) S.; m. John Howard Schwarz, Sept. 17, 1983; 1 child, Luke Alexander. BS in Chemistry, Chestnut Hill Coll., 1971; MD, Mich. State U., 1976; diploma of Tropical Medicine and Hygiene, U. London, 1980. Diplomate Am. Bd. Family Medicine. With Soc. Cath. Med. Missionaries, Phila., 1966-82; ward clk., nursing asst. Holy Family Hosp., Atlanta, 1971-72; resident in family practice Somerset Family Med. Residency Program, Somerville, NJ, 1976-79; physician East Coast Migrant Health Project, Newton Grove, NC, 1980; physician, missionary SCMM, Diocese of Sunyani, Berekum, Ghana, 1980-81; emergency rm. physician Northeast Emergency Med. Assn., Quakertown, Pa., 1981-82; founder, physician Family Health Care Ctr., Inc., Pennsburg, Pa., 1982-90; physician Lifequest Med. Group, Pennsburg, 1990-93; pvt. practice Pennsburg, 1993-99; physician Tri-Valley Primary Care Group, 1999—. Fellow Royal Soc. Tropical Medicine and Hygiene; mem. Am. Acad. Family Practice, Am. Bd. Family Practice, Am. Med. Women Assn. Pa. Acad. Family Practice, Lehigh Valley Women Med. Assn. Roman Catholic. Avocations: guitar, reading, bicycling, hiking. Office: 101 W 7th St Ste 2C Pennsburg PA 18073-1512

SHULER, CAROLETTA ALEXIS, psychologist, educator; b. Orangeburg, SC, Mar. 17, 1967; d. Tom and Bernadean Shuler. BA, U. SC, Columbia, 1989, BS, 1994, M of Criminal Justice, 1996; EdD, U. SD, Vermillion, 1998. Asst. mgr. Fast Mart Store, Orangeburg, SC, 1990—92; parking enforcement officer SC State U., Orangeburg, 1992—93; resident adv. divsn. student affairs U. SC, Columbia, 1993—94, asst. hall dir. divsn. of student affairs, 1994, grad. asst. coll. criminal justice, 1995—96, tchg. intern coll. criminal justice, 1996; grad. asst. higher edn. program U. SD, Vermillion, 1997—98; vis. asst. prof. SC State U., Orangeburg, 1998—99, asst. prof., 1999—. Campus dir. SC Tchg. Fellows Program, Orangeburg, 2000—. Mem.: Am. Study of Higher Edn., SC Coun. for the Social Studies, Philosopy Edn. Soc., Nat. Coun. for History Edn., Nat. Coun. for the Social Studies, Pi Lambda Theta (faculty liaison 1999), Kappa Delta Pi (faculty counselor 1999), Alpha Kappa Alpha. Democrat. Roman Catholic. Office: SC State Univ 300 College St NE Orangeburg SC 29117 Office Phone: 803-536-8793. Office Fax: 803-516-4568. Personal E-mail: calexisshuler@msn.com. Business E-Mail: cshuler@scsu.edu.

SHULER, SALLY ANN SMITH, retired media consultant; b. Mt. Olive, N.C., June 11, 1934; d. Leon Joseph and Ludia Irene (Montague) Simmons; m. Henry Ralph Smith Jr., Mar. 1, 1957 (div. Jan. 1976); children: Molly Montague, Barbara Ellen, Sara Ann, Mary Kathryn; m. Harold Robert Shuler,

Aug. 2, 1987 (div. Mar. 1997). BA in Math., Duke U., 1956; student, U. Liège, Belgium, 1956-57; postgrad., Claremont Grad Sch., 1970-72. Mgr. fed. systems GE Info. Svcs. Co., Washington, 1976-78, mgr. mktg. support Rockville, Md., 1978-81; dir. bus. devel. info. tech. group Electronic Data Sys., Bethesda, Md., 1981-82, v.p. mktg. optimum systems div. Rockville, 1982-83, v.p. planning and comm. Dallas, 1983-84; exec. dir. comml. devel. U.S. West Inc., Englewood, Colo., 1984-90; v.p. mktg. devel. Cin. Bell Info. Sys. Inc., 1990-92; mgmt. cons. in mergers and acquisitions Denver, 1992-93, 1995—2002; v.p. major accounts U.S. Computer Svcs., Denver, 1993-95; ret., 2002. Bd. dirs. Rotary-Denver Tech. Ctr., 1999—2006, Seeking Common Ground, 2001—02. Recipient GE Centennial award, Rockville, 1978. Mem. Women in Telecommunications, Rotary (Found. fellow, prest. Denver Tech. Ctr. 1999-2000, amb. scholar 1956-57), Phi Beta Kappa, Tau Psi Omega, Pi Mu Epsilon, Sigma Kappa. Democrat. Presbyterian. Personal E-mail: sallysss@aol.com.

SHULER DONNER, LAUREN, film producer; BS in Film and Broadcasting, Boston U. Assoc. prodr.: (films) Thank God It's Friday, 1978; Mr. Mom, 1983; Ladyhawke, 1985; St. Elmo's Fire, 1985; Pretty in Pink, 1986; Three Fugitives, 1989; Radio Flyer, 1992; Dave, 1993; Free Willy, 1993; prodr.: (TV films) Amateur Night at the Dixie Bar and Grill, 1979; (films) Free Willy 2: The Adventure Home, 1995, You've Got Mail, 1998, Any Given Sunday, 1999, X-Men, 2000, X2: X-Men United, 2003, Timeline, 2003, Constantine, 2005; exec. prodr.: Assassins, 1995; Free Willy 3, 1997; Volcano, 1997; Out Cold, 2001; Just Married, 2003; prodr.: She's The Man, 2006, X-3, 2006, Unaccompanied Minors, 2006. Office: The Donners' Co 9465 Wilshire Blvd Ste 430 Beverly Hills CA 90212

SHULGASSER-PARKER, BARBARA, critic, writer; b. Manhasset, N.Y., Apr. 10, 1954; d. Lew and Luba (Golante) S.; m. Norman Parker, Sept. 1999; 1 child: Atticus. Student, Sarah Lawrence Coll., 1973-74; BA magna cum laude, CUNY, 1977; MS, Columbia U., 1978. Feature writer Waterbury (Conn.) Rep., 1978-81; reporter, feature writer Chgo. Sun Times, 1981-84; film critic San Francisco Examiner, 1984-98; freelance book critic N.Y. Times Book Rev., N.Y.C., 1983—; film critic Chgo. Tribune, 1999—2001. Author: Funny Accent, 2001; co-author: (screenplay, with Robert Altman) Ready to Wear, 1994; freelance video columnist N.Y. Times Sunday Arts & Leisure, 1989, features for Vanity Fair, Glamour and Mirabella mags.

SHULL, CLAIRE, documentary film producer, casting director; b. NYC, Oct. 26, 1925; d. Barnet Joseph and Fannie (Florea) Klar; m. Leo Shull, Aug. 8, 1948; children: Lee Shull Pearlstein, David. Student, Am. Acad. Dramatic Arts, NYC, 1943—44, NYU, 1973—74. Editor, assoc. pub. Show Bus. Publs., NYC, 1957-85; owner, founder Claire/Casting, NYC and Miami, Fla., 1972—, Claire/Casting Film Prodns., NYC and Miami, 1978—; cons. dir., prodr., dir. film and TV The Bass Mus., Miami Beach, Fla., 1992—. Miami corr. film, TV, theatre Show Bus. Weekly, 1999—; curator archives Show Bus. Pubs. Performing Arts Theatre Collection, N.Y. Pub. Libr., 2005—. Actress in The Front Page, USO European tour, 1945-46, (on Broadway) Tenting Tonight, 1947; prodr., dir. HBO TV series How To Break into Show Business, 1980-81, Cable-TV series, Join Us at the Bass, 1993-97. Recipient gold award and distinctive merit TV award Advt. Club. Hartford, Conn., 1984, Clio award, 1989. Mem.: Drama Desk, Actors Equity Assn., Ind. Casting Dirs. Assn. NY, South Fla. Internat. Press Club, Miami Internat. Press Club.

SHULL, MIKKI, media consultant; b. Cleve. d. Lois Biles; life ptnr. Jerome China. BS, Carnegie-Mellon U., 1983. Bus. transformation cons. PriceWaterhouseCoopers, N.Y.C., 1986-97; media and entertainment cons. IBM Global Svcs., N.Y.C., 1997—. Mem. Advt. Women N.Y. Republican. Office: IBM 590 Madison Ave New York NY 10022 Home: 180 Belmont Ave Jersey City NJ 07304-2002 E-mail: shull@us.ibm.com.

SHULMAN, ALIX KATES, writer; b. Cleve., Aug. 17, 1932; d. Samuel Simon and Dorothy (Davis) Kates; m. Martin Shulman, June 1959 (div. 1985); children: Ted, Polly; m. Scott York, Apr. 1989. BA, Case Western Res. U., 1953, LHD (hon.), 2001; MA, NYU, 1978. Instr. New Sch. for Social Rsch., N.Y.C., 1972-74, NYU Sch. of Continuing Edn., 1976-79, Yale U., New Haven, Conn., 1979-81, NYU, 1981-84; writer-in-residence U. Colo., Boulder, 1984-86; vis. writer-in-residence Ohio State U., Columbus, 1987; citizen's chair of lit. U. Hawaii at Manoa, Honolulu, 1991-92; vis. writer-in-residence U. Ariz., Tucson, 1994. Author: Bosley on the Number Line, 1970, Finders Keeper, 1971, Awake or Asleep, 1971, To the Barricades: The Anarchist Life of Emma Goldman, 1971, Memoirs of an Ex-Prom Queen, 1972, Red Emma Speaks, 1972, Burning Questions, 1978, On the Stroll, 1981, In Every Woman's Life., 1987, Drinking the Rain, 1995, A Good Enough Daughter, 1999. Feminist activist Redstockings, NY, 1969-71, Carasa, NYC, 1971-82, No More Nice Girls, NYC and Honolulu, 1986-92, Women's Action Coalition, NYC, 1992-94, Vet. Feminists Am., 1998-05, Feminist Futures, N.Y.C., 2001-05. Fellowship in fiction Nat. Endowment for the Arts, 1983, DeWitt Wallace/Reader's Digest fellow, 1979, MacDowell Colony for the Arts, 1975-77, 79, 81, Body Mind Spirit award of excellence, 1996, Rockefeller Found. Bellagio Ctr. resident, 1997. Mem. Poets Essayists Novelists (exec. bd. 1974-91, v.p. 1982-83), Nat. Writers Union, Author's Guild and Author's League, Columbia U. Seminar on Women and Soc. (exec. bd. 1980-82).

SHULMAN, MILDRED, artist; b. Perth Amboy, N.J., Aug. 13, 1927; d. Abraham and Estelle Shulman; m. Ben Spina, Feb. 20, 1947 (div. Aug. 1954). Student, Sch. Indsl. Arts, N.Y.C., 1942—45, McDowell Sch. Art, 1946—47, NYU, 1961—62, Art Student's League, 1991—95. Contr. Continental Mdse. Co., Inc., N.Y.C., 1959-65, Famous Fashion Shops, N.Y.C., 1966-69; owner, pres. Luminere Creations, Inc., N.Y.C., 1969-91; self-employed artist N.Y.C., 1991—. Author: Barter "The Silent Giant", 1985. Mem.: Midtown West Art Assn., Am. Soc. Portrait Artists, Nat. Mus. Women in Arts, Art Students League, New Art Ctr., Salmagundi Club. Achievements include 3 patents flexible screen partitions, electrical lighting design, sculpting method. Avocations: hiking, swimming. Office Phone: 212-242-2846.

SHULTZ, LINDA JOYCE, retired library director; b. South Bend, Ind., Aug. 25, 1931; d. Justin Russell and Gladys Ernstine (Miller) Nash; m. Dale Jay Shultz, Apr. 20, 1952; children: Donald Jay, Sally Janine, William Justin, Alan Joel, Kent Jon. AA, Stephens Coll., 1951; BS in Edn., Ind. U., Ft. Wayne, 1971, Cert. I in Libr. Edn., 1975. Sec. John R. Worthman, Inc., Ft. Wayne, 1951-54; farm wife, mother Noble County, Ind., 1954-68; libr. Noble County Pub. Libr., Albion, Ind., 1968-97; ret., 1997. Exec. bd. Tri-Alsa Libr. Svc. Authority, Ft. Wayne, 1988—90; sec. James M. Prickett, Albion, Ind., 2003—. Editor: Albion Memories, 1977. Mem. Albion Local Devel. Corp., 1989-92; sec. Cen. Noble Jr. Achievement, 1988-92. Named Albion Citizen of the Yr. Albion Rotary Club, 1977. Mem. DAR, Order Ea. Star, Rotary (pres. Albion club 1993-94, Paul Harris fellow 1999), Toastmasters (pres. U.S. Six Shooters chpt. 1988-89), Gene Stratton Porter Meml. Soc., Ind. Soc. Mayflower Descendants, Geneal. Soc., Noble County Hist. Soc., Noble County Geneal. Soc. (sec. 1985-95, pres. 1997—). Republican. Methodist. Avocation: genealogy. E-mail: lindales@ligtel.com.

SHULTZ, LOIS FRANCES CASHO, nursing supervisor; b. Phila., Apr. 29, 1936; d. Ellwood Francis Casho and Beatrice Mae Gunther Casho; m. Thomas Eugene Shultz, Aug. 15, 1959 (div. June 1983); children: David T., Patricia Shultz Bichefsky, Jeffrey A. Nursing diploma, Temple U. Hosp., 1957; BSN, U. Pa., 1961. RN Pa., 2003, bd. cert. gerontol. nursing, ANCC, 2001. Staff nurse Temple U. Hosp., Phila., 1957, pvt. duty nurse, 1958-59; nursing instr. St. Luke's Hosp. Sch. Nursing, Bethlehem, Pa., 1959-61, Reading (Pa.) Area C.C., 1985-88; asst. DON Reading Nursing Ctr., West Reading, 1988-89; night supr. Berks County Home-BerksHeim, Leesport, Pa., 1989—2004; ret., 2004. Mem. Berks County Bd. Assistance, Reading, 1980—, chmn., 1988-2001, chmn. cmty. rels. com., 2001—; pres., dir. Berks County Med. Soc. Aux.; bd. dirs., chmn., mem. children and youth com. Berks County Mental Health Assn.; bd. dirs., past bd. chmn. Berks County Children and Youth Svcs.; organizer, past dir. Reading Is Fun-damental for Berks County; past mem., chmn., mem. programs and svcs. sub-com. United Way Home Health Care Study Com.; bd. dirs. Berks-Schuylkill unit Arthritis Found., 2005—, sec., 2006—. Mem. Nat. Soc. DAR (1st vice-regent br. Berks County chpt. 1977-80). Republican. Presbyterian. Home: 5 Wendy Rd Reading PA 19601-1031 Personal E-mail: templenurse@1usa.com.

SHUMADINE, ANNE BALLARD, financial advisor, lawyer; b. Norfolk, Va., Mar. 8, 1943; d. William Pierce Ballard and Helen Caulfield Ballard Hoffman; m. Conrad Moss Shumadine, Sept. 1, 1965; children: John Ballard, James Hunter. AB, Wellesley Coll., 1965; JD, Coll. William and Mary, 1983. Bar: Va. 1983. Assoc. McGuire Woods Battle & Boothe, Norfolk, 1983-88; ptnr. Shumadine & Rose, P.C., 1988-94, McCandlish Kaine & Grant, 1994—; pres. Signature Fin. Mgmt., 1994—. Bd. dirs. CENIT Bancorp, Norfolk; co-chmn. Old Dominion Tax Conf., Norfolk, 1992; mem. adv. coun. William and Mary Tax Conf., 1997—. Trustee William and Mary Law Sch. Found., 1992—; chmn. Tidewater Scholarship Found., Norfolk, 1995—; rector, bd. visitors Old Dominion U., 1996-97. Fellow Va. Law Found., 1999—; named Vol. of Yr., Downtown Norfolk Coun., 1995. Office: Signature Financial Management Inc 150 W Main St Ste 1550 Norfolk VA 23510-1676

SHUMAKER, TARA L., performing arts educator; b. N. Wildesboro, N.C., Nov. 11, 1973; d. Bobby Lee and Shirley Ann (Pipes) Shumaker. BFA in Dance, E. Carolina U., 1997; MFA in Dance, U. N.C., 2001. Tchg. asst. U. N.C., Greensboro, 1998—2001; tchr., choreographer J.H. Rose H.S., 2001—05. Guest lectr. U. N.C., Greensboro, 1998—2001. Dancer Wilkes Cmty. Coll. Theatre, Powder Horn Theater, High County Youth Ballet, Burklyn Ballet Theatre, Horn In The West, 1996, 1998, Dancing for Friends, 1999, Internat. Dance Conf., 1999, N.C. Dance Festival, 1999, John Gamble Dance Theater, 2000, Dance Nova Dance Co., 2000, Am. Dance Festival, 2001, Dance Collective, 2002. Artistic dir. Pitt County Contemporary Dance Co. Avocations: martial arts, yoga, pilates. Home: PO Box 99 North Wilkesboro NC 28659

SHUMAN, ANN, investment company executive; b. 1968; BA in Eng., Trinity Univ., San Antonio, Tex.; JD, Univ. Chgo. Atty., derivatives, investments products group Sidley & Austin, Chgo.; with Chgo. Merc. Exch. Holdings, Inc., Chgo., 2000—, dir., co-head corp. devel., 2005—. Named one of 40 Under Forty, Crain's Bus. Chgo., 2005. Office: Chgo Merc Exch Holdings Inc 20 Wacker Dr Chicago IL 60606 Office Phone: 312-930-1000.*

SHUMAN, LOIS ANNA, educational coordinator; b. Anderson, Ind., Oct. 31, 1952; d. Lester Herman and Ruby Irene (Reavis) S. Student, Modesto (Calif.) Jr. Coll., 1974-76. Head lay-a-way dept. Weiler's Dept. Store, Anderson, 1973-74; med. records clk. Meml. Hosps., Modesto, 1974-76; med. transcriptionist Gould Med. Group, Modesto, 1975-76, Ind. U. Hosps. Nuclear Medicine, Indpls., 1976-79, prin. sec., 1979-82, sr. adminstrv. sec. radiology dept., 1982-89. Residency selection and edn1. coord. dept. radiology Ind. U. Sch. Medicine, Indpls., 1989—, word processing cons., 1982—. Proofreader, editor: Highlights & Heartaches, 1984, The Communion, The Passover and the Last Supper, 1986, The Country Preacher, 1992. Mem. Indpls. Computer Soc. Baptist. Avocations: photography, portraiture, travel, sewing, computers. Home: 4893 S 525 W Pendleton IN 46064-9020 Office: Ind U Sch of Medicine Rm 1143 1001 W 10th St Indianapolis IN 46202-2879 Business E-Mail: lshuman@iupui.edu.

SHUMAN-MILLER, NANCY, education educator, department chairman; d. Louis Edward and Alma Gill Brandenburg; m. Russell G. Miller, Oct. 25, 1985; children: Mark, Raeanne, Kara, Zachary. BS in Psychology, Tex. A&M U., Commerce, 1979, MS in Psychology, 1982, PhD, 1995; PhD in Christian counseling, Am. Bible Coll. and Seminary, Okla. City, 1998. Doctoral tchg. asst. Tex. A&M U., Commerce, 1984—85; psychology lectr. U. Md., Assn. Divsn., Seoul, Republic of Korea, 1986—90; psychology adj. faculty Okla. State U., 1992—2001, full time faculty, dept. head, 2001—02, dept. head, asst. prof., 2002—. Adv. bd. mem. Alcohol & Substance Abuse Degree, Oklahoma City, 1997—98, Pub. Svc. Degree Bd., Oklahoma City, 2002—06. Contbr. Okla. State U. Found. Fund, Oklahoma City, 2001—, Habitat for Humanity, Midwest City, Okla., 1995—. Mem.: Christian Assn. for Psychological Studies (assoc.), APA (assoc.). Avocations: travel, old books, gardening, pets. Office: Okla State Univ 900 N Portland Ave Oklahoma City OK 73107 Personal E-mail: shuman@osuokc.edu.

SHUMATE, DONNA LARSEN, engineering educator, department chairman; d. Carl and Ruth B. Larsen; m. Thomas A. Shumate, Oct. 3, 1981; 1 child, Nathan. DSc, N.C. State U., Raleigh, 2001. Tel. switching and computer maintenance sys. specialist USAF, 1981—90; computer tech. instr. ECPI Tech. Coll., Raleigh, NC, 1991—97; mem. electronics engrng. tech. faculty Johnston C.C., Smithfield, 1997—99, chair applied indsl. tech. dept., 1999—. Contbr. articles to profl. jours. Decorated Meritorius Unit citation USN, Commendation medal USAF; named Instr. of Yr., ECPI Tech. Coll., 1993; fellow, Nat. Initiative Leadership and Instl. Effectiveness, 1998—2001; Joseph D. Moore fellow, NC State U., 1998—2000. Mem.: Rotary (pres. Ctrl. Johnston County chpt. 2001, centennial pres. Ctrl. Johnston County chpt. 2004—05, Rotarian of Yr. Ctrl. Johnston County chpt. 2004—05, Paul Harris fellow 2003). Avocations: music, singing, sudoku, gardening, writing. Office: Johnston CC 245 Coll Tech Rd Smithfield NC 27577 Office Phone: 919-209-2163.

SHUMICK, DIANA LYNN, retired computer executive; b. Canton, Ohio, Feb. 10, 1951; d. Frank A. and Mary J. (Mari) S.; 1 child, Tina Elyse. Student, Walsh Coll., 1969—70, Ohio U., 1970—71, Kent State U., 1971—77. Clk. data entry Ohio Power Co., Canton, 1969—70; clk. City of Canton Police Dept., 1971—73; sys. engr. IBM, Canton, 1973—81, adv. market support rep. Dallas, 1981—89, sys. engr. mgr. Madison, Wis., 1989—93, mgr. mktg. customer satisfaction Research Triangle Park, NC, 1993; HelpCenter mgr. desktop and consumer sys. support IBM Personal Computer Co., Research Triangle Park, 1993—96, mgr. call ctr. brand ops., 1996—97; solution mgr. product support svcs. IBM Global Svcs., Cary, NC, 1997—98, tech. solutions mgr. strategic outsourcing Boulder, Colo., 1999—2006; ret., 2006. Author: Technical Coordinator Guidelines, 1984. Mem. Western Stark County Red Cross, Canton, 1980; v.p. Parents Without Ptnrs., Madison, 1991; vol. ARC, 1985—2005, Paint-A-Thon, Dane County, 1990, Badger State Games Challenge, 1992, Cystic Fibrosis Found. Gt. Strides, 1992—, Cystic Fibrosis Found. Mother's Day Tea, 1991, 1992, 1993, 1994, 1995, 1996, 1998, 2002, 2004, 2005, N.C. Sr. Olympics, 1998—2005, The Dorcas Shop, Cary, 1999—2005, Susan G. Komen Race for the Cure, 2000—04, Habitat for Humanity Global Village Project, Jacksonville, Fla., 2003; active Strong Women Organizing Outrageous Projects, 1998—2001; vol. Coastal Wildlife Club, Ret. Sr. Vol. Program; mem. St. Philip Parish Coun., Lewisville, Tex., 1988—89; pres., bd. dirs. Big Bros. and Sisters of Denton (Tex.) County, 1989, v.p., 1988, sec., 1987; founding bd. mem. Single Parents Network, 1991; mem. bd. dirs. Rape Crisis Ctr., Dane County, sec., 1990—91; bd. dirs. Carolina chpt. Cystic Fibrosis, 1996—2005. E-mail: dshumick@verizon.net, dshumick@comcast.net.

SHUPP, KARLEN S., language educator; b. Bridgeport, Conn., Dec. 10, 1976; d. Sean Brian Stanziale and Karen Lois Hovan; m. Jon Peter Shupp, Aug. 21, 1999; children: Jaden Kenneth, Tanner Andrew. BA in English, Boston Coll., Chestnut Hill, Mass., 1998, MEd in Secondary Edn., 1999. Cert. tchr. Conn. English tchr. Trumbull HS, Conn., 1999—2006, varsity gymnastics coach, 2000—05; adj. prof. English Western Conn. State U., Danbury, Conn., 2006—. Mem.: Nat. Coun. Tchrs. English. Home: 82 Old Church Rd Oxford CT 06478

SHURE, MYRNA BETH, psychologist, educator; b. Chgo., Sept. 11, 1937; d. Sidney Natkin and Frances (Laufman) Shure. Student, U. Colo., 1955; BS, U. Ill., 1959; MS, Cornell U., 1961, PhD, 1966. Lic. psychologist Pa. Asst. prof. U. R.I.; head tchr. Nursery Sch., Kingston, 1961-62; asst. prof. Temple U., Phila., 1966-67, assoc. prof., 1967-68; instr. Hahnemann Med. Coll., Phila., 1968-69, sr. instr. psychology, 1969-70, asst. prof., 1970—73, assoc. prof., 1973—80, prof., 1980—2002, Drexel U., Phila., 2002—. Spl. cons. PBS Children's TV Show The Puzzle Place; adv. bd. Parents Mag., 2004—. Author (with George Spivack): Social Adjustment of Young Children, 1974; author: (with George Spivack and Jerome Platt) The Problem Solving Approach to Adjustment, 1976; author: (with George Spivack) Problem Solving Techniques in Childrearing, 1978; author: (child curricula manual) I Can Problem Solve, 1992; author: (trade book) Raising a Thinking Child, 1994; author: (audiotape, workbook, paperback) Raising a Thinking Preteen, 2000 (Parents' Choice award, 2001, Parent's Guide Classic award, 2001); author: Thinking Parent, Thinking Child, 2004; mem. editl. bd. Jour. Applied Devel. Psychology. Recipient Lela Rowland Prevention award, Nat. Mental Health Assn., 1982, Sarah award, Women in Comm. (Phila. chpt., 1998, Psychology in the Media award, Pa. Psychol. Assn., 1999, award, Ctr. for Substance Abuse Prevention, 2001; rsch. grantee, NIMH, 1971—75, 1977—79, 1982—85, 1987, 1988—93, NJ Gov.'s Juvenile Justice and Delinquency Prevention grantee. Fellow: APA (divsn. clin. psychology, child sect. 1994, Disting. Contbn. award divsn. cmty. psychology 1984, Task Force on Prevention award 1987, Task Force on Model Programs award 1994, U. Utah and Juvenile Justice Dept. of Delinquency Prevention award 1996, U.S. Dept. Edn. award 2001); mem.: Phila. Soc. Clin. Psychologists, Soc. Rsch. in Child Devel., Nat. Assn. Edn. Young Children, Nat. Assn. Sch. Psychologists. Home: 1500 Locust St Apt 3311 Philadelphia PA 19102-4323 Office: Drexel U Dept Psychology 245 N 15th St MS 626 Philadelphia PA 19102 Office Phone: 215-762-7205. Business E-Mail: mshure@drexel.edu.

SHURE, PATRICIA D., mathematician, education educator; Dir. Math. and Sci. Comprehensive Studies Program200 U. Mich., Ann Arbor, 1982—2000, lectr. math. Coll. Lit., Sci. and Arts, 2000—. Author (with B. Black, D. Shaw): Michigan Calculus Program Instructor Training Materials. Recipient Louise Hay award, Assn. Women in Math., 2001, Sarah Goddard Power award, Acad. Women's Caucus, 2000; grantee, Sloan Found., 1990—95, NSF. Office: Math Dept 3832 East Hall 1109 Univ Michigan Ann Arbor MI 48109 E-mail: pshure@umich.edu.

SHURKIN, LORNA GREENE, writer, publicist; b. N.Y.C., Mar. 5, 1944; d. Morris and Rita Rose (Cohen) Greene; m. Joel N. Shurkin, July 4, 1966 (div. Nov. 1981); children: Jonathan Greene, Michael Robert BA, Bklyn. Coll., CUNY, 1964; postgrad., NYU, 1965—66; fundraising cert., U. Pa., 1997. Tchr. English N.Y.C. Schs., 1963—64; asst. to articles editor Womans Day mag., N.Y.C., 1964—66; reporter, columnist News-Herald, Willoughby, Ohio, 1966—68; reporter, reviewer Phila. Inquirer, Reuters and others, 1974—76; pub. rels. rep., editor Thomas Jefferson U., Phila., 1976—79; account exec. Sommers/Rosen Pub. Rels., Phila., 1979—81; dir. pub. rels. Swarthmore Coll., Pa., 1981—84; writer, publicist, fund raiser St. Davids, Pa., 1995—99; corr. Delaware County Daily Times, 1998—2000; dir. media rels. Dickinson Coll., Pa., 2000—04. Advt. mgr. STAGE: A Theater Monthly, 1997-2000 Coord. pub. rels. Pa. Resources Coun., 1999; v.p. Footlighters Theater, Berwyn, Pa., 1985—88; ofcl. pronouncer Delaware County Spelling Bee, Pa., 1986—2000; candidate Radnor Twp. Sch. Bd., Pa., 1987; mem. Radnor Dem. Com., 1988—99, vice chair, 1998—99; twp. rep. Dem. County Coun., 1994; mem. adv. bd. Ea. Pa. Theater Coun., 1986—2000; bd. dirs. Anti-Violence Partnership Phila., 1989—97; movie com. Carlisle Theater, 2001—05; bd. dirs. Cantate Carlisle, 2002—04. Mem.: Coun. Advancement and Support Edn., Coll. and Univ. Pub. Rels. Assn. Pa., Del. County Press Club (program chmn. 1991—93, bd. dirs. 1991—). Jewish. Home: 23 Old Forge Crossing Devon PA 19333 Personal E-mail: lornags@comast.net.

SHURLING, ANNE MARLOWE, psychology educator, consultant; b. Lexington, Ky., Jan. 25, 1947; d. Charles Franklin and Margaret Helen (Crossfield) Marlowe; m. Thomas Lennard Shurling, June 25, 1982; 1 child, Jayne-Margaret. B.M., U. Ky., 1969, M.S., Fla. State U., 1970, Ph.D., 1979. Lic. counseling psychologist, Ky. Asst. dir. student activities Eastern Ky. U., Richmond, 1971-73; mental health specialist Ky. Dept. for Human Resources, Frankfort, 1973-76; personnel research analyst IBM, Lexington, Ky., 1976-79, sr. assoc. instr., 1979-81; asst. v.p. C & S Georgia Corp., Atlanta, 1981-82; prof. psychology Transylvania U., Lexington, 1982-91, psychologist Ea. State Hosp., 1989-90; clin. therapist United Behavioral Clinics, Lexington, 1991—; ind. psychology practice, 1991—; cons. and guest presenter to various groups. Author: Greek Membership: Its Impact on the Value Orientations and Moral Development of College Freshmen, 1979. Contbr. articles in field of psychology to profl. jours. Bd. dirs. Inst. for Social Change, Lexington, 1979-86. Mem. Am. Psychol. Assn., Ky. Psychol. Assn., Phi Delta Kappa. Republican. Mem. Christian Ch. (Disciples of Christ). Avocations: gardening; music; cooking. Home: 326 Curtin Dr Lexington KY 40503-2608 Office: 2505 Larkin Rd Ste 104 Lexington KY 40503

SHURTLEFF, AKIKO AOYAGI, artist, consultant; b. Tokyo, Jan. 24, 1950; d. Kinjiro and Fumiyo (Sugata) Aoyagi; m. William Roy Shurtleff, Mar. 10, 1977 (div. Jan. 1995); 1 child, Joseph Aoyagi. Grad., Women's Coll. Art, Tokyo, 1971; student, Acad. Art, San Francisco, 1991—92. Fashion designer, illustrator Marimura Co. and Hayakawa Shoji, Inc., Tokyo, 1970-72; co-founder, art dir. Soyfoods Ctr. consulting svcs., Lafayette, Calif., 1976-94; freelance illustrator, graphic designer. Lectr. U.S. Internat. Christian U., Tokyo, 1977, Japanese Tofu Mfrs. Conv., Osaka, 1978; presenter cooking demonstrations; tchr. cooking classes. Co-author, illustrator: The Book of Tempeh, 1979, Tofu and Soymilk Production, 1979, Miso Production, 1979, Tempeh Production, 1980, The Book of Tofu and Miso, 2001, The Book of Tofu, 2005, The Book of Miso, 2005, co-author, illustrator: Chinese edit., 2005, illustrator: Spirulina, 1982, The Book of Shiatsu-The Healing Art of Finger Pressure, 1990, Staying Healthy with Nutrition, 1992, Culinary Treasures of Japan, 1992, Yookoso, An Invitation to Contemporary Japanese, vols. 1 and 2, 1994—95, Blue Collar and Beyond, 1995, Damn Good Ready to Go Resumes, 1995, Homework, 1995, Vegetarian's A to Z Guide to Fruits and Vegetables, 1996, Hubert Keller's Cuisine, 1996, Doctor Generic Will See You Now, 1996, Everyday Pediatrics for Parents, 1996, Angels in My Kitchen-Devine Desserts Recipes, 1997; The Shurtleff and Lawton Families: Genealogy and History, 2005; designer co. logos, greeting cards:. Office: PO Box 443 Lafayette CA 94549-0443

SHUSS, JANE MARGARET, artist; b. Ost, Kans., Feb. 15, 1936; d. Leo and Mary Catharine Nett; m. Robert Hamilton Shuss, Feb. 19, 1954; children: Patric, Andrea, Matt, Lisa, Robert, Eric. Student, Otis Art Inst., L.A. Sec. Found. for Plein Air Painting, Avalon, Calif., 1995-97. One-woman shows include Challis Galleries, Laguna Beach, Calif., 1981—83, Esther Wells Gallery, 1984—87, exhibited in group shows at Plein Air Painters of Am., 1985—2005, Western Acad. Women Artists, 1996, O'Brien's Gallery, Scottsdale, Ariz., 1996, Desert Caballeros Mus., 1997, 1998, Caesar's, Tahoe, Nev., 2004—05. Mem. Am. Acad. Women Artists (signature mem.), Soc. Am. Impressionists, Plein Air Painters Am. (signature mem.), Calif. Art Club. Republican.

SHUSTER, DONNALYN E. (DONALYN EATON SHUSTER), secondary school educator, artist; d. Donald C. Eaton and Carolyn S. Donald; m. Arthur T. Shuster. AS in Advt., Design and Prodn., Mohawk Valley C.C., 1976; BA in Art, SUNY, Potsdam, N.Y., 1978, MS in Edn., 1985. Cert. tchr. art K- 12 N.Y., 1985, tchr. K-6 N.Y., 1985. Tchr. art grades 6, 8 Phoenix (N.Y.) Ctrl. Sch. Dist., Phoenix, NY, 1980—82; tchr. art grades K - 12 St. Johnsville (N.Y.) Ctrl. Sch. Dist., 1983—90; tchr. art grades 6 - 12 Frankfort- Schuyler (N.Y.) Ctrl. Sch., 1990—. Mem. edn. adv. com. Munson Williams Proctor Inst., Utica, NY; mem. model sch. art com. Madison - Oneida BOCES, Verona, NY; mem. art bid award com. Herkimer Count BOCES, Herkimer, NY; mem. adv. bd. greek alumni coun. Potsdam (N.Y.) Coll.; designer talented and gifted program 1 - 6 St. Johnsville Ctrl. Sch. Dist. One-woman shows include Cooperstown Art Assn., N.Y., 2005 (award, 2005), exhibitions include N.Y. State Art Tchrs. Assn., 1994 (Peoples Choice award, 1994), Herkimer County C.C., 1994, N.Y. State Fedn. China Painters, Albany, 1994 (Best In Show scholarship, 1994), Mohawk Valley Ctr. Arts, Little Falls, 1998 (Second Pl. Watercolor award, 1998), 2000 (Second Pl. Mixed Media award, 2000). Sec. Margaret Reaney Meml. Libr., St. Johnsville, NY, 1996. Mem.:

Nat. Art Edn. Assn. (assoc.), N.Y. State Art Tchrs. Assn. (assoc.; sec. capital region 1988), Frankfort-Schuyler Tchrs. Assn. (assoc.; v.p. 2004—05), St. Johnsville Tchrs. Assn. (assoc.; sec. 1987—89), Delta Kappa Gamma (assoc.), Omega Delta Phi (life; pres. 2004—06). Democrat. Avocations: illustrator, gardening, photography. Home: 1527 Kennedy Rd Saint Johnsville NY 13452 Office: Frankfort-Schuyler Middle/HS 605 Palmer St Frankfort NY 13340

SHUSTERMAN, LINDA, ceramist, educator; d. Meyer and Julia Shusterman; m. Alan Willoughby, Oct. 15, 1982; 1 child, Lianna Shusterman-Willoughby. BA, Goddard Coll., 1972; MFA, Clemson U., 1984. Cert. art tchr. Pvt. practice, Deptford, NJ, 1982—; ceramics instr. C.C. Phila., 1991—; instr. ceramics and design Gloucester County Coll., Deptford, 1998—. Ceramic workshop Peters Valley Craft Ctr., Layton, NJ, 2002—04; chair Perkins Ctr. for Arts Pottery Sale, 1999—. Exhibitions include Matt Burton Gallery, Clay Studio, Pa., 2000, ACC Balt. Craft Show, 1993—2001; contbr. to 500 Bowls, 2003, to Ceramics Art and Perception, 2005, to Ceramics Monthly, 1999. Grantee, NJ State Coun. of Arts, 1991. Mem.: Nat. Coun. for Edn. Ceramic Arts, Am. Crafts Coun. (juror 1998—2001). Home: 1805 Almonesson Rd Deptford NJ 08096

SHUTICH, TINA LYNN, mathematics educator; b. Nuerenburg, Germany, Nov. 27, 1971; d. Kitty L Rogers; m. Daniel G. Shutich, Nov. 16, 2001. BS in Math., Grand Valley State U., Allendale, Mich., 1997; MEd in Leadership, Grand Valley State U. Cert. tchr. secondary math. Mich., 1997. Math. tchr. Rockford Pub. Schs., Mich., 1998—. Math. dept. head Rockford H.S., 2005—, nat. honor soc. advisor, 2005—. With USAF, 1989—94. Home: 520 Oakhurst Ave NW Grand Rapids MI 49504 Office: Rockford High School 4100 Kroes Rd Rockford MI 49341 Personal E-mail: tshutich@rockford.k12.mi.us.

SHUTLER, MARY ELIZABETH, academic administrator; b. Oakland, Calif., Nov. 14, 1929; d. Hal Wilfred and Elizabeth Frances (Gimbel) Hall; m. Richard Shutler Jr., Sept. 8, 1951 (div. 1975); children: Kathryn Allice (dec.), John Hall, Richard Burnett. BA, U. Calif., Berkeley, 1951; MA, U. Ariz., 1958, PhD, 1967. Asst., assoc., full prof. anthropology, chmn. dept. San Diego State U., 1967-75; prof. anthropology, dept. chmn. Wash. State U., Pullman, 1975-80; dean Coll. Arts and Scis., prof. anthropology U. Alaska, Fairbanks, 1980-84; vice chancellor, dean of faculty, prof. anthropology U. Wis. Parkside, Kenosha, 1984-88; provost, v.p. for acad. affairs, prof. anthropology Calif. State U., L.A., 1988-94; provost West Coast U., L.A., 1994-97; dean Sch. of Arts and Scis. Nat. U., La Jolla, Calif., 1997—2004, dean emeritus, 2004—. Mem. core staff Lahav Rsch. Project, Miss. State U., 1975-92. Co-author: Oceanic Prehistory, 1975, Deer Creek Cave, 1964, Archaeological Survey of Southern Nevada, 1963, Stuart Rockshelter, 1962; contbr. articles to jours. in field. Mem. coun. Gamble House. Fellow Am. Anthropol. Assn.; mem. Soc. for Am. Archaeology, Am. Schs. for Oriental Rsch., Am. Coun. Edn., Am. Assn. for Higher Edn., Am. Assn. State Colls. and Univs., Delta Zeta. Republican. Roman Catholic. Avocations: travel, gardening. E-mail: bullet18@netzero.com.

SHUTTER, CHRISTINE, psychologist; d. Jack and Donna Shutter. BS, Coastal Carolina U., Conway, SC, 1994; MS, Francis Marion U., Florence, SC, 1998. Cert. sch. psychologist II State Dept. Edn., SC, lic. psycho-ednl. specialist SC. Sch. psychologist level II Florence County Sch. Dist. 5, Johnsonville, SC, 1998—; tchg. assoc. Coastal Carolina U., 2000—. Recipient Alumni of Yr. award Sch. of Natural and Applied Scis., Coastal Carolina U., 2005. Mem.: SC Assn. Sch. Psychologists, Nat. Assn. Sch. Psychologists. Business E-Mail: cshutter@flo5.k12.sc.us.

SHUY, TANYA RUSSELL, educational association administrator; BS, Syracuse U., 1980; MEd, U. Md., 2004. Rsch. scientist Nat. Inst. Child Health and Human Devel., Bethesda, Md., 2001—03; sr. program officer adolesent literacy Nat. Inst. for Literacy, Washington, 2003—. Co-editor: (spl. issue) Scientific Studies of Reading, 2006, Perspectives, 2006. Office: Nat Inst Literacy 1775 I St NW Ste 730 Washington DC 20006 Office Phone: 202-233-2031. E-mail: tshuy@nifl.gov.

SHWARTZ, SIMA M., music educator; arrived in U.S., 1995; d. Michael Shwartz and Sophia Leshchiner; m. Vladimir A. Shpachenko, June 7, 1975 (div. Oct. 1978); 1 child, Nadia Shpachenko. Grad., Music Sch. for Gifted Youth, Kharkov, 1964; MusM in Tchg. Piano, Accompanist, Performer, State Inst. Arts, Kharkov, 1969. Piano faculty Kharkov Music Schs., 1964—91; accompanist Kharkov State Philharm., 1964—91, Kharkov Inst. Arts, 1964—65; piano faculty Severodonetsk State Music Coll., 1969—72; founder, condr. Jewish Children Orch., Kharkov, 1990—91; piano tchr. Gilloh Dalled Sch., Jerusalem, 1992—95; founder, piano tchr. Sima's Music Club, Cambridge, Mass., 1996—2000; piano faculty The Music Sch., Providence, 1999—2000; founder, piano tchr. Shwartz Piano Sch., Marlborough, Mass., 2000—02; piano faculty Performing Arts Sch., Worcester, Mass., 2003—04. Mem.: Mass. Music Tchrs. Assn. (v.p. membership), Music Tchrs. Nat. Assn. Avocations: walking, ping pong/table tennis, reading, theater.

SHWAYDER, ELIZABETH YANISH, sculptor; b. St. Louis; d. Sam and Fannie May (Weil) Yaffe; m. Nathan Yanish, July 5, 1944 (dec.); children: Ronald, Marilyn Ginsburg, Mindy; m. M.C. Shwayder, 1988 (dec.). Student, Washington U., 1941, Denver U., 1961; pvt. studies. One-woman shows include Woodstock Gallery, London, 1973, Internat. House, Denver, 1963, Colo. Women's Coll., Denver, 1975, Contemporaries Gallery, Santa Fe, 1963, So. Colo. State Coll. Pueblo, 1967, others; group shows include Salt Lake City Mus., 1964, 71, Denver Art Mus., 1961-75, Oklahoma City Mus., 1969, Joslyn Mus., Omaha, 1964-68, Lucca (Italy) Invitational, 1971, Denver Art Mus., Mus. Natural History, Mizel Mus., Eden Theatrical Workshop, Rose Hosp. Aux., Nat. Mus. Women in the Arts, Colo. Chpt. 8th Air Force Aux., Women's Art Ctr., others; represented in permanent collections Colo. State Bank, Bmh Synagogue, Denver., Colo. Women's Coll., Har Ha Shem Congregation, Boulder, Colo., Faith Bible Chapel, Denver, others. Chmn. visual arts Colo. Centennial-Bicentennial, 1974-75; pres. Denver Coun. Arts and Humanities, 1973-75; co-chmn. visual arts spree Denver Pub. Schs., 1975; trustee Denver Ctr. Performing Arts, 1973-75; chmn. Concerned Citizens for the Arts, 1976; pres. Beth Israel Hosp. Aux., 1985-87; organizer Coat Drive for the Needy, Denver, N.Y.C., 1982-87, Common Cents penny drive for homeless, 1991-93; bd. dirs. Mizel Mus., Srs., Inc.; active Mayor's Com. on Cultural Affairs, Denver Art Mus., Mus. Natural History, Freedom Found. at Valley Forge, Hospice of Metro. Denver; bd. dirs. Rainbow Bridge; bd. dirs. Diabetes Found., Asian Arts Assn. Denver Art Mus., also pres.; historian Childrens Diabetes Found., Univ. Colo. Found. Inc. Humanities scholar Auraria Librs.-U. Colo.; recipient McCormick award Ball State U., Muncie, Ind., 1964, purchase award color Women's Coll., Denver, 1963, Tyler (Tex.) Mus., 1963, 1st prize in sculpture 1st Nat. Space Art Show, 1971, humanitarian award Milehi Denver Sertoma, 1994, The Gleitsman Found., 1994, svc. to mankind awards Freedom Found. at Valley Forge, Mile Hi Sertoma Club, Minoruyasui Found., Gleitsman Found. Mem. Denver Art Mus., Asian Arts Assn. (pres.). Home: Unit 503 2400 Cherry Creek South Dr Denver CO 80209-3259

SIAHPOOSH, FARIDEH TAMADDON, librarian; b. Eshghabad, Turkestan, Russia, Nov. 15, 1928; came to U.S., 1964; d. Hosane and Ghamar (Ramzi) Tamaddon; m. Ismail Siahpoosh, Nov. 30, 1952. BA, Tehran U., Iran, 1962; student, Columbia U., 1967; MLS, Queens Coll., Flushing, N.Y., 1972. Cert. librarian, N.Y. Reference libr. Queens Borough-Pub. Libr. Brs., N.Y.C., 1974-85, asst. br. mgr., 1985—94; part-time libr. Baha'i Internat. Cmty., N.Y.C., 1994—. Intern Baha'i World Ctr. Libr., Haifa, Israel, 1998; mem. L.I. Multi-Faith Forum; part-time ref. libr. Shelter Rock Pub. Libr., 1998—. Mem. ALA. Mem. Baha'i Faith. Home and Office: 19 Ridge Dr E Roslyn NY 11576-1443 Office Phone: 516-627-1919. Personal E-mail: fsiahpoosh@hotmail.com.

SIANO, JONNA TEEN, small business owner; b. Battle Creek, Mich., June 5, 1964; d. John James and Marjo Linda Diane Siano; m. John Nelson Whitaker; 1 child, Jonathan Siano Bowen. AA, Kellogg C.C., Battle Creek, 1987, AAS, 2007; BS, Western Mich. U., Kalamazoo, 1989. Lic. cosmetologist Mich. Owner/operator Cool Mama's Ice Cream, Battle Creek, 2002—. Dir. Battle Creek Postal Credit Union, 2003. Founder Neighborhood Watch Program, Galion, Ohio, 1995; organizer citywide coat dr. Galion, 1997. Recipient Spl. Achievement award for Outstanding Cmty. Svc., 1996. Mem.: DAR, AAUW. Home and Office: 32 Woodmer Ln Battle Creek MI 49017 Office Phone: 269-209-8712.

SIAS, MARY, university president; b. Jackson, Miss., July 2, 1950; d. Augusta and Ada Lee (Hill) Evans; m. Shadrach Sherman Sias III, Mar. 20, 1976; 1 child, Adrienne Marie. BA, Tougaloo Coll., 1972; MS, U. Wis., 1974, PhD, 1980; MBA, Abilene Christian U., 1983. Instr. sociology Grambling (La.) State U., 1977-79; asst. prof. sociology U. Tex. at Dallas, Richardson, 1980-81, So. Meth. U., Highland Park, Tex., 1981-82; dir. women's resource ctr. YWCA Met. Dallas, 1982-83, asst. mgr. ctrl. br., 1983-84, exec. dir., 1984-95; sr. v.p. U. Tex., Dallas, 1995—2004; pres. Ky. State U., Frankfort, 2004—. Bd. dirs. Oaks Bank & Trust, Dallas Co-author: Planned Resettlement in Nepal's Terrain, 1976. Bd. dirs. King Found. Doctoral fellow Ford Found., 1972; recipient Maura award Women's Ctr., 1988, Trailblazer award South Dallas Bus. and Profl. Club, 1989, Outstanding Texan award State of Tex., 1989, She Knows Where She's Going award Girls, Inc., 1994, award of distinction Girl Scouts U.S.A., 1997, Women of Excellence award Women's Enterprise mag., 1998, Lance of Champions award Women of Enterprise mag., 2004, Profiles in Leadership award So. Meth. U., 2004. Mem. Nat. Assn. YWCA Execs., Greater Dallas C. of C., State Bar Tex. Avocations: reading, upholstering, refinishing furniture. Home: 201 Cold Harbor Dr Frankfort KY 40601-3009 Office: Ky State U Hume Hall 400 E Main St Frankfort KY 40601 Office Phone: 502-597-6260. Business E-Mail: msias@kysu.edu.

SIATRA, ELENI, English educator; b. Kozani, Greece, Oct. 22, 1961; came to U.S., 1985; d. Athanasios and Alexandra (Lanaras) S.; m. Todd Alan Reda, May 30, 1991. B of English, Aristotle U., 1983; MLS, Kent State U., 1986; MA in English, Miami U., 1990. Tchr. English as a 2d lang. Fgn. Langs. Inst., Kozani, Greece, 1983-85; asst. to dir. of ethnic studies ctr. Kent (Ohio) State U., 1986, student reference asst., 1985-86, instr., libr. adminstr., 1987; libr. readers' svcs. Bloomsburg (Pa.) U., 1987-88; grad. rsch. asst. Miami U., Oxford, Ohio, 1988-90, King Libr., Miami U., Oxford, Ohio, 1990-91; coord., portfolio rater Miami U., Oxford, Ohio, 1994-97, teaching assoc., 1991-94; instr. English Ind. U. East, Richmond, 2003—05, reading lab. coord. tutorial svcs., 2005—. Vis. instr. Miami U., 1994-97, tchr. ESL, Synchronon, Kozani, Greece, 1999-2001; mem. Coll. of Arts and Scis. Comparative Lit. Com., Miami U., 1995-96. Sinclair Meml. scholar, 1995-96. Fulbright scholar, 1985-86; recipient Gordon Wilson award, 1994. Fellow Phi Kappa Phi; mem. ALA, Am. Soc. 18th Century Studies, Nat. Coun. Tchrs. English, Modern Lang. Assn., Internat. Soc. Study of European Ideas (workshop chair, 1996. Greek Orthodox. Home: PO Box 416 West College Corner IN 47003-0416 Office: Tutorial Svcs 202 Springwood IU East 2325 Chester Blvd Richmond IN 47374 Office Phone: 765-973-8575. Business E-Mail: esiatra@indiana.edu.

SIBERT, POLLY LOU, conductor, music educator; b. Washington, Pa., Sept. 22, 1962; d. Earl Richard and Virginia Gray Sibert. B in Music Edn., James Madison U., Harrisonburg, Va., 1984, MusM in Orchestral Conducting, 1996; D in Music Edn., Shenandoah Conservatory of Shenandoah U., Winchester, Va., 1999. Orch. dir. Chesterfield (Va.) County Schs., 1985—92; violin maker, restorer self-employed, Chester, Va., 1989—92, Charlottesville, Va., 1992—; orch. dir. Charlottesville (Va.) City Schs., 1992—; first violinist Lynchburg (Va.) Symphony, 2002—. Expert panelist mid. sch. music AECT Project Pa. State U. Edn. Sch., 2002—; cons. music publ. Frank J. Hackinson Music Co., Inc., Ft. Lauderdale, 2003—. Bowing editor (music) Nancy's Waltz, 1997; author: (dissertation) A Study of the Violin Bow: Identification and Application of Criteria and Tchg. Strategies, 1999; contbr. author (book) Strategies for Teaching: Technology, 2001; author: (jour. article) The Am. String Tchr., 2001. Mem.: NEA, Nat. Sch. Orch. Assn., Am. String Tchrs. Assn., Va. Music Educators Assn. Methodist. Achievements include Built two stringed instruments: a violin and a viola. Avocations: golf, antiques, crocheting. Home: 3003 Colonial Dr Charlottesville VA 22911-9109 Office: Charlottesville City Schs 1564 Dairy Rd Charlottesville VA 22903 E-mail: PLSibert@aol.com.

SIBLEY, REBECCA LEIGH CARDWELL, dietician; b. Starkville, Miss., Dec. 29, 1955; d. Joe Thomas and Leota (Patterson) Cardwell; m. Daniel Paul Sibley, May 22, 1976; children: John Paul, Jennifer Leigh. BS, Miss. State U., 1977, MS, 1978. Dietary supr. Oktibbeha County Hosp., Starkville, Miss., 1975-76; nutrition instr. Miss. State Dept. Pub. Welfare, Starkville, 1978-80; univ. food service mgr. Miss. U. for Women, Columbus, 1978, instr. foods, nutrition, 1979; dietary cons. Martha Coker Convalescent Home, Yazoo City, Miss., 1981-86, Yazoo Community Action, 1984-90, King's Daughters Hosp., Yazoo City, 1981-82, 88—, dir. dietary div., 1982-88, Profl. Nutrition Svcs., 1988—; dir. nutrition Regional Med. Ctr., Orangeburg, SC, 1992-93; dietitian Gambro Healthcare, 1993—2001; dietitian cardiac and pulmonary rehab. Regional Med. Ctr., Orangeburg, SC, 1992—. Dietary cons. various civic orgns., lectr. in field. Author: Through It All God Reigns My Battle with Cushing's Disease, 1988, 94. Active Yazoo County Extension Gen. Service Adv. Bd., 1984-90; pres. chmn. Yazoo Extension Home Econs. Adv., 1984-90; food chmn. Miss. State U. Alumni, Yazoo City, 1985-86; mem. Orangeburg-Wilkinson H.S. Athletic Booster Club, Chorus Booster Club. Named One of Outstanding Young Women of Am., 1987, Agriculture and Home Econs. scholar Miss. State U., 1974-77, Miss. Home Econ. Assn. scholar, 1974; recipient Gamma Sigma Delta Alumni award of Merit, 1996. Mem. Am. Dietetic Assn., Phi Kappa Phi, Phi Tau Sigma, Gamma Sigma Delta, Kappa Omicron Phi, Alpha Zeta, Alpha Lambda Delta. Republican. Presbyterian. Avocations: knitting, needlecrafts, cooking, reading, singing. Home and Office: 3387 Hart St NE Orangeburg SC 29118-1938 E-mail: sibley76@oburg.net.

SIBO, ELSA LYNETTE, secondary school educator; d. Lawrence E. and V. Azalee Chapman; m. Richard J. Sibo, Feb. 8, 1964 (dec. Mar. 1, 1986). BA, Blue Mountain Coll., 1962; MEd, U. Nev., 1978. Tchg. cert. Miss., 1962, Tex., 1972, Ga., 1973, Nev., 2002. Tchr. English Greenville H.S., Miss., 1962—64, Schertz-Cibolo Ind. Sch. Dist., Schertz, Tex., 1964—65; tchr. English, speech Randolph Field Ind. Sch. Dist., Universal City, Tex., 1965—72, Clayton County Sch. Dist., Jonesboro, Ga., 1973—74; tchr. English St. Yves H.S., Las Vegas, 1975—76; grad. asst. reading ctr. part time staff U. Nev., 1976—78; tchr. English Clark County Sch. Dist., 1978—2002, CC of So. Nev., Henderson, 2003—. Mem., pres., sec., treas., com. mem. Gamma Chpt., Delta Kappa Gamma, Las Vegas, 1972—2005. Fellow Study Stipend, Delta Kappa Gamma, 1982. Mem.: NEA (life), Delta Kappa Gamma (Rose of Recognition 1983), Kappa Delta Pi (assoc.). Independent. Methodist. Avocations: travel, hiking, ballroom dancing. Personal E-mail: lsibo@earthlink.net.

SIBOLSKI, ELIZABETH HAWLEY, academic administrator; b. Gt. Barrington, Mass., Aug. 18, 1950; d. William Snyder and Frances Harrington (Smith) Gallup; m. John Alfred Sibolski Jr., Aug. 15, 1970. BA, The Am. U., 1973, MPA, 1975, PhD, 1984. Acting dir. acad. adminstrn. Am. U., Washington, 1974, planning analyst, 1974—79, asst. dir. budget and planning, 1980—83, dir. instl. rsch., 1984—85, exec. dir. univ. planning and rsch., 1985—2000; exec. assoc. dir. Middle States Commn. on Higher Edn., Phila., 2000—. Trustee Mortar Bd. Nat. Found., 1989—95. Recipient Comencement award, Am. U. Women's Club, 1973. Mem. Soc. Coll. and Univ. Planning (bd. dirs. 1995-2000, pres. 1998-99), Mortar Bd. (sect. coord. 1975-82), Pi Alpha Alpha, Phi Kappa Phi (chpt. officer 1986-92), Pi Sigma Alpha, Omicron Delta Kappa. Avocations: breed, raise and show morgan horses. Home: 565 Wayward Dr Annapolis MD 21401-6747 Office: Middle States Commn on Higher Edn 3624 Market St Philadelphia PA 19104-2614 Business E-Mail: esibolski@msche.org.

SICH, GLORIA JEAN, elementary school educator; b. Isabella, Pa., June 5, 1949; d. James Edward and Betty Mae Rable; children: Chantel Janine Angelo, Vincent Louis Angelo Jr. BS in Secondary Edn., Calif. State Coll., Pa., 1970, BS in Elem. Edn., 1976. Math tchr. Brownsville Area Sch. Dist., Hiller, Pa., 1981—. Mem.: Brownsville Edn. Assn. Lutheran. Avocations: reading, travel, crafts.

SICHOK, MARYANNE M., art educator; d. Michael and Agnes Sirokman Mosorjak; m. Frank Richard Sichok, Aug. 3, 1968; children: Michael Ian, Christopher J. BA in Art Edn., George Washington U., Washington, 1969; M in Adult Edn. with honors, Pa. State U., University Park, 1994. Cert. tchr. Pa. Art tchr. Johnstown Sch. Dist., 1969—70, Wilkinsburg (Pa.) Sch. Dist., 1970—72, Mt. Pleasant (Pa.) Sch. Dist., 1991—92, Yough Sch. Dist., Herminie, Pa., 1994—. Recipient Great Ideas grant, Mon Valley Edn. Consortium, McDonald's Achievement grant, Pa. Sch. Bds. grant; grantee, Pa. Alliance Arts Edn. Mem.: AAUW (bd. dirs.), Pa. State Edn. Assn., Yough Edn. Assn. (bd. dirs.), Pa. Art Edn. Assn., Nat. Art Edn. Assn., Pi Lambda Theta. Office: Yough Sch Dist Herminie PA 15637 Office Phone: 724-872-5164. Business E-Mail: sichokm@yough.k12.pa.us.

SICILIANO, ELIZABETH MARIE, secondary school educator; b. Mansfield, Ohio, Apr. 22, 1934; d. Samuel Sevario and Lucy (Sferro) S. BS in Edn., Ohio State U., 1957; MA in Edn., Ea. Mich. U., 1971; MFA, Bowling Green U., 1975. Cert. tchr., Mich. Instr. adult edn. The Toledo (Ohio) Mus. Art, 1972-81; tchr. art Monroe (Mich.) Pub. Schs., 1975-2001. Workshop facilitator; presenter in field; art tchr. computer graphics. Artist, working in oils, pastels and fabricating jewelry. Judge Monroe Bicentennial, Monroe Arts and Crafts League, other shows. Mem. NEA, Mich. Edn. Assn., Nat. Art Edn. Assn., Mich. Art Edn. Assn., Stratford Festival for the Arts, Toledo Craft Club, Toledo Fedn. Art Socs., Toledo Mus. Art. Avocations: swimming, skiing, classic cars, designing and creating jewelry, portraiture and landscape in oils. Office: Monroe High Sch 901 Herr Rd Monroe MI 48161-9744

SICOLI, MARY LOUISE CORBIN, psychologist, educator; b. Delaware County, Pa., Nov. 15, 1944; d. C.M. Lewis and Lucille (Weber) Corbin; m. Thomas Sicoli, Aug. 27, 1967; children: Michael, Kathryn Francesca. BS, West Chester U., Pa., 1966, MS, 1974, U. Wis., Madison, 1967; PhD, Bryn Mawr Coll., Pa., 1977. Tchr. music, supr. Unionville-Chadds Ford (Pa.) Sch. Dist., 1967-70; supr. student tchrs. Rosemont (Pa.) Coll., 1976-78; prof. psychology, campus psychologist, coord. psychol. svcs. Cabrini Coll., Radnor, Pa., 1974—. Cons. Children's Svcs. Southea. Pa., 1974-80; supr. doctoral interns in psychology Bryn Mawr Coll., 1979-86; presenter in field. Contbr. articles to profl. jours., scientific papers at profl. Confs. Founding mem. bd. dirs. Maternal Support Sys. Chester County, 1981—; mem. Citizens Action for Better TV, 1981—; founder, chair Psychol. Aspects Popular Culture, Popular Culture Assn. Recipient Legion of Honor award Chapel of the Four Chaplains, 1980, Christian and Mary Lindback award for Disting. Coll. Tchg., 1984; named hon. alumnus Cabrini Coll., 2005. Fellow Pa. Psychol. Assn. (founder campus psychologist network); mem. AAUP, Am. Psychol. Assn., Ea. Psychol. Assn., Jean Piaget Soc., Assn. Moral Devel., Kappa Delta Pi, Psi Chi (founding adv., Ea. Region Chptr. award 2005), Delta Epsilon Sigma. Home: 404 Darlington Dr West Chester PA 19382-2139 Office: Cabrini Coll Dept Psychology Radnor PA 19087 Office Phone: 610-902-8310. Business E-Mail: mlsicoli@cabrini.edu.

SIDAMON-ERISTOFF, ANNE PHIPPS, not-for-profit developer; b. NYC, Sept. 12, 1932; d. Howard and Harriet Dyer (Price) Phipps; m. Constantine Sidamon-Eristoff, June 29, 1957; children: Simon, Elizabeth, Andrew. BA, Bryn Mawr Coll., 1954. Chairwoman emerita Am. Mus. Natural History, N.Y.C.; dir.-at-large Black Rock Forest Consortium; mem. distbn. com. N.Y. Cmty. Trust. Trustee God Bless Am. Fund, Storm King Art Ctr., Mountainville, NY; hon. trustee World Wildlife Fund; bd. dirs. Greenacre Found., Highland Falls (N.Y.) Libr.; past bd. dirs. Scenic Hudson, St. Bernard's Sch., N.Y.C., Mus. Modern Art, N.Y.C., Mus. Hudson Highlands, Hudson River Found. Address: 120 E End Ave New York NY 10028-7552

SIDDALL, PAM, publishing executive; b. Phenix City, Ga. m. Greg Siddall; 2 children. B in Acctg., Columbus State U., 1991. CPA Ga. Sr. fin. analyst W.C. Bradley Co., Columbus, Ga., 1991—94; contr. lic. product divsn. Russell Corp., 1994—97; CFO Columbus Ledger-Enquirer, 1997—2001, v.p., gen. mgr., 2003—04, pres., pub., 2004—; CFO to v.p., CFO The Macon Telegraph, Ga., 2001—03. Office: Columbus Ledger-Enquirer 17 W 12th St Columbus GA 31902

SIDDAYAO, CORAZÓN MORALES, economist, educator, consultant; b. Manila, July 26, 1932; came to U.S., 1968; d. Crispulo S. and Catalina T. (Morales) S. Cert. in elem. teaching, Philippine Normal Coll., 1951; BBA, U. East, Manila, 1962; MA in Econs., George Washington U., 1971, MPhil, PhD, 1975. Cert. Inst. de Francais, France. Tchr. pub. schs., Manila, 1951-53; exec. asst. multinational oil corps., 1953-68; asst. pensions officer IMF, Washington, 1968-71; cons. economist Washington, 1971-75; rsch. assoc. Policy Studies in Sci. and Tech. George Washington U., Washington, 1971-72, teaching fellow dept. econs., 1972-75; natural gas specialist U.S. Fed. Energy Adminstrn., Washington, 1974-75; sr. rsch. economist, assoc. prof. Inst. S.E.A. Studies, Singapore, 1975-78; sr. rsch. fellow energy/economist East-West Ctr., 1978-81, project dir. energy and industrialization, 1981-86; vis. fellow London Sch. Econ., 1984-85; sr. energy economist in charge energy program Econ. Devel. Inst., World Bank, Washington, 1986-94, ret., 1994. Affiliate prof. econs. U. Hawaii, 1979—94; co-dir. UPecon Inst. Resource Studies, 1995—; vis. prof. econs. U. Montpellier, France, 1992, France, 1995—96, France, 1997—; vis. prof. pub. policy Duke U., 1997; lectr. pub. policy George Mason U., 2000; tchr. coord. English for Hispanic program Parish, 2002; cons., spkr. in field. Author or co-author: Increasing the Supply of Medical Personnel, 1973, The Offshore Petroleum Resources of Southeast Asia: Some Potential Conflicts and Related Economic Factors, 1978, Round Table Discussion on Asian and Multinational Corporations, 1978, The Supply of Petroleum Resources in Southeast Asia: Economic Implications of Evolving Property Rights Arrangements, 1980, Critical Energy Issues in Asia and the Pacific: The Next Twenty Years, 1982, Criteria for Energy Pricing Policy, 1985, Energy Demand and Economic Growth, 1986; editor, co-author: Energy Policy and Planning series, 1990-92, Energy Investments and the Environment, 1993; co-editor: Investissements Energetiques et Environnement, 1993; co-editor: (series) Energy Project Analysis for the CIS Countries (Russian), 1993, Politique d'Efficacité de l'Énergie et Environnement, Expérience pratiques, 1994, Matérial Pedagogique sur la Politique d'Efficacité de l'Energie et Environnement, 1994; contbr. chpts. to books, articles to profl. jours. Grantee in field; recipient Outstanding Alumni award Arellano Pub. H.S., 1998, Philippine Normal U., 2003 Mem.: Alliance Francaise, Internat. Assn. Energy Economists (charter 1986—2003), Am. Econ. Assn., Les Amis de l'Abbaye de Chancelade, Eucharistic Frat. 3d Order of St. P.J. Eymard, World Bank 1818 Soc. (bd. dirs. 1999—2000), John Carroll Soc., Chorale de St. Louis de France, Perpetual Adoration Soc. of St. Agnes (Arlington), Omicron Delta Epsilon. Roman Catholic. Office: 1201 S Eads St Ste 1712 Arlington VA 22202-2845

SIDDEEQ, BAIYINAH NAWAL RUBYE, secondary school educator; AA, Emory U., 1995, BA in Elem. Edn., 1997. Asst. tchr. Sister Clara Muhammad Sch., Indpls., 1993; co-founder, jr. counselor A Step Up! Summer Enrichment Program, Stone Mountain, Ga., 1995; tutor for academically challenged Cook Elem., Atlanta, 1995; math specialist Medlock Elem., Decatur, Ga., 1996; tchr. Fernbank Elem., Decatur, Ga., 1997; instr. essay, creative writing Md. Homeschoolers, Gaithersburg, Md., 1999—2000; tchr. English Washington Homeschoolers, College Park, Md., 1999—2005; prep instr. English, SAT Muslimah's Alt. to Pub. H.S. (MAPHS), Beltsville, Md., 2001—02; tchr. English Sch. Knowledge, Indpls., 2003; lit./social studies tchr., grades 6-8

Al-Hada Sch., College Park, Md., 2003—. Author: (novels) If I Should Speak, 2001, (children's book) Amir's Cap is Green, 1999, The Show and Tell, 1997, (novels) A Voice, 2003. Recipient Academic Excellence award, Delta Sigma Theta, 1996—97; scholar Phi Theta Kappa scholar, 1993—94. Personal E-mail: baiyinah@hotmail.com.

SIDDIQUI, RAZIA SULTANA, retired psychotherapisst, educator; d. Gurcharan Singh and Bhupinder Kaur Sangha; m. Mohammed Sadiq Siddiqui, May 2, 1963; children: Niloufer Siddiqi Dennis, Adeeba Sultana Siddiqi, Khalid Mohammed Siddiqi. BA, D.M. Coll., Moga, India, 1956; MA in Psychology, Lucknow U., India, 1958; BT, D.M. Tng. Coll., Moga, 1959; DM and SP, Mysore U., Bangalore, India, 1962; cert. in psychotherapy, Southwestern Med. Sch., Dallas, 1972; PhD in Neuropsychology, Postgrad. Inst. Med. Edn. and Rsch., Chandigarh, India, 1994. Asst. prof. ednl. psychology Saraswati Tng. Coll., Amritsar, India, 1959—60; clin. psychologist Niloufer Pediat. Hosp., Hyderabad, India, 1962—65; asst. prof. med. psychology Nangrahar Med. Sch., Jalalabad, Afghanistan, 1965—80, dir. publs., 1968—80; assoc. prof. psychology Kabul U., Afghanistan, 1980—88, assoc. prof. ednl. psychology Faculty Edn., 1980—88, dir. fgn. rels., 1982—88. Asst. editor Kabul Times, 1967—68. Election officer tech. Registrar of Voters, San Diego, 2006—. Home: 2162 Crystal Clear Dr Spring Valley CA 91978 E-mail: goodie65@hotmail.com.

SIDDONS, ANNE RIVERS (SYBIL ANNE RIVERS SIDDONS), writer; b. Fairburn, Ga., Jan. 9, 1936; m. Heyward Siddons, 1966; 4 stepchildren. BA Auburn U., 1958, student Atlanta Sch. Art, 1958. Mem. advt. dept. bank; sr. editor Atlanta mag., 1960. Author: (novels) John Chancellor Makes Me Cry, 1975, Heartbreak Hotel, 1976, The House Next Door, 1978, Fox's Earth, 1981, Homeplace, 1987, Peachtree Road, 1988, Kings Oak, 1990, Outer Banks, 1991, Colony, 1992, Hill Towns, 1993, Downtown, 1994, Fault Lines, 1995, Up Island, 1997, Low Country, 1998, Nora, Nora, 2000, Islands, 2003, Sweetwater Creek, 2005.

SIDDONS, JOY GARBEE, music educator; b. Lynchburg, Va., July 18, 1952; d. Clyde Lewis and Julia Schmitt Garbee; m. James Siddons, July 2, 1977. BS, Liberty U., 1984; MEd, Lynchburg Coll., 1996; MusEdM, Shenandoah U., 1998. Music educator Bedford County Pub. Schools, Bedford, Va., 1989—2003, Fairfax County Pub. Schools, Springfield, Va., 2003—. Dir. of music United Meth. churches, 1988—. Dir.: children's choirs and musical theater prodns. Mem.: Music Educators Nat. Conf., Phi Delta Kappa. United Methodist. Home: 6020 Woodland Ter Mc Lean VA 22101 Office: Fairhill Elem Sch 3001 Chichester Ln Fairfax VA 22116 Office Phone: 703-208-8100.

SIDEL, ENID RUTH, retired literature and language professor; b. N.Y.C., Apr. 15, 1936; d. Jerome and Mae (Sklaroff) Lipskin; m. H. David Sidel (div. May 1970). AB, Hunter Coll., 1958; MEd, U. Buffalo, 1961; postgrad., Rutgers U., 1978--. Grad. asst. U. Buffalo (N.Y.), 1958-59; English tchr. Buffalo City Bd. Edn., 1959-60; tchr. Matawan (N.J.) Bd. Edn., 1969-70; field faculty Goddard Coll., Plainfield, Vt., 1977—78; prof. and coord. honors program Brookdale C.C., Lincroft, NJ, 1970—2001, prof. emeritus English, 2001—. Freelance cons. Matawan, 1970—; spkr. Am. Assn. Higher Edn. Author, editor Bayshore Community Hosp. Newsletter, Holmdel, 1968-70. Mem. Nat. Council Tchrs. English, Pi Lambda Theta. Democrat. Jewish. Avocations: reading, theater, opera, writing. Office: Brookdale CC 765 Newman Springs Rd Lincroft NJ 07738-1543

SIDES, I. RUTH S., retired music educator; d. John Daniel Donald and I. Ruth Schulmeyer; m. Anthony Fred Sides, May 25, 1972 (dec. Sept. 7, 1997); children: Rebecca Ruth Desenti, Connie Susanne Moore. BA, Baldwin Wallace Coll., 1968. Cert. tchg. Ohio, 1968. Dir. band, choruses Ridgemont Local Schs., Ridgeway, Ohio, 1967—71; dir. choral music Groveland H.S., Fla., 1972—93, South Lake H.S., 1993—2005, chair dept. fine arts and fgn. langs., 2002—05. Cert. judge Fla. BBQ Assn., Fla., 2002—. Nominee Disney's Am. Tchr., Walt Disney World, 2001; recipient Tchr. Of The Yr., Hardin County Schools, 1969-1970, Outstanding Young Women Am., 1973, Teacherific - Judge's Choice, Walt Disney World, 2000. Mem.: Fla. Vocal Assn., Fla. Music Educators Assn. Avocations: cooking, sewing, travel. Home: 11844 Lake Minneola Shores Clermont FL 34715

SIDLER, MICHELLE ANN, literature and language professor; b. Nuremberg, Germany, Oct. 7, 1968; BA in English, Oglethorpe U., Atlanta, 1991; MA in English, Purdue U., West Lafayette, Ind., 1993, PhD, 1998. Grad. tchg. asst. Purdue U., West Lafayette, 1992—98; asst. prof. Pa. State U.-Berks, Reading, 1998—2000, Auburn U., Auburn University, Ala., 2000—. Office: Auburn Univ Dept English 9030 Haley Ctr Auburn University AL 36849 Business E-Mail: sidlema@auburn.edu.

SIDNEY, CORINNE ENTRATTER, retired journalist, actress; b. L.A., Apr. 13, 1937; d. Carl Smith and Alice (Polk) Kegley; m. Jack Entratter (dec. 1971); m. Robert Heffron, 1973 (div. 1980); 1 child, Benjamin Jack; m. George Sidney, Oct. 12, 1991 (dec. 2002). Student, U. Calif., Berkeley; Grad., U. Judaism, L.A., 1971; postgrad., UCLA, 1983; fine arts grad., UNLV, 2002—. Feature editor Univ. Man fashion mag., 1972-86; columnist Beverly Hills, 1986-89; writer syndicated entertainment column Real to Real Capital News Svc., 1988-91; chmn. fine arts com. U. (Las Vegas) Nev., 2003, 2004. Stringer USA Today, People weekly, Beverly Hills (Calif.) Post, 1990-91; pub. rels. cons., 1972-86. Film appearances include Murderers' Row, North to Alaska, Speed Limit 65, That Funny Feeling, The Big Mouth, The Journey, (with Peter Sellers) The Party, Road House, (George Sidney's film) The Swinger, Who's Minding the Mint?; TV appearances include Steve Allen, Caine's 100, Cannon, Bob Hope, Hazel, Home Show, Ironside, Monkees, Ozzie and Harriet, Bachelor Father, Tennessee Ernie Ford, General Hospital, FBI, Larry King, Bob Newhart, Shower of Stars, Johnny Carson Players, This is Alice; stage appearances include Born Yesterday, Seven Year Itch, Ninety Day Mistress, Tender Trap, Who Was That Lady I Saw You With?, Getting It; toured with Las Vegas New Frontier Hotel Lounge act, The New Yorkers, also toured 1990-TV cir. with Playboy's playmates of each decade; hostess TV talk show Westcoasting.with Corinne, 1991; co-host Real to Reel. Active civic orgns.; candidate Beverly Hills City Coun., 1980; mem. El Rodeo Sch. PTA, El Rodeo YMCA; established George Sidney award, 5 full 4 yr. student scholarships UNLV. 1st runner-up Miss U.S.A. Contest; named Playboy Ctr. Fold of 50's Decade, 1958; named Pin-up Girl of Atomic Nuclear Submarine Nautilus, 1958, one of 7 Top Playmates Fox-TV Am. Chronicles., 1990. Mem. AFTRA (women's com.), SAG, LWV, Women in Film, Am. Film Inst., C. of C. and Civic Assn. (pres. 1997), Hollywood Women's Press Club (pres. 1997), Bus. and Profl. Women (conv. del., Olympic com., program chmn., founder West Side chpt. 1985), Hadassah (v.p., membership chmn., co-chmn. ann. ball honoring Barbara Sinatra, founder, pres. Haifa chpt.), Israel Tennis Ctrs., UCLA Theatre Arts Alumni Assn, Beverly Hills Cannes' Sister City, Corinne's Beverly Hills Salon (founder). Office Phone: 702-894-5298. Office Fax: 702-894-5291.

SIDRAN, MIRIAM, retired physicist; b. Washington, May 25, 1920; d. Morris Samson and Theresa Rena (Gottlieb) S. BA, Bklyn. Coll., 1942; MA, Columbia U., N.Y.C., 1949; PhD, NYU, 1956. Rsch. assoc. dept. physics NYU, N.Y.C., 1950-55, postdoctoral fellow, 1955-57; asst. prof. Staten Island Community Coll., Richmond, NY, 1957-59; rsch. scientist Grumman Aerospace Corp., Bethpage, NY, 1959-67; prof. N.Y. Inst. Tech., N.Y.C., 1967-72; NSF rsch. fellow Nat. Marine Fisheries Svc., Miami, Fla., 1971-72; assoc. prof. then prof. physics Baruch Coll., N.Y.C., 1972-89, chmn. dept. natural scis., 1983-89, prof. emerita, 1990—. V.p. Baruch chpt. Profl. Staff Congress, 1983-89. Contbr. numerous articles to profl. and govtl. publs., chpts. to books. N.Y. State Regents scholar, 1937-41; NSF summer fellow, Miami, 1970. Mem. N.Y. Acad. Scis., Am. Assn. Physics Tchrs., Physics Club N.Y., N.Y. Gilbert and Sullivan Soc., Wynmoor Computer Club, Friends of Mozart, Sigma Xi, Sigma Pi Sigma. Avocations: french and hebrew languages, music, bicycling, poetry, opera. Home: 210 W 19th St Apt 5G New York NY 10011-4009

SIEBEN, KAREN K., philosopher, educator; b. Chgo., Oct. 24, 1943; d. John and Mary Anderson; children: Christopher, Elizabeth, Jeffrey, Jeanne. MA in Philosophy, West Chester U., Pa., 2001. Lectr. NYU, NYC; philosophy instr. Brookdale C.C., Lincroft, NJ, 1996—, Ocean County C.C., Toms River, NJ, 2005—. Mem.: Am. Philos. Assn. (assoc.). Home: 615 Rt 524 Allentown NJ 08501 Office: Brookdale Community College 765 Newman Springs Rd Lincroft NJ 07738 Office Phone: 732-224-2533. Business E-Mail: ksieben@brookdalecc.edu.

SIEBENALER, RITA REILLY, clinical social worker, consultant; b. Bklyn., June 12, 1943; d. Edward Thomas and Rita (Farrell) Reilly; m. Donald L. Siebenaler, June 12, 1965; children: Sharon L., Kristin R. BA, St. Joseph's Coll., Bklyn., 1964; MSW, NYU, 1966. Lic. clin. social worker, Va. Social worker Child and Adolescent Clin. Kings County Hosp., Bklyn., 1966; sch. social worker Internat. Sch., Bangkok, 1969-70; social worker Child Guidance Clinic, Heidelberg, Fed. Republic of Germany, 1975-76, No. Va. Family Svc., Falls Ch., 1966-67, 76-77; sch. social worker Fairfax (Va.) County Pub. Schs., 1977-78, 89-90; dir. Cmty. Mental Health Program, Moscow, 1980-82; family counselor Luth. Svcs., Camp Hill, Pa., 1982-84, Family Life Ctr., Ft. Leavenworth, Kans., 1988-89; clin. social worker med. div. U.S. Dept. State, Washington, 1984-94; social worker, counselor Arlington (Va.) Pub. Schs., 1994—2005. Lectr. Foreign Svc. Inst. Overseas Briefing Ctr. Rosslyn, Va., 1984-94, cons. 1989—. Mem. adv. bd. Fairfax County Juvenile and Domestic Rels. Ct., 1986-89; counselor Borromeo Housing, Inc., Arlington, Va., 1990. Grantee, HEW, 1964, '65. Fellow Am. Orthopsychiatry Assn.; mem. Acad. Cert. Social Workers (bd. cert. diplomate).

SIEBER, ANGELA R., social studies educator; d. Sheila A. Harshbarger and Gerald L. Sieber. B in History, Wash. & Jefferson Coll., Washington, Pa., 1993—97; M in Curriculum & Design Instrn., Wilkes U., Wilkes-Barre, Pa., 1999—2001. Cert. Tchr. Pa. Dept. Edn., 2000. Social studies tchr. Juniata HS, Mifflintown, Pa., 1997—. Field hockey coach Juniata HS, 1998—2005. Team mem. Am. Cancer Soc.-Relay for Life, Lewistown, 2003. Mem.: Juniata County Edn. Assn. (v.p. 2006). Republican. Avocations: travel, reading, gardening, physical fitness, auto racing. Home: RR 4 Box 1010 Mifflintown PA 17059 Office Phone: 717-436-2111.

SIEBER JOHNSON, RUTH E., music educator; b. Houston, Aug. 22, 1952; d. Glen P. and Martha N. (Grumbles) Armstrong; m. Richard E. Sieber, Mar. 21, 1982; children: Andrea, Jami, Kurt, Liesle, Jenny, Beth. MusB, U. Ark., 1983. Voice instr. at pvt. studio, Little Rock, 1975-88; soprano Ark. Opera Theater, Little Rock, 1977-88; music dir. Jubilee! Cmty. Ch., Asheville, 1989—; nat. exec. sec. Sigma Alpha Iota Internat. Music Fraternity, Asheville, 1992—. Premiered opera songs by the composer Robert Boury, U. Ark., Litte Rock, 1989; concert soloist and recitalist/soprano. Pres. PTA Booker Magnet Sch., Little Rock, 1986-88; music. dir. Westminster Presbyn. Ch. Singing fellow Stonybrook Bach Aria Festival, 1985. Mem. NAFE, Nat. Assn. Tchrs. Singing (nat. finalist Young Artist Awards 1987), Am. Guild Organists, Ptnrs. of the Americas (arts com. 1986—), Sigma Alpha Iota (state pres. 1984-88, exec. dir., 1992—, nat. bd., Sword of Honor, Rose of Honor, Ring of Excellence). Home: PO Box 1137 Asheville NC 28802-1137 Office: Sigma Alpha Iota 1 Tunnel Rd Asheville NC 28805-1229

SIEBERT, DIANE DOLORES, author, poet; b. Chgo., Mar. 18, 1948; m. Robert William Siebert, Sept. 21, 1969. RN. Author: Truck Song, 1984 (Notable Childrens Book award ALA 1984, Sch. Libr. Jour. one of Best Books 1984, Outstanding Childrens Book award NY Times Book Rev. 1984, Reading Rainbow Selection book 1991), Mojave, 1988 (Childrens Editors Choice 1988, Internat. Reading Assn. Tchr. Choice award 1989, others), Heartland, 1989 (award Nat. Coun. for Social Studies/Childrens Book Coun. 1989, on John Burroughs List Nature Book for Young Readers 1989, Ohio Farm Bur. Women award 1991), Train Song, 1990 (Notable Childrens Book award ALA, 1990, Redbook Mag. one of Top Ten Picture Books 1990, one of Best Books award Sch. Libr. Jour. 1990, others), Sierra, 1991 (Outstanding Sci. Trade Book for Children award NSTA 1991, Notable Childrens Trade Book in Field Social Studies award Nat. Coun. Social Studies 1991, Beatty award Calif. Libr. Assn. 1992), Plane Song, 1993 (Outstanding Sci. Trade Book for Children 1994, Reading Rainbow Selection book, Platinum award Oppenheim Toy Portfolio, Tchrs. Choice award Internat. Reading Assn. 1994), Cave, 2000 (Notable children's Book in the english Language Arts, 2001, Nat. Coun. of English Tchr., named to John Burroughs List of Nature Books for Young Readers 2000), Mississippi (named to John Burroughs List 2001), 2001, Motorcycle Song, 2002, Rhyolite, 2003, Tour America, 2006. Avocations: environmental affairs, running, classical guitar, motorcycle, animals. Home: 9676 SW Jordan Rd Culver OR 97734-9567 Personal E-mail: dsiebert48@msn.com.

SIEBERT, MURIEL (MICKIE), brokerage house executive, retired bank executive; b. Cleve., 1932; d. Irwin J. and Margaret Eunice (Roseman) Siebert. Student, Western Res. U., 1949-52; DCS (hon.), St. John's U., St. Bonaventure U., Molloy Coll., Adelphi U., St. Francis Coll., Mercy Coll., Coll. New Rochelle, St. Lawrence U., Manhattan Coll., Seton Hall Coll., Case Western Res. U., Marymount Manhattan Coll., Hofstra U., U. Rochester, U. NC, Asheville, 2004, U. NC, Greensboro, 2005. Security analyst Bache & Co., 1954-57; analyst Utilities & Industries Mgmt. Corp., 1958, Shields & Co., 1959-60; ptnr. Stearns & Co., 1961, Finkle & Co., 1962-65, Brimberg & Co., NYC, 1965-67; individual mem. (first woman mem.) NY Stock Exch., 1967; chmn., pres. Muriel Siebert & Co., Inc., 1969-77; trustee Manhattan Savs. Bank, 1975-77; supt. banks, dept. banking State of NY, 1977-82; dir. Urban Devel. Corp., NYC, 1977-82, Job Devel. Authority, NYC, 1977-82, State of NY Mortgage Agy., 1977-82; chmn., pres. Muriel Siebert & Co., Inc., NYC, 1983—. Former assoc. in mgmt. Simmons Coll.; former mem. adv. com. Fin. Acctg. Stds. Bd., 1981-84; former mem. adv. bd. Minority and Women-Owned Bus. Enterprise; guest lectr. numerous colls. Author: Changing the Rules - Adventures of a Wall Street Maverick, 2002. Ran for Rep. nomination, U.S. Senate, 1982; former mem. women's adv. com. Econ. Devel. Adminstrn., NYC; former trustee Manhattan Coll.; former v.p., current mem. exec. com. Greater NY Area coun. Boy Scouts Am.; former mem. NY State Econ. Devel. Bd., NY Coun. Economy; bd. overseers NYU Sch. Bus., 1984-88; former bd. dirs. United Way of NYC; former trustee Citizens Budget Commn., LI U.; mem. bus. com. Met. Mus., bus. com. of NY State Bus. Coun.; adv. coun. Women's Campaign Fund.; bd. dirs., past pres. NY Women's Agenda; trustee Guild Hall Mus. EH; current appointee Commn. Jud. Nomination; founding mem. The Mus. Women-The Leadership Coun; founder, bd. dirs. The WISH List; bd. dirs. Breast Cancer Rsch. Found., Animal Rescue Fund of the Hamptons; mem. Bretton Woods Com.; former Tokyo adv. com. Sister City Program NYC Recipient Spirit of Achievement award Albert Einstein Coll. Medicine, 1977, Women's Equity Action League award, 1978, Outstanding Contbns. to Equal Oppty. for Women award Bus. Coun. UN Decade for Women, 1979, Silver Beaver award Boy Scouts Am., 1981, Elizabeth Cutter Morrow award YWCA, 1983, Emily Roebling award Nat. Women's Hall of Fame, 1984, Entrepreneurial Excellence award White House Conf. on Small Bus., 1986, NOW Legal Def. and Edn. Fund award, 1981, Brotherhood award NCCJ. 1989, Women on the Move award Anti-Defamation League, 1990, Bus. Philanthropist of Yr. award So. Calif. Conf. for Women Bus. Owner's, 1990, award Borough of Manhattan, 1991, Benjamin Botwinick prize Columbia Bus. Sch., 1992, Women in Bus. Making History award Women's Bus. Coun. NY C. of C., 1993, Disting. Woman of Yr. award Greater NY Boy Scouts of Am., 1993, Corning Excellence award NYC Bus. Coun., 1993, Woman of Yr. award Fin. Women's Assn. NY, 1994, Medal of Honor award Ellis Island, 1994, Star award N.Y. Women's Agenda, 1994, NY Urban Coalition's Achievement award, 1994, Women of Distinction award Crohn's and Colitis Found., 1994, Entrepreneurial Leadership award Nat. Found. Tchg. Entrepreneurship, 1994, Athena award, 1997, USO Women of Yr. award, 1998, Sara Lee Frontrunner award, 1998, Mattel/Barbie Ambassador of Dreams award, 1999, Town Hall Friend of Arts award, 2000, Pride of NY (PONY) award, 2001, I.O. Salzberger award, 2001, Friars Found. Applause award, 2003, numerous others; honoree Am Bankers Assn., 2003, Enterprising Women's Mag. Lifetime Achiev. award, 2003, Lifetime Achievement award US China Women Bus. Leaders, 2005; inductee Nat. Woman's Hall of Fame, Seneca Falls, NY, 1994, Internat. Women's Forum Hall of Fame, 1994, Ohio Women's Hall Fame, 1994; NY Univ.'s Stern Sch. Bus. 1st Woman Stovall fellow, 1992; established Siebert Entrepreneurial Philanthropic Program, 1990. Mem. Women's Forum (founding mem., pres.), Com. 200, Fin. Women's Assn. (Cmty. Svc. award 1993), Coun. on Fgn. Rels, Nat. Assn. Women Bus. Owners (NAWBO's Veuve Clicquot Bus. Women of Yr. award 1992, Mayor's Lifetime Achievement award for Women Bus. Owners 1993), Econ. Club (exec. com.), Southampton Bath and Tennis Club (founding mem., bd. dirs.), Women's Campaign Fund, Fashion Group Internat., Friars Club, River Club, Doubles Club, Westchester Country Club, Breakers Country Club of Palm Beach. Office: Muriel Siebert & Co Inc 885 3rd Ave Ste 1720 New York NY 10022-4834 Personal E-mail: MSiebert@siebertnet.com.

SIEBERT-FREUND, DEBORAH ANN, public relations and marketing executive; b. Hoisington, Kans., Nov. 12, 1952; d. Kenneth Theodore and Mildred Marie (Steiner) Siebert; m. Donald Raymond McLaughlin, July 17, 1976 (div. Oct. 2001); 1 child, Kalla Dawn; m. Michael Edward Freund, Feb. 14, 2005. AS, Barton County Coll., Great Bend, Kans., 1972; BS, Kans. State U., Manhattan, 1975. News editor Great Bend Tribune, 1975-76; deposition indexer Turner & Boisseau, Great Bend, 1976-77; feature editor Mid-Kans. Ruralist, Hoisington, 1977-78; copywriter, audio-editor Advt. Assocs., Great Bend, 1978-79; photographer, sales mgr. Clay Ward Color Portraits, Great Bend, 1979-80; news editor, photographer St. John (Kans.) News, 1980-83; freelance writer, photographer Great Bend, 1984-85; pres., owner McLaughlin Pub. Rels. Agy., Great Bend, 1985-87; owner Cen. Kans. Sunrise mag., Great Bend, 1987-88, Creative Mktg. Svcs., Great Bend, 1988—; dir. pub. info. Unified Sch. Dist. 428, Great Bend, 1991-93; editor Ellinwood Leader, 1995-97; acct. exec. Multimedia Cable Ad Sales, 1998-99, Cox Comms., 2000—03; realtor assoc. Help-U-Sell Real Estate, 2005; mktg. cons. NRG Media, 2004—. Realtor assoc. Help-U-Sell Real Estate, 2005—. Contbr. articles and photographs to various publs. Mem. Coalition for Prevention Child Abuse, Great Bend, 1986-87; mem. 75th anniversary com. Kansas State U. Coll. Journalism and Mass Communications, Manhattan, 1986. Mem. Kans. State U. Alumni Assn., Kans. Bd. Realtors, Great Bend Bd. Realtors. Roman Catholic. Avocations: gardening, gourmet cooking, interior decorating, swimming. Home: 381 Grove Ter Great Bend KS 67530-9710

SIEBKE, LORETTA BELLE, retired elementary school educator; b. Grinnell, Iowa, July 22, 1936; d. Earl Eli and Laura Belle (Copeland) Graham; m. Vergil Elmer Ihms, June 9, 1957 (dec. Nov. 1975); children: Kevin Lee, Karen Belle; m. Marvin Carl Siebke, June 15, 1979. Diploma, Iowa State Tchrs. Coll., 1956; BA, Marycrest Coll., 1975. Sec. Durant (Iowa) Edn. Assn., 1980-81, pres., 1983, chmn. Instrnl. and Profl. Devel., 1984—96; mem. exec. bd. Miss. Bend Uniserv Unit, Davenport, Iowa, 1982, 89, chmn. instrnl. devel., 1990—96; ret. Presenter Iowa Math. Conf., 1983; participant NASA Endl. Workshop for Elem. Sch. Tchrs., 1992. Recipient Nat. Kids Network award Carver Trust, 1990-91; Carver Trust Grant III grantee Am. On Line, 1992-93. Mem. DAR, Nat. Coun. Tchrs. Math., Iowa State Edn. Assn., Iowa Reading Assn., Ladies of Moose, Am. Legion Aux., Pythian Sisters (sec. 1968-69, Most Excellent Chief 1963—). Repulican. Methodist. Avocations: reading, sewing, cake decorating, crafts. Office: Durant Community Sch 408 7th St Durant IA 52747-9700

SIEFERT-KAZANJIAN, DONNA, corporate librarian; b. NYC; d. Merrill Emil and Esther (Levins) Siefert; m. George John Kazanjian, June 15, 1974; 1 child, Merrill George. BA, NYU, 1969; MSLS, Columbia U., 1973; MBA, Fordham U., 1977. Asst. librarian Dun & Bradstreet, N.Y.C., 1969-73; research assoc. William E. Hill & Co., N.Y.C., 1973-76; sr. info. analyst Info. for Bus., N.Y.C., 1976-77; librarian Handy Assocs., N.Y.C., 1979-90; mgr. Infoserve Fuchs Cuthrell & Co., Inc., N.Y.C., 1991-94; info. specialist Heidrick & Struggles, Inc., N.Y.C., 1994-2001; learning media specialist St. Mary's Elem. Sch., Manhasset, NY, 2002—03; libr. I Manhasset Pub. Libr., 2003—. Mem.: Rsch. Roundtable, Spl. Librs. Assn., Mensa, Am. Mensa Ltd. Roman Catholic.

SIEFKER, JUDITH MARIE, writer; b. St. Louis, Nov. 12, 1946; d. Joseph Alphonse and Mary Gertrude Siefker; m. Darrell R. Dobson, Mar. 16, 1984. BA in Psychology, Quincy Coll., 1967; MA in Clin. Psychology, Bradley U., 1971. Registered counselor Wash., 1988, cert. rehab. counselor 1981, profl. guardian 2002. Intern Peoria State Hosp., Ill., 1971—72; psychologist Divsn. Vocat. Rehab., 1973—74; vocat. evaluator Seattle Hearing & Speech Ctr., 1977—80; br. mgr. Intracorp, 1980—86, Crawford & Co., 1987—89; counselor, cons. pvt. practice, 1989—. Author: Vocational Evaluation in Private Sector Rehabilitation, 1992, Tests and Test Use in Vocational Evaluation and Assessment, 1996, Fundamentals of Case Measurement, 1997; mem. editl. bd.: Vocat. Evaluation and Work Adjustment Bulletin, 1988—96. Vol. Idaho Pk. Found., Boise, 1977, Farmers India, Hyderabad, 1994; del. UN Fourth World Conf. Women, Beijing, 1995. Mem.: Wash. Assn. Profl. Guardians. Democrat. Avocations: travel, needlecrafts, sailing, skiing. Office Phone: 206-772-6497.

SIEGAL, RITA GORAN, engineering company executive; b. Chgo., July 16, 1934; d. Leonard and Anabelle (Soloway) Goran; m. Burton L. Siegal, Apr. 11, 1954; children: Norman, Laurence Scott. Student, U. Ill., 1951-53; BA, DePaul U., 1956. Cert. elem. tchr., Ill. Tchr. Chgo. Public Schs., 1956-58; founder, chief exec. officer Budd Engring. Corp., Skokie, Ill., 1959—; founder, pres. Easy Living Products Co., Skokie, 1960—; pvt. practice in interior design, Chgo., 1968-73; dist. sales mgr. Super Girls, Skokie, 1976. Lectr. Northwestern U., 1983; guest speaker nat. radio and TV, 1979—. Contbr. to profl. jours. Mem. adv. bd. Skokie High Schs., 1975-79; advisor Cub Scouts Skokie coun. Boy Scouts Am., 1975; bus. mgr. Nutrition for Optimal Health Assn., Winnetka, Ill., 1980-82, pres., 1982-84, v.p. med./profl., 1985-93; leader Great Books Found., 1972; founder Profit Plus Investment, 1970; bd. dirs. Noha, Internat. Named Prominent Alumni, Sullivan HS, 2001; recipient Cub Scout awards, Boy Scouts Am., 1971—72, Nat. Charlotte Danstrom award, Nat. Women of Achievement, 1988, Corp. Achievement award, 1988, Frannie Award, U. Ill., 1998. Mem. North Shore Women in Mgmt. (pres, 1987-88), Presidents Assn. Ill. (bd. dirs 1990-94, membership chair 1991-93), Inventors Coun., Oriental Art Soc. Chgo. (publicity chair).

SIEGEL, BETTY LENTZ, university president; b. Cumberland, Ky., Jan. 24, 1931; d. Carl N. and Vera (Hogg) Lentz; m. Joel H. Siegel, June 6; children: David Jonathan, Michael Jeremy. BA, Wake Forest U., 1952; M in Edn., U. NC, 1953; PhD, Fla. State U., 1961; postgrad., Ind. U., 1964-66; doctorate (hon.), Miami U., 1985, Cumberland Coll., 1985, Ea. Ky. U., 1992, Morehead State U., 2002; degree (hon.), Lynchburg Coll., So. Conn. State U. Asst. prof. Lenoir Rhyne Coll., Hickory, N.C., 1956-59; assoc. prof., 1961-64; asst. prof. U. Fla., Gainesville, 1967-70, assoc. prof., 1970-72, prof., 1973-76, dean acad. affairs for continuing edn., 1972-76; dean Sch. Edn. and Psychology Western Carolina U., Cullowhee, N.C., 1976-81; pres. Kennesaw State U., Marietta, Ga., 1981—. Bd. dirs. Nat. Services Industries; cons. numerous sch. systems. Author: Problem Situations in Teaching, 1971, Becoming An Invitational Leader, 2002; contbr. articles to profl. jours. Bd. dirs. United Way Atlanta, Ga. Partnership for Excellence in Edn., Ga. Coun. Econ. Edn., Northside Hosp. Found., Atlanta Ballet; Ga. rep. so. growth policy bd. Commn. on Future of South, 1998. Recipient Disting. Tchr. of Yr. award U. Fla., 1969; Mortar Bd. Woman of Yr. award U. Fla., 1973, Mortar Bd. Educator of Yr., Ga. State U., 1983, CASE award, 1986, Aluma of Yr. award Wake Forest U., 1987, "Grad Made Good" award Fla. State U. Alumni Assn, Omicron Delta Kappa, 1991, Spirit of Life award City of Hope, 1992, Woman of Achievement award Cobb Chamber YWCA, 1992, First Lifetime Achievement award YWCA, N.W. Ga., Oak award outstanding Alumni Ky., 1998, Adminstrv. Leadership award Assn. Gerontology in Higher Edn., 2001, Women in Bus. Lifetime Achievement award, 2001, Peabody award UNC-Chapel Hill Sch. Edn., 2003, Justice Robert Benham award outstanding leadership, svc. and commitment equality of all citizens Black's United for Youth of Cobb County, 2004, Howard Washington Thurman Ecumenical award Morehouse Coll.'s Martin Luther King, Jr. Internat. Chapel, 2005,

Leita Thompson Lifetime Achievement award; named 50 Most Influential Women in Ga., One of 100 Most Influential People in State of Ga., Ga. Trend Mag., Outstanding Alumni, Fla. State U. Coll. Edn. Alumni Assn., 1992, Cobb Citizen of Yr., 1996, Ga. Woman of Yr. Ga. Commn. Women, 1997, Divas for Life Bus. to Bus. Mag., 2001, 100 Most Disting. Alumni Cumberland Coll.; named to Jr. Achievement Hall of Fame, 1999, 20 Women Making a Mark on Atlanta Atlanta mag., 20 Yrs., 20 Leaders Ga. Trend mag. Mem. Am. Psychol. Assn., Am. Assn. State Colls. and Univs. (bd. dirs., chmn. 1990), Am. Coun. Edn. (bd. dirs., bd. advisors), Am. Inst. Mng. Diversity (bd. dis.), Soc. Internat. Bus. Fellows, Commn. on Women in Higher Edn., Internat. Alliance Invitational Edn. (co-founder, co-dir.), Nat. Ctr. Study of Freshman Yr. Experience, So. Inst. Bus. and Profl. Ethics (mem. gov. bd.), Am. Cancer Soc. (Cobb chpt.), Cobb Exec. Women (founder), Ga. Exec. Women's Network, Internat. Bus. Forum, State Bar Ga., Found. Freedom, Bus./Higher Edn. Forum, mem. exec. com.), Cobb C. of C. (chair 1996), Kiwanis (Atlanta chpt.), Am. Humaries, Inc., Phi Alpha Theta, Pi Kappa Delta, Alpha Psi Omega, Kappa Delta Pi, Pi Lambda Theta, Phi Delta Kappa, Delta Kappa Gamma. Office: Kennesaw State Univ Office of the President 1000 Chastain Rd NW Kennesaw GA 30144-5591

SIEGEL, CAROLE ETHEL, mathematician; b. N.Y., Sept. 29, 1936; d. David and Helen (Mayer) Schore; m. Bertram Siegel, Aug. 18, 1957; children: Sharon, David. BA in Math., NYU, 1957, MS in Math., 1959, PhD in Math., 1963. With computer dept. Atomic Energy Commn., 1957-59; rsch. asst. Courant Inst. of Math. Sci., 1959-63; rsch. scientist dept. of engring. NYU, N.Y.C., 1963-64; rsch. math. Info. Scis. Div. Rockland Rsch. Inst., Orangeburg, NY, 1965-74; head Epidemiology and Health Svcs. Rsch. Lab., Stat. Scis., Epidemiology divsn. Nathan S. Kline Inst. Psychiat. Rsch., Orangeburg, NY, 1974—2003, dir. Stats. and Health Svcs. Rsch. Divsn., 2003—. Adj. assoc. prof. Wagner Grad. Sch. Pub. Svc., NYU; rsch. prof. dept. psychiatry NYU, 1987—; dep. dir. WHO Collaborating Ctr., Nathan S. Kline Inst., 1987—; grant reviewer NIHM, 1988—; prin. investigator Ctr. for Study of Issues in Public Mental Health, NIMH, 1993--, prin. investigator, dir., 1995—. Editor: (with S. Fischer) Psychiatric Records in Mental Health Care, 1981; contbr. articles to profl. jours. Recipient Carl Taube award, mental health sect. APHA, 2001; grantee SAMHSA, CMHS, 1997—, NIMH, 1993—, 1988—91, Nat. Ctr. for Health Svcs. Rsch., 1979—82, Nat. Inst. Alcohol Abuse, 1978—82. Mem. Assn. for Health Svcs. Rsch., Am. Soc. Clin. Pharmacology and Therapeutics, Assn. Women in Math., Am. Statis. Assn. Avocations: pottery, gardening, cooking. Office: Nathan S Kline Inst Orangeburg NY 10962

SIEGEL, CAROLYN AUGUSTA, judge, lawyer, social worker; b. Buffalo, Dec. 29, 1943; d. Joseph Frederick and Louise Augusta (Knecht) S.; m. Roger John Fenlon, Feb. 15, 1969 (div. Nov. 1, 1989); children: Kristin M. Jaeger, Jocelyn N. Walsh. BA, St. Bonaventure U., 1965; MS, SUNY, Buffalo, 1973, MSW, JD, SUNY, Buffalo, 1999. Bar: N.Y. 2000; cert. elem. and exceptional tchr., lic. Master Social Worker N.Y. Indsl. investigator N.Y. Dept. Labor, Buffalo, 1966-67; tchr. St. Bonaventure Grammar Sch., Buffalo, 1967; adminstrv. analyst N.Y. State Dept. Law, Albany, 1967-68; caseworker N.Y. State Dept. Social Svcs., Buffalo, 1968-72; resource agent N.Y. State Dept. Mental Hygiene, Buffalo, 1972-73; resource and reimbursement agt. N.Y. State Office Mental Retardation and Developmental Disabilities, Buffalo, 1982—2001; coord. policy svcs. Erie 1 BOCES, West Seneca, NY, 2001—; town justice Town of Colden, 2004—. Mem. surrogate decision-making panel N.Y. State Commn. on Quality of Care; adj. instr. SUNY, Buffalo, 2004—; cert. instr. Mandated Child Abuse Reporters, 2005—. Contbr. articles to profl. jours. Pres. Bd. Edn. Springville (N.Y.)-Griffith Inst. Ctrl. Sch. Dist., 1980-95; bd. visitors Buffalo Psychiat. Ctr., 1994—, pres., 1998—; bd. dirs. Erie County Mental Health Assn., Buffalo; 4H Group Leader Erie County Coop. Extension, East Aurora, N.Y., 1974-92; town chmn. Am. Cancer Soc., Buffalo. Mem.: ABA, Erie County Magistrates Assn., N.Y. Magistrates Assn., Erie County Bar Assn., Women's Bar Assn., N.Y. State Bar Assn. Home: PO Box 360 West Falls NY 14170-9624 Office: Erie 1 BOCES 355 Harlem Rd West Seneca NY 14224 Business E-Mail: csiegel@e1b.org.

SIEGEL, ERIKA JANET, psychologist; b. N.Y.C., Apr. 26, 1962; d. Joel Robert and Anne (Shuttleworth) S. AB in Art History with distinction, Swarthmore Coll., 1984; MA in Psychology with honors, Cath. U., 1993, PhD in Psychology, 2001. Asst. Galerie St. Etienne, N.Y.C., 1984-86; asst. art dir. Promotion Solutions, N.Y.C., 1986-87; graphic designer Corp. Graphics, Inc, N.Y.C., 1987-89; designer Lintas Mktg. Communications, N.Y.C., 1989-91; sr. graphic designer Sparkman & Assocs., Washington, 1991; clin. psychologist The Family Ctr., Falls Ch., Va., 2004—; resident in clin. psychology Emergency Svcs. Woodburn Ctr. for Cmty. Mental Health, Annadale, Va., 2003—04. Recipient award Am. Inst. Graphic Arts, Type Dirs. Club. Mem. APA, Phi Beta Kappa

SIEGEL, HEIDI ELLEN, neurologist, researcher; b. Buffalo, Apr. 4, 1965; d. Allan and Carla Siegel; children: David Oletsky, Jennifer Oletsky. BA in Biophysics, Brandeis U., 1987; MD with spl. distinction rsch. in neuro., Albert Einstein Coll. Medicine, 1991. Diplomate Am. Bd. Psychiatry and Neurology, Am. Bd. Clin. Neurophysiology. Intern in internal medicine U. Md. Hosp., Balt., 1991-92, resident in neurology, 1992-95; fellow in EEG, epilepsy, sleep NIH, Bethesda, Md., 1995-98; asst. prof. neurology Mt. Sinai Sch. Medicine, N.Y.C., 1998—, NYU Sch. Medicine, N.Y.C., 1999—. Author: Pretest: Neuroscience, 3d edit., 1998; contbr. numerous articles, abstracts to profl. jours. Mem. Jewish Cmty. Ctr., West Orange, N.J., 1998—. Lt. comdr. USPHS, 1995-98. Recipient Richter award for Excellence in Rsch. in Neurosci., Brandeis U., 1984; Cyberonics Rsch. grantee, 1999. Mem. AMA, Am. Acad. Neurology (sleep section, epilepsy section, history section), Am. Epilepsy Soc., Am. Sleep Disorders Assn., Soc. for Neurosci. Office: Mount Sinai Med Ctr Box 1052 1 Gustave L Levy Pl New York NY 10025 E-mail: heidi_siegel@mssm.edu.

SIEGEL, JUDITH S., music educator; b. Richmond, Va., June 27, 1940; d. Meyer Harry and Mildred (Meyers) Salsbury; m. Murray Siegel, June 18, 1960; children: Lisa Siegel Machlin, Sheri Siegel Cohen, Harry. Student, U. N.C., Greensboro, 1958-60, Smithdeal-Massey Coll., Richmond, 1960-61, Columbia U. Tchrs. Coll., 1965-68, U. Richmond, 1968-79, Columbia U. Tchrs. Coll., 1970. Nat. cert. tchr. of music. Dir. The Pianoforte Sch. of Music, Va., Md., 1965—. Contbr. over 300 articles to profl. jours. and 25 books; composer of music and poetry. Avocations: performing arts, journalism, gourmet cooking. Home: 143 Dragonfly Dr Titusville FL 32780-2587 E-mail: pianolessons@bellsouth.net.

SIEGEL, LAURIE, human resources specialist; married; 2 children. B of Gen. Studies, U. Mich.; MBA, Harvard U. Dir. global compensation Avon Products; prin. Strategic Compensation Assocs.; various positions in human resources Honeywell Internat., 1995—2003; sr. v.p. human resources Tyco Internat. Ltd., Princeton, NJ, 2003—. Bd. dirs. Hayes Lemmerz Internat., Inc. Office: Tyco International PO Box 5260 Princeton NJ 08543-5260 Office Phone: 609-720-4200. Office Fax: 603-720-4208.

SIEGEL, LAURIE F., accountant, painter; b. Chgo., Aug. 25, 1959; d. Phil P. and Carol Siegel; life ptnr. Mary Ruth Cadwallader. BA, U. Wis., 1982. CPA Va., 1989. Freelance writer, Chgo., 1982—83; investigative reporter, intern with Jack Anderson Washington, 1983; investigative reporter, intern CNN, Washington, 1984; reporter Washington Times, 1984; acct. various firms, Md., 1984—89; pvt. practice Arlington, Va., 1989—. Contbr. columns in newspapers. Mem.: AICPA, Nat. Assn. Tax Profls., Md. Soc. Accts., Va. Soc. CPA's. Independent. Avocations: running, travel, racquetball. Office: Laurie F Siegel CPA PC 1307 S Monroe St Arlington VA 22204 Office Phone: 703-920-9444. Business E-Mail: siegel@lsiegelcpa.com.

SIEGEL, LUCY BOSWELL, public relations executive; b. NYC, July 5, 1950; d. Werner Leiser and Carol (Fleischer) Boswell; m. Henry Winter Siegel, Nov. 11, 1979 (div.); children: David Alan Siegel, Joshua Adam Siegel. BA, Conn. Coll., 1972. Assoc. editor Conn. Western, Litchfield, Conn., 1972-73; assoc. editor, editor United Bus. Publ., NYC, 1974—78; mgr. external communications Equitable Life Assurance Soc., NYC, 1978—86; mgr. internat. affairs Cosmo Pub. Rels. Corp., Tokyo, 1986-87, dir. internat. affairs, 1987-88, pres. NYC, 1988—90, Siegel Assocs. Internat., NYC, 1990—97; sr. v.p. Lobsenz Stevens, NYC, 1997—99; sr. prin., mng. dir. Publicis Dialog, NYC, 1999—2000, exec. v.p., group mng. dir., 2000—04; pres., CEO Bridge Global Strategies LLC, NYC, 2004—. Contbr. articles to jours. and mags. Bd. dirs. NYC chpt. Am. Jewish Com., 1993—, sec. 1993-05. Mem. Pub. Rels. Soc. Am. (treas., exec. com. bd., N.Y.C. chpt. 2004—, exec. bd. internat. sect. 2004), Women Execs. in Pub. Rels. (bd. dirs. 1997-99), Inst. Pub. Rels. (mktg. com. mem., 2004-). Democrat. Jewish. Home: 41 W 96th St Apt 12B New York NY 10025-6519 Office: 15th Fl 575 Lexington Ave New York NY 10022

SIEGEL, MARY ANN GARVIN, writer; b. Louisville, Apr. 3, 1944; d. Samuel Hughes and Ann Wendell (Smith) Garvin; m. Charles Holladay Siegel, Sept. 2, 1967 (div.); children: Emily Hughes, Charles Holladay, Jr., Margaret Shafer. BA, Conn. Coll., 1966. Photog. rschr. Time Inc., NYC, 1966—67, Nat. Geog. Soc., Washington, 1967—68; content author and editor FundraisingINFO.com, 2000—01. Leadership Atlanta, 1993-94, exec. com., 1995-96. Trustee Conn. Coll., New London, 1985-90; chair Friends of Spelman Coll., Atlanta, 1990-92; active Atlanta/Fulton County adv. bd. United Way Met. Atlanta, 1994-96; Olympic Envoy to Republic of Nauru, Atlanta Com. Olympic Games, 1994-96; formerly active adv. bd. N.C. Outward Bound Sch., Asheville. Recipient Agnes Berkeley Leahy award Conn. Coll. Alumni Assn., 1991. Personal E-mail: seagullwrite@yahoo.com.

SIEGEL, REVA, law educator; BA, Yale U., 1978, MPhil, 1982, JD, 1986. Law clk. for Hon. Spottswood W. Robinson, III, US Ct. Appeals, Washington, DC, 1986—87; acting prof. U. Calif., Berkeley, 1988—94; vis. prof. Yale U., New Haven, 1993—94, prof. law, 1994—99, Nicholas deB. Katzenbach prof., 1999—. Vis. prof. Harvard Law Sch., 1998—99, Columbia U., 2001—02. Co-editor: Directions in Sexual Harassment Law, 2004; contbr. articles to law jours. Office: Yale Law Sch PO Box 208215 New Haven CT 06520 E-mail: reva.siegel@yale.edu.

SIEGEL, STEPHANIE S., mathematics professor; d. Marvin and Gerry Siegel. BA in Math. with honors, Herbert H. Lehman Coll., 1977; MS in Quantitative Math., NYU, 1980. Adj. instr. math. Herbert H. Lehman Coll., Bronx, NY, 1978—79, 1991; adj. instr. stats. NYU, NYC, 1991—96; instr. math. Touro Coll., Bklyn., 1997—. Mem.: Am. Math. Soc. Avocations: chess, poetry, puzzles. Office: Touro Coll 1602 Ave J Brooklyn NY 11230 Business E-Mail: ssiegel@touro.edu.

SIEGEL-HINSON, ROBYN LEE, psychologist, consultant, clinic director; d. Robert Donald and Elizabeth Helen Siegel; m. Tony Hinson, Jan. 1, 1981; 1 child, Rhys. AA cum laude, Rochester Coll., 1981; BA in Psychology and Sociology with honors, U. Mich., 1991; MA, U. Toledo, 1996, PhD, 1999. Licensed Clin. Psychologist Mich., 1998. Psychology intern U. of Mich. Med. Ctr., Ann Arbor, Mich., 1996—97; staff psychologist Advanced Counseling Ctr., Taylor, Mich., 1997—2000; clinic dir. Agape Counseling Ctr., Plymouth, Mich., 2003—, Lawrence Technol. U., Southfield, Mich., 2004—; clin. psychologist, pvt. practice Dr. Siegel-Hinson, Allen Park, Mich., 2003—. Assessment cons. Lawrence Technol. U., Southfield, Mich., 2004. Contbr. articles to publs. and jours. Pres. Neighborhood, Cmty. Outreach, Wyandotte, Mich., 1995—97; com. mem. Healthy Downriver, Guidance Ctr., Southgate, Mich., 1996—2002; mem., tchr. Ch. of Christ, Allen Park, Mich., 1985—2005; bd. mem. Thunderers Drum and Bugle Corps, Ypsilanti, Mich., 1993—97. Grantee Rsch. Grant, NIMH Grant-Group Rsch. Project, 1995, Returning Woman scholar, U. of Mich., 1990; scholar Acad. Merit scholar, 1989; Rsch. Asst. fellow, U. of Toledo, 1992-1996, Honors Psychology Rsch. grant, U. of Mich., 1990, Mich. Coll. scholar, State of Mich., Rochester Coll., 1979-1981. Mem.: APA (assoc.). Achievements include Elected First Female President of Student Body Association in the history of Rochester College; patents for Patent on Tachistoscope test of Spatial Ability. Office: Lawrence Technol Univ Ten Mile Rd Southfield MI Office Phone: 248-204-4116. E-mail: hinson@ltu.edu.

SIEGENTHALER, DENISE L., lawyer; b. Rochester, NY, Aug. 22, 1969; d. William Thomas Siegenthaler and Cheryl Rocki Israel. BA, SUNY, Oswego, 1992; JD, Ariz. State U. Coll. Law, Tempe, 1998. Bar: Ariz. 1999, U.S. Dist. Ct. Ariz. 2003. Staff atty. Cmty. Legal Svcs., Kingman, Ariz., 1999; asst. atty. gen. State of Ariz., Phoenix, 1999—2001; mng. atty. Denise L. Siegenthaler & Assoc./ The Hartford, 2001—. Vol. Phoenix Children's Hosp., 2004—05; mem. Ariz. Gov.'s Domestic Violence Task Force, 1999. Mem.: ABA (mem. young lawyers divsn. 1999—2000), Ariz. State Bar Assn. Office: Law Offices Ste 205 10050 N 25th Ave Phoenix AZ 85021 Fax: 602-997-4266.

SIEGMAN, MARION JOYCE, physiologist, educator; b. Bklyn., Sept. 7, 1933; d. C. Joseph and Helen Siegman. BA, Tulane U., 1954; PhD, SUNY, Bklyn., 1966. Instr. physiology Med. Coll. Thomas Jefferson U., Phila., 1967-68, asst. prof., 1968-71, assoc. prof., 1971-77, prof., 1977—, chair dept. physiology, 2001—. Mem. physiology study sect. NIH. Editor: Regulation and Contraction of Smooth Muscle, 1987. Recipient award for excellence in rsch. and teaching Burlington No. Found., 1986, award for excellence in teaching Lindback Found., 1987, Outstanding Alumna award, Newcomb Coll./Tulane U., 1990; grantee NIH, 1967—. Mem. Am. Physiol. Soc., Biophys. Soc. Avocation: photography. Office: Jefferson Med Coll 1020 Locust St Philadelphia PA 19107-6731 Office Phone: 215-503-7761. E-mail: marion.siegman@jefferson.edu.

SIEGMUND, MARY KAY, priest, counselor, marriage and family therapist; b. Kans. City, Mo., Aug. 18, 1953; d. John Riley Thompson and Agnes Ann Purcell; m. Mark Steven Siegmund, Dec. 27, 1979; children: Melissa, Michael. BA, Park Coll., 1977; MA, U. Mo., 1988; MDiv, Midwestern Bapt. Theol. Sem., 1995. Lic. profl. counselor. Chaplain Independence (Mo.) Regional Hosp., 1985—88, therapist, 1985—88; chaplain Marillac Ctr., Kansas City, 1995—98, therapist, 1995—98; vicar St. John's Northland, Kansas City, 1987—2001; asst. rector Ch. of Good Shepherd, Nashua, NH, 2001—. Episc.

SIEKIERSKI, KAMILLA MALGORZATA, dental laboratory technician; b. Warsaw, Poland, Aug. 4, 1938; came to U.S., 1963, naturalized, 1970; d. Tomasz and Janina W. (Sendzimir) Piotrowski; cert. dental technician Sch. Dental Technicians, Krakow, Poland, 1957; m. Kazimierz Siekierski, Nov. 25, 1959; children: Marzanna, Eva. Owner, operator Kama's Dental Lab., Krakow, 1963; dental technician Dan's Dental Lab., Waterbury, Conn., 1963-65, Wilcox Dental Lab., Wethersfield, Conn., 1965-68; pres. Dentek, Inc., Milford, Conn., 1980—; lectr. Smile Seminars, 1990—; lectr. in field of dental prosthetics. Mem. Conn. Dental Lab. Assn. (pres. 1977-79), Nat. Assn. Dental Labs., Conf. Dental Labs. Office: PO Box 3649 233 Research Dr Milford CT 06460-8540 Home: 1155 Warburton Ave 12S Yonkers NY 10701 Office Phone: 914-751-5495. E-mail: kamakamilla@hotmail.com.

SIEMER, DEANNE CLEMENCE, lawyer; d. Edward D. and Dorothy J. (Helsdon) S.; m. Howard P. Willens; 1 child, Jason L. BA, George Washington U., 1962; LLB, Harvard U., 1968. Bar: N.Y. 1968, D.C. 1969, Md. 1972, Commonwealth of No. Mariana Islands 1976. Economist Office of Mgmt. and Budget, Washington, 1964-67; assoc., then ptnr. Wilmer, Cutler & Pickering, Washington, 1968-77, 80-90; ptnr. Pillsbury, Madison & Sutro, Washington, 1990-95; mng. dir. Wilsie Co., Washington and Saipan, 1995—. Gen. counsel U.S. Dept. of Def., Washington, 1977—79; spl. asst. to sec. U.S. Dept. of Energy, Washington, 1979—80. Author: Tangible Evidence, 3d edit., 1996, National Security and Self-Determination: United States Policy in Micronesia, 1999, Corel Presentations for Litigators, 2000, PowerPoint for Litigators, 2000, Effective Use of Courtroom Technology: A Judge's Guide to Pretrial and Trial, 2001, An Honorable Accord: The Covenant Between the Northern Mariana Islands and the United States, 2001, Effective Use of Courtroom Technology: A Lawyer's Guide to Pretrial and Trial, 2002, Easy Tech: Cases and Materials on Courtroom Technology, 2002, The Patronus Technique: A Practical Proposal In Asbestos-Driven Bankruptcies, 2002, Power Point 2002 for Litigators, 2002, Basic Power Point Slides, 2003, Argument Slides, 2003, The Evidence Camera, 2004, Oral Histories of the Northern Mariana Islands: Political Life and Developments 1945-1995, 2004, The Digital Projector and Laptop Computer, 2005, PowerPoint 2003: 50 Great Tips for Better, Easier Slides, 2005, From the White House: Documents on the Northern Mariana Islands and Micronesia (1945-1995) Collected from the Presidential Libraries, 2005, The Secret Guam Study: The Documents, 2005, Asbestos Prepackaged Bankruptcies: Apply the Brakes But Retain Flexibility for Debtors, 2005. Mem. Lawyers Com. Civil Rights, Washington, 1973—; mediator U.S. Ct. Appeals, Washington, 1988—; trustee Nat. Inst. Trial Advocacy, 1989—, Am. Law Inst., 1988—; arbitrator Atty. Client Arbitration Bd., 1990-, NASD, 2001-; mem. com. sci. and nat. security NAS, 2002-. Recipient citation Air Force Assn., 1977, Dist. Pub. Svc. medal Sec. of Def., 1979, Commendation Pres. of U.S. 1981; grantee Nat. Endowment Humanities, Commonwealth of No. Mariana Islands Divsn. Hist. Preservation, No. Mariana Islands Coun. Humanities. Mem. D.C. Bar Assn. (Disting. Svc. award 2006), No. Marianas Bar Assn. Episcopalian. Business E-Mail: wilsieco@aol.com.

SIERRA, DOLORES, communications educator; b. Dunlap, Ill., Aug. 4, 1954; d. Mark and Burnette Hill; m. George Sierra, Mar. 13, 1999; children: Abigail Honold, Nicholas Honold, Catherine Honold. AA, Ill. Ctrl. Coll., East Peoria, 1974; BS in Mass Comm., Ill. State U., Normal, 1976, M in Speech Comm., 1981. Asst. prof. Ill. Ctrl. Coll., East Peoria, 1980—86; instr. Western Ky. U., Bowling Green, 1986—87; assoc. prof. broadcasting and speech Black Hawk Coll., Moline, Ill., 1987—. Spkrs. bur. Black Hawk Coll., 1996—, coord. broadcast adv. bd., 1987—, new faculty mentor, 2000—, advisor chieftain newspaper, 1998—2002, co-advisor broadcast club, 1991—2000; vol. WQPT Pub. TV, 1989—2003. Actor: (plays) Fiddler on the Roof;, singer cantor/music ministry. Bd. edn. Sacred Heart Cathedral, Davenport, Iowa, 1990—93, reader, 2004; bd. mem., newsletter editor Celtic Heritage Trail, 2005; m.c. Mullane Irish Dance Acad., Quad Cities area, 1990—92. Mem.: Am. Film Inst., Internat. Assn. Media and History, Am. Conf. Irish Studies. Roman Catholic. Avocations: theater, reading, counted cross stitch, baseball. Office: Black Hawk Coll 6600 34th Ave Moline IL 61265 Office Phone: 309-796-5367. E-mail: sierrad@bhc.edu.

SIERRA, MARIA PATRICIA, special education educator; b. Laredo, Tex., Aug. 14, 1977; d. Juan and Maria Luisa Vargas; m. Salome Sierra, July 30, 2005. BS, Tex. A&M U., College Sta., 1999; MEd, Tex. A&M U., 2002. Self-contained tchr. UISD, Laredo, 2001—. Rep. DEIC, Laredo, 2003—. Mem.: ATPE, Alpha Delta Kappa. Office: UISD 8501 Curly Ln Laredo TX 78045 Office Phone: 956-473-7460. E-mail: patriciabriones@yahoo.com.

SIERRA, REGINA AURELIA, science educator; b. Austin, Tex., Mar. 10, 1973; d. Rick and Alice Brinnel; m. Juan Sierra, June 16, 1968; 1 child, Juan. BS, Tex. A&M U., College Station, 1996; M in Interdisciplinary Sci., U. Tex., Arlington, 2004. Cert. in geology Tex., 1997. Sci. tchr. Garland Ind. Sch. Dist., Tex., 1997—98, Mansfield Ind. Sch. Dist., Tex., 1998—. Social worker Salvation Army, Bryan, Tex., 1994—96. Named First Class Tchr., Minyard Food Stores, Inc, 1997; grantee, Mansfield Ind. Sch. Dist. Edn. Found., 1999, 2000, 2002, 2003, 2005. Mem.: UEA, Tex. Sci. Tchrs. Assn. Office: Mansfield Ind Sch Dist 500 Pleasant Ridge Arlington TX 76002 Office Phone: 817-473-5668. E-mail: sierre@mansfieldisd.org.

SIESS, JUDITH ANN, librarian; b. Urbana, Ill., Sept. 28, 1947; d. Chester Paul and Helen (Kranson) Siess; m. Stephen Paul Bremseth, Aug. 27, 1983. BA cum laude, Beloit Coll., 1969; MA, Ea. N.Mex. U., 1973; MS in Libr. Info. sci., U. Ill., 1982. Asst. extension agrl. economist dept. agrl. econs. U. Ill., Urbana, 1976-83; librarian Enzyme Tech. Corp., Ashland, Ohio, 1983-86, North Coast Biotechnology, Warrensville Heights, Ohio, 1986-87, NASA Lewis Rsch. Ctr., Cleve., 1987-88; corp. libr. Bailey Controls Co., Wickliffe, Ohio, 1988—96; pres. Bridges Internat., Inc., Cleve., 1996—. Editor: Price Forecasting and Sales Management, 1978; pub., editor: The One-Person Libr.: A Newsletter for Librs. and Mgmt., 1998—; author: The SOLO Librarian's Sourcebook, 1997, The OPL Sourcebook: A Guide for Solo and Small Libraries, 2001, Time Managment, Planning and Prioritization for Librarians, 2002, The Visible Librarian: Asserting Your Value with Marketing and Advocacy, 2003, The Essential OPL: 1998-2004, The Best of Seven Years of the One-Person Libr., 2005, The New OPL Sourcebook, 2006. Mem.: Libr. and Info. Assn. South Africa, Libr. and Info. Assn. New Zealand, Australian Libr. and Info. Assn., Chartered Inst. Libr. and Info. Profls., Am. Assn. Law Librs., Med. Librs. Assn., Spl. Librs. Assn. Avocation: reading. Home: 477 Harris Rd Richmond Heights OH 44143-2537 Office: 477 Harris Rd Cleveland OH 44143-2537 Business E-Mail: jsiess@ibi-opl.com.

SIEVERT, MARY ELIZABETH, small business owner, retired secondary school educator; b. Sioux City, Iowa, Sept. 28, 1939; d. Arthur Harry and Bertha Busboom Sievert. BS, Morningside Coll., 1960; MA, U. Nebr., 1962; postgrad., U. Iowa, Hope Coll., U. Calif., Irvine. Instr. chemistry lab. Morningside Coll., Sioux City, Iowa, 1959—60; tchr. chemistry Davenport Schs., Iowa, 1962—86, Blackhawk Coll., Moline, Ill.; admissions officer St. Luke's Hosp., Davenport; SSTP counselor U. Iowa, Iowa City; computer instr. Grinnell Coll., Iowa, 1983; P/K-12/A sci. coord. Davenport Schs., 1986—96, AGATE dept. chair, 1995—99; pres., CEO Memorabilia ExtraOrdinaire, Davenport, 1996—. Exchange tchr. Rowley Regis Coll., Birmingham, England, 1975; pres., CEO Quad Cities Sci. and Engring. Fair, Davenport, 1962—99; adv. evaluation coun. Antique Am., Davenport, 2000—01; antiques and collectibles lectr. Ea. Iowa C.C., Davenport, 2001—, Blackhawk Coll., Moline, Ill., 2002—. Contbr. articles to profl. jours. Fundraising v.p. Miss Iowa Bd., Davenport, 1999—2001; mem. plan and zone commn. City of Davenport, 1988—94; WelcomeAires mem. QC vol. bur. QC Internat. Airport, 2000—; charter mem. 1st in the Nation in Edn. Rschr. Found., 1986—97; 63 com. woman Scott County Rep. Party; handbell ringer, former dir. vacation Bible sch. Holy Cross Luth. Ch., Davenport; mem. bd. Christ Lutheran Ch., 2002—. Named Outstanding H.S. Chemistry Tchr. of Yr. in Iowa, Iowa Acad. Scis., 1969, Outstanding Young Educator, Davenport Jaycees, Centennial Tchr. of Yr. in Iowa, NIH, 1987; named to Iowa Sci. Tchrs. Hall of Fame, 2002; recipient Regional Catalyst award for outstanding chemistry tchr., Chem. Mfg. Assn., 1985, Golden Apple award for top educator, Scott County Edn. Orgn., 1998; fellow Woodrow Wilson fellow for outstanding H.S. chemistry tchrs., Princeton U., 1982; scholar NSF. Mem.: AAUW (past pres. local br. and Iowa State), NEA (life), U. Nebr. Alumni Assn. (life), Morningside Alumni Assn. (life), Delta Kappa Gamma (former local and state parliamentarian, mem. Hapke scholarship com.), Pi Lambda Theta (life; mem. charter alumni chpt.), Sigma Kappa (life). Avocations: bridge, gardening, travel, theater, symphony. Office: Memorabilia ExtraOrdinaire Inc 2707 East Hayes St Davenport IA 52803

SIEVERT, VICKI LEE, retired music educator; d. Joe Sproul and Ruby Baughman-Sproul; m. Richard Paul Sievert, Mar. 16, 1974; children: Michael William, Cassandra Ruth. MusB, Bowling Green State U., 1970. Profl. tchg. cert. Ohio, cert. Level 1 Am. Orff Schulwerk Assn., cert. Level II Am. Orff Schulwerk Assn. Music specialist pub. sch. Benton/Carroll/Salem Sch. Dist., Oak Harbor, Ohio, 1970—2003; elem. music specialist Genoa (Ohio) Local Sch. Dist., 2003—04; music dir. Oak Harbor United Meth. Ch., 2002—. Music dept. chair Benton/Carroll/Salem Sch. Dist., Oak Harbor, Ohio, 1989—98, co-chair curriculum update com. dept. music, 2001—03, chair curriculum and nat. standards com. music strategic plan, 2002—04. Com. chair Oak Harbor (Ohio) United Meth. Ch., choir dir., 2000—, bd. mem. Mem.: Music Educators Nat. Conf. (assoc.), Ohio Educators Assn. (assoc.; sec. 1996—98), Ohio Music Educators Assn. (life; mentor). Avocations: handcrafts, playing piano. Home: 8845 W State Rt 163 Oak Harbor OH 43449

SIFF, MARLENE IDA, artist, designer; b. N.Y.C. d. Irving Louis and Dorothy Gertrude (Lahn) Marmer; m. Elliott Justin Siff, July 11, 1959; children: Bradford Evan, Brian Douglas. BA, Hunter Coll., 1957. Cert. tchr. elem. edn., N.Y., N.J. Tchr. Stewart Manor (N.Y.) Sch. Sys., 1957-59, Teaneck (N.J.) Sch. Sys., 1959-60; freelance interior designer Westport, Conn., 1966-70; designer Varo Inertial Products, Trumbull, Conn., 1970; designer signature collections J.P. Stevens & Co. Inc., N.Y., 1974-78, J.C. Penney Co., N.Y., 1978, C.R. Gibson Co., Norwalk, Conn., 1980. Corp. sec., treas., bd. dirs. Belmar Corp., Westport, 1972—; chmn. bd. Marlene Designs Inc., Westport, 1973-77; owner Marlene Siff Design Studio, Westport, 1978—; aesthetic cons. Alcide Corp., Norwalk, 1980-88. One-person shows include David Segal Gallery, N.Y.C., 1987, Conn. Pub. TV Gallery, Hartford, 1987, Paul Mellon Art Ctr., Choate Rosemary Hall, Wallingford, Conn., 1989, Conn. Nat. Bank Hdqs., Norwalk, 1990, Michael Stone Collection, Washington, 1992, Bergdorf Goodman Men, N.Y.C., 1993, Joel Kessler Fine Art, Miami Beach, Fla., 1994, Park Pl., Stamford, Conn., 1995, Westport Arts Ctr., 1995, Mitchells, Westport, 1998, NIH, Bethesda, Md., 1999, Durst Lobby Gallery, N.Y.C., 1999, Rosenthal Gallery at Rich Forum, Stamford, Conn., 2005; represented in permanent collections B'nai Brith Klutznick Nat. Jewish Mus., Washington, 1997. Decorator Easter Seal Home Svc. Charity Ball, 1976; bd. dirs. United Jewish Appeal, Westport, 1982-86; com. mem. Levitt Pavillion of the Performing Arts, Westport, 1982-89. Recipient award for creating the most beautiful working environment in an indsl. facility in lower Conn., Lower Conn. Mfrs. Assn., 1970. Mem.: LVW, Art Adv. Coun. Herbert F. Johnson Mus. Art at Cornell U. NY, Anti Defamation League, Nat. Coun. Jewish Women, Kappa Pi. Jewish. Avocations: tennis, swimming, race walking, gardening. Home: 15 Broadview Rd Westport CT 06880-2303 Office Phone: 203-226-8557. Business E-Mail: marlene@marlenesiff.com.

SIFTON, KAREN MARIE, mathematics professor; d. Wilbert Ray and Frances Alverda Sifton; m. Cecil Roger Hornsby, July 8, 1986. BS, Thiel Coll., Greenville, Pa, 1968; MEd, West Ga. Coll., Carrollton, 1998. Cert. 500-Hour Yoga Teacher Yoga Alliance, 2000. With Social Security Adminstrn., Atlanta, 1968—79, dep. regional commr., 1979—81; math instr. U. West Ga., Carrollton, Ga., 1981—. Author: Energy, A Practical Guide to Personal Achievement, Health, and Transformation, 1998. V.p. and treas. Zachariah Found., Carrollton, Ga., 2004—06. Office: Univ W Ga Maple St Carrollton GA 30118 Office Phone: 678-839-0696. E-mail: ksifton@westga.edu.

SIGAL, JILL L., federal agency administrator; BA, Vermont U.; JD, George Washington U. Advisor office of gen. counsel Dept. of Energy; pres. Jill Sigal Assocs.; dep. asst. sec. for environ. and sci. Office Congl. and Intergovernmental Affairs US Dept. Energy, 2003—04, prin. dep. asst. sec., 2004—05, acting asst. sec., 2005, asst. sec., 2005—. Office: US Dept Energy Forrestal Bldg 1000 Independence Ave SW Rm 7B-138 Washington DC 20585 Office Phone: 202-586-5450.

SIGAL-IBSEN, ROSE, artist; b. Bucharest, Romania, Aug. 22; arrived in U.S., 1957; d. Joseph and Tilly (Eckstein) Cohen; m. Albert D. Sigal, Dec. 25, 1941 (dec. May 1970); 1 child, Daniel M.; m. Joseph Ibsen, Oct. 1973 Diploma, Fashion Inst. Technology, N.Y.C., 1978; Parson, Sch. of Design, N.Y.C., 1985—86; student, Koho Sch. of Sumi-E, N.Y.C., 1979—90, Zhejiang Acad. Fine Arts, China, 1990. Curator Metro N.Y. Chpt. of Sumi-E Soc., 1990—, v.p., 1990—. One-woman shows include China-Gallery Weizhi Schubert, Hanover, Germany, 1991, Manhattan Savs. Bank, N.Y.C., 1993—94, Chem. Bank, 1993—95, N.Y. Pub. Libr., 1996, Bankers Fed., N.Y.C., 1996, Rep. Bank for Savs., 1996, Roumanian Cultural Found., Bucharest, 1998, World Fine Art Gallery, N.Y.C., 1998, Romanian Embassy, Washington, 2000, Berkeley Coll. Gallery, 2006, others, numerous group shows including most recently, exhibited in group shows at Broome St. Gallery, NYC, 2001—02, 2005—06, Sumi-e Soc. Am. Inc. at Courthouse Galleries of Portsmouth Va., 2001 (Hallie Hazen Meml. award, 2001), Pen and Brush Ann. Mixed Media, 2002, Korean Cultural Ctr., L.A., 2002, Japanese Artists Assn. N.Y., 2002, Mobile Mus. Art, 2004, NY Hall of Sci., 2005, Hammond Mus., 2005, Keith and Janet Kelly U. Art Gallery, Calif. State Poly. U., Pomona, 2005, Courage Card design, 1998. Recipient Manhattan Arts award Cover Art Competition, N.Y.C., 1992, 94, 95, 97, King Point award, Fla., 1991, Tenth Japanese Internat. Calligraphy Exhbn. award, N.Y.C., 1996, Manhattan Arts Internat. Showcase award, Emily N. Hatch Meml. award Pen and Brush, Inc., Spring Watercolor Exhbn., 1998, Hallie Hazen Meml. award Sumi-e Soc. Am., Inc., 2001. Mem. Nat. Mus. of Women in the Arts, Artist Equity of N.Y., Am. Soc. Contemporary Artists, Art of Ink in Am., The Oriental Brushwork Soc. of Am., Sumi-e Soc. (hon.). Avocations: sculptor in clay, dance. Home: One Irving Pl Apt 2-22B New York NY 10003-9741

SIGLER, JAMIE-LYNN, actress; b. Jericho, NY, May 15, 1981; m. A.J. DiScala (separated). Student, NYU. Actor: (films) A Brooklyn State of Mind, 1997, Campfire Stories, 2001, Death of a Dynasty, 2003; (TV films) Call Me: The Rise and Fall of Heidi Fleiss, 2004; (TV series) The Sopranos, 1999—; (Broadway plays) Beauty and the Beast, 2002—03; singer: (albums) Here to Heaven, 2001; author: (autobiography) Wise Girl, 2002. Achievements include started acting at NY regional theaters; starred in over two dozen theatrical prodns. including Annie, The Wizard of Oz, The Sound of Music, The Wiz, and Gypsy.

SIGMOND, CAROL ANN, lawyer; b. Phila., Jan. 9, 1951; d. Irwin and Mary Florence (Vollmer) S. BA, Grinnell Coll., 1972; JD, Cath. U., 1975. Bar: Va. 1975, D.C. 1980, Md. 1988, N.Y. 1990, U.S. Dist. Ct. (ea. dist.) Va. 1975, U.S. Dist. Ct. (so. and ea. dist.) N.Y. 1991, U.S. Ct. Appeals (4th cir.) 1976, U.S. Ct. Appeals (fed. cir.) 1987, U.S. Ct. Appeals (2d cir.) 2000, Fed. Claims Ct. 2002, Ct. Internat. Trade 2006. Asst. gen. counsel Washington Met. Area Transit Authority, 1978-85; acting assoc. gen. counsel for appeals and gen. law, 1985-86; assoc. Patterson, Belknap, Webb & Tyler, Washington, 1986-89, Berman, Paley, Goldstein & Kannry, NYC, 1991—93; prin. Law Offices of Carol A. Sigmond, NYC, 1993—97; of counsel Pollack & Greene, LLP, NYC, 1998—2000; pvt. practice NYC, 2000—03; ptnr. Kehl, Katzive, & Sigmond, NYC, 2004—05, Dunnington, Bartholomew & Miller, LLP, NYC, 2005—. Mem. ABA, D.C. Bar Assn., Assn. Bar City N.Y., N.Y. County Lawyers Assn., Women's Nat. Dem. Club. Democrat. Mem. Lds Ch. Avocations: piano, bridge. Office: Dunnington Bartholow & Miller LLP 477 Madison Ave 12th Fl New York NY 10022 Office Phone: 212-682-8811. Business E-Mail: csigmond@dunnington.com.

SIGMUND, DIANE WEISS, judge; b. NYC, Mar. 1, 1943; BS, Pa. State U., 1963; JD magna cum laude, Temple U., 1977. Bar: Pa. 1977. Atty. Blank, Rome, Cominsky & McCauley, Phila.; judge U.S. Bankruptcy Ct. (Pa. ea. dist.), 3rd circuit, Phila., 1993—, chief judge, 2004—. Mem. steering com. Ea. Dist. Pa. Bankruptcy Conf., 1995—, 3d Cir. Task Force Equal Treatment in Cts., Gender Commn., 1995-97; chmn. endowment edn. Nat. Conf. Bankruptcy Judges., 1996—, bd. govs., 1998-2002; mem. com. on automation and tech. Jud. Conf. U.S., 1997-2004. Fellow Am. Coll. Bankruptcy. Office: Robert NC Nix Courthouse 900 Market St Rm 203 Philadelphia PA 19107-4237

SIKANDER, SHAHZIA, artist; b. Lahore, Pakistan, 1969; BFA, Nat. Coll. Arts, Lahore, Pakistan, 1992; MFA, RISD, Providence, 1995. Artist-in-residence Otis Coll. Art and Design, LA, 2005. Work represented in numerous newspapers and mags., represented in solo and group exhibitions at MoMA, NY, Hirshhorn Mus. and Sculpture Garden, Nat. Gallery Canada, Musée d'Art moderne de la Ville de Paris, one-woman shows include Barbara Davis Gallery, Houston, 1996, Hosfelt Gallery, San Francisco, 1997, Deitch Project, N.Y.C., 1997, Renaissance Soc. U. Chgo., 1998, Kemper Mus. Contemporary Art and Design, Kansas City, Mo., 1998—88, Hirshhorn Mus., Washington, 1999, exhibited in group shows at Rhotas Gallery, Islamabad, Pakistan, 1992, Pacific Asia Mus., Pasadena, Calif., 1994—95, Bradford (Eng.) City Mus., 1996, Glassell Sch. Art Mus. Fine Arts, 1996, 1997, Laing Gallery, Newcastle, Eng., 1997, Whitney Mus. Am. Art, 1997, Queens Mus. Art, Flushing Meadows, N.Y., 1997, Yerba Buena Gardens Ctr. Arts, San Francisco, Forum for Contemporary Art, St. Louis, 1998, Bard Coll., Annandale-on-Hudson, N.Y., 1998, Ludwig (Austria) Mus., 1998, Aldrich Mus. Contemporary Art, Conn., 1998, also exhbns. in Portugal, Johannesburg, South Africa, Mexico City, Drawing to Drawing, Hosfelt Gallery, 2003, Vancouver Art Gallery, 2003, Venice Biennale, 2005, Queens Mus. Art, 2006. Recipient Haji Sharif award for miniature painting, Shakik Ali award and Kipling award, Nat. Coll. Art, Lahore, 1993; grad. fellow, RISD, 1993—95, core program fellow, Glassel Sch. Art Mus. Fine Arts, Houston, 1995—97, grantee, Louis Comfort Tiffany Found., 1997, Joan Mitchell grantee, 1998—99, MacArthur Fellow, John D. and Catherine T. MacArthur Found., 2006. Address: care Deitch Projects 76 Grand St New York NY 10013-2220*

SIKES, CYNTHIA LEE, actress, children's advocate, singer; b. Coffeyville, Kans., Jan. 2, 1954; d. Neil and Pat (Scott) S.; m. Alan Bud Yorkin, June 24, 1989. Student, Am. Conservatory Theater, San Francisco, 1977-79. Actor: (TV series) St. Elsewhere, 1981—83, L.A. Law, 1989, JAG, 2000—01, (TV movies) Oceans of Fire, 1986, His Mistress, 1990; prodr., actor: Sins of Silence, 1996; actor: (films) Man Who Loved Women, That's Life, Arthur on the Rocks, Love Hurts, 1988, Possums, 1998, Going Shopping, 2005, (Broadway musical) Into the Woods, 1988—89. Active Hollywood Women's Polit. Com.; apptd. Pres. Clinton's Adv. Com. on Arts John F. Kennedy Ctr. for Performing Arts, 1999; apptd. commr. Calif. Svc. Corps, 2005—. Recipient Gov.'s Medal of Merit, Kans., 1986. Democrat. Avocations: hiking, writing, reading.

SIKORA, BARBARA JEAN, library director; b. Passaic, NJ, Apr. 12, 1943; d. Stanley Francis and Jean (Sobczyk) S. BA in Edn., English, William Paterson Coll., 1969, MEd in Learning Disabilities, 1978; MLS, Rutgers U., 1978; Cert. in Fundraising Mgmt., Fairleigh Dickinson U., 1990. Profl. libr. N.J. Tchr. Clifton (N.J.) Pub. Schs., 1969-73; office mgr. Singer/TRW, Fairfield, NJ, 1974-76; prin. libr. Passaic Pub. Libr., 1978-88; asst. libr. dir. Pub. Libr. Livingston, NJ, 1989-90, libr. dir., 1991—. Adj. faculty William Paterson Coll., 1977-90; trustee Wayne Pub. Libr., 1986-88; bd. dirs. Polish and Slavic Fed. Credit Union, 1999—. Mem. Polish Heritage Festival Com., Holmdel, N.J., 1987—, gen. chmn., 1999; trustee, bd. dirs. Livingston Area C. of C., 1998—; pres. Libr. Pub. Rels. Coun., 1997; West Essex br. YMCA of the Oranges, 1997—; mem. Polish Children's Heartline, Inc. Grantee U.S. Dept. Edn. libr. literacy program, 1987, N.J. State Libr. Leadership Inst., 1988, Christopher Leadership Inst., 1997; Paul Harris fellow Rotary Internat., 1999. Mem. ALA (ethics com. 1995-99), AAUW, N.J. Libr. Assn., Nat. Spkrs.' Assn., Rotary (pres. Livingston chpt. 1994-96, 2000), Rutgers Sch. Comm. and Info. Libr. Studies Alumni Assn. (pres. 1991-94), Beta Phi Mu. Avocation: writing. Home: The Mill 300 Main St Apt 314 Little Falls NJ 07424-1359 Office: Pub Libr Livingston 10 Robert Harp Dr Livingston NJ 07039 E-mail: sikora@bcols.org.

SIKORA, DIANA MARIE, elementary school educator; b. St. Louis, June 13, 1945; d. Roy K. and Margaret Anne (Heffner) Hennen; m. Theodore George Sikora, Nov. 12, 1966; children: Christine Ann Fix, Elizabeth Jane Pritchard. BS in Edn., So. Ill. U., Edwardsville, 1967; MEd in Counseling, U. Mo., St. Louis, 1996. Cert. counseling Mo. Tchr. grade 1 Commons Lane Sch. Ferguson Florissant Sch. Dist., Florissant, Mo., 1967—69; tchr. grade 2-3 Graham Sch. Ferguson Florissant Sch. Dist., 1971—74; tchr. St. Ferdinand Cath. Sch., 1974—86, Ferguson Mid. Sch. Ferguson Florissant Sch. Dist., Ferguson, 1986—92; tchr. Vogt grade 4-5 Ferguson Florissant Sch. Dist., 1992—99; guidance counselor grades k-6 Halls Ferry Sch. Ferguson Florissant Sch. Dist., Florissant, 1999—. Supt. Salem Sunday Sch., 2000—. Named Bldg. Tchr. of Yr., Graham Sch., 1973, Ferguson Mid. Sch., 1989. Mem.: Chi Iota, Alpha Delta Kappa (chaplain 1999). Avocations: singing, nature, reading. Home: 1800 Layven Ave Florissant MO 63031 Office Phone: 314-831-1023 ext. 1500. Personal E-mail: dsikora@mindspring.com.

SIKORA, GLORIA JEAN, social studies educator, department chairman; d. Joseph Anthony and Margaret Julia Di Marco; m. David John Sikora, June 29, 1963; children: Craig Joseph, Dean David. BE, Ind. U., Pa., 1963. Tchr. West Mifflin Area Schs., West Mifflin, Pa., 1963—69, James Lavelle Sch., West Mifflin, Pa., Campus Sch. Carlow U., Pitts., 1987—. Mem.: Assn. for Supr. amd Cirriculm Devel., Pa. Coun. for the Social Studies, Nat. Coun. for the Social Studies. Office: Campus Sch Carlow U 3333 Fifth Ave Pittsburgh PA 15213 Business E-Mail: sikoragj@carlow.edu.

SIKORA, ROSANNA DAWN, emergency physician, educator; b. Weirton, W.Va., Nov. 16, 1955; d. Edward and Dorothy Ann (Wade) S.; m. Odus E. Brown, Nov. 25, 1994; stepchildren: Aza, Katherine, Hannah. AB in Biology, W.Va. U., 1978, MD, 1982. Cert. in emergency medicine; cert. in pediats., specialty in pediat. emergency medicine; cert. in internal medicine. Resident in pediat. internal medicine W.Va. U. Hosps. Inc., Morgantown, 1982-86, with. Assoc. prof. emergency medicine, pediats., internal medicine W.Va. U. Sch. Medicine, 1996—; mem. pediat. advanced life support subcom. Am. Heart Assn., Charleston, 1987-97, mem. pediat. advanced life support affiliate faculty, 1987-97. Physician men's/women's varsity swim/diving team W.Va. U., Morgantown, 1994—. Fellow Am. Coll. Emergency Physicians (bd. dirs. 1990—, sec.-treas. 1995-96, v.p. 1996-97, pres.-elect 1997-98); mem. AMA, ACP, Am. Acad. Pediats., Alpha Omega Alpha. Democrat. Roman Catholic. Office: W Va U Dept Emergency Medicine PO Box 9149 Morgantown WV 26506-9149

SIKULA, CHRISTINE LYNN, legal association administrator, education educator; b. Detroit, Aug. 30, 1957; d. Robert Lee and Patricia Ann Sabine; m. Otto Sikula, June 27, 1976. BA summa cum laude, Wayne State U., Detroit, 1991, MA Speech Comm., 1997. Legal adminstr. Charfoos & Christensen, P.C., Detroit, 1997—; adj. prof. Baker Coll., Clinton Twp., Mich., 1998—. Paralegal adv. bd. mem. Baker Coll., Clinton Twp., Mich., 2004—; legal sec. adv. bd. mem. Warren Consol. Sch. Dist. Career Preparation Ctr., Warren, Mich., 1989—99. Guest spkr. Oakland C.C. Ctr. for Displaced Workers, Pontiac, Mich., 1993—93, Exploring Divsn. of Detroit Area Coun., Detroit, Mich., 1990—90, Warren Consol. Sch. Dist. Career Preparation Ctr., Warren, Mich., 1986—87; tour guide Preservation Wayne Hist. Soc., Detroit, Mich., 1992—93. Recipient, Nat. Dean's List, 1985-1986. Mem.: Assn. of Legal Adminstrs., Detroit Chpt., Pub. Rels. Student Soc. of Am., Golden Key. Roman Cath. Avocations: travel, reading, bicycling. Office: Charfoos & Christensen PC 5510 Woodward Ave Detroit MI 48202 Office Phone: 313-875-8080.

SILA, CATHY ANN, neurologist; b. Cleve., Apr. 21, 1955; d. Andrew Lee and Mary Florence (Patrick) S.; m. Gene H. Barnett, Dec. 9, 1990; children: Austin Andrew, Addison Edgar. BA Chemistry, Zoology summa cum laude, Miami U., 1977; MD, Case Western Res. Sch. Med., 1981. Intern, resident in neurology Cleve. Clinic, 1981-83; resident in neurology Mayo Clinic, Rochester, Minn., 1983-85; rsch. fellow in cerebrovascular rsch. studies Cleve. Clinic, 1985-86; assoc. med. dir. cerebrovascular ctr. Cleve. Clin. Found., 1987—. Examiner Am. Bd. Psychiatry and Neurology, 1987—; mem. expert panel Agy. for Health Care Policy and Rsch., 1995-96; presenter in field; mem. stroke adv. bd. several pharm. firms; clin. events com. mem. multiple clin. trials; chmn. clin. events com. Abest9; mem. adv. bd. Nat. Women's Health Resource Ctr. Mem. editl. bd. Stroke, Jour. Stroke and Cerebrovascular Disease, Jour. Thrombosis and Thrombolysis, Cleve. Clinic Jour. Medicine; contbr. articles to profl. jours., chpts. to books. Mem. adv. bd. Astra-Zeneca Stroke Specialists; mem. BMS-Sanofi Stroke Adv. Bd. Fellow Am. Heart Assn. (brain-stroke peer rev. com. 1998-2001, women and minorities com. 1993-95, operaton stroke med. subcom. 1999—, sci. programs com. 1999-2000, sci. programs com. 2001-), Am. Acad. Neurology (editl. panel Brain Matters Stroke Initiative 1997-98, exec. com. Vascular Neurology section, quality stds. subcom. 1989-98); mem. AMA (name bank for divsn. rsch. grants 1995—, cons. file project 1996—), Nat. Stroke Assn., Internat. Stroke Soc., Phi Kappa Phi. Office: Cleve Clinic Found S91 9500 Euclid Ave Cleveland OH 44195-0001 E-mail: silac@ccf.org.

SILAGI, BARBARA WEIBLER, corporate officer; b. Chgo., June 26, 1930; d. Carleton Thomas and Catherine Josephine (Wolph) Weibler; m. Joseph Edward Sturgulewski (Sturgus), Feb. 12, 1953 (div. Aug. 1954); 1 child, Mariann Catherine; m. John Louis Silagi, Jr., July 2, 1960 (div. July 1968). BM in Edn., Northwestern U., 1958; MS in Edn., No. Ill. U., 1965. Cert. K-14 supervisory teaching, spl. edn. tchr., airline transport pilot, FAA dispatcher. Elem. sch. tchr. St. Mary's Sch., Chgo., 1947-49, Kingman, Ariz., 1949-52; legal sec. Judge Edward J. Mahoney, Quincy, Ill., 1954-55; elem. sch. tchr. C.M. Bardwell Sch., Aurora, Ill., 1955-76; flight instr. flight schs. Chgo., Aurora and Frankfort, Ill., Clinton, Iowa, 1970-77; aircraft dispatcher Transcontinental Airlines, Zantop Internat. Airlines, Ypsilanti, Mich., 1977-81; airline pilot Mannion Air Charter, Ypsilanti, 1977-80; head night auditor Howard Johnson, Quality Inn, Travelodge, BestWestern, others, Ocala, Fla., Silver Springs, Fla., 1983-87; sec.-treas. Diamond Design Svcs., Inc., Ocklawaha, Fla., 1985—. Pub. Forest Shopper, Springs Shopper, Belle Shopper. Author: Dispatch Training, 1989; editor tng. manuals, 1977-85. Violist Chgo. Suburban Symphony, Naperville, Ill., 1956-60; contralto Palestrina A capella Choir, Aurora, Ill., 1956-60; life mem. Ill. PTA, Aurora, 1974—; apptd. vice chmn. adv. bd. Dunellon Airport and Indsl. Park, 1992-96. Recipient 1st place Suburban Aviation Assn., Chgo., 1975, 5th place Illi-Nines Air Derby, Chgo., Moline, Ill., 1973, 2d place Leg prize Powder Puff Derby, McLean to Lincoln, Nebr., 1971; Eckstein scholar Northwestern U., 1952; inducted into Internat. Forest of Friendship, 2006. Mem. AAUW (life), NEA (life), Ill. Edn. Assn., Ninety Nines Internat. (life), Illi-Nines Air Derby (handicap chmn. 1972-76, air marking chmn. 99's Chgo. chpt. 1972-76, corr. sec. Chgo. chpt. 1976-77, 1st pl. achievement awards 1972-78), Pi Lambda Theta (charter, life, rsch. chmn. Beta Delta chpt. 1962-63). Roman Catholic. Avocations: needlecrafts, gardening, reading, music. Home: 6305 SE 158th Ct Ocklawaha FL 32179-2988 Office: Diamond Design Svcs Inc PO Box 186 Ocklawaha FL 32183-0186

SILAK, CATHY R., lawyer, former state supreme court justice; b. Astoria, NY, May 25, 1950; d. Michael John and Rose Marie (Janor) S.; m. Nicholas G. Miller, Aug. 9, 1980; 3 children. BA, NYU, 1971; M in City Planning, Harvard U., 1973; JD, U. Calif., 1976. Bar: Calif. 1977, U.S. Dist. Ct. (no. dist.) Calif. 1977, D.C. 1979, U.S. Ct. Appeals (D.C. cir.) 1979, U.S. Dist. Ct. (so. dist.) N.Y. 1980, Idaho 1983, U.S. Dist. Ct. Idaho 1983, U.S. Ct. Appeals (2nd cir.) 1983, U.S. Ct. Appeals (9th cir.) 1985. Law clk. to Hon. William W. Schwarzer U.S. Dist. Ct. (no dist.), Calif., 1976-77; pvt. practice San Francisco, 1977-79, Washington, 1979-80; asst. U.S. atty. So. Dist. of N.Y., 1980-83; spl. asst. U.S. atty. Dist. of Idaho, 1983-84; pvt. practice Boise, Idaho, 1984-90; judge Idaho Ct. Appeals, 1990-93; justice Idaho Supreme Ct., Boise, 1993—2000; ptnr. Hawley, Troxell, Ennis, and Hawley, 2001—. Assoc. gen. counsel Morrison Knudsen Corp., 1989-90; mem. fairness com. Idaho Supreme Ct. and Gov.'s Task Force on Alternative Dispute Resolution; instr. and lectr. in field. Assoc. note and comment editor Calif. Law Rev., 1975-76. Land use planner Mass. Dept. Natural Resources, 1973; founder Idaho Coalition for Adult Literacy; bd. dirs. Literacy Lab., Inc.; mem. adv. bd. Boise State U. Legal Asst. Program. Recipient Jouce Stein award Boise YWCA, 1992, Women Helping Women award Soroptimist, Boise, 1993. Fellow Idaho Law Found (ann., lectr.); mem. ABA (rat. conf. state trial judges jud. adminstrn. divsn.), Nat. Assn. Women Judges, Idaho State Bar (corp./securities sect., instr.), Am. Law Inst., Fellows of the Am. Bar Found, Am. Judicature Soc. (bd. dirs.). Office: Hawley Troxell Ennis & Hawley PO Box 1617 Boise ID 83702-1617

SILBERBERG, INGA, dermatologist; b. Kassel, Germany, Sept. 16, 1934; arrived in U.S., 1938; d. Willi and Erna (Rosenbaum) S.; m. Herbert M. Sinakin, Feb. 16, 1969; 1 child, William Elias. BA, Hunter Coll., 1955; MD, SUNY, 1959; MS in Dermatology, NYU, 1965. Diplomate Am. Bd. Dermatologists, 1964. Instr., clin. dermatology NYU Med. Ctr., N.Y.C., 1963-65, clin. asst. prof., 1965-66, asst. prof. dermatology, 1966-71, clin. assoc. prof. dermatology, 1971-76; cons., dermatology Newcomb Hosp., Vineland, N.J., 1975-98. Recipient Henry Silver award Dermatologic Soc. Greater N.Y., 1962, 65, Dermatology Found. Discovery award, 1993, Dr. Rose Hirschler award Women's Dermatologic Soc., 1999; Jonas Salk scholar, City of N.Y., 1955-59. Fellow Am. Acad. Dermatology; mem. AMA. E-mail: hmsina@aol.com.

SILBERG, LOUISE BARBARA, physician, anesthesiologist; b. Bklyn., Apr. 13, 1958; m. David J. Lazar. BA, Rutgers U., 1981; MS, Seton Hall U., 1986; DO, U. Health Scis., 1990. Diplomate Am. Bd. Anesthesia. Intern Union (N.J.) Hosp., 1990-91; resident in anesthesiology Albany (N.Y.) Med. Ctr., 1991-94, fellow in obstet. anesthesiology, 1994-95; anesthesiologist Anesthesia Consultants Assocs., El Paso, Tex., 1995—. Chair dept. anesthesia, Providence Meml. Hosp., El Paso, 1998—. Bd. dirs. El Paso Symphony Chorale, 1996—; mem. Nat. Coun. Jewish Women, 1996—. Mem. AMA, Am. Soc. Anesthesiologists, Soc. Obstet. Anesthesia and Perinatology. Office: Anesthesia Consultants Assoc 2400 N Oregon St Ste D El Paso TX 79902-3135

SILBERGELD, ELLEN KOVNER, epidemiologist, researcher, toxicologist; b. Washington, July 29, 1945; d. Joseph and Mary (Gion) Kovner; m. Alan Mark Silbergeld, 1969; children: Sophia, Nicholas. AB, Vassar Coll., 1967; PhD, Johns Hopkins U., 1972. Kennedy fellow Johns Hopkins Med. Sch., Balt., 1974—75; scientist NIH, Bethesda, Md., 1975—81; chief toxics scientist Environ. Def. Fund, Washington, 1982—90; prof. epidemiology, toxicology and pharmacology U.Md., Balt., 1990—2001, affil. prof. environ. law, 1990—2001, dir. program in human health and environ., 1996—2000, prof. dept. pathology, 1995—2000, adj. prof. dept. pharmacology and exptl. therapeutics, 1995—2000; prof. environ. health scis. epidemiology, and health policy and mgmt. Bloomberg School Public Health, Johns Hopkins U., Balt., 2001—. Mem. sci. adv. bd. EPA, 1983—89, 1993—99, Dept. Energy, 1994—95; mem. bd. on environ. sci. and toxicology NAS-NRC, 1983—89; mem. Com. Geosci. Environ. and Resources, 1994—98; mem. bd. biotech. and agr., 1999—2004; mem. bd. sci. councellors Nat. Inst. Environ. Health Scis., 1987—93; cons. Oil and Chem. Atomic Workers, 1970, NSF, 1974—75, OECD, 1987—90. Mem. editl. bd.: Neurobehavioral Toxicology, 1979—87, Am. Jour. Medicine, 1980—, Neurotoxicology, 1981—86, Environ. Rsch., 1983—, editor-in-chief:, 1994—. Mem. Homewood Friends Meeting. Recipient Wolman award, Md. Pub. Health Assn., 1991, Barsky award, APHA, 1992, Md. Gov. Excellence citation, 1990, 1993; Fulbright fellow, London, 1967, Woodrow Wilson and Danforth fellow, 1967, NAS Exch. fellow, Yugoslavia, 1976, MacArthur Found. fellow, 1993—98, Baldwin scholar, Coll. Notre Dame. Mem.: APHA, AAAS, Soc. for Neurosci., Soc. Toxicology, Soc. for Occupl. and Environ. Health (sec.-treas. 1983—85, pres. 1987—89), Am. Soc. Tropical Med. Hygiene, Collegium Ramazzini (councillor), Phi Beta Kappa. Office: Bloomberg Sch Pub Health 615 N Wolfe St Baltimore MD 21205

SILBERMAN, LINDA JOY, law educator; b. 1944. BA, U. Mich., 1965, JD, 1968. Bar: Ill. 1969. Fulbright scholar U. London, 1968-69; assoc. Sonnenschein, Levinson, Carlin, Nath & Rosenthal, 1969-71; asst. prof. law NYU Sch. Law, 1971-74, assoc. prof., 1974-77, prof., 1977—, now Martin Lipton prof. law, assoc. dir. Inst. Jud. Adminstrn., 1991-95; vis. prof., U. Pa., 1981, 1984-85, Columbia U., 1982-83, prof.-in-residence appellate staff, Dept. Justice, 1985-86; cons. NY Law Revision Commn., 1983-85, Hague Conv. Civic Aspects Internat. Child Abduction. Mem. Am. Law Inst, Order of Coif. Author: Non-Attorney Justice in the United States, 1979; co-author: (with Foster & Freed) Family Law: Cases and Materials, 1977; contbr. articles to legal journals. Achievements: first woman to receive full-time tenure track appt. and first woman to be tenured a full professor at NYU Sch. Law. Office: NYU Sch Law Vanderbilt Hall Rm 339 40 Washington Sq S New York NY 10012-1099 Office Phone: 212-998-6204. E-mail: silberml@juris.law.nyu.edu.

SILBERSTEIN, ALLEGRA JOSTAD, retired elementary school educator; b. Holmen, Wis., Dec. 4, 1930; d. Ray and Esther Jostad; children: Dawn Abigail, Maia Naomi, Eden Anne. Grad. with distinction, LaCrosse State Coll., 1950; BA in Speech and Dramatic Art, U. Iowa, 1957. Cert. adminstr., reading specialist Wis. Elem. tchr. Mindoro (Wis.) Sch., 1955—56, Lauderdale Lake Sch., Elkhorn, Wis., 1951—53, Holmen (Wis.) Area Schs., 1950—51, NYC Schs., 1960—63, Pioneer and North Davis Schs., Davis, Calif., 1977—80; reading specialist Birchland Elem. Sch., Davis, 1980—95; ret., 1995. Author: (poetry) Acceptance, 1999, In the Folds, 2005; contbr. poetry to lit. publs. Vol. Sacramento Food Bank, 2001—; mem. Sacramento U. Chorus, 2000—02; leader liturgical dance group Unitarian Ch., Davis, 2000—06. Mem.: Calif. State Poetry Soc., Ina Coolbrith Cir. Home: 1248 Drummond S Davis CA 95618 E-mail: allegras@dcn.org.

SILER, VIRGINIA CARLISLE, retired elementary school educator; d. Stanley Gordon and Jane Carlisle Volbrecht; m. David Colin Beckman, July 31, 1990;; children: Scott Q., Christina Carlisle. BA, U. Pacific, 1975, cert. in Tchg., 1985. Tchr. Stockton (Calif.) Unified Sch. Dist., 1986—97, 2001—04, ret., 2004. Counselor gang determent City Lodi, Calif., 2000. Avocations: gardening, fishing, camping. Home: 215 Donner Dr Lodi CA 95240-0668

SILL, LINDA DEHART, science educator; d. William and Helen DeHart; m. Wayne R. Sill; children: Amy Tobey, Karyn Francois. BEd, Wagner Coll., S.I., 1970; MEd, SUNY, Stony Brook, 1975. Tchr. sci. and tech. grade 6 Mt. Sinai Mid. Sch., NY, 1970—. Drama advisor Mt. Sinai Mid. Sch. Drama Club, 1970—. Involved with preservation and adoption of area beaches Mt. Sinai Sch. Dist., 1999—; involved with breast cancer awareness Fortunato Breast Ctr., Port Jefferson, NY. Grantee, Mideast Suffolk Tchr. Ctr., 1982, 1983, 1984. Mem.: N.Y. State United Tchrs. (assoc.). Avocations: theater, travel, music. Office: Mt Sinai Mid Sch North Country Rd Mount Sinai NY 11766 Office Phone: 631-870-2700. Business E-Mail: lsill@mtsinai.k12.ny.us.

SILL, MELANIE, editor; m. Bennett Groshong. Grad. in journalism, U. N.C., 1981. Mng. editor, 1998; asst. metro editor, 1988; with The Transylvania Times, Brevard, NC, United Press Internat., Raleigh; project editor Boss Hog; exec. editor, sr. v.p. The News & Observer, Raleigh, NC, 2002—. Recipient Pulitzer prize, Boss Hog, 1996; fellow Nieman, Harvard U., 1993—94. Office: 215 S McDowell St Raleigh NC 27601

SILLER, PAMELA PEARL, psychiatrist; b. NY, Sept. 1, 1977; d. Joseph Jacob and Beverly Joan Siller. BA, Bklyn. Coll., Bklyn., 1999; MD, Downstate Med. Sch., Bklyn., 2003. Resident in psychiatry North Shore U. Hosp., Manhasset, NY, 2003—06, chief resident in psychiatry, 2006—. Grantee Phizer grant for Edn., NY, 2003. Office: N Shore Univ Hosp 400 Cmty Dr Manhasset NY 11030

SILLMAN, AMY, painter, art educator; b. Oct. 1955; Student, Beloit Coll., NYU; BFA, Sch. Visual Arts, Manhattan; MFA, Bard Coll. Milton Avery prof. arts, faculty Milton Avery Grad. Sch. Arts, Bard Coll., 1996—. One-man shows include Brent Sikkema Gallery, 2000, exhibitions include Casey Kaplan Gallery, Manhattan, N.Y., 1996, 1998, White Columns, 1996, Postmasters Gallery, N.Y.C., 1997, Sixth@Prince Fine Art, 1999, Exit Art, 2000, Whitney Biennial, Whitney Mus. Am. Art, NY, 2004. Recipient Tiffany Found. award, 1999—2000; Guggenheim fellow, 2001—02. Personal E-mail: amyfelix@aol.com.

SILLMAN, DENISE MARIE, music educator, small business owner; b. Wooster, Ohio, Dec. 17, 1964; d. Carol Ann Kauffman; m. Dana Alan Sillman, Oct. 27, 2001; children: Felicia, Zach. BS in Elem. Edn., Ashland U., Ohio, 1987. Band dir., music tchr. Green Local Schs., Smithville, Ohio, 1989—, after-sch. tutor, 2004—. Musical dir. Greene Mid. Sch. Drama, Smithville, Ohio, 2001—. Mem. Ctrl. Fire Aux., Smithville, 2001—; dir. ch. choir Smithville Brethren Ch., 1999—. Mem.: Ohio Edn. Assn., Ohio Music Edn. Assn., Music Edn. Nat. Conf. Brethren. Avocations: reading, travel, crafts, flower and vegetable gardening. Home: 334 E Prospect St Smithville OH 44677 Office Phone: 330-669-9109. E-mail: danetrain940@sssnet.com.

SILLMAN, EDLYNNE MINA, caseworker, consultant; b. Bklyn., July 25, 1943; d. Israel and Frances L. (Katz) S. BS, N.Y.U., 1965; MA, Bklyn. Coll., 1968; certificate Mediation, Ill. Psychol. Inst., 1985. Licensed realtor, Ill. Tchr. art Lefferts Jr. High Sch., Bklyn., 1965-69, Ridge High Sch., Basking Ridge, N.J., 1969-72; tchr. art history Middlesex City Jr. Coll., Edison, N.J., 1973; owner, mgr. Edlynne and Friends Inc., New Brunswick, N.J., 1972-73; instr. travel and sales Wal-Mar Hobby Distbr., Boston, 1973-74; mgr. sales Halperin Galleries, Chgo., 1975; instr., salesperson Lanier Bus. Systems, Chgo., 1974-76; with real estate sales Kaplan Real Estate, Chgo., 1977-79; caseworker Dept. Supportive Services Cook County, Chgo., 1979—; owner Sillman Advt. Design, Chgo., 1985-88; loan originator Attys. Nat. Mortgage Network Inc., Chgo., 1987-88, Gt. Chgo. Mortgage, 1988-90; salesperson Daniel & Assocs., 1988—, Lincoln Mortgage and Funding, 1990-95; ret., 2003. Playbill designer Victory Gardens Benefit, Chgo., 1986-89. Asst. pub. Key Line and Design Mag., 1985-86. Vol. Chgo. Symphony Marathon, 1987. Mem. NAFE, HAKAFA (sec. 1989-90), Women's Advt. Chgo. (edn. com. 1985-88, pub. svc. com. 1985-88), Bklyn. Coll. Alumni Assn. Chgo. chpt. (pres. 1981-84, co-chmn. 1988-90), Am. Adoption Congress, Assn. Family Cts. and Conciliators. Democrat. Jewish. Home: 7667 W Cathedral Canyon Dr Tucson AZ 85743-5144

SILLS, BEVERLY (MRS. PETER B. GREENOUGH), performing company executive, singer; b. Bklyn., May 25, 1929; d. Morris and Sonia (Bahn) Silverman; m. Peter B. Greenough, 1956 (dec. Sept. 7, 2006); children: Meredith, Peter B.; stepchildren: Lindley, Nancy, Diana. Studied with Estelle Leibling, studied with Paolo Gallico, studied with Desire Defrere; doctorate (hon.), Harvard U., NYU, New Eng. Conservatory, Temple U.; degree (hon.), Harvard U., NYU, Calif. Inst. Arts. Gen. dir. N.Y.C. Opera, 1979-1989; pres. N.Y.C. Opera Bd., 1989-90; mng. dir. Met. Opera, N.Y.C., 1991-94; chairwoman Lincoln Ctr. for Performing Arts, Inc., N.Y.C., 1994—2002, Met. Opera, N.Y.C., 2002—05. Bd. dirs. Met. Opera, 1991-2005; cons. Nat. Coun. on Arts. Radio debut as Bubbles Silverman on Uncle Bob's Rainbow House, 1932; appeared on Major Bowes Capitol Family Hour, 1934-41, on Our Gal Sunday; toured with Shubert Tours, Charles Wagner Opera Co., 1950, 51; operatic debut Phila. Civic Opera, 1947; debut, N.Y.C. Opera Co. as Rosalinda in Die Fledermaus, 1955; debut San Francisco Opera, 1953; debut La Scala, Milan as Pamira in Siege of Corinth, 1969, Royal Opera, Covent Garden in Lucia di Lammermoor, London, 1971, Met. Opera, N.Y.C., 1975, Vienna State Opera, 1967, Teatro Fenice in La Traviata, Venice; appeared Teatro Colon, Buenos Aires; recital debut Paris, 1971, London Symphony Orch., 1971; appeared throughout U.S., Europe, S. Am. including Boston Symphony, Tanglewood Festival, 1968, 69, Robin Hood Dell, Phila., 1969; title roles in: Don Pasquale, Norma, Ballad of Baby Doe, Thais, La Traviata, Anna Bolena, Maria Stuarda, Lucia de Lammermoor, Barber of Seville, Manon, Louise, Tales of Hoffmann, Daughter of the Regiment, The Magic Flute, Elizabeth in Roberto Devereaux, I Puritana, Julius Caesar, Suor Angelica, Il Tabarro, Gianni Schicchi, Faust, La Loca, Merry Widow, Turk in Italy, Rigoletto, I Capuleti e I Montecchi, Lucrezia Borgia, Ariodante, Le Coq D'Or, others; recordings include The Art of Beverly Sills, Welcome to Vienna, Great Scores (with Placido Domingo); ret. from opera and concert stage, 1980; numerous TV spls; author: Bubbles:A Self-Portrait, 1976, Bubbles: An Encore, Beverly: An Autobiography. Active with March of Dimes, 1971- (Past chmn. bd., past nat. chmn. Mothers' March on Birth Defects); bd. dirs. Apollo Theatre Found., 1999-2001. Recipient Handel medallion, 1973, Pearl S. Buck Women's award, 1979, Emmy award for Profiles in Music, 1976, Emmy award for Lifestyles with Beverly Sills, 1978, Presdl. Medal of Freedom, 1980, Kennedy Ctr. Honors award, 1980, Heinz award in Arts and Humanities, 1995, Grammy award for Best Classical Vocal Soloist Performance, 1976, Best Opera Recording, 1978, Bess Wallace Truman award, March of Dimes, 1994, Juanita Kreps award, JC Penny Co., 1996, MS Hope award, Nat. Multiple Sclerosis Soc., 1998, Medal of the Order of Arts and Letters, Min. French Culture, 2000. Office: Met Opera Lincoln Ctr Performing Arts 140 W 65th St New York NY 10023

SILMAN, ROBERTA KARPEL, writer, critic; b. Bklyn., Dec. 29, 1934; d. Herman and Phoebe Karpel; m. Robert Silman, June 14, 1956; children: Miriam, Joshua, Ruth. BA, Cornell U., 1956; MFA, Sarah Lawrence Coll., 1975. Sec. Saturday Rev. Mag., N.Y.C., 1957, sci. writer, 1958—60; freelance fiction writer Ardsley, NY, 1961—. Author: Somebody Else's Child, 1976 (award Child Study Assn.), Blood Relations, 1977 (Hon. Mention Pen Hemingway prize, Hon. Mention Janet Kafka prize), (novels) Boundaries, 1979 (Hon. Mention Janet Kafka prize), The Dream Dredger, 1986, Beginning The World Again, 1990; contbr. numerous short stories to lit. publs., book reviews to newspapers. Mem. adv. coun. Coll. Arts & Scis. Cornell U. Fellow, Guggenheim Found., 1979—80, Nat. Endowment for Arts, 1982—83. Mem.: PEN, Poets and Writers, Authors Guild, Phi Beta Kappa. Democrat. Jewish. Avocations: piano, classical music, hiking, travel. Home: 18 Larchmont St Ardsley NY 10502 Office Phone: 914-693-2816. E-mail: r.silman@verizon.net.

SILSBY, PAULA D., prosecutor; b. Ellsworth, Maine, 1951; JD, U. Maine, 1976; BA, Mt. Holyoke Coll. Bar: Maine 1976. US atty. (dist. Maine) US Dept. Justice, Portland, 2001—. Fellow: Maine Bar Found. Office: US Attys Office 100 Middle St Ste 6 Portland ME 04101-4182*

SILVA, ALBERTINA, computer company executive; b. Providence, Feb. 23, 1964; d. Manuel R. and Mary P. Silva. BS in Bus. Adminstrn., Bryant Coll., 1986, MBA, 1992. Cert. PMP. Programmer Gen. Dynamics, Norwich, Conn., 1986-87; cons. Orbis, East Providence, R.I., 1987-88; mgr., cons. Early Cloud & Co., Middletown, R.I., 1988-96; project mgr. IBM, Middletown, 1996—. Ptnr. R.I. Sports Exch., Warwick. Mem. PMI.

SILVA, JOAN YVONNE, writer; b. Bloomfield, Nebr. d. Leslie and Rosamond (Stephens) Downie; m. Robert Silva, Mar. 28, 1950 (div. Aug. 1973); children: Diane, Robert, Gregory; m. Ralph M. Kniseley, Oct. 16, 1973. Student, U. Oreg., 1949-50, U. Tenn., 1963-66. Freelance writer, Oak Ridge, Tenn., 1958-73, Vienna, Austria, 1973-75, Emmett, Idaho, 1975—. Organizer Thursday Writers Group, Vienna, 1973-75. Author: Attila, 1976; editor, pub. (literary mag.) The Signal, 1987-92, Kreka-Barbarian Queen, 2000; contbr. articles, essays and poetry to profl. publs. Active Cmty. Rels. Coun., Oak Ridge; facilitator Mothers United Sexual Abuse Program, Boise; organizer, facilitator Women's Conciousness Raising Group, Boise and Emmett, 1990-94. Named Poet of the Yr., Idaho Writer's League, 1989. Mem. NOW, Nat. Writers Union, Nat. Writers Assn., Poets and Writers Inc. Democrat. Avocations: dog training, animal rights, travel, textiles. Address: 1118 W Outer Dr Oak Ridge TN 37830-8611

SILVA, MARY BARNES, retired elementary school educator; d. Walter Howard and Rosalinda M. Barnes. BS Edn., Kent State U., 1964; M Edn., U. Hawaii, 1976. Provisional Ohio, profl. Hawaii. Tchr. St. Louis Sch., Louisville, Ohio, 1960—62, Elyria Pub. Schs., Ohio, 1962—68, Kailua Elem., Hawaii, 1968—78, tchr. academically gifted and talented, 1978—88; tech. coord. Royal Sch., Honolulu, 1988—2001; ret., 2001. Adviser student coun., newspaper, yearbook Kailua Elem., 1979—88, chair grade level, 1975—78, Royal Sch., Honolulu, 1993—2001, chair sch. cmty.-based mgmt., 1994—99, sch. facilitator, 1995—99, tech. trainer, 1996—2001. Pres., vp., sec., treas. Assn. of Apt. Owners, Honolulu, 1979—2004. Named Tchr. of Yr., Honolulu Dist., 1997. Mem.: NEA (life), Hawaii State Ret. Tchrs. Assn., Hawaii Edn. Assn. (life), Contemporary Mus., Bishop Mus., Acad. Arts. Avocations: travel, the arts. Home: 410 Magellan Ave 808 Honolulu HI 96813 Personal E-mail: malia.aloha@hawaiiantel.net.

SILVA, OMEGA LOGAN, physician; b. Washington, Dec. 14, 1936; d. Louis Jasper and Ruth (Dickerson) Logan; m. C. Francis A. Silva, Oct. 25, 1958 (div. 1981); 1 child, Frances Cecile; m. Harold Bryant Webb, Nov. 28, 1982. BS cum laude with honors in chemistry, Howard U., Washington, 1958, MD, 1967. Bio-chemist NIH, Bethesda, Md., 1958-63; resident in medicine Vets. Affairs Med. Ctr., Washington, 1967—70, fellow in endocrinology, 1970—71, rsch. assoc., 1971—74, clin. investigator, 1974—77, asst. chief endocrinology, 1977-96, dir. diabetes clin., 1977—96; assoc. prof. medicine George Washington U., Washington, 1975-91; physician Mitchell-Trotman Med. Group, P.C., Washington, 1996-97; prof. George Washington U., Washington, 1991-98, prof. emeritus, 1999—; prof. Howard U., Washington, 1977-96. Mem. exec. com. Health Care Coun. Nat. Capital Area, 1995—, bd. dirs.; med. rev. officer Employee Health Programs, Bethesda, 1998-2004 Author: (with others) Endocrinology, 1990; featured Nat. Libr. Medicine's Changing the Face of Medicine, an Exhibition on America's Women Physicians, 2003; contbr. articles to profl. jours. Charter mem. Nat. Mus. of Women in the Arts, Washington, 1986; trustee Howard U., 1991-97. Recipient Disting. Alumni award Howard U. Coll. Medicine, 1997. Master ACP (mem. com. 2003-06, Best Sci. Presentation award 1974); mem. Am. Chem. Soc., Am. Med. Women's Assn. (br. I v.p. 1986-87, pres. 1987-88, anti-smoking task force 1989-92, chair govtl. affairs, 1992-96, mem. nominations com. 1992, gov. region III 1996-97, v.p. program 1997-99, chmn. leadership com. 1996-97, pres. elect 1999-00, pres. 2000-02, founder Internat. Women in Medicine Hall of Fame, 2001), Howard U. Med. Alumni (pres. 1983-88, bd. dirs. 1983-), Alpha Omega Alpha. Avocations: dress and hat design, furniture design, home construction.

SILVER, AUDREY WILMA, nurse, educator; b. Nashville, Nov. 29, 1945; d. David and Roslyn Silver; m. Lawrence Claster Falk (div. June 1973); children: Wendy Falk MacGregor, Laurie Falk Fields, PJ Falk MacGregor, Jason Falk Fields; m. Stuart Alan Berney, May 20, 1988; stepchildren: Elizabeth Berney Weiskopf, Joshua Forrest Berney. AS in Nursing, Tenn. State U., Nashville, 1992, BS in Psychology cum laude, 1997. RN Tenn., Fla., cert. case mgr.; lic. real estate broker Tenn., Fla. Consumer health writer, editor Healthy Earth Comms., Nashville, Columbia/Hosp. Corp. Am., Nashville; nurse educator, case mgr., disease mgr. Health Integrated, Tampa Healthways, Nashville, 1999—. Contbr. articles to profl. publs., ency. Vol. Great Harvest Food Bank; precinct county chmn. Kerry for Pres., Pinellas County, Fla.; health edn. coord. Hadassah, 2006. Recipient Top Internet Site award, US News and World Report, 1996, Top Health Content award, AOL and Dow Jones, 1997, award, USA Today; grantee Virtual Body feature award, CNN, 1997. Mem.: LWV, Sierra Club, Fla. Assn. Realtors, Nat. Assn. Realtors, Case Mgmt. Soc. Am., Mensa, Planned Parenthood, Habitat for Humanity, So. Poverty Law Ctr. Jewish. Avocations: bicycling, photography, reading, exercise.

SILVER, JOAN MICKLIN, film director, screenwriter; b. Omaha, May 24, 1935; d. Maurice David and Doris (Shoshone) Micklin; m. Raphael D. Silver, June 28, 1956; children: Dina, Marisa, Claudia. BA, Sarah Lawrence Coll., 1956. Writer, dir. (movies) Hester Street, 1975 (Writers Guild best screenplay nomination), Chilly Scenes of Winter, 1981, (TV film PBS) Bernice Bobs Her Hair starring Shelly Du Vall, 1975; dir. (documentary) Only Faster: Six Legendary Jewish Comediennes, 2005; dir. (TV films HBO) Finnegan, Begin Again with Robert Preston and Mary Tyler Moore, Parole Board, A Private Matter with Sissy Spacek and Aidan Quinn, (TV film Showtime) In The Presence of Mine Enemies, 1997, (films) Between the Lines, 1976, Crossing Delancey with Amy Irving, 1988, Loverboy, 1989, Stepkids, 1991; dir. stage plays and musicals including Album, Maybe I'm Doing It Wrong, Off-Broaday prodn. A.My Name is Alice; prod. On The Yard, (radio) Great Jewish Stories from Eastern Europe and Beyond, 1995; dir. (feature film) A Fish in the Bathtub, 1998, (TV film Lifetime) Invisible Child, 1999, (TV film Showtime) Charms for the Easy Life, 2001, TV film LifeTime) Hunger Point, 2003. Office: Silverfilm Prodns Inc 510 Park Ave New York NY 10022-1105 Office Phone: 646-282-0312.

SILVER, KATHRYN, health services executive; b. Belleville, Ill. d. Oliver and Bernice Knepper; m. Jules A. Silver (div. July 1986); children: Brett, Ryan. B of Health Care Adminstrn., U. Nev., 1994; MBA, U. Phoenix, 1996. Regional dir. Maxi-Health IPA, Las Vegas, Nev., 1984-88; sr. assoc. adminstr. U. Med. Ctr., Las Vegas, 1988-94; COO Lake Mead Hosp., North Las Vegas, Nev., 1994-96; CEO Oasis Health Sys., Las Vegas, 1996—2001; assoc. adminstr. U. Med. Ctr., 2001—. Clin. asst. prof. hosp. adminstrn. U. Nev. Sch. Medicine, Reno. Fellow Healthcare Fin. Mgmt. Assn.; mem. Am. Coll. Healthcare Execs. (diplomate). Republican. Roman Catholic. Avocations: golf, travel, shopping, gourmet dining. Office: Univ Med Ctr 1800 W Charleston Blvd Las Vegas NV 89102-4356 Office Phone: 702-383-3695. Business E-Mail: kathy.silver@umcsn.com.

SILVER, KYLA MARIE, music educator; b. Denver, Oct. 3, 1968; d. Oneil Joseph and Beverly Ann Fontenot; children: David, Emma. Student, Loretto Heights Coll., Englewood, Colo., 1985—87; BA, Oral Robert U., Tulsa, 1995. Cert. tchr. vocal performance Va. Exec. asst. Denver Ctr. for Performing Arts Complex, 1986—90; sales cons. Franchise Distbn., Inc., Denver, 1990—92; founder, CEO Children's Charities, Denver, 1992—; promotions coord., model Maximum Talent Agy., Denver, 1992—97; v.p. ops., multi media mgmt. B.A.M. Cos., Denver, 1994—98; field mgr. Innova Mktg., L.A., 1997—98; choral tchr. Lunenbura City Schs., Victoria, Va., 2001—. Owner, entrepreneur DHT Mgmt., Keysville, Va., 2003—; soprano soloist Denver Opera Co., 1993; guest artist Colo. Concert Chorale, Denver, 1992; founder Voices of Essence Choir, Victoria, 2001—; prin. vocal artist Gethsemane Presbyn. Ch., 2001—; music minister Holy Manor Nursing Home, Farmville, Va., 2001—, Brookview Retirement Home, Farmville, 2001—; actress numerous roles film and TV including Bedazzled, Monkey Bone, Nothing is Easy, Reverend Do Wrong, Days of Our Lives, Asteroid, Dying to be Perfect, Perry Mason, The Price is Right; actress TV commls. including Allstate, Plastic Surgeon, Inc., Saturn Dearlership, Billy Blues Restaurant; exec. dir. Miss So. Va. Pageant Miss Am. Orgn. Inc., 2004. Composer (CD) Straight From the Heart, 1997, songwriter various sheet music pieces, 1987—2002; actor: (plays) Oru Theatre Co., 1987—90, Oru Dinner Theatre, 1987—88. Named Runner up, Mrs. Photogenic, Mrs. Congeniality, Mrs. Colo. Am. Pageant, 1994; scholar, Bayview Conservatory scholar, 1994, acad. scholar, Sachs Found., Colorado Springs, Colo., 1990—93. Mem.: Sigma Gamma Rho, Alpha Kappa Alpha. Republican. Christian Ch. Avocations: travel, music, gardening. Home and Office: PO Box 211 Keysville VA 23947

SILVER, LYNN ELLEN, music educator; b. Elmira, N.Y., Mar. 3, 1952; d. Charles G. and June E. Hunter; m. Ramon R. Silver, Jan. 26, 1974; children: Jason, Matthew. BA in Music, English, Fresno State U., Calif., 1975; MS in Edn. Adminstrn., Nat. U., Costa Mesa, Calif., 1998. Cert. tchr. Calif., 1980. Music specialist Madera Unified Sch. Dist., Calif., 1975—77, Escondido Union Sch. Dist., Calif., 1977—89, Upland Unified Sch. Dist., Calif., 1989—99; music specialist, tchr. English, Ocean View Sch. Dist., Huntington Beach, Calif., 1994—. Choir dir. United Meth. Ch., Madera, Calif., 1975—77, St. Paul's Meth. Ch., Coronado, Calif., 1982—85, St. Peter's By-the-Sea Presbyn. Ch., Huntington Beach, Calif., 1993—. Recipient Intermediate Tchr. of Yr. award, Ocean View Sch. Dist., 1997—98, Educator of Yr. award, Orange County Arts, 2001, Disting. Arts Educator award, Allied Arts Bd., 2001, Exceptional Educator award, Calif. State Assembly, 2003, Vol. of Yr. award, Orange County Philharmonic, 2006. Mem.: Calif. Tchr.'s Assn. Avocations: cooking, spending time with family. Home: 17021 Westport Dr Huntington Beach CA 92649 Office: Marine View Mid Sch 5682 Tilburg Dr Huntington Beach CA 92649 E-mail: rljmsilver@g.mail.

SILVER, ROSLYN OLSON, federal judge; b. Phoenix, Feb. 28, 1946; BA, U. Calif. Santa Barbara, 1968; JD cum laude, Ariz. State U., 1971. Bar: Ariz. 1971, U.S. Ct. Appeals (9th cir.) 1980, U.S. Supreme Ct. 1984. Law clk. Hon. Lorna E. Lockwood Ariz. Supreme Ct., Phoenix, 1971-72; advisor, litigator Navajo Nation Native Am. Rights Fund, Phoenix, 1974-76; legal labor counsel Dial Corp., Phoenix, 1976-78; ptnr. Logan and Aguirre, Phoenix, 1978-79; legal counsel EEOC, Phoenix, 1979-80; asst. U.S. Atty. Dist. Ariz., Phoenix, 1980-84; asst. atty. gen. Ariz. Atty. Gen.'s Office, Phoenix, 1984-86; acting 1st asst., chief criminal divsn. dist. Ariz. U.S. Atty. Office, Phoenix, 1986-94; judge Dist. Ariz. U.S. Dist. Ct., Phoenix, 1994—. Chair local rules com. Ariz. Dist. Ct.; mem. regional sect. panel Harry S Truman Scholarship Found. Contbg. editor: Rutter Group Practice Guide; contbr. articles to profl. jours. Mem. bd. visitors U. Ariz. Law Sch.; mem. adv. panel Lodestar Mediation Clinic, Ariz. State U. Law Sch. Named one of 100 Significant Women and Minorities in Ariz.'s Legal History, 2000. Mem. ABA, Fed. Bar Assn., Nat. Assn. Women Judges, Ariz. Bar Assn. (Pub. Lawyer of Yr. 1990), Ariz. Women Lawyers Assn. (outstanding legal practitioner award 1999), Ariz. State U. Alumni Assn. (outstanding alumnus award 1996). Office: US Dist Ct 401 W Washington SPC 59 Phoenix AZ 85003 Office Phone: 602-322-7520.

SILVER, SALLY, minister; b. Farmington, Maine, July 8, 1943; d. Edwin Raymond and Ethel Elizabeth Pearson; children: Gregory, Peter. Spiritual min., Fairfield Spiritual Ch., 1990—92. Tchr. Tangwala Healing Ctr., Oquossoc, Maine, 1973—80; founder, tchr. Western Maine Woman's Meditation Soc., Kingfield, Maine, 1979—85, Crystalmaineia, Eustis, Maine, 1980—86; reader, min. tchr. Light of the Moon, Portland, Maine, 1993—98; min., bd. mem. Ctr. of Eternal Light, Cape Coral, Fla., 1994—97; min., clairvoyant tchr. Planet Earth Book Ctr., Ft. Myers, Fla., 1997—2005. Bd. mem. Ctr. of Eternal Light, Cape Coral, Fla., 1994—97. Min. Universal Brotherhood Movement, 1994—, Fla. Assn. of Spiritual Ministers, 1994. Avocations: reading, painting. Home: 99 W Kingfield Rd Kingfield ME 04947-4252 Office Phone: 239-272-9165.

SILVER, SHELLY ANDREA, artist; b. N.Y.C., July 16, 1957; d. Reuben and Anita (Kuriloff) S. BA, BFA, Cornell U., 1980. Program fellow Japan/U.S. Friendship Commn. Artist Exch., 1994, Deutscher Akademischer Austauschdienst Berliner Kunstlerprogramm, 1992; vis. prof. Deutsche Film und Fernsehakadamie, 1992; vis. artist Art Inst. Chgo., 1991; prof. Sch. Visual Arts grad. dept. photo and related media; Yaddo residency, 1999; freelance editor Sesame St., Frontline, Saturday Night Live, HBO, MTV, Showtime, others. Represented in exhbns. including The New Mus., N.Y.C., 1987, The Mus. of Modern Art, 1991, 95, 96, 97, The N.Y. Film Festival (video sect.), 1994, 96, The Mus. of Kyoto, Japan, 1994, The London Film Festival, 1991, Internat. Ctr. Photography, N.Y.C., 1989, 91, Portrait Gallery, Smithsonian Inst., 1998, Pulse, Serpentine Gallery, London, 1998, Mus. Art and History, Fribourg, Switzerland, 2000, Stadtgalerie Bern, Switzerland, Mus. Contemporary Art, Mexico City, 2001, Yokohama Portroid Gallery, 2002, Singapore Internat. Film Festival, 2002, Musée de L'Elysée, Lausanne, Switzerland, 2001. Grantee Japan Found. Film & Video, 1995, N.Y. State Coun. Arts Project, 1987, 89, 95, Checkerboard Found., 1990, Media Bur. Finishing Funds, Anonymous Was A Woman, 1998, Jerome Found.; fellow U.S./Japan Artists Exch., 1993, NEA, 1989, 91, N.Y. Found. Arts, 1986, 91, 99, John Simon Guggenheim Found., 2005 E-mail: info@ahellysilver.com.

SILVER, THELMA, social worker; b. Nfld., Can., Nov. 17, 1948; d. Mike and Monya Silver. BA, McGill U., 1969, MSW, 1971; PhD in Social Welfare, Case Western Res. U., 1995. Clin. supr. Neighboring: Supporting Svcs. for Mental Health, Mentor, Ohio, 1983-94; lectr. Case Western Res. U. Sch. Applied Social Sci., Cleve., 1990; asst. prof. social work D'Youville Coll., Buffalo, 1994-99; asst. prof. Youngstown State U., 1999—. Mem. Lake County Cmty. Crisis Intervention Team, Painesville, 1985-94; bd. dirs. Solomon Schechter Day Sch., Cleve., 1980-85. Mem. citizen's adv. bd. Northcoast Behavioral Healthcare Ctr., 2000—. Mem. NASW, Coun. on Social Work Edn., Am. Assn. for Advancement of Social Work with Groups. Avocations: walking, reading, gardening. Home: 24525 Penshurst Dr Cleveland OH 44122-1386 Office: Humanistic Counseling Ctr 4979 Mayfield Rd Lyndhurst OH 44124-2601 Office Phone: 440-734-7880. E-mail: doovil@aol.com.

SILVERBERG, KRISTEN L., federal agency administrator; BA, Harvard U.; JD, Tex. U. Law clk. to Justice Clarence Thomas US Supreme Ct.; atty. Williams & Connolly, LLP; spl. asst. to Pres. office of chief of staff Exec. Office of Pres., dep. asst. to Pres. for domestic policy, advisor to chief of staff for policy; sr. advisor to amb. Paul Bremer US Embassy to Iraq, 2003; asst. sec. internat. orgn. affairs US Dept State, 2005—. Office: US Dept State Harry S Truman Bldg 2201 C St NW Rm 6323 Washington DC 20520 Office Phone: 202-647-9602. Office Fax: 202-736-4116.

SILVERHART, JOY E., retired elementary school educator; d. Charles Arthur and Jennie Rose (Moser) Colley; m. Glenn Silverhart, June 29, 1984; stepchildren: Jerry Allen, Gary Norman, Julie Ann; m. Michael A. Untch (dec.). Student, Ohio State U., Columbus, 1955; BS, Mt. Union Coll., Alliance, Ohio, 1958; MEd in Counseling and Supervision, Kent State U., Ohio, 1965, postgrad. spl. degree, 1975. Cert. elem. tchr., spl. edn. tchr., supr., gidance counselor, prin. Ohio. Elem. tchr. Marlington Local Sch. Dist., Alliance, 1958—64; tchr. cons. Stark County Bd. Edn., Canton, Ohio, 1964—66; tchr. learning disabled Canton City Schs., Ohio, 1966—71, 1982—89, spr. behavioral disorder programs, learning disabilites and educably challenged student ednl. programs, 1971—82; ret., 1989. Mem. adv. bd. Kent State U., Akron U., Ohio Dept. Spl. Edn., Columbus, 1971—82; v.p. Symphony League Canton, 1995—2005, sec., 2005—; trustee Canton Symphony, 2006; mem. 1846 Soc., Mt. Union Coll., Alliance, 2000—. Mem.: Phi Delta Kappa. Avocations: travel, golf, tennis, theater, music.

SILVERMAN, AMY JOCELYN, psychiatrist; b. Royal Oak, Mich., Apr. 6, 1972; d. Fredrick and Evelyn Simon; m. Stephen Silverman, Sept. 15, 2001; 1 child, Alexandra Joy. BA in Psychology, Brandeis U., Waltham, Mass., 1994; MD, Mt. Sinai, NYC, 1998. Resident Harvard Longwood Psychiatry Residency Tng. Program, Boston, 1998—2001; fellow Ny Presbyn. Hosp.-Payne Whitney, Manhattan, 2001—03; psychiatrist NY Presbyn. Hosp., Weill Cornell Med. Ctr., White Plains, NY, 2003—. Recipient Physician of Yr., NY Presbyn. Hosp.-Westchester Divsn., 2005. Mem.: Am. Acad. Child and Adolescent Psychiatry, Am. Psychiat. Assn. Office: New York Presbyterian Hospital 21 Bloomingdale Rd White Plains NY 10605 Office Phone: 914-997-5991. Personal E-mail: ams9012@med.cornell.edu.

SILVERMAN, BEATRICE TOLTZ, retired psychiatrist; b. Boston, Mar. 20, 1922; d. Hyman Silverman and Jennie Gertrude Toltz; m. Norman Mailer (div.); 1 child, Susan Mailer; m. Salvador Sanchez Valdez; 1 child, Salvador Sanchez. BA in Psychology, Boston U., 1944; diploma in French studies, Sorbonne, Paris, 1948; MD, Nat. Autonomous U. Mexico, Mexico City, 1959. Diplomate Am. Bd. Psychiatry and Neurology. Intern State Mental Hosp., Mexico City, 1957—58; pvt. practice psychiatry Mexico City, 1959—62, 1964—69, Daytona Beach, 1975—96; psychiat. resident Mental Health Inst., Cherokee, Iowa, 1963—64; sr. psychiatrist Mil. Hosp., Mexico City, 1964—69; psychiat. resident Worcester State Hosp., Mass., 1969—71, sr. psychiatrist, 1971—74, dir. drug unit, 1971—74; med. dir. Guidance Ctr., Daytona Beach, Fla., 1974—80; ret., 1996. Psychiat. cons. Tropical Disease Hosp., Mexico City, 1959—62; asst. clin. prof. psychiatry Tufts U. Med. Sch., Boston, 1972—74; mem. tchg. staff, psychotherapy supr. residency program State Hosp., Worcester, 1971—74. Author: Woman Well at Ease, 2004, Mexican Passages, 2004. Lt. jr. grade U.S. Naval Res., 1944—46. Mem.: Am. Med. Women;s Assn. (founder, 1st pres.). Home: 1023 Bel Aire Dr Daytona Beach FL 32118-3636

SILVERMAN, EILEEN R., elementary school educator; b. Bronx, NY, July 20, 1954; d. Stanley and Evelyn Silverman. BS in Edn., Hofstra U., Hempstead, NY; MS in Edn., Nova U., Davie, Fla. Cert. tchr. NY, Fla. Tchr. Dade County Pub. Schs., Miami, Fla. Home: 1100 SE 5th Ct Apt 81 Pompano Beach FL 33060-8162

SILVERMAN, ELAINE ANN, mathematics educator; b. Cin., Aug. 22, 1951; d. Samuel David and Freda Miller; children: Jennifer, Mindy, Brandon. BS magna cum laude, U. Cin., 1973. Cert. tchr. Nev. Math. tchr., dept. chair Quannah McCall Sixth Grade Ctr., Las Vegas, Nev., 1973—75; third grade tchr. Harvey Dondero Elem. Sch., Las Vegas, 1975—78; middle sch. math. tchr., head tchr., master tchr. The Meadows Sch., Las Vegas, 1992—. Pvt. math. tutor, Las Vegas. Bd. dirs., v.p. Jewish Fedn. Women's Divsn., 1979—86; presch. dir. Temple Beth Sholom, 1980—85; bd. dirs. Jewish Family Svcs., 1985—86, Solomon Schechter Day Sch., 2006. Recipient Excellence in Leadership, Jewish Fedn. of Las Vegas. Mem.: Math. Assn. Am. (Edyth May Sliffe award for disting. jr. high sch. math. tchg. 2003), Nat. Coun. Tchrs. Math. Avocation: travel. Office: The Meadows Sch 8601 Scholar Ln Las Vegas NV 89128 Business E-Mail: esilverman@themeadowsschool.org.

SILVERMAN, ELLEN-MARIE, speech and language pathologist; b. Milw., Oct. 12, 1942; d. Roy and Bettie (Schlaeger) Loebel; m. Feb. 5, 1967 (div.); 1 child, Catherine Bette. BS, U. Wis., Milw., 1964; MA, U. Iowa, 1967, PhD, 1970. Rsch. assoc. U. Ill., Urbana, 1969-71; asst. prof. speech pathology Marquette U., Milw., 1973-79; assoc. clin. prof. otolaryngology Med. Coll. Wis., 1980—83; assoc. prof. speech pathology Marquette U., 1979-85; pvt. practice speech and lang. pathology, Milw., 1985—. Founder, CEO TSS-The Speech Source, Inc., 1995—. Author, illustrator: Jason's Secret; contbr. articles to profl. jours., chpts. to books. Marquette U. grantee, 1982. Fellow Am. Speech, Hearing, Lang. Assn.; mem. Wis. Speech, Hearing, Lang. Assn., Sigma Xi, Delta Kappa Gamma. Avocations: photography, painting, gardening, writing. E-mail: tsss920499@aol.com.

SILVERMAN, ENID, painter, stained glass artist, muralist; b. Chgo., Mar. 15, 1931; d. Frank Herbert and Idelle (Makowsky) Levy; m. Irv Silverman, Aug. 24, 1952 (dec.); children: Dan E., Susan Pritzker. BS, Ill. Inst. Tech., 1953; postgrad., Chgo. Acad. Fine Arts, 1951, Evanston Art Ctr., 1961-62, Northshore Acad. Art, 1963-68. Art instr. Steiner Gallery, Lincolnwood, Ill., 1971-80, Centre East Art Ctr., Skokie, Ill., 1980-92, Cambridge-on-the-Lake, Buffalo Grove, Ill., 1987-2001, Wheeling (Ill.) Park Dist., 1995—, Buffalo Grove Park Dist., 1998—. Host cable TV show Artist to Artist, 1989—. Stained glass windows designer A.G. Beth Israel, Chgo., 1991, Lincolnwood Jewish Congregation, 1992-97, Sanctuary-B'nai Jehoshua Beth Elohim, Glenview, Ill., 1992, Ark-Beth Tikvah Congregation, Hoffman Estates, Ill., 1995, Ner Tamid Congregation of North Town, Chgo., 2001; represented in Oak Brook (Ill.) Fine Art Invitational, Old Orchard (Ill.) Fine Art Promenade, Northwestern U. Dittmar Gallery, Ill., Harold Washington Cultural Ctr., Chgo., James Thompson Ctr., Chgo.; created murals in oper. rms. and adjacent hallways Children's Meml. Hosp., Chgo., 1998. Charter mem. Nat. Mus. Women Arts. Grantee Skokie Cable Found., 1989. Mem. Oil Painters Am. (charter), Chgo. Artists Coalition, Am. Jewish Artists Club. Avocations: theater, travel, music, dance. Home: 724 Picardy Cir Northbrook IL 60062-1719 E-mail: enidartist@aol.com.

SILVERMAN, JOAN L., historian, consultant; b. Bklyn., July 30, 1925; d. Morris and Anne E. Levinson; m. Richard A. Silverman, June 4, 1948; children: Michael, Elizabeth, Katharine. BA with distinction, Cornell U., Ithaca, N.Y., 1946; MA in Russian Studies, Columbia U., N.Y.U., 1949; MA in Tchg. Social Studies, Columbia U., N.Y.C., 1953; PhD in Am. Civilization, NYU, 1979. Rschr./translator Army Security Agy., Washington, 1947—48, Harvard Russian Rsch. Ctr., Cambridge, Mass., 1949—50; instr. Highland Sch., Jamaica, NY, 1963—77; adj. asst. prof., Am. and bus. history Stevens Inst. Tech., NYU, Rutgers U., 1979—83; pub. affairs officer Citibank, NA, N.Y.C., 1983—92. Cons. Citibank, NA, N.Y.C., 1979—83, Citicorp, Citigroup, N.Y.C., 1992—, Mus. Am. Fin. History, 1992—93. Co-translator: books Tolstoy as I Knew Him, 1948, contbr.: books Citibank - 1812-1970, 1985; editor: (book) Wriston: Rise & Fall of American Financial Supremacy, 1995; editl. svcs.: Women at Risk, Columbia Presbyn. Hosp. Breast Cancer Newsletter, 1996—, contbr.: Encyc. of N.Y.C., contbr.: Encyc. of So. Culture; contbr. articles to profl. jours. Mem.: Phi Beta Kappa. Avocations: reading, 20th century classical music.

SILVERMAN, LESLIE E., commissioner; b. Needham, Mass. Grad., U. Vt.; JD, Am. U.; M with distinction, Georgetown U. Bar: D.C., Mass. Law clk. U.S. Atty.'s Office; assoc. Keller & Heckman, 1990—97; labor counsel Senate Health, Edn., Labor and Pensions Com., 1997—2002; commr. US Equal Employment Opportunity Commn., Washington, 2002—. Office: US Equal Employment Opportunity Commn 1801 L St NW Washington DC 20507*

SILVERMAN, SARAH, actress, comedian, writer; b. Bedford, NH, Dec. 1, 1970; Actor: (TV series) Saturday Night Live, 1993—94, Mr. Show with Bob and David, 1995—97, Greg the Bunny, 2002; (TV miniseries) Pilot Season, 2004, (voice): (TV series) Crank Yankers, 2002,: (TV films) Mr. Show and the Incredible, Fantastical News Report, 1998, Smog, 1999, Late Last Night, 1999, Rocky Times, 2000, (voice) Saddle Rush, 2002,: (films) Overnight Delivery, 1998, Bulworth, 1998, There's Something About Mary, 1998, The Bachelor, 1999, The Way of the Gun, 2000, Black Days, 2001, Say It Isn't So, 2001, Heartbreakers, 2001, Evolution, 2001, Run Ronnie Run, 2002, The School of Rock, 2003, Nobody's Perfect, 2004, (voice) Hair High, 2004, Rent, 2005, I Want Someone to Eat Cheese with, 2005, School for Scoundrels, 2006; actor, co-prodr.: Who's the Caboose?, 1997; writer, actor: Sarah Silverman: Jesus is Magic, 2005; actor: (TV series, guest appearance) Star Trek: Voyager, 1996, The Larry Sanders Show, 1996, Seinfeld, 1997, Brotherly Love, 1997, JAG, 1997, The Naked Truth, 1997, Futurama, 2000, V.I.P., 2002, Frasier, 2003, Monk, 2004, Entourage, 2004, (voice) Aqua Teen Hunger Force, 2004, Drawn Together, 2004, American Dad, 2005. Office: Creative Artists Agy Inc 9830 Wilshire Blvd Beverly Hills CA 90212*

SILVERMAN, SYDEL FINFER, anthropologist; b. Chgo., May 20, 1933; d. Joseph and Elizabeth (Bassman) Finfer; m. Mel Silverman, Dec. 27, 1953 (dec. Sept. 1966); children: Eve Rachel, Julie Beth; m. Eric R. Wolf, Mar. 18, 1972 (dec. Mar. 1999). MA, U. Chgo., 1957; PhD, Columbia U., 1963. From lectr. to prof. anthropology Queens Coll., CUNY, Flushing, 1963-75; prof., exec. officer PhD program anthropology Grad. Sch. CUNY, N.Y.C., 1975-86, acting dean of Grad. Sch., 1982-83; pres. Wenner-Gren Found. for Anthropol. Rsch., N.Y.C., 1987-99. Spkr. and writer in field; bd. dirs. Social Sci. Rsch. Coun., N.Y.C., 1984-87. Author: Three Bells of Civilization, 1975; editor: Totems and Teachers, 1981, Inquiry and Debate in the Human Sciences, 1992, Preserving the Anthropological Record, 1995, Pathways of Power, 2001, One Discipline, Four Ways, 2005, Complexities, 2005; contbr. articles to profl. jours. Recipient Franz Boas award Am. Anthropol. Assn., 1999; fellowship Am. Coun. Learned Socs., 1986, NEH, 1973-74, NIH, 1960-63, NSF, 1959; grantee Am. Phil. Soc., 1985. Jewish. E-mail: ssilwolf@aol.com.

SILVERMAN, WENDY K., psychologist, educator; PhD, Case Western Reserve Univ. Prof., psychology Fla. Internat. Univ., Miami. Author: 4 books; editor: Journ. Clin. Child and Adolescent Psychology. Mem.: Soc. Clin. Child and Adolescent Psychology (pres. 2005—06), Am. Psychological Assn. Office: Dept Psychology Fla Internat Univ- DM256 11200 SW 8th St Miami FL 33199 Business E-Mail: silverw@fiu.edu.

SILVERNELL, KERRI ANNE, artist, educator; b. Battle Creek, Mich., Jan. 1, 1953; d. Orrie Milton and Mary Lou Korporal; m. Donald Alan Silvernell, July 30, 1971; children: Ashley Lauren, Shelby Aerin. AA, St. Petersburg Coll., Fla., 1993; BA, U. South Fla., Tampa, 1995. Cert. prof. Nat. Bd. Cert. Art tchr. Forsyth Pub. Schs., Mont., 1995—2000, Pinellas County Schs., Palm Harbor, Fla., 2000—. Paintings, 1971—. Mem.: Pinellas Art Edn. Assn., Fla. Art Edn. Assn. Personal E-mail: silvernelldk@juno.com.

SILVERS, ANN, peri-operative nurse, educator; b. Omaha, Mar. 1, 1943; d. John Stephen and M. Georgina Marie Mary McNeil; m. Ralph L. Silvers, Oct. 30, 1993. Diploma, St. Joseph Hosp. Sch. Nursing, Phoenix, 1966; BS in Health Care Scis., Chapman Coll., Travis AFB, Calif., 1979. RN Ariz. Pvt. scrub nurse Drs. Nelson, Brown, Cornell, Phoenix, 1969; staff nurse operating room St. Joseph Hosp., Phoenix, 1966-69, 70, Tucson, 1970—71, Washoe Med. Ctr., Reno, 1976—77; staff nurse U. Ariz. Med. Ctr., Tucson, 1971—75, asst. oper. rm. supr., 1975—76; oper. rm. staff nurse David Grant Med. Ctr., Travis AFB, Calif., 1977—81; coord. oper. rm. edn. Seton Med. Ctr., Daly City, Calif., 1981—85; staff nurse operating room Yavapai Regional Med. Ctr., Prescott, Ariz., 1985—88, John C. Lincoln Hosp., Phoenix, 1988—2000. Instr. surg. technician program and perioperative nurse program Gateway C.C., Phoenix, 1989-91, also extern preceptor. Capt. USAF, 1977-81. Mem. Assn. Operating Room Nurses (cert.), Sigma Theta Tau.

SILVERS, SALLY, choreographer, performing company executive; b. Greeneville, Tenn., June 19, 1952; d. Herbert Ralston and Sara Elizabeth (Buchanan) S.; life ptnr. Bruce Erroll Andrews. BA in Dance and Polit. Sci., Antioch Coll., 1975. Artistic dir. Sally Silvers & Dancers, N.Y.C., 1980—. Mem. faculty Leicester Poly., 1986, 87, 89, summer choreography project Bennington Coll., 1988-92, Chisenhale Dance Space, London, 1989, 91, Am. Dance Festival, Durham, N.C., 1990, 92; guest tchr. European Dance Devel. Ctr., Arnhem, The Netherlands, 1992—. Choreographer (performances) Politics of the Body Microscope of Conduct, 1980, Social Movement, 1981, Connective Tissue, 1981, Less Time You Know Praxis, 1981, Don't No Do And This, 1981, Lack of Entrepreneurial Thrift, 1982, Celluoid Sally and Mr. E, 1982, Mutate, 1982, Being Red Enough, 1982, Disgusting, 1982, Bedtime at the Reformatory, 1982, Eat the Rich, 1982, They Can't Get It in the Shopping Cart, 1982, Blazing Forceps, 1982, And Find Out Why, 1983, Choose Your Weapons, 1984, Extend the Wish for Entire, 1985, No Best Better Way, 1985, Every All Which is Not Us, 1986, Swaps Ego Say So, 1986, Be Careful Now, You Know Sugar Melts in Water, 1987, Fact Confected, 1987, Both, Both, 1987, Tizzy boost, 1988, Moebius, 1988, Whatever Ever, 1989, Get Tough, Sports and Divertissement, 1989, Flap, 1989, Swan's Crayon, 1989, Fanfare Tripwire, 1990, Harry Meets Sally, 1990, Along the Skid Mark of Recorded History, 1990, Matinee Double-You, 1991, Grand Guignol, 1991, Dash Dash Slang Plural Plus, 1992, The Bubble Cut, 1992, Vigilant Corsage, 1992, Oops Fact, 1992, Small Room, 1993, Exwhyzee, 1993, Elegy, 1993, Now That It Is Now, 1994, Give Em Enough Rope, Swoon Noir, 1994, Radio Rouge, 1995, Braceletizing, 1995, Hush Comet, 1995, Bite the Pillow, 1995, Pandora's Cake Stain, 1996, Secrets Of, 1997, HUSHHUSH, Sugar Raised, 1998 Capture, Teddy Growl, 1999, Storming Heaven, 2000, Swaphot Trouble, 2001, Strike Me Lightning, 2002, Spaced Out, 2003, Dreams Do Come True, 2004, Dang Me, 2004; video and performance filmmaker: (films) Little Lieutenant, 1993 (Silver); N.Y. Dance on Camera Festival, Mechanics of the Brain, 1997; co-author: (book) Resurgant New Writings By Women, 1992; contbr. articles to profl. jours.; choreographer RUPT, Versus, Oven Rack Professionals, 2005. Grantee Nat. Endowment Arts, 1987, 89, 90, 91, 98, Jerome Found., 1993, 1996, Meet the Composer N.Y. Found. for the Arts, 1995; Guggenheim Found. fellow, 1988; Found. Contemporary Performance Arts, 2001. Mem. Segue Found. (bd. dirs. Segue Performance Space 1992-2002). Avocations: reading, writing, art events, costume design. Home: 303 E 8th St Apt 4F New York NY 10009-5212

SILVERSTEIN, JUDITH LYNN, clinical psychologist; b. Phila., Oct. 19, 1946; d. Arthur J. and Ruth L. (Lieberman) Handelsman. PhD, Tufts U., 1975, Fielding Inst., 1985. Lic. psychologist; cert. sex therapist and supr.; diplomate Am. Bd. Sexology; cert. group psychotherapist; cert. life coach, Internat. Coach Fedn. Psychotherapist Boston Psychol. Ctr. for Women, 1977-81, New Eng. Inst., Framingham, Mass., 1977-81, Next Step Counseling, Newton, Mass., 1983-86; psychologist Boston Inst. Psychotherapies, 1986-91; pvt. practice psychologist Needham, Mass., 1981—. Cons. Newton Wellesley Hosp.; coord. continuing edn. Boston Inst. for Psychotherapies, 1985-92, assoc. dir. tng., 1993-95. Author: Sexual Enhancement for Women, 1978, Sexual Enhancement for Men, 1986. Mem. Mass. Psychol. Assn. Am. Psychol. Assn., Am. Group Psychotherapy Assn., Ineternat. Coach Fedn. Democrat. Jewish. Avocation: ballroom dancing. Home: 29 Briarwood Cir Needham MA 02494-1829 Office Phone: 781-449-6211.

SILVERSTEIN, SUZANNE, art therapist; b. L.A., Jan. 14, 1948; d. Lita (Factor) Kilpatrick; m. Andrew Chiaramonte, July 4, 1988; 1 child, Jaysen Pascal. BFA, Calif. Inst. of the Arts, L.A., 1971; MA, Immaculate Heart Coll., L.A., 1975. Art therapy coord., supr. family and child program Thalians Mental Health Ctr., L.A., 1977—; art therapy coord., supr. famil and child program dept. psychiatry Cedars-Sinai Med. Ctr., L.A., 1977—; pres., co-founder Psychol. Trauma Ctr., L.A., 1981—. Faculty clin. art therapy dept. Immaculate Heart Coll., 1975-81, Loyola Marymount U., 1981-82, leader, group dynamics class, 1975-82; adminstr. Psychol. Trauma Ctr., 1981—, pres. 1981—. Author: (with others) Expanding Mental Health Interventions in Schools, 1988. Fellowship Thalians Mental Health Ctr./Cedars Sinai Med. Ctr., L.A., 1975-76. Mem. Am. Art Therapy Assn., So. Calif. Art Therapy Assn. Office: Psychol Trauma Ctr 8730 Alden Dr Rm C212 Los Angeles CA 90048-3811 Office Phone: 310-423-3541. Business E-Mail: suzanne.silverstein@cshs.org.

SILVERSTONE, ALICIA, actress; b. San Francisco, Oct. 4, 1976; d. Monty and Didi Silverstone; m. Christopher Jarecki, June 11, 2005. Stage debut in Carol's Eve at Met Theater, L.A.; starred in three Aerosmith videos, including Cryin', Amazing, Crazy; actress (films): The Crush, 1993, True Crime, 1995, Le Nouveau Monde, 1995, Hideaway, 1995, Clueless, 1995, The Babysitter, 1995, Batman & Robin, 1997, Blast from the Past, 1999, Love's Labour Lost, 2000, Scorched, 2002, Global Heresy, 2002, Scooby-Doo 2: Monsters Unleashed, 2004, Beauty Shop, 2005; actress, prodr.(film) Excess Baggage, 1997; exec. prodr. (TV Series) Braceface, 2001; appeared in TV programs including Torch Song, 1993, Scattered Dreams, 1993, The Cool and the Crazy, 1994; appeared in TV series: The Wonder Years, 1992, Braceface (voice only), 2001, Miss Match, 2003.

SILVERTHORN, LAURA LYNNE, secondary school educator; d. William Franklin and Charlotte Raye Meyer; m. Larry Gene Silverthorn, July 20, 1984; children: Tyler Ray, Derek Gene. Bachelors, Simpson Coll., Indianola, Iowa, 1987. Tchr. Indianola Cmty. Schs., 1992—2000, Winterset Cmty. Schs., Iowa, 2000—. Elder First United Presbyn. Ch., Winterset, 2006. Avocations: reading, travel, boating. Home: 1410 W Jefferson St Winterset IA 50273 Office Phone: 515-462-3320.

SILVESTRI, GINA, lawyer; b. NJ, Feb. 18, 1972; BA magna cum laude, Seton Hall U., NJ, 1994; JD, Thomas M. Cooley Law Sch., Mich., 1995. Bar: NY 1999, NJ 2001, U.s. Dist. Ct. of NJ (Dist. Ct. NJ) 2001. Atty. Gina Silvestri, Esq., Jackson, NJ, 2003—04; assoc. atty. Law Office Of Terence G. Van Dzura, Edison, NJ, 2001—03, William J. Leininger, PC, SI, 2000—01, Law Office Of Mahipal Singh, PC, Jackson Heights, NY, 1999—2000. Fla. notary pub., Fla., 2004—. Mem.: NJ Bar Assn., NY Bar Assn., Alpha Phi (life). Personal E-mail: gsilvst@prodigy.net.

SILVESTRI, HEATHER L., psychologist; b. Passaic, N.J., Mar. 3, 1972; d. Philip J and Dorothy J Silvestri; m. Christopher M Ferguson, Sept. 23, 2000. PhD, LI U., 1997—2002. Lic. Psychologist NY, 2003, cert. Hospice Vol. Hospice of NJ., Bergen County Agy., 1994. Vol. supr. psychologist Beth Israel Med. Ctr., NYC, 2004—. Psychology instr. Coll. New Rochelle, Bronx, 1999—2000; pvt. practice psychologist, N.Y.C., 2003—; asst. adj. prof. John Jay Coll., 2003—04. Mem. Greenpeace, 2001, Amnesty Internat., New Yorkers Against the Death Penalty, The Nature Conservancy, Habitat for Humanity, Nat. Resources Def. Coun., World Wildlife Fedn. Fellow, NYU, NYC, 2002—03; Tchg. Fellowship, LI U., 2000, Garden State Disting. scholar, State of NJ., 1994, Rotary Scholarship, Rotary Club of Nutley, NJ., 1990—94, Italian-American Scholarship for Proficiency in the Italian Lang., Italian-American Club of Nutley, NJ., 1990, PTA scholarship, PTA of Nutley, NJ, 1990. Mem.: APA (assoc.), Internat. Soc. for Theoretical Psychology, Phi Beta Kappa, Phi Eta Sigma, Alpha Lambda Delta, Psi Chi, Pi Beta Phi. Avocations: travel, jogging. Home: 95 Tuscan Rd Maplewood NJ 07040 Office: 103 St Mark's Pl Ste A New York NY 10009 Office Phone: 212-614-9600 Ext. 207.

SILVEY, ANITA LYNNE, editor; b. Bridgeport, Conn., Sept. 3, 1947; d. John Oscar and Juanita Lucille (McKitrick) Silvey. BS in Edn., Ind. U., 1969; MA in Comm. Arts, U. Wis., 1970. Editorial asst. children's book dept. Little Brown and Co., Boston, 1970-71; asst. editor Horn Book Mag., Boston, 1971-75; mng. editor, founder New Boston Rev., 1975-76; mktg. mgr. children's books, libr. svcs. mgr. trade divsn. Houghton Mifflin, Boston, 1976-84; editor-in-chief Horn Book Mag., Boston, 1985-95; v.p., pub. Children's Books Houghton Mifflin Co., Boston, 1995—2001. Editor: Children's Books and Their Creators, 1995, Help Wanted: Stories About Young People and Work, 1997, Essential Guide to Children's Books and their Creators, 2002, 100 Best Books for Children, 2004, 500 Great Books for Teens, 2006. Named one of 70 Women Who Have Made a Difference, Women's Nat. Book Assn., 1987. Mem.: ALA (chmn. children's librs., Laura Ingalls Wilder award 1987—89), Assn. Am. Pubs. (mem. libr. com.), Internat. Reading Assn. (mem. IRA Book award com. 1985—87), New Eng. Round Table (chmn. 1978—79). Personal E-mail: anitasilvey@aol.com.

SILVEY, MARSHA K., elementary school educator; b. Arlington Heights, Ill., Mar. 30, 1964; m. Craig L. Silvey, June 24, 2000; children: Chelsea, Brian. BS in Elem. Edn. and Hearing Impaired, MacMurray Coll., Jacksonville, Fla., 1986; MS in Elem. Adminstrn., William Wood U., Fulton, Mo., 2005. Hearing impaired spl. edn. specialist Horace Mann, Sedalia, Mo., Hebor Hunt, Sedalia, Skyline Elem., Sedalia, 1986—2000, leading specialist, 2000—05, reading recovery/title I tchr., 2005—. Comm. mem., merit badge counselor Boy Scouts Am., Sedalia. Mem.: Sedalia Cmty. Edn. Assn., Mo. State Tchrs. Assn. Office: Skyline Elem 2505 W 32d Sedalia MO 65301

SIMANSKI, CLAIRE DVORAK, art educator; d. George James and Gertrude Louise Dvorak; m. Robert Simanski, June 20, 1970 (div. Sept. 2000); children: Joseph Brian, John Francis. BFA, Md. Inst. Coll. Arts, Balt., 1968. Cert. art tchr. K-12 Va. Dept. Edn. Tchr. Ann Arundle County Bd. Edn., Annapolis, 1969—71; day care provider Andover, 1973—77; fine arts instr. Bolling AF Base, Md.; sales Md. Nat. Capital Parks, 1981—84, Loudon Jewelers, Loudon, 1989—90; vol. coord. Telecom. Exch. for Deaf, Great Falls, Va., 1990; tchr. Fairfax County Schs., Herndon, Va., 1992—. Mem. character counts com. Herndon Mid. Sch., 1999—2001; prodr., writer, bd. dirs. Herndon Cable TV, 1999—2006, sec., 2001, 03, 05; dept. chair Fine & Performing Arts, Herndon, 2000—06; mem. P.A.R. com. Johns Hopkins U., Balt., 2003—06. Active Art in Pub. Places, Herndon, Reston, 1998—2006; com. mem. Cmty. Arts Ctr., Herndon, 2001—02. Recipient Partnership in Edn. award, Optomists of Herndon, 1998, Fairfax County Police Dept. award, 2001, Outsanding Vol. award, Mayor, Herndon, Va., 2003, 2005, Hon. Commn., Congl. Youth Leadership Coun., Outstanding Vol. award, Herndon Cable TV, 2003. Mem.: Va. Edn. Assn., Fairfax Educators Assn. Avocations: antiques, writing. Office: Herndon Mid Sch Herndon VA 20170

SIMECKA, BETTY JEAN, marketing executive; b. Topeka, Apr. 15, 1935; d. William Bryan and Regina Marie (Rezac) S.; m. Alex Pappas, Jan. 15, 1956 (div. Apr. 1983); 1 child, Alex William. Student, Butler County C.C., 1983—85. Freelance writer and photographer, L.A., also St. Marys, Kans., 1969-77; co-owner Creative Enterprises, El Dorado, Kans., 1977-83; coord. excursions into history Butler County C.C., El Dorado, 1983-84; dir. Hutchinson (Kans.) Conv. & Visitors Bur., 1984-85; dir. mktg. divsn. Exec. Mgmt., Inc., Wichita, 1985-87; exec. dir. Topeka Conv. and Visitors Bur., 1987-91, pres., CEO, 1991-96; pres. Internat. Connections, Inc., 1996-97, Simecka and Assoc., 1996-99, Pinnacle Prodns., L.L.C., 1997-99; pres., CEO Cultural Exhbns. and Events, L.L.C., 1999—2003; organizer Czars: 400 Years of Imperial Grandeur exhbn., 2002—04; v.p. mktg. Sunflower Exhbns., L.L.C., 2003—04; mktg. cons., 2003—. Dir. promotion El Dorado Thunderboat Races, 1977-78. Contbr. articles to jours. and mags.; columnist St. Marys Star, 1973-79. Pres. El Dorado Art Assn., 1984; chair Santa Fe Trail Bike Assn., Kans., 1988-90; co-dir. St. Marys Summer Track Festival, 1973-81; chair spl. events Mulvane Art Mus., 1990, sec., 1991-92; membership chair, 1993-94, bd. dirs., 1995-96; bd. dirs. Topeka Civic Theater, 1991-96, co-chair spl. events, 1992; Kans. chair Russian Festival Com., 1992-93; vice-chair Kans. Film Commn., 1993-94, chair, 1994; bd. dirs. Kans. Expoctr. Adv. Bd., 1990-96, Brain Injury Assn. Greater Kansas City, Concerned Citizens Topeka, 1998-2000; pres. Kans. Internat. Mus., 1994-96. Recipient Kans. Gov.'s Outstanding Tourism award Kans. Broadcaster's Assn., 1993, Disting. Svc award City of Topeka, 1995, Hist. Ward Meade Disting. award Topeka Parks and Recreation Dept., 1995; named Kansan of Yr., Topeka Capitol-Jour., 1995, Sales and Mktg. Exec. of Yr., 1995, Internat. Soroptomists, Topeka chpt., Woman of Distinction, 1996. Mem. Nat. Tour Assn., Sales and Mktg. execs. (bd. dirs. 1991-92), Internat. Assn. Conv. and Visitors Burs. (co-chair rural tourism com. 1994), Am. Soc. Assn. Execs., Travel Industry Assn. Kans. (membership chair 1988-89, sec. 1990, pres. 1991-92, Outstanding Merit award 1994), St. Marys C. of C. (pres. 1975), I-70 Assn. (v.p. 1989, pres. 1990), Optimists (social sec. Topeka chpt. 1988-89). Republican. Methodist. Holder Nat. AAU record for 100-yard dash, 1974.

SIMEONE, HELEN LILLI, retired elementary school educator; b. Astoria, N.Y., June 24, 1934; d. George J. and Angelina C. (Stravino) Lilli; m. Edward Simeone, Apr. 19, 1958; children: Edward J., George M., Carolyn M. BS, Immaculata Coll., 1956. Clin. dietitian St. John's Hosp., N.Y.C., 1956-59; instr. dietitian St. John's Sch. Nursing, N.Y.C., 1956-59, 62-64; instr. remedial reading St. Francis of Assisi Sch., Astoria, N.Y., 1972-74; substitute tchr. Diocese of Bklyn. and Queens, N.Y., 1974-79; elem. tchr. St. Joan of Arc Sch., Jackson Heights, N.Y., 1979—, primary coord., 1983—2000; ret., 2000. Vol. Children's Liturgy and Bible Study St. Francis of Assisi. Mem. Nat. Cath. Edn. Assn. Avocations: travel, cooking. Home: 22-02 73rd St Flushing NY 11370-1014 Office: Saint Joan of Arc Sch 35-27 82nd St Jackson Heights NY 11372-5128

SIMJEE, AISHA, ophthalmologist, educator; b. Surat, India, Jan. 23, 1944; came to U.S., 1970; d. Yusuf Esmail Simjee and Amina Ahmed Badat; m. Sabbir A. Dadabhai, Apr. 28, 1978; children: Alia Dadabhai, Sufia Dadabhai. Intermediate Sci. degree, Rangoon (Burma) U., 1963; MB, BS, Inst. Medicine, Rangoon, 1968. Diplomate Am. Bd. Ophthalmology. Intern Rangoon Gen. Hosp., 1968-69, South Balt. Gen. Hosp., 1970-71; rschr. in ophthalmology Johns Hopkins Hosp., Balt., 1971-72; resident in ophthalmology Eye Dept. Howard U. Hosp., D.C. Gen. Hosp., Armed Forces Inst. Pathology, Washington, 1972-75; fellow in cornea external diseases Wills Eye Hosp., Phila., 1975-76; fellow in ophthalmic pathology and med. retina Scheie Eye Inst., Phila., 1976-77; asst. prof. ophthalmology Howard U., Washington, 1977-78; clin. assoc. prof. ophthalmology U. Calif., Irvine, 1978—; pvt. practice Orange, Calif. Mem. med. adv. bd. Orange County Eye & Tissue Bank, 1990—; attending physician St. Joseph Hosp., Orange, 1978—, U. Calif. Irvine Med. Ctr., 1978—. Contbr. articles to profl. jours. Vol. ophthalmologist La Amistad de Jose Clinic, Sponsor Care Program of St. Joseph Hosp., 1988—, Testing 1-2-3 Screening Clinic St. Joseph Hosp., ann. eye screening for local sch. children, Project Orbis, S.E.E. Internat., Santa Barbara, Am. Eye Care Project, Hope World Wide, 2002—, Internat. Asst. Mission, 2002—. Named Woman of Achievement, Rancho Santiago Coll., Santa Ana, 1990; recipient certs. of recognition Calif. state senator John Seymour, Calif. congressman Christopher Cox, Calif., lt. gov. Leo McCarthy; recipient Pride in the Profession award AMA Found., 2005, Woman of Vision award We Give Thanks or Orange County, 2006. Fellow ACS, Am. Acad. Ophthalmology (Nat. Eye Care Project 1986—); mem. AMA (Pride in Profession award 2005), Calif. Med. Assn., Orange County Med. Assn. (bd. dirs. 1995-02), Orange County Soc. Ophthalmology (exec. com. 1992-02). Office: 1310 W Stewart Dr Ste 501 Orange CA 92868-3856 Office Phone: 714-771-2020. Personal E-mail: drsimjee@sbcglobal.net.

SIMMERS, ANDREA JEAN, elementary school educator; b. Boston, Sept. 20, 1953; d. Richard Wesley Steenburg and Doris Ann Marshall; m. Stephan George Simmers, May 29, 1993. BA, Coll. Wooster, Ohio, 1975; MSc, U. Nebr., Omaha, 1981. Tchr. phys. edn., health Brownell Talbot Sch., Omaha, 1975—84; tchr., chmn. Dept. Sci. McDonagh Sch., Owings Mills, Md., 1984—2002; tchr. sci. Ruxton Country Sch., Owings Mills, 2002—. Sec., mgr. track meet Logan Valley Conf., Omaha, 1978—84. Historian Chestnut Ridge Vol. Fire Co., Owings Mills, 1996. Recipient Barrett award, Coll. Wooster, 2000. Mem.: Nat. Sci. Tchrs. Assn. Episc. Avocations: horseback riding, beagle dogs, outdoor activities, crafts, flute, fitness. Home: 2121 Breeds Ln Owings Mills MD 21117-1661 Office: Ruxton County Sch 11202 Garrison Forest Rd Owings Mills MD 21117-1661

SIMMONDS, RAE NICHOLS, musician, composer, educator; b. Lynn, Mass., Feb. 25, 1919; d. Raymond Edward and Abbie Iola (Spinney) Nichols; m. Carter Fillebrown, Jr., June 27, 1941 (div. May 15, 1971); children: Douglas C. (dec.), Richard A., Mary L., Donald E.; m. Ronald John Simmonds, Oct. 9, 1971 (dec. Nov. 1995). AA, Westbrook Coll., Portland, Maine, 1981; B in Music Performance summa cum laude, U. Maine, 1984; MS in Edn., U. So. Maine, 1989; PhD, Walden U., 1994. Founder, dir. Studio of Music/Children's Studio of Drama, Portsmouth, NH, 1964-71, Studio of Music, Bromley, England, 1971-73, Bromley Children's Theatre, 1971-73, Oughterard Children's Theatre, County Galway, Ireland, 1973-74, Studio of Music, Portland, Maine, 1977-96, West Baldwin, Maine, 1997—; resident playwright Children's Theatre of Maine, Portland, 1979-81; organist, choir dir. Stevens Ave. Congl. Ch., Portland, 1987-95; field faculty advisor Norwich U., Montpelier, Vt., 1995. Field advisor grad. program Vt. Coll., Norwich U., 1995; cons./educator mus. tng. for disabled vets. VA, Portsmouth, N.H., 1966-69; show pianist and organist, mainland U.S.A., 1939-59, Hawaii, 1959-62, Rae Nichols Trio, 1962—; mus. dir. Theatre By the Sea, Portsmouth, N.H., 1969-70. Author/composer children's musical: Shamrock Road, 1980 (Blue Stocking award 1980), Glooscap, 1980; author/composer original scripts and music: Cinderella, If I Were a Princess, Beauty and the Beast, Baba Yaga - A Russian Folk Tale, The Journey - Musical Bible Story, The Perfect Gift - A Christmas Legend; original stories set to music include: Heidi, A Little Princess, Tom Sawyer, Jungle Book, Treasure Island; compositions include: London Jazz Suite, Bitter Suite, Jazz Suite for Trio, Sea Dream, Easter (chorale), Rae Simmonds Jazz Trio Songbook Series, (CD) Fascinatin' Gershwin Rae Simmonds Jazz Trio, 2000; contbr. Maine Women Writers Collection. Recipient Am. Theatre Wing Svc. award, 1944, Pease AFB Svc. Club award, 1967, Bumpus award Westbrook Coll., 1980; Nat. Endowment for Arts grantee, 1969-70; Women's Lit. scholar, 1980, Westbrook scholar, 1980-81, Nason scholar, 1983; Kelaniya U. (Colombo, Sri Lanka) rsch. fellow, 1985-86. Mem. ASCAP, Internat. Soc. Poets, Internat. League Women Composers, Music Tchrs. of Maine, Am. Guild of Organists, Music Tchrs. Nat. Assn., Internat. Alliance for Women in Music, Doctorate Assn. N.Y. Educators, Inc., Delta Omicron, Phi Kappa Phi. Democrat. Episcopalian. Avocations: travel, stamp collecting/philately. Home: 230 Douglas Hill Rd West Baldwin ME 04091-9715

SIMMONS, ADELE SMITH, foundation executive, former educator; b. Lake Forest, Ill., June 21, 1941; d. Hermon Dunlap and Ellen T. (Thorne) Smith; m. John L. Simmons; children— Ian, Erica, Kevin BA in Social Studies with honors, Radcliffe Coll., 1963; PhD, Oxford U., Eng., 1969; LHD (hon.), Lake Forest Coll., 1976, Amherst Coll., 1977, Franklin Pierce Coll., 1978, U. Mass., 1978, Alverno Coll., 1982, Marlboro Coll., 1987, Smith Coll., 1988, Mt. Holyoke Coll., 1989, Am. U., 1992, Tufts U., 1994. Asst. prof. Tufts U., Boston, 1969-72; dean Jackson Coll., Medford, Mass., 1970-72; asst. prof. history, dean student affairs Princeton U., NJ, 1972-77; pres. Hampshire Coll., Amherst, Mass., 1977-89, John D. and Catherine T. MacArthur Found., Chgo., 1989—99; vice chair, sr. exec. Chgo. Metropolis 2020, 1999—; sr. assoc. Ctr. for Internat. Studies U. Chgo., 1999—2005. Bd. dirs. Marsh & McLennan Cos., N.Y.C., Shorebank Corp., Chgo., Union Concerned Scientists, Synergos Inst., Environ. Def., bd. mem., Am. Prospect; bd. dirs. Global Fund for Women, Field Mus., Chgo., Mexican Fine Arts Ctr. Mus., Chgo. Coun. on Fgn. Rels.; emeritus mem. bd. dirs. Rocky Mountain Inst.; former corr. in Mauritius and Tunisia for N.Y. Times, The Economist; high level adv. bd. UN, 1993—; mem. adv. com. World Bank Inst.; mem. bd. overseers Harvard U., 1972-78; chair Fair Labor Assn.; sr. advisor World Econ. Forum. Co-author: (with Freeman, Dunkle, Blau) Exploitation from 9 to 5: Twentieth Century Fund Task Force Report on Working Women, 1975; author: Modern Mauritius, 1982; contbr. articles on edn. and pub. policy in The N.Y. Times, Christian Sci. Monitor, The Bulletin of Atomic Scientist, Harper's, The Atlantic Monthly and others. Commr. Pres.'s Commn. on World Hunger, Washington, 1978-80, Pres.'s Commn. on Environ. Quality, 1991-92; mem. Commn. Global Governance; trustee Carnegie Found. for Advancement Teaching, 1978-86; chair Mayor Richard Daley's Youth Devel. Task Force, 1993-95. Named one of Chgos. 100 Most Influential Women, Crain's Chgo. Bus., 2004. Fellow Am. Acad. Arts and Scis.; mem. Phi Beta Kappa. Office: Chgo Metropolis 2020 30 W Monroe St Chicago IL 60603 Office Phone: 312-332-8161. Business E-Mail: adele.simmons@cm2020.org.

SIMMONS, ANN LORRAINE, actress, educator; b. Kansas City, Mo., Feb. 8, 1952; d. Ronald Lee and Frances Jean (Smith) S.; m. Mithcell Duane Duckworth, Mar. 20, 1971 (div. Feb. 21, 1978); 1 child, Jason Bartholomew Duckworth; m. Russel Yates Mulock, July 25, 1986. BA, U. Calif., 1987; MFA, Calif. Inst. of the Arts, 1995. Adult mentor Virginia Ave. Project. Appeared in plays Love's Labours Lost, Macbeth, The Comedy of Errors, Dancing at Lughnasa, Agamemnon, Twelfth Night, The Glass Menagerie, The Rose Tattoo, Merchant of Venice, The Bacchae, The Real Inspector Hound, Hamlet, All's Well That Ends Well, The Birds, Love's Labour's Lost, (films) Simple Gifts, Stranger Than Fiction, All That You Love. Mem. Actors Network, Theatre Comms. Group. Home: 1603 1/2 N Harvard Blvd Los Angeles CA 90027

SIMMONS, ANNE L., federal official; b. Spencer, Iowa, Jan. 4, 1964; d. Donald Lewis and Lois Amber (Blass) S. B in Spl. Studies, Cornell Coll., 1986. Intern for Congressman Berkley Bedell, Washington, 1986; field staff Iowans for Clayton Hodgson, Sioux City, Iowa, 1986; exec. sec. Atomic Indsl. Forum, Bethesda, Md., 1986-87; staff asst. House Armed Svcs. Com., Washington, 1987; legis. asst. to Congressman Tim Johnson Washington, 1988-93; staff dir. gen. farms commodities subcom. House Agriculture Com., Washington, 1993, staff dir. environ., credit and rural devel. subcom., 1994, minority resource conservation rsch. and forestry subcom., 1995-96. Profl. Staff Ho. Com. on Agrl., 1997—. Music scholar Cornell Coll., 1982-86. Mem. Delta Phi Alpha. Democrat. Office: House Agriculture Com 1301 Longworth House Ofc Bldg Washington DC 20515-0001 E-mail: anne.simmons@mail.house.gov.

SIMMONS, BARBARA ANN, music educator; b. Bellefonte, Pa., Feb. 21, 1965; d. Edward Alfred Miller and Cathy Nan Hoffman; m. William Clark Simmons, June 17, 2000; 1 child, Reid William. BS in Music Edn., West Chester U., 1987, MusM in Music Edn., 1993. Cert. tchr. Pa. Elem. music specialist Coatesville (Pa.) Area Sch. Dist., 1987—. Coop. tchr. West Chester (Pa.) U., 1991—99; presenter workshops in field. Recipient Outstanding Svc. award, Coatesville Area Parent Coun., 1990, 1999, Gift of Time Tribute, Am. Family Inst., 1992. Mem.: Pa. Music Educators Assn. (citation of excellence 2000), Am. Orff Schulwerk Assn., Music Educators Edn. Assn., NEA. Democrat. Lutheran. Avocations: boating, skiing, travel, cooking. Home: 160 Park St Honey Brook PA 19344 Office: Coatesville Area School District 545 E Lincoln Hwy Coatesville PA 19320-5404

SIMMONS, BARBARA LOUISE, school system administrator, language educator; b. Boston, Mar. 20, 1948; d. Dorothy Mankowich Furne; children: James, Bradley. BA, Wellesley Coll., Wellesley, Mass., 1969; MA in Writing Seminars, John Hopkins, Balt., Md., 1970; MA in Ednl. Adminstrn., Santa Clara Univ., Calif., 1983. English tchr. Northfield Mount Hermon, Northfield, Mass., 1970—72, Waltham H.S., Waltham, Mass., 1972—74; asst. dir. admissions Wellesley Coll., Wellesley, Mass., 1974—75; dir. tng. Gap Stores, Burlingame, Calif., 1975—78; asst. dean grad sch. Santa Clara Univ., Santa Clara, Calif., 1983—2000; coll. counselor, tchr. Bellamine Coll. Prep., San Jose, Calif., 2000—. Ednl. com. St. Jude the Apostle, Cupertino, Calif., 2005—. Contbr. poetry pub. to profl. jour. Libr. tutor San Jose Pub. Libr., San Jose, Calif., 1990—95. Recipient Outstanding Employee, Santa Clara Univ., 2000, Outstanding Alumni, 2001. Mem.: Calif. Assn. English Tchrs., Coll. Bd., Nat. Assn. of Coll. Admissions Counselors. Avocations: reading, hiking, poetry, writing.

SIMMONS, DEBORAH ANNE, environmental educator; b. Oroville, Calif., Oct. 9, 1950; d. Daniel Fredrick and Jeanne (Marlow) Simmons; m. Ronald Eugene Widmar, May 17, 1980. BA in Anthropology, U. Calif., Berkeley, 1972; MS, Humboldt State U., Arcata, Calif., 1977, PhD in Natural Resources, 1983. Cert. secondary tchr., Calif. TESOL instr. U.S. Peace Corps, South Korea, 1973-75; postdoctoral scholar U. Mich., Ann Arbor, 1983-84; asst. prof. Montclair State Coll., Upper Montclair, N.J., 1984-87; asst. prof. Dept. Teaching and Learning No. Ill. U., DeKalb, 1987-92, assoc. prof., 1992-98, prof., 1998—. Dir. Nat. Project for Excellence in Environ. Edn., 1994—; exec. editor Jour. Environ. Edn., 1999—; cons. in field. Author monograph; contbr. articles to profl. jours. Recipient Rsch. award Progressive Architecture, 1987, 88, Outstanding Rsch. award N.Am. Assn. Environ. Edn., 1996; U.S. Forest Svc. grantee, 1991-1997, 2006—, U.S. Fish and Wildlife Svcs., 1999-2004; Environ. Edn. and Tng. Partnership grantee, 1995—. Mem. N.Am. Assn. for Environ. Edn. (treas. 1991-95, pres. 1996, Walter Jeske Outstanding Achievement award 2000). Avocation: backpacking. Office: No Ill U Dept Tchg Lng Dekalb IL 60115

SIMMONS, DEBRA ADAMS, editor; m. Jonathan Simmons; children: Jacob, Jonathan. BA, Syracuse U., NY; diploma in Advanced Exec. Program, Northwestern U. Reporter Syracuse (N.Y.) Herald-Jour., The Hartford (Conn.) Courant; metro editor The Virginian Post; asst. metro editor and reporter Detroit (Mich.) Free Press; dep. mng. editor The Virginian-Pilot, Norfolk, Va., 2000—03; mng. editor Akron (Ohio) Beacon Jour., 2003, editor, 2003—, v.p., 2003—. Office: Akron Beacon Journal 44 E Exchange St PO Box 640 Akron OH 44309-0640

SIMMONS, DEIDRE WARNER, retired performing company executive, arts consultant; b. Easton, Pa., May 11, 1955; d. Francis Joseph and Irene Carol (Burd) Mooney; m. Robert D. Jacobson, June 27, 1981 (div. Mar. 1989); m. William Richard Simmons, Aug. 18, 1990; children: Caitlin Dawn, Abigail Patricia, Samantha Irene. BA in Music, Montclair State Coll., 1978. Music tchr. Warren Hills Regional Sch., Washington, NJ, 1978-80; devel. dir. N.J. Shakespeare Festival, Madison, 1981-83; dir. contbns. Parent Found., Lancaster, Pa., 1983-86; exec. dir. Fulton Opera House, Lancaster, 1986—95, capital campaign counsel, 1995—2000, dir. theatre advancement, 2000—03; arts cons., 2003—. Bd. dirs. WITF, vice chmn., 2005—; chmn. Lancaster Arts, 2005; bd. dirs. Lancaster Country Day Sch. Vice chmn. bd. dirs. Ind. Eye, Lancaster, 1986—89; bd. dirs. Pa. Dutch Conv. and Visitors Bur., Lancaster Campaign; chair Destination Downtown. Recipient Exemplar award, Lancaster C. of C. and Industry, 2003. Mem.: League Hist. Theatres, Theatre Comm. Group. Avocations: piano, singing. E-mail: dwsimmons@comcast.net.

SIMMONS, DONNA MARIE, neuroscientist, histotechnologist, neuroendocrine anatomist, researcher; b. Hartford, Conn., Oct. 13, 1943; d. John Henry and Ellen Louise (Meehl) Strayer; m. Corvin Gale Simmons, Sept. 17, 1964. Student, U. Wash., We. Wash. State U.; PhD, U. So. Calif., 2005. Histologic technician, instr. Tacoma Gen. Hosp. Sch. Med. Tech., Tacoma, 1963; lab. technician Med. Sch. U. Wash., 1964; histologic technician Northgate Med. Lab., Seattle, 1964—67; rsch. technologist in neuroanatomy Regional Primate Rsch. Ctr. U. Wash., 1967—82; rsch. asst. Devel. Neurobiology Lab. Salk Inst., La Jolla, Calif., 1982—85, sr. technician. lab. mgr. Neural Sys. Lab. Howard Hughes Med. Inst., 1985—90; vis. faculty neurosciences dept. Baylor U. Med. Sch., 1990; rsch. assoc. dept. biol. scis.-neurobiology U. So. Calif., L.A., 1990—, Neurosci. Rsch. Inst., 2002—. Cons., lectr. in field; judge Greater San Diego Sci. and Engring. Fair, 1987-89, Calif. Sci. Fair, 1992—; leader sci. del. to People's Rep. of China, 1986; chair China Scientist Exch. Fund, 1986-87; mem. Swiss Histology Meeting Exch., 1990. Author tech. articles, revs. in field; mem. editl. bd. Jour. Histotech, 1982-2002. Recipient Diamond Cover award Jour. Histotech., 1990; various svcs. awards; best non-clin. pub. in field, 1985; Hudson Hoagland USA-Australia Exch. Med. Rsch. fellow Prince Henry's Rsch. Inst. Monash U., 1996. Mem. AAAS, APA, Am. Soc. Clin. Pathologists (affiliate), Am. Physiol. Soc., Wash. State Histology Soc. (past pres., histology liason Am. Soc. Med. Tech.), Nat. Soc. Histotech. (charter, regional dir. 1980-82, jud. chair 1983-86), Calif. Soc. Histotech. (San Diego dir. protem 1985-86), Assn. Women in Sci. (San Diego charter, bd. dirs. 1985-90), Soc. for Neurosci., Women in Neurosci., NY Acad. Sci., J.B. Johnston Club, Cajal Club, Sierra Club, NOW, Am. Alpine Club, Sigma Xi. Office: U So Calif Mc 2520 Los Angeles CA 90089-0001

SIMMONS, DOREEN ANNE, lawyer; b. Dec. 22, 1949; d. Samuel and Gloria (Jensen) Buranich; m. Harvey O. Simmons III, Oct. 12, 1974; children: Olivia, Grace, Harvey. BA, Purdue U., 1971; JD, Union U., 1974. Bar: NY 1975, U.S. Dist. Ct. (No., So., Ea. and We. dists.) N.Y. Sr. asst. dist. atty. Onondaga County (N.Y.), Syracuse, 1975-80; ptnr. Hancock & Estabrook, Syracuse, 1980—. Chair com. on character and fitness 5th Jud. Dist. N.Y. State Appellate Divsn., 1984—. Fellow: N.Y. State Bar Found.; mem.: No. Dist. N.Y. Fed. Ct. Bar Assn., Inc. (pres.), N.Y. State Bar Assn. (environ. and trial coms.). Office: Hancock & Estabrook Mony Tower I PO Box 4976 Syracuse NY 13221-4976 Office Phone: 315-471-3151. Business E-Mail: dsimmons@hancocklaw.com.

SIMMONS, EMMY B., former federal agency administrator; b. Suring, Wis., Oct. 26, 1941; m. Roger Simmons. BA in Internat. Rels., U. Wis., Milw., 1965; MS in Agrl. Econs., Cornell U., Ithaca, NY, 1968. Rsch. fellow Ahmadu Bello U., Zaria, Nigeria, 1969—73; economist Ministry Planning and Econ. Affairs, Monrovia, Liberia, 1974—77; agr. economist US Agency Internat. Devel., 1978—91; supervisory program economist US Agency Internat. Devel. Regional Office East and South Africa, 1991—94; sr. program officer US Agency Internat. Devel. Regional Office Moscow, 1995—97; deputy asst. admin. Global Bureau US Agency Internat. Devel., Washington, 1997—2001; asst. admin. US Agency Internat. Devel. Wash., 2002—05. Vol. Peace Corps., Philippines, 1962—64; bd. mem. Soc. Internat. Devel., Wash. chapter, Internat. Inst. Tropical Agr., Ibadan, Nigeria, Internat. Livestock Rsch. Inst., Nairobi, Kenya; mem. Nat. Acad. Sci. Roundtable on Sci. Tech. for Sustainability. Personal E-mail: emmybsimmons@aol.com.

SIMMONS, GAIL LINDSAY, lawyer; b. NYC, June 15, 1949; d. James Lambert Simmons and Jacqueline (Chambers) Cook; m. Allen Howard Feldman, Jan. 5, 1980; children: Andrew Feldman, Thomas Feldman, Alexandra Feldman. Student, U. London, 1968, Harvard U., 1970; BA, Carnegie-Tech., Pitts., 1971; JD, Case Western Res. U., 1974. Bar: Ohio 1974, DC 1975. Law clk. Thurlow Smoot, Cleve., 1972—74; atty. US Customs, Washington, 1974—75, US Dept. Labor, Washington, 1975—79; asst. corp. counsel DC Govt., Washington, 1979—81; ptnr. Cotten, Day & Doyle, Washington, 1981—87, Doyle & Savit, Washington, 1987—. Active Jr. League Washington, Don't Tear It Down, Preservation of Assateague Nat. Seashore, Va. Mem.: ABA, Trial Lawyers Assn. Am., DC Bar Assn., Fed. Bar Assn. Republican. Presbyterian. Home: 3708 Morrison St NW Washington DC 20015-1734 Office: Jackson & Kelly 2401 Pennsylvania Ave NW Washington DC 20037-1730

SIMMONS, JANET BRYANT, writer, publishing executive; b. Oakland, Calif., Apr. 22, 1925; d. Howard Pelton and Janet Horn (McNab) Bryant; m. William Ellis Simmons, May 17, 1944 (div. 1979); children: William Howard, Janet Margaret Simmons McAlpine. BA, San Jose State U., Calif., 1965; MA, U. San Francisco, 1979. Social worker Santa Clara County Social Svcs., San Jose, Calif., 1965-91; editor, pub. Enlightenment Press, Santa Clara, 1994—. Author: The Mystical Child, 1996. Mem. AAUW, Am. Booksellers Assn., Pubs. Mktg. Assn., Bay Area Ind. Pubs. Assn., Audubon Soc., Jacques Cousteau Soc. Avocations: playing piano, swimming, tai chi, travel, gardening. Office: Enlightenment Press PO Box 3314 Santa Clara CA 95055-3314 Office Fax: 408-248-3222. Personal E-mail: simmonssj@aol.com.

SIMMONS, JEAN BYERS, academic administrator, director; b. Ft. Worth, July 29, 1956; d. James Clifford and Don Jean Carter; m. Jim Allen Simmons, Sept. 20, 1973; children: Jeffrey Brent, Joshua Allen. B of Arts History magna cum laude, Columbia Coll., Mo., 2002; M of History, Tarleton State U., 2004. DataTel Columbia Coll., 2000. Office mgr. Columbia Coll., 2002—03, acad. advisor, 2003—05; dir. Embry Riddle Aeronautical U., 2005—. Trainer Columbia Coll., Columbia, Mo., 2000—05. Fund raising Little League, White Settlement, Tex., 1984—90; mem. PTA, 1980—93; treas. Brewer Bear Athletic Booster Club, 1990—93. Mem.: Phi Alpha Theta (life), Alpha Sigma Lambda (life). Democrat-Npl. Baptist. Avocations: travel, reading, swimming, researching. Home: 508 Meadow Park Dr White Settlement TX 76108 Office: Embry-Riddle Aeronautical Univ NAS JRB Bldg 1525 Fort Worth TX 76127 Office Phone: 817-737-8180. Personal E-mail: js114729@sbcglobal.net. Business E-Mail: jean.simmons@erau.edu.

SIMMONS, KARLA PEAVY, researcher, educator; b. Las Vegas, July 17, 1970; d. John Lester and Patricia Vail Peavy; m. Gill Simmons, Aug. 1, 1998. BS, Auburn U., 1992, MS, 1996; PhD, N.C. State U., 2002. Quality control mgr. Oneita Industries, Andrews, SC, 1992—93; asst. prof. U. Mo., Columbia, 2002—05, Auburn U., Ala., 2005—. Adv. bd. mem. Lori Coulter True Measure, St. Louis, 2002—. Mem. Howard County Christian Women's Orgn., Fayette, Mo., 2004—06, Friends of Mo. Hist. Costume Collection, Columbia, 2005—. Grantee, USDA, 2004—, Nat. Textile Ctr., 2006—. Mem.: DAR, ASTM, Internat. Textile and Apparel Assn., Kappa Alpha Theta (adv. bd. 1994—97). Conservative. Achievements include research in 3D Body Scanning and Site Manager of SizeUSA National Sizing Study. Avocations: sewing, crafts. Office: Auburn U 308 Spidle Hall Auburn University AL 36849 Office Phone: 334-844-1345. Office Fax: 334-844-1340. E-mail: ksimmons@auburn.edu.

SIMMONS, KIMORA LEE, apparel designer, television personality, model; b. St. Louis, May 3, 1975; d. Vernon Whitlock and Joanne Perkins; m. Russell Simmons, 1998; 2 children. Former model Chanel; founder, CEO, dir. Baby Phat Clothing. Appearances include (films) Unzipped, 1995, Catwalk, 1996, Brown Sugar, 2002, The Big Tease, 1999, Beauty Shop, 2005, Rebound, 2005, (TV series) America's Next Top Model, 2003, Life & Style, 2004—, Fashion Week Diaries, 2005; exec. prodr.: (Broadway plays) Def Poetry Jam, 2003 (Tony award). Established Kimora Lee Simmons Scholarship Fund, Kimora Lee Simmons Foundation. Named Vibe Vixen, Vibe mag., 2005, Outstanding Stylemaker, Asian Excellence Awards, 2006. Office: Sony Pictures Entertainment 10202 W Washington Blvd Culver City CA 90232*

SIMMONS, LAURA, religious studies educator; PhD, Fuller Theol. Sem., Pasadena, Calif., 1999. Assoc. prof. Christian ministries George Fox Sem., Portland, Oreg., 2001—. Author: Creed without Chaos: Exploring Theology in the Writings of Dorothy L. Sayers. Mem.: Dorothy L. Sayers Soc. Office: George Fox Sem 12753 SW 68th Ave Portland OR 97223 Office Phone: 503-554-6157. Business E-Mail: lsimmons@georgefox.edu.

SIMMONS, LYNDA MERRILL MILLS, retired principal; b. Salt Lake City, Aug. 31, 1940; d. Alanson Soper and Madeline Helene (Merrill) Mills; m. Mark Carl Simmons, Nov. 17, 1962; children: Lisa Lynn Simmons Morley, William Mark, Jennifer Louise, Robert Thomas. BS, U. Utah, Salt Lake City, 1961, MS, 1983. Cert. sch. adminstr., Utah. Tchr. Wasatch Jr. H.S./Granite Dist., Salt Lake City, 1961-64, Altamont (Utah) H.S./Duchesne Dist., 1964-66; tchr. spl. edn. Park City (Utah) H.S., 1971-73; resource tchr. Eisenhower Jr. H.S., Salt Lake City, 1979-88; tchr. specialist Granite Sch. Dist., Salt Lake City, 1985-90; asst. prin. Bennion Jr. H.S., Salt Lake City, 1990-93; prin. Hartvigsen Sch., Salt Lake City, 1993—2002; ret., 2002. Adj. prof. spl. edn. U. Utah, Salt Lake City, 1987—, Utah Prin. Acad., 1994-95, co-chair Utah Spl. Educators for Computer Tech., Salt Lake City, 1988-90; adv. com. on handicapped Utah State Office Edn., 1990-93; presenter in field; edtl. cons. 2006-. Author: Setting Up Effective Secondary Resource Program, 1985; contbr. articles to profl. jours. Dist. chmn. Heart Fund, Cancer Dr., Summit Park, Utah, 1970-82; pack leader Park City area Boy Scouts Am., 1976-80; bd. dirs. Jr. League Salt Lake City, 1977-80, cmty. bd., 1997—; cookie chmn. Park City area Girl Scouts U.S., 1981; dist. chmn. March of Dimes, 1982—. Recipient Amb. award Salt Lake Conv. and Vis. Bur., 1993; named Bus. Woman of Yr., South Salt Lake C. of C., 2001. Mem. Nat. Assn. Secondary Sch. Prins., Park City Young Women's Mut. (pres. 1989-93, family history cons. 1993-95), Women's Athanaeum (v.p. 1990-93, pres. 1994-2001), Gen. Fedn. Women's Clubs (pres. Salt Lake dist. 1998-02, cmty.-improvement chairperson Utah 1996-98, chairperson Woman of Yr. 1998—, state treas. 2006-) Coun. for Exceptional Children (pres. Salt Lake chpt. 1989-90, pres. Utah Fedn. 1991-93, Spl. Educator of Yr. 1995), Granite Assn.

Sch. Adminstrs. (sec.-treas. 1992-94); Mission for Ch. of Jesus Christ of Latter Day Saints, Blacksburg, Va., 2003-04. Mem. Lds Ch. Avocations: reading, cooking, writing, sports, handiwork.

SIMMONS, LYNDA TEEL, nurse, healthcare executive; d. A. Stokes. A in Nursing, Columbus Coll., 1969, BA in Psychology, 1973; BSN, Troy State U., 1984, MSN magna cum laude, 1986. RN State Med. Agy., Clin. Nurse Specialist. Head nurse emergency room Columbus Med. Ctr., Ga., 1972—75; hosp. supr. Drs. Hosp. Hosp. Corp. Am., 1975—80; dir. surgical nursing divsn. Columbus Med. Ctr., 1980—82; critical care instr. BSN Program Auburn U., Auburn, Ala., 1985; RN State Med. Agy., Columbus, Ga., 1988—93; CEO Simmons Healthcare Enterprises, 1996—. Lectr. seminars, 2004. Mem.: Am. Assn. Critical Care Nurses, Emergency Nurse Assn., Soc. Critical Care Medicine, Am. Assn. Legal Nurse Cons., Sigma Theta Tau. Avocations: horseback riding, fencing, tennis, swimming. Office: Simmons Healthcare Enterprises 1303 Pagoda Dr Columbus GA 31907

SIMMONS, MARGUERITE SAFFOLD, pharmaceutical sales professional; b. Montgomery, Ala., Oct. 21, 1954; d. Arthur Edward and Gwendolyn Jane (Saffold) S. BS in Communications, U. Tenn., 1976. Press sec. Met. Mayor's Office, Nashville, 1977-78; advt. copywriter United Meth. Pub. House, Nashville, 1976-77; sales rep. No Nonsense Pantyhose, Houston, 1978-81, Breon Labs., Houston, 1981-82; profl. sales rep. Janssen Pharmaceutica, Inc., Houston, 1982-88, sr. sales rep., 1988-97; territory sales mgr. Bristol-Myers Squibb Co., Atlanta, 1997-2001, sr. territory bus. mgr., 2001—02, long-term care specialty rep., 2002—. Vol. Dem. Nat. Conv., Atlanta, 1988. Named to Outstanding Young Women in Am., 1981, 87. Mem. NAFE, U. Tenn. Alumni Assn. (bd. dirs. Atlanta chpt. 1989-90, v.p. 2000—), U. Tenn. Black Alumni Assn. (bd. dirs. Atlanta chpt. 1989—, pres. Atlanta chpt. 1995-96, bd. govs. dist. 5 rep. 1995-2000), Ga. Trust Hist. Soc., Ala. Geneal. Soc., Ga. Geneal. Soc., Nat. Trust Hist. Preservation, Delta Sigma Theta. Baptist. Avocations: reading, genealogy, personal computing. Personal E-mail: marguerite.s@usa.net.

SIMMONS, MARTHA R., mortgage company executive; Grad., Am. Bankers Assn. Nat. Trust Sch., Northwestern U., Am. Bankers Assn. Nat. Commercial Lending Sch., U. Okla., Sch. for Exec. Develop., U. Ga. Former bus. mgr. SunTrust Bank; former pres., Gainesville, Ga. market SunTrust Mortgage, Inc (subsidiary of SunTrust Bank), bus. mgr., central region Richmond, Va., 2002—04, exec. v.p., nat. retail production mgr., 2004—. Former vice chair of exec. Greater Hall Chamber of Commerce, former chmn., co-chair, HALLmark Initiative campaign, 2001. Named one of 25 Women to Watch, US Banker mag., 2005. Office: SunTrust Mortgage Inc 901 Semmes Ave Richmond VA 23224-2270*

SIMMONS, MARTI J. JOHNSON, gifted and talented education educator; b. Gt. Lakes, Ill., Aug. 30, 1948; d. William Ernest and Martha Aliene (Jones) Johnson; m. Ernest Lee Simmons, Jr., June 14, 1970; children: Scott Ernest, Leah Kathleen. Student, Pitzer Coll., Claremont, Calif., 1978; BS in Edn., Minot (N.D.) State U., 1980; gifted credential, Moorhead (Minn.) State U., 1980, elem. endorsement, 1986. Tutor, paraprofl. Agassiz Jr. High Sch., Fargo, N.D., 1980-84; tchr., coord. gifted program West Fargo (N.D.) Mid. Sch., 1984-90; tchr. English, West Fargo Mid. Sch., 1990—. Insvc. speaker in field; conf. presenter in field. Mem. N.D. Edn. Assn., West Fargo Edn. Assn. (bldg. rep.), Valley Reading Coun. (bldg. rep., literacy com. 1988-90), Valley Tchrs. Gifted Network, Alpha Delta Kappa (chpt. pres., staff officer 1986-88). Democrat. Lutheran. Avocation: gourmet cooking. Home: 2714 Rivershore Dr Moorhead MN 56560-4219 Office: West Fargo Mid Sch 109 3rd St E West Fargo ND 58078-1817

SIMMONS, PATRICIA ANN, pharmacist, consultant; b. Monroe, Wis., Apr. 17, 1964; d. Wendell Louis and Gladys Lemae (Casey) S. Student, Mercer U., Macon, Ga., 1982-84; PharmD, Mercer So. Sch. Pharmacy, Atlanta, 1990. Registered pharmacist, Ga., Fla.; cons. pharmacist, Fla.; cert. geriat. pharmacist. Intern in pharmacy Joel N Jerry's Pharmacy, Clearwater, Fla., 1987-90, staff pharmacist, 1990-96, mgr., 1991-92; resident in pharmacy VA Med. Ctr., Gainesville, Fla., 1990-91; cons., staff pharmacist Sun Pharmacy, Largo, Fla., 1991—2002; pharmacist Lesco and Pharmacistance, Tampa and Largo, Fla., 1993—2001, Medicine Shop in Kash-n-Karry, 2001—. Vol. pharmacist Pasco County Free Clinic, Hudson, Fla., 1994-99, mgr., 1996-97. Author: Drugs of Abuse for Non-Medical Professional, 1993. Sec. Choice Single Friends in Faith, Tampa, 1994-95, svc. coord., 1995-97, asst. coord., 1996-97, coord., 1997-2006; eucharist minister St. Luke Ch., Palm Harbor, Fla., 1995-99, youth ministry asst., 1995-98. Mem. Young Reps., 1982-85; instr. CPR ARC, 1982-91, mem. local disaster team, 1986-90; spkr. poison prevention elem. schs., Pinellas County, Fla., 1993-97; svc. coord. Mercer U. Circle-K, 1983-84. Named Disting. Young Pharmacist, Hoechst-Marion Roussel, Inc., Fla., 1996. Mem. Am. Pharm. Assn., Pinellas Pharmacy Assn. (chair poison prevention 1993-97, sec. 1994-95, pres. 1996-97, Pharmacist of Yr. 1994). Roman Catholic. Office: Simmons Realty 1780 Main St Dunedin FL 34698-6427

SIMMONS, RUTH J., academic administrator; b. Grapeland, Tex., July 3, 1945; d. Isaac and Fannie Stubblefield; m. Norbert Simmons, 1968 (div. 1989); children: Khari, Maya. Student, Universidad Internacional, Saltillo, Mex., 1965, Wellesley Coll., 1965—66; BA, Dillard U., 1967; postgrad., Universite de Lyon, 1967—68, George Washington U., 1968—69; AM, Harvard U., 1970, PhD in Romance Langs., 1973; LLD (hon.), Amherst Coll., 1995; LHD (hon.), Howard U., 1996, Dillard U., 1996; LLD (hon.), Princeton U., 1996, Lake Forest Coll., 1997; LHD (hon.), U. Mass., 1997; LLD (hon.), Dartmouth Coll., 1997, Mt. Holyoke Coll., 2001, U. Pa., 2001, Harvard U., 2002, George Washington U., 2002, Columbia U., 2002, Washington U., 2002, U. So. Calif., 2003, Boston U., Rensselaer Polytechnic Inst., N.Y. U., Northeastern; D of Women's Studies (hon.), Ewha Woman's U., Rep. of Korea, 2002; LittD (hon.), U. Toronto, 2004; LHD, Jewish Theol. Sem., 2004, Taugaloo Coll., 2004. Interpreter lang. svcs. divsn. U.S. Dept. State, Washington, 1968—69; instr. French George Washington U., 1968—69; admissions officer Radcliffe Coll., 1970—72; asst. prof. French U. New Orleans, 1973—75, asst. dean coll. liberal arts, asst. prof. French, 1975—76; adminstrv. coord. NEH liberal studies project Calif. State U., Northridge, 1977—78, acting dir. internat. programs, vis. assoc. prof. Pan-African studies, 1978—79; asst. dean grad. sch. U. So. Calif., 1979—82, assoc. dean grad. sch., 1982—83; dir. studies Butler Coll. Princeton U., NJ, 1983—85, acting. dir. Afro-Am. studies, 1985—87, asst. dean faculty, 1986—87, assoc. dean faculty, 1986—90, vice provost, 1992—95; provost Spelman Coll., 1990—91; pres. Smith Coll., Northampton, Mass., 1995—2001; pres Brown U., Providence, 2001—, prof. comparative lit. and African studies. Peer reviewer higher edn. divsn. NEH, 1980—83, bd. cons., 1981; mem. grad. adv. bd. Calif. Student Aid Commn., 1981—83; chair com. to visit dept. African-Am. studies Harvard U., 1991; mem. strategic planning task force N.J. Dept. Higher Edn., 1992—93; mem. nat. adv. commn. EQUITY 2000 Coll. Bd., 1992—95; mem. adv. bd. ctrl. N.J. NAACP Legal Def. Fund, 1992—95; mem. Mid. States Assn. Accreditation Team, Johns Hopkins U., 1993; chmn. accreditation team Bryn Mawr Coll., 1999; chair rev. panel for model instns. planning grants NSF, 1993; mem. Conf. Bd., 1995; bd. dirs. MetLife, JSTOR, Pfizer Inc., 1997—, COFHE, Com. Econ. Devel., Goldman Sachs, 1999—, Tex. Instruments, 1999—; mem. adv. coun. dept. Romance Langs. and Lit. Princeton U., 1996; trustee Carnegie Corp., 1999—; presenter, spkr. and panelist in field. Mem. editl. bd.: World Edn. series Am. Assn. Collegiate Registrars and Admissions Officers, 1984—86; contbr. articles to profl. jours. Named mem. Women's Progress Commemoration Commn. by Pres. Bill Clinton, 1999; mem. adv. coun. Bill and Melinda Gates Millennium Scholars Found.; chmn. Congl. Black Caucus Found. Washington, 2004; mem. adv. bd. N.J. Master Faculty Program Woodrow Wilson Nat. Fellowship Found., 1987—90, trustee, 1991—96, Inst. Advances Study, 1995—98, The Clarke Sch. for Deaf, 1995—; chmn. bd. trustees Acad. Music, 1995—98; mem. adv. com. Healthy Steps for Young Children Program, 1996—98; mem. bd. advisors 1st Internat. Conf. on AIDS, Ethiopia, 1998. Named Women of Yr., CBS, 1996, Glamour Mag., 1996, Disting. Fulbright Alumna, Inst. Internat. Edn., 1997, Woman of World, NASA, 1998, Am. Best Coll. Pres., Time mag., 2001, Woman Yr., Ms. mag., 2002; named one of Newsweek Person to Watch, 2002; recipient Disting. Svc. award, Assn. Black Princeton Alumni, 1989, Dillard U., 1992, Pres.'s Recognition award, Bloomfield Coll., 1993, TWIN award, Princeton Area YWCA, 1993, Women's orgn. Tribute award, Princeton U., 1994, Leadership award, Third World Ctr. Princeton U., 1995, Tex. Excellence award, Leap Program, 1995, Benjamin E. Mays award, A Better Chance, 1995, Centennial medal, Harvard U. Grad. Sch. Arts & Scis., 1997, Achievement award, Nat. Urban League, 1998, Tchr. Coll. Medal for Disting. Svc., Columbia U., 1999, Pres. award, United Negro Coll. Fund, 2001, "Drum Major for Justice" Edn. award, So. Christian Leadership Conf./W.O.M.E.N., 2002, Fulbright Lifetime Achievement Medal, 2002, R.I. History Makers award, 2002, Amelia Earhart award, 2002, ROBIE Humanitarian award, The Jackie Robinson Found., 2004, The Eleanor Roosevelt Val-Kill medal, 2004, fellowship, DAAD, Presdl. Medal of Honor, Dillard U., 2006; fellow, Danforth Found., 1967—73, Sr. Fulbright fellow, 1981; scholar, KYOK, 1963, Worthing Found., 1963—67, Fulbright scholar, U. de Lyon, 1967—68. Fellow: Am. Acad. Arts & Scis.; mem.: AAAS, Coun. Foreign Rels., Am. Philos. Soc. Office: Office of Pres Brown U One Prospect Street, Campus Box 1860 Providence RI 02912 Office Phone: 401-863-2234. Office Fax: 401-863-7737. E-mail: president@brown.edu.*

SIMMONS, SARAH R., lawyer; b. Ducktown, Tenn., Jan. 23, 1948; BA magna cum laude, U. Ariz., 1970, postgrad.; JD magna cum laude, U. Denver, 1973. Bar: Colo. 1974, Ariz. 1975. Mem. Molloy, Jones & Donahue, Tucson, Brown & Bain, P.A., Lewis & Roca LLP, 2002—05; judge Ariz. Supreme Ct. Pima County, 2006—. Mem. Davis Monthan 50, 1991—, pres., 1998-2000; trustee Tohono Club Park, 1995-2004, sec., 1997-99, v.p. 1999-2001, pres., 2001-03; trustee Tucson Airport Authority, 1996-2006, bd. dir., 2005-06; mem. Law Coll. Assn. Bd., 1996—, sec. 1998-99, pres. 2000-01; 4th R bd. Tucson Unified Sch., 1996-2003; bd. dir. United Way Tucson, 1995-2000, Family Advocacy Resource and Wellness Ctrs., Resources Women, 1995-2000; bd. dir. Ariz. Town Hall, 1998-2003; mem. adv. bd. Ariz. Drug Free Workplace, 1991-2002, So. Ariz. Sports Devel. Corp., U. Ariz. Social and Behavioral Scis., 1994-96; sec. So. Ariz. Minutemen, 1996-98; mem. bd. visitors Coll. Law, chair, 2002-06; v.p. Met. Tucson Conv. and Visitors Bur., 2003-05, pres. 2005-06. Recipient Outstanding Alumni award U. Ariz. Coll. of Law, 1993, Tucson Woman of Yr. of C. of C., 1994, Women on the Move award YWCA, 1995, Alice Truman Leadership award, 2003; named one of 100 Women and Minorities in the Law, 2000, Women Who Lead, U. Ariz. Women's Studies Adv. Coun., 2003. Fellow ABA, Ariz. Bar Assn.; mem. Nat. Assn. Bond Lawyers, State Bar Ariz. (bd. govs. 1987-95, sec.-treas. 1989-90, 2d v.p. 1990-91, 1st v.p. 1991-92, pres.-elect 1992-93, pres. 1993-94, employment law sect., profl. conduct com., fee arbitration com., co- mem. of yr. 2004), Ariz. Women Lawyers Assn. (charter), Colo. Bar Assn., Pima County Bar Assn. (bd. dirs. 1985-94), Am. Judicature Soc., So. Ariz. Legal Aid (bd. dir. 1990-93), Lawyers Against Hunger (v.p. D-M 50 1996-98, pres. 1998-2000), Order St. Ives, Phi Beta Kappa, Phi Kappa Phi, Phi Alpha Theta, Kappa Beta Pi. Office: Ariz Supreme Ct in Pima County 110 W Congress Tucson AZ 85701 Office Phone: 520-740-8441. E-mail: ssimmons@sc.pima.gov.

SIMMONS, SUE, newscaster; b. NY, May 27, 1943; d. John Simmons. Corr. WTNH-TV, New Haven, 1973-74, WBAL-TV, Balt., 1974, anchor, host Balt. at One, 1975—76; corr./anchor. WRC-TV, Washington, 1976—80; co-anchor News Channel 4/Live at Five/News Channel 4 at 11 p.m WNBC News, NYC, 1980—; host Images: A Year in Review, WNBC, 2002—. Recipient four Emmy awards, award for Outstanding Performance by a News Commentator, Barnabus McHenry, Vice-Chmn. Pres.'s Task Force on Arts and Humanities, 1981; named to the NY State Broadcasters Assn. Hall of Fame, 2005 Office: WNBC-TV 30 Rockefeller Plz New York NY 10112-0002*

SIMMONS, SYLVIA (SYLVIA SIMMONS NEUMANN), advertising executive, writer; b. NYC; m. Hans H. Neumann, 1962. BA cum laude, Bklyn. Coll.; MA in English Lit., Columbia U. Dir. sales promotion and direct mail divsn. McCann Erickson, Inc., N.Y.C., 1958-62; v.p., asst. to pres. Young & Rubicam, Inc., N.Y.C., 1962-73; sr. v.p., dir. spl. projects Kenyon & Eckhardt, Inc., N.Y.C., 1975-86; sr. v.p., dir. corp. comms. Bozell, Jacobs, Kenyon & Eckhardt, 1985-86, cons., 1986-88; free-lance speech writer, 1987—. Author: New Speakers Handbook, 1972, The Great Garage Sale Book, 1982, 2d edit. 2000, (with Hans H. Neumann) The Straight Story on VD, 1974, 2d edit., 2000; Dr. Neumann's Guide to the New Sexually Transmitted Diseases, 1983; co-author: (with Thomas D. Rees) More Than Just a Pretty Face, 1987, How to be the Life of the Podium, 1991; contbr. articles to profl. jours., nat. and local newspapers. Recipient Medal of Freedom, 1946, award for best radio comml. NY Radio Broadcasters Assn., 1976-77, Sales Promotion Execs. Assn. award. Mem. Nat. League Am. Pen Women, Authors Guild, Propylaea, Exec. for Peace (founding mem.), Sigma Tau Delta.

SIMMONS, SYLVIA JEANNE QUARLES (MRS. HERBERT G. SIMMONS JR.), academic administrator, educator; b. Boston, May 8, 1935; d. Lorenzo Christopher and Margaret Mary (Thomas) Quarles; m. Herbert G. Simmons, Jr., Oct. 26, 1957; children: Stephen, Alison, Lisa. BA, Manhattanville Coll., 1957; MEd, Boston Coll., 1962, PhD, 1990; DHL (hon.), St. Joseph's Coll., 1994; EdD (hon.), Merrimack Coll., 1999. Montessori tchr. Charles River Park Nursery Sch., Boston, 1970-76; registrar Boston Coll. Sch. Mgmt., Chestnut Hill, 1966-70; dir. fin. aid Radcliffe Coll., Cambridge, Mass., 1970-75, assoc. dean admissions and fin. aid, 1972-75, assoc. dean admissions, fin. aid and women's edn., 1975; assoc. dean admissions and fin. aid Harvard and Radcliffe, from 1975; assoc. v.p. for acad. affairs ctrl. adminstrn. U. Mass., Boston, 1976-79, spl. asst. to chancellor, 1979; v.p. field svcs. Am. Student Assistance, 1982-84, sr. v.p., 1984-93, exec. v.p., 1983-95, pres., 1996; mem. faculty Harvard U., 1970-77, pres. faculty, 1995-96; lectr. Boston U., 1991—. Cons. Mass. Bd. Higher Edn., 1973—77. Co-editor: Student Loans Riches and Realities. Past bd. dirs. Rivers Country Day Sch., Weston, Mass., Simons's Rock Coll., Great Barrington, Mass., Wayland (Mass.) Fair Housing, Cambridge Mental Health Assn., Family Svcs. Greater Boston, Concerts in Black and White, Mass., Higher Edn. Assistance Corp.; chmn. bd. dirs. North Shore Cmty. Coll., 1986-88, mem. bd. dirs., 1985—; trustee and alumnae bd. dirs. Manhattanville Coll., 1986—; mem. adv. com. Upward Bound, Chestnut Hill Boston Coll., 1972-74, Women in Politics John McCormick Inst., 1994-2000; Camp Chimney Corners, Becket, Mass., 1971-77; bd. dirs. Am. Cancer Soc. Mass., 1987-89, Boston Coll., 1990-98, Merrimack Coll., 1992-2000, Mass. Found. for Humanities, 1990-92, Mass. Bay United Way, 1990-94, Grimes King Found., 1992—, St. Elizabeta's Hosp., 1991—, Anna Stearns Found., 1996—, Regis Coll., 1997—, Edn. Resources Inst., 1998—, Supreme Ct. Jud. Hist. Soc., 2001—, Newton Country Day Sch., 2002—, Shirley Eustes House, 2002—; overseer Mt. Ida Coll., 1990—, Exec. Svc. Corp., 1997—, Supreme Ct. Judicial Hist. Soc., 2001-, Newton County Day Sch., 2002-, Shirely Euestes House, 2002, The Edn. Resources Inst., 1998, Mus. Fine Arts, Boston, Mass., 2002—; chair Coll. Club Scholarship com., 1997. Recipient Educator of Yr. award Boston and Vicinity Club, 1989, Bicentennial medal Boston Coll., 1976, Achievement award Greater Boston YMCA, 1977, Human Rights awsard Mass. Tchrs. Assn., 1988, Pres'. award Mass. Ednl. Opportunity Assn., 1988, Archbishop Timothy Healy award, 1997, Outstanding Alumna award Girl's Latin Sch., 1998; named One of Ten Outstanding Yung Leaders, Boston Jr. C. of C., 1971, Sojourner's Daus.: 25 African women who have made a difference, 1991. Mem. Eastern Assns. Fin. Aid Officers (2st v.p. 1973), Coll. Scholarship Svc. Coun., Links (pres. local chpt. 1967-69), Nat. Inst. Fin. Aid Adminstrs. (dir. 1975-77), Jack and Jill Am. (pres. Newton chpt. 1972-74), Manhattanville Club (pres. Boston 1966-68), Delta Sigma Theta, Delta Kappa Gamma (pres. 1988-90). Home: 19 Clifford St Roxbury MA 02119-2120 Office: 330 Stuart St Boston MA 02116-5237 Personal E-mail: ssimm38414@aol.com.

SIMMS, ADRIENNE ELAINE, pre-school educator, consultant; b. Chgo., Mar. 2, 1952; d. James Steven and Elaine J. Simms; children: Paul James, Andrew Theodore. MA, U. of No. Colo., 1998; BA in Sociology, Western Ill. U., 1976. Director Qualification State of Colo., 1998. Cons./trainer The Sandbox, Greeley, Colo., 2002—; site dir. Head Start, Greeley, Colo., 2003—04; coord. ECE, Parent Edn. Metro State Coll. Denver, 2005—. Mem. Children's Festival Planning Com., Greeley, Colo., 2000—, Child Care and Youth Program Task Force, Greeley, Colo., 1999—2000. Recipient Pinnacle Honor Soc., U. of No. Colo., 8. Mem.: Nat. Assn. for the Edn. of Young Children (assoc.). Greek Orthodox. Achievements include research in the business of child care in Northern Colorado. Avocations: spinning wool, nature walking, travel.

SIMMS, AMY LANG, writer, educator; b. Bryn Mawr, Pa., Sept. 21, 1964; d. Eben Caldwell and Anna Mary L.; children: Harrison Lang, Maud Whittington. BA in French and Sociology, Bucknell U., 1986; postgrad., Sch. Mus. Fine Arts, 1988, Bryn Mawr Coll., 1988, Vassar Coll., 1993, U. Pa., 1995-97, Villanova U., 2001. Assoc. dir. pub. rels. Haverford (Pa.) Coll., 1995-96; copywriter, media and prodn. asst. DBM Assocs., Cambridge, Mass., 1986-88; tchg. asst. sociology dept. Bucknell U., Lewisburg, Pa., 1989; staff reporter Lewisburg Daily Jour., 1989-92, asst. editor, 1991, Milton (Pa.) Standard, 1991; tchr. Gt. Valley Sch. Dist., Malvern, Pa., 1997—2006; tchr. elem. gifted Colonial Sch. Dist., Plymouth Meeting, Pa., 2006—. Co-founder, co-editor Lewisburg Holiday Herald, 1990; co-founder Environ. Advisor Newsletter, Lewisburg, 1990-91. Assoc. editor: Main Line Life, 1996-97. Media corr. Elem. Related Arts Com., Lewisburg, 1989; mem. adv. bd. Union County Children and Youth Svcs., Lewisburg, 1991-92; trustee Sarah Hull Hallock Meml. Libr., Milton, N.Y., 1993-95. Recipient Hon. Speakers award Lewisburg Lions Club, 1990. Mem. AAUW. Avocations: books, travel, photography. Home: 8020 Saint Martins Ln Philadelphia PA 19118 Business E-Mail: asimms@colonialsd.org.

SIMMS, MARIA KAY, small business owner, writer, artist; b. Princeton, Ill., Nov. 18, 1940; d. Frank B. and Anna (Haurberg) S.; m. Neil F. Michelsen, Oct. 2, 1987 (dec. 1990); children: Shannon Sullivan Stillings, Molly A. Sullivan, Elizabeth Maria Jossick; m. James L. Jossick, July 12, 1998. BFA, Ill. Wesleyan U., 1962. Cert. cons. profl. astrologer; ordained min. L.A. Cmty. Ch. of Religious Sci. Elder priestess Covenant of the Goddess; tchr. art Dundee, Northbrook, Ill., 1962-65; tchr. H.S. art Danbury, Conn., 1975-76; freelance artist, 1966—75; owner Mystic Arts and Cafe Boheme, New Milford, Conn., 1976—79; prin., owner Gallery, Conn., 1976-79; art dir. ACS Pubs., Inc., San Diego, 1987-90; pres. Astro Comm. Svcs., Inc. (formerly ACS Pubs.), San Diego, 1990-98, dir., 1990-2000, acquisitions editor, 1998—2000; owner, mgr. Starcrafts Publishing, Starcrafts LLC, 2004—. Bd. dirs. Omni Techs. Corp.; lectr., cons. in field. Author: Twelve Wings of the Eagle, 1988, Dial Detective, 1989, 2d edit., 2001; co-author: Search for the Christmas Star, 1989, Circle of the Cosmic Muse, 1994, Your Magical Child, 1994, Future Signs, 1996, The Witch's Circle, 1996, Millenium: Fears, Fantasies and Facts, 1998, A Time for Magick, 2001, Moon Tides, Soul Passages, 2004, 2006; contbr. articles to popular mags. High priestess Cir. of the Cosmic Muse; elder priestess Covenant of the Goddess, 2d officer Calafia Local Coun., 1995-96, pub. info. officer, 1996-98; mem. adv. bd. Kepler Coll., 1998—. Recipient numerous art awards. Mem. Nat. Coun. Geocosmic Rsch. Inc. (dir., pubs. dir. 1981-92, editor jour. 1984-92, chmn. bd. 1999-2004, mem. advt. bd. 2005—, chair adv. bd., 2005-06), Am. Fedn. Astrologers, Internat. Soc. Astrol. Rsch., New Age Pubs. Assn., Assn. for Profl. Astrologers Internat., Seacoast Art Assn., Alpha Gamma Delta. Personal E-mail: maria@starcraftspublishing.com.

SIMMS, MARSHA E., lawyer; b. St. Louis, Sept. 15, 1952; AB, Barnard Coll., 1974; JD, Stanford U., 1977. Bar: NY 1978. Ptnr., corp. dept. Weil, Gotshal & Manges LLP, NYC. Bd. trustees Lawyers' Com. Civil Rights Under Law, Ednl. Broadcasting Corp. (Channel 13). Mem. editl. bd.: Bus. Lawyer. Former trustee Stanford Alumni Assn.; former mem. campaign steering com. Stanford Law Sch. Named one of Am. Top Black Atty., Black Enterprise, 2003. Mem.: ABA, Am. Law Inst., Met. Black Bar Assn., NY State Bar Assn., Am. Arbitration Assn. (past bd. dirs.). Office: Weil Gotshal & Manges LLP 767 Fifth Ave New York NY 10153 Office Phone: 212-310-8116. Office Fax: 212-310-3007. Business E-Mail: marsha.simms@weil.com.

SIMON, BERNECE KERN, retired social worker; b. Denver, Nov. 27, 1914; d. Maurice Meyer and Jennie (Bloch) Kern; m. Marvin L. Simon, Feb. 26, 1939; 1 child, Anne Elizabeth. BA, U. Chgo., 1936, MA, 1942. Social worker Jewish Children's Bur. Chgo., 1938-40, U. Chgo. Hosps. and Clinics, 1940-44; mem. faculty U. Chgo., 1944-81, instr., 1944-48, asst. prof., 1948-60, prof. social casework, 1960—81, prof. emeritus, 1981—. Samuel Deutsch prof. Sch. Social Service Adminstrn., 1960-81. Mem. bd. editors 17th Edit. Ency. Social Work, 1975—77, Social Svc. Rev., 1975—99, Social Work, 1978—82; book rev. editor: Social Work, 1982—87, cons. editor: Jour. Social Work Edn., 1991—94; contbr. articles to profl. jours., chapters to books. Mem.: NASW, Nat. Acads. Practice Social Work, Acad. Cert. Social Workers, Coun. Social Work Edn. (mem. nat. bd. dirs., sec. 1972—74).

SIMON, CARLY, singer, composer, author; b. NYC, June 25, 1945; d. Richard S.; m. James Taylor, 1972 (div. 1983); children: Sarah Maria, Benjamin Simon; m. James Hart, Dec. 23, 1987. Studied with Pete Seeger. Singer, composer, rec. artist, 1971—. Albums include Carly Simon, 1971, Anticipation, 1972, No Secrets, 1973, Hotcakes, 1974, Playing Possum, 1975, The Best of Carly Simon, 1975, Another Passenger, 1976, Boys in the Trees, 1978, Spy, 1979, Come Upstairs, 1980, Torch, 1981, Hello Big Man, 1983, Spoiled Girl, 1985, Coming Around Again, 1987, Greatest Hits Live, 1988, My Romance, 1990, Have You Seen Me Lately?, 1990, Carly Simon, This Is My Life, 1992, Carly Simon's Romulus Hunt: A Family Opera, 1993, Bells Bears & Fishermen, 1994, Letters Never Sent, 1994, Film Noir, 1997, Bedroom Tapes, 2000, Christmas Is Almost Here, 2002, Christmas Is Almost Here Again, 2003, Moonlight Serenade, 2005, Into White, 2006; single records: You're So Vain/Nobody Does It Better, 1977, Let the River Run, 1988 (Academy award best original song, 1989), (with Frank Sinatra) In the Wee Small Hours of the Morning, 1993, Clouds in My Coffee, 1995; TV appearance: Carly in Concert: My Romance, 1990; singer & composer(films) Torchlight, 1985, Postcards from the Edge, 1990, This Is My Life, 1992, Marvin's Room, 1996, Primary Colors, 1998, Madeline, 1998, Piglet's big Movie, 2003, Pooh's Heffalump Movie, 2005; actor No Nukes, 1980, In Our Hands, 1984, Perfect, 1985, Little Black Book, 2004; author: (children's books) Amy the Dancing Bear, The Boy of the Bells, Fisherman's Song, The Nighttime Chauffeur. Recipient Best New Artist award, Grammy Awards, 1971.*

SIMON, DEBORAH BLICK, educational consultant, retired secondary school educator; b. Akron, Ohio, Sept. 25, 1951; d. Danley Ward and Ruth Failor Wilcox; m. Morris Simon, July 21, 2003; m. Barry Allan Blick, Dec. 27, 1972 (div. Apr. 18, 1997); children: Adam Lee Blick, Stephen Andrew Blick. B of Edn., U. N.C., 1972, MEd, 1986. Bd. cert. in exceptional needs Nat. Bd. Profl. Tchg. Stds., 2000, cert. in spl. edn./early childhood edn. State of N.C., 2006. Tchr., spl. edn. dept. chair Millbrook H.S., Raleigh, NC, 1987—97; tchr., coord. spl. programs SE Raleigh H.S., 1997—99; tchr., spl. edn. dept. chair East Millbrook Magnet Mid. Sch., 1999—2002; ednl. advisor, mentor Jill Broder's Tutoring Ctr., Rockville, Md., 2002—; adj. prof., rsch. assoc. George Washington U., Washington, 2003—. Ednl. cons. Simon Assocs., Falls Church, Va., 2002—. Del. People to People Tour of Republic of China, 1993. Mem.: ASCD, NEA (life), Coun. Exceptional Children, N.C. Assn. Ret. Educators, Phi Delta Kappa. Jewish. Avocation: travel. Home: 7967 Yancey Dr Falls Church VA 22042 Office Phone: 703-560-5239. Personal E-mail: dwbsimon@aol.com.

SIMON, DEBORAH ELIZABETH, private school educator; b. San Francisco, Sept. 20, 1949; d. Louis Sherwin and Gladys Harriet (Herst) Simon. BA in Drama and Speech, U. of the Pacific, Stockton, Calif., 1971, MA in Comm., 1973. Cert. tchr. Calif. Tchr. Pelton Jr. High, San Francisco, 1973—74, Lincoln HS, Stockton, 1974—80, Milton Acad., Mass., 1980—. Instr. Nat. Forensic Inst./Am. U., Washington, 1986—91, Nova Southeastern U., Ft. Lauderdale, Fla., 1995—2001; guest prof. theatre and speech Northwestern U., Evanston, 1988, assoc. dir., 1990—94; curriculum dir. interpretation U. Tex., Austin, 1994—2006; dir. coaches symposium, interpretation instr. George Mason U., Fairfax, Va., 2005—06. Edn. coord., vol. Seattle Children's Theatre, Seattle Repertory; past adv. bd. Calif. State Speech Assn. Named Tchr. of Yr., Lincoln HS, 1980, Bruno Jacob Coach, Nat. Forensic League Hall of Fame, 1988; named to, 2003, Mass. Hall of Fame, 2005; fellow, Northwestern U., Evanston, Ill., 1980. Avocations: theater, reading. Home: 170 Centre St Milton MA 02186 Office: Milton Acad Milton MA 02186

SIMON, DOLORES DALY, copy editor; b. San Francisco, Nov. 18, 1928; d. Francis Edward and Jeannette (Cooke) Daly; m. Sidney Blair Simon, Aug. 24, 1952 (div. Nov. 1955); children: John Roderick, Douglas Brian. BA in Journalism, Pa. State U., 1950. County editor Centre Daily Times, State College, Pa., 1950-51; soc. editor Bradford (Pa.) Era, 1951-52; copy editor Harper & Bros., Pubs., N.Y.C., 1955-60; copy chief Harper & Row, Pubs., N.Y.C., 1960-88; freelance editor, copy editor Warwick, NY, 1988—. Co-author: Recipes into Type, 1993 (Best Food Reference 1994). Mem. James Beard Found., Phi Mu. Democrat. Avocation: book collecting. Office: Editl Svcs 63 Blooms Corners Rd Warwick NY 10990-2403 Office Phone: 845-986-4442.

SIMON, DORIS MARIE TYLER, nurse; b. Akron, Ohio, Jan. 24, 1932; d. Gabriel James and Nannie Eliza (Harris) Tyler; m. Matthew Hamilton Simon, Apr. 20, 1952; children: Matthew Derek, Denise Nanette, Gayle Machele, Doris Elizabeth. ADN, El Paso (Tex.) Coll. Media, 1969, El Paso Community Coll., 1976; BSPA in Health Care Adminstrn., St. Joseph's Coll., North Windham, Maine, 1991. RN, Tex. Med. asst. Dr. Melvin Farris, Akron, 1962-63, Dr. Samuel Watt, Akron, 1967-68, Drs. May, Fox and Buchwald, El Paso, 1972-76; head nurse, home dialysis and transplant and CAPD Hotel Dieu Med. Ctr., El Paso, 1977-87; nurse mgr., transplant coord. Providence Meml. Hosp., El Paso, 1987-95, nurse clinician nephrology, 1995; transplant coord. Sierra Med. Ctr., El Paso, 1995—. Med. asst. instr. Bryman Sch. Med. Assts., El Paso, 1970-72. Youth choir dir. Ft. Sill, Okla., 1964-67; choir dir. Ft. Sill area and Ft. Bliss, Tex., 1964-74; instr. in piano and music theory, Ft. Sill, 1964-67; leader Ft. Sill coun. Girl Scouts U.S., 1965-67; instr. Sch. for Handicapped, Lawton, Okla., 1965-67; nephrology nurse del. to People's Republic China Citizen Amb. Program, People to People Internat., 1988, to Russia and the Baltics Citizen Amb. Group Project Asst. Healthcare, 1992. Recipient Molly Pitcher award U.S. Army, 1963-67, Martin Luther King Jr. Share a Dream Svc. award, 1993, Delta Sigma Theta Outstanding Profl. of 1993 award; named One of 12 Outstanding Personalities of El Paso El Paso Times, 1993. Mem. ANA, Am. Med. Assts. Assn., Am. Nephrology Nurses Assn., Les Charmantes (Akron) (pres./sec. 1950-52), Links Inc. (pres. El Paso chpt. 1992-96), Interclub Coun. (pres. 1992—), Donor Awareness Coalition, Trid-Transplant Recipients Internat. Orgn. Baptist. Avocations: piano, organ, singing, sewing, bowling. Office: Transplant Dept Sierra Med Ctr 1625 Medical Center St El Paso TX 79902-5005 Home: 558 Scioto Meadows Blvd Grove City OH 43123-8660

SIMON, DOROTHY ELAINE, retired elementary school educator; b. Madison, Wis., Nov. 17, 1931; d. William Rees and Beatrice Helena (Reque) Beckett; m. William Henry Simon, Oct. 1, 1955; children: Stephen Eric, William Edward. BS, So. Conn. State U., 1954. Cert. elem. tchr. Conn. Tchr. grade 1 Ctr. St. Sch., North Haven, Conn., 1954—57; tchr. grades 3-4 Clover St. Sch., Windsor, 1968—87; ret., 1987. Cooperating tchr. internship programs U. Hartford, Ctrl. Conn. State U., 1973—85; unit leader Multi Unit Sch., Windsor, 1972—87. V.p. PTO, Windsor, 1965—68; co-chmn. Windsor ARC Drive, 1969; corr. sec. Women's Aux. of Hartford Symphony, 1966—70. Recipient honorarium, So. New Eng. Tel., Piedmont award, 2003, 2005. Mem.: Wis. Historical Soc., Green Mountain Club (Vt.), Sierra Club, Nat. Arbor Day Found., Nat. Wildlife Fedn., Ctr. Marine Conservation, Windsor Palette and Brush Club, Women's Club First Ch. of Windsor. Episcopalian. Home: 17 Priscilla Rd Windsor CT 06095-1945 Personal E-mail: debs1931@hotmail.com.

SIMON, EVELYN, lawyer; b. N.Y.C., May 13, 1943; d. Joseph and Adele (Holzschlag) Berkman; m. Fredrick Simon, Aug. 18, 1963; children: Amy Jocelyn, Marcie Ann. AB in Physics, Barnard Coll., 1963; MS in Physics, U. Pitts., 1964; JD, Wayne State U., 1978; LLB, Monash U., Melbourne, Australia, 1980. Bar: Mich. 1980, Victoria (Australia) 1981. Supr. engring. Chrysler Corp., Detroit, 1964-72; edn. and profl. mgr. Engring. Soc. Detroit, 1972-78; solicitor Arthur Robinson & Co., Melbourne, 1980-81; sr. atty. Ford Motor Co., Detroit, 1981-89; assoc. gen. counsel Sheller-Globe Corp., Detroit, 1989-90; v.p. planning, gen. counsel United Techs. Automotive Inc., Dearborn, Mich., 1991-94, v.p. bus. devel. and legal affairs, 1995-96, v.p. Asian bus. devel., 1997-98; pvt. practice, 1999—. Cons. internat. bus. devel., 1998—. Mem.: Mich. Bar Assn. Office: 1787 Alexander Dr Bloomfield Hills MI 48302-1204 Office Phone: 248-539-0969. E-mail: evelynsimon@prodigy.net.

SIMON, JACQUELINE ALBERT, political scientist, writer; d. Louis and Rose (Axelroad) Albert; m. Pierre Simon; children: Lisette, Orville. BA cum laude, NYU, MA, 1972, PhD, 1977. Adj. assoc. prof. Southampton Coll., 1977-79; mng. editor Point of Contact, NYC, 1975-76; assoc. editor, US bur. chief Politique Internationale, Paris, 1979—. Sr. fellow Inst. French Studies, NYU, 1980—, adj. assoc. prof., 1982-85; assoc. prof. govt. Southampton Coll., 1982-83; frequent appearances French TV and radio. Author: A Century of Artists' Letters: Delacroix to Leger, 2004; contbg. editor: Harper's mag., 1984—92; contbr. numerous articles to French mag., revs., books on internat. affairs. Bd. dirs. Fresh Air Fund, 1984—, Overseas Press Club Found. Mem. Overseas Press Club of Am. (bd. dirs., treas. 2000-04), Phi Beta Kappa. Home: 988 5th Ave New York NY 10021-0143 Personal E-mail: jasimon@verizon.net.

SIMON, KARLA W., law educator; b. New Haven, May 30, 1947; d. Frederick Tyler and Irene Marianne (Schoening) S.; m. Leon E. Irish. BA, Western Coll., Oxford, Ohio, 1969; JD, Duke U., 1972; LLM in Taxation, NYU, 1976. Bar: N.C. 1972, U.S. Dist. Ct. (mid. dist.) N.C. 1973, U.S. Ct. Appeals (4th cir.) 1974, U.S. Supreme Ct. 1991. Ptnr. Hobbet & Simon, Durham, NC, 1972-76; rsch. fellow Yale U. Law Sch., New Haven, 1976-78; asst. prof., assoc. prof. Seton Hall U. Sch. Law, Newark, 1978-84; prof. U. San Diego Sch. Law, 1984-89, coord. L.A. grad. tax program, 1984-88; prof. Cath. U. Am. Sch. Law, Washington, 1989—. Instr. U. Fla. Coll. Law, Gainesville, 1975; adj. asst. prof. Yeshiva U. Benjamin Cardozo Sch. Law, N.Y.C., 1977-78; vis. prof. UCLA Sch. Law, 1982-84, Ctrl. European U., 1997—, Peking Law Sch. 2005; vis. fellow Yale Law Sch., 1993-95; cons. O'Melveny & Myers, Washington, 1988-93; exec. dir. Am. Tax Policy Inst., Washington, 1990-92; pres., CEO Internat. Ctr. for Non-for-Profit Law, 1992-97, exec. v.p., 1997-2001; chair Internat. Ctr. Civil Soc. Law, 2002—. Editor in chief: Inter. Jour. Civil Soc. Law, 2003—. Mem. ABA (vice chmn. spl. project com. sect. taxation 1994-95, tax procedure com. sect. adminstrv. law 1989-94 sect. internat. law 2003—), Am. Coll. Tax Counsel, Am. Law Inst. Democrat. Avocations: reading, collecting art and antiques. Office: Cath U Am Sch Law 3600 John Mccormack Rd NE Washington DC 20064-0001 Home: 304 Kyle Rd Crownsville MD 21032 Office Phone: 202-319-5140. Business E-Mail: simon@law.edu.

SIMON, KINDRA LEE, language educator, translator; b. Cheraw, SS, Jan. 09; d. Lee N. and Dianne Crawford Simon. BA in English & Psychology, Clemson U., SC, 1993—97. Cert. English tchr. SC Dept. Edn., 2005, ESOL SC Dept. Edn., 2005. Sales rep., trainer ALLTEL Comm., Charlotte, NC, 2000—02; ESOL tchr. Chesterfield County Sch. Dist., SC, 2002—. Translator Chesterfield County Sch. Dist., 2002—. Singer ch. choir singer Jesus Christ Ch. Jubilee, Pageland, SC, 2004. Recipient Ednl. Testing Svc. award of excellence; Rsch. grant, Office English Lang. Acquisition, 2003—05. Mem.: Golden Key Honor Soc. (life). Avocations: photography, singing, travel, reading, writing. Home: 695 Virgil Griffin Rd Pageland SC 29728 Personal E-mail: kindrasimon@yahoo.com.

SIMON, LOIS PREM, interior designer, artist; b. N.Y.C., Apr. 27, 1933; d. Frank Herbert and Sybil Gertrude (Nichols) Prem; m. William Patterson Simon, Mar. 24, 1956; children: William Patterson, Beth Hanson, Stuart Prem. BA, Wells Coll., 1955; postgrad., Parsons Sch. Design, N.Y.C., 1955. Self-employed portrait painter, Pitts., 1954-72; self-employed guitar tchr., 1972-76; designer Lois Simon Interior Designs, Pitts., 1976—. Self-employed writer, illustrator, 1972—; freelance designer, Pitts., 1972—78; curator Cultural Ctr. of Ponte Vedra, 2000—. Author, artist: (children's book) Moo Moo, 1971, Lefty and Righty, 1975; landscape artist. Mem. Pitts. Opera Guild, 1968-72; coach Spl. Olympics, Pitts., 1985—; chair various coms., mem. exec. bd. Jr. League Pitts., 1958—; bd. dirs., program designer South Hills Performing Arts, Upper St. Clair, 1966-70; mem. exec. bd., program and pub. relations chair Three Rivers Art Festival, Pitts., 1967-77; bd. dirs. Pitts. Plan for Arts, 1968-70; Sunday Sch. tchr., Pitts., 1972—; mem. Younglife Adult Com., 1973-83; mem. session, elder, Southminster ch., 1982-84. Named Vol. of Yr., Jr. League Pitts., 1962, Jr. League Show House Designer, 1985. Mem.: Am. Soc. Interior Designers, Associated Artists, Sawgrass Country (Ponte Vedra Beach, Fla.), Ponte Vedra Club (founder, pres. 1999—). Republican. Presbyterian. Avocations: running, tennis, hiking, golf, painting. Home and Office: 201 Settlers Row N Ponte Vedra Beach FL 32082-3941

SIMON, LOU ANNA KIMSEY, academic administrator; BA in Math., Ind. State U., 1969, MS in Student Personnel and Counseling, 1970; PhD in Higher Edn., Mich. State U., 1974. Faculty mem. Mich. State U., asst. dir. Office Instl. Rsch., 1974—78, asst. provost gen. academic adminstrn., 1981—87, assoc. provost, 1987—92, v.p. acad. affairs, 1993—2004, interim pres., 2003, pres., 2005—. Office: Mich State U 450 Administration Bldg East Lansing MI 48824-1046 Office Phone: 517-355-6560. Business E-Mail: presmail@msu.edu.

SIMON, MARGARET BALLIF, elementary school educator, writer; b. Washington, Sept. 12, 1942; d. Paul Shirvington and Lucy White (Grasty) Ballif; m. Roger Tillison, 1964 (div. 1965); 1 child, Melle Broaderick; m. Bruce Boston, Apr. 7, 2001. BA, U. No. Colo., 1969, MA, 1970. Art tchr. Marion County Sch. Sys., Ocala, Fla., 1973—2004. Author: Eonian Variations, 1995, Night Smoke, 2002, Artist of Anthithesis, 2003; illustrator Pitchblende (Bram Stoker award, 2004); illustrator: CD-ROM Extremes 2, 2001 (Bram Stoker award, 2002); illustrator Consumed, Reduced to Beautiful Gray Ashes, 2001 (Bram Stoker award, 2002); illustrator: Thy Kingdom Come, 2002; illustrator Pitchblende, 2003 (Bram Stoker award, 2004); illustrator, editor: Mystic Hoofbeats, 1988; editor: Poets of the Fantastic, 1992; art/poetry editor: Small Press Writers/Artists Orgn. Internat. Showcase, 1987—92. V.p. Marion Art Educators Assn., Ocala, 1987. Mem.: Horror Writers Assn. (membership chmn. 1999—2004), Sci. Fiction Poetry Assn. Internat. (editor Star*Line 1993—96, pres. 1996—2000, editor Star*Line 2004—, Rhysling Best Long Poem award 1995), Small Press Writers/Artists Orgn. Internat. (pres. 1988—90, Best Artist award 1991, Dale Donaldson award 1991). Home: 1412 NE 35th St Ocala FL 34479

SIMON, MARY B., primary school educator; b. Port Arthur, Tex., July 1, 1950; d. Henry Thomas Beebe, Jr. and Mary Frances Beebe; m. Raywood Joseph Simon, Jan. 10, 1941; children: Brian, Cody. BS in Elem. Edn., Lamar U., 1972, cert. in minimally brain injured and physically handicapped, 1972. Self contained spl. edn. tchr. C.O. Wilson Jr. High, Nederland, Tex., 1972—75, Highland Park Elem., 1975—81; self contained resource tchr. Van Buren Elem., Groves, Tex., 1982—, 1st grade tchr., 1982—. Master supervising tchr. edn. dept. Lamar U., Beaumont, Tex., 2000—; dist. ednl. improvement com. Port Neches Groves Ind. Sch. Dist., 2002—05, com. mem. to select new asst. supt. instrn., 2004—05. CCD tchr. St. Peter's the Apostle Cath. Ch., Groves, Tex., 1986—95. Recipient Spotlight on Excellence award, Port Neches Groves Ind. Sch. Dist., 1995, 2000. Mem.: Tex. Classroom Tchrs. Assn. (bldg. rep. 1972—76), Alpha Delta (corr. sec. Beta Alpha chpt. 2003—04), Delta Kappa Gamma Soc. Internat. (pres. Delta Theta chpt. 2000—04, state yearbook com., state constitution/byaws com., sec. stering com. 2006). Democrat. Avocations: reading, computers, gardening. Home: 5349 Grant Groves TX 77619

SIMON, NORMA PLAVNICK, psychologist; d. Mark and Mary Plavnick; m. Robert G. Simon, Dec. 18, 1949; children: Mark Allan, Susan. BA, NYU, 1952, cert. in psychoanalysis, 1977; MA, Columbia U., 1953, EdD, 1968. Diplomate Am. Bd. Profl. Psychology, Am. Bd. Counseling Psychology, Am. Bd. Psychoanalysis. Psychologist Queens Coll. Counseling Ctr., Flushing, NY, 1968-70, asst. dir., 1970-76, dir., 1976; gen. practice psychology N.Y.C., 1970—. Faculty, supr. New Hope Guild, Bklyn., 1976—, dir. child and adolescent tng. prog., 1988-98; adj. prof. clin. psychology Columbia U., N.Y.C., 1986-2002; supr. NYU Postdoctoral Prog. in Psychoanalysis, 1988—; mem. com. on profl. practice and ethics Nat. Register Health Svc. Providers, 1998-2003. Author: (with Robert G. Simon): Choosing a College Major: Social Science, 1981; co-author 3 book chpts. on licensure and ethics in psychology; mem. editl. bd. The Counseling Psychologist jour., 1986-89, Profl. Practice and Rsch. in Psychology, 1994-99, Jour. Infant, Child and Adolescent Psych Therapy, 1999—. Vice chair N.Y. State Bd. for Psychology State Edn. Dept., Albany, 1978-82, chair, 1982-88; bd. dirs. Pelham (N.Y.) Guidance Coun., 1980-83; pres.-elect Assn. State and Provincial Psychology Bds., 1990, pres., 1991. Recipient Morton Berger award, Assn. State and Provincial Psychology Bds., 1998, Outstanding Psychologist award, Acad. Counseling Psychology, 2003. Fellow: APA (mem. bd. profl. affairs 1987—89, chair bd. profl. affairs 1988—89, policy and planning bd. 1991—93, mem. ethics com. 1995—97, vice chair ethics com. 1996—97, chair ethics com. 1997, workgroup on telehealth 1998—2000, mem. accreditation com. 2004—, non-govtl. orgnl. UN team assoc. mem. 2006—, John Black award 1994, Disting. Psychologist of Yr., Divsn. Ind. Practice 2004, Karl Heiser award 1993), Am. Bd. Counseling Psychology (bd. dirs. 1992—2000, pres.-elect 1999, pres. 2001—03), Nat. Acads. of Practice (elected disting. practitioner), Am. Bd. Profl. Psychology (trustee 1998—2001, pres.-elect 2001—, pres. 2004—05).

SIMON, PATRICIA ANN, art educator; b. East St. Louis; m. Craig Martin Simon; children: Jacob B., Zachary M., Benjamin A. BS in Art Edn., So. Ill. U., Edwardsville, 1977. Art tchr. Hazelwood Schs., Mo., 1980—82; tchr. Learning Tree Presch., Collinsville, Ill., 1994—98; guest art tchr. Collinsville Unified Sch. Dist., 1994—98; art tchr. Livingston Sch. Dist., Ill., 1998—99, Collinsville H.S., 1999—2002, Collinsville Mid. Sch., 2002—. Pvt. art tchr., Collinsville, 1993—2002. Avocations: drawing, painting, gardening, reading. Office: Collinsville Mid Sch 9649 Collinsville Rd Collinsville IL 62234 Business E-Mail: psimon@kahoks.org.

SIMON, SANDRA RUTH WALDMAN, state agency administrator; b. N.Y.C., May 11, 1943; d. Jacob S. and Ann Waldman; m. Sanford R. Simon, Aug. 23, 1964 (div.); m. F. Jerry Lucia, Apr. 30, 1989; children: Hilary G., Taylor M., Pamela Lucia, David Lucia. BA, Barnard Coll., 1965; PhD, Rockefeller U., 1972; MSW, SUNY, Stony Brook, 1985. Postdoctoral rsch. assoc. Brookhaven (N.Y.) Nat. Lab., 1972; rsch. assoc. SUNY, Stony Brook, 1972; cons. Developed and Directed Health Edn. Programs, Islip Town, N.Y., 1977-81; coord. Suffolk County creative learning program L.I. Regional Adv. Coun. Higher Edn., 1979-80; mng. dir. Pandion Stony Brook Assocs., 1984-87; evaluation and planning specialist Tex. Dept. Human Svcs., Austin, 1987-91, supr. planning and evaluation, 1991-93, dir. policy analysis and program evaluation, 1993—. Lectr., conf. coord. Women's Health Alliance L.I., St. James, N.Y., 1975-77; cons., 1998—; field instr. U. Tex. Sch. Social Work, 1989, 2000-01. Welfare Reform Evaluation grantee, 1997—. Mem. Nat. Coun. Jewish Women. Avocations: walking, opera. Office: Tex Dept Human Svcs 701 W 51st St # MC W-340 Austin TX 78751-2312 Fax: 512-438-4675.

SIMON, SARAH MARIE, elementary school educator; b. Macomb, Ill., Mar. 17, 1976; d. Paul Michael Sr. and Barbara Ann Flynn; m. Christopher J. Simon, Sept. 27, 2003. BS in Phys. Edn., No. Ill. U., DeKalb, 1999; tchg. cert. adapted phys. edn., U. Wis., Madison, 2004. Head athletic trainer Stoughton HS, Wis., 2001—; elem. phys. edn. tchr. New Century Charter Sch., Verona, Wis., 2004—05, Eagle Sch., Madison, 2004—. Pers. trainer Harbor Athletic Club, Middleton, Wis., 2005—. Author website for profl. tchrs. Recipient Equipment award, Wis. Alliance for Health, Phys. Edn., Recreation and Dance, 2005, 2006. Mem.: AAHPERD, Nat. Athletic Trainers Assn. Home: 1109 Holiday Dr Waunakee WI 53597 Personal E-mail: sarah.peteacher@gmail.com.

SIMONDS, MARIE CELESTE, architect; b. Miami, Fla., Mar. 30, 1947; d. Hinton Joseph and Frances Olivia (Burnett) Baker; m. Albert Rhett Simonds, Jr., Oct. 9, 1974; children: Caroline Lamar, Frances Rhett. BA, U. Pa., 1968; BArch, U. Md., 1973. Registered architect, Va. Architect Harry Weese & Assocs., Washington, 1973-75; pvt. practice Alexandria, Va., 1976—. Mem. Jr. League Washington, 1978—. NSF grantee, 1972; recipient Design award No. Va. Chpt. AIA, 1990. Mem. AIA (scholar 1971, Design award No. Va. 1990), Va. Soc. AIA, Severn Sailing Assn. (Annapolis, Md.). Episcopalian. Avocations: sailboat racing, horseback riding. Home and Office: 624 S Lee St Alexandria VA 22314-3820

SIMONDS, THERESA M. TROEGNER, accountant; b. Flemington, N.J., Apr. 15, 1958; d. William and Theresa E. Troegner; m. Raymond E. Simonds, Oct. 25, 1980; children: Ben, Jason, Gregory. BS in Acctg., U. Vt., 1980; MBA in Fin., Rider Coll., 1990. CPA, N.J. Staff level I Amper, Politziner & Mattia, Flemington, 1980, sr. through to supr., 1982-88, mgr., 1988-93, ptnr., 1993—. Spkr. N.J. Bar Assn., ATLA. Contbg. author: Income Reconstruction: A Guide to Discovering Unreported Income, 1999. Bd. trustees Mid Jersey chpt. Nat. M.S. Soc., 1998—; founding mem. Carpe Diem, Flemington, 1985; mem. planned giving com. Hunterdon Med. Ctr., Flemington, 1998. Named One of 1st Ladies of Hunterdon, Flemington C. of C., 1999. Mem. Am. Inst. CPAs, Am. Soc. Appraisers, N.J. Soc. CPAs, Inst. Bus. Appraisers. Roman Catholic. Avocations: tennis, bike riding, swimming. Office: Amper Politziner Mattia 750 US Highway 202 Ste 500 Bridgewater NJ 08807-5530

SIMONE, BEVERLY SUE, academic administrator; b. Evansville, Ind., Aug. 11, 1946; d. Lloyd C. and Edna Margaret (Steckler) Miller; 1 child, Andrellia Christina Acheson-Rupert. BA in Speech and Theatre, Butler U., 1969; MS in Edn. and Communications, Ind. U., 1973, EdD in Adult Edn., 1986. Co-owner, mgr. Tres Bien Catering, Indpls., 1969-71; instr. communications Ind. Vocat. Tech. Coll., Indpls., 1970-72, dir. learning resources, 1972-75, chair div. gen. edn., 1975-79, dir. external svcs., 1979-80; v.p. community and govtl. rels. Milw. Area Tech. Coll., 1980-85, provost, 1985-87; pres. Western Wis. Tech. Coll., La Crosse, 1987-89; pres., chief exec. officer Madison Area Tech. Coll., 1989—. Nat. bd. dirs. Am. Family Ins. Mem. Milw. Jr. League, 1980-94, past v.p.; mem. Madison Jr. League, 1994—; bd. dirs. United Way Dane County, Madison, Wis., 1991-96, Am. Players Theatre, Madison Cmty. Found. Recipient Nat. Recognition award Am. Coun. Edn., 1981, 85, 86, Outstanding Alumnus award Ind. U. Sch. Edn., 1993; named Woman of Achievement La Crosse Regional Bus. Assn., 1988, Woman Who Makes a Difference, Internat. Women's Forum, 1994. Mem. Am. Assn. Community and Jr. Colls. (chair 1992-93, chair elect 1991-92, bd. dirs. 1989-94, Futures Commn.), Am. Assn. Women in Community and Jr. Colls. (pres. 1985-87), Am. Coun. on Edn. (bd. dirs. 1994-97), Assn. C.C. Trustees (adv. mem. 1985-87), Internat. Women's Forum, Greater Madison C. of C. (bd. dirs.), Tempo, Vantage Point, Rotary. Office: Madison Area Tech Coll 3550 Anderson St Madison WI 53704-2520

SIMONE, GAIL ELISABETH, manufacturing executive; b. Boston, Dec. 3, 1944; d. Hugh Nelson and Louise Amelia (Shedrick) Saunders; m. Edburne R. Hare, Sept. 7, 1968 (div. 1974); m. Joseph R. Simone, June 27, 1987. BA, The King's Coll., 1966; postgrad., Harvard U., 1976-77, N.H. Coll., 1991—92. Placement dir. Boston Bar Assn., 1966-67; pub. relations Emerson Coll., Boston, 1967-69; asst. to v.p. Vance, Sanders, Inc., Boston, 1969-70; office mgr. Trans. Displays, Inc., Boston, 1970-71; seminar coordinator Assn. Trial Lawyers Am., Cambridge, Mass., 1971-74; writer, researcher Ednl. Expeditions Internat., Belmont, Mass., 1975-76; analyst United Brands Co., N.Y.C., 1976-80, Mil. Sealift Commd., USN, Washington, 1980-84, legis. affairs officer, 1984-88; rsch. analyst Bath (Maine) Iron Works Corp., 1988—. Freelance writer, editor, Boston, 1970—73. Active New Missions, Haiti, 2000—; mem. Amnesty Internat., N.Y.C., 1987—; bd. dirs. Coastal Transp.; various other orgns. Mem.: NAFE, AAUW, People for Ethical Treatment Animals. Avocations: ballet, writing, gardening. Office: Bath Iron Works 700 Washington St Stop 1 Bath ME 04530-2556 Business E-Mail: gail.simone@biw.com.

SIMONEAU, CYNTHIA LAMBERT, editor, educator; b. Central Falls, R.I., May 18, 1958; d. Roland and L. Jean Simoneau; m. Paul E. Lambert, Oct. 24, 1981; children: Thomas S. Lambert, Marc S. Lambert. BA, U. R.I., 1980. Asst. news editor Newtown (Conn.) Bee, 1980-82; reporter Bridgeport (Conn.) Post & Telegram, 1982-83, bur. chief, 1983-91; editor Woman Wise Conn. Post, Bridgeport, 1991-97, asst. mng. editor, 1997—2004, cons. newspaper editor, 2004—. Adj. prof. So. Conn. State U., New Haven, 1993—, Fairfield (Conn.) 2003—, Sacred Heart U., Fairfield, Conn., 2004, Quinnipiac U., Hamden, Conn., 2005—. Eucharistic min., mem. parish adv. coun., former religious edn. tchr., St. Thomas Aquinas Ch., Fairfield, Conn. Mem. Soc. Profl. Journalists (bd. dirs. Conn. chpt. 1983-2003, treas. Conn. chpt. 1985-95, 2003—, pres. Conn. chpt. 1995-97, Journalism Excellence awards for news stories and columns, 2 Pres.'s award Conn. chpt., Women of Dist. award Girl Scout Coun.). Avocation: reading. Office: Conn Post 410 State St Bridgeport CT 06604 E-mail: csimonea@aol.com.

SIMONS, AUDREY KAY, music educator; b. Allentown, Pa., Feb. 9, 1967; d. Edward Wilson and Claire Christine Buss; m. Anthony Russell Simons; 1 child, Luke Edward. MusM, Temple U., Philadelphia, Pa., 1989—92; MusB, Susquehanna U., Selinsgrove, Pa., 1985—89. Cello & piano instr. Susquehanna U. Cmity Music Program, Selinsgrove, Pa., 1986—89; instr. music history Temple U. Tchg. Assistantship, Philadelphia, Pa., 1989—91, Montgomery County Cmty. Coll., Blue Bell, Pa., 1993—98; artist/lectr. Moravian Coll., Bethlehem, Pa., 1993—; asst. music dir. Pocono Youth Orchestra, Stroudsburg, Pa., 1993—. Cellist Allentown Symphony Orchestra, Allentown, 1992—, Classical Attitude String Quartet, Bethlehem, 1993—, Chestnut Hill Chamber Players, Center Valley, 2003—, Pocono Chamber Music Soc., East Stroudsburg, Pa., 2005—. Recipient Presser Found. music scholarship, Susquehanna U., 1988, Elizabeth G. Eyster award music, 1987, music scholarship, 1985—89; scholar dean's list, 1985—89. Mem.: Internet Cello Soc., Violoncello Soc., Music Tchrs. Nat. Assn., Am. String Tchrs. Assn., Sigma Alpha Iota. Home: 4955 Chestnut Hill Rd Center Valley PA 18034 Office: Moravian Coll 1200 Main St Bethlehem PA 18018 Personal E-mail: asimons94@aol.com.

SIMONS, CAROL LENORE, magazine editor; b. Bklyn., Feb. 2, 1942; d. Paul and Grace (Rotwein) Seiderman; m. Lewis M. Simons, Feb. 7, 1965; children: Justine, Rebecca, Adam. BA, Tufts U., 1963; MS, Columbia U., 1964. Rschr. Newsweek mag., N.Y.C., 1964-65, CBS News, N.Y.C. and Saigon, Vietnam, 1967-68; reporter Denver Post, 1965-67; editor Pres. Commn. on Marijuana and Drug Abuse, Washington, 1971-72; assoc. editor Smithsonian mag., Washington, 1978-82; dir. publs. Am. C. of C. in Japan, Tokyo, 1991-96; exec. editor AARP The Mag., Washington, 2003—, AARP Bull., Washington, 2005—. Office: AARP The Bulletin 601 E St NW Washington DC 20049-0001

SIMONS, ELIZABETH R(EIMAN), biochemist, educator; b. Vienna, Sept. 1, 1929; came to U.S., 1941, naturalized, 1948; d. William and Erna Engle (Weisselberg) Reiman; m. Harold Lee Simons, Aug. 12, 1951; children: Leslie Ann Mulert, Robert David. BChemE, Cooper Union, N.Y.C., 1950; MS, Yale U., 1951, PhD, 1954. Rsch. chemist Tech. Ops., Arlington, Mass., 1953-54; instr. chemistry Wellesley (Mass.) Coll., 1954-57; rsch. asst. Children's Hosp. Med. Ctr. and Cancer Rsch. Found., Boston, 1957-59, rsch. assoc. pathology, 1959-62; rsch. assoc. Harvard Med. Sch., 1962-66, lectr. biol. chemistry, 1966-72; tutor biochem. scis. Harvard Coll., 1971-94; assoc. prof. biochemistry Boston (Mass.) U., 1972-78, prof., 1978—, asst. dir. Office

Med. Edn., 2000—. Contbr. articles to profl. jours. Grantee in field. Mem.: AAAS, Soc. for Neurosci., Biophys. Soc., Am. Soc. Hematology, Am. Soc. Cell Biology, Am. Soc. Biol. Chemists, Am. Chem. Soc. Office: Boston U Sch Medicine 80 E Concord St Roxbury MA 02118-2307 Office Phone: 617-638-4332. Business E-Mail: esimons@bu.edu.

SIMONS, GAIL S., artist, educator, librarian; b. Elgin, Ill., Aug. 13, 1963; d. James Philip and Vivian Faith (Ewalt) S. Cert. Christian edn., Lincoln Christian Coll., 1986; BFA, Judson Coll., 1991. Tchg. asst. Pub. Sch. Dist. 300, Dundee, Ill., 1986-89; illustrator computer clip art Media Mktg. Svcs., St. Charles, Ill., 1989; computer data plant ops. Judson Coll., Elgin, Ill., 1990-91, watercolor painting instr., 1991—; libr. Dundee Twp. Pub. Libr., East Dundee, Ill., 1994—, staff artist, 1997—. Youth/adult choral dir. First Congl. Ch., Carpentersville, Ill., 1986-96; stop motion animator, Chgo., 1991. Exhibited works at Ruth M. Wendt Gallery, East Dundee, 1997-99, Agora Gallery, N.Y.C., 1999—, Incognito Gallery, Fox Lake, Ill., 2001, art-exchange.com, 2003; actress, asst. dir., set/prop designer various musicals and plays. Deaconess/Sunday sch. dir. Congl. Ch., Carpentersville, 1986-96; watercolor/craft tchr. Pub. Libr, East Dundee, 1997—; wildlife adv.; youth leader. Mem. Christians in the Visual Arts, N.W. Area Arts Coun., Dundee Twp. Fine Arts Coun., Alpha Chi Soc. Avocations: collecting, gardening, writing, entomology, old movies. Office: Dundee Twp Pub Libr Dist 555 Barrington Ave East Dundee IL 60118-1422 E-mail: gailmominsect@msn.com.

SIMONS, HELEN, school psychologist, psychotherapist, educator; b. Chgo., Feb. 13, 1930; d. Leo and Sarah (Shrayer) Pomper; m. Broudy Simons, May 20, 1956 (div. May 1972); children: Larry, Sheri. BA in Biol., Lake Forest Coll., 1951; MA in Clin. Psychology, Roosevelt U., 1972; D of Psychology, Ill. Sch. Profl. Psychology, 1980. Intern Cook County Hosp., Chgo., 1979-80; pvt. practice psychotherapist Chgo., 1980—; sch. psychologist Chgo. Bd. Edn., 1974-79, 80—. Faculty Internat. Soc. for Prevention of Child Abuse and Neglect; lectr., presenter at workshops. Contbr. articles to profl. jours. Mem.: APA, Internat. Sch. Psychologists Assn., Internat. Assn. Applied Psychology, Internat. Soc. for Prevention of Child Abuse and Neglect, Internat. Coun. Psychologists, Chgo. Sch. Psychol. Assn., Chgo. Psychol. Assn., Ill. Sch. Psychologists Assn., Nat. Sch. Psychologists Assn. Avocations: music, dance, reading. Home: 6145 N Sheridan Rd Apt 29D Chicago IL 60660-6855 Office: Gladstone Sch 1231 S Damen Ave Chicago IL 60608 Personal E-mail: hpompers@aol.com.

SIMONS, JULIO MERREDITH, psychotherapist, social worker; b. Miami, Fla., Sept. 15, 1968; d. Marshall Douglass and Arita Rynning Simons; m. Walter Wade Botkin, Apr. 16, 2005; children: Sydney, Andrew. BA, U. South Fla., Tampa, 1990, MSW, 1994. Cert. bioenergetic therapist. Therapist Florida Sheriff's Youth Ranches, Bradenton, Fla., 1994—96; adoption specialist Cithatic Charities, Sarasota, Fla., 1996—2004; pvt. practice Mind Body Assn., Inc., Sarasota, Fla., 1996—. Home: 3773 Parkridge Cir Sarasota FL 34243

SIMONS, LYNN OSBORN, educational consultant; b. Havre, Mont., June 1, 1934; d. Robert Blair and Dorothy (Briggs) Osborn; m. John Powell Simons, Jan. 19, 1957; children: Clayton Osborn, William Blair. BA, U. Colo., 1956. Tchr. Midvale (Utah) Jr. H.S., 1956-57, Sweetwater county Sch. Dist. 1, Rock Springs, Wyo., 1957-58, U. Wyo., 1959-61, Natrona County Sch. Dist. 1, Casper, Wyo., 1963-64; credit mgr. Gallery 323, Casper, 1972-77; Wyo. state supt. pub. instrn. Cheyenne, 1979-91; sec.'s regional rep. region VIII U.S. Dept. Edn., Denver, 1993—2001; mem. Denver Fed. Exec. Bd., 1995-2001; mem. exec. bd. combined Fed. campaign, 1994—2001; ednl. cons., 2001—03; state planning coord. Capitol Bldg., Cheyenne, Wyo., 2003. Mem. State Bds. Charities and Reform, Land Commrs., Farm Loan, 1979-91; mem. State Commns. Capitol Bldg., Liquor, 1979-91; Ex-officio mem. bd. trustees U. Wyo., 1979-91; ex-officio mem. Wyo. Community Coll. Commn., 1979-91; mem. steering com. Edn. Commn. of the States, 1988-90; mem. State Bd. Edn., 1971-77, chmn., 1976-77; advisor Nat. Trust for Hist. Preservation, 1980-86. Bd. dirs. Cheyenne Bot. Gardens Found., 2004—. Mem. LWV (pres. 1970-71). Democrat. Episcopalian.

SIMONSON, DONNA JEANNE, accountant; b. Malden, Mass., Sept. 6, 1947; d. George Francis and Dorothy Josephine (Bridges) Yost; m. Scott N. Simonson, June 30, 1967 (div. Feb. 1989); children: Stephanie Louise Burke, Kelly Lynn Pratt. AA Bus. Adminstrn., Corning Community Coll., 1979; BS in Mgmt., Keuka Coll., 1981. Bus. office supr. Steuben Allegany B.O.C.E.S., Bath, N.Y., 1969-75; staff acct. David L. Snyderwine & Co. CPA's, Bath, 1979-82; fin. dir. Steuben Assoc. for Retarded Children, Inc., Bath, 1982-98; owner Donna J. Simonson, Taxes, & Acctg., Bath, 1982--. Pres. Pulteney Vol. Firemen's Auxiliary, 1973. Mem. Am. Assn. Univ. Women, Bath Area Humane Soc., Pulteney Free Library Assn., Fiscal Mgrs. Assn. Democrat. Presbyterian. Home and Office: 1 Ellis Ave Bath NY 14810-1107

SIMPSON, ALFREDA GAIL, music educator; d. James A. and Edith H. Wilson; 1 child from previous marriage, Nancy. BA in Music, Okla. Coll. Liberal Arts, Chickasha, 1969; EdM, Southwest Okla. State U., Weatherford, 1981, MusM, 1987. USOESEA tchr. Bitburg H.S., Germany, 1971; tchr. Oak Valley Sch., Tulare, Calif., 1973—79, Broxton Sch., Apache, Okla., 1979—90, Weatherford Schs., 1990—. Mem. negotiations team WACT, Weatherford, Okla., 2001—03. Named Tchr. of Yr., Burcham Elem. Sch., 1999. Mem.: Okla. Music Edn. Assn. (regional audition chair 1999—), Okla. Choral Dirs. Assn. (chair women's chorus 2005), Kappa Kappa Iota (pres. 1994—96). Democrat. Baptist. Avocations: reading, computers, board games, card games. Office Phone: 580-772-3385.

SIMPSON, ANDREA LYNN, communications executive; b. Altadena, Calif., Feb. 10, 1948; d. Kenneth and Barbara Simpson; 1 child, Christopher Ryan Myrdal. BA, U. So. Calif., 1969, MS, 1983; postgrad., U. Colo., Boulder Sch. Bank Mktg., 1977. Mktg. officer United Calif. Bank, L.A., 1969-73; asst. v.p. mktg. 1st Hawaiian Bank, Honolulu, 1973-78; v.p. corp. comms. Pacific Resources Inc., Honolulu, 1978-89, BHP Hawaii, Inc., 1989-98; v.p. corp. rels. Tesoro Petroleum Corp., San Antonio, 1998-2000; v.p. corp. comms. Edison Internat., Rosemead, Calif., 2000—01; pres. Simpson Comm., 2001—. Bd. dirs. Arts Coun., Hawaii, 1977-81, Hawaii Heart Assn., 1978-83, Coun. Pacific Girls Scouts USA, 1982-85, Child and Family Svcs., 1984-86, Honolulu Symphony Soc., 1985-91, Sta. KHPR Hawaii Pub. Radio, 1988-92, Kapiolani Found., 1990-95, Hanahauoli Sch., 1991-98, Hawaii Strategic Devel. Corp., 1991-98, Children's Discovery Ctr., 1994-98, Pacific Asian Affairs Coun., 1994-96, Hawaii MADD, 1992-96, Girl Scout Coun. Mt. Wilson Dist., 2005—; adv. dir. Hawaii Kids at Work, 1991-98; bd. dirs., 2d v.p. Girl Scout Coun. Hawaii, 1994-96, mem. adv. bd., 1996-98; trustee Hawaii Loa Coll., 1984-86, Kapiolani Women's and Children's Hosp., 1988-97, Hawaii Sch. for Girls at LaPietra, 1989-91, Kapiolani Med. Ctr. at Pali Momi, 1994-98; bd. dirs. Aloha coun. Boy Scouts Am., 1998, Alamo coun., 1998-2000; found. bd. dirs. Hawaii Pub. TV, 1998, bd. dirs., San Pedro Playhouse, 1999-2000; bd. dirs. Red Cross of San Antonio, 1999-2000; commr. Hawaii State Commn. on Status of Women, 1985-87, State Sesquecentennial of Pub. Schs. Commn., 1990-91; bd. dirs. Art Wilson coun. Girl Scouts Am., 2005—. Named Advt. Woman of Yr., Honolulu Advt. Fedn., 1982, Pub. Rels. Profl. of Yr., Honolulu Pub. Rels. Soc., 1993, Communicator of Yr., Utilities Communicators Internat., 1983; recipient Silver Anvil award Pub. Rels. Soc. Am., 1983, 97. Mem. Internat. Pub. Rels. Assn. (Golden World award 1997), Am. Mktg. Assn., Pub. Rels. Soc. Am. (bd. dirs. Honolulu chpt. 1984-86, Silver Anvil award 1984, Pub. Rels. Profl. Yr. 1991), U. So. Calif. Alumni Assn. (bd. dirs. Hawaii 1981-83), Outrigger Canoe Club, Rotary (pub. rels. chmn. 1988-97, Honolulu chpt., bd. dirs. 1998), Rotary Club of San Antonio, Alpha Phi (past pres., dir. Hawaii), Hawaii Jaycees (Outstanding Young Person of Hawaii 1978.

SIMPSON, ASHLEE NICOLE, vocalist, actress; b. Dallas, Oct. 3, 1984; d. Joe and Tina Simpson. Studied, Sch. of Am. Ballet. Singer: (albums) Autobiography, 2004, I Am Me, 2005; performer: (songs) "Just Let Me Cry", Freaky Friday Soundtrack, 2003; actor: (films) The Hot Chick, 2002, Raise Your Voice, 2004, Undiscovered, 2005; (TV series) 7th Heaven, 2002—04, The Ashlee Simpson Show, 2004—05; musical guest appearance Saturday Night Live, 2004, guest appearance Saved By the Bell: The New Class, 1993, The View, 1997, Malcom in the Middle, 2001, 60 Minutes, 2004, Newlyweds: Nick & Jessica, 2003, 2004; actor: (plays) Chicago, 2006. Recipient Female New Artist of Yr., Billboard Music Awards, 2004. Avocations: vintage shopping, writing and recording music, spending time with family and friends.*

SIMPSON, BERYL BRINTNALL, botany educator; b. Dallas, Apr. 28, 1942; d. Edward Everett and Barbara Frances (Brintnall) S.; children: Jonathan, Meghan. AB, Radcliffe Coll., 1964; MA, PhD, Harvard U., 1968. Rsch. fellow Arnold Arboretum/Gray Herbarium, Cambridge, Mass., 1969-71; curator Smithsonian Instn., Washington, 1971-78; prof. U. Tex., Austin, 1978—. Chmn. U.S. Com. to IUBS, 1985-88; co-pres. Internat. Congress Systematic and Evolutionary Biology, 1980-85. Author: Economic Botany, 1994, 3d edit., 2001; editor: Mesquite, 1977; contbr. over 160 articles and notes to profl. jours. Recipient Greenman award Mo. Bot. Garden, 1970. Fellow AAAS, Am. Acad. Arts and Sci., Soc. for Study Evolution (coun. 1975-80, pres. 1985-86), Bot. Soc. Am. (pres. 1990-91, Merit award 1992), Bot. Soc. Washington (v.p. 1975), Am. Soc. Plant Taxonomists (pres. 1994, Cooley award, Asa Gray award), Am. Inst. Biol. Scis. (bd. dirs. 1993-95), U.S.-Mex. Found. for Sci. (bd. govs.), Soc. Econ. Botany (pres. 1999). Office: 1 University Station A6700 Univ Tex Sect Integrative Biology Austin TX 78712 Business E-Mail: beryl@mail.utexas.edu.

SIMPSON, CAROL LOUISE, investment company executive; b. Phila., Jan. 30, 1937; d. William Huffington and Hilda Agnes (Johnston) S. Student, Phila. C.C., 1985—87. Cert. Nat. Assn. Securities Dealers, Inc., Washington; registered options, mcpl. securities, gen. securities, fin. and ops. prin.; lic. life, accident, health ins. Exec. asst. Germantown Fed. Savs., Phila., 1954-67; asst. sec. Am. Med. Investment Co., Inc. (formerly Cannon and Co., Inc.), Blue Bell, Pa., 1967-91; v.p., sec. AMA Investment Advisers, Inc. (formerly Pro Svcs., Inc.), Blue Bell, Pa., 1967-91; exec. v.p., sec. Rutherford Fin. Corp., Phila., 1991-2000, Rutherford, Brown & Catherwood Inc., Phila., 1991-2000, Walnut Asset Mgmt. Inc., Phila., 1991-98. Mem. Investment Co. Inst. (fed. legis. com. 1984-91, investment advisers com. 1988-2000, compliance com. 1990-2000), VNA Cmty. Svcs. Found. (bd. dirs. 1995-2001), Vis. Nurse Assn. Cmty. Svcs. (bd. dirs. 1997-2000), Whitemarsh Valley Country Club. Republican. Home: 7701 Lawnton St Philadelphia PA 19128-3105

SIMPSON, CAROL MANN, librarian, educator, editor; b. Aberdeen, Md., Nov. 28, 1949; d. Joey Mathew and Grace Winifred (Fielman) Pirrung; m. Robert Smith Mann, Jan. 4, 1969 (div. May 1986); children: Stephen, David (dec.), Sarah; m. Douglas Michael Simpson, Jan. 18, 1992; stepchildren, Brian, Kevin. BS in Edn., Southwestern U., 1971; MA, U. Tex., 1975, MLS, 1977; EdD, East Tex. State U., 1987. Cert. art and French tchr., libr., learning resources specialist, supr., Tex. Tchr. Round Rock (Tex.) Ind. Sch. Dist., 1970-74; libr. Mesquite (Tex.) Ind. Sch. Dist., 1977-90, coord. libr. and media svcs., 1990-92, facilitator libr. tech., 1992—98; assoc. prof. U. North Tex. Sch. Libr. and Info. Scis., Denton, 1998—2006; adj. prof. Tex. Women's U., 1992-93. Fellow Tex. Ctr. for Digital Knowledge, 2000—; cons. Orex Petroleum, Dallas, 1988, Mesquite Pub. Libr., 1989-90, HBW Assocs., Dallas, 1988-89; reviewer Booklist, 1984-95, Sch. Libr. Jour., 1984-95, Video Rating Guide for Librs., 1989-92. Author: Copyright for School Libraries, 1994, Internet for Library Media Specialists, 1995, Copyright for Schools, 1997, 2005, Copyright Catechism, 2005, Internet for Schools, 1997, 2003, Ethics for School Librarianship, 2003; editor: Technology Connection, 1995—99, The Book Report, 1999—2003, Library Talk, 1999—2003, Library Media Connection, 2003—; contbr. articles to profl. jours. Mem. ALA, Assn. for Ednl. Comms. and Tech., Tex. Libr. Assn., Am. Assn. Sch. Librs., Tex. Assn. Sch. Librs. Methodist. Avocations: genealogy, computers, gardening. Home: 1086 Holly Ln Lewisville TX 75067-5710 Office: U North Tex Sch Libr and Info Scis PO Box 311068 Denton TX 76203

SIMPSON, CHARLENE JOAN, elementary school educator; b. Lincoln, Nebr., Mar. 25, 1952; d. Victor Hadley Sr. and Lois Maxine (Brittain) Wright; m. James Edward Simpson, June 15, 1974; children: Matthew James, Kelly Charlene. BS in Edn. and English, U. Nebr., 1975. Cert. tchr., Nebr. Transcriber Nebr. Legis., Lincoln, 1982-85; sec. Nebr. Dept. Agriculture, Lincoln, 1985-87; tchr. Lincoln Pub. Schs., 1988—. Instr. water safety ARC, Lincoln, 1971-90; den leader Cub Scouts, Lincoln, 1985-87; asst. Brownie leader Girl Scouts U.S., Lincoln, 1986-87; sec.-treas., newsletter editor Lakeview Neighborhood Orgn., 1983-87; mem. parent adv. bd. Lakeview Sch., 1982-91; pres. Lakeview/Yankee Hill Sch. Orgn., 1987-88. Recipient Outstanding Community Vol. award United Way, Lincoln, 1986. Mem. Phi Mu (alumnae pres. 1976-77, adv. bd. 1977-89, 1993-2001, corp. bd., 2003-04, Betty Vlasnik award). Democrat. Methodist. Avocations: reading, needle-crafts, golf. Home: 810 W R St Lincoln NE 68528-1354 Office Phone: 402-436-1170. Business E-Mail: csimpson@lps.org.

SIMPSON, DEBRA BRASHEAR, artist; b. Tulsa, Dec. 4, 1938; d. Chapman Claude Brashear and Ruby Maxine (Muck Brashear) Speed; m. Robert Thomas Oedamer, Aug. 27, 1957 (div. May 1969); 1 child, Demetra Suzanne Oedamer Haymes; m. John Garlington III Simpson, Aug. 9, 1976; 1 child, Zachary Claude Taliaferro. Student, U. Ala., 1961—77, Broward C.C., Melboourne, Fla., 1970—71, Tyler Sch. Fine Art, Phila., Temple U., Art Students League, N.Y.C., 1998. Writer/editor Chrysler Corp., Huntsville, Ala., 1958—61, NASA, Huntsville, Ala., 1961—62, personal sec., 1962—67; adminstrv. asst. Life Support, Melbourne, Fla., 1970—71; sec., editor U.S. Army, Huntsville, 1972—78; fashion designer Betty Grisham Inc., Huntsville, 1981—83. Art instr. Huntsville Mus. Art, 1995—97; art instr., color cons. Simpson Assocs., Huntsville, 1997—; dir. adv. bd. Monte Sano Art Assn., Huntsville, 1999—; pvt. tchr. art. Exhibitions include Huntsville Art League and Mus. Assn., 1973—76, Birmingham Art Guild Exhbn., 1979, Birmingham Bot. Gardens, 1980, Woodlawn Plantation Show, Washington, 1982 (award), Decatur Art Guild, 1985, Huntsville Mus. of Art Partnership Gallery, 1985—86, Panoply of the Arts, Huntsville, 1985—89 (merit, purchase and monetary awards), Huntsville Mus. Art, 1986 (award), Acad. of Arts and Acad., Huntsville, 1990, Marilyn Wilson Gallery, Birmingham, 1990, Connie Ulrich Gallery, Huntsville, 1991, Salon France-America, Paris, 1991 (Kabeltechnik Dietz award for portraiture), Oklahoma City, 1991, Huntsville Art League, 1995, one-woman shows include Kennedy Douglas Ctr., Florence, Ala., 1996, 1998, exhibitions include Tenn. Valley Art Ctr., 1998, Cornell Grisham Art Gallery, Decatur, 1998, numerous other shows. Fellow mem. Monte Sano Civic Assn., Huntsville, 1979—. Fellow: Internat. Assn. Exptl. Artists; mem.: Am. Soc. Portrait Artists. Avocations: hiking, gardening, swimming, jewelry designing. Home: 3415 Highland Plz SE Huntsville AL 35801

SIMPSON, DOROTHY AUDREY, retired speech educator; b. Las Vegas, N.Mex., Feb. 29, 1944; d. Clyde Joseph and Audrey Shirley (Clements) Simpson; m. Gary Alan Beimer, May 13, 1972 (div. Apr. 1986); children: Laura Lea Beimer Mitchell, Rose; m. Ian B. Croxton, Dec. 27, 1992 (div. Oct. 1993); m. Doyle W. Hauschulz, Feb. 23, 2001 (div. June 2003). BA, N.Mex. Highlands U., 1965; MS, U. Utah, 1968; EdD, U. N.Mex., 1989. Cert. secondary edn., N.Mex. Tchr. West Las Vegas (N.Mex.) H.S., 1966-67, Santa Rosa (N.Mex.) H.S., 1968-71, Questa (N.Mex.) Consol. Schs., 1972-73; prof. speech comm., assoc. dean coll. arts and scis. N.Mex. Highlands U., Las Vegas, 1975—2003, prof. emeritus, 2003—. Ednl. cons. Rancho Valmora, 2003—. Author: Hovels, Haciendas, and House Calls: The Life of Carl H. Gellenthien, M.D., 1986, Speaking for Life: A Speech Communication Guide for Adults, 1990, Wreck of the Destiny Train, 1993; From Pajarito to Lungchow, 2003. Active 1st Bapt. Ch., Las Vegas, 1959—. Recipient Educator of Yr. award Pub. Svc. Co. of N.Mex., Albuquerque, 1990. Mem. P.E.O. Republican. Avocation: writing. Home: PO Box 778 Las Vegas NM 87701-0778

SIMPSON, INDIA.ARIE, musician; b. Denver, Oct. 3, 1976; d. Ralph and Joyce Simpson, Gary Harris (Stepfather). Student, Savannah Coll. Art and Design. With Motown Records, 1999—. Musician: (recordings) Acoustic Soul, 1999 (Cert. Gold), (songs) Peaceful World (with John Mellencamp), Just Another Parade, Just Another Parade (with Cassandra Wilson), Good Man for film We Were Soldiers, (tour) Women in Hip-Hop and Soul, 2001, (recordings) Voyage to India (Gest R&B Album Grammy, 03); contbg. musician (compilation) Conceptions: Musical Tribute to Stevie Wonder, 2003. Nominee 7 Grammy awards, 2002; named Best New Artist, Vibe Mag., 2001, MTV2, 2001, Billboard Video Awards, 2001, Best R&B Female Artist, BET, 2002, Best Female R&B Artist, 2003; named one of Top 100 It Entertainers, Entertainment Weekly mag., 2001; recipient Essence award, 2002, Best Urban/Alternative Performance for Little Things, Grammy Awards, 2003. Office: Universal Music Enterprises Motown Records 2220 Colorado Ave Santa Monica CA 90404

SIMPSON, JAYNE LOU, retired academic administrator; b. Pekin, Ill., Dec. 10, 1947; d. Robert George and Bernadine Carrie (Weyhrich) Meeker; m. Charles Nichols Orton, Feb. 3, 1968 (div. 1977); children: Dawn Annette, Michelle Diane; m. John Niehaus Simpson, Apr. 11, 1981; 1 child, Ashley Elizabeth. BA, Bradley U., 1976, MA, 1979; EdD in Ednl. Adminstrn., Ill. State U., 1994. Cert. sch. psychologist, nat. and Ill.; cert. supt., adminstr. spl. edn. Sch. psychologist Spl. Edn. Assn. Peoria (Ill.) County, 1979-84, Mid. Cen. Assn. Child Find, Peoria, 1984-85, Peoria Pub. Schs., Peoria, 1985-87, Lisle (Ill.) Community Unit Sch. Dist., 1987-92, adminstr., 1992—2003; ret., 2003. Cons. North Cen. Evaluation Com., 1990. James scholar U. Ill., 1966. Mem. ASCD, Coun. for Exceptional Children, Nat. Assn. Sch. Psychologists, Ill. Sch. Psychologists Assn., Ill. ASCD, Phi Delta Kappa, Pi Lambda Theta. Lutheran. Avocations: golf, tennis, bowling, bridge, softball. Home: 1458 W Flint Ln Romeoville IL 60446-5239 Personal E-mail: jane1210@aol.com.

SIMPSON, JESSICA ANN, singer, actress; b. Abilene, Tex., July 10, 1980; d. Joe and Tina Simpson; m. Nick Lachey, Oct. 26, 2002 (div. June 30, 2006). Launched edible fragrance, cosmetic and body care line, Dessert Beauty, 2004; co-creator and launched, edible fragrance, cosmetic, and body care line, Taste, 04; nat. spokesperson for Operation Smile. Singer: (albums) Sweet Kisses, 1999, Irresistible, 2001, In This Skin, 2004, Rejoyce: The Christmas Album, 2004, A Public Affair, 2006, (songs) These Boots are Made for Walkin', 2005 (People's Choice award for Favorite Song from a Movie (The Dukes of Hazzard), 2006); actor: (films) The Dukes of Hazzard, 2005, Employee of the Month, 2006; (TV series) Newlyweds: Nick and Jessica, 2003—05, (TV) Nick & Jessica's Variety Hour, 2004, Nick & Jessica's Family Christmas, 2004, Nick & Jessica's Tour of Duty, 2005; co-author: I Do: Achieving Your Dream Wedding, 2003; co-host with husband: Saturday Night Live, 2004; co-host with Dane Cook Teen Choice Awards, 2006, guest appearances (TV series) MadTV, 2000, 2001, That '70s Show, 2002, 2003, Punk'd, 2003, Twilight Zone, 2003, Top of the Pops, 2004, Ashlee Simpson Show, 2004, The Apprentice, 2004. Recipient Movies-Choice Breakout (Female), Teen Choice Awards, 2006. Office: c/o Creative Artists Agy 9830 Wilshire Blvd Beverly Hills CA 90212-1825 also: Epic Records 550 Madison Ave New York NY 10022-3211*

SIMPSON, JOANNE MALKUS, meteorologist; b. Boston, Mar. 23, 1923; d. Russell and Virginia (Vaughan) Gerould; m. Robert H. Simpson, Jan. 6, 1965; children by previous marriage: David Starr Malkus, Steven Willem Malkus, Karen Elizabeth Malkus. BS, U. Chgo., 1943, MS, 1945, PhD, 1949; DSc (hon.), SUNY, Albany, 1991. Instr. physics and meteorology Ill. Inst. Tech., 1946-49, asst. prof., 1949-51; meteorologist Woods Hole Oceanographic Instn., 1951-61; prof. meteorology UCLA, 1961-65; dir. exptl. meteorology lab. NOAA, Dept. Commerce, Washington, 1965-74; prof. environ. scis. U. Va., Charlottesville, 1974—79, W.W. Corcoran prof. environ. scis., 1974—79; head Severe Storms br. Goddard Lab. Atmospheres, NASA, Greenbelt, Md., 1979—88; chief scientist for meteorology, earth scis. dir. Goddard Space Flight Ctr., NASA, 1988—2004, chief scientist emeritus for meteorology, 2004—; project scientist tropical rainfall measuring mission, 1986—98. Mem. Bd. on Atmospheric Scis. and Climate, NRC/NAS, 1990-93, 97-2000, Bd. on Geophys. and Environ. Data, 1993-96, com. on climate, ecosystems, infectious diseases and human health, 1998-2000; mem. sr. adv. bd. NOAA, 1998-2003. Author: (with Herbert Riehl) Cloud Structure and Distributions Over the Tropical Pacific Ocean; assoc. editor: Revs. Geophysics and Space Physics, 1964-72, 75-77; contbr. articles to profl. jours. Mem. Fla. Gov.'s Environ. Coordinating Coun., 1971-74. Recipient Disting. Authorship award NOAA, 1969, Silver medal Dept. Commerce, 1967, Gold medal, 1972, Vincent J. Schaefer award Weather Modification Assn., 1979, Cmty. Headliner award Women in Comm., 1973, Profl. Achievement award U. Chgo. Alumni Assn., 1975, 92, Lifetime Achievement award Women in Sci. Engring., 1990, Exceptional Sci. Achievement award NASA, 1982, William Nordberg award NASA, 1994, NASA Medal Outstanding Leadership, 1998, I.M.O. prize World Meteorol. Orgn., 2002, U.S. Gov. Presdl. Rank award, 2003, 04; named Woman of Yr., L.A. Times, 1963; Guggenheim fellow, 1954-55, Goddard Sr. fellow, 1988-2004. Fellow Am. Geophys. Union, Am. Meterol. Soc. (mem. coun. 1975-77, 79-81, mem. exec. com. 1977, 79-81, commr. sci. and tech. activities 1982-88, pres.-elect 1988, pres. 1989, publs. commr. 1992-98, hon. mem. 1995, Meisinger award 1962, Rossby Rsch. medal 1983, Charles Franklin Brooks award 1992, Charles E. Anderson award 2001), World Meterol. Orgn. (IMO prize 2002), Explorers Club, Nat. Acad. Engring., Am. Acad. Arts & Sciences; mem. Royal Meterol. Soc. (hon.), Cosmos Club, Phi Beta Kappa, Sigma Xi. Home: 540 N St SW Washington DC 20024-4557 Office: NASA Goddard Space Flight Ctr Earth Scis Greenbelt MD 20771-0001 Personal E-mail: nasajoanne@earthlink.net. Business E-Mail: simpson@agnes.gsfc.nasa.gov, joanne.simpson_1@nasa.gov.

SIMPSON, KAREN CRANDALL, artist, educator; b. Newport, R.I., Mar. 31, 1944; d. Jack Conway and Elizabeth Ann (McLyman) Crandall; m. Donal Robertson Simpson, Mar. 30, 1968. BA, U. R. I., 1966; MFA, Tex. Womans U., 1992. Cert. Tchr. Pa., Md., Conn., R.I. Spl. issues editor Phoenix Times Newspaper, Bristol, R.I., 1975-81; newsletter editor Trinity Ch., Newport, R.I., 1980-83; pub. editor St. Matthews Episcopal Ch., Austin, Tex., 1984-86; exhibiting artist Tex., 1988—2001. Adj. faculty Mt. View Coll., Dallas, 1993-95, U. Tex., Arlington, 1999-2001; tchr. of record Tex. Womens U., 1990-92; exhibiting artist, NC, 2002-. One-woman shows include Brookhaven Coll., Farmers Branch, Tex., 1994, Sam Houston State U., 1995, Eastfield Coll., Dallas, 1998, Rock Hill Art Ctr., 2005, others; exhibited in group shows including Mus. of the Southwest, Beaumont, 1999, Old Jail Art Ctr. and Mus., 1998, Mint Mus. Art, 2002, Fayetteville Mus. Art, 2006, others; curator Mountain View Coll., Dallas, 1994, Handley-Hicks Gallery, Ft. Worth, 1996. Mem. Dallas Visual Art Ctr., Dallas Womens Caucus for Art (v.p. 1993, pres. 1994-95, bd. advisors 1996-98), Nat. Womens Caucus for Art, Coll. Art Assn. Lutheran. Avocations: drawing, reading, walking, travel, gardening. Home: 231 Bentley Oaks Ln Charlotte NC 28270-6004

SIMPSON, LINDA SUE, elementary school educator; b. Rogers, Ark., Oct. 13, 1947; d. Richard Eugene and Shirley Joan (Kilpatrick) S. BS in Edn., Ohio State U., 1969, postgrad., 1989-91; MA in Edn., Ea. Ky. U., 1978. Cert. elem. tchr. Tchr. Conrad Sch., Newark, Ohio, 1969-71; tchr. 1-6 North Elem. Sch., Newark, 1971-89; tchr. K-3 Cherry Valley Elem., Newark, 1989—; primary literacy coordinator Cherry Valley Sch., 1999—. Adv. bd. Ohio Coun. of Social Studies, Columbus, 1994—; planning team Ctrl. Ohio Regional Profl. Devel., Columbus, 1994-95. Elder 1st Presbyn. Ch., Newark, 1990-93; tutor Licking County Children's Home, Newark, 1969-73. Jenning scholar Martha H. Found., 1987; named Newark Tchr. of the Yr., 1981; recipient Ashland Oil Tchg. award Ashland Oil Co., 1995. Mem.: DAR (history and scholarship chair 1982—), Delta Kappa Gamma. Presbyterian. Avocations: genealogy, golf, bowling. Home: 579 Manor Dr Newark OH 43055-2119 Office: Cherry Valley Sch 1040 W Main St Newark OH 43055-2556

SIMPSON, LISA ANN, physician, educator; b. Lagos, Nigeria, Feb. 9, 1958; (parents Am. citizens); d. Howard Russell and Mary Alice (Turner) Simpson; m. Richard L. Wittenberg; children: Ethan Simpson Wittenberg, Sydney Simpson Wittenberg. MB, B of Surgery, Trinity Coll., Dublin, Ireland, 1981; MPH, U. Hawaii, 1986. Diplomate Am. Bd. Pediat. Resident in pediat. U. Hawaii, Honolulu, 1982-85; resident in preventive medicine U. NC, Chapel Hill, 1987-88; dir. Maternal and Child Health Bur. State Dept. Health, Honolulu, 1988-90, acting dir. family health svcs. divsn., 1990; policy advisor Office of Asst. Sec. for Health HHS, Washington, 1993-94, sr. advisor Agy. for Health Care Policy and Rsch. Rockville, Md., 1994-95, acting dep. adminstr. Agy. for Health Care Policy and Rsch., 1995-96, dep. adminstr. Agy. for Health Care Policy and Rsch., 1996-99, dep. dir. Agy. Healthcare Rsch. and Quality, 1999—2002; prof., All Children's Hosp. Guild endowed chair child health policy dept. pediat. U. South Fla., St. Petersburg, 2003—. Mid-career fellow Inst. Health Policy Studies, San Francisco, 1991-93; adj. faculty dept. health policy and mgmt. Johns Hopkins U., Balt., 1995—; vis. prof. U. Wash., 2000, U. Mich., 2000; nat. dir. child health policy, Nat. Initiative Children's Healthcare Quality, 2004-. Mem. editl. bd. Future Children, Maternal and Child Health Jour., 1996-2005; contbr. articles to profl. jours. Recipient Preventive Medicine traineeship Pub. Health Svc., 1986, Sec. Disting. Svcs. award Dept. HHS, 2000, Dir. Disting. Svc. award AHRQ, 2001, Meritorious Rank SES Presdl. award, 2002. Fellow: Am. Acad. Pediat. (Excellence in Pub. Svc. award 2002); mem.: APHA (governing coun. 1994—96), Nat. Acad. for Social Ins., Ambulatory Pediat. Assn. (chair pub. policy and advocacy com. 2005—), Acad. Health. Avocations: hiking, cuisine, gardening. Address: 601 4th St South CRI 1008 Saint Petersburg FL 33701 Office Phone: 727-553-3672. Business E-Mail: lsimpso1@hsc.usf.edu.

SIMPSON, MARY MICHAEL, priest, psychotherapist; b. Evansville, Ind., 1925; d. Link Wilson and Mary Garrett (Price) S. BA, BS, Tex. Women's U., 1946; grad., N.Y. Tng. Sch. Deaconesses, 1949, Westchester Inst. Tng. in Psychoanalysis and Psychotherapy, 1976; S.T.M., Gen. Theol. Seminary, 1982. ordained priest Episcopal Ch., 1977. Missionary Holy Cross Mission, Bolahun, Liberia, 1950-52; mem. Order of St. Helena, 1952—; acad. head Margaret Hall Sch., Versailles, Ky., 1958-61; sister in charge Convent of St. Helena, Bolahan, 1962-67, dir. novices, 1968-74; pastoral counselor on staff St. John the Divine, N.Y.C., 1974-87, canon residentiary, canon counselor, 1977-87, hon. canon, 1988—. Pvt. practice psychoanalyst, 1974—; dir. Cathedral Counseling Svc., 1975-87; cons. psychotherapist Union Theol. Seminary, 1980-83; bd. dirs. Westchester Inst. Tng. in Psychoanalysis and Psychotherapy, 1982-84; priest-in-charge St. John's Ch., Wilmot, New Rochelle, N.Y., 1987-88; trustee Coun. Internat. and Pub. Affairs, 1983-87;interim pastor St. Michael's Ch., Manhattan, 1992-94; cons. Diocese of N.Y., 1990—. Author: The Ordination of Women in the American Episcopal Church: The Present Situation, 1981; contbg. author: Yes to Women Priests, 1978. Mem. Nat. Assn. Advancement of Psychoanalysis, N.Y. State Assn. Practicing Psychotherapists, N.Y. Soc. Clin. Psychologists. Home and Office: 151 E 31st St Apt 8H New York NY 10016-9502 Office Phone: 212-951-4316. Personal E-mail: mmsimpson@rcn.com.

SIMPSON, MILDRED KATHLEEN, health facility administrator; b. Balt., Jan. 4, 1950; d. John Green and Mildred Elizabeth Green-Bieard; children: Sabrina, David, Derek. AA, C.C. of Balt., 1989, cert. of gerontology, 1991; BA, Towson State U., 1998. Program dir. Balt. City Health Dept., 1974—99, acting dir., 1999—2000, project coord., 2000—02, program dir., 2002—. Mem. morale com. Balt. City Health Dept., 2003—; adviser Police Athletic League, Balt., 2002—. Vol. Habitat for Humanity, Balt., 2003—04; booster 4-H Club, Balt., 1999—2003; sponsor So. Law Ctr. Nat. Campaign for Tolerance. Recipient Outstanding Contbn. to Sandtown Comty., 2002, Outstanding Support to Rosemont Comty., 2003. Mem.: NAACP, Towson State U. Active Alumni (adviser to students 2000—02), Madison Ave. Head Start (comty. organizer 2001—03, Outstanding Svc. award 2003). Avocations: travel, reading, community activist, star gazing. Home: 540 Wyanoke Ave Baltimore MD 21218

SIMPSON, NANCY IDA, nursing educator; b. Belfast, Maine, Feb. 14, 1952; d. C. D. and M. Lillian Simpson; m. Gary R. Sprague, Mar. 9, 1991; children: Ivan, Amos, Ely, Ezra, Logan LeBlanc-Simpson, India Sprague. MSN, U. So. Maine, Portland, 1987. RN Maine, 1974, Bahamas, 2001. Commd. 2d lt. US Army Nurse Corps, 1972, advanced through grades to lt. col. Portland, Maine, ret., 1997; vis. lectr. in nursing Coll. of Bahamas, Nassau, 2003—04; nursing prof. U. New Eng., Portland, Maine, 1986—. Mem.: Caribbean Curses' Orgn., Nurses Assn. Commonwealth of Bahamas, Nat. League Nursing (cert. nurse educator 2005). Office: U New Eng 716 Stevens Ave Portland ME 04103 Office Phone: 207-221-4488. Office Fax: 207-221-4895. Business E-Mail: nsimpson@une.edu.

SIMPSON, SANDRA KAY, operations research specialist; b. Rutland, Vt., Feb. 26, 1949; d. Freeman Edward and Ruth Gail (Smith) Campbell. BA, U. Vt., Burlington, 1971; M of Pub. Adminstrn., Troy State U., Europe, 1988, MSc in Internat. Rels., 1991. Isntr., trainer U.S. Govt., Ft. McClellan, Ala., 1975-79, asst. logistics officer Kitzingen, Germany, 1979-82, property acctg. officer Ft. Hood, Tex., 1982-86, Wiesbaden, Germany, 1986-93; exec. mgmt. asst. Sport and Sound, Mainz Kastel, Germany, 1993-94; maintenance mgmt. coord. U.S. Govt., Wiesbaden, 1994—, dep. dir. internal logistics, 1999—2002, theater level logistics mgr., 2002—03, 2005—06, def. logistics agy., 2003—05, theater level logistics mgr., 2005—. Cons. U.S. Govt., Heidelberg, Germany, 1994—. With U.S. Army, 1973—93. Mem. Women in Mil. Svc. to Am. Found. (charter mem.), USAREUR Retiree Coun., Wiesbaden/Mainz Retiree Coun. (sec. 1994—), Oxford Club. Avocations: photography, marathons. Home: Cmr 467 Box 1505 APO AE 09096-1505 Office Phone: 49-631-4138063. Business E-Mail: sandy.simpson@us.army.mil.

SIMPSON, ZELMA ALENE, retired librarian; b. Bristow, Okla., Nov. 2, 1923; d. Robert E. and Zelma (Wolfe) Tidrow; m. Eugene Lester Simpson, Dec. 26, 1945 (dec. 1967); 1 son, Lantz Eugene. BS in Edn., Central State U., Edmond, Okla., 1948, postgrad., 1961—. Sch. tchr., Oklahoma County, Okla., 1948-65; library dir. Okla. Hist. Soc., Oklahoma City, 1965-79; tchr. Oscar Rose Junior Coll., Midwest City, Okla., 1972-73; librarian Lawton (Okla.) Pub. Library, 1982-89, ret., 1989; family history cons., researcher, 1989—. Lectr. history and geneaology. Chmn. Hist. and Geneal. Fair Oklahoma City, 1976; sec.-treas. Broncho Basketball Booster Club, Central State U., 1967-78. Recipient Certificate of Recognition D.A.R., 1975, Award of Honor Oklahoma City Bicentennial Commn., 1975; named Distinguished Former Student Central State U., 1977 Mem. Okla. Geneal. Soc. (life, past acquisition's chmn., past 1st v.p., pres. 1972-73), DAR (lineage rsch. chmn. Samuel King chpt. 1977—, regent 1978-80, geneal. chmn. 1978-85, registrar Lawton chpt. 1986-88, co-chmn. family history fair in Lawton mall 1988), Okla. Hist. Soc., Central State U. Alumni Assn. (life), S.W. Okla. Geneal. Soc. (libr. rep. 1982-88), Edmond Geneal. Soc. (charter 1991—).

SIMPSON-JEFF, WILMA, social worker; b. Chapel Hill, Tex., Oct. 19, 1939; d. Robert Dell and Pearline (Collins) Simpson. BA, Wiley Coll., 1960; MSW, Atlanta U., 1962; postgrad., NYU, 1970-73, Hunter Coll., 1984. Cert. social work adminstrn. Asst. teen supr. Bronx (N.Y.) River Neighborhood Ctr., 1962-64; asst. dir. program Claremont Neighborhood Ctr., Bronx, 1964-66; program planning and rev. specialist N.Y.C. Youth Svc. Agy./Youth Bd., 1966-69; social worker, 1969-73; instr., counselor N.Y. Tech. Coll., Bklyn., 1973-75; parent coord. regional Deaf-Blind Ctr., Bronx, 1975-84; program social worker N.Y. Inst. for Spl. Edn., 1984-87, coord. parent edn. Bronx., 1987—. Instr. Lehman Coll., Bronx, 1984-86, Boro Manhattan C.c., N.Y.C., 1986-91. Bd. dirs. Parenting Coalition Internat., 1999. Mem. Clark Atlanta U. Nat. Alumni Assn. (v.p. 1995—, fin. sec. 1990-95, v.p. Sch. Social Work 1975-79, 85-87), CAUA of Greater N.Y. (pres. 1992—), Alpha Kappa Alpha. Avocations: reading, bowling, painting, writing. Home: 3001 Henry Hudson Pky Bronx NY 10463-4717 Office: NY Inst for Spl Edn 999 Pelham Pky N Bronx NY 10469-4905

SIMS, DARCIE DITTBERNER, grief management specialist, psychotherapist, clinical hypnotherapist; b. Milw., May 20, 1947; d. Van F. and Alicia (Haake) Dittberner; m. Robert A. Sims, Aug. 19, 1970; children: Alicia, Austin (dec.). BA in Journalism, U. N.Mex., 1969, MEd, 1971; MA in Mental Health Counseling, St. Mary's U., San Antonio, 1980; PhD, LaSalle U., 1991. Cert. counselor, N.Mex., Mich., Kans., Mo., La.; nationally cert. grief counselor, clin. hypnotherapist; diplomate Am. Psychotherapy Assn., Nat. Bd. Cert. Clin. Hypnotherapist; nat. cert. Thanatologist. Adj. prof. death and dying No. Mich. U., Marquette, 1978-79; cons. crisis mgmt. Northside Ind. Sch. Dist., San Antonio, 1981-82; adj. prof. sociology McMurry Coll., Abilene, Tex., 1983; psychotherapist Pastoral Care & Counseling Ctr., Abilene, 1983-84; dir. social svc. Hospice Abilene, 1983-84; counselor, therapist Albuquerque Pub. Sch. System, 1984-85, mental health specialist, 1985-88; dir. prevention program Crittenton Children's Psychotherapy Ctr., Kansas City, Mo., 1988-89; pvt. practice Slidell, La., 1989-91; pvt. practice, trainer N.D., 1991-92; pvt. practice, psychotherapist Albuquerque, 1992-94; hypnotherapist, psychotherapist Wenatchee, Wash., 1994—; dir. tng. and program devel. Accord Aftercare Svcs., Louisville, 1995—2000; founder and pres. Grief Inc., Louisville, 2000, Seattle, 2005—; dir. Am. Grief acad., Seattle, 2005—. V.p. nat. bd. dirs. Compassionate Friends, Inc., Chgo.; dir. Big A and Co. Cons., Albuquerque; bd. v.p. Widowed Person's Svc. D. Dirs., Kansas City; co-chmn., keynote speaker World Gathering on Bereavement, Seattle, 1991; chair World Gathering on Bereavement, 1991, 96, 2005; nat. trustee Nat. Cath. Ministries to the Bereaved, 1992-2000; v.p. EduVisions, Inc.; cons. in the field of grief mgmt. Author: Why Are the Casseroles Always Tuna?, 1990, Footsteps Through the Valley, 1993, Touchstones, 1993, The Other Side of Grief, 1993, Finding Your Way Through Grief, 1993, If I Could Just See Hope, 1994, A Place for Me: Guided Imagery for Kids Age 8-80; author: (with others) Dear Parents; We Need Not Walk Alone, 1990, Young People and Death, 1991; author monthly column Bereavement Mag.: Grief and Humor Dept., 1987-2001, Coping Editor, 1987-2001. Troop cons. Girl Scouts Am.; state sec. Associated Care Children's Health, Albuquerque, 1985-87. Named Vol. of Yr. USAF Family Svcs., 1975. Mem. ACA, Am. Mental Health Counselor Assn., Assn. for Death Edn. and Counseling (cert. grief counselor 1983—, nat. bd. dirs. 1995-98), Make Today Count Inc. (cons. 1975—, Nat. Appreciation award 1988). Avocations: art, canoeing, writing. Office: Grief Inc 4227 S Meridian Ste C-363 Puyallup WA 98373-9112 Office Phone: 253-929-0649.

SIMS, LENNIE COLEMAN, public relations consultant; b. Wellington, Tex., July 31, 1930; d. John Scott Jr. and Ethel Breeding Coleman; m. Billy Mac (William McDowell) Sims, Sept. 1, 1956; children: Richard McDowell Sims, Randall Coleman Sims (twins).* BBA, Abilene Christian U., 1950. Author, choreographer, music arranger (U.S. BiCentennial hist. play) Man & Land & Love, 1972, (all musical) 1976, Collingsworth County Centennial Links of Our Legacy, 1991. Appointed as 1st woman to bd. regents West Tex. State U., 1974 (reappointed 1982, 1st vice chmn., v.p. merger com., W. Tex. A&M U., 1998, Crime Stoppers Adv. Coun. (chair edn. steering com., 1999); Collingsworth County chair Dem. party; 1st v.p. Tex. Dem. Party County Chairs Assn.; appt. State Bar Tex. Mem. Fedn. Women's Clubs (state pres. 1980-82, region Tex., Colo., N. Mex., La., Ariz., Ark.), Internat. Gen. Fedn. Women's Clubs (pres.), 1st chmn. Women's History/Resource Ctr. Internat. Gen. Fedn. Women's Clubs), Tex. Fedn. Music Clubs (state 1st v.p. 1968-70, editor state mag. Lines & Spaces, 1964-75). Home: PO Box 248 Wellington TX 79095-0248

SIMS, LOWERY STOKES, museum curator, museum administrator, writer, educator; b. Washington, Feb. 13, 1949; d. John Jacob and Bernice Marion (Banks) S. BA in Art History, Queens Coll., 1970, MPhil, 1989; PhD in Art History, CUNY, 1995; MA in Art History, Johns Hopkins U., 1972; LHD (hon.), Md. Coll. Art, Balt., 1988; ArtsD (hon.), Moore Coll. Art, Phila., 1990; ArtsD, Brown U., Providence, 2003. Mus. edn. assoc. Met. Mus. Art, NYC, 1972-75, asst. curator, 1975-79, assoc. curator, 1979-95, curator, 1995—99; exec. dir. Studio Mus. in Harlem, NYC, 1999—2005, pres., 2005—06, adj. curator, 2006—. Prin. author: (catalogue) Stuart Davis, American Painting, 1991; co-author: (book) Wifredo Lam and the International Avant Guide, 1923, 1982, (catalogue) Wifredo Lam and His Contemporaries, 1992, (catalogue) Challenge of the Modern: African American Arts, 1925-1945, 2002-03, Persistence of Geometry, Cleve. Mus. Art, 2006. Bd. dirs. Caribbean Cultural Ctr., N.Y.C., 1975-80, 90—, Tiffany Found., N.Y.C., 2005—, Met. Mus. Art, 2005—. Recipient award of distinction Am. Women's Econ. Devel., 1993. Mem. Internat. Assn. Art Critics, Coll. Art Assn. (bd. dirs. 1993-97, Mather award for art criticism 1991). Democrat. Avocations: needlepoint, collecting black memorabilia. Office: Studio Museum in Harlem 144 West 125th St New York NY 10027 Personal E-mail: lsimssmh@aol.com. Business E-Mail: lsims@studiomuseum.org.

SIMS, MARCIE LYNNE, language educator, writer; b. Monrovia, Calif., Feb. 22, 1963; d. Charles Eugene and Delores May (Wonert) S.; m. Douglas Todd Cole; children: Marcus Anthony Cole, Thomas Halvor Cole. BA in English, Calif. State Poly., 1986; MA in English, San Diego State U., 1990. Page U.S. Senate, Washington, 1979; instr. Calif. Conservation Corps, San Diego, 1990; instr. in English Shoreline C.C., Seattle, 1990-94, Seattle Ctrl. C.C., 1990-94, Green River C.C., Auburn, Wash., 1994—. Founder Wild Mind Women Writers Workshop, Seattle, 1992—. Author: Soul-Making: John Keats and the Stages of Death, 1990; contbg. author Moms on Line, 1996-; editor Espial Lit. Jour. Vol. cons. Camp Fire, Wash., 1994-96. Mem. Am. Fedn. Tchrs., The Keats-Shelley Orgn., Wash. Fed. Tchrs. (exec. bd. mem. 1993-94), Phi Kappa Phi, Sigma Tau Delta. Democrat. Avocations: cooking, tennis. Office: Green River CC 12401 SE 320th St Auburn WA 98092-3622

SIMS, PAMELA JAN (CERUSSI), writer, minister; b. Little Rock, Sept. 10, 1933; 2 children. Attended, Mt. St. Mary's Acad., St. Scholastica's Coll., Sydney, Delgado Coll., Nola, Tulane U., 1951; DD (hon.). Lic. rev. in Christian ministry, in specialized svcs. Fla., 2006. Past pres. Ikebana Internat., Le Gals, Inc., 1979—89; pres. Titanic Bead Co.; journalist, notary pub. Fla., 1986—. Tchr. legal secretarial classes, Nola; support writer Pres. George W. Bush, 1999—2007. Author: Pensacola Today mag., Climate mag., introduction to Bonsai & Basic Ikebana; featured on local TV Guide mag. cover Anskebara Design; prin. works include Ikebana design articles; contbr. articles in mags. and newspapers. Vol. Pensacola Art Mus.; team leader Bush/Cheney Inc., 2002—; mem. Rep. Nat. Com., Rep. Woman's Club, Pensacola Christian Women's Club, United Intercessors Inc. Recipient Cert. of Recognition, Rep. Nat. Party, 2002, Congl. Award of Merit, 2004, Blue and Tri-Color Ribbon awar, Fla. Fedn. Garden Clubs, 2004, Cert. of Appreciation, Rep. Nat. Com., 2005. Mem.: Pensacola Camellia Club. Achievements include patents pending for AIDS cure. Office Phone: 850-607-1786. Office Fax: 850-457-1022.

SIMS, SANDRA, elementary school educator; b. Oakland, Calif., Oct. 12, 1944; d. Harry Oscar and Lucille Rice; children: Curt, Derek; m. Terеence Sims Sr. BS in Human Devel., Calif. State U., Hayward, 1972; MA, U.S. Internat. Univ., San Diego, 1988. Tchr. Oakland (Calif.) Pub. Schs., 1973-88, tchr. on spl. assignment, 1988—2004; ret. Cons. Calif. Literacy Project, Hayward, 1990—, Bay Area Writing, Berkeley, Calif., 1991—. Tutorial program grantee Marcus Foster Inst., 1994. Mem. Calif. Ret. Tchrs. Assn., Phi Delta Kappa. Democrat. Baptist. Avocation: reading. Home: 455 59th St Oakland CA 94609-1503

SIMS, TERRE LYNN, insurance company executive; b. Madison, Wis., Dec. 26, 1951; d. Roy Charles and Ruth Marie (McCloskey) Pierstorff; m. Gary Peter Laufenberg, Feb. 15, 1969 (div.); children: Amie, Monte, Tawna; m. Perry Allen Sims, May 3, 1994 (dec. Aug. 2000). Sales agt. Bankers Life and Casualty, Madison, 1977-80, asst. mgr., 1981-84, br. mgr. Peoria, 1984-91; co-owner Complete Ins. Svcs., Inc., Madison, Wis., 1991—; owner, operator Ohio Tavern, Madison, 1993—; co-owner Nu Brick Inn Bar and Grill, Madison, 2000—01. Office: 4521 Stein Ave Madison WI 53714-1731 Office Phone: 608-245-0007. Personal E-mail: terres123@aol.com.

SIMS, VERONICA GAIL, literature educator; b. Detroit, Jan. 8, 1959; d. Eura Dell Sims; 1 child, Vernon. Grad., Wayne State U., Detroit, 1985. Unit clerk Grace Hosp., Detroit, 1977—91; substitute tchr. Detroit Pub. Schs., 1984—86; reading specialist, English tchr. Detroit Pub. Sch., 1987—. Mentor Detroit Pub. Schs., 2004—, tchr., tutorial instr., 2006—. Parent vol. Wayne State U., 2006. Recipient Mentoring Program Cert. award, Detroit Pub. Schs., 2005. Mem.: Detroit Reading Counc., Mich. Reading Assn., Metropolitan Reading Council, Internat. Reading Assn., Women of Wayne State, Nat. Tchrs. of English, Assn. Supr. and Curriculum Devel. Avocations: travel, reading, music, porcelain doll collection. Home: 18520 Asbury Park Detroit MI 48235 Office: Detroit Pub Schs Northern HS 9026 Woodward Detroit MI 48202

SIMS-NESMITH, CAROLYN SANDRA, cultural arts association administrator; b. Phila., July 16, 1950; d. Robert Lee and Laura Sims; m. Henry Luther Nesmith, Sept. 15, 1985. B in Social Scis., Pa. State U., 1971. Program coord. YWCA of Kensington, Phila., 1980—82; asst. exec. dir. Human Resources Forum, Phila., 1982—83; program dir. YWCA of Germantown, Phila., 1983—85; mgr. Pvt. Industry Coun., Phila., 1985—93, assessment counselor, 1993—98; facilitator Transitional Work Corp., Phila., 1998—. Cons. YWCA of Germantown, Phila., 1978—79. Composer: Hats on the Vine, 1999, Ushers, 2002; author: (plays) The Journey, 2000; prodr.: (CD collection of original music) The Journey, 2000; (plays) Women of Distinction, 2002, Men of Distinction, 2003, Sky is the Limit Youth Jamboree, 2003, (album) Believe, 1983. Founder Pa. State Gospel Choir, Capitol Campus, Middletown, 1970—72; founder, dir. Freedom Choir of Phila., 1969—; resident musical dir. Rainbow Connection, Prince Music Theater on the Ave. of the Arts, Phila., 2004—; music dir. Calvary Bapt. Ch. Youth Mass Choir, Phila., 2000—; founder, dir. Freedom Youth Mass Choir, Phila., 1993—; founder Slippery Rock (Pa.) State Coll. Gospel Choir, 1971—2002. Recipient Outstanding Cmty. Svc. award, State of Pa, 1986, City of Phila., 1999, 2002, 2003, 2004, 2005, 1st Pl., PathMark Gospel Choir Competition (Youth Divsn.), 2002. Mem.: Gospel Music Workshop of Am. Avocations: gym/spa activities, writing, sketching, travel, reading. Home: 3882 Conshohocken Ave Philadelphia PA 19131 Office: Freedom Choir of Phila 3882 Conshohocken Ave Philadelphia PA 19131 Office Phone: 215-965-3000. Personal E-mail: simsnesmith@aol.com.

SIMSON, RENATE MARIA, English and African American studies professor; b. Vienna, Mar. 13, 1934; d. Erwin Rheinhold and Margaret Ludmilla (Horel) Biel; m. Brian William Simson, June 18, 1966; children: Thomas, Bonnie. BA, Syracuse U., 1956; MA, Rutgers U., 1959; PhD, Syracuse U., 1974. Cert. tchr. N.J., N.Y. Prof. English coll. agr. and tech. SUNY, Morrisville, 1965—. Adj. prof. African Am. studies Syracuse (N.Y.) U., 1975—; speaker N.Y. State Coun. on Humanities, 1988—. NYU Women's Studies Coun., 1990—. Author book chpts.; contbr. articles numerous profl. publs. NEH grantee, 1978, Am. Philos. Soc. grantee, 1979, 82, Morrisville Coll. Found. grantee, 1983; recipient Outstanding Faculty Woman of Yr. Student Govt. Orgn. Morrisville Coll., 1980-81, travel award United Univ. Professions, 1990. Mem. Nat. Assn. Ethnic Studies, Nat. Coun. Tchrs. of Eng., Nat. Coll. Eng. Assn., N.Y. State Coun. Tchrs. of Eng. Roman Catholic. Avocations: travel, swimming. Home: 350 Summerhaven Dr N East Syracuse NY 13057-3142

SIMUN, PATRICIA BATES, education educator, consultant; b. Pitts., Apr. 20, 1931; d. A.E. Griffith and Mary Effa (Casey) Bates; m. Richard Vincent Simun, Dec. 31, 1961; children: Mary Bates, Ann Eugenia Simun-Park. BS in Edn., W.Va. U., 1952; MA, U. Pitts., 1962, PhD, 1967. Cert. tchr., Calif., Pa., W.Va.; cert. counselor, Pa. Tchr. Avonworth Union Sch. Dist., Ben Avon, Pa., 1955-57; tchr. placement dir. Carnegie-Mellon U., 1957-61; rsch. asst. U. Pitts., 1961-62, rsch. assoc., 1962-63; chair ednl. founds. Calif. State U., L.A., 1983-84, assoc. chair adminstrn., counseling and founds. dept., 1985, prof. edn., 1967-91, dir. Costa Rica travel study, 1988-98, prof. emerita, 1991—. Vis. disting. prof. Universidad Autonoma, Guadalajara, Mex., summer 1975; cons., evaluation project support Calif. State U./L.A. Unified Sch. Dist., 1992-95; cons., evaluation integration L.A. Unified Sch.Dist., 1981-91; cons. ACLU, L.A., 1976-80; participant Alternative Edn. Exch., 1975, Internat. Options in Pub. Edn., Pasadena, Calif., 1975, others; discussion leader Am. Edn. Rsch. Assn. evaluation conf., San Francisco, 1977; speaker in field. Editor Excellence Through Equity, 1984-87; contbr. articles to profl. jours. Bd. dirs. Cmty. Child Care, Inc., L.A., 1985-88; mem. L.A. High Cmty. Adv. Voun., 1980-84; advisor Inst. Tchr. Leadership, L.A., 1978-80; mem. edn. com. Cmty. Rels. Conf. So. Calif., L.A., 1980-84; docent Page Mus. of La Brea Discoveries, 2001—. Recipient Cert. of Merit Human Rels. Commn., L.A., 1978, Cert. of Outstanding Svc. So. Poverty Law Ctr., 1984, Cert. of Appreciation L.A. Unified Sch. Dist., 1977, Outstanding Svc. award Mid-City Alternative Sch., 1982; Docent George C. Page Mus., 2001—. Mem. Am. Ednl. Rsch. Assn. (SIG com. chair 1983-84, sec. 1984-89), Calif. Edn. Rsch. Assn., Phi Lambda Theta, Kappa Delta Pi, Phi Beta Delta. Avocations: knitting, hiking, stamp collecting/philately, reading. Home: 522 S Genesee Ave Los Angeles CA 90036-3241 Personal E-mail: psimun@pacbell.net.

SINCLAIR, CAROL ANN, accountant, consultant; d. Edward Norman and Doris Mae Nowicki; m. Harold Richard Sinclair, Apr. 7, 1972; children: Matthew John, Catherine Carol, Elizabeth Ann. BA in Acctg. with honors, St. Leo U., Fla., 2004; BA in Art Direction/Design with honors, Coll. Creative Studies, Detroit, 1990. Art dir., designer and illustrator Young & Rubicam Ltd., Detroit, 1992—94, Stone & Simon Advt. Agy., Southfield, 1994—96; acct. accounts receivable nat. accounts Manpower Metro Detroit, Inc., Southfield, 1996—99; acct. Lincare, Inc., Clearwater, Fla., 2000—. Cons. Grosse Pointe Artists Assn., Grosse Pointe, Mich., 1980—95, Assistance League to NE Guidance Ctr., Detroit, 1982—96. Supporting mem. Gulf Coast Mus. Arts, Largo, Fla., 2000—. Recipient Tiffany award, Manpower Metro Detroit, Inc., 1999, Eagle award, 1999, Peer award. Mem.: Nat. Mus. Women in the Arts, Founders Soc. Detroit Inst. Arts, Grosse Pointe Arts Coun. (bd. mem.), Detroit Soc. Women Painters and Sculptors (bd. mem.), Mich. Watercolor Soc. (bd. mem.), Grosse Pointe Artists Assn. (bd. mem.). Avocations: genealogy, reading, travel. Office Phone: 727-431-8316.

SINCLAIR, CAROLE, publishing executive, editor; b. Haddonfield, N.J., May 13, 1942; d. Earl Walter and Ruth (Sinclair) Dunham; 1 child, Wendy. Student, U. Florence, Italy, 1963; BA in Polit. Sci., Bucknell U, 1964. Advt. copywriter BBD&O Advertising, N.Y.C., 1966-67; sales promotion mgr. Macmillan Pub. Co., N.Y.C., 1967-71; mktg. mgr. Doubleday & Co., Inc., N.Y.C., 1972-74, promotion dir., 1974-76, advt. mgr., sales and promotion, chmn. mktg. com., 1976-80; v.p. mktg., editorial dir. Davis Pubs., N.Y.C., 1980-83; founder, pub., editorial dir., sr. v.p. Sylvia Porter's Personal Fin. Mag., N.Y.C., 1983-90; pres. The Sylvia Porter Orgn., Inc., N.Y.C., 1980—; founder, pres. Sinclair Media Inc., N.Y.C., 1990—. Mktg. dir. Denver Pub. Inst., summers 1975-78; lectr. Columbia U. Bus. Sch. and Sch. of Journalism, 1976; host nationally syndicated TV show, Sylvia Porter's Money Tips, syndicated daily radio show, Sylvia Porter's Personal Fin. Report, audio cassette series on fin. topics. Author: Keys for Women Starting and Owning a Business, 1991, Keys to Women's Basic Professional Needs, 1991, When Women Retire, 1992; contbg. editor Pushcart Prize, 1977; contbr. The Business of Publishing, 1980. Renaissance Art Program fellow, Florence, Italy, 1963; White House intern, 1962. Mem. Women's Forum, Intercorp. Communications Group, Mag. Pubs.' Assn., Advt. Women in N.Y., Spence Sch. Parent's League. Clubs: Pubs. Lunch. Presbyterian. Avocation: boating.

SINCLAIR, CLARA MILL, retired science educator; b. Cranbrook, BC, Can., May 2, 1920; d. John Peat Sinclair and Clara Anna Mill; m. Baxter C. Hurn Jr. (div.); children: Paula H. Zeitlin, C. Jane Stegmaier, Maren S. Hurn, Joanna S. Matetich. BA in Biology, Park Coll., Parkville, Mo., 1942; MA in Edn., Ariz. State U., Tempe, 1957; MA in Humanistic Edn., Boston U., 1975. HS sci. tchr. Avoca Sch. Dist., Iowa, 1942—43; lab. asst. Colony, Va., 1943—44; mid. sch. sci. and math. tchr. Scottsdale Pub. Schs., Ariz., 1957—72; sci. tchr. Olney Friends Sch., Barnesville, Ohio, 1972—74; dir. presch. project refugee camps Am. Friends Svc. Com., Gaza Strip, Palestine, 1975—79, liaison for sceondary schs. East Africa Kenya, 1979—81; head resident Pendle Hill, Quaker Study Ctr., Wallingford, Pa., 1981—83; field sec. Western Region Quakers Am., 1983—87; coord. religious activities Mountain View Sch. for Girls, Helena, Mont., 1990; Howard and Ann Brinton Meml. fellow Soc. of Friends, 1991. Mem. Peace Action, Montgomery County, Md., 2001—; active Drs. Without Borders, Am. Friend Svc. Com., Heifer Project; vol. Friends Com. on Nat. Legislation, Washington, 2001—. Recipient Jeannette Rankin Peace award, INst. Peace Studies, Rocky Mountain Coll., Billings, Mont., 2001. Mem.: ACLU, Amnest Internat. (Bruce Collmar award 2000, Jeanette Rankur Civil Liberties award 2001). Avocations: reading, gardening. Home: 12310 Quaker Ln C-17 Sandy Spring MD 20860

SINCLAIR, DAISY, communications executive; b. Perth Amboy, N.J., Mar. 22, 1941; d. James Patrick and Margaret Mary (McAniff) Nieland; m. James Pratt Sinclair, May 25, 1978; children: Duncan, Gibbons. BA, Caldwell Coll., 1962. Jr. copywriter Young & Rubican, N.Y.C., 1962-64; various positions in casting dept. Ogilvy & Mather, N.Y.C., 1964-90, sr. v.p., dir. casting, 1990—. Mem.: Drama League N.Y. (3d v.p. 1982—), Am. Assn. Advt. (talent agt. com. 1972—), N.Y. Yacht Club, Union Club, Tuxedo Club, Chapaquoit Yacht Club, Edgartown Yacht Club, Knickerbocker Greys (pres.). Republican. Episcopalian. Avocations: opera, theater, sailing, skiing. Home: 4 E 95th St New York NY 10128-0705

SINCLAIR, FRANCES TERESA, music educator, musician; d. Joe Neal Sinclair, Jr. and Ruth Spears Smith; m. John Jay Galland, July 31, 1999; 1 stepchild, Hill Autumn Galland. MusB with distinction, U. N.C., Chapel Hill, 1986; MusM, Fla. State U., Talahassee, 1989; DMA, U. N.C., Greensboro, 1997. Choral dir. Pinecrest HS, Southern Pines, NC, 1989—93; asst. prof. and asst. dir. choral activities Clemson U., SC, 1998—2000; instr. music applied and class piano Sandhill's CC, Pinehurst, NC, 2000—03; asst. prof., interim dir choral activities U. NC, Charlotte, 2003—04, dir. choral music, coord. vocal studies Asheville, 2005; asst. prof., dir. choral activities Coastal Carolina U., Conway, SC, 2005—. Guest condr.; clinician; adjudicator local to regional festivals. competitions and clinics. Contbr. articles to profl. jours. Mem. Moore County Choral Soc., Pinehurst, NC, 1989—91, Moore County Music Soc., 1989—93, So. Pines Bus. and Profl. Women, 2000—02; dir. music Cmty. Presbyn. Ch., Pinehurst, 1991—; mem. bd. dir. Moore County chpt. N.C. Symphony, So. Pines, 1989—93. Finalist Tchr. of Yr., Pinecrest H.S., 1991, Prof. of Yr., Coastal Carolina U., 2006; recipient Outstanding Young Musician of Yr., Moore County Music Soc., 1991. Mem.: Am. Choral Dir. Assn. (exec. bd. N.C. and S.C. chpt. 1998—), Coll. Music Soc., Music Educators Nat. Conf. (sec. jr. high exec. bd. 1991—93). Home: 5 Wampanoag Ln Pinehurst NC 28374 Office: Coastal Carolina U Conway SC 29528

SINCLAIR, LINDA DRUMWRIGHT, educational consultant; b. Norfolk, Va., Aug. 4, 1942; d. Raymond Edward and Evelyn Elizabeth (Edwards) Drumwright; m. Charles Armstrong Sinclair, Oct. 5, 1962; children: William, Dianne, Sandy. BS, U. S.C., 1974, MA, 1976, postgrad. Cert. tchr. in biology, chemistry, physics. Sci. tchr. Keenan H.S., Columbia, S.C., 1976-77; chemistry/physics tchr. Lexington (S.C.) H.S., 1977-93; talented/gifted tchr. U. S.C., Columbia, 1988; tchr. rsch. program Oak Ridge (Tenn.) Nat. Lab., 1989; rschr. Savannah River Ecology Lab., Aiken, S.C., 1991-92; state sci. edn. cons. S.C. Dept. Edn., Columbia, 1993—. Cons. Prentice Hall Pub., Princeton, N.J., 1992-93. Author: Operation Radon, 1993. Adv. bd. S.C. Forestry Commn., Columbia, 1993—, S.C. Environ. Coalition, Columbia, 1993—, S.C. Sci. Coun., Columbia, 1989—; mem., com. chair Lexington Woman's Club, 1986—; v.p. Lexington Garden Club, 1983—. Named S.C. Sci. Tchr. of the Yr., S.C. Acad. Sci., 1986, Sigma Xi, 1986, S.C. Chemistry Tchr. of the Yr., S.C. Chem. Soc., 1992; recipient Presdl. Award for Excellence in Sci. Teaching, NSF, 1993. Mem. S.C. Sci. Coun. (v.p., pres.), S.C. Chemistry Tchrs. Assn. (bd. dirs. 1987—), S.C. Acad. Sci. (bd. dirs. 1982—), S.C. Jr. Acad. Sci. (bd. dirs. 1980—), S.C. Environ. Edn. Assn. (bd. dirs. 1990—), Nat. Sci. Tchrs. Assn. (bd. dirs. 1992-94). Lutheran. Avocations: horseback riding, gardening, swimming, water sports. Home: 107 Hermitage Rd Lexington SC 29072-2221 Office: SC Dept Edn 801-B Rutledge Bldg 1429 Senate St Columbia SC 29201-3730 Office Phone: 803-734-0887. Business E-Mail: lsinclai@sde.state.sc.us.

SINCLAIR, LISA, science educator; BS in Elem. Edn. (hon.), Southwestern Okla. State U., Weatherford, 2002, BS (hon.) in Health Sci., 2002. Lic. tchr. Colo., 2003, Okla., 2005. Instr. sci., math. Springfield Jr./Sr. H.S., Colo., 2002—05; instr. sci. Yuma Mid. Sch., 2005—. Grantee, St. Patties Found., 2006. Mem.: NSTA. Conservative. Southern Baptist. Avocations: travel, photography, scrapbooks. Home: 700 W 3rd Ave #108 Yuma CO 80759 Office Phone: 970-848-2000.

SINCLAIR, MARY L., science educator; b. Calgary, Alberta, Canada, Nov. 14, 1960; d. John Lawrence and Anne Erica Sinclair; m. Graham J. Cox, Aug. 4, 1984; children: Aaron Michael Sinclair Cox, Sean Stuart Sinclair Cox, Joshua Mathias Sinclair Cox, Samantha Marie Sinclair Cox. BS, U. Sask., Saskatoon, Canada, 1985, MS, 1995. Asst. prof. Nebr. Meth. Coll. Josie Harper Campus, Omaha, 2003—. Grad. scholar, U. Sask., 1991—94. Mem.: Human Anatomy and Physiology Soc. Office: Nebraska Meth Coll 720 North 87th St Omaha NE 68114 Office Phone: 402-354-7060. Personal E-mail: m.sinclair@methodistcollege.edu.

SINCLAIR, PATRICIA WHITE, literature educator; b. Selma, Ala., Feb. 26, 1963; d. Lorenzo Vaughn and Elizabeth Morrison Sinclair. BA, U. of N. Tex., Denton, 1991. Lic. tchr. English, ESL(PreK-12), Gifted, and Earth/Space Science Va., 2006, cert. tchr. secondary edn., ESL and gifted edn. Tex., 2005. H.s. tchr. English, 9-12, TAAS remediation, creative and practical writing, reading The Colony HS/Lewisville ISD, The Colony/Flower Mound, 1995—99; tchr. English, SAT prep., TAKS remediation, and creative writing Lewisville ISD/Hebron H.S., Carrollton, LISD in Flower Mound, Tex., 1999—. Acad. decathlon coach Hebron H.S., Carrollton, Tex., 2001—05; co-author, collaborator on English curriculum, grades 9-12 and creative writing Lewisville ISD, Flower Mound, Tex., 1997—2003, presenter, English/lang. arts tchr. inservices on state testing strategies, incorportating media to meet the teks, & questioning strategies, 1997—2003. Author: (short story) Death by Natural Causes (Second Pl., Fiction, U. of North Tex. Green Fuse Lit. Competition, 1988), Drink Entire Against the World (Publ. in The Green Fuse, 1987), Briar Patch (Publ. in The Elk River Rev., 1991), (poem) Heroes for Breakfast (Publ. in The Elk River Rev., 1991). Mem.: Nat. Coun. Tchrs. English (state leader Tex. program to recognize excellence in student lit. mags), Va. Tchrs. ESOL, Delta Kappa Gamma, Tex. Fedn. of Tchrs., ASCD. Democrat-Npl. Humanistic-Methodist. Avocations: writing, photography, horseback riding, reading, films. Office Phone: 972-539-1551.

SINCLAIR, RUTH SPEARS SMITH, music educator; b. Rowland, N.C., Apr. 21, 1931; d. Charles McDuffie and Frances Paul Smith; m. Joe N. Sinclair Jr., Dec. 30, 1954; children: Frances T. Sinclair-Galland, David Neal Sinclair. MusB, Flora MacDonald Coll., 1953. Pvt. piano tchr., NC, 1953—; chmn. So. Pines chpt. Nat. Guild Auditions, Southern Pines, NC, 1975—. Pres. music dept. Fayetteville Presbytery, 1968-70; mem. Weymouth Festival for Young Musicians, Southern Pines, 1988-92; deacon Bethesda Presbyn. Ch., Aberdeen, 1996-98; bd. dirs. Moore County N.C. Symphony, 1997—. Mem. N.C. Music Tchrs. Assn. (state contest dir. 1997-99, coll. audition chair 2000—2002), Nat. Guild Piano Tchrs. (chmn. Fairmont chpt. 1955-56, Maxton chpt. 1962-67), Moore Music Soc. (chmn. and performer young musicians concert), Cardinal Book Club. Republican. Presbyterian. Avocations: bridge, water aerobics, reading, gardening, walking. Home: 604 Mcqueen Rd Aberdeen NC 28315-2106

SINCLAIR, SARA VORIS, health facility administrator, nurse; b. Kansas City, Mo., Apr. 13, 1942; d. Franklin Defenbaugh and Inez Estelle (Figenbaum) Voris; m. James W. Sinclair, June 13, 1964; children: Thomas James, Elizabeth Kathleen, Joan Sara. BSN, UCLA, 1965. RN, Utah; lic. health care facility adminstr.; cert. health care adminstr. Staff nurse UCLA Med. Ctr. Hosp., 1964-65; charge nurse Boulder (Colo.) Meml. Hosp., 1966, Boulder Manor Nursing Home, 1974-75, Four Seasons Nursing Home, Joliet, Ill., 1975-76; dir. nursing Home Health Agy of Olympia Fields, Joliet, Ill., 1977-79, Sunshine Terr. Found., Inc., Logan, Utah, 1980, asst. adminstr., 1980-81, adminstr., 1981-93; dir. divsn. health systems improvement Utah Dept. Health, Salt Lake City, 1993-97; CEO Sunshine Terr. Found., 1997—. Long term care profl. and tech. adv. com. Joint Commn. on Accreditation Healthcare Orgns., Chgo., 1987—91, chmn., 1990—91; adj. lectr. Utah State U., 1991—93, search com. for dir. major gifts, 2001; adj. clin. faculty Weber State U., Ogden, Utah; moderator radio program Healthwise Sta. KUSU-FM, 1985—93; del. White House Conf. on Aging, 1995; chmn. Utah Dept. of Health's Ethics, Instl. Rev. Bd. Com., 1995—97, Utah Dept. Health Rist Mgmt. Com., 1995—97; exec. com. Utah Long Term Care Coalition, 1995, chmn., 1997—2001; oversight com. and long term care tech. adv. group Utah Health Policy Commn., 1996—2000, Health Insight Utah State Coun., 1996—2001; adj. vol. faculty U. Utah Gerontology Ctr., 1997—; moderator Living Well Longer Utah Pub. Radio weekly program, 1998—; bd. dirs. Logan Regional Hosp., chair quality assurance, 2001—; mem. regional adv. bd. Zions Bank, 2001—; chair quality subcom. Am. Health Care Assn., 2003—05, chair clin. practice com., 2006; chmn. adv. bd. No. Utah Arca Health Edn. Ctr., 2004—; spkr., presenter in field. Contbg. author: Associate Degree Nursing and The Nursing Home, 1988; contbr. articles to profl. jours. Deans adv. coun. Coll. Bus. Utah State U., Logan, 1989—91, mem. presdl. search com., 1991—92; chmn., co-founder Cache Cmty. Health Coun., 1985, chair, 2000; bd. dirs. Bridgerland Area Tech. Coll., 2001—, Utah Assistive Tech. Found., 2001—04, vice chair; chmn. bd. Hospice of Cache Valley, Logan, 1986; apptd. chmn. Utah Health Facilities Com., 1989—91; chmn. health and human svcs. subcom. Cache 2010, 1992—93; mem. long term care tech. adv. group oversight com. Utah Health Policy Commn., 1997; dir. Health Insight, 1996; trustee Utah State U., 1997—2001; chmn. Utah State U. Trustee's Acad. Affairs Com., 1999—2001; co-chair Living Well Longer Coun., 1997—2004, Cache Cmty. Health Coun., 2000—; apptd. Utah State Bd. Regents, 2001; apptd. mem. Utah State Bd. Edn., 2002, officer, 2006; chair Am. Coll. of Health Care Adminstrs., 2005; bd. dirs. Utah Higher Edn. Assistance Authority, 2002—03; govtl. appointee Utah Commn. on Aging, 2005, vice chmn., 2005—; mem. bd. trustees Utah Coll. Applied Tech., 2006—; mem. exec. com. Utah Partnership Edn., Inc., 2006, bd. trustees, 2006. Named Rotarian of Yr., Logan Rotary Club, 2002; named one of Those Who Dare to Care, U. Utah Coll. Nursing Alumni Assn., 2005; recipient Disting. Svc. award, Utah State U., 1989, Total Citizen award, Cache C. of C., 2002, Pioneer award, Utah Area Health Edn. Ctr., 2003, Utah AHEC Pioneer award, 2003, Mary Meredith Dist. Pub. Health Nurse award, Utah Pub. Health Assn., 2004. Fellow: Am. Coll. Health Care Adminstrs. (convocation and edn. coms. 1992—93, v.p. Utah chpt. 1992—94, bylaws com. 1996—2000, region IX vice gov. 1998—2000, chmn. bylaws com. 1999—2000, chair edn. com. 2000, nominating com. 2000, bd. dirs. 2002—, chmn. bd. 2005—06, immediate past chair 2006—); mem.: Logan Bus. and Profl. Women's Club (pres. 1989, Woman of Achievement award 1982, Woman of Yr. 1982), Utah Gerontol. Soc. (bd. dirs. 1992—93, chmn. nominating com. 1993—94, bd. dirs. 1995—97, chmn. ann. conf. 1996, pres. 1997), Utah Health Care Assn. (pres. 1983—85, treas. 1991—93, pres. 2000—01, Disting. Svc. award 1991, Sv. award for long term care 1996), Am. Health Care Assn. (non-proprietary v.p. 1986—87, region v.p. 1987—89, exec. com. 1993, cert. facilitator 2002, chmn. quality subcom. 2003—05, chmn. clin. practice com. 2006), Cache C. of C. (pres. 1991, named Total Citizen of Yr. 2002), Rotary (Logan chpt. chair cmty. svc. com. 1989—90, pres. Logan club 1999—2000, Rotarian of Yr. 2002), Golden Key Nat. Honor Soc. (hon.). Avocations: walking, reading. Office Phone: 435-754-0216. Business E-Mail: sarasinclair@sunshineterrace.com.

SINCLAIRE, ESTELLE FOSTER, appraiser, writer, former educator; b. Trenton, N.J. d. Douglas Cumming and Lydia (Foster) Sinclaire; m. Frederic Breakspear Farrar, March 14, 1942 (div.); 1 child: Frederic Douglas. BA, Rutgers U.; MA, Hofstra U. Cert. Grant Writing. Libr., tchr. Waldorf Sch., Adelphi Coll.; adjunt assoc. prof. Art Dept. Hofstra U. Tchr., lectr. glass courses Hofstra, Cooper-Hewitt, Rider Coll., Internat. Assn. History Glass Spain. Writer for N.J. Art Princeton Packet "Time Off", 1986-90; author H.P. Sinclaire Jr. Glassmaker Vol. 1, Vol. 11, 1975; co-author (with Jane Spillman) The Cut and Engraved Glass of Corning, 1868-1940, (1st and 2d edition), 1997; author: American Fine Glass: The Birmingham Connection, A Century of Misconceptions European Fine Glass Sold as American. Appraiser, fundraiser On Air Hofstra Annual Art History Dept. Auction, Princeton Packet. Mem. Appraisers Assn. Am. (cert.), Nat. Am. Glass Club (founder empire branch).

SINCONOLFI, DEBORAH, medical/surgical nurse; b. Bklyn., Sept. 26, 1952; d. Edward W. and Thelma (LaVella) Pontorno; m. Anthony Sinconolfi, Aug. 18, 1973; 1 child, Marcus. Diploma, Westchester Sch. Nursing, 1973. RN, N.Y.; cert. ACLS; cert. med./surg. nurse ANCC. Nurse Westchester U. Hosp. Med. Ctr., Valhalla, NY, 1973—75, Staff Builders, White Plains, NY, 1976; asst. head nurse Yonkers Profl. Hosp., Yonkers, NY, 1976—77; nurse Upjohn, 1979—83, Kimberly Nurses, 1983—88; staff nurse Vassar Bros. Hosp., Poughkeepsie, NY, 1988—, nurse pulmonary care unit, 1995—. Mem. N.Y. State Nurses Assn.

SINGER, BARBARA HELEN, photographer, radiographer; b. NYC, Jan. 29, 1927; d. Robert and Rose (Kaplowitz) S.; m. Nat Herz, Jan. 15, 1956 (dec. Nov. 1964); m. Melvin C. Zalkan, Sept. 7, 1983 (dec. Nov. 1993). BA in Biology, NYU, 1947; studied with Eli Siegel, 1944-76. Registered in diagnostic radiography, in mammography, cert. Women's Bus. Enterprise, 2001, NYC Dept. Small Bus. Svcs., 2005. Radiographer, 1951—; instr. Meth. Hosp. Sch. Radiologic Tech., Bklyn., 1968-72; asst. to Benedict J. Fernandez N.Y.C., 1985-91; asst. to Lucien Clergue New Sch., Parsons, N.Y.C., 1989; photographer N.Y.C., 1983—. Lectr. NY Film Acad., NYC, 2000; panel mem. Phoenix Gallery, NYC, 1999, St. Francis Coll., NYC, 2001. Represented by John Stevenson Gallery, Bridgeman Art Library Internat. Ltd., Getty Images, workbookstock.com, Getty Images; exhibited in numerous group shows including most recently John Stevenson Gallery, N.Y.C., 1999, 2003, Pietra di Luna Gallery, Fla., 1999, 2000, Park Ave. Armory, N.Y.C., 1999, AIPAD, N.Y.C., 1999, George A. Spiva Ctr. for the Arts, Mo., 2000, Hist. Yellow Springs, Chester, Pa., 2000, Nat. League Am. Pen Women Art Exhbn., N.Y.C., 2000, AIR Gallery, NYC, 2000, Pietra di Luna Gall., Hollywood FL., 2000, St. Francis Coll., NYC, 2001, Modernage, N.Y.C., 2001, Ashforth-Warburg Downtown, N.Y.C., 2002, The Gallery in Stamford, Conn., 2003, WBENC Conf. and Bus. Fair, N.Y.C., 2003, Photo-Plus Expo, N.Y.C., 2003, 04, APA, N.Y.C., 2003, John Stevenson Gallery, 2003, MFA Exhibn. Space, 2005-06, MFA Exhbn. Space, NJ, 2005; CD-ROM Urbane Photography, 1996; photography published in The Murray Hill News, 1983, Profl. Women Photographers Newsletter, 1985, 95, Light and Shade, 1985, Best of Photography Annual 1990, Women of Vision, 1990, Tear Sheet, 1995, Wildlife Conservation Soc. Annual Report, Photonica 21, 1996, In Shape, 1996, Summer of Betrayal, Farrar Straus Giroux, 1997, Wildlife Conservation Mag., 1997, Worldcare Annual Report, 1997, Svenska Missions, 1997, Photonica 25, 1997, Fotophile, 1997, Photonica 34, 1998, Photonica 38, 44, 1999, 49, 2000, Shots, vol. 63, 1999, Photo Dist. News Online, 2003, How Success Happens, 2003, The Picture Professional, 2003, Women's Winners Circle, 2004, Breaking Through, 2004, Roseanne Backstedt, 2005, Partnering For Profit, 2005, www.modernwomentoday.com, 2004, www.thejewishpost.com, 2004, www.montlyherald.net, 2004, Fancy Living mag., 2005; lit. published in PWP Newsletter, 2001, Tear Sheet, vol. 3, 1995, Today's Great Poems, 1994, Evangelism in America, 1988, Radiologic Tech., 1969, 71; editor, pub. The Impossible Landscapes of Nat Herz and Kurt Seligmann, 1999; appeared in website video, 2003, Manhattan Neighborhood Network TV, 2004; contbr. articles to profl. jours. Photographers' Forum Finalist, 1990; recipient Photography award Beaux Arts Soc., 1994, fiscal sponsorship N.Y. Found. for the Arts, 2000, 2d pl. winner for poetry E.F.S. 1999 Ann. Writing Competition, 2000. Cert. by Women Pres. Ednl. Orgn., 2002, named to Jewish Post list of American's Brightest, Most Talented and Hottest Women of the Yr., 2004, Outstanding Jewish Woman of the Yr., 2004, others; subject of articles ARRT Ann. Report, N.Y. Monthy Herald. Mem.: Am. Soc. Radiologic Technologists, Advt. Photographers Am., Acad. Am. Poets, Poetry Soc. Am., Am. Soc. Media Photographers, Am. Soc. Picture Profls. Avocation: ballroom dancing. Office: 319 East 24 St #3A New York NY 10010 Fax: 212-684-1051. Office Phone: 212-689-0395. Personal E-mail: barbara@barbarasinger.com.

SINGER, CECILE DORIS, bank executive, former state legislator; BA, Queens Coll.; DHL (hon.), Pace U., 1997. Past rep. Spl. Svcs. for Children, N.Y.C.; past exec. dir. N.Y. State Assembly Social Svcs. and Judiciary Coms., Joint Legis. Com. on Corps., Authorities and Commns.; past pub. rep. Yonkers (N.Y.) Emergency Control Bd.; past coord. Westchester County Assembly Dels.; past chief of staff for dep. minority leader; mem. N.Y. State Assembly, Albany, 1988—94, leadership sec. Rep. Conf., mem. assembly children & families com., mem. various other coms.; bd. dirs. Hudson Valley Bank; prin. Cecile D. Singer Cons. Past rep. Temp. Commn. to Revise Social Svcs. Law; mem. Presdl. Commn. on Privacy Conf., N.Y. State Senate Transp. Conf.; task force on substance abuse Am. Legis. Exch. Coun., task force on econ. devel., crime victims' rights, hosp. crisis, women's issues, com. on mass transit; sec. Rep. Conf. Nat. Adv. Panel Child Care Action Campaign; chmn. Westchester County Commn. on Pub. Financing of Campaigns; chmn. Lower Hudson Valley Adv. Com. N.Y. State Divsn. for Women.; past dir. commn. on poverty and pregnancy, Yonkers IDA, N.Y.; treas. Riverside Corp.; chair, N.Y. State Hudson Valley Coun.; pres. Women's Enterprise Devel. Ctr.; bd. dirs. Hudson Valley Bank, N.Y.; prin. Cecile D. Singer Cons. Chair adv. com. Westchester C.C. Found., Westchester 2000 Rsch., Womens Adv. Bd. Westchester County; task force on certiorari Westchester County Sch. Bds. Assn.; sch. and cmty. chmn. Yonkers PTA; bd. dirs. Yonkers chpt. United Jewish Appeal; v.p. Westchester Sr. Housing; chair Women's Networking, Women in Bus. and the Professions; v.p. Westchester Srs. Housing; trustee, treas. St. John Hosp. Recipient Jenkins Meml. award, Nat. PTA award, Bus. and Profl. award Yonkers C. of C., Millian Vernon award WAWBD, Star award Mental Health Assn., Trustee award St. Johns Hosp., 2005; inducted into Women's Hall of Fame, 1996, Sr. Citizens Hall of Fame, 1996. Mem. Mental Health Assn. (bd. dirs., v.p., nominating and pub. affairs coms. Westchester County chpt.), Rotary. Office: 21 Scarsdale Rd Yonkers NY 10707-3204 Home: 1 Scarsdale Rd Tuckahoe NY 10707-3215

SINGER, DEBRA, curator; b. 1968; BA, Princeton U. Intern CNN; assoc. curator Whitney Mus. Am. Art, NYC, 2001—04; exec. dir., chief curator The Kitchen, NYC, 2004—. Spkr. in field. Graphic designer: Cutting Ball Theatre; contbr. articles to numerous prof. jours.; Whitney Mus. 2004 Biennial Exhibition, 2004. Named one of Forty Under 40, Crain's NY Bus., 2005. Office: The Kitchen 512 W 19th St New York NY 10011 Office Phone: 212-255-5793.

SINGER, DINAH S., federal agency administrator, immunologist, researcher; Grad., MIT, 1969; MPhil, PhD, Columbia U. Post-doctoral fellow Lab. Biochemistry Nat. Cancer Inst., sr. investigator Immunology Branch; sr. scientific officer Howard Hughes Med. Inst., 1998—99; dir. Divsn. Cancer Biology Nat. Cancer Inst., 1999—, also chief Molecular Regulation Sect. of Exptl. Immunology Branch. Mem.: Am. Assn. Immunologists. Office: Nat Cancer Inst Divsn Cancer Biology Executive Plaza North Ste 5000 Bethesda MD 20892-7390 Office Phone: 301-496-8636. E-mail: ds13j@nih.gov.*

SINGER, DONNA LEA, writer, editor, educator; b. Wilmington, Del., Oct. 6, 1944; d. Marshall Richard and Sara Emma (Eppihimer) S. BA in English cum laude, Gettysburg Coll., 1966; postgrad., Montclair State Coll., 1972-73, U. Birmingham, Eng., 1977; M of Letters, Drew U., 1985. Asst. to dir. student activities Fairleigh Dickinson U., Madison, crw., 1966-68; tchr., drama coach Morris Hills High Sch., Rockaway, N.J., 1968-84; free-lance editor Basic Books, Inc., N.Y.C., 1983-86; adj. instr. Fairleigh Dickinson U., Madison, 1986-87; free-lance writer, editor Visual Edn. Corp., Princeton, N.J., 1988—, Fact's on File, Bantam, Random House, Fodor's Travel Books, N.Y.C., 1990—, John Wiley & Sons, N.Y.C., 1990—; tchr. Sylvan Learning and Tech. Ctr., Sarasota, Fla., 1999—. Co-founder, co-dir. Traveling Hist. Troupe, Rockaway, 1976-78; tour leader Am. Leadership Study Groups, 1976, 78, 82; theatre studies participant Royal Shakespeare Co., Stratford, Eng., 1978-79, 81; docent, lectr. acting co. Hist. Spanish Point, Osprey, Fla., 1989-2001; grant facilitator NEA, Sarasota, Fla. Author: numerous poems; contbr. chapters to books, articles to profl. jours. Big sister Big Bros./Big Sisters, Sarasota, Fla., 1990-98; NEA grant facilitator Asolo Theater, Sarosota, Fla. Mem. Internat. Women's Writing Guild, West Coast Writers, Met. Mus. Art, Royal Shakespeare Company Assocs., Emerald Coast Writers, Travel Writers Internat. Network. Avocations: dance, theater, travel, antiques. E-mail: shakesds@aol.com.

SINGER, ELEANOR, sociologist, editor; b. Vienna, Mar. 4, 1930; arrived in U.S., 1938; d. Alfons and Anna (Troedl) Schwarzbart; m. Alan Gerard Singer, Sept. 8, 1949; children: Emily Ann, Lawrence Alexander. BA, Queens Coll., 1951; PhD, Columbia U., 1966. Asst. editor Am. Scholar, Williamsburg, Va., 1951-52; editor Tchrs. Coll. Press, N.Y.C., 1952-56, Dryden-Holt, N.Y.C., 1956-57; rsch. assoc., sr. rsch. assoc., sr. rsch. scholar Columbia U., N.Y.C., 1966-94; sr. rsch. scientist Inst. for Social Rsch. U. Mich., Ann Arbor, 1994—2003, acting assoc. dir., 1998-99, assoc. dir., 1999—2002, rsch. prof., 2004—06, prof. emeritus, 2006—; editor Pub. Opinion Quar., N.Y.C., 1975-86. Author (with Carol Weiss): The Reporting of Social Science in the Mass Media, 1988; author: (with Phyllis Endreny) Reporting On Risk, 1993; author: (with Robert M. Groves et. al.) Survey Methodology, 2004; editor (with Herbert H. Hyman): Readings in Reference Group Theory and Research, 1968; editor: (with Stanley Presser) Survey Research Methods: A Reader, 1989; editor: (with Stanley Presser, others) Methods for Testing and Evaluating Survey Questionnaires, 2004; editor: (with James S. House, others) A Telescope on Society, 2004; contbr. articles to profl. jours. Mem. Am. Assn. Pub. Opinion Rsch. (pres. N.Y.C. chpt. 1983-84, pres. 1987-88, Exceptionally Disting. Achievement award 1996), Am. Sociol. Assn., Am. Statis. Assn. Office: U Mich Inst Social Rsch PO Box 1248 Ann Arbor MI 48106-1248 Office Phone: 734-647-4599.

SINGER, EMEL, staffing industry executive; b. Gaziantep, Turkey, Apr. 7, 1944; came to U.S., 1960; d. Mehmet Resit and Nesrin (Kescioglu) Tuzun; m. James Michael Singer, Apr. 28, 1968 (dec. 1987); children: Justin Michael, Jodi Michelle. BBA, Bradley U., 1968. Adminstrv. asst. U. Ky. Med. Ctr., Lexington, 1968; exec. sec. Hoffman Products/Cortron Industries, Chgo., 1968-70; co-founder, adminstr. Banner Pers. Svc., Inc., Chgo., 1970-87, chmn., CEO, 1988—; co-founder Banner Temp. Svc., 1982—; founder Banner Tng. Ctrs., 1996—, Banner Acctg. and Fin., 1999—. Guest spkr. Chgo. Entrepreneurship Program, U. Ill., Chgo., 1993—; fund-raising co-chair U. Chgo., Divsn. Mid. Ea. Studies, 1993-95. Mem. parents bd. Bradley U., Peoria, Ill., 1989-90, assoc. trustee, 1992-93, alumni master, 1993, mem. Bradley coun., 1993-95, bd. trustees, 1995—. Listed in Crains Chgo. Bus. as a Top Woman-Owned Firm, 1989, 90, 91, Today's Chgo. Woman as one of 100 Women Making a Difference, 1997; named to Entrepreneurship Hall of Fame, 1993. Mem. ASTD, Chgo. Orgn. Data Processing Educators, Nat. Assn. Pers. Svcs., Nat. Assn. Temp. Svcs., Ill. Assn. Pers. Svcs., Ill. Assn. Temporary Svcs. Avocations: skiing, scuba diving, travel, sailing. Home: 3750 N Lake Shore Dr Chicago IL 60613-4238 Office: Banner Personnel Service Inc 125 S Wacker Dr #1250 Chicago IL 60606-4424

SINGER, JOY DANIELS, journalist, consultant; b. N.Y.C., Feb. 22, 1928; d. Maurice Blumberg and Anna S. (Kleegman) Daniels; m. Jack Singer, July 30, 1955; children: Meriamne B., Daniel C., Richard K. BA, Cornell U., 1948; postgrad., The Sorbonne, Paris, 1949. Advt. copywriter Franklin Spier, George Knoerr & Assocs., Parents Mag., Diener & Dorskind, March Advt., N.Y.C., 1950-68; CEO J.D. Singer, N.Y.C., 1968—. Scriptwriter Can. TV show, Magistrate's Court, 1968-69; syndicated columnist with Marlies Wolf, Women at Work, Feature Assocs., San Rafael, Calif., 1979—. Author: My Mother, The Doctor, 1970. Dem. County committeewoman, 1960-61. Mem. Direct Mktg. Creative Guild (v.p., corp. sec.), Friends Com., Gen. Soc. Libr. (chmn.), NATAS. Home and Office: 1725 York Ave Apt 19F New York NY 10128-7811 Office Phone: 212-348-0881. E-mail: imrejoysing@aol.com.

SINGER, MAXINE FRANK, retired biochemist, science association director; b. N.Y.C., Feb. 15, 1931; d. Hyman S. and Henrietta (Perlowitz) Frank; m. Daniel Morris Singer, June 15, 1952; children: Amy Elizabeth, Ellen Ruth, David Byrd, Stephanie Frank. AB, Swarthmore Coll., 1952, DSc (hon.), 1978; PhD, Yale U., 1957, DSc (hon.), 1994, Wesleyan U., 1977, U. Md.-Baltimore County, 1985, Cedar Crest Coll., 1986, CUNY, 1988, Brandeis U., 1988, Radcliffe Coll., 2000, Williams Coll., 1990, Franklin and Marshall Coll., 1991, George Washington U., 1991, NYU, 1992, Lehigh U., 1992, Dartmouth Coll., 1993, Harvard U., 1994, Yale U., 1994, U. Nebr., 2004; PhD honoris causa (hon.), Weizmann Inst. Sci., 1995. USPHS postdoctoral fellow NIH, Bethesda, Md., 1956—58, rsch. chemist biochemistry, 1958—74; head sect. on nucleic acid enzymology Nat. Cancer Inst., 1974—79; chief Lab. of Biochemistry, Nat. Cancer Inst., 1979—87, rsch. chemist, 1987—88; pres. Carnegie Inst. Washington, 1988—2002. Regents vis. lectr. U. Calif., Berkeley, 1981; bd. dirs. Perlegen Sci., Inc. Mem. editl. bd.: Jour. Biol. Chemistry, 1968—74, Sci. mag, 1972—82, chmn. editl. bd.: Procs. of NAS, 1985—88; co-author (with Paul Berg): 3 books on molecular biology and a sci. biog.; contbr. articles to scholarly jours. Chmn. Smithsonian Coun., 1992—93; trustee Wesleyan U., Middletown, Conn., 1972—75, Yale Corp., New Haven, 1975—90, Carnegie Inst. Wash., 2002—; bd. govs. Weizmann Inst. Sci., Rehovot, Israel, 1978—; bd. dirs. Whitehead Inst., 1985—94, chmn. bd., 2003—04. Named to Washington D.C. Hall of Fame, 2000; recipient award for achievement in biol. scis., Washington Acad. Scis., 1969, award for rsch. in biol. scis., Yale Sci. and Engring. Assn., 1974, Superior Svc. Honor award, HEW, 1975, Dirs. award, NIH, 1977, Disting. Svc. medal, HHS, 1983, Presdl. Disting. Exec. Rank award, 1987, U.S. Disting. Exec. Rank award, 1987, Mory's Cup, Bd. Govs. Mory's Assn., 1991, Wilbur Lucius Cross Medal for Honor, Yale Grad. Sch. Assn., 1991, Nat. Medal Sci., NSF, 1992, Pub. Svc. award, NIH Alumni Assn., 1995, Vannevar Bush award, Nat. Sci. Bd., 1999. Fellow: Am. Acad. Arts and Scis.; mem.: AAAS (Sci. Freedom and Responsibility award 1982, Philip Hauge Abelson prize 2004), NAS (coun. 1982—85, com. sci., engring. and pub. policy 1989—91, chmn. 1999—2005), Am. Soc. Cell Biology, Pontifical Acad. of Scis., Inst. Medicine of NAS, Am. Philos. Soc., Am. Chem. Soc., Am. Soc. Microbiologists, Am. Soc. Biol. Chemists. Home: 5410 39th St NW Washington DC 20015-2902 Office: Carnegie Inst Washington 1530 P St NW Washington DC 20005-1933

SINGER, NIKI, media consultant; b. Rochester, NY, Sept. 10, 1937; d. Goodman A. and Evelyn (Simon) Sarachan; m. Michael J. Sheets, 1973; children: Romaine Kitty, Nicholas Simon Feramorz. BA cum laude, U. Mich., 1959. Mgr. advt. sales promotion Fairchild Publ., NYC, 1959-67; acct. exec., acct. supr. Vernon Pope Co., NYC, 1967-69, v.p., 1969-71; pres. Niki Singer, Inc., NYC, 1971-93; sr. v.p. M. Shanken Comm., Cigar Aficionado, Wine Spectator, 1994—2002; founder Niki Singer, LLC, 2003—. Mem.: Les Dames d'Escoffier (bd. dirs.), Am. Inst. Wine and Food (bd. dirs.). Office: 1035 5th Ave New York NY 10028-0135 E-mail: sheets@nyc.rr.com.

SINGER, PAULA M., management consultant; b. Bronx, N.Y., 1953; m. Michael Pearlman; stepchildren: Stewart, Louis. BS, Cornell U., 1973; MAS, Johns Hopkins U., 1976; MA, Fielding Inst., 1993, PhD, 1995. Sr. compensation analyst Comml. Credit Co., 1973—75; minority bus. devel. specialist Mass Transit Adminstrn., 1975—77; exc. dir. Classified Mcpl. Employees Assn., 1977—79; mgr. human resources Bendix Corp., 1979—81; exec. dir. Md. Nurses Assn., 1981—83; nat. faculty Nova Southeastern U., 1997—; faculty assoc. Johns Hopkins U., 1996—; pres., prin. cons. The Singer Group Inc., 1983—. Mem. adv. bd. MA in Orgn. Mgmt. Fielding Inst., 1999; mem. internat. adv. bd. govs. for career devel. Maine Tech. Coll., 1999; mem. pres.'s adv. and planning com. Fielding Inst., 1996—98, mem. governance task force, 1996—98. V.p. Myerberg N.W. Sr. Ctr., 1995—; co-chair Strategic Planning Com., 1997—98, The Girls's Project, Jewish Big Brother and Big Sister League, 1996—99; grad. Leadership Md., 1999; bd. dirs. Jewish Big Brother and Big Sister League, 1997—98, Jewish Family Svcs., 1987—93. Named one of Md.'s Top 100 Women, Daily Record, 1997, 1999. Office: 12915 Dover Rd Reisterstown MD 21136

SINGER, PHYLLIS, editor-in-chief; b. Newark, May 22, 1947; d. Carl N. and Marion (Heller) Singer; children: James, Daniel. BS, Boston U., 1969. Mgr. print and broadcast traffic F. William Free & Co., NYC, 1969—70; rschr., reporter, editor L.I. Comml. Rev., Syosset, NY, 1970—72; from asst. editor to sr. editor viewpoints Newsday, LI, NY, 1972—; asst. mng. editor NY Newsday, NY, 1985—95, asst. mng. editor features NY, 1995—. Bd. dirs. Newspaper Features Coun. Mem.: Am. Assn. Sunday and Feature Editors. Office: Newsday Inc 235 Pinelawn Rd Melville NY 11747-4250

SINGER, SANDRA MANES, university administrator; b. Washington, Jan. 24, 1942; d. Joseph Gabriel and Rebekah Mary (Miller) Manes; m. Malcolm Singer; children: Cathryn, Scott; m. Allan Robert Kuse, July 5, 1978. BA, U. Colo., 1969, MA, 1972, PhD, 1975. Instr. dept. psychology U. Colo., Boulder, 1975-77, mem. rsch. faculty Inst. for Behavioral Genetics, 1978-80; postdoctoral fellow in psychiat. genetics U. Iowa, Iowa City, 1977-78; prof. psychology U. So. Ind., Evansville, 1980-92, chair dept. psychology, 1985-86, dir. grad. studies, 1986-92, asst. v.p. acad. affairs, 1987-92; vice chancellor for acad. affairs Purdue U., Hammond, Ind., 1992—2002, prof. psychology, 1992—. Mem. adv. bd. Ind. Resource Ctr. for Autism, Bloomington, 1987-93; cons. to youth leadership programs Nat. Crime Prevention Coun., Washington, 1987-93. Author: Heredity of Behavior Disorders in Adults and Children, 1986; reviewer Teaching of Psychology, 1986-1993; contbr. articles to profl. jours. Bd. dirs., mem. exec. com. Greater Evansville Cmty. Found., 1991-93; bd. dirs. St. Anthony's Med. Ctr., Crown Point, Ind., 1995-2001, Calumet coun. Girl Scouts U.S., 1993-1998, Ind. Humanities Coun., 1993—, Lake Area United Way, Lake County, 1994-2000, Citizens' Commn. for the Future of Ind. Cts., 1994-1998; chair No. Ind. Region Sisters St. Francis Health Care, Inc., 2000—, bd. dirs., 2000—; peer educator North Ctrl. Assn. Accredation Post-Secondary Instns., 2002— NIMH postdoctoral fellow, 1977-78. Mem. Am. Psychol. Soc., Behavior Genetics Assn., Sigma Xi. Office: Purdue Univ-Calumet 213 Porter Hall Hammond IN 46323 Business E-Mail: smsinger@calumet.purdue.edu.

SINGER, SUZANNE FRIED, editor; b. NYC, July 9, 1935; d. Maurice Aaron and Augusta G. (Ginsberg) Fried; m. Max Singer, Feb. 12, 1959; children: Saul, Alexander (dec.), Daniel, Benjamin. BA with honors, Swarthmore Coll., 1956; MA, Columbia U., 1958. Program asst. NSF, Washington, 1958-60; assoc. editor Bibl. Archaeology Rev., Washington, 1979-84, mng. editor, 1984-96, exec. editor, 1996-99, contbg. editor, 1999—; mng. editor Bibl. Rev., Washington, 1984-96, exec. editor, 1994-99; mng. editor Moment, Washington, 1990-99, editor, 1999—2004, contbg. editor, 2004—; exec. editor Archaeology Odyssey, 1998-99, contbg. editor, 1999—2005. Jewish. Address: Barak 1 Jerusalem Israel 93502 Personal E-mail: suzsinger@bogriver.net.

SINGH, DEANN COATES, small business owner, artist, educator; d. Nathan Devere and Maxcine Coates; m. Rajendra Singh, July 30, 1977; children: Jonathan Ray, Donavan Ray, Hailey Rae. Student, Weber State Coll., Santa Monica Coll., Cerritos College. Master calligrapher Apprenticeship to Master Calligraphers, 1988. Art and calligraphy tchr., 1981—; calligrapher for county suprs. County L.A., 1987—91; owner Designing Letters Studio, L.A., 1988—. Calligraphy and lettering arts, Calligraph Mag. Cub scout den leader Boy Scouts Am., L.A. Mem.: Soc. for Calligraphy (pres. 2000—). Democrat. Mem. L.D.S. Ch. Avocations: art history, paleography, art, painting, poetry. Personal E-mail: designingletters.com. E-mail: societyforcalligraphy.org, describe25@aol.com.

SINGH, SANGITA, information technology and marketing executive; With HCL Technologies, Wipro Technologies, Mountain View, Calif., 1992—, jr. exec., mktg. mgr. e-bus. portfolio, 1999, chief mktg. officer, 2001—, v.p. strategic mktg. Office: Wipro Technologies 2nd Fl 1300 Crittenden Lane Mountain View CA 94043 Office Phone: 650-316-3555. Office Fax: 650-316-3468.*

SINGH-KNIGHTS, DOOLARIE, education educator; d. Ranchate and Parbatie Singh; m. Marlon Knights; 1 child, Marleah J. Knights. PhD, W.Va. U., Morgantown, 2003. Asst. prof. Potomac State Coll., Keyser, W.Va., 2002—04, W.Va. U., Morgantown, 2004—. Agrl. ext. agt. Ministry of Agr., Port-of-Spain, Trinidad and Tobago, 1989—98. Chair Coun. for Women's Concerns, Morgantown, W.Va., 2004—06. Fellow, OAS, 1998. Mem.: Am. Agrl. Economics Assn. (assoc.; reviewer 2005—06). Achievements include research in sustainable rural devel. Office Phone: 304-293-4832.

SINGLETARY, DEJUAN THERESA, child and adolescent psychiatrist; b. Berkeley, Calif., Apr. 7, 1965; d. Wilbert Paul and Frances Mahala Thomas; m. Craig Singletary, Jan. 31, 2003. AA in Gen. Edn., Chalot Coll., Hayward, Calif., 1986; BS in Physiology, U. Calif., Davis, 1989; MD, U. So. Calif., L.A., 1995. Diplomate Am. Bd. Psychiatry and Neurology. Intern LAC/USC Med. Ctr., L.A., 1995—96; resident U. Calif.-Davis Dept. Psychiatry, 1996—98; fellow U. Ariz. Health Sci. Ctr., Tucson, 1998—2000; child and adolescent psychiatrist Carmel Psychiatric Assocs., Charlotte, NC, 2001—03, N.E. Psychiat. and Psychol. Inst., Concord/Harrisburg, NC, 2003—05, Elon Homes for Children, 2005, The Keys of the Carolinas, Charlotte, 2005, DeJuan T. Singletary LLC/St. Charles Med. Ctr., Bend, Oreg., 2005—. Cons. Best Care Treatment Svcs., Madras, Oreg., 2006—, Luth. Family Svcs., 2006—. Mem.: AMA (polit. action com. 2000—), Am. Acad. Child and Adolescent Psychiatrists, Am. Psychiat. Assn. (Psychiatry Resident of the Yr. 1999), Golden Key (life). Avocations: gourmet cooking, antiques, travel. Office: 2100 NE Wyatt Ct Ste 202 Bend OR 97701

SINGLETARY, ELOISE, business educator; b. Lake City, S.C., Aug. 21, 1942; d. Otto and Lillie (Barr) S. BS, Fayetteville U., 1969; postgrad., Winthrop U., 1973, U. Va., 1974; EdM in Cmty. and Occup. Programs in Edn., U. S.C., 1978, EdM in Sch. Adminstrn., 1982, postgrad., 1995. Nat. bd. cert. tchr., 2002. Bus. tchr. Lake View (S.C.) High Sch., 1969-76, Hemingway (S.C.) High Sch., 1976-83, Florence (S.C.) Career Ctr., 1983—. Advisor Hemingway High Sch. Newspaper, 1976-83, Future Bus. Leaders Am., Hemingway, 1976-79. Pres. Dem. Caucus, Lake City, 1984-85, Dem. precinct 2, Lake City, 1984-90; del. State and Local Convs., Columbia and Florence, S.C., 1984-85. Named Lifetime Dep. Gov., 1989, Two Thousand Notable Am. Women Hall of Fame, 1989, Most Admired Decade, Am. Biog. Inst., 1992. Mem. NEA, ASCD, NAFE, NAACP, Nat. Bus. Edn. Assn. (Merit award 1969), So. Bus. Edn. Assn., S.C. Bus. Edn. Assn., Fayetteville State U. Alumni Assn., U. S.C. Alumni Assn., Joint Stock Lodge #151 (sec. 1972—), Alpha Kappa Alpha. Baptist. Avocations: reading, spectator sports, tennis, sewing and collecting patterns. Home: PO Box 208 Lake City SC 29560-0208 Office: Florence Career Ctr 126 E Howe Springs Rd Florence SC 29505-5004

SINGLETARY, PATRICIA ANN, minister; b. N.Y.C., Mar. 3, 1948; d. George and Minnie Juanita (Williams) Nickens; m. Edward Franklin Singletary, Feb. 5, 1966 (dec.); children: Erik Franklin, Don Andre. BTh, New World Bible Inst. & Sem., 1984, MRE, 1986; AS, BS, SUNY-Empire State Coll., 1991; AA, Va. Sem. and Coll., 1995; MDiv, New Brunswick Theol. Sem., 1995; DD, Tenn. Bapt. Sch. Religion, 1989. Sr. reorgn. underwriter Depository Trust Co., N.Y.C., 1968-90, acct. coord., 1990—98, security specialist, 1998—2003; ret., 2003. Nat. corr. sec. Nat. Bapt. Conv. U.S.A. Inc., 1984-87; vice chair Spiritual Life Commn. of Clergywomen, 1987—; assoc. minister Morning Star Missionsry Bapt. Ch. of Jamaica, N.Y. CEO, founder Adoni Econ. Enterprises, Inc., v.p. Queens County Young Pastors, Mins. Evangelist Ea. Bapt. Assn. Author: African-American Guide to Buying Stock Without a Broker; nat editor: Ekklesia, 1986. Pastor Elmendorf Reformed Ch., East Harlem, NY. Recipient Vol. Svcs. award City of N.Y., 1980. Mem. NAFE, Nat. Assn. Negro Bus. and Profl. Women, Interdenominational Bd. Clergywoman (gen. sec. 1985-91), Nat. Bapt. Women Ministers Conv. (bd. mgrs. 1983-91), Ea. Bapt. Assn. (instr. 1981-83, v.p. evangelistic unit 1982-83, gen. dir. women's aux. 1988-91), Nat. Coun. Women U.S., Internat. Platform Assn., Bronx Bapt. Ministers Evening Conf. Greater N.Y. and Vicinity, Queens Bapt. Mins. Conf. Greater N.Y. and Vicinity, Assn. Black Seminarians (pres. 1993-95). Office Phone: 212-534-5856.

SINGLETON, JOAN VIETOR, publishing executive, writer, film producer; b. LA, Nov. 8, 1951; d. Carl William and Elizabeth Anne (Caulfield) Vietor; m. W. Alexander Sheafe, Apr. 23, 1977 (div. 1981); m. Ralph Stuart Singleton, Dec. 21, 1984. Premiere degre, Universite de Paris, 1971; BA, Hollins Coll., 1972. Asst. to pres. Calif. Fed. Savs., Los Angeles, 1972-73, dir. promotion, publicity, 1973-74; publicist Dave Mirisch Enterprises, Beverly Hills, Calif., 1974-75; owner, pres. Joan Vietor Enterprises, Los Angeles, 1975-79; bus. affairs staff Warner Bros., Inc., Burbank, Calif., 1979-80; pres. Lone Eagle Pub. Co., Los Angeles, 1981—. Assoc. prodr. Stephen King's Graveyard Shift, 1990; prodr., writer Because of Winn-Dixie, 2005. Bd. dirs. The Curtis Sch., 1993—, Crestwood Hills Sch., 1993-95. Mem. Pubs. Mktg. Assn. (bd. dirs. 1984-87). Democrat. Presbyterian. Avocations: skiing, needlepoint, tennis, scuba diving, reading. Office: Lone Eagle Pub Co 2337 Roscomare Rd Los Angeles CA 90077-1851

SINGLETON, SHIRLEY, software development executive; Faculty mem. Mass. pub. schs.; v.p., gen. mgr. N.E. region Logica North Am.; co-founder, pres., CEO Edgewater Tech., Inc., 1992—. Office: Edgewater Technology Inc 20 Harvard Mill Sq Wakefield MA 01880-3209

SINGLETON, STELLA WOOD, nurse; b. Moore County, NC, Nov. 3, 1948; d. Jay and Thelma A. Wood; children: Jennifer, Mike. Diploma, Hamlet Hosp. Sch. Nursing, Hamlet, N.C., 1975; postgrad., Appalachian State U., Boone, N.C., 1990—. RN, N.C. Dir. Hospice of Boone (N.C.) Area, 1982-83; Hospice dir. Hospice of Avery County, Newland, N.C., 1983-85; DON Toe River Health Dist., Newland, N.C., 1983-84; mental health nurse II New River Mental Health, Newland, N.C., 1977-82, 85-95; beauty cons. Mary Kay Cosmetics, 1986—; habilitation asst. Devl. Disabilities Svcs., Boone, N.C., 1995-98; personal care supr. HomeCare Mgmt. Corp., Boone, N.C., 1996-98; co-assoc., program mgr. Avery Citizens Against Domestic Abuse, 1998-2000; nurse Broughton Hosp., Morganton, N.C., 2000—. Instr. Mayland C.C., Spruce Pine, N.C., 1996-99. Co-facilitator Avery County Alzheimer's Support Group; group facilitator Cancer Support Group Svc., 1985-98; rehab. chmn. Am. Cancer Soc., 1977-99, cmty. amb. Celebration on the Hill, 2002; HIV counselor. Recipient Gov.'s. award for adminstrv. vol. Home: PO Box 483 Crossnore NC 28616-0483 Office: Broughton Hosp Morganton NC 28655 Office Phone: 828-433-2207. Personal E-mail: sane2b@yahoo.com.

SINIS, ELAINE M., personnel director; m. Barry Sinis; children: Sondra, Robin. Pres. Omne Staffing, Inc., Cranford, NJ, 1992—. Mem.: N.Y. Chase WPO. Office: Omne Staffing Ii Iii Iv Inc 218 State Rt 17 N Ste 13 Rochelle Park NJ 07662-3398

SINKFORD, JEANNE CRAIG, dental association administrator, retired dentist, dean, educator; b. Washington, Jan. 30, 1933; d. Richard E. and Geneva (Jefferson) Craig; m. Stanley M. Sinkford, Dec. 8, 1951; children: Dianne Sylvia, Janet Lynn, Stanley M. III. BS, Howard U., 1953, MS, 1962, DDS, 1958, PhD, 1963; DSc (hon.), Georgetown U., 1978, U. Med. and Dentistry of N.J., 1992, Detroit Mercy U., 1996. Instr. prosthodontics Sch. Dentistry Howard U., Washington, 1958—60, faculty dentistry, 1964—, rsch. coord., co-chmn. dept. restorative dentistry, assoc. dean, 1968—75, dean, 1975—91, prof. Prosthodontics Grad. Sch., 1977—91, dean emeritus, prof., 1991—; spl. asst. Am. Assn. Dental Schs., 1991—93, dir. office women and minority affairs, 1993—97, assoc. exec. dir., 1998—. Instr. rsch. and crown and bridge Northwestern U. Sch. Dentistry, 1963—64; cons. prosthodontics and rsch. VA Hosp., Washington, 1965—; resident Children's Hosp. Nat. Med. Ctr., 1974—75; cons. St. Elizabeth's Hosp.; mem. attending staff Freedman's Hosp., Washington, 1964—; adv. bd. DC Gen. Hosp., 1975—; mem. nat. adv. dental rsch. coun. Nat. Bd. Dental Examiners; mem. ad hoc adv. panel Tuskegee Syphilis Study for HEW; sponsor DC Pub. Health Apprentice Program; mem. adv. coun. to dir. NIH; adv. com. NIH/NIDR/NIA Aging Rsch. Coun.; mem. dental devices classification panel FDA; mem. select panel for promotion child health, 1979—80; mem. spl. med. adv. group VA; bd. overseers U. Pa. Dental Sch., Boston U. Dental Sch.; bd. advisors U. Pitts. Dental Sch.; mem. bd. visitors Temple U. Sch. Dentistry, Howard U Coll. Dentistry, Ind. U. Sch. Dentistry, W.Va. U. Health Ctr.; mem. anat. rev. bd. DC NRC Governing Bd.; cons. FDA; mem. Nat. Adv. Dental Rsch. Coun., 1993—96; active NRC Governing Bd. Mem. editl. bd. Jour. Am. Coll. Dentists, 1988—. Mem. Mayor's Block Grant Adv. Com., 1982; mem. parents' coun. Sidwell Friends, 1983; adv. bd. United Negro Coll. Fund, Robert Wood Johnson Health Policy Fellowships; mem. women's health task force NIH; bd. dirs. Girl Scouts U.S.A., 1993—95; bd. visitors Temple U. Sch. Dentistry, W.Va. U. health Scis. Ctr., Howard U. Coll. Dentistry. Fellow Louise C. Ball fellow grad. tng., 1960—63. Fellow: Internat. Coll. Dentists (Merit award), Am. Coll. Dentists (sec.-treas. Wash. met. sect.); mem.: ADA (chmn. appeal bd. coun. on dental edn. 1975—82), Fedn. Dentistry Internat., Links Inc., Dean's Coun. (chair), Smithsonian Assocs., NY Acad. Scis., Am. Soc. Dentistry for Children, Inst. Medicine of NAS (coun.), Nat. Dental Assn., Fed. Prosthodontic Orgn., Am. Prosthodontic Soc., Am. Pedodontic Soc., Leadership in Acad. Medicine (adv. bd.), Health Professions Partnership Initiative (adv. bd.), Assn. Am. Women Dentists, Wash. Coun. Adminstrv. Women, So. Conf. Dental Deans (chmn.), Inst. Grad. Dentists (trustee), Am. Inst. Oral Biology, Dist. Dental Soc., Internat. Assn. Dental Rsch., Am. Soc. for Geriatric Dentistry (bd. dirs.), North Portal Civic League, Golden Key, Beta Kappa Chi, Psi Chi, Omicron Kappa Upsilon, Phi Beta Kappa, Sigma Xi (pres.). Achievements include first female dental dean at Howard U., and in the U.S.A.

SINNARD, ELAINE JANICE, painter, sculptor; b. Fort Collins, Colo., Feb. 14, 1926; d. Elven Orestes and Catherine (Bennet) S. Student, Art Students League, 1948, NYU, 1953, Sculpture Ctr., NYC, 1954, Academie Grande Chaumiere, Paris, 1956. Painter, sculptor. Works exhibited Riverside Mus., NYC, 1955, City Ctr., NYC, 1954-56, Nat. Arts Club, NYC, 1959-90, Lord & Taylor, NYC, 1963-78, Bergdorf Goodman, NYC, 1980-90, Zantman Art Galleries, Carmel-by-the-Sea, Calif., 1970-73, Chevy Chase Gallery, Washington, 1981-88; one woman shows and group exhbns. include: Bergdorf Goodman Nena's Choice Gallery, Sinnard Art Studios; tchr. open workshop for artists, (murals) Trinity Assembly of GOD, Middletown, NY. Mem. Nat. Arts Club NYC. Home: PO Box 304 New Hampton NY 10958-0304 Office Phone: 845-374-8128. Personal E-mail: sinnard@warwick.net.

SINSABAUGH, MARIE ELIZABETH DIENER, retired nurse, massage therapist; b. Cleve., Nov. 15, 1927; d. Gottlieb John and Tess Resepal Diener; children: Susan Elizabeth Edwards, Kathryn Louise S. Grange, Nancy, Barbara Ann S. Tolman, Joseph Charles. BSN, Ohio State U., Columbus, 1949, MSN, 1987. RN Ohio; lic. massage therapist Fla. Staff nurse Ohio State U. Hosp., Columbus, 1949—50, asst. head nurse, 1950—51; office mgr. Newark Family Physicians, Ohio, 1952—80; med. inspector nursing homes Ohio Dept. Health, Columbus, 1987—93; massage therapist Curative Massage, New Smyrna Beach, Fla., 1996—99; office nurse Office of Lisa Reimer MD, Armond Beach, Fla., 2003; ret., 2003. Home: 431 Middleton Ave Granville OH 43023

SIPES, KAREN KAY, communications executive; b. Higginsville, Mo., Jan. 8, 1947; d. Walter John and Katherine Marie (McLelland) Heins; m. Joel Rodney Sipes, Sept. 24, 1971; 1 child, Lesley Katherine. BS in Edn., Ctrl. Mo. State U., 1970. Reporter/news editor Newton Kansan, 1973—76; sports writer Capital-Jour., Topeka, 1976—83, spl. sects. editor, 1983—85, editl. page editor, 1985—92, mng. editor/features, 1992—2002, asst. editl. page editor, 2002—03; dir. commn. Kans. Dept. Aging, Topeka, 2003—. Co-chair Mayor's Commn. on Literacy, Topeka, 1995-96; mem. Act Against Violence Com., Topeka, 1995-96, Mayor's Task Force on Race Rels., 1998; mem. planning com. Leadership Greater Topeka, 1997; Great Am. Cleanup, 1999-2001, ERC/Resource and Referral, 2001—; mem. Martin Luther King Living the Dream Bus. Ptnrs. Com., 2001-2004; mem. Centennial planning com. Family Svc. and Guidance Ctr., 2003-04; mem. Project Topeka Com., 2004—, Arthritis Walk Com., 2004-05, Faith in Action-No Place Like Home Coalition, 2003—; bd. dirs. Western Swing Music Soc. Kans., 2003—. Mem. Ctrl. Mo. State U. Alumni Assn. (bd. dirs. 1996-2002, v.p. 1999, pres. 2000). Avocations: music, gardening, art. Office: Kans Dept Aging New England Bldg 503 S Kans Ave Topeka KS 66603-3404 Office Phone: 785-368-7196. Personal E-mail: critterkaren@aol.com. Business E-Mail: karen.sipes@aging.state.ks.us.

SIPPEL-WETMORE, FRANCES MARIE, microbiologist, retired business owner; b. Phila., Apr. 17, 1930; d. Jacob Harry Jr. and Catharine Seachrist (Hershey) Pickle; m. Roy Joseph Sippel, Feb. 8, 1958 (div. June 1979); m. Orville Chase Wetmore, June 14, 1997. BA Biology and Chemistry with honors, Hood Coll., 1952; postgrad., Women's Med. Coll., Pa., 1952—54; MS Microbiology, U. Pitts., 1956. Rsch. asst. to Dr. Jonas Salk U. Pitts., 1955; rsch. asst. to Dr. T.S. Danowski Children's Hosp., Pitts., 1956; bacteriologist Shadyside Hosp., Pitts., 1956—57; rsch. asst. to Dr. Leonard Hayflick Wistar Inst., Phila., 1958—59; asst. editor Biol. Abstracts, Phila., 1959—60; lit. chemist E.I. du Pont de Nemours & Co., Wilmington, Del., 1960—66; sec.-treas. Can-Am Sales Corp., West Chester, Pa., 1972—73; sales rep. Quick Courier Svc., Phila., 1977—82; owner Color Profile, West Chester, 1982—97. Bd. dirs. Chester County Emergency Med. Svcs., Pa., 1980-97; co-chair Holiday House Tour, 1989-93, chair House Acquisitions, 1995; vol. YWCA. Mem. AAUW (Outstanding Woman from West Chester br. 1991), LWV (chmn. Chester County coun. 1993-95), Am. Soc. Microbiologists, Phila. Hood Coll. Club (past pres.), Chester County Hist. Soc. (antiques show com.), Wilmington Country Club, Sigma Xi Republican. Unitarian Universalist. Avocations: art, music, downhill skiing, travel. Home: 1007 Oriente Ave Wilmington DE 19807-2260

SIPSKI, MARY LEONIDE, physiatrist, health facility administrator; b. Somerville, N.J., July 6, 1950; d. Joseph John and Sophia Barbara (Marcewicz) Sipski; m. Thomas Edward Lammertse, June 16, 1979; children: Meredith, Matthew, Evan. AB, Rutgers U., 1972; PhD in Phys. Biochemistry, Ohio U., 1976; MD, Ohio State U., 1979; M in Med. Mgmt., U. So. Calif., 2003. Diplomate Am. Bd. Phys. Medicine and Rehab., Am. Bd. Managed Care Medicine, cert. in med. mgmt. Am. Coll. Physician Execs. and U. So. Calif., 2001. Intern, resident in phys. medicine and rehab. Ohio State U. Hosps., 1979-83; dir. phys. medicine and rehab. Gaylord Hosp., Wallingford, Conn., 1983-90; dir. brain injury program, dir. outpatient svcs. Kessler Inst. Rehab., Chester, NJ, 1990-97; chief med. officer Consumer Health Network Solutions, South Plainfield, NJ, 1997—2005, Selective Ins. Managed Care Solutions, Hamilton, NJ, 2002—05. Med. dir. Gaylord/Yale-New haven Ctr. at Long Wharf, 1989-90; asst. clin. prof. dept. orthopedics and rehab. Yale U., New Haven, 1989-90; cons. Bur. Disability Determination, Columbus, Ohio, 1982-83; pvt. practice cons. in brain injury, disability, and expert medico-legal testimony, Far Hills, 1991—. Fellow Am. Acad. Phys. Medicine and Rehab. (sec. Conn. soc.); mem. AMA, Am. Coll. Physician Execs., Am. Coll. Managed Care Medicine, Consumer Health Network Solutions. Office: CHN Solutions 3525 Quakerbridge Rd Hamilton NJ 08619 Office Phone: 800-225-4246. E-mail: dr.sipski@chn.com.

SIRGADO, JO ANNE E., lawyer; b. Meadville, Pa., May 16, 1960; BA magna cum laude, Villa Maria Coll., 1982; JD, Pace Univ., 1990. Bar: NY 1991. Ptnr., project devel., fin., leasing Hunton & Williams LLP, NYC, and co-chmn. recruitment com. Office: Hunton & Williams LLP 43rd Fl 200 Park Ave New York NY 10166-0136 Office Phone: 212-309-1093. Office Fax: 212-309-1100. Business E-Mail: jsirgado@hunton.com.

SIRIGNANO, MONICA ANN, performing company executive, playwright; b. Princeton, N.J., May 18, 1971; d. William Alfonso and Molly Wilhelmina Sirignano. BA in English, Stetson U., 1993; postgrad., CUNY. Mng. editor Encore Mag., Miami, Fla., 1993—95; asst. mng. editor PC Mag., N.Y.C., 1995—2000; performer, playwright N.Y.C., 1995—; artistic dir., pres. Screaming Venus Prodns., N.Y.C., 1999—, also bd. dirs. Adjudicator Fringe NYC, 2000, 01; mem. adv. bd. Blue Allied Theatre Co., N.Y.C., 2002—. Contbr. articles to jours.; author: On Zither & Autobiography, 2004, short story publs. Mem. membership com., mem. creative black tie invitation com.

Am. Cancer Soc., Miami, 1993—94; mem. Habitat for Humanity, Ft. Lauderdale, Fla., 1994. Recipient award, Off-Off Broadway Rev., 2001; grantee, Harburg Found., 2000. Mem.: Theatre Comm. Group, Dramatists Guild. Avocations: photography, painting, graphic design. Office: Screaming Venus Prodns 29-22 Hoyt Ave S # 21 Astoria NY 11102 Personal E-mail: nicasiri@gmail.com.

SIRLIN, DEANNA LOUISE, artist; b. Bklyn., Mar. 7, 1958; d. Robert and Sylvia (Goldsmith) S.; m. Philip Auslander, Aug. 29, 1990. BA, SUNY at Albany, 1978; MFA, CUNY, 1980. Bd. dir. Contemporary Art Soc., High Mus. Art, Atlanta, Nexus Contemporary Art Ctr., Atlanta. One-woman shows include Fay Gold Gallery, 1993, 95, Cheekwood Fine Arts Ctr., 1995, Nexus Contemporary Arts Ctr., 1996, Solomon Projects, 1998, High Mus. Art, Atlanta, 1999, Ca Foscari Venezia, Venice, 2001, Saltworks Gallery, Atlanta, 2003, Ty Stokes Gallery, Atlanta, 2004, 2005, Antalya Cultural Ctr., 2004, Hartsfield-Jackson Internat. Airport, 2005, Plus Gallery, Denver, 2006, Ferst Ctr. Ga. Tech., Atlanta, 2006, Ctr. 4 Recent Drawing, London, 2006; represented in permanent collections High Mus. Art, Ca Foscari Venezia, Kunsthaus, Nurnberg, Germany, Macon (Ga.) Mus. Arts and Scis., Ga. Pacific, United Airlines, CSX Corp., Egleston Hosp., Shenzhen (China) Inst. Fine Arts; commd. pub. art N.E. Regional Libr. Fulton County, 1998. Recipient Yaddo fellowship, 1983, Artist grant Artist's Space, 1987, Artist award Fulton County Arts Coun., 1994, Ga. Coun. for the Arts, 1994. Home and Office: 120 N Christophers Run Alpharetta GA 30004-3100 Office Phone: 770-475-4960. E-mail: deannasirlin@yahoo.com.

SIRNA, GAIL CAROLYN, artist, educator, writer; b. Detroit, Apr. 7, 1943; d. John Arthur and Viola Rose McKeown; m. Robert G. Sirna, May 28, 1966; children: Michele Lee Grace, Cheryl Lynn, Anthony McKeown. AB, St. Louis U., 1965; MA, U. Mich., 1969. Tchr., counselor Hazel Park (Mich.) Pub. Schs., 1972—82; shopowner The Fancyworks, Sterling Heights, Mich., 1982—85. Author: (bi-monthly column) Needlepoint Now, 2001—, (book) In Praise of the Needlewoman: Embroiderers, Knitters, Lacemakers, & Weavers in Art, 2006. Mem.: Am. Needlepoint Guild (nominating com. 2000—03, Best of Show 1999), Nat. Embroidery Tchrs. Assn. (sec. 2002—05, pres. 1985—88), Embroiderers' Guild Am. (region dir. 1990—92, chmn. cert. grad. tchr. program 2001—04, cert. grad. tchr.), Nat. Acad. Needlearts (dir. 1990—2000, treas. 2000—, cert. tchr. needlearts, cert. judge, Lifetime Achievement award 2004), Phi Kappa Phi. Roman Catholic. E-mail: gigigail@speakeasy.net.

SIRTAK, MELISSA ANNE, mathematics educator; BS in Edn., Ill. State U., Bloomington; MS in Edn., So. Ill. U., Edwardsville. Math. instr. Masocutah H.S., Ill., 1987—. Office Phone: 618-566-8523.

SISAKIAN, MARINA, psychiatrist; b. Spitak, Armenia, Feb. 1, 1964; arrived in U.S., 1995; d. Sargis Sisakyan and Jenny Torosyan; m. David Grigorian (dec. Dec. 7, 1988). Med Diploma, Yerevan State Inst. Med., Yerevan, Armenia, 1987; diploma gen psychiatry, NY Med. Coll., NY, 2005. Lic. gen. psychiatry Kirovakan First Hosp., 1989, cert. Psychotherapy NY Med. Coll. Attending physician Yerevan Physical Therapy Rehab. Inst., Yerevan, Armenia, 1990—99; fellowship Columbian Presbyn. Hosp., NY, 1992; chief physician therapy and rehab. medicine Finish Polit. Norweigian Hosp., Spitak, Armenia, 1992—95; vis. prof. NYU Med. Ctr., NY, 1995; MD resident NY Med. Coll., NY, 2000—05, attending physician, 2005—. Co-author: Crush 1988: Earthquake in Spitak, 1990. Office: Met Hosp Ctr 1901 E 97th St New York NY 10002

SISCHY, INGRID BARBARA, editor, art critic; b. Johannesburg, Republic of South Africa, Mar. 2, 1952; came to U.S., 1967; d. Benjamin and Claire S. BS, Sarah Lawrence Coll., 1973; PhD (hon.), Moore Coll. Art, 1987. Assoc. editor Print Collector's Newsletter, N.Y.C., 1974-77; dir. Printed Matter, N.Y.C., 1977-78; curatorial intern Mus. Modern Art, N.Y.C., 1978-79; editor ArtForum Mag., N.Y.C., 1979-88; editor-in-chief Interview, N.Y.C., 1989—. Office: Interview Magazine 575 Broadway Fl 5 New York NY 10012-3230

SISCO, MELISSA ANN, history educator; b. Oneonta, NY, May 25, 1970; d. Nancy Elizabeth Tweedale; m. Bill Sisco, Sept. 9, 1995; children: Shannon Elizabeth, Matthew William. MA in Reading Edn., Oswego State U., NY, 2001. Permanent cert. in secondary edn. NY. Tchr. G Ray Bodley HS, Fulton, NY, 1997—. Named Most Spirited Tchr., 1999, 2000, 2001, Most Influential Tchr., 2006, Rookie Tchr. of the Yr., 2001. Avocations: reading, walking, travel. Office: G Ray Bodley HS 6 William Gillard Dr Fulton NY 13069 Office Phone: 315-593-5400. Business E-Mail: msisco@fulton.cnyric.org.

SISEMORE, CLAUDIA, educational films and videos producer, director; b. Salt Lake City, Sept. 16, 1937; d. Darrell Daniel and Alice Larril (Barton) S. BS in English, Brigham Young U., 1959; MFA in Filmmaking, U. Utah, 1976. Cert. secondary tchr., Utah. Tchr. English, drama and writing Salt Lake Sch. Dist., Salt Lake City, 1959-66; tchr. English Davis Sch. Dist., Bountiful, Utah, 1966-68; ind. filmmaker Salt Lake City, 1972—. Filmmaker-in-residence Wyo. Coun. for Arts and Nat. Endowment for Arts, Dubois, Wyo., 1977-78; prodr., dir. ednl. films Utah Office Edn., Salt Lake City, 1979-93, Canyon Video, 1993—. Prodr., dir. Beginning of Winning, 1984 (film festival award 1984), Dancing through the Magic Eye, 1986, Se Hable Espanol, 1986-87, Alvin Giffins, Realist, 1980, Maestro Maruice Abravanel, 1982; writer, dir., editor (film) Building on a Legacy, 1988, (videos) Energy Conservation, 1990, Alternative Energy Sources, 1990, Restructuring Learning, 1991, Kidsercise, 1991, Traditional Energy Sources, 1992, Canyon Video, 1993—; videos Western Mountains and Basins, 1994, Ramps and Rails, 1994, Fitness After 50, 1995, Timescape, 1996, A Winter's Hush: Understanding Depression, 1996, Your Guide to the Internet, 1997, Desert Southwest, 1998, Utah Landscape and the Arts, 2001, Repertory Dance Theater, 2003, Ririe Woodbury Dance, 2003, Civil Defense, 2006, Lee Deffekach Abstractionist, 2006; exhibited in group show Phillips Gallery; represented in pvt. and pub. collections. Juror Park City (Utah) Arts Festival, 1982, Utah Arts Festival, Salt Lake City, 1982, Am. Film Festival, 1985-86, Best of West Film Festival, 1985-86; bd. dirs. Utah Media Ctr., Salt Lake City, 1981-87; mem. multidisciplinary program Utah Arts Coun., Salt Lake City, 1983-87. Recipient award Utah Media Ctr., 1984, 85; Nat. Endowment for Arts grantee, 1978, Utah Arts Coun. grantee, 1980. Mem. Lds Ch. Avocations: writing, reading, music.

SISK, CHERYL, neuroscientist, educator; b. Waco, Tex., July 4, 1954; BA in Psych., Baylor U., Waco, Tex., 1974; MS in Psych., Fla. State U., Tallahassee, 1976, PhD in Psychobiology/Neuroscience, 1980. Postdoctoral rschr. dept. neurobiology and physiology Northwestern U., 1980—82; rsch. assoc. dept. zoology U. Tex. Inst. Reproductive Biology, Austin, 1983—85; asst. prof. dept. psych. and neuroscience prog. Mich. State U., 1985—89, assoc. prof., 1989, prof., 1995—, adj. assoc. prof., prof. dept. physiology, 1990—. Dir. Interdepartmental Grad. Neuroscience Prog. Mich. State U., 1998—. Contbr. articles to profl. jours., chapters to books; mem. adv. bd.: Jour. Biol. Rhythms, 1995—97, mem. editl. bd.: Endocrinology, 1999—2002, Jour. Exptl. Biology and Medicine, 2004—. Mem.: Soc. Study Reproduction, Soc. Neuroscience, Soc. Behavioral Neuroendocrinology (treas. 2004—), Endocrine Soc., AAAS, Am. Neuroendocrine Soc. Office: Dept Psych Neuroscience Prog Mich State U East Lansing MI 48824 Office Phone: 517-355-5253. Office Fax: 517-432-2744. E-mail: sisk@msu.edu.*

SISK, JANE ELIZABETH, economist, educator; b. West Reading, Pa., Sept. 23, 1942; 2 children. BA with honors, Brown U., 1963; MA, George Washington U., 1965; PhD, McGill U., Montreal, Que., Can., 1976. Cons. Nat. Planning Assn., Washington, 1976; scholar VA, Washington, 1978-81; rsch. dir. Office Tech. Assessment, U.S. Congress, Washington, 1976-78, sr. analyst, 1981-84, sr. assoc., 1984-91. Vis. prof. Columbia U. Sch. Pub. Health, N.Y.C., 1990-91, prof., 1992—99; prof. Mt. Sinai Sch. Medicine, N.Y.C., 1999—, dir. divsn. health care stats. Nat. Ctr. for Health Stats., Ctrs. for Disease Control, Hyattsville, Md., 2004—. Co-author: Toward Rational Technology in Medicine, 1981; mem. editl. bd. Internat. Jour. Tech. Assessment in Health Care, 1987—, vol. editor, 1990, 98; asst. editor Am. Jour. Pub. Health, 1990-91; mem. editl. bd. Health Svcs. Rsch., 1994—; contbr. articles to profl. jours. Pres. Internat Soc. Tech. Assessment in Health Care, 1991-93, bd. dirs., 1987-95; mem. N.Y. State Task Force on Clin. Guidelines & Med. Tech. Assessment, 1994-96; mem. study sect. on health care quality and effectiveness rsch. U.S. Agy. for Health Care Policy and Rsch., 1997-2001. Elisah Benjamin Andrews scholar Brown U., 1961, 63; Bronfman fellow McGill U., 1971. Fellow Assn. for Health Svcs. Rsch.; mem. Inst. of Medicine, NAS (mem. cancer policy bd. 1997-2000, inst. medicine, 2001—), Phi Beta Kappa. Office Phone: 301-458-4157.

SISK, KRISTIN CARRINGTON, secondary school educator; b. Danville, Ill., May 7, 1961; d. Arthur Ernest and Jodell Carrington (Brewster) Berg; m. Rex Alan Sisk, June 18, 1994. BS in Edn. and Math., U. Ill., 1984; MS in Instrnl. Systems Design, U. N. Tex., 1989. Math. and reading tchr. North Ridge Jr. H.S., Danville, Ill., 1984-85; math. tchr. Carpenter Middle Sch., Plano, Tex., 1985—2003, Pioneer Heritage Mid. Sch., Frisco, Tex., 2003—. Tchr. gifted program Plano Jr. U., summers 1985-92. Named Tchr. of Yr. Carpenter Mid. Sch., Plano, 1994-95. Mem. Plano Civic Chorus (sec. 1990-95, singer select chorus measure for measure 1990-96). Methodist. Avocations: scuba diving, swimming, golf, singing, sailing. Office: Pioneer Heritage Mid Sch 1649 High Schools Dr Frisco TX 75034

SISK, REBECCA BENEFIELD, retired secondary school educator, small business owner; b. Roanoke, Ala., Aug. 22, 1936; d. Arthur D. Benefield and Sollie Florence (Adcock) Riley; m. Rodney Ray Sisk, Jan. 8, 1931; children: Carlotta Rae, Kenneth Lamar. BS, Auburn U., 1957, MS, 1961. Tchr. Brentwood Jr. H.S., Pensacola, Fla., 1959-67, Woodham H.S., Pensacola, 1967; instr. Pensacola Jr. Coll., 1967-93, coord. fashion merchandising program, 1981-93; owner, sec., treas., bd. dirs. Electronic Commns. South, Inc., Pensacola, 1977-93, ret., 1993. Author: Textiles Lab Manual and Study Guide, 1982, Fashion Internship Manual, 1983, Clothing Design, A Programmed Manual, 1990. Mem. Am. Home Econs. Assn. (del. 11th Lake Placid conf.), Am. Vocat. Assn., Am. Assn. Coll. Profs. of Textiles and Clothing, West Fla. Home Econs. Assn. (pres. 1982-84), AAUW, Omicron Nu, Delta Kappa Gamma, Phi Delta Kappa. Democrat. Mem. Christian Ch. (Disciples Of Christ). Avocations: remodeling older homes, tailoring, gardening, reading. Home: 1608 Spalding Cir Pensacola FL 32514-8301

SISKE, REGINA, artist; b. Varen Muritz, Germany, Oct. 11, 1944; d. Peter Paul and Olga Vanda Markunas; m. Roger Charles Siske, May 31, 1969; children: Kelly, Jennifer, Kimberly. BSN, U. Ill., 1966; postgrad. in MSN program, U. Mich., 1968—69; ind. fine art studies, North Shore Art League, Winnetka, Ill., 1970s, Alain Gavin, Art Inst. Chgo., 1980s, Tom James, Wilmette, Ill., 2000—; Asian brush painting and calligraphy studies Lampo Leong, U. Mo., 1998—; Asian brush painting and Chinese calligraphy studies Madeleine Jossem and Qi-Gu Jiang, Art Inst., Chgo., 1999—2002; Asian brush painting and Chinese calligraphy studies Moon Yan Huen, City Coll., San Francisco, 1999—2002; Asian brush painting and Chinese calligraphy studies, Charles Liu, Westmont, Ill., 1999—, numerous workshops, N.Y.C. and Chgo. RN Ill., 1966. Staff med.-surg. nurse Presbyn.-St. Luke's Hosp., Chgo., 1966—67, Mass. Gen. Hosp., Boston, 1967—68; nursing staff devel. VA Rsch. Hosp., Chgo., 1969—70, Evanston/Northwestern Hosp., Evanston, Ill., 1971, St. Francis Hosp., Evanston, Ill., 1971—73; nursing cons. Evanston Hosp., 1971; rsch. and quality control studies VA Hosp., Chgo., 1969—70; cmty. outreach and edn. Evanston and St. Francis Hosps., 1971—73. Chair Asian art exhibit and workshop Suburban Fine Arts Ctr., 2004. Exhibitions include Mobile (Ala.) Mus. Art, 1998, Bayard Cutting Arboretum, Long Island, N.Y., 1999, Suburban Fine Arts Ctr., Highland Pk., Ill., 1999—2006 (award, 2001), Alliance Gallery, Indpls. Mus. Art, 2000—01, Strathmore Hall of Arts, Bethesda, Md., 2000 (award, 2000), 2003 (award, 2003), Courthouse Gallery, Norfolk, Va., 2001, Nat. Juried Virtual Exhbn., Internet, 2002, 2004, Chinese Fine Arts Soc., Westmont, Ill., 2001, Virtual Exhbn., Internet, 2002, 2004, Chgo. Bot. Gardens, Art League Alliance, 2004, J. Harrison Smith Fine Art Gallery, Clearwater, Fla., 2005, Represented in permanent collections. Vol. Kellogg Cancer Rsch. Ctr., Evanston Hosp., 1988—89; bd. dir. St. Elizabeth Nursery Sch., Glencoe, Ill., 1981—82, Josselyn Ctr. for Mental Health, Northfield, Ill., 1989—93, devel. chmn., 1992—93. Named hon. lifetime trustee, Josselyn Ctr. Mental Health, 1993—. Mem.: Nat. Sumi-e Soc. Am., Midwest Sumi-e Soc. (program dir. 2000—06). Avocations: piano, jewelry design, skiing, swimming, tennis. Home and Studio: 248 Hawthorn Ave Glencoe IL 60022 Fax: 847-835-2836. E-mail: sisker@aol.com.

SISLEY, BECKY LYNN, physical education educator; b. Seattle, May 10, 1939; d. Leslie James and Blanche (Howe) S.; m. Jerry Newcomb, 1994. BA, U. Wash., 1961; MSPE, U. N.C., Greensboro, 1964, EdD, 1973. Tchr. Lake Washington H.S., Kirkland, Wash., 1961-62; instr. U. Wis., Madison, 1963-65, U. Oreg., Eugene, 1965-68, prof. phys. edn., 1968—2004, women's athletic dir., 1973-79, head undergrad. studies in phys. edn., 1985-92. Co-author: Softball for Girls, 1971; contbr. over 70 articles to profl. jours. Mem. athletic adv. bd. Women's Sports Found., 1993-96. Named to Hall of Fame, U. Oreg. Athletics, 1998, Hall Fame, N.W. Women's Sports Found., Seattle, 1981, Nat. Masters Track and Field Hall of Fame, 2001; recipient Honor award, N.W. Dist. AAHPERD, 1988, Nat. Assn. for Girls and Women in Sports, 1995, Disting. Alumni award, Sch. Health and Human Performance, U. N.C., Greensboro, 1996. Mem. AAHPERD, Oreg. Alliance Health, Phys. Edn., Recreation and Dance (hon. life mem.), Western Soc. for Phys. Edn. of Coll. Women (hon. mem., exec. bd. 1982-85), Oreg. High Sch. Coaches Assn., N.W. Coll. Women's Sports Assn. (pres. 1977-78), Oreg. Women's Sports Leadership Network (dir. 1987-97), Phi Epsilon Kappa, others. Office: U Oreg Phys Activity & Recreation Svcs Eugene OR 97403

SISLEY, EMILY LUCRETIA, psychologist, writer; b. North Charleroi, Pa., May 7, 1930; d. Frederick William and Harriet Watkins (Litman) S. PhD in Clin. Psychology, L.I. U., 1972. Diplomate Am. Bd. Med. Psychotherapists. Mng. editor Med. Jours., Harper & Row, N.Y.C., 1960-67; freelance med. writer-editor N.Y.C., 1967-95; supervising psychologist, dept. psychiatry Roosevelt Hosp., N.Y.C., 1972-77; clin. instr. Columbia Univ. Coll. Physicians and Surgeons, N.Y.C., 1975-77; chief psychologist Gramercy Park Inst., N.Y.C., 1978-84; staff therapist MedcoBehavioral Care Sys., N.Y.C., 1984-95; ret., 1995. Cons. Internat. Jour. Group Tensions, N.Y.C., 1968-72. Illustrator: You and Your Brain, 1963, Thomas Alva Edison award, 1963; co-author: The Vitamin C Connection, 1983; contbr. articles to profl. and lit. jours. Fellow Am. Bd. Med. Psychotherapists; mem. APA, N.Y. Acad. Scis. Democrat. Episcopalian. Avocations: music, golf, skiing, sailing.

SISLEY, NINA MAE, physician, public health service officer; b. Jacksonville, Fla., Aug. 19, 1924; d. Leonard Percy and Vera (Martin) S.; m. George W. Fischer, May 16, 1962 (dec. 1990). BA, Tex. State Coll. for Women, 1944; MD, U. Tex., Galveston, 1950; MPH, U. Mich., 1963. Intern City of Detroit Receiving Hosp., 1950-51; resident in gen. practice St. Mary's Infirmary, Galveston, Tex., 1951-52; sch. physician Galveston Ind. Sch. Dist., 1953-56; dir. med. svcs. San Antonio Health Dept., 1960-63, acting dir., 1963-64; resident in pub. health Tex. Dept. Pub. Health, San Antonio, 1963-65; dir. cmty. health svcs. Corpus Christi-Nueces County Dept. Health, Tex., 1964-67; dir. Tb control region 5 Tex. Dept. Health, Corpus Christi, 1967-73; chief chronic illness control City of Houston Health Dept., 1973-78; dir. pub. health region 11 Tex. Dept. Health, Rosenberg, 1978-87; dir. Corpus Christi-Nueces County Dept. Pub. Health, 1987—2002. Lectr. Incarnate Word Coll., San Antonio, 1963-64; adj. prof. U. Tex. Sch. Pub. Health, Houston, 1980—2002; adj. prof. Tex. A&M U., Corpus Christi, 1997—2002; pvt. practice Galveston, Stockdale, Hereford and Borger, Tex., 1952-59; mem. adv. bd. Cmty. Adv. Coun.; clin. instr. U. Tex. Health Sci. Ctr., San Antonio, 1997-2002 Bd. dirs. Coastal Bend chpt. ARC, Corpus Christi, 1990-94, 2003—, pres., 1990-91; bd. dirs. United Way-Coastal Bend, Coastal Bend Coalition on AIDS, 1988-94; mem. Nueces County Child Fatality Rev. Com.; mem. adv. com. Nueces County Hosp. Dist.; mem. adv. bd. Alzheimers Assn.; mem. health adv. bd. Corpus Christi Ind. Sch. Dist.; bd. dirs. Charlie's Place Alcohol and Drug Rehab. Ctr. Fellow Am. Coll. Preventive Medicine; mem. Tex. Med. Assn., Nueces County Med. Soc. (pres. 1997-98), Tex. Assn. Pub. Health Physicians, Tex. Pub. Health Assn. (pres. 1991-92), Local Emergency Planning Assn., Long Term Health Assn., Asthma Coalition. Episcopalian. Avocations: fishing, crossword puzzles, raising african violets. Home: 62 Rock Creek Dr Corpus Christi TX 78412-4214 E-mail: nsisley@sbcglobal.org.

SISON, MICHELE J., ambassador; b. Arlington, Va., May 27, 1959; BA, Wellesley Coll.; studied at, London Sch. Econs. Joined Fgn. Svc., US Dept. State, assigned to US missions Port-au-Prince, Haiti, 1982—84, Lome, Togo, 1984—88, Cotonou, Benin, 1988—91, Douala, Cameroon, 1991—93, Abidjan, Cote d'Ivoire, 1993—96, consul gen. US Consulate Gen. Chennai, India, 1996—99, dep. chief of mission, chargé d'affaires US Embassy Islamabad, Pakistan, 1999—2002, prin. dep. asst. sec. Bur. of South Asian Affairs, 2002—04, US amb. to United Arab Emirates, 2004—. Office: US Embassy United Arab Emirates 6010 Abu Dhabi Pl Washington DC 20521-6010

SISSELSKY, SHARON LEE, travel company executive, secondary school educator; b. Rochester, N.Y., July 13, 1957; d. Julian and Carol (Fritt) Lee; m. Lee Sisselsky, Dec. 21, 1985; 1 child, Carla Beth. Student, Endicott Coll., Beverly, Mass., 1975-76; BS, Ithaca Coll., NY, 1979; MS, Nazareth Coll. Rochester, 1985; student travel program, Am. Travel Inst., 1997. Cert. in physical edn. and driver edn., N.Y., cert. math tchr.; cert. travel agt. Inst. Cert. Travel Agts.; cert. LET trainer, Hadassah. Driver edn. tchr. Rush-Henrietta (N.Y.) Cen. Sch., 1979-80, Hilton (N.Y.) Cen. Sch., 1980-81, Herkimer (N.Y.) Cen. Sch., 1981-87; math. tutor, Utica, N.Y., 1987-94; math. tutor Longwood, Fla., 1995—97; pres. Longwood Travel, 2001—. Curriculum cons. N.Y. State Edn. Dept., Albany, 1987; advisor student coun. Herkimer H.S., 1984-87, students against drunk driving orgn., 1985-87, pep club, 1985-87; v.p. Bootyfull Baskets, 1988-93; chair math. superstars Sabal Point Elem. Sch., Longwood, 1995-97; travel cons. Travel Matters, 1997-98. Vol. vote cope program Mario Cuomo campaign N.Y. Stat United Tchrs., Utica, 1982; advisor youth group Temple Emanu-El, 1987-90, chmn. publicity Hadassah, 1987-89, treas., 1989-91, pres. Utica chpt. 1992-93, fin. sec. Sabra group, Orlando, 1995-97; mem. Hughes Elem. Sch. PTA, New Hartford, N.Y. Mem. Am. Driver and Traffic Safety Educators Assn., N.Y. State United Tchrs. Driver Educators of N.Y. State (sec.-treas. Mohawk Valley chpt. 1985-90), Herkimer Faculty Assn. (sec. 1984-87), Hadassah (pres. Sabra group, Orlando 1998-99, pres. Orlando chpt. 2000-03, v.p. leadership Fla. Ctrl. region 2003-05, v.p. Fla. Ctrl. region 2005-06, pres.-eclect 2006), Bus. Network Internat., Temple Israel Sisterhood (fin. sec. 2005, recording sec. 2006). Democrat. Jewish. Avocations: counted cross-stitch, reading, skiing, tennis, travel. Home and Office: 808 Riverbend Blvd Longwood FL 32779-2327 Office Phone: 407-869-6888. E-mail: longwoodtrvl@aol.com.

SISSON, BERNICE BELAIR, advocate; b. St. Paul, Oct. 25, 1922; d. Kenneth Theodore Belair and Bernadette Josephine Cormier; m. John McCormick Sisson, May 8, 1948 (dec. Feb. 12, 2005); children: Hilde, Lydwine, John, Catherine, Angela, Paul, Kenneth, David, Marie, Joseph. BA, Minn. Met. State U., St. Paul, 1986. Maternity nurse Miller Hosp./United Hosp., St. Paul, 1966—80; dir. Region XI Battered Women's Consortium, St. Paul, 1980—84; co-founder, early pres., bd. mem. Women's Advocate Shelter, St. Paul, 1974—84; co-founder, first chairperson Minn. Network on Abuse in Later Life, St. Paul, 2002, bd. dirs., 2002—; co-coordinator, legal adv. Older Battered Women's Program. Developer, facilitator Home Free Shelter Support Groups, Plymouth, Golden Valley, Minn., 1984—87. Author: (book/manual) Old Women: Breaking the Silence, 1987. Tutor reading East Side Literacy, St. Paul, 2001—03. Named Marvelous Minn. Woman, Minn. Gov., Minn. Women's Consortium, 1993, Woman of Vision and Courage award, Minn. Met. State U., 2001; recipient Sunshine Peace award, Nat. Coalition Against Domestic Violence, 1998, Disting. Svc. award, Office of Justice, Dept. Pub. Safety, 2005. Mem.: Minn. Women's Consortium, Minn. Coalition Against Domestic Violence. Avocations: reading, music, Sudoku, card and board games, theater. Home: 932 Westminster St Saint Paul MN 55130-4038 Office: St Paul Intervention Project 1509 Marshall Ave Saint Paul MN 55104

SISSON, JEAN CRALLE, retired elementary school educator; b. Village, Va., Nov. 16, 1941; d. Willard Andrew and Carolyn (Headley) Cralle; m. James B. Sisson, June 20, 1964 (div. Oct. 1994); 1 child, Kimberly Carol; m. donald Wimer (div. 1998). BS in Elem. Edn., Longwood Coll., 1964; MA in Adminstrn. and Supervision, Va. Commonwealth U., 1979. Tchr. 2nd grade Tappahannock (Va.) Elem. Sch., 1964-67; tchr. 2nd and 4th grades Farnham (Va.) Elem. Sch., 1967-71; tchr. 6th grade Callao (Va.) Elem. Sch., 1971-81; tchr. 6th and 7th grades Northumberland Mid. Sch., Heathsville, Va., 1981—2003; ret., 2003. Sr. mem. Supt. Adv. Com., Heathsville, 1986-93; exercise instr. Riverside Wellness Ctr., Tappahannock. Author: My Survival, 1994; author of children's books, short stories and poetry. Lifetime mem. Gibeon Bapt. Ch., Village, Va., 1942—. Mem.: AFFA Aerobics Inst., AARP, PETA, IDEA, NEA, ASCD, Nat. Geographic Soc., Aquatic Fitness Assn., Nat. Wildlife Fedn., Nat. Coun. English Tchrs., Exercise Safety Assn., Va. Mid. Sch. Assn., Aerobics and Fitness Assn., Alpha Delta Kappa. Avocations: aerobics, dance, music, art, travel. Home: 1068 Lodge Rd Callao VA 22435-2105 Personal E-mail: jcrallesisson@w.m.connect.com.

SISSON, VIRGINIA BAKER, geology educator; b. Boston, Apr. 8, 1957; d. Thomas Kingsford and Edith Virginia (Arnold) S.; m. William Bronson Maze, Oct. 14, 1989. AB, Bryn Mawr Coll., 1979; MA, Princeton U., 1981, PhD, 1985. Rsch. assoc. Princeton (N.J.) U., 1985-86, Rice U., Houston, 1986-87, lectr., 1987-92, asst. prof. geology, 1992-99, clin. prof., 1999-2001, rsch. scientist, 2001—05. Cons. U.S. Geol. Survey, Anchorage, 1984-95; rsch. assoc. Am. Mus. Natural History, 2001—; rsch. assoc. prof. U. Utah, 2001—. Contbr. over 40 articles to profl. jours.; co-editor: Geology of Transpressioned Ridge Trench Interaction in the Northern Cordillean, 2003, South American/Caribbean Plate Interactions in Northern Venezuela, 2005. Trustee Geol. Soc. Am. Found. Rsch. grantee, NSF, Houston and Calif., 1988, Houston and Scotland, 1990, Alaska, 1990, Venezuela, 1996, Alaska, 1998, Nat. Geographic, 1998. Fellow Geol. Soc. Am.; mem. Assn. Women Geoscientists, Am. Women in Sci., Am. Geophys. Union, Mineral Soc. of Am., Mineral Assn. Can., Yellowstone Rsch. Assn. (pres. 2004—) Avocations: pilot, cross country skiing, recorder playing, warbirds. Home: 4118 Lanark Ln Houston TX 77025-1115 Personal E-mail: j_sisson@netzero.com.

SISTO, ELENA, artist, educator; b. Boston, Jan. 11, 1952; d. Fernando Jr. and Grace Sisto; m. John David Kirkpatrick. BA in Art & Art History, Brown U., 1975; grad., N.Y. Studio Sch., 1977; postgrad., Yale U., Norfolk, Conn., 1975, Skowhegan (Maine) Sch., 1976. Gallery artist Vanderwoude Tanabaum, NYC, 1983-89; gallery artist Damon Brandt Gallery, NYC, 1989-91, Germans Van Eck, NYC, 1991-94. Tchr. RI Sch. Design, Providence, 1987—, NY Studio Sch., NYC, 1987—, SUNY-Purchase, 1988, Bard Coll., summer, 1990, Columbia U., NYC, Yale U., Chautauqua Inst., Sch. Visual Arts. Exhibited in one-man shows at Vanderwoude Tananbaum Gallery, 1984, 1986, Damon Brandt Gallery, 1990, Germans Van Eck Gallery, 1991, 1992, Gallery 210, U. Mo., 1991, Stephen Wirtz Gallery, 1993, David Beitzel Gallery, 1995, Greenville County Mus., SC, 1997, Wurtz Gallerie, San Francisco, Littlejohn Contemporary, 1998, 2001, 2002, 2005, Maier Mus., Va, 1999, Bucheon Gallery, San Francisco, 2003; represented in various pub. and pvt. collections. Fellow Skowhegan Sch., 1970, Yale Norfolk, 1975, NEA, 1983, 89-90, Millary Colony, 1987, Fine Arts Work Ctr., Handhollow Found., Provincetown, Mass., 1995. Address: Littlejohn Gallery 41 East 57th St New York NY 10022 E-mail: elena_sisto@yahoo.com.

SITARZ, ANNELIESE LOTTE, pediatrician, educator, physician; b. Medellin, Colombia, Aug. 31, 1928; came to U.S., 1935; d. Hans and Elisabeth (Noll) S. BA cum laude, Bryn Mawr (Pa.) Coll., 1950; MD, Columbia U., 1954. Diplomate Nat. Bd. Med. Examiners, Am. Bd. Pediatrics, Am. Bd. Pediatric Hematology and Oncology. Intern Children's Med. Ctr., Boston, 1954—55; resident in pediat. Babies Hosp.-Columbia-Presbyn. Med. Ctr., N.Y.C., 1955—57; mem. faculty Columbia U., N.Y.C., 1957—74, assoc. prof. clin. pediat., 1974—83, prof. clin. pediat., 1983—2000, prof. emerita clin. pediat., spl. lectr. in pediat., 2000—; attending in pediat. Babies and Children's Hosp., N.Y.C., 1983—. Cons. pediatrics, hematology and oncology Harlem Hosp., N.Y.C., 1967—72, Overlook Hosp., Summit, NJ, 1975—2001. Contbr. articles to profl. jours. Pres. Mt. Prospect Assn., Summit, 1987—. Fellow Am. Acad. Pediatrics; mem. Am. Assn. Cancer Rsch., Am. Soc. Clin. Oncology, Am. Soc. Hematology, Internat. Soc. Hematology, Harvey Soc. Republican. Episcopalian. Avocations: gardening, sewing, hiking, stamp collecting/philately, photography. Office: Childrens Hosp of NY Presbyn Irving Pavilion 161 Ft Washington Ave New York NY 10032-3710 Office Phone: 212-305-5808. Business E-Mail: als4@columbia.edu.

SITARZ, PAULA GAJ, writer; b. New Bedford, Mass., May 25, 1955; d. Stanley Mitchell and Pauline (Rocha) Gaj; m. Michael James Sitarz, Aug. 26, 1978; children: Andrew Michael, Kate Elizabeth. BA, Smith Coll., 1977; MLS, Simmons Coll., 1978. Children's libr. Thomas Crane Pub. Libr., Quincy, Mass., 1978—84; libr. Dartmouth Pub. Libr., 2000—. Dir. Reader's Theatre Workshop Thomas Crane Pub. Library, Quincy Mass., 1985. Author: (book) Picture Book Story Hours: From Birthdays to Bears, 1986, More Picture Book Story Hours, 1989, The Curtain Rises: A History of Theater From Its Origins in Greece and Rome Through the English Restoration, 1991, The Curtain Rises Volume II: A History of European Theater from the Eighteenth Century to the Present, 1993, Story Time Sampler: Read Alouds, Book Talks, and Activities for Children, 1997; contbr. monthly column Bristol County Baby Jour., 1992-98, South Shore Baby Jour., 1992-98, First Tchr., 1992-98, Kidding Around, 2004—. Mem. New Eng. Libr. Assn., Libr. Sci. Honor Soc., Smith Club of Southeastern Mass. (v.p. 1987-89, pres. 1989-91), Dartmouth (Mass.) Arts Coun., Beta Phi Mu. Roman Catholic. Avocation: singer. Home and Office: 25 Stratford Dr North Dartmouth MA 02747-3843 E-mail: msitarz@comcast.net.

SITOMER, SHEILA MARIE, television producer, television director; b. Hartford, Conn., Aug. 25, 1951; d. George W. and Mary E. (Chaponis) Bowe; m. Daniel J. Sitomer, Aug. 25, 1985. BA, Smith Coll., 1973. Field producer, dir. Good Morning Am., ABC-TV, N.Y.C., 1981-86; field producer Evening Magazine, WWOR-TV, KDKA-TV, Pitts. and Secaucus, NJ, 1978-79, 88; supervising producer The Reporters, Fox Broadcasting, N.Y.C., 1988; producer Inside Edition, King World Prodns., N.Y.C., 1988-95; co-exec. prodr. Inside Edition and Am. Jour., 1995-98; exec. prodr. Extra, 1998-2000; exec. prodr. program devel. ABC News, N.Y.C., 2000—. Recipient Peabody award, Columbia Dupont award, AWRT Gracie award, 3 Emmys, New England chpt. TV Acad. Arts & Scis., 1975-78, 2 Emmys, N.Y. chpt. TV Acad. Arts & Scis., 1979, 89, recipient first prize Internat. Film & TV Festival N.Y., 1988, No. N.J. Press Club award, 1988, George Polk award, Sigma Delta Chi award, IRE award Nat. Headliners, Columbus Film Festival. Mem. Dirs. Guild Am., Actors Equity Assn. Office: ABC News 47 W 66th St New York NY 10023 E-mail: sheila.sitomer@abc.com.

SITTERLY, CONNIE S., small business owner, writer, management consultant; b. Fairfax, Okla., Oct. 9, 1953; d. Claude O. and Virda (Smith) S. AA, Frank Phillips Coll., 1973; BS, West Tex. State U., 1975, MA, 1978; EdD, Tex. Woman's U., 1991. Cert. mgmt. cons. 1993. Instr. Frank Phillips Coll., Borger, Tex., 1978-83; pres. Sittcom, Inc., Mgmt. Tng. Specialists, Ft. Worth, 1983—. Asst. prof. Amarillo (Tex.) Coll., 1980-85; assoc. adj. prof. Tex. Woman's U., Denton, 1986-2004; trainer, speaker, author, mediator, expert fact witness, exec. coach and cons. in field. Co-author: A Woman's Place: Management, 1988; author: The Woman Manager, 1993, The Female Entrepreneur, 1993; contbr. more than 350 articles to newspapers and profl. jours. Named Disting. Alumni, Tex. Women's U., 2005. Mem.: Inst. Mgmt. Cons. (bd. dirs.). Office: Sittcom Inc PO Box 470695 Fort Worth TX 76147 Office Phone: 817-737-2893. Business E-Mail: president@sittcom.com.

SIVCO, DEBORAH LEE, materials scientist, researcher; b. Somerville, NJ, Dec. 21, 1957; d. Lawrence M. Skurkay and Elizabeth J. McCulla; m. Gregory Charles Sivco, July 11, 1981; children: Scott Gregory, Michelle Elizabeth, Carolyn Suzanne, David Charles. BA in chem. edn., Rutgers U., 1980; MS in material sci., Stevens Inst., 1988. III-V processing tech. Laser Diode Labs, New Brunswick, NJ, 1980-81; materials scientist Bell Labs. Lucent Technologies, Murray Hill, NJ, 1981—. Contbr. articles to profl. jours. Recipient Newcomb Cleveland prize AAAS, 1993-94, Electronics Letters premium Instn. Elec. Engrs. U.K., 1995, Group Achievement award NASA, 2000. Achievements include 30 patents in field. Office: Bell Labs Lucent Technologies 600 Mountain Ave New Providence NJ 07974-2008 Office Phone: 908-582-2041. Business E-Mail: dls@lucent.com.

SIVE, REBECCA ANNE, public relations executive; b. Jan. 29, 1950; d. David and Mary (Robinson) S.; m. Clark Steven Tomashefsky. BA, Carleton Coll., 1972; MA in Am. History, U. Ill., Chgo., 1975. Asst. to chmn. of pres.' task force on vocations Carleton Coll., Northfield, Minn., 1972; rsch. asst. Jane Addams Hull House, Chgo., 1974; instr. Loop Coll., Chgo., 1975, Columbia Coll., Chgo., 1975-76; dir. Ill. Women's History Project, 1975-76; founder, exec. dir. Midwest Women's Ctr., Chgo., 1977-81; exec. dir. Playboy Found., 1981-84; v.p. pub. affairs/pub. rels. Playboy Video Corp., 1985—85; v.p. pub. affairs Playboy Enterprises, Inc., Chgo., 1985-86; pres. The Sive Group, Inc., Chgo., 1986—. Instr. Roosevelt U., Chgo., 1977-78; dir. spl. projects Inst. on Pluralism and Group Identity, Am. Jewish Com.; trainer Midwest Acad. Contbr. articles to profl. jours. Commr. Chgo. Park Dist., 1986-88; del.-at-large Nat. Women's conf., 1977; mem. Ill. Human Rights Commn., 1980-87, Ill. coordinating com., Internat Womens Yr.; coord. Ill. Bicentennial Photog. Exhbn., 1977; mem. Ill. Employment and Tng. Coun.; bd dirs. Nat. Abortion Rights Action League and NARAL Found., Ill. div. ACLU, Midwest Women's Ctr. Recipient award for outstanding cmty. leadership YWCA Met. Chgo., 1979, award for outstanding cmty. leadership Chgo. Jaycees, 1988. Office: The Sive Group Inc 1235 N Astor St Chicago IL 60610-5213

SIVINSKI, TINA M., human resources specialist; Grad. magna cum laude, Springfield Coll. Various positions including v.p. Data Gen. Corp., 1980—99; corp. v.p. mktg. and innovation Sci. Applications Internat. Corp., 2000; v.p. strategic mktg., sales and bus. devel. GrandBasin, 2000—01; pres. energy glow industry solutions group Elec. Data Systems, Plano, Tex., 2001—02, sr. v.p., 2002—03, exec. v.p. human resources, 2003—. Bd. dirs. Tranxition. Office: Elec Data Systems 5400 Legacy Dr Plano TX 75024-3199 Office Phone: 972-604-6000. Office Fax: 972-605-2643.

SKADDEN, VANDA SUE, retired music educator; b. Salida, Colo., Jan. 10, 1942; d. Clarence Walter and Lulu Corinne (Van Fossen) Sydenham; m. James Timothy Skadden, June 8, 1964; children: Javan Marie Skadden Carson, Gayla Sue Skadden Flack. BMus Edn., U. Denver, 1964; Music Cert., Internat. Culture Symposium, Neuberg, Austria, 1977. Cert. tchr. Ill., 1964, Colo., 1967. Tchr. instrumental music Rantoul City Schs., Ill., 1964—67; tchr., strings specialist Widefield Sch. Dist. #3, Colorado Springs, 1967—69, orch. dir., 1975—99; ret., 1999; pvt. tchr. violin, viola, piano. Bd. dirs. Colo. All State Orch., Colorado Springs, 1996—98; judge various music contests; clinician Pueblo Pub. Schs. All City Orch. Music editor (newspaper) Clarion, U. Denver, 1962—64; editor: (newsletter) String Vibrations, 1991—94 (cert., 1994). Mem. Emerald City Opera Orch., 2005; choir dir. Good Shepherd United Meth. Ch., 1983—92; violinist Colorado Springs Symphony, 1967—77; concert master Cmty. Orch./Pikes Peak Civic, Colorado Springs, 1979—85; violinist Chamber Orch. of Springs, Colorado Springs, 1979—, bd. sec., 2000—; cmty. mem. Colo. Coll. Orch., 2005. Recipient Outstanding Tchr. awards, Colo. Music Educators, 1986, 1987, 1989, 1996; scholar, U. Denver, 1960—64. Mem.: Am. String Tchrs. Assn. (state bd. 1985—90, state bd. pres., editor 1991—94, Lifetime Achievement award 1999), Mu Phi Epsilon. Republican. Methodist. Avocations: painting, sewing, travel, genealogy, history. Home: 7025 Defoe Ave Colorado Springs CO 80911 E-mail: jvskadden@earthlink.net.

SKAGGS, KAREN GAYLE, elementary school educator; b. Campbellsville, Ky., Sept. 29, 1956; d. E. Edward and Mary Virginia (Kearney) Davis; m. Stephen Douglas Skaggs, July 30, 1976. BA in English, French and Journalism, Campbellsville Coll., 1977, elem. edn. endorsement 1-8, 1989; MA in Secondary Edn. and Psychology, Western Ky. U., 1980, reading specialist degree, 1986, rank 1 in edn., 1990. Cert. secondary tchr., Ky. Tchr. English, French, journalism Taylor County Bd. Edn., Campbellsville, 1978-81, adult edn. tchr., 1981-89; elem. tchr. Campbellsville Bd. Edn., 1989—. Bdlg. coord. Extended Sch. Svcs., 1998—. Mem. Campbellsville Site Based Coun., 1993-98, 99-2002. Recipient Outstanding Tchr. award State Dept. of Edn. Mem. Internat. Reading Assn., Taylor County Lit. Coun. (pres.), Taylor County Bus. and Profl. Women's Club (chmn. young careerist com. 1987-88, Outstanding Young Career Woman award 1987, Tchr. of Yr. award 1993, Excellence in Tchg. award 1994). Democrat. Baptist. Avocations: reading, country music, decorating, internet. Home: 901 S Columbia Ave Campbellsville KY 42718-2410 Office Phone: 270-465-4561. Personal E-mail: sskaggs01@alltel.net. Business E-Mail: kjkaggs@cville.kyschools.com.

SKAINE, ROSEMARIE KELLER, writer, consultant, publisher; d. Warren V Keller and Marie W Kuehner Keller; m. James Cole Skaine, June 4, 1957; children: James Keller, Forrest Todd. BA, U. S.D., Vermillion, 1958; MA, U. No. Iowa, Cedar Falls, 1977. Cert. secondary edn. tchr. NY, 1959, SD, 1958. English tchr. Ovid Ctrl. Sch., NY, 1958—60; adminstrv. and legislative asst. Pres. Kennedy's Consumer Adv. Coun. Chairperson, Ithaca, NY, 1963; adj. instr., sociology Wartburg Coll., Waverly, Iowa, 1979—80; adj. instr., composition Hawkeye C.C., Waterloo, Iowa, 1998—98. Cons., institutes on sexual harassment Adult Edn. Bd. YWCA, Waterloo, Iowa, 1992; cons., sexual harassment KCET Pub. TV, Los Angeles, Calif., 1991—94; ct. testimony, sexual harassment Dist. Ct., Waterloo, Iowa, 1989—99; US del. XII Internat. Congress on Family Law, Havana, Cuba, 2002; speaking tour, women of Afghanistan under the Taliban SD Ctr. for the Book's three day program, Maintaining Democracy in an Unstable World, Aberdeen, Brookings, Mitchell and Sioux Falls, SD, 2002; presenter, Am. family, Guilin, Shijiazhuang, Xian, China U. No. Iowa, Cedar Falls, 1993. Co-author (with Warren V. Keller and James C. Skaine): (book) A Man of the Twentieth Century: Recollections of Warren V. Keller, A Nebraskan, 1999; author: Women at War: Gender Issues of Americans in Combat, 1999, Power and Gender: Issues in Sexual Dominance and Harassment, 1996 (Gustavus Myers Ctr. award for the study of human rights in N.Am. for the outstanding work on intolerance in N.Am., 1997), Sexual Harassment: Questions and Answers, 2d revised edit., 1990, (nonfiction book) Female Genital Mutilation: Legal, Cultural and Medical Issues, 2005, (short stories) Lessons in Love and Life, (book) The Cuban Family: Custom and Change in an Era of Hardship, 2004, Questions and Answers about Sexual Harassment, 1980, Paternity and American Law, 2003, The Women of Afghanistan Under the Taliban, 2002, Women College Basketball Coaches, 2001, Female Suicide Bombers, 2006; contbr. articles to profl. jours. Panel mem., women in Afghanistan Cable TV Here and There, Cedar Falls, Iowa, 2001; voters svc. chair, pres. LWV of Waterloo-Cedar Falls, Cedar Falls, Iowa, 1964—69; nat. steering com., hon. mem. Gore 2000 Presdl. Campaign, 2000, Clinton-Gore Presdl. Campaign, 1996; campaign mgr. James Skaine for U.S. Congress, Cedar Falls, Iowa, 1972—74. Recipient award, Women's Studies Undergraduate and Grad. Programs, U. of No. Iowa, Cedar Falls, 1998, So. Poverty Law Ctr., Montgomery, Ala., 2003—. Mem.: Alpha Kappa Delta, Pi Kappa Delta (life). Office: Author's Castle Publishing PO Box 1044 Cedar Falls IA 50613 Office Phone: 319-266-8163. Home Fax: 319-266-1406; Office Fax: 319-266-1406. Personal E-mail: rskaine@cfu.net.

SKAISTIS, RACHEL G., lawyer; b. Phila., June 7, 1970; BA, Yale Coll., 1992; JD cum laude, Cornell U., 1997. Bar: NY 1998, US Dist. Ct., So and Ea. Dists. NY 2000. Reporter Fort Worth Star-Telegram, Tex.; assoc. Cravath, Swaine & Moore LLP, NYC, 1997—99, 2000—05, ptnr., litig., 2005—; law clk., Hon. Shira Ann Scheindlin US Dist. Ct., So. Dist. NY, 1999. Mng. editor Cornell Law Rev. Mem.: NY State Bar Assn. Office: Cravath Swaine & Moore LLP Worldwide Plz 825 Eighth Ave New York NY 10019-7475 Office Phone: 212-474-1934. Office Fax: 212-474-3700. Business E-Mail: rskaistis@cravath.com.

SKANDERA TROMBLEY, LAURA ELISE, academic administrator, literature educator; b. LA, Nov. 1, 1960; d. John and Mary Ruth (Chaney) S.; m. Nelson Edmund Trombley, July 13, 1991. BA, Pepperdine U., 1981, MA summa cum laude, 1993; PhD in English Lit., U. So. Calif., 1989. Asst. prof. Dept. English SUNY, Potsdam, 1990—92, assoc. prof., 1993—97, spl. asst. to pres., 1994—97, dir. Tchg., Tenure and Promotion Assistance Program, 1994—97, asst. provost, 1995—97; v.p. academic affairs, dean faculty Coe Coll., Cedar Rapids, Iowa, 1997—2002; pres. Pitzer Coll., Claremont, Calif., 2002—. Asst. lectr. writing program U. So. Calif., 1983—85, 1987; vis. prof. Am. studies U. Eichstaett, Bavaria, Germany, 1985—86, Bavaria, 1987—88; vis. asst. prof. Dept. English Pepperdine U., 1988—90. Author: Epistemology: Turning Points in the History of Poetic Knowledge, 1986, Mark Twain's Literary Marriage, 1992, Mark Twain in the Company of Women, 1994; editor: Critical Essays on Maxine Hong Kingston, 1998; co-editor: Constructing Mark Twain: New Directions in Scholarship, 2001; contbr. articles to profl. jours. Named Quarry Farm fellow Ctr. for Mark Twain Studies, 1988, Finklestein fellow U. Soc. Calif., 1988. Mem.: Internat. Assn. Univ. Prof. English, Internat. Assn. Univ. Pres., Am. Assn. Univ. Women, Mark Twain Circle of Am. Office: Office of Pres Pitzer Coll 1050 N Mills Ave Claremont CA 91711 Office Phone: 909-621-8198. E-mail: president@pitzer.edu.*

SKAVLEM, MELISSA KLINE, publisher; Pres. Hanser Gardner Pub., Cin.

SKEEN, JUDY L., religious studies educator; b. Milford, NJ, Dec. 13, 1957; d. Max Verne and Mae Corliss Skeen. BA, Samford U., Birmingham, Ala., 1979; MA, Vanderbilt U., Nashville, 1987; MDiv, So. Sem. pre Mohler, Louisville, 1983, PhD, 1993. Min. Immanuel Bapt. Ch., Nashville, 1993—96; ops. mgr. Garland Log Homes, Victor, Mont., 1996—98; prof. religion Belmont U., Nashville, 1996—. Contbr. chapters to books, articles to profl. jours. Co-founder and organizer Blvd. Bolt, Nashville, 1994—2006. Mem.: Nat. Assn. Bapt. Profs. of Religion, Am. Acad. Religion, Soc. Bibl. Lit. Office: Belmont University Sch Religion 1900 Belmont Blvd Nashville TN 37212 Office Phone: 615-460-6273.

SKEETE, HELEN WATKINS, minister, counselor; b. Wallace, N.C., Mar. 2, 1938; d. James Edward Newkirk, Edith Newkirk; m. Paul Louis, Sr. Watkins, Aug. 31, 1958; children: Paul Jr. Watkins, Stella Ross Finch, Trina Joy Gatlin. BTh, Calvary Grace Inst., Columbus, Ohio, 1977. Cert. crisis counselor. Internat. evangelist Soul Saving Sta. Every Nation, N.Y.C., 1959—84; asst. adminstr., assoc. min. Grace Ch. All Nations, Boston, 1983—88; founder, CEO Love Unlimited Drug Rehab. Outreach Programs, Inc., Boston, 1988—; founder, dir. Love U God's Gang, Brookline, Mass., 1991—; founder, CEO, pastor Love Unlimited Outreach Ministries, Inc., Boston, 1991—; overseer Men & Women of Crossroads Ministries, Dorchester, Mass., 1996—, Gospel Truth Ministries. Mem. adv. bd. New Eng. Med. Ctr. Hosp., Boston, 1981—83, Boston Against Drugs, 1991—96, Living After Murder Program, Inc., Roxbury, Mass., 1993—95. Author: (plays) Life on the Streets in a World of Drugs, 1990 (Proclamation from Mayor Flynn of Boston, 1990), Matriac of Ministry, 2002, Official Resolution - Boston City Council, 2002; co-author: Boston Area Violence Prevention Resource Directory, 1993 (Hon. Cmty. Svc. award, 1993). Facilitator Healthy Boston, 1997—99; mem. AIDS Action Com., Boston, 1995—2001; counselor Boston Safe Neighborhood, 1990—97; mem. evaluation team Boston Against Drugs, 1993—97; dir. March Against Violence, 1991. Recipient Recognition of Achievement, Gov. Paul Cellucci of Mass., 1997, Ofcl. Resolution, Boston City Coun., Recognition of Achievement, Commonwealth of Mass. Ho. Reps., 1997, Letter of Recognition, U.S. Pres. George Bush, 1990, Letter of Appreciation, U.S. Pres. Bill Clinton, 1997, cert. of Appreciation, Boston Police Dept., 1997, Proclamation, City of Boston Mayor Menino, 1997, Letter of Recognition, U.S. Pres. Ronald Regan, 1983; grantee, Boston Safe Neighborhood, 1991. Mem.: Grandparents Raising Their Grandchildren (facilitator 1996—99, cert. of Appreciation 1997). Democrat. Avocations: travel, reading, sewing, singing, writing. Home: 99 Kent St Ste 7-317 Brookline MA 02445-7955 Office: Love Unlimited Drug Rehabilitation Out Brookline MA 02445-7955 Personal E-mail: revhelenwatkinsskeete@yahoo.com.

SKEETER, SHARYN JEANNE, literature educator, writer; b. Yonkers, NY, July 12, 1945; d. Clarence Doyle and Jeanne Althea (Ryerson) Skeeter; m. Clarence Major, July 11, 1975 (div. 1978); m. Michael Thomas Tucker, Oct. 16, 1982. BA, CCNY, 1966; postgrad., Sch. Edn., 1966—68, Sch. Liberal Arts, 1973—75; MBA, Anna Maria Coll., Paxton, Mass., 1981. Tchr. NYC Bd. Edn., 1966—68; editl. asst. Mademoiselle mag., NYC, 1969—70; fiction, poetry and books editor Essence mag., NYC, 1970—76; asst. prof. writing, lit. and pub. Emerson Coll., Boston, 1980—. Poetry/fiction reader, lectr. in field. Co-editor: Departures, 1979; author: numerous poems; contbr. articles to profl. jours. Judge poetry competition United Negro Coll. Fund, NYC, 1972; press rep. Phillis Wheatley Poetry Festival, Jackson, Miss., 1972. Mem.: Women in Comm., Nat. Coun. Tchrs. English. Democrat. Unitarian-Universalist. Office: Black Elegance Starlog Telecommunications Inc 475 Park Ave S Rm 801 New York NY 10016-6989

SKELTON, KRISTEN JOY, music educator; d. LeRoy Charles and Sally Lou Kling; married, Dec. 22, 2001; 1 child, Lennon Paul. B in Music Edn., U. Mo., Kans. City, 1995. Cert. vocal & instrumental music tchr. K-12 Mo., 1990. Tchr. music Golden City Sch. Dist., Mo., 1995—.

SKERL, DIANA M., stockbroker; b. Zagreb, Croatia, Aug. 17, 1959; d. Damir Steven and Zdenka (Klaric) S.; m. Michael Karakasians, June 14, 1986. BBA, Texas Christian, 1981; MBA, Columbia U., 1999. Dept. mngr. Lord & Taylor, N.Y.C., 1981-1985; buyer Bloomingdales, N.Y.C., 1985-1987; stockbroker Gruntal & Co., N.Y.C., 1987-1989, Donaldson, Lufkin & Jenrette, N.Y.C., 1989—. Dir. Marquis Studios. Treas. Children in Crisis. Mem. Women's Nat. Rep. Club, N.Y. Jr. League (Mentoring Ptnrs. 1998—, Children in Crisis 1995-98, Heartsong 1992-95). Rupublican. Roman Catholic. Avocations: music, diving, literature, travel. Home: 120 E 87th St New York NY 10128-1116 E-mail: dskerl@dlj.com.

SKIBINSKI, OLGA, artist, art conservator; b. Bucharest, Romania, Sept. 15, 1939; came to U.S., 1986; d. Alois Skibinski and Marina Barbulescu; divorced; 1 child, Stefan. BA, Fine Arts Coll., 1963; diploma in art conservation, Nat. Mus. Art, 1967. Sr. art conservator Nat. Mus. Art, Bucharest, 1964-86; freelance artist and art conservator N.Y.C., 1986—. Lectr. on art conservation. One woman shows at Orizont Gallery, Bucharest, Romania, 1978, Mus. Fine Arts, Craiova, Romania, 1981, Simeza Gallery, Bucharest, 1984, Romanian Cultural Ctr., N.Y.C., 1993; group shows in N.Y., Washington, Chgo.; contbr. articles to art mags. Mem. Internat. Inst. for Conservation London, Am. Inst. for Conservation. Democrat. Avocations: classical music, history, literature. Home: 40 W Point Hwy # 21 Highland Falls NY 10928-2317

SKIDMORE, MICHELLE MARIE, elementary school educator, principal; b. Newport Beach, Calif., Oct. 11, 1969; d. Rene and Jan Sommer; m. James Jonathan Skidmore, June 28, 2002. BA in Psychology, U. Calif., Davis, 1991; MS in Edn., Calif. State U., Fullerton, 2002. Tchr. 4th & 5th grade, tchg. asst. prin. Capistrano Unified Sch. Dist., San Juan Capistrano, Calif., 1996—; faculty reading dept. Calif. State U., Coll. Edn., Fullerton, 2003—. Coord. Ladera Ranch Sch. Improvement Coun., Calif., 2003—; beginning tchr. support & assistance support provider Calif. Commn. for Tchr. Credentialing, 2003—; asst. dir. CSUF Coll. Kids Reading Clinic, Mission Viejo, 2002—02. Keynote spkr. conf. Contitutional Rights Found., Irvine, Calif., 2006—06; vol. Ladera Ranch Ednl. Found., Ladera Ranch, 2003—06; dir. Change Change Program, 2004—06. Recipient Tchr. Yr., Capistrano Unified Sch. Dist., 2005, Orange County Dept. Edn., 2006, award, Hines Found., 2006; grantee, Capistrano Unified Sch. Dist., 2005, Ladera Ranch Edn. Found., 2006; Japan Fulbright Meml. scholar, 2005. Mem.: Calif. Assn. Gifted, Computer Using Educators, Internat. Reading Assn., Calif. Tchrs. Assn., Golden Key, Phi Beta Kappa, Pi Beta Phi. Home: 112 Sellas Road South Ladera Ranch CA 92694 Office: Ladera Ranch School 29551 Sienna Parkway Ladera Ranch CA 92694 Office Phone: 949-234-5915. Home Fax: 949-218-4795. Personal E-mail: mmskidmore@capousd.org.

SKIGEN, PATRICIA SUE, lawyer; d. David P. and Gertrude H. (Hirschhaut) Skigen; m. Irwin J. Sugarman, May 1973 (div. Nov. 1994); 1 child, Alexander David Sugarman; m. Gary W. Guttman, May 2001. BA with distinction, Cornell U., 1964; LLB, Yale U., 1968. Bar: NY 1968, US Dist. Ct. (so. dist.) NY 1969. Law clk. Anderson, Mori & Rabinowitz, Tokyo, 1966-67; assoc. Rosenman Colin Kaye Petschek Freund & Emil, NYC, 1968-70, Willkie Farr & Gallagher, NYC, 1970-75, ptnr., 1977-95, J.P. Morgan Chase & Co., NYC, 1995—2002, mng. dir., assoc. gen. counsel, 2002—04; gen. coun. fin. svcs. Am. Internat. Group, Inc., 2005—. Dep. supt., gen. counsel NY State Banking Dept., NYC, 1975-77, first dep. supt. banks, 1977; adj. prof. Benjamin Cardozo Law Sch. Yeshiva U., 1979. Contbr. articles to profl. jours. Cornell U. Dean's scholar, 1960-64, Regent's scholar, 1960-64, Yale Law Sch. scholar, 1964-68. Mem.: ABA (corp. banking and bus. law sect.), Assn. of Bar of City of N.Y. (chmn. com. banking 1991—94, long range planning com. 1994—96, audit com. 1994—2001), Phi Kappa Phi, Phi Beta Kappa. Office Phone: 212-770-8805. Business E-Mail: patricia.skigen@aig.com.

SKILLING, MARIE L., music educator; b. Alma, Mich., Aug. 26, 1931; d. Dan Ernest and Florence Marie (Tolles) Harper; m. Darroll Dean Skilling, June 10, 1951; children: Ann Marie, James Dean, Stephen Richard. BS cum laude, U. Minn., 1974. Piano tchr., St. Paul. Scout leader Girl Scouts USA, St. Paul, 1958-64; ch. nursery dir. Presbyn. Ch., Wausau, Wis., 1956-60, ch. youth evening dir. weekly program, 1963-68. Mem. Nat. Music Tchrs. Assn., Minn. Music Tchrs. Assn. (test ctr. chmn., treas., constn. chair 1993-99, Disting. Svc. award 1998), St. Paul Piano Tchrs. Assn. (treas. 1975-78, pres. 1984-86, 1st v.p. 1982-84, 3d v.p. 1978-82). Avocations: sewing, needlecrafts, sailing, camping, backpacking.

SKILLINGSTAD, CONSTANCE YVONNE, social services administrator, educator; b. Portland, Oreg., Nov. 18, 1944; d. Irving Elmer and Beulah Ruby (Aleckson) Erickson; m. David W. Skillingstad, Jan. 12, 1968 (div. Mar. 1981); children: Michael, Brian. BA in Sociology, U. Minn., 1966; MBA, U. St. Thomas, St. Paul, 1982. Lic. social worker; cert. vol. adminstr., lic. real estate agt. Social worker Rock County Welfare Dept., Luverne, Minn., 1966-68, Hennepin County Social Svc., Mpls., 1968-70, vol. coord., 1970-78, St. Joseph's Home for Children, Mpls., 1978-89, mgr. cmty. resources, 1989-94; exec. dir. Mpls. Crisis Nursery, 1994-97; mem. cmty. faculty Met. State U., St. Paul and Mpls., 1980-97; faculty U. St. Thomas Ctr. Non Profit Mgmt., 1990—2001; asst. adminstr. St. Joseph's Home Children, Mpls., 1997-98; asst. dir. Cath. Charities Archdiocese of St. Paul and Mpls., 1998-2000; dir. mem. svc. Minn. Coun. Fedns., 2001—02; pres. Golden Girl Homes, Inc., 2001—; exec. dir. Prevent Child Abuse Minn., St. Paul, 2002—. Trainer, mem. adv. commn. Mpls. Vol. Ctr., 1978—90, cons., 1980—, chmn. Contbr. articles to profl. jours. Mem. adv. bd. MADD, Minn., 1986—88, Congregations Concerned for Children, 2002—, Stop It Now!, Minn., 2003—, Grandkids and Me; bd. dirs. Survivors Network Minn., 2005—, Authentic Voices Internat., Ctr. Giref, Loss and Transition, U. Minn. Children Youth and Family Consortium; vice chmn., chmn. adminstrv. coun., lay leader Hobart United Meth. Ch.; lay rep. Minn. Ann. Conf. Meth. Chs., 1989—92; chmn. social concerns commn. Park Ave. United Meth. Ch., 1992—. Named Woman of Distinction, Mpls. St. Paul Mag./Sta. KARE-TV, 1995; named one of Outstanding Young Women in Am., 1974; recipient Vol. of Yr. 2001, Boca Ballet. Mem.: Minn. Social Svcs. Assn. (pres. 1981, 1998—99, bd. dirs. 1996—2001, mem. legis. com., Disting. Svc. award 1987), Assn. Vol. Adminstrn. (v.p. regional affairs 1985—87, mem. assessment panel 1986—94, coord. nat. tng. team, cert. process vol. adminstr. 1986—92, profl. devel. chair 1990—92), Minn. Assn. Vol. Dirs. (pres. 1975, sec., ethics chmn.

1987—). Dfl. Avocations: bridge, volleyball, travel, reading, accordion. Office: Prevent Child Abuse Minn Ste 202 S 1821 University Ave Saint Paul MN 55104 Home: 28544 Lakewood Dr NW Isanti MN 55040 Business E-Mail: cskillingstad@pcamn.org.

SKILLMAN, BECKY SUE, lieutenant governor, former state legislator; b. Bedford, Ind., Sept. 26, 1950; d. Jack Delmar and Catherine Louise (Flinn) Foddrill; m. Stephen E. Skillman, 1969; 1 child, Aaron. Dep. recorder Lawrence County, 1971-76, county recorder, 1977-84; clerk Lawrence County crct. ct., 1985—92; mem. Ind. Senate from 44th dist., 1992—2005; lt. gov. State of Ind., Indpls., 2005—. Co-dir. Lawrence County Young Reps., 1973-78; co-chmn. State Young Reps. Conv., 1975, 77; vice chmn. Lawrence County Rep. Ctrl. Com. Named The Outstanding Elected Official of 2000, Ind. Assn. Area Agencies, "Legislator of the Year", Ind. Library Found., 2002; recipient "Champion of Small Bus." award, Small Bus. Coun, 1995, Disting. Pub. Policy award, Ind. Rural Health Policy award, 2003. Republican. Office: Office Lt Governor State Capitol Rm 333 Indianapolis IN 46204 Office Phone: 317-232-4545. Office Fax: 317-232-4788.*

SKINNER, HELEN CATHERINE WILD, biomineralogist; b. Bklyn., Jan. 25, 1931; d. Edward Herman and Minnie (Bertsch) Wild; m. Brian John Skinner, Oct. 9, 1954; children: Adrienne, Stephanie, Thalassa. BA, Mt. Holyoke Coll., 1952; MA, Radcliffe/Harvard, 1954; PhD, Adelaide (Australia) U., 1959. Mineralogist sect. molecular structure Nat. Inst. Arthritis and Metabolic Diseases, NIH, 1961-65; with sect. crystal chemistry Lab. Histology and Pathology Nat. Inst. Dental Rsch., NIH, 1965-66; lectr. dept. geology and geophysics Yale U., 1967-69, rsch. assoc. dept. surgery, 1967-72, sr. rsch. assoc. dept. surgery Medical Sch., 1972-75; Alexander Agassiz vis. lectr. dept. biology Harvard U., 1976-77; lectr. dept. biology Yale U., 1977-83, assoc. prof. biochemistry in surgery, Medical Sch. New Haven, 1978-84, lectr. dept. orthopaedic surgery, 1972—, lectr., rsch. affiliate in geology and geophysics, 1987—. Pres. Conn. Acad. Arts and Scis., 1984—94, publs. chair, 1994—2001; faculty affiliate in mineralogy Yale U. Peabody Mus., 2001—; mineralogist AEC, summer, 1953; master Jonathan Edwards Coll., Yale U., 1977—82; Alexander Agassiz vis. lectr. dept. biology Harvard U., 1976—77; vis. prof. sect. ecology and systematics dept. biology Cornell U., 1980, 83; disting. prof. geology Adelaide U., 1990—91, disting. lectr., 1993; disting. prof. geology U. Wyo., 1996; Alan Cox vis. prof. Stanford U., 2003; mem. dental adv. com. Yale-New Haven Hosp., 1973—80, Yale-New Haven Tchrs. Inst., 1983—99; chmn. site visit team Nat. Inst. Dental Rsch., 1974—75; mem. publs. com. Yale U. Press., 1979—84, Am. Geol. Inst., 1993—96, 2000—05; MSA del. Internat. Mineral. Commn. Applied Mineralogy, 1992—; chair Nat. Acad. Sci./NRC Com. on Earth Sci. and Pub. Health, 2004—06. Author: Asbestos and Other Fibrous Materials, 1988, Biomineralization: Iron and Manganese, 1992, Dana's New Mineralogy, 8th edit., 1997, Geology and Health, 2003; contbr. articles to profl. jours. and mags., chpts. to 4 books. Mem. bd. edn. com. Conn. Fund for Environ., 1983—89, mem. sci. adv. com., 1989—92; founder, pres. Investor's Strategy Inst., New Haven, 1983—85; trustee Miss Porter's Sch., Farmington, Conn., 1984—91, mem. edn. com., 1986—88, mem. salaries and benefits com., 1988—91; treas. YWCA, New Haven, 1983—84; trustee Geol. Soc. Am. Found., 1998—. Fellow: AAAS, Geol. Soc. Am., Mineralogical Soc. Am.; mem.: Conn. Acad. Arts and Sci. (dir., past pres.). Home: 39 Temple Ct New Haven CT 06511-6820 Office: Yale U Dept Geology Geophysics PO Box 208109 New Haven CT 06520-8109 Office Phone: 203-432-3787. Business E-Mail: catherine.skinner@yale.edu.

SKINNER, MARY JACOBS, lawyer; b. 1957; m. Sam Skinner, Aug. 17, 1989; stepchildren: Thomas, Steven, Jane. BA cum laude, Harvard U., 1978; JD, Northwestern U., 1981. Bar: Ill. 1981, D.C. 1990, U.S. Supreme Ct. 1990. With Sidley Austin Brown & Wood, Chgo., 1981—, ptnr., 1989—; counsel to spkr. Ill. Ho. of Reps., Springfield, Ill., 1983—85. Intern White House, 1979. Former trustee RAdcliffe Coll.; participant leadership coun. Greater Chgo. Fellowship Program, 1984. Named One of Forty under 40 Most Outstanding Leaders in Chco., Crain's Chgo. Bus. Mem. Harvard Alumni Assn. (bd. dirs.), Radcliffe Coll. Alumni Assn. (past pres.). Office: Sidley Austin Brown and Wood Bank One Plz 10 S Dearborn St Chicago IL 60603

SKINNER, NANCY JO, municipal recreation executive; b. Ogallala, Nebr., Nov. 5, 1956; d. Dale Warren Skinner and Beverly Jane (Fister) Berry. AA, Platte Community Coll., 1977; BS, U. Ariz., 1981; MBA, U. Phoenix, 1990; diploma, Nat. Exec. Devel. Sch., 1992. Cert. leisure profl. Sports specialist YWCA, Tucson, 1981, asst. dir. summer day camp, 1981, dir. health, phys. edn. and recreation, 1981-82; sr. recreation specialist Pima County Parks and Recreation Dept., Tucson, 1983, recreation program coord., 1983-90; recreation coord. III Phoenix Parks, Recreation and Libr. Dept., 1990-94, recreation supr., 1994—. Labor mgmt. quality of work life rep. Pima County Govt., 1987; dist. coord. Atlantic Richfield Co. Jesse Owens Games, Tucson, 1986-89; adv. Pima County Health Dept. Better Health Through Self Awareness, 1982-83. Dir. tournament Sportsman Fund-Send a Kid to Camp, Tucson, 1984, 85, 86; mem. labor mgmt. quality of working life com. Pima County Govt., 1987; dist. coord. Nat. Health Screening Coun., Tucson, 1982-85; event coord. Tucson Women's Commn. Saguaro Classic, 1984; com. mem. United Way, Tucson, 1982-83; panelist Quality Conf. City of Phoenix, 1992. Musco/APRf Grad. scholar; recipient City of Phoenix Excellence award, 1994. Mem.: Ariz. Pks. and Recreation Assn. (treas. dist. IV 1987, pres. 1988, 1989, state treas. 1990, pub. rels. chair 1993, co-chair state conf. ednl. program com. 1995, nat. cert. bd. rep. Ariz. C.P.R.P. cert. program coord. 1997, cert., Am. Register of Outstanding Profl. 2002, Tenderfoot award 1984), Nat. Recreation and Pks. Assn., Delta Psi Kappa. Democrat. Avocations: music, reading, travel, tennis, golf. Office: Phoenix Pks Recreation & Libr Dept 3901 W Glendale Ave Phoenix AZ 85051-8132

SKINNER, PATRICIA MORAG, state legislator; b. Glasgow, Scotland, Dec. 3, 1932; d. John Stuart and Frances Charlotte (Swann) Robertson; m. Robert A. Skinner, Dec. 28, 1957; children: Robin Ann, Pamela. BA, NYU, 1953. Mdse. trainee Lord & Taylor, N.Y.C.; adminstrv. asst. Atlantic Products, N.Y.C.; newspaper corr. Salem Observer, NH, 1964-84; mem. N.H. Ho. of Reps., 1972-94, chmn. labor, human resources, and rehab. com., 1975-86, mem. House edn. com., 1987, chmn., 1989-94, exec. com. Nat. Conf. State Legislatures, 1987-90; chmn. N.H. Adv. Coun. Unemployment Compensation, 1984-94. Mem. State Libr. Adv. Coun., 2001—. Bd. dirs. Castle Jr. Coll., 1975, chmn. bd., 1988-96; v.p. bd. Swift Water coun. Girl Scouts U.S., v.p., 1987-92; N.H. Voc-Tech. Coll., Nashua, 1978-83; trustee Nesmith Libr., Windham, N.H., 1982—, chmn. bd. trustees, 1994-99; pres. N.H. Fedn. Rep. Women's Clubs, parliamentarian, legis. chmn., 1984-86, 94-96. Mem. Windham Woman's Club (pres. 1981-83), Order Ea. Star. Christian Scientist.

SKINNER, SUE DOSSETT, retired director; b. Geneva, Ky., Dec. 4, 1928; d. Ural Morrison and Nellie Susan (Long) Dossett; m. William Thomas Skinner III, Sept. 7, 1952 (dec.); children: William Thomas IV, John Little Clay. BS, U. Ky., Lexington, 1951; EdM, N.C. State U., Raleigh, 1972. Asst. home demonstration agt. N.C. Ext. Svc., Warren County, 1952—60; food svcs. dir. Warren County Schs., 1968—72, tchr. home econ., 1972—88, dir. vocat. edn., 1988—92; ret., 1992. Past chair and vice chair Region III Home Econ. Leadership Coun.; v.p. N.C. Assn. Educators, Warren County, NC, sec., past pres. home econ. tchrs. sect.; Warren County del. N.C. Vocat. Assn.; past state sec. N.C. Home Econ. Assn., past state scholarship chair; mem. state scholarship com. N.C. Sch. Food Svc. Assn.; past advisor Region III Future Homemakers Am. Contbr. articles to periodicals. Participant Internat. Farm Youth Exch., Finland; local club leader 4-H; past dist. pres. Fedn. Woman's Clubs; past pres., com. chair Warrenton Woman's Club; v.p. Valley Investors; past pres. Littleton Womans Club; elder, choir dir. Presbyn. Ch. Finalist runner-up, Mrs. N.C. Contest; named county and state winner, 4-H Alumni Recognition Program; recipient state poetry prizes (4), Fedn. Woman's Clubs. Mem.: DAR (pres. 2004—06, state chaplain 1997—2000), Gavel Soc., Am. Assn. Career and Tech. Edn., Order of the Merovingian Dynasty, Sons and Daus. Pilgrims, Order Ancient Planters (nat. sec. 2005—), Jamestowne Soc. (hon. gov. 1st N.C. chpt. 2005—), Dau. Colonial Wars (state chaplain 2005—), Dames Ct. Honor (state chaplain 2006—, state sec. 2006), Charlemagne Soc., Colonial Dames Am., Little Garden Club, Delta Kappa Gamma (past pres.). Presbyterian. Avocations: knitting, antiques. Home: PO Drawer 520 Littleton NC 27850-0520

SKIRBOLL, LANA R., federal health policy director; b. Balt., Dec. 7, 1948; m. Leonard Taylor, Feb. 19, 1986; 2 children. BA, NYU, 1970; MS in Zoology and Physiology, Miami U., 1972; PhD in Pharmacology, Georgetown U., 1977. Postdoctoral tng. in psychiatry and pharmacology Yale U. Sch. Medicine, New Haven, 1977-79; vis. scientist dept. histology and neurobiology Karolinska Inst., Stockholm, 1979-81; chief electrophysiology unit NIMH, 1981—86; dep. sci. advisor Alcohol Drug Abuse and Mental Health Adminstrn., 1986—88, exec. asst. to administr., 1989-91, assoc. adminstr. for sci., 1990—92; dir. office of sci. policy and program planning NIMH, 1992-95, 95—. Cons. Ctr. Environ. Health and Human Toxicology, 1985-87. Author: Pharmacology of Biochemical Behavior, 1988, Neuroanatomical Tract-Tracing Methods II: 1981-86, 1990, (with T. Hokfelt, G. Foster, O. Johannsson et alCentral Phenylethanolamine N-Methyltransferase Immunoreactive Neurons: Distribution Projections, Fine Structure, Ontogeny and Co-Existing Peptides, 1988, (with G.Stoner, S. Werkman, D. Hommer) Effects of Caffeine on the Substania Nigra, Biological Psychiatry, 1988, (with J.A. Stivers, R. Long, J. Crawley) Anatomical Analysis of Frontal Cortex Sites at Which Carbachol Induces Moteor Seizures in the Rat, (with T. Hokfelt, B. Robertson) Retrograde Flourescent Tracers with Immunohistochemistry, (with M. Palkovits, E. Mezey, T. Hokfelt) Adrenergic Projections from the Lower Brainstem to the Hypothalamic Paraventricular Nucleus, the Lateral Hypothalamic Area and the Central Nucleus of the Amygdala in Rats, vol. 1020, 1992. Biol. Scis. fellow in in psychiatry NIMH, 1977-79, Fogarty fellow, Internat. fellow Swedish Med. Rsch. Coun., 1979-81. Mem. AAAS, Am. Coll. Neuropsychopharmacology (Mead Johnson award), N.Y. Acad. Scis., Nat. Com. Edn. (Potomac chpt. pres. 1988-89), European Neurosci. Soc., Soc. Neurosci. Office: HHS NIH 9000 Rockville Pike Bldg 1 Bethesda MD 20892-0001

SKJERVOLD, GERALDINE REID See REID, GERALDINE

SKLADAL, ELIZABETH LEE, retired elementary school educator; b. NYC, May 23, 1937; d. Angier Joseph and Julia May (Roberts) Gallo; m. George Wayne Skladal, Dec. 26, 1956; children: George Wayne Jr., Joseph Lee. BA, Sweet Briar Coll., 1958; postgrad., U. Kans., 1966-67; EdM, U. Alaska, 1976. Choir dir. Main Chapel, Camp Zama, Japan, 1958-59, Ft. Lee, Va., 1963-65, Main Chapel and Snowhawk, Ft. Richardson, Alaska, 1968-70; tchr. Anchorage (Alaska) Sch. Dist., 1970-98; ret. Active Citizen's Adv. Com. Gifted and Talented, Anchorage, 1981-83; mem. music com. Anchorage Sch. Dist., 1983-86; soloist Anchorage Opera Chorus, 1969-80, Cmty. Chorus, Anchorage, 1968-80; mem. choir First Presbyn. Ch., Anchorage, 1971—, deacon, 1988—, elder, 1996—, mission com. chair, 1996-99, mem. pastoral nominating com., 1982-83, 2001-03, moderator, Presbyn. Women, 2005-; participant 1st cultural exch. Alaska Chamber Singers, Magadan, Russia, 1992; participant summer mission trip First Presbyn. Ch., Swaziland, 1995. Named Am. Coll. Theater Festival winner Amoco Oil Co., 1974; recipient Cmty. Svc. award Anchorage U. Alaska Alumni Assn., 1994-95. Mem. AAUW, Anchorage Concert Assn. Patron Soc. (assocs. coun. of dirs.), Alaska Chamber Singers, Anchorage Concert Chorus, Anchorage Woman's Club (1st v.p.), Alaska Prospectors (pres.), Am. Guild Organists (former dean, former treas., mem.-at-large), Local Delta Kappa Gamma (1st v.p., pres.). Republican. Avocations: camping, travel, bicycling, fishing, cross country skiing. Home: 1841 S Salem Dr Anchorage AK 99508-5156

SKLAR, ETHEL (DUSTY SKLAR), writer; b. Sokol, Poland, Mar. 11, 1928; came to U.S., 1930; d. Max and Lena (Charap) K.; m. David Sklar, Nov. 27, 1949 (div. June 1988); children: Steven, Leeza, Joseph Grad. high sch., 1945. Author: Gods and Beasts, 1977, The Nazis and the Occult, 1990 Mem. Am. Soc. Journalists and Authors, Investigative Reporters and Editors Home: 1275 15th St Apt 17i Fort Lee NJ 07024-1933

SKLAR, GAIL JANICE, special education educator; b. Phila., Nov. 10, 1949; d. Harold and Irma (Lusky) S.; m. David William Tucker, May 30, 1976 (div. May 1984); 1 child, Benjamin; m. Howard Rod Cohen, Jan. 2, 1997. BS in Edn., Temple U., 1971, MEd, 1974. Tchr. Simon Gratz High Sch., Phila., 1971—; ednl. diagnostician Phila./Ardmore, Pa., 1980—. Prin., owner Native Am. Arts, Etc. Recipient Dr. Ruth Hayre Svc. award. Mem. Phila. Writing Project, Greater Phila. Orchid Soc., Southeastern Pa. Orchid Soc. Avocations: reading, researching women in history, orchid growing. Home: 402 Marple Rd Broomall PA 19008-2044 Office: Simon Gratz High Sch 18th & Hunting Park Ave Philadelphia PA 19140 Office Phone: 610-325-3108. E-mail: gailjsklar@erol.com.

SKLAR, HOLLY L., writer, columnist; b. N.Y.C., May 6, 1955; BA, Oberlin Coll., 1977; MA in Polit. Sci., Columbia U., 1980. Rschr. UN Ctr. Transnat. Corps., N.Y., 1978; writer, rschr. N. Am. Congress Latin Am., N.Y., 1981-82; exec. dir. Inst. New Communications, N.Y., 1982-84; writer, lectr. N.Y., Boston. Review panelist NEH, Washington, 1989; del. Soviet-Am. Women's Summit, N.Y., Washington, 1990. Author, co-author (books) Trilateralism, 1980, Poverty in the American Dream: Women and Children First, 1983, Washington's War on Nicaragua, 1988, Streets of Hope: The Fall and Rise of an Urban Neighborhood, 1994, Chaos or Community? Seeking Solutions, Not Scapegoats for Bad Economics, 1995, Shifting Fortunes: The Perils of the Growing American Wealth Gap, 1999, Raise the Floor: Wages and Policies that Work for All of Us, 2001, A Just Minimum Wage: Good for Workers, Business and Our Future, 2005. Mem. adv. bd. The Progressive Media Project, Polit. Rsch. Assocs.; bd. dirs. United for a Fair Economy, 1996-2000; mem. steering com. Caribbean Basin Info. Project, 1982-85; mem. working group on global econs. Am. Friends Svc. Com., 2002-04. Recipient Outstanding Book award Gustavus Myers Ctr. for Study Human Rights in U.S., 1988, Assocs. award Polit. Rsch. Assocs., Cambridge, 1991-97; fellow Columbia U. Grad. Sch. Arts and Scis., 1978-80. Mem. Nat. Writers Union, Acad. Polit. Sci. Office Phone: 617-522-2923. Personal E-mail: hsklar@aol.com.

SKLAR, KATHRYN KISH, historian, educator; b. Columbus, Ohio, Dec. 26, 1939; d. William Edward and Elizabeth Sue (Rhodes) Kish; m. Robert A. Sklar, 1958 (div. 1978); children: Leonard Scott, Susan Rebecca Sklar Friedman; m. Thomas L. Dublin, Apr. 30, 1988. BA magna cum laude, Radcliffe Coll., 1965; PhD, U. Mich., 1969. Asst. prof., lectr. U. Mich., Ann Arbor, 1969-74; assoc. prof. history UCLA, 1974-81, chmn. com. to administer program in women's studies Coll. Letters and Sci., 1974-81, prof., 1981-88; Disting. prof. history SUNY, Binghamton, 1988—, co-dir. Ctr. Hist. Study of Women and Gender, 1998—; Harmsworth prof. U.S. history U. Oxford, 2005—. Pulitzer juror in history, 1976; fellow Newberry Libr. Family and Community History Seminar, 1973; active Calif. Coun. for Humanities, 1981-85, N.Y. Coun. for Humanities, 1992—; Harmsworth prof. Am. history Oxford U., 2005—. Author: Catharine Beecher: A Study in American Domesticity, 1973 (Berkshire pri e 1974); editor: Catharine Beecher: A Treatise on Domestic Economy, 1977, Harriet Beecher Stowe: Uncle Tom's Cabin, or Life Among the Lowly: The Minister's Wooing, Oldtown Folks, 1981, Notes of Sixty Years: The Autobiography of Florence Kelley, 1849-1926, 1984, (with Thomas Dublin) Women and Power in American History: A Reader (2 vols.), 1991, (with Linda Kerber and Alice Kessler-Harris) U.S. History as Women's History: New Feminist Essays, 1995, Women's Rights Emerges within the Antislavery Movement: A Short History with Documents, 1830-1870, 2000; co-editor: The Social Survey Movement in Historical Perspective, 1992, Florence Kelley and the Nation's Work: The Rise of Women's Political Culture, 1830-1900, 1995 (Berkshire prize 1996). Social Justice Feminists in the United States and Germany: A Dialogue in Documents, 1885-1933, 1998; mem. editl. bd. Jour. Women's History, 1987—, Women's History Rev., 1990—, Jour. Am. History, 1978-81; contbr. chpts. to books; co-dir. Women and Social Movements in the U.S. 1600-2000: An Online Jour. and Datebase, 1997—. Fellow Woodrow Wilson Found., 1965-67, Danforth Found., 1967-69, Radcliffe Inst., 1973-74, Nat. Humanities Inst., 1975-76, Rockefeller Found. Humanities, 1981-82, Woodrow Wilson Internat. Ctr. for Scholars, 1982, 1992-93, Guggenheim Found., 1984, Ctr. Advanced Study Behavioral and Social Scis., Stanford U., 1987-88, AAUW, 1990-91; Daniels fellow Am. Antiquarian Soc., 1976, NEH fellow Newberry Library, 1982-83; Ford Found. faculty rsch. grantee, 1973-74; grantee NEH, 1976-78, UCLA Coun. for Internat. and Comparative Studies, 1983. Mem. Am. Hist. Assn. (chmn. com. on women historians 1980-83, v.p. Pacific Coast br. 1986-87, pres. 1987-88), Orgn. Am. Historians (exec. bd. 1983-86, Merle Curti award com. 1978-79, lectr. 1982—), Am. Studies Assn. (coun. mem.-at-large 1978-80), Berkshire Conf. Women Historians, Am. Antiquarian Soc., Phi Beta Kappa. Avocation: photography. Office: SUNY Dept History Binghamton NY 13902 Office Phone: 607-777-6202.

SKLENARIK, DENISE LAUREN, science educator; b. Peekskill, N.Y., Aug. 12, 1982; d. Dennis John and Katherine Mary Sklenarik. BA, Rider U., Lawrenceville, N.J., 2004. Tchr. aid Putnam Valley (N.Y.) Sch. Dist., 2003—04; sci. tchr. Mid. Sch. 143, Bronx, NY, 2004—05, E. Bronx Acad., NY, 2005—06. Alumni scholar, Rider U., 2000. Mem.: Nat. Sci. Tchrs. Assn., Sierra Cluc, Order of Omega, Delta Phi Epsilon, Omicron Delta Kappa, Phi Delta Kappa. Office Phone: 718-861-8641. Office Fax: 718-861-8634. Personal E-mail: denisesklenarik@aol.com.

SKLYAR, ADELINA M., lawyer; d. Joseph and Klafira Sklar. BA, NYU, NYC, 1993, JD, 1998. Bar: US Dist. Ct. (ea. dist.) NY 2001. Assoc. Ferro & Kuba, P.C., NYC, 1998—2001, Ferro, Kuba, Bloom, Mangano, Gacovino & Lake, P.C., NYC, 2001—05; ptnr. Ferro, Kuba, Mangano, Sklyar, Gacovino & Lake, P.C., NYC, 2005—. Mem.: ACLU, ATLA, NY State Bar Assn., NY County Lawyers' Assn. (assoc.). Office: Ferro Kuba Mangano Sklyar Ste 1100 360 West 31st St New York NY 10001 Office Phone: 212-244-7676. Office Fax: 212-244-9393. Business E-Mail: asklyar@ferrokuba.com.

SKOGLUND, MARILYN, state supreme court justice; b. Chgo., Aug. 28, 1946; BA, So. Ill. U., 1971; clerkship, 1977-81. Bar: Vt. 1981, U.S. Dist. Ct. Vt. 1981, U.S. Ct. Appeals (2d cir.) 1983. Asst. atty. gen. Civil Law Divsn., 1981—89, chief, 1988—93, Pub. Protection Divsn., 1993-94; judge Vt. Dist. Ct., 1994-97; assoc. justice Vt. Supreme Ct., 1997—. Office: Vt Supreme Ct 109 State St Montpelier VT 05609-0001*

SKOGLUND, SANDRA LOUISE, artist, educator; b. Boston, Sept. 11, 1946; d. Walter and Dorothy Ramsey (Bowes) S.; m. Albert Baccili, July 3, 1980. B.A., Smith Coll, 1968; M.F.A., U. Iowa, 1972. Instr. U. Hartford, West Hartford, Conn., 1973-76; assoc. prof. Rutgers U., Newark, 1976—. One-woman shows include Castelli Gallery, N.Y.C., 1981, 83, 87, Ft. Worth Art Mus., 1981, Mpls. Inst. Art, 1982, Wadsworth Atheneum, Hartford, Conn., 1982, Sharpe Gallery, 1987; exhibited in group shows at Fogg Art Mus., 1980, Mus. Am. Art, N.Y.C., 1981, Inst. Contemporary Art, London, 1981, Internat. Mus. Photography, 1982, Castelli Gallery, 1980, 84, 85, Walker Art Ctr., Mpls., 1987. Nat. Endowment for Arts grantee, 1980. Studio: 241 Eldridge St Apt 3F New York NY 10002-1388

SKOLAN-LOGUE, AMANDA NICOLE, lawyer, consultant; b. Los Angeles, Feb. 19, 1954; d. Carl Charles and Estelle (Lubin) Skolan; m. James Edward Logue, Dec. 10, 1983. BS, U. Calif., Los Angeles, 1973; MBA, U. So. Calif., 1976; JD, Southwestern U., Los Angeles, 1982. Bar: Calif. 1982, U.S. Dist. Ct. (cen., no. and ea. dists.) Calif. 1982, N.Y. 1986. Sr. internal cons. Getty Oil Co., Los Angeles, 1976-80; atty. litigation ACLU of So. Calif., Los Angeles, 1982-83; corp. atty. Am. Can Co., Greenwich, Conn., 1983-86; assoc. Shereff, Friedman, Hoffman & Goodman, N.Y.C., 1986-88; region counsel Gen. Electric Capital Corp., Danbury, Conn., 1988—. Mem. ABA, N.Y. State Bar Assn. Republican. Home: 33 Musket Ridge Rd New Fairfield CT 06812-5101 Office: Gen Electric Capital Corp 44 Old Ridgebury Rd Danbury CT 06810-5107

SKOLDBERG, PHYLLIS LINNEA, musician, educator; d. August Theodore Skoldberg and Esther Amanda Carlson. MusB with honors, New Eng. Conservatory, 1955, MusM, 1957; M in Music Edn. with high distinction, Ind. U., 1964, Mus D in Performance, 1967. Violinist Houston Symphony Orch., 1957—59, Cin. Symphony Orch., 1959—62; assoc. instr. Ind. U., Bloomington, 1962—64; prof. music SUNY, Oswego, 1964—77; asst. dean fine arts Ariz. State U., Tempe, 1977—84, prof. music, 1977—2001, prof. emeritus, 2001—. Vis. artist Paris Conservatoire, 1973; vis. prof., cons. Australian String Tchrs. Assn., Brisbane and Sydney, 1984, Shanghai Conservatory Music, 1984; artist-in-residence U. Hong Kong, 1984; adj. prof., coord. string dept. Mesa (Ariz.) CC, 2001—. Author: The Strings: A Comparative View, Vol. I, 1981, Vol. 2, 1982; performer: (solos) Reston (Va.) Music Festival, 1972, 1973, Charles Ives Music Festival, 1975, 1976, Western Music Festival, 1980, (1st violin) Concert Quartet, 2003; soloist Philharmonic. Named winner performance competition, Seattle Philharm. Orch., 1952; recipient Boston Civic Music award, 1954. Mem.: The Phoenix Inst. of Music (founding dir. 2005), Red Rock Music Festival (bd. dirs. 2002—), Music Tchrs. Nat. Assn., Am. String Tchrs. Assn. (adv. bds. 1970—84, Ariz. pres. 1984—86). Home: 12002 S Tuzigoot Ct Phoenix AZ 85044-3467 Office: Mesa CC 1833 W Southern Ave Mesa AZ 85202 Office Phone: 480-461-7575. Office Fax: 480-461-7422. Business E-Mail: phyllis.skoldberg@asu.edu.

SKOLNICK, HOLLY R., lawyer; b. NYC, May 7, 1954; BA, Univ. Wis., 1976; JD, Harvard Univ., 1980. Bar: DC 1980, Fla. 1984. Law clk. Hon. Eugene P. Spellman US Dist. Judge (so. dist.) Fla.; staff atty. public defender svc., Washington; shareholder, litig., chair pro bono com. Greenberg Traurig LLP, Miami, Fla. Editor: Harvard Civil Rights-Civil Liberties Law Rev. Bd. dir. Florida Immigrant Advocacy Ctr., Equal Justice Works. Named one of one of the top 250 lawyers in So. Fla., So. Fla. Legal Guide. Office: Greenberg Traurig LLP 1221 Brickell Ave Miami FL 33131 Office Phone: 305-579-0500. Office Fax: 305-579-0717. Business E-Mail: skolnickh@gtlaw.com.

SKOLNIK, SANDRA J., educational association administrator; b. N.Y.C., Jan. 23, 1938; m. Leonard Skolnik; children: Rachel Cogan, Adam. Student, Balt. Jr. Coll., U. Md. Exec. dir. Md. Com. for Children Inc., 1994—. Mem. Nat. Child Care Policy Rsch. Consortium; founding pres. Md. Assn. Non-profit Orgns.; mem. Friends of the Family Inc., Leadership Network on Children and Welfare Reform, U. Md. Hosp. for Children; mem. fund adv. bd. Md. After-Sch. Opportunity; mem. adv. bd., com. mem. Md. State Dept. Edn., Jr. League Balt.; mem. Judith P. Hoyer Blue Ribbon Commn. on Funding of Early Child Care and Edn.; mem. adv. bd., com. mem. Md. State Dept. Human Resources. Named one of Md.'s Top 100 Women, Daily Record, 1998, one of Balt. Power Couples, Balt. Mag., 2000; recipient $5,000 Leadership Distinction award for mgmt. excellence, United Way Cen. Md., Woman of Excellence award, Nat. Assn. Women Bus. Owners, Pres.'s award, Healthy Mothers, Healthy Babies, honoree, NA'AMAT USA, Celebration of Women. Mem.: Nat. Assn. Resource and Referral Agys. (treas., bd. dirs., leadership coun.). Office: 608 Water St Baltimore MD 21202

SKONEY, SOPHIE ESSA, educational administrator; b. Detroit, Jan. 29, 1929; d. George Essa and Helena (Dihmes) Cokalay; m. Daniel J. Skoney, Dec. 28, 1957; children: Joseph Anthony, James Francis, Carol Anne. PhB, U. Detroit, 1951; MEd, Wayne State U., 1960, EdD, 1975; postgrad., Ednl. Inst. Harvard Grad. Sch., 1986—. Tchr. elem. sch. Detroit Bd. Edn., 1952-69, remedial reading specialist, 1969-70, curriculum coord., 1970-71, region 6 article 3 title I coord., 1971-83, area achievement specialist, 1984-88; adminstrv. asst. Office Grant Procurement and Compliance, 1988-2000. Mem. dean's adv. coun. Coll. Edn. Wayne State U., 1995—; cons. in field. Editor newsletter Alliance to the Mich. Dental Assn., 1993-2000. Recipient Disting. Alumni award Wayne State U., 1993. Mem. ASCD, Wayne State U. Edn. Alumni Assn. (pres. bd. govs. 1979-80, newsletter editor 1975-77, 80—), Macomb Dental Aux. (pres. 1969-70), Mich. Dental Aux. (pres. 1980-81), Alliance Mich. Dental Assn. (pres. 1998-2000), Am. Assn. Sch. Adminstrs., Wayne State U. Alumni Assn. (dir., v.p. 1985-86), Internat. Reading Assn., Mich. Reading Assn., Mich. Assn. State and Fed. Program Specialists, Profl. Women's Network (newsletter editor 1981-83, pres. 1985-87, Anthony

Wayne award for leadership 1981), Retirees Orgn. Sch. Adminstrs. and Suprs. (pres. 2003—), Anthony Wayne Soc., Delta Kappa Gamma, Beta Sigma Phi, Phi Delta Kappa (v.p. 1988-90, pres. 1990-91, Educator of Yr. 1985, 91, 96, 2000). Roman Catholic. Home: 20813 Lakeland St Saint Clair Shores MI 48081-2104 Personal E-mail: skoneys@aol.com.

SKONSKY, CAROLINE TRESCHOW, marriage and family therapist; b. Pitts., Mar. 13, 1942; d. Godfrey Augustine Treschow and Lillian Marguerite Burns; m. William Lawrence Skonsky, Oct. 14, 1964; children: Sharon Louise, William Lawrence, Bradley James. BA in psychology, Carlow U., 1998; MSW, U. Pitts., 2001. LCSW Pa., 2001. Asst. to dir. New Choices-New Options, Pitts.; vol. mgr. Hospice Care of Pitts., 1998; social worker St. Margaret Senceca Pl., Verona, Pa., 1999; sr. adv. Step by Step, Pitts., 2000; family therapist Holy Family Soc. Svcs., Pitts., 2001—03; dual diagnosis therapist Mercy Behavioral Health, Pitts., 2004—. Vol. Women's Ctr. and Shelter, 1999—2000. Mem.: Pa. Psychological Assn., Nat. Assn. Social Workers. Avocations: genealogy, writing. Home: 116 4th Ave West Mifflin PA 15122 Business E-Mail: ctskonsky01@libcom.com.

SKOP, KATHY, art educator; b. Huntington, N.Y., July 14, 1946; d. William and Josephine (Raymond) Prince; m. Michael Skop, Oct. 5, 1968; children: Ahna Renee, Tarsia Daria, Zesha Leah, Damien. BS, So. Conn. State U., 1969, MS, 1972. Cert. tchr., Conn., Ohio, Ky. Chair art dept. Highland High Sch., Ft. Thomas, 1981—. Dir. Meadowlands Summer Art, Covington, Ky., 1982-84; juror Orange (Conn.) Art Show, 1972. Solo exhbns. include Wesleyan Hills Gallery, Middletown, Conn., 1971; group shows at Art Acad. Gallery, 1986, Downtown Gallery, 1986, Carnegie Art Ctr., 1988, Manuel High Sch., Louisville, 1989, Sealboch Hotel, 1991, Louisville Pub. Libr., 1990, Heart for Art, 1990-93. Chmn. cultural art com. Woodfill Sch. PTA, Ft. Thomas, 1981-82; chmn. Italian Festival Art, Covington, 1982. Mem. Nat. Art Edn. Assn., Ky. Art Edn. Assn. (exec. coun.), Ft. Thomas Edn. Assn., Cin. Art Mus. Home: 70 Hawthorne Ave Fort Thomas KY 41075-2413 Office Phone: 859-781-5900 11207. E-mail: kathy.skop@fortthomas.kyschools.us.

SKORKA, DARLENE MCDONALD, psychologist; b. Downey, Calif., June 4, 1942; d. Winfred ASA and Rose Muriel McDonald; m. Don T. Skorka, Nov. 25, 1972. BS in Psychology, U. Idaho, 1964; PhD in Clin. Psychology, U. Houston, 1971. Lic. psychologist, Calif. Clin. psychologist VA Hosp., Houston, 1971-74, asst. dir. drug abuse program, 1972-74; clin. psycholologist Kaiser Permanent, L.A., 1974-85; pvt. practice Rolling Hills Estates, Calif., 1975—. Mem. med. staff Del Amo Hosp., Torrance, Calif., 1986-2000; cons. Kaiser Mental Health Ctr., L.A., 1989. Contbr. articles to profl. jours. Mem. Am. Psychol. Assn., Calif. Psychol. Assn., Phi Beta Kappa. Home: 32203 Schooner Dr Palos Verdes Peninsula CA 90275-6017 Office: 827 Deep Valley Dr Ste 309 Palos Verdes Peninsula CA 90274-3655

SKORY, JANEL LYNN, English and speech educator; b. Manistee, Mich., Jan. 18, 1973; d. Wayne Allen and Nancy Ann Skory. BS in Math. Edn., Ferris State U., Big Rapids, Mich., 1995; EX in English Edn., Western Mich. U., Kalamazoo, 1996. Cert. profl. tchr. State of Mich., 1995. English and speech tchr. Pine River H.S., LeRoy, Mich., 1997—. Mem.: Pine River Edn. Assn. (v.p. 2005—06). Lutheran. Avocations: camping, fishing, gardening, travel. Office Phone: 231-829-3841.

SKOWRONSKI, NANCY, library director; m. Dennis Skowronski. Acting dir. Detroit Pub. Libr., 2001—02, interim dir., 2002, now dir., CEO. Bd. dirs. ProLiteracy Detroit, 2006—. Mem.: ALA, Univ. Cultural Ctr. Assn. (bd. mem.), Mich. Libr. Assn. Office: Cetroit Pub Libr 5201 Woodward Ave Detroit MI 48202 Office Phone: 313-833-3997. Office Fax: 313-833-2327. E-mail: nskowro@detroit.lib.mi.us.*

SKREDSVIG, JANICE B., information technology executive; Sr. dir. tech. & ops. PACCAR Inc., Bellevue, Wash., sr. dir. applications & global ops., 2001—04, gen. mgr., chief info. officer, 2004, v.p., chief info. officer, 2005—. Office: PACCAR Inc 777 106th Ave NE Bellevue WA 98004*

SKRIP, CATHY LEE, psychologist; b. Berwyn, Ill., July 19, 1948; d. Raymond Joseph and Gladys Catherine (Mazanec) Jirsa; m. Paul Joseph Skrip, Aug. 29, 1970; children: Carrie Anne, Christie Ellen, Jonathan Paul. AB in English, Miami (Ohio) U., 1969; MS in Counseling, Calif. State U., L.A., 1971. Cert. counselor, Calif.; lic. psychologist Minn. 1990. Counselor, instr. Rio Hondo Coll., Whittier, Calif., 1971-73; instr. N. Shore Community Coll., Beverly, Mass., 1974-75, counselor, dir. of placement, 1973-75; instr. Western Wis. Tech. Inst., La Crosse, Wis., 1975; asst. dir. Community Care Orgn. of La Crosse (Wis.) County, Inc., 1976-79; planning analyst Dept. Health and Social Svcs., Madison, Wis., 1979-80; vol. co-facilitator battered women's support group Alexandra House, Circle Pines, Minn., 1985-88; pvt. practice Hugo, Minn., 1992—98, Crystal, Minn., 1993—98, New Hope, Minn., 1998—2003, Forest Lake, Minn., 1998—. Charter trustee 621 Found., Shoreview, Minn., 1988-91, co-chair, 1990-91, chair, 1991-92; sec. Rio Hondo Coll. Faculty Assn., Whittier Calif., 1972-73. Author: (with Kristin Kunzman) Women With Secrets: Dealing With Domestic Abuse and Childhood Sexual Abuse in Treatment, 1991. Treas. LWV, La Crosse, 1978-81; mem. Ramsey County Cmty. Initiative to End Family Violence, 1990—, Family Violence Tng. Task Force, St. Paul, 1991, Mounds View Violence Prevention Coun., 1993—, Anoka County Domestic Violence Coun., 1994—, Forest Lake C. of C., 2003-; chair sch. adv. com. Chippewa Elem. Ctr., St. Paul, 1986-87; bd. dirs. YWCA, La Crosse, 1980-81; adv. com. Social Work Dept. U. Wis., La Crosse, 1981-82; bd. dirs. Ret. Sr. Vol. Program, La Crosse, 1980-82; founder, exec. dir. Abuse Resource Ctr., St. Paul, 1988-92; exec. dir. Abuse Resource Ctr. Hugo, 1992-93. Recipient Bertha Provine Oxford Coll. scholarship, Miami (Ohio) U., Oxford, 1968, Alumni Assn. Departmental Hons. award, Calif. State U., L.A., 1971. Mem. Minn. Women in Psychology, Minn. Women Psychologists (social action chair 1992-94, Greater Minn. co-chair 1993-94, steering com. 1992—, vice-chair 1994-95, chair 1995-97), Minn. Psychol. Assn., Minn. Soc. Clin. Hypnosis, Alpha Omicron Pi. Roman Catholic. Avocations: sewing, bicycling, crafts, running, canoeing. Office: 20 North Lake St Ste 308 Forest Lake MN 55025 Office Phone: 651-464-8918, 651-468-8918.

SKRIP, LINDA JEAN, nurse; b. Neenah, Wis., Apr. 16, 1963; d. Donald Charles and Kathryn Amelia Patrikus; m. Stephen Michael, May 21, 1988. BSN, U. Wis., 1986. RN Va. Staff nurse U. Hosp. Ill., Chgo., 1986-87; asst. clin. nurse mgr. Northwestern Meml. Hosp., Chgo., 1987-88; nursing coord. Pitt County Meml. Hosp., Greenville, N.C., 1988-91; nursing supr. Chesapeake (Va.) Gen. Hosp., 1991-92, case mgmt. coord., 1992—2000, cert. case mgr., 1993-2000, dir. care mgmt., 2000—02. Roman Catholic. Avocations: tennis, travel. Home: 1253 Smokey Mountain Trail Chesapeake VA 23320-8187 E-mail: ljsccm@msn.com.

SKRUPKY, ELAINE CHARLOTTE, art educator; b. Amery, Wis., Nov. 11, 1927; d. Herbert Roy Peterson and Nina Louise Olson; m. Hartferd Gay Elaine Charlotte Peterson, June 24, 1950 (dec. Aug. 2, 1982); children: Lynn, Jenene, Van(dec.), Renée, Shawndel(dec.). BSc in Art and English, River Falls U., 1949. Art supr. Rice Lake (Wis.) Schs., 1949—50; art tchr. U. Wis. Ctr., Rice Lake, 1968—69, VIII Pk., Jensen Beach, Fla., 1993—. Author: Poetry Guild Anthology, 1996 (Editors Choice award, 1996), The Best Poems of the 90's, 1997 (named Internat. Poet of Merit, Internat. Soc. Poetry, 1997), Of Moonlight and Wishes, 1997, A Celebration of Poets, 1998, sound of Poetry, 1998. Chmn. and organizer Aquafest Art Show, Rice Lake, 1960—75; chmn. state fine arts Wis. Fedn. Women's Clubs, 1972—74, state drama chmn., 1974—76, dist. art chmn., 1976; pres. Daubers Guild, Rice Lake, 1976—77; chmn. Am. Cancer Dr., Rice Lake, 1979—80, Heart Drive, Rice Lake, 1980; organizer The Red Barn Theatre, Rice Lake. Named Outstanding Woman in Arts, Wis. Federated Woman's Club, 2000; named to Internat. Hall of Fame, Internat. Soc. Poetry, 2000; recipient State Art award, Rural Artists Wis., 1979, 4th runner-up, Ms. Nat. Sr Queen Contest, 1998, State Achievement award, Wis. Federated Woman's Club, 2000, 2001. Mem.: Art League, Alpha Psi Omega, Art Gallery Coop, Poetry Club. Avocations: painting, writing, piano, singing, acting. Home (Summer): 1310 D Orchard Beach Ln Rice Lake WI 54868 Home (Winter): 10701 S Ocean Dr Jensen Beach FL 34957 Personal E-mail: peterson@mailstation.com.

SKRZYCKI, MARYANN, physics educator; d. John and Dorothy Krywcun; m. Lawrence Robert Skrzycki, July 28, 1973; children: Kristin S., Jeffrey A., Jonathan M. BS in Edn., Physics, SUNY, Buffalo, 1972, MS in Edn., Physics, 1975. Sci. tchr. Kenmore West Sr. H.S., Kenmore, NY, 1972—73, Cheektowaga Ctrl. H.S., Cheektowaga, NY, 1975—77, Loudoun Valley H.S., Purcellville, Va., 1982—84; sci. tchr. & sci. dept. chair Pk. View H.S., Sterling, Va., 1985—. Mem.: Loudoun Edn. Assn. (assoc.), Phi Delta Kappa. Office: Park View High School 400 West Laurel Ave Sterling VA 20164 Office Phone: 703-444-7500.

SKURDENIS, JULIANN VERONICA, librarian, educator, writer, editor; b. July 13, 1942; d. Julius J. and Anna M. (Zilys) S.; m. Lawrence J. Smircich, Aug. 21, 1965 (div. July 1978); m. Paul J. Lalli, Oct. 1, 1978; 1 adopted child, Kathryn Leila Skurdenis-Lalli. AB with honors, Coll. New Rochelle, 1964; MS, Columbia U., 1966; MA, Hunter Coll., 1974. Young adult libr. Bklyn. Pub. Libr., 1964-66; periodicals libr., instr. Kingsborough C.C., Bklyn., 1966-67; acquisitions libr. Pratt Inst., Bklyn., 1967-68; acquisitions libr., asst. prof. Bronx (N.Y.) C.C., 1968-75, head tech. svcs., assoc. prof., 1975-97, prof., 1998—. Acting dir. Libr. Resource Learning Ctr., 1994-97, dep. dir., 1997—. Author: Walk Straight Through the Square, 1976, More Walk Straight Through the Square, 1977; contbg. editor Internat. Travel News, 1989—, Travel Your Way/N.Y. Times, 1996-98; travel editor Archaeology mag., 1986-89; contbr. over 500 travel, hist., and archaeol. pieces. N.Y. State fellow, 1960-66, Columbia U. fellow, 1964-66, Pratt Inst. fellow, 1965. Mem. AAUP, Libr. Assn. CUNY (chairwoman numerous coms.), Archaeol. Inst. Am. Avocations: archaeology, travel, travel writing. Office: CUNY Bronx CC University Ave Bronx NY 10453-6994 Office Phone: 718-289-5436. Personal E-mail: julie.skurdenis@optonline.net. Business E-Mail: julie.skurdenis@bcc.cuny.edu.

SKY, ALISON, artist, designer; b. N.Y.C. BFA, Adelphi U., 1967; student, Art Students League, 1967-69, Columbia U. Co-founder, v.p. Sculpture in the Environ./SITE, N.Y.C., 1969-91; co-founder, prin. SITE Projects, N.Y.C., 1970-91. Adj. faculty mem. Parsons Sch. Design, N.Y.C., 1994-95, Cooper Union, N.Y.C., 1995; vis. artist Purchase Coll., SUNY, 1994-95; artist-in-residence Urban Glass, 1995; lectr. in field. Exhbns. include The Venice Biennale, 1975, The Pompidou Ctr. and Louvre, Paris, 1975, The Mus. Modern Art, N.Y.C., 1979, 84, Ronald Feldman Fine Arts, N.Y.C., 1980, 83, The Wadsworth Atheneum, Hartford, Conn., 1980, The Va. Mus. Fine Arts, Richmond, Va., 1980, Neuer Berliner Kunstverein, 1982, Castello Sforzesco, Sala Viscontea, 1983, Victoria and Albert Mus., London, 1984, Nat. Mus. Modern Art, Tokyo, 1985-86, The Triennale di Milano, Italy, 1985, Whitney Mus. Am. Art, N.Y.C., 1985-86, Grey Art Gallery, N.Y.C., 1987-88, Documenta 8, Kassel, Germany, 1987, Am. Craft Mus., N.Y.C., 1996; permanent collections include, Smithsonian Instns., Washington, Mus. Modern Art, N.Y.C., Avery Libr., Columbia U., N.Y.C., Formica Corp., N.J., GSA, Pharr, Tex.; projects include BEST Products, 1979-84, Williwear Ltd., N.Y.C. and London, 1982-89, SITE Studio, 1984, The Mus. Borough of Bklyn., N.Y.C., 1985, Laurie Mallet House Memories, N.Y.C., 1986, Hwy. 86, Vancouver, Can., 1986, Pershing Sq., L.A., 1986, MTV Sets, N.Y.C., 1988, SWATCH, N.Y.C. and Zurich, Switzerland, 1988-90, N.Y.C. Pub. Libr., 1990, Grove Hotel, Boise, Idaho, 1999, U. Conn., 2001, Independence Nat. Hist. Park, Phila., 2003; author: (series of Books) ON SITE, 1971-76, Unbuilt America, 1976; pub. numerous books on art, 1971-76. Design fellow NEA, 1984, 90, Pollock-Krasner Found. fellow, 1991, Fulbright Indo-Am. fellow, 1992. Fellow Am. Acad. Rome. Studio: 60 Greene St New York NY 10012-5139

SKYLAR, ALAYNE, television producer, writer, educator, talent scout, agent; b. N.Y.C., July 12, 1957; BA, Hunter Coll., 1979. Talent agent Funny Face, N.Y.C., 1984-85; owner, pres. Skylar Talent, N.Y.C., 1985-91; freelance TV prodr. various mag. and talk shows, N.Y.C., 1991—; owner, pres. Skylar Prodn., 1997—; owner Automat Cafe, 2003. Spkr. in field.

SLABY, KRISTI LYNN, secondary school educator; b. Rensselaer, Ind., Oct. 30, 1949; d. LaMarr Courtright and Wini Bryant; m. Frank Slaby, May 18, 1978; children: Cami Lynn Nail, Kerianne Lee, Joy Marie Mendenhall. BA, Ball State U., 1971; MLA, Valparaiso U., 1984. Cert. tchr. Ind. HS sci. tchr. Kankakee Valley Sch. Corp, Wheatfield, Ind., 1984—. Author edn. materials. Clk. of session Presbyn. Ch., Rensselaer, 1999—2003. Recipient RadioShack Nat. Tchr. award, 2000. Home: 5669 W 200 N Rensselaer IN 47978 Office: Kankakee Valley HS 3923 W 200 N Rensselaer IN 46392 Office Phone: 219-956-3143. Business E-Mail: kslaby@kv.k12.in.us.

SLACK, CLEMONTENE, education educator; m. Milton Slack. D in Edn., Nova Southeastern U., 1995. Tchr., counselor Rome City Schs., Ga., 1969—99; dir. Reach-A-Youth Mentor Svc., Rome, 1990—95. ESL instr. Consortium Global Edn., 2004—; spkr. in field. Ministries bd. North Rome Church of God; mem. Rome/Floyd Parks and Recreation Assn., 1996—2004. Named Cmty. Resource Person of Yr., Rome Minority Bus. Assn., 1992. Mem.: AAUW (assoc.). Achievements include research in counseling techniques. Office: Shorter Coll 315 Shorter Ave Rome GA 30165 Office Phone: 706-233-7268. Office Fax: 706-233-7437.

SLACK, MOLLY JOHANNA, theater educator; b. Baytown, Tex., Dec. 1, 1951; d. Thomas Edward and Bonnie Burkman Slack. AA, Lon Morris Coll., Jacksonville, Tex., 1972; BA, Trinity U., San Antonio, 1975; M in Liberal Arts, Houston Bapt. U., 1994. Asst. program dir. Houston Bapt. U., 1994—96; tchr. theatre arts Lamar Consol. Sch. Dist., Rosenberg, 1996—. Supts. secondary adv. com. Lamar Consol. Ind. Sch. Dist., Rosenberg, Tex., 1999—2001; site-based mgmt. com. Wessendorff Mid. Sch., 1997—2001, chair dept. fine arts, 2003—, campus coord. U. Interscholastic League, 1996—, bd. mem. PTO, dist. coord. U. Interscholastic League, 2005—. Dir.(designer): Beauty & the Beast, The Pirates of Penzance, Cinderella, H.M.S. Pinafore, Reynard the Fox (Superior One Act Play Festival, 1999), The Adventures of Tom Sawyer, Peter Pan, You're A Good Man, Charlie Brown; set designer Annie, Once Upon a Mattress, Bye, Bye Birdie, Rodger's and Hammerstein's Cinderella, Guys and Dolls. Coord. fine arts related activities Wessendorff Parent/Tchr. Orgn., 2003—06. Recipient Tchr. Yr., Wessendorff Faculty and Staff, 2001; grantee, Lamar Ednl. Found., 2001—02. Mem.: Tex. Ednl. Theatre Assn., Tex. Assn. Gifted and Talented. Avocations: travel, reading, painting, orchids. Home: 14207 Whitecross Drive Houston TX 77083 Office: Wessendorff Middle Sch 5201 Mustang Rosenberg TX 77471 Office Phone: 832-223-3300. E-mail: mslack@lcisd.org.

SLACK, VICKIE, human services administrator; b. Monroe, La., Mar. 27; d. Rufus J. and Minnie (Starr) S. BS, Sacramento State U., 1988; MPA, Golden Gate U., 1989. Phys. therapy asst. Easter Seals, Sacramento, 1983-84; intern aide to Congresswoman Barbara Boxer, Vallejo, Calif., 1986-87; phys. therapist asst. U. Calif.-Davis Med. Ctr., Sacramento, 1984-85; adminstrv. asst. St. Luke Hosp., San Francisco, 1987-88; ins. rep. Am. Nat. Ins. Co., Vallejo, 1988-89; health info. specialist Solano County Health Dept., Vallejo, Calif., 1990-93; supr., health educator, dir. tobacco edn. programs Bay Area Urban League, Oakland, Calif., 1993-95, health and human svc. dir., 1995—. Mem. Housing and Redevel. Commn., Cultural Commn., Commn. on Aging and Sister City Assn., City of Vallejo. Mem. NAFE, NAACP, Nat. Assn. Pub. Adminstrs., Nat. Council Negro Women, Delta Sigma Theta. Democrat. Baptist. Office: Bay Area Urban League 2201 Broadway Ste 100A Oakland CA 94612-3039 Home: #120 55 Springstowne CTR Vallejo CA 94591-5566

SLACK-BEARD, KAY LANE, secondary school educator; d. Harlan Murl and Patsy Ray Lane; m. Barry Beard, July 20, 2005; children: John Hatfield, Jayson Hatfield, Sam Beard. BS in Edn., U. Houston, 1979, MS in Health Edn., 1992; postgrad., Baylor Coll. Medicine, Dallas. Tchr. health and peer assistance leadership Dulles H.S., Suger Land, Tex., 1981—. Instr. CPR Am. Heart Assn., bd. dirs. Sugar Land, 2000—01, Habitat for Humanity, Fort Bend County, Tex., 2000—02. Named Fort Bend County Woman of Yr., 2005; named one of 100 Women, Eckerd, 2000; recipient Tchr. award, Disney, 2000, Tchr. of Yr. award, Walmart, 2003. Mem.: Delta Kappa Gamma. Republican. Avocation: golf. Office: Dulles High School 550 Dulles Ave Sugar Land TX 77478

SLADE, BARBARA ANN, art educator; b. Bklyn., May 15, 1941; d. Steve Licata, Margie Licata; m. George Drakos, Sept. 16, 1961 (div.); 1 child, Matthew Drakos; m. Fred Slade, Aug. 18, 1996. Student, Sch. Art and Design, N.Y., 1955—59; AAS, Fash Inst. Tech., N.Y., 1961; student, Art Student League, N.Y., 1975—83. Instr. art U. Nev., Las Vegas, 1992—93, Las Vegas Art Mus., Las Vegas, 1993—97, Sun City Summerlin Art Club, Las Vegas, 1995—. Lectr., demo in pastel Sun City DelWeb Art Club, 2001. One-woman shows include Sunrize Libr. Gallery, 1993, Las Vegas Art Mus., 1991, 2005, exhibitions include Sapienza Art Gallery, 1995; contbr. Mem.: Nev. Pastel Soc. (pres., co-founder 1998—2006). Avocation: birdwatching. Home: 1775 Montessouri St Las Vegas NV 89117-1623 Office Phone: 702-254-1935.

SLADE, BARBIE EVETTE DELK, special education educator; b. Orlando, Fla., Sept. 5, 1961; d. Jack Everett and Barbara Nell (Corley) Delk; m. Mark Anthony Slade, Sept. 22, 1984; children: Nicholas Mark, Wesley Evan. BS with honors, U. So. Miss., 1992, MS, 2000, postgrad. in spl. edn., 2001—. Tchr. specific learning disability K-12 North Forrest HS, Hattiesburg, Miss., 1992—2006; tchr. specific learning disability 7-12 Bronx Cmty. Sch. Social Justice, 2006—. Mem. various coms. and couns. North Forrest H.S., 1996—. Vol. Spl. Olympics, cmty. elderly, Civitan Camp; vol. cmty theatre. Mem.: U. So. Miss. Alumni Assn., Am. Fedn. Tchrs., Coun. Exceptional Children. Baptist. Avocation: reading. Office: Bronx Cmty Sch Social Justice 350 Gerard Ave Bronx NY 10451 Office Phone: 718-402-8481. Personal E-mail: sladebl@hotmail.com.

SLADE, MARGOT S., editor; d. Melvin S.; m. Nicholas Baxter, Apr. 26, 1981. BA, Wellesley Coll.; MA, Columbia Univ. Various positions NY Times, 1981—2001; editor, sr. dir. Consumer Reports, 2001—. Mem.: Phi Beta Kappa. Office: Consumer Reports 101 Truman Ave Yonkers NY 10703-1044 Office Phone: 914-378-2665. Office Fax: 914-378-2900.*

SLADE-REDDEN, DEBRA KAY, biology educator; b. Lake Jackson, Tex., May 13, 1960; d. James Ewell and Gladyne Bell Slade; children: James Slade Redden, Cory Wain Redden, Daniel Gene Redden. BAT, Sam Houston State U., Huntsville, Tex., 1981. Cert. elem. educator Tex., spl. edn. educator Tex., biology educator Tex., driver's edn. educator Tex. Biology/aquatic sci. tchr. New Caney HS, Tex., 1983—; waitress Black-Eyed Pea, Conroe, Tex., 1986—. Master tchr. ARMADA project, Narragansett, RI, 2005—. Named Secondary Tchr. of Yr., New Caney Ind. Sch. Dist., 2005—06. Mem.: Tex. Marine Educators Assn., Sci. Tchrs. Assn. Tex., Nat. Sci. Tchrs. Assn., Nat. Marine Educators Assn. Presbyterian. Avocation: texas marine educators association. Home: 201 Forest Way Conroe TX 77304 Office: New Caney HS 21650 Loop 494 New Caney TX 77357 Office Phone: 281-577-2800. Office Fax: 281-354-0816. Personal E-mail: dsladeredden@hotmail.com. E-mail: dredden@newcaneyisd.org.

SLAGLE, JUDITH BAILEY, literature/language educator; b. Kingsport, Tenn., Nov. 20, 1949; d. Dewey Bert and Louise (McGlothlin) Bailey; m. Donald Clarence Slagle, Dec. 27, 1969. BS in English, East Tenn. State U., 1983, MA, 1985; PhD, U. Tenn., 1991. Writer, prodr. Tenn. Eastman Co., Kingsport, 1968-87; grad. teaching asst. East Tenn. State U., Johnson City, 1984-85; teaching assoc. U. Tenn., Knoxville, 1987-91, dir. Writing Ctr., 1991-92; instr. English lit. and lang. Carson-Newman Coll., 1992-93; asst. prof. English lit. and lang. Middle Tenn. State U., Murfreesboro, 1993—. Editor of plays, author critical material: (books) Thomas Shadwell's The Lancashire Witches, and Tegue o Divelly the Irish-Priest: A Critical Old Spelling Edition, 1991, Thomas Shadwell's The Woman-Captain: A Critical Old-Spelling Edition, 1993. Violinist Kingsport Symphony Orch., 1971-87, U. Tenn. Civic Orch., Knoxville, 1988-91, Middle Tenn. State U. Orch., 1993—; bd. dirs. Kingsport Fine Arts Ctr., 1986-87. John C. Hodges Competitive Dissertation fellow U. Tenn., 1990; recipient Chancellor's award U. Tenn., 1991; summer grantee NEH, 1994. Mem. MLA, South Atlantic MLA, Am. Soc. 18th-Century Studies. Avocation: music.

SLAGLE, LUSETTA, librarian; b. Johnson City, Tenn., Oct. 31, 1959; d. Jimmie S. and Margaret Lamira (Francis) Slagle. BS in Bible and Christian Edn., Roanoke Bible Coll., 1981; MLS, Vanderbilt U., 1982. Libr. Roanoke Bible Coll., Elizabeth City, N.C., 1982-86; reference libr. Milligan College, Tenn., 1986-88; dir. libr. svcs., registrar Bristol (Tenn.) U., 1988-90; br. libr. Scott Co. (Va.) Pub. Libr., 1991-94, Washington County/Gray Libr., Tenn., 1994—. Mem. Assn. Christian Librs., Tenn. Libr. Assn., Boone Tree Libr. Assn., Fellowship of Christian Librs. and Info. Specialists. Avocations: cross stitch, reading, crafts. Office: Gray Libr 5026 Bobby Hicks Hwy Gray TN 37615

SLAGLE, PENNY LEE, physical education educator; b. Williston, N.D., Aug. 18, 1954; d. Stafford S. Johnson and Bertha Grenz-Johnson; m. Rich Glen Slagle, Dec. 27, 1980; children: Lacey Lee Hendrickson, Jordan David, Tucker John. BA, Williston State Coll., ND, 1974; BS, Dickinson State U., ND, 1976; M in Ednl. Leadership, N.D. State U., Fargo, 2000. Phys. edn. instr. Williston State Coll., 1978—83, women's basketball coach, 1976—92; elem. phys. edn. instr. Williston Pub. Sch. Dist. #1, 1993—95, h.s. phys. edn. instr., 1995—. Women's basketball team mgr. Olympics Sports Com., 1984—85, women's basketball mgr. south team, 1984—85. Named Coach of Yr., Nat. Jr. Coll. Athletic Assn., Region 13, 1979, 1980, 1981, 1982, 1984, Coll. Coach of Yr., N.D. Sportswriters and Sportscasters, 1981—82, 1983—84, Nat. Jr. Coll. Coach of Yr., Women's Basketball Coaches Assn., 1983—84, Women in Sports Program, 1983—84. Mem.: Nat. Jr. Coll. Women's Basketball Coaches Assn. (v.p. 1983—86, pres. 1986—92), Jr. Coll. Women's Basketball Coaches Assn. (sec. 1980—83). Democrat-Npl. Lutheran. Home: 3021 13th Ave E Williston ND 58801 Office: Willsiton High Sch 502 W Highland Dr Williston ND 58801 Office Phone: 701-572-0967. Office Fax: 701-572-5449. Personal E-mail: penny.slagle@sendit.nodak.edu.

SLATE, MARY ELIZABETH, real estate agent, medical/surgical nurse; b. Ashburn, Ga., Jan. 9, 1938; d. Jacob and Mary Elizabeth Hampton; m. Robert W. Slate; children: Robert W. Jr., Elizabeth A. Cook, G. Brian, Benjamin W., RN St. Joseph's Hosp., Atlanta, 1961; cert. real estate agt. North Ga. Tech. Sch., 1986. Surg. nurse St. Joseph's Hosp., Atlanta, 1961—64, Stephens County Hosp., Toccoa, 1971—78; real estate agt. Prudential Key Realty, 1986—. Recipient Over One Million in Sales award, Prudential Key Realty, 2000—05. Roman Catholic. Home and Office: 172 Pine Valley Dr Toccoa GA 30577-1838 Office Phone: 706-886-3404.

SLATER, CATHRYN BUFORD, former federal agency administrator; married; 5 children. BSE in English with honors, U. Ark., 1969, MA in English with high honors, 1972; postgrad., Duke U., 1990. Spl. asst., liaison natural & cultural resources State Ark., Little Rock, 1984-88; state hist. preservation officer, dir. Ark. Hist. Preservation Program, Little Rock, 1988—2000; coun. chmn. Adv. Coun. on Historic Preservation, 1997—2001. Lectr. English dept. U. Ark., Little Rock, 1975-84, 88—. Bd. dirs. Nat. Conf. State Hist. Preservation Officers, 1990-94, exec. com., 1992-94, chmn. critical issues com., 1992-94, sec., 1993-95; bd. dirs. Shelter Battered Women, Pulaski County, Ark., Ctrl. H.S. Parent Tchr. Student Assn., Little Rock, Pulaski Heights United Meth. Ch. Mem. Nat. Pks. & Conservation Assn., Nature Conservancy, Nat. Trust Hist. Preservation, Sierra Club, Wilderness Soc., Audubon Soc. Avocations: reading, hiking, canoeing, camping, backpacking.

SLATER, LORI ANNETTE, project manager; b. Houston, Aug. 8, 1964; d. Ted Gerald Patterson, JoAnn Patterson. AAS in Bus., Blinn Coll., 1984; BA in Applied Behavioral Sci., Nat. Louis U., 2000. Cert. profl. project mgr. Sec. Century Coating, Houston, 1984—85; asst. Ted's Pool Svc., Houston,

1985—88; sec. Freestone County Attorney's Office, Fairfield, Tex., 1989—90; dispatcher Tex. Instruments, Inc., Houston, 1990—93, Hewlett Packard Co., Atlanta, 1993—95; global accounts tech. adminstr. Hewlett Packard Co., Atlanta, 1995—98; bus. process analyst Hewlett Packard Co., Atlanta, 1998—2000, project/program mgr., 2000—. Mem. Friends of the Ctr. So. Poverty Law Ctr., Montgomery, 2001—, founding mem. Nat. Campaign for Tolerance, 2001—. Mem.: Project Mgmt. Inst. Avocations: reading, tennis, watching old movies. Business E-Mail: lori.slater@hp.com.

SLATER, REBECCA ANNE, music educator, director; b. Milw., Wis., Nov. 28, 1962; d. Delbert Edwin and Margaret Gene Lins; m. Jeffrey A. Slater, Aug. 16, 1986; children: Daniel, Paul. BS, Ball State U., Muncie, Ind., 1984; MM, U. Cin., Ohio, 1990. Adj. prof. Xavier U., Cin., Ohio, 1989; dir., owner Slater Music Acad., Ft. Thomas, Ky., 1996—; music specialist Summit County Day Sch., Cin., 2000—; music dir. St. Pius X Ch., Edgewood, Ky., 2006—. Mem.: Am. Schulwerk Assn., Nat. Assn. Pastoral Musicians, Mu Phi Epsilon. Home: 40 Brigadier Ct Wilder KY 41076 Office: Slater Music Acad PO Box 75049 Fort Thomas KY 41075

SLATER, VALERIE A., lawyer; b. Passaic, NJ, Oct. 13, 1952; BA magna cum laude, Allegheny Coll., 1974; JD, Cath. U. Am., 1977. Bar: DC 1977, US Ct. Appeals (DC cir.) 1978, US Dist. Ct. (DC dist.) 1982, US Ct. Internat. Trade 1984, US Ct. Appeals (fed. cir.) 1984. Ptnr. Akin Gump Strauss Hauer & Feld LLP, Washington, 1990—2003, ptnr., chair internat. trade practice group, 2003—. Mem.: Phi Beta Kappa. Office: Akin Gump Strauss Hauer & Feld LLP 1333 New Hampshire Ave NW Washington DC 20036-1564 Office Phone: 202-887-4112. Office Fax: 202-887-4288. Business E-Mail: vslater@akingump.com.

SLATER, VALERIE PERIOLAT, volunteer; b. Michigan City, Ind., May 6, 1949; d. Emmett Gerard and Alma Rosalee (Keys) Wozniak; m. John Grey Periolat, Jan. 24, 1970 (div. Aug. 1975); 1 child, Jason; m. Donald Joseph Slater, Mar. 30, 1976; stepchildren: Meredith M., Julie. Cert. in French, L'Inst. De'Catholique, Paris, 1968; student, Western Mich. U., 1968-69, U. South Fla., 1973-75. Registrar Tampa (Fla.) Bus. Coll., 1971-75; adminstrv. asst. Crown Ins., Tampa, 1975-77; key employee S&A Restaurant Corp., Atlanta and Miami, Fla., 1977-82; realtor Century 21, Atlanta, 1982-84; owner Horizon Concepts, Plano, Tex., 1988-89. Co-owner Horizon Properties, Plano, 1979-89. Vol. HCA Med. Ctr., Plano, 1986-95; bd. dirs. Cystic Fibrosis Found., Dallas, 1988, 89, 2000. Republican. Roman Catholic. Home: 5785 Stony Point Rd Barboursville VA 22923-1804

SLATER, WANDA MARIE WORTH, property manager; b. Thurston, Ohio, Feb. 18, 1927; adopted d. Daniel Harrison and Grace Marie (Neel) Worth; m. Charles Edwin Slater (dec. Sept. 2005); children: Margaret Grace(dec.), Daniel Worthington(dec.), Donald Edwin. Student, Denison U., 1941-45, Bethany Coll., 1945-46. Recipient certs. Ohio Ho. Reps. and Senate, 116th Ohio Assembly, Creative Living, Columbus. Sub. tchr. Licking County Schs., Union Twp., Ohio, 1946; clerical typist Farm Bur. Ins. Co., Columbus, Ohio, 1947-49; salesperson Avon Co., Clyde, Ohio, 1954-63; dep. registrar Sandusky County, Ohio, 1960-64; notary pub. State of Ohio, Clyde, 1965-78, Hebron-Buckeye Lake, Ohio, 1978-98. Owner, mgr. rental property. Editor OFWC Buckeye mag., 1970-74, 88-98. Pres. Welcome Wagon, Clyde, 1957, Clyde Jr. League of Women, 1966, Leads-Licking County Cmty. Action Com., 1988, 94, 2000-01. Recipient Disting. Leadership award 1992, certificate of appreciation CARE. Mem.: Twentieth Century Club (pres. 1976—77), Order Eastern Star (worthy matron Clyde chpt. 1965, 1978, Hebron Eagon chpt. 1989, 1994, 2001), Mut. and Civic Improvement Club (pres. 1994—), Ohio Fedn. Women's Clubs (pres. 1986—88), Gen. Fedn. Women's Clubs Marionettes (pres. 1988—). Republican. Avocations: monologues, flower arranging, travel, crafts. Home and Office: 36 Worth Dr Hebron OH 43025-9760

SLATER-FREEDBERG, JILL REBECCA, dermatologist; b. Utica, N.Y., Mar. 27, 1955; d. Howard Jay and Judith Dube Slater; m. Paul David Freedberg, June 5, 1988; children: Abraham, Agatha. MD, Tufts Sch. Medicine, Boston, 1988. Dermatologist Lexington Dermatology, Mass., 1998—. Mem.: Mass. Acad. Dermatology, New Eng. Dermatology, Am. Acad. Dermatology.

SLATON, DANIELLE VICTORIA, professional soccer player; b. San Jose, Calif., June 10, 1980; Majored in psychology, Santa Clara U., Calif., 1998—2001. Capt. U.S. Under-16 Nat. Team, 1996—97; mem. U.S. Under-21 Nat. Team, 1999, starter, Nordic Cup championship team, 1999; soccer player, defender U.S. Women's Nat. Team, 1999—; mem. U.S. soccer team Summer Olympics, Sydney, Australia, 2000; team mem. Carolina Courage, WUSA. Finalist Mo. Athletic Club award, 2000, 2001, Hermann trophy, 2001; named third team All-Am., NSCAA, 1998, first team All-Am., 1999, 2001, 2002. Office: US Soccer Fedn 1801 S Prairie Ave Chicago IL 60616

SLATTER, MICHELE DENISE, science educator; BS, Spelman Coll., Atlanta, 1993; MEd, U. Buffalo, 1996. Cert. sci. edn. Ga. Profl. Stds. Commn. Sci. tchr. Dekalb County Bd. Edn., Decatur, Ga., 1997—2004, 2005—. E-mail: mdslatter@bellsouth.net.

SLATTERY, KATHLEEN MILICENT, language educator; b. Riverside, Calif., Mar. 25, 1952; d. Donald Joseph and Mary Joan Mawn; m. Peter Nial Slattery (div.); 1 child, Noah Michael. BA in Biology, U. Calif., Riverside, 1974; MA in Marine Biology, Moss Landing Marine Lab., 1980; MA, Sch. Internat. Tng., 1999. Biologist, ecologist Moss Landing (Calif.) Marine Lab., 1976—78; ESL instr., tech. coord. Salinas (Calif.) Adult Sch., 1989—. Contbr. articles to profl. jours. Coord., cmty. organizer Nuc. Weapons Freeze, Monterey County, Calif., 1983—85. Mem.: ACLU, TESOL, LWV (nat. security com. chair, action com. chair, v.p.), Calif. TESOL, Salinas Valley Fedn. Tchrs. (negotiator 1999—2004, union v.p. 2003—04), Sierra Club. Democrat. Office: Salinas Adult Sch 20 Sherwood Pl Salinas CA 93906 E-mail: kslattery@salinas.ca.us.k12.edu.

SLATTERY, MICHELE G., research scientist; b. Lawrence, Kans., May 19, 1944; d. Jefferson Briscoe and Hope Hunn Goldman; m. Ronald J. Slattery, Aug. 24, 1990; m. Frank C. English (div.). BA, U. Tex., 1966. Staff rsch. tech. M.D. Anderson Hosp., Houston, 1966—70; engr. Honeywell, Inc., San Diego, 1970—73; sr. rsch. assoc. Scripps Rsch. Inst., La Jolla, Calif., 1973—76; sr. staff rsch. assoc. U. Calif., San Diego, 1976—89; rsch. assoc. Ochsner Med. Found., New Orleans, 1989—93; rsch. specialist, coord. Tulane U. Sch. Medicine, New Orleans, 1993—96; owner, mgr. Cunral Rsch. Specialists, Metairie, La., 1997—. Compliance officer Clin. Rsch. Specialist, Metairie, La., 1997—. Contbr. articles to profl. jours. Mem. Diamondhead Performers Act, 2005—; Krewe of Diamondhead Soc., 2000—; mem. Lions Club, 1999—2003. Mem.: Diamondhead Yacht Club. Republican. Avocations: gardening, travel, walking. Home: 948 Kalikimaka Pl Diamondhead MS 39525 Office: Clin Rsch Assoc 3939 Houma Blvd Metairie LA 70006

SLATTON, BARBARA, secondary school educator; b. Haleyville, Ala., Mar. 24, 1948; d. Hosie S. Cagle and L.V. Sartin; m. Terry Lynn Slatton, Sept. 14, 1968; children: Kimberly Dawn Howell, Christy Lynn Cagle, Scott Alan, Holly Diane. MS, U. of North Ala., Florence, 1990; BS in Biology, U. North Ala., 1992. Sci. tchr. Winston County H.S., Double Springs, Ala., 1987—; social worker II Dept. of Human Resources. Upward Bound tutor/coord. Bevill State C.C., Hamilton, Ala., 1999—; sponsor Future Teachers of Ala., Double Springs, Ala., 1990—. Sunday sch. tchr. Ch. of Christ, Haleyville, Ala., 1995—2006. Scholar Fulbright Meml. Tchrs. Program scholar, Fulbright Found., 2001. Mem.: Alpha Delta Kappa (assoc.; pres. 2006). R-Consevative. Christian. Office: Winston County High School Holly Grove Rd Double Springs AL 35553 Office Phone: 205-489-5593. Personal E-mail: wchs_slatton@yahoo.com.

SLAUGHTER, ANNE-MARIE, dean; m. Andrew Moravcsik; children: Edward, Alexander. Grad. magna cum laude, Princeton U., 1980; JD cum laude, Harvard U., 1985; MPhil, Oxford U., 1982, DPhil, 1992. Tchr. law U. Chgo.; rschr. Harvard U., J. Sinclair Armstrong prof. internat., fgn., and comparative law, dir. internat. legal studies program; Bert G. Kerstetter univ. prof. politics and internat. affairs Princeton U., dean Woodrow Wilson sch. pub. and internat. affairs, 2002—. Bd. dirs. McDonalds Corp., Coun. Fgn. Rels., New Am. Found., Can. Inst. Internat. Governance Innovation; spkr. in field. Author: (book) A New World Order; contbr. articles to profl. jours. Covener, acad. co-chair Princeton Project on Nat. Security. Recipient Francis Deak Prize, Am. Jour. Internat. Law, 1990, 1994. Fellow: Am. Acad. Arts and Scis.; mem.: Am. Soc. Internat. Law (pres. 2002—04). Office: Princeton Univ 424 Robertson Hall Princeton NJ 08544-1013 E-mail: slaughtr@princeton.edu.

SLAUGHTER, GLORIA JEAN, elementary school educator; b. Norfolk, Va., Nov. 20, 1940; d. Cloyce Miner and Mary Leatrice (McClure) McClurkin; m. John Wilson Slaughter, June 4, 1961; children: Hugh Leland, Lara Lee BS, U. South Ala., 1972; MEd, Ga. State U., 1984. Tchr. first grade Ocean Gate Elem., NJ, 1968—70, Old Shell Rd. Sch., Mobile, Ala., 1972—80; tchr.second grade Columbia Elem., Decatur, Ga., 1980—2002; ret., 2002. Participant DeKalb Neighborhood Leadership Inst., Decatur, 1986; exec. com. Dem. Party, Decatur, 1990—; mem. Up and Out of Poverty, Atlanta, 1990-94, Jobs With Peace, Atlanta, 1981-89; bd. mem. WRFG Radio Mem. Orgn. DeKalb Educators (pres. 1984-86, pub. rels. 1986—), Ga. Assn. Educators (governing bd. 1991-94, resolution com. 1992-94, Hall of Fame award 2002) Methodist. Avocations: reading, gardening. Home: 567 Raven Springs Trl Stone Mountain GA 30087-4835

SLAUGHTER, LOUISE MCINTOSH, congresswoman; b. Lynch, Ky., Aug. 14, 1929; d. Oscar Lewis and Grace (Byers) McIntosh; m. Robert Slaughter, 1956; children: Megan Rae, Amy Louise, Emily Robin. BS in Microbiol., U. Ky., Lexington, 1951, MPH, 1953; D (hon.), U. Ky., 2006. Bacteriologist Ky. Dept. Health, Louisville, 1951-52, U. Ky., 1952-53; market rschr. Procter & Gamble, Cin., 1953-56; mem. Monroe County Legislature, NY, 1976—79; regional coord. Staff of Sec. State Mario Cuomo, NY, 1976—78, Staff of Lt. Gov. Mario Cuomo, NY, 1979—82; mem. NY State Assembly, 1982—86, US Congress from 28th NY dist., 1987—, ranking minority mem. rules com., Dem. chair Congl. Arts Caucus, Dem. chair Congl. Pro-Choice Caucus, mem. Dem. steering and policy com., mem. Commn. Security and Cooperation in Europe. Del. Dem. Nat. Conv., 1972, 76, 80, 88, 92, 96; mem. Nat. Ctr. for Policy Alternatives Adv. Bd., League of Women Voters, Nat. Women's Polit. Caucus. Named Lay Educator of Yr., Phi Delta Kappa Internat., Rochester chpt., 1999; recipient Disting. Pub. Health Legislator award, Pub. Health Assn., 1997, Award for Outstanding Arts Leadership in the US Ho. Reps., US Conf. Mayors and Ams. for the Arts, 1998, Humane Legislator of Yr., Am. Humane Assn., 2003, Woman of Vision award, Women in Film and Vision, 2004, Sidney R. Yates Nat. Arts Advocacy award, Nat. Assembly State Arts Agencies. Democrat. Episcopalian. Office: US Ho Reps 2469 Rayburn Ho Office Bldg Washington DC 20515-3228 Office Phone: 202-225-3615.*

SLAUGHTER-DEFOE, DIANA TRESA, education educator, psychologist; b. Chgo., Oct. 28, 1941; d. John Ison and Gwendolyn Malva (Armstead) S.; m. Michael Defoe (div.). BA, U. Chgo., 1962, MA, 1964, PhD, 1968. Instr. dept. psychiatry Howard U., Washington, 1967-68; rsch. assoc., asst. prof. Yale U. Child Study Ctr., New Haven, 1968-70; asst. prof. dept. behavioral scis. and edn. U. Chgo., 1970-77; asst. to assoc. prof. edn. and African Am. studies and Ctr. for Urban Affairs and Policy Rsch. (now Inst. for Policy Rsch.) Northwestern U., Evanston, Ill., 1977-90, prof., 1990-97; Constance E. Clayton prof. urban edn. Grad. Sch. Edn. U. Pa., 1998—. Nat. adv. bd. Fed. Ctr. for Child Abuse & Neglect, 1979-82, coord. Human Devel. and Social Policy Program, 1994-97; nat. adv. bd. Learning Rsch. and Devel. Ctr. U. Pitts., Ednl. Rsch. & Devel. Ctr., U. Tex., Austin; formerly chmn., dir. public policy program com. Chgo. Black Child Devel. Inst., 1982-84; dir. Ill. Infant Mental Health Com., 1982-83; res. adv. bd. Chgo. Urban League, 1986-97. Mem. editl. bd.: Ednl. Rschr., 2004—06, NHSA Dialog, 2004—. Human Development, 2006—; contbr. articles to profl. jours. Fellow APA (mem. divsn. ethnic and minority affairs, com. on children, youth and families, devel. psychology, sch. psychology, bd. sci. affairs 1995-97, bd. advancement psychology pub. interest 2003-06, assoc. editor, mem. editl. bd. Child Devel. 1995-98, Disting. Contbn. to Rsch. in Pub. Policy award 1993); mem. Soc. for Rsch. in Child Devel. (governing coun. 1981-87), Am. Ednl. Rsch. Assn. (editl. bds. Rev. Ednl. Rsch., Ednl. Rschr.), Nat. Assn. Edn. Young Children, Assn. Study African Ams. and History, Nat. Head Start (past Rsch. and edn. adv. bd.), Nat. Acad. Scis. (com. on child devel. and publ. policy 1987-93), Delta Sigma Theta. Office: U Pa Grad Sch Edn 3700 Walnut St Philadelphia PA 19104-6216 Office Phone: 215-573-3947. Business E-Mail: dianasd@gse.upenn.edu.

SLAVEN, BETTYE DEJON, psychotherapist; b. New Orleans, Sept. 27, 1946; d. Edward William and Bettye (Ray) DeJ.; m. Richard W. Slaven, Nov. 28, 1968; children: Kelly DeJon Slaven, Richard Daniel. BA, Tex. Tech U., 1969; MA, U. Houston, 1974; postgrad. N. Tex. State U., 1974-76. Lic. counselor, Tex.; lic. marriage and family therapist, Tex. Tchr. Somerville Pub. Schs., Mass., 1971-72, Trinity Episc. Sch., New Orleans, 1972-73, Richardson Ind. Sch. Dist., Tex., 73-74, with Goals for Dallas-Devel., 1975—; pvt. practice psychotherapy, Dallas, 1979-86; therapist family crisis intervention Dallas Ind. Sch. Dist., 1986-97. Bd. dirs. Way Back House-Vol., 1979-82, Freedom Rides Found., bylaws com., 1987-88, Foster Child Advocate Svcs., 1987-90, sec. 1989-90, v.p., pers. chmn., 1990—; founder, project chmn. Women's Way Back House, 1979; project chmn., bd. dirs. Interfaith Housing Coalition, 1987-88; pres. living bible class Highland Park Meth. Ch., Dallas, 1982, 90-91, mem. adminstrv. bd., 1986, also bd. dirs.; adv. bd.; bd. dirs. Dallas County Mental Health Assn., 1989, Dallas Coun. Alcoholism, 1989-90; mem. Communities Found. Tex. Networking, 1986—, Letot task force, 1986, nominating com. Camp Fire Girls Inc., 1987-90; city chmn. Dallas Area Rapid Transit, 1983; pub. affairs chmn. Jr. League Dallas, 1984, resch. and devel. chmn., 1985-86, cmty. v.p., 1986-87, exec. and pub. rels. coms., 1986-87, grantee sr. mentor program at N. Dallas HS, 1995-96; chmn. Camp Task Force for Chronically Ill Children, 1986-87, Spl. Camps for Spl. Kids, 1987-88, bd. dirs. 1988-89, adv. bd., 1989-92; pres. McCulloch Mid. Sch. PTA, 1987—; chmn. Career Day Highland HS PTA, 1990, coll. night chair, 1991; assoc. Pathways to Prevention, 1989-91; pers. chmn. bd. dirs. Foster Child Advocates Svcs., 1989-93; bd. dirs. Dallas Mental Health Assn., 1990-95; co-chmn. Jr. Symphony Ball, 1993; mem. Leadership Dallas Curriculum Planning Com. Edn. Area, 1997-98, chpt. advisor VPO Kappa Kappa Gamma, 1998-98, Ctr. for Brain Health, 2001-; bldg. coord. Safe Haven grant, 1995-96. Named one of Outstanding Young Women in Am., 1980, Leadership Dallas, 1996. Avocations: sailing, swimming, reading.

SLAVICK, ANN LILLIAN, retired art educator; b. Chgo., Sept. 29, 1933; d. Irving and Goldie (Bernstein) Friedman; m. Lester Irwin Slavick, Nov. 21, 1954 (div. Mar. 1987); children: Jack, Rachel. BFA, Sch. of Art Inst. of Chgo., 1973, MA in Art History, Theory, Criticism, 1991. Dir. art gallery South Shore Commn., Chgo., 1963-67; tchr. painting, drawing, crafts Halfway House, Chgo., 1972-73; tchr. studio art Conant H.S., Hoffman Estates, Ill., 1973-74; tchr. art history and studio arts New Trier H.S., Winnetka and Northfield, Ill., 1974-80; tchr. 20th century art history New Trier Adult Edn. Program, Winnetka, 1980-81; tchr. art adult edn. program H.S. Dist. 113, Highland Park, Ill., 1980-81; rschr., writer Art History Notes McDougall-Littel Pub., Evanston, Ill., 1984-85; tchr. art and art history Highland Park and Deerfield (Ill.) H.S., 1980-2000; tchr. art history Coll. of Lake County, Grayslake, Ill., 1986-88; ret., 2000. Faculty chair for visual arts Focus on the Arts, Highland Park H.S., 1981-85, faculty coord. Focus on the Arts, 1987-2005; panelist Ill. Arts Coun. Arts Tour, 1999, Evanston Arts Coun., 2000-02, Ill. Arts Coun. Multidisciplinary Grant Awards, 2001-03; reader advanced placement art history exams, 2003, 04, 06. One woman show Bernal Gallery, 1979, U. Ill., Chgo., 1983, Ann Brierly Gallery, Winnetka, 1984; exhibited paintings, drawings, prints and constrns. throughout Chgo. area; work represented by Art Rental and Sales Gallery, Art Inst. Chgo., 1960-87, Bernal Gallery, 1978-82; group shows at Bernal Gallery; work in pvt. collections in Ill., N.Y., Calif., Ariz., Ohio. Recipient Outstanding Svc. in Art Edn. award Ea. Ill. U., 1992, Mayors award for contbn. to the arts, Highland Park, 1995. Mem.: Ill. Art Edn. Assn., Nat. Art Edn. Assn. Avocations: cooking, reading, theater. Home: 5057 N Sheridan Rd Chicago IL 60640-3127 Office: Highland Park High Sch 433 Vine Ave Highland Park IL 60035-2099 E-mail: annlslavick@aol.com.

SLAVIN, ARLENE, artist; b. N.Y.C., Oct. 26, 1942; d. Louis and Sally (Bryck) Eisenberg; m. Neal Slavin, May 24, 1964 (div. 1979); m. Eric Bregman, Sept. 21, 1980; 1 child, Ethan. BFA, Cooper Union for the Advancement of Sci. and Art, 1964; MFA, Pratt Inst., 1967. One-woman shows include Fischbach Gallery, N.Y., 1973, 1974, 2003, Brooke Alexander Gallery, 1976, Alexander Milliken Gallery, N.Y.C., 1979, 1980, 1981, 1983, U. Colo., 1981, Pratt Inst., N.Y.C., 1981, Am. Embassy, Belgrad, Yugoslavia, 1984, Heckscher Mus., Huntington, N.Y., 1987, Katherine Rich Perlow Gallery, 1988, Chauncey Gallery, Princeton, N.J., 1990, The Gallery Benjamin N. Cardoza Sch. Law, 1991, Norton Ctr. for Arts, Danville, Ky., 1992, Kavesh Gallery, Ketchum, Idaho, 1993, exhibited in group shows at Bass Mus. Art, Fla., Whitney Museum of Art, 1973, The Contempory Arts Center, Cin., 1974, Indpls. Mus. Art, 1974, Madison (Wis.) Art Ctr., Santa Barbara (Calif.) Mus., Winnipeg (Can.) Art Gallery, Gensler Assocs., San Francisco, 1986, Eliane Benson Gallery, Bridgehampton, N.Y., 1987, 1989, 1991, 1993, 2004, City of N.Y. Parks and Recreation Central Park, N.Y.C., 1989, Benton Gallery, Southampton, N.Y., 1991, Parish Mus., Southampton, 1991, Michele Miller Fine Art, 1993, Dillon Gallery, N.Y.C., 1998, Hebrew Union Coll., 2000—01, Fischbach Gallery, 2003, Am. Inst. Archs., 2003, Represented in permanent collections Met. Mus. of Art, N.Y.C., Fogg Art Mus., Cambridge, Mass., Hudson River Mus., Yonkers, N.Y., Heckscher Mus., Huntington, N.Y., Cin. Art Mus., Readers' Digest, Pleasantville, N.Y., pub. commns., N.C. Zoo, 1999, N.Y.C. Parks and Recreation, 1999, NJ Transit, Hoboken Terminal and Middletown Station, NJ, 1999—2002, Forest City Ratner, Ct. St Devel., 2000, Assunpink (NJ) Wildlife Ctr., 2004; subject: bibliography Arlene Slavin: Mediating Public Space, 2001; pub. commns., Town of Chapel Hill, N.C., 2002, PS 89, NYC, 2003, Island Beach State Pk., N.J., 2006, one-woman shows include Fischbach Gallery, N.Y., 2003; artist mem. design team Hillsborough Area Regional Transit, Tampa, Fla., 2003—05. Grantee, Nat. Endowment for Arts, 1977—78, Threshold Found., 1991. Home: 119 E 18th St New York NY 10003-2107 Office Phone: 212-777-3042. E-mail: slavin@arleneslavin.com.

SLAVIN, ROSANNE SINGER, textile converter; b. N.Y.C., Mar. 24, 1930; d. Lee H. and Rose (Winkler) Singer; divorced; children: Laurie Jo, Sharon Lee. Student, U. Ill. Prodn. converter Doucet Fabrics, silk prints, N.Y.C., 1953-57; sales mgr., mdse. mgr. print divsn. Crown Fabrics, N.Y.C., 1957-65; owner Matisse Fabrics, Inc. printed fabrics (now Hottmomma Inc.), N.Y.C., 1965—. Recipient Tommy award Am. Printed Fabrics Coun., 1978, 93; designated ofcl. printed fabric supplier for U.S. Olympic swimteam, 1984. Office: 1412 Broadway Ste 1975 New York NY 10018 Office Phone: 212-354-9118.

SLAVOFF, HARRIET EMONDS, learning disabilities teacher, consultant; b. Elmer, N.J., Mar. 18, 1931; d. Lewis Arthur and Margaret (Miles) Emonds; m. Eugene Victor Slavoff, Feb. 3, 1951; children: Stephen, Stephanie Slavoff Perry, Eugene Jr. BA, Glassboro Coll., 1969, MA, 1976. Cert. tchr., N.J. Tchr. kindergarten Olivet Sch., Pittsgrove Twp., N.J., 1953; remedial tchr. Upper Pittsgrove Sch., 1964-74; learning disabilities tchr. cons. Salem County Schs., Woodstown, N.J., 1976, Pittsgrove Twp. Sch., 1977-78, Oldmans Twp. Sch., Pedricktown, N.J., 1979-83, Logan Sch., Bridgeport, N.J., 1985; child study team coord. East Greenwich Schs., Mickleton, N.J., 1987-93; supr. student tchrs. Rowan Coll., 1992-94. Learning disabilties cons.; ct. clk., Elmer, N.J., 1976, chair Juvenile Conf. Com., 1976-82; adj. prof. Rowan Coll., 1993-96. Pub. History of Elmer, 1893-1993, 1993. Mem. election bd. Dem. com., Elmer; mem. ch. choir; pres. Elmer PTA. Mem.: DAR, Country Garden Club (pres. 2002—03). Avocations: library work, flowers, crafts, reading. Home: 111 Front St Elmer NJ 08318-2138

SLAWSKY, DONNA SUSAN, librarian, singer; b. N.Y.C., Jan. 18, 1956; d. Samuel Slawsky and Lillian (Freizer) Alexander. BA, City Coll. N.Y., 1977; M of Infor. Libr. Sci., Pratt Inst., 1998. Coord. NYNEX Market Info. Ctr., White Plains, NY, 1985—87; dir. Info. Ctr./Archives, exhbns. curator HarperCollins Pubs., N.Y.C., 1988—99; singer N.Y.C., 1987—; dir. content devel. BuyerWeb, Inc., N.Y.C., 1999—2000; founder Info Diva, N.Y.C., 2001—02, Mixed Beadia Jewelry, 2004—; mgr. indexing for digital archive Scholastic, Inc., N.Y.C., 2002—. Contbr. articles to profl. jours. Pres. Assn. HarperCollins Employees, N.Y.C., 1990-94; dir. Tenants Assn., N.Y.C., 1994. Recipient Schubertiade Lieder Competition award 92d St. Y, N.Y.C., 1990. Mem.: Am. Soc. Info. Sci. and Tech., Assn. Ind. Info. Profls., Profl. Women Singers Assn. (treas. 1992—96, mem.-at-large 1997—, webmaster 2001—), Spl. Librs. Assn., Beta Phi Mu. Avocations: bicycling, theater, jewelry designing. Office: Scholastic Inc 568 Broadway Rm 1045 New York NY 10012 Office Phone: 212-343-7716. E-mail: dslawsky@scholastic.com.

SLAYMAN, CAROLYN WALCH, geneticist, educator; b. Portland, Maine, Mar. 11, 1937; d. John Weston and Ruth Dyer (Sanborn) Walch; m. Clifford L. Slayman; children: Andrew, Rachel BA with highest honors, Swarthmore Coll., 1958; PhD, Rockefeller U., 1963; DSc (hon.), Bowdoin Coll., 1985. Instr., then asst. prof. Case Western Res. U., Cleve., 1967; from asst. prof. to prof. genetics Yale U. Sch. Medicine, New Haven, 1967—, Sterling prof. genetics, 1991—, chmn. dept. genetics, 1984-95, dep. dean acad. and sci. affairs, 1995—. Chmn. genetic basis of disease rev. commn. NIH, 1981—85, nat. adv. gen. med. scis. coun., 1989—93; bd. dirs. J. Weston Walch Pub., Portland, Maine, Applera Corp.; mem. sci. rev. bd. Howard Hughes Med. Inst., 1992—97. Mem. editl. bd. Jour. Biol. Chemistry, 1989-94; contbr. articles to sci. jours. Trustee Foote Sch., New Haven, 1983—89, Hopkins Sch., New Haven, 1988—93; bd. overseers Dartmouth Med. Sch., 1997—, Woods Hole Oceanographic Instn., 1997—, Bowdoin Coll., Brunswick, Maine, 1976—88, trustee, 1988—2001. Recipient Deborah Morton award Westbrook Coll., 1986. Mem. Am. Soc. Biol. Chemists, Genetics Soc. Am., Soc. Gen. Physiologists, Am. Soc. Microbiology, Inst. Medicine, Phi Beta Kappa

SLEDGE, CARLA ELISSA, county official; b. Detroit, July 20, 1952; d. Thomas Biggs Sr. and Zephrie (Heard) Griffin; m. Willie Frank Sledge, July 20, 1974; children: Arian Darkell, Ryan Marcel. B in Acctg., Wayne State U., 1973; MA, Eastern Mich. U., 1982. Tchr. Taylor (Mich.) Bd. Edn., 1974-81, Met. Detroit Youth Found., 1981-86; auditor Deloitte & Touche, Detroit, 1982—95; chief dep. fin. officer Wayne County, Mich., 1995—2002; CFO, 2002, 2005—; pres. Govt. Fin. Officers Assn. Bd. dirs. Mich. Assn. Cert. Pub. Accountants. Coordinator Tiger Cub Boy Scouts Am., Detroit, 1985—. Mem. Nat. Assn. Black Accountants. Democrat. Avocations: reading, music, travel. Office: Govt Fin Officers Assn 203 N LaSalle St Suite 2700 Chicago IL 60601

SLEDGE, LELA BELL, minister; b. Madisonville, Tenn., July 8, 1938; d. Henry and Hattie Louella (Freeman) Bowers; m. Fred Thomas Sledge, Aug. 8, 1953 (dec.); children: Benny Ray, Wanda Faye Pico, Timothy Fred, Pamela Darlene McKee. DDiv, United Christian Bible Inst., Cleveland, Tenn., 1997; D.Bible Knowledge, United Christian Bible Inst., 1985. Ordained to ministry United Christian Ch., 1969. Minister, evangelist, missionary Full Gospel Bible Ch., Cleveland, Tenn., 2000—. Author: The Girl Who Found Life in the Graveyard, 1978. Mem.: Full Gospel Bible Ministries (pres.). Avocations: reading, travel, sewing, puzzles, exercise. Office Phone: 423-472-6237.

SLEEMAN, MARY (MRS. JOHN PAUL SLEEMAN), retired librarian; b. Cleve., June 28, 1928; d. John and Mary Lillian (Jakub) Gerba; m. John Paul Sleeman, Apr. 27, 1946; children: Sandra (Sleeman) Swyrydenko, Robert, Gary, Linda. BS, Kent State U., 1965, MLS. Children's libr. Twinsburg Pub. Libr., Twinsburg, Ohio, 1965—66; supr. libr. mid. sch. Nordonia Hills Bd.

Edn., Northfield, Ohio, 1965—93, ret., 1993. Mem.: No. Eastern Ohio Tchr. Assn., Storytellers Assn., Summit County Librarians Assn., ALA. Meth. Home: 18171 Logan Dr Cleveland OH 44146-5236 Office: 72 Leonard Ave Northfield OH 44067-1945

SLEEPER, CHERI ACOSTA, music educator; b. Honolulu, Aug. 15, 1963; d. John and Mary Ann Acosta; m. Brent Eric Sleeper, July 23, 1998; children: James Eric, Paul David. MusB in Edn., Fla. State U., Tallahassee, 1986; MA in Music Edn., U. South Fla., Tampa, 2001. Cert. profl. tchr. Fla. Dir. of bands Charlotte HS, Punta Gorda, Fla., 1986—90, Webb Jr. HS, Tampa, 1990—91, Marshall Jr. HS, Tampa, 1991—92; music specialist Woodbridge Elem. Sch., Tampa, 1992—93; dir. of bands Middleton Mid. Sch. of Tech., Tampa, 1993—96, C. Leon King HS, Tampa, 1996—. Nominee Disney Tchr. award, 2006; recipient Nat. Honor Roll Outstanding Am. Tchr.'s award, 2006. Mem.: Fla. Music Educators Assn. (Tri-M Honor Soc. state chair 1999—2002), Fla. Bandmasters Assn. (dist. sec. 1999—2002), Music Educators Nat. Conf. Office: C Leon King King HS 6815 N 56th St Tampa FL 33610 Office Phone: 813-744-8333 ext 266. E-mail: cheri.sleeper@sdhc.k12.fl.us.

SLEEPER, NANCY JOANN, mental health services professional; d. John Harold and Helen Amelia Sagdahl; m. John Edward Tracy (div.); children: Christopher Tracy, Heidi Thorley, Jeffrey Tracy, Scott Tracy; m. Richard Edwin Sleeper, Jan. 26. BS in Psychology, Wash. State U., Pullman, 1977; MA in Clin. Psychology, John F. Kennedy U., Orinda, Calif., 1985. LPC Ill., LMHC Wash., lic. clin. social worker Wis., MAC NAFC, NCR Wash. Mental health profl. KTSAP Mental Health Svcs., Bremerton, 1988—90; exceptional family mem. program coord. Army Comty. Svc., Schofield Barracks, Hawaii, 1991—93; new parent support team counselor Navy Family Svc. Ctr., Great Lakes, Ill., 1993—95; therapist Luth. Social Svcs., Bremerton, 1995—96; MICA specialist, older adults therapist KTSAP Mental Health Svcs., Bremerton, 1996—2000; substance abuse counselor Dept. Army, 104th ASG, Germany, 2000—03, Dept. Army, Ft. Huachuca, Ariz., 2003—. Mem. Comty. Emergency Response Team, Sierra Vista, Ariz., 2004—. Mem.: ACA, Am. Psychotherapy Assn. (diplomate). Mem. Lds Ch. Office: Army Substance Abuse Program Bldg 22414 Fort Huachuca AZ 85613 Business E-Mail: nancy.sleeper@us.army.mil.

SLEIGH, SYLVIA, artist, educator; b. Llandudno, North Wales; came to U.S., 1961; d. John Harold and Katherine Amy (Miller) S.; m. Lawrence Alloway, June 28, 1954. Student, Sch. Art, Brighton, Sussex, Eng., 1932-36; diploma, U. London Extra-Mural Dept., 1947. Vis. asst. prof. SUNY-Stony Brook, 1978; instr. New Sch. Social Research, N.Y.C., 1974-77, 78-80; Edith Kreeger Wolf disting. prof. Northwestern U., Evanston, Ill., 1977; vis. artist Baldwin Seminar Oberlin Coll., Ohio, 1982, New Sch. Social Rsch., N.Y.C. One person shows include Bennington (Vt.) Coll., 1963, Soho 20 Art Gallery, N.Y.C., 1974, 76, 80, 82, A.I.R. Gallery, N.Y.C., 1974, 76, 78, Ohio State U., Columbus, 1976, Matrix, Wadsworth Atheneum, Hartford, Conn., 1976, Marianne Deson Gallery, Chgo., 1990, G.W. Einstein, Inc., N.Y.C., 1980, 83, 85, U. Mo., Saint Louis, 1981, Zaks Gallery, Chgo., 1985, 95, Milw. Art Mus., Butler Inst., Youngstown, Ohio, 1990, Stiebel Modern, N.Y.C., 1992, 94, Gallery 609, Denver, Canton (Ohio) Art Inst., Soho 20 Gallery, 1999, Deven Golden Fine Arts, N.Y., 1999, The Art of Sylvia Sleigh and Lawrence Alloway Phila. Art Alliance, Phila., 2001; exhibited in group shows: Newhouse Gallery, S.I., N.Y., Stamford (Conn.) Mus., 1985, Albany (N.Y.) Inst. Art, Cin. Art Mus., New Orleans Mus. Art, Denver Art Mus., Pa. Acad. Fine Arts, 1989, Carlsten Art Gallery, Stevens Point, Wis., 1993, Stiebel Modern, N.Y.C., 1994, Soho 20, N.Y.C., 1993, 96, Katzen Brown Gallery, N.Y.C., 1989, Zaks Gallery, Chgo., 1986, Steinbaum Krauss Gallery, 1997, Deven Golden Fine Arts, Ltd., N.Y.C., 1997, Rutgers U., New Brunswick, N.J., 1984, 86, RioArriba Gallery, Abiquiu, N.Mex., 1996, Milw. Art Mus., 1996, Steinbaum Krauss Gallery, 1997, N.Y. Mus. exhbn. traveling until 2001, David and Alfred Smart Mus., Chgo., Broome St. Gallery, N.Y.C., Deven Golden Fine Arts, N.Y.C., A.I.R. Gallery, N.Y.C., Apex Art Co., N.Y.C., 1998, McKee Gallery, N.Y.C., 1998, Royal Coll. Art, London, 1998, Heckscher Mus. Art, Huntington, N.Y., 1999, Printworks Gallery, 2000, SoHo 20, N.Y.C., 2004, Snug Harbor Cultural Ctr., N.Y.C., 2005, Mason Gross at Rutgers U., N.J., 2005, Mus. Contemp. Art, L.A., 2006. Panelist Creative Artists Pub. Service Program, N.Y.C., 1976. Nat. Endowment for Arts grantee, 1982, Pollock-Krasner Found. grantee, 1985. Home: 330 W 20th St New York NY 10011-3302 Personal E-mail: ssallway@verizon.net.

SLIKER, SHIRLEY J. BROCKER, bookseller; b. Irwin, Pa., Sept. 5, 1929; d. Robert John and Hannah Alberta (McGrew) Brocker; m. Alan Sliker, June 23, 1956; children: Mark Alan (dec.), William James, Barbara Louise Sliker-Seewer. BS, Syracuse U., 1951, MS, 1954. Owner Shirley's Book Svcs., Okemos, Mich., 1987—; tchr. evening coll. Mich. State U., East Lansing, 1988—2000. Mgr. Book Burrow, Friends of Lansing (Mich.) Pub. Libr., 1985-86. Commr. Lansing Charter Commn., 1976-78. Mem. Mid-Mich. Antiquarian Bookdealers Assn., Zonta (chmn. various coms. 1992—), Lansing Woman's Club. Avocations: collector of glass artistry, paperweights. Office: Shirleys Book Services 4330 Hulett Rd Okemos MI 48864-2434

SLINGERLAND, MARY JO, writing educator; b. Lansing, Mich., Oct. 19, 1958; d. Thomas James and Maxine Margaret Slingerland; 1 child, Nicole Charisse Ballesteros. BA in English/Journalism, Mich. State U., 1983; MA in Tchg., Wayne State U., 2005. Owner, writer, editor Vision Decisions, SCS, Mich., 1982—; proposal writer Mich. State U., 1989—90; writer, editor Daimler-Chrysler Corp., Auburn Hills, Mich., 1995—99; writer, editor for CDI Ford Motor Co., Livonia, Mich., 1999—2001; instr. English lit./composition, tech. writing/speaking Wayne County Coll., Detroit, 2002—; coord. Tutorial Lab. Baker Coll., Detroit, 2006—. Instr. Baker Coll., 2005—. Editor: Arthroscopic Surgery, 1986; contbr. articles to profl. jours. Scholar, Wayne State U., 2004—05, Grad. Profl. scholar, 2005; Wheaton Tutor scholar, Mich. State U., 1980. Mem.: Internat. Reading Assn., Mich. Reading Assn., Nat. Coun. Tchrs. English, Mich. Coun. Tchrs. English, Mich. Assn. Computer Users Learners, Internat. Tech. Assn., Nat. Orgn. Women Bus. Owners. Avocations: golf, tennis, sailing, fishing. Home: 17771 Feather Ln Brownstown MI 48193-8460 Office Phone: 586-764-8630. Personal E-mail: mslinger2@netzero.net.

SLITKIN, BARBARA ANN, artist; b. Newark, Oct. 15, 1948; d. Lewis Leonard Small and Charlotte Deborah Rothgessor Small; m. Kenneth Bernard Slitkin, Sept. 23, 1967 (div. July 12, 1991); 1 child, Tiffany Simone. Faculty Art Sch. Ednl. Alliance, NYC, 1999—; presenter in field. Actor: (plays) Dolly Pardon Me, 1999; one-woman shows include Ortho Diagnostics, Raritan, N.J., 1986, Tompkins Sq. Gallery, NYC, 1992—93, 1998, 2001, 2004, exhibited in group shows at Paterson (N.J.) Mus., 1987, Krasdale Gallery Bronx (NY) Mus., 1989, Blue Mountain Gallery, NYC, 1997—98, 2000—02, 2004—06, exhibitions include Avanian Awards Gallery, NY, 1988—90, N.Y.C., 2004, Bass Mus. Broward C.C., 1996, 1997, Represented in permanent collections Franklin Furnace Archive Mus. Modern Art, NYC, Mid Hudson Arts Ctr., Poughkeepsie, N.Y., New Eng. Ctr. Contemporary Art, Conn., Das Deutsche Gartenzwerg Mus., Germany, Sharajah Mus., United Arab Emigrates, Willem Coll., Tilberg, Internat. Mus. Collage and Assemblage Construction, Mex. Scholar, Internat. Fine Arts, 1966—67. Mem.: The Nat. Mural Soc. Office: 175 East 96 St 12-0 New York NY 10128 Personal E-mail: barbaraslitkin@yahoo.com. E-mail: slitkin@msn.com.

SLIVKA, THOMASINA, secondary school educator; b. Cleve., Oct. 27, 1954; d. Thomas J. and Mary J. Casadonte; m. Steven J. Slivka; children: David, Stephanie. BS in Edn., Cleve. State U., Ohio, 1976, MS in Curriculum, 2002. 7th & 8th grade sci. & English tchr. St. Monica Sch., Garfield Heights, Ohio, 1976—85; 9th grade phys. sci. tchr. Trinity HS, Garfield Heights, 1985—98; 8th grade sci. & reading, 7th gr. sci. tchr. Independence Local Schs., Ohio, 1998—. Recipient Making the Grade award, Channel 5 News, 2003. Mem.: NSTA, NEA, Ohio Educator's Assn. Office: Independence Mid Sch 6111 Archwood Independence OH 44131

SLOAN, ANNE ELIZABETH, food scientist, writer; d. Thomas and Anne Sloan; m. James Murtland, June 14, 2003. BS, Rutgers U., 1973; PhD, U. Minn., 1976. Mgr. nutrition comm. Gen. Mills, Mpls., 1976—78; dir. Good Housekeeping Inst., N.Y.C., 1978—85; editor-in-chief McCall's Mag., N.Y.C., 1985—92; pres. Sloan Trends and Solution, Stuart, Fla., 1993—2003, Sloan Trends, Escondido, Calif., 2004—. Author: Food For Thoughts, 1977, Contemporary Nutrition Controversies, 1979; contbr. articles to numerous profl. jours. and mag. Recipient Pub. Rels. award, John W. Hill Found.; George Cook scholar, Rutgers U., 1973. Office: Sloan Trends PO Box 461149 Escondido CA 92046

SLOAN, CAROLYN, music educator, composer, lyricist; d. Myron and Susanne Sloan; m. Stuart Zagnit; 1 child, Sam Zagnit. BA, N.Y. U., N.Y.C., 1982. Cert. Orff instr. N.J., 2004. K-12 music chair Berkeley Carroll Sch., Bklyn., 2005—. Author: (book) Finding Your Voice-A Practical and Spiritual Approach to Singing and Living, Hyperion, 1999; composer (lyricist): (theatrical) I Have Found Home, 1986, My Name is Still Alice, 1992—, Pets, 1992—93, That's Life, 1993—94. Recipient Founder's Day Acad. Excellence award, N.Y. U., 1981, 1982. Mem.: ASCAP (assoc.). Achievements include development of new voice technique for singers and actors; two volumes of children's songs currently being used around the country. Avocations: cooking, travel, swimming, bicycling. Personal E-mail: sloantone@aol.com.

SLOAN, JEANETTE PASIN, artist; b. Chgo., Mar. 18, 1946; d. Antonio and Anna (Baggio) Pasin; children: Eugene Blakely, Anna Jeanette. BFA, Marymount Coll., Tarrytown, N.Y., 1967; MFA, U. Chgo., 1969. One-woman shows include G.W. Einstein Gallery, N.Y.C., 1977—85, Landfall Press Gallery, Chgo., N.Y.C., 1978, 1987, Roger Ramsay Gallery, Chgo., 1987, 1989, 1992, Tatischeff Gallery, Santa Monica, Calif., 1989, Steven Scott Gallery, Balt., 1989, Butters Gallery, Portland, Oreg., 1989, 1991, 1994, 1996, 1999, Tatistcheff & Co. Inc., 1995, 1997, 1999, Quartet Editions, N.Y.C., 1995, Elliot Smith Gallery, St. Louis, 1994, Peltz Gallery, Milw., 1994—95, 1999, 2006, Gerhard Wurzer Gallery, Houston, 1997, 2001, Cline Fine Arts Gallery, Santa Fe, 1998, 2001, J. Cacciola Gallery, N.Y.C., 2004—05, Amarillo Mus. Art, Tex., 2006, Represented in permanent collections Art Mus. Chgo., Cleve. Mus. Art, Ill. State Mus., Indpls. Mus. Art, Canton (Ohio) Art Inst., Ball State Bus., Mpls. Inst. Art, Fogg Mus. Harvard U., Yale U. Art Gallery, Snite Mus. U. Notre Dame, Met. Mus. Art, N.Y.C., Herbert F. Johnson Mus. Cornell U., Ithaca, N.Y., Valpariaso (Ind.) Mus. Art, Nat. Gallery Art, Washington, exhibited in group shows; subject of book by Gerritt Henry Jeanette Pasin Sloan, 2000, subject of book by by James Yood The Prints of Jeanette Pasin Sloan, 2003. Studio: 301 Loma Arisco Santa Fe NM 87501 Office Phone: 505-699-9234. Personal E-mail: jeanettepasin@aol.com.

SLOAN, JUDY BECKNER, law educator; b. Cochran Field AFB, Ga., Jan. 9, 1945; d. Edward Lee and Peggy Joyce (Adkins) Beckner; m. William R. Sloan, Apr. 4, 1965; children— Anita Lee, Jacqueline H. B.A., U. Chgo., 1967; J.D., U. Md., 1975. Bar: Ohio 1976, U.S. Dist. Ct. (no. dist.) Ohio 1979, U.S. Dist. Ct. (no. dist.) Ill. 1989, Supreme Ct. Bar, 1987. Law clk. firm Miles & Stockbridge, Balt., 1973-74; Asper fellow to R. Dorsey Watkins, Balt., 1974-75; asst. prof. law U. Toledo Coll. Law, 1975-77, assoc. prof., 1978-90, prof., 1990-91; vis. prof. Southwestern Sch. Law, L.A., 1991—, prof. law, 1992—; Jud. fellow U.S. Supreme Ct. Fed. judicial ctr. rsch. div., 1987-88; cons. firm Sonnenschein, Carlin, Nath & Rosenthal, Chgo., summer 1978, firm Schwartz, Cooper, Kolb & Gaynor, 1989; auditor internat. law World Ct.-Acad. Internat. Law, The Hague, Netherlands, summer 1972; arbitrator Toledo Elec. Welfare Trust and Local # 8 Retirement Plan. Contbr. articles to profl. jours. Conductor Orange County Jewish Community Ctr. Orch.; composer music performed by Jewish Community Orch. Toledo, 1983, 84; performed with Toledo Opera, 1982. Trustee, Toledo Symphony Orch. 1979—, Toledo Ballet, 1977-81; mem. citizens adv. bd. N.W. Ohio Devel. Ctr., Toledo, 1979-84, chmn. pub. relations Jr. League, Toledo, 1981-84; trustee Ohio Citizens Commn. for Arts, 1980—. Recipient Toledo Arts Commn. award, 1982; NEH fellow Columbia U., summer 1981. Mem. ABA, Ohio Bar Assn., Toledo Bar Assn. (law inst. com. 1977—, med.-legal com. 1976-79), Supreme Ct. Fellows Commn., Phi Kappa Phi, Delta Theta Phi. Jewish. Club: University (pres. 1980-81) (Toledo). Home: 2252 Cheswic Ln Los Angeles CA 90027-1134 Office: Southwestern U Sch Law 675 S Westmoreland Ave Los Angeles CA 90005-3905

SLOAN, KATHERINE (KAY SLOAN), college president; DArts in English, Carnegie Mellon U. Pres. Greenfield C.C., 1988—94, North Hennepin C.C., Mpls., 1994—96, Mass. Coll. Art, Boston, 0199—. Office: Office of President Mass College of Art 621 Huntington Ave Boston MA 02115 Office Phone: 617-879-7100.

SLOAN, MARY JEAN, retired media specialist; b. Lakeland, Fla., Nov. 29, 1927; d. Marion Wilder and Elba (Jinks) Sloan. BS, Peabody Coll., Nashville, 1949; MLS, Atlanta U., 1978, SLS, 1980. Cert. libr. media specialist. Music dir. Pinecrest Sch., Tampa, Fla., 1949-50, Polk County Schs., Bartow, Fla., 1950-54; pvt. music tchr. Lakeland, 1954-58; tchr. Clayton County Schs., Jonesboro, Ga., 1958-59; media specialist Eastualley Sch., Marietta, Ga., 1959-89; ret., 1989. Coord. conf. Ga. Libr. Media Dept., Jekyll Island, 1982-83, sec., Atlanta, 1982-83, com. chmn. ethnic conf., Atlanta, 1978, pres., 1984-85, state pres., 1985-86; program chmn. Ga. Media Orgns. Conf, Jekyll Island, 1988. Contbr. to bibliographies. Recipient Walter Bell award Ga. Assn. Instrnl. Tech., 1988, Disting. Svc. award, 1991. Mem. ALA (del. 1984, 85, 90), NEA, Southeastern Libr. Assn., Am. Assn. Sch. Librs., Soc. for Sch. Librs., Internat., Ga. Assn. Educators (polit. action com. 1983), Beta Phi Mu, Phi Delta Kappa. Republican. Methodist. Home: 797 Yorkshire Rd NE Atlanta GA 30306-3264

SLOAN, NINA, language educator; b. Volcheyarovka, Lugansk region, Ukraine, Mar. 18, 1956; d. Ivan and Praskovya Borisovich; m. Paul M. Sloan, Jan. 29, 1999; children: Olena Sambucci, Tanya. MA, Kharkov State U., Ukraine, 1981. Cert. ESL K-12; bilingual edn. K-12; English grades 6-12 Idaho State Dept. Edn., 2002. Tchr. English and French Sch. 146, Kharkov; tchr. English as fgn. lang., Am. studies Sch. 169, Kharkov, 1992—98; instr. English prep program Internat. Christian U., Kiev, Ukraine, 1999—2001; tchr. Frontier Elem. Sch., Boise, 2001—02, Centennial H.S., Boise, 2002—. Chair English lang. and country studies Sch. 169, 1992—98, vice prin. fgn. langs., 1996—97; chair English lang. prep program Internat. Christian U., Kiev, 1999—2001. Recipient Excellence in Tchg., Ukraine Ministry Edn. and USAID, 1997, Nat. Winner-Excellence in Tchg. English and Am. Studies, 1998. Mem.: NEA, Meridian Ednl. Assn. Home: 903 W Highland View Dr Boise ID 83702 Office: Centennial HS 12400 W Macmillan Rd Boise ID 83713 Office Phone: 208-855-4250. Personal E-mail: pnsloan@aol.com.

SLOAN, SAUNDRA JENNINGS, real estate company executive; b. Prosperity, S.C., June 30, 1961; d. Denny Jennings and Kay Hyler Green; m. Lowell Evan Sloan, Mar. 14, 1998. Student, Midlands Tech. Coll., Airport Location/Columbia, 1979—82. Lic. real estate. Pres. Southpark Svcs., Inc., Columbia, SC, 1990—95; mgr. sales and leasing Foster, Saad & Co., Columbia, SC, 1995—. Pres. BNI Midlands Chpt., Columbia, SC, 1999—2000. Recipient Gold Club award, Bus. Network Internat., 2001. Avocations: dance, travel, sewing. Office: Foster Saad & Co Ste 2A 1201 Hampton St Columbia SC 29201 Business E-Mail: SaunJenSloan@aol.com.

SLOANE, BEVERLY LEBOV, writer, consultant, writing instructor; b. NYC, May 26, 1936; d. Benjamin S. and Anne (Weinberg) LeBov; m. Robert Malcolm Sloane, Sept. 27, 1959 (dec. May 16, 2002); 1 child, Alison Lori Sloane Gaylin. AB, Vassar Coll., 1958; MA, Claremont Grad. U., 1975, postgrad., 1975—76; cert. in exec. mgmt., UCLA Grad. Sch. Mgmt., 1982, grad. exec. mgmt. program, 1982, cert. in advanced exec. mgmt., 1995, grad. advanced exec. mgmt. program, 1995; grad. profl. pub. course, Stanford U., 1982, grad. exec. refresher course in profl. pub., 1994; grad. intensive bioethics course Kennedy Inst. Ethics, Georgetown U., 1987, advanced bioethics course, 1988; grad. Summer Bioethics Inst., Loyola Marymount U., 1990; grad. Annual Summer Inst. on Teaching of Writing, Columbia U. Tchrs. Coll., 1990; grad. Annual Summer Inst. on Advanced Teaching of Writing, Columbia Tchrs. Coll., 1993; grad. Annual Inst. Pub. Health and Human Rights, Harvard U. Sch. Pub. Health, 1994; grad. women's campaign sch., Yale U., 1998; grad. writing and thinking course, Inst. Writing and Thinking, Bard Coll., 2005; Ethics Fellow, Loma Linda U. Med. Ctr., 1989. Circulation libr. Harvard Med. Libr., Boston, 1958-59; social worker Conn. State Welfare, New Haven, 1960-61; tchr. English Hebrew Day Sch., New Haven, 1961-64; instr. creative writing and English lit. Monmouth Coll., West Long Branch, NJ, 1967-69; writer, cons., 1970—. V.p. coun. grad. students, Claremont Grad. U., 1971-72, adj. dir. Writing Ctr. Speaker Series, 1993-2000, spkr., 1996-98, Claremont Grad. U.; mem. Strategic Planning Task Force Com. Campaign Pre-eminence. 1986-87, Alumni Coun., bd. dirs. Alumni Assn., 1993-96; mem. Vol. Devel. Com., 1994-96, Alumni Awards Com., 1993-96; bd. visitors Claremont Grad. U. Ctrs. for Arts and Humanities, 2001—; adv. coun. tech. and profl. writing Dept. English, Calif. State U., Long Beach, 1980-82; adv. bd. Calif. Health Rev., 1982-83; mem. Foothill Health Dist. Adv. Coun. LA County Dept. Health Svcs., 1987-93, pres., 1989-91; vis. scholar Hastings Ctr., 1996; spkr. NY State Task Force on Life and the Law, 1996; panel spkr. Annual Conf. Am. Assn. Suicidology, 1998; adj. instr. English composition Marist Coll., Poughkeepsie, NY, 2005—. Author: From Vassar to Kitchen, 1967, A Guide to Health Facilities: Personnel and Management, 1971, 2nd edit., 1977, 3d edit., 1992, Introduction to Healthcare Delivery Organization: Functions and Management, 4th edit., 1999. Co-chmn. Vassar Christmas Showcase Vassar Club, New Haven, 1965—66; pub. rels. bd. Monmouth County Mental Health Assn., 1968—69; co-chmn. Vassar Club So. Calif. Annual Book Fair Vassar Coll., 1970—71; chmn. creative writing group Calif. Inst. Tech. Woman's Club, 1975—79; mem. task force edn. and cultural activities City of Duarte, 1987—88; class rep. Vassar Coll. Alumnae Assn., 1989; chmn. creative writing group Yale U. Newcomers, 1965—66; dir. creative writing group Yale U. Women's Orgn., 1966—67; mem. Exec. Program Network UCLA Grad. Sch. Mgmt., 1987—2000; trustee Ctr. Improvement Child Caring, 1981—83; mem. League Crippled Children, 1982—, treas. for gen. meetings, 1990—91, chmn. hostesses com., 1988—89, pub. rels. com., 1990—91; del. Task Force on Minorities in Newspaper Bus., 1987—89; rep. cmty. County Health Network Tobacco Control Program, 1991; mem. NY Citizens Com. Health Care Decisions, bd. dirs., 2005—; mem. Vassar Coll. Class Gift Com., 1998; chmn. 1st ann. Rabbi Camillus Angel Interfaith Svc. Temple Beth David, 1978, v.p., 1983—86; cmty. rels. com. Jewish Fedn. Coun. Greater LA, 1985—87; bd. dirs. League Crippled Children, 1988—91; ethics com., human subjects protection com. Jewish Home for Aging, Reseda, Calif., 1994—97; various positions and coms. Claremont Grad. U., 1986—; bd. visitors Claremont Grad. U. Ctr. Arts and Humanities, 2001—; bd. dirs. LA Commn. Assaults Against Women, 1983—84; class corr. Vassar Coll. Quar. Alumnae Mag., 1993—98; class of 1958 coms. Vassar Coll., class v.p., 1998—2000, class co-pres., 2000—01, class pres., 2001—03, program chmn. 40th reunion, 1998. Recipient cert. of appreciation City of Duarte, 1988, County of LA, 1988, Ann. Key Mem. award LA Dept. Health Svcs., 1990, cert. of appreciation Alumni Coun. Claremont Grad Sch., 1996; Coro Found. fellow, 1979, Ethics fellow Loma Linda U. Med. Ctr., 1989; named Calif. Communicator of Achievement, Woman of Yr. Calif. Press Women, 1992. Fellow: Am. Med. Writers Asn. (Pacific S.W. del. to nat. bd. 1980—87, dir. 1980—93, chmn. nat. book awards trade category 1982—83, chmn. Nat. Networking Luncheon 1983—84, nat. chmn. freelance sect. 1984—85, workshop leader, Nat. Ann. Conf. 1984—89, gen. chmn. Asilomar Western Regional Conf. 1985, workshop leader, Asilomar Western Regional Conf. 1985, nat. exec. bd. dirs. 1985—86, nat. adminr. sects. 1985—86, pres.-elect Pacific Southwest chpt. 1985—87, chmn. gen. session nat. conf. 1986—87, chmn. Walter C. Alvarez Mem. Found award 1986—87, program co-chmn. 1987, program chmn. nat. conf. 1987, moderator gen. session. nat. conf. 1987, pres. Pacific S.W. chap. 1987—89, workshop leader, Asilomar Western Nat. Conf. 1988, spkr. Pacific S.W. chpt. 1988—89, program co-chmn. 1989, workshop leader, Asilomar Western Nat. Conf. 1989, Pacific Southwest deleg. to nat. bd. 1989—91, immediate past pres. 1989—91, workshop leader, Nat. Ann. Conf. 1990—92, bd. dirs. 1991—93, workshop leader, Nat. Ann. Conf. 1995, chmn. conv. coms., Appreciation award for outstanding leadership 1989, named to Workshop Leaders Honor Roll 1991); mem.: AAUP, APHA, AAUW (creative writing chmn. 1969—70, books and plays chmn. Arcadia Br. 1973—74, 1st v.p. program dir. 1975—76, legis. chmn. Arcadia Br. 1976—77, networking chmn. 1981—82, spkr. 1987, chmn. task force promoting individual liberties 1987—88, pres.-elect 1998—99, educ. equity chmn. 1998—99, chmn. deleg. to national conv. 1999, chmn. Technical Trek Sci. Camp Scholarship for Girls 1999, Career Day 1999, pres. Arcadia br. 1999—2000, writer in res Calif. State Am. Assn. Univ. Women 1999—2000, diversity chmn. Arcadia br. 2000—01, LA Interbr. Coun. Arcadia br. repr. 2000—02, Calif. State diversity com. 2000—02, program vice-chmn. LA County Interbr. Coun. 2000—02, Woman of Achievement Arcadia br. 1986, cert. of appreciation 1987), Calif. State AAUW (program co-v.p. 2002), Town Hall Calif. (vice chmn. cmty. affairs sect. 1982—87, faculty-instr. Exec. Breakfast Inst. 1985—86, Exec. Breakfast Inst. spkr. 1986), Pasadena Athletic, Claremont Cols. Faculty House, Women's City (Pasadena), Nat. Writer's Union, Authors Guild, Assn. Writing Programs, NY Acad. Medicine (met. NY Ethics Network), Soc. Health and Human Values, Kennedy Inst. Ethics, Nat. Fedn. Press Women (chmn. state women of achievement comt. 1986—87, nat. co-chmn. task force recruitment minorities 1987—89, del. 1987—89, bd. dirs. 1987—93, nat. dir. spkrs. bur. 1989—93, Plenary past pres. state 1989—, workshop leader, spkr. annual nat. conf. 1990, editor spkrs. bur. directory 1991—92, editor spkrs. bur. addendum dir. 1992, cert. of appreciation 1991, 1st runner up, Nat. Communicator of Achievement 1992, cert. of appreciation 1993), Hastings Cent. (vis. scholar 1996), Ind. Writers So. Calif. (bd. dirs. corp. 1988—89, bd. dirs. 1989—90, dir. at large 1989—90, dir. specialized groups 1989—90, dir. speech writing group 1991—92), NY Acad. Scis., Calif. Press Women (v.p. programs L.A. chpt. 1982—85, pres. 1985—87, state pres. 1987—89, immediate past state pres. 1989—91, chmn. state speakers bur. 1989—95, deleg. nat. bd. 1989—95, dir. family literacy day Calif. 1990, moderator, ann. spring conv. 1990, chmn. nominating comt. 1990—91, Calif. literacy dir. 1990—92, dir. state literacy com. 1990—92, moderator, ann. spring conv. 1992, Cert. of Appreciation 1991, Calif. Communicator of Achievement 1992), Am. Soc. Law, Medicine, Ethics, AAUW Calif. State Comns. Comt. (writer in residence 1999—2000), Coro Nat. Alumni Assn. (bd. dirs. 1999—, continuing edn. com. 2003—), Am. Assn. Higher Edn., Women in Comm. Inc. (N.E. area rep. 1980—81, bd. dirs. 1980—82, v.p. cmty. affairs 1981—82, chmn. awards banquet 1982, chmn. LA chpt. Agnes Underwood Freedom Info. Awards banquet 1982, nominating com. 1982—83, seminar leader, spkr., ann. nat. profl. conf. 1985, program adv. com. LA chpt. 1987, com. Women of the Press awards luncheon 1988, bd. dirs. 1989—90, v.p. activities 1989—90, Recognition award 1983), Duarte Rotary Club. Home and Office: 22 East Knoll Rhinebeck NY 12572 Office Phone: 845-876-0738. Business E-mail: beverly.sloane@marist.edu.

SLOANE, BRENDA SUE, language educator; b. Terre Haute, Ind., June 11, 1953; d. Leon and Bertha Jackson; m. Stephen Richard Sloane, Aug. 7, 1984; children: Scott MacKenzie, Stephen Arthur, Sean Anthony, Philip Lee Marlowe. AA, Lincoln Trail Coll., Robinson, Ill., 1973; BA, Ind. State U., Terre Haute, 1975; MA, Ind. State U., 1980. Tchr. Wiesbaden Am. Mid. Sch., Germany, 1988—92, Gettysburg Area Sr. H.S., Pa., 1994—99, Sch. for Ednl. Enrichment, El Paso, Tex., 1999—2001; lectr. U. of Tex. at El Paso, 2001—. Asst. to the dir. of the composition program U. of Tex. at El Paso, 2001—. Mem.: Nat. Bus. Edn. Assn., Nat. Coun. of Tchrs. of English, MLA. Office: The University of Texas at El Paso 500 W University Ave El Paso TX 79968 Office Phone: 915-747-6243. E-mail: bssloane@utep.edu.

SLOAT, BARBARA FURIN, cell biologist, educator; b. Youngstown, Ohio, Jan. 20, 1942; d. Walter and Mary Helen (Maceyko) Furin; m. John Barry Sloat, Nov. 2, 1968; children: John Andrew, Eric Furin. BS, Denison U., Granville, Ohio, 1963; MS, U. Mich., Ann ARbor, 1966, PhD, 1968. Lic. and cert. emergency med. technician, paramedic. Lab. asst. U. Ghent, Belgium, 1964; tchg. fellow, lectr. U. Mich., Ann Arbor, 1964-66, 68-70, asst. rsch. biologist Mental Health Rsch. Inst., 1972-74, vis. asst. prof., lectr. Ann Arbor and Dearborn, 1974-76, dir. women in sci. Ann Arbor, 1980-84, assoc. dir. honors, 1986-87, rsch. scientist, 1976—, lectr. Residential Coll., 1984—, assoc. Inst. Humanities, 1991—. Author: Laboratory Guide for Zoology, 1979, Summer Internships in the Sciences for High School Women (CASE Silver medal, 1985, Excellence in Edn. award, U. Mich., 1993). Bd. dirs. Jewel Heart Tibetan Cultural Ctr., Ann Arbor, Mich., 2005—, Jewel Heart Health Ctr. and Cmty. Hospice, Ann Arbor, 2003—, HIV/AIDS Resource Ctr., Ypsilanti, Mich., 1994—2000. Recipient Sarah Goddard Power award U. Mich., 1984, Grace Lyon Alumnae award Denison U., 1988; grantee NSF, U.S. Dept. Edn., Warner Lambert Found., others. Mem. AAAS, Am. Soc. Cell Biology, N.Y. Acad. Scis., Nat. Assn. Women Deans, Adminstrs. and Counselors, Assn. for Women in Sci. (councilor 1988-90, pres. elect 1990, mentor of yr. award Detroit area chpt. 1994), Phi Beta Kappa, Sigma Xi. Avocations: hiking, yoga, tibetology. Home: 240 Indian River Pl Ann Arbor MI 48104-1825 Office: U Mich Residential Coll 216 Tyler East Quad Ann Arbor MI 48109-1245 Business E-Mail: bsloat@umich.edu.

SLOCUM, LAURA ELIZABETH, chemistry educator; AS in Respiratory Therapy, Ind. U., 1981; BA in Chemistry, Western Conn. State U., 1990; MS in Chemistry, Ball State U., 2001. Chemistry instr. Greens Farms (Conn.) Acad., 1992—99, Univ. HS of Ind., Carmel, Ind., 2001—. Mem.: Am. Chem. Soc. (chmn. local sect. 2004—05, trustee Examinations Inst. 2004—). Office: University HS Ind 2825 W 116th St Carmel IN 46032 Office Phone: 317-733-4475 203.

SLOCUM, SUSANNE TUNNO, medical/surgical nurse; b. Atlanta, Aug. 28, 1962; d. Dean Dunwody and Patricia Murphey Tunno; m. Everett Ward Hogsed, May 14, 1988 (div. Feb. 1991); m. Robert Daniell Slocum, May 11, 1996. BSN, Emory U., 1987. Staff nurse St. Joseph's Hosp. Atlanta, 1987—98, mgr. neurovas. unit, 1998—2000, coord. CV screening & prevention, 2000—. Spkr. in field. Mem. St. Joseph's Edn. Coun., Atlanta, 1992—98, St. Joseph's Practice Coun., Atlanta, 1992—93; nurse Camp Breathe Easy, Atlanta Lung Assn., 1990—2001, Atlanta Olympics, 1996. Recipient Key Vol. award, Am. Stroke Assn., 2001—03. Mem.: Preventative Cardiology Nurses Assn., Acad. Med.-Surg. Nurses (immediate past pres. immediate past pres. 2002—03). Methodist. Avocations: boating, reading, four-wheeling. Home: 540 Old Preston Tr Alpharetta GA 30022 Office: St Joseph's Hosp Atlanta 5665 Peachtree Dunwoody Rd Atlanta GA 30342

SLOMINSKI, ELENA GREGORYEVNA, mathematics educator; b. Vilnius, Lithuania, Feb. 25, 1959; arrived in U.S., 1989, naturalized, 1996; d. Gregory Andreyevich and Irina Andreyevna Maciura; m. Alexander Nicholas Slominski, July 26, 1980; children: Etalia, Elina, Emily, Zachary, Samuel, Elizabetta. MS Math., Vilnius U., 1981. Cert. tchr. Ariz. Tchr. math. H.S. # 10, Vilnius, 1980—81; substitute tchr. math. Painted Pony Ranch Charter Sch., Prescott, Ariz., 1999—2001; part-time tchr. math. Prep H.S. Tri-City Coll., Prescott, 2001—03, tchr. math. Prep H.S., 2003—. Adj. instr. math. Graceland U., Lamoni, 2003—, Embry Riddle Aero. U., Prescott, 2006; chair dept. math. and sci. Prep H.S. Tri-City Coll., Prescott, 2004—. Nominee Presdl. Math. award, USA Today Math. Team, 2005, Yarapai County Tchr. of Yr., 2005; named Yarapai County H.S. Tchr. of Yr., Yarapai County Ednl. Found., 2006. Mem.: Ariz. Assn. Tchrs. Math., Math. Assn. Am., Nat. Coun. Tchrs. Math. Avocations: languages, dance, vegetarian cooking. Office: Tri-City Coll Prep HS 5522 Side Rd Prescott AZ 86301

SLONAKER, MARY JOANNA KING, columnist; b. Richmond, Ind., July 18, 1930; d. Claiborn F. and Carlyle (Diffendenfer) King; divorced; children: Mary Sue Hosey, Steven, Allis Ann Fox. Student, Earlham Coll., 1948-49; BS, Ball State U., 1969; MA in Teaching, Ind. U., 1974. Cert. residential child care worker. Home econs. tchr. Lewisville (Ind.) Sch., 1978-79, Morton Meml. Sch., Knightstown, Ind., 1970-83; town coun. mem. Cambridge City, Ind., 1991-2001. Mem. Ind. U. Chancellor's Medallion Dinner Com., 2001. Recipient Kiwanis Cmty. award, 1983-84, 95, Appreciation award Am. Bus. Women, 1985, Appreciation award Waseda U. Japanese Exch. Program, 1986-88. Mem. AAUW, Soc. Profl. Journalists, Ind. U. Alumni Club, Ind. U. Varsity Club, The Woman's Club, Psi Iota Xi, Alpha Delta Kappa, Pi Beta Phi. Democrat. Presbyterian. Avocations: basketball, football, harness racing, walking, gardening. Home: 36 W Church St Cambridge City IN 47327-1615 Office: 127 N Foote St Cambridge City IN 47327-1144

SLOSBURG-ACKERMAN, JILL ROSE, artist, educator; b. Omaha, Aug. 28, 1948; d. Harold Walter and Marion (Gill) Slosburg; m. James Sloss Ackerman, Aug. 8, 1987; 1 child, Jesse August Ackerman. Diploma, Boston Mus. Sch., 1971; BFA, Tufts U., 1971, MFA, 1983. Prof. art Mass. Coll. Art, Boston, 1973—; vis. artist Cranbrook Acad. Art, Bloomfield, Mich., 1993. One-woman shows include Harcus-Krakow-Rosen-Sonnabend Gallery, Boston, 1978, 1980, Helen Shlien Gallery, 1980, 1982, Cohen Arts Ctr., Tufts U., Medford, Mass., 1982, Van Buren/Brazellon/Cutting Gallery, Cambridge, Mass., 1985, Genovese Gallery, Boston, 1995, Manwaring Gallery Cumings Art Ctr., Conn. Coll., New London, 1995, Rose Art Mus., Brandeis U., Waltham, Mass., 1996, Atrium Gallery, U. Mass., Dartmouth, 1999, Judy Ann Goldman Fine Art, Boston, 1999, 2004, exhibited in group shows at Naga Gallery, 1980, DeCordova Mus., Lincoln, Mass., 1980, Jewett Art Ctr., Wellesley, Mass., 1982, Helen Shlien Gallery, Boston, 1982, Cherry Stone Gallery, Wellfleet, Mass., 1984, Quadrum Gallery, Chestnut Hill, Mass., 1985, Fed. Res. Gallery, Boston, 1986, Danforth Mus., 1986, Conseil de la Sculpture, Montreal, 1986, North Hall Gallery, Boston, 1987, Artists Found. Gallery, 1990, Mus. Decorative Arts, Prague, 1991, Nancy Margolis Gallery, N.Y.C., 1991, Bellevue (Wash.) Art Mus., 1992, Artwear, N.Y., 1992, Genovese Gallery, Albany, N.Y., 1992, Judy Ann Goldman Fine Art, Boston, 1997, 2002, Mills Gallery, 1997—98, 2004, Boston Mus. Fine Arts, 1999, DeCordova Mus., Lincoln, 2000, Nat. Art Mus. China, Beijing, 2001, Forest Hills Cemetery, Boston, 2002, 2004, Coll. Holy Cross, Worcester, Mass., 2003, Fuller Craft Mus., 2005, Represented in permanent collections J. L. Brandeis & Sons, Omaha, Mass. Coll. Art, Boston, Boston Pub. Libr., City of Cambridge, Forest Hills Cemetery, Jamaica Plain, Mass.; contbr. articles to profl. jours. Founder, mem. Boston Women's Action Coalition; bd. dirs. Cambridge (Mass.) Multi-Cultural Ctr., Gallery at Green St., 1993. Recipient Patricia Jellinek Hallowell prize for Jewelry, 1984, Disting. Svc. award, Mass. Coll. Art, 1980, 4th prize sterling silver design competition, Nat. Guild Sterling Silversmiths, 1970; fellow, Haystack Mountain Sch. Crafts, 1972, 1976, Nat. Endowment Arts, 1974, 1986, The Artists Found., 1984, Mary Ingraham Bunting Inst., 1985—86; grantee, Artist's Resource Trust, 2001, New Eng. Art Critics Assn., 2004, 2006; Profl. Devel. grantee, Mass. Coll. Art, 1987, Polaroid Corp. Photography grantee, 1988, New Eng. Found. Arts fellow, 1998, Mass. Cultural Coun. Artist's grantee, 1999, 2006. Jewish. Home: 12 Coolidge Hill Rd Cambridge MA 02138-5510 Studio: One Fitchburg St Apt C415 Somerville MA 02143-2128 Office Phone: 617-625-4056. Personal E-mail: jsackerman44@comcast.net.

SLOTKIN, ALMA ISOBEL, artist; b. Kellettville, Pa., Apr. 18, 1914; d. Otto and Bertha (Anderson) Rosenquist; m. Edgar Slotkin (dec.); children: Edgar, Ellen Slotkin Lauber. RN, Buffalo Gen. Hosp., 1936; student in Medicine, Montreal Neurol. Hosp., Can., 1938; studied with Robert Blair. Art chmn. Temple Br'th Zion, Buffalo, 1969—79; donor in rental gallery Albright Knox Gallery, Buffalo, 1970—. One-woman shows include Cole Gallery Medaile Coll. Art Dialogue, 1963, exhibited in group shows at Buffalo Soc. Arts, 1960—66, Albright Knox Gallery, Buffalo, Butler Inst. Am., Ohio, 1975—86, Springfield Art Gallery, Mo., 1964—65, Cole Gallery, Medaile Coll., 1970—98, Art Dialogue, 2002, Burchfield Penny Gallery, 2004, exhibitions include US Dept. State. Mem.: Western N.Y. Artist Group, Buffalo Soc. Artists (pres. 1960—2005), Buffalo Club. Avocations: gardening, golf, reading. Home: 33 Burbank Terr Buffalo NY 14214

SLOUGH, SANDRA OLLIE, secondary school educator; b. Fries, Va., Oct. 14, 1949; d. John Columbus and Opal Faye (Bond) Phibbs; m. William Fred Slough, June 27, 1970; children: Sonya Michelle, William Alexander. BS, East Tenn. State U., 1972. Teaching Cert. English, Speech, Drama, S.C. 1st grade tchr. Our Saviour Luth. Ch. Sch., Greenville, SC, 1975; English drama tchr. Travelers Rest HS, SC, 1976-79; English tchr. Wade Hampton HS, Greenville, SC, 1981-92, Carolina HS, Greenville, SC, 1992—95; computer specialist Life Long Learning, 1995—96; computer specialist, souncelor Parker Acad., 1996—2003; guidance counselor Carolina Acad., 2003—. Tchr. rep. to PTSA, Greenville, S.C., 1990-92; sec. tchrs. chmn. S. C. Internat. Reading Assn., 1989-90, 90-91; on bd. human rights chmn. State SCSCA Bd., 2001-04. Bd. PTA Taylors (S.C.) Elem. Sch., 1985-86; del. Dem. State Conv., S.C., 1988; v.p. Local Precinct Dem. Party, Taylors, S.C., 1988,89. Mem. Greenville Coun. S. C. Internat. Reading Assn. (v.p. 1990-91, pres. 1991-92, del. 1990-93), IRA Conv. Democrat. Presbyterian. Avocations: reading, painting, arts and crafts. Office: Carolina High School 2725 Anderson Rd Greenville SC 29611 Office Phone: 803-355-2359. Business E-Mail: sslough@greenville.k12.sc.edu.

SLOVENSKY, DEBORAH WILBANKS, secondary school educator; b. Birmingham, Ala., Nov. 9, 1951; d. Euel Wilburn and Mildred Louise (Canoles) Wilbanks; m. Ron R. Slovensky, Aug. 3, 1973; children: Adam R., Andrew T. BS in English, U. Montevallo, 1985. Cert. tchr. secondary lang. arts. Enrichment tchr. Birmingham City Schs./Glen Iris, Birmingham, Ala., 1985-86, Shelby County Schs./Riverchase Middle Sch., Columbiana, Ala., 1986-89; lang. arts tchr. 7th grade Hoover (Ala.) City Schs. - Simmons Middle Sch., 1989-91, enrichment tchr., 1991-96, lang. arts 7th grade tchr., 1996—. Governing bd. mem. Inservice and Rsch. Ctr., U. Montevallo, 1994—; presenter Ala. Insvc. Annual Conf., Huntsville, 1995; dist. curriculum facilitator for lang. arts Hoover City Schs., 1993-95. Faculty rep. to nominating com. PTA for Simmons Middle Sch., 1994; co-capt.-mini-parish St. Peter's Cath. Ch., Hoover, 1993-95; mem. Our Lady of Sorrows Cath. Ch., Homewood, Ala., presenter State of Ala. Dept. of Edn., 2002, 2004—. Recipient Outstanding Alumna in Secondary Edn. U. Montevallo, 1996; grantee Hoover Found., 1996. Mem. ASCD, Nat. Coun. of Tchrs. of English. Democrat. Roman Catholic. Avocations: gardening, writing, photography. Home: 1813 Napier Dr Hoover AL 35226-2624 Office: Hoover City Schs Simmons Middle Sch 1575 Patton Chapel Rd Hoover AL 35226-2257 Office Phone: 205-439-2115. E-mail: dslovensky@charter.net.

SLOVIK, SANDRA LEE, retired art educator; b. Elizabeth, N.J., Mar. 22, 1943; d. Edward Stanley and Frances (Garbus) S. BA, Newark State Coll., 1965, MA, 1970. Cert. art tchr. Art tchr. Holmdel (N.J.) Twp. Bd. Edn., 1965-99, ret., 1999. Computer art in-sv. tng. Holmdel Bd. Edn., 1990; computer art workshop Madison (N.J.) Bd. Edn., 1991; presenter Nat. Edn. Computer Conv., 1999. Charter supporter, mem. Statue of Liberty/Ellis Island Found., 1976—; charter supporter Sheriffs' Assn. N.J., 1993—; mem. PTA, Holmdel, 1965—. Recipient Curriculum award N.J. ASCD, 1992; grantee Holmdel Bd. Edn., 1989, 90, N.J. Bus., Industry, Sci., Edn. Consortium, 1990. Mem. NEA, Nat. Art Edn., Assn., N.J. Art Educators Assn., N.J. Edn. Assn., Monmouth County Edn. Assn., Holmdel Twp. Edn. Assn. (sr. bldg. rep. 1977-79). Avocations: travel, sports. Office: Village Sch 67 Mccampbell Rd Holmdel NJ 07733-2299 E-mail: sslovik@hotmail.com.

SLOVITER, DOLORES KORMAN, federal judge; b. Phila., Sept. 5, 1932; d. David and Tillie Korman; m. Henry A. Sloviter, Apr. 3, 1969 (dec. May 2003); 1 child, Vikki Amanda. AB in Econs. with distinction, Temple U., 1953, LHD (hon.), 1986; LLB magna cum laude, U. Pa., 1956; LLD (hon.), Dickinson Sch. Law, 1984, U. Richmond, 1992, Widener U., 1994. Bar: Pa. 1957. From assoc. to ptnr. Dilworth, Paxson, Kalish, Kohn & Levy, Phila., 1956—69; mem. Harold E. Kohn PA, Phila., 1969—72; assoc. prof. Temple U. Law Sch., Phila., 1972—74, prof., 1974—79; judge U.S. Ct. Appeals (3rd cir.), Phila., 1979—, chief judge, 1991—98. Bd. overseers U. Pa. Law Sch., 1993—99; bd. trustees Nat. Constitution Ctr., 1998—; mem. Jud. Conf. of U.S., 1991—98. Chair Pa. Rhodes Scholarship Selection Com., 2003—04; mem. S.E. region Pa. Gov.'s Conf. on Aging, 1976—79, Com. of 70, 1976—79; U.S. com. Bicentennial Constn., 1987—90; com. on Rules of Practice and Procedure, 1990—93; com. to Rev. Cir. Coun. Conduct and Disability Orders, 2004—; mem. Dist. IV Selection Com., Rhodes Scholarship Competitions, 2005—; trustee The Pa. Women's Forum, 1996—, Jewish Publ. Soc. Am., 1983—89. Recipient Juliette Low medal, Girl Scouts Greater Phila., Inc., 1990, Honor award, Girls High Alumnae Assn., 1991, Jud. award, Pa. Bar Assn., 1994, James Wilson award, U. Pa., 1996, Cert. of Honor award, Temple U., 1996; Disting. Fulbright scholar, Chile, 1990. Mem.: ABA, Phila. Bar Assn. (gov. 1976—78, Sandra Day O'Connor award 1997), Am. Judicature Soc. (bd. dirs. 1990—95), Nat. Assn. Women Judges, Am. Law Inst., Fed. Judges Assn., Fed. Bar Assn., The Pa. Women's Forum, Order of Coif (pres. U. Pa. chpt. 1975—77), Phi Beta Kappa. Office: US Ct Appeals 18614 US Courthouse 601 Market St Philadelphia PA 19106-1713*

SLOWIK, SHARON A., real estate agent; b. Rochester, NY, Apr. 23, 1944; d. Edward and Evelyn (McGillis) Schreiner; m. William G. Slowik, Sept. 12, 1970; children: Heather, Elizabeth, Michael, Matthew. A, Lab. Inst. Mdse., 1964. Agent Long & Foster Real Estate Inc., Vienna, Va., 1990—. Mem. Nat. Realtors Assn., Graduate Realtor Inst. (cert.), Cert. Residential Specialist (cert.), No. Va. Bd. Realtors (top prodr. sales club 1993-, polit. action com. 1991—, top prodr. 2002-06). Home: 10901 Treeview Ct Great Falls VA 22066-1639 Office: Long & Foster Real Estate Inc 8227 Old Courthouse Rd Ste 100 Vienna VA 22182-3815 Office Phone: 703-472-3593. Personal E-mail: slowik@erols.com.

SLUSHER, KIMBERLY GOODE, researcher; b. Benham, Ky., Oct. 4, 1960; d. Herschel James and Nevelyn Faye (Hayes) Goode; m. Joe Allan Slusher, May 1, 1985; children: Tarah Rena, Preston Cole. BS in Agr., Ea. Ky. U., 1982; MS in Agr., U. Tenn., 1989. Rsch. asst. U. Tenn., Knoxville, 1983-89; info. analyst Oak Ridge (Tenn.) Nat. Lab., 1989—, tchr., cons. sci. honors program, 1993. Author: (army study) Drinking Water Contamination Study, 1995; contbr. chpt.: Teratogens: Chemicals Which Cause Birth Defects, 1993. Methodist. Avocations: gardening, piano. Office: Human Gene Info Analysis Sect 1060 Commerce Park Dr # Ms6480 Oak Ridge TN 37830-8043 Business E-Mail: kfg@ornl.gov.

SLUTSKY, BERNICE, agricultural products executive; PhD, U. Iowa. Rsch. asst. Plant Genetic Sys., Gent, Belgium; rsch. assoc. plant rsch. labs. Mich. State U.; with biotech. staff EPA, sci. policy advisor fgn. agrl. svc.; asst. v.p. internat. and regulatory affairs Pharm. Rsch. and Mfrs. Am.; sr. advisor to sec. USDA, 2004—06, spl. asst. to sec. biotech., 2004—06; v.p. sci. and internat. affairs Am. Seed Trade Assn. Inc., 2006—. Office: Am Seed Trade Assn Inc 225 Reinekers Ln Ste 650 Alexandria VA 22314-2875 Office Phone: 703-837-8140. Office Fax: 703-837-9365.*

SLUTSKY, LORIE A(NN), foundation executive; b. NYC, Jan. 5, 1953; d. Edward and Adele (Moskowitz) S. BA, Colgate U., 1975; MA in Urban Policy Analysis, New Sch. Social Rsch., NYC, 1977. Program officer NY Cmty. Trust, NYC, 1977-83, v.p., 1983-87, exec. v.p., 1987-89, pres., CEO, 1990—. Former mem. and chmn. bd. Coun. on Founds., Inc., Washington, 1986-95. Trustee emerita, former chmn. budget com. Colgate U., Hamilton, N.Y., 1989-98; former mem. bd. dirs. Found. Ctr., Inc., N.Y.C., L.A. Wallace Fund for Met. Mus. Art, N.Y.C., D. Wallace Fund for Meml. Sloan Kettering, United Way of N.Y.C.; bd. dirs. BoardSource, Alliance Capital; trustee New Sch. U. Office: NY Community Trust 22d Fl 909 3d Ave New York NY 10022

SLUTZ, PAMELA JO HOWELL, ambassador; b. Chgo., 1949; d. Robert and Rose Slutz; m. Ronald Deutch; 2 children. B in Politics, Hollins U., 1970; M in Asian Studies and Polit. Sci., U. Hawaii, 1972. Office of Korean Affairs Bur. East Asian and Pacific Affairs US Dept. of State (FSO), 1981—82, Office of China and Mongolia Affairs Bur. East Asian and Pacific Affairs, 1995—97, Office of East Asian and Pacific Regional Security and Policy Planning Bur. East Asian and Pacific Affairs, 1997—99, amb., fgn. svc. officer Shanghai, 1991—94, Am. Inst. Taiwan, 2001—03. Mem. U.S. Del. to Nuc. and Space Talks with Russia, Geneva, 1987—89. Fellow, East West Ctr., 1970—72. Home and Office: 4410 Ulaanbaatar Pl Washington DC 20521-4410 Fax: 976-11-320776.

SLYGH, CAROLYN V., biologist, educator; b. Ravenna, Ohio, Dec. 13, 1953; d. Charles Robert and Sue (Miller) Vajner; m. Robert G. Slygh, Sept. 17, 1988; children: Kari Michelle Forrest, Lauren Gayle. BS, Kent State U., Ohio, 1977; MS, Nova Southeastern U., Ft. Lauderdale, Fla., 1996. Cert. Nat. Bd. Profl. Tchg. Stds., 2002. Biology/AP biology tchr. Lake Worth HS, Fla., 1986—2005; lead tchr., biotech. acad. Seminole Ridge HS, Loxahatchee, Fla., 2005—. Faculty cons./table leader Ednl. Testing Svc., Princeton, NJ, 1996—2005. Contbr. articles to profl. jours. Recipient Dwyer Award for H.S. Edn., Econ. Coun. of Palm Beaches, 2002. Mem.: NSTA, Nat. Assn. Biology Tchrs. (Outstanding Biology Tchr. Award 2004). Avocations: eventing, dressage. Office: Seminole Ridge High School 4601 Seminole Pratt Whitney Rd Loxahatchee FL 33470 Office Phone: 561-422-2600. Office Fax: 561-422-2764. E-mail: slyghc@palmbeach.k12.fl.us.

SMAGALSKI, CAROLYN M., publishing executive, webmaster, director; b. Phila., Aug. 28, 1952; d. Raymond L and Mary K Hanisco; children: Michael M, Tyler A. BA Cum Laude, Temple U., Philadelphia, 1971—75. Lic. private pilot SEL with IFR rating and Complex Aircraft Rating US Dept. of Transp./Fed. Aviation Adminstrn., 1996. Account mgr. Brown Printing Co., East Greenville, Pa., 1996—; exec. dir., author, webmaster, internetwork marketer CQ Web Wide LLC, Harleysville, Pa., 2002—. Beer and brewing advisor Gluten Free Beer Festival U.K., 2006—. Author (editor): (website mag.) Beer and Brewing, 2004—; creator Beer Fox, 2004, guest appearance Beer Fox/Beer Chef, Beer Radio. Beer and brewing advisor Gluten Free Beer Festival, England, 2006—. Mem.: Better Internet Bur., Internat. Assn. Home Bus. Entrepreneurs, Internat. Orgn. Women Pilots, Aircraft Owners & Pilot's Assn. Avocations: information technology, aviation, psychology of brain & socio-emotional challenges, gourmet cooking, public relations & travel. Home: 805 Continental Drive Harleysville PA 19438 Office: CQ Web Wide LLC 805 Continental Drive Harleysville PA 19438 Office Phone: 215-541-2723. Personal E-mail: carolsmagalski@comcast.net. E-mail: cs1@cqwebwide.com.

SMALBEIN, DOROTHY ANN, guidance counselor; b. Rochester, N.Y. d. Karl Taylor and Virginia (Woodcock) Howard; m. June 27, 1954 (div.); children: William Paul, John Allen. Student, St. Lawrence U., Canton, N.Y., 1952-54; BA, U. Cen. Fla., 1971, MEd in Counseling, 1978. Guidance counselor Pine Trail Elem. Sch., Volusia County Sch. Bd., Fla., 1978—. Recipient Outstanding Svc. award, Volusia County Counselors, 1979. Mem. AACD, Fla. Sch. Counselors Assn., Fla. Assn. for Counseling and Devel. (conv. presenter 1981-88), Volusia Assn. for Counseling and Devel. (sunshine chmn. 1980-81, treas. 1988-90), Volusia County Elementary Counselors Assn. (chmn. 1981-82), Jr. League, Pi Beta Phi. Methodist. Avocations: piano, singing. Office: Pine Trail Elem Sch 300 Airport Rd Ormond Beach FL 32174-8725

SMALL, BERTRICE W., writer; b. N.Y.C., Dec. 9, 1937; d. David Roger Williams, Doris Melissa (Maud) Steen; m. George Sumner Small, Oct. 5, 1963; 1 child, Thomas David. Student, Western Coll. for Women, Oxford, Ohio, Katherine Gibbs Sectl. Sch., N.Y.C., 1959. With Young & Rubicon, N.Y.C., 1959—60, Weed Radio & TV, N.Y.C., 1960—61, Edward Petry & Co., N.Y.C., 1961—63. Author: The Kadin, 1978, Sky O'Malley, 1980, All The Sweet Tomorrows, 1984, Amount In Time, 1991, Betrayal, 1998, The Innocent, 1999, Rosamund, 2002, 25 others. Vestrywoman Redeemer Episc. Ch., Mattituck, NY, 1998—2001. Recipient Career Achievement Reviewers Choice award, Romantic Times Mag., 1983, 1988, 1995, 2001. Mem.: L.I. Romance Writers (bd. dirs. 1999—2001), Romance Writers of Am., Authors Guild. Episcopalian. Avocation: gardening. Mailing: PO Box 765 Southold NY 11971

SMALL, ELISABETH CHAN, psychiatrist, educator; b. Beijing, July 11, 1934; came to U.S., 1937; d. Stanley Hong and Lily Luella (Lum) Chan; m. Donald M. Small, July 8, 1957 (div. 1980); children Geoffrey Brooks, Philip Willard Stanley; m. H. Sidney Robinson, Jan. 12, 1991 (div. 2001). Student, Immaculate Heart Coll., L.A., 1951-52; BA in Polit. Sci., UCLA, 1955, MD, 1960. Intern Newton-Wellesley Hosp., Mass., 1960-61; asst. dir. for venereal diseases Mass. Dept. Pub. Health, 1961-63; resident in psychiatry Boston State Hosp., Mattapan, Mass., 1965-66, Tufts New Eng. Med. Ctr. Hosps., 1966-69, psychiat. cons. dept. gynecology, 1973-75; asst. clin. prof. psychiatry Sch. Medicine Tufts U., 1973-75, assoc. clin. prof., 1975-82, asst. clin. prof. ob-gyn, 1977-80, assoc. clin. prof. ob-gyn, 1980-82; from assoc. prof. to prof. psychiatry U. Nev. Sch. Med., Reno, 1982-95; practice psychiatry specializing in psychological effects of bodily changes on women, 1969—; emeritus prof. psychiatry and behavioral scis. U. Nev. Sch. Medicine, Reno, 1995—, from assoc. prof. to clin. assoc. prof. ob-gyn, 1982-88; mem. staff Tufts New Eng. Med. Ctr. Hosps., 1977-82, St. Margaret's Hosps., Boston, 1977-82, Washoe Med. Ctr., Reno, 1983—2006, St. Mary's Regional Med. Ctr., Reno, Truckee Meadows Hosp., Reno, St. Mary's Hosp., Reno; chief psychiatry svc. Reno VA Med. Ctr., 1989-94. Lectr., cons. in field; mem. psychiatry adv. panel Hosp. Satellite Network; mem. office external peer rev. NIMH, HEW; psychiat. cons. to Boston Redevelopment Authority on Relocation of Chinese Families of South Cove Area, 1968-70; mem. New Eng. Med. Ctr. Hosps. Cancer Ctr. Com., 1979-80, Pain Control Com., 1981-82; reproductive sys. curriculum com. Tufts Univ. Sch. Medicine, 1975-82. Mem. editorial bd. Psychiat. Update Am. (Psychiat. Assn. ann. rev.), 1983-85; reviewer Psychosomatics and Hosp. Community Psychiatry, New Eng. Jour. of Medicine, Am. Jour. of Psychiatry Psychosomatic Medicine; contbr. articles to profl. jours. Immaculate Heart Coll. scholar, 1951-52, Mira Hershey scholar UCLA, 1955; fellow Radcliffe Inst., 1967-70. Fellow Am. Coll. Psychiatrists (sci. program com. 1989-98); mem. AMA, Am. Psychiat. Assn. (life, rep. to sect. com. AAAS, chmn. ad hoc com. Asian-Am. Psychiatrists 1975, task force 1975-77, task force cost effectiveness in consultation 1984—, caucus chmn. 1981-82, sci. program com. 1982-88, courses subcom. chmn. sci. program com. 1986-88), Nev. Psychiat. Assn., Assn. for Acad. Psychiatry (fellowship com. 1982), Washoe County Med. Assn., Nev. Med. Soc. Avocations: skiing, cooking. Home and Office: 825 Caughlin Crossing Reno NV 89509-0647

SMALL, JOYCE GRAHAM, psychiatrist, educator; b. Edmonton, Alta., Can., June 12, 1931; came to U.S., 1956; d. John Earl and Rachel C. (Redmond) Graham; m. Iver Francis Small, May 26, 1954; children: Michael, Jeffrey. BA, U. Sask., Saskatoon, Can., 1951; MD, U. Man., Alta., Can., 1956; MS, U. Mich., 1959. Diplomat Am. Bd. Psychiatry and Neurology, Am. Bd. Electroencephalography. Instr. in psychiatry Neuropsychiat. Inst. U. Mich., Ann Arbor, 1959-60; instr. in psychiatry med. sch. U. Oreg., Portland, 1960-61, asst. prof. in psychiatry med. sch., 1961-62; asst. prof. in psychiatry sch. of medicine Washington U., St. Louis, 1962-65; assoc. prof. in psychiatry sch. of medicine Ind. U., Indpls., 1965—69, prof. psychiatry sch. of medicine, 1969—2004, prof. emerita, 2004—. Mem. initial rev. groups NIMH, Washington, 1972-76, 79-82, 87-91; assoc. mem. Inst. Psychiat. Rsch., Indpls., 1974—. Mem. editl. bd. Quar. Jour. Convulsive Therapy, 1984-2000, Clin. EEG, 1990—; contbr. articles to profl. jours. Rsch. grantee NIMH, Portland, Oreg., 1961-62, St. Louis, 1962-64, Indpls., 1967-95, Epilepsy Found., Dreyfus Found., Indpls., 1965; recipient Merit award NIMH, Indpls., 1990, Career award EEG and Clin. Neurosci. Soc., 2003. Fellow Am. Psychiat. Assn., Am. EEG Soc. (councillor 1972-75, 1982); mem. Soc. Biol. Psychiatry, Cen. Assn. Electroencephalographers (sec., treas. 1967-68, pres. 1970, councillor 1971-72). Business E-Mail: jgsmall@iupui.edu.

SMALL, NATALIE SETTIMELLI, retired pediatric mental health counselor; b. Quincy, Mass., June 2, 1933; d. Joseph Peter and Edmea Natalie (Bagnaschi) Settimelli; m. Parker Adams Small, Jr., Aug. 26, 1956; children: Parker Adams III, Peter McMichael, Carla Edmea. BA, Tufts U., 1955; MA, EdS, U. Fla., 1976, PhD, 1987. Cert. child life specialist. Pediatric counselor U. Fla. Coll. Medicine, Gainesville, 1976-80, Shands Hosp.-U. Fla., Gainesville, 1980-87, supr. child life dept. patient and family resources, 1987—2003; pres. Small Group Cons.com, 2003—. Adminstrv. liaison for self-dir. work teams, mem. faculty Ctr. for Coop. Learning for Health and Sci. Edn., Gainesville, 1988-2003, assoc. dir., 1996, supr. pastoral svcs., 1998-2003; cons. and lectr. in field. Author: Parents Know Best, 1991; co-author team packs series for teaching at risk adolescent health edn. Building Strong Families, 1998. Bd. dirs. Ronald McDonald House, Gainesville, 1980—, mem. exec. com., 1991-05; bd. dirs. Gainesville Assn. Creative Arts, 1994—;

mem. health profl. adv. com. March of Dimes, Gainesville, 1986-96, HIV prevention planning partnership, 1995-96; mem. Teen Pregnancy Prevention Action Com., 1998-00, exec. com. Children's Hosp., 1998-03. Recipient Thayer Acad. Humanitarian award, 2006, Caring and Sharing award Ronald McDonald House, 1995, Appreciation award March of Dimes, 1996; Boston Stewart Club scholar, Florence, Italy, 1955; grantee Jessie Ball Du Pont Fund, 1978, Children's Miracle Network, 1990, 92-95, 97, 2000, 01-03. Mem. ACA. Roman Catholic. Avocations: travel, reading, swimming. Home: 3454 NW 12th Ave Gainesville FL 32605-4811 E-mail: smallgroup2@aol.com.

SMALL, SARAH MAE, volunteer; b. Salisbury, N.C., Nov. 16, 1923; d. Clint and Lillie Mae (Wilbourn) Evans; m. Jesse Small Sr., May 4, 1941; children: Jesse Jr., Jean Carol Small Bell. Cert., Cortez Bus. Sch., 1948. File clk. gen. acctg. office Fed. Govt., Washington, 1941—47; sec., stenographer CIA, Washington, 1948—52, adminstrv. asst. McLean, Va., 1952—65, ret., 1965. Elected pres. Energetic Crusaders, Inc., 1993—. Pres. Energetic Crusaders, Inc., 1993; bd. dirs. ARC, Washington, 1986-87, Children's Edn. Found., Inc., 1989—. Recipient Outstanding and Dedicated Vol. Svc. award Kiwanis Club of Capital Centre, 1985, Plaque in Recognition of Dedicated and Outstanding Vol. Svc. to the Corps and Washington D.C., Cmty. Jr. Citizen's Corps., 1989, Appreciation award for Outstanding and Dedicated Vol. Svc. to Corps, Jr. Citizens Corps., Inc., 1990, Appreciation award Jr. Citizens Corp., Inc., 1990, Cmty. Svc. award for leadership and youth advocacy Bus. and Profl. Women's League, Inc., 1991, Vol. award achievement excellence svc. youths of Jr. Citizens Corps., Inc., 1992, others. Mem. Jr. Citizens Corps (life, pres. 1985—, Dedicated Cmty. Svc. award 1983, Bus. and Cmty. Svc. award 1986), Bus. and Profl. Women's League (treas. 1982-86), Women in Arts (chartered, pres. 1984—), Nat. Coun. Negro Women, World Affairs Coun. Washington, Agrl. Coun. Am. Democrat. Baptist. Avocations: travel, photography, walking, swimming. Home: 2010 Upshur St NE Washington DC 20018-3244

SMALLEY, PENNY JUDITH, healthcare technology consultant; b. Chgo., Feb. 20, 1947; d. Ernest Rich and Muriel L. (Touff) Brown; m. Ivan H. Smalley, Jan. 11, 1972; children: Cherie Ann, Michael John, Geoffry Paul. Grad., Evanston Hosp. Sch. Nursing, Ill., 1980. Diplomate Am. Bd. Laser Surgery. Staff nurse Evanston Hosp., 1979-81, laser coord., 1981-83; office mgr. Women's Health Group, 1981; laser nurse specialist Cooper Lasersonics, various, 1983-86; pres., CEO Technology Concepts Internat., Inc., Chgo., 1986—. Lectr., writer Sino Fgn. Laser Conf., People's Republic of China, 1987; bd. dirs. Laser Inst. Am.; rep. Assn. Perioperative RN's. Contbg. author: Nursing Clinics of North America, 1990; mem. editl. bd. Clin. Laser Monthly, Laser Nursing mag., 1989—, Minimally Invasive Surg. Nursing, Photodiagnosis and Photodynamics Therapy; contbr. articles to profl. jours. Mem. Am. Soc. Laser Medicine and Surgery (chmn. edn. com. 1987-90, standards of practice com. 1990, quality assurance com., nursing sect. chmn. 1992-94, chair safety com.), award for Excellence in Laser Nursing 1993), Laser Inst. Am. (bd. dirs.), Am. Nat. Standards Com., Inst. Com. Lasers in Health Care, Brit. Med. Laser Assn. (course dir. first laser nursing conf. in U.K., 1990), Assn. Perioperative Registered Nurses (tchr. nat. seminars, spl. com. on internat. issues, liaison to ANSI Z136, Australian/N.Z. 4173 laser safety stds.), Internat. Soc. Laser Surgery and Medicine (chmn. nursing 1988—, chmn. safety com. 2002), Internat. Electrotech. Commn. (Am. delegation tech. com. 76 for internat. stds. regarding lasers and electromed. equipment). Democrat. Avocations: music, community theater, travel, photography. Home and Office: 1444 W Farwell Ave Chicago IL 60626-3410 Office Phone: 773-262-2810. Personal E-mail: pennyjs@aol.com.

SMALLWOOD, CAROL, writer; b. Cheboygan, Mich., May 3, 1939; d. Lloyd Gouine and Lucille Drozdowska; m. T.M. Smallwood, 1963 (div. 1976); children: Michael, Ann. BS, Ea. Mich. U., 1961, M in History, 1963; MLS, We. Mich. U., 1976. Tchr. Mich. Pub. Sch., 1961—64; grad. asst. Western Mich. U., Kalamazoo, 1975-76; Title I libr. cons. Northland (Mich.), Grand Traverse (Mich.) Library Systems, 1976-77; head media dir. Pellston (Mich.) Pub. Schs., 1977—97; writer, libr. cons. classes Mt. Pleasant, 1998—. Asst. dir. Northland Libr. System, Alpena, Mich., 1977; developer, operator ednl. materials clearinghouse, 1981-83; adult edn. tchr. Cheboygan Area Schs., 1985-86. Author: Free Michigan Materials for Educators, 1980, 2nd edit., 1986, Free Materials Resource Disk, 1983, Exceptional Free Library Resource Materials, 1984, Free Resource Builder, 1985, 2d edit., 1992, A Guide to Selected Federal Agency Programs and Publications for Librarians and Teachers, 1986, Health Resource Builder, 1988, An Educational Guide to the National Park System, 1989, Current Issues Builder, 1989, Library Puzzles and Word Games, for Grades 7-12, 1990, Reference Puzzles and Word Games for Grades 7-12, 1991, Michigan Authors, 1993, Helpful Hints for the School Library, 1993, Recycling Tips for Teachers and Librarians, 1995, An Insider's Guide to Libraries, 1997, Free or Low-Cost Health Information, 1998; (with S. McElmeel) WWW Almanac, 1999; (with B. Hudson, A. Riedling, J. Rotole) Internet Sources on Each U.S. State, 2005, Educators as Writers: Publishing for Personal and Professional Development, 2006; author 100 poems in English Jour., Poesia, others; contbr; columnist Detroit News; others. Charter bd. mem., publicity chmn. Cheboygan Area Arts Coun.; founder, pres. Cheboygan County Humane Soc.; co-founder Humane Animal Treatment Soc. Recipient 1st prize for fiction, Byline Mag., 2004. Mem.: Doris Day Animal Found. Mailing: PO Box 1485 Mount Pleasant MI 48804 E-mail: smallwood@tm.net.

SMALLWOOD, REBECCA RUTH, elementary school educator; b. Greenville, SC, Nov. 9, 1970; d. Tom and Judy White; m. Chadrick Gray Smallwood, May 5, 1990; children: Gray, Bryson. BS cum laude, Presbyn. Coll., Clinton, SC, 1996. Cert. tchr. SC Dept. Edn., 1996. Tchr. Laurens (SC) 55 Sch. Dist., 1997—2005, sci. coach, 2005—. Mem.: NEA (assoc.). Home: 228 Peachtree St Gray Court SC 29645 Office: Gray Court-Owings School 9210 Hwy 14 Gray Court SC 29645 Office Phone: 864-876-2171. Office Fax: 864-876-2965. Business E-Mail: rsmallwood@laurens55.k12.sc.us.

SMALLWOOD, SANDRA DENISE, pastor, daycare administrator; b. Buffalo, Feb. 28, 1953; d. Harl and Dorothy Mae Smallwood; children: Samuel Hayes II, Dorinda Hayes, Deana Hayes, Aaron Hayes, Eric Hayes. Student, Erie C.C., 1992—94, Child Devel. Assoc., 2001—02. Ordained pastor 1993. Evangelist prison ministry Eric County Holding Ctr., Buffalo, 1977—80; tchr., evangelist Concerned Citizens Against Violence and Crime, 1990—92; chaplain Shoreline Apts. Block Club, 1995—98; pastor, founder Kingdom of Heaven Light House Growth Min. Ch., 1995—; mem. Buffalo Pub. Access Media, 1995—; dir., owner Kingdom of Heaven Little Ones Day Care, 2003—; chaplain svcs. Mary Agnes & Conerstone Manor, 2003—. Founder TV ministry Bibical Morals & Truth, Buffalo, 1995—; tchr. daycare Cmty. Action Orgn., 1999—2002; dist. parent coord. McKinley High Sch., 2002—04; mem. Child Care Coalition, 2005—; residential coord. Cornerstone Manor, 2006—. Avocations: story telling, swimming, reading, singing. Home: 117 Virgil Ave Buffalo NY 14216 Office: Kingdom of Heaven Light House Growth Ministry 117 Virgil Ave Buffalo NY 14216 Office Phone: 716-871-0957.

SMALLWOOD, VIRGINIA N., special education educator; d. Felton L. and Bulah L. Smallwood. AB in Psychology and Spl.Edn., Ctrl. Wesleyan Coll., Central, S.C., 1975; MA in Secondary Guidance, Clemson U., S.C., 1983; EdSp in Spl. Edn., U. S.C., Columbia, 1988. Cert. tchr. S.C. Spl. ednl. tchr., cheerleader coach Ninety-Six H.S., Ninety-Six, SC, 1976—86, Gilbert H.S., SC, 1986—. Grantee Recycling grantee, Dept. Health and Environ. Control, 2005. Mem.: Coun. for Exceptional Children, S.C. Cheerleader Coaches Assn. (treas. 1990—96, bd. dirs. 1996—). Democrat. Methodist. Avocations: reading, travel, house plants, raising cats.

SMARGIASSI, REBECCA SUE, secondary school educator; b. Marceline, Mo., Mar. 12, 1967; d. Garry Amen; m. Michael Lawrence Smargiassi, Aug. 1, 1965; children: Mariah, Payne. BS in Edn., Truman State U., Kirksville, Mo., 1989. H.s. English tchr. Morrison (Ill.) H.S., 1989—99, Triad H.S., Troy, Ill., 1999—. Student amb. leader People to People, Ill., 2003—03; advisor Future Teachers Am., Troy, 2002—06; mission trip participant Bethel Bapt. Ch., Troy, 2002—02. Mem.: Nat. Coun. Tchrs. English. Avocations: reading, travel. Office: Triad High School 703 E Hwy 40 Troy IL 62294 Office Phone: 618-667-8851 7133. Business E-Mail: rsmargiassi@triad.madison.k12.il.us.

SMART, JILL BELLAVIA, financial consultant; b. Chgo., Oct. 16, 1959; d. Salvatore and patricia (Foran) B.; m. Stephen D. Smart; two children. BS, U. Ill., 1981; MBA, U. Chgo., 1991. Assoc. ptnr. Accenture Ltd., Chgo., 1981—89, mng. ptnr. human resource delivery/Chgo. office, lead ptnr., 1989—. Bd. trustee Accenture Found. Vol. Treehouse Animal Found., Chgo., 1986-90, Chgo. Area Runners Assn., 1986—; bd. dirs. Goodman Theater, Chgo.; dir. United Way Met. Chgo.; mem. pres. adv. com. U. Ill. Named one of Chgos. 100 Most Influential Women, Crain's Chgo. Bus., 2004. Republican. Roman Catholic. Avocations: jogging, aerobics, travel, reading, skiing. Office Phone: 312-693-0161.

SMART, MARY-LEIGH CALL (MRS. J. SCOTT SMART), civic worker; b. Springfield, Ill., Feb. 27, 1917; d. S(amuel) Leigh and Mary (Bradish) Call; m. J. Scott Smart, Sept. 11, 1951 (dec. 1960). Diploma, Monticello Coll., 1934; student, Oxford U., 1935; BA, Wellesley Coll., 1937; MA, Columbia U., 1939, postgrad., 1940—41, NYU, 1940—41; painting student, with Bernard Karfiol, 1937—38. Dir. mgmt. Cen. Ill. Grain Farms, Logan County, 1939—; owner Lowtrek Kennel, Ogunquit, Maine, 1957-73, Cove Studio Art Gallery, Ogunquit, 1961-68; art collector, patron, publicist, 1954—. Cons. in field. Editor: Hamilton Easter Field Art Found. Collection Catalog, 1966; originator, dir. show, compiler of catalog Art: Ogunquit, 1967; Peggy Bacon-A Celebration, Barn Gallery, Ogunquit, 1979. Program dir., sec. bd. Barn Gallery Assoc., Inc., 1958-69, pres., 1969-70, 82-87, asst. treas., 1987-92, hon. dir., 1970-78, adv. trustee, 1992-94, v.p., 1994-2003; curator Hamilton Easter Field Art Found. Collection, 1978-79, curator exhbn., 1979-86, chair exhbn. com., 1987-94; acquisition com. DeCordova Mus., Lincoln, Mass., 1966-78; chancellor's coun. U. Tex., 1972—; pres. coun. U. NH, 1978—; bd. dir. Ogunquit C. of C., 1966, treas., 1966-67, hon. life mem., 1968—; bd. overseers Strawbery Banke, Inc., Portsmouth, NH, 1972-75, 3d vice chmn., 1973, 2d vice-chmn., 1974; bd. advisors U. Art Galleries, U. NH, 1973-89; pres., 1981-89; bd. dir. Old York Hist. and Improvement Soc., York, Maine, 1979-81, v.p., 1981-82; adv. com. Bowdoin Coll. Mus. Art Invitational exhibit, 1975, '76 Maine Artists Invitational Exhbn., Maine State Mus., Maine Coast Artists, Rockport, 1975-78, All Maine Biennial '79, Bowdoin Coll. Mus. Art juried exhbn.; mem. jury for scholarship awards Maine com. Skowhegan Sch. Painting & Sculpture, 1982-84; nat. com. Wellesley Coll. Friends of Art, 1983—; adv. trustee Portland Mus. Art, 1983-85, fellow, 1985—; mus. panel Maine State Commn. on Arts and Humanities, 1983-86; adv. com. Maine Biennial, Colby Coll. Mus. Art, 1983; coun. advisors Farnsworth Art Mus., Rockland, Maine, 1986-98; collections com. Payson Gallery, Westbrook Coll., Portland, 1987-91; dir. Greater Piscataqua Cmty. Found., NH Charitable Fund, 1991-97; com. to establish artist's advancement grant, 2001; mem. corp. Ogunquit Mus. Am. Art, 1988-90, 95-2000; active Maine Women's Forum, 1993—; mem. art com. York Pub. Libr., 2002—; pres. Class of 1937, Wellesley Coll., 2001—. Lt. (j.g.) WAVES, 1942-45. Recipient Deborah Morton award Westbrook Coll., 1988, Friend of the Arts award Maine Art Dealers Assn., 1993. Mem. Springfield Art Assn., Jr. League Springfield Ill., Western Maine Wellesley Club. Episcopalian. Address: 30 Surf Point Rd York ME 03909-5053

SMART, ROBIN MCDANIEL, music educator; b. Atlanta, Nov. 2, 1961; d. John Robert and Virginia Gann McDaniel; m. James Anthony Smart; children: Laurel Morgan, Andrew Forrest. B Ch. Music, Shorter Coll., Rome, Ga., 1984, MusB Edn., 2004; M Ch. Music, So. Bapt. Theol. Sem., Louisville, 1988. Cert. music tchr. Ga. Children's min. First Bapt. Ch., Lithia Springs, Ga., 1995—2004; music tchr. Smitha Mid. Sch., Marietta, Ga., 2005—. Mem.: Ga. Music Edn. Assn., Am. Choral Dirs. Assn. (pres. 2000—), Music Educators Nat. Conf.

SMEAL, JANIS LEA, psychiatrist; b. Johnstown, Pa., Aug. 31, 1953; d. Charles Truman S. and Clara Belle (Smeal) Satterlee. RN, Mercy Hosp. Sch. Nursing, 1974; BS summa cum laude, U. Houston, 1996; DO, U. North Tex., 2001. RN, Tex.; cert. oper. rm. nurse; cert. ACLS. Staff, relief charge nurse emergency rm. Mercy Hosp., Altoona, Pa., 1974—85; staff nurse oper. rm. McAllen Med. Ctr., Tex., 1985—87, Rio Grande Regional Hosp., McAllen, 1987—88; co-owner Associated Hypnotherapy and Pain Mgmt. Svcs. Tex., Bellaire, 1991—97; staff nurse oper. rm. Meml. City Hosp., Houston, 1992—97; psychiatry resident U. Tex. Health Sci. Ctr., Houston, 2001—05, asst. prof. psychiatry, 2005—. Co-owner, cons. J.L. Med. Svcs., McAllen, Tex., 1988-94. Recognition Golden Key Nat. Honor Soc., 1993, Phi Kappa Phi, 1994, Natural Sci. and Math. Scholars and Fellows, 1995. Mem.: Tex. Med. Assn., Tex. Osteo. Med. Assn., Am. Psychiat. Assn., Golden Key, Alpha Omega Alpha, Phi Kappa Phi. Avocations: travel, dog training, interior design. Office: 2800 S MacGregor Ste 3D-08 Houston TX 77021

SMELSER, JUNE, librarian; b. Portland, Oreg., June 1, 1919; d. George and Kathryn Ellen (Reynolds) England; m. Richard O. Williams Jan. 30, 1942 (wid. 1944); m. Lawrence C. Smelser, June 30, 1950 (wid. 1987); children: Jean, Kenneth, Gail, Rosanne, Marianne, Duane, Michael. BA, U. Oreg., 1941; BLS, Columbia U., 1946. Children's librarian Oregon City Pub. Library, 1946-51; librarian David Douglas High Sch., Portland, 1957-69, Lake Oswego (Oreg.) Jr. High Sch., 1969-71; mgr. Food for Thought (Food Coop), Oregon City; cons., distbr. Golden Neo-Life Diamite Internat., Milw., 1976—. Editor newsletter Weedy Acres Gazette, 1988—. Mem. Am. Assn. Ret. Persons (Oreg. state coord. ret. tchrs. 1988-91, dist. dir. Oreg. 1992—), Toastmasters Internat. (pres. club 1988), Trails Club of Oreg. Avocations: hiking, backpacking, cross-country, skiing, reading.

SMELSER, RUTH MALONE, volunteer; b. Tescott, Kans., Dec. 20, 1917; d. Dial Pete and Mamie Evelyn (Donbarger) Moss; m. Raymond U. Schoonover, 1939 (div. 1950); children: Marion, Karen, Linda; m. Charles Fay Stiles, Nov. 15, 1951 (dec. June 1960); children: Vicki, Rhonda, Bonnie; m. Everett Frey, 1962 (div. 1963); m. Stanley Malone, 1964 (div. 1981); m. Hershel Smelser, 1982. Grad., Custer County Jr. Coll., Miles City, Mont., 1936; student, Mont. U., 1977, 78. Tchr., Campbell County, Wyo., 1936-37; rancher Johnson County, Wyo., 1939-51; owner Cattle and Irrigated Farm, Custer County, Mont., 1951-70; mgr. House of Fabrics, Tempo Store, Miles City, Mont., 1970-77; owner Ruth's Draperies, Miles City, 1978-80; builder Passive Solar-Earth Sheltered Home, Buffalo, Wyo., 1982-85; organizer recycling program Buffalo, 1990-95. Leader 4-H Club Willing Workers, Miles City, 1965-75; pres. Buffalo/Johnson County Recycling Bd., 1990-97. Recipient Cert. of award as Wyo. Recycler of Yr., 1997. Democrat. Methodist. Avocations: sewing, fine arts painting.

SMELSER, THELMA ANN, writer, tax specialist; b. Piedmont, Ala., June 7, 1941; d. Rufus Milton and Florence Inez Steward; m. William Guy Smelser, Jr., June 11; children: Joseph Milton, William Preston. BA in English, Huntingdon Coll., 1964; postgrad., U. Ga., 1973—77. Lic. SEC. Tchr. Montgomery (Ala.) Bd. Edn., 1964—66, DeKalb County Bd. Edn., Decatur, Ga., 1966—85; owner Everlasting Images Wholesale, Snellville, Ga., 1985—98; tax profl. H&R Block, Loganville, Ga., 1998—; owner TAS Publs., 2004—. SEC fin. advisor H&R Block, Loganville, Ga., 2003—. Author: Strawberries & Honeysuckle, 1985; columnist: Loganville Post, 2004—. Tax advisor The Loganville Post, 2004; team mom Little League Baseball Team, Gwinnett County, Ga., 1986; mem. charity com. First Bapt. Ch., Loganville, 1997. Recipient Yearbook award, Walker H.S., 1977, Scrapbook award, Snellville Middle Sch., 1988. Republican. Baptist. Avocations: wildlife, boating, rug hooking, painting, reading. Home: 4201 Cannon Rd Loganville GA 30052 Office: H&R Block 4325 Atlanta Hwy Loganville GA 30052 Office Phone: 404-444-7279. E-mail: asmelser@bellsouth.net.

SMELTZER, KATHY ANN, mathematics educator; b. Wyandotte, Mich., Sept. 2, 1954; d. F. David and Ruth D. Charles; m. Joseph M. Charles, Nov. 17, 1979; children: Caralyn K., Benjamin J., Rebekah B. BS, Ea. Mich. U., Ypsilanti, 1975; MS, Westerm Mich. U., Kalamazoo, 1997. Math. tchr. Milan Area Schs., Mich., 1976—78; math./physics tchr. Lake Fenton Schs., Mich., 1978—80, Bethel Schs., Tipp City, Mich., 1980—81, Jefferson Schs., Monroe, Mich., 1981—. Mem.: MCTM, NCTM. Avocations: singing in gospel group, puppetry.

SMETANA, KRISTINE SAMARIA, chemistry professor, consultant; b. Arlington, Mass., Dec. 26, 1968; d. Nancy Joan and Richard Angelo Samaria; m. Christopher Danial Smetana, Oct. 10, 1998; children: Alexander Nial, Andrew Nicholas. PhD in Inorganic Chemistry, Va. Commonwealth U., Richmond, 1997; BA in Chemistry, Wheaton Coll., Norton, Mass., 1990. Sci. and economics instr., rsch. coord. Governor's Sch. for Global Economics and Tech., Alberta, Va., 1997—99; sci. tchr., coord. Appomattox Regional Governor's Sch., Petersburg, Va., 1999—2000; prof. chemistry John Tyler C.C., Chester, Va., 2000—. Cons., sci. instr. sys. career switchers program Va. C.C., Richmond, 2004—05. Recipient Donna Ingemie Sorenson prize, Wheaton Coll., 1989; grantee, Am. Chem. Soc. Va. Sect., 2006. Mem.: NSTA (life), Am. Chem. Soc. (life; exec. com. Va. sect. 2000). Home: 4501 Fitzhugh Ave Richmond VA 23230-3730 Office: John Tyler Cmty Coll 13101 Jefferson Davis Hwy Chester VA 23831 Office Phone: 804-706-5143. Office Fax: 804-796-4361. Business E-Mail: ksmetana@jtcc.edu.

SMETANKA, MARY JANE, reporter; Grad., U. Minn.-Twin Cities. Reporter, Minn., ND, Conn.; higher edn. reporter Mpls. Star Tribune, Mpls. Mem.: Edn. Writers Assn. (pres.). Achievements include being a Minn. Master Gardener. Office: Mpls Star Tribune 425 Portland Ave Minneapolis MN 55488-1511

SMETANKA, SALLY S., small business owner; b. Athens, NY, Aug. 26, 1944; AS, Valencia C.C., Orlando, Fla., 1981; BA, Rollins Coll., Winter Park, Fla., 1991. With labor rels. Walt Disney World, Orlando, Fla., 1978—81, asst. to pres., 1983—2005; owner Carriage Ho. Antiques, Orlando, Fla., 2005—. Home and Office: 1253 Nottingham St Orlando FL 32803 Office Phone: 321-217-1687.

SMIDA, MARY AGNES, counselor; b. Pitts., Oct. 19, 1953; d. Harry Edward and Grace Ceclia (Kehlenbeck) Baum; m. Michael Richard Smida Jr., Aug. 6, 1983; 1 child, Joette Andrea. Student, Seton Hill Coll.; BFA in Art, Edinboro State Coll., 1975; MS in Community Agy. Counseling, Calif. U. of Pa., 1992. Lic. profl. counselor, nat. cert. counselor. Dispensing and lab. optician Pearle Vision Ctr., West Mifflin, Pa., 1981-84, dispensing optician Belle Vernon, Pa., 1987-91; counselor New Choices, YWCA, Washington, Pa., 1992-94, Crosskeys Human Svcs., Inc., 1994—97, Centerville Clin., Fredericktown, Pa., 1998, Wash. Communities, 1999—2004, Family Behavioral Resources, 2004—. Organist St. Joseph Ch., Roscoe, Pa., 1985-2002, liturgy planner, 1985-. Presdl. scholar Calif. U. Pa. Mem. ACA, Am. Mental Health Counselor's Assn., Assn. for Spiritual, Ethical & Religious Values in Counseling. Democrat. Roman Catholic. Avocation: reading. Home: 520 1st St Monessen PA 15062-1509

SMILEY, CAROL ANNE, health facility administrator, sculptor; b. Cedar Rapids, Iowa, Sept. 11, 1937; d. Ralph Derold and Mary C. Miller; m. Donald Victor Smiley, June 29, 1956 (div. Aug. 1970); children: Donald Victor Jr., Julie Ann, Joseph Charles, Thomas Wayne; m. Douglas Brewster Reed, Aug. 6, 1976 (div. Jan. 1988); 1 child, Brook (dec.). Co-founder, v.p., sec., treas. Anvic Enterprise, Cedar Rapids, 1963-70; co-founder, dir. Yankee Horse Trader, Bennington, Vt., 1974; organic farmer Solon, Iowa, Argyle, N.Y., 1970-86; fiber sculptor, 1970-86; tchr. Solon H.S., 1973-74; caregiver, coord. Home Health Care and Hospice, Brattleboro, Vt., 1986—; cons. in grassroots home health. Sculpture shows include Green Mt. Collaborative, Bennington, 1974-78, Woman Art Gallery, N.Y.C., 1977-78, Lincoln Ctr. Group Show, N.Y.C., 1978; exhbns. various group shows. Mem. GOP ctrl. com. for Johnson County, Iowa, 1971-72. Mem.: ACLU. Office: Home Health Care Hospice 142 Green St Brattleboro VT 05301-6054 Office Phone: 802-254-8564.

SMILEY, CINDY YORK, psychotherapist educator; b. Pasadena, Tex., Oct. 6, 1956; d. Clem T. and Sharon G. (Mead) York; m. Richard E. Smiley, June 7, 1975 (div. Apr. 1989); 1 child, Matthew J.; Lee Allen Moore, Jr., May 22, 1993. AA in Bus. Adminstrn., San Jacinto Coll., 1986; BS in Psychology, U. Houston-Clear Lake, 1988, MA in Clin. Psychology, 1993. Lic. profl. counselor; cert. group therapist, mediator. Proprietor Custom Tinting, Pasadena, Tex., 1980-92; co-developer, founder Innovative Alternatives, Houston, 1986-92; coord., exptl. therapy Intracare Hosp., Houston, 1993-94, case mgr., therapist children and adult svcs., 1994-95; pvt. practitioner psychotherapy Cindy Y. Smiley, M.A., LPC, Houston, 1994—; dir. mediation and sexual abuse tng. programs Innovative Alternatives, Houston, 1995—. Adj. prof. mediation U. Houston-Clear Lake, Houston, 1991-92; trainer, conflict resolution Innovative Alternatives, Houston, 1988—. Spkr., presenter for workshops and seminars, Houston, 1989—. Named to Nat. Dean's List, 1988. Mem. Am. Counseling Assn., Am. Assn. Specialist GroupWork, U.S. Assn. Victim/Offender Mediation. Avocations: reading, stained glass, outdoor activities, computers. Home: 604 Yorkshire Ave Pasadena TX 77503-1456 Office: Innovative Alternatives 18301 Egret Bay Blvd Houston TX 77058-3253

SMILEY, DENISA ANN, music educator; d. Tom and Kathleen Smiley; m. John I. Interpreter, Apr. 25, 1992; 1 child, Annissa J. Interpreter. MA in Music, No. Ariz. U., Flagstaff, 1992—98. Cert. music tchr. K-12 Ariz. Dept. Edn. Band tchr. Pinon Unified Sch., Ariz., 1999—2000, Laveen Unified Sch., 2000—01; music/band tchr. Pendergast Unified Sch., Phoenix, 2001—02; music tchr. Thomas J. Pappas Elem. Sch., Phoenix, 2002—03, Cartwright Unified Schs., Phoenix, 2003—. After-sch. chorus club tchr. Spitalny Elem., Phoenix, 2003—06, after sch. piano club tchr., 2004—06; adv. bd. Cartwright Music Dept., Phoenix, 2006. Mem.: Ariz. Music Educator's Assn., Ariz. Educator's Assn., Am. Orff-Schulwerk Assn. (scholarship 2006). Mem. Native Am. Ch. Avocations: running, cake decorating, saxophone, piano. Home: 4118 E Frye Rd Phoenix AZ 85048 Office: Spitalny Elem Sch 3201 N 46th Dr Phoenix AZ 85031

SMILEY, JANE GRAVES, author, educator; b. LA, Sept. 26, 1949; d. James La Verne and Frances Nuelle (Graves) S.; m. John Whiston, Sept. 4, 1970 (div.); m. William Silag, May 1, 1978 (div.); children: Phoebe Silag, Lucy Silag; m. Stephen Mark Mortensen, July 25, 1987; 1 child, Axel James Mortensen. BA, Vassar Coll., 1971; MFA, U. Iowa, 1976, MA, PhD, U. Iowa, 1978. Asst. prof. Iowa State U., Ames, 1981-84, assoc. prof., 1984-89, prof., 1989-90, Disting. prof., 1992-96. Vis. asst. prof. U. Iowa, Iowa City, 1981, 87. Author: (fiction) Barn Blind, 1980, At Paradise Gate, 1981 (Friends of American Writers prize 1981), Duplicate Keys, 1984, The Age of Grief, 1987 (Nat. Book Critics Cirle award nomination 1987), The Greenlanders, 1988, Ordinary Love and Goodwill, 1989, A Thousand Acres, 1991 (Pulitzer Prize for fiction 1992, Nat. Book Critics Cirle award 1992, Midland Authors award 1992, Amb. award 1992, Heartland prize 1992), Moo: A Novel, 1995; (non-fiction) Catskill Crafts: Artisans of the Catskill Mountains, 1987, The All-True Travels and Adventures of Lidie Newton, 1998, Horse Heaven, 2001, Good Faith, 2003, Thirteen Ways of Looking at the Novel, 2005. Grantee Fulbright U.S. Govt., Iceland, 1976-77, NEA, 1978, 87; recipient O. Henry award, 1982, 85, 88. Mem. Author's Guild, Screenwriters Guild. Avocations: cooking, swimming, playing piano, quilting. Office: c/o Molly Friedrich Dept English 708 3rd Ave Fl 23 New York NY 10017-4201

SMILEY, MARILYNN JEAN, musicologist; b. Columbia City, Ind., June 5, 1932; d. Orla Raymond and Mary Jane (Bailey) S. BS (State scholar), Ball State U., 1954; MusM, Northwestern U., 1958; cert., Ecoles d'Art Americaines, Fontainebleau, France, 1959; PhD (Grad. scholar, Delta Kampa Gamma scholar), U. Ill., 1970. Public sch. music tchr., Logansport, Ind., 1954-61; faculty music dept. SUNY-Oswego, 1961—, Disting. Teaching prof., 1974—, chmn. dept., 1976-81. Presenter papers at confs. Contbr. articles to profl. jours. Bd. dirs. Oswego Opera Theatre, 1978—, Oswego Orch. Soc., 1978—, Penfield Libr. Assocs., 1985—. Recipient Chancellor's award for Excellence in Tchg., 1973; SUNY Rsch. Found. fellow, summers, 1971, 1972, 1974, NEH grantee, 1990—91. Mem.: AAUW (grantee 1984, pres. Oswego br. 1984—86, br. coun. rep. dist. III, N.Y. State divsn. 1986—88, br. coun. coord. N.Y. State divsn. 1988—90, N.Y. divsn. area interest rep. cultural interests 1990—92, N.Y. divsn. diversity dir. 1993—96, Oswego br. diversity chair 1995—, N.Y. state unofcl. historian 2000—04, N.Y. state historian 2004—), NOW, Oswego County Hist. Soc., Early Music Am., Am. Recorder Soc., Soc. Am. Music (membership chair 1998—2003), Renaissance Soc. Am., Coll. Music Soc., Music Libr. Assn., Medieval Acad. Am., Am. Musicol. Soc. (chmn. N.Y. chpt. 1975—77, chpt. rep. to AMS coun. 1993—96, bd. dirs. N.Y. State-St. Lawrence chpt. 1993—96, mem. status of women com. 1997—2000), Oswego Recorder Consort, Ontario Singers, Heritage Found. of Oswego, Phi Kappa Phi, Kappa Delta Pi, Sigma Tau Delta, Sigma Alpha Iota, Pi Kappa Lambda, Delta Phi Alpha, Phi Delta Kappa, Delta Kappa Gamma (music chair State of Ind. 1961, music chair State of N.Y. 1968). Methodist. Office: SUNY Dept Music Oswego NY 13126 Office Phone: 315-312-3054. Business E-Mail: smiley@oswego.edu.

SMITH, ABBIE OLIVER, college administrator, educator; b. Augusta, Ga., Jan. 31, 1931; d. Rowland Sheppard and Abigail Seabrook (Hanahan) Oliver; m. William Parkhurst Smith, Jr., July 2, 1953; children: William Parkhurst Smith, III, Oliver Hamilton. BS, George Washington U., 1953, MEd, 1958, EdDin Higher Edn., 1986. Tchr. St. Mary's Acad., Monroe, Mich., 1954-55; tchr., coach Washington-Lee H.S., Arlington, Va., 1955-58; homemaker, cmty. vol. Bethesda, Md., 1959-64; asst. professorial lectr. George Washington U., Washington, 1965-69, adminstr. continuing edn., 1969-80, asst. dean, dir., 1981-89, acting dean divsn. continuing edn., 1989-93, asst. v.p., asst. to dean institutional advancement, 1993—. Panelist TV series WETA, Washington; mem. exec. bd., newsletter editor Tng. Officers Conf., 1989—, chair charter expansion 1992—. Co-author: (workbook) Developing New Horizons for Women, 1975, Manual for Counselors for Developing New Horizons for Women, 1975. Mem. adv. bd. Washington Bd. Trade, 1975-77, women's branch adv. bd. State Nat. Bank, Bethesda, Md., 1978-81; collegiate adv. bd. Episcopal Diocese of Washington, 1977-79. Recipient Leadership in Adult Edn. award, 1976, GW award for outstanding contbn. to univ. life Office of GW Pres., 1991, Washington Women of Achievement, Washington Edn. TV Assn., 1980. Mem. Nat. U. Continuing Edn. Assn. (awards chair divsn. women's edn. 1977-78, nat. chair 1977-78, chair-elect divsn. part-time students program 1984-86, nat. chair 1984-86, chair coun. human resources 1985-86, nat. spl. com. on couns. and divsn. 1984-86, nat. exec. bd. 1984-86, nat. bd. dirs. 1984-98, nat. charters and bylaws coms. 1987-89, sec.-elect divsn. cert. and nontraditional degree programs 1987-89, chair-elect 1989-90, nat. chair 1990-91, nat. ann. planning coms. 1987, 92, sec. region II 1989-90, chair-elect, ann. conf. chair, single host instn. ann. conf. region II 1990-91, chair region II 1991-92, awards com. chair 1992, Walton S. Bittner Svc. Citation 1994, hon. mention for program catalog nat. divsn. mktg. 1988, Floyd B. Fisher Leadership award 1996), Phi Delta Kappa Internat. (G.W. chpt., v.p. for programs 1995-96, pres. 1996-97, newsletter editor 1977—, Newsletter Award Merit 1998-99, Outstanding Newsletter award 1999-2000, 2000-01). Democrat. Episcopalian. Avocations: writing, painting, swimming, dance, travel. Home: 3751 Jocelyn St NW Washington DC 20015-1836 Office: George Washington U 2134 G St NW Washington DC 20037-2797 E-mail: asmith@gwu.edu.

SMITH, ADA LAVERNE, state legislator; b. Amherst County, Va. d. Thomas and Lillian Smith. Grad., CUNY. Dep. clk. N.Y.C.; state senator N.Y. Legislature, Albany, 1988—, mem. various coms., ranking corp. commn. and authorities, 1994, minority whip, 1994—2003, chair Senate Dem. Conf., 2003—05, asst. Dem. leader, policy and adminstrn., 2005—. Mem. Senate Minority Puerto Rican and Hispanic Task Force. Trustee, life dir. Coll. Fund Baruch Coll. Recipient Outstanding Alumni award Baruch Coll. Mem. NY Assn. State Black and Puerto Rican Legislators, Baruch Coll. Alumni Assn. (pres., Disting. Svc. award, Outstanding Achievement award), Nat. Black Caucus of State Legislators (bd. dirs., vice chair telecomms. com.), Women in Govt. (state bd. dirs.). Office: NY State Senate Rm 808 Legis Office Bldg Albany NY 12247 also: Queens Dist Office 11643 Sutphin Blvd Jamaica NY 11434-1526 Office Phone: 518-455-3531. E-mail: smith@senate.state.ny.us.

SMITH, AGNES MONROE, history professor; b. Hiram, Ohio, Aug. 8, 1920; d. Bernie Alfred and Joyce (Messenger) Monroe; m. Stanley Blair Smith; children: David, Doris, Darl, Diane. BA, Hiram Coll., 1940; MA, W.Va. U., 1945; PhD, Western Res. U., 1966. Social sci. tchr. Freedom (Ohio) High Sch., 1940-44; instr. of history W.Va. U., Morgantown, 1945; instr. of social sci. Hiram Coll., 1946; inst. history and social sci. Youngstown (Ohio) State U., 1964-66, asst. prof. to prof. of history, 1966-84, prof. history emeritus, 1984—; vis. prof. history Hiram Coll., 1988-90. Co-editor: Bourgeois, Sans Culottes and Other Frenchmen, 1981; contbr. articles to profl. jours. Mem. Ohio Acad. History, Delta Kappa Gamma, Phi Alpha Theta, Pi Gamma Mu. Mem. Christian Ch. (Disciples Of Christ). Home: 16759 Main Market Rd West Farmington OH 44491-9608

SMITH, ALICE DAVIS, retired biology and art educator; b. Hill City, SD, Feb. 25, 1917; d. John Oliver Davis and Medora Alice Morehouse; m. Dwaine Casey Smith, June 21, 1941 (dec. 1991); children: Richard, Ronald, Brian, Dee, Doreen. BSc, ND State Coll., 1940; degree in art, Black Hills Tchg. Sch., 1960. Botany lab instr. S.D. State U., 1946—48; jr. high. gen. svc. Pierre Sch. Dist., 1953—56, biology tchr., 1955—65, art and biology tchr., 1965—70, art tchr., 1970—75; ret., 1975. Mem. Hill City Arts Coun., SD, We. Women in the Arts, Black Hills Writers; presenter in field. Author: (poetry) Potpourri, Medley of Life, (plays) A Port and Points in Time; contbr. articles to profl. jours. Mem. H-Camp; mem., trustee Friends of Libr. Nominee Spirit of Dakota award, Gov.'s Art award, 2000; recipient Award of Honor, Nat. Coun. State Garden Clubs, 1999. Mem.: AAUW, Pierre Edn. Assn., Hill City C of C (life), SD State Poetry Soc. (bd. dirs.), Canvas Backs Art Club, Hill City Garden Club. Avocations: fishing, swimming, photography, gardening, writing.

SMITH, ALICE F., medical/surgical, critical care, and home health nurse; b. Albertville, Ala., Dec. 25, 1955; d. Brownlow Tilton and Dorothy Lavelle (Teal) Smith; m. Grady D. Smith, Nov. 18, 1978; children: Scott Allan, Christopher Brownlow. AD, Gadsden (Ala.) State Jr. Coll., 1984; BSN, U. Ala., Huntsville, 1990. Obstetrics nurse, med.-surg. nurse Guntersville Hosp., Ala., 1984—88, ICU supr., 1988-90; med.-surg. coord. Guntersville-Arab Med. Ctr., 1990-92; part time emergency rm. nurse Marshall Med. Ctr. North, 1992—2005; with ALACARE Home Health Svcs., 1992-97; br. mgr. Riverview Reg. Med. Ctr. Home Health Agy., 1997—2004, MidSouth Home Health, 2004—05; SICU nurse Jackson Madison County Gen. Hosp., 2005—. Mem. Phi Theta Kappa. Home: 1210 US Hwy 45 Byp N Lot 29 Trenton TN 38382-0015

SMITH, ALISON LEIGH, lawyer; b. Brownsville, Tex., Sept. 24, 1952; d. Arthur Lee and June (Allen) Smith; m. Dean A. Burkhardt, Apr. 24, 1981. B in Journalism summa cum laude, U. Tex., 1974, JD cum laude, 1977. Bar: Tex. 1977, U.S. Dist. Ct. (so. dist.) Tex. (1978), U.S. Ct. Appeals (5th cir.) 1981, U.S. Dist. Ct. (no. dist.) Tex. 1987, U.S. Ct. Appeals (D.C. cir.) 1989. Assoc. Vinson & Elkins LLP, Houston, 1977-84, ptnr., 1984—89, 1991—2004; dep. asst. atty. gen. antitrust divsn. U.S. Dept. Justice, Washington, 1989-91; ptnr. Dewey Ballantine LLP, Houston, 2004—05, Haynes and Boone, LLP, Houston, 2005—. Adj. prof. law U. Tex., Austin, 1992-93. Alternate del. Rep. Nat. Conv., New Orleans, 1988; mem. ethics com. City of Houston, 1988-89; chair Mayor's Animal Protection Task Force, 2005. Mem. ABA (antitrust law sect., chair transp. industry com., 1992-95, co-chmn. pvt. antitrust litig. com. 2001-04, vice chmn. Sherman Act sect. one com. 2004-05, econ. evidence task force 2005-06, ed. bd. state antitrust practice and procedure), Am. Law Inst., Tex. Bar Found., Houston Bar Assn. Home: 2125 Bolsover St Houston TX 77005-1617 Office: Haynes and Boone LLP 1221 McKinney Ste 2100 Houston TX 77010 Office Phone: 713-547-2673. Business E-Mail: alison.smith@haynesboone.com.

SMITH, AMANDA R., secondary school educator; d. Paul F and Cheryl A Smith. BS, So. Conn. State U., New Haven, 2002. Cert. phys. edn. tchr. Mass., Conn., 2002, health educator Conn., 2002. Health educator Hamden Mid. Sch., Hamden, Conn., 2002; gymnastics coach So. Conn. State U., New Haven; phys. edn. tchr. Wilson Mid. Sch., Natick, Mass.; gymnastics asst. coach Natick H.S., 2004—05; gymnastics head coach Holliston/Ashland High Sch., Holliston, 2005—. Grantee Jump Up and Go grantee, Blue Cross and Blue Shield, 2005—. Achievements include fitness competitor with Savage Choreography. Office: Wilson Middle School Rutledge Rd Natick MA 01760 Personal E-mail: diesel9128@aol.com.

SMITH, AMY B., mechanical engineer, educator; BSc, MIT, 1984, MSE, 1995. Vol. Peace Corps, Botswana, 1986—90; inventor, instr. MIT Edgerton Ctr., Cambridge, Mass., 2000—. Co-founder MIT IDEAS competition (Innovation, Devel., Enterprise, Action, Svc.); and co-founder Internat. Devel. Initiative. Named a MacArthur Fellow, 2004; recipient Lemelson-MIT Student prize, 2000. Office: MIT Edgerton Ctr Rm 4-405 77 Mass Ave Cambridge MA 02139*

SMITH, ANNA NICOLE (VICKIE LYNN HOGAN), television personality, model; b. Mexia, Tex., Nov. 28, 1967; d. Donald Eugene and Virgie (Hart) Hogan; m. Billie Smith, Apr. 4, 1985 (div. 1987); 1 child, Daniel (dec.); m. J. Howard Marshall II, June 27, 1994 (dec. Aug. 4, 1995); m. Howard K. Stern, Sept. 28, 2006; 1 child, Dannie Lynn Hope Former model for Guess? jeans; weekly gossip columnist Nat. Enquirer, 2005—. Spokesperson Trim Spa X32 (Ephedra Free), 2003—. Actress (films) Naked Gun 33 1/3: The Final Insult, 1994, The Hudsucker Proxy, 1994, To the Limit, 1995, Skyscraper, 1997 (also assoc. prodr.), Be Cool, 2005; (TV series) N.Y.U.K., 2000, The Anna Nicole Smith Show, 2002-04 (also creative cons.); prodr., screenwriter, dir. (video) Anna Nicole Smith: Exposed, 1988; guest TV appearance include MadTV, 1998, Veronica's Closet, 1999, Ally McBeal, 1999, and several talk show appearances. Named Playmate of the Month, 1992, Playmate of the Yr., 1993.

SMITH, ANNE DAY, writer; b. Bath, Maine, Oct. 14, 1937; d. Harry L. Day; m. Gerald H. Smith, Dec. 21, 1957; children: David, Frederick, Stephen. AA, Lasell Coll., Auburndale, Mass., 1957. Contbg. editor Nutshell News Mag., 1979-96; freelance writer various newspapers and mags., 1979—. Author: Interior Design in Miniature, 1986, Masters in Miniature, 1987, The Andrews Collection, 1988, The Period Rooms of Ruth McChesney, 1997; contbg. editor Dollhouse Miniatures mag., 1996—; contbr. articles to publs. Mem. Nat. Assn. Miniature Enthusiasts, Acad. Honor (chmn. 1996-2000), Internat. Guild Miniature Artisans. Avocations: reading, research, travel, antique collecting.

SMITH, ANNE SISSON, private school educator; d. Howard and Margaret Sisson; m. Robert Herschel Smith; children: Margaret, Katherine Langham, Claire Taylor. BA, Birmingham-So. Coll., 1966; MA, U. Mobile, Ala., 1989. Cert. tchr. Ala. Tchr. UMS-Wright Prep. Sch., Mobile, 1990—. Former pres. Mobile Opera Guild, 1987—88. Named Nobel Tchr. of Distinction, Nat. Soc. H.S. Scholars, 2004. Mem.: Nat. Sci. Tchrs. Assn. (assoc.), Am. Chem. Soc. (assoc.), Mortar Bd. (assoc.), Kappa Delta Epsilon (assoc.). Office: UMS-Wright Prep Sch 65 N Mobile St Mobile AL 36607 Office Phone: 251-479-6551.

SMITH, ANNICK, writer; b. Paris, May 11, 1936; came to U.S., 1937; d. Stephen and Helene Deutch; m. David James Smith (dec. 1974); children: Eric, Stephen, Alex, Andrew. Student, Cornell Univ., 1954-55, U. Chgo., 1955-57; BA, U. Wash., 1961. Editor U. Wash. Press, Seattle, 1961-64, Montana Bus. Quarterly, U. Montana, Missoula, 1971-72; founding bd. mem. Sundance Film Inst., Sundance, Utah, 1981-85; founding mem. Ind. Film Project, N.Y.C., 1981-84; acting dir. Montana Com. for the Humanities, Missoula, 1983-84; devel. dir. Hellgate Writers, Inc., Missoula, 1986-96; creative dir. Yellow Bay Writers Workshop, U. Montana Continuing Edn. Dept, Missoula, 1987-98. Freelance filmmaker, producer, arts administrator, writer, Mont., 1974—; past H.S. tchr., cmty. organizer, environ. worker. Exec. prodr. Heartland, 1981; co-prodr. A River Runs Through It, 1992; co-editor: (with William Kittredge) The Last Best Place; author: Homestead, 1994, Big BlueStem A Journey into the Tall Grass, 1996, In This We Are Native, 2001; contbr. to anthologies including Best Am. Short Stories, 1992. Recipient Western Heritage award Cowboy Hall of Fame, 1981; Mont. Humanites award Mont. Com. for Humanities, 1988, Okla. Book award, 1997, Bancroft Prize Denver Pub. Libr., 1998. Mem. Trout Unlimited, Blackfoot Challenge. Democrat. Office: 898 Bear Creek Rd Bonner MT 59823

SMITH, BARBARA, camping administrator; b. Fox Point, Wis., Apr. 17, 1952; d. Robert Wayne and Katherine Mary (Neuzerling) S. BS, U. Wis., 1975; EdM, SUNY, Amherst, 1978. Cert. N.Y. State Swim Official. Camp dir. Patriot's Trail Girl Scout Council, Boston, 1976-77; field and camp dir. Sparand Spindle Girl Scout Council, Middleton, Mass., 1978-79; adult edn. dir. Niagara County Council of Girl Scouts, Inc., Niagara Falls, N.Y., 1979-80; camping services dir. Girl Scout Council of Buffalo and Erie County, Inc., Buffalo, 1980—. Mem. Am. Camping Assn. (planner 1985—), N.Y. State Outdoor Edn. Assn., Assn. Girl Scout Exec. Staff, Girl Scouts of U.S.A., ARC (lifeguard instr. 1969—, trainer 1980—). Mem. Society of Friends Ch. Avocations: downhill skiing, whitewater canoeing, running, swimming, horseback riding, camping, photography, writing. Office: Girl Scout Coun Buffalo/Erie 70 Jewett Pkwy Buffalo NY 14214-2322

SMITH, BARBARA, food service executive, model; b. Everson, Pa., Aug. 24, 1949; m. Dan Gasby; 1 stepdaughter. Owner B. Smith Restaurant Group; former model. Mem. adv. bd. Culinary Inst. Am., 1995—. Author: B. Smith's Cooking and Entertaining for Friends, 1995; host (syndicated weekly TV show) B. Smith With Style; founder B. Smith Style mag. Mem.: Screen Actors Guild, Feminist Press (founding bd. mem.), NY Women's Found. (founding bd. mem.), Times Sq. Bus. Improvement Dist. (founding bd. mem.). Achievements include appeared in over 100 radio, print, and TV ads; First African Am. woman elected to bd. trustees Culinary Inst. Am. Avocation: family activities. Mailing: 320 W 46th St New York NY 10036

SMITH, BARBARA ANNE, health facility administrator, consultant; b. N.Y.C., Oct. 10, 1946; d. John Allen and Lelia Maria (De Silva) Santoro; m. Joseph Newton Smith, Feb. 5, 1966 (div. Sept. 1984); children: J. Michael, Robert Lawrence. Student, Oceanside/Carlsbad Coll. Real estate agt. Routh Robbins, Inc., Washington, 1973-75; gen. mgr. Mall Shops, Inc., Kansas City, Kans., 1975-80; regional mgr. FAO Schwarz, N.Y.C., 1980-84; clin. adminstr. North Denver Med. Ctr., Thornton, Colo., 1984-88; adminstrv. dir. Country Side Ambulatory Surgery Ctr., Leesburg, Va., 1989-91; pres. SCS Healthcare Mgmt. Inc., Washington, 1991—. Bd. dirs. Franz Carl Weber Internat., Geneva, 1982-84; mng. dir. Nat. Healthcare Consortium, 1997—; mng. assoc. Monarch Assocs. in Healthcare. Pres. Am. Women Chile, 1968; v.p. Oak Park Assn., Kansas City, 1977-78, pres., 1978-79; vol. Visitor Info. and Assn. Reception Ctr. program Smithsonian Instn., Washington. Mem. NAFE, Network Colo., Profl. Bus. Women Assn., Med. Group Mgmt. Assn., Federated Ambulatory Surgery Assn.

SMITH, BARBARA GAIL, economist; b. Phoenix, June 6, 1957; d. Loren Leonard Smith and Geneva May (Gabbert) Hewlett; m. Loren L. Farrell, 1999; children: Lori L. Farrell, Lynda S. Farrell, Jason L. Farrell. BS in Environ. Sci., Grand Canyon Coll., 1979; postgrad., Ariz. State U. Power supply analyst Ariz. Pub. Svc., Phoenix, 1981-84, rate devel. analyst, 1984-86, regulatory economist, 1986-93, sr. rate analyst, 1993—99, rate cons., 1999—. Profl. pianist, Phoenix, 1976—; team supr. RGIS Inventory Svcs., 1981—83, tng. cons., 1982—85; freelance arranger, Phoenix, 1981—. Vol. Nat. Cancer Soc., Nat. Red Cross, Ariz. Humane Soc., Westside Food Bank; bd. dirs. Valley of Sun United Way. Named Girl of the Yr., Ariz. Red Cross, 1974; named one of Outstanding Young Women Am., 1979. Mem.: NAFE, Ariz. Bus. Women's Assn., Alpha Chi. Republican. Baptist. Avocation: gourmet cooking. Home: 4145 W Charter Oak Rd Phoenix AZ 85029-6104 Office: PO Box 53999 Phoenix AZ 85072-3999 Office Phone: 602-250-2030. Business E-Mail: Barbara.Smith@aps.con.

SMITH, BARBARA J., music educator; b. LA, June 1, 1954; adopted d. Orville Dane and Golda Marie Cotten; children: Meagan Ashley, Caitlin Brooke. MusB in Edn., Loma Linda U., 1976. Cert. Tchg. Credential Calif. Dental asst. Calvin R. Devnich, DDS, Inc., Glendale, Calif., 1979—82; substitute tchr. Glendora (Calif.) Unified Sch. Dist., 1999—2004; music tchr. Rowland Unified Sch. Dist., Rowland Heights, Calif., 2004—. Pres. La Fetra Elem. Sch., PTA, Glendora. Soloist: Calvary Presbyn. Ch. Active Reflections fine arts program San Gabriel Valley First Dist. PTA, Alhambra, Calif., 1999—2001. Recipient award, Glendora Coun. PTA. Mem.: MENC. Home: 311 E Meda Ave 1 Glendora CA 91741 Office: Rowland Unified Sch Dist 1830 S Nogales St Rowland Heights CA 91748 Personal E-mail: barbarasmith1@verizon.net.

SMITH, BARBARA JANE, computer scientist, educator; d. Kenneth O. and Jane Louise Campbell; m. Douglas Brian Smith, Dec. 29, 1984; children: Michael Douglas, James Kenneth. MS in Math., Purdue U., 1981. Assoc. prof. Purdue U., Ft. Wayne, Ind., 1979—84; pres. Software Profls., Inc, Ft. Wayne, 1980—84; sr. sys. analyst Burroughs Corp., Camarillo, Calif., 1984—86, W. L. Gore, Flagstaff, Ariz., 1986—89; instr. Cochise Coll., Sierra Vista, Ariz., 1989—, U. Ariz., South, Sierra Vista, 1996—. Author: Programming Logic and Design. Mem. White Cross, Ft. Wayne, 2005—. Office: Cochise Coll 901 N Colombo Sierra Vista AZ 85635 Office Phone: 520-515-5441. Personal E-mail: barbaraj@email.arizona.edu.

SMITH, BARBARA JEAN, lawyer; b. Washington, Jan. 9, 1947; d. Harry Wallace and Jean (Fraser) S.; m. Philip R. Chall, July 13, 1991; children: Brian C.S. Brown, Craig F.S. Brown, Amy E. Spiers, Carrie A. Chall. BA, Old Dominion Coll., 1968; MBA, Pepperdine U., 1974; JD, Case Western Res. U., 1977. Bar: Ohio 1977. Assoc. Squire, Sanders & Dempsey, Cleve., 1977—88, ptnr., 1988—93; shareholder McDonald, Hopkins, Burke & Haber Co., L.P.A., Cleve., 1993—2003; ptnr. Shottenstein, Zox & Dunn Co., LPA, Cleve., 2003—05; founding mem. Smith & Hultin LLC, Chagrin Falls, Ohio, 2005—. Bd. editors Health Law Jour. of Ohio, 1989-95; contbr. articles to health jours. and periodicals. Trustee Urban Community Sch., Cleve., 1984-86, Alzheimer's Assn. Greater Cleve., 2000-2005. Mem. Ohio Women's Bar Assn. (pres. 1994-95), Cleve. Bar Assn. (pres. 1998-99, trustee 1992-95, chair health law sect. 1991-92), Am. Health Lawyers Assn., Ohio State Bar Assn. (health law com. 1991—), Soc. Ohio Hosp. Attys., Sci. Edn. Coun. Ohio. Democrat. Mem. United Ch. of Christ. Avocations: reading, hiking. Home: 416 Fairway Vw Chagrin Falls OH 44023-6718 Office: Smith & Hultin LLC 100 N Main St Ste 350 Chagrin Falls OH 44022 Office Phone: 440-247-2620. Business E-Mail: smith@smithhultin.com.

SMITH, BARBARA RATH, foundation executive; b. Washington, Oct. 22, 1946; d. Gunnar Emil and Mary (Faux) Rath; m. Stanley Sherrel Smith, Mar. 29, 1969; children: Trevor Eli, Whitney Marin, Kendall Risa Elisabeth. BA in Psychology, Fed. City Coll., 1970; postgrad., U. Md., 1976-77. Psychodramatist St. Elizabeth's Hosp., Washington, 1972-73; psychology technician VA Hosp., Washington, 1971-74; vol. Cedar Lane Unitarian Ch., Bethesda, Md., 1979-88; exec. adminstr. Am. Thyroid Assn., Washington, 1988-94, now exec. dir. Falls Church, Va., 2001—; assoc. dir. Nat. Assn. Hispanic Journalists, Washington, 1994-97; dir. found. and govt. rels. Assn. for Healthcare Philanthropy, Falls Church, Va., 1997—. Chair religious edn. coun. Cedar Lane Unitarian Ch., Bethesda, Md., 1987-89; v.p. ways and means Oakland Terr. Elem. Sch., Kensington, Md., 1982-84; pastoral caregiver St. Mark's Episcopal Ch., Washington. Mem. Am. Soc. Assn. Execs., Grtr. Washington Soc. Assn. Execs., Nat. Soc. Fundraising Execs. Democrat. Avocations: religious education leader, literacy and english teacher to speakers of other languages. Office: Am Thyroid Assn Ste 650 6066 Leesburg Pike Falls Church VA 22041 Office Phone: 703-998-8890.*

SMITH, BARBARA RUTHJENA DRUCKER, writer, educator; b. Newport News, Va., June 5, 1936; d. Abraham Louis and Loraine Blechman Drucker; children: Lisa Lorraine, Eric Drucker. BA in English, Speech and Journalism, Coll. William and Mary, 1964. Cert. hypnotherapist Ea. Va. Hypnotherapy Inst., 1999, Nat. Assn. Transpersonal Hypnotherapists, 2003. Freelance writer, Newport News, 1960—; pvt. practice hypnotherapy, 1999—; hypnotist Positive Changes Hypnosis Neurolinguistic Programming, Newport News, 2000—04. Workshop leader various pub. schs., Newport News, 1976—; tchr. in English and remedial reading various schs., Newport News, 1966—; mem. adv. bd. Christopher Newport Writer's Conf., Newport News, 1989—2006. Author: Darling Loraine The Story of A. Louis Drucker A Grateful Jewish Immigrant, 2000 (Nominated Best Non-Fiction Book of 2000 award Libr. Va., 2001), A Poetic Journey, 2004 (Nominated Best Poetry Book of 2004 award Libr. Va.), Prose From the Old Century to the New: Vignettes, Petite Petites, Epistles, Points of View, 2006; contbr. Poet's Domain 4 Others, 1987—2000. Crisis teleph. worker Contact Peninsula, Newport News, 1981—2005; docent Mariner's Mus., Newport News, 1982—. Mem.: Soc. for Historians, Authorship, Reading and Publishing, Nat. Assn. Transpersonal Hypnotherapists, Poetry Soc. Va., Tidewater Writers Assn., Va. Choral Soc., Va. Writers Club. Avocations: bicycling, swimming, piano, travel. Home and Office: 120 Selden Road Newport News VA 23606

SMITH, BARBARA T., artist, educator; b. Pasadena, Calif., July 6, 1931; d. Max Harvey and Margaret Helen (Didricksen) Turner; children: Richard Allen, Julie Lynn Johnson, Katherine Marie Norman. BFA, Pomona Coll., Claremont, Calif., 1953; MFA, U. Calif., Irvine, 1971. Curatorial adminstr. New Gallery, Santa Monica, Calif., 1994—95. Guest faculty Humbolt (Calif.) State U., 1993; lectr. U. Calif., La Jolla, 1993; guest lectr., cons. Linz U., Austria, 1999; vis. artist Ohio State U., Columbus, 1990, Otis Coll. Arts and Design, LA, 1996—. Exhibitions include Mus. Contemporary Art, LA, 1998, Pomona Coll. Mus. Art, 2005, Ctr. Georges Pompidou, Paris, 2006. Rev. com. Dorland Mountain Art Colony, Calif., 1988—; bd. dirs. LA Poverty Dept., 1997—. Grantee Individual Artist grant, Nat. Endowment for the Arts, 1979, 1981, 1985. Mem.: Mus. Contemporary Art, So. Calif. Womens Caucus of Art (Nat. Honor award 1999), Santa Monica Mus. Art (hon.). Avocations: exercise, reading, travel. Home: 801 Coeur d'Alene Ave Venice CA 90291

SMITH, BECKY, charitable organizations consultant; b. LA, July 21, 1945; d. Burchard Rutherford and Evelyn Keach; m. Ray Hunt, July 21, 1963 (div. Feb. 1990); children: Vickie Jan Hunt, Jeffry K. Hunt. Student, Wichita State U. Cert. fund raising exec. Cons. to charitable orgns. including ARC, Am. Hosp. Assn., Child Welfare League Am., Nat. Assn. Homes for Children, Duke Endowment. Author: How to Raise the Money You Need Now! 1986, 3d edit., 1999. Mem. Nat. Assn. Fundraising Execs. Avocations: watercolor painting, decorative painting, murals. Home: 581 Powers Ferry Rd Se Marietta GA 30067-7355

SMITH, BETTY, writer, not-for-profit developer; b. Bonham, Tex., Sept. 16; d. Sim and Gertrude (Dearing) S. Student, Stephens Coll.; BJ, U. Tex. Women's editor Daily Texan; pres. Hope Assocs. Corp., N.Y.C.; pres., owner Betty Smith Assocs., N.Y.C. Author: A Matter of Heart, 1969, Journey to Valhalla: The Life of Lauritz Melchoir, 2006 Bd. dirs. Melchior Heldentenor Found., N.Y.C., 1968—, pres., 1987-97; pres., CEO Gerda Lissner Found., 1994—; bd. dirs. Herman Lissner Found., 1990—, CEO, 2004—. Mem. Author's Guild. Office: care Lissner Found 135 E 55th St 8th Fl New York NY 10022-4049 Office Phone: 212-826-6100. E-mail: bsmithassocs@aol.com.

SMITH, BETTY ANN INGRAM, elementary school educator; b. Newnan, Ga., Apr. 23, 1951; d. William C. and Frances H. (Hubbard) I.; m. James Michael Smith, Aug. 5, 1972; children: Joseph Michael Smith, Frances Ann Smith. BS in Elem. Edn. summa cum laude, Shorter Coll., 1973; MEd, West Ga. Coll., 1985. Tchr. Putnam County (Ga.) Schs., Eatonton, 1973-74, Coweta County (Ga.) Schs., Newman, 1974-77, 1982—. Cons. in field; tchr.

Ga. Youth Sci. & Tech. Ctr., Newnan, Summer, 1995; mem. com. Ga. Power First Grade Environ. Edn. Program, 1995. Recipient: Presdl. award Excellence in Sci. Tchg. NSF, 1993; Honor Tchr. award Atlanta Jour. Constitution, 1992. Mem. Profl. Assn. Ga. Educators, Nat. Tchrs. Assn., Ga. Tchrs. Assn., Newnan Pilot Club, Alpha Delta Kappa (pres. Chi chpt. 1992-94), Coun. Elem. Sci. Baptist. Avocation: internet. Home: 139 Lagrange St Newnan GA 30263-2939 Office: Elm Street Sch 46 Elm St Newnan GA 30263-1540

SMITH, BETTY DENNY, county official, administrator, fashion executive; b. Centralia, Ill., Nov. 12, 1932; d. Otto and Ferne Elizabeth (Beier) Hasenfuss; m. Peter S. Smith, Dec. 5, 1964; children: Carla Kip, Bruce Kimball. Student, U. Ill., 1950-52; student, L.A. City Coll., 1953-57, UCLA, 1965, U. San Francisco, 1982-84. Freelance fashion coordinator, L.A., N.Y.C., 1953-58; tchr. fashion Rita LeRoy Internat. Studios, 1959-60; mgr. Mo Nadler Fashion, L.A., 1961-64; showroom dir. Jean of Calif. Fashions, L.A., 1965—. Freelance polit. book reviewer for community newspapers, 1961-62; staff writer Valley Citizen News, 1963. Bd. dirs. Pet Assistance Found., 1969-76; founder, pres., dir. Vol. Services to Animals L.A., 1972-76; mem. County Com. To Discuss Animals in Rsch., 1973-74; mem. blue ribbon com. on animal control L.A. County, 1973-74; dir. L.A. County Animal Care and Control, 1976-82; mem. Calif. Animal Health Technician Exam. Com., 1975-82, chmn., 1979; bd. dirs. L.A. Soc. for Prevention Cruelty to Animals, 1984-94, Calif. Coun. Companion Animal Advocates, 1993-97; dir. West Coast Regional Office, Am. Humane Assn., 1988-97; mem. adv. com. Moorepark Coll., 1988-97; CFO Coalition for Pet Population Control, 1987-92; trustee Gladys W. Sargent Found., 1997—, Coalition to End Pet Overpopulation, 1998—; cons. Jungle Book II, Disney Studios, 1997; mem. adv. com. Wishbone Prodn., 1995-97; mem. govt. rels. and pub. affairs com. Motion Picture & TV Industry Assn., 1992-97; mem. Coalition to Protect Calif. Wildlife, 1996-97, Spl. Commn. Spay/Neuter City L.A., 1998-99; adv. com. La. Dept. of Animal Reg. 2000; mem. adv. com. Calif. Dept. Fish & Game Animal Care, 2003; pres., bd. dirs. Fauna Found., 2004-; mem. Calif. Rep. Cen. Com., 1964-72, mem. exec. com., 1971-73; mem. L.A. County Rep. Cen. Com., 1964-70, mem. exec. com., 1966-70; chmn. 29th Congl. Cen. Com., 1969-70; sec. 28th Senatorial Cen. Com., 1967-68; mem. speakers bur. George Murphy for U.S. Senate, 1970; campaign mgr. Los Angeles County for Spencer Williams for Atty. Gen., 1966; mem. L.A. County Art Mus., L.A. Libr. Assn. Mem. Internat. Platform Assn., Mannequins Assn. (bd. dirs. 1967-68), Lawyer's Wives San Gabriel Valley (bd. dirs. 1971-74, pres. 1972-73), L.A. Athletic Club, Town Hall. Home: 1766 Bluffhill Dr Monterey Park CA 91754-4533 Office Phone: 323-262-1815.

SMITH, BETTY MALLETT, philosopher, educator; b. Tulsa, Dec. 4, 1924; d. James L. and Eula (Gravitt) Mallett; m. Myron Chawner Smith, Aug. 28, 1948; children: Marston, Shelley, Shonti. BA, William Jewell Coll., Liberty, Mo., 1947; MA, Brown U., Providence, R.I., 1949. Instr. philosophy Baylor U., Waco, Tex., 1950-51, Santa Monica (Calif.) Coll., 1968-69; lectr. philosophy Mt. St. Mary's Coll., L.A., 1963-64, 66-67, Calif. Luth. U., Thousand Oaks, 1969-73; instr. C.G. Jung Inst., L.A., 1974—90, Jung Study Ctr., L.A., 2004—. Founder, dir. Poiesis, Malibu, Calif., 1966-; lectr.-dir. mythology tours to Greece, 1973-2005; lectr. in field Author: (book on audio casette) Loved by a God, 1997. Mem. LWV. Marston scholar Brown U., 1947-48. Mem. AAUW, C.G. Jung Inst. L.A. (assoc.). Mem. Soc. Of Friends. Avocations: poetry, writing, philosophy.

SMITH, BETTY PAULINE, television producer; b. Benton, Ill., Nov. 27, 1926; d. Roy Herman and Goldie Ada (Rodgers) Keen; m. Richard Caldwell Smith, Jan. 11, 1946; children: Constance Raelene, Elana Gayle, Jill Christina. AA in Mgmt., U. Nev., 1982; cert., Ikenbo Sch. Floral Art, 1985; student, Hawaii Pacific U., 1994. Lic. real estate broker, Nev.; cert. real estate salesperson, Hawaii. TV producer Old Plantation Prodns., Inc. Active Coalition of Women-Legis., Domestic Violence Divsn., State of Hawaii, 1994-96; pres. NaKupuna U. Hawaii, 1999. Exec. prodr. Hawaiin Music, 1985; prodr. (TV) The Open Door, 1992, 95, 96, Health Issues: Issues for Women over 55 Years Old, 1992, Honolulu Police Dept., 1995, There's No Excuse for Abuse, 1995, Gang Violence in the Schools, 1995, Women Against Violence, 1996; poem carried by 2002 Olympic Torchbearers who were firefighters at World Trade Center, Sept. 11, 2001; author numerous poems. Recipient Comm. Svc. award Aloha State Assn. of the Deaf, 1993, scholarship Americorps, 1996, cert. Hope Domestic Violence Counselor, 1996, Oahu Unsung Angel award, 1998, Internat. Poet merit Internat. Soc. Poets, 1999, Mayor's Proclomation award City of Honolulu, 1999, seal City and County Honolulu, 1999, Pres. award Nat. Authors Registry, 1999, Powers of Expression Through Poetry commendation Gov. of Hawaii, 2000 Prometheus Trophy award The Famous Soc. Poets, 2000; named Poet of Merit The Famous Soc. Poets, 2000, Muse of Fire, 2000, Internat. Poet of Merit Internat. Soc. Poets, 2002, Poet Laureate, 2003. Mem. Ind. TV Producers Assn., Hometown Media Alliance TV Producers, Elks, LWV, OES, Mason/White Shrine of Jerusalem, Toastmasters (Hall of Fame), others. Avocations: swimming, bicycling, walking, kayaking, hawaiian music. Personal E-mail: chasin.rainbows@hotmail.com.

SMITH, BETTY ROBINSON, retired elementary school educator; b. Athens, Ga., Jan. 31, 1941; d. Willie Martin and Leila Mary Robinson; m. Freddie Smith; children: Natalie Yvonne, Rewa Patrice. BSEd, Tuskegee (Ala.) Inst., 1964; MS in Early Childhood Edn., Nova U., Ft. Lauderdale, Fla., 1979; cert. early childhood, U. S. Fla. Head tchr. in headstart program Perkins Elem. Sch., St. Petersburg, Fla., 1965; tchr. Orange Grove Elem. Sch., Tampa, Fla., 1967-68, Largo (Fla.) Ctrl. Elem. Sch., 1970-71, North Shore Elem. Sch., St. Petersburg, Fla., 1971-99, Gulfport Elem. Montessori Acad., 2000—06; resource cons., bd. dirs. Mt. Zion Christain Acad., 1999—. Head tchr. Early Success Program; active Appreciate Cultures Program for sch. improvement plan Pinellas County; chair Multicultural Club; organizer ann. Elem. workshop; network trainer, Gulfport Elem., 2000—; head mutlicultural com., acad network trainer Gulfport Elem. Montessori Acad., 2002-2004; head multicultural liason, 2000-05. Dir. youth choir, active community and religious roles; mem. mass choir Mt. Zion Progressive Baptist Ch.; organizer 55+ Club; head multicultural com. North Shore Elem. Sch. Mem. PCTA, Am. Montessori Soc., Zeta Gamma Zta, PREP (rep. for Pinellas County, Fla.). Home: 4301 Cortez Way S Saint Petersburg FL 33712-4024 Office Phone: 727-893-2643.

SMITH, BETTY W., librarian; b. Lincoln, Nebr., June 29, 1919; d. Clem and Edith Margaret (Stanley) Wilder; m. Dulaney Dale Smith, Mar. 20, 1946; children: Douglas D., Diane E., Richard W. BA, Wayne U., 1940; BS, U. Minn., 1941; MA, Mich. State U., 1955. Cert. libr. Br. libr. Pub. Libr., Park Ridge, Ill., 1941-42, reference libr. Dearborn, Mich., 1942-44; U.S.C.G. SPAR, libr. asst. U.S.C.G. Acad., New London, Conn., 1945-46; reference libr. Libr. Hawaii, Honolulu, 1946-47; libr. Hawaiian Econ. Found., Honolulu, 1947-49; reference libr. Lansing Pub. Libr., Mich., 1967-86, substitute libr., 1986-98. Mem. Citizens for Actions in Mental Health, 1980—86; steering com. Long-Range Planning Mich. Dept. Mental Health, 1986—90; bd. dirs. Tri-Co. Cmty. Mental Health, Lansing, 1992—98; founding and exec. com. mem. Alliance for Mentally Ill, Mich., 1985—2003, now v.p.; adv. coun. Mich. Forensic Ctr., 1988—, Lafayette Clinic, Detroit, 1986—92. Mem. LWV, Mental Health Assn., Mich. Assn. Emotionally Disturbed Children (bd. dirs. 1963-68), Mich. Mental Health (adv. coun. 1986-90), Phi Alpha Theta. Home: 1782 Eifert Rd Holt MI 48842-1976

SMITH, BEULAH MAE, music educator; b. Okmulgee, Okla., Aug. 14, 1920; d. Willie Arthur Geller and Pearl Oretha Miears; m. Jodie C. Smith, May 16, 1943; 1 child, Joni Smith Levinson. BA in Music Edn., Ctrl. State U., 1942; MA in Music Edn., Okla. U., 1948. Cert. piano specialist. H.S. music tchr., Lindsay, Okla., Newkirk, Okla.; jr. high music tchr. Guthrie, Okla.; H.S. music tchr. Purcell, Okla.; elem. music tchr. Norman, Okla.; tchr. North Ea. U., Tahlequah, Okla.; jr. high music tchr. Hobbs, N.Mex.; piano specialist Norman. Piano cons. Warner (Okla.) State Coll., 1980. Recipient Cert. of Achievement, Howell-Aretta Conservatory Music, 1955; Beulah Mae Smith Day named in honor Town of Hobbs, 1978. Democrat. Methodist. Avocations: travel, fishing, musicals, interior decorating. Home: 2007 Creighton Dr Norman OK 73071-7338

SMITH, BEVERLY HARRIETT, elementary school educator; b. Cleve. d. William Nathaniel and Tommie Lee (Hooks) Stovall; m. Levi Smith, July 3, 1970; children: Kimberly Varese, Tommy Levi. BA in Edn., Ky. State U., 1970; MA in Curriculum and Instrn., Cleve. State U., 1975. Guidance liaison Almira Elem. Sch., Cleve., 1986—2002, drug liaison, 1988—2002, sci. lead tchr., 1993—2002; bldg. chairperson Cleve. Tchr. Union, 1990—2002, exec. bd. dirs., 1996—2002, chair salary and benefits, 1996—2002. Supt. tchr. for practicum tchrs., 1989-2000, supt tchr. for student tchrs., 1990-2001. Fin. sec. Shiloh Bapt. Ch. Ednl. Bd., Cleve., 1984-86. Recipient career edn. grant, 1989-90, Sunshine Energy award East Ohio Gas Co., 1984-85, 1988-89; named Educator of Yr., 1995; Martha Holden Jennings scholar, 1997. Mem. ASCD. Avocations: reading, arts and crafts, travel. Office: Almira Elem Sch 3380 W 98th St Cleveland OH 44102-4639

SMITH, CARLA ANNE, music educator; b. Albany, N.Y., Feb. 1, 1955; d. William Anthony and Florence Emma Africano; m. Gil Raymond Smith, Aug. 18, 1974; children: Alycia Erin(dec.), Turner Anthony. Student Ithaca (N.Y.) Coll., 1973—74; student, Potsdam (N.Y.) State U., 1974—75; BS magna cum laude, Pa. State U., 1977, MEd, 1983; postgrad., Ea. Ky. U., 2001—. Music tchr. Park Forest Jr. H.S., State College, Pa., 1978; chorus and music tchr. Bellefonte Mid. Sch., Pa., 1978—82; piano tchr. Muncie, Ind., 1985—95; choir dir. United Meth. Ch., Cammack, Ind., 1986—95; elem. music tchr. Model Lab Sch., Richmond, Ky., 1997—98; piano/oboe tchr. Richmond, Ky., 1995—; band dir., music tchr. Madison Bd. of Edn., Richmond, Ky., 1998—. Accompanist Madison Bd. Edn., Richmond, 1996—; keyboardist St. Mark's Ch., Richmond, 1995—. Mem. Friend of the Fine Arts, Richmond, 1996—; sch. counselor 4H Talent Show Club, Richmond, 2000—; founding mem. Wall of Tolerance, 2003. Named an Outstanding Am. Tchr., Nat. Honor Roll, 2005—06; recipient Arts in Edn. award, Richmond Area Arts Coun., 1999, Achievement award, Muncie Matinee Musicals, 1995, Vivian Conley award, AAUW, 1994, Madison County Internat. Artist Exch. Japan, 2003; grantee Fine Arts Mini grantee, Madison Bd. Edn., 1998—2001. Mem.: NEA, Ky. Edn. Assn., Ky. Fedn. of Music Clubs (jr. counselor 1996—), Ky. Music Educators Assn., Madison Music Makers Club (founder, counselor 1996—), Cecilian Music Club (jr. counselor 1996—), Mortar Bd., Phi Kappa Phi. Avocations: attending art galleries, reading. Home: 1104 Valley Run Dr Richmond KY 40475 Office: Clark-Moores Middle Sch 1143 Berea Rd Richmond KY 40475

SMITH, CARMELA VITO, administrator, counselor, educator; b. Riverdale, Md., Aug. 2, 1950; d. Samuele G. and Bertha Gray (McNeil) V.; m. Rodney Charles Smith, Nov. 25, 1983. BS, Frostburg State Coll., 1972; MEd, U. Md., 1978. Nat. cert. counselor; cert. profl. counselor, Md. Tchr. Prince George's County Bd. Edn., Upper Marlboro, Md., 1972-78, counselor, 1978-91, tchr. coord. talented and gifted magnet sch., 1991-94; pvt. practice counseling Bowie, Md., 1982-90; adminstr. Prince George's County Bd. Edn., Upper Marlboro, Md., 1994—99, prin., 1999—. Mem. AACD, ASCD (profl. conf. com. Md. unit), Am. Sch. Counselors Assn., Md. Assn. Counseling and Devel. (sec., exec. bd. 1989-90, com. chair profl. conf. 1990), Md. Mental Health Counselors, Phi Delta Kappa, Alpha Xi Delta. Office: Riverdale Elem Sch 5006 Riverdale Rd Riverdale MD 20737

SMITH, CAROL ANNE, retired physical education educator; d. James M. and Alice M. Gillan; m. Mark S. Smith, Jan. 21, 1983. BS in Phys. Edn./Tchr. Edn., U. Mass., Amherst, 1977—81; MEd in Phys. Edn. & Health, Frostburg State U., Md., 1981—82; PhD in Kinesiology, Tex. A&M U., College Station, 1990—97; MS in Curriculum & Instrn., Black Hills State U., Spearfish, SD, 1997—99. Cert. Adapted Phys. Educator APENS/Nat., 1999. Tchg. assoc. U. Tex., San Antonio, 1985—90; asst. lectr. Tex. A&M U., College Station, 1990—92, 1994—97, lectr. Koriyama, Japan, 1992—94; asst. prof. Black Hills State U., Spearfish, 1997—99, Elon U., 1999—2006, assoc. dir., N.C. Tchg. Fellows, 2005—, assoc. prof., 2006—. Author: (book) Country & Western Partner Dancing, Jitterbug Dancing; contbr. articles. Vol. Gibsonville Pub. Libr., NC, 2000; donations SPCA of the TRIAD, Triad, NC, 2002. Mem.: Am. Alliance for Health, Phys. Edn., Recreation & Dance (assoc.), N.C. Alliance for Athletics, Health, Phys. Edn., Recreation & Dance (assoc.; pres. elect 2005—06). Avocations: gardening, exercise, travel, cross stitch. Office: Elon Univ 2105 Campus Box Elon NC 27244 Office Phone: 336-278-5872.

SMITH, CAROL C., elementary school educator; BS in elem. edn., Castleton State Coll., 1968; MED, U. Vt., 1976. Tchr. 4th grade Williston (Vt.) Ctrl. Sch., 1969-73, Shelburne (Vt.) Cmty. Sch., 1974-75, tchr. alpha program, 1975—. Contbr. articles to profl. jours.; presenter of numerous presentations and workshops. Recipient Vt. Tchr. of the Year, 1995. Mem. The Nat. Edn. Assn., Nat. Middle Sch. Assn., Nat. Coun. Tchrs. of Math., Assn. Supr. and Curr. Devel., Vt. Assn. for Middle Level Edn., New England League of Middle Sch., Vt. Assn. for Supr. and Curr. Devel., Vt. Edn. Assn., Chittened S. Edn. Assn., Shelburne Parent, Tchr. Organ.

SMITH, CAROL LEE, science educator; BA in Chemistry, U. Tex., Arlington, 1993. Sci. tchr. Van Alstyne H.S., Van Alstyne, Tex., 1997—. Office: Van Alstyne High School 2001 N Waco Dr Van Alstyne TX 75495 Office Phone: 903-482-8803. E-mail: clsmith@ednet10.net.

SMITH, CAROLE DIANNE, retired lawyer, editor, writer, product developer; b. Seattle, June 12, 1945; d. Glaude Francis and Elaine Claire (Finkenstein) S.; m. Stephen Bruce Presser, June 18, 1968 (div. June 1987); children: David Carter, Elisabeth Catherine. AB cum laude, Harvard U., Radcliffe Coll., 1968; JD, Georgetown U., 1974. Bar: Pa. 1974. Law clk. Hon. Judith Jamison, Phila., 1974—75; assoc. Gratz, Tate, Spiegel, Ervin & Ruthrouff, Phila., 1975—76; freelance editor, writer Evanston, Ill., 1983—87; editor Ill. Inst. Tech., Chgo., 1987—88; mng. editor LawLetters, Inc., Chgo., 1988—89; editor ABA, Chgo., 1989—95; product devel. dir. Gt. Lakes divsn. Lawyers Coop. Pub., Deerfield, Ill., 1995—96; product devel. mgr. Midwest Market Ctr. West Group, Deerfield, Ill., 1996—97; mgr acquisitions, bus. and fin. group CCH, Inc., Riverwoods, Ill., 1997—2002; ret. Author Jour. of Legal Medicine, 1975, Selling and the Law: Advertising and Promotion, 1987; (under pseudonym Sarah Toast) 79 children's books and stories, 1994-2002; editor The Brief, 1990-95, Criminal Justice, 1989-90, 92-95 (Gen. Excellence award Soc. Nat. Assn. Pubs. 1990, Feature Article award-bronze Soc. Nat. Assn. Pubs. 1994), Franchise Law Jour., 1995; mem. editl. bd. The Brief, 1995-2000, editor-in-chief, 1998-2000. Dir. Radcliffe Club of Chgo., 1990-93; mem. parents coun. Latin Sch. Chgo., 1995-96; trustee Winnetka-Northfield Libr. Dist., 2003—, pres. trustees, 2005-; mem. Winnetka Plan Commn. 2003-05, Winnetka Forestry Commn., 2004-05 Mem. ABA (editor-in-chief The Brief 1998-2000, mem. publs. editl. bd. tort trial and ins. practice sect. 2003-05, chair 2005—).

SMITH, CAROLYN J(ANE) HOSTETTER, psychologist, educator; b. Indpls., Mar. 29, 1938; d. John Daniel and Louise Margaret (Reiber) Hostetter; m. Thomas Tomasian, June 18, 1988. BA, DePauw U., 1959; MS in Teaching-Guidance & Counseling, U. Chgo., 1962, PhD, 1981. Lic. psychologist, Mass. Guidance counselor Blue Island (Ill.) High Sch., 1962-63, Univ. Chgo. (Ill.) Lab. Schs., 1963-66; counseling dir. Upward Bound, Mundeline Coll., Chgo., 1966-68; assoc. prof. counseling Kennedy-King Coll., Chgo., 1968-82; psychotherapist Worcester County Counseling Associates., Bolton, Mass., 1982-87; clin. supr. Valley Adult Counseling Svc., Bellingham, Mass., 1982-84; cons. psychologist Mass. Dept. Edn., Bur. of Instl. Schs., Boston, 1984-90; dir., psychotherapist Ea. Shore Assocs., Shrewsbury, Mass., 1987—. Psychologist Dept. Pediatrics and Psychiatry, St. Vincent's Hosp., Worcester, 1986—; cons., educator various schs. and orgns., Mass., Ill., 1962—; workshop presenter. Bd. mem., chair children's com. Worcester (Mass.) Area Mental Health & Retardation Bd., 1984-87; bd. alumni affairs DePauw U., 2003-; coord. Ctrl. Mass. disaster response network Mass. Psych Assoc., 1999-2005; mem. Local CISM Team, comm. on ministry Dioceses Western Mass., 1995-2005. Recipient Improvement Edn. grant Ford Found., Univ. Chgo., 1962. Fellow Am. Assn. Orthopsychiatry; mem. APA, Eye Movement Desensitization Reprocessing Internat. Assn., Mass. Psychol. Assn., New Eng. Soc. for Study Dissociative Disorders, Pi Lambda Theta, Psi Chi, Delta theta Chi. Episcopalian. Avocations: attending plays, jazz, swimming, travel. Office: Ea Shore Assocs 586 Main St Shrewsbury MA 01545-2920 Office Phone: 508-842-3100 14.

SMITH, CATHERINE MARIE, science educator; b. Bridgeport, Conn., Dec. 28, 1958; d. Arthur Vincent Giles, Sr. and Lila Catherine (Auger) Giles; m. Roger K. Smith, July 16, 1982. BS, U. Bridgeport, 1980; MBA, Sacred Heart U., 1994. Cert. Med. Technologist Am. Soc. Clin. Pathologists, 1981. Medical technician Bridgeport Hosp., Conn., 1980—88; med. technologist St. Joseph Med. Ctr., Stamford, Conn., 1988—94; lab. mgr. Stamford Medical Group, Stamford, 1994—99; chemistry and biology tchr. Wilbur Cross HS, New Haven, 1999—2003, New Canaan HS, Conn., 2003—. Donor Am. Red Cross, Conn., 1984—; tchr. participant Jr. Sci. & Humanities Symposium, U. Conn., 2000—03; youth min. Our Lady of Assumption, Fairfield, Conn., 1989—2004; emmaus team mem. Holy Family, Fairfield, Conn., 2000—, St. Aloysius, New Canaan, Conn., 2004—. Mem.: NSTA, So. Poverty Law, Am. Soc. Clin. Pathologists, Conn. Nat. Sci. Tchrs. Assn., Pi Lambda Theta, Delta Mu Delta. Roman Catholic. Avocations: car racing, dog training. Personal E-mail: cmbgs@aol.com.

SMITH, CECE, venture capitalist; b. Washington, Nov. 16, 1944; d. Linn Charles and Grace Inez (Walker) S.; m. John Ford Lacy, Apr. 22, 1978. BBA, U. Mich., 1966; M in Liberal Arts, So. Meth. U., 1974. CPA, Tex. Staff acct. Arthur Young & Co. (CPAs), Boston, 1966-68; staff acct., then asst. to contr. Wyly Corp., Dallas, 1969-72; contr., treas. subs. Univ. Computing Co., Dallas, 1972-74; contr. Steak and Ale Restaurants Am., Inc., Dallas, 1974-76, v.p. fin., 1976-80, exec. v.p., 1980-81, Pearle Health Services, Inc., 1981-84, pres. Primacare divsn., 1984-86; gen. ptnr. Phillips-Smith-Machens Venture Ptnrs., 1986—; pres. Le Sportsac Dallas, Inc., 1981-87. Bd. dirs. Brinker Internat. Inc., Michaels Stores, Inc.; chmn. Fed. Res. Bank Dallas, 1994—96; past v.p., dir. IWF-Dallas; mem. pres. adv. group U. Mich.; treas, mem. exec. bd. Dallas Symphony Assn. Past co-chmn. pres.'s rsch. coun. U. Tex. S.W. Med. Ctr. Dallas; past vis. com. U. Mich. Bus. Sch.; exec. bd. So. Meth. U. Cox Sch. Bus.; past v.p., bd. dirs. Jr. Achievement Dallas; past pres. Charter 100; past treas. Dallas Assembly; exec. bd., treas. Dallas Symphony Assn. Mem.: Com. of 200. Home: 3710 Shenandoah St Dallas TX 75205-2121 Office: 5080 Spectrum Dr Ste 805 W Addison TX 75001-4648 Office Phone: 972-387-0725.

SMITH, CECILIA MAY, hospital official; b. Oakland, Calif., Feb. 18, 1933; d. Frederick Arthur and Inez Calista Small; m. Harold Joseph Smith, June 17, 1957 (dec. June 18, 1966); children: Harold Frederick, Estelle Marie. BS, Holy Name Coll., 1956; MS, U. Calif., San Francisco, 1966; postgrad., U. Calif., Berkeley, 1972. RN Calif. Asst. prof. U. Nev., Reno, 1966-69; instr. U. Wash., Seattle, 1972-74; dir. continuing edn. Wash. State Nurses Assn., Seattle, 1974-78; pres., ptnr. World of Continuing Edn., Seattle, 1975-85; continuing edn. specialist U. Calif., San Francisco, 1979-82; asst. adminstr. Cordilleras Mental Health Ctr., Redwood City, Calif., 1984-86, adminstr., 1986-90; dir. psychiat. svcs. St. Luke's Hosp., San Francisco, 1990—. Mem. ANA Nat. Accreditation Bd., Kansas City, 1974-7; sec., workshop leader Nat. Staffing Systems, San Francisco, 1981-82; cons. WHO, New Delhi, 1985. Editor ind. study courses for nurses and nursing home adminstrs., 1975-85; author AIDS ind. study courses, 1984; contbr. articles to Jour. of Continuing Edn. Recipient Marie Durocher scholarship Coll. of Holy Name, 1952, NIMH traineeship U. Calif. San Francisco, 1963, Nursing Rsch. fellowship U. Calif. Berkeley, 1969-71. Mem.: Sigma Theta Tau. E-mail: ceciliams33@hotmail.com.

SMITH, CHARLOTTE REED, retired music educator; b. Eubank, Ky., Sept. 15, 1921; d. Joseph Lumpkin and Cornelia Elizabeth (Spenser) Reed; m. Walter Lindsay Smith, Aug. 24, 1949; children— Walter Lindsay IV, Elizabeth Reed. B.A. in Music, Tift Coll., 1941; M.A. in Mus. Theory, Eastman Sch. of Music, 1946; postgrad. Juilliard Sch., 1949. Asst. prof. theory Okla. Bapt. U., 1944-45, Washburn U., 1946-48; prof. music Furman U., Greenville, S.C., 1948-92; chmn. dept. music, 1987-92. Editor: Seven Penitential Psalms with Two Laudate Psalms, 1983; author: Manual of Sixteenth-Century Contrapuntal Style, 1989. Mem. Internat. Musicological Soc., Am. Musicological Soc., Soc. for Music Theory, AAUP (sec.-treas. Furman chpt. 1984-85), Nat. Fedn. Music Clubs, Pi Kappa Lambda. Republican. Baptist.

SMITH, CHERYL A., science educator; b. New Rochelle, N.Y., Jan. 3, 1962; d. Charles William and Linda Carpenter; m. Stephen Daniel Smith, June 1, 1985; children: Stephen Daniel Jr., Christian Anthony. BS in Edn. and Biology, Concordia Coll., 1985; MS in Secondary Sci. Edn. with honors, Iona Coll., 1990. Sci. tchr. New Rochelle Cen. Sch. Dist., 1987—. Mem. bd. trustees Somers Sch. Bd., 1992—. Recipient Environ. Educator award, Texaco Corp., 1996. Mem.: Planned Parenthood of Am., Nat. Wildlife Fedn., Sierra Club. Democrat. Home: 9 Valley Dr Yorktown Heights NY 10598

SMITH, CHERYL ANN, secondary school educator; d. Andrew and Anna May Smithy. Student, SUNY, Suffern, N.Y., 1990—92; BA in Fine Arts Edn., St. Thomas Aquinas Coll., Sparkill, N.Y., 1995; MS in Edn. Counseling Psychology, Fordham U., Bronx, N.Y., 2003. Cert. in art edn. K-12 N.Y., N.J., sch. counselor N.Y., N.J. Coord. program Internat. Edn. Forum, Bayshare, NY, 1991; office mgr. Paldades Interstate Pk. Commn., Bean Mountain, NY, 1991—96; tchr. Beacon City Sch. Dist., NY, 1996—97, South Drangertown Ctrl. Sch. Dist., Blavrelt, NY, 1997—98, Clarkstown Ctrl. Sch. Dist., West Nyack, NY, 1999—2000, Highland Falls Ctrl. Sch. Dist., NY, 2000—. Office: James O'Neill High Sch PO Box 287 Highland Falls NY 10928-0287

SMITH, CHERYL DIANE, music educator; b. Princeton, Ind., Jan. 17, 1952; d. Ralph Eugene and Beulah J. Smith. BA, Oakland City U., 1974; MS, Ind. State U., 1980. Substitute tchr. North Gibson Sch. Corp., Princeton, Ind., 1974—77, South Gibson Sch. Corp., Ft. Branch, 1974—77; tchr. choral, gen. music South Knox Sch. Corp., Vincennes, 1977, North Knox Sch. Corp., Birknell, 1977—. Co-author: Introduction to Theater, 1999. Mem. exec. com. North Knox Social Mins., 1997—. Mem.: Choral Dirs. Nat. Assn., Nat. Music Educators Assn. Avocations: cross stitch, piano, reading. Personal E-mail: resox6x4@yahoo.com.

SMITH, CHERYL JAN, language educator; d. Robert Beryl and Cindy Jean Hogue (Stepmother); m. S. Craig Smith, May 18, 1990. PhD, U. Calif., Santa Barbara, 2006. Cert. writing Calif. State U., Bakersfield, 1999. Lectr. Calif. State U., Bakersfield, 1999—. Cfo Agri Pest Mgmt. Svcs., Inc., Bakersfield, 1993—. Instr. Bakersfield Homeless Shelter, 2004—06. Fellow: South Coast Writing Project (life); mem.: Nat. Coun. Tchrs. of English, Internat. Reading Assn., MLA. Office: Calif State Univ Bakersfield 9001 Stockdale Hwy Bakersfield CA 93311-1099 Office Phone: 661-654-2086. Office Fax: 661-654-2063.

SMITH, CHRISTINE MOORE, literature and language professor, writer; b. Anderson, Ind., July 12, 1944; d. Robert Lee Moore and Mary Audrey Estes; m. Harold Vaughn Smith; children: Tammy (Tamara) Joy Martin, Gregory Scott. MA in English, Ea. Ky. U., Richmond, 1977. Adj. instr. writing and lit. dept. English Butler U., Indpls., 1995—. Bd. dirs. Diocese of Indpls. Home: 4530 N 850 E Greenfield IN 46140 Office: Butler U Dept English 4600 Sunset Indianapolis IN 46208 E-mail: cmsmith@butler.edu.

SMITH, CLAIRE LAREMONT, language educator; b. Panama City, Panama, Dec. 30, 1939; came to U.S., 1965; d. Sebastian Hamlet and Ambrozine Beatriz (Simon) Laremont; m. Stephen E. Greaves, Nov. 29, 1961 (div. 1968); children: Liza N. Greaves Smith, Katia T. Laremont Smith; m.

James Elliott Smith, Dec. 20, 1969; 1 child, Raquel J. Student, U. Panama, Panama City, 1959-62; BA, SUNY, Fredonia, 1968, MS, 1970; postgrad., SUNY, Buffalo, 1983-93. Cert. tchr. secondary social studies, elem. bilingual edn., secondary Spanish and ESL, N.Y. Bilingual stenographer, bookkeeper, cashier Foto Internat., Panama City, 1960-65; tchr. secondary social studies and Spanish Forestville (N.Y.) Cen. Schs., 1968-69; grad. asst. dept. history SUNY, Fredonia, 1969-70; substitute tchr. Am. Overseas Schs. of Army Dependents, Camp Livorno, Italy, 1983-95; tchr. early childhood bilingual Dunkirk (N.Y.) Migrant Daycare Ctr., 1972-73; tchr., home instr. Head Start program Durkirk Schs., 1973-74; tchr. adult basic edn. N.Y. State Migrant Workers Opportunities, Dunkirk, 1977-80; tchr. social studies, bilingual, Spanish and ESL Dunkirk Mid. Sch., 1973-98; adj. instr. ESL SUNY, Fredonia, 1992, 93. Mem. affirmative action com. on cultural ethnic rels. SUNY, Fredonia, 1989-98; mem. com. on discipline Dunkirk Sch. Dist., 1991-98, compact learning com., 1993-98, Youth Empowerment System, wellness com.; mem. sch. improvement team Dunkirk Med. Sch., 1991-92; presenter profl. confs., U.S., Mex.; guest speaker Hispanic Heritage Week Celebration, N.Y. State Migrant Daycare, Fredonia, 1991. Bd. dirs. North County Counseling Svc., Dunkirk, 1992-96, People's Action Coaliton, Dunkirk, 1992-95, v.p., 1993-94, 95—; chairperson cultural awareness task force Dunkirk Cmty. Challenge, 1993-95; bd. dirs. Chautauqua County Connections, 1993-96, First Night Internat. Alliance, Boston, 1994-99; chair First Night Dunkirk, 1994-96, exec. dir., 1996-97; harborfest com. City of Dunkirk, 1992-96; vol. ARC fundraiser, 1995; founder, advisor Dunkirk H.S. ASPIRA Leadership Club, 1994-98, Dunkirk Schs. Step and Drill Team, 1994-97; N.Y. State advisor, trainer Hispanic Youth Leadership Inst. Conf., Albany, 1994-98. Named Person of Yr., Dunkirk Kiwanis, 1995; recipient Cmty. Svc. award N.Y. State Senator Jess Present, 1997. Mem. AAUW, NAAPC (edn. com. 1976), N.Y. State Assn. Bilingual Educators, Tchrs. of English to Speakers of Other Langs., Nat. Assn. Bilingual Edn., Dunkirk Tchrs. Assn. (bilingual scholarship fund, annual dinner awards program, 1979-92, active voter registration drive 1992), N.Y. State United Tchrs., SUNY Buffalo Grad. Student Assn. (senator 1990-92, co-pres. dept. learning and instrn. 1991-92), Phi Delta Kappa (SUNY Buffalo chpt.). Democrat. Roman Catholic. Avocations: jogging, reading, travel. Office: SUNY Coll Fredonia Dept Edn Fredonia NY 14048-1328

SMITH, CLARE, art appraiser; Grad, Oxford Univ., Courtauld Inst. Art, London. Specialist, Victorian picture dept. Christie's, NYC, 1999, now specialist, sporting art, also US rep. for British & Irish art. Project coord., sale, Forbes collection, Victorian art Christie's, 2003. Office: Christie's 20 Rockefeller Plz New York NY 10020 Office Phone: 212-636-2084. Office Fax: 212-636-4925. Business E-Mail: claresmith@christies.com.

SMITH, CORA ADELE, author; b. Bklyn., Oct. 14, 1939; d. Gabriel and Gemma (DeMartino) Garofalo; m. Mel Warren Smith, July 22, 1967; children— Charles Edward, Dorothy Rose. B.S. in Elem. Edn., Fordham U., 1967; postgrad. N.Y. Inst. Tech., 1979-81, U. Mass., Amherst, 1982. Tchr. pvt. and parochial schs., 1960-72; data processor IRS, Holtsville, N.Y., 1984-87; staff writer monthly Our Voice, Holbrook, N.Y. Author serialized stories for Organian Quest mag. including: Emotions Double Edge, 1979; Contemptable Struggle, 1980; By Appearances Deceiving, 1980; Sweetness in the Air, 1981; Shuttle Ark, 1982; Sweet Times, 1983; A Child Fantasy-Freckles Mother's Day Surprise, 1984. Mem. com. Boy Scouts Am., 1980-85; asst. Girl Scouts U.S.A., 1983-85. Mem. Am. Film Inst., Air Force Sgts. Assn. Aux. Democrat.

SMITH, CORINNE ROTH, psychologist; b. Reading, Pa., May 22, 1945; d. Zoltan and Elizabeth (Foldes) Roth; m. Lynn Helden Smith, June 9, 1968; children: Juliette Sarah, Rachael Eliza. BA in Psychology cum laude, Syracuse U., 1967, PhD, 1973; MA, Temple U., Phila., 1969. Lic. psychologist, N.Y. Psychologist experimental presch. program Syracuse City Schs., 1970-71; psychologist reading clinic Syracuse (NY) U., 1969-70, coordinator lab. sch. and clinic, 1971-72, founder, dir. psychoedul. teaching lab., asst. prof., 1971—84, founder, dir. comprehensive assessment ctr., 1981-83, psychologist experimental presch. program, 1984—96, assoc. dean edn., 1992—2000, prof., 1997—, dean, 2000—02. Mem. Coun. for Exceptional Children; reviewer Aspen, Ablex, Mc Graw Hill, Little Brown & Co., N.Y., Allyn & Bacon, Pergammon, 1985—; apptd. mem. Gov. N.Y. Coun. for Youth, Albany, 1984-91; speaker in field. Author: Learning Disabilities: The Interaction of Learner, Task and Setting, 1983, 2d edit., 1991, 3rd edit, 1994, 4th edit., 1998, 5th edit., 2004, The People's Guide to Drug Education, 1992, Learning Disabilities A to Z: The Complete Parent Guide to Learning Disabiltities from Preschool to Adulthood, 1997; contbr. articles to profl. jours. and chpts. to books. Bd. dirs. Ctrl. N.Y. United Way, 1987-93, leadership giving chair, 2003-06; pres. Jewish Comm. Ctr., Syracuse, 1978-81; bd. dirs., chair career womens network Syracuse Jewish Fedn., 1985-87, womens campaign chair, 1987-89, gen. campaign chair, 1990-92. Recipient Disting. Svc. award Jewish Comm. Ctr., 1976, Comm. Leadership award Syracuse Jewish Fedn., 1986, 89, Jewish Family Svc. Humanitarian award, 1991, Roth Humanitarian award, 1992, Citizen of Yr. award, 2000; named Woman of Yr. Post Std., 1990; grantee N.Y. State Office Mental Retardation and Devel. Disabilities, 1985-93; Leadership award Coun. Jewish Women, 1999. Mem. Am. Psych. Assn., Nat. Assn. Sch. Psychologists, N.Y. State Learning Disabilities Assn., Learning Disability Assn. Am., Winnick Hillel (pres. nat. bd. 2003-06). Avocations: tennis, gardening. Office: Syracuse U 236 Huntington Hl Syracuse NY 13244-0001

SMITH, D(AISY) MULLETT, publisher; b. Washington, Aug. 17, 1948; d. Gordon Hunt and Suzanne Myrick (Mullett) Smith. BA, Am. U., 1970; cert. computer programming, U. So. Calif., Arlington, Va., 1986; cert. in records mgmt., Assn. Records Mgrs. Am., Prairie Village, Kans., 1987. Christian Sci. practitioner The First Ch. of Christ, Scientist, Boston, 1970-86; clk. Fifth Ch. of Christ, Scientist, Washington, 1971-74; Christian Sci. campus counsellor The Am. U., Washington, 1976-81; editor, computer specialist, desktop pub. Mullett-Smith Press, Washington, 1984-89, owner, pub., 1989—, music copyist, pub. on computer, 1990—, web weaver, 1996—, pub., typesetting, 2004—; ptnr. James Enterprises, Inc. and JonathanJames. Cons., spkr. in field; started webhosting svc. partnership with H. James Enterprises and Bluebirdartworks.com. Author: AB Mullett, His Relevance in American Architecture, 1990 (Printers award 1990); editor: AB Mullett, Architect Engineer 1862-90, 1985; contbr. articles to profl. jours. Participant White House Conf. on Children, 1970; active Save Pioneer Post Office, Portland, Oreg., 1996—; fundraising com. U.S. Treasury Bill Restoration Fund, 1998-2000; libr. Christian Sci. Reading Rm., 1999-2002; renovator TH-7, 2003, Hist. Townhouse Wheat Row, 2003-06; commrs. Jefferson County, W.Va., 2003; interviewer PBS radio, saving Jefferson County Jail. Recipient Key to the City, Mayor Lincoln, Nebr., 1989. Mem. Nat. Soc. Arts and Letters (editor/pub. directory 1971-2006, treas. 1988-90, web weaver 1996—, web host 2006—), Nat. Trust for Hist. Preservation, Assn. Records Mgrs. and Adminstrs., Assn. for Info. and Image Mgmt. Internat., U.S. Treasury Hist. Assn., U.S. Capitol Hist. Soc. Avocations: art, design, guitar, windsurfing, computers. Office Phone: 202-479-4333. Business E-Mail: mspress@mullett-smithpress.com.

SMITH, DEBBIE ILEE RANDALL, elementary school educator; b. Pampa, Tex., Oct. 8, 1955; d. Lester R. and Launa I. (Elmner) Randall; m. Jimmie E. Smith, July 20, 1974; children: Christi I., James R., Stacy L. AA, Seward County Community Coll., Liberal, Kans.; student, Panhandle State U., Goodwell, Okla. Paraprofl. High Plains Edn. Coop., Garden City, Kans.; tchr. USD 480, Liberal; TESOL DISD, Dumas, Tex. Mem. Phi Theta Kappa.

SMITH, DEBRA FARWELL, school librarian; b. Lock Haven, Pa., Sept. 9, 1950; d. James Samuel and Betty (Jackson) Farwell; m. James L. Smith, Oct. 4, 1977; children: Jason James, Joshua Jordan. BS, Lock Haven U., 1972. Cert. elem. tchr., libr., early childhood instr. Kindergarten tchr. Follow-Through, Lock Haven, 1972—83; elem. libr. Keystone Cen. Sch. Dist., Lock Haven, 1983—99; mid. sch. libr. Ctrl. Mountain Mid. Sch., Lock Haven, 1999—. Mem.: ALA, Pa. State Libr. Assn. Republican. Avocations: computers, skiing, golf, reading. Home: 1389 Cardinal Dr W Lock Haven PA 17745-9517 Office: Ctrl Mountain Mid Sch 200 Ben Ave Mill Hall PA 17751

SMITH, DEBRA L., band director; b. Fort Benning, Ga., Feb. 8, 1969; d. Jack H. and Pauline Leveillee Smith. BS in Music Edn., Troy State U., 1992, MS in Music Edn., 1994. Cert. tchr. grades N-12 Ala., 1992. Band dir. Pacelli H.S., Columbus, Ga., 1992—93; educator humanities and band Escambia County Mid. Sch., Atmore, Ala., 1995—. Clinician various music programs, 1990—; mem. Escambia County Grant Com., 2000—; student/cmty. liason and tchr. Learn and Serve, Atmore, 2000—; after-school tutor Smart-Links, Atmore, 2001—. Mem. Relay for Life, Atmore, 2000—02; bd. mem. Atmore Arts Coun., 1999—2003. Mem.: NEA (assoc.), Music Educators Nat. Conf. (assoc.), Ala. Bandmasters Assn. (assoc.), Ala. Educators Assn. (assoc.), Omicron Delta Kappa, Gamma Beta Phi, Pi Kappa Phi, Sigma Alpha Iota, Tau Beta Sigma. Avocations: travel, reading, politics, music, theater. Office: Escambia County Middle School PO Drawer 1236 Atmore AL 36504 Personal E-mail: educ8or@frontiernet.net.

SMITH, DENA MICHELE, physical education educator; d. Edward I. Smith and Beverly M. Metz. BS, U. Wis., La Crosse, 1992. Tchr. phys. edn. and health Shell Lake Schs., Wis., 1993—2000, Sch. Dist. Jefferson, Jefferson, Wis., 2000—. Head coach girls basketball Shell Lake Schs., 1993—2000, head coach girls softball, 1994—2000; head coach girls basketball Sch. Dist. Jefferson, 2000—. Mem.: Wis. Basketball Coaches Assn. Office: Sch Dist Jefferson 700 W Milwaukee St Jefferson WI 53549 Office Phone: 920-675-1185.

SMITH, DENISE GROLEAU, data processing professional; b. Worcester, Mass., Feb. 7, 1951; d. Edmond Laurence and Audrey Mildred (Paquin) Groleau; m. Wayne Marshall Smith, Apr. 17, 1976; 1 child, Andrew. BSBA, Fitchburg State U., 1983. Bindery worker Atlantic Bus. Forms, Hudson, Mass., 1969-73; proofreader New Eng. Bus., Townsend, Mass., 1974-75, computer operator Groton, Mass., 1975-80, adminstrv. asst. bus. systems, 1980-82, adminstrv. asst. info. ctr., 1982-85; info. ctr. analyst Wright Line Inc., Worcester, 1985-88; personal computer coord. Thom McAn Shoe Co., Worcester, 1988-91. Cons. personal computer Buckingham Transp., Groton, 1987-2001, Software Mgr. Moppet Sch., 1993—; Maple Dene Elem. Sch., 1993—, software mgr. Avocations: reading, sewing, quilting. Home: 14 Cedar Cir Townsend MA 01469-1336 E-mail: dpgesmith@verizon.net.

SMITH, DIANA MARIE, business educator; b. Des Moines, Oct. 25, 1940; d. Nathan Henry and Helen (Hall) Kitchen; m. Robert Nelson Smith, Jan. 26, 1971 (dec. 12-7-2004); 1 child, Stephen BA, Drake U., Des Moines, Iowa, 1968, MA, 1971. Cert. tchr., Iowa. Stenographer Polk County Welfare Dept., Des Moines, 1960—67; typist Polk County Auditor, Des Moines, 1968, Ctrl. Life Assurance Co., Des Moines, 1976—79; computer oper. IRS, Des Moines, 1988; lead specialist II Norwest Bank, Des Moines, 1978—2002; sec. Shive-Hattery Engrs., Des Moines, 1976—90; instr. adult edn. Des Moines Ind. Dist., 1969—2001; tchr. bus., computers Des Moines Pub. Schs., 1968—2000; instr. computers St. Paul Ch. and Saks Inc., Des Moines, 2000—04. Ind. computer cons.; instr.-authorized tng. assoc. program for Word Perfect, 1994; Mary Kay beauty cons., 1993— Chair meml. com. Burns United Meth. Ch., Des Moines, 1988—, Sunday sch. tchr., 1961-83, 92-98, 2006—, sec. adminstrv. bd., 1983-2004 Democrat. Avocations: reading, computers. Office: Saks Inc 701 Walnut Des Moines IA 50309 Office Phone: 515-246-3189. Personal E-mail: dsmith1034@aol.com.

SMITH, DIANE JANS, librarian, educator; b. Chgo., May 10, 1951; d. Steven Fred and Lillian Ann Jans; m. John H. Smith, July 22, 1989; stepchildren: Laurie, Tammy. BA in English, Calif. State U., Fullerton, 1973; MLS, U. So. Calif., L.A., 1974. Children's libr. Riverside Co. Libr. Sys., Indio, Calif., 1979—81, Orange Co. Pub. Libr., Mission Viejo, Calif., 1981—85, br. mgr., 1987—89, Laguna Beach, 1985—87, bibliog. svcs. supr. Santa Ana, 1990—94, program adminstr., 1994—2002; ref. libr., br. mgr. Riverside Co. Libr. Sys., San Jacinto, Calif., 2002—. Libr., faculty mem. U. N.D., Williston, 1974—77. Mem. City of Mission Viejo Libr. Design Task Force, Calif., 1994—96; tchr. Ch. on Northside, La Habra, Calif., 1987—90, El Toro Baptist Ch., Lake Forest, Calif., 1992—2002, Hemet Valley Baptist Ch., Calif., 2002—. Recipient Cmty. Svc. Award, City of Mission Viejo, Calif., 1989. Baptist. Avocations: hiking, canoeing, kayaking, dance, reading. Office: Riverside Co Libr Sys San Jacinto Libr 500 Idyllwild Dr San Jacinto CA 92583

SMITH, DOLORES T., language educator, consultant; b. Pearsall, Tex., June 19, 1943; d. Lucas and Leocadia Coronado Trevino; m. David Stowe Smith, Jr., Dec. 22, 1968; children: Yvette Marie, David Lucas, Richard Todd. BA in English and History, Incarnate World Coll. (now U.), San Antonio, Tex., 1965. Cert. tchr. Tex., 1965, family devel. U. Iowa. Tchr. Dowagiac Pub. Sch., Mich., 1965—66; vol. Peace Corps, Colombia, 1966—69; tchr. homebound students Delaware Pub. Sch. System, Delaware, Ohio, 1983—86; clerk Delaware Dist. Libr., Delaware, Ohio, 1986—88; translator Dr. Harry Bahrick psych. project Ohio Wesleyan U., Delaware, 1985—89; program dir. emergency svcs. People In Need, Delaware, Ohio, 1994—97; translator Spanish/English Job/Family Svcs. and Delaware County Health Dept., Ohio, 1997—2006; tchr. Spanish St. Mary Sch., Delaware, 2001—06; self-employed, 2006—. Tchr. suicide prevention Help Anonymous, Delaware, 1986—91; vol. Delaware City Schs. Levy Campaigns, 1992—93; mem. Chenoweth scholarship com. Delaware City Schs., 1993—; mem. adv. bd. Summer Lang. Program, Delaware, 2005—. Mem. Big Bros./Big Sisters, Delaware, 1995—99; mem. Delaware County chpt. Red Cross, 1997—; bd. dirs. Ch. Women United, Delaware, 1997—; mem. bd. Ecumenical Youth Coun., 2003—, Common Ground Free Store Ministries, 2006; bd. dirs. Rahway Day Care Ctr., NJ, 1970—75; bd. dirs./tchr. Help Anonymous 24 hr. Crisis Line, Delaware, 1986—92. Finalist Cmty. Svc. award, The Columbus Dispatch, Ohio, 1989; recipient Citizen of Yr. Achievement award, Del. C. of C., 1990, Cmty. Svc. award, 1999, Wayne Hilborn Lifetime Achievement award, 2003. Catholic. Avocations: travel, piano, reading, refinishing furniture.

SMITH, DORIS IRENE, music educator; b. Cleve., Sept. 22, 1950; d. Erwin John and Irene Janet Sladewski; m. Jerrold J. Smith, May 19, 1973 (div. Mar. 2002); children: Laura Diane, Carolyn Joy, Michael Everett, Rebecca Ann, Matthew William. Student, Otterbein Coll., 1968—69; B in Music Edn., Baldwin-Wallace Coll., 1972; MFA in Music Edn., U. Akron, 2002. Pvt. flute tchr., Lyndhurst, Ohio, 1968—; music tchr. Garfield Heights (Ohio) Schs., 1973—75; flute tchr. Cleve. Music Settlement, 1992—96; music tchr., band dir. Kenston Schs., Bainbridge, Ohio, 1996—. Flutist Cleve. Women's Orch., 1971—72. Mem.: NEA, No. Ohio Flute Assn., Ohio Music Educator Assn. Republican. Evangelical. Avocations: calligraphy, crafts, stained glass. Personal E-mail: musiclady5@adelphia.net. E-mail: ke_dsmith@lgca.org.

SMITH, DOROTHY OTTINGER, apparel designer, volunteer; b. Indpls., 1922; d. Albert Ellsworth and Leona Aurelia (Waller) Ottinger; m. James Emory Smith, June 25, 1943 (div. 1984); children: Michael Ottinger, Sarah Anne, Theodore Arnold, Lisa Marie. Student, Herron Art Sch. of Purdue U. and Ind. U., 1941-42. Comml. artist William H. Block Co., Indpls., 1942-43, H.P. Wasson Co., 1943-44; dir. Riverside (Calif.) Art Ctr., 1963-64; jewelry designer Riverside, 1970—; numerous design commns. Adviser Riverside chpt. Freedom's Found. of Valley Forge; co-chmn. fund raising com. Riverside Art Ctr. and Mus., 1966-67, bd. dirs. Art Alliance, 1980-81; mem. Riverside City Hall sculpture selection panel Nat. Endowment for the Arts, 1974-75; chmn. fundraising benefit Riverside Art Ctr. and Mus., 1973-74, trustee, 1980-84, chmn. permanent collection, 1981-84, co-chmn. fund drive, 1982-84, trustee, 1998—; chmn. Riverside Mcpl. Arts Commn., 1974-76, Silver Anniversary Gala, 1992; juror Riverside Civic Ctr. Purchase Prize Art Show, 1975; mem. pub. bldgs. and grounds subcom., gen. plan citizens com. City of Riverside, 1965-66; mem. Mayor's Commn. on Civic Beauty, Mayor's Commn. on Sister City Sendai, 1965-66; bd. dirs., chmn. spl. events Children's League of Riverside Community Hosp., 1952-53; bd. dirs. Crippled Children's Soc. of Riverside, spl. events. chmn., 1952-53; bd. dirs. Nat. Charity League, pres. Riverside chpt., 1965-66; mem. exec. com. bd. trustees Riverside Arts Found., 1977-91, fund drive chmn., 1978-79, project rev. chmn., 1978-79, advisor Eveing for the Arts, 1998, juror Gemco Charitable and Scholarship Found., 1977-85; mem. bd. women deacons Calvary Presbyn. Ch., 1978-80, elder, 1989-92; mem. incorporating bd. Inland Empire United Fund for the Arts, 1980-81; bd dirs. Hospice Orgn. Riverside County, 1982-84; trustee Riverside Art Mus., 1998—; mem. Calif. Coun. Humanities, 1982-86. Recipient cert. Riverside City Coun., 1977, plaque Mayor of Riverside, 1977, Spl. Recognition Riverside Cultural Arts Coun., 1981, Disting. Svc. plaque Riverside Art Ctr. and Mus., Jr. League Silver Raincross Community Svc. award, 1989, Cert Appreciation Outstanding Svc. to the Arts Community Riverside Arts Found., 1990, Top Dog award Riverside Art Mus., 1999. Mem. Riverside Art Assn. (pres. 1961-63, 1st. v.p. 1964-65, 67-68, trustee 1959-70, 80-84, 87-92), Art Alliance of Riverside Art Ctr. and Museum (founder 1964, pres. 1969-70). Address: 3979 Chapman Pl Riverside CA 92506-1150

SMITH, E. FOLLIN, corporate financial executive; b. Miss. m. John Gerdy; children: E. Wallace Gerdy, James F. Gerdy. BA, Davidson Coll.; MBA, U. Va. With treas.'s office GM, NYC, 1985; treas. GM Canada Ltd., 1994-97; v.p. fin. GMAC; asst. treas. GM, 1994-97; CFO Delphi Cahssis, Dayton, Ohio, 1997-98; v.p., treas. Armstrong World Industries, Inc., Lancaster, Pa., 1998-2000, sr. v.p., CFO, 2000—01, Constellation Energy, Balt., 2001—03, exec. v.p., CFO, CAO, 2003—. Bd. dir. Ryder Sys. Inc. Trustee, chair audit com. Darden Sch., Univ. Va.; mem. bd. vis. Davidson Coll.; bd. dir. Balt. Mus. Art. Office: Constellation Energy 750 E Pratt St Baltimore MD 21202*

SMITH, ELAINE DIANA, foreign service officer; b. Glencoe, Ill., Sept. 15, 1924; d. John Raymond and Elsie (Gelbard) S. BA, Grinnell Coll., 1946; MA, Johns Hopkins U., 1947; PhD, Am. U., 1959. Commd. fgn. svc. officer U.S. Dept. State, 1947; assigned to Brussels, 1947-50, Tehran, Iran, 1951-53, Wellington, New Zealand, 1954-56, Dept. State, Washington, 1956-60, Ankara, Turkey, 1960-69, Istanbul, Turkey, 1969-72, Dept. Commerce Exch., 1972-73; dep. examiner Fgn. Svc. Bd. Examiners, 1974-75; Turkish desk officer Dept. State, Washington, 1975-78. Consul gen., Izmir, Turkey, 1978—. Author: Origins of the Kemalist Movement, 1919-1923, 1959. Recipient Alumni award Grinnell Coll., 1957. Mem. U.S. Fgn. Svc. Assn., Phi Beta Kappa. Home: The Plaza 800 25th St NW Apt 306 Washington DC 20037-2207

SMITH, ELAINE JANET, social worker; b. Albert Lea, Minn., Nov. 25, 1939; d. Manville Frederick Arthur and Laura Bertha Louise (Hintz) Pestorious; m. John Vernon Smith, Nov. 27, 1968; stepchildren: E. Michelle, John M., Thomas M., James M. BA, U. Minn., 1960; MSW, U. Denver, 1965. Lic. social worker II, Colo. Social worker Rochester (Minn.) State Hosp., 1961-63, Denver pub. schs., 1965-67, Denver Gen. Hosp., 1967-78; real estate agt. Century 21, Denver, 1978-80; social worker Adams County Social Services, Commerce City, Colo., 1980-85, Children's Hosp., Denver, 1985-87, Adult Care Mgmt., Denver, 1987-88; with property mgmt. A-Action Realty, Denver, 1988-89, The Charlton Co., Aurora, Colo., 1989—. Field instr. Community Coll. Denver, 1980-84. Organist United Ch. Montbello, Denver, 1978-89; pres. Green Valley Ranch Homeowners Assn., 2002-06. Recipient Outstanding Achievement Merit Increase award Denver Gen. Hosp., 1974. Mem. NASW, Alliance for Mentally Ill (asst. sec. local chpt. 1985-86). Democrat. Avocations: bowling, sewing, reading, bicycling, travel. Home: 18996 E 43rd Ave Denver CO 80249-7145 Office: CharltonCo 1010 JOliet #105 Aurora CO 80012 Personal E-mail: johnandelainesmith@comcast.net.

SMITH, ELEANOR JANE, retired university chancellor, consultant; b. Circleville, Ohio, Jan. 10, 1933; d. John Allen and Eleanor Jane (Dade) Lewis; m. James L. Banner, Aug. 10, 1957 (div. 1972); 1 child, Teresa M. Banner Watters; m. Paul M. Smith Jr. (dec. Apr. 30, 2004). BS, Capital U., 1955; PhD, The Union Inst., Cin., 1972. Tchr. Columbus (Ohio) Pub. Schs., 1956-64, Worthington (Ohio) Pub. Schs., 1964-72; from faculty to administrator U. Cin., 1972-88; dean Smith Coll., Northampton, Mass., 1988-90; v.p. acad. affairs, provost William Paterson Coll., Wayne, NJ, 1990-94; chancellor U. Wis.-Parkside, Kenosha, 1994-97, ret., 1997; ind. cons. in higher edn. Dir. Afrikan Am. Inst., Cin., 1977-84; adv. bd. Edwina Bookwalter Gantz Undergrad. Studies Ctr., Cin.; mem. Gov.'s Tobacco Tax adv. coun.; lectr. in field. Performances include (concert) Black Heritage: History, Music and Dance, 1972—. Spl. Arts Night Com., Northampton, 1988-89; bd. dirs. Planned Parenthood No. and Ctrl. Ariz., Am. Lung Assn. Ariz./N.Mex. Named career woman of achievement YWCA, Cin., 1983. Mem. AAUW, Nat. Assn. Women in Higher Edn., Am. Assn. for Higher Edn., Leadership Am. (bd. dirs., treas. 1993-95), Nat. Assn. Black Women Historians (co-founder, co-dir. 1979-82), Am. Coun. on Edn. (mem. com. on internat. edn. 1994-97, bd. dirs. 1995-97), Am. Assn. State Colls. and Univs. (mem. com. on policies and purposes 1994-97). Avocations: music, pen and ink drawing, travel, reading. Home: 1208 Verona Way Keller TX 76248

SMITH, ELISE FIBER, international non-profit development agency administrator; b. Detroit, June 14, 1932; d. Guy and Mildred Geneva (Johnson) Fiber; m. James Frederick Smith, Aug. 11, 1956 (div. 1983); children: Gregory Douglas, Guy Charles; life ptnr. Jac Smit, 1990. BA, U. Mich., 1954; postgrad., U. Strasbourg, France, 1954-55; MA, Case Western Res. U., 1956. Tchr. U.S. Binat. Ctr., Caracas, Venezuela, 1964-66; instr. English Am. U., 1966-68; prof. lang. faculty Catholic U., Lima, Peru, 1968-70; coord. English lang. and culture program, lang. faculty El Rosario U., Bogota, Colombia, 1971-73; lang. specialist, mem. faculty Am. U., English Lang. Inst., 1975-78; exec. dir. OEF Internat. (name formerly Overseas Edn. Fund), Washington, 1978-89, bd. dirs.; dir. Global Women's Leadership Program Winrock Internat., 1989-98, sr. policy advisor on gender, 1998—. Co-founder, founding chair Women's EDGE, 1997—; v.p. Pvt. Agys. Collaborating Together, NYC, 1983-89; trustee Internat. Devel. Conf., Washington, 1983-2001, exec. com., 1985-90; hon. com. for Global Crossroads Nat. Assembly, Global Perspectives in Edn., Inc., NYC, 1984, Washington, 1984-92, gen. assembly, 1992; nat. com. Focus on Hunger '84, LA; ofcl. observer UN Conf. on Status Women, 1980, UN 3rd World Conf. on Women, 1985, del. NGO Forum, UN 4th World Conf. on Women, del. NGO Forum, 1995; mental health adv. com. Dept. State, 1974-76; U.S. del. planning seminar integration women in devel. OAS, 1978; participant Women, Law and Devel. Forum; exec. com., chair commn. advancement women interaction Am. Coun. for Vol. Internat. Action, co-founder, co-chair, 1982-84, exec. com., 1985-88; adv. bd. Global Links Devel. Edn., Washington, 1985-86; adv. coun. Global Fund for Women, 1988-93; US del. Vital Voices Conf. Women and Democracy, Iceland, 1999, Women in Democracy Conf., Lithuania, 2000, Baltic Women in Democracy Conf., Estonia, 2003. Co-editor: Toward Internationalism: Readings in Cross-cultural Communication, 1979, 2d edit. 1986; author: (book chpt.) Developing Power: How Women Transformed International Development, 2004. Bd. dirs. Internat. Ctr. Rsch. on Women, 1992-2001, Sudan-Am. Found.; adv. com. on vol. fgn. aid US AID, 1994—; women and conservation adv. com. World Wildlife Fund, 1998-2002; state dept. adv. com. US Internat. Econ. Policy, 2000—. Rotary Internat. ambassadorial scholar Strasbourg, France, 1954-55; grantee Dept. State, 1975. Mem. Assn. Women in Devel., UNIFEM, Coalition Women in Internat. Devel. (co-founder 1979, chair 1993-96),pvt. Agys. in Internat. Devel. (co-chmn. 1980-82, pres. 1982-85), Nat. Assn. Fgn. Student Affairs (grantee 1975), U. Mich. Alumni Assn., Women's Fgn. Policy Group, Rotary Internat. (mem. global com. Women in Future Soc. 1996). Unitarian Universalist. Home: 4701 Connecticut Ave NW Apt 304 Washington DC 20008-5617 Office Phone: 202-362-6234. Business E-Mail: esmith@winrock.org.

SMITH, ELIZABETH ANGELE TAFT, curator; Degree in Art History, Columbia U. Curator Mus. Contemporary Art, LA, 1983—99, James W. Alsdorf Chief Curator Chgo., 1999—. Adj. prof. pub. art studies program U. So. Calif., 1992—98; bd. advisors Independent Curators Internat., NYC; bd. overseers, Sch. Architecture, Ill. Inst. Tech., Chgo. Curator (exhibitions) Blueprints for Modern Living: History and Legacy of the Case Study Houses, Mus. Contemporary Art, LA, 1989, Urban Revisions: Current Projects for the Public Realm, 1994, Cindy Sherman: Retrospective, 1997, At the End of the Century: One Hundred Years of Architecture, 1998, The Architecture of R.M. Schindler, 2001 (Named Best Architecture or Design Exhibition of Yr.,

Internat. Assn. Art Critics/USA, 2001), Matta in America: Painting and Drawings of the 1940s, Mus. Contemporary Art, Chgo., 2001, Donald Moffett: What Barbara Jordan Wore, 2002, Lee Bontecou: A Retrospective, 2003 (Named Best Monographic Mus. Show Nationally, Internat. Assn. Art Critics/USA, 2004); author: (books) Techno Architecture, 2000, Case Study Houses: The Complete CSH Program 1945-66, 2002; co-editor: Lee Bontecou: A Retrospective of Sculpture and Drawing, 1958-2000, 2003. Named Woman of Yr., Chgo. Soc. Artists, 2004. Office: Mus Contemporary Art 220 E Chgo Ave Chicago IL 60611

SMITH, ELIZABETH MACKEY, retired financial consultant; b. Phila., Mar. 23, 1941; d. William Norman and Celeste (Parvin) Mackey; m. George Van Riper Smith, Aug. 15, 1964; children: Douglas George, Todd Mackey. BA, Gettysburg Coll., 1963; MAT in French, Ga. State U., 1978. ChFC. Tchr. fgn. lang. Haverford (Pa.) H.S., 1963-65; registered rep. Am. Express Fin. Advisors, Inc., Macon and Savannah, Ga., 1979-2000, br. mgr. Tybee Island, Ga., 2000—05, ret., 2005. Reader Atlanta Serv for the Blind, 1968; hostess Atlanta Coun Int Visitors, 1972—74; foreign exchange student coord Loisirs Culturels a l'Etranger, 1990; staff protocol vol sailing venue Olympic Games, Savannah, 1996. Mem.: Delta Gamma, Delta Phi Alpha, Phi Sigma Iota. Avocations: tennis, swimming. Home: 104 Landings Way North Savannah GA 31411-1512 Personal E-mail: islandwoman64@earthlink.net.

SMITH, ELIZABETH TURNER, mathematician, educator; d. David Chester and Jane Ellen Turner; m. Lon Albert Smith; children: James David, Jane Marie. BS in Computer Sci., La. State U., Shreveport, La., 1986; MEd in Secondary Edn., U. La., Monroe, La., 1988. Cert. secondary edn. in math., computer sci., computer literacy La. Instr. math. U. La., Monroe, 1988—. Editor: Mathematics 093, Math 110 Workbook. Recipient Outstanding Devel. Educator award, La. Assn. Devel. Educators, 2002; grantee, U. La., Monroe, 2003, La. Systemic Initiatives Program, 2003—04, 2004—05; MERLOT Scholar, La. Bd. Regents, 2004—06. Mem.: Internat. Soc. Tech. Edn., Northeastern La. Assn. Tchrs. Math. (pres. 2006—, founding mem.), La. Assn. Computer Using Educators, La. Assn. Tchrs. Math. (v.p. univs. 2006—, Outstanding Coll. Tchr. award 2006), Math. Assn. Am., Nat. Coun. Tchrs. Math. Republican. Episcopalian.

SMITH, ELSKE VAN PANHUYS, retired academic administrator, astronomer; b. Monte Carlo, Monaco, Nov. 9, 1929; came to U.S., 1943; d. Johan AE Abraham and Vera (Craven) van Panhuys; m. Henry J. Smith, Sept. 10, 1950 (dec. July 1983); children: Ralph A., Kenneth A. BA, Radcliffe Coll., 1950, MS, 1951, PhD, 1956. Rsch. assoc. Sacramento Peak Observatory, Sunspot, N.Mex., 1955-62; rsch. fellow Joint Inst. for Lab. Astrophysics, Boulder, Colo., 1962-63; assoc. to prof. U. Md., College Park, 1963-80, asst. provost, 1973-78, asst. vice chancellor, 1978-80; dean, coll. humanities and scis. Va. Commonwealth U., Richmond, 1980-92, interim dir. environ. studies, 1992-95; ret., 1995. Cons. NASA, Greenbelt, Md., 1964-76, reviewer NSF, Washington, 1970, 86; vis com. Assn. of Univ.'s for Rsch. in Astronomy, Tucson, 1975-78. Author: (with others) Solar Flares, 1963, Introductory Astronomy and Astrophysics, 1973, 3d edit., 1992; contbr. articles to profl. jours. Instr., bd. dirs. Berkshire Inst. for Lifetime Learning, 1997-2001; bd. dirs. Ctrl. Berkshire Habitat for Humanity, 1997-2004; pres. Unitarian Universalist Ch., Pittsfield, 2004—. Rsch. grantee Rsch. Corp., 1956-57, NSF, 1966-69, 90, NIH, 1981-90, NASA, 1974-78; program grantee Va. Found. for Humanities, 1985, NEH, 1987, Assn. Am. Colls., 1987, EPA, 1994. Fellow AAAS; mem. Am. Astron. Soc. (counselor 1977-80, vis. prof. 1975-78), Internat. Astron. Union (chief U.S. del. 1979, U.S. Nat. com.), Coun. Colls. of Arts and Scis. (bd. dirs. 1989), Phi Beta Kappa. Democrat. Avocations: hiking, travel, environmental issues. Home: 68 Old Stockbridge Rd Lenox MA 01240-2810

SMITH, EVA JOYCE, retired social worker; b. Coleman, Tex., Feb. 7, 1939; d. Thomas Charles and Donnie Mae (Herring) Bomar; children: George William, Melissa Jo Means. BS, Sam Houston U., Huntsville, Tex., 1961; M, Sul Ross U., Alpine, Tex., 1988. Cert. Teaching Tarleton State, 1977. Juvenile probation officer Bexan County Jud. Dept., San Antonio, 1961—62; social worker McKnight State Hosp., Carlsbad, Tex., 1965—66; elem. tchr. S.H.A.P.E. Elem. Dept. Def., Belgium, 1973—76; social studies tchr. Lampases Jr. H.S., Tex., 1976—84; secondary social studies tchr. Seoul Am. Sch., Republic of Korea, 1984—86; social studies tchr. Uvalde Jr. H.S., Tex., 1986—88; counselor k-8 Coleman Intermed. Sch. Dist., Tex., 1988—92; itinerant rural counselor Yukon Koyukok Sch. Dist., Fairbanks, Alaska, 1992—93; elem. sch. counselor Northwest Elem. Sch., Brownwood, Tex., 1993—95, Ballinger Elem., Tex., 1995—2002; ret. Editor: (plays) Little Bit of History Never Hurt Anyone, 1990. Adv. Girl Scouts of Am., San Angelo, 1963—66; spring ho.chmn. Lampasas C. of C., Tex., 1979—82; cancer dr. chmn. United Fund, Lampasas, 1978; med. records Operation Smile, Norfolk, Va., 2003—; ct. apptd. spl. adv., 2002—. Recipient History Fair award, Hist. Assn. of Tex., 1976—80, Ms. Congeniality, Tex. Sr. Am. Pageant, 2002, for Outstanding Work, State Legislator in History, 1978. Mem.: Kiwanis Club. Presbyn. Avocations: horseback riding, travel, gardening. Home: 1251 County Rd 411 Coleman TX 76834 Personal E-mail: lilranch@web-access.net.

SMITH, F. LOUISE, elementary school educator; b. Balt., Nov. 4, 1946; d. Joseph L. and Catherine L. Lilley; m. Wayne F. Smith, Aug. 7, 1976; 1 child, Ryan. BA, Mt. St. Agnes Coll., 1968; MEd, Loyola Coll. Elem. tchr. St. Clement Sch. Diocese Balt., 1966—68, elem. tchr. St. Mark Sch., 1968—71; elem. tchr. Longfellow Elem. Howard County, Columbia, Md., 1971—72, elem. tchr. Hammond Elem. Laurel, Md., 1972—2002. Tutor, Catonsville, Md. Named Tchr. of Yr., Am. Legion, 1997, Sunpapers All-Star Reading Tchr., Balt. Sun, 2001. Mem.: State Md. Reading Assn., Md. Congress Parents and Tchrs. (life), State Md. Internat. Reading Coun. Home and Office: 312 Locust Dr Catonsville MD 21228

SMITH, FAY G.N., literature and language educator; b. Peekskill, N.Y., Apr. 29, 1946; d. Raymond S. and K. Margaret Nelson; m. Charles C. Smith, July 6, 1968; children: Paul C., Robert M., Christine R. Landrigan. BA, Morningside Coll., Sioux City, Iowa, 1968. HS French tchr. Emerson-Hubbard Schs., Emerson, Nebr., 1968—69; HS English tchr. Knightstown Schs., Ind., 1986; English tchr. New Castle Chrysler HS, 1987—89, IKM HS, Manilla, Iowa, 1989—. Mem.: Nat. Coun. Tchrs. of English. Independent. Avocations: quilting, reading, piano. Office: IKM Schs 755 Main St Manilla IA 51454

SMITH, FERN M., judge; b. San Francisco; children: Susan, Julie. AA, Foothill Coll., 1970; BA, Stanford U., 1972, JD, 1975. Bar: Calif. 1975. Assoc. Bronson, Bronson & McKlinnon, San Francisco, 1975-81, ptnr., 1981—86; judge San Francisco County Superior Ct., 1986-88, U.S. Dist. Ct. (no. dist.) Calif., 1988—. Dir. Fed. Jud. Ctr., Wash., 1999-2003; mem. adv. com. on Jud. Conf. U.S., Rules of Evidence, 1993-96, chair, 1996-99; mem. exec. com. Ninth Cir. Jud. Conf., 1994-96, Ninth Cir. State-Fed. Jud. Coun., 1990-93, Calif. Jud. Coun. 1987-88, mem. adv. Task Force on Gender Bias, 1988-90, hiring, mgmt. and pers. coms., active recruiting various law schs.; faculty Inst. Study and Devel. Legal Sys., 1992, Egypt & Bolivia, 1994, Mexico and Tunisia, 1995, Israel, Jordan, Greece and Egypt, 1996, India, 1998, Jordan and Italy, 1998, Italy, Israel and France, 2000, India, Israel and Russia, 2001, Morocco, Thailand and China, 2002, Turkey, Bahrain, the Netherlands and Russia, 2003, Jordan and Brazil, 2004, ISDLS Rule of Law Conf., Berkeley, Calif.; bd. vis. Law Sch. Stanford U., 1990-92, 99—; chair U.S. Jud. Conf. Com. on Internat. Jud. Rels., 2003—. Contbr. articles to legal publ. Mem. ABA, Queen's Br. Nat. Assn. Women Judges, Calif. Women Lawyers Assn., Bar Assn. San Francisco, Fed. Judges Assn., 9th Cir. Dist. Judges Assn., Am. Judicature Soc., Calif. State Fed. Jud. Coun., Phi Beta Kappa.

SMITH, FREDRICA EMRICH, rheumatologist, internist; b. Princeton, NJ, Apr. 28, 1945; d. Raymond Jay and Carolyn Sarah (Schleicher) Emrich; m. Paul David Smith, June 10, 1967. AB, Bryn Mawr Coll., 1967; MD, Duke U., 1971. Intern, resident U. N.Mex. Affiliated Hosps., 1971-73; fellow U. Va. Hosp., Charlottesville, 1974-75; pvt. practice, Los Alamos, N.Mex., 1975—. Chmn. credentials com. Los Alamos Med. Ctr., 1983—, chief staff, 1990, 2003; bd. dirs. N.Mex. Physicians Mut. Liability Ins. Co., Albuquerque, 1988-97; regional adv. bd. Am. Physicians Assurance, 1997-. Contbr. articles to med. jours. Mem. bass sect. Los Alamos Symphony, 1975—; mem. Los Alamos County Parks and Recreation Bd., 1984-88, 92-96, Los Alamos County Med. Indigent Health Care Task Force, 1989—2003; mem. ops. subcom. Aquatic Ctr., Los Alamos County, 1988—. Fellow ACP, Am. Coll. Rheumatology; mem. N.Mex. Soc. Internal Medicine (pres. 1993-96), Friends of Bandelier. Democrat. Avocations: swimming, music, reading, hiking. Office: Los Alamos Med Ctr 3917 West Rd Los Alamos NM 87544-2275 Office Phone: 505-662-9400.

SMITH, FREDRIKA PATCHETT, retired pediatrician; b. Berkeley, Calif., June 30, 1915; d. Philip Edward and Irene Amy (Patchett) Smith. BS, Wilson Coll., Chambersburg, Pa., 1938; MA, Smith Coll., Northampton, Mass., 1940; MD, Columbia Coll. Physicians and Surgeons, N.Y.C., 1949. Dir. corrective phys. edn. Radcliffe Coll., Cambridge, Mass., 1940—42, Duke U. Women's Coll., Durham, NC, 1942—43; med. intern Strong Meml. Hosp., Rochester, NY, 1949—50, pediat. intern, 1950—51; asst. resident pediatrician Stanford Ln. Hosp., San Francisco, 1951—52; chief resident pediatrician Strong Meml. Hosp., Rochester, 1952—53; pvt. practice Northampton, Mass., 1953—74; dir. children's svcs. Sonoma County Pub. Health Dept., Santa Rosa, Calif., 1975—80, pediatrician, 1980—83; ret., 1983. Mem.: Am. Acad. Pediatricians (emeritus mem.). Avocations: photography, travel, hiking, sewing, tennis. Home: # J107 5555 Montgomery Dr Santa Rosa CA 95409

SMITH, GAIL HUNTER, artist; b. Nashville, Mar. 18, 1948; d. Walter Gray Smith and Eleanor Theresa (Cregar) Egan. Student, Memphis State U., 1966-67; BFA in Advt. Design, Memphis Acad. Arts, 1971. Prodn. asst. Visual Studios, Phila., 1970; asst. art dir. Eric Ericson and Assocs. and Ken White Design, Inc., Nashville, 1971-72; art dir. Contemporary Mktg., Inc., Ivan Stiles Advt., Bala Cynwyd (Pa.), Phila., 1972-74; specialist publs. design Temple U., Phila., 1974-75. Graphic designer pvt. practice, 1969-85; judge Haddonfield (N.J.) Artists' Exhbn., 1976; tchr. in field. Editor: Artists' USA, 7th edit., Yacht Portraits, 1987, The Art of the Sea, 1990; one woman show Dow Jones Co., Inc., Princeton, N.J., 1987, Johnson & Johnson, Inc., New Brunswick, N.Y.,1990; exhibited in group shows at 12 and 17th Tenn. All-State Artist Exhbn., Nashville, 1972, 77, Arnold Art Gallery, Newport, 1986, 87, 88, 89, 90, 91, Wildfowl Festival, Easton, Md., 1987, Mystic Maritime Gallery, 1984-86, 88-90, Capricorn Gallery, 1986-92, Quester Gallery, 1992, 93, 94; represented by Mystic (Conn.) Maritime Gallery, 1984-90, Capricorn Gallery, Bethesda, Md., 1986-92, Cumberland Gallery, Nashville, 1982-83, The Studio L'Atelier, Nashville, 1983-85, Ambiance Fine Arts, Nashville, 1985, Arnold Art Gallery, Newport, R.I., 1986-92, Quester Gallery, 1992-94. Recipient awards Nashville Ad Fedn., 1973. Mem. NAFE, Am. Inst. Graphic Arts, Am. Soc. Marine Artists, Met. Mus. N.Y.C., Artists Equity Assn., Soc. Illustrators, Soc. Scribes, Mus. Women in Arts. Avocations: bicycling, boating, fishing, hiking, swimming.

SMITH, GLORIA S., local commissioner, educator; b. Midland, SD, July 25, 1924; d. John and Hattie Leora Saucerman; m. Albert Francis Smith, July 21, 1945; children: Gregory, Bradley, Karen. Grad., Dakota Wesleyan U., 1942, U. Minn., 1945. Cert. elem. edn. Elem. tchr. Sansarc (S.D.) Sch. Dist., 1943-44; ins. underwriter Firemans Fund Ins. Co., San Francisco, 1945-46; supr. disability ins. General Electric Co., Schenectady, NY, 1947-49; v.p., then pres. bd. edn. Upper St. Clair (Pa.) Sch. Dist., 1964-77; from bd. dir. to v.p. elect South Hills Area Coun. of Govs., Pitts., 1994—2003, pres. elect, 2003; commr., v.p. Upper St. Clair (Pa.) Twp., 1994—. Mem. Upper St. Clair Bd. Commrs., Pa., 1994—; bd. dir. special edn. Allegheny County Intermediate Unit, Pitts., 1974-77; bd. dir. Outreach Teen and Family Svcs., Mt. Lebanon, Pa., 1979—, treas. 1990—. Americans Abroad selection com. Am. Field Svc. Upper St. Clair, Pa., 1970-77; ch. sch. tchr. United Methodist Ch., Bethel Park, Pa., 1960—; mem. Advisory Com. to Establish Home Rule Charter dists., Allegheny Cty., Pa., 1998. Recipient Outstanding Citizen award Upper St. Clair Repub. Com., Pa., 1967. Republican. Methodist. Avocations: travel, home decorating, community block parties. Home: 529 Long Dr Upper Saint Clair PA 15241 Office: Twp Bd of Commissioners 1820 Mclaughlin Run Rd Upper Saint Clair PA 15241 Office Phone: 412-833-1284.

SMITH, GLORIA YOUNG, retired graphics designer; b. N.Y.C., Jan. 15, 1926; d. Frederick William and Anastasia Margaret (Regan) Young; m. Henry George Smith, Oct. 1, 1949; children: Stephanie, Kevin, Brian, Robert, Sean. Student, Art Students League, N.Y.C., 1944, 45, Nat. Acad. Design, 1946, 47, 48, Nassau C.C., Uniondale, N.Y., 1971, 72. Artist Lynn Mfg. Co., Astoria, N.Y., 1947-50; forms designer, graphic artist Mercy Hosp., Rockville Centre, N.Y., 1972-81; art tchr. Art Inst. & Gallery, Salisbury, Md., 1992-98, Art League of Ocean City, Md., 1995—. Mem. com. Nat. Juried Art Show, Salisbury, 1996-2000. Artist numerous paintings. Pres. Artists Co-op, Salisbury, 1998—; bd. dirs. Art League of Ocean City, Md., 1997--; sec., bd. dirs. Art Inst. & Gallery, Salisbury, 1991-95; hdqrs. mgr. congl. campaign Rep. Orgn., Baldwin, N.Y., 1968; treas. Conservative Women, L.I., 1971; judge Nat. Seashore Poster Art Contest, Assateague Island, Md., 1992. Recipient Best in Category award Ann. Arts and Crafts Show, Indian Harbour Beach, Fla., 1987, 2d pl. award Arts Atlantica-Worcester County Heritage, 1996, 1st pl. award Art League Ocean City, 1992, Mem.'s award Fells Point Art Gallery, 1993. Mem. Nat. League Am. Pen Women, Portrait Soc. Am., Inc., Art Students League N.Y. (life), Miniature Art Soc. Fla. Republican. Roman Catholic. Avocations: reading, music, foreign travel, walking. Home: 260 Ocean Pkwy Berlin MD 21811-1525

SMITH, HEATHER ANN, elementary school educator; b. Lima, Ohio, Aug. 5, 1973; d. Harvey Davidson and Linda Jane Burkholder; m. Robert Andrew Smith, June 20, 1998; children: Zoe, Samantha. BS, Bowling Green State U., Ohio, 1996; M, U. Dayton, Ohio, 2002. Cert. ednl. leadership. sch. adminstrn. Ohio. Tchr. Perry Local Schs., Lima, 1997—98, 1999—, Spencerville Local Schs., 1998—99. Mem.: NW Ohio Edn. Assn. (awards com., Promising Leader 2005), Ohio Edn. Assn., Perry Edn. Assn. (bldg. rep., social chair). Home: 222 S Dale Lima OH 45805 Office: Perry Elem Sch 2770 E Broese Rd Lima OH 45806

SMITH, HEATHER CLARK, academic administrator; b. Quincy, Mass., Oct. 5, 1951; d. Keith Fales and Mildred Louise (Dodge) Clark; m. Mark Henry Smith, Aug. 21, 1971 AA, Chipola Jr. Coll., 1971; BS Comm. Disorders, Worcester State Coll., 1976; MBA, Anna Maria Coll., 1987; EdD, Johnson and Wales U., 1999. Asst. dean student svcs. Ctrl. New Eng. Coll., Worcester, Mass., 1980—89; registrar Middlesex C.C., Bedford, Mass., 1989—90; asst. dean admissions and records C.C. R.I., Lincoln, 1990—96, assoc. dean enrollment svcs. admissions/fin. aid, 1999—2005; assoc. v.p. acad. affairs for enrollment svcs. Bridgewater State Coll., Mass., 2005—. V.p. prof. devel. and publicity Am. Assn. Collegiate Registrars Admissions Officers, 1997-2000, pres., 2002-03, 2004— Mem. Am. Assn. Collegiate Registrars and Admissions Officers (chair placement com. 1994, phys. arrangements com. ann. mtg. 1994, nominations and elections com. 1995-96), New Eng. Assn. Collegiate Registrars and Admissions Officers (chair orgn. com. 1991—, pres.-elect 1992, pres. 1993, past pres. 1994), Bus. and Profl. Women (state, fin. chair 1995—, local past pres. 1990, nominations and elections com. 1995—), Profl. Devel. Rsch. & Publications (v.p. 1997—) Home: 229 W Main St Westborough MA 01581-3558 Office: Bridgewater State Coll Boyden Hall 104 Boston MA 02297 Office Phone: 508-531-2553. Business E-Mail: hzsmith@bridgew.edu.

SMITH, HEATHER LEE, psychologist; d. Wayne Allan and Sherron Ann Smith. BA in Psychology, U. N.C., Wilmington, 1997; MA with distinction in Psychology, Hofstra U., Hempstead, N.Y., 1998; PhD in Clin. and Sch. Psychology, Hofstra U., 2003. Lic. clin. psychologist N.Y., 2005. Postdoctoral fellow in clin. child psychology Schneider Children's Hosp. Divsn. of Child and Adolescent Psychiatry, New Hyde Park, NY, 2003—04; applied behavior sci. specialist Epilepsy Found. of LI, Garden City, NY, 1998—2005; clin. child psychologist North Shore LI Jewish Health Sys.: Zucker Hillside Hosp. Child and Adolescent Day Program, Glen Oaks, NY, 2005—. Adj. prof. of psychology Hofstra U., Hempstead, 1999—2001; lectr. in field. Recipient Chancellor's Achievement award, U. N.C., Wilmington, 1996—97; scholar Batchelder scholar, Alpha Xi Delta Nat. Alumna Assn., 2001. Mem.: APA, Assn. for the Advancement of Behavior Therapy, Psi Chi, Alpha Xi Delta (v.p., alumna rels., philanthropy 1994—96). Methodist. Avocations: running, aerobics, art. Home: 210-19 41st Ave Bayside NY 11361 Office: NorthShore LIJ: Zucker Hillside Hospital Child&Adol Day Program 75-59 263rd St Glen Oaks NY 11004 Office Phone: 718-470-8052. Personal E-mail: hleesmith1@aol.com.

SMITH, HELEN ELIZABETH, retired career officer; b. San Rafael, Calif., Aug. 11, 1946; d. Jack Dillard and Marian Elizabeth (Miller) S. BA in Geography, Calif. State U., Northridge, 1968; MA in Internat. Rels., Salve Regina, Newport, R.I., 1983; MS in Tech. Comm., Rensselaer Poly. Inst., 1988; postgrad., Naval War Coll., 1982-83. Commd. ensign USN, 1968, advanced through grades to capt., 1989; adminstrv. asst. USN Fighter Squadron 101, Key West, Fla., 1969-70; adminstrv. officer Fleet Operational Tng. Group, Mountain View, Calif., 1970-72; leader human resource team Human Resource Ctr., Rota, Spain, 1977-79; adminstrv. officer Pearl Harbor (Hawaii) Naval Sta., 1979-80; dir. Family Svc. Ctr., Pearl Harbor, 1980-82; officer-in-charge R&D lab. Naval Ocean Systems Ctr., Kaneohe, Hawaii, 1983-85; exec. officer Naval ROTC, assoc. prof. Rensselaer Poly. Inst., Troy, N.Y., 1985-88; comdg. officer Navy Alcohol Rehab. Ctr., Norfolk, Va., 1988-90; faculty mem., commanding officer Naval Adminstrv. Command, dean adminstrv. support, comptr. Armed Forces Staff Coll., Norfolk, Va., 1990-93; ret., 1993; exec. dir. Calif. for Drug-Free Youth, 1995-96. Author: (walking tour) Albany's Historic Pastures, 1987; composer (cantata) Night of Wonder, 1983. Chair Hawaii State Childcare Com., Honolulu, 1981-82; coun. mem. Hist. Pastures Neighborhood Assn., Albany, N.Y., 1985-88; mem. working group Mayors Task Force on Drugs, Norfolk, 1989-90; chair, bd. dirs. Va. Coun. on Alcoholism, 1989-92, Calif. for Drug Free Youth, 1995-96; singer North County Baroque Ensemble; assoc. Westar Inst. Avocation: writing. Home: 952 Frederico Blvd Belen NM 87002-7027 E-mail: capthelen@webeworld.com.

SMITH, IRENE HELEN-NORDINE, music educator; d. John J. and Dorothy J. Horzepa; m. Thomas Carlyle Smith, Dec. 19, 1982; children: Julie Ann Nordine, Ryan Carlyle. AA in Music Edn. K-12, Broward C.C., Fort Lauderdale, Fla., 1973; BA in Music Edn. K-12, Fla. Atlantic U., 1975; BA in Elem. Edn., Kennesaw State U., 1991. Cert. tchr. Ga. Profl. Stds. Commn., 2003. Elem. music tchr. Tedder Elem. Broward County Sch. Sys., Pompano, Fla., 1976—77, elem. music tchr. Harbordale Elem. Fort Lauderdale, 1979—83, elem. music tchr. Meadowbrook Elem., 1979—83, elem. music tchr. Banyan Elem., 1979—83; pvt. piano and voice tchr. Roswell, Ga., 1983—; tchr. Mabry Mid. Sch. Cobb County Bd. Edn., Marietta, Ga., 1993—. Organist, choir dir. Coral Springs (Fla.) United Meth. Ch., 1976—83; organist / choir dir. Birmingham United Meth. Ch., Alpharetta, Ga., 1994—99; accompanist Ga. Music Educators Assn. Dist. 12 Mid. Sch. Honor Chorus, Marietta, 1999—. Composer: (Rocky Mount Elem. spirit song) Rocky Mountain Warriors, (Shallowford Falls Elem. spirit song) The Foxy Foxes, (Tritt Elem. Sch. spirit song) I Am A Tritt Tiger, (music high school alma mater) Alan Pope High School Alma Mater. Dir., accompanist Roswell United Meth. Ch., 1983—90. Scholar, Broward C.C., 1971—73, Fla. Atlantic U., 1973—75. Mem.: Music Educators Nat. Conf., Ga. Music Educators Assn., Phi Theta Kappa. Republican. Methodist. Avocations: travel, piano, art, reading, football. Office: Mabry Middle School 2700 Jims Rd Marietta GA 30066 Personal E-mail: irenesmith@bellsouth.net.

SMITH, JACLYN, actress; b. Houston, Oct. 26, 1947; d. Jack and Margaret Ellen S.; m. Dennis Cole (div. 1981); m. Tony Richmond, Aug. 4, 1981; 1 dau., Spencer Margaret. Student, Trinity U., San Antonio. Worked as model. Motion picture appearances include The Adventurers, 1970, Bootleggers, Deja Vu; TV film appearances include Bogen County, 1977, The Users, 1978, Rage of Angels, 1980, Nightkill, 1980, Jacqueline Bouvier Kennedy, 1981, Sentimental Journey, 1984, George Washington (miniseries), 1984, Florence Nightingale, 1985, The Night They Saved Christmas, 1986, Wind Mills of the Gods (miniseries), 1988, The Bourne Identity, 1988, Settle the Score, 1989, Danielle Steele's Kaleidoscope, 1990, Lies Before Kisses, 1991, The Rape of Dr. Willis, 1991, In The Arms Of A Killer, 1992, Love Can Be Murder, 1992, Family Album, 1994, Cries Unheard: The Donna Yaklich Story, 1994, My Very Best Friend, 1996, Married to a Stranger, 1997, Before He Wakes, 1998, Three Secrets, 1999, Freefall, 1999; one of prin. roles TV series Charlie's Angels, 1976-80, (ABC Saturday Night Movie) Christine Cromwell, 1989-90; other TV appearances include Get Christy Love, McCloud, The Rookies, Love Boat, Switch, Navigating the Heart, 2000, The District, 2000; appeared in numerous TV commls. Mem. AFTRA. Office: ICM 8942 Wilshire Blvd Beverly Hills CA 90211-1934

SMITH, JAMESETTA DELORISE, author; b. Chgo., Jan. 26, 1942; d. James Gilbert and Ora Mae (Roberts) Howell; m. Leroy Smith, June 2, 1962; children: Leroy, Darryll Keith. Student, Oxford Bus. Coll., Chgo., 1961-62. Office clerk Justice of the Peace, Gary, Ind., 1966-69; bookkeeper, office mgr. Jones Electric, Gary, Ind., 1971-85. Author: How Strong is Strong, 1988; contbr. articles to profl. jours., newspapers. Treas., bd. dirs. N.W. Ind. Lupus Found., Gary, 1988-92; co-founder, pres. Ark. chpt. Lupus Found., 1993—, mem., race organizer, 1995; facilitator Gary Meth. Hosp. for Lupus Found., 1991-92; pastor's aide Bible study leader Greater St. Paul Bapt. Ch., 1995, sec. ch. food com., 1994-2000, ch. trustee, 1994, hostess and announcing clk., 1997—, spl. recognition trustee, 1998, Sunday sch. tchr., 1998; Bible enrichment instr., 1996—; pastor's aide sec. Clark Rd. M.B. Ch., 1990-92; mem. nomination com. Nat. Lupus Found. Am. Named Vol. of Yr., Ark. chpt. Lupus Found., 1995, Woman of Yr., Hot Springs C. of C., 2005; recipient Legacy award pin AARP, 1998, Growth award, Lupus Found. Am., 1995-96, 98-99, 2002-2003, Nat. Fleur-De-Lis award for outstanding svc., 2001, award for fin. support Ark. chpt., 2001, award for Dedicated work with Ark. chpt. Lupus Found. Am. Dreams of Heartland; nominated while pres. as Outstanding Organizer of Yr., Lupus Found. Am., 2002; nominated Woman of Yr., C. of C., 2005; recipient African Am. Trail Blazers award 2002. Mem. Jones Electric Gary Ind. (Sec. 1986). Democratic. Baptist. Avocations: writing, cooking, numbers, crafts. Office Phone: 501-525-9380. E-mail: lupusarkhs@direclynx.net.

SMITH, JANET HUGIE, lawyer; b. Logan, Utah, Aug. 1, 1945; BA magna cum laude, Utah State U., 1967; MA cum laude, Stanford U., 1969; JD, U. Utah, 1976. Bar: Utah 1976, US Supreme Ct. 1992, U.S. Ct. Appeals (10th cir.) 1977, (9th cir.) 2003, US Dist. Ct. Colo. 2004. Shareholder, exec. com. Ray, Quinney & Nebeker, Salt Lake City, 1983—. Mem. ABA (labor and employment law sect.), Utah State Bar (labor and employment law sect.), CUE (labor lawyers adv. coun.), Am. Law Coun., Am. Coll. Trial Lawyers, Aldon J. Anderson Am. Inns of Ct. Office: Ray Quinney & Nebeker 36 S State St Ste 1400 Salt Lake City UT 84111-1431 Business E-Mail: jhsmith@rqn.com.

SMITH, JANET MARIE, sports executive; b. Jackson, Miss., Dec. 13, 1957; d. Thomas Henry and Nellie Brown (Smith) S. BArch, Miss. State U., 1981; MA in Urban Planning, CCNY, 1984. Draftsman Thomas H. Smith and Assocs. Architects, Jackson, 1979; mktg. coord. The Eggers Group, P.C. Architects and Planners, N.Y.C., 1980; program assoc. Ptnrs. for Livable Places, Washington, 1980-82; coord. asst. Lance Jay Brown, Architect and Urban Planner, N.Y.C., 1983-84; coord. architecture and design Battery Park City Authority, N.Y.C., 1982-84; pres., chief exec. officer Pershing Sq. Mgmt. Assn., L.A., 1985-89; v.p. stadium planning and devel. Balt. Orioles Oriole Park at Camden Yard, 1989-94; v.p. sports facilities Turner Properties, Atlanta, 1994-97; v.p. planning and devel. Atlanta Braves, Braves, 1994—; pres. TBS Sports Devel., Inc., 1997-2000; with Struever Brothers, Eccles & Rouse, Inc., Balt., 2000—; sr. v.p. planning Boston Red Sox, 2002—. Bd. dirs. Assn. Collegiate Schs. Architecture, Washington, 1979-82, Assn. Student Chpts. AIA, Washington, 1979-82. Guest editor: Urban Design Internat., 1985; assoc. editor: Crit, 1979-82; contbr. articles to profl. jours. Named

Disting. Grad., Nat. Assn. State Univs. and Land Grant Colls., 1988, One of Outstanding Young Women of Am., 1982; recipient Spirit of Miss. award, Sta. WLBT, Jackson, 1987, Disting. Grad. award Nat. Assn. State Univs., 1988, Outstanding Alumni award Miss. State U., 1994, Andrew White medal Loyola Coll., 1997, Ptnrs. Livable Cmtys. award, 1998, City Coll. N.Y. award, 1998. Mem. AIA (assoc.), Urban Land Inst. Democrat. Episcopalian. Office Phone: 443-573-4342. E-mail: jm.smith@sber.com.

SMITH, JANET NEWMAN, retired physical education educator; b. Florence, Ala., Aug. 27, 1946; d. Glyndon Oliver and Azile Lee Newman; m. Glenn Wylie Smith, Dec. 28, 1995; 1 child, Brian Michael. BSc in Edn., Athens Coll., 1968; M, U. Ala., 1971, Edn. Specialist degree, 1980. Physical edn. tchr. Clements H.S., Ala., 1968, Gardendale H.S., Ala., 1968—70; tchr. Spl. Sch. for the Deaf, Ala., 1974—80; adapted physical edn. tchr. Helen Keller Sch. of Ala., 1980—94, dir., motor develop. dept., 1993—94; ret. Coach Spl. Olympics, 1974—97; pres. Optimist Internat., Talladega, Ala., 2001—03, lt. gov. zone 1, 2004—05, lt. gov. zone 4, 2005—06. Recipient Mid. Sch. Educator of Yr., Ala. State Assn., 1990, Alumni Loyalty award, Athens State U., 2003, Coach of Yr., Spl. Olympics, 1991, Alumni Achievement award, Athens State Coll., 1992, Alumni Spirit award, Athens State U., 2002. Mem.: Zeta Tau Alpha. Home: 200 Allen Rd Pell City AL 35128

SMITH, JANET SUSANNAH, literature and language educator, department chairman; b. Waynesville, N.C., Aug. 1, 1956; d. Jerry Liner, Jr. and Patricia Ruth Cooper; m. Fletcher Wade Smith, Apr. 23, 1996; children from previous marriage: Jessica Music Tripp, Allysen Alexis, Aimee Ruth Tripp. BS summa cum laude, Fla. State U., Tallahassee, 1992; EdM, State U. Ga., Carrollton, 1994; EdS, Lincoln Meml. U., Knoxville, Tenn., 1999. Cert. gifted edn. Internat. Baccalaureate Tng., 2001, tchr. English grades 7-12, adminstrn. and supervision, nat. bd. cert. adolescent young adult in English and lang. arts 2003, cert. Advanced Placement Tng., 2001. Instr. English S.E. Whitfield HS, Dalton, Ga., 1992—, dept. chair lang. arts, 2006. Mem. content adv. com. Profl. Stds. Commn., Atlanta; chair Ann. Yearly Progress Com.; region literary sponsor, 2004—; polit. speechwriter. Nominee Tchr. of Yr., Southeast Whitfield H.S., 1992—2006; recipient Golden Apple award, 1995, 1998; scholar, So. Scholarship Found. Mem.: NEA, Nat. Coun. Tchrs. English, Ga. Assn. Educators, Golden Key, Phi Kappa Phi, Phi Theta Kappa. Office: Southeast Whitfield HS 1954 Riverbend Rd Dalton GA 30721-5547

SMITH, JANICE ALFREDA, secondary school educator; b. San Pedro, Calif., Jan. 4, 1938; d. Willis Alfred and Elsie Ann (Moser) S. AA, Compton (Calif) Jr. Coll., 1957; BA, Calif. State U., Long Beach, 1960. Tchr. Mayfair H.S., Lakewood, Calif., 1960-85, Redmond (Oreg.) H.S., Sch. Dist. 2J, 1985-98, O'Callaghan Middle Sch., Las Vegas, 2000—. Drill team instr. Mayfair H.S. Athletic Dept., Lakewood, Calif., 1962-71, coach volleyball, basketball, softball, 1974-85. Coach 10 league championship teams, Mayfair H.S., Lakewood, Calif., 1974-82, 1 Calif. Interscholastic Fedn. So. Divsn. League Champion, 1979; recipient Youth Sports award Lakewood (Calif.) Youth Hall of Fame, 1983; named Tchr. of Yr., Wal-Mart Found., 1999. Mem. NEA, Redmond Edn. Assn. (bargaining chmn. 1996-97, co-pres. 1997-98). Avocations: travel, golf, dogs. Home: 5848 Sassa St Las Vegas NV 89130-7235

SMITH, JEAN, interior design firm executive; b. Oklahoma City; d. A. H. and Goldy K. (Engle) Hearn; m. W. D. Smith; children: Kaye Smith Hunt, Sidney P. Student Chgo. Sch. Interior Design, 1970. v.p. Billco-Aladdin Wholesale, Albuquerque, 1950-92, v.p. Billco Carpet One of Am, 1970. Pres. Opera Southwest, 1979-83, advisor to bd. dirs.; active Civic Chorus, 1st Meth. Ch.; pres. Inez PTA, 1954-55, life mem.; hon. life mem. Albuquerque Little Theater, bd. dirs. Republican. Clubs: Albuquerque County, Four Hills Country, Daus. of the Nile (soloist Yucca Temple). Home: 1417 Wagon Train Dr SE Albuquerque NM 87123-4295 Office: 1417 Wagon Train Dr SE Albuquerque NM 87123-4295

SMITH, JEAN KENNEDY, former ambassador; b. Brookline, Mass., Feb. 20, 1928; d. Joseph P. and Rose Kennedy; m. Stephen E. Smith (dec. 1990); 4 children. BA, Manhattanville Coll.; Degree (hon.), NYU, Fordham U., Nat. U. Ireland, Dublin City U. Founder, dir., chair Very Spl. Arts, 1974—; amb. to Ireland Dublin, 1993-98. Author: (with George Plimpton) Chronicles of Courage, 1993; contbr. articles on the disabled to profl. jours. Trustee John F. Kennedy Ctr. Performing Arts, 1964— Recipient Sec.'s award Dept. Vets. Affairs, Vol. of Yr. award People-to-People Com. Handicapped, Margaret Mead Humanitarian award Coun. Cerebral Palsy Auxs., Jefferson award Am. Inst. Pub. Svc., Spirit of Achievement award Yeshiva U., Humanitarian award Capital Children's Mus., Irish Am. of Yr. award Irish Am. Mag., 1995, Rotary One Internat. award Rotary Club Chgo., 1997, Terence Cardinal Cooke Humanitarian award, 1997.

SMITH, JEAN WEBB (MRS. WILLIAM FRENCH SMITH), civic worker; b. LA; d. James Ellwood and Violet (Hughes) Webb; m. George William Vaughan, Mar. 14, 1942 (dec. Sept. 1963); children: George William Vaughan, Merry Vaughan; m. William French Smith, Nov. 6, 1964. BA summa cum laude, Stanford U., Calif., 1940. Mem. Nat. Vol. Svc. Adv. Coun., 1973—76, vice chmn., 1974—76; dir. Beneficial Std. Corp., 1976—85; bd. dirs. Cmty. TV So. Calif., 1979—93. Bd. dirs. United Way, Inc., 1973—80, Nat. Symphony Orch., 1980—85; nat. bd. dirs. Boys' Club Am., 1977—80; mem. Pres.'s Commn. White House Fellowships, 1980—90, Nat. Coun. Humanities, 1987—90, Calif. Arts Commn., 1971—74, vice chmn., 1973—74; bd. dirs. The Founders, Music Ctr., LA, 1971—74; bd. dirs. costume coun. Los Angeles County Mus. Art, 1971—73; bd. dirs. LA chpt. NCCJ, 1977—80, LA World Affairs Coun., 1990, LA chpt. ARC, 1994—95; mem. adv. bd. Salvation Army, 1979—; bd. overseers Hoover Instn. War, Revolution and Peace, 1989—94; bd. govs. Calif. Cmty. Found., 1990—; bd. dirs. Hosp. Good Samaritan, 1973—80, mem. exec. com., 1975—80; bd. fellows Claremont U. Ctr. and Grad. Sch., 1987—; bd. regents Children's Hops. LA, 1993—. Named Woman of the Yr. for Cmty. Svc., LA Times, 1958; recipient Citizens of the Yr. award, Boys Clubs Greater LA, 1982, Life Achievement award, LA Coun. Boy Scouts Am., 1985. Mem.: Kappa Kappa Gamma, Assn. Jr. Leagues Am. (dir. region XII 1956—58, pres. 1958—60), Jr. League LA (pres. 1954—55, Spirit of Volunteerism award 1996), Phi Beta Kappa. Home: 11718 Wetherby Ln Los Angeles CA 90077-1348

SMITH, JENNIE, artist; b. San Francisco, 1981; Student, Burren Coll Art, Ireland, 2002; BFA in Drawing, Mpls. Coll. Art & Design, 2004. Prin. works include Migration, 2003, Animal Its Habitat, 2004, Animals Slumber, 2004, Kite Wars, 2004, We'll Never Tell You Where We Have Gone, 2004, exhibited in group shows at Made at MCAD, Mpls., 2005, Sr. Exhbn., Mpls. Coll. Art & Design, 2005, Drawing Show, Soo Vac Gallery, Mpls., 2005, Grp. Drawing Show, The Gen. Store, Milw., 2005, Four Color Drawing Show, Van Harrison Gallery, Chgo., 2005, Whitney Biennial: Day for Night, Whitney Mus. Am. Art, 2006, exhibitions include Bull. Bd. Project 008, Calif. Coll. Arts Wattis Inst. Contemporary Arts, San Francisco, 2006, Rena Bransten Gallery, San Francisco, 2006. Mailing: c/o Rena Bransten Gallery 77 Geary St San Francisco CA 94108*

SMITH, JENNIFER C., insurance company executive; b. Boston, Nov. 3, 1952; d. Herman J. and Margaree L. Smith. BA in English, Union Coll., 1974; MA, Fairfield U., 1982. Claim rep. Travelers Ins. Co., Boston, 1974—75, supr., 1976—78, from regional asst., acct. exec. to sec. casualty and property depts. Hartford, Conn., 1979—85; from pers. dir. to asst. city mgr. City of Hartford, Hartford, 1984—87; dir. mktg. Travelers Cos., 1987; from asst. v.p. corp. human resources to v.p. corp. mktg. Aetna Life and Casualty Co., 1987—91; v.p., chief of staff Aetna Health Group, 1992—93; v.p., COO Aetna Profl. Mgmt. Co., 1993—94; v.p. Occupl. Managed Care Aetna, 1994—. Claim rep. Sentry Ins. Co., NJ, 1975—76; bd. dirs., exec. com., nominating com Hartford Stage Co. Contbr. articles to local newspapers. Trustee St. Joseph's Coll., Martin Luther King Jr. Scholarship Fund, U. Conn.; bd. dirs. Boys Club Hartford.

SMITH, JESSIE P. DOWLING, retired social services administrator; b. Sturgills, NC, June 15, 1918; d. Rohe V. and Stella Pennington (Eller) Smith; m. F. P. Smith, July 22, 1983. AB, Berea Coll., 1939; MSW, Columbia U., 1945. Social work assignments WPA, Ky., 1939—43; social worker ARC, New Orleans, 1943—45, Bklyn., 1943—45, Huntington, W.Va., 1946—56, Washington, 1946—56; instr. Sch. Social Work W.Va. U., Morgantown, 1953—54; cons. W.Va. Dept. Mental Health, Charleston, 1954—55; program supr. USPHS Clin. Ctr., Bethesda, Md., 1956—62; cons., social work NIMH, Chgo., 1962—66, NYC, 1962—66; assoc. regional health dir. Mental Health Programs, NYC, 1966—81; ret., 1981; v.p. adv. bd. Mental Retardation Substance Abuse Programs Davidson County Mental Health, NC, 1987—89, pres., 1988—89. Mem.: NASW (exec. bd. 1968—70, pres. Washington Met. Area chpt., pioneer steering com. 1999—), Columbia U. Alumni Fedn. Bd., Columbia U. Sch. Social Work Alumni Assn. (pres. 1979—81), Columbia U. Sch. Social Work (adv. coun.), Social Casework (editl. adv. bd. 1968—70), NC Coun. of Cmty. Mental Health Programs (adv. bd. 1987—92). Home: Apt 703 1330 Massachusetts Ave NW Washington DC 20005-4154

SMITH, JO ANNE, writer, retired communications educator; b. Mpls., Mar. 18, 1930; d. Robert Bradburn and Virginia Mae S. BA, U. Minn., 1951, MA, 1957. Wire and sports editor Rhinelander (Wis.) Daily News, 1951-52; staff corr., night mgr. UPI, Mpls., 1952-56; interim instr. U. N.C., Chapel Hill, 1957-58; instr. U. Fla., Gainesville, 1959-65, asst. prof. journalism, communications, 1965-68, assoc. prof., 1968-76, prof., 1976-88, disting. lectr., 1977, prof. emeritus. Author: JM409 Casebook and Study Guide, 1976, Mass Communications Law Casebook, 1979, 3d edit., 1985. Active, Friends of Libr., Alachua County Humane Soc. Recipient outstanding Prof. award Fla. Blue Key, 1976; Danforth assoc., 1976-85. Mem. Women in Communications, Assn. Edn. in Journalism, Phi Beta Kappa, Kappa Tau Alpha. Democrat. Unitarian Universalist. Home: 208 NW 21st Ter Gainesville FL 32603-1732

SMITH, JOAN ADDISON, priest; b. Beckley, W. Va., Sept. 18, 1948; d. John Wesley Smith and Dorothy Claire Sheffler Smith. BA, Randolph Macon Woman's Coll., Lynchburg, Va., 1971; MDiv, Va. Theol. Seminary, Alexandria, Va., 1982. Interim rector Episc. Ch. of the Nativity, Maysville, Ky., 1998—99; interim asst. Ch. of the Good Shepherd, Lexington, Ky., 1999—2000; interim rector St. Raphael's Episc. Ch., Lexington, Ky., 2000—02, St. Paul's Episc. Ch., Louisville, 2002—03, Episc. Ch. of the Advent, Louisville, 2003—04, St. Philip's Episc. Ch., Harrodsburg, Ky., 2004—05, St. Pauls Episc. Ch., Henderson, Ky., 2006—. Commn. on ministry Diocese of Lexington, 2004—; field edn. mentor Interim Ministry Network, Balt., 2004; founder Episc. Peace Fellowship Chpt., Cin., 1985. Pres. alumni assn. Va. Theol. Sem., 1984—85, bd. trustees, 1981—82, 1984—85; bd. pub. affairs Planned Parenthood, Cin., 1991—94; bd. mem. East End Learning Ctr., Cin., 1991—94. Recipient Emerging Young Woman award, Jr. Women's Club, 1978. Mem.: Randolph-Macon Alumnae Chpt., Girl Scouts of Am. (life). Democrat. Episc. Office Phone: 270-826-2937.

SMITH, JOAN H., retired women's health nurse, educator; b. Akron, Ohio; d. Joseph A. and Troynette M. (Lower) McDonald; m. William G. Smith; children: Sue Ann, Priscilla, Timothy. Diploma, Akron City Hosp., 1948; BSN in Edn., U. Akron, 1972, MA in Family Devel., 1980. Cert. in inpatient obstetric nursing. Mem. faculty Akron Gen. Med. Ctr. Sch. Nursing, 1964; former dir. obstet. spl. procedures Speakers Bur., Women's Health Ctrs. Akron Gen. Med. Ctr., 1988; ret., 1990. Cons., speaker women's health care. Mem. Assn. Women's Health, Obstet. and Neonatal Nursing (charter, past sec.-treas., past vice chmn. Ohio sect., chmn. program various confs.). Home: 873 Kirkwall Dr Copley OH 44321-1751

SMITH, JOBETH, elementary school educator; b. Houston, Tex., Sept. 3, 1955; d. Fred Tillman and JoBeth Lambert; m. Norman Kendall Smith, June 15, 1979; children: Amy Leeanne Hancock Smith, Kelli Elizabeth. AA, Lon Morris Coll., Jacksonville, Tex., 1975; BS, Tex. Wesleyan Coll., Ft. Worth, 1978. Cert. Provisional Elem. and Music Tex., 1978. Tchr. Aldine Ind. Sch. Dist., Houston, 1978—79, Everman Ind. Sch. Dist., Ft.Worth, 1979—80, Kate Burgess Elem. Sch., Wichita Falls, Tex., 1980—82; music specialist Austin Elem. Sch., Wichita Falls, 1982—87, Jefferson Elem. Sch., Wichita Falls, 1987—97, Maedgen Elem. Sch., Lubbock, Tex., 1997—2006. Dir. elem. choral Jefferson Honor Choir, Wichita Falls, 1987—97, Maedgen Elem., Lubbock, 1997—, dir. elem. chimes & boomwhacker ensemble, 1997—; dir. all city elem. choir Lubbock Ind. Sch. Dist., 1998—2000, Wichita Falls Ind. Sch. Dist., 1990—97. Composer: (elem. music composition) Parting Song (Music K-8 Mag. Contbr., 2000). Musician City Of Lubbock Newcomers & Christmas Tour, 2000—01, Sweet Adelines, Wichita Falls, 1980—82; dir. Miracle on 34th St. Parade, Tex., 2004—05; musician Civic Chorus, Wichita Falls, 1980—82, Wesly United Meth. Ch., Wichita Falls, 1983—97, St. Luke's United Meth. Ch., Lubbock, 1997—2006. Named Tchr. of Yr., Wichita Fall Ind. Sch. Dist., 1991, KLUR Tchr. of Week, Wichita Falls, 1996, 1987, 1988; named to Who's Who Among Am. Tchrs., Former Students, 1996, 1994, 1998, 2006; recipient Lubbock Avalanche- Jour., Best Elem. Music Tchr., City of Lubbock, 2004, Extra Mile Award, United Meth. Ch., 1982, Lubbock Ind. Sch. Dist. Tchr. Spotlight, Glen Teal, Prin. Maedgen Elem., 2006, West Found. Excellence in Tchg. award, Wichita Falls Ind. Sch. Dist., 1990, Wichita Falls. Ind. Sch. Dist., 1994, Tchr. of Yr., Ladies Aux. VFW, 1992, KLUR Tchr. of Yr., Wichita Falls, 1987; scholar Harvard U. Grad. Sch. of Edn. Assessment, Wichita Falls Ind. Sch. Dist., 1991. Mem.: Tex. Music Educators Assn. (assoc.), Tex. Congress Parent and Tchr. (life). R-Consevative. Methodist. Avocations: travel, music. Home: 10220 Renwick Cove Keller TX 76248 Office: Maedgen Elementary Sch 4401 Nashville Lubbock TX 79413

SMITH, JOELLEN, dean, literature and language educator; b. Johnstown, Pa., May 1, 1957; d. Joseph J. and Ellen I. Piskura; m. Edward Smith, July 18, 1981 (div. Apr. 1, 2005); 1 child, Matthew Edward. BS in Elem. Edn., U. Pitts., 1981; MEd in Instrnl. Tech., Am. Intercontinental U., 2004. Cert. tchr. Tex., 1988, user specialist Microsoft Office, 2005. Tchr. St. Thomas More Parish Sch., Houston, 1986—, dean of students, lang. arts coord., 1993—. Mem. critical thinking curriculum Diocese of Galveston-Houston, 1988—89, accreditation team mem., 1996—2004, mem. lang. arts curriculum, 1996—2003; trainer, presenter Profile Approach to Writing Evaluation, College Station, Tex., 1998—99. Grantee Tech. Grant, U. St. Thomas, Houston Endowment, 2004-2005. Mem.: ASCD, Am. Classical League, Internat. Reading Assn., Nat. Mid. Sch. Assn., Nat. Coun. Teachers English. Home: 2210 Mustang Springs Dr Missouri City TX 77459 Office: St Thomas More Parish Sch 5927 Wigton St Houston TX 77096 Business E-Mail: jsmith@stmorenews.com.

SMITH, JUANITA BÉRARD, lawyer, artist; b. St. Martinsville, La., Oct. 23, 1947; d. Zachary Joseph and Lucille Bourque Bérard; m. Mark Christian Smith III, Mar. 16 (dec. 2003); children: Mark IV, Brett, Robyn, Tara. BA in History, Loyola U., 1979, JD, 1982. Bar: La. 1982. Pvt. practice, New Orleans, 1982—; pres. 730 Bienville Inc., New Orleans, 2003—, TSL Properties Inc., New Orleans, 2003—, Century Hotels Inc., New Orleans, 2003—; owner, pres. St. Louis Hotel, New Orleans, 2003—, St. Ann Hotel, New Orleans, 2003—, Louis XVI Restaurant, New Orleans, 2003—, La Louisiane Restaurant, New Orleans, 2003—, Woodstone Subdivsn., Mandeville, 2003—, McCrory's, New Orleans, 2003—, Hotel Marie Antoinette, New Orleans, Mark Smith Enterprises, New Orleans, 2004. Exhibited in group shows at Alexander and Victor Gallery Fine Art, New Orleans, Alexander and Victor Gallery, Coral Gables, Fla., Palma Gallery, New Orleans, one-woman shows include La. Gallery, 2004. Named one of Women of Yr., New Orleans City Bus., 2004. Mem.: La. State Bar Assn., New Orleans Bar Assn. Avocations: skiing, theology. Home: 730 Rue Bienville St New Orleans LA 70130 Office: 730 Bienville Partners Ltd 1000 Iberville St New Orleans LA 70130 Studio: 106 Mariners Island Mandeville LA 70448 Mailing: PO Box 57929 New Orleans LA 70157 Personal E-mail: jbsmith1947@charter.net.

SMITH, JUDITH A., legal analyst; d. Thomas Goldsberry and Dorothy Marie Smith; 1 child, David Sheldon. BA in Psychology, U. Maine, Portland, 1975; JD, McGeorge Sch. Law, Sacramento, 1979. Cert. vocat. instr. 1980. Pvt. rsch. cons., Sacramento, 1980—84; rsch. asst. Severaid & Nauman, Sacramento, 1984—96; sr. legal analyst State Calif. Dept. Transp., Sacramento, 1997—. Instr. Los Rios C.C. Dist., Am. River Coll., Sacramento, 1980—2006. Pres. McGeorge Alumni Assn., Sacramento, 1980—86, Sacramento Children's Home Guild and Bd., 1981—2000; treas. Donegal Terr. Homeowners Assn., Citrus Heights, Calif., 1992—. Avocations: reading, horseback riding, knitting. Home: 6241 Louth Way Citrus Heights CA 95621 Office: State Calif Dept Transp 1120 N St Sacramento CA 95814

SMITH, JUDITH LYNN, physical education educator; b. Newton, N.J., Mar. 12, 1955; d. Thomas Saint Smith and Joan Joss Mitchell. BS, Ithaca Coll., N.Y., 1977; MA, U. Md., College Park, 1983; PhD, Temple U., Phila., Pa., 1998. Cert. tchr. N.Y., N.J., Pa. Tchr., coach West Canada Valley Sch. Sys., Newport, NY, 1978—81, Newton H.S., NJ, 1983—86; prof. Kutztown U., Pa., 1986—. Home: 65 Pine St Breinigsville PA 18031-1712

SMITH, JULIA LADD, oncologist, physician; b. Rochester, N.Y., July 26, 1951; d. John Herbert and Isabel (Walcott) Ladd; m. Stephen Slade Smith; 1 child. BA, Smith Coll., 1973; MD, N.Y. Med. Coll., 1976. Diplomate Am. Bd. Internal Medicine, Am. Bd. Med. Oncology, Am. Bd. Hospice and Palliative Medicine. Intern in medicine N.Y. Med. Coll., N.Y.C., 1976-77; resident in medicine Rochester Gen. Hosp., 1977-79; internist Genesee Valley Group Health, Rochester, 1979-80; oncology fellow U. Rochester, 1980-82, asst. prof. oncology in medicine sch. medicine and dentistry, 1986—2003; oncologist Med. Ctr. Clinic, Ltd., Pitts., 1982-83; oncologist, internist Rutgers Community Health Plan, New Brunswick, N.J., 1983-86; med. dir. Genesse Region Home Care Assn./Hospice, Rochester, 1988—; med. oncologist Genesee Hosp., Rochester, 1996—2001, chief hematology/oncology, 1996—2001; med. oncologist Rochester Gen. Hosp., 2001—. Bd. dirs. Am. Cancer Soc., Monroe County, 1988-92. Nat. Cancer Inst. rsch. grantee, 1993—95. Fellow Acad. Hospice Physicians; mem. ACP, Am. Soc. Clin. Oncology. Unitarian-Universalist. Avocations: sailing, reading, movies, bridge. Office: Lipson Blood and Cancer Ctr 1425 Portland Ave Rochester NY 14621 Office Phone: 585-922-4020.

SMITH, JULIE ANN, pharmaceutical executive; BS, Cornell Univ. Mktg. div. Bristol-Myers Squibb; comml. team Novazyme Pharmaceutical Corp.; v.p. product strategy and devel. Genzyme Corp., v.p. global mktg.; v.p., mktg. Jazz Pharmaceuticals, 2006—. Clinical rschr. neuroendocrinology Mass. Gen. Hosp. Named one of 40 Under 40, Boston Bus. Jour., 2005. Office: Jazz Pahrmaceuticals 3180 Porter Dr Palo Alto CA 94304*

SMITH, JUNE BURLINGAME, English educator; b. Barrington, NJ, June 1, 1935; d. Leslie Grant and Esther (Bellini) Burlingame; m. Gregory Lloyd Smith, July 6, 1963; children: Gilia Cobb Burlingame Smith, Cyrus Comstock. BA, Reed Coll., 1956; MS, Ind. U., 1959; MA, Calif. State U., Dominquez Hills, 1986. Sec. to dean Reed Coll., 1956-57; residence hall supr. Ind. U., 1957-59; buyer Macy's Calif., 1959-63; residence hall supr. U. Wash., 1963, interviewer Tchr. Placement Bur., 1964; music tchr. Chinook Jr. High Sch., Bellevue, Wash., 1964-68; pvt. practice music tchr., 1971-83; gifted grant coord. South Shores/CSUDH Magnet Sch., 1981; tchr. cons. L.A. Unified Sch. Dist., 1981-82; prof. English LA CC, Harbor Coll., Wilmington, Calif., 1989—; sexual harrassment officer Harbor Coll., Wilmington, Calif., 1991-92, pres. acad. senate, 1997—2000, staff devel. coord., 2001—02. Chair Sex Equity Commn., L.A. Unified Sch. Dist., 1988-91; bd. dirs. Harbor Inter Faith Shelter, 1994-2005; chair San Pedro Coordinated Plan Com. for the Port of L.A.; mem., parliamentarian, v.p. Coastal San Pedro Neighborhood Coun.; pres. Point Fermin Residents Assn., 2003—. Mem. AAUW (pres. San Pedro, Calif. br. 1989-90, mem. task force Initiative for Equity in Edn. 1991-95), Am. Acad. Poets, Phi Kappa Phi,. Democrat. Home: 3915 S Carolina St San Pedro CA 90731-7115 Office: LA CC Harbor 1111 Figueroa Pl Wilmington CA 90744-2311

SMITH, JUSTINE TOWNSEND, recreational association executive; b. Evanston, Ill., June 28, 1936; d. William West and Justine Wilhelmina (Laituri) Townsend; m. Edward Charles Smith, Oct. 15, 1955 (div. 1983); 1 child, Leigh Ann. Student, Evanston Bus. Coll., 1954. Cert. asm. exec. Chief proofreader Melville series dept. English, 1965—70; asst. editor Libr. of Living Philosophers Northwestern U., 1959—64; owner J.J. Creations, Buffalo Grove, Ill., 1972—79; ice skating profl. Northbrook Sports Complex, Ill., 1974, Watts Ice Rink, Glencoe, Ill., 1975; exec. dir. Ice Skating Inst. Am., Wilmette, Ill., 1981—; v.p. Women in Mgmt., Downers Grove, Ill., 1986. V.p. Shelter Inc., Arlington Heights, Ill., 1980; trustee Ice Skating Inst. Am. Edn. Found., 1988—; mem. adv. coun. Wheeling H.S., 1993—. Mem.: Nat. Coun. Youth Sports (pres. 1987—89), Am. Soc. Assn. Execs. (cert.). Office: Ice Skating Inst Am Ste 140 17120 Dallas Pkwy Dallas TX 75248-1140

SMITH, KAREN A., lawyer; b. Newark, May 26, 1962; BA, Lafayette Coll., 1984; JD, Cornell U., 1987. Bar: NJ 1987, NY 1988, DC 1989. Ptnr., co-head Bus. & Internat. Sect. Vinson & Elkins LLP, NYC. Mem.: ABA. Office: Vinson & Elkins LLP 666 Fifth Ave, 26 Fl New York NY 10103-0040

SMITH, KAREN ANN, visual artist; b. Trenton, NJ, May 25, 1964; d. James Roy and Clara Patricia (Walton) S. A in Comml. Art, Art Inst. Phila., 1984; BFA in Graphic Design and Art Therapy, U. Arts, Phila., 1989; grad. in graphic design, Basel Sch. for Design, 1991; MA in Expressive Therapies, Lesley Coll., 1993. Graphic designer Mercer County C.C., Trenton, 1984-86; mural painter, supr. Anti-Graffiti Network, Phila., 1988; tchr. drawing and set design Chestnut Hill (Mass.) Sch., 1995, 96; freelance graphic designer Swiss Fed. Rys., Bern, 1993-95; tchr. drawing Wentworth Inst. Tech., Boston, 1996, 97; tchr. design Northeastern U., Boston, 1997. Fireworks crew Pyrotech. Inc., Boston, 1997; apprentice Johnson Atelier Tech. Inst. of Sculpture, Trenton, 1997-99; artist Airtex Interiors, Fallsington, 2000-03; artist, instr. intergenerational program Pennswood Village and Newtown Friends Sch., 2003-; visual artist. Author numerous poems; one-woman shows include Contempo Galerie, Bern, Switzerland, 1994, Boston Archtl. Ctr. Atelier, 1997, George Sch., Newtown, Pa., 1997, exhibited in group shows at Howard Yezerski Gallery, Boston, 1994, Kingston Gallery, 1995, Phillips' Mill, New Hope, Pa., 1997, Woodmere Art Mus., Chestnut Hill, Pa., 1998, Princeton (NJ) Day Sch., 1999, Trenton City Mus., 1999, Vorpal Gallery, N.Y.C., 2000—02, Artsbridge, Prallsville Mills, N.J., 2000, Riverbank Arts, Stockton, N.J., 2000—, iTheo.com, San Francisco, 2000—01, Nat. Bottle Mus., Ballston Spa, N.Y., 2001, Artsbridge Photography Exhbn., Lamberville, NJ, 2003, Artists at the Farm, Langhorne, Pa., 2003—, Rosenberg-Wila, Switzerland, 1994, 2005, 2006. Scholar Women in Graphic Arts, 1987-89; grantee Mystic Studios Trust, 1994-97, Artists at the Farm, Langhorne, Pa., 2003—. Mem. Coll. Art Assn., Soc. Artists in Healthcare, Origami USA, Artsbridge. E-mail: sunbellsmith@msn.com.

SMITH, KAREN E., mathematician, educator; b. Red Bank, New Jersey, May 9, 1965; married; children: Sanelma, Tapio, Helena. BA in Math., Princeton U., 1987; PhD, U. Mich., 1993. Tchr. math. N.J. Pub. Schs., 1987—88; NSF postdoctoral fellow Purdue U., West Lafayette, Ind., 1993—94; Moore instr., asst. prof. MIT, Cambridge, 1994—97; prof. math. U. Mich., Ann Arbor, 1997—. Vis. prof. U. Jyvaskyla, Finland, 2001. Author: An Invitation to Algebraic Geometry, 2000; assoc. editor Jour. Am. Math. Soc., mem. editl. bd. Am. Math. Monthly. Recipient Ruth Lyttle Satter prize, 2001; fellow, Fulbright Found.; grantee, NSF, Alfred P. Sloan Found. Mem.: Nat. Rsch. Coun. (bd. dirs. Math. Scis.). Office: Dept Math Rm 2832 East Hall Univ Michigan 530 Church St Ann Arbor MI 48109 Office Phone: 734-763-5048. Fax: 734-763-0937. E-mail: kesmith@umich.edu.*

SMITH, KAREN GIL, social studies educator; b. Denver, July 12, 1971; d. Larry F. and Mercedes A. Gil; m. Christopher Ron Smith, Oct. 8, 1994; children: Emma Adele, Leah Alexander. BEd, U. Ga., Athens, 1993. Tchr. Wheeler H.S., Marietta, Ga., 1997—2001, basketball asst. coach,

1997—2001; tchr. Starr's Mill H.S., Fayetteville, Ga., 2002—06, tennis coach, 2002—06. Basketball asst. coach Sandy Creek H.S., Tyrone, Ga., 1993—97. Office Phone: 770-486-2710. Office Fax: 770-486-2716. Business E-Mail: smith.karen@fcboe.org.

SMITH, KAREN LYNNE, elementary school educator; b. Aurora, Mo., May 29, 1956; d. William Kenneth Faucett and Norma Lee (Rhodes) Stockton; m. James Paul Smith, Sept. 14, 1974; children: Jami Lynne, Jason Paul. BA, S.W. Bapt. U., Bolivar, Mo., 1974—78; tchr. cert., Drury U., Springfield, Mo., 1996—98; MS, S.W. Bapt. U., 1998—2002. Title I communication arts tchr. Golden City Schs., Mo., 1993—. Dir. Title I, Golden City, 2000—. Mem.: Mo. State Tchrs. Assn., Delta Kappa Gamma. Baptist. Avocations: reading, travel. Home: 10738 Lawrence Rd Miller MO 65707 Office: Golden City Elem 1208 Walnut St Golden City MO 64748

SMITH, KATHRYN J., music educator, conductor; d. Joy Clarke; m. Luke Smith, June 8, 1968; children: Joshua, Kimberly Borchard. BA in Music Edn., U. No. Colo., Greeley, 1969. Music tchr. various pub. and pvt. instns., Salt Lake City, 1979—89; instrumental music dir. Heritage Christian Sch., Milw., 1989—2004; music/string instr. Seward County C.C., Liberal, Kans., 2004—. Condr./dir. S.W. Symphony Orch., Liberal, Kans., 2004—. Choir dir. Valley West Bapt. Ch., Salt Lake City, 1979—89. Named Tchr. of Yr., Euclid Jr. HS, Littleton, Colo., 1973, Heritage Christian Sch., 2002. Avocations: travel, knitting, bicycling.

SMITH, KATHRYN LEE, artist, educator; b. Washington, Aug. 31, 1953; d. Jay Lloyd and Sibyl (Warthen) Smith; m. Joseph Thayer Papaleo (div.); 1 child, Liana Angele. BFA, U. Md., College Park, 1975; coursework, Md. Inst. Art, Balt., 1976, Colo. State U., Ft. Collins, 1984, U. Colo., Boulder, 1984. Ednl. coord. Provincetown Art Assn., Mass., 1998—99; program designer PIAI, Mass., 1998—99; mem. faculty Herman and Mary Robinson Mus. Sch., Provincetown, 1998—; coord. dept continuing edn. Cape Cod C.C., Provincetown, 1999—2000; coord. Dept Acad. Affairs, Provincetown, 2000—01; instr. prints and drawing Cape Cod CC, Provincetown, 1999—2002; printmaking instr. Herman and Mary Robinson Mus. Sch., Provincetown, 1991—; current rep. The Schoolhouse Ctr., Provincetown, Mass., Comenos Fine Arts, Boston. Trustee PAAM, Provincetown, 1996—2000, chmn. Mus. Sch., 1999—2001. Exhibited in group shows at Cape Mus. Fine Arts, Dennis, Mass., 1999, exhibitions include Schoolhouse Ctr., Silas Kenyon Gallery, Provincetown, Mass., 1998, Fitzwilliam Mus., Cambridge, Eng., 1999, Comenos Fine Arts, Boston, 1999, Lamia, Inc., NYC, 1999, C3TV Gallery, Yarmouthport, Mass., 2000, Davis Gallery, Wellfleet, Mass., 2000, 2004, Schoolhouse Ctr., Provincetown, Mass., 2001—02, SAGA, NYC, 2002, Harmony, LamiaInk and Handmade Culture Club, Japan, 2003, DNA Gallery, Provincetown, Mass., 2003, Corcoran Gallery Art, Washington, 2004, Silas Kenyon Gallery, Provincetown, 2004, 2006, 29 Newbury St., Boston, 2005, Represented in permanent collections Provincetown Art Assn. and Mus., Fitzwilliam Mus., Cambridge, Eng., Boston Pub. Libr. Recipient First recipient Art Bridge Workshop Residency, Lamia Ink, N.Y.C., Kami Gori, Japan, 2003, award, Nat. Soc. Arts and Letters, Washington, 1972; grantee, Provincetown Cultural Coun., Mass. Cultural Coun., 1994. Mem.: Provincetown Arts Assn. & Mus., Washington Print Club. Personal E-mail: ksmithart@aol.com.

SMITH, KATHY L., elementary school educator, cosmetics executive, consultant; b. Gillespie, Ill., Mar. 8, 1959; d. William G. and Phyllis L. Russell; m. Thomas A. Smith, Aug. 30, 1980; children: Ashley M., Blake T. BA, So. Ill. U., Edwardsville, 1981, MA, 1988. Cert. Nat. Bd. Cert. Tchr. Fla., 2002. Tchr. 1st, 4, th and 6th Bunker Hill Sch. Dist., Bunker Hill, Ill., 1984—89; tchr. kindergarten, 1st, and 2nd Marion County Sch. Dist., Weirsdale, Fla., 1989—96; tchr. 1st grade Lake County Sch. Dist., Eustis, Fla., 1996—99, intensive reading tchr. Leesburg, Fla., 1999—; beauty cons. Mary Kay, Fruitland Park, Fla., 2003—. Facilitator U. Ctrl. Fla., Orlando, Fla., 2004—. Author: (novels) Powerful Classroom Stories from Accomplished Teachers. Family fun Women of the Moose, Leesburg, Fla., 2005—; vol. Morrison United Meth. Ch., Leesburg, Fla., 1989—2001. Mem.: Cert. Accomplished Tchrs. (assoc.), So. Ill. U. Alumni Assn. (life), Women of the Moose (assoc.). Avocations: reading, travel, swimming. Home: 4209 Idlewild Dr Fruitland Park FL 34731 Office: Carver Mid Sch 1200 N Beecher St Leesburg FL 34748 Office Phone: 352-787-7868. Personal E-mail: kathysmarykay4u@aol.com.

SMITH, KATHY WOSNITZER, psychiatrist; b. Paterson, NJ, May 30, 1970; d. Albert Abraham and Arlene Ann Wosnitzer; m. Timothy Alan Smith, Apr. 28, 2001; 1 child, Nicholas Rearden. MD, U. Ariz., Tucson, 2001. Resident U. Ariz. Coll. Medicine, Tucson, 2001—04, child and adolescent psychiatry fellow, 2004—; asst. prof. clin. psychiatry U. Ariz., 2006. Co-program dir. Regional Coun. Am. Acad. Child and Adolescent Psychiatry, Tucson, 2006—, resident rep., 2005—; regional rep. Am. Psychiat. Assn. Com. Residents and Fellows, 2002—05. Recipient Boris Zemsky award Excellence Psychiatry, U. Ariz., Coll. Medicine, 2000, Roy N. Killingsworth, M.D. Meml. award Excellence Psychiatry, 2001. Mem.: Ariz. Psychiat. Soc., Am. Acad. Child and Adolescent Psychiatry (resident rep. 2005—06, co-program dir. 2006—), Am. Psychiat. Assn. (resident rep., sec. com. residents and fellows 2002—05). Independent. Avocations: hiking, literature. Office: University of AZ College of Medicine 1501 North Campbell Avenue Tucson AZ 85724 Office Phone: 520-694-6000. Home Fax: 520-626-2004; Office Fax: 520-626-2004. Personal E-mail: kathywsmith@comcast.net.

SMITH, KATIE (KATHERINE MAY SMITH), professional basketball player; b. Logan, Ohio, June 4, 1974; d. Don Smith. Degree in zoology, Ohio State U., 1996. Profl. basketball player Columbus Quest, ABL, 1997—98, Minn. Lynx, WNBA, 1999—, Lotos VBW Clima, EuroLeague, Gdynia, Poland, 2001—02. Named Ohio State Female Athlete of the Century, Columbus Touchdown Club, 2002; named to ABL All-Star Team, 1997, 1998, All-ABL First Team, 1998, WNBA All-Star Team, 2000, 2001, 2002, 2003, All-WNBA First Team, 2001, 2003. Achievements include mem., Columbus Quest ABL Championship Team, 1997, 98; mem., US Women's Basketball Gold Medal Team, FIBA World Championships, 1998, 2002; mem., US Women's Basketball Gold Medal Team, Sydney Olympics, 2000; mem., US Women's Basketball Team, Athens Olympics, 2004; first female in history of Ohio State U. to have number retired, Jan. 21, 2001. Office: Minn Lynx 600 First Ave North Minneapolis MN 55403

SMITH, KATRINA DIANE, writer; b. Oakland, Calif., Dec. 23, 1957; d. Mack Edward and Mary Jean Smith; children: Rose, Jason Larenzo. Student, Alameda Coll., Calif., Laney Coll., Oakland, Calif., Careercom Bus. Coll., Oakland, 1998. Author: The Founders Guide of Girl Scouting, 1994, The Floral Factor of the Cotton Mill, 1998, The History of the War in Theatrical Genology, 1997. Vol. So. Poverty Law Ctr., Montgomery, Ala., 1996, Sr. Citizens League, Washington, 1996, Notch Reform Campaign, Washington, 1996; adv. bd. Missing Persons, Oakland, Calif., 1999, Consular Search Statistics, Dept. State, 2001; mem. U.S. Olympic Com., 1996. Named to Internet Poetry Hall of Fame; recipient Colgate Youth for Am. award, Colgate Palmolive Co., 1993—94, Editor's Choice award, Internet Libr. Poetry. Mem.: AARP (bd. dirs. 2001—02), Nat. Geog. Soc. (bd. dirs. 1989), TWA Club (SFO bd. 1991). Avocation: reading. Home: 1699 70th Ave Oakland CA 94621 Office: Internet Library of Poetry 1 Poetry Plz Owings Mills MD 21117 Office Phone: 510-562-6059.

SMITH, KAYE TRAIN, artist; b. Camden, NJ, July 15, 1927; d. William Matthew Biddle and Jennie May Leibensperger; m. Robert L. Smith, Aug. 18, 1995; m. John Martin Train, June 3, 1945 (dec. Jan. 2, 1993); children: Jeanne Carole Train, Suzanne Kathryn Coffee, Kurt Robert Train. Airbrush artist Norcross Greetings Corp., N.Y.C., 1945—46; profl. in-house model Jo Collins Sportswear Corp., St. Louis, 1947—48; freelance artist Fremont, Roseville, Calif., 1967—2005. Exhibit coord. Placerville Art Assn., 1971—72. Recipient Nat. Design award, Am. Greetings Corp., 1966. Mem.: Roseville Arts Ctr., Sun City Roseville Art Club (pres. 1996—97, various coms., signature painting, 8th ann. show 2003). Home: 7260 Timberrose Way Roseville CA 95747

SMITH, KELLY MCCOIG, assistant principal; b. Hampton, Va., Nov. 5, 1977; d. Forrest Daniel and Janet Ward McCoig; m. Chris Steven Smith, July 26, 2003; 1 child, Emma. BA, Coll. William and Mary, 2000; Ednl. Leadership/Adminstrn., Old Dominion U., 2002. Tchr. English, advisor yearbook Denbigh H.S., Newport News, Va., 2000—05; asst. prin. Beachville H.S., Newport News, Va., 2005—. Mem./sec. UDC, Hampton, Va., 2000—03. Mem.: ASCD, NEA, Va. Educator's Assn., Nat. Coun. Tchrs. English, Phi Kappa Phi, Phi Delta Kappa. Baptist. Avocations: health and fitness, music, dance. Office: Beachville High School 675 Beachville Rd Newport News VA 23602

SMITH, KERI A., literature and language educator; b. Jamestown, ND, Nov. 23, 1975; d. Jimmy W. and Julie A. Carson; m. Bryan S. Smith, Nov. 21, 1998; 1 child, Hayden Kristoffer. B in Elem. Edn. Grades 1-8, Southeastern La. U., Hammond, 1998. Nat. bd. cert. in early adolescence and English lang. arts Nat. Bd. Profl. Tchg. Stds. Tchr. Springfield (La.) Mid. Sch., 1999—. Nat. bd. mentor Nat. Bd. Profl. Tchg. Stds., Hammond, La., 2006—. Chairperson Vets.' History Project, Springfield, 2004—. Mem.: Pi Lambda Theta. Republican. Lutheran. Avocations: travel, reading. Office: Springfield Mid Sch 24145 Coats Rd Springfield LA 70462 Office Phone: 225-294-3306. E-mail: keri.smith@lpsb.org.

SMITH, KIKI, artist; b. Nuremberg, Germany, Jan. 18, 1954; d. Tony Smith. One-woman shows include The Kitchen, N.Y.C., 1982, Fawbush Gallery, 1988, 1992, 1993, Galerie René Blouin, Montreal, 1989, 1991—92, 1994, Dallas Mus. Art, 1989, Ezra and Cecile Zilkha Gallery Ctr. for the Arts Wesleyan U., Middletown, Conn., 1989, Tyler Gallery Tyler Sch. Art Temple U., Phila., 1990, Ctr. d'Arte Contemporaine, Geneva, 1990, Inst. Art and Urban Resources The Clocktower, Long Island, N.Y., 1990, Inst. Contemporary Art, Amsterdam, 1990, Mus. Modern Art, N.Y.C., 1990—91, Shoshana Wayne Gallery, Santa Monica, Calif., 1991, 1992, 1992—93, MAK Galerie, Vienna, 1991, U. Art Mus., Berkeley, Calif., 1991, Art Awareness, Inc., Lexington, N.Y., 1991, Corcoran Gallery Art, Washington, 1991, Greg Kucera Gallery, Seattle, 1991, Rose Art Mus. Brandeis U., Waltham, Mass., 1992, Österreichisches Mus. angewandte Kunst, Vienna, 1992, Moderna Mus., Stockholm, 1992, Bonner Kunstverein, Bonn, 1992, Galerie M & R Fricke, Düsseldorf, Germany, 1992—93, Williams Coll. Mus. Art, Williamstown, Mass., 1992—93, Ohio State U., Columbus, 1992—93, Anthony d'Offay Gallery, London, 1993, 1995, Phoenix Art Mus., 1993, U. Art Mus., Santa Barbara, Calif., 1994, La. Mus. Modern Art, Humlebaek, Denmark, 1994, The Israel Mus., Jerusalem, 1994, Barbara Gross Galerie, Munich, 1994, Laura Carpenter Fine Art, Santa Fe, 1994, Pace Wildenstein, N.Y., 1994, Royal LePage Gallery, Toronto, 1994—95, Barbara Krakow Gallery, Boston, 1994—96, Whitechapel Art Gallery, London, 1995, San Francisco Mus. Modern Art, 2005, Contemporary Art Mus., Houston, 2006, numerous others, exhibited in group shows at Brooke Alexander Gallery, N.Y., 1980, 1991, White Columns, N.Y., 1981, 1983, 1990, Artists Space, 1981, 1990, Barbara Gladstone Gallery, 1982, Hallwalls, Buffalo, N.Y., 1983, Susan Caldwell Gallery, N.Y., 1984, 1987, Galerie Engstrom, Stockholm, 1984, Art City, N.Y., 1985, Moderna Mus., Stockholm, 1985, Cin. Art Mus., 1985, Bklyn. Mus., 1986, 1989, Curt Marcus Gallery, N.Y., 1986, Fawbush Gallery, 1987, 1989, 1990, Mus. Modern Art, N.Y.C., 1988, 1992, IBM Gallery, N.Y., 1988, Arch Gallery, Amsterdam, 1988, Tom Cugliani Gallery, 1989, Simon Watson Gallery, N.Y., 0190, Mus. Fine Arts, Boston, 1990, Hunter Coll. Art Gallery, 1991, Milw. Art Mus., 1992, Paula Cooper Gallery, 1993, Serpentine Gallery, London, 1994, PaceWildenstein, N.Y., 1995, 1997, 1998, Ace Gallery, Mex., 1997, Yale U. Art Gallery, New Haven, Conn., 1998, John Berggruen Gallery, San Francisco, 2005, numerous others. Named one of 100 Most Influential People, Time Mag., 2006. Mem.: AAAL. Office: c/o Pace Wildenstein 32 E 57th St New York NY 10022-2513*

SMITH, KIMMIE CHRISTINE, small business owner; b. Redding, Calif., Apr. 28, 1971; d. Steven Burton Tyler and Kim Kassina Hern; m. Kenneth Thomas Smith, Nov. 12, 1988; 1 foster child, Savannah children: Stephanie, Shannon, Steven, Shelby, Danika. AAS, U. Alaska, Sitka, 2003, AA, 2004, BLA, 2005; postgrad. in Psychology, Walden U. Owner, adminstr. Krissy's Playland Childcare Ctr., Wrangell, Alaska, 1995—. Sec., treas., com. mem. Cub Scouts Am., Wrangell, Alaska, 2000—04; v.p. Emblem Club #87, 2006—. Named Family Childcare Provider of Year, AEYC-SEA, 2005. Avocations: hunting, scrapbooks, fishing. Home: PO Box 615 Wrangell AK 99929 Office: Krissy's Playland PO Box 615 Wrangell AK 99929 Office Phone: 907-874-4307. Business E-Mail: krissysplayland@aptalaska.net.

SMITH, LAURA DOSSETT, art dealer; d. Walter Brown Dossett and Alethea Halbert Sleeper; m. Curtis Cullen Smith, Mar. 6, 1948; children: Sallie Chesnutt Smith Wright, Alethea Risher Smith Gilbert, Elizabeth Brient. Student, Mary Baldwin Coll., Staunton, Va., 1943—44, U. Tex., 1945—46; BA, Baylor U., Waco, Tex., 1948. Prin. St. Alban's Sch., Waco, 1948—49; owner Festoon Galleries, Waco, 1982—2003. Art curator Amb. Lyndon Olson, Stockholm, 1998—2001. Bd. mem. Waco Art Ctr., 1961—68, McLennan C.C., Waco, 1975, pres. bd., 1978. Recipient Path Finders award, YWCA of McLennan County, 1991. Mem.: Colonial Dames in State of Tex., Assocs. Royal Acad. Avocations: reading, travel, walking. Home: 447 Meandering Way China Spring TX 76633

SMITH, LEILA HENTZEN, artist; b. Milw., May 20, 1932; d. Erwin Albert and Marian Leila (Austin) Hentzen; m. Richard Howard Smith, Sept. 12, 1959; 1 child, Jennie. BFA, Miami U., 1955; cert., Famous Artists Schs., 1959. Quilting tchr. Milw. Pub. Schs., 1975-79. One-woman shows include Boerner Bot. Gardens, Whitnall Park, Wis., 1995, 2 person show, Firefly Gallery, Wauwatosa, Wis., 2003, exhibited in group shows at Milw. Art Ctr., 1961, West Bend Gallery Fine Arts, 1963, 1993, 1996, 1999, 2002, 2005, Wustum Mus. Art, Racine, Wis., 1966, Mount Mary Coll., Milw., 1969—2001, Mapledale Sch. Gallery, Bayside, Wis., 1977, 1981, Artist's World Gallery, Cedarburg, Wis., 1975, Ozaukee Art Ctr, 1982—86, John Michael Kohler Arts Ctr., Sheboygan, Wis., 1984, 1987, 1989—2002, 2005, Cedarburg Cultural Ctr., 1988—2001, Ozaukee Art Ctr, Cedarburg, Wis., 1993, Rahr-West Art Mus., Manitowoc, Wis., 1994, Gallery 110 North, Plymouth, Wis., 1996, Rahr-West Art Mus., Manitowoc, Wis., 1997, Cardinal Stritch U., 1998—2003, Represented in permanent collections Milw. County Art Commn. Women's aux. vol. Salvation Army, Milw.; mem. dean's adv. coun. U. Wis. Milw. Sch. Arts. Recipient Honorable Mention for painting Bayshore Merchants Assn, 1969, Delta Gamma Art Fair, 1981, Best of Show for painting John Michael Kohler Arts Ctr., 1988. Mem. AAUW, Cedarburg Artists Guild, Wis. Watercolor Soc., Seven Arts Soc. Milw. (pres. 1967-68, painters group chmn. 1962-63), DAR (Milw. chpt. Holiday Folk Fair chmn. 1965-76, libr. historian 1974-77, corr. sec. 1977-80, dir. 1983-86, rec. sec. 1992-95, regent 1995-98, Outstanding Jr. Mem. 1966), Wis. Soc. Daus. of Founders and Patriots of Am. (pres. 1964-66, 2d v.p. 1966-68, 70-73, corr. sec. 1976-79), Wis. Ct. Assts., Nat. Soc. Women Descendants Ancient and Hon. Arty. Co. Boston, Wis. Soc. Mayflower Descendants (sec. 1999-02), Delta Zeta. Congregationalist. Avocations: needlecrafts, swimming, quilting.

SMITH, LEONIE C.R., healthcare educator; b. St. Johns, Antigua, West Indies, May 4, 1975; arrived in U.S., 1987; d. Robert Leonard and Rosalind Rebecca Smith; 1 child, Shivani. BA, Hamilton Coll., Clinton, N.Y., 1997; MPH, Hunter Coll., N.Y.C., 2000; post-grad., Kent State U., Ohio, 2001—. Cert. health edn. specialist Nat. Commn. Health Edn. Credentialing, 2000. Tchr. grade 6th-8th Mid. Sch. 61, Bklyn., 1998—99; tchr. Cmty. Sch. Dist. 18, 1999—2000, Canarsie H.S. and Sheepshead, 2000—01; doctoral tchg. fellow Kent State U., Ohio, 2000—01, grad. rsch. asst., 2002—05, part time faculty, 2005; adj. faculty Cuyahuga CC, Cleve., 2006—. Cardiovasc. disease coord. Lorain City Health Dept., Ohio, 2002. Contbr. chapters to books, poems to anthologies. Mem.: Am. Assn. Health Edn., Phi Beta Delta, Eta Sigma Gamma. Avocations: poetry, reading, movies, rollerblading, piano. Personal E-mail: leonie_south867@hotmail.com.

SMITH, LEONORE RAE, artist; b. Chgo. d. Leon and Rose (Hershfield) Goodman; m. Paul Carl Smith, Apr. 17, 1943; children: Jill Henderson, Laurie Christman. Student, Chgo. Art Inst., 1935-40, U. Chgo., 1939—. Performer in many Broadway shows, with Met. Opera Quartet, Carnegie Hall, nat. concerts; portrait, landscape painter; signature artist Oil Painters of Am., Chgo., 1992-2006, Am. Acad. of Women Artists, 1997-98; ofcl. artist U.S. Coast Guard, Washington, 1989-2000; cert. artist Am. Portrait Soc., Huntington Harbor, Calif., 1985; nat. adv. bd. The Portrait Club, N.Y.C., 1983. Pres. Pacific Palisades Rep. Women, Calif. Named one of Master Artists of the World, Internat. Artist Mag., 1996; recipient Best of Show awards, Salamagundi U.S. Coast Guard, 1989, Pacific Palisades Art Assn., 1987, 1st prize in oils, Greater L.A. Art Competition, Santa Monica, Calif., 1995, prize, The Artist's Mag., 1995, Internat. Soc. Artists, 1977, 1st pl. award, Dream Studio competition, 1996, 1st pl. in portrait, O.P.A. Nat. Show, 2001, award, Northlight Art Mag., 2002, Internat. Artist Mag., 2002, several awards, Calif. Art Club, shown at Nat. Mus. Naval Aviation, Carnegie Mus., Frederick Weisman Mus., Malibu, Calif. Mem. Am. Acad. Women Artists (signature), Salmagundi Club, Pacific Palisades Art Assn. (past pres.), Calif. Art Club, Oil Painters Am. (signature, 1st Pl. 2001), Am. Portrait Soc. (cert.). Achievements include moer than 50 oil paintings of fallen military in Iraq and Afghanistan. Avocations: singing, acting, poetry. Office Phone: 310-454-4096. E-mail: leonorpaul@aol.com.

SMITH, LESLIE M., lawyer; BA, Georgetown U., 1984, JD magna cum laude, 1987. Bar: Ill. 1987. Ptnr., antitrust & competition litig. Kirkland & Ellis LLP, Chgo. Named one of 40 Ill. Attys. Under 40 to Watch, The Law Bulleting Printing Co., 2001, 21 Women Litigators on the Rise, Diversity & the Bar mag., 2004. Mem.: Order of Coif. Office: Kirkland & Ellis Aon Ctr 200 E Randolph Dr Chicago IL 60601 Office Phone: 312-861-2141. Office Fax: 312-861-2200. Business E-Mail: lsmith@kirkland.com.

SMITH, LESLIE MORROW, counselor; b. Ft. Wayne, Ind., Nov. 10, 1958; d. Don Stuart and Sharon Kay (Morris) Morrow; children, Emily Kristen Linnea, Erwin, Brandun Eugene, Kyle David; m. Rick Eugene Smith, Feb. 5, 2000. Student, Ind. State U., Evansville, 1979; BS in Psychology, Western Ky. U., 1980; MS in Clin. Psychology, U. Evansville, 1989. Grad. asst. psychology U. Evansville, 1987, rsch. asst. psychology, acad. advisor, 1987-88; vocat. evaluator Assn. for Retarded Citizens, Evansville, 1988; program dir. Work Able, Inc., Evansville, 1988-89; psychol. evaluator Developmental Diagnostics, Inc., Evansville, 1988-89; asst. dir. counseling disability specialist children's program U. So. Ind., Evansville, mem. enrollment mgmt. team, 1992, mem. Am. with Disabilities task force, 1992, mem. adv. com., 1991, mem. disabled student adv. com., 1989—. Cons. Henderson (Ky.) Psychol. Assocs., 1988-92. Vol. Evansville State Hosp., 1979; leadership tng. participant Ind. Gov.'s Planning Coun., Indpls., 1992; mem. Cmty. Counseling Resource Com., Evansville, 1992, Ind. Gov.'s Planning Coun. Com., Evansville, 1992. Mem. APA (assoc.), Southwestern Ind. Psychol. Assn., Assn. on Higher Edn. and Disability, Ind. Assn. on Higher Edn. and Disability (pres., chair 1993-94). Democrat. Presbyterian. Avocations: theater, classical music, creative writing, reading, weightlifting. Office: U So Ind Counseling Ctr 8600 University Blvd Evansville IN 47712-3534 E-mail: lmsmith@usi.edu.

SMITH, LILLIAN LOUISE, biology educator, librarian; b. Garner, NC, Feb. 14, 1930; d. Charlie and Queen Esther Jones; m. Matthew Smith (dec.); 1 child, Matthew L. BSc, Shaw U., Garner, NC, 1954; M in Edn., Wayne State U., Detroit, 1971, MLS, 2001. Sci. tchr. Speight H.S., Ft. Gaines, Ga., 1955—57; ins. agent Diggs and Mammoth Ins. Co., Detroit, 1959—62; biology tchr. Lillington Pub. H.S., NC, 1962—65, Detroit Pub. H.S., 1965—91; judge Met. Sci. Fair, Detroit, 1991—2000; pres. Det. Assn. of Women's Clubs, 1997—2004, exec. dir., 2002—04. Owner Concerned Parents and Citizens of Northwest Detroit, 1980. Dir. Ebenezer Meth. Ch. Vacation Bible Sch., 1982—86; pres. Century of Progress Club, 1983—86, Dorcas Soc. Club, 1993—95; treas. Pal Little Leaguers, Detroit, 1980; vol. ch. libr. Ebenezer A.M.E. Ch., Detroit, 2002—. Recipient Cmty. Svc. award, Wayne County Exec., Detroit, 1986, Profl. Growth award, State Bd. Edn., 1990, Cmty. Svc. award, Nat. Assn. of Negro Bus. and Profl. Women's Club, 2004, Achievement award, Wayne County Intermed. Sch. Dist., 1990, Worthy Matron Appreciation, Internat. Free and Accepted Masons and Order of the Eastern Star, 1991, Cert. of Appreciation, Mich. State Assn. of Colored Women's Clubs, 1994. Mem.: ALA, 21st Century Women's Club. Avocations: quilting, golf, reading, computers. Home: 1300 East Lafayette Apt 812 Detroit MI 48207

SMITH, LINDA ANN GLIDEWELL, accountant; b. Birmingham, Ala., Aug. 11, 1944; d. Emmett O'Neal and Iola Florence (Harris) Glidewell; m. Lindsey Stribling Smith, Nov. 5, 1966 (div. Dec. 1990); 1 child, Lindsey Nelson; m. Charles G. Espey, Sept. 11, 1997 (div. Sept. 2001). BA cum laude, Birmingham-So. Coll., 1984. Stenographer Cook's Pest Control, Decatur, Ala., 1962, Nelson-Weaver Cos., Birmingham, Ala., 1963-69; resident mgr. Twin Homes of Mt. Brook, Ala., 1966-69; bookkeeper, sect. to v.p. Molton, Allen & Williams, 1969-72; sec. quality assurance dept. So. Co. Svc., Birmingham, 1972-74, sec. sys. constrn. budget, 1974-82, sr. sec. treasury dept., 1982-83; jr. acct. major projects-acctg. Ala. Power Co., Birmingham, 1983-87, sr. acct. fuel dept., 1987-90, sr. acct. stats. dept., 1990-92; fin. adminstr., comptr. Ala. Bapt., Inc., Birmingham, 1992-99; bus. revenue tax compliance officer Shelby County, 1999—2002. Dep. clk. Bay County, Panama City, Fla., 2002—06; pvt. practice acct. Quick Books, 2006—. Asst. treas. So. Co. Svcs. State and Fed. PAC, Ala. PowerCo. State and Fed. PAC. Mem. Am. Soc. Women Accts., Am. Bus. Women's Assn., The Club, Inc., Alpha Lambda Delta, Birmingham So. Alumni Assn. (coun. mem.). Avocations: travel, culinary art, walking, fishing.

SMITH, LINDA JEANE, allied health educator; b. Alton, Ill., Mar. 22, 1952; d. LeRoy Homer and Jeane (Garrett) Campbell; m. Gary L. Smith, Mar. 14, 1998; children: Mary Jeane, Barbara Jo. BSN, St. Louis U., 1974, MS in Nursing of Children, 1976; EdD, So. Ill. U., 1993. RN, Ill., Mo. Staff nurse St. Louis Children's Hosp., 1973-75; faculty allied health Lewis and Clark C.C., Godfrey, Ill., 1976-87, coord. assoc. deg. nursing program, 1987—2000. Pres. Am. Lung Assn. of Ill., Springfield, 1994-95. Mem. Coun. of Deans and Dirs. of Assoc. Deg. Nursing Programs (chair 1990-92), Nat. League for Nursing, Order Ea. Star, Sigma Theta Tau, Kappa Delta Pi. Presbyterian. Home: 226 Forest Ct Edwardsville IL 62025-5389 Office: Lewis & Clark C C 5800 Godfrey Rd Godfrey IL 62035-2426

SMITH, LINDA S., musician, educator; b. Topeka, Kans., Oct. 8, 1955; d. Wilbur Porter and Esther Nadine (Faith) Smith. MusB, Oklahoma City U., 1977; MusM, Eastman Sch. Music, 1979; postgrad., EAstman Sch. Music, 1979—81; degree preparatoire superieur, Conservatoire Nat. de Region, Paris, 1982. Organist Calvary Bapt. Ch., Topeka, 1965—73, Ctrl. Presbyn. Ch., Oklahoma City, 1973—77, 1st Reformed Ch., Rochester, NY, 1977—81, St. Michael's Ch., Paris, 1981—83, West Side Christian Ch., Topeka, 1983—; dir. music Accent Acad., Topeka, 1997—99. CEO, pres., founder Genesis Music Found., Inc., 1999—. Editor: Kids Music Jour., 1999—, composer more than 400 songs. Piano tchr. Salvation Army, Topeka, 1999. Mem.: Music Tchrs. Nat. Assn., N.E. Kans. Music Tchrs. Assn., Topeka Music Tchrs. Assn. (v.p. 2000—, publicist 1998—99, sec. 1999—2000, pres. 2001—). Home: 2416 SE Monroe Topeka KS 66605 E-mail: Smithlinmu@aol.com.

SMITH, LINDA WINES, government official; b. Charleston, W.Va., Dec. 27, 1949; BA, W.Va. U., 1971, MPA, 1973; postgrad., U. So. Calif., 2000—. With N.E. Regional Office, U.S. Parole Commn., Phila., 1976-79, with Ctrl. Office, Washington, 1979-91; with Fed. Correctional Inst., Fed. Bur. Prisons, Dept. Justice, Morgantown, W.Va., 1972-76, chief pub. affairs, info., policy and pub. affairs divsn. Washington, 1991—.

SMITH, LISA MARGARET, federal judge; b. Hamilton, NY, Apr. 25, 1955; d. Robert Virgil and Rosalind E. (Walls) S.; m. Joseph L. Hedrick, May 19, 1979. BA, Earlham Coll., 1977; JD, Duke U., 1980. Bar: N.Y. 1981, U.S. Dist. Ct. (ea. and so. dists.) N.Y. 1984, U.S. Ct. Appeals (2d cir.) 1984, U.S. Dist. Ct. (no. dist.) N.Y. 1985, U.S. Supreme Ct. 1985. Asst. dist. atty. Kings County Dist. Atty.'s Office, Bklyn., 1980-85; asst. atty. gen. NY Dept. of Law, Albany, NY, 1985-86; supervising sr. asst. dist. atty. Kings County Dist. Atty.'s Office, Bklyn., 1986-87; asst. US atty. So. Dist. NY, NYC, 1987—95; magistrate judge US Dist. Ct. (So. Dist.) NY, NYC, 1995—. Mem. ABA, N.Y. State Bar Assn. Democrat. Methodist. Office: US Courthouse Rm 428 300 Quarropas St White Plains NY 10601-4150

SMITH, LIZ (MARY ELIZABETH SMITH), columnist, newscaster; b. Ft. Worth, Feb. 2, 1923; d. Sloan and Sarah Elizabeth (McCall) S. B.J., U. Tex., 1948. Editor Dell Publns., N.Y.C., 1950-53; assoc. producer CBS Radio, 1953-55, NBC-TV, 1955-59; assoc. Cholly Knickerbocker newspaper column, N.Y.C., 1959-64; film critic Cosmpolitan mag., 1966; columnist Chgo. Tribune-N.Y. Daily News Syndicate (now Tribune Media Services), 1976-91; TV commentator WNBC-TV, N.Y.C., 1978-91; commentator Fox-TV, N.Y.C., 1991—; columnist Newsday, L.A. Times Syndicate, 1991—, Family Circle mag., 1993—; freelance mag. writer; commentator Gossip Show E! Entertainment, 1993—; columnist N.Y. Post, N.Y.C., 1995—, 1995—. Author: The Mother Book, 1978, Natural Blonde, 2000, Munich at Your Door, 2003, Dishing, 2005. Home and Office: 160 E 38th St New York NY 10016-2651

SMITH, LOIS ANN, real estate company executive; b. Chgo., Jan. 1, 1941; d. Alburn M. and Ruth A. (Beaver) Beaudoin; m. Dickson K. Smith, Mar. 24, 1962 (div. May 1982); children: Michelle D., Jeffrey D. BA, U. Utah, 1962; MBA, Marquette U., 1972. Asst. mgr. prodn. Northwestern Mut. Life Ins. Co., Milw., 1979—83, asst. mgr., asset mgr., 1983—88, assoc. dir. Asset Mgmt., 1988—89, dir. asset mgmt. Milw., 1990—95, dir. real estate equities, 1995—2003; ret., 2003. Cons. Girl Scouts Am., Milw., 1986, YWCA, Milw., 1986, bd. dirs., 1981-87; bd. dirs. YWCA, Planned Parenthood of Wis., 1998-2005, Present Music, Renaissance Theatres Mem. Internat. Coun. Shopping Ctrs., Profl. Dimensions, Beta Gamma Sigma. Unitarian Universalist. Home: 808 E Kilbourn Ave Milwaukee WI 53202-3462 Office: Northwestern Mut Life Ins Co 720 E Wisconsin Ave Milwaukee WI 53202-4703 E-mail: lolosmi@aol.com.

SMITH, LOIS ARLENE, actress, writer; b. Topeka, Kans., Nov. 3, 1930; d. William Oren and Carrie D. (Gottshalk) Humbert; m. Wesley Dale Smith, Nov. 5, 1948 (div. 1973); 1 child, Moon Elizabeth. Student, U. Wash., 1948-50; studied with Lee Strasberg, Actor's Studio, NYC, 1955—. Guest dir. Juilliard Sch., 1987; Clarence Ross fellow Am. Theater Wing at Eugene O'Neill Theater Ctr., 1983; mem. adv. panel program fund Pub. Broadcasting Service, 1981-82; hon. founder Harold Clurman Theatre Artists Fund, Ctr. for Arts, SUNY-Purchase, 1981 Author: play All There Is, 1982; debut in Time Out for Ginger, 1952; actress Broadway and off-Broadway prodns., 1952—; stage appearances include Theater of the Living Arts, Mark Taper Forum, Long Wharf Theater, Balt. Centerstage and Steppenwolf Theater Co.; appears on network and pub. TV programs; stage appearances include, The Young and the Beautiful, 1955, The Glass Menagerie, 1956, Blues for Mr. Charlie, 1964, Orpheus Descending, 1957, Miss Julie, 1966, Uncle Vanya, 1965, 69, The Iceman Cometh, 1973, Harry Outside, 1975, Hillbilly Women, 1979, 81, the Vienna Notes, 1985, The Stick Wife, April Snow, 1987, The Grapes of Wrath, 1988-89, 90, Measure for Measure, Beside Herself, 1989, Escape from Happiness, 1993, Buried Child, 1995-96, Defying Gravity, 1997, Impossible Marriage, 1998, Mrs. Warren's Profession, 1999, Give Me Your Answer, Do, 1999, Mother Courage, 2001, The Trip to Bountiful, 2005 (Lucille Lortel award, outstanding actress 2006, Outer Critics' Cir. award outstanding actress in a play 2006, OBIE award Village Voice 2006, Drama Desk award outstanding actress in a play, 2006, Kingsley-Evans award, 2006); films include East of Eden, 1955, Five Easy Pieces, 1970, Next Stop Greenwich Village, 1975, Resurrection, 1980, Green Card, 1990, Fried Green Tomatoes, 1991, Falling Down, 1993, How to Make an American Quilt, 1995, Dead Man Walking, 1995, Larger than Life, 1996, Twister, 1996, Tumbleweeds, 1998, Minority Report, 2002, The Laramie Project, 2002, Iron-Jawed Angels, 2004, Best Thief in the World, 2004, P.S., 2004, Sweet Land, 2005, Little Fugitive, 2006, Hollywoodland, 2006, Kill Shot, 2006. Named Best Supporting Actress for Five Easy Pieces, Nat. Soc. Film Critics, 1971; named to named to Filmdom's Famous Fives for East of Eden, Failm Daily mag., 1955; recipient Tony nominations, for Grapes of Wrath, 1990, Buried Child, 1996, Steppenwolf Ensemble Nat. Medal of Arts, 1998. Mem. SAG, AFTRA, Actors Equity Assn., Dramatists Guild, Actors Studio, Ensemble Studio Theater, Steppenwolf Theatre Co. Ensemble, Acad. Motion Picture Arts and Scis.

SMITH, LOIS C., university administrator; b. Hawthorne, N.J., Jan. 14, 1935; d. Frank Phillip and Clara (Bosland) Crisbacher; m. Jan. 29, 1960; children— Paul, Philip, Jennifer, Stephen. BA, Douglass Coll., 1955; MA, U. Ill., 1957; PhD, Rutgers U., 1960. Chemist Hoffmann-LaRoche, Inc., Nutley, N.J., 1959; prof. chemistry Russell Sage Coll., Troy, N.Y., 1964-80, Ithaca (N.Y.) Coll., 1980-85, provost, 1980-84; dean continuing edn. Utah Tech. Coll., Provo, 1985-87; assoc. v.p. acad. affairs Utah Valley Community Coll., Orem, 1987-88; v.p. for acad. affairs East Stroudsburg U., Pa., 1988—, provost Pa., 1989—. Mem. Am. Chem. Soc., Phi Beta Kappa, Sigma Xi. Republican. Mem. Lds Ch.

SMITH, LYNDA MITCHELL, science educator; b. St. Joseph, Mich., Apr. 8, 1959; d. Larry Burton and Marlene Burke Mitchell; m. Fredrick J. Smith, July 18, 1981; children: Rachael, Laura. BS in Secondary Edn., Ctrl. Mich. U., Mt. Pleasant, 1981; MS in Biology, Mich. State U., East Lansing, 1995. Sci. tchr. Lake Michigan Cath. H.S., St. Joseph, 1981—91, Lakeshore Pub. Sch., Stevensville, Mich., 1991—. Named R.J. Johnson Dist. Educator, Lakeshore Sch., 1997. Mem.: Nat. Consortium Specialized Secondary Schs. Math, Sci. and Tech. (bd. dirs. 2005—), Nat. Assn. Bioloby Tchrs. (Mich. Outstanding Biology Tchr. award 2002), Mich. Sci. Tchrs. Assn. (Tchr. of Yr. 2003). Avocations: reading, travel, hiking.

SMITH, MABEL HARGIS, retired secondary school educator, musician; b. Ruby, La., Sept. 29, 1917; d. Ildephonso Albinos Hargis and Stella Gertrude Baker; m. Thomas Leonard Smith, Jr., Dec. 29, 1950; 1 child, Susan Claire Smith McLaughlin. BA, La. Coll., 1938; MusM, Northwestern U., 1952. Tchr. Tioga H.S., La., 1938—75; pianist-organist children's choir Tioga First Bapt. Ch., Tioga, 1941—2002. Named Sr. Adult of Yr., First Bapt. Ch., 1989, Disting. Alumna, La. Coll., 1977; named one of Women of Century, Daily Town Talk, Alexandria, La., 1999; recipient Cmty. Svc. award, Matinee Music Club, 1953—54, Recognition for musical contbns., Curtis T. Hines Masonic Lodge, 1997. Mem.: La. Music Educators (Hall of Fame 1999), Music Educator's Nat. Conf., Delta Omicron Internat., Delta Kappa Gamma. Baptist. Avocations: sewing, cooking, reading, gardening. Home: 27 Purser Pineville LA 71360

SMITH, MABLE COGDELL, retired county official; d. Thurman V. and Rosa W. Cogdell; 1 child, Denise Smith Paye. Tax clk., asst. register of deeds Cumberland County, Fayetteville, 1981—96; ret., 1996. Chairperson Human Rels. Adv. Bd., Fayetteville, 1978. Chairperson, mem. Cumberland Cmty. Action, Fayetteville, 1967—77; elected ofcl. city coun. City of Fayetteville, 1999—2005; chairperson Cumberland County Dem. Party, Fayetteville, 1989—91; trustee, usher, Sunday sch. sec., choir mem., asst. clk. Falling Run Missionary Bapt. Ch. Recipient Invisible Giant award, So. Christian Leadership, Ala., 1995, Govs. Long Leaf Pine award, Gov. Jim Hunt, NC, 1996. Mem.: NOW, NAACP (life), NC Ret. Govtl. Employees Assn. Avocations: walking, singing. Home: 1606 Deep Creek Rd Fayetteville NC 28312

SMITH, MADELEINE T., medical products executive; BA, Northwestern U., 1973; MA, U. Rochester, 1978, PhD, 1984. Computer programmer Sears Roebuck and Co., 1974—75; tchg. asst. U. Rochester, 1977—80, rsch. asst., 1979—80; cons. Black and Regenstreif Assocs., 1977—78; adminstrv. asst. Bur. Budget and Efficiency Evaluation Unit, Rochester, NY, 1978—79; program evaluation asst., Dept. Mental Health State of Mo., 1982—84; sr. analyst, cons. DBS Corp., 1985—89; social legis. specialist congl. rsch. svc. Library Congress, 1989—94, 1998—2002, cons., 1995—98; mgr. Barents Group, LLC, 1994—95; staff mem. subcom. on health, ways and means com. U.S. Ho. of Reps., 2002—06; sr. v.p. payment and health care delivery Advanced Med. Tech. Assn., 2006—. Office: Advanced Med Tech Assn 1200 G St NW Ste 400 Washington DC 20005-3814 Office Phone: 202-783-8700. Office Fax: 202-783-8750.*

SMITH, MARCIA J., pastor; b. Columbus, Ohio, Apr. 7, 1958; d. William Wilson and Mary Anna Gibbs, adopted d. Bill and Anna Lee Sutton; m. George E. Smith, Sept. 27, 1975 (div. May 1985); children: Eugenia Marie, Todd Jefferson; m. George E. Smith, June 16, 2003. Degree in bus. mgmt., Ohio Dept. Transportation, 1988; degree in law, Scott Inst., 1989. Ministerial ordination Higher Ground Always Abounding Assemblies, 1994. Evangelist Higher Ground Always Abounding Assemblies, Columbus, Ohio, 1991—94; founder, pastor Living Water Chosen Generation, Circleville, Ohio, 1994—. Dean of students Prophecy Ctr., Columbus, 2001—, with, 2000—. Profl. football player Cleve. Fusion, 2002. Achievements include first only woman pastor in Columbus Ohio to also be a profl. football player. Avocations: computer games, fishing, photography, musician. Office: Living Water Bible Fellow Worldwide Chosen Gen Ch 5393 Sinclair Rd Columbus OH 43229

SMITH, MARGARET A., secondary school educator; b. Queens, NY, May 28, 1957; d. Harris McLain and Mary Davis Applewhite; m. Thomas John Smith; children: Russell, Elizabeth, Abigail, Nathanael. AAS in Physical Therapy Asst., N.Va. CC, Annandale, 1995; BS in Liberal Studies, Excelsoir Coll., 1998; MEd, Liberty U., 2005. Cert.; tchr., spll. edn. tchr., secondary sci. tchr. Va. Mid. and secondary phys. edn. tchr. Emmanuel Christian Sch., Manassas, Va., 1997—99, mid. phys. edn. and history tchr., 1999—2000, mid. sch. history and sci. tchr., 2000—03, secondary sci. tchr., 2004—; spl. edn. tchr. learning disabled Prince William County Pub. Sch., Prince William, Va., 2003—04. Office: Emmanuel Christian Sch 8302 Sprice St Manassas VA 20111

SMITH, MARGARET ANN, retired art educator; b. Floyd, Va., May 27, 1930; d. Floyd Patterson and Annie Mallie (William) Smith. BA in Art Edn., Radford Coll., 1951; M in Elem. Edn., U. Va., 1973. Cert. tchg. State of Va. Counselor Camp Carysbrook, Riner, Va., 1950—51; tchr. Marion (Va.) HS, 1951—52, Floyd (Va.) Elem. Sch., 1952—53; clerk Floyd Municipal Bldg., 1953—54; tchr. Check (Va.) HS, 1954—56, Patrick Henry Elem. Sch., Martinsville, Va., 1956—59, Draid Hills Sch., Martinsville, 1958—80, Albert Harris Mid. Sch., Martinsville, 1980—90; ret., 1990. Com. mem. State of Va., Lang. Art Dept., Richmond, Va., 1978—79. Exhibitions include Chains of Modern Man, 1973 (1st prize junk sculpture, 1973), Alaskan Triangle, 1982 (2d prize, 1982), In The Manner of Matisse, 1988. Named Vol. of Month, Piedmont Arts Assn.; recipient War Bond Poster Contest award, County of Floyd, Va., 1942, Purchase award, Foot of Hills Show, 1993, Pres. award, Lynwood Artists Show, 1994, Purchase award, Expressions Show, 2002. Mem.: DAR (treas. 2000—, former regent, vice regent), Martinsville Edn. Assn. (v.p., chmn. polit. action com.), Va. Edn. Assn. (chmn. dist. 7 polit. action com., bd. of dir.), Nat. Edn. Assn., Floyd Hist. Soc. (v.p. 2004—), Jacksonville Art and Design Ctr., Sawtooth Ctr. for Visual Design, Danville Fine Arts Mus., Piedmont Arts Assn. (bd. of dirs. sec. 1973—76, 1st prize 1973, 2d prize 1982, Hon. Mention 1988, award 2002, Purchase award 2003, Hon. Mention 1996, Pres.' award 1996, Purchase award 2001), Docent Guild of Piedmonts Arts Assn. (program com. 2005), Lynwood Artists of Piedmont Arts Assn., Va. Mus. of Fine Arts, Colonial Dames of 17th Century, Weavers Exchange (v.p.), United Daughters of the Confederacy (sec. 1998—2005), Delta Kappa Gamma (v.p. 1973). Democrat. Presbyterian. Avocations: weaving, watercolor painting, silver jewelry fabrication.

SMITH, MARGARET TAYLOR, volunteer; b. Roanoke Rapids, N.C., May 31, 1925; d. George Napoleon and Sarah Luella (Waller) T.; m. Sidney William Smith Jr., Aug. 15, 1947; children: Sarah Smith, Sidney William Smith III, Susan Smith, Amy Smith. BA in Sociology, Duke U., 1947. Chair emeritus bd. trustees Kresge Found., Troy, Mich., 1985—; chmn. Nat. Coun. for Women's Studies Duke U., NC, 1986—, chmn. Trinity Bd. Visitors NC, 1988-98; chair emeritus. Chmn. bd. visitors Wayne State U. Med. Sch., 1993; bd. dirs., mem. exec. com. Detroit Med. Ctr.; mem. bd. govs. Detroit Med. Ctr. Recipient the Merrill-Palmer award Wayne State U., Detroit, 1987, Zimmerman award Gtr. Detroit Health Coun., Athena award C. of C., 1998, Women of Achievement award Mich. Women's Fedn., 1999, disting. svc. award Wayne State U., 1999; named disting. alumna award Duke U. Mem. The Village Club, Internat. Women's Forum, Pi Beta Phi, Phi Beta Kappa. Methodist. E-mail: sidmyth@aol.com.

SMITH, MARGHERITA, writer, editor; b. Chgo., May 24, 1922; d. Henry Christian and Alicia (Koke) Steinhoff; m. Rufus Zartman Smith, June 26, 1943; children: Matthew Benjamin, Timothy Rufus. AB, Ill. Coll., 1943. Proofreader Editl. Experts, Inc., Alexandria, Va., 1974, mgr. proofreading divsn., 1978-79, mgr. publs. divsn., 1979-81, asst. to pres., 1980-81; freelance editor, cons. Annandale, Va., 1981-97. Instr. proofreading and copy editing, George Washington U., Washington, 1978-82; presenter workshops on proofreading for various profl. orgns., 1981-95. Author: (as Peggy Smith) Simplified Proofreading, 1980, Proofreading Manual and Reference Guide, 1981, Proofreading Workbook, 1981, The Proof Is In the Reading: A Comprehensive Guide to Staffing and Management of Typographic Proofreading, 1986, Mark My Words: Instructions and Practice in Proofreading, 1987, rev. edit., 1993, 98, 2003, 06, Letter Perfect: A Guide to Practical Proofreading, 1995; contbr. articles to revs. to various publs. Recipient Best Instrnl. Reporting award Newsletter Assn. Am., 1980, Disting. Achievement award for excellence in ednl. journalism Ednl. Press Assn. Am., 1981, Disting. Citizen award Ill. Coll., 1992. Avocation: writing. Home and Office: 9120 Belvoir Woods Pkwy Apt 110 Fort Belvoir VA 22060-2722 Office Phone: 703-360-1557. Personal E-mail: mssmss@pobox.com.

SMITH, MARGUERITE IRENE, gifted and talented educator; b. Duryea, Pa., Aug. 10, 1950; d. John Sylvester and Irene Anne Morris; m. James Michael Smith, June 9, 1973; children: Jennifer Lynn Smith Ruth, Kimberly Ann Smith Ikeler. BS in Secondary Edn., Bloomsburg U., 1972, EdM in Reading, 1995. Tchr. head start, home visitor Ctrl. Susquehanna Intermediate Unit 16, Montandon, Pa., 1987—91, intervention specialist, 1993; tchr. Spanish H.S. Lewisburg Area Sch. Dist., 1991—92, aide, 1992—94; tchr. reading Lewisburg Area Sch. Dist., Donald H. Eichhorn Mid. Sch., 1994—98, specialist reading, coord. gifted, 1998—. Mem. Am. Legion Post #841 Marching Band, Montandon; sec., treas. No. Deanery Coun. of Cath. Women, Sacred Heart Coun. of Cath. Women, Lewisburg, 1984—88; pres. Parish Coun. Sacred Heart, 1988—89; eucharistic min. Sacred Heart Jesus Ch., 1989—2003; asst. to Cath. chaplain Geisinger Med. Ctr., Danville, 1988—91. Mem.: AAUW (v.p. membership 1988—89), ASCD, Keystone State Reading Assn., Susquehanna Valley Reading Coun., Internat. Reading Assn., Buffalo Valley Singers (pres. 2001—02), Mifflinburg Buggy Mus. Roman Catholic. Avocations: French horn, singing, reading, needlecrafts, gardening. Office: Donald H Eichhorn Mid Sch 2057 Washington Ave Lewisburg PA 17837

SMITH, MARIA CARMEN, retired science educator; b. Santiago de Cuba, Cuba, Jan. 14, 1954; d. Mario Lao and Maria Sam; m. Dwight Hamilton Smith, Dec. 17, 1977; children: David Dwight, Cesar Allen. BS in Chemistry, Recinto U. Mayaguez, PR, 1977. Analytical chemist Winthrop Lab, Barceloneta, PR, 1977; chemistry tchr. Caribbean Sch., Ponce, PR, 1992—2005; ret., 2005. Nat. honor soc. advisor Caribbean Sch., 1992—98. Recipient Tchr. of Yr., Caribbean Sch., 1993, 1995. Mem.: Am. Chem. Soc. Home: 1680 Calle Marquesa Ponce PR Personal E-mail: smithlao54@yahoo.com.

SMITH, MARIA LYNN, school system administrator; b. Salisbury, Md., July 20, 1952; d. Benhamin Jones Sr. and Beulah Jones; children: Eric Wood, Brian. BS, U. Md., 1974; MEd, Bowie State U., 1990, ABD in Ednl. Leadership, 2003. Tchr. Prince George's County Pub. Schs., counselor, staff developer, regional instructional supr. Chair instructional chair Nicolas Orem Mid. Sch., Hyattsville, Md., 1992—94; curriculum writer Prince George's County Pub. Schs., Upper Marlboro, 1976—80. Sec. campaign Friends of Ken Johnson, Largo, Md., 1990—2000. Mem.: ASCD. Democrat. Baptist. Avocations: movies, reading, singing, cooking. Office: Prince George's County Pub Schs 10001 Ardwick/Archmore Rd Harwood MD 20776 E-mail: msmith1@pgcps.org.

SMITH, MARIE EDMONDS, real estate agent, property manager; b. Quapaw, Okla., Oct. 5, 1927; d. Thomas Joseph and Maud Ethel Edmonds; m. Robert Lee Smith, Aug. 14, 1966 (dec. 1983). Grad. vocat. nurse, Hoag Hosp., Costa Mesa, Calif., 1953; BA, Vanguard U., 1955; MS, U. Alaska, 1963. Lic. vocat. nurse, Calif.; cert. sci. tchr., Alaska. Nurse Calif. Dept. Nurses, Costa Mesa, 1952-60; tchr. Alaska Dept. Edn., Aniak and Anchorage, 1955-60; tchr. sci. Garden Grove (Calif.) Sch. Dist., 1960-87; property mgr. Huntington Beach, Calif., 1970—; agent Sterling Realtors, Huntington Beach, 1988—. Author: Ocean Biology, 1969. Bd. dirs., tchr. Newport Mesa Christian Ctr., Costa Mesa, 1983-2001; com. chmn. Garden Grove Unified Sch. Dist. PTA, 1977. NSF grantee, 1960-62. Mem. AAUW, Vanguard U. Alumnae Assn. Republican. Avocations: skin diving, travel. Home: 8311 Reilly Dr Huntington Beach CA 92646 Office: L8153 Brookhurst St Fountain Valley CA 92708

SMITH, MARIE F., lobbyist, small business owner, writer, retirement association executive; b. East St. Louis, Ill., Mar. 12, 1939; d. David and Christina Ford; m. Richard Stanley Smith, Dec. 13, 1986; stepchildren: Jeffrey, Reginald, Laurie Debrotz. BA, Fisk U., 1961. Dir. manpower mgmt. and orgn. planning Social Security Adminstrn.; realtor assoc., 1987—; small bus. owner, 1987—; freelance writer, 1987—; commr. Status of Women; chair Nat. Legis. Coun. AARP, Washington, spokesperson Women's Initiative Program, mem. audit and fin. com., 2000—02, mem. exec. dir. search com., 2000—02, treas. found. bd. dirs., 2000—02, pres. elect, 2002—04, pres., 2004—. Active Interfaith Vol. Caregivers; sec. bd. dirs. Maui Adult Day Care Ctr.; pres. bd. dirs. Maui Vol. Ctr. Named one of Am.'s 100 most influential African Am. leaders, Ebony mag., Most Influential Black Americans, 2006; recipient Woman of Excellence award, Commn. on the Status of Women, Circle of Women award, County Commn. on the Status of Women. Mem.: Zonta Internat., Nat. Assn. Ret. Fed. Employees (pres.), African Am. Heritage Found. Maui (pres.). Avocations: writing, travel, golf. Office: AARP 601 E St NW Rm A10-331 Washington DC 20049 E-mail: mfsmith@aarp.org.*

SMITH, MARJORIE, music educator, conductor; d. Robert and Evelyn Drick; m. Mark Smith, Oct. 1, 1994. BS in Music Edn., U. South Fla., 1972, MA in Music Edn., 1976. Cert. Nat. Bd. Profl. Tchrs., 2002. Elem. music tchr. Schwarzkopf Elem. Sch., Lutz, Fla., 1992—; condr. children's choir Gulf Coast Youth Choirs, Tampa, 1995—; music specialist The Spring of Tampa Bay, 2000—. Mentor tchr. Hillsborough Elem. Music Tchrs., Tampa, 2002—. Author: (series on active listening lessons) Listen and Learn, (elementary music series) Music Connections. Celebration choir singer Idlewild Bapt. Ch., Tampa, 1993—2005, pre-school ministry tchr. Recipient Hillsborough County Tchr. of Yr., Hillsborough County, 1989—90, Fla. Music Educator of Yr., Fla. Music Educator's Assn., 2001—02, Music Demonstration Sch. award, Fla. Dept. of Edn., 2001—. Mem.: Am. Orff Schulwerk Assn. (assoc.), Hillsborough County Elem. Music Educator's Coun. (assoc.), Fla. Elem. Music Educator's Assn. (assoc.), Fla. Music Educator's Assn. (assoc.), Am. Choral Dirs. Assn. (assoc.), Music Educator's Nat. Conf. (assoc.). Office: Schwarzkopf Elem Sch 18333 Calusa Trace Blvd Lutz FL 33558 Office Phone: 813-975-6945. Office Fax: 813-975-6948. Business E-Mail: margie.smith@sdhc.k12.fl.us.

SMITH, MARJORIE HAGANS, retired librarian; b. Atlanta, Nov. 24, 1936; d. Simon Peter and Erma Ruth (Miller) Hagans; m. Jimmie L. Smith, Dec. 26, 1959; children: Jimmie Marquette, Jocelyn Marcella, Jevon Marcel. BA, Clark Coll., 1959; MS in Libr. Sci., Atlanta U., 1969, specializing in libr. sci., 1980. Cataloger Livingstone Coll., Salisbury, N.C., 1961-62; tchr., librarian Berean Jr. Acad., Atlanta, 1965-68; media specialist, libr. Atlanta Bd. Edn., 1968—97; ret., 1997. Co-author: Ethnic Book Bibliography. Sec. West Manor PTA, Atlanta, 1976-77, corr. sec., 1977-78; sec. SW High Sch. Band Parents Club. Mem. Am. Library Assn., Ga. Library Assn., Metro Atlanta Library Assn., Atlanta Assn. Educators. Home: 3176 Kingsdale Dr SW Atlanta GA 30311-3639

SMITH, MARSHA ANN, literature and language educator; b. San Antonio, Jan. 20, 1956; d. Rogelio Guadalupe and Elsa Lopez Colunga; m. John C. Smith, July 25, 2003; m. David W. Millis (div.); children: David W. Millis Jr., Suzanne A. Millis. BS in Edn., U. Tex., Austin, 1978. Cert. secondary tchr. Tex. Exec. sec. Lamar Savings, Dallas, 1985—88; tchr. English Spruce H.S. Dallas Ind. Sch. Dist, 1988—90, Robstown H.S. Robstown Ind. Sch., 1990—95; dept. chair English A. Marco Smith H.S. Dallas Ind. Sch. Dist., 1995—2000, Sunset H.S., 2000—02, tchr. Reconnect, 2002—. Office: Sunset HS 2120 W Jefferson Blvd Dallas TX 75208 Office Phone: 972-502-1609.

SMITH, MARSHA H., state agency administrator, lawyer; b. Boise, Idaho, Mar. 24, 1950; d. Eugene F. and Joyce (Ross) Hatch; 2 children. BS in Biology/Edn., Idaho State U., 1973; MLS, Brigham Young U., 1975; JD, U. Wash., 1980. Bar: Idaho, U.S. Dist. Ct. Idaho, U.S. Ct. Appeals (9th cir.), U.S. Ct. Appeals (D.C. cir.). Dep. atty. gen. Bus./Consumer Protection Divsn., Boise, 1980-81, Idaho Pub. Utilities Commn., Boise, 1981-89, dir. policy and external rels., 1989-91, commr., 1991—, pres., 1991-95. Mem. Harvard Electricity Policy Group, Nat. Coun. on Electricity Policy; com. for regional electric power coop. Western Interstate Energy Bd., 1999-2005; dir. Western Electricity Coordinating Coun., 2002—; mem. adv. coun. Electric Power Rsch. Inst. Legis. dist. chair Ada County Democrats, Idaho, 1986-89. Mem. Nat. Assn. Regulatory Utility Commrs. (bd. dirs. 1999—, chair electricity com. 2000-03, 2nd v.p. 2005). Office: Idaho Pub Utilities Commn PO Box 83720 Boise ID 83720-0074 Office Phone: 208-334-3912.

SMITH, MARTHA A., academic administrator; b. Bradford, Pa., Aug. 31, 1948; BA, Slippery Rock State U., Pa., 1970; MEd, U. Hawaii, 1972; PhD, U. No. Colo., 1974. Dir. Hawaii Open program U. Hawaii, 1975—77; v.p. student affairs Coll. of St. Teresa, 1977—81; dean of students Dundalk CC, 1982—87, acting pres., 1987, pres., 1988—94, Anne Arundel CC, Arnold, Md., 1994—. Bd. dir. Inst. CC Devel. at Cornell U.; mem. Gov.'s Workforce Investment Bd., Md. Ednl. Coun., Nat. Edn. Commn. of the States; charter mem. Nat. Cmty. Coll. Adv. Bd. Campaign chair Anne Arundel County United Way, 1999; mem. adv bd. Chesapeake Innovation Ctr.; mem ACE Commn. on Adult Learning and Ednl. Credentials; bd. dirs. League for Innovation in the C.C., Leadership Anne Arundel, Greater Balt. Com. Named Bus. Leader of Yr., Anne Arundel Trade Coun., 1996—97, Power Elite, Daily Record, 2003; named one of Md.'s Top 100 Women, 1998, 2000, 2002; recipient First Women award, YWCA of Annapolis and Anne Arundel County, 1995, Tribute to Women in Industry award, YWCA, 1995, Cmty Trustee award, Leadership Anne Arundel, 2001, Inside the Field Nat. Leadership award, Nat. Coun. Continuing Edn., 2001, Fannie Lou Hamer award, Dr. Martin Luther King awards com., 2002, Kathleen Kennedy Townsend award of excellence, Women in Govt. Studies, 2001, Employer of the Yr., BWI Bus. Partnership, 2004. Mem.: Md.Assn. of CC (exec. com.). Office: Anne Arundel CC 101 College Pkwy Arnold MD 21012-2222 Office Phone: 410-777-1177. E-mail: masmith@aacc.edu.

SMITH, MARTHA ANN, retired special education educator; b. Wallis, Tex., May 2, 1938; foster d. Bert Randolph Abendroth Sr. and Ruby Faye Ayers; m. Homer Alvin Smith Jr., Aug. 26, 1959; children: Melinda Anne, Matthew Brian. BA in Speech and Dramatics, Okla. State U., 1961; MS in Spl. Edn., Ind. U., 1978. Cert. tchr. pre-sch. handicapped, Va., learning disabilities, Va., Ill., Dramatics and costume design, Va., speech and pub. speaking, Va., Mo. Substitute tchr. Prince Edward County Pub. Schs., Farmville, Va., 1969-75; tchr. handicapped presch. Buckingham Pub. Schs., Dillwyn, Va., 1979-85; tchr. learning disabilities Decatur (Ill.) Pub. Schs., 1985-86; tchr. early childhood spl. edn. Tuscola (Ill.) Pub. Schs., 1986-87; tchr. presch. handicap Portsmouth (Va.) Pub. Schs., 1989—2004; ret., 2004. Mem. Monroe County Parent Adv. Bd. for Exceptional Children, Bloomington, Ind., 1977-78; vol. regional rep. Devel. Disabilities Protection and Advocacy Office, Va., 1978-80. Deacon, mem. numerous coms. Coll. Prebyn. Ch., Hampden-Sydney, Va., elder Green Acres Presbyn. Ch. Grantee Portsmouth Sch. Found., Portsmouth Gen. Hosp., Portsmouth City Tchr. of Yr., 2001. Mem. Ill. Edn. Assn., Millikin Assn. Women, Kappa Kappa Iota. Avocations: quilting, reading. Home: 3608 Linnet Ln Portsmouth VA 23703-2261

SMITH, MARTHA LEE, lawyer; b. Austin, Tex., 1968; BA in English, cum laude, Washington & Lee U., 1990; JD, U. Tex., 1993. Bar: Tex. 1993. Ptnr., Banking/Fin. Andrews Kurth LLP, Houston, chmn. recruiting com., mem. policy com. Mem.: Houston Bar Assn., ABA, State Bar Tex. Office: Andrews Kurth LLP 600 Travis St Ste 4200 Houston TX 77002-3090 Office Phone: 713-220-4372. Office Fax: 713-238-7202. Business E-Mail: martysmith@andrewskurth.com.

SMITH, MARTHA VIRGINIA BARNES, retired elementary school educator; b. Camden, Ark., Oct. 12, 1940; d. William Victor and Lillian Louise (Givens) Barnes; m. Basil Loren Smith, Oct. 11, 1975; children: Jennifer Frost, Sean Barnes. BS in Edn., Ouachita Bapt. U., 1963; postgrad., Auburn U., 1974, Henderson State U., 1975. Cert. tchr., Mo. 2d and 1st grade tchr. Brevard County Schs., Titusville and Cocoa, Fla., 1963-65, 69-70; 1st grade tchr. Lakeside Sch. Dist., Hot Springs, Ark., 1965-66, Harmony Grove Sch., Camden, 1972-76; 1st and 5th grade tchr. Cumberland County Schs., Fayetteville, NC, 1966-69; kindergarten tchr. Pulaski County Schs., Ft. Leonard Wood, Mo., 1970-72; 3d grade tchr. Mountain Grove (Mo.) Schs., 1976-99; ret., 1999. Chmn. career ladder com. Mountain Grove Dist., 1991-99. Children's pastor 1st Bapt. Ch., Vanzant, Mo., 1984-88. Mem. NEA (pres.-elect Mountain Grove chpt. 1995-97, pres. Mountain Grove chpt. 1997-99), Kappa Kappa Iota. Avocation: antique and classic cars.

SMITH, MARY ELLEN, educational program facilitator; b. Provo, Utah, Aug. 2, 1954; d. Lloyd Coltrin McEwan and Barbara Jean Saxey; m. Samuel Adam Smith, Oct. 4, 1988; children: Brandy Lee Wilbur, Jeremy Mark Penrod. BS in Elem. Edn., So. Utah U., 1987; MA in Elem. Edn. Diverse Learners, U. Phoenix, Provo, Utah, 1998. Spl. edn./resource tchr. Jordan Sch. Dist., Eastmont Mid. Sch., Sandy, Utah, 1987—90; 6th grade tchr. Jordan Sch. Dist., Sprucewood Elem., Sandy, 1990—95, kindergarten tchr., 1995—98; clin. faculty assoc. Brigham Young U., Provo, Utah, 1998—2002; partnership facilitator Brigham Young U./Jordan Sch. Dist., Midvale, Utah, 2002—. Conf. co-chair Univ. Partnership, Sandy, 2005—. Judge State Geography Bee, Lehi, Utah, 1999—. Named Tchr. of Month, Jordan Edn. Assn., 1995; grantee, Jordan Edn. Found., 2005. Mem.: ASCD (assoc.), Internat. Reading Assn. (assoc.), Assn. Childhood Edn. Internat. (assoc.), Phi Delta Kappa (assoc.; constl. conv. rep. 2002—03). Mem. Lds Ch. Avocations: reading, travel, children and youth activities. Home: 675 N 1150 E Lehi UT 84043 Office: Copperview Elem 8449 S 150 W Midvale UT 84047 Office Phone: 801-565-7440. Office Fax: 801-302-4912. Personal E-mail: marysunshine73@hotmail.com. E-mail: mary.smith@jordan.k12.ut.us.

SMITH, MARY HILL, volunteer; b. Dallas, Jan. 14, 1943; d. Wendell Tennyson and Laura Leta (Massey) Hill; m. Andrew Jeptha Kincannon Smith, July 10, 1965; children: Emily Catherine Smith McGrath, Andrew III, Bradley Tennyson. BA with Volunteer Adminstrn. Cert., Metro. State U., 1987. Pres., mem. Raggedy Ann chpt. Children's Health Ctr. Assn., Mpls., 1972-83; pres. exec. com. Jr. League Mpls., 1973-84; dir. 75th Anniversary bd. Minn. Orchestral Assn., Mpls., 1977-78; dir. Guthrie Theater Bd., Mpls., 1979-83; bd. dirs. YWCA, 1981-82; pres. Wayzata (Minn.) Cmty. Edn. Bd., 1981-83; mem. adv. bd. N. Hennepin C.C., Brooklyn Center, Minn., 1982-84; chair, sec. Wayzata Sch. Bd., 1984-92; chair Minn. Women's Polit. Caucus, St. Paul, 1984-92; bd. dirs. Hennepin Tech. Coll., Plymouth, Minn., 1985-92; chair. bd. dirs. Art Ctr. Minn., Orono, 1985-92; mem. Metro. Coun., St. Paul, 1993—; chmn. Trans. Com., WestChamber Leadership Com., Minnetonka, 1994—98, 1999—, vice chmn., 1996—2002, sec., 2003—. Bd. mem. Hennepin County Libr. Found., 1996—99, Sheltering Arms Found., 1996—2002, pres., 1999—2000; del. Orono (Minn.) Rep. Party, 1992; mem. Twin State Ethical Practice Bd., St. Paul, 1986—91, Gov. Carlson's Re-election com., 1994—95, State Adv. Coun. on Metro Airports, St. Paul, 1995; bd. dirs. Minn. Women's Campaign Fund, 1996—2003, pres., 2000—02; mem. exec. com. U. Minn. Ctr. for Transp. Studies, 1995—2001, 2003—; bd. dirs. Met. State U. Found., St. Paul, 2000—; chair Met. Airports Commn. Joint Zoning Bd., 2001—04, Ripley Meml. Found., 2003—, rec. sec., 2005. Named Woman of the Yr., Women's Transp. Seminar, Minn., 2001; recipient Disting. Pub. Leadership award, U. Minn. Ctr. Transp. Studies, 2002. Republican. Episcopalian. Avocations: reading, gardening, cooking. Home: 515 Ferndale Rd N Wayzata MN 55391-1008 Office: Metro Commuter Services 560 6th Ave N Minneapolis MN 55411-4332 E-mail: maryhillsmith@aol.com, mary.smith@metc.state.mn.us.

SMITH, MARY LOUISE, real estate broker; b. Eldorado, Ill., May 29, 1935; d. Joseph Henry Smith and Opal Marie (Smith) Hungerford; m. David Lee Smith, June 18, 1961; children: Ricky Eugene, Brenda Sue Smith Millsap. Student, So. Ill. U., 1954-56, 57-58. Cert. substitute tchr., Mo.; cert. real estate broker, Mo. With acctg. dept. Cen. Hardware Co., St. Louis, 1958-61; mgr. income tax office Tax Teller Inc., St. Louis, 1967-69; substitute tchr. Mo., 1967—; mgr. income tax office H&R Block Co., St. Louis, 1970—76, tax preparer, 1992—2001; with acctg. dept. Weis Neumann Co., St. Louis, 1976-79; broker/salesperson Century 21 Neubauer Realty Inc., St. Louis, 1980-83, 88-90; sales assoc. John R. Green Realtor, Inc., St. Louis, 1983-85, Century 21 Action Properties, St. Louis, 1985-88, real estate broker/salesperson, 1986-88, Century 21 Neubauer Realty, Inc., St. Louis, 1988-90, L.K. Wood Realtors, 1992-96; security officer Reliance Security, 1995-97; tax preparer H&R Block Co., St. Louis, 1983, 1992—2001. Younger children's dir. Lafayette Park Bapt. Ch., St. Louis, 1981-95; children dir. Kingshwy. Bapt. Ch., 1999-01; vol. tax preparer for UAW Local 136 retirees, 2000-04. Mem. Am. Fedn. Tchrs., St. Louis Real Estate Bd. (equal rights com. 1986-88). Baptist. Avocation: writing children's stories.

SMITH, MARY SCOTT, elementary school and education educator; b. Fordyce, Ark., Sept. 16, 1926; d. Arthur and Jo Anna Scott; m. Joe Cephas Smith, Apr. 13, 1952; children: Marylyn Joe Anna Washington, Reginald Joseá. BS, Ark. Bapt. Coll., Little Rock, 1949; MA, U. Wis., Madison, 1952; postgrad., U. Ark., Fayetteville, 1966—70. Tchr. Childs' Sch. Dist., Banks, Ark., 1944—48; registrar Ark. Bapt. Coll., 1950—52, bus. mgr., 1952—54; tchr. Dallas County Tng. Sch., Fordyce, Ark., 1954—66, Little Rock Sch. Dist., 1966—86; asst. prof. edn. Ark. Bapt. Coll., 1986—93. Bd. dirs. Ark Tchrs. Credit Union, Little Rock, 1985—90. Mem.: Ark. Edn. Assn., Nat. Edn. Assn., Classroom Tchrs. Assn. (bldg. rep. 1974—80), Am. Retired Educator Assn. (chairperson 1997—), AAUW, Order of Eastern Star (state treas. 1979—, worthy matron), Fed. Womans' Club (pres. 1995—), Pi Lambda Theta, Zeta Phi Beta (Outstanding Educator 1996). Democrat. Baptist. Avocations: reading, travel, singing, crossword puzzles. Home: 2400 Howard St Little Rock AR 72206

SMITH, MARYA JEAN, writer; b. Youngstown, Ohio, Nov. 12, 1945; d. Cameron Reynolds and Jean Rose (Sause) Argetsinger; m. Arthur Beverly Smith Jr., Dec. 30, 1968 (div. 1996); children: Arthur Cameron, Sarah Reynolds. BA, Cornell U., 1967. Editorial asst. Seventeen Mag., N.Y.C., 1967-68; promotion writer U. Chgo. Press, 1968-70; asst. account exec. Drucilla Handy Co., Chgo., 1970-72; feature writer various mags. Chgo., 1972-74; freelance writer Cornell U., Ithaca, N.Y., 1975-76, lectr., 1976-77; playwright Playwrights' Ctr. Prodn., Chgo., 1978; humor columnist various jours. Chgo., 1979-81; freelance writer, 1982—. Author: Across the Creek, 1989, Winter-Broken, 1990, Danish edit., 1991, (play) Hire Power, 1998; contbr. poetry Primavera, Ariel VI and VIII, 1974, 87, 89; contbr. articles and essays to mags. and papers, 1984—. Vol. reading tutor Literacy Vols. Western Cook County, Oak Park, Ill., 1988-89, Oak Park Pub. Libr. Reading Program, 1990-94. Recipient 1st place for news writing Assoc. Ch. Press, 1986, poetry award Poets and Patrons, 1986, Triton Coll. Salute to Arts, 1987, 89, 2d Grand prize Mississippi Valley Poetry Contest, 2003. Mem. Authors Guild, Soc. Midland Authors, Am. Soc. Journalists and Authors. Roman Catholic.

SMITH, MARY-ANN TIRONE, writer; b. Hartford, Conn., Feb. 6, 1944; d. Maurice Paul and Florence Marie (Deslauriers) Tirone; m. Jere Patrick Smith, Sept. 2, 1968; children: Jene Maria, Jere Paul. BA, Cen. Conn. State U., 1965. Vol. Peace Corps, Cameroon, 1965-67; librarian Stamford (Conn.) Pub. Libraries, 1968-69; tchr. Norwalk (Conn.) pub. schs., 1968-72; instr. Fairfield (Conn.) U., 1986—. Author (novels): The Book of Phoebe, 1985, Lament for a Silver-Eyed Woman, 1987, The Port of Missing Men, 1989, Masters of Illusion: A Novel of the Connecticut Circus Fire, 1994, An American Killing, 1998, Love Her Madly, 2002, She's Not There, 2003, She Smiled Sweetly, 2004, (memoir) Girls of Tender Age, 2005; editor: Long Ridge Writers Group, 1990—; book critic N.Y. Times Book Rev., 1986—, Readers Digest Books, 1986-88. Active Nat. Abortion Rights, NYC, 1989—, MADD, NYC, 1987—, PTA, Ridgefield, Conn., 1977—; officer Ridgefield Little League, 1981—. Mem. PEN, The Authors Guild. Democrat. Avocations: swimming, hiking, strength training. Mailing: care Molly Friedrich Aaron Priest Lit Agy 708 Third Ave New York NY 10017

SMITH, MAURA ABELN, lawyer, paper company executive; b. Reading, Pa., Oct. 3, 1955; d. Henry Joseph and Lynn (Blashe) Abeln; children: Gwendolyn Casebeer, Karl Casebeer; m. Steven A. Smith, Dec. 18, 1999. AB, Vassar Coll., 1977; M Philosophy, Oxford U., 1979; JD, U. Miami, 1982. Bar: Fla. 1982, Ohio 1999. Assoc. Steel, Hector & Davis, Miami, 1982—87; ptnr. Baker & McKenzie, Miami, 1987-91; v.p., gen. counsel GE Co./Plastics, Pittsfield, Mass., 1991-98; sr. v.p., gen. counsel, sec. Owens Corning, Toledo, 1998-2000, chief restructuring officer, sr. v.p., gen. counsel, sec., 2000—03, bd. dirs.; sr. v.p., gen. counsel, sec., pub. affairs Internat. Paper, Memphis, 2003—. Rhodes scholar, Oxford, Eng., 1977-79; John M. Olin fellow in law and econs., Olin Found., 1979-82. Mem.: Phi Beta Kappa. Avocations: skiing, horseback riding, tennis, golf. Office: 6400 Poplar Ave Memphis TN 38197 Office Phone: 901-419-3829. E-mail: maura.abelnsmith@ipaper.com.

SMITH, MELODY KENNON, mathematics professor; b. Quonset Point, RI, Aug. 23, 1949; d. Robert Lawrence and Mary Louise Kennon; m. James Douglas Smith, Aug. 17, 1974; children: Myla Ann, Luke Townsend, Aaron Kennon. BS, Memphis State U., 1970, MS, 1972, EdD, 1976. Tchr. Immaculate Conception HS, Memphis, 1975—79; hs tchr. Harding Acad. Memphis, 1979—80; assoc. prof. math. Dyersburg State CC, Covington, Tenn., 1999—. Adj. instr. SW Tenn. CC, Memphis, 1981—99, Shelby State CC, Memphis, 1981—99, State Tech. Inst., Memphis, 1981—99, U. Memphis, 1981—99. Home: 9141 Delachmit Rd Millington TN 38053 Office: Dyersburg State Cmty Coll 3149 Hwy 51 S Covington TN 38019

SMITH, MERILYN ROBERTA, art educator; b. Tolley, N.D., July 24, 1933; d. Robert Coleman and Mathilda Marie (Staael) S. BA, Concordia Coll., Minn., 1953; MA, State U. of Iowa, Iowa City, 1956, MFA, 1966. Tchr. Badger (Minn.) High Sch., 1954; instr. in art Valley City (N.D.) State Tchrs. Coll., 1957, 58, U. Wis., Oshkosh, 1967, asst. prof. art, 1969, assoc. prof., 1977-91, prof., 1991-93, prof. emeritus, 1993—; represented by Miriam Perlman Gallery, Chgo. Counselor Luth. Student Ctr., U. Iowa, 1959-65, rsch. asst. in printmaking, 1960-65; owner, dir. James House Gallery, Oshkosh, 1972-77; dir. Allen Priebe Gallery, U. Wis., Oshkosh, 1975. Exhibited in group shows at N.W. Printmakers Internat., Seattle and Portland, Oreg., 1964, Ultimate Concerns 6th Nat. Exhbn., Athens, Ohio, 1965, 55th Nat. Exhbn., Springfield, Mass., 1974, 11th An. So. Tier Arts and Crafts, Corning, N.Y., 1974, Soc. of the Four Arts, Palm Beach, Fla., 1974, Appalachian Nat. Drawing Competition, Boone, N.C., 1975, Rutgers Nat. Drawing Exhbn., Camden, N.J., 1975, 8th and 9th Biennial Nat. Art Exhibit, Valley City, N.D., 1973, 75, Clary-Miner Gallery, Buffalo, 1988, Nat. Art Show, Redding, Calif., 1989, Internat. Printmaker, Buffalo, 1990, Westmoreland Nat. Juried Competition, Youngwood, Pa., 1990, Ariel Gallery, Soho, N.Y., 1990, Grand Prix de Paris Internat., Chapelle De La Sorbonne, Paris, 1990, Nat. Juried Exhbn., Rockford, Ill., 1991, Nat. Invitational Exhbn., Buffalo, 1991, East Coast Artists Nat. Invitational Art Exhbn., Havre de Grace, Md., 1991, Ariel Gallery, Soho, N.Y., 1991, N.Y. Art Expo, 1991, Milw. Art for AIDS Auction, 1991, 92, 94, Oshkosh 150, 2003, Three Perspectives Gallery, Plymouth, Wis., 2004. Mem. Winnebago Hist. Soc., Oshkosh, 1987—. Lutheran. Avocation: gardening. Home: 226 High Ave Oshkosh WI 54901-4734

SMITH, MICHELE, lawyer; b. Ogden, Utah, Feb. 12, 1955; d. Max S. and Grace B. (Gerstman) Smith. BA, SUNY, Buffalo, 1976; JD, U. Chgo., 1979. Law clk. U.S. Ct. Appeals (7th cir.), Chgo., 1979-81; asst. atty. no. dist. U.S. Atty's Office, Chgo., 1981-89; assoc. gen. counsel Internat. Truck and Engine Corp., Chgo., 1989-2001, gen. counsel engine group, 2001—. Mem. Am. Corp. Counsel Assn., Phi Beta Kappa. Office: Internat Truck and Engine Corp 4201 N Winfield Rd Warrenville IL 60555 E-mail: michele.smith@nav-international.com.

SMITH, MICHELLE SUN, psychologist; b. Balt., June 9, 1971; d. Nelson Cang and Laura Gamber Sun; m. Michael Timothy Smith, Nov. 22, 1997; children: Nolan Sean, Hailey Elizabeth. PhD, Calif. Sch. of Profl. Psychology, Berkeley, 1998. Lic. psychologist Md., 2001, N.Y., 1999. Staff psychologist, sr. instr. psychiatry U. Rochester, NY, 1999—2001; staff psychologist, coord. eating disorder svcs. Johns Hopkins U. Counseling Ctr., Balt., 2001—03; clin. psychologist MedPsych Assocs., Lutherville, Md., 2003—; asst. prof. U. Md. Dental Sch., Md., 2004—. V.p. program devel. bMed Techs., Rochester, NY, 2001—; cons. Ruxton Orthop. Assocs., Towson, Md., 2004—. Contbr. articles to profl. jours. Recipient Ruth C. Wylie prize in psychology, Goucher Coll., 1993; fellow, Okura Mental Health Leadership Found., 1997. Mem.: APA, Md. Psychol. Assn., Interdisciplinary Coun. of Learning Disorders, Psi Chi. Avocation: autism awareness & early intervention. Office: 2324 West Joppa Rd Ste 220 Lutherville MD 21093 Office Phone: 410-583-2623. Business E-Mail: msunsmith@comcast.net.

SMITH, MOLLY D., theater director; b. Yakima, Wash. d. Kay. BA, Cath. U.; MA in Theatre, Am. U., PhD (hon.), 2001. Founder Perserverance Theatre, Juneau, Alaska, 1979—98; artistic dir. Arena Stage, Washington, 1998—. Creative advisor Sundance Inst. New Plays; lit. advisor Banff Playwright's Colony, Canada; bd. dir. Theatre Comms. Group; panelist Ctr. Internat. Theatre Devel.; spkr. in field; prof. Arts, Music and Theatre Dept. Georgetown U.; judge Susan B. Blackburn Prize. Dir.: (plays). Named Artist of Yr., Alaska State Coun. Arts; named one of 100 Most Powerful Women, Washingtonian Mag., 2001; recipient Cmty. Leader award, U. Alaska Southeast. Office: Arena Stage 1101 6th St SW Washington DC 20024

SMITH, MONA RILEY, psychotherapist; b. Sioux City, Iowa, Nov. 17, 1943; d. John Collins and Mary Mc Hugh Riley; m. Scot Edward Smith II, June 17, 1967 (div. Dec. 1975). BA, U. Iowa, 1965; degree, Sorbonne U., Paris, 1964; MS, Calif. State U., Hayward, 1981. Lic. marriage, family, child psychotherapist Calif., cert. hypnotherapist. Founder and pres. Incest Help, Inc., Albany, Calif., 1976—; psychotherapist Psychol. Svcs. Dublin, Calif., 1985—. Lectr. and trainer Parents United Internat., San Jose and San Leandro, Calif., 1977—81, co-head of staff, San Leandro, 1980; life skills trainer, San Francisco, 1994—; grief counselor and post trauma stress trainer, San Francisco, 2001; lectr. in field. Co-founder A.I.M., San Francisco, 1980. Recipient reception and luncheon honor, Commonwealth Club, 1987, Women Helping Women awards, Soroptimist Internat. Ams., Inc., 1989. Mem.: St. Laurence Inst. Hypnotherapy (co-trainer), Calif. Assn. Family Therapists (Cert. of Appreciation 1983), Nat. Exch. Club (Spl. Svc. award 1987), Delta Gamma. Avocations: films, literature, visiting eldercare homes. Address: 2635 Mt Pleasant St Unit 103 Burlington IA 52601-2194

SMITH, MONIKA ROSE, researcher; b. Vienna, Mar. 23, 1941; 010d. August G. and Gertrude A. (Kleinman) Smith; m. Frank Gutowski (div. Aug. 1985); children: Leila, Robert, Nadja, Stephan. BA, Clarion U. Pa., 1976; MSW, Va. Commonwealth U., 1979; MS, Loyola Coll., Balt., 1994, CAS, 2000; PhD, Somerset U., Eng., 1995. Cert. Nat. Bd. Cert. Counselors. Coord. Family Crisis Ctr., Richmond, Va., 1977-78; dir., exec. dir. Employment Program Epilepsy Assn. Va., Richmond, 1979-81; coord. for brokerage Life Ins. Co. Va., Richmond, 1982-85; state dir. VOKAL, Richmond, 1985-86; assoc. Geerdes Internat. Inc., Richmond, 1986-93, Columbia, Md., 1993-98; cons. U.S. Dept. HHS, Washington, 1995—. Author: Enough, 1999, also articles. Bd. dirs. Va. Opera, Richmond, 1979-82, mem. adv. bd., 1982-85; apptd. by gov. to Va. Vols. Against Child Abuse, Richmond, 1977-79; apptd. by mayor to Richmond Youth Svc., 1980-85. Recipient Ralph Bunche citation UN, 1968; Am. Acad. Experts in Traumatic Stress fellow, 1998—. Mem. NASW, Am. Assn. Pastoral Counselors. Roman Catholic. Avocations: opera, symphony, museums. Home and Office: 378 Fleeton Point Cir Reedville VA 22539-4216

SMITH, NANCY ANGELYNN, federal agency administrator; b. Nashville, Mar. 28, 1950; d. Russell Monroe and Louise (Stephenson) Smith; m. Richard Christian Egan, Jan. 1, 1999. Student, Vanderbilt U., Nashville, 1966, Am. Internat. Acad. Europe, 1970; BA in Psychology with distinction, Rhodes Coll., Memphis, Tenn., 1972; MS with honors, U. Tenn., Knoxville, 1974; cert. in acctg., U. New Orleans, 1985, U. SC, Aiken, 1987. Contract adminstr. State of Tex. Dept. Health and Human Svcs., Houston, 1976-78; dept. Head Coop. Edn. Program No. Va. C.C., Annandale, 1978-81; revenue agt. IRS Dept. of Treasury, Nashville, 1988-99, mgr., adminstr. IRS, 1999—. Faculty rep. Faculty Senate No. Va. C.C., Annandale, 1979—81; comm. rep. IRS, 2002—. Author: numerous poems; contbr. articles to profl. jours. Vol. Voter Registration program, Denver, 1981—84, Adopt-a-Sch., Nashville, 1993—97, Tenn. State Guard; disaster relief coord. Ky. and Tenn., 1998—99, Red Cross Inst., 1976—78, VITA, 1990—95; vol. Congresswoman Pat Shroeder, Denver, 1981—84, Al Gore for Senate, Nashville, 1987—88, Federica Pena for Mayor, Denver, 1981—; bd. dirs. No. Va. C.C., Annandale, 1978—81. Mem.: DAR, Advancement Individual Minorities, Profl. Mgrs. Assn., Cert. Fraud Examiners Assn., Gamma Beta Phi, Alpha Omicron Pi (chmn. bd. dirs. Colo. chpt.), Omicron Nu (hon.), Phi Kappa Pi (hon.). Avocations: painting, skeet shooting, camping, historical battlefields, collecting edged weapons.

SMITH, NANCY HOHENDORF, sales executive, marketing professional; b. Detroit, Jan. 30, 1943; d. Donald Gerald and Lucille Marie (Kopp) Hohendorf; m. Richard Harold Smith, Aug. 21, 1978 (div. Jan. 1984). BA, U. Detroit, 1965; MA, Wayne State U., 1969. Customer rep. Xerox Corp., Detroit, 1965-67, mktg. rep. Univ. Microfilms subs. Ann Arbor, Mich., 1967-73, mktg. coord., 1973-74, mgr. dir. mktg., 1975-76, mgr. mktg. Can., 1976-77, major account mktg. exec. Hartford, Conn., 1978-79, New Haven, 1979-80, account exec. State of N.Y. N.Y.C., 1981, N.Y. region mgr. customer support Greenwich, Conn., 1982, N.Y. region sales ops. mgr., 1982, State of Ohio account exec. Columbus, 1983, new bus. sales mgr. Dayton, Ohio, 1983, major accounts sales mgr., 1984, info. systems sales and support mgr., quality specialist Detroit, 1985-87, new product launch mgr., ops. quality mgr., 1988, dist. mktg. mgr., 1989-92, major accounts sales mgr., 1992—; graphics arts industry sales mgr., 1998—; sales mgr. corp. accounts Sprint- Nextel Comms., Farmington Hills, Mich., 2005—. Reg. graphic arts industry cons. mgr., 1999. Mem. exec. leadership team Am. Heart Assn. Named to Outstanding Young Women of Am., 1968, Outstanding Bus. Woman, Dayton C. of C., 1984, Women's Inner Circle of Achievement, 1990. Mem. NAFE, Am. Mgmt. Assn., Am. Heart Assn. (mem. exec. leadership team 2005-06), Women's Econ. Club Detroit, Detroit Inst. Arts Founders' Soc., Detroit Hist. Soc., Detroit Hist. Soc., Greater Detroit C. of C. Republican. Roman Catholic. Avocations: interior decorating, reading, music, art. Home: 6462 West Oaks Dr West Bloomfield MI 48324-3269 Office Phone: 248-866-0601. Personal E-mail: nancyhsmith@sbcglobal.net.

SMITH, NANCY L., information technology executive; BS in Mgmt. and Orgnl. Behavior, U. San Francisco. Western regional sales mgr., nat. sales mgr. Electronic Arts, Redwood City, Calif., 1984, v.p. sales, 1988—93, sr. v.p. N.Am. sales and distbn., 1993—96, exec. v.p. N.Am. sales, 1996—98, exec. v.p., gen. mgr. N.AM. pub., 1998—. Office: Electronic Arts Inc 209 Redwood Shores Pkwy Redwood City CA 94065-1175

SMITH, NANCY LEE, communications official; b. Junction City, Kans., May 10, 1953; d. James Emerson and Donna Lee (Cousins) Smith. BA with hons., Stephens Coll., Columbia, Mo., 1975; MPA with hons., Am. U., 1990. Appt. sec. to chief of staff The White House, Washington, 1975; appt. sec. to sec. of def. Dept. Def., Washington, 1975-77; sec., office mgr. to various congressmen U.S. Ho. of Reps., Washington, 1977-83; Congl. specialist U.S. Geol. Survey, Washington, 1983-84; staff asst. to sec. of land and mineral mgmt. U.S. Dept. Interior, Washington, 1984-85; Congl. liaison officer Office of Surface Mining, Reclamation and Enforcement, Washington, 1985-95, comms. officer, 1995-2000; group mgr. legis. affairs Bur. of Land Mgmt., Washington, 2000—. Mem.: Pi Alpha Alpha, Alpha Lambda Delta. Avocations: white-water rafting, photography, reading, origami, exercise. Office: Bur of Land Mgmt 1849 C St NW 401L5 Washington DC 20240-0001

SMITH, NANCY WOOLVERTON, journalist, real estate agent, antique appraiser; b. San Antonio, July 31, 1947; d. Tillman Louis and Enid Maxine (Woolverton) Brown; 1 dau., Christina Elizabeth Woolverton Jones; m. William F. Pry II, Mar. 7, 1998 (div. July 31, 2003). Student, Ecole Nouvelle de la Suisse, Romande, Lausanne, Switzerland, 1962, Vanderbilt U., 1964; BA, So. Meth. U., 1968, postgrad., 1969-70. Cert. S.E. Paralegal Inst., Ancien Regime Christie's (London), antiques and residential contents. Tchr. spl. edn. Hot Springs Sch. Dist. (Ark.), 1970-72; reporter, soc. editor Dallas Morning News, 1974-82; soc./celebrity columnist Dallas Times Herald, 1982-91; owner, pub. High Society, Society Fax; bus. editor DFW Cmty. Newspapers divsn. Lionheart Newspapers Inc., Plano, Tex., 1999—2003; co-founder Decorative Arts Soc. Dallas, For Worth; pub. Decorative Arts Mag.; owner Personal Property Appraisal Svc., 2005—; realtor Keller Williams. Realtor, Ebby Halliday Realtors; stringer Washington Post, 1978; owner Nancy Smith Pub. Rels. Contbg. editor Ultra mag., Houston, 1981-82, Tex. Woman mag., Dallas, 1979-80, Profl. Woman mag., Dallas, 1979-80; mem. bd. advisors Ultra Mag., 1985—; columnist North Dallas People; appeared on TV series Jocelyn's Weekend, Sta. KDFI-TV, 1985. Bd. dirs. TACA arts support orgn., Dallas, 1980—, asst. chmn. custom auction, 1978-83; judge Miss Tex. USA Contest, 1984; bd. dirs. Am. Parkinson Disease Assn. (Dallas chpt.), mem. adv. bd. Cattle Baron's Ball Com., Dallas Symphony Debutante presentations; mem. bd. dirs. Dallas Opera Women's Bd., Northwood Inst. Women's Bd., Dallas Symphony Leauge; mem. Friends of Winston Churchill Meml. and libr., Dallas Theatre Ctr. Women's Guild, Childrens' Med. Ctr. Aux.; mem. women's com. Dallas Theatre Ctr.; hon. mem. Crystal Charity Ball Com.; mem. Cmty. Coun. Greater Dallas Cmty. Awareness Goals Com. Impact '88, 1985—; com. mem. Dallas Arboretum, Preservation Dallas; co-chmn. Multiple Sclerosis San Simeon Gala, 1988; celebrity co-chmn. Greer Garson Gala of Hope 1990-91; gala chmn. Greer Garson Gala of Hope for Am. Parkinson's Disease Assn., 1991-93; chmn. gala benefit Northwood U., 1994; co-chmn. star-studded stomp Mar. Dimes, 1994; mem. Femmes du Monde spl. activities com., 1999 luncheon com., com. Dallas Coun. World Affairs; bd. dirs. Dallas Ballet's Lone Star Adagio; pub. rels. vol. Habitat for Humanity, 2005. Mem.: DAR, Internat. Soc. Appraisers (accredited; antiques and residential contents cert.), Nat. Press Club, Soc. Profl. Journalists (v.p. coms. 1978—79), Mis Amis, Preservation Soc. Newport County, Decorative Arts Soc. Dallas/Ft. Worth (CEO, appraiser, co-founder), French Heritage Soc., Lancaster Hist. Soc., Daus. of Republic of Tex. (registrar 1972), Dallas So. Meml. Assn., Dallas County Heritage Soc. (bd. dirs.), Dallas Mus. Art League, Dallas Opera Guild, City of Plano Sister Cities Com., Flagler Mus., Dallas Glass Club, Rotary Club (gala chmn. North Tex. dist. 5810 2007, dist. 5810 gala chmn. 2007), Park Cities Rotary Club, Bent Tree Country Club, Dallas Knife and Fork Club, S'Amuser, Kermis Club, Coterie Club, Thalia Club, Rondo/Carrousel Club, The 500 Club (Dallas), Argyle Club (sec. 1983—84, 1st v.p. 2005—), Pub. Affairs Luncheon Club, Trippers Club, Tower Club. Home: 5727 Covehaven Dr Dallas TX 75252-4934 Office Phone: 214-625-1162. Personal E-mail: nancywoolvertonsmith@comcast.net, nancysmithpry@aol.com.

SMITH, NINA MARIE, music educator; d. Smith James Roy and Bernice Smith. MA in Edn., Washington U., Clayton, Mo., 1993; postgrad., Am. U., Washington. Music tchr. Alexandria City Pub. Schs., Va., 1995—. Leadership cohort George Mason U., Fairfax, Va., 2005—. Named one of Outstanding Young Women of Am., 1986; Parsons Blewett scholar, St. Louis Pub. Schs., 1990—93. Mem.: Alpha Kappa Delta, Tri Rho (assoc.), Delta Sigma Theta (life). Achievements include research in education and socialization of Black girls. Office Phone: 703-933-6300. Office Fax: 703-212-8465. E-mail: nsmith1@acps.k12.va.us.

SMITH, NONA COATES, academic administrator; b. West Grove, Pa., Apr. 1, 1942; d. John Truman and Elizabeth Zane (Trumbo) Coates; m. David Smith, Oct. 12, 1968 (div. May 1986); children: Kirth Ayrl, Del Kerry, Michael Sargent, Sherri Lee. BA, West Chester (Pa.) U., 1988; PhD, Temple U., 1998. Legal sec. Gawthrop & Greenwood, West Chester, 1968-73, MacElree, Gallagher, O'Donnell, West Chester, 1981-84; social sec. Mrs. John B. Hannum, Unionville, Pa., 1975-81; rsch. asst. West Chester U., 1984-88, cons., 1988; dir. sponsored rsch. Bryn Mawr (Pa.) Coll., 1989—, chair rsch./tchg. evaluation, 1993-95. Treas. Kennett Vol. Fire Co., Kennett Square, Pa., 1984-86; founding mem. Colls. of Liberal Arts-Sponsored Programs. Recipient Scholastic All-Am. award U.S. Achievement Acad., 1988, Rsch. award Truman Libr., 1992, Goldsmith Rsch. award Harvard U., 1993; fellow Truman Dissertation, 1997—. Fellow Phi Alpha Theta; mem. AAUW, Am. Hist. Assn., Soc. Historians of Am. Fgn. Rels., Nat. Coun. Univ. Rsch. Adminstrs. (mem. nat. conf. com. 1995-96). Republican. Presbyterian. Avocations: reading, gardening, travel, cultural events. Home: PO Box 239 Unionville PA 19375-0239 Office: Bryn Mawr Coll 101 N Merion Ave Bryn Mawr PA 19010-2859 Business E-Mail: nsmith@brynmawr.edu.

SMITH, PAMELA HYDE, ambassador; b. Tacoma, July 1945; m. Sidney G. Smith (dec.); 2 children. BA in Art History, Wellesley Coll., 1967. Joined US Info. Agy., 1975; asst. & cultural attaché US Embassy, Bucharest, 1976—77; special asst. to USIA Dir., 1977—81; cultural asst. US Embassy, Belgrade, 1982—86; dep. chief Acad. Exch. Program USIA, 1986—91; press attaché US Embassy, Jakarta, 1991—95; dir. Office Geog. Liaison U.S. Info. Agy., 1995—97; pub. affairs officer US Embassy, London, 1997—2001; U.S. amb. to Moldova Dept. State, 2001—.

SMITH, PAMELA LATRICE, school psychologist; b. Monroe, La., Jan. 11, 1975; d. Tommy Lee Smith and Lovely Marie Bams. BA, N.E. La. U., Monroe, 1997, MS, 1999. Cert. specialist in sch. psychology 2000, supr. sch. psychol. svcs. 2004. Sch. psychologist Westside Alternative Sch., Tallulah, La., 1999—2000; sch. psychologist Office Spl. Ednl. Svcs. Monroe City Schs., 2000—. Instr. psychology U. La., Monroe, 2002—; instr. Crisis Prevention Inst., Monroe, 2001. Founding mem. Wall of Tolerance, Montgomery, Ala., 2002—; mem. Southern Poverty Law Ctr., 2005—. Recipient Outstanding Academic Achievement, 1992—93; scholar La. Honor's Scholarship award, 1993. Mem.: AAUW, La. Sch. Psychol. Assn., So. Property Law Ctr., Cooking Club of Am. (life), Mortar Bd. Honor Soc., Phi Kappa Phi, Psi Chi Nat. Honor Soc., Delta Sigma Theta Sorority Inc. Democrat. Avocations: travel, reading, music, shopping. Home: 507 Auburn Ave Monroe LA 71201 Office: Divsn Student Support Svcs PO Box 4180 Monroe LA 71211 Personal E-mail: psmith@bayou.com.

SMITH, PAMELA ROSEVEAR, air transportation executive; b. Corvallis, Oreg., Nov. 26, 1953; BS, U. Oreg., 1977; MBA, valedictorian, C.W. Post Coll., L.I. U., 2003. V.p. inflight customer svc. Air America, L.A., 1984—90, MGM Grand Air, L.A., 1990—95; dir. sales Ogden Aviation, New York, 1995—; pres., owner Sader-Smith Mktg., Inc., 1995—; v.p. sales, the americas Pourshins P/C, New York, 1998—; v.p. sales, mem. mgmt. bd. Pourshins Inc., 2004—. Bd. dirs. Pourshins Mgmt., 2004—. Recipient Dean's Award for acad. Excellence, L.I. U., 2003. Mem.: Inflight Food Svc. Assn. (bd. dirs. 1999—), Greater L.I. Running Club, Kappa Alpha Theta (N.Y. Alumni chpt.) (v.p. 1998—99). Avocations: sports, travel, education, cooking, Japanese language. Office: 63 Tooker Ave Oyster Bay NY 11771 Office Phone: 516-624-0207. Personal E-mail: pampplc@optonline.net.

SMITH, PATRICIA CRAWFORD, elementary school educator; d. Billy Monroe and Jewel Ann Crawford; m. John William Smith, June 16, 1978; children: Stephanie D'Ann, Whitney Lauren. Degree in elem. edn., Athens State Coll., Ala., 1994; M in elem. edn., U. N.Ala., Florence, 2000, degree in adminstrv. leadership, 2006. Cert. elem. edn. K-6 Ala., 1994. Tchr. Athens City Sch., Ala., 1989—2006, amsti trainer, 2004—06. Named Tchr. of Yr., 2000—01. Mem.: Adminstrv. Leadership. Office: Athens Intermediate Sch 1916 Hwy 72 W Athens AL 35611 Office Phone: 256-230-2880.

SMITH, PATRICIA GRACE, federal official; b. Nov. 10, 1947; d. Douglas and Wilhelmina (Griffin) Jones; m. J. Clay Smith, Jr., June 25, 1983; children: Eugene Douglas, Stager Clay, Michelle L., Michael L. BA in English, Tuskegee Inst., 1968; postgrad., Auburn U., 1969-71, Harvard U., 1974, George Washington U., 1983, Fed. Exec. Inst., 1997. Cert. exec. mgmt. tng. devel. assignments Dept. Def., 1986, U.S. Senate Commerce Com., 1987. Instr. Tuskegee Inst., Ala., 1969-71; program mgr. Curber Assocs., Washington, 1971-73; dir. placement Nat. Assn. Broadcasters, Washington, 1973-74, dir. pub. affairs, 1974-77; assoc. prodr. Group W Broadcasting, Balt., 1977, prodr., 1977-78; dir. affiliate rels. and programming Sheridan Broadcasting Network, Crystal City, Va., 1978-80; dep. dir. policy, assoc. mng. dir. pub. info./reference svc. FCC, Washington, 1992-94, acting assoc. mng. dir., pub. info. and reference svcs., 1994—. Chief of staff office assoc. adminstr. for comml. space transp. FAA, U.S. Dept. Transp., 1994-96, dep. assoc. adminstr. for comml. space transp., 1996-97, acting assoc. adminstr., 1997, assoc. adminstr., 1998—. Vice-chmn. Nat. Conf. Black Lawyers Task Force on Comms., Washington, 1975-87; trustee, mem. exec. com., nominating com., youth adv. com. Nat. Urban League, 1976-81; mem. comms. com. Cancer Coordinating Coun., 1977-84; mem. Braintrust Subcom. on Children's Programming, Congl. Black Caucus, 1976—; mem. adv. bd. Black Arts Celebration, 1978-83; mem. NAACP; mem. journalism and comms. adv. coun. Auburn U., 1976-78; mem. Washington Urban League, 1985—; bd. dirs. Black Film Rev., 1989-91; mem. D.C. Commn. on Human Rights, 1986-88, chmn., 1988-91; mem. adv. coun. NIH, 1992-96; mem. bd. advisors The Salvation Army, 1993-2000. Named Outstanding Young Woman of Yr., Washington, 1975, 78; recipient Sustained Superior Performance award FCC, Washington, 1982-95, Disting. Alumnus award Tuskegee U., 1996, C. Alfred Anderson award, 2002. Mem. Women in Comms., Inc. (mem. nat. adv. com.), Broadcasters Club (bd. dirs. 1976-77), Lambda Iota Tau. Democrat. Baptist. Avocations: writing, swimming. Home: 4010 16th St NW Washington DC 20011-7002 Office: DOT/AST 800 Independence Ave SW Rm 331 Washington DC 20591-0001 Office Phone: 202-267-7793.

SMITH, PATRICIA LAURA, literature and language educator; b. East St. Louis, Ill., Dec. 6, 1950; d. Paul James Larsen and Laura Mae Anderson; m. Jon Dean Smith; children: Jende Kristi, Jairus Dathan, Jamin Laura Fisher, Janah Elise. BA in English, SE Mo. State U., Cape Girardeau, 1971, MA English, 1972, BS English, 1974; MA History, NW Mo. State U., Maryville, 1995; ABD, U. Mo. Kansas City, 2003. Cert. EMT Mo., 2003. Tchr. Benton H.S., St. Joseph, Mo., 1998—. Instr. Mo. We. State U., St. Joseph, 2000—. Office: Benton HS 5655 South 4th St Saint Joseph MO 64504 Home Fax: 816-324-3163.

SMITH, PATRICIA LYNNE, artist; b. Camden, NJ, Nov. 3, 1955; d. Thomas Patrick Connelly and Elizabeth Jean (Swope) Shober; m. William Clarence Smith, Nov. 30, 1973 (div. June 1980); children: Travis, Taryn. BA, Rutgers U., Camden, N.J., 1980; MFA, Rutgers U., New Brunswick, N.J., 1984. Adj. instr. Rutgers U., New Brunswick, NJ, 1983-84, Trenton State Coll., 1989-90. One-woman shows include Piezo Electric Gallery, N.Y.C., 1986, S.O.M.A. Gallery, Berlin, 1994, A.I.R. Gallery, N.Y.C., 1994, St. Peter's Ch., 1994, Croxhapox Gallery, Belgium, 1995, Black and Herron Gallery, N.Y.C., 1996, Studio Five Beekman, 1997, Front Room Gallery, Bklyn., 2006, others, exhibited in group shows at Art Exch. Fair, NYC, 1996—97, Bklyn. Mus. Art, 1997, Cornerhouse, Manchester, Eng., 1997, Gas Works, London, 1997, Gramercy Art Fair, 1997, Rotunda Gallery, 1997, Kunstlerhause, Vienna, 1998, Vassar Coll., Poughkeepsie, N.Y., 1998, Bard Coll., Rheinbeck, N.Y., 1998, Eyewash Gallery, Bklyn., 1994, 1999—2000, Project Space, Toronto, Can., 2001, Sideshow Gallery, Bklyn., 2001, Exit Art, N.Y.C., 2002, Voorkamer, Lier, Belgium, 2002, 2006, Art Ctr. Coll. Design, Pasadena, Calif., 2002, U. Md., College Park, 2003, Solway Jones Gallery, LA, 2003, Carlsbad Mus., N.Mex, 2003, Krasdale Gallery, N.Y., 2004, Stadt Mus., Lier, Belgium, 2004, Stedelijk Mus., Aalst, Belgium, 2004, 2006, Ill. State U., 2004, Gallery 32, London, 2004, Shore Inst. Contemporary Art, Long Branch, N.J., 2005, Pierogi, N.Y., 2005, Galerie In Situ, Aalst, Belgium, 2006, Weatherspoon Art Mus., Greensboro, NC, 2006. Recipient Stedman Purchase prize, Rutgers U., 1980; Garden State fellow, 1982—84, Exhbn. grantee, Artist's Space, 1988, 1990. E-mail: smithpl@frontiernet.net.

SMITH, PATRICIA M. (PATTI SMITH), state supreme court justice; married; 2 children. BA, Troy State U., 1973; JD, Jones Sch. of Law, 1976. Atty. Bell, Johnson and Medaris; asst. dist. atty. Shelby County, Ala., 1976—80, dist. judge Ala., 1980—2004; assoc. justice Ala. Supreme Ct., 2005—. Organized Shelby County's Children's Policy Council; mem. Governor's Commn. on Crime, Commn. on Future of Juvenile Justice System, Ala. Jud. System Study Commn. on Sentencing; chmn. Task Force on Dependency, Interagency Conference on Youth. Named Judge of the Yr., Nat. Ct. Appointed Special Advocates, 2001. Mem.: Ala. State Bar Assn., Shelby County Bar Assn., Ala. Assn. of Juvenile and Family Ct. Judges, Ala. Assn. of Dist. Ct. Judges. Office: Ala Supreme Ct 300 Dexter Ave Montgomery AL 36104 Office Phone: 205-670-6400.*

SMITH, PATSY JUANITA, financial executive; b. Dallas, Aug. 3, 1939; d. Roland Murl and Ruby Esther (Whiteside) Stephens; m. Jerry Arlin Kerby, June 7, 1957 (div. Nov. 1971); children: Timmy Wayne, Pamela Anita; m. Charles Albert Smith, June 17, 1977. Student, Ins. Inst., Dale Carnegie Sch. Claims adjuster Crum & Forster, Dallas, 1967—77, Atlantic Mut. Co., Dallas, 1978—79, Am. States Ins. Co., Dallas, 1979—81, Trinity Adjusting Co., Dallas, 1981—83; beauty cons. Mary Kay Cosmetics, Dallas, 1980—83, sales dir., 1983—84; loan officer Westco Fin. Svcs., Dallas, 1984—. Precinct chmn. Dem. Party, Dallas, 1981, election judge, 1981, 1982. Named Queen of Recruiting, 1982; recipient Claims Profl. of Yr. award, Ins. Women Dallas, 1998, Ins. Woman of Yr. award, 1999. Mem.: Am. Bus. Womans Assn., Dallas (Tex.) Claims Assn. (pres. 2002—03), Women's Coun. Realtors (state pub. rels. com.), Greater Dallas Bd. Realtors, Mortgage Bankers Assn., Am. Bus. Women Assn. (sec. 1980), Ins. Women of Dallas (pres. 1981—82, 2000—02, Claimswoman of Yr. 1979, 1980, Ins. Woman of Year 1998), Order Blue Goose. Home: 9922 Burnham Dr Dallas TX 75243-2412 E-mail: patjsmith1@sbcglobal.net.

SMITH, PAULETTE W., secondary school educator; d. Robert and Irene M. Weatherwax; m. Michael C. Smith; children: Ellen Elizabeth, Deborah Lindsay, Stephen Michael. BS, SUNY, Oneonta, 1970; MEd, Pa. State U., State College, 1972. Dale Carnegie instr. Ralph Nichols Group, Livonia, Mich., 1987—; social studies tchr. Clawson Pub. Sch., Mich., 1989—; mem. bias and sensitivity com., content com. Mich. Dept. Edn., Lansing, 2004—. Inspirational workshop leader, spkr.; presenter in field. Author: (travel guide) Las Vegas on the Cheap!. Speech contest coach Clawson- Troy Optimist Club, Clawson, Mich., 1994—2004; recycling coord. Abitibi Recycling, Clawson, 2004—. Mem.: NEA, Mich. Assn. Mid. Sch. Educators (conf. presenter), Mich. Edn. Assn., Clawson Edn. Assn. (rep. NEA 2001—, Mich. Edn. Assn. rep.), Pa. State Alumni Assn. (life). Avocation: travel. Home: 31072 Pickwick Ln Franklin MI 48025 Office: Clawson Pub Schs 150 John M Clawson MI 48017

SMITH, PHYLLIS ELIZABETH, community volunteer; b. Cedar Rapids, Iowa, Aug. 3, 1928; d. Elza Raymond and Wilma Grace (Walrath) Potter; m. Willard Gregg Smith, June 11, 1949; children: Willard Mark, Kevin, Sara Blair, Andrew, David. BA, U. Kans. City, 1950. Personnel asst. The Jones Store Co., Kansas City, Mo., 1950-51; purchasing clk. Hallmark Cards, Kansas City, Mo., 1950-52; ptnr., owner, cons. Doncaster Clothing, Overland Park, Kans., 1990—2000. Bd. dirs. Am. Cancer Soc., 1987-93, 79, 1987-93; trustee St. Paul Sch. Theology, Kansas City, 1983-2000; adv. bd. breast cancer ctr. U. Kans. Med. Ctr., 1993-97. Mem. PEO, Kappa Delta. Democrat. Methodist. Home: 5118 W 120th Ter Overland Park KS 66209-3550

SMITH, PRISCILLA R., social sciences educator; b. Pasadena, CA, Oct. 27, 1949; d. Aldric Joseph and Ruth Chenoweth Smith; m. H. Russell Searight, Sept. 10, 1977 (div. Nov. 1988). AB, Indiana U., 1972; MSW, Wash. U., 1980; PhD, Saint Louis U., 1988. A.C.S.W., L.C.S.W., L.S.W. Social worker Special Svcs. Co-op., Imperial, MO, 1984-86; adj. prof. St. Louis (Mo.) U., 1990-91; asst. prof. Southern Ill. U., Edwardsville, 1987-94; adj. prof. U. Kans., 1994-95; sch. social worker Wichita (Kans.) Pub. Schs., 1994-95; therapist Lakepoint Psychiatry, Wichita, KS, 1994-95; asst. prof. U. Akron, OH, 1995—. Family therapist Children's Ctr. Behavioral Devel., E. St. Louis, Ill., 1982-84; therapist Logos Sch. St. Louis, Mo., 1980-82; social worker Consol. Neighborhood Svcs., Inc., St. Louis, Mo, 1980, therapist MADD Belleville, Ill., 1991-93. Contbr. articles, chpts. to profl. publs. Adv. bd. mem. Salvation Army St. Louis, Mo., 1990-94; petitioner Dollars & Democracy Akron, Ohio, 1998-99, Akron Clean Money, 2000; bd. mem. Coop. Market, Akron, 1997-99; Econ. Justice and Empowerment bd. mem. Am. Friends Svc. Com. Akron, 1999-2003. Mem. Nat. Assn. Social Workers, Acad. Cert. Social Workers. Avocations: the arts, acting, volunteering. Office: Univ Akron Polsky Bldg Akron OH 44325-8001 E-mail: psmith@uakron.edu.

SMITH, REBECCA L., musician; b. Atlanta, July 14, 1961; d. Lowell E. and Lil R. Smith. EdS, Piedmont Coll., Demorest, Ga., 2006; B Music Edn., Brenau Coll., 1983; MA, U. Phoenix, 2004. Cert. tchr. Ga., 2006. Band dir. Towns County, 1984—86, Lumpkin County, 1986—87, Banks Co. Sch. Sys., Homer, Ga., 1987—2001; tchr. Buford (Ga.) H.S., 2001—. Mem.: NEA, Ga. Assn. Educators. Home: 5194 Clarks Br Rd Gainesville GA 30506 Office: Buford High School 2750 Sawnee Ave Buford GA 30518 Office Phone: 770-945-6768. Personal E-mail: beckysmith7@bellsouth.net.

SMITH, REBECCA MCCULLOCH, social sciences educator; b. Greensboro, N.C., Feb. 29, 1928; d. David Martin and Virginia Pearl (Woodburn) McCulloch; m. George Clarence Smith Jr., Mar. 30, 1945; 1 child, John Randolph. BS, Woman's Coll., U. N.C., 1947, MS, 1952; PhD, U. N.C., Greensboro, 1967; postgrad., Harvard U., 1989. Tchr. pub. schs., N.C., S.C.; instr. U. N.C., Greensboro, 1958—91, asst. prof. to prof. emeritus human devel./family studies. Dir. grad. program, 1975-82; ednl. cons. depts. edn. N.C., S.C., Ind., Ont., Man.; vis. prof. N.W. La. State U., 1965, 67, U. Wash., 1970, Hood Coll., 1976, 86. Author: Teaching About Family Relationships, 1975, Klemer's Marriage and Family Relationships, 2d edit., 1975, Resources for Teaching About Family Life Education, 1976, Family Matters: Concepts in Marriage and Personal Relationships, 1982; co-author: History of the School of Human Environmental Sciences: 1892-1992, 1992, assoc. editor Jour. Applied Family and Child Studies, 1980-90; ednl. cons. Current Life Studies, 1977-84. Bd. dirs. Sch. HES Alumni, 1997-99. Named Outstanding Alumna Sch. Home Econs., 1976; recipient Sperry award for service to families N.C. Family Life Coun., 1979. Mem. Nat. Coun. Family Rels. (exec. com. 1974-76, treas. 1987-89, Osborne award 1973), U. N.C. at Greensboro Alumni Assn. (chair membership recruitment com. 1994-96). Home: 1212 Ritters Lake Rd Greensboro NC 27406-7816 Office: U NC Dept Human Devel Sch Human Environ Scis Greensboro NC 27412-0001

SMITH, ROBERTA HAWKINS, plant physiologist; b. Tulare, Calif., May 3, 1945; d. William Brevard and Freda Lois Hawkins; m. James Willie Smith, Jr., Sept. 17, 1968; children: James Willie III, Christine. BS, U. Calif., Riverside, 1967, MS, 1968, PhD, 1970. Postdoctoral fellow dept. plant sci. Tex. A&M U., College Station, 1972-73; asst. prof. Sam Houston State U., Huntsville, 1973—74; asst. prof. dept. plant sci. Tex. A&M U., College Station, 1974-79, assoc. prof. dept. plant sci., 1979-85, prof. dept. soil and crop sci., 1985-89; Eugene Butler prof., 1989—; ret., 2002. Editor (editl. bd.): (sci. jour. review) In Vitro Cellular and Developmental Biology, 1991—96; editor: (jour.) Plant Physiology, 1994—; co-editor (assoc. editor): Journal Crop Science, 1995—. Fellow: Am. Soc. Agronomy; mem.: Soc. In Vitro Biology (chmn. plant divsn. 1983—86, pres. 1994—96), Faculty of Plant Physiology (chmn. 1987—89), Internat. Crops Rsch. Inst. Semi-Arid Tropics (bd. govs. 1989—95), Crop Sci. Soc. Am. (chmn. C-7 divsn. 1990—91). Avocations: horseback riding, gardening, reading. Home: 16475 FM 1159 Clarksville TX 75426-9710 Personal E-mail: bobbyjean@1starnet.com.

SMITH, ROBIN L., municipal official; b. Buffalo, July 22, 1955; d. Vernon Myron and Lois Alice (Kerr) Dean; m. Rickie J. Chilson, Nov. 24, 1973 (div. Dec. 1980); m. Garry Edward Smith, Apr. 17, 1982; children: Kevin Michael, Steven Garry. Asst. dir. civil def. Allegany County, Belmont, 1980; exec. sec. pers. CVC Products, Rochester, NY, 1980—81; inside sales Atlas Alloys, Rochester, NY, 1981—82; office mgr. Nasco Carpets & Rugs, Waverly, NY, 1992—99; twp. supr. Athens Twp., Pa., 1998—2003, twp. sec., 1999—, asst. permit officer, 2004—. Asst. emergency coord. Athens (Pa.) Township, 2004—. Mem., pres. Belmont Fireman's Aux., 1976—80; treas. Cmty. Chest, Belmont, 1977; EMT Amity Rescue Squad, Belmont, 1979—80; mem. mitigation com. Valley Project Impact, 1999—; sec. Athens Twp. Authority, 1999—2002, Satterlee Creek Watershed Assn., 2000—. Mem.: Pa. State Assn. Twp. Suprs. Democrat. Baptist. Avocations: knitting, crafts, family. Home: RD #1 Box 12-A Sayre PA 18840 Office: Athens Twp 184 Herrick Ave Sayre PA 18840

SMITH, ROBYN, secondary school educator; b. Huntsville, Ala., July 15, 1969; d. George Darrell and Elizabeth Ray; m. Paul M. Smith, Jan. 31, 1997; 1 child, Cameron Patricia Malone. BA, Stephen F. Austin State U., Nacogdoches, Tex., 1994. Cert. tchg. La. State Dept. Edn., 2002, Tex. Edn. Agy., 1994. Tchr. Huntington H.S., Tex., 1995—2000, Bolton H.S., Alexandria, La., 2000—01, Jena H.S., La., 2001—. Youth tchr. Midway Bapt. Ch., Jena, 2003. Mem.: Delta Kappa Gamma. R-Conservative. Baptist. Avocations: reading, travel, movies. Office: Jena High Sch PO Box 89 Jena LA 71342 Office Phone: 318-992-5195. Office Fax: 318-992-4797. Personal E-mail: rsmith@lasallepsb.com.

SMITH, RUTH HODGES, city clerk; b. Roanoke, Va., Jan. 15, 1931; d. James Elpherson and Ruth Elizabeth (Morgan) Hodges; m. Leon Menaclus Smith, June 18, 1978 (dec.); children: Dorothy Ruth Smith Swift, Marvis Frances Smith Mills. Student, Potomac State Coll., 1949-51. Cert. mcpl. clk. Va. Legal sec. Commonwealth Atty., Woodstock, Va., 1952-54; adminstrv. asst. Nelson Oil Corp., Mt. Jackson, Va., 1954-56; exec. sec., office mgr. Tidewater Va. Devel. Co., Norfolk, Va., 1956-72; from corp. sec. to purchasing agt. Nepratex Industries, Virginia Beach, Va., 1972-77; realtor, life agt. Real Estate/Ins., 1977—; city clk. City of Virginia Beach, 1978—. Sec.-treas. Hospice Virginia Beach, 1981-86; liaison, coord. Mayor's Sister City Commn., 1993—; mem. IIMC Acad. Advanced Edn., 1984-87, 87— (Quill award 1991); founder Z House shelter for battered spouses; state coord. Sister Cities Internat., 2005—. Mem. Internat. Mcpl. Clks. (bd. dirs. 1986-89, chair internat. com. 1989-91, chair year 2000 planning com. 1998—), Va. Mcpl. Clks. Assn. (pres. 1982-84, master mcpl. clk. 2000—, treas. 2002), Lifelong Acad. Advanced Edn., 1996—. Club: Pilot (officer 1960-72). Lodges: Zonta Internat. (dir. 1983-90), Order Eastern Star (worthy grand matron grand chpt. Va. 1993-94, worthy matron Westminster chpt. #99 2000—), Daus. of Nile, Shriners. Avocations: crafts, bicycling, skating, travel. Home: 1153 Belvoir Ln Virginia Beach VA 23464-6766 Office: City of Virginia Beach Room 281 City Hall Virginia Beach VA 23456

SMITH, SALLYE WRYE, librarian; b. Birmingham, Ala., Nov. 11, 1923; d. William Florin and Margaret (Howard) Wrye; m. Stuart Werner Smith, Sept. 20, 1947 (dec. June 1981); children: Carol Ann, Susan Patricia, Michael Christopher, Julie Lynn, Lori Kathleen. BA, U. Ala., 1945; MA, U. Denver, 1969. Psychometrician U.S. Army, Deshon Gen. Hosp., Butler, Pa., 1945-46, U.S. Vet. Adminstrn. Vocat. Guidance, U. Ala., Tuscaloosa, 1946; clin. psychologist U.S. Army, Walter Reed Gen. Hosp., Washington, 1946-47, U.S. Army, Fitzsimons Gen. Hosp., Denver, 1948, U.S. Vets. Adminstrn., Ft. Logan, Colo., 1948-50; head sci.-enging. libr. U. Denver, Colo., 1969-72; instr., reference libr. Penrose Libr., U. Denver, 1972-80, asst. prof., reference libr., 1980-90, interim dir., 1990-92, asst. prof. emerita, 1992—. Vis. prof. U. Denver Grad. Sch. Libr. Info. Mgmt., 1975-77, 83; info. broker Colo. Rschrs., Denver, 1979—; cons., presenter The Indsl. Info. Workshop Inst. de Investigaciones Tecnologicas, Bogota, Colombia, 1979, LIPI-DRI-PDIN workshop on R&D mgmt., Jakarta, Indonesia, 1982; mem. BRS User Adv. Bd., Latham, N.Y., 1983-86. Indexer: Statistical Abstract of Colorado 1976-77, 1977. Recipient Cert. of Recognition, Sigma Xi, U. Denver chpt., 1983. Mem. ALA, Spl. Libr. Assn., Colo. Assn. Librs., Phi Beta Kappa, Beta Phi Mu. Office: Colo Researchers PO Box 22779 Denver CO 80222-0779

SMITH, SARAH SEELIG, mathematics professor; b. El Paso, Tex., Apr. 22, 1967; d. William Lawrence and Catalina Seelig; m. Ferlin Andre Smith, June 15, 1999; 1 child, Dana; children: Christopher, Brandon. BS in Edn., U. Tex., El Paso, 1990. Tchr. El Paso Ind. Sch. Dist., 1991—. Roman Catholic. Avocation: reading. Home: 3308 Zircon Dr El Paso TX 79904 Office: Magoffin Mid Sch 4931 Hercules Ave El Paso TX 79904

SMITH, SARAH T., educational specialist; b. Lebanon, Pa., Feb. 18, 1970; d. Warren K.A. and Ann S. Thompson; m. Robert J. Smith Jr., Nov. 25, 1995; 1 child, Dylan. BA, Lebanon Valley Coll., Annville, Pa., 1992. Cert. reading specialist. Edn. dir. Kinder Care Learning, Lebanon, Pa., 1993—2000; reading specialist Derry Twp. Sch., Hershey, Pa., 2001—. Play dir. Hershey Mid. Sch., 2003—. Mem.: Internat. Reading Assn. Lutheran. Avocations: reading, travel. Office Phone: 717-531-2222. Business E-Mail: ssmith@hershey.k12.pa.us.

SMITH, SELMA MOIDEL, lawyer, composer; b. Warren, Ohio, Apr. 3, 1919; d. Louis and Mary (Oyer) Moidel; 1 child, Mark Lee. Student, UCLA, 1936-39, U. So. Calif. Law School, 1939-41; JD, Pacific Coast U., 1942. Bar: Calif. 1943, U.S. Dist. Ct. 1943, U.S. Supreme Ct. 1958. Gen. practice law; mem. firm Moidel, Moidel, Moidel & Smith, 1943—. Field dir. civilian adv. com. WAC, 1943—45; charter mem. nat. bd. Med. Coll. Pa. (formerly Woman's Med. Coll. Pa.), 1953—, mem. exec. bd., 1976—80, pres., 1980—82, chmn, past pres. com., 1990—92, spkr., honoree 50th anniversary gala, 2003. Author: A Century of Achievement: The National Association of Women Lawyers, 1998, The First Women Members of the ABA, 1999; composer: Espressivo-Four Piano Pieces (orchestral premiere, 1987, performance Nat. Mus. Women in the Arts, 1989), numerous works. Decorated La Orden del Merito Juan Pablo Duarte (Dominican Republic), 1956. Fellow Am. Bar Found. (life); mem. ASCAP, ABA (jr. bar. conf., 1946-52, activities com., 1948-49), Sr. Lawyers divsn. ABA (vice-chair editl. bd. Experience mag. 1997-99, chair arts com. 1998-99, chair editl. bd. Experience Mag. 1999-2001, exec. coun. 1999-2003, Experience mag. adv. bd. 2001—, nominating com. 2003-04, co-chair newsletter 2003-04, chair 2004-05, asst. sec., 2005—, Dist. Svc. award 2003-05), Calif. Supreme Ct. Hist. Soc. (bd. dirs. 2001—, programs and pubs. com., 2004—, State Bar program coord., 2006), Assn. Learning in Retirement Orgns. in West (pres. 1993-94, exec. com. 1994-95, Disting. Svc. award 1995), Plato Soc. UCLA (discussion leader Constitution Bicentennial Project 1985-87, moderator extension lecture series 1990, Toga editor 1990-93, sec. 1991-92, chmn. colloquium com. 1992-93, Exceptional Leadership award 1994), Euterpe Opera Club (chair auditions 1972, chair awards 1973-75, v.p. 1974-75), Docents L.A. Philharm. (press and pub. rels. 1972-75, cons. coord. 1973-75, v.p. 1973-83, chair Latin Am. Cmty. Rels., Recognition and Honor award, 1978), Calif. Fedn. Music Clubs (chair Am. music 1971-75, conv. chair 1972), Nat. Fedn. Music Clubs (vice-chair Western region 1973-78), Nat. Assn. Composers USA (dir. 1974-79, luncheon chair 1975), Calif. Pres. Coun. (1st v.p.), L.A. Bus. Women's Coun. (pres. 1952), Calif. Bus. Women's Coun. (dir. 1951), Coun. Bar Assns. L.A. County (charter sec. 1950), Inter-Am. Bar Assn., League of Ams. (dir.), Nat. Assn. Women Lawyers (regional dir. western states, Hawaii

1949-51, jud. adminstrn. com. 1960, nat. chair world peace through law com. 1966-67, liaison to ABA Sr. Lawyers Divsn. 1996—, chair bd. elections 1997-98, centennial com. 1997-99, chair com. unauthorized practice of law, social commn. UN, Lifetime Svc. award 1999, honoree annual Selma Moidel Smith law student writing competition 2005—), L.A. Lawyers Club (pub. defenders com. 1951), L.A. Bar Assn. (servicemen's legal aid com. 1944-45, psychopathic ct. com. 1948-53, Outstanding Svc. award 1993), State Bar Calif. (conf. com. on unauthorized practice of medicine 1964, Disting. Svc. award 1993), Women Lawyers Assn. LA (formerly So. Calif. Women Lawyers Assn.)(hon life; pres., 1947, 48, chair law day com. 1966, subject of oral hist. project 1986, 2001), Iota Tau Tau Legal Scholastic Soc. (1st prize 1942, dean L.A. 1947, supreme treas. 1959-62). Home: 5272 Lindley Ave Encino CA 91316-3518

SMITH, SHANNON DIANE, elementary school educator; b. Canton, Ohio, June 15, 1975; d. Kevin Wynn and Lillian Diane Marshall; m. Douglas Joseph Smith, June 19, 1999. BS in Edn. summa cum laude, Ohio U., Athens, 1997; MA in Edn. summa cum laude, Muskingum Coll., New Concord, Ohio, 2004. Tchr. New Philadelphia City Schs., Ohio, 1998—; online tchr. Quaker Digital Acad., New Philadelphia, Ohio, 2004—. Tchr. Collaborative Lang. and Literacy Instrnl. Project, Ohio, 2000—02; presenter in field. Mem. team Relay for Life, Dover, Ohio, 2005, 2006; mem. Little Theatre of Tuscarawas County, 2006. Recipient Educator of Yr. award, New Philadelphia City Schs., 2005—06. Mem.: Ohio Edn. Assn., Ladies Aux.-VFW (life), Phi Kappa Phi, Alpha Lambda Delta, Kappa Delta Pi, Golden Key Nat. Honor Soc. Democrat. Presbyterian. Avocations: dance, theater. Office: Welty Mid Sch 315 Fourth St NW New Philadelphia OH 44663 Office Phone: 330-364-0645. E-mail: smiths@npschools.org.

SMITH, SHARMAN BRIDGES, state librarian; b. Lambert, Miss. BS, Miss. U. for Women, Columbus, 1972; MLS, George Peabody Coll., Nashville, 1975. Head libr. Clinton (Miss.) Pub. Libr., 1972-74; asst. dir. Lincoln-Lawrence-Franklin Regional Libr., Brookhaven, Miss., 1975-77, dir., 1977-78; info. svcs. mgr. Miss. Libr. Commn., Jackson, 1978-87, asst. dir. libr. ops., 1987-89, dir. libr. svcs. div., 1989-92; state libr. State Libr. Iowa, Des Moines, 1992—2001; exec. dir. Miss. Libr. Commn., Jackson, Miss., 2001—. Recipient Iowa Computer Using Educators Friend of Edn. award, 1995, Iowa Libr. Assn. Mem. of Yr. award, 1996. Office: Miss Libr Commn 3881 Eastwood Dr Jackson MS 39211 Office Phone: 601-432-4039. Business E-Mail: sharman@mlc.lib.ms.us.

SMITH, SHARRON WILLIAMS, chemistry professor; b. Ashland, Ky., Apr. 3, 1941; d. James Archie and May (Waggoner) Williams; m. William Owen Smith, Jr., Aug. 16, 1964; children: Leslie Dyan, Kevin Andrew. BA, Transylvania U., 1963; PhD, U. Ky., 1975. Chemist Proctor & Gamble, Cin., 1963-64, NIH, Bethesda, Md., 1974-75; tchr. sci. Lexington (Ky.) Pub. Schs., Bethesda, Md., 1964-67; asst. prof. chemistry Hood Coll., Frederick, Md., 1975-81, assoc. prof., 1981-87, prof., 1987—, chair dept. chemistry and physics, 1982-86, 95-99, acting dean grad. sch., 1989-91, Whitaker prof. chemistry, 1993—. NDEA fellow, 1967-70, Beneficial-Hodson faculty fellow Hood Coll., 1984, 92; grantee Hood Coll. Bd. Assocs., 1981, 85, 91, NSF, 1986, 2001. Mem. AAAS, Am. Chem. Soc. (E. Emmet Reid award 2001), Mid.-Atlantic Assn. Liberal Arts and Chemistry Tchrs. (pres. 1984-85). Democrat. Office: Hood Coll Dept Chemistry Frederick MD 21701 Office Phone: 301-696-3675. E-mail: ssmith@hood.edu.

SMITH, SHEILA ROBERTSON, laboratory technician; b. Washington, Jan. 4, 1945; d. Philip Franklin and Emelyn Fiske Smith. AS, Penn Hall Coll., 1965. Hematology technician Duke U. Med. Ctr., Durham, NC, 1966—72, North Arundel Hosp., Glen Burnie, Md., 1972—73, Anne Arundel Med. Ctr., Annapolis, Md., 1973—93. Rep. on employees coun. Duke U. Med. Ctr., Durham, 1968—72. Bd. dirs. Smallwood Found., LaPlata, Md., 1997—. Mem.: Soc. for Restoration Port Tobacco (bd. dirs. 1997—), Charles County Hist. Soc., Charles County Garden Club. Republican. Episcopalian. Avocations: gardening, needlepoint, travel. Home: PO Box 365 Port Tobacco MD 20677-0365

SMITH, SHERRI LEE, law educator; b. Dec. 30, 1964; PhD, Fla. State U. Adj. prof. Fla. Agrl. and Mech. U., Tallahassee, 1992-94; asst. prof. U. South Fla., Ft. Myers, 1995-97; asst. prof., vis. faculty cons. for instrnl. tech. Fla. Gulf Coast U., Ft. Myers, 1995—. Assoc. editor: Encyclopedia of Women and Crime, 1997-99. Mem. edn. com. Lee County Domestic Violence Coun., Ft. Myers, 1995—; bd. dirs. girls initiative workgroup dist. 8 State of Fla., Ft. Myers, 1997—. Mem. U.S. Distance Learning Assn., Am. Acad. Criminal Justice, Am. Soc. Criminology, Fla. Coun. on Crime and Delinquincy.

SMITH, SHIRLEY, artist; b. Wichita, Kans., Apr. 17, 1929; d. Harold Marvin and Blanche Carrie (Alexander) S. BFA, Kans. State U., 1951; postgrad., Provincetown (Mass.) Workshop, 1962-66. One-woman shows include 55 Mercer St. Gallery, N.Y.C., 1973, Wichita Art Mus., Kanas, 1978, Stamford Mus. and Nature Ctr., Conn., 1987, Aaron Gallery, Washington, 1987, 1988, Joan Hodgell Gallery, Sarasota, Fla., 1987, Marianna Kistler Beach Mus. 38 Yr. Retrospective, Kans. State U., 1999—2000, John Jay Gallery, NYC, 2000, Represented in permanent collections Whitney Mus. Am. Art, Phoenix Art Mus., The Aldrich Mus. Contemporary Art, Ridgefield, Conn., Ulrich Mus., Wichita State U., Kans., Everson Mus., Syracuse, N.Y., U. Calif. Berkeley Art Mus., Marianna Kistler Beach Mus., Kans. State U., Manhattan, Telfair Mus. of Art, Savannah, Ga. Recipient Grumbacher Cash award for mixed media New Eng. Exhibition, Silvermine, Conn., 1967, Acad. Inst. award Am. Acad. Arts and Letters, N.Y.C., 1991, Richard Florsheim Art Funds grantee, 1998, Retrospective Opening grantee, 1999. Mem. Artist Equity. Democrat. Presbyterian. Home: 141 Wooster St New York NY 10012-3163

SMITH, SHIRLEY A., state legislator, state representative; b. 1950; 2 children. AA, Cuyahoga CC; BA, Cleve. State U. Rep. Ohio State Ho. Reps., Columbus, 1998—. Mem. banking, pensions and securities com. Ohio State Ho. Reps., mem. juvenile and family law com., mem. fin. instns., real estate and securities com., ranking minority mem. health com., mem. joint legis. com. on health care oversight. Vice chair Ohio Women's Dem. Caucus; chair region IX exec. com. Nat. Black Caucus of State Legislators; sec. Ohio Legis. Black Caucus; active Cuyahoga County Dem. Del. Mem.: NOW, Ohio Legis. Women's Caucus, Nat. Black Caucus of State Legis., Women in Govt., Emily's List. Democrat. Office: Ohio State House Reps 77 South High Street 10th Floor Columbus OH 43215-6111

SMITH, STEPHANIE RENAE, middle school educator; b. Atlanta, Apr. 25, 1969; d. Jasper and Dianna H. Smith; 1 child, Kare K. Greene. BS, Tuskegee U., Ala., 1993; MA, Ctrl. Mich. U., Mount Pleasant, 2002; EdS, Argosy U., Sarasota, Fla., 2003, EdD, 2006. Cert. tchr., gifted edn. and reading tchr. Ga. Tchr. grad. sci. lab. Atlanta Pub. Sch. Sys., 1997—99, 8th grade phys. sci. tchr., 1999—2004, after sch. tutor, 2000—, 8th grade earth sci. tchr., 2003—04, tutor 21st century aftersch. program, 2004—05, gifted/challenged tchr. L. Judson Price Mid. Sch., 2004—. Mem. exec. bd. Worthy's Christian Acad.; active sci. instr. Antioch Bapt. Ch. North, Atlanta, tchr. Adult Christian Class. Named Tchr. of Yr., W. L. Parks Mid. Sch., Atlanta, 2001—02. Mem.: NSTA, Ga. Assn. Gifted, Argosy U. Alumni Assn., Central Mich. Alumni Assn., Tuskegee Alumni Assn., Hall of Tolerance, Stopping Hate, Sheriff Assn. Home: 2805 Amber Forest Dr Douglasville GA 30135-7306 Personal E-mail: ksrs69@aol.com.

SMITH, STUART LEWIS, community volunteer; b. Richmond, Va., Mar. 28, 1936; d. John Minor Botts Lewis Jr. and Elise Davis Deyerle; m. Isaac Noyes Smith IV, Apr. 30, 1960; children: Isaac Noyes V, Minor Botts, Lyle Davis, Lisa Lewis. BA in Sociology, Hollins Coll., 1958. Home svc. caseworker ARC, Richmond, 1958—60; kindergarten tchr. First Presbyn. Ch. Sch., Charleston, W.Va., 1960—61; W.Va. sales assoc. Stanmar Homes, Sudbury, Mass., 1974—81; sales assoc., clothes cons. The Worth Collection, Charleston, 1992—2002. Mem. devel. com. Hollins Coll., Roanoke, Va., 1985—88; mem. legis. adv. com. Charleston Meml. Hosp., 1975—76; mem. budget and adv. coms. United Way, Charleston, 1965—77, resdl. chair, trustee, 1977—92; mem. legis. adv. com. Cmty. Coun.-Children's Svcs., Charleston, 1985—92; master gardener vol. pks. and hosp. planting Wonderful W.Va. Mag.; chairperson cmty. opportunity for study book and author series U. Charleston; contbr., local documentor Smithsonian Archive Am. Gardens; pks. commr., chair long range planning com. Kanawha County Pks. Sys., 1986—; mem. steering com. Kanawha County Cares for Youth, 2004—06; charter mem. Nat. Mus. Women in Arts; mem. collectors club Avanpata Mus.; mem. com. YWCA High Hopes, 2004—06; elder Kanawha United Presbyn. Ch., Charleston, 1968; past pres., bd. dirs. U. Charleston Builders, 1973, Kanawha Garden Club, Charleston, 1973, Briar Hills Garden Club, Charleston, 1969; bd. dirs. Sunrise Mus., 1973—80. Recipient award, W.Va. State Garden Club, 1985, 20 Yrs. of Bd. Svc. award, Ronald McDonald Ho., 2002. Mem.: Robert E. Lee Meml. Assn. (W.Va. dir., sec. to the bd. 1975, v.p. 2005—), Garden Club Am. (nat. vice chair, scholarship com. 1990, Outstanding Cmty. Leadership award 2000). Avocations: tennis, travel, gardening, fishing, reading. Home: 153 Abney Cir Charleston WV 25314

SMITH, SUE FRANCES, newspaper editor; b. Lockhart, Tex., July 4, 1940; d. Monroe John Baylor and Myrtle (Krause) Mueck; m. Michael Vogtel Smith, Apr. 20, 1963 (div. July 1977); 1 child, Jordan Meredith; m. Kirkland Gideon Smith, Apr. 17, 1999. B of Journalism, U. Tex., 1962. Feature writer, photographer Corpus Christi Caller Times, 1962-64; feature writer, editor Chgo. Tribune, 1964-76; features editor Dallas Times Herald, 1976-82; sales assoc. Bumpas Assocs., Dallas, 1982-83; asst. mng. editor for features Denver Post, 1983-84, assoc. editor, 1984-91; asst. mng. editor in charge of Sunday paper Dallas Morning News, 1991-94, asst. mng. editor Lifestyles, 1994-96, dep. mng. editor Lifestyles, 1996—2001, dep. mng. editor recruiting/devel., 2001—. Active Coun. Pres., 1993; juror Pulitzer Prize, 2002, 03. Mem. Am. Assn. Sunday and Feature Editors (pres. 1993), Newspaper Features Coun. (pres. 2002), Tex. AP Mng. Editors (pres. 1999-00, Jack Douglas award disting. svc. 2005, adv. com. conf. 2005, 06), Delta Gamma. Home: 6241 Park Meadow Ln Plano TX 75093-8863 Office: 508 Young St Dallas TX 75202-4893 E-mail: ssmith@dallasnews.com.

SMITH, SURVILLA MARIE, social services administrator, artist, poet; b. Chattanooga, Oct. 17, 1933; d. Charlie and LeGusta (Robinson) Prater; children: Charles, Calvin, Robin. Student, Mass. Bay C.C., Boston, 1965—66, Northeastern U., 1967-79, Mus. Sch. Fine Arts, 1989—91, U. Mass., 1989—96, Simmons Grad. Sch. Mgmt., 1995—97. Exec. sec. The Ecumenical Ctr., Roxbury, Mass., 1965-67, Roxbury Fedn. of Neighborhoods, 1965-68; bus. mgr. Coun. of Elders, Inc., Boston, 1969-72; exec. sec., asst. bookkeeper Edn. Renewal, Inc., Boston, 1972-73; asst. dir. METCO Inter-Dist. Transfer Inc., Roxbury, 1973-75; pupil pers. coord. Met. Coun. for Ednl. Opportunity, Roxbury, 1975-78; with Vis. Nurse Assn. of Boston, 1978-79; sec. Bay State Banner Newspaper, Roxbury, 1980; sr. outreach coord. Mattahunt Community Sch Sr. Outreach, Mattapan, Mass., 1989-95. Founder, chmn., CEO S.P.A.C.E. An Artistic Comty., Inc.; founder., chmn., CEO LED, 1995—. Exhibitions include Steppin Out, Boston, 1993, Treasured Legacy Gallery, 1995, Urban League Ea. Mass., Roxbury, 1997—98, Codman Sq. Br. Libr., Dorchester, Mass., 1997—2002, New Art N.Eng. Libr. Arts Ctr., Newport, N.H., 1997, Dorchester Hist. Soc., 1996, 1997, 1998, Dorchester Art Assn., Boston, 1996, 1997, 1998, Open Studios, South End, Mass., 1998, Roxbury Cmty. Coll. Media Arts Ctr., 1998, Reggie Lewis Ctr., Roxbury, 1998, Rothschild Gallery, Radcliffe Coll., Cambridge, Mass., 1998, Boston City Hall Scollay Sq. Gallery, Boston, 1998, 1999, 2000, Pan African Historical Mus., Springfield, Mass., 1999, Grove Hall Br. Libr., Roxbury, 2000, Egleston Br. Libr., Mass., 2000, Parker Hill Br. Libr., Roxbury, 2000, South End (Mass.) Open Studios, 2000, CVS Windows-The Mall at Grove Hall, Roxbury, 2002, Codman Sq. Br. Libr., Dorchester, 2004—05, CVS Window Porter Sq., Cambridge, 2002—05, Macy's Windows, 2000, 1999, Codman Sq. Libr., Mass., 2004—, North River Cmty. Ch., 2006—, Boston Bus. Assistance Ctr., Roxbury, Mass., 2005—, Represented in permanent collections N.Eng. Zoo, pvt. collections, artwork published, Art New Eng., Art News, ArtsMedia, Art & Antiques; author: (poetry book) Days, Years to Remember: A Collection of Poems, 2003. Active Women's Caucus Art, Boston chpt., Coalition Black Women, Nat. Coun. Negro Women; chmn. health campaign Grove Hall/Franklin Park AARP, Boston, 1990—; vol. Experiment in Internat. Living, Mass., Mattapan/Franklin Park Jubilee Task Force, WGBH, Am. Cancer Soc.; artwork auction donor various orgns. Grantee, New Eng. Found. for the Arts; scholar, U. Mass., Amherst, 1999; Americans for the Arts scholar, 1999. Mem.: PEN N.E., NAACP, Boston Afro-Am. Artists, Nat. Poetry Soc., South End Artists, Mass. Advocates for the Arts, Scis. & Humanities, Dorchester Art Assn., Am. for the Arts, Nat. Writer's Assn., Poetry Soc. Am. Avocations: writing, painting, reading. Home: 4 Wentworth St Dorchester MA 02124-3517 Office Phone: 617-436-1063. E-mail: 1space@gte.net, 1space@verizon.net.

SMITH, SUSAN, bank executive; b. 1961; Exec. Boatmen's Ark. Bank (now Regions Bank); sr. exec. v.p., CFO Met. Nat. Bank. Chmn. Arkansas Commitment Scholarship Program. Named one of 25 Most Powerful Women in Banking, Fortune Mag., 2004. Office: Metropolitan National Bank 425 W Capitol Little Rock AR 72201 Office Phone: 501-377-7600. Office Fax: 501-377-7608.

SMITH, SUSAN CARLTON, artist, illustrator; b. Athens, Ga., June 30, 1923; d. Edward Inglis and Hart Wylie Smith; m. George Stanley Terence Cavanagh, Oct. 25, 1977. BS in Zoology, U. Ga., 1947, MFA in Drama, 1961. Sci. illustrator US Pub. Health Communicable Disease Ctr., Atlanta, 1952; artist archeology dept. U. Ga., 1953—, costume designer, speech tchr., drama dept, 1956—61, sci. illustrator biology dept., 1964—65; conservator, asst. curator Med. Ctr. Libr., Duke U., Durham, NC, 1967—90; biological and botanical illustrator Duke U., 1967—90; botanical illustrator U. NC, 1967—90. Lectr. in field. Illustrator Jack & Jill Magazine, 1960—62, (book) Plant Variations and Classification, 1967, Wildflowers of NC, 1968, A Child's Book of Flowers, 1976, A Book of Flowers, 1987, illustrator, text contr. (book) Lady Bug, Lady Bug, 1969 (Top 50 Best Children's Books of Yr., 1969), (Book) Hey Bug!, and Other Poems About Little Things, 1972 (Printers Industries of Am. award), 3 Famous Artists-Naturalists of the Colonial Period, John Abbot, William Bartram, Mark Catesby- A Coloring Book for all Ages, 2002; contbr. various sci. jours.; exhibitions include eleventh Internat. Botanical Congress, Seattle, 1969, Internat. Exhbn. Botanical Art, Johannesburg, South Africa, Second Internat. Exhbn. Twentieth Cent. Botanical Art and Illustration, Carnegie-Mellon U., 1968—69, Duke U. Mus. Art, U. Ga. Mus. Art, State Botanical Garden, Ga. Vol. U. NC Botanical Gardens, 1967—89, State Botanical Gardens, Ga., 1989—2006. Mem.: Trent Soc. History of Med., Duke U., Am. Assn. History of Med., Nat. Soc. Colonial Dames, Jr. Ladies Garden Club, Garden Club Am. (Eloise Payne Lequer medal 1989), Puppeteers of Am., Chi Omega, Phi Kappa Phi. Episcopalian. Avocation: sculpting. Home: 755 EPPS Bridge Pky #404 Athens GA 30606 Address: 755 Eppa Bridge Pkwy Cottage 404 Athens GA 30606 Personal E-mail: gotcavan@regis.net.

SMITH, SUSAN ELIZABETH, guidance director; b. Phila., Mar. 24, 1950; d. E. Burke Hogue and Janet Coffin Hogue Ebert; m. J. Russell Smith, June 17, 1972 (div. June 1989); 1 child, Drew Russell. BS in Elem. Edn., E. Stroudsburg Coll., 1972; MEd in Counseling, U. Okla., 1974, postgrad., 1976-77, Trenton State Coll., 1989-90; EdM in Devel. Disabilities, Rutgers U., 1992, postgrad., 1994—. Cert. elem. tchr., N.C.; cert. elem. tchr., early childhood edn. tchr., guidance and counseling, Okla.; cert. elem. tchr., guidance and counseling, tchr. of handicapped, psychology tchr., supr. instrn., dir. student pers. svcs., N.J. Elem. tchr. Morton Elem. Sch. Onslow County Schs., Jacksonville, NC, 1971-72; instr. U. Isfahan, Iran, 1974-76; guidance counselor Moore (Okla.) Pub. Schs., 1976-77; counselor Johnstone Tng. Ctr. N.J. Divsn. Devel. Disabilities, Bordentown, 1988-90; spl. edn. tchr. Willingboro (N.J.) Schs., 1990-91; guidance counselor Haledon (N.J.) Pub. Schs., 1991-92; spl. edn. adj. tchr. Gateway Sch., Carteret, NJ, 1991-93; guidance counselor Bloomfield (N.J.) Pub. Schs., 1992-94; dir. guidance Somerville (N.J.) Pub. Schs., 1994-95. Adj. prof. in spl. edn. Essex County (N.J.) Coll., 1994; guidance Ft. Lee (N.J.) Schs., 1995-2001; guidance dir. Bogota Schs., N.J., 2001-02, Closter Schs., Closter, N.J., 2002—; cons., seminar and workshop presenter on behavior mgmt., parenting skills, and behavior modification techniques; cons. N.J. Fragile X Assn. Author: Motivational Awards for ESL Students, 1993, Parent Contracts to Improve School Behaviors, 1996; contbr. articles to profl. jours. Leader Boy Scouts Am., Oklahoma City, 1983-87, com. chmn., Redmond, Wash., 1987-88. Recipient Rsch. award ERIC/CAPS, 1992, Svc. award N.J. Fragile X Assn., 1993. Mem. ACA, Am. Sch. Counselor Assn. (grantee 1992), N.J. Counseling Assn., N.J. Sch. Counseling Assn., Assn. for Multicultural Counseling and Devel., AAUW, Assn. for Counselor Edn. and Supervision, N.J. Assn. for Counselor Edn. and Supervision, N.J. Prins. and Suprs. Assn., Nat. Assn. Coll. Admissions Counselors (grantee 1995), Alpha Omicron Pi. Episcopalian. Home: 916 Lincoln Pl Teaneck NJ 07666-2572

SMITH, SUSAN K., musician, educator; d. Richard Allen and Doree Ann Smith; m. Joseph William Stegemann, Dec. 27, 2003. MusB, U. Kans., 1980; MusM, U North Tex., 1983. Trombone instr., tchg. fellow U. North Tex., 1980—83; trombone instr. Mcneese State U., 1984—85, Notre Dame, 1992—93, U. Tenn., Chattanooga, Austin Peay State U., 1994—; asst. prin., second trombonist Nashville Symphony Orch., 1994—. Musician: Balt. Symphony, Fla. Orchestra, Grant Park Symphony, Springfield Symphony, South Bend Symphony, various symphonies. Mem.: Music Educators Nat. Conv., Internat. Trombone Assoc. (faculty, soloist clinician 1997, coll. tchrs. trombone choir 1998, faculty, soloist clinician 2000, Frank Smith Solo award 1982).

SMITH, SUSAN K., director; b. Dayton, Ohio, Jan. 28, 1959; d. Thomas Hugh Westfall and Carol Ann Lorton; m. Robert H. Smith, Jr., June 27, 1992; stepchildren: Matthew, Marcus; 1 child from previous marriage, Jennifer Bitzer. BA in Comm., Wright State U., Dayton, Ohio, 1984. Cataloguer Wright State U., Dayton, Ohio, 1980—92, dir. devel. rsch., 1992—95, assoc. dir. corp. and found. rels., 1995—97, dir. ann. giving, 1997—98, exec. dir. alumni rels., 1998—. Grad. Leadership Dayton, Ohio, 2004; dir. Clothes That Work, 2004—. Mem.: Ohio Alumni Dirs. (pres. 2002), Coun. Advancement and Support of Edn. Independent. Methodist. Avocations: reading, golf. Office: Exec Dir Alumni Rels Wright State U 3640 Col Glenn Hwy Dayton OH 45435-0002 Office Phone: 937-775-2536.

SMITH, SUSAN LOUISE, special educator; b. Council Bluffs, Iowa, Apr. 22; d. Louis Edgar and Mary (Maughan) Sahn; children: Mary E. Coons, Stephen F. II. BS Edn., U. Nebr., Lincoln; MA Edn., Concordia U., Seward, Nebr., 1993. Cert. tchr. Nebr. Tchr. Idaho Falls Schs., 1962—66, Dist. #66, Omaha, 1966—67; reading specialist, head tchr. Seward Pub. Schs., 1968—71; reading resource tchr. Lincoln Pub. Schs., 1994—97; trainer Learning PX, Lincoln, 2002—03; dir. Performance Based Learning Ctr., Lincoln, 2004—. Instr. Southeast C.C., Lincoln, 2002—. Author: Cognitive Training Skills, 2004; contbr. articles to profl. jours. Named Citizen of Month, Seward C. of C. Mem.: ASCD, Nebr. Edn. Assn., Nebr. Dyslexia Assn., Internat. Dyslexia Assn. Avocation: interior decorating. Office: Performance Based Learning Ctr 7200 Old Post Rd #12 Lincoln NE 68506

SMITH, SUSANN RENEE See FLETCHER, SUSANN

SMITH, SUSANNAH, clinical and organizational development consulting psychologist; b. Jackson, Miss., Mar. 15, 1949; d. Sydney Allen and Frances Smith Darden (Witty) S.; children: Nathan Walter, Erik Sydney, Christopher Pemberton. A.B., Vassar Coll., 1970; M.S., San Jose State U., 1973; Ph.D., Calif. Sch. Profl. Psychology, San Diego, 1975. Lic. psychologist Miss., Calif., Colo. Child and family worker Child and Family Clinic and Counseling Ctr., San Jose (Calif.) State U., 1970-72, Peninsula Children's Ctr., Palo Alto, Calif., 1970-72; psychotherapist, psychologist Family Services Assoc., San Diego, 1973-74; intern, post-doctoral fellow Mercy Hosp., San Diego, 1974-75; dir. research and program evaluation, dir. day treatment and srs. program San Luis Obispo (Calif.) Mental Health, 1976-80; pvt. practice clin. and cons. psychology, Gulfport, Miss., 1980—; founder, co-dir. Coast Psychotherapy Assocs; dir. Susannah Smith & Assocs.; cons. staff Gulf Coast Community Hosp., Gulfport Meml. Hosp., Sand Hill Hosp., Garden park Hosp., Hancock Gen. Hosp., co-founder Inst. Life Enrichment: Wellness Ctr. mem. faculty U. So. Miss. Bd. dirs., co-founder Anred (Anorexia Nervosa and Related Eating Disorders), San Luis Obispo, 1979—; condr. workshops, lectr. Rape Crisis Ctr.; mem. cons. staff Gulfport Meml., Garden Park, Biloxi Regional hosps.; bd. dirs., cons., v.p. internal affairs Aesculapius Internat. Medicine. Author: The Choice. Mem. APA, Colo. Psychol. Assn., Miss. Psychol. Assn., Calif. Psychol. Assn. Democrat. Episcopalian. Contbr. articles to profl. jours.; columnist Practical Psychology: What's On Your Mind?, Tupelo (Miss.) N.E., Miss. Daily Jour.; composer several songs.

SMITH, SUSIE IRENE, cytologist, histologist; b. Oct. 10, 1942; d. Taft and Evelyn (Samuels) Woodford; m. Eugene Smith, Dec. 2, 1960; children: Regina Marie, Kimberly Denise, Teresa Yvette, Stacia Ann. Student, Boston State coll., 1975—80. Med. worker Boston City Hosp., 1970, lab asst., 1970—75; lab. tech. hematopathology lab Mallory Inst. Pathology, 1975—80, chief med. technologist, 1982—90; owner, pres. Easy Travel Internat., Inc., 2000—. Lectr. and cons. in field; rsch. assoc., health & safety officer CytoLogix Corp., 1998—2004. Contbr. articles to sci. jours. Treas. Whittier St. Tenants Assn., 1985—86, pres., 1987—88, Tenants United for Pub. Housing Progress, 1985—87, Com. Boston Pub. Housing, 1987—88; sec. Com. to Elect Jesse L. Corbin for State Rep., 1981—82. Mem.: Am. Soc. Clin. Pathologists (notary pub. 1988—). Office: 54 Annunciation Rd Apt L Roxbury Crossing MA 02120-1871 Office Phone: 617-314-6297. E-mail: etii@comcast.net.

SMITH, SUZANNE M., federal agency administrator; b. Jan. 5, 1950; BA, Pa. State U., 1970; MD, Med. Coll. Pa., 1976; MPH, Emory U., 1991; MPA, Harvard U., 2000. Resident in internal medicine Morristown (NJ) Hosp., 1977—80; infectious disease fellow Med. Coll. Va., 1980—83; with CDC, Atlanta, 1983—, chief Health Care and Aging Studies br., Divsn. Adult and Cmty. Health, 1997—2003, acting dir. pub. health practice program office, 2003—04, spl. asst. for strategy and innovation, Office of the Dir., 2005—.

SMITH, TARA MICHELLE, counselor; b. Aurora, Colo., May 18, 1979; d. Terry M. and Meredith J. Smith. BA in Psychology, U. No. Colo., Greeley, 2001; MA in Social Work, U. Denver, Colo., 2006—. On-call counselor Alternative Homes for Youth, Greeley, Colo., 2000—01; youth treatment counselor Denver Children's Home, Denver, 2001—06; clinician Arts Cross Point, Denver, 2006—. Recipient Nat. Dean's List, Ednl. Comm., Inc., 2000-2001, UNC's Next Challengers, U. No. Colo., 1998-1999; scholar GSSW High Merit Scholarship, U. Denver Grad. Sch. of Social Work, 2004-2005, GSSW Tuition Scholarship, 2004-2005, Provost Scholarship, U. No. Colo., 1997-2001. Mem.: NASW, Phi Alpha Honor Soc., Mortar Bd. Nat. Honors Soc., Golden Key Nat. Honors Soc., Psy Chi. Avocations: travel, writing, music, reading. Home: 3364 S Quintero St Aurora CO 80013 Office: Denver Children's Home 1501 Albion St Denver CO 80220 Office Phone: 303-399-4890. Personal E-mail: tsmith24@du.edu.

SMITH, TERESA HUNT, elementary school educator, counselor; b. Gastonia, NC, Dec. 10, 1947; d. Forrest William and Katherine Faux Hunt; m. Charles William Smith; 1 child, Lindsey Rebecca. BA in Edn., U. N.C., Greensboro, 1970; BS in Counseling Psychology, Nova U., Ft. Lauderdale, Fla. Tchr. Jefferson Elem. Sch., Shelby, NC, Pasadena Lakes Elem. Sch., Hollywood, Fla., Ramblewood Middle Sch., Coral Springs, Fla., Residence Park Elem. Sch., Dayton, Ohio, Ellenboro Elem. Sch., NC, East Rutherford Middle Sch., Bostic, NC, guidance counselor. Counselor in pvt. practice, Ft. Lauderdale. Named Tchr. of Yr., Ellenboro Ele. and East Rutherford Middle; recipient Top Tchr. award, Dayton, Ohio. Mem.: NC Counseling Assn., NC Edn. Assn. Baptist. Avocation: reading. Home: 2095 Big Island Rd Rutherfordton NC 28139 Office: East Rutherford Middle Sch 259 E Church St Bostic NC

SMITH, THELMA CHERYL, principal, minister; d. Junius Edmund and Mildred Celestine Cromartie; m. Pierce Alexander Smith, Apr. 6, 1974; children: Cheri Nicole, Dawn Alexandra, Pierce Alexander II. BS in Premedicine, U. Dayton, Ohio, 1975; MS in Ednl. Leadership, Hood Coll., Frederick, Md., 1996. Cert. adminstrn. and supervision 1995. Sci. tchr. Seneca Valley H.S., Germantown, Md., 1983—95; resource tchr. Roberto Clemente, Germantown, 1995; asst. prin. Dr. M.L. King Middle Sch., Germantown, 1995—98, N.W. H.S., Germantown, 1998—2000; prin. Gaithersburg Middle Sch., Md., 2000—05, Coastal Christian Acad., 2006—. Assoc. pastor New Life Bapt. Ch., Gaithersburg, 2000—05. Mem.: Nat. Assn. Secondary Sch. Prins. Home: 3041 Egyptian Ln Virginia Beach VA 23456

SMITH, THERESA JOANNE, research scientist, educator; b. Corona, N.Y., Aug. 22, 1959; d. Felix Adolph and Norma Alberta Smith. BA, CUNY, Flushing, N.Y., 1982; MS, Tex. Woman's U., Denton, Tex., 1984, PhD, 1988. Lic. practical nurse, NY, 1978. Postdoctoral rsch. assoc. Rutgers, The State U. N.J., Piscataway, 1988—92, rsch. assoc., 1992—96, rsch. asst. prof., 1996—99; asst. prof. U. S.C., Columbia, 1999—2005, assoc. prof., 2005—. Cons. NIH, Ctr. for Sci. Rev., Bethesda, Md., 2001—. Contbr. chapters to books, articles to profl. jours. Named Rschr. of Yr., Coll. Pharmacy, U. S.C., 2002; grantee, Am. Cancer Soc., 1998—2002, NIH, 2002—, 2003—06. Mem.: AAAS, Women in Cancer Rsch., S.C. Alliance for Cancer Chemoprevention, Soc. for Nutrition Edn., Am. Assn. for Cancer Rsch. Democrat. Roman Catholic. Avocations: gardening, travel, fishing. Office: University of South Carolina College of Pharmacy 700 Sumter St Columbia SC 29208 Office Phone: 803-777-0857. Office Fax: 803-777-8356. Personal E-mail: tjsmith822@aol.com. Business E-Mail: smithtj@cop.sc.edu.

SMITH, TRINA, academic administrator; b. Rogersville, Ala., Sept. 18, 1971; d. Will Buford and Margaret Cannon Smith. BS, Athens State U., 1993; MS, U. Ala., Huntsville, 2000; M of Accountancy, U. Ala., 2001. Cert. Notary Pub. Br. ops. supr. Union Planters Bank, Athens, Ala., 1994—2000; acct. Calhoun Coll., Decatur, Ala., 2000—. Dir. Habitat for Humanity, Athens, 1994—2000; mem. adv. bd. Dogwood Festival Com., Athens, 1999. Vol. Jr. Achievement, Decatur, Ala., 1997—2000, Care Assurance Sys. for Aging and Homebound, Athens, 1995—99, Found. of Aging, Athens, 1999—2002. Recipient Outstanding Support award, Habitat for Humanity, 1996. Mem.: NAFE, NAACP, Am. Inst. of Cert. Pub. Accts., Nat. Assn. Black Accts., Am. Acctg. Assn., Am. Soc. Women Accts., Nat. Notary Assn., Inst. Mgmt. Accts. Baptist. Avocations: gardening, photography, collecting antiques, investments, outdoor activities. Home: 13708 Dart Cir Athens AL 35611 Office: Calhoun Cmty Coll Hwy 31 S Decatur AL 35609 Personal E-mail: TSmith3671@aol.com.

SMITH, VALENE LUCY, anthropologist, educator; b. Spokane, Wash., Feb. 14, 1926; d. Ernest Frank and Lucy (Blachly) S.; m. Edwin Chesteen Golay, June 7, 1970 (dec. June 1980); m. Stanley George McIntyre, Nov. 26, 1983 (dec. Oct. 2000); m. George Addison Posey, Oct. 5, 2005. BA in Geography, U. Calif., 1946, MA in Geography, 1950; PhD in Anthropology, U. Utah, 1966. Cert. travel counselor. Prof. earth sci. L.A. City Coll., 1947-67; prof. anthropology Calif. State U., Chico, 1967—. Cons. World Tourism Orgn., Madrid, 1987. Editor: Hosts and Guests: The Anthrop, 1989, Tourism Alternatives: Potentials and Problems in the Development of Tourism, 1992, Hosts and Guests Revisited, 2001. Mem. Soroptimist Internat., Chico, 1968—; founding pres. Chico Mus. Assn., 1978. Named Fulbright prof., Peshawar, Pakistan, 1953—54; recipient Athena award, U.S.C. of C., 1988. Mem. Internat. Acad. for Study Tourism, Cert. Travel Counselors, Am. Anthrop. Assn., AAUW, Canyon Oaks Country Club, Soroptimists. Republican. Avocations: travel, aviation, photography. Office: U Calif Dept Anthropology Chico CA 95929-0004 Office Phone: 530-891-1155. Business E-Mail: vsmith@csuchico.edu.

SMITH, VALERIE, curator; Curator Artists Space, NYC; curator, dir. exhibitions Queens Mus. Art, NYC. Curator (exhibitions) Sonsbeek Sculpture Exhbn., Arnhem, The Netherlands, 1993 (Named one of the top 10 shows of the 1990s, Artforum mag.), Joan Jonas: Five Works, Queens Art Mus., 2003—04 (Award for Best Exhbn. of Time Based Art, Internat. Assn. Art Critics/USA, 2005). Office: Queens Mus Art NYC Bldg Flushing Meadows Corona Pk Corona NY 11368

SMITH, VANGY EDITH, accountant, consultant, artist, writer; b. Saskatoon, Can., Dec. 17, 1937; d. Wilhelm and Anne Ellen (Hartshorne) Gogel: m. Clifford Wilson, May 12, 1958 (de. Dec. 1978); children: Kenneth, Koral, Kevin, Korey, Kyle; m. Terrence Raymond Smith, Dec. 14, 1979. Student, Saskatoon Tech. Collegiate Inst., 1956, BBA, 1958, MBA, 1987, PhD in English with honors, 1988. Prin. Vangy Enterprises, Springfield, Oreg., 1960—; accounts payable clk. Maxwell Labs., Inc., San Diego, 1978; invoice clk. Davies Electric, Saskatoon, 1980-81; office mgr. Ladee Bug Ceramics, Saskatoon, 1981-87, Lazars Investments Corp., Eugene, Oreg., 1987; bookkeeper accounts payable Pop Geer, Eugene, Oreg., 1987; office mgr., bookkeeper Willamette Sports Ctr., Inc., Eugene, Oreg., 1985-89; clk. I Lane C.C., Springfield, Oreg., 1992-96. Self-employed Vangy Enterprises, 1992—; circulation mgr. Nat. WCTU, 1990-92, UN rep. for World WCTUm 1989-91; appointed mem. Parliament for the U. for Peace, Holland, 1991; adv. chair Lane C.C. Ctr. for Leisure and Learning, 1999-2001. Contbr. articles to profl. jours. (recipient doctoral award 1987). Counselor Drug and Rehab. Ctr., Eugene, 1970—88; trustee Children's Farm Home, Corvallis, Oreg., 1989—91, 3d v.p., 1989—90; co-pres. Lane County UN Assn., 1989—90; mem. artist Nat. Bd. Edn., 1989, 1990; mem. adv. com. Dept. Pub. Safety for City of Eugene, 1989—90; exec. dir. H.E.L.P., 1993—; pres. Lane County Coun. of Orgns., 1994—96; treas. Cascade/Coast chpt. Alzheimers Assn., 1994; mem. UN Devel. Fund for Women, mem. exec. com., 1999; chair adv. com. Ctr. for Leisure and Learning, Lane C.C., 1999—2001; state pres. Rebekah Assembly Oreg., 2004—05; mem. Found. Christian Living; pres. Oreg. State Christian Temperance Union, 1989—90. Recipient 3d and 4th place artists' awards Lane County Fair, 1987, 1st and 2d place awards Nat. Writing Contest, 1987-91, Oasis Vol. Model award, 1998; named City of Eugene Hometown Hero, 1998, named Woman of Yr., Am. Bus. Women's Assn., 1999-00. Mem. WCTU (life, pres., state bd. dirs. projection methods circulation 1987-90, Appreciation award 1982, Presdl. award 1985, Lane County Eugene Woman of Yr. 1990), UNIFEM (chpt. pres. 1997—, exec. bd. 1999—, Women in Leadership award 1997), Am. Soc. Writers, Alzheimers Assn. (treas. Cascade/Coast chpt. 1994), Rebekah Lodge (Noble Grand 1995-99), Rebekah Assembly Oreg.-Odd Fellows (pres. 2004-05), Lions (sec. 1994), Oasis (adv. coun. chair 1993-98), Am. Bus. Women's Assn. (pres. 2000—). Democrat. Avocations: needlecrafts, rug hooking, reading, writing, painting. Home and Office: 1235 Charmelton Eugene OR 97401 Office Phone: 541-747-1237. Personal E-mail: vsmith3237@aol.com.

SMITH, VERONICA LATTA, real estate company officer; b. Wyandotte, Mich., Jan. 13, 1925; d. Jan August and Helena (Hulak) Latta; m. Stewart Gene Smith, Apr. 12, 1952; children: Stewart Gregory, Patrick Allen, Paul Donald, Alison Veronica Hurley, Alisa Margaret Lyons, Glenn Laurence. BA in Sociology, U. Mich., 1948. Tchr. Coral Gables (Fla.) Pub. Sch. Sys., 1949—50; COO Latta Ins. Agy, Wyandotte, 1950—62; treas. L & S Devel. Co., Grosse Ile, Mich., 1963—84; v.p. Regency Devel., Riverview, Mich., 1984—. Active U. Mich. Bd. Regents, 1985-92, regent emeritus, 1993—; mem. Martha Cook Bd. Govs., U. Mich., pres., 1976-78; del. Rep. County Conv., Grand Rapids, Mich., 1985, 87, 89, 91, 92, 94, 96, Lansing, Mich., 1996, Detroit, 1986, 88, 90, 92, 97; mem. pres. adv. com. Campaign for Mich., 1992-97, mem. campaign steering com., 1992-97. Mem. Mich. Lawyers Aux. (treas. 1975, chmn. 1976, 77, 78, 79), Nat. Assn. Ins. Women (cert.), Faculty Women's Club U. Mich. (hon.), Radrick Farms Golf Club (Ann Arbor), Pres.'s Club U. Mich., Investment Club (pres. 1976, sec. 1974-75, treas. 1975-76), Alpha Kappa Delta. Home: 22225 Balmoral Dr Grosse Ile MI 48138-1403

SMITH, VICKIE M., chemicals executive; Asst. contr. Helena Chem. Co., sr. dir. info. tech., 2000—. Named one of Premier 100 IT Leaders, Computerworld, 2005. Office: Helena Chem Co 225 Schilling Blvd Collierville TN 38017

SMITH, VICTORIA WEILEPP, educator; b. Decatur, Ill., Jan. 6, 1951; d. James Redmon Weilepp and Anna Ruth (Sewell) Porter; m. Richard Vickers Smith, June 9, 1972 (div. 1986); children: John Vickers, Emily Anne BS, U. So. Miss., 1973; MEd, William Carey Coll., 1977; postgrad., Nicholls State U., 1997. Tchr. math. Ocean Springs Jr. H.S., Miss., 1973—77, St. Martin H.S., Ocean Springs, 1979—80; instr. Tarrant County Jr. Coll., Ft. Worth, 1981—83; lectr. Nicholls State U., Thibodaux, La., 1984—93, instr., 1994—. Mem. Nat. Coun. Tchrs. Math., La. Assn. Tchrs. Math., Lit. Club Avocations: travel, history. Home: 105 Parlange St Thibodaux LA 70301-6434 Office: Nicholls State U Math Dept Thibodaux LA 70310-0001

SMITH, VIRGINIA, real estate broker; b. N.y.C., Oct. 24, 1928; d. John Harvey Woodhull and Sally Horton Hurd Warren; m. Ward William Smith III, June 28, 1952 (div. Aug. 1977); children: Ward William IV, Sally Hurd, Carluie Farnsworth, George M., Judy McCourbrey. AA, Green Mt. Coll., 1948. Asst. to buyer Gourmets Bazaar, N.Y.C., 1948-49, rschr. food articles, 1949-50; asst. editor Table Topics, N.Y.C., 1950-51; asst. mktg. editor House & Garden, N.Y.C., 1951-52; real estate broker DeVre Realty, Kent, Conn., 1973-95, asst. mgr. Cornwall, Conn., 1976-77; broker, owner Virginia Smith Real Estate, New Milford, Conn., 1997—. Theatre critic Sharon Playhouse, 1977-78. Active Christmas Bazaar, St. Andrews Ch., Kent, 1977-97, Bd. Assessment Appeals, New Milford, 1992—, Dem. Town Com., New Milford, 1992—. Episcopalian. Avocations: reading, swimming, gardening, cooking, antiques. Home: 55 Curtiss Rd New Preston Marble Dale CT 06777-1003 Office: 52 Squire Hill Rd New Milford CT 06776-5013

SMITH, VIRGINIA ELEANORE, psychologist, educator; b. Bklyn., Aug. 12, 1940; d. Valentine A. and Katherine V. (Angold) Pajer; m. Albert G. Smith, Aug. 12, 1961; children: Daniel, Douglas, Andrew, Katherine, James. BA, Neumann Coll., 1978; MS, Drexel U., 1984; PhD, Union Inst., Cin., 1994; postgrad. clin. tng., Gestalt Therapy Inst. Phila., 1991—. Lic. mental health counselor, Del., Pa. Med. social worker Delaware County Commn. Nursing Svc., Chester, Pa., 1983-84; counselor Manatee County Mental Health Agy., Bradenton, Fla., 1984-85; pvt. practice Wilmington, Del., 1990—; mental health counselor Correctional Med. Systems, Wilmington, Del., 1990—, AIDS Delaware, Wilmington, 2004—. Adj. prof. Delaware County CC, Media, Pa., 1985—, Widener U., Goldey Beacon Coll., Wilmington, 1987—, Neumann Coll., 2001-; assoc. dir. assessments CATCH, Phila., 1995-2003. Mem. AACD, Am. Sociol. Assn., Mental Health Counselors Assn., Assn. Humanistic Psychologists. Roman Catholic. Avocations: travel, hiking, photography, writing. Home: 830 S Walnut St Kennett Square PA 19348 Personal E-mail: virginiasmith173@comcast.net.

SMITH, VIVIAN, elementary school educator; b. Clarksville, Tenn., Oct. 30, 1950; BS in Biology and Chemistry, Berry Coll., Rome, Ga., 1976; MS in Anatomy and Physiology, U. Ga., Athens, 1978, MEd in Secondary Sci. Edn., 1981. Tchr. Oconee Pub. Schs., Watkinsville, Ga., 1978—. Team leader Oconee Mid. Sch., 2000—; instr. fitness YWCO, Athens, 1978—, YMCA, 1978—, Omni Club, 1978—, Eastside Fitness, 1978—. V.p. Friendship Recreation, Watkinsville, 2005—06. Grantee, Oconee Edn. Found., 2001—06. Mem.: Nat. Sci. Tchrs. Assn., Sigma Xi, Gamma Sigma Delta. Office: Oconee County Middle School 1101 Mars Hill Rd Watkinsville GA 30677 Office Phone: 706-769-0074. Business E-Mail: vsmith@oconee.k12.ga.us.

SMITH, VIVIAN BLAINE, elementary school educator; b. Lynchburg, Va., Feb. 22, 1947; d. Hugh Allison and Virginia Blaine Cobb. B Music Edn., Va. Commonwealth U., Richmond, 1970; MS, Marshall U., Huntington, W.Va., 1972. Cert. tchr. Ohio, 2005. Tchr. Dayton Pub. Schs., Ohio, 1984—. Trustee Showcase Am. Unltd., Westerville, Ohio, 2004—06. Home: 2723 Rugby Rd Dayton OH 45406 Office: Wilbur Wright Mid Sch 1361 Huffman Ave Dayton OH 45403 Office Fax: 937-542-6381. Business E-Mail: vbsmith@dps.k12.oh.us.

SMITH, VME EDOM (VERNA MAE EDOM SMITH), social sciences educator, freelance photographer, freelance writer; b. Marshfield, Wis., June 19, 1929; d. Clifton Cedric and Vilia Clarissa (Patefield) Edom; children: Teri Smith Freas, Anthony Thomas. AB in Sociology, U. Mo., 1951; MA in Sociology, George Washington, 1965; PhD in Human Devel., U. Md., 1981. Tchr. Alcohol Safety Action Program Fairfax County, Va., 1973-75; instr. sociology No. Va. C.C., Manassas, 1975-77, asst. prof., 1977-81, assoc. prof., 1981-84, prof., 1984-94, prof. emerita, 1995, coord. coop. edn., 1983-89, Chancellor's Commonwealth prof., 1991-93; adj. faculty Tidewater C.C., 1996—; freelance writer, editor and photographer, 1965—; dir. Clifton and Vi Edom Truth With a Camera (photography workshops), 1994—. Asst. prodr. history of photography program Sta. WETA-TV, Washington, 1965; rsch. and prodn. asst., photographer, publs. editor No. Va. Ednl. TV, Sta. WNVT, 1970—71; cons. migrant divsn. Md. Dept. Edn., Balt., 1977; rschr. photographer Roundabout presch. high sch. series Am. Values Sta. WNVT, 1970—71; documentary photographer Portsmouth (Va.) Redevel. and Housing Authority, 1998—2000; dir. Edom Found. Photojournalism Edn. Author, photographer Middleburg and Nearby, 1988; co-author: Small Town America, 1993; contbr. photographs to various publs. Mem. ednl. adv. com. Head Start, Warrenton, Va. Recipient Emmy, Ohio State Children's Programming award; Fulbright-Hays Rsch. grantee, 1963, Va. Found. Humanities and Pub. Policy grantee, 1997—99. Mem.: Va. Assn. Coop. Edn. (com. mem.). Democrat. E-mail: vme@macs.net.

SMITH, WENDY HAIMES, federal agency administrator; b. Tex. m. Jay L. Smith. BA in Econs., U. Mich.; postgrad., Ohio State U., Am. U., Washington Studio Sch., Aspen Inst., Wye, Md., 1997. Cert. real estate agt. Office mgr. Haimes Travel Agy., Ohio, 1972-73; mgmt. intern US Dept. Commerce, Washington, 1973-75, country specialist for Korea, 1973, spl. asst. to dep. asst. sec. for internat. commerce, 1973-74, project officer, maj. projects divsn., 1974-75, project mgr. indsl. sys., maj. projects divsn., 1975-77, country specialist for Brazil, 1978, project mgr., hydrocarbons and chem. process plants, maj. export projects divsn., 1977-79, exec. asst. to dep. asst. sec. of commerce for export devel. and staff dir. Pres. Export Coun., 1979-81, dir. Pres. Export Coun., 1981-92, acting dir. Office Planning and Coordination, 1988-89, dir. adv. coms. and pvt. sector programs Internat. Trade Adminstrn., 1992-97; dir. Trade Info. Ctr., Washington, 1997—, acting dir. office of export promotion, 1999, 2000-01; acting dir. Office Export Assistance and Bus. Outreach, 2003—04; deputy dir. U.S.A. Trade Promotion, 2005—; sr. advisor Nat. Acad. Pub. Adminstrn., 2005—. Author, editor US Trade in Transition: Maintaining the Gains, 1988, co-author, editor The Export Imperative, 1980, Coping with the Dynamics of World Trade in the 1980s, 1984; Exhibited in group shows at Courtyard Gallery, Brian Logan Artspace, Artists Mus., Washington, Designer's Art Gallery, Bethesda, Md., one-woman shows include Courtyard Gallery, Washington, 2001. Active Art League, Smithsonian Instn., Washington Opera Guild; bd. dir. Washington Studio Sch; one man show Courtyard Gallery, 2001.

SMITH, WENDY L., foundation executive; b. Chgo., Sept. 12, 1950; d. John Arthur and Dolores Mae (Webb) Rothenberger; m. Alan Richard Smith; children: Angela Fuhs, Erica Smith. Student, Oakton CC, Des Plaines, Ill., 1986, Mundelein Coll., 1990. Purchasing clk. AIT Industries, Skokie, Ill., 1975-76; purchasing agt. MCC Powers, Skokie, 1976-78; office mgr. Spartan Engring., Skokie, 1978-80, Brunswick Corp., Skokie, 1980—; successively sr. sec., coord. indsl. rels., dir. Brunswick Found., Lake Forest, Ill., 1982-89, pres., 1989—. Asst. sec. Brunswick Pub. Charitable Found., Lake Forest, 1989—; mem. adv. com. Found. for Ind. Higher Edn., Stamford, Conn., 1989—, Coun. Better Bus. Burs., Arlington, Va., 1988-90; bd. dirs. Associated Colls. of Ill., 1991—; bd. dirs., mem. trustees com., mem. compensation and benefits com. Donors Forum of Chgo., 1988-93. Bd. dirs. INROADS/Chgo., Inc., 1994—; mem. steering com. Dist. 57 Edn. Found., Mt. Prospect, Ill., 1996—. Recipient Pvt. Sector Initiative Commendation, U.S. Pres., 1987-89. Mem. Donors Forum Chgo. (treas. 1988-91, bd. dirs., mem. exec. com., chairperson audit and fin. com., mem. trustees com. 1992—), Coun. on Founds., Ind. Sector Suburban Contbns. Network (chairperson 1987-89), Women in Philanthropy Corp. Founds. (mem. cmty. rels. com. 1985-87), Chgo. Women in Philanthropy. Avocations: antique restoration, pleasure reading, bowling, golf.

SMITH, YEARDLEY, actress; b. Paris, July 3, 1964; Voice of Lisa Simpson, Maggie Simpson and others The Simpsons, 1989—. Actor: (films) Heaven Help Us, 1985, The Legend of Billie Jean, 1985, Maximum Overdrive, 1986, Three O'Clock High, 1987, Listen to Me, 1989, Zwei Frauen, 1989, City Slickers, 1989, Toys, 1992, Jingle All the Way, 1996, Just Write, 1997, As Good As It Gets, 1997, (voice only) We're Back! A Dinosaur's Story, 1993,; (TV films) Mom's On Strike, 1984, Tickets, Please, 1988; (TV series) Brothers, 1984, The Tracey Ullman Show, 1987—89, Herman's Head, 1991, Dharma & Greg, 1997—99, 2001—02, (TV guest appearance) Tales from the Darkside, 1986, Mama's Family, 1986, Mathnet, 1987, Sydney, 1990, Likely Suspects, 1992, Hey Hey, It's Sunday, 1994, Empty Nest, 1994, Smart Guy, 1997, Teen Angel, 1997, Sports Night, 1998, Nash Bridges, 1999, Becker, 2003, (theatre) More, 2004.

SMITH, ZULEIKA, art educator; d. Eronomy and Phyllis Smith. BS in Art Edn., NC A&T State U., Greensboro, 1998; MS in Bus. Tech., Marymount U., Arlington, Va., 2004. Art Education, K-12 DC Pub. Schools, 2006. Tchr. art Cresthaven Elem. Sch., Silver Spring, Md., 2000—04, Birney Elem. Sch., Washington, 2004—. Art exhibit planner and facilitator Birney Elem. Sch., Washington, 2004—. Wash. Post Grant For The Arts, Wash. Post, 1999.

SMITH ALDER, ANGELA GRACE, education educator; b. Omaha, Nebr., Sept. 8, 1960; d. Alfred Kingsley and Donna Jean Smith; m. Robert Currier Alder, Sept. 30, 1995; children: Julie Renee Lewis, Ryan James Alder, Mari Lyn Ballentine. BA, U. Nebr., 1982, MS, 1985; JD, Creighton Law Sch., Omaha, Nebr., 1988; LLM, Harvard Law Sch., Cambridge, Mass., 1994. Bar: Nebr. 1988. Jud. clk. U.S. Ct. of Appeals - 8th Circuit, Lincoln, Nebr., 1988—89; asst. prof., dir. of legal writing Creighton Law Sch., Omaha, 1990—93; dir. of advising U. Nebr. Teachers Coll., 1994—95; prof., dir. of legal studies Mt. Union Coll., Alliance, Ohio, 2001—. Recipient 2005 Gt. Tchr. award, Mt. Union Coll., 2005. Avocations: gardening, music, travel. Office: Mount Union Coll 1972 Clark Ave Alliance OH 44601 Office Phone: 330-823-2473. E-mail: smithaag@muc.edu.

SMITHART-OGLESBY, DEBRA LYNN, food service executive; b. Apr. 24, 1959; BA in Acctg., U. Tex.; MBA, So. Methodist U. Asst. contr. Brinker Internat., Inc., Dallas, 1985—86, contr., 1986—88, v.p., contr., 1988—91, v.p. fin., 1991, exec. v.p., CFO, 1991—97; pres. corp. services, CFO First Am. Autootive Inc., 1997—99; pres. Dekor, Inc., 1999—2000, O/S Partners, 2000—06; chmn. Denny's Corp., Spartanburg, SC, 2006—. Bd. dirs. Brinker Internat., Inc., 1991—97, Denny's Corp., 2003—, Noodles & Co. Office: Dennys Corp 203 E Main St Spartanburg SC 29319*

SMITH BRINTON, MARCIA, psychologist, consultant; b. Miami, Fla., Feb. 19, 1945; d. Clarence Hall and Felicia (Trombetta) Smith; m. James Conrad Hilderbrand, Aug. 3, 1964 (div. Mar. 1978); children: Mark Gregory, James Christopher; m. George Albert Brinton, Aug. 31, 1986. BA, U. Miami, 1970; MA, Montclair State U., 1982; PhD, NYU, 1996. Rsch. assoc. Metro Ctr., NYU, 1983-85; sch. psychologist Frankford Twp. (N.J.) Pub. Sch. Sys., 1985, Green Twp. (N.J.) Pub. Schs., 1985-86; mental health clinician emergency svcs. Newton (N.J.) Meml. Hosp. Ctr. for Mental Health, 1989-92; intern in psychology Queens Childrens Psychiat. Ctr., Bellerose, N.Y., 1992-93; psychologist St. Christopher Ottilie Residential Treatment Facility, Briarwood, N.J., 1996-98; clin. specialist Inhealth Assocs., Sparta, N.J., 1998—. Cons. Gifted/Talented parent Counseling program, Green Twp. Elem. Sch., 1985-86, Sussex County Assn. for Retarded Citizens, 1998—. Co-author: Finding, Loving and Marrying Your Lifetime Partner, 1988; contbr. articles to profl. jours. Vol. summer program dir. Sunray, Bristol, Vt., 1994, 95, 96, advisor to bd. trustees, 1995-96. Mem. APA, NYU Alumni Assn. Democrat. Unitarian Universalist. Avocations: gardening, hiking, canoeing, horseback ridng, flute.

SMITH-CAMPBELL, CHARMAINE, secondary school educator; b. Kingston, Jamaica, West Indies, Jan. 6, 1956; d. Orville Clifford and Mabel Rebecca Smith; m. Carnel Charles Campbell, Apr. 20, 1978; children: Damali, Jelani, Pschopelia. BA in history, U. West Indies, 1982; MA in history, Queens Coll., 1989. Cert. tchr. social studies, N.Y. Instr. high sch. John Bowne H.S., Flushing, N.Y., 1979-83, high sch. tchr., 1981-87, special edn. tchr., 1984-91, social studies tchr., 1991—, grade advisor, 1997—. Advisor and coord. Caribbean Club, John Bowne H.S., Queens, N.Y., 1985-95, Am. History Month Activities, 1996—. Mem. Jamaica Progessive Club, Brooklyn, 1984-91, bd. dirs. Rosedale Condominium, 1998—. Democrat. Methodist. Avocations: sewing, gardening, reading, travel. Office: 6325 Main St Flushing NY 11367-1303 E-mail: charmsoup@aol.com.

SMITHERAM, MARGARET ETHERIDGE, health facility administrator, director; b. Atlanta, Jan. 5, 1938; d. Philip Fitzgerald and Mary Catharine (Dwyer) E.; m. Roy Charles McCracken, May 5, 1975; m. William Bertram Smitheram, Aug. 17, 1985. BA, Emory U., 1960; M in Health Adminstrn., Washington U., St. Louis, 1973. Registered record adminstr., 1960-71; spl. asst. to dir. VA Med. Ctr., Roseburg, Oreg., 1973-74; hosp. administrn, specialist VA Central Office, Washington, 1974-75; asst. dir. trainee VA Med. Ctr., Phila., 1976, assoc. dir. Hampton, Va., 1976--80, Buffalo, 1980-81; presdl. exchange exec. Kimberly Clark Corp., Neenah, Wis., 1981-82, Roswell, Ga., 1981-82; dir. VA Med. Ctr., Grand Island, Nebr., 1982-94; interim dir. Grand Island-Hall County Health Dept., 1996-97; instr. Cerritos Coll., 1969-70. Bd. dirs. Project 2M Coordinating Coun., Inc., Grand Island, 1985-87, Hall County Leadership Unlimited, Inc., 1990. Bd. dirs. Grand Island Area United Way, 1987-90 (pres. 1989), Grand Island Concert Assn, 1987-92, Ctrl. Nebr. Goodwill Industries, Inc., 1987-93 (pres. 1991-92). Fellow Am. Coll. Healthcare Execs. (life); mem. rev. bd. State of Nebr. Foster Care, Am. Hosp. Assn., Fed. Exec. Assn. (pres. Grand Island chpt. 1987), Nebr. Hosp. Assn., Grand Island C. of C. (bd. dirs. 1988-92, legis. affairs com 1984-85, priorities com. 1984-85, govtl. affairs com. 1984-88, nominating com. 1991-92, 94-95, audit com. 1992-93, pres. club 1993-94), Rotary Internat. Club #1485 (v.p. 1998-2000, pres. 2000-2001, District 5630 Group Study Exchange Team Leader to South Korea District 3710, 1999, Paul Harris fellow). Home: 221 Trail of the Flowers Georgetown TX 78628

SMITHGALL, JUDY LEE, music educator, director; b. Wellsboro, Pa., Oct. 28, 1955; d. Carl Leroy Smith and Dorothy Anna Krause; m. Edward Gee Smithgall; children: Marcus Leon Myers, Shelley Lynne Myers, Heather, LeAnne. BS in Music Edn., Mansfield U., Pa., 1973—77, MusM, 1994—98. Pvt. musical instrument tchr. Smith's Pianos & Organs, Wellsboro, Pa., 1972—93; ptnr. in retail bus. numerous bus.'s, Wellsboro, 1977—97; music tchr. No. Tioga Sch. Dist., Pa., 1987—88, band dir., 1988—93; choral dir. Wellsboro Area Sch. Dist., 1993—. Musician: Ole Bull Festival Performance Competition (Advanced Piano award, 1969). Accompanist Wellsboro Women's Chorus; organist Coolidge Hollow United Meth. Ch., Wellsboro, 1969—2006. Nominee Woman of Yr. award, 1992, 1993, Personalities of Am. award, 1992, Two Thousand Notable Am. Women award, 1992. Mem.: Music Educator's Nat. Conf., Pa. Music Educator's Assn., Pa. State Edn. Assn. United Methodist. Avocations: 4-wheeling, travel. Home: 749 Charleston Rd Wellsboro PA 16901 Office: Wellsboro Area HS 225 Nichols St Wellsboro PA 16901 Office Fax: 570-724-3027.

SMITH-INGRAM, KAREN CAMILLE, reading specialist, educator; d. Winnifred H. Smith and Bobbie J. Tatum-Anglin; m. Darrell Lynn Ingram, Mar. 20, 1982; children: Candiz Ingram, Bryce Ingram. BA in Elem. Edn., East Tex. State U., Commerce, 1981, M in Bilingual Edn., 1987; PhD in

Christian Edn., Aspen Theol. U., Colo., 2003. Cert. Spanish tchr. Tex. Tchr. reading demonstration Dallas Pub. Schs., 1981—98; sales cons. Harcourt Sch. Pubs., 1998—2000; ednl. cons., owern Profl. Tchg. Tng. Methods, 1998—2000; instr. Spanish lang. Paul Quinn Coll., 2000—03; tchr. reading Dallas Ind. Sch. Dist., 2003—. Active Mt. Tabor Bapt. Ch. Recipient Campus Tchr. of Yr. award, 1989, 1994, 1998, Svc. award, Head Start Dallas, 1991. Baptist. Office: Dallas Ind Sch Dist Dept Reading/Lang Arts 408 N Haskell Dallas TX 75346 Office Phone: 972-925-3022. E-mail: ProJesus17@yahoo.com.

SMITH-LEINS, TERRI L., mathematics instructor; b. Salina, Kans., Sept. 19, 1950; d. John W. and Myldred M. (Hays) Smith. BS, Ft. Hays (Kans.) U., 1973, MS, 1976; AA, Stephen Coll., Columbia, Mo., 1970. Math tchr. Scott City (Kans.) Jr. H.S., Howard (Kans.) Schs.; instr. math. U. Ark., Ft. Smith. Contbr. chapters to books, articles to profl. jours. Mem. AADE, ASCD, Nat. Assn. Devel. Edn. (state sec. 1986-88, computer access com. 1980-85), Phi Delta Kappa (Kappan of Yr. 1985), Delta Kappa Gamma (state chair women in art 1993-95, area one leader 1999-2001, Kappa state corr. sec., 2003-05, rec. sec. 2005—). Home: PO Box 3446 Fort Smith AR 72913-3446 Office Phone: 479-788-7665. Business E-Mail: tleins@uafortsmith.edu.

SMITH-LOEB, MARGARET, marketing educator; b. Columbus, Ohio, Apr. 17, 1932; d. Frederick James Church and Margaret MacWhannell; m. Dennis Patrick Delaney, Aug. 7, 1954 (div. Apr. 1959); m. Curtis Malchman Smith, Oct. 15, 1959 (div. Jan. 1967); 1 child, Jean Delaney Smith; m. John Meltzer Loeb, July 9, 1976 (dec. Jan. 1995). BA, Hood Coll., 1953; postgrad., St. Johns, Santa Fe, N.Mex, 1969. Buyer, asst. buyer Malchman's, Falmouth, Mass., 1960-63; tchr. Sandia Middle Sch., Albuquerque, 1963-67; dean Kent Middle Sch., Englewood, Colo., 1967-69; buyer intimate apparel May D&F, Denver, 1969-73; buyer young jr. dept. Gertz, Jamaica, N.Y., 1973-74; buyer, product developer Belk Store Svcs., N.Y.C., 1974-76; divsnl. mdse. mgr. Kirby Block/Irene Johns, N.Y.C., 1976-79; buyer, dept. mgr. Bloomingdale's, N.Y.C., 1979-81; asst. prof. fashion buying and mdsg. dept. Fashion Inst. Tech., N.Y.C., 1981-88, asst. prof., chairperson cosmetics and fragrance mkgt. dept., 1988—. Chairperson cert. bd. Fragrance Found., N.Y.C., 1993—; participant confs. Inst. Supervision Harvard Sch. Edn., 1969, workshop Am. Mgmt. Assn., 1974, Excellence in Coll. Tchg. Lilly Conf., Oxford, Ohio, 1990. Mem. Cosmetic Exec. Women. Avocations: reading, music, travel, theater. Office: Fashion Inst Tech 7th Ave at 27th St New York NY 10001-5992

SMITH LONG, CARYN LEANN, elementary school educator; d. Birch L. Smith and Carol K. Adams Smith; m. Steve Long, June 28, 1998; children: Randolph Lyle Long children: Forest Calvin Long. B of Edn., Queens U., Charlotte, NC, 1988; M of Edn., U. NC, 1990. 4th grade tchr. Matthews Elem., NC, 1988—89; tchr. 4th and 6th grade Billingsville Elem., Charlotte, NC, 1989—92; tchr. 5th grade U. Meadows Elem., 1992—97; sci., tech. facilitator Winterfield Elem., 1997—2002; adj. prof. U. NC, 1996—2004; Einstein fellow NASA-HQ, Washington, 2002—03; tchr. elem. sci. lead Charlotte-Meck Schs., Charlotte, 2003—04; NASA explorer schs. coord. NASA Stennis Space Ctr., Stennis Space Ctr., Miss., 2004—. Bscs rep. BSCS, Colorado Springs, Colo., 2001—; chairperson Winterfield Sch. Leadership Team, Charlotte, 1997—2002; sci. lead U. Meadows and Winterfield Elem. Schs., 1992—2002; reviewer NSTA, Arlington, Va., 2003—04. Recipient NC Sci. Teachers Assn. Dist. Tchr. Yr., NCSTA, 2002, Disting. Tchr. Yr., NSTA, 2001, Featured Tchr., PC TeachIT, 2001, Presdl. award for Excellence in Math and Sci. Tchg., NSF, 2000, NC Presdl. award for Excellence in Math and Sci. Tchg., NC Dept. of Pub. Instrn., 1999, Outstanding Educator, Sigma Xi, 2000; Albert Einstein Disting. Educator fellow, Triangle Coalition Math and Sci., 2002-2003, Eleanor Roosevelt Tchg. fellow, AAUW, 1999, Harris Found. grant, Harris Found., 1999. Mem.: NCSTA, NCTM, NSTA, ITEA, SEPA (life), APAST. Independent. Christian Church Disciples Of Christ. Avocations: dance, reading, travel, cross stitch.

SMITH-MCLAUGHLIN, AMY ELIZABETH, psychologist; b. Norristown, Pa., Apr. 6, 1976; d. James John and Theresa Catherine Smith; m. Edward Joseph McLaughlin III, July 10, 2004. BA in Psychology, Villanova U., Pa., 1998; MA in Counseling Psychology, Immaculata U., Pa., 2003; student in Psychology, Phila. Coll. Osteo. Medicine, 2005—. Lic. sch. psychologist Pa., 2003. Sch. psychologist Phoenixville (Pa.) Area Sch. Dist., 2003—. Employment tng. specialist Devereux Day Sch., Downingtown, Pa., 1998—2001, transition coord., 2001—02; residential counselor Devereux Whitlock Ctr., Berwyn, Pa., 1998—2004; transition specialist Devereux Mapleton, Malvern, Pa., 2002—03. Scholar, Immaculata (Pa.) U., 2000—01. Mem.: NEA, APA, Pa. State Edn. Assn., ABCT, Nat. Assn. Sch. Psycholgists, PCOM Psychology Club (treas. 2006, historian 2006—), Chi Sigma Iota. Roman Catholic. Avocations: aerobics, scrapbooks. Office: Phoenixville Area School District 301 Gay Street Phoenixville PA 19460 Office Phone: 610-917-3032. Personal E-mail: amy_mclaughlin@comcast.net.

SMITH-MEYER, LINDA HELENE (LINDA SMITH), artist; b. Manhattan, Nov. 18, 1947; d. Murray and Beatrice Victory (Waters) Smith; m. Charles Emil Meyer, Oct. 28, 1995. BFA, SUNY, 1969; MFA, NYU, 1973. One-woman shows include Sushi Gallery, West Hollywood, Calif., 1983, The Ivey Gallery, L.A., 1987, Schwartz Cierlak Gallery, Santa Monica, Calif., 1990; group shows include Cicchinelli Gallery, N.Y.C., 1981, Proteus Gallery, Beverly Hills, Calif., 1981, Elizalde Gallery Internat., Laguna Beach, Calif., 1981, 82, Gallery Helene, West Hollywood, 1982, Factory Place Gallery, L.A., 1983, 84, The Ivey Gallery, 1986, Ratliff-Williams Gallery, Sedona, Ariz., 1990-91, Spago Restaurant, Hollywood, Calif., 1985-2001, Orlando Gallery, Tarzana, Calif., Craft and Folk Art Mus. Shop, L.A., 2005, Beatrice Wood Ctr. Arts, Ojai, Calif., 2006, others; represented in permanent collections at Peter Selz, Berkeley, Calif., Cedars-Sinai Med. Ctr., L.A., Martin Blinder/Barry Levine-Martin Lawrence Galleries, L.A., Ms. Found. for Women, N.Y.C., also pvt. collections; contbr. articles to profl. jours. Home: 1261 S Highland Ave Los Angeles CA 90019-1731 Personal E-mail: linda@lindasmithceramicsplus.net.

SMITH-MOONEY, MARILYN PATRICIA, city government official, management consultant; b. Jamaica, NY, July 5, 1942; d. Raymond Lionel and Katherine Marie (Doepp) Cowan; m. Jack (John) J. Mooney, Sept. 1, 2002; 1 child, Paul William Hibner. Student various aviation schs., St. Joseph's Coll., N.Y. cert. in Leadership and Human Resources Devel., Goldratt Inst., Conn., JONAH cert. Inst. Elected Ofcls., Advanced Inst. for Elected Ofcls., Leadership Charlotte Class of 97-98, Local Govt. Leadership Fla., Class IV-99. Exec. sec. to chief design Wiedersum Assoc., Arch. and Engr., Valley Stream, NY, 1960-61; office mgr., arch. apprentice, interior designer Keith I. Hibner, Arch., Hicksville, Garden City, NY, 1961-73; owner, pres. Hibner Atelier, Ltd., Garden City, 1968-75; interior design and gen. constrn. Garden City, 1968-76; office mgr., tech. planning, manual writer for county dept. structure & operation Ward Assoc./Planning Assoc., Arch. and Engr., Bohemia, NY, 1975-76; chief pilot, flight/ground aviation instr. Islip Aviation Ltd., NY, 1974-77; exec. asst. to pres. Arkay Packaging Corp., Hauppauge, NY, 1977-86; in-house constrn. mgr., 1980-82; adminstrn. and human resources mgr. Arkay Packaging Corp., Hauppauge, NY, 1986-89, dir. corp. devel., 1989, dir. materials mgmt., 1989-90. Cert. assoc. Goldratt Inst. for LI/Metro NY area, 1990-92; owner Concepts for Constructive Change, Educators and Facilitators for Continuous Improvement, Lake Grove, NY, 1990-92; ind. aviation flight/ground instr. airplane and instrument, 1977—; safety counselor FAA, 1974-92, FAA Ea. region counselors coord., 1985-86; mem. city charter rev. com. City Punta Gorda, Fla., 1996; mem. city coun. City of Punta Gorda, Fla., 1996—, vice mayor, 1998-99, 2000-01, first woman mayor, 2001-02, 2002-03; selected "top 100" west influential in Charlotte County by "Charlotte SUN", 2002, 2003; past bd. dir., officer Aviation Coun. LI; founder Seminar on Air Travel for Everyone (S.A.F.E.), 1975, Fly-C-Cure/We Air Condition People, 1979; city coun. appointee to S.W. Fla. Regional Planning Coun., 1999—, Charlotte County tourist devel. coun., 1998—, Charlotte County Assembly, 1998, 2001, Punta Gorda Historic Mural Soc., past mem. bd. dir.; county appointee Enterprise Charlotte Econ. Devel. team. Author articles, seminar syllabus. Past mem. nat. panel Consumer Arbitrators, Nat. Consumer Arbitration Program, Better Bus. Bur.; lic. comml. pilot, flight and ground instr.; chmn. bd. Charlotte Skatepark, Inc.; past Bd. mem., past officer Punta Gorda Elks Lodge 2606. Past chmn. ninety-nines L.I. chpt., founding internat. chmn. safety edn.; Amelia Earhart Bronze medal 1975, Old Punta Gorda, Inc.; mem. various cmty. non-profit org., (past mem. bd. dir.). Home: 654 Andros Ct Punta Gorda FL 33950-5809

SMITH-PORTER, SUZANNE CLARE, mathematics educator; b. Roseau, Minn., Apr. 26, 1964; d. William Harvey and Helen Ann Wagner; m. Jeffrey Allen Porter, Feb. 18, 2006; children: Courtney Elizabeth Smith, Jordan Clare Smith, Shelby Elizabeth Hutcherson-Porter, Alexis Summer Porter. BS, Ea. Ill. U., Charleston, 1986. Lic. tchr. Profl. Stds. Commn. Ga., 1997, Ill., 1986, Nev., 1991, Ariz., 1987. Math tchr. Kingman Unified Sch. Dist., Ariz., 1987—91, Clarke County Schools, Las Vegas, Nev., 1991—94; secondary math tchr. Nye County Schools, Pahrump, Nev., 1994—97; advanced math tchr. The Walker Sch., Marietta, Ga., 1998—99; secondary advanced placement calculus tchr. Paulding County Schs., Hiram, Ga., 1999—2002; secondary calculus tchr. Douglas County Schs., Douglasville, Ga., 2002—04; mid. sch. math tchr. Cobb County Sch. Sys., Marietta, Ga., 2004—05; secondary math tchr. Rockdale County Sch. Sys., Conyers, Ga., 2005—. Mem.: NEA (life). Home: 1509 WIndy Oaks Ct SE Conyers GA 30013 Office: Salem High School 3551 Underwood Rd Conyers GA 30013 Office Phone: 770-929-0176. Personal E-mail: smith1509@comcast.net. Business E-Mail: ssmith4@rockdale.k12.ga.us.

SMITH-SMITH, PEOLA, principal, not-for-profit executive; Prin. Neptune Middle Sch., NJ. Named one of Most Influential Black Americans, Ebony mag., 2005, 2006. Mem.: Nat. Assn. of Negro Bus. & Profl. Women's Clubs (nat. pres.). Office: NANBPWC, Inc 1806 New Hampshire Ave, NW Washington DC 20009 Office Phone: 202-483-4206. E-mail: PSmith@nanbpwc.org.*

SMITH-VALLEJO, LORA LEE, elementary school educator; d. Juan Carlos and Graciela Vallejo; m. Derek Jason Smith, Mar. 15, 2004. B in Edn., Baylor U., Waco, Tex., 2003. Cert. tchr. Tex. Coord. Waco Reads, 2001—; history tchr. Sharpstown Mid. Sch., Houston, 2003—. Basketball coach Sharpstown Mid. Sch., Houston, 2004—, volleyball coach, 2005—. Children ministry tchr. Awakenings Movement Ch., Houston, 2004—06. Hispanic Future Leaders scholar, Hispanic Assn., 2003. Mem.: ATPE (assoc.). Avocations: reading, camping, travel. Home: 1025 Dulles Ave # 1328 Stafford TX 77477 Office: Sharpstown Mid Sch 8330 Triola Ln Houston TX 77036 Office Phone: 713-778-3440. Business E-Mail: lvallej1@houstonisd.org.

SMITS, HELEN LIDA, medical association administrator, educator; b. Long Beach, Calif., Dec. 3, 1936; d. Theodore Richard Smits and Anna Mary Wells; m. Roger LeCompte, Aug. 28, 1976; 1 child, Theodore. BA with honors, Swarthmore Coll., 1958; MA, Yale U., 1961, MD cum laude, 1967. Intern, asst. resident Hosp. U. Pa., 1967—69; fellow Beth Israel Hosp., Boston, 1969-70; chief resident Hosp. U. Pa., 1970-71; chief med. clinic U. Pa., 1971-75; assoc. adminstr. for patient care svcs. U. Pa. Hosp., 1975-77; v.p. med. affairs Community Health Plan Georgetown U., Washington, 1977; dir. health standards and quality bur. Health Care Financing Adminstrn., HHS, Washington, 1977-80; sr. rsch. assoc. The Urban Inst., Washington, 1980-81; assoc. prof. Yale U. Med. Sch., New Haven, 1981-85; assoc. v.p. for health affairs U. Conn. Health Ctr., Farmington, 1985-87; prof. community medicine U. Conn. Sch. Medicine, Farmington, 1985-93; hosp. dir. John Dempsey Hosp., Farmington, 1987-93; dep. adminstr. Health Care Financing Adminstrn., Washington, 1993-96; pres., chmn. Health Right, Inc., Meriden, Conn., 1996-99; vis. prof. Robert F. Wagner Grad. Sch. Pub. Svc., NYU, 1999—2001. Commr. Joint Com. on Accreditation Hosps., Chgo., 1989-93, chair, 1991-92; mem., co-chair strategic framework bd. Nat. Forum on Health Care Quality Measurement and Reporting, 2000—01; Fulbright lectr. faculty medicine Eduardo Mondlane U., Maputo, Mozambique, 2001-04. Contbr. numerous articles to profl. jours. Bd. dirs. The Ivoryton Playhouse Fedn., Inc., 1990-92, The Connecticut River Mus., 1990-93, Hartford Stage, 1990-93; mem. Dem. Town Com., Essex, Conn., 1982-89; vol. The William J. Clinton Found., Mozambique, 2000-04. Recipient Superior Svc. award HHS, Washington, 1982; Royal Soc. Medicine Found. fellow, London, 1973; Fulbright scholar, 1959-60. Mem. ACP (master, regent 1984-90), Inst. Medicine (vice chmn. com. for evaluation of PEPPAR implementation 2005—), Nat. Acad. Scis., Phi Beta Kappa, Alpha Omega Alpha. Episcopalian. Avocations: sailing, cooking, gardening.

SMOLENSKI, LISABETH ANN, physician; b. Pitts., Oct. 1, 1950; d. Anthony Edward and Betty Jean (Gross) S.; m. William Ward Daniels, May 24, 1980; 1 child, Kathryn Elizabeth. BA, Carlow Coll., Pitts., 1972; MD, Hahnemann U., Phila., 1982. Diplomate Am. Bd. Family Practice. Resident in family practice West Jersey Health Sys., Voorhees, N.J., 1982-85; pvt. practice, Somerville, Tenn., 1985-90, Memphis, 1990—2003; with Spectrum Pain Clinics, Franklin-Nashville, Tenn., 2003—04, Cumberland Back Pain Clinic PC, Cookeville, Tenn., 2005—, Clarksville, Tenn., 2005—. Sec. exec. com. med. staff Meth. Hosp. Somerville, 1988-90. Fellow: Am. Acad. Family Physicians. Republican. Avocation: reading. Office: Cumberland Back Pain Clinic PC 480 Neal St Cookeville TN 38501 also: Cumberland Back Pain Clinic PC 271 Med Park Dr Clarksville TN 37043-6310 Office Phone: 931-520-8104, 931-647-5747.

SMOLKE, CHRISTINA, chemical engineer; BSChemE summa cum laude, U. So. Calif., 1997; PhD in Chem. Engring., U. Calif., Berkeley, 2001. Postdoctoral rschr. U. Calif., Berkeley, 2001—03; asst. prof. chem. engring. Calif. Inst. Tech. Contbr. articles to profl. jours. Named one of Top 100 Young Innovators, MIT Tech. Review, 2004; Postdoctoral fellow, NIH, 2001. Office: Calif Inst Tech Bioengring Faculty MC 210-41 236 A Spalding Pasadena CA 91125

SMOLYANSKY, JULIE, consumer products company executive; b. Russia; arrived in US, 1976; d. Michael and Ludmila Smolyansky. BA, U. Ill., 1996. Dir. sales and mktg. Lifeway Foods Inc., Morton Grove, Ill., 1997—2002, pres., 2002—, CEO, 2002—, CFO, 2002—, treas., 2002—, dir. Avocation: running. Office: Lifeway Foods Inc 6431 West Oakton Ave Morton Grove IL 60053*

SMOOKLER, MAURRISSA, elementary school educator; b. El Paso, Jan. 11, 1950; d. David and Rachael Dichter; children: Lisa, Maureen, Eugene. BS, U. Tex., El Paso, 1989. Tchr. El Paso Ind. Sch. Dist., 1989—. Avocations: bridge, reading, dance. Office: Cordova Mid Sch 2231 Arizona El Paso TX 79930

SMOOT, NATALIE MARIE, lawyer; b. Las Vegas, Nev., Sept. 6, 1980; d. Lawrence James Smoot and Nancy Lee Williams. BA in English, U. Nev., Las Vegas, 2000, JD, 2004. Bar: Nev. 2004. Atty. Palazzo Law Firm, Las Vegas, Nev., 2004, Tharpe & Howell Law Firm, 2005, Bremer, Whyte, Brown & Omeara, 2006—. Avocations: rollerhockey, kickboxing.

SMOOT, SKIPI LUNDQUIST, psychologist; b. Aberdeen, Wash., Apr. 10, 1934; d. Warren Duncan and Miriam Stephen (Bishop) Dobbins; m. Harold Richard Lundquist, June 2, 1951 (div. Mar. 1973); children: Kurt Richard, Mark David, Ted Douglas, Blake Donald; m. Edward Lee Smoot, June 14, 1975. BA in Psychology, Coll. of William and Mary, 1978; MA, Pepperdine U., 1980; PhD, Calif. Sch. of Profl., Psychology, San Diego, 1985. Lic. clin. psychologist, Calif.; lic. marriage and family therapist, Calif. Owner, operator McDonald's Restaurants, San Pedro and Torrance, Calif., 1965-76, Williamsburg, Va., 1965-76; psychotherapist Coll. Hosp., Cerritos, Calif., 1979-81, Orange County Child Guidance, Laguna Hills, Calif., 1981-82, Calif. State Police, Costa Mesa, 1982-83, Anaheim, 1983-84; psychologist Orange County Mental Health, Santa Ana, Calif., 1984-85, Psychol. Ctr., Orange and El Toro, Calif., 1985-91; clin. dir. Career Ambitions, Lake Forest, Calif., 1991-98, Psychol. Decisions, Irvine-Laguna Hills, Calif., 1991-94. Psychol. cons. seminars and workshops for bus., Irvine and Laguna Hills, 1991-98. Mem. APA, Calif. Psychol. Assn. Democrat. Avocations: music, travel, rsch. Office: Psychol Decisions Career Ambitions Unltd 23832 Rockfield Blvd # 165 Lake Forest CA 92630-6822 Office Phone: 949-770-2675. Personal E-mail: skipilsmootphd@cox.net.

SMOTHERMON, PEGGI STERLING, middle school educator; b. Dallas, Nov. 11, 1948; d. Kiel Sterling and Ann C. (Wolfe) Sterling; m. William C. Smothermon Jr., June 20, 1981; children: Kirsten, Melinda, William III. BA, So. Meth. U., Dallas, 1973; MLA, So. Meth. U., 1978. Tchr. Richardson (Tex.) Ind. Sch. Dist., 1973-90, Coppell (Tex.) Ind. Sch. Dist., 1990-96, 2002—. J.J. Pearce scholar. Mem. NEA (faculty rep., membership chmn., sec.), Nat. Coun. Tchrs. Math., Tex. Tchrs. Assn., Assn. Coppell Educators, Tex. Computer Edn. Assn., Tex. Coun. Tchrs. Math., Kappa Delta Pi. Home: 408 Greenridge Dr Coppell TX 75019-5714 Office: Coppell Mid Sch N 120 Natches Trace Dr Coppell TX 75019

SMOTHERMON, REBA MAXINE, elementary school educator; b. Liberal, Kans., July 8, 1933; d. Albert Isaac and Georga Maxine (Long) Shank; m. Wendell Scott Smothermon, Sept. 6, 1953; children: Jennifer Lynn Smothermon Kirby, Wendell Brent Smothermon. BA in Edn., Wichita State U., 1955; MA in Ednl. Psychology and Guidance, U. No. Colo., 1959. Cert. tchr. Kans., Calif., Colo., arthritis instr. Tchr. second grade Unified Sch. Dist. 480/Washington Sch., Liberal, Kans., 1955-57, Adams County Dist. Skyline Vista Sch., Westminster, Colo., 1957-61; elem. tchr. Ventura Unified Santa Ana Sch., Ojai, Calif., 1964-80, Unified Sch. Dist. #480, Southlawn McKinley Schs., Liberal, 1980-95; ret., 1995. Literary coun. mem. Southwest Reading Coun., Liberal, 1985-95. Participant devel. sch. curriculum, 1977-79. Sec. to pres. Evergreen Garden Club, Liberal, 1980-05; youth sponsor, pres. women's group 1st United Meth. Ch., Liberal, 1945—; mem. Liberal Panhellenic, 1980-96; bd. dir., pres. Community Concerts of Liberal, 1987-91; pres. Liberal Woman's Club, 1995—; mem. Kans. Coun. on Travel and Tourism, 2002-05; pres. Book Club I, sec.-treas., tchr. swimming, arthritis support groups. Recipient Lifetime Achievement award, Southwest Daily Times, 2006. Mem. AAUW (pres. local chpt. 1980—, Woman of Yr. 1985, state chmn. internat. rels. com. 1985-90),DAR (regent chaplain 1972-), PEO (various to pres. 1985—), Aurora Club, Ladies' Oriental Shrine N.Am., Delta Kappa Gamma (various to pres. 1981—). Republican. Avocations: music, reading. Home: 830 S Clay F3 PO Box 470 Liberal KS 67905-0470 Personal E-mail: smutsmut@swko.net.

SMOTHERS, DELORIS RICE, computer career educator; d. Bill Junior and Mamie Ford Rice; m. William Douglas Smothers, June 13, 1998; children: Jemeana Roberson, Knegleshia, Terra, Canderiah. MEd, Ala. A&M U., Normal, 1992—95. Computer & office careers instr. North Ala. Skills Ctr., Huntsville, 1981—2001; cis/oad instr. J. F. Drake State Tech. Coll., Huntsville, 2001—; office sys. mgmt. dept. instr. Ala. A&M U. Recipient Master Tchr. Participant award, Ala. Coll. Sys., 2006. Mem.: Nat. Bus. Edn. Assn., Delta Sigma Theta Sorority, Inc. (life; rec. & corr. sec. 2001—). Home: 6607 Willow Springs Blvd Huntsville AL 35806 Office: J F Drake State Tech Coll 3421 Meridian St N Huntsville AL 35811

SMOYAK, SHIRLEY ANNE, psychiatric nurse practitioner, educator; b. Peth Amboy, NJ, June 22, 1935; d. Stephen and Mary Nemeth Soos; m. Cornelius Stephen Smoyak, June 27, 1954; children: Deborah Anne Parrinello, Karen Gail Hoffman, Mark Stephen, Lisa Marie. BSN, Rutgers U., Newark, 1957; MS in Psychiat. Nursing, Rutgers U., New Brunswick, NJ, 1959, PhD in Sociology, 1970. RN NJ., 1957. Disting. prof. Rutgers U., New Brunswick, 2005—. Cons. Jewish Renaissance Found., Peth Amboy; rschr. Network Psychiat. Nurse Rschrs., Oxford, England, 1990—; vis. prof. various univs. Author 4 books; contbr. articles to profl. jours. Rundraiser Diocese of Metuchen, Piscataway, NJ; ct. appointed monitor Morris County Ct., 1977—; bd.dirs., treas. Raritan Millstone Heritage Alliance, Highland Park, NJ, 2004. Recipient Pres.' award for Tchg. Excellence, Rutgers U., 1985, Presdl. award for Commnity Svc., 1995. American Heritage. Home: 4 Roney Rd Edison NJ 08820-3208 Office: Rutgers State U NJ 55 Commercial Ave DCEO New Brunswick NJ 08901 Office Phone: 732-932-4727. Office Fax: 732-235-4004. Business E-Mail: smoyak@rci.rutgers.edu.

SMULLENS, SARAKAY COHEN, psychotherapist, writer; b. Balt. m. Stanton N. Smullens; children: Elizabeth R. Smullens, Douglas R. Smullens, Elisabeth J. Cohen, Kathyanne S. Cohen. Student, Skidmore Coll., 1958-60, Goucher Coll., 1960-62, Cath. U., 1963-64, U. pa., 1964-65. Cert. social worker, group therapist, family life educator; diplomate Am. Bd. Examiners in Clin. Social Work. Regional coord. for Young Dems. Dem. Nat. Com., Washington, 1962-63; protective svc. counselor Soc. to Protect Children from Cruelty, Phila., 1965-66; family therapist Phila. Psychiat. Hosp., 1966-68; marriage and family counselor Jewish Family Svc. of Phila., 1968-73, dir. family life edn., 1971-73; pvt. practice marital, couple, family, group psychotherapy Phila., 1973—. Instr. mental health tech. Hahnemann Med. U., 1974-78, sr. instr., 1978-90, clin. asst. prof., 1990-97; presenter, lectr. in field; appearances on local and nat. TV and radio programs. Author: Whoever Said Life is Fair?, 1982, 2d edit., 1988, Japanese edit., 1985, Setting Yourself Free: Breaking the Cycles of Emotional Abuse in Family, Friendship, Love and Work, 2002; columnist Phila. Inquirer, 1976-81, Phila. Bull., 1981-82. Mem. Goucher Com. for Towson Integration, 1960-62; 8th ward committeewoman Dem. Party, 1967-71; co-founder Women's Way, 1971; mem. cmty. edn. and pub. rels. com. Jewish Family and Children's Agy., 1977-86; bd. dirs. Family Svc. Phila., 1987-92; mem. women's bd. Thomas Jefferson U. Hosp., 1984—, sec., 1989-95; bd. overseers Sch. Social Work, originator of Crystal Stair award U. Pa., 1990—; bd. dirs. Center City Resident's Assn., 1990-94, Phila. chpt. Am. Jewish Congress, 1994—; vice chair Child Welfare Adv. Bd. Phila., 1994, chair, 1994-97; mem. Interdisciplinary Task Force of Child Welfare Sys., 1997; founding co-chair Sabbath of Domestic Peace, 1995. Recipient Peace medal Women's Internat. League for Peace and Freedom, 1962, Louise Waterman Wise award Am. Jewish Congress, 1996.. Mem. NASW, Acad. Cert. Social Workers, Am. Assn. Marriage and Family Therapy, Nat. Coun. Family Rels., Am. Group Therapy Assn., Pa. Assn. marriage and Family Therapy, Authors' Guild. Home and Office: 1710 Pine St Philadelphia PA 19103-6702 Fax: 215-732-4603.

SMULYAN, LISA, educator; b. Syracuse, N.Y., Dec. 5, 1954; d. Harold and Ruth (Finkelstein) S.; m. Michael Steven Langton Markowicz, June 13, 1982; children: Benjamin Markowicz Smulyan, Amanda Smulyan Markowicz. BA, Swarthmore (Pa.) Coll., 1976; MAT, Brown U., 1977; EdD, Harvard U., 1984. Tchr. Brookline (Mass.) Pub. Schs., 1977-80, 84; lectr. U. N.H., Durham, 1983; adj. faculty Lesley Coll., Cambridge, Mass., 1983; lectr. Lincoln-Sudbury (Mass.) Pub. Schs., 1984-85; asst. prof. Program in Edn., Swarthmore Coll., 1985-90, acting dir., 1988—, assoc. prof., 1990—. Cons. HM Study Skills Program, Cambridge, 1982-89; dir. Adventures in Math and Sci., Swarthmore, 1986-88. Co-author: Adolescent Portraits, 1992, Collaborative Action Research, 1989; editor HM Study Skills Program, 1982-83; contbr. articles to profl. jours. Bd. dirs. ABC Swarthmore, 1988-91. Recipient Fulbright fellowship U. Warwick, Eng., 1989, Joel Dean grant Swarthmore Coll., 1987, 89, Faculty Rsch. grant, 1986—, Brown U. fellowship, 1976. Mem. AAUW, Am. Ednl. Rsch. Assn., Consortium for Excellence in Tchr. Edn., Educators for Social Responsibility, Phi Delta Kappa, Phi Beta Kappa.

SMUTNY, JOAN FRANKLIN, academic director, educator; b. Chgo. d. Eugene and Mabel (Lind) Franklin; m. Herbert Paul Smutny; 1 child, Cheryl Anne. BS, MA, Northwestern U. Tchr. New Trier H.S., Winnetka, Ill.; mem. faculty, founder, dir. Nat. H.S. Inst. Northwestern U. Sch. Edn., Chgo.; faculty, founder, dir. h.s. workshop critical thinking/edn. Nat. Coll. Edn., Evanston, Ill., exec. dir. h.s. workshops, 1970-75; founder, dir. Woman Power Through Edn. Seminar, 1969-74; dir. Right to Read Seminar in critical reading, 1973-74; dir. seminar gifted h.s. students, 1973; dir. gifted programs for 6th, 7th, 8th graders Evanston pub. schs., 1978-79; dir. gifted programs 1st-8th grade Glenview (Ill.) pub. schs., 1979—. Dir. gifted programs Nat.-Louis U., Evanston, 1980-82, dir. Ctr. for Gifted, 1982—; dir. Bright and Talented Project, 1986—, North Shore Country Day Sch., Winnetka, 1982—; dir. Job Creation Project, 1980-82; dir. New Dimensions for Women, 1973;

dir. Thinking for Action in Career Edn. Program 1976-79; dir. TACE, dir. Humanities Program for Verbally Precocious Youth, 1978-79; co-dir., instr. seminars in critical thinking Ill. Family Svc., 1972-75; writer edn. filmstrips in lang. arts and lit. Soc. Visual Edn., 1970-74; spkrs. bur. Coun. Fgn. Rels., 1968-69; adv. com. edn. professions devel. act U.S. Office Edn., 1969—; state team for gifted, Ill. Office Edn., Office of Gifted, Springfield, Ill., 1977; writer, cons. Radiant Ednl. Corp., 1969-71; cons. ALA, 1969-71, workshop leader and spkr. gifted edn., 1971—; coord. career edn. Nat. Coll.Edn., 1976-78, dir. Project 1987—, dir. Summer Wonders, 1986—, Creative Children's Acad., bd. dirs., Worlds of Wisdom and Wonder, 1978—; dir. Future Tchrs. Am. Seminar in Coll. and Career, 1970-72; cons. rsch. & devel. Ill. Dept. Vocat. Edn., 1973—; evaluation cons. DAVTE, IOE, Springfield, Ill., 1977, mem. Leadership Tng. Inst. Gifted, U.S. Office Edn., 1973-74; dir. workshops for h.s. students; cons., spkr. in field; dir. Gifted Young Writers and Young Writers confs., 1978, 79; dir. Project '92 The White House Conf. on Children and Youth; mem. adv. bd. Educating Able Learners, 1991—; chmn. bd. dirs. Barbereux Sch., Evanston, 1992—; asst. editor, editl. bd. Understanding our Gifted, 1994—. Author: (with others) Job Creation: Creative Materials, Activities and Strategies for the Classroom, 1982, A Thoughtful Overview of Gifted Education, 1990, Your Gifted Child—How to Recognize and Develop the Special Talents in Your Child from Birth to Age Seven, 1987, paperback, 1991, Education of the Gifted: Programs and Perspectives, 1990, Teaching Gifted Young Children in the Regular Classroom, 1997, Gifted Girls, 1998, Stand Up For Your Gifted Child, 2001, Gifted Education: Promising Practices, 2003, Differentiated Instruction, 2003, Differentiating For the Young Child, 2004; editor: The Young Gifted Child: Potential and Promise: An Anthology, 1998, Underserved Gifted Populations, 2003; contbg. editor Roper Rev., 1994—; asst. editor Understanding Our Gifted, 1995—; editor, contbr. Maturity in Teching; writer ednl. filmstrips The Brothers Grimm, How the West Was Won, Mutiny on the Bounty, Dr. Zhivago, Space Odyssey 2001, Christmas Around the World; editor IAGC Jour. for Gifted, 1994—; adv. bd. Gifted Edn. Press Quar., 1995—; contbr. editor numerous books in field; contbr. articles to profl. jours. including Chgo. Parent Mag.; reviewer programs for Gifted and Talented, U.S. Office Edn., 1976-78; editor Creativity Series Ablex, 1998—. Mem. AAUP, Nat. Assn. Gifted Child (nat. membership chmn. 1991—, co-chmn. schs. and programs, co-editor newsletter early childhood divsn.), Nat. Soc. Arts & Letters (nat. bd., 1st and 3d v.p. Evanston chpt. 1990-92), Mortar Bd., Outstanding Educators of Am. 1974, Pi Lambda Theta, Phi Delta Kappa (v.p. Evanston chpt. rsch. chmn. 1990-92). Home: 633 Forest Ave Wilmette IL 60091-1713

SNAPP, ELIZABETH, librarian, educator; b. Lubbock, Tex., Mar. 31, 1937; d. William James and Louise (Lanham) Mitchell; m. Henry Franklin Snapp, June 1, 1956 (div. Dec. 2001). BA magna cum laude, North Tex. State U., Denton, 1968, MLS, 1969, MA, 1977. Asst. to archivist Archive of New Orleans Jazz Tulane U., 1960-63; catalog libr. Tex. Woman's U., Denton, 1969-71, head acquisitions dept., 1971-74, coord. readers svcs., 1974-77, asst. to dean Grad. Sch., 1977-79, instr. libr. sci., 1977-88, acting Univ. libr., 1979-82, dir. librs., 1982—2002, dir. librs. emeritus, 2002—, univ. historian, 1995—2002; adj. prof. dept. history and govt. Tex. Woman's U., Denton, 2002—; rsch. assoc. Tex. Woman's U. Libr., Denton, 2002—. Chair-elect Tex. Coun. State U. Librs., 1988—90, chmn., 1990—92; adv. com. on libr. formula Coord. Bd. Tex. Coll. and Univ. Sys., 1981—92; Libr. Sys. Act adv. bd. Tex. State Libr. and Archives Commn., 1999—2002; del. OCLC Nat. Users Coun., 1985—87, by-laws com., 1985—86, com. on less-than-full-svcs. networks, 1986—87; trustee AMIGOS Libr. Svcs., 1994—2000, sec. bd. trustees, 1996—97, vice-chmn. bd. trustees, 1997—99, chair bd. trustees, 1999—2000; project dir. NEH consultancy grant on devel. core curriculum for women's studies, 1981—82; chmn. Blue Ribbon com. 1986 Gov.'s Commn. for Women to select 150 outstanding women in Tex. History; project dir. math./sci. anthology project Tex. Found. Women's Resources; co-sponsor Irish Lecture Series, Denton, 1968, 70, 73, 78. Asst. editor Tex. Academe, 1973—76; co-editor: Read All About Her! Texas Women's History: A Working Bibliography, 1995; contbg. author Women in Special Collections, 1984, Special Collections, 1986, book reviewer Libr. Resources and Tech. Svcs., 1973—2002; contbr. articles to profl. jours. Trustee, treas. Adult Day Care of North Tex., 2002—04, v.p., 2004; sec. Denton County Dem. Caucus, 1970. Recipient Ann. Pioneer award, Tex. Woman's U., 1986, Women's Studies Vision award, 1998. Mem.: AAUW (legis. br. chmn. 1973—74, br. v.p. 1975—76, br. pres. 1979—80, state historian 1986—88, treas. 1998—99), ALA (stds. com. 1983—85), AAUP, Tex. Assn. Coll. Tchrs. (pres. Tex. Woman's U. chpt. 1976—77), So. Conf. Brit. Studies, Women's Collecting Group (chmn. ad hoc com. 1984—86), Tex. Hist. Commn. (judge for Farenbach History prize 1990—93), Tex. Libr. Assn. (program com. 1978, Dist. VII chmn. 1985—86, archives and oral history com. 1990—92, co-chair conf. program com. 1994, Tall Texan selection com. 1995—96, treas. exec. bd. 1996—99, Centennial com. 2000—02), AAUW Ednl. Found. (rsch. and awards panel 1990—94), Alliance Higher Edn. (chair coun. libr. dirs. 1993—95), Rotary Internat. (sec. local chpt. 1999—2002), Soroptimist Internat. (pres. Denton chpt. 1986—88), Women's Shakespeare Club (pres. 1967—69), Pi Delta Phi, Alpha Lambda Sigma (pres. 1970—71), Alpha Chi, Beta Phi Mu (pres. chpt. 1976 1978, sec. nat. adv. assembly 1978—79, pres. 1979—80, nat. dir. 1981—83). Methodist. Office: TWU Sta PO Box 424093 Denton TX 76204-4093 Personal E-mail: esnapp@verizon.net.

SNAVELY, DEANNE LYNN, chemistry professor; b. Columbus, Ohio, Nov. 16, 1951; d. Cloyd Arten and Ruth Helen Snavely; 1 child, Evangelia Sophia Leontis. PhD in Chemistry, Yale U., New Haven, Conn., 1979—83. Prof. chemistry Bowling Green State U., Ohio, 1998—2006, chair dept. chemistry, 1999—2003, assoc. dean grad. coll., 2003—. Recipient Naval Young Investigator award, 1988. Mem.: Am. Chem. Soc. Office: Bowling Green State Univ Bowling Green Bolwing Green OH 43403 Business E-Mail: snavely@bgnet.bgsu.edu.

SNEDAKER, CATHERINE RAUPAGH (KIT SNEDAKER), editor; d. Paul and Charity (Primmer) Raupagh; m. William Brooks; children: Eleanor, Peter William; m. 2d Weldon Snedaker. BA, Duke U. Promotion mgr. Sta. WINR-TV and WNBF-TV, Binghamton, N.Y.; TV editor, feature writer Binghamton Sun, 1960-68; mem. staff, food editor, restaurant critic L.A. Herald Examiner, 1978-80, food and travel editor. Author: The Great Convertibles; editor: The Food Package; guest editor: Mademoiselle mag., 1942; contbr. numerous articles on food and travel to nat. mags. and newspapers. Recipient 3 awards L.A. Press Club, VISTA award, 1979. Democrat. Home: 140 San Vicente Blvd Apt A Santa Monica CA 90402-1533 E-mail: kitsnedaker@verizon.net.

SNEED, ELLOUISE BRUCE, retired nursing administrator, educator; b. Monroe, La., June 21, 1945; d. Wesley Newton Bruce and Oza Celeste Parker; m. Gary Arnold, Aug. 10, 1978. RN, Mather Sch. Nursing, New Orleans, 1966; BS in Nursing, William Carey Coll., Hattiesburg, Miss., 1975; MS in Nursing, Med. Coll. Ga., Augusta, 1978; EdD, U. So. Miss., Hattiesburg, 1981. Instr. comm.-psychiat. nursing Charity Hosp. Sch. Nursing, New Orleans, 1975-77; family nurse cons. Drs. R. Gregory and G. Keller, Mandeville, La., 1978-83; assoc. prof. Sch. Nursing William Carey Coll., New Orleans, 1980-88; employee well health and health fair cons. St. Tammany Parish Hosp., Covington, La., 1987-88; prof., Holder Coughlin Sanders chair divsn. nursing La. Coll., Pineville, 1988—95, prof. emeritus, 1999—. Ednl. program cons., 1984-85; speaker-presenter for profl. orgns. and instns. throughout La. Contbg. author: Crisis Intervention Theory and Practice: A Clinical Handbook, 1980, Mosby's 1988, 92 Secured Assess Test: A Practice Test Exam for RN Licensure, 1988, 92. Trustee and Deacon Emmanuel Bapt. Ch. Alexandria. Named A Great One Hundred Nurse, New Orleans Dist. Nurses Assn., 1987. Mem. ARC, Friend of Nursing of La. (coll. divsn. of nursing 1997), Sigma Theta Tau (treas. Nu Tau chpt.). Home: PO Box 13467 Alexandria LA 71315-3467

SNEED, PAULA ANN, food products executive; b. Everett, Mass., Nov. 10, 1947; d. Thomas Edwin and F. Mary (Turner) S.; m. Lawrence Paul Bass, Sept. 2, 1978; children: Courtney Jameson. BA, Simmons Coll., 1969; MBA, Harvard U., 1977; D Bus. Adminstrn. (hon.), Johnson & Wales U., 1991. Ednl. supr., femal coord. Outreach Program for Problem Drinkers, 1969-71; dir. plans, program devel. and evaluations Ecumenical Ctr. in Roxbury, Mass., 1971-72; program coord. Boston Sickle Cell Ctr., 1972-75; asst. product mgr. Gen. Food Corp., White Plains, N.Y., 1977-79, assoc. product mgr., 1979-80; product mgr. Gen. Foods Corp., White Plains, N.Y., 1980-82, sr. product mgr., 1982-83, product group mgr., 1983-86, category mgr., 1986-87, v.p. consumer affairs, 1986-90, pres. food svc. div., sr. v.p., 1990-95; sr. v.p. mktg. svcs. Kraft Foods N.Am., 1995, group v.p., pres. e-commerce and mktg. services, 2000—04; sr. v.p. global mktg. resources Kraft Foods Inc., 2004—05, exec. v.p. global mktg. resources & initiatives, 2005—. Mem. bd. dirs. Hercules Inc., 1994-2002, Airgas Inc., 99-, Charles Schwab Corp., 2002-. Bd. dirs. Crispus Attucks Scholarship Fund, Ridgewood, N.J., 1982, Westchester/Fairfield Inroads; trustee Simmons Coll., Teach for Am., Chgo. Children's Museum. Recipient Benevolent Heart award Graham-Windham, 1987, Black Achiever award Harlem YWCA, 1982, MBA of Yr. Harvard Bus. Sch., 1987, Benevolent Heart award Graham Windham Soc., 1987; named MBA of Yr. Harvard Bus. Sch. Black Alumni Orgn., 1987; named one of 100 Top Black Women in Corp. Am. Ebony Mag., 1990, 91, 21 Most Influential African Ams. in Corp. Am., 1991, 97 (One of 40 Most Influential, 1993), Breakthrough 50 Exec. Female Mag., 50 Most Powerful Women Mgrs., 1994, 25 Most Influential Mothers Working Mother Mag., 1998; inducted Acad. Women Achievers N.Y. YWCA, 1990. Mem. AAUW, Exec. Leadership Coun., Chgo. Network, adv. coun. to dean Howard U. Bus. Sch., Nat. Assn. Negro Bus. and Profl. Women, Coalition of 100 Black Women, Soc. Consumer Affairs Profls., Women's Forum. Office: Kraft Foods Inc Three Lakes Dr Northfield IL 60093-2753

SNELL, COURTNEY LYNN, academic administrator; d. Lester Anthony, Jr. and Sandra Lynn Snell. BS, Miss. Valley State U., Itta Bena, 1999; MS, Grambling State U., La., 2001. Tchg. asst. Grambling State U., 2000—01; US Golf Assn. P. J. Boatwright intern Nat. Minority Golf Found., Phoenix, 2001—02; asst. to mountain region dir. First Tee, Albuquerque, 2002—03; sr. acad. and athletic advisor U. N.Mex, Albuquerque, 2003—. Com. mem. U. N.Mex Grad. and Profl. Student Conflict Resolution Com., Albuquerque, 2004—. Mem.: Nat. Assn. Girls and Women in Sports, Am. Alliance Health, Phys. Edn., Recreation and Dance, N.Mex Am. Alliance Health, Phys. Edn., Recreation and Dance, Alpha Kappa Alpha. Office Phone: 505-277-0721.

SNELL, JENNIFER LYNN, literature and language educator; b. Oklahoma City, Jan. 11, 1972; d. Kenneth Ray and Susan Kaye Davis; m. Steven Christopher Snell, Oct. 24, 1992; children: Laura, Patrick. BA, East Cen. U., Ada, Okla., 1994, MA in Edn., 1998. Tchr. English, libr. Pittsburg (Okla.) H.S., 1996—2000; tchr. English, speech coach Stonewall (Okla.) H.S., 2000—. Team adviser Curriculum Alignment, Stonewall, 2006—. Named Local Tchr. of Yr., 1999, 2003. Mem.: Okla. Coun. Tchrs. English, Nat. Coun. Tchrs. English.

SNELL, MARILYN NELSON, psychologist, researcher; b. American Fork, Utah, Feb. 11, 1951; d. Ray C. and Affra M. Nelson; m. Paul Decker Snell, Aug. 13, 1969; children: Ben, Matt, Scott, Nelson, Jeff, Robby. BS in Psychology, Brigham Young U., 1972; MS in Counseling Psychology, U. Utah, 1996, PhD in Counseling Psychology, 1999. Postdoc. fellow, resident U. Counseling Ctr. and Dept. Family Preventive Medicine, U. Utah, Salt Lake City, 1999—2000; vis. asst. prof. U. Utah, Salt Lake City, 2000—02; pvt. practice Sandy (Utah) Counseling Ctrs., 2001—05, dir. rsch., 2001—05; chief psychologist Journey at Willow Creek, Utah, 2003—; prin., owner Snell Psychol. Svcs., Sandy, 2004—; co-owner Counseling and Assessments, LLC, Sandy, 2005—. Presenter in field; rev. manuscripts Covenant Pub., American Fork, 2002—; bd. dirs. Nat. Coalition for Emotional Abuse Awareness, 2005—; adj. faculty mem. dept. counseling psychology U. Utah, 2004—. Co-author: Quality Assurance in Residential Care: Organizational Assessment, 2001. Acad. scholar, Brigham Young U., 1969—72. Mem.: Assn. Women Psychologists, Utah Psychol. Assn., Am. Psychol. Assn. Mem. Lds Ch. Avocations: gardening, sports, travel, reading. Office: Counseling and Assessments LLC 11075 S State Ste 28 Sandy UT 84070 Office Phone: 801-501-8444. Business E-Mail: msnell@uofu.net.

SNELL, PATRICIA POLDERVAART, librarian, consultant; b. Santa Fe, Apr. 11, 1943; d. Arie and Edna Beryl (Kerchmar) Poldervaart; m. Charles Eliot Snell, June 7, 1966. BA in Edn., U. N.M., 1965; MSLS, U. So. Calif., 1966. Asst. edn. libr. U. So. Calif., L.A., 1966—68; med. libr. Bedford (Mass.) VA Hosp., 1968—69; asst. law libr. U. Miami, Coral Gables, Fla., 1970—71; acquistions libr. U. N.Mex. Law Sch. Libr., Albuquerque, 1971—72; order libr. Los Angeles County Law Libr., 1972—76, cataloguer, 1976—90; libr. Parks Coll., Albuquerque, 1990—92; records technician Technadyne Engrng. Cons. to Sandia Nat. Labs., 1992—93; libr. Tireman Learning Materials Ctr. U. N.Mex., Albuquerque, 1993—96, instr. libr. sci. program Coll. Edn., 1991—; rsch. technician City of Albuquerque, 1996—2006; legal rsch. techn. Bernalillo County, 2006—. Ch. libr. Beverly Hills Presbyn. Ch., 1974-90, ch. choir libr., 1976-90. Southwestern Library Assn. scholar, 1965. Mem.: ALA, N.Mex. Libr. Assn., Pi Lambda Theta. Avocations: travel, reading. Office: Law Libr BCMDC 5800 Shelly Rd SW Albuquerque NM 87151 Business E-Mail: psnell@bernco.gov.

SNELL, VICKI L., chemistry and physics educator; d. Howard W. and Jeanette M. Popham; m. Richard E. Snell, Jan. 26, 2001; children: Jennifer L. Morgan, Jason P. Morgan. MA in Gen. Sci., Ball State U., Muncie, Ind., 2004. Lic. tchr. chemistry and physics Ind. Dept. Edn., 2004. Tchr. sci. St. Matthew's Sch., Alton, Ill., 1976—77; tchr. biology, chemistry, and physics West End Christian Sch., Tuscaloosa, Ala., 1978—86; tchr. chemistry and physics Aliceville (Ala.) H.S., 1977—78; tchr. chemistry Delta H.S., Muncie, Ind., 1994—97; tchr. chemistry and physics Monroe Ctrl. Jr-Sr H.S., Parker City, Ind., 1997—. Election pole worker Rep. Party, Muncie, Ind., 1990—96; active bible sch. Ctr. Chapel United Meth. Ch., Muncie, 1988—90; tchr. Sunday Sch. 1st Presbyn. Ch., Muncie, 1986—87. Finalist Educator of Yr. award, Tuscaloosa (Ala.) Jaycees, 1983; named Most Accessible Educator, Disabled Student Assn. Ivy Tech Coll., 1994. Mem.: Hoosier Assn. Sci. Tchrs., Inc., Ind. Alliance Chemistry Tchrs. (assoc.; area rep. 2003—05). Meth. Avocations: jewelry making, painting, stained glass, reading, walking. Office Phone: 765-468-7545.

SNELLING, BARBARA W., retired state legislator; b. Fall River, Mass., Mar. 22, 1928; d. Frank Taylor and Hazel (Mitchell) Weil; m. Richard Arkwright Snelling, June 14, 1947 (dec. Aug. 1991); children: Jacqueline, Mark, Diane, Andrew. AB magna cum laude, Radcliffe Coll., 1950; D of Pub. Svc. (hon.), Norwich U., 1981; LLD (hon.), Middlebury Coll., 1997; LLD (hon.), St. Michaels Coll., 2002. Pres. Snelling and Kolb, Inc., 1982-95; lt. gov. State of Vt., 1993-97; mem. Vt. Senate, Montpelier, Vt., 1997—99, 2001—02, ret., 2002. Bd. dirs. U.S. Inst. Peace; mem. adv. bd. Westaff Inc. Vt., 1997—. Mem. bd. sch. dirs. Champlain Valley Union HS, 1962—69, chmn., 1962—68, others; mem. Vt. Edn. Adv. Coun., 1968—71, New Eng. Tchr. Edn. Adv. Com., 1968—70, Shelburne Sch. Bd., 1958—73, Vt. Alcohol and Drug Rehab., 1970—73, Vt. State Bd. Edn., 1971—77, Vt. Ednl. Partnerships, 1992—2000, New. Eng. Bd. Dollars for Scholars, 1997—2002, Champlain Valley Area Health Edn. Coun., 1997—2002; bd. dirs. Vt. Cmty. Found., 1986—94, Shelburne Mus., 1988—98, Vt. Program Quality, 1997—2002; trustee Champlain Coll., 1971—74, Radcliffe Coll., 1990—95; v.p. devel. and external affairs U. Vt., 1974—82. Named Vt. Citizen of the Yr., Vt. State C. of C., 2002; recipient Laymen's award, Vt. Edn. Assn., 1965, Fanny G. Shaw award for Disting. Cmty. Svc., Burlington Cmty. Coun., 1972, Hope award, MS Cmty. Champion, 1996, Philanthropy Day award, Nat. Soc. Fundraising Execs., 1997, Susan B. Anthony award, YWCA Vt., 2001, Robert Skiff Cmty. Svc. award, Lake Champlain C. of C., 2002, Vt. Children's Trust Found. award, 2002, Patricia S. Walton award, Vt. Soc. Pub. Adminstrn., 2002, AHEC Bi State Primary Care Assn. award, 2002, Vt. Alzheimer's Assn. award, 2002, Gold heart, Am. Heart Assn., 2002. Office Phone: 802-985-2121. Personal E-mail: ulfkiel@aol.com.

SNIDER, BEVERLY ANNETTE, mathematics educator; b. Sulphur, Okla., May 24, 1951; d. Leon William and Verbie Mae Richards; m. David Michael Snider, Aug. 6, 1972; children: Michael John, Melinda LuAnn. BS in Edn., East Ctrl. U., Ada, Okla., 1972; MA in Edn., Cameron U., Lawton, Okla., 2003. Tchr. math. Eisenhower H.S., Lawton, Okla., 1986—. Mem. grad. adv. com. Cameron U., Lawton, Okla., 2002—03. Mem.: Phi Kappa Phi.

SNIDER, JANE ANN, retired elementary school educator; b. Inglewood, Calif., Nov. 18, 1939; d. Percy E. and Mamie D. (Gorman) S. MusB, U. So. Calif., 1962; MS, Azusa Pacific U., 1987. Cert. gen. elem. and spl. secondary music tchr. Tchr. 6th grade Centralia Sch. Dist., Buena Park, Calif., 1963—2004, mentor, tchr. computer tech., 1983-97; ret. Home: 24597 Glen Eagles Dr Corona CA 92883 E-mail: jasnider@sbcglobal.net.

SNIDER, KAREN, human services administrator; b. Reading, Pa., Jan. 4, 1940; d. Howard Calvin and Margaret (Davis) Goeringer; m. Jack F. Snider, Sep. 2, 1961; children: Todd Jefferey, Kipp David. BA, Susquehanna U., Selinsgrove, Pa., 1961. Civil rights program dir. Office of Mental Health, Harrisburg, Pa., 1974-75; acting dep. sec., dir. field ops., spl. asst. to dep. Office of Mental REtardation, Harrisburg, 1975-82; exec. asst. to exec. dep. sec. Pa. Dept. Pub. Welfare, Harrisburg, 1982-83, area mgr. income maintenance, 1983-85, spl. asst. to sec., 1985-89, dep. sec. for mental health, 1989-91, sec., 1991-95; pvt. cons. Human Svcs. Innovations, Mechanicsburg, Pa., 1995-97; chief oper. officer Northwestern Human Svcs., Lafayette Hill, Pa., 1997—. Chair fin. campaign Pa. Alliance for Mentally Ill, Harrisburg, 1995-99. Recipient Human Svcs. award The Northwesetern Corp., 1990, Pres.'s award Pa. Assn. County Human Svcs. Adminstrs., 1993, Pres.'s award Domestic Rels. Assn. Pa., 1993, Outstanding Pub. Svc. award Assn. for Retarded Citizens Pa., 1994, Leadership award Shippensburg State U., 1994, Outstanding Leadership award Pa. Assn. Residences for People with Mental Retardation, 1994, others. Avocations: gardening, interior design. Home: 20 Manor Dr Mechanicsburg PA 17055-6133

SNIDER, LOIS A. PHILLIPS, educator; b. Keokuk, Iowa, July 9, 1949; d. Forrest W. and Dorothy J. (Sisson) Phillips; m. Duane E. Snider, Apr. 3, 1970; children: David Duane, Leigh Anne. AA, Hannibal-LaGrange Coll., 1969; BA, Okla. Baptist U., Shawnee, 1971; MA, Northeast Mo. State U., Kirksville, 1985. Bus. tchr. Ind. Pub. Schs., Mo., 1971-77; bus. instr. Ind. Adult Edn., Mo., 1973-82; instr. Hannibal-LaGrange Coll., Mo., 1982-85, asst. prof. of bus. Mo., 1985—, chair. bus. dept. Mo., 1992—, divsn. chair bus/cis, 2003—. Mem., past chairperson Bus. Edn. Adv. Com. of the Hannibal Area Vocat. Tech. Sch., 1982-88. Sun. sch. tchr. Fifth St. Bapt. Ch., 2001—03, 2005—. Recipient Govs. award Excellence in Tchg., 2001. Mem. DAR, Mo. Assn. Acctg. Educators, Nat. Bus. Edn. Assn., Delta Pi Epsilon. Republican. Avocations: reading, gardening. Office: Hannibal-LaGrange Coll 2800 Palmyra Rd Hannibal MO 63401-1940 Home: 416 Lake Apollo Dr Hannibal MO 63401-6203

SNIDER, MARIE ANNA, syndicated columnist; b. Croghan, N.Y., Aug. 9, 1927; d. Nicholas and Dorothy (Moser) Gingerich; m. Howard Mervin, Nov. 27, 1954; children: Vada Marie, Conrad Howard. BS, Goshen Coll., 1949; M in Religious Edn., Mennonite Bibl. Sem., 1957; MS, Kans. State U., 1980. High sch. tchr. Rockway Collegiate, Kitchener, Ont., Can., 1949-53; free-lance writer, 1953-54; pub. rels. Goshen Coll., Ind., 1955-57; free-lance writer, homemaker, 1957-67; info. editor Prairie View, Inc., Newton, Kans., 1967-76, dir., pub. info. & edn., 1976-85, dir. communications, 1985-91; freelance writer, columnist North Newton, 1991—; syndicated columnist "This Side of 60", 1992—. Bd. dirs. Health Systems Agy. of S.E. Kans., 1981-86, v.p., 1986-87; workshop presenter Nat. Coun. of Community Mental Health Ctrs., Atlanta, 1980, N.Y., 1982, 89, Miami, 1987. Editor: Media and Terrorism--The Psychological Impact, 1976; columnist: This Side of 60. Pres. City Council, N Newton, 1977-79, pres. 1980. Recipient 1st Pl. MacEachern award Assn. of Hosp. Pub. Rels., 1981, 1st Pl. Media award Nat. Coun. Community Mental Health Ctrs., 1977, 84, runner-up Pub. Rels. award Nat. Assn. Pvt. Psychiat. Hosps., 1980. Mem. Nat. Soc. Newspaper Columnists. Democrat. Avocations: research on role of women in american comics (speaker and media interviews on this topic), empowerment in aging. Home and Office: PO Box 332 North Newton KS 67117-0332 E-mail: thisside60@aol.com.

SNIDER, STACEY, film company executive; b. Phila., Apr. 29, 1961; m. Gary Jones; children: Katie, Natalie. BA, U. Penn., 1982; JD, U. Calif. LA, 1985. Dir. of devel. Guber-Peters Entertainment Co., 1986—90, exec. v.p., 1990—92; pres. prodn. TriStar Pictures, 1992-96; co-pres. prodn. Universal Pictures, Universal City, Calif., 1996—98, pres. prodn., 1998—99, chmn., CEO, 1999—2006; co-chmn., CEO DreamWorks SKG, Glendale, Calif., 2006—. Bd. dirs. Am. Film Inst. Bd. dirs. Spl. Olympics of So. Calif.; bd. trustees Art Ctr. Coll. of Design, Pasadena, Calif. Named one of 100 Most Powerful Women in Entertainment, Hollywood Reporter, 2005, Most Powerful Women, Forbes mag., 2005, 50 Most Powerful People in Hollywood, Premiere mag., 2004—05, 100 Most Powerful Women in Bus., Fortune mag., 2005—06; recipient Dorothy and Sherrill C. Corwin Human Rels. Award, Am. Jewish Com., 2003. Office: DreamWorks SKG 1000 Flower St Glendale CA 91201*

SNIDER, VIRGINIA L., antitrust consultant; b. Chgo., July 17, 1946; d. Edwin Gaines and Sue (Kemmer) Lansford; m. L. Britt Snider, Aug. 24, 1974; 1 child, Britt Arnold. BA, Wash. State U., Pullman, 1971. Merger analyst U.S. Fed. Trade Commn., Washington, 1973-89, spl. projects dir., 1989-94; antitrust cons. Clifford Chance US LLP, N.Y.C. and Washington, 1994—2003; antitrust conts. Weil, Gotshal & Manges LLP, NYCand Washington, 2003—. Co-author of U.S. merger guidelines for U.S. Govt., 1992; contbr. articles to profl. jours. Mem. bd. visitors Washington Episcopal Sch., 1988—, founding trustee, 1986. Recipient Disting. Svc. award U.S. Govt., 1994. Episcopalian. Office: Weil Gotshal & Manges 1300 Eye St NW Washington DC 20005 Office Phone: 202-682-7006. Business E-Mail: ginger.snider@weil.com.

SNIFFEN, FRANCES P., artist; d. Esther Wade; m. Richard Sniffen; children: William, Kevin, Jeffrey, John, Caroline. BFA, Corcoran Coll. Art and Design, 1996. Resident artist Arlington Arts Ctr., Arlington, Va., 2001—, tchr. art summer workshop; studio Millennium Art Ctr., Washington, 2003. Mem. women's com. Nat. Mus. Women in Arts, Washington, 2001—. Author (with Caroline Sniffen): Coloring Shadows, 1994 (Dorothy Tabak Meml. award NAWA, 2002); exhibitions include Artscape 97, Balt., Md., 1997, WPA Space, Washington, 1998, Bristol (RI) Art Mus., 2001, The DCCA, Wilmington, Del., 2002, Russian Embassy Cultural Ctr., Washington, 2002, Attleboro (Mass.) Mus., 2002, IASG, 2002, Tsinghua U., Bejing, China, Gallery K, Washington, 2002, Biennale Internazionale Dell'Arte Contemporanea Citta di Firenze, 2003, one-woman shows include Gallery K, Wash., 2003, mentioned in critical review by John Blee, Art Critics Rev., Georgetowner Newspaper, 2003. Mem. gala com. Imperial Collections, State Hermitage Mus. for Nat. Mus. Women in the Arts, Washington, 2003; vol. White House, Washington, 1992—93; mem. art com., event chmn. Hospitality Info. Svc. Meridian House Internat., Washington, 1986—; mem. women's com., event chair Nat. Symphony Orch. Kennedy Ctr., Washington, 1986—; women's bd. exec. vol. Georgetown U. Hosp., Washington, 1988—2002. Mem.: Nat. Assn. Women Artists, Inc. (juried membership, N.Y.C.). Avocations: creative writing, music, sports, politics, nutrition.

SNODDERLY, LOUISE DAVIS, librarian; b. Polk County, Oreg., Feb. 1, 1925; d. Charles Benjamin Franklin and Grace L. (Cassady) Davis; m. Charles Hugh Snodderly, May 19, 1949; 1 son, Lynn Jerome. BS, E. Tenn. State U., 1946; MS, U. Tenn., 1962, postgrad., 1979, 82. Tchr., girls' coach Rush Strong HS, Strawberry Plains, Tenn., 1946-49, libr., 1954-62; tchr., girls' coach Cosby HS, Tenn., 1949-50; tchr., libr. Maury HS, Dandridge, Tenn., 1951-54; cataloger City of Knoxville, Tenn., 1962-67; periodicals libr. Carson-Newman Coll., Jefferson City, Tenn., 1967-90; cons. Jefferson County Libr., Tenn., 1976—2003. Sch. commr. Jefferson County, 1976—2004; com.

woman Nat. Fedn. Rep. Women, Jefferson County, 1976—. Mem. Southeastern Libr. Assn., Tenn. Libr. Assn., Am. Sch. Bd. Assn., Tenn. Sch. Bd. Assn., PTA, Les Aimes Club. Baptist. Home: 2131 W Highway 11E Strawberry Plains TN 37871-3556

SNODGRASS, CONNIE SUE, secondary school educator; b. Sparta, Wis., Jan. 2, 1952; d. E.L. and Kathleen Travis; m. Robert L. Snodgrass, Aug. 4, 1973; children: Clayton, Erin. BS in Bus. Edn., Mo. So. State Coll., Joplin, 1973; MS in Edn., Ctrl. Mo. State U., Warrensburg, 1984; cert., Emporia (Kans.) State U., 1991. Tchr. Hickman Mills H.S., Kansas City, Mo., 1973-83, Blue Valley H.S., Stilwell, Kans., 1984—. KAN LEAD fellow Dept. Edn. State of Kans., 1990. Mem. ASCD, Nat. Bus. Edn. Assn., Phi Delta Kappa. Avocations: water sports, reading, computer activities. Office: Blue Valley H S 6001 W 159th St Stilwell KS 66085-8808 E-mail: connies@sound.net.

SNODGRASS, LYNN, small business owner, former state legislator; married; children: Jenne, Megan. BS in Elem. Edn., Oreg. State U., 1973; degree, Portland State U., 1975. Owner Drake's 7 Dees Nursery & Landscape Co., Oreg.; mem. Oreg. Ho. of Reps., 1995—2000; dep. majority leader, 1995-97; majority leader, 1997—2000; speaker of the house Oregon House of Reps, Salem, 1998—2000. Mem. Damascus (Oreg.) Sch. Dist. Budget Com., 1985-88, Damascus Sch. Bd., 1991-94; mem. Oreg. Ho. of Reps. Human Resources and Edn. Com. (Edn. sub-com.), 1995-97, Labor Com., 1995-97, Commerce Com. (Bus. sub-com.), 1995-97, Children and Families Com., 1995-97, Emergency Bd. Com. (Edn. sub-com.), 1995-97, Interim Edn. Com., 1995-97, Legis. Adminstrn. Com., 1995—, Rules and Election Com., 1997—. Mem., past pres. Mt. Hood Med. Ctr. Found.; bd. dirs. Specialized Housing, Inc., Metro Home Builder; mem. Good Shepherd Cmty. Ch.; tchr. Jr. Achievement; classroom vol. Avocations: racquetball, reading, singing, camping, cooking. Fax: 503-986-1347.

SNOOK, BEVERLY JEAN, elementary school educator; b. Fort Dodge, Iowa, Feb. 7, 1947; d. Francis B. Collins and Juanita Faye Bowers; m. Francis K. Snook, Aug. 9, 1969; children: Katherine, Jennifer, Megan, Ashley. AA, Centerville Community Coll., Iowa, 1967; BA, U. No. Iowa, 1969; MA, Marycrest Coll., Davenport, Iowa, 1990. Tchr. Wayne Community Sch., Corydon, Iowa, 1969-70; spl. edn. instr. Chariton (Iowa) Community Sch., 1972-75, Wayne County Schs., Corydon, Iowa, 1977—. Rsch. in field. Mem. PTA, Rural Schs. Network Project NCREL. Mem. NEA, Iowa Edn. Assn., Wayne Cmty. Edn. Assn. Home: 1403 90th St Corydon IA 50060-8863 Office: Wayne Jr High Wayne Cmty Sch Wayne Cmty Sch Corydon IA 50060

SNORTLAND, ELLEN BARBARA, writer; b. Denver, Aug. 27, 1953; d. Arnold Morton and Barbara Marie (Klabo) Snortland; m. Laurence David Rebhun, Dec. 19, 1977 (div. Mar. 1984); m. Gregory William Dowden, Mar. 23, 1988 (div. Mar. 1997). BA, U. Calif., Irvine, 1972; JD, Loyola U., L.A., 1977. Bar: Calif. 1978. Pres. Theatre of Process, Santa Barbara and L.A., 1974—80; actor various TV shows L.A., 1980—87; reporter for TV Lite KCRA, Sacramento, 1987; freelance commentator L.A. Times, Phila. Inquirer, KNBC L.A., others, 1992—. Author: Beauty Bites Beast: Awakening the Warrior Within Women and Girls, 1998; columnist Pasadena Weekly, 1993—; contbr. On the Issues Mag., 1995; performer: (one woman show) Now That She's Gone, 2005. Del. UN Assn., Pasadena and Beijing Women's Conf., 1995. Office: 2460 N Lake Altadena CA 91001 E-mail: ellensnortland@cs.com.

SNOW, MARINA, writer; b. Boston, Apr. 9, 1937; d. Charles Ernest Snow and Katherine Alice Townsend; m. Richard DeVere Horton, 1958 (div. 1968); children: Heather Kertchem, James Horton; m. Charles A. Washburn, 1978 (div. 1979). BA, U. Iowa, 1958; MA in Speech Pathology, N.Mex. State U., 1967; MA in Librarianship, San Jose State U., 1976; MA in Theatre Arts, Calif. State U., Sacramento, 1979. Cert. clin. competence Am. Speech and Hearing Assn. Tchr. ESL Inst. Colombo-Americano, Cali, Colombia, 1958-59; tchr. Las Cruces (N.Mex.) Pub. Schs., 1964-66; speech therapist Sutter County Schs., Yuba City, Calif., 1967-72; reference libr. Calif. State U., Sacramento, 1976-95. Author: (novels) The Walking Wounded, 2001 (Best First Novel of 2001-2002 award Bay Area Ind. Pub. Assn., 2001), Look No Further, 2004, (plays) Apricot Coffee, Alkali Flat, (short stories) (in Artisan) The Black Iris, 1999, The Masthead, 2006; contbr. articles to profl. jours. Pres. Alkali Flat Neighborhood Assn., Sacramento, 1987—94. Mem.: Calif. Writer's Club, Sacramento Old City Assn. Avocations: theater, historic preservation, gardening.

SNOW, SANDRA INEZ, mortgage company executive; b. Detroit, Aug. 8, 1960; d. Teddy and Phyllis B. (Marlowe) Rowland; children: Jason P., Shannon B. Comml. lending diploma, Am. Inst. of Banking, 1987; AS cum laude, Oakland Cmty. Coll., 1990. Credit analyst Huntington Banks of Mich., Troy, 1984-93; loan officer The Huntington Mortgage Co., Troy, 1992-93; v.p. Suburban Mortgage Corp., Rochester Hills, Mich., 1993-94; pres., CEO The Mortgage Store, Inc., Clarkston, Mich., 1994—. Fund raiser Easter Seals, Clinton Twp., 1994. Named among Top 10 Women Owned Businesses, Dun & Bradstreet and Entrepreneur Mag., 1998. Mem. NAFE, Womens Coun. of Realtors (assoc. mem., mem. state chpt.), Profl. Assn. Svcs. (South Oakland bd. realtors), Davisburg Rotary. Republican. Avocations: boating, exercise, camping. Office: Mortgage Store Inc 5896 Dixie Hwy Clarkston MI 48346-3358

SNOWDEN, BERNICE RIVES, former construction company executive; b. Houston, Mar. 21, 1923; d. Charles Samuel and Annie Pearl (Rorex) Rives; m. Walter G. Snowden; 1 child. Grad., Smalley Comml. Coll., 1941; student, U. Houston, 1965. With Houston Pipe Line Co., 1944-45; clk.-typist Charles G. Heyne & Co., Inc., Houston, 1951-53, payroll asst., 1953-56, sec. to pres., also office mgr., 1956-62, sec. to pres., also controller, 1962-70, sec.-treas., 1970-77, CFO, also dir. Mem. Women in Constrn., Nat. Assn. Women in Constrn. (past pres.), San Leon C. of C., Lord and Ladies Dance Club. Methodist. Home: 6611 Kury Ln Houston TX 77008-5101

SNOWDEN, RUTH, artist, educator, executive secretary; b. Quincy, Ill., Apr. 29, 1939; d. Emil G. and Edith M. Pfaffe; m. Howard L. Snowden; children: Jim, David, Sam, Amy. BS, Quincy U., 1964, BFA, 1989; MFA, U. So. Ill., 1991. Math. tchr. Notre Dame H.S., Quincy, 1964-67; math. lectr. Quincy U., 1974-83; legal sec. Snowden & Snowden Attys., Quincy, 1983—. Curator Significant Arch. in Quincy, Bell Tel., Chgo., 1986; mem. multi-arts panel Ill. Arts Coun., Chgo., 1986-89; art lectr. Quincy U., 1994—. Artist, editor: Visualizing Revelation, 1993; artist: Artists of Illinois, 1995, Quincy Women, 1838-1996, 1996; exhbns. include Biblical Arts Ctr., Dallas, The Michael Stone Collection Gallery, Washington, Art and The Law at Kennedy Galleries, N.Y.C., Loyola Law Sch., L.A., Minn. Mus. Am. Art, St. Paul, State of Ill. Ctr., Chgo., Oak Knoll, St. Louis, Overland Park, Kans. Bd. dirs. YMCA and YWCA, Quincy, 1978-96, Quincy Mus., 1984; Adams County campaign coord. U.S. Senator Dick Durbin, Quincy, 1980. Mem. Quincy Art Ctr. (pres. 1984-86, chair exhbn. com. 1995-96, adv. bd.). Democrat. Lutheran. Avocations: international travel, bible study.

SNOWDEN, RUTH O'DELL GILLESPIE, artist; b. Gary, W.Va., Apr. 16, 1926; d. Haynes Thornton and Blanche Beaula (Boling) Gillespie; m. Eugene Louis Snowden, Dec. 21, 1946; children: Wanda Snowden Ballard, Eugene III, Ronald, Marian Snowden Warren, Jeffry. RN, Natharith Coll., 1946; student Sch. Art, Transylvania U., 1983-84, U. Ky., 1985-89. RN. Painter, publicity chmn. Artist's Attic Inc., Lexington, Ky., 1988-89. Exhibited in group shows at U. Ky. Art Mus., Lexington, 1988, 5th Internat. Juried Exhibition Pastels, Nyack, N.Y., 1988, Small Paintings Nat., Ky. Highlands Mus., Ashland, 1988, The Appalachian Cen., U. Ky., 1988, Ft. Wayne (Ind.) Mus. Art, 1986, John Howard Sanden Nat. Artists Seminar, Washington, Nat. Artists' Seminar, Chgo., Huntington (W.Va.) Galleries, Nat. Nursing Art Exhibit, Meth. Med. Cen., Peoria, Ill., Chautauqua Art Assn. Galleries, N.Y., 1990, Central Bank gallery, Chatauqua, 1990, Pastel & Chisel Acad. Fine Arts, 1990, Opera House Gallery, 1990, Sacramento Fine Arts Ctr., 1990, Ariel Gallery, Soho, N.Y., 1990, 91, Sumi-e Soc. Am., Inc., 1993, Watercolor Soc. Ala., 1994; represented in the Director of American Portrait Artists, Am. Portrait Soc., Huntington Harbour, Calif., Audubon Artists Exhibit, N.Y.C., 2003, 2004; numerous local and nat. shows; in pvt. collections. Recipient Assn. Alliance award Am. Frame Co., 1993, Elizabeth Morris Genious award, 2002, Winsor Newton Merchandising award Summie Soc. Am., 2002. Mem. Oil Pastel Assn., Winchester Art Guild, Lexington Art League, Ky. Watercolor Assn. (Bluegrass regional dir. 1988, 89, 90, 91, 92), Ky. Guild Artists and Craftsmen, Inc., Northwest Pastel Soc., Degas Pastel Soc., Pen & Brush Soc. (Perfect Proportion award). Avocations: golf, bowling. Home and Studio: 2800 Old Boonesboro Rd Winchester KY 40391-8805 Office Phone: 859-744-6693.

SNOWE, OLYMPIA J., senator; b. Augusta, Maine, Feb. 21, 1947; d. George John and Georgia G. Bouchles; m. John McKernan. BA, U. Maine, 1969; LLD (hon.), U. Maine, Orono, 1981, Nasson Coll., 1981, U. Maine, Machias, 1982, Bowdoin Coll., 1982, Colby Coll., 1985; LHD (hon.), Thomas Coll., 1987; LLD (hon.), Suffolk U., 1994; DSc (hon.), Maine Maritime Acad., 1995; LLD (hon.), Colby Coll., 1996, U. New England, 1996; degree (hon.), Harvard U., 1997; LLD (hon.), Bates Coll., 1998. Businesswoman; mem. Maine Ho. of Reps., 1973-76, Maine Senate, 1976-78, 96th-103d Congresses from 2d Maine Dist., 1979-94, mem. budget com., foreign affairs com., com. on aging, 1979-94; co-chair Congl. Caucus for Women's Issues, 1983-94; U.S. senator from Maine, 1995—. Mem. Senate com. armed svcs., 1997-2001, chair, seapower subcom., Senate com. on commerce, sci. and transp., 1995—, chair, oceans and fisheries subcom., Senate Budget com., 1995—, Senate com. small business, 1995—, Senate com. Fgn. Rels., 1995-97; counsel to asst. majority leader, 1997—. House Budget com., 1991-95, House Fgn. Affairs com., 1979-95, House Aging com. 1979-95, Congl. Caucus on Women's Issues 1979-84, co-chair 1983-95; dep. Repub. Whip, 1984-95; dep. Whip, 1996-97; corporator Mechanics Savs. Bank. Recipient Homeric award for adv. of human rights Chian Fedn., 1999, award for "Excelling in Standing up for Choice" Women's Campaign Fund, 1999, Spirit of Enterprise award U.S. Chamber of Commerce, 1997, 99, Woman of Yr. award Glamour Mag., 1998, David and Sherry Huber award for leadership on family planning, women's health issues, Family Planning Assn. of ME, 1998, Golden Bulldog award Watchdogs of the Treasury, Inc., Wash., 1994, 96, 98, Guardian of Small Business award Nat. Fedn. Indep. Bus., Wash., 1994, 96, 98, Responsible Choices award Planned Parenthood of Am., 1998, Spl. honor Nat. Assn. Devel. Orgns., 1998, Disting. Pub. Svc. award Am. Legion, Wash., 1998, Neil W. Allen award Greater Portland Chamber of Commerce, 1997, Legis. award for outstanding svc. to schs. and pub. librs., White Ho. Conf. on Libr. and Info. Svcs. Task Force, Wash., 1997, Pub. Leadership award, Nat. Breast Cancer Coalition, 1997, Magnificent Seven award Bus. & Profl. Women/USA, Wash., 1997, Deborah Morton award Westbrook Coll., Portland, ME, 1997, Golden Gavel award U.S. Senate Leadership, Wash., 1996, Nat. Osteoporosis Assn. award for leadership, Wash., 1996, award for leadership U.S. Distance Learning Assn., Crystal City, Va., 1996, award for leadership United Hellenic Am. Cong., 1995, William H. Natcher Disting. Svc. award Com. for Edn. Funding, 1995, Pub. Svc. award Am. Coll. Obstetricians and Gynecologists, 1995, Nat. Security Leadership award Am. Security Coun., Wash., 1994, Thomas Jefferson award Nat. Am. Wholesale Grocers Assn./Internat. Foodsvc. Distbrs. Assn., 1994, Grace Caucus award Citizens Against Govt. Waste, 1994, Sound Dollar award Free Cong. Found., 1994, Appreciation award Agrl. Stblzn. and Conservation Com. Somerset County chpt., Lifetime Achievement award Am. Hellenic Inst., 1994, Golden Heart award Assn. for Children for Enforcement of Support, ME chpt., 1993, Am. Social Health Assn. award on behalf of women's health issues, 1993, Medal of St. Andrew presented by His All Holiness Dimitrios Ecumenical Patriarch of Constantinople, Wash., 1990, Congrl. Waste Watchers award Coalition to Reform the Davis-Bacon Act, 1990; named to "CQ 50" Congrl. Quarterly Mag., Wash., 1999, Maine Women's Hall of Fame, 1999, Washingtonian Mag. 100 Most Powerful Women, 1997, All Maine Women Honor Soc. U. Maine, 1996, Deficit Reduction Honor Roll Concord Coalition, 1994, Honor Roll for dairy farmer support Associated Milk Prodrs., 1993; named Taxpayer's Hero for preventing govt. waste Citizens Against Govt. Waste, 1997, No Nonsense Am. Women, No Nonsense Coun. on Women's Issues, 1995, Congresswoman of Yr. Nat. Assn. for Transp. Alternatives, 1986; honored by Nat. Coalition for Osteoporosis and Related Bone Diseases, 1999, Edn. and Libr. Networks Coalition, 1997, Am. Assn. Univ. Pres., 1996, Pub. Policy Com. for Hellenic-Am. Women, 1995, Nat. Vietnam Vet. Coalition, 1994; named one of most powerful women, Forbes mag., 2005. Mem.: Philoptochos Soc. Republican. Greek Orthodox. Office: US Senate 154 Russell Senate Bldg Washington DC 20510-1903 E-mail: olympia@snowe.senate.gov.*

SNOWHOOK, ANN LAFERTY, social services administrator; b. N.Y.C., May 25, 1929; d. Paul Gause and Anna Gladys (Braun) Laferty; m. John David Snowhook, Sept. 13, 1952; children: Eileen M., Elizabeth J., David P., J. Jordan, Nancy P. BA in Math., UCLA, 1953, postgrad., 1965, 70. Mathematician missiles divsn. The Rand Corp., L.A., 1951-52; substitute tchr. math. Spastic Children's Found., L.A., 1958-60; sec. women's aux. Exceptional Children's Found., L.A., 1960-63; chmn. and treas. parents group, chmn. fundraising, subsitute tchr. Exceptional Children's Class Pacific Palisades, L.A., 1963-73; chmn. area guild, mgr. sch. lunch program Corpus Christi Ch., L.A., 1972-74; statistician, rsch. asst. in mental retardation, family therapy and anorexia nervosa Neuropsychiatric Inst. UCLA, 1974-90; mem. program/policy bd. Kennedy Regional Ctr. for Developmentally Disabled, L.A., 1974-78; del. program devel. fund grants review Los Angeles County Area Bd. X, 1978-82; del. We. Regional Ctr. Assn. Regional Ctr. Contracting Agys., L.A., 1981-82; bd. dirs., pres., corp. sec. We. Regional Ctr. for Developmentally Disabled, L.A., 1978-82; founding dir., corp. sec., treas. Home Ownership Made Easy, L.A., 1988-91; bd. dirs., corp. sec., treas. Found. for Developmentally Disabled, L.A., 1982—; bd. dirs., corp. treas. Marian Homes for Physically Handicapped and Devel. Disabled, L.A., 1992—95. Rsch. assoc. Family Therapy: An Overview, 1980, Anorexia Nervosa: A Body Image Disturbance, 1978, Autism: A Study for Chromosomal Abnormalities, 1979, Family Therapy Today, Estrogen Therapy in Menopausal Women, 1991; rsch. cons. Estrogen Therapy in Menopausal Women, Family Therapy Today; bd. mem. Programs for the Developmentally Handicapped, 1995—, v.p. 1997-98, 2003-; bd. mem. Jay Nolan Cmty. Svcs., 1995-, v.p. 1997-98, chmn. human resources, 2001—, Jay Nolan v.p. 2005—, sec. 2003-05; program chair and bd. dirs. Easter Seals So. Calif., 1996—, treas., 2002—. Mem. Autism Soc. L.A. (v.p., program chair 1993-95, pres. 1995-99, 2001-02). Roman Catholic. Avocations: reading, swimming, antiques. Home: 901 Iliff St Pacific Palisades CA 90272-3826

SNOW-SMITH, JOANNE INLOES, art history educator; b. Balt. d. Henry Williams and Elsie Orrick (Bagley) Snow; m. Robert Porter Smith (dec.); children: Joanne Tyndale Darby, Henry Webster Smith, III (dec.), Constance Elizabeth Bagley, Cynthia Porter Bloom, Robert Porter Smith, Jr.; m. Robert Edward Willstadter (dec.) BA, Goucher Coll.; MA, U. Ariz., 1968; PhD, UCLA, 1976. Prof. Italian Renaissance art history U. Wash., Seattle, 1981—. Program dir. of art history U. Wash. Rome Ctr. in Palazzo Pio, Rome, 1998, 2000, 2002. Author: (book) The Salvator Mundi of Leonardo da Vinci, 1982 (Internat. award 1983), The Primavera of Sandro Botticelli: A Neoplatonic Interpretaion, 1993; contbr. numerous articles to profl. jours. Recipient Rsch. Professorship to study in Oxford and London, U. Wash. Grad. Sch., 1986. Mem. Nat. Soc. Colonial Dames of Am., Renaissance Soc. of Am., Leonardo Soc./U. London, Coll. Art Assn., Seattle Art Mus., Met. Mus. Art, Ashmolean Mus. (Oxford, Eng.). Home: 1414 Shenandoah Dr E Seattle WA 98112-3730 Office: Univ Wash PO Box 353440 Seattle WA 98195-3440 E-mail: jsnowsmi@u.washington.edu.

SNYDER, A. MICHELLE, federal agency administrator; Mgr. health benefits and income security Office of Asst. Sec. Mgmt. and Budget, HHS, 1989—94; dir. Office Fin. Mgmt., CFO Centers for Medicare and Medicaid Services, HHS, 1994—2003; assoc. adminstr. Health Care Systems Bur., Health Resources and Services Adminstrn., HHS, 2003—05, Bur. Primary Health Care, Health Resources and Services Admstrn., HHS, 2005—. Office: Bur Primary Health Care Parklawn Bldg 5600 Fishers Ln Rockville MD 20857 Office Phone: 301-594-4110.

SNYDER, ANDREA JILL, psychologist; b. Salem, Ohio, Apr. 8, 1980; d. Lowell Emerson and Cheryl Ann Snyder. BSAS, Younstown State U., Ohio, 2002; MSED, Fordham U., N.Y.C., 2005. Intern Youth Devel. Ctr., New Castle, Pa., 2001—01; extern Pub. Sch. 99, Kew Gardens, NY, 2003—04, Kings County Hosp., N.Y.C., 2004—05, Coler-Goldwater Speciality Hosp. and Nursing Facility, N.Y.C., 2005—06. Mem.: ACA, Am. Psychol. Soc., Psi Chi, Golden Key, Phi Kappa Phi. Avocations: reading, travel.

SNYDER, BARBARA K., pediatrician, educator; MD, George Washington U., 1979. Diplomate in pediatrics and adolescent medicine Am. Bd. Pediatrics. Intern Children's Nat. Med. Ctr., Washington, 1979—80, resident in pediatrics, 1980—82; fellow in adolescent medicine U. Rochester (N.Y.) Sch. Medicine, 1986—88; chief divsn. adolescent medicine, dept. pediatrics Robert Wood Johnson Med. Sch., New Brunswick, NJ, 1990—, assoc. prof., 1994—, dir. eating disorders program, adolescent medicine program, 1990—. Office: U Medicine and Dentistry NJ-Robert Wood Johnson Med Sch Dept Pediats New Brunswick NJ 08903-0019 Office Phone: 732-235-7896.

SNYDER, BARBARA LOU, retired educational association administrator; b. Denison, Iowa, July 13, 1935; d. Alfred Howard and Elsie May Bowen; children: Steven, Terry, Richard, Jonathan. BA, Simpson Coll., 1957; MEd, Mid. Tenn. State U., 1975. Cert. insurance agent TN. Tchr. Huntsville City Schs., Huntsville, Ala., 1966—68, Huntsville Achiev. Sch., 1968—70; resource tchr. Tullahoma City Schs., Tullahoma, Tenn., 1971—95; ins. agent Nat. Health Administr., 1996—2004; lobbyist Tenn. Retired Tchrs. Assn., Nashville, 2001—, assoc. exec. dir. to exec. dir., 2003—04. Legislative chair Tenn Retired Tchrs. Assn., Nashville, 1995—2001. Treas. Tenn. Federation Democratic Women, Nashville, 1997—99, cooresponding sec., 1995—97; convention co-chair 41st Annual Tenn. Federation Democratic Women, Manchester, Tenn., 1998; recording sec. Tenn. Federation Democratic Women, Nashville, 1999—2001; mem. Coffee County Dem. Exec. Com., 1992—, sec., 1998—. Named First Hometown Hero, Tullahoma News, 2001, Mrs. Democrat, Highland Rim Democratic Club, 2000. Mem.: Coffee County Retired Tchrs., Tenn. Retired Tchrs. Assn., Nat. Retired Tchrs. Assn. Democrat. Unitarian. Avocations: reading, gardening, walking, politics. Home: 320 E Fort St Tullahoma TN 37388 Office: Tenn Retired Tchrs Assn 801 Second Ave N Nashville TN 37201 Office Phone: 615-242-8392 x 330. Personal E-mail: bsnyder@cafes.net.

SNYDER, BARBARA LOUISE, language arts educator; b. Hartford, Conn., Apr. 30, 1946; d. Ely and Marie Ruth (Shalett) Shor; m. Philip Harvey Snyder (div.); children: Jeremy David, Rebecca Amy. BS, Cen. Conn. State U., New Britain, 1968, MS, 1971; 6th yr. cert., U. Conn. and Cen. Conn. State U., Storrs and New Britain, 2000. Cert. reading cons. Conn., reading recovery tchr., writing project cons. Conn. Tchr. grade 1 Milner Sch. Hartford Pub. Schs., 1968—71; tutor English spkrs. of other langs. Glastonbury Pub. Schs., 1980—84, tchr. lang. arts, cons., 1984—. Adj. instr. U. New Haven, 2005—; tchr. reading recovery Reading Recovery Coun. Am., Glastonbury, 1995—; writing cons. Conn. Writing Project, Storrs, 1999—. Contbr. articles to profl. jours. Pres. Glastonbury chpt. Hadassah, 2004—06; pres. Hopewell Sch. PTO, Glastonbury, 1983—84; leader La Leche League, Glastonbury, 1972—76; mem.Glastonbury Reads a Book com. Welles Turner Libr., Glastonbury, 2000—04. Grantee, George Ensworth Found., 1993, 2003. Mem.: Conn. Reading Assn., Conn. Assn. Reading Rsch., Internat. Reading Assn. Democrat. Jewish. Avocations: reading, writing, walking, tennis, theater. Home: 250 Leigh Gate Rd Glastonbury CT 06033 Office Phone: 860-652-7276.

SNYDER, BARBARA ROOK, academic administrator; BA, Ohio State U., 1976; JD, U. Chgo., 1980. Bar: Ill. 1980. Law clk. for Judge Luther M. Swygert U.S. Ct. Appeals for the Seventh Cir.; with Sidley & Austin, Chgo.; joined law faculty Case Western Res. U., 1983, Ohio State U., Columbus, 1988, assoc. dean for acad. affairs, 2000—01, vice provost for acad. policy and human resources, 2001—03, interim provost, 2003—04, exec. v.p., provost, 2004—, Joanne W. Murphy/Class of 1965 professorship Moritz Coll. Law. Office: Ohio State U Office Acad Affairs 203 Bricker Hall 190 N Oval Mall Columbus OH 43210 Office Phone: 614-292-5881. Business E-Mail: snyder.7@osu.edu.

SNYDER, CAROLYN ANN, education educator, librarian, director; b. Elgin, Nebr., Nov. 5, 1942; d. Ralph and Florence Wagner. Student, Nebr. Wesleyan U., 1960—61; BS cum laude, Kearney State Coll., 1964; MS in Librarianship, U. Denver, 1965. Asst. libr. sci. and tech. U. Nebr., Lincoln, 1965—67, asst. pub. svc. libr., 1967—68, 1970—73; from pers. libr. to interim dean Ind. U. Librs., Bloomington, 1973—89, interim dean, 1989—91; adminstrv. army libr. Spl. Svcs. Agy., Europe, 1968—70; dean libr. affairs So. Ill. U., Carbondale, 1991—2000, prof. libr. affairs, 2000—, dir. found. rels., 2000—. Team leader Midwest Univs. Consortium for Internat. Activities-World Bank IX project to develop libr. sys. and implement automation U. Indonesia, Jakarta, 1984-86; libr. devel. cons. Inst. Tech. MARA/Midwest Univs. Consortium for Internat. Activities Program in Malaysia, 1985; ofcl. rep. EDUCAUSE, 1996-2000; mem. working group on scholarly comm. Nat. Commn. on Librs. and Info. Sci., 1998-2000. Editor: Library and Other Academic Support Services for Distance Learning, 1997; contbr. chpt. to book and articles to profl. jours. Active Carbondale Pub. Libr. Friends, 1991-, Morris Libr. Friends, 1991—; br. pres. AAUW, Carbondale, 2004-05; bd. dirs. Carbondale Cmty. Arts Bd., 2006-, Carbondale Info. and Telecomm. Commn., 2006-. Cooperative Rsch. grant Coun. on Libr. Resources, Washington, 1984. Mem. ALA (councilor 1985-89, Bogle Internat. Travel award 1988, H.W. Wilson Libr. Staff devel. grant 1981), Libr. Adminstrn./Mgmt. Assn. (pres. 1981-82, numerous others), Com. on Instnl. Coop./Resource Sharing (chair 1987-91), Coalition for Networked Info. (So. Ill. U. at Carbondale rep. 1991-00), Coun. Dirs. State Univ. Librs. in Ill. (chair 1992-93, 99-00), Coun. on Libr. and Info. Resources Digital Leadership Inst. Steering Com. (Assn. Rsch. Librs. rep. 1998-00), Ill. Assn. Coll. and Rsch. Librs. (chair Ill. Bd. Higher Edn. liaison com. 1993-94), Ill. Network (bd. dirs.), Ind. Libr. Assn. (chair coll./univ. divsn. 1982-83), U.S. Grant Assn. (bd. dirs. 1992—), Ill. Libr. Computer Sys. Orgn. (policy coun. 1992-95, 96-00), Nat. Assn. State Univs. and Land-Grant Colls. (commn. on info. tech. and its distance learning and libr. bds. 1994-96), NetIllinois (bd. dirs. 1994-96), OCLC Users Coun. (elected rep. 1995-98), Big 12 Plus Libr. Consortium (chair 1997-98), Nat. Commn. on Librs. and Info. Sci. Working Group on Scholarly Comm., Assn. Rsch. Libr. (vis. program officer 2000-01). Avocations: antiques, theater, movies, reading. Office: So Ill U Ctrl Devel Carbondale IL 62901-6632 Office Phone: 618-453-1447.

SNYDER, CAROLYN SWICK (CARRIE SNYDER), special education educator, vocational program administrator; b. Rapid City, S.D., May 15, 1949; d. Calvin A. and Eula B. (Sharp) Swick; m. Robert R. Snyder, Aug. 15, 1969; children: Sara, Shawn. Student, Sioux Falls Coll., 1967-68; BS in Edn., Augustana Coll., 1971, postgrad.; MS in Counseling and Pers. Svcs., Drake U., 1987, postgrad., U. Calif., Ctrl. Bapt. Theol. Seminary, Kans. State U., Iowa State U., U. No. Colo. Cert. spl. edn. tchr., ednl. cons., secondary sch. counselor, work experience coord., tchr. to mentally disabled, Iowa. Lead tchr. spl. edn. Kans. City (Kans.) Pub. Schs., 1971-73; tchr. spl. edn. Meade (Kans.) Pub. Schs., 1975-79; tchr. spl. edn., coord. work experience Arrowhead Area Ednl. Agy., Ft. Dodge, Iowa, 1980-82; coord. spl. edn. work experience Des Moines Ind. Pub. Schs., 1982—. Developer, coord. Neighbors Youth Monitoring Program, Des Moines; facilitator HIV/AIDS spl. edn. curriculum, social skills curriculum Des Moines Pub. Schs.; mem. 11 county multi-agy. transition adv. com., 1992. Co-treas. Ankeny (Iowa) High Sch. Boosters; min. counseling Westover Bapt. Ch.; active leadership tng. program Mid-Am. Bapt. Chs. Recipient Utilization award Outstanding Pub. Educator Nat. Assn. Industry Edn., 1992. Mem. NEA, Iowa State Edn. Assn., Des

Moines Edn. Assn., Nat. Coun. Exceptional Children, Iowa Coun. Exceptional Children, Iowa Counseling Assn. Office: Des Moines Pub Schs 1800 Grand Ave Des Moines IA 50309-3310

SNYDER, DOLORES WILMA, culinary educator; b. Oakwood, Tex., June 18, 1933; d. James Clyde and Frances Wilma Simmons; m. Richard Hepburn Snyder, Feb. 26, 1956; children: Emily June, Richard Henry. BS summa cum laude, U. Tex., 1954. Dir. Gourmet & Cookery Sch., Irving, Tex., 1976—2004; pres. DWS Pub., Irving, 2003—. Dir. French wine and food tour Neiman Marcus, Dallas, 1978. Author: Tea Time Entertaining, 2004. Mem. adv. bd. food and hospitality program El Centro C.C., Dallas, 1986—2005; vis. com. dept. human ecology U. Tex., Austin, 2002—06. Mem.: James Beard Found. (founder, Best Cooking Tchr. award 1990), Les Dames d'Escoffier (pres. 1984—86, 1989—91, mem. adv. com. 1998—2006), Internat. Assn. Culinary Profls. (cert. culinary profl.). Home: 3409 Hidalgo Irving TX 75062 Office: DWS Pub 3409 Hidalgo Irving TX 75062 E-mail: rhs629@aol.com.

SNYDER, DOROTHY Z., social worker; b. Detroit, June 26, 1952; d. William Edward and Ann Mildred Zynda; m. Edward William Snyder, Sept. 4,1 976; children: Julie Ann, Janey Lee. BA, Mich. State U., 1974; MSW, U. Mich., 1981. Cert. social worker. Foster care worker Cath. Social Svcs., Detroit, 1974-81, pregnancy counselor, 1984-87, psychotherapist Livonia, Mich., 1987-99; mem. staff devel. com., 1997-99; psychotherapist, dir. Bridgewood Clinic, Farmington, Mich., 1999—. Chair yearbook com. PTA, Farmington, Mich., 1986-95; mem. Cheerleader Backers, Farmington, 1999-2002; mem. Booster Club, Farmington, 1995-2002. Fellow Nat. Assn. Social Workers; mem. Farmington Glen Aquatic Club, Our Money Making Investment Club (sec. 1998-99). Republican. Roman Catholic. Avocations: gardening, exercise, walking, restaurants. Office Phone: 248-426-0079. E-mail: dzsnyder@hotmail.com.

SNYDER, JAN LOUISE, administrative aide; b. Warrington Twp., Pa., Sept. 15, 1935; d. Wilbert Adam and Alice (Myers) March; divorced; children: Steven Michael Krone, David Sylvan Snyder. Grad. H.S., Dover, Pa. Employment sec. personnel dept. stores divsn. McCrory Corp., York, 1966—94, receptionist exec. buying divsn., 1994—97; receptionist, switchboard operator human resources Healthsouth Rehab. Hosp., York, Pa., 1997-99; gen. office specialist, shared svcs. Dentsply Internat., 2002—. Active Northwestern region York Hosp. Aux., 1970—, mem. membership com. and administer II, 2002; active York Symphony Assn., 1990—, membership com., 1992—; active York chpt. Am. Cancer Soc. Am., 1990—. York Chorus, 1988-90; Dover Twp. Fire Co. Aux. for Women, 1975—, Harrisburg Jr. League Lectr. Series, 1980-95, York Jr. League Lectr. series, 1989-96, Messiah United Meth. Ch., 2003—.; womens aux. Johns Hopkins Hosp., 1999—; mem. Md. House and Garden Pilgrimage House Tours, 1968—; mem. Interfaith Alliance, Inc., Washington. Mem. Am. Bus. Women's Assn. (pres. Colonial York charter chpt. 1980, mem. adv. bd. 1980-89), nat. Trust for Historic Preservation. Democrat. Avocations: travel, music, educational lecturing series, flower and vegetable gardening. Home: 2823 Grandview Ave York PA 17404-3905 Office: 570 West College Ave York PA 17404

SNYDER, JEAN MACLEAN, lawyer; b. Chgo., Jan. 26, 1942; d. Norman Fitzroy and Jessie (Burns) Maclean; m. Joel Martin Snyder, Sept. 4, 1964; children: Jacob Samuel, Noah Scot. BA, U. Chgo., 1963, JD, 1979. Bar: Ill. 1979, U.S. Dist. Ct. (no. dist.) Ill. 1979, U.S. Ct. Appeals (7th cir.) 1981. Ptnr. D'Ancona & Pflaum, Chgo., 1979-92; prin. Law Office of Jean Maclean Snyder, Chgo., 1993-97, 2004—; trial counsel The MacArthur Justice Ctr. U. Chgo. Law Sch., 1997—2004, of counsel, 2004—05. Contbr. articles to profl. jours. Bd. dirs. Citizens Alert, 2005—. Mem.: Lawyers for the Creative Arts (bd. dirs. 1995—97), ACLU of Ill. (bd. dirs. 1996—99), ABA (mem. coun. on litigation sect. 1989—92, editor-in-chief Litigation mag. 1987—88, co-chair First Amendment and media litigation com. 1995—96, co-chair sect. litigation task force on gender, racial and ethnic bias 1998—2001, standing com. on strategic comms. 1996—2001). Office Phone: 773-285-5100. Business E-Mail: jeansnyder@sbcglobal.net.

SNYDER, JILL, museum director; b. Trenton, N.J., June 28, 1957; d. Barry and Arline (Gellar) S. BA, Wesleyan U., Middletown, Conn., 1979. Exec. assoc. Guggenheim Mus., N.Y.C., 1983-88, edn. assoc., 1989-91; dir./curator Freedman Gallery, Albright Coll., Reading, Pa., 1993-95; dir. The Aldrich Mus. of Contemporary Art, Ridgefield, Conn., 1995—96; exec. dir. Mus. Contemporary Art Cleve., 1996—. Mem. curatorial rev. panel Abington Art Ctr., Jenkintown, Pa., 1995; staff lectr. Mus. of Modern Art, N.Y.C., 1989-94, Guggenheim Mus., 1988-92; adj. faculty N.Y. Sch. Interior Design, 1988-92, Mary Schiller Myers Sch. Art, U. Akron. Author: Caring for Your Art, 1991, In the Flesh (catalogue), 1996, Impossible Evidence: Contemporary Artists View the Holocaust (catalogue), 1994, Against the Stream: Milton Avery, Adolph Gottlieb and Mark Rothko in the 1930s (catalogue), 1994. Bd. dirs. Forum for U.S.-Soviet Dialogue, Washington, 1990-91. Milton and Sally Avery Found. fellow, 1990, Shelby and Leon Levy fellow, 1988. Mem. Art Table, Am. Assn. Mus., Coll. Art Assn. Office: Mus Contemporary Art Cleve 8501 Carnegie Ave Cleveland OH 44106 E-mail: jsnyder@MOCAcleveland.org.

SNYDER, JOAN, artist; b. Highland Park, N.J., Apr. 16, 1940; d. Leon D. and Edythe A. (Cohen) S.; 1 child, Molly Fink. AB in Sociology, Douglass Coll., 1962; M.F.A., Rutgers U., 1966. Mem. faculty SUNY, Stony Brook, 1967-69, Yale U., 1974, U. Calif., Irvine, 1975, San Francisco Art Inst., 1976, Princeton U., 1975-77, Parsons, 1992, 93. One-woman exhbns. include, Paley and Lowe, New Brunswick, N.J., 1971, 73, Michael Walls Gallery, San Francisco, 1971, Parker 470, Boston, 1972, Los Angeles Inst. Contempory Art, 1976, Portland (Oreg.) Center Visual Arts, 1976, Carl Solway Gallery, NYC, 1976, Neuberger Mus., Purchase, N.Y., 1978, Hamilton Gallery Contemporary Art, 1978, 79, 82, 83, Nielson Gallery, Boston, 1983, 86, 91, Hirshl & Adler Modern Art Mus., NYC, 1985-87, 88, 90, 92, Compass Rose Gallery, Chgo., 1988, 89, Victoria Munroe, N.Y., 1990, Gibbs Mus. Art, Charleston, N.C., 1992, Artists Space, N.Y., 1992, Michael Walls Gallery, N.Y., 1992, Victoria Monroe Gallery, N.Y., 1993, Richard Anderson Gallery, N.Y., 1993, Nielson Gallery, 1993, 2002, Fine Arts Work Ctr., Mass., 1993, Allentown Art Mus., Pa., 1993, Nina Bransten Gallery, Calif., 1993, Jay Gorney Modern Art, NYC, 1993, Hirschl/Adler Modern, NYC, 1994, Nielsen Gallery, Mass., 1994, Rose Art Mus. Brandeis U., Waltham, Mass., 1994, Brooklyn Mus. Art, 1998, Robert Miller Gallery, NY, 2001, Elena Zang Gallery, NY, 2003, Betty Cuningham Gallery, 2004, Alexandre Gallery, NY, 2004, Sawhill Gallery, James Madison Univ., Harrisburg, Va., 2005; travelling one-woman show, San Francisco Art Inst., Grand Rapids Art Mus., Renaissance Soc., U. Chgo., Anderson Gallery, Va. Commonwealth U., Richmond, 1979-80, The Jewish Mus., NYC, Danforth Mus., Framington, Mass., 2005—, group exhbns. include Whitney Ann., 1972, Whitney Bienniel, 1974, 80, Corcoran Bienniel, 1975, 87, Mus. Modern Art, NYC, Ann Jaffe Gallery, Bay Harbor Island, Fla., 1991, Cynthia Mcallister Gallery, NYC, Bixler Gallery, NYC, Parrish Art Mus., Southampton, N.Y., Acad. Arts and Letters, NYC, Tribeca 148 Gallery, NYC. Grantee Nat. Endowment Art, 1974; Guggenheim fellow, 1981-82

SNYDER, KATHLEEN THERESA, state agency administrator; b. Balt., Oct. 8, 1951; children: Jay, Matt, Carrie. BS, U. Md., 1973; MS, Am. U., 1978. Info. specialist Prince George's Pub. Sch., 1981—84, exec. v.p. adv. coun., 1984—87; exec. v.p. Prince George's Md. Chamber, 1987—92; pres., CEO Alexandria (Va.) Chamber, 1992—99, Md. C. of C., 1999—. V.p. Va. Assn. C. of C., 1996—99; bd. mem. Am. C. of C. Execs., 2000—01; pres. Mo. Assn. Ch. Execs., 2003. Mem. Scholarship Fund Alexandria, 1994—99; founding bd. First Night Alexandria, 1994—99; chair employers adv. com. Alexandria Works, 1996—99. Named Chamber Exec. of Yr., Va. Assn. Chamber Execs., 1996, Bus. Woman of Yr., Alexandria Commn. on Women, 1996, Cert. Chamber Exec., Am. C. of C. Execs., 2000, Md. Top 100 Women, 2001, 2003; recipient Brotherhood/Sisterhood award, Nat. Conf. Christians and Jews Prince George's chpt., 1992. Office: Md C of C Ste 100 60 West St Annapolis MD 21401

SNYDER, LESLIE CROCKER, lawyer; b. NYC, Mar. 8, 1942; AB, Radcliffe Coll., 1962; cert., Harvard-Radcliffe Program in Bus. Adminstrn., 1963; JD with honors, Case-Western Reserve Law Sch., 1966. Bar: Ohio 1966, NY 1967, US Ct. Appeals, Second Circuit 1967, US Dist. Ct. 1974, Ea. and So. Dist. NY 1974, US Supreme Ct. 1974. Justice NY Supreme State Ct., Criminal Term, 1986—2000; apptd. to Ct. Claims, 2000; chief trials Office Spl. Prosecutor against Corruption in the Criminal Justice Sys.; dep. criminal justice coord., head of the Arson Strike Force Office NYC Criminal Justice Coord.; chief and founder Sex Crimes Prosecution Bureau; atty. criminal law/litigation, ptnr. Kasowitz, Benson, Torres & Friedman LLP, 2003—. Order of the Coif assoc. editor Case-Western Law Review; immediate past chair Criminal Procedure Law Adv. Com. to Chief Judge NY State, 1992—98. Author: 25 To Life: The Truth, the Whole Truth, and Nothing But the Truth, 2002; co-author: New York's Rape Shield Law. Trustee Kips Bay Boys and Girls Club, Bronx; bd. mem. NY Police Fire Widows' and Children's Orgn., DARE, NYC; mem. Citizen's Crime Commn., Moot Ct. Team. Mem.: Women's Bar Assn. (pres. 1982—83, past first v.p and third v.p.), Assn. Bar City NY (past mem. criminal justice counsel, past mem. com. on criminal advocacy, criminal cts., sex and law). Office: Kasowitz Benson Torres & Friedman LLP 1633 Broadway New York NY 10019 Office Phone: 212-506-1754. Office Fax: 212-506-1800. Business E-Mail: lsnyder@kasowitz.com.

SNYDER, LINDA ANN, editor; b. Pitts., Feb. 24, 1957; d. Arthur Anthony and Patricia Ann (Balzer) Krysinski; m. Christopher Lee Snyder, June 1, 1996. BFA, Carnegie Mellon U., 1979. Lic. real estate salesperson Pa., 2004. Systems adminstr. Duncan, Lagnese & Assocs. (now known as Killam Assocs.), Pitts., 1979-86; editorial office supr. Materials Rsch. Soc., Pitts., 1986-94; monographs editor Air & Waste Mgmt. Assn., Pitts., 1994-95; mktg. specialist Killam Assocs., Warrendale, Pa., 1995-96; mng. editor Soc. of Automotive Engrs., Warrendale, Pa., 1996—; sales exec. Northwood Realty Svcs., Pitts., 2004—. Freelance corr. Pitts. Post-Gazette, 1990-93. Vol. Animal Friends, Pitts., 2006—. Named Jaycee of Quar., North Hills Jaycees, 1990. Republican. Roman Catholic. Avocations: photography, gardening, hiking, writing. Home: 210 Hillendale Rd Pittsburgh PA 15237-1804 Office: Soc of Automotive Engrs 400 Commonwealth Dr Warrendale PA 15096-0001 Business E-Mail: lsnyder@sae.org.

SNYDER, LIZA, actress; b. Northampton, Mass., Mar. 20, 1968; Appeared in T.V. movie Race Against Time: The Search for Sarah, 1996; T.V. series Sirens, 1993, Jesse, 1998-2000, Yes, Dear, 2000-; T.V. guest appearance Chgo. Hope, 1996; Film appearance in Pay it Forward, 2001. Office: William Morris Agency One William Morris Pl Beverly Hills CA 90212

SNYDER (MACKLEY), LOUISE MARIE, speech pathology/audiology services professional, consultant; d. Gordon Joseph and Audrey Augusta (Garvelman) Mackley. BS, Western Mich. U., 1972; MA, 1972; PhD, Mich. State U., 1993. Cert. tchg. elem. edn., speech pathology Dept. Edn., Mich., 1972, clin. competence Am. Speech-Lang.-Hearing Assn., 1975, myofunctional therapy Inst. Myofunctional Therapy, 1986, pre-primary impaired tchg. endorsement Office of Spl. Edn./Dept. Edn., Mich., 1993, lic. speech-lang. pathology Ind., 1995. Speech-lang. pathologist Port Huron Area Sch. Dist., Mich., 1974—75, Br. Intermediate Sch. Dist., Coldwater, Mich., 1975—, Speech and Lang. Svcs., Coldwater, 1992—; cons. Pines Behavioral Health Svcs., Coldwater, 1993—2003; speech-lang. pathologist Laurels Health Care, Coldwater, 1999—, Sundance Rehab., Angola, Ind., 2000—; instr. Kellogg CC, Battle Creek, 2001—03. Cons. speech pathology Office Spl. Edn.-Dept. Edn., Lansing, 1993—96, Venture Behavioral Health, Battle Creek, 1997—2003. Author: (doctoral dissertation) Contextual Factors in Receptive Vocabulary Development of Three-Year-Old Children in Homogeneous and Heterogeneous Day Care. Pres. Early Bird Exch. Club, Coldwater, Mich., 1997—98, 2000—01, 2004—. Recipient Exchangite of Yr., Early Bird Exch. Club, 1995, 2004, ACE, Am. Speech-Lang.-Hearing Assn., 1996. Mem.: Am. Speech-Lang.-Hearing Assn. (licentiate), Nat. Exch. Club. Avocations: miniature pinschers, Norman Rockwell memorabilia, gardening.

SNYDER, NADINE ELDORA, music educator; d. Clair Ernest and Eldora Irene Snyder. BA in Music, Moravian Coll., 1982; MS in Edn., Temple U., 1987. Cert. music tchr. N.J. Dept. Edn., 1982, music tchr. instrnl. I Pa. Dept. Edn., 1982, music tchr. instrn. II Pa. Dept. Edn., 1989. Music tchr. Voorhees H.S., Glen Gardner, NJ, 1982—83, Palisades Jr./Sr. H.S., Ottsville, Pa., 1983—84, Lehighton (Pa.) Area Schs., 1984—85; supr. Wee Care Nursery Sch., Palmerton, Pa., 1985—88; music tchr. Pleasant Valley Schs., Brodheadsville, Pa., 1988—, music dept. chair, 1992—. Mem. curriculum coun. Pleasant Valley Sch. Dist., Brodheadsville, 1992—, mem. prin. adv. coun., 2000—; pvt. music instr., Pa., 1980—; organist, choir dir. various chs., Allentown, Pa., 1983—93. Recipient Lioness award, Lehigh Twp. Lioness Club, 1994; Thursby scholar, Moravian Coll., 1979, 1980, 1981. Mem.: ASCD, Kimmel Ctr. for the Performing Arts, Am. Choral Dirs. Assn., State Theater Easton, Moravian Coll. Music Alliance, Monroe County Arts Coun., Monroe County Arts Coun., Pa. State Edn. Assn., Pa. Music Educators Assn., Music Educators Nat. Conf., Moravian Coll. Alumni Assn., Order Ea. Star (Gnaden Huetten chpt.), Phi Delta Kappa (Recognition award 2001). Democrat. Avocations: walking, reading, swimming, travel, drama/musicals. Office: Pleasant Valley Sch Dist School Ln Brodheadsville PA 18322 Office Phone: 570-402-1000 x3152.

SNYDER, PATRICIA, volunteer; b. Fox, Ark., Nov. 3, 1948; d. Burton Joseph and Mary Mottinger May; m. Neil N. Snyder III, May 4, 1968; 1 child, Neil N. IV. BS, U. Ark., 1971. Chmn. tours Officers' Wives Club, Heidelberg, Germany, 1981-82, pres., Frankfurt, 1982-83, Ft. Jackson, S.C., 1987-88, second v.p., Heidelberg, 1993-94, hon. v.p., Ft. Jackson, 1994-96; dental vol. ARC, Ft. Jackson, 1987-88, chpt. advisor, 1994-96, chmn. vols., Ft. Monroe, Va., 1996; publicity chmn. PTA, Frankfurt, 1990-91; Am. liaison Steuben-Schurz Damengruppe, Frankfurt, 1990-91; mem. bazaar com. Am. Women's Club, Frankfurt, 1990-92, pres., 1991-92; spl. events com. Heidelberg Bazaar, 1992-94; mem. Sch. Adv. Com., Heidelberg, 1992-94; chmn. Sr. Parents, Heidelberg, 1993-94; pres. Heidelberg 2000, 1993-94; chmn. family support group Soldier Support Inst., Ft. Jackson, 1994-96. Recipient Caroline Scott Harrison award Ft. Benjamin Harrison, Indpls., 1975, Scroll of Appreciation, 1st Pers. Command, Heidelberg, 1982, Scroll of Appreciation, U.S. Army V Corps, Frankfurt, 1992, Heidelberg Star, Heidelberg Cmty., 1994, Scroll of Appreciation, 411th Base Support Bn., Heidelberg, 1994, Cert. Appreciation, Heidelberg H.S., 1994, Soaring Eagle award U.S. Army Europe, Heidelberg, 1994, Outstanding Civilian Svc. medal U.S. Dept. Army, Ft. Monroe, 1996, Commdrs. award for pub. svc. U.S. Dept. Army, Ft. Jackson, 1996, Cert. Appreciation, U.S. Dept. Army, Washington, 1996. Republican. Episcopalian. Avocations: writing, reading, dogs.

SNYDER, REBECCA, literature and language educator; b. Peckville, Pa., May 15, 1974; d. Thomas John and Carol Ann Lopatofsky; m. William Christopher Snyder, Aug. 10, 1996; 1 child, William Vincent. BA English, St. Vincent Coll., Latrobe, Pa., 1996. Cert. Secondary English Tchr. Pa., 1996. Tchr. English/lang. arts Greater Latrobe Sr. H.S., Pa., 1998—. Prodr., dir. musical prodns. Greater Latrobe Sr. H.S., 1998—; instr. elem. drama Greater Latrobe Sch. Dist., 1998—2004; instr. continuing profl. edn. course Westmoreland Intermediate Unit, Greensburg, Pa., 2003—; instr. Challenge Program course St. Vincent Coll., Latrobe, 1998—2000. Dir.: (musical prodn.) Joseph and the Amazing Technicolor Dream Coat, Good News, Anything Goes, Godspell; dir., dir.: Bye Bye Birdie; musician: (piano accompanist) Man of LaMancha, The Fantasticks, (pit orch. condr.) Cinderella, (piano accompaniment) Working, You're a Good Man Charlie Brown, Guys and Dolls, Celebration; dir.: (musical prodn.) The Music Man, Return to the Forbidden Planet. Named All-American Scholar, U.S. Achievement Acad., 1996; named to Who's Who Among America's H.S. Tchrs., Who's Who, 2002, 2004, Nat. Dean's List, 1996, Who's Who Among America's Coll. Students, Who's Who, 1996; recipient Outstanding Am. Tchr., Nat. Honor Roll, 2005—06, Excellence in Edn. award, Latrobe C. of C., 2001, 2004; Arts Integration Grant, McFeely-Rogers Found., 2000, Academic Merit and Hugh O'Brien Leadership Scholarships, St. Vincent Coll., 1992—96. Mem.: Greater Latrobe Edn. Assn. (exec. com. bldg. rep. 2004—06), Nat. Coun. Tchrs. English. Avocations: classically trained pianist, gardening. Office: Greater Latrobe Senior High School 131 High School Road Latrobe PA 15650 Office Phone: 724-539-4225. Office Fax: 724-539-4295. Business E-Mail: snyder@wiu.k12.pa.us.

SNYDER, SUSAN R., music educator; b. Tokyo, Jan. 25, 1949; came to U.S., 1949; d. Sidney and Ruth (Blassberg) Cohen; m. Alan Jay Snyder, June 20, 1971; 1 child, Aaron. BS in Music Edn., U. Conn., 1970; MA in Music Edn., Montclair State Coll., 1973; PhD in Curriculum and Instrn., U. Conn., 1986. Orff master tchr., coop. learning trainer. Tchr. vocal music. elem. and mid. schs. Terryville, Greenwich, Conn., Ringwood, Bergenfield, N.J., 1970-90; music educator various schs. and colls. including C.W. Post, CUNY, Wichita State U., U. Minn., U. South Fla., 1970—; asst. prof. Hunter Coll. CUNY, 1993; pres. Inventive Designs in Edn. and the Arts, 1995—. Coord. Orff levels I, II and III, U. Conn., Storrs, 1976-79; dir. Ridgewood Orff summer workshops Tchrs. Coll., Columbia U., 1973-86; program team chair Hamilton Ave. Sch., Greenwich, Conn., 1986-90; presenter workshops on topics including cooperative learning, early childhood music, multicultural edn., integrated lang. arts; selected as one of four model U.S. music tchrs. as rep. of Orff Inst., Salzburf, Austria, 1985; opened St. John (V.I.) Sch. for the Arts, 1990; guest condr. Ft. Worth ISD; ednl. cons. PBS pilot, 1996; edn. cons. ready to learn partnership evaluation team US Dept. Edn., 2005—. Contbg. author: (book series) Music and You, 1988; coord. author: (book series) Share the Music, 1995; rsch. collaborator A Comparative Study Between the Creative Musical Compositions of Second Grade Gifted and Talented Students and Average Second Grade Students Utilizing the Orff-Schulwerk Music Edn. Method and the Xylophone Instrumentation, 1988; creator: (video series) In the Music Room with Dr. Sue Snyder; author: Integrate With Integrity: Music Across the Curriculum, 1996, ArtSmart: Art Activities for Classroom Teachers, 1997; arts editor Early Childhood Edn. Jour., Total Literacy, 2002; contbr. articles on music edn. to profl. jours.; presenter in field. Gunild Keetman scholar, 1988. Mem. Am. Orff Schulwerk Assn. (founder, pres. No. N.J. chpt. 1975-80, rsch. adv. rev. panel 1987—, rsch. panel nat. conf. Detroit 1988, rsch. strand facilitator nat. conf. Atlanta 1989), Music Educators Nat. Conf., N.J. Music Educators Assn., Conn. Music Educators Assn., N.J. Am. Orff Schulwerk Assn. (pres. 1977-80), Conn. Am. Orff Schulwerk Assn., NEA, Conn. Edn. Assn., ASCD, Internat. Reading Assn. (co-chair reading excellence through the arts), Friends of Kodaly, Pi Lambda Theta.

SNYDER, VIRGINIA ARTRIP, writer; b. Winchester, Va., Nov. 27, 1920; d. William Franklin and Leota Motsey (Dean) Artrip; m. Hendrix C. Royston, Jan. 28, 1939 (div. 1952); m. Ross S. Snyder, July 20, 1954. BA in Govt. & Politics, Fla. Atlantic U., Boca Raton, 1965. Reporter Ft. Lauderdale (Fla.) News, 1966-70, Boca Raton (Fla.) News, 1971-74; pres., pvt. eye Virginia Snyder, Inc., Delray Beach, 1976-98; ret., 1998. Author: Poems of Fact and Fantasy, 1999, numerous poems. Founder So. County Neighborhood Ctr., Boca Raton, 1968. Named one of 14 Outstanding Women of Fla., Gov. Reuben Askew, 1975, one of Fla.'s Finest, Gov. Lawton Chiles, 1996, Sr. Poet Laureate Fla., Angels Without Wings Found., 2004. Mem. NOW (Susan B. Anthony award 1990), Fla. Poetry Soc., Va. Poetry Soc., W.Va. Poetry Soc., Poets of the Palm Beaches, Profl. & Bus. Forum (Profl. of Yr. 1997). Democrat. Unitarian Universalist. Home: 200 S Swinton Ave Delray Beach FL 33444-3658 Personal E-mail: nyknott@bellsouth.net.

SNYDERMAN, SELMA ELEANORE, pediatrician, educator; b. Phila., July 22, 1916; d. Harry Samuel and Rose (Koss) S.; m. Joseph Schein, Aug. 4, 1939; children: Roland M. H., Oliver Douglas. AB, U. Pa., 1937, MD, 1940. Diplomate Am. Bd. of Physican Nutrition Specialists, Am. Bd. Pediatrics. Intern Einstein Med. Ctr., Phila., 1940-42; resident Bellevue Hosp., N.Y.C., 1944-45; fellow NYU Med. Ctr., N.Y.C., 1945-46; from instr. to prof. pediat. NYU Sch. Medicine, N.Y.C., 1946—95, prof. emerita pediat., 1995—; assoc. prof. U. Tex. Med. Br., Galveston, 1952-53; attending physician Bellevue Hosp., 1947—95; dir. Pediatric Metabolic Disease Ctr. Bellevue Med. Ctr., 1965-95; attending physician Tisch Hosp., N.Y.C., 1947-95; prof. human genetics and pediat., attending physician Mt. Sinai Med. Ctr., N.Y.C., 1995—, dir. Metabolic Disease Ctr., 1995—. Mem. nutrition study sect. NIH, Bethesda, Md., 1973-77. Contbr. numerous med. articles to profl. jours. Named career scientist, Health Rsch. Coun., 1961—75; recipient Disting. Grad. award, U. Pa. Sch. Medicine, 2004. Fellow Am. Acad. Pediatrics (Borden award 1975); mem. Am. Inst. Nutrition, Am. Pediatric Soc., Soc. for Pediatric Rsch., Am. Soc. Clin. Nutrition, Soc. Inherited Metabolic Disorders (v.p. 1978, pres. 1979, bd. dirs. 1980-83), Soc. Parenteral and Enteral Nutrition, Soc. for Study of Inborn Errors of Metabolism, Phi Beta Kappa. Jewish. Avocations: gardening, orchid growing, reading. Office: Mount Sinai Med Ctr Dept Human Genetics Fifth Ave & 100th St New York NY 10029 Office Phone: 212-241-4161. Business E-Mail: selma.snyderman@mssm.edu.

SNYDER-SOWERS, MARY ANNE SARAH, performing arts educator, performing company executive, choreographer; b. Bristol, Tenn., Jan. 26, 1956; d. John Calvin and Pauline June Snyder; m. Lee E. Sowers, June 29, 1991; children: Mark Jason Sowers, Jeffrey Lee Sowers. BA, Va. Intermont Coll., Bristol, 1978; MEd, Milligan Coll., Tenn., 1997. Artistic dir. Bristol Ballet Co., Va., 1978—95; cert. tchr., first dance specialist Johnson City Schs., Tenn., 1995—. Dance grant rev. panelist Tenn. Arts Commn., Nashville, 2005—; prin. dancer Bristol Ballet Co., Va., 1968—82; regional evaluator Southeastern Regional Ballet Assn./Regional Dance Am., Atlanta, 1992—95; facutly mem. ballet dept. Va. Intermont Coll., Bristol, 1978—90; faculty summer arts camp Milligan Coll., 2000—; dir. Hardinge Ballet Ctr./Bristol Sch. Ballet, 1978—95; creative movement and dance specialist, artistic dir. ballet ensemble Mt. View Elem. Sch., Johnson City, 1995—. Dir.: (artisitc director) several ballet cos. Founding bd. mem. A! Mag. For The Arts, Bristol, Va., 1984—86; instr. liturgical dance St. Anne's Cath. Ch., Bristol; assoc. mem., dir. Southeastern Regional Ballet Assn./Regional Dance Am., Atlanta, 1991—95. Grantee, Johnson City Sports Found., 2005—06, Johnson City Area Arts Coun., 2005—06. Mem.: NEA, Tenn. Edn. Assn., Nat. Dance Edn. Orgn., Nat. Dance Edn. Assn. (assoc.), Tenn. Arts Commn. (assoc.; dance grant rev. panelist 2005), Johnson City Edn. Assn. (assoc.; com. chair 1992—2006, negotiating panel 2006). Home: 2859 Carroll Creek Road Johnson City TN 37615 Office: Johnson City Schools/Mountain View Elem 907 King Springs Road Johnson City TN 37601 Office Phone: 423-434-5260. Home Fax: 423-913-8183; Office Fax: 423-434-5596. Personal E-mail: maryanne@maryannesowers.com. E-mail: sowersm@jcschools.org.

SOAVE, ROSEMARY, internist; b. NYC, Jan. 23, 1949; BS, Fordham U., 1970; MD, Cornell Med. Coll., 1976. Diplomate Am. Bd. Internal Medicine, Subspecialty Bd. in Infectious Diseases. Intern, resident N.Y. Hosp., N.Y.C., 1976-79; chief med. resident Meml.-Sloan Kettering Cancer Ctr., N.Y.C., 1979-80; fellow infectious diseases N.Y. Hosp., N.Y.C., 1980-82, asst. prof. medicine, 1982-89, assoc. prof. medicine and pub. health, 1989—. Spkr. in field; mem. Nat. Insts. Allergy and Infectious Diseases-AIDS and Related Diseases Study Sect. Contbr. numerous articles to profl. jours., chpts. to books, reviews and abstracts to profl. jours. Recipient Mary Putnam Jacobi fellowship for rsch., 1981-82, Leopold Schepp Rsch. fellowship, 1983-84, Nat. Found. for Infectious Diseases Young Investigator Matching Grant award, 1984-85; NIH grantee, 1986-89, 83-86, 87-90, 99-00. Fellow ACP, Infectious Diseases Soc. Am.; mem. AAAS, Am. Fedn. Med. Rsch., N.Y. Acad. Scis., Am. Soc. for Microbiology, Harvey Soc., Sigma Xi. Office: NY Presbyn Hosp Weill Cornell Med Ctr Box 125 1300 York Ave New York NY 10021-4805 Office Phone: 212-746-6319.

SOBEL, FAYE WALTON, elementary school educator; d. Richard Lee and Margaret Walton; m. Bryant Blain Goodloe, July 9, 1966 (div.); children: Jason Cameron, Elizabeth Blaine; m. Ronald Sobel, June 25, 1994. BS, Radford Coll., 1966; MS, Madison Coll., 1971. Cert. reading specialist, elem. sch. adminstr. Tchr. Nelson County Sch. Bd., Lovington, Va., 1966—68, Augusta County Sch. Bd., Fishersville, Va., 1968—71; reading specialist, asst. prin., parent rels. coord. Suffolk Pub. Sch. Bd., Va., 1972—2003. Mem.: Internat. Dyslexic Assn., Internat. Reading Assn., AAUW, Va. Ed. Assn., Nat. Ed. Assn., Am. Assn. of Univ. of Women, DAR, Phi Delta Kappa. Avocations: bridge, bowling, quilting, genealogy.

SOBERAL, ISABEL M., minister, music educator, social worker; b. Arecibo, PR, Aug. 22, 1940; d. Jesús Soberal and Justina Román; children: Isabel M., Maria T., Ana M., Miguel A. Rodriguez. BA, Catholic U., 1962; MDiv, Evangelical Sem., 1997, MA in Religion, 2001; postgrad., Instituto Teologico Internacional de Puerto Rico, 2002—. Ordained min. Meth. Ch., 2005; LCSW 1963. Social worker Health Dept., PR, 1963—88; handbell choir dir. Samuel Aun Weor handbell choir, PR, 1986—2004; music tchr. Dept. Edn., PR, 1994—2004; pastor United Meth. Ch., Hopkinsville, Ky., 2004—05, Meth. Ch., PR, 2002—04. Hand bell choir dir. Sala Festivales-Centro Bellas Artes, 2002—04; interpreter Cabinet for Health and Family Svcs. Disability Determination Svcs. Named one of, Musicians Arts Corp., 2003. Mem.: Assn. de Maestros de PR, Am. Guild English Handbell Ringers. Home: 2820 S Virginia St Hopkinsville KY 42240 Office: St John Corona de Vida 2808 S Virginia St Hopkinsville KY 42240 Office Phone: 270-886-1049. Office Fax: 270-886-0391. E-mail: isabelm@hesenergy.net, isbsb@aol.com.

SOBERON, PRESENTACION ZABLAN, state bar administrator; b. Cabambangan, Bacolor, Pampanga, Philippines, Feb. 23, 1935; came to U.S., 1977; naturalized, 1984; d. Pioquinto Yalung and Lourdes (David) Zablan; m. Damaso Reyes Soberon, Apr. 2, 1961; children: Shirley, Sherman, Sidney, Sedwin. Office mgmt., stenography, typing cert., East Cen. Colls., Philippies, 1953; profl. sec. diploma, Internat. Corr. Schs., 1971; A in Mgmt. Supervision, Skyline and Diablo Coll., 1979, LaSalle Ext. U., 1980-82; AA, cert. in Mgmt. and Supervision, Diablo Valley Coll. With U.S. Fed. Svc. Naval Base, Subic Bay, Philippines, 22 yrs, clerical, stenography and secretarial positions, 1955-73, adminstrv. asst., 1973-77; secretarial positions Mt. Zion Hosp. and Med. Ctr., San Francisco, 1977, City Hall, Oakland, Calif., 1978; with State Bar Calif., San Francisco, 1978-79; secretarial positions gen. counsel divsn. and state bar ct. divsn., adminstrv. asst. fin. and ops. divsn., 1979-81; office mgr. sects. and coms. dept., profl. and pub. svcs., 1981-83; appointment adminstr. office of bar rels., 1983-86; adminstr. state bar sects. bus. law sect., estate planning, trust and probate law sect., labor and employment law sect., office of bar rels., 1986-89; adminstr. antitrust and trade regulation law sect., labor and employment law sect., workers' compensation sect., edn. and meeting svcs., 1989-96; adminstr. criminal law sect., 1996—; labor and law employment law sect., 1996—; internat. law sect., 1996—; workers' compensation sect., 1996—; edn. and meeting svcs., 1996-98; ret., 1998. Lectr., min. Our Lady of the Queen of the World Ch.; disc jockey, announcer Radio Sta. DZYZ, DZOR and DWHL, Philippines, 1966-77. Organizer Neighborhood Alert Program, South Catamaran Circle, Pittsburg, Calif., 1979-80. Recipient 13 commendation certs. and outstanding pers. monetary awards U.S. Fed. Svc., 1964-77, 20 Yr. U.S. Fed. Svc. cert., 1975, Nat. 1st prize award Nat. Inner Wheel Clubs Philippines, 1975, Kaiser Vol. Svc. Mem.: NAFE, Am. Soc. Assn. Execs., Our Lady Queen Ch. Filipino Assn., SRF Tigers No. Calif., Castillejos Assn. No. Calif., Olongapo-Subic Bay Assn. Am. (Pitts. rep. 1982—87, bus. mgr. 1988—89, pub. rels. officer 1993—94, bus. mgr. 1997—, bus. mgr. Ulo Ng Apo chpt. 2003—). Roman Catholic. Home: 207 South Catamaran Circle Pittsburg CA 94565-3613 Office: State Bar of Calif 180 Howard St San Francisco CA 94105-1639 Personal E-mail: pzsoberon@comcast.net.

SOBKOWICZ, HANNA MARIA, neurologist, researcher; b. Warsaw, Jan. 1, 1931; arrived in U.S., 1963; d. Stanislaw and Jadwiga (Ignaczak) S.; m. Jerzy E. Rose, Mar. 12, 1972. BA, Girls State Lyceum, Gilwice, Poland, 1949; M.D, Med. Acad., Warsaw, 1954, PhD, 1962. Intern. 1st Internal Med. Clinic Med. Acad., Warsaw, 1954-55; resident 1st Internal Med. Clinic, Med. Acad., Warsaw, 1955-59, Neurol. Clinic, Med. Acad., 1959, jr. asst., 1959-61, sr. asst., 1961-63; research fellow neurology Mt. Sinai Hosp., N.Y.C., 1963-65; Nat. Multiple Sclerosis Soc. fellow Columbia U., N.Y.C., 1965-66; asst. prof. neurology U. Wis., Madison, 1966-72, assoc. prof., 1972-79, prof., 1979—2006, prof. emerita, 2006—. Contbr. articles to profl. jours. NIH rsch. grantee, 1968—2002. Mem. Internat. Brain Rsch. Orgn., Soc. Neurosci., Internat. Soc. Devel. Neurosci. (editl. bd. 1984—). Office: U Wis Dept Neurology 1300 University Ave Madison WI 53706-1510 Office Phone: 608-262-1246. Business E-Mail: hmsobkow@wisc.edu.

SOBOL, ELISE SCHWARCZ, music educator; b. Chgo., June 12, 1951; d. Morton and Harriet Jacobsohn Schwarcz; m. Lawrence Paul Sobol, Aug. 21, 1977 (div. Sept. 1989); children: Marlon I., Aaron L. AA, Simon's Rock Bard Coll., 1971; student, Mannes Coll. Music, 1971—73, Juillard Sch. Music, 1973—74; BA, New Sch. Social Rsch., 1985; MA, Columbia U., 1987. Staff auditorium events, concerts, lectures Met. Mus. Art, 1972-73; sec. to pres. Harry Beall Mgmt. Inc., N.Y.C., 1973-76; sales rep. M.L. Falcone Pub. Rels., N.Y.C., 1976-77; asst. to pres. Jacques Leiser Artist Mgmt., N.Y.C., 1977-78; artist rep. Elise Sobol Mgmt. Inc., South Huntington, NY, 1978-82; dir. early musical devel. program children Calling All Kids, South Huntington, 1981—86; tchr. music Roslyn Mid. Sch., 1987—88, Nassau Boces Divsn. Spl. Edn., 1988—; dir. LI Music Workshop, 1992—. Tchr. young and adult piano students, 1968—; instr. SUNY, Farmingdale, 1993—98; piano adjudicator, NY, 1993—; guest lectr. NYU, N.Y.C., 1999; adj. prof. NYU, Steinhardt Sch. Edn., N.Y.C., 2000—; advisor arts and humanities Internat. Biog. Ctr., Cambridge, England; guest lectr. Hofstra, 2000; adj. faculty C.W. Post Coll. LI U., 2000. Musician: (piano concerts) Chamber Music series at U.S. Mil. Acad., N.Y./N.J. met. area concerts, Disting. Artists series, 2002—03, Met. Area Concerts, 2003, Am. Assn. Univ. Women Commentary and Concerts, 2003; musician: (commentary and concert) A Gentlewoman's Pursuit, AAUW, 2003, concerts in New Zealand, Australia, Eng., Ireland, Can. and U.S.; contbg. author: Spotlight in Making Music with Special Learners, 2004; author: (signature series) A Gentleman's Pursuit, 2003—04; author: An Attitude and Approach for Teaching Music to Special Learners, 2001. Active Nassau Boces Elem. Program PTA, cultural arts coord., 1988—. Nominee N.Y. Senate Women of Distinction Program, 2003; named Internat. Musician of the Yr., 2004; recipient award of Honor, LI Very Spl. Arts Festival, 1993, Spl. citation, N.Y. State Assembly Ames Elem. Program, 1998, Spl. recognition, Nassau Music Educators Assn., 1999, 1st prize, Dr. Martin Luther King Jr. Performing Arts Competition Exceptional Students Nassau County, 1999—2001, Internat. Peace prize, United Cultural Conv., 2002, citation, Town of Oyster Bay, 2002, award, Ernest Kay Internat. Found., 2004. Mem.: AAUW, ASCD, NAFE, Music Educators Nat. Conf., N.Y. State Sch. Music Assn. (chair music spl. learners 1993—). Home: 21 Saxon St Melville NY 11747 E-mail: ESSOBOL@aol.com.

SOBRERO, KATE (KATHRYN MICHELE SOBRERO), professional soccer player; b. Pontiac, Mich., Aug. 23, 1976; BA in Bus., U. Notre Dame, 1997. Mem. U.S. Nat. Women's Soccer Team, 1995—2001; profl. soccer player Boston Breakers (WUSA), 2001—03. Mem. U.S. Under-20 Nat. Team, 1993—. Named Defensive Most Valuable Player, NCAA Final Four, 1995. Achievements include on cover of Soccer Am. mag., 1995; member Notre Dame NCAA National Championship Team, 1995; member U.S. World Cup Championship Team, 1999; member U.S. Olympic Silver Medal Team, 2000. Office: US Soccer Fedn 1801-1811 S Prairie Ave Chicago IL 60616

SOBUS, KERSTIN MARYLOUISE, physician, physical therapist; b. Washington, June 16, 1960; d. Earl Francis and Dolores Jane (Gill) G.; m. Paul John Jr., March 10, 1990; children: Darlene Marie, Julieann Marie, Gwendolyn Rose Marie. BS in Phys. Therapy summa cum laude, U. N.D., 1981, MD, 1987. Clinic instr. pediatric physical therapy U.N.D. Sch. Medicine, Grand Forks, 1981-83; pediat. phys. theraist child evaluation-treatment program Med. Rehab. Ctr., Grand Forks, 1981-83, med. dir. program, 1997—; asst. prof. dept. pediatrics, asst. prof. dept. physical medicine and rehab. U. Ark. for Med. Scis., Little Rock, 1992-96; resident in internal medicine Sinai Hosp. Balt., 1987-88; resident in phys. medicine and rehab. Johns Hopkins program Sinai Hosp., Balt., 1988-91; pediatric rehab. clin. and rsch. fellow Alfred I. DuPont Inst., Wilmington, Del., 1991-92; pediatric pysiatrist Altru Health System, Grand Forks, 1997—. Contbr. articles to med. jours. Mem. Am. Acad. Cerebral Palsy and Devel. Medicine, Alpha Omega Alpha Honor Soc. Office: Altru Health Sys PO Box 6002 1300 S Columbia Rd Grand Forks ND 58201-4012 Home: 7451 S 25th St Grand Forks ND 58201 Office Phone: 701-780-2482.

SOCHA, CINDY L., secondary school educator; b. Worcester, Mass., Oct. 16, 1954; d. Robert B. and Gloria M. David; m. Edward J. Socha, Aug. 30, 1986. BS in elem. edn., Worcester State Coll., Mass., 1976, MS in edn., 1983. Cert. elem. K-8 tchr. Dept. Edn., math 7-12 tchr., prin., asst. prin., K-12. Tchr. Webster Pub. Schs., Mass., 1976—99; adj. prof. Nichols Coll., Dudley, Mass., 1986—2005; asst. prin. Douglas Mid. HS, Mass., 1999—2001; tchr. Douglas HS, Mass., 2001—. Cheerleading coach Bartlett H.S., 1983—91, Nichols Coll., Dudley, Mass., 1993—2005, Douglas Pub. Schs., Mass., 1999—2006; math. dept. chair Douglas HS, Mass., 1999—2006. Yearbook advisor Bartlett High, 1983—99, Douglas H.S., Mass., 2001—. Mem.: NEASC (mem. steering com. 2006), Nat. Coun. Tchrs. of Math., Mass. Tchrs. Assn., Douglas Tchrs. Assn. Avocations: photography, boating, gardening. Home: 2 Scenic Ave Webster MA 01570 Office: Douglas HS 33 Davis St Douglas MA 01516 Business E-Mail: csocha@douglas.k12.ma.us.

SOCHA, MAUREEN PATRICIA, elementary school educator; b. Chgo., Feb. 13, 1934; d. Daniel Patrick and Eva (Disko) O'Connell; m. Joseph Kenneth Socha, Aug. 14, 1954; children: Patricia, Kenneth, James, William. BA, St. Xavier Coll., 1971. Tchr. elem. schs. Archdiocese of Chgo., 1971—2000. Sci. resource and cons. Our Lady of the Ridge Sch., Chicago Ridge, 1990-2000. Trustee Village of Chicago Ridge, Ill., 1989-2005, co-chmn. Village Fest com., 1991-2005, chmn. beautification com., 1994-1998, youth svc. bur., 1989-2005, firedept., 1996-2005; mem. Police and Fire Commn., Vilage Chgo. Ridge, 2006—. Mem. Nat. Cath. Edn. Assn., Ill. Mcpl. League, Chicago Ridge C. of C. Roman Catholic. Avocations: reading, word puzzles, boating, grandchildren. Home: 11001 Lombard Ave Chicago Ridge IL 60415-2114 Office: Village of Chicago Ridge 10655 Oak Ave Chicago Ridge IL 60415-1999

SOCHEN, JUNE, history professor; b. Chgo., Nov. 26, 1937; d. Sam and Ruth (Finkelstein) S. BA, U. Chgo., 1958; MA, Northwestern U., 1960, PhD, 1967. Project editor Chgo. Superior and Talented Student Project, 1959-60; high sch. tchr. English and history North Shore Country Day Sch., Winnetka, Ill., 1961-64; instr. history Northeastern Ill. U., 1964-67, asst. prof., 1967-69, assoc. prof., 1969-72, prof., 1972—. Author: The New Woman, 1971, Movers and Shakers, 1973, Herstory: A Woman's View of American History, 1975, 2d edit., 1981, Consecrate Every Day: The Public Lives of Jewish American Women, 1981, Enduring Values: Women in Popular Culture, 1987, Cafeteria America: New Identities in Contemporary Life, 1988, Mae West: She Who Laughs Lasts, 1992, From Mae to Madonna: Women Entertainers in 20th Century America, 1999; editor: The New Feminism in 20th Century America, 1972, Women's Comic Visions, 1991; contbr. articles to profl. jours. Nat. Endowment for Humanities grantee, 1971-72 Office: Northeastern Ill U 5500 N Saint Louis Ave Chicago IL 60625-4679 Office Phone: 773-442-5607. Business E-Mail: j-sochen@neiu.edu.

SOCHET, MARY ALLEN, psychotherapist, educator, writer; b. Plattsburgh, N.Y., Feb. 10, 1938; d. Edwin Elisha and Mary Elizabeth (Thomson) Allen; m. Marvin J. Sochet, 1963; children: Melorra, David. BS in Childhood Edn., SUNY, Plattsburgh, 1958; MA in Human Rels., NYU, 1961, PhD in Human Devel., 1963. Tchr. kindergarten L.I. Pub. Schs., 1958-62; tchr. N.Y.C. Pub. Schs., 1962-64; prof. early childhood edn., child devel. and psychology Bklyn. Coll., 1964-71; program dir., acting exec. dir. Newark Pre-Sch. Coun., 1965-66; psychotherapist N.Y.C. Community Guidance Svc., 1966-78; staff cons. Human Resources Inst., 1966—; pvt. practice psychotherapy N.Y.C., 1966—. Writer, lectr., ednl. cons. and editorial cons. in field. Author: (with Robert Allen) Toward a Caring Community, 1980; contbr. articles on edn., community orgns., peace and mental health to various jours. Founding mem. Community Loft, 1971-74, Neighbor's Network, 1979—; organizing mem. Children's Free Sch., 1969-81; co-chair Perhaps Kids Meeting Kids Can Make a Difference, 1982—. NCCJ fellow, 1961-61; recipient Founder's Day award NYU, 1963. Mem. Am. Psychol. Assn., Soc. Psychol. Study Social Issues, Psychologists for Social Responsibility. Home and Office: 380 Riverside Dr New York NY 10025-1858 Business E-Mail: kidsmtgkids@igc.org.

SOCOLOW, ELIZABETH ANNE, poet, educator, artist, writer; b. NYC, June 15, 1940; d. Ralph Maurice and Frances Irene (Goldberg) Sussman; m. Robert H. Socolow, June 10, 1962 (div. Apr. 1982); children: David Jacob, Seth Louis. BA, Vassar Coll., 1962; MA, Harvard U., 1963, PhD, 1967. Lectr. in English and composition U. Mich., Dearborn, 1993—99; lectr. in English Wayne State U., 1993—99, Lawrence Technol. U., Southfield, Mich., 1994—98; lectr. Bucks County C.C., 1999—2001, Rutgers/Camden at Freehold, 2001—. Poetry editor newsletter Soc. for Lit. and Sci., Athens, Ga., 1989—. Author: Laughing at Gravity: Conversations With Isaac Newton, 1988 (Barnard Women Poets Series prize 1987). Avocations: computer, graphics, cards.

SODERBERG, NANCY, former court official, writer; b. San Turce, P.R., Mar. 13, 1958; d. Lars Olof and Nancy (MacGilvrey) S. BA in French and Econs., Vanderbilt U., 1980; MS in Fgn. Svc., Georgetown U., 1984. Del. selection asst. Mondale-Ferraro Com., Washington, 1983, fgn. policy advisor, 1984; dep. issues dir. fgn. policy Dukakis for Pres. Com., Boston, 1988; fgn. policy advisor Senator Edward M. Kennedy, Washington, 1985-88, 89-92; fgn. policy dir. Clinton/ Gore Campaign, Little Rock, 1992; dep. asst. dir. transition nat. security Clinton/ Gore Transition, Little Rock, 1992-93; dep. asst. to Pres. for nat. security affairs Nat. Security Coun., Washington, 1993—97; amb. (alt. rep.) UN, NYC, 1997—2001; v.p., dir. NY office Internat Crisis Group, 2001—05; dist. vis. scholar U. North Fla., Jacksonville, 2006—. TV and radio commentator MSNBC; mem. Coun. Fgn. Rels. Author: The Superpower Myth: The Use and Misuse of American Might, 2005. Home: 121 Lanternwich Pl Ponte Vedra Beach FL 32082 Office Phone: 212-813-0820, 646-591-0912. Office Fax: 212-813-0825. Personal E-mail: nsoderberg@aol.com.

SODETZ, CAROL JEAN, aquatic fitness educator; b. Chgo., Aug. 24, 1943; d. Frank John Shamel and Stella Mary Wozniak; m. Frank Jack Sodetz Jr., Aug. 24, 1963; children: Lynn, Frank, Diane. Student, Fenger Jr. Coll., 1962—63, Montgomery Coll., 1999—. Typist Fed. Sign & Signal, Blue Island, Ill., 1961; sec. Verson All Steel, Chgo., 1962; office mgr. Tri-State Elec., 1963; fitness instr. Silver Spring YMCA, Silver Spring, Md., 1975—84, aquatic dir., 1980—84; owner, CEO Swimming Sch., Bangkok, 1984—94; lesson coord. Montgomery County OSC, Olney, Md., 1998—; fitness expert Wellness Network, 2000—. Sec. Tomorrow Group Assocs., Silver Spring, Md., 1998—; mem. Niams, Washington, 2000—; chair Internat. Women's Club, Bangkok, 1987—94; pres. Scleroderma Found. Greater Washington, 2002—. Pres. Am. Women's Club, Bangkok, 1992—93; sec. Reps. Abroad, 1986—94. Republican. Roman Catholic. Avocations: reading, gardening, travel. Office: Olney Swim Ctr 16601 Georgia Ave Olney MD 20832 Business E-Mail: csod@t-grp.com.

SODEY, ANGELA ANN, gifted and talented educator; b. Freeport, Ill., Sept. 26, 1949; d. John Francis and Carolyn Lola McKenna; m. James Carleton Sodey, Sept. 5, 1970; children: Jay Carleton, Christopher John. BA, U. Iowa, Iowa City, 1971; MSE Reading Specialist, Drake U., Des Moines, Iowa, 1978. Tchr. grade 4 Ottumwa (Iowa) Schs., 1971; tchr. grades 5,6 Des Moines Pub. Schs., 1972—75, reading specialist, 1975—77, tchr. grade 3, 1977—79, tchr. grades 4, 5, 6 lang. arts, 1980; kindergarten tchr. Boone (Iowa) Pub. Schs., 1980; tchr. h.s. reading Jefferson County Schs., Denver, 1981—83; elem. talented and gifted tchr. Spencer (Iowa) Pub. Schs., 1984—85, Ft. Madison (Iowa) Pub. Schs., 1985—88, TAG coord., reading coord., 1988—92, tchr. mid. sch. reading, 1992—98, tchr. grade 6, 1998—2004, elem. talented and gifted tchr., 2004—. Bd. dirs. Shining Trail coun. Girl Scouts Am., Burlington, Iowa, 2003—07. Grantee, Wal-Mart, 2004—05. Mem.: Lee County Reading Assn., Iowa Reading Assn. (pres.-elect, pres. 2003—05), Ft. Madison Country Club (bd. dirs. 1994—96), Delta Kappa Gamma (sec. 1992). Independent. Methodist. Avocations: boating, reading, knitting, bicycling, hiking, exercise, travel. Home: 612 Ave G Fort Madison IA 52627

SOETEBER, ELLEN, journalist, editor; b. East St. Louis, Ill., June 14, 1950; d. Lyle Potter and Norma Elizabeth (Osborn) S.; m. Richard M. Martins, Mar. 16, 1974. BJ, Northwestern U., 1972. Edn. writer, copy editor Chgo. Today, 1972-74; reporter Chgo. Tribune, 1974-76, asst. met. editor, 1976-84, assoc. met. editor, 1984-86, TV and media editor, 1986, met. editor, 1987-89, assoc. mng. editor for met. news, 1989-91, dep. editor editorial page, 1991-94; mng. editor South Fla. Sun-Sentinel, Ft. Lauderdale, 1994-2001; editor St. Louis Post-Dispatch, 2001—05. Fellow journalism U. Mich., Ann Arbor, 1986-87; guest instr. Poynter Inst. Journalism Studies and other profl. seminars, vis. faculty, 2006-; leader mgmt. seminars, 2006-. Named to Hall of Achievement, Medill Sch. of Journalism, 2003. Office Phone: 954-522-9287. Personal E-mail: ellsoeteber@aol.com.

SOFFA, MARY LOU, computer science and engineering educator; PhD in Computer Sci., Univ. Pitts., 1977. Former prof., Dept. Computer Sci. Univ. Pitts.; Owen R. Cheatham Prof., Dept. Computer Sci. Univ. Va., Charlottesville, Va., 2004—, chair, Dept. Computer Sci., 2004—. Mem. exec. com. SIGSOFT, SIGPLAN. Contbr. articles to numerous profl. jours. Mem.: ACM (edl. bd., Transactions on Software Engineering Methodology, edl. bd., Transactions on Programming Languages and Sys.), Computer Rsch. Assn. (mem. bd.). Office: Univ Va Dept Computer Sci Sch Engring and Applied Sci 151 Engineers Way Box 400740 Charlottesville VA 22904-4740 Office Phone: 434-982-2277. Office Fax: 434-982-2214. E-mail: soffa@cs.virginia.edu.*

SOFFER, GRACE FLOREY, retired elementary school educator, artist; b. Jeannette, Pa. d. James Paul Florey and Mary Ann Winewski; m. Rubin Soffer, Mar. 16, 1946; 1 child, Jerry Paul. BA, Ohio State U., 1944; MA, Adelphi U., 1975. Tchr. common br. N.Y.C. Bd. of Edn., 1966-85. One women shows include N.Y. Poly. U., Farmingdale, 1995, South Nassau Unitarian Ch., 1989, Parlor Gallery Cmty. Ch., 1989, Malverne Pub. Lib., 1985; exhibited in group shows at Fine Arts Mus. of L.I., Art Circa 2100, 1995, Inter-Media Art Ctr., Huntington, Art Circa 2100, 1995, 97, South Nassau Cmty. Hosp., 1990, TriCounty Arts Invitational Small Group Fine Arts exhibit, N.Y., 1999, N.Y. Tech. U., Wisser Libr., Old Westbury, 1990, Shelter Rock Gallery, Manhasset, 1994, Adelphi Art and Art History Alumni Assn., N.Y.C., 1990, Five Towns Music and Art Found., Woodmere, 1990, others, Village Art Club, 1988-91 (prizes), Lee Scarfone Gallery, 1998, Guild Hall East Hampton, 1992, Fine Arts Mus. of L.I., 1997 (3d pl. winner 1998), Nassau County Mus. of FIne Art, 1992, Long Beach Art League, 1999, 2002 (prize), South Nassau Unitarian Ch., 1989, 92 (prizes), Village Art Club at Chelsea Ctr., 1991, others. Mem. Nat. Assn. Women Artists, Long Beach Art Leauge, Nat. League Am. Pen Women (exhibits chair 1995-2001), Nat. Mus. Women in the Arts (charter), Village Art Club, Tri County Artists of L.I. (newsletter 1980-95, prizes), Art Circa 2100, Adelphi Art Hist. Alumni Assn., Mensa. Home: 56 Dickson St Inwood NY 11096-1004

SOH, CHUNGHEE SARAH, anthropology educator; b. Taegu, Korea, May 1, 1947; came to U.S., 1970; d. Sang Yung and Ock Yun (Choi) S.; m. Jerry Dee Boucher. BA in English summa cum laude, Sogang U., 1971; postgrad., U. Calif., Berkeley, 1971; MA in Anthropology, U. Hawaii, 1983, PhD in Anthropology, 1987. Staff instr. English Korean Air Lines, Edn. & Tng. Ctr., Seoul, 1978-79; instr. anthropology Ewha Womans U., Seoul, 1985; postdoctoral assoc. Inst. of Culture and Comm., East-West Ctr., Honolulu, 1987; asst. prof. U. Hawaii, 1990; asst. prof. anthropology Southwest Tex. State U., San Marcos, 1991-94, San Francisco State U., 1994-96, assoc. prof. anthropology, 1996—2006, prof., 2006—. Guest lectr. Chaminade U. Honolulu, 1988; vis. asst. prof. anthropology U. Ariz., 1990-91; adj. prof. Intercultural Inst. Calif., 1996-98; cons. in field. Author: The Chosen Women in Korean Politics: An Anthropological Study, 1991, Women in Korean Politics, 1993; contbr. articles to profl. jour. Bd. dirs. Women Devel. Inst. Internat., 2000—. Grantee East-West Ctr., 1981-87, NSF, 1985-86; fellow Korea Found., 1993, Japan Found., 1997-98, Inst. Social Sci., U. Tokyo, 1997-98, Leiden U. Internat. Inst. for Asian Studies, The Netherlands, 1998, Inst. for Corean-Am. Studies, 1998—; Hoover Inst. scholar, 1996-97, Stanford U. Inst. for Rsch. on Women and Gender scholar, 2000-01; Rsch. and Writing grantee John D. and Catherine T. MacArthur Found., 2000-01. Fellow Am. Anthrop. Assn. (treas. East Asia sect. 2001-03), Inst. for Corean-Am. Studies; mem. Am. Ethnological Soc., Soc. Psychol. Anthropology, Assn. Asian Studies (exec. bd. Com. Women Asian Studies 1995-97), Korean Assn. Womens Studies, Royal Asiatic Soc. Korean Br. Office: San Francisco State U Dept Anthropology 1600 Holloway Ave San Francisco CA 94132-1722 Business E-Mail: soh@sfsu.edu.

SOHAILI, MONIRA, retired special education educator; b. Pune, India, Nov. 4, 1933; d. Ispandiar and Keshvar Yaganegi; m. Shahpur Sohaili, Oct. 15, 1953 (dec. Dec. 2000). BA in Edn., Northeastern Ill. U., 1981, MA, 1982. Cert. behavioral therapy Behavioral Therapy Tng. Ctr., L.A., 1996. Tchr. Parramalta Marist H.S., Australia, 1970—71; guide Bahai House of Worship, Chgo., 1973—83; ESL instr. Cuban/Hatian Refugee Program, Chgo., 1983—84, Chgo. Bd. Edn., 1984—87; ESL and Eng. instr. Santa Monica (Calif.) City Coll., 1987—89; ESL, Eng. and reading tchr. Le Conte Mid. Sch., L.A., 1989—96; head dept. Ctr. Mid. Sch., 1994—96, spl. edn. tchr. L.A., 1996—2005, dept. head, 1996—2000; tchr. spl. edn. J. Burroughs Mid. Sch., L.A., 2000—05; ret., 2005. Storyteller in field, 2002—. Author: Monira's Fables, 2000, From Earth and Beyond, 2003, Spotty the Wonder Dog, Family History. Coord. childproof medicine vials donation, Papua New Guinea, 1995—97. Recipient Cert. of Achievement, L.A. USD Lang. Acquisition, 1993, I Made a Difference award, L.A. Dept. Edn., 1995. Mem.: NEA (reading and writing program 1990—), Calif. Tchrs. Assn. (assisted in program 1990—). Avocations: reading, writing, travel, swimming. Home: PO Box 590 Santa Monica CA 90406-0590

SOHN, CATHERINE ANGELL, pharmaceutical executive, pharmacist; b. San Francisco, Mar. 21, 1953; d. Vincent Herbert and Margaret Ann Ware Angell; m. John Edwin Sohn, Aug. 10, 1974; children: Karen Elizabeth, Jennifer Michele. Student, U. Calif., Davis; PharmD, U. Calif., San Francisco, 1977. Registered pharmacist, Calif., Pa. Pharmacist Kaiser Permanent, San Francisco, 1977-78; asst. prof. pharmacy Phila. Coll. Pharmacy and Sci., 1978-82; mgr. med. affairs Smith Kline & French, Phila., 1982-86; assoc. dir. bus. devel. pharm. divsn. Smith Kline Beecham, Phila., 1986-88, product dir., 1988-93, v.p. worldwide strategic product devel., 1994-97; v.p. worldwide bus. devel. Glaxo Smith Kline Consumer Healthcare, Phila., 1998—. Lectr. St. Andrew the Apostle, Gibbsboro, NJ, 1989—; adv. bd. Healthcare Bus. Women's Assn., N.Y.C., NY, 1996—; bd. overseers U. Calif. Sch. Pharmacy, San Francisco, 1997—; health adv. bd. Johns Hopkins U. Sch. Pub. Health, Balt., 1998—. Author: (with others) Applied Clinical Therapeutics, 1980, Handbook of Non-Prescription Drugs, 1980, rev. edit., 1982; contbr. chpts. to profl. pubs. Mem. Am. Pharm. Assn., Calif. Pharmacists Assn., Consumer Healthcare Products Assn. (chmn. internat. affairs com. 1998—, bd. dirs. 1999—), Licensing Exec. Soc., Rho Chi. Roman Catholic. Avocations: swimming, bicycling. Office: GlaxoSmithKline FP1370 200 N 16th St Philadelphia PA 19102-1282

SOHN, JEANNE, librarian; b. Milton, Pa. d. Robert Wilson and Juliette Lightner (Hedenberg) Gift; m. Steven Neil Sohn, Nov. 23, 1962. BA, Temple U., 1966; MSLS, Drexel U., 1971. Lit. bibliographer Temple U., Phila., 1971-75, chief of collection devel., 1975-81; asst. dean for collection devel.

U. N.Mex., Albuquerque, 1981-86, assoc. dean for libr. svcs., 1986-89; dir. libr. svcs. Cen. Conn. State U., New Britain, 1989—. Cons. New Eng. Assn. Schs. and Colls., Winchester, Mass., 1991—. Mem. editorial bd. Collection Mgmt., 1984—; contbr. articles to profl. jours. Mem. Gov.'s Blue Ribbon Commn. on the Future of Libraries, 1994-96. Mem. ALA, New Eng. Libr. Assn., Conn. Libr. Assn., Assn. Coll. and Rsch. Librs., Beta Phi Mu. Office: Cen Conn State Univ Elihu Burritt Libr New Britain CT 06050

SOHNEN-MOE, CHERIE MARILYN, business consultant; b. Tucson, Jan. 2, 1956; d. D. Ralph and Angelina Helen (Spiro) Sohnen; m. James Madison Moe, Jr., May 23, 1981. BA, UCLA, 1977. Rsch. asst. UCLA, 1975-77; ind. cons. L.A., 1978-83; cons. Sohnen-Moe Assocs., Inc., Tucson, 1984—. Author: Business Mastery, 1988, 2d edit., 1991, 3d edit., 1998; co-author: The Ethics of Touch, 2003; contbr. to Compendium mag., 1987-90, Massage Mag., 1992-94, 96-97, Am. Massage Therapy Assn. Jour., 1989—2003; bus. editor Massage Therapy Jour., 1998-2002. Vol. Am. Cancer Soc., Tucson, 1984—; mem. Ariz. Sonora Desert Mus., Tucson; pres. Women in Tucson, 1989. Recipient Outstanding Instr. award Desert Inst. of Healing Arts, 1992. Mem. NOW, ASTD (dir. mem. svcs. 1988, dir. mktg., Disting. Svc. award 1988, Profl. Achievement award 1997), Nat. Fed. Independent Bus., Nat. Assn. Women Bus. Owners, Small Pubs. Assn. N.Am., Pubs. Mktg. Assn. Avocations: reading, swimming, crossword puzzles, board games, singing. Office: Sohnen-Moe Assocs Inc 3906 W Ina Rd #200-367 Tucson AZ 85741-2295 Office Phone: 520-743-3936.

SOHONYAY, LISA CELLA, orthopedic nurse; b. N.Y.C., June 27, 1961; d. Mario and Frances (Miletich) Cella. BSN, Coll. of Mt. St. Vincent, 1983; MPS, New Sch. Social Rsch., 1990. Cert. med.-surg. ANA. Staff nurse St. Vincent's Hosp. and Med. Ctr., N.Y.C., 1983-86, asst. nursing care coord., 1986-88, staff edn. instr., 1988-91; asst. nurse mgr. orthopedics Danbury (Conn.) Hosp., 1991—97, case coord., 1997—. Office Phone: 203-739-6246.

SOILEAU, VERONICA DEMORUELLE, counselor, educator; d. Joseph Edison Demoruelle and Vernice Marie La Haye-Demoruelle; m. Robert B. Soileau (div.); children: Blaine Philip, Alyson Camille, Shanon Gerard. BA, U. Southwestern La., Lafayette, 1963; MEd, McNeese State U., La., 1992. Lic. profl. counselor LA Bd. Examiners, 1994, nat. cert. counselor Nat. Bd. Cert. Counselors, N.C., 1995, lic. profl. counselor Tex. Bd. Examiners of LPC, 2005. Dir. counseling ctr. Charter Lake Charles, Lake Charles, La.; clin. mgr. Vol. of Am., Lake Charles, La.; sch. counselor Goose Creek Ind. Sch. Dist., Baytown, Tex., 2002—. Avocations: travel, reading. Office: Robert E Lee HS 1809 Market St Baytown TX 77520 Personal E-mail: vsoileau@msn.com. Business E-Mail: vdsoileau@gccisd.net.

SOKOL, JENNIFER MARIE, musician; b. Seattle, Wash., Mar. 26, 1958; d. Vilem and Agatha Sokol. BA in violin performance, Ind. U. Founder, first violinist, mgr. Cameo String Quartet. Contbr. articles various profl. jours. Recipient Pres. award for Literary Excellence, Nat. Authors Registry, 2004. Roman Cath. Avocations: reading, ballet, outdoor recreation. Home: 6303 NE 185th St Kenmore WA 98028 Office Phone: 425-485-8380. E-mail: jennifermsokol@aol.com.

SOKOL, MARIAN, medical association administrator; PhD in Early Childhood Spl. Edn., Univ. Tex., Austin; postdoctoral M in Pub. Health, Univ. Tex. Health Sci. Ctr., Houston. Founding dir. Any Baby Can Inc., 1982—2003; pres. First Candle/SIDS Alliance, 2003—; vice chair Gov. Commn. for Women, 1991—93. Vice chair Gov. (Tex.) Commn. for Women, 1991—93; commr. Nat. Adv. Commn. on Childhood Vaccines, 1995, chair., 97, 98; bd. chair Nat. SIDS Alliance. Founding chair Tex. Network for Medically Fragile and Chronically Ill Children. Named to San Antonio Women's Hall of Fame; recipient Imagineeer award, Mind Sci. Found., 1987, Excellence 90 Health Care Profl. award, Women's Coalition, Prudential HealthCare's Salute to San Antonio's Good Health award, 1996, San Antonio Cmty. of Churches award, 2001. Office: First Candle/SIDS Alliance Ste 210 1314 Bedford Ave Pikesville MD 21208 Office Phone: 800-221-7437. Business E-Mail: marian.sokol@firstcandle.org.*

SOKOLOFF, AUDREY L., lawyer; b. Providence, R.I., 1966; AB, Dartmouth Coll., 1987; JD, UCLA, 1990. Bar: Calif. 1990, N.Y. 1999. Atty. Skadden, Arps, Slate, Meagher & Flom LLP, New York, 1999—. Office: Skadden Arps Slate Meagher & Flom LLP Four Times Sq New York NY 10036

SOKOLOW, ISOBEL FOLB, sculptor; b. Bklyn. d. Henry Folb and Betty Forshaw; m. Gilbert Sokolow (dec.); children: Helene, Cheryl. Student, Silvermine Coll. Art, 1965-68, Art Students League, Nat. Acad. Design, Westchester C.C., N.Y., Ednl. Alliance Art Sch. Tchr., art therapist Jewish Guild for the Blind, Yonkers, N.Y., 1974-76; dir. Westchester Art & Culture Assn., Ardsley, NY, 1984—86; coord. sculpture workshops Pietrasanta, Italy, 1984-86; coord. summer workshop Pratt U., Venice, Italy, 1987. Artist in residence Nat. Woman's Com., Brandeis U., 1995; prodr., host cable TV show Art Scene Thru An Artist's Eye, 1995—. One-woman shows include Bell Gallery, Greenwich, Conn., 1977, River View Gallery, Dobbs Ferry, N.Y., 1978, North Shore Sculpture Ctr., Great Neck, N.Y., 1980, Harkness House, N.Y.C., 1981, Musavi Art Ctr., N.Y.C., 1984, Atlantic Gallery, N.Y.C., 1988, 90, 92, 94, 96, 98, 2000, 2002, Sara Lawrence Coll., 1995-96, 2002, Shelter Rock Art Gallery, 1997, La Lac Gallery, Lake Lugano, Switzerland, 2002; exhibited in group shows at Monmouth Mus. Art, Red Bank, N.J., 1990, Westbeth Gallery, N.Y.C., 1991, Capital Bldg. Gallery, Tallahassee, 1991, Atlantic Gallery, N.Y.C., 1991, N.Y. Acad. Sci., N.Y.C., 1991, Broome St. Gallery, N.Y.C., 1991, Gallery Stendahl, N.Y.C., 1991, 97, 2002, Raleigh Gallery, Dania, Fla., 1993, Casa d'arte Gadiva Gallery, Forte dei Marmi, Italy, 1993, Bigi Art Gallery, Florence, Italy, 1993, Living Arts Gallery, Milan, Italy, 1994, Steiner Gallery, Bal Harbor, Fla., 1995, 97, Atlantic Gallery, 2002, Galleria Faustini, Florence, Italy, 2000, Gallery Art, Aventura, Fla., 2003; permanent collections include Mus. Vitomele, S. Maria de Finibus Terrae, Italy, Mus. dei Bozzetti, Pietrasonta, Italy; selected exhibits include Yonkers Art Assn., 1978, Audubon Artists Guild, 1978-80, N.J. Painters and Sculptors, 1980, Sculptors Alliance, 1982, Nat. Assn. Women Artists, 1984, N.Y. Soc. Women Artists, 1986, Am. Soc. Contemporary Artists, 1992; spl. exhibits include Dancer, GM Bldg., N.Y.C., 1978-79, Torso, Schulman Realty Group, N.Y.C., 1983-85, Dancer I, Westchester C.C., Valhalla, N.Y., 1982-92, Dancer Reborn, Roosevelt H.S., Yonkers, N.Y., 1992-98. Recipient Silver medal Audubon Artists, 1978, Sculpture award Mamaroneck (N.Y.) Artists Guild; Tres Jolle des Arts award Nat. Assn. Women Artists, 1984, Best in Show award, 1993, David Pece Meml. prize, 2001. Mem.: Art Students League, Artists Equity (past bd. dirs., past v.p.), Am. Soc. Contemporary Artists (v.p., Meml. award 2001). Avocations: music, literature, travel. Home: 498 Winding Rd N Ardsley NY 10502-2702 E-mail: csokolaw@artnet.com.

SOKOLOWSKI, DENISE GEORGIA, librarian, academic administrator; b. Oceanside, NY, Nov. 2, 1951; d. Charles John and Georgia Denis (Papadam) Sokolowski; m. Robert Harald Munoz, May 21, 1983. AA, Modesto Jr. Coll., 1971; BA, Calif. State Coll., Stanislaus, 1974; MLIS, U. Calif., Berkeley, 1982. Sec. to support svcs. officer Stanislaus State Coll., Turlock, Calif., 1973—75; vet. asst. U. Md. European Div., Heidelberg, Germany, 1976—77, publs. asst., 1983—85, libr., 1985—. Tour guide, escort Great Pacific Tour Co., San Francisco, 1978—81; word processor Telegraph Ave. Geotechn. Assocs., Berkeley, 1982—83. Mem.: ALA, Assn. Coll. Rsch. Librs., Calif. Library Assn., Beta Phi Mu. Democrat. Office: U Md Unit 29216 APO AE 09102 E-mail: dsoko@ed.umuc.edu.

SOLA, CARIDAD MARIA, architect; b. Miami, Fla., Aug. 27, 1980; d. Manuel and Lidia Sola. BFA, BArch, U. Miami, 2003; MFA, Parsons Sch. Design, N.Y.C., 2006; grad. in constrn. engring., Columbia U., 2006. Intern architect Bermello, Ajamil & Partners, Miami, 2001—04. Dean's Grad. Fellowship, NYU, 2005—. Mem.: Nat. Mus. Woman Artists (assoc.), AIA (assoc.). Home: 4880 Granada Blvd Coral Gables FL 33146 also: 250 Mercer St #C-611 New York NY 10012

SOLA, JANET ELAINE, retired secondary school educator; b. New Britain, Conn., Oct. 23, 1935; d. Walter Andrew and Helen (Mandl) Sinkiewicz; m. Raymond Albert Sola. BS, Ctrl. Conn. State U., 1957; MS, So. Conn. State U., 1962; postgrad., U. Conn, 1969. Tchr. bus. Amity Regional High Sch., Woodbridge, Conn., 1957-60; bus. instr. Stone Coll., New Haven, 1962; instr. Manpower Devel. and Tng. Act, New Britain, 1970-74, So. Ctrl. C.C., New Haven, 1977, lectr., 1987; mgmt. lectr. II, Quinnipiac Coll., Hamden, Conn., 1981-87; mayor's aide Town of Hamden, 1987-89, recycling coord., 1989-92; tchr. bus. edn. Hamden H.S., 1992—2005, coord. coop. work experience and diversified occupations, 1992—2005. Assessor credit for life Quinn Coll., Hamden, 1986-89; advisor Hamden Hub Student Interns, 2000-05. Author: (poetry) Flights of Fancy, 1991, Recycled Thoughts, 1992; contbr. poetry to Contemporary, The Hamden Chronicle, Treasured Poems of Am., Nat. Arts Soc. Campaigner Sola for Town Clk. Com., Hamden, 1981; community liaison Carusone for Mayor Com., Hamden, 1981-87; v.p., Am. Legion Aux. Unit 88, Hamden, 1985-95; treas. Green Dragon Enterprises, Inc., 2002-05; chmn. unit 88 Laurel Girl States. Named Tchr. Yr., Hamden H.S., 2000—01. Mem.: AAUW, NAFE, ASCD, Conn. Bus. Educators Assn. (bd. dirs. 2003—05), Nat. Bus. Educators, Assn. Ret. Tchrs. Conn. (life), Internat. Platform Assn., Nat. Assn. Italian Women, Internat. Soc. Poetry (disting. mem.), Lions Internat. Hamden chpt., Ctrl. Conn. U. State Alumni Assn. (bd. dirs., Disting. Alumni Svc. award 2003), Delta Pi Epsilon Nat. Bus. Educators Hon. Soc. Avocations: bowling, swimming. Home: 186 Deepwood Dr Lebanon CT 06249-2117 Personal E-mail: osdamia@yahoo.com.

SOLÁ, VICTORIA M., announcer, writer; b. Englewood, N.J., Nov. 11, 1952; d. Salvador Felix and Hedda Blanc (Westhead) Solá; 1 child, Frank Salvador Solá Grillo. Student, Fairleigh Dickinson U., N.J., 1970—72. Radio host and prodr. jazz WFDU-FM Radio, Teaneck, NJ, 1981—83, jazz dir., 1982—86, radio host and prodr. Latin, 1983—, Latin music dir., 1983—. Contbg. editor Descarga Catalog, N.Y.C., 1996—2002; columnist Latin Beat Mag., Gardena, Calif., 1998, Latin London Mag., 1999; Latin jazz planning com. adv. Smithsonian Inst. Traveling Exhbn. Svc., Washington, 1999—2002, narrator, 2002. Coord. ann. on-air fundraiser for Latin music programming WFDU-FM, Teaneck, NJ, 1983—; participant on-air blood donor drive Bergen Cmty. Regional Blood Ctrs., Paramus, NJ, 1986; vol. fund raiser Operation Rescue North Shore Animal League Am., 2006. Mem.: Internat. Latin Music Hall of Fame (adv. com. 1999—, Spl. Recognition award 2001). Democrat. Avocations: reading, photography, drawing, writing. Office: WFDU-FM 1000 River Rd Teaneck NJ 07666 Office Phone: 201-692-2806 ext. 10. Office Fax: 201-692-2807. E-mail: vickisola1@aol.com.

SOLANTO, MARY VICTORIA, psychologist; b. N.Y.C., Sept. 8, 1951; d. Gregory Albert and Geraldine (Ricciardelli) S BA, Princeton U., N.J., 1973; MS, Cornell U., 1977; PhD, SUNY, Buffalo, 1981. Lic. psychologist, N.Y. Postdoctoral fellow dept. psychiatry Albert Einstein Coll. Medicine, Bronx, 1981—83, asst. prof. dept. pediat., 1983—89, assoc. prof. dept pediat., 1989—98; assoc. prof. dept. psychiatry Mt. Sinai Med. Ctr., N.Y.C., 1998—. Sr. psychologist L.I. Jewish Med. Ctr., New Hyde Park, N.Y., 1989-98; dir. Attention Deficit and Hypertension Disorder Ctr. Mt. Sinai Med. Ctr., 1998—; guest reviewer various profl. publs Author articles on psychopharmacology, attention deficit/hyperactivity disorder, eating disorders Grantee NIH, 1984, 98—, NIMH, 1986-89 Mem. APA, Soc. for Rsch. in Child and Adolescent Psychopathology Roman Catholic. Avocations: travel, tennis, classical music, singing, art spectator. Office: Mt Sinai Med Ctr PO Box 1230 New York NY 10029-0313

SOLBERG, AMY KATHLEEN, director; b. Chester, Mont., Mar. 11, 1977; d. Timothy and Kathleen Solberg. MusB, Concordia Coll., Moorhead, Minn., 1999; MusM, U. Houston, 2005. Cert. tchr. Tex., N.Mex. Choir dir. Valley HS, Albuquerque, 1999—2003; music dir. Minot State U. Theatre, ND, 1999—2003; tchg. asst. U. Houston, 2003—05; choir dir. Bellaire HS, 2005—. Singer St. John's Episcopal Cathedral, Albuquerque, 2001—03. Singer: Cantare Houston, Mercury Baroque, Santa Fe Desert Chorale; mus. dir.: Guys and Dolls, Oklahoma, Anything Goes!, Into the Woods; mus. dir.: Children of Eden.; mus. dir.: Forever Plaid, Nunsense, Music Man, Oliver, Funny Thing Happened on the Way to the Forum, Fantasticks. Sect. leader Bellaire (Tex.) Presbyn. Ch., 2003—06. Named Most Inspirational Tchr., Valley HS Acad., 2002; recipient Excellence in Tchg. award, Valley HS, 2002; fellow, U. Houston, 2003—05; Music Performance scholar, Concordia Coll., 1995—99, Faculty scholar, 1995—99, Music scholar, U. Houston, 2003—05. Mem.: Tex. Music Educators' Assn., Music Educators' Nat. Conf., Tex. Choral Directors' Assn., Am. Choral Directors' Assn. Avocations: reading, travel, dance. Office Phone: 713-295-3753.

SOLBERG, DI ANNE, retired secondary school educator; d. David Allen and Dorothy Alice Dougherty; children: Denell Ra'lee, Joel David. BA in English, Wash. State U., Pullman, 1973; MA in Edn., Whitworth Coll., Spokane, Wash., 1986. Cert. tchr. Wash., N.Y., Oreg., ESOL tchr. 1999. Tchr. Southold Union Free Schs., Southold, NY, 1986—87, Triangle Lake Sch. Dist., Triangle Lake, Oreg., 1993—94, Adrian Sch. Dist., Adrian, Oreg., 1994—97, Nyssa Sch. Dist., Nyssa, Oreg., 1997—. Site coun. mem. Adrian H.S., 1996—97, Nyssa H.S., Oreg., 1999—2001. Named Most Inspirational Tchr., Ea. Oreg. U., 2002. Mem.: Nat. Coun. of Tchrs. of English (assoc.). Home: 1245 N Farragut St Portland OR 97197

SOLBERG, ELIZABETH TRANSOU, public relations executive; b. Dallas, Aug. 10, 1939; d. Ross W. and Josephine V. (Perkins) Transou; m. Frederick M. Solberg Jr., Mar. 8, 1969; 1 son, Frederick W. BJ, U. Mo., 1961. Reporter Kansas City (Mo.) Star, 1963-70, asst. city editor, 1970-73; reporter spl. events, documentaries Sta. WDAF-TV, Kansas City, Mo., 1973-74; prof. dept. journalism Park Coll., Kansas City, Mo., 1975-76, advisor, 1976-79; mng. ptnr. Fleishman-Hillard Inc., Kansas City, Mo., then exec. v.p., sr. ptnr., gen. mgr. Kansas City br., now regional pres., sr. ptnr.; pres. Fleishman-Hillard/Can., 1994—99. Mem. Kansas City Commn. Planned Indsl. Expansion Authority, 1974-91; bd. dirs. Ferrellgas, Midwest Airlines. Mem. long range planning com. Heart of Am. coun. Boy Scouts Am., 1980-82, bd. dirs., 1986-89; mem. Clay County (Mo.) Devel. Commn., 1979-88; bd. govs. Citizens Assn., 1975—; mem. exec. com. bd. Kansas City Area Devel. Coun., 1989-96, co-chair, 1991-93; trustee Pembroke Hill Sch., 1987-93, U. Kansas City, 1990-2002, exec. com., 1992-2002, Midwest Rsch. Inst., 1995-2002; bd. dirs. Greater Kansas City Cmty. Found. and Affiliated Trusts, 1996-2005, Starlight Theatre, 1996-2002, Union Sta. Bd., 1998-2002, Mo. Devel. Fin. Bd., 2000—, chair, 2003—; regent Rockhurst Coll., 1984-96; active Bus. Coun., Nelson Gallery Found., Nelson-Atkins Mus. Art, 1990—; bd. dirs. Civic Coun. Greater Kansas City, 1992—, chair civic coun., 2003-2005; mem. Jr. League Kansas City. Recipient award for contbn. to mental health Mo. Psychiat. Assn., 1973, Arthur E. Lowell award for excellence in orgn. comm. Kansas City/IABC, 1985, Kansas City Spirit award Gillis Ctr., 1994. Mem. Pub. Rels. Soc. Am. (nat. honors and awards com., co-chmn. SilverAnvil com. 1983, Silver Anvil award 1979-82, chair nat. membership com. 1989-91, assembly del.-at-large 1995-96), Counselor's Acad. (exec. com. 1991-92), Mo. C. of C. Pub. Rels. Coun., Greater Kans. City C. of C. (chair 1994-95, bd. exec. com.), River Club, Carriage Club. Office: Fleishman Hillard Inc 2405 Grand Blvd Ste 700 Kansas City MO 64108-2522

SOLBERG, MARY ANN, federal official; Grad., Western Mich. U. Dep. dir. Office Nat. Drug Control Policy Exec. Office of Pres., Washington, 2001—; exec. dir. Coalition of Health Cmtys., Troy (Mich.) Cmty. Coalition for Prevention of Drug and Alcohol Abuse; various positions Troy Adult and Cmty. Edn., 1977—91. Mem. adv. com. to develop a nat. prevention sys. Nat. Ctr. for Substance Abuse Prevention; mem. adv. com. Nat. Ad Coun.'s Cmty. Anti-Drug Campaign; mem. Pres.'s Commn. on Drug-Free Cmtys., 1998, co-chairperson. Office: Exec Office of Pres Office Nat Drug Control Policy 750 17th St NW Washington DC 20503

SOLBERG, NELLIE FLORENCE COAD, artist; b. Sault Ste. Marie, Mich.; d. Sanford and Mary (McDonald) Coad; m. Ingvald Solberg, Aug. 24, 1930; children: Jeanne Elaine Solberg Unruh, Walter Eugene, Kay Louise Solberg Link. BA, Minot State U., 1930; MA, N.D. State U., 1963; postgrad. Wash. State U., 1960, U. Wyo., 1964, St. Cloud Coll., 1971. Tchr. Bismarck Elem. Schs., N.D., 1954-63, art dir. high sch., 1963-72; instr. art Bismarck Jr. Coll., 1964-67; cons. Bismarck Art Assn. Galleries, 1973-79, State Capitol Galleries, 1973-78; dir. arts festivals including Statewide Religious Arts Festival, Bismarck, 1969-85, State Treas.'s Gallery, 1977, N.D. State Capitol, Bismarck, 1973-78; co-dir. Indian Art Show, Nat. Congress Am. Indians, Bismarck, 1963. Artist: (print) Prairie Rose for N.D. centennial, 1989; one-woman shows include Minot State Coll., 1963, Dickinson State Coll., 1964, Jamestown Coll., 1964, U. N.D., Valley City State Coll., Bismarck Jr. Coll., 1963, 65, 68, 69, N.D. State U., 1970, 74, Linha Gallery, Minot N.D., 1972, 74-77, Bank of N.D., 1972-74, 76-77, Elan Gallery, 1982; exhibited in group shows at Gov. John Davis Mansion, 1960, Concordia Coll., Moorhead, Minn., 1965, N.D. Capitol, 1968, 69, Internat. Peace Gardens, 1969, Gov. William Guy Mansion, 1971, Gov. George Sinner Mansion, 1991. Mem. Indian Culture Found., 1964—. Civic Music Assn., 1942-89; works included in numerous pvt. collections U.S., Can., Europe; religious arts com. Conf. Chs., 1973; bd. dirs. Citizens for Arts, 1978-81; mem. The Statue of Liberty/Ellis Island Found., 1984-89. Recipient numerous awards including Gov.'s award for arts, 1977, Gov. Allen Olson award, 1982, Gov.'s award Bismarck Art Show, 1982, Dakota Northwestern Bank award, 1983, Dr. Shari Orser Purchase award Religious Arts Festival, 1984, William Murray award Religious Arts Festival, 1984, Mandan Art Assn. award, 1986, 18th ann. 3d prize weaving Festival of Arts, 1987, Dr. Cy Rinkel watercolor purchase award, 1987, Heritage Centennial Art award Heritage Arts, Inc., 1988; named N.D. Woman Artist of Yr., 1974, Heritage Centennial award, 1989; the New Visual Arts Gallery named the Children's Gallery in name of Nellie Solberg; Mem. Bismarck Arts and Galleries Assn. (membership com., mem. Gallery 522, mem. Visual Arts Ctr.), Bismarck Art Assn. (charter, Honor award 1960, pres. 1963-64, 71-72), Jamestown Art Assn., Linha Gallery (Minot), Nat. League Am. Pen Women (pres. N.D. 1964-66, pres. Medora br. 1972-74, treas. 1975-86), Mpls. Soc. Fine Arts, P.E.O. (pres. chpts. 1967-69), Bismarck Vets., Meml. Library (life), Soc. Preservation Gov.'s Mansion (charter, bd. dirs.), Women in the Arts Nat. Mus. (charter), Zonta, Order of Ea. Star, Sigma Sigma Sigma. Republican. Home: 925 N 6th St Bismarck ND 58501-3922

SOLBRIG, INGEBORG HILDEGARD, literature educator, writer; b. Weissenfels, Germany, July 31, 1923; arrived in U.S., 1961, naturalized, 1966; d. Reinhold J. and Hildegard M. A. (Ferchland) Solbrig. Grad. in chemistry, U. Halle, Germany, 1948; student, Delmar Coll., 1961; BA summa cum laude, San Francisco State U., 1964; postgrad., U. Calif., Berkeley, 1964-65; MA, Stanford U., 1966, PhD in Humanities and German, 1969. Asst. prof. U. R.I., 1969-70, U. Tenn., Chattanooga, 1970-72, U. Ky., Lexington, 1972-75; assoc. prof. German U. Iowa, 1975-81, prof., 1981-93, prof. emerita, 1993—. Domestic and abroad lectr.; former presenter The Light from the East, Coptic Christians/Egypt, 2004. Author: Hammer-Purgstall und Goethe, 1973, Orient-Rezeption, 1996, Orient-Rezeption, Fischer Lexikon Literatur, 1996, 2d edit., 2000, Modulationen von Gold und Licht in Goethes Kunstmärchen, 1997, Momentaufnahmen, 2000, J.G. Herder: Echo of the Cultural Philospher's Ideas in Early African-American Intellectual Writing, 2000, Maria Sibylla Merian., 2001; main editor: Rilke Heute, Beziehungen und Wirkungen, 1975; editor (and translator): Reinhard Goering: Seeschlacht/Seabattle, 1977; mem. editl. bd.: Kairoer Germanistische Studien, vol. 9 & 10, 1998; contbr. articles to profl. jours., chpts. to books. Mem. Iowa Gov.'s Com. 300th Anniversary German-Am. Rels. 1683-1983, 1983. Named Ky. Col., 1975; recipient Hammer-Purgstall Gold medal, Austria, 1974; fellow, Stanford U., 1965—66, 1968—69, Austrian Ministry Edn., 1968—69; Delta Phi Alpha Deutsche Ehrenverbindung, U. Ky., 1973, Old Gold fellow, Iowa, 1977, Am. Coun. Learned Socs. grantee, German Acad. Exch. Svc. grantee, 1980, Sr. Faculty Rsch. fellow in humanities, 1983, NEH grantee, 1985, May Brodbeck fellow in humanities, 1989, numerous summer faculty rsch. grants. Mem.: MLA (life), Soc. for History Alchemy and Chemistry, Internat. Herder Soc. (founding mem.), Goethe Soc. N.Am., Inc., Can. Soc. 18th Century Studies, Am. Soc. 18th Century Studies, Deutsche Schiller Gesellschaft, Goethe Gesellschaft, Internat. Vereinigung fur Germanische Sprach und Lit. Wiss., Egyptian Soc. Lit. Criticism (hon.), World Peace and Diplomacy Forum (life). Avocations: horseback riding, photography, writing, travel, theology. Home and Office: 1126 Pine St Iowa City IA 52240-5711

SOLCHANY, JOANNE ELIZABETH, psychotherapist, nursing educator; b. New Westminister, British Columbia, Canada, Apr. 21, 1958; d. Jerry Emil and Swanhild Solchany; children: Anna Swanhild, Nicolas Francisco. AAS, Everett C.C., Wash., 1979; BA, Western Wash. U., Bellingham, 1981; BSN, U. Alaska, Anchorage, 1989; MSN, U. Calif., San Francisco, 1991; PhD, U. Wash., Seattle, 2000. RN State of Wash., 1989, registered advanced nurse practitioner, State of Wash., 1992, bd. cert. infant and child psychiatry and mental health, ANCC, 1993, cert. infant mental health, Ctr. Infant Mental Health & Devel. U Wash., 2002. Pvt. practice psychotherapist, and nurse practitioner, Seattle, 1992—; asst. prof. Sch. Nursing U. Wash., 2001—. Cons. in field, Seattle, 1991—; adv. bd. Ctr. Infant Mental Health & Devel., Seattle, 2002—06. Author: Promoting Maternal Mental Health During Pregnancy, 2001 (Sigma Theta Tau Internat. Nursing Print Media award); contbr. chapters to books, articles to periodicals and profl. jours. Expert panel Bright Futures, 2004—06; adv. bd. ABA Ctr. Children, Washington, 2006. Recipient Dissertation award, Pediatric Nursing, 2000, Cmty. Contribution award, Head Start, 2006; Solnit fellow, Zero to Three: Clin. Infant Programs, 2000—01. Mem.: Infant, Child and Adolescent Psychiat. Nurse Practitioner Group. Achievements include research in nature of mothers' developing relationships with adopted daughters. Avocations: travel, music, camping, playing, soccer mom. Office: Univ Wash Box 357262 Seattle WA 98195 Office Phone: 206-543-8238. Office Fax: 206-543-6656.

SOLDAY, ALIDRA (LINDA BROWN), psychotherapist, filmmaker; b. Mineola, NY, Feb. 18, 1941; d. Charles Harold and Helen (Golbach) Brown. Student, Smith Coll., Northampton, Mass., 1958—60; BA, Barnard Coll., N.Y.C., 1962; MPS in Art Therapy, Pratt Inst., Bklyn., 1973; MSW, Hunter Coll., N.Y.C., 1976. Cert. social worker, psychoanalyst, N.Y.; lic. clin. social worker, Calif.; diplomate clin. social work Am. Bd. Examiners in Clin. Social Work. Singer, actress Broadway theatres, N.Y.C., 1962-65, pub. rels./community rels. specialist, real estate, publicist/editor, pub., edn. cons., 1965-71; art therapist Bronx (N.Y.) Psychiat. Ctr., 1972-74; clin. social worker North Richmond Community Mental Health Ctr., S.I., N.Y., 1977-79; staff therapist Lincoln Inst. Psychotherapy, N.Y.C., 1978-80; sr. staff therapist Ctr. for Study Anorexia and Bulimia, N.Y.C., 1983-85; staff therapist Inst. Contemporary Psychotherapy, N.Y.C., 1988-95; pvt. practice psychotherapy N.Y.C., 1978—. Human svc. faculty Tristate Inst. Traditional Chinese Acupuncture, NYC, 1986—89; faculty NY Open Ctr., NYC, 1987—98; adj. faculty Health Choices Ctr. for Healing Arts, Princeton, NJ, 1987—90; pvt. practice, San Francisco, 2003—; presenter, cons. in field. Prodr., dir.: (documentaries) Granny Goes to Washington, 2006. Mem.: NASW. Office: 3195 California St San Francisco CA 94115 Office Phone: 415-289-9501. E-mail: asolday@earthlink.net.

SOLDUNIAS, BERNADETTE LOUISE, psychiatrist; b. Buffalo, 1948; d. Louis James and Geraldine Mary Merlino; m. Stuart Alan Tiegel, June 12, 1993; children from previous marriage: Alexander, Jason. BS, Cornell U., 1970, MS, 1974; MD, U. Conn., 1985. Med. dir. Ashley Inc., Havre de Grace, 1995—. Mem.: Am. Acad. Addiction Psychiatrists, Am. Soc. Addiction Medicine, Am. Psychiat. Assn. (Nancy Roeske Tchg. award 1995). Office: Ashley Inc 800 Tydings Ln Havre De Grace MD 21078

SOLEIMANPOUR, MOJGAN, language educator; arrived in U.S., 1995; d. Hassan Shahim and Haydei Tagizadeh; m. Aziz Soleimanpouv, Dec. 20, 1993; children: Amir A. Soleimanpouv, Omid Soleimanpouv. B in French Lang., Theran U., 1994; EdM, U. Dayton, Ohio, 2004. Lic. tchr. Ohio. French tchr., Theran, 1988—94; French tutor Sinclair Coll., Dayton, 1994—96; French and Persian interpreter Vocalink, Dayton, 2000—06; ESL and French tchr. West Carrollton Schs., Dayton, 2004—06. Mem.: West Carrollton Internat. Club.

SOLER, ESTA, foundation administrator; Founder, pres. Family Violence Prevention Fund, 1980—. Cons. and adv. Dept. Justice, U.S. Dept. Health and Human Svcs., CDC, others; bd. dirs. The Ctr. on Fathers, Families and Pub. Policy. Co-author: Ending Domestic Violence: Changing Public Perceptions/Halting the Epidemic, 1997. Bd. dirs. Blue Shield Calif. Found., Bay Area United Way Safe Cmtys. Cabinet. Recipient Koret Israel Prize, 1989, Public Health Heroes award, U. Calif., 1998; fellow, Kellogg Found. Nat. Leadership, 1990. Office: 383 Rhode Island St Ste 304 San Francisco CA 94103-5133

SOLEYMANI, NANCY, psychologist, researcher; b. N.Y.C., May 20, 1972; d. Yosef and Louise Soleymani. BA in Psychology magna cum laude, Columbia U., 1994; MA in Psychology with distinction, Hofstra U., 1995, PhD in Combined Clin. & Sch. Psychology, 1999. Cert. of qualification in sch. psychology, N.Y. Rsch. asst. Barnard Toddler Ctr., N.Y.C., 1993-94, Columbia Presbyn. Med. Ctr., N.Y.C., 1994; tchrs. asst. Little Village Sch., Garden City, N.Y., 1994; sch. psychology intern JLM Great Neck (N.Y.) North High Sch., 1996-97; sch. psychologist Port Washington Sch. Dist., 1997; counselor S.E. Nassau Guidance Ctr., Seaford, N.Y., 1997-99; asst. psychologist, rschr. Inst. for Bio-Behavioral Therapy & Rsch., Great Neck, 1999—. Invited guest lectr. Hofstra U., Hempstead, N.Y., 1998-99, Hunter Coll., Grad. Sch. Social Work, N.Y.C., 1998, Adelphi U., Garden City, 1999. Mem. fund raising com. Juvenile Diabetes Found., N.Y.C., 1994—. Mem. APA, Assn. for Advancement of Behavior Therapy. Jewish. Avocations: volleyball, painting, pottery, ice-skating. Office: Inst for Bio-Behavioral Therapy & Rsch 935 Northern Blvd Great Neck NY 11021-5309 E-mail: nsoleymani@aol.com.

SOLIS, HILDA LUCIA, congresswoman, educational administrator; b. LA, Oct. 20, 1957; d. Raul and Juana (Sequiera) S.; m. Sam H. Sayyad, June 26, 1982. BA in Polit. Sci., Calif. State Poly U., 1979; MA in Pub. Adminstrn., U. So. Calif., 1981. Interpreter Immigration and Naturalization Service, Los Angeles, 1977-79; editor in chief Office Hispanic Affairs, The White House, Washington, 1980-81; mgmt. analyst Office Mgmt. and Budget, Washington, 1981-82; field rep. Office Assemblyman Art Torres, L.A., 1982; dir. Calif. Student Opportunity and Access, Whittier, 1982—; rep. 57th assembly dist. Calif. State Assembly, Sacramento, 1992-94; mem. Calif. Senate from 24th dist., 1994-2000, U.S. Congress from Calif. 32nd dist., Washington, 2001—; mem. resources com., energy & commerce com., former mem. edn. and workforce com. Cons. South Coast Consortium, L.A., 1986—; mem. South Coast Ednl. Opportunity Pers. Consortium. Bd. dirs. Calif. Commn. on Status of Women, 1993—; corr. pres. Friendly El Monte (Calif.) Dem. Club, 1986—; mem. credentials com. Calif. Dem. Com., 1987-88; trustee Rio Hondo C.C., 1985-92. Recipient Meritorious Svc. award Dept. Def., 1981, Young Careerist award El Monte Bus. and Profl. Women, 1987; fellow Nat. Edn. Inst., Kellogg Found., 1984-85. Mem. Western Assn. Ednl. Opportunity Pers. (sec. bd. dirs. 1986—), Comision Feminil de Los Angeles (bd. dirs. 1983-84, edn. chmn.), Women of Moose. Democrat. Roman Catholic. Office: 1725 Longworth House Office Bldg Washington DC 20515-0532 also: Ste 211 4401 Santa Anita Ave El Monte CA 91731

SOLLENBERGER, DONNA KAY FITZPATRICK, hospital and clinics executive; b. Tuscola, Ill., Jan. 13, 1949; d. Vincent Norman and Marian Louise (Mumbower) Fitzpatrick; m. Kent T. Sollenberger, Dec. 30, 1983; children: Shannon, Blake, Bradley. Student, U. Kans., 1968-70; BA in English and Chemistry, U. Ill., Springfield, 1970, MA in English, 1974. With pub. info. office Ill. Dept. Transp., Springfield, 1974-75; exec. III, dir. pub. info., strategic planning/spl. programs Ill. Dept. Conservation, Springfield, 1975-76; prof. Lincoln Land C.C., Springfield, 1980-84; chief adminstrv. officer surgery So. Ill. U. Sch. Medicine, Springfield, 1976-80, 85-91; divsn. adminstr., chief adminstrv. officer divsn. surgery U. Tex. M.D. Anderson Cancer Ctr., Houston, 1991-93, v.p. for hosps. and clinics, 1993-96; exec. v.p., COO, City of Hope Nat. Med. Ctr., Duarte, Calif., 1997-99; pres., CEO, U. Wis. Hosp. and Clins., 2000—. Mem. bd. dirs., audit com. Madison Gas and Electric; bd. dir., chmn. governance com. Inacom; mem. ops. com. Univ. Health Sys. Consortium. Co-chmn. Heart Assn. Walk, 2001—02. Recipient Conservation Merit award State of Ill., 1976, Alumni Achievement award U. Ill., 2005; named one of Outstanding Young Women in Am., 1980. Mem. Am. Coll. Healthcare Execs., Acad. Practice Assembly (instnl. membership coord. 1992—), Assn. Acad. Surgery Adminstrs. (exec. com. 1992-94, mem.-at-large so. region 1992-93, membership chairperson 1993-94), Med. Group Mgmt. Assn., Am. Hosp. Assn. (nominating com., reg. policy bd.), Wis. Hosp. Assn. (mem. policy coun., so. region alt. to bd. dirs.), L.A. Area Delta Gamma Alumnae Assn., U. Ill. Alumni Assn. (bd. dirs.). Office: U Wis Hosp & Clinics 600 Highland Ave Madison WI 53792-0001 Home: 3938 Caribou Rd Verona WI 53593-8407 E-mail: clksoll@charter.net.

SOLNIT, REBECCA, writer, critic; Author: Secret Exhibition: Six California Artists of the Cold War Era, 1994, Savage Dreams: A Journey into the Landscape Wars of the American West, 1995, A Book of Migrations: Some Passages in Ireland, 1998, Wanderlust: A History of Walking, 2001, As Eve Said to the Serpent: On Landscape, Gender and Art, 2001, Hollow City: The Siege of San Francisco and the Crisis of American Urbanism, 2002, Motion Studies: Time, Space and Eadweard Muybridge, 2003, River of Shadows, 2003 (Nat. Book Critics Circle award, 2004). Grantee Guggenheim Fellowship, NEA Fellowship. Office: c/o Bloomsbury USA 175 5th Ave New York NY 10010

SOLO, JOYCE RUBENSTEIN, volunteer; b. Buffalo, N.Y., Feb. 14, 1924; d. Jay Harry and Rose (Maisel) Rubenstein; m. Richard D. Solo, Jan. 6, 1946; children: Harry Jay Solo, Eleanor Solo, Sally Solo. BA, Wellesley Coll., 1945. Mem. S.E. Pa. Health Coord. Coun., 1978—84; chair reach to recovery Phila. divsn. Am. Cancer Soc., 1985—87; sec. Sarasota County Health Care Coord. Adv. Coun., Fla., 1993—95; chair sr. adv. com. Sarasota Meml. Hosp., 1996—98; vol. Reach to Recovery Breast Cancer Task Force, Manatee County Am. Cancer Soc.; mem. numerous other health and civic orgn. activities; pres. women's bd. Temple Beth Israel, 1996—98, bd. dirs., 1998—2000; mem. governing bd. Health Systems Agy. S.E. Pa., 1977—86. Mem.: LWV (v.p. Pa. chpt. 1969—73, pres. Phila. 1975—77, pres. Sarasota County 1990—92, healthcare com. chair 1988—90, 1992—), Phi Beta Kappa. Personal E-mail: rjoysolo14@comcast.net.

SOLOD, LISA, writer; b. Knoxville, Tenn., Jan. 3, 1956; d. Jay Lawrence and Fredlyn Kovitch Solod; m. John Addison Lambeth, June 23, 1985 (div.); children: Philip Stanhope Lambeth, Grace Amelia Lambeth. AB in Semiotics with honors, Brown U., 1978. Pub. info. officer Mus. Fine Arts, Boston, 1978-79; asst. editor Boston Mag., 1979-80; editor Moviegoer Mag. Whittle Comms., 1980-83; chief advt. copywriter Parsons, Friedman and Cen. Advt. Agy., Boston, 1984-85; pub. rels. dir. So. Va. Coll. for Women, Buena Vista, Va., 1985-86; pub. info. dir. The George C. Marshall Found., Lexington, Va., 1986-88. Instr. expository writing U. R.I., 1984; editl. cons. TeenAge Mag., Cambridge Free Press, The Illustrated, 1983-85; bd. dirs. Project Horizon, 1988-90. Bd. dirs. Montessori Ctr. for Children, Lexington, 1995-99, sec., 1996-98; bd. dirs. Lexington City Sch. Bd., 1997—2001, v.p., 1998—2001; sec. Valley region Va. Sch. Bd. Assn., 1997-98, v.p. Valley region, 1998-99, chmn. Valley region, 1999-2001, bd. dirs. Temple House of Israel, 2004-05, pres. 2006. Recipient 12 fellowships/residencies Va. Ctr. for Creative Arts, Mt. San Angelo, 1989-2004. Democrat. Jewish. Home: 310 Enfield Rd Lexington VA 24450-1756 E-mail: lisa@rockbridge.net.

SOLOFF, LAURA J., academic administrator; BA in English, minor in Art History, UCLA. Human resources position Broadway Dept. Stores; dir. career planning & placement Fashion Inst. Design & Merchandising, Calif., campus dir. Calif., regional dir. Calif., dir. student financial svcs. Calif.; dir. human resources & adminstrn. Sony Pictures Entertainment, Culver City, Calif.; mem. Edn. Mgmt. Corp., 1998—; pres. Art Inst. Calif.-Orange County, 2000—03, Art Inst. Calif.-LA, 2003—; regional v.p. Edn. Mgmt. Corp., 2004—. Office: Office Pres Art Institute California LA 2900 31st St Santa Monica CA 90405-3035

SOLOMON, DEBORAH, application developer, educator, lawyer; JD, Harvard Law Sch., Cambridge, Mass., 1996. Asst. prof. computer applications Montgomery Coll., Rockville, Md., 2002—. Office: Montgomery Coll Computer Apps 51 Mannakee St Rockville MD 20850 Office Phone: 301-279-5136.

SOLOMON, ELINOR HARRIS, economics professor; b. Boston, Feb. 26, 1923; d. Ralph and Linna Harris; m. Richard A. Solomon, Mar. 30, 1957; children: Joan S. Griffin, Robert H., Thomas H. AB, Mt. Holyoke Coll., 1944; MA, Radcliffe U., 1945; PhD, Harvard U., 1948. Jr. economist Fed. Res. Bank Boston, 1945-48; economist Fed. Res. Bd. Govs., Washington, 1949-56; internat. economist U.S. State Dept., Washington, 1957-58; professorial lectr. Am. U., Washington, 1964-66; sr. economist antitrust div. U.S. Dept. Justice, Washington, 1966-82; prof. econs. George Washington U., Washington, 1982—. Econ. cons., Washington, 1982—; expert witness antitrust, fin. networks, electronic funds transfer cases, Washington, 1988—. Author: Virtual Money, 1997; author, editor: Electronic Funds Transfers and Payments, 1987, Electronic Money Flows, 1991; contbr. articles on econs., banking and law to profl. jours. Mem. Am. Econs. Assn., Nat. Economists Club (bd. govs. 1997-98), The Cosmos Club (chmn. Frontiers of Sci. 2001-04, chmn. program com. 2004-06, bd. mgmt. 2006—). Home: 6805 Delaware St Chevy Chase MD 20815-4164 Office: George Washington U Dept Econ Washington DC 20052-0001 Personal E-mail: rsolomonhome@earthlink.net.

SOLOMON, ELLEN JOAN, business owner, consultant; b. Orange, N.J., Aug. 26, 1943; d. Abram Shrier and Mildred Elizabeth (Berger) Solomon. BA in Psychology, U. NC, 1965; MS in Human Resource Devel., Am. U., 1985. Cert. Women owned bus. enterprise 2004. Contract writer Conn. Gen. Life Ins. Co., Bloomfield, 1965—66; mgmt. trainee, asst. buyer G. Fox & Co., Hartford, Conn., 1966—68; account exec. WLAE-FM, Hartford, 1968; sr. analyst Travelers Ins. Co., Hartford, 1968—70; job analyst Conn. Blue Cross, New Haven, 1970—71; sr. ops. auditor Govt. Employees Ins. Co., Washington, 1972—75; employee devel. specialist Employment Stds. Adminstrn., U.S. Dept. Labor, Washington, 1975—81, mgmt. analyst, 1981—82, supervisory mgmt. analyst, 1982—87; program designer, cons. Eastman Kodak Co., Rochester, NY, 1987—89, mgr., 1989, sr. orgnl. cons., 1990—93; pres., CEO Strategic Change, Inc., Fairfax, 1993—. Adj. faculty Rochester Inst. Tech., 1993—2001; conf. spkr.; workshop leader; cons. Named Women in Bus. Advocate of Yr., SBA NC, 2003; named one of Bus. Leaders Impact 100, Bus. Leader Mag., 2003; recipient spl. achievement award, U.S. Dept. Labor, 1977, 1978, 1983, 1985. Mem.: NOW, Rochester Women's Network (bd. dirs. 1990—92, v.p. 1991—92, Pres.'s award 1992), NAWBO (chpt. pres. 2002—03), NTL Inst. Applied Behavioral Sci., Leadership Am. NC, Leadership Am., OD Network, Leadership Triangle, U. N.C. Alumni, Alpha Gamma Delta. Democrat. Jewish. Home: 13200 Parson Ln Fairfax VA 22033 Office: Strategic Change Inc 4094 Majestic Ln Fairfax VA 22033 Office Phone: 703-263-2702. Business E-Mail: catalyst@strategicchangeinc.com.

SOLOMON, GAIL ELLEN, physician; b. Bklyn., May 26, 1938; d. Samuel and Estelle (Suffin) S.; m. Harvey Hecht, Oct. 28, 1962; children: Daniel, Jonathan, Elizabeth. AB, Smith Coll., 1958; MD, Albert Einstein Coll. Medicine, 1962. Diplomate Am. Bd. Pediats., Am. Bd. Psychiatry and Neurology (assoc. examiner), Am. Bd. Electroencephalography, Am. Bd. Electroencephalography and Neurophysiology, Am. Bd. Clin. Neurophysiology. Intern in pediat. Bronx Mcpl. Hosp. Ctr., 1962—63, resident in pediat., 1963—64, N.Y. Hosp.-Cornell U. Med. Coll., N.Y.C., 1964—65; NIH vis. fellow in neurology and child neurology Columbia-Presbyn. Med. Ctr., N.Y.C., 1965—68, NIH vis. fellow in clin. neurophysiology and electroenceph.; instr. neurology Columbia U. Coll. of Physicians and Surgeons, N.Y.C., 1968—69, asst. prof. neurology and pediat., 1970—76, assoc. prof. clin. neurology and pediat., 1976—2004, prof. clin. neurology and pediat., 2004—; asst. prof. Cornell U. Med. Coll., 1969—70, prof. clin. neurology and and pediat., 2004—; asst. attending in neurology and pediat. N.Y. Hosp., N.Y.C., 1969—76, dir. electroencephalography, 1969—, assoc. attending in neurology and pediat., 1976—, assoc. attending neurologist in psychiatry, 1983—. Mem. joint com. for stroke facilities NIH; mem. FDA Peripheral and CNS Adv. Com., 1979-83, chmn., 1983, cons., 1983-84; mem. med. audit com. N.Y. Hosp., mem. utilization rev. com.; mem. profl. adv. bd. N.Y. State Epilepsy Assn.; adj. attending physician in neurology Meml.-Sloan Kettering Cancer Ctr., 1982-93; assoc. attending pediatrician Hosp. Spl. Surgery, 1987—; neurology cons. Blythedale Children's Hosp., Valhalla, N.Y., 1991—, Meml.-Sloan Kettering Cancer Ctr., 1993—. Author: (with F. Plum) Clinical Management of Seizures: A Guide for the Physician, 1976, (with Plum and Kutt) 2d edit., 1983; editor: (with Kaufman and Pfeffer) Child and Adolescent Neurology for Psychiatrists, 1992, Neurologic Disorders: Developmental and Behavioral Sequelae, 1999; contbr. articles to profl. jours., chpts. to med. books. Fellow: Am. Acad. Neurology, Am. Acad. Pediats., Am. Electroencephalographic Soc.; mem.: AMA (Physician's Recognition award in Continuing Med. Edn.)), NY State Med. Soc., NY County Med. Soc., Am. Med. Women's Assn., Am. Epilepsy Soc., Am. Acad. Clin. Neurophysiology, Eastern EEG Soc., Am. Med. EEG Assn., Child Neurology Soc., Internat. Child Neurology Assn., Tristate Child Neurology Soc., Assn. for Rsch. in Nervous and Mental Diseases, NY Acad. Sci. Avocations: art museums, reading literature, french language, travel. Office: NY Presbyn Hosp Cornell U Med Coll 525 E 68th St New York NY 10021-4870

SOLOMON, MARILYN KAY, primary school educator, consultant, small business owner; b. Marshall, Mo., Oct. 16, 1947; d. John W. and Della M. (Dille) S. BS, Ctrl. Mo. State U., 1969; MS, Ind. U., 1974. Cert. in early childhood and nursery sch. edn., Mo., Ind. Tchr. Indpls. Pub. Schs., 1969—74; dir. Singer Learning Ctrs., Indpls., 1974—78; v.p. ECLC Learning Ctrs., Inc., Indpls., 1978—95; pres., CEO, owner Early Learning Ctrs., Inc., Indpls., 1995—; owner, pres., CEO Solomon Antique Restoration, Inc., Indpls., 1996—. The Shoppes at Guilford Junction, 2002—; pres., CEO Woodbridge Group, 1995—. Mem. OJT tng. task force Dept. Labor, Washington; mem. nat. task force for parenting edn. HEW, Washington; cons. to numerous corps. on corp. child care; built 29 child care ctrs. for corps., hosps. and govt. Co-author curricula. Founding bd. dirs. Mid City Pioneer, Indpls., 1977; mem. adv. bd. Enterprise Zone Small Bus. Incubator, Indpls., 1995-2002; founding bd. dirs. Family Support Ctr., Indpls., 1983, pres. bd. dirs., 1985-87; founding mem., co-chair Voices for Children, 1996—2004; mem. White Rivers Gardens State Park, Indpls. Mus. Art, 500 Festival Assn. Recipient Outstanding Leadership award Ind. Conf. on Social Concerns, 1975, 76, 77, Children's Mus. Edn. award, 1974; named to Outstanding Young Women of Am., 1984. Mem. Indpls. Mus. Art, Ind. Lic. Child Care Assn. (v.p. 1992, pres. 1974, 75), State of Ind. Quality and Tng. Coun. (chair 1992), Step Ahead-Marion County (rep. for child care 1992—2005, co-chair educare com. 1999—2005), Ind. Alliance for Better Child Care (bd. dirs. 1992, adv. bd. 1990-95), Pub. Broadcasting (tng. com. 1992-99, child devel. tng. com. 1996-99), Indpls. Zool. Soc. (charter), Order Eastern Star. Office: Early Learning Ctrs Inc 1315 S Sherman Dr Indianapolis IN 46203-2210 E-mail: earlylearn@indy.rr.com.

SOLOMON, MARSHA HARRIS, draftsman, artist; b. Tulsa, Oct. 21, 1940; d. Ruel Sutton and Anna May (Fellows) Harris; m. Robert E. Collier, Aug. 13, 1960 (div. Dec. 1968); 1 child, Craig Robert Collier; m. Louis G. Solomon, Sept. 5, 1984. Student, U. Tex., 1958-61; BFA, U. Houston, 1966. Chief draftsman Internat. Paper, Petroleum and Minerals Divsn., Houston, 1985—2003; artist, ptnr. Archway Gallery, Houston, 1994. Mem. Nat. Mus. Women in Art (charter). Mem. Watercolor Art Soc. Houston (bd. dirs. 1984-91, treas. 1987-89, pres. 1990-91), Tex. Watercolor Soc. (signature mem., Purple Sagebrush), N.Mex. Watercolor Soc. (signature mem.), Okla. Watercolor Soc. (signature mem.), Ariz. Watercolor Soc. (signature mem., Royal Scorpion mem.). Home: 5832 Valley Forge Dr Houston TX 77057-2248

SOLOMON, MARY-JO KELLEHER, mathematics educator; d. Joseph Aloysious Kelleher and Mary Agnes Fitzgerald; m. Arnold Solomon, Aug. 25, 1972; children: Scott, Eric. BA, Rutgers U., Newark, N.J., 1971. Cert. math. tchr. N.J. Tchr. Hawthorne, NJ, 1971—80, Parsippany Hills, Parsippany, NJ, 1991—. Treas. Morris Knolls Marching Band, Denville, NJ, 2002—06. Named Tchr. of the Yr., Cen. Mid. Sch., 1998. Avocations: genealogy, Karate. Home: 83 Ford Rd Denville NJ 07834 Office: Cen Mid Sch 1620 Rte 46 W Parsippany NJ 07054 Personal E-mail: nomolos@optonline.net.

SOLOMON, PATTY JO, elementary school educator; b. Richmond, Mo., Mar. 25, 1965; d. Glen B. and Joyce A. (Briggs) Solomon. AA Bus., Wentworth Jr. Coll., 1985; B Elem. Edn., Ctrl. Mo. State U., 1987; M Elem. Edn., N.W. Mo. State U., 1996. Cert. lifetime tchg. grades 1-8 Mo. Dept. Elem. and Secondary Edn. Tchr. 3d grade Richmond R-XVI Sch. Dist., 1988—98, tchr. 2d grade, 1998—. Coach Mo. Accelerated Schs., Richmond, 1998—. Mem. exec. bd. Federated Women's Dem. Club Ray County, Richmond, 1986—96. Mem.: AAUW (treas. 1988—98), PTA (exec. bd. 1992—), Richmond Cmty. Tchr's Assn. (exec. bd. 1988—, Outstanding Leader of Yr. 1993—94, Outstanding Educator of Yr. 2003—04), Mo. State Tchrs. Assn. (del. to conv. 1987—, Profl. Devel. Com. ctrl. region 1996—2002), Phi Kappa Phi, Delta Kappa Gamma (chpt. Beta Tau 1997—2000), Kappa Delta Pi. Democrat. Baptist. Achievements include helping to formulate a MSTA resolution that led to the passage of legislation in the Missouri Assembly, that returned lifetime certification to Missouri teachers. Avocations: reading, walking, travel, collecting historical artifacts. Office: Sunrise Elem Sch 401 Matt Waller Dr Richmond MO 64085

SOLOMON, PENNY GOREN, artist, designer; b. Phila., Mar. 4, 1941; d. Samuel Edward and Frances Lillian (Hellman) Goren; m. Sheldon Dubrow Solomon, June 2, 1963; children: Peter Lindsay, Kenneth Garrett, Jennifer Ann, Emily Lauren. BFA cum laude, BS in Edn., Temple U., 1963. Cert. tchr., Pa., N.J. Art tchr., head dept. art Collingsdale (Pa.) Sch., 1963-65; artist, 1963—; fashion designer, fabric designer, bus. owner, 1990—. Curator art show Pavillion Gallery, Mt. Holly, N.J., 1993. One-woman shows include Pavilion Gallery, Mt. Holly, N.J., 1984, 93, Home for Contemporary Theatre and Art, N.Y.C., 1987, Artifacts, Haddonfield, N.J., 1989; two-women shows include DaVinci Soc., Pa., 1985; exhibited in group shows at Stedman Art Gallery, Camden, N.J., 1989, The Noyes Mus., Oceanville, N.J., 1990, Pavilion Gallery, Mt. Holly, 1991, 93 (Dir.'s Choice award 1991), Long Beach Island Art Ctr., Loveladies, N.J., 1991 (Grand prize), Hopkins House Gallery, Haddon Twp., N.J., 1993, Stedman Gallery Rutgers U., 1993, Glouster County Community Coll., Sewell, N.J., 1993, First St. Gallery, N.Y.C., 1993, N.J. Designer Craftsman Gallery, New Brunswick, N.J., 1994, Beaux Arts, Media, Pa., 1994, Westby Art Gallery Rowan Coll., N.J., 1994; TV interviews featured artist: NJN State of the Arts, 1993, PBS State of the Arts, 1994; fashions modeled Phila. Mus. Art, 1993, 94. Bd. dirs. Arthritis Found. South Jersey Art Show, 1984—. Avocations: reading, skiing, dogs, travel, opera. Home: 302 Wexford Dr Cherry Hill NJ 08003-1829

SOLOMON, PHYLLIS LINDA, social work educator, researcher; b. Hartford, Conn., Dec. 6, 1945; d. Louis Calvin and Annabell Lee (Nitzberg) S. BA in Sociology, Russell Sage Coll., 1968; MA in Sociology, Case Western Res. U., 1970, PhD in Social Welfare, 1978. Lic. social worker Pa. Rsch. assoc. Inst. Urban Studies Cleve. State U., 1970-71; program evaluator Cleve. State Hosp., 1971-74; project dir. Ohio Mental Health and Mental Retardation Rsch. Ctr., Cleve., 1974-75; rsch. assoc. Psychiat. Rsch. Found. of Cleve., 1975; project dir. Ohio Mental Health and Mental Retardation Rsch. Ctr., 1977-78; rsch. assoc. dirs. rsch. and mental health planning Fedn. for Cmty. Planning, 1978-88; prof. dept. mental health scis., dir. sect. mental health svcs. and systems rsch. Hahnemann U., Phila., 1988-94; prof. Sch. Social Work U. Pa., Phila., 1994—. Secondary appointment Prof. Social Work in Psychiatry U. Pa. Sch. Medicine, 1994—; adj. prof. dept. psychiatry Allegheny U., 1994—97. Author: (with others) Community Services to Discharged Psychiatric Patients, 1984; co-editor: New Developments in Psychiatric Rehabilitation, 1990, Psychiatric Rehabilitation in Practice, 1993, Research Process in the Human Services, 2005; editl. adv. bd. Community Mental Health Jour., 1988—; editl. bd. Jour. Rsch. in Social Work, 1997-2000, Social Work Forum, 1997—, Health and Social Work, 1998-2000, Psychiat. Rehab. Jour., 1999—, Mental Health Svcs. Rsch. Jour., 2001—, Brief Treatment and Crisis Intervention, 2001—, Social Work, 2003—; contbr. articles to profl. jours. Trustee Cleve. Rape Crisis Ctr., 1981-84, CIT Mental Health Svcs., Cleve., 1985-88; mem. citizen's adv. bd. Sagamore Hills (Ohio) Children's Psychiat. Hosp., 1984-88; bd. dirs. Plan of Pa., 2004—. Named Evaluator of the Yr., Ohio Program Evaluators Group, 1987; recipient Ann. award Cuyahoga County Cmty. Mental Health Bd., 1988, Armin Loeb award Internat. Assn. Psychosocial Rehab. Svcs., 1999, Outstanding Non-Psychiatrist award Am. Assn. Cmty. Psychiatrists, 2002, Knee/Wittman Outstanding Lifetime Achievement award Nat. Assn. Social Workers Found., 2005. Mem. NASW, U.S. Psychiat. Rehab. Assn., Soc. for Social Work and Rsch. (1st place award for pub. article 1997). Jewish. Home: 205 Governor's Ct Philadelphia PA 19146 Office: U Pa Sch Social Policy & Practice 3701 Locust Walk Philadelphia PA 19104-6214 Business E-Mail: solomonp@sp2.upenn.edu.

SOLOMON, RISA GREENBERG, clinical social worker, child and family therapist, former entertainment industry executive; b. NYC, June 22, 1948; d. Nathan and Frances (Guttman) Greenberg; m. Philip Howard Solomon, June 21, 1970 (dec. 1994); children: Elycia Beth, Cynthia Gayle. BA, NYU, 1969, MA, 1970, MSSW, 1996. Asst. editor Redbook Mag., N.Y.C., 1969-70; assoc. editor Greenwood Press, Westport, Conn., 1970-71; mng. editor Dushkin Pub., Guilford, Conn., 1971-72; freelance editor Yale U. Press, New Haven, 1972-75; v.p. ops. Videoland, Inc., Dallas, 1980-82; v.p. Video Software Dealers Assn., Cherry Hill, N.J. and Dallas, 1981-83; pres. Videodome Enterprises, Dallas, 1983-94; clin. social worker, child and family therapist pvt. practice, Dallas, 1994—. Cons. Home Rec. Rights Coalition, Washington, 1983—84; spkr. in field of child and adolescent therapy. Bd. dirs. Congregation Anshai Emet, Dallas, 1985-86. Mem. Video Software Dealers Assn. (founder, dir. 1981-82). Democrat. Jewish. Avocations: skiing, travel, tennis, scuba diving. Office: 17103 Preston Rd Ste 100 Dallas TX 75248 Personal E-mail: rgs8961@msn.com.

SOLOMON, SUSANNE NINA, podiatrist, surgeon; b. Buffalo, Aug. 1, 1956; d. Joseph Michael and Olga (Kyzmir) S.; m. Jack M. Thompson, July 8, 1989; 1 child, Katherine Olga. AB cum laude, Cornell U., 1978; D of Podiatric Medicine, Pa. Coll., 1984. Diplomate Am. Bd. Podiatric Orthopedics, Am. Bd. Acad. of Wound Mgmt.; cert. wound specialist. Chief resident dept. podiatry Cambridge Hosp./Harvard Med. Sch., 1984-85; chief podiatric medicine and surgery Lemuel Shattuck Hosp., Jamaica Plain, Mass., 1986-89; podiatrist Deaconess Hosp., Cin., 1989—, Jewish Hosp., Cin., Bethesda Hosp., Cin., Miami Valley Hosp., Dayton, Ohio, 1999—; pediatric dir. Wound Care Ctr. Wright State Sch. of Medicine, Ohio, 1999—. Chief podiatric medicine and surgery Deaconess Hosp., Cin., 1996—, lectr. diabetes and athletes tchg. team, 1990—; dance medicine dir. Am. Acad. Podiatric Sports Medicine, 1993-94; dance medicine physician Met. Classical Ballet Co., Cin., 1991-93; supr. in podiatry Boston Marathon, 1985—; spokesperson women's health issues; U.S. Olympic com., Jacobs Inst. of Women's Health; com. mem. Impact of Tng. on Early Menarchal Athletes; pres., CEO Baby Greek, Inc. Co-author: (one act play) Courting Falia, 1997. Spokesperson Health Care Reform, Washington, 1994-95; health care task force Pres. Coun. of Cornell Women, 1995—. Fellow Am. Coll. Foot and Ankle Orthop. and Medicine, Am. Acad. Podiatric Sports Medicine; mem. Internat. Marathon Med. Dirs. Assn., Am. Med. Womens Assn. (Cin. chpt.), Am. Coll. Sports Medicine, Am. Podiatric Med. Assn., Cornell U. Club S.W. Ohio (pres. 1994-97), Alpha Phi (pres. Cin. chpt. 1992-95, trustee Cornell chpt. 1995—). Democrat. Russian Orthodox. Avocations: gardening, art, theater, gourmet cooking, music. Home: 5241 Wandering Way Mason OH 45040-9184 also: 2600 Stratford Ave Cincinnati OH 45219-1027

SOLOMONSON, KATHERINE, architecture educator; PhD in History of Art, Stanford U. Prof. Stanford U.; co-dir. study of cultural landscape of East Palo Alto, Calif.; assoc. prof., dept. co-head U. Minn., Coll. Arch. and Landscape Arch., Mpls. Mem. nat. register nominations com. Minn. State Rev. Bd.; mem. bd. bldgs. of U.S. Soc. Archtl. Historians; mem. com. on the press U. Minn. Press. Author: The Chicago Tribune Tower Competition: Skyscraper Design and Cultural Change in the 1920s, 2001. Recipient Ralph Rapson award for disting. tchg., Roy Jones award for outstanding rsch. Office: Univ Minn CALA 145F Rapson Hall 89 Church St SE Minneapolis MN 55455

SOLOVEI, MARION, clinical psychologist; b. Marburg, Germany, Dec. 20, 1936; came to U.S., 1964; d. Erwin Isaac and Henni (Walldorf) Hoechster; m. Norman Solovei, Jan. 11, 1959; children: Howard, Robyn. BA, Witwatersrand U., Johannesburg, Republic South Africa, 1958, Calif. State U., Long Beach, 1973; MA, Chapman Coll., 1975; PhD, U.S. Internat. U., 1987. Lic. psychologist, marriage, family and child counselor, Calif. Rsch. officer Franklin Rsch., Johannesburg, 1957-61; contract counselor Family Svc. Long Beach, 1975-80, supr., 1980-82, clin. dir., 1982—. Mem. adv. bd. Child Care Ctr., Long Beach City Coll., 1986—; mem. at large Long Beach Child Trauma Coun. Chmn. Long Beach Community Mental Health Com., 1988—. Mem. Am. Psychol. Assn., Calif. Assn. Marriage and Family Therapists, Long Beach Child Trauma Coun. (pres. 1983-84), Phi Kappa Phi. Jewish. Avocations: travel, reading. Office: Family Svc Long Beach 5500 E Atherton St Ste 416 Long Beach CA 90815-4017

SOLOWAY, ROSE ANN GOULD, clinical toxicologist; b. Plainfield, N.J., Apr. 19, 1949; d. George Spencer Jr. and Rose Emma (Frank) Gould; m. Irving H. Soloway, Dec. 13, 1979. BSN, Villanova U., 1971; MS in Edn., U. Pa., 1976. Diplomate Am. Bd. Applied Toxicology. Staff nurse Hosp. of U. Pa., Phila., 1971-73; asst. clin. instr. Hosp. of U. Pa. Sch. Nursing, Phila., 1973-77; staff devel. instr. Hosp. of Med. Coll. Pa., Phila., 1977-78; dir. emergency nurse tng. program Ctr. for Study of Emergency Health Svcs., U. Pa., Phila., 1979-80; edn./comms. coord. Nat. Capital Poison Ctr. Georgetown U. Hosp., Washington, 1980-94; clin. toxicologist Nat. Capital Poison Ctr. George Washington U. Med. Ctr., Washington, 1994—; adminstr. Am. Assn. Poison Control Ctrs., Washington, 1994-99, assoc. dir., 1999—2005. Mem. clin. toxicology and substance abuse adv. panel U.S. Pharmacopeial Conv., Inc., Washington, 1990—2000, mem. expert panel clin. toxicology and substance abuse, 2000—05. Contbr. articles to profl. jours. Mem.: APHA, Poison Prevention Week Coun. (vice-chair 1988—91, chair 1991—93, vice-chair 2001—03, chair 2003—05), Am. Acad. Clin. Toxicology (edn. com. 2000—), Am. Assn. Poison Control Ctrs. (co-chmn. pub. edn. com. 1985—90). Avocations: reading, cooking, knitting, jewelry making. Office: Nat Capital Poison Ctr Ste 310 3201 New Mexico Ave NW Washington DC 20016-2756

SOLTAN, MARGARET, literature and language professor; b. Balt., Aug. 15, 1953; d. Herbert Joseph and Marion Rapp; m. Karol Edward Soltan; 1 child, Ania Livia. PhD, U. Chgo., 1983. Assoc. prof. George Washington U., Washington, 1985—. Reporter Garrett Park (Md.) Bugle Newspaper, 2001—05. Recipient Univ. Advising award, George Washington U., 2004. Mem.: Assn. Lit. Scholars and Critics. Democrat. Home: Box 518 11121 Rokeby Ave Garrett Park MD 20896 Office: George Washington U English Dept Washington DC 20052

SOLTERO, MICHELLE DOLORES, director; b. San Diego, Calif., Mar. 25, 1960; d. Albert Lloyd and Dolores Luque Cardenas; m. Richard Soltero, Dec. 31, 1985; children: Cecilio Miguel(dec.), Patrick Anthony. BS in child develop., San Diego State U., 1978—83; M in human develop., Pacific Oaks Coll., 1990—95. Regular Children's Ctr. Supervision Permit State of Calif. Commn. on Tchr. Credentialing, 1996. Site dir. Child Devel. Associates, Inc., Chula Vista, Calif., 1985—89; program dir. YMCA of San Diego County, 1989—90; resource specialist YMCA of San Diego County Childcare Resource Svc., 1990—93; edn. and profl. devel. coord. Ednl. Enrichment Systems, Inc, San Diego, 1993—98; hsqic infant toddler specialist Devel. Associates, Inc, Walnut Creek, Calif., 1998—99; regional trainer/coord. WestED, Sausalito, Calif., 1999—. Pres. San Diego Assn. for the Edn. of Young Children, 1996—98; coun. mem. San Diego County Child Care and Devel. Planning Coun., 1997—; state pres. Calif. Assn. for the Edn. of Young Children, 2001—03; co-chmn. PFA Leadership Coun., Fist 5 Commn., San Diego, 2006—. Marcia Fochler Grad./Post Grad. award, Calif. Assn. for the Edn. of Young Children, 1994. Mem.: Chicano Fedn. San Diego County, Nat. Assn. Edn. Young Children (gov. bd. 2004—). Avocations: hinge box collector, memory books. Home: 10157 Tres Lagos Court Spring Valley CA 91977 Office Phone: 619-644-7717. E-mail: msolter@wested.org.

SOLTES, JOANN MARGARET, retired music educator, realtor; b. Sewickley, Pa., Nov. 11, 1942; d. Mary Ann Soltes. BS in Music Edn., Duquesne U., 1964; MA, Mich. State U., 1977; student, Goethe Institut, Germany, 1992, Big Bend Coll., 1992. Music tchr. grades K-12 Ctr. Twp. Schs., Monaca, Pa., 1964—69; facilitator of masters program Nat.-Louis U., Heidelberg, Germany, 1995—99; music tchr., classroom tchr. Dept. Def. Dependent Schools Overseas, Okinawa, Turkey, Germany, Japan, 1969—99; realtor Coldwell Banker, Monaca, Pa., 1999—2006; substitute tchr.; adminstrv. assessor Nat. Assessment Ednl. Progress, 2005. Facilitator The Study of Teaching Study Groups, Schweinufirt, Germany, 1992—95; presenter in field, Germany and Japan, 1992, Germany and Japan, 85. Mem. sch. advisory coun. Schweinfurt Am. Sch., Germany, 1995—96, mem. fine arts com., 1987—, chair grade level com., 1990—91, mem. sch. improvement com., 1989—90; vol. Adult Literacy Action, Beaver, Pa., 1999—2002; ch. organist; bd. dirs. Cmty. Concert. Mem.: AAUW (co-pres. 2006—), Beaver Falls Bus. and Career Women's Club (program chmn.), Outlook Club, Phi Delta Kappa. Roman Catholic. Avocations: reading, cooking, bridge, singing, theatrical performance.

SOLTIS, KATHERINE, editor; b. Pitts., Apr. 15, 1950; d. John Andrew and Katherine (Hnidec) Goidich; m. Patrick T. Soltis, July 27, 1973 (div. 1998). BA, Mich. State U., 1972; MA in English/Linguistics, Case Western Res. U., 1982. Part time clk. Case Western Res. U., Cleve., 1974-83; lexicographer Webster's New World Dictionaries, Wiley Pub., Cleve., 1983—. Freelance copy editor. Editor: Webster's New World Vest Pocket Dictionary, 2nd edit., 1994; style guide editor, Webster's New World Desk Dictionary and Style Guide, 2d edit. Trustee Cleve.- Volgograd Ptnr. Cities, 1990-2001; pres. Women Speak Out for Peace & Justice/Women's Internat. League for Peace & Freedom, 1993-95, chair program com., 1995-2001; orgn. rep. Cleve. Coalition Against the Death Penalty, 1981-, chair, 2002-; supporter Ariz. death row inmate, 1981-; former mem. Cleve. Pro-Choice Action League, 1996—, Windsong Cleve. Feminist Chorus, 1998-, Ohioans to Stop Executions. Mellon fellow Case Western Res. U. Mem.: Phi Beta Kappa. Soc. Of Friends. Avocations: reading, music, gardening, composting/recycling, foreign travel. Home: 896 Englewood Rd Cleveland Heights OH 44121-2042 Office: Webster's New World Dictionaries 850 Euclid Ave Ste 306 Cleveland OH 44114-3304 E-mail: kssoltis@yahoo.com.

SOLTZ, JUDITH E., insurance company executive, retired lawyer; BA, Barnard Coll., 1968; JD cum laude, Boston Coll., 1971; LLM in Taxation, NYU, 1978. Tax atty. Conn. Gen. Corp., 1973—85; from asst. gen. counsel to exec. v.p., gen. counsel Cigna Corp., Phila., 1985—2001, sr. v.p., assoc. gen. counsel, 1998—2001, exec. v.p., gen. counsel, 2001—06, ret., 2006. Trustee Acad. Natural Scis. Phila. Mem.: ABA (tax and bus. law sects.).

SOLYMOSY, HATTIE MAY, writer, educator; b. Kew Gardens, N.Y., Apr. 1, 1945; d. Julius and Sylvia Becky (Glantz) Fuld (dec.); m. Abraham Edward Solymosy, Apr. 21, 1974 (div., Sept. 2000). BA, Queens Coll., 1966, MS in Edn., 1973. Cert. tchr., N.Y.C. and N.Y. Actress, model, 1950-60; elem. tchr. N.Y.C. Bd. of Edn., 1966—; owner Ultimate Jewelry, N.Y.C., 1976-80; tutor N.Y.C., 1983-91; children's writer N.Y., 1991—; romance writer N.Y., 1993—; owner Hatties' Tales, Cedarhurst, N.Y., 1993—, Cigar Box Factory, Cedarhurst, N.Y., 1993—. Bd. dirs. Hamajama Gifts; co-owner Cigar Box Factory, 1996—, Spouse-For-Hire, 1999—, Pen Pal psychic advisor, 1999, Psychic Line, 1999—, ATM Mktg., 1999—, Credit Card Machines, 2000—; Ads-in Motion, Hot Nuts, Teaching Kids to Cook!, 2003, Ally-for-Hire, 2003, Cool Kids Cook!, 2003; del. People to People Internat. Missions in Understanding. Author: (sound recs.) Delancy Dolphin, 1993, Thaddius Thoroughbred, 1993, Willie's War, 1993, Noodles-An Autobiography, 1993, (with Jared Marc Milk) Trapped With The Past, 1993, Thick Slick Tangled Webs, 1993, Cinderella Cockroach, 1993, A Christmas Tale, 1993, Chanukah Tale, 1993, Doc Simon, 1995, Mr. Music, 1996, Women on Film, 1996, Buying a Dream, 1996, Rock and Roll, 1996, The Psycho Line, 1999, Legally Raped, 1999; author: Myster of the Old Fishing Shack, 1999. Social sec., fundraiser Children's Med. Ctr., N.Y.C., 1969-79; aux. mem. St. John's Hosp., N.Y., 1987—; storyteller children's stories Oklahoma City Fed. Bldg. bombing victims, Mo. flood victims, children's hosps.; assoc. mem. Mus. Natural History; fundraiser Lung Assn., 1997—, Am. Heart Assn., 1998—. Mem. Romance Writers Am., Soc. Children's Writers and Illustrators, Simon Wiesenthal Ctr., World Jewish Congress. Democrat. Jewish. Avocations: music, tennis, movies, gardening, dance. Home: 133 Eldorado St Atlantic Beach NY 11509 Office: Hatties Tales Cigar Box Factory and Spouse-for-Hire Psychic Line Pen Pal Psych PO Box 24 Cedarhurst NY 11516-0024 Office Phone: 212-920-7151.

SOMBURU, ZAKIYA NETIFNET T., physician; b. Montclair, NJ, Aug. 30, 1951; d. Clarence Clinton Jones and Margaret Cleo (Hilliard) Hilliard-Jones; m. Kwame Montsho Ajamu Somburu, Dec. 19, 1979; children: Khalid Lateef Sheffield, Asi-Yahola Mauri Kayin. AA, Fashion Inst. Design Merchandising, LA, 1972; student, Calif. State U., Hayward, 1991; MPH, U. Calif., Berkeley, 1994. Adj. faculty San Francisco State U., 1995—96; mgmt. program analyst San Francisco Dept. Social Svc., 1996—97; adj. faculty Calif. Inst. Integral Studies, 1996—97, John F. Kennedy U., Pleasant Hill, 2006—; program mgr. Alameda County Pub. Health Dept., Oakland, Calif., 1999—2002; pub. health educator San Joaquin County, Stockton, Calif., 2002—05. Project dir. Families United Against Crack Cocaine, Oakland, 1990—92; cons. in field. Co-dir., co-founder Bay Area Black Woman's Health Project, Oakland, 1983—91; adv. bd. Grandmothers as Caregivers Rsch./U. Calif., Berkeley, 1990—92; cand. for city coun. Oakland, 1979; cand. for mayor City of Oakland, 1981. Recipient Recognition cert., 13th Assembly Dist., Oakland, 1991. Mem.: APHA, AAUW, Black Women's Health Imperative. Avocations: reading, politics, violin, singing, art.

SOMER-GREIF, PENNY LYNN, lawyer; b. New Hyde Park, NY, Mar. 30, 1970; d. Stanley Jerome and Janice Somer; m. Brian Scott Greif; 1 child, David Joseph Somer Greif. BS, SUNY, Binghamton, 1992; JD, Am. U., 1995. Bar: N.J. 1996, N.Y. 1996, D.C. 2000. Atty.-advisor U.S. SEC, Washington, 1995-2000; assoc. Arnold & Porter, Washington, 2000—06, Ober, Kaler, Grimes & Shriver, Balt., 2006—. Avocations: reading, exercise. Office: 120 E Baltimore St Baltimore MD 21202-1643 Business E-Mail: psomergreif@ober.com.

SOMERMAN, MARTHA J., dean, dental educator; m. Norm Schiff. DDS, NYU, 1975; PhD, U. Rochester, 1980. Diplomate Am. Acad. Periodontology. Asst. prof., periodontics and pharmacology Balt. Coll. Dental Surgery, 1984—87, assoc. prof., pharmacology, 1987—91; William K. and Mary Anne Najjar prof., dept. periodontics, prevention and periodontics U. Mich. Sch. Dentistry, 1991—2002, chair dept. periodontics, prevention and geriatrics, 1991—2001, assoc. dean rsch., 2001—02; assoc. prof., pharmacology U. Mich. Med. Sch., 1991—95, prof., pharmacology, 1995—2002; dean U. Wash. Sch. Dentistry, 2002—. Adv. coun. mem. Nat. Inst. of Dental and Craniofacial Rsch. Contbr. articles to profl. jours. Recipient Rsch in Oral Biology Award, Internat. Assn. Dental Rsch., 2005. Fellow: AAAS; mem.: Am. Assn. Dental Rsch. (past pres.). Office: RM D-322 Box 356365 Seattle WA 98195 Office Phone: 206-543-5982. Office Fax: 206-616-2612. Business E-Mail: somerman@u.washington.edu.*

SOMERS, ANNE RAMSAY, retired medical educator; b. Memphis, Sept. 9, 1913; d. Henry Ashton and Amanda Vick (Woolfolk) Somers; m. Herman Miles Somers, Aug. 31, 1946; children: Sara Ramsay, Margaret Ramsay. BA, Vassar Coll., 1935; postgrad., U. N.C., 1939—40; DSc (hon.), Med. Coll. Wis., 1975. Ednl. dir. Internat. Ladies Garment Workers Union, 1937—42; labor economist U.S. Dept. Labor, 1943—46; rsch. assoc. Haverford Coll., 1957—63; rsch. assoc. indsl. rels. sect. Princeton U., 1964—84; prof. U. Medicine and Dentistry of N.J.-R. Wood Johnson Med. Sch. (formerly Rutgers Med. Sch.), 1971—84, adj. prof., 1984—2002. Adj. prof. geriat. medicine U. Pa. Sch. Medicine, 1990—2002; mem. Nat. Bd. Med. Examiners, 1983—86; cons. in health econs., health edn., geriats., gerontology, realted areas. Author: Hospital Regulation: The Dilemma of Public Policy, 1969, Health Care in Transition: Directions for the Future, 1971; author: (with H.M. Somers) Workmen's Compensation: The Prevention, Rehabilitation and Financing of Occupational Disability, 1954; author: Medicare and the Hospitals, 1967, Doctors, Patients and Health Insurance, 1961, Health and Health Care: Policies in Perspective, 1971; author: (with N.L. Spears) The Continuing Care Retirement Community: A Significant Option for Long Care?, 1992; editor (with D.R. Fabian): he Geriatric Imperative: An Introduction to Gerontology and Clinical Geriatrics, 1981. Mem. bd. visitors Duke U. Med. Ctr., 1972—77, U. Tex. Health Scis. Ctr., Houston, 1982—86. Named to Health Care Hall of Fame, 1993; recipient Elizur Wright award, Am. Risk and Ins. Assn., 1962. Fellow: Coll. Physicians Phila. (hon.), Am. Coll. Hosp. Adminstrs. (hon.); mem.: Nat. Acad. Social Ins., Inst. Medicine of NAS, Soc. Tchrs. of Family Medicine (hon.). Home: Pennswood Village # C-202 Newtown PA 18940-2401

SOMERS, JANICE A., elementary school educator; b. Washington, Nov. 18, 1951; d. Wilber and Sarah Patsy Somers. BS, U. Rochester, Rochester, NY, 1973. Cert. Tchr. K-7 gifted edn. Va. Tchr. 2nd grade Fairhill Elem., Fairfax, Va., 1973—75; tchr. 2nd, 6th grade Woodburn Elem., Fairfax, Va., 1975—91; tchr. 6th grade Edagr Allan Poe Mid., Fairfax, Va., 1991—. Chmn. black history com. Warner Bapt. Ch., Falls Ch., Va., 1996—. Mem.: NEA, Fairfax Edn. Assn., Va. Edn. Assn. Avocations: cross stitch, quilting, sewing, reading, travel. Office: Edgar Allan Poe Mid Sch 7000 Cindy Ln Annandale VA 22003

SOMERS, MARION, gerontologist, family therapist; children: Lynne, Randy, Cortney, Jessica, Craig, Matthew. M in Neuro Linguistic Programming, The Fielding Inst., PhD. Lic. nursing home adminstr. N.Y. Dir. profl. geriatric care mgrs. Brookdale Ctr. on Aging Hunter Coll. Grant reader HHS, Washington; observer White House Conf. on Aging. Author: The Home: A Brief Moment in Time, —. Office: 50 Bridge St Ste 515 Brooklyn NY 11201-1181

SOMERS, SUZANNE MARIE, actress, writer, singer; b. San Bruno, Calif., Oct. 16, 1946; d. Frank and Marion Mahoney; m. Greg Somers (div.); 1 child; m. Alan Hamel, 1977. Student, Lone Mountain Sch., San Francisco Coll. for Women; studies with Charles Conrad. Owner, founder Suzanne Somers Collection. Actress: (theater) The Blonde in the Thunderbird, 2004; (films) American Graffiti, 1973, Billy Jack Goes to Washington, 1977, Yesterday's Hero, 1979, Nothing Personal, 1980, Rusty: A Dog's Tale, 1997; (TV films) Sky Heist, 1975, It Happened at Lakewood Manor, 1977, Happily Ever After, 1978, Zuma Beach, 1978, Goodbye Charlie, 1985, Totally Minnie, 1988, Rich Men, Single Women, 1990, Seduced by Evil, 1994, Devil's Food, 1996, Love-Struck, 1997, No Laughing Matter, 1998, The Darklings, 1999; (TV series) Anniversary Game, 1969, High Rollers, 1974, Three's Company, 1977-81, She's the Sheriff, 1987-89, Step by Step, 1991—98; (TV mini-series) Hollywood Wives, 1985; actress, co-exec. prodr.: (films) Exclusive, 1992; host: (TV series) The Suzanne Somers Show, 1994, VH1's 8-Track Flashback, 1995, Candid Camera (co-host), 1997-2000; performer Las Vegas (Nev.) Hilton, MGM Grand, Las Vegas, Sands Hotel, Atlantic City, USO, various TV commls.; author: Touch Me Again, 1973, Keeping Secrets (autobiography), 1988, Suzanne Somers' Eat Great, Lose Weight, 1997, After the Fall: How I Picked Myself Up, Dusted Myself Off and Started All Over Again (autobiography), 1998, Suzanne Somers' Get Skinny on Fabulous Food, 1999, Suzanne Somers 365 Ways to Change Your Life, 1999, Eat, Cheat, and Melt the Fat Away, 2001, The Sexy Years: Discover the Hormone Connection, 2004. Named Las Vegas Entertainer of Yr., 1986; named an hon. mem., US Military, 2005; recipient Humanitarian award, Nat. Council on Alcoholism, 1992, President's award, Nat. Assoc. of American Drug Counselors.

SOMERVILLE, DAPHINE HOLMES, retired elementary school educator; b. Clinton, N.C., Jan. 19, 1940; d. George Henry and Mamie Estelle (Streeter) Holmes; m. Kalford Burton Somerville, Dec. 26, 1970 (div. Sept. 1992); 1 child, Daria Lynn. AA, Blackburn Coll., 1959, BA, 1961; MS in Edn., Hofstra U., 1967; postgrad., Columbia U., 1971, SUNY, Farmingdale, 1999-2000. Permanent tchg. cert. common br. subjects grades 1-8. Tchr. East Islip (N.Y.) Sch. Dist., 1961-99, ret., 1999; tchr. computer/writing Opportunities Industrialization Ctr., 1998—2003, cert. webmaster, 2000—04; field supr. dept. edn. Dowling Coll., 2006. Mem., instr. Outcome Based/Mastery Learning/Excellence in Learning Com., East Islip, 1984—89; mentor East Islip Sch. Dist., 1987—88, mem. sch. improvement team, 1989—91, staff devel. com., 1992—96; chair Ptnrs. in Edn., 1991—2001; instr. AARP's Driver Safety, 2001—03; election insp., 2001—. Author: Beaman Family Reunion Journal, 2001, Baptist Training Union Study Guide; founder, co-author: tutoring program Adopt-A-School Child/Family, 1990. A founding mem. Nat. Dr. Martin L. King Jr. Meml., Washington, 2005; Mem. Bay Shore (N.Y.) Civic Assn. and Bay Shore Pub. Schs. Task Force for Advancement Equality Ednl. Opportunity, 1967—69; sec. Islip Town NAACP, Bay Shore, 1965—90; dir. Bapt. Tng. Union, 1974—81; trustee First Bapt. Ch., Bay Shore, 1972—90, vice chair revitalization com., 2000—04. Named Silver Life Member, NAACP, 2006; recipient Cmty. Svc. award, Town Bd.-Town of Islip, Suffolk County, 1982, Recognition award, Islip Town NAACP, 1987, Disting. Svc. award, L.I. Region NAACP, 1993, Dedicated Svc. award, Ptnrs. in Edn. First Bapt. Ch. Bay Shore, 1995, 1996, recognition, Congressman Rick Lazio, 1997, African-Am. Educators award, Martin L. king Commn. Suffolk County, 1997, Editors Choice award, Nat. Libr. Poetry, 1999, citation, Town of Islip, 1999; L.I. Sch. to Career Partnership for Proposed Sch./Bus. Govt. Project grantee, 1996. Mem.: NAACP (silver life mem. 2006), N.Y. State United Tchrs., East Islip Tchrs. Assn. (past bldg. rep.), Nat. Coun. Negro Women (life Ednl. Involvement award 1993), Huntington Christian Women's Club (fin. coord. 2003—). Democrat. Avocations: theater, writing, tennis, reading, working with children, travel. Home: 130 Carman Rd Dix Hills NY 11746-5648 Personal E-mail: dsomer@optonline.net.

SOMERVILLE, DIANA ELIZABETH, author; b. Lincoln, Nebr., June 12, 1942; d. Edward John and Eunice Louise (Johnson) Wagner; m. Dale Springer Johnson, Aug. 7, 1961 (div. 1971); children: Carlyle Johnson Lee, Kelmie Blake. BA in English Lit., Centenary Coll., 1967. Dir. info. office Nat. Ctr. Atmospheric Rsch., Boulder, Colo., 1969-81; mgr. info. svcs. RDD Cons., Boulder, 1981-82; sci. writer U. Colo., Boulder, 1983-87; mgr. comm. Optoelectronic Computing Sys. Ctr., Boulder, 1987-88; columnist Daily Camera, Boulder, 1992—99; lectr. Peninsula Coll., 2001—. Lectr. U. Colo., 1996-99; founder Colo. Mag. Writers Inst. Author: Inside Out Down Under: Stories fom a Spiritual Sabbatical, 2006; editor: Optimum Utilization of Human Knowledge, 1983, Artful Meditation, 1995; contbr. numerous articles to profl. jour. Mem. women's caucus AAAS, 1969-75; mem. com. on pub. info. Am. Geophys. Union, 1977-78; mem. ednl. programs com. Am. Meteorol. Soc., 1978-80; mem. Turning the Wheel Dance/Theatre Co.; bd. dirs. Womanfest. Recipient Exceptional Achievement award Coun. for the Advancement and Support of Edn., Gold medal, 1986, Gold Pick award Pub. Rels. Soc. Am., 1985, Gold Quill award Internat. Assn. Bus. Comms., 1985. Mem. Nat. Assn. Sci. Writers, Am. Soc. Journalists and Authors, Boulder Media Women. Avocations: theater, dance, jungian dreamwork, healing rituals. E-mail: writer@olypen.com.

SOMERVILLE, VIRGINIA PAULINE WINTERS, executive assistant; b. Jo Daviess County, Ill., Jan. 14, 1936; d. Roy and Effie Winters; m. Thomas C. Somerville, June 8, 1957; children: Tod Andrew, Ian Winter. BMus magna cum laude, U. Dubuque, 1957; MMus with honors, Roosevelt U., 1964. Music tchr. pub. sch., Jessup, Iowa, 1959-60; music tchr. pvt. sch. P.R., Puerto Rico, 1960-61; prof. music St. Andrews Presbyn. Coll., Laurinburg, N.C., 1966-71; pvt. music tchr. Glendale, Calif., 1976-86; exec. asst. to sr. min. First Congl. Ch. L.A., 1986—2001; ret., 2001. Workshop and seminar leader Chapman Coll. Ch. Sec.'s Seminar, Orange, Calif., 1991, 92. Performer one-woman musical shows. Active PTA, Canoga Park, Calif., Glendale, 1972-84, Glendale Assistance League, 1975—. Recipient Citizen Appreciation award PTA-Verdugo Woodlands, Glendale, 1980, various music awards. Mem. Nat. Exec. Secs., Nat. Assn. Tchrs. of Singing. Avocations: concert going, reading, films, travel, theater.

SOMES, JOAN MARIE, critical care nurse; b. St. Paul, Aug. 17, 1952; d. Richard and Jane (Blaiser) Friesen; m. Michael Somes, Nov. 15, 1975. BA in Nursing, Coll. of St. Catherine, St. Paul, 1974; paramedic cert., Inver Hills C.C., Inver Grove Heights, Minn., 1976; MSN, U. Minn., 1989; PhD in Health Adminstrn., Columbia So. U., Orange Beach, Ala., 2002. RN, Minn.; cert. emergency nurse, getiatrics nurse; nat. registered EMT-paramedic; cert. ACLS instr., PALS instr.; cert. TNCC instr.; cert. CATN instr., ENPC instr.; cert. ACLS-EP instr. Paramedic A.L.F. Ambulance, Apple Valley, Minn., 1987-97; charge nurse emergency dept. Divine Redeemer Hosp., South St. Paul, Minn., 1974-94; staff nurse emergency dept. St. Joseph's Hosp., St. Paul, 1994—, emergency dept. educator/staff nurse, 1999—. Instr. numerous local cmty. colls., hosps. and ambulance svcs.; item writer CEN exam., 1994-96, 96-98; edn. specialist Regions Emergency Med. Svcs., 1994—; spkr. in field; co-chair Cornerstones Emergency Nursing Conf., 2000; mem. regional faculty PALS Am. Heart Assn., 2004—; mem. magnet steering com. Health East, 2005—. Author nursing home study courses; consulting editor Man. of Emergency Dept. and Urgent Care Instrns., 2001--; contbr. articles to profl. jour. Grantee Glaxo Pharm. Co., 1989, Health East Found. 1991, 94, 97, 98, recipient Mary Piner award Minn. Emergency Nurses Assn. State Coun. 1994-2006 Fellow: Acad. Emergency Nurses; mem.: Vision Coun. for Profl. Devel., Nat. Emergency Nurses Assn. (chair geriatric com. 2003—04, mem. exam item writer com. 2003—, mem. geriat. com. 2005—), Emergency Nurses Assn. (chair state trauma com. 1994—95, sec. treas. Minn. state coun. 1994—95, sec. 1996—98, sec. treas. Minn. state coun. 1997—98, 1999—2000, pres. Greater Twin Cities chpt. 2001—02, state coun. rep. 2001—03, sec.-treas. Minn. state coun. 2004—, dir./state coun. liaison Greater Twin Cities chpt., Nurse Competency in Aging award 2005, Deanna Earle award Greater Twin Cities chpt.).

SOMMER, ALICIA PINE, flight attendant, performing company executive; b. Guadalajara, Mexico, Jan. 16, 1966; d. Robert Floyd and Bea Pine; m. Mark Flemming Sommer, Apr. 8, 1995; children: Sydney Alicia, Sienna Julieanne. BA, U. Tex., Austin, 1989; student Lang. and Culture of Spain, U. Aliciante, Spain, 1988—89. Cert. FAA U.S. Dept. Transp., 2004, Geneva Convention card U.S. Dept. Def., 2006. Flight attendant United Airlines, Reston, Va., 1984—; artistic dir. and dept. head Harmony Sch. Creative Arts, Marble Falls, Tex., 2006—. Cast mem. Up With People, Tucson, 1986—87, bd. of govs., 1997—99. Performer: Fantasy Nutcracker. Named to Top 15, Miss Tex. T.E.E.N, 1985; recipient Winner, Miss Austin T.E.E. N Pageant, 1984, cert. of Appreciation, United Airlines, 1991, Achievement award, United Airlines Tng. Dept., 1991, Achievment award, Dance Tchr. Mag., 2005; scholar, U. Tex., 1984, Rotary Club, 1984. Mem.: Alpha Gamma Delta (life). Home: PO Box 8449 Horseshoe Bay TX 78657 Office Phone: 512-470-8464. Personal E-mail: amsommer@zeecon.com. E-mail: aliciasommer@yahoo.com.

SOMMER, MIRIAM GOLDSTEIN (MIMI G. SOMMER), writer, photographer; b. Springfield, Mass., May 2, 1929; d. Nathan E. and Anna (Ginsberg) Goldstein; children: Babette, Anne. BA, Wells Coll., 1950; rsch. cert., London Sch. Econs., 1953; MS in Art History, So. Conn. State U., 1977. Music dept. adminstr. Yale U., 1963-83; free-lance travel writer, photographer New Haven, 1984—. Mem. Creative Arts Workshop, New Haven, 1960—; mem. New Haven Arts Coun., 1970—, Met. Mus. Art/Yale U. Art Galleries; guest lectr. Journalism dept., So. Conn. State U., 1989-2005. Contbr. articles to profl. mags. including Colonial Homes Mag., Family Fun Mag., Touring

Am. mag., Coastal Living mag., Conn. mag., Travel Agent mag.; also newspapers including N.Y. Times, L.A. Times, New Haven Register. V.p. Decade Alumni Coun., Williston Northampton Sch., Easthampton, Mass., 1989, co-founder, panelist career day; bd. mem., co-dir. Assn. for Handicapped Artists, New Haven, 1989; co-founder Creative Arts Workshop course for handicapped artists; commr. and vice-chmn. cultural affairs City of New Haven. Mem. Soc. Profl. Journalists (Excellence in Journalism First Prize Winner 1991 for best mag. spl. supplement feature "Designing Woman, Conn. Mag.), Am. Soc. Journalists and Authors, Soc. Profl. Journalists (Excellence in Journalism, 2002, 1st Pl. and 2nd Pl. Mag. Featured Photo awards competition), Rockport Art Assn. Avocations: pottery, movies, theater, museum. Home: 603 Prospect St New Haven CT 06511-2146 E-mail: miriam.sommer@yale.edu.

SOMMERFELD, MARIANNA, retired social worker, writer; b. Frankfurt, Germany, Jan. 25, 1920; d. Martin and Helene (Schott) S. BA, Smith Coll., 1940; MA, Radcliffe Coll., 1946; MSW, Simmons Coll., 1957. Lic. ind. social worker. Tchr. Latin, German, English Burnham Sch. Girls, Northampton, Mass., 1940-43; German translator Yale Inst. Human Rels., New Haven, 1943-44; tchr. Northfield (Mass.) Sch. Girls, 1944-45; psychiat. social worker McLean Hosp., Belmont, Mass., 1957-59, Gaebler Children's Unit/Met. State Hosp., Waltham, Mass., 1959-62, Boston U./Boston City Hosp., 1962-67, New Eng. Med. Ctr., Boston, 1967-71; pvt. practice Cambridge, Mass., 1962-68; supr. clin. social work Erich Lindemann Mental Health Ctr., Boston, 1971-90; writer, 1976—. Author: Marianna Sommerfeld: Diary of a Single Woman, 1991. Vol. Cambridge Sch., 1993. Mem. NOW, AFL-CIO, Planned Parenthood, Nat. Writers Union, Women's Nat. Book Assn., PEN New Eng. (assoc.). Office Phone: 617-354-1803.

SOMVILLE, MARILYN F., retired dean; Dean Mason Gross Sch. Arts, New Brunswick, NJ; ret., 2000. Bd. dirs. Opus 118 Harlem Ctr. Strings.

SONDAY, ARLENE W., educational consultant; d. Rudolph Anselm and Ebba Isabelle Linnea Waxlax; m. Ralph E. Sonday, July 30, 1955; children: Barbara Ann Sonday Neafus, Bradley Allen, Karen Lee, David Ralph. BA, Gustavus Adolphus Coll., 1954; MA, U. St. Thomas, 1976. Cert. learning disabilities State of Minn., 1973. Founder, academic dir. summer sch. St. Paul Acad., 1975—93, faculty, 1975—85; tchr. educator Scottish Rite Children's Learning Ctr., various cities in Pa and Ohio, 1997—2003; tchr. tng. Winsor Learning, Inc., St. Paul, 1999—. Lectr., workshop leader, 1972—; adj. faculty Fairleigh Dickinson U., Teaneck, 1988—, adv. com. dyslexia specialist cert. program, 1988—; adj. faculty Hamline U., St. Paul, 1988—; adv. bd. curriculum stds. Scottish Rite Children's Learning Ctr., Lexington, Mass., 1997—2003; conf. workshop leader Egyptian Learning Disabilities Assn., Cairo, 2005—. Author: (curriculum writer) Sonday System-Let's Play Learn; Sonday System Learning to Read; Sonday System II. V.p., bd. dirs. Internat. Dyslexia Assn., Balt., 1982—93, pres., bd. dirs., bd. advisors upper midwest br. Mpls., 1969—2005. Recipient Betty Jones Dedicated Svc. award, Minn. Assn. Children with Learning Disabilities, 1989. Fellow: Acad. Orton-Gillingham Practitioners and Educators (bd. dirs., chair organizing com. 1993—2000, pres. 1996—97); mem.: Coun. for Exceptional Children, Learning Disabilities Am., Internat. Reading Assn., Internat. Dyslexia Assn. (v.p. 1987—93, Outstanding Svc. award 1993). Avocations: travel, reading, needlecrafts, exercise. Home: 1585 Dodd Rd #303 Saint Paul MN 55118 Office: Winsor Learning 1620 W 7th St Saint Paul MN 55102 Office Phone: 800-321-7585. Home Fax: 651-455-9361; Office Fax: 651-222-3969. Personal E-mail: sonday@sprynet.com.

SONDE, SUSAN, writer; b. N.Y.C., Nov. 17, 1940; d. John Walter and Elizabeth (Frant) Kolisch; m. Theodore Irwin Sonde, Sept. 12, 1964; children: Andrea Hawthorne, David. MA in German Lit., Johns Hopkins U., 1967; MA in Studio Art, U. Md., 1970. Poetry instr. U. Md., College Park, 1970—72; instr. Writer's Ctr., Glen Echo Park and Bethesda, Md. Author: (poetry) Inland Is Parenthetical, 1979, (fiction) Say It, 1999 (Peregrine prize), My Scout, My River Baby, 1993 (Writer's Digest award); assoc. editor The Crescent Rev. Recipient Capricorn Book award West Side YMCA, Md. State Arts award in Poetry Md. State Arts Coun., 2001; fellow Va. Ctr for Arts. Mem. Acad. Am. Poets, Writer's Voice, Poetry Soc. Am. (Gordon Barber Meml. award 1985). Avocation: pottery. Home: 2011 St Stephens Woods Dr Crownsville MD 21032 Office Phone: 301-858-1528. E-mail: susansonde@msn.com.

SONDERBY, SUSAN PIERSON, federal judge; b. Chgo., May 15, 1947; d. George W. and Shirley L. (Eckstrom) Pierson; m. James A. De Witt, June 14, 1975 (dec. 1978); m. Peter R. Sonderby, Apr. 7, 1990. AA, Joliet Jr. Coll., Joliet, Ill., 1967; BA, U. Ill., 1969; JD, John Marshall Law Sch., 1973. Bar: Ill., 1973; U.S. Dist. Ct. (cen. and so. dists.) Ill., 1978,; U.S. Dist. Ct. (no. dist.) Ill., 1984; U.S. Ct. Appeals (7th Cir.), 1984. Assoc. O'Brien, Garrison, Berard, Kusta, and De Witt, Joliet, Ill., 1973-75, ptnr., 1975-77; asst. atty. gen. consumer protection div., litig. sect. Office of the Atty. Gen., Chgo., 1977-78, asst. atty. gen., chief consumer protection divsn. Springfield, Ill., 1978-83; U.S. trustee (no. dist.) Ill. Chgo., 1983-86; judge U.S. Bankruptcy Ct. (no. dist.) Ill., Chgo., 1986—, chief fed. bankruptcy judge, 1998—2002. Mem. law faculty Fed. Jud. Tng. Ctr., Ill., Practicing Law Inst., Ill., U.S. Dept. Justice, Ill., Nat. Bankruptcy Inst., Ill., Ill. Continuing Edn.; spl. asst. atty. gen., Ill., 1972—78; adj. faculty De Paul U. Coll. Law, Chgo., 1986; past mem. U.S. Trustee adv. com., Ill.; consumer adv. coun. Fed. Res. Bd., Ill.; past sec. of State Fraudulent I.D. com. Dept. of Ins. Task Force on Improper Claims Practices, Ill.; former chair pers. rev. bd., mem. task force race and gender bias, U.S. Dist. Ct.; jud. conf. planning com. 7th Cir. Jud. Conf.; former mem. Civil Justice Reform Act Adv. Com., Adminstrv. Office of the U.S. Cts. Bankruptcy Judges Adv. Group, Ct. Security com., Adminstrv. Office of the U.S. Cts. Budget and Fin. Coun. Contbr. articles to profl. jour. Mem. Fourth Presbyn. Ch., Art Inst. Chgo.; past mem. Westminster Presbyn. Ch., Chgo. Coun. of Fgn. Rels.; past bd. dirs. Land of Lincoln Coun. Girl Scouts U.S.; past mem. individual guarantors com. Goodman Theatre, Chgo.; past chair clubs and orgns. Sangamon County United Way Capital campaign; past bd. dirs., chair house rules com. and legal subcom. Lake Point Tower; past mem. Family Svc. Ctr., Aid to Retarded Citizens, Henson Robinson Zoo. Named Young Career Woman, Bus. and Profl. Women, One of Ten Outstanding Bankruptcy Judges, Turnarounds and Workouts, 2002; named one of 500 Leading Judges in Am., Law Dragon mag., 2006; recipient Spl. Achievement Award, Dept. Justice, 1984, Disting. Svc. Alumni Award, Joliet Jr. Coll., 1987, Disting. Alumni Award, John Marshall Law Sch., 1988, Dir. Award, Exec. Office U.S. Trustee, Leadership Award, Internat. Orgn. Women Exec., Outstanding Svc. to Bench, Am. Bankruptcy Inst., 1990. Master: Abraham Lincoln Marovitz Inn of Ct. (former pres., membership com.); fellow: Am. Coll. Bankruptcy (circuit admissions com.); mem.: ATLA, Comml. Law League Am. (former exec. coun. mem., bankruptcy and insolvency sect., coord. with nat. conf. bankruptcy judges com.), Nat. Conf. Bankruptcy Judges (co-chair ednl. program com. conf. 2001, liaison with bankruptcy rev. commn. com.), Bar Assn. (7th cir.) (former treas., judicial conf. planning com.), Am. Bankruptcy Inst. (bd. dirs. Chgo. chpt.), Fed. Bar Assn., Chgo. Archtl. Found., John Marshall Law Sch. Alumni Assn. (bd. dirs.), Nordic Law Club (past legis. com.), Lawyers Club Chgo. (hon.). Avocations: travel, flying, interior decorating. Office: US Bankruptcy Ct 219 S Dearborn St Ste 638 Chicago IL 60604-1702

SONDERMAN, ELIZABETH LOUISE, literature and language educator, writer; b. Manila, Philippines, Feb. 20, 1938; arrived in U.S., 1945; d. Charles Joseph Cushing and Mercedes (Ortensia) Kane; m. Armandus Werner (dec.); m. Robert Ramon MacGavin (div.); children: Charles Richard MacGavin, Brian Robert MacGavin, James Raymond MacGavin, Judith Mercedes MacGavin, Ramona Angela MacGavin. AA Liberal Arts, San Bernardino Valley Coll., San Bernardino, Calif., 1972; BAin Comparative Lit. cum laude, U. Calif. Riverside, 1974. Cert. tchr. Calif. Substitute tchr. Rialto Sch. Dist., Calif., 1982—84; opportunity tchr. Sierra H.S., San Bernardino, Calif., 1984—86; substitute tchr. Colton H.S., Calif., 1986—98; home tchr. Sonora H.S., Calif., 1998—2001; ret., 2001. Tchr. 7th grade St. Anthony's Sch., San Bernardino, 1980—82; substitute tchr. San Bernardino Sch. Dist., 1982—84. Author: By the East Wind Driven, 2005; author: (poetry) Crest of the Cedar, 2003, Sweet and Bitter, 1975. Vol. Interfaith Cmty. Svcs., Tuolumne, Calif., 1998—2006. Mem.: Twain Harte Calif., All Saints Ladies Guild (treas. 2004—06), Secular Franciscan Order (sec. 2002—06). Roman Catholic. Home: 19859 Via Redonda Rd Sonora CA 95370

SONDOCK, RUBY KLESS, retired judge; b. Apr. 26, 1926; d. Herman Lewis and Celia (Juran) Kless; m. Melvin Adolph Sondock, Apr. 22, 1944; children: Marcia Cohen, Sandra Marcus. AA, Cottey Coll., Nevada, Mo., 1944; BS, U. Houston, 1959, LLB, 1961. Bar: Tex. 1961, U.S. Supreme Ct. 1977. Pvt. practice, Houston, 1961-73, 89—; judge Harris County Ct. Domestic Rels. (312th Dist.), 1973-77, 234th Jud. Dist. Ct., Houston, 1977-82, 83-89; justice Tex. Supreme Ct., Austin, 1982; of counsel Weil Gotshal and Manges, 1989-93, Houston Ctr., 1993—. Mem. ABA, Tex. Bar Assn., Houston Bar Assn., Houston Assn. Women Lawyers, Order of Barons, Phi Theta Phi, Kappa Beta Pi, Phi Kappa Phi, Alpha Epsilon Pi. Address: 550 Westcott #220 Houston TX 77007 Office Phone: 713-655-1111. Personal E-mail: sondock@airmail.net.

SONI, JAYSHRI, science educator, director; arrived in U.S., 1989; d. Mangilal and Krishnabai Soni; m. Komal Soni, May 28, 1988; children: Kishen K., Reema K. MSc in Botany, Sagar U., Khandwa, India, 1989, BSc in Biology, 1987; BSc in Edn., Lander U., Greenwood, S.C., 1995. Cert. tchr. biology S.C., 1995. Tutor McCormick County Literacy Assn., SC, 1989—95; tchr. sci. Long Cane Acad., McCormick, SC, 1996—98; tchr. math. John de la Howe Sch., McCormick, SC, 2002—04, tchr. sci., 2004—; program dir. Gurukul L.L.C., McCormick, 2005—. Mentor to mid. sch. sci. tchrs. John de la Howe Sch., 2004—. Grantee, Am. Aeronautics Assn., 2004-05, Donorschoose.org, 2005-06. Mem.: S.C. State Employees Assn. Home: 4098 Hwy 378 W Mc Cormick SC 29835 Office: John de la Howe Sch Box 154 Hwy 81 Mc Cormick SC 29835 Office Phone: 864-391-2131 110. Home Fax: 864-852-2865. Personal E-mail: ksoni@wctel.net. Business E-Mail: sonij@delahowe.k12.sc.us.

SONMOR, MARILYN IDELLE, music educator; b. Wilson, Wis., Jan. 18, 1933; d. John Reuben and Mary (Feldhahn) Haglund; m. Stephen Malcom Sonmor, Aug. 3, 1957; children: Tamara Lynn and Terri Lee (twins), Stephen Mark MusB, Northwe. Coll., Roseville, Minn., 1958; postgrad. music studies, Ariz. State U., 1985—86; MA, Fuller Theol. Sem., 1992. Tchr. Mesquite H.S., Tex., 1959—60, Dallas Christian Grade Sch., 1960—61; prof. Dallas Bible Coll., 1960—62; missionary Conservative Bapt. Fgn. Mission Soc., Manila, 1965—75; prof. Conservative Bapt. Bible Coll., Manila, 1973—75; prof., dean women Southwe. Coll., Phoenix, 1976—95. Dir. mus. and outreach ministry Conservative Bapt. Bible Coll., 1971-75; dir. women's work Campariza Assn. Philippines, Manila, 1973-75; spkr. Conservative Bapt. Assn., 1964-75 Named First Pl. Winner voice Minn. Vocal Tchrs. Assn., 1957 Mem. Am. Assn. Christian Counselors, Southwe. Women's Aux. (pres. 1980-82) Republican. Avocations: vocalist, pianist, needlecrafts, interior decorating. Home: 2305 N 127th Ave Avondale AZ 85323-6583

SONNEK, BONNIE KAY, education educator; b. Wells, Minn., Oct. 15, 1953; d. Albert Peter and Mary Jane Sonnek; life ptnr. Steven Walter Nelson, Nov. 22, 1949. BS, Winona State U., Minn., 1976; MA, Tex. State U., San Marcos, 1995; PhD, U. Iowa, Iowa City, 2003. Hs tchr., Alexandria, Minn., 1976—78, Dept. Def., Germany, 1979—82; tchr. NATO Base, Ketlavik, Iceland, 1978—79; reporter, editor Rsch. & Planning Cons., Inc., 1982—90; coord. student learning ctr. Tex. State U., San Marcos, 1993—95; prof. U. Tex., Austin, 1995—98; student tchg. supr. U. Iowa, Iowa City, 2000—03; English edn. coord. Western Ill. U., Macomb, 2002—, asst. prof., 2003—. Ednl. dir. Operation Springboard, Canyon Lake, Tex., 1990—92; presenter in field. Bd. mem. San Marcos Youth Svcs., 1994—96. Named Devel. Edn. Grad. Student of Yr., Tex. State U., 1995. Mem.: Nat. Coun. Tchrs. English (assoc.; advisor 2003, Outstanding Advisor 2004). Achievements include research in writing remediation. Home: 732 S McArthur St Macomb IL 61455 Office: Western Illinois University English and Journalism Dept Macomb IL 61455 Office Phone: 309-298-1511. Home Fax: 309-298-2974; Office Fax: 309-298-2974. Business E-Mail: bk-sonnek@wiu.edu.

SONNEMAKER, SUSAN S., music educator; b. Fairbanks, Alaska, Jan. 22, 1975; d. Robert Charles Benefield and Edna Sue Chapman; m. J. Andrew Sonnemaker, June 13, 1998; 1 child, A. Wesley. MusB in Music Edn., U. Nev., Reno, 1998; postgrad., Calif. State U., LA. Cert. tchr. Nev., Ind. Elem. music tchr. Carson Sch. Dist., Carson City, Nev., Washoe County Schs., Reno; mid. sch., HS music tchr. E.V. Sch. Corp., Evansville, Ind.; HS music tchr. Carson City Schs. Mem. United Meth. Women, Reno, 2005—. Mem.: NEA, Nev. Music Educators, Am. Choral Dirs. Assn. (chmn. women's choirs Ind. chpt. 2004—05), U. Nev.-Reno Alumni Assn. Democrat. Methodist. Avocations: singing, piano, antiques.

SONNEMAN, EVE, artist; b. Chgo., 1946; d. Eric O. and Edith S. BFA, U. Ill., 1967; MFA, U. N.Mex., 1969. One-woman shows include Castelli Gallery, N.Y.C., 1976, 78, 80, 82, 84-86, Tex. Gallery, Houston, 1976, 78, 80, 82, 85, Galerie Farideh Cadot, Paris, 1978, 80, 83, François Lambert Gallery, Milan, Italy, 1980, 87, Mpls. Inst. Arts, 1980, La Noveau Musèe, Lyon, France, 1980, Musèe de Toulon, France, 1983, Centre Georges Pompidou, Paris, 1984, Circus Gallery, L.A., 1989, 97, Jones Troyer Fitzpatrick, Washington, 1989, Zabriskie Gallery, N.Y., 1990, Gloria Luria Gallery, Miami, 1990, Grand Central Terminal, N.Y.C., 1991, Charles Cowles Gallery, 1992, Sidney Janis Gallery, N.Y.C., 1996, La Geode Mus., Paris, 1996, Cirrus Gallery, 1997, Bruce Silverstein Gallery, N.Y., 2002, Jadite Gallery, N.Y., 2002, 03, 04, 05, 06, Galeria Turchi, Siena, Italy, 2002, I Space, Chgo., 2005, Mingle Salon, Tokyo, 2005; author: America's Cottage Gardens, 1990, Where Birds Live, 1992; co-author: How To Touch What, 2000; photographs subject of book Real Time, 1976. Grantee Nat. Endowment Arts, 1971, 78, Polaroid Corp., 1978; Cartier fellowship, France, 1989. Address: 446 W 47th St Apt 5C New York NY 10036-2381 Office Phone: 212-582-9375. Personal E-mail: evesonneman@earthlink.net.

SONNENBERG, LINDA L., literacy educator; b. Milw., Mar. 20, 1952; d. James Charles and Bernice Mary Sonnenberg; m. Michael J. Ziegenhagen, Aug. 20, 1989; stepchildren: Nicole Multauf, Gina Ziegenhagen. BS in Early Childhood, U. Milw., Wis., 1974, MS in Curriculum Instrn., 1979. Tchr. nursery sch. Jewish Cmty. Ctr., Milw., 1974—76; reading tchr. Milw. Pub. Schs., 1977—83, tchr. kindergarten, 1985—86, tchr. 1st grade, 1986—97, reading source tchr., 1997—2002, literacy specialist, 2002—05, grant literacy support tchr., 2005—. Adj. prof. U. Milw., 1998—; presenter Internat. Reading Assn., Reno, 2004, Chgo., 06. Mem.: Wis. State Reading Assn., Internat. Reading Assn. Avocations: reading, walking. Office: Milw Pub Schs 5225 W Vliet Milwaukee WI 53208 E-mail: llsathome@wi.rr.com.

SONNENFELD, SANDI, writer; b. Queens, N.Y., May 22, 1963; d. Fred I. and Myra G. (Gever) S.; m. Warren A. Berry, Sept. 6, 1992. BA in English/Dance, Mount Holyoke Coll., 1985; MFA in Creative Writing, U. Wash., Seattle, 1989. Adj. English instr. Seattle Cmty. Coll., 1989-91, Pierce Coll., Puyallup, Wash., 1991-95; devel. coord. Hope Heart Inst., Seattle, 1995-96; dir. devel. Tacoma Actors Guild, 1996-97; media rels. dir. Publicis Dialog, Seattle, 1998—2002; media rels. mgr. White & Case LLP, N.Y.C., 2002—. Freelance writer, Seattle, 1989-2002; planning com. co-chair Northwest Bookfest, Seattle, 1995-97. Author: Case Study Harvard Bus. Rev., 1994, 95, Memoir: This Is How I Speak, 2002; contbg. author Literary Anthology, 1995, (short story) Sex and the City, 1992, Family: A Celebration, This Is How I Speak, 2002; contbr. feature articles to Wall St. Jour., Nat. Bus. Employment Weekly, Animals Mag. Recipient award David Dornstein Nat. Fiction Writing Contest, Coalition for the Advancement of Jewish Edn., 1998; named Celebration Author, Pacific N.W. Booksellers Assn., 2002. Mem. Pen Ctr. West, PEN Washington (pres. 2002), Author's Guild, Mount Holyoke Coll. Club Puget Sound (pres. alumnae club 1996-97). Democrat. Jewish. Home: 483 78th St #2 Brooklyn NY 11209-3011

SONNHALTER, CAROLYN THERESE, physical therapist, consultant; b. Bedford, Ohio, Apr. 26, 1942; d. Gabriel Edward Jr. and Josephine Irene (Kubera) Farkas; m. Donald Joseph Lippert, June 11, 1966 (div. June 1981); 1 child, Kevin Michael; m. Robert Louis Sonnhalter, Aug. 31, 1985. BS, Ohio State U., 1964. Lic. phys. therapist, Ohio. Staff and sr. phys. therapist Akron (Ohio) City Hosp., 1964-69; asst. dir. phys. therapy Akron Gen. Med. Ctr., 1975-82; dir. phys. therapy Litchfield Rehab. Ctr., Akron, 1983-87; phys. therapist HMO Health Ohio, Akron, 1987-97, Phoenix-Hudson Corp., Middleburg Heights, Ohio, 1993-98; dir. phys. therapy Tri-County Home Nursing, Mogadore, Ohio, 1997-99; phys. therapist VNS, Kent, Ohio, 1999—. Revel. phys. therapy first outpatient Chronic Pain Mgmt. Program, Ohio, 1983; cons. video animation on mechanism of whiplash for use by med. and legal profls., Ohio, 1996. Mem. Am. Phys. Therapy Assn., Alpha Gamma Delta. Avocations: traveling ohio and nearby states in search of antiques, gardening. Home: 3631 Oak Rd Stow OH 44224-3934 Office: VNS 234 S Water St Kent OH 44240-3526

SONNIER, PATRICIA BENNETT, business management educator; b. Park River, ND, Mar. 25, 1935; d. Benjamin Beekman Bennett and Alice Catherine (Peerboom) Bennett Brenckinridge; m. William McGregor Castellini (dec.); m. Cecil Sherwood Sonnier (dec.); m. Joseph N. Pagano; children: Bruce Bennett Wells (Nabil Subhani), Barbara Lea Ragland. AA, Allan Handcock Coll., Santa Maria, Calif., 1964; BS magna cum laude, U. Great Falls, 1966; MS, U. N.D., 1967, PhD, 1971. Fiscal acct. USIA, Washington, 1954-56; pub. acct. Bremerton, Wash., 1956; statistician USN, Bremerton, Wash., 1957-59; med. svcs. accounts officer USAF, Vandenberg AFB, Calif., 1962-64; instr. bus. adminstrn. Western New Eng. U., 1967—69; vis. prof. econs. Chapman Coll., 1970; vis. prof. U. So. Calif. Sys., Griffith AFB, NY, 1971-72; assoc. prof., dir. adminstrv. mgmt. program Va. State U., 1973-74; assoc. prof. bus. adminstrn. Oreg. State U., Corvallis, 1974-81, prof. mgmt., 1982-90, emeritus prof. mgmt., 1990—, univ. curriculum coord., 1984-86, dir. adminstrv. mgmt. program, 1974-81, pres. Faculty Senate, 1981. Mem. Interinstl. Faculty Senate, 1986-90, pres., 1989-90; exec. dir. Bus. Enterprise Ctr., 1990-92, Enterprise Ctr. LA, Inc., 1992-95; commr. Lafayette Econ. Devel. Authority, 1994-2000, treas., 1995-96, vice chmn., 1996-97, chmn., 1997-98, past chmn., 1998-99, sec., chmn. bldg. com., 1999-2000; cons. process tch. devel. Digital Equipment Corp., 1981. Pres., chmn. bd. dirs. Adminstrv. Orgnl. Svcs., Inc., Corvallis, 1976—83, Dynamic Achivement, Inc., 1983—92; cons. Oregonians in Action, 1990—91, sec., 1999, 2000; cert. adminstrv. mng. pres. TYEE Mobile Home Park, Inc., 1987—92; mem. Leadership LA, 1986; del various convs.; mem. parish coun. St. Patrick's Cath. Ch., 1998—2000, Risen Savior Ch., 2005—06. Fellow: Assn. Bus. Comm. (internat. bd. 1980—86, v.p. Northwest 1981, 2d v.p. 1982—83, 1st v.p. 1983—84, pres. 1984—85); mem.: AAUP (chpt. sec. 1973, chpt. bd. dirs. 1982, pres. Oreg. conf. 1983—85, chpt. bd. dirs. 1984—89, pres. chpt. 1985—86), Corvallis Area C. of C. (v.p. chamber devel. 1987—88, pres. 1988—89, chair bd. 1989—90, Pres.'s award 1986), La. Bus. Incubation Assn. (sec.-treas. 1993—95), Nat. Assn. Tchr. Edn. for Bus. Office Edn. (pres. 1976—77, chair pub. rels. com. 1978—81), Better Bus. Bur. (sec. 1994, treas. 1995, vice-chair 1996, chair 1997, past chair 1998, sec. 1999, chair nominating com. 1999, chair pub. rels., Lafayette Blue Ribbon 1999—2000), Nat. Bus. Edn. Assn., Associated Oreg. Faculties, Am. Vocat. Assn. (nominating com. 1976), Adminstrv. Mgmt. Soc., Assn. Info. Sys. Profls. (chpt. v.p. 1977, chpt. pres. 1978—81), Am. Bus. Women's Assn. (chpt. v.p. 1979, pres. 1980, Top Businesswoman in Nation 1980, Bus. Assoc. of Yr. 1986), Albuquerque Federated Rep. Women (hospitality chair 2003—04, 1st v.p. 2004—), Acadiana Rep. Women (gen. chmn. La. Fedn. Rep. Women's Clubs State Conv. 1997, 1st v.p. 1997—98, pres. 1998—2000, asst. state CAP chmn. 1999—2000, Ahrens for Gov. Com. 2002), Rotary (co-chmn. fundraiser com. 2002), Boys and Girls Club of Corvallis (pres. 1991—92), Lafayette Rotary (cmty. svc. dir. 1993—94, bd. dirs. 1993—2000, treas. 1995—96, sec. 1996—97, v.p. 1997—98, pres. 1998—99, Dist. 6200 Found. award 2000), Rotary of Albuquerque del Norte (silent auction chair 2001—02, dep. dir. internat. svc. com. 2002, dist. 5520 dep. dir. permanent fund, asst. gov. 2003—04, dist. 5520 found. chair 2003—06, dist. 5520 internat. chmn. 2004—06, chmn. shrimp fiesta 2005, Dist. 5520 Found. award 2003, 2004, Dist. 5520 Svc. Above Self award 2004—05, Dist. 5520 Found. award 2005, Dist. 5520 Svc. Above Self award 2005—06), Sigma Kappa. Personal E-mail: patriciasonnier@aol.com.

SONNIKSEN, JANET W., education educator; b. Portland, Oreg., Nov. 7, 1942; d. Edward Conrad and Edith Geneve (Matson) Wyss; m. Scott Thomas Sonniksen, Nov.18, 1967 (div. 1976); 1 child, Lara W. Student architecture, U. Oreg., 1960-62; BS, Portland State U., 1963-66, postgrad., 1971-72; MAT, Lewis & Clark Coll., 1995. Cert. tchr., Oreg. Art tchr. Beaverton (Oreg.) Sch. Dist. #48, 1966-69, 76-83, art tchr., 1985—; chair fine arts and applied arts dept. Beaverton H.S., 1990—; designer J & J Designs, Concord, Calif., 1983—, ptnr., 1985—; art tchr. Westview H.S., 1994—2003; ret. Chair Kidspace Artquake, Portland, 1990, 91; adj. instr. art edn. Pacific U., 1997-2003. Artist: sculpture, Useful Objects, NW Exhibit '76, Jurors' Award. Art tchr. coord. Congl. Student Art Exhibn., Les Aucoin Dist., 1988-93, coord. Oreg. Art Edn. Student art exhibit "Youth Art Month", Portland, 1988-93. Named Mentor Tchr., Oreg. State U., 1987-88; recipient Oreg. Secondary Art Educator of Yr. award, 1989, Pacific Regional Secondary Art Educator of Yr. award, 1990, Oreg. Art Educator of Yr. award, 1994, Outstanding Educator Arts award, Beaverton Arts Commn., 2002, Art Cmty. award, 2000. Mem. NEA, Oreg. Art Edn. Assn. (co-dir. state conf. 1991, pres.-elect 1990-92, pres. 1992-94, mus. edn. rep. 1988-90), Nat. Art Edn., Beaverton Edn. Assn., Oreg. Edn. Assn. Republican. Avocations: sewing, reading, travel, calligraphy. Office: Westview High Sch 4200 NW 185th Ave Portland OR 97229-3050

SONS, LINDA RUTH, mathematician, educator; b. Chicago Heights, Ill., Oct. 31, 1939; d. Robert and Ruth (Diekelman) Sons. AB in Math., Ind. U., 1961; MS in Math., Cornell U., 1963, PhD in Math., 1966. Tchg. asst. Cornell U., Ithaca, NY, 1961-63, instr. math., summer 1963, rsch. asst., 1963-65; from asst. prof. to assoc. prof. math. No. Ill. U., De Kalb, 1965—78, prof., 1978—, presdl. tchg. prof., 1994-98, disting. tchg. prof., 1998—, dir. undergrad. studies math. dept., 1971—77, exec. sec. univ. coun., 1978—79, chair faculty fund, 1982—. Author (with others): A Study Guide for Introduction to Mathematics, 1976, Mathematical Thinking in a Quantitative World, 1990, 2003; contbr. articles to profl. jours. Bd. dirs., treas. DeKalb County Migrant Ministry, 1967—78; pres. Luth. Women's Missionary League, 1974—87; mem. campus ministry com. No. Ill. Dist. Luth. Ch./Mo. Synod, Hillside, 1977—2001; mem. ch. coun. Immanuel Luth. Ch., DeKalb, 1978—85, 1987—89, 2005—. Recipient Excellence in Coll. Tchg. award, Ill. Coun. Tchrs. Math., 1991; NSF Rsch. grantee, 1970—72, 1974—75. Mem.: London Math. Soc., Ill. Sect. Math. Assn. Am. (past pres. 1982—87, bd. dirs. 1989—92, v.p. sect., pres., pres.-elect, Disting. Svc. award 1988), Math. Assn. Am. (mem. nat. bd. govs. 1989—92, mem. com. undergrad. program math. 1990—96, chmn. subcom. on quantitative literacy 1990—96, chmn. coun. awards 1997—2003, chmn. Adler award com. 2004—, Disting. Coll. or Univ. Tchg. Math. Sect. award 1995, Cert. Meritorious Svc. Nat. award 1998), Assn. Women in Math., Am. Math. Soc., Sigma Xi (past chpt. pres.), Phi Beta Kappa (pres. No. Ill. assn. 1981—85). Achievements include research in mathematics education and classical complex analysis, especially value distribution for meromorphic functions with unbounded characteristic in the unit disc. Office: No Ill U Dept Math Scis Dekalb IL 60115 Office Phone: 815-753-6760.

SOOD, ARADHANA AVASTHY, psychiatrist, director; arrived in U.S., 1983; m. Rakesh Sood; children: Richi, Shalin, Asherin. BSI, Jiwaji U., India, 1974; MD, Jiwaji U., India, 1979; MSHA, VCU, Va., 2006. Diplomate Fed. Licensing Examination, Am. Bd. Psychiatry and Neurology. Clinical instr. Ohio State U., Columbus, 1986—88; asst. prof. psychiatry VCU, Richmond, Va., 1988—95, assoc. prof. psychiatry, 1995—2005, prof. psychiatry, 2005—, dir. tng. child and adolescent psychiatry, 1994—, chair child and adolescent psychiatry, 2002—; dir. mood disorders clinic VTCC, Richmond, Va., 1996—, dir. ADHD clinic, 1996—. Med. dir. Va. Treatment Ctr. for Children, Richmond, 2001—; divsn. chair child psychiatry VCISHS, Richmond, 2001—, prof. psychiatry, 2005—. Author scientific book chpts. Mem.: Am.

Acad. Child Adolescent Psychiatry (councilor at large 2005—), Am. Med. Assn. (rep. 2004—). Avocations: gardening, reading, music, dance, movies. Office: VCUHS PO Box 980489 515 N 10th St Richmond VA 23298

SOPER, JEANNINE, real estate agent; b. N.Y.C., Nov. 24, 1929; d. Antonio Bruno and Marie Kapuscinski; widowed; children: Erik, Wayne. Grad., Scudder Secretarial Coll., 1948, Realtors Inst., 1970. Sec. Std. Brands Inc., N.Y.C., 1948—52, Armstrong Rubber Co., Norwalk, Conn., 1952—53; real estate sales assoc. V, Ducale Real Estate, Norwalk, 1960—63; owner Sopers Real Estate, Norwalk, 1963—66; owner, ptnr. Siegel and Soper, Realtors, Norwalk, 1966—86; realtor, sales mgr. Prudential Real Estate, Norwalk, 1986—91; realtor Wm. Pitt Real Estate, Norwalk, 1991—. Pres. Women's Coun. Realtors, Conn., 1970, Norwalk Bd. Realtors, 1979. Exhibited in group shows at Rowayton Art Ctr., Darien Art Ctr., others. Chmn. Bd. Assessment Appeals, Norwalk, 1989—; pres., treas. Rowayton (Conn.) Art Ctr., 2000—. Mem.: Wilson Cove Yacht Club (life 1st Woman Commodore 1991). Office: Wm Pitt Sothebys Internat Real Estate 162 East Ave Norwalk CT 06851 Office Phone: 203-838-0018. Personal E-mail: jlsoper@optonline.net.

SOPER, MARSHA ANN PAULSON, counselor; b. Monroe, Wis., Sept. 21, 1954; d. Merlin O. and Priscilla (Peterson) Paulson; m. John B. Soper, June 24, 1978; children: Lachlyn, Sarah, Anna. BS, U. Wis., 1977; MS in Edn., U. Wis., Platteville, 1991. Faculty asst. dept. biochemistry U. Wis., Madison, 1977-78; adminstrv. asst. Rochester (Victoria, Australia) High Sch., 1979-81; project asst. U. Wis. Extension-Green County, Monroe, 1987-90, home economist, 1990; guidance counselor Monroe Pub. Schs., 1991—. EMT Argyle (Wis.) Vol. Ambulance, 1985-2000; Brownie troop leader Girl Scouts Am., 1988-90; pres. bd. dirs. Argyle Libr., 1985-88; mem. Argyle Women's Club, 1984-93, treas., 1987-89; treas. Sunday Sch., Argyle Luth. Ch., 1987-96, ch. coun., 2001—; founding mem Cmty Theater, 1999—; bd. mem. Hist. Argyle, 2001—. Democrat. Avocations: exercise, golf, reading.

SOPHER, VICKI ELAINE, appraiser; b. Streator, Ill., May 22, 1943; d. Donald Bird and Thelma Elsie (Saxton) Watson; m. Terry Ray Sr., Jan. 20, 1962 (div. July 1982); 1 child, Terry Ray Jr. AA, No. Va. Community Coll., 1973; BA, Am. U., 1976; MS, Bank State Coll. Edn., 1986; Cert., Getty Mus. Mgmt. Inst., 1998. Cert. in appraisal courses George Washington U., 2004. Adminstrv. asst. Decatur & Wilson House, Washington, 1977-81; asst. dir. Decatur House/Nat. Trust for Hist. Preservation, Washington, 1981-84, dir., 1984-95; exec. dir. Hammond-Harwood House Assn., Annapolis, Md., 1996-98; curator Nat. Am. Red Cross, Washington, 1999—2004; pres. Vintage Appraisals, Inc., Tampa, Fla., 2005—. Cons.; founder, pres. Historic House Mus. Met. Washington. Mem. Am. Assn. Mus., Mid-Atlantic Assn. Mus., Am. Assn. State and Local History, Victorian Soc. Am. (bd. dirs.), Am. Soc. Appraisers. Home and Office: Vintage Appraisals 3116 W Wallcraft Ave Tampa FL 33611-1943 Office Phone: 815-300-9200. Personal E-mail: vsopher@verizon.net.

SOPKIN, CAROLE A., realtor; b. Chgo., Feb. 26, 1934; d. Earle E. and Pauline M. Zahn; children: Dawn Glaser, Terry, April, Rob, Greg. Realtor, Harper, 1978. Cert. realtor. Importer Tamp Internat., Schaumburg, Ill., 1973—84, Leidecker, Elk Grove, Ill., 1984—85; realtor Century 21 Cambridge, Schaumburg, 1986—97, Century 21 1st Class, Schaumburg, 1998—2000, Coldwell Banker, Schaumburg, 2000—03. Election judge Republican Hoff, Ill., 1980—90. Mem.: Million Dollar Club. Avocations: aerobics, dance.

SORELL STEHR, DEBORAH K., lawyer; b. NYC, 1962; m. Mark Stehr; children: Daniel, Julia. AB, Princeton U., 1984; JD, Northwestern U., 1987. Bar: 1987. With Kronish Lieb Weiner & Hellman, O'Sullivan Graev & Karabell; assoc. gen. counsel Nine West Group Inc., 1996—98; gen. counsel Iconix Brand Group, Inc., 1998—, v.p., 1998—99, sr. v.p., 1999—. Office: Iconix Brand Group Inc 215 W 40th St New York NY 10018 Office Phone: 212-730-0030. Office Fax: 212-391-2057.*

SORENSEN, ELIZABETH JULIA, retired cultural administrator; b. Kenora, Ont., Can., Nov. 24, 1934; d. John Frederick and Irene Margaret (Dowd) MacKellar; m. O. Leo P. Sorensen, July 7, 1956 (div. 1963); children: Lianne Kim Sorensen Kruger. BA, Lakehead U., 1970; MA, Brigham Young U., 1972; Assoc. Royal Conservatory, U. Toronto, 1978; Assoc., Mt. Royal Coll., Calgary, AB, 1978. Sec. Canadian Med. Assn. Manitoba, Winnipeg, 1956-59; legal sec. Filmore, Riley & Co., Winnipeg, 1961-63; tchr. Fort Frances (Ont.) High Sch., 1963-70; instr. drama, speech, English Lethbridge (Alta.) C.C., 1972-77; tchr. bus. edn. Henderson Coll. Bus., Lethbridge, 1978-80; supt. cultural svcs. City Medicine Hat, Alta., 1980-99; ret., 1999. Mem. Stirling Hist. Soc. (sec.). Mem. Lds Ch. Avocations: directing plays, writing, genealogy, storytelling, scrapbooking.

SORENSEN, JACKI FAYE, choreographer, aerobic dance company executive; b. Oakland, Calif., Dec. 10, 1942; d. Roy C. and Juanita F. (Bullon) Mills; m. Neil A. Sorensen, Jan. 3, 1965. BA, U. Calif., 1964. Cert. tchr., Calif. Ptnr., Big Spring Sch. Dance, 1965; tchr. Pasadena Ave. Sch., Sacramento, 1968; founder, pres., choreographer Jacki's Inc., DeLand, Fla., 1990—; cons., lectr. on phys. fitness. Author: Aerobic Dancing, 1979, Jacki Sorensen's Aerobic Lifestyle Book, 1983; choreographer numerous dance exercises for records and videocassettes. Trustee Women's Sports Found. Recipient Diamond Pin award Am. Heart Assn., 1979, Individual Contbn. award Am. Assn. Fitness Dirs. in Bus. and Industry, 1981, Spl. Olympics Contbn. award, 1982, Contbn. to Women's Fitness award Pres.'s Coun. Phys. Fitness and Sports, 1982, Healthy Am. Fitness Leader award U.S. Jaycees, 1984, Lifetime Achievement award Internat. Dance Exercise Assn., 1985, New Horizons award Caldwell (N.J.) Coll., 1985, Legend of Aerobics award City Sports mag., 1985; Pres. Coun. award Calif. Womens' Leadership Conf., 1986, Hall of Fame award Club Industry mag., 1986, IDEA, 1992. Mem. AAHPERD, AFTRA, Am. Coll. Sports Medicine, Nat. Intramural and Recreation Assn. Office: care Jacki's Inc 129 1/2 N Woodland Blvd Ste 5 Deland FL 32720-4269 Home and Office: 2578 Enterprise Rd # 155 Orange City FL 32763-7904

SORENSEN, LINDA, lawyer; b. Eureka, Calif., Mar. 3, 1945; BS, U. Wis., 1967; JD, U. Calif., 1976. Bar: Calif. 1976, U.S. Dist. Ct. (no. dist.) Calif. 1976, U.S. Ct. Appeals (9th cir.) 1976, U.S. Dist. Ct. (ea. dist.) Calif. 1977. Assoc., ptnr. Rothschild, Phelan & Mortali, San Francisco, 1976-88; dir. Howard, Rice, Nemerovski, Canady, Falk & Rabkin, San Francisco, 1988-95; shareholder Feldman, Waldman & Kline, P.C., San Francisco, 1997-99; pvt. practice Berkeley, Calif., 1999—; of counsel Stromsheim & Assoc., 2001—. Mem. ABA (mem. subcom. on avoiding powers, bus. bankruptcy com. 1983-95), Bar Assn. of San Francisco (chmn. comml. law and bankruptcy sect. 1984, editor fed. cts. com., no. dist. Calif. digest 1979-82). Office: PO Box 325 Bodega Bay CA 94923 Office Fax: 707-875-9287. Personal E-mail: lindasorensen@earthlink.net.

SORENSEN, SHEILA, state legislator; b. Chgo., Sept. 20, 1947; d. Martin Thomas Moloney and Elizabeth (Koehr) Paulus; m. Wayne B. Slaughter, May, 1969 (div. 1976); 1 child, Wayne Benjamin III; m. Dean E. Sorensen, Feb. 14, 1977; (stepchildren) Michael, Debbie, Kevin, Dean C. BS, Loretto Heights Coll., Denver, 1965; postgrad. pediatric nurse practicioner, U. Colo., Denver, 1969-70. Pediatric nurse practicioner Pub. Health Dept., Denver, 1970-71, Boise, Idaho, 1971-72, Boise (Idaho) Pediatric Group, 1972-74, Pediatric Assocs., Boise, 1974-77; mem. Idaho Ho. Reps., 1987-92, Idaho Senate, Dist. 13, Boise, 1992—; chair senate health and welfare com. Idaho Senate, 1992-94, chair senate majority caucus, 1994-96, vice chair state affairs com., 1996-98, chair state affairs, 1998—. State chair Am. Legis. Exchange Coun. Precinct committeeman Ada County Rep. Ctrl. Com., Boise, 1982-86, dist. vice chair, 1985-88; polit. chair Idaho Med. Assn. Aux., 1984-87, Ada County Med. Assocs., 1986-87; bd. dirs. Family Practice Residency Program, 1992-94, Univ./Cmty. Health Sci. Assn., Bishop Kelly Found., 1993—99; chair Senate Majority Caucus, 1995-96, chair state affairs com., 1999—; mem. adv. com. on health care edn. and workforce devel. State Bd. Edn., mem. adv. bd. Drug Free Idaho., Boise State U. Master of Health Sci. Recipient AMA Nathan Davis award for Outstanding State Legislator, 1994. Mem. Nat. Conf. State Legislators, Nat. Orgn. Women Legislators (state chair), Am. Legis. Exch. Coun. (Legis of Yr. award 1999). Roman Catholic. Office Phone: 208-870-8081. Personal E-mail: sheilasorensen@hawaii.rr.com.

SORENSON, GEORGIA LYNN JONES, political science professor; b. Abilene, Tex., Aug. 23, 1947; d. Wyly King and Olive M. (Sorenson) Jones; 1 child, Suzanna Simmonds Strasburg. BA, Am. U., 1974; MA, Hood Coll., 1976; PhD, U. Md., 1992. Social scientist Nat. Inst. Edn., Washington, 1978-79, U.S. Commn. Civil Rights, Washington, 1976-79; sr. policy analyst The White House, Washington, 1979-80; founder, sr. scholar James MacGregor Burns Acad. Leadership U. Md., College Park, 1980—; Inaugural chair and prof. transformation U.S. Army, Army War Coll., 2005—. Adv. mem. W.K. Kellogg Found. Nat Fellows, Battle Creek, Mich., 1996-99; inaugural choir, prof. transformation U.S. Army, U.S. Army War Coll., 2005-06. Co-author: (with James MacGregor Burns) Dead-Center: Clinton-Gore Leadership and the Perils of Moderation, 1999; editor: (with George Goethals and James MacGregor Burns) Encyclopedia of Leadership, 2004; contbr. articles to profl. jours. Chair Md. Women's Polit. Caucus, 1991-94; mem. White House Productivity Coun., Washington, 1979; mem. V.P. Youth Employment Task Force, 1979-80. Mem. Am. Polit. Sci. Assn., Internat. Soc. Polit. Psychologists, A.K. Rice Inst. Office: James MacGregor Burns Acad Leadership Univ Md College Park MD 20742-0001 Office Phone: 301-405-6100. Business E-Mail: gsorenson@academy.umd.edu.

SORENSON, GRETCHEN HARTLEY, elementary school educator; b. Muncie, Ind., Dec. 3, 1935; d. James Ross and Lois (Reed) Hartley; m. Ray L. Valour, June 6, 1959 (div. June 1988); 1 child, Virginia; m. George W. Sorenson, June 17, 1988. BFA, Colo. U., 1957; MA in Edn., Ball State U., 1961; cert. elem. edn. administrn., Ariz. State U., 1980. Cert. elem. art, elem. classroom, elem. administrn. Art tchr. Jefferson County (Colo.) Schs., Jefferson County, Colo., 1957-59; tchr. Delaware County Schs., Selma, Ind., 1959-60, Beverly (Mass.) Schs., 1960-61, Delaware County Schs., Muncie, Ind., 1961-66, Park Forest (Ill.) Schs., 1966-68, Scottsdale (Ariz.) Pub. Schs., 1968—95, Trinity Luth. Sch., Fountain Hills, Ariz., 1995—. Trainer of tchrs. Ariz. Bar Found., Phoenix, 1988-93; mem. site-based mgmt. team Laguna Sch., 1990-91. Author: (book) Fifth of Fun, 1986. Mem. ch. bd. Paradise Valley (Ariz.) United Meth. Ch., 1970-74, Desert Hills Presbyn. Ch., Carefree, Ariz., 1975-87, Shepherd Desert Luth. Ch., Scottsdale, 1988—; mem. exec. bd. Luth. Hispanic Ministry; mem. Scottsdale Bicentennial Commn., 1987-90. Recipient Outstanding Young Educator, C. of C., Park Forest, 1968. Mem. Phi Delta Kappa (treas. 1988-91, Outstanding Educator award 1992). Lutheran. Avocations: travel, reading. Home: 15043 E Greene Valley Dr Fountain Hills AZ 85268-1339 E-mail: g2sorenson@att.net.

SORENSON, KATHERINE ANN, elementary school educator; b. Hastings, Minn., Aug. 30, 1947; d. Fredrick William Nearing and Marguerite Lucille Keene-Nearing; m. Michael Alfred Sorenson; children: Brock, Scott. BS in Edn., Black Hills State Coll., 1972; MA in Early Childhood Edn., U. Colo., Denver, 1995. Profl. tchr. lic. Colo., cert. reading recover tchr. Tchr. Maternity Mary Cath. Sch., St. Paul, 1967—68, St. Andrew's Cath. Sch., St. Paul, 1968—70, Hill City Pub. Sch., 1972—73, Groton Pub. Sch., 1973—75; substitute tchr. Billings Pub. Sch., 1975—76; tchr. Livingston Pub. Sch., 1977—85; asst. dir. childcare Children's Creative Encounters, Littleton, Colo., 1986—87; tchr. Cherry Creek Sch. Dist., Eastridge Elem., Aurora, Colo., 1987—96, 1996—; creator immerson program for mobile at risk students, edn. cons., 2004—. Co-author: Blue Ribbon Application, 1998 (Blue Ribbon School, 1999), Reading Recovery Longitudinal Analysis, National Association for Year Round Education Application. Pack leader Boy Scouts Am., Parker, 1988—94, bd. dirs., 1988—94; mem. Cherry Creek Schs. North Area Task Force, Aurora, 2001—03; Sunday sch. tchr. St. Mary's Cath. Ch., Livingston, 1978—84, religious edn. coord., 1981—82; Sunday sch. tchr. Ave Maria Cath. Ch., Parker, 1992—94; mem. team fundraising Parker Baseball, 1989—92; sec. Moorhead Foster Parent Assn., 1976—77. Recipient Dewitt Wallace Libr. Power award, Dewitt Wallace Found., 1997, Exemplary Reading Program award, Colo. Coun. Internat. Reading, 1998-1999, Tchr. of the Yr. award, Cherry Creek Sch.-Eastridge Elem., 2003, Reading Recovery Excellence award, Morgridge, 2004. Mem.: Cherry Creek Edn. Assn., Reading Recovery Assn., Colo. Coun. Internat. Reading Assn. Avocations: reading, travel, southwest history, quilting. Home: 11182 Cambridge Ct Parker CO 80138 Office: Eastridge Elem Sch 11777 E Wesley Ave Aurora CO 80014

SORENSON, LIANE BETH MCDOWELL, director, state legislator; b. Chgo., Aug. 13, 1947; d. Harold Davidson McDowell and Frances Elanor (Williams) Daisey Van Kleeck; m. Boyd Wayne Sorenson, June 30, 1973; children: Nathan, Matthew, Dana. BS in Edn., U. Del., 1969, M in Counseling with honors, 1986. Tchr. Avon Grove Sch. Dist., West Grove, Pa., 1969-70, Alexis I. duPont Sch. Dist., Wilmington, Del., 1970-73, Barrington (Ill.) Sch. Dist., 1973-75; counseling intern Medill Intensive Learning Ctr.-Christina Sch. Dist., Newark, Del., 1985; counselor Family Violence Shelter CHILD, Inc., Wilmington, 1985, 86-87, dir. parent edn. programs, 1987-88; dir. Office Women's Affairs, exec. dir. Commn. on Status of Women U. Del., Newark, 1988—; mem. Dist. 6 Del. Senate, Dover, 1992—, minority whip. Chair Del. Ho. Edn. Com., 1992—, Adv. Bd. Del. Breast Cancer Coalition, 1998—; commr. Edn. Commn. State Del.; mem. tng. com. Nat. Conf. State Legislatures; mem. Bd. Women's Network Nat. Conf. State Legislatures; mem. joint sunset com. Del. Legislature, Del. House of Reps., 1992-94, Del. Senate, 1994—, Del. Legis. Joint Fin. Com. Del. Legis., 1994—, Coun. State Govts. Toll Fellowship. Presenter papers various meetings & confs. Pres. bd. dirs. Nursing Mothers, Inc., 1980-81; trustee Hockessin Montessori Sch., 1982-84, enrollment chair, 1982-83; trustee Hockessin Pub. Libr., 1982-84, pres. bd., 1982-84; bd. dirs. Del. Coalition for Children, 1986-88; bd. dirs. Children's Bur. Del., 1984-87, sec., 1985-87; pres. Jr. League Wilmington, 1986-87, rsch. coun. v.p., 1985-86; bd. dirs. YWCA New Castle County, 1989-91; pres. Del. Women's Agenda, 1986-88; vice-chair Women's Leadership Ctr., 1992—; mem. Del. Work Family Coalition; bd. dirs. Del. divsn. Am. Cancer Soc., 1993—. Grantee Del. Dept. Svcs. to Children, Youth and Their Families, 1987-88, 1988, State of Del. Gen. Assembly, 1992; recipient Disting. Legis. Svc. award Del. State Bar Assn., 1997, Del Tufo award Delaware Humanities Forum, 1999. Mem.: Hockessin Hist. Soc. (bd. mem. 2000—), Del. Family Law Commn., Del. Alliance for Arts in Edn., Del. Greenway and Trails Coun., Am. Assn. for Higher Edn. (chair women's caucus 1991—92, program chair women's caucus 1990—91, pre-conf. workshop coord. women's caucus 1990 Ann. Conf.), Rotary (charter mem. Hackessin Pike Creek club 1994—). Republican. Methodist. Avocations: camping, hiking. Office: State of Delaware Legislative Hall Rm 210 PO Box 1401 Dover DE 19903-1401

SORENSON, LYNETTE EVELYN, librarian; b. Bellingham, Wash., Mar. 13, 1955; d. Floyd Theodore and Evelyn Marie (Askland) Sorenson. B in Religious Edn., Prairie Bible Coll., Can., 1977; B in Liberal Studies, Master's Coll., 1989; MLS, U. Wash., 1992; MA in Ednl. Tech., Pepperdine U., 2004. User svcs. libr. NW U., Kirkland, Wash., 1993—. Libr. tech adv. bd. mem. Lake Wash. Tech. Coll., Kirkland, 1998—2001. Vol. usher Bellevue (Wash.) Philharm. Orch., 1997—2002. Mem.: Assn. Christian Librs. (asst. conf. coord. 2002, conf. presentation coord. 2000—, outstanding vol. svc. award 2002). Avocations: walking, quilting, reading. Office: NW U 5520 108th Ave NE Kirkland WA 98033 Office Phone: 425-889-5302. Business E-Mail: lynette.sorenson@northwestu.edu.

SORENSON, SANDRA LOUISE, retired retail executive; b. Santa Monica, Calif., Nov. 30, 1948; d. Edward John and Gordon Dudley (Pollock) S. BA in Telecommunications, BS in Mktg., U. So. Calif., 1970. Merchandiser Montgomery Ward Inc., Los Angeles, 1970-82; sr. fin. planner Plums Co., Los Angeles, 1982-84; mgr. merchandising systems devel. and tng. Millers Outpost, Ontario, Calif., 1984-89; merchandising systems specialist Oshmans Sporting Goods, Santa Ana, Calif., 1989-90; sr. dir. planning and allocations Clothestime, Anaheim, Calif., 1990-96; dir. planning and allocation Pacific Sunwear, Anaheim, 1996-97; sr. dir. planning and allocation Clothestime Anaheim, 1997—2003; ret., 2003. Vol. Pomona Valley Hosp. Aux.; officer in charge of grants Assistance League Pomona Valley. Recipient Achievement award Bicentennial Com. Norwalk, Calif., 1976. Mem. Commerce Assocs., Internat. Platform Soc., Mensa, Chi Omega, Phi Chi Theta, Alpha Epsilon Rho. Republican. Mem. Reformed Ch. Am. Home: 14913 Little Bend Rd Chino Hills CA 91709-3494 Personal E-mail: ssorenso@aol.com.

SORENSTAM, ANNIKA, professional golfer; b. Stockholm, Oct. 9, 1970; m. David Esch. Student, U. Ariz. With Women's Profl. Golf European Tour, 1992—, LPGA, 1993—, Swedish Nat. Team, 1987-92, Solheim Cup Team, 1994, 96, 98; playing editor Golf Digest, 2006—, Golf for Women, 2006—. Recipient Vare Trophy award, 1998, Espy Awards for Best Female Golfer, ESPN, 1996, 1998, 1999, 2002-2004, Espy Award for Best Female Athlete, 2006; named Rolex Player of Yr., 1995, 97, 98, 2000-2003, Female Athlete of Yr., AP, 2003. Achievements in Tournaments won include: Australian Ladies Open, 1994, U.S. Women's Open, 1995, 96, 2006, Ladies Masters, 1995, 2000, 2002, LPGA Championship, 1997, 2002-2004, Women's British Open, 2003, first woman since 1945 to appear in a PGA Tour event, 2003, inducted into World Golf Hall of Fame, 2003, 61 career LPGA Tour victories, topped $2 million in earnings 2001-2004, only woman in LPGA history to ever go over $2 million in one season. Office: LPGA 100 International Golf Dr Daytona Beach FL 32124-1092

SORGE, KAREN LEE, printing company executive, consultant; b. Warwick, N.Y., May 27, 1958; d. Wesley Thomas and Margaret Anne (Storms) Kervatt; m. David W. Farquhar, July 16, 1982 (div. Feb. 1990); 1 child: Lauren Nicole; m. Thomas E. Sorge, May 16, 1997; children: Natalie MaKalen Sorge, Ryan Thomas. AS, Roger Williams Coll., 1978, BS cum laude, 1980. Office mgr. Price-Rite Printing Co., Dover, NJ, 1975—76; cons. SBA, Bristol, RI, 1978—80; account exec. P.M. Press Inc., Dallas, 1980—90, sales trainer, 1984—85; v.p. KDF Bus. Forms Inc., Dallas, 1984—90; account exec. Jarvis Press, Dallas, 1990—; pres. Print Trends, Dallas, 1990—. Printer Tex. Aux. Charity Auction Orgn., Dallas, 1985, Cystic Fibrosis, Dallas, 1989—93, Life Enhancement Assn. Programs Found., 1992—, Dallas Soc. Visual Comm., 1992, AIDS Resources Com., Dallas chpt. Cerebral Palsy, 1994, Lloyd-Paxton AIDS Benefit, 1994, Feast for the Eyes Gala-Benefit to Prevent Blindness, 2001, Genesis Women's Shelter, 2002, others. Recipient award, Clampitt Paper Co., Dallas, 1982, P.M. Press Inc., 1983—89, Mead Paper Co., 1985—96, Feast for the Eyes Gala, 2001, Gold award, Adrian Advt., 2004, Silver award, 2005, 2006. Mem. Printing Industry in Am. (recipient Judges Favorite award 1992, Best of Show Hon. Mention award 1994, gold award Best of Tex. 1996), Internat. Assn. Bus. Communicators, Nat. Bus. Forms Assn. Republican. Baptist. Avocation: piano. Home: 2600 Raintree Dr Southlake TX 76092-5536 Office Phone: 817-424-5252. E-mail: printtrends@aol.com.

SORGEN, ELIZABETH ANN, retired elementary school educator; b. Ft. Wayne, Ind., Aug. 21, 1931; d. Lee E. and Miriam N. (Bixler) Walker; m. Don DuWayne Sorgen, Mar. 8, 1952; children: Kevin D., Karen Lee Sorgen Hoeppner, Keith Alan. BS in Edn., Ind. U., 1953; MS in Edn., St. Francis Coll., Ft. Wayne, 1967. Tchr., bldg. rep. and math. book adoption rep. East Allen County Schs., Monroeville, Ind., 1953-94, ret., 1994. Founder nursery sch., choir mem. St. Marks Luth. Ch., Monroeville, 1960—; vol. Sci. Ctrl.; pres. Heritage Homemakers, 1990-2000; substitute tchr. Recipient Golden Apple award East Allen County Schs., 1976, Monroeville Tchr. of Yr. award, 1993. Mem.: AAUW, Ft. Wayne Ret. Tchrs. Assn. Avocations: square and line dancing, camping, gardening. Home: 25214 Lincoln Hwy E Monroeville IN 46773-9710 Personal E-mail: dubeth@webtv.net.

SORIANO, NANCY MERNIT, editor-in-chief; married; 1 child. Degree in Art History, Bard Coll. Former editor Good Food; former contbg. editor Cosmopolitan, Food & Wine, Brides; joined Country Living, 1982, assoc. decorating editor, home bldg. and arch. editor, exec. editor, 1995—98, editor-in-chief, 1998—. Founder Country Living Restoration Mag., 1996. Design editor (book series) American Country Design, Time Life Books, editor spl. interest publ. Country Living Dream Homes; co-author: (books) Country Living Decorating Style: The New Look of Country, 1999, Country Living Decorating with Baskets: Accents for Every Room, 2000, Country Living Decorating with Candles, 2000, Country Living Handmade Christmas: Decorating Your Tree and Home, 2001, Country Living Handmade Halloween, 2002, Stylish Renovations: Design Ideas for Old and New Houses, 2002. Office: Heart Corp Country Living 224 W 57th St Fl 7 New York NY 10019-3212*

SORKIN, JENNI, curator, critic; b. Chgo. BFA, Sch. of Art Inst. of Chgo., 1999; MA, Bard Coll., 2002; student PhD program in History of Art, Yale U., 2004—. Former curatorial rsch. asst., project coord. Mus. Contemporary Art, LA; former rsch. asst. Dept. Contemporary Programs and Rsch. Getty Rsch. Inst. Curator (exhibitions include) High Performance: The First Five Years, 1978-1982, Bard Coll., 2002, LA Contemporary Exhibitions, 2003, Judy Chicago: Minimalism, 1965-1973, LewAllen Contemporary, Santa Fe, 2004. Recipient Art Jour. Award for article Envisioning High Performance, Coll. Art Assn., 2004. Mem.: Queer Caucus for Art (co-chair 2004—). Office: Yale U Hist of Art Dept 56 High St New Haven CT 06520

SOROSKY, JERI P., academic administrator; b. Chgo. d. Hans S. and Florence J. (Hurwitz) Pakula; m. Gene E. Sorosky; children: Cindi, Dana, Lesli. BA, Roosevelt U., Chgo., 1952; MEd, Fla. Atlantic U., Boca Raton, 1967; EdS, Nova Southeastern U., Ft. Lauderdale, Fla., 1972; EdD, MS, Nova Southeastern U., 1981. Cert. adminstr., supr., media specialist, gifted and elem. educator, Fla. Chairperson Elem. Highland Oaks, North Miami Beach, Fla., 1967-75; mem. faculty gifted program Highland Oaks Gifted Ctr., North Miami Beach, 1975-85; chairperson gifted program Miami (Fla.) Dade C.C., 1985-2000; site adminstr. grad. tchr. edn. program Nova. Southeastern U., Ft. Lauderdale, 1992—2004. Adj. prof. Nova Southeastern U., Ft. Lauderdale, 1979-87, adv. doctoral practicums, 1985-00, cluster coord., 1987-03, admissions com. doctoral programs Tech. and Distance Edn. and Child and Youth Studies, 1996-03, adj. prof. innovative math, 2004-, adj. prof. early childhood, 2004-; chairperson gifted edn. Dade County Schs., Miami, 1990-93; mem. com. State Gifted Task Force, Tallahassee, 1992; presenter in field. Author: GEM Major Module in Gifted Education, 1981, Ideas Unlimited, 1985, Guide for Elementary Educators, 1995, Technology in the Curriculum, 1998; editor: Readings: Gifted Education, 1991, Early Childhood Education, 1982. Project chairperson Kids in Distress, Ft. Lauderdale, 1989. Named Woman of Yr. Bus. Profl. Women, 1985. Mem. Fla. Assn. Gifted (charter, v.p. 1975-97), Nova Southeastern U. Alumni (bd. dirs. 1981-97), AAUW, Phi Delta Kappa (chairperson newsletter 1985-97). Avocations: dance, technology. Office: Nova Southeastern U 1750 NE 167th St North Miami Beach FL 33162-3017 Business E-Mail: jeris@nova.edu.

SORRELL, ROZLYN, singer, actress, educator, theater director; b. Bklyn. d. Nathaniel Otis and Cupid Viola (Logan) S. BA in Theatre, CUNY, 1976, MS in Edn., 1985. Cert. tchr. Calif., NY. Tchr. LA Unified Sch. Dist., 1997, Sylvan Learning Ctr., LA, 1998, Westmark Sch., Encino, Calif., 2000, Achievement Sch., Raleigh, NC, 2002, Easter Seals UCP, NC, 2006. Bus. cons., LA, 1989—; voice tchr., LA, 1992—; mem. Albert McNeil Jubilee Singers, LA, 1994—2000. Actress various TV programs, commls., stage prodn. and films, 1986—; soloist Temple of Music and Art, Tucson, 1990, El San Juan (PR) Hotel, 1985, Hour of Power, Glory of Christmas, Glory of Easter, Garden Grove, Calif., 1994—, Miyazaki Civic Culture Hall, Japan, 1996, Anaheim Pond, Calif., 1997, Honolulu Symphony, 1998, Hollywood Bowl, Calif., 1998, Gospel Recording Artist, 2000, Harris Teeter Harvest Festival, Raleigh Conv. Ctr., 2004, Carolina Theatre, Durham, NC, 2005, Spiritual Awakening, WRAL-TV, N.C., 2004, Pops in the Park, Regency Theatre, Cary, NC, 2004, 05, 06, African Am. Cultural Ctr., Raleigh, NC, 2004, Greensboro Coliseum, 2005, Progress Energy Ctr. Performing Arts, Meymandi Concert Hall, Raleigh, NC, 2006, N.C. Fairgrounds, 2006; guest artist, soloist N.C.

Symphony, 2006; dir. Storms of Life, 2005. Mem. AFTRA, SAG, Actors Equity Assn. Avocations: dance, walking, theater, exercise. Office Phone: 866-686-0713. Personal E-mail: rozlyn@rozlynsorrell.com. Business E-Mail: sorrell@sorrell-intl.com.

SORRELLS, KRISTEEN, violinist, music therapist; b. Mt. Pleasant, Mich., Mar. 28, 1956; d. Daniel Jackson and Eleanor Kathryn Sorrells; m. Ernest Fillmore Windsor, Sept. 2, 1959. BA, U. Ga., Athens, 1978; MusM, U. Ga., 1985. Registered music therapist Ga., 1985, cert. tchr. Ga., 2001. Violist Atlanta Ballet Orch., 1986—, Atlanta Opera Orch., 1986—2006. Pvt. viola and violin tchr. Lovett Sch., Atlanta. Mem.: Am. String Tchrs. Assn. (chamber music workshop chair 1999—2005). Home: 222 Flora Ave Atlanta GA 30307 Office: Ridgeview Middle Schoo 5340 Trimble Rd Atlanta GA 30342 Office Phone: 404-843-7710. E-mail: sorrells@fulton.k12.ga.us.

SORRENTI, RUSHIE GOWAN, literature and language educator; b. Union, SC, Sept. 14, 1951; d. Donald Mansel and Frances Lawson Gowan; m. Larry Sorrenti, Mar. 29, 1986; m. Richard Bedenbaugh, June 17, 1973 (div. Aug. 21, 1981); 1 child, Jason Wesley Bedenbaugh. BS, Winthrop U., 1973. Cert. Elem. Edn. SC. Tchr. Howe Hall Mid. Sch., Goose Creek, SC, 1973—76, Pine Ridge Mid. Sch., W. Columbia, SC, 1977—86, Dacusville Mid., Easley, SC, 1986—, mentor, 1996—; adept evaluator Pickens Sch. Dist., Easley, 2005—. Beta club sponsor Howe Hall Mid., 1973—76, student coun. sponsor, 1973—75, newspaper reporter, 1974—76; cheerleader sponsor Pine Ridge Mid., W. Columbia, 1977—82, Dacusville Mid., 1986—91, English dept. chair, 1992—2001, sch. comm. team, 2005—. Singer: Wizard of Oz, PACT Pep Rallies; dir.: Queen of the Dacusville Doosies. Bd. mem., sec. Midlands Baseball League, W. Columbia, 1984—86. Recipient Tchr. of Yr., Dacusville Mid., 1991—92; grantee, State Dept. Ed., 1997-1999. Bapt. Avocations: travel, reading. Home: 135 Lakeshore Dr Easley SC 29642 Office: Dacusville Mid Sch 899 Thomas Mill Rd Easley SC 29640 Office Phone: 864-859-6049. Personal E-mail: rsorr34015@aol.com. Business E-Mail: sorrentr@pickens.k12.sc.us.

SORRENTINO, RENATE MARIA, illustrator; b. Mallnitz, Carinthia, Austria, June 21, 1942; came to the U.S., 1962; d. Johann and Theresia (Kritzer) Weinberger; m. Philip Rosenberg, Nov. 22, 1968 (dec. 1982); m. Francis J. Sorrentino, Sept. 4, 1988. Grad. gold and silversmith artist, Höhere Technische Lehranstalt, Austria, 1961. Draftswoman Elecon Inc., N.Y.C., 1962-65; jr. designer Automatics Metal Prod. Corp., N.Y.C., 1965-70; designer, art dir. Autosplice, Inc., Woodside, NY, 1970-90; freelance artist Jupiter, Fla., 1990—. Patentee Quick Disconnect from Continuous Wire, 1977. Home: 2301 Marina Isle Way Apt 404 Jupiter FL 33477-9423 Office: Autosplice Inc 10121 Barnes Canyon Rd San Diego CA 92121-5797 E-mail: sorrenate@adelphia.net.

SORSTOKKE, ELLEN KATHLEEN, marketing executive, educator; b. Seattle, Mar. 31, 1954; d. Harold William and Carrol Jean (Russ) Sorstokke. MusB with distinction, U. Ariz., 1976; postgrad., UCLA Extension, 1979-83, L.A. Valley Coll., 1984-85, Juilliard Extension, fall 1987, U. Calif. Berkeley Extension, 1992-93. Pvt. practice music tchr., Tucson, 1975—77, Whiteriver, Ariz., 1977—78, L.A., 1980—85, S.I., N.Y.C., 1986—89; music tchr. Eloy (Ariz.) Elem. Schs., 1976-77, Whiteriver (Ariz.) Pub. Schs., 1977-78; svc. writer, asst. svc. mgr. Alfa of Santa Monica, Calif., 1978-79; purchasing agt. Advance Machine Corp., L.A., 1979-80; asst. mgr. Atlantic Nuclear Svcs., Gardena, Calif., 1980-81; mgr. Blue Lady's World Music Ctr., L.A., 1981-83; instrument specialist Baxter-Northup Music Co., Sherman Oaks, Calif., 1983-85; dir. mktg. Mandolin Bros., Ltd., S.I., N.Y., 1985-89; product mgr. Gibson Guitar Corp., Nashville, 1989; sales mgr. Saga Musical Instruments, South San Francisco, Calif., 1990-91, mktg. dir., 1991-95, mktg. analyst, 2002—. Freelance mktg. cons., S.I., Foster City, Atlanta, 1986—; freelance cons. www.fussycats.com, 2002; music cons. 20th Century Fox, L.A., 1984; freelance music copyist and orchestrator, Tucson, L.A., N.Y.C., 1972-89; freelance graphic designer and advt., N.Y.C., S.I., Foster City, Atlanta, 1986—. Contbr. articles to profl. jours. Campaign worker Richard Jones for Supr., Tucson, 1972; mem., program book designer Marina Del Rey-Westchester Symphony Orch., L.A., 1981-83. Scholar U. Ariz., 1973-76, ASCAP scholar UCLA, 1980-81. Mem. Tucson Flute Club (publicity chmn. 1974-75, v.p. 1975-76). Republican. Personal E-mail: esorstok@bellsouth.net.

SORSTOKKE, SUSAN EILEEN, systems engineer; b. Seattle, May 2, 1955; d. Harold William and Carrol Jean (Russ) Sorstokke. BS in Systems Engrng., U. Ariz., 1976; MBA, U. Wash., Richland, 1983. Warehouse team mgr. Procter and Gamble Paper Products, Modesto, Calif., 1976-78; quality assurance engr. Westinghouse Hanford Co., Richland, Wash., 1978-80, supr. engrng. document ctr., 1980-81; mgr. data control and adminstrn. Westinghouse Electric Corp., Madison, Pa., 1981-82, mgr. data control and records mgmt., 1982-84; prin. engr. Westinghouse Elevator Co., Morristown, NJ, 1984-87, region adminstrn. mgr. Arleta, Calif., 1987-90; ops. rsch. analyst Am. Honda Motor Co. Inc., Torrance, Calif., 1990-95; project leader parts sys. Am. Honda Motor Co., Inc., Torrance, Calif., 1995-96, mgr. parts systems and part number adminstrn., 1996-97, mgr. parts systems, 1997-2000, mgr. supply chain mgmt., 2000—02, mgr. process control and regulatory issues, 2002—. Adj. prof. U. LaVerne, Calif., 1991—92; pres. Fussy Cuts Inc., Torrance, Calif., 2000—05. Advisor Jr. Achievement, 1982—83; literacy tutor Westmoreland Literacy Coun., 1983—84; host parent EF Found., Saugus, Calif., 1987—88, Am. Edn. Connection, Saugus, 1988—89, 1991; instr. Excell, L.A., 1991—92; mem. Calif. Acad. Math. and Sci., 1996—97. Mem.: Am. Inst. Indsl. Engrs., Soc. Women Engrs., Optomists Charities Inc. (bd. dirs. Acton, Calif. 1991—94). Republican. Methodist. Home: 2567 Plaza Del Amo Unit 205 Torrance CA 90503-8962 Office: Am Honda Motor Co Inc Dept Parts 100 5C 3B 1919 Torrance Blvd Torrance CA 90501-2722 Office Phone: 310-783-2854. Personal E-mail: ssorstokke@msn.com.

SORTUN, ANA, food service executive; b. Seattle; Fluency degree, L'Ecole Francais; grand diplome, La Varenne Ecole de Cuisine, Paris; diploma in Wine Studies, L'Academie du Vin. Pastry asst. and rounds cook with chef Tom Douglas Café Sport, Seattle; exec. chef Aigo Bistro, Concord, Mass., 1990; co-opener with Moncef Medeb 8 Holyoke, Cambridge, Mass.; exec. chef Casablanca, Cambridge; chef, owner Oleana, Cambridge, 2001—. Nominee Best New Restaurant, James Beard, 2002, Best Chef, Northeast, 2003, 2004; named Best New Chef, Boston Mag., Rising Star in the city's restaurant cmty., Esquire Mag.; recipient Best Chef, Northeast, 2005. Avocation: travel. Office: Oleana 134 Hampshire St Cambridge MA 02139 Office Phone: 617-661-0505. Business E-Mail: oleanarestaurant@earthlink.net.*

SORVINO, MIRA, actress; b. Tenafly, N.J., Sept. 28, 1967; d. Paul Sorvino and Lorraine Davis; m. Christopher Backus, June 11, 2004, children: Mattea Angel, Johnny BA in Asian Studies, Harvard U., 1990. Actor (films) New York Cop, 1993, The Obit Writer, 1993, Barcelone, 1994, Quiz Show, 1994, The Dutch Master, 1994, Mighty Aphrodite, 1995 (Acad. award for Best Supporting Actress), Blue in the Face, 1995, Beautiful Girls, 1996, Tarantella, 1996, Sweet Nothing, 1996, Tales of Erotica, 1996, New York Cop, 1996, Romy and Michele's High School Reunion, 1997, Mimic, 1997 The Replacement Killers, 1998, Too Tired to Die, 1998, Lulu on the Bridge, 1998, Free Money, 1998, Summer of Sam, 1999, At First Sight, 1999, Joan of Arc: The Virgin Warrior, 2000, Triumph of Love, 2001, The Grey Zone, 2001, Wise Girls, 2002, Semana Santa, 2002, Between Strangers, 2002, Gods and Generals, 2003, The Final Cut, 2003; actor, assoc. prodr., Amongst Friends, 1993; actor (TV movies) Parallel Lives, 1994, The Second Greatest Story Ever Told, 1994, Jake's Women, 1996, Norma Jean and Marilyn, 1996, The Great Gatsby, 2001, Human Tafficking, 2005; (TV mini-series) The Buccaneers, 1995, Covert One: The Hades Factor, 2006; (TV appearances) The Guiding Light, 1991, The Swans Crossing, 1992, 1995, Will & Grace, 2003; prodr. (films) Famous, 2000 Office: The William Morris Agy 151 El Camino Dr Beverly Hills CA 90212*

SOSA, RITA SLADEN, social sciences educator; b. Providence, Apr. 27, 1947; d. Sidney B. and Margaret (Casey) Sladen; m. Alejandro A. Sosa Sr., Nov. 22, 1969; 1 child, Alejandro A. Jr. BS, Wheelock Coll., Boston, 1969; MA, U. Okla., 1975. Elem. tchr. Teaneck (N.J.) Pub. Schs., 1969-70, Panama Canal Schs., Panama Region, 1970-82; coord. Panama Canal Coll., Panama Region, 1982-83; tchr., chair dept. social studies Balboa High Sch., Panama Region, 1983—. Mem. Balboa Leadership Team. Leadership roles in numerous civic orgns. Recipient Voice of Democracy Coord. award V.F.W., 1992. Mem. ASCD, Am. Fedn. Tchrs., Nat. Coun. Social Studies, Am. Soc. (exec. bd. dirs. 1993—), Phi Delta Kappa (pres. 1993—, Kappan of Yr. 1992). Home: Psc 2 Box 2284 APO AA 34002-2284 Office: Balboa High Sch DODDS Panama Region Psc 2 APO AA 34002-9998

SOSEMAN, ELEANOR DOUGLASS, volunteer; b. Creston, Iowa, May 7, 1930; d. John Wayne and Ruby Neill Douglass; m. Floyd William Soseman, Jr., Aug. 17, 1952 (dec. Aug. 2003); children: Douglass John, Amy Lynn Stover, Elizabeth Kistenmacher, Thomas William. BA, Grinnell Coll., Iowa, 1952. Past mem. We. Iowa Tech. Adv. Bd., Sioux City. Co-editor: Holstein Centennial Book, 1982. Acative Girl Scouts USA, 1938—; trustee Stubbs Meml. Libr., Holstein, 1959—94; vol. Holstein Cmty. Betterment, 1984—87. Recipient Gov.'s Leadership award, Planning Coun., Holstein, 1982, Gov.'s Vol. award, Gov.'s Office, Des Moines, 2002. Mem.: AAUW, United Meth. Women, Gen. Fedn. Women Clubs, Philanthropic Ednl. Orgn. Sisterhood. Democrat. United Methodist. Avocations: reading, doll collecting, travel. Home: 510 E 2nd Box 470 Holstein IA 51025 Office: Agnew-Soseman Ins Holstein IA 51025

SOSMAN, MARTHA B., state supreme court justice; b. Boston, Oct. 20, 1950; BA Middlebury Coll, JD U. Mich. Assoc. Foley, Hoag & Eliot, Boston, 1979—84; with U.S. Atty.'s Office, Boston, 1984—89; founding ptnr. Kern, Sosman, Hagerty, Roach & Carpenter, Boston, 1989—93; apptd. judge Superior Ct., Concord, 1993—2000; assoc. justice Mass. Supreme Jud. Ct., 2000—. Mem. bd. directors Planned Parenthood League of Mass. Mem.: Mass. Bar Assn., Mass. Women's Bar Assn. Office: Supreme Judicial Court 1 Pemberton Sq Ste 2-500 Boston MA 02108-1717*

SOSNICK, AMANDA JOY, social studies educator; d. John E. and Barbara D. Wallace; m. Michael Scott Sosnick, Oct. 27, 2001. BA, SUNY, New Paltz, 2001. Cert. tchr. NY, 2001. 8th grade social studies tchr. Wappingers Jr. H.S., Wappingers Falls, NY, 2001—. Avocations: aerobics, travel. Office Phone: 845-298-5200.

SOSSAMON, NANCY H., city official; b. Concord, N.C. m. D.H. Sossamon, Jr., 1980; 4 children: David, Kathy, Jill, Kelly. Student, U. N.C., Chapel Hill, cert. govt. purchase officer. Life cert. local govt. purchasing officer. Collections clk. City of Concord, N.C., 1967-68, customer svc. rep. N.C., 1968-69, accounts payable, inventory and payroll clk. N.C., 1970-74, purchasing and records agt. N.C., 1975-86, purchasing agt. N.C., 1986-92, buyer N.C., 1992-98, purchasing officer N.C., 1998—. Mem. Nat. Assn. Purchasing Mgmt., Am. Purchasing Soc., Nat. Notary Assn., Carolina Assn. Govtl. Purchasing. Avocations: computer applications and new technology, cooking, spending time with her grandchildren. Office: City of Concord PO Box 308 26 Union St S Concord NC 28025-5010 Fax: 704-786-7818.

SOTIRIOU-LEVENTIS, CHARIKLIA, chemist, educator, researcher; b. Nicosia, Cyprus, Jan. 20, 1960; came to U.S., 1982; d. Sotiris and Eleni (Papakyriacou) S.; m. Nicholas Leventis, Nov. 12, 1988; children: Theodora, Helen, Julia. BS in Chemistry summa cum laude, U. Athens, Greece, 1982; PhD in Organic Chemistry, Mich. State U., 1987. Grad. asst. Mich. State U., East Lansing, 1982-87; rsch. assoc. Northeastern U., Boston, 1987-89, Harvard U., Cambridge, Mass., 1989-92; rsch. scientist Ciba Corning Diagnostics, East Walpole, Mass., 1992-93, sr. rsch. scientist, 1993; adj. asst. prof. U. Mo., Rolla, 1994-95, asst. prof., 1995-2001, assoc. prof., 2001—05, prof., 2005—. Contbr. articles to profl. jours. including Jour. Am. Chem. Soc., Jour. Organic Chemistry, Tetrahedron, Chem. Materials, Nanoletters Fellow SOHIO, 1986; recipient Greek Inst. State scholarship awards, 1978-82, Gustel Giessen Advanced Rsch. award Barnett Inst. Chem. Analysis and Materials Sci., 1988, Outstanding Tchg. award U. Mo., Rolla, 1996-97, 99-2000, 01-02, 05-06. Mem. AAAS, Am. Chem. Soc. Achievements include patents for hydrophilic acridinium esters, strong silica aerogels. Office: U Mo-Rolla Dept Chemistry Rolla MO 65409-0001 Business E-Mail: cslevent@umr.edu.

SOTO, NELL, state senator; b. Pomona, Calif., June 16, 1926; children: Philip, Robert, Michael, Patrick, Anna, Tom. Grad., Pomona High Sch., 1944; student, Mt. San Antonio Jr. Coll., 1946—47, UCLA. Govt. affairs rep. Equal Opportunity Agy., 1971—73; commr. status of women L.A. County, 1972—74; pers. dir. Rest Haven Hosp., 1973—76; govt. affairs rep. Health Sys. Agy., 1976—80; commr. cmty. life commn. City of Pomona, 1979—83, mem. city coun., 1987—98; govt. affairs rep. Rapid Transit Dist., 1984—94; mem., dist. 61 Calif. State Assembly, 1998—2000; mem., dist. 32 Calif. State Senate, 2000—. Mem. Air Quality Mgmt. Dist., 1993—99, Vets. Affairs Com., Transp. Com., Local Govt. Com., Ins Com., Govtl. Orgn. Com.; chair Pub. Employment and Retirement Com. Mem. PTA St. Joseph Sch. and Giano Sch., Nogales HS, La Puente, 1955—78. Democrat. Roman Catholic. Mailing: State Capitol Rm 4074 Sacramento CA 95814 Office: 822 N Euclid Ave Ontario CA 91762

SOTOMAYOR, SONIA, federal judge; b. Bronx, June 25, 1954; d. Sonia and Celina (Baez) Sotomayor; m. Kevin Edward Noonan, Aug. 14, 1976 (div. 1983). BA summa cum laude, Princeton U., 1976; JD, Yale U., 1979; LLD honoris causa (hon.), 1999, JD (hon.) honoris causa, 2001. Bar: N.Y. 1980, U.S. Dist. Ct. (ea. and so. dists.) N.Y. 1984. Asst. dist. atty. Office of Dist. Atty. County of NY, NYC, 1979—84; assoc., ptnr. Pavia & Harcourt, NYC, 1984—92; fed. judge US Dist. Ct. (so. dist.) NY, NYC, 1992—98; cir. judge US Ct. Appeals (2d Cir.), NYC, 1998—. Adj. prof. NYU Sch. Law, 1998, lectr. law Columbia Law Sch., 1999. Editor: Yale U. Law Rev., 1979. Mem. State Adv. Panel on Inter-Group Rels., N.Y.C., 1990—92, 1990—91; bd. dirs. P.R. Legal Def. and Edn. Fund, N.Y.C., 1980—92, State of N.Y. Mortgage Agy., N.Y.C., 1987—92, N.Y.C. Campaign Fin. Bd., 1988—92. Mem.: ABA, Assn. Hispanic Judges, Am. Philos. Soc., NY Women's Bar Assn., P.R. Bar Assn., Hispanic Bar Assn., Phi Beta Kappa. Office: US Courthouse 40 Foley Sq Rm 401 New York NY 10007*

SOUCH, MARY PAULINE, gifted and talented educator; b. Columbus, Ohio, Jan. 31, 1945; d. Peter Souch Suciu and Mary Savko Souch; children: Sarah Louise Scurlock, Lawrence Daniel Scurlock. BE, Old Dominion U., 1968; MEd, OH State U., 1991. Cert. OH Dept. Edn., Elem. K-8 Gifted Talented OH Pub. Sch., Reading K-12 OH Pub. Sch. Tchr. Norfolk Pub. Sch., 1968—69, Indian Harbor Beach Pub. Sch, Fla., 1969, Archdiocese Cin., Springfield, Ohio, 1969—72, Archdiocese Cleve., 1972—75, Columbus Pub. Sch., 1986—89, 1991—2000, reading specialist, 1989—91, gifted talented specialist, 2000—05. Sr. faculty rep. Columbus Edn. Assn., 1996—98, 2000—01; svc. lectr. gifted edn., 2000—05. Author: Curriculum Guide in Gifted Reading Extensions, 2000. Ch. organist St. Peter and St. John Baptist Ch. Mem.: Nat. Assoc. Gifted Children, Columbus Edn. Assoc., OH Edn. Assoc., Nat. Edn. Assoc. Roman Catholic. Avocations: music, piano, travel, voice. Home: 2361 Sutter Pkwy Dublin OH 43016

SOUCY, ERIN C., nursing educator; d. Millard O. Carlson and Shirlee Connors-carlson; m. Mark E. Soucy, Sept. 7, 1996; children: Taylor, Leah. BSN, U. Maine, Fort Kent, Maine, 1995; MSN, St. Joseph's Coll. Maine, 2004. RN Maine State Bd. Nursing, 1995. Nurse No. Maine Med. Ctr., Fort Kent, 1995—2005; mgr. Nursing Resource Ctr. U. Maine, Fort Kent, 2000—04, instr. nursing, 2004—. Amb. Nursing Spectrum Amb. Program, 2004—; mem. Nursing Adv. Coun., Fort Kent, 2000—. Mem.: ANA (continuing edn. com., mem. 2002—06, mem. continuing edn. com. Maine chpt. 2002—), Am. Heart Assn. (instr. 2003—), Internat. Nursing Assn. Clin. Nursing Simulation and Learning, Student Nurses Orgn. (adv. 2003—05), U. Maine Nursing Hon. Soc., Sigma Theta Tau.

SOUDERS, JEAN SWEDELL, artist, educator; b. Braham, Minn., July 13, 1922; d. John Almond and Frances Johanna (Alm) Swedell; m. Robert Livingston Souders, Sep. 22, 1945 (dec. 1985). BA, Duluth (Minn.) State Coll., 1944; postgrad., Minn. Sch. of Art, 1944, Walker Sch. of Art, 1948; MA, U. Iowa, 1955, MFA, 1956. Instr. art St. Olaf Coll., Northfield, Minn., 1947-50; instr. craft U. Minn., 1951; prof. art history painting Calif. State U., Chico, Calif., 1957-74, prof. art history, 1959-60, faculty gen. studies, 1971-73. Exhbn. Creative Art Ctr., 1975, Des Moines Art Ctr., Crocker Mus. of Art, Chico State U. and Chico Art Gallery, 1994, and various others; paintings in over 200 collections. Mem.: Women Artists Assn. San Francisco, Mus. of Women in the Arts, Nat. Archives (work and exhibit records). Lutheran. Avocations: photography, hiking, backpacking, classical music.

SOUDERS, ROBERTA BELSHAW, literature and language educator; b. Bethlehem, Pa., Sept. 25, 1954; d. Samuel James and Josephine Porazzi Belshaw; m. Peter Malcolm Souders, Feb. 27, 1986; children: Zac Peter, Samantha Jo. M in Secondary Edn./Reading, West Chester U., Pa., 1978. Project Discovery ptnr. Peoples' Light and Theatre, Malvern, Pa., 1996—; comm. arts dept. chair Octorara HS, Atglen, Pa., 1999—. Vol. March of Dimes, Parkesburg, Pa., 2000—; Sunday sch. tchr. Episc. Ch., Parkesburg, 1992—2001. Mem.: Nat. Orgn. Tchrs. (life). Episcopalian. Avocations: dogs, reading, writing, swimming, gardening. Office: Octorara HS 226 Highland Rd Atglen PA 19310 Office Phone: 610-593-8251. E-mail: rsouders@octorara.org.

SOULE, LUCILE SNYDER, musician, educator; b. Fargo, N.D., Sept. 21, 1922; d. Roy Henry and Gene (McGhee) Snyder; m. Leon Cyprian Soule Jr., Sept. 1, 1954 (dec. Dec. 1994); children: Robert Leon, Anne Lucile. MusB, MusB in Edn., MacPhail Coll. Music, 1943; MA, Smith Coll., Northampton, Mass., 1945; postgrad. diploma, Juilliard Sch. Music, 1948. Organist various chs., Mont., La., and Ohio, 1935-68; instr. Smith Coll., Northampton, 1945-46; freelance pianist, accompanist Juilliard Sch. Music, also pvt. groups and individuals, N.Y.C., 1946-49; from instr. to assoc. prof. Newcomb Coll., Tulane U., New Orleans, 1949-61; staff pianist, soloist New Orleans Symphony, 1954-61; guest artist Contemporary Music Festival La. State U., Baton Rouge, 1953-61; lectr. Lakewood br. Ohio State U., 1964-66; music tchr. East Cleveland (Ohio) Pub. Schs., 1969-85; music dir. East Cleveland Theater, 1985—2001; cons. and mgr. of spl. programs East Cleve. (Ohio) Theater, 2001—03; pianist Zhao Rong Chun, Cleve., 1995—2002; pianist for William Dempsey, Cleve., 1997—. Pres. New Orleans Music Tchrs. Assn., 1958-59; publicity chair Rocky River (Ohio) Chamber Music Soc., 1963-67; v.p. Cleve. chpt. Am. Orff Schluwerk Assn., 1974-75, mem. The Trio, 1998-2004, The Thesmacher Trio, 2004—; presenter in field. Pianist (compact disc with Zhao) Master of the Erhu, 1996; debut recital with Zhao at Weill Recital Hall, Carnegie Hall, 1999; composer Serenity Prayer, 1998, The Crown of Life, 1999. Mem. Citizens Adv. Group, East Cleveland, 1967-69; vocal coach, 1946—. Woolley Found. fellow, 1950-51, Tchg. fellow Case Western Res. U., 1967-68, Smith Coll., 1943-45; Juilliard Sch. Music scholar, 1946-48. Mem. Darius Millhaud Soc. (bd. dirs. 1984—), Fortnightly Mus. Club (corr. sec. 1996-2000, pres. 2004—), Lecture Recital Club (bd. dirs. 1993-95), Mu Phi Epsilon. Democrat. Christian Scientist. Avocations: church work, gourmet cooking, travel, art. Home and Office: 15617 Hazel Rd East Cleveland OH 44112-2904 Office Phone: 216-268-2824. E-mail: l.soule@earthlink.net.

SOULES, ALINE, librarian, writer; arrived in U.S., 1971; d. Stanley and Harriet Flora (Craig) Stannard; m. Donald Keith Soules (dec.); 1 child, Craig. BA with honors, U. Windsor, Can., 1969, MA, 1970; MLS, Wayne State U., 1973; MFA, Antioch U., 2003. Libr. Lawrence Tech. U., Southfield, Mich., 1974—76; dept. head U. Windsor, Ont., Canada, 1976—88; mgr. tech. svc. and automation U. Mich. Bus. Sch., Ann Arbor, 1988—93, dir. libr., 1993—2000, mgr. rsch. support, 2000—02; assoc. univ. libr. Calif. State U., Hayward, 2002—06, prof. East Bay, 2006—. Presenter in field; guest lectr. Sch. Info., U. Mich., 1995; mem. adv. bd. NSF, Washington, 2001; cons. Cleary Coll. Libr, 1995, 99. Author: Meditation on Woman, 2004; co-author (with Nancy Ryan): The Size of the World/The Shape of the Heart, 2000; co-author: Variations on the Ordinary, 1995; contbr. poetry to anthologies, articles to profl. jours. Recipient Dist. Svc. award, U. Mich., 2003, 3rd pl. Poetry award, Inland Empire Br. Calif. Writers Club, 2004, 2d pl. open short story award, N.Am. Internat. Auto Show, 3d pl., Poet Hunt, 1993. Mem.: Mich. Libr. Assn. (bd. dirs. acad. and rsch. libr. divsn. 1989—91, chair-elect acad. and rsch. libr. divsn. 1992—93, chair acad. endowment fund com. 1992—94, chair acad. and rsch. libr. divsn. 1993—94, past chair acad. and rsch. libr. divsn. 1994—95, leadership acad. oversight com. 1994—95, long range planning com. 1994—95, conf. planning com. 2000—01, pub. chair 2000—01, pub. policy com. 2000—02), Am. Assn. U. Prof., ALA (libr. higher edn. and campus adminstrn. com. 1994—96, mem. current topics planning com. 1997—99, subcom. intellectual property 2001—), ACRL (govt. rel. com. 1997—2001, legis. network rep. to Mich. 1998—2002, chair current topics planning com. 1999—2001, conf. planning com. 1999—2002, copyright com. 2001—05, legis. network rep. to Calif. 2002—), Calif. Acad. Rsch. Libr. (legis. liaison, ex-officio mem. bd. 2002—), Beta Phi Mu. Avocation: singing. E-mail: aline.soules@csueastbay.edu.

SOUPATA, LEA N., human resources specialist; b. NYC; With UPS, Atlanta, 1969—, various positions in human resources and customer service, dist. mgr. NY, 1990—94, mem. mgmt. com. Atlanta, 1995—, v.p. to sr. v.p. human resources. Bd. dirs. UPS. Chair UPS Found.; trustee Annie E. Casey Found.; bd. dirs. Jr. Achievement Ga., St. Basil's Acad. Recipient Human Capital award, Hunt-Scanlon Advisors, 2005. Fellow: Nat. Human Resources Acad.; mem.: Human Resources Policy Assn. (bd. dirs.). Office: UPS 55 Glenlake Pkwy NE Atlanta GA 30328

SOURK, CATHERINE CLEARY, educational consultant; b. Washington, Oct. 20, 1949; d. John Francis and Catherine Schueller Cleary; m. Geroge Kamp Sourk, Apr. 7, 1979; children: John Michael, Kyle George, Kevin Cleary. BS, Russell Sage Coll., 1971; MEd, Towson State Coll., 1975. Tchr. Balt. City Pub. Schs., 1971—73, Archdiocese Balt., 1973—76; reading specialist Montgomery County Pub. Schs., Rockville, Md., 1976—2005, staff devel. content specialist, Office Orgnl. Devel., 2005—. Sec. Flower Valley Citizen's Assn., Rockville, Md., 1996—98; treas. Flower Valley PTA, 1991—93. Mem.: ASCD, Md. Assn. Supervision, Curriculum Devel., Nat. Staff Devel. Coun., State Md. Reading Assn., Internat. Reading Assn. Roman Cath. Avocations: reading, photography, travel, creative arts. Home: 15400 Narcissus Way Rockville MD 20853 Office: Office Orgnl Devel 20010 Century Blvd Germantown MD 20874

SOURWINE, CLAIRE ELAINE, retired music educator, conductor; d. Raymond C. and Irene L. Sourwine. BS in Music Edn., Ind. U. of Pa., 1970. Music tchr. North Clarion County Schs., Tionesta, Pa., 1970—2006; condr. Clarion Cmty. Choir, Pa., 1995—2006; ret., 2006. Actor: Nuncrackers. Mem.: Schubert Musical and Lit. Soc. Oil City (pres. 2004—06). Home: 14204 Pine Valley Rd Orlando FL 32826

SOUSA, JULIE, biomedical engineer; b. New Bedford, Mass., Apr. 5, 1975; d. Franklin and Laura (Mateus) Sousa; m. Kevin Summers, Jan. 15, 2002. BS Biomed. Engrng., Boston U., 1998, BA Chemistry, 1998; postgrad., Tufts U., 2001—. Applications specialist Advanced Surface Tech., Billerica, Mass., 1998—99; database developer Smarterkids.com, Needham, Mass., 1999—2001; biomed. engr. Siemens Med. Sys., Danvers, Mass., 2001—02; validation compliance specialist Abbott Bid Fund, Mass., 2002—.

SOUTHALL, VIRGINIA LAWRENCE, retired artist; b. Portsmouth, Va., Aug. 25, 1927; d. Malachi Ashley Lewis and Bessie (Oliver) Lawrence; m. Junius Nathan Southall, Apr. 18, 1959; children: Lawrence Nathan. Student

Norfolk divsn., Va. State Coll., 1945-46; student, Prince George's C.C., Largo, Md., 1988—. Sec. to dean sch. engring. Tuskegee (Ala.) Inst., 1949-51; passport clk., ID clk. dept. army The Pentagon, Washington, 1951-62; pers. clk. AID, Dept. State, Washington, 1963-67. Exhibited in group shows including U. Md. Coll. Arts Program Gallery, College Park, 1993, Prince Georges C.C., Marlboro Gallery, Largo, Md., 1993-94, Montpelier Cultural Art Ctr., Laurel, Md., 1996, Md. State Ho., Annapolis, 1998, Children's Nat. Med. Ctr. Atrium Gallery 1, Washington, 1999, Mary McCleod Bethune Coun. Ho., Washington, 1999; one-woman shows include Outreach and Devel. Ctr. Ebenezer United Meth. Ch., Lanham, Md., Art Atrium II Gallery, Portsmouth, Va., 1998. Concert choir mem. Prince Georges C.C.; Chancel Choir mem. Ebenezer United Meth. Ch., vol. art tchr. for youth programs. Mem. Nat. Mus. Women in the Arts, Md. Choral Soc. Avocations: arts and crafts, music, singing. Home: 9015 Wallace Rd Lanham Seabrook MD 20706-4211

SOUTHER, LISA, music educator; b. Syracuse, N.Y., Apr. 24, 1967; d. William Arthur Ours, Jr. and Jeannette Pauline Ours; m. Brian Keith Souther, May 20, 1989; children: Ashley, Deanna, Keri, Jared. BS in Acctg., Liberty U., Lynchburg, Va., 1989. Accounts payable clk. Kewani Plant, Statesville, NC, 1989—90; pvt. music tchr. Melody Studio, Statesville, NC, 1992—; fine arts dir. Southview Christian Sch., Statesville, 1995—2003; music tchr. Fairview Fine Arts Acad., Statesville, 1999—. Substitute tchr. Southview Christian Sch., Statesville, 1995—. Composer, arranger many band and orch. pieces. Vol. Right to Life, 1990—, WRA, 1990—. Mem.: Nat. Fedn. Music Clubs, McDowell Music Club (counselor 1995—). Republican. Baptist. Avocations: scrapbooks, skiing, reading, painting, rock climbing.

SOUTHWARD, PATRICIA ANN, school psychologist; b. Circleville, Ohio, Jan. 17, 1942; d. Stanley Pearl and Orpha Josephine (Eveland) Frazier; m. Rodger Lee Southward, June 5, 1966; children: Nichol Jocinda, Teratia Jo, Rebecca Leigh-Ann. BS, Ohio State U., 1964, MA, 1967. Cert. tchr. English, speech, Ohio; lic. sch. counselor Ohio; lic. sch. psychologist, Ohio. Tchr. Teays Valley H.S., Ashville, Ohio, 1964-67; sch. psychologist South-Western City Schs., Grove City, Ohio, 1967-71, 78—, Circleville City Schs., 1972-77, ret., 1995; with Pickaway County Ednl. Svcs., Circleville, 1995—2000; ret. Mem. governing bd. Pickaway County Edl. Svcs., 2006. Named Outstanding Young Educator, Sertoma, 1975. Mem. Ohio Sch. Psychologists Assn. (F. Peter Gross Best Practices award 1995), Sch. Psychologists of Ctrl. Ohio (Best Practices award 1994), Nat. Assn. Sch. Psychologists, Coun. of Exceptional Children, Ohio State U. Alumni Assn. (pres. Pickaway County chpt. 1995—), Kiwanis (v.p. 1994-95, sec. 1992-94, pres. 1996-97), Delta Kappa Gamma (historian Theta chpt.), Ret. Tchrs. Assn. Methodist. Home: 125 Maple St Ashville OH 43103-1569 Office: Pickaway County Ednl Svcs Ctr Franklin St Circleville OH 43113

SOUTHWARD, PATRICIA C., volunteer; b. Alexandria, La., Mar. 9, 1942; d. George Emerson and Mary Alice (Boland) Cilley; m. Arnold Lester Greenfield, May 18, 1963 (div. June 1968); m. Ernest Merritt Southward, Mar. 1970 (dec. 2002); 1 daughter. BA, U. Fla., Gainesville, 1963; MS, Fla. State U., Tallahassee, 1966; postgrad., U. Ctrl. Fla. Office mgr. Southward Gardens, Lake Mary, Fla., 1977-84, Southward Investment and Realty, Lake Mary, Fla., 1970—2001. Adj. instr. Caldwell C.C., Boone, NC, 1999—, Seminole C.C., Lake Mary, Fla., 2001—; city commr. Lake Mary, 1977-79, 82. Com. mem. Fla. Govs. Coun. on Housing Goals, 1980; sponsor, vol. and social worker Refugee Resettlement Office, Cath., 1980-95; bd. dirs., sec. Ctrl. Fla. Migrant and Community Health Clinic, Sanford, 1981-89. Mem.: LWV (bd. dirs. Seminole County, Fla. 1982—92, 1st v.p. Seminole County 1990—94, 2004—05, pres. 2005—06). Republican. Avocation: anthropology. Home: 316 Oak Leaf Cir Lake Mary FL 32746-3059 Office: PO Box 950730 Lake Mary FL 32795-0730 also: 161 Meadow Avenue Loop Rd Banner Elk NC 28604-9659 E-mail: psouthward@earthlink.net.

SOUTHWORTH, JAMIE MACINTYRE, retired education educator; b. Ironton, Ohio, Oct. 16, 1931; d. Gaylord and Lydia Marcum (Adkins) MacIntyre; m. Horton C. Southworth; children: Jaye, Brad, Alexandra, Sueann, Janet, Jim. BS, Ball State U., 1952, MA, 1961; EdD, U. Pitts., 1981; attended, Oxford (Eng.) U., 1997. Cert. adminstr. and tchr., reading specialist, Pa. Instr. Mich. State U., East Lansing, 1964-67; instr., coord. U. Minn., Mpls., 1967-71; rsch. assoc. Pitts. Pub. Schs., 1971-80; assoc. prof. California U., Pitts., 1988, prof. edn., 1993—, state grants educator, 1990-95, dir. leadership tng. proposal, 1996-00; ret., 2000. Chancellor state adv. com., California U. rep., 1994—, faculty profl. devel. com. state rep., 1991-99; invited participant Oxford (Eng.) U. Leadership Studies, 1995, 97; cons. TITL project Duquesne U.; CEO Learning Tree Corp., 1975-2000; presenter, rsch. conf. 2000, Waikato U., New Zealand, rsch. young childrens conf. 2000-02, San Diego; chair-IRA, internat. conf. nat. Fulbright scholars, San Francisco, 2002. Contbr. articles to profl. jours. Recipient Seal of St. Peter's Coll., Oxford, 1997; U.S. Office of Edn. title III & IVC grantee; grantee Pa. Vocat. Tech. State, 1990-91, 93, Bibliotherapy Project California Univ. Pa., 1992, Pa. State, 1993, Pa. Campus Compac, 1993. Mem. Am. Assn. Colls. Tchr. Edn., NEA Young Children, Kappa Delta Pi (counselor), Phi Delta Kappa.

SOUZA, BLASE CAMACHO, librarian, educator; b. Kohala, Hawaii, Feb. 3, 1918; d. Lawrence Lorenzo Ramos and Mary Maria (Caravalho) Camacho; m. Alfred Patrick Souza, Nov. 26, 1949; children: Michelle Louise, Patricia Ann. EdB, U. Hawaii, 1939, PhD, 1940; MLS with honors, Pratt Inst., 1947. Cert. tchr., Hawaii. Tchr. Honolulu Dept. Pub. Instrn., 1940—42, Lahaina Dept. Pub. Instrn., Maui, Hawaii, 1941—42, Waialua Dept. Pub. Instrn., Oahu, Hawaii, 1943—46, libr., 1947—66; rsch. libr. dept. of edn. U. Hawaii, Honolulu, 1967—68, adminstr., rsch. libr. dept. of edn., 1968—70; edn. officer, program specialist media svcs. Hawaii Dept. of Edn., Honolulu, 1970—75; local historian P.R. Heritage Soc. of Hawaii, Honolulu, 1976—. Cons. Hawaii Multi-Cultural Ctr., Honolulu, 1976-80, Hawaii Heritage Ctr., Honolulu, 1981—; lectr., cons. P.R. Heritage Soc. of Hawaii, Honolulu, 1984—. Author: Boricua Hawaiiana: Puerto Ricans of Hawaii, Reflections of the Past and Mirror of the Future, 1983, De Borinquen a Hawaii, 1985, A Puerto Rican Poet On The Sugar Plantations of Hawaii, 2000; co-author: Legacy of Diversity, 1975, MONTAGE-An Ethnic History of Women in Hawaii, 1977, A Puerto Rican Poet on the Super Plantations of Hawaii, 2000; contbr. articles to profl. jours. Bd. dirs. Friends of Waipahu Cultural Garden Park, 1983-92; active Hist. Hawaii Found., Honolulu, 1984, Bishop Mus., Honolulu, 1985—. Hawaii Com. for the Humanities grantee, 1980, 91. Mem. Hawaii Assn. Sch. Librs. (pres. 1965), Hawaii Libr. Assn. (pres. 1975), Hawaii Mus. Assn., P.R. Heritage Soc. Hawaii (founder, pres. 1980-84, 93-99), AAUW. Roman Catholic. Achievements include All materials collected by Blase Comacho Souza donated and housed at Centro de Estudios Puertorriguenos/Hunter Coll. archived for research use. Avocations: collect sculpture, music, reading. Home: 3042 Kromer Ave Everett WA 98201-4123

SOUZA, DIANE D, corporate financial executive; BS in acctg. with high honors, U. Mass.; AS in dental hygiene, Forsyth Sch. at Northeastern U. CPA. Dir. northeast ins. Price Waterhouse; sr. mgr. Deloitte Haskins & Sells; asst. v.p. Aetna Inc., 1994—96; v.p., CFO Large Case Pensions divsn. of Aetna Inc., 1996—98; v.p., dir. of internal audit Aetna Inc., 1998—2001, v.p., nat. customer ops., 2001—. Mem.: Conn. Soc. of CPA's (mem. ins. com.), Am. Inst. Cert. Pub. Accountants. Office: Aetna Inc 151 Farmington Ave Hartford CT 06156

SOWALD, DEBRA KAY, psychologist; b. Columbus, Ohio, Sept. 28, 1951; d. Martin Michael and Beatrice Fay (Kronick) S.; children: Chad, Piper, Jody. BS, Case Western Res. U., 1973; MA, Ohio State U., 1975; D Psychology, Wright State U., 1982. Lic. psychologist, counselor, Ohio; cert. tchr., Ohio. Tchr. Groveport (Ohio)-Madison Schs., 1973-76; sch. counselor Centerville (Ohio) City Schs., 1976-79; tchr. Sinclair Community Coll., Dayton, Ohio, 1982-86; pvt. practice Dayton, 1984—. Guest on TV programs including The Today Show. Mem. adv. bd. Make Today Count, Dayton, 1982—. Mem. APA, Internat. Transactional Analysis Assn., Ohio Psychol. Assn., Ohio Women in Psychology (v.p. 1983-86, mem.-at-large 1986—), Am. Assn. Counseling and Devel., Miami Valley Assn. Counseling and Devel., Dayton Area Psychol. Assn. (treas. 1988-89), Single Mothers by Choice, La Leche League Internat. Avocation: gardening. Office: 28 E Rahn Rd Ste 105 Dayton OH 45429-5460

SOWALD, HEATHER GAY, lawyer; b. Columbus, Ohio, Dec. 26, 1954; d. Martin M. and Beatrice (Kronick) S.; m. Robert Marc Kaplan, June 12, 1977; children: Andrew Scott, Alexis Beth. BA, Case Western Res. U., 1976; JD, Capital U., 1979. Bar: Ohio 1979, U.S. Dist. Ct. (so. dist.) Ohio 1980, U.S. Ct. Appeals (6th cir.) 1981, U.S. Supreme Ct., 1987. Ptnr. Sowald & Sowald, Columbus, 1979-85, Sowald & Daneman, Columbus, 1985-1987, Sowald, Sowald & Mas, Columbus, 1988, Sowald, Sowald & Clouse, Columbus. Hearing officer Cert. Need Rev. Bd. State of Ohio, 1982—, Dept. Adminstrv. Services, 1982—, Dept. Mental Health, 1986—, Dept. Mental Retardation, 1986-88, Dept. Health, 1986-89, Ohio Dept. Liquor Control, 1989—. Bd. dirs. Wilderness Bond, Inc., Franklin County, Ohio, 1982-86, Youth Svcs. Adv. Bd., Franklin County, 1984—, chmn. 1987—, Ohio Bd. of Nursing, 1988—; legal advisor United Way League Against Child Abuse, Franklin County, 1986-87. Mem. Ohio State Bar Assn. (council of dels. 1986, pres. 2004, mem. family law com.), Columbus Bar Assn. (chmn. juvenile law com. 1982-84, chmn. admissions to bar 1984-86, chmn. publications com., 1987-88, chmn. family law com. 1988—, ethics com. 1988—, pres. 19998-99), Franklin County Trial Lawyers Assn. (trustee 1985-88, treas. 1988-89. pres.-elect 1989—, pres. 1989-90), Women Lawyers of Franklin County (pres. 1984-85), Capital U. Law Sch. Alumni Assn. (pres. 1984-86). Democrat. Jewish. Office: Sowald Sowald & Clouse One Americana 400 S 5th St Ste 101 Columbus OH 43215

SOWALSKY, PATTI LURIE, author; b. Hartford, Conn., Oct. 16, 1940; d. Joseph Aaron and Mildred (Weisinger) Lurie; m. Jerome Saul Sowalsky, Oct. 22, 1961; children: Richard, John, Susan. Cert. dental hygiene, U. Pa., 1960. Author, pub. On Exhibit Fine Art Publs., Potomac, Md., 1992-98. Author, publisher: (art travel guide) On Exhibit: The Art Lover's Travel Guide to American Museums, 1992-98, The Blanced Way To Cook Courmet, 2003. Docent Corcoran Mus., Washington, 1985-90; cert. in Braille, Libr. of Congress, Washington; bd. mem. Signature Theater, Va. Recipient Docent of Yr. award Corcoran Mus., Washington, 1989. Avocations: art collector, rosearian. Home: 8613 Chateau Dr Potomac MD 20854-4528

SOWANDE, BEVERLY FOLASADE, lawyer, educator; d. Olufela Charles and Mildred Bernice (Marshall) Sowande. BA, CUNY, 1963, MS, 1966; PhD, NYU, 1974; JD, Yeshiva U., 1980. Bar: N.Y., U.S. Dist. Ct. (so. dist., ea. dist.), U.S. Ct. Appeals (2d cir.), U.S. Supreme Ct. Pvt. practice, N.Y.C., 1986—88, 1992—; assoc. counsel Office Gen. Counsel CUNY, 1988—90; 1st dep. gen. counsel Human Resources Adminstrn., N.Y.C., 1990—92. From. lectr. to assoc. prof., dept. academic skills Hunter Coll. CUNY, 1970—92, adj. assoc. prof., women's studies program and dept. polit. sci., 1982—86, N.Y.C., 1995—96, adj. assoc. prof., dept. comm., 1995—96; adj. assoc. prof., consortium for worker edn. City Coll. CUNY, 1987—88; panel mem. departmental disciplinary com. 1st Jud. Dept., 1993—98; presenter in field. Pro bono atty. for indigent and abused women and men Coun. N.Y. Law Assocs. and NYU Law Project for Battered Women, 1986—88; adv. bd. Sanctuary Families Legal Advocacy Ctr., N.Y.C., 1988—90; coord. pro bono domestic violence panel Family Ct. Project, with Victim Svcs. Agy., 1989—93; mem. N.Y.C. Conditional Release Commn., 1989—96; bd. dirs. Lenox Hill Neighborhood Assn., Inc., N.Y.C., 1993—96; trustee Urban Resource Inst., Bklyn., 1994—97, sec. bd. trustees, 1997—98; adv. bd. Rosen Scholars Program, N.Y.C., 1996—97; cert. rape crisis counselor, sexual assault and violence intervention program Mt. Sinai Med. Ctr., N.Y.C., 2004—. Named to Hunter Coll. Hall of Fame, CUNY, 1987; recipient Cert. Appreciation, Urban Women's Retreat, 1991; Univ. Founder's scholar, NYU, 1974, Danforth Found. fellow, 1974. Mem.: N.Y. State Bar Assn. (Pres.'s Pro Bono Svc. award 1989, Merit award 1990), Assn. Bar City of N.Y. (crime victims com. 1992, matrimonial law com. 1992—93, dir. lawyer's com. violence 1994—96, com. profl. responsibility 1997—98), N.Y. Women's Bar Assn. (chair com. battered women 1987—91, coord. pro bono domestic violence project 1987—93, bd. dirs. 1988—92, chair continuing legal edn. com. 1991—94, corr. sec. 1992—93, rec. sec. 1993—94), N.Y. County Lawyers Assn. (com. minorities 1992), Coun. N.Y. Law Assocs. (bd. dirs. 1986—92, chair bd. com. not-for-profit law project 1988—92, Cert. of Appreciation for Pro Bono Activities 1988), Wistarians Alumni Hunter Coll. CUNY (v.p. 1986—88, pres. 1988—90), Alumni Assn. Hunter Coll. CUNY (bd. dirs. 1977—78, sec. 1978—81, 2d v.p. 1981—84, 4th v.p. 1984—87, 2d v.p. 1987—90, chair bylaws revision com. 1987—93, 1st v.p. 1990—93, pres. 1993—96). Personal E-mail: bsowande@aol.com.

SOWER, MILENE A., nursing educator; b. LaCrosse, Wis., Oct. 14, 1939; d. Miles Marcus and Dorethea Rose (Cox) Morrison; children: Karlene A. Mrosko, Paula B. Utley. BSN, Coll. St. Scholastica, Duluth, Minn., 1961; MA, U. Iowa, 1972, PhD, 1980. Dir. nursing edn. Moline (Ill.) Pub. Hosp. Sch. Nursing; dir. nursing adminstrn. grad. prog. U. S.C., Columbia; dean nursing Coastal Carolina Coll., Conway, S.C.; exec. sec. N.Y. State Bd. for Nursing, N.Y. State Edn. Dept., Albany; ret., 2001. Contbr. articles to profl. jours. Mem. Am. Nurses Assn., Am. Bus. Women's Assn. Home: 1960 Bell Rd Crossville TN 38571-7476

SOYSTER, MARGARET BLAIR, lawyer; b. Washington, Aug. 5, 1951; d. Peter and Eliza (Shumaker) S. AB magna cum laude, Smith Coll., 1973; JD, U. Va., 1976. Bar: N.Y. 1977, U.S. Dist. Ct. (so. and ea. dists.) N.Y. 1977, U.S. Ct. Appeals (2nd cir.) 1979, U.S. Supreme Ct. 1981, U.S. Ct. Appeals (4th cir.) 1982, U.S. ct. Appeals (11th cir.) 1987, U.S. Ct. Appeals (7th cir.) 1991, U.S. Ct. Appeals (3d cir.) 1992. Assoc. Rogers & Wells, N.Y.C., 1976-84, ptnr., 1984-99, Clifford Chance U.S. LLP, N.Y.C., 2000—. Mem. ABA, Assn. of Bar of City of N.Y., Nat. Assn. Coll. and Univ. Attys., Phi Beta Kappa. Office: Clifford Chance US LLP 31 W 52nd St New York NY 10019 Office Phone: 212-878-8479. Business E-Mail: blair.soyster@cliffordchance.com.

SPACEK, SISSY (MARY ELIZABETH SPACEK), actress; b. Quitman, Tex., Dec. 25, 1949; d. Edwin S. and Virginia S.; m. Jack Fisk, 1974; children: Schuyler Elizabeth, Virginia Madison. Attended, Lee Strasberg Theatrical Inst. Motion picture appearances include Prime Cut, 1972, Badlands, 1974, Carrie, 1976 (Acad. award nomination for best actress 1976), Three Women, 1977 (Best Supporting Actress 1977), Welcome to L.A., 1977, Heartbeat, 1980, Coal Miner's Daughter, 1980 (Acad. award best actress 1980, Golden Globe best actress 1980, Brit. Acad. award nomination best actress 1980, L.A. Film Critics for best actress 1980, Nat. Soc. Film Critics best actress 1980), Raggedy Man (Golden Globe nomination best actress 1981), 1981, Missing, 1982 (Acad. award nomination best actress, Golden Globe nomination best actress 1982, Brit. Acad. award nomination best actress 1982), The River, 1984 (Acad. award nomination best actress), Marie, 1985, Night Mother, 1986, Crimes of the Heart, 1986 (Acad. award nomination best actress, Golden Globe best actress 1986), Violets Are Blue, 1986, JFK, 1991, The Long Walk Home, 1990, Hard Promises, 1992, Trading Mom, 1994, The Grass Harp, 1995, Affliction, 1997, Blast From the Past, 1998, Songs in Ordinary Time, 2000, In the Bedroom, 2001 (Best Actress in Drama Golden Globe 2001, Am. Film Inst. award, Ind. Spirit award, Broadcast Critics award, Chgo. Film Critics award, Fla. Film Critics award, Golden Satellite award, Sundance Film Festival award, Southeastern Film award, N.Y. Film Critics award, L.A. Film Critics award 2001), Last Call, 2002 (nominee Outstanding Supporting Actress in Miniseries or Movie Emmy award) Tuck Everlasting, 2002, A Home at the End of the World, 2004, Nine Lives, 2005, The Ring Two, 2005, Summer Racing: The Race to Cure Breast Cancer, 2005, North Country, 2005, An American Hauntig, 2006; TV movie appearances include Straight Story, 1999, In the Bedroom, 2001 (Acad. award nomination best actress 2001, Brit. Acad. award nomination best actress 2001, Brit. Film Critics Choice award best actress 2001, Sundance Film Festival Spl. prize 2001, Golden Globe best actress 2001, Ind. Spirit award best felmale lead 2001, AFI, Actress of Yr. 2001, L.A. Film Critics best actress 2001, N.Y. Film Critics best actress 2001, SAG nomination best actress 2001, nominee Best Actress Acad. award 2001), The Migrants, 1973, Katherine, 1975, Verna: USO Girl, 1978, A Private Matter, 1992, A Place for Annie, 1994, The Good Old Boys, 1995, Streets of Laredo, 1995, If These Walls Could Talk, 1996, Beyond the Call, 1996, Songs in Ordinary Time, 2000, Midwives (SAG nomination best actress 2001), 2001; guest host TV show Saturday Night Live, 1977; appeared in episode TV show The Waltons. Office: care Creative Artists Agy LLC c/o Steve Tellez 9830 Wilshire Blvd Beverly Hills CA 90212-1804*

SPADE, KATE (KATHERINE NOEL SPADE), apparel designer; b. Kansas City, Mo., 1962; m. Andy Spade, 1994. BA in journalism and broadcasting, Arizona State U., 1985. From asst. to accessories editor Mademoiselle mag., 1985—92; co-founder, designer Kate Spade Inc., N.Y.C., 1993—; designer Kate Spade paper and social stationary, 1998—, Kate Spade shoe collection, 1999—, Kate Spade glasses, 2001, Kate Spade beauty, 2002—; co-founder Jack Spade, 1999—, Kate Spade Home, 2002—. Designer (uniforms) Song Airlines (subs. Delta Airlines), 2004. Recipient Perry Ellis award, New Fashion Talent, Coun. Fashion Designers of Am., 1996, Accessory Designer of the Year, 1998, FiFi award for Bath & Body Star of the Year, U.S. Fragrance Found., 2003, FiFi award for Best Fragrance in Ltd. Distribution, U.K. Fragrance Found., 2003. Achievements include stores opening in N.Y.C. in 1996, Boston and LA in 1998, and Chicago and San Francisco in 2000. Office: Kate Spade Inc 48 W 25th St New York NY 10010

SPADORA, HOPE GEORGEANNE, real estate company executive; b. Long Branch, N.J., May 13, 1965; d. Joseph Vincent and Gladys Beatrice (Clayton) S.; life ptnr. Rebecca Elise DeAnda; 1 child, Clayton Vincent Spadora. Cert. in Mktg. Comm., San Jose State U., 1988; AA in Biology with hons., Cabrillo Coll., Aptos, Calif., 1991; BA in Sociology with hons., U. Calif., Santa Cruz, 1993; M in Corp. Real Estate, Inst. Corp. Real Estate, 1998. Lic. real estate broker, Calif. Fin. analyst Lam Rsch., Fremont, Calif., 1993-94, portfolio mgr., 1994-96; v.p. internat. svcs. Cawley Internat., San Jose, Calif., 1996-97; v.p. real estate facilities Sybase Corp., Emeryville, Calif., 1997—. Bd. dirs. Emeryville (Calif.) Industries Assn., 1997-98. Mem. editl. bd. Jour. of Corporate Real Estate. Mem. Human Rights Campaign, San Francisco, 1997, The Commonwealth Club of Calif., San Francisco, 1998, Calif. Elected Womens Assn. for Edn. and Rsch., Sacramento, 1998; bd. dirs. Emeryville Cmty. Action Program. Mem. Internat. Assn. Corp. Real Estate Executives, Nat. Assn. Corp. Real Estate Execs., Bldg. Owners and Mgrs. Assn. Democrat. Avocations: golf, fishing, sailing, boating.

SPADY, JOANNE SMITH, secondary school educator; b. Phila., Jan. 17, 1935; d. Houston Thomas and Odeas Frances (Ewell) Savage; m. Sydney thomas Smith, June 1, 1963 (dec. July 1989); children: Deborah, Gregory; m. Lester Herbert Spady Sr., Apr. 3, 1994. AS, Norfolk State U., 1954; BA, U. Md., 1956. Choral, band tchr. Worcester County H.S., Snow Hill, Md., 1956-57; tchr. choral, history Acomac County, Mary N. Smith H.S., Accomac, Va., 1957-73; part-time tchr. Montgomerycounty Dept. Edn., Rockville, Md., 1973-76; asst. mgr. csh office Bradlees Inc., Rockville, 1976-86; tchr. fine arts Northampton County Dept. Edn., Eastville, Va., 1987-97. Vice chmn. planning commn. City of Cape Charles; sec. Arts Coun.; me. AFS BlackCoalition; bd. dirs. Eastern Shore C.C., Melfa, Va., 1989—. Mem. NEA, NAACP, Northampton County Edn. Ass., Edn.Assn. Va., Assn. Am. Choral Dirs., Va. Music Educators Assn., Nat. Music Educators Assn., Nat. Assn. Female Execs. Democrat. Methodist-Episcopalian. Avocations: music teaching, creative needle work. Home: PO Box 170 Capeville VA 23313-0170

SPAETH, JAN MILLS, jury consultant; b. Grinnell, Iowa, July 17, 1951; d. Paul Herbert and Joyce Carol Broadwell; m. Paul Vincent Spaeth, May 26, 1988. BA with honors, U. Wis., Madison, 1973; MA, U. Ariz., 1996; PhD, Calif. Coast U., 1999. Social worker Cass County Dept. Social Svcs., Walker, Minn., 1973—75; dir. rsch. Lakehead Social Planning Coun., Thunder Bay, Ont., Canada, 1975—76; social worker Thunder Bay Social Svcs. Dept., 1976—78; free-lance workshop coord. Duluth, Minn., 1979; freelance litig. cons. Tucson, 1980—. Educator Tucson Free U., 1980, Pima County Jail, Tucson, 1981, Pima County Juvenile Ct. Ctr., Tucson, 1981; instr. U. Ariz., Tuscon, 1980—94, Pima C.C., Tucson, 1990—94, Cochise C.C., Sierra Vista, Ariz., 1991; supplemental juror questionnaire subcom. Supreme Ct. Ariz., Phoenix, 1995; spkr. in field. Contbr. articles to profl. jours. Recipient Appreciation award, Pima County Juvenile Ct. Ctr., 1982. Mem.: APA, Ariz. Attys. for Criminal Justice, Am. Coll. Forensic Examiners, Am. Soc. Trial Cons. Avocations: hiking, travel, golf, research, writing. Office: Ariz Jury Rsch PO Box 91410 Tucson AZ 85752 Office Phone: 520-297-4131.

SPAFFORD, SUZANNE LEE, biology educator; b. Callicoon, NY, Apr. 23, 1961; d. Mary Louise and Lee Howard Andrews; m. Michael Spafford, July 10, 1999 (separated); 1 child, Caleb Andrews Mall. BS, State U. of NY Coll. at Plattsburgh, 1984—86; MS, LI U., 1990—92. Biology, chemistry, and rsch. tchr. Narrowburg Ctrl. Sch., Narrowsburg, NY, 1995—2001; biology tchr. Sullivan West Ctrl. Sch., Lake Huntington, NY, 2001—. Sci. club advisor Sullivan West Ctrl. Sch., Lake Huntington, NY, 2003—. Vol. Protection Hose Co. No. 1 of Jeffersonville, NY, 2000. Mem.: Sci. Teachers Assn. of NY State. Achievements include research in marine science. Home: 5026 Rte 52 Jeffersonville NY 12748 Office: Sulllivan West Ctrl Sch Dist 6604 Rte 52 Lake Huntington NY 12752 Office Phone: 845-932-8401 1138. Office Fax: 845-932-8425. Business E-Mail: spaffordsuz@swcsd.org.

SPAGNOLI, DEBORAH ANN, commissioner; b. 1964; BA, U. Calif.; JD, McGeorge Sch. Law. Chief counsel Assembly Pub. Safety Subcom. on Juvenile Justice; dep. dist. attorney Kern County, Calif.; spl. asst. to the Pres. White House, dep. dir. intergovernmental affairs; liaison to state and local elected officials; advisor Cmty. Oriented Policing Svices Office (COPS); commr. U.S. Parole Commn., 2004—. Co-founder Stonecreek Group. Mem.: DC Bar Assn., Calif. Bar Assn. Office: US Parole Commn 5550 Friendship Blvd Ste 420 Chevy Chase MD 20815-7286 Office Phone: 301-492-5990. Office Fax: 301-492-6694.

SPAHR, BERTHA E., chemistry educator, department chairman; b. York, Pa., Apr. 20, 1943; d. Joseph Anthony and Marie Evelyn Campanelli; children: Michael, Matthew. BS in Chemistry, Elizabethtown Coll., Pa., 1965; MEd in Chemistry, Shippensburg U., Pa., 1969. Chemistry tchr. Dover Area HS, Dover, Pa., 1965—, sci. dept. chair, 1993—. New tchr. mentor Dover HS, curriculum com. Judge York County Jr. Miss; EMT Spring Ambulance Club, Spring Grove; vol. York Hosp. Emergency Rm. Recipient O.F. Stambaugh award in Chemistry, Elizabethtown Coll., 1988, Whalen award, Outstanding Chemistry Tchr., ACS, York, Pa., 2003. Mem.: NEA, NSTA, Dover Area Edn. Assn. (chair, meet and discuss), PSEA. Avocations: travel, antiques, reading. Office: Dover Area HS 46 W Canal St Dover PA 17315

SPAHR, ELIZABETH, environmental research administrator; b. Warren, Ohio, Nov. 12, 1930; d. Sullivan and Elizabeth (St. Clair) Spahr; children: Gretchen, Carolyn. BS, Case Western Res. U., 1952, MS, 1954, PhD, 1957, MBA, 1973. Sr. rsch. scientist NASA, Cleve., 1956-71; mgr. internat. ops., mgr. spl. projects The Std. Oil Co., Cleve., 1973-86; v.p. strategic planning Ameritrust Corp., Cleve., 1987-92; dir. fin. & adminstrn. AAUW, Washington, 1993-98; CEO Technol. Exec. Inst., 1998—2002; pres. AcromaTech Group, Inc., 1999—2002; assoc. dir. U. Md. Ctr. for Environ. Scis. Horn Point Lab., Cambridge, 2002—. Dir. supply emergency team Internat. Energy Agy., Paris, 1984-86; chair fed. women's program Fed. Exec. Bd., Cleve., 1969-71. Trustee Case Western Res. U., Cleve., 1988-92, chair ann. fund, 1989-93; pres. bd. dirs. Cuyahoga City Hosp. Found., Cleve., 1983-85. Grantee USPHS, 1952-56. Mem. Women in Tech., Arlington C. of C., Strategic Alliance Va. Employers, Strategic Alliance Md. Employers. Office: Univ Md Ctr Environ Sci Horn Point Lab PO Box 775 Cambridge MD 21613-0775 Home: PO Box 352 Trappe MD 21673-0352 E-mail: espahr@hpl.umces.edu.

SPAIN, MARY ANN, realtor, educator, historian, writer; b. Nashville, May 31, 1950; d. James Ivan Spain and Mary Lou Crocker; m. Don Quitman Reynolds II (div.); m. James Clifford Miller, Oct. 15, 1988 (dec. Aug. 10, 1990). BS, Mid. Tenn. State U., 1972; postgrad., U. Ark., 1982; MAT, Mid.

Tenn. State U., 1975, MAT, 1977. Lic. realtor Tenn. Counselor State of Tenn. Dept. Human Svcs., 1972—76; grad. tchg. asst. Mid. Tenn. State U., Murfreesboro, 1974—77; instr. Vol. State C.C., Gallatin, Tenn., 1974—92; grad. tchg. fellow U. Ark., Fayetteville, 1977—82; staff sgt. Chem. Corps, I Corp., 2d Infantry Divsn. U.S. Army, 1983—87; realtor Folk-Jordan Better Homes and Gardens, Nashville, 1987—99; instr. State of Tenn. Real Estate Commn., Nashville, 1995—; realtor Crye-Leike Realtors, Nashville, 1999—. Editor: U.S. Mil. Manuals on Chem. Warfare, Chem. Def., Chem. Ops. Newsletter. Charter mem., founder U.S. Army Nat. Mus., 2004. Decorated Army Commendation medal, Good Conduct medal, Army Achievement medal, Overseas medal; recipient Best Article in State or Local Publ. award, Ark. Hist. Commn., 1981. Mem.: PETA, ASPCA, VFW, Sumner County Realtors Assn. (edn. com. dir., Excellence in Real Estate award 1992—2004, nominee Realtor of Yr. 2003), Tenn. Assn. Realtors, Nat. Assn. Realtors, Women in Mil. Svc. for Am. Meml. Found. (charter), Realtors Polit. Action Group Tenn. Avocations: gardening, fishing, animals, travel, reading. Office: Crye-Leike Realtors 383 Johnny Cash Pky Hendersonville TN 37075 Office Phone: 615-824-8008. E-mail: spainma@realtracs.com.

SPAIN-SAVAGE, CHRISTI LYNN, secondary school educator; b. Lubbock, Tex., Dec. 8, 1971; d. Harold Russell Spain and Kathy Davis; m. Obadiah Savage. BFA, Southwest Tex. State, 1994; student in English Lit., NY U. Actress, 1995—; reading, writing tutor Hunter Coll., NY, 2005—; h.s. tutor Am. Reads, NY, 2005; SAT tutor Comsuccess Acad., NY, 2005. Mem.: Theatre Commn. Group. Avocations: reading, acting, movies. Home: 63-11 Queens Blvd Apt G 11 Woodside NY 11377

SPAKE, MARY BARBARA, music educator; b. Mpls., Apr. 7, 1919; d. Donald Nivison Ferguson and Arline Calista (Folsom); m. Virgil F. Spake, July 2, 1978. BS, U. Minn., 1942, M. Music Edn., 1949. Tchr. Grand Marais (Minn.) Pub. Schs., 1942-43, Litchfield (Minn.) Pub. Schs., 1943-45, Mpls. Pub. Schs., 1945-79, Mpls. Coll. Music, 1949-55, Macalestar Coll., St. Paul, 1950-56; pvt. music tchr. Golden Valley, Minn., 1949—. Asst. choir dir. Cen. Luth. Ch., Mpls., 1946-56; choir dir. Grace U. Luth. Ch., Mpls., 1950-55. Mem. Retired Tchrs. Mpls., Music Educators Nat. Conf., Nat. Assn. Tchrs. of Singing, Sigma Alpha Iota. Avocation: dress making. Home and Office: Apt C227 5800 Saint Croix Ave N Golden Valley MN 55422-4763

SPAKOSKI, MARCIA, insurance agent; b. Bklyn., Oct. 8, 1936; d. Matthew Dabrowski and Helen Tomaszewski; m. Francis L. Spakoski, Apr. 16, 1955 (div. Feb. 1969); children: Francis L. Jr., Evelyn M., Louise A. A in Bus., Mohegan Coll., 1977. CLU; ChFC; comml. pilot; cert. flight instr. Cert. flight instr. Coastal Airways, Groton, Conn., 1967—76; real estate sales staff Century 21, Groton, 1977-80; tax preparer H&R Block, 1977-78; ins. sales staff Allstate Ins., Groton, 1980-99; ret., 1999. Dist. leader Rep. Town Com., Groton, 1973—74; majority leader Rep. Town Meeting, Groton, 1974—75; mem. City Planning and Zoning Commn., Groton, 1979—87; support group leader Multiple Sclerosis Soc., 1983—91; mem. mystic River Chorale, 1991—99; vol. Spl. Olympics, Groton Food Bank, Mary Elizabeth Nursing Home, Child and Family Agy., Nutmeg Pavilion, Meals on Wheels; bd. dirs. Habitat for Humanity, 1993—96, site selection chmn., 1993—96; chmn. Conn. Chpt. 99s, 1978—80, 1980 New Eng. Air Race, 1980. Shirley Mann Aviation scholar New Eng. Sect. 99s, 1977. Mem. Mensa (area cood. 1980-82). Democrat. Congregationalist. Avocations: flying, sailing, volunteering, travel. Home (Summer): 16 Whitehall Pond Mystic CT 06355-1954 Home (Winter): 5955 30th Ave So #301 Gulfport FL 33707 Personal E-mail: marciactfla@aol.com.

SPALDING, ALMUT MARIANNE, minister; b. Heidelberg, Fed. Republic Germany, July 19, 1957; came to U.S., 1979; d. Heinz-Peter Georg Alexander and Helga Käthe Ruth (Könnecke) Grützner; m. Paul Stuart Spalding, May 27, 1978; children: Peter James, Eckhart Arthur, Alex John. BA, U. Heidelberg, 1979; MDiv, McCormick Theol. Sem., 1984; MA, U. Iowa, 1985, U. Ill., Urbana, 1994; PhD, U. Ill., Champaign, 2001. Ordained to ministry Presbyn. Ch., 1984. Co-pastor Elba (N.Y.) Presbyn. Ch., 1984-88; asst. prof. Ill. Coll., Jacksonville, 2002—. Instr. Ill. Coll., Jacksonville, 1988—. Avocations: travel, hiking, music.

SPALDING, RITA LEE, artist; b. Pitts., Nov. 30, 1928; d. Clarence E. and Irene Francis (Israel) McEldowney; m. Willard Perkins Spalding, Sept. 15, 1956; children: Gregory Scott, Laura Lee Dooley. BA, Chatham Coll., 1950. Artist IDL, Inc., Pitts., 1950-56; tchr. West Pa. Sch. for Deaf, Pitts., 1970-82; dir. family daycare Beulah Presbyn. Ch., Pitts., 1983-87. Sec. Penn Hills Arts Coun, Pa., 1989—91, 1998, Pa., 2004. Exhibited in many one-woman shows and group shows including Three Rivers Arts Festival, West Va. U., Chatham Coll., Pitts. Ctr. for the Arts, Scaife Gallery, Westmoreland Mus. of Art, Studio Z. Vol. Meals on Wheels, Churchill, 1995—2001, 2004—; judge of elections Penn Hills 5-5, 1993—2001; mem. Penn Hills Arts Coun., 1991—2001, sec., 1991—2001, 2004—; elder, trustee Beulah Presbyn. Ch., Churchill, Pa., 1979—82, pres. deacons, 1976—79. Recipient Jean Thoburn award, Aqueous Open, 1979, Jurors award, Pitts. Watercolor Soc., 1988, Merit award, Westmoreland Art Nats., 1993, awards, Wilkins Art Festival, 1991—98, 2000, 1st Place award, Saxonburg Arts Festival, 1996—98, awards, Penn Hills Arts Festival, 1988—, S.W. Regional award of excellence, Westmoreland Mus. Art, 2001, many local awards. Mem.: Pitts. Soc. Artists, Pitts. Watercolor Soc. (membership chair 1993—97), Pitts. Print Group, Assoc. Artists Pitts., Pa. Art Assn. (bd. govs. 1994—, pres. 1989—94, scholarship 2000—). Republican. Avocations: reading, crafts, bridge, swimming. Home: 611 Dixie Dr Pittsburgh PA 15235-4529

SPALLONE, SHARON LEE, secondary school educator; b. Hazleton, Pa., Sept. 18, 1946; d. Joseph Raymond and Helen Irene (Purcell) Bergeron; m. Robert Charles Spallone, Dec. 26, 1970. BS in Secondary Edn., Bloomsburg State Coll., Pa., 1968; MA, Pa. State U., 1970; postgrad., U. Alaska, Carlow Coll., Ind. Wesleyan U., Coll. of St. Rose; MS, Bloomsburg U. Cert. comm. and speech tchr., Pa. Instr. speech Bloomsburg State U., 1970; mentor Weatherly (Pa.) Area H.S., 1987, tchr. comm. and English, 1970—2000; ret. Adj. instr. Luzerne County C.C., Nanticoke, Pa., 1980. Author: Elephant Stew, 1972; contbr. poetry to various anthologies and mags. Mem. adv. com. Pocono Renaissance Fiare, Mt. Pocono, Pa., 1993, 94, Dem. Steering Com., 1995; sponsor Women to Women Internat., Washington, DC. Mem. AARP, NEA, Pa. Edn. Assn., Weatherly Area Edn. Assn. (chmn. publicity com.), Nat. Women's Mus. (charter mem.), Nat. Mus. Am. Indian (charter mem.). Avocations: poetry, collecting antiques, reading, gardening, decorating.

SPANDER, DEBORAH L., lawyer; b. 1969; BA in polit. sci. with honors and distinction, Stanford U., 1991; JD, UCLA Sch. Law, 1995. Bar: Calif. 1995. Mgr. bus. and legal affairs BLT Prodn., Inc., LA, 1994—96; assoc. Law Offices of Maidie E. Oliveaa, 1996—97; dir. bus. and legal affairs Fox Sports Network, LA, 1998—2001; v.p. bus. and legal affairs Fox Cable Networks Group, LA, 2002—. Guest lectr. UCLA Sch. Law, 1999—2001; adv. bd. mem. Nat. Sports Law Inst., Marquette U. Law Sch. Vol. Friends of Break The Cycle, LA, 1996—. Mem.: Stanford West LA Club, Westcoast Sports Assoc., Women's Entertainment Network, Sports Lawyers Assn. (bd. mem., mem. program com., moderator and spkr. Nat. Conf. 2003—04, spkr. Nat. Conf. 1997—2002). Avocations: tennis, swimming, skiing, travel, cooking. Office: 12100 Sunset Hills Rd Ste 130 Reston VA 20190 Office Phone: 703-437-4377. Business E-Mail: debspander1@yahoo.com.

SPANDORFER, MERLE SUE, artist, educator, writer; b. Balt., Sept. 4, 1934; d. Simon Louis and Bernice P. (Jacobson) S.; m. Lester M. Spandorfer, June 17, 1956; children: Cathy, John. Student, Syracuse U., 1952-54; BS, U. Md., 1956. Mem. faculty Cheltenham (Pa.) Sch. Fine Arts, 1969—; instr. printmaking Tyler Sch. Art Temple U., Phila., 1980-84; faculty Pratt Graphics Ctr., N.Y.C., 1985-86. One woman shows include Richard Feigen Gallery, N.Y.C., 1970, U. Pa., 1974, Phila. Coll. Textiles and Sci., 1977, Ericson Gallery, N.Y.C., 1978, 79, R.I. Sch. Design, 1980, Syracuse U., 1981, Marian Locks Gallery, Phila., 1973, 78, 82, Temple U., 1984, Tyler Sch. Art, 1985, University City Sci. Ctr., 1987, Gov.'s Residence, 1988, Wenninger Graphics Gallery, Provincetown, Mass., 1989, Widener U. Art Mus., 1995, Gloucester County Coll., 1996, Mangel Gallery, 1992, 97, 2000, 03, 06, Cabrini Coll., 1999, Mangel Gallery, 2006; group shows Bklyn. Mus. Art, 1973, San Francisco Mus. Art, 1973, Balt. Mus. Art, 1970, 71, 74, Phila. Mus. Art, 1972, 77, Fundacio Joan Miro. Barcelona, Spain, 1977, Del. Mus. Art, Wilmington, 1978, Carlsberg Glyptotek Mus., Copenhagen, 1980, Moore Coll. Art, Phila., 1982, Tyler Sch. Art, 1983, William Penn Meml. Mus., Harrisburg, Pa., 1984, Ariz. State U., 1985, Tiajin Fine Arts Coll., China, 1986, Beaver Coll., Phila., 1988, The Port of History Mus., Phils., 1987, Sichuan Fine Arts Inst., Chong Qing, China, 1988, Glynn Vivian Mus., Swansea, Wales, 1989, Phila. Mus. Art, 1990, Fgn. Mus., Riga, Latvia, 1995, Woodmere Art Mus., Phila., 1996, Am. Coll., 1997, Cheltenham Ctr. for the Arts, Phila., 1997, Rowan Coll., 1997, Villanova U., 1998, U. Pa., 1999, U. of the Arts, 2001, others; represented in permanent collections Met. Mus. Art, N.Y.C., Whitney Mus. Am. Art, N.Y.C., Mus. Modern Art, N.Y.C., The Israel Mus., Balt. Mus. (gov.'s prize and purchase award 1970), Phila. Mus. Art (purchase award 1977), Toyoh Bijutsu Gakko, Tokyo, Library of Congress, Temple U.; commd. works represented in U. Pa. Inst. Comtemporary Art, 1991; co-author: Making Art Safely, 1993 Recipient award Balt. Mus. Art/Md. Inst. Art, 1971, Govs. prize and Purchase award Balt. Mus. Art, 1970, Outstanding Art Educators award Pa. Art Edn. Assn., 1982, Purchase award Berman Mus., 1995, Artist Equity award, 1996; grantee Pa. Coun. Arts, 1989. Mem. Am. Color Print Soc., Pa. Art Edn. Assn. Jewish. Office: 307 E Gowen Ave Philadelphia PA 19119-1023 Personal E-mail: merlespandorfer@comcast.net.

SPANEL, HARRIET, state legislator; b. Audubon, Iowa, Jan. 15, 1939; 3 children. BS in Math., Iowa State U., 1961. Mem. Wash. Ho. of Reps., 1987-93, Wash. Senate, Dist. 40, Olympia, 1993—. Cath. Office: Wash Senate PO Box 40440 Olympia WA 98504-0440

SPANGENBERG, KRISTIN LOUISE, curator; b. Palo Alto, Calif, June 3, 1944; d. Rudolph Karl and Ruth Fay (Beahrs) Spangenberg; m. John E. Gilmore III, Aug. 13, 1988. BA, U. Calif., Davis, 1967; MA, U. Mich., Ann Arbor, 1971. Curator prints, drawings and photographs Cin. Art Mus., 1971—. Author: Photographic Treasure from the Cincinnati Art Museum, 1989, Six Centuries of Master Prints, 1993, (catalog) Innovation and Tradition: Twentieth Century Japanese Prints, 1990. Mem.: Circus Hist. Soc., Print Coun. Am. Avocation: gardening. Office: Cin Art Mus 953 Eden Park Dr Cincinnati OH 45202 Office Phone: 513-639-2948. E-mail: kspang@cincyart.org.

SPANGLER, DIANNE MARIE, physical education educator; d. Chester Eugene Spangler Jr. and Marie Anne Kimber. AA, Glendale C.C., Calif., 1971; BA, Calif. State U., LA, 1974, MA, 1979. Cert. C.C. tchr. Calif., 1976. Tchr. phys. edn. Hoover H.S., Glendale, Calif., 1974—76, head coach girl's volleyball, basketball, badminton, 1974—76; prof. phys. edn. Glendale C.C., 1976—, coach women's volleyball team, 1976—90, coach coed volleyball team, 1976, coach women's track and field team, 1977—81, head coach women's cross-country team, 1977. Named Women's Sr. Divsn. Volleyball All-American, US Volleyball Assn., 1984, 1989, 1990, Nat. Women's Sr. Volleyball Champion, 1984, 1990; recipient Calif. State Champion 80 meter hurdles, AAU, 1969, 2d Pl. in Women's Nat. Pentathlon Track and Field championship, 1969, Carried Olympic Torch in Olympic Track & Field Trials, 1968, 2nd Pl. in Nat. Pentathlon Track & Field Championship, 1969; scholar, Glendale Women's Athletic Club, 1971. Mem.: So. Calif. Orgn. Phys. Edn. (assoc.), Calif. Assn. Health, Phys. Edn., Recreation and Dance (assoc.), PGA Tour Partner's Club (assoc.). Republican. Avocations: travel, fitness. Office: Glendale cc 1500N Verdugo Rd Glendale CA 91208 Office Phone: 818-240-1000 5645. E-mail: dianes@glendale.edu.

SPANGLER, EDRA MILDRED, psychologist; b. Webbville, Ky., Sept. 6, 1941; d. Chester A. and Laura B. (Webb) Sawyer; m. Robert Noel Spangler, Sept. 6, 1959; children: Robert Mark Spangler, Kendra Lynn Lovett. AS in Bus. Adminstrn., Franklin U., 1975; BA in Social Psychology, Park Coll., 1979; MA in Mgmt. and Supervision, Ctrl. Mich. U., 1980; D in Psychology, Wright State U., 1989. Lic. psychologist Ohio, Fla.; diplomate clin. hypnotherapy; diplomate Am. Bd. Psychol. Specialties in Med. Psychology, Forensic Clin. Psychology and Neuropsychology. With adminstrn., mgmt., fin. and computer sys. design various pvt. and govt. orgns., 1958-85; psychology assoc. Stonegate Psychol. Assocs., Columbus, Ohio, 1989-91; dir. pain & stress program The Rehab. Ctr., Columbus, 1991-94; pvt. practice, 1991—; mem. med. staff Riverside Meth. Hosps., Columbus, 1992—; health psychologist Mind/Body Med. Inst., 1993-95; mem. med. staff Grady Meml. Hosp., Delaware, Ohio, 1997—2004. Fellow Biofeedback Cert. Inst. of Am.; mem. Am. Coll. Forensic Examiners, Ohio Psychol. Assn., Fla. Psychol. Assn., Assn. Applied Psychophysiology and Biofeedback. Avocations: reading, travel, hiking, research in mind/body.

SPANGLER, NITA REIFSCHNEIDER, volunteer; b. Ukiah, Calif., Apr. 17, 1923; d. John Charles and Olga Augusta (Wuertz) Reifschneider; m. Raymond Luper Spangler, Sept. 22, 1946 (dec.); children: Jon Martin, Mary Raymond, Thor Raymond. BA, Univ. Nev., 1944. News reporter Redwood (Calif.) City Tribune, 1944-46, Country Almanac, Woodside, Calif., 1969-77. Mem. bd. dirs. San Mateo (Calif.) County Hist. Assn., 1961-68, pres., 1964-66; founder, 1st pres. Portolá Expedition Bicentennial Found., 1966-70; chmn. San Mateo County Scenic Rds. Com., 1967-76; mem. San Mateo County Hist. Resource Adv.; mem. commn. San Mateo County Parks and Recreation, 1983-97, past chmn.; cons. hwy. aesthetics Cal Trans., 1981-83; mem. sch. coms. Recipient Commendation, County Bd. Suprs., 1968, 1977, 92. Mem. Sierra Club, Western History Assn., Mormon History Assn., Nev. State Hist. Soc. (life), San Mateo County Hist. Assn. (life), Resolution of Thanks 1968, 76, 94), Friends Redwood City, Kappa Alpha Theta. Democrat. Episcopalian. Avocation: historic preservation. Home: 970 Edgewood Rd Redwood City CA 94062-1818

SPANIER, DEANNE A., music educator; d. Wilbur Claire and Marcelle Love Sloan; children: Justin Bradly, Shane Andrew, Adam Michael. MusB in Edn. summa cum laude, Ft. Hays State U., Hays, Kans., 1997. Profl. lic. Kans. State Bd. Edn., 1998. Dir. of bands Unified Sch. Dist. 318 Atwood Schs., Kans., 1998—2001; dir. of bands Unified Sch. Dist. 452 Stanton County Schs., Johnson City, Kans., 2001—02; dir. of bands Unified Sch. Dist. 294 Decatur Cmty. Schs., Oberlin, Kans., 2002—05; dir. of bands Unified Sch. Dist. 352 Goodland Schs., Kans., 2005—. Dir. Christian edn. Sonrise Christian Ch., Goodland, Kans., 2006; dir. choir/music First United Meth. Ch., Hays, 1996—97, bell choir, 1995—97; Christian edn. dir. United Meth. Ch., Lakin, Kans., 1992—95, dir. choir/music, 1992—95, Herndon Covenant Ch., Kans., 1999—2005, United Meth. Ch., Atwod, Kans., 1998—99, missionary Vols. in Missions Hays, 1998. Mem.: Internat. Clarinet Assn., Music Educators Nat. Coalition, Kans. Music Educators Assn. (asst. chair dist. bands 2003—05), Phi Theta Kappa, Phi Kappa Phi, Sigma Alpha Iota (treas. 1996—97, v.p. membership 1997, Sword 1997). Office Phone: 785-890-5656.

SPANN, WILMA NADENE, retired principal; b. Austin, Tex., Apr. 24, 1938; d. Frank Jamison and Nadene (Burns) Jamison Plummer; m. James W. Spann II, Aug. 2, 1958 (dec.); children: James III, Timothy, Terrance, Kemberly, Kelby, Elverta, Peter, Margo. BA, Marquette U., 1974; MS, U. Wis., 1985; PhD, Tenn. Sch. Religion. Sec. Spandagle Coop., Milw., 1969-89; tchr. adult basic edn. Milw. area Tech. Coll., Milw., 1975-80; tchr. Milw. Pub. Sch. System, 1975-90, adminstrv. intern, 1990-91; asst. prin. Clara Barton Elem. Sch., Milw., 1992-93; asst. prin. in charge Greenfield Montessori Sch., Milw., 1993-94, 1993-94, prin., 1993—2003; ret., 2003—. Del. Inter Group Coun.; instr. Nat. Baptist Congress Christian Edn., Milw. Area Tech. Coll. (MATC); lectr. German Baptist Congress, Wiesbaden, Germany, 2003—. Contbr. articles to profl. jours. Dir. Vacation Bible Sch., Tabernacle Cmty. Bapt. Ch., Milw., 1977-80, bd. dirs. Christian edn., 1981-90; v.p. women's aux. Wis. Gen. Bapt. State Conv., 1985-95, pres. women's aux., 1995—; instr. Wis. Congress Christian Edn., 1982—; asst. dean Wis. Gen. Bapt. State Congress Christian Edn., 1985; mem. sr. retreat com. Nat. Bapt. Youth Camp; fin. sec. Interdenominational Min.'s Wives Wis; CEO Rev. James W. Spann Found. Recipient cert. of Recognition, women's auxiliary Wis. Gen. Bapt. State Conv., 1986, Bd. Edn. Tabernacle Bapt. Ch., 1990, Leadership award, NAACP, 2003; named Educator Yr., Career Youth Develop. (CYD), 2003; named one of Milw. 28 Women of Hon., Galilee Baptist Ch., 2003. Mem. NAACP, Internat. Assn. Childhood Edn. (sec. 1990-92), Met. Milw. Alliance Black Sch. Educators, Nat. Bapt. Conv. (life, del. intergroup coun., Myra Taylor scholar com.), Marquette U. Alumni Assn., Interdenominational Alliance Minister's Wives & Widows of Wis. (fin. sec.), Assn. Women in Adminstrn., N.Am. Baptist Women's Union, Ch. Women United (life, del. to intergroup), Milw. Elem. Principal's Assn., Phi Delta Kappa, Eta Phi Beta. Democrat. Avocations: writing, public speaking, travel, reading. Home: 1906 W Cherry St Milwaukee WI 53205-2046 Office: Greenfield Montessori Sch 3239 S Pennsylvania Ave Milwaukee WI 53207-3131 E-mail: wnlspann@sbcglobal.com.

SPANN-COOPER, MELODY, broadcast executive; b. Aug. 1964; d. Pervis (Blues Man) Spann; m. Pierre Spann. BA in Criminal Justice, Loyola Univ. With WVON-AM, Chgo., 1980—, news dir., 1986—94, pres., gen. mgr., 1994—; owner, chairwoman Midway Broadcasting Corp., Chgo., 1999—. Past v.p. broadcast affairs Chgo. Assn. Black Journalists. Named one of Chicago's Most Influential Women, Crain's Chicago Business mag., 2004; recipient Barrister's Award, Cook County Bar Assn. Office: Office of President WVON Midway Broadcasting 3350 S Kedzie Ave Chicago IL 60623

SPANNINGER, BETH ANNE, lawyer; b. Bucks County, Pa., July 3, 1950; d. Feryl Louis and Nancy Elizabeth (Hendricks) S. AB magna cum laude, Muhlenberg Coll., 1972; MA, MEd, Lehigh U., 1975; JD, Temple U., 1979. Bar: Pa. 1979. Asst. dist. atty. Phila. Dist. Atty.'s Office, 1979-81; assoc. Bolger, Picker, Hankin & Tannenbaum, Phila., 1981-86, ptnr., 1986-88; sr. counsel SmithKline Beecham Corp., Phila., 1988-96; v.p., assoc. gen. counsel Glaxosmithkline, Phila., 1996—. Mem. ABA, Pa. Bar Assn., Phila. Bar Assn. (law com. 1992—), Phi Beta Kappa. Avocations: literature, jogging, theater, piano. Business E-Mail: beth.a.spanninger@gsk.com.

SPARACINO, JOANN, lawyer, consultant; b. Passaic, N.J., Feb. 25, 1956; d. Carlo and Lillian Ida (Thinschmidt) S.; 1 child, Jason Alexander Leshner. BA cum laude, NYU, 1978; JD, U. Miami, 1989. Bar: Fla. 1989. Contract atty. pvt. firms, Miami and Washington, 1989-94; pres., gen. counsel Alexis Internat., Inc., Washington, 1994—. Cons., spkr. SADC Ambs. Workshop on Trade and Investment, Washington, 1998; participant meetings on the devel. of the African Growth and Opportunity Act, Washington, 1994-99; del. U.S. Presdl. Mission to the African-African Am. Summit, Harare, Zimbabwe, 1997; cons. White House Roundtables on Trade and Investment in Africa, Washington, 1998. Contbr. articles to profl. jours. Recipient scholarship NYU, 1977. Mem. ABA (co-chair subcom. on African trade and investment 1994-98), Fla. Bar. Avocations: world culture, international travel. Office: Alexis Internat Inc 1730 K St NW Ste 304 Washington DC 20006-3839 Address: Ste 600 1133 20th St NW Washington DC 20036-3450 E-mail: jsparacino@alexisint.com.

SPARE, MELANIE KIM, management consultant; b. Lorain, Ohio, Feb. 25, 1971; d. Charles E. Reynolds and Estelene Rathburn; m. Scott Allen Spare, Aug. 8, 1992; children: Colton, Branson, Katie. BSc, Cleve. State U., 1994; MBA, Alpharetta, Ga., 2004. From tng. specialist to global agreement cons. Siemens, Alpharetta, 1996—2004, global agreement cons., 2004—. V.p. Riverbend Homes, Inc., Cumming, Ga., 1997—2004; mem. customer care adv. com. Siemens, Norcross, Ga., 2005—06; divsn. rep. Valveing People Coun., Norcross, 2005—06. Leader mission com. Meth. Ch., Cumming, 2002—04; lay spkr. Bethelview United Meth. Ch., Cumming, 2001—02, bd. dirs. preschool, 2001—03. Republican. Meth. Avocations: motorcycling, riding ATVs, camping. Home: 101 Hightower Lake Tr Ball Ground GA 30107

SPARKS, DONNA L., school librarian; d. Howard W. and Betty J. Pollock; m. David Malcolm Sparks, Jan. 7, 1972; 1 child, Jamie Michelle Ingolia. BS, Tex. A&M U., Commerce, 1976; MEd, Rivier Coll., Nashua, NH, 1990. Cert. learning resource specialist Tex., 1999, tchr. Tex., 1976. Kindergarten tchr. Huntsville City Schs., Ala., 1979—81, Okla. Pub. Schs., Oklahoma City, 1981—83, Nashua City Schs., NH, 1988—90; 2d grade tchr. Jaffrey/Rindge Schs., Rindge, NH, 1985—88; 2d and 4th grade tchr. Katy Ind. Sch. Dist., Tex., 1990—98, libr. media specialist, 1999—. Named Tchr. of Yr., Diane Winborn Elem. Sch., 1995. Mem.: Tex. Libr. Assn., Am. Contract Bridge League. Methodist. Home: 16539 Chalk Maple Ln Houston TX 77095 Office: Pattison Elem Sch 16539 Chalk Maple Ln Houston TX 77095-3876 Office Phone: 281-237-5478. Personal E-mail: dlsparks@houston.rr.com. Business E-Mail: donnasparks@katyisd.org.

SPARKS, JEANNE, columnist, photographer, educator; b. Melbourne, Fla., Aug. 26, 1960; d. William Frank and Armintha Viola Sparks. BA, U. So. Calif., 1982. Reporter City News Svc., L.A., 1984-85; reporter, announcer WNMB Radio Sta., North Myrtle Beach, S.C., 1985-86; reporter, photographer Santa Maria (Calif.) Times, 1987-90; county supr.'s exec. asst. County of Santa Barbara, Fifth Dist. Office, Santa Maria, 1991—2003; newspaper columnist Santa Maria Times, 1999—. Founder, bd. dirs. No. Santa Barbara County Habitat for Humanity, Santa Maria, 1994, Santa Maria Valley Sustainable Garden, 1994—, No. Santa Barbara County Women's Polit. Com., 1997—; grad. Leadership Santa Maria Valley, 1997; a founder, coord. Livable Cmtys. Group, Santa Maria, 1999-2002; bd. dirs. Natural History Mus., Santa Maria, 1999-2000, Santa Maria Valley YMCA, 1992-99, People for Nonviolence, Santa Maria, 1997-2000, Santa Maria Valley Water Conservation Dist., 2002—, Santa Maria Valley Beautiful, v.p., pres., mem., 1996—; founder, pres. Winners of Off-leash Freedom, 2001—. Recipient Pres.'s Cup, U.S. Jaycees, 1991, Presdl. medallion Calif. Jaycees, 1991, Women of Excellence/Women of Spirit award Santa Maria Women's Network, 1998. Avocations: theater sports, photography, art, hiking, soccer. Home: PO Box 6437 Santa Maria CA 93456-6437 E-mail: sparkie@sparkie.us.

SPARKS, MILDRED THOMAS, state agency administrator, educator; b. Montgomery, Ala., Oct. 2, 1942; d. Leon and Annie Lee (Johnson) Thomas; m. John H. Sparks, Aug. 29, 1964; children: Melanie J. Thomas Bosak, Jennifer L. Gerhartz, Regina F. BS, Ala. State U., 1964; MS, Pepperdine U., 1978; postgrad., Claremont Coll., Calif. State U., Boston Coll. Cert. reading specialist, contract mgmt., U. Phoenix, U. Wyo. Tchr. Dayton (Ohio) Schs., 1964-66, Oxon Hill (Md.) Schs., 1966-70; techncian Reading Lab. Grambling (La.) State U., 1972; reading lab. aide Calif. City (Calif.) Schs., 1975; reading instr. Cerro Coso So. Outreach, Edwards AFB, Calif., 1976-78; substitute tchr. San Bernardino City Schs., 1979, Aquinas H.S., San Bernardino, 1978-79; reading lab. tchr. San Bernardino H.S., 1979; instr. reading lab. San Bernardino Valley Coll., 1980-81, assoc. prof. reading, dept. head, 1981-86; contract adminstr. Hercules Missile Ordinance and Space Group, Magna, Utah, 1986, Alliant Techsys. (formerly Hercules Missile Ordinance and Space Group), 1987-97; dir. Office of Black Affairs State of Utah, 1997—2000; assoc. prof. Salt Lake CC, Salt Lake City, 2003—. Mem. Pres.'s Diversity Coun. Tchg. Cir. - Courage Teach Salt Lake City (Utah) C.C., 2003—, mem. gen. edn. com. Mem. Black Adv. Coun., Office of Black Affairs, AARP (mem. Utah bd., safety program instr.); presenter workshops, cmty. events; troop vol. Girl Scouts U.S.; vol. The March of Dimes, Am. Heart Assn., Visitation of the Elderly Homebound, Am. Cancer Soc. and Marriage and Family Workshop for Teens, Cath. Cmty. Svcs.; civil rights movement participant Ala. Bus Boycott; mem. minority health adv. bd. Utah Health Dept.; mem. Cath. Women League, Black Caths. Utah, Salt Lake City, African Am. Task Force, Gov.'s Initiative on Family Today, Anti-Discrimination Com.; planning com. United Way Greater Salt Lake, vol.; past pres. Salt Lake Diocesan Pastoral Coun., vol.; mem. Americorp Legacy program, Salt Lake County, Utah State Bd. Aging and Adult Svcs. Mem. Calif Tchrs. Assn., Nat. Coun. Tchrs. English, Assn. Supervision and Curriculum Devel., Western Coll. Reading Assn., Bus. and Profl. Women's Club, Link's, Jack and Jill of Am. Inc., Delta Kappa Gamma, Alpha Kappa Alpha. Roman

Catholic (Norton lav lector). Avocations: reading, writing, gardening, cross country skiing. Home: 3790 Becky Cir Salt Lake City UT 84109-3302 Office: Salt Lake CC Coll Devel Edn 4600 S Redwood Rd Salt Lake City UT 84123

SPARKS, PAMELA SHEPHERD, music educator; b. Jackson, Miss., May 13, 1954; d. Henry F and Martha W Shepherd; m. Richard C Sparks, June 10, 1978; 1 child, Richard Ryan. MusB, Miss. Coll., 1977, MusM, 1982. Elem. music tchr. Rankin County Sch. Dist., Brandon, Miss., 1977—. Mem. Music Edn. Nat. Conf., 1975—. Pianist Eastside Bapt. Ch., Pearl, Miss., 1992—. Recipient Tchr. of Yr., Stevens Elem. Sch., 1990—91, Tchr. of the Month, Rouse Elem. Sch., 1998, 1998, 2004. Mem.: Music Educators Nat. Conf., Alpha Delta Kappa (nat. registered music educator). Home: 506 Daniel Lane Brandon MS 39042

SPARKS, TELITHA ELAINE, music educator, director; b. Chattanooga, Tenn., Aug. 14, 1981; d. Sheila and Richard Sparks. BS in Music Edn., U. Ala., Tuscaloosa, 2003—03; MS in Music Edn., Troy State, Ala., 2005. Music Educator Class A P-12 Ala., 2003. Band dir. Limestone County Sch., Lester, Ala., 2003—05, Calhoun County Sch., Anniston, Ala., 2005—. Mem. Sparkys Helping Hand, Anniston, 2000—01; choir dir. Southwind Christian Ctr., Athens, Ala., 2003—05; childrens ch. Sotuhwind Christian Ctr., Athens, 2003—05; bass player Oxford Ch. of God, Ala., 2006; tchr. Lionhear Christian Acad., Athens, 1999—2005. Mem.: Ala. Bandmasters, Ala. Bandmasters Assn., Internat. Tuba Euphonium Assn., Women's Band Dir., Music Educators Nat. Assn., Gamma Beta Phi, Sigma Alpha Iota (life). Home: 1716 Hillyer Robinson Pky S Apt H62 Oxford AL 36203 Office: White Plains HS 250 White Plains Rd Anniston AL 36207 Office Phone: 256-741-7811. Business E-Mail: tsparks.wp@calhoun.k12.al.us.

SPARROW, ALISON KIDDER, painter, sculptor; b. Grosse Pointe, Mich., Feb. 13, 1974; d. Herbert George and Nancy Woodruff Sparrow. BFA, RISD, 1997. Fellow Va. Ctr. for the Creative Arts, Lynchburg, 2002, 2004; artist in residence Mary Anderson Ctr. for the Arts, Mt. St Francis, Ind., 2002—05; Hambidge fellow, 2003; artist in residence Contemporary Artist Ctr., North Adams, Mass., 2006, Ragdale, Lake Forest, Ill., 2006. Exhibitions include Inst. for Unpopular Culture of San Francisco, Detroit Artists Market, Scarab Club of Detroit, Moore Art Gallery of St. Clair, Nat. Scholastic Hallmark award (Best of Show (Mich. region), Internat. Salon Exhbn. of Small Works, 2002—06, Mike Kelley Selects, 2004, Member Show, 2006, Represented in permanent collections Mary Anderson Ctr., Mt. St. Francis, Ind., Vt. Studio Ctr., Johnson. Tchr. Literacy Volunteers of Am., Detroit, 2000—03; vol. Inst. for Unpopular Culture, San Francisco, 1999—2002, Providence Pub. Schools, 2001, Detroit Inst. of Arts. Recipient Advanced Standing, RISD, 1996; fellow, Woodstock Guild, 2002, 2003, 2006; grantee, Vt. Studio Ctr., 2002, 2004, 2006. Fellow: Scarab Club (assoc.); mem.: Nat. Mus. of Women in the Arts (records stored in archives). Green Party. Protestant. Avocation: writing. Office Phone: 313-300-0971. Personal E-mail: painteraksparrow@yahoo.com.

SPARROW, KATHLEEN GAIL, elementary school educator; b. Akron, Ohio, Apr. 20, 1948; d. Richard Donald and Eldean Kathryn Kraft Sparrow; m. Philip Heiner Gross, May 5, 1988. BA, Miami U., Oxford, Ohio, 1970; MA, U. Akron, 1974, PhD, 1987. Sci. tchr. Akron Pub. Schs., 1970—92, sci. learning specialist k-12, 1992—. Praxis III evaluator Ohio Dept. Edn., Columbus, 2003—; nat. selection com. presdl. awards math. and sci. NSF, Washington, 1998—98; mem. global polymer acad. steering com. U. Akron, 2001—; co-prin. investigator NSF gk-12 grant U. Akron and Akron Pub. Schs., 2001—04; co-prin. investigator NSF comprehensive partnership math. and sci. achievement Akron Pub. Schs., 1996—2001; mem. content rev. com. Ohio graduation test Ohio Dept. Edn., Columbus, 2003—, mem. sci. content rev. com.ohio graduation test, 1999—2000, mem. sci. content standards adv. bd., 2001—02, mem. sci. program model writing com., 2005—; adj. prof. U. Akron, 1994—2005, Ashland U., 1996—. Mem. humane commn. County of Summit, Akron; leadership cir., mem. Humane Soc. Greater Akron, Peninsula. Recipient Nat. Sci. Supr. award, Nat. Sci. Ednl. Leadership Assn., 1999, Disting. award Coun., Akron Coun. Engring. and Sci. Socs., 2001, Friend Sci. award, Sci. Edn. Coun. Ohio, 2001; scholar, Martha Holden Jennings Found., 2002. Mem.: ASCD (assoc.), Nat. Sci. Ednl. Leadership Assn. (assoc.; pres. 2000—01, dir. region E 1996—99, coun. mem. 1999—2001), Nat. Sci. Tchrs. Assn. (assoc.), Phi Delta Kappa (pres. 1987—88, 1996—99, Svc. Key 1989). Independent. Home: 2267 W Bath Road Akron OH 44333-2074 Office: Akron Public Schools 65 Steiner Ave Akron OH 44308 Office Phone: 330-761-3117. Office Fax: 330-761-3252. Personal E-mail: ksparrow@adelphia.net. E-mail: ksparrow@akron.k12.oh.us.

SPARROW, LAURA, secondary school educator; b. Boston, June 15, 1947; d. John Henry Jr. and Laura Josephine (Thickens) Halford; m. William Talbot Sparrow, July 11, 1970. BA, U. Mich., Ann Arbor; MAT, Johns Hopkins U., Balt., 1970. Cert. secondary tchr. Instr. social sci. C.C. of Balt., 1970; English tchr. North Farmington H.S., Farmington Hills, Mich., 1970-71; tchr. English and humanities and philosophy Harrison H.S., Farmington Hills, 1971—2006, tchr. English, chair dept., 1995—2005. Author: The White Wave, 1983, Hostages to Fortune, 1984, Firesigns, 1986, Seaswept, 1990. Named Oakland County Secondary Tchr. of Yr., Newsweek/WDIV-TV, 1998; Shakespeare study grantee NEH, 1992, Galileo leader Kellogg Found., 1999. Mem. ASCD, Nat. Coun. Tchrs. English, Detroit Working Writers, Authors Guild. Avocations: travel, music, kayaking, writing. Office: Harrison HS 29995 W 12 Mile Rd Farmington Hills MI 48334-3901 Office Phone: 248-489-3501. Personal E-mail: laurasparrow@aol.com.

SPATAFORA, GRACE ANN, biology professor; b. Hoboken, N.J., Sept. 19, 1958; m. Douglas Edward Rooney, Feb. 8, 1996; 1 child, Olivia Grace Rooney. PhD, St. Louis U., St. Louis, Mo., 1988. Prof. Middlebury Coll., Vt., 2004—, chmn. Dept. Biology, 2004—. Grant rev. NIH, DC, 2002—06. Contbr. articles to profl. jours. Grantee, Nat. Inst. Dental and Craniofacial Rsch., 1991—, NIH, 1991—. Mem.: The Sigma Xi, Internat. Assn. Dental and Craniofacial Rsch., Am. Soc. Microbiology. Office: Middlebury College 276 Bicentennial Way MBH354 Middlebury VT 05753 Office Phone: 802-443-5431.

SPATARO, JANIE DEMPSEY WATTS, freelance/self-employed writer; b. Chattanooga, May 17, 1951; d. Ray Dean and Anne America (Dempsey) Watts; m. Stephen Anthony Spataro, June 18, 1977; children: Anthony Dempsey, Stephen Jackson. BS in Journalism, U. Calif., Berkeley, 1974; MA in Broadcast Journalism, U. So. Calif., 1982. Writer, editor McGiffin Newspapers, South Gate, Calif., 1976; news bur. mgr. Loyola Marymount U., Westchester, Calif., 1976; asst. dir. pub. relations Hawthorne Cmty. Hosp., Calif., 1977—78; pub. rels. cons. Security Pacific Bank, LA, 1978—82; writer Cable Card, Inc., Marina del Rey, Calif., 1983—86; pres. Write Path, Inc., 1997—. Writer, prodr., editor (TV documentary) Who's Minding the Children?, 1983, screenwriter, Monkey Doll, Fireworks, Oatmania, Soft Shoe, Hard World; contbr. chapters to books. Office: 100 Wilshire Blvd Ste 200 Santa Monica CA 90401-1111 Business E-Mail: janie@spataro.com.

SPATCHER, DIANNE MARIE, finance executive; b. Reading, Pa., Feb. 1, 1959; d. Frederick Jacob and Claire Marie (Paskey) Seidel; m. Peter D. Spatcher. ASBA, Pa. State U., 1986; BA, Alvernia Coll., Reading, Pa., 1988. Office asst. Berks-Lehigh Valley Farm Credit Service, Fogelsville, Pa., 1977-80, sr. office asst., 1980, office supr., 1980-83, office mgr., 1983-86; chief fin. officer, 1986-88; exec. v.p. Keystone Farm Credit ACA, Lancaster, 1989-92, sr. v.p. fin. svcs., CFO, 1992-2000; treas. AAA Reading-Berks, Wyomissing, Pa., 2001—, corp. sec., 2003—. Avocations: travel, classic cars, collectibles. Office: 920 Van Reed Rd Wyomissing PA 19610 Home: 1965 Meadow Ln Reading PA 19610-2710 E-mail: pdspatch@aol.com.

SPATZ, MEAGEN SORENSEN, music educator, director; b. Rahway, NJ, Sept. 27, 1978; d. Alfred Joseph and Diane Carol Sorensen; m. Matthew Leon Spatz, Aug. 14, 2005. MusB in Music Edn., Mansfield U., Pa., 1996—2000, MA in Music. Edn., 2001—03. Cert. music tchr. NJ, K-12 music tchr. Pa. Instrumental music tchr. So. Bd. Edn., Cranford, NJ, 2000—01; band dir. Cranford Bd. Edn., 2003—; music dir. Beattystown Presbyn., Hackettstown, NJ, 2003—. Prin. bassoon Whitehouse Wind Symphony, Peapack, NJ, 2003—; bassoon tchr. Ea. Conservatory Music, Bernardsville, NJ, 2005—. Choir arranger hymns/choral works Ch.; dir. vacation bible sch. Hackettstown area Presbyn. Chs., 2006—. Integration Tech. grant for educational excellence, Cranford, 2005. Mem.: NEA, Music Educator's Nat. Conf., Skyliners Drum & Bugle Corps. Democrat. Presbyn. Avocation: outdoor activities. Home: 621 Lincoln Ave Manville NJ 08835

SPAULDING, HELEN BOWDOIN, former foundation administrator; m. Josiah Augustus Spaulding. HHD (hon.), Rocky Mt. Coll. Pres. and chair New England Aquarium; mem. The Boston Found., 1992—2002, chair, 1997—2002; dir. emeritus Mus. Trustee Assn. Bd. dirs. Georgetown U., Boston U., Mus. Sci., Huntington Theatre, Wang Ctr. Performing Arts, United Way Mass. Bay, World Wildlife Found., Nat. Conf. Christians and Jews, Children's Hosp. Med. Ctr., Spaulding Rehabilitation Hosp.; adv. coun. Malcolm Weiner Sch. Social Policy; adv. coun. Hauser Ctr. for Non-profits Kennedy Sch. Govt., Harvard U. Recipient Disting. Citizen award, Greater Boston C. of C., Lifetime Achievement award, Arthritis Found. Fellow: Am. Acad. Arts and Sciences.*

SPAULDING, NANCY KELLY, elementary school educator, small business owner; b. Hartford, Conn., Oct. 10, 1945; d. Russell James Kelly, Sr. and Miriam Harriet Kelly; m. Victor B. Spaulding, June 29, 1974 (dec.); children: Joshua Butler, Jared Butler. Degree in Legal Secretarial, Bryant Coll., 1965; BA in Phys. Edn., Plymouth State Coll., NH, 1971; BA in Elem. Edn., Rivier Coll., 1987. Legal sec. Robinson Robinson & Cole, Hartford, Conn., 1965—68; tchr. phys. edn. Oxford (Mass.) Mid. Sch., 1971—74; tutor E.G. Sherburne Sch., Pelham, NH, 1984—87; head tchr. Stark (N.H.) Village Sch., 1987—94, tchr., 1994—. Supr. checklist Town Stark, asst. treas., trustee libr.; vol. Am. Red Cross Bloodmobile, Berlin, NH, 1997—; active Adopt A Hwy. Program State N.H.; staff devel. com. NH Assn. Health, Phys. Edn., Recreation and Dance; sec. bd. dirs. Weeks State Pk., Lancaster, NH. Mem.: NEA, Stark (N.H.) Meth. Ch. Women. Avocations: sports, dance, reading, cooking. Home: 16 Northside Rd Stark NH 03582 Office: Stark School Dist 1192 Stark Hwy Stark NH 03582

SPEAR, LAURINDA HOPE, architect; m. Bernardo Fort-Brescia. BFA, Brown U., 1972; MArch, Columbia U., 1975. Registered architect, Fla., N.Y.; cert. Nat. Coun. Archtl. Registration. Founding prin. Arquitectonica (ARQ), Miami, Fla., 1977—. Lectr. in field. Prin. works include Pink Ho., Miami, Fla., 1978, The Palace, Miami, 1982 (Honor award Miami chpt. AIA 1982), The Atlantis, Miami, 1982 (Miami chpt. AIA award 1983), The Imperial, Miami, 1983, Casa los Andes (Record Hos. award Archtl. Record 1986), North Dade Justice Ctr., Miami, 1987 (Honor award Miami chpt. AIA 1989), Rio, Atlanta, 1988 (Honor award Miami chpt. AIA 1989), Banco de Credito del Peru, Lima, 1988 (Honor award Miami chpt. AIA 1989), The Ctr. Innovative Tech., Herndon, Va., 1988 (Honor award Va. chpt. AIA 1989, Honor award Miami chpt. 1990, Merit award Fairfax, Va., County Exceptional Design Awards Program 1990), Sawgrass Mills (Merit award Miami chpt. AIA 1990, Honor award Fla. chpt. 1991), Miracle Ctr. (Honor award Miami chpt. AIA 1989), Internat. Swimming Hall of Fame, Ft. Lauderdale, Fla., 1991, Banque de Luxembourg, 1993, Disney All-Star Resorts, Orlando, Fla., 1994, U.S. Embassy, Lima, 1994, USCG Family Housing, Bayamon, P.R., 1994, Altamira Ctr., Caracas, Venezuela, 1994, Festival Walk, Hong Kong, 1998, Miami Fed. Courthouse, Am. Airlines Arena, Miami, 1999, Philips Arena, Atlanta, 1999, Miami Internat. Airport D-E-F Wrap. Mem. beaux arts support group Lowe Art Mus., Miami; bd. dirs. Miami Youth Mus. Recipient Design Awards citation Progressive Architecture, 1975, 80, Rome Prize in Architecture, 1978, Award of Excellence, Atlanta Urban Design Commn., 1989; inductee Interior Design Hall of Fame, 1999. Fellow AIA (Silver medal for design 1998); mem. Internat. Womens Forum, NAD (academician, 1994-). Office: Arquitectonica International Corp 801 Brickell Ave Ste 1100 Miami FL 33131-2945 Office Phone: 305-372-1812. Office Fax: 305-372-1175. Business E-Mail: lspear@arqintl.com.

SPEAR, PATRICIA ANN, principal; d. Herbert N. and Madeline E. Urmson; m. George G. Spear, Aug. 5, 1972; children: Ryan, Stephen, Anastasia. BS, Portland State U., Oreg., 1970, MS, 1972; grad. in Ednl. Adminstrn., Ctrl. Wash. U., Ellensburg, 1987. Tchr. Vancouver Sch. Dist., Wash., 1970—90; asst. prin. mid. level Battle Ground Sch. Dist., Wash., 1990—92; asst. prin. H.S., Evergreen Sch. Dist., Vancouver, Wash., 1992—2000; prin. H.S., Kelso Sch. Dist., Wash., 2000—. Office: Kelso HS 1904 Allen St Kelso WA 98626-1999

SPEAR, SARAH G., county administrator; b. Montgomery, Ala., Apr. 23, 1939; d. Penson Raybon and Dora Nell (McLauchin) Graham; m. James Rufus Spear, Nov. 8, 1996; children: Deborah, Connie, Beth. Cert. in tax adminstrn., Auburn U. From clk. to chief clk. Montgomery County Office of Tax Collections, Montgomery, 1958-91, tax collector, 1991-97, revenue commr., 1997—. Active Easter Seals, Mothers March of Dimes, Am. Heart Assn.; bd. dirs. Montgomery Area United Way, mem. budget and allocation com.; bd. dirs. Leadership Montgomery, co-chmn. program com.; past pres., exec. bd. dirs. Montgomery Coun. on Aging; numerous officers Frazer United Meth. Ch., Montgomery.; past bd. dirs. Ala. Credit Union Adminstrn., past bd. dirs., vice-chmn., sec. Ala. Credit Union League. Mem. Nat. Assn. Female Execs., Nat. Assn. County Officers, LWV, Internat. Assn. Assessing Officers, Tax Assessors and Tax Collectors of Ala. (pres., mem. exec. bd.), Ala. Assn. Assessing Ofcls., Fellowship of Christian Athletics, Kiwanis, Montgomery Auburn Club. Democrat. Avocations: family, friends, college football, bridge, fishing. Home: 648 Pimblico Rd Montgomery AL 36109-4646 Office: Montgomery Cty Office Revenue Commr 1005 S Lawrence St Montgomery AL 36104-5035

SPEARING, KAREN MARIE, retired physical education educator, coach; b. Chgo., Apr. 17, 1949; d. John Richard and Naomi (Allen) Miller; m. Edward B. Spearing III, Apr. 28, 1973. BS in Phys. Edn., U. Wis., Whitewater, 1972; MS in Outdoor Edn., No. Ill. U., 1978. Cert. phys. edn. tchr., Ill.; cert. CPR instr., master hunter safety instr., boating safety instr., master snowmobile instr., Ill. Tchr., coach Glenside Mid. Sch., Glendale Heights, Ill., 1973—2006, athletic dir., 1981—92, 1995—98, 2003—06, chair dept., 1992-93; ret., 2006. Hunter safety instr. State of Ill., 1988—, water safety instr., 1989—, snowmobile instr., 1990-2000, master snowmobile instr., 1995, CPR instr., 1996—, level I sporting clays instr., 2000—; range and shotgun instr. NRA, 2001; pres. Allied Ill. Workswomen, 2004. Amb. People to People Citizen Amb. Program, Russia and Belarus, 1993; awards chairperson U.S. Power Squadron, Chgo., 1987—93; mem. exec. com. DuPage Power Squadron., 1993—96, comdr., 2000—01, edn. officer, 1996—98, Adminst. Officer, 1998; mem. com. Ill. Hunting and Fishing Days, Silver Springs State Pk., 1993; mem. Outdoor Wilderness Leadership Class, 1997; pres. Allied Ill. Markswomen, 2001—02. Mem. AAHPERD, Ill. Assn. Health, Phys. Edn., Recreation and Dance, Ill. H.S. Assn. (volleyball referee). Avocations: clock collecting, hunting, fishing, boating.

SPEARMAN, DIANE NEGROTTO, art/special education educator; b. New Orleans, Nov. 22, 1949; d. Allen Jules and Constance Lenora (Hinkel) Negrotto; m. Joe Dalton Spearman, June 26, 1971; children Brett Dalton, Eric Clayton, Scott Brandon. BS in Art Edn., La. State U., 1971, MA in Art Edn., 1991, Ed. Spl. Education, 1994. Cert. tchr. La. art, English, spl. edn., 1-12, supr. student tchrs. Art tchr. E. Baton Rouge Schs., 1971-72, 1973-78, 1981-83, 1990—2007. Presenter state confs. gifted and spl. edn., Baton Rouge, 1985, 94; mem. com. to write art edn. and to revise art edn. curriculum Holmes Program La. State U., Baton Rouge, 1988, supr. student tchrs., 1992-96, cons. art and spl. edn., 1991-96. Products of students sold to fund art program have been featured in newspaper and mag. articles. Leadership positions Cub Scouts Pack 37, Boy Scouts Troop 478, Boy Scouts Am., 1982-95; scoutmaster Troop 93 (handicapped boys), Baton Rouge, 1992-2006. Named Arlington Tchr. of Yr. East Baton Rouge Parish Schs., 1993-94; grantee Arts Coun. of Greater Baton Rouge, Jr. League, 1991, 92, 93. Mem. Nat. Art Edn. Assn., Am. Legion Auxiliary. Republican. Roman Catholic. Avocations: travel, pokeno, motorcycling. Home: 14628 Bailey Dr Baton Rouge LA 70816-1201 Office: Arlington Prep Acad 931 Dean Lee Dr Baton Rouge LA 70820-5102

SPEARS, ANGELA RAY, science educator; b. Danville, Ky., May 10, 1973; d. Donald Ray and Kathy Jo Godbey; 1 child, Isaiah Seth. BSc in Mid. Grade Edn. Emphasis Sci. & S., Ea. Ky. U., Richmond, Ky., 2002; MAED in Instrnl. Leadership, Ea. Ky. U., 2006. Cert. Mid. Grades Tchr. Emphasis in Sci. and Social Studies Ky., 2002. 8th grade sci. tchr. Russell County Mid. Sch., Russell Springs, 2002—. Aceadmic team coach Russell County Mid. Sch., Russell Springs, 2004—. Sec. Ky. Young Rep., Liberty, Ky. Scholar Scholarhip, Ky. Farm Bur. Mem.: Kappa Kappa Iota Gamma. Home: 2482 Hwy 3525 Russell Springs KY 42642 Office: Russell County Mid Sch 2258 S Hwy 127 Russell Springs KY 42642 Office Phone: 270-866-2224. Personal E-mail: zabug@duo-county.com.

SPEARS, BRITNEY, singer; b. McComb, Miss., Dec. 2, 1981; d. Jamie and Lynne Spears; m. Jason Alexander, Jan. 2, 2004 (annulled Jan. 5, 2004); m. Kevin Federline, Sept. 18, 2004; children: Sean Preston, Jayden James stepchildren: Kori, Kaleb. Released signature fragrance Curious BRITNEY SPEARS, 2004, Britney Spears: Fantasy, 2005; release of fragrance In Control, 2006. Singer: (albums) Baby One More Time, 1999, Oops! I Did It Again, 2000 (Billboard Album artist of the Year, 2000), Britney, 2001, In the Zone, 2003, Britney Spears Greatest Hits: My Prerogative, 2004, B In The Mix, The Remixes, 2005; actor(voice only): (TV films) Hooves of Fire, 1999, Legends of the Lost Tribe, 2002,: (films) Longshot, 2000, Crossroads, 2002, (TV reality show) Britney And Kevin: Chaotic, 2005; guest appearance with husband (reading a top 10 list on The Late Show with David Letterman), 2005; composer: (songs) (for film Drive Me Crazy) You Drive Me Crazy, 1999, (for film Pokémon the First Movie: Mewtwo Strikes Back) Soda Pop, 1999, (for film On The Line) Let Me Be, 2001, (for film Jimmy Neutron: Boy Genius) Intimidated, 2001, (for film Austin Powers in Goldmember) Boys, 2002. Britney Spears Found. Recipient Female Artist of the Year, Billboard, 1999, New Artist of the Year, 1999, Hot Dance Sales Single of Yr. for "Me Against the Music" featuring Madonna, 2004, Choice Music Single "Baby One More Time", Teen Choice award, 1999, Choice Hottie Female & Choice Female Artist, 2000, 2002, Choice Female Artist, 2001, Choice Music Single "Toxic", 2004, Best New Artist, Am. Music Awards, 2000, Grammy for Best Dance Recording for Toxic, 2005. Mailing: Jive Records 137 W 25th St New York NY 10001-7216

SPEARS, DIANE SHIELDS, art director, elementary school educator; b. Seattle, May 21, 1942; d. Richard Keene McKinney and Dorothy Jean (Shields) Thacker; m. Howard Truman Spears, Sept. 3, 1977; 1 child, Truman Eugene. BA in Art, English, Edn., Trinity U., 1964; MA in Christian Counseling, San Antonio Theol. Sem., 1986, D of Christian Edn., 1988. Cert. tchr. secondary edn., elem. edn., ednl. supervision, Tex. Instr. ESL Dliel-Geb (Def. Lang. Inst.), San Antonio, 1973-74, Ceta/Ace Bexar County Sch. Bd., San Antonio, 1975-78; tchr. elem. edn., art, music New Covenant Faith Acad., San Antonio, 1983-89; instr. ESL Jewish Family Svc., San Antonio, 1991; from tchr. elem. art to dir. visual arts Edgewood Ind. Sch. Dist., San Antonio, 1992—2002, dir. visual arts, 2002—04; tchr. Pipe Creek Christian Sch., Tex., 2004—06. Owner, operator Art for Kings, San Antonio, 1985—2004, Spears Art Studio, Inco., 2004—05. Illustrator teacher-created materials-lit. activities for young children, 1989-90; author: (art curriculum) Art for Kings, 1987; editor: (art curriculum) Edgewood Ind. Sch. Dist. Elem. Art Curriculum, 1993; exhibited in group shows at Charles and Emma Frye Mus., Seattle, 1966, 68, Centro Cultural Aztlan Galerie Expression, 1998 (Best of Show 1998). Dir. intercessory prayer New Covenant Fellowship, San Antonio, 1980-90. Recipient awards for painting and graphics, San Antonio, 1996-98. Mem.: San Antonio Art Edn. Assn. (1st pl. 1995), Tex. Art Edn. Assn. (1st pl. graphics divsn. 1995), Nat. Mus. for Women in Arts (charter). Republican. Avocations: water-skiing, motorcycle riding, sewing, writing. Home: 264 Mountain Dr Lakehills TX 78063-6725 Office Phone: 830-612-2585. E-mail: shieldsandspears@earthlink.net.

SPEARS, GINA MARIE, elementary school educator; b. Butler, Pa., Oct. 12, 1971; d. Michael Joseph and Mary Lou D'Antonio; m. Scott Douglas Spears, Aug. 5, 2000; 1 child, James Rocco. BFA in Dance Edn., Shenandoah U., Winchester, Va., 1993. Cert. tchr. K-12 dance edn. IL, 1998. Profl. dancer Syncopated Inc. Dance Co., Lexington, Ky., 1994—95; dance tchr. Northtown Arts Ctr., Chgo., 1999—2004, Boone Elem. Sch., Chgo., 1999—2004, Whitney Young Magnet H.S., Chgo., 2004—06; tchr. Boone Elem. Sch., Chgo., 2006—. Guest educator IAHPERD, Ill., 2003—. Dir., producer, head choreographer: Traditions and Tributes. Dir. of liturgical dance ministry St. Benedict Parish, Chgo., 2001—06; bd. dirs. Northtown Arts Ctr., Chgo., 2002—04. Named Barbie Arts Tchr. of the Yr., Entertainment Industry Found., 2002, Alumni of Excellence, Shenandoah U., 2003; recipient Awesome Tchr. award, AT&T, 2002; Tchr. Incentive grant, Oppenheimer Family Found., 2001—03, 2005, Jordan Fundamentals grant, Michael Jordan Found., 2003. Mem.: Ill. Dance Assn. (assoc.), Nat. Dance Edn. Orgn. (assoc.), Ill. Assn. for Health, PE, Recreation and Dance (assoc.). Roman Catholic. Avocations: singing, reading, cooking. Personal E-mail: gina.luv2dance@gmail.com.

SPEARS, JAE, state legislator; b. Latonia, Ky. d. James and Sylvia (Fox) Marshall; m. Lawrence E. Spears; children: Katherine Spears Cooper, Marsha Spears-Duncan, Lawrence M., James W. Student, U. Ky. Reporter Cin. Post, Cin. Enquirer newspapers; rschr. Stas. WLW-WSAI, Cin.; tchr. Jiya Gakuen Sch., Japan; lectr. U.S. Mil. installations East Anglia, England; del. State of W.Va., Charleston, 1974-80; mem. W.Va. Senate, Charleston, 1980-1993. Mem. vis. com. W.Va. Extension and Continuing Edn., Morgantown, 1993-2000, W.Va. U. Sch. Medicine, 1992—; with state sen., 1980-93; apptd. to Jud. Hearing Bd., 1993-2000. Chmn. adv bd. Sta. WNPB, 1992-94; congl. liaison Am. Pub. TV Stas. and Sta. WNPB-TV, 1992-97; mem. coun. W.Va. Autism Task Force, Huntington, 1981-90; mem. W.Va. exec. bd. Literacy Vols. Am., 1986-90, 94—, pres., 1990-92; mem. Gov.'s State Literacy Coun., 1991-97; bd. dirs. Found. Ind. Colls. W.Va., 1986—; mem. regional adv. com. W.Va. Gov.'s Task Force for Children, Youth and Family, 1989; mem. USS W.Va. Commn., 1989; mem. exec. com. W.Va. Employer Support Group for Guard and Res., 1989, mem. steering com., 1990-92. Decorated Purple Heart (hon.); recipient Susan B. Anthony award NOW, 1982, edn. award Profl. Educators Assn. W.Va., 1986, ann. award W.Va. Assn. Ret. Sch. Employees, 1985, Meritorious Svc. award W.Va. State Vets. Commn., 1984, Vets. Employment and Tng. Svc. award U.S. Dept. Labor, 1984, award W.Va. Vets. Coun., 1984; named Admiral in N.C. Navy, Gov. of N.C., 1982, hon. Brigadier Gen. W.Va. N.G., 1984, One of 11 Women Pioneers of W.Va. Legislature, W.Va. U. Inst. for Pub. Affairs, 1997, Disting. West Virginian, Gov. W.Va., 2005, Comm. award W.Va. Womens Comm., 2006. Mem. DAR, VFW (aux.), Bus. and Profl. Women (Woman of Yr. award 1978), Nat. League Am. Pen Women (Pen Woman of Yr. 1984), Nat. Order Women Legislators, Am. Legion (aux.), Delta Kappa Gamma, Alpha Xi Delta. Democrat. Home and Office: PO Box 98 Shinnston WV 26431 Office Phone: 304-558-0070.

SPEARS, JULIA BUCKNER, psychologist; b. San Antonio, Tex., June 5, 1932; d. Noa and Emy (King) Spears. BA, Hollins Coll., 1954; MA, New Sch. for Social Rsch., 1962; PhD, NYU, 1971. Lic. psychologist, N.J., Tex. Staff psychologist Westchester Cmty. Mental Health Svcs., Mt. Kisco, N.Y., 1964-66, Rockland State Hosp., Orangeburg, N.Y., 1966-68; ward adminstr. Bronx (N.Y.) State HOsp., 1968-70; dir. dept. psychology Rockland Children's Psychiat. Ctr., Orangeburg, 1970-80; psychologist in pvt. practice, Bergen County, N.J., 1976-86, San Antonio, 1988-95; dir. psychol. svcs. Correctional Health Care Svcs., Univ. Health Sys., San Antonio, 1991-98; psychologist, vol. Disaster Svc. Response Network/ARC, 1999—. Bd. dirs. Unitarian Universalist Counseling and Edn. Svc., N.J., 1977-79; founding mem. N.J. Psychol. Trust; bd. dirs. Mental Health Assn. San Antonio, 1988-89. Psychologist-cons. to hostage negotiations team Bexar County

Sheriff's Dept., San Antonio, 1992-95; mem. Disaster Response Team, ARC, 1999— Mem. APA, N.J. Psychol. Assn., Am. Coll. Forensic Psychology, Bexar County Psychol. Assn. Democrat. Unitarian Universalist. Home: 1113 Apache Dr Brenham TX 77833-5731

SPEARS, LOUISE ELIZABETH, minister, secondary school educator; b. Liberty, Miss., Feb. 2, 1945; d. Willie and Alice Gray Spears; 1 child, Guy Alice. BSc, Alcorn State U., 1966; MSc, Ind. U., 1969; PhD, U. N. Colo., 1975; MDiv, Garrett-Evang. Theol. Sem., 1983. Cert. African Meth. Episcopal Ch., 90; Tchr. Ga. Tchr. Hazlehurst H.S., Hazlehurst, Miss., 1967—68; tchg. asst. Ind. U., Bloomington, Ind., 1968—70; tchr. Ala. State U., Montgomery, Ala., 1970—72, Ky. State U., Frankfort, Ky., 1972—73, Jackson State U., Jackson, Miss., 1975—81; pastor United Meth. Ch., Keosauqua, Iowa, 1983—85, Detroit, 1985—88; tchr. Clarke County Sch. Dist., Athens, Ga., 1998—2004; pastor African Meth. Episcopal Ch., various, Ga., 2000—. Realtor Ga. Real Estate, Atlanta, 1989—92; academic adminstr. Emmanuel Bible Coll., Macon, Ga., 1992—93; substitute tchr. Atlanta Pub. Sch., Atlanta, 1994—98; co-chmn. Augusta Ga. Conf., Augusta, Ga., 2001, mem. stewardship commn.; fin. coord. Reach Out and Touch Club, Inc., 2002—03; mem. Athens-Clarke County Commn. on Disability, 2003; mem. career and tech. edn. exec. adv. bd. Athens-Clarke County Commn. on Disability; mem. career and tech. edn. adv. bd. Tech. Prep Awareness, 2003, mem. sub-com., 03. Co-author: National Poetry Book, 1995; featured cover story: Zebra Mag., 2001. Bd. dir. Reach Out & Touch Club, Inc., Athens, 2001—. Recipient Cmty. Svc. award, Reach Out & Touch Club, Inc., 2000. Mem.: NEA, Nat. Assn. Social Studies, Reach Out and Touch Club (fin. coord.). Democrat. African Meth. Episcopal. Avocations: reading, travel, writing. Home: 10 Huntington Ln Crawford GA 30630-2333

SPEARS, SALLY, lawyer; b. San Antonio, Aug. 29, 1938; d. Adrian Anthony and Elizabeth (Wylie) S.; m. Tor Hultgreen, July 15, 1961 (div. Jan. 1983); children: Dagny Elizabeth, Sara Kirsten, Kara Spears. BA, U. Tex., 1960, LLB, 1965. Bar: Tex. 1961, Ill. 1971. Practice law, Stamford, Conn., 1966-67, Chgo., 1970-71, Northbrook, Ill., 1972-73, Toronto, Ont., Canada, 1973-81; assoc. firm Cummings & Lockwood, Stamford, 1966-67, Kirkland & Ellis, Chgo., 1970-71; sr. atty. Allstate Ins. Co., Northbrook, Ill., 1971-73; gen. counsel, sec. Reed Paper Ltd., Reed Ltd., Toronto, 1973-78, Denison Mines Ltd., Toronto, 1978-81; pvt. practice law San Antonio, 1981—. Apptd. by Sec. of Def. to serve on Def. Adv. Com., Women in the Svcs., 1997—99. Author: Call Sign Revlon: The Life and Death of Navy Fighter Pilot Kara Hultgreen, 1998. Mem. Tex. Bar Assn., San Antonio Bar Assn., Bankruptcy Bar Assn., Bexar County Women's Bar Assn., San Antonio Country Club, The Club at Sonterra. Home: 433 Evans Ave San Antonio TX 78209-3725 Office: Ste 106 8151 Broadway San Antonio TX 78209-1938 Office Phone: 210-826-7020. Personal E-mail: sespears@swbell.net.

SPECHT, LISA, lawyer; m. Ronald J. Rogers, Oct. 17, 1982. JD, U. Laverne, 1976. Bar: Calif. 1976. Assoc. Manatt, Phelps & Phillips, LA, 1976—82, ptnr., 1982—. Legal reporter Sta. KABC-TV, LA, 1979—89; host Trial Watch, Sta. NBC-TV; co-chair, Govt. Practice Group Manatt, Phelps & Phillips, chair, Land Use Practice Group. Chair, commissioner LA Meml. Coliseum Commn.; chair LA Recreation & Parks Commn.; chief coun. Dem. Nat. Convention, LA, 2000; mem. Women's Leadership Bd. John F. Kennedy Sch. Govt. Harvard U.; mem., exec. bd. Am. Jewish Com.; hon. dir. NOW Legal Defense & Edn. Fund Bd. (now Legal Momentum); bd. dirs. Bet Tzedek Legal Svcs.; mem. US Dept. Commerce Industry Policy Advisory Com.; co-founder, chair Women's Polit. Comm.; co-chmn. Women's Polit. Com. LA, 1982—; exec. bd. mem. Ctrl. City Assn.; exec. bd. trustees Pitzer Coll.; exec. bd. mem. Town Hall LA; bd. dirs. LA Sports & Entertainment Commn., Urban League; trustee LA Sports Coun. Named one of Top 100 Attys. in Calif., Calif. Law Bus., Most Prominent Attys. in LA County, LA Bus. Journ., Top Influential Laywers in Calif., Calif. Law Bus.; recipient Learned Hand award, Am. Jewish Com., Women of Achievement award, Calif. Legis., Woman of Achievement award, Big Sisters, Nat. Orgn. Women, Women of Achievement award, Bus. & Profl. Women's Club. Mem.: LA Women's Lawyers Assn., Calif. Women Lawyers Assn. (bd. dirs.), Calif. Bar Assn., LA County Bar Assn. Office Phone: 310-312-4298. Business E-Mail: lspecht@manatt.com.

SPECHT, LOIS DARLENE, volunteer; b. Clinton, Iowa, June 4, 1931; d. Carl Andrew and Viola Emma (Andresen) Johnson; m. Joseph H. Smith, Sept. 2, 1951 (dec. 1963); m. Paul A. Specht, Nov. 26, 1965; children: Linda Marie Janson, Susan Jo Swanson. AA, Clinton Community Coll., 1951, Mt. St. Clare Coll., 1960; BA, Marycrest Coll., 1967. Cert. elem. sch. tchr., art tchr., Iowa. Tchr. Clinton Community Schs., 1960-88. Active State Adv. Com. on Tchr. Cert., Des Moines, 1980-86. Bd. dirs. Clinton Community Coll., 1982—; vol. Clinton Main St. Program, 1986-89, 1991—, Symphony Aux., Clinton, 1989; com. woman Rep. Cen. Com., Clinton. Named Best Vol. State of Iowa Dept. Econ. Devel., 1991. Mem. AAUW, Clinton C.C. Assn., Delta Kappa Gamma (pres. Alpha Beta chpt. 1992-96). Lutheran. Home: 1005 7th Ave Fulton IL 61252-1249

SPECK, HEIDI, philosopher, educator; d. Bruce and Carmen Speck. B in Profl. Studies, U. Memphis, 1999, MA, 2001; postgrad., Ariz. State U., Tempe, 2002—. Intern Tenn. Gen. Assembly, Nashville, 1996; legal aide Armstrong, Allen, Prewitt, Gentry, Johnston, & Holmes P.L.L.C., Memphis, 1996—98; intern US Senate, Washington, 1997; grad. asst. Lincoln Ctr. for Applied Ethics, Tempe, Ariz., 2002—03; instr. philosophy and religion Scottsdale C.C., Ariz., 2003—; editl. asst. Philos. Studies, Tempe, 2003—04. Chair univ. tchg. award com. Ctr. for Academic Excellence, U. Memphis, 1999—2000. Vol. Meals on Wheels, Fayetteville, 2001—02. Recipient Alumni Assn. award, U. Memphis, 1999, Outstanding Legal Rsch. award, 2000, Outstanding Paralegal Student award, 2000, U. Grad. Scholar award, Ariz. State U., 2002—04, Philosophy Grad. Student award, 2005—06; Regents scholar, U. Memphis, 1994—98. Mem.: Am. Philos. Assn. Personal E-mail: heidi.speck@asu.edu.

SPECKHART, DAWN SEIDNER, bone marrow transplant/leukemia psychologist; b. Miami, Fla., Mar. 8, 1971; d. Jack Edward and Judith Naomi Seidner; m. Michael Alan Speckhart, June 25, 1995; children: Logan Shay, Jordan Elizabeth. BA, Ind. U., 1989—93, MS, 1993—95, PhD, 1995—99. Licensed Psychologist GA, 2000. Clin. psychologist Medlin Treatment Ctr., Stockbridge, Ga., 2000—02; bone marrow transplant/leukemia psychologist Northside Hosp., Atlanta, 2002—. Rsch. psychologist Northside Hosp., Atlanta, 2004—. Mem.: APA, Southeastern Psychol. Assn., Am. Psychosocial Oncology Soc., Alpha Chi Omega (social chair 1991—92, Alumni). Office: Northside Hosp 1000 Johnson Ferry Rd BMT Unit Atlanta GA 30342 Office Phone: 404-255-1930. Office Fax: 404-255-1939. E-mail: dawn.speckhart@northside.com.

SPECTOR, ELEANOR RUTH, manufacturing executive; b. NYC, Dec. 2, 1943; d. Sidney and Helen Lebost; m. Mel Alan Spector, Dec. 10, 1966; children: Nancy, Kenneth. BA, Barnard Coll., 1964; postgrad. sch. pub. adminstrn., George Washington U., 1965-67; postgrad sch. edn., Nazareth Coll., 1974. Indsl. investigator N.Y. State Dept. Labor, White Plains, 1964-65; mgmt. intern Navy Dept., Washington, 1965, contract negotiator, 1965-68, contract specialist, 1975-78, contracting officer/br. head, 1978-82, dir. div. cost estimating, 1982-84; dep. asst. sec. def. for procurement Washington, 1984-91; dir. Def. Procurement, Washington, 1991-2000; v.p. contracts Lockheed Martin Corp., Bethesda, Md., 2000—. Advisor Nat. Contract Mgmt. Assn., 1984—, Fed. Contracts Report, 2000—. Recipient Def. Meritoroius Civilian Svc. medal, 1986, 93, 96, Meritorious Svc. Presdl. award, 1989, 94, Disting. Civilian Svc. Presdl. award, 1990, 97, Def. Disting. Civilian Svc. medal, 1991, 94, 2000, Nat. Pub. Svc. award, 1998, Sec. Def. award for Excellence, 1997. Office: Lockheed Martin Corp MP 110 6801 Rockledge Dr Bethesda MD 20817-1877

SPECTOR, JOHANNA LICHTENBERG, ethnomusicologist, former educator; b. Libau, Latvia; came to U.S., 1947, naturalized, 1954; d. Jacob C. and Anna (Meyer) Lichtenberg; m. Robert Spector, Nov. 20, 1939 (dec. Dec. 1941). DHS, Hebrew Union Coll., 1950; MA, Columbia U., 1960. Rsch. fellow Hebrew U., Jerusalem, 1951-53; faculty Jewish Theol. Sem. Am., N.Y.C., 1954—, dir., founder dept. ethnomusicology, 1962-85, assoc. prof. musicology, 1966-70, Sem. prof., 1970-85, prof. emeritus, 1985—. Author: Ghetto-und Kzlieder, 1947, Samaritan Chant, 1965, Musical Tradition and Innovation in Central Asia, 1966, Bridal Songs from Sana Yemen, 1960, Jewish Music in a Changing World Vol. 1, 2001; documentary films The Samaritans, 1971, Chicago International, 1973, Middle Eastern Music, 1973, About the Jews of India: Cochin, 1976 (Cine Golden Eagle 1979), The Shanwar Telis or Bene Israel of India, 1978 (Cine Golden Eagle 1979), About the Jews of Yemen, A Vanishing Culture, 1986 (Cine Golden Eagle 1986, Blue Ribbon, Am. Film Festival 1986), 2000 Years of Freedom and Honor: The Cochin Jews of India, 1992, Margaret Mead, 1992, Columbus International, 1993; religious and folk recs. number over 10,000; contbr. articles to encys., various jours.; editorial bd. Asian Music. Fellow Am. Anthrop. Assn.; mem. Am. Ethnol. Soc., Am. Musicol. Soc., Internat. Folks Music Coun., World Assn. Jewish Studies, Yivo, Asian Mus. Soc. (v.p. 1964—, pres. 1974-78), Soc. Ethnomusicology (sec.-treas. N.Y.C. chpt. 1960-64). Home: 400 W 119th St New York NY 10027-7125

SPECTOR, MAGALY, telecommunications industry executive; MS in Elec. Engr., PhD in Elec. Engr., Lehigh Univ., Bethlehem, Penn.; MBA, Harvard Bus. Sch.; degree (hon.), Bloomfield Coll. With Bell Labs, 1981, tech. innovator; global dir., quality and process improvement Lucent Technologies. Office: Lucent Technologies Inc 600 Mountain Ave New Providence NJ 07974-0636

SPECTOR, ROSE, former state supreme court justice; BA, Columbia U.; JD, St. Mary's Sch. Law, 1965. Judge County Ct. at Law 5, 1975-80, 131st Dist. Ct., 1981-92; justice Tex. Supreme Ct., 1993-98; atty. Bickerstaff, Heath, Pollan, Kever & McDaniel, L.L.P., Austin, Tex., 1998—. Office Phone: 512-404-7867.

SPEED, LYNN ELIZABETH, nurse practitioner; b. Houston, Mar. 23, 1954; d. Thomas R. and Kathryn M. Schmidt; m. David L. Speed, Sept. 11, 1982; children: Barbara Kay, William David. BSN, U. Tex., Houston, 1977; M Nursing, U. Wash., 1983; cert. nurse practitioner, U. Colo., 1987. RN, N. Mex.; cert. family nurse practitioner. Nurse practitioner Family Practice Office, Carlsbad, N.Mex., 2003—. Contbr. articles to nursing jours. Mem. ANA. Home: 1618 Mission Ave Carlsbad NM 88220-9644 Office: 2402 W Pierce Ste 4A Carlsbad NM 88220 Office Phone: 505-234-9964.

SPEEGLE, LAURA ANN, elementary school educator; d. James William and Mary Lou Speegle; 1 child, Kimberly Lynn Akers. MA in Edn., Wayne State U., 2003. Cert. tchr. Mich. Educator Detroit Pub. Schs., 1993—. Sch. improvement com. Carl T. Rowan Elem., Detroit, 1994—2001; team leader NASA Explorer Schs., 2005—; sci. adv. com. Mich. Dept. Edn., Lansing, 2004—. Constrn. com. vol. Habitat for Humanity, Detroit, 1998—2005; tutor Macomb (Mich.) Reading Ptnrs., 2001—02. Recipient Educator Achievement award, Booker T. Washington Bus. Assn., 1998; Target Tchr. scholar, Target Inc., 1999, Detroit Urban Systemic Initiative grantee, Detroit Pub. Schs., 1999—2000, Explorer Sch. grantee, NASA, 2005—. Mem.: Nat. Assn. for Edn. of Young Child, Mich. Sci. Tchr. Assn., Courville Girls Running Club (leader 2004—05). Democrat. Avocations: running, volleyball, weightlifting. Office: Detroit Pub Schs Courville Elem 18040 St Aubin Detroit MI 48234 Office Phone: 313-866-3000. Home Fax: 586-754-4106; Office Fax: 313-866-3011. Personal E-mail: lauraspeegle@sbcglobal.net.

SPEER, LEONA BETTINA, secondary school educator; b. Lakeland, Fla., June 22, 1953; d. James Leon and Rosemarie Margaretha (VonArnim) MacCartney; m. William J. Smith, Sr., July 12, 2003; children: Stephanie Bettina, Grant Michael. BS in Clinical Chemistry with honors, U. South Fla., Tampa, 1975, BS in Med. Tech., 1976; MS, Fla. Atlantic U., Boca Raton, 1984. Med. technologist Tampa Gen. Hosp., 1975—78; sales rep. lab. equipment Helena Labs., Beaumont, Tex., 1981—83; tchg. cons. Ednl. Resource Ctr., Boca Raton, 1985—93; sci. tchr. Omni Mid. Sch., Boca Raton, 1987—. Rsch. asst. U. South Fla., Tampa, 1977—80; sci. dept. chair Palm Beach County Sch. Bd., Fla., 1987—90. Vol. Advent Luth. Ch., Boca Raton, 1995—96, active women's group, 1997—2000. Mem.: Classroom Tchrs. Assn., Nat. Educators Am., Am. Chem. Soc. Avocations: reading, gardening, fishing. Home: 263 NW 70th St Boca Raton FL 33487 Office: Omni Mid Sch 5775 Jog Rd Boca Raton FL 33496

SPEICHER, HILDA, psychologist, educator; b. N.Y.C., Apr. 17, 1959; d. John Francis Speicher and Mary Cicely Nichols. BA in Psychology with honors, CUNY, 1989; MA in Social Psychology, U. Del., 1996, PhD in Social Psychology, 1998. Prin. Speicher Rsch. Cons., East Haven, Conn., 1988—; asst. to coord. undergrad. rsch. U. Del., 1989—98; project dir. Tandem Rsch., Mahwah, NJ, 1998—2000, sr. project dir., 2000, acct. group dir., 2000—02; sr. assoc. dir. Ctr. Rsch. Edn. and Practice, Nat. Alliance for Mentally Ill., Washington, 2002—03; dir. rsch. Inst. Rsch. to Practice, Peconic, NY, 2002—03; asst. prof. psychology, coord. psychology accelerated degree program Albertus Magnus Coll., New Haven, 2003—. Presenter in field. Contbr. articles to profl. jours. Activist MoveOn.org, Conn., 2003—, Conn. Carcinoid Initiative, 2004—. Grantee, Wellness, Inc., 1997, U. Del., 1997—98, NAMI, 2002, Janssen Pharmaceutica, 2002; Youth Found. scholar, 1988. Mem.: Assn. Psychological Sci., New Eng. Psychol. Assn., Ea. Psychol. Assn. Democrat. Avocations: nature photography, creative writing, bird-watching, hiking, sailing. Home: 223 Thompson St D East Haven CT 06513 Office: Albertus Magnus Coll 700 Prospect St New Haven CT 06511 Business E-Mail: hspeicher@cc.albertus.edu.

SPEIGHTS, LILLIE, elementary school educator; b. Marianna, Fla., July 20, 1951; AA, Chipola Jr. Coll., 1973; BS, U. West Fla., 1975; MA, Troy State U., 1977, edn. specialist, 1990. Prin. Marianna Mid. Sch., 1986—89; parent edn. specialist Jackson Co. Sch. Bd., Marianna, 1989—90, dir. title I, 1990—2003, dir. title I, early childhood/elem. edn., 2003—06; ret., 2006. Office: Jackson Co Sch Bd 2903 Jefferson St Marianna FL 32446 E-mail: lillie.speights@jcsb.org.

SPEIR, MARCIA ANN, retired accountant; b. Tulsa, Oct. 20, 1935; d. Charles Henry and Pearl Jewell (Palmer) Hall; m. Jack Wesley Speir, June 17, 1955; 1 child, Andrea Renee. Student, Northeastern State Coll., Tahlequah, Okla., 1953-56, Am. River Coll., Sacramento, Calif., 1974-76. Acct. Commonwealth Life Ins. Co., Tulsa, 1953-56, Okla. Natural Gas Co., Tulsa, 1957-62; acct., systems analyst Shell Oil Co., Tulsa, 1962-69; staff acct. Trane Heating and Air Conditioning, Sacramento, 1975-79; owner Arapahoe County Steamway Carpet & Upholstery Cleaning Co., Denver, 1969-74; acct., office mgr. Sureway Corp., Sacramento, 1980-89; on med. leave, 1989—. Career counselor Am. River Coll., 1974-76; active in cancer support groups. Mem. NAFE, Sacramento Employer Adv. Group. Republican. Mem. Christian Ch. Avocations: tennis, walking, sewing, piano. Home: 4930 Andrew Cir Sacramento CA 95841

SPELBRING, BRANDI D., language educator, writer; b. Dieterich, Ill., Jan. 8, 1977; d. Nancy and Ernest Spelbring. M in English, Ea. Ill. U., Charleston, 2001. Instr. Lake Land Coll., Mattoon, Ill., 2001—. Home: 20 Easy Breeze Effingham IL 62401 Office: Lake Land Coll 1204 Network Centre Blvd Effingham IL 62401 Office Phone: 217-540-3555. Business E-Mail: bspelbri@lakeland.cc.il.us.

SPELLING, TORI (VICTORIA DAVEY SPELLING), actress; b. LA, May 16, 1973; d. Aaron and Carol Jean Spelling; m. Charlie Shanian, July 3, 2004 (div. Apr. 20, 2006); m. Dean McDermott, May 7, 2006. Actor: (TV films) Shooting Stars, 1983, The Three Kings, 1987, A Friend to Die For, 1994, Awake to Danger, 1995, Deadly Pursuits, 1996, Co-ed Call Girl, 1996, Mother, May I Sleep with Danger?, 1996, The Alibi, 1997, Way Downtown, 2002, A Carol Christmas, 2003, Hush, 2005, The Family Plan, 2005, Mind Over Murder, 2006; (TV series) Beverly Hills, 90210, 1990—2000, So Downtown, 2003, The Help, 2004, So noTORIous (also co-exec. prodr.), 2006—; (films) Troop Beverly Hills, 1989, The House of Yes, 1997, Scream 2, 1997, Perpetrators of the Crime, 1998, Trick, 1999, Sol Goode, 2001, Scary Movie 2, 2001, Evil Alien Conquerors, 2002, 50 Ways to Leave Your Lover, 2004, Cthulhu, 2006. Office: c/o United Talent Agy Ste 500 9560 Wilshire Blvd Beverly Hills CA 90212-2401*

SPELLINGS, MARGARET LAMONTAGNE, secretary of education; b. Ann Arbor, Mich., Nov. 30, 1957; d. John and Peg Dudar; m. Robert Spellings, 2001; children: Mary, Grace. BA in polit. sci. & jornalism, U. Houston, 1979. Worked for Tex. Gov. William P. Clements; assoc. exec. dir. Tex. Assn. Sch. Bds.; polit. dir. Gov. George W. Bush gubernatorial campaign, Tex., 1994; sr. advisor to Gov. George W. Bush State of Tex., 1994—2000; asst. to Pres. for domestic policy The White House, Washington, 2001—05; sec. US Dept. Edn., Washington, 2005—. Host online interactive forum Ask the White House. Named one of 100 Most Powerful Women in Wash., Washingtonian mag., 2001. Achievements include one of the principal authors of the No Child Left Behind Act, 2001. Office: US Dept Edn 400 Maryland Ave SW Washington DC 20202*

SPELLMAN, ELIZABETH MAY, education administrator; b. Waterbury, Conn., June 23, 1933; d. William Joseph and Beatrice Louella (Hill) Dunn; d. John Franklin Spellman Jr., Aug. 11, 1951 (dec. Mar. 1979); children: John Franklin III, Adam Lyons. BA, U. R.I., 1971; MA, Calif. State U., Northridge, 1972. Instr. Bristol Community Coll., Fall River, Mass., 1972-74, R.I. Sch. for Deaf, Providence, 1972-74, supr., instr., 1974-76, dir. adult svcs., 1977-86, dir. sign lang., 1977—91, transition coord., 1986—91. Mem. R.I. Commn. on Deaf and Hearing Impaired, Providence, 1979-91; mem. adv. bd. Nat. Captioning Inst., Falls Church, Va., 1981-88; facilitator Nat. Conf. on Deaf and Hard of Hearing People, El Paso, Tex., 1988. Editor newsletter Voice, 1990-92; author pamphlet Words From a Deaf Parent, 1973. Named Deaf Woman of yr., 15th Dist. Quota Club, 1978. Mem. Am. Deafness and Rehab. Assn., Nat. Assn. of Deaf, Registry of Interpreters for Deaf Inc. (life, cert.), Nat. Rehab. Assn. Unitarian Universalist. Avocations: needlecrafts, reading.

SPELLMAN SWEET, JULIA T., lawyer; b. Orange, Calif., Oct. 11, 1967; BA, Claremont McKenna Coll., 1989; JD, Columbia Univ., 1992. Bar: NY 1993. Assoc. Cravath Swaine & Moore LLP, NYC, 1992—2000, ptnr., corp., 2000—. Bd. trustees Claremont McKenna Coll.; bd. dir. Drew Found. Recipient Harlan Fiske Stone Scholar, 1992. Mem.: NY Lawyers for the Pub. Interest, Disability Rights Task Force, Phi Beta Kappa. Fluent in Mandarin Chinese. Office: Cravath Swaine & Moore LLP Worldwide Plz 825 Eighth Ave New York NY 10019-7475 Office Phone: 212-474-1572. Office Fax: 212-474-3700. Business E-Mail: jspellmansweet@cravath.com.*

SPELMAN, LUCY H., zoological park administrator; b. Bridgeport, Conn. BS in Biology, Brown U., 1985; DVM, U. Calif., Davis, 1990. Intern in small animal medicine and cardiology Dr. S. Ettinger and Assocs., L.A., 1990—91; resident in zool. medicine NC State Coll. Vet. Medicine/NC State Zool. Park, Asheboro, 1991—94; assoc. vet. med. officer Nat. Zool. Pk., Washington, 1995—99, sr. vet. med. officer, 1999—2000, dir., 2000—. Vet. advisor giant panda species survival plan Am. Zoo and Aquarium Assn., 1998—. Editor: Jour. Zoo and Wildlife Medicine, 1994—. Mem.: Am. Coll. Zool. Medicine (mem. exam. com. 1995—). Office: Nat Zool Park 3001 Connecticut Ave NW Washington DC 20008

SPENARD, PATRICIA ANN, science educator; b. Fort Meade, Md., Apr. 26, 1958; d. Napoleon Louis and Mitsuko Miyajima Spenard. BS in Biology, Columbus Coll., Ga., 1989; MEd in Sci. Edn., Ga. State U., 1994. Science education T-5 Ga., 1997. Tchr. Hardaway H.S., 1996—97, Jordan H.S., 1997—99, Shaw H.S., 2000—. Mem. sci. acad. team Jordan H.S., tennis coach, 2000—01, 2003—; tchr. support specialist, curriculum coun., 2003—. Mem. Nat. Arbor Day Found., Help the Hooch River Clean Up, 2000—, tech. com., 2001. Mem.: Nat. Educator Assn., Ga. Assn. of Educators, Nat. Sci. Tchrs. Assn., Cousteau Soc., Am. Forest Assn., Arbor Day Found., Audubon Soc., U.S. Tennis Assn., Nat. Home Gardening Assn., Kappa Delta Pi. Home: 4705 20th Ave Apt 2 Columbus GA 31904 Office: Muscogee County School District/ Shaw Hs 7601 Schomburg Road Columbus GA 31909 Office Phone: 706-569-3638. Personal E-mail: p.spenard@worldnet.att.net.

SPENCE, BARBARA E., former publishing company executive; b. Bryn Mawr, Pa., July 8, 1921; d. Geoffrey Strange and Mary (Harrington) Earnshaw; m. Kenneth M. Spence Jr., June 29, 1944; children: Kenneth M. III, Christopher E., Hilary B. Grad. high sch. Movie, radio editor Parade Mag., N.Y.C., 1941-45; with Merchandising Group, N.Y.C., 1946-47; exec. dir. Greenfield Hill Congl. Ch., Fairfield, Conn., 1958-74, dir. religious edn., 1968-74; assoc. Ten Eyck-Emerich Antiques, 1974-76; personnel dir. William Morrow & Co., Inc., N.Y.C., 1976-91; ret., 1991. Chmn. pub. relations, bd. dirs. ARC, 1951-56, Family Service Soc., Fairfield, 1956-57, 61-63; chmn. pub. relations Citizens for Eisenhower, 1952, Fairfield Teens Players, 1968-71; bd. dirs. Fairfield Teens, Inc., 1965-70, Planned Parenthood of Greater Bridgeport, 1969-75, chmn. pub. affairs, 1971-72, chmn. personnel, 1972-73, chpt. vice chmn., 1973-75; pres. steering com. Am. Playwrights Festival Theatre, Inc., Fairfield, 1969-70, v.p., bd. dirs., 1971—; bd. govs. Unquowa Sch., Fairfield, 1963-69; bd. dirs. Fairfield U. Playhouse, 1971-73, Downtown Cabaret Theatre, Bridgeport, 1975-76; bd. missions Southport Congl. Ch., 1998. Mem. AAP (compensation survey com.), Fairfield Women's Exch. (bd. dirs. 1993). Home: 101 Twin Brooks Ln Fairfield CT 06430-2834

SPENCE, DIANNA JEANNENE, software engineer, educator; b. Mountain View, Calif., June 5, 1964; d. Ronald Kenneth and Susan (Durham) S. BA, Coll. William and Mary, 1985; MS, Ga. State U., 1996; PhD, Emory U., 2004. Tchr. math. and computers Woodward Acad., College Park, Ga., 1985-90; software engr. Computer Comm. Specialists, Inc., Norcross, Ga., 1990-98; ind. cons., 1998—2003; instr. math. and computer sci. Ga. Perimeter Coll., 1999, 2002—04; software engr. Knowlagent, Inc., Alpharetta, Ga., 2003—05; prof. math. North Ga. Coll. and State U., 2005—. Tutor, 1994-. Mem. Pi Kappa Phi, Pi Mu Epsilon. Jewish. Avocations: travel, writing, music, theater.

SPENCE, FAY FRANCES, lawyer, educator; b. Charlottesville, Va., June 15, 1962; d. Ronald Kenneth and Susan (Durham) S. AA, St. Leo Coll., 1980, BA summa cum laude, 1983; JD, Coll. of William & Mary, 1987. Bar: Va. 1987, U.S. Dist. Ct. (ea. dist.) Va. 1987, U.S. Ct. Appeals (4th cir.) 1987, U.S. Supreme Ct., 1991, Ga. 1997. Electrician Newport News (Va.) Shipbuilding, 1980-84; assoc. Knight, Dudley, Dezern & Clarke, Norfolk, Va., 1987-92; ptnr. Gaidies, Young & Spence, Norfolk, 1992-95, Spence & Whitlow, Norfolk, 1995—. Adj. prof. law St. Leo Coll.-Langley AFB, Hampton, Va., 1989-95. Mem. Lawyers Helping Lawyers, Norfolk, 1988—, chmn., 1992-97. Mem. Va. Bar Assn. (substance abuse com.), VADA, Norfolk-Portsmouth (Va.) Bar Assn. (CLE com.), Am. Corp. Counsel. Assn., Order of Coif. Lutheran. Avocations: writing, tennis, needlecrafts, cooking. Office: Spence & Whitlow 1630 Dominion Tower 999 Waterside Dr Norfolk VA 23510-3300

SPENCE, MARY LEE, historian, educator; b. Kyle, Tex., Aug. 4, 1927; d. Jeremiah Milton and Mary Louise (Hutchison) Nance; m. Clark Christian Spence, Sept. 12, 1953; children: Thomas Christian, Ann Leslie. BA, U. Tex., 1947, MA, 1948; PhD, U. Minn., 1957. Instr., asst. prof. S.W. Tex. State U., San Marcos, 1948-53; lectr. Pa. State U., State College, 1955-58; mem. faculty U. Ill., Urbana-Champaign, 1973—, asst. prof., assoc. prof., 1973-81, 81-89, prof. history, 1989-90, prof. emerita, 1990—. Editor (with Donald Jackson) The Expeditions of John Charles Fremont, 3 vols., 1970-84, (with Clark Spence) Fanny Kelly's Narrative of Her Captivity Among the Sioux Indians, 1990, (with Pamela Herr) The Letters of Jessie Benton Fremont, 1993, The Arizona Diary of Lily Fremont, 1878-1881, 1997; contbr. articles to profl. jours. Mem. Children's Theater Bd., Urbana-Champaign, 1965-73. Grantee Nat. Hist. Pub. and Records Commn., Washington, 1977-78, 87-90,

Huntington Libr., 1992; recipient Excellent Advisor award Liberal Arts and Sci. Coll./U. Ill., 1986. Mem. Western History Assn. (pres. 1981-82), Phi Beta Kappa (exec. sect. Gamma chpt. 1985-89, pres. 1991-92), Phi Alpha Theta. Episcopalian. Home: 101 W Windsor Rd #1211 Urbana IL 61802-6663 Office: U Ill Dept History 810 S Wright St Urbana IL 61801-3644

SPENCE, SANDRA, retired trade association administrator; b. McKeesport, Pa., Mar. 25, 1941; d. Cedric Leroy and Suzanne (Haudenshield) S. BA, Allegheny Coll., 1963; MA, Rutgers U., 1964. With Pa. State Govt., Harrisburg, 1964-68, Appalachian Regional Commn., Washington, 1968-75; legis. rep. Nat. Assn. Counties, Washington, 1975-77; fed. rep. Calif. Dept. Transp., Washington, 1977-78; dir. congl. affairs Amtrak, Washington, 1978-81, corp. sec., 1981-83, dir. comml. svcs., 1983-84; co-owner Parkhurst-Spence Inc., 1985; owner The Spence Group, 1986-90; v.p. Bostrom Corp., Washington, 1990-92; exec. dir. Soc. Glass and Ceramic Decorators, 1992-2000. Chmn. legis. com. Womens Transp. Seminar, 1977-79, dir., 1982-83, v.p., 1983-84, chmn. edn. com., 1982-83; com. on edn. and tng. Transp. Rsch. Bd., 1982-85; mng. ptnr. Cambio Capital Club, 1996. Contbr. articles to profl. jours. Commnr. DC Commn. for Women, 1983—88, sec., 1983—88; pres. Found. for Work of Laity, 2001—06; del. Ward III Dem. Com., 1982—90, 1st vice chmn., 1987—88; bd. dir. DC Habitat for Humanity, 1998—2002, chmn. devel. com., 1998—2000, sec., 2000—01, Sussex County (Del.) Habitat for Humanity, 2003—05, bd. dirs., 2003—, treas., 2005—. Fellow Eagleton Inst. Politics, 1963-64; recipient Achievement award Transp. Seminar, 1982, 83 Mem. Greater Washington Soc. Assn. Execs. (vice-chair law and legis. com. 1989-90, chmn. 1990-91, chmn. scholarship com. 1992-93, bd. dirs. 1993-96, Rising Star award 1989, Chmn.'s award for Govt. Rels. 1991), Am. Soc. Assn. Execs. (mgmt. cert. 1987), Phi Beta Kappa. Home: 18471 Seashell Blvd Lewes DE 19958 Personal E-mail: sandy_s@juno.com.

SPENCE, SIQUE (MARY STEWART SPENCE), art dealer; b. Balt., Aug. 16, 1946; d. Joseph Adolphus and Nell Orum (Jones) Stoll; m. Ronald A. Kuchta, Nov. 2, 1969 (div. 1975); m. Andrew R. Spence, June 24, 1977. Dir. Galeria del Sol/Fairtree Fine Crafts Inst., Santa Barbara, Calif., 1970-75; asst. to dir. Arco Ctr. for the Visual Arts, L.A., 1975-77; registrar Droll/Kolbert Gallery, N.Y.C., 1977-78; gallery asst. Nancy Hoffman Gallery, N.Y.C., 1978-81, dir., 1981—. Office: Nancy Hoffman Gallery 429 W Broadway New York NY 10012-3799 Fax: 212-334-5078.

SPENCER, ANGELA, physician assistant; b. Zilah, Hungary, Feb. 24, 1943; came to U.S., 1964; d. Janos Sreter and Iren Both; m. Egon S. Fabian, June 20, 1966 (div.); children: Thomas Fabian, Gabor Fabian; m. Donald Lynn Spencer, May 7, 1994. BSN, Szegedi Vedonokepzo Iskola, Szeged, Hungary, 1963; BS, Hahnemann U., 1982; MSN, Gwynedd Mercy Coll., 1994. RN, cert. physician asst. Physician asst. Germantown Orthopedics, Phila., 1990-93, Campus Med. Ctr., Chester, Penn., 1993—. Dir. A&M Home Health Care, Gwynedd Valley, Penn.; asst. adminstr. Pinewood Acres Nursing & Rehab. Ctr., Maple Shade, N.J. Mem. Assn. Am. Phys. Assts., Nat. Commn. Cert. Phys. Assts., Penn. Soc. Phys. Assts., Sigma Theta Tau. Republican. Roman Catholic. Avocations: gardening, teaching, arts & crafts, painting. Home: 710 Elm Tree Ln Boca Raton FL 33486-5655 E-mail: docspenc@aol.com.

SPENCER, ANNA KATHLEEN, mathematics educator; b. Anderson, Ind., May 21, 1978; d. Debra Ann Spencer. BS in Elem. Edn., Anderson U., 2001. Cert. tchr. mid. sch. math. Ind. Tchr. 7th grade math. Wilson Mid. Sch. Muncie Cmty. Schs., Ind., 2001—. Asst. program dir. Camp Crosley YMCA Camp, North Webster, Ind., 1999—2003. Recipient Tchr. of Yr. Sch. Level award, Muncie Cmty. Schs., 2005. Mem.: Kappa Delta Pi (assoc.). Home: 2401 Holden Dr Anderson IN 46012 Office: Muncie Comty Schs Wilson Mid Sch 3100 S Tillotson Ave Muncie IN 47302 Office Phone: 765-747-5370. Business E-Mail: aspencer@muncie.k12.in.us.

SPENCER, CAROL BROWN, retired educational association administrator; b. Normal, Ill., Aug. 26, 1936; d. Fred William and Sorado (Gross) B.; m. James Calvin Spencer, Dec. 18, 1965 (div. July 1978); children: James Calvin Jr., Anne Elizabeth. BA English, Calif. State U., L.A., 1964, MA Pub. Adminstrn., 1986. Cert. secondary edn. tchr., Calif. Tchr. English Seneca Vocat. H.S., Buffalo, 1966—70; pub. info. officer City of Pasadena, Calif., 1979—90, City of Mountain View, Calif., 1990—93; exec. dir. Calif. Assn. for Gifted, 1993—98; ret., 1998. Owner PR to Go, 1994— Sec., bd. dirs. Calif. Music Theatre, 1987-90; bd. dirs. Pasadena Beautiful Found., 1984-90, Pasadena Cultural Festival Found., 1983-86, Palo Alto-Stanford Heritage, 1990-93, Mountain View Libr. Found., 1997-98; mayoral appointee Strategic Planning Adv. Com., Pasadena, 1985-86; active Nev. Arts Advocates; trainer Clark County Election Dept., 1997-2004; centennial com. City of Las Vegas, 2004-06 Mem. NOW, Pub. Rels. Soc. Am., Calif. Assn. Pub. Info. Ofcls. (Paul Clark Achievement award 1986, Mktg. award 1990), City/County Comm. and Mktg. Assn. (bd. dirs. 1988-90, Savvy award for mktg. 1990), Las Vegas Art Mus Democrat. Episcopalian. Home: 7915 Laurena Ave Las Vegas NV 89147-5064

SPENCER, CAROLE A., medical association administrator, medical educator; BSc in Applied Biochemistry, Bath U. Tech., Bath, Somerset, Eng., 1969; PhD, Glasgow U., Scotland, 1972. Lic. clin. chemist med. technologist Calif., 1985. Lectr. in biochemistry Glasgow U., Scotland, 1972—73; asst. prof. rsch. medicine U. So. Calif., L.A., 1980—88, assoc. prof. rsch. medicine, 1988—94, prof. rsch. medicine, 1995—, dir. Endocrine Svcs. Lab., 1980—, GCRC Core Lab. dir. Clin. Rsch. Ctr., 1977—, GCRC Core Low Level Ligand Detection lab. dir., 1993—. Biochemist dept. pathol. biochemistry Glasgow Royal Infirmary, 1973—77; lectr. in field; cons. in field. Editl. bd. Jour. Clin. endocrinology and Metabolism, 1984—88, Am. Assn. Clin. Chemistry Jours., 1996—, Hormone and Metabolic Rsch., 1996—, reviewer Annals of Internal Medicine, —, Clin. Chemistry, —, Gerontology, —, Hormone and Metabolic Rsch., —, Jour. of Clin. Endocrinology and Metabolism, —, Jour. of Clin. Investigation, —, Jour. of Endocrinol. Investigation, —; contbr. articles to profl. jours. Mem.: European Thyroid Assn., Assn. Clin. Biochemists U.K., Endocrine Soc., Clin. Ligand Assay Soc. (Disting. Scientist award 1998), Am. Thyroid Assn. (pub. health com. 1991—, pres., exec. coun. 1995—), Am. Fedn. Clin. Rsch., Am. Assn. Clin. endocrinologists, Am. Assn. Clin. Chemists (Outstanding Spkr. award 1992, 1997), Cross-Town Endocrine Club. Achievements include research in includes thyroid physiology and pathology; thyroglobulin and thyroid cancer; thyroid hormone metabolism; immunoassay techniques. Office: U Southern Calif EDM111 9560 Los Angeles CA 90089

SPENCER, CHERYL L., literature and language educator; BA, Edgewood Coll., 1969; MA in Theater and Drama, U. Wis., Madison, 1993. Cert. tchr. secondary education, English Wis., 1974. Affirmative action asst. officer City of Madison, Wis., 1985—86; English tchr. Madison Met. Sch. Dist., 1969—, English tchr. diploma completion program, 1977—84, English tchr. summer sch., 1975. Sys. strategic planning in tchr. edn. com. U. of Wis., 1989—92; minority student achievement com. Madison Met. Sch. Dist., 1977—79, graduation stds. com., 1999—2000; pres. faculty senate Madison Meml. H.S., 1980—84, scholarship com., 2003—; tchr. edn. rev. panel U. Wis.-Plattville Dept. of Pub. Instrn., State of Wis., Madison, 2003. Producer- organizer, media person (traveling theatre group performances); dir.: (high school play) Plautus' The Captives. Bd. dirs. Urban League of Greater Madison, 1992—94. Recipient Outstanding H.S. Tchr. award, U. of Chgo., 1998. Mem.: Nat. Coun. of Tchrs. of English, Wis. Edn. Assn. Coun. (rep. to state rep. assembly 1977—80), Madison Tchrs. Inc. (bd. dirs., com. chair 1980—94). Office: Madison Memorial High School 201 S Gammon Rd Madison WI 53717 Office Phone: 608-663-5990. E-mail: cspencer@madison.k12.wi.us.

SPENCER, ELIZABETH, writer; b. Carrollton, Miss., 1921; d. James Luther and Mary James (McCain) S.; m. John Arthur Blackwood Rusher, Sept. 29, 1956. BA, Belhaven Coll., 1942; MA, Vanderbilt U., 1943; LittD (hon.), Southwestern U. at Memphis, 1968; LLD (hon.), Concordia U. at Montreal, 1988; LittD (hon.), U. of the South, 1992; DLitt (hon.), U. NC, Chapel Hill, 1998, Belhaven Coll., 1999. Instr. N.W. Miss. Jr. Coll., 1943-44, Ward-Belmont, Nashville, 1944-45; reporter The Nashville Tennessean, 1945-46; instr. U. Miss., Oxford, 1948-51, 52-53. Vis. prof. Concordia U., Montreal, Que., Can., 1976-81, adj. prof., 1981-86; vis. prof. U. NC, Chapel Hill, 1986-92. Author: Fire in the Morning, 1948, This Crooked Way, 1952, The Voice at the Back Door, 1956, The Light in the Piazza, 1960, Knights and Dragons, 1965, No Place for an Angel, 1967, Ship Island and Other Stories, 1968, The Snare, 1972, The Stories of Elizabeth Spencer, 1981, Marilee, 1981, The Salt Line, 1984, Jack of Diamonds and Other Stories, 1988, (play) For Lease or Sale, 1989, On the Gulf, 1991, The Night Travellers, 1991, (memoir) Landscapes of the Heart, 1998, The Southern Woman, 2001; contbr. short stories to mags. and anthologies. Named to NC Hall of Fame, 2002; recipient Women's Dem. Com. award, 1949, recognition award, Nat. Inst. Arts and Letters, 1952, Richard and Hinda Rosenthal Found. award, Am. Acad. Arts and Letters, 1957, Fortner award for lit., 1998, Award of Merit medal for the short story, 1983, 1st McGraw-Hill Fiction award, 1960, Henry Bellamann award for creative writing, 1968, Salem award for lit., 1992, Dos Passos award for fiction, 1992, NC Gov.'s award for lit., 1994, Corrington award for lit., 1997, Richard Wright award for lit., 1997, award for non-fiction, Miss. Libr. Assn., 1999, Brooks medal, Fellowship of So. Writers, 2001, Thomas Wolfe award for lit., 2002, William Faulkner award for lit. excellence, 2002, Miss. Gov.'s award for excellence in the arts, 2006; fellow, Guggenheim Found., 1953; Kenyon Rev. fellow in fiction, 1957, Bryn Mawr Coll. Donnelly fellow, 1962, Nat. Endowment for Arts grantee in lit., 1983, Sr. Arts Award grantee, Nat. Endowment for the Arts, 1988. Mem. Am. Acad. Arts and Letters, Fellowship of So. Writers (charter; vice chancellor 1993-97). Home: 402 Longleaf Dr Chapel Hill NC 27517-3042 Office Phone: 919-929-2115. E-mail: elizabeth0222@earthlink.net.

SPENCER, HEIDI HONNOLD, psychotherapist, writer, educator; b. Washington, June 30, 1943; d. John Otis and Annamarie (Kunz) Honnold; m. Charles David Spencer, Dec. 28, 1962; children: Hans Steven, Jason John, Tanya Anna BA, U. Pa., 1965; MA, Columbia U., 1966; MSW, Cath. U., 1982; PhD Adult and Family Psychology, Union Inst., Cin., 1990. Cert. clin. social worker, cert. nat. bd. addictions examiners; lic. social worker, D.C., Md., W.Va. Tchr. h.s. Peace Corps, Yap Island, 1966—68; faculty instr. Ctrl. Wash. State Coll., Ellensburg, 1972—75; parent group facilitator Individual Psychology Assocs., Chevy Chase, Md., 1975—79; group facilitator Georgetown U. Med. Sch., Washington, 1977—80; staff clinician D.C. Inst. Mental Health, 1980—86; pvt. practice in adult psychotherapy Bethesda, Md., 1985—; faculty Cath. U. Psychoanalytic Found., 1989—91; bd. dirs., cons., faculty, supr. Clin. Social Work Inst.; pvt. practice, 2006—. Mem. bd. doctoral program for clin. social workers; counselor, tchr. Spl. Sch. for Pregnant Teenagers, Seattle, 1969-71; crisis intervention counselor Montgomery County (Md.) Hotline, 1975-79; mental health intern No. Va. Mental Health Inst., Falls Church, 1979-80; faculty Cath. U., Washington, 1991; cons., counselor Christ Child Soc., Rockville, Md., 1985-86; cons. Jewish Cmty. Ctr., Rockville, 1992, Brooklane Psychiat. Ctr., Hagerstown, Md., 1992, AmeriCorps, Washington, 1996, Affiliated Cmty. Counselors, Inc., Rockville, 1996—; instr. insvc. psychol. and learning ctr. Am. U., Washington, 1990—; chair, Conf. Washington Psychoanalytic Found., 1989-90; cons. The Bilingual Project/Project BUILD, Yakima, Wash., 1973-75; curriculum com. Clin. Social Work Inst., 1991-94; spkr., presenter in field; with recovery work Charles Town Race Traces Office of Chaplain; clinician Shenandoah Valley Free Clinic, Charles Tocon, W.Va.; cons., primary clinican HIV/AIDS Network Tristate, Martinsburg, W.Va Author: (2 vols. book and record) Our Valley-Our Song, 1974, (book) Did I Do Something Wrong? A Supportive Guide for Parents and Loved Ones or People in Psychotherapy, 1995; columnist Family Therapy Acad., 1996-97 Trainer, cons. cmty.-based overflow shelters for homeless, Bethesda, 1989-94; vice chair bd. social concerns Cedar Ln. Unitarian Ch., 1986-87; active dr.-lawyer anti-drug program Fairfax Bar Assn., 1997 Mem. Greater Washington Soc. Clin. Social Work (v.p. for edn. 1992-94, at-large 1994-96, membership task force 1995-96) Baha'I. Avocations: violin, piano, accordion, gardening, writing. Office: PO Box 3008 Shepherdstown WV 25443-3008 Office Phone: 304-876-8203. Personal E-mail: motherheidi@aol.com, spenceinc@aol.com.

SPENCER, JOANN NORA, retired education educator; b. Allentown, Pa., Mar. 27, 1939; d. James Wilson and Elizabeth (Farmer) S.; 1 child, Jacque Christian Spencer Darrell. BS, Cheyney U., Pa., 1961; MS, Lehigh U., Bethlehem, Pa., 1963, PhD, 1971. Cert. elem. edn., spl. edn., reading and supervision. Elem. tchr. Allentown (Pa.) Sch. Dist.; prof. Moravian Coll., Bethlehem, Pa., Cheyney U., Lehigh U., Bethlehem, Kutztown (Pa.) U., 1974—2005, prof. emeritus, 2005—. Cons. Dyslexic Clinic, Children's Learning Ctr., Allentown; bd. mem. Kidspeace-Nat. Hosp. for Children in Crisis, Orefield, Pa. Pres. This Is Your Life Assn., Allentown, 1984—, Soroptimist Internat. Women's Club, Allentown, Pa.; benefit coord. Ebony Fashion Show, Allentown, Pa., 2005; chmn. Ebony Fashion Fair for Children/Youth of Lehigh Valley, Allentown; bd. dirs. Lehigh Valley coun. Girl Scouts US, Allentown; bd. edn. Swain Sch., Allentown, 2004—; bd. dirs. YWCA/YMCA, Allentown, Kidspeace Nat. Hosp. for Children/Youth in Crisis. Named Educator of Yr., Valley Forge Awards, 1971, Women of Yr., Women Unlimited, Allentown, 1985, Womencare Lehigh Valley Hosp., 1995, Educator of Yr., NAACP, 2002, Educator Honoree, NAACP, Allentown, Pa., 2000; recipient Kidspeak Nat. Hosp. Children and Youth in Crisis award, 2005. Mem. Order Ea. Star (past Worthy Matron), Delta Sigma Theta, Delta Kappan Gamma Honor Soc., Phi Beta Kappa.

SPENCER, JUDITH, retired secondary school educator, writer; b. Parkersburg, W.Va., Sept. 17, 1949; d. Avon Lockard and Christine (Burns) Elder; m. Ronald Eugene Randolph, June 5, 1970 (div. June 1986); children: Jennifer Rowena Randolph Babich, Nicola Christine Randolph; m. Peter Spencer, Dec. 23, 1987. BA with high distinction, Ariz. State U., 1970. Cert. secondary tchr. in history, Ariz. Grad. tchg. asst. dept. history Ariz. State U., Tempe, 1970-72; tchr. U.S. Army B.S.E.P. Program, Ft. Lewis, Wash., 1985; tutor Stilwell Reading Clinic, Sierra Vista, Ariz., 1986-87; journalist The Friday Times, Sierra Vista, 1986-87; tchr. world history Buena H.S., Sierra Vista, Ariz., 1987—2001. Active RIF, 1990—2001. Editor, contbr.: Writers of the Desert Sage, 1996—, author numerous poems. Mem.: NEA, Ariz. Edn. Assn., Nat. Soc. Collegiate Scholars, Phi Alpha Theta, Phi Kappa Phi. Avocations: reading, writing, poetry, painting, needlecrafts. Home: 1701 Sunview Way Sierra Vista AZ 85635-6422 Personal E-mail: spencer.pete@cox.net.

SPENCER, KATHRYN ROSE, secondary school educator; b. Waukegan, Ill., Sept. 8, 1943; d. James Durley and Magdalena Rose Curran; m. Colin Todd Spencer, Jan. 31, 1970; children: Heather Ann, Colin Todd Jr. BA, U. Ill., 1961. Cert. tchr. Ill. Latin tchr. United Twp. H.S., East Moline, 1965—67; Latin/history tchr. Geneva (Ill.) Cmty. H.S., 1967—70, Rosary H.S., Aurora, Ill., 1987—. Dist. pres. Am. Legion Aux., 1981; pres. Irish Water Spaniel Club Am., 1983. Recipient Tchg. award, Knox Coll., 1993. Mem.: Vergilian Soc., Ill. Classics Conf. (mem. nominating com. 1996—98), Am. Classical League. Roman Catholic. Avocations: travel, reading, needlecrafts. Home: 53 Cebold Dr Oswego IL 60543 Office: Rosary High Sch 901 N Edgelawn Dr Aurora IL 60506 Personal E-mail: kathyspencer@yahoo.com.

SPENCER, LARA, television personality, journalist; married, 2000; 1 child. BA in Journalism, Pa. State U. Reporter WDEF-TV, Chattanooga, News 12, L.I., NY, WABC, NY Eyewitness News, 1995—99; nat. corr. ABC News' Good Morning Am., 1999—2001, corr., 2001—04; host Antiques Roadshow, WGBH-PBS, 2004—; co-host, NY anchor Paramount TV The Insider, NYC, 2004—. Office: Antiques Roadshow-WGBH 125 Western Ave Allston MA 02134 Studio: Paramount Studios 5555 Melrose Ave Los Angeles CA 90038

SPENCER, LINDA ANNE, history professor; b. Albany, NY, Mar. 24, 1944; d. Richard Earl and Lorraine Clares (Barney) S. AB in History, Guilford Coll., 1972; MA in History, U. N.C., 1974; MLS, U. N.C., Greensboro, 1977; MA in History/Archival Mgmt., N.C. State U., 1991. Rsch. assoc., adminstrv. asst. U. N.C., Greensboro, 1978—79; librarian N.C. Hosp. Assn., Raleigh, 1982—91; cons. librarian SunHealth Svcs., 1982—84; with provost's office N.C. State U., 1984—88, circulation and sys. libr., 1988—91. Adj. instr. history Greensboro Coll., 2000—06, Guilford Tech. C.C., 2000—; reader advanced placement world history exams. Coll. Bd. Contbr. articles to profl. jours. Avocations: reading, travel, computers. Home: 2104 Starlight Dr Greensboro NC 27407-3048

SPENCER, LINDA B., painter; b. Oceanside, NY, June 22, 1943; d. William Thomas and Catharine Christine (Randall) Bushell; m. William Sherrick (div.); m. Karl Leopold Herbst, Feb. 14, 1980; 1 child, Lorene Quail. AA magna cum laude, San Jose City Coll., 1988; BA magna cum laude, San Jose State U., 1990; Masters, Inst. Transpersonal Psychology, Calif., 1993, PhD, 1995. Realtor Cabrillo Co., San Jose, 1975—87; artist, owner Spencer Arts, Los Gatos, Calif., 1980—97, Tavares, Fla., 1995—. Author: Heal Abuse and Trauma Through Art, 1995. Recipient Best of Show, Springfield, Mo., 2005. Mem.: Nat. Assn. Women in Arts, Nat. League Am. Pen Women (pres. Orlando Br. 2006—). Independent. Home and Office: Spencer Arts 32850 Lakeshore Dr Tavares FL 32778 Office Phone: 408-205-8385. Business E-Mail: linda@spencerarts.com.

SPENCER, LINDA LOU, elementary school educator; b. Balt., Sept. 22, 1949; d. Key Kynette and Brownie Helen (Shisler) S. BS, W.Va. Wesleyan Coll., 1972; MA, W.Va. U., 1985. Cert. early childhood, elem., bus. edn. tchr., W.Va. 5th and 6th grade tchr. Smoot Elem. Sch., W.Va., 1973; 6th grade tchr. White Sulphur Springs Elem. Sch., W.Va., 1973-74, 2d grade tchr. W.Va., 1974-95, kindergarten tchr., 1995—2006. Participant Summer Inst. for W.Va. Tchrs., Glenville, 1992, Martinsburg, 1995. Edn. chmn. Lewisburg United Meth. Ch., 1990-92, mem. adminstrv. bd., 1995—. Named First Runner Up Tchg. award Greenbrier County Reading Coun., 1994; W.Va. Edn. Fund grantee, 1993, 94, 2002, 04-06; recipient Ideas That Work award W.Va. Devel. for Profl. Growth, 1993. Mem. PEO Sisterhood (chpt. corr. sec. and chaplain 1987-93, v.p. 1995—, chptr. pres., P.E.O. siderhood), DAR, Bluebell Garden Club (co-chmn. 1993—), Delta Kappa Gamma (2d v.p. and rec. sec. 1989-92). Avocations: gardening, drying flowers, walking, lawn work. Office: White Sulphur Elem Sch 150 Reed St White Sulphur Springs WV 24986-2598

SPENCER, LISA ANN, special education educator; d. Jack and Betty Jean Spencer. BS, Bowie State Coll., 1983; M, Howard U., 1989, George Wash. U., 2004. Tchr. PGCPS, Mitchellville, Md., 1988—90, spl. edn. tchr. Bowie, Md., 1990—97, tech. coord. Hyattsville, Md., 1997—99, regional tech. coord. Oxon Hill, Md., 1999—2004, tng. and support mgr. Upper Marlboro, Md., 2004—. Mem.: NEA, Internat. Soc. Tech. Edn., Assn. Info. Tech. Profls. Democrat. Office Phone: 301-952-6251. Business E-Mail: lspencer@pgcps.org.

SPENCER, LONABELLE (KAPPIE SPENCER), political agency administrator, lobbyist; b. Owatonna, Minn., Aug. 3, 1925; d. Reuben Alvin and Florence Elizabeth (Wells) Kaplan; m. Mark Rodney Spencer, Sept. 14, 1947 (dec. May 1986); children: Gregory Mark, Gary Alan, Carol Ann, Dane Kaplan. BA, Grinnell Coll., 1947. State bd. legis. chair Am. Assn. Univ. Women, Iowa, 1978-82, nat. legis. com. Washington, 1980-83, nat. bd. legis. chair, 1982-83, nat. legis. and program coms., 1985-89, nat. bd. dir. for women's issues, 1985-89; founder, dir. Nat. Gender Balance Project, Sarasota, Fla., 1988—; bd. dirs., nat. steering com. Nat. Women's Political Caucus, Washington, 1992-97. Lobbyist, cmty. activist state legis. and congress, Fla. Iowa, Washington, 1974—; rep. Fla. women's pol. caucus ERA summit, Washington, 1992—; cons., presenter in field. Author: (manuals) Don't Leave It All to the Experts, 1981, Take An Unratified State to Launch, 1981, I Think We Need a Woman, 1982, It's a Man's World Unless Women Vote, 1983, Woman Power: It's a Capitol Idea, 1995, Gender Balance Project-USA: Politics and Decision Making, 1995, Whose Money Is It Anyway: Wills and Trusts for Women, 1999. U.S. rep. World Assn. Girl Guides Girl Scouts U.S., Acapulco, Mex., 1965, bd. dirs. Moingona Coun. Girl Scouts U.S., 1965-75; Rep. candidate Iowa Senate, Des Moines, 1976; del. Internat. Fedn. U. Women, Netherlands, New Zealand, Finland, Sweden, 1983, 86, 89,; trustee Grinnell (Iowa) Coll., 1993—; Iowa del. to Nat. Women's Conf., 1977; founder Fla. Women's Consortium, 1989; active People to People Internat.; tour leader Mission in Understanding to Cuba, 2001. Recipient Girl Scout awards Moingona Girl Scout Coun., Des Moines, 1969, 73, 78, Christine Wilson medal for Equality and Justice, Iowa Women's Hall of Fame, Des Moines, 1990; named gift honoree Am. Assn. Univ. Women, Des Moines and Sarasota, Fla. branches, Iowa and Vt. divsns., 1980, 82, 87, 92; named in National Women's Hall of Fame Book of Lives and Legacies, 2002. Mem. AAUW (leader corps, com. mem. 1975—89), UN Fund for Women (UNIFEM), Nat. Assn. Commns. for Women, Vet. Feminists of Am. (Medal of Honor 2000), Women in Senate and House WISH-LIST (founder 1992). Republican. Avocation: travel.

SPENCER, MARGARET GILLIAM, lawyer; b. Spokane, Wash., Aug. 30, 1951; d. Jackson Earl and Margaret Kathleen (Hindley) Gilliam; m. John Bernard Spencer, Feb. 21, 1993. BA in Sociology, U. Mont., 1974, MA in Sociology, 1978, JD, 1982. Bar: Mont. 1982, Colo. 1982. Assoc. Holland & Hart, Denver, 1982-84, Rauth & Brega, P.C., Denver, 1984-88, shareholder, dir., 1988-89; spl. counsel Brega & Winters, P.C., Denver, 1989; corp. counsel CH2M Hill, Inc., Denver, 1989—. Democrat. Episcopalian. Avocations: skiing, scuba diving. Office: CH2M Hill Inc 9191 S Jamaica St Englewood CO 80112 Business E-Mail: pspencer01@msn.com.

SPENCER, MARY MILLER, civic worker; b. Comanche, Tex., May 25, 1924; d. Aaron Gaynor and Alma (Grissom) Miller; 1 child, Mara Lynn. BS, U. North Tex., 1943. Cafeteria dir. Mercedes (Tex.) Pub. Schs., 1943-46; home economist coord. All-Orange Dessert Contest Fla. Citrus Commn., Lakeland, 1959-62, 64; tchr. purchasing sch. lunch dept. Fla. Dept. Edn., 1960. Clothing judge Polk County (Fla.) Youth Fair, 1951-68, Polk County Federated Women's Clubs, 1964-66; pres. Dixieland Elem. Sch. PTA, 1955-57, Polk County Coun. PTA's, 1958-60; chmn. pub. edn. com. Polk County unit Am. Cancer Soc., 1959-60, bd. dirs., 1962-70; charter mem., bd. dirs. Lakeland YMCA, 1962-72; sec. Greater Lakeland Cmty. Nursing Coun., 1965-72; trustee, vice-chmn. Polk County Eye Clinic, Inc., 1962-64, pres., 1964-82; bd. dirs. Polk County Scholarship and Loan Fund, 1962-70; mem. exec. com. West Polk County (Fla.) Cmty. Welfare Coun., 1960-62, 65-68; mem. budget and audit com. Greater Lakeland United Fund, 1960-62, bd. dirs., 1967-70, residential chmn. fund drive, 1968; mem. adv. bd. Polk County Juvenile and Domestic Rels. Ct., 1960-69; sec. bd. dirs. Fla. West Coast Ednl. TV, 1960-81; mem. Polk County Home Econs. Adv. Com., 1965-71; mem. exec. com. Suncoast Health Coun., 1968-71; worker children's svcs. divsn. family svcs. Dept. Health and Rehab. Svcs., State of Fla., 1969-70, social worker, 1970-72, 74-82, social worker Overpayment Fraud Recoupment unit, 1977-81, with other pers. svcs., 1981-82, supr. Overpayment Fraud Recoupment unit, 1982-83, pub. assistance specialist IV, 1984-89; bd. dirs. Lake Region United Way, Winter Haven, 1976-81; mem. Polk County Cmty. Svcs. Coun., 1978-88; with other pers. svcs. Emergency Fin. Assistance Housing Program, 1990-96. Mem. AAUW (pres. Lakeland br. 1960-61), Nat. Welfare Fraud Assn., Fla. Congress Parents and Tchrs. (hon. life, pres. dist. 7 1961-63, chmn. pub. rels. 1962-66), Fla. Health and Welfare Coun., Fla. Health and Social Svc. Coun., Polk County Mental Health Assn., U. North Tex. Alumni Assn., Order Ea. Star. Democrat. Methodist. Home: 1639 Crystal Lake Dr Lakeland FL 33801-5915

SPENCER, MELISSA FISCHER, science educator; b. Hinsdale, Ill., Aug. 18, 1979; d. George and Pamela Heintz Fischer; m. Christopher Stephen Spencer, July 5, 2003. BA in Math., Drake U., Des Moines, Iowa, 2001, BS in Physics, 2001, BSE in Secondary Edn., 2001. Summer intern Syngenta Seeds, Inc., Downers Grove, Ill., 1997—2000; mus. educator Sci. Ctr. Iowa, Des Moines, 2000—02; chemistry tchr. North H.S., Des Moines, 2002—. Author: (article) Young Children Jour. V.p. Des Moines Edn. Assn., 2006—. Recipient Presdl. scholarship, Drake U., 1997—2001. Mem.: NSTA, NEA (local v.p. 2006—). Avocations: knitting, scrapbooks, travel. Office: North HS 501 Holcomb Ave Des Moines IA 50313 Office Phone: 515-242-7200. Office Fax: 515-242-7360. Business E-Mail: melissa.spencer@dmps.k12.ia.us.

SPENCER, MELISSA JOHANNA, psychotherapist, special education educator; b. Durham, NC, Sept. 13, 1951; d. Joseph Whitney and Regina Colleen (Barnett) Spencer; m. Charles Ray Barrow, Aug. 21, 1972; children: Matthew R. Barrow, Christine N. Gonzales, Charlotte D. Barrow. Attended, U. Hawaii-Manoa, 1986—88; BA in Psychology, Tex. Tech. U., Lubbock, 1990, MEd in Counseling, 1994, EdD in Counselor Edn., 1999. Lic. profl. counselor NC, 2000. Dir. vols. Rappahannock Coun. Domestic Violence, Fredericksburg, Va., 1999—2000; asst. prof. U. NC-Pembroke, 2000—02; pvt. practice psychotherapy Southeastern Psychol. Svcs., Fairmont, NC, 2002—; tchr. exceptional children with autism Seventy-First HS, Fayetteville, NC, 2003—06, Magnolia Sch., Lumberton, NC. Adv. bd. Substance Abuse & Traumatic Brain Injury Linking Svcs., Fairmont, 2005—06. Recipient Tchg. Excellence award, Jiffy Lube, 2005. Mem.: Assn. Counselor Edn. and Supervision, Assn. Specialists Group Work, Internat. Assn. Marriage & Family Counselors, Am. Counseling Assn. Office: Southeastern Psychol Svcs 302 N Main Fairmont NC 28340 Personal E-mail: dr_melissajspencer@yahoo.com.

SPENCER, RENEE A., social worker, educator, researcher; b. Toronto, Can. BA, Austin Coll., 1987; MSSW, U. Tex., 1991; EdD, Harvard U., 2002. Lic. ind. clin. social worker Mass. Asst. prof. Boston U. Sch. Social Work, 2002—. Grantee, Radcliffe Inst. for Advanced Study, Harvard U., 2001—02; scholar, William T. Grant Found., 2005—. Mem.: Am. Ednl. Rsch. Assn., APA, Soc. Rsch. on Adolescence, Soc. Rsch. in Child Devel., Soc. Social Work and Rsch. Office: Boston Univ Sch Social Work 264 Bay State Rd Boston MA 02215

SPENCER, RUTH, announcer; b. San Diego; m. Jerry Aaron Spencer, 1992; 1 child, Amy. BS in Broadcast Journalism, San Francisco State U. With KSTP-TV, Mpls., 1985—89, WDIV-TV, Detroit, 1990—. Office: WDIV-TV 550 W Lafayette Blvd Detroit MI 48226

SPENCER, RUTH ALBERT, music educator; b. NYC, Sept. 13; d. Jack and Pearl Ray Albert; 1 child, Joanna Albert. BS, Mannes Coll. Music, N.Y.C., 1963. Mem. faculty music dept 92d St. Y Sch. Music, N.Y.C., 1987—; adj. lectr. CCNY, 1998—. Lectr. N.Y. Coun. Humanities, 2003—. Author: (textbook) Early Learning Music Program. Vol. Ground Zero (World Trade Ctr.), N.Y.C. Avocations: cooking and entertaining, swimming, biking, reading. Home: 107 W 86th St #6C New York NY 10024-3409 Office: City College New York Shepard #72 138 St and Convent Ave New York NY 10033 Office Fax: 212-650-5428. Business E-Mail: rspencer@ccny.cuny.edu.

SPENCER, TERESA ANN, music educator; b. Lima, Ohio, Oct. 6, 1959; d. John Ralph and Janice Ann Crosina; m. Bradley Carl Spencer, Dec. 23, 1988. MusB, Miami U., Oxford, Ohio, 1987; Master of Ednl. Adminstrn., U. Dayton, Ohio, 1995. Cert. spl. K-12 Bd. of Edn. State of Ohio, 1982, H.S. prin. Bd. of Edn. State of Ohio, 2002, asst. supt. Bd. of Edn. State of Ohio, 2002. Tchr. Allen East Local Schs., Harrod, Ohio, 1983—95, 1997—. Ext. agt. 4-H youth devel. The Ohio State U., Lima, 1995—97; mem. worship team Grace United Meth. Ch., Piqua, Ohio, 2001—06. Dunlap scholar, Sch. Music Miami U., 1981. Mem.: NEA, AEEA (pres. 2003—05), OEA (com. chmn. 2003—05), OMEA, Music Educators Nat. Conf., Delta Omicron (hon.). Home: 18170 County Rd 25-A Wapakoneta OH 45895 Office: Allen East High School 105 N Washington St Lafayette OH 45854 Office Phone: 419-649-6311. Office Fax: 418-648-8900. Business E-Mail: spencert@ae.noacsc.org.

SPENCER, TRICIA JANE, writer; b. Springfield, Ill., Dec. 8, 1952; d. Frank Edward and LaWanda (Edwards) Bell; m. Mark Edward Spencer, Aug. 21, 1982. Student pub. schs. Instr. Falcons Drum & Bugle Corps, Springfield, 1969-72; concert, stage, TV performer, 1970-82; guest dir. Sing Out, Salem, Ohio, 1973; legal sec. to pvt. atty. Tustin, Calif., 1980-82; owner Am. Dream Balloons & Svcs., Orange, Calif., 1982-89; founder, corp. pres. Am. Dream Limousine Svc., Inc., Orange, 1983-90; founder, designer Am. Dream Creations Co., Inc., Irvine, Calif., 1988—96; founder Am. Dream Bride's Mus., 1992; established Lilac Bloom Press, Riverside, Calif., 2002. Designer greeting cards, t-shirts, wedding related gifts, one-of-a-kind automobile; mediator Limousine and Chauffeur Coun., Orange County, 1984-85. Author: TIPS - The Server's Guide to Bringing Home the Bacon, 1987 (Winner 1999 Best Non-Fiction Book S.W. Writers Workshop Ann. Competition 1999), There's a Bunny in the House, 1992, Real Rabbits Don't Eat Lettuce, 1992, Elysium, 1996, Miracle Man, 1997, (winner Cloak and Dagger Mystery Shor Story Contest, 2005), Deviled Eggs, 1998 (winner L. Ron Hubbard's Writer's of the Future Competition for Sci. Fiction award 2000, Winner Crossquarter Publish Competition 2002), Tourist Attraction, 2004, Shamrock, 2004, DMV, 2004, Brave Destiny, 2005, Noses, Toes and Elbows, 2005 (winner Scribes Valley Publ. Short Story Competition, 2005), Once Upon an eBay Moon, 2005; performer Up With People, 1972-73; contbr. Saddle Tramps Wild West Revue, 1977-79. Organizer Bicentennial Com. Springfield, 1976; vol. Orange County Performing Arts Soc. Recipient Appreciation, Achievement awards Muscular Dystrophy Assn., 1977-79, Transp. Partnership award, 1988, 7 songwriting and vocal performance awards Music City Song Festival, 1989, Outstanding Booth Display award Chgo. Gift Show, 1991; named one of top 10 Bridal Cos. Assn. Bridal Cons. Mem. Greenpeace, World Wildlife Fedn., Nature Conservancy. Avocations: music, writing. E-mail: lilacbloompress@aol.com.

SPENCER CHAPPELL, PINKIE MAE, secondary school educator, actress; b. Hillsboro, N.C., May 14, 1956; d. Theodore Roosevelt and Sarah Idell Spencer; m. Larry Chappell, June 27, 1987. BA, U. Md., 1978; MA, Hampton U., 1985. Cert. secondary sch. prin. Va. Asst. bookkeeper Va. Mutual Benefit Life Ins. Co., Norfolk, 1978—80; paralegal Wm. P. Williams, PC-Legal, Norfolk, 1980—82; tchr. Forestville HS, Md., 1987—89, Lake Taylor Middle Pub. Sch., Norfolk, 1980—98, Azalea Gardens Middle Pub. Sch., Norfolk, 1999—2003, Coronado Sch. Alternative Sch., Norfolk, 2001—. Theater dir.'s asst. Ctr. Stage Children's Theater, Norfolk, 1989—98; dept. chairperson Lake Taylor Middle Sch., 1991—94, Azalea Gardens Middle Sch., 1997—2000. Treas. Georgetown Civic League, Chesapeake, Va., 2002—03. Recipient Best Supporting Actress, The Eye, Va. Beach, 1998. Mem.: Nat. Coun. of Tchrs. of English, Va. Assn. of Sec. Sch. Prin., Assn. Supervision and Curriculum Devel. (pres. 1990). Republican. Avocations: travel, directing and producing plays, puzzles, tennis, power walking. Office Phone: 757-409-3298. E-mail: act4paint@Q-express.net.

SPENCER-FLEMING, JULIA, writer; married; 3 children. Graduate, Ithaca Coll., George Washington Univ.; JD, Univ. Maine. Former atty., Portland, Maine. Author: (novels) In the Bleak Midwinter, 2003 (St. Martin's/Malice Domestic award, 2001, Dilys award, Independent Mystery Booksellers Assn., Agatha, Anthony, Macavity, Barry awards for Best First Novel), A Fountain Filled with Blood, 2004 (Borders Original Voices selection, nominee Barry award for Best Mystery Novel, Deadly Pleasures Mag.), Out of the Deep I Cry, 2004 (St. Martin's Minotaur's lead title, nominee Reviewers' Choice award, Romantic Times Book Club, 2005, nominee Edgar award for Best Mystery, 2004, nominee Anthony award for Best Mystery, 2004), To Darkness and to Death, 2005. Episcopalian. Mailing: c/o Jimmy Vines The Vines Agy Ste 901 648 Broadway New York NY 10012

SPENIER, JOANNE B., secondary school educator; b. Reading, Pa., June 7, 1953; d. Joseph Ralph and Bernice Mary Pietrobane; m. John Joseph Spenier, June 17, 1989; 1 child, Lydia Lee. BA in English, Kutztown U., Pa., 1985. Cert. K-6 Secondary English Aluemia Coll., 2000. Reading, math tchr. Cobra Acad., 2000—01; 6th grade tchr. St. Peters, 2001—04, Sacred Heart Sch., West Reading, Pa., 2004—. Admin. asst. Savage, Sinking Springs, Pa., 1974—2000. Mem.: Pa. Assn. of Notaries. Democrat. Cath. Home: 2306 Bell Dr Reading PA 19607 Office: Sacred Heart Sch Franklin St West Reading PA 19611

SPERLING, IRENE R., publishing executive; Asst. mktg. coord. seminars and trade shows Security World Publ., 1979—80; asst. show mgr. Cahners Expn. Group Kitchen and Bath and Office Product Shows, 1980—83, co-pub., 1983—86, v.p. sales and mktg., 1986—2000, publ., 2000—; publisher Tradeshow Week, LA, 2000—02; v.p. spl. projects and internat. sales Trade Show Exec. Mag., 2003—05, v.p., assoc. pub., 2005—. Office: Trade Show Exec 701 Palomar Airport Rd #300 Carlsbad CA 92009 Office Phone: 818-990-1050. E-mail: irenesperling@tradeshowexecutive.com.

SPERLING, RANDI A., pediatrician; b. Hempstead, N.Y., Mar. 19, 1964; d. Harold and Sandra Irene S.; m. Jason A. Schulman, Sept. 1, 1996. BA, Vassar Coll., 1986; DO, N.Y. Coll. Osteo. Medicine, 1990. Diplomate Am Bd. Pediatrics. Intern, resident Schneider Childrens Hosp., New Hyde Park, N.Y., 1990-94, chief resident, 1994-95; dir. pediat. svcs. and med. edn. Long Beach (N.Y.) Med. Ctr., 1995-98; asst. prof. pediat. Nova Southeastern Coll. Osteo. Medicine, Ft. Lauderdale, Fla., 1998-99. Pediat. cons. for parenting website Robyns nest, 1999. Mem. Bikor Cholim, Hollywood, Fla., 1999; Broward program svcs. com. mem. March of Dimes, Broward County, Fla., 1999. Fellow Am. Acad. Pediatrics. Office: Oakland Park Med Ctr Inc 2701 W Oakland Park Blvd Fort Lauderdale FL 33311-1330

SPERO, JOAN EDELMAN, foundation administrator; b. Davenport, Iowa, Oct. 2, 1944; d. Samuel and Sylvia (Halpern) Edelman; m. C. Michael Spero, Nov. 9, 1969; children: Jason, Benjamin. Student, L'Inst. d'Etudes Politiques, Paris, 1964-65; BA in Internat. Rels. with honors, U. Wis., 1966; MA, Columbia U., 1968, PhD, 1973; LLD (hon.), Amherst Coll., 1997. Asst. prof. Columbia U., N.Y.C., 1973-79; amb. of U.S. to UN Econ. and Social Coun., N.Y.C., 1980-81; v.p. Am. Express Co., N.Y.C., 1981-83, sr. v.p. internat. corp. affairs, 1983-89; treas., sr. v.p., 1989-91; exec. v.p. corp. affairs and communications Am. Express Co., 1991-93; under sec. for econ., bus. and agrl. affairs Dept. of State, Washington, 1993-97; pres. Doris Duke Charitable Found., N.Y.C., 1997—. Vis. scholar Fed. Res. Bank NY, 1976—77; bd. dirs. IBM Corp., 1st Data Corp.; hon. trustee The Brookings Inst. Author: The Politics of International Economic Relations, 6th edit., 2003, The Failure of the Franklin National Bank, 1980; contbr. articles to profl. jours. Trustee Wis. Alumni Rsch. Found., 1997—, Columbia U., 1998; trustee emeritus Amherst Coll.; mem. Coun. Am. Ambs. Named to Acad. Women Achievers, YWCA, 1983; named Fin. Woman of Yr., Fin. Women's Assn., 1990; recipient George Washington U. Disting. Statesperson award, 1994; Woodrow Wilson fellow. Mem. Am. Acad. Diplomacy, Found. Execs. Group, Coun. on Fgn. Rels. (bd. dirs.), Am. Philos. Soc., Phi Beta Kappa. Democrat. Jewish. Avocations: writing, swimming. Office: Doris Duke Charitable Found 650 5th Ave 19th Fl New York NY 10019-6108 Office Phone: 212-974-7000.

SPERO, NANCY, artist; b. Cleve., 1926; BFA, Sch. Art Inst. Chgo., 1949; student, Ecole des Beaux-Arts, Paris, 1950, Atelier Andre l'Hote, 1950. One-woman shows include Hewlett Gallery, Carnegie-Mellon U., Pitts., 1989, Rhona Hoffman Gallery, Chgo., 1986, 94, Inst. Contemporary Art, London, 1987, Everson Mus. Art, Syracuse, N.Y., 1987, Mus. Contemporary Art, L.A., 1988, Smith Coll. Mus. Art, Northampton, Mass., 1990, Haus am Walsee, Berlin, Germany, 1990, Barbara Gross Galerie, Munich, 1991, 95, 97-98, Salzburger Kunstverein, Austria, 1991, Christine König Gallery, Vienna, Austria, 1992, Ulmer Mus., Ulm, Germany, 1992, Josh Baer Gallery, N.Y.C., 1993, Nat. Gallery Can., Ottowa, 1993, Greenville (S.C.) County Mus. Art, 1993, Printworks, Chgo., 1994, Kunststichting Kanaal Art Found., Kortrijk, Belgium, 1994, Malmö (Sweden) Konsthall, 1994, Am. Ctr., Paris, MIT List Visual Arts Ctr., Cambridge, 1994, Arthur M. Sackler Mus., Harvard U., 1995, Fine Arts Gallery, U. Md. Baltimore County, 1995, N.Y. Kunsthalle, 1996, Vancouver Art Gallery, 1996, Hiroshima City Mus. Contemporary Art, 1996, Jüdisches Mus. der Stadt Wien, 1996, Heeresspital, Innsbruck, Tyrol, 1996, Jack Tilton Gallery, N.Y.C., 1996, PPOW Gallery, N.Y.C., 1996, Galerie im Taxispalais, Innsbruck, 1996, Elaine C. Jacob Gallery, Wayne State U., Detroit, 1997, Documenta X, Kassel, Germany, 1997, Crown Gallery, Brussels, 1997-98, Ikon Gallery, Birmingham, Eng., 1997-98, Internat. Biennale of Cairo, 1998, Festpielhaus Hellerau, Dresden, 1998, Galerie Montenay-Giroux, Paris, 1998, Barbara Gross Galerie, Munich, 1998, Miami U., Oxford, Ohio, 2000, others; exhibited in group shows at The Biennial of Sydney, Australia, 1986, Mus. Modern Art, N.Y.C., 1988, The Bertha and Karl Leubsdorf Art Gallery, Hunter Coll., N.Y.C., 1988, Le Grande Halle de La Villette, Paris, 1989, Bullet Space, N.Y.C., 1989, Ctr. Internat. d'Art Contemporain, Montreal, 1990, Dum Umeni Mesta Brna, Brünn, Czechoslovakia, 1991, Boston (Mass.) U. Art Gallery, 1991, Mus. der Stadtentwässerung, Zurich, 1994, Stichting Artimo, Beurs van Berlage, Amsterdam, 1994, Sch. Art Inst. Chgo., Betty Rymer Gallery, Chgo., 1994, MIT List Visual Arts Ctr., Cambridge, 1995, Southeastern Ctr. for Contemporary Art, Winston-Salem, N.C., 1995, Ctr. Georges Pompidou, Paris, 1995, Uffizi Gallery, Florence, Italy, 1995, Mus. Modern Art, N.Y.C., 1996, The Whitney Museum of Am. Art, N.Y., 1999, numerous others; represented in permanent collections Art Inst. Chgo., Australian Nat. Gallery, Boston Museum of Fine Arts, Brooklyn Museum, N.Y., Centro Cultural, Mex. City, Frac Nord Pas de Calais, France, Harvard U. Art Museums, Hiroshima City Museum of Contemporary Art, MIT List Visual Arts Ctr., Madison Art Ctr., Musée des Beaux-Arts de Montreal, Nat. Gallery of Canada, Ottowa, Phil. Museum of Art, The Museum of Modern Art, N.Y., U. Art Museum, Berkeley, Calif., Vancouver Art Gallery, Whitney Museum of Am. Art, N.Y., Subway Station, N.Y.C.; publs. include Nancy Spero: Rebirth of Venus, 1989, Nancy Spero: Woman Breathing, 1992, Nancy Spero, 1996. Mem.: Am. Acad. Arts and Letters.*

SPEROTTO, ANGELA DIANE, secondary school educator; b. Wheatridge, Colo., Sept. 6, 1975; d. Gloria Castaneda and John Stephen Sudela, Genero Castaneda (Stepfather) and Cynthia Sudela (Stepmother); m. Adriano Sperotto, June 13, 2006. BA, U. Houston, 1999. Tchr. Elsik HS, Alief, Tex., 1999—2001, Bellaire (Tex.) HS, 2001—. Ap coll. bd. table leader Coll. Bd., Nebr., 2003—; SAT ii world history test devel. com. ETS, NH, 2004—; cons. in field. Named Bellaire Tchr. of Yr., 2003. Mem.: World History Assn. Office: 5100 Maple Bellaire TX 77401 Office Phone: 713-667-2064. Business E-Mail: asperott@houstonisd.org.

SPETSIERIS, PHOEBE GEORGE, physicist, application developer, researcher; b. Athens, Greece, Apr. 26, 1944; came to U.S., 1947; d. Elis P. and Helen Elis George; m. Spyridon Spetsieris, June 30, 1972; 1 child, Zoe. BS in Physics, U. Athens, 1968; MA in Physics, CCNY, 1970; MPhil in Physics, CUNY, 1979, PhD in Physics, 1980. Adj. lectr. in physics and math. CCNY, N.Y.C., 1968—77; rsch. asst. in physics CUNY, N.Y.C., 1972—79; engr., sys. analyst Am. Electric Power Svc. Corp., N.Y.C., 1979—83; sr. sci. programmer analyst Meml. Sloan-Kettering Cancer Ctr., N.Y.C., 1984—89; sys. analyst, assoc. investigator Ctr. Neurosci. Functional Brain Imaging Lab. North Shore L.I. Jewish Rsch. Inst., Manhasset, NY, 1990—; rsch. assoc. prof. neurology NYU Sch. Medicine, 2001—. Presenter, cons. in field; adj. asst. prof. bioengring. Sch. Health Scis., Touro Coll., Dix Hills, NY, 1994—95. Contbr. articles to profl. publs. Recipient Alumni Achievement award, CUNY, 2005; N.Y. State Regents scholar, 1962, CUNY scholar, 1971, CUNY rsch. fellow, 1976. Mem. IEEE Enging. in Medicine and Biology. Democrat. Greek Orthodox. Avocations: art, computer graphics, scientific visualization. Office: North Shore U Hosp Dept Neurology 350 Community Dr Manhasset NY 11030-3849

SPHEERIS, PENELOPE, film director; b. New Orleans, Dec. 2, 1945; MFA, UCLA Film Sch. Film dir. The Gersh Agy. Inc., 1993—. Producer: TV series of shorts for Saturday Night Live; films include: Real Life, 1979; dir. The Decline of Western Civilization, 1981, The Boys Next Door, 1985, Hollywood Vice Squad, 1986, Dudes, 1987, Wayne's World, 1992, Black Sheep, 1996, The Thing in Bob's Garage, 1998, The Decline of Western Civilization Part II, 1998, Senseless, 1998, Hollywierd, 1999, Posers, 2001, (TV series) Danger Theater, 1993; dir., prodr. The Beverly Hillbillies, 1993, The Kid & I, 2005; dir., writer, prodr. The Decline of Western Civilization, 1981; dir., writer Suburbia, 1984, The Little Rascals, 1994; screenwriter: Summer Camp Nightmare, 1987; actress: Wedding Band, 1990; TV films directed include: Prison Stories: Women on the Inside, 1991, Applewood 911, 1998, Dear Doughboy, 2000, The Crooked E: The Unshredded Truth About Enron, 2003. Office: The Gersh Agency Inc 232 N Canon Dr Beverly Hills CA 90210-5302*

SPICER, JEAN UHL, art educator; b. Phila., Nov. 5, 1935; d. George Louis Uhl and Bertha Evelyn Mann; m. Ronald Edwin Spicer, Feb. 6, 1960; children: Scott, Jeffery. Diploma, Phila. Mus. Sch. Art, 1957. Instr. art Cmty. Art Ctr., Wallingford, Pa., 1984—87, Wayne Art Ctr., Pa., 1987—90. Instr. travel workshop painting Wallendra Art Ctr., Sydney, 1985, Bermuda, 1990—2000, England, 1990—94, Hawaiian Watercolor Soc., 2006, United States, 1980—2006; rec. sec. Phila. Watercolor Soc., 1985—95; bd. dirs. Rittenhouse Sq. Art Show, Phila., 1990—95; artist-in-residence Haverford Sch. Dist., Havertown, Pa., 1978—82. Author: Bright and Beautiful Flowers in Watercolor, 2004; contbr. articles to profl. jours. Mem.: Pa. Watercolor Club Soc., Balt. Watercolor Soc., We. Colo. Watercolor Soc. (signature), Pa. Watercolor Soc. (signature, 2d Pl. award 2004), Nat. Watercolor Soc. (signature), Am. Watercolor Soc. (signature, Edgar Whitney award 1995, 2001), Catherine Lorillard Wolfe Art Club. Avocation: shell designs. Home: 11 Tenby Rd Havertown PA 19083 Office Phone: 610-449-5639.

SPICKNALL, JOAN, music educator; b. Arlington, Va., Feb. 13, 1942; d. Joseph Richard and Rhoda Louise (Beran) Singer; m. Marvin Herbert Spitz, Dec. 12, 1992; children from previus marriage: Lisa Sharon Spicknall Fruth, Richard Mark Spicknall. B of Mus, Peabody Conservatory, 1962, MusM, 1963; D of Musical Arts, U.Md., 1974. Grad. asst. U. Md., College Park, 1966-69; asst. prof. St. Mary of the Woods (Ind.) Coll., 1971-83; instr. piano pvt. practice, Columbia, Md., 1983-88; instr. Essex C.C., Balt., 1983-84, Loyola Coll., Balt., 1983-84, Howard C.C., Columbia, 1983-86; pres., dir. Suzuki Music Sch. Md., Inc., Columbia, 1988—. Adj. prof. Rose-Hulman Inst. Tech., Terre Haute, Ind., 1973-83; piano tchr. Howard County Schs., 1986—; guest faculty, lectr. nat. and internat. music convs., 1991-; mem. music educators delegations to South Africa, 2003, Russia, 2005. Pianist (new 2 CD album): The Piano Music of Aaron Copland, 2004; contbr. articles to profl. articles, newspapers, jours., and mags. Mem. MTNA, SAA, Inc., ISA, AAUW, SAGWA, MENC, CMS, People to People Amb. Programs, Mu Phi Epsilon, Delta Kappa Gamma. Home: 10659 Green Mt Cir Columbia MD 21044 Office: Suzuki Music Sch Md Inc PO Box 1284 Columbia MD 21044-0284 E-mail: director@suzukimusicschool.com.

SPIEGEL, ANDREA, marketing executive; Mktg. and advt. mgr. Avis Rent A Car; dir. mktg. Virgin Atlantic Airways; v.p. mktg. Cunard Line; owner AKS Comms.; mktg. cons. Virgin USA; chief mktg. officer JetBlue Airways, Forest Hills, NY, 2005—. Office: JetBlue Airways 118-29 Queens Blvd Forest Hills NY 11375*

SPIEGEL, EDNA Z., lawyer; b. Oct. 27; m. Rubin E. Spiegel; children: Linda F. Spiegel Duboff, Joyce I., Bennett L. BS, MA, NYU; JD, Seton Hall U. Bar: N.J. 1988, U.S. Dist. Ct. N.J. 1988, U.S. Supreme Ct. 1993. Pvt. legal practice, River Edge, NJ, 1990—2004, New Milford, 2004—. Atty. River Edge Environ. Protection Commn., 1987—96; with cmty. outreach on advance directives Holy Name Hosp., Teaneck, NJ, 1994—97; trustee Bergen County Legal Svcs., Hackensack, 1999—2002; lawyer law day Divsn. Human Svcs. Bergen County, Hackensack, 1988—2004. Mem. Nat. Acad. Elder Law Attys. (charter mem. N.J. chpt.), N.J. Women Lawyers' Assn., N.J. State Bar Assn. (charter, elder law sect.), Bergen County Bar Assn. (charter, elder law com.), Women Lawyers in Bergen County, Hadassah/The Womens Zionist Orgn. of Am. (River Dell chpt., v.p. programs 1978-80, 96-03, chmn. Am. affairs 1979—, Woman of the Yr. 1996, Nat. Leadership award 1997), Elderlawanswers.com Avocations: gardening, painting, cooking, swimming, collectibles. Office: 1106 Roosevelt Ave New Milford NJ 07646 E-mail: ezsesq@aol.com.

SPIEGEL, EVELYN SCLUFER, biology professor; b. Phila., Mar. 20, 1924; d. George and Helen (Laurantos) Sclufer; m. Melvin Spiegel, Apr. 16, 1955; children: Judith Ellen, Rebecca Ann. BA, Temple U., 1947; MA, Bryn Mawr Coll., 1951; PhD, U. Pa., 1954. Asst. program dir. for regulatory biology NSF, Washington, 1954-55; instr. in biology Colby Coll., Waterville, Maine, 1955-59; rsch. assoc. Dartmouth Coll., Hanover, N.H., 1961-74, rsch. assoc. prof. biology, 1974-78, rsch. prof. biology, 1978-91; rsch. prof. biology emerita, 1991—. Vis. scholar Calif. Inst. Tech., Pasadena, 1964-65, U. Calif.-San Diego, La Jolla, 1970, Nat. Inst. for Med. Rsch., Mill Hill, Eng., 1971, NIH, Washington, 1975-76, U. Basel (Switzerland) Biocenter, 1979, 80, 81, 82, 85. Contbr. numerous articles to profl. jours., chpts. to books and book reviews. Mem. Soc. for Devel. Biology, Marine Biol. Lab. Corp. (trustee 1981-86, 88-92). Office: Dartmouth Coll Dept Biol Scis Hanover NH 03755

SPIEGEL, PHYLLIS, public relations consultant, journalist; b. Bronx, N.Y. d. Bernard and Lillian (Horowitz) Finkelberg; m. Stanley Spiegel, Sept. 20, 1959 (div. 1981); children: Mark, Adam. BA, NYU. Feature writer various newspapers, pubs., 1960's-70's; dir. pub. rels. Mort Barish Assocs., Princeton, NJ, 1975-80; account exec. pub. rels. Keyes Martin, Springfield, NJ, 1980-84; pres. Phyllis Spiegel Assocs., Plainsboro, NJ, 1984—. Pub. rels. dir., founder Red Oak Coop. Nursery Sch., Middletown, N.J., 1960's, Matawan (N.J.) Student Enrichment Program, 1960s-70s; pub. rels. cons., event organizer New Philharm. of N.J., Morristown, 1991-93; mem. Child Placement Rev. Bd. of Family Ct., Mercer County, N.J., 1994-98. Recipient Commendation from Gov. N.J. for U. Med. and Dentistry of N.J. campaign, 1983, Commendation for N.J. Pharm. Assn. campaign Pub. Rels. News Assn., 1979. Mem.: Soc. Humanistic Judaism (bd. dir. 1983—85). Avocations: film and theatre, classical music, reading, travel, walks. Office: Phyllis Spiegel Assocs PO Box 243 Plainsboro NJ 08536-0243

SPIEGELBERG, EMMA JO, business education educator, academic administrator; b. Mt. View, Wyo., Nov. 22, 1936; d. Joseph Clyde and Dorcas (Reese) Hatch; m. James Walter Spiegelberg, June 22, 1957; children: William L., Emory Walter, Joseph John. BA with honors, U. Wyo., 1958, MEd, 1985; EdD, Boston U., 1990. Tchr. bus. edn. Laramie H.S., Wyo., 1960—61, 1965—93, adminstr., 1993—97; prin. McCormick Jr. H.S., Cheyenne, 1997—2002; exec. dir. Wyo. Assn. Secondary Sch. Prins., 2001—. Author: Branigan's Accounting Simulation, 1986, London & Co. II, 1993; co-author: Glencoe Computerized Accounting, 1993, 2d edit., 1995, Microcomputer Accounting: Daceasy, 1994, Microcomputer Accounting: Peachtree, 1994, 3d edit., 2000, Microcomputer Accounting: Accpac, 1994, Computerized Accounting with Peachtree, 1995, 2000, 02. Bd. dir. Cathedral Home for Children, Laramie, 1967-70, 72—, pres., 1985-88, Laramie Plains Mus., 1970-79. Named Wyo. Bus. Tchr. of Yr., 1982, Wyo. Asst. Prin. of Yr., 1997. Mem.: NASSP, NEA, Wyo. Assn. Secondary Sch. Prins. (sec., treas. 1997—2001), Albany County Edn. Assn. (sec. 1970—71), Wyo. Edn. Assn., Wyo. Bus. Edn. Assn. (pres. 1979—80), Internat. Soc. Bus. Edn. (rep. Mt. Plains chpt. 2006—), Mt. Plains Bus. Edn. Assn. (Wyo. rep. to bd. dirs. 1982—85, pres. 1987—88, Sec. Tchr. of Yr. 1991, Leadership award 1992), Nat. Bus. Edn. Assn. (bd. dir. 1987—88, 1991—96, Sec. Tchr. of Yr. 1991), Wyo. Vocat. Assn. (exec. bd. 1978—80, pres. 1981—82, exec. sec. 1986—89, Outstanding Contbns. to Vocat. Edn. award 1983, Tchr. of Yr. 1985), Am. Vocat. Assn. (policy com. region V 1984—87, region V Tchr. of Yr. 1986), U. Wyo. Alumni Assn. (bd. dir. 1985—90, pres. 1988—89), Laramie C. of C. (bd. dir. 1985—88), Zonta Internat. (Laramie) (v.p. 2002—03, pres. 2003—04, dist. 12 parliamentarian 2004—06), Delta Pi Epsilon, Pi Lambda Theta, Chi Omega, Alpha Delta Kappa (state pres. 1978—82), Phi Delta Kappa, Kappa Delta Pi. Episcopalian. Home: 3301 Grays Gable Rd Laramie WY 82072-5031 Office Phone: 307-745-5468. Personal E-mail: jwejspiegelberg@aol.com.

SPIELER, EMILY A., dean, law educator; AB, Radcliffe Coll., Harvard U., 1969; JD, Yale U., 1973. Ptnr. Women's Law Collective, Cambridge, Mass.; spl. asst. atty. gen. Mass. Dept. Pub. Health's Lead Poisoning Prevention Div.; commr. W.Va. Workers' Compensation Fund; first dep. atty. gen. for civil rights Govt. W.Va., mem. Human Rights Commn.; Hale J. and Roscoe P.

Posten Prof. Law W.Va. U., 1990—2002; dean Northeastern U. Sch. Law, 2002—. Com. mem. U.S. Department of Energy, Nat. Inst. Occupl. Safety and Health. Contbr. articles to law jours. Recipient Fulbright award, 2001, Martin Luther King Jr. Advocacy of Justice Award. Mem.: NAS, Nat. Acad. Soc. Insurance. Office: Northeastern U Sch Law 120 Knowles Ctr 400 Huntington Ave Boston MA 02115 Office Phone: 617-373-3307. Office Fax: 617-373-8793. Business E-Mail: e.spieler@neu.edu.

SPIGENER, SUSAN ARNOLD, science educator; b. Anderson, S.C., June 6, 1959; d. Emily McCallum and Thaddeus Roy Arnold; children: Marion Bruce, Laney Shuler. BS, Coll. of Charleston, S.C., 1981. Cert. sci. tchr. S.C., 1981, Va., 1985. Rsch. asst. SC Marine Resources, Charleston, SC, 1980—81; phlebotomist Roper Hosp., Charleston, SC, 1980—81; sci. tchr., varsity soccer coach Bishop Eng. H.S., Charleston, SC, 1981—84; tchr. sci. Lake Taylor Mid. Sch., Norfolk, Va., 1985—86; tchr. biology Lake Taylor H.S., Norfolk, Va., 1985—85; tchr. sci. Notre Dame H.S., Guam, 1986—88; tchr. biology, chemistry Beaufort H.S., SC, 1990—91; tchr. sci. Powdersville Mid. Sch., SC, 1991—95; tchr. biology, chemistry, anatomy, physiology, AP Biology T.L. Hanna H.S., Anderson, SC, 1995—, new tchr. mentor, 1995—. Dept. head Powdersville Mid. Sch., SC, 1991—95; sci. olympiad head coach T.L. Hanna H.S., Anderson, SC, 2000—04, Astra Club sponsor, 2005—; curriculum cons. Anderson Sch. Dist. Five, SC, 2001—05. Vol. Salvation Army, Anderson, SC, 1999—2000, Anderson Interfaith Ministries, SC, 1998; deacon, Sunday sch. tchr. First Presbyn. Ch., Anderson, SC, 2000—03; tchr. Sunday sch. Trinity Methodist Ch.; mem. United Methodist Women Handbell Choir. Named 1st woman to coach an all-male soccer team to a H.S. championship in SC., SC. Athletic Hall of Fame, 1984; Edn. Improvement Act grant, SC. Dept. of Edn., 1993, Circuit grant, Clemson U., 2004. Mem.: S.C. Edn. Assn. Methodist. Achievements include Started the junior varsity and varsity soccer program at Bishop England High School. Varsity team won state championship after only 3 years; Coached Science Olympiad Team who placed in the top six teams in the state for four years in a row. Avocations: gardening, reading, church work. Home: 114 Kingswood Ter Anderson SC 29621 Office: TL Hanna HS 2600 Hwy 81 N Anderson SC 29621 Office Phone: 864-260-5110. Business E-Mail: susanspigener@anderson5.net.

SPIKES, PATRICIA WHITE, medical technologist; b. Houston, Nov. 30, 1951; d. Albert Carr and Willie Mae (Sneed) White; m. Herbert Charles Pete, May 24, 1980 (div.); 1 dau., Sheatri Denise; m. John Ray Spikes, Sept. 7, 1991; 1 child, John Ray II. BS Tex. Christian U., Ft. Worth, 1974. Med. technologist, edn. coordinator Riverside Gen. Hosp., Houston, 1974-76; chief lab. technologist Almeda Med. Lab., Houston, 1976-80; med. technologist Jefferson Davis Hosp., Harris County Hosp. Dist., Houston, 1980—, Lyndon B. Johnson Hosp., Harris City Hosp. Dist. Founder Coalition of Pre-Sch. Dirs., 1982—; dir. Parents Calling Parents, Houston, 1980—; and 3d v.p. Vols. in Pub. Sch. Adv. Bd., Houston, 1981, 2d v.p., 1983, pres. 1986-89, v.p. tng. chair, 1990-92, v.p. community coalitions, 1993; mem. Tex. State Bd. for Vols. in Pub. Sch., 1982—, sec., 1988—, 1st v.p., 1985, pres., 1986, sec. 1987—; chairperson Bucks for Belts Coalition for Sch. Bus Seat Belts, 1985; chair awards com. Salute to Sch. Vols.; mem. Mayor's Task Force on Edn., Houston, Mayor's Com. on Child Abuse Prevention; panelist Regional IV Svc. Ctr. State Seminar; mem. adv. bd. Blueridge Health Dept., Attucks Community Coll.; pres. Reynolds Elem. Parent Tchr. Orgn., 1982, treas., 1984; sec. Pershing Middle Sch., PTO, 1985, Class of 1969 Worthing High Sch. Reunion; candidate for Houston Ind. Sch. Dist. Bd. Edn., 1989; pres. Kings Row Child Care Parent Tchrs. Orgn., 1978; mem. Nat. Sch. Vol. Program 1982—, Mo. City Space; panelist Houston Area Black Sch. Educators, 1987; bd. dirs. Women in Action, 1984-85; mediator Dispute Resolution Ctr., 1984—, Women of Vision, Chs. Interested in Premature Parentage; city wide adv. com. Houston Ind. Sch. Dist., 1988; edn. adv. com. Family Life; pres. adv. com. Inner City 4-H, 1989—; chmn. adult leaders adv. bd. Harris County 4-H, 1989-91, treas. 1890 program, 1991-93; chmn. Northeast Adolescent Program, 1990-92; computer maintenance adv. com. Reagan High Sch., 1988—; chair Salute to Sch. Vols., 1984-86; speaker career day Houston Ind. Sch. Dist., 1989—; chmn. adv. bd. Sunnyside Multi-Svc. Ctr./Health Ctr., 1991—; mem. steering com. Tex. Cancer Coun., 1992—; spkr., active Teen Health Symposium Prairie View Adminstrn. 1980 4-H Program, 1992, 93; coord. baby buddy program Sunnyside Clinic City of Houston Health Dept., 1989—; mem. S.E. br. adv. bd. ARC, 2000-, chair, 2004-06, membership com. Greater Houston coun., 2004-; mem. membership com. Nat. Healthy Start Assn., 1974—; consortium chmn. Sunny Futures Healthy Start Program, Houston, 1998-2003; coord. Girls Rite of Passage, 2000-02; chmn. Prairie View A&M Coll. Coop. Extension Project H.O.P.E., 2001—; cons. Families Under Urban and Social Attack Non Profit Devel., 2002—; CEO, founder S&J Literary Works, 2003, Rewriting the Script Through Connections, 2005; mem. Syphilis Elimination Adv. Task Force, 2003—; chair Syphilis Elimination Bd., ARC, 2004-06; mem. program svcs. com.; mem. Sunnyside Pride, 2005; mem. Healthy Minority Marriage Initiative, 2006; mem. City of Houston HIV/AIDS Task Force, 2003—; workshop trainer Families Under Urban and Social Attack, 2004-; presenter, cons., spkr. in field. Recipient Vols. in Pub. Sch. Spl. Service cert., 1984; recipient numerous certs. of appreciation. Mem. NAACP, Delta Sigma Theta. Recipient Cert. of Appreciation, Vols. Am., 1980, Vols. in Pub. Schs., 1986, 87, Houston Ind. Sch. Dist., 1981, 82, 83, pres.' award Vols. in Pub. Schs., 1986-95; Outstanding Service award Reynolds Sch., 1982, cert. recognition Training Tchrs. and Adminstrs. Parent Involvment, 1986, Kay On-going Edn. Ctr., Pershing Mid. Schs., 1987, Neighborhood Ctrs. Crystal House Cmty. Svc. award, 2005, Vol. award Prairie View A&M U. project H.O.P.E. Democrat. Baptist. Mem. Top Ladies of Distinction. Home: 3134 Sunbeam St Houston TX 77051-3526 Personal E-mail: pspikes30@aol.com.

SPIKOL, EILEEN, artist; b. Sarasota, Fla. 1 child, Hannah. BA in Fine Arts, Fordham U., 1975; MFA in Sculpture, City Coll., N.Y., 1977. Supr. reproduction studio Am. Mus. Natural History, N.Y.C., 1971-78; tchr. painting and drawing grades 7-12 Fieldston Sch., Riverdale, N.Y., 1977-79; tchr. molding, casting, patina workshop Children's Mus. Manhattan, N.Y.C., 1979-80; tchr. art spl. edn. Sch. Visual Arts, N.Y.C., 1982; tchr. drawing, painting, sculpture, printmaking Studio in a Sch., N.Y.C., 1987-90; instr. Bronx (N.Y.) Mus. Arts, 1990-91. Tchr. sculpture Md. Ctr. Arts Goucher Coll., Towson, 1986; adj. prof. art edn., spl. edn. Bkyln. (N.Y.) Coll., 1979-85, field supr.; adj. prof. fine arts St. Johns U., Queens, N.Y., 1991-93; artist in residence Found. Michel Karolyi, Vence, France, 1989, Domiciliary Care Program for Homeless Vets., St. Albans (N.Y.) VA Ctr., 1997—; adj. prof. in art edn., spl. edn. Nat. History N.Y.C., 1979-85; lectr. in field. One woman exhbns. include Soho 20 Gallery, N.Y.C., 1974, 75, 77, 78, Maples Gallery Fairleigh Dickinson U., Teaneck, N.J., 1980, 84, Islip Art Mus., E. Islip, N.Y., 1986, Bronx (N.Y.) Mus. Arts, 1988; group exhbns. include One Hundred Acres Gallery, N.Y.C., 1972, Aldrich Mus., Ridgefield, Conn., 1974, New Britain (Conn.) Mus., 1974, Hera Gallery, Wakefield, R.I., 1976, Bronx (N.Y.) Mus. Arts, 1979, 1980, Landmark Gallery, N.Y.C., 1979, Nobe' Gallery, N.Y.C., 1979, Walnut St. Galleries, Phila., 1979, Blaffer Gallery U. Houston, 1980, Mus. Natural History, N.Y.C., 1982, The Fine Arts Ctr. SUNY, Stony Brook, 1982, Fed. Plz., N.Y.C., 1982, Freedman Gallery Albright Coll., Reading, Pa., 1982, The New Mus., N.Y.C., 1984, Henry Street Settlement, N.Y.C., 1986, Artspace Gallery, New Haven, Conn., 1992, Leopold-Hoesch-Mus., Duren, Ger., 1992, B4A Gallery, N.Y.C., 1993; featured in Arts Mag., Soho Weekly News, Womanart, The Nation, The Village Voice, Coll. Art Jour., N.Y. Times, Newsday, New Haven Register. Home: 175 W 72nd St New York NY 10023-3203

SPILIOTIS, JOYCE A., state legislator; State rep. Mass. House, 2003—. Mem. Mass. Dem. State Com., N. Shore Labor Coun.; counilor-at-large City of Peabody; trustee City of Peabody Libr., 1986—88. Democrat. Office: State House Rm 236 Boston MA 02133

SPILKER, LINDA JOYCE, aerospace scientist; b. Mpls., Apr. 26, 1955; d. Arthur Elzear and Bonnie Joy (Jansen) Bies; m. John Leonard Horn, Jr., July 31, 1976 (div.); children: Jennifer, Jessica; m. Thomas Richard Spilker, 1997. BA in Physics, Calif. State U., Fullerton, 1977; MS in Physics, Calif. State U., L.A., 1983; PhD in Geophysics and Space Physics, UCLA, 1992. Rep. Voyager Infrared Radiometer and Spectrometer expt. Jet Propulsion Lab., Pasadena, Calif., 1977-90, sci. assoc. Voyager Photopolarimeter, 1984-90, sc. assoc. Voyager Infrared Radiometer and Spectrometer, 1988-90, study scientist Cassini asst., 1988-90, co-investigator Cassini Composite Infrared Spectrometer, 1990—, dep. project scientist Cassini mission, 1990—, prin. investigator planetary geology and geophysics, 1993—. Mem. planetary sci. data steering group NASA, Washington, 1991-95, adv. coun. for planetary data sys. ring node, Moffett Field, Calif., 1990—. Contbr. chpt. Van Nostrand Encyclopedia of Planetary Science, 1994; contbr. jour. articles Icarus. Pres. North San Gabriel Valley Dem. Club, Monrovia, Calif., 1992-94. Named one of Hottest 25 in Orange County, Orange County Metro mag., 2004; named to Hall of Fame, Placentia-Yorba Linda Unified Sch. Dist., 1998—99; recipient Exceptional Svc. medal, NASA, 1990, Sci. Achievement award, 1992, Disting. Alumna award, Calif. State U., L.A., 1996, Calif. State U., Fullerton, 2005. Mem. AAAS, AAUW, Divsn. of Planetary Sci. Democrat. Presbyterian. Avocations: hiking, astronomical observing, piano, jogging. Home: 457 Granite Ave Monrovia CA 91016-2324 Office: Jet Propulsion Lab MS 230-205 4800 Oak Grove Dr Pasadena CA 91109-8001 Business E-Mail: Linda.J.Spilker@jpl.nasa.gov.

SPILKER, YVONNE WAILES, mathematics educator; d. Charles David and Shannon Adrienne Wailes; m. Jeffrey C. Spilker, Jan. 19, 1991; children: Charles Christopher Scott, Wesley David Scott, Jeffrey Logan. BS in Math., U. Pacific, Stockton, Calif., 1982. Tchr. math. Monte Vista H.S., Danville, Calif., 1983—. Office: Monte Vista High School 3131 Stone Valley Rd Danville CA 94526 Office Phone: 925-552-5530. E-mail: mvhigh.net.

SPILLANE, BARBARA ANN, secondary school educator; b. Scranton, Pa., Aug. 1, 1943; d. Michael Kuratnick and Catherine Tomachick; m. Thomas Joseph Spillane, Sr., Nov. 21, 1964; children: Patricia Catherine Schaffer, Thomas Joseph Jr., Melanie Lynn. BS in Edn., Kent State U., Ohio, 1964; MA in Edn., Montclair State U., NJ, 1968. Cert. social studies, English, reading, supr. Tchr. English Orange HS, NJ, 1964—67; tchr. social studies Green Ridge Mid. Sch., NJ, 1967—69, Belleville Mid. Sch., NJ, 1983—2006. Sec. West Caldwell (N.J.) Hist. Soc., 2005—. Named Belleville Woman of Yr., Belleville C. of C., Mid. Sch. Tchr. of Yr., Belleville Bd. Edn., 1993; recipient Cmty. Svc. award, Belleville C. of C., 1988, Lifetime Achievement award, Belleville Pub. Libr., 2004. Mem.: NEA, NJ Coun. for Social Studies (workshop presenter), Nat. Coun. for Social Studies, Belleville Edn. Assn. (assn. rep.), NJ Edn. Assn., NJ State Fedn. Women's Clubs (state bd. 2006—, Woman of Achievement award 2005). Avocations: travel, reading, antiques. Personal E-mail: baspill@aol.com.

SPILLETT, ROXANNE, social services administrator; 1 son, Keith. BA in Edn., SUNY; postgrad., St. Lawrence U., Hunter Coll., N.Y. Tchr., curriculum writer NY State Schs., 1971-73; program specialist Girl Scouts USA, 1973; dir. nat. health project Boys & Girls Clubs Am., Atlanta, 1978-79, dir. program svcs., 1979-91, asst. nat. dir. program svcs., 1991-1995, v.p. N.E. regional office, 1995, acting pres., 1995-96, pres., 1996—. Vice chair bd. dirs. Nat. Assembly of Health and Human Svc. Orgns. Office: Boys & Girls Clubs Am 1230 W Peachtree St NW Atlanta GA 30309-3404*

SPILLMAN, JANE SHADEL, curator, writer, researcher; b. Huntsville, Ala., Apr. 30, 1942; d. Marvin and Elizabeth (Russell) Shadel; m. Don Lewis Spillman, Feb. 18, 1973 (dec. Jan. 1999); children: K. Elizabeth, Samuel Shadel. AB, Vassar Coll., 1964; MA, Cooperstown Grad. Program, 1965. Rsch. asst. Corning (N.Y.) Mus. Glass, 1965-70, asst. curator, 1971-73, assoc. curator Am. glass, 1974-77, curator, 1978—, head of curatorial dept., 1994-99, dep. dir. collections, 1999—2004. Cons. The White House Curator's Office, Washington, 1987-90, other museums. Author: Complete Cut and Engraved Glass of Corning, 1979, rev. edit., 1997, Knopf Collectors Guide to Glass, Vol. 1, 1982, Vol. 2, 1983, White House Glassware, 1989, Masterpieces of American Glass, 1990, The American Cut Glass Industry: T.G. Hawkes and His Competitors, 1996, Glass of the Maharajahs: European Cut Glass Furnishings for Eastern Palaces, 2006, also 6 other books, numerous articles; editor The Glass Club Bull., 1999—. Mem. Am. Assn. Mus. (chair curators com. 1989-93), Nat. Early Am. Glass Club (bd. dirs. 1989-95), Glass Circle of London, Internat. Assn. for the History of Glass (gen. sec. 2003—). Office: Corning Mus Glass 1 Museum Way Corning NY 14830-2253

SPILLMAN, MARJORIE ROSE, theater producer, dancer; b. Norfork, Va., Jan. 5, 1958; d. William Bert and Rose Marjorie (Naperski) S.; m. David E. Marks, Apr. 4, 1985 (dec. July 1997); children: F. Oscar Marks, Miranda Rose. AS, Mt. Ida Jr. Coll., 1974; CT, Northeastern U., 1975; BS in Nursing, U. Mass., 1977; MAT, Our Lady of Elms Coll., 2005; postgrad. in Applied Theology, Elms Coll., Chicopee, Mass., 2006—. RN, Mass. Charge nurse VA Med. Ctr., Northampton, Mass., 1977-82; dancer N.E. Am. Ballet, Northampton, 1982, Ballet Theater Sch., Springfield, Mass., 1982-84, Smith Coll., Northampton, 1984-96; sales rep. Winthrop Pharm., N.Y.C., 1982-94, Nycomed, N.Y.C., 1994-96; dir. mktg. and devel. The Northampton Ctr. for the Arts, 1997. Prin. dancer Project Opera, Northampton, 1984—86; dancer Polobulus East St. Dance, Hadley, Mass., 1985; dance and theatre reviewer Holyoke T. Telegram, 1991—92; theater critic Daily Hampshire Gazette, 1993—96; dance panelist Mass. Cultural Coun., 1998; curator The Refrigerator Door art exhibit Smith Coll., 1999—2001; prodr. Pioneer Valley Performing Arts H.S., 1998; founder Open Door Prodns., 1999; cons. Organic Trade Assn., 1999, New Eng. Artist Trust, 1999—; organizer Congl. Edn. Day in Washington, D.C.; tchr. Easthampton HS, 2000—. Dancer, creator part of Carmen in Carmen, 1985, Ruth St. Denis in the House of Ruth Ted and Martha, 1994; dancer, choreographer A Victorian Evening, 1986; dancer Nutcracker Ballet, Pioneer Valley Ballet, 1988; creator, prodr. The Halloween House at Sunnyside, 1990, producing dir., 1991-92; actor, author play Mary P. Wells Smith Narrates, 1987; founder, prodr., dir. Northampton Children's Theater, 1993—; prodr. Northampton's First Night Children's Parade, 1996, dir. First Night Northampton, 1997-98, Saturday As a Work of Art—Summer Series, 1997; contbg. writer Healthy & Natural Mag. Theater panelist Mass. Cultural Coun., 1997, 2000; devel. com. Cooley Dickerson Hosp., 1999; religious tchr. St. Mary of the Assumption, 2001-04, 2005—; dir. Nothing Scary Halloween House, East St. Studios, 2004. Democrat. Roman Catholic.

SPILMAN, JANET LYNNE, special education educator; b. Marysville, Calif., Nov. 29, 1957; d. Mary Elizabeth and James Maurice Spilman. BA in Hist. and Polit. Sci., Jamestown Coll., ND, 1980; BS in Spl. Edn., Moorhead State U., Minn., 1983; MEd, U. La Verne, Calif., 2004. Specialist Instrn. Credential: Learning Handicapped Commn. on Tchr. Credentialing, Calif., 1989, Single Subject Tchg. Credential: Soc.Sci. Commn. on Tchr. Credentialing, Calif., 1989, Resource Specialist Cert. Commn. on Tchr. Credentialing, Calif., 2000, Nat. Cert. In Assistive Tech. Calif. State U. Northridge, 2000. Case mgr., behavior analyst Fraser Hall, Inc, Fargo, ND, 1983—85; spl. edn. tchr. Yuma Union H.S. Dist. - Kofa H.S., Yuma, Ariz., 1985—89; job coord. Job Tng. Partnership Act - Summer Youth Program, 1986—88; tchr. (govt.) Yuma Union H.S. Dist., Migrant Edn. Dept., Yuma, Ariz., 1987—89; resource specialist Live Oak Unified Sch. Dist., Calif., 1989—94; ind. living instr. Cmty. Resource Svcs., Marysville, Calif., 1994—96; spl. day class tchr., emotionally disturbed program Milhous Sch., Inc., Sacramento, 1996—97; resource specialist Wash. Unified Sch. Dist., West Sacramento, Calif., 1997—2002, Sacramento City Unified Sch. Dist., Sacramento, 2002—. Mem.: ASCD, Vocat. Evaluation and Work Adjustment Assn., Nat. Rehab. Assn., Assn. for Children and Adults with Learning Disabilities, Coun. for Children with Behavioral Disorders, Calif. Assn. for Resource Specialists, Phi Delta Kappa, Assn. Calif. Sch. Adminstrs., Am. Assn. Sch. Adminstrs., Prader Willi Assn., Coun. For Exceptional Children. Avocations: working cattle, packing (horse and burro), hiking, photography, gardening, horseback riding. Home: 9524 North Butte Rd Live Oak CA 95953 Personal E-mail: spilmanrsp@comcast.net.

SPILMAN, PATRICIA, artist, educator; b. Charlottesville, Va., Oct. 3, 1930; d. Harry Franklin and Katherine Elizabeth (Alexander) Black; m. William Bruce Spilman, Feb. 3, 1951 (dec. May 1987); children: Rebecca, Elizabeth, Barbara, William. BA, Madison Coll., 1969, MEd, 1971. Art tchr. Stuarts Draft (Va.) H.S., 1969-86; artist in residence Augusta County Schs., Fishersville, Va., 1987—. Pvt. tchr. art, Waynesboro, Va., 1986—; docent Shenandoah Valley Art Ctr., Waynesboro, 1986—. Mem. Main St. U. Meth. Ch., Waynesboro; troop leader Girl Scouts U.S., 1958-66. Mem. Nat. Assn. Women Artists, Am. Inst. Fgn. Study (travel tchr. 1977-83), Va. Watercolor Soc., Shenandoah Valley Art Ctr., Shenandoah Valley Watercolor Soc., Delta Kappa Gamma. Avocations: gardening, travel. Home: 1837 Cherokee Rd Waynesboro VA 22980-2228

SPINAK, JANE M., law educator; BA, Smith Coll., 1974; JD, NYU, 1979. Staff atty. Juvenile Rights Div., Legal Aid Soc. of NY, 1980—82, atty.-in-charge, 1995—98; co-founder Child Advocacy Clinic Columbia Law Sch., NYC, 1982—, Edward Ross Aranow Clin. Prof. of Law, dir., clin. progs. Steering com. Columbia U. Inst. on Child and Family Policy. Contbr. articles to law jours. Mem.: NY State Permanent Judicial Commn. on Justice for Children. Office: Columbia Law Sch 435 W 116th St New York NY 10027 E-mail: spinak@law.columbia.edu.

SPINELLA, JUDY LYNN, health facility administrator; b. Ft. Worth, Apr. 8, 1948; d. Gettis Breon and Velrea Inez (Webb) Prothro; children: Scott Slater, Jennifer. BS, U. Tex., 1971; MS, Tex. Woman's U., 1973; MBA, Vanderbilt U., 1993. RN, Tex., Calif., Tenn. Asst. prof. U. Tex., Arlington, 1976-81; dir. emergency svcs. San Francisco Gen. Hosp., 1981-84, assoc. adminstr. for clin. svcs., 1984-88; exec. dir. for nursing svcs. Vanderbilt U. Med. Ctr., Nashville, 1988-93, dir. patient care svcs., 1993-94; dir., COO Vanderbilt U. Hosp., Nashville, 1994-96; healthcare cons. APM, Inc., N.Y.C., 1996—98; health care cons. The Meth. Hosp., Houston, 1998—2001, v.p. ops., 2001—04; pres., CEO Gunnison Valley Hosp., Colo., 2004—05; chief nursing officer U. N. Mex. Hosp., 2005—. Wharton fellow Johnson & Johnson, 1987. Mem. Am. Orgn. Nurse Execs., Am. Coll. Healthcare Execs., Emergency Nurses Assn. (bd. dirs., treas. 1979-86), Tenn. Orgn. Nurse Execs. (bd. dirs. 1989-91), Sigma Theta Tau. Avocations: hiking, skiing, travel. Office: U N Mex Hosp Chief Nursing Office 2211 Lomas Blvd NE Albuquerque NM 87106 Office Phone: 970-641-1456. Business E-Mail: jspinella@gvh-colorado.org. E-mail: jlspinella@aol.com.

SPINNER, PAMELA MARIE, special education educator; b. Cleve., Feb. 11, 1956; d. Henry Joseph and Frances Rita (Riegelsberger) Jaros; children: Joshua Lowell, Matthew Joseph. BS in Edn., Kent State U., 1977, MEd, 2000. Cert. tchr. elem. edn., educable mentally retarded, moderate, severe, profoundly retarded. Tchr. East Cleveland (Ohio) City Schs., 1977-89; tchr., counselor Positive Edn. Program, Cleve., 1989—94, case mgr., 1994—97, asst. program coord., 1997—. Curriculum writer East Cleveland City Schs., 1983-88; freelancer Perma-Bound, Jacksonville, 1989-90; speaker/presenter Am. Re-edn. Assn., Norfolk, Va., 1990; regional trainer devel. therapy, devel. tchg. Martha Holden Jennings Found. grantee, Cleve., 1980; named Model Tchr./Counselor, Positive Edn. Program, Cleve., 1990. Mem. Ohio Tchrs. Assn., Ohio Edn. Assn. Avocations: bicycling, swimming, crafts. Home: 1357 Gladys Ave Lakewood OH 44107-2511 Office: Positive Edn Program 5209 Detroit Ave Cleveland OH 44102 Office Phone: 216-939-2200. E-mail: pspinner@pepcleve.org.

SPIRAKUS, KAREN ANN, elementary school educator, researcher; m. Art J. Spirakus; 1 child, Kelly K. Stazyk. M in Outdoor Edn., Akron U., Ohio, 1991. Elem. tchr., 1975—81; math tchr. Willetts Mid. Sch., Brunswick, Oreg., 1981—2005, rsch. tchr., 2005—. Avocations: music, singing. Office: Willetts Mid Sch 1045 Hadcock Rd Brunswick OH 44212 Office Phone: 330-273-0489. Business E-Mail: kspirakus@bcsoh.org.

SPIRN, MICHELE SOBEL, communications professional, writer; b. Newark, Jan. 26, 1943; d. Jack and Sylvia (Cohen) Sobel; m. Steven Frederick Spirn, Jan. 27, 1968; 1 child, Joshua. BA, Syracuse U., 1965; MFA, The New Sch., 1999. Creative dir. Planned Communications Svcs., N.Y.C., 1966-72, EDL Prodns., N.Y.C., 1972-73; free-lance writer Bklyn., 1973-83; dir. pub. rels. Nat. Coun. Jewish Women, N.Y.C., 1983-90, dir. communications, 1990-95; freelance writer Bklyn., 1995—. Adj. lectr. CUNY, Bklyn., 1977—81; instr. The New Sch., N.Y.C., 1999—, NYU, 2002—. Author: The Fast Shoes, 1985, The Boy Who Liked Green, 1985, The Know-Nothings, 1995; co-author: A Man Can Be., 1981, A Know-Nothing Birthday, 1997, Birth Celebrations, 1998, New Year Celebrations, 1998; co-author: The Nutcracker, 1998, A Know-Nothing Halloween, 2000, The Know-Nothings Talk Turkey, 2000, The Bridges in London, 2000, All Washed Up, 2000, Racing To The Light, 2000, Wait Til The Midnight Hour, 2000, Jackie Joyner-Kersee, 2000, The Bridges in Paris, 2000, Race to the Sea, 2001, A Twist in Time, 2001, I Am the Turkey, 2004, The Bridges in Edinburgh, 2004, Cold-Blooded Creatures, 2004, Arachnids, 2004, Great Teams, 2005, Mysterious People, 2005, Mysterious Places, 2006, Poisoned Plate, 2006, Great Days in Harlem: The Harlem Renaissance, 2006, Missing Dad, 2006, Spies and Pies, 2006, Octopuses, 2006; editor, columnist Children's Entertainment Rev. mag., N.Y.C., 1982; columnist The Phoenix newspaper, Bklyn., 1983. Pres. Tenth St. Block Assn., Bklyn., 1989-91, Friends of the Park Slope Libr.; vol. Model Media Program, Bklyn., 1985—. Recipient Silver medal for pub. svc. film N.Y. Internat. Film and TV Festival, 1972. Mem.: Authors Guild, Soc. Children's Book Writers and Illustrators, Mystery Writers Am. Avocations: reading, gardening. E-mail: michelesteve21@hotmail.com.

SPIRO, ROSANN LEE, marketing professional, educator; b. Fort Wayne, Ind., Oct. 13, 1945; d. Samuel G. and Vivian Marie Spiro; m. Rockney G. Walters, June 10, 1990; children: Samantha G., Jennifer Lauren Walters, Christi Marie Walters. AB, Ind. U., 1967, MBA, 1969; PhD, U. of Ga., 1976. Prof. and chairperson Dept. of Mktg., Kelley Sch. of Bus., Ind. U., Bloomington, Ind., 1992—; vis. prof. Insitute of Mgmt., U. of Aarhus, Aarhus, Denmark, 1991—92, I.E.S.E., Barcelona, 2000. Author: (textbook) Management of a Salesforce, 11th edition; contbr. articles to profl. jours. Recipient Outstanding Article award, Pi Sigma Epsilon, 1981, 1996. Mem.: Am. Mktg. Assn. (chairperson of the bd. 1994—95, Ann. Excellence in Rsch. award 2002). Office: Kelley Sch of Business Indiana University Bloomington IN 47405

SPITZ, BARBARA SALOMON, artist; b. Chgo., Jan. 8, 1926; d. Fred B. and Sadie (Lorch) Salomon; m. Lawrence S. Spitz, Mar. 19, 1949; children—Thomas R., Linda J., Joanne L. Student, Art Inst. Chgo., 1942—43, R.I. Sch. Design, 1945; AB, Brown U., 1947. One-woman exhbns. include Benjamin Galleries, Chgo., 1971, 73, Kunsthaus Buhler, Stuttgart, Germany, 1973, Van Straaten Gallery, Chgo., 1976, 80, Elca London Studio, Montreal, Que., Can., 1977, Loyola U. Chgo., 1988, Schneider, Bluhm, Loeb gallery, Chgo., 1993, Newport Beach Pub. Lib., 2002, The Ctr. Gallery, 1994; group exhibitions include Am. Acad. Arts and Letters, Library of Congress traveling print exhbn., Tokyo Cen. Mus. Arts, Nat. Acad. Design, NYC, Pratt Graphic Ctr., Honolulu Acad. Arts, Wadsworth Atheneum, Nat. Aperture, 1986—, Laguna Art Mus., others; represented in permanent collections Phila. Mus. Art, DeCordova Mus., Okla. Art Ctr., Milw. Art Ctr., Los Angeles County Mus. Art, Art Inst. Chgo., Portland Mus. Art, Wadsworth Atheneum, med. arts programs UCLA, Block Mus./Northwestern U., Smart Mus./U. Chgo. Vice-chmn. Chgo. area Brown U. Bicentennial Drive; treas. Hearing and Speech Rehab. Ctr., Michael Reese Hosp., 1960; fine arts patron bd. Newport Harbor Art Mus. Mem. Print Club Phila., Boston Printmakers, Arts Club of Chgo., Soc. Am. Graphic Artists. Address: 1106 Somerset Ln Newport Beach CA 92660-5629 E-mail: bsslss@adelphia.net.

SPITZ, MARGARET R., epidemiologist, researcher; Grad., U. Witwatersand Med. Sch.; M in pub. health, U. Tex. Prof. divsn. cancer prevention MD Anderson Cancer Ctr., U. Tex., Houston, chmn. dept. epidemiology, 1998—. Bd. sci. advisors Nat. Cancer Inst., cons.; professorship in cancer prevention Mesa Petroleum Co.; served on study sections NIH. Contbr. articles to profl. jour. Recipient Am. Cancer Soc. award for rsch. excellence in cancer epidemiology and prevention, Am. Assn. Cancer Rsch., 2002. Mem.: Am. Soc. Preventive Oncology (past pres.). Achievements include research in genetic susceptibility to cancer devel; discovery of possible hereditary component to nicotine addiciton. Office: U Tex MD Anderson Cancer Ctr 1515 Holcombe Blvd Houston TX 77030 Office Phone: 713-792-3020. Office Fax: 713-792-0807. Business E-Mail: mspitz@mail.mdanderson.org.

SPITZE, GLENYS SMITH, retired teacher and counselor; b. Rozel, Kans., May 20, 1919; d. Harry H. and Mary Louisa (Mishler) Smith; m. LeRoy A. Spitze, Dec. 31, 1942 (dec. Nov. 1995); children: Randall LeRoy, Kevin Lance, Kimett Alvin, Terril Christian, Shawn Smith; 1 fosterchild, Theo Ritz-Spitze. Cert. tchg., U. Kans., 1939; AA, San Jose (Calif.) City Coll., 1963; BA in Psychology, San Jose State U., 1965, MA in Child Devel., 1968. Cert. tchr., counselor, Calif. Elem. sch. tchr. Topeka County Schs., Richland, Kans., 1939-40, Kinsley (Kans.) Pub. Schs., 1940-42; presch. substitute tchr. AAUW Kindergarten, Newark, Ohio, 1945—46; presch. tchr. Meth. Ch. Facility, Campbell, Calif., 1956-58; guest lectr. Govt. Sch. Social Work, Colombo, Sri Lanka, 1965-66; instr. man-woman relationship San Jose State Free U., 1966-67; child devel. lab. psychol. examiner Child Labs San Jose State U., 1967-68; pvt. informal practice tchr., counselor, cons. San Jose, Kailua-Kona, Hawaii. Vocal music dir. grades 1-3 Southside Sch., 1940-41; 6th dist. Calif. Congress Parent-Tchrs. Social Welfare dir., officer 6th dist. com. Calif. Coun. on Crime and Delinquency, San Jose, 1956-62; mem. kindergarten com. AAUW, Newark, Ohio, 1945-46; coord. Sangha Symposium, Asian Philosophy Club, San Jose State U., 1964-65; lectr. in field. Contbr. articles, poems to profl. publs. Hon. del. Gov. Brown's Conf. on Prevention of Juvenile Delinquency, Sacramento, 1963; co-organizer Post Polio Support Group, Kailua-Kona, HI, 2000. Mem.: Psi Chi. Avocations: writing, reading, swimming, snorkeling, anthropology. Home: 78-6800 Alii Dr KKSRC 5-103 Kailua Kona HI 96740-4421 Home (Summer): 311 E Bowman Woodland Park CO 80863 also: PO Gen Delivery Woodland Park CO 80863 Personal E-mail: gmglenys@webtv.net.

SPIVACK, KATHLEEN ROMOLA DRUCKER, writer, educator; b. N.Y.C. d. Peter and Doris Drucker; children: Nova, Marin. BA, Oberlin (Ohio) Coll., 1959; MA, Boston U., 1963. Prof. U. Paris VII and VIII, 1991-96, U. St. Quentin, Versailles, Paris, 1995—, Ecole Polytechnique, Paris, 1995—, U. Francois Rabelais, Tours, France, 2001; dir. Advanced Writing Workshop, Boston. Author: Flying Inland, 1971, The Jane Poems, 1973, Swimmer in the Spreading Dawn, 1986, The Honeymoon, The Beds We Lie In, 1986, The Breakup Variations, 2002. Bunting fellow Radcliffe Coll., 1969-71; Nat. Endowment Arts fellow, 1978; Sr. Fulbright prof., Paris, 1993. Home: 53 Spruce St Watertown MA 02472-1902 Office Phone: 617-926-1637. E-mail: kspivack@earthlink.net.

SPIVAK, CAROL, investment company executive, volunteer; b. L.A., Dec. 27, 1934; d. Ralph and Muriel Dorothy (Wexler) DeSure; m. Roy Andrew Moss, Feb. 14, 1954 (dec. Dec. 1982); 1 child, Steven Moss; m. Julius Spivak, Mar. 28, 1987. AA, Santa Monica Coll., 1983; BA, UCLA, 1998. Established trust fund Guide Dogs for the Blind, Inc., San Rafael, Calif., 1989—; major. contbr. Guide Dogs of the Desert, Palm Springs, Calif., 1995—; established Carol Moss Spivak Cell Imaging Facility, Brain Rsch. Inst. of UCLA, 1998—. Established cancer care unit at Stanford U. Hosp., Palo Alto, Calif., 1991. Author: Cathy's Sandy, 1947. Trustee UCLA Found., 1992; bd. dirs. United Hostesses' Charities; rec. sec. cardiology rsch. support group at Cedars Sinai Hosp. Avocation: raising orchids.

SPIVAK, JOAN CAROL, communications executive; b. Phila., May 12, 1950; d. Jack and Evelyn Lee (Copelman) S.; m. John D. Goldman, May 17, 1980; children: Jesse, Marcus. AB, Barnard Coll., 1972; M of Health Scis., Johns Hopkins U., 1980. Freelance writer, N.Y.C., 1980-84; project dir. Impact Med. Communication, N.Y.C., 1984-87; exec. v.p., gen. mgr. health and sci. strategies Edelman Worldwide, N.Y.C., 1987—2002; pres. Prime Medica, Inc., 2002—. Co-author: (pamphlet) Lead: New Perspectives on an Old Problem, 1978; contbr. The Book of Health, 1981, articles to profl. jours. Bd. dirs. May O'Donnell Dance Co., N.Y.C., 1983-85, Chamber Ballet U.S.A., N.Y.C., 1985-87, Nat. Child Labor Commn., 1991-2000, Cases, 1995-2001, Learning Through an Expanded Arts Program, 2004—. Mem. N.Y. Acad. Sci. Democrat. Jewish. Avocations: pottery, boating. Office Phone: 212-921-1250. E-mail: joan.spivak@prime-medica.com.

SPLITTSTOESSER, SHIRLEY O., elementary school educator; b. Rochester, Minn., June 21, 1937; d. Edward and Rose (Kruger) O'Connor; m. Walter Splittstoesser; children: Pamela, Sheryl, Riley. BS with honors, Mankato State U., 1960; MEd, Purdue U., 1962; postgrad., U. Calif., Berkeley, U. Ill. Tchr. Dist. 2148, Steele County, Minn., 1956—59, Chrysler Sch., Modesto, Calif., 1963—64, North Davis Pub. Schs., Calif., 1964—65, Delphi Pub. Schs., Ind., 1960—61, 1962—63, Dist. 116-Yankee Ridge Sch., Urbana, Ill., 1965—89, Wiley Sch., 1989—94; dir. Howard Hughes Med. Inst. Sci., Urbana, 1994—2002. Rsch. in field; dir. sci. fairs, nature ctrs. Author: Hooray! A Cookbook for Single Me, 2006. Recipient Disting. Educator awrd Milken Family Found., 1990. Mem. Univ. Women's Club (chair 1996—, Delta Kappa Gamma (pres. 1998-2000). Home: 2006 Cureton Dr Urbana IL 61801-6226 Business E-Mail: splitts@life.uiuc.edu.

SPOFFORD, SALLY (SALLY HYSLOP), artist; b. NYC, Aug. 20, 1929; d. George Hall and Esther (McNaull) Hyslop; m. Gavin Spofford, Mar. 11, 1950 (dec. Jan. 1976); children: Lizabeth Spofford Smith, Leslie Spofford Russell. Student, The China Inst., N.Y.C., 1949, The Art Students League, 1950; BA with high honors, Swarthmore Coll., 1952. Instr. Somerset Art Assn., Peapack, N.J., 1978-95, Hunterdon Mus. Art, Clinton, N.J., 1985—; adv. bd., lectr. Apollo Muses, Inc., Gladstone, N.J.; trustee Artshowcase, Inc. One-woman shows include Riverside Studio, Pottersville, N.J., 1985, Morris Mus., Morristown, N.J. 1989, Schering-Plough Gallery, Madison, N.J., 1989, Phoenix Gallery, N.Y.C., 1990, Robin Hutchins Gallery, Maplewood, N.J., 1992, Berlex Labs. Corp. Office, Wayne, N.J., 1992, Hunterdon Mus. Art, Clinton, 1993, 2003, Newark Acad., Livingston, N.J., 1997, Simon Gallery, Morristown, 2004; exhibited in group shows at Hickory (N.C.) Mus., 1983, Purdue U., 1983, Monmouth (N.J.), 1984, Nabisco Brands Gallery, East Hanover, N.J., 1985, 89, Hunterdon Mus. Art, 1988, 93, 99, Schering-Plough Gallery, Madison, 1988, Morris Mus., Morristown, 1989, Montclair (N.J.) State U., 1995, Williams Gallery, Princeton, N.J., 1997, Monmouth Mus., Lincroft, N.J., 1998, Newark Acad., Livingston, 2000, Bristol-Myers Squibb Gallery, Princeton, N.J., 2005; represented in permanent collections N.J. State Mus., Trenton, Newark Mus., Morris Mus., Morristown. Painting residency fellow Vt. Studio Ctr., 1992. Mem. Assoc. Artists N.J. (pres. 1985-87), N.J. Watercolor Soc., Federated Art Assns. of N.J. (panel mem. 1985, demonstrator 1991). Home: PO Box 443 Bernardsville NJ 07924-0443 Office Phone: 908-766-1219.

SPOHN, DOROTHY M., retired elementary school educator; b. Bloomington, Ind., Dec. 31, 1929; d. Charles L. and Martha V. (Staley) Mc Conville; m. Charles L. Spohn, Sept. 23,1949; children: Charles David, Steven Michael. BA, Wichita State U., 1973; MEd, Miami U., 1978. Cert. tchr. Ohio. Tchr. Ross Local Sch. Dist., Hamilton, Ohio, until 1995. Marth Holden Jennings Found. scholar, 1986; recipient Southwestern Ohio Spl. Edn. cert. of recognition, 1987, Golden Apple Achievement award Ashland Oil Co., 1990. Mem. AAUW, NEA, NSTA, Nat. Assn. Gifted Children, Ohio Assn. Gifted Children, Ohio Edn. Assn., Ross Edn. Assn. Home: 8407 Barnesburg Rd Cincinnati OH 45247-3551

SPOHN, NOR RAE, computer company executive; married; 2 children. BS in Computer Sci., Iowa State U.; MEE, Stanford U. R&D engr. Hewlett Packard, 1980, R&D mgr. LaserJet Divsn., 1998, v.p., gen. mgr. Personal LaserJet Solutions. Chair Idaho Sci., Math. and Tech. Coalition; bd. mem. Treasure Vallet Math. & Sci. Ctr.; bd. adv. Sch. Engring. Boise State U. Named to WITI Hall of Fame, Women in Tech. Internat., 2006. Office: Personal LaserJet Solutions Divsn. Hewlett Packard Co 3000 Hanover St Palo Alto CA 94304-1185*

SPOMER, PENNY SUE, elementary school educator; d. Pete and Pat Tuckness; m. Vernon Lee Spomer, June 29, 1974; children: Nicole Lea Lopez, Leslie Ann Buddecke. BA, Mesa State Coll., Grand Junction, Colo., 1991; M in Tech. in Edn., Lesley Coll., 2000. Sixth grade tchr. Orchard Mesa Mid. Sch., Grand Junction, 1993—. Sponsor Welcome Everybody 8th Grade Mentors, Grand Junction, 1988—, 8th Grade Fla. Ednl. Trip, Grand Junction, 1998—. Mem.: Delta Kappa Gamma (assoc.; 2nd v.p. 2004). Business E-Mail: xfile@mesa.k12.co.us.

SPOOLSTRA, LINDA CAROL, minister, educator, religious organization administrator; b. Hillsdale, Mich., July 11, 1947; d. Jay Carroll and Carol Elsa (Linstrom) Lehmann; m. Gerald William Spoolstra, Feb. 17, 1973. BA, Bethel Coll., 1969; MA, Fla. State U., 1970; M of Div., McCormick Theol. Sem., Chgo., 1978; DD (hon.), Cen Bapt. Theol. Sem., Kansas City, Kans., 1988. Ordained Am. Bapt. Clergywoman. Tchr. Dade County Pub. Schs., Miami, Fla., 1970-71; ins. claims adjustor Safeco Ins. Co., Chgo., 1971-72; dir. of community outreach and edn. N. Shore Bapt. Ch., Chgo., 1972-78, assoc. pastor, 1978; pastor First Bapt. Ch., Swansea, Mass., 1978-84; exec. dir. commn. on the ministry Am. Bapt. Chs. U.S.A., Valley Forge, Pa., 1984-90; exec. minister Am. Bapt. Chs. Mass., Dedham, 1990—2003; pastor Calvary Bapt. Ch., Providence, 2003—. Mem. Nat. Coun. Chs. Profl. Ch. Leadership, N.Y.C., 1984-90; mem. commn. on pastoral leadership Bapt. World Alliance, McLean, Va., 1986-90; mem. gen. bd. Nat. Coun. Chs. of Christ, 1990-96. Trustee Andover-Newton Theol. Sch., 1990—2003. Avocations: sailing, reading, travel, classical music. Office: Calvary Bapt Ch 747 Broad St Providence RI 02907 Personal E-mail: spoolstra@msn.com.

SPOONER, DONNA, management consultant; b. Deland, Fla. d. Michael and Ruth Elizabeth Linkovich. BS, Fla. State U., 1971, MPA, 1993, PhD in Pub. Adminstrn. and Policy, 2001. Budget analyst Dept. Adminstrn./Exec. Office of Gov. State of Fla., Tallahassee, 1977-80, spl. projects adminstr./acting chief, Bur. of Employee Cert., 1980-81, sr. govtl. analyst Exec. Office of Gov., 1981-85, pub. and legis. affairs dir. Dept. Adminstrn., 1985-87, asst. dir. Gov.'s Drug and Crime Policy Office, 1987-90; statewide planning coord. alcohol, drug abuse, mental health Fla. Dept. Health and Rehab. Svcs., Tallahassee, 1990-95; owner Spooner Energy Assocs., Tallahassee, 1996—2000; dir., founder Ctr. for Policy and Mgmt. Strategies, Tallahassee, 2001—; co-founder, co-dir. CE Studies LLC, Tallahassee, 2005—. Mem. Am. Soc. Pub. Adminstrn., S.E. Evaluation Assn., Capital Women's Network, Pi Alpha Alpha. Avocations: reading, hiking, dance. Office: Ctr for Policy and Mgmt Studies PO Box 14595 Tallahassee FL 32317 also: CE Studies LLC PO Box 12337 Tallahassee FL 32317 E-mail: cpmstrategies@att.net.

SPOONER, SUSAN ELIZABETH, counseling psychologist, educator, retired; b. Indpls., Feb. 14, 1939; d. Hugh J. and Dorothy (Genung) Baker; m. John A. Spooner, June 30, 1962; 1 child, Kevin. BS, Purdue U., 1960; MS, U. Wis.-Madison, 1961; PhD, Purdue U., 1975. Exec. dir. Sycamore council Girl Scouts U.S.A., Lafayette, Ind., 1970-72; asst. to dir. U. Placement Svc., Purdue U., W. Lafayette, Ind., 1974-75, vis. asst. prof. Counseling and Personnel Svcs., 1975-76; asst. prof. counselor edn. U. Wis.-Oshkosh, 1976-81, assoc. prof., 1981-83; assoc. prof. Coll. student personnel adminstrn. U. No. Colo., Greeley, 1983-93, prof., 1993-2000, ret., 2000; cons. Manpower Lab., Denver, 1968-72, Evergreen Retirement Cmty., Oshkosh, 1980, Trenton State Coll., 1984. Contbr. articles to profl. jours. Exploring chair dist. 7 Bay Lakes counc., Winnebago County, Oshkosh, Wis., 1980-83, dist. com. Longs Peak Coun., 1984—; mem. Nat. Exploring Program com. Boy Scouts Am., 1985—. Mem. Assn. for Counseling and Devel. (senator 1980-84), Assn. Counselor Educators and Suprs. (com. chair 1982-84, treas. 1986-89, 92-96), Colo. Assn. Counselor Educators and Suprs. (pres. 1984-85, pres. Rocky Mountain Aces 1987-88), Am. Coll. Personnel Assn. (exec. council 1982-85, commn. XII directorate 1978-81, 84—), Am. Psychol. Assn., Phi Theta Kappa, Omicron Nu, Rho Delta Gamma. Congregationalist.

SPOSATO, AIMÉ, music educator, opera singer; b. Pitts., Aug. 19, 1965; d. Joseph Louis and Cecilia (Gur) S. BA in voice, U. Pitts., 1987; MM, Duquesne U., 1989; DMA in voice, W.Va. U., 1993. Freelance opera singer, Washington, Pa., 1989—. Adj. prof. voice Thiel Coll., Greenville, Pa., 1992-93, Shenandoah U., Winchester, Va., 1992—. Soloist debut John F. Kennedy Ctr. Performing Arts, Washington, 1997. Cantor Immaculate Conception Ch., Washington, Pa., 1989—. Competition winner Palm Beach Opera Vocal Competition, 1989, Pitts. Concert Soc. Competition, 1990. Mem. Nat. Assn. Tchrs. Singing, Tuesday Musical Club (scholarship 1998), Sigma Alpha Iota (soloist 1983-85). Republican. Roman Catholic. Office: Shenandoah U College Ave Winchester VA 22601 Home: 600 Lakeview Dr Cross Junction VA 22625-2425 Office Phone: 540-665-4524. Business E-Mail: asposato@su.edu.

SPOSET, BARBARA ANN, secondary school educator; b. Cleve., Ohio, Oct. 14, 1947; d. Arthur John and Angela Marie (Rutkowski) Hille; m. Raymond Wilbur Sposet, Aug. 19, 1972; 1 child, Michael Samuel. BA, Kent State U., 1968; MEd, Millersville State U., 1974; PhD, Kent State U., 1997. Cert. tchr., prin., asst. supt., Ohio. Tchr. and dept. chair pub. rels. Brooklyn (Ohio) City Schs., 1968—2000; asst. to assoc. prof. edn. Notre Dame Coll., Notre Dame, 2000—05; assoc. prof. mid. childhood coord. Baldwin-Wallace Coll., 2005—. Exch. tchr. AFS, Cen. Am., 1976; instr. Kent State U., 1996-1999; instr. edn. Walsh U., Ohio, 1996—. Recipient Disting. Faculty award, Notre Dame Coll.; Rockefeller Found. fellow, 1987; Jennings scholar, 1997; Jennings Tchr. grantee, 1988. Mem. ASCD, NEA, Am. Edn. Rsch. Assn., Nat. Coun. Accreditation of Tchr. Edn. (coord., dept. chair), Ohio Mid. Sch. Assn., Phi Delta Kappa. Home: 18175 Trailside Pl Cleveland OH 44136-4247 Office Phone: 440-826-8173. E-mail: bspost@bw.edu.

SPOTTSWOOD, LYDIA CAROL, nurse, health facility administrator; b. N.Y.C., N.Y., May 6, 1951; d. Rudolph Messerschmidt and Eleanor Schlesinger; m. Paul Gregory Spottswood, Feb. 17, 1989; children: Mark Philip, Jayne Alexander, Erin Lenore. BS in Nursing, U. Va., Charlottesville, 1972. RN Va., Colo., D.C. Head nurse operating room U. Va. Hosp., Charlottesville, Va., 1974—77; nurse Children's Hosp., Washington, 1978—79, Wurzburg Army Med. Hosp., Germany, 1979—80; mem. city coun. City of Kenosha, Wis., 1990—98; dir. New Start Cmty. Health Ctr. (now Kenosha Cmty. Health Ctr.), Wis., 1994—95; mem. bd. U. Wis. Benevolent Found., 2000—. State and regional bd. mem. Area Health Edn. Ctr. Sys., Wis., 1996—2000; columnist Kenosha News, Wis., 2001—02. Past chair 1st Dist. Dem. Party Wis., congl. cand., 1996—98; mem. First Presbyn. Ch., Kenosha, Wis. Recipient Congl. Svc. Recognition award, Rep. Peter Barca, 1996, Svc. award, Kenosha County Med. Soc., 1996; grantee, HHS, 1994. Avocations: skiing, horseback riding, interior decorating, travel.

SPRACHER, NANCY A., psychotherapist; b. Seattle, Wash., July 4, 1940; d. Walter Joseph and Anita Kathleen Brown; m. Larry Frazier, Aug 24, 1962 (div. Nov. 1979); children: Larry K., Jay W., Susannah J.; m. Thomas Peter Utterback, July 24, 1999. RN, Sacred Heart Sch. Nursing, 1961; BA in Commn., Marylhurst Coll., 1979; MA in Counseling Psychology, Vt. Coll./Norwich U., 1992. RN; cert. mental health counselor. RN various hosps. and clinics, 1961-85; coll. instr. Portland State U., 1979-81; psychiat. nurse Yakima (Wash.) Valley Meml. Hosp., 1990—; psychiatric nurse Ctrl. Wash. Comprehensive Mental Health, Yakima, 1987-92; psychotherapist pvt. practice, Yakima, 1993—. Cons. Womens Health Ctr., Yakima, 1994—; instr. Yakima Valley Cmty. Coll., 1988-94; pub. spkr. women's issues. Co-author: (workbook) Structured Experiences in Human Communications, 1979; author: (manual) How to Teach the Adult Learner, 1983. Adv. bd. Womens Program, Yakima Valley Cmty. Coll., 1999; founder Women Together, Yakima, Wash., 1994—. Recipient tchg. asst. Portland State U., 1979-80. Avocations: drawing, painting, reading, theater.

SPRADLEY, PAMELA CLAIRE, art educator; b. Amarillo, Feb. 23, 1955; d. Leon Herman and Winifred Claire Skidgel; 1 child, Jordan Leon. BSE in art and Spanish, U. Ctrl. Ark., 1980. Cert. tchr. Art tchr. Smith Mid. Sch., Killeen, Tex., 1983—84; Spanish tchr. Killeen (Tex.) HS, 1984—85; art/Spanish tchr. North Little Rock (Ark.) Pub. Sch., 1985—87; Spanish tchr. Northwood Jr. HS, 1987—88; art/Spanish tchr. Rose Bud Pub. Schs., 1989—, art edn. instr. K-12, 2005—06. Avocations: drawing, painting, printmaking. Home: 3000 John Harden Dr #142 Jacksonville AR 72076 Office: Rose Bud Pub Schs 124 Sch Rd Rose Bud AR 72137

SPRADLIN, REBECCA L., art educator; b. Bismarck, Ark., Sept. 30, 1952; d. Coy D. Tims and Bobbie R. Thornton; m. Larry D. Spradlin, Oct. 21, 1970; children: Amanda Pundam, Chad. BSE in Art, Henderson State U., Arkadelphia, Ark., 1988, MSE, 2001. Tchr. Goza Mid. Sch., Arkadelphia, 1988—95, Bismarck Pub. Sch., Ark., 1995—. Adj. tchr. Ouachita Bapt. U., Arkadelphia, 1997. Personal E-mail: spradlp@hotmail.com.

SPRAGUE, ANN LOUISE, aerospace scientist; b. Bellfonte, Pa., Feb. 25, 1946; d. David Carpenter and Opal (Wheat) S.; m. Donald M. Hunten, 1995. BA Geology, Syracuse U., 1969; MA, Boston U., 1980; PhD, U. Ariz., 1990. Tchr. sci. Selinsgrove Mid. Sch., 1970—79; space scientist Lunar and Planetary Lab. U. Ariz., Tucson, 1990—. Mem. Lunar and Planetary Exploration com. NRC, 2000— Contbg. author: Caloris Basin: An Enhanced Source for Potassium in Mercury's Atmosphere, 1990, Sulfur at Mercury, Elemental at the Poles and Sulfides in the Regolith, 1995, Water Brought In to Jupiter's Atmosphere by Fragments R and W of Comet SL-9, 1996, Distribution and Abundance of Sodium in Mercury's Atmosphere, 1985-1988, 1997, Exploring Mercury: The Iron Planet, 2003; editl. bd. ICARUS Mem. AAAS, Internat. Astron. Union, Am. Astron. Soc. (com. divsn. planetary scis.), Am. Geophys. Union Office: U Ariz Lunar & Planetary Lab Tucson AZ 85721-0001 Business E-Mail: sprague@lpl.arizona.edu.

SPRAGUE, ELIZABETH ANNE, chemistry professor, researcher; b. Albany, N.Y., July 28, 1964; d. Thomas T., Jr. and Katherine Frances Van Wagenen; m. James P. Sprague, Aug. 17, 1991. AS, Jr. Coll. Albany, N.Y., 1989; BS, Russell Sage Coll., Troy, N.Y., 1991; PhD in Chemistry, Rensselaer Poly. Inst., Troy, N.Y., 2001. Recipient VanderVoort award, Russell Sage Coll., 1991, Excellence in Svc. award, Questar III Rensselaer Poly. Inst., 2001—04. Mem.: Am. Chem. Soc. (northeast chpt. affiliate 2000—), Phi Theta Kappa. Avocations: horseback riding, gardening, birdwatching. Office Phone: 518-276-2115.

SPRAGUE, MARCIA SCOVEL, small business owner; b. Rockford, Ill., Aug. 4, 1957; d. Mary Alice and Ward Norman Scovel; m. Tom K Sprague, Nov. 2, 1991; children: Kayla Rachon, Devi Mackenzie. BS in sociology, Ctrl. Mich. U., 1975—79. Teaching K-12 Music State of NH., 2003, lic. Massage Therapist Conn., 1993, Neuro-Linguistic Programming Mass., 1988, Touch for Health Practitioner Touch for Health, Internat., Switzerland, 1996, lic. Massage Therapist NH., 1995, Reike I John Harvey Gray, Mass., 1992, Foot Reflexology Inst. of Foot Reflexology, Fla., 1981, Bach Flower Practitioner Ellon, USA, 1983, Reike 2 NH., 1996. Tchr. Peace Corps, Sierra Leone, 1979—80; psychiat. counselor Battle Creek Sanitarium, Battle Creek, Mich., 1981—82; educator - developed and taught assertiveness classes at mt. holyoke coll., amherst coll., belchertown state sch., and cmty. edn. Self-employed, Hadley, Mass., 1985—86; program dir. Gardner Social Services, Gardner, Mass., 1986—88; counselor Conn. Halfway Ho., Hartford, Conn., 1989—90, Beech Hill Hosp., Dublin, NH, 1990—91; lic. massage therapist self-employed, New Haven, 1993—94, Self-employed, Concord, NH, 1995—99; music tchr. Pembroke Sch. Dist., Pembroke, NH, 1999—2003; educator/cons. Self-employed, Concord, NH, 2002—. Educator - touch for health self-employed, Concord, NH, 1996—98; educator - pregnancy massage Yale-New Haven Hosp., New Haven, 1992—93; family mediator Northampton Social Services, Mass., 1985—87; educator - profl. tng. for mental health agencies United Way Goodwill, Grand Rapids, Mich., 1984—85. Dir. (kids are authors - book writing contest for second and fourth graders) Scholastic, Concord, NH, 2001—02; editor and writer of cmty. newsletter Lamplighters, Concord, NH, 1995—97; mentor to a six week speechcrafters class Toastmasters Internat., Concord, NH, 2003—03; educator - commn. and pub. speaking classes Cinderella Modeling, Manchester, NH, 2003—03; girl scout leader Girl Scouts, Concord, NH, 2000—02; bell choir dir. for adult and youth handbell choirs Wesley United Meth. Ch., Concord, NH, 1995—2001; bell choir dir. Branford United Meth. Ch., Conn., 1993—94; lay spkr. First United Meth. Ch., Concord, NH, 1998—, youth leader, 2000—01; camp program dir. Wanakee Meth. Camp, Meredith, NH, 2000—03. Recipient Advanced Toastmaster, Silver level, Competent Leader, Toastmasters Internat. Mem.: Toastmasters Internat. (sec.club #2112 2002—03, v.p. of membership, club #6954 2003—, recipient first place Eval. and Humorous Speech contests Area Level 2003). Avocations: biking, writing, storytelling. Home: 157 Mountain Rd Concord NH 03301 Personal E-mail: mtkdo@aol.com.

SPRAGUE, MARY GABRIELLE, lawyer; b. Phila., Pa., Oct. 7, 1957; AB summa cum laude, Harvard U., 1979; JD, Yale U., 1983. Bar: Colo. 1984, D.C. 1992. Law clk. to Hon. Jim R. Carrigan US Dist. Ct. Colo., 1984-85; law clk. to Hon. Byron R. White US Supreme Ct., Washington, 1986-87; ptnr. Arnold & Porter, Washington. Mem. Phi Beta Kappa. Office: Arnold & Porter 555 12th St NW Washington DC 20004-1206 Office Phone: 202-942-5773. Office Fax: 202-942-5999. E-mail: Mary.Gay.Sprague@aporter.com.

SPRAKER, DEANNA KING, biology educator; m. Scott Spraker. BS in Edn., Bluefield State Coll., 1996; MA in Curriculum and Instrn., Va. Tech, 2001. Lic. profl. tchr. Va. Dept. Edn., 1996. Tchr. biology, earth sci. Pulaski County HS, Dublin, Va., 1998—2003, biology and honors biology tchr., 2004—05; life sci. tchr. Wythe County Schs./Rural Retreat Mid. Sch., Va., 2003—04; biology tchr. Smyth County Schs./Marion Sr. HS, 1996—98. Mentor new sci. tchrs. Pulaski County HS, 1999—2001. Named Tchr. of Month, Pulaski County Schs., 2006. Mem.: Nat. and Va. Edn. Assn., Gamma Beta Phi. Office: Pulaski County HS 5414 Cougar Trail Rd Dublin VA 24084 Office Phone: 540-643-0264. Personal E-mail: dspraker@vt.edu. Business E-Mail: dspraker@pcva.us. E-mail: dspraker@gmail.com.

SPRAYBERRY, ROSLYN RAYE, retired secondary school educator; b. Newnan, Ga., June 29, 1942; d. Henry Ray and Grace (Bernhard) S. BA, Valdosta State Coll., 1964; MA in Teaching, Ga. State U., 1976, EdS in Spanish, 1988; EdD, Nova U., 1993. Cert. tchr., Ga. Tchr. history Griffin (Ga.) High Sch., 1964-65; tchr. 6th grade Beaverbrook Elem Sch., Griffin, 1965-66; tchr. Spanish, chair fgn. lang. dept. Forest Park (Ga.) High Sch., 1969-77, Riverdale (Ga.) High Sch., 1977-99; ret., 1999. Correlator Harcourt, Brace, Jovanovich, 1989; adv. bd. So. Conf. Lang. Teaching, 1992-99; lectr. and speaker in field. Contbr. articles to The Ednl. Resource Info. Ctr. Clearinghouse on Langs. and Linguistics, Ctr. for Applied Linguistics, Washington; designed courses for the Gifted, Ga. Dept. of Edn. Cnvener Acad. Alliances-Atlanta II, Clayton County, Ga., 1982-99; advisor, workshop leader Ga. Fgn. Lang. Camp, Atlanta, 1983; dir. Clayton County Fgn. Lang. Festival, 1990-91. Recipient STAR Tchr. award Ga. C. of C., 1982; Fulbright-Hays scholar, 1978; NEH grantee, 1977, 84. Mem. NEA, Am. Coun. Tchrs. Fgn. Langs., Am. Assn. Tchrs. Spanish and Portuguese, Ga. Assn. Educators, Fgn. Lang. Assn. Ga. (treas. 1977-85, assoc. editor jour. 1981-86, Tchr. of Yr. award 1976), Clayton County Edn. Assn., So. Conf. Lang. Teaching, KPS Leadership Specialists (co-founder 1993). Methodist. Avocations: guitar playing, travel, reading, writing. Home: 104 Hickory Trail Stockbridge GA 30281-7361

SPRIESER, JUDITH A., former software company executive; BA in Linguistics, Northwestern U., MBA in Fin. CPA, Ill., 1982. Comml. banker Harris Bank, Chgo., 1974-81; dir. treasury ops. Esmark, 1981-84; asst. treas. internat. Nalco Chem. Co., 1984-87; asst. treas. corp. fin. Sara Lee Corp., 1987-90; sr. v.p., CFO Sara Lee Bakery N.Am., 1990-93, pres., CEO, 1993-94; sr. v.p., CFO Sara Lee Corp., 1994-99, CEO, Foods and Food Svc., 2000-2001; CEO Transora, Chgo., 2001—05. Bd. dirs. USG Corp., Reckitt Benckiser, Allstate Corp., 1999-, Kohl's Corp., 2003-, CBS Corp., 2005- Bd.

dirs. Hinsdale Hosp. Found.; trustee Northwestern U. Mem. AICPA, Chgo. Network, Young Pres. Orgn., Chgo. coun. Fgn. Rels., Econ. Club, Conf. Bd. Coun. Fin. Execs. Mailing: Bd Dir Allstate Corp 2775 Sanders Rd Northbrook IL 60062-6127*

SPRINCE, LEILA JOY, retired librarian; b. Toronto, Ont., Can., July 10, 1936; came to U.S., 1981; d. Harry and Anna Helen Caller; children: Alan Rosenthal, Joel Rosenthal; m. Arnold Joel Sprince, Feb. 16, 1982 BA, U. Toronto, 1957, B of Edn., 1962; MA, U. South Fla., 1987. Cert. tchr., Ont. Ballet dancer Volkoff Can. Ballet, Toronto, 1953-54; tchr. h.s. North York Bd. Edn., Toronto, 1958-60; libr. Broward County Libr. Sys., Plantation, Fla., 1987-88, 91-93, Margate, Fla., 1988-91, head youth svcs. Coconut Creek, Fla., 1996—2001; ret., 2001. Advisor Omnigraphics Pub., Detroit, 1993—; cons. Gale/U*X*L* Pubs., N.Y.C., 1996—; state facilitator summer programs State Libr. Fla., 1993. Contbr. articles to profl. jours. Mem. nat. children and youth membership orgns. outreach com. ALA/ALSC, 2001—; mem. adv. bd. Broward County Libr., 2006—. Mem. ALA (Best Books for Young Adult Cmty. spkr. 1989, 90), Fla. Libr. Assn. (spkr.), B'nai B'rith Women (fin. sec. 1983, pres. 1984, 85), Phi Kappa Phi, Beta Phi Mu. Democrat. Jewish. Avocations: music/dance, computers, travel, history. Personal E-mail: ajsprince@aol.com.

SPRING, KATHLEEN MARIE, musical program director, educator; b. L.A., Apr. 6, 1951; d. James David and Mabel Katherine (Nobbe) Klein; m. Glenn Ernest Spring, Dec. 16, 1973; children: Christopher, Heidi, Brian. BA in Music, Walla Walla Coll., 1974; student, Hochschule für Musik, Vienna, Austria, 1970-71, 85, 88; Mus M, U. Denver, 2000. Registered tchr. trainer, Suzuki Assn. of Ams. Violin instr., College Place, Wash., 1977—2001; string techniques instr., 1977—2001; string and orchs. tchr. Rogers Elem., College Place, 1980—2001, Est. Spring Violin Studio, Auroria, Colo., 2001—. Dir. Walla Walla Suzuki Program, Wash., 1984-2001; asst. prin. first violin Walla Walla Symphony, 1986-91, prin. second violin, 1991-99. Performer: (duo recital) Duo LeClair, Switzerland, Austria, 1983, (solo) Walla Walla, 1985, 88, WWC Centenial Chamber Music Series, 1992. Dir. Rogers String Ensembles, 1985-2001; co-conductor Cantabile Walla Walla area youth string ensemble, 1994-2001. Mem. Am. String Tchrs. Assn. (Studio Tchr. of Yr. Wash. state chpt. 1996), Internat. Suzuki Assn., Suzuki Assn. of Ams. (cert.), Suzuki Assn. Colo. Seventh-day Adventist. Home: 20442 E Union Cir Aurora CO 80015-5451

SPRINGER, LINDA M., federal official; BS, Ursinus Coll., 1977. Staff assoc. Coopers and Lybrand, 1977—79; actuary Penn Mut. Life Ins. Co., Phila., 1979—86, exec. asst. to pres., 1986—87, asst. v.p. & prod. mgr., 1987—90, v.p. & prod. mgr., 1990—92; actuary Provident Mut. Life Ins. Co., Berwyn, Pa., 1992—95, asst. v.p. & actuary, 1995—96, v.p. and contr., 1996—2000, sr. v.p. & contr., 2001—02; counselor to the dep. dir. for mgmt. Office Fed. Fin. Mgmt., Office Mgmt. & Budget, Washington, 2002—03, contr., 2003—05; dir. US Office Pers. Mgmt., Washington, 2005—. Avocations: golf, gardening, cello. Office: US Office Pers Mgmt Theodore Roosevelt Fed Bldg 1900 E St NW Rm 5A09 Washington DC 20415*

SPRINGER, MARLENE, university administrator, educator; b. Murfreesboro, Tenn., Nov. 16, 1937; d. Foster V. and Josephine Jones; children: Ann Springer, Rebecca Springer. BA in English and Bus. Adminstrn., Centre Coll., 1959; MA in Am. Lit., Ind. U., 1963, PhD in English Lit., 1969. Chair English dept. U. Mo., Kansas City, 1980-81, acting assoc. dean grad. sch., 1982; Am. Coun. of Edn. Adminstrn. fellow U. Kans., Lawrence, 1982-83; dean of grad. sch. U. Mo., Kansas City, 1983-84, assoc. vice chancellor for acad. affairs and grad. studies, 1985-89; vice chancellor for acad. affairs East Carolina U., Greenville, NC, 1989-94; pres. CUNY Coll., Staten Island, 1994—. Author: Edith Wharton and Kate Chopin: A Reference Guide, 1976; What Manner of Woman: Essays, 1977, Thomas Hardy's Use of Allusion, 1983, Plains Woman: The Diary of Martha Farnsworth, 1986 (Choice award 1986), Ethan Frome: A Nightmare of Need, 1993. Huntington Libr. fellow, 1988. Mem.: Coun. Grad. Schs. (chair 1986—88), Assn. Tchr. Educators (chair 1992), Acad. Leadership Acad. (exec. com. 1992—94), Am. Assn. State Colls. and Univs., Am. Coun. on Edn. (profl. devel. com. 1991—, invited participant Nat. Forum 1984, bd. dirs. 2001—). Office: Coll Staten Island 2800 Victory Blvd Rm 1a-404 Staten Island NY 10314-6609

SPRINGER, RUTH WIREN, music educator; b. Bronx, N.Y., July 17, 1956; d. Bror Stanley Wiren and Ingrid Katerina Walderman; life ptnr. Dominick Frank Lettera. BS in Music Edn., Taylor U., 1978; MA in Music Edn., Ball State U., 1981. Cert. tchr. Am. Orff Schulwerk Assn., 1980. Music educator Maconaquah Sch. Corp., Bunker Hill, Ind., 1978—2001, Darien (Conn.) Pub. Schs., 2001—. Pvt. piano tchr., Kokomo, Ind., 1978—94; area coord. Cir. State With Song, Ind. Children's Choral Festival, Muncie, 1996—97; pianist Svea Lodge 253, Vasa Order Am., Indpls., 1996—2001. Actress, singer, rehearsal accompanist and vocal music dir. Kokomo Civic Theatre, 1983—2001; dir., actress, singer, accompanist and stage crew mem. Curtain Call Children's Theatre, Kokomo, 1988—91; singer Kokomo Symphonic Chorus. Named Outstanding Ind. Elem. Music Educator of Yr., Ind. Music Educators Assn., 2000—01; recipient 25 Years of Service in Music Education award, CT Music Educators Assn., 2004; grantee, Sydnor and Miriam Reiss Tchr's. Fund for Further Study, 2003. Mem.: NEA, Am. Guild Organists, Am. Choral Dirs. Assn., Darien Edn. Assn., Conn. State Tchrs. Assn., Conn. Music Educators Assn., Music Educators Nat. Conf., Theatre 308 (rehearsal and performance pianist 2002—). Conservative-R. Protestant. Achievements include being selected as one of four educators from across the United States to participate in the Singers On Stage Broadway Workshop and performed in the chorus of On Broadway 1998, NYC; Randall School Choir performed, under my direction, for First Lady, Barbara Bush in 1991; Randall School Choir and Holmes School Choir performed on television in The World's Largest Concert in 1990 and 2004; Randall School Choir, under my direction, were featured performers at the Indiana Children's Choral Festival, 1989; Pipe Creek School Choir, under my direction, performed twice for Youth Art Month at the Indiana State Capitol building. Avocations: theater, dance, gardening, travel, tennis. Office: Holmes Sch 18 Hoyt St Darien CT 06820

SPRINGER, WILMA MARIE, retired elementary school educator; b. Goshen, Ind., Jan. 13, 1933; d. Noah A. and Laura D. (Miller) Kaufman; m. Walter Frederick Springer, May 25, 1957; children: Anita Daniel, Timothy, Mark. BA, Goshen Coll., 1956; MS, Bradley U., 1960. Tchr. Topeka Elem. Sch., Ind., 1956—57, Metamora Grade Sch., Ill., 1957—59, Bellflower Unified Sch. Dist., Calif., 1960—61, 1968—2001, Lindstrom Elem. Sch., 1970—89, Jefferson Elem. Sch., Bellflower, 1989—92, Woodruff Elem., 1992—93, Williams Elem. Sch., Lakewood, Calif., 1993—96, Baxter Elem. Sch., Bellflower, 1996—2001; ret., 2001. Chmn. gifted and talented edn. Lindstrom Elem. Sch., Lakewood, 1986—89, Jefferson Elem. Sch., Bellflower, 1989—91, Baxter Elem., 1996—2001; stage mgr. Hour of Power TV Crystal Cathedral, 1983—; mem. program quality rev. team State of Calif., 1989—91; mem. adv. bd. Weekly Reader, 1989—96. Contbr. articles to profl. jours. Active sch. bd. campaign, 1984, Bellflower City Coun., 1988, state senator and assemblyman campaigns, 1986-87; petition circulator various state initiatives, 1987-88; bd. dirs. Women's Ministries of Crystal Cathedral, Garden Grove, Calif., 1978-88; educator del. People to People Ambassadors Program, South Africa, 2003, Russia, 2004. Instructional Improvement Program grantee State of Calif., 1986-87; recipient Recognition award Regional Edn. TV Adv. Coun., 1986, Cathedral Star award Women's Ministries of Crystal Cathedral, 1985. Mem.: AAUW, NEA (del. nat. conv. 1986, 1987, 1990, 1992, 1993, 1994, 1995), Calif. Tchrs. Assn. (del. 1986, 1994), Bellflower Edn. Assn. (elem. dir. 1986—88, treas. 1988—89, v.p. 1989—91, pres. 1991—95), Toastmasters (Founder's Dist. Gov. 2001—02, Disting. Toastmaster, Disting. Dist.), Delta Kappa Gamma. Republican. Mem. Reformed Churches of Am. Avocations: quilting, painting. Home: 3180 Marna Ave Long Beach CA 90808-3246 Personal E-mail: wmspr@aol.com.

SPRINGFIELD, SANYA A., federal agency administrator; BS in zoology, Howard U., PhD in physiology and biophysics. Fellow Dept. Pharmacology Robert Wood Johnson Sch. Medicine, Piscataway, NJ; asst. prof. to assoc. prof. Dept. Biology CCNY, 1985—95; program dir. Divsn. Integrative Biology and Neurosiences NSF; participant NIH Grants Assoc. Program; sci. rev. adminstr. Grants Rev. Br. Nat. Cancer Inst., dir. Comprehensive Minority Biomedical Br., 1999—, acting dir. Ctr. to Reduce Cancer Health Disparities. Office: Comprehensive Minority Biomedical Br Nat Cancer Inst 6116 Executive Blvd Ste 7028 Bethesda MD 20892-8350 also: Ctr to Reduce Cancer Health Disparities Nat Cancer Inst 6116 Executive Blvd Ste 602 MSC 8341 Bethesda MD 20892 Office Phone: 301-496-7344. Office Fax: 301-402-4551. E-mail: springfs@mail.nih.gov.

SPRINGSTEAD, MARTHA WYATT, voice educator; b. Temple, Tex., Apr. 10, 1954; d. Gerald D. and Sylvia H. Wyatt; m. David Bruce Springstead, July 5, 1980; children: Robert, Jane, Paul, David Jr. B in Music Edn., Mt. Union Coll., 1976; M in Music Edn., Shenandoah U., 1999, D of Music Edn., 2006. Vocal music tchr. Am.Sch.of Tangler, Tangler, Morocco, 1977—78; piano instr. Town and Country Theatre, 1978—79; vocal music tchr. Cloverleaf Local Schools, Lodi, Ohio, 1979—84, City of Va. Beach Schools, 1984—. Choral accompanist Salem H.S. Choirs, Va. Beach, 1997—; mentor Old Dominion U., Norfolk, Va., 2002, Norfolk, 06. Music dir. Cmty. United Meth. Ch., 1991—; accompanist Voices of Youth Mission Choir, Va., 2002, Miss., 2002; dir. Norfolk Dist. Choir United Meth. Men's, 1999—. Mem.: NEA, Am.Choral Dir. Assn., Music Educators Nat. Conf. Avocations: theater, needlecrafts, reading. Office: Landstown HS 2001 Concert Dr Virginia Beach VA 23456 Business E-Mail: mwspring@vbschools.com.

SPRINKLE, DENISE L., science educator; d. Frank A. and Ann S. Linkenauger; m. Peter D. Sprinkle, Aug. 26, 1972; children: Jason, Amy, Michael, Jenna. BS in Chemistry, Roanoke Coll., Va., 1975. Tchr. Botetourt County Schs., Fincastle, Va., 1976—. Chair sci. dept. Ctrl. Acad., Fincastle, 1996—; tchr., leader Content Literacy Grant, 2005—. Mem. Botetourt County Planning Commn., Fincastle, 1991—92. Mem.: Botetourt Ednl. Assn., Va. Ednl. Assn., Nat. Sci. Tchrs. Assn., Va. Assn. Sci. Tchrs. (life). Office: Ctrl Acad Mid Sch 367 Poor Farm Rd Fincastle VA 24090

SPRINKLE, MARTHA CLARE, elementary school educator; b. Tehachapi, Calif., Oct. 17, 1944; d. William Foote and Mildred Sprinkle; BA, U. Calif., Santa Barbara, 1966; MA in Orgn. Mgmt., U. Phoenix, 2000. Cert. tchr. Calif., water aerobics instr. 1986. Tchr. Muroc Unified Sch. Dist., Edwards, Calif., 1966—71, Elk Hills Sch., Tupman, Calif., 1971—79, Tehachapi Valley Recreation and Pks., 1979—, So. Kern Unified Sch., Rosamond, Calif., 1984—2003. Planning commr. City of Tehachapi, Calif., 1984—. Home: PO Box 852 Tehachapi CA 93581

SPROAT, RUTH C., retired director, consultant; b. Lake Forest, Ill., Aug. 22, 1930; d. Christian Peter and Anna Elsa Christensen; m. Robert M. Volpe (div.); m. John Gerald Sproat, Mar. 18, 1967; 1 stepchild, Barbara Jeanne. BA in History, Lake Forest Coll., 1952; MA in History, Northwestern U., 1962. Registrar, admissions counselor Lake Forest Coll., 1948—68, dir. alumni affairs, 1972—74; dir. Master's Degree Program, asst. to pres. Lake Forest Coll. Grad. Sch. Mgmt., 1968—70, asst. to pres., 1971—72; dir. higher edn. SC Ednl. TV Network, Columbia, 1974—80, asst. dir. programming, exec. prodr., prodr., 1980—82, dir. higher edn., project dir., prodr., exec. prodr., 1982—87, asst. to pres. for devel. Satellite Ednl. Resources Consortium, 1988—92, exec. staff, dir. planning, grants and rsch., project dir., exec. prodr., 1992—97, cons. and asst. to pres., 2000—02; dir. devel. U. SC, Columbia, 1997—99; ret., 2002; cons. in field, 2002—. V.p. S.C. chpt. Am. Women in Radio and TV, 1983; co-prodr. with Am. Film Inst. Am. TV and Video Festival, India, 1985, prodr., presenter, India, 1986—91. Project dir., grant writer: (PBS TV series) Voices and Visions; U.S. project dir. Spaceship Earth; coordinating prodr. Cinematic Eye (Day Time Emmy award). Mentor to devel. staff Columbia Mus. Art, 2002. Recipient Alumni Disting. Svc. citation, Lake Forest Coll., 1987. Mem.: Hist. Columbia Found., Ill. Assn. Coll. Registrars and Admissions Officers (hon.; pres. 1965), Am. Assn. Collegiate Registrars and Admissions Officers (hon.; sec. 1966—68), Riverbanks Zoo Soc., Friends of U. S.C. Sch. Music (sec. 2001—03, dir. publicity for ann. fundraiser 2002—03, 2003—04, v.p. 2005—), State Mus. S.C., Sierra Club. Democrat. Avocations: gardening, writing, photography, travel. Home: 1686 Woodlake Dr Columbia SC 29206 E-mail: rcsproat@sc.rr.com.

SPROUL, JOAN HEENEY, retired elementary school educator; b. Johnstown, Pa., July 17, 1932; d. James L. and Grace M. (Dunn) Heeney; m. Robert Sproul, July 31, 1957 (dec.); 1 child, Mary Claire. BS, Clarion U., 1954; MA, George Wash. U., 1963; postgrad., U. Va., 1966-88. Cert. tchr., Va. Kindergarten tchr. Jefferson Sch., Warren, Pa., 1954-55; primary grades tchr. Alexandria (Va.) Pub. Schs., 1955-64; elem. tchr. Fairfax County Schs., Springfield, Va., 1965-97; math. lead tchr. West Springfield (Va.) Sch., 1987-97, ret., 1997. Contbr. (with others) Virginia History, 1988. Advisor Springfield Young Organists Assn., 1971-83; mem. Fairfax County Dem. Com., 1988-94, West Springfield Civic Assn., 1965—, Women's Aux. Fairfax Co. Salvation Army. Grantee Impact II, 1985-86. Mem. AAUW, NEA, Nat. Fedn. Bus. and Profl. Women (pres., dir., dist. VIII 1984—, Woman of Yr. 1985, 88), Delta Kappa Gamma (2d v.p. Va. chpt. 1963—), Phi Delta Kappa, Sigma Sigma Sigma. Episcopalian. Avocations: reading, music, gardening, fashion design. Home: # 124 1881 Harvest Dr Winchester VA 22601 Personal E-mail: joanh.sproul@yahoo.com.

SPROUL, SARAH LEE, conductor, musician, educator; b. NJ, Mar. 16, 1976; d. George and Sandra Lee Sproul. MusB, So. Meth. U., 1998, MusM, 2000. Cert. Tex. Bd. Edn. Orch. dir. Forestwood Mid. Sch., Flower Mound, Tex., 2000—; condr. Lone Star Youth Orch., Las Colinas, 2001—; asst. condr. Las Colinas Symphony Orch., 2001—, Garland (Tex.) Symphony Orch., 2001—, Symphony Arlington, Tex., 2001—; orch. dir. Shadow Ridge Mid. Sch., Flower Mound, Tex., 2005—. Recipient Don Nobles Meml. award, Meadows Sch. Arts, So. Meth. U., 1999, Sigma Alpha Iota award, 1999; Meadows Artistic scholar, 1994—98, Algur H. Meadows Grad. Conducting and Tchg. fellow, 1998—2000. Mem.: ASPCA, Tex. Music Edn. Assn., Am. Symphony Orch. League (guardian), Condr.'s Guild. Avocation: music. Personal E-mail: sproulsl@lisd.net.

SPRUDE, MARGARET, credit services company executive; b. 1946; BS in Bus., Western Ill. U., 1977, MS of Accountancy, 1982. CPA, CMA. Various fin.-exec.-level positions card divsn. including CFO card svcs. Bank of Am., 1986—2000, mng. dir., CFO HSC Card Svcs. divsn., 2000—. Office: HSBC 1441 Schilling Pl Salinas CA 93901-4543 Business E-Mail: margaret.a.sprude@us.hcbc.com. E-mail: masprude@household.com.

SPRUNGER, LESLIE KAREN, physiologist, educator; b. Palo Alto, Calif., Aug. 29, 1961; d. Richard Marmion and Patricia Joann (Sprunger) Oldacre; 1 child, Katherine Elyse Traynor. BS, U. Alaska, 1983; DVM, Wash. State U., 1987; PhD, U. Minn., 1995. Vet. Alder Trail Animal Hosp., Bremerton, Wash., 1987-88; vet. med. assoc. U. Minn. Dept. Vet. Pathobiology, St. Paul, 1988-94; rsch. assoc. U. Minn. Dept. Physiology, Mpls., 1994-95; rsch. investigator human genetics U. Mich., Ann Arbor, 1995—2000; asst. prof. Wash. State U., 2000—. Howard Huges Med. Inst. cons., 2003—. Contbr. articles to profl. jours. including Jour. Vet. Med. Edn., Jour. Comparative Neurology, Neuron, Jour. Neurosci. Cell & Tissue Rsch., Human Molecular Genetics. Tutor ESL Project Literacy, Mpls., 1988-89. Grantee NIH, 1994-2000; Howard Hughes Med. Inst. fellow, 1989-94. Mem. Am. Assn. Anatomists, Soc. Gen. Physiologists, Soc. for Neurosci., Internat. Mouse Genome Soc., Sigma Xi, Phi Zeta. Democrat. Avocations: reading, music, exercise. Office: Dept of Veterinary and Comparative Anatomy Pharmacology and Physiology Wash State U 205 Wegner Hall Pullman WA 99164-6520 Office Phone: 509-335-7071. Business E-Mail: lsprunger@wsu.edu.

SPRUNGL, JANICE MARIE, nurse; b. Brooklyn, Ohio, Mar. 9, 1960; d. Donald Edward and Dolores Jane (Slys) Sprungl. BS in Nursing, U. Akron, 1982. RN, Ohio. Commd. 2nd lt. USAF, 1982, advanced through grades to maj., 1994, clin. nurse Med. Ctr. Keesler Biloxi, Miss., 1982-86, charge nurse Med. Ctr. Keesler, 1986-88, charge nurse ambulatory med. svcs. USAF Acad. Hosp. Colorado Springs, Colo., 1988-91; charge nurse primary care clinic ambulance svcs. Lowry Clinic USAF, 1991-94; clin. nurse, educator Family Practice Clinic, USAF Acad. Hosp., 1994-97; telehealth nurse Metrohealth Med. Ctr., Cleve., 2000—. Magnet chairperson Metrohealth Med. Ctr., Cleve. Vol. Spl. Olympics, Keesler AFB, 1983—87; fundraiser Nat. Multiple Sclerosis Soc. Mem.: Ret. Officers Assn., Ohio Nursing Assn. Avocations: swimming, skiing, bicycling.

SPRY, BARBARA DIANE, elementary school educator; BS in Edn., U. Kans., Lawrence, 1970—73. Lic. Tchr. Colo. Dept. Edn., 1979. Tchr. Ohio County Schs., Horse Branch, Ky., 1974—78, Aurora Pub. Schs., Colo., 1978—. Office Phone: 303-750-2836.

SPUNGIN, CHARLOTTE ISABELLE, retired secondary school educator, writer; b. Providence, June 12, 1929; d. Abraham Spungin and Golde Morrison. BA, U. RI, 1951; MEd, U. Fla., 1966; EdS, Nova Southeastern U., Davie, Fla., 1981. Tchr., head dept. social sci. South Broward HS, Hollywood, Fla., 1962-90. Cons. Fla. Atlantic U., Boca Raton, 1985-90, U. Miami, Fla., 1980-90, Broward County Sch. Dist., Ft. Lauderdale, Fla., 1990-96; tchr. trainer Fla. Performance Measurement Sys.; instr. psychology and sociology Broward C.C. Co-author: (books) (with N. Tallent) Psychology: Understanding Ourselves and Others, 1977, (with H. Besner) Gay and Lesbian Students: Understanding Their Needs, 1995, Training for Professionals Who Work with Gays and Lesbians in Educational and Workplace Settings, 1997, (curriculum guides) Creativity with Bill Moyers, 1984, World of Difference, 1987, Holocaust Curriculum Guide for the State of Florida, 1990, The Holocaust Remembered, 1986, (monograph) Southeast Asian Monograph on Comparative Educational School Systems: Singapore, Malaysia and the Indonesian Islands, 1971. Cons., bd. dirs. Holocaust Documentation Ctr., North Miami, Fla., 1985-90; bd. dirs. Fla. Coun. for Social Studies, Orlando and Tallahassee, 1979-85. Recipient Spirit of Excellence award Miami Herald, 1985, Skretting award Fla. Coun. for Social Studies, Wilma Simmons Golden Svc. award, 1985, Outstanding Svc. in Mental Health award Fla. divsn. Nat. Assn. Mental Health, Woman of Yr. in Edn. award Women in Comm., 1990; Fulbright fellow, 1970, 76; scholar NSF, 1965. Mem. APA, ASCD, Nat. Coun. on Social Studies, Fla. Coun. for Social Studies, Phi Delta Kappa, Phi Alpha Theta. Democrat. Jewish. Avocations: travel, writing, reading. Office: PO Box 8833 Fort Lauderdale FL 33310-8833 E-mail: spunbar@comcast.net.

SPURLOCK, EVELYN HARVEY, retired elementary school educator, minister; b. June 25, 1914; d. Forrest and Maude Hunter Harvey; m. Junius White; 1 child, Matona; m. Richard Spurlock; 1 child, Maxella. Grad., Storer Coll., 1934, Miner Tchrs. Coll., Hampton Inst.; postgrad., NYU. Ordained min. Cross Bapt. Ch., 1994. Tchr. Carver H.S., Mt. Olive, NC, Watson H.S., Covington; ret., 1979. Home: 332 S Marion Ave Covington VA 24426-1717

SPURR, DAWN M., special education educator; b. Marietta, Ohio, Oct. 26, 1970; d. William Barse and Carol Forbes; m. Timothy Spurr, June 12, 1994; 1 child, Nicholas. BA in Edn., Ohio U., Athens, 1991; MA, Muskingum Coll., New Concord, Ohio, 2001. Cert. tchr. Ohio, 1991. Intervention specialist Ft. Frye Schs., Beverly, Ohio, 1998—; v.p. C2C2learn.com. Volleyball and softball coach. Recipient Tchr. of Yr. Mem.: NEA (assoc.; president local chpt. 2004—06). Achievements include development of tutoring website; research in misdiagnosis of ADHD. Home: 111 Pineview Dr Marietta OH 45750 Office: Fort Frye Schs 215 5th St Beverly OH 45715 Office Phone: 740-984-2376. E-mail: ff_dspurr@seovec.org.

SPURRIER, MARY EILEEN, investment advisor, financial planner; b. Mpls., Sept. 16, 1943; d. Charles Joseph and Ruth Eileen (Rowles) Dickman; m. Joseph Leo Spurrier, Jan. 16, 1965 (div. Aug. 1976); 1 child, Christopher Jude; m. Gary Albert Gutfrucht, July 8, 1988. BS, U. Minn., 1965. CFP; CDP; registered prin., registered investment advisor. Rsch. fellow, libr. Sch. Bus. Adminstrn. U. Minn., Mpls., 1965-68; exec. dir. Zero Population Growth, N.Y., 1972-76; fin. cons. Merrill Lynch, Rochester, N.Y., 1977-84, Shearson/Smith Barney, 1984-89; investment cons. CitiCorp, Rochester, 1989-91; assoc. v.p. Essex Investment, Rochester, 1991-95; pres. M. Spurrier Fin. Svcs., Rochester, 1995—. Bd. dirs. Micro Bus. Alliance, Rochester; cons. Fund Devel. Rochester Women's Network, 1995-97, Women's Coun. C. of C., Rochester, 1992-97; spkr. in field. Advisor Blue Jean Mag.; contbr. articles to newspapers. Chmn. endowment campaign YWCA, Rochester, 1994-98, bd. dirs., mem. fin. com. 1997—; mentor Wilson Commencement Park, Rochester, 1993—; v.p., bd. dirs. N.Y. State Environ. Planning Lobby, 1973-75; bd. dirs. N.Y. State Family Planning Coalition, 1973-75; fin. dir. LWV, Rochester, 1989-90; capital campaign com. Susan B. Anthony House, 1997-99. Recipient Eminent Rochester Women award Upstate Mag., 1974. Mem. NAFE (spkr. 1990-95), Rochester Women's Network (bd. dirs. 1997—, v.p. 1999—), Women's Coun. C. of C. (chair W award 2000, nominee W award 1999), Nat. Assn. Women Bus. Owners (bd. dirs. Greater Rochester chpt. 1997-2000, chair Top Women's Bus. Owners Awards 1997-2000). Avocations: gardening, reading, walking. Office: 315 Westminster Rd Rochester NY 14607-3230

SPYKER, LEOLA EDITH, missionary; b. Wallace, Mich., Mar. 15, 1925; d. Oscar Eugene Anderson and Edith Ragnhild Nelson; m. George Spyker, Feb. 16, 1951 (div. June 1967); children: Marilyn Joy, John George, Thomas Oscar, Sandra Lee. AA, N. Park U., Chgo., 1944; BA, Bob Jones U., Greenville, S.C., 1947; postgrad. in Counseling, Seattle Pacific U., Seattle, Wash., 1969—70. Cert. in ESL Upton Coll., Pasadena, Calif., 1961, in French and Italian, Academia Uruapan, Michoacan, Mex. 1965, in Secondary Edn. Mich., Wis., Wash., Tex. Instr. King's Garden Sch., Seattle, 1969—71; lectr. Seminario El Calvario, El Carmen, Nuevo Leon, Mexico, 1971—74, 1977—80; lectr. in missionary outreach, anthropology, history, comparative religions Inst. Misionera Morelia, Michoacan, 1983—92; prof. U. Michoacan, Uruapan, Michoacan, Mexico, 1975—77, Mexico, 1982—84. Founder, dir. Casa Hogar La Esparanza, Uruapan, Michoacda, Mexico, Hogar la Esperanza, Utuapan, 1953—93; conf. spkr. Vida Abundante, Morelia, Mexico, 1980—2003; coord. student groups to Honduras, Nicaragua and Spain, 1995, 99, 2002; Spanish translator internat. conf. for Billy Graham, Amsterdam, Netherlands, 1996; worker refugee rehab. and outreach, Honduras, Nicaragua, 84, Honduras, Nicaragua, 86, Honduras, Nicaragua, 87. Contbr. 40 articles in profl. publications. Avocations: painting, travel, reading, ornithology. Home: PO Box 2050 2021 Harvey Dr Mcallen TX 78501 Office Phone: 956-682-6774. Personal E-mail: leolas@juno.com.

SQUAZZO, MILDRED KATHERINE (MILDRED KATHERINE OETTING), corporate executive; b. Bklyn., Dec. 22, 1927; d. William John and Marie M. Oetting. Student, L.I. U. Sec.-treas. Stanley Engrng., Inc., 1960—68; v.p. Stanley Chems., Inc., 1960—68; founder, pres. Chem-Dynamics Corp., Scotch Plains, NJ, 1964—68; gen. adminstr., purchasing dir. Richardson Chem. Co., Metuchen, NJ, 1968—69; owner Berkeley Employment Agy. and Berkeley Temp. Help Svc., Berkeley Heights, NJ, 1969—91, Berkeley Employment Agy., Morristown, NJ, 1982—91, Bridgewater, NJ, 1987—91; pres. M.K.S. Bus. Group, Inc., Berkeley Heights, 1980—91; mgmt. cons.; pers. fin.; lectr. With Nurse Corps U.S. Army, 1946—47. Mem.: Nat. Bus. and Profl. Women's Club.

SQUIER, RITA ANN HOLMBERG, graphic designer; b. Norwalk, Conn., Jan. 4, 1967; d. Stig H. and Julia Mildred Tjader Holmberg; m. Michael Craig Squier, May 19, 1990. BS in Visual Arts, U. Bridgeport, 1988. Art dir., web designer Squier Design, Chatham, NY, 1995—; graphic designer, owner Studio 46, Chatham, 1990-99. Mem. Mooresville Artist Guild, Columbia County Coun. on the Arts. Republican. Avocations: watercolor, pen and ink, gardening, acrylics, photography. Office: Squier Design 46 Payn Ave Chatham NY 12037-1427

SQUIRE, ANNE MARGUERITE, retired humanities educator; b. Amherstburg, Ont., Can., Oct. 17, 1920; d. Alexander Samuel and Coral Marguerite Park; m. William Robert Squire, June 24, 1943; children: Frances, Laura, Margaret. BA, Carleton U., Ottawa, 1972, BA with honors, 1974, MA, 1975; LLD (hon.), Carleton U., 1988; DD (hon.), United Theol. Coll., 1979, Queen's U., 1985. Cert. tchr., Ont. Adj. prof. Carleton U., 1975-82; sec. div. ministry personnel and edn. United Ch. Can., Toronto, 1982-85, moderator, 1986-88; ret., 1988. Author curriculum materials, 1959—; contbr. articles to profl. jours. Mem. bd. mgmt. St. Andrew's Coll., Saskatoon, Sask., 1982, Queens Theol. Coll., Kingston, Ont., 1999-2005; founding mem. Muslim-Christian Dialogue Group; patron MultiFaith Housing Initiative; hon. advisor Can. Ctr. for Progressive Christianity. Recipient Senate medal Carleton U., 1972. Mem. Can. Research Inst. for Advancement Women, Delta Kappa Gamma (pres. 1978-79). Mem. United Ch. Can. Office: 731 Weston Dr Ottawa ON Canada K1G 1W1 E-mail: a.squire@sympatico.ca.

SQUIRE, BEVERLY, entrepreneur, business owner; b. San Antonio, Sept. 11, 1947; d. Orville Herbert and Theda Lenora Atkinson; m. Roger W. Squire, Apr. 10, 1970; children: Ryan Christopher, Suzanne Louise. Grad. H.S., Escondido, Calif. Owner, entrepreneur, pres. Inventory Control Sys., Arcadia, Calif., 1971—. Active L.A. County Mus. Art, 1992, L.A. World Affairs Coun., 1993, Nat. Fedn. Ind. Bus., Washington, 1995; donor U. Calif. Riverside Found., 1997; co-chmn. bus. adv. coun. Rep. Congl. Com., 1999. Recipient Medal of Merit, Rep. Congl. Com., 1999; named Bus. Woman of the Yr., Rep. Congl. Com., 1998. Mem. Nat. Watercolor Soc. (assoc.), Nat. Mus. Women in the Arts, Am. Watercolor Soc. (assoc.), U.S. Lighthouse Soc. Roman Catholic. Avocations: visual arts, playing piano, lighthouse history.

SQUIRE, GILDA N., publishing executive, writer; b. Balt., July 11, 1969; d. Gilbert Squire. BA in Comms., George Mason U., 1995. Adminstrv. sec. FBI, Washington, 1987—90; adminstrv. asst. Office Tech. Assessment U.S. Congress, Washington, 1990—95; mktg. mgr. Goldman Sachs, N.Y.C., 1996—2001; publicist Penguin Putnam, Inc., N.Y.C., 2001—. Freelance writer Sister 2 Sister Mag., Washington, 1992—93, Black Elegance and Belle Mags., N.Y.C., 1995—2000, Upscale Mag., N.Y.C., 1999—. Author: Dark Eros: Black Erotic Writings, 1998. Mem.: Dance Theatre of Harlem Jr. Coun. (treas. 2000—01). Home: 422 W 160th St #3 New York NY 10032 Personal E-mail: gnsquire@aol.com.

SQUIRE, SHERI MARIE, science educator; b. Ft. Rucker, Ala., July 5, 1965; d. Joseph William and Mitzi Jane Squire; 1 child, Jordan Baker Gross. BA, U. N.C., Chapel Hill, 1989; MEd, East Carolina U., Greenville, N.C., 1991. Cert. Nat. Athletic Trainers, 1992; tchr. N.C., 1992. Anatomy/physiology tchr. Douglas Byrd H.S., Fayetteville, NC, 1992—95; tchr. sci. grade 7 Anne Chesnutt Mid. Sch., Fayetteville, 1997—2003; tchr. sci. grade 6 Westover Mid. Sch., Fayetteville, 2003—. Recipient Tchr. of Yr., Westover Mid. Sch., 2005—06. Mem.: Nat. Athletic Trainers Assn. (licentiate), N.C. Assn. Educators (assoc.), Chi Omega Frat. (life). Catholic. Avocations: crafts, reading. Home: 400 Gleneagles Ct Fayetteville NC 28311 Office: Westover Mid Sch 275 Bonanza Dr Fayetteville NC 28311 Office Phone: 910-864-0813. Office Fax: 910-864-7906. Business E-Mail: sherisquire@ccs.k12.nc.us.

SQUIRES, NANCY, psychology professor; PhD, U. Calif., San Diego, 1972. Prof. biopsychology SUNY, Stony Brook, chairperson Dept. Psychology. Office: Dept Psychology SUNY Stony Brook Psychology B154 Stony Brook NY 11794 Office Phone: 631-632-7808. E-mail: nancy.squires@stonybrook.edu.*

SQUIRES, SANDRA KAY, special education educator; b. Glendive, Mont., June 3, 1944; d. Ralph E. and M. Elouise (Cabbage) S.; m. James A. Boland, June 19, 1965 (div. May 1, 1980); children: Michael F., Tatiana L. BS in Elem. Edn., Eastern Mont. Coll., 1966; MA in Mental Retardation, Colo. State Coll., 1969; EdD in Mental Retardation, U. No. Colo., 1972. Cert. elem. tchr., Mont., Okla., Colo. First grade tchr. Billings Pub. Sch., Mont., 1966-67; spl. edn. tchr. Ft. Benning Children's Schs., Ga., 1967-68, Comanche County United Cerebral Palsy Assn., Lawton, Okla., Weld Bd. Coop. Services, Ault, Colo., 1970; instr. Loretto Heights Coll., Denver, 1972; instructional materials specialist Rocky Mountain Instructional Materials Ctr., Greeley, Colo., 1971-72, asst. prof., 1973-74; dir. career edn. for Mentally Handicapped Weld Bd. Coop. Svcs., LaSalle, Colo., 1974-77; asst. prof. Colo. State U., Ft. Collins, 1978; sr. project assoc. Pa. State U., Bur. of Edn. for Handicapped, Washington, 1979; asst. prof. Wash. State U., Pullman, 1979-81; assoc. prof., chmn. counseling and spl. edn. U. Nebr. Omaha, 1981-88, assoc. prof. dept. scp. edn. and communication disorders, 1988-98, prof., 1998-2000, coord. women's studies, 1995-97; pres. Ednl. Cons. Enterprises Inc., Greeley, 1974-79; speaker, cons. univs., local, state, and federal agencies, profl. orgns. U.S. and Canada, 1972—; sec., treas. Squires, Inc., Glendive, Mont., 1980—. Co-editor, editor: (newsletter) Inservice Consultant, 1974-77; author tng. manuals, monograph, children's books; contbr. articles to profl. jours. Polit. action network coordinator Nebr. Fedn. Council for Exceptional Children, Omaha, 1982-85, 87-89, 95-; youth coord. Episcopal Diocese of Nebr., 1987-94. Recipient Robert G. Sando award Eastern Mont. Coll., 1966, Outstanding Achievement award Chancellor's Commn. on Status of Women, 2001. Mem. Internat. Coun. Exceptional Children, Internat. Divsn. on Career Devel. (sec. 1976-79, v.p. 1979-80, pres.-elect 1980-81, pres. 1981-82), Tchr. Edn. Divsn. (dir. behavioral divsn.), Pioneer Divsn. Home: 681 S 85th St Omaha NE 68114-4205 Office: U Nebr Dept Spl Edn and Communication Disorders Omaha NE 68182 Office Phone: 402-554-3582. Personal E-mail: sksquires@earthlink.net. Business E-Mail: ssquires@mail.unomaha.edu.

SQUIRES, SHELLY MARX, retired special education educator; b. Bronx, N.Y., Nov. 23, 1950; d. Martin and Helen Ruth (Kaufman) Marx; m. Harold Ira Edelson, Aug. 27, 1972 (div.); children: Melissa Ivy, Alanna Gail. AAS, Rockland C.C., Suffern, N.Y., 1970; BS in Edn. magna cum laude, SUNY, Buffalo, 1972; MS in Edn. with honors, Binghamton (N.Y.) U., 1980. Cert. permanent spl. edn. tchr., N.Y. Tchr. spl. edn. Broward County Schs., Ft. Lauderdale, Fla., 1973-74, Broome-Tioga Bd. Coop. Ednl. Svcs., Binghamton, 1980-85; tchr. spl. edn., cons. outcomes-based edn. Johnson City (N.Y.) Ctrl. Schs., 1985—99; tchr. spl. edn. Monroe #1 BOCES, 1999—2004; ret., 2004. Cons. Spl. Edn. Tng. and Resource Ctr., Binghamton, 1980—; community-based edn. program developer and specialist Johnson City Ctrl. Schs., 1991-1999. Leader Girl Scouts U.S.A., Vestal, N.Y., 1985-86; del. NEA N.Y. State Assembly, 1991—. Mem. Coun. for Exceptional Children (pres. 1986-88), So. Tier Assn. Resource Room Tchrs. (charter), Kappa Delta Pi. Home: 799 Lauren Ct Webster NY 14580-2454

SRIKANTIAH, JAYASHRI, law educator; BSEE, Univ. Calif., Berkeley, 1991; JC magna cum laude, NYU, 1996. Bar: Calif., US Ct. Appeals (fed., 5th, 9th. cir.), US Dist. Ct. (no., ea., so. dists.) Calif., US Supreme Ct. Graduate rotation engr. Intel Corp., Santa Clara, Calif., 1991—92, tech. mktg. engr., 1992—93; law clk., Hon. David R. Thompson US Ct. Appeals (9th cir.), 1996—97; assoc., litig. Howard, Rice, Nemerovski, Canady, Falk & Rabkin, San Francisco, 1997—98; staff atty. ACLU Immigrants' Rights Project, 1998—2001, ACLU No. Calif., 2001—03, assoc. legal dir., 2003—04; assoc. prof. law Stanford Univ. Law Sch., 2004—, and dir. Immigrants' Rights Clin., 2004—. Sr. note & comment editor NYU Law Rev. Named one of 40 Indian-Am. Faces of the Future, India Today, 2000, Best Lawyers Under 40, Nat. Asian Pacific Am. Bar Assn., 2004. Mem.: Clin. Legal Edn. Assn., Nat. Lawyers Guild, Am. Immigration Lawyers Assn., Assn. Am. Law Schs., S. Asian Bar Assn. and Minority Bar Coalition (Outstanding Svc. to Legal Cmty. award 2000), Asian Law Alliance (Cmty. Impact award 2002), Asian Am. Bar Assn. (bd. dir. 2002—, co-chair civil rights com. 2001), Order of Coif. Office: Crown Quadrangle Stanford Law Sch 559 Nathan Abbot Way Stanford CA 94305-8610 Office Phone: 650-724-2442. Business E-Mail: jsrikantiah@law.stanford.edu.

SRINATH, LATHA, physician; b. Bangalore, India, Jan. 1, 1958; came to U.S., 1985; d. Krishna and Shamanthaka (Ananthachar) Iyengar; m. Sampath Holevanahalli Srinath, Jan. 22, 1984; children: Shilpa, Preetha. BS, Bangalore U., 1978; MB, BChir, Bangalore Med. Coll., 1984; MD, Georgetown U., 1990. Diplomate Am. Bd. Internal Medicine. Fellow in infectious diseases U. Louisville, 1992-94; pvt. practice Boynton Beach, Fla., 1994—. Staff Bethesda Meml. Hosp., Boynton Beach, 1994—, JFK Med. Ctr., Boynton Beach, 1994—; cons. HIV Adv. Bd., Fla., 1997—. Contbr. articles to profl. jours. Nat. Merit scholar, India, 1975. Mem. Am. Assn. Physicians from India, Fla. Med. Assn., Palm Beach Med. Soc. Hindu. Avocations: travel, yoga, tennis, painting, athletics. Office: ID Cons Inc 2623 S Seacrest Blvd Boynton Beach FL 33435-7501 Home: 125 Turnberry Dr Lake Worth FL 33462-1024 Office Phone: 561-735-7531. E-mail: lsrinath@idconsults.net.

STAAB, DIANE D., lawyer; BA, CUNY Hunter Coll., 1977; JD, Yeshiva U., 1980. Bar: N.Y. 1981. Assoc. atty. Hall, McNicol, Hamilton & Clark, 1980-84, Patterson, Belknap, Webb & Tyler, 1984-87; corp. counsel Internat. Paper Co., 1987—95; v.p., gen. counsel, corp. ethics/environ. compliance officer Ariz. Chem., Panama City, 1996—2001; gen. counsel Internat. Paper Europe, 2001—. Mem. ABA (mem. bus. law sect. fed. ref. of securities com. 1988-2001, vice-chmn. com. on corp. & bus. legis. subcom. on corp. governance 1992-98), Assn. of the Bar of the City of N.Y. (mem. spl. com. on election law 1987-89, mem. corp. law com. 1989-92, sec. com. on corp. law dept. 1992-93). Office: Internat Paper 400 Atlantic St Stamford CT 06921 Office Phone: 32 02 774 1254.

STABENOW, DEBORAH ANN, senator, former congresswoman; b. Gladwin, Mich., Apr. 29, 1950; d. Robert Lee and Anna Merle (Hallmark) Greer; m. Tom Athans; children: Todd Dennis, Michelle Deborah. BS magna cum laude, Mich. State U., 1972, MSW magna cum laude, 1975. With spl. svcs. Lansing (Mich.) Sch. Dist., 1972-73; county commr. Ingham County, Mason, Mich., 1975-78; state rep. State of Mich., Lansing, 1979—91, state senator, 1991—94; mem. 103rd-106th Congress from Mich. 8th dist. U.S. Ho. Reps., 1997—2001; US Senator from Mich., 2001—. Founder Ingham County Women's Commn.; co-founder Council Against Domestic Assault. Recipient Service to Children award Council for Prevention of Child Abuse and Neglect, 1983, Disting. Service to Mich. Families award Mich. Council Family Relations, 1983, Outstanding Leadership award Nat. Council Community Mental Health Ctrs., 1983, Snyder-Kok award Mental Health Assn. Mich., Awareness Leader of Yr. award Awareness Communications Team Developmentally Disabled, 1984, Communicator of Yr. award Woman in Communications, 1984, Lawmaker of Yr. award Nat. Child Support Enforcement Assn., 1985, Disting. Service award Lansing Jaycees, 1985, Disting. Service in Govt. award Retarded Citizens of Mich., 1986, Cmty. award Mich. Mental Health, 1988, Boxing Glove award Nat. Com. to Preserve Social Security and Medicare, 1999, Home Health Hero Nat. Assn. for Home Care, 1999, Friend of Farm Bur. Mich. Farm Bur., 1999, Leadership award Nat. Coun. of Space Grant Dirs., 1998, Outstanding Achievement Nat. Farmers Union, 1998, Legislator of Yr. award Nat. Multiple Sclerosis Soc., 1992, Assn. for Children's Mental Health, 1991, Mich. Assn. of Vol. Adminstrs., 1989, Citizens Alliance to Uphold Spl. Edn., 1989, Recognition award State 4-H Alumni, 1991, Public. Elected Ofcl. award Nat. Assn. Social Workers, 2004, Congressional Support for Sci. award Inst. Food Technologists, 2004, Cmty. Health Defender award Nat. Assn. Cmty. Health Centers, 2005; named One of Ten Outstanding Young Ams. Jaycees, 1986. Mem. NAACP, Nat. Assn. Social Workers, Lansing Regional C. of C., Delta Kappa Gamma. Democrat. Meth. Office: US Senate 702 Hart Senate Office Bldg Washington DC 20510 also: District Office Ste 100 221 W Lake Lansing Rd East Lansing MI 48823-8661 Office Phone: 202-224-4822, 517-203-1760. Office Fax: 202-228-0325, 517-203-1778. E-mail: senator@stabenow.senate.gov.*

STABER, JUDY WHITE, retired performing arts association administrator, writer, director; b. London, Eng., Jan. 3, 1943; arrived in U.S., 1959; d. Archibald Patrick Moore and Joan White; m. Colgate Salsbury, June 10, 1964 (div. Nov. 1982); children: Abigail Salsbury Pulver, Sherrod Louise Salsbury Bailey; m. John Hermann Staber, July 13, 1991. Studied, HB Studio, N.Y.C., 1961—63. Sec., asst. Equity Libr. Theatre, N.Y.C., 1961—63; rschr. Dept. Mental Health, Berkshire County, Mass., 1974—75; journalist Berkshire Courier, Great Barrington, Mass., 1976—79; mktg. dir. Shakespeare & Co., Lenox, Mass., 1979—85; publicist Berkshire County, Mass., 1985—92; cultural tourism dir. Mass. Cultural Alliance & Tourism, Boston, 1987—88; exec. dir. Spencertown Acad. Arts Ctr., NY, 1996—2004; ret. Pub. rels. cons. Williamstown Conservation Lab., Mass., 1988—92, Berkshire Mus., Pittsfield, Mass., 1987—93. Writer, prodr. (TV series) Grovers Corner, Hanukkaht, 1990—92 (Emmy nom., 1992), (plays) Pantomimes, 2000—03. Democrat. Episcopalian. Avocations: gardening, reading, acting, poetry, play reviewing.

STABILE, PATRICE CHRISTINE, mathematics educator; b. Bronx, Aug. 19, 1956; d. Herman and Dolores Hansen; m. Stephen Lawrence Stabile, Aug. 11, 1979; children: Kristen Patrice, Robert Lawrence. BA, Iona Coll., New Rochelle, N.Y., 1978; MA, We. Conn. State U., Danbury, 2006. Math tchr. Msgr. Scanlan H.S., Bronx, NY, 1978—84, Wappingers Jr. H.S., Wappingers Falls, NY, 2001—. Substitute tchr. Wappingers Ctrl. Sch. Dist., NY, 1998—2001. Pres. Oak Grove PTA, Poughkeepsie, NY, 1993—97; cheerleading coach Wappingers Pop Warner, Wappingers Falls, NY, 2001—06. Named Rotary Club Tchr. of the Yr., Rotary Club, 2005. Home: 66 Helen Dr Wappingers Falls NY 12590 Office: Wappingers Junior High School 30 Major Macdonald Way Wappingers Falls NY 12590-3740 Office Phone: 845-298-5200. Office Fax: 845-298-5156. Personal E-mail: btm819@msn.com.

STABIN, ALICE MARIE, administrative assistant; b. Boston, Mass., May 10, 1932; d. Fred and Martha Annette Stabin. A in Comml. Sci., Boston U., 1951, BS, 1953, postgrad., 1974—75. Cert. in tchg. Mass., 1954, in human rels. Heidelberg U., Germany, 1960. Exec. med. sec. Harvard Med. Sch., Boston, 1953—55; club dir. Spl. Svcs., Frankfurt, Germany, 1959—61; social security disability claims MA Rehabilitation Commn., Boston; alt. supr., 1974—78; ombudsman, nursing homes, 1999—. Instr. Eastern MA Literacy Coun., Medford, Mass., 2004; mem. Claflin Soc., Boston U., 1990—. Mem.: Coun. on Aging, Am. Soc. U. Women, Sierra Club. Independent. Avocation: travel. Home: 11 Village Rock Lane Natick MA 01760 Personal E-mail: alexus4@verizon.net.

STABINSKY, JEAN, elementary school educator; BA, U. Albany, N.Y., 1977, MA, 1978. Tchr. N.Y.C. Dept. Edn., 1990—. Recipient Master Composter certificate, Bklyn. Botanic Gardens and N.Y.C. Dept. Sanitation, 2005, Robert P. Porter Scholar award, Am. Fedn. Tchrs., Washington, 2003, Rsch. Incentive Pilot Project award, Equity Studies Rsch. Ctr., Queens Coll., CUNY, 2005. Mem.: Wildlife Conservation Soc., Bklyn. Botanic Gardens, Park Slope Food Corp. Avocation: indoor gardening.

STABINSKY, SUSAN, psychiatrist; b. N.Y.C., Aug. 8, 1946; d. Milton and Mary Graeber; m. Harvey Stabinsky, July 3, 1967; 1 child, Caryn. AB, Hunter Coll., N.Y.C., 1967; MD, U. Noreste, Tampico, Mex., 1978. Lic. N.Y., cert. Am. Bd. Psychiatry and Neurology, qualification in geriatrics Am. Bd. Psychiatry and Neurology, qualification in addictions Am. Bd. Psychiatry and Neurology, lic. N.Y. State, (inactive) Nev. Elem. sch. tchr. N.Y.C. Bd. Edn., 1967—71; intern psychiatry L.I. Jewish- Hillside Med. Ctr., Queens, 1980—81; resident psychiatry Montefiore Med. Ctr. Albert Einstein Coll. Medicine, Bronx, 1981—83, chief resident outpatient and consultation-liaison psychiatry, 1983—84, fellow in consultation- liaison psychiatry dept. psychiatry, 1984—85; dir. outpatient mental health North Ctrl. Bronx Hosp., 1989—95; coord. ambulatory psycho-geriatrics St. Vincent's Hosp., Harrison, 1995; chief physician mental health clinic Grand Concourse Clinic Bronx-Lebanon Hosp. Ctr., 1995—97; acting chief and dir. edn. Lincoln Med. and Mental Health Ctr., 1998, dir. residency tng. and edn., 1998, chmn., chief of svc. and dir. edn. dept. psychiatry, 1999—2003; mental health care line mgr. Hudson Valley VA Health Care Sys., Armonk, 2003—. Pvt. practice, Westchester and Bronx, NY, 1984—; clin. instr. psychiatry Albert Einstein Coll. Medicine, Bronx, 1985—89, clin. prof. psychiatry, 1988, asst. prof. psychiatry, 1989—98, mem. faculty senate, 1997; med. dir. project crisis Jewish Assn. Svcs. Aged Mobile Geriatric Psychiatric Crisis Team, 1985—89; psychiatric cons. Med. Geriatric Assoc. Plan Montefiore Med. Ctr., Bronx, 1987—89; dir. psychiatry outpatient dept. North Ctrl. Bronx Hosp. affiliated with Albert Einstein Sch. Medicine, 1989—95; cons. North Ctrl. Bronx Hosp. Med. Ambulatory Clinic, 1989—95; assoc. dir. residency tng. psychiatry Albert Einstein Sch. Medicine, 1990—94; faculty internal medicine ambulatory care psychiatric tchg. program Montefiore Med. Ctr. and North Ctrl. Bronx Hosp., Bronx, NY, 1994—95; extended faculty gen. internal medicine Women's Health Track Bronx Mcpl. Hosp. Ctr., 1994—96; clin. asst. prof. psychiatry Weill Med. Coll. Cornell U., N.Y.C., 1998—2003; cons. Office Profl. Med. Conduct N.Y. State Dept. Health, 1998—; mem. hosp.-wide committees Lincoln Med. and Mental Health Ctr., Bronx, 1998—2003; exec. com. Downtown Bronx Med. Assoc., 2000—02; clin. asst. prof. psychiatry and behavioral scis. N.Y. Med. Coll., N.Y.C., 2003—; examiner pt. II psychiatry boards Am. Bd. Psychiatry and Neurology, 2002, 04; chair and presenter profl. workshops and seminars. Cons.: APA Practice Guidelines for the Treatment of Psychiatric Disorders- Compendium 2002, APA Quick Reference Practice Guidelines for the Treatment of Psychiatric Disorders, 2002; contbr. chapters to books, scientific papers, articles to profl. jours. Mem. Bronx Mental Health Coalition, 1994—2003. Named Ho. Officer of Yr., Montefiore Hosp., 1984; recipient Excellence in Practice award, N.Y.C. Health and Hosps. Corp. Com. Med. and Profl. Affairs, 2001, cert. appreciation, N.Y.C. Health and Hosps. Corp. World Trade Ctr. Disaster Assistance Svcs., 2002. Fellow: Am. Psychiatric Assn. (sec. Bronx dist. br. 1993—96, chair com. on women Bronx dist. br. 1994—96, chair membership com. Bronx dist. br. 1994—98, pres. elect Bronx dist. br. 1996—98, steering com. practice guidelines 1996—2003, exec. com. Bronx dist. br. 2000—03, disting. fellow, Meritorious Svc. Bronx dist. br. 2000); mem.: Am. Assn. Geriatric Psychiatry, Am. Assn. Psychiatric Adminstrn., Am. Assn. Addiction Psychiatry, Assn. Academic Psychiatry (chair exec. coun. 1996—2000, regional network com. 1996—2000, region II coord. with Am. Assn. Geriatric Psychiatry), N.Y. State Psychiatric Assn. (task force on strategic planning 1998—2003), Westchester Psychiatric Soc. (exec. com. 2005—, treas. 2005—).

STACEY, SUSAN STEPHANIE, education administrator; b. N.Y.C., Feb. 9, 1953; d. William John and Margaret Elke Stacey. BFA, Pratt Inst., 1974; MS, Northwestern U., 1975; MA, Columbia U., 1985. Freelance editor N.Y.C., 1975-76; head publs. dept. Christie's, 1976-77; editor Newsbank, New Canaan, Conn., 1977-80; editor Columbia Sch. Press Assn., 1983; tchr. art history and fine arts King Sch., Stamford, Conn., 1980-85, adj. faculty mem., asst. prof. communication arts Murphy Ctr. Iona Coll., New Rochelle, N.Y., 1987—; adminstr., dir. pub. rels./devel., St. Mary's High Sch., New Haven, 1987-89. Mem. Am. Film Inst., Am. Assn. Museums, Nat. Mus. of Women in the Arts (charter), Friends of Ferguson Library (dir.), Stamford Art Assn. (dir.), Columbia Scholastic Press. Adv. Assn., Assn. Tchrs. in Ind. Schs. (dir.), AAUW, Coll. Art Assn., Am. Soc. for Aesthetics, Northwestern U. Alumni Admissions Council, Kappa Delta Pi. Republican. Episcopalian.

STACK, ANGELA JOHANN, artist; b. St. Louis, Nov. 22, 1946; d. Daniel O'Connell and Angela Elizabeth (Bonn) S. BFA, Washington U., St. Louis, 1969; MFA, Cranbrook Acad., 1972. Dir., gallery, tchr. Florissant Valley Community Coll., St. Louis, 1973-74; tchr., art St. Louis Bd. Edn., 1976; instr., art U. Md., Heidelberg, Germany, 1977-78; graphic artist Cosmetic Speciality Labs. Inc., Lawton, Okla., 1980, 87-88; art specialist Dept. Army, Ft. Sill, Okla., 1983-85; tech. illustrator Mössner Konstrukteur Betriebswirt, Schwäbisch Gmünd, Germany, 1986; instr., art Community Adult Edn. Program, Lawton, 1987-88; tchr. Rite of Passage Sch., Minden, Nev., 1990-92. Master tchr. Adult Basic Edn. Program, St. Louis, 1974-76; interviewer Westat, Rockville, Md., 1988; edn. dir. Yerington Paiute Tribe, Indian counselor Yerington (Nev.) H.S., 1992-1998, acad. specialist, Nev. Dept. Corrections, 1998; caseworker, We. Nev. C. C., 1998-2006. Exhibited in group shows, 1970-86; one-woman shows, 1972, 74, 84, 86, 87, 97. Recipient Tchr. of Yr. award Rite of Passage Schs., 1991; Fulbright fellow, 1972. Democrat. Roman Catholic. Avocations: photography, gardening.

STACK, MAY ELIZABETH, retired library director; b. Jackson, Miss., Nov. 10, 1940; d. James William and Irene Thelma (Baldwin) Garrett; m. Richard Gardiner, Apr. 15, 1962; children: Elinor, Harley David. BS, Miss. State Coll. for Women, 1962; MBA, Western New Eng. Coll., 1981; MLS, So. Conn. State U., 1989. Clk. Western New Eng. Coll., Springfield, Mass., 1965-66, acquisitions staff, 1966-72, cataloger, 1972-84, asst. dir., 1984-89, acting dir., 1989-90, dir., 1990—2005. Chair Ctrl./Western Mass. Automated Resource Sharing Collection Devel. Com., Paxton, Mass., 1993-95, exec. bd., 1993-96. Mem. East Longmeadow (Mass.) Hist. Soc., 1989-92. Mem. ALA, Mass. Libr. Assn., Assn. Coll. and Rsch. Librs., Libr. and Mgmt. Assn., Libr. Info. and Technology Assn. Methodist. Avocations: horseback riding, show dogs. Office: Western New Eng Coll D'Amour Libr 1215 Wilbraham Rd Springfield MA 01119-2612 Business E-Mail: mstack@wnec.edu.

STACY, RUTH CLAIR, counselor, consultant; b. Trenton, N.J., July 6, 1929; d. Ervin Case and Edith (Watson) Smith; m. James Erwin Stacy, June 24, 1950; 1 child, Richard E. BS in Edn., U. Cin., 1950; EdM, Indiana U. Pa., 1965, EdD, 1980; postgrad., Pa. State U., 1983. Nat. cert. counselor, Pa., N.Y.; nat. cert. sch. counselor, Pa., N.Y. Tchr. Maple Shade (N.J.) Schs., 1950-52; sch. counselor Yough Sch. Dist., Herminie, Pa., 1965-75; supr. of counseling, adminstr., supr. guidance svcs. Indiana (Pa.) Area Sch. Dist., 1975-91; counselor Westfield (N.Y.) Counseling Svcs., 1991-93, bd. dirs., 1993—. Part time asst. prof. counseling dept. Indiana U. of Pa., 1971-84; cons. Gateway Sch. Dist., Monroeville, Pa., 1991-92, Indiana (Pa.) Sch. Dist., 1993; past pres., pers. chair, cons. The Indiana County Guidance Ctr., Mental Health Agy. Bd. Dirs.; nat. adv. apptd. Am. Coll. Testing Program; chair ad-hoc adv. com. Gifted of the Indiana Area Sch. Dist. Part-time asst. prof. dept. counseling Indiana U. of Pa., 1971-84; cons. Gateway Sch. Dist., Monroeville, Pa., 1991-92, Indiana (Pa.) Sch. Dist., 1993; past pres., pers. chair, cons. The Indiana County Guidance Ctr., Mental Agy. Bd. Dirs.; nat. adv. apptd. Am. Coll. Testing Program, 1986-89; chair ad hoc adv. com. Gifted of the Indiana Area Sch. Dist.; mem. The College Bd., 1983-86; author 30 Year History of First Presbyterian Church. Community rep. Long Range Plan Com. of Local Schs., Mayville, N.Y., 1991—, Chautaugua Lake Sch.; elder First Presbyn. Ch., 1996-99; moderator Presbyn. of Western NY, 2000-02; coun. chair Presbrytery, 2002-03, synod rep., 2006-; active vol. ARC, Hospice; deaconess First Presbyn. Ch., Westfield, N.Y., 1993-95. Recipient Outstanding Practitioner of Yr. award The Pa. Assn. Counselor Educators and Suprs., 1986, GE Found. fellowship, 1967. Mem. ACA, AAUW (gender equity chair 1994-95), Am. Sch. Counseling Assn. (coord. retirement issues 1991—), Am. Assn. Counselor Educators and Suprs., Am. Assn. Group Workers, Pa. Counseling Assn., Pa. Sch. Counselors Assn. (pres. 1989-90), Zonta (charter mem., v.p., bd. dirs. 1993-94), Mayville Tuesday Club, Kappa Delta Pi, Phi Delta Kappa (10 Yr. Recognition award 1986), Delta Zeta Sorority (life). Avocations: camping, boating, needlepoint, copper enameling, gardening. Home: 32 E Whallon St Mayville NY 14757-1227 Personal E-mail: rcstacy32@adelphia.net.

STACY, TRUDY L., elementary school educator; b. Malone, N.Y., Apr. 3, 1953; d. John P. Keefe and Rita B. Bushey; m. Ronald W. Stacy, July 1, 1978; children: Nicole L., Steven J. BS, SUNY, Potsdam, 1975. Tchr. grade 6 E. Side Elem. Sch., Gouverneur, NY. Mem.: AAUW (sec., treas. 1997—2001). Avocations: travel, reading. Home: 2106 County Route 35 Norwood NY 13668 Office: East Side Elem Sch 111 Gleason St Gouverneur NY 13642

STADLER, KATHERINE LOY, advertising executive, consultant; b. N.Y.C., Mar. 26, 1930; d. William L. and Catherine Stadler. Student, St. John's U., 1948—49, Hunter Coll., 1957—59, NYU Mgmt. Inst., 1963—69. Br. mgr. Hull Travel Svc., Inc., N.Y.C., 1959—63; with Loire Imports, Inc., N.Y.C., 1963—69; dist. mgr. Sweet's divsn. McGraw-Hill Info. Sys. Co., N.Y.C., 1969—74; mgr. nat. sales Floor Covering Weekly, N.Y.C., 1974—76; account exec. Hotel and Travel Index Ziff-Davis Pub. Co., L.A., 1976—81; founder Katherine Stadler & Assocs., 1981—83; regional mgr. Modern Salon,

1984—94; founder, CEO Bone Cancer Internat., Inc., 1999—2006. Mem. Nat. Cancer Inst./Consumer Advocates in Rsch. and Related Activities. Mem. Med. Mission Sisters, Roman Catholic. Ch., 1949-57; mem. Early Music Ensemble L.A., 1985-87; mem. Thousand Oaks Coun. on Aging, 2003-04. Named Sweet's Ea. Region Salesman of Yr., 1972, Salesman of Yr., Vance Pub., 1992; recipient Pres.'s Vol. Svc. award, 2004. Mem. Nat. Assn. Profl. Saleswomen, L.A. Ad Club, Toastmasters.

STADLER, SELISE MCNEILL, laboratory and x-ray technician; b. Portsmouth, Va., Dec. 27, 1960; d. William M. and Jorja Lee (Rigg) Gaidos; m. Stephen Michael McNeill, Feb. 29, 1988 (div. July 1993); 1 child, Stephen Michael Jr.; m. David Robert Stadler, June 15, 1996. Cert. chiropractic asst., Practice Mgmt. Assn., 1983; student, Tarrant County Coll., 2000—01. Cert. radiologic technologist, instr. cert. World Modeling Assn., artificial external defibrilator, cardiopulmonary resuscitation and breath alcohol technician, bone scan technician, lab. technician. Chiropractic asst. Dr. Brad Hayes, D.C., Tulsa, Okla., 1982-84; adminstrv. asst. Dr. Wallace Gauntner, M.D., Pitts., 1984, sec., 1985-87; traffic mgr., office mgr. WVBS-AM/FM, Wilmington, NC, 1985-87; med. asst. Dr. J. Bailey Bland, D.C., Wilmington, 1988-90; therapy/radiology supr. Dr. Roy L. Creasy Jr., D.C., Wilmington, 1990-91; med. asst., radiologist Westside Clinic, Dallas, 1991-94; model, exec. instr. Aleksaundra's Prodns., Ft. Worth, 1994-96; med. asst., radiologist Dr. Wayne R. English Jr., D.O., Ft. Worth, 1994-2000; lab/x-ray technician, med. asst. Care Now, Ft. Worth, 2001—02; x-ray/bone scan technician Kaner Med. Group, Bedford, Tex., 2001—02; med. asst., x-ray tech. Premier Orthopedics, Dr. Craig Saunders, MD and Dr. Marvin Van Hal, MD, 2002—. Author published poetry. Vol. Holy Family Cath. Ch., Ft. Worth, 1997-99. Mem. Tex. Soc. Radiologic Technologists (cert. in CPR and automated external defibrillation program). Episcopalian. Avocations: scuba diving, horseback riding, horse breeding, tennis, rollerblading. Office Phone: 817-267-4492. E-mail: selise@charter.net.

STADTMAN, THRESSA CAMPBELL, biochemist; b. Sterling, NY, Feb. 12, 1920; d. Earl and Bessie (Waldron) Campbell; m. Earl Reece Stadtman, Oct. 19, 1943. BS, Cornell U., 1940, MS, 1942; PhD, U. Calif., Berkeley, 1949. Rsch. assoc. U. Calif., Berkeley, 1942-47, Harvard U. Med. Sch., Boston, 1949-50; biochemist Nat. Heart, Lung and Blood Inst. NIH, USPHS, HHS, Bethesda, Md., 1950—. Mem. Burroughs-Wellcome Fund Toxicology Adv. Commn., 1994-97; pres. Internat. Soc. Vitamins and Related BioFactors, 1998-2001. Editor Jour. Biol. Chemistry, Archives Biochemistry and Biophysics, Molecular and Cellular Biochemistry; editor-in-chief Bio Factors, 1991-95; contbr. articles on amino acid metabolism, methane biosynthesis, vitamin B12 biochemistry, selenium biochemistry to profl. jours. Helen Haye Whitney fellow Oxford U., Eng., 1954-55; Rockefeller Found. grantee U. Munich, 1959-60; recipient Rose award, 1987, Klaus Schwarz medal, 1988, Life Achievement Women in Sci. award L'Oreal-UNESCO, 2000, Bertrand medal and prize Assn. European Trace Elements and Metals in Biology and Medicine, Venice, 2001. Mem. NAS, Am. Soc. Microbiology, Biochem. Soc., Soc. Am. Biochemists, Am. Chem. Soc., Am. Acad. Arts and Scis., Sigma Delta Epsilon (hon.). Home: 16907 Redland Rd Derwood MD 20855-1954 Office Phone: 301-496-3002. Business E-Mail: tcstadtman@nih.gov.

STAFFIER, PAMELA MOORMAN, psychologist; b. Passaic, NJ, Dec. 7, 1942; d. Wynant Clair and Jeannette Frances (Rentzsch) Moorman; m. John Staffier, Jr., Apr. 5, 1975; children: M. Anthony, C. Matthew. BA, Bucknell U., 1964; MA in Psychology, Assumption Coll., Worcester, Mass., 1970, CAGS, 1977; PhD, Union Inst., 1978. Psychologist Westboro (Mass.) State Hosp., 1965, prin. psychologist, asst. to supt., 1973—76; rsch. psychologist Wrentham (Mass.) State Sch., 1966, Cushing Hosp., Framingham, Mass., 1967; prin. psychologist, asst. to supt. Grafton (Mass.) State Hosp., 1967—72; dir. Staffier Clinic, 1978—; psychologist Moriarty Mental Health Clinic; psychiat. cons. local gen. hosp. Mem.: APA (assoc.), Nat. Register Health Svc. Providers Psychology, Mass. Psychol. Assn., Am. Psychol. Practitioners Assn. (founding mem.). Achievements include research in state hospital closings; biochemical basis of schizophrenia. Home: 68 Adams St Westborough MA 01581 Office: 57 E Main St Westborough MA 01581-1464 Office Phone: 508-366-0406. E-mail: johnstaffier@charter.net.

STAFFORD, ABI, ballerina; b. Carlisle, Pa. Studied with, Ctrl. Pa. Youth Ballet, Carlisle; studied, Sch. Am. Ballet Summer Program, 1996—97, Sch. Am. Ballet, 1998. Apprentice N.Y.C. Ballet, 1999—2000, mem. corps de ballet, 2000—02, soloist, 2002—. Dancer prin. roles (ballets) George Balanchine's Ballo Della Regina, Divertimento No. 15, The Nutcracker, La Source, Symphony in C, Symphony in Three Movements, Tschaikovsky Pas de Deux, Valse-Fantaisie, Theme and Variations, Square Dance, Who Cares?, featured roles Stars and Stripes, Swan Lake, Walpurgisnacht Ballet, Peter Martin's Sleeping Beauty, Miriam Mahdaviani's Appalachia Waltz, Fanfare, Martins' Viva Verdi, Swerve Poems, Mercurial Manoeuvres, Organon, Coppelia, Raymonda Variations, Cortege Hongrois. Named Janice Levine dancer, 2000—01. Office: NYC Ballet NY State Theatre 20 Lincoln Ctr Plz New York NY 10023-6913 Personal E-mail: aistafford@hotmail.com.

STAFFORD, REBECCA, retired academic administrator, sociologist, consultant; b. Topeka, July 9, 1936; d. Frank C. and Anne Elizabeth (Larrick) S.; m. Willard Van Hazel. AB magna cum laude, Radcliffe Coll., 1958, MA, 1961; PhD, Harvard U., 1964. Sociology lectr., dept. social rels. Sch. Edn., Harvard U., Cambridge, Mass., 1964-70, mem. vis. com. bd. overseers, 1973-79; assoc. prof. sociology U. Nev., Reno, 1970-74, prof., 1973-80, chmn. dept. sociology, 1974-77, dean Coll. Arts and Scis., 1977-80; pres. Bemidji (Minn.) State U., 1980-82; exec. v.p., prof. sociology Colo. State U., Ft. Collins, 1982-83; pres. Chatham Coll., Pitts., 1983-91, prof. sociology, 1992-93; pres. Monmouth U., West Long Branch, NJ, 1993—2003. Cons. higher edn., 1992—, U.S. Internat. U. on Acad. Planning, 1992-94, USDA, 1992-93, Integra Bank, 1992-93, Millsaps Coll, Jackson, Miss., 1991, U. Pitts. Med. Sch., 1992-93; co-dir. acad. leadership inst. Carnegie Mellon U., 1991-93, U. Tenn., Knoxville, 1992-93; vis. scholar dept. sociology Harvard U., 1991; mem. faculty coll. mgmt. program. Carnegie Mellon U., Pitts., 1984-93; cons. adult devel. grant Harvard U. Health Svcs., Cambridge, 1979, rsch. sociologist, 1964-69; dir. ednl. enrichment project Harvard Sch. Edn., 1966-67, 69-70. Mem. editl. bd. Sociometry, 1974-77, Sociol. Focus., 1974-77; contbr. articles to profl. jours.; presenter papers at profl. confs. Trustee Monmouth Med. Ctr., 1993—, Winchester-Thurston Sch., Pitts., 1986-91, Montefiore Hosp., Pitts., 1990-93; trustee Presbyn.-Univ. Hosp., Pitts., 1984-93, exec. planning com., 1986-89, fin. com., 1989-93; pres. Pitts. Coun. Higher Edn., 1990; mem. Found. Ind. Colls. Inc. Pa., 1984-91, sec., 1986; mem. Colo. Commn. Higher Edn. Task Force on Quality, 1981; mem. adv. bd. Animal Rescue League, Pitts., 1989-93; founder Bemidji Area Women's Network, Minn., 1980-82; mem. intergovtl. planning steering com. Bemidji, 1980-82; mem. cmty. rels. com. Girl Scouts Southwestern Pa., 1983-86; mem. brotherhood dinner coun. Nat. Conf. Christians and Jews, 1985; mem. hon. centennial com. Pa. Sch. Blind Children, Pitts., 1986; mem. citizens sponsoring com. Allegheny Conf. Cmty. Devel., Pitts., 1983-91; mem. five state regional bd. First Union Nat. Bank, 1996—; bd. dirs. Pitts. Symphony, 1984-93, First Fidelity Bank, N.A., N.J., 1993-95, Integra Bank, Pitts., 1987-97, Urban League, Pitts., 1984-87, Women's Ctr., Ft. Collins, Colo., 1982-83, Coun. Colls. Arts and Scis., 1978-81; chmn. Harvard U. Grad. Soc. Coun., 1987-93. Recipient McCurdy-Rinkle prize for rsch. Eastern Psychiat. Assn., 1970; named Woman of Yr. in Edn., City of Pitts., 1986, Vectors/Pitts., 1987, Woman of Yr. in Edn., YWCA Tribute to Women, 1989, Women of Distinction award Muscular Dystrophy Assn., 1999, Women of Leadership award Monmouth County Girl Scouts Am., 1995, Woman of Achievement in Edn. award Monmouth County Adv. Commn. on Status of Women, 1994, Salute to Policymakers award Exec. Women in N.J., 1994; grantee Am. Coun. Edn. Inst. Acad. Deans, 1979, Inst. Ednl. Mgmt., Harvard U., 1984. Mem. Assn. Ind. Colls. and Univs. of N.J. (v.p. 1999—, sec. 1998-99, treas. 1994-98, pres. northeastern conf. 1995-99, bd. dirs. 1993—), Am. Coun. on Edn., Assn. Am. Colls., Soc. for Coll. and Univ. Planning (mem. instl. decision making and resource planning acad. 1994—), Ind. Coll. Fund (treas. 1995-96, bd. dirs. 1993—), Nat. Coun. Family Rels., Harvard U. Alumni Assn. (bd. dirs. 1985-87), Phi Beta Kappa, Phi Kappa Phi. Business E-Mail: Becky@monmouth.edu.

STAGE, GINGER ROOKS, psychologist; b. Allentown, Pa., Sept. 23, 1946; d. John Myers Rooks and Catherine Estelle (Graser) Rooks Bistritz; m. Robert Roy Stage, Aug. 23, 1969; 1 child, Stephen. BA in Psychology magna cum laude, Moravian Coll., Bethlehem, Pa., 1968; MA in Psychology, Temple U., Phila., 1969. Lic. psychologist, Pa.; cert. clin. hypnotherapist Nat. Bd. Clin. Hypnotherapists. Instr. Beaver campus Pa. State U., Monaca, 1969-74; staff psychologist St. Francis Cmty. Mental Health Ctr., Pitts., 1974-83; pvt. practice family therapy Coraopolis, Pa., 1977—. Mem. Greenstein Family Therapy Consultation Group, Pitts., 1981-2000; mem., spkr. Human Sexuality Alliance, Pitts., 1989-91; spkr. in field. Mem. APA, Greater Pitts. Psychol. Assn., Western Pa. Family Ctr. Episcopalian. Avocations: needlecrafts, guitar, exercise, walking. Home: 112 Wessex Hills Dr Coraopolis PA 15108-1021 Office: 409 Mill St Coraopolis PA 15108-1607

STAGGE, KAREN M., elementary school educator; b. East St. Louis, Ill., Nov. 5, 1952; d. Mike and Evelyn Magac; m. Herb Stagge, Aug. 16, 1975; 1 child, Hope-Ann. BA, MacMurray Coll., Jacksonville, Ill., 1974; M in Curriculum and Instrn., Nat. Louis U., Evanston, Ill., 2001. Tchr. 7th grade math. Avon Ctr. Sch., Grayslake, Ill., 1974—79, Highland Mid. Sch., Libertyville, 1990—. Mem. standardized testing edn. com. Ill. State Bd. Edn., Springfield; staff rep. Dist. 70 Profl. Devel. Com., Libertyville, Dist. 70 Math. Com., 1990—2006. Pres. Rockland Sch. Family Assn., Libertyville, 1988—90; staff liaison Highland Mid. Sch. Family Assn., 1992—2000. Mem.: Am. Assn. Univ. Women, Nat. Coun. Tchrs. Math. Home: 2818 Gateway Circle Grayslake IL 60030 Office: Highland Middle School 310 W Rockland Road Libertyville IL 60048 Office Phone: 847-362-9020. Business E-Mail: kstagge@d70schools.org.

STAGGERS, MARY E., minister; b. Rocky Mount, N.C., Sept. 28, 1923; d. John and Emma Jane White; m. Calvin Staggers, Jr., May 18, 1938; children: Luther, Gervis, Earlie Mae, Curtis, Herbert, Betty Joann, Yvonne. BA, Coll. New Rochelle, 1983; M in Profl. Studies, N.Y. Theol. Sem., 1985; M in Humanities, Ctr. Humanities N.Y., 1985; D of Theology of Bible, Internat. Sem. Fla., 1990; DD, Balt. Coll. Bible, 1988. Pastor Holy Redeemer Bapt. Ch., Bklyn., 1961—. Family therapist Beth Israel Hosp., N.Y.C., 1980—98; min. N.Y.C. World's Fair. Author: It's Seed Time, 1999, The Spirit Supercedes Nature, 2003. Liaison N.Y.C. Cmty. Bd. Dist. 16; v.p. Women's Nat. Evang. and Missionary Conf., 1996—2001; pres. World Conf. Gospel Explosion, 1994—, United Ladies Ministers Counsel, 1978—99; pres. Ea. N.Y. br. Women's Nat. Evang. and Missionary Conf., 1997—2001; pres. Mother's Bd. Cedar Grove Bapt. Ch., 1940—51. Mem.: N.Y.C. Clergy Conf., Ea. Bapt. Conf., So. Bapt. Conf., Nat. Bapt. Conf. Democrat. Avocations: cooking, reading, writing. Office Phone: 718-816-5181.

STAGGS, BARBARA ANNETTE, state representative; b. Hulbert, Okla., July 18, 1940; d. Truman and Veleria (Trapp) Masterson; m. Ross Staggs; children: Rick, Matt. BA in Edn., Northeastern U., 1963; MA, U. Tulsa, 1968, EdD, 1987. Tchr., adminstr.; mem. Okla. Ho. of Reps., 1995—. Named Outstanding Adminstr., Okla. Schs. Adv. Coun., 1993, Woman of Distinction, Muskogee Soroptimist's, 1996. Democrat. Office: State Capitol 2300 N Lincoln Blvd Rm 302 Oklahoma City OK 73105 Home: PO Box 1545 Muskogee OK 74402 Office Phone: 405-557-7310.

STAGGS, BARBARA J., vice mayor; b. Trotwood, Ohio, Aug. 25, 1944; d. Campbell Cester and Zelma Ann (Barlow) Phillips; m. Edward Lowell Staggs, June 10, 1961; children: Terrence Lee, Deann Lorraine Staggs Roediger, Eric Justin. Lic. real estate salesperson, Ohio. In retail sales, Dayton; secretarial aide, tchrs. aide Trotwood (Ohio) Sch. Sys.; real estate agt. Hussman Realty, Dayton, 1988-90, Dever-Schenk Realty, Trotwood, 1990-93; mem. city coun. City of Trotwood, 1994—; exec. dir. Trotwood C. of C., 1990—2001. Advisor Civil Svc. Commn., Trotwood; bd. dirs. Miami Valley Career Tech. Ctr., Job Adv. Bd., Clayton, Choices in Cmty. Living, Dayton. Pres. Cmty. Investment, Trotwood; bd. dirs. Northwest Devel. Assn., Trotwood, Resolution Commn., Nat. League of Cities, human devel. policy com., info. tech. and comm. steering com., coun. re. zoning appeals bd., program planning com., NLC first tier suburbs com. Recognized Gold Level in Leadership Tng. Mem.: Women in Govt., Trotwood Rotary. Avocations: doll collecting, building doll houses, sewing and crafts. Home: 19 W Sunrise Ave Trotwood OH 45426-3525 Office: City of Trotwood 35 Olive Rd Ste 2 Trotwood OH 45426-2698 E-mail: bbs19ws@aol.com.

STAHELI, LINDA ANNE, social science executive; b. Salt Lake City, Dec. 9, 1959; m. David Samuel Abramowitz, May 17, 1992. BA, U. Wash., 1983; M in Pub. Mgmt., U. Md., 1988. Consumer rels. intern Atty. Gen.'s Office, Seattle, 1981; project coord. Metrocenter YMCA, Seattle, 1983; lobbyist Coun. for a Livable World, Washington, 1984-86; MacArthur fellow Ctr. for Internat. Security Studies U. Md., College Park, 1986—88; coord. for constituency outreach Dem. Nat. Com., Washington, 1988; rsch. analyst Pacific Sierra Rsch. Corp., Arlington, Va., 1989; fgn. affairs officer Bur. of Oceans, Environment and Sci. Affairs, Dept. of State, Washington, 1990-93; sr. policy advisor for internat. affairs White House Office of Sci. and Tech. Policy, Washington, 1993-95; acting dir. divsn. internat. rels. Fogarty Internat. Ctr., NIH, Washington, 1995-98; pres. Staheli and Assocs. Consulting, Washington, 1998—2002; sr. staff assoc. U.S. Civilian R&D Found., 2001—. Mem. adv. bd. Yosemite Nat. Insts., San Francisco, 1996-99; mem. internat. adv. com. Global HELP, 2001—; bd. dirs. Internat. Network for Cancer Treatment and Rsch., 1999-2002, bd. Women in Internat. Security, 2006.

STAHL, ANNE LOUISE, statistics educator, researcher; b. Somerset, Pa., Dec. 12, 1955; d. Glenn E. and Leona B. Stahl; m. Christopher J. Laubach, Jan. 28, 1978 (div. Apr. 1986); children: Michael Christopher Laubach, Joseph Edward Laubach; m. Robert L. Aughenbaugh, Aug. 9, 1986 (div. Aug. 1996); 1 child, Julia Anne Aughenbaugh. Degree in social welfare, Seton Hill U., 1977, degree in math. edn., 1986; M Pub. Mgmt., Carnegie Mellon U., 1992; postgrad., U. Pitts., 2001. Cert. secondary math. tchr. Pa. Group home direct care provider Pan Am Group Homes, Greensburg, 1979—84; respite worker trainer Westmoreland Hosp. MH/MR Unit, Greensburg, Pa., 1984—85; math. instr. Greensburg Ctrl. Cath. HS, 1985—86; rsch. assoc. Nat. Ctr. for Juvenile Justice, Pittsburgh, Pa., 1993—; adj. prof. stats. Seton Hill U., Greensburg, 2002—. Part-time prof. Westmoreland County Single Point of Contact Program, New Kensington, PR, 1986—88, Westmoreland CC Job Tng. Ctr., Youngwood, Pa., 1986—88. Mem.: Am. Math. Soc. (assoc.), Am. Soc. Criminology (assoc.). Roman Catholic. Avocations: golf, travel, theater, symphony, football. Office Phone: 412-227-6950.

STAHL, BARBARA E., school counselor, consultant; b. Sydney, Australia, Dec. 26, 1940; arrived in US, 1965; d. Maurie and Helen Konn; children: Roger, Andrew, Warren, Wendy. AA, Pasadena City Coll., Calif., 1971; BA, spl. edn. credential, Calif. State U., LA, 1985; MA, Xavier U., Cin., 1985. Lic. counselor Ohio, std. tchg. credential Calif., Ohio, spl. edn. credential Calif., Ohio, cert. ednl. planner. Spl. edn. tchr. Warner Union Sch. Dist., San Diego, 1973—74; mid. sch. tchr. Alhambra (Calif.) Sch. Dist., 1974—79; tchr., counselor Madeira Sch. Dist., Cin., 1979—82; cons., counselor Right Assocs., Cin., 1983—88; HS counselor Taipei (Taiwan) Am. Sch., 1988—93; HS counselor, head dept. Internat. Sch. of Singapore, 1993—94, Ruamrudee Internat. Sch., Bangkok, 1994—97; student support svcs. dir. Harare Internat. Sch., 1997—2001. Cons. Zimbabwe U., Harare, 1999—2001. V.p. Com. for Transit, Santa Clara, 2004; mem. Mayor's Commn., San Jose, Calif., 2004. Recipient Tchr. of Yr. award, Alhambra City Schs, 1979, Counseling and Devel. award, Nat. Disting. Svc. Registry, 1979, Exceptional Leadership award, United Appeal and Cmty. Chest, 1985, Recognition of Outstanding Svc. award, Jr. Achievement, 1988. Mem.: ACA, Ind. Ednl. Consultants Assn., Soc. Children's Writers and Illustrators, Pi Lambda Theta, Phi Delta Kappa. Home: 1675 Scott Blvd # 321 Santa Clara CA 95050 Personal E-mail: barbaraestahl@earthlink.net.

STAHL, LESLEY R., news correspondent; b. Lynn, Mass., Dec. 16, 1941; d. Louis and Dorothy J. (Tishler) Stahl; m. Aaron Latham; 1 child, Taylor. BA cum laude, Wheaton Coll., Norton, Mass., 1963. Asst. to speechwriter Mayor Lindsay's Office, N.Y.C., 1966—67; rschr. N.Y. Election unit CBS News, 1967—68; rschr. London-Huntley Brinkley Report, NBC News, 1969; prodr., reporter WHDH-TV, Boston, 1970—72; news corr. CBS News, Washington, 1972—; co-anchor CBS Morning News, 1977—79; White House corr. CBS News, 1979-91; moderator Face the Nation, 1983-91; anchor America Tonight, 1990—91; co-editor, corr. CBS News, 60 Minutes, 1991—; host 48 Hours, 2002—04. Notable TV appearances include: Murphy Brown, 1993, 1995; Frasier, 1997. Trustee Wheaton Coll. Named Best White House Corr., Washington Journalism Rev., 1991; named to Broadcasting Mag. Hall of Fame, 1992; recipient Tex. Headliners award, 1973, Dennis Kauff award for lifetime achievement in journalism, Fifth Estate award, Fred Friendly First Amendment award, 1996.

STAHLECKER, BARBARA JEAN, marketing professional, consultant; b. Stamford, Conn., Jan. 22, 1958; d. Roger Francis and Lillian Ann Beauleau; m. Richard Walter Stahlecker; children: Shannon Lee Banks, Brande Lauren Beach; children: Cori, Cara. Grad., Brien McMahon H.S., Norwalk, Conn., 1975. New bus. adminstr. Mutual of Omaha Ins. Co., L.A., 1983—85; ind. ins. agt. L.A., 1985—88; mktg. coord. LifeCare Assurance Corp., Canoga Park, Calif., 1988—96; v.p., nat. mktg. dir. Centrelink Ins. & Fin. Svcs., Woodland, Calif., 1996—. Author: (Continuing Education Courses) Everything You've Always Wanted to Know about LTC - and Then Some, 1998, (Continuing Education Course) The Nuts and Bolts of Long Term Care Insurance, 2000, TQ vs. NTQ LTCi, 2001; contbr. articles to profl. jours., 2001. Recipient Million Dollar Prodr. award, UNUM/Provident, 2001. Mem.: Soc. Cert. Sr. Advisors (cert. sr. advisor), Long-Term Care Profl., Am. Assn. Long-Term Care Ins. (Top Prodr. award 2000, 2001, BRAMCO Million Dollar Club award 2002), Nat. Assn. Health Underwriters (cons. 1999—). Office: Centrelink Ins & Fin Svc 20750 Ventura Blvd #300 Woodland Hills CA 91364 Business E-Mail: barbara@centrelink.com.

STAHLMAN, MILDRED THORNTON, pediatrician, pathologist, educator, medical researcher; b. Nashville, July 31, 1922; d. James Geddes and Mildred (Thornton) Stahlman. AB, Vanderbilt U., 1943, MD, 1946; MD (hon.), U. Goteborg, Sweden, 1973, U. Nancy, France, 1982. Diplomate Am. Bd. Pediat., Am. Bd. Neonatology. Intern Boston Children's Hosp., 1947—48; resident Vanderbilt Univ. Hosp., 1948—49; fellow Royal Caroline Inst. Medicine, Sweden, 1949—50; cardiac resident La Rabida Sanitarium, Chgo., 1951; instr. pediat. Vanderbilt U., Nashville, 1951—58, instr. physiology, 1954—60, asst. prof. pediat., 1959—64, asst. prof. physiology, 1960—62, assoc. prof. pediat., 1964—70, prof., 1970—, prof. pathology, 1982—, Harvie Branscomb Disting. prof., 1984, dir. divsn. neonatology, 1961—89, prof. pediat. and pathology. Editor: Respiratory Distress Syndromes, 1989; contbr. over 175 articles to profl. publs., chpts. to books. Recipient Apgar award, Am. Acad. Pediat., 1987; grantee NIH, 1954—. Mem.: AAAS, Inst. Medicine NAS, Royal Swedish Acad. Scis., So. Soc. Pediatric Rsch. (pres. 1961—62), Am. Physiology Soc., Soc. Pediatric Rsch., Am. Pediatric Soc. (pres. 1984, John Howland award 1996). Episcopalian. Home: 538 Beech Creek Rd S Brentwood TN 37027-3421 Office: Vanderbilt Univ Med Ctr 2215 B Garland Ave 1125 MRB IV LH Nashville TN 37232-0656 E-mail: mildred.stahlman@vanderbilt.edu.

STAHR, BETH A., librarian; b. Elmhurst, Ill., June 13, 1951; d. John H. Pohlmann and Mary Anne Price; m. Charles Ward Stahr, Aug. 25, 1973; children: Margaret L., Andrew J. BS Engring., Purdue U., 1973; MLS, Syracuse U., 1999. Environ. specialist Owens Corning Fiberglas, Toledo, 1973—78; genealogical rschr. pvt. practice, Wausau, Wis., 1988—98; libr. Southeastern La. U., Hammond, La., 1999—, asst. prof., 2000—06, assoc. prof., 2006—. V.p., trustee Wis. Genealogical Coun., 1992—98; treas., trustee Assn. Profl. Genealogists, Washington, 1994—95, Bd. Cert. Genealogists, Washington, 1998—, pres., 2004—05. Vol. Birch Trails coun. Girl Scouts Am., Tomahawk, Wis., 1980—91; v.p., trustee La. Genealogical and Hist. Soc., La., 2001—. Mem.: ALA, La. Geneal. and Hist. Soc. (v.p. 2001—05), ACRL. Episcopalian. Home: 55 Dogwood Ln Covington LA 70435 E-mail: bstahr@selu.edu.

STAHR, CELIA SUZANNE, art educator; d. Carl Wolfganag and Illene Louise Stahr; m. Gary Allen Lee, May 21, 2000; children: Mei Lin, Miriam Lee-Stahr. BA, San Francisco State U., 1980, MA, 1989; PhD, U. Iowa, Iowa City, 1997. Adj. prof. Sonoma State U., Cotati, Calif., 1998—99, Coll. of Marin, 1999—2000, Calif. Coll. of Arts, Oakland, 1999—2003, San Francisco Art Inst., 2004—05, U. San Francisco, 2004—06, San Francisco State U., 1997—. Affiliated scholar Inst. for Women & Gender, Stanford U., 2000—02; presenter in field. Contbr. essays to books, articles to profl. pubs. Vol. Women's Resource & Action Ctr., Iowa City, 1991—95; active Women Against Racism, 1994—95; vol. Rape Victim Advocacy, Iowa City, 1995. Grantee Schumacher scholarship, U. Iowa, 1996, Seashore Dissertation fellowship, 1996, USA Rsch. grant, 1996. Mem.: Coll. Art Assn/. Avocations: tai chi, salsa dance. Office: San Francisco State Univ 1600 Holloway Ave San Francisco CA 94132

STAIANO-JOHANNES, BARBARA ANN, physician assistant, chiropractor; b. Manhasset, NY, Oct. 4, 1966; d. Ralph Joseph and Margaret Angelina Staiano; m. Barry Glenn Johannes, Apr. 30, 1999. D in Chiropractic, N.Y. Chiropractic Coll., 1991; AS in Paramedicine, La Guardia C.C., L.I. City, 1996; BS in Physician Asst., Touro Coll., 1998. Paramedic, paramedic instr. N.Y. Hosp. Med. Ctr. Queens, Flushing, 1993-98; lifeguard supr. Town of North Hempstead, New Hyde Park, N.Y., 1984—; coll. lab. technician Queensborough C.C., Bayside, N.Y., 1995—; physician asst. in surgery Elmhurst (N.Y.) Hosp. Ctr., 1998—. Adj. faculty L.I. U., C.W. Post, Brookville, N.Y., 1990-93; cert. instr. coord. N.Y. State Dept. Health, 1993—; vol. instr. ARC, Nassau County, 1984—. Recipient scholarship Am. Chiropractic Assn., 1990. Fellow Am. Acad. Physician Assts.; mem. Phi Theta Kappa. Republican. Roman Catholic. Avocations: swimming, hiking. Office: Elmhurst Hosp Ctr Dept Surgery E 2-27 79-01 Broadway Elmhurst NY 11373 Personal E-mail: bstaiano@aol.com.

STAINBACK, SUSAN BRAY, education educator; b. Balt., May 22, 1947; d. William Devaughn and Cleo Margaret (Selig) Bray; m. William Clarence Stainback, Dec. 16,1967. BS, Radford Coll., 1968; MEd, U. Va., 1970, EdD, 1973. Tchr. Albemarle County Schs., Crozet, Va., 1968-70; edn. specialist Hope Haven Children's Hosp., Jacksonville, Fla., 1973-74; prof. edn. U. No. Iowa, Cedar Falls, 1974—; Matthew J. Gujlielmo Endowed Chair Dept. Spl. Edn., Calif. State U., L.A., 1988-89. Speaker at profl. confs.; cons. in field. Co-author: Establishing a Token Economy in the Classroom, 1973, Classroom Discipline: A Positive Approach, 1974, Educating Students eith Severe Maladaptive Behavior, 1980, The Severely Motorically Impaired Child: A Handbook for Classroom Teachers, 1980, Teaching Eating Skills, 1982, Integration of Students with Severe Handicaps into Regular Schools, 1985, Qualitative Research, 1988, Making the Grade, 1989, others; co-editor: Educating All Students in the Mainstream of Regular Education, 1989, Support Networks for Inclusive Schools, 1990, Curriculum Considerations in Inclusive Classrooms, 1992, Restructuring for Caring and Effective Education, 1992, Controversial Issues Confronting Special Education, 1992. Mem. Coun. Exceptional Children, Am. Assn. Ednl. Rsch., Nat. Soc. Autistic Children, Assn. for Edn. of Persons with Severe Handicaps, Coun. for Children with Behavior Disorders, Tchr. Educators in Severe Behavior Disorders, Am. Assn. Mental Deficiency, Can. Assn. Community Living, Schools Are For Everyone. Democrat. Avocations: care and protection of animals, biking, skating, country/western dancing. Home: 8616 Rippling Waters Rd Blairsville GA 30512-8015

STAIVISKY, JEANNE LOUISE, counselor, alcohol/drug abuse services professional; b. Hughesville, Pa., Dec. 30, 1947; d. Charolotte Bowen and John Staivisky. AA in Psychology, Palm Beach Jr. Coll., 1981; BS in Gen. Psychology, Nova U., 1984, M in Sci. in Counseling Psychology, 1987. Lic. profl. counselor Ill., 2003, nat. cert. psychologist Psychology Profl. Bd., 2000, lic. mental health counselor Ind., 1999, cert. Nat. Bd. Cert. Counselors, 1996, Am. Acad. Health Providers Addictive Disorders, 1995. Program mgr., counselor Hugs Not Drugs Treatment Program, Boca Raton, Fla., 1987—87; clin. supr., counselor The Starting Pl., Hollywood, Fla., 1987—89; counselor, clin. supr. Adolescent Substance Abuse Counseling Svc., Kaiserslautern and Hanau, Army Military Bases, Germany, 1987—89, clin. supr., counselor Kaiserslauter and Hanau, 1989—97, counselor, acting clin. supr. Camp Zama, 1997—2002, counselor Schofield Barracks/Wahiawa, Hawaii, 2002—. Cons. Crisis Intervention Team, Kaiserslauter; sponsor Teen Peer Facilitator Programs, Kaiserslautern; chair Character Edn. Program in Schools, Camp Zama, Japan, 2000—02; team mem. Camp Zama HS Crisis Intervention Team, 1997—2002; yean mem. WMS Crisis Intervention Team Wheeler Army Airfield Middle School, 2002—; youth 2 youth group Youth 2 Youth Internat. Group Camp Zama, 1998—2002; sponsor S.A.D.D., Kaiserslautern and Camp Zama, 1987—2002; chairperson Jorney Into Adulthood for Teens Risk, 1996—97; sponsor ASACS Role Model Club, Wheeler Army Air Base/WMS, Hawaii, 2002—05, Teen Panell educationing parents on teen issues, Schofield Barracks/Wahiawa, 2002—. Author: Looking For The Pot of Gold at The End of The Rainbow, poems; contbr. articles to profl. jours. Sponsoring mem. So. Law Poverty-Wall of Tolerance Civil Rights, Alabama, Ga., 2004—05. Mem.: Nat. Assn. Master Psychologists, Nat. Alcohol and Drug Abuse Counselors, Hawaii Alcohol and Drug Abuse Counselors, Am. Mental Health Cousnelors, Am. Assn. Counseling. Achievements include include 1990 letter of Commendation from Gerneral Crosbie E. Saint; SAIC 1990 Environmental Achievement Award for Single Superior Performance; 1997 415th Base Support Battalion Community Coin; SAIC 2000 Founders Award; Y2Y group nominated to represnt the Army in the first DoD Youth Alcohol and Drug Awareness Program Award; 2002 Legendary Service Award for the Army Military Community in Hawaii. Avocations: needlecrafts, stamp'in up-making cards, designing clothes, collecting poreclain dolls from all over the world. Home: 226 Cullom Way Clarksville TN 37043 Personal E-mail: jeanne123047@yahoo.com.

STAKOE, LINDSEY ANN, actor, educator; b. Southfield, Mich., Apr. 16, 1980; d. Ted and Carla Stakoe. BA in Theatre, Mich. State U., East Lansing, 2002. Cert. nat. enrichment tchr. CBEST. Substitute tchr. Tchrs. On Res., Burbank, Calif., 2003—; choreographer, acting tchr. Performing Arts Workshops, Marina Del Rey, Calif., 2004—; dance tchr. James Jordan Mid. Sch., Chatsworth, Calif., 2005—, Studio Experience, Tarzana, Calif., 2005—. Choreographer, tchr. Interlochen Ctr. for Arts, Mich., summers; choreographer, dir. Adderly Sch. for Performing Arts. Dancer Satin Dollz, LA, 2005—; actor: (plays) Diary of Anne Frank, 2002, many plays in LA theatres, A Faery Hunt, 2005—, Miracle Man, 2006—; dir./writer (sketch show) An Ode to Bill Maher, 2005 (acting award Lansing, Mich.). Mem.: AFTRA. Avocations: painting, sewing, running, dance. Personal E-mail: lindseystakoe@yahoo.com.

STALEY, DAWN MICHELLE, professional basketball player; b. Phila., May 4, 1970; d. Estelle. Grad., U. Va., 1992. Profl. basketball player Brazil, France, Italy, Spain, Richmond Rage, ABL, 1996—98, Charlotte Sting, WNBA, 1999—; head women's basketball coach Temple U., 2000—. Mem. USA Basketball Teams, 1989—. Founder Dawn Staley Found. Named USA Basketball Female Athlete of Yr., 1994, MVP, Goodwill Games, 1994, Phila. Big Five Coach of Yr., 2002, Atlantic 10 Coach of Yr., 2004; named to First Team All-ABL, 1997, WNBA All-Star Team, 2001, 2002, 2003; recipient Spectrum Award, ARC, 1998, Entrepreneurial Spirit Award, WNBA, 1999, Sportsmanship Award, 1999. Achievements include being a member of US Women's Basketball gold medal team, Atlanta, 1996; being a member of US Women's Basketball gold medal team, Sydney Olympics, 2000; being a member of US Women's Basketball Team, Athens Olympics, 2004; having her number retired at U. Va; being the first women in professional basketball history to record 1,000 career assists; serving as Olympic Flag bearer, Athens Olympic Games, 2004. Office: 100 Hive Dr Charlotte NC 28208-7707

STALEY, LYNN, literature educator; b. Madisonville, Ky., Dec. 24, 1947; d. James Mulford and Florine (Hurt) Staley. AB, U. Ky., 1969; MA, PhD, Princeton U., 1973. Grad. asst. Princeton (N.J.) U., 1971-73; instr. English Colgate U., Hamilton, NY, 1974-75, from asst. to assoc. prof., 1975-86, prof., 1986—. Author: The Voice of the Gawain-Poet, 1984, The Shepheardes Calendar: An Introduction, 1990, Margery Kempe's Dissenting Fictions, 1994; author: (with David Aers) The Powers of the Holy: Religion, Politics and Gender in, 1996;, 1996; editor: The Book of Margery Kempe, 1996; translator, 2001, Dictionary of the Middle Ages, 2004, Languages of Power in the Age of Richard II, 2005; contbr. articles to profl. jours. NEH fellow, 2003—04, Guggenheim fellow, 2003—04. Mem. MLA, Medieval Acad. Am., Renaissance Soc. Am., New Chaucer Soc., Spenser Soc. Office: Colgate U Dept English 13 Oak Dr Dept English Hamilton NY 13346-1383 Office Phone: 315-228-7667. Business E-Mail: lstaley@mail.colgate.edu.

STALEY, MINDI K., information technology manager, educator; d. James A. and Susan C. Staley. BBA in Mktg., Ohio U., Athens, 1998; MBA summa cum laude, Franklin U., Columbus, Ohio, 2005. Cert. Webmaster U. of Cin., 2001. Mktg. devel. mgr. SARCOM, Columbus, 2002—04; program mgr. Manifest Cos., Columbus, 2003—04; web mgr. Franklin U., Columbus, 2004—06; mgr. online customer support Nationwide Corp., Columbus, 2006—; adj. prof. Columbus State Coll., 2002—. Editor: (tech. mag.) intuITion. Big sister Big Bros., Big Sisters, Columbus, 2005. Named Outstanding Grad., Ohio U., 1998. Mem.: Am. Mktg. Assn., eMktg. Assn.

STALHEIM-SMITH, ANN, biology educator; b. Garretson, S.D., Oct. 19, 1936; d. Oliver Theodore and O'dessa Beldina (Olson) Stalheim; m. Christopher Carlisle Smith, Aug. 24, 1960; children: Heather, Andrea, Jamie. BS, Augustana Coll., Sioux Falls, S.D., 1958; MS, U. Colo., 1960; PhD, No. Ariz. U., 1982. Teaching asst. Augustana Coll., 1955-58; teaching fellow U. Colo., Boulder, 1958-59, rsch. asst., 1959-60; instr. Pacific Luth. U., Tacoma, 1960-61, Fisk U., Nashville, 1967, Kans. State U., Manahattan, 1970-86, asst. prof. biology, 1986-94, assoc. prof., 1994—2003, emeritus prof., 2003. Mem. grant rev. panel NSF, Washington, 1979, 81, 91; textbook reviewer Harper & Row Pub., West Pub., Saunders, others, 1975-87. Author: (with Greg K. Fitch) Understanding Human Anatomy and Physiology, 1993; contbr. articles to profl. jours. Grantee NSF, 1979-81, 90—, Howard Hughes Found., 1992—. Mem. AAAS, Am. Soc. Zoologists, Sigma Xi. Democrat. Lutheran. Home: 1328 Fremont St Manhattan KS 66502-4001

STALKER, JACQUELINE D'AOUST, academic administrator, educator; b. Penetang, Ont., Can., Oct. 16, 1933; d. Phillip and Rose (Eaton) D'Aoust; m. Robert Stalker; children: Patricia, Lynn, Roberta. Teaching cert., U. Ottawa, 1952; tchr. music, Royal Toronto Conservatory Music, 1952; teaching cert., Lakeshore Tchrs. Coll., 1958; BEd with honors, U. Manitoba, 1977, MEd, 1979; EdD, Nova U., 1985. Cert. tchr. Ont., Man., Can. Adminstr., tchr., prin. various schs., Ont. and Que., 1952-65; area commr. Girl Guides of Can., throughout Europe, 1965-69; administr., tchr. Algonquin Community Coll., Ottawa, Ont., 1970-74; tchr., program devel. Frontenac County Bd. Edn., Kingston, Ont., 1974-75; lectr., faculty advisor dept. curriculum, edn. U. Man., Can., 1977-79; lectr. U. Winnipeg, Man., Can., 1977-79; cons. colls. div. Man. Dept. Edn., 1980-81, sr. cons. programming br., 1981-84, sr. cons. post secondary, adult and continuing edn. div., 1985-88, dir. post secondary career devel. br. and adult and continuing edn. br., 1989; asst. prof. higher edn., coord. grad. program in higher edn. U. Man., 1989-92, assoc. prof., coord. grad. program in higher edn., 1992-95. Cons. lectures, seminars, workshops throughout Can. Contbr. articles to profl. jours.; mng. editor Can. Jour. of Higher Edn., 1989-93. Mem. U. Man. Senate, 1976-81, 86-89, bd. govs., 1979-82; Can. rep. Internat. Youth Conf., Garmisch, Fed. Republic of Germany, 1968; vol. Can. Cancer Soc.; mem. Assn. RN Accreditation Coun., 1980-85; chair Child Care Accreditation Com., Man., 1983-90; chair Task Force Post-Secondary Accessibility, Man., 1983; vol. United Way Planning and Allocations; provincial dir., mem. nat. bd. Can. Congress for Learning Opportunities for Women. Recipient award for enhancing the Outreach activities of the univ. U. Man., 1994. Mem. Can. Soc. Study Higher Edn., Man. Tchrs. Soc., U. Man. Alumni Assn., Women's Legal Edn. and Action Fund.

STALLING, JANET KITTS, music educator; b. Waycross, Ga., Apr. 6, 1960; d. Kenneth Kermit and Nancy Buckner Kitts; m. James Reed Bethel, Dec. 20, 1986 (div. Dec. 1998); children: Rachel Allison, Stuart Reed, Mary Susan, Victoria Elizabeth; m. Jeffrey Bryant Stalling, Apr. 16, 2004. B in Music Edn., U. N.C., 1982; MusM, Notre Dame U., 1984. Cert. tchr. N.C., Ga., nat. bd. cert. music Nat. Bd. Profl. Tchg. Stds. Educator State Bridge Crossing Elem., Alpharetta, 2002—. Mem. leadership team State Bridge Crossing Elem., Alpharetta, 2002—; prin. Johns Creek Bapt. Ch. Orch., Alpharetta, 2003—. Mem.: Ga. Music Assn., Music Educators Nat. Conf. Baptist. Home: 3790 Crescent Walk Ln Suwanee GA 30024 Office: State Bridge Crossing Elem 5530 State Bridge Rd Alpharetta GA 30022 Office Phone: 770-497-3850.

STALLINGS, PHYLLIS ANN, music educator; b. Little Rock, Feb. 24, 1944; d. Roy Edwin and Helen Lavern (Waters) Moseley; m. Paul Harold Stallings, Jan. 22, 1966; children: Kevin Scott, Michael Shane, Natasha Lynette, Clayton Lane. B in Music Edn., Ouachita Bapt. U., 1966; M in Music Edn., Ark. State U., 1971. Cert. vocal and band music tchr., Ark., Mo. Tchr. elem. music Glenwood Pub. Sch., Ark., 1966—67; tchr. elem. music DeSoto vocal music Glenwood Pub. Sch., Ark., 1966—67; tchr. elem. music DeSoto (Mo.) Pub. Sch., Mo., 1967—69; tchr. secondary music Richland Pub. Sch., Essex, Mo., 1969—71; tchr. elem. music Augusta (Ark.) Pub. Sch., Ark., 1971—82; tchr. vocal music Independence Christian Sch., Mo., 1982—87; tchr. secondary music Doniphan Region I Pub. Sch., Mo., 1988—91; dir. vocal and band grades K-12 Delaplaine H.S., Ark., 1992, Stanford H.S., Ark., 1992—93; dir. band and choir grades K-12 Delaplaine Schs., 1993—94; dir. K-12 vocal and band Southland C-9 Schs., Cardwell, Mo., 1994—2001; organist 1st Bapt. Ch., Paragould, Ark., 1998—; substitute tchr. six local sch., 2001—. Camp music dir. YWCA/Camp Burgess Glen, Cedar Mountain, N.C., summer 1964; interum min. music First Bapt. Ch., Paragould, 1988-89; pvt. piano and voice tchr., 1967—. Active PTA. Am. Coll. Musicians scholar, 1962; acad. and music scholar. Mem. Music Educators Nat. Conf., Ctrl. Tchrs. Assn., Mo. Tchrs. Assn. Avocations: cooking, composing, reading, vocal solo singing. Home: Sunset Hills Subdivsn 1700 Hillcrest Dr Paragould AR 72450-4057

STALLINGS, VALERIE A., physician, state agency administrator; b. N.Y.C., Nov. 27, 1943; BS in Zoology, Duke U., 1964; MD, U. N.C., 1968, MPH, 1988. Intern, resident Pediat. Med. Coll. Va., 1968-71; physician Va. Dept. Health Bur. Crippled Children, Norfolk, 1972—75, Portsmouth (Va.) Health Dept., 1972—77; dir. Tidewater Child Devel. Clin., Norfolk, 1977-82; dep. dir. Norfolk Dept. Pub. Health, 1982-89, dir., 1989—. Office: Norfolk Dept Pub Health 830 Southampton Ave Norfolk VA 23510-1001

STALLINGS, VIRGINIA A., pediatric gastroenterologist; BS, Auburn U.; MS, Cornell U.; MD, U. Ala. Cert. pediatrics, clin. nutrition. Pediat. resident U. Va.; nutrition fellow Hosp. for Sick Children, Toronto; prof. pediatrics U. Pa. Sch. Med., Phila.; with Children's Hosp. Phila., 1985, attending physician, div. gastroenterology & nutrition, chief of nutrition sect., prof. pediatrics, Jean Cortner Endowed Chair in Pediat. Gastroenetology, dir. Nutrition Ctr., dep. dir. Joseph Stokes Rsch. Inst. Mem.: APA, Inst. Medicine (chair food & nutrition bd. 1999). Office: Children's Hosp of Philadelphia 34th St & Civic Ctr Blvd Philadelphia PA 19104*

STALLWORTH, MONICA LAVAUGHN, geriatrician; b. Savannah, Ga., July 29, 1952; d. William D. and Betty Lou Stallworth; m. Robert J. Kolimas, Oct. 17, 1955; 1 child, Catherine. BS in Biology, St. Mary's Coll., Notre Dame, Inc., 1974; MA in Biology and Health Edn., Ball State U., 1975; MD, Mayo Med. Sch., 1980. Diplomate Am. Bd. Family Practice; cert. Am. Bd. Hospice and Palliative Medicine; bd. cert. Geriatric Medicine. Family practitioner MacGregor Med. Assn., Houston, 1983-97; asst. prof. family medicine Georgetown U. Sch. Medicine, Washington, 1997—; geriatrician Washington Home and Hospice, 1998-99; dir. geriatric assessment clinic Georgetown Family Practice Residency, Md., 1999—. Dir. home care program Georgetown Residency Family Practice, 1998—. Recipient Civic Svc. award City of West University Place, 1994, Svc. award Rotary Club, 1994, 95. Bd. dirs. Newcomers Club, Houston, 1995-97, Rotary Club, Tex., 1995-97, U. Tex.; chmn. Innunization Project, Houston, 1995-97; mem. pres. adv. coun. SMC. Fellow Am. Acad. Family Practice; mem. Am. Geriatric Soc. (bd. dirs. D.C. chpt. 1998—). Avocations: ice skating, reading. Office: 4151 Bladensburg Rd Colmar Manor MD 20722-1928 E-mail: lavonnie_20002@yahoo.com.

STALLWORTH-ALLEN, ELIZABETH ANN, business and computer science educator; d. Kenneth and Catherine Stallworth; m. Irving Henry Allen, Aug. 17, 1991; children: DonTeus Holtz, Jasmine Stallworth, LaNaria Allen. AA, Pensacola (Fla.) Jr. Coll., 1983; BS in Computer Info. Systems, Troy State U., Fort Walton Beach, Fla., 1994. Sr. tech. sales specialist Mfg. Tech. Inc., Ft. Walton Beach, 1994—96; sr. computer programmer analyst State U. Bd. of Regents, Tallahassee, 1997—98; sys. project analyst Dept. of Transp., Tallahassee, 1998; sr. programmer analyst Escambia County Sch. Bd., Pensacola, Fla., 1998—2000; bus./requirements analyst BTG Inc., Niceville, Fla., 2000—01; prof. computer sci. Okalossa Walton Coll., Niceville, 2001—. Computer cons. Allens Ednl. Svcs., Ft. Walton Beach, 2000—; mem. coll.-wide coun. Okalossa Walton Coll., 2005—06, mem. coll. tech. com., 2006—. Regional mem. judging panel Exellence in IT Leadership Award for South Fla. Businesses, 2004. Recipient Spot award, BTG Inc., 2001. Mem.: Nat. Coalition 100 Black Women, Inc. (chair Sisters Reaching Out, co-chair constn. and bylaws 1995), Alpha Sigma Lambda. Office: Okaloosa Walton Coll 100 College Blvd Niceville FL 32578 Office Phone: 850-729-5223.

STALNAKER, JUDITH ANN, education educator; b. San Diego, Sept. 3, 1942; d. Harold Willard and Dorothy Ione (Maxwell) Growcock; m. Archie LaVern Stalnaker, Aug. 31, 1963; children: Dena Lyn Garcia, Keri Leigh Hale. BA, teaching credential, Calif. State U., San Diego, 1973; MA, reading specialist credential, San Diego State U., 1985. Cert. tchr., reading specialist. Tchr. El Centro Sch. Dist., Calif., 1976—98; prof. San Diego State U., Calexico, Calif., 1987—89; ret. Presenter critical thinking skills, Imperial County, Calif., 1986, El Centro, 1986, English/lang. arts framework, El Centro, 1989. Mem. Young Democrats, San Diego, 1962-63; mem. McKinley Sch. PTA, 1969-75, pres., 1971-72. Mem. AAUW, Imperial County Reading Coun. (v.p. 1988-89), Internat. Reading Assn., Lang. Arts Leadership Team, Jr. Women's 10,000 Club (pres. 1971-72), Calif. Fedn. Women's Clubs (jr. mem. De Anza dist., v.p. 1972-73, Calif. Jr. Citizen of Yr. 1972), Del Rio Ladies Golf Assn. (officer, 1998-02, Pres. Cup winner, 2005), B.P.O Elks El Centro (officer, 1999-02, chmn., vet. affairs nat. hon., 2003). Lutheran. Avocations: world travel, reading, golf.

STALSBERG, GERALDINE MCEWEN, accountant; b. Springfield, Mo., May 10, 1936; d. Gerald Earl and Marie LaVerne (Pennington); m. Bill Eugene Bottolfson, Mar. 10, 1956 (div. 1978); children: Bill Earl, Robert Edward, Brian Everett, Michelle Marie; m. Arvid Ray Stalsberg, Sept. 21, 1979; stepchildren: Angelite Renae, Neil Ray, Terry Jay. Diploma Hastings Beauty Acad., 1955; cert. in interior design, Cen. Tech. Community Coll., 1975; student Doane Coll., 1982; cert. computer programmer Lincoln Sch. Commerce, Nebr., 1984. Cosmetologist, Marinello Beauty Shop, Hastings, 1955-57; owner Nursery Sch. for Toddlers, 1958-67; acct. grain dept. Morrison-Quirk Elevator, Hastings, Nebr., 1968-69; acct., exec. sec., interior decorator Uerling's Home Furnishings, Hastings, 1970-79; acct., computer programmer, Lincoln Transp., Nebr., 1980-86, systems analyst, 1984-86; tax cons. H&R Block, Lincoln, 1983-86; programmer, tax cons., controller EBKO Industries, Hastings, 1987-90; pvt. practice acctg. and tax cons., 1987—. Emergency radio dispatcher Adams County Civil Def., Hastings, 1973-78; active YWCA, Girl Scouts USA, PTA, 4-H Clubs Am. Recipient Civic Achievement award City of Hastings, 1974. Mem. Nat. Assn. Govt. Employees, Bus. Profl. Women, Library Assn., Nat. Am. Mfrs. Assn., NAFE, Nat. Assn. Mfrs., Soroptimists Internat., Beta Sigma Phi (Woman of Yr. 1978, Order of Rose). Republican. Lutheran. Avocations: reading, bowling, fishing, swimming, jogging. Home and Office: 1602 W 12th St Hastings NE 68901-3745

STALVEY, CHERYL B., elementary school educator; d. Alexander and Joann Brigman; m. Franklin A. Stalvey, June 23, 1979; 1 child, Jason R. BS in Elem. Edn., Francis Marion U., Florence, SC, 1982, M of Secondary Edn., 1988. Tchr. mid. sch. math. Marion Sch. Dist. I, SC, 1982—. Chair youth com. First Bapt. Ch., Mullins, SC, 2004—06. Toyota grantee, 2002. Mem.: S.C. Coun. Tchrs. Math., Nat. Coun. Tchrs. Math.

STAMATAKIS, CAROL MARIE, lawyer, former state legislator; m. Michael Shklar. BA in Criminology and Criminal Justice, Ohio State U., 1982; JD, Case Western Res., 1985. Bar: N.H. 1985, U.S. Dist. Ct. N.H. 1985. Atty. Elliott, Jasper & Stamatakis, Newport, NH, 1990-93; state rep. N.H. State Legislature, 1988-94; atty. N.H. Dept. Health and Human Svcs., Concord, 1994—. Instr. Am. Inst. Banking, Claremont, 1987-88, 91-92, 95. Treas., mem. Town of Lempster N.H. Conservation Commn., 1987—; town chair N.H. Dem. Party, 1987—. Mem. N.H. Bar Assn., Sierra Club, Upper Valley Group (former vice chair and solid waste chair). Avocations: drawing, painting. Home: PO Box 807 Newport NH 03773-0807

STAMBERG, SUSAN LEVITT, radio personality; b. Newark, Sept. 7, 1938; d. Robert I. and Anne (Rosenberg) Levitt; m. Louis Collins Stamberg, Apr. 14, 1962; 1 child, Joshua Collins BA, Barnard Coll, 1959; DHL (hon.), Gettysburg Coll., 1982, Dartmouth Coll., 1984, Knox Coll., U. N.H., SUNY, Brockport. Editorial asst. Daedalus, Cambridge, Mass., 1960-62; editorial asst. The New Republic, Washington, 1962-63; host, producer, mgr., program dir. Sta. WAMU-FM, Washington, 1963-69; host All Things Considered Washington, 1971-86; host Weekend Edition Nat Pub. Radio, Washington, 1987-89; spl. corr. Nat. Pub. Radio, 1990—. Bd. dirs. AIA, Washington, 1983-85, PEN/Faulkner Fiction Award Found., 1985—. Author: Every Night at Five, 1982, The Wedding Cake in the Middle of the Road, 1992, Talk: NPR's Susan Stamberg Considers All Things, 1993. Recipient Honor award Ohio U., 1977, Edward R. Murrow award Corp. for Pub. Broadcasting, 1980; named Woman of Yr., Barnard Coll., 1984; fellow Silliman Coll. Yale U., 1984—; inducted Broadcasting Hall of Fame, 1994, Radio Hall of Fame, 1996. Avocations: drawing, piano, knitting. Office: Nat Pub Radio 635 Massachusetts Ave NW Washington DC 20001-3753 Office Phone: 202-513-2000.

STAMM, BARBARA MARIE, elementary school educator, interior designer; b. Oakland, Calif., June 11, 1937; d. Reuben Anders Anderson and Helen Francis Sjogren-Anderson; m. George F. Stamm, July 26, 1959; children: George Anders, Anne-Marie. AA, U. Calif., Berkeley, 1957, BA, 1959. Tchr. Antioch Unified Sch. Dist., Calif., 1959—62, 1966—68, 1976—95; interior designer San Francisco Bay Area, 1975—. Author: (classroom trial) People v. Missoin Mouse, 1987; dir.: (choral reading) T.S. Eliot's Cats, 1992. Pres. Delta Meml. Hosp. Aux., Antioch, 1970; bd. trustees Delta Meml. Hosp. Bd., Antioch, 1973; v.p. Citizens for Responsible Active Waterfront Design and Devel., Antioch, 1987. Republican. Lutheran. Avocations: travel, gardening, reading, cooking. Home: 501 B St Antioch CA 94509-1202 Personal E-mail: bstamm501@aol.com.

STAMM, CAROL ANN, obstetrician, gynecologist; b. Denver, Aug. 8, 1959; d. Robert L. and Mary Ellen Stamm. BA in Biology cum laude, U. Colo., 1981, cert. in elem. tchg., 1985; MD with honors, U. Colo., Denver, 1991. Diplomate Am. Bd. Ob-Gyn. Bilingual elem. tchr. Denver Pub. Schs., 1986—87; intern in ob-gyn U. Colo. Sch. Medicine, Denver, 1991—92, resident in ob-gyn, 1992—95, asst. prof., 1997—2003; staff ob-gyn, asst. prof. Denver Health Med. Ctr., 1995—2003; dir. women's health rotation Colo. Health Found. (formerly High St. Primary Care Clinic), Denver, 2003—, asst. prof. clin. medicine, 2003—, dir. women's svcs., 2004—. Mem. Patient and Family Edn. Work Group, 1996—97; mem. ob-gyn edn. com. U. Colo. Health Scis. Ctr., 1997—2003; dir. ob-gyn Grand Rounds, 1997—2001; provider design team Lifetime Clin. Record Project, 1998—2001; alt. mem. Colo. Multiple Instl. Rev. Bd., 1998—2003; presenter in field. Co-author: (book) Management of High-Risk Pregnancy, 4th edit., 1999, Medical Care of the Pregnant Patient, 2000, The Female Athlete, 2002, Contemporary Therapy in Obstetrics and Gynecology, 2002; contbr. articles to profl. jours.; peer reviewer Jour. Obstetrics and Gynecology, 1999—, Am. Jour. Obstetrics and Gynecology, 1999—. Recipient Richard Whitehead award, Phi Rho Sigma, 1989; grantee, March of Dimes, 2000—01; Trust fellow, Am. Cancer Soc. Brooks, 1988, Acad. Enrichment grantee, U. Colo. Health Scis. Ctr., 1993—95, NIH subcontract grantee, U. Pitts., 2000—03, NIH grantee, IBBEX, 2002. Fellow: ACOG (History fellow 2006); mem.: N.Am. Menopause Soc, Golden Key, Phi Beta Kappa (mem. mortar bd.). Avocations: reading, running, pilates, symphony, opera. Home: 155 S Jackson St Unit C Denver CO 80209 Office: Health One Alliance/High St Primary Care Clinic 1801 High St Denver CO 80218 Office Phone: 303-869-2158. Business E-Mail: cstamm@health1.org.

STAMMER, NANCY A., travel company executive; b. Manning, Iowa, June 19, 1951; d. Reuben A. and Edith M. Stoberl; m. Calvin F. Stammer, Sept. 20, 1975; children: Clinton F., Chad F. BA, U. Iowa, Iowa City, 1972; MA, Viterebo U., LaCrosse, Wis., 1999. Reporter Sarasota Newspapers, Fla., 1973—74, Manning Monitor, Iowa, 1974—81; owner Stammer's Personalized Printing, 1981—86; tchr. Wall Lake View Auburn Schs., Lake View, 1986—94; tchr. gifted and talented and title I IKM Cmty. Schs., Manilla, Iowa, 1995—2006; tour planner Star Destinations, Carroll, Iowa, 2006—. Cons. in field. Ctrl. com. RAGBRAI (R) Bicycle Visit, Manning, Iowa, 2006; asst. editor Centennial History Book, Manning, Iowa, 1980—81, editor Aspinwall, Iowa, 1982. Home: 2897 380th St Manning IA 51455 Office: Star Destinations PO Box 456 Manilla IA 51401

STAMOS, KATHRYN ELIZABETH, secondary school educator; b. Walnut Creek, Calif., May 27, 1978; d. Richard Gordon and Nancy Jane Plath; m. Alexander Charles Stamos, Dec. 28, 2003. BA in History, U. Calif., L.A., Calif., 2000; MA in Edn., Pepperdine U., Malibu, Calif., 2001. Cert. tchr. Calif. Commn. Tchr. Credentialing, 2001. Tchr. El Dorado (Calif.) Union H.S. Dist., El Dorado Hills, 2001—03, San Mateo Union H.S. Dist., Millbrae, Calif., 2003—. Home: 170 Positano Circle Redwood Shores CA 94065 Office: Mills High School 400 Murchison Dr Millbrae CA 94065 Home Fax: 415-242-5229. Personal E-mail: katie@stamos.org.

STAMPER, EWA SZUMOTALSKA, psychologist; b. Warsaw, Sept. 8, 1954; came to U.S., 1984; d. Tadeusz and Regina S.Szumotalska MA in Clin. Psychology, U. Warsaw, Poland, 1978; PhD in Psychology, New Sch. U., N.Y.C., 1992. Staff therapist Marital Therapy Counseling Ctr., Warsaw, 1978—79, Ctr. for Psychotherapy and Personality Growth, Warsaw, 1978—80; sr. staff therapist Lab. for Psychoedn. Polish Psychol. Assn., Warsaw, 1981—85; postgrad. affiliate Washington Sq. Inst. for Psychotherapy, N.Y.C., 1990—92; police psychologist Honolulu Police Dept., 1993—98; pvt. practice, Honolulu, 1994—. With Tng. Ctr. for Family Therapy, Warsaw, 1976—78, Stuyvesant Poly., N.Y.C., 1988—89, North Ctrl. Bronx (N.Y.) Hosp., 1988—89, Yale Psychiat. Inst., 1989—90, Castle Med. Ctr., Kailua, Hawaii, 1993—94; co-chmn. Crystal Methampetamine Forum, Honolulu, 1996—99. Mem. APA, Am. Acad. Experts in Traumatic Stress, Hawaii Psychol. Assn. (clin. divsn. rep. 1998-99, coord. for Disaster Response Network 2005—). Avocations: horseback riding, raising German Shorthaired Pointers and Siamese cats, gardening, fiction and poetry writing, running. Office: 30 Aulike St Ste 308 Kailua HI 96734 Office Phone: 808-261-5555. E-mail: ewastamper@aol.com.

STAMPS, LAURA ANNE, writer, poet; b. Indpls., Apr. 2, 1957; d. James Oliver and Isabelle Anne (Holland) Smith; m. Carl Thomas Stamps, Jr., June 30, 1979. Student, Dalton (Ga.) Jr. Coll., 1977, Coll. of Charleston, S.C., 1979. Owner Kittyfeather Press, Columbia, SC, 1985—. Author: Art Marketing Manual, 1988, How to Create the Life You Desire, 1995, How to Become a Prosperous Woman, 1995, Songs of Power, 1996, (fiction) Earth Lessons, 1995, Tuning Out, 1996, The Way of Love, 1998, I Can Do Anything, vol. 1, 2000, vol. 2, 2000, Restore my Soul, 2002, In the Company of Cats, 2002, Joy Unspeakable, 2003, Evergreen, 2003, Cat Daze, 2004, Angel, 2004, In the Garden, 2004, Cats and Chrysanthemums: New and Collected Poems 1987-2005, 2005, The Year of the Cat, 2005 (nominated Pulitzer Prize), The Tarot Cats, 2006, Blue Moon, 2006, The Cat Lady, 2006; editor The Artist's Forum, 1989-94, Laura's Letter for Women, 1996-97 Avocations: gardening, cats. Office: Kittyfeather Press PO Box 212534 Columbia SC 29221-2534 E-mail: laurastamps@mindspring.com.

STAMSTA, JEAN F., artist; b. Sheboygan, Wis., Nov. 2, 1936; d. Herbert R. and Lucile Caroline (Malwitz) Nagel; m. Duane R. Stamsta, Aug. 18, 1956; children: Marc, David. BS, BA, U. Wis., 1958. Guest curator Milw. Art Mus., 1986; resident artist Leighton Artist Colony, Banff, Alta., Can., 1987. One-woman shows include Am. Craft Mus., N.Y.C., 1971, Winona (Minn.) State U., 1986, Lawrence U., Appleton, Wis., 1990, Walkers Point Ctr. Arts, Milw., 1990, U. Wis. Ctr., Sheboygan, 1998, Wis. Luth. Coll., Milw., 1999, Carroll Coll., Waukesha, Wis., 2006, exhibited in group shows at Cleve. Mus. Art, 1977, Milw. Art Mus., 1986, 1988, Nat. Air and Space Mus., Smithsonian Instn., Washington, 1986, Madison (Wis.) Art Ctr., 1987, 1990, Paper Press Gallery, Chgo., 1988, North Arts Ctr., Atlanta, 1990, Dairy Barn Cultural Arts Ctr., Athens, Ohio, 1991, Paper Arts Festival, Appleton, 1992, Fine Arts Mus., Budapest, Hungary, 1992, Tilburg Textile Mus., Netherlands, 1993, U. Wis. Union Gallery, 1994, Holland Area Arts Coun. Gallery, U. Mich., Ann Arbor, 1996, Charles Allis Art Mus., Milw., 1996, Bergstrom-Mahler Mus., Neenah, Wis., 1998, West Bend Mus. Art, Wis., 2000, Three Rivers Arts Festival, Pitts., 2001, U. Wis. Alumni Assn., Milw., 2002, Racine (Wis.) Art Mus., 2003, 2005, Rochester Art Ctr., 2004. Fellow Craftsman fellow, NEA, 1974. Avocations: swimming, travel. Home: 9313 Center Oak Rd Hartland WI 53029 E-mail: jstamsta@aol.com.

STANAWAY, LORETTA SUSAN, small business owner; b. Selfridge AFB, Mich., Jan. 1, 1954; d. Vincent Carl and Carolyn Jane (Grasser) Pizzo; m. Thomas Lee Stanaway, Apr. 23, 1983; stepchildren: Todd Richard, Toni Marie. Student, Ctrl. Mich. U., 1972-75. Intern, reporter Daily Times-News, Mt. Pleasant, Mich., 1974; editorial asst. Bar Jour. Mich., Lansing, 1975-76; with prodn. control dept. Dart Container Corp., Mason, Mich., 1976-80; mgr. Payless Shoes, Lansing, 1980; shift supr. Greyhound Food Mgmt., Lansing, 1980-82; owner, mgr. L.S. Distbg., Lansing, 1982-89, Send Out Svcs. S.O.S., Lansing, 1989-98; owner, mgr. lawn care divsn., snow removal divsn. Send Out Svcs., 1993-98; owner, mgr. Stanaway's Outstanding Svcs. S.O.S., 1998—. Meml. Minders, 2000—. Mem. focus group on customer svc. Small Bus. Devel. Ctr., Lansing, 1991—. Treas. Mich. Coalition on Smoking or Health, Lansing, 1987-89; bd. dirs. Am. Cancer Soc. Mich., Lansing, 1988-89; mem. custodial svcs. com. Ingham Intermediate Sch. Dist., 1991—; mem. adminstrv. bd., fin. chair cert., lay spkr., sunday sch. supt., Grovenburg United Meth. Ch., 1994—. Recipient Outstanding Svc. award Am. Cancer Soc. Mich., 1988. Mem. NAFE, Nat. Assn. Self-Employed, Nat. Fedn. Ind. Bus., Internat. Platform Assn. Republican. Methodist. Avocations: camping, fishing, gardening, birdwatching, travel. Home and Office: 546 Armstrong Rd Lansing MI 48911-3811

STANBERRY, D(OSI) ELAINE, English literature educator, writer; b. Elk Park, N.C. m. Earl Stanberry; 1 child, Anita St. Lawrence. Student in Bus. Edn., Steed Coll. Tech., 1956; BS in Bus. and English, East Tenn. State U., 1961, MA in Shakespearean Lit., 1962; PhD, Tex. A&M U., 1975; postgrad., North Tex. State U., U. South Fla., NYU, Duke U., U. N.C. Prof. Manatee Jr. Coll., Bradenton, Fla., 1964-67; Disting. prof. English Dickinson State U., ND, 1967-81; retired, 1981. Author: Poetic Heartstrings, Mountain Echoes, Love's Perplexing Obsession Experienced by Heinrich Heine and Percy Bysshe Shelley, Poetry from the Ancients to Moderns: A Critical Anthology, Finley Forest, Chapel Hill's Tree-lined Tuck, (plays) The Big Toe, The Funeral Factory; contbr. articles, poetry to jours., mags. Recipient Editor's Choice award Nat. Libr. Poetry, 1988, 95, Distinguished Professor of English Award, Dickinson State U., 1981; included in Best Poems of 1995. Mem. Acad. Am. Poets, N.C. Writers Network, N.C. Poetry Soc. (Carl Sandburg Poetry award 1988), Poetic Page, Writers Jour., Poets and Writers, Friday-Noon Poets, Delta Kappa Gamma.

STANCIL, DONIELLE LAVELLE, nursing administrator; b. Washington, May 18, 1971; d. Cedric Lorenzo and Lula Yvonne (Curry) Jackson; m. LeKeith Don Stancil, Sept. 29, 2001; children: Bianca, Jalexis, Keith. BSN, Pitts. State U., 1993; MS in Health Care Mgmt., Marymount U., 2002. Team leader Kaiser Permanente, Washington, 1996—; clin. nurse mgr. Profl. Healthcare Resources, Falls Church, Va., 2003—04; nurse coord. Lockheed Martin Svcs., 2004—. Vol. Va. Emergency Vol. Svcs., 2003—. Mem.: Chi Eta Phi. Home: 15002 Plum Tree Way Bowie MD 20721 Office Phone: 301-458-4783.

STANCIL, IRENE MACK, family counselor; b. St. Helena Island, Sept. 29, 1938; d. Rufus and Irene (Wilson) Mack; m. Nesby Stancil, Dec. 29, 1968; 1 child, Steve Lamar. BA, Benedict Coll., 1960, CUNY, 1983; MA, New World Bible Coll., 1984; SSD, United Christian Coll., 1985; cert., Mercy Coll., 1993. Supr. City of New York; tchr. local bd. edn., SC; supr, case worker, counselor City of New York. Mem. Am. Ctr. for Law & Justice.

STANDERFORD, CATHERINE ANN, school nurse practitioner, director; b. Lufkin, Tex., Aug. 5, 1967; d. E. W. and Paterica Ann Cross; m. Robert Micheal Standerford, Feb. 14, 1986; children: Robert Jacoby, Amanda Lyn, Micah Wyatt. Bus. cert., Angelina Coll., 1985; RN, Angelina Coll., Lufkin Texas, 1994. RN; Registered Nurse RSN, Bd. of Nurse Examiners for the State of Tex., 1994. RN critical care Meml. Med. Ctr. of East Tex., Lufkin, Tex., 1994—97; sch. nurse dir. Hudson ISD, Lufkin, Tex., 1997—. Pub. rels. dir., medifast diet LiveWell Athletic Club, Lufkin, 1990—92; chmn. Social Health Adv. Coun., 2003—05. Author (training): (policy manual) Blood Pathens. Mem. First Assembly of God, Lufkin, 1998—2005, lay pastor, 1999—2005, host home group, 2004—05. Tobacco Compliance Edn. grant, Tex. Dept. of Health, 2002-2004. Mem.: Nat. Sch. Nurse Adminstrn. Assn. (hon.), Tex. Assn. Sch. Nurses (hon.), Nat. Assn. of Sch. Nurses (hon.). Assembly Of God. Achievements include first to Advanced Cardiac Life support 1995; Instructor Caridac rounds. Avocations: time with family, travel, entaining guest, decorating home. Office: Hudson ISD 6735 Ted Trout Dr Lufkin TX 75904 Office Phone: 936-875-9207.

STANDIFORD, NATALIE ANNE, writer; b. Balt., Nov. 20, 1961; d. John Willard Eagleston and Natalie Elizabeth Standiford; m. Robert Craig Tracy, Apr. 29, 1989. BA, Brown Univ., 1983. Clerk Shakespeare and Co. Bookstore, N.Y.C., 1983; editl. asst. Random House, N.Y.C., 1984-85, asst. editor books for young readers divsn., 1985-87; freelance writer N.Y.C., 1987—. Author: The Best Little Monkeys in the World, 1987, The Bravest Dog Ever: The True Story of Balto, 1989 (Puffin award Alaska Assn. Sch. Libr. 1992), The Headless Horseman, 1992, Brave Maddie Egg, 1995, Space Dog and Roy, 1990, Space Dog and the Pet Show, 1990, Space Dog in Trouble, 1991, Space Dog the Hero, 1991 (Fifty Books of Yr. citation Fedn. Children's Book Groups 1992), The Power #2: The Witness, 1992, The Power #4: The Diary, 1992, The Power #7: Vampire's Kiss, 1992, (picture book) Dollhouse Mouse, 1989, (as Emily James) Fifteen: Hillside Live!, 1993, Jafar's Curse, 1993, (picture book) Santa's Surprise, 1992, The Mixed-Up Witch, 1993, Astronauts are Sleeping, 1996, The Stone Giant, 2000. Reader, N.Y.C. Author Read-Aloud Program, 1992—. Mem. Soc. Children's Book Writers and Illustrators, Author's Guild, Authors League Am. Avocations: travel, movies, music.

STANDING, KIMBERLY ANNA, researcher; b. Hagerstown, Md., Mar. 24, 1965; d. Thomas Townsend and Ruth Annadeane (Powell) Stone; m. Christopher G. Standing, May 20, 1989; children: Iain Christopher, Leah Elizabeth. BA in Math., St. Mary's Coll., 1988; MA in Higher Edn. Adminstrn., George Washington U., 1996, postgrad. Sr. analyst Westat, Inc., Rockville, Md., 1988—. Mem. Am. Ednl. Rsch. Assn., Assn. Study Higher Edn. Office: Westat Inc RW2564 1650 Research Blvd Rockville MD 20850-3195 Home: 23 Sheridan Ln Knoxville MD 21758-8901 E-mail: KimStanding@westat.com.

STANDLEY, SHERRIANNE MADDOX, bank executive; b. Biloxi, Miss., Apr. 12, 1945; d. Tom Smith and Mary Anna (Jenkins) Maddox; m. Barry Layne Standley, Dec. 18, 1971; 1 child, Sloane. BS, Ind. U., 1967; MPA, Ind. State U., 1980. Dir. pub. rels. Ind. Dem. State Cen. Com., Indpls., 1967-71, Ind. Motor Truck Assn., Indpls., 1971, No. Ky. U., Highland Heights, 1972-76; dir. publs. U. So. Ind., Evansville, 1976-78, asst. to pres., 1978-86, v.p. advancement, 1986—2006; pres. Bond Bank Evansville, Ind., 2006—. Precinct committeman Dem. Party of Marion County, Indpls., 1969, Vanderburgh County, Evansville, 1978; pres. Vanderburgh County Sheriff's Bd. and Pension Bd., 2004-2005; chair Operation City Beautiful, Evansville, 1990-92; trustee Trinity United Meth. Ch., 2002-03; bd. dirs., pres. Evansville YWCA, 2006. Recipient Disting. Master Pub. Adminstrn. Alumni award, Ind. State U., 1994. Mem. Ind. Coun. for Advancement and Support Edn. (pres. 1988-89), Evansville Kennel Club, Pub. Edn. Found. (bd. dirs. and adv. council). Methodist. Home: 117 Woodward Dr Evansville IN 47712-7301 Office: U So Ind 8600 University Blvd Evansville IN 47712-3534

STANDRIDGE, JEAN, real estate company executive, broker; b. Danville, Ala., July 14, 1931; d. Elbert Eugene and Pearl May Rogers Brown; m. Arch Standridge, Jr., June 21, 1952; 1 child, Terry Brian. Grad., Burroughs Bus. Sch., Birmingham, 1951, Am. Real Estate Inst., 1975; student, Jefferson State Coll., Birmingham, 1980. Cert. real estate broker. Bookkeeper Mac Wates Coal Co., Birmingham, Ala., 1952-57; music tchr. County Schs., Blount County, Ala., 1957-75; real estate broker, owner Standridge Realty, Hayden, Ala., 1977—. Organist Meth. Ch., Hayden, 1957-77; sponsor Young Boys Soft Ball, Hayden, 1985-86; city coun. mem. Town of Hayden, 1988-92. Mem. Nat. Assn. Realtors, Ala. Assn. Realtors, Birmingham Assn. Realtors. Avocations: photography, indoor gardening, reading, music. Home: 177 Main St Hayden AL 35079-6452 Office: Standridge Realty Inc 177 Main St Hayden AL 35079-6452 also: 177 Main St Hayden AL 35079-6452

STANFEL, JANE ELLEN, artist, adult education educator; b. Chgo., Mar. 7, 1941; d. Raymond Roy and Lucille Pauline Yetter; m. Larry Eugene Stanfel, Sept. 1, 1962; children: Kenneth, Larry, Christine, Rebecca. Student, Dominican U., 1959—61, Loyola U., 1961, U. Fla., 1968—70, Colo. State U., 1970, U. Tex., Arlington, 1978—80. Grade sch. tchr. St. William's Sch., Oak Park, Ill., 1961—62; H.S. tchr. East Baton Rouge Parish, Greenwell Springs, La., 1985—88; office mgr. Def. Comm. Agy., Arlington, Va., 1989—90; adult basic edn. specialist Tuscaloosa (Ala.) County Sch. Bd., 1990—94; contractor Kelly Svcs., Reston, Va., 1996, Tuscaloosa, 1996; workplace edn. specialist Tuscaloosa County Sch. Bd., 1997—2002; artist Tuscaloosa, 1995—, Roundup, Mont., 1995—. One-woman shows include Downtown Gallery, Tuscaloosa, 1997—98, Christina's Art Gallery, 1998, Nordic Heritage Mus., Seattle, 2000—02, Royal Norwegian Embassy, Washington, 2001, 2001—02, exhibitions include Montmartre, Brussels, 2002, Represented in permanent collections Royal Norwegian Embassy, Washington, exhibitions include variuos juried art shows, Mont.; contbr. articles to profl. jours. and newspapers. Tutor literacy program Tuscaloosa County Sch. Bd., 1988—89; designer, head vol. literacy program Def. Comm. Agy., Arlington, 1989—90. Recipient First prize internat. logo competition, Def. Comm. Agy., 1989, Presdl. Points of Light award, Office of the U.S. Pres., 1991. Mem.: Archives on Women Artists, Nat. Mus. Women in the Arts. Avocations: cross country skiing, ballet, mineralogy, lapidary arts, hiking. Home: PO Box 348 Roundup MT 59072 E-mail: j-barre-lranch@hughes.net.

STANFIELD, MARGARET HELENE, nursing educator, administrator; b. Roswell, N.Mex., July 3, 1951; d. Shelby E. Stanfield and Frances Berry Stanfield. PhD, Tex. Woman's U., Denton, 1991. RN Tex. Bd. Nurse Examiners, 2005. Staff nurse to head nurse and inservice instr. Parkland Meml. Hosp., Dallas, 1979—81; instr. Tex. Woman's U., Denton, 1983—84; dir. Wichita Home Health, Wichita Falls, 1984—88; instr. El Centro Coll., Dallas, 1999—. Avocation: needlepoint. Home: 2260 Colony Ct Dallas TX 75235 Office: El Centro Coll Main at Lamar Dallas TX 75201 Office Phone: 214-630-6133.

STANFIELD-MADDOX, ELIZABETH, language educator, translator; b. Jacksonville, Fla., Aug. 9, 1930; d. Thomas William and Mattie Olene (Padgett) Poplin; m. William Thomas Stanfield, June 30, 1956; children: C. Freeman, William Thomas III; m. Houston Noble Maddox, June 26, 2004. BA in English magna cum laude, U. N.C., Greensboro, 1952; MA, Emory U., 1966. Tchr. fgn. langs. Atlanta City Schs., 1952—57, Fulton County H.S., 1963—65; instr. Spanish Ga. State U., Atlanta, 1968—78, asst. prof., 1978—95, asst. prof. emerita, 1995—. Lectr. Learning Resources Ctr., 1975—95, Spkrs. Bur., 1979—95, Elderhostel, 1990—93, so. culture and living, 1992—95; cons. Internat. Bus. Coun. Inst. Internat. Cons. Directory, 1984; coll. supr. student tchrs. Ga. State Dept. Edn.; adv. coun. Internat. Quarterly. Author: From Plantation to Peachtree: A Century and a Half of Atlanta Classic Homes, 1987; contbg. author: The University Bookman, 1984, 2004; translator: Carolina Coronado's, My Cousin Angela, 1995; contbr. articles to profl. jours. and mags. Founder New Hanover County Libr. Found., NC, 2006; donor Friends of New Hanover County Pub. Libr., NC, 2006; mem. adv. bd. New Hanover County Pub. Libr., 2002—, mem. centennial com., 2006. Fellow, AAUW, 1964—65. Mem.: SAMLA, DAR, AAUP, AAUW, Carteret Writers Assn., So. Assn. Women Historians, N.C. Libr. Assn., Am. Lit. Translators Assn. (conf. coord. 1993, sec.-treas. 1994), Atlanta Assn. Interpreters and Translators (bd. dir. 1985—95, chair accreditations 1986—95), 19th Century Studies Assn., Am. Assn. Tchrs. Spanish and Portuguese (pres. Ga. chpt. 1979—81), Smithsonian, Nat. Trust Hist. Preservation, United Daus. Confederacy, Phi Sigma Iota, Sigma Delta Pi, Omicron Delta Kappa, Phi Beta Kappa. Mem. Ch. Of Christ. Office: 2912 Park Ave Wilmington NC 28403

STANFORD, DIANA L., librarian; b. East St. Louis, Ill., Feb. 22, 1952; d. Richard Leland and Helen Jeanette (Hoy) Ninness; children: James Kent LeBlanc Jr., Jonathan Brice LeBlanc; m. John C. Stanford, June 1999. Grad. high sch., Collinsville, Ill. Dir. & head libr. Caseyville (Ill.) Pub. Libr. Sec. 1st Bapt. Ch. Caseyville, 1986-95, treas., 1974-89. Recipient Hardees Home Town Award for Public Service, 1999. Republican. Avocations: painting, cross stitch, gardening, sewing, crafts, baking. Office: 419 S 2nd St Caseyville IL 62232-1525

STANFORD, (FRANCES) JANE HERRING, management consultant, educator, writer; b. Lockhart, Tex., Dec. 17, 1939; d. John William and Frances Argyra (Cheatham) Jr.; m. Rube V. Stanford; children: (Steven) Scott, Lisa Ann. BS, Texas A&M U., Kingsville; MS in Counseling, Texas A&M U., Corpus Christi; MBA, Texas A&M U., Kingsville; PhD in Orgn. Theory and Strategic Mgmt., U. North Tex. Tchg. fellow U. North Tex., Denton; prof. bus. policy and strategic mgmt., pres. faculty senate Texas A&M U., Kingsville, 1990—, grad. rsch. advisor, MBA/MPA program, Coll. Bus., 1992-98, 2004—, asst. v.p. Acad. Affairs, 1997—99, ret., 1999, vis. assoc. prof. mgmt. Corpus Christi, Tex., 2000—04, Kingsville, 2004—, chair dept. mgmt. and mktg. Coll. Bus., 1993—97, current mem. grad. faculty, Coll. Bus. grad. rsch. advisor; mgmt. cons. Strategic Mgmt. Solutions, Inc., 1999—. Chair univ. assessment, budgeting and planning com. Tex. A&M U., 1997—98; internat. lectr. strategic mgmt. within internat. context, Colombia, Argentina; workshop leader and participant in acad. issues. Author: Building Competitiveness: U.S. Expatriate Management Strategies in Mexico, 1995; contbr. articles to profl. jours. and conf. procs. Apptd. to water resources adv. com. City of Corpus Christi, 2003—. Named Leadership Corpus Christi Class of XXX, 2001—02; fellow Sys. Chancellor's fellow in leadership in higher edn. program, Tex. A&M U., 1997. Mem.: Univ. Grad. Faculty, Soc. Advancement Mgmt., Acad. Mgmt., Inst. Mgmt. Cons., Strategic Mgmt. Soc., Delta Sigma Pi, Kappa Delta Pi (life). Presbyterian. Avocations: book collecting, photography, travel. Home: 13526 Carlos Fifth Ct Corpus Christi TX 78418 Office: 212 Coll Bus Admin TAMUK Kingsville TX 78363 Office Phone: 361-593-3939. E-mail: jhstanford@aol.com.

STANGE, SHARON (SHERRI), science educator; d. Edwin and Thelma Lowry; life ptnr. Donald Domenigoni; children: Brian, Karla Sluis. AA, Mt. San Jacinto Coll., 1972—77; BSc, U. of Calif., 1978—81; M, LaVerne U., 1995—96. Teaching Credential Calif. State U., San Bernardino, 1982. Tchg. asst. Kiddie Korners Preschool, Hemet, Calif., 1972—74; biology lab asst. Mt. San Jacinto Coll., San Jacinto, Calif., 1973—82; sci. tchr. San Jacinto Unified Sch. Dist., Calif., 1982—; sub. tchr. Hemet Unified Sch. Dist., Calif., 1979—82; environ. sci. tchr. Mt. San Jacinto Coll., 1989—90. Mentor tchr. San Jacinto Unified Sch. Dist., 1998—, green schools coord., 2004—; profl. affairs/scholarship chair Delta Kappa Gamma/Gamma Theta chpt., 1999—; scholarship chair Gene Lombard Meml. Scholarship, 2001—; sci. club advisor Monte Vista and North Mountain Mid. Sch., San Jacinto, 1982—98; cheerleading advisor Monte Vista Mid. Sch., San Jacinto, 1984—92; sci. fair coord. Monte Vista Mid. Sch./North Mountain Mid. Sch., San Jacinto, 1982—2001; sci. dept. chair Monte Vista and North Mountain Mid. Sch., San Jacinto, 1982—. Co-founder Valley Youth Task Force, Hemet/San Jacinto, Calif., 1991—93; leader Neighborhood Watch, Hemet/San Jacinto, 1991—98; mem. PTA, Hemet/San Jacinto, 1973—2005, Friends of the No. San Jacinto Valley, 1995—2005. Recipient Calif. Environ. Edn. award, State of Calif., 1995, Inland Empire Environ. Educator of the Yr., Calif. State U. San Bernardino, 1994, Outstanding Biology Achievement, Mt. San Jacinto Coll., 1976, Environ. Edn. award, Nat. Audubon Soc., 1991, We Honor Ours award, Calif. Teachers Assn., 1992, 1994; Audubon Naturalist grant, Hemet Valley Women's Club, 1995. Mem.: NSTA, San Jacinto Teachers Assn./CTA/NEA (pres., v.p., site rep, San Gorgonia coun. rep 1983—2005), Mt. San Jacinto Coll. Alumni Assn. (life; v.p.), Living Desert Assn., Nat. Audubon Soc./San Bernardino Valley chpt. (v.p./edn. chair/idyllwild christmas bird count compiler 1980—2005). Avocations: fishing, camping, travel, birdwatching. Office: North Mountain Middle Sch 1202 E 7th St San Jacinto CA 92583 Office Phone: 951-487-7797.

STANGER, ILA, editor-in-chief; b. NYC; d. Jack Simon and Shirley Ruth (Nadelson) S. BA, Bklyn. Coll., 1961. Feature and travel editor Harpers Bazaar, N.Y.C., 1969-75; exec. editor Travel and Leisure mag., N.Y.C., 1975-85; editor in chief Food and Wine Mag., N.Y.C., 1985-89, Travel and Leisure mag., N.Y.C., 1990-93; mng. editor More mag., N.Y.C., 1993—. Writer on arts, features and travel. Mem. Am. Soc. Mag. Editors Office: More Magazine 375 Lexington New York NY 10017 Business E-Mail: ila.stanger@meredith.com.

STANIAR, LINDA BURTON, retired communications executive; b. Glen Ridge, N.J., July 6, 1948; d. Harold Burton and Helen (Kintzing) Staniar; m. William Glasgow Bergh, Jan. 21, 1978; 1 child, Courtney Christian Bergh. BA, Briarcliff Coll., 1970; MA, NYU, 1974. From pub. rels. asst. to v.p. corp. comm. N.Y. Life Ins. Co., N.Y.C., 1977-96, sr. v.p. corp. comm., 1996—. Mem. Advt. Women of N.Y., PRSA and YWCA Acad. of Women Achieves.

STANKAVAGE, AMY L., physical therapist, athletic trainer; b. Pottsville, Pa., May 28, 1977; d. Charles and Lucy Snukis; m. Brian J. Stankavage, May 28, 2005. BS in Athletic Tng. magna cum laude, West Chester U., Pa., 1999; MS in Phys. Therapy magna cum laude, Thomas Jefferson U., Phila., 2002. Lic. physical therapist Bd. Phys. Therapy, 2002; cert. athletic trainer Nataboc, Pa., 1999. Head acute care phys. therapist Good Samaritan Regional Med. Ctr., Pottsville, Pa., 2002—; head athletic trainer Nativity BVM HS, 2002—. Head jr. varsity girls basketball coach Nativity B.V.M. HS, Pottsville, 2005—; aerobics instr. Champs Fitness, Minersville, Pa., 2005—. Lector Sacred Heart Ch., New Phila., Pa., 1992. Mem.: APTA (assoc.), NATA (assoc.). Conservative. Roman Catholic. Avocations: running, aerobics, weightlifting, sailing. Home: 266 Louisa Ave Pottsville PA 17901

STANKEVITZ, DIANE LYNN, athletic trainer; b. West Covina, Calif., May 7, 1963; d. Richard Joseph Stankevitz and Geraldine Ann Vezzuso. BS, UCLA, 1996; MS, Calif. State U., Long Beach, 1998. Cert. athletic trainer Nat. Athletic Trainer's Assn., 2000, strength and conditioning specialist NSCA, 1999, MT L.A. County Dept. of Health, 1998. Athletic trainer East L.A. Coll., Monterey Park, Calif., 2000—, instr., 2000—, Rio Hondo Coll., Whittier, Calif., 2001—. Prodr.(stand-up comedienne): (comedy) The Comedy Train. Scholarship fundraiser The Comedy Train, West Covina, Calif., 2001. Recipient Faculty Appreciation award, Student Body of Rio Hondo Coll., 2004. Mem.: Nat. Strength and Conditioning Assn. (assoc.), Nat. Athletic Trainer's Assn. (assoc.), Phi Kappa Phi (life). Home: 1818 Sam Diego St West Covina CA 91790 Office: East Los Angeles College 1301 Avenida Cesar Chavez Monterey Park CA 91754 Office Phone: 323-265-8611. Office Fax: 323-265-8909. E-mail: distanky@hotmail.com.

STANKIEWICZ, MARY ANN, art educator; b. Keene, N.H., May 5, 1948; d. Napoleon Joseph and Annette (Vadeboncoeur) S.; m. David Mackinnon Ebitz, Jan. 1, 1983; children: Rebecca Aemilia, Cecilia Charlotte. BFA in Art Edn., Syracuse U., 1970, MFA in Art Edn., 1976; PhD in Art Edn., Ohio State U., 1979. Lic. art specialist, Mass., N.Y. Elem. art tchr. Pub. Schs. of Lenox, Mass., 1970-74; resident advisor Syracuse U., NY, 1974—75, student tchg. supr. NY, 1974—75, grad. tng. asst. NY, 1975—76; grad. adminstrv. asst. Ohio State U., Columbus, 1977—79; cooperating asst. prof., Coll. Edn. U. Maine, Orono, 1979-85, asst. prof. art edn., dept. art, 1979—85, cooperating assoc. prof., Coll. Edn., 1985—87, assoc. prof., art edn., dept. art; assoc. prof., dept. art Calif. State U., Long Beach, 1988-90; program officer Getty Ctr. for Edn. in Arts, Santa Monica, Calif., 1990-92; asst. v.p. acad. affairs Ringling Sch. Art and Design, Sarasota, Fla., 1992—94; assoc. prof., art edn., Sch. Visual Arts Pa. State U., University Park, Pa., 1999—2000, 2000—04, prof. art edn., 2004—. Cons. Getty Ctr. for Edn. in Arts, L.A., 1984—; ind. scholar, cons. 1994-; spkr., presenter, and invited lectr. in field; svcs. at Pa. State U. include: adviser, Pa. Art Edn. Assn. student chapter, 2000-01; judge, 15th Ann. Grad. Exhbn., 2000; chair, Art Edn. Program Grad. Recruitment and Admissions, 2001-02, Sch. Visual Arts Diversity Com., 2000-01, 2001-02; mem. adv. com., Palmer Mus. of Art Education, 2001-02; mem. Graduate Coun. Com. on Programs and Course, 2001-02, Grad. Coun. Subcommittee on Program Review and Evaluation, 2000-01, Review Com. for 2001 NEH Summer Stipends, 2000, Art Edn. Search Com., 2001; elected rep., Grad. Coun., Coll. Arts & Architecture, 2001-03; alternate mem., Behavioral Com., Institutional Review Bd., 2001-04. Co-editor: Framing the Past, 1990; editor, Art Education, Nat. Art Edn. Assn., 1995-98; author Roots of Art Education Practice, 2001; edited books and monographs; contbr. articles to profl. jours. and book chpts. Grantee NEH, 1986, Spencer Found., 1987; recipient Kenneth Marantz Disting. Alumni award Grad. Students Dept. Art Edn., Ohio State U., 1992; Grad. Fellowship, 1976-77, Grad. Student Alumni Rsch. award, 1978; summer rsch. fellowship, Oreg. Ctr. for Humanities, U. Oreg., 1995. Mem. Coun. Policy Studies in Art Edn., Nat. Art Edn. Assn. (pres. women's caucus 1984-85 (June King McFee award, 2003, historian/archivist 1980-88, Maine Art Educator of Yr. 1983, pres.-elect 2001-03, pres. 2003-, Maine Art Educator Yr., and Maine Art Edn. Assn., 1983), Philosophy of Edn. Soc., History of Edn. Soc., Phi Kappa Phi, Nat. Art Edn. Assn. (pres.-elect 2001-2003, pres. 2003-2005, past pres. 2005—2007), Nat. Art Edn. Found. (bd. trustees 2005—). Office: Pa State U Art Edn Program 207 Arts Cottage University Park PA 16802-2905 Office Phone: 814-863-7307. Office Fax: 814-863-8664. Business E-Mail: mas53@psu.edu.

STANLEY, CONNIE, medical/surgical nurse; b. Tonasket, Wash., Nov. 15, 1939; d. Albert Leroy and Lilly May (Davis) Johnson; m. Earl Leroy Stanley, Oct. 29, 1984; children: Loretta June, Janette Sue, Arthur Charles. BS, San Jose (Calif.) State U., 1973. RN, Wash.; cert. med.-surg. nurse. Nursing adminstrv. supr. coord. Walla Walla (Wash.) Gen. Hosp. Mem. Assn. Seventh Day Adventist Nurses, Sigma Theta Tau.

STANLEY, COURTENAY TURNER, secondary school educator; b. Charlottesville, Va., July 15, 1942; d. Courtenay Eldridge and Virginia Dare (McCarthy) Turner; m. Richard Arthur Stanley, Apr. 30, 1971. BA, Coll. of William and Mary, 1962; MEd, U. Va., 1964. Cert. tchr., Va. Math. tchr. Charlottesville Ednl. Found., Va., 1962-66, Albemarle County Schs., Albemarle HS, Charlottesville, 1966—2002; ret., 2002. Tchr., researcher innovative HS scheduling rsch. project James Madison U., Harrisonburg, Va., 1994-96; chair math. dept. Albemarle HS, Charlottesville, 1992-98. Asst. sec., bd. dirs. Laurelwood Condominium Assn., Wintergreen, Va., 1993—. Mem. NEA, DAR, Colonial Dames XVII Century, Nat. Soc. United State Daughters of 1812 (sec. 1995—), Va. Edn. Assn. (Uniserv stds. adv. com. 1978-85, chair 1982-84, profl. rights and responsibilities com. 1992-96), Albemarle Edn. Assn. (sec. 1988-89, treas. 1972-76, pres. 1976-77, v.p. 1994-95), Jamestowne Soc., Delta Kappa Gamma (pres. 1982-84), Phi Delta Kappa. Avocations: skiing, travel, auto rallying, bridge, genealogy. Home: 110 Oakhurst Cir Charlottesville VA 22903-3215

STANLEY, DEIRDRE, lawyer; b. Huntsville, Ala. BA, Duke U.; JD, Harvard U., 1989. With Cravath, Swaine & Moore, NYC and London, 1990—97; assoc. gen. counsel, head mergers and acquisitions group GTE Corp., 1997—99; dep. gen. counsel USA Networks, Inc. (now InterActive Corp.), 1999—2002; sr. v.p., gen. counsel The Thomson Corp., 2002—. Office: The Thomson Corp Toronto-Dominion Bank Tower 66 Wellington St W Toronto Canada M5K 1A1*

STANLEY, DENISE YVONNE, art educator; b. Modesto, Calif., Sept. 20, 1973; d. Henry Maria and Janice Rae Leer. BA, Calif. State U., Sacramento, 1995; MA in Edn., So. Oreg. U., 1999. Cert. tchr. Tchr. computer graphics Encina H.S., Sacramento, 1999—2000; tchr. art Medford Sch. Dist., Oreg., 2000—. Pvt. tchr. music, Rogue Valley, Oreg., 1991—, Sacramento, 1991—; spkr. in field; dir. Entomology Corp., Ashland, Oreg., 1998; guest artist Brisco Elem. Sch., Ashland, 1999, Talent Mid. Sch., Oreg., 1999, Sam's Valley Elem. Sch., Oreg., 2001; mentor sr. projects Phoenix H.S., 1999; participant confs. in field; art com. leader Oktoberfest, Phoenix, 1998. Mem. visual arts judging panel Best of the Best Rogue Valley Art Show, 1999. Rep. Intel Teach to Future Program, Medford, 2001; active Non-Crisis Prevention Workshop, Medford, 2000, Schneider Mus. Children Workshops, 1999. Recipient Tchr. Edn. award, Sigma Fi, 1999, Raymond and Joyce Witt Fellowship Artist award, 1995, Peyser prize in painting, 1995; grantee team tchg. project in culinary arts, Wal Mart, 2001; scholar Frank Mancini scholar for music edn., Mancini Family, 1995, Modesto Tchrs. scholar, Outdoor Edn. scholar, Fulbright Found., 2002. Mem.: Medford Edn. Assn., Oreg. Edn. Assn., Oreg. Music Tchrs. Assn., Oreg. Arts Edn. Assn., Music Tchrs. Nat. Assn., Nat. Arts Edn. Assn. Avocations: piano, singing, cooking, hiking, entomology. Home: 1049 N Dakota Ave Modesto CA 95358-9206 Address: 2 10 Ocean Rd Manly NSW 295 Australia Personal E-mail: dylart@yahoo.com. Business E-Mail: studio.stanley@yahoo.com.

STANLEY, ELLEN MAY, historian, consultant; b. Dighton, Kans., Feb. 3, 1921; d. Delmar Orange and Lena May (Bobb) Durr; m. Max Neal Stanley, Nov. 5, 1939; children: Ann Y. Stanley Epps, Janet M. Stanley Horsky, Gail L. Stanley Peck, Kenneth D., Neal M., Mary E. Stanley McEniry. BA in English and Journalism, Ft. Hays State U., Kans., 1972, MA in History, 1984. Pvt. practice local/state historian, cons., writer local history, Dighton, 1973—; cons. genealogy, 1980—. Vice chmn. State Preservation Bd. Rev., Kans., 1980-87; area rep. Kans. State Mus. Assn., 1978-84. Author: Early Lane County History: 12,000 B.C.--A.D. 1884, 1993 (Cert. of Commendation, Am. Assn. for State and Local History, 1994), Cowboy Josh: Adventures of a Real Cowboy, 1996, Early Lane County Development, 1993, Golden Age, Great Depression and Dust Bowl, 2001 (Ferguson Kans. History Book award Kans. Author Club, 2002); contbr. articles to profl. jours. Precinct woman com. Alamota Township, Kans., 1962-86; mem. Dem. State Affirmative Action Com., 1975. Recipient hon. mention for photography Ann. Christian Arts Festival, 1974, Artist of Month award Dane G. Hansen Mus., 1975. Mem. Kans. State Hist. Soc. (pres. 1990-91), Lane County Hist. Soc. (sec. 1970-78). Methodist. Avocations: fossil hunting, walking, photography, antiques. Home: 100 N 4th Dighton KS 67839 Office: 110 E Pearl St Dighton KS 67839

STANLEY, GWEN G., elementary school educator; b. Abbington, Pa., Feb. 11, 1954; d. Richard A. and Doris K. Guba; m. Ray L. Stanley, June 6, 1976; children: R. L., Sarah Rae. BA, Maryville Coll., 1977; MA in Edn., Ga. State U., 2002, D of Edn., 2003. Nat. Bd. Cert. Tchr. US, 2001, cert. asst. tchr. 2005. Libr. educator Whittier County Schs., Calif., 1976—79; tchr. Montessori Sch. of Ligonier, Ligonier, Pa., 1981—83, Ligonier Bd. of Edn., 1985—88, Perston Ridge Monetssori Sch., Alpharetta, Ga., 1990—92, Forsyth County Bd. of Edn., Cumming, Ga., 1992—, Ga. State U., Atlanta, 2004—. Presentor Internat. Reading Assn., Reno, 2003—04; standards and benchmarks contbr. Forsyth County Schs., Ga., 2000—01. Contbr. seminar on literacy. Recipient Tchr. of Yr., 2002. Office: Forsyth County Schs 1670 James Burgess Rd Suwanee GA 30024 Home: 434 Winfield Blf Dawsonville GA 30534-8634 Office Phone: 770-888-7511. Personal E-mail: gstanley@forsyth.k12.ga.us.

STANLEY, HEIDI, bank executive; Grad., Wash. State U., 1979. With IBM, San Francisco, Tucson; joined Sterling Savings Bank, Spokane, Wash., 1985, exec. v.p. Corp. Adminstrn., vice chair, COO, 2003—. Vice chmn. Am.'s Cmty. Banker's Membership Com.; mem. Govt. Affairs Steering Com.; bd. govs. WSU Found., chmn. planning com. Mem.: Spokane C. of C. (bd. mem.). Office: Sterling Savings Bank 111 N Wall St Spokane WA 99201

STANLEY, LILA GAIL, political science professor, art appraiser; b. Marietta, Ga., Mar. 23, 1941; d. James Miller and Louise (Land) S. AB cum laude, Randolph-Macon Woman's Coll., 1963; MA in Polit. Sci., Emory U., 1964; cert. appraisal studies decorative arts, George Washington U., 1997. Polit. sci. instr. U. West Ga., Carrollton, 1964-66; Am. history tcrh. Foxcroft Sch., Middleburg, Va., 1966-67; staff asst. Rep. John J. Flynt U.S. Ho. Reps., Washington, 1967-74; legis. asst. Sen. Robert C. Byrd U.S. Senate, Washington, 1974-80; asst. to arch. Arch. of the Capitol, Washington, 1980-97; appraiser Gail Stanley Appraisers, Washington, 1997—. Participation Winter Inst., Winterthur (Del.) Mus., 2000. Vol. worker various nat. polit. campaigns Dem. Orgn., Washington, 1968-80; bd. dirs., 1st v.p., treas. Watergate East Inc., Washington, 1986-96; vol. rsch. asst. Nat. Mus. Am. History, Smithsonian Instn., Washington, 1999—; docent, curatorial vol. Tudor Pl., Washington, 1999—. Mem. DAR, Am. Soc. Appraisers, Appraisers Assn. Am., Washington Decorative Arts Forum, Zeta Tau Alpha. Democrat. Methodist. Home and Office: Ste 814 19375 Cypress Ridge Terr Lansdowne VA 20176

STANLEY, MARGARET KING, performing arts association administrator; b. San Antonio, Dec. 11, 1929; d. Creston Alexander and Margaret (Haymore) King; children: Torrey Margaret, Jean Cullen. Student, Mary Baldwin Coll., 1948-50; BA, U. Tex., Austin, 1952; MA, U. Incarnate Word, 1959. Cert. elem. tchr. Tex. Elem. tchr. San Antonio Ind. Sch. Dist., 1953-54, 55-56, Arlington County Schs., Va., 1954-55, Ft. Sam Houston Schs., San Antonio, 1956—58; art and art history tchr. St. Pius X Sch., San Antonio, 1959-60; originator, founding chairwoman Student Music Fair, San Antonio, 1963; English tchr. Trinity U., 1963-65; designer-mfr., owner CrisStan Clothes, Inc., San Antonio, 1967-73; founder, exec. dir. San Antonio Performing Arts Assn., 1976-92; founding chmn. Joffrey Workshop, San Antonio, 1979; host On Stage with Margaret Stanley Sta. KTRU-FM, San Antonio, 1983-98. Orginator (with the Joffrey Ballet) Jamboree, 1984. Mem. Met. Opera Nat. Coun., 1969—80; founder Arts Coun. San Antonio, 1962, v.p., 1975; pres. San Antonio Symphony League, 1971—74; v.p., founder San Antonio Opera Guild, 1974—, pres., 2002—05; bd. govs. Artists Alliance San Antonio, 1982; founder San Antonio Early Music Festival, 1990—92; artistic advisor, dir. presentation, dir. devel. San Antonio Symphony, 1992—94; founding organizer Musica San Antonio, 1997—98; v.p. Instnl. Devel. Carver Cultural Ctr., 1998—2000; adv. bd. Hertzberg Circus Collection, San Antonio Dance Umbrella, Houston Early Music, Morgan-Scott Ballet; pres. Univ. Roundtable, 1995—97. Named to Women's Hall of Fame, San Antonio, 1984, Disting. Alumnae, St. Mary's Hall, 1990; recipient Outstanding Tchr. award, Arlington County Sch. Dist., 1954, Emily Smith award for outstanding alumni, Mary Baldwin Coll., 1973, Today's Woman award, San Antonio Light Newspaper, 1980, Woman of the Yr. in Arts award, San Antonio Express News, 1983, Erasmus medal, Dutch Consulate, 1992, Mary Baldwin Sesquicentennial medallion, 1992, Opera Guild Founder's award, 2000, Vol. award, Opera Vols. Internat., 2005, Music Support award, Cactus Pear Festival, 2006; Tchg. fellow, Trinity U., San Antonio, 1964—66. Mem.: S.W. Performing Arts Presenters (chmn. 1988—92), Battle Flowers Assn., Jr. League San Antonio (Vol. Extraodinaire 2001), Women in Comm. (Headliner award 1982), Assn. Performing Arts Presenters (award for commn.of Jamboree 1984), Internat. Soc. for Performing Arts (hon.; regional rep. 1982—85, bd. dirs. 1991—97). Avocations: travel, reading, cooking, music, dance.

STANLEY, MARIANNE, professional athletics coach; 1 child, Michelle. BS in Sociology, Immaculata Coll., 1976. Asst. coach women's basketball Old Dominion U., Norfolk, Va., 1976—77, head coach, 1977—87; coach women's basketball U. Pa., 1987—89, U. So. Calif., 1989—93, Stanford U., Calif., 1995—96, U. Calif., Berkeley, 1996—2000; asst. L.A. Sparks, 2000—01; asst. coach Washington Mystics, Washington, 2001—02, head coach, 2002—. Mem. coaching staff US Nat. Team, 1981—93. Named Conf. Coach of the Yr., Nat. Coach of the Yr.; named to Women's Basketball Hall of Fame, 2002. Office: Washington Mystics MCI Ctr 601 F St NW Washington DC 20004

STANLEY, MARLYSE REED, horse breeder; b. Fairmont, Minn., Sept. 19, 1934; d. Glenn Orson and Lura Mabel (Ross) Reed; m. James Arthur Stapleton, 1956 (div. 1976); 1 child, Elisabeth Katharene; m. John David Stanley, Oct. 22, 1982. BA, U. Minn., 1957. Registered breeder Arabian horses in Spain, 1976-94. Chmn. bd. dirs. Sitting Rock Spanish Arabians, Inc., Greensboro, N.C., 1978-81, pres. Hollister, Calif., 1981-91, Stanley Ranch, Yerington, Nev., 1991—. Bd. dirs. Glenn Reed Tire Co., Fairmont, Minn. Author Arabian hunter/jumper rules Am. Horse Shows Assn.; contbr. articles to horse jours. Named Palomino Queen of Minn., 1951, Miss Fairmont, 1954, Miss Minn., 1955. Mem.: AAUW, World Arabian Horse Assn., Assn. Española de Criadores de Caballos Arabes (Spain), Am. Paint Horse Assn. (nat. bd. dirs. 1967—70), Minn. Arabian Assn. (bd. dirs. 1972—75), Internat. Arabian Assn. (Minn. and Wis. 1973—76, nat. chmn. hunter-jumper com. 1976—81, chair IAHA sport horse rules com. 1998—2001, bd. dirs. region 10), Arabian Horse Registry Am., U.S. Nat. Arabian Sport Horse Finals--Show Commn., Alpha Xi Delta. Republican. Episcopalian. Avocations: fox hunting, fishing, breeding and importing Arabian horses. Office Phone: 775-849-8655. E-mail: stanleyranch@charter.net.

STANLEY, MARTHA BARBEE, music educator; b. Panama Canal Zone, 1950; d. Henry Quinton and Kathleen Barbee; m. Ray H Stanley. MusB in Edn., Fla. State U., 1971, MusM in Edn., 1978. Cert. Orff-Schulwerk III Am. Orff-Schulwerk Assn., 1985, tchr. 2002. Elem. music tchr. Leon Dist. Schs., Tallahassee, 1972—, tchr. of gifted students, 1989—99. Ednl. cons., clinician Tallahassee Symphony Orch., 1999—; co-author of district's first music scope and sequence Leon County Schs., Tallahassee, 1981; clinician Very Spl. Arts Festival, Tallahassee, 1983—85; chair, instrnl. and profl. devel. Leon Classroom Teachers Assn., Tallahassee, 1981—83; facilitator, sch. improvement team Hartsfield Elem. Sch., Tallahassee, 1983—85; facilitating coun., tchr. edn. ctr. Leon Dist. Schs., Tallahassee, 1978—83; clinician Tallahassee Area Orff Chpt., 2000—01, pres., 1986—87, v.p., 1995—2001; elem. rep. to tchr. competency com. Fla. Music Educators Assn., Tallahassee; pres. Tallahassee Area Orff Chpt., Tallahassee, 2001—02; clinician, presenter Fla. Elem. Music Educators Assn., Tampa, Fla., 2002—. Author (co-author with Margaret Van Every): (jazz curriculum) Open Ears Curriculum; creator and webmaster (ednl. website) Tallahassee Symphony Orch. Ednl. Site; contbr. articles to profl. jours. Musician, asst. music dir., accompanist Tallahassee Little Theater; dir. of reps. and pubs./website author VOICES, Inc., Tallahassee, 2001—03. Named Music Tchr. of Yr., Tallahassee Symphony Orch., 2004; grantee Tech. and Classroom grantee, Leon County Schools, Leon Schools Found., 1986, 1992, 1997, 2000, 2002. Mem.: Fla. Music Educators Assn., Am. Fedn. Tchrs., Am. Orff-Shulwerk Assn., Music Educators Nat. Conf. Avocations: reading, mandolin.

STANLEY, MARY ELIZABETH, judge; AB, Mt. Holyoke Coll., 1970; JD, Univ. of Va., 1973. Bar: W.Va., U.S. Dist. Ct. (so. dist.) W.Va., U.S. Ct. Appeals (4th cir.). Atty. Columbia Gas Transmission Corp., 1973-76; law clk. to Judge Dennis R. Knapp, 1976-77; asst. U.S. atty. Charleston, W. Va., 1977-92; magistrate judge U.S. Dist. Ct. (so. dist.) W. Va., Bluefield, W. Va., 1992-01, Charleston, W. Va., 2001—. Office: Robert C Byrd US Courthouse Rm 5408 300 Virginia St E Charleston WV 25301

STANLEY, SHERRY A., lawyer; b. Buffalo, Oct. 17, 1955; d. Arthur A. and Irene S. Stanley. BA, U. West Fla., 1975; JD, U. Fla., 1978. Bar: Fla. 1978. Assoc. Mahoney, Hadlow & Adams, Miami, Fla., 1978-80; ptnr. Steel, Hector & Davis, Miami, 1980-87, Weil, Gotshal & Manges, Miami, 1987-92; sr. counsel Barnett Banks, Inc., Miami, 1992-94; ptnr. Coll, Davidson, Carter, Smith, Salter & Barkett, P.A./Shook, Hardy Bacon, Miami, Fla., 1994—2000; exec. v.p., gen. counsel Greenstreet Ptnrs., 2001—; dir. Semeo Energy, Inc., 2004—05. Dir. SEMCO Energy, Inc., 2004—05. Mem.: Fla. Bar, Order of Coif, Phi Theta Kappa. Republican. Roman Catholic. Office: 2601 S Bayshore Dr Ste 800 Miami FL 33133 Office Phone: 305-858-8119. Business E-Mail: sas@greenstreetpartners.com.

STANLEY, SHIRLEY DAVIS, artist; b. Mt. Vernon, NY, Dec. 5, 1929; d. Walter Thompson and Elsie Viola (Lumpp) Davis; m. Charles B. Coble Jr., June 11, 1951 (div. 1968); children: Jennifer Susan Farmer, Charles B. Coble III; m. Marvin M. Stanley, Dec. 18, 1983 (dec.). BA in Home Econs. and Gen. Sci., Greensboro Coll., 1951; grad., Real Estate Inst., 1962. Tchr. Dryher H.S., Columbia, SC, 1951-52, Haw River (N.C.) Sch., 1954-56, Alexander Wilson Sch., Graham, NC, 1957-58; guest essayist for news Mebane (N.C.) Enterprise, 1955-56; pres. Shirley, Inc., Burlington, NC, 1962—2004. One woman show Art Gallery Originals, Winston-Salem, 1976, Olive Garden Gallery, 21st Century Gallery, Williamsburg, Va., galleries in Fla., N.C. Bd. dirs. Girl Scouts Am. Kings Daus., Burlington, 1961, Williamsburg Libr. Found., 1997—; life mem. Rep. Inner Cir., Washington, 1990—; active Salvation Army; com. mem. York County Rep. Party, 1995; vol. disaster & blood banks ARC, 1990—; founding mem. Am. Air Force Mus.; bd. dirs. William Burg Libr. Found., 1997—; pres. Burlington Coun. Garden Clubs, 1955-56. Recipient Rep. Medal of Freedom, 1994, 2002, 2003. Mem. AAUW, Am. Watercolor Soc. (assoc.), Va. Watercolor Soc., Sierra Club, Williamsburg Bibliophiles, Raleigh Tavern Soc. Colonial Williamsburg, Christopher Wren Soc., Williamsburg C. of C., Williamsburg Photography Soc., Mil. Officers Assn. (life), Army-Navy Country Club. Episcopalian. Avocations: travel, gardening, writing, dance, reading. Home: 103 Little John Rd Williamsburg VA 23185-4907 also: 1953 Shirley Dr Burlington NC 27215-4831

STANNY, CLAUDIA J., psychology professor; b. Detroit, Aug. 9, 1950; d. Joseph H. and Virginia R. Hoffman; m. Robert R. Stanny, Sept. 1, 1970; 1 child, Margaret E. BA, Fla. State U., 1976, MS, 1978, PhD, 1981. Asst. prof. Coe Coll., Cedar Rapids, Iowa, 1981—82; lectr., hon. fellow U. Wis., Madison, 1982—84; faculty assoc., adj. faculty U. West Fla., Pensacola, 1985—93, asst. prof. psychology, 1993—2003, assoc. prof., 2003—, fellow for assessment Ctr. for Univ. Tchg., Learning and Assessment, 2005—06; interim dir. Ctr. U. Tchg., Learning and Assessment. Contbr. articles to profl. jours. Mem.: APA, Soc. Applied Rsch. in Memory and Cognition, Psychonomic Soc. (assoc.), Phi Kappa Phi. Office: U W Fla 11000 University Pky Pensacola FL 32514 Office Phone: 850-857-6355. E-mail: cstanny@uwf.edu.

STANO, SISTER DIANA, academic administrator; AB, Ursuline Coll.; PhD, Ohio State U. Prof. edn. Ursuline Coll., Pepper Pike, Ohio, chair edn. dept., dir. grad. program in non-pub. sch. adminstrn., dir. master's degree program, dean of grad. studies, dir. of instl. rsch., pres., 1996—. Bd. trustees Coll. of New Rochelle; sec. bd. trustees Ohio Found. Ind. Coll.; cons. in field. Recipient YWCA Women of Profl. Excellence award, No. Ohio Live Rainmaker in Edn. award. Mem.: In Counsel With Women, Exec. Women's Leadership Forum. Office: Ursuline Coll 2550 Lander Rd Pepper Pike OH 44124-4398

STANOVSKY, ELAINE J.W., minister, church organization administrator; b. Vancouver, Wash., Oct. 12, 1953; d. Robert Byron and Edith Vernie Woodworth; m. Clinton Sebastian Stanovsky, June 11, 1977; children: Walker, Micah, C. Axel. BA, U. Puget Sound, Tacoma, 1976; MDiv, Harvard U., 1981. Ordained elder Pacific N.W. Conf. United Meth. Ch., 1983. Pastor Kennydale United Meth. Ch., Renton, Wash., 1981-88, Crown Hill United Meth. Ch., Seattle, 1988-90; pres., dir. Ch. Coun. of Greater Seattle, 1990-95; dist. supt. Puget Sound Dist. United Meth. Ch., Everett, Wash., 1995—2002; dir. coun. min. Pacific N.W. Conf., United Meth. Ch., 2002—05; dist. supt. Seattle Tacoma Dist., United Meth. Ch., 2005—. Co-author: Generation to Generation: Church Council of Greater Seattle, 1996. Trustee U. Puget Sound, 1995—; del. World Coun. of Chs., Canberra, Australia, 1991, Gen. Conf. United Meth. Ch., Portland, Oreg. and Denver, 1976, 96, Cleve., 2000, 2004, Sister Ch. Program, Seattle and St. Petersburg, Russia, 1991; del. or alt. Consultation on Ch. Union, N.J., 1976-88; co-chair Seattle Holocaust Conf., 1982; mem. Mayor's Partnership for Homeless, Seattle, 1992. Avocations: gardening, hiking, reading. Office: Ste 300 2112 3d Ave Seattle WA 98121

STANSBERRY, JOETTA LEE, special education educator; b. Boone, NC, Oct. 2, 1955; d. Joseph Walter McConnell and Lillie Florence Lyons; children: Delaina Ann, Julie Marie. BS in Early Childhood Devel., East Tenn. State U., 1997, M in Early Childhood Spl. Edn., 2006. Nurse's aide Mt. Care Facilities, Boone, NC, 1989—96; tchr. Lynhill Child Devel. Ctr., Boone, 1996—2003; tchr.-dir. Merryland Acad., Boone, 2000—02; caregiver in clients home Elizabethton, Tenn., 2003—05; residential direct support profl. Dawn of Hope, Johnson City, Tenn., 2005; special edn. tchr. Johnson County Sch. Sys. Tenn., Tenn., 2006—. Mem.: Student Tchr. Edn. Assn., Council for Exceptional Children. Avocation: hiking. Home: 488 Tester Rd Butler TN 37640 Personal E-mail: msjols@earthlink.net.

STANSFIELD, CLAIRE, apparel designer; b. London, Aug. 27, 1964; Co-founder C&C California, 2003—. Actor: (films) The Doors, 1991, Nervous Ticks, 1992, Best of the Best II, 1993, The Swordsman, 1993, The Favor, 1994, Drop Zone, 1994, Gladiator Cop, 1994, Sensation, 1995, Red Shoe Diaries 5: Weekend Pass, 1995, The Outpost, 1995, Darkdrive, 1996, Steel, 1997, Sweepers, 1999; (TV series) Xena The Warrior Princess, Frasier, Twin Peaks. Office: c/o Lela Tillem #705 127 E 9th St Los Angeles CA 90015

STANSON, KAY V., elementary school educator, consultant; b. Laurel, Nebr., Aug. 21, 1952; d. Dee W. and Edna C. Rasmussen; 1 child, Shawn McDonald. BA, Midland Coll., Fremont, Nebr., 1973; MEd, Tex. State U., San Marcos, Tex., 1987, Our Lady of Lake U., San Antonio, Tex., 2005. Tchr. Rose Garden Elem., Universal City, Tex., 1979—84, Schertz Elem., Schertz, Tex., 1984—85, Dobie Mid. Sch., Schertz, 1985, Spring Meadow's Elem., Converse, Tex., 1985—88, Miller's Point Elem., Converse, 1988—96, Woodlake Hills Mid. Sch., San Antonio, 1996—. Mem. master sci. tchr. com. Tex. Edn. Agy., Austin, Tex., 2005—; master tchr. for tchrs. as mentors Our Lady of Lake U., 2001—, globe regional trainer, 2001—. Nominee Excellence in Math and Sci. Presdl. award, Tex. Edn. Agy., U.S. Dept. Edn., 2004; grantee 4 different Sci. Grants, Judson Edn. Found., 2002-2005. Mem.: ASCD, Tex. Mariene Edn. Assn., Nat. Sci. Educators Leadership Assn., Sci. Tchrs. Assn. Tex., Nat. Sci. Tchrs. Assn. Home: 7514 Old Spanish Trail San Antonio TX 78233 Office: Woodlake Hills Middle School 6625 Woodlake Parkway San Antonio TX 78244 Office Phone: 210-661-1110. Personal E-mail: ibteacher@hotmail.com. Business E-Mail: kstanson@judson.k12.tx.us.

STANTON, AMY, marketing executive; BA; M in Mktg., U. Pa. Account dir. Bartle Bogle Hegarty, NYC; dir. mktg. & comm. NYC2012; chief mktg. officer, sr. v.p. Martha Stewart Living Omnimedia, 2005—. Office: Martha Steward Living Omnimedia 11 W 42nd St New York NY 10036 Office Phone: 212-827-8000.*

STANTON, DOROTHY MARIE, special education educator, tax specialist; b. Beacon, NY, May 14, 1951; d. Benjamin Earl and Edna Mae Stanton. AAS, Dutchess C.C., Poughkeepsie, NY, 1972; BA, Lenior Rhyne Coll., Hickory, NY, 1974; MS, SUNY, New Paltz, 1991. Cert. in spl. edn. NY. Acct. Roy C. Knapp & Sons, Inc, Beacon, 1974—78; bus. tchr. Beacon City Sch. Dist., 1982—87; spl. ed tchr. Nausau County Schs., Fernindina Beach, Fla., 1987—88; spl. edn. tchr. Monticello (NY) Ctrl. Sch. Dist., 1988—; tax advisor H & R Block, Beacon, 1998—. Chmn. Christian edn. First Presbyn. Ch., Beacon, 1988—2006, handbell choir dir., 2002—; multi-county camp bd. Presbyn. Camp and Conf. Ctr., Holmes, NY, 1990—95; dist. dep. grand matron Order of Ea. Star, State of NY, Beacon, 2001—02. Mem.: Am. Legion Aux. (50 yr. mem. 2005). Conservative. Presbyterian. Avocations: travel, swimming. Home: 153 N Elm St Beacon NY 12508 Office: Monticello Mid Sch 40 Breaky Ave Monticello NY 12701 Office Phone: 845-796-3058.

STANTON, PAMELA FREEMAN, interior designer, writer; b. Jacksonville, Tex., July 18, 1941; d. William Thomas and Ruth Ethel (Branton) Freeman; m. Karl F. Edmonds, Jr., Jan. 28, 1961 (div. 1966); m. Charles Calvin Stanton, Sept. 1, 1973; 1 child, Julie Anne. AA in Bus., Kilgore Coll., 1961. Design cons., Denver, Boston and Salem, Oreg., 1963-69; exec. sec. Alexander: Alexander of Tex. Inc., Dallas, 1967-69; interior designer Milmac Furniture, Dallas, 1969-73, Homestead House, Denver, 1973-76; case aide counselor Eliot Cmty. Mental Health Ctr., Concord, Mass., 1980-82; pres., owner Stancom Designs, Virginia Beach, Va., 1990-2000; interior designer Willis Furniture Co., 2000—. Author: I Am That I Am, 1994 (Best Book of Yr. N.Am. Bookdealers Exch., 1995). Recipient Cert. of Appreciation for vol. work Emerson Hosp., Concord, 1981; named Internat. Writer of Yr., 2003. Republican. Avocations: collecting art, travel, gardening, theatre-plays, entertaining. Home and Office: 4401 Leatherwood Dr Virginia Beach VA 23462-5704 Office Phone: 757-499-3432.

STANTON, SYLVIA DOUCET, artist, gallery owner; b. New Orleans, Sept. 21, 1935; d. Clifton Leo Sr. and Maria Delbert (Alfonso Swiber) Doucet; m. Robert Elmer Stanton, Jan. 3, 1953; children: Robert, Sylvia, Barbara, Richard, Laura, Cheri. Grad. high sch., New Orleans, 1952. Real estate agt. Century 21, Slidell, La., 1982-88; ptnr. Doucet's Jewelry, Slidell, 1969-82; owner Plantation Antiques, Slidell, 1974-88, Magnolia Plantation, Slidell, 1988-97, Doucet-Stanton Ltd., Slidell, 1988-97, Gallery at Milbrook, Picayune, Miss., 2001—05; co-owner Lott Stanton Gallery, Jackson, Miss., 2006—. Appraiser jewelry, antiques, real estate, 1969—; artist, painter, 1950—. Exhibited in group shows at Montserrat Gallery, N.Y.C., Abita Gallery, Abita Springs, La., The Gallery at Millbrook, Picayune, Miss., Serenity Gallery, Bay St. Louis, Miss., Sterling Art Gallery, New Orleans, Represented in permanent collections Montserrat Salon, NY. Founder Le cotillion, Slidell, 1975; founding chmn. Pres. Coun. of Le Cotillion, 1987. Recieved title of nobility Countess De Miron Delbert, Greece, 1988. Mem.: Allied Artists of Am., New Orleans Art Assn., Inner Wheel (dist chmn. 6840 1990—91, founding pres. Slidell 1989), World Trade Ctr., Albuquerque Art League, Bayou Liberty Garden Club (sec. 1988—), Picayune Garden Club, Ozone Camellia Club. Republican. Roman Catholic. Avocations: art, antiques, gardening, interior decorating. Home: 615 E Lakeshore Dr Carriere MS 39426 Office: Lott Stanton Gallery 1800 N State St Jackson MS 39202 Personal E-mail: stanfam2@bellsouth.net. Business E-Mail: lottstantongallery@homestead.com.

STANTON, VIVIAN BRENNAN (MRS. ERNEST STANTON), retired guidance counselor; b. Waterbury, Conn.; d. Francis P. and Josephine (Ryan) Brennan; B.A., Albertus Magnus Coll.; M.S., So. Conn. State Coll., 1962, 6th yr. degree, 1965; postgrad. Columbia U.; m. Ernest Stanton, May 31, 1947; children— Pamela L., Bonita F., Kim Ernest. Tchr. English, history, govt. Milford (Conn.) High Sch., 1940-48; tchr. English, history, fgn. Born Night

Sch., New Haven, 1948-54, Simon Lake Sch., Milford, 1960-62; guidance counselor, psychol. examiner Jonathan Law High Sch., Milford, 1962-73, Nat. Honor Soc. adv., 1966-73, mem. Curriculum Councils, Graduation Requirement Council, Gifted Child Com., others, 1940-48, 60-73; guidance dir. Foran High Sch., Milford, 1973-79, career center coordinator, 1976-79, ret., 1979. Active various community drives; mem. exec. bd. Ridge Rd PTA, 1956-59; mem. Parent-Tchr. council Hopkins Grammer Sch., New Haven; mem. Human Relations Council, North Haven, 1967-69; vol., patient rep. surg. waiting rm. Fawcett Meml. Hosp., P.C., Sun City Ctr. Emergency Squad, Good Samaritans. Mem. Nat. Assn. Secondary Schs. and Colls. (evaluation com.; chmn. testing com.), AAUW, LWV, Conn. Personnel and Guidance Assn., Conn. Sch. Counselors Assn., Conn. Assn. Sch. Psychol. Personnel, Conn., Milford (pres. 1945-47) edn. assns. Clubs: Univ., Charlotte Harbor Yacht, Sun City Ctr. Golf and Racquet. Home: 1716 Wroxton Ct Houston TX 77005-1717

STAPLES, HEIDI L, poet, writer; b. Dade County, Fla., Dec. 12, 1971; d. Jeaniene Eddye Cole and Robert Wesley Kitchen; m. John V. Staples, May 16, 2004. PhD in English Lit. and Creative Writing, U. Ga., 2003. Edn. assoc. Planned Parenthood, Syracuse, 1994—95; writing instr. Syracuse U., 1996—98; tefl instr. The Lang. Ho., Prague, Czech Republic, 1998—99; asst. to the editors Ga. Rev., Athens, 2002—03; writing instr. U. Ga., 2002—03; part-time faculty Syracuse U., NY, 2003—. Co-founder and co-editor Parakeet, Syracuse, NY, 2003—05; asst. editor Verse, Athens, Ga., 2001—03; asst. coord. Helen Lanier Speaker's Series, Chaired Series of the UGA English Dept., Athens, Ga., 2001—03; asst. editor Salt Hill, Syracuse, 1997—98, poetry editor, 1995—97. Founder and moderator Grad. Student Reading Series, Athens, Ga., 2002—03; judge Ga. Scholastic Assn., Athens, Ga., 2001; mentor Syracuse Mentor and Youth in Learning Program, 1995—98; hotline counselor Athens Rape Crisis Line, Ga., 1992—93. Scholar Grad. Sch. scholarship, Syracuse U., 1995—98; Grad. assistantship, U. of Ga., 2002—03, Tchg. assistantship, 2000—02, Summer Rsch. grant, Syracuse U., 1996, fellowship, 1995—96. Mem.: PEN, Assoc. Writing Programs. D-Liberal. Avocations: baking, piano, canoeing. Home: 115 Roosevelt Avenuse Syracuse NY 13210 Office: Syracuse Univ 240 Hbc Syracuse NY 13210 Office Phone: 315-443-9314. Personal E-mail: hlkitche@syr.edu.

STAPLES, KAREN ELEANOR, special education educator; b. Lady Grey, South Africa, Sept. 25, 1943; arrived in US, 1965; d. Alpheus Marais and Sarah Mary (Cooks) Cloete; m. Thomas George Staples, July 25, 1965; children: Thomas, Gaelen, Kristopher. Student, Helderberg Coll., Somerset West, South Africa, 1963; BA, Mid. East Coll., Beirut, 1974; MA, Mich. State U., Lansing, 1987; EdS, La Sierra U., Riverside, Calif., 1993. Spl. edn. tchg. credential Calif., clear tchg. credential Calif. Tchr. Trans Africa Dvisn. SDA, Harare, Zimbabwe, 1964; bookkeeper, acct. Pacific Union Coll., Angwin, Calif., 1965—67, San Francisco, 1967—68; tchr. Beirut Overseas Sch., 1974—75, 1978—83; tchr., prin. Addis Overseas Sch., Addis Ababa, Ethiopia, 1975—78; acct. Far Ea. Dvisn. SDA, Singapore, 1983; tchr. Far Ea. Elem. Sch., Singapore, 1984—91, SE Asia UN Coll., Singapore, 1991—92, Alvord Unified Sch. Dist., Riverside, 1994—. Foster parent Riverside County Social Svcs., 1995—. Named Tchr. of Yr., Alvord Unified Sch. Dist., Riverside County, Parent of Yr., Caregivers Assn. of Calif. Mem.: Learning Disabilities Assn., Internat. Reading Assn., Inland Empire Foster Parent Assn., Internat. Wildlife. Seventh Day Adventist. Avocations: bicycling, sailing, sewing, writing, decorating. Home: 11240 Yearling St Riverside CA 92503 Office: Alvord Unified Sch Dist 10436 Keller Ave Riverside CA 92505 Office Phone: 951-351-9261. E-mail: kestaples@hotmail.com.

STAPLES, LYNNE LIVINGSTON MILLS, retired psychologist, educator, consultant; b. Detroit, Sept. 18, 1934; d. Robert Livingston Mills Staples and Lyda Charlotte (Diehr) Staples; m. Lee Edward Burmeister, July 16, 1955 (div. 1982); children: Benjamin Lee, Lynne Ann. BS, Ctrl. Mich. U., 1957; MA, U. Mich., 1965; student, Marygrove Coll., Cen. Mich. U., 1971-74. Ltd. lic. psychologist, sch. psychologist; cert. social worker, elem. permanent cons. and tchr. for mentally handicapped. First grade tchr. Shepherd (Mich) Schs., 1957-59; tchr. Kingston (Mich.) Schs., 1959-65; tchr. educationally handicapped Rialto (Calif.) Unified Sch. Dist., 1965-66; tchr., cons. Tuscola Int. Sch. Dist., Caro, Mich., 1966-71; sch. psychologist Huron Int. Sch. Dist., Bad Axe, Mich., 1971-74, Tuscola Int. Sch. Dist., Caro, 1974-89; instr. Delta Coll., University Center, Mich., 1976-88; tchr. spl. day classes Victorville (Calif.) High Sch., 1989; sch. psychologist Bedford (Ind.) Schs., 1990-91; clin. psychologist ACT team and outpatient therapy Sanilac County Mental Health Svcs., Sandusky, Mich., 1991-99; ret., 1999. Cons. sch. psychologist Marlette (Mich.) Schs., 1982-86, Bartholomew Pub. Schs., Columbus, Ind., 1989, Johnson County Schs., Franklin, Ind., 1990; clin. psychologist Thumb Family Counseling, Caro, 1985-88; personnel com. Team One Credit Union, 1993; instr. St. Clair C.C., 1993; court cons. Samlac County, 1991-99; exec. bd. sec. Team One Credit Union, 2004, bd. dirs.; presenter in field. Del. NEA-Mich. Edn. Assn. Rep. Assemblies, 1970—89; pres., auction chmn. Altrusa Club, Marlette, 1982—88; style show chmn. Marlette Band Boosters, 1983; exec. bd. Lawrence County Tchrs. Assn., Bedford, 1991; active Sanilac Symphonic Band, 1993—2000, Vassar City Band, 1998—2006, Meth. Choir, 2000—03, Sanilac Three-Minute Band, 2001—03, Vassar Pit Orch., 2002—05, Frankenstrost Band, 2006; tour guide Gagetown Octagon Barn, 2003—04; horn quartet Frankenmuth Wind Ensemble, 2005; mem. Saginaw Classic Heritage Band, 2005—06; precinct del. Dem. Party, 2000—06; dist. dir. social action United Meth. Women, 1999—2002, v.p., 2003—05, pres., 2006—; active Marlette First United Meth. Praise Band, 1999—2004; social action office Marlette First United Meth. Women, 1999—2006; coord. peace and justice Port Huron dist. United Meth. Ch., 2006; bd. dirs. Flint Concert Band, 2000—05, Bay City Concert Band, 2000—02, Unionville-Sebewaing Cmty. Band, 2001—02, Honsinger Wind Ensemble, 2001—05, Mott CC Band, 2004—06, Saglnaw Classic Heritage Band, 2005—06. Fed. govt. grantee Wayne State U., 1968. Mem.: Ind. Assn. Sch. Psychologists (pub. rels. bd. 1990—91), Ind. State Tchrs. Assn. (rep. assembly del. 1991), Am. Federated State and Mcpl. Employees (chairperson #15 chpt. 1993—96), Mich. Edn. Assn-Ret. Thumb Area (sec. 1996—2002, exec. bd. 2002—03), Emmaus Reunion Group, Lions (bd. dirs. 1996—99, 2d v.p. 1999). Democrat. Avocations: antiques, swimming, gardening, travel. Home: 6726 Clothier Rd Clifford MI 48727-9501

STAPLETON, BEVERLY COOPER, aerospace executive; b. Birmingham, Ala., June 4, 1933; d. Herston MacAger and Virginia (Averyt) Cooper; m. John Parker Stapleton, Aug. 31, 1959 (div. July 1981); children: Lisa Karen, Lawrence Cooper BBA magna cum laude, U. Miami, 1954; MA, U. Ala., 1960. Tchr. Miami Beach H.S. Dade County Pub. Schs., Fla., 1956—59; mem. behavior R & D program U. Ala., Tuscaloosa, 1959—61; contracts adminstr. Houghton Mifflin Co., Palo Alto, Calif., 1974—78; Calif. sales rep. Prentice-Hall Inc., San Jose, 1978; contract adminstr., cost analyst United Techs., Sunnyvale, Calif., 1978—82; mgr. contract adminstrn. Echo Sci. Corp., Mountain View, Calif., 1982; contracts mgr. Lockheed Martin Corp. Missiles & Space, Sunnyvale, 1982—98; ret., 1998. Instr. master's program in contracts and material mgmt. St. Mary's Coll., Moraga, Calif., 1984—86; mem. adv. bd. grad. program in contracts and acquisition mgmt. Golden Gate U., San Francisco, 1984—85; contracts mgr. Hubble Space Telescope Program, 1983—85. Fellow polit. sci. U. Ala., 1954-55; recipient Women of Achievement award Santa Clara County Commn. on Status of Women, 1985 Fellow Nat. Contract Mgmt. Assn. (cert., pres. San Francisco area chpt. 1984-85, nat. coun. fellows 1983—, nat. exec. com. 1986-88, nat. bd. dirs. 1985-86, 97-98, nat. v.p. 1987-88), Mgmt. Assn. (treas. Chem. Systems divsn., 1981), Beta Gamma Sigma, Delta Delta Delta Democrat. Presbyterian. Home: 3728 Rhoda Dr San Jose CA 95117-3421

STAPLETON, CLAUDIA ANN, academic administrator; b. Memphis, July 14, 1947; m. Mark Phillip Stapleton, Sept. 18, 1985. AS, Amarillo Coll., 1995; BS, Wayland Bapt. U., 1997, postgrad., 1997-98. Campus pres. High Tech. Inst., Irving, Tex., 2005—. Republican. Methodist. Office: High Tech Inst 4250 N Beltline Rd Irving TX 75038-4201 Business E-Mail: cstapleton@hightechinstitute.com.

STAPLETON, JEAN (JEANNE MURRAY), actress; b. N.Y.C., Jan. 19, 1923; d. Joseph E. and Marie (Stapleton) Murray; m. William H. Putch (dec.); 2 children. Student, Hunter Coll., NYC, Am. Apprentice Theatre, Am. Actors Co., Am. Theatre Wing; studied with Harold Clurman; LHD (hon.), Emerson Coll.; degree (hon.), Hood Coll., Monmouth Coll. Opera debut in Candide with Balt. Opera Co.; appeared in The Italian Lesson with Balt. Opera; first N.Y. stage role in The Corn is Green, Equity Library Theatre; starred as mother in Am. Gothic, Circle-in-the-Sq.; Broadway debut with Judith Anderson In The Summer House; also appeared on Broadway in Damn Yankees, Bells Are Ringing, Juno, Rhinoceros and Funny Girl, Arsenic & Old Lace, Bwax & On Tour; first major break in comic ingenue role as Myrtle Mae with Frank Fay in Harvey on-tour; played with nat. tour of Come Back, Little Sheba starring Shirley Booth; starred in tour of Morning's at Seven, The Show-Off, Daisy Mayme; (Films) Damn Yankees, 1958, Bells Are Ringin, 1960, Something Wild, 1961, Up the Down Staircase, 1967, Cold Turkey, 1971, Klute, 1971, The Buddy System, 1984, Michael, 1996, You've Got Mail, 1998, Pursuit of Happiness, 2001; (TV series) All in the Family, 1968-79, Archie Buncker's Place, 1979, Beakman's World, 1995-96; (TV Films) Tail Gunner Joe, 1977, You Can't Take It With You, 1979, Aunt Mary, 1979, Angel Dusted, 1981, Isabel's Choice, 1981, Eleanor, First Lady of the World, 1982, Something Afoot, 1984, A Matter of Sex, 1984, Grown-Ups, 1985, Dead Man's Folly, 1986, Tender Places, 1987, Mother Goose Rock 'n' Rhyme, 1990, Fire in the Dark, 1991, The Habitation of Dragons, 1992, The Parallax Garden, 1993, Ghost Mom, 1993, Lily Dale, 1996, Chance of a Lifetime, 1998, Baby, 2000, Like Mother Like Son: The Strange Story of Sante and Kenny Kimes, 2001; (guest appearances) Robert Montgomery Presents, 1952, Women with a Past, 1954, The Phileo TV Playhouse, Dr. Kildare, 1961, Dennis the Menace, 1962, The Nurses, 1962, The Defenders, 1962, Car 54, Where Are You?, 1962, Studio One, Naked City, 1963, Armstrong Circle Theatre, Jackie Gleason Show, The Eleventh Hour, 1963, Route 55, 1963, My Three Sons, 1964, The Patty Duke Show, 1965, Scarecrow and Mrs. King, 1984, Faerie Tale Theatre, 1983, 1985, The Love Boat, 1986, Shelley Duvall's Bedtime Stories, 1992, Ray Bradbury Theatre, Grace Under Fire, 1994 (Emmy nomination), Caroline in the City, 1995, Murphy Brown, 1996, Everybody Loves Raymond, 1996, Style and Substance, 1998, Touched by an Angel, 2000; performances include The Matchmaker at A.C.T., San Francisco, Trying Times Shakespeare Co. D.C., 1994, Night Seasons, Signature Theatre N.Y., 1994, Blithe Spirit, Costa Mesa, Calif., Mrs. Piggle-Wiggle on Showtime, stepmother in N.Y.C. Opera's Cinderella, 1995, On Tour: Eleanor: Her Secret Journey, 1998-99, Indian Ink by Tom Stoppard, A.C.T., Geary Theater, San Francisco, 1999, The Habitation of Dragon's on TNT, Roads to Home, Night Seasons, The Birthday Party, Mountain Language, Classic Stage Co., N.Y.C., The Death of Papa, Hartford Stage, 1999, Eleanor: Her Secret Journey, Coconut Grove Playhouse, Miami, Fla., 1999, Canon Theatre, L.A., Royal Poinciana, Palm Beach, Fla., Spreckles Theatre, San Diego, Paramount Theatre, Austin, Tex., Marines Meml. Theatre, San Francisco, 2000, Smithsonian Inst., Washington, 2000, Hartford (Conn.) Stage, 2000, Syracuse (N.Y.) Stage, 2000; CD-Rom Grandma Ollie's Morphabet Soup, 1996. U.S. commr. to Internat. Woman's Yr. Commn. and Nat. Conf. Women, Houston, 1977; bd. dirs. Women's Rsch. and Edn. Inst.; trustee Actors' Fund Am. Recipient Emmy award for best performance in comedy series All in the Family 1970-71, 71-72, 78, Golden Globe awards Hollywood Fgn. Press Assn. 1972, 73, Obie award, 1990, Cable Ace award. Mem. AFTRA, SAG, Actors Equity Assn. Office: care Bauman & Assocs 5757 Wilshire Blvd Los Angeles CA 90036-3635*

STAPLETON, KATHARINE HALL (KATIE STAPLETON), commentator, writer; m. Benjamin Franklin Stapleton; children: Benjamin Franklin III, Craig Roberts, Katharine Hall. BA, Vassar Coll., 1941. Prodr., writer, host Cooking with Katie Sta. KOA, 1979—89. Author: Denver Delicious, 1980, 3d edit., 1983, High Notes, 1985. Chmn. women's divsn. United Fund, 1955-56; founder, chmn. Denver Debutante Ball, 1955, 56; hon. chmn. Nat. Travelers Aid Assn., 1952-56 95-; commr. Denver Centennial Authority, 1958-60; trustee Washington Cathedral, regional v.p., 1967-73; trustee Colo. Women's Coll., 1975-80; sole trustee Harmes C. Fishback Found., 1989-; hon. chmn. Le Bal à Versailles, 2000, 02, 04, Rocky Mountain Planned Parenthood Campaign, 2006. Decorated Chevalier de L'Etoile Noire (France); recipient People-to-People citations, 1960, 66, Beautiful Activist award, Colo.-Wyo. Restaurant Assn. award, 1981, Humanitarian of Yr. award Arthritis Found., 1995, Arts award Colo. Symphony, 1998; Outstanding Vol. Fundraiser, Nat. Philanthropy Day, 1995, Outstanding Alumna, Barstow Sch., 2003, Girl Scout award, 2006. Mem. Denver Country Club. Republican. Episcopalian. Home: 8 Village Rd Cherry Hills Village CO 80113-4908 E-mail: kties8@aol.com.

STAPLETON, MARYLYN ALECIA, diplomat; b. St. Thomas, V.I., Sept. 25, 1936; d. Lambert George and Aletha C. (Callendar) John; m. Frank Stapleton, Oct. 22, 1967 (div. Apr. 1983); 1 child, Linda E. Student, Washington Bus. Inst., 1959. Reservations agt. Caribair Airlines, St. Thomas, 1954-56; sales clk. Macy's Dept. Store, N.Y.C., 1956-57, Gift Shop, N.Y.C., 1957-63; supr. Ea. Airlines, Inc., N.Y.C. and St. Thomas, 1964-86; travel cons. Caribbean Travel Agy., St. Thomas, 1986-87; asst. commr. Dept. Licensing and Consumer Affairs, Govt. of V.I., St. Thomas, 1987-95, dep. of planning and natural resources, 1995—, small bus. tech. assistance program coord., 1995—; state exec. dir. Internat. Assn. Plumbing Mech. Officials, 1999—; environ. program mgr. Dept. Planning and Natural Resources, 2004. Owner, pres. Stapleton Enterprises, St. Thomas, 1989—. Pub. rels. officer Nevis Benevolent Soc., St. Thomas, 1966-85; state chair Dem. party V.I., 1986—, dist. chair, 1984-86; small bus. ombudsman Clean Air Act of 1990, 1998—. Recipient Legis. Resolution V.I. Legislature, St. Thomas, 1986. Mem. Internat. Assn. Plumbing and Mech. Ofcls., Nat. Assn. Plumbing, Heating and Cooling Contrs., St. Thomas/St. John Plumbing Assn. (pres. 1995—), St. Thomas Lioness Club (treas. 1985-86, pagent chair 1986-87, pres. 1987-88, mem. chair 1988-89, Melvin Jones fellow 1989), Lions Club of Charlotte Amalie (bd. dirs.). Democrat. Anglican. Home: 148-87 Est Annas Retreat PO Box 303739 St Thomas VI 00803-3739 Office: Democratic Party of Virgin Islns PO Box 3739 Saint Thomas Charlotte Amalie VI 00801 Office Phone: 340-774-3320.

STAPLETON, ROMAYNE HUCZEK, secondary school educator; b. Detroit, May 7, 1943; d. Joseph and Lucia Teresa Huczek; m. Robert John Stapleton (dec.); children: Elena, Sally. BA, Wayne State U., 1965; MEd Leadership, Saginaw Valley State U., University Ctr., Mich., 1999; postgrad., Wayne State U., 1966—72, Mercy Coll., Detroit, 1969. Cert. secondary tchr. Mich. Lit. and drama tchr. Hamtramack H.S., Mich., 1967—68; lit. and libr. tchr. Kosciuscko Elem. Sch., Mich., 1968—69; swimming instr., dir. Warren Consol. Sch. Dist., Mich., 1961—72; remedial reading and honors English tchr. Kelly Jr. H.S., Eastpointe, Mich., 1969—78; tchr. lit., composition, advanced placement East Detroit H.S., Eastpointe, 1982—2003; tchr. biology Oakwood Jr. H.S., Eastpointe, Mich., 1980—82. Instr. world lit. Rochester Coll., Rochester Hills, Mich., 2004; sponsor, organizer ann. student field trips to Shakespeare Festival in Can.; mem. accreditation com. Macomb County, Mich. Rec. sec., pres. elect Bi-County Hosp. Guild, Warren, Mich., 1968—71; sec. Romeo Park and Recreation Commn., Washington, Mich., 1975—84; docent Hist. 19th Century Homes Tour, 1979—84. Recipient Citation for Heroism, Madison Hghts., Mich. Police Dept., 1985. Mem.: AAUW (sec. Romeo, Mich. chpt. 1979—85). Avocations: gardening, swimming, writing, tai chi. E-mail: romaynestapleton@comcast.net.

STARCHER-DELL'AQUILA, JUDY LYNN, special education educator; b. Cuyahoga Falls, Ohio, Sept. 20, 1956; d. James Calvin and Jane Yvonne (Hart) Starcher; m. Richard Paul Dell'Aquila, July 16, 1983; 1 child, Jessica Lynn Dell'Aquila. BS in Hearing & Speech Scis., Ohio U., 1978; MEd in Deaf Edn., U. Cin., 1980; PhD in Spl. Edn., Kent State U., 1996. Cert. supr. and tchr., Ohio. Tchr. deaf parma (Ohio) City Schs., 1978-79, Mayfield (Ohio) City Schs., 1980-81; tchr. deaf, low incidence work study coord. Trumbull County Ednl. Svc. Ctr., Warren, Ohio, 1981-84; work study coord. Cuyahoga Ednl. Svc. Ctr., Valley View, Ohio, 1984-88; instr., student tchg. supr. Kent (Ohio) State U., 1993-95; project dir. Children's Hosp. Med. Ctr./Family Child Learning Ctr., Tallmadge, Ohio, 1995-2000; coord. spl. edn. Cleveland Heights/University Heights (Ohio) City Sch. System, 2000—. Am. Sign Lang. instr. Cuyahoga C.C., Cleve., 1993-2000; dir. adv. bd. Hearing Impaired Toddler Infant & Families Program, Tallmadge, 1995-2000; mem. County Collaborative Group, Medina, Summit counties, Ohio, 1995-2000; state trainer SKI—HI, Logan, Utah, 1997—. Mem. Coun. Exceptional Children. Grantee Job Tng. & Partnership Act, Cleve., 1982, 86-88; Univ. fellow Kent State U., 1991. Democrat. Avocations: antique collector, exercise, reading. Home: 151 E Pleasant Valley Rd Seven Hills OH 44131-5601 Office: Cleveland Hgts/Univ Hgts Bd Edn 2155 Miramar Blvd University Heights OH 44118 Office Phone: 216-371-7435. Personal E-mail: jdellaqu@yahoo.com.

STARER, RUANA MAXINE, clinical psychologist; b. N.Y.C., Dec. 30, 1946; d. Emanuel and Zoe (Cibul) S.; B.A. in Psychology summa cum laude, Hunter Coll., CUNY, 1974; M.A., Calif. Sch. Profl. Psychology, 1977, Ph.D., 1980; m. Jed H. Weitzen, Oct. 27, 1979; children— Jason Seth, Mia Elyse. Psychol. asst. in pvt. practice, Upland, Calif., 1977-79; parent tng. specialist Via Avanta, Didi Hirsch Community Mental Health Center, Pacoima, Calif., 1979-80; staff clin. psychologist So. Reception Center and Clinic, Calif. Dept. Youth Authority, Norwalk, 1980-82; pvt. practice, Riverdale, N.Y., 1982-86; supervising psychologist Children's Village, Dobbs Ferry, N.Y., 1985-86, pvt. practice, co-dir. Calif. Comprehensive Psychological Ctr., Ithaca, N.Y., 1986—. Mem. APA, Ctrl. N.Y. Psychol. Assn., Psi Chi. Office: 416 N Tioga St Ithaca NY 14850-4229 Office Phone: 607-273-0690.

STARFIELD, BARBARA HELEN, pediatrician, educator; b. Bklyn., Dec. 18, 1932; d. Martin and Eva (Illions) Starfield; m. Neil A. Holtzman, June 12, 1955; children: Robert, Jon, Steven, Deborah. AB, Swarthmore Coll., 1954; MD, SUNY, 1959; MPH, Johns Hopkins U., 1963. Tchg. asst. in anatomy Downstate Med. Ctr., N.Y.C., 1955—57; intern in pediat. Johns Hopkins U., 1959—60, resident, 1960—62, dir. pediatric med. care clinic, 1963—66, dir. cmty. staff comprehensive child care project, 1966—67, dir. pediatric clin. scholars program, 1971—76, prof. health policy, joint appointment in pediat., 1975—, disting. univ. prof., 1994—. Mem. Nat. Com. Vital Stats., 1994—2002; cons. DHHS; mem. nat. adv. coun. Agy. for Health Care Policy and Rsch., 1990—94; adv. subcom. on Health Systems and Svcs. Rsch. Pan Am. Health Orgn., 1988—92, 1995—; cons. Health Care Fin. Adminstrn., 1980—. Editl. bd. Med. Care, 1977—79, Pediat., 1977—82, Internat. Jour. Health Svcs., 1978—, Med. Care Rev., 1980—84, Health Svc. Rsch., 1996—, assoc. editor Ann. Rev. Pub. Health, 1996—2001; contbr. articles to profl. jours. Recipient Dave Luckman Meml. award, 1958, HEW Career Devel. award, 1970—75, Disting. Investigator award, Assn. Health Svcs. Rsch., 1995, 1st Primary Care Achievement award, Pew Charitable Trust Fund, 1994, 1st Ann. Rsch. award, Ambulatory Pediatric Assn., 1990, Baxter prize, 2004. Fellow: Am. Acad. Pediat.; mem.: APHA (Martha May Eliot award 1995), Internat. Soc. for Equity in Health (pres. 2000—02), Ambulatory Pediatric Assn. (pres. 1980), Internat. Epidemiologic Assn., Soc. Pediatric Rsch., Inst. Medicine of NAS (governing coun. 1981—83), Alpha Omega Alpha, Sigma Xi. Office: Johns Hopkins Sch Hygiene 624 N Broadway Baltimore MD 21205-1900 Business E-Mail: bstarfie@jhsph.edu.

STARGER, VICTORIA GONDEK, artist; Diploma in Art (hon.), du Cret Sch. Arts, Plainfield, NJ, 1976. Instr. drawing and painting Joe Kubert Sch. of Cartoon and Graphic Art, Dover, NJ, Morris County Art Assn., Morristown and Boonton, NJ, Somerset Art Assn., Bedminster, NJ. Exhibitions include numerous, including Galerie Le Carre d'Or, Eloge du petit Format dans l'art d'aujourd'hui, Paris, 2000—03, exhibitions include The Art of the Portrait, Cerulean Gallery, 2000, 12th Internat. Book and Press Fair, Geneva, Switzerland, 1998, Artworks, The Visual Art Sch. of Princeton and Trenton, 1997, Lever House, Park Ave., N.Y.C., 1991, Salon d'Automne 1988, Paris, Morris Mus., Morristown, N.J., 2003, Ctr. Culturel Christiane Peugeot, Paris, 2003—04, 2006. Office: Victoria Starger Art Studio 6 Vale Dr Mountain Lakes NJ 07046 Office Phone: 973-476-8574.

STARK, DIANA, public relations executive; b. NYC, July 01; d. Benjamin and Sara (Zelasny) S. BA, Hunter Coll. Promotion mgr. TV Guide mag., N.Y.C., 1950-61, Show Bus. Illustrated, N.Y.C., 1961-62; broadcast specialist Young & Rubicam, N.Y.C., 1962-69; pres. Stark Comms. Inc., N.Y.C., 1969-76; pub. svc. publicity account exec. Y & R E, N.Y.C., 1976-77; pres. Stark Comms. Internat., N.Y.C., 1978—. Pub. rels. workshop leader Chgo. Econ. Devel. Corp., 1973-76; cons. to Asahi Shimbun for English Language Newsletter. 1991-92, columnist Host mag., 1960-65; writer, producer programs for women's TV shows, 1962—. Book developer Ellis Island: The First Experience With Liberty, 1991. Coord. We Have Arrived, Portraits at Ellis Island, Augustus Sherman Photographs, 1902-24. Mem. NATAS (trustee 1974-78, publicity com., chmn., chpt. gov. 1972-76, 82-86, 87-91, editor N.Y. TV Directory 1987-90). Office Phone: 212-582-5619. Office Fax: 212-765-3670. Personal E-mail: dstarkny@aol.com.

STARK, EVELYN BRILL, poet, musician; b. N.Y.C., Sept. 12, 1913; d. Henry Brill and Rae Hessberg; m. Morton W. Stark, Apr. 27, 1933; 1 child, Henry. BA, Barnard Coll., 1933; artist student of Edouard Dethier, Juilliard Sch. Music, 1933-40. Bd. dirs., violinist Nat. Found. Mus. Therapy, N.Y.C., 1940-50; violinist ARC Hosp. Music Unit, N.Y.C., 1950-70, Hosp. Music Unit, Protestant Coun. Chs., N.Y.C., 1950-70; bd. dirs., violinist Music Therapy Ctr., N.Y.C., 1960-80; founder, sponsor Nora Hellen Music Friends, N.Y.C., 1970-80; ret., 1980. Author: My Search for the Infinite, 2002; mem. editl. bd. Music Jour., 1969-70; recorded tapes with original programs; author: (poetry) Never Apart, 1992, 2003; (autobiography) Life is a Poem, 1999; dramatic presentations of Life is a Poem, Hartford, Conn., 2000, Essex, Conn., 2000, Brooklyn, Conn., East Haddam, Conn., Middleton, Conn.; performer (record) All About the Violin, 1969; (CD) Journey of a Soul in Music via the Infinite Way, 2003; contbr. articles to profl. jours.; author numerous poems. Donated 3 violins (Amati, Carcassi, Gragnani) to the Met. Mus. Art, N.Y.C., 1974, 80, 97. Recipient 1st prize poetry award Altrusa Internat. Middletown, Conn., 1997-98; named Poet Laureate of Conn. Gilbert and Sullivan Soc., 1998; named to Internat. Poetry Hall of Fame, 1998. Mem. Internat. Soc. Poets. Address: 317 W Main St Chester CT 06412-1057

STARK, JANICE ANN, elementary school educator; b. Oelwein, Iowa, July 25, 1940; d. Wilbert George and Martha Isabelle (Bulgur) Brown; widowed; children: Stephanie, Brad. BA, U. No. Iowa, 1962; MA, St. Thomas U., 1991. Lic. tchr. Tchr. 5th grade Roseville (Minn.) Schs., 1962-63; tchr. 4th grade Iowa City Schs., 1963-64, Calumet City (Ill.) Schs., 1964-65; tchr. 3d grade, substitute tchf. 6th grade Robbinsdale (Minn.) Schs., 1965-69, 74-78; tutor, W.I.S.E. vol. Mpls. Pub. Schs., 1969-72, 79-86, tchr. grades 3-5 Putnam Elem., 1986-92, tchr. 4th grade Hamilton Elem., 1992-93; guest tchr. Koln (Germany) Holweide Sch., 1993-94; with Tchr. Inst. Minn. Humanities Commn., Mpls., 1995; tchr. Burroughs Cmty. Sch., Mpls., 1995—; internat. teaching exchange grades 5 and 6 Manorvale Primary Sch., Werribeo, Australia, 1997. Mem. City-Wide Tchr. Adv. Com., 1987-89; bldg. contact rep. Lang. Arts and Social Studies, 1986-89; mem. Site Coun. Leadership Team, 1989-92; N.E. Mplw. tchr. contact person Whole Lang., 1991-92; mem. Mpls. Pub. Schs. Profl. Devel. Com., 1992-93, Local 59 Leadership Consortium, 1992-93. Mem. AAUW, Pi Lambda Theta. Avocations: travel, reading. Home: 3000 North Douglas Dr #104 Crystal MN 55422

STARK, JOAN SCISM, education educator; b. Hudson, N.Y., Jan. 6, 1937; d. Ormonde F. and Myrtle Margaret (Kirkey) S.; m. William L. Stark, June 28, 1958 (dec.); children: Eugene William, Susan Elizabeth, Linda Anne, Ellen Scism; m. Malcolm A. Lowther, Jan. 31, 1981. BS, Syracuse U., 1957; MA (Hoadly fellow), Columbia U., 1960; Ed.D., SUNY, Albany, 1971. Tchr. Ossining (N.Y.) High Sch., 1957-59; free-lance editor Holt, Rinehart & Winston, Harcourt, Brace & World, 1960-70; lectr. Ulster County Community Coll., Stone Ridge, NY, 1968-70; asst. dean Goucher Coll., Balt., 1970-73, asso. dean, 1973-74; assoc. prof., chmn. dept. higher postsecondary edn. Syracuse (N.Y.) U., 1974-78; dean Sch. Edn. U. Mich., Ann Arbor, 1978-83, prof., 1983-2001, prof. and dean emeritus, 2001—; dir. Nat. Ctr. for Improving Postsecondary Teaching and Learning, 1986—91. Editor: Rev. of Higher Edn., 1991-96; contbr. articles to various publs. Leader Girl Scouts

U.S.A., Cub Scouts Am.; coach girls Little League; dist. officer PTA, intermittently, 1968-80; mem. adv. com. Gerald R. Ford Library, U. Mich., 1980-83; trustee Kalamazoo Coll., 1979-85; mem. exec. com. Inst. Social Research, U. Mich., 1979-81; bd. dirs. Mich. Assn. Colls. Tchr. Edn., 1979-81. Mem. Am. Assn. for Higher Edn., Am. Ednl. Rsch. Assn. (Div. J. Rsch. award 1998), Assn. Study Higher Edn. (dir. 1977-79, v.p. 1983, pres. 1984, Rsch. Achievement award 1992, svc. award 1998, Disting. Career award 1999), Assn. Innovation Higher Edn. (nat. chmn. 1974-75), Assn. Instl. Rsch. (disting. mem., Sidney Suslow award 1999), Assn. Colls. and Schs. Edn. State Univs. and Land Grant Colls. (dir. 1981-83), Acctg. Edn. Change Commn., Phi Beta Kappa, Phi Kappa Phi, Sigma Pi Sigma, Eta Pi Upsilon, Lambda Sigma Sigma, Phi Delta Kappa, Pi Lambda Theta.

STARK, MARTHA, psychiatrist, environmental medicine physician; d. Martin Charles and Elizabeth Fite Stark. AB, Harvard U., 1969, MD, 1974; postgrad., Boston Psychoanalytic Inst. Resident in adult psychiatry Cambridge (Mass.) Hosp., 1974—77; child fellow Mass. Mental Health Ctr., Boston, 1977—79; clin. instr. in psychiatry Harvard Med. Sch., Boston, 1979—. Dir. Three Ripley St.: Continuing Med. Edn. for Mental Health Profls., Newton, Mass., 1990—2002; mem. faculty Boston Psychoanalytic Inst., 1990—, Mass. Inst. for Psychoanalysis, Boston, 1990—; mem. faculty continuing edn. program Mass. Mental Health Ctr., Harvard Med. Sch., Boston, 1992—; mem. faculty Ctr. for Psychoanalytic Studies Mass. Gen. Hosp., 1998—. Author: Working with Resistance, 1994, A Primer on Working with Resistance, 1994, Modes of Therapeutic Action, 1999 (Pub.'s Book of Yr., 2000). Mem.: Am. Acad. Environ. Medicine (bd. dirs. 2005—), Environ. Health Found. (sec. 2004—). Democrat. Unitarian. Achievements include renovation and design of environmentally safe, chemical-free, award winning kitchen. Avocations: dance, travel, bridge, music, kitchen design. Office: 3 Ripley St Newton MA 02459 Office Phone: 617-244-7188. Business E-Mail: marthastarkmd@hms.harvard.edu.

STARK, NELLIE MAY, forester, ecologist, educator; b. Norwich, Conn., Nov. 20, 1933; d. Theodore Benjamin and Dorothy Josephine (Pendleton) Beetham; m. Oscar Elder Stark, Oct. 1962 (dec.). BA, Conn. Coll., 1956; AM, Duke U., 1958, PhD, 1962. Botanist Exptl. Sta., U.S. Forest Svc., Old Strawberry, Calif., 1958-66; botanist, ecologist Desert Rsch. Inst., Reno, 1966-72; prof. forest ecology Sch. Forestry, U. Mont., Missoula, 1972-92; pvt. cons. Philomath, Oreg. Pres. Camas Analytical Lab., Inc., Missoula, 1987—92. Author: Will Your Family Survive the 21st Century, 1997, Memories of Wren, Oregon, 1998, So You Want to Build a Little Log Cabin in the Woods, 2002, Thirteen Days of Christmas, 2005; contbr. articles to profl. jours. Named Disting. Dau. Norwich, Conn., 1985; recipient Conn. award Conn. Coll., 1986, 54 grants. Mem. Ecol. Soc. Am. (chair ethics com. 1974, 76), Soc. Am. Foresters (taskforce 1987-88).

STARK, PATRICIA ANN, psychologist; b. Ames, Iowa, Apr. 21, 1937; d. Keith C. and Mary L. (Johnston) Moore. BS, So. Ill. U., Edwardsville, 1970, MS, 1972; PhD, St. Louis U., 1976. Counselor to alcoholics Bapt. Rescue Mission, East St. Louis, Ill., 1969; rschr. alcoholics Gateway Rehab. Ctr., East St. Louis, 1972; psychologist intern Henry-Stark Counties Spl. Edn. Dist. and Galesburg State Rsch. Hosp., Ill., 1972—73; instr. Lewis and Clark C.C., Godfrey, Ill., 1973—76, asst. prof., 1976—84, assoc. prof., 1994, coord. child care svcs., 1974—84; mem. staff dept. psychiatry Meml. Hosp., St. Elizabeth's Hosp., 1979—2001; supr. students interns, 1974—94. Dir. child and family svc. Collinsville Counseling Ctr., 1977-82; clin. dir., owner Empas-Complete Family Psychol. and Hypnosis Svcs., Collinsville, 1982—; cons. cmty. agys., 1974—; mem. adv. bd. Madison County Coun. on Alcoholism and Drug Dependency, 1977-80. Mem. APA, Ill. Psychol. Assn., Midwestern Psychol. Assn., Am. Soc. Clin. Hypnosis, Internat. Soc. Hypnosis. Office: 2802 Maryville Rd Maryville IL 62062 Office Phone: 618-345-6632.

STARK, ROBIN CARYL, psychotherapist, consultant; d. Louis and Bernice Stark. BA in Psychology cum laude with honors, Hunter Coll., 1979; MSW, NYU, 1982. Diplomate Am. Bd. Clin. Social Work; LCSW, N.Y.; cert. psychoanalytic psychotherapy, psychotherapy of eating disorders, trauma tng. for mental health profls., ARC. Pvt. practice psychotherapy, N.Y.C., 1983—. Mem. adj. field faculty Grad. Sch. Social Svc. Fordham U., N.Y.C., 1986—87, Grad. Sch. Social Work, Hunter Coll., N.Y.C., 1987—88; coord. patient care svcs. Achievement and Guidance Ctrs. Am., Inc., N.Y.C., 1988—89; staff psychotherapist Ctr. for Study of Anorexia and Bulimia, 1990—94, facilitator wellness support chronic & life-challenging illness, 1993—; bd. dirs. N.Y. Met. Cmty. of Mindfulness, 1999—2000; pro bono svc. provider Project Liberty's post Sept. 11 trauma counseling program, N.Y.C., 2001—; mem. Operation Comfort, 2004—. Recipient service award Young Adult Inst., 1987; N.Y.C. Youth Bur. grantee, 1983-85. Mem. NASW, Acad. Cert. Social Workers. Office: 410 E 57th St Ste 1A New York NY 10022-3059

STARKEY, LAURIE SHAFFER, chemistry professor; b. NJ, Sept. 24, 1969; PhD in Chemistry, UCLA, 1996. Asst. prof. Cal Poly Pomona, Calif., 1996—2001, assoc. prof., 2001—. Office: Cal Poly Pomona Chemistry Dept 3801 W Temple Ave Pomona CA 91768 Office Phone: 909-869-3670.

STARKEY, SHIRLEY CONDIT, writer, artist; b. Tucson, Dec. 25, 1933; d. Edwin Carmichael and Mabel (Votaw) Condit; m. James Edward Starkey, Sept. 28, 1956; children: James Edward Jr., Patrick Joseph, Peggy Musselmann, Richard Carmichael. BA, U. Ariz., Tucson, 1955. Cert. tchr. k-8. Tchr. elem. various states, 1956—75; agt. real estate Tucson, 1976—2002; owner Columbia Estate Appraisals, Tucson, 1978—80, LaCasa Esperanza Supervisory Care Home, Tucson, 1979—2001. Author: The Scorpion Stings, 2005. Mem.: Asst. League of Tucson, AU PEO (pres. Ariz. chpt.), Soc. Southwestern Authors, Ariz. Watercolor Assn., So. Ariz. Watercolor Guild (signature mem.). Republican. Presbyterian. Home: 7270 E Ventana Canyon Dr Tucson AZ 85750

STARKMAN, BETTY PROVIZER, genealogist, writer, educator; b. Detroit, July 18, 1929; d. Jack and Rose (Bodenstein) Provizer; m. Morris Starkman, Dec. 25, 1952; children: Susan Lynn Starkman Rott, Robert David Starkman. AB, Wayne State U., 1951; postgrad., U. Wis., 1949; MA, Wayne U., 1954. Cert. social worker, Mich. Social worker Wayne County Social Aid, Detroit, 1951-54, B'nai B'rith Youth Orgn., Detroit, 1951-54; genealogist, historian Birmingham, Mich., 1979—. Tchr. Midrasha Coll., Southfield, Mich., 1986-88, Coll. Jewish Studies, Birmingham, 1986-88; lectr. Jewish Cmty. Ctr., West Bloomfield, Mich., 1986-89. Editor jour. Generations, 1986; contbr. articles to Jwish News, Generations, Search, others. Bd. dirs. Anti Defamation League,Detroit, 1980—, Jewish Cmty. Coun., Southfield, 1980—, Tribute Fund, Detroit, 1979-85; v.p. Maimonides, Detroit, 1966-67; bd. dirs. Am. Mogen David for Israel, Mich. br.; del. 1st conf. Jews of Old China, Harvard U., 1992; mem. archives com. Jewish Welfare Fedn. Mich., 1993—. Recipient Humanitarian award State of Israel Bonds, 1980; Helping Hand award Israel Red Cross, 1980, Humanitarian award, 1991; honored by Mich. region Am. Red Mogen Dovid for Israel, 1997, Jewish Geneal. Soc. Mich., 1997. Mem. Jewish Genealogy Soc. Mich. (founder, pres. 1982-84, bd. dirs. 1995—), Jewish Genealogy Soc. Ill., Jewish Genealogy Soc. Inc., Jewish Hist. Soc. (Mich. bd. dirs. 1986-88), Jewish Genealogy Soc. L.A., Jewish Genealogy Soc. Phila., Jewish Genealogy Soc. Washington, Jewish Genealogy Soc. Toronto, Polish Genealogy Soc. Mich. Avocations: travel, reading, collecting art, music, archaeology. Home and Office: 1260 Stuyvessant Rd Bloomfield Hills MI 48301-2141

STARKS, CAROL ELIZABETH, retired principal; b. Elizabeth, N.J., Oct. 16, 1941; d. Arthur E. and Argetha P. (Henderson) Starks. AA, Graceland Coll., 1961; BA in Elem. Edn., Mich. State U., 1963; MA in Elem. Adminstrn., San Jose State U., 1972. Cert. elem. sch. tchr. Calif., life diploma for elem. edn. Calif., specialist tchr. in reading Calif., std. svc. credential in supervision Calif., elem. sch. tchr. N.J., elem. edn. Mo., early childhood edn. Mo. Tchr. grade 3 Hayes Sch., Monterey, Calif., 1963—65; tchr. grade 2 Woodruff Sch., Berkeley Heights, NJ, 1965—67; tchr. remedial reading and educationally handicapped Ord Terrace Sch., Monterey, 1967—68, asst. prin., 1975—77, prin., 1984—88; tchr. grade 3 Manzanita Sch., Monterey, 1968—73; asst. prin. La Mesa Sch., Monterey, 1973—74, tchr. grade 6, 1974—75; prin. Foothill Sch., Monterey, 1977—80, Olson Sch., Monterey, 1980—84, Highland Sch., Monterey, 1988—95, Bay View Sch., Monterey, 1995—99; career ladder asst. Kansas City Sch. Dist., Mo., 2000—. Interviewed as representative of elementary principals Calif. Commn. on the Tchg. Profession, 1984—85. Mem. world ch. pubs. com. Remnant Ch. Jesus Christ of Latter Day Saints, 2001—05, music dir. Blue Springs congregation, 2001—05, mem. world ch. hymnbook com., 2003—. Recipient Calif. Disting. Sch. Prin.'s award, 1989, 1993, Proclamation for profl. accomplishments and 19 yrs. of svc., City of Seaside (Calif.), 1995. Mem.: AAUW (sec. Independence br. 2003—05), Monterey Bay Sch. Adminstr. Assn. (pres. 1997—98), Assn. Calif. Sch. Adminstr. (sec./treas. Monterey Peninsula charter 1977—78, v.p. 1978—79, pres. 1979—80, treas. region X 1979—81, pres. region X 1981—82, elem. adminstrn. com. 1982—86, del. to Nat. Assn. Elem. Sch.Prins. Convention 1983—84, state facilitator Elem. Adminstrn. Acad. North 1984—85, state dir. Elem. Adminstrn. Acad. North 1985—86, state del. to rep. assembly 1986—91, Region X Blanche Montague award for Outstanding Sch. Adminstr. 1987), Delta Kappa Gamma (pres. Delta Lambda chpt. 1990—92, Calif. membership task force 1991—93, Calif. personal growth and svcs. com. 1993—95, dir. area V Calif. 1995—97, state chair comms. com. 1997—99, scholarship com. Kansas City coun. 2000—01, pres. Phi chpt. 2000—02, state comm. com. 2001—03, treas. Kansas City coun. 2002—, chair state comm. com. 2003—05). Republican. Avocations: travel, reading, music, computers, quilting. Home: 3341 S Cochise Ave Independence MO 64057

STARKS, DORIS N., retired nursing educator, administrator; b. Conecuh County, Ala., July 30, 1937; m. Wilbert L. Starks Sr., Dec. 25, 1961; children: Wilbert L. Jr., Garrick Edward. BS in Nursing, Tuskegee U., 1958; MS in Nursing, The Cath. U. of Am., 1965; PhD, Union Grad. Sch., 1978. Lic. nurse, Md. Staff nurse VA Hosp. Ctr., Tuskegee, Ala., 1958-61, insvc. edn. instr., 1965-66; staff nurse Washington Hosp. Ctr., 1963-65; asst. prof. med./surg. nursing Tuskegee U., 1966-68; prof. Community Coll. Balt, 1968, asst. chair dept. nursing, 1980-84, chair, 1984-86, chair dept. nursing and health scis., 1986-89, dir. nursing program, 1989; asst. dean, prof. nursing div. Coppin State Coll., Balt., 1990-91, dean nursing, div. nursing, 1991-98; ret., 1998. Item writer Nat. State Bd. Exam. Test Pool. Author bi-weekly health issues column Christian World, 1976-77. Mem. adv. coun. on vocat. edn. City of Balt. 1nd lt. US Army Nurse Corps., 1959-62. Recipient plaque and commendation Tuskegee Inst. Alumni Assn., 1983, Leadership in Nursing award Md. Found. for Nursing, 1994, Strong Blacks in Health Care award, Balt., 1995; honoree Black Nurses Assn., 1984; inducted Tuskegee U. Sch. Nursing Hall of Fame, 1992. Fellow Am. Acad. Nursing; mem. ANA, Tuskegee U. Nurses Alumni Assn. (Balt. met. area chpt.), Nat. Coalition of 100 Black Women, Alpha Kappa Alpha, Sigma Theta Tau, Chi Eta Phi. Home: 318 Bullskin St Charles Town WV 25414

STARKS, FLORENCE ELIZABETH, retired special education educator; b. Summit, N.J., Dec. 6, 1932; d. Edward and Winnie (Morris) S. BA, Morgan State U., 1956; MS in Edn., CUNY, 1962; postgrad., Fairleigh Dickinson U., 1962—63, Seton Hall U., 1963, Newark State Coll. Cert. blind and visually handicapped and social studies tchr., N.J. Tchr. adult edn. Newark Bd. of Edn.; ret., 1995; tchr. N.Y. Inst. for Edn. of the Blind, Bronx. Developer first class for multiple handicapped blind children in pub. sch. system, Newark, 1960; ptnr. World Vision Internat. Mem. ASCD, AFL-CIO, AAUW, Coun. Exceptional Children, Am. Assn. U. Women, Nat. Assn. Negro Bus. and Profl. Women's Club Inc., N.J. Edn. Assn., Newark Tchrs. Assn., Newark Tchrs. Union-Am. Fedn. Tchrs., World Vision Internat. (ptnr.). Home: 4 Park Ave Summit NJ 07901-3942

STARLING, VIRGINIA R., music educator, consultant; b. Loraine, TX, Apr. 26, 1929; d. Lawrence Livingston and Ruth Cleo (Martin) Trott; widowed; children: Catherine, Caroline, Randall. B of Music Edn., Mary Hardin Baylor U., 1950; MusM, 1976; BS in Psychology, Coll. of Southwest, 1989. Choir dir. Methodist Ch., Belton, TX, 1949-50; music instr. Monahans (Tex.) Pub. Schs., 1950-52, Lovington (N.Mex.) Pub. Schs., 1952-54, N.M. Jr. Coll., Hobbs, 1976-79; pvt. sch. music tchr. Hobbs, N.M., 1987-93; ch. organist, pvt. tchr. Lovington, Hobbs, N.M., 1952-99; ch. organist, cons. Cloudcroft, N.Mex., 1999—2005. Bd. dirs. Clauderoft Dance Acad. Soloist: (CD) Enduring Devotion; composer piano solos for children, Just For You, 2000; concert performances in Hobbs, N. Mex., Carnegie Hall. Bd. dirs. Southwest Symphony. Mem. Music Tchrs. Nat. Assn., Profl. Music Tchrs. of N.Mex. (bd. dirs.), Lea County Music Forum, Sigma Alpha Iota. Baptist. Avocations: gardening, travel, history, music. Home: 3003 North Houston Hobbs NM 88240 E-mail: skyhigh@zianet.com.

STARNER, BARBARA KAZMARK, marketing, advertising and export sales executive; b. Detroit, Sept. 2, 1940; d. Eugene Anthony and Lucille Ann Kazmark; m. G. Frederick Starner, June 30, 1962; 1 child, Natasha Lucienne. BA with honors, U. Mich., 1962; BS, Ohio State U., 1965. Tchr. art Columbus (Ohio) Pub. Schs., 1965-68, Mt. Olive Pub. Schs., Budd Lake, N.J., 1968-71; stained glass designer Barbara Designs, LaCrosse, Wis., 1975-87; from trade show mgr. to v.p. advt., mktg., export sales Kart-A-Bag divsn. Remin, Joliet, Ill., 1978—. Advt. and mktg. cons. Starner Mktg., L.A., 1987-95; ptnr. PreciousGem, L.A., 1999—. Mem., pres. East Bank Artists, LaCrosse, 1979-86; co-founder, dir. crafts Great River Traditional Music & Crafts Festival, LaCrosse, 1975-87; chmn. Spiritual Frontiers Fellowship, Mpls., 1979-85, 85-87; co-chmn. Spiritual Sci. Fellowship, 1985-87; fund raiser, mem./cook 1st crew Sloop Clearwater Restoration, Maine-N.Y., 1969 (Hudson River pollution clean-up). Democrat. Mem. Universalist Ch. Avocation: landscape and portrait painting. Office: Kart-A-Bag 510 Manhattan Rd Joliet IL 60433-3099 E-mail: bks@kart-a-bag.com.

STARNES, SUSAN SMITH, elementary school educator; b. Grinnell, Iowa, Oct. 8, 1942; d. Edwin Fay Smith Jr. and Miriam Jane (Spaulding) Smith Simms; m. Wayman J. Starnes, Apr. 25, 1964; children: Michele Ann Starnes Hoffman, Mary Shannon Starnes Zornes. BS Edn. summa cum laude, Mo. Bapt. U., 1991. Cert. early childhood tchr., elem. tchr. 1-8. Adminstr. Presbyn. Ch. in Am. Hist. Ctr., St. Louis, 1985—90; tchr. 3d grade Ctrl. Christian Sch., St. Louis, 1991—98; substitute tchr. Ctrl. Christian Sch., Kirk Day Sch., St. Louis, 1998—. Mem. chapel com. Ctrl. Christian Sch., St. Louis, 1991-98 Children's dir. Canaan Bapt. Ch., St. Louis, 1991—96, Bible Study Fellowship children's leader, 1986—89, mission trip vol., 1992, 1993, 1999—2006; camp counselor Youth for Christ, Kansas City, 1992, 1993, Awana leader, 1996—; mem. Mo. Bapt. Conv. Disaster Relief Childcare Unit, 1997—. Mem. Kappa Delta Pi Avocations: biking, swimming, hiking.

STAROST, DIANE JOAN, music educator; b. Huntington, NY, June 27, 1963; d. Frank Basil and Therese Basile Castrogivanni; m. Alan Francis Starost, May 20, 1990; children: Nicholas Francis, Arianna Marie. MusB in Music Edn., SUNY, 1985; MusM in Music Performance, Manhattan Sch. Music, 1988. Cert. tchr. N.Y. Pvt. practice, Greenlawn, NY, 1980—; vocal music tchr. Manetuck & Oquenock Elem. Schs., West Islip, NY, 1985—92, Udall Mid. Sch., West Islip, NY, 1992—97; dir. youth music Old First Presbyn. Ch., Huntington, NY, 1997—. String tchr. Northport (N.Y.)-East Northport Schs., 1987—91, summer music coord., 1991; colorguard dir., choreographer West Islip (N.Y.) Schs., 1987—91, all dist. chorus dir., 1991—94; musical theater dir., adv. Udall Middle Sch., West Islip, 1992—97, West Side Elem., Syosset, NY, 2000—01, Cold Spring Harbor Schs. Soloist Old First Ch., Huntington, NY, 1984—. Recipient Crane Performers cert., Crane Student Tchg. award; Crane Merit scholar, SUNY, 1985. Mem.: Music Educators Nat. Conf., N.Y. State Sch. Music Assn., Suffolk County Music Educators Assn. Roman Catholic. Avocations: music, art, cooking, gardening. Home: 16 Geneva Pl Greenlawn NY 11740 E-mail: dialstar@yahoo.com.

STARR, SANDRA SCHJELDAHL, music educator; b. Torrance, Calif., Oct. 19, 1941; d. Norris Goodwin Schjeldahl and Zora Ellen Shearer; m. Kenneth Ray Starr, Aug. 18, 1974; 1 child, Rebecca Ellen. BA, St. Olaf Coll., 1963; MME, U. N.D., 1966. Cert. tchr. N.D. Vocal music tchr. Lake Mills Cmty. Schs., Iowa, 1963—67; music edn. prof. Minot State U., ND, 1967—, chair divsn. music, 2005—. Dir. of music 1st Luth. Ch., Minot, 1972—2003; founder, dir. Western Plains Children's Choir, Western Plains Opera Co., Minot, 1991—; chair divsn. music Minot State U., 2004—. Contbr. articles. Adjudicator various music festivals, N.D. and Mont., 1972—; clinician N.D. Music Educators Assn. Confs.; hon, life mem. PTA. Mem.: Orgn. of Am. Kodaly Educators, Coll. Music Soc., Music Educators Nat. Conf. (bd. dirs. 1970—74, 1982—86), Am. Choral Dirs. Assn. (life), Delta Kappa Gamma (chpt. pres. 2006—), Sigma Alpha Iota (life). Lutheran. Avocations: travel, sewing, music, computer, games. Home: 1118 Valley View Dr Minot ND 58703 Office: Minot State Univ 500 W University Ave Minot ND 58707 Office Phone: 701-858-3185. Business E-Mail: sandra.starr@minotstateu.edu.

STARR, SHARON DIANE, elementary school educator; b. Newton, Kans., Aug. 1, 1953; d. Warner Grey and Dorothy Louise (Schlup) Williams; m. Fredric Ross Starr, oct. 8, 1976; children: Caleb, Kristi. BS Elem. Edn., BS History, Coll. of the Ozarks, 1975. Elem. tchr. Tulsa (Okla.) Christian Acad., 1975-78; tchr. kindergarten La Petite Acad., Tulsa, 1979-81; tchr. first and second grades Tulsa Christian Sch., 1985-91, Trinity Christian Sch., Broken Arrow, Okla., 1991; tchr. first grade Southpark Christian Sch., Tulsa, 1991—. Numerous activities at Eastland Bapt. Ch., Tulsa, including: Sunday Sch. tchr., children's choir dir., ch. organist, vocalist, ch. camp counselor, Vacation Bible Sch. tchr. Named Tchr. of Yr., Southpark Christian Sch., 2004—05, Wal-Mart Tchr. of Yr., 2002. Republican. Avocations: reading, playing piano, riding motorcyle. Home: 10584 E 2nd St Claremore OK 74019-5465 Office: Southpark Christian Sch 10811 E 41st St Tulsa OK 74146-2710

STARRATT, JEANETTE ELLEN, elementary school educator; b. San Jose, Calif., Oct. 27, 1943; d. Raymond Walter Huston and Lee Ellen (Smith) Huston-Schwarzbach; m. Norman D. Starratt, Nov. 23, 1962 (div. 1998); children: Mark Todd, Wendy Ellen. AA, Foothill Coll., 1974; BA with honors, San Jose State U., 1978. Tchr./tchr. aide Palo Alto (Calif.) Unified Sch. Dist., 1979-87; tchr. Challenger Sch., San Jose, Calif., 1987-88; owner Starratt Enterprises, Los Altos Hills, Calif., 1983—97; mgr. Clark's Book Store, Palo Alto, 1988-91; co-owner Secret Staircase Bookshop, Redwood City, Calif., 1992—97; tchr. 4th grade Cupertino Union Sch. Dist., 1999—. Pres. Sequoyah Elem. Sch. PTA, Palo Alto, 1976; co-pres. Wilbur Mid. Sch. PTA, Palo Alto, 1978; rep. Supts. Com. for Sch. Closure, Palo Alto, 1975, former mem. Mem. AAUW (mentor), No. Calif. Children's Booksellers Assn. (sec. 1990-91), No. Calif. Ind. Booksellers Assn., Redwood City Merchant's Group (sec. 1993), Hewlett Packard Sailing Club (Posadero award 1983), Assn. of Booksellers for Children, Redwood City San Mateo County C. of C., Cupertino Edn. Assn., Nat. Edn. Assn., Calif. Tchrs. Assn. Home: Jasmine Cottage 84 Murray Ct Redwood City CA 94061-3827 Office: Faria Acads Plus Sch 10155 Barbara Ln Cupertino CA 95014

STARRETT, LUCINDA, lawyer; b. Washington, June 21, 1957; BA magna cum laude, Princeton U., 1979; student, U. Nigeria, Nsukka, 1980-84; JD cum laude, U. Pa., 1984. Bar: Calif. 1986. Law clerk to Hon. Dorothy W. Nelson U.S. Ct. Appeals (9th cir), 1984-85; ptnr. Latham & Watkins, L.A., 1991—. Chief comment editor Jour. Capital Markets and Securities Regulation, 1983. Mem. bd. alternative dispute resolution Western Justice Ctr. Fulbright scholar, Nigeria, 1980—81. Mem. ABA, L.A. County Bar Assn. Office: Latham & Watkins 633 W 5th St Ste 4000 Los Angeles CA 90071-2005 E-mail: cindy.starrett@lw.com.

STARR-WILSON, CAROL ANN, small business owner, retired researcher and genealogist; b. Camp Mackall, N.C., Dec. 22, 1943; d. Hinkle Melvin Starr and Katie Ruth Holcombe-Starr; m. Neil Elmo Rizzotto, Jan. 12, 1967 (div. Mar. 1972); children: Tab Anthoney, Tammy Ann, Scotti Ivan, Kimberly Kay Johnson-Rizzotto-Grace; m. James Edward Wilson, May 14, 1988. Student, Long Beach City Coll., Calif., 1983, Marrinellos Beauty Coll., 1983, Herald Bus. Coll., Walnut Creek, Calif., 1984—85. Sec. Peavy Automotive, Hayward, Calif., 1980—81, Clinic for Adults and Children, San Leandro, Calif., 1981, Baca & Sons Painting, San Francisco, 1981—85; sec. to dir. Naval Supply Ctr., Oakland, Calif., 1985—86; sec. Mil-Spec Industries, Brisbane, Calif., 1986; genealogist, rschr. Amonsoquath Tribe of Cherokee, 1996—2000; owner, genealogist, rschr. Rsch. Desk of Tat-su-hwa (The Redbird), 2000—. Genealogist, rschr. Amonsoquath Tribe of Cherokee, 1996—2000; owner, genealogist, rschr. Rsch. Desk of Tat-su-hwa. Mem.: Lost Dutchman's Mining Assn., Little Rock Hist. Soc., Pope/Faulkner Counties Hist. Soc., Beta Sigma Chi. Democrat. Seventh Day Adventist. E-mail: tatsuhwa@direcway.com, tatsuhwa03@yahoo.com.

STARUCH, ELIZABETH, theater educator; d. Stephen and Helen Staruch. BA with honors, Coll. Wooster, Ohio, 1995; MFA, U. NC, Greensboro, 1999. Grad. tchg. asst. U. NC, Greensboro, 1996—99; mem. faculty theater and dance West Chester U., Pa. Choreographer (musical) Hair (Nat. Commendation for choreography, Kennedy Ctr. Am. Coll. Theatre Festival, 2005), (dance) Bach Follies (Am. Coll. Dance Festival selection, 1997). Avocations: tennis, swimming, billiards, theater. Office: West Chester Univ EO Bull Ctr Rosedale Ave West Chester PA 19383 Office Phone: 610-436-3356. Business E-Mail: estaruch@wcupa.edu.

STASI, LINDA, writer, television producer, editor, scriptwriter; b. NYC, Apr. 14, 1947; d. Anthony John and Florence (Barbara) Stasi; m. John Rovello, Nov. 22, 1970 (div.); 1 child, Jessica Stasi Rovello. BFA, NY Inst. Tech., 1970; postgrad., Hofstra U., 1971. Pres. Linda Stasi & Assocs., Inc., 1978—84; editor beauty and health New Woman mag., 1984—86; editor-in-chief Beauty Digest mag., 1986—88; editor health and beauty Elle mag., 1987—88; beauty editor Cosmopolitan mag., 1988—. Prodr., creator, host Good Looks Line, 1979—81; editor: Seventeen mag., 1970—74; columnist Inside NY, 1989—, NY Newsday, 1989—, contract screenwriter, 1989—; author: Simply Beautiful, 1983, Looking Good is the Best Revenge, 1984, A Fieldguide to Impossible Men, 1987; syndicated writer NY Daily News, 1984—, Tribune Syndicate, 1984—, Times of London, feature writer Redbook, Mademoiselle, Cosmopolitan, Elle, Harper's Bazaar, Newsday, Washington Post, host, prodr. (TV series) Disney Channel, 1983. Home: 20 Waterside Plz New York NY 10010-2612 Office: Newsday 235 Pinelawn Rd Melville NY 11747-4250

STASKO, ANDREA ALOIA, physical education instructor; b. Sommerville, NJ, Mar. 13, 1955; d. Attilio Saturn and Catherine Loretta Aloia; m. Michael Edward Stasko, Oct. 9, 1977; children: Peter Michael, Michael Edward II, Paul Andrew. BS in Phys. Edn., Niagara U., NY, 1977. Physical Education Teaching K-12 NY State, 1989. Elem. and adaptive phy. ed. instr. Byron-Bergen Ctrl. Sch., Bergen, NY, 1977—, varsity girls soccer coach, 1978—81, jv girls basketball coach, 1977—78, girls jv softball coach, 1978—81, ski club advisor, 1987—. Phys. edn., health curriculum coord. Byron-Bergen Ctrl. Sch., 1999—2002. Youth soccer league Genesee Area Soccer Assn., Batavia, NY, 1989—99. Recipient Genesee County Coach of the Yr., Genesee soccer league, 1980, 1981. Mem.: AAHPERD (assoc.). Free Methodist. Avocations: travel, skiing, sailing. Home: 16 Woodland Dr Batavia NY 14020 Office: Byron-Bergen Elem Sch 6971 W Bergen Rd Bergen NY 14416 Office Phone: 585-494-1220 1308. Business E-Mail: astasko@bbcs.k12kny.us.

STASSINOPOULOS, ARIANNA See HUFFINGTON, ARIANNA

STATEN, DONNA KAY, elementary school educator; b. Temple, Tex., Apr. 17, 1958; d. Paul James and Doris Mary (Kleypas) Hoelscher; 1 child, Ryan. BS in Edn., U. Mary Hardin-Baylor, Belton, Tex., 1980. Cert. tchr. in art, elem. edn., health, phys. edn., recreation, gifted and talented edn., Tex. Art tchr. Meridith Magnet Sch., Temple, 1980-84, 1991—2000; bank officer mktg. Tex. Am. Bank, Houston, 1985-88; pvt. practice art tchr., designer Houston, 1989; tchr. ESL Aldine Ind. Sch. Dist., Houston, 1990; art tchr. Kennedy-Powell Acad., Temple, 2000—. Exec. dir. Visual Arts Friends of the Cultural Activities Ctr., Temple, 1993-95, Temple Sister Cities Corp., Temple,

1994-97; chmn. fine arts team Meridith Campus, 1993-96; state rev. panelist Tex. Edn. Agy., 1997; curator Artsonia.com student art gallery, 2002—; dir. Binney & Smith Camp Crayola, 2003; presenter in field. Curator Internat. Children's Art Exhbn., 1996, 2003, 04, 05, art exhibit From Russia with Love, 1992-95. Mem. Contemporaries, Temple, 1994—2001; treas. Oaks Homeowners Assn., Temple, 1994—95, sec. bd. dirs., 1997—99; mem. Temple Mayor's Panel; bd. sec. Keep Temple Beautiful, 1997—99; Tchr.'s Honor Scroll Internat. Project, 2001—02; pres. Assn. Tex. Profl. Educators; singer St. Luke's Ch. Choir, Temple, 1991—; mem. St. Luke's Women's Soc., 1993—. Recipient honorable mention in Christmas Decorating Contest Women's Day mag., 1989, cert. of recognition Crayola/Binney & Smith, 1993-94, 95-96, 97-2001, 03-04, 04-05, Golden Apple Tchr. award Sta. KWTX-TV, 2002; named Rotary Club Educator of the Month, 2004; Focus on Edn. grantee, Wal-Mart, 2001. Mem. ASCD, AAUW, Fine Arts Network, Internat. Soc. for Edn. Through Art, Nat. Art Edn. Assn., Tex. Classrm. Tchrs. Assn., Am. Craft Coun., Soc. Craft Designers, Tex. Computer Edn. Assn., Tex. Fine Arts Assn., Tex. Art Edn. Assn. (presenter 2005 conf.), Nat. Mus. of Women in the Arts, Cultural Activities Ctr., Temple Assn. for the Gifted, Electronic Media Interest Group, Tex. Alliance Edn. and the Arts., Friends of the Temple Libr., Tex. Assn. Gifted and Talented. Roman Catholic. Avocations: gardening, painting and drawing, singing. Office: Kennedy-Powell Acad 3707 W Nugent Ave Temple TX 76504 Address: 2420 Holly Ln Temple TX 76502-2669 Office Phone: 254-215-6000. Personal E-mail: donna.staten@tisd.org.

STATHAKOPOULOS, MELISSA, recreation director; b. San Mateo, Calif., Apr. 3, 1977; d. Dennis Forrest and Heather Taylor; m. Kris Stathakopoulos, June 3, 2006. BA in liberal Studies, San Francisco State U., 2001. Kinder accreditation for tchrs. USA Gymnastics, Calif., cert. movement edn. and lesson plan devel. USA Gymnastics, Calif., safety USA Gymnastics, CPR and first aid Red Cross. Preschool dir. Jr. Gym, San Mateo, Calif., 1996—2002; gymnastics coord. City of San Mateo, 2002—. Mem. Wall of Tolerance, Montgomery, Ala. Recipient Customer Svc. award, City of San Mateo, 2005. Mem.: Caifornia Parks & Recreation Soc. (assoc.), USA Gymnastics (assoc.). Avocation: photography. Personal E-mail: pnkin71@hotmail.com.

STATHOS, ANASTASIA, retired elementary school educator; b. Cambridge, Mass., Apr. 8, 1918; d. Anthony John nad Panzy Stathos. Diploma, Lesley Coll., 1939; BEd, Boston U., 1941, MEd, 1960. Tchr. grades 1-5 Berlin (Mass.) Sch. Dept., 1943-44; tchr. grade 4 Kingston (Mass.) Sch. Dept., 1944-46, Winchester (Mass.) Sch. Dept., 1946-48, Belmont (Mass.) Sch. Dept., 1948-93, ret., 1993. Co-author and developer social studies curricula. Mem. Nat. Tchrs. Assn., Mass. Tchrs. Assn., Belmont Tchrs. Assn. Greek Orthodox. Avocations: music, reading, travel. Home: 13 Goodman Rd Cambridge MA 02139-1608

STATHOS, DONNA LEE, mathematics educator; b. Exeter, N.H., Oct. 27, 1953; d. Herman and Catherine Elizabeth Bohle; children: Erica Spechuilli, Christina. BS, Plymouth State Coll., N.H., 1975; MEd, Notre Dame Coll., N.H., 1997. Math tchr. SAU #15, Candia, NH, 1975—2006. Advisor 8th grade graduation, Candia, NH, 1977—2006; 8th grade yearbook advisor, Candia, 1980—2006. Pres. Candia Edn. Assn., NH, 1978—85, treas., 1985—2006. Avocations: quilting, gardening, scrapbooks, sports. Home: 25 Old Fremont Rd Raymond NH 03077

STATHOS, LIFTERIA K., retired educational association administrator; b. Hartford, Conn. d. Peter Karlames and Nota Politis; AA with honors, Tunxis CC, Farmington, Conn., 1971; BA, BS, Ctrl. Conn. State U., New Britain, 1980, MA, 1982. Edn. sec. Bur. Pupil Pers. and Spl. Edn. Svcs., State Dept. Edn., Hartford, 1959—69, edn. acct., 1969—80, edn. adminstr., 1980—89. Co-chmn. St. George Ch. Libr., New Britain; New Britain Gen. Hosp. Aux.; mem. planning com. Hospice of Greater New Britain; founder ch. libr. St. George Ch., New Britain, 1993—. Mem.: AAUW, Daus. Penelope (life), New Britain Indsl. Mus., Ladies Philoptochos Soc. (bd. dirs., former pres., v.p., sec., treas.), New Britain Mus. Am. Art, Coll. Club New Britain (mem. scholarship com. 1989). Republican. Greek Orthodox. Avocations: piano, stamp collecting/philately, gardening, cooking, reading. Home: 40 Knollwood Dr New Britain CT 06052-1123

STAUBER, MARILYN JEAN, retired elementary and secondary school educator; b. Duluth, Minn., Feb. 5, 1938; d. Harold Milton and Dorothy Florence (Thompson) Froehlich; children: Kenneth D. and James H. Atkinson; m. Lawrence B. Stauber Sr., Jan. 11, 1991 (dec.). BS in Edn., U. Minn., Duluth, 1969, MEd in Math., 1977. Cert. elem. and secondary reading tchr., remedial reading specialist, devel. reading tchr., reading cons. Sec. div. vocat. rehab. State Minn., Duluth, 1956-59; sec. Travelers Ins. Co., Duluth, 1962-66; lead tchr. Title 1 reading and math. Proctor, Minn., 1969-98; ret. Mem. choirs and Choral Soc. John Duss Music, chairperson Outreach, Forbes Meth. Ch., proctor. Mem. NEA, VFW, Internat. Reading Assn., Nat. Reading Assn., Minn. Arrowhead Reading Coun., Elem. Coun. (pres. 1983-84, 86-87), Proctor Fedn. Tchrs. (recert. com. 1980—, treas. 1981-86), Proctor Edn. Assn. (chairperson recert. com.), Am. Legion, Euclid Ea. Star, Phi Delta Kappa. Home: 6713 Grand Lake Rd Saginaw MN 55779-9782

STAUBER-JOHNSON, ELIZABETH JANE, retired elementary school educator; b. Duluth, Minn., Apr. 7, 1950; d. Edward James and Kathleen Mary (LeBlanc) Stauber; m. A(lden) Ronald Johnson, July 26, 1975; children: Todd Alden, Heidi Ann, Dean Edward, Shane Ronald. BS summa cum laude, Coll. St. Scholastica, 1972; MEd summa cum laude, U. Minn., Duluth, 1982; PhD in Curric./Instrn. Elem. Math. Edn., U. Minn., 1996. Cert. tchr., Minn. Tchr. Ind. Sch. Dist. 709/Duluth Pub. Schs., 1972-88; tchr. elem. math. Nettleton Math./Sci./Computer Magnet Sch., Duluth, 1988-93; asst. prof. math. edn. U. Wis., Superior, 1993-97; ret., 1997. Pres. Equine Attire, Inc., 2004—; trainer Success Understanding Math. Project, Des Moines, gender-ethnic excellence student achievement GESA, 1991—; instr. tchr. Family Math., Mpls., 1988—; mem. project for reforming and improving math. edn. com. Minn. Dept. Edn., math. framework team, 1992—; com. mem. Gov.'s Nat. Sci. Found. Statewide Systemic Initiative, 1991—, Coll. of St. Scholastica Ctr. for Promotion of Underrepresented in Sci., 1990—; desegregation adv. com. Duluth Schs., 1987—; initiative com. Gov.'s Nat. Sci. Found.; team mem. Minn. Dept. Edn. Math. Frameworks; presenter in field Trustee Coll. St. Scholastica, Duluth, chair acad. affairs; bd. dirs. Marshal Coll. Prep. Sch., 2003—, v.p., 2004—; pres. Equine Allies, Inc., 2004—. Mem. Minn. Coun. Tchrs. Math., Nat. Assn. Tchrs. Math., Minn. Reading Assn., Arrowhead Reading Coun. (bd. dirs. 1984—, pres. 1988-89), Assn. Childhood Edn. (pres. Duluth chpt. 1980-81, state bd. dirs. 1982-83), Phi Kappa Phi, Alpha Delta Kappa (pres. 1982-84), Phi Delta Kappa. Avocations: reading, children's pop-up books, orchid collecting/growing, showing and breeding quarter horses. Home: 2400 Minnesota Ave Duluth MN 55802-2518

STAUFFER, JOANNE ROGAN, steel company official; b. Coatesville, Pa., Oct. 15, 1956; d. Joseph Chester and Anne Mary (Kauffman) Rogan; m. Robert Lee Marvin Stauffer, Oct. 15, 1988. AS in Bus. Adminstrn., Harrisburg Area C.C., 1979, student, 1986—88; BS in Leadership, Duquesne U., 2000, MA in Leadership, 2004. Store acct. Giant Foods, Harrisburg, Pa., 1977—79; payroll clk. Bethlehem Steel (name changed to Pa. Steel Techs., bankrupt 2003, co. sold to Mittal Steel USA, Chgo.), Steelton, Pa., 1980—83, material and cost acct., 1983—86, cost analyst, 1986—96, bus. mgr. for gen. mech. dept., 1996—2002, coord. steelmaking dept., 2002—. Treas. Pot of Gold Investors, 1997—. Mem. Internat. Platform Assn., Am. Bus. Women's Assn. (corr. sec. Rainbow Valley charter chpt. 1991-92, v.p. 1992-93, pres. 1993-94, 2005—), Steelton Plant Engrs. Club (sec. 1982-85, v.p. 1985-86, pres. 1986-87). Republican. Avocations: outdoor activities, swimming, horses, reading, crafts. Home: 401 Sheetz Rd Halifax PA 17032-9695 E-mail: JRStauffer@yahoo.com.

STAUTBERG, SUSAN SCHIFFER, communications executive; b. Nov. 9, 1945; d. Herbert F. and Margaret (Berwind) Schiffer; m. T. Aubrey Stautberg, Jr., Dec. 10, 1979. BA, Wheaton Coll., 1967; MA, George Washington U., 1970. Nat. TV corr., Washington, 1970-74; fellow White Ho., Washington, 1974-75; dir. comm. U.S. Consumer Products Safety Commn., Washington, 1976-78, McNeil Consumer Products Co., 1978-80; v.p. Fraser Assocs., Washintgon, 1980; exec. asst. to pres. Morgan Stanley & Co., NYC, 1980-82; dir. comm. Deloitte & Touche, NYC, 1982; pres. MasterMedia Ltd., 1986—, PartnerCom, NYC. Bd. dirs. States Inc. Author: Making It in Less Than an Hour, 1976, Pregnancy Nine to Five: The Career Woman's Guide to Pregnancy and Motherhood, 1985, The Pregnancy and Motherhood Diary: Planning the First Year of Your Second Career, 1988, Managing It All, 1989, Balancing Act, 1992. Mem. nat. chmn. adv. coun. Ctr. Study Presidency, 1976—; mem. Phila. Regional Panel Selection White Ho. Fellows; bd. dirs. Schiffer Pub., Berwind Found.; mem. Reagan-Bush Presdl. Transition Team; mem. Commn. Presdl. Scholars; State Dept. spkr. Selected One of Wheaton's 10 Most Oustanding Grads. Alumnea Assn. Wheaton Coll., 1982. Mem. Pub. Rels. Soc. Am. (bd. dirs.), Pub. Affairs Profls., Nat. Soc. Colonial Dames, Acorn Club, City Tavern Club, Cosmopolitan Club, Colony Club, Radnor Hunt Club. Office: PartnerCom 17 E 89th St Ste 7D New York NY 10128-0615

STAVES, SUSAN, humanities educator; b. N.Y.C., Oct. 5, 1942; d. Henry Tracy and Margaret (McClemon) Staves. AB, U. Chgo., 1963; MA, U. Va., 1964, PhD, 1967. Woodrow Wilson intern Bennett Coll., Greensboro, NC, 1965-66; from asst. prof. to prof. Brandeis U., Waltham, Mass., 1967-93, Paul Proswimmer prof. of Humanities, 1993—2001, dept. chair, 1986-89, 95-98, prof. emerita, 2001—. Clark prof. UCLA, 1989—90. Author: Players' Scepters: Fictions of Authority in the Restoration, 1979, Married Women's Separate Property in England, 1660-1833, 1990, A Literary History of Women's Writing in Britain, 2005, Studies on Voltaire and the 18th Century, (essays) Fetter'd or Free?: Collected Essays on 18th Century Women Novelists, 1986, History, Gender, and 18th Century Literature, 1994, Woman and Political Writing, 1998, Enchanted Ground: Reimagining John Dryden, 2004, Cambridge Companion to Aphra Behn, 2004; co-author (with John Brewer): Early Modern Conceptions of Property, 1994; co-editor (with Cynthia Ricciardi): Elizabeth Griffith's Delicate Distress, 1997; contbr. articles to profl. jours. Mem. ACLU, 1967—; assoc. mem. Belmont Dem. Town Com., Belmont, Mass. Woodrow Wilson fellow, 1963—64, Woodrow Wilson Dissertation fellow, 1966—67, Harvard Liberal Arts fellow, 1980—81, John Simon Guggenheim fellow, 1981—82. Mem.: AAUP, MLA (exec. com. divsn. on late 18th century English lit. 1984—86), English Inst., Am. Soc. for 18th Century Studies (exec. bd. 1987—90). Episcopalian. Avocations: hiking, harpsichord. Office: Brandeis U Dept English MS 023 Waltham MA 02454 Office Phone: 781-736-2161. Business E-Mail: staves@brandeis.edu.

STAVISKY, TOBY ANN, state legislator; b. NYC; m. Leonard Stavisky, 1964 (dec. 1999); 1 child, Evan. BA, Syracuse U.; Grad. Degree, Hunter Coll., Queens Coll. Social studies tchr. N.Y.C. Pub. High Schs.; dist. mgr. N.E. Queens 1980 Census; mem. N.Y. Senate from 16th Dist., Albany, 1999—, asst. minority whip, 2003—. Mem. legis. commns. fin., tourism, recreation and sports devel. N.Y. State Sen. 16th Dist., ranking minority mem., mem. aging com., mem. civil svc. and pensions com., mem. edn. com. Founder North Flushing Sr. Ctr., bd. dirs.; trustee Whitestone Hebrew Ctr. Named Worthy Woman of Forest Hills; recipient Claire Shulman award, Top 10 Women in Bus., 2004, award, Neurol. Impaired Brain Injured Children, 2002, Counseling, Admissions and Fin. Aid Legis. Consortium, 2003, Flushing C. of C. and Bus. Assn., Taiwanese Assn. Am., CUNY, Korean-Am. Assn. Flushing. Democrat. Office: Rm 504 Legislative Office Bldg Albany NY 12247 also: 14436 Willets Point Blvd Flushing NY 11357-3411 Office Phone: 718-445-0004. Business E-Mail: stavisky@senate.state.ny.us.

STAVOLE, JANET M., librarian, director; b. Cleve., Nov. 25, 1949; d. Frank A and Gertrude E Stavole. BA, Kent State U., 1972, MLS, 1972—77. Children's libr. Kent Free Libr., Ohio, 1973—78, Main Children's Rm. Akron-Summit County Pub. Libr., Akron, Ohio, 1979—85; br. mgr. & early childhood libr. Nordonia Hills Br. Akron-Summit County Pub. Libr., Northfield Ctr., Ohio, 1985—. Pres. Akron-Summit County Pub. Libr. Staff Assn., 1984—85. Mem.: Ohio Libr. Coun. Avocations: reading, gardening, art. Office: Akron-Summit County Pub Libr 9458 Olde Eight Rd Northfield OH 44067 Office Phone: 330-467-8595. Office Fax: 330-467-4332. E-mail: jstavole@akronlibrary.org.

STAVROPOULOS, ROSE MARY GRANT, community activist, volunteer; b. Decatur, Ill. d. Walter Edwin and Ora Lenore (Kepler) Grant; m. Stan Stavropoulos; children: Becky Ann Stavropoulos Betian, Stephanie Diane. BS, Ea. Ill. U. Cert. elem. edn. Tchr. 2nd grade Garfield Sch., Decatur; bd. dirs. Wilmot Sch. Bd. PTA, Deerfield, Moraine Girl Scout Coun., Deerfield, also bd. dirs.; chmn. Human Rels. Commn., Deerfield; mem. sr. citizen adv. com. Deerfield Park Dist.; pres. Lake County (Ill.) LWV; chmn. Deerfield Village Caucus; pres. Caring For Others, Inc., Deerfield, Deerfield Area LWV; bd. mem., pres. Deerfield Area United Way, pres. Mem. Deerfield Village Caucus Adv. Coun. Recipient Deerfield Human Rels. Humanitarian award, Lerner Life's Citizen of Month. Mem. Deerfield Area Hist. Soc., Highland Park Hosp. Aux, Legacy at Bryant Ranch Home Assn. (bd. dirs., treas., sec.), Delta Zeta. Home: 23959 Sanctuary Pkwy Yorba Linda CA 92887 Personal E-mail: jjjjgrandma@aol.com.

STAY, BARBARA, zoologist, educator; b. Cleve., Aug. 31, 1926; d. Theron David and Florence (Finley) S. AB, Vassar Coll., 1947; MA, Radcliffe Coll., 1949, PhD, 1953. Entomologist Army Research Center, Natick, Mass., 1954-60; vis. asst. prof. Pomona Coll., 1960; asst. prof. biology U. Pa., 1961-67; asso. prof. zoology U. Iowa, Iowa City, 1967-77, prof., 1977—. Fulbright fellow to Australia, 1953; Lalor fellow Harvard U., 1960 Fellow AAAS, Entomol. Soc. Am.; mem. Soc. Comparative and Integrative Biology, Am. Inst. Biol. Scis., Am. Soc. Cell Biology, Iowa Acad. Scis., Sigma Xi. Office: U Iowa Dept Biological Scis Iowa City IA 52242 E-mail: barbara-stay@uiowa.edu.

STCHUR, MARY NANORTA, literature and language professor; d. John Edward and Marian Moore Nanorta; children: Suzanne Marian Jones, Diane Marie Bray, Peter, Julianne Cote, Joanne Shultz, Michael John, Marianne. BA in English, Coll. Misericordia, Dallas, Pa; M in English Edn., Wilkes U., Pa., 1998. Asst. prof. English Luzerne County C.C., Nanticoke, Pa., 1989—. Advisor lit. arts soc. Luzerne County C.C., Nanticoke, Pa., 2001—. Office: Luzerne County CC 1333 S Prospect St Nanticoke PA 18634 Office Phone: 570-740-0600.

STEA, MARY LUCILLE, secondary school educator; d. William and Mary deFelice; divorced; 1 child, Daniel III. MA, CW Post, NY, 1974; BFA, NY IT, 1969. Art tchr. Hicksville HS, NY, 1969—. Facilitator sociology Suffolk CC, NY, 1987—88. Active MADD, NY, 1987—. Avocations: poetry, music.

STEADMAN, LYDIA DUFF, symphony violinist, retired elementary school educator; b. Hollywood, Calif., Dec. 31, 1934; d. Lewis Marshall and Margaret Seville (Williams) Duff; m. John Gilford Steadman, Apr. 14, 1961 (dec.). Student, Pepperdine U., 1952-55; BA in Music Edn., U. So. Calif., 1957. Cert. spl. secondary music, edn. tchr., Calif. Instrumental music tchr. Lancaster (Calif.) Sch. Dist., 1957-62, Simi Sch. Dist., Simi Valley, Calif., 1962-70, elem. tchr., 1970—2001. Tchr. Polynesian culture, dances, games, 1970—; hist. play wright for elem. grades, organizer elem. sch. dance festivals; dir. All Dist. Orch., Lancaster, Simi Valley Schs., 1957-70; compile Japanese Culture Study Unit for elem. grades Ventura County. Musician (1st violinist) San Fernando Valley Symphony, Sherman Oaks, Calif., 1962-75, Valley Symphony, Van Nuys, 2001—, Simi Valley's Santa Susana Symphony, Conejo Valley Symphony, Thousand Oaks, 1975-81, tour concert mistress, 1980; (2d violinist) Ventura County Symphony, Santa Susana Symphony, 1981-95, Young Artists Ensemble, Civic Arts Plaza, 2001-05, 2006, LA Drs. Symphony, 2001-, sec., Kenai Peninsula Orch., Alaska, Camarillo HS Theatre Orch., 2003-04, Loyola Marymount Orch., 2003, 04, 06; (violinist) Calif. Luth. U. Orch Pres. San Fernando Cmty. Concerts, Van Nuys, Calif., 1982-94; free lancing with pit orch. Cabrillo Music Theatre, Conejo Players Theater, Moorpark Coll. Theatre, Newbury Park H.S. Theater Orch., 2001—; coun. mem. LA Doctors Symphony, 2001—, bd. dirs. and sec.; sec. 1st and 2d violins Kenai Peninsula Orch., Alaska; organizer ann. sch. Jump Rope-a-Thon for Am. Heart Assn., Nat. Geog. Geography Bee; bd. dirs. East Ventura County Cmty. Concert Assn.; organ completion com. Ascension LUth. Ch., Thousand Oaks Mem. AAUW, NAFE, L.A. World Affairs Coun., Bus. and Profl. Women of Conejo Valley (pres. Golden Triangle chpg. 1988-90, 95-96, issues and mgmt. chair 1990, ways and means chair Coast chpt. 1990, editor Golden Triangle newsletter 1988-90, treas. 1992-93, sec. 1993-94, v.p. 1994—, organizing spkr. 2005), Pacific Asia Mus., Armand Hammer Mus., Sigma Xi. Republican. Lutheran. Avocations: hula dancing, walking, coin collecting/numismatics, travel, violin. Home: 32016 Allenby Ct Westlake Village CA 91361-4001

STEARMAN, SHERRI LYNN, physical education educator; d. Mark Dillon and Barbara Ann Jones; m. John Patrick Stearman, Aug. 8, 1966; children: Anna Marion, Patrick Dillon. BS in History and Dance, Tex. Woman's U., Denton, 1994. Cert. tchr. Tex., 1995. Tchr. phys. edn. James L. Collins Cath. Sch., Corsicana, Tex., 1995—97; tchr. H.S. dance Sunset H.S. Dallas Ind. Sch. Dist., 1998—. Mem. Daus. of The King, 2005—06. Mem.: Dallas Dance Educators (v.p. 2003—04). Episcopalian. Avocations: scrapbooking, dance, travel, Bible study. Office: Sunset HS 2120 W Jefferson Blvd Dallas TX 75208 Office Phone: 972-502-1500.

STEARNS, ANN KAISER, psychologist, educator, writer; b. Thomas, Okla., Sept. 7, 1942; d. E. A. and Margaret O. Kaiser; m. James Larry Stearns (div.); children: Amanda Asha, Ashley Anjali. BA, Okla. City U., 1964; MDiv, Duke U., Durham, N.C., 1967; PhD, Union Inst. U., Cin., 1977. Assoc. chaplain United Ministries Mich. State U., Lansing, Mich., 1969; prof. psychology C.C. of Balt. County, Md., 1970—; adj. prof. Loyola Coll., Balt., 1977—84, Police Exec. Leader Program, Johns Hopkins U., Balt., 1999—; faculty behavioral scientist Family Practice Residency Program Franklin Squares Hosp., Balt. County, Md., 1975—85. Author: (Book) Living Through Personal Crisis, 1985, Coming Back: Rebuilding Lives After Crisis and Loss, 1988, Living Through Job Loss, 1995; contbr. articles to profl. jour. Recipient Pastoral Care and Counseling award, Loyola Coll., 1985, Disting. Alumna award, Okla. City U., 1985, Service award, Compassionate Friends, 1992, 2003, Alumni award for Tchg. Excellence, Johns Hopkins U., 2004. Fellow: Md. Psychol. Assn. (Md. Psychology Tchr. of the Yr. 2004); mem.: APA, Am. Assn. Pastoral Counselors. Democrat. Methodist. Avocations: bridge, golf, travel. Office: CC Balt County Essex Campus Rosedale MD 21237 Office Phone: 410-780-6736.

STEARNS, ANN NICHOLSON, education educator; d. Frank M. and Anne Blair Stearns; children: Nancy, Elizabeth, Howard. BA, Hood Coll., 1960; MEd, U. Va., 1974, PhD, 1997. Head of acquisitions Nova U., Ft. Lauderdale, Fla., 1967—68; pres. Aurora Sch., Inc., Waynesboro, Va., 1970—73; supr. Augusta County Pub. Schs., Fishersville, Va., 1974—80, Va. Dept. Edn., Richmond, 1980—86, Augusta County Schs., Fishersville, 1986—94; instr. James Madison U., Harrisonburg, Pa., 1995—97; asst. prof. Clarion (Pa.) U., 1997—. Faculty adv. Spl. Olympics, Va., 1974—2004, Pa., 1974—2004; active Va. Spl. Edn. Adv. Commn., 1970—73, Va. Ind. Spl. Edn. Facilities, 1972—73; bd. dirs. emeritus Waynesboro (Va.) Players, 1964—2005. Mem.: PEO, Coun. for Exceptional Children. Methodist. Avocations: acting, theater, camping. Home: 244 Wood St Clarion PA 16214 Office: Clarion Univ Clarion PA 16214 E-mail: astearns@clarion.edu.

STEARNS, LINDA BREWSTER, sociologist, educator; d. Herbert Kenneth and Evelyn Brewster; m. Stephen Aronson, Aug. 16, 1992; children from previous marriage: Ronald M., Danielle Marie stepchildren: Peter Aronson, Elizabeth Aronson. BA, SUNY, Stony Brook, 1975, MA, 1978, PhD, 1983. Prof. and chair sociology U. Calif., Riverside, 1989—2003, So. Meth. U., Dallas, 2003—. Mem. editl. bd. Socio-Economic Rev., Rsch. in Political Sociology, Calif. Mgmt. Rev. Contbr. articles to profl. jours. Fellow, George A. and Eliza Howard Found., 1988—89, Ctr. Social Scis., Columbia U., 1989; grantee, NSF, 1993—95, Citicorp Behavior Sci. Rsch. Coun., 1997—2001; vis. scholar, Russell Sage Found., 1988, 2000. Mem.: Am. Sociol. Assn. (chair program com. organizations and occupation sect. 1990—91), So. Sociol. Soc. (program com. 1987—88), Soc. Advancement of Socio-Econ. (exec. coun. mem. 1991—96), Acad. of Mgmt., Internat. Sociology Assn., World Affairs Coun. Greater Dallas (assoc.). Achievements include research in mergers and acquisition, and intracorporate and intercorporate networks. Office: So Meth Univ PO Box 750192 Dallas TX 75275 Office Phone: 214-768-4179.

STEARNS, MARILYN TARPY, music educator; b. Peoria, Ill., Aug. 3, 1936; d. Roger Maynard Tarpy and Nellie Mae Livingston; m. Gordon Woodburn Stearns, June 13, 1958; children: Gordon Schuyler, Jennifer Maye, William Livingston. Student, Ohio Wesleyan U., 1954—56; BA, Mt. Holyoke Coll., 1958; MA, Goddard Coll., 1988. Instr. piano, vocal pvt. practice, 1959—98; substitute tchr. Portslade Schs. C.C., England, 1973—75; owner Grain Weaving, Inc., Springfield, Vt., 1976—85; tchr. Head Start, 1977—78; instr. spl. edn., 1980—81; mission/stewardship cons. Vt. Conf. of United Ch. of Christ, 1982—90; soprano soloist, 1954—; adminstrv. asst. Epilepsy Found. Greater Chgo., 1991; tchr., adminstr., devel. officer Stechman Studio Music, Chgo., 1991—95, Oak Park, 1991—95; tutor voice, piano, music literacy pvt. practice, Chgo., 1995—98, Oak Park, 1995—98. Performed numerous recitals; soloist, oratorio works with choirs throughout New Eng.; soloist Vt. Symphony Orch.; mem. Sounds of Joy Choristers, Burlington Oriana Singers, Vt. Chamber Singers, Arts Acad. Chorale of Shenandoah U. Author: Sunday's Child, 1978, (workbook) The Art of Grain Weaving, 1978, A Handbook on Our Churches, 1990; editor: Don't Throw it Away, Through A Glass Darkly, Children's Sermons for Young Stewards, Reflections on Tithing, Simply Christmas - Good Stewardship, Stewards of History, Stewardship Lenten Devotions, A Church Treasurer's Handbook. Trustee Vt. Hist. Soc., Montpelier, 1983—90; bd. dirs. Epilepsy Found. Vt., Rutland, 1979—83; mission, stewardship, cons. Vt. Conf. United Ch. Christ, 1982—90. Independent. Avocations: archaeology, poetry, travel, art, reading. E-mail: gmstearns@aol.com.

STEARNS, SHEILA MACDONALD, academic administrator; b. Ft. Snelling, Minn., Aug. 30, 1946; d. Alexander Colin and Marie Kristine (Peterson) MacD.; m. Hal Stearns, June 22, 1968; children: Scott, Malin. BA, Univ. Mont., Missoula, 1968, MA, 1969, EdD, 1983. English and history tchr. Wiesbaden (Germany) Jr. High Sch., 1969-72; libr. media specialist Missoula Pub. Schs., 1975-77; dir. alumni rels. Univ. Mont., Missoula, 1983-87, v.p. univ. rels., 1987-93; chancellor Univ. Mont. Western, Dillon, 1993—99; pres. Wayne State Coll., Mich., 1999—2003; commr. higher ed. State of Mont., Helena, 2003—. Contbr. articles to profl. publs. Chair gov. bd. dirs. St. Patrick Hosp., Missoula, 1991-93; mem. Mayor's Adv. Bd., Missoula; nat. chair NAIA Coun. of Pres., 1996-97; chair NAIA Gender Equity com. Mem. Missoula C. of C. (v.p. exec. com.), Rotary (bd. dirs.) Alpha Phi (Chi chpt.), Phi Delta Kappa. Roman Catholic. Avocations: golf, reading, writing. Office: Commissioner Of Higher Education 46 N Last Chance Gulch St Helena MT 59601-4122 Office Phone: 406-444-0311.

STEARNS, SUSAN A., education educator; b. Fresno, Calif. PhD, U. Okla., 1990. Prof., comm. studies Ea. Wash. U., Cheney, 2001—, chair, comm. studies, 2002—. Exec. sec. Ctr. for Academic Integrity, Durham, NC, 2001—04. Mem. Ctr. for Academic Integrity, Durham, NC, 2000—. Rsch. grant, Ea. Wash. U., 2002. Mem.: Internat. Comm. Assn. (life), Nat. Comm. Assn. (life). Office Phone: 504-939-1753. Business E-Mail: sstearns@mail.ewu.edu.

STEARNS, SUSAN TRACEY, lighting design company executive, lawyer; b. Seattle, Oct. 28, 1957; d. Arthur Thomas and Roberta Jane (Arrowood) S.; m. Ross Alan De Alessi, Aug. 11, 1990; 1 child, Chase Arthur. AA, Stephens Coll., 1977, BA, 1979; JD, U. Wash., Seattle, 1990. Bar: Calif. 1990, U.S. Ct. Appeals (9th cir.) 1990, U.S. Dist. Ct. (no. dist.) Calif 1990, U.S. Dist. Ct. (we. dist.) Wash. 1991, Wash. 1991. TV news prodr. KOMO, Seattle, 1980-86; atty. Brobeck, Phleger & Harrison, San Francisco, 1990-92; pres. Ross De Alessi Lighting Design, Seattle, 1993—. Author periodicals in field. Alumnae Assn. Coun. Stephens Coll., Columbia, Mo., 1995—. Named Nat. Order of Barristers, U. Washington, Seattle, 1990. Mem. ABA (mem. state labor and employment law subcom.), Wash. State Bar Assn. (mem. bench-bar-press com.), State Bar Calif., King County Bar Assn., Bar Assn.San Francisco, Wash. Athletic Club. Avocations: travel, dance. Office: Ross De Alessi Lighting Des 2330 Magnolia Blvd W Seattle WA 98199-3813

STEBLETON, MICHELLE MARIE, musician, educator; b. Midland, Mich., Apr. 10, 1966; d. Leo Frederick and Sally Joanne (Brosman) Stebleton. MusB in Horn Performance, U. Mich., 1988, MusM in Horn Performance, 1989; diploma, European Mozart Found., Prague, Czech Republic, 1993. Third horn Ann Arbor (Mich.) Symphony, 1986-89, Saginaw (Mich.) Symphony, 1988-89; hornist Lone Star Brass Quintet, Midland, Tex., 1989-90; prin. horn Midland (Tex.)/Odessa Symphony, 1989-90; adj. prof. horn Odessa (Tex.) Coll., 1990; assoc. prof. horn Fla. State U., Tallahassee, 1990—. Clinician First Internat. Swiss Horn Workshop, 1994, Nove Straseci Internat. Interpreters Course, 1996, 2001; bd. dirs., co. pres. RM Williams Pub., Tallahassee, 1997—; chair faculty senate profl. devel. and welfare com. Fla. State U., Tallahassee, 1999—; lectr. in field. Performer Internat. Mozart Festival, 1991, Orquesta Filarmonica de la UNAM, Mexico City, 1992, Vienna Philharm. Chamber Players, Sapporo, Japan, 1994, 95, Pacific Music Festival, Sapporo, Tokyo, 1994, Sapporo, Hiroshima, Tokyo, 1995, Vienna Chamber Players, Santo Domingo, Dominican Republic, 1997, Internat. Orch. Festival Santo Domingo, 1997, 99, others; soloist (concert tour Vietnam) Fla. State U. Singers, 1999. Fin. advisor Sigma Alpha Iota, Fla. State U., Tallahassee, 1994—; performer Peace Concert, Pacific Music Festival, Hiroshima, Japan, 1995; coord. dept. fundraising United Way Big Bend, Tallahassee, 1998. Recipient second prize Am. Horn Competition-Natural Horn Divsn., 1989, second prize Am. Horn Competition-Profl. Divsn., 1994, 99, Tchg. Incentive Program award State of Fla., Fla. State U., 1996; com. on faculty rsch. support grantee Fla. State U., 1992, 97. Mem. Internat. Horn Soc. (life, co-host, lectr., bd. mem. S.E. region conf. adv. bd. 1991—, first prize solo competition 1987), Nat. Assn. Coll. Wind and Percussion Instrs., Music Educators Nat. Conf., Music Tchrs. Nat. Assn., Pi Kappa Lambda. Avocations: travel, photography, T'ai Chi teaching. Home: 2519 Prest Ct Tallahassee FL 32301-3386 Office: Fla State Univ HMU 127 Tallahassee FL 32306-1180

STECHER, PAULINE, painter, educator; b. Bklyn. d. Helen Solomon; m. Bernard Stecher; children: Martin Alan, David Joseph. Attended, pvt. studio instrn. with Paul Puzinas, NYC, 1961—63. Oil painting instr., Bellerose, Bellerose Village, Little Neck, New Hyde Park, NY, 1965—85. Judge, lecture demonstrator American Pen Women, Floral Park Art League, Flushing Art League, Ind. Art Soc., Island Art Guild, Rockville Ctr. Art Club, Tri-County Artists, Queens Alliance Artists, Suburban Art League, 1978—. Exhibitions include Newington-Cropsey Found. Gallery Art, Hastings-on-Hudson, NY, Westchester County Ctr., NY, Salmagundi Club, NYC, Nat. Arts Club, N.Y.C., N.Y., Nassau County Mus. Art, Roslyn, N.Y., Roslyn, NY; contbr. articles to mags. and books. Recipient Jane Peterson Meml. First Pl. Still Life award, 2004, John R. Grabach Meml. award, 1994, Helen De Cozen award, 1997. Fellow: Hudson Valley Art Assn. (Dumond Meml. award Best Light and Atmospheric Effect, First prize 1998, Georgie Read Barton Meml. award 2002, Jane Peterson Still Life Meml. award, First Pl. Still-Life award 2004), Am. Artists Profl. League (bd. dirs. 1985—2002, Dir.'s award 1991, John R. Grabach Meml. award 1994, Helen De Cozen award 1997, Pres.'s award 1999, 2001); mem.: Coun. Am. Artists Soc. (Painting award 1993), Nat. Art League (Gold medal 1973), Art. League Nassau County (Coun. Am. Artists Soc. Painting award 1993). Avocation: painting. Home: 80 30 250th St Bellerose NY 11426

STECKEL, JULIE RASKIN, psychotherapist, lecturer, consultant; b. Los Angeles, Jan. 3, 1940; d. Edward M. and Selma (Romm-Rosby) Raskin; m. Richard Jay Steckel, June 16, 1960; children: Jan Marie, David Matthew. BA, UCLA, 1960, MSW, 1975; MA in Teaching., Harvard U., 1961. Lic. clin. social worker; Bd. Cert. Diplomate in Clin. Social Work. Music tchr., Los Angeles, Beverly Hills and Santa Monica, Calif., 1968-70; psychol. cons. BMA Dialysis Units, Torrance, Calif., 1976-83; pvt. practice psychotherapy Los Angeles, 1975—. Affiliate staff Del Amo Hosp., Torrance, 1983-90; lectr., cons. UCLA Dental Sch., 1984—; lectr. social welfare UCLA Grad. Sch., 1985-90. Mem. editorial bd. Comtemporary Dialysis and Nephrology Jour.; contbr. articles to jours. Bd. dirs. Palisades Dem. Hdqrs., Pacific Palisades, Calif., 1972; credentials currier Dem. Conv., Miami, Fla., 1972; mem. L.A. Women's Consortium Task Force on Child Abuse, 1990—. Fellow Soc. Clin. Social Workers; mem. Nat. Assn. Social Workers, Acad. Psychosomatic Medicine, Am. Orthopsychiat. Assn. Home: 1126 Bel Air Dr Santa Barbara CA 93105-4642 Office: 3250 Lomita Blvd Ste 304 Torrance CA 90505-5006 also: 1126 Bel Air Dr Santa Barbara CA 93105-4642

STECKER, SUZANNE LOUISE, business executive; b. Orange, Calif., Apr. 22, 1976; d. George Russell and Etta Louise Stecker. BA, Gallaudet U., Washington, 1998; MA, U. Balt., 2000, MFA, 2005—. Pres., creative dir. Design Actually, LLC, Costa Mesa, Calif., 1999—; interactive media mgr. CSD, Sioux Falls, SD, 2003—05; mng. ptnr. InterpreterQuest, LLC, Glenview, Ill., 2004—. Founding mem. DeafRepublicans.com, L.A., 2004. Pres. fellow, Gallaudet U., 2005—. Liberal. Achievements include design of one-of-a-kind Web-based scheduling, billing and request software for sign language interpreting agencies and businesses. Home: 1111 Visalia Dr Costa Mesa CA 92626

STECKLER, PHYLLIS BETTY, publishing consultant; b. NYC; d. Irwin H. and Bertha (Fellner) Schwartzbard; m. Stuart J. Steckler; children: Randall, Sharon Steckler-Slotky. BA, Hunter Coll.; MA, NYU. Editl. dir. R.R. Bowker Co., NYC, Crowell Collier Macmillan Info. Pub. Co., NYC, Holt Rinehart & Winston Info. Systems, NYC; pres., CEO Oryx Press, Scottsdale, Ariz., 1973-76, Phoenix, 1976—2000, Zephyr Info., Phoenix, 2001—; publ. cons., 2001—. Adj. prof. mktg. scholarly publs. Grad. History dept., Ariz. State U., Tempe; mem. dean's coun. Coll. of Extended Edn., Ariz. State U., Phoenix; mem. adv. coun. Republic Bank Ariz., NA. Past chmn. Info. Industry Assn.; past chair Ariz. Ctr. for the Book; past pres. Contemporary Forum of Phoenix Art Mus.; founding mem. Nat. Edn. Network, U.S. Dept. Edn.; past pres. Friends of the Libr., U.S.A.; mem. Ariz. Women's Forum; bd. dirs. Ariz. region Com. for the Weizmann Inst. Sci.; mem. order coun. Republic Bank, Ariz. Recipient Women Who Make a Difference award The Internat. Women's Forum, 1995, Excellence in Pub. award Ariz. Book Pub. Assn., 1997, The Pub. History Program Ariz. State U. Founding Friend award, 2000; elected to Hunter Coll. Hall of Fame. Mem.: ALA, Ariz. Libr. Assn., Univ. Club of Phoenix. Home and Office: 6446 N 28th St Phoenix AZ 85016-8946 E-mail: pbs.zephyr@cox.net.

STEDMAN, MOLLY RENEE, special education educator, researcher; b. Peoria, Ill., Aug. 29, 1972; d. Gary Paul and Kathryn Ann Stedman. BS in Edn., Ill. State U., 1996; MS in Edn., U. Nebr., 1999, postgrad., 2000—. Tchr. Cert. Ill., 1996, Iowa, 1996, Nebr., 2000. Asst. prof., project dir. - deaf and hard of hearing program Marshall U. Grad. Coll., South Charleston, W.Va., 2003—; doctoral grad. tchg. asst. U. Nebr., Lincoln, 2000—03; resource tchr. Nebr. Dept. Edn., Lincoln, 2001—03; tchr. Iowa Sch. for Deaf, Council Bluffs, 1996—2000. Cons. tech. support W.Va. Dept. Edn., Charleston, 2003—. Mem.: W. Va. Deaf-blind Project Adv. Com., Commn. on Multiculturalism Com. (Disabled Student Com.), W. Va. Speech-Language-Hearing Assn., W. Va. Commn. Deaf and Hard of Hearing, W.Va. Assn. of the Deaf, Newborn Hearing Adv. Com., Early Childhood Focus Com., Assn. Coll. Educators-Deaf and Hard of Hearing, Coun. on Edn. of Deaf, Coun. for Exceptional Children. Roman Catholic. Achievements include researching the literacy practices in the homes and preschools of young deaf and hard of hearing children. Office: Marshall University Graduate School 100 Angus E Peyton Drive South Charleston WV 25303-1600 Office Phone: 304-746-1957. E-mail: stedman@marshall.edu.

STEED, CONNIE MANTLE, nurse; b. Ft. Riley, Kans., Oct. 6, 1956; d. Ronald James Jr. and Ivey Coene (Jenkins) Mantle; m. Thomas Joseph Steed, Jr., Aug. 27, 1979; children: Christopher Michael, Robert James. ADN, Columbus Coll., 1976; postgrad. RN, S.C.; cert. in infection control. Nurse aide Bradley Ctr. Psychiatric Hosp., Columbus, Ga., 1975-76; staff nurse West Ga. Med. CTr., LaGrange, 1976-78, nurse epidemiologist, 1978-87, nurse edn. coord., 1987-88; employee health coord. Spartanburg Regional Med. Ctr., S.C., 1988-89; nurse epidemiologist Greenville Meml. Hosp., S.C., 1989—. Nat. infection control adv. bd. mem. SmithKline and Beecham, Inc., 1991-92; nat. adv. com. mem. Standard Textiles, Inc., Cin., 1993-94; cons. Kimberly Clark Healthcare Divsn., Roswell, Ga., 1992, B. Braun, Inc., Bethlehem, Pa., 1992-93; mem. regulatory affairs com. S.C. Hosp. Assn., 1995, 96; chmn. S.C. TB Task Force, 1993-98. Co-author: Home Health Infection Control Manual, 1988; contbr. articles to profl. jours. Recipient scholarship for abstract devel. Palmetto Hosp. Trust, Inc., 1995. Mem. Am. Heart Assn. (dist. 4 chmn. 1984-87, Ray Johnson award for edn. achievement Ga. affiliate 1987), Assn. for Profls. in Infection Control and Epidemiology, Inc. (Horizon award Palmetto chpt. 1995, nat. govt. affairs com. mem. 1994, 95), Nat. Assn. for Profls. in Infection Control and Epidemiology, Ga. Infection Control Network (mem. of yr. award 1988), Inc. (chmn. bd. 1982-91, award 1988). Republican. Avocations: reading, softball. Office: Greenville Meml Hosp 701 Grove Rd Greenville SC 29605-4295

STEED, MICHELLE ELNORA, special education educator, consultant; b. Raleigh, N.C., Sept. 23, 1967; d. Johnnie Wilbert and Ednell (Thornton) S. BA, N.C. State U., 1989, MEd, 1990. Cert. spl. edn. Tchr. Franklin County Schs., Youngsville, NC, 1999—. N.C. State U. fellow, 1989-90, All Am. scholar N.C. State U. Democrat. Baptist. Avocations: pianist, organist. Home: 5512 Thornton Rd Raleigh NC 27616-5728

STEED, THERESA JEAN, manufacturing executive; b. Grapeland, Tex., Mar. 10, 1932; d. Robert Tresband and Alma Inez (Denson) Bobbitt; m. Jarvis Lacy Steed, July 8, 1950; children: Judy Karen, Pamela Kay, Kim Lacy. Grad., Elliott Bus. Sch., Houston, 1949; BMus. Edn., So. Coll. Fine Arts, Houston, 1956; postgrad., U. Tex., 1961, Sul Ross U., Alpine, Tex., 1962, U. Wis., 1962; M Rhymes (hon.), Duke U., 1961. Exec. sec. various cos., Houston, 1950—57; tchr. elem. sch. Rosenburg Ind. Sch. Dist., Tex., 1957—58; tchr. kindergarten/music edn. Sonora Ind. Sch. Dist., Tex., 1959—65; tchr. elem. sch. Houston Ind. Sch. Dist., 1965—67, Conroe Ind. Sch. Dist., Tex., 1968—70; co-founder, co-owner Steed Tile & Mfg. Co., Conroe, 1965—. Author: Audio-Visual Curriculums for Music Education: Kindergarten Through Eighth Grade, 1962 Mem. Dem. Nat. Com., Washington, 1993—, Dem. Senatorial Campaign Com., Washington, 1996 Recipient Presdl. Letter of Commendation, Pres. Lyndon B. Johnson, 1969. Mem.: Am.'s Nat. World War II Mus. (charter), Nat. Women's History Mus. (charter), Nat. Trust for Hist. Preservation, Order Ea. Star (assoc. matron 1963), Women in Constrn. (charter) (reporter 1970—75, publicity chmn.), Nat. Federated Music Clubs Am., Pilot Club, Delta Kappa Gamma (publicity chmn. 1962—65). Methodist. Avocations: cooking, gardening, politicking. Home: 452 Lexington Ct Conroe TX 77302-3050 E-mail: quechick007@yahoo.com.

STEEDMAN, DORIA LYNNE SILBERBERG, foundation administrator; b. LA; d. Mendel B. and Dorothy H. (Howell) Silberberg; m. Richard Cantey Steedman, Feb. 19, 1966; 1 child, Alexandra Loren. BA summa cum laude, UCLA. Producer EUE/Screen Gems, N.Y.C., 1963-66, Jack Tinker & Ptnrs., N.Y.C., 1966-68, Telpac Mgmt., N.Y.C., 1968-72; v.p. broadcast prodn. Geer DuBois Advt., N.Y.C., 1973-78, account mgr., dir. ops., 1979-92; exec. v.p., creative dir. Partnership for a Drug-Free America, N.Y.C., 1992—. Bd. dirs. Friends of the Earth. Recipient Andy award Art Dirs. Club, 1968, 71; named one of 100 Best and Brightest Women in Advt., Advt. Age mag.; named Advt. Woman of Yr., 1996. Mem. Advt. Women N.Y. (pres. 1993-95), Advt. Women N.Y. Found. (pres. 1995-97), Phi Beta Kappa. Office: Partnership for a Drug-Free Am 405 Lexington Ave New York NY 10174-0002 Business E-Mail: doria_steedman@drugfree.org.

STEEL, CLAUDIA WILLIAMSON, artist; b. Van Nuys, Calif., Mar. 19, 1918; d. James Gordon and Ella (Livingston) Williamson; m. Lowell F. Steel, Aug. 15, 1941; children: Claudia Steel Rosen, Douglas Lowell, roger Conant. BA in Art, U. Calif., Berkeley, 1939, secondary credential, 1940; MFA, Mills Coll., 1967. Tchr. art Greenville Jr./Sr. High Sch., Calif., 1940-42; faculty Calif. State U., Chico, 1967-69; pvt. tchr. art, Chico; one-woman shows include Laboudt Gallery, San Francisco, 1958, Witherspoon Bldg., Phila., 1959, traveling show with Old Bergen Guild to nat. galleries, 1971-84, Redding (Calif.) Mus., 1973, Central Wyo. Mus. Art, Casper, 1976, U. Portland 1976, U. Wis., LaCrosse, 1978, Purdue U., West Lafayette, Ind., 1979, Pratt Inst., Manhatten Gallery, N.Y.C., 1980, Creative Arts Ctr., Chico, Calif., 1980, 84; exhibited in group shows Santa Barbara Art Mus., 1951, San Francisco Arts Festival (award), 1953, Oakland Art Mus., 1954, San Francisco Women Artists juried shows, 1958, 68 (award), 72, 73, 75, 76, Crocker Mus., Sacramento, 1958, 59, 60, 65, 67 (award), 73, Richmond Mus. (Calif.), 1960, DeYoung Mus. Art, San Francisco, 1960, San Francisco Mus. Art, 1959, 61 (award), Legion of Honor Mus., San Francisco, 1960, Mills Coll. Gallery, 1962, 67, 78, Berkeley Art Ctr. Gallery, 1969, San Francisco Art Commn. Gallery, 1972, Brandeis U., Mass., 1973, Ohio State U., Columbus, 1973, Brandt Gallery, Glendale, Calif., 1978, 1987, Chico State U., 1979, 1987, Fisher Gallery, Chico, Walnut Creek Art Gallery and Sonoma State U., 1979, Pratt Inst., Manhattan Gallery, N.Y.C., 1980, 1980, Calif. Soc. Printmakers traveling show, 1981, juried show, Singapore and Switzerland, 1984, Purdue U., 1982, U. Wis.-Eau Claire, 1982, Nat. Gallery, Bangkok, Malmo, Sweden, 1984-86, gallery show, Tokyo, 1985, Pacific Art League Gallery, Palo Alto, Calif., 1986, Tokyo Met. Mus., 1986, U.S.-U.K. Print Connection Barbican Ctr., London, 1989, others. Bd. dirs. Creative Art Ctr., Chico, 1977-81, Omni Arts, Chico, 1979-82. Recipient San Francisco Mus. of Art Serigraphy award, 1961; trustees' scholar Mills Coll., 1935, others. Mem. Calif. Soc. Printmakers (v.p., dir. 1973-77), L.A. Printmakers Soc.

STEEL, DANIELLE FERNANDE, author; b. NYC, Aug. 14, 1947; d. John and Norma Schuelein-Steel; 9 children. Student, Parsons Sch. Design, 1963, NYU, 1963-67. Vice pres. pub. relations and new bus. Supergirls Ltd., NYC, 1968-71; copywriter Grey Advt., San Francisco, 1973-74; founder Steel Gallery of Contemporary Art, San Francisco, 2003—. Author: (novels) Going Home, 1973, Passion's Promise, 1977, Now and Forever, 1978, The Promise, 1978, Season of Passion, 1980, Summers End, 1980, To Love Again, 1981, Remembrance, 1981, Once in a Lifetime, 1981, The Ring, 1981, Palomino, 1981, To Love Again, 1981, Remembrance, 1981, Loving, 1981, Once In A Lifetime, 1982, Crossings, 1982, A Perfect Stranger, 1982, Thurston House, 1983, Changes, 1983, Full Circle, 1984, Family Album, 1985, Secrets, 1985, Wanderlust, 1986, Fine Things, 1987, Kaleidoscope, 1987, Zoya, 1988, Star, 1988, Daddy, 1989, Message from Nam, 1990, Heartbeat, 1991, No Greater Love, 1991, Jewels, 1992, Mixed Blessings, 1992, Vanished, 1993, Accident, 1994, The Gift, 1994, Wings, 1994, Lightning, 1995, Five Days in Paris, 1995, Malice, 1996, Silent Honor, 1997, The Ranch, 1998, Special Delivery, 1997, The Ghost, 1997, The Long Road Home, 1998, The Klone And I, 1998, His Bright Light, 1998, Mirror Image, 1998, Bittersweet, 1999, Granny Dan, 1999, Irresistible Forces, 1999, The Wedding, 2000, The House on Hope Street, 2000, Journey, 2000, Lone Eagle, 2001, Leap of Faith, 2001, The Kiss, 2001, The Cottage, 2002, Sunset in St. Tropez, 2002, Answered Prayers, 2002, Dating Game, 2003, Johnny Angel, 2003, Safe Harbour, 2003, Ransom, 2004, Second Chance, 2004, Echoes, 2004, Impossible, 2005, Miracle, 2005, Toxic Bachelors, 2005, The House, 2006, Coming Out, 2006, Bungalow Two, 2006, H.R.H., 2006, Sisters, 2007; (children's books) Martha's Best Friend, Martha's New School, Martha's New Daddy, Max's New Daddy, Max and The Babysitter, Max's Daddy Goes To The Hospital; contbr. poetry to mags., including Cosmopolitan, McCall's, Ladies Home Jour., Good Housekeeping. Chevalier of the Disting. Order of Arts & Letters, France, 2002. Home: PO Box 1637 New York NY 10156-1637 Office: care Dell Publishing 1540 Broadway New York NY 10036-4039*

STEELE, ANA MERCEDES, retired federal agency administrator; b. Jan. 18, 1939; d. Sydney and Mercedes (Hernandez) S.; m. John Hunter Clark, June 2, 1979. AB magna cum laude, Marywood Coll., 1958. Actress, 1959-64; sec. Nat. Endowment for Arts, Washington, 1965-67, dir. budget and rsch., 1968-75, dir. planning, 1976-78, dir. program coordination, sr. exec. svc., 1979-81, assoc. dep. chmn. programs, dir. program coordination, 1982-93, acting chmn., acting sr. dep. chmn., 1993, sr. dep. chmn., sr. exec. svc., 1993-96, dep. chmn. mgmt. and budget, sr. exec. svc., 1996-98; ret., 1998. Guest lectr. George Washington U., 1987; trustee Marywood Coll., 1989-96, Marywood U., 1997-98. Author, editor report: History of the National Council on the Arts and National Endowment for the Arts During the Johnson Administration, 1968; editor: Museums USA (Fed. Design Coun. award of Excellence 1975), 1974, National Endowment Arts, 1965-85: A Brief Chronology of Federal Involvement in the Arts, 1985. Former reader Rec. for the Blind, N.Y.C.; former tutor Future for Jimmy, Washington; judge Helen Hayes Awards, 2003—. Named Disting. Grad. in Field of Arts, Marywood Coll., 1976; recipient Sustained Superior Performance award Nat. Endowment for Arts, 1980, Disting. Svc. award, 1983-85, 89, 92, 96, Presdl. medal Marywood U., 2000; named to Disting. Alumnae Hall of Fame, Ursuline Acad., 2001. Mem. Actors' Equity Assn., Screen Actors Guild, Delta Epsilon Sigma, Kappa Gamma Pi. Home: 2475 Virginia Ave NW Apt 604 Washington DC 20037-2639

STEELE, BEVERLY J., elementary school educator; b. Gary, Ind., June 16, 1948; d. Earl Robert S. and Mandy Pearl Hearon; stepfather: James T. Hearon. BS in Edn., Lincoln U., 1970; MEd, Ind. U., 1974. Cert. elem. sch. tchr. Tchr. grades 2, 4, 6 Norton Sch. Gary (Ind.) Cmty. Sch. Corp., 1970-72, tchr. grades 3-5 Vohr Sch., 1972-83; tchr. grade 1 Vohr Sch., 1983-95; tchr. grade 4, 1995—. Tchr. challenge grant program Gary Cmty. Sch. Corp., 1997, 98. Asst. min. music United Male Chorus Gary-Calumet Region, Gary, 1989—; mem. The Sounds of Peace Singing Ensemble, Gary and Calumet, 1974—; dir. Voices of Praise Children's Choir; min. music Carter Meml. Christian Meth. Episcopal Ch., 1997, past bd. dirs. Recipient numerous plaques Carter Meml. CME Ch., Gary, 1993, 99. Mem. Sorority, Inc., Delta Sigma Theta, Phi Delta Kappa. Democrat. Avocations: computers, piano and organ, teaching. Office: Vohr Elem Sch 1900 W 7th Ave Gary IN 46404-1408 E-mail: bjsteele51@hotmail.com.

STEELE, JOAN DOROTHY, retired academic administrator; b. Portland, Oreg., Jan. 13, 1930; d. Joseph Hirsch Friedenthal and Faye Genevieve Jaloff; m. Edward Steele, Apr. 17, 1949 (div.); children: Martin Frederic, Cheryl Roberta Latif. AB, UCLA, 1961, MA, 1963, PhD, 1970. Dir. rsch. and grants Calif. State U. Stanislaus, Turlock, Calif., 1976—91, dir. academic advising, 1981—91, ret., 1991. Author: Captain Mayne Reid, 1978; editor: Calif. State U.-Stanislaus Catalogue. Mem. Hist. Commn., Ashland, Oreg., 1996—2001. Mem.: Phi Beta Kappa. Jewish. Avocations: gardening, needlecrafts, travel.

STEELE, JUDITH MCCONNELL, writer; b. Lamar, Colo., Oct. 5, 1945; d. Taylor and Elva June (Buchtel) McC.; m. Richard M. Steele, Nov. 14, 1975. BA, Cornell Coll., 1967; MA, Northwestern U., 1972. Vol. Peace Corps, Sergipe, Brazil, 1968-70; translator office Project Hope, Rio Grande do Norte, Brazil, 1972; reporter, columnist The Idaho Statesman, Boise, 1978-93; freelance writer fiction, poetry Boise, 1993—. Chair young writers competition IJA Prodns., Boise, 1994. Author: Stories From Home, 1989, More Stories From Home, 1993, (anthology) Family, 1998, Woven on the Wind, 2001; collaborative work with Sun Valley Ctr. Arts, 1999, Balance Dance Co., 2003, Dance Forum, 2003; group exhibits with Chris Binion, 1998-99; poetry duet, 2000-2002. Mem. Snake River Writers, Log Cabin Literary Ctr., Treas. Valley Pub. Access TV, Acad. Am. Poets.

STEELE, KAREN DORN, journalist; b. Portland, Oreg., Oct. 27, 1943; d. Ronald and Margaret Elizabeth (Cates) Moxness; m. Charles Stuart Dorn, Oct. 30, 1965 (div. Oct. 1982); children: Trilby Constance Elizabeth Dorn, Blythe Estella Dorn; m. Richard Donald Steele, July 4, 1983. BA, Stanford U., 1965; MA, U. Calif., Berkeley, 1967. Prodr. Sta. KSPS-TV, Spokane, Wash., 1970—72, dir. news and pub. affairs, 1972—82; reporter Spokesman-Rev., Spokane, 1982—87, environ./spl. projects reporter, 1987—. Contbr. articles to sci. publs. (Olive Br. award NYU Ctr. War, Peace & The Media, 1989). Bd. dirs. Women Helping Women, Spokane, 1994; trustee St. George's Sch., Spokane, 1988-92. Mid-career fellow Stanford Knight Fellowship Program, 1986-87, Arms Control fellow Ctr. for Internat. Security and Arms Control, Stanford U., 1986-87; Japan Travel grant Japan Press Found., Tokyo, 1987, Rsch. grantee John D. and Catherine T. MacArthur Found., 1992; recipient Gerald Loeb award Anderson Sch. Mgmt. UCLA, 1995, George Polk award L.I. U., 1995, William Stokes award U. Mo., 1988, Nat. Headliner award, Excellence in Legal Journalism award Wash. State Bar Assn., 2000, Payne award U. Oreg., 2006; named to State Hall of Journalistic Achievement, Wash. State U., Pullman, 1995. Unitarian Universalist. Office: Spokesman Review 999 W Riverside Ave Spokane WA 99210-2160 Office Phone: 509-459-5462. Business E-Mail: karend@spokesman.com.

STEELE, KATHLEEN PATRICIA, science educator; b. Staten Island, N.Y., Sept. 18, 1950; d. Thomas Leo and Patricia Marguerite (Hinman) S. BA, Caldwell Coll., 1972; PhD, W.Va. U., 1977. Postdoctoral trainee Inst. for Cancer Research, Phila., 1977-79; asst. prof. biology Moravian Coll., Bethlehem, Pa., 1979-86; sci. tchr. Pius X High Sch., Bangor, Pa., 1986—. Book reviewer coll. textbook pubs., 1983-86; book and manuscript reviewer Nat. Assn. Biology Tchrs. and NSTA, 1990—. Mem. Audubon Soc., Nat. Wildlife Fedn., Hawk Mt. Wildlife Sanctuary, Lehigh Valley Conservancy; assoc. Sisters Mercy, Merion, Pa., 1997—. Named Hame Fame, DiVinci Discovery Ctr., 2005; recipient Tchr. Yr., Nat. Assn. Biology Tchrs., 1997; Woodrow Wilson fellow, 1987. Mem. AAAS, Nat. Assn. Biology Tchrs., Nat. Sci. Tchrs. Assn., Am. Assn. Physics Tchrs., Am. Chem. Soc., Sigma Xi. Clubs: Great Books (co-leader 1980-1990). Republican. Roman Catholic. Avocations: music, softball, hiking, reading. Office: Pius X High Sch 580 3rd Ave Bangor PA 18013-1399

STEELE, MILDRED ROMEDAHL, educator; b. Boone, Iowa, Jan. 13, 1924; d. Joe and Gladys Madeline (Bonebright/Cree) Romedahl; m. Otto Scott Steele Jr., Sept. 4, 1947; children: Martha Steele Knepper, John Joseph, Timothy Scott. BA, Simpson Coll., 1946; MA, Drake U., 1968; Edn. Specialist, U. Iowa, 1973, PhD, 1982. Instr. Des Moines Area Community Coll., Ankeny, 1972-73, Drake U., Des Moines, 1973, 77; coord. communication Cen. Coll., Pella, Iowa, 1977-90, emirita, 1990. Lectr. Iowa Humanities Bd., 1991—. Co-author: 101 Voices and Guide, 1973; editor: An Iowa Soldier in World War I, 1993, 15 volumes Romedahl Family History (CD), 1996, 3 volumes Steele Family History, 2005; author numerous poems and contbr. numerous articles to profl. jours. Chmn. Higher Edn. and Campus Ministry, Iowa, 1984-88; vice chmn. adminstrv. coun. Pella United Meth. Ch., 1988—, chmn. bd. trustees, 1990-92, cons. to bldg. com.; bd. dirs., bd. fellows Sch. Religion U. Iowa, 1986-88. Recipient Alumni Achievement award Simpson Coll., 1991, Stars in Our Crown award, 1992. Mem. AAUW, Nat. Assn. Devel. Edn. (nat. sec. 1988-90, chmn. 1987-88, Outstanding Svc. award 1988, Nat. Rsch. award 1986, 95), Nat. Simpson Coll. Alumni Bd., Pi Lambda Theta, Sigma Tau Delta, Delta Delta Delta. Democrat. Home and Office: Vriendschap Village 2604 Fifield Rd Apt A103 Pella IA 50219

STEELE, NANCY EDEN ROGERS, nonprofit corporate executive, retired principal; b. Elgin, Ill., Aug. 18, 1946; d. Vance Donald and Barbara Marie (Yarwood) Rogers; m. James Frederick Steele, Apr. 12, 1976; children: Justin Vance Jabari, Barbara Marie Noni. BS, Centenary Coll., 1968; MA, U. Nebr., 1971; EdS, Pt. Loma Nazarene U., 1999. Program asst. Head Start & Follow Through, Lincoln, Nebr., 1971-74; K-12 resource tchr. Nantucket (Mass.) Pub. Schs., 1975-77; kindergarten lead tchr. Parkville Sch., Guaynabo, P.R.,

1977-79; instr. in gen. psychology L.A. C.C., Sebana Seca, P.R., 1978-79; lang. arts and parent edn. tchr. Sweetwater Union H.S. Dist., Chula Vista, Calif., 1980-86; upper grade team leader Park View Elem. Sch., Chula Vista, 1986-91; upper grade tchr. Clear View Elem. Sch., Chula Vista, 1991-94; mentor tchr. Chula Vista Elem. Sch. Dist., 1990-94; acad. dir. AmeriCorps Nat. Civilian Cmty. Corps, San Diego, 1994-96; asst. prin. Harborside Elem. Sch., Chula Vista, 1996-98; prin. Burton C. Tiffany Elem. Sch., Chula Vista, 1998-2000; exec. dir. Interactions for Peace, 2000—. Cons. in field. Author: Peace Patrol: A Guide for Creating a New Generation of Problem Solvers, 1994 (Golden Bell award 1993), Primary Peacemakers, 2001; co-author: Power Teaching for the 21st Century, 1991. Recipient Peacemaker of Yr. award San Diego Mediation Ctr., 1993, Champion for Children award Children's Hosp. and San Diego Office of Edn., 1994, Leadership award San Diego Channel 10, 1998. Mem. ASCD, AAUW, Nat. Coun. for Social Studies, Assn. Calif. Sch. Adminstrs., Chula Vista Aquatics Assn. (bd. dirs. 1986-96), Optimist Club. Home: 1551 Malibu Point Ct Chula Vista CA 91911-6116

STEELE, PATRICIA ANN, dean, librarian; b. Columbus, Ohio, Mar. 28, 1943; d. Gerald Henry and June Eileen (McCullough) Costlow; m. Charles Nolan Steele, Aug. 31, 1963; children: Kelly Colleen, Ryan Charles. AB in English, Ind. U., 1966, MLS, 1981. Cert. tchr., Mich. Tchr. Chippewa Valley Schs., Mt. Clemens, Mich., 1966-67; br. head, extension asst. Lansing Pub. Library, Mich., 1967-74; head librarian, Atomic Energy Commn. plant research lab. Mich. State U., East Lansing, 1969-73; head librarian, Health, Physical Edn. and Recreation Library Ind. U., Bloomington, 1979-81, head librarian sch. of library and info. sci., 1981, exec. assoc. dean, head customer and access svcs., coord. academic info. and customer svc., Ruth Lilly interim dean of univ. libraries, 2005—. Chmn. faculty council ednl. task force on pornography Ind. U., 1985—; cons., specialist conspectus Research Libraries Group, 1985-86. Editor Library Sci. Nat. Newsletter, 1984-86; columnist Library Bookshelf, 1981—, InULA Innuendo, 1984—. Mem. ALA (v. chmn. library sci. librarians discussion group 1984-86), Ind. Library Assn. (chmn. exec. com. div. on women 1983-86), Ind. U. Librarian's Assn., Stone Hills Area Library Sci. Authority. Avocations: swimming, jogging, hiking. Home: 4791 N Benton Dr Bloomington IN 47408-9503 Office: Herman B Wells Libr Ind U 1320 E Tenth St Bloomington IN 47405*

STEELE, SHARI, think-tank executive; Grad., Widener U.; LLM in Advocacy, Georgetown U.; MS in Instrnl. Media, West Chester U. Legal dir. Electronic Frontier Found., San Francisco, 1992—2000, exec. dir., pres., 2000—. Spkr. in field; tchg. fellow Georgetown U. Law Ctr. Office: Electronic Frontier Found 454 Shotwell St San Francisco CA 94110-1914

STEELE, SHIRLEY SUE, retired special resource educator; b. Shelbyville, Tenn., Apr. 10, 1939; d. Clarence Sr. and Laura Ocie (Marr) McCullough; m. James Harold Levi Steele, June 23, 1957; children: Tonya Sue, Michaele Ann. BS magna cum laude, U. Tenn., 1973. Cert. spl. edn. tchr., Tenn. Spl. resource tchr. Chattanooga City Schs., ret.; tchr. spl. edn. Orange Grove Ctr., Chattanooga. Bd. dirs. Scouting for Spl. Citizens; leader Explorers Club for the Retarded; bd. mem. Freedom Found. Mem. Alpha Soc. (tchr. Sunday sch. autistic children), Kappa Delta Pi. Home: 5720 Laurel Ridge Rd Chattanooga TN 37416-1050 E-mail: shirstill@aol.com.

STEELE, VICKI LYNN, educator; d. Myron Cecil and Ora Mae McClain; m. Roger Leonard Steele, Oct. 7, 1972; children: David Roger, Andy McClain. BS cum laude, Piedmont Coll., Demorest, Ga., 1975; MEd, North Ga. Coll., Dahlonega, Ga., 1978; EdS, Clemson U., S.C., 1998. Faculty Stephens Co. Jr. H.S., Toccoa, Ga., 1975—80, Truett-McConnell Coll., Cleve., Ga., 1990—. Dir. acad. advising Truett-McConnell Coll., Cleve., 2000—03. Program chairperson AMICAE Scholarship, Cleve., Ga., 1997—98, pres.-elect, 1998—99, pres., 1999—2001, program chair, 2003—06. Recipient Faculty Excellence award, Truett-McConnell Coll., 1995. Mem.: Nat. Acad. Advising Assn. Baptist. Avocations: camping, spending time with family and friends. Office: Truett McConnell Coll 100 Alumni Dr Cleveland GA 30528 Office Phone: 706-864-2134. Office Fax: 706-865-5135. E-mail: vsteele@truett.edu.

STEELEY, DOLORES ANN, music educator; b. Middletown, N.Y., Sept. 14, 1956; d. Richard and Martha Steeley. AAS in Music, Orange County C.C., Middletown, N.Y., 1977; BA in Music, West Chester U., Pa., 1980; MS in Music Edn., Coll. St. Rose, Albany, N.Y., 1991. Cert. tchr. music edn., nat. bd. cert. tchr. Pvt. music tchr., Albany, NY, 1986—; music tchr. Town of Colonie, Latham, NY, 1986—93, Coxsackie-Athens Sch. Dist., NY, 1986—93, Niskayuna Sch. Dist., NY, 1993—. Mem.: N.Y. State Sch. Music Assn., Music Educators Nat. Conf. Home: 95 Southbury Rd Clifton Park NY 12065 Office: Iroquois Mid Sch 2495 Rosendale Rd Niskayuna NY 12309

STEEN, MARY FROST, literature and language professor; b. Mpls., July 7, 1940; d. Reuben Bernhard Frost and Jean Elizabeth Timmons; m. Lynn Arthur Steen, June 22, 1963; children: Margaret Elizabeth, Catherine Mary Wille. BA, Luther Coll., Decorah, Iowa, 1962; MA in Tchg., Harvard U., Cambridge, Mass., 1965. Instr. English St. Olaf Coll., Northfield, Minn., 1965—88, asst. prof. English, 1988—, chair dept. English, 2004—. 2nd v.p., editor, writer LWV, St. Paul, 1987—2006. Scholar, Nat. Merit Found., 1958—62. Democrat. Lutheran. Avocations: reading, travel, fiber arts. Home: 716 St Olaf Ave Northfield MN 55057 Office: St Olaf Coll 1520 StOlaf Ave Northfield MN 55057 Office Phone: 507-646-3200.

STEENBURGEN, MARY, actress; b. Newport, Ark., Feb. 8, 1953; m. Malcolm McDowell, 1980 (div. 1990); children: Lilly, Charlie; m. Ted. Danson, Oct. 7, 1995. Student, Neighborhood Playhouse. Films: Goin' South, 1978, Time After Time, 1979, Melvin and Howard, 1980 (Academy award best supporting actress 1981), Ragtime, 1981, A Midsummer Night's Sex Comedy, 1982, Cross Creek, 1983, Romantic Comedy, 1983, One Magic Christmas, 1985, Dead of Winter, 1987, End of the Line, 1987 (also exec. prodr.), The Whales of August, 1987, Miss Firecracker, 1989, Parenthood, 1989, Back to the Future III, 1990, The Long Walk Home, 1990 (narrator), The Butcher's Wife, 1991, Philadelphia, 1993, What's Eating Gilbert Grape, 1993, Clifford, 1994, It Runs in the Family, 1994, Pontiac Moon, 1994, Powder, 1995, Nixon, 1995, My Family, 1995, The Grass Harp, 1995, About Sarah, 1995, Trumpet of the Swan (voice), 1999, Life as a House, 2001, I Am Sam, 2001, Sunshine State, 2002, Wish You Were Dead, 2002, Hope Springs, 2003, Casa de los babys, 2003, Elf, 2003; appeared in Showtime TV's Faerie Tale Theatre prodn. of Little Red Riding Hood and (miniseries) Tender Is the Night, 1985, Gulliver's Travels, 1996;, (miniseries) Noah's Ark, 1999, Living with the Dead, 2002; TV series: Ink, 1996, Joan of Arcadia, 2003-; TV films: The Attic: The Hiding of Anne Frank, 1988, About Sarah, 1998, Picnic, 2000, Nobody's Baby, 2001, It Must Be Love, 2004, Capital City, 2004; theater appearances include: Holiday, Old Vic, London, 1987, Candida, Broadway, 1993. Nat. spokesperson Elizabeth Glaser Pediatric AIDS Found. Office: The Gersh Agency 232 N Canon Dr Beverly Hills CA 90210

STEEN-HINDERLIE, DIANE EVELYN, social worker, musician; b. Duluth, Minn., June 13, 1947; d. Julian Sem and Evelyn Synnove (Helgaas) Steen; m. John Peter Hinderlie, June 27, 1971 (div. Sept. 1987); children: Peder Donald, Erik Steen; m. John Richard Olson, July 21, 1989. BA in Asian Studies/Social Psychology cum laude, St. Olaf Coll., 1969; postgrad., U. Minn. and other instns., 1991, Hamline U., 1989—91. Lic. social worker, Minn.; cert. music tchr. Music Tchrs. Nat. Assn. Social worker child care licensing Hennepin County Welfare Dept., Mpls., 1970—73; mem. clergy team exch. program Luth. World Fedn., Göppingen, Germany, 1973—77; mem. clergy team, music dir. Jubilation Singers Bethel Luth. Ch., Rochester, Minn., 1978—83; mem. clergy team, music dir. youth choir First Luth. Ch., St. Louis Park, Minn., 1983—86; adminstr. Family Child Care facility, St. Louis Park, 1986—90; faculty, tchr. Stenson Suzuki Studios and Home Studio, St. Louis Park, 1988—92; small group leader, tchr. vol. Mt. Olive Ch., Children's Hosp., Mpls., 1993, 1996—98; workshop and children's ministry Augsburg Coll. Youth and Family Inst., Trinity Cong., 1998—; founding dir. Fair Pay Inst., Mpls., 1995—; trainer United for a Fair Economy, 1997—. Founder orgn. and curriculum Early Childhood Orgn. for Edn. with Singing, 1993—, co-leader German-Am. youth group exch., 1979-82; co-founder Family DayCare Cert. Program and Babygarten (B-12 edn.) classes, 1970-73; bd. dirs. Midwest Coun., Nat. Peace Inst. Found., Grinnell, Iowa, 1991; presenter in field.; mem. root causes of violence action team Initiative for Violence-Free Families, 4th Jud. Dist. Minn., 1997—. Author: (tng. manual) Mother Tongue Singing/Voice Method, 1988, (study packet) School Start Time/Teen Sleep Deprivation, 1996-97, A+=Baby Church School, 2002; rec. artist, mem. ensemble record/cassettes Nowell Sing We, 1986; performer Nordic Am. Psalmodikon Forbundet, 1997—. Vol. People of Faith Peacemakers, Feminists in Faith/ReImagining and Jewish Cmty. Rels. Coun., 1992-2003, Muslim-Christian Rels. Coun., Joint Religious Legis. Coalition, Bread for the World; founder People for Reforming Early Start Time for Teens Orgn., Mpls., 1993—; mem. steering com. Progressive Cmty. and FairVote, Minn., 1994-99; local host youth com. NAACP Conv., Mpls., 1995; vol. Common Cause, St. Paul and Washington; charter mem. U.S. Holocaust Mus., 1993; cofounder antitorture com. Women Against Mil. Madness, 2005. Recipient appreciation plaque Christian Boy/Girl Scouts Germany; Svc. pin Am. Luth. Ch. Women; listed in Minn. Profiles, Minn. Hist. Soc. A Tribute to Outstanding Minn. Women by Marilyn Chelstrom, 2001; named Asset Builder of Month, St. Louis Park Children First Initiative, 1997; named to Honor Roll, Mendota Mdewakanton Dakota Cmty., 1999. Mem.: MADD, Minn. Music Tchrs. Assn. (first early childhood music chair 2001—03), Assn. Pre- and Perinatal Psychology and Health, Wash. Nat. Cathedral, Soc. for Psychol. Studies of Social Issues, Interfaith Alliance Minn., Nat. Luth. Choir Acad., Suzuki Assn. Americas (study area co-organizer, editl. adviser), Internat. Suzuki Assn., Nat. Assn. Tchrs. Singing and VoiceCare Network, UN Assn., Sojourner Project, Inc., Am.'s Jr. Miss. Coun., Germanic-Am. Inst., Nat. Peace Found., Amnesty Internat., Minn. Parenting Assn., Ctr. for Victims of Torture, World Wildlife Fund, Sons of Norway (lodge trustee 1991—), Phi Beta Kappa, Am. Mensa. Green. Lutheran. Avocations: reading, political activism, concerts, travel, memory albums. Office: Fair Pay Inst PO Box 16031 Minneapolis MN 55416-0031

STEFANE, CLARA JOAN, finance educator; b. Trenton, N.J., Apr. 08; d. Joseph and Rose M. (Bonfanti) Raymond; m. John E. Stefane, July 19, 1975. BS in Bus. Adminstrn., Georgian Ct. Coll., Lakewood, N.J., 1968. Cert. tchr. gen. bus. and secretarial studies, N.J. Tchr. bus. Camden Cath. High Sch., Cherry Hill, N.J., 1960-68, Cathedral High Sch., Trenton, 1970-72; tchr., bus., chair dept. McCorristin Cath. High Sch., Trenton, 1972-95—; ret., 2004. Mem. Mercer County Task Force for Bus. Edn., Trenton, 1989-90. Sustaining mem. Rep. Nat. Com.; del. mem. 1992 Presdl. Trust; mem. Rosary Altar Soc., Incarnation Ch. Named Tchr. of Yr., The Cittone Inst., Princeton, N.J., 1991. Mem. ASCD, N.J. Bus. Edn. Assn., Nat. Cath. Edn. Assn., Sisters of Mercy of the Ams. (assoc.). Roman Catholic. Avocations: reading, creative writing, attending operas and yankee baseball games. Home: 278 Weber Ave Trenton NJ 08638-3638

STEFANEK, MEGAN LYNN, elementary school educator; b. Tucson, Mar. 10, 1972; d. Thomas Anthony and Donna Joy Stefanek; children: Hayley Atraya Fester, Eleanor Ada Fester. Degree in elem. edn., Concordia U., Irvine, Calif., 1994. Elem. tchr. Sunnyside Unified Sch. Dist., Tucson, 1998—. Recipient Rodel Tchg. award, 2005. Office Phone: 520-545-2900.

STEFANI, GWEN RENEE, singer; b. Anaheim, Calif., Oct. 3, 1969; d. Dennis and Patti Stefani; m. Gavin McGregor Rossdale, Sept. 14, 2002; 1 child, Kingston James McGregor. Student, Calif. State U., Fullerton. Musician No Doubt, 1987—. Designer, creator fashion line L.A.M.B. (Love. Angel. Music. Baby.), 2004—; launched toy doll line (8 dolls) Love. Angel. Music. Baby. Fashion Dolls, 2006. Singer: (albums) No Doubt, 1992, Tragic Kingdom, 1995, Beacon Street Collection, 1995, Collector's Orange Crate, 1997, Return of Saturn, 2000, Rock Steady, 2001 (Grammy awards: Best Pop Performance By A Duo Or Group With Vocal for song "Hey Baby", 2002, Best Pop Performance By A Duo Or Group With Vocal for song "Underneath it All", 2003), The Singles 1992-2003, 2004, Love, Angel, Music, Baby, 2004, Everything In Time, 2005, (songs) Let Me Blow Your Mind (with Eve), 2001 (Grammy award, Best Rap/Song Collaboration, 2001), It's My Life (MTV Video Music award Best Group Video, 2004, MTV Video Music award Best Pop Video, 2004), Hollaback Girl, 2005 (Billboard awards, Digital Song of Yr., 2005); actor: (voice) Malice; A Kat's Tale, 2002, (film) Zoolander, 2001, (TV guest appearances) Saturday Night Live, 1996, 2001, Mad TV, 2000, Dawson's Creek, 2002, (Voice) King of the Hill, 2001; (films) The Aviator, 2004. Recipient Best Choreography In a Video for Hollaback Girl, MTV Video Music Awards, 2005, Best Art Direction In a Video for What You Waiting For?, Favorite Female Artist, Am. Music Awards, 2005, New Artist of Yr., Billboard Music Awards, 2005, Best-Selling New Female Artist, World Music Awards, 2005.*

STEFANIK-BRANDT, JANET RUTH, retired realtor; b. Harrisville, W.Va., Apr. 25, 1938; d. John Jack Davis Jr. and Helen Virginia (Waller) D.; m. Robert John Stefanik, Oct. 13, 1956 (div. Apr. 1977); children: Robert Mark, Deborah Ruth, Perry Wayne, David Lee, Susan Irene; m. Joseph Brandt, June 14, 2005. Grad., Midview High Sch., Grafton, Ohio; student, Lorain County Community Coll., Elyria, Ohio, 1982, 85, 90-91. Salesperson Demby Real Estate, Elyria, 1970-71, Schwed Real Estate, Elyria, 1971-93; ret., 2003. Mem. women's coun. Lorain County Bd. Realtors, 1971—74, pres., 1974; toll collector, Ohio Turnpike Commn., 1975—2000. Mem. Amherst Cmty. Chorus. Mem.: AARP, Travel Resorts Am., VFW Aux., Eagles Aux., Women of the Moose. Roman Catholic. Avocations: travel, dancing, computer.

STEFANOV, IVANKA, music educator; d. Miodrag and Jozefa Zivkovic; m. Petar Stefanov; 1 child, Emi. B, Acad. of Musical Art, 1967—71. Treas. Jr. Friday Morning Musicale Club, Tampa, Fla., 1997—2004. Ch. pianist and choir dir. Presbyn. Ch. of Seffner, Seffner, Fla., 1992—98. Recipient Honor Roll, Nat. Guild of Piano Tchr., 2004. Mem.: Nat. Guild of Piano Teachers (assoc.), Nat. Fedn. of Musical Clubs (assoc.), Music Tchr. Nat. Assn (assoc.). Home: 9005 Bana Villa Ct Tampa FL 33635

STEFANOWICZ, JANUS, costume designer; MA in Theatre, Villanova U.; MFA in Costume Design, Temple U., 1989. Prof. costume design U. Pa.; prof. costume design grad. theatre dept. Villanova U., costume shop mgr., 1980—. Costume designer Phila. Theatre Co., The Wilma Theatre, The People's Light & Theatre Co., Arden Theatre Co., Phila. Young Playwrights Festival, Phila. Theatre Festival for New Plays. Costume designer (films) Philadelphia, 1992, Beloved, 1997, (plays) Loot, Patience, Passion, Perfect Pie, The Invention of Love, Intimate Apparel (Earl Gish awards outstanding costume design Barrymore awards, 2006), On the Razzle, 1998 (Barymore award, 1998), Les Liaisons Dangereuses, Black Comedy, The Real Inspector Hound, Spin, Orpheus Descending, Love and Anger, The Cripple of Inishmaan, Arcadia, How I Learned to Drive, Seven Guitars, Love! Valour! Compassion!, Broken Glass, The Woods, All in the Timing, Minutes from the Blue Route, Vilna's Got a Golem, Three Sisters, Uncle Vanya, Straight Men; exhibitions include Theatrical Threads: The Art of Costume Design, Art Gallery, Villanova U. Recipient Certificate of Merit, Am. Coll. Theatre Festival. Office: Villanova Univ Theatre Dept Vasey Hall Room 205 800 Lancaster Ave Villanova PA 19085 Office Phone: 610-519-4394. E-mail: janus.stefanowicz@villanova.edu.*

STEFANSSON, WANDA GAE, language educator, literature educator; b. Tucson, Ariz., Dec. 3, 1936; d. Alva Harold and Beryl Eaks Roberson; m. Joseph Robert Henry, Dec. 28, 1963 (div. Dec. 1997); 1 child, Michael Joseph Henry; m. Rafn Stefansson, Apr. 25, 1998. AA, Stephens Coll., 1956; BA, U. Oreg., 1958; MA, U. Wash., 1961. Instr. German lang. and lit. Pomona Coll., Calif., 1961—66; acad. studies counselor Art Ctr. Coll. Design, Pasadena, Calif., 1980—87; registrar Art Ctr. Europe, La Tour-de-Peilz, Switzerland, 1987—90; develop. officer Huntington Libr., San Marino, Calif., 1995—98. Mem., officer PEO, 2001—06; leader creative christian cmty San Marino Cmty. Ch., 1975—77, chair adult edn., 1977—80, chair pastor search com., 1981—82; tchr. disciple bible study 1st United Meth. Ch., Pasadena, 1993—94, 1996—99, chair adminstrv. coun., 1998—2001, founder ongoing journey, 1999—2001, membership sec., 1999—, tchr. spiritual growth, 2001—03, chair info. program chapel restoration campaign, 2002—05, chmn. adult ministries com., 2005—06, mentor H.S. students, 2005—, chmn. homeless dinners program, ch. publicist; rep. UMC Annual Conf., 2005—06. Home: 1825 Alpine Dr San Marino CA 91108

STEFANYSHYN-PIPER, HEIDEMARIE M., astronaut; b. St. Paul, Minn., Feb. 7, 1963; d. Michael and Adelheid Stefanyshyn; m. Glenn A. Piper; 1 child. BS in Mech. Engring., MIT, 1984, MS in Mech. Engring., 1985. Tng. as Navy basic diving officer and salvage officer Naval Diving and Salvage Tng. Ctr., Panama City, Fla.; several tours of duty as an engring. duty officer in area of ship repair and maintenance; underwater ship husbandry ops. officer for the supr. of salvage and diving Naval Sea Systems Command; astronaut, mission specialist NASA Johnson Space Ctr., 1996—. Crew mem., will perform spacewalks Space Shuttle Atlantis (STS-115), 2006. Recipient Meritorious Svc. medal, Navy Commendation medal (2), Navy Achievement medal (2). Mem.: Am. Soc. Mech. Engineers. Avocations: scuba diving, swimming, running, rollerblading, ice skating. Office: Astronaut Office CB NASA Lyndon B Johnson Space Ctr Houston TX 77058*

STEFFE, CYNTHIA, fashion designer; m. Richard Roberts. Grad., Parsons Sch. of Design, 1981. Asst. to Donna Karan and Louis Dell'Olio Anne Klein & Co., 1981—83; designed sportswear line Spitalnick & Co., 1983—88; prin., owner Cynthia Steffe Collection, 1988—, Francess & Rita, Cynthia's Closet. Featured as one of the "New Majors" Women's Wear Daily, one of "Fifty Most Beautiful People" People Mag. Avocations: auctions, tennis, gardening. Office: 550 7th Ave Fl 21 New York NY 10018-3203*

STEFFEE, NINA DEAN, publisher; b. Mahopac, N.Y., Apr. 11, 1917; d. Henry Jackson and Eliza May (Willson) Dean; m. Clay Runels Steffee, June 21, 1942; children: Eliza May Steffee Karpook, Clay Jackson, Henry Morgan. Student, Cornell U., 1934-36. Sec., asst. editor Fla. Audubon Soc., Maitland, 1965-71; owner/mgr. Flying Carpet Tours, Orlando, Fla., 1971-80, Russ's Natural History Tours, Kissimmee, Fla., 1980-83, Lake Helen, Fla., 1983-94; pub., compiler Nina Steffee Pub., Lake Helen, 1994—. Compiler bird checklists; contbr. articles to profl. jours. Mem.: West Volusia Audubon (pres.), Kissimmee Valley Audibon (pres.). Avocation: birding. Home: 3839 NW 48th PL Gainesville FL 32606-4426

STEFFEY, A KAY, accountant; b. Decatur, Ind., Sept. 26, 1959; d. Marvin Chester and Barbara Ellen (Merkle) DeBolt; m. Richard Lee Steffey II, Jan. 1, 1986; children: Brittaney Nicole, Luke Vaughn. AAS with acctg. certs., U. Alaska, 2000. Customer svc. agent Northwest Airlines, Traverse City, Mich., 1989-93; supr. ERA Aviation, Kodiak, Alaska, 1993-95; staff acct. Shaffer & Harrington CPAs, Sitka, Alaska, 1995-97, Sheldon Jackson Coll., Sitka, 1997-99; acct. tech. Altman, Rogers & Co. CPA, Anchorage, 1999-2000, USCG ISC Kodiak, Kodiak, 2000—. Editor ROTORWASH Coast Guard Family Newsletter, 1988 (Alex Haley award excellence in info. 1988). Treas. Girl Scouts Tongass Coun. Sitka Cmty., 1997-98. Lutheran. Avocations: fishing, wilderness camping, hiking, swimming. Office: ISC Kodiak Comptr Divsn Kodiak AK 99615-7300 Fax: 907-486-5696. E-mail: steffey@gci.net.

STEFFEY, LELA, state legislator, banker; b. Idaho Falls, Idaho, Aug. 8, 1928; d. Orawell and Mary Ethel (Owen) Gardner; m. Carl A. Hendershott, Jr., Apr. 16, 1949 (div. 1961); children: Barry G. Hendershott, Bradley Carl Hendershott, Barton P. Hendershott; m. Warren D. Steffey, July 13, 1973; children: Dean, Wayne, Luann, Scott, Susan. Grad., Am. Inst. Banking, 1972. With Pacific Tel. & Tel., San Diego, 1948—49, Bank of Am., San Diego, 1949—52, escrow officer, mgr. consumer loans, 1961—63; with Gen. Dynamics/Astro, San Diego, 1960—61; real estate agt. Steffey Realty, Mesa, Ariz., 1978—. Mem. Ariz. Ho. of Reps, Phoenix, 1982—86, vice-chmn. banking and ins. com., 1982—86, house appropriations, judiciary, counties and municipalities coms., 1986—90, chmn. counties and municipalities com., 1987—90, chmn. transp., 1991—, multi-state hwy. transp. commn., 1993—94. Founder Citizens Com. Against Domestic Abuse; chmn. adv. bd. Mesa Mus., 1981—83; precinct com., dep. registrar Legis. Dist. 29, 1978—; pres. Mesa (Ariz.) Rep. Women, 1980; del. to Rep. Nat. Conv., Dallas, 1984; bd. dirs. Mesa Cmty. Coun., 1985—, Ariz. Hist. Soc., Ariz., Ariz. Life Found., Aide to Women Ctr. Mem.: Am. Legis. Exchange Coun., Ariz. Fedn. Rep. Women (bd. dirs.), Nat. Fedn. Rep. Women, Nat. Order Women Legislators (v.p. 1987—88, pres. 1989—90), Ariz. Assn. of Women (bd. dirs.), Am. Mothers Assn., Pi Beta Phi. Mem. Ch. Lds Ch. Office: Ariz Ho of Reps 1700 W Washington St Phoenix AZ 85007-2812

STEFFY, MARION NANCY, state agency administrator; b. Fairport Harbor, Ohio, Sept. 23, 1937; d. Felix and Anna (Kosaber) Jackopin; 1 child, Christopher C. BA, Ohio State U., 1959; postgrad., Butler U., 1962-65, Ind. U., 1983. Exec. sec. Franklin County Mental Health Assn., Columbus, Ohio, 1959-61; caseworker Marion County Dept. Pub. Welfare, Indpls., 1961-63, supr., 1963-66, asst. chief supr., 1966-73; dir. divsn. pub. assistance Ind. Dept. Pub. Welfare, Indpls., 1973-77, asst. adminstr., 1977-85; regional adminstr. Adminstrn. Children and Families Ill. Dept. Health and Human Svcs., Chgo., 1985-98; nat. dir. Performance Initiative, 1998—. Lectr. Ball State U., Lockyear Coll., Ind. U. Grad. Sch. Social Work; mem. Ind. Devel. Disabilities Coun., 1979-81, Ind. Cmty. Svcs. Adv. Coun., 1978-81; Ind. Child Support Adv. Coun., 1976-82, Welfare Svc. League, 1968—; chmn. rules com. Ind. Health Facilities Coun., 1974-81; chmn. Lawrence Twp. Roundtable, 1983—; dir. Palette and Chisel Acad. Fine Arts, 2003. Mem. Nat. Assn. State Pub. Welfare Adminstrs., Am. Pub. Welfare Assn., Network of Women in Bus. Roman Catholic.

STEGER, DONNA ANN, printing company executive, broker; b. Manhasset, Dec. 13, 1958; d. Paul Wilcof and Lisel Spielman Bernstein; m. Eric Daniel Steger, May 19, 1985; children: Simone, Madeleine, Daniel. BS in Graphic Comms., Calif. Poly., San Luis Obispo, 1981. Estimator Warren's Waller Press, South San Francisco, Calif., 1981—82, sales rep., 1982—99; ptnr. p.s. Print Smart, LLC, San Bruno, 1999—2003; pres. and owner p.s. Print Smart, Inc., Calif., 2003—. Recipient Premier Print award, Printing Indistries Am., 2005. Mem.: Women's Bus. Enterprise, Printing Industries No. Calif. Office Phone: 650-588-4200.

STEGGE, DIANE FAYE, counselor; b. Cedar Rapids, Iowa, Jan. 21, 1948; d. Ivor and Anna Ella Matilda (Wardenburg) Mumm; married; children: Joseph, James BS, Iowa State U., 1970; MS, Drake U., 1990. Tchr. Havelock-Plover Cmty. Sch., Havelock, Iowa, 1973—77, Ayrshire Consol. Sch., Iowa, 1977—81, Sioux Valley Cmty. Sch., Peterson, Iowa, 1981—90, elem. counselor, 1990—2000; counselor Pocahontas Area Cmty. H.S., Iowa, 2000—. Adj. faculty Iowa Ctrl. C.C., 2000—, Buena Vista U., 2006. Mem. Am. Sch. Counseling Assn., Iowa Sch. Counseling Assn. (pres. 1998-2000, v.p. secondary level), Iowa Girls H.S. Athletic Assn (ofcl) Democrat. Lutheran. Avocations: photography, reading, archery.

STEGMULLER, AGNES LEONORE, physical education educator; b. Phila., Jan. 24, 1923; d. George August and Agnes B. Stegmuller. BS in Edn., Temple U., Phila., 1945, MS in Edn., 1948; postgrad., Sorbonne U., Paris, 1954, Brigham Young U., Laie, Hawaii, Pa. State U. From tchr. to dept. head health and phys. edn. Sch. Dist. Phila., 1946—93; adj. prof. Temple U., Phila., 1993—. Pres. Dist. I Track Offcls., Abington, Pa., 2004—06. Vol. Spl. Olympics, Phila., March of Dimes, Pa.; mem. U.S. Women's Basketball Olympic Com., 1978—79; pres. Temple U. Coll. Health, Physical Edn., Recreation and Dance Alumni, 1998—99. Named Agnes L. Stegmuller scholarship in her honor, Temple U., 1994; named to Temple U. Hall of Fame, 1989, Pa. Sports Hall of Fame, 1999, Pa. Lacrosse Hall of Fame, 2002; recipient Steoher award, Phila. Sch. Dist., 1986, Coach of Yr., Women's Sports Fedn., 1988, Pathfinder award, Am. Alliance Health, Physical Edn., Recreation and Dance, 1990, Conwell award, Temple U., 2000, Meritorious

Svc. award, Pa. Interscholastic Athletic Assn., 2004. Mem.: AAHPERD (Pa. liason), Pa. AAHPERD (v.p. 1988—92, girls sports chmn.), Phi Delta Kappa. Home: 27 Jeffrey Rd Aldan PA 19018

STEHLE, CHERYL DIANE FRENCH, language educator; b. Latrobe, Pa., July 15, 1946; d. George Edward and Eleanor (Evans) French. BA, SUNY, Brockport, 1969, MA, 1973, cert. advanced study in ednl. adminstrn., 1979; Doctorate, U. Rochester, 1981. Permanent tchg. cert., N.Y.; cert. sch. dist. adminstr. and sch. adminstr. and supr. Instr. English and elem. Batavia (N.Y.) City Schs., 1969-86; prof. English U. S.C., Hilton Head, 1986—, adj. grad. faculty, 1986—. Prof. English and comm. Genesee C.C., Batavia, 1983-86; pvt. practice ednl. cons., Hilton Head, 1986—. Contbr. articles to profl. publs. Active Hilton Head Island Town Coun. Task Force for Higher Edn.; vestry mem., lay reader, eucharistic min. St. Luke's Episcopal Ch., Hilton Head. Mem. Internat. Alliance for Invitational Learning (bd. dirs. 1985—). Avocations: travel, power walking, swimming, tennis, cinema. Home: 25 Myrtle Bank Rd Hilton Head Island SC 29926-1809

STEHN, LORRAINE STRELNICK, physician; b. Richmond, Ind., Aug. 27, 1950; d. Daniel H. and Eleanor Gayle (Robertson) Strelnick; m. Thomas Veasey Stehn, June 16, 1973; children: Alexander Veasey, Andrew Thomas. BA, Carleton Coll., 1972; DO, Coll. Osteo. Medicine & Surg., 1976. Diplomate Am. Bd. Family Practice. Intern Pontiac (Mich.) Osteo. Hosp., 1976-77; vol. med. officer U.S. Peace Corps, Swaziland, 1977-79; resident family practice St. Mary's Hosp., Port Arthur, Tex., 1980-82; family practice osteo. medicine Aransas Pass, Tex., 1982—; med. adv. Christian Svc. Ctr., Aransas Pass, Tex., 1983—. Chief staff Coastal Bend Hosp., Aransas Pass, 1985, 90, 95, North Bay Hosp., 2003, chief of staff elect, 2006. Pres. bd. dirs. Corpus Christi (Tex.) Chorale, 1995-96; pres. Aransas Pass H.S. Band Booster, 1998-2000. Recipient Svc. award Aransas Pass Jr. High, 1984. Fellow Am. Acad. Family Practice (pres. bd. dirs. profl. counseling svcs.); mem. Tex. Med. Assn., SPAR County Med. Soc. (pres. 2006—). Democrat. Home: 1613 S Saunders St Aransas Pass TX 78336-3107 Office Phone: 361-758-2799. E-mail: stehn@cableone.net.

STEICHEN, JOANNA T(AUB), psychotherapist, writer; b. N.Y.C., Feb. 22, 1933; d. William James and Edna (Notice) Taub; m. Edward Steichen, Mar. 19, 1960 (dec. 1973). BA, Smith Coll., 1954; MS, Columbia U., 1973. Diplomate Am. Bd. Social Work. Copywriter Young & Rubicam, Inc., N.Y.C., 1955-60; asst. social worker Mount Sinai Hosp., N.Y.C., 1970-71; pvt. practice N.Y.C., 1975—2001; cons. supr. Baltic St. Svc., South Beach Psychiat. Ctr., Bklyn., 1976-77; supr. psychotherapy New Hope Guild Ctrs., Bklyn., 1977—88, dir. group therapy tng., 1980-88; dir. acad. tng. Ctr. for Group Studies, NYC, 1989—90, faculty, supr., 1989—99. Author: Marrying Up: An American Dream-and Reality, 1983, Steichen's Legacy, 2000; contbr. articles to mags. Task force schs. self-study Columbia U. Sch. Social Work, N.Y.C., 1972-75; trustee Internat. Mus. Photography, Rochester, N.Y., 1980-1996, trustee emeritus, 1996—; active Creative Arts Awards Commn., Brandeis U., 1985-91, Long House Res. Arts Com., 1996—; bd. dirs. Edward F. Albee Found., 1980—, Hampton Day Sch., 1994-97. Mem. NASW (diplomate), N.Y. State Soc. Clin. Social Work Psychotherapists, Authors Guild Democrat. Episcopalian. Avocations: architecture, theater, opera, piano. Office: Apt 14F 252 7th Ave New York NY 10001-7347

STEIDER, DORIS, artist; b. Decatur, Ill., Apr. 10, 1924; d. Rudy C. and Helen (Regan) Sleeter; m. Robert E. Steider, Nov. 16, 1944 (div.); children: Kristen (Mrs. Gerald Latham), Robert S., Tim D; m. Carroll B. McCampbell, May 19, 1972. BS, Purdue U.; MA, U. N.Mex. Exhibited in more than 190 maj. juried shows including Smithsonian Instn., Washington, Gilcrease Inst., Tulsa, Army Traveling Print Shows, 1963, 64, Witte Mus. Western Art, San Antonio, Mont. State Hist. Soc. Mus., Helena, Mus. N.Mex. Biennials, N.Mex. State Fair Profl. Show, Nat. Art Shows, La Junta, Colo., 1978, 81, 83, Nebraskaland Days Invitational Art Exhbn., 1976—; exhibited in over 100 one-woman shows; represented in permanent collections Holt Rinehart and Winston, Purdue U. Galleries, Time Inc., Loewen Group British Columbia, West Tex. Mus., U. N.Mex. Art Mus., N.Mex. State Fair Collection, Albuquerque Pub. Libr., over 2500 in pvt. collections; Book (by Mary Carroll Nelson) A Vision of Silence: The Egg Tempera Landscapes of Doris Steider, 1997. Mem. Albuquerque Fine Arts Adv. Bd., 1966-72; chmn. standards com. N.Mex. Arts and Crafts Bd., 1964-70; chmn. invitational rev. bd. SW Arts and Crafts Fair, 1977-78. Doris Steider St. named in her honor Albuquerque, 1989; recipient over 85 local, regional, nat. and internat. awards, Disting. Alumni honor Purdue U., 2000. Mem.: Soc. of Layerists in Multi-Media. Home: 12905 Sunrise Trail Pl NE Albuquerque NM 87111-8194 Personal E-mail: steiderart@cs.com.

STEIDL, MARY CATHERINE, food service executive; b. Saratoga, N.Y., Dec. 13, 1961; d. Peter Anthony Fabbozzi and Catherine Mary Moody; m. Scott Vincent Steidl Sr., July 7, 1986 (div. Dec. 1995); children: Scott Jr., Martin C. Student, Seton Hall U., 1980—81. Dir. ops. McDonalds Corp., Oakbrook, Ill., 1980—; trustee Ronald McDonald House, Long Branch, NJ, 2000—; bd. dirs. Queens (NY) Cmty. Cadet Corp. Pres. emeritus Sacred Heart Grammar Sch. PTA, Clifton, NJ, 2000. Roman Catholic. Avocations: backgammon, gardening. Office: McDonalds NY Region 105 Eisenhower Pkwy Roseland NJ 07068

STEIER, AUDREY KELLER, music educator; b. Newark; d. Solomon Charles and Tillie (Tomarin) Keller; m. Herbert Steier (dec.); children: Marcy Byer, Lisa Moore, David. BS in Music Edn., NYU, 1956; Hebrew cert. and religious edn., Hebrew Union Coll. Jewish Inst. Religion. Music tchr. Elizabeth Bd. Edn., NJ, 1956—57; religious sch. music tchr. Temple B'Nai Jesurun, Short Hills, NJ, 1957—80, pre-sch. dir., 1966—91, youth group adv., 1980—82; pre-sch. dir. Temple Has Shalom, Warren, NJ, 1992—97. Cons. Various Pre-Sch., Essex County, 1990. Mem.: Nat. Coun. Jewish Women (life; v.p. 1980—93). Avocations: knitting, needlecrafts, travel, reading. Home: 4200 Cleveland Lane Rockaway NJ 07866

STEIGER, BETTIE ALEXANDER, information industry specialist; b. Spirit Lake, Idaho, Jan. 27, 1934; d. Walter and Velma Esteline (Williamson) Alexander; m. Donald Wayne Steiger, Nov. 10, 1956; children: Craig Alexander Scott, Ann Alexander Carla. BS in Polit. Sci., Wash. State U., 1956, postgrad., 1957; MBA, Harvard U., 1987. V.p. Gartner Group, Inc., Stamford, Conn., Reference Tech. Inc.; exec. dir. Assn. for Info and Image Mgmt., Silver Spring, Md.; dir. to prin. Worldwide Mktg. Xerox Corp., McLean, Va.; prin. tech. and market devel. v.p. Xerox Palo Alto Rsch. Ctr., Palo Alto, Calif.; pres. Power Image Making, 2005—. Founder online system The Source; vis. prof. Wash. State U., 2003. Founder Army Family Symposium, 1979; class sec. Harvard Bus. Sch., 1987—; bd. dirs. B-Llinked, Inc., Internat. Mus. Women. Recipient Outstanding Alumni award Wash. State U., 1988; named Woman of Yr., Wash. State, 2003. Mem. Internat. Women's Forum, Women's Forum West, Army Officers Wives (pres. Greater Washington Area 1976), Info. Industry Assn., Videotex Industry Assn. (bd. dirs.), Am. Women's Club (pres. 1971), Pi Beta Phi (pres. alumnae prov. 1965). Republican. Presbyterian. Avocations: poetry, tennis, swimming. Home and Office: Steiger Assocs 1370 Trinity Dr Menlo Park CA 94025-6680 Office Phone: 650-854-7500. Personal E-mail: bsteiger@earthlink.net.

STEIGERWALD-CLAUSEN, BEVERLY, sculptor, educator; b. Akron, Ohio, Nov. 15, 1934; d. Benjamin Wilford and Marion Eleanor (Ion) Betz; m. James Carl Steigerwald, June 21, 1958 (dec. 1988); children: Mary Jo, Michael, James, Denise, Michelle, Suzanne, Beth; m. Kenneth E. Clausen, Feb. 14, 1997. Attended, Cleve. Inst. Art, 1952-54. Sculpture tchr. Art Students League, Denver, 1995—2005. Chmn. organizing com. Foothills Art Ctr., N.Am. Sculpture Exhbn., Golden, Colo., 1985-92; presenter Interfaith Forum on Religion, Art and Architecture, Brno, Czechoslovakia, 1992; presenter Exposition des Artistes Americains, Auvillar, France, 1996; lectr. Cath. City Women's Club, Akron, Ohio, 1995; presenter Lancaster Theological Sem., Lancaster, Pa., 2000; juror, Internat. Snow Sculpture Championships, Breckenridge, Colo., 2003, Art Students League, Denver, 2004, Summer Sculpture Competition, Hammer and Pen Prodns., 2006. Prin. works include life-size bronze figures St. Michael the Archangel Ch., Aurora, Colo., 1990, 15 relief bronze plaques St. Patrick Ch., Colorado Springs, Colo., 1991, bronze relief figure and wall Mercy Hosp. Chapel, Denver, 1992, outdoor life-size bronze Queen of Peace Ch., Aurora, Colo., 1993, lobby bronze Queen of Peace Ch., Aurora, 1999, outdoor bronze Lancaster (Pa.) Theol. Sem., 2000, lobby life-size bronze Northside Hosp., Atlanta, 2001, outdoor life-size bronze Lakewood, Colo., 2004. Vol. Foothills Art Ctr., 1976-92. Recipient Excalibur Bronze award Catherine Lorillard Wolfe Art Club, 1986, Roman Bronze award Pen and Brush, 1987, Internat. Visual Arts Citation award Interfaith Forum on Religion, Art and Architecture, 1991, Colo. Best of Show Colo. Art Exhbn., 1999, Calif. Best of Show, Ministry & Liturgy Mag., 2002, 2nd pl., 2004. Mem.: No. Colo. Artist Assn. Home and Office: 782 S Emporia St Denver CO 80247-1908 Office Phone: 303-364-8498.

STEIKER, CAROL S., law educator; b. Phila., May 31, 1961; AB in History and Lit., Harvard-Radcliffe, 1982; JD, Harvard U., 1986. Bar: NY 1987, DC 1988. Law clk. to Judge J. Skelly Wright US Ct. Appeals DC Cir.; law clk. to Justice Thurgood Marshall US Supreme Ct.; asst. prof. law Harvard Law Sch., Cambridge, Mass., 1992—98, prof., 1998—, assoc. dean academic affairs, 1998—2001. Office: Harvard Law Sch 1563 Massachusetts Ave Cambridge MA 02138 Office Phone: 617-496-5457. Office Fax: 617-496-5156. Business E-Mail: steiker@law.harvard.edu.

STEIL, JANICE M., social psychology educator; b. Fall River, Mass., Mar. 1, 1941; d. Alfred Edward Ingham and Rita Hindle; m. M. Peter Steil Jr., June 28, 1970; children: Justin Peter, Alexis Ingham. BA, U. Mass., 1962; EdM, Boston U., 1965; PhD, Columbia U., 1979. Lectr. Boston U., 1966, Brandeis Coll., Waltham, Mass., 1967, 69; project dir. Nat. Commn. on Resources for Youth, N.Y.C., 1971-73; rsch. scientist State of N.Y., N.Y.C., 1978-79; prof. social psychology Adelphi U., Garden City, N.Y., 1979—, dir. rsch. tng., 1997—, chair univ.-wide self-study for re-accreditation, 1997-99. Presenter in field.; scholar in-residence Catalyst, N.Y.C., 1997-98; mem. steering com. Feminist Conf. Series, 1993-94. Assoc. editor Psychology of Women Quar., 1993-98; author: Marital Equality: Its relationship to the well-being of husbands and wives, 1997; contbr. numerous articles to profl. jours., chpts. to books; ad hoc reviewer numerous jours. in field. Fellow APA; mem. Am. Psychol. Soc., Internat. Soc. for Study of Personal Relationships, Internat. Network on Personal Relationships, Ea. Psychol. Assn. (program com. 1988-91). Office: Adelphi U Derner Inst Garden City NY 11530

STEIMLE, JAMI P., elementary school educator; b. Lansing, Mich., July 26, 1980; d. Pamela and Douglas Reeves; m. Joseph Steimle, Jan. 15, 2005. BA in edn., Mich. State U., East Lansing, 2003; MA in edn., No. Ariz. U., Phoenix, 2006. K-8 Edn. tchr. Ariz., 2003. 3d grade tchr. Lansing Sch. Dist., 2002—03; 5th grade tchr. Cartwright Elem. Sch. Dist., Phoenix, 2003—06, Dysart Sch. Dist., El Mirage, Ariz., 2006—. Curriculum rev. com. Cartwright Elem. Sch. Dist., Phoenix, 2003—06; extended leadership com. Cartwright Elem. Sch., Phoenix, 2005—06. Mem.: NSTA, Ariz. Reading Assn., Phoenix West Reading Coun. (assoc.). Avocations: travel, bicycling. Office: Ashton Ranch Elem Sch 14898 W Acoma Dr Surprise AZ 85379

STEIN, AMY RENEE, elementary school educator; b. Great Bend, Kans., Aug. 16, 1977; d. Charles Earl and Cheryl Ann Richardson; m. Troy Allen Stein, July 19, 1997; children: Aaron Michael, Tyler Alan. BS in Edn., U. Kans., Lawrence, 1995—2000. Cert. Tchr., Elem K-9 Kans. Dept. Edn., 2002. 7th grade sci. & health tchr. USD 450 Shawnee Heights Mid. Sch., Tecumseh, Kans., 2002—04; 7th & 8th grade math tchr. USD 331 Kingman-Norwich Pub. Schs., Kingman, 2004—05, 6th grade math & sci. tchr., 2005—. Head mid. sch. girls' track coach USD 331 Kingman-Norwich Pub. Schs., 2004—. Mem.: Kans. Nat. Edn. Assn.

STEIN, CHERYL DENISE, lawyer; b. N.Y.C., Nov. 3, 1953; d. Arthur Earl and Joyce (Weitzman) S. BA magna cum laude, Yale U., 1974; postgrad., U. Chgo., 1974-75; JD, Yale U., 1977. Bar: D.C. 1978, U.S. Dist. Ct. D.C. 1983, U.S. Dist. Ct. Md. 1995, U.S. Ct. Appeals (D.C. cir.) 1988. Atty. advisor CAB, Washington, 1978-79; assoc. Cohn & Marks, Washington, 1979-82; pvt. practice Washington, 1982—. Vol. reader radio reading svc. for the blind Washignton Ear, Silver Spring, Md., 1982-91; vol. tutor Friends of Tyler Sch., 1992-95, Habitat for Humanity, Washington, 1997-99; pvt. vol. tutor, 1995-97. Mem. Nat. Assn. Criminal Def. Lawyers, D.C. Assn. Criminal Def. Lawyers. Democrat. Jewish. Avocations: horseback riding, gardening. Home: 706 12th St Ne Washington DC 20002-4434

STEIN, DAWN MARIE, science educator; b. St. Louis, Mo., July 16, 1980; d. Tammy Sue and Dean Gerald Stein. M in Ednl. Adminstrn., Lindenwood U., St. Louis, Mo., 2006; B in Secondary Edn. Unified Sci., SW Mo. State U., 2002. Chemistry and chem. systems tchr. Hazelwood Ctrl. H.S., Florissant, Mo., 2002—04; chemistry and phys. sci. tchr. Lindbergh H.S., St. Louis, Mo., 2004—05; math and sci. tchr. Seckman H.S., Imperial, Mo., 2005—. Mem.: NEA. Personal E-mail: stein@fox.k12.mo.us.

STEIN, JANE WALLISON, lawyer; b. Mar. 23, 1947; AB, Barnard Coll., 1968; MA, NYU, 1969; JD magna cum laude, Bklyn. Law Sch., 1974. Bar: NY 1975. Ptnr., co-leader Project Fin. practice Pillsbury Wiinthrop Shaw Pittman, NYC. Editor (in chief): Bklyn. Law Rev. Mem.: Nat. Assn. Bond Lawyers, NY State Bar Assn., Assn. Bar City of NY (chmn. com. on Project Fin. 2002—). Office: Pillsbury Winthrop Shaw Pittman 1540 Broadway New York NY 10036 Office Phone: 212-858-1225. Office Fax: 212-858-1500. Business E-Mail: jane.stein@pillsburylaw.com.

STEIN, JOAN DOROTHY, nurse anesthetist; b. Meadville, Pa., Mar. 6, 1941; d. Oakley Lycurgus and Helen Chamberlain Kistner; m. Bernard Harold Stein, June 20, 1963; children: Robert, Jeanne Thorndike, Jack. Diploma, St. Elizabeth Hosp. Sch. Nursing, Youngstown, Ohio, 1961; cert., St. Elizabeth Hosp. Sch. Anesthesia, Youngstown, Ohio, 1963; BS in Anesthesia, Edinboro U., 1980, EdM in Psychology, 1983. RN Ohio, Pa., N.C. Staff nurse anesthetist Spencer Hosp., Meadville, Pa., 1965—80, Hamot Med. Ctr., Erie, Pa., 1980—81, asst. dir. Sch. Nurse Anesthesia, 1981—91; staff nurse anesthetist Meadville Med. Ctr., 1991—2001, New Hanover Regional Med. Ctr., Wilmington, NC, 2001—. Mem.: N.C. Assn. Nurse Anesthetists, Am. Assn. Nurse Anethetists (cert.). Independent. Roman Catholic. Avocations: reading, walking, gardening, classical music, opera. Home: 622 Robert E Lee Dr Wilmington NC 28412-0824

STEIN, JULIE ESTHER, piano instructor; b. Kingman, Ariz., June 23, 1975; d. John Michael and Eloise Margaret Cook; m. Scott Anthony Stein, Sept. 27, 1997; children: Anthony John, Ellie June, Amber Lindy. BS in Music Performance, U. Wis., Superior, 1998. Pianist Superior Sch. Dist., 1995-97; pvt. piano instr. Julie Stein's Studio, Duluth, Minn., 1994—; organist, choir dir., 1997—2005; piano instr. John Duss Music Conservatory, Duluth, 1997—2001; bell choir dir. Zion Lutheran, Superior, 2002—05; conductor Founder Hibbing Youth Orchestra, 2006—. Contbr. musical revs. Daily Telegram and Budgeteer, 1998—. Mem. Itasca Symphony 2003-06, Wis. Superior orchestra 2006-. Avocations: writing, running, cooking, art, reading. Personal E-mail: scottnjulie03@yahoo.com.

STEIN, KAREN LEE, critical care nurse; d. Roy and Elizabeth; m. Richard Stein; children: Tara, Chelsea. BSc in Nursing, U. Pitts., 1984; MSc in Edn., Duquesne U., 1998. RN Pa., 1984, cert. critical care nurse, Am. Assn. Critical Care Nurses, 1986. Staff nurse Intensive Care Unit Magee Women's Hosp., Pitts., 1984—87, nurse educator, 1987—92, clinical specialist, 1992—. Vol. story hour CC Mellor Libr., Edgewood, Pa., 1998—; coach tng. Pitts. Harlequin Found., Indianola, Pa., 2000—. Mem.: Am. Assn. Critical Care Nurses, Am. Heart Assn. (instr. 1987—). Avocations: painting, photography, landscaping, skiing, boating.

STEIN, KIRA D., psychiatrist; d. David H. and Vivien Y. Burt; m. Michel R. Stein, Aug. 18, 1996. BA in Polit. Sci., UCLA, 1991; Post-Baccalaureate Premedical Cert., Bryn Mawr Coll., Pa., 1993; MD, U. Rochester, N.Y., 1997. Bd. cert. psychiatry Am. Bd. Psychiatry and Neurology, 2003, registered Drug Enforcement Agy., 1999, cert. in cognitive behavioral therapy UCLA Anxiety Disorders Clinic, 2000, in interpersonal psychotherapy UCLA Interpersonal Psychotherapy Clinic, 2001. Intern internal medicine Huntington Meml. Hosp., L.A., 1997—98; resident adult psychiatry program UCLA Neuropsychiatric Inst., 1998—2001; pvt. practice Kira Stein, MD, APC, Sherman Oaks, Calif., 2001—; clin. instr. UCLA Neuropsychiatric Inst., David Geffen Sch. Medicine, 2001—. Contbr. chapters to books, articles to profl. jours. Mem.: So. Calif. Psychiat. Soc., Calif. Psychiat. Assn., Am. Psychiat. Assn. Avocations: travel, camping, hiking, swimming, theater. Office: Ste 410 15300 Ventura Blvd Sherman Oaks CA 91403 Office Phone: 818-990-5901.

STEIN, LAURA, food products executive; b. 1961; children: Amanda, Christopher. BA, Dartmouth Coll., 1983; JD, Harvard Law Sch., 1987; MA, Dartmouth Coll. Bar: Calif., 1987. Tracsactional corp. lawyer Morrison & Foerster, San Francisco; asst. gen. counsel, regulatory affairs The Clorox Co., 1992—99; sr. v.p., gen. counsel The Heinz Co., Pittsburgh, Pa., 2000—. Mem. ABA (chmn. Commn. on Domestic Violence), Calif. State Bar, Assn. Am. Corp. Counsel Assn., Am. Soc. Corp. Sect. Office: H J Heinz Co 600 Grant St Ste 6000 Pittsburgh PA 15219-2857

STEIN, MARY KATHERINE, photographer, communications executive; b. Denver, Sept. 7, 1944; d. Robert Addison and Minta Mary (MacDonald) Dunlap; m. Lawrence Bronstein, June 29, 1970 (div. 1974); m. Donald L. Stein, Aug. 16, 1982. BS in Journalism, U. Kans., 1966. Sr. editor Am Family Physician mag., Kansas City, Mo., 1967-78; editor-in-chief Current Prescribing mag., Oradell, N.J., 1978-79; sr. editor Diagnosis mag., Oradell, 1979-83; mng. editor Advances in Reproductive Medicine, Bolton, Conn., 1983-85; pres. MD Comm., Tucson, 1983—; pres. Desert Light Photography, Tucson. Author: Child Abuse, 1987, Caring for the AIDS Patient, 1987, Lifetime Weight Control, 1988, Substance Abuse, 1988, An Overview of HIV Infections and AIDS, 1989, Cardiovascular Disease: Evaluation and Prevention, 1989, Substance Abuse: A Guide for Healthcare Professionals, 1997; mng. editor: Eating Disorders Rev., 1990—; editor Nutrition and the M.D., 1992-95; contbr. articles to mags. Mem. Women in Comm. (pres. Greater Kansas City chpt. 1977-78, pres. Orange County chpt. 1990-92), Am. Med. Writers Assn., Profl. Photographers Am. Democrat. Lutheran. Avocation: photography. Office: MD Comm Inc and Desert Light Photography 302 S Pinto Pl Tucson AZ 85748-6902 E-mail: marykaystein1@aol.com.

STEIN, MIRIAM, social worker, training services executive; b. Boston, Sept. 25, 1941; d. Ernest and Grete Hamburger; m. William Mark Stein, July 11, 1965; children: Adam, Amelle. MSW, Boston U., 1965. Lic. ind. clin. social worker Mass. Program dir. Mass. Human Services Coalition, Boston, 1978—82; free-lance journalist, 1980—; dir. comm. Mass. Immigrant and Refugee Advocacy Coalition, Boston, 1998—2001; advocacy and media trainer, cons. Stein Consulting, Arlington, Mass., 2001—; project dir. Coop. Met. Ministries, Newton, Mass., 2002—. Interfaith religious task force on welfare Campaign for Real Welfare Reform, Boston, 1994—96; mem. adv. bd. Office of Justice and Peace, Sisters of St. Joseph, Boston, 1994—2002; guest lectr. Sch. Social Work, Simmons Coll., 2003—; pres. Mass. Human Services Coalition, Boston, 2005—. Author: (memoir) To Trust The Future. Co-chair Vision 2020 Diversity Task Group, Arlington, Mass., 1994—2004; mem. Arlington Fair Housing Adv. Com., 1983—94. Recipient Citizen award, Arlington Fair Housing Adv. Com., 1998, Spl. award, Foster Kids' Caucus of the Mass. Legislature, 1998, MLK Jr. Cmty. Svc. award, 2003, Social Worker of the Yr., Nat. Assn. Social Workers, Mass. Chpt., 2006. Mem.: NASW (dir. of govtl. affairs Mass chpt. 1984—98, recognition award 1996). Jewish. Home: 17 Oak Knoll Arlington MA 02476 Office: Stein Consulting 17 Oak Knoll Arlington MA 02476 Office Phone: 781-648-0255. E-mail: miriam.stein@comcast.net.

STEIN, PAULA JEAN ANNE BARTON, hotel real estate company executive, real estate broker; b. Chgo., July 29, 1929; m. Marshall L. Stein; children: Guy G., George L.; guardian of Bradley Stein, Gregory Stein. BA, Lake Forest (Ill.) U., 1951; postgrad., Roosevelt U., Chgo., 1955—77, UCLA, 1978—79. Adminstrv. asst. publicity Kefauver for Pres., Chgo., 1951; adminstrv. asst. Wells Orgns., Chgo., 1952; rschr., writer Employers Assn. Am., Chgo., 1951-52; writer Woodworking Jobbers Assn., Chgo., 1953; cons. L.A., 1978-80; pres., broker Steinvest, Inc., Chgo., 1980—; freelance writer, 1996—. Cons., hotels Nat. Diversified Svcs., Inc., Chgo., 1990—, Beach Hotel, Inc., Monterey, Calif., IBA Women's Adv. Bd., 1999; advocate for learning disorder solutions. Script for first TV bus. prog. on WGN-TV, 1951-52. Mem. Ragdale Found., Lake Forest, Ill. IBA fellow, 1990. Mem. World Future Soc. (profl.), Sisters in Crime, Mystery Writers, So. Poverty Law Ctr., others. Avocations: painting, writing. Home and Office: Steinvest Inc 2291 Hybernia Dr Highland Park IL 60035-5509 Personal E-mail: steinvest@msn.com.

STEIN, PAULA NANCY, psychologist, educator; b. N.Y.C., Aug. 23, 1963; d. Michael and Evelyn (Graber) S.; m. Andreas Howard Smoller, Sept. 2, 1991; children: Rebecca Leigh Smoller, Rachel Jordan Smoller. BA, Skidmore Coll., 1985; MA with distinction, Hofstra U., 1986, PhD, 1989. Lic. clin. psychologist, N.Y.; cert. in sch. psychology, N.Y. Intern NYU Med. Ctr.-Rusk Inst., N.Y.C., 1988-89; instr. Mt. Sinai Med. Ctr., N.Y.C., 1989-93, asst. prof. rehab. medicine, 1993-95. Psychologist Fishkill (N.Y.) Consultation Group, 1991—. Contbr. chpt. to book, articles to profl. jours. Kraewic scholar Skidmore Coll., 1985. Mem. APA, Assn. for Advancement of Behavior Therapy, Phi Beta Kappa. Jewish. Avocations: skiing, swimming. Office: Fishkill Consultation Group 1064 Main St Fishkill NY 12524-0446 Office Phone: 845-896-6751.

STEIN, RUTH ELIZABETH KLEIN, physician; b. NYC, Nov. 2, 1941; d. Theodore and Mimi (Foges) Klein; m. H. David Stein, June 9, 1963; children: Lynn Andrea Stein Melnick, Sharon Lisa, Deborah Michelle. AB, Barnard Coll., 1962; MD, Albert Einstein Coll. Medicine, 1966. Diplomate Am. Bd. Pediat. Intern, then resident Bronx Mcpl. Hosp. Ctr., 1966—68; sr. resident, fellow; 1968instr. dept. pediats. George Washington U., Washington, 1968—70; with Albert Einstein Coll. of Medicine, Bronx, 1970—77, assoc. prof. pediats., 1977—83, prof., 1983—; vice-chmn. dept. pediats. Albert Einstein Coll., 1992—2002, dir. office of acad. affairs, dept. pediats., 1997—2002; pediatrician-in-chief, dir. pediats. Jacobi Med. Ctr. (formerly Bronx Mcpl. Hosp. Ctr.), 1992—97. Vis. prof. pub. health dept. epidemiology Yale U. Sch. Medicine, New Haven, 1986-87; scholar-in-residence United Hosp. Fund, NY, 1995-97; dir., prin. investigator Preventive Intervention Rsch. Ctr. for Child Health, NY, 1983-94, Nat. Child Health Assessment Planning Project, NY, Behavioral Pediatric Tng. Program, NY; dir. gen. pediatrics Pediat. Divsn., NY, 1992-97; apptd. to Montefiore Med. Ctr., North Ctrl. Bronx Hosp., Jacobi Med. Ctr.; bd. dirs. Ctr. for Child Health Rsch. of Am. Acad. Pediatrics, mem. exec. com., 1999-2004; co-chmn. com. on evaluation of child health 2002-04, NRC/Inst. Medicine, 1999-2005; bd. sci. counselors Nat. Ctr. Health Stats. of CDC, 2006-. Editor: Caring for Children with Chronic Illness: Issues and Strategies, 1989, Health Care for Children: What's Right, What's Wrong, What's Next, 1997; mem. editorial bd. Jour. Behavioral and Devel. Pediatrics; contbr. articles to profl. jours. Fellow Am. Acad. Pediats.; mem. APHA, Am. Pediatric Soc., Soc. for Pediat. Rsch., Ambulatory Pediat. Assn. (bd. dirs. 1982-89, pres. 1987-88, rsch. award 1995, Ray Helfer award 1999), NY Acad. Medicine (chmn. NY forum on child health 2001-05), Soc. for Devel. and Behavioral Pediats., Alpha Omega Alpha. Jewish. Home: 91 Larchmont Ave Larchmont NY 10538-3748 Office: Albert Einstein Coll Med Montefiore Med Ctr Dept Pediat 111 E 210 St Bronx NY 10467-2804 Office Phone: 718-920-7932. Business E-Mail: rstein@aecom.yu.edu.

STEIN, SANDRA LOU, educational psychology professor; b. Freeport, Ill., Oct. 6, 1942; d. William Kenneth and Marien Elizabeth Stein. BS, U. Wis., Madison, 1964; MS Edn., No. Ill. U., 1967, EdD, 1969. Tchr. English

Rockford Sch. Dist., Ill., 1964—65; tchr. Russian Jefferson County Sch. Dist., Lakewood, Colo., 1965—66; asst. prof. edn. U. S.C., Columbia, 1969—71, No. Ill. U., DeKalb, 1971—72, Rider U., Lawrenceville, NJ, 1972—75, assoc. prof. edn., 1975—81; prof. edn. Rider Coll., Lawrenceville, 1981—, dept. chair, 1983—91, 2003—06. Cons. on measurement and evaluation, women's edn., 1973— Contbr. articles to ednl. publs Deacon Presbyn. Ch. Lawrenceville, 1984—87. Recipient Disting. Tchg. award Rider Coll. and Lindback Found., 1981 Mem. APA, AAUP (chpt. pres. 2000-01, negotiating team 2002, Outstanding Achievement award Rider Coll. chpt. 1988), Am. Ednl. Rsch. Assn., Phi Delta Kappa (chpt. pres. 1986-87, Svc. Key award 1991, faculty advisor 1994—99) Office: Rider U 2083 Lawrenceville Rd Lawrenceville NJ 08648-3099 Office Phone: 609-896-5348. E-mail: stein@rider.edu.

STEIN, SHERYL E., lawyer; b. Bklyn., Apr. 20, 1952; BA cum laude, Univ. Miami, 1974; JD, Southwestern Univ., 1978. Bar: Calif. 1979. Ptnr., office mng. ptnr., leader office Corp. & Securities practice sect. Pillsbury Winthrop Shaw Pittman, LA. Mem.: LA County Bar Found. (bd. mem.), LA County Bar Assn., Org. Women Exec. Office: Pillsbury Winthrop Shaw Pittman Suite 2800 725 S Figueroa St Los Angeles CA 90017 Office Phone: 213-488-7194. Office Fax: 213-629-1033. Business E-Mail: sheryl.stein@pillsburylaw.com.

STEIN, TRISHA, advocate; b. 1971; Commn. analyst Mich. House, House of Commons, London; dir., millage campaign Suburban Mobility Authority for Regional Transp., 1996; exec. asst. Wayne County executive's office, 1998; campaign mgr. Mike Duggan, Wayne County prosecutor, 2000; exec. dir. One United Mich., 2004—. Named one of 40 Under 40, Crain's Detroit Bus., 2006. Office: One United Michigan PO Box 81156 Lansing MI 48908 Office Phone: 877-482-1438.*

STEIN, ZENA A., retired epidemiologist, educator; b. Durban, South Africa, July 7, 1922; married; 3 children. BA in History, U. Capetown, 1941, MA in History with honors, 1942; MB, BChir, U. Witwatersrand, 1950, DSc (hon.), 1993. Med. officer Alexandra Health Ctr. & U. Clinic, Johannesburg, 1952—55; registrar psychiatry Shenley Mental Hosp., England, 1956; rsch. assoc. Dept. Social & Preventive Medicine U. Manchester, 1959—62, sr. rsch. fellow Mental Health Rsch. Fund, Dept. Social & Preventive Medicine, 1959—62, rsch. fellow, Medical Rsch. Coun., Dept. Social & Preventive Medicine, 1962—65; rsch. assoc. Assn. for Aid Crippled Children, NYC, 1965—66; assoc. prof. epidemiology Columbia U. Sch. Pub. Health, NYC, 1966—73, prof. pub. health epidemiology, 1973—92, prof. pub. health epidemiology, Gertrude H. Sergievsky Ctr., 1977—, assoc. dir. rsch. and acad. affairs N.Y.C., 1986—; dir. epidemiology of brain disorders rsch. dept. NY State Psychiat. Inst., NYC, 1968—98, co-dir. HIV Ctr. for Clin. and Behavioral Studies, 1987—; co-dir. HIV Ctr. for Clin. and Behavioral Studies, NY State Psychiatric Inst. Columbia U., NYC, 1987—, prof. psychiatry dept. psychiatry, 1991—92, acting chair divsn. epidemiology, sch. pub. health, 1993—95, prof. emerita dept. epidemiology & psychiatry, sch. pub. health, 1993—. Cons. Pan Am. Health Orgn., 1972, WHO, 1978, 83, 86, 91, UNICEF, South African Med. Rsch. Coun., 1992-93, Robert Wood Johnson Found., 1993-94; vis. prof. U. Sydney, 1975, Nat. Inst. Mental Health, Lima, Peru, 1988, Inst. Sukperiore de Sanita, Rome, 1989; hon. prof. Nat. Sch. Pub. Health, Madrid, Spain, 1999; co-dir. Africa Ctr. Population Studies & Reproductive Health, Mtubatuba, South Africa, 1999; spkr. in field. Co-editor: (with Hatch, M.) Reproduction at the Workplace, 1986, (with M. Wright, J. Scandlyn) Women's Health and Apartheid: The Health of Women and Children and the Future of Progressive Health Care in Southern Africa, 1988, (with A. Zwi) Action on AIDS in Southern Africa: Maputo Conference on Health in Transition in Southern Africa, 1990; co-author: (with Kline, J.) Conception to Birth: Epidemiology of Prenatal Development, 1989; edit. bd. Am. Journal of Public Health, Genetic Epidemiology, Teratogenesis, Carcinogenesis & Mutagenesis, Reproductive Toxicology, American Journal of Human Genetics; contbr. chpts. to books and articles to profl. jours. Lt. South African Defense Force, 1943—45. Recipient Physicians & Surgeons Disting. Svc. award, Coll. Physicians & Surgeons, Columbia U., 1994, 75th Jubilee medal, U. Witwatersrand Med. Sch., 1997, Tribute to Zena Stein award, Internat. Conf. Microbicides Organizing Com., 2002; grantee Fogarty Ctr., NIMH. Mem.: NAS, NIMH (mem. study sects.), Joint Commn. Internat. Aspects Mental Retardation, Am. Soc. Human Genetics, Am. Epidemiological Soc., Soc. Study of Social Biology, Soc. Life History Rsch. Psychiatric Epidemiology, Internat. Epidemiological Assn., Soc. Epidemiologic Rsch., Am. Pub. Health Assn. (Wade Hampton Frost award & lecture 1992, John Snow award 1999), Am. Assn. Mental Deficiency, Inst. Medicine (sr. mem. 1998), Nat. Inst. Child Health & Human Devel., Nat. Inst. Occupl. Safety & Health, Nat. Inst. Environ. Health Scis. Office: HIV Ctr NY State Psychiat Inst 722 W 168th St New York NY 10032-2603 Business E-Mail: zas2@columbia.edu.

STEINBACH, LYNNE SUSAN, radiologist, educator; b. San Francisco, Dec. 28, 1953; d. Howard Lynne and Ilse (Rosengarten) S.; m. Eric Franklin Tepper, Aug. 14, 1977; 1 child, Mark Evan. Student, Vassar Coll.; BA, Stanford U., 1975; MD, Med. Coll. Pa., 1979. Intern Coll. Medicine and Dentistry N.J., Newark, 1979—80; resident radiology N.Y. Hosp.-Cornell Med. Ctr., N.Y.C., 1980—83; fellow musculoskeletal radiology Hosp. Spl. Surgery Cornell Med. Ctr., N.Y.C., 1983—84; asst. prof. radiology U. Calif., San Francisco, 1984—92, assoc. prof., 1992—98, prof., 1998—. Chief musculoskeletal imaging U. Calif. San Francisco. Editor 4 books; contbr. articles 130 on radiology, chpts. on musculoskeletal radiology to profl. pubs. Fellow Am. Coll. Radiology; mem. Internat. Skeletal Soc. (mem.-at-large 2002-03, asst. sec. 2003-04, Pres. medal), San Francisco Radiol. Soc. (sec. treas. 1994, pres. 1996), Radiol. Soc. N.Am., Am. Assn. Women Radiologists (mem.-at-large 1987-88, sec. 1989-91, v.p. 1991-92, pres.-elect 1992-93, pres. 1993-94), Am. Roentgen Ray Soc., Assn. U. Radiologists, Soc. Skeletal Radiology. Avocations: swimming, piano, travel, gardening. E-mail: lynne.steinbach@radiology.ucsf.edu.

STEINBAUM, BERNICE, art dealer; b. Flushing, NY, Jan. 3, 1941; d. Julius Dov and Sarah (Lasker) Aptowitz; m. Harold Steinbaum; children: Jeremy, Sara, Carrie. BA, Queens Coll., 1961; MA, Hofstra U., 1965; PhD in Art Edn., Columbia U., 1977. Tchr. Iowa Pub. Sch. System; assoc. prof. Drake U., Iowa; prof. Hofstra U., N.Y.C.; gallery dir. Bernice Steinbaum Gallery, N.Y.C. Curator numerous exhbns. and traveling mus. shows; speaker in field; juror numerous art shows. Host: Art Time with Mrs. Steinbaum, Iowa; contbr. articles to profl. publs., mags., and newspapers; author: The Rocker, 1992. Named Woman of Yr. NOW, 1988. Office: Bernice Steinbaum Gallery 3550 N Miami Ave Miami FL 33127-3112 Office Phone: 305-573-2700. Business E-Mail: info@berniesteinbaumgallery.com.

STEINBERG, AMY WISHNER, dermatologist; b. N.Y.C., Nov. 19, 1959; d. Arnold Blaine and Sylvia Fay (Bernoff) Wishner; m. Alan Lloyd Steinberg, June 15, 1986; children: Joshua Darren, Arielle Dana, Natalie Tara. BS, Northwestern U., Evanston, Ill., 1981; MD, Northwestern U., Chgo., 1983. Clin. instr. Univ. Hosp., Stony Brook, N.Y., 1987—; pvt. practice Stony Brook, 1987—. Fellow Am. Acad. Dermatology; mem. Suffolk Dermatology Soc., Internat. Soc. Dermatology, N.Y. State Dermatology Soc. Office: 2500 Route 347 Bldg 5 Stony Brook NY 11790-2555 Office Phone: 631-689-7683.

STEINBERG, BETH AILEEN, employee assistance manager; b. N.Y.C., Jan. 30, 1952; d. Henry Steinberg and Frances Marion Sokolovsky; m. Andrew Franklin Hudnall, Oct. 18, 1997. BA, Bklyn. Coll., 1973; MSW, U. Ky., 1986. Cert. employee assistance profl; cert. clin. addiction counselor; master cert. addiction counselor; lic. ind. clin. social worker. Social worker Valley Clinic, St. Albans, W.Va., 1976-80; clinical coord., substance abouse counselor Housing Authority of City of Charleston, W.Va., 1980-82; clin. coord. Our Lady of Bellefonte, Ashland, Ky., 1982-89; family therapist Thomas Meml. Hosp. Southway, South Charleston, W.Va., 1989-97; employee assistance counselor Union Carbide, 1997—2001; U.S. EAP ops. specialist Dow Chem. Co., 2001—. Mem. Nat. Assn. Alcohol/Drug Abuse Counselors, W.Va. Assn. Alcohol/Drug Abuse Counselors (Counselor of Yr. 1996), Employee Assistance Profls. Assn. (W.Va. chpt.), Sisterhood Temple B'nai Israel (v.p.). Democrat. Jewish. Avocations: travel, music. Office: Dow Employee Counseling Svcs Bldg 82 Rm 121 437 MacCorkle Ave South Charleston WV 25303 E-mail: bshnyer104@charter.net.

STEINBERG, BLEMA, political science professor; m. H. Arnold Steinberg; children: Margot, Donna, Adam. BA, McGill Univ., 1955; MA, Cornell Univ.; PhD, McGill Univ., 1961. Cert. psychoanalyst 1989. Assoc. prof. McGill Univ., prof., 1996—2001, prof. emeritus, 2001—. Author: Shame & Humiliation: Presidential Decision Making on Vietnam, 1996 (Quebec Writers Federation award, 1996, QSPELL First Book award, 1996); co-editor: Superpower Involvement in the Middle East, 1985; contbr. articles to profl. jours. Named one of Top 200 Collectors, ARTnews Mag., 2004, 2005, 2006. Avocation: collector of modern & contemporary art. Mailing: McGill Univ Political Science Dept 855 Sherbrooke St W Montreal PQ H3A 2T7 Canada*

STEINBERG, DEBRA BROWN, lawyer; b. Nashville, May 16, 1954; AB, Smith Coll., 1976; JD cum laude, Boston Coll., 1979. Bar: N.Y. 1980, U.S. Dist. Ct. (so. and ea. dists.) N.Y., 1981, U.S. Ct. Appeals (2d cir.) 1987, U.S. Supreme Ct. 1994. Ptnr. Cadwalader, Wickersham and Taft, N.Y.C., 1990—. Recipient Pro Bono Svc. award, N.Y. State Bar Assn., 2003. Mem.: ABA, Assn. Bar City of N.Y., N.Y. Women's Bar Assn. Achievements include leading her firm's pro bono representation of families of World Trade Center victims, with her work recognized by U.S. House Rep.(2004) and N.Y. State Senate (2003) resolutions. Office: Cadwalader Wickersham Taft 1 World Financial Ctr # 6 New York NY 10281-1003 Office Phone: 212-504-6598. Business E-Mail: debra.steinberg@cwt.com.

STEINBERG, JANET ECKSTEIN, journalist; d. Charles and Adele (Ehrenfeld) Eckstein; m. Irvin S. Silverstein, Oct. 22, 1988; children: Susan Carole Steinberg Somerstein, Jody Lynn Steinberg Lazarow. BS, U. Cin., 1964. Travel cons., 1994—; pub. Paine Webber Vantage Living website, 2000—02; guest lectr. Tri State Travel Sch., 1999—2001. Freelance writer:; guest appearance Braun & Co., Sta. WLW-TV, Sta. WMKV-TV, travel editor Am. Israelite, 1996—, Jewish News, 1996—, N.J. Jewish News, 1997—; travel editor: Miami Herald Jewish Star Times, 2002—03; travel editor S. Fla. Single Living, 1988—92, Cin. Post, 1978—86, Ky. Post, 1978—86, Cin. Enquirer, 1986—94, MetroWest Jewish News, N.J., 1996—, Jewish News-New Orleans, 1996—, L.A. Jewish Jour., 1997—; contbg. editor: Travel Agt., 1986—88, Birnbaum Travel Guides, 1988—98, The Writer, 1988, 1992, 1998, Entree, 1986—97; travel columnist Northeast Mag., 1986—88, South Fla. Single Living, 1984—92, Eastside Weekend Mag., 1994—96; contbr. articles to newspapers, mags., and books. Recipient Lowell Thomas Travel Journalism award, 1984, 1985, 1990, Henry E. Bradshaw travel journalism award, 1st pl., best of show, 1988, Buckeye Travel award, Ohio Divsn. Travl & Tourism, 1992, Cipriani Best Overall WRiter award, 1981, 13 awards, Soc. Am. Travel Writers, 1981—96, 16 awards, Midwest Travel Writers, 1981—2004. Home: 900 Adams Xing Ste 9200 Cincinnati OH 45202-1677 E-mail: jxs4travel@aol.com.

STEINBERG, JOAN EMILY, retired secondary school educator; b. San Francisco, Dec. 9, 1932; d. John Emil and Kathleen Helen (Montgomery) S. BA, U. Calif., Berkeley, 1954; EdD, U. San Francisco, 1981. Tchr. Vallejo (Calif.) Unified Sch. Dist., 1959-61, San Francisco Unified Sch. Dist., 1961-93, elem. tchr., 1961-78, tchr. life and phys. sci. jr. high sch., 1978-85, 87-93, sci. cons., 1985-87; lectr. elem. edn. San Francisco State U., 1993-94. Ind. sci. edn. cons., 1993-2002. Contbr. articles to zool. and edn. books and profl. jours. Recipient Calif. Educator award, 1988, Outstanding Educator in Tchg. award U. San Francisco Alumni Soc., 1989; Fulbright scholar U. Sydney, Australia, 1955-56. Mem. San Francisco Zool. Soc., Exploratorium, Am. Fedn. Tchrs., Calif. Acad. Scis., Calif. Malacozool. Soc., Nat. Sci. Tchrs. Assn., Elem. Sch. Sci. Assn. (sec. 1984-85, pres. 1986-87, newsletter editor 1994-99), Sigma Xi. Democrat.

STEINBERG, LAURA, lawyer; b. Phila., Feb. 3, 1948; d. Leonard and Pearl (Zeid) S.; children: Seth, Adam, Bree. BA magna cum laude with honors, Bryn Mawr Coll., 1968; JD cum laude, Harvard U., 1972. Bar: Mass. 1972, U.S. Dist. Ct. Mass. 1972, U.S. Dist. Ct. R.I. 1974, U.S. Ct. Appeals (1st cir.) 1973, U.S. Ct. Appeals (10th and D.C. cirs.) 1986, U.S. Ct. Appeals (4th cir.) 1988, U.S. Claims Ct. 1979, U.S. Supreme Ct. 1988. Assoc. Sullivan & Worcester, Boston, 1972-79, ptnr., 1979—, mem. mgmt. com., 1988-2000, head litigation dept., 1987—99, chair complex bus. fiduciary litigation group, 2004—. Dir. Greater Boston Legal Svcs., 1987-90. Bd. dirs. Law Firm Resources Project, Boston, 1980-86, Lawyers Com. for Civil Rights Under Law, 1998—; pres. Peirce Extended Day Program, Inc., West Newton, Mass., 1983-86. Spl. career fellow U. Calif., Berkeley, 1968-69; Fulbright scholar, 1968. Mem. Boston Bar Assn. (vice-chmn. litigation sect. 1992-94, chmn. 1994-95). Avocations: reading, tennis. Office: Sullivan & Worcester LLP One Post Office Sq Ste 2100 Boston MA 02109-2129 Office Phone: 617-338-2800. E-mail: lsteinberg@sandw.com.

STEINBERG, MARILYN MARIE, psychotherapist; b. Hammond, Ind., July 13, 1965; d. Willard and Lorraine Cassity; BA, Purdue U., 1993, MS, 1999. Psychology intern Southlake Ctr. for Mental Health, Schererville, Ind., 1992, St. Margaret Mercy, Dyer, Ind., 1993; mental health counselor Charter Behavioral Health Systems, Hobart, Ind., 1994—95; and family therapy intern Purdue U. MFT Ctr., Hammond, 1996; psychology instr. Purdue U., 1995—96; and family therapy intern Thornton Twp. Youth Com., South Holland, Ill., 1997; psychotherapist Willowglen Acad., Gary, Ind., 1999—. Lectr. in field. Contbr. articles to profl. jours., chpt. to book. Mem.: Internat. Family Therapy Assn., Ind. Assn. Marriage and Family therapy, Am. Assn. Marriage and Family therapy, Golden Harvest Condominium Assn. (pres. 2002—06), Alpha Chi. Democrat. Roman Catholic. Avocations: travel, cooking, scrapbooking, Chicago White Sox, Purdue football. Office: Willowglen Acad 308 E 21st Ave Gary IN 46407 Personal E-mail: msteinbergmslmft@aol.com.

STEINBERG, SALME ELIZABETH HARJU, academic administrator, historian; b. N.Y.C. d. Johan Edward and Jenny Lydia (Peltonen) Harju; m. Michael Stephen Steinberg, Sept. 15, 1963; children: William, Katharine Lovisa. BA, Hunter Coll., 1960; MA, CCNY, 1962; PhD, Johns Hopkins U., 1971. Lectr. history Goucher Coll., Towson, Md., 1971—72; asst. prof. history Northwestern U., Evanston, Ill., 1972—75; prof. Northeastern Ill. U., Chgo., 1975—83, chmn. dept., 1983—87, assoc. provost then acting provost, 1987—92, provost, v.p. for acad. affairs, 1992—95, pres., 1995—. Author: Reformer in the Marketplace: Edward W. Bok and The Ladies' Home Journal, 1979; contbr. articles to profl. jours. Named to, Hunter Coll. Hall of Fame, 1997; recipient 14th Ann. award Appreciation, Asian Am. Coalition Chgo., 1997; grantee, Danforth Found., 1967—68. Episcopalian. Avocations: opera, theater. Office: Northeastern Ill U Office of President 5500 N Saint Louis Ave Chicago IL 60625-4679

STEINEM, GLORIA, writer, editor, advocate; b. Toledo, Mar. 25, 1934; d. Leo and Ruth (Nuneviller) S.; granddaughter of suffragette Pauline Steinem; m. David Bale, Sept. 3, 2000 (dec. Dec. 30, 2003); step-son Christian Bale. BA in Govt., magna cum laude (hon.), Smith Coll., 1956; postgrad. (Chester Bowles Asian fellow), India, 1957-58; D. Human Justice, Simmons Coll., 1973, PhD (hon.). Co-dir., dir. edn. found. Ind. Rsch. Svc., Cambridge, Mass. and N.Y.C., 1959-60; contbg. editor Glamour Mag., N.Y.C., 1962-69; co-founder, contbg. editor New York Mag., 1968-72; feminist lectr., 1969—; co-founder, editor Ms. Mag., 1971-87, columnist, 1980-87, cons. editor, 1987—. Active various civil rights and peace campaigns including United Farmworkers, Vietnam War Tax Protest, Com. for the Legal Def. of Angela Davis (treas., 1971-72); active polit. campaigns of Adlai Stevenson, Robert Kennedy, Eugene McCarthy, Shirley Chisholm, George McGovern; Co-founder, bd. dirs. Women's Action Alliance, 1970-2001, (now Feminist Majority Found.); co-founder, convenor, mem. nat. adv. com. Nat. Women's Polit. Caucus, 1971; co-founder, pres. bd. dirs. Ms. Found. for Women, 1972-1990; founding mem. Coalition of Labor Union Women, 1974, Pres. Voters for Choice, 1979; mem. Internat. Women's Year Commn., 1977, pres. Choice USA, co-founder, chmn. Liberty Media for Women, 1998 (current owner and operator Ms. mag); editorial cons., Conde Nast Publications, 1962-69, Curtis Publishing, 1964-65, Random House Publishing, 1988-, McCall Publishing. Author: The Thousand Indias, 1957, The Beach Book, 1963, Wonder Woman, 1972, Outrageous Acts and Everyday Rebellions, 1982, Marilyn: Norma Jeane, 1986, Revolution from Within: A Book of Self-Esteem, 1992; contbg. corr. NBC Today Show, 1987—88; author: Moving Beyond Words: Age, Rage, Sex, Power, Money, Muscles - Breaking the Boundaries of Gender, 1994; contbr. to various anthologies. Named Woman of Yr., McCall's mag., 1972; named to Nat. Women's Hall of Fame, 1993; recipient Penney-Missouri Journalism award, 1970, Award for Journalism, Gov. Ohio, 1972, Bill of Rights award, ACLU of So. Calif., 1975, Mo. Honor Medal for Disting. Svc. in Journalism, U. Mo. Sch. Journalism, 2005; Woodrow Wilson Internat. Ctr. for Scholars Fellow, 1977. Mem.: Author's Guild, Soc. Mag. Writers, Nat. Press Club, AFTRA, NOW, Phi Beta Kappa. Coined phrase "reproductive freedom" during 1972 nat. abortion debate. Office: MS Magazine 433 S Beverly Dr Beverly Hills CA 90212-4401 also: Choice USA 712 Hershey Ave Monterey Park CA 91755-1473

STEINER, FRANCES JOSEPHINE, conductor, musician, educator; b. Portland, Oreg., Feb. 25, 1937; d. Ferenz Joseph and Elizabeth (Levy) Steiner; m. Mervin Israel Tarlow, June 8, 1965; 1 child, Sarah Leah Tarlow. EdB with hon., Temple U., 1956; MusB, Curtis Inst. Music, 1956; student with Nadia Boulanger, France, 1957; MA, Radcliffe Coll., 1958; Mus D arts, U. So. Calif., 1969; student with Hans Beer, 1972—82. Tchr., orch. dir. Roosevelt Jr. HS, Phila., 1956, Brown Jr. HS, Malden, Mass., 1957—58; mem. faculty Newton Jr., Sr. HS, 1958—62; instr. Bklyn. Coll., 1962—65; mem. faculty Fullerton Jr. Coll., Calif., 1966—67; soloist Glendale Symphony, 1970—71; asst. prin. cellist Pasadena Symphony, 1970—71, L.A. Chamber Orch., 1970—73; prin. cellist Calif. Chamber Symphony, 1970—76; condr., music dir. Baroque Consortium Chamber Orch. (now named Chamber Orch. of the So. Bay), 1974—; mem. faculty Calif. State U., Dominguez Hills, 1967—2005, prof., 1975—2005, prof. emeritus, 2005—, chmn. Dept. Music, 1978—84; condr., music dir. Carson-Dominguez Hills Symphony Orch., 1977—; prin. cellist Glendale Symphony Orch., 1975—85, asst. condr. Calif., 1984—85. Guest condr. MIT Orch., Cambridge, Mass., 1980, Maracaibo Symphony, Venezuela, 1984, Nat. Symphony Orch. of Dominican Republic, Brevard (County) Symphony Orch., 1986, Bay Area Women's Philharm., 1986, Billings (Mont.) Symphony, 1987, Wis. Chamber Orch., Calif. All-State Honor Orch., 2005, Wis. Chamber Orch., 1994, Sofia Chamber Orch., Nizhny Nougorod, Russia, 2003. Co-editor: Introduction to Music, 1964; co-author (with Max Kaplan): Musicianship for the Classroom, 1966; arranger: menuets Six Minuets in Two Celli (Haydn), 1967. Recipient citation Nat. Fedn. Music Clubs, 1975—76, Elizabeth Mathias award, CSUDH Status of Women award, 1991, Mu Phi Epsilon award of merit; fellow Thomas Dana fellow, 1956—57; scholar, Temple U., 1952—56; Curtis Inst. Music scholar, 1945—56, Russell Kingman scholar, 1957. Mem.: Am. Symphony Orch. League, Condrs. Guild. Democrat. Jewish. Avocations: gourmet, wines. Home and Office: 21 La Vista Verde Dr Rancho Palos Verdes CA 90275 Business E-Mail: fsteiner@csudh.edu.

STEINER, GLORIA LITWIN, psychologist; b. Newark, Oct. 21, 1922; d. David Milton and Minna (Krasner) Litwin; m. Charles Steiner, Aug. 29, 1942; children: Charles Jr., Susan Steiner Sher, Jeanne. BA, U. Pa., 1944; MS, CCNY, 1956; EdD, Columbia U., 1965. Psychologist St. Michael's Hosp. and Mt. Carmel, Newark, 1956-62; chief psychologist Children's Hosp., Newark, 1965-78; prof. psychology, dir. psychol. svc. Child Study Ctr., Kean Coll., Union, N.J., 1971-78; vis. assoc. prof. grad. sch. applied and profl. psychology Rutgers U., Piscataway, N.J., 1976-94; clin. assoc. prof., former dir. psychology tng. U. Medicine and Dentistry N.J.-N.J. Med. Sch., Newark, 1978—. Psychology cons. Nat. Pediatric HIV Resource Ctr., 1991-94; trustee Sister Rose Thering endowment dept. Jewish Christian studies Seton Hall U., 1992—. Co-author: Traumatic Abuse/Children, 1980; co-editor: Children, Families and HIV/AIDS: Psychosocial and Psychotherapeutic Issues, 1995; contbr. articles to profl. jours.; mem. editl. bd. Jour. Psychotherapy, 1981-96. Mem. N.J. State Task Force on AIDS, 1986-89, N.J. State Bd. Psychol. Exam., 1978-84, Regional Health Planning Coun., N.J., 1984-85, child adv. com. Mental Health Assn., N.J., 1974-80; trustee, founder N.J. Acad. Psychology, 1978-83, bd. trustees, 1994-97; bd. govs. Metro N.J. chpt. Am. Jewish. Com., 1996—. Grantee tng. health care workers Regional AIDS Edn. and Tng. Ctr. U. Medicine and Dentistry N.J., Newark, 1990, Nat. Pediat. HIV Resource Ctr., Newark, 1991-94. Fellow Am. Orthopsychiat. Assn.; mem. N.Y. Acad. Scis., N.J. Assn. for the Advancement Family Therapy (vice-chmn. 1979-81), Am. Psychol. Assn. Home and Office: 321 N Wyoming Ave Apt 4D South Orange NJ 07079-1671 Office Phone: 973-763-7472. E-mail: charglorsteiner@verizon.net.

STEINER, JANET JOY, educational consultant; d. John Simon and Mildred (Metzler) Steiner; m. Michael Francis O'Malley, 1991. BA, Goshen Coll., 1966; MEd, U. Va., 1970. Reading Recovery tchr. cert. Va. Poly. Inst. and State U., 1990. Classroom tchr. Goshen City Schs., Ind., 1966—67, Harrisonburg City Schs., Va., 1967—69; adult edn. tchr. Charlottesville City Schs., Va., 1972; reading tchr. Arlington Pub. Schs., Va., 1972—2000, Reading Recovery tchr.; co-developer, co-instr. Emergent Reading Strategies Inst. Arlington Pub. Schs., 1993—2000. Organizer, adult basic and Gen. Equivalency Degree programs Vol. In Svc. To Am., Phila., 1970—71; bd. dirs. Greater Washington Reading Coun., Va., 1986—93; program devel. team Nat. Reading Rsch. Ctr., College Park, Md., 1991—96, Arlington, Va., 1991—96; lectr. edn. Marymount U., Arlington, 1993; presenter Internat. Reading Rsch. Conf., New Orleans, 1993; cons. curriculum and staff devel. Alief Ind. Sch. Dist., Tex., 1994; presenter N.Y. State Reading Assn. Conf., Albany, 1994, 1st Combined Internat. Reading Assn. Regional Conf., Nashville, 1995, Nat. Reading Conf., Charleston, 1996, Va. State Reading Assn., Crystal City, 1997; cons. program devel. schools Montgomery County Schs., Md., 1997; textbook cons. Shortland Pub. Co. (U.S.A.), Inc, Denver, 1997—98; cons. curriculum and staff developement Monroe Bd. Coop. and Ednl. Svcs., Rochester, 1998; textbook cons. Newbridge Ednl. Pub., N.Y.C., 1998—2004, Heinemann Pub. Co., Chgo., 2001—02. Co-editor: Greater Washington Reading Council Journal, 1988—92; editor, 1992—93; contbg. narrative author: Coming Together As Readers by Donna Ogle; co-author, steering com. Family Focus: Reading and Learning Together, 1988—89. Bd. dirs. Washington Reading Coun., Va., 1986—93; vol. Children's Def. Fund, Wash., 2002—04; steering com. Interfaith Children's Advocacy Network of Greater Wash., 2002—05. Mem.: Delta Kappa Gamma, Internat. Reading Assn. Avocations: writing, cooking, entertaining, travel, bicycling. Personal E-mail: janmo5225@aol.com.

STEINER, JUDITH MARIE, elementary school educator; b. Catskill, NY, May 15, 1948; d. Roger and Madeline Steiner; children: Benton James Miller, Abigail Marie Miller. Student, Ithaca Coll., NY, 1968; BS, U. Ill., Chgo., 1971; MS in Edn., Drake U., Des Moines, 1976. Cert. tchr. Iowa, NY. Elem. tchr. Muscatine Schs., Iowa, 1971—73, Carlisle Elem. Sch., Iowa, 1974—78; tchr. Moulton Elem. Sch., Des Moines, 1978—89, Mid. Sch., Des Moines, 1990—91; drama tchr. Gifted Inst., Des Moines Pub. Schs., 1978—90; land. arts tchr. Cooperstown Elem. Sch., NY, 1991—. Adj. prof. divsn. edn. SUNY, Oneonta, 2001—. Contbr. essays to lit. publs. Developer, performer History Sings ballad workshop, 2002—; singer Ah Coopella, Cooperstown, 2003—; mem. acoustic/vocal trio Grin & the T's. Recipient Behind Women in Aviation award, 2003. Mem.: ASCD. Avocations: poetry, children's books, writing. Home: 948 Wiley Town Rd Fly Creek NY 13337

STEINER, SALLY ANN, psychiatric nurse practitioner; b. Bayshore, NY, Oct. 21, 1968; d. Richard and Carol Julia (Rotter) Hendershot; m. Michael Francis Steiner, July 6, 2002. BSN, USNY; MSN in pediatric nurse practitioner, U. So. Fla., 2001; post master's cert. family nurse practitioner, U. South Fla., 2002, post master's cert. psychiat. and mental health nurse practitioner, 2003. RN NY State, Fla. State, Advanced Reg. Nurse Practitioner, Fla. State. Grad. tchg. asst. U. So. Fla., Coll. of Nursing, Tampa, 2000—02; parttime prof. U. So. Fla., Coll. of Medicine, Tampa, 2003; psychiat. advanced registered nurse practitioner Hillsborough County Dept.

of Children's Svcs., Tampa, 2003—. Social skills counselor Tampa Children's Devel. Ctr., Tampa, 2002—; cons. U. So. Fla., 2003—. Vol. nurse Boggy Creek Camp, Eustis, Fla., 2000—; vol. activities related to med. care underpriviledged. Mem.: Nat. Assn. Pediat. Nurses and Advanced Practitioners, Am. Acad. of Nurse Practitioners, Am. Psychiat. Nurses Assn., Tampa Bay Advance Practice Nurses Coun. Avocations: swimming, reading, travel, writing poetry and short stories, rollerblading. Office: Hillsborough County Dept of Childrens Svcs 3110 Clay Mangum Ln Tampa FL 33618 E-mail: sallyrn@tampabay.rr.com.

STEINER, SHARI YVONNE, editor, journalist; b. Colorado Springs, Colo., Mar. 3, 1941; d. Evan Keith and Blanche Marie (Ketzner) Montgomery; m. Clyde Lionel Steiner, June 16, 1962; children: Vienna Kay, Marco Romano. BA, Adams State Coll., 1962; cert. in sociology, London Sch. Econs., 1978; postgrad., U. Calif., Berkeley, 1988—. Lic. real estate broker, Calif. Freelance journalist various publs., 1964—; owner, mgr. SREI Group, San Francisco, 1985—; tng. design developer 1st Nationwide Bank, San Francisco, 1987-90; pub., editor Ind. Info. Publs., San Francisco, 1990—; pres. The SREI Group, San Francisco. Feature writer Internat. Herald Tribune, Rome, 1964-79; acct. exec. Allen, Ingersol & Weber, Rome, 1970-72; gen. ptnr. Greenhaven Park, Sacramento, 1990-2003, Port Chicago Indsl., Concord, Calif., 1991-98, Star/Steiner, 1997—. Author: The Female Factor: A Report on Women in Europe, 1972, 2d edit., 1996, Steiners' Complete How to Move Handbook, 1997, 2d edit., 1999, Steiners' Complete How to Talk Mortgage Talk, 1998, 3d edit., 1999, Relocation Guru, 2000; editor The Bottom Line newsletter, 1985-92; assoc. editor The Semaphore, 1990-92; columnist Country's Best Log Homes and Vacation Homes, 1999—. Coord. urban reforestation Friends of Urban Forest, San Francisco, 1989; co-founder New Sch. for Internat. Elem. Students, Rome, 1970. Recipient internat. journalism award Guida Monaci, 1970, award of merit Lotus Club, N.Y.C., 1975; corr. in archives Am. Heritage Ctr., U. Wyo. Mem. Nat. Assn. Realtors (multiple listing svc. selection com. 1986, 91, investment real estate group 1991), Comml. Real Estate Women (editor, bd. dirs. 1985-2001), Am. Soc. Journalists and Authors (exec. bd. dirs. 1998—), PEN Internat., Employee Relocation Coun. Avocation: gardening. Office Phone: 415-643-6100.

STEINER-HOUCK, SANDRA LYNN, interior designer; b. Columbia, Pa., May 29, 1962; d. Howard Jr. and Mary Louise Steiner; children: Brandon Paul, Brittany Leigh. AA in Interior Design, Bauder Fashion Coll., 1981. Cert. kitchen designer. Designer Bob Harry's Kitchen Ctr., Inc., York, Pa., 1982-87, Leggett, Inc., Camp Hill, Pa., 1987-90, Mother Hubbard's Kitchen Ctr., Mechanicsburg, Pa., 1990-93; owner ind. design svc., 1994—. Designer: Bath Industry Technical Manuals Vol.3, 1993; contbr. designs to profl. jours. Recipient 1st pl. award and Best of Show Resdl. Bath Design, 1986, Showroom Design, 1989, 3d pl. award Resdl. Kitchen, 1992, Resdl. Bath Design, 1992, Heritage Custom Kitchens Mfr.'s Design award, 1986, 94, 3 Nat. Design. awards Resdl. Kitchen, 1994, Kasmar Kitchen Design award 1994, 95, 96, 2d pl. Nat. Design award Kitchen Design, 1997, 1st pl. Nat. Design award Bath Design, 1997, 2000. Mem. Am. Soc. Interior Design, Soc. Cert. Kitchen Designers. Home: 515 Mockingbird Dr Columbia PA 17512-8438 Office: Steiner & Houck Inc 515 Mockingbird Dr Columbia PA 17512-8438 Fax: 717-591-0563.

STEINGASS, SUSAN R., lawyer; b. Cambridge, Mass., Dec. 18, 1941; BA in English Lit., Denison U., 1963; MA in English Lit. with honors, Northwestern U., 1965; JD with honors, U. Wis., 1976. Bar: Wis. 1976, US Dist. Ct. Wis. 1976. Instr. dept. English La. State U., 1965—66, Calif. State Coll., LA, 1966—68, U. Wis., Stevens Point, 1968—72; law clk. Hon. Nathan S. Heffernan Wis. Supreme Ct., 1976—77; ptnr. Stafford, Rosenbaum, Reiser and Hansen, 1977—85; judge Dane County Cir. Ct., Wis., 1985—93; ptnr. Habush, Habush & Rottier, S.C., Madison, Wis., 1993—. Lectr. civil procedure, environ. law, evidence, trial advocacy Law Sch., U. Wis., 1981—, dir. comm. and advocacy programs, 2003—; instr. Nat. Inst. for Trial Advocacy, 1987—, trustee, 2002—; instr. Nat. Jud. Coll., 1993—. Note and comment editor Wis. Law Rev., 1974-76; co-editor: Wisconsin Civil Procedure Before Trial, 1994, The Wisconsin Rules of Evidence: A Courtroom Handbook, 1998—. Chair Wis. Equal Justice Task Force, 1989—91, Wis. Sentencing Commn., 2003—; mem., chair Wis. Jud. Selection Com., 2003—. Recipient Disting. Svc. award Am. Assn. Mediators, 1991, Presdl. award of excellence State Bar Wis., 2000; named Wis. Trial Judge of Yr. Am. Bd. Trial Advocates, 1992. Fellow Wis. Bar Found.; mem. ATLA, ABA (ho. dels. 2000—06), Am. Bar Found., Am. Law Inst., Wis. Bar Assn. (pres. 1998-99), Wis. Law Alumni Assn. (bd. dirs., pres. 2001-05), Wis. Acad. Trial Lawyers, Wis. Equal Justice Fund (pres. 2000-05), Wis. Trust Account Found. (bd. dirs. 1999), Order of the Coif (Marygold Melli Achievement award 2001). Office: Habush Habush Davis & Rottier SC 150 E Gilman St Ste 2000 Madison WI 53703-1481 also: Univ Wis Law School 975 Bascom Mall Madison WI 53706 Business E-Mail: ssteingass@habush.com.

STEINHARDT GUTMAN, BERTHA, artist, educator; b. N.Y.C., N.Y., July 2, 1951; d. Max E. Steinhardt and Irene Goldberg; m. Irving Gutman, June 25, 1972; children: Micah, Simeon, Shanah. BA, CUNY-Queens Coll., 1972; MFA, SUNY, Stony Brook, 1991. Adj. assoc. prof. Suffolk County C.C., Selden, NY, 1991—2001; adj. lectr. St. Joseph's Coll., Patchogue, NY, 1993—97, Adelphi U., Garden City, NY, 1995—2001, Nassau County C.C., Garden City, 2000—01; adj. instr. Montgomery County C.C., Blue Bell, Pa., 2001—02; tenured asst. prof. art Delaware County C.C., Media, Pa., 2002—. Mus. shop mgr. The Jewish Mus., N.Y.C., 1973—77; faculty cons. The Coll. Bd., Phila., 1999—2003, Ednl. Testing Svcs., Trenton, NJ, 1995—2003; artist-in-residence Mishkenot Sha'ananim, Jerusalem, 1994. Recipient Spl. Opportunity stipend, N.Y. State Found. on Arts, 1992—94, Grumbacher Gold medallion in painting, 1995. Home: 165 Somerset Dr Blue Bell PA 19422 Office: Delaware County C C 901 S Media Line Rd Media PA 19063 Office Phone: 610-359-5382. Business E-Mail: bgutman@dccc.edu.

STEINHAUER, GILLIAN, lawyer; b. Aylesbury, Bucks, Eng., Oct. 6, 1938; d. Eric Frederick and Maisie Kathleen (Yeates) Pearson; m. Bruce William Steinhauer, Jan. 2, 1960; children: Alison (Humphrey) Eric, John, Elspeth. AB cum laude, Bryn Mawr (Pa.) Coll., 1959; JD cum laude, U. Mich., 1976. Bar: Tenn. 1998, U.S. Dist. Ct. (ea. dist.) Mich. 1976, U.S. Ct. Appeals (6th cir.) 1982. From assoc. to sr. ptnr. Miller, Canfield, Paddock & Stone, Detroit, 1976-92; dir. Commonwealth of Mass. Workers' Compensation Litigation Unit, Boston, 1992—2002; atty. U.S. Postal Svc., 2002—. Chancellor Cath. Ch. St. Paul, Detroit, 1976-83, 91; pres. bd. trustees Cath. Cmty. Svcs. Inc., 1989-92; bd. dirs. Spaulding for Children, 1991-92, Davenport House, 1992-96, chair 1995-96, vestry mem. St. Michael's Ch., Marblehead, Mass., 1994-97; chpt. mem. St. Mary's Cathedral, Memphis, 2005—. Mem. Mich. State Bar Found. (life), Fed. Jud. Conf. 6th Cir. (life). Home: 4010 S Galloway Dr Memphis TN 38111-6842

STEINHAUER, LUANN, retired learning disabilities educator; b. Camden, N.J., Dec. 25, 1934; d. Ralph John and Ethel May(Spangler) Steinhauer; m. Harry John Sheetz III, June 22, 1957 (div. 1970); children: Ralph John (dec.), Deborah Ann, H. Kevin. BS, Wagner Coll., 1957; postgrad., Pa. State U., 1972-75, Kutztown U., 1987. Tchr. 1st grade Miss Haig Sch., Maple Shade, N.J., 1957; tchr. 4th grade Strawbridge Sch., Haddon Twp., N.J., 1957-59; kindergarten tchr. Swain Sch., Allentown, Pa., 1972-74; learning disabilities tchr. Allentown (Pa.) Sch. Dist., 1975—99, ret., 1999. Homebound tchr., pvt. tutor. Mem. ch. coun. Christ Luth. Ch., Allentown, 1987-93, vacation ch. sch. and Sunday sch. tchr.; mem. Lehigh County Hist. Soc.; vol. Lehigh Valley Hosp., 2000—; ct. appounted spl. adv. neglected or abused children, 2003—. Mem. Learning Disabilities Assn. of Lehigh Valley (Apple for the Tchr. award 1991), Allentown Art Mus., AAUW. Avocations: antiques, gardening, reading. Home: 1052 N 22nd St Allentown PA 18104-3625

STEINHAUER, SHERRI, professional golfer; b. Madison, Wis., Dec. 27, 1962; Student, U. Tex. Mem. Futures Tour, LPGA Tour, 1986—; mem. US Team Solheim Cup, 1994, 1998, 2000. Achievements include winning LPGA Tour events including du Maurier Ltd. Classic, 1992, Sprint Championship, 1994, Weetabix Women's British Open, 1998, 99, Japan Airlines Big Apple Classic, 1999, Sybase Classic Presented by Lincoln Mercury, Women's British Open, 2006; 4 LPGA career holes-in-one. Office: c/o LPGA 100 Internat Golf Dr Daytona Beach FL 32124-1092*

STEINHAUSER, JANICE MAUREEN, arts administrator, educator, artist; b. Oklahoma City, Okla., Apr. 3, 1935; d. Max Charles and Charlotte (Gold) Glass; m. Stuart Z. Hirschman, Dec. 30, 1954 (div. 1965); children: Shayle, David, Susan; m. Sheldon Steinhauser, May 2, 1965; children: Karen, Lisa Steinhauser Hackel. Student, U. Mich., 1953—55; BFA, U. Colo., 1972. Adminstr. cmty. affairs United Bank Denver, 1973—76; dir. visual arts program We. States Arts Found., Denver, 1976—79; exec. dir. Artreach, Inc., Denver, 1980—82; v.p. mktg. Mammoth Gardens, Denver, 1982—83; dir. pub. rels. Denver Ctr. for Performing Arts, 1983—86; founder, pres. Resource Co., Denver, 1986—88; dir. liberal studies divsn. Univ. Coll. U. Denver, 1992—97; sculptor, 1997—. Bd. dirs. Met. Denver Arts Alliance, 1982-85, Denver Internat. Film Festival, 1983-86, Colo. Nat. Abortion Rights Action League, 1991-95, Mizel Mus. Judaica, 1995-2000; mem. Women's Forum of Colo., 1981-2002. Mem. Nat. Assn. Women Artists, Colo. New Music Assn. (bd. dirs. 1987-91), Asian Performing Arts Colo. (bd. dirs.), Phi Beta Kappa, Kappa Delta Phi. Democrat. Jewish. Avocations: travel, reading, films. E-mail: jansart3@aol.com.

STEINHERZ, LAUREL JUDITH, pediatric cardiologist; b. NYC, Jan. 5, 1947; d. Bernard and Adeline Weinberger; m. Peter Gustav Steinherz, July 4, 1967; children: Jennifer, Jonathan, Daniel, David. Student, Hebrew U., Jersualem, 1966; BA with distinction, U. Rochester, 1967; MD, Albert Einstein Coll. Medicine, 1970. Diplomate Am. Bd. Pediatrics, sub-bd. pediatric cardiology. Intern in pediatrics N.Y. Hosp.-Cornell Med. Ctr., N.Y.C., 1970-71; pediatric cardiology fellow N.Y. Presbyn. Hosp.-N.Y. Weill Cornell Med. Ctr. (formerly N.Y. Hosp. Cornell U. Med. Ctr.), N.Y.C., 1973-75, asst. attending pediatrician, 1978-85, assoc. attending pediatrician, 1985—; resident in pediatrics St. Louis Children's Hosp., 1971-72; attending pediatrician State U. Hosp. and King County Med. Ctr., Bklyn., 1975-77; asst. prof. pediatrics SUNY Downstate, 1975-77, Cornell U. Med. Coll., N.Y.C., 1977-85, assoc. prof. pediatrics, 1985—; from asst. to attending pediatrician Meml. Sloan Kettering Cancer Ctr., N.Y.C., 1997—, dir. pediatric cardiology, 1977, asst. clin. mem., 1984-92, assoc. mem., 1997—2006, mem., 2006—. Contbg. author Adolescent Medicine II, 1976, Principles and Practice of Oncology, 1992, 1996, 2001, Supportive Care of Children With Cancer, 1993, 1997, Cardiac Toxicity After Treatment for Childhood Cancer, 1993, Progress in Pediat. Cardiology, 1998; contbr. articles to profl. jours. Hutzler Found. grantee, 1987. Fellow: Am. Coll. Cardiology, Am. Acad. Pediatrics; mem.: Children's Oncology Group, Am. Heart Assn. Avocations: photography, swimming, science fiction. Office: Meml Sloan Kettering Cancer Ctr 1275 York Ave New York NY 10021-6094 Office Phone: 212-639-8103.

STEINHOFF, JUDITH B., art history educator; d. Reynold and Rose Steinhoff; m. Donald R. Morrison, Nov. 1, 1987; children: Noah Theodore Steinhoff Morrison, Adam Nathan Steinhoff Morrison. BA, Sarah Lawrence Coll., 1977; PhD, Princeton U., 1990. Vis. lectr. Trinity Coll., Hartford, Conn., 1987—88; vis. asst. prof. Rice U., Houston, 1988—93; rsch. asst. dept. so. Italian painting Nat. Gallery of Art, Washington, 1995; asst. prof. U. Houston, 1996—2005, assoc. prof., 2005—. Vis. scholar dept. art and archaeology Princeton U., 1997; vis. scholar Ohio State U., Columbus, 1992. Author: Sienese Painting After the Black Death: Artistic Pluralism, Politics, and the New Art Market, 2006; contbg. author: Coming About.A Festschrift for John Shearman, 2001, Renaissance Siena: Art in Context, 2005, Between the Picture and the Word, 2005; contbr. articles to profl. jours. Fellow, NEH, 1993; grantee, Fulbright/Italian Govt., 1983—84, U. Houston, 1997. Mem.: Internat. Ctr. Medieval Studies, Tex. Medieval Assn., Internat. Ctr. Medieval Art, Italian Art Soc., Coll. Art Assn., 14th Century Soc. Office: Sch of Art U Houston Houston TX 77204-4019 Office Phone: 713-743-2839. E-mail: jsteinhoff@uh.edu.

STEINHORN, ROBIN H., neonatologist, educator; b. Akron, Ohio, June 12, 1956; d. Paul Henry and Marion Robinson Heise; m. David Marc Steinhorn; children: Rachel, Benjamin. BS, U. Akron, 1976; MD, Washington U., 1980. Bd. cert. pediat. Am. Bd. Pediat., bd. cert. neonatal-perinatal medicine. Neonatologist Children's Hosp. Buffalo, 1991—99; chief neonatology Children's Meml. Hosp., Chgo., 1999—; intern Wash. U., St. Louis, 1980—81; resident, fellow U. Minn., 1982—88. Assoc. prof. pediat. SUNY, Buffalo, 1991—99; prof. pediat. Northwestern U., Chgo., 1999—. Editor: (book) Extracorporeal Cardiopulmonary Support in Critical Care, 2000; contbr. articles to profl. jours. Grantee, NIH, 1995—. Mem.: Soc. for Pediat. Rsch., Am. Thoracic Soc., Am. Acad. Pediat., Am. Heart Assn. (Established Investigator award 1998). Office: Childrens Meml Hosp Neonatology #45 2300 Childrens Plaza Chicago IL 60614 Office Phone: 773-880-4142. Business E-Mail: r-steinhorn@northwestern.edu.

STEINKE, CAROLYN JOYCE, artist, educator; d. Edward Gerhart and Selma Martha (Schkade) Wagner; m. Peter Louis Steinke; children: Rene, Timoty, Krista, Matthew. BS in Edn., Valparaiso U., Ind.; MA in Humanities, U. Houston, Clear Lake City; MA in Art History, U. Tex., Austin; MFA in Painting and Drawing, Sch. Art Inst., Chgo. Cert. tchr. art Tex. Tchr. Concord Luth. Sch., St. Charles, Ill., Redeemer Luth. Sch., Dallas, Zion Luth. Sch., Dallas; tchr. art Carollton Sch. Dist., Tex.; profl. fine artist Austin, 1994—95, NYC, 1995—99, Austin, 1999—; adj. prof. Austin CC, 1999—, Concordia U., Austin, 2002. Pre-sch. dir. Hope Luth. Sch., Friendswood, Tex., 1978—80; lectr. arts Brauer Mus. Art Valparaiso U., 2001. Manhattan Arts Internat., 1996 (Showcase award, 1996), Bond & Market Assn. catalog, 2000, cover art, The Lit. Rev., 2004, Represented in permanent collections Brower Mus. Art, Lessedra Internat. Art Print Collection, Sofia, Bulgaria. Vol. Am. Cancer Soc.; choral mem. Bach Soc., St. Louis, 1960—64. Grantee, Sch. of Art Inst., Chgo., 1993—94. Mem.: Women Printmakers of Austin, Coll. Art Assn., So. Graphics Coun., Phi Kappa Phi. Avocations: travel, reading, gardening, hiking.

STEINMAN, LISA MALINOWSKI, English literature educator, writer; b. Willimantic, Conn., Apr. 8, 1950; d. Zenon Stanislaus and Shirley Belle Malinowski; m. James A. Steinman, Apr. 1968 (div. 1980); m. James L. Shugrue, July 23, 1984. BA, Cornell U., 1971, MFA, 1973, PhD, 1976. Asst. prof. English Reed Coll., Portland, Oreg., 1976-82, assoc. prof., 1982-90, prof., 1990—, Kenan prof. English lit. and humanities, 1993—. Cons. NEH, Washington, 1984—85. Author: Lost Poems, 1976, Made in America, 1987, All That Comes to Light, 1989, A Book of Other Days, 1992, Ordinary Songs, 1996, Masters of Repetition, 1998, Carslaw's Sequences, 2003; editor: Hubbub Mag., 1983—; mem. editl. bd. Williams Rev., 1991—, Stevens Jour., 1994—; contbr. articles to profl. jours. Appt. adv. com. Publ. of the Modern Lang. Assn., 2006—. Fellow Danforth Found., 1971-75, NEH, 1983, 96, 2006, Oreg. Arts Commn., 1983, Nat. Endowment for Arts, 1984; Rockefeller Found. scholar, 1987-88; recipient Pablo Neruda award, 1987, Oreg. Inst. Lit. Arts award, 1993. Mem. MLA, Poets and Writers, PEN (N.W. chpt., co-founder, officer 1989-93). Home: 5344 SE 38th Ave Portland OR 97202-4208 Office: Reed Coll Dept English 3203 SE Woodstock Blvd Portland OR 97202-8138 Business E-Mail: lisa.steinman@reed.edu.

STEINMAYER, JANET L., food service executive, lawyer; b. 1955; Grad., Bryn Mawr Coll. Sr. v.p. external affairs, gen. counsel TWA, Inc., Mt. Kisco, N.Y.; pres. Centerplate, Inc., Spartanburg, SC, 2005—06, COO, 2005—06, CEO, 2006—. Bd. dirs. Centerplate, Inc., 2005—. Trustee Bryn Mawr Coll. Office: Centerplate Inc 201 E Broad St Spartanburg SC 29306*

STEINMETZ, DEBORAH SUSAN, interior designer; b. New Orleans, Nov. 29, 1951; d. Donald Frederick and Estelle Margaret (Ulmer) Tossell; m. Robert Steinmetz, Dec. 29, 1973. BFA, La. State U., 1973. Interior designer David Grinnell Architect, 1973—75; pvt. practice Columbus, Ga., 1975—77; designer Dameron-Pierson, New Orleans, 1977—79; v.p. interior design Interior Environments, Inc., New Orleans, 1979—83; pres., owner Steinmetz & Assocs., 1983—. Interior design curriculum com. Dominican Coll., New Orleans, 1981—82; interior design adv. com. Delgado CC, New Orleans, 1982—; chmn. membership Preservatin Resource Ctr., 1988. Dir. profl. devel. Nat. Coun. Interior Design Qualification, 1994—95; Visual arts com. Contemporary Art Ctr., 1980—81. Mem.: La. State Interior Design Alumni (sec. 1987), Interior Designers of La. (treas. 1987), La. State Bd. Interior Design Examiners, Internat. Interior Design Assn., Am. Soc. Interior Designers (bd. dirs. 1993—94, bd. dirs. La. chpt. 1982—, newsletter editor 1982, chain membership/admissions 1984, treas. 1985—87, sec. 1988, chmn. New Orleans chpt. 1980—81, Presdl. citation), La. Landmarks Soc., Nat. Trust Hist. Preservation. Roman Catholic. Office: 225 Baronne St Ste 207 New Orleans LA 70112-1704

STEITZ, JOAN ARGETSINGER, biochemistry professor; b. Mpls., Jan. 26, 1941; d. Glenn D. and Elaine (Magnusson) Argetsinger; m. Thomas A. Steitz, Aug. 20, 1966; 1 child, Jon. BS, Antioch Coll., 1963; PhD, Harvard U., 1967; DSc (hon.), Lawrence U., Appleton, Wis., 1981, Rochester U. Sch. Medicine, 1984, Mt. Sinai Sch. Medicine, 1989, Bates Coll., 1990, Trinity Coll., 1992, Harvard U., 1992, Brandeis U., 2002, Brown U., 2003, Princeton U., 2003, Watson Sch. Biol. Sciences, Cold Spring Harbor Lab., 2004. NSF postdoctoral fellow, Andorra, 1967—69; Jane Coffin Childs Meml. Fund Fellow, Divsn. Cell Biology Med. Rsch. Coun. Lab. Molecular Biology, Cambridge, England, 1967—70; asst. prof. molecular biophysics and biochemistry Yale U., New Haven, 1970-74, assoc. prof., molecular biophysics and biochemistry, 1974-78, prof., molecular biophysics and biochemistry, 1978—92, Henry Ford II prof. molecular biophysics and biochemistry, 1992—98, chmn. dept. molecular biophysics and biochemistry, 1996—99, dir. molecular genetics program Boyer Ctr. Molecular Medicine, Sterling prof. molecular biophysics and biochemistry, 1998—. Josiah Macy Scholar Max Planck Inst. fur Biophysikalische Chemie (Göttingen), Germany and Med. Coun. Ctr., Lab. of Molecular Biology, Cambridge, England, 1976—77; Fairchild Disting. Fellow Calif. Inst. Technology, Pasadena, Calif., 1984—85; investigator Howard Hughes Med. Inst, Yale Univ., 1986—; scientific dir. Jane Coffin Child Fund for Med. Rsch., 1991—2002; dir., molecular genetics program Boyer Center for Molecular Medicine; mem. vis. com. for biology divsn. Caltech, Calif. Inst. Technology, 1999—; mem. basic sciences scientific adv. bd. Fred Hutchinson Cancer Ctr., 2001—; mem. scientific adv. bd., biology divsn. Molecular Biology Dept., Princeton Univ., Max Planck Inst. for Biophysical Chemistry (Göttingen), 1999—; mem. Lasker Awards Jury, 2001—, Jury for L'Oréal UNESCO award, 2001—; mem. scientific adv. com. Sci. Found. Ireland, 2002—. Mem. editl. bd. Genes and Development, 1994—, assoc. editor RNA, 1994—, bd. reviewing editors Science, 2004—. Bd. overseers Harvard Univ., 2003—. Co-recipient (with Thomas R. Cech) Warren Triennial Prize, Mass. Gen. Hosp., 1989; named Fritz Lipmann Lectr., Am. Soc. for Biochemistry and Molecular Biology, 1989, 11th Ann. Keith Porter Lectr. on Cell Biology, Am. Soc. for Cell Biology, 1992; recipient Young Scientist award, Passano Found., 1975, Eli Lilly Award in Biol. Chemistry, 1976, U.S. Steel Found. Award in Molecular Biology, 1982, Lee Hawley, Sr. Award for Arthritis Rsch., 1983, Nat. Medal Sci., 1986, Radcliffe Grad. Soc. Medal for Disting. Achievement, 1987, Dickson Prize for Sci., Carnegie-Mellon U., 1988, Christopher Columbus Discovery Award in Biomed. Rsch., 1992, Rebecca Rice award for Disting. Achievement, Antioch Coll. Alumni Assn., 1993, Weizmann Women and Sci. Award, 1994, City of Medicine Award, 1996, Disting. Svc. award, Miami Bio/Technology Winter Symposium, 1996, Novartis Drew Award in Biomed. Rsch., 1999, UNESCO-L'Oreal Women in Sci. Award, 2001, Lewis S. Rosenstiel for Distinguished Work in Basic Medical Rsch. Award, 2002, FASEB Excellence in Sci. Award, 2003, Howard Taylor Ricketts Award, U. Chgo., 2004, Caledonian Rsch. Found. Prize Lectureship, Royal Soc. Edinburgh, 2004, The RNA Soc. Lifetime Achievement Award, 2004, Gairdner award for achievement in med. rsch., Gairdner Found., 2006. Fellow: AAAS, Am. Acad. Microbiology; mem.: NAS, Inst. Medicine, Academia Europaea, Japanese Biochemical Soc. (hon.), European Molecular Biology Orgn. (assoc.), Conn. Acad. Sciences and Engring., Am. Philos. Soc., Am. Acad. Arts and Sciences. Office: Yale Univ Rm BCMM 136E Dept Mol Biophys & Biochem 189 Elm St New Haven CT 06520 Office Phone: 203-737-4418. Business E-Mail: joan.steitz@yale.edu.*

STELCK, MICKIE JOANN, technologist; b. Des Moines, Nov. 12, 1959; d. Richard Findley and Betty Marie Woolsey; m. Michael Lowell Stelck, July 29, 1978. Cert. in surg. tech., Des Moines Area C.C., 1980. Cert. surg. technologist Mayo Clinic, Rochester, Minn., 1980—. Mem. surg. tech. adv. bd. Rochester C.C., 1995—. Co-author: (book) Bronchoscopy, 1994; contbr. articles to profl. jours. Mentor Family Y, Rochester, 1997—. Mem.: Assn. Surg. Technologists (cert.), Lambda Beta. Office: Mayo Clinic Saint Marys Hosp 1216 2d St SW Rochester MN 55902

STELK, VIRGINIA HORN, retired language educator; b. Salina, Kans., Apr. 17, 1939; d. David Horn and Georgia May Zimmerman; m. Lincoln Frank Stelk, June 17, 1960; children: Kirsten Virginia Frazier, Sara Georgianna, Marla Josephine. BA in Spanish, Bethany Coll., Kans., 1960; MA in Reading, Ohio State U., 1981. Cert. in Adminstrn. SUNY, 1992, ESL endorsement U. So. Maine, 2001. Tchr. Suitland Schs., Md., 1960—61, Brookline Schs., Mass., 1961—64, St. Mary's Sch., Delaware, Ohio, 1974—77, Mount Vernon Schs., Ohio, 1978—87, Lakeland Pub. Schs., Shrub Oak, NY, 1987—99, Portland Pub. Schs., Maine, 2000—04; adj. prof. U. So. Maine, 2001—. Adj. prof. Manhattanville Coll., Purchase, NY, 1995—99; instr. Westchester and Putnam Bd. Coop. Ednl. Svcs., Yorktown, NY, 1987—95; presenter in field. Author: Writing Charlotte's Web, 1989, When I Was Young., 2005; contbr. articles to profl. jours. Cellist Mid. Coast Symphony, Topsham, Maine, 2003—. Named Tchr. of Yr., Ohio Ho. Rep., 1982; scholar Martha Holden Jennings Found., 1984. Mem.: FLAME, NCTE, Am. Assn. Tchrs. Spanish and Portuguese, Internat. Reading Assn. Democrat. Episcopalian. Avocations: travel, reading, walking, music groups. Home: 141 Island Ave Peaks Island ME 04108 Personal E-mail: stelk2@aol.com.

STELLA, MARIE VITA, retired engineer, consultant, homeland and information security; b. Bklyn., N.Y., Mar. 27, 1943; d. Joseph Domenico and Maria (Savino) Stella. BA, CCNY, 1965—70; MS, U. of Colo. Sch. of Engring., 1978—80. Cert. info. sys. security profl. Cons. IBM, White Plains, NY, 1980—82; telecommunication engr. Port Authority of NY and NJ, NYC, 1982—84; dep. dir. govt. systems Network Mgmt., Fairfax, Va., 1984—85; lead engr., group leader MITRE Corp, McLean, Va., 1985—90; dep. dir. Network Strategies, Fairfax, Va., 1990—91; lead security engr. FAA, Washington, 1991—2005; sr. rsch. fellow Ctr. For Tech. and Nat. Security Policy, Nat. Def. U., Washington, 2003—04; ret. Cons. in field. Vol. Ct. Apptd. Spl. Adv. (CASA), Spotsylvania, Va., 1998—2004. Personal E-mail: mvstella_99@yahoo.com.

STELLA, ROBIN LYNN, psychologist; b. New Britain, Conn., Mar. 24, 1976; d. Kenneth C. and Nancy A. Stella. BA in Psychology and Anthropology magna cum laude, U. Conn., 1997; MS in Sch. Psychology, So. Conn. State U., 2000, 6th yr. profl. diploma in Sch. Psychology, 2001. Cert. tchr. Conn. Psychologist Waterbury Pub. Schs., Conn., 2002—. Mem.: Conn. Assn. Sch. Psychologists (assoc.), Nat. Assn. Sch. Psychology (assoc.; cert.). Independent. Avocations: travel, theater, museums, snowboarding. Office: Waterbury Pub Schs Driggs Sch 77 Woodlawn Terr Waterbury CT 06710 Office Phone: 203-574-8160. Business E-Mail: rstella@waterburyk12.ct.us.

STELLUTO, SHARON RENEE, apparel designer, painter; b. West Trenton, NJ, Apr. 17, 1981; d. Joseph Fernando and Barbara Ann Stelluto. BFA, SUNY, New Paltz, 2003. Asst. to profl. artist Andrew Braitman Art Studio, Charlotte, NC, 1995—98; server, barista, hostess Xando's Coffee, Bar, Bryn Mawr, Pa., 1999—2000; display designer, sales assoc. Illuminations, King of Prussia, Pa., 2001—01; sales assoc. Health and Nutrition Ctr., New Paltz, 2002—02; customer svc. rep. Certa Pro Painters, Oaks, Pa., 2003—03; handbag designer, office mgr., pub. rels. Debbie Brooks Designs, Gardiner, NY, 2003—04; asst. designer of handbags, quality supr., office mgr. L'egent Internat., Newburgh, NY, 2004. Fashion vendor Accessories Show at Jacob Javitts Ctr., Manhattan, NY, 2004—04; invitation Internat. Biennial of Contemporary Art, Ferrara, Italy, 2004—04. Official 2004 olympics pop art,

Splash To Victory, one-woman shows include Living Seed Gallery, exhibitions include Samual Dorsky Mus., Backstage Studio Productions, Kingston Libr., online art exhibit, www. projekt30.com. Avocations: steel welder, piano, hiking, oil painting. Personal E-mail: sstelluto@yahoo.com.

STELTON, SUSAN DIANE, nursing specialist, educator; b. Erie, Pa., Oct. 28, 1951; d. Philip Clair and Elizabeth Ruth (Kaufmann) Wilcox; m. Peter Jon Stelton, Dec. 8, 1973; 1 child, Christa Marie. ADN, Morton Coll., 1972; BSN, U. Ill., Chgo., 1975; MSN, Loyola U., 1977; dilpoma enterostomal therapy nursing edn. program, Emory U., 1991. Med./surgical advanced practice nurse, wound, ostomy and continence nurse. Staff nurse Loyola U. Hosp., Maywood, Ill.; instr. nursing Coll. DuPage, Glen Ellyn, Ill., Southwestern Mich. Coll., Dowagiac; advanced practice nurse Meml. Hosp., South Bend, Ind. Contbr. articles to profl. jours. Mabel Wilen scholar, 1970. Mem. ANA (v.p. dist. 7), Nursing Rsch. Consortium North Central Ind., Wound Ostomy and Continence Nurses Soc. (accreditation com. mem.), World Coun. Enterostomal Therapy Nurses (exec. bd. mem., sec. v.p.), Phi Theta Kappa, Sigma Theta Tau. Home: 2433 Yankee St Niles MI 49120-3905 Office: Meml Hosp 615 N Michigan St South Bend IN 46601-1087 Office Phone: 574-647-3156. E-mail: notlets@aol.com.

STELZER, PATRICIA JACOBS, retired secondary school educator; b. Springfield, Ohio, Sept. 7, 1936; d. George Kenneth and Beatrice Snook Jacobs; m. James Glea Stelzer, May 12, 1956; children: Michael G., Samantha S. Moehn, James Todd. BS in Edn., Wright State U., 1973, MA in History, 1997. Reporter, features writer, columnist Springfield News-Sun, 1962—65; social studies tchr. Schaefer Jr. H.S., Springfield, 1975—77, 1978—81, South H.S., Springfield, 1977—78, 1981—2000; ret., 2000; chmn. social studies dept. South H.S., Springfield, 1991—2000. Adj. prof. history Clark State C.C., Springfield, 2001—; cons. Ohio test scholastic achievement State of Ohio Dept. Edn., Columbus, 1985—87; participant cert. assessment pilot program social studies program Nat. Bd. Profl. Tchg. Stds., 1998. Author (book): Dangerous Research, By George!, Deadly Research By George!. Pres. Springfield Civic Theater, 1984—85; performer, mem. pub. rels. com. Music-Stage Theater, Springfield, 1964—68, 1975; dir., choreographer Northwestern H.S. and South H.S., Springfield, 1977—91; advt. dir. Choral Arts Springfield, 2004—05. Lutheran. Avocations: golf, travel, theater, writing. Home: 6541 Troy Rd Springfield OH 45502 Office: Clark State CC 570 E Leffel Ln Springfield OH 45501

STEMBEL, MARGERY JOAN, elementary school educator; b. Mankato, Minn., May 11, 1948; d. Arnold Jens and Patricia Evelyn (Johnson) Fossum; m. Oren E. Stembel Jr., Aug. 8, 1970 (div. July 1991); children: Sophia Faulkner, Kelsi N., Jeffrey W BS, Mankato State U., 1970. cert. advanced profl. Md. State Dept. Edn. Tchr. grade 4 Elkhart County Schs., Ind., 1970—71, Spencer County Schs., Ind., 1971—73; tchr. grades 5 and 6 D.C. Pub. Schs., Washington, 1973—76; tchr. grade 3, 4 and 5 Montgomery County Pub. Sch., Garrett Park, Md., 1976—. Master tchr. social studies Montgomery County Schs., 2003, Intel master tchr. tech., 2001—; computer coord. Garrett Park Elem. Sch., 1986-98; presenter in field Mem. Md. Instrnl. Computer Consortium Assn., Woodmoor/Pinecrest Citizens Assn., Woodmoor Garden Club (pres. 1987-89, 92-94, 98-99) Avocations: gardening, travel, crafts, reading, camping. Home: 127 Eastmoor Dr Silver Spring MD 20901-1508 Office: Garrett Park Elem Sch 4810 Oxford St #219 Garrett Park MD 20896 Office Phone: 301-929-2170. Business E-Mail: margery_j_stembel@mcpsmd.org.

STENDAHL, BRITA KRISTINA, humanities educator, social studies educator; b. Stockholm, Jan. 10, 1925; came to U.S., 1954; d. Johan Victor and Ingeborg (Normann) Johnsson; m. Krister Stendahl, Sept. 7, 1946; children: Johan, Anna, Dan. Cand. Theology, Uppsala U., Sweden, 1949, cand. Philosophy, 1954, PhD (hon.), 1981. Hist. and lit. tchr. Gymnasium, Uppsala, Sweden, 1949-54; hist. and lit. tchr. extension program Harvard U., Cambridge, Mass., 1956-59, hist. and lit. tchr. freshman program, 1964-74; hist. and lit. tchr. seminar program Radcliffe Coll., Cambridge, 1976-84; cultural sec. Ch. of Sweden, Stockholm, 1984-88. Mem. Govt. Coun. for Coord. and Planning of Rsch., Stockholm, 1985-88. Author: (monographs) Søren Kierkegaard, 1976, The Force of Tradition, 1984, The Education of a Self-Made Woman, Fredrika Bremer, 1801-1865, 1994, (autobiography) Sabbatical Reflections, 1978; contbr. Multicultural Writers from Antiquity to 1945, 2002; book reviewer.; Co-chair Fellowship in Israel for Arab-Jewish Youth, Boston, 1972-84, 88-95; bd. dirs. The Abraham Fund, N.Y.C., 1996—. Bunting fellow, Radcliffe Coll., Cambridge, Mass., 1961-63; assoc. fellow Henry A. Murray Ctr. at Radcliffe, 1981-82; recipient Myron B. Bloy award The Assn. for Religion and Intellectual Life, 1993. Mem. Arstasallskapet for Fredika Bremer-Studier (chmn. 1985—89). Democrat. Lutheran. Avocations: walking, Tai Chi.

STENNETT, KATHY ELAINE, elementary school educator; b. Hattiesburg, Miss., Apr. 24, 1956; d. Charles Norman and Patricia Marie (Moss) Bryant; m. Milton Stennett, July 15, 1978; children: Lauren, Katy. AA, Jones County Jr. Coll., Ellisville, Miss., 1976; BS, U. Miss., 1978; MEd, U. So. Miss., 1984, MEd in Ednl. Leadership, 1999. Cert. tchr., Miss. Tchr. 6th grade Laurel (Miss.) City Schs., 1980—99, prin., 1999—. Mem. Delta Kappa Gamma. Office: Nora Davis Elem Sch 1305 Martin Luther King Dr Laurel MS 39440-3134

STENSAAS, STARLA A., education educator, artist; b. Madison, S.D., Aug. 1, 1956; d. Harlan and Vianne (Schooler) Stensaas; life ptnr. Ann Marie McBreen. BA, Ea. Ill. U., 1975—79, MA, 1979—80; MFA, U. of Wis.-Milw., 1990. Asst. prof. So. Ill. U., 1998—2000; assoc. prof. Nebr. Wesleyan U., 2000—03; tenured assoc. prof. Dana Coll., Blair, 1992—98, 2003—. On-line tchg./distance learning So. Ill. U., 1998—2000; curriculum design, BFA in edesign Nebr. Wesleyan U., 2000—03; cross-disciplinary iMedia program devel. Dana Coll., 2003—05. Grantee Tchg. Fellowship in Graphics, Poynter Inst., 1989, Audience Feedback on the Web, Pontikes Ctr. for Mgmt. of Info., 1999, Graphic Reproduction On-Line, Multimedia Instrnl. Grant, So. Ill. U., 1999, Interactive Hyperlinks to Illuminate Texts, Office of R & D, So. Ill. U., 2001, ITC Summer Tech. Inst. fellowship, Nebr. Wesleyan U., 2001, Ameritas Faculty fellowship, 2002, White Endowment Faculty grant for Internationalization, 2002. Office: Dana Coll 2838 Coll Dr Blair NE 68008 E-mail: sstensaa@dana.edu.

STENSGAARD, KAREN J., brokerage house executive; b. Dayton, Ohio, Feb. 5, 1959; d. Karl Josef and Ann Andrews Springer; m. Michael K. Stensgaard, May 16, 1987. BA, U. Tex., Austin, 1981; MBA, U. St. Thomas, Houston, 1986. CPA N.Y., cert. internal auditor; lic. series 7 and 55. Banker Post Oak Bank, Houston, 1981—83, Banc Tex. Westheimer, Houston, 1983—86; bank holding co. examiner Fed. Res. Bank, San Francisco, 1986—93; v.p. wholesale and global capital mkts. audit group, audit cons. Bank of Am., San Francisco, 1993—98; sr. mgr. internal audit svc. divsn. Price Waterhouse Corp., N.Y.C., 1999—2003; broker, dealer Knight Capital Group, Jersey City, 2003—. Mem.: AICPA, Assn. Cert. Fraud Examiners, Inst. Internal Auditors, Securities Industry Assn. (v.p. internal audit divsn. N.Y.C. chpt., mem. exec. com.). Avocations: reading, travel, theater, museums. Office: Knight Capital Group Inc 545 Washington Blvd Jersey City NJ 07310 Business E-Mail: kstensgaard@knight.com.

STENZ, JESSICA LYNN, administrative associate; b. Milw., Apr. 7, 1979; d. Truman Wayne and Darlene Cheryl Turall; m. Andrew Patrick Stenz, May 16, 2003. BA in Music, Luther Coll., Decorah, Iowa, 2001. Cert. K-12 music tchr. Wis. K-8 music tchr. Swallow Sch., Hartland, Wis., 2001—06; adminstrv. assoc. Kaztex Cos., Pewaukee, Wis., 2006—. Alto singer Milw. Symphony Orch., 2001—02; sect. leader, alto 1st. Congl. Ch., Wauwatosa, Wis., 2004; singer Bel Canto Chorus, Milw., 2006—. Worship team musician, hospitality coord. New Vision Ch., Pewaukee, Wis., 2004—. Avocations: pottery, cooking, travel. Business E-Mail: jstenz@kaztexcos.com.

STENZEL, MARY FRANCIS, social worker; b. Milw., Apr. 9, 1960; d. Joseph Edward and Betty Josephine (Andracki) Gronowski; m. Paul Anthony Stenzel, Oct. 17, 1997. BSW, Marian Coll., 1982; MBA, Cardinal Stritch Coll. U., 1992. Geriatric social worker various nursing homes, Milw., 1984—86; youth care specialist Child and Adolescent Treatment Ctr., Milw. County, 1988—94. Pres. Milw. Area Self Help, W. Milw., 1997—. Cpl. USMC, 1976—80. Mem.: Brain Injury Assn. (mem. Brain Injury Support Group). Roman Catholic. Avocations: crafts, gardening, scrapbooks, woodworking. Home: 3115 W Plaza Dr Franklin WI 53132 Office Phone: 414-761-3186.

STEPENOFF, BONNIE MARIE, history professor; b. Allentown, Pa., July 18, 1949; d. Ernest W. and Nancy Owens Steckel; m. Jerald Sheldon Stepenoff, Feb. 14, 1986; m. Peter L. Wright, 1977 (div.); m. Francis M. Ryck, 1969 (div.); children: Samantha Marie Wright, Hannah Evelyn. BA, Ohio State U., Columbus, 1971; MA, U. Mo., Columbia, 1978, MA in Libr. Sci., 1981, PhD, 1992. Acquisitions specialist State Hist. Soc. Mo., Columbia, 1978—84; cultural resource preservationist Mo. Dept. Natural Resources, Jefferson City, 1984—92; prof. history SE Mo. State U., Cape Girardeau, 1993—. Author: Their Fathers' Daughters: Silk Mill Workers in Northeastern Pennsylvania, 1999, Thad Snow: A Life of Social Reform in the Missouri Bootheel, 2003, From French Community to Missouri Town: Ste. Genevieve in the Nineteenth Century, 2006; contbr. articles to profl. jours.;, author short stories. Active Mo. Adv. Coun. on Hist. Preservation, 2004. Sullivan fellow, Mus. Am. Textile History, 1991, Short-term Rsch. grantee, Hagley Mus. and Libr., 1991. Mem.: State Hist. Soc. Mo. (trustee, Best Article award 1991, Richard S. Brownlee grantee 1992, 1997). Office: Southeast Missouri State University One University Plaza Cape Girardeau MO 63701 Office Phone: 573-651-2831. Business E-Mail: bstepenoff@hotmail.com.

STEPHANI, NANCY JEAN, social worker, journalist; b. Garden City, Mich., Feb. 19, 1955; d. Ernest Helmut Schulz and Margaret Mary Fowler Thompson; m. Edward Jeffrey Stephani, Aug. 29, 1975; children: Edward J., Margaret J., James E. AA, Northwood Inst., Midland, Mich., 1975; student in theology, Boston Coll., 1991; BS summa cum laude, Lourdes Coll., Sylvania, Ohio, 1992; MSW, Ohio State U., 1995. Lic. ind. social worker; cert. cognitive behavioral therapist, master addictions counselor. Profl. facilitator Parents United, Findlay, Ohio, 1989-94; contbg. writer Cath. Chronicle, Toledo, 1988-95; mem. ministry formation faculty Cath. Diocese of Toledo, 1992-96; crisis intervention specialist John C. Hutson Ctr., 1994-98; contbg. writer Sunset Gazette, Findlay, Ohio, 1996-98; mgr. Century Health Svcs., Findlay, Ohio, 1998, dir. emergency mental health svcs., 1998—, co-chair strategic planning action team, 1999-00; prof., field coord. MSW program Ohio State U., Lima, 2000—. Social work clinician Family Svc. Hancock County, coord. clin. svcs. Family Svc., 1997—98, Blanchard Valley Home Health Social Svc.; trustee, bd. dirs. Hope House for Homeless, Findlay, 1990—99, v.p., 1996—97, pres., 1997—99; mem. Hancock County Cluster on Elderly; v.p., pres. parish coun. St. Michael Parish, Findlay, 1985—89, adult edn. coord., 1986—93, mem. strategic plan core com., 1989—91; program planning com. Family Life Conf., Cath. Diocese, 1994—95, mem. accreditation com. ministry formation dept.; profl. facilitator Hope Plus Program through Hancock County Common Pleas Ct., 1996—; coord. critical incident stress mgmt. team Hancock County, 1997—; profl. facilitator Hancock County Survivors of Suicide group, 1997—2000; coord. Hancock County Survivors of Suicide Group, 1997—; field instr. dept. social work U. Findlay, Ohio, 1996—, mem. social work adv. coun., 1998—, adj. faculty, 2003—; field instr. Capital U., Bowling Green State U., Heidelberg U., 1997—98; mem. adj. faculty Owens Tech. Coll., Findlay; trustee City Mission, 2000—04; co-program coord., field edn. coord. MSW program Ohio State U., Lima, 2001—; profl. facilitator Persons Affected by a Loved one's Suicide, 2002—. Founder Food Coop., MPBA, Findlay, 1981; founding mem. Chopin Hall, Findlay, 1983; mem. Hancock County AIDS Task Force, 1994-98; strategic planning com. mem., co-chair goal setting com. Findlay Pub. Schs., 1994, steering com., Call to Action Northwest Ohio, 1997—; trustee City Mission, 1999—; clin. dir. Hancock County CISM Team; mem. Red Cross Disaster Svcs. Team; mem. BURHC Pandemic Flue Preparedness Com., 2006—; mem. Ohio State U.-Lima campus disaster team, pandemic flu preparedness team, 2006—. Nat. Inst. Food Svcs. grantee, 1974; Diocese of Toledo grantee, 1991; Ohio State U. Coll. Social Work grantee, 1994. Mem. NOW, NASW (ethics com. Ohio 1997—, v.p. bd. trustees 2000-02, nat. com. on nominations and leadership 2001—, region VII rep. nat. leadership identification com. 2001-04, treas.-elect 2003—, program planning com., Social Worker of Yr. Region 1, 2000), AAUW (legis. chair Findlay chpt.), Internat. Critical Incident Stress Found., Am. Assn. on Child Abuse, Transpsychol. Assn., Friends of Creation Spirituality, Cognitive/Behavioral Profl. Soc., Call to Action, Pax Christi, Women in Ch. Leadership, Green Cross (clin. mem.). Avocations: jogging, hiking, cooking, travel. Home: 2615 Goldenrod Ln Findlay OH 45840-1025 Office Phone: 419-422-3711. E-mail: NancyStephani@hotmail.com.

STEPHANIC, BARBARA JEAN, art historian, writer, curator, researcher; b. L.A., Sept. 1, 1937; d. Frank Cecil (Stepfather) and Ethel Louise Jones; m. Jeffery Lynn Stephanic, May 4, 1985; children: Deborah Louise Arnold, Lorraine Marie Ward, Charles Frank Ward. AA, Antelope Valley Coll., Lancaster, Calif., 1978; BA, George Washington U., Washington, 1981, MA, 1985; PhD, U. Md., College Park, 1997. Art history lectr. Montgomery Coll., Rockville, Md., 1986—87, No. Va. C.C., Alexandria, 1987—90; assoc. prof. art history Charles County C.C., La Plata, Md., 1990—97; prof. art history Coll. So. Md., La Plata, 1997—. Art history lectr. Georgetown U., Washington, 1990—97; curator Fine Arts Ctr. Gallery Coll. So. Md., La Plata, 1993—; adj. prof. Parsons Sch. Design and Smithsonian Instn., Washington, 1993—2000; study abroad lectr. Coll. So. Md., La Plata, 2003—; faculty cons. Ednl. Testing Svc., Princeton, NJ, 1993—2004; adj. prof. Am. U., Washington, 1995—96; academic advisor Parsons Sch. Design, Washington, 1996—97; mem. art adv. bd. U. Md. U. Coll., Adelphi, 2003—, vice chmn. art adv. bd., 2006—; guest lectr. in field. Contbr. exhibition catalogue; author: (exhibition catalogue) The Graphic Work of Joseph Pennell From the Permanent Collection of The George Washington University; contbr. exhibition catalogue; author: (exhibition catalogue) Dialogue in Color and Form: The Art of Joseph Holston, Dynamic Spaces: Abstract Form Within and Beyond the Landscape: Painting, Collage, and Assemblage by Larry Chappelear, Color in Freedom: Journey Along the Underground Railroad, Paintings and Graphics by Joseph Holston. Founding mem. Nat. Mus. Am. Indian, Washington, 2000—06; mentor Literacy Coun. No. Va., Alexandria, Va., 1998—2000; mem. Sewell-Belmont Ho., Washington, 2005—06. Recipient Faculty Svc. award, Coll. So. Md., 1996, 1999, Faculty Excellence award, Faculty Senate, Coll. So. Md., 1999, Nat. Inst. for Staff and Orgnl. Devel., C.C. Leadership Program, 2000; Outstanding Scholar in the Field of Humanities, Antelope Valley Coll., 1978, Outstanding Scholar, Alliance Francaises, 1978, Faculty Devel. grantee, Coll. So. Md., 2004, 2006. Mem.: Nat. Assn. U. Women, Assn. Historians Am. Art, Assn. Faculty for Advancement C.C. Tchg., Am. Studies Assn., Coll. Art Assn., C.C. Profs. Art and Art History (treas. 1999—2000), George Wash. U. Alumni (life), Literacy Coun. Am., Alliance Francaises (Outstanding Scholarship 1978), Phi Delta Gamma (Beta chpt., Scholastic Achievement award 1983, 1986). Office: College Southern Maryland 8730 Mitchell Rd La Plata MD 20646 Office Phone: 301-934-7860. Business E-Mail: barbaras@csmd.edu.

STEPHANSEN, STEPHANIE, elementary school educator; d. Russell Henry and Jane Flesner Brown; children: Lauren Nicole, Sean Patrick. BS, Clemson U., SC, 1986. Tchr. Dekalb County Pub. Schs., Decatur, Ga., 1986—96, Gwinnett County Pub. Schs., Lawrenceville, Ga., 1996—. Office Phone: 770-682-4100.

STEPHEN, ANNE MARIE DIIORIO, music educator; b. Trenton, N.J., July 30, 1952; d. Roland Joseph DiIorio and Mary Clementina Angelini; m. C. R. "Bud" Stephen, Aug. 6, 1982; stepchildren: Daniel, Tim Stephen. BA, U. Nev., 1974, M of Music Edn., 1987. Music specialist Mabel Hoggard 6th Grade Ctr., Clark County Sch. Dist., Las Vegas, Nev., 1982—84; dir. choral studies Las Vegas H.S., Clark County Sch. Dist., 1984—. Part-time instr. music dept. U. Nev., Las Vegas, 2002, Las Vegas, 04; chair, co-chair honor choir Clark County Sch. Dist., Las Vegas, 1991—95, mem. curriculum com. for madrigals, 2000—01, choral clinician, adjudicator, adjudicator, vocal coach. Named Educator of Yr., Kiwanis Club, 1993, N.W. Chpt. Optimists, 2001, Disting. Tchr., White House Commn. on Presdl. Scholars, 1993; recipient Woman Musician of the Month award, Las Vegas Alumnae chpt. Sigma Alpha Iota. Mem.: Nev. Music Educators Assn. (chair, co-chair all-state choir 1998—2001, Nev. Music Educator of Yr. 2003), Am. Choral Dirs. Assn (Nev. state treas. 1991—95, chair for show choirs Nev. R&D 2001—), Las Vegas Philharmonic Chorus, Lamplight Carolers. Democrat. Roman Catholic. Avocations: golf, sailing, reading, singing, dance. Home: 10769 Hawes End Ct Las Vegas NV 89123 Office: Las Vegas HS 6500 E Sahara Ave Las Vegas NV 89142 Office Phone: 702-799-0180 x4050. Personal E-mail: missanan@aol.com.

STEPHEN, DORIS MOYER, music educator; b. Buffalo, Nov. 27, 1928; d. Arthur Burness and Helen May Moyer; m. Robert Mill Stephen Jr., Aug. 30, 1952 (dec. June 1999); children: Robert Mill III, Elizabeth Lynn Stephen Benck. Student, Bethany Coll., 1946—48, NYU, 1948—49. Tchr. piano, Naperville, Ill., 1958—70, 1991—2006. Editor (newspaper) Lake Wildwood Sunbeam, 1971-76; newswriter, reporter Naperville Sun, 1971-74; author of stories and poetry. Various positions ending with pres. LWV, Naperville, 1958-68. Mem. Music Tchrs. Assn. Republican. Methodist. Avocations: writing, painting, bridge, piano. Home: The Devonshire Apt 410 1700 Robin Ln Lisle IL 60532

STEPHEN, TINA MARIE, elementary school educator; b. Keyser, W.Va., Dec. 11, 1964; d. John Lee and Margaret Jean Stephen; 1 child, Derek Todd. AA in Phys. Edn. and Health, Potomac State Coll., Keyser, W.Va., 1983—85; BS in Phys. Edn. and Health, Frostburg U., Md., 1988. Health and phys. edn. tchr. Frankfort H.S., Ridgeley, W.Va., 1999—2000; health tchr. Keyser Mid. Sch., Keyser, W.Va., 2000—. Mem.: Moose. Home: 1015 Carolina Ave Keyser WV 26726 Office: Keyser Primary Mid Sch 700 Harley O Staggers Dr Keyser WV 26726 Office Phone: 304-788-4220. Personal E-mail: tina_355@hotmail.com.

STEPHENS, AMY E., middle school educator; BS magna cum laude in Edn., U. Ala., Tuscaloosa, 2000; MS summa cum laude in Edn., U. Ala., Birmingham, 2003. 7th grade sci. tchr. Pizitz Mid. Sch., Vestavia Hills, Ala., 2000—. Mem.: Am. Assn. Educators.

STEPHENS, B. CONSUELA, minister, consultant; b. Bklyn., May 12, 1947; d. Montiphus (Mortimer King) DeReyes and Bernadine Whitley. PhD Religion, Clayton Theol. Inst., 1983. Pastor Chenaniah Missionary Ch., Hollis, NY, 1986—. Cons. Chenaniah Missionary Ch., Hollis, United States, 1986—. Author: (book) Behold, I Shew You A Mystery, 1998. Dir. CASE Group, Inc., 2003—. Avocation: gardening. Home: 515 Mount Prospect Ave Newark NJ 07104-2964 E-mail: consuelastephens@yahoo.com.

STEPHENS, BRENDA WILSON, librarian; b. Durham, N.C., Oct. 22, 1952; d. Leroy Thomas and Lucy Mae (Umstead) Wilson; m. Gregory Frederick Stephens, Mar. 6, 1977; children: Seth, Sara. Student, Vincennes U., 1970-71; BA, Winston-Salem State U., 1974; MLS, N.C. Cen. U., 1981. Cert. pub. libr., N.C. From bookmobile coord. to county libr. Orange County Pub. Libr., Hillsborough, NC, 1976-92, regional libr. dir., 1992—. Sec. United Way of Greater Orange County, 1991—93; elected mem. Orange County Sch. Bd., 1998—, chair, 2001—03, vice chair, 2003—; sec. Lipscomb Bapt. Ch., 1998—2002. With U.S. Army, 1974—76. Mem.: ALA, N.C. Pub. Libr. Dirs. Assn. (officer, pres. 2001), N.C. Libr. Assn. (chair adult sect. 1987—93, co-chair 1985—87, lit. com. 1983—85), A.L. Stanback Mid. Sch. PTO (pres. 1991—92), Kiwanis Club (pres. 1992—93). Democrat. Baptist. Avocation: quilting. Home: 5807 Craig Rd Durham NC 27712-1008 Office: Orange County Pub Libr 300 W Tryon St Hillsborough NC 27278-2438

STEPHENS, BROOKE, financial commentator, writer; BA, Fisk U.; MA, Western Mich. U.; mktg. and fin. student, Harvard Bus. Sch. Cert. fin. planner, stockbroker, registered investment adv.; cert. insurance agent. Internat. trade officer Chase Manhattan Bank; sr. investment cons. Citicorp Investment Svcs., NY; personal fin. adv.; personal fin. commentator NPR's The Tavis Smiley Show, PBS's Nightly Bus. Report, Bloomberg Morning Report. Regular guest CNBC's Power Lunch, CNNfn's It's Only Money, CNN's Your Money with Stuart Varney; former weekly personal fin. expert FX Cable's Breakfast Time; tchr. fin. seminars Am. Mgmt. Assn., Inst. Internat. Rsch., Everywoman's Money Conf., Coalition Black Investors, Coalition 100 Black Women, Nat. Alliance Black Sch. Educators, Nat. Black MBA Assn., Nat. Assn. Black Journalists. Author: Talking Dollars & Making Sense: A Wealth Building Guide for African-Americans, 1996, Men We Cherish: African-American Women Praise the Men in their Lives, 1997, Wealth Happens One Day at a Time: 365 Days to a Brighter Future, 1999; contbr. articles to profl. pubs. including Black Enterprise, Essence, Self, and MS. Mem.: NY Soc. Cert. Fin. Planners (former bd. dirs.), Girls, Inc. (mem. adv. bd., chairwoman econ. lit. com.). E-mail: stephensnn@aol.com.

STEPHENS, CONNIE E., secondary school educator; b. Tuscaloosa, Ala., Oct. 7, 1952; d. Maxine S. Stephens. BS, U. Ala., Tuscaloosa, 1975. Tchr. Lisman Jr. H.S., Butler County, Ala., 1975—76; tchr., coach Huntsville (Ala.) City Schs., 1976—. Mem.: Ala. H.S. Athletic Assn. (assoc.). Avocations: tennis, camping, gardening, water sports. Home: 2008 Hackberry Green Huntsville AL 35803 Office: Grissom High School 7901 Bailey Cove Rd Huntsville AL 35802 Office Phone: 256-428-8000.

STEPHENS, DEBRA YOUNG, elementary school educator; d. Robert Adam Young and Joan Cope French; m. John Blunt Stephens Jr., June 28, 1981; 1 child, Robert Daniel. BA, Elon U., NC, 1979; M in Elem. Admin., The Citadel, Charleston, SC, 1983. Tchr. Whitesville Elem. Sch., Moncks Corner, SC, 1979—87, Coll. Pk. Elem. Sch., Ladson, 1987—. Neighborhood chair Am. Cancer Soc., Atlanta, 2005. Named Tchr. of Yr., Coll. Pk. Elem. Sch., 1998. Mem.: SC Reading Assn., Coll. Pk. PTA, Berkeley Reading Coun. (pres. 2001—02, Disting. Reading Tchr. 1993, 1997), SC Internat. Reading Assn. (grantee 1998, 1999, 2006), Kappa Kappa Iota. Episcopalian. Avocations: reading, exercise, water aerobics. Office: Coll Pk Elem Sch 100 Davidson Dr Ladson SC 29456

STEPHENS, ELISA, college president; d. Richard A. Stephens. Pres. Acad. of Art Coll., San Francisco, 1992—. Office: 79 New Montgomery St 6th Fl San Francisco CA 94105-3410

STEPHENS, H. JEANNETTE, mathematics educator; d. Clarence Francisis and Harriette Josephine Stephens. BS, SUNY, Geneseo, 1965, MS, 1969; PhD, U. Iowa, Iowa City, 1979. Cert. tchr. Tchr. math. West Jr. HS, Binghamton, NY, 1966—69; grad. asst. math. edn. U. Iowa, Iowa City, 1970—73; tchr. math. West HS, Iowa City, 1975—80, Lane CC, Eugene, Oreg., 1980—84; tchr. math., math. edn. U. Oreg., Eugene, 1980—84, Western Wash. U., Bellingham, 1987—90, Whatcom CC, Bellingham, 1986—. Mem.: Am. Math. Assn. Two Yr. Colls., Math. Assn. Am., Nat. Coun. Tchrs. Math. Jewish. Avocations: sewing, music, puzzles. Home: 1118 N Forest St #200 Bellingham WA 98225-5141

STEPHENS, KATHRYN J., science educator; d. Randy Howard and Anita Rae Bassham; m. Ernest Lee Stephens, June 4, 2004. BSc, Union U., Jackson, Tenn., 1998; MSc in Natural Sci., S.E. Mo. State U., Cape Girardeau, Mo., 2002. Tchr. Poplar Bluff Schs., 1998—2000; asst. prof. North Ctrl. Mo. Coll., Trenton, Mo., 2002—04, C.C. Aurora, Denver, 2004—. Bd. dirs. Birthright Crisis Pregnancy Ctr., Chillicothe, Mo., 2002—04. Republican. So. Bapt. Avocations: reading, needlepoint, hiking. Office: Community Coll Aurora Bldg 903 710 Alton Way Denver CO 80230

STEPHENS, LEONORA, psychiatrist; b. Dallas, Jan. 14, 1951; d. Joseph and Marjorie Stephens; m. Lonald Shapiro (div.); children: Alex Shapiro,

Kate Shapiro. BA in molecular biophysics, Yale U., 1974; MD (hons.), U. Tex., Dallas, 1978. Diplomate Nat. Bd. Med. Examiners, 1979, Am. Bd. Psychiatry and Neurology, 1986, lic. N.C., 1982, Tex., 1983. Instr. dept. psychiatry U. Tex., Dallas, 1982—84; individual, group and family psychotherapy pvt. practice, 1982—; dir. Family Psychiatric Group, 1984—2000; tng. dir. Southwest Family Inst., 1987—91; contract psychiatrist MHMR to Youth and Family Ctr. at Cary Mid. Sch., 1995—98, Dallas Pub. Schs., 2000—. Family sys. cons. Episcopal Diocese of Dallas, 1991—93; cons. Boude Storey Mid. Sch., 1991—94, Family Ctr. at Carey Mid. Sch., 1995—98; cons. psychiatrist Dallas Ind. Sch. Dist. Youth and Family Ctrs., 2000—. Social svcs. com. The Family Place, 1983—85; bd. dirs. Southwest Family Inst., 1984—86. Grantee Falk Fellowship, Am. Psychiatric Assn., 1980—82; Distinguished Fellow, 2003. Home: 4606 Sugar Mill Rd Dallas TX 75244 Office: 3303 Lee Pkwy Ste 220 Dallas TX 75219

STEPHENS, LINDAGRACE, artist, educator; b. Washington, Feb. 20, 1942; d. Allen Carroll and Rose Ellen (Mattern) Stephens. BFA, Boston U., 1964; MAT, Oklahoma City U., 1965. Tchr. Dexter (Kans.) Pub. Sch., 1966; secondary art tchr. Unified Sch. Dist. 210, Hugoton, Kans., 1967—. Judge Wichita Garden Show, 2004—06, Barton County 5 State Show, 2006, Watercolor Soc. Wichita, 2006. One-woman shows include Baker Arts Found., Liberal, Kans., 1991, 1998, 2005, Carnegie Ctr. for Arts, 2006. Lay spkr. United Meth. Ch. Recipient Purchase award, Barton County C.C., 2006. Home: PO Box 385 Hugoton KS 67951 Office Phone: 620-544-4311. Business E-Mail: Lstephens@usd210.org.

STEPHENS, LOREN M., publishing executive, writer; b. NYC, Mar. 8, 1944; d. Seymour and Carol Meyer; m. Dana Miyoshi; 1 child, Joshua. BA, Cornell U., 1965; MA in Internat. Affairs, Columbia U., 1967. Editor Houghton Mifflin, Boston, 1969—71; assoc. Berg & Co./Mortgage Bankes, Boston, 1971—73, sr. v.p., 1973—80; asst. v.p. Nat. Med. Enterprises, LA, 1980—82; prin. Stephens & Hyde, LA, 1982—84, One Step Prodns., Studio City, 1984—97; asst. devel. officer Anti Defamation League, LA, 1990—94, dir. devel., 1994—2000, dir. planned giving & endowments, 2000—05; dir. devel. U. Judaism, 2005—06. Pres. Write Wisdom, Inc.; founder, owner Provenance Press, 2000—. Exec. prodr.: (documentaries) Legacy of the Hollywood Black List, 1985 (Cine Gold Eagle, 1985), Sojourner Truth: Ain't I a Woman, 1987 (Golden Apple, 1987), Los Pastores (Cine Gold Eagle, 1997). Alice Stetton Fellow, Columbia U., 1966, 1967. Avocations: skiing, hiking, teaching writing classes. Home: 847 S Bundy Dr Los Angeles CA 90049 Office Phone: 310-820-2052. Business E-Mail: loren@writewisdom.com.

STEPHENS, NICHELE WILIAMS, elementary school educator, assistant principal; b. New Orleans, Oct. 3, 1967; d. Michael Joseph and Sarah Lee Williams; m. Dewitt Lee Stephens, Nov. 29, 2003; children: Joshua Joseph-Lee, Nicole Alexandria. BA, Dillard U., 1989; MA, Fla. Atlantic U., 2004. Cert. ednl. leadership k-12 Fla., 2006, tchr. sci. Fla., 2006. Tchr. mid. grades sci. Alachua County Schs., Gainesville, Fla., 1990—97; tchr. Broward County Schs., Ft. Lauderdale, Fla., 1997—, curriculum specialist, 1997—, asst. prin., 1997—. Dist. trainer reading program Broward County Schs., 1999—2001, lead explorer, Costa Rica, 2000; presenter League Mid. Sch. Teachers, Davie, Fla., 1999—2001. Active Universal Truth Ctr., Miami Gardens, Fla., 1999—2006. Named Tchr. of Year, Forest Glen, 2000; grantee, U. Fla., 1996. Mem.: NEA (licentiate). Democrat. Avocations: reading, travel, quilting, writing. Office Phone: 754-321-0000. Personal E-mail: nawfau@yahoo.com. Business E-Mail: nichele.williams@browardschools.com.

STEPHENS, PATRICIA ANN, marketing professional; b. Gulfport, Miss., Feb. 1, 1945; d. James Marshall and Edna Mathilda (Hogan) Stephens. BA, St. Louis U., 1967; MA, Memphis State U., 1971. Lic. secondary educator speech, theatre, English, religion. Exec. v.p. Prodns. Unltd., Memphis, 1971—73; chairperson speech dept. Southaven HS, Miss., 1973-77; instr. speech N.W. Jr. Coll., Southaven, 1974-76; pub. rels. dir., instr. St. Agnes Acad., Memphis, 1977-78; religion and English instr. Memphis Cath. HS, 1978-82; resource tchr. comm. Mobile City Schs., Ala., 1982-84; mktg. devel. specialist/mktg. mgr. Prime Health Ala., Mobile, 1984-85; mktg. mgr. Blue Cross Blue Shield Fla./Health Options, Lakeland and Orlando, Fla., 1986-92; ind. agt., 1992-94; nat. mktg. and svc. coord. Delta Care, PMI, Tampa, Fla., 1994—2002, dir. account svcs. eastern region, 2002—. Speech instr. Keiser Coll., Lakeland, Orlando. Bd. dirs. Red Balloon Players, Memphis, 1971—73, Cir. Playhouse/Playhouse on the Sq., Memphis, 1980—82, WIFS Ctrl. Fla., 2002—04. Recipient Pres.'s Club BCBSF/Health Options Sales Mgr. award, Health Options Polk County, 1987; Wall St. Jour. Newspaper Fund fellow, U. Oreg., 1968, Writing fellow, Memphis State U., 1980, Part-Time Masters fellow, 1981—82. Democrat. Roman Catholic. Home: 4128 Sunny Land Dr Lakeland FL 33813-3946 Office: Delta Dental Ins Co Ste 350 258 Southhall Ln Maitland FL 32751-7427 Office Phone: 407-660-9034. Business E-Mail: pstephens@pmi.delta.org.

STEPHENS, RACHEL DE-VORE, finance company executive, educator; b. Akron, Ohio, Feb. 18, 1954; d. William Wallace; m. Charles Richard Stephens; children: Kirk children: Reginald Louis Young Jr., Demetrius Azxandra Young. BA, Malone Coll., 1990; MA, U. Akron, Akron, Oh, 1997; PhD, Ctrl. State, Riverside, Calif., 1999; DD, Summit Bible Seminary. Account mgr. Goodyear Tire & Rubber Co, Akron, Ohio, 1973—2005. Author: (dessertation) Managing Workforce Diversity. Bd. mem. The Coming Together Project, Akron, Ohio, 1997—2002. Mem.: Alpha Kappa Alpha (v.p. 1996—). Home: 1589 S Plainview Dr Copley OH 44321 Office: Goodyear Tire & Rubber Co 1144 E Market St Akron OH 44316 Office Phone: 330-730-7918. Home Fax: 330-666-6280; Office Fax: 330-666-6280. Personal E-mail: ryoung2048@aol.com.

STEPHENS, SALLIE L., retired assistant principal, commissioner; b. Crawfordville, Ga., May 23, 1931; d. Columbus and Bertha (Swain) Stephens; 1 child, Marilyn E. BA in Elem. Edn., Clark Coll., 1954; MS, Nova Southeastern U., 1975, EdD, 1998. Tchr. elem. sch. Broward County Sch. Dist., Ft. Lauderdale, Fla., 1954—78, asst. prin., 1978—2001. City commr. City of Miramar, Fla., 1999—, vice mayor, 1999—; vol., mentor Broward County Sch. Dist., 2002—. Mem.: Miramar Pembroke C. of C. (bd. dirs. 1982—), Phi Delta Kappa (bd. dirs. 1995—). Democrat. Baptist. Avocations: golf, dance. Home: 2740 Huron Way Miramar FL 33025 Office: City of Miramar 6700 Miramar Pkwy Miramar FL 33023

STEPHENS, SHERYL LYNNE, physician; b. Huntington, W.Va., Dec. 11, 1949; d. William Clayton Stephens and Virginia Eleanor (Hatten) Stephens Terry; 1 child, William Earl Hicks III (dec.); m. Lannie Dale Rowe, Jan. 17, 1981; 1 child, Seton Christopher. BA, U. Ky., 1972; MA, Marshall U., 1982, MD, 1988. Tchr. Wayne County Bd. Edn., Ceredo, W.Va., 1973—83; real estate developer Huntington, 1981—88; resident in family practice Grant Med. Ctr., Columbus, Ohio, 1988—91; gen. practice indigent care physician Columbus (Ohio) Health Dept., 1991—; med. dir. St. Stephens Health Care Ctr., Columbus, 1995—98, Billie Brown Jones Family Health Care Ctr., Columbus, 1993—2003, lead physician, 1998—2002; staff physician East Ctrl. Family Health Ctr., Columbus, 2003—04, Health Care for the Homeless, 2004—, John Maloney Health Ctr., 2004—; med. dir. Health Care for the Homeless, 2005—. Chair Coll. Health Dept. Com. on Pharmacy and Therapeutics, 1994-2000; rschr., 1976-81. Counselor, instr. Contact of Huntington, 1975-88; polit. activist pro choice movement and ratification of equal rights amemdment, 1976-81. Recipient Leadership award Marshall U., 1985. Mem. Am. Assn. Family Practitioners (pres. 1984-85, Leadership award 1985), Am. Med. Women's Assn. (sec. 1985-86), NOW (pres. 1976-78, 79-81, v.p. Huntington 1978-79, sec. 1981-82), Nat. Abortion Rights Action League. Democrat. Avocations: horseback riding, reading, boating, skiing (snow and water), travel. Home: 9323 Mccord Rd Orient OH 43146-9518 Office: John Malony South Side Health Ctr 1833 Parsons Ave Columbus OH 43207

STEPHENS, TRACY LEE, music educator; b. Colorado Springs, Colo., Apr. 12, 1975; d. Wayne Douglas and Pauline Stephens; 1 child, Jonah Gabriel. BE in Music, U. Ill., Urbana-Champaign, 1999; MEd, Lesley U., Colorado Springs, 2002. Orch. dir. Russell Mid. Sch., Colorado Springs, 1999—2000; vocal music tchr. Wilson Elem., Colorado Springs, 1999—. Mem.: Colo. Music Educator Assn. Roman Catholic.

STEPHENS, WANDA BREWER, social services administrator, investor; b. Bolckow, Mo., Nov. 6, 1932; d. Perry Clark and Mary Carolyn (Fisher) Brewer; m. Lloyd Wesley Stephens, June 19, 1954; children: Ruth Ann, Susie Jo, John Allen, Donna Lynn. BS in home econs., U. Ark., 1954, MS, 1958. Cert. secondary edn. Tchr. home economics West Fork H.S., Ark., 1954—58; pres. Devel. Child Care Assn., Fayetteville, Ark., 1971—74; pres., founding bd. Infant Devel. Ctr., Fayetteville, 1972—75, treas., 1975—81; edn. chmn., fin. com., admin. bd. Cen. United Meth. Ch., Fayetteville, 1976—79; pres. LWV, Fayetteville, 1979—83, NOW, Fayetteville, 1983—89, state legis. v.p., 1985—90, 1993—98; state pres. NOW Ark., Fayetteville, 1991—93, 1998—2004. Bd. sec., headstart, Econ. Opportunity Agy., Fayetteville, 1969-70; treas. Mama's Mink Investment Club, 1970-72. Co-author: Bylaws for Economic Opportunity Agy., 1969; co-editor: Washington County, Ark., 1982. Fundraiser United Fund, 1972-75; polit. organizer NOW, 1986; treas. Washington County Dem. Women, 1990-92; organizer/staff/fund Women's Libr., 1982-91, 99-2000; cons./organizer Ctrl. Child Care Ctr., 1977-78. Recipient Internat. 4-H Youth Exch., 1953-54, Infant Devel. Ctr. Founders Plaque Univ. Ark., 1987; Fayetteville Women's History honoree, 2001; named Lay Person of Yr., Ctrl. United Meth. Ch., 1977. Mem. Mental Health Assn. (Cmty. Svc. award 1972), AAUW (pres. Fayetteville 1975-77, state treas. 1996-2000, Edn. Found. fellow 1984), ACLU (Susan B. Anthony award 1985, Disting. Svc. award 1999), Ark. Women's Polit. Caucus (Uppity Woman award 1987, 92). Democrat. Methodist. Avocations: genealogy, reading, investing. Home: 1177 E Ridgeway Dr Fayetteville AR 72701-2612 Personal E-mail: wandasteph@aol.com.

STEPHENSON, CATHERINE, education educator; b. Johnstown, Pa. m. Charles Howard, Apr. 9, 1988. BS in Elem. Edn., U. Pitts., Pa., 1971, MEd, 1975, EdD, 1985. Cert. tchr. Pa. Tchr. elem./mid. sch. Westmont Hilltop Sch. Dist., Johnstown, Pa., 1972—96; assoc. prof. edn. Ind. U. Pa., Indiana, 1996—. Presenter in field. Regional U.S. editor: Green Tchr. Mag., 1998—. Mem.: NSTA, Keystone State Reading Assn., Nat. Assn. for Devel. Edn., Nat. Coun. for Social Studies, Pa. Sci. Tchrs. Assn. (state conv. chair, v.p. 2004, pres. 2005, immediate past pres. 2006), Kappa Delta Pi (Svc. to Chpt. award 2003), Delta Kappa Gamma. Avocations: gardening, travel, music, reading, studying hummingbirds. E-mail: cstephen@atlanticbb.net.

STEPHENSON, IRENE HAMLEN, biomedical researcher, consultant, editor, educator; b. Chgo., Oct. 7, 1923; d. Charles Martin and Carolyn Hilda (Hilgers) Hamlin; m. Edgar B. Stephenson, Sr., Aug. 16, 1941 (div. 1946); 1 child, Edgar B. Author biorhythm compatibilities column Nat. Singles Register, Norwalk, Calif., 1979-81; instr. biorhythm Learning Tree Open U., Canoga Park, Calif., 1982-83, instr. biorhythm personality analysis, 1980—, instr. biorhythm compatibility, 1982—; owner, pres. matchmaking svc. Pen Pals Using Biorhythm, Chatsworth, Calif., 1979—. Editor newsletter The Truth, 1979-85, Mini Examiner, Chatsworth, 1985—; rschr. biorhythm personality and compatibility, 1974—, biorhythm columnist Psyhic Astrology Horoscope, 1989-94, True Astrology Forecast, 1989-94, Psychic Astrology Predictions, 1990-94, Con Artist Types, 1995, Pedophile (child molester) Types, 1995-2000, Personality Types, 1996, Trouble-Addict (Suicide) Types, 1997, Domineering/Nag Types, 1998, Con Artists, Sweetheart Swindlers, Super Con Artist Types, 1998, Bully types, 2000, Deadly Compatibility Combination, 2000, Fatal Attraction Types, 2000, Sadism, Sadistic, Sadistic Predators, 2000, Salesperson, Practical Joker Types, 2000, Doormat Types, 2000, Famous/Queen Bee/Rescuer Types, 2000, Prostitution, 2000. Author: Learn Biorhythm Personality Analysis, 1980, Do-It-Yourself Biorhythm Compatibilities, 1982; contbr. numerous articles to mags. Office: PO Box 3893 Chatsworth CA 91313-3893

STEPHENSON, JANE CONNELL, artist, educator; b. Ruston, La., Feb. 23, 1932; m. Alvis Doyle Stephenson, June 28, 1957; children: John Thomas, Deborah Lynn, Mary Elizabeth, Ann Liddell. BA, La. Tech. U., 1953; degree in art edn., U. Colo., 1955. Art instr. Clarksdale (Miss.) Ind. Sch. Dist., Clarksdale; art tchr. Dallas Ind. Sch. Dist., 1955—58; designer Atelier Stephenson, Dallas, 1977—85; artist Artisan Studio, Dallas, 1989—99; asst., 1989—; faculty art dept. La. Tech. U., Ruston, 1989—95; faculty art North Lake masters class in figure La. Tech. U., Ruston, 1989—95; faculty art North Lake Coll. Continuing Edn., Dallas, 1983—93; faculty art dept. Creative Art Ctr., Dallas, 2001—04. Leader drawing tours, The Netherlands, Belgium, France, 1992—96, 1998—99, Italy, 1999. Exhibitions include Found. Fighting Blindness, 1990—92, 1994, Irving Art Ctr., 1992, Goodrich Gallery, 2001, Art in the Metro Plex, Ft. Worth, Represented in permanent collections Miss. Art Mus., Jackson, Jackson Art Mus., Sr. Voice, 2004. Named one of Nation's Top 50 Experimental Artists, Artist Mag., 1991; recipient Exxon Mobile Award of Excellence, Tex. Neighbors Exhibit, 2002. Mem.: Irving Art Assn. (recipient over 150 awards in 200 nat. exhbns.; featured in article in Sr. Voice, 2004), Nat. Women's Mus. Washington, Nat. Watercolor Soc. Calif. (signature mem.), Watercolor Soc. Miss. (signature mem.), Watercolor Soc. La. (signature mem.), Watercolor Soc. Tex. (signature mem.), Okla. Watercolor Soc., Western Fedn. Watercolor Socs., Southwestern Art Soc. (signature mem., bd. dirs.), Tex. Visual Art Assn. (signature mem., bd. dirs., show chmn.). Avocations: travel, music, anthropology, gardening, reading. Home: 3524 Northaven Rd Dallas TX 75229 Office Phone: 469-766-1617. Personal E-mail: jane.stephenson@sbcglobal.net.

STEPHENSON, JANE PHILLIPS, librarian; b. Malvern, Ark., July 28, 1945; d. Heuel Devoy and Addie Adealia (Perry) Phillips; m. Josiah Stephenson, June 24, 1967. BS in Edn., Henderson State Tchrs. Coll., 1966; MA, S.E. Mo. State U., 1978. Cert. K-12 libr., 7-12 secondary English tchr., Mo. Tchr. Thayer (Mo.) R-I Schs., 1969-71; legal sec. Fay Swan Atty.-at-Law, Sacramento, Calif., 1972-73; libr., tchr. Mountain View (Mo.) Birch Tree Schs., 1973-82; mem. distbr. rels. staff Eagle Internat. Mktg., Oklahoma City, 1982-86; libr. Okla. Christian Sch., Edmond, 1986-87; English tchr. Altamonte Christian Sch., Altamonte Springs, Fla., 1988; children's libr. Seminole County Libr., Casselberry, Fla., 1988-90; br. libr. Tulsa City-County Libr., 1990-91; elem. libr. Fredericktown (Mo.) Elem. Sch., 1991—. Grantee Mo. Dept. Elem. and Secondary Edn., 1994-95. Mem. Mo. State Tchrs. Assn., Mo. Assn. Sch. Librs. Baptist. Avocations: needlecraft, gardening, genealogy. Home: 1060 Highway C Fredericktown MO 63645-7176

STEPHENSON, NANCY LOUISE, medical products company professional; b. Bemidji, Minn., Nov. 7, 1945; d. Raymond Julian and Dorothy Marion Stephenson. BSN, Pacific Luth. U., 1972. RN, Wash., Minn. ICU/CCU nurse various hosps., Tacoma and Mpls., 1967-72; instr. med. nursing Luth. Deaconess Hosp., Mpls., 1972-73; clin. rsch. assoc. Medtronic, Mpls., 1973-76, clin. evaluation mgr., 1976-82, sr. clin. evaluation mgr., 1982-86, mgr. physicians rels., 1986-98, dir. physician rels., 1998—2005; ret., 2005. Vol. Big Bros./Big Sisters Am., St. Paul, 1978-82, N. Hawaii Cmty. Hosp., Kamuela, 2005— bd. dirs. Sight and Hearing Assn., Mpls., 1998-2005, Heartbeat Internat., Tampa, 2000—. Mem. Heart Rhythym Soc., Am. Heart Assn. Coun. Cardiovasc. Nursing, Am. Coll. Cardiology (corp. liaison bd. mem. 1996-2002, 50th Anniv. com. 1998-99), Order of Eastern Star, Rotary. Democrat. Methodist. Avocations: travel, reading, writing, poetry. Home: 67-5123 Yutaka Pen Pl Kamuela HI 96743 E-mail: nancynparadise@yahoo.com.

STEPHENSON, SUSAN MARIE, English educator; b. Butler, Pa., Sept. 15, 1954; d. Mark R. and Virginia R. (McBride) S. BS in Edn., Clarion (Pa.) State U., 1976; MEd, Indiana U. Pa., 1989. Journalism tchr. Amelia (Va.) County Pub. Schs., 1976-80; tchr. English Seneca Valley Sch. Dist., Harmony, Pa., 1981—. Mem. NEA, Nat. Coun. Tchrs. English, Pa. State Edn. Assn., Seneca Valley Edn. Assn. Democrat. Roman Catholic. Avocations: guitar, tennis, calligraphy, graphic designs, photography. Home: 408 Franklin St Slippery Rock PA 16057-1107 Office: Seneca Valley High 128 Seneca School Rd Harmony PA 16037-9198

STEPHENSON, SYLVIA, elementary school educator; Tchr. Crockett County Mid. Sch., Alamo, Tenn., 1993—. Organist First United Meth. Ch., Bells, Tenn., 1986—2006. Named Educator of Yr., Crockett County C. of C., 2005. Mem.: Crockett County Edn. Assn. (pres. 2005—). Methodist. Home: 2543 Cherryville Rd Bells TN 38006

STEPHENSON, TONI EDWARDS, publishing executive, investment company executive, communications executive; b. Bastrop, La., July 23, 1945; d. Sidney Crawford and Grace Erleene Little; m. Arthur Emmet Stephenson Jr., June 17, 1967; 1 child, Tessa Lyn. Grad. owner/pres. mgmt. program, Harvard Bus. Sch. Pres., dir. Gen. Comm., Inc., Denver; sr. v.p., founder Stephenson & Co., Denver, 1971—; ptnr. Stephenson Properties, Stephenson Ventures. Past. pres. Children's Hosp. Assn. Vols.; past troop leader Girl Scouts Am.; past dir. Anchor Ctr. for Blind Children; dir. bd. dean's advisors Harvard U. Bus. Sch.; past dir. The Children's Hosp., St. Joseph's Hosp., Cherry Creek H.S. Parent Tchr. Conf. Orgn. Mem. Harvard Bus. Sch. Club Colo., DAR, Delta Gamma, Jonathan Club, Annabel's (London), Thunderbird Country Club.

STEPHENSON-BENNETT, MICHELLE ANNETTE, music educator; b. Hillsdale, Mich., Apr. 4, 1967; d. Robert Marcus and Carol Ann Stephenson. BMus, We. Mich. U., 1990, postgrad., 1994—2000; MusM, Oreg. State U., 2004. Cert. profl. tchr. Dir. band Edwardsburg Pub. Schs., Mich., 1990—94, Wayland Union Schs., Mich., 1994—. Past mem. sch. improvement com. Wayland Schs. Recipient Disney Tchr. award, 2001. Mem.: Mich. Edn. Assn., Mich. State Band and Orch. Assn. (state solo/ensemble adjudicator 2000—, past officer dist. 6, officer dist. 10 2005—, pres. mid. sch. solo and ensemble 2005—), We. Mich. U. Alumni Assn., Sigma Alpha Iota (mem. alumni, past officer). Avocations: motorcycling, gardening. Office: Wayland Union Schs 870 E Superior Wayland MI 49348 E-mail: dubussi@yahoo.com.

STEPHENSON-WOOLWINE, PENNY G., music educator; b. Joliet, Ill., Oct. 11, 1977; d. Haney Joe and Brenda Gale Stephenson; m. Mark P. Woolwine, July 10, 2004. BA, postgrad., Ea. Ill. U., Charleston. Childrens' and youth choral dir. Wesley United Meth. Ch., Charleston, 2000—; choral dir. CHS and Jefferson Elem., Charleston, 2005—. Piano tchr., Charleston, 1995—. Youth music dir. Wesley United Meth. Ch., Charleston, 2001. Recipient Talented Student award, Ea. Ill. U., 2001—03. Office Phone: 217-639-5050.

STEPHENS-RICH, BARBARA E., religious studies educator; Adj. faculty Drew Theological Sch., Madison, NJ, 1983—85. Contbr. Mem. Bd. of Ordained Min., E. Ohio, Ohio, 1992—2000, No. NJ, 1977—84; clergy United Meth. Methodist. Avocations: reading, hiking, swimming, cross country skiing, travel. Office: Lakeside Assn 236 Walnut Lakeside OH 43440 Office Phone: 419-798-4461 239. Office Fax: 419-798-5033. E-mail: bstephensrich@aol.com.

STEPNICK, ARLENE ALICE, nursing education administrator; b. Phila. MS, Old Dominion U., 1982; PhD, U. Tex., 1987. Assoc. prof. nursing Hampton (Va.) U., 1982-89; chair dept. nursing Christopher Newport U., Newport News, Va., 1989—. Nursing cons. various hosps., Va., 1982—. Contbr. articles to profl. publs. Mem. ANA (coun. nurse researchers), Nat. League Nursing, So. Nursing Rsch. Soc., Sigma Theta Tau. Avocations: opera, symphony music, non-fiction books.

STEPP, PATRICIA JOANN, middle school educator; b. Madison, W.Va., Jan. 12, 1954; d. Albert Junior and Ruby Mae Stowers; m. Clifton Tad Gale Stepp, Apr. 23, 1971; children: Kevin Dale, Craig Alden. BA in Edn., Marshall U., Huntington, W.Va., 1981. Cert. profl. educator. Tchr. Henlawson Grade Sch., Logan, W.Va., 1981—86, Okeechobee 5th/6th Grade Ctr., Fla., 1986—87, Lake Placid Mid. Sch., Fla., 1987—97, Kathleen Mid. Sch., Lakeland, Fla., 1997—. Office: Kathleen Mid Sch/Polk County Sch 3627 Kathleen Pines Lakeland FL 33810 Office Phone: 863-853-6040. E-mail: patricia.stepp@polk-fl.net.

STEPS, BARBARA JILL, lawyer; b. Springfield, Mo., June 19, 1945; d. Louis Edward and Margaret Pearl (Stiver) Bredeman; m. Robert William Steps, Dec. 21, 1968; children: Rebecca Harper, Aaron Andrew, Jessica Anne. BA in Psychology, St. Louis U., 1966; JD, U. Mo., 1969; MBA, U. Conn., 1983. Atty. Ralston Purina Co., St. Louis, 1969; law clerk U.S. Dist. Ct., St. Louis, 1969-72; assoc. Stone, Keck & Staser, Evansville, Ind., 1973-75, Cline & Callahan, Indpls., 1975-77, Law Office, Herbert V. Camp, Ridgefield, Conn., 1978-81; from comml. counsel to corp. counsel, sec. Framatome Connectors USA, Inc. (now FCI USA, Inc.), Fairfield, Conn., 1981-93; v.p., counsel, sec. FCI USA, Inc. (formerly Framatome Connectors USA, Inc.), Etters, Pa., 1993—2002, sr. v.p. adminstrn., counsel, sec., 2002—. Mem.: ABA, Am. Corp. Counsel Assn. Home: 23 Emlyn Ln Mechanicsburg PA 17055-8017 Office: FCI USA Inc 825 Old Trail Rd Etters PA 17319-9392

STEPTOE, MARY LOU, lawyer; b. Washington, July 15, 1949; d. Philip Pendleton and Irene (Hellen) S.; m. Peter E. Carson, Sept. 1986; children: Elizabeth Maud, Julia Grace. BA, Occidental Coll., 1971; JD, U. Va., 1974. Bar: Va., 1974, Supreme Ct., 1987, D.C. 1996. Staff atty., Bur. of Competition FTC, Washington, 1974-79, atty. advisor to commr., 1979-86, exec. asst. to chmn., 1988-89, assoc. dir., Bur. of Competition, 1989-90, dep. dir., 1990-92, acting dir., 1992-95, dep. dir., 1995-96; ptnr. Skadden Arps Slate Meagher & Flom LLP, Washington. Office Phone: 202-371-7020. Business E-Mail: msteptoe@skadden.com.

STEPTOE, SONJA, journalist; b. Lutcher, La., June 16, 1960; d. Eldridge Willie and Rosa Jane Steptoe. BA in Econs., U. Mo., 1982, B in Journalism, 1982; JD, Duke U. Law Sch., 1985. Staff reporter Wall St. Jour., N.Y.C., 1985—90; sr. editor Sports Illustrated, N.Y.C., 1990—2001, People Mag., N.Y.C., 2001—02; nat. corr. CNN Sports, N.Y.C., 1999—2001; corr. HBO Sports, 1995—2001; sr. corr. Time Mag., L.A., 2002—. Editl. adv. bd. U. Mo. Alumni Mag., Columbia, Mo., 1991—96; alumni bd. Duke U. Law Sch., Durham, NC, 1996—98; mem. U. Mo. Strategic Develop. Bd., 1988—. Co-author: (book) Guide to Women's Golf, 1993, A Kind of Grace" The Autobiography of the World's Greatest Female Athlete, 1997. Bd. mem. Alvin Ailey Dance Sch., NYC, 2001—02, Assoc. Black Charities, NYC, 1989—97. Recipient Emmy award, Nat. Assn. TV Arts and Sci., 1998, Nat. Headliner award, Press Club of Atlantic City, 1999, Disting. Alumni award, U. Mo., Duke Law Sch. Young Alumni award, 1994, 2000. Mem.: ABA, Nat. Assn. Black Journalists, World Affairs Coun.

STERCHI, MARY ELIZABETH, social worker; b. Terre Haute, Ind., Jan. 31, 1960; d. Herbert Franklin and Patricia Ann (Lamb) Griffith; m. David Allen Sterchi, Sept. 18, 1982; children: Malcolm Grant, Gavin Maxwell. BA, Purdue U., 1982; MSW, Ind. U., 1988. Cert. clin. social worker, sch. social worker, Ind., sch. social work specialist, Nat.; cert. Acad. Cert. Social Workers; cert. LCSW. Agy. social worker Shelter, Inc., Arlington Heights, Ill., 1983-85; psychiat. social worker Midtown Cmty. Mental Health Ctr., Indpls., 1985-88; sch. outreach program coord. Southside Youth Coun., Indpls., 1988-92; pvt. practice family therapy Family Interventions, Indpls., 1988-92; clin. social worker, dir. Greenwood (Ind.) Cmty. Sch. Corp., 1992—97; founder, exec. dir. Adoptions Ind., 1995—. Adj. faculty Sch. Social Work, Ind. U., Indpls., 1990-91, 95—; peer facilitation advisor Greenwood H.S., 1992-1996. Vol. leader Young Life, Indpls., 1985-90, West Lafayette, Ind., 1979-82; vol. Moselle Sanders Thanksgiving Offering, Indpls., 1988—, Habitat for Humanity, Ky., 1990, Caulk of the Town, Indpls., 1990, 91; deacon Tabernacle Presbyn. Ch., 1985—, young life com., 2005—. Mem.

NASW, Alpha Omicron Pi. Republican. Avocations: sailing, travel, swimming, bicycling. Home: 11707 Tidewater Dr S Indianapolis IN 46236-8580 Office: Adoptions Ind 1980 East 116th St Ste 325 Carmel IN 46032

STERLING, COLLEEN, artist; b. Sterling, Ill., Dec. 17, 1951; d. Gordon Dennis and Ruth Mary (Lendman) McKee. Student, Mundelein Coll., Chgo., 1970—72, Sch. of the Art Inst., 1973—74, U. Cin., 1974, Mass. Coll. Art, Boston, 1980, student, 1985. Mem. staff Mus. of the Art Inst., Chgo., 1973—74, Mus. Fine Arts, Boston, 1974—76; owner, operator Sterling Graphics, Blairsville, Ga., 1989—92; visual artist Blairsville, 1989—. Dir. Studio Epona, Cambridge, 1980—83. One-woman shows include Amarillo (Tex.) Art Ctr. and Mus., 1993, Atlanta Bur. Cultural Affairs, 1996, exhibited in group shows at Riverside (Calif.) Art Mus., 1992, An Art Place, Chgo., 1993, Telfair Mus. Art, Savannah, Ga., 1995, Vanderbilt U., Nashville, 1995, Hunter Mus. Am. Art, Chattanooga, 1998, major commn., Hyatt Roissy, Paris, 1992, Hartsfield Internat. Airport, Atlanta, 1998. Mem. Nat. M us. Women in the Arts, Ga. Citizens for the Arts, Atlanta, 1995—98, Calif. Lawyers for the Arts, San Francisco, 1994—95; bd. dirs. S.A.F.E. House, Blairsville, 1996—98. Recipient 2d pl., Hunter Mus. Am. Art, Donald Kuspit, juror, 1998; grantee individual arts grantee, Ga. Women in the Visual Arts, Ga. Commn. on Women, 1997;, Ga. Coun. for Arts, Atlanta, 1995. Democrat. Avocations: herb gardening, trout fishing, canoeing, hiking. Home: 3529 Mason Rd Blairsville GA 30512-5256 Office Phone: 706-745-7900. Personal E-mail: csinbville@yahoo.com.

STERLING, LISA ANNE, psychologist; b. Boise, Aug. 18, 1977; d. Eva Louise Harris; m. Justin Brian Sterling, July 14, 2001. BS in Psychology, Boise State U., Idaho, 2000; MS in Spl. Edn., U. Oreg., Eugene, 2003, PhD in Sch. Psychology, 2005. Cert. sch. psychologist Idaho, Oreg. Sch. psychologist Boise (Idaho) Sch. Dist., 2004—. Scholarship, U. Oregon, 2004, Claire Wilkins Meml. scholarship, U. Coll. Edn., 2004, Liz Gullian Meml. scholarship, Oreg. Assn. Sch. Psychologists, 2004. Mem.: Idaho Sch. Psychologists Assn., Nat. Assn. Sch. Psychologists. Avocations: travel, photography, skiing. Office: Boise Sch Dist 8100 W Victory Rd Boise ID 83709 Office Phone: 208-322-3758. Business E-Mail: lisa.sterling@boiseschools.org.

STERLING, LORRAINE, volunteer; b. So. Norwalk, Conn., Apr. 22, 1923; d. Edward and Irene Terris; m. Alvin Sterling, Nov. 11, 1946 (dec. Jan. 1981); children: Richard, Kenneth, Glenn. BA, Bklyn. Coll., 1945. From bd. adv. to v.p. trustees Nassau County Mus., Roslyn, NY, 1986—90, v.p. trustees, 1990—91. Artists expn. Fashion Inst. Tech., N.Y.C., 1994—96; design cons. Lisette Lingerie, N.Y.C., 1970—80, Sterling Sophisticates, N.Y.C., 1982—87. Bd. dir. L.I. Opera Co., L.I., NY, 1991—93; mem. fin. bd. Nassau C.C., N.Y.C., 1993—94. Mem.: Lake Success Club, Boca West Club. Home: 20031 Waters Edge Cir Boca Raton FL 33434 also: 20031 Waters Edge Cir Unt1204 Boca Raton FL 33434-3586

STERLING, MARCIA KEMP, lawyer; b. Texarkana, Ark. m. Nathaniel Sterling. Grad., Vanderbilt U., 1965, Stanford U., 1982. Ptnr. Wilson, Sonsini, Goodrich & Rosati, Palo Alto, Calif.; sr. v.p., gen. counsel, sec. Autodesk, Inc., San Rafael, Calif. Lectr. Calif. Continuing Edn. of the Bar, Practicing Law Inst.; bd. dirs. Bus. Software Alliance. Bd. dirs. Nat. Spasmodic Dysphonia Assn.; mem. advisory coun. program in law sci. and tech. Stanford U.; mem. bd. trustees First United Methodist Ch., Palo Alto, Calif. Mem.: ABA, Santa Clara County Bar Assn., Palo Alto Bar Assn. Office: Autodesk Inc 111 McInnis Pkwy San Rafael CA 94903-2773*

STERLING, SARAH L., archaeologist, educator; b. Portland, Oreg., Apr. 12, 1964; d. Donald J. and Julie C. Sterling. BA, Barnard Coll., N.Y., 1987; MA, U. Wash., Seattle, Wash., 1995; PhD, U. Wash., 2004. Lectr. Portland State U., Portland, Oreg., 2000—. Editor: (book) Posing Questions for a Scientific Archaeology; contbr. articles to profl. jour. Recipient Yeager award, U. Wash., 2004; Niles fellow, U. Wash., 1997-1998. Mem.: Am. Rsch. Ctr. in Egypt, Soc. Am. Archaeology. Democrat-Npl. E-mail: ssterl@myuw.net.

STERLING, SHIRLEY FRAMPTON, artist, educator; b. L.A., Oct. 9, 1920; d. James Alexander and Elizabeth Mary (Herman) F.; m. Edwin Leigh Sterling, Mar. 26, 1942; children: Michael Leigh, Marianne. BA, Occidental Coll., 1942; postgrad., La. Tech. U., 1979-89. Cert. tchr. Tchr., Glendale, Calif., 1942-45; artist, tchr. Watercolor Art Soc., Houston, Pasadena, Kemah, Tex., 1973—. Lectr., demonstrator various art socs. Active as Gray Lady Internat. Red Cross, Wiesbaden, Fed. Republic Germany, 1960-61, Honolulu, 1968-69. Mem. Nat. Watercolor Soc.(elected signature mem.), Knickerbocker Artists, Southwestern Watercolor Soc., Tex. Watercolor Soc. (Patron of Arts award), So. Watercolor Soc., Watercolor Art Soc.-Houston, Western Fedn. Watercolor Soc., Phi Beta Kappa. Republican. Home: 4011 Manorfield Dr Seabrook TX 77586-4209

STERLING ST. JOHN, VICKI LYNN, lawyer; BS magna cum laude, Dana Coll., 1984; JD, U. Denver, 1987. Nebr. 1987, Calif. 1989, U.S. Ct. Appeals (9th cir.), U.S. Dist. Ct. (no. dist.) Calif. Analyst U.S. West Comm., Denver, 1975-86; assoc. Kutak Rock & Campbell, Omaha, 1987-88, Irell & Manella, Menlo Park, Calif., 1988-91, Fenwick & West, Palo Alto, Calif., 1991-92; sr. counsel Walt Disney Co., Burbank, Calif., 1992-93; asst. gen. counsel SunSoft, Inc., Mountain View, Calif., 1993-97; gen. counsel Quickturn Design Systems, Inc., San Jose, Calif., 1997-98; sr. mgr., counsel Accenture (formerly Andersen Cons.), Palo Alto, 1998—. Cons. Calif. Com. Bar Examiners, San Francisco, 1989-92; spkr., AIPLA Mid-Winter Inst., Jan. 2000. Contbr. articles to profl. jours.; spkr. U. So. Calif. 17th Computer Law Inst., May, 1996. Bd. dirs. Palo Alto Humane Soc., 1991-92. Mem. ABA (vice chair sci. and tech. sect.), Calif. Bar Assn., Am. Intellectual Property Law Assn., Computer Law Assn., Order of St. Ives Office: Accenture LLP 1661 Page Mill Rd Palo Alto CA 94304 Office Phone: 650-213-2254. Business E-Mail: vicki.st.john@accenture.com.

STERN, JOAN NAOMI, lawyer; b. Phila., Mar. 7, 1944; d. Clarence J. and Diana D. (Goldberg) S. BA, U. Pa., 1965; JD, Temple U., 1977. Bar: Pa. 1977. Assoc. Blank Rome LLP, Phila., 1977—83, ptnr., 1983—, co-chair pub. fin. group, 1983-92, chair pub. fin. group, 1993, chair pub. fin. dept., 1994—. Cons. counsel Phila. Charter Commn., 1993-94. Contbr. articles to profl. jours. Mem. Sch. Dist. Task Force on Regulatory Reform, Phila., 1987, Tax Policy and Budget Com., Phila., 1989, Phila. Mayor's Fiscal Adv. Com., 1990; chair Sch. Dist. of Phila. Task Force on Alternate Financing Strategies, 1995; bd. mgrs. Moore Coll. Art and Design, Phila., 1993—, vice chair bd. trustees, bd. mgrs., 1995—; bd. dirs. Police Athletic League, Phila., 1994—, Jewish Fedn. of Greater Phila., 2000—, Am. Jewish Congress, 1995—, Urban Tree Connection, 2000-; trustee The Franklin Inst., 2004—. Fellow Am. Bar Found. (life); mem. ABA, Nat. Assn. Bond Lawyers, Phila. Bar Assn., Phila. Bar Assn. (chmn. mcpl. govt. com. 1983-97), Pa. Assn. Bond Lawyers. Office: Blank Rome LLP One Logan Square Philadelphia PA 19103-6998 Office Phone: 215-569-5526. E-mail: stern@blankrome.com.

STERN, JUDITH SCHNEIDER, nutritionist, researcher, educator; b. Bklyn. d. Sidney and Lillian (Rosen) Schneider; m. Richard C. Stern; 1 child, Daniel Arthur. BS, Cornell U., 1964; MS, Harvard U. Sch. Pub. Health, 1966, ScD, 1970. Rsch. asst., dept. food sci. and nutrition MIT, Cambridge, 1964—65; rsch. assoc. dept. human behavior and metabolism The Rockefeller U., NYC, 1968—72, asst. prof. dept. human behavior and metabolism, 1972—74; contbg. editor Vogue Mag., Conde Nast Publs., NYC, 1974; asst. prof. nutrition U. Calif., Davis, 1975—77, assoc. prof. dept. nutrition, 1977—82, dir. food intake lab. group, 1980—2001, prof. dept. nutrition, 1982—, prof. divsn. endocrinology, clin. nutrition and vascular biology, 1988—, disting. prof., 2003—. Mem. editl. bd. Internat. Jour. Obesity, 1976-85, Appetite, 1990, Obesity Rsch., 1993—2002, Nutrition Today, 1999—. Bd. sci. advisors Am. Coun. Sci. and Health, 1980—; mem. U.S. Dept. Agr. Dietary Guidelines Adv. Com., 1983—85; mem. obesity task force NIDDK, 1996—2002, AAAS; mem. expert com. U.S. Pharmacopeia Bioavailability and Nutrient Absorption, 2000—03; mem. adv. bd. USDA Nat. Agrl. Rsch. Ext., Edn. and Econs., 2000—03. Recipient Sec.'s Honor award USDA, 2004; NIH tng. grantee, 1979-2006. Fellow Am. Heart Assn.; mem. Am. Soc. Clin. Nutirition (pres. 1995-96), Am. Dietetic Assn., Am. Diabetes Assn., Am. Obesity Assn. (co-founder, v.p. 1995-), N.Am. Assn. for Study of Obesity (pres. 1992-93), Inst. Medicine of NAS, Inst. Food Technologists, Am. Soc. Nutrition Sci. (chair pub. info. com. 1992-94), Sigma Xi, Delta Omega. Office: U Calif Dept Nutrition 1 Shields Ave Davis CA 95616-5271 Office Phone: 530-752-6575. Business E-Mail: jsstern@ucdavis.edu.

STERN, MADELEINE BETTINA, rare book dealer, writer; b. N.Y.C., July 1, 1912; d. Moses Roland and Lillie (Mack) S. BA, Barnard Coll., 1932; MA, Columbia U., 1934. Tchr. English N.Y.C. High Schs., 1934-43; ptnr. Leona Rostenberg Rare Books, N.Y.C., 1945—, Leona Rostenberg and Madeleine B. Stern Rare Books, N.Y.C., 1980—. Lectr. history of book, feminism, pub. history, lt. Author: We Are Taken, 1935, The Life of Margaret Fuller, 1942, Louisa May Alcott, 1950, new edit., 1996, Purple Passage: The Life of Mrs. Frank Leslie, 1953, Imprints on History: Book Publishers and American Frontiers, 1956, We the Women: Career Firsts of Nineteenth Century America, 1962, new edit., 1994, So Much in a Lifetime: The Story of Dr. Isabel Barrows, 1965, Queen of Publishers' Row: Mrs. Frank Leslie, 1966, The Pantarch: A Biography of Stephen Pearl Andrews, 1968, Heads and Headlines: The Phrenological Fowlers, 1971, Books and Book People in 19th-Century America, 1978, Antiquarian Bookselling in the United States: A History from the Origins to the 1940s, 1985, Nicholas Gouin Dufief of Philadelphia Franco-American Bookseller, 1776-1834, 1988, The Life of Margaret Fuller: A Revised Second Edition, 1991, Louisa May Alcott: From Blood & Thunder to Hearth & Home, 1998; (with Leona Rostenberg) Old and Rare: Forty Years in the Book Business, 1974, rev. edit. 1988, Between Boards: New Thoughts on Old Books, 1978, Bookman's Quintet: Five Catalogues about Books, 1980, Quest Book-Guest Book: A Biblio-Folly, 1993, Connections: Our Selves-Our Books, 1994, Old Books in the Old World: Reminiscences of Book Buying Abroad, 1996, Old Books, Rare Friends: Two Literary Sleuths and Their Shared Passion, 1997, New Worlds in Old Books, 1999, Books Have Their Fates, 2001, Bookends: Two Women, One Enduring Friendship, 2001, From Revolution to Revolution: Perspectives on Publishing and Bookselling, 2002; editor: Women on the Move, 4 vols., 1972, Victoria Woodhull Reader, 1974, Louisa's Wonder Book-An Unknown Alcott Juvenile, 1975, Behind a Mask: The Unknown Thrillers of Louisa May Alcott, 1975, new edit., 1995, Plots and Counterplots: More Unknown Thrillers of Louisa May Alcott, 1976, Publishers for Mass Entertainment in 19th-Century America, 1980, A Phrenological Dictionary of 19th-Century Americans, 1982, Critical Essays on Louisa May Alcott, 1984, A Modern Mephistopheles and Taming a Tartar by Louisa May Alcott, 1987, Louisa May Alcott Unmasked: Collected Thrillers, 1995, Modern Magic by Louisa May Alcott, 1995, The Feminist Alcott: Stories of a Woman's Power, 1996, Louisa May Alcott: Signature of Reform, 2002; co-editor: Selected Letters of Louisa May Alcott, 1987, A Double Life: Newly Discovered Thrillers of Louisa May Alcott, 1988, The Journals of Louisa May Alcott, 1989, Louisa May Alcott: Selected Fiction, 1990, (co-editor) Freaks of Genius: Unknown Thrillers of Louisa May Alcott, 1991, From Jo March's Attic: Stories of Intrigue and Suspense, 1993 (Victorian Soc. award), The Lost Stories of Louisa May Alcott, 1995. Recipient Medalie award, Barnard Coll., 1982, Victorian Soc. award, Disting. Alumna award, 1997;, Guggenheim fellow, 1943—45. Mem. Antiquarian Booksellers Assn. Am. (gov. 1966-68, 78-80), Internat. League Antiquarian Booksellers, MLA, Am. Printing History Assn. (co-recipient award 1983), Authors League, Manuscript Soc. (former trustee), Phi Beta Kappa. Jewish. Home: 40 E 88th St New York NY 10128-1176

STERN, MARGARET BASSETT, retired special education educator, author; b. Bklyn., June 6, 1920; d. Preston Rogers and Jeanne (Mordorf) Bassett; m. Fritz R. Stern Oct. 11, 1947 (div. Dec. 1992); children: Frederick Preston, Katherine Stern Brennan. BA, Wellesley Coll., 1942; MEd, Bank Street Coll. Edn., N.Y.C., 1943, MEd, 1974. Propr. Castle Sch., N.Y.C., 1944-51; dir. Mothers' Coop. Nursery Sch., Ithaca, N.Y., 1952-54; tchr. sci. and math. The Brearley Sch., N.Y.C, 1956-57. Cons., lectr. Head Start, Tuskegee, Ala., 1964; cons. in math. The Gateway Sch., N.Y.C., 1967-90; spl. lectr. Columbia U. Tchrs. Coll., N.Y.C., 1990-94; condr. workshops in Eng., 1960-88. Author: (with Catherine Stern and Toni Gould) Structural Reading Program, Workbooks and Teachers Guides A through E, 1963, 3d edit., 1978, Structural Arithmetic Workbooks and Teachers Guides Grades 1-3, 1965, 2d edit., 1966, (with Stern) Children Discover Arithmetic, 1971, (with Gould) Spotlight on Phonics, Four Workbooks and Teachers Guides, 1980, Sound/Symbol Activities and Decoding Activities, 1980, 2d edit., 1994; Experimenting with Numbers, 1988, 2004, Structural Arithmetic, 1-3, 1992, 2006. Recipient award, Orton Dyslexia Soc. N.Y., 1989, Bank St. Coll. Edn., 1998. Mem.: Nat. Coun. Tchrs. Math., Internat. Dyslexia Assn. Home: 3204 River Crescent Dr Annapolis MD 21401 Personal E-mail: structuralarith@aol.com.

STERN, MARILYN, photographer, editor, writer; b. Detroit, Nov. 8, 1953; d. Julian and Phyllis Stern. BA, Brown U., 1976. Photographer's asst., N.Y.C., 1976-82; freelance photographer, 1976—; freelance writer, 1985—; picture editor Across the Board mag., N.Y.C., 1990-96; faculty Internat. Ctr. of Photography, 2001, NYU, 2004—. Photographer, organizer: (book) Masked Culture: The Greenwich Village Halloween Parade, 1994; author, photographer: Kval! Die Walfänger der Lofoten, 1990; solo exhbns. Profil Gallery, Bratislava, 2001, Scandinavia House, N.Y.C., 2003; several group exhbns., 1976--; represented in permanent collection Detroit Inst. Arts, also numerous pvt. collections. Travel Study grantee Royal Norwegian Consulate to Norway in the U.S., 1987, Am.-Scandinavian Found., 1986. E-mail: mstern@sternphoto.com.

STERN, MARILYN JEAN, special education educator; b. Akron, Ohio, Oct. 7, 1937; d. Walter Keith Pallage and Betty Jane Freeman-Pallage; m. Robert Stern, June 14, 1974 (dec.); children: John Daily, Anne Tunney, Jane Henault, Andrew Daily. BS in Elem. Edn., U. Akron, 1961, MS in Spl. Edn., 1978. Cert. in tchg. Ohio, 1974, Penn., 1963, in tchg. spl. edn. 1978. Tchr. Phila. Sch. Dist., 1963—64; spl. edn. tchr. Summit County Bd. Mental Health, Tallmadge, Ohio, 1974—78, Girard Sch. Dist., Pa., 1999—2004; spl. edn. Learning Disabilities tchr. NW Tri-County Intermediate Unit, Girard, 1978—88, county computer advisor edn. Erie County, Pa., 1988—90, ret., 2004. Computer cons. NW Tri-County Intermediate Unit, 1985—90; vol. reading tutor Hooked-On-Books, Erie County, 2004—; presenter in field; leader spl. programs 4th grade level. Mem. Lake Erie Ballet Bd., Erie, Pa., 1980—92; polit. action chair Girard Fedn. Tchrs., 2000—04; past pres. Local Ridge Coun., nominating chmn., act 48 hours chairperson, spl. projects chair; vol. Hooked on Books; reader Erie Zoo. Mem.: Keystone State Reading Assn. (exec. bd. mem. 2003—), Internat. Reading Assn. (chair 2000—, del. to conf. 2005), Reading Tchrs. Orgn. (pres. 2003—05). Avocations: reading, gardening, quilting, fiber arts, quilting. Home: 1420 Lord Rd Fairview PA 16415

STERN, NANCY FORTGANG, mathematics and computer science, educator; b. N.Y.C., July 15, 1944; d. Murray and Selma (Karp) Fortgang; m. Robert A Stern, Sept. 3, 1964; children: Lori Anne, Melanie. AB, Barnard Coll., 1965; MS, NYU, 1968; MA, SUNY, 1974, PhD, 1978. Programmer analyst ATT, N.Y.C., 1965—67; asst. prof. Nassau C.C., Garden City, NY, 1965—68; adj. prof. Dowling Coll. SUNY, 1968—77; disting. prof. Hofstra U., Hempstead, NY, 1977—. Spkr. in field, rsch. cons. Am. Inst. Physics, N.Y.C., 1976-77; adv. editor John Wiley & Sons, 1977— Author 12 textbooks on computing; asst. editor in chief Annals of the History of Computing, 1977-87; contbr. articles to profl. jours Mem. Charles Babbage Inst., Nat. Computing Com., BCIS Dept. Pers. Com., U. Pioneer Program E-mail: nancy.stern@hofstra.edu.

STERN, PAULA, international trade consultant; b. Chgo., Mar. 31, 1945; d. Lloyd and Fan (Wener) Stern; m. Paul A. London; children: Gabriel Stern London, Genevieve Stern London. BA, Goucher Coll., 1967; MA in Middle Eastern Studies, Harvard U., 1969; MA in Internat. Affairs, Fletcher Sch. of Law and Diplomacy, 1970, MA in Law and Diplomacy, 1970, PhD, 1976; D Comml. Sci. (hon.), Babson Coll., 1985; LLD (hon.), Goucher Coll., 1985. From legis. asst. to sr. legis. asst. to U.S. Sen. Gaylord Nelson U.S. Senate, Washington, 1972—74, 1976; guest scholar Brookings Inst., Washington, 1975-76; policy analyst Pres. Carter-V.P. Mondale Transition Team, Washington, 1977-78; internat. affairs fellow Council on Fgn. Rels., Washington, 1977-78; commr. Internat. Trade Commn., Washington, 1978-87, chair, 1984-86; sr. assoc. Carnegie Endowment for Internat. Peace, Washington, 1986-88; sr. fellow Progressive Policy Inst., 1994—95. Howard W. Aikire chmn. internat. bus. and econs. Hamline U., 1994—2000; chairwoman The Stern Group, Inc., 1988—; bd. dirs. Avaya, Inc., Avon Products, Inc., Hasbro, Inc.; mem., sr. advisor U.S. trade policy coun. Competition Policy Inst., 1991—93; sr. fellow Progressive Policy Inst., 1994—95; pub. vice chairwoman Atlantic Coun. U.S.; trustee Com. Econ. Devel.; mem. Inter-Am. Dialogue, Coun. Fgn. Rels.; mem. high level adv. group Global Subsidies Initiative Project; past co-chair Internat. Competition Adv. Com.; antitrust divsn. U.S. Dept. Justice; past chmn. US Export-Import Bank; past mem. U.S. Pres. Adv. Com. on Trade Policy and Negotiation; bd. dirs. Carnegie Coun. Ethics and Internat. Affairs. Author: Water's Edge--Domestic Politics and the Making of American Foreign Policy, 1979; contbg. author newspapers; contbr. articles to profl. jours. Recipient Journalism award, Alicia Patterson Fund, 1971, Joseph Papp Award for Racial Harmony, Found. Ethnic Understanding, 2004. Democrat. Jewish. Avocations: sculpting, tennis, dance. Office: 3314 Ross Pl NW Washington DC 20008-3332 Office Phone: 202-966-7894. Business E-Mail: pstern@sterngroup.biz.

STERN, ROSLYNE PAIGE, magazine publisher; b. Chgo., May 26, 1926; d. Benjamin Gross and Clara (Sniderman) Roer; m. William E. Weber, May 3, 1944 (div. Mar. 1956); m. Richard S. Paige, June 28, 1958 (div. Apr. 1978); children: Sandra Weber Porr, Barbara Paige Kaplan, Elizabeth Paige (dec.); m. Robert D. Stern, June 5, 1978. Cert., U. Chgo., 1945. Profl. model, singer, 1947-53; account exec. Interstate United, Chgo., 1955-58; sales mgr. Getting To Know You Internat., Great Neck, NY, 1963-71, exec. v.p., 1971-78; pub. After Dark Mag., N.Y.C., 1978-82; assoc. pub. Dance Mag., N.Y.C., 1978-85, pres., pub., 1985—2001, pres. emeritus, 2001—. Bd. dirs. Rudor Consol. Industries, Inc., N.Y.C., AGC/Sedgwick, Inc., Princeton, N.J. Founding pres. Dance Mag. Found., NYC, 1984-86 chair Dance Mag. awards, 1986-2004; life mem. nat. women's com. Brandeis U., Waltham, Mass., 1958—; bd. dirs. Westport Arts Ctr.; The Internation Com. for Dance Libr. of Israel. Recipient Disting. Svc. award Dance Notation Bur., 1996, Am. Coll. Dance Festival award, 1998, Pres.'s award Dance Masters of Am., Inc., 1998, Documents of Dance award Dance Library of Israel, 1999. Mem. Pub. Relations Soc. Am., LWV, Am. Theatre Wing, Nat. Arts Club. Democrat. Jewish. Avocations: dance, theater, opera, visual arts, travel. Home: 2 Imperial Lndg Westport CT 06880-4934 Office: 1930 Broadway Ste 25C New York NY 10023 Office Phone: 212-724-4909. Personal E-mail: sterndance@aol.com.

STERN, RUTH SZOLD, artist; b. Bronx, N.Y., Oct. 14, 1929; d. Albert and Margaret (Karl) Nussbacher; m. Martin Szold, Apr. 10, 1949 (div. Sept. 1978); children: Lauren, Terry; m. James C. Stern, Aug. 22, 1982. Student, Hunter Coll., N.Y.C., 1947; cert. in writing, UCLA, 1988; BFA, Calif. Inst. Arts, 1994, MFA, 1996. Exec. legal sec. to sr. ptnr. Paul, Weiss, Rifkind, Wharton & Garrison, N.Y.C., 1958-62; asst. to pres. M.E. Green & Co. brokerage, N.Y.C., 1962-65; demonstrator, cons. various cosmetic cos., 1965-85; founder, pres. Ruth Szold Promotional Models, 1968-84, Cosmetic Art, Inc., 1979-85, founder, pres., designer, promoter cosmetic line, 1979-85; columnist Fire Island News, Ocean Beach, N.Y., 1985-89; asst. to pres., CEO Gladden Entertainment, L.A., 1989-90; exec. adminstr. C&O Cogent Light and Techs., 1990-91. Demonstrator-lectr. TV, videotapes; condr. cosmetic workshops N.Y. Salute to Fashion Industries, 1981; chmn. earthquake com. Fountainview Assn., 1989-98, bd. dir., 1997-98; cons. in field; tchr. art to homeless Found. House, West Hollywood, Calif., 2000, on-site mgr., 2001-05. One-woman shows include Fire Island Transmission, 1997; group exhbns. include SPLICE Side St. Projects, Santa Monica, Calif., 1997-98, 5th Ann. Miracle on 18th St. Side St. Projects, Santa Monica, 1997, (videos) Mel and Alice's Wedding 1950, 2000, Santa Barbara Contemporary Arts Forum, 2002, others, (edible books) Occidental Coll., 2002, (armory N.W. installation) "24 Hours", Pasadena, Calif., 2004; N.Y.C. Internat. Film & Video Fest. "Mel & Alice's Wedding", West Hollywood, 2004, N.Y.C. 2004, 05, Champagne and Chocolate Exhbn. and Installation, L.A., 2005; photos appear in membership drive brochure Mus. Contemporary Art, 2004. Mem. coun. Girl Scouts U.S.A., 1964-69; bd. dir. Bleecker Tower Tenants Corp., N.Y.C., 1979-80, chmn. architecture and design com., 1979-80, chmn. maintenance, 1980-85, pres., 1981-82; mem. Hunger Project, Fin. Family; lectr., panelist Am. Women's Econ. Devel. Corp., 1981; nom. bd. dir. alumni assn., Calif. Inst. of the Arts, 2002, benefit exhbn. Habitat Katrina, 2005. Recipient gold medal Deborah Fund Raising Dinner, 1955, othres. Mem. Foragers of Am., Nat. Retail Mchts. Assn., Fragrance Found., Cosmetic Exec. Women, Brandeis U. Club, Hadassah Club. Home: 1855 Industrial St 419 Los Angeles CA 90021 Personal E-mail: ruthszoldstern@netscape.net.

STERN, S(EESA) BEATRICE, executive secretary, medical/surgical nurse; b. Atlantic City, Feb. 13, 1919; d. Max and Gussie (Thierman) Rosen; m. Francis H. Stern, June 29, 1958 (dec. Feb. 1973); m. Bernard N. Abelson, Dec. 5, 1973 (div. Feb. 1992). AA, Miami-Dade C.C., Fla., 1982, AS in Nursing, 1982. RN Fla., NJ, Nev. Profl. dancer, 1928—32; sec. N.J. State Highway Dept., Trenton, 1938-41; columnist N.J. Herald, Trenton, 1939-41; sec. U.S. Army, various locations, 1941-46; legal sec. Gus Feuer, Atty. at Law, Miami, 1946-47; exec. sec. to pres. Pharms., Inc., N.Y.C., 1947-58; med. sec. Phila., 1958-72; nurse Mt. Sinai Med. Ctr., Miami Beach, Fla., 1982-83, Atlantic City Med. Ctr., 1983-84. Vol. Hollywood Med. Ctr., 1992-96, Aventura Med. Ctr., 1992—; mem. bd. govs. Brith Sholom, 1970—. Mem. Brith Sholom Women (nat. pres. 1970-72), Four Chaplains Legion of Hon., Phi Theta Kappa. Avocations: swimming, handcrafts, reading, crossword puzzles.

STERN, SHERRY ANN, journalist; b. Paterson, N.J., June 27, 1954; d. Richard Norman and Norma (Davidowitz). BA, U.S. Calif., Los Angeles, 1876; MS, Northwestern U., Evanston, 1982. Reporter Ariz. Daily Star, Tucson, 1976-79, TV critic, 1979-81; news editor The Morning Press, Vista, Calif., 1982-83, mng. editor, editor in chief, 1983-84; copy editor The Orange County Register, Calif., 1984-85, asst. features news editor Santa Ana, Calif., 1985-86; features news editor Orange County Register, Santa Ana, Calif., 1986--. Journalism instr. Mira Costa Coll., Oceanside, 1983-84. Vol. Lit. Vols. of Am., Huntington Beach, 1988--. Named Best Headling Portfolio Orange County Press Club, 1985, Best Student Feature Los Angeles Press Club. Mem. Orange County, Press Club. Democrat. Jewish. Office: The Orange County Register 625 N Grand Ave Santa Ana CA 92701-4347

STERN, SUSAN TOY, human resources specialist; BA in Sociology, UCLA, 1974. Chief dep. dir. LA County Dept. Human Resources. Co-chair UCLA Fund; spkr. in field. Mem.: So. Calif. Personnel Mgmt. Assn. Human Resources (past pres.), Internat. Pub. Mgmt. Assn. Human Resources (life; pres. 2001, former mem. exec. coun., former chair Conf. rev. task force). Office: LA County Dept Human Resources 3333 Wilshire Blvd Ste 100 Los Angeles CA 90010

STERNBERG, BETTY J., school system administrator; b. N.Y., Jan. 30, 1950; d. Julius and Edith Jane (Meyer) Levin; m. Robert Jeffrey Sternberg, June 18, 1972 (div. Jan. 13, 1987); children: Seth, Sara. BA, Brandeis U., 1971; MA, Columbia U., 1972; PhD, Stanford U., 1978. Bur. chief Dept. Edn., Hartford, Conn., 1980-85, divsn. dir., 1985-92, assoc. commr., 1992—2003, commr. edn., 2003—. Cons. Nat. Bd. for Profl. Teaching Standards, Washington, 1992. Co-author: (textbook) Metric Multibase Mathematics, 1973, Attribute Acrobatics, 1973, People Pieces Primer, 1975; (textbook series) Math In Stride, 1987. Mem. bd. dirs. William Benton Mus. of Art U. Conn., 1989—; mem. adv. coun. Ct. for Ednl. Excellence, 1992-93. Recipient Disting. Managerial Svc. award State of Conn., 1986. Mem. ASCD (sec. 1975-80), Conn. Assn. Suprs. of Curriculum Devel. Avocations: tennis, interior design, gardening. Home: 2 Squirrel Hill Rd West Hartford CT 06107-1036 Office: Conn Dept Edn 165 Capitol Ave Hartford CT 06106-1659

STERNBERG, ESTHER MAY, neuroendocrinologist, immunologist, hematologist; b. Montreal, May 9, 1951; came to U.S., 1980, naturalized, 1991; d. Joseph and Ghitta (Wexler) Sternberg; 1 child, Penny Rebecca Herscovitch. BSc with great distinction, McGill U., 1972, MD, 1974. Diplomate Nat. Bd. Med. Examiners; lic. physician, Can., Mo. Intern Royal Victoria Hosp./McGill U., Montreal, 1974-75, resident II in medicine, 1977-78, clin. fellow rheumatology, 1978-79, clin. and rsch. fellow rheumatology, 1979-80; gen. practice medicine Mount Royal, Que., 1975-77; rsch. assoc. divsn. allergy/clin. immunology Washington U., St. Louis, 1981-83, rsch. assoc. Howard Hughes Med. Inst., 1983-84, assoc. Howard Hughes Med. Inst., 1984-86, instr. divs. rheumatology, 1984-86; attending physician Barnes Hosp., St. Louis, 1984-86; tenured sr. scientist NIMH/NIH, Bethesda, 1991—, med. officer, chief unit on neuroendocrine immunology, 1991-95, assoc. br. chief clin. neuroendocrinology br., 1994-2000, med. officer, chief sect. neuroendocrine immunology, 1995—, dir. integrative neural-immune program, 1999—. Vis. scientist Nat. Inst. Arthritis Musculoskeletal and Skin Disease, NIH and head Inter-Inst. Unit on Neuroendocrine Immunology and Behavior, NIMH and Nat. Inst. Arthritis, Musculoskeletal and Skin Diseases, Bethesda, 1989-90; rsch. full prof. Am. U., Washington, 1995—; temporary advisor WHO, 1991; ad hoc mem. NIH/NIMH/Libr. Congress Human Genome Project liaison com., 1990-91; invited expert CDC, Atlanta, 1989-93; spl. cons. Inst. Health (Hygienic) Scis., Min. of Health, Japan, 1992-94; med. adv. bd. Scleroderma Fedn., 1993-95; cons. John D. and Catherine T. MacArthur Found. Network on Mind-Body Interactions, 1994—; participant WHO/Pan Am. Health Orgn. Collaborating Ctr. for Health of the Elderly Work Group meeting, 1995; mem. com. on military nutrition rsch. Inst. of Medicine of NAS, 1998—; advisor Nat. Libr. of Medicine Planning Com., Breath of Life: An Exhbn. on Asthma, 1997-98, NIMH/NIH Ctr. for Sci. Rev., 1998; reviewer FDA's Office of Women's Health, 1998; co-dir. Exhibition on Emotions and Disease Nat. Libr. Medicine, 1996-97, others; dir. NIMH Program on Integrative Neural-Immune, 1999—; co-chair/chair/organizer numerous confs. Author: The Balance Within. The Science Connecting Health and Emotions; editl. bd. Brain, Behavior and Immunity, Jour. Neuroimmunology, Neuroimmunomodulation, Molecular Psychiatry, Immunologic Rsch.; invited guest series editor Jour. Clin. Investigation, 1997; reviewer Jour. Clin. Investigation, New Eng. Jour. Medicine, Jour. Immunology, Endocrinology, Jour. Clin. Endocrinology and Metabolism, Arthritis and Rheumatism, Am. Jour. Physiology, Jour. Neuroimmunology, Brain, Behavior and Immunity; editor: Stress: Mechanisms and Clinical Implications, 1995, Neuroimmune Interactions: Molecular, Integrative Systems and Clinical Implications, 1998; assoc. editor Brain, Behavior and Immunity, Neuroimmunomodulation; contbr. chpts. to books and articles to profl. jours.; patentee in field. Recipient Arthritis Found. Met. Washington William R. Felts award for excellence in rheumatology rsch. pubs., 1991, FDA's Commr.'s Spl. Citation, 1991, USPHS Superior Svc. award, 1994; McGill U. scholar, 1967-68, 68-71; Am. Acad. Allergy/Schering Travel grantee, 1982, United Scleroderma Found. grantee, 1985-86, 86-87, Scleroderma Found. Greater Washington, 1987, 88; NIH New Investigator awardee, 1985-88, others. Fellow Am. Coll. Rheumatology; mem. AAAS, Soc. Neurosci., Am. Soc. Clin. Investigation, Am. Assn. Immunologists, N.Y. Acad. Scis., Can. Med. Assn., Internat. Soc. Neuroimmunology (mem. internat. adv. com. 1995), PsychoNeuroImmunology Rsch. Soc. (councillor 1997—), Soc. for Neuroimmunomodulation (sec. 1997-99, pres. 1999—). Office: NIMH/NIH Bldg 10 10 Center Dr MSC-1284 Bethesda MD 20892-1284 Fax: 301-496-6095. E-mail: ems@codon.nih.gov.

STERNHAGEN, FRANCES, actress; b. Washington, Jan. 13, 1930; Student, Vassar Coll., Perry-Mansfield Sch. Theatre; studied with Sanford Meisner, NY. Tchr. Milton Acad., Cath. U.; actress Arena Stage, Washington, DC, 1953-54. Debut Thieves Carnival, NY, 1955; plays include The Carefree Tree, The Admirable Bashville (Clarence Derwent award, Obie award), Ulysses in Night Town, Red Eye of Love, Misalliance, The Return of Herbert Bracewell, Laughing Stock, The Displaced Person, The Pinter Plays (Obie award); Broadway shows include The Skin of Our Teeth, Viva Madison Avenue, Great Day in the Morning, The Right Honorable Gentleman, The Cocktail Party, Cock-a-Doodle Dandy, Playboy of the Western World, The Sign in Sidney Brustein's Window, The Good Doctor (Tony award 1973), Equus (Drama Desk award), Angel, On Golden Pond (Drama League award), The Father, Grownups, Summer, You Can't Take It With You, Home Front, Driving Miss Daisy, Remembrance, A Perfect Ganesh, The Heiress (Tony award 1995), Long Day's Journey into Night, 1998, The Exact Center of the Universe, 1999, Morning's at Seven, 2003, The Foreigner, 2003, Echoes of the War, 2004, Seascape, 2005, Steel Magnolias, 2005; actress (films) Up The Down Staircase, 1967, Starting Over, 1979, Outland, 1981, Independence Day, 1983, Romantic Comedy, 1983, Bright Lights, Big City, 1988, See You in the Morning, 1989, Communion, 1989, Misery, 1990, Doc Hollywood, 1991, Raising Cain, 1992, Curtain Call, Land Fall, 1997, The Rising Place, 1998; (TV series) Love of Life, The Doctors, Secret Storm, Cheers, Golden Years, Under One Roof, The Road Home, E.R., Sex and the City, The Closer; (TV movies) Who Will Save Our Children?, 1978, Prototype, 1982, Resting Place, 1986, Follow Your Heart, 1990, She Woke Up, 1992, Labor of Love: The Arlette Schweitzer Story, 1993, Reunion, 1994, Tales from the Crypt, Outer Limits, Law and Order, 1990, 96, The Con, 1997, To Live Again, 1997, New York: A Documentary Film, 1999, The Laramie Project, 2001. Recipient Edith Oliver Award for Sustained Excellence, 2005.

STERN-LAROSA, CARYL M., advocate, educational association administrator; married; 3 children. BA in Studio Art, SUNY, Oneonta; MD in Student Personnel Adminstrn., We. Ill. U.; postgrad., Loyola U. Dean students Polytecn. U.; former sr. mgmt. World of Difference Inst., 1991, former dir. spl. tng. program, dir.; dir. edn. divsn. Anti-Defamation League, COO, sr. assoc. nat. dir. Nat. chairperson Nat. Assn. Campus Activites; former chairperson Boroughof Bklyn. Unity Task Forcce; lectr. in field. Co-author: Future Perfect: A Model for Professional Development, 1987, Hate Hurts: How Children Learn and Unlearn Prejudice, 2000; contbr. articles to profl. jours.; regularly appears on national news programs. Named one of 25 Moms We Love, Working Mother, 2000; recipient Founder's award, Nat. Assn. Campus Activities, 1992, Borough of Bklyn. Unity award, Borough of Queen's Citation for Contbn. to Racial and Religious Harmony, Oneonta Alumni Recognition award, SUNY, Alumni Achievement award, We. Ill. U., Senn award for profl. excellence. Office: Anti-Defamation League 823 United Nations Plz New York NY 10017

STETINA, PAMELA ELEANOR, nursing educator; b. Cambridge, Mass., Nov. 11, 1964; d. Charles and Eleanor Mary (Jennison) Toth; m. Francis Lee Stetina Jr., Aug. 15, 1987. BSN, Salisbury (Md.) State U., 1987; cert. in gerontology, U. Denver, 1990; M in Nursing, U. Phoenix, Englewood, Colo., 1996. RN. Grad. nurse, RN Dorchester Gen. Hosp., Cambridge, Md., 1987-89; staff nurse Salisbury Med. Ctr., 1988-89; staff/charge nurse Porter Care Hosp., Denver, 1989-91; float nurse Summit Health Profls., Denver, 1991—96; clin. nurse NMC Home Care, Englewood, 1992-95; mem. faculty, asst. dir. nursing Concorde Career Inst., Denver, 1994-96; coord. nursing Pueblo C.C.-S.W., Durango, Colo., 1996-2000; asst. prof. Tex. A&M U., Corpus Christi, 2000—. Mem. curriculum com., faculty whole com., libr. com. Tex. A&M U., Corpus Christi, 2000—. Contbr. Jour. Nursing Jocularity. Instr. CPR Am. Heart Assn., Colo., 1994-2004. Named Educator of Yr., Colo. Pvt. Sch. Assn., Denver, 1995. Mem. Nat. League for Nursing, Oncology Nursing Soc., So. Nursing Rsch. Soc., Sigma Theta Tau. Avocations: reading, hiking. Office: Tex A&M U Sch Nursing 6300 Ocean Dr Corpus Christi TX 78412 Personal E-mail: pstetina@juno.com.

STETSON, NANCY EMILY, retired academic administrator; b. Kitty Hawk, N.C., Sept. 24, 1936; d. Harold Clifton Stetson and Nannie Temperance (White) Mattern; children: Laurel Kroon Hair, Nancy Lee Kroon AA, Wenatchee Valley Coll., Wash., 1973; BA, Evergreen State Coll., Olympia, Wash., 1976; MS, Ctrl. Wash. U., 1990; EdD, Nova Southea. U., 1985. Info. specialist, pub. info. officer, dir. info. and devel. Wenatchee Valley Coll., 1972—80, interim dean North Campus Omak, Wash., 1991, asst. to pres., 1980—82; dir. pub. affairs and devel. Marin C.C. Dist., Kentfield, Calif., 1982—86, dean devel. and info. svcs., 1986—87, acting v.p. student and spl. svcs., 1987—88, v.p. planning and devel., 1988—91, mem. faculty, 1991—97; pres. Company of Experts.net, San Anselmo, Santa Rosa, and Dillon Beach, Calif., 1989—2005, expert on call, cons., 1989—. Appreciative inquiry facilitator, trainer, 2001-; faculty mentor Walden U., 2005-; instr. Wenatchee Valley Coll., 1972-79; interim adminstr. student svcs. Marin C.C. Dist., Kentfield, 1984 Contbr. several books and numerous articles to profl. jours., also verse, short stories and poetry Recipient We. Region John Fry Ind. Merit award Nat. Coun. Staff, Program, and Orgnl. Devel., Nat. Leadership award, Appreciation Cert. for Svc. Cmty. Trustees and Staff Devel. C.C. League Calif., Exec. Bd. Outstanding Svc. award, Appreciation Cert. Small Bus. Ctr. Coll. Marin, Dedicated Svc. award, Svc. award City Wenatchee Parks Bd., Oustanding Svc. and Dedication to Students awards Wenatchee Valley Coll. and Coll. Marin, Individual Supporting the Arts award Allied Arts Coun. North Ctrl. Washington, Ervin S. Fulop Pub. Spkg. award Commencement Address Union H.S., N.J.; named to Practitioners Hall of Fame Nova Southea. U. Mem. Appreciative Inquiry Consulting Avocations: beachcombing, jazz, reading, writing. Home and Office: 300 Enterprise Dr #411 Rohnert Park CA 94928 Office Phone: 707-878-9340.

STEUART, SYBIL JEAN, elementary school educator; b. New Orleans, Aug. 6, 1954; d. John Thompson and Sybil Rose (Cousans) S. BS in Elem. Edn., Loyola U. of the South, New Orleans, 1976; postgrad., U. So. Miss., William Carey Coll.; M in Theol. Studies, Spring Hill Coll., 2004. Cert. elem. sch. tchr., Miss. Tchr. 6th grade St. Rita Elem. Sch., New Orleans; tchr. kindergarten, religion coord. Sacred Heart Elem. Sch., D'Iberville, Miss. Presenter ednl. workshops. Author of poems. Lay mem. Mercy Assocs., St. Louis, 1985—; vol. aide VA Hosp., Biloxi, Miss., 1989, various civic and ch. orgns.; commentator, lectr., kindergarten tchr. Christian doctrine St. Elizabeth Seton Ch., Ocean Springs, Miss., 1982—; commentator, lectr., eucharistic min., liturgist Sacred Heart Ch., D'Iberville, 1988—; v.p. Friends of Ocean Springs Libr., 1983-91; mem. Diocese of Biloxi-Commn. on Women; mem. Christus Ecumenical, Mobile. Recipient Cert. of Appreciation, New Orleans Pub. Schs., 1984, Bishop's Svc. Cross award Diocese of Biloxi, 1985, 18 Yr. Catechist Svc. award St. Elizabeth Seton Ch.; named Outstanding Young Educator of Biloxi, Jaycees, 1986; named Catechist of Yr. Knights of Columbus, Ocean Springs, 1994, Order of St. Louis, Archdiocese of New Orleans, 1980. Mem. Nat. Cath. Educators Assn., Mississippians for Ednl. Broadcasting, St. Elizabeth Seton Altar Soc. (chmn. spiritual com. 1988-92), St. Mary's Dominican High Sch. Alumni Assn. (developer ednl. advancement programs), Loyola U. Alumni Assn. (developer ednl. advancement programs), Theol. Inst., Sacred Heart Automobile League. Avocations: art, crafts, gardening, cooking, photography, reading, poetry. Office: 10482 Lemoyne Blvd Diberville MS 39540-5911

STEUTERMAN, ERIKA C., government agency administrator; Student Air Force Res. Officer Tng. Corps program, Purdue U., West Lafayette, Ind. Commd. USAF, 1977, advanced through grades to brig. gen., individual mobilization asst. to commdr. of Air Intelligence Agy. Lackland AFB, Tex.

STEVENS, AMY, history educator; d. Mark and Barbie Hendricks; m. Richard Adam Stevens, July 8, 2000; 1 child, Jordan. Bachelor's, Warner So. Coll., Lake Wales, Fla., 2001. Cert. tchr. Va. Dept. Edn., 2006. Tchr. govt. Blacksburg H.S., Va., 2003—. Instr. flag corps/color guard Blacksburg H.S., 2003—05, student coun. sponsor, 2005—. Office Phone: 540-951-5706.

STEVENS, ANNE L., metal products executive, retired automotive executive; b. Reading, PA, Dec. 1948; BS in mechanical & materials engring., Drexel U., 1980; Grad. Level Business student, Rutgers U; PhD (hon.), Ctrl. Mich. U. With Exxon Corp.; mktg. specialist plastic products divsn. Ford Motor Co., 1990—92, mgr., Quality Services Dept., 1992—95, mfr. mgr., Automotive Components Divsn., 1995, Plant mgr., Automotive Components Div. Enfield, England, 1995—97, asst. vehicle line dir., Ford Automotive Operations Dunton, England, 1997—99, dir., Manufacturing Business Office, N. Am., 1999—2000, v.p. N. Am. Assembly Ops., 2000—01, v.p. N. Am. Vehicle Ops., 2001—03, group v.p., Canada, Mexico, and S. Am., 2003—05, exec. v.p., COO, The Americas, 2005—06; chmn., CEO, pres. Carpenter Tech. Corp., Wyomissing, Pa., 2006—. Bd. dirs. Lockheed Martin Corp., 2002—, Coun. Americas; bd. trustees Drexel U.; trustee Women's Automotive Assn. Internat.; mem. advisory bd. Mexico Inst., Woodrow Wilson Internat. Ctr. for Scholars; mem. exec. advisory bd. Juran Ctr. for Leadership in Quality, U. Minn. Named one of Most Powerful Women in Bus., Fortune mag., 2005; recipient Shingo Leadership award, 2000, Circle of Distinction award, Drexel U. Coll. Engring., 2001, Eli Whitney award, Soc. Mfg. Engineers, 2003. Mem.: NAE. Office: Carpenter Tech Corp 2 Meridian Blvd Wyomissing PA 19610-1339*

STEVENS, ANNIE BICKETT PARKER, retired architect; b. Marshville, N.C., Dec. 25, 1921; d. Benjiman Carl and Rosa Mae (Blakeney) Parker; m. Jack Elmer Stevens, Mar. 31, 1945 (dec.); children: Susan, Barbara, Martha. Student, U. N.C., Greensboro, 1938—40, Syracuse U., 1940—42; BArch, Columbia U., 1945; postgrad., U. N.C., 1971—75. Archtl. draftsman J.N. Pease & Co., Charlotte, NC, 1942, draftsman, 1944, So. Mapping and Engr., Greensboro, NC, 1943, Charles and Edward Stotz, Pitts., 1945—51; ptnr. Jack E. Stevens Builder, Pitts., 1951—68, Chapel Hill, NC, 1969—74, Charlotte, 1975—77, Pinehurst, NC, 1978—82; pvt. practice Parker Stevens Builder, Pinehurst, 1983—84, Anne P. Stevens Builder, Surf City, NC, 1984—2001; ret., 2001. Avocations: art, painting. Home: Apt 2 14482 Tramore Dr Chesterfield MO 63017 Office Phone: 636-227-2113.

STEVENS, CHERITA WYMAN, social sciences educator, writer; b. Erick, Okla., Jan. 12, 1938; d. Forrest Clarence and Wilma Peter Wyman; m. Paul Donald Stevens, May 30, 1958 (div. Nov. 10, 1978); children: Paul McDonald, Mark Liu. BA in Social Sci., Phillips U., 1961; MA in Sch. Law and Fin., Calif. State U., LA, 1976; cert. in ESL, U. Calif., LA. Adminstrv. credential K-12 and adult; LA, Calif. Classroom tchr. grades 7-9 South Pasadena (Calif.) Unified, 1966—74; assoc. regional pastor Disciples of Christ, Pacific Southwest, 1976—82; computer store owner Claremont (Calif.) Computer, 1982—87; tchr., prin., grant writer Cabrillo Unified Sch. Dist., Half Moon Bay, Calif., 1987—97; ESL computer lab. media instr. Chapman Edn. Ctr., Garden Grove, Calif., 1997—2005. Legis. intern Calif. State Assembly, Sacramento, 1978—80; NASD registered rep. Primerica Life/Citigroup, Orange, Calif., 2000—05; grant reviewer U.S. Dept. Edn., Washington, 2002; presenter in field; grant writer Calif. Dept. Edn./Joint Partnership Training Act, Half Moon Bay, 1996. Editor: Direction Newspaper, 1976—82; author: (software) Apartment Maintenance, 1988, Grants Tracking, 1989, Financial Management, 1991, Curriculum and Lesson Plans for the Independent Learning Lab, 1995; designer, lesson plan builder: OTAN Website, 2002—05; contributor KOCE (PBS) Schoolhouse Video Project, 2004; contbr. articles to newspapers and mag. Mem. Ams. for Dem. Action, Pasadena, 1963—80; civil rights activist, 1960—69; organizer first Martin Luther King Jr. celebration in U.S. L.A., 1972; active First Christian Ch., Orange, 1963—2005, Pasadena, Calif. Mem.: Assn. Calif. Sch. Adminstrs. (site rep. 1993—97, state presenter 2005, state workshop presenter). Avocations: golf, photography, genealogy. Home: 401 W La Veta Ave #220 Orange CA 92866-2649 Personal E-mail: cheri1066@msn.com.

STEVENS, CHRISTINA LEA, film director, writer, film producer; b. Sydney, NSW, Australia, Apr. 9, 1948; arrived in US, 1971; d. William James and Margaret Diana (Young) Stevens. Writer Young & Rubicam, Inc., NYC, 1971—76; sr. writer Wells Rich Green, LA, 1977—79; sr. v.p. creative dir. Ogilvy & Mather, LA, 1981-84, LA, 1981—84; pres. Blue Sky Prodns., Inc., Santa Paula, Calif., 1984—; creative dir., cons. Ogilvy & Mather, Inc., 1984—. Cons. in field. Author: Vic the Viking, 1968, Illuminations, 1984; prodr., dir. Voices from the Heart, 1996. Founder, pres. Angel Found., LA, 1983. Recipient Gold Lion, Cannes Film Festival, 1975, Lulu award, LA Advt. Women, 1977, 1980, Clio award, 1978—79, IBA awards, Internat. Advt. Bur., 1978, 1981—82. Mem.: SAG, Dirs. Guild Am. (spl. projects com.).

STEVENS, DIANA LYNN, elementary school educator; b. Waterloo, Iowa, Dec. 12, 1950; d. Marcus Henry and Clarissa Ann (Funk) Carr; m. Paul John Stevens; 1 child, Drew Spencer. BS, Mid Am. Nazarene Coll., 1973; M in Liberal Arts, Baker U., 1989. Elem. tchr. Olathe (Kans.) Sch. Dist. #233, 1975—. Artwork appeared in traveling exhibit ARC/Nat. Art Edn. Assn., 1968, Delta Kappa Gamma Bull., 2001. Olathe Sch. Dist. Action grantee, 1996-97; recipient Excellence in Edn. award Olathe Pub. Schs. Found., 2002. Mem. NEA, Kans. Edn. Assn., Olathe Edn. Assn. (social com. Olathe chpt.), Coll. Ch. of the Nazarene, Delta Kappa Gamma (profl. affairs com. mem., chpt. membership chair 2006-, Excellence in Edn. award 2002), Beta Omega (membership chair, 2d v.p. 2006-). Avocations: portrait art, reading, walking. Home: 217 S Montclaire Dr Olathe KS 66061-3828

STEVENS, DOROTHY FROST, retired television producer; b. Rockville Centre, NY, June 18, 1924; d. George Sanford Frost and Theodora Barbara Emmanuel; m. Kenneth Hayes Stevens, Aug. 14, 1949 (dec. Apr. 1967). BA, Stanford U., Calif., 1945. Tchr. adult edn., San Jose, Calif., 1945—49; various offices Folk Dance Fedn. Calif., 1945—61; tchr. Los Gatos H.S. Dist., Calif., 1946—51; various positions Calif. State. E.D.D., 1966—82; host, prodr., exec. prodr. Cupertino (Calif) Sr. TV Prodns., 1983—2001; ret., 2001. Prodr.: The Better Part, 1983—2001. Named Vol. of Yr., Retired Sr. Vol. Program Santa Clara County, 1994; recipient Civic Svc. award, City of Cupertino, 1984, Vol. award, Calif. Parks & Recreation Soc., 1988, Golden Rule award, J.C. Penney, 1993, Outstanding Prodr. award, City of Cupertino, 1997, Ripp King Meml. award, Bay Area Cable Excellence, 1998. Presbyterian. Avocations: travel, reading, sewing, gardening. Home: 15243 Clydelle Ave San Jose CA 95124

STEVENS, ELISABETH GOSS (MRS. ROBERT SCHLEUSSNER JR.), journalist, writer, graphic artist; b. Rome, N.Y., Aug. 11, 1929; d. George May and Elisabeth (Stryker) Stevens; m. Robert Schleussner, Jr., Mar. 12, 1966 (dec. 1977); 1 child, Laura Stevens BA, Wellesley Coll., 1951; MA with high honors, Columbia U., 1956. Editl. assoc. Art News Mag., 1964-65; art critic and reporter Washington Post, Washington, 1965-66; freelance art critic and reporter Balt., 1966—; contbg. art critic Wall Street Jour., N.Y.C., 1969-72; art critic Trenton (NJ) Times, 1974-77; art and architecture critic The Balt. Sun, 1978-86; critic-at-large srqradio.com, 2004—; art correspondent Sarasota Herald Tribune, 2005—. Author: Elisabeth Stevens' Guide to Baltimore's Inner Harbor, 1981, Fire and Water: Six Short Stories, 1982, Children of Dust: Portraits and Preludes, 1985, Horse and Cart: Stories from the Country, 1990, The Night Lover: Art & Poetry, 1995, In Foreign Parts, 1997, Household Words, 1999, 2000, Eranos, 2000, Cherry Pie & Other Stories, 2001; one-woman shows include Coll. Notre Dame of Md., 1997, Galerie Francoise, Lutherville, Md., 2000, exhibited in group shows at The Corcoran Gallery of Art, Washington, Towson State U., Balt., Atelier A/E, N.Y.C., Stephen Gang Gallery, Govt. Ho., Annapolis, U. Minn., Morris, Cooperstown (N.Y.) Art Assn., Armory Art Ctr., West Palm Beach, Fla., Venice (Fla.) Art Ctr., Ft. Meyers (Fla.) Alliance for the Art, Katharine Butler Gallery, Sarasota, Fla., 2004, Combined Talents: Fla. Internat., Tallahassee, 2005, Mus. Fine Arts, Tallahassee, 2005; contbr. articles, poetry and short stories to jours., nat. newspapers and popular mags. Recipient A.D. Emmart award for journalism, 1980, Critical Writing citation Balt.-Washington Newspaper Guild, 1980, fiction awards Md. Poetry Rev., 1992, 93, 94, 2d prize Lite Circle, 1994, 1st prize in fiction Lite Circle, 1995, 96, Balt. Writers Alliance Play Writing Contest award, 1994; art critics' fellow NEA, 1973-74, fellow MacDowell Colony, 1981, Va. Ctr. for Creative Arts, 1982-85, 88-90, 92, 93, 95, 97, 2000, Ragdale Found., 1984, 89, Yaddo, 1991, Villa Montalvo, 1995; Work-in-Progress grantee for poetry Md. Art Coun., 1986, Creative Devel. grantee for short fiction collection Balt. Mayor's Com. on Art and Culture, 1986. Mem. Coll. Art Assn., Authors Guild, Fla. Printmakers Assn., Poetry Soc. Am., Am. Soc. Graphic Artists, Nat. Book Critics Circle, Women Contemporary Artists Sarasota. Home: Bards Castle 5353 Creekside Trail Sarasota FL 34243

STEVENS, ELIZABETH MCCARTHA, secondary school educator; m. James Gordon Stevens; children: Jay Stone, Grant Stone; m. James W. Stone II (div.). BS in Secondary Edn., Auburn U., Ala., 1977; M in Secondary Edn., U. Ala., Birmingham, 1979. Cert. sci. tchr. Ala. Tchr. biology McAdory H.S., McCalla, Ala., 1971—75, Leeds H.S., Ala., 1975—84; tchr. 7th grade sci. Pizitz Mid. Sch., Vestavia Hills, Ala., 2002—04, tchr. 8th grade sci., 2004—. Chmn. sci. dept. Pizitz Mid. Sch., Vestavia Hills, Ala., 2004—; chmn. sci. curriculum review com. Vestavia Hills City Schs., 2005—. Mem., donor Birmingham Mus. Art, Ala., 1999—. Recipient grant, Legacy, Ptnrs. in Environ. Edn., 2003. Mem.: Ala. Nat. Bd. Cert. Tchrs. Network, Pi Lambda Theta. Avocations: scuba diving, photography, golf, tennis, travel. Home: 6535 Harper's Dairy Loop Bessemer AL 35022 E-mail: bethstevens7@aol.com.

STEVENS, HELEN JEAN, music educator; b. Nevada, Iowa, July 11, 1934; d. Paul Ellison and Helen Margaret (Ives) Stevens. MusB, U. So. Calif., 1956. Cert. secondary music tchr. Calif. Tchr. San Francisco Sch. Dist., 1956-58; prin. oboist Marin Symphony Orch., San Rafael, Calif., 1956-94, Santa Rosa (Calif.) Symphony, 1956-86; tchr. Santa Venetia Mid. Sch., San Rafael, 1958-83; asst. prof. music Sonoma State Coll., Rohnert Park, Calif., 1963-76; tchr. Davidson Mid. Sch., San Rafael, 1984-89; pvt. tchr. oboe. Oboist Evenings on the Roof Series, LA, 1953—56, Debut TV Show, L.A., 1954—56, Carmel (Calif.) Bach Festival, 1954—82; prin. oboist Light Opera Curren Theatre, San Francisco, 1966—67, Marin Opera Co., San Rafael, 1980—84. Leader Sonoma County 4-H Guide Dog Project Guide Dogs for Blind, Inc., 1974—87; organist, choir dir. Korean Meth. Ch., L.A., 1953—56; music dir. United Meth. Ch., St. James, Mo., 2002—. Named Outstanding Tchr., Marin Edn. Found., 1986; recipient Svc. award, PTA, 1974, Golden Bell award, Marin County Office Edn., 1984, Continuing Svc. award, Calif. Congress Parents, Tchrs. and Students, Inc., 1989. Mem.: German Shepherd Dog Club Am. Avocations: computers, animals. Home: 14713 State Rt BB Saint James MO 65559 E-mail: stevfam@fidnet.com.

STEVENS, JANE SEXTON, psychologist; b. Topeka, Apr. 3, 1947; d. Earl Luther and H. Eileen (Miller) Sexton; m. Robert David Stevens, Dec. 27, 1969; 1 child, James Robert. BA magna cum laude, Duke U., 1969, MEd, 1972, PhD, 1975. Lic. psychologist, N.C. Staff psychologist Children's Psychiat. Inst., Butner, NC, 1971-76, 1989—2002, psychology program mgr., 1976-82, rsch. coord., 1982-88, dir. psychology, 2002—; pvt. practice Durham, NC, 1982—2002. Mem. adv. bd. Bragtown Project, Durham, N.C., 1976-82. Mem. Am. Psychol. Assn., N.C. Psychol. Assn. Home: 3439 Rugby Rd Durham NC 27707-5431

STEVENS, JOANN A., textile, political leader, author, minister; b. Snow Hill, NC, May 15, 1957; d. Moses Lee and Annie Iola Artis; m. Willard Ray Stevens, Apr. 3, 1993; children: Thyais Artis, Jorel, Shakira. Student, Wayne C.C., Goldsboro, N.C., 1983; student in criminal justice, Lenoir C.C., Kinston, N.C., 1984. Ordained elder Bapt. Ch., 1983; cert. substance abuse counselor N.C., 1986, Min. Inst. Shaw Divinity Sch., 1987, protective intervention Caswell Ctr., Dept. Human Resource, 1988, Safety E.I. Dupont, 1989. Founder, owner JoAnn's Christian Supply, Bibile and Bookstore, Snow Hill, NC, 1989—93; founder, counselor Spectrum's Substance Abuse, N/A, A/A Group, Snow Hill, NC, 1991—94; founder Rosenwald Ctr. Cultural Enrichment, 2001—; co-founder Power of Prayer Bible Inst. and Sem., 2002—04. Incorporator Spectrum for Living, Snow Hill, NC, 1990—93; assoc. pastor Cry Out Loud Ministries, 2006—; presenter in field. Author: The Holy Spirit, Is He a Stranger in Your House?, 1997 (1999), Could it Be I'm Chosen? (Fear, Peer Pressure, Rejection), 1999; host (TV Show) Appearances on various morning TV shows., 2002—03; singer: You Can Love Again, 1985; author: Fear, Peer Pressure Rejection- Could it be I'm Chosen. Policy coun. chair person Greene Lamp Headstart Inc., Kinston, NC; v.p. Greene County Interfaith Vols., Snow Hill, NC, 1999—2001; host Parad in Honor Local Africa. Am. Heroes, 2004; cert. grantwriter HUD; press sec. Com. To Elect Don Davis for Mayor, Snow Hill, NC, 2002; sec. Snow Hill Dem. Party, Snow Hill, NC; asst. regional chmn. Dem. Get Out to Vote Campaign, 2002; coord. ticket sales Mal Williams Gospel World Tour, Germany, 1996; bd. dirs. Legal Aide, NC, 2002—. Recipient Cert. of Achievement, Goshen Rubber

Co., 1984, Cert. of Award, Snow Hill Primary Sch., 1985, Cert. of Appreciation, State of NC, Dept. of Correction & Human Resources, 1985 -1986, Award of Merit, East Carolina U. Sch. of Medicine / Project Concern Internat., 1988 - 1990, Cert. of Recognition, Self Image Bldg. Program, 1989, Letter of Appreciation, First Lady Hillary Rodham Clinton, 1998, Letter of Recognition, N.C. Gen. Assembly - Marian McLawhorn 9th Dist., 1999 -2001, Friends of Project Head Start award, 1999, cert. of Excellence, N.C. Hist. Preservation Office, 2003; Nat. Trust Diversity scholar, 2004. Mem.: N.C. Ctr. for Non Profit Gifts In Kind Internat., Nat. Trust. for Hist. Preservation, Greene County Arts & Hist. Soc. (bd. dirs. 2001—03, neighborhood affairs com., vice chmn. hist. commn. 2002—03). Achievements include initiated process of Nat. Register Nomination for Snow Hill Colored, Greene Co. Sch; partnering with Vocational Rehabilitation to open first transitional house in Greene County, NC; Established Rosenwald Center, counties first community development corporation. Avocations: travel, reading, counseling, research, history. Home: PO Box 343 Snow Hill NC 28580 Office Phone: 252-747-4912. Personal E-mail: rcenter@earthlink.net.

STEVENS, KATHERINE, secondary school educator; b. Ypsilanti, Mich., July 21, 1942; d. Francis Raymond and Eileen Agnes Simkins; m. Jack Alan Stevens, Nov. 11, 1962 (dec.); children: John Alan, Merry Margaret. BS in English and History, U. Dubuque, Iowa, 1974; MA in English, Middlebury Coll., 1985. Cert. tchr., Iowa. Tchr. Dubuque Cmty. Schs., 1976—. Facilitator of planning insts., mem. nat. faculty Expeditionary Learning Outward Bound, Cambridge, Mass., 1993—. Contbr. poetry to publs. Pres., Dubuque Fine Arts Soc., 1988-94, 2000-03; bd. dirs. Dubuque Mus. Arts, 1985-89, 90-93; mem Dubuque Human Rights Commn., 1993-96, 2000-03. Named Dubuque Comty. Schs. Tchr. of Yr., 2004. Mem. Iowa Poetry Assn. (area rep.), Nat. Coun. Tchrs. English. Roman Catholic. Avocations: reading, gardening, writing.

STEVENS, KRISTINA DIANE, art educator; b. Park Ridge, Ill., Nov. 26, 1972; d. Kenneth Warren and Janet Lee Kloss; m. Todd Edward Stevens, July 27, 2002. AA, Coll. of DuPage, 1992; BS in Art Edn., No. Ill. U., 1994; M Curriculum and Instrn., U. Ill., 2001. Cert. art tchr. Ill. Art tchr. Cmty. Unit Sch. Dist., Oswego, Ill., 1995—2000, Geneva, Ill., 2000—. Art dir. Sandwich (Ill.) Park Dist., 1993; part-time mgr. Health Track Sports Wellness, Glen Ellyn, Ill., 2005—06; owner Kidz Dezign Kreationz, Glen Ellyn, 2000—; presenter in field. Sch. murals. Vol. art program TLC Camp, Lombard, Ill., 2004, 2006; religious edn. tchr. St. Petronille Ch., Glen Ellyn, 2002—05. Peg Bond scholar, No. Ill. U., 1994. Mem.: Art Inst. Chgo., Ill. Art Edn. Assn., Nat. Art Edn. Assn. Avocations: painting, gardening. Office: Harrison St Sch 201 N Harrison St Geneva IL 60134

STEVENS, LINDA K., lawyer; BA cum laude, Kalamazoo Coll., 1984; JD cum laude, Univ. Mich., 1987. Bar: Ill. 1987, U.S. Dist. Ct. No. Ill. 1987, U.S. Dist. Ct. Ctrl. Ill., U.S. Ct. Appeals 7th cir. 1993, U.S. Ct. Appeals 4th cir. Ptnr. Schiff Hardin, Chgo. Adj. faculty Northwestern U. Sch. Law, Nat. Inst. Trial Advocacy. Contbr. articles law jour. Mem.: ABA. Office: Schiff Hardin 6600 Sears Tower Chicago IL 60606-6473

STEVENS, LIZBETH JANE, special education educator, researcher; b. Angola, Ind., Oct. 31, 1949; d. Gilbert Emmett Curme and Billie Jean Bassett; m. John Alden Stevens, Feb. 11, 1947; children: Kimberly Jean Steiner, Joshua Alexander, Miranda Christine. BA, U. Mich., 1974, MS, 1976; PhD, Wayne State U., 1992. Cert. clin. competence in speech-language pathology Am. Speech-Language-Hearing Assn., 1977. Speech-lang. pathologist Warren Woods Pub. Schs., Mich., 1978—98; assoc. prof. dept. spl. edn. Ea. Mich. U., Ypsilanti, 1998—; speech-lang. pathologist Daly's Speech & Lang. Ctr., Farmington, 2002, Northville Pub. Schs. Adj. instr. Wayne State U., Detroit, 1997—98, Marygrove Coll., 1990—95; presentor, spkr. William Beaumont Parenting Program, Beaumont Hosp., Royal Oak, 1989—94. Contbr. articles to profl. jours. Pres. bd. dirs. Mich. Speech-Lang.-Hearing Found., 2006. Recipient Continuing Edn. award, Am. Speech-Lang.-Hearing Assn., 1983, 1987, 1990, 1993, 1996, 1998, 2000, 2002, 2004, Clara B. Stoddard award, Wayne State U., 1987; scholar James B. Angell scholar, U. Mich., 1975. Mem.: Am. Speech-Lang.-Hearing Assn. (legis. councilor 1995—2000, leader state edn. advocacy 2000—04, asha-aspiire cadre 2001—04, legis. councilor 2005—), Mich. Speech-Lang.-Hearing Assn. (v.p. for pub. schs. 2000—03, pres.-elect 2004, pres. 2006). Office: Eastern Michgan University 128L Porter Ypsilanti MI 48197 Office Phone: 734-487-3300. Business E-Mail: lizbeth.stevens@emich.edu.

STEVENS, LORETTA MARIE, special education educator; b. Bethpage, N.Y., Nov. 26, 1955; d. Hamilton Thomas and Evelyn Barbara Pendergast; m. Louis C. Stevens, Apr. 2, 1987; children: Erin Michelle Cook, Megan Colleen Oneill. BS, Shenandoah U., Winchester, Va., 1995; MEd, James Madison U., Harrisonburg, Va., 1997; M of Ednl. Adminstrn., Shenandoah U., Winchester, Va., 2005. Cert. elem. edn. tchr. Va., 1995, spl. edn. tchr. Va., 1997, ednl. adminstr. Va., 2005. Learning disabilities specialist Warren County Pub. Schs., Front Royal, Va., 1995—2004, ednl. diagnostician, 2004—06, supr. spl. edn., 2006—. Lead tchr. for learning disabilities Warren County Pub. Schs., Front Royal, Va., 1996—2004, spl. edn. dept. chairperson, 1997—2004; individual edn. plan coord. Warren County Pub. Schools, Front Royal, Va., 1999—; mentor new spl. educators Old Dominion U., Newport News, Va., 1997—. Pres. PTA, Manassas Park, Va., 1986—89; mem./advisor 4-H Club, Warren County, Va., 2002—04; dir. children's choir St. John the Bapt. Cath. Ch., Front Royal, Va., 1989—93, dir. adult modern music choir, 1993—98. Mem.: ASCD, Therapeutic Riding Assn., Internat. Reading Assn., Learning Disabilities Assn., Coun. for Exceptional Children (Professionall Recognized Spl. Educator 200-2005). Achievements include development of Educational program to improve learning for students who are slow learners. Avocations: horseback riding, hiking. Office: Warren County Public Schs 210 N Commerce Ave Front Royal VA 22630 Office Phone: 540-635-2171 ext. 247.

STEVENS, LORI ANN LABEAU, school librarian, educator; b. Yakima, Wash., Dec. 31, 1959; d. Raymond L. and Irene A. LaBeau; m. Mark D. Stevens, Apr. 24, 1981; children: Elisabeth A., Jared S., Mark D., Jonathan R. BMus, Brigham Young U., 1983; MLS, Emporia State U., 1999. Pub. svcs.-media ref. libr. Orem Pub. Libr., Utah, 1991—99; media instrn. libr. Utah Valley State Coll., Orem, 1999—. Contbr. chapters to books. Chair libr. adv. commn. City of Orem, 2002. Recipient Merit award, Utah Humanities Coun., 2001, Trustees award Excellence, Utah Valley State Coll. Bd. Trustees, 2002. Mem.: ALA (assoc.; chair 2001—05), Video Round Table ALA (assoc.; program chair 2004—), Music Libr. Assn., Mountain Plains Chpt. (assoc.; mem. at large 2002—03), Utah Libr. Assn. (assoc.; mem. at large 2002—, Spl. Recognition award 2005), Music Libr. Assn. (assoc.; chair film music roundtable 2005—). Mem. Lds Ch. Avocations: singing, piano, hiking, travel, gardening. Office: Utah Valley State Coll Libr 800 W University Pky Orem UT 84058 Home Fax: 801-863-7065. Personal E-mail: stevenlo@uvsc.edu.

STEVENS, LYDIA HASTINGS, community volunteer; b. Highland Park, Ill., Aug. 2, 1918; d. Rolland T.R. and Ruth Shotwell (Beebe) Hastings; m. George Cooke Stevens, Nov. 2, 1940; children: Lydia Stevens Gustin, Priscilla Stevens Goldfarb, Frederick S., Elizabeth Stevens MacLeod, George H., Ruth Stevens Stellard. BA, Vassar Coll., 1939. State rep. 151st Dist. of Conn., Greenwich, 1988-92. Cons. Nat. Exec. Svc. Corps, N.Y.C., 1985. Pres. Greenwich YWCA, 1971-74, Greenwich Housing Coalition, 1982-86; v.p. planning Greenwich United Way, 1973-76; sr. warden Greenwich Christ Episcopal Ch., 1981-86; chmn. rev. commn. Episcopal Diocese of Conn., 1985-87; bd. dirs. Greenwich Libr., 1985-93; chmn. Greenwich Commn. Aging, 1986-88; pres., bd. dirs. Greenwich Broadcasting Corp., 1977-79; bd. dirs. Fairfield County Cmty. Found., 1992, United Way of Greenwich, Save the Sound, 1996—, League Conservation Voters Conn., 1999. Recipient Golden Rule award J.C. Penney, 1987, President's award Greenwich YWCA, 1992, Brava award, 1994, Conn. Assn. for Human Svc. Dirs. award, 1992; named Layperson of Yr., Coun. Chs. and Synagogues, 1995. Republican. Episcopalian. Avocations: sailing, organic gardening. Home: 125 West Ln Guilford CT 06437-3230

STEVENS, MARILYN RUTH, editor; b. Wooster, Ohio, May 30, 1943; d. Glenn Willard and Gretchen Elizabeth (Ihrig) Amstutz; m. Bryan J. Stevens, Oct. 11, 1969; children: Jennifer Marie, Gretchen Anna. BA, Coll. Wooster, 1965; MAT, Harvard U., 1966; JD, Suffolk U., 1975. Bar: Mass. 1975. Tchr. Lexington (Mass.) Pub. Schs., 1966-69; with Houghton Mifflin Co., Boston, 1969—, editl. dir. sch. depts., 1978-81, editl. dir. math. scies. sch. divsn., 1981-84, mng. editor sch. pub., 1984—2005. Mem.: Cosmopolitan Neighborhood Assn.

STEVENS, MAY, artist; b. Boston, June 9, 1924; d. Ralph Stanley and Alice Margaret (Dick) S.; m. Rudolf Baranik, June 5, 1948; 1 child, Steven. BFA, Mass. Coll. Art, 1946; postgrad., Academie Julian, Paris, 1948-49, Art Students League, 1948. Mem. faculty Sch. Visual Arts, N.Y.C., 1964-96, Skowhegan Sch. Painting and Sculpture, 1992, Vt. Studio Ctr., 1997, 2005, Santa Fe Art Inst., 2000, 2003. Lectr. Royal Coll. Art, London, 1981, U. Wis.-Racine, 1973, Coll. Art Assn., Washington, 1975; sole juror Am. Drawing Biennial, Coll. William and Mary, Williamsburg, Va., 2000; lectr. Coll. Santa Fe, 1998, Santa Fe Art Inst., 2003. One-woman shows: Terry Dintenfass Gallery, N.Y.C., 1971, Cornell U., 1973, Douglass Coll., Rutgers U., 1974, Lerner-Heller Gallery, N.Y.C., 1975, 76, 78, 81, Clark U., 1982, Boston U. Art Gallery, 1984, Frederick S. Wight Gallery, UCLA, 1985, U. Md., College Park, 1985, Real Art Ways, Hartford, Conn., 1988, New Mus. Contemporary Art, 1988, Orchard Gallery, Derry, No. Ireland, 1988, Kenyon Coll., Gambier, Ohio, 1988, Greenville County (S.C.) Art Mus., 1991, Herter Gallery, U. Mass., Amherst, 1991, U. Colo., Boulder, 1993, U. N.Mex., Albuquerque, 1996, Mary Ryan Gallery, N.Y.C., 1996, 97, 99, 2001, 2003, 2005, Mus. Fine Arts, Boston, 1999, LewAllen Contemporary, Santa Fe, 1998, Minn. Inst. Art, 2005, Nat. Mus. Women in the Arts, Washington, 2005, Springfield (Mo.) Art Mus., 2006; exhibited in numerous group shows including most recently: Santa Fe Art Inst., 2002, Mus. Fine Art, Santa Fe, 2002, Guild Hall, East Hampton, N.Y., 2002, Hobart & William Smith Colls., 2002, We. Wash. U. Bellingham, 2002, UBS Paine Webber Art Gallery, N.Y.C., 2002, Deutsche Bank, N.Y.C., 2002, Bass Mus. Art, Miami Beach, Fla., 2002, Bklyn. Mus., 2003, Nat. Mus. Women in the Arts, Washington, 2003, Danese Gallery, N.Y.C., 2003, Tamarind Inst., Albuquerque, N.Mex., 2004, Harwood Mus., Taos, N.Mex., 2004, Ctr. Contemporary Arts Warehouse, Santa Fe, N.Mex., 2004, Nat. Acad. Design, N.Y.C., 2004, Evo Gallery, Santa Fe, N. Mex., 2005, Mason Gross Sch. of Arts, Rutgers U., New Brunswick, NJ, 2006; represented in permanent collections: Met. Mus. Art, N.Y.C., Mus. Modern Art, N.Y.C., Moca, L.A., San Francisco Mus. Art, New Mus. Contemporary Art, Whitney Mus., Bklyn. Mus., Herbert F. Johnson Mus., Cornell U., Mus. Fine Arts Boston, De Cordova Mus., Lincoln, Mass., Harwood Mus., Taos, N.Mex., Joslyn Art Mus., Omaha, Nat. Mus. Women in Arts, Washington, Minn. Inst. Art, Mpls., Springfield Mus. Art, Mo., Mcnhy Art Mus., San Antonio, Tex., McCormick Pl. Ctr. Art Coll., Chgo., Jacksonville Art Mus., Fla., Cleve. Mus. Art, Ill., U. Miami, Fla.; contbr. articles to various mags. Recipient Childe Hassam Purchase awards Nat. Inst. Arts and Letters, 1968, 69, 75, N.Y. State Coun. on Arts award, 1974, Disting. Alumna award Mass. Coll. Art, 1997, Disting. Artist award Coll. Art Assn., 2001, Edwin Palmer Meml. prize NAD, 2004; Andy Warhol Found. grantee for project space Headlands Ctr. for Arts, Sausalito, Calif., 2001; MacDowell Colony fellow, 1971, 72, 74, 75, 81, 82, 84, Bunting Inst. fellow Radcliffe Coll., 1988-89; Line Assn. grantee for artists books, 1978; grantee NEA, 1983, Guggenheim, 1986; honoree Women's Caucus for Art, 1990. Mem.: NAT, Coll. Art Assn.

STEVENS, MURIEL KAUIMAEOLE LEE, elementary school educator; b. Hana, Hawaii, May 29, 1942; d. Charles Pohaku and Violet Leimamo (Wahihako) Lee; m. James Gary Stevens, 1964 (div. 1976); 1 child, James Todd (dec.). AS, Ch. Coll. Hawaii, 1962; BS in Edn., Brigham Young U., 1964; postgrad., U. Utah, 1969, U. Hawaii, 1974—. Cert. and lic. elem. tchr., Hawaii. 1st grade tchr. Woodstock Elem. Sch., Salt Lake City, 1965-69; kindergarten-1st grade team tchr. Ewa (Hawaii) Elem. Sch., 1971-78; tchr. Honowai Elem. Sch., Waipahu, Hawaii, 1978—99, Hana Elem.-HS, 1999—. Aerospace tchr., coord. after sch. improvement program Honowai Elem. Sch., 1991, 95; mem. Citizen Amb. Program, Spokane, 1987-95; participant Tchr. in Space program NASA, 1985-86. Spiritual living tchr. LDS Ch., Kaneohe, 1994, choir mem., 1992-94, sem. tchr., single adult rep. Waipahu II ward, 1996; tchr. and music leader LDS Primary at Hana Branch, 1999-2001; amb. People to People Internat., Spokane, Wash., 1987-95. With CAP, 1985-95. Recipient Aerospace Edn. Achievement award Aux. USAF CAP, 1985. Mem. ASCD, Hawaii Parent, Tchr., Student Assn., NEA, Hawaii State Tchrs. Assn., Wilson Ctr. Assocs., Acad. Polit. Sci., World Aerospace Edn. Orgn. Republican. Avocations: hula dancing, swimming, sewing, baking, arts and crafts. Home: PO Box 879 Hana HI 96713-0879

STEVENS, NICOLE TANYA, music educator; b. Fort Hood, Tex., Sept. 18, 1964; d. Kenneth Sterling Stevens. MusB, U. Tex., Austin, 1988. Cert. music tchr. Tex., 1988, spl. edn. tchr. Tex., 1996. Band dir. Comal Ind. Sch. Dist., New Braunfels, Tex., 1989—90, Sharyland Ind. Sch. Dist., Mission, Tex., 1990—92, Seguin Ind. Sch. Dist., Tex., 1992—93; head injury specialist Tangram, San Marcos, Tex., 1993—94; ADL counselor Brown-Karhan Head Injury and Psychiat. Care, Dripping Springs, Tex., 1994—97; spl. edn. tchr. Temple Ind. Sch. Dist., Tex., 1998—99; ADLK counselor MHMR, San Marcos, 1998—2000; music tchr. St. Cyril and Methodius Sch., Granger, Tex., 2001—02; nurses aide Will-o-Bell Nursing Home, Bartlett, Tex., 2001—02; band dir. St. Joseph Cath. Sch., Bryan, Tex., 2002—05; elem. music tchr. La Marque Ind. Sch. Dist., Tex., 2005—; studio tchr. Sing & Play Fine Arts Studio, Pearland, Tex., 2005—. Pres. music dist. 2 Tex. Assn. Pvt. and Parochial Schs., 2004—05. Episcopalian. Avocations: hiking, travel. Home: 801 E Nasa Rd 1 #2700 Webster TX 77598

STEVENS, PAULETTE, daycare administrator; b. Cleve., Jan. 26, 1947; d. Joseph George and Mildred Margie Henderson; m. David Leon Stevens, Jan. 28; children: Dewayne, Fred, Derrick, Lisa, Shaun Knox. Degree, Pitts. C.C., 1976, Calif. State U., 1977, Allegheny C.C., 1976. Dir., owner, asst. tchr. Sewickley (Pa.) Care and Devel. Ctr., 1973-81, Family Day Care, Coraopolis, Pa., 1982-91; dir., owner Mt. Olive Day Care, Coraopolis, Pa., 1991—. Mem. Kiwanis, Women in Christian Ministries (bd. dirs. 1992—). Baptist. Avocations: reading, sewing. Home: 1413 5th Ave Coraopolis PA 15108-2025

STEVENS, PHYLLIS A., conceptual artist; b. Washington, June 14, 1931; d. Carle Wright Stevens and Maybelle Bayley Whiting; 1 child, Karen. Student, Antioch Coll., 1953, Art Students League, Acad. of Realist Art. Self employed free lance artist, 1956—; set designer Eccentric Circles Theater, N.Y.C.; stage sets dir. Theater Genesis, N.Y.C.; designer CBS Network, Shadow Puppet Productions, N.Y.C., Am. Opera Soc., Shadow Puppet Production, N.Y.C. Exhibitions include Salmagundi Club, NYC, Philmont Ranch, N. Mex., Art Expo, NYC, Artist and Artisans, NJ, Hunter Crafts Show, NYC, Living Handcrafts, Mus. of Contemporary Crafts, Mus. of Fine Arts, Del., Bonwit-Teller, N.Y.C., Bratta Gallery, Antioch Coll., Ohio, prin. works include Mural in Lobby, Internat. Longshoreman's Union, Anthony Anastasia Med. Ctr., NY, Four built-in panels, Private home, NY; contbr. articles to profl. jours. Mem.: Writers Guild of Am. East, N.Y. Artists Equity Assn., Graphic Artists Guild, Chatham (N.C.) Plein Air, Salmagundi Club. Home: 214 Weaver Mine Trail Chapel Hill NC 27517 Personal E-mail: phyllisstevens@earthlink.net.

STEVENS, RHEA CHRISTINA, lawyer; b. Chgo., Dec. 25, 1964; d. Samuel Nowell and Rhea Mae (Lipham) S.; m. Peter Linzer, June 20, 1992; 1 child, Grayson Nowell. BS in Psychology, U. Houston, 1989; MEd, Cambridge Coll., 1987; JD, U. Houston, 1992. Bar: Tex. 1992. Instr., client liaison Hippocrates Health Inst., Boston, 1985-86; reorganization cons. Psychotechnics, Inc., Cary, Glenview, Ill., 1987-88; pvt. practice law Houston, 1992—. Founder, owner Aristic Enterprises I and II, 1995, breeder Great Danes, Anatolian Shepherds, Papillons and Dobermans for svc. orgns. and show-August Kennels, 1988—; canine behaviorist; founder DemiSance Ctr., 1999. Rep. mid-Am. chpt. ARC to Nat. Conv., 1980; bd. dirs., treas. Clark Rd. Found., Houston, 1990-92, Houston ACLU, 1990-92; counsellor Boston Area Rape Crisis Ctr., 1986-87. Recipient cert. commendation ARC, 1979-80. Mem. State Bar Tex. (disability issues com. 1996—, Pro Bono Coll. 1995—). Avocations: training and exhibiting dogs, locksmithing, computer consulting. Office: 6655 Arabia Ln Ste 100 Sealy TX 77474

STEVENS, RISË, performing arts association administrator; b. NYC; m. Walter Surovy; 1 child, Nicolas. Student, Juilliard Sch.; Hon. Degree Smith Coll., Coll. of Senecas, Russell Sage Coll., Rider Coll., U. Pa., Baylor U., Rice U., Mercy Coll., Mannes Coll Music, Hobart Coll., Cleve. Inst. Music, Va. Commonwealth U. Co-gen. mgr. Met. Opera Nat. Co., N.Y.C., 1980-88; pres. The Mannes Coll. Music, N.Y.C., 1975-78; mng. dir. Met. Opera Bd., N.Y.C. Performer Prague Opera, Vienna State Opera, Royal Opera, NY Met. Opera, 1938-61; starred in films, concerts, TV, and radio. Mem. Nat. Endowment for Arts (co-chair music panel 1981-83), N.Y. State Coun. on Arts (chmn. music panel), Met. Opera Guild (bd. dirs.), Wagnerian Soc. Buenos Aires, Sigma Alpha Iota. Office: Met Opera Assn Lincoln Ctr New York NY 10023

STEVENS, ROSEMARY A., medicine and public health historian, artist; b. Bourne, Eng. came to U.S., 1961, naturalized, 1968; d. William Edward and Mary Agnes (Tricks) Wallace; m. Robert B. Stevens, Jan. 28, 1961 (div. 1983); children: Carey, Richard; m. Jack D. Barchas, Aug. 9, 1994. BA, Oxford U., Eng., 1957; Diploma in Social Adminstrn., Manchester U., Eng., 1959; MPH, Yale U., 1963, PhD, 1968; LHD (hon.), Hahnemann U., 1988; DSc (hon.), Northeastern Ohio U. Coll. Medicine, 1995; DSc, Rutgers U., 1995. Various hosp. adminstrv. positions, Eng., 1959-61; rsch. assoc. Med. Sch. Yale U., 1962-68, asst. prof. Med. Sch., 1968-71, assoc. prof. Med. Sch., 1971-74, prof. pub. health Med. Sch., 1974-76; master Jonathan Edwards Coll., 1974-75; prof. dept. health systems mgmt. and polit. sci. Tulane U., New Orleans, 1976-78, chmn. dept. health systems mgmt., 1977-78; prof. history and sociology of sci. U. Pa., Phila., 1979—2002, chmn. dept., 1980-83, 86-91, UPS Found. prof., 1990-91, dean Sch. Arts and Scis., Thomas S. Gates prof., 1991-96, Stanley I. Sheerr prof., 1997—2001, prof. emeritus, 2002—. Prof. emeritus U. Pa., Phila., 2002-; vis. lectr. Johns Hopkins U., 1967-68; guest scholar Brookings Instn., Washington, 1967-68; acad. visitor London Sch. Econs., 1962-64, 1973-74; DeWitt Wallace disting. scholar social medicine and pub. policy, dept. psychiatry Weill Cornell Med. Coll., 2005—. Author: Medical Practice in Modern England: The Impact of Specialization and State Medicine, 1966, new edit., 2003, American Medicine and the Public Interest, 1971, rev. edit., 1998, In Sickness and in Wealth: American Hospitals in the Twentieth Century, 1989, rev. edit., 1999, (with others) Foreign Trained Physicians and American Medicine, 1972, Welfare Medicine in America, 1974, new edit., 2003, Alien-Doctors: Foreign Medical Graduates in American Hospitals, 1978. Bd. dirs. Milbank Meml. Fund. Rockefeller Humanities fellow, 1982-83, Guggenheim fellow, 1984-85; Bellagio Study and Conf. scholar, 1984; recipient Frohlich medal Royal Soc. Medicine, London, 1986, Baxter Found. prize distinction in health svcs. rsch., 1990, James A. Hamilton Book award Am. Coll. Healthcare Execs. best book, 1990, Welch medal distinction in history of medicine Am. Assn. History Medicine, 1990, Arthur Viseltear award history pub. health Am. Pub. Health Assn., 1990, Nicholas E. Davies award Piedmont Hosp., Atlanta, 1997, Investigator award in health policy rsch. Robert Wood Johnson Found., 1998-2003, Carlson award for extraordinary contbns. to history of medicine Cornell U., Weill Med. Coll, 2000., Lifetime Achievement award Am. Assn. History Medicine, 2002. Fellow Am. Acad. Arts and Scis.; mem. AAAS (chmn. sect. history and philosophy of sci., 2002-03), Inst. Medicine of Nat. Acad. Sci., Am. Sociol. Assn., Am. Assn. for History of Medicine, Coll. Physicians of Phila.Am. Bd. Med. Specialties (pub. mem., bd. dirs.), Cosmopolitan Club. Home: 500 E 77th St Apt 419 New York NY 10162 Office Phone: 212-746-5798. E-mail: ras2023@medcornell.edu.

STEVENS, SHARON COX, lawyer; b. 1948; m. Michael Callahan. BA, Washington State Univ.; JD, McGeorge Sch. Law. Bar: Oreg. 1977. Ptnr. Callahan & Stevens, Keizer, Oreg. Mem.: ABA (bd. gov. 2004—). Office: Callahan & Stevens 5845 Shoreview Lane N PO Box 20937 Keizer OR 97307-0937

STEVENS, SUSAN SELTENREICH CIRILLO, special education educator; b. Rockville Centre, NY, Apr. 16, 1962; d. Richard Paul and Estelle Duboise Seltenreich; m. John Stafford Cirillo (div.); children: Adam Cirillo, Jeremy Cirillo, Nicholas Cirillo; m. Peter Stevens, Oct. 4, 2003. AS in Early Childhood Edn., SUNY, Farmingdale, 1982; BS in Edn., SUNY, Geneseo, 1986; MEd, U. North Tex., 1992. Cert. lay min. United Meth. Ch. of N.Y., local lay min. United Meth. Ch. of N.Y.; spl. edn. tchr. N.Y., tchr. nursery, kindergarten, grades 1-6 N.Y., spl. edn. tchr. K-12 Wash., tchr. ESL Wash., elem. edn. tchr. Wash., early childhood educator Wash., spl. edn. tchr. Tex., tchr. ESL Tex., elem. edn. tchr. Tex., kindergarten tchr. Tex. Spl. edn. tchr. United Cerebral Palsy of Queens, Jamaica, NY, 1987—88; elem. and ESL educator Herbert Marcus Elem. Sch., Dallas Ind. Sch. Dist., 1988—92, spl. edn. educator Hillcrest H.S., 1994—96; enrichment educator The Huntington Learning Ctr., Issaquah, Wash., 1999—2000; spl. edn. educator Beaver Lake Mid. Sch., Issaquah Sch. Dist., 2000—02; spl. edn. educator Silas Wood 6th Grade Ctr., South Huntington Union Free Sch. Dist., Huntington Sta., NY, 2000—. Author: (poetry) Mellie the Muskrat, 2004. Lay min., mem. edn. com., Sunday sch. educator, children's sermon min. Dix Hills (N.Y.) United Meth. Ch., 2002—05; Sunday sch. educator Faith United Meth. Ch., Issaquah, 2000—02, St. John's Luth. Ch., Columbia, Md., 1996—98; Sunday sch. educator, mem. worship and music coun. Preston Meadow Luth. Ch., Plano, Tex., 1988—96. Fellow ednl. grantee, South Huntington Parent Tchr. Ctr., 2004. Mem.: Coun. Exceptional Children (assoc.). Avocations: poetry, travel. Home: 3 Wexford St Huntington NY 11743 Office: Silas Wood 6th Grade Ctr 23 Harding Pl Huntington Station NY 11746 Office Phone: 631-425-5515. Personal E-mail: susanc001@msn.com. E-mail: sstevens@shufsd.org.

STEVENS, YVETTE MARIE See KHAN, CHAKA

STEVENSON, ALEXANDRA, professional tennis player; b. San Diego, Calif., Dec. 15, 1980; d. Samantha. Student, U. Colo. Mem. U.S. Fed Cup Team, 2003. Winner ITF/Midland, Mich., 1998, 13 of 15 grass court matches, 1999; semifinalist Wimbledon, 1999, U.S. Open, 1999; mem. U.S. Pan Am Games Team, 1999; jr. competition winner U.S. Open Jr., 1997, USTA Nat. Girls' 18s, 1997; jr. competition singles finalist USTA Nat. Girls' 18 Clay Courts, 1996; named Roles Rookie of the Yr., Tennis Mag., 1999. Avocations: singing, ballet, swimming, dance.

STEVENSON, AMANDA (SANDY STEVENS), librettist, composer, songwriter; b. Bklyn., Oct. 24, 1943; d. Haakon and Grace Svendsen. Cert. Nat. Bur. Document Examiners. Composer, librettist, Nellie Bly, Victorine, (screenplay) The Last Assignment Mem. Actors Equity Assn., BMI, Songwriters Guild. Democrat. Avocations: chess, art history, songwriting. Home and Office: 35-43 84th St Jackson Heights NY 11372 Office Phone: 718-429-5998.

STEVENSON, ANDREA J. (ANDI STEVENSON), not-for-profit executive; m. John H. Hewett. V.p. venue sales and client mgmt. Kimmel Ctr. Inc., Phila. Named one of 40 Under 40, Phila. Bus. Jour., 2006. Office: Kimmel Ctr, Inc 260 S Broad St, Ste 901 Philadelphia PA 19102 Office Fax: 215-790-5801. E-mail: astevenson@kimmelcenter.org.*

STEVENSON, CYNTHIA, actress; b. Piedmont, Calif., Aug. 2, 1962; Actor: (films) The Player, 1992, Watch It, 1993, Forget Paris, 1995, Home for the Holidays, 1995, Happiness, 1998, Air Bud: Golden Receiver, 1998, Agent Cody Banks, 2003, Agent Cody Banks 2: Destination London, 2004, Neverwas, 2005, (TV films) A Father's Homecoming, 1988, Double Your Pleasure, 1989, To the Moon, Alice, 1990, (TV series) Off the Wall, 1986-87, My Talk Show, 1990-91, Bob, 1992-93, Hope & Gloria, 1995-96, Dead Like Me, 2003-04, Men in Trees, 2006, (theater) Ladies Room.*

STEVENSON, DENISE L., diversified financial services company executive, consultant, realtor; b. Washington, Sept. 18, 1946; d. Pierre and Alice (Mardrus) D'Auga; m. Walter Henry Stevenson, Oct. 17, 1970 (div. 1990). AA, Montgomery Coll., 1967; BA in Econs./Bus. Mgmt., N.C. State U., 1983; cert. legal asst., Meredith Coll., 1989; cert. in mgmt., Fin. Women Internat., 1990. Lic. ins. agt.; accredited buyer rep. Nat. Assn. of Realtors, grad. Realtor Inst., sr. real estate specialist, e-PRO Coun. of Residential Speclaists, cert. new home specialist. Savs. counselor Perpetual Bldg. Assn. (now Crestar Bank), Washington, 1968—70; regional asst. v.p. 1st Fed. Savs. (now Centura Bank, Rocky Mount), NC, 1971—83; pres., owner Diversified Learning Svcs., Raleigh, 1983—; pres., treas. Daily Life Svcs., Inc., 1994—99; realtor Prudential Carolinas Realty, 2002—. Instr. Inst. Fin. Edn., Raleigh, 1983—89, Am. Inst. Banking, 1986. Mem. Am. Bus. Women's Assn. (Woman of Yr. 1982), Fin. Women Internat. (cert. leader 1987, Mem. of Yr. award 1992, N.C. Woman of Yr. 1992), Laurel Hills Women's Club (pres. 1974-75, Raleigh), Omicron Delta Epsilon, Broker Assoc. Hon. Soc. Avocation: fishing. Office: Diversified Learning Svcs PO Box 33231 Raleigh NC 27636-3231 E-mail: divlrnserv@aol.com.

STEVENSON, ELIZABETH, author, educator; b. Ancon, Panama, C.Z., June 13, 1919; d. John Thurman and Bernice (Upshaw) S. BA magna cum laude, PBK Agnes Scott Coll., 1941. With war time agys. U.S. Govt., Atlanta, 1942-47; order asst. Atlanta Pub. Library, 1948-56; asst. to coll. dean Emory U., Atlanta, 1960-74; from research assoc. to Candler prof. Grad. Inst. Liberal Arts, Emory U., Atlanta, 1974-87. Author: The Crooked Corridor: A Study of Henry James, 1949, Henry Adams, 1955, 98 (Bancroft prize 1956), Lafcadio Hearn, 1961, reissued as The Grass Lark, A Study of Lafcadio Hearn, 1998, Babbitts and Bohemians, 1967, 98, Park Maker: A Life of Frederick Law Olmsted, 1977, Figures in a Western Landscape: Men and Women of the Northern Rockies, 1994; editor: A Henry Adams Reader, 1958. Guggenheim fellow, 1950-51, 58-59; grantee Rockefeller Found., 1958-59, Am. Coun. Learned Socs., 1975; recipient Faculty Rsch. Fund award Emory U., 1960s, 70s, summer stipend NEH, 1974. Mem. Authors Guild, Phi Beta Kappa. Democrat.

STEVENSON, FRANCES KELLOGG, retired museum program director; b. Boston; d. Charles Summers and Alice deGueldry (Stevens) S.; m. James Richard Wein, 1971 (div. 1989). BA, Wells Coll., Aurora, N.Y., 1967; MA, Oxford U., England, 1972; MBA, U. Pa., Phila., 1992. Publs. officer Nat. Portrait Gallery Smithsonian Instn., Washington, 1974—2001, strategic planning officer, 2001—06; ret., 2006. Bd. mem. Am. Friends of St. Hilda's Coll., Oxford U.; mem. St. John's Episcopal Ch., Georgetown. James E. Webb fellow Smithsonian Instn., 1988-89. Mem. Sulgrave Club, Am. Friends St. Hilda's coll., Oxford U. (bd. mem.). Home: 2724 Ordway St NW Apt 4 Washington DC 20008-5047

STEVENSON, GALE, librarian; b. Bklyn., Oct. 8, 1942; d. Clifford Edwin and Ruth Helen (Davis) Spates; m. Andrew Kenneth Stevenson Jr., Aug. 28, 1988. BA, Drew U., 1964; MLS, Pratt Inst., 1970. Reference asst. Purdue U., West Lafayette, Ind., 1964-68; libr. Yonkers Pub. Libr., Yonkers, N.Y., 1968-71; adminstrv. svcs. libr. Westchester Community Coll., Valhalla, N.Y., 1971-78; libr. Tompkins County Pub. Libr., Ithaca, N.Y., 1978-88, Bus. Libr., Bklyn. Pub. Libr., Bklyn., 1988—, sr. bus. libr., 1988-93; divsn. chief social scis. Bklyn. Pub. Libr., Bklyn., 1993-94, asst. bus/ libr., 1994—. Office: Bklyn Pub Libr Bus Libr 280 Cadman Plz W Brooklyn NY 11201-2701

STEVENSON, JO ANN C., federal bankruptcy judge; b. 1942; AB, Rutgers U., 1965; JD cum laude, Detroit Coll. Law, 1979. Bar: Mich. 1979. Law clk. to Vincent J. Brennan, Mich. Ct. Appeals, Detroit, 1979; law clk. to Cornelia G. Kennedy, U.S. Ct. Appeals for 6th Cir., Detroit, 1980; assoc. Hertzberg, Jacob & Weingarten, P.C., Detroit, 1980-87; chief judge U.S. Bankruptcy Ct., Grand Rapids, Mich., 1987—. Office: US Bankruptcy Ct NW1 1 Divsn Grand Rapids MI 49503

STEVENSON, JOYCE R.L., psychologist; d. Harry Woodson Lamberston and Rosetta P. Lamberston; m. William J. Stevenson, Aug. 30, 1957 (dec. 2006); children: Cathy A. Hansell, Jeffrey L. Steveson. BA in Law justice, Glassboro State Coll., Glassboro, NJ, 1979; MA Sch. Psychologist, Glassboro State Coll., 1985. Cert. Sch. Psychologist NJ. Sr. probation officer Camden County Probation Dept., Camden, NJ, 1976—89; sch. psychologist Gloucester County Spl. Svc. Sch. Dist., Sewell, NJ, 1991—92, Edgewood Sch. HS, Sicklerville, NJ, 1992—94; chairperson and child study team sch. psychologist Vineland Bd. Edn., Vineland, NJ, 1994—2003. Contbr. scientific papers. Mem.: MENSA, DAR (treas.), Colonial Dames Seventeenth Century, Swedish Colonial Soc. Avocations: genealogy, tai chi. Personal E-mail: joycerls@earthlink.net.

STEVENSON, MARSHA JOAN, librarian; b. Moline, Ill., July 10, 1953; d. Theodore Thomas Stevenson, Laverne Joan Stevenson; m. George King Rugg; 1 child, Gwendolyn Rugg. MA in Libr. Sci., U. Wis., 1976. Ref. libr. Ohio State U., Newark, Ohio, 1976—79; catalog/ref. libr. U. Pitts., 1979—83; head access svc. divsn. U. Mo., Columbia, Mo., 1984—89; head ref. dept. U. Notre Dame, Ind., 1990—. Contbr. chapters to books What is Written Remains: Historical Essays on the Libraries of Notre Dame, 1994, Technical Services Today and Tomorrow, 1990, articles to profl. jours. Bd. dirs. Holy Cross Athletic Assn., South Bend, Ind., 1997—2002. Mem.: ALA (vice chair/chair LAMA bldg. and equipment sect. 2001—03), Beta Phi Mu. Home: 127 E North Shore Dr South Bend IN 46617 Office: Univ Notre Dame 243 Hesburgh Libr Notre Dame IN 46556 Business E-Mail: stevenson.2@nd.edu.

STEVENSON, MARY COMPHER, pharmacist, educator; b. Blanton, Fla., Apr. 13, 1932; d. Robert Grubb and Frances Parker Compher; m. Bill Stevenson (dec.); children: Will, Paul, Mike. BS in Pharmacy, U. Ga., Athens, 1953. Pharmacist Emory U. Hosp., Atlanta, 1954; dir. of pharmacy Kennestone Hosp., Marietta, Ga., 1955—57; pharmacist Pharmerica, Smyrna, Ga., 1975—80, Emory Adventist Hosp., Smyrna, 1980—. Mem. sch. bd. Covenant Christian, Smyrna, 1985—2006. Mem.: Ga. Pharmacy Assn. Republican. Presbyn. Avocations: coin collecting/numismatics, stamp collecting/philately, travel, swimming. Home: 3880 Ridgewood Dr Smyrna GA 30080 Office: Emory Adventist Hosp 3949 S Cobb Dr Smyrna GA 30080

STEVENSON, NANCY NELSON, museum director; b. Annapolis, Md., Oct. 23, 1950; d. Perry Waldemar and Grace Anne Nelson; m. Roger Stevenson Jr., Nov. 18, 1972; children: Jennifer Loren, Matthew Austin. BA, Sarah Lawrence Coll., 1972. Tchr. Montgomery County (Md.) Pub. Schs., 1972—76; bd. dirs. Jr. League of Washington, 1988—89, 1990—92; trustee Nat. Mus. Women in the Arts, Washington, 1996—, sec. bd. of trustees, 1997—98, treas. bd. of trustees, 1998—2002, v.p. bd. trustees, 2002—04, pres. bd. trustees, 2004—. Co-author French immersion curriculum, 1974. Pres. Country Pl. Citizens Assn., Potomac, Md., 1983-84. Office: Nat Mus Women in the Arts 1250 New York Ave NW Washington DC 20005-3970

STEVENSON, NORMA ANN, elementary school educator, real estate agent, property manager; b. Detroit, Aug. 10, 1931; d. Austin Sipple and Viola (Anderson) Neeb; m. Thomas J. Stevenson Jr., June 20, 1953 (div. Feb. 1983); children: Mark, Lori Ann Smith, Thomas J. III; m. Gordon E. Sawyers, July 6, 2003. BS, Mich. State U., 1953; MA, Wayne State U., 1972. Tchr. Grosse Pointe Schs., Mich., 1969—87; real estate sales staff Schweitzer, Prudential, Grosse Pointe, 1979—2000; owner, pres., real estate developer Thompson Marlor Fin. Mgmt. Co., Grosse Pointe, 1980—. Bridge dir. Celebrity Cruise Line, 2001—, Norweigian Cruise Line, 2001—; developer condominium conversion Stevenson Condominium, Grosse Pointe, 1995; lectr., spkr. in field. Treas. PTA, Grosse Pointe, 1968; vol. Hospice, Grosse Pointe, 1990—94, Meals on Wheels, Grosse Pointe, 1999—2003; mem. St. James Luth. Ch., Grosse Pointe, 1940—2006. Mem.: PEO, Am. Contract Bridge League (dir.), Delta Kappa Gamma (Woman of Distinction 1980). Republican. Avocations: sailing, bridge, bicycling, travel, exercise. Home (Winter): 16236 W Tuscany Way Surprise AZ 85374 Home (Summer): 225 N Maloney Dr North Platte NE 69101-8901

STEVENSON, RUTH CARTER, art patron; b. Ft. Worth, Oct. 19, 1923; d. Amon Giles and Nenetta (Wiess) Carter; m. J. Lee Johnson III, June 8, 1946 (div. Feb. 1978); children: Sheila Broderick Johnson, J. Lee, Karen Carter Johnson Hixon, Catherine Johnson, Mark Lehane; m. John R. Stevenson, May 21, 1983 BA, Sarah Lawrence Coll., 1945. Pres. Ft. Worth Jr. League, 1954—55, Amon Carter Mus., Ft. Worth, 1961—, Amon G. Carter Found., 1982—, Arts Coun. Greater Ft. Worth, 1963—64; bd. regents U. Tex. Austin, 1963—69; v.p. internat. coun. Mus. Modern Art, 1965—72; bd. dirs. Nat. Trust Hist. Preservation, 1968—74; bd. dirs. Nat. Coll. Fine Arts Smithsonian Instn., Washington, 1966—70; bd. dirs. U. Dallas, 1971—74; trustee Tex. Christian U., 1974—86, Nat. Gallery Art, Washington, 1979—97; bd. dirs. Nat. Trust Hist. Preservation. Pres. Ft. Worth City Art Commn., 1960-80; nat. chmn. collector's com. Nat. Gallery Art, Washington, 1975—97; mem. vis. com. Fogg Mus., Cambridge, Mass., 1978-83 Roman Catholic. Office: Amon Carter Mus 3501 Camp Bowie Blvd Fort Worth TX 76107 Office Phone: 817-989-5095.

STEVENS-SOLLMAN, JEANNE LEE, artist; d. Ernest and Virginia; m. Philippus Steven Sollman, Oct. 16, 1971 BS, R.I. Coll., 1968, BFA, 1970; MFA Ceramics, Pa. State U., 1972, postgrad., 1986—87. Artist in residence, instr. ceramics Juniata Coll., Huntington, Pa., 1975—76; artist in residence State College Area H.S., Pa., 1995; instr. ceramics Haystack Mountain Sch. Crafts, Deer Isle, Maine, 1977, Pa. State U., University Park, 1978. Coord., dir. Trout Run Medallic Symposium, St. Marys, Pa., 1997, 99, 2001; juror Ctrl. Pa. Festival Arts, 2005, Polish Art Union Exhibit, Colorado Springs, 2001, Polish medals from Collection of Medallic Mus. Art, Wraclaw, Hands Across the Sea exhibit, 2002, F.I.D.E.M., Paris Mint; curator invitational Medallic Sculptors, Altoona, Pa., 2004; cons. in field One-person shows include Handcrafters Gallery, Portland, Maine, 1984, Soc. Arts and Crafts, Boston, 1984, Susan McLeod Gallery, Sarasota, Fla., 1984, Palisander Gallery, Taos, N.Mex., 1986, 15 Steps, Ithaca, N.Y., 1987, Shippensburg (Pa.) U., 2001, Am. Philatelic Ctr., Bellefonte, Pa., 2004; recent group exhbns. include The Pen and Brush Club, N.Y., 1997, 98 (Medallic Art Co. award), 99, 2000, 01, 02 (Charlotte Dunwiddie Meml. award, III Internat. Biennial Contemporary medal, Seixal, Portugal, 2003), Art Show at the Dog Show, Wichita, 2002, Rack and Hamper Gallery, N.Y., 1997, 99, 2000, 2003, Gallery Heian, Kyoto, Japan, 1997, Art Alliance Gallery, Lemont, Pa., 1997, 2d pl., 2005, Campus Mall Pa. State U., University Park, 1998, 99, 2000, Sculptures at Sea Mus., The Hague, 1998, Benson Park, Loveland, Colo., 1997, 98, 99, 2000, Bedford (Pa.) Art Arts Coun., 1999, So. Alleghenies Mus. Art, Loretto, Pa., 1999, 2001, Mus. of the Dog, St. Louis, 1999, Altoona Campus Pa. State U., 1999, Queensboro (N.Y.) C.C., 2000, Goethe Nat. Mus., Weimar, Germany, 2000, HUB Pa. State U., 2001, Shippensburg U., 2001, Maguro Mus. Art, Kyoto, 2001, AMSA Ornamental Metal Mus. Art, Memphis, 2003, Ottawa War Mus., 2002, West Sylvania Art Exhibit (First Prize award), 2003, (Hon. Mention), 2005, Bienal Internacionale Medalha Comtemporanea, Seixal, 2003, Animals in Art, Baton Rouge, 2004, Antigos Fefeitorios da Mundet, Seixal, 2004, Arts Alliance, Pa. (2d Pl. award), others; represented in permanent collection at State Mus., Harrisburg, Pa., So. Allegheneis Mus. Art, Loretto, Pa., Brit. Mus., London, Medallic Mus., Warsaw, Poland, Smithonian Inst.; commd. completion of Presdl. Mace, Iowa State U., 2004, Hon. Alumni award, Alumni Fellow award Pa. State Alumni Assn., 2005, Arts and Humanities award of distinction Pa. State U., 2006 Co-partitioner Patton Concerned Citizens, Centre County, Pa., 1990 Recipient Distinction in Sculpture award So. Allegheneis Mus. Art, Loretto, 1997, Dutch Art Metal award Dutch Art Metal Soc., The Hague, 1998, 1st prize sculpture Rural Am. 2000, Harrisburg, Pa., 2000, J. Sanford award for Signal Achievement in Art of Medal; Designer Hon. Alumni award, Alumni Fellow Pa. State U. Alumni Assn., 2005, Designer for Arts and Humanities award, 2006 Fellow Am. Numismatic Soc. (J. Sanford Saltus award 1999, group show 2001); mem. Am. Sculpture Assn., Am. Numismatic Assn., Nat. Sculpture Soc., Pen and Brush (Margaret Sussman Meml. award 1999), Fedn. Internat. de la Medaille (juror Am. delegation, vice del. for USA 1999—), Am. Medallic Sculpture Assn. (juror, coord., 2d v.p. 1997—2000, pres. 2000-02, advisor 2002—), Medallic Art Soc. Can., Art in Common Avocations: gardening, dogtrials & showing, shepherding. Studio: Stevens Sollman Studios 318 N Fillmore Rd Bellefonte PA 16823-9047 E-mail: stevsollmn@aol.com.

STEVER, MARGO TAFT, poet; b. Cin., Mar. 4, 1950; d. David Gibson and Katharine Longworth (Whittaker) Taft; m. Donald Winfred Stever Jr., July 31, 1976; children: David Whittaker, James Taft. AB, Radcliffe Coll., 1972; EdM, Harvard U., 1974; MFA, Sarah Lawrence Coll., 1988. Asst. dir. N.H. Civil Liberties Union, Concord, 1976-77, dir. women's rights project, 1976-77; classroom tchr. learning disabled children The Krebs Sch., Lexington, Mass., 1975-76; staff asst. Senator Ted Stevens, U.S. Senate, Washington, 1974-75; founder, dir. Sleepy Hollow Poetry Series, Warner Library, Tarrytown, N.Y., 1983-89;m founder Hudson Valley Writers' Ctr., 1988, chair, 1988-2002; founder, co-editor: Slapering Hol Press, 1991—. Contbr. poetry and critical revs. to pub. mags., anthologies; author: Reading the Night Sky, 1996, Frozen Spring, 2002. Mem. Acad. Am. Poets, Poetry Soc. Am., Adirondack League Club, Abenakee Club, Sleepy Hollow Country Club, Mill Reef Club. Democrat. Episcopalian. Avocations: riding, showing. Home: 157 Millard Ave Sleepy Hollow NY 10591-1412

STEVES, GALE C., marketing professional, writer, editor-in-chief, publishing executive; b. Mineola, N.Y., Dec. 20, 1942; d. William Harry and Ruth (May) Steves; m. David B. Stocker, Mar. 31, 1972 (div. Apr. 1978); m. Philip L. Perrone, Aug. 14, 1983. BS, Cornell U., 1964; MA, NYU, 1966. Editl. asst. Ladies Home Jour., N.Y.C., 1966-69; seafood consumer specialist U.S. Dept. Commerce, N.Y.C., 1969-73; editor food Homelife mag., N.Y.C., 1973-74; editor food and equipment Co-Ed mag., N.Y.C., 1974-76, Am. Home mag., N.Y.C., 1976-78; editor kitchen design and equipment Woman's Day mag., N.Y.C., 1979-83; editor-in-chief Woman's Day Spls., N.Y.C., 1983-91; v.p., editor-in-chief Home Mag. Group, N.Y.C., 1991—2001; pres. Open House Prodns., N.Y.C., 2001—03, 2005—; v.p., editl. dir., pub. AMI Mini Mags. Group, N.Y.C., 2003—05. Bd. dirs. Les Dames d'Escoffier, Coun. Sr. Ctrs. and Svcs. N.Y.C., Catskill Ctr. Cons. and Econ. Devel. Author: Game Cookery, 1974, The International Cook, 1980, Creative Microwave Cooking, 1981; author: (with Lee M. Elman) Country Weekend Cooking, Home Magazine's Best Little Houses, 1998; mem. editl. bd. Sr. Summary, N.Y.C., 1982—88. Co-chmn. Alder Lake Restoration Soc.; chmn. alumni adv. bd. Coll. Human Ecology, Cornell U., 1993—97, mem. univ. coun., 1996—2000, mem. pres.'s coun. Cornell Women; mem. adv. bd. Cornell Plantations, 1998—2005; bd. mem. Catskill Ctr. Conservation and Econ. Devel. Mem.: Garden Writers Assn. Am., Am. Soc. Mag. Editors, Internat. Furnishings and Design Assn., Acad. Women Achievers YWCA N.Y.C. Address: 185 West End Ave Ste 26C New York NY 10023-5551

STEVISON, WENDY, personal trainer; b. Euclid, Ohio, Feb. 3, 1971; d. Frank Howard and Linda Sue Stevison. BA in Athletic Trng., John Carroll U., University Heights, Ohio, 1995; MS, Ohio U., Athens, 1996. Cert. athletic trainer Fla. Cert. athletic trainer Leesburg HS, Fla., 1996—2002, FOI, Tampa, Fla., 2002—04, Sports & Orthop. Rehab., Tampa, 2004—05, Eckerd Coll., St. Petersburg, Fla., 2005—. Ins. agt. Orlando Regional, Fla., 2000—02; athletic ins. coord. Eckerd Coll., St. Petersburg, 2005—. Mem.: Athletic Trainer Assn. Fla., Nat. Athletic Trainers Assn. (cert. athletic trainer). Republican. Roman Catholic. Avocations: running, bicycling, swimming, triathlons. Home: 11601 4th St N # 2716 Saint Petersburg FL 33716 Office: Eckerd Coll 4200 54th Ave S Saint Petersburg FL 33711

STEWART, ANN BURGESS, elementary school educator; b. Fairbanks, Alaska, Jan. 28, 1951; d. Clinton Briggs and Marion Burgess Stewart. BA in Phys. Edn., U. No. Colo., Greeley, 1973, MA in Mid. Level Edn., 1990; student, Mankato State U., Minn., 1986—88. Phys. edn. tchr., coach Rangely Mid. Sch., Rangely HS, Colo., 1973—77, Basalt Mid. Sch., 1977—. Outdoor edn. coord. Aspen Camp Sch. for Deaf, Snowmass, Colo., 1978—82; phys. edn. dept. head Roaring Fork Sch. Dist., Glenwood Springs; presenter in field. Contbr. articles to profl. jours. and pubs. Pledge bike ride across U.S. St. Jude Children's Hosp., Tenn., 1976; pledge climb for asthma Basalt Mid. Sch., 1993. Recipient Tchr. of Yr. award, Roaring Fork Sch. Dist., 2000, Phys. Edn. Tchr. of Yr. award, Colo. Mid. Sch., 2006; grantee Phys. Edn. grant, Basalt Edn. Found., Basalt Mid. Sch., 1977—. Mem.: NEA, Colo. Assn. Health, Phys. Edn., Recreation & Dance (mid. sch. rep. 1985—95, bd. mem. 1989—94), Am. Alliance Health, Phys. Edn., Recreation & Dance. Avocations: bicycling, skiing, counted cross stitch, hiking, travel. Office: Basalt Mid Sch 51 School St Basalt CO 81621

STEWART, ANN S., music educator, director; b. Connersville, Ind., Nov. 24, 1930; d. Carl John Schoenholtz and Teresa Eugenia Schoonover; m. Thomas Hill Stewart, Dec. 27, 1951 (dec.); children: Jay, Jan, Todd. MusB, Ind. U., Bloomington, 1952; student, Miami U., Ohio, 1952—54. Vocal music tchr. Connersville HS, Ind., 1952—54, Webster Groves, Mo., 1954—55, Wauconda HS, Ill., 1979—80; pres. music dir. Music on Stage, Palatine, Ill., 1979—. Treas. Music on Stage, Palatine, Ill., 1979—, head workshops, 2004, scholarsip com. for coll. students, 2005, 2006. Republican. Roman Catholic. Avocations: golf, bowling, crafts, bridge, cooking. Home: 410 E Oakwood Dr Barrington IL 60010 Office: Music on Stage Inc 410 E Oakwood Dr Barrington IL 60010 Personal E-mail: musicann@aol.com.

STEWART, ANNE WILLIAMS, historian, writer, researcher; b. New Haven, Oct. 13, 1933; d. Howard Dudley and Minnie Victoria (Rattelsdorfer) Williams; m. Kenneth Neal Stewart (div. Oct. 1985); children: Elizabeth Anne Stewart-Marshall, Kenneth Neal Jr., David Bradley. BA, Allegheny Coll., Meadville, Pa., 1955. Coord. hist. sites survey Crawford County Planning, Meadville, 1976-80; chmn. hist. sites survey Meadville Redevel. Authority, 1980-83; program coord. Crawford County Hist. Soc., Meadville, 1981-88; bd. dirs. Meadville Bicentennial, 1986-88; dir. Academy Theater restoration Meadville Redevel. Authority, 1988-90; gen. reporter Meadville Tribune, 1990-92; grantsman Meadville Redevel. Authority, 1991—; adminstr. The Col. Inc., Drake Well Mus., Titusville, Pa., 1992-95. Historian, advisor Meadville Main St., 1986—90; historian Meadville Comprehensive Plan, 1992—93. Author: John A. Mather: Legacy of Pennsylvania's Oil Region Photographer, 1995, A Concise History of Meadville, 1995, 4th edit., 2002; author: (with Jonathan Miller Design) Meadville: Heart of the French Creek Valley, 1997; author: (with William B. Moore) Images of America, Meadville, 2001; editor: A Guide to City and County, 1972, Meadville: Yesterday and Today, 1976, Gentle Giants: Stories of Ballooning, 1992, George Washington's French Creek Trip, 1999, The Oilfield Barker, 1993—96, Market Square Messenger, 1996—99, Crawford County History, 2001—; contbr. articles to mags.; editor: John Brown: From the Record, 1999, Erie: Jour. of Erie Studies, 2002; author (with Steven Utz): Meadville Architectural Heritage, 2005. Planning commr. Crawford County, Meadville, 1971—95, City of Meadville, 2000—; bd. dirs. Meadville Area Meml., 1983—95; chmn. bd. dirs. Health Svcs. Inc. Crawford County, 1976—81; coord. Meadville Area Coalition; chair The Founders Forum, 1997—. Mem.: Pa. Planning Assn. (bd. dirs. 1974—80), Crawford County Hist. Soc. (bd. dirs. 2003—), Woman's Lit. Club (lectr.). Avocations: travel, research, textile crafts. Office: 443 Byllesby Ave Meadville PA 16335-1411 Business E-Mail: byllesby@alltel.net.

STEWART, ANNETTE, judge; b. Paris, Tex., Jan. 1, 1928; d. Ray Bryan and Mary Christene (Plumer) Stewart. BA, U. Tex., Austin, 1949; MEd, U. Tex., 1952; LLB summa cum laude, So. Meth. U., 1966. Bar: Tex. 1966. Assoc. Parnass, McGuire & Handy, 1966-67; ct. reporter Ct. Domestic Rels., Dallas, 1957-66, 67-74, judge, 1975-77, 301st Dist. Ct., Dallas, 1977-83, 305th Dist. Ct., 1985-86, Ct. Appeals, Dallas, 1983-84, 86-92, sr. judge, 1993—. Fellow Tex. Bar Found.; mem. State Bar Tex., Tex. Bar Found., Dallas Bar Assn., P.E.O., Phi Beta Kappa. Democrat. Presbyterian.

STEWART, ARLENE JEAN GOLDEN, art director; b. Chgo., Nov. 26, 1943; d. Alexander Emerald and Nettie (Rosen) Golden; m. Randall Edward Stewart, Nov. 6, 1970; 1 child, Alexis Anne. BFA, Sch. of Art Inst. Chgo., 1966; postgrad., Ox Bow Summer Sch. Painting, Saugatuck, Mich., 1966. Designer, stylist Formica Corp., Cin., 1966; with Armstrong World Industries, Inc., Lancaster, Pa., 1968—96, interior furnishings analyst, 1974—76, internat. staff project stylist, 1976—78, sr. stylist Corlon flooring, 1979—80, sr. exptl. project stylist, 1980—89, sr. project stylist residential DIY flooring floor divsn., 1989—96, master stylist DIY residential tile, 1992—96; creative dir. Stewart Graphics, Lancaster, Pa., 1996—. Mem. Exhibitions include Art Inst. Chgo., 1966, Ox-Bow Gallery, Saugatuck, Mich., 1966. Home and Office: 114 E Vine St Lancaster PA 17602-3550 Personal E-mail: stewartgraphics@redrose.net.

STEWART, BARBARA LYNN, church administrator; b. Billings, Mont., May 13, 1954; d. Joseph Isacc and Ima Evelyn (Daugherty) Gates; m. Forrest Y. Stewart, Nov. 15, 1997. BS in Elem. Edn., Eastern Mont. Coll., 1976. Cert. tchr. Mont. Tchr. Union Sch., Lindsay, Mont., 1976-79, Greycliff Sch., Mont., 1979-80; supr. Alliance Christian Sch., Lewistown, Mont., 1981-83, prin., supr., 1983-86, Paradise Christian Acad., Lewistown, 1986-91; driver, dispatcher, contracts and svcs. coord. Spl. Transp. Inc., Billings, Mont., 1991-94; in-home caregiver Billings, 1994-97; tax preparer H&R Block, Carbondale, Ill., 1999, Herrin, Ill., 1999—2000; adminstrv. asst. First Presbyn. Ch., Carbondale, 2000—.

STEWART, BONNIE LOUISE, psychologist; b. Pittsfield, Mass., Nov. 9, 1952; d. Alan Perkins and Suzanne R. (Forster) S.; m. Allen Arthur Meyer, Sept. 13, 1975 (div. 1997). BS, Springfield Coll., 1975; MEd, U. Pa., 1983, PhD, 1990. Asst. payroll mgr. G. Fox & Co., Hartford, Conn., 1973-77; territory mgr. Certain Teed Corp., Valley Forge, Pa., 1977-81; rsch. coord. U. Pa. Counseling Ctr., Phila., 1985-88, U. Pa. Ctr. for Cognitive Therapy, Phila., 1988-90; project coord. Dave Garroway Lab., Phila., 1990-92; psychologist pvt. practice, Lafayette Hill, Pa., 1995—. Psychotherapist Psych Resource Assocs., Havertown, Pa., 1990-95. Contbr. articles to profl. jours. Avocations: book collecting, walking, gardening, watercolor.

STEWART, CANDRA L., lawyer; d. Louis E. and Sandra C. Stewart; 1 child, Theodore. BA in Polit. Sci. and Psychology, Fisk U., Nashville, 1997; JD, Southern U., Baton Rouge, 1999. Bar: La. 2005. Dir. Girls Only B&G Clubs Am., Ft. Worth, 1997—99; legal clk. Blaies & Hightower LLP, Ft. Worth, 1999—2002; tchg. asst. SULC, 2002—05; liaison Katrina Legal Relief, Legal Aid NW Tex., Ft. Worth, 2005—. Analyst civil rights Dept Health and Human Svcs., Dallas, 2003. Asst. editor, writer and copy editor The Pub. Defender, 2004; contbr. articles to newspapers. Scholar, J.L. Turner Assn., 2004; J.L. Dawson scholar, Mt. Olive Missionary Bapt. Ch., 1992. Mem.: ABA, ATLA (mem. mock trial team), LWV, Delta Theta Phi.

STEWART, CONNIE WARD, retired academic administrator; b. Athens, Ga., Nov. 19, 1938; d. Fred Tendal and Elsie (James) Ward; m. D.G. Stewart, l960 (div. 1967); 1 child, Sheri Lyn; m. Nick Vista, Apr. 16, 1982. AB in Journalism, U. Ga., 1959, MA, 1968; postgrad., George Washington U., 1979; cert. in ednl. mgmt., Harvard U., 1985. Cert. elem. and secondary tchr., Ga. Promotion-pub. rels. staff Sta. WSB-TV, Atlanta, 1959—61; assoc. dir. Ga. Scholarship Commn., Atlanta, 1967; faculty U. Ga. Journalism Sch., Athens, 1967—70; dir. orientation U. Ga., Athens, 1970—71; project mgr. Planned Mgmt. Corp., Tampa, Fla., 1976—77; dir. policy comm., mem., Carter-Mondale adminstrn. HEW, Washington, 1977—79; orgnl. staff U.S. Dept. Edn., Washington, 1979; v.p. Mich. State U., East Lansing, 1980—87; assoc. v.p. Emory U., Atlanta, 1987—93; ret., 1993. Dir. Cmty. Forum on Children and Families Ga. State U., 1995; mil. acad. screening com. Office U.S. Senator Donald Riegle, Lansing, Mich., 1984-86. Editor, columnist Oconee Enterprise, 1971-72. Steering com. Carter for Pres. Campaign, Fla., 1975—76; exec. com. Mich. Sesquicentennial Celebratoin, 1985—87; mem. Ga. Scholarship Commn., 1965—67, Ga. Motion Picture-TV Adv. Bd., 1972—76, Ga. Gov.'s Commn. on Edn., 1965—67, Mich. Film and TV Coun., 1984—86; exec. com. Comm. Coun., The Atlanta Project, 1992—94; vol. mentor in pub. schs. Success-by-Six program, 1993—96; trainer vols. United Way, 1993—96, Big Bros./Bis Sisters Teach One program, 1997—99; docent Carter Presdl. Libr./Mus., 1998—; bd. councilors Carter Presdl. Ctr., 2005—; bd. dirs. Olympic Acad., 1987—88, Atlanta Olympics Organizing Com. for

Olympic Games, 1991—93. Recipient Outstanding Alumna award Henry W. Grady Coll. of Journalism and Mass Communications, U. Ga., 1993, hon. alumnus award Mich. State U., 1987; disting. svc. award Ga. Edn. Advancement Coun., 1990. Mem. Coun. for Advancement and Support Edn., Nat. Assn. State Univs. and Land Grant Colls. (univ. rels. coun. 1984-87), Atlanta C. of C. (Forward Atlanta 1989), Soc. Profl. Journalists, Nat. Press Club (Washington), Pub. Rels. Soc. Am., Phi Beta Kappa (v.p. Mich. State U. chpt. 1986, pres. 1987), Phi Kappa Phi, Sigma Delta Chi, Theta Sigma Phi, Di Gamma Kappa, Zeta Tau Alpha. Democrat. Avocations: travel, reading, poetry. Home: 2848 Warrington Close Tucker GA 30084-2598

STEWART, CYNTHIA WILLIS, minister; b. Friendship, Guyana, Dec. 13, 1944; arrived in U.S., 1985; d. William Nathaniel and Hilloise Isola Willis; m. Ronald Eustace Stewart, June 3, 1990. BSc magna cum laude, Mich. State Univ., 1973; MA in Comm. Arts, Cornell Univ., 1980; MDiv, Hood Theol. Sem., 1983; DD, Drew Univ., 1990. Lic. local preacher 1979, admitted on trial 1981, Deacon's Orders 1982, Elder's Orders 1983; cert. Pub. Rels. Sch. of Pub. Rels., Eng., 1975. Pastor Alleyne A.M.E. Zion Ch., Guyana, South America, 1982—85; bishop's adminstrv. asst., presiding elder, advisor Guyana Conf., 1982—88, bishop's adminstrv. asst., presiding elder, 1992—96, Guyana, Barbados, Trinidad, Tobago Conf., 1996—98; assoc. min. First A.M.E. Zion Ch., Bklyn., 1986—92; pastor Westbury A.M.E. Zion Ch., NY, 1992—2000; presiding elder L.I. Dist., N.Y. Conf., 2000—01, Westchester Dist., N.Y. Conf., 2001—. Editor, design and layout artist, contbg. writer: Missionary Seer; contbr. articles pub. to non-profit jours. Bd. dirs. Harriet Tubman Home Inc.; adminstrv. bds. Theol. Sem., Christian Edn., Sch. and Coll.; pres. elder's coun. A.M.E. Zion Ch., first v.p.; chmn. bd. Christian Edn. and Admission Com.; mem. Budget Com., Holy Orders Com., N.Y. Conf.; bd. trustees N.Y. Conf., M. Ardelle Shaw Retreat Ctr. Recipient Excellence in Christian Life and Conduct, GW Griffin Meml. Preaching award, Hood Theol. Sem., Nat. Sojourner Truth Meritorious Svc. award, Nat. Assn. of Negro Bus. and Profl. Women's Club. Mem.: NAACP, Ch. Women United, World Fedn. of Meth. and Uniting Ch. Women, Ministerial Alliance, Nat. Coun. of Negro Women (life), Assn. of Christian Educators (life), A.M.E. Zion Ch. Min. and Lay Assn. (life). Home: 1129 Pembrooke St Uniondale NY 11553-1408

STEWART, DEBORAH CLAIRE, dean; b. Freeport, Ill., Sept. 14, 1951; Student, Monterey Peninsula Coll., 1969-71; BS in Zoology, U. Calif., Davis, 1973; MD, U. Calif., San Francisco, 1977. Diplomate Am. Bd. Peds. Intern Children's Hosp. L.A., 1977-78, resident in peds., 1978-79, fellow in adolescent medicine, 1979-81, attending physician emergency med. svcs., 1980-81; med. dir. comprehensive adolescent program dept. ob-gyn. Charles R. Drew Postgrad. Med. Sch., L.A., 1981-83; asst. prof. dept. ob-gyn. UCLA/Charles R. Drew Postgrad. Med. Sch., 1982-83; mem. ped. staff Children's Hosp. of Orange County, Orange, Calif., 1983-86, U. Calif. Irvine Med. Ctr., Orange, 1983-99; assoc. prof. ob-gyn., assoc. prof. medicine U. Calif., Irvine, 1983-99, dir. child sexual abuse program, 1983-99, assoc. prof. clin. peds., chief divsn. gen. peds., dir. adol. 1988-95, assoc. dean for med. student and resident affairs, 1992-99; med. dir. child protection ctr. Meml. Miller Children's Hosp., Long Beach, Calif., 1995-99; assoc. dean med. edn. program U. Calif.-San Francisco, Fresno, 1999—. Project dir. South Ctrl. L.A. Sexual Trauma Program, 1983; med. cons. L.A. Commn. on Assaults Against Women, 1982-84, Calif. Children's Svcs., 1980-85, Sexual Assault Protocol Office of Criminal Justice Planning, 1984-86, Sexual Assault Protocol L.A. County, 1984-86; med. dir. Child Abuse Svcs. Team County of Orange, 1987—; physician mem. Calif. State Atty. Gen.'s Investigative Pilot Projects Rsch. and Evaluation Adv. Panel; cons. County of Orange Coroner's Office, 1994-99. Contbr. articles to profl. jours.; presenter in field; reviewer: Ped. and Adolescent Gyn., 1988—, Jour. Adolescent Health Care, 1986—, Peds., 1988—, Am. Jour. Obs. and Gyn., 1991— Mem. med. adv. bd. Planned Parenthood, 1983-94. Fellow Am. Acad. Pediatrics (pres. Dist. IX Chpt. 4, 1995-97, sec. chpt. IV, chair chpt. IV com. on child abuse 1983—); mem. N.Am. Soc. Pediatric And Adolescent Gynecology (co-chair collaborative rsch. com. 1988—), Orange County Ped. Assn. Office: U Calif San Francisco-Fresno Med Edn Program 2615 E Clinton Ave Fresno CA 93703-2223 E-mail: deborah.stewart@ucsfresno.edu.

STEWART, DEBRA WEHRLE, academic administrator; b. Petersburg, Va., May 22, 1943; BA in Philosophy and Polit. Sci., Marquette U., 1965; MA in Govt., U. Md., 1967; PhD in Polit. Sci., U. N.C., 1975. Instr. polit. sci. European divsn. U. Md., Nuremberg, Germany, 1967-69; instr. polit. sci. and pub. adminstrn. N.C. State U., Raleigh, 1974-75, asst. prof., 1975-78, assoc. prof., 1979-83, prof., 1984—, acting dir. MPA program, 1978, assoc. dean Grad. Sch., 1983-86, interim vice provost and dean Grad. Sch., 1986-88, dean Grad. Sch., 1988-2000, vice provost, 1995-98, vice chancellor, dean Grad. Sch., 1998-2000; pres. Coun. Grad. Schs., Washington, 2000—. Interim chancellor U. N.C., Greensboro, 1994; mem. com. on assessment of rsch. doctorate NRC, 1992-95; mem. Grad. Record Exam. Bd., 1992-96, chmn.-elect, 1994-95, chmn., 1995-96; bd. dirs. Coun. Grad. Schs., 1990—, chmn.-elect, 1992-93, chmn., 1993-94; mem. Test English as Fgn. Lang. Bd., 1992-95; councilor Oak Ridge Assoc. Univs., 1988-92, bd. dirs., 1993—, chair-elect 1997—; bd. dirs. Nat. Phys. Scis. Consortium, 1998—; mem. exec. com. Coun. So. Grad. Schs., 1989-91; trustee Triangle U. Ctr. for Advanced Studies, 1989—; mem. Commn. on Peer Rev. and Accreditation, Nat. Assn. of Schs. of Pub. Affairs and Adminstrn., 1997-99. Author: The Women's Movement in Community Politics: The Role of Local Commissions on the Status of Women, 1980, (with G. David Garson) Organizational Behavior and Public Management, 1983, 3d edit. (with Vasu and Garson), 1998; editor: Women in Local Politics, 1980; mem. editl. bd. Rev. Pub. Pres. Adminstrn., 1981-89, Annals Pub. Adminstrn., 1982-84, Women and Politics, 1980-88, Politics and Policy, 1983-86; contbr. articles to profl. jours., chpts. to books. Recipient edn. award YWCA Acad. Women, 1988 Mem. Nat. Assn. State Univs. and Land-Grant Colls. (bd. dirs. 1992-94, exec. com. coun. on rsch. policy and grad. edn. 1989-92, chmn. 1990-91), Am. Soc. for Pub. Adminstrn. (com. on status of women in pub. adminstrn. 1976-78, com. on profl. stds. and ethics 1980-89, chmn. com. on whistle blowing and dissent channels of profl. stds. and ethics com. 1985-86, Burchfield award 1976), So. Polit. Sci. Assn. (nominating com. 1978, coord. pub. adminstrn. sect. 1979), Women's Forum N.C., Phi Kappa Phi, Pi Sigma Alpha, Pi Alpha Alpha. Office: Coun Grad Schs Grad Sch 1 Dupont Cir NW Ste 430 Washington DC 20036-1136 Office Phone: 202-223-3791. Business E-Mail: dstewart@cgs.nche.edu.

STEWART, DORIS MAE, biology professor; b. Sandsprings, Mont., Dec. 12, 1927; d. Virgil E. and Violet M. (Weaver) S.; m. Felix Loren Powell, Oct. 8, 1956; children: Leslie, Loren. BS, Coll. Puget Sound, 1948, MS, 1949; PhD, U. Wash., 1953. Instr. U. Mont., Missoula, 1954-56, asst. prof., 1956-57, U. Puget Sound, Tacoma, 1957-58; head sci. dept. Am. Kiz Lisesi, Istanbul, Turkey, 1958-62; rsch. asst. prof. U. Wash., Seattle, 1963-67, rsch. assoc. prof., 1967-68; assoc. prof. Cen. Mich. U., Mt. Pleasant, 1970-72, U. Balt., 1973-81, prof., 1981-95, prof. emeritus, 1995—. Contbr. numerous articles to profl. jours. Mem. Am. Physiol. Soc., Sigma Xi. Home: 1103 Frederick Rd Baltimore MD 21228-5032

STEWART, DOROTHY K., librarian; b. Bristol, Conn., Sept. 28, 1928; d. Robert and Anna Esther (Schwitz) Konopask; m. David Benjamin Stewart, Sept. 27, 1952 (div. Nov. 1979); children: Douglas Neil, Diane Alison. BA in Romance Langs. and Lit. cum laude, Boston U., 1950; MSLS, Cath. U. Am., 1959. Children's libr. Brookline (Mass.) Pub. Libr., 1953-55, Takoma Park (Md.) Libr., 1955-57; reference libr. U.S. Geol. Survey, 1961; libr. Washington Internat. Sch., 1979-80, Office Sea Grant NOAA, Rockville, Md., 1980-82; info. specialist Life Ring, Inc., Silver Spring, Md., 1983-84; pub. svc. libr. Urban Inst., Washington, 1984-85; user svcs. coord. ERIC Clearinghouse on Tchg. and Tchr. Edn., Washington, 1985-97; ret., 1997. Active, past pres. PTA, Rockville, Md., 1973-78; chmn., mem. com. Potomac (Md.) Libr. Adv. Com., 1975-85. Mem. Capital PC User Group, French lang. clubs, Phi Beta Kappa, Beta Phi Mu. Democrat. Avocations: travel, hiking, birding, computers. Personal E-mail: dkstewart24@comcast.net.

STEWART, ELLEN D., theater producer; Former fashion designer; founder, dir. La MaMa Exptl. Theatre Club, NYC, 1961—. Vis. prof. Inst. Drama, Republic of Korea. Prodr. innovative theatre, most recently Antigone, a part of SEVEN: Seven Greek Plays in Repertory; dir., most recently Perseus, Great Jones Rep. Co.; active in internet theatre exch. Named Officer Ordre des Arts et Lettres, Republic France; named to Theatre Hall of Fame, 1993; recipient Margo Jones award, 1969, MacArthur Genius award, Les Kurbas award disting. svc. to art and culture, Ukraine, Order of Sacred Treasure Gold Rays with Rossette, Emperor Japan, 1994, Human Rights award, Philippines. Mem.: Seoul Internat. Theatre Inst. Office: La MaMa ETC 74A E 4th St New York NY 10003-8903 Office Phone: 212-254-6468. Business E-Mail: lamama@lamama.org.*

STEWART, GEORGIANA LICCIONE, writer; b. Mount Vernon, N.Y., May 18, 1943; d. Arthur Alfred and Grace Marie (Zuzzolo) Liccione; m. William Lawrence Stewart, July 18, 1975. BA, Columbia U., 1971; MA, Columbia Tchr.'s Coll., N.Y.C., 1973; MAT, Manhattanville Coll., 1973. Author, cons. Kimbo Ednl., Long Branch, NJ, 1970—; spl. edn. tchr. Bronxville (N.Y.) H.S., 1989—. Cons. NAEYC, SACUS, 1975-89, Pres.'s Coun. on Physical Fitness, 1979-81. Author: (69 children's musical activity records and books including) Adaptive Motor Learning, 1982, Bean Bag Activities, 1983, Preschool Aerobic Fun, 1989, Children of the World, 1991, ulticultural Rhythm Stick Fun, 1992, Toddlerific, 1993, World of Parachute Play, 1997, Children's Folk Dances, 1998, Moving with Mozart, 1999 (Early Childhood Dir.'s Choice award NAEYC), Nursery Rhyme Time, 2000, Cool Aerobics for Kids, 2001, Musical Scarves, 2002, Circle Time, 2004. Recipient Student Advocacy Overcoming the Odds award, 1997. Mem. AAHPERD, Nat. Assn. for Edn. of Young Children, So. Assn. for Children Under Six, Faculty Dance Educators Am., Assn. for Retarded Citizens, Columbia Club, Women's Nat. Rep. Club. Avocations: Heatsong music and art therapy program, organizing local benefit programs. Home: 81 Pondfield Rd # 328 Bronxville NY 10708-3818 Office: Kimbo Ednl PO Box 477 Long Branch NJ 07740-0477

STEWART, GHISLAINE LYNNE, music educator, conductor; d. Walter and Katherine Kubica; m. Fitzroy A. Stewart, Oct. 24, 1971. BS in Music Edn., SUNY, Potsdam. Cert. elem. tchr. N.Y., 1972. String tchr. Maine Endwell Schs., NY, 1970—76, Jugendmusikschule, Frankfurt am Main, Germany, 1979—87. Elem. vocal tchr. Cath. Sch. Broome County, Binghamton, NY, 1987—93; vocal & string tchr. Benjamin Franklin Elem. Sch., Binghamton, NY, 1993—. Mem.: ACDA. Office: Benjamin Franklin School 262 Conklin Rd Binghamton NY Office Phone: 607-762-8344. Business E-Mail: stewartg@bcsd.org.

STEWART, GWENDOLYN JOHNS, music educator; b. Winston-Salem, N.C., Feb. 11, 1926; d. Island Lemuel Johns and Vandelia Trumilla Perry-Johns; m. Jason Hawkins, Sr. (dec.); 1 child, Jason Hawkins Jr.; m. George Sturgis (dec.); 1 child, Daryl Sturgis; m. Robert H. Stewart, Jan. 20, 1979 (dec.). Student, Spelman Coll., 1943—46, Juilliard Sch. Music, 1947; BS in Edn., Winston-Salem Tchrs. Coll., 1950; postgrad., A & T State U., Greensboro, N.C., 1955. Tchr. Pub. Sch. Sys., Gastonia, NC, 1951—57, Mooresville, NC, 1957—61, Forsyth County Pub. Sch. Sys., Winston-Salem, 1961—65; owner-oper. Jack & Jill Kindergarten #2, Winston-Salem, 1965—68; dir. chancel choir Friendship Bapt. Ch., Winston-Salem, 1961—79; pianist, organist, dir. Grace Presbyn. Ch. USA, Winston-Salem, 1997—; pianist, organist Gen. Bapt. State Conv. N.C., Winston-Salem, 1982—86, dir. music, 1986—90. Chmn. music dept. Shiloh Bapt. Ch., Winston-Salem, 1997—2002. Author: The Gwen Johns Basic Music Guide, 2000, Bells Alive Book One, 2003, composer song collection; contbr. poetry to anthologies. Avocations: sewing, cooking. Home: 2795 Bethabara Rd Winston Salem NC 27106-9604 E-mail: gjstewart12@triad.rr.com.

STEWART, HEATHER MERI, painter, sculptor; b. Appleton, Wis., Oct. 12, 1964; d. Paul James and Josephine Pauline (Smania) S BA Archaeol. Studies cum laude, Boston U., 1988, BFA Painting, 1988; MA, Harvard U., 2006. Cert. tchr., Mass. Tchr., vol. arts and crafts The Hole in the Wall Gang Camp, Ashford, Conn., 1995-97; cons., critic thesis revs. Boston Archtl. Ctr., 1998-99, collaboration on pub. art project with Harvard's Union of Clerical & Tech. Workers, 2002 One-woman shows include Curry Ctr. Art Gallery, Boston, 1999, Boston Archtl. Ctr. Atelier Gallery, 1999, Someday Cafe, 2005, Holyoke Gallery, Harvard U., 2006, exhibited in group shows at Colby Coll. Art Mus., Waterville, Maine, 1991, Boston Archtl. Ctr., 1994, Boston Mus. Sch., 1989, 1992, 1995, 1999, 2001, 2002, Boston Ctr. for the Arts, 1997, 2004, Bunting Inst., Cambridge, Mass., 1998, 1999, 2000, Brickbottom Gallery, Somerville, Mass., 1998—2001, The Discovery Mus., Bridgeport, Conn., 1999, Catherine Lorillard Wolfe Art Club, N.Y.C., 1999, 2000, 2001, 2003, Arlington Ctr. for the Arts, 1999—2002 (First prize, 2000), Harvard Neighbors, Loeb House, Harvard U., 2002, Stamford Art Assn., Conn., 2002, Rocky Nede Artist Colony, 2005, exhibitions include Aidekman Arts Ctr., Tufts U., 2003, Chelsea Theatre Works, 2003, Mass. Gen. Hosp., 2003, Somerville Arts Windows Project, 2004, Soprafina Gallery, 2004, Holyoke Ctr. Gallery, Harvard U., 2005, others; web designer: Women's Caucus for Art, Boston chpt., 2005—; illustrator for mystery writer Dana Cameron, —, 96 Inc. mag., 1998—2005, organizer (exhibit) Harvard U. Holyoke Gallery, 2005, curator and co-juror Casella Gallery, Wentworth Inst., 2006, web designer Harvard Coll., Harvard U. Mem.: Internat. Registry Artists and Artwork, 96 Inc Writers/Artists Collaborative (bd. dirs.), Women's Caucus for Art (treas. steering com. Boston chpt. 2000—, web designer 2005—). Personal E-mail: hms_studio@yahoo.com.

STEWART, IDALEE ADEL, educational administrator, consultant; b. Chgo., Aug. 11, 1941; d. Jack and Rose Adel; m. David Henry Stewart, Mar. 16, 2002; children: Stacey Elyn Garrison, Douglas Joel Lusky, Zoe Claire Alvarez. BA, UCLA, 1978; MA, Calif. State U., Dominguez Hills, 2002. Cert. tchr. Calif., adminstr. Calif., lang. devel. specialist Calif. Tchr. L.A. Unified Sch. Dist., 1979—98, mentor, 1984—98, cons., 1998—, profl. expert, 1999—2001; pub. rep. Great Source Edn. Group, HoughtonMifflin, L.A., 2001—02; textbook reviewer Ballard & Tighe, Brea, Calif., 1996—98; supr. Loyola Marymount U., 2003—, Nova Southeastern U., North Miami Beach, Fla., 2003—. Cons./event coord. L.A. Unified Sch. Dist., 1998—2002; profl. test developer Calif. Dept. Edn., 1986—91; spl. edn. adviser East L.A. Coll., Monterey Park, Calif., 1976—80. Vol. Camp Ronald McDonald for Good-Times, L.A., 2000—03. Integrated History and Art Tchg. Unit grantee, LA Ednl. Partnership, 1987—88. Mem.: Women in Ednl. Leadership (assoc.), Assn. for Profl. and Curriculum Devel. (assoc.). Avocations: travel, reading, fashion development, outdoors. Personal E-mail: iastewart2@hotmail.com.

STEWART, JANET, artist; b. Des Moines, July 5, 1931; d. Joseph Kenneth Siberz and Bertha Schiltz; m. Clifford Charles Russell, Oct. 3, 1950 (div. 1967); children: Lynn Marie, Wayne Kenneth; m. Donald Roy Stewart, Feb. 7, 1969 (dec. May 1996). Represented by Wyland Gallery of Las Vegas, 1996—2002, Wyland Galleries of Hawaii, 1988—98, Wyland Galleries of Fla., 1997—, Aloha Fine Arts Kapas, Kauai, 1999, Island Art Galleries, Honolulu, 1999—, Dreams of Paradise, Hilo, Hawaii, 1999—, Pictures Plus and Diamondhead Galleries, 1999—2002, Rift Zone, Kona, 2001—04, Waikiki Beach Gallery, Honolulu, 2003—, HB Gallery at the Huntington Beach Hyatt, 2004—, Art-Broker.com, 1996—. Commissions include Ariz. Aloha Festival, Epilepsy Found. Hawaii, Fremont Ctr. Theatre, Girl Scouts Hawaii 75th Anniversary poster, Hawaii Air Lines 85th Anniversary poster, Ho'olaulea, L.A., Calif., Lahainaluna H.S., Maui, L.A. Family Guidance Ctr. 160th Anniversary Poster, Weinberg Trust, Honolulu and Oahu. Author: Ohana O Janet Stewart, 1997; prin. works include Portrait Series of Harry and Jeanette Weinberg, Oahu, Official Centennial Paintings Samoa Amerika, Pago Pago. Mem. Women Painters West, Pasadena Soc. Artists, Calif. Art Club. Avocations: reading, dance, singing.

STEWART, JANICE MAE, federal judge; b. Medford, Oreg., Feb. 13, 1951; d. Glenn Logan and Eathel Mae (Jones) S.; m. F. Gordon Allen III, Aug. 10, 1975; children: Benjamin Stewart, Rebecca Mae. AB in Econs., Stanford U., 1972; JD, U. Chgo., 1975. Bar: Ill. 1976, Oreg. 1977, U.S. Dist. Ct. Oreg. 1977, U.S. Ct. Appeals (9th cir.) 1978. Assoc. Winston & Strawn, Chgo., 1975-76, McEwen, Gisvold, Rankin & Stewart, Portland, Oreg., 1976-81, ptnr., 1981-93; U.S. Magistrate Judge Portland, 1993—. Mem. law rev. Fed. Ct., 2003—; mem. exec. com. 9th Cir. Conf., 2005—; magistrate judge 9th Cir. Exec. Com. Mem. Multonomah County Profl. Responsbility Com., Portland, 1979-82, Oreg. Profl. Responsibility Bd., 1982-85, Oreg. State Bar Practice and Procedure Com., 1985-88, Profl. Liability Fund Def. Panel, Portland, 1985-93, Multnomah County Jud. Selection Com., 1985-88, Oreg. State Bar Professionalism Com., 1989-91, Oreg. State Bar Fed. Practice and Procedure Com., 1996-99, 2004-, Coun. Ct. Procedures, 1991-93, lawyer rep. 9th Cir. Jud. Conf., 1990-93, Multnomah County Professionalism Com., 1997-2000. Mem. ABA, Am. Arbitration Assn. (arbitrator 1990-93), Oreg. Bar Assn., Multnomah County Bar Assn. (dir. 1990-93), Phi Beta Kappa. Democrat. Office: 1027 US Courthouse 1000 SW 3rd Ave Portland OR 97204-2930 Office Phone: 503-326-8260.

STEWART, JENNIFER, advertising executive; b. Sutton Coldfield, Eng., May 30, 1940; d. Eric Laughlan and Rita Joan (Taylor) Stewart. BA in Philosophy and Econs. with honors, U. Coll., U. London, 1961. With Cement Mktg. Co., London, 1961—63, ICI Fibres Ltd., London, 1963—65, Rsch. Svcs. Ltd., London, 1965—68, Batton, Barton, Durstine & Osborne, Inc., NYC, 1968—69, Ogilvy & Mather Inc., NYC, 1969—; exec. v.p., dir. branding and strategic svcs. Ogilvy and Mather Worldwide; with with Desktop Strategy, NYC, 1989—. Mem.: Conf. Bd. (trustee), Copy Rsch. Coun. (past pres.), Comm. Rsch. Coun. (past pres.), Market Rsch. Coun., Am. Assn. Advt. Agencies (rsch. com.), Am. Mktg. Assn. (past dir. NY, past chmn. Effie awards com.). Home: 130 W 67th St New York NY 10023-5909

STEWART, JOAN HINDE, academic administrator; b. NYC, Aug. 11, 1944; d. Wade and Dorothy (Ronning) H.; m. Philip Robert Stewart, Jan. 31, 1970; children: Anna Faye, Justin. Student, Université Laval Summer Sch., Quebec, 1963, Middlebury Coll. Summer Sch., 1964-65; BA summa cum laude, St. Joseph's Coll., 1965; student, Salzburg Summer Sch., Austria, 1966; MPhil, Yale U., 1969, PhD, 1970. Tchg. assoc. French Yale U., New Haven, 1967—69, acting instr. French, 1969—70; instr. French Wellesley Coll., 1970—71, asst. prof. French, 1971—72, NC State U., Raleigh, 1973—77, assoc. prof. French, 1977—81, prof. French, 1981—99, asst. head dept. fgn. langs. and lits., 1978—82, asst. dean rsch. and grad. programs, 1983—85, acting head dept. fgn. langs. and lits., 1984—85, head dept. fgn. langs. and lit., 1985—97; prof., dean liberal arts U. SC, 1999—2003; prof. French, pres. Hamilton Coll., Clinton, NY, 2003—. Author: The Novels of Mme Riccoboni, 1976, Colette, 1983, 1996, Gynographs: French Novels by Women of the Late Eighteenth Century, 1993; editor: Mme Riccoboni's Lettres de Mistriss Fanni Butlerd, 1979; co-editor: Isabelle de Charrière's Lettres de Mistriss Henley, 1993, Marie Riccoboni's Histoire d'Ernestine, 1998. Chmn. N.C. Humanities Coun., 1988-89. Fellow Camargo Found., Cassis, France, 1979, Nat. Humanities Ctr., 1982-83, (sr.) ctr. for humanities Wesleyan U., 1990; NEH summer seminar fellowship, Princeton U., 1980; NEH fellowship Coll. Tchrs. and Ind. Scholars, 1990-91, 1994-95; fellow Ctr. d'Etude du XVIII Siecle, U. Paul Valery, Montpellier, France, 1995, Liguria Study Ctr. for the Arts and Scis., Bogliasco, Italy, 1997, Beinecke Rare Book and Manuscript Libr., Yale U., 1997; stipend younger humanists NEH, 1973; travel grantee ACLS, 1983; travel to collections grantee NEH, 1984; vis. scholar European Humanities Rsch. Ctr., Oxford U., 1995. Mem. AAUP, MLA, Am. Assn. Tchrs. French. Address: Hamilton Coll Pres Office 198 College Hill Rd Clinton NY 13323 Office Phone: 315-859-4104. E-mail: jstewart@hamilton.edu.

STEWART, JOANNE, retired director; b. Vancouver, Wash., Mar. 10, 1944; d. Edward Charles and Claudine Marie Spencer; m. William Lemley Stewart, Sept. 2, 1966 (dec. June 1983); children: Amy Diane Stemple, Nicholas William. BS, Wash. State U., 1966, MA, 1973. Cert. tchr., Mont., Idaho, Wash., Calif. Tchr. foods Seaside High Sch., Monterey, Calif., 1966-67; tchr. home econs. Marysville (Wash.) High Sch., 1967-68, Palouse (Wash.) High Sch., 1968-73, Ennis (Mont.) High Sch., 1973-76, Genesee (Idaho) High Sch., 1976-77; instr. young family Missoula (Mont.) County High Sch., 1983-84; tchr. home econs. Woodman Sch., Lolo, Mont., 1985-86; travel cons. Travel Masters, Missoula, 1984-87; ticketing mgr. Blue Caboose Travel, Missoula, 1987-91; tchr. family and consumer scis. Victor (Mont.) High Sch., 1991-2001; dir. Victor 21st Century Learning Ctr., 2001—04; project dir. Reaching Out for Positive Edn. Success (ROPES) program After Sch. Learning Ctr. Co-pres. Lolo PTO, 1980-81; v.p. Lolo Cmty. Ctr., 1981, team of leaders, 2004—06; sec. Lolo Mosquito Control Bd., 1988—; mem. telecommunications com. Conrad Burns & Gov. Racicot; sec. state supt. edn. task force on vocat. edn., 1995-96; coord. Health Rocks!, Nat. 4-H Program, 2000-01 Recipient Wash. State U. Alumni Achievement award, 2005; Marysville Edn. Assn. scholar, 1962, Future Homemakers Am. scholar, 1962. Mem. AAUW (sec. 1986, program chmn. 1987), Forestry Triangle (pres. 1981, editor cookbook 1982), Washington State Future Homemakers Am. (hon.), Am. Family and Consumer Scis. Assn., Mont. Family and Consumer Scis. Assn. (bylaws chair 1994, pres. elect 1995-96, pres. 1996-97, Profl. of Yr. 1997), Mont. Vocat. Tchrs. Assn. (returning Rookie of Yr. 1992, Am. Federated Tchrs., Mont. Vocat. Family and Consumer Scis. Tchrs. (v.p. 1993-94, pres. 1994-95, Tchr. of Yr. 1998), Sassy, Intelligent Lolo Ladies in Excellent Shape (Queen team of Lolo Red Hat chpt. 2002-), Am. Cancer Soc. Relay for Life (team capt. 2005-06, chmn. surviorship, 2006). Republican. Methodist. Avocation: swimming. Home: 1200 Lakeside Dr Lolo MT 59847-9705

STEWART, JULIA A., food service executive; m. Jon Greenawalt (div.); 2 children. BA in Communications, San Diego State U., 1977. Regional mktg. dir. Carl's Jr. Restaurant, 1978—80; regional mktg. mgr. Burger King Corp., 1980—84; mktg. dir. Spoons Grill & Bar Stuart Anderson's Black Angus/Cattle Co. Restaurants, 1985, mktg. v.p., 1986—91; western region v.p. operations Taco Bell Yum! Brands, 1991, nat. v.p. franchise, license Taco Bell, 1997—98; pres. domestic div. Applebee's Internat., Inc., 1998—2001; pres, COO Internat. House Pancakes (IHOP), 2001—, CEO, 2002—, chmn., 2006—. Bd. dirs. Avery Denison, Town Hall, LA, Women's Franchise and Distbn. Forum; mem. Elliott Inst. Leadership Coun.; bd. visitors UCLA Anderson Sch. Mgmt.; trustee Calif. Sci. Ctr. Found. Named one of Top Fifty Women in foodservice, Nation's Restaurant. Mem.: Nat. Restaurant Assn. (pres. mktg. executives group), Calif. Restaurant Assn. (exec. bd. mem.), Women's Foodservice Forum (past pres., founding mem.). Avocations: cooking, skiing. Office: IHOP 450 N Brand Blvd Glendale CA 91203-1903*

STEWART, KATHERINE WOOD, middle school educator; b. Fort Belvoir; BME, U. Montevallo, 1977, MEd, 1978. Tchr. Bibb County Sch., Centreville, Ala., 1978—80; art & music tchr. Shelby County Sch., Columbiana, Ala., 1989—. Choir dir., organist U. Bapt. Ch., Montevallo, Ala., 1998—. Mem.: NAEA, ACDA, Music Educators Nat. Conf., Centrala Garden Club (assoc.; pres. 1990—93). Avocations: designing jewelry, gardening. Home: 260 Creek St Montevallo AL 35115 Office: Montevallo Mid Sch 235 Samford St Montevallo AL 35115 Personal E-mail: kathy01204@aol.com.

STEWART, KAY BOONE, writer, retired academic administrator; b. Amarillo, Tex., Feb. 2, 1934; d. Howard Taft and Olive Eugenia (Greer) Boone; m. Robert N. Alkire, July 22, 1952 (div. Aug. 1971); children: Shelley Kay Alkire, Kristin Lynne Alkire Porter; m. Elmer Donald Stewart, July 16, 1978. Student, Phoenix Coll., 1957-64, Glendale (Ariz.) C.C., 1967; BA in Elem. Edn. with distinction, Ariz. State U., 1969; postgrad., Seattle Pacific U., 1988-90. Cert. tchr. elem. edn., Ariz. Tchr. Glendale (Ariz.) Meth. Day Sch., 1960-63, Trinity Meth. Day Sch., Glendale, 1966-67, Ctrl. Meth. Day Sch., Phoenix, 1967-68, Catalina Elem. Sch., Phoenix, 1969-70, Valencia Elem. Sch., Phoenix, 1970-71, Palo Alto Pre-Sch., Tempe, Ariz., 1971-73; sales rep., ednl. program Western Pub., southwestern states, 1972-75; dist. mgr. Brittanica Films Divsn., 1975—78; adminstr., program developer, thcr. Palo Alto and Glendale Meth. Day Sch. Adminstr. Skytech Cons., Inc., Elk Grove, Calif., 1999; prin., owner Kay's Kards, 2001—, Glass Painting, 2002—; watercolor artist, glass painting Kay's Kards: Giftware, 2003. Author: (novel) Chariots of Dawn, 1992, (poetry) Sunrise Over Galilee, 1993, Here's Help, A

Management System for Chronic Fatigue Syndrome, 1996. (poetry) The Color Red, 1994; editor Writers Info. Network, 1986-99; composer and lyricist children's and adults' choir music. Mem. Am. Penwomen (pres. 1990-92), Writers Info. Network, Kappa Delta Phi. Republican. Presbyterian. Avocations: storytelling, singing, harp, directing children's choir. Office: Writers Info Network PO Box 11337 Bainbridge Island WA 98110 E-mail: kstew2234@aol.com, ksb@mymailstation.com.

STEWART, KENNETTE NOWELL, music educator; d. Kenneth and Kay Nowell; m. Scott Lee Stewart, July 30, 1994; 1 child, Kara. BA in History and English, U. N.C., Chapel Hill, 1980; MA in Music Edn., Calif. State U., L.A., 1994. Cert. K-12 music N.C. Tchr. elem. sch. music L.A. Unified Sch. Dist., L.A., 1987—93; tchr. elem. and mid. sch. music Johnston County Schs., Smithfield, NC, 1993—. Coord. mid. sch. honors chorus Johnston County Schs., Smithfield, 1997—2000. Recipient Target Tchr. scholarship, Target, 1998, Ray Boyette Visual Arts/Music grant, Johnston County Edn. Found., 1998, Showcase of Stars grant, 1998; grantee, 2002—03, 2003—04. Avocations: reading, gardening. Office: McGee's Crossroads Mid Sch 13353 NC Hwy 210 Benson NC 27504 Office Phone: 919-894-6003. Office Fax: 919-894-6008. Business E-Mail: kennettestewart@johnston.k12.nc.us.

STEWART, LEORA KLAYMER, textile artist, educator; b. Jerusalem, June 5, 1943; came to the U.S., 1952; d. Errol and Reva (Svirsky) Klaymer. BFA, Art Inst. Chgo., 1962, MFA, 1968. Asst. prof. Tyler Sch. Art, Phila., 1970-72, New Sch. Parsons, N.Y.C., 1974-77; prof. art Baruch Coll., N.Y.C., 1977-96, Fashion Inst. Tech., N.Y.C., 1987—. Textile designer LLAMA Studios, Palm Beach, Fla., 1990-2005, FIT-Textile Surface Design Dept. B521 N.Y.C., 2005-; guest artist Textile Study Group N.Y., 1992, Textile Arts Conf., Chgo., 1993, Textile Conservation Group, 1990; juror/curator of numerous exhbns.; lectr. in field One-woman exhibits include Hadler/Rodriguez Galleries, N.Y.C., 1976, 79, 2/20 Gallery, NYC, 2001, Gayle Willson Gallery, Sothampton, NY, Helsinki Mus. Art & Design, Helen Drutt Gallery, Phila.; two-person shows include Gayle Wilson Gallery, Southampton, L.I., N.Y., 1988, 2/20 Gallery, N.Y.C., 2004; group exhibits include Gayle Wilson Gallery, Southampton, 1993-94, Pres.'s Office-FIT, N.Y., 1993-94, Colonial House Gallery, N.Y., 1994, Faculty Exhbn.-FIT Galleries, N.Y., 1995-2005, Acad. of the Arts, Easton, Md., 1996, Armory Art Ctr., West Palm Beach, Fla, 2004; archtl. commn. Knoll Internat. Showrooms, World Trade Ctr., Dallas, Gotaas-Larsen Shipping Corp., N.Y.C., Bank of Hong Kong, World Trade Ctr., N.Y.C., Bullock's Corp., Christown Mall, Phoenix; represented in permanent collections Prudential Life Ins., Chase Manhattan Bank, Continental Wheat and Grain Corp., S.E. Banking Corp., Becton-Dickson Pharm. Corp Travel grantee Art Inst. Chgo., 1968-69; craftsman fellow Nat. Endowment for the Arts, Washington, 1972-73, 76-77. Avocations: travel, hiking, bicycling, swimming. Office: Fashion Inst Tech 27th St & 7th Ave New York NY 10001 Office Phone: 212-217-7037. Personal E-mail: klaymer1@aol.com.

STEWART, LINDA BERENFIELD, librarian; b. Warren, Pa., June 10, 1942; d. Myer and Ida Belle (Samuels) Berenfield; m. Roger H. Stewart, May 23, 1964; children: Sheri Lynne, Michael Lee. BA, U. Mich., 1964; media specialist, Fla. Atlantic U., 1980; MLS, U. South Fla., 1981. Tchr., Garden City, Mich., 1964-66, Charlottesville, Va., 1967-68; libr. cons. Hosp. Librs., Fort Lauderdale, Fla., 1981-82; reference libr. Hebrew Day Sch. Fort Lauderdale, 1982—. Reference libr. Pompano Beach (Fla.) Pub. Libr., 1983-85. Active Jewish Fedn. Fort Lauderdale, bd. dirs. women's div., 1990-91; pres. Fort Lauderdale Jewish Adoption and Foster Care Orgn. Mem. ALA, Broward County Libr. Assn., Fla. Libr. Assn., Jewish Libr. Assn., Ft. Lauderdale Symphony Soc., Broward Womens Investment Club (past pres.), Ft. Lauderdale Golf Club, Phi Beta Mu. Avocations: travel, reading, tennis. Home: 2350 Sunrise Key Blvd Fort Lauderdale FL 33304-3826 Office: David Posnack Hebrew Day 6511 W Sunrise Blvd Fort Lauderdale FL 33313-6036 E-mail: lbstew@bellsouth.net.

STEWART, LUCILLE MARIE, retired special education coordinator, educator; b. Pitts., Feb. 24; d. William H. and Edna (Hoffman) S. BEd, Duquesne U.; MEd, U. Pitts.; postgrad., Columbia U., U. Calif., Calif. State U. Cert. elem. and secondary tchr., spl. edn. tchr., supr., adminstr. Tchr., group leader mentally retarded Ednl. Alliance, N.Y.C., 1950—53; tchr. Lincoln (Ill.) State Sch., 1953; tchr., program leader, sec. Edn. Alliance, N.Y.C., 1954-58; tchr. mentally retarded Ramapo Ctrl. Sch. Dist., Spring Valley, NY, 1958-60, tchr. seriously emotionally disturbed, 1960-64, supr. presch. program for educationally disadvantaged, 1965-67; program dir. Pomona (N.Y.) Camp for Retarded, summers 1960-63; tchr. mentally retarded Stockton Sch., San Diego, 1964-65; tchr. mentally retarded sch. Cathedral City Sch., 1967-78; program specialist spl. edn. Palm Springs (Calif.) Unified Sch. Dist., 1978-95, prin. elem. summer schs., 1971-72; tchr. elem. mentally retarded sch. Palm Springs (Calif.) Unified; prin.-tchr. Summer Extended Sch. for Spl. Students, summer 1979-99. Exec. com. U. Calif. Extension, area adv. com.; spl. edn. surrogate parent Palm Springs Unified Sch. Dist. Mem. NEA, AAUW, ASCD, Calif. Adminstrs. Spl. Edn. (desert cmty. mental health childrens com.), Coun. Exceptional Children (adminstrn. divsn., early childhood-learning handicap divsns.), Am. Assn. Childhood Edn., Autism Soc., Coachella Valley, Learning Disabilities Assn., Creative Desert, Desert Theater League, Alpha Kappa Alpha, Phi Delta Kappa, Delta Kappa Gamma.

STEWART, MARCIA KATHRYN, music educator; b. Lafayette, La., Dec. 18, 1946; d. Seaborn Buffard and CoraLee (Herndon) Young; m. G. Carter Stewart, June 29; children: Melanie Maxwell, Ben Steward, Stephanie Christiansen. BS in Music Edn., McMurry Coll., Abilene, Tex., 1968. Music tchr. Taylor County Schs., Abilene, 1968—69, Reagen Elem. Sch., Abilene, 1969—72, Hollis Elem. Sch., Okla., 1991—; ch. sec. Southside Bapt. Ch., Abilene, 1972—79, 1st Bapt. Ch., Hollis, 1989—91; switchboard operator Vernon Savs. & Loan, Tex., 1986—89. Office: Gillentine Elem Sch PO Box 193 Hollis OK 73550-0193

STEWART, MARGARET MCBRIDE, biology professor, researcher; b. Guilford County, NC, Feb. 6, 1927; d. David Henry and Mary Ellen (Morrow) S.; m. Paul C. Lemon, June 1962 (div. 1968); m. George Edward Martin, Dec. 19, 1969. AB, U. N.C.-Greensboro, 1948; MA, U. N.C.-Chapel Hill, 1951; PhD, Cornell U., 1956; DSc (hon.), U. P.R., Mayaquez, 1996. Instr. biology Greensboro Evening Coll. U. N.C., Greensboro, 1950-51; instr. biology Catawba Coll., Salisbury, N.C., 1951-53; extension botanist Cornell U., Ithaca, N.Y., 1954-56; asst. prof. biology SUNY, Albany, 1956-59, assoc. prof., 1959-65, prof. vertebrate biology, 1965-97, disting. tchg. prof., 1977—, disting. tchg. prof. emerita, 1997; dir. Program in Biodiversity Conservation and Policy, 1997-2000. Faculty rsch. participant Oak Ridge Assoc. Univs., 1983. Author: (with A.H. Benton) Keys to the Vertebrates of the Northeastern States, 1964, Amphibians of Malawi, 1967; contbr. numerous articles and revs. to profl. jours. Bd. dirs. E.N. Huyck Nature Preserve, Rensselaerville, N.Y., 1976-86; bd. dirs. Ea. N.Y. chpt. Nature Conservancy, 1983-88, 90-96, 97-2004, N.Y. State chpt., 1987-90; mem. Albany Pine Bush Commn., 1993-2004. Recipient Citizen Laureate award SUNY Found., 1987, Oak Leaf award Nature Conservancy, 1997; Am. Philos. Soc. rsch. grantee, 1975, 81, NSF grantee, 1978-80, Oak Ridge Assocs. Univs. grantee, 1983-97. Fellow Herpetologists' League (bd. dirs. 1978-80); mem. Soc. for Study of Amphibians and Reptiles (pres. 1979), Am. Soc. Ichthyologists and Herpetologists (bd. govs. 1975-80, 87-90, 96—, herpetology editor 1983-85, pres. 1996, historian 1999-2004, Johnson award 2005, Fitch award 2005), Ecol. Soc. Am., Assn. for Tropical Biologists, Soc. Study of Evolution, III World Congress of Herpetology (mem. exec. com. 1995-01), Sigma Xi, Sigma Delta Epsilon, Phi Beta Kappa (emeritus), Phi Kappa Phi. Democrat. Presbyterian. Avocations: photography, gardening, reading, travel. Office: SUNY Dept Biol Scis 1400 Washington Ave Albany NY 12222-1000

STEWART, MARSHA BEACH, performing arts educator; b. Memphis, Jan. 17, 1952; d. Bruce Charles and Marjorie Hudson (Campbell) Stewart; 1 child, Myra Grace. BBA in Internat. Bus., U. Tex., 1982; MFA in Arts Adminstrn./Dance Mgmt., Yale Sch. Drama, 1985; MS in Ednl. Adminstrn., CUNY, 2004. Mng. dir. Yale Cabaret, New Haven, 1984-85; agt. Columbia Artists Mgmt., Inc., NYC, 1985-90; v.p., dir. sales SATRA Arts Internat. (formerly Classical Artists), NYC, 1990-92; pres. Beach Internat. Enterprises, Inc., NYC, 1993—95; tchr. NYC Dept. Edn., 1999—, Fulbright Meml. Fund, 2003—. Dancer with Louisville Ballet (formerly Civic Ballet), 1967-70, Actor's Theatre of Louisville, 1972, Arena Stage, Washington, 1972, Disney on Parade, NBC, S.Am., Europe, Africa, 1974, 75, 76, Geneva Ballet Co., 1975, 76; dance chairwoman cultural entertainment com. U. Tex., Austin, 1981-82. NEA fellow, 1983, assoc., 1984. Mem. Yale U. Alumni Assn., Kentuckians of NYC, Scottish Heritage Soc., NY Caledonian Club. Avocations: travel, languages.

STEWART, MARSHA K., science educator; d. Robert and Dee Sewell; m. Lynn Stewart, Dec. 6, 1997; children: Heath, Kyle, Abby. AA, NECC, Norfolk, 1971; BS in Edn., Wayne State Coll., Nebr., 1973; MA, U. Nebr., Kearney, 1991. Cert. profl. tchr. Nebr., 1973. Sci. tchr. Petersburg (Nebr.) Pub. Sch., 1973—75; tchr. Dist. #19 Stanton, Nebr., 1975—80, Dist.#25, Norfolk, 1980—81; jr. high tchr. Hadar (Nebr.) Pub. Schs., 1981—87; sci. tchr. Norfolk Cath. Schs., 1987—. Sci. chmn. Norfolk Cath. HS, Norfolk, 1994—. Named Tchr. of Yr., Omaha Archdiocese, 1992, Norfolk Kiwanis Tchr. of Yr., Kiwanis of Norfolk, 1992, Crystal Apple Tchr. of Yr., Norfolk Cath. HS, 2000; recipient Treck of the Mammoth Tchr. award, Chadron State Coll., 1992, Presdl. Award for Excellence in Sci. Tchg. Honoree, Nebr. Dept. Edn., 1993; NEWMAST Summer Rsch. grantee, NASA, 1993, Beloit Summer Rsch. grantee, Beloit U., 1999. Mem.: NE CC, NSTA, Nebr. Assn. Tchrs. Sci. Home: 107 South 16th St Norfolk NE 68701 Office: Norfolk Catholic Schools 2300 Madison Ave Norfolk NE 68701 Office Phone: 402-371-2784. Personal E-mail: mkaystewart@yahoo.com. Business E-Mail: marshastewart@ncknights.com.

STEWART, MARTHA KOSTYRA, entrepreneur, lecturer, author; b. Jersey City, Aug. 3, 1941; d. Edward and Martha (Ruszkowski) Kostyra; m. Andy Stewart, July 1, 1961 (div. 1990); 1 child, Alexis Gilbert. BA European History and Archtl. History, Barnard Coll. Former model; former stockbroker N.Y.C.; former profl. caterer; mag. owner, editor-in-chief Martha Stewart Living, 1990—97; CEO Martha Stewart Living Omnimedia, 1997—2003, chief creative officer, 2003—04, chmn., 1997—2004, founding editl. dir., 2004—. Lifestyle cons. for K-Mart Corp., 1987; bd. dirs., NYSE, 2002-04. Host (TV show) Martha Stewart Living, 1993-2004, The Apprentice: Martha Stewart, 2005, (TV talk show) Martha 2005-; Author: (with Elizabeth Hawes) Entertaining, 1982, Weddings, 1987; Martha Stewart Hors d'Oeurvres: The Creation and Presentation of Fabulous Finger Food, 1984, Martha Stewart's Pies and Tarts, 1985, Martha Stewart's Quick Cook Menus: Fifty-two Meals You Can Make in Under an Hour, 1988, The Wedding Planner, 1988, Martha Stewart's Gardening: Month by Month, 1991, Martha Stewart's New Old House: Restoration, Renovation, Decoration, 1992, Martha Stewart's Christmas, 1993, Martha Stewart's Menus for Entertaining, 1994, Holidays, 1994, Good Things: The Best of Martha Stewart Living, 1997, Four Seasons of Great Menus to Make Every Day, 1997, Hors D'Oeuvres Handbook, 1999, The Best of Martha Stewart Living: Weddings, 1999, The Barefoot Contessa Cookbook: Secrets from the East Hampton Specialty Food Store for Simple Food and Party Platters You Can Make at Home, 1999, (with Ina Garten) Favorite Comfort Food, 1999, The Martha Stewart Living Cookbook, 2000, Halloween: The Best of Martha Stewart Living, 2001, Classic Crafts and Recipes Inspired by the Songs of Christmas, 2002, Martha Stewart Living 2003, Recipes, 2002, Simple Home Solutions, 2004, The Martha Rules, 2005, Martha Stewart's Baking Handbook, 2005, Martha Stewart's Homekeeping Handbook: The Essential Guide to Caring for Everything in Your Home, 2006; appeared in semi-monthly cooking segment on Today Show; syndicated columnist, NY Times. Named one of World's 100 Most Influential People, Time Mag., 2005, 50 Most Powerful Women in Bus., Fortune mag., 2006. Office: 10 Saugatuck Ave Westport CT 06880-5720 also: care Susan Magrino Agy 40 W 57th St Fl 31 New York NY 10019-4001*

STEWART, MARY R., artist, educator; BFA, U. New Mex., 1975; MFA, Ind. U., 1980. Asst. prof. U. of Ark., 1980—81; instr. Santa Rosa Jr. Coll., Calif., 1981—82; asst. prof. Dickinson Coll., Carlisle, Pa., 1982—85; assoc. prof. Syracuse U., 1985—2001, No. Ill. U., 2001—. Cons. SUNY, Oswego, NY, 2000, U. Tenn., Knoxville, 2000; scholarly artist in residence Colo. Coll., 2000; artists fellowship Va. Ctr. for the Creative Arts, 1994, 95, 98, 99, 2003, artist fellowship, 05; artists fellowship Ore. Coll. of Art and Craft, 1993; v.p. conf. program Found. in Art Theory and Edn., 1995—97, v.p. for regional programming, 2001—03. Exhibitions include St. Bonaventure U., 2001, Everson Mus. of Art, 1993, U. of Richmond, 2003; author: Launching the Imagination: A Comprehensive Guide to Basic Design, Launching the Imagination: 2D Design, Launching the Imagination: 3D Design, Sucess Stragegies in Art and Design. Office: Sch of Art No Ill U 314D Ahrends Hall Dekalb IL 60115 E-mail: mstewart@niu.edu.

STEWART, MARY TOMLINSON, science educator, researcher; b. San Francisco, Aug. 27, 1944; d. John Reid and Evelyn M. (Munro) Tomlinson; children: David Christophere, Mary Cameron. BA, Goddard Coll., 1966; MLS, U. Okla., 1990; MSMSE, U. Tulsa, 1996. Tchr. Hyde Park (Vt.) Elem., 1966—78; reading tchr. Marlow (Okla.) Elem., 1978—84; tchr. Monte Casino Elem., Tulsa, 1984—88; tchr. gifted Emerson Elem., Tulsa, 1988—93; adminstr. sci. Okla State Dept. Edn., Okla. City, 1993—96, Tulsa Pub. Schs., 1996—2002; rsch. assoc. U. Tulsa, 2002—. Co-author: Fossils to Fuel, 1995, Petro Active, 1998. Corr. sec. PEO, Tulsa, 1997—. Named Support Person of Yr., Tulsa Pub. Schs., 2001; recipient Jack Renner award, Okla. Sci. Tchrs. Assn., 1998. Mem.: Nat. Math. Sci. Tchrs. Assn. (chair 1990—), Coalition for Advancement Sci. (pres., v.p., bd. mem. 1995—2006). Democrat. Unitaria. Avocations: reading, travel. Home: 4638 S Quincy Pl Tulsa OK 74105 Office: U Tulsa 600S Coll Tulsa OK 74104 Business E-Mail: marytstewart1@netzero.net.

STEWART, MIRIAM KAY (MIMI STEWART), state legislator, educator; b. Sarasota, Fla., Jan. 27, 1947; d. Wilbur H. Stewart and Alice Miriam Beck; children: Boris Nathan Margolin, Hannah Beck Margolin. BA cum laude, Boston U., 1971; MS, Wheelock Coll., 1977. Spl. educator, 1977—2004; mem. N. Mex. Ho. of Reps., Albuquerque, 1994—. Democrat. Address: 313 Moon St NE Albuquerque NM 87123-1151 Office Phone: 505-880-8249 ext. 113. E-mail: mstewart@osogrande.com.

STEWART, PATRICIA CARRY, foundation administrator; b. Bklyn., May 19, 1928; d. William J. and Eleanor (Murphy) Carry; m. Charles Thorp Stewart, May 30, 1976. Student, U. Paris, 1948—49; BA, Cornell U., 1950. Fgn. corr. Irving Trust Co., N.Y.C., 1950-51; with Janeway Rsch. Co., N.Y.C., 1951-60, sec., treas., 1955-60; with Buckner & Co. and successor firms, N.Y.C., 1961-73, ptnr., 1962-70, v.p., treas., 1970-71, pres., treas., 1971-73, Knight, Carry, Bliss & Co., Inc., N.Y.C., 1971-73, G. Tsai & Co., Inc., 1973; v.p. Edna McConnell Clark Found. Inc., 1974-92. Dir. Cmty. Found. Palm Beach and Martin Counties, 1993-2001, chair, 1998, 2000; allied mem. N.Y. Stock Exch., 1962-73; past mem. nominating com. Am. Stock Exch., N.Y. Stock Exch., N.Y.C. Fin. Svcs. Corp.; dir. emeritus, past chmn. Investor Responsibility Rsch. Ctr. Trustee emerita, vice chair Cornell U., mem. bd. life overseers Cornell Med. Coll.; mem. vis. com. Grad. Sch Bus., Harvard U., 1974-80; bd. dirs. NOW Legal Def. and Edn. Fund, 1984-92, Women in Founds./Corp. Philanthropy, 1980-86; v.p. fin. com. Women's Forum, 1982-90; vice chmn. CUNY, 1976-80; bd. dirs. United Way of Tri-State, 1977-81, Inst. for Edn. and Rsch. on Women and Work; voting mem. Blue Cross and Blue Shield Greater N.Y., 1975-82; trustee N.Y. State 4-H Found., 1970-76, Internt. Inst. Rural Reconstrn., 1974-79; mem. N.Y.C. panel White House Fellows, 1976-78; mem. bus. adv. coun. The Hosp. Chaplaincy. Recipient Elizabeth Cutter Morrow award YWCA, 1977, Catalyst award Women Dirs. in Corps., 1978, Trustee medal CUNY, 1983, Acomplishment award Wings Club N.Y. 1984, Women's Funding Coalition Innovators for Women$hare award, 1986, Banking Industry Achievement award Nat. Assn. Bank Women, 1987, Cert. Disting. Accomplishments Barnard Coll., 1989; named to YWCA Acad. Women Achievers. Mem. Fin. Women's Assn. N.Y., Country Club of Fla. (bd. dirs.), Univ. Club (N.Y.C), Gullane Golf Club (Scotland), North Berwick Golf Club (Scotland), Dunbar Golf Club (Scotland), St. Andrews Club (Delray Beach, Fla.), Phi Beta Phi. Home and Office: 2613 N Ocean Blvd Delray Beach FL 33483-7367 also: Halfland Barns North Berwick EH395PW Scotland Personal E-mail: stewartpc@aol.com.

STEWART, PATRICIA KIMBRIEL, retired legal assistant; b. Memphis, Apr. 4, 1939; d. Albert Lafayette Kimbriel and Mildred Inez McKinney; m. Benjamin Franklin Stewart, Oct. 21, 1972 (div. Mar. 4, 1993); children: Benjamin Franklin III, Patrick Kimbriel. BA, Belmont U., Nashville, 1963. Cert. Fed. Income Tax Course II, H&R Block, 1985; Inst. of Children's Lit. Conn., 2006. Investor rels. Tyler Corp., Dallas, 1993—97; legal asst. Gardere Wynne Sewell, Dallas, 1997—2004. Computer consulting Arlington Ind. Sch. Dist, Tex., 1985—86. Participant Sanctuary Choir, Arlington, Tex., 2005—06. Mem.: Soc. of Children's Book Writers & Illustrators. Conservative. Baptist. Avocations: travel, reading, gardening, writing. Home: 2447 N Graham Dr Arlington TX 76013 Personal E-mail: pstew4439@sbcglobal.net.

STEWART, PATRICIA RHODES, former clinical psychologist, researcher; b. Vallejo, Calif., Feb. 11, 1910; d. Butler Young Rhodes and Sarah Virginia (Ryan) Rhodes; m. John Kenneth Stewart (div.); children: John K., Nancy Rush. AB summa cum laude, Stanford U., 1930; MA, San Jose State U., 1959; PhD, U. London, 1963. Tchg. asst. San Jose State U., 1959—60; staff psychologist Napa State Hosp., 1964—77; pvt. practice in psychotherapy Berkeley, Calif., 1978—94; pvt. rsch. in adolescent deviance, 1979—85. Staff psychologist Westwood Mental Health Facility, Fremont, Calif., 1985-88. Author: Children in Distress: American and English Perspectives, 1976. Chair criminal justice com. No. Calif. region Am. Friends Svc. com., San Francisco, 1977-80, chair exec. com. 1970-74, 80-83, bd. dirs., 1980-83; bd. dirs. Friends Com. on Legis., Sacramento, 1985-88, No. Calif. Ecumenical Coun., Oakland, Calif., 1989-95. Mem. APA, AAAS, Phi Beta Kappa. Mem. Soc. Of Friends. Home: 1225 Monterey Ave Berkeley CA 94707-2718

STEWART, PHILLIS, museum official; Pres. Nev. State Mus., Carson City. Office: Nev State Mus 600 N Carson St Carson City NV 89701-4004

STEWART, RITA JOAN, academic administrator; b. Muncie, Ind., June 6, 1945; d. John Marion and Crystalee Masterson; children: Jon Lewis, Robert Forrest. BS, Ball State U., 1967, MA, 1974. Tchr. Blue River H.S., Mt. Summit, Ind., 1968-69, Sunnyside Elem. Sch., New Castle, Ind., 1967-68; copywriter, announcer Sta. WTIM, Taylorville, Ill., 1974-75; dir. Kitselman Conf. Ctr. Ball State U., Muncie, Ind., 1978-2000, dir. conf. and spl. events, 2000—. Contbr. articles to profl. jours. Precinct committeewoman Henry County Dem. Party, New Castle, Ind., 1969-70; precinct chmn. March of Dimes, New Castle, Ind., 1974-75; chmn. edn. com. West Viwe Sch. Coun., Muncie, 1987-88; sec., bd. dirs. PAL Club, Muncie, 1988-93; pres., bd. dirs. Altrusa Club Found., Muncie, 1997-98, v.p., 2001-01, pres., 2002. Mem.: AAUW (v.p. 1984—85), Ind. Conf. Dirs. Assn., Assn. Collegiate Conf. and Event Dirs. Internat. (dir. region 8 1999—2000, pres. elect 2006—, internat. bd. dirs., Mentor Yr. award 2004), Altrusa Club of Muncie (pres. 2002—03), Kappa Delta Pi (Disting. Svc. award 1995). Methodist. Office: Ball State U Confs and Spl Events Muncie IN 47306 Home: # 1-203 4501 N Wheeling Ave Muncie IN 47304-1277 Office Phone: 765-285-1396. Office Fax: 765-285-5457. Business E-Mail: conferences@bsu.edu.

STEWART, RUTH ANN, public policy educator; b. Chgo., Apr. 4, 1942; d. Elmer Ashton and Ann (Mitchell) Stewart; m. David Levering Lewis; children: Allegra Stewart, Jason Lewis, Allison Lewis, Eric Lewis. Student, U. Chgo., 1960-61, Simmons Coll., 1963; BA, Wheaton Coll., Norton, Mass., 1963; MS, Columbia U., 1965; postgrad., Fisk U., 1970, Harvard U., 1976, postgrad., 1987. Mktg. mgr. Macmillan Co., N.Y.C., 1968-70; asst. chief Schomburg Ctr. Rsch. Black Culture, N.Y.C., 1970-80; assoc. dir. external svcs. N.Y. Pub. Libr., 1980-86; asst. Libr. Congress Nat. Programs, Washington, 1986-89; assoc. Dir. Resource Devel., Washington, 1989-95; sr. policy analyst arts, humanities & social legis. Congl. Rsch. Svc., Washington, 1989-97; rsch. prof. cultural policy Ctr. Urban Policy Rsch. Bloustein Sch. Planning and Pub. Policy, Rutgers U., New Brunswick, NJ, 1997—2003; clin. prof. Wagner Grad. Sch. Pub. Svc., NYU, N.Y.C., 2003—. Trustee, sec. Wheaton Coll., Norton, 1980—99; mem. libr. vis. com. Harvard U., 1975—88, MIT, 1986—90. Cons. editor: Jour. Arts Mgmt. Law and Soc., 1998—, founding co-editor: book series Public Life of the Arts, 1998—. Bd. dirs. Nat. Pk. Found., Washington, 1978—84, Fund Folk Culture, Santa Fe, 1991—2003, Lab. Sch. Washington, 1992—94, Women's Fgn. Policy Group, 1999—2003, Bklyn. Bot. Garden, 2000—, Studio in Sch., 2000—, Cooper-Hewitt Nat. Design Mus., Smithsonian Instn., 2003—; mem. rsch. adv. coun. Ctr. Arts and Culture, Washington, 1997—2006; sch. com. Alvin Ailey Sch., 1998—. Fellow, NY State Coun. Arts. Mem.: Coun. Fgn. Rels., ArtTable (nat. bd. dirs. 2002—03), Friends of Edn., Mus. Modern Art. Office: NYU Wagner Sch 295 Lafayette St New York NY 10012 Office Phone: 212-998-7480.

STEWART, SANDRA KAY, music educator; b. New Albany, Ind., Dec. 24, 1947; d. Dale F. and June V. (Martin) Byrne; m. William Lee Stewart, June 25, 1971. B Music Edn., Ind. U., 1969; MusM, Norfolk State U., 1992; D Mus. Arts, U. S.C., 1995. Cert. vocal music tchr., N.Y., Mo.; nat. cert., state cert. piano tchr. Vocal music tchr., choral dir. Ritenour Sch. Dist., St. Louis, 1969-75, Sch. Dist. # 54, Chgo., 1975-76, Waverly (N.Y.) Jr./Sr. H.S., 1977-78, Clarence (N.Y.) H.S., 1978-82; piano instr., show choir dir. Inst. Fine Arts, Reading, Pa., 1982-85; piano accompanist Berks Grand Opera Co., Reading, Pa., 1982-85, Va. Opera Co., Norfolk, 1986, U. S.C., Columbia, 1992-95, Jacksonville Masterworks Sr. Chorale, 1996-99, Bolles Sr. H.S., 1996-98, Pinewood Presbyn. Ch., 1996-98; piano and music theory instr. Acad. of Music, Virginia Beach, Va., 1986-91, 2002—03; piano instr., choral dir., vocal jazz dir., accompanist Jacksonville (Fla.) U., 1995—2000; chair vocal music dept. Douglas Anderson Sch. of Arts, 1998—2000; prof. music U. North Fla., Jacksonville, 2000—. Editor: Florida Music Teacher, 1999-2000; contbr. articles to profl. publs. Mem. Virginia Beach Pops Orch., 1989-91; founder, dir. North Fla. Piano Camp, 2000-2006. Recipient Fla. First Lady's Art Scholar award, 2000. Mem. AAUW (numerous offices 1975—), Am. Choral Dirs. Assn., Coll. Music Soc., Nat. Piano Found., Music Educators Nat. Conf., Nat. Guild Piano Tchrs., Music Tchrs. Nat. Assn., Delius Assn. Fla. (bd. dirs. 1997-99), Phi Kappa Lambda, Mu Phi Epsilon, Delta Kappa Gamma Soc. Internat., TRI-M Music Honor Soc. Home: 4782 Harpers Ferry Ln Jacksonville FL 32257-4544 Office: U North Fla 4567 St Johns Bluff Rd S Jacksonville FL 32224 Office Phone: 904-620-3854.

STEWART, SUE S., lawyer; b. Oct. 9, 1942; d. Fraizer McVale and Carolyn Eliabeth (Hunt) S.; m. Arthur L. Stern, III, July 31, 1965 (div.); m. children: Anne, Mark Alan; m. John A. Ciampa, Sept. 1, 1985 (div.); m. Stephen L. Raymond (dec.). BA, Wellesley Coll., 1964; postgrad., Harvard U. Law Sch., 1964-65; JD, Georgetown U., 1967. Bar: N.Y. 1968. Clk. to judges Juvenile Ct., Washington, 1967-68; mem. Nixon, Hargrave, Devans & Doyle (now Nixon Peabody LLP), Rochester, NY, 1968-74, ptnr., 1975—2001, mng. ptnr., 1998—2001, ret., 2001; v.p., gen. counsel U. Rochester, 2003—. Lectr. in field; trustee Found. of Monroe County (N.Y.) Bar, 1976-78; v.p. & Gen. Counsel Univ. Rochester, NY, 2003-. Author: Charitable Giving and Solicitation. Sec., dir. United Cmty. Chest of Greater Rochester, 1973-87, 1992-; trustee, sec. Internat. Mus. Photography at George Eastman House, Rochester, 1974-97, 2000-03, Genesee Country Mus., Mumford, N.Y., 1976-2002; bd. dirs. Ctr. for Govtl. Rsch., 1990-97; trustee, chmn. United Neighborhood Ctr. of Greater Rochester Found., 1991-2003; trustee, chmn. exec. com. Nat. Ctr. Edn. and Economy, 1997-; dir. Canandaigua (N.H.) Nat. Bank, 2000-. Mem. ABA (chmn. task force on charitable giving, exempt orgs. com. tax sect. 1981-2003), N.Y. State Bar (exec. com. tax sect. 1974-76, chmn. com. exempt orgns. 1975-76), Monroe County Bar Assn. (trustee 1974-75), BNA Portfolio, Pvt. Found. Distbns. (Athena award 2000, de Tocqueville award 2003). Office: Office of Counsel 266 Wallis Hall PO Box 270040 Rochester NY 14627-0040 Office Phone: 585-273-2167.

STEWART, SUSAN, writer; b. 1952; BA, Dickinson Coll., 1973; MA, Johns Hopkins U., 1975; PhD, U. Pa., 1978. Asst. prof. dept. English Temple U., Phila., 1978—81, assoc. prof., 1981—85, prof., 1986—87; Regan prof.

English U. Pa., Phila., 1997—. Vis. scholar Getty Ctr. for the History of Art and the Humanities, Santa Monica, Calif., 1995. Author: Nonsense: Aspects of Intertextuality in Folklore and Literature, 1979, On Longing: Narratives of the Miniature, the Gigantic, the Souvenir, the Collection, 1984, Crimes of Writing: Problems in the Containment of Representation, 1991, poetry. Recipient Individual Writer's award, Lila Wallace-Reader's Digest Found., 1996; fellow, Nat. Endowment for the Arts, 1982, 1990, Pa. Coun. on the Arts, 1984, 1988, John Simon Guggenheim Meml. Found., 1987; MacArthur fellow, 1997. Office: Univ Pa Dept English 119 Bennett Hall 3340 Walnut St Philadelphia PA 19104-6273

STEWART, SUSAN HAMILTON, medical/surgical and oncological nurse; b. Williamson, W.Va., May 11, 1963; d. Graydon Alexander and Frances (Oakes) Hamilton; 1 child, Kenna Leigh. ADN, So. W.Va. C.C., Williamson, 1983; BSN summa cum laude, W.Va. U., 1990, MSN, 1994. RN, Ky.; cert. family nurse practitioner; cert. nursing adminstrn., advanced. Instr. Mingo County Bd. Edn., Williamson, 1988; pediatric staff charge nurse Appalachian Regional Healthcare, Inc., South Williamson, Ky., 1983, med.-surg. charge nurse, 1989, emergency room staff nurse, 1989-90, pediatric advanced life support, 1991—98; family nurse practitioner Pikeville Meth. Hosp., 1995—2000, dir. ambulatory clinics, 1998-99; dir. Leonard Lawson Cancer Care Ctr., 1999-2000. Mem. advanced nursing practice coun. Ky. Bd. Nursing, 1997-2000. Mem. ANA, Ky. Nurses Assn., Ky. Coalition of Nurse Practioners and Nurse Midwives, Sigma Theta Tau.

STEWART, TERRY, lawyer; b. San Francisco; life ptnr. Carole Scagnetti; 1 adopted child. Diploma, Cornell U., 1981; JD, Boalt Hall Sch. Law, 1981. Law clk. 11th cir. Ct. Appeals, Savannah, Ga., 1981—82; ptnr. Howard, Rice, Nemerovski, Canady, Robertson, & Falk; chief dep. city attorney San Francisco, 2002—. Pro bono counsel Internat. Dog Racing Assn.; vol. asst. Iditarod. Mem.: Bar Assn. San Francisco (founder Sch.-to-Coll. program 1999—, pres. 1999). Known for representing same-sex marriage rights in San Francisco. Office: City Hall Rm 234 1 Dr Carlton B Goodlet Pl San Francisco CA 94102-4682

STEWART, TRACY FLOOD, social studies educator; b. Hereford, Tex., Oct. 31, 1971; d. Darrell L. and Jackie S. Flood; m. Douglas Duane Stewart, July 29, 1995. BS in Govt., W. Tex. A&M U., Canyon, 1995, M in Edn. Adminstrn., 2005. Cert. Tex. Dept. Edn., 1995. Tchr. Hereford (Tex.) Jr. High, 1995—, social studies dept. chair, 2003—06. Panhandle area collaboration for excellence in tchg. Am. history Edn. Svc. Ctr., Amarillo, Tex. Independent. Methodist. Avocations: travel, reading. Office: Hereford Jr High Sch 704 La Plata Dr Hereford TX 79045 Office Phone: 806-363-7630.

STEWART, VERLINDSEY LAQUETTA, accounting educator; b. Birmingham, Ala., Dec. 27, 1965; d. Nathan Jr. and Shirley Ruth Brown; m. Kelvin Lorenzo Stewart I, June 22, 1991 (div. Feb. 1999); 1 child, Kelvin Lorenzo II. BS in Acctg., Ala. A&M U., 1988, MS in Bus. Edn., 1995, AA Cert. in Bus. Edn., 1997; EdD in Higher Edn. Leadership, Nova Southeastern U., 2004. Cert. tchr. bus. 7-12 Ala. Jr. acct. Childress Acctg., Huntsville, Ala., 1990-93; acctg. clk. Appeal Beauty Salon, Huntsville, 1988-94; receptionist Coop. Ext., Normal, Ala., 1992-94; grad. asst. Ala. A&M U., Normal, 1995; student tchr. J.O. Johnson H.S., Huntsville, Ala., 1995; acctg. instr. J.F. Drake State Tech., Huntsville, 1996—. Cons. Jr. Achievement, Huntsville, 1995—96. Post-reviewer: (book) College Accounting 9th, 1999 (Honorarium 1999). Vol. Habitat for Humanity, Huntsville, 1995-97; vol. asst. leader Girl Scouts North Ala., Huntsville, 1995-96. Recipient Adminstrv. Acad. award Rust Coll., 1999, Emerging Leaders Sch. award Ala. Edn. Assn., 1994, Ala. Master Tchr. Seminar, 2001. Mem. Nat. Bus. Edn., Ea. Star Mitzpah Ctr., Phi Beta Lambda (adviser 1998—), Delta Sigma Theta. Democrat. Baptist. Avocations: aerobics, weights, reading, listening to jazz music. Office: JF Drake State Tech Coll 3421 Meridian St N Huntsville AL 35811-1544 Personal E-mail: vbdst28@aol.com.

STEWART SIMPSON, DONNAMAY ANGELA, interior designer; b. Mandeville, Jamaica, W.I., Dec. 31, 1965; d. Ermine Stewart and Mary Ester Stewart Bromfield; m. Everton Seymour Simpson (div.); 1 child, Dimitre Andre Simpson. Student, Miami Dade C.C., 1986. Sec. Jamaica Transformer Co., 1986—87; secretarial clk. Pat Thompson Constrn. Co., Jamaica, 1987—89; ops. mgr. Blaise Trust, Mandeville, Jamaica, 1989, Nat. Car Rental, Mandeville, Jamaica, 1989—90; sec., accounts clk. Simpsons Wholesale Co., Elizabeth, Jamaica, 1990—91; ops. mgr. Simpson Supermarket, Elizabeth, Jamaica, 1991—94, Wesley Plz., Mandeville, Jamaica, 1995—97; owner Angelique Enterprises, Miramar, Fla., 1997—; fgn. exch. teller Ft. Lauderdale Internat. Airport, 1999—2001. Songwriter: Hill Top Records, 2006, Amerecord. Interior decorator, stage performer Perfect Praise Sch. Dance, Fla., 2002; conf. spkr. Women's Empowerment Conf. Believers and Achievers Internat., 1998. Mem.: Reagan Ranch Found., Paralyzed Vets. Am., USO, U.S. Navy Meml., Internat. Poetry Soc. Avocations: dance, writing, design, motivational speaking. Home: 1980 SW 103d Terr Miramar FL 33025 Office: Angelique Enterprises 1980 SW 103d Terr Miramar FL 33025 Office Phone: 954-295-8694. E-mail: Dimitre01@aol.com.

STEWART TYLER, VIVIAN DELOIS, primary school educator; b. Birmingham, Ala., June 30, 1940; d. Hessie Stewart and Johnnie Lee Bell Stewart; children: Evelyn, Elizabeth, Felicia. BA, Shaw U., Raleigh, N.C., 1976; MA, Governor's State U., Park Forest South, Ill., 1985. Tchr. St. Mary's Alternative HS, Chgo., 1976—81; commr. State Ill. Human Rights Commn., Ill., 1993—99; tchr., k-9th grades Chgo. Bd. Edn., Chgo., 1976—. Cons. Midwest Cmty. Coun.; mem. Midwest Cmty. Coun. Women Aux.; sec. Introspect Youth Services; unit chairperson & co-chairperson Chgo. LWV, Unit 11, Chgo. Recipient Westside Jewel award, Midwest Cmty. Coun., 1970, Svc. in Leadership award, 1997, Legacy award, Martin Luther King Jr. Boys and Girls Clubs of Chgo., 1995, Everyday Hero award, Lt. Gov., 2000. Mem.: The Excellentia (v.p., polit. affairs, Mem. of the Yr. 1997, 1998).

STEYTLER, C. ANNE WEBSTER, clinical social worker; b. Milw., Jan. 10, 1921; d. Royden Erastus and Jessie Emily (Beebe) Webster; m. Walter David Stimple, Dec. 31, 1941 (dec. May 1951); children: Jeanne Elizabeth Pitz, Alan Lee Steytler, Margaret Anne Rosenfield; m. Edmund John Steytler, Dec. 25, 1951 (dec. May 1998); 1 child, Carolyn Sue. BS, U. Wis., 1943, MA, 1945; MSSA, Western Res. U., Cleve., 1967. LSW, Pa. Instr. U. Wis., Madison, Wis., 1946-47; pediatric aide Wis. Gen. Hosp., Madison, 1947-49; tchr. Blacksburg (Va.) High Sch., 1951-52; order clerk med. libr. U. N.C., Chapel Hill, 1953-55; caseworker children's svcs. Lake County Welfare Dept., Painesville, Ohio, 1964-65; psychiatric social worker Lake County MH-MR Ctr., Mentor, Ohio, 1967-69; psychiatric unit dir. Southeastern MH-MR Ctr., Pitts., 1969-77; pvt. practice Pitts., 1974-95; staff therapist Persad Ctr., Inc., Pitts., 1983-95; sex educator Family Health Coun., Pitts., 1991—. In house therapist Dr. John Morocca, Sewickley, Pa., 1981-83; cons. Project Headstart, Pitts., 1980-83; cons., educator Parent and Child Guidance Ctr., Pitts., 1984-86; sex educator, Women's Health Svcs., Pitts., 1978-90. Co-founder Pub. Library, ad hoc com., Murray, Ky., 1962, Family Planning Svcs., Lake and Geauga Counties, Ohio, 1968, Women's Ctr. and Shelter, Pitts., 1974; lay leader Unitarian Universalist Ch. South Hills, Pitts., 1975-77; bd. dir., troop leader, day camp dir., Girl Scouts U.S., Murray, 1957; bd. dirs. Thomas Merton Ctr., Alliance for Progressive Action, 1995—. Mem. NASW (diplomate), Internat. Transactional Analysis Assn., Am. Assn. Marriage and Family Therapists. Democrat. Avocations: reading, theater, camping, gardening.

STICH, ROBERTA LYNN, not-for-profit fundraiser, social worker; b. N.Y.C., N.Y., May 23, 1948; d. Melvin Harold Stich and Shirley Pearl Kaplan-Stich. Student, U. Rochester, 1965—67; BA, Bklyn. Coll., 1970; MSW, Hunter Coll., 1972; postgrad., Stanford Law Sch., 1980—85. Lic. master social worker N.Y. Legal asst. Howard Deutsch Atty. at Law, N.Y.C., 1977—80, Donald Lindover Atty. at Law, N.Y.C., 1982; rsch. asst. sociology dept. Stanford (Calif.) U., 1986—87; rsch. asst. Merit Co., Jerusalem, 1989—91; fundraiser Nat. Symphony Orch. Assn., Washington, 1991—95, Nat. Rep. Senatorial Com., Washington, 1995—97, Nat. Capital Teleservices, LLC, Washington, 1997—. Telephone solicitor Nat. Children's Ctr. Value Village Project Inc., Adelphi, Md., 1992—. Mem. Smithsonian Instn., Washington, 1996—, Phillips Collection, 2005, U.S. Holocaust Mus., Washington, 2000—, Rep. Nat. Com., 2002—. Mem.: Nat. Trust Historic Preservation, Stanford Alumni Assn. (life). Republican. Jewish. Avocations: surfing the Internet, cassettes and videos, casino gambling, travel, fashion. Home: Apt 208 1255 New Hampshire Ave NW Washington DC 20036 Office: CAPTEL 300 5th St NE Washington DC 20002 Office Phone: 202-547-4614. E-mail: robersti@aol.com.

STICHT, MIRANDA, music educator; b. Payson, Utah, July 22, 1972; d. Danny J. Loveless and Sharon Turner, Wayne Lloyd Hicks (Stepfather) and Karen Loveless (Stepmother); m. Alan K. Sticht, Apr. 18, 1992; children: Stephanie, Katie, Melanie, Aaron Daniel. MusB, U. Utah, Salt Lake City, 1994; MEd Curriculum and Instrn., U. Phoenix, 2005. Music educator Weber Sch. Dist., Ogden, Utah, 1994—2000, Davis Sch. Dist., Farmington, Utah, 2000—. Recipient Apple for Tchr., Std. Examiner, 1996; Utah Career Tchg. Scholarship, State of Utah, 1994. Mem.: Utah Music Teacher's Assn., Am. String Teacher's Assn., Collegiate Music Educators Nat. Conf. (pres. 1993—94), Music Educators Nat. Conf. R-Consevative. Mem. Lds Ch. Avocations: music, needlepoint, cooking.

STICK, ALYCE CUSHING, systems administrator, consultant; b. N.J., July 13, 1944; d. George William and Adele Margaret (Wilderotter) Cushing; m. James McAlpin Easter, July 1970 (div. Aug. 1986); m. T. Howard F. Stick, June 1989. AA, Colby-Sawyer Coll., 1964; student, Boston U., 1964-65, Johns Hopkins U., 1972-74; cert., Control Data Inst. and Life Office Mgmt. Assn., 1976. Claims investigator Continental Casualty Co., Phila., 1967-69; data processing coord. Chesapeake Life Ins. Co., Balt., 1970-72; sr. systems analyst Comml. Credit Computer Corp., Balt., 1972-80; v.p. Shawmut Computer Systems, Inc., Owings Mills, Md., 1980-85; pres. Computer Relevance, Inc., Gladwyne, Pa., 1985—. Cons. Sinai Hosp., Balt., 1982—85, AT&T, Reading, Pa., 1987—88, Dun and Bradstreet, Allentown, Pa., 1988, Arco Chem. Co., Newtown Square, Pa., 1990—91, Rohm and Haas Co., Phila., 1992—. Designer, author (computer software systems) Claim-Track, 1977, Property-Profiles, 1979, Stat-Model, 1989, co-designer, author Patient-Profiles, 1983. Treas. Sales and Rental Gallery Balt. Mus. Art, 1984. Mem.: Ind. Computer Cons. Assn., Data Processing Mgmt. Assn., Assn. Sys. Mgmt., Merion Cricket Club (Haverford, Pa.). Republican. Avocations: American antiques, Chinese export porcelain dealer. Office: Computer Relevance Inc 1501 Monticello Dr Gladwyne PA 19035-1206

STICKELER, CARL ANN LOUISE, legislator; b. Plant City, Fla., Dec. 26, 1930; d. Carl Ulysses and Marian Lucille (Churchill) Sangster; m. Nickolas Joseph Stickeler, May 14, 1949; children: Nickolas J., Juliann E., Carl A., John C., Katherine M. Profl. registered parliamentarian. Bus. mgr. Kendall Automobile Sales, Inc., Miami, 1967-82; parliamentarian Stickeler & Assocs., P.A., Miami, 1982-88, Ocala, Fla., 1988—. Editor: The Answer, 1983-89, 97-2002, The Florida Parliamentarian, 1983-87. Recipient Internat. Woman of Distinction Beta Sigma Phi Internat., 1980, Order of the Rose award Beta Sigma Phi Internat., 1969. Mem. Nat. Assn. Parliamentarians (bd. dirs. 1979-83, 91-93, 95-97, 99-2002, v.p. 1983-89, pres. 1989-91, parliamentarian 1997-99), Acad. Parliamentary Procedure and Law (bd. dirs. 1979—, pres. 1985-87), Gen. Fedn. Women's Clubs, Fla. Fedn. of Women's Clubs (parliamentarian 1992-98, 2000--), DAR (parliamentarian Fla. state soc. 1997-98), Beta Sigma Phi. Republican. Roman Catholic. Avocation: parliamentary research. Office: Stickeler & Assocs 102 Almond Rd Ocala FL 34472-8634 Office Phone: 352-624-2794. Personal E-mail: castickeler@aol.com. E-mail: CAStickeler@earthlink.net.

STICKLES, LINDA COCHRAN, elementary school educator; b. Abbeville, SC, Feb. 16, 1949; d. Julius Eakin and Rucella Ray Cochran; m. Van Abram Stickles; children: Amy, Sharie, Pete. BS in Edn., Lander U., Greenwood, SC, 1971. Tchr. Cateechee-Norris Sch., Central, SC, 1971—73, Wachamaw Elem. Sch., Pawleys Island, SC, 1975—77, Elloree Acad., SC, 1979—82, Elloree Elem. Sch., 1982—. Named Tchr. of Yr., Elloree Elem. Sch., 2005—06, Orangeburg Consol. Sch. Dist., 2005—06; named to Manchester's Who's Who Among Exec. and Profl. Women In Edn. Mem.: Internat. Reading Assn., SC Sci. Coun., Mentor Book Club (v.p. 2004—06). Avocations: church work, sewing, reading, cooking. Home: 341 Barkley St Elloree SC 29047 Office: Elloree Elem Sch 200 Warrior Dr Elloree SC 29047

STICKLES, PAULA RENEE, mathematics educator; b. Quincy, Ill., Aug. 7, 1972; d. Imogene Strahlman; m. Joe Stickles, June 16, 2001. BS in Math., Millikin U., Decatur, Ill., 1994; MS in Math., No. Ill. U., 1996; PhD in Math. Edn., Ind. U., 2006. Math. instr. Springfield Coll. in Ill., 1996—99, Marshall U., Hungtington, W.Va., 1999—2000; chair math. dept. Evansville Day Sch., Ind., 2000—02; math. instr. U. So. Ind., Evansville, 2002—03; asst. prof. Millikin U., 2006—. Head basketball coach Evansville Day Sch., 2000—02. Recipient Dean's fellowship, Ind. U., 2003—06. Mem.: Math. Assn. of Am., Nat. Coun. Tchrs. of Math.

STICKNEY, JESSICA, former state legislator; b. Duluth, Minn., May 16, 1929; d. Ralph Emerson and Claudia Alice (Cox) Page; m. Edwin Levi Stickney, June 17, 1951; children: Claudia, Laura, Jeffrey. BA, Macalester Coll., St. Paul, Minn., 1951; PhD (hon), Rocky Mtn. Coll., Billings, Mont., 1986. Rep. State of Mont., 1989-92. Mem. Gov.'s Commn. on Post-Sec. Edn., Mont., 1973-75. Mem. Sch. Bd. Trustees, Miles City, Mont., 1968-74; mem., chmn. zoning bd., Miles City, 1975-89; mem. Govt. Study Commn., Miles City, 1974-76, United Ch. Christ Bd. Homeland Ministries, 1975-81; chmn., conf. moderator United Ch. Christ Bd. Mont.-Northern Wyo. Conf., 1980-82; chmn. Town Meeting on the Arts, Mont., 1980; mem., chmn. Miles Community Coll. Bd., 1975-89, chmn. 1978-80. Recipient Disting. Citizen's award, Macalester Coll., 2006. Mem. Mont. Arts Coun. (chmn. 1982-85), Western States Arts Found. (vice chmn. 1984), Nat. Assembly State Arts Agys. (bd. dirs. 1982-88), AAUW (pres. 1964-66). Democrat. Avocations: writing, sewing, painting, reading.

STICKNEY, LORRAINE PHYLLIS OSBERG, retired librarian; b. Spicer, Minn., Sept. 2, 1936; d. Edgar Albin and Ella Sophie (Orson) Osberg; m. Frederic Haskell Stickney, June 25, 1960. BA, Augsburg Coll., 1958; MLS, U. Maine, 1967. Cert. secondary tchr. English tchr., libr. Thornton Acad., Saco, Maine, 1958-59; libr. Kenyon Pub. Schs., Minn., 1959-60; English tchr., libr. Falmouth HS, Maine, 1960-61; libr. Gorham HS, Maine, 1961—99; ret., 1999. Sec. Maine Sch. Libr. Assn., 1963-65. Named Lorriane O. Stickney Library in her honor, Gorham HS Library, 2002; recipient Excellence in Edn. award, U. So. Maine, 1989. Mem. Maine Ednl. Media Assn. (sec. 1985-89), Gorham Tchrs. Assn., Maine Tchrs. Assn. Democrat. Lutheran. Avocations: hiking, reading, swimming, knitting.

STICKNEY, NANCY CARVER, state legislator; b. Bethel, Maine, July 20, 1936; d. Irving L. and Ruth W. (Homsted) Carver; m. Wallace E. Stickney, 1957; children: Peter, Christopher J., Daniel C., Adam K. BS, U. NH, 1960. Mem. NH Ho. of Reps. (dist. 26), Concord, Maine, 1997—2000. Methodist. Home: PO Box 177 North Salem NH 03073-0177 Office: NH State Legis State House Concord NH 03301

STIEBER, TAMAR, journalist; b. Bklyn., Sept. 15, 1955; d. Alfred and Florence (Spector) Stieber. Student, Rockland C.C., 1972—75, West London (Eng.) Coll., 1973—74; BA in Film cum laude, U. Calif., Berkeley, 1985, postgrad. in comparative lit., 1985—86; grad. Police Res. Acad. cum laude, Napa Valley Coll., 1988. Office mgr., confidential sec. AP, San Francisco, 1981—83; stringer Daily Californian, Berkeley, Calif., 1983—84; film rsch. tchg. asst. U. Calif., Berkeley, 1984—86; libr. and rsch. asst. Pacific Film Archive, Berkeley, 1984—86; intern San Francisco Examiner, 1984; reporter Sonoma (Calif.) Index-Tribune, 1987—88; Vallejo (Calif.) Times-Herald, 1988—89, Albuquerque Jour., 1989—94, freelancer, 1994—. Recipient Pulitzer Prize for specialized reporting, 1990, 1st pl. pub. svc. divsn., N.Mex. Press Assn., 1990, Pub. Svc. award, Albuquerque Press Club, 1990, 1st pl. newswriting, N.Mex. Press Assn., 1991, Hon. Mention, AP Mng. Editors, 1994. Mem.: AAUW, Phi Beta Kappa. Home: PO Box 9835 Santa Fe NM 87504-9835 E-mail: tstieber@isp.com.

STIEGLITZ, IMOGENE L., intravenous therapy nurse; b. McLean County, Ill., Sept. 23, 1926; d. George H. and Elizabeth S. AS, Purdue U., 1973. Staff nurse Turtle Creek Nursing Home, Fort Wayne, Ind.; IV therapy nurse Parkview Hosp., Fort Wayne. Home: 7529 Westerlin Dr Woodburn IN 46797-9722

STIEHM, JUDITH HICKS, director, political scientist, educator; b. Madison, Wis., Oct. 9, 1935; d. Stratton Elson and Eleanor Spencer (Kilbourn) Hicks; m. E. Richard Stiehm, July 12, 1958; children: Jamie Elizabeth, Carrie Eleanor, Meredith Ellen. Student, Oberlin Coll., 1953; BA in E. Asian Studies, U. Wis., 1957; MA in Am. History, Temple U., 1961; PhD in Polit. Theory, Columbia U., 1969. Dir. resident hons. program U. So. Calif., LA, 1970-73, asst. prof., 1970-74, assoc. prof., 1974-83, dir. program for study of women and men in soc., 1975-81, prof. polit. sci., 1983, vice provost, 1984-87; provost Fla. Internat. U., Miami, 1987-91, prof. polit. sci., 1987—. Vis. prof. U. Wis., 1994, U.S. Army Peacekeeping Inst., U.S. Army War Coll., 1995-96, U.S. Army Strategic Studies Inst., U.S. Army War Coll., 1996, U. So. Calif., 2002-; lectr. U. Wis., Madison, 1966-69, UCLA, 1969-70; vis. lectr. San Francisco State U., 1965-66; affiliate NAS Project, 1981-82; cons. UN Div. for the Advancement of Women, Calif. Elected Women, Dept. HEW, AAUW, LWV L.A., UN Lessons Learned Unit, Dept. Peacekeeping Ops. Author: Nonviolent Power: Active and Passive Resistance in America, 1972, Bring Me Men and Women., 1981, Arms and the Enlisted Woman, 1989, The U.S. Army War College: Military Education in a Democracy, 2002, Champions for Peace: Women Winners of the Nobel Peace Prize, 2006; editor: The Frontiers of Knowledge, 1976, Women and Men's Wars, 1983, Women's Views of the Political World of Men, 1984, It's Our Military, Too!, 1996, The U.S. Army War College: Military Education in a Democracy, 2002, Champions for Peace: Women Winners of the Nobel Peace Prize, 2006; mem. editorial bd. Western Polit. Quar., 1972-75, Signs, 1981-84, Women and Politics, 1986-88, 2000-. Mem. Calif. Postsecondary Edn. Commn., 1978, Calif. Adv. Coun. on Vocat. Edn., 1978-82, Def. Adv. Com. on Women in Svcs., 1979-82; bd. dirs. So. Calif. and Miami chpts. ACLU. Named Woman of Yr., Santa Monica YWCA, 1981; recipient Outstanding Civilian Svc. medal U.S. Army, 1996, U. Wis. Disting Alumni award, 2006. Mem. Am. Polit. Sci. Assn. (exec. coun. 1989, sec. 2000), Western Polit. Sci. Assn. (pres. 1986), Women's Caucus Polit. Sci. (pres. 1996-97), Nat. Council for Research on Women (exec. council 1982), Council on Fgn. Relations, Phi Beta Kappa, Phi Kappa Phi (Victoria Schuck Book award 1990). Avocations: tennis, skiing, stained glass. Office: Fla Internat U Dept Polit Sci Tamiami Trl Miami FL 33199-0001 E-mail: stiehmj@fiu.edu.

STIEHR, LIZETTE ESTELLE, special education educator, director; b. Chgo., Sept. 23, 1946; d. Benton Hoooper and Georgialou Fleager Burns; children: Jesse Hopper, Auguste Micah, Magayr Alexia. BA in Psychology, Ind. U., 1969, MA in Spl. Edn., 1970. Cert. tchr. Dept. of Edn., Alaska, 1974. Spl. edn. instr. Brown County (Ind.) Sch. Dist., 1971—74; dir. profl. svcs. Hope Cmty. Resources, Anchorage, 1974—77; mental health clinician South Ctrl. Counseling, Anchorage, 1978—81; project coord. Communicative Disorders Prog., Anchorage, 1983—85; health program mgr. Sect. of Maternal Child Health, Anchorage, 1988—99; exec. dir. Family Outreach Ctr. for Understanding Spl. Needs, Chugiak, Alaska, 1999—. Officer Divsn. Early Childhood, Anchorage, 1994—2000. Pres. bd. dirs. Child Care Connection, Anchorage, 1995—2000. Recipient Early Intervention Appreciation award, Alaska Assn. Infant Learning Programs, 1997, Plaque of Appreciation award, Hope Cmty. Resources, 1978, Plaque of Recognition award, Alaska Speech Lang. Hearing Assn., 1990; fellow, Ind. U., 1970. Mem.: Anchorage (Alaska) Assn. Edn. Young Children, Eagle River C. of C. (assoc.). Independent. Avocations: travel, astrology, camping, hiking, bicycling. Home: PO Box 671902 Chugiak AK 99567 Office: Focus PO Box 671750 Chugiak AK 99567 E-mail: lizette-stiehr@gci.net.

STIENMIER, SAUNDRA KAY YOUNG, aviation educator; b. Abilene, Kans., Apr. 27, 1938; d. Bruce Waring and Helen E. (Rutz) Young; m. Richard H. Stienmier, Dec. 20, 1958; children: Richard, Susan, Julia, Laura. AA, Colo. Women's Coll., 1957; postgrad., U. Colo., 1959, 69; BS, Temple Buell Coll., 1969; student, Embre Riddle Aviation U., Ramstein, Germany. Cert. FAA pilot. Dir. Beaumont Gallery, El Paso, Tex., 1972-77; mem. grad. studies faculty Embre Riddle Aviation U., 1979-80; mgr. Ramstein Aero Club, USAF, 1977-80, Peterson Flight Tng. Ctr., Peterson AFB, Colo., 1980-97, Flight Tng. Ctr., Rocky Mtn. AFB, Colo., 1997—. Named Outstanding S.W. Artist. Mem.: AAUW, Assn. Profl. Flight Tng. Ctrs., Soc. Arts and Letters, Women in Aviation, Colo. Pilots Assn., Nat. Pilot Assn., Aircraft Owners and Pilots Assn., Nat. Air Transp. Assn., Interant. Women Pilots Assn., Scots Heritage Soc., Scottish Soc. Pikes' Peak, 99's Club, Order Eastern Star, Delta Psi Omega, Beta Sigma Phi. E-mail: saundra@viawest.net.

STIENSTRA, STEPHANI ANN, editor, writer; b. Baytown, Tex., Aug. 6, 1955; d. Herbert Howard and Janice Faye (Stowe) Cruickshank; m. George Keyston III, Oct. 8, 1983 (div. Mar. 1997); children: Jeremy George, Kristopher Samuel; m. Thomas Frank Stienstra, Dec. 4, 1998. AA with honors, Merced Coll., Calif., 1975; BA in Journalism with distinction, San Jose State U., 1976. Reporter Fresno (Calif.) Bee, 1974-75; reporter, photographer Merced (Calif.) Sun-Star, 1974-77; pub. info. officer Fresno City Coll., 1977—80; dir. comms. Aerojet Tactical Sys. Co., Sacramento, 1980—83; co-owner, v.p. Keyco Landscape Contractor Inc., Loomis, Calif., 1984—96; co-owner Stienstra Outdoor Books, Inc., 2003—. Co-author (with Tom Stienstra): (book) Northern California Cabins and Cottages, 2002 (Hon. Mention Book award Outdoor Writers Assn. Calif., 2002), Washington Camping, 2002. Co-coord. Aerojet United Way Campaign, 1981; Aerojet Tactical Sys. Co. coord. West Coast Nat. Derby Rallies, 1981-83; co-founder, pres. Calif. Lion Awareness. Mem.: Internat. Assn. Bus. Communicators (dir. Sacramento chpt. 1983), Citrus Heights C. of C. (v.p. 1983). Office: PO Box 151 Mount Shasta CA 96067-0151 Personal E-mail: stienstra@jps.net.

STIER, MARY P., publishing executive; b. Memphis, Nov. 9, 1956; m. Jeff Stier; 2 children. Grad. in comm., broadcasting, U. Iowa. With Gannett Co., 1982—; retail advt. mgr. Iowa City Press-Citizen, 1982—84, advt. dir., 1984—87, pres., pub., 1987—91; v.p. Ctrl. Region Newspaper Divsn., 1990—93; pres., pub. Rockford (Ill.) Register Star, 1991—2000; pres. Midwest Newspaper Group, 1993—2000; pres., pub. The Des Moines Register, 2000—; sr. group pres. Midwest Newspaper Group, 2000—. Bd. trustees Drake U. Mem.: The Greater Des Moines Partnership, Am. Press Inst., Iowa Newspaper Assn., Newspaper Assn. Am., Phi Beta Kappa. Office: Des Moines Register PO Box 957 Des Moines IA 50304-0957

STIFFLER, ERMA DELORES, minister, retired elementary school educator; b. Blairsville, Pa., June 26, 1942; d. Harry Reuben and Dorothy Velma (Buterbaugh) Berenbrok; m. Charles Harry Stiffler, July 15, 1966; children: Barbara Wojichowski, Dee-ann Bollinger, Crissy, Rebecca Stewart. BS in Edn. cum laude, Indiana State Coll., Pa., 1964; MTh, Christian Bible Coll., 1999, ThD, 2000; Bible diploma, Liberty U., 1996; pvt. investigator diploma, Harcourt Learning Direct, 2000; postgrad., Ctr. Biblical Counseling, 2001, postgrad., 2003. Ordained min. Gospel Revelation, Inc., 2001. Elem. tchr. Armstrong County Sch. Dist., Elderton, Pa., 1964—67, Purchase Line Sch. Dist., Commodore, Pa., 1968—70; pastor, founder Lighthouse Gospel Revelation Fellowship, Blairsville, Pa., 1995—. Intercessory prayer Breakthrough Internat., Lincoln, Va., 1997—; vol. Prison Fellowship Ministries, Washington, 1999—2000; outreach person Lighthouse Neighborhood Prayer Movement, Edina, Minn. and Blairsville, 1999—; prayer Mastermedia Internat., Redlands, Calif., 2001—03. Contbr. articles to mags. Contact person Nat. Day of Prayer, Blairsville, Pa.; active PTA, Blairsville; col. March of Dimes, Heart Assn.; spkr. cmty. luminary svc. Blairsville, Pa., 2003; Bible studies tchr., youth group leader, tchr., Sunday sch. supt., 1966—; tchr. Child Evangelism Fellowship, Indiana County, Pa.; Christian edn. dir. Missionary

Alliance Ch., Blairsville; vol. Blairsville Sch. Dist. Mem.: Am. Assn. Christian Counselors, Kappa Delta Pi. Republican. Avocations: collecting old books, collecting figurines, reading, walking. Home: 216 N Walnut St Blairsville PA 15717 Office: Lighthouse Gospel Revelation Fellowship Blairsville PA 15717

STIFLER, VENETIA CHAKOS, dancer, educator, choreographer; b. Chgo., Feb. 27, 1950; d. Theodore and Ruth (Pastirsky) Chakos; m. John G. Stifler, Jan. 28, 1972 (dec. 1977); m. Michael Hugos, 1994. BA, U. Ill., Chgo., 1983; MFA equivalency, Union Inst., Cin., 1987, PhD, 1992. Tchr. workshops Urban Gateways, Chgo., 1977; tchr. Chgo. Dance Ctr., Chgo., 1971-78, Smith Coll., Northampton, Mass., 1975, Wilson Coll., Chambersburg, Pa., 1984; gusest tchr., artistic dir. composition/improvisation U. Wis., Madison, 1980-81, 85, 87; tchr. modern, jazz and ballet Venetia Stifler & Concert Dance, Inc., Chgo., 1978—; tchr. choreography workshop Bell Elem. Sch., Chgo., 1987; tchr./artist in residence Mundelein Coll., Chgo., 1982-90; asst. prof., chair dance program Northeastern Ill. U., Chgo., 1987—; tchr. modern technique So. Ill. U., Carbondale, 1975. Lectr. Mundelein Coll., Chgo., 1983, 84, 85, 86, Mayor's Office of Spl. Events, Chgo., 1980program dir. and choreogrpaher spl. programs Chgo. Symphony Orch., 1985, 87; pres. bd. dirs. Chgo. Dance Arts Coalition, 1983-85; adv. dance panel Ill. Arts Coun., 1983-85, Chgo. Office of Fine Arts, 1983-86; guest speaker Chgo. Office of Fine Arts, 1987; choreographer Sears Fashion Files, BoMay Prodns., 1983, 84, 86; prodn. asst. Audio Visual Prodns., 1970-71; artistic dir. Ruth Page Dance Series, 1992—; centennial dir. Ruth Page Found. Centennial, 1999; exec. dir. Ruth Page Found., 2000-. Choreographer Between Us, 1991, Magic Spaces, 1985, 86, Fugues, 1981, 82, Corporate Cases, 1988, Private places, 1987, Bell School Scrimmage, 1987, Blessings, 1986, Don't Dance with Your Back to the Moon, 1986, Imagery & Concept in the Dances of Venetia Stifler, 1985, Rhymes, 1984, Arriving at Onion, 1984, Pulse, 1983, Haiku, 1982, Mundelein Madness, 1981, Solo Crane, 1981, Tales of a Winter's Night, 1980, Jackson Park-Howard, 1979, La Gaite Parisienne (opera), 1976, Chicago Sketches, 1995, Veils, 1996, Over Weight Over Wrought Over You, 1997, Three German Songs, 1999, Shenandoah. Recipient Ruth Page award; named for Outstanding Artistic Achievement, Chgo. Dance Coalition, 1985. Avocations: films, art. Office: Northeastern Ill U 5500 N Saint Louis Ave Chicago IL 60625-4679 also: Ruth Page Ctr Arts 1016 N Dearborn Parkway Chicago IL 60610 E-mail: Venetia@ruthpage.org, V-Stifler@neiu.edu.

STILES, CAROL M., plant pathologist, educator; AAS, U. S.D., Springfield, 1984; BS, S.D. State U., Brookings, 1986; MS, U. Ill., Champaign, 1989; PhD, Wash. State U., Pullman, 1994. Postdoctoral rsch. assoc. Blueberry and Cranberry Rsch. Ctr., Rutgers State U., Chatsworth, NJ, 1994—96; asst. prof. Valdosta State U., Ga., 1996—99, U. Fla., Gainesville, 2000—. Mem.: Mycol. Soc. Am., Am. Phytopathol. Soc.

STILES, DORIS D., elementary school educator; b. Portland, Tenn., Feb. 6, 1948; d. Frank Nacy and Ethel Graves Douglas; m. Harold Robert Stiles, Sept. 7, 1968; children: Vonnie, Robert, Katrina, Kevin. Student, George Peabody Vanderbilt, Nashville, 1966—68; BS in Edn., Ga. State U., Atlanta, 1971; MS in Classroom Tchg., No. State U., Aberdeen, S.D., 1997, MS in Ednl. Adminstrn., 1999; doctoral studies, U. S.D., Vermillon, 2004—. Remedial reading tchr. Pierre Pub. Schs., SD, 1988—95, gifted edn. elem. coord. & tchr., 1995—2001, 4th grade tchr., 2001—04, reading first coach, 2004—. Mem.: Assn. Supervision & Curriculum Devel., Nat. Assn. Gifted Children, Internat. Reading Assn. Mem. Nazarene Ch. Avocation: reading. Home: 329 N Euclid Pierre SD 57501 Office: Pierre Pub Schs 100 N Buchanan Pierre SD 57501

STILES, JULIA, actress; b. NYC, Mar. 28, 1981; d. John O'Hara and Judith Stiles. B in English, Columbia U., 2005. Actor: (TV films) Before Women Had Wings, 1997, The '60s, 1999; (films) I Love You, I Love You Not, 1996, The Devil's Own, 1997, Wicked, 1998, Wide Awake, 1998, 10 Things I Hate About You, 1999, Down to You, 2000, Hamlet, 2000, State and Main, 2000, Save the Last Dance, 2001 (Teens Choice Drama award, 2001), The Business of Strangers, 2001, O, 2001, The Bourne Identity, 2002, A Guy Thing, 2003, Carolina, 2003, Mona Lisa Smile, 2003, The Prince & Me, 2004, The Bourne Supremacy, 2004, Edmond, 2005, A Little Trip to Heaven, 2005, The Omen, 2006; TV guest appearances include Ghostwriter, 1992, Promised Land, 1996, Chicago Hope, 1994; actor: (plays) Fran's Bed, 2005. Volunteer Habitat for Humanity, Costa Rica, Amnesty Internat. Named one of 25 Hottest Stars under 25, Teen People mag., 2002; voted one of, People Mag.'s 50 Most Beautiful People, 2001. Democrat. Office: Clare Ryu c/o United Talent Agy 9560 Wilshire Blvd Beverly Hills CA 90212*

STILES, MARY ANN, lawyer, writer, lobbyist; b. Tampa, Fla., Nov. 16, 1944; d. Ralph A. and Bonnie (Smith) S.; m. Barry Smith. AA, Hills Community Coll., 1973; BS, Fla. State U., 1975; JD, Antioch Sch. Law, 1978. Bar: Fla. 1978. Legis. analyst Fla. Ho. of Reps., Tallahassee, 1973-74, 74-75; intern U.S. Senate, Washington, 1977; v.p., gen. counsel Associated Industries Fla., Tallahassee, 1978-81, gen. counsel, 1981-84, spl. counsel, 1986-97; assoc. Deschler, Reed & Crichfield, Boca Raton, Fla., 1980-81; founding ptnr. Stiles, Taylor, & Grace, P.A., Boca Raton, Tampa, Orlando, Jacksonville, Talahassee, and Miami, Fla., 1982—, shareholder, dir. Tampa; gen. counsel Associated Industries Ins. Co., Inc., 1996—, Associated Industries Fla., Inc., 1997—, Associated Industries Ins. Svcs., Inc., 1997—. Shareholder, dir. Six Stars Devel. Co. of Fla., Inc. Platnum Bank; dr. Eclipse, Inc.; owner, pres. Styles by Stiles; shareholder, pres. 42nd St., The Bistro; mem. Workers' Compensation Task Force, 2000-01. Author: Workers' Compensation Law Handbook, 1980-94 edit. Bd. dirs., sec. Hillsborough C.C. Found., Tampa, 1985-87, 94-96; bd. dirs. Hillsborough Area Regional Transit Authority, Tampa, 1986-89, Boys and Girls Club of Tampa, 1986—; The Spring, 1992-93, What's My Chance, 1992-94; mem. Gov.'s Oversite Bd. on Workers' Compensation, 1989-90, Workers' Compensation Rules Com., Fla. Bar, 1990-95, 2000—, Workers' Compensation Exec. Counsel Fla. Bar, 1990-95, Jud. Nominating Commn. for Workers' Compensation Cts., 1990-93, trustee Hillsborough Cmty. Coll., 1994-99, vice-chair, 1995-96, chair, 1996-97; bd. dirs. Seminole Boosters, Inc., Fla. State U., 1996—. Mem. ABA, Fla. Bar Assn., Hillsborough County Bar Assn., Hillsborough Assn. Women Lawyers, Fla. Assn. Women Lawyers, Fla. Women's Alliance, Hillsborough County Seminole Boosters (past pres.), Tiger Bay Club (Tampa, past. pres., sec.). Republican. Baptist. Avocations: boating, reading. Office: 315 S Plant Ave Tampa FL 33606-2325 also: 317 N Calhoun St Tallahassee FL 32301-7605 also: PO Box 310397 Miami FL 33231-0397 Address: PO Box 294349 Boca Raton FL 33429 also: PO Box 48190 Jacksonville FL 32247

STILLER, JENNIFER ANNE, lawyer; b. Washington, May 4, 1948; d. Ralph Sophian and Joy (Dancis) Stiller. AB in Econs. and History, U. Mich., 1970; JD, NYU, 1973. Bar: Pa. 1973, U.S. Dist. Ct. (mid. dist.) Pa. 1977, U.S. Supreme Ct. 1978, U.S. Dist. Ct. (ea. dist.) Pa. 1983, U.S. Ct. Appeals (3rd cir.) 1983, U.S. Ct. Appeals (D.C. cir.), 1996. Dep. atty. gen. Pa. Dept. Justice, Harrisburg, 1973-75, Pa. Dept. Health, Harrisburg, 1975-78; sr. staff atty. Am. Hosp. Assn., Chgo., 1978-80, mgr., dept. fed. law, 1980-81; gen. counsel Ill. Health Fin. Authority, 1981-82; sr. assoc. Berriman & Schwartz, King of Prussia, Pa., 1983-85, Wolf, Block, Schorr & Solis-Cohen, Phila., 1985-88, Montgomery, McCracken, Walker & Rhoads, LLP, Phila., 1988-90; ptnr. Montgomery, McCracken, Walker & Rhoads, Phila., 1990-2000, chair health law group, 1991-2000; sr. counsel Tenet Healthcare Corp., Phila., 2000-2001; pvt. practice Haverford, Pa., 2001—. Contbr. articles to profl. jours. Fellow Am. Health Lawyers Assn. (bd. dirs. 1997-2003, exec. com. 2002-03); mem. ABA (gov. com. Health Law Forum 1994-95), Pa. Soc. Healthcare Attys. (pres. 1995). Avocations: gardening, bicycling, hiking, music. Office: Law Office Jennifer A Stiller 625 Haydock Ln Haverford PA 19041-1207 Office Phone: 610-642-3366. Business E-Mail: stiller@healthregs.com.

STILLER, SHARON PAULA, lawyer; b. Rochester, N.Y., Mar. 31, 1951; d. Alfred Stiller and Hilda (Silver) Ring; 1 child, Sierra Alexandra. Ptnr. Jaeckle Fleischman & Mugel LLP, Rochester, NY. Office: Jaeckle Fleischman & Mugel LLP 190 Linden Oaks Rochester NY 14625 Office Phone: 585-899-2934. Business E-Mail: sstiller@jaeckle.com. E-mail: sstiller@rochester.rr.com.

STILLINGS, IRENE ELLA GRACE CORDINER, retired foundation executive; b. Boston, Aug. 17, 1918; d. Matthew Wilson and Susan F. (Mason) Cordiner; m. Gordon A. Stillings, May 13, 1945; children: David Gordon, Susan Irene. Student, Radcliffe Coll., 1936-39; diploma, Burdett Coll., 1941. Sec., bookkeeper Boston Refrigerator Co., 1941-42; sec., tchr. Burdett Coll., 1942-44; sec., bookkeeper Gertrude Rittenburg, Boston, 1944-46. Town chmn. Heart Fund, Woodland, Maine, 1953-61; Brownie leader Girl Scouts U.S., 1954-58; pres. Woodland Woman's Club 1961-63; sec. PTA, 1961-62; chmn. Baileyville Superintending Sch. Com., 1962-64; chmn. women's activities Nat. Found., East Washington County, 1959-61; pres. Hosp. Aid, 1961-63; chmn. Newcomers Coll. group YWCA, 1965-66, chmn. theatre group, 1968-70, pres. Suburbanites, 1970-71; Stamford (Conn.) chmn. Expt. in Internat. Living, 1965-68; bd. dirs. YWCA of Stamford, 1969-78, chmn. antique show, 1960-77, chmn. devotion, 1970-92, ann. Antique Show benefit, 1970-77; pres. New Suburbanites, Stamford, 1994-95, ret. 1996. Mem. Mass. Hort. Soc., St. Luke's Guild (treas. 1954-63), Radcliffe Club, Stamford Woman's Club (treas. 1975-79, program com., co-chmn. Am. home dept. 1974, 75, pres. 1981-83, bd. dirs. 1981—, 2d v.p. fin. 1979-81, 83-85, 87-89, chmn. bldg. investment 1979-81, parliamentarian 1990—, pres., newcomers/suburbanites, 1994-95), Theta Alpha Chi. Episcopalian. Home: 277 W Hill Rd Stamford CT 06902-1708

STILLMAN, BELINDA ANN, psychiatrist; b. North Hills, Pa., May 18, 1977; d. Robert E. and Betty Louise Snyder; m. Bryan K. Stillman, Aug. 18, 2002; children: Ashley Marie, Eli Benjamin. BS in Molecular Biology, Grove City Coll., 1999; DO, Lake Erie Coll. Osteo. Medicine, 2003. Med. coll. admission test instr. Kaplan Edn. Ctr., Erie, Pa., 2001—03; jr. faculty Lake Erie Coll. Osteo. Medicine, Erie, Pa., 2003—; gen. psychiatry resident Millcreek Cmty. Hosp., Erie, 2003—; psychiatrist Multi-Cultural Health Evaluation Clinic, Erie, 2005—, Ctr. for Personal and Family Growth, Erie, 2005—, Erie Homes for Children and Adults, 2006—. Jr. faculty intern coord. Lake Erie Coll. Osteo. Medicine, Erie, 2003—04, psychiatry and neurology club resident advisor, 2003—04. Vol. Women's Care Ctr., Erie, 1999, Ind. Venture, Erie, 1999—2000; girl scouts troop leader Erie Housing Authority, 1999—2001; promoter child awareness of dental health careers Area Health Edn. Ctr., Healthy Smiles, Erie, 2000; vol. Mercy Ctr. on Aging, Erie, 2000; vol.,d coord. Erie Hotline, 2000—05; pediatric bereavement counseling The Caring Pl., Erie, 2003—05; prison ministry Kairos, Conneaut, Ohio, 2004—06; lay ministry Koinonia, Erie, 2004—06; small group leader Millcreek Cmty. Ch., Erie, 1999—2006; health ministry Bridging the Gaps Cmty. Health Internship Program, Erie, 2000; spirituality and medicine intern Hamot Med. Ctr., Erie, 2000; vacation bible sch. missions leader Millcreek Cmty. Ch., Erie, 2005. Scholar, Am. Coll. Osteo. Family Physicians, 2003, Am. Acad. Child and Adolescent Psychiatrists, 2004; Amb. scholar, Lake Erie Coll. Osteo. Medicine, 2000—03. Mem.: Christian Med. and Dental Soc. (assoc.), Am. Assn. Christian Counselors (assoc.), Pa. Osteo. Med. Assn. (assoc.; intern and resident rep. 2003—05, resident del. 2004—05), Am. Coll. Osteo. Neurologists and Psychiatrists (assoc.), Am. Acad. Child and Adolescent Psychiatry (assoc.), Pa. Psychiat. Soc. (assoc.), Am. Osteo. Assn. (assoc.; bur. interns and residents continuing med. edn. com. rep. 2004—05, pres. lecom chpt. 1999—2001), Am. Psychiat. Assn. (assoc.). R-Consevative. Avocations: reading, crafts. Office Phone: 814-459-9300.

STILLMAN, ELINOR HADLEY, retired lawyer; b. Kansas City, Mo., Oct. 12, 1938; d. Hugh Gordon and Freda (Brooks) Hadley; m. Richard C. Stillman, June 25, 1965 (div. Apr. 1975). BA, U. Kans., 1960; MA, Yale U., 1961; JD, George Washington U., 1972. Bar: D.C. 1973, U.S. Ct. Appeals (10th cir.) 1975, U.S. Ct. Appeals (9th cir.) 1976, U.S. Ct. Appeals (2d cir.) 1976, U.S. Ct. Appeals (5th cir.) 1983, U.S. Ct. Appeals (4th cir.) 1985, U.S. Supreme Ct. 1976. Lectr. in English CUNY, 1963-65; asst. editor Stanford (Calif.) U. Press, 1967-69; law clk. to judge U.S. Dist. Ct. D.C., Washington, 1972-73; appellate atty. NLRB, Washington, 1973-78; asst. to solicitor gen. U.S. Dept. Justice, Washington, 1978-82; supr. appellate atty. NLRB, Washington, 1982-86, chief counsel to mem. bd., 1986-88, 94-00, chief counsel to chmn. bd., 1988-94; ret., 2000. Mem.: D.C. Bar Assn., Order of Coif, Phi Beta Kappa. Democrat.

STILLMAN, MARY ELIZABETH, librarian, administrator, educator; b. Phila., Oct. 31, 1929; d. Ernest E. and Rosalie (Burhans) Stillman; B.A., Wilson Coll., Chambersburg, Pa., 1950; M.S., Drexel U., Phila., 1952; Ph.D. (fellow), U. Ill., 1966. Librarian, USAF, 1953-63, Export-Import Bank U.S., 1965-68; asst. prof. Drexel U., 1968-72; mem. faculty Albright Coll., Reading, Pa., 1972-87, prof., librarian, 1975-87, spl. asst. to pres., 1987—; editor Drexel Library Quar., 1969-72; cons. research info. system Social and Rehab. Service, 1972-74; del. Pa. Gov.'s Conf. on Libraries, 1977; chmn. Pa. Library Week, 1978, 79; shareholder Reading Library Co., 1980—; mem. long-range planning com. Reading Pub. Library, 1982—, trustee, 1985—; pres. Reading Library, 1985—. Bd. dirs. Reading YWCA, 1981-83. Mem. ALA (reviewer Subscription Books Bull. 1969—), Pa. Library Assn. (dir. pub. relations task force 1974-79, editor bull. 1973-79, treas. colloquium on info. retrieval 1978-79), AAUP. Contbr. articles to profl. jours. Home: 416 Benjamin Dr Chambersburg PA 17201-1490

STILLMAN, NINA GIDDEN, lawyer; b. N.Y.C., Apr. 3, 1948; d. Melvin and Joyce Audrey (Gidden) S. AB with distinction, Smith Coll., 1970; JD cum laude, Northwestern U., 1973. Bar: Ill. 1973, U.S. Dist. Ct. (no. dist.) Ill. 1973, U.S. Dist. Ct. (ea. dist.) Wis. 1979, U.S. Dist. Ct. (no. dist. trial bar) Ill. 1983, U.S. Ct. Appeals (7th cir.) 1974, U.S. Supreme Ct. 1981, U.S. Dist. Ct. (ctrl. dist.) Ill. 1994, U.S. Dist. Ct. (ea. dist.) Tex., 1996, U.S. Dist. Ct. (Colo.), 1999, U.S. Dist. Ct. (ND) 2002. Assoc. Vedder, Price, Kaufman & Kammholz, Chgo., 1973-79, ptnr., 1980—2004, Morgan, Lewis and Bockius, LLP, Chgo., 2004—. Adv. bd. occupational health and safety tng. program U. Mich., Ann Arbor, 1980-83; adj. faculty Inst. Human Resources and Indsl. Rels., Loyola U., Chgo., 1983-86, bd. advisors, 1986—. Author: (with others) Women, Work, and Health: Challenge to Corporate Policy, 1979, Occupational Health Law: A Guide for Industry, 1981, Employment Discrimination, 1981, Personnel Management: Labor Relations, 1981, Occupational Safety and Health Law, 1988; contbg. author: Occupational Medicine: State of the Art Reviews, 1996; contbr. articles to profl. jours. Legal advisor, v.p. Planned Parenthood Assn. Chgo., 1979—81; sec. jr. governing bd. Chgo. Symphony Orch., 1983; trustee Merit Sch. Music, 2000—, vice chmn. bd. trustees, 2001—. Recipient Svc. award Northwestern U., 1994. Mem.: ABA (occupl. safety and health law com. 1978—), Human Resources Mgmt. Assn. Chgo (bd. dirs. 1986—88, officer), Am. Inns of Ct. (v.p. Wigmore chpt. 1988—89), Chgo. Bar Assn. (chmn. labor and employment law com. 1986—87), Northwestern U. Sch. Law Alumni Assn. (pres. 1991—92), Univ. Club Chgo. (bd. dirs. 1988—2001, sec. 1999—2000, v.p. 2000—01), The Chgo. Com., Econ. Club Chgo., Lawyers Club, Smith Coll. Club Chgo. (pres. 1972). Avocations: travel, reading, the arts, collecting art. Office: Morgan Lewis and Bockius LLP 77 W Wacker Dr Ste 600 Chicago IL 60601 Office Phone: 312-324-1150. Business E-Mail: nstillman@morganlewis.com.

STILLMAN, SHARON J., real estate broker; b. Milw., May 17, 1949; Mktg. and sales cons. Haddonstone, Brighton Ridge Subdivsns., 1988-92; dir. career devel. Overlake Condominium, Greendale, Wis. Contbr. articles to The Christian Courier. Dir., bd. co-founder Whitefish Bay 4th July Parade and Festivities, 1976-79; develpoer short term mission project Eastbrook Ch., Miw., 1980's; vol. Discipleship Unltd. Taycheetah Prison, 1990-98. Mem. Met. Bd. Realtors, Urban Day Sch., Alliance Francaise, AIWF. Republican. Avocations: watercolors, interior design, reading, travel. Office: Realty Executives 409 E Silver Spring Dr Milwaukee WI 53217-5226

STILLMAN-MYERS, JOYCE L., artist, educator, writer, illustrator, consultant; b. N.Y.C., Jan. 19, 1943; d. Murray W. and Evelyn (Berger) Stillman. BA, NYU, 1964; student, Art Students League, 1965, Pratt Inst., 1972; MFA, L.I. U., 1975; postgrad., Calif. Inst. Integral Studies, 1994—. Tchr. N.Y.C. Pub. Schs., 1964-71; artist, 1974-76, Louis K. Meisel Gallery, N.Y.C., 1975-84, Tolarno Gallery, Melbourne, Australia, 1976—, Allan Stone Gallery, N.Y.C., 1990—; founder CoCreative Inst. Art, Fingerlakes Region, NY. Assoc. prof. Towson U., Md., 1981; vis. assoc. prof. Towson State U., 1982; tchr. Tompkins Cortland C.C., 1988; lectr. Cornell U., 1990; founder Ithaca Women Artists Salon, Artistic Applications Decorative Arts Ctr.; prof. art studies Tompkins County C.C., 1986; pvt. art instr., Odessa, NY, 1986—. One-woman shows include Ctrl. Hall Gallery, Port Washington, 1975, Tolarno Gallery, Melbourne, 1976, Louis K. Meisel Gallery, N.Y.C., 1977, 1980—82, Heckscher Mus., Huntington, N.Y., 1980, Holtzman Gallery, Towson (Md.) State U., 1982, Roslyn Oxley Gallery, Sydney, 1976, 1982, Tomasulo Gallery, Union Coll., N.J., 1983, Stages Keuka Coll., Keuka Park, N.Y., 1985, New Visions, Ithaca, N.Y., 1989, Her-Chambliss, Hot Springs, Ark., 1990, Artist on the Lake, Hector, N.Y., 1992, Arnot Mus., Elmira, N.Y., Mus. Modern Art Christmas Card Collection, 1994, Arnot Mus., Elmira, N.Y., 2002, over 75 group shows, designer, Mus. Modern Art Christmas Card Collection, 1978—81, 1994, Time-Life Poster, 1978, Doing Dionysos, Arts of the So. Trees, 2000—02. Mem. Literacy Vols. Am. Recipient Flower Painting award, Artist's Mag., 1986, Distinctive Merit award, Art Dir.'s Club 58th Ann., 1979; grantee Pub. Svc., N.Y. State Creative Artist's, 1979. Mem.: AAUW, Nat. Assn. Women Artists. Home: PO Box 131 Odessa NY 14869-0131 Office Phone: 607-330-4542. Personal E-mail: stillmanart@gmail.com.

STILWELL, CONNIE KAY, retired elementary school educator; b. Frontenac, Kans., Feb. 26, 1947; d. Jerry Albert and Ann (Zortz) Scavezze; m. Richard W. Stilwell, June 7, 1969; 1 child, John Thomas. BS in Edn., Pittsburg State U., Kans., 1970; MS in Curriculum/Guidance, U. Kans., Lawrence, 1975. Tchr. Shawnee Mission (Kans.) Pub. Schs., 1970—2005; CEO Bluestem Learning LLC, 2005—. Adminstrv. asst. Learning Exch., Kansas City, Mo., 1976-77; instr. Webster Coll., Kansas City, 1978, U. Mo., Kansas City, 1979, Kans. U.-N.E. Kans. Math. Dissemination Project, summer 1993, curriculum coun. in lang. arts, 1992, mem. supt. coun., 1993-94, mem. math. coun., 1993-95, mem. science curriculum coun., 1994—, mem. profl. devel. coun., 2001-03; mem. regional conf. U.S. Dept. Edn., 1995; program advisor math curriculum Kansas City Pub. TV, 1993-95; curriculum writer Shawnee Mission (Kans.) Pub. Schs., 1977-93, math. mentor, 1995—; instr. Avila Coll., 2000-01; presenter in field Co-author: Language Arts, 1979, Science Curriculum, 1983, Curriculum-Math., 1977-87, Social Studies Curriculum, 1990, Power Pack-Math Enrichment Activities, 1990 Mem. steering com. Imagination Celebration, Kennedy Ctr., Kansas City, 1983-84; mem. QPA Site Coun., Kans., 1993, Westwood View Ednl. Enhancement Fund Coun., mem. bldg. team, 1994-95; mem. long range planning team PTA; Co-chmn. fundraising Folly Theatre, Kansas City, 1986; mem. tchr. mentoring planning team SMSD, 2005-06. Recipient Presdl. award for Excellence in Sci. and Math. Tchg., Kans. State Level, 1990, Tchrs. Who Make a Difference award Kansas City Chiefs, 1992; named Shawnee Mission Tchr. of Yr., 2003, Golden Ruler award Westwood View PTA, 1999, Alumni Meritorious award Pitts. State U., 2006; finalist for Tchr. of Yr., Kans. Region III. Mem. NEA, ASCD, Nat. Assn. Tchrs. Math., Mainstream Coalition, U. Kans. Alumni Assn., Pitts. (Pa.) State Alumni Assn. (edn. adv. coun.), Friends of Art-Nelson Art Gallery, sec., Sigma Chi Mother's Club, Delta Kappa Gamma, Alpha Gamma Delta Alumni, Am. Cancer Soc. (adv. chmn. gala) Republican. Avocations: bicycling, walking, reading. Home: 3911 Homestead Dr Shawnee Mission KS 66208-1545 Office: Bluestem Learning LLC Box 9101 Shawnee Mission KS 66201-1701 Office Phone: 913-522-8864. Business E-Mail: cstilwell@bluestarlearning.com, cstilwell@bluestemlearning.com.

STILWELL, CYNTHIA ANN, secondary school educator; d. Floyd Taylor and Ann Royal Bell; m. David Allen Stilwell, June 27, 1998; children: Ethan, Jason. BA, Georgetown Coll., Ky., 1990; MA in US History, U. SC, Columbia, 1994; MEd, Western Ky. U., Bowling Green, 1998. Cert. tchr. Ky. Tchr. Ohio County HS, Harford, Ky., 1991—92, Breckinridge County HS, Harned, Ky., 1994—98, Daviess County HS, Owensboro, Ky., 1998—.

STIMMELL, ANNE KRUEGER, special education educator; b. Stuart, Fla., Mar. 7, 1959; d. Karl John Krueger, Jr. and Geraldine Koestner Krueger; m. William Andrew Stimmell, May 29, 1977; children: Melissa Anne, William Andrew Stimmell, Jr. AA in Pre-Med, Indian River C.C., Ft. Pierce, Fla., 1978; BS in Spl. Edn., Fla. Atlantic U., 1998. Cert. tchr. K-12, varying exceptionalities Fla., 1998, tchr. grades 5-9 math Fla., 2005. Mgr. Krueger's Florist, Inc., Stuart, Fla., 1978—86; office mgr. Britt-Britt Constructors, Inc., Stuart, Fla., 1986—95; teacher's aide Martin Co. Sch. Dist., Stuart, Fla., 1995—96; tchr., spl. edn. Martin County Sch. Dist., Stuart, Fla., 1998—2006; property mgr. Krueger Trust, Stuart, Fla., 2006—. Mem.: Coun. for Exceptional Children, Kappa Delta Pi. Republican. Avocations: antiques, genealogy, gardening, camping, fishing. Home: 1170 SE Ocean Blvd Stuart FL 34996

STIMMELL, TAMARA, special education educator; b. Charleroi, Pa., Apr. 4, 1958; d. John R. and Patricia (Strenske) Stimmell. BA in Edn., Westminster Coll., 1980; MEd, Calif. U. of Pa., 1982; PhD, U. Pitts., 1990. Cert. elem. tchr., reading specialist, curriculum and supervision; supt. letter of eligibility. Reading specialist Somerset Area Sch. Dist., Pa., 1982-92, gifted and talented edn. educator, 1982-92, dir. spl. edn., 1992—. Mem. student assistance core team Somerset Area Sch. Dist., 1986-94, active drug adv. commn., 1989-92; dir. drug and alcohol edn. program Twin Lakes, 1992—; peer monitor Dept. of Edn., Pa., 1992—. Active drug and alcohol exec. commn. Somerset County, chair edn. rep. 1987—, chair planned courses and instructional practice com. Recipient award for Outstanding Contbn. Twin Lakes Rehab. Ctr., Red Ribbon Campaign for Drug Prevention, 1990, 94, 97. Mem. Coun. Exceptional Children, Phi Delta Kappa, Kappa Delta Pi. Home: 515 Rostraver Rd Belle Vernon PA 15012-1926

STIMPSON, CATHARINE ROSALIND, literature educator, writer; b. Bellingham, Wash., June 4, 1936; d. Edward Keown and Catharine (Watts) Stimpson. AB, Bryn Mawr Coll., 1958; BA, MA, Cambridge U., Eng., 1960; PhD, Columbia U., 1967. Mem. faculty Barnard Coll., N.Y.C., 1963—80; prof. English, dean of grad. sch., vice provost grad. edn. Rutgers U., New Brunswick, NJ, 1980—92, univ. prof., 1991—; chmn. bd. scholars Ms. Mag., N.Y.C., 1981—92; dir. fellows program MacArthur Found., 1994—97; univ. prof., dean Grad. Sch. Arts and Sci. NYU, N.Y.C., 1998—. Author: Class Notes, 1979, Where the Meanings Are, 1988; editor: Signs: Jour. Women in Culture and Soc., 1974—81, Women in Culture and Society book series, 1981; contbr. Change Mag., 1992—93. Chmn. N.Y. Coun. Humanites, 1984—87, Nat. Coun. Rsch. on Women, 1984—89; trustee Bates Coll., 1990—; pres. Assn. Grad. Schs., 2000—01; bd. dir. Stephens Coll., Columbia, Mo., 1982—85, Legal Def. and Edn. Fund, 1991—96. Fellow, Woodrow Wilson Found., 1958, Nat. Humanities Inst., 1975—76; Fulbright fellow, 1958—60, Rockefeller Humanities fellow, 1983—84. Mem.: PBS (bd. dirs. 1994—2000), NOW, PEN, MLA (exec. coun., chmn. acad. freedom com., 1st v.p., pres. 1990). Democrat. Home: 29 Washington Sq W Apt 15C New York NY 10011-9199 Office: NYU 6 Washington Sq N New York NY 10003-6668 Office Phone: 212-998-8040. Business E-Mail: catharine.stimpson@nyu.edu.

STINCHCOMB, AUDREY THOMPSON, respiratory care educator; b. Phila., May 2, 1944; d. Lewis and Theresa (Thompson) James; divorced; children: Davida, Dawn. ASc, Midlands Tech. Coll., 1976; BSc, U. S.C., 1991; MSc, So. Wesleyan U., 1997. Registered respiratory therapist. Therapist Baptist Med. Ctr., Columbia, S.C., 1976-78; supr. pulmonary lab. Dorn Med. Ctr., Columbia, S.C., 1978-90; dept. head Orangeburg (S.C.)-Calhoun Tech. Coll., 1990—. Cons. Manor Care Nursing Home, Columbia, 1981-90. Mem. Am. Assn. Respiratory Care. Baptist. Avocations: exercise, sewing, reading. Office: Orangeburg Calhoun Tech Coll 3250 Saint Matthews Rd NE Orangeburg SC 29118-8299 E-mail: stinchcomba@org.tec.sc.us.

STINE, ANNA MAE, publishing company executive; b. Monongahela, Pa., Sept. 6, 1938; d. Carlton Lee and Martha Regina (Graham) Stine. BS in Edn., Calif. State Coll., Pa., 1959; M in Elem. Edn., 1962; postgrad., U. Pitts., 1963—65. Cert. Elem. Prin. Duquesne U., 1962, Reading Specialist U. Pitts., 1963. Tchr., student tchr. supr. Upper St. Clair Sch. Dist., Pitts., 1959—65; nat. lang. arts cons. Macmillan Pub. Co., N.Y.C., 1965—75, regional mgr. Riverside, NJ, 1975—78; v.p., nat. sales mgr. East of Macmillan Pub. Co., 1978—89, v.p., nat. sales mgr. McGraw Hill Sch. divsn., 1989—92, sr. v.p., 1992—. Recipient Robert Hann award, Macmillan Pub. Co., 1965, Donald McGrew award, 1967, NJRA award, 1985. Mem.: NEA, Upper St. Clair Tchrs. Orgn. (pres.), Keystone Reading Assn., Regional Edn. Svc. Agy., Internat. Reading Assn. Republican. Roman Catholic. Home: 51 Foxwood Dr Moorestown NJ 08057-4102

STINE, CATHERINE MORRIS, artist; b. Roanoke, Va., Jan. 12, 1953; d. Richard Dengler and Dorothy Geraldine (Cornog) S.; m. Norris Jewett Chumley, Oct. 22, 1983; children: Jack H.M., Nathaniel B. BFA, Mus. Sch. Fine Arts, Boston, 1975; MFA in Creative Writing, New Sch., NYC, 2002. Art dir. Ear Mag., N.Y.C., 1980-83; asst. art dir. Jacmel Jewelry, N.Y.C., 1984-88; textile designer Style Coun., N.Y.C., 1989-90, Ruvetta Designs, N.Y.C., 1990—; represented by Margaret Bodell Gallery, N.Y.C., 1999—, Red Piano Gallery, Saint Helena, S.C. Curator Bratton Gallery, NYC, 1989; tchr. creative writing New Sch., N.Y.C., 2006. Author: Wild at Heart/End of the Race, 2002, Refugees, 2005; one-woman shows include Plant Factory, Boston, 1974, Sixth Sense Gallery, NYC, 1986, Pinnacle Awards/Am. Women in Radio and TV, NYC, 1987, Limelight Club, NYC, 1987, Parker-Bratton Gallery, NYC, 1987, Bratton Gallery, NYC, 1988, Carol Getz Gallery, Miami, Fla., 1990, Sunnen Gallery, NYC, 1993-94, Galley B.A.I., NYC, 1996, Margaret Bodell Gallery, NYC, 2000; group shows include Mus. Fine Arts Gallery, Boston, 1974, Williamsburg, Bklyn., 1982, ABC No Rio, NYC, 1983, 85, City Without Walls Gallery, Newark, 1984-85, Parsons Gallery, NYC, 1985, author, illustrator: The Halcyon, 1984, Hudson Valley Exhbn., Poughkeepsie, 1985, Parker-Bratton Gallery, NYC, 1986, Bratton Gallery, 1989, Neo Persona, NYC, 1990, Tribeca 148, NYC, 1991, Helio Gallery, NYC, 1991, S. Bitter Larkin, NYC, 1992, Sarah Rentschler Gallery, NYC, 1992, Dooley-Le Cappellaine, NYC, 1993, NYU Law Sch., 1994, Margaret Bodell Gallery, NYC, 2001; reviewed by Art in Am., 2001; represented in permanent collections Art Mus. Western Va., Paramount Pictures, others; represented by Margaret Bodell Gall., NYC Mem. Fifteenth St. Quaker Meeting, N.Y.C. Curatorial grantee Artist Space, N.Y.C., 1989. Mem. Soc. Childrens' Book Writers and Illustrators. Avocation: writing for young readers. Home: 214 E 17th St Apt 2 New York NY 10003-3647

STINE, KATIE KRATZ, state legislator; b. Dec. 6, 1956; BS, U. Cin.; JD, No. Ky. U. Atty.; mem. Ky. Ho. of Reps., Frankfort, 1995-98; senate pres. pro-tempore Ky. Senate, Frankfort, 1999—, mem. judiciary com. on com. rules. Active Jr. League Cin., Episcopal Ch. Women, No. Ky. Right to Life; former vice chair Ft. Thomas Bd. Adjustments. Mem. DAR, Ky. Bar Assn., Ft. Thomas Garden Club. Republican. Office: Ky Senate 24th Dist 702 Capitol Ave Rm 204 Frankfort KY 40601-3448 Home: 21 Fairway Dr Southgate KY 41071-3023

STINES, BETTY IRENE PARHAM, artist; b. Stinesville, Ind., May 3, 1918; d. Claude Everett Parham and Helen Bryan Acuff Parham; m. Willard Russell Elliott, Oct. 11, 1936 (dec. Aug. 1969); children: Jerry Lee Elliott, Gillespie-Kathy Lyn Elliott Holtsclaw, Willard Keith Elliott; m. Edmond Glen Stines, Feb. 19, 1972. Grad. high sch., Bloomington, Ind. Organizer, mem. Hoosier Hills Art Guild, Bloomington, Ind., 1963—80; organizer Hoosier Hills Art Guild Ann. Student Art Exhibit, 1963—73; floral designer Unique Florist Shoppe, Ellettsville, Ind., 1963—69; hon. dir. Internat. Biog. Ctr., Cambridge, England. Oil and water color paintings, 1950—2001, exhibited in group shows at Ind. U., Manchester Coll., Swope Art Gallery, Terre Haute, Ind., Hoosier Hills Art Gallery, Bloomington, Ind., Owen County Art Gallery, Spencer, Ind., Represented in permanent collections, exhibited in group shows at Ind. State House Art Salon. Chmn., co-chair art exhibits Monroe County Festival, Ellettsville, Ind., 1950—60; Sunday sch. tchr. Gave Chalk Talks Bapt. Ch., 1950; leader Brownie Scouts, 1943—47. Recipient numerous First, Best in Show and Champion Exhibitor awards. Mem.: Ind. Women in Arts, Nat. Mus. Women in Arts. Baptist. Avocations: genealogy, antiques. Home: 7935 W Ratliff Rd Bloomington IN 47404-9685

STINSMUEHLEN-AMEND, SUSAN, artist; b. Balt., Nov. 5, 1948; d. William I. and Geraldine S. (Dodds) Hamilton; m. Richard E. Amend, Nov. 27, 1987; children: Jason Stinsmuehlen, Wyatt Amend. Student, Hood Coll., U. Tex. Designer, owner Renaissance Glass Co., Austin, 1973-87; artist, glass, paint and mixed media dba Impresa, Inc., L.A. and Ojai, Calif., 1987—. Mem. Art in Pub. Places Panel, Austin, 1986-87; cons. Nat. Endowment for the Arts, Washington, 1986, 87, Cmty. Redevel. Agy., L.A., 1990-92; artist trustee Am. Craft Coun., 1988-92; lectr., lead artist Hollywood Blvd. Streetscape Team, Hollywood, Calif., 1991-94; lead artist Canoga Park, Calif., Pedestrianscape and Madrid Theater Project, City of L.A., 1996-2000; mem. Arts Commn., Ojai, Calif., 2000—; mem. Hollywood Art and Design Adv. Panel, 1994-2003; head artist Canoga Pk., Calif., 1996-2000; guest lectr., artist Puchuck Glass Sch., 1980-92, 94-95, 97, 2005, R.I. Sch. Design, 1980, 2006, Mass. Coll. Art, 1980, Dallas Mus. Art, 1981, Japanese Glass Conf., 1985, Calif. Coll. Arts, Oakland, 1985, 89, Australian Glass Conf., 1987, Penland Sch. Craft, N.C., 1996; artist-in-residence Pilchuck Glass Sch., Wash., 2005; educator in field. One-woman shows include Mattingly Baker Gallery, Dallas, 1984, Kurland Summers Gallery, L.A., 1985, 88, 90, 92, Traver Sutton Gallery, Seattle, 1986, Habatat Galleries, Detroit, 1991, The Nest Gallery, Ojai, Calif., 1997, The Glass Gallery, Bethesda, Md., 2000, Carnegie Mus. Art, Oxnard, Calif., 2004, Sandy Carson Gallery, Denver, 2005, D&A Fine Arts, L.A., 2005; exhibited in group shows at Whatcom Mus., Bellingham, Wash., 1992, 94, Finegood Art Gallery, West Hills, Calif., 1993-94, Miller Gallery, N.Y.C., 1994, The Wignall Mus., Chaffey Coll., Rancho Cucamonga, Calif., 1995, Traver Gallery, Seattle, 1995, Smithsonian Inst. Travelling Exhbn., 1999, Muckenthaler Cultural Arts Ctr., Calif., 1999, Loveland (Colo.) Mus. Gallery, 1998, 99, Fresno Art Mus., 1998, SOFA Chgo., 1998, Santa Cruz Mus. Art and History, 1999, Smithsonian Inst., 1998-2000, L.A. County Mus. Art, 1999, Orange County Mus. Art, 1999, L.A. Mcpl. Art Gallery, 2003, Reynolds Gallery, Richmond, Va., 2003, Nathan Larramendy Gallery, 2004, Ojai Valley Mus., 2003-05, San Francisco Mus. Craft & Design, 2005, L.A. Mcpl.Art Gallery, 2005, Beatrice Wood Ctr. Arts, 2005, others; represented in permanent collection Am. Airlines, Dallas, Renwick Gallery Nat. Mus. Art, Washington, The Jewish Mus., N.Y.C., The Corning (N.Y.) Mus. Glass, Detroit Inst. Arts, Leigh Yawkey Woodson Mus., Wausau, Wis., Oakland (Calif.) Mus., Wagga Wagga City Art Gallery, NSW, Australia, Nishida Mus., Toyoma, Japan, Pilchuck Glass Ctr., Stanwood, Wash., Mus. Art & Design, N.Y.C., L.A. (Calif.) County Mus. Art, Radisson Hotel, Austin, AT&T, Dallas, AT&T, N.Y.C., Marshall Fields Corp. Collection, Chgo., City of L.A., Mus. Am. Art/Smithsonian Instn., Carnegie Art Mus., Beatrice Wood Ctr. for Arts, Ojas Valley Cmty. Hosp., others plus numerous pvt. collections. Nat. Endowment for the Arts grantee, Washington, 1982, 88; Hauberg fellowship Pilchuck Glass Sch., 2001. Mem. Glass Art Soc. (hon. life; bd. dirs. 1982-86, pres. 1984-86), Mus. Contemporary Art (L.A.), L.A. County Mus. Avocations: gardening, swimming, walking, hiking, golf. E-mail: impresa@pobox.com.

STINSON, ANDREA MARIA, professional basketball player; b. Mooresville, N.C., Nov. 25, 1967; BA, N.C. State U., 1991. Guard Charlotte Sting, 1997—. Named Kodak All-Am., 1990, 1991, MVP, ACC Tournament, ACC Player of Yr., 1991, lead scorer, Charlotte Sting, 1997—2001; named to All-ACC Tournament Team, Italian League All-Star Team, Ea. Conf. All-Star Team, 2001; recipient Gold medal, 1992 Jones Cup Team, Bronze medal, 1991 Pan Am. Team playing overseas for Thiene in Italy, 1996—97. Office: Charlotte Sting 100 Hive Dr Charlotte NC 28208-7707

STINSON, MARY FLORENCE, retired nursing educator; b. Wheeling, W.Va., Feb. 11, 1931; d. Rolland Francis and Mary Angela (Voellinger) Kellogg; m. Charles Walter Stinson, Feb. 12, 1955; children: Kenneth Charles, Karen Marie Wiberg, Kathryn Anne Kartye. BSN, Coll. Mt. St. Joseph, 1953, postgrad., 1983; MEd, Xavier U., Cin., 1967; postgrad., U. Cin., 1981. Staff nurse contagious disease ward Cin. Gen. Hosp., 1953-54, asst. head nurse med. and polio wards, 1955, acting head nurse, clin. instr., 1955-56; instr. St. Francis Hosp. Sch. Practical Nursing, Cin., 1956-57, Good Samaritan Hosp. Sch. Nursing, Cin., 1957—66; instr. refresher courses for nurses Cin. Bd. Edn. and Ohio State Nurses Assn. Dist. 8, 1967-70; coord. sch. health office Coll. Mt. St. Joseph, Ohio, 1969-72, instr. dept. nursing, 1974-79, asst. prof., 1979-89; RN assessor pre-admission screening sys. providing options & resources today Coun. on Aging Southwestern Ohio, 1989-90, quality assurance coord. pre-admission screen sys. providing options & resources today program, 1990-93, quality assurance supr. pre-admission screen sys. providing options & resources today and elderly svcs. programs, 1993-94; quality assurance mgr. Coun. Aging Southwestern Ohio, 1995-2000; ret., 2000. Staff nurse St. Francis/St. George Hosp., Cin., 1988-89; vol. ombudsman Pro Srs. of S.W. Ohio, 2005—. Charter mem. Adoptive Parents Assn. St. Joseph Infant and Maternity Home, 1966—70; women's com. for performing arts series Coll. Mt. St. Joseph; chmn. by-law com. Coll. Mt. St. Joseph Nursing Honor Soc., 1996—98; active St. Antoninus Rosary Altar and Sch. Soc., 1973—84, St. Antoninus Athletic Club, com. chmn., 1969—70; bd. dirs. Coll. Mt. St. Joseph Alumni Assn., 1982—84, sec., 1968—69, v.p., 1969—70, pres., 1970—71, chmn. revision of constn., 1976—77; homecoming chmn. Coll. Mt. St. Joseph, 1970, co-chmn., 1977, co-chair com. to celebrate 75 years of nursing edn., 2001—02; mem. com. to plan 50th ann. of graduation Coll. Mt. St. Joseph Alumni Assn., 2003. Mem. River Squares Club (v.p. 1967), Sigma Theta Tau (charter Omicron Omicron chpt. 1998—), St. Antonious Adult Social Group (pres. 2005—). Democrat. Roman Catholic. Home: 5549 Cleander Dr Cincinnati OH 45238-4266 Personal E-mail: flostinson@current.net.

STINSON, SUSAN ELIZABETH, director, writer; b. Amarillo, Tex., Oct. 17, 1960; d. Billy Ray and Mollie Elizabeth (Jordan) S. BA, U. Colo., Boulder, 1983. Dir. devel. Ctr. for Popular Econs., Amherst, Mass., 1990—99. Editor Orogeny Press, Northampton, 1992-97. Author: Belly Songs, 1993, Fat Girl Dances with Rocks, 1994, Martha Moody, 1995 (Benjamin Franklin award 1996), Venus of Chalk, 2004 Fiction fellow The Millay Colony, Austerlitz, N.Y., 1991, Helene Wurlitzer Found., Taos, N.M., 1991, Blue Mountain Ctr., Blue Mountain Lake, N.Y., 1994, Norcroft, Lutson, Minn., 2005; fiction grantee Ludwig Vogelstein Found., N.Y.C., 1992, Mass. Arts lottery grantee, 1993, 97. Home: PO Box 1272 Northampton MA 01061-0433 Personal E-mail: susan@susanstinson.net.

STIPEK, DEBORAH JANE, dean, education educator; BS in Psychology, U. Wash., 1972; PhD in Devel. Psychology, Yale U., 1977. Prof. Grad. Sch. Edn. UCLA, 1977—2000; co-dir. NIMH Tng. Program in Applied Human Devel.; dir. Corinne Seeds U. Elme. Sch., Urban Edn. Studies Ctr.; I. James Quillen dean, prof. edn. Stanford (Calif.) U. Grad. Sch. Edn., 2001—. Mem. bd. on children, youth and families NRC; dir. MacArthur Found. Network on Tchg. and Learning. Author: Motivation to Learn: From Theory to Practice, 2002; author: (with A. Bohart) Constructive and Destructive Behavior: Implications for Family, School, and Society, 2001; author: (with K. Seal) Motivated Minds: Raising Children to Love Learning, 2001. Congl. Sci. fellow, Soc. for Rsch. in Child Devel., Office Senator Bill Bradley, 1983—84. Office: Stanford Univ Sch Edn 485 Lasuen Mall Stanford CA 94305-3096

STIPEK, KATHLEEN, reference librarian; b. Oakland, Calif., Nov. 14, 1946; d. William Antone and Geraldine Catherine (Cullen) S. BA, Fla. Atlantic U., 1967; MLS, Fla. State U., 1982. Clerical/secretarial positions U. Fla., Gainesville, 1968-81; dir. Haines City (Fla.) Pub. Libr., 1982-86; adult svcs. coord. Ctrl. Fla. Regional Libr., Ocala, 1986-89; reference libr. Hernando County Libr. Sys., Brooksville, Fla., 1989; freelance writer and editor, 1989-91; reference libr. Alachua County Libr. Dist., Gainesville, 1991—. Contbr. chpt. to book, articles to profl. jours. Higher Edn. Act Title IIB fellow, 1981-82. Mem. ALA, Fla. Libr. Assn., Fla. Pub. Libr. Assn., Am. Mensa. Avocations: reading, cookery, embroidery. Office: Alachua County Libr Dist 401 E University Ave Gainesville FL 32601-5453 Personal E-mail: afn05848@yahoo.com.

STIRL, WILMA JEAN, mathematics educator; BS, Angelo State U., San Angelo, Tex., 1977. Coach/math tchr. Crane HS, Tex., 1977—83; math tchr., student coun. advisor Stanton HS, Tex., 1983—. Named Tchr. of Yr., Martin County C. of C., 2001. Mem.: Assn. Tex. Profl. Educators (life).

STIRLING, ELLEN ADAIR, retail executive; b. Chgo., June 21, 1949; d. Volney W. and Ellen Adair (Orr) Foster; m. James P. Stirling, June 6, 1970; children: Elizabeth Ginevra, Diana Leslie, Alexandra Curtiss. Student, U. Chgo., 1970-71; BA, Wheaton Coll., Norton, Mass., 1971; postgrad., U. London, 1974. Pres., CEO, The Lake Forest Shop, 1986—; CEO Zita, 2005—. Bd. dirs. Lake Forest Bank and Trust. Founder, v.p. aux. bd. Art Inst. Chgo., 1972-91; dir. Friends of Ryerson Woods, 1992—; mem. women's bd. Lyric Opera, Chgo., 1992—, Lake Forest Coll., 1989—; mem. adv. bd. Hope C. McCormick Costume Ctr.; mem. costume coun. Chgo. Hist. Soc.; trustee Nat. Louis U., 1999—; bd. dirs. Lake Forest OPen Lands, 1990—. Mem. Onwentsia Club, Racquet Club, Chgo. Club, Econ. Club Chgo. Office: The Lake Forest Shop 165 E Market Sq Lake Forest IL 60045

STIRLING, ISABEL ANN, science librarian; b. San Jose, Calif., Dec. 4, 1948; d. James H. and Betty Stirling. BA, U. Calif., Riverside, 1970; MLS, Western Mich. U., 1977. Head bio-agrl. library U. Calif., Riverside, 1977-82; head sci. libr., prof. U. Oreg., Eugene, 1982—. Author: Self-Paced Library Instruction Workbook for the Sciences, 1981; contbr. articles to jours. Mem. ALA (Libr./Book fellow Ankara, Turkey 1988-89), Assn. Coll. and Rsch. Libr. of ALA (various coms.), Internat. Fedn. Libr. Assn., Oreg. Library Assn. Avocations: handloom, fiber arts. Office: U Oreg Sci Library Eugene OR 97403-5201

STIRM, DORIS ELIZABETH, artist; b. Binghamton, N.Y., U.S.A., July 25, 1919; d. Williamh and Amanda Maria (Hall) Wusthof. B.A., Stanford U., 1941; Grad. Work (hon.), Coll. San Mateo, Calif., 1951. Passenger agent TWA Airlines, SanFrancisco, Calif., 1942—46; art instr. Recreation Dept., Calif., 1970—99; dir. Redwood City Art Gallery, Redwood, Calif., 1998—2003. Pres. Soc. West Artists, San Francisco, 1990—91. Chmn. Cancer Soc. Drive, Calif., 1951; co-chmn. Art in Pub. Places, Calif., 1990—95. Recipient Artist of The Yr., Burcwcame Art Soc., 1979. Mem.: Western Pastel Soc. Democrat. Protestant. Avocations: painting, aerobics, gardening. Home: 442 Cumberland Dr Burlingame CA 94010

STIRRATT, BETSY, artist, gallery director; b. New Orleans, Sept. 22, 1958; d. Avery and Betty Lou (Chadwick) S.; m. Jeffrey Alan Wolin, Aug. 20, 1983; children: Benjamin, Andrew. BFA, La. State U., 1980; MFA, Ind. U., 1983. Gallery dir. Fine Arts Gallery, Ind. U., Bloomington, 1987—. Exhibited works at Salon Show, Art in Gen., 1992, Meat, White, Columns, 1993, Between Mind and Body, Air Gallery, 1994, Physical Affinities, Carl Hammer Gallery, 1994, In Situ Gallery, 1995. Masters fellow Ind. Arts Commn., 1989, Arts Midwest fellow Arts Midwest, 1989, NEA fellow, 1990. Office: Fine Arts Gallery Ind Univ Bloomington IN 47405

STITELY, KAREN RICHARDSON, performing arts educator; b. Lakewood, N.J., Aug. 23, 1967; d. Glen Allen and Eileen Strunk Richardson; m. Wilton Francis Stitely III, Oct. 30, 1993; children: Noah Allen, Alec Michael. BA in Acting, Shenandoah U., Winchester, Va, 1989; Advanced Cert. in Edn., Mt. St. Mary's U., Emmitsburg, Md, 2000. Cert. advanced profl. in tchg. Md. Tchr. drama, dance and English Catoctin H.S., Thurmont, Md., 1998—. Actor, dir. and choreographer sch. and cmty. musicals and plays. Home: 6309 Towncrest Ct Frederick MD 21703 Office: Catoctin HS Sabillasville Rd Thurmont MD 21788 Office Phone: 240-236-8141. E-mail: karen.stitely@fcps.org.

STITES, M(ARY) ELIZABETH, architecture educator; b. N.Y.C., July 28, 1915; d. Otto and Olivia (Stites) Gaertner; m. Raymond S. Stites, Jul. 29, 1938; 1 child: Mary Elizabeth. BArch, NYU, 1940; postgrad., U. Vienna, 1961. Instr. U. Md. Coll. Arts & Scis., College Park, 1949-67, adminstrv. asst., 1959-76, assoc. prof., 1967-76; cons. Md. Coll. Art and Design, Silver Spring, 1976-89; asst. organist St. Luke's Ch., Bethesda, Md., 1976—95. Lectr. religious architecture, history architecture, archtl. studies of Leonardo da Vinci. Contbr. articles to Book of Knowledge Grolier Soc., 1952, New Cath. Ency., 1965. Past mem. Yellow Springs Town Planning Commn.; mem. Montgomery County com. Md. Hist. Trust for Archtl. Preservation. Mem. Coll. Art Assn., Soc. Archtl. Historians, Archaeol. Inst. Am., AIA. Episcopalian. Home: PO Box 98 Garrett Park MD 20896-0098

STITES, SUSAN KAY, writer, human resources specialist; b. Colorado Springs, Colo., Sept. 20, 1952; d. William Wallace and Betty Jane (Kosley) Stites; m. Gerald Frederick Simon, Aug. 14, 1988. BA, Wichita State U., 1974; MA, Northwestern U., 1979. Benefits authorizer Social Security Adminstrn., Chgo., 1974-77; trainer Chgo. Urban Skills Inst., 1977-79; human resources mgr. Montgomery Ward, Chgo., 1979-83; mgr. tng. Lands' End, Dodgeville, Wis., 1983-87; dir. human resources Ctrl. Life Assurance, Madison, Wis., 1988-90; owner Mgmt. Allegories, Madison, 1987—. Author: Delegating for Results, 1992, Business Communications, 1992, Managing with a Quality Focus, 1994, Training Orientation for the Small Business, 1994, Powerful Performance Management, 1994, Safety Management Techniques, 1995, Teaching First Aid and CPR, 1995, Alive at 25, 1995, Strategic Thinking and Planning, 1995, Teaching Alice at 25, 1996, Fundamentals of Industrial Hygiene, 1996, Recruiting, Developing and Retaining Volunteers, 1996, Creating a Credit Union University: An Administrator's Guide, 1997, 2d. edit., 2001, Creating a Corporate University, 1997, Strategic Thinking for the Automotive Industry, 1997, Managing Sales and Service, 1997, Sales and Service Management in Credit Unions, 1997, Provide Training Without Straining Your Budget, 1997, Car America Sales Training Manual, 1998, Introduction to Community Organizing, 1998, Car America Leader's Guide, 1998, Effective Loan Interviewing, 1999, Driven to Extremes, 2000, Safety Inspections, 2001, Job Safety Analysis, 2001, Incident Investigations, 2001, Ergonomics for the Small Business, 2003, Creating a Safety Culture: Strategies for Small Business, 2004, Preventing Slips, Trips and Falls, 2006, How May I Help You? Service with a Smile and a Story, 2006; editor: Backstay, 1999—2001. Vol. tutor Japanese students in English, Evanston, Ill., 1977—80; reader to the blind Chgo. Coun. for Blind, 1974—76. Named Outstanding Woman of the Yr., Wichita State U., 1974. Mem.: ASTD (v.p. membership 1986, chpt. pres. 1988, Region V awards chair 1992), Assn. Quality and Participation, Madison Area Quality Improvement Network, Soc. Applied Learning Tech., Mendota Yacht Club (treas. 1990—94), Rotary (vol. fundraiser). Avocations: sailing, windsurfing, gardening, cooking, travel. Office: Mgmt Allegories 3788 Highridge Rd Madison WI 53718-6206

STITH, LAURA DENVIR, state supreme court justice; b. St. Louis, Oct. 30, 1953; m. Donald George Scott; children: Lisa, Rebecca, Cynthia. BA magna cum laude, Tufts U., 1975; JD magna cum laude, Georgetown U., 1978. Law clk. to Hon. Robert E. Seiler, Mo. Supreme Ct., 1978—79; assoc. Shook, Hardy & Bacon, Kansas City, Mo., 1979—84, ptnr., 1984—94; judge. Mo. Ct. Appeals (we. dist.), 1994—2001; judge Mo. Supreme Ct., 2001—. Speaker Mo. New Judges Sch. Author: articles on appellate practice, products liability and civil procedure. Tutor, mentor Operation Breakthrough, St. Vincent's Sch.; founding dir., mem. Lawyers Encouraging Academic Performance. Mem.: Assn. Women Lawyers of Greater Kansas City (speaker, past pres.), Mo. Bar Assn., Kansas City Metropolitan Bar Assn. Office: Supreme Ct Mo PO Box 150 Jefferson City MO 65102

STITH-CABRANES, KATE, law educator; b. St. Louis, Mar. 16, 1951; d. Richard Taylor and Ann Carter (See) Stith; m. Jeffrey Leonard Pressman, Dec. 23, 1970 (dec. Mar. 1977); m. José Alberto Cabranes, Sept. 15, 1984; children: Alejo, Benjamin José; stepchildren: Jennifer, Amy. BA, Dartmouth Coll., 1973; MPP, J.F.K. Sch. of Govt., 1977; JD, Harvard U., 1977. Bar: D.C. 1979. Law clk. to Judge Carl McGowan US Ct. of Appeals, Washington, 1977-78; law clk. to Justice Byron White US Supreme Ct., Washington, 1978-79; staff economist Coun. of Econ. Advisers, Washington, 1979-80; spl. asst. Dept. of Justice, Washington, 1980-81, asst. U.S. atty. NYC, 1981-84; assoc. prof. Yale Law Sch., New Haven, 1985-90, prof. of law, 1990—97, Lafayette S. Foster prof. law, 1998—, dep. dean, 1999—2001, 2003—04; mem. adv com. Fed. Rules of Criminal Procedure, 1995—2001. Mem. Permanent Commn. on the Status of Women, State of Conn., Hartford, 1990-96. Author: (with José A. Cabranes) Fear of Judging: Sentencing Guidelines in the Federal Courts, 1998 (Cert. of Merit ABA); contbr. articles on criminal law and constl. law to profl. jours. Trustee Dartmouth Coll., Hanover, N.H., 1989-2000, Women's Campaign Sch., 1994—, Fed. Bar Found., 1998-2004. Mem. Am. Law Inst., Coun. Fgn. Rels., Conn. Bar Found. (bd. dirs. 1987—, chair 1999-2002). Office: Yale Law Sch PO Box 208215 New Haven CT 06520-8215 E-mail: kate.stith@yale.edu.

STITT, DOROTHY JEWETT, journalist; b. Houston, Sept. 4, 1914; d. Harry Berkey and Gladys (Norfleet) Jewett; m. James Wilson Stitt, Feb. 14, 1939; children: James Harry (dec. 1999), Thomas Paul. AB, Rice U., 1937; MS, Columbia U., 1938. Reporter Houston Post, 1936-38, asst. city editor, 1938; editor of publs. Jewett Family of Am., 1971-94, editor emeritus, 1994—. Spl. asst. to pub. Jewett Genealogy Vols. III and IV, 1995-97; Jewett family Dir.-for-Life, 1995—; gen. chair Jewett Family Reunion, 1996; exec. com. Jewett 2000 Millennium Reunion. Author, editor: The 100th Anniversary Yearbook and History of the George Taylor Chapter, DAR, 1895-1995, 1994, Easton Red Cross Fiftieth Anniversary Booklet and History—Fifty Years of Service, 1967. Adv. bd. Easton Salvation Army, pub. chmn., 1956—, chmn. bd. dirs., 1964, bd. treas., 1981; bd. dirs., pub. chmn. Easton chpt. ARC, 1952-67, vol. Lehigh Valley chpt., 1995-96, 98; founding chmn., pres. Easton JC Wives, 1950-53; fin. com. Little Stone House Mus. Assn., 1974-76, 80, organizing bd. dirs. sec. and pub. chmn., 1974-91; bd. dirs. Easton United Comty. Chest/United Way, 1957-60, publicity chmn. for United Way 1st campaign, 1960; active Easton Civil Def. Comms., 1956-60; charter mem. bd. Montgomery County Pa. Girl Scouts USA, 1946-48, publicity chmn., initiator and editor county newsletter; den mother cub scouts Easton Boy Scouts Am., 1948-55; capt. renovation campaign area YWCA, 1956; mem. March Sch., Easton PTA, 1948-57, sec., 1952-54, v.p., 1954-56, bylaws chmn., 1953, Easton H.S., 1954-61, membership chmn., 1955-57, 59-60; bd. dirs. Easton Young Woman's Christian Assn., 1965-68, publicity chmn. Y-Teen com., 1953-68; sponsoring dir. Easton area H.S. Students weekly TV 30-minute news program, 1955-56; class agent 60th reunion Pulitzer Grad. Sch. Journalism Class of 1938 Columbia U., 1998 Recipient citation, United Way of Easton, 1960, cited for outstanding svcs., Easton chpt. ARC, 1967, cert. for outstanding svc. and support, 1997, Molly Pitcher Gold medal, SAR, 1980, plaques, Salvation Army, 1982, 1991, 2005, Vol. Svc. cert., 2005, plaques, Jewett Family of Am., 1993, citation for outstanding svc. in restoration and pub. of Little Stone Ho. Mus., Hist. and Geneal. Soc. Northampton County, 1993, cert. of recognition, State Senate of Pa., 2005. Mem. AAUW (treas. Easton br. 1950-52, newsletter initiator and editor 1951-60, rep. of br. to UN N.Y.C. conf. 1961-68, internat. rels. chair 1960-68; Pa. achievement award 2000), UDC (Jefferson Davis chpt./Houston), DAR (George Taylor chpt. regent 1974-80, 89-95, vice regent 1980-83, historian 1971-74, 95—, pub. chair 1969—, Pa. state chair vol. svcs. 1995-98, DAR chmn. Kressler Meml. Garden, Easton, 1999—), DAR, PEO (chpt. AF Houston), Easton Tavern House Soc., World Affairs Coun. Phila., Woman's Club of Easton (pres. 1961-64, bd. dirs. 1957—, pub. chair 1952-68, 70-82, 92-96, parliamentarian 1984-92, 2000—, spl. fin. chair 1969-78, legis. chair 1982-84, internat. affairs chair 1996-2000, history update chair 1997—, Outstanding Woman of Yr. 1992, Gold Medal of Honor 1992), Pa. Northeastern Dist. Regents Club (pres. 1980-83, treas. 1997—2003), Northampton Country Club (Niners' Golf chair 1957-91), Women's Golf Assn. (constn. and bylaws chair, publicity chmn. 1957-92, parliamentarian 1960-92), Libr. of Congress Assn. (founding nat. mem., charter assoc.). Republican. Episcopalian. Avocations: history, antiques, golf, swimming. Home: 110 Upper Shawnee Ave Easton PA 18042-1356

STITT, MARI LEIPPER, poet; b. Salem, Ohio, May 1, 1923; d. Robert and Myrtle (Cost) Leipper; m. Rodney Dean Stitt, Apr. 22, 1944; children: Dana Lovelace, Rodney D. Jr. BA in Music, San Diego State U., 1946; MA in Human Rels., Calif. Western U., 1966. Dir. religious edn. Ctrl. Congl. Ch., 1941-50; tchr. sociology San Diego Evening Coll., 1966-84; writer poetry, 1984—. Home: The Academy Village 7761 S Vivaldi Ct Tucson AZ 85747-9632 Personal E-mail: marilstitt@cox.net.

STIVERS, CAROL URBAN, retired music educator, consultant; b. Orlando, Fla., Aug. 10, 1938; d. Sanford W. and Ada R. Padgett; m. James D. Stivers, July 16, 1989; m. Bela Urban (dec.); 1 child, Suzanne Urban Zamberlan. MusM in Performance, Fla. State U., Tallahassee, 1962. Nat. cert. music tchr. Music Tchrs. Nat. Assn., 1980. Asst. prof. piano U. Nev., Las Vegas, 1989—95, assoc. prof. piano, 1995—2004; ret., 2004. Founding mem. Mariposa Trio, 1989—2003; concert pianist, 1970—; profl. accompanist, 1970—; pianist Las Vegas Philharmonic, 1972—. Named Outstanding Tchr. of Yr., U. Nev. Las Vegas Coll. Fine Arts, 1998. Mem.: Music Tchrs. Nat. Assn. (nat. bd. dirs. 2000—02, SW divsn. pres. 1998—2000, Outstanding Tchr. of Competition Winners 2003). Avocations: horseback riding, gardening, sewing, hiking, travel. Home: HC 38 Box 288 Las Vegas NV 89124

STOBB, MARY JEAN, retired association administrator; b. Winnipeg, Man., Can., Oct. 16, 1934; came to U.S., 1955; d. Rudolph Edwin and Milla Elida (Corneliussen) Rasmussen; m. Gordon Wesley Stobb, June 14, 1958; children: Barbara Jean, David Gordon, William Eric. BS in Home Econs., U. Man., 1955. Cert. home economist. County home agt. U. Minn. at Stearns County, St. Cloud, 1955-58, U. Minn. at Mille Lacs County, Milaca, 1962-67; pvt. practice home economist Little Falls, Minn., 1967-71; interviewer Mid-Continent Surveys, Inc., Mpls., 1971-78, Rsch. Triangle Inst., Inc., Research Triangle Park, NC, 1976-78; dir. nutrition Region V Elderly Nutrition Program, Little Falls, Minn., 1978-80; dist. dir. Minn. unit Green Thumb, Inc., Wadena, Minn., 1980—89, mgr. field ops., 1989—95; field ops. coord. Green Thumb, Inc. (now Experience Works, Inc.), Minn., 1995—2003, ret., 2003. Key leader Riverwood Ramblers 4-H Club, Little Falls, 1968—70, 1971—79; county clothing leader Morrison County, Little Falls, 1974—75; chair adv. com. North Ctrl. Minn. Coun. on Aging, 2003—05; chair Ctrl. Minn. Coun. Aging, 2006—; commr. Little Falls Housing and Devel. Authority, 2005—; mem. adv. bd. Morrison County Interfaith Hospitality Network, 2004—06; pres. United Ch. Women's Assn., Little Falls, 1977—79; lay leader First United Ch., 2003—05, outreach chair, 1976—78, fin. chair, 1987—93, chair mission and ministry com., 1996—2002, mem. mission and ministry com., 2006—. Named 4-H Leader of Yr. Morrison County 4-H Leaders, 1974. Mem.: Minn. Home Econs. Assn. (dist. pres. 1969—71, chmn. home economists in homemaking 1972—73, by-laws chair 1977—78, del. 1981, 1982, dist. pres. 1986—87), Am. Assn. Family and Consumer Scientists (dist. pres. 1986—87), Internat. Fedn. Home Economists, Morrison Coast Interfaith Hospitality Network (host coord. 2005—), Mid-Sota Home Economists in Homemaking Club (Little Falls) (pres.). Methodist. Avocations: singing, gardening, walking. E-mail: maryjeans@charter.net.

STOCK, ANN, federal official; m. Stuart C. Stock; 1 child. Grad., Purdue U. Dep. press sec. to V.p. Walter F. Mondale, 1980, 84; regional dir. pub. rels. Bloomingdales Dept. Stores, 1982—86, ops. v.p., 1986—89, v.p. pub. rels., 1989—93; dep. asst. to Pres. and Social Sec. The White House, Washington, 1993-97; v.p. institutional affairs The Kennedy Ctr., Washington, 1997—. Asst. sec. Kennedy Ctr. Bd. Trustees; bd. dirs. Young Concert Artists, Cultural Alliance Greater Washington, United Artists. Mem. Capital Children's Mus. (co-founder), The Women's Forum, N.Y. Fashion Group (former program chmn.), Washington Woman Roundtable (founder), "Race for the Cure" (co-founder). Office: Institutional Affairs The Kennedy Ctr Washington DC 20566-0001 Office Phone: 202-416-8703.

STOCK, PATRICIA D., literature, language and history educator; b. Little Falls, N.Y., Dec. 26, 1950; d. Doloris J. and Doris Horender Masi; m. Roger N. Stock, Aug. 10, 1974; children: Jason M., Johanna S. BA, Eisenhower Coll., Rochester, N.Y., 1973. Cert. secondary social studies and English N.Y., 1977. Secondary tchr. English and history Oppenheim-Ephratah Ctrl. Sch., St. Johnsville, NY, 1974—. Student coun. advisor Oppenheim-Ephratah Ctrl. Sch., 1978—, yearbook advisor, 2003—. Parade co-chairperson Canal Day's Com., Little Falls, 1985—; counselor Boy Scouts Am., Little Falls, 1990; com. person Rep. Party of Little Falls, Herkimer County, Little Falls, 1998—. Mem.: Oppeheim-Ephratah Ctrl. Sch. Tchrs. Assn. (assoc.; v.p. 1999—). R-Liberal. Roman Catholic. Avocations: sewing, reading, writing, genealogy. Office: Oppenheim-Ephratah Ctrl Sch 6486 St Hwy 29 Saint Johnsville NY 13452 Office Phone: 518-568-2014.

STOCKAR, HELENA MARIE MAGDALENA, artist; b. Bratislava, Czechoslovakia, Mar. 22, 1933; came to the U.S., 1968; d. Arnost J. and Helen R. (Strakova) Kubasek; m. Ivo J. Stockar, Oct. 31, 1959; children: David, Laura Bates. Diploma, Graficka Skola, Prague, 1952, Music Conservatory, 1954. Piano tchr. Music Sch., Prague, 1954-68; company pianist State Ballet/Breacrest Sch., R.I., 1968-74; piano tchr. Music Tchr. Assn., R.I., 1968-86. One-woman shows include Warwick (RI) Mus., 1986, Brown U., Providence, 1987, Westerly (RI) Art Gallery, 1987, Westerly Art Gallery/Morin-Miller, 1988—89, Galerie Horizon, Paris, 1989, Barnes & Noble, Warwick, 1999—2000, Bohemian Gallery, NYC, 1999, Hoxie Gallery, Westerly, 2000, Happy White Gallery, Barrington, R.I., 2000, C.C. R.I., Lincoln, 2000, 2004, Pittenween Art Festival, Scotland, 2001, 2004, Pawtucket Congl. Ch., 2002, Bell St. Chapel, Providence, 2002, Courthouse Ctr. Arts, West Kingston, R.I., 2003, two-person shows, RI State Com. Nat. Mus. Women in the Arts, Triboro Studio, 1995, Bush Gallery, Bryce Studio, Providence, 2001, Monserat Gallery, Soho, 2002, Courthouse Ctr. for the Arts, West Kingston, R.I., 2002, De Blois Gallery, Newport, 2002, Stonington Vineyards Gallery, Conn., 2002, Teichman Gallery, Cape Cod, Mass., 2003, Gallery Z, Providence, 2003—04, one-man shows include McGrath Courthouse, Wakefield, RI, 2005, exhibited in group shows at World Congress Czechoslovak Soc. Art and Sci., Washington, 1988, Prague, 1992, Morin-Miller Internat., N.Y.C., 1989, Ariel Gallery, Soho, N.Y.C., 1989, Art Expo N.Y.C., 1989, New Eng. Internat. Art Expo, 1993, R.I. State Com. Nat. Mus. Women Arts, 1995, Providence Art Club, 1996—97, Sarah Doyle Gallery, Brown U., Providence, 1997, Visions, Newport, 2001—02, Gallery Z, Providence, 2003—05, Krause Gallery, 2003, 2005, Breslin Fine Arts, Inc., Warwick, RI, 2003—05, Warwick Mus., 2003, Charmed Gallery, East Greenwich, RI, 2004—05, BFA Boston Internat. Fine Art Show, 2005, BFA Art Expo, N.Y.C., N.Y., 2005, BFA Contemporary Art Fair, Edinburgh, 2005, BFA Art Ireland, Dublin, 2005, Real Art Ways, Hartford, Conn., 2006, Ct. House Ctr. for the Arts, West Kingston, RI, 2006, Represented in permanent collections; featured on TV shows. Participant Art in Public Places: Convention Ctr., Providence, 1994. Recipient Second prize Nat. Competition of Children's Book Illustration, Prague, 1965. Mem.: Czechoslovak Soc. Art and Sci. Avocations: travel, gardening. Personal E-mail: istockar@aol.com.

STOCKARD, SUSAN ANTONIA WILLIAMS See CHANNING, STOCKARD

STOCKBURGER, JEAN DAWSON, lawyer; b. Scottsboro, Ala., Feb. 4, 1936; d. Joseph Mathis Scott and Mary Frances (Alley) Dawson; m. John Calvin Stockburger, Mar. 23, 1963; children: John Scott, Mary Staci, Christopher Sean. Student, Gulf Park Coll., 1954-55; BA, Auburn U., 1958; M in Social Work, Tulane U., 1962; JD, U. Ark., Little Rock, 1979. Bar: Ark. 1979, U.S. Dist. Ct. (ea. dist.) Ark. 1980. Assoc. Mitchell, Williams, Selig, Gates & Woodyard and predecessor, Little Rock, 1979-85, ptnr., 1985-94, of counsel, 1994—. Bd. dirs., sec. Cen. Ark. Estate Coun., Little Rock, 1984—85, 2d v.p., 1985—86, pres., 1987—88. Assoc. editor: U. Ark. Law Rev., 1978—79. Bd. dirs. Little Rock Cmty. Mental Health Ctr., 1994—, v.p., 1996—99, pres., 1999—2001; bd. dirs. Sr. Citizens Activities Today, Little Rock, 1983—88, treas., 1986—88; bd. dirs. Vol. Orgn. for Ctrl. Ark. Legal Svcs., 1986—91, sec., 1987—88, chmn., 1989—91, H.I.R.E. Inc., 1994—2001. Mem. ABA, Ark. Bar Assn. (chmn. probate and trust law sect. 1986-88), Pulaski County Bar Assn. (bd. dirs. 1994-97), Ark. Bar Found., Am. Coll. Trust and Estate Counsel. Democrat. Methodist. Office: Mitchell Williams Selig Gates & Woodyard 425 W Capitol Ave Ste 1800 Little Rock AR 72201-3525 Office Phone: 501-688-8818. E-mail: jstockburger@mwsgw.com.

STOCKER, CHRISTINE MARIE, language educator; b. Detroit, Oct. 14, 1946; d. Norman Robert and Verna Mary. BA in English, U. Windsor, Ont., Can., 1968; MA in Comparative Lit., U. Mich., Ann Arbor, 1969; cert. in Paralegal, Oakland C.C., 1993. Designer Inst. Continuing Legal Edn., Ann Arbor, Mich., 1968—70; mgr. Donaldson Lufkin and Jenerette, N.Y.C., 1980—82; cons. Warner Comms., N.Y., 1982—83; assoc. prof. Madonna U., Livonia, Mich., 1986; pvt. practice tutor lang. Farmington Hills, Mich., 1994—. Tchr. ESL Lang. Ctr. Internat., Southfield, Mich., 1996—2000; assoc. prof. Oakland C.C., Farmington Hills, Mich., 2000, tutor, 2004—05; assoc. prof. St. Mary's Coll., Orchard Lake, Mich., 2002. E-mail: mysticalrosesig@yahoo.com.

STOCKHOLDER, JESSICA, sculptor; b. Seattle, 1959; BFA, Univ. Victoria, 1982; MFA, Yale Univ., New Haven, Conn., 1985. Instr., dept. Sculpture NYU, 1992, Bard Coll., 1993. Exhibited in group shows at Contingent Realms: Four Contemporary Sculptors, Whitney Mus. Am. Art, NYC, 1990, Whitney Biennial, 1991, Perfume, Dia Ctr. Arts, NYC, 1995, La Biennale di Venezia: 47th Esposizione Internazionale d'arte, Venice, Italy, 1997, Blaffer Gallery, Art Mus. Houston, 1999, 2004. Grantee NEA award for Sculpture, 1988, NY Found. Arts grant in Painting, 1989. Office: c/o Blaffer Gallery 120 Fine Arts Building Univ Houston Houston TX 77204*

STOCKMAN, CAROLE ANN, elementary school educator; BS, Mankato State U., Minn., 1969. Educator Prior Lake Sch., Prior Lake, Minn., Bloomington Pub. Sch, Mich., Shakopee Jr. High, Minn., 1994—. Mem.: NEA, Nat. Coun. Social Studies, Alpha Omicron Pi. Office Phone: 952-496-5752.

STOCKMAN, JENNIFER BLEI, political organization administrator; b. Phila., Dec. 5, 1954; d. William Harry and Florence (Sussberg) Blei; m. David. A. Stockman, Nov. 10, 1983; children: Rachel, Victoria. BS, U. Md., 1976; MBA in Fin., George Washington U., 1983. Systems engr. IBM Corp., Washington, 1976-78, mktg. rep., 1978-81, staff mktg. mgr., 1981-83; dir. tech. trade Sears World Trade, Washington, 1983-84, v.p. tech. investment, 1984-85; founder Stockman & Associates Inc., Greenwich, Conn., 1985, past pres., CEO. Co-chair Rep. Majority for Choice (formerly Rep. Pro-Choice Coalition); bd. mem. WISH List. Pres. Solomon R. Guggenheim Mus., NYC, 2003—; phography com. MOMA; co-chair Bruce Mus. Council; nat. adv. bd. Aspen Art Mus. Named Republican Woman of Year award, Conn. Women's Forum; recipient Heart of Greenwich, YMCA. Republican. Avocations: tennis, swimming, children. Office: Republican Majority For Choice 1660 L St NW Ste 609 Washington DC 20036-5676 Home: 1850 Henry Cowgill Rd Camden Wyoming DE 19934 Business E-Mail: jbstockman@aol.com.

STOCKMAN, KATHLEEN HELEN, elementary school educator; b. Hazleton, Pa., Aug. 29, 1954; d. John and Mildred Ann (Rick) Polak; m. Martin F. Stockman, Aug. 27, 1977; children: Martin Andrew, Alexander John. AA, Northampton C.C., Bethlehem, Pa., 1974; BA, Moravian Coll., Bethlehem, 1977; permanent cert., Lehigh U., Bethlehem, 1985. Permanent tchg. cert. Pa., 1985. Elem. tchr. Christ the King Sch., Whitehall, Pa., 1979—. Group facilitator Rainbows Program, Whitehall, Pa. Nominee Disney Tchr. of Yr., 2006; named Tchr. of Week, Local Radio Show. Mem.: Nat. Cath. Educators Assn. Roman Catholic. Avocations: travel, music, reading, gardening. Home: 3212 Highfield Dr Bethlehem PA 18020 Office: Christ the King School 22 S 5th St Coplay PA 18037 E-mail: katkas@aol.com.

STOCKS, ELIZABETH LUNN, retired art educator; b. Phila., May 14, 1936; d. Edwin DeMoss and Lillian May (Robelen) Lunn; m. David Lowell Stocks, Aug. 22, 1959 (div. 1984); 1 child, Susan Merle. BA, Tulane U., 1958; MA, Claremont (Calif.) Grad. Sch., 1965; postgrad., Calif. State Poly. Coll., Pomona, 1968, Calif. State Coll., L.A., 1969, UCLA, 1969-72, Goethe Inst., Kochel, Fed. Republic Germany, 1971, Internat. U., Puebla, Mex., 1993. Cert. secondary edn. tchr., lang. devel. specialist, Calif., jr. coll. teaching credential, Calif. Instr. evening div. Mt. San Antonio Community Coll., Walnut, Calif., 1966-74; chmn. art dept. Ontario (Calif.) High Sch./Chaffey Jt. Union High Sch. Dist., 1967-86; tchr. fine arts dept. Ontario High Sch./Chaffey Dist., 1986—, mem. restructure com., mem. accreditation com., 1993-94. Mem. Prin.'s Coun., 1967-86; mem. curriculum steering com., rep. Ontario High Sch. Dist., 1967-86, sponsor Art Club, dir. art exhibits, 1967—, sponsor, 1991—; mem. High Sch. Architects Com. on Visual and Performing Arts, Rancho Cucamonga, Calif., 1988-89; originator art dept. Ontario High Sch., 1967, co-chmn. Internat. Heritage Week, 1996-97; mem. spl. exptl. program Systematic Sociometry, 1970. Art work in acrylic, ceramics, silver, bronze, stained glass and mixed media. Originated "Sheltered" Art for limited English speaking and non-English speaking students, 1990; mentor-tchr. supervising student tchr. Calif. State U., Fullerton, 1994-95; mem. Dem. Party, Ontario, Pomona and San Juan Capistrano, Calif., 1960—. Honnold fellow Claremont Grad. Sch., 1958-59; Hockaday Presp. Sch. scholar, 1952-53, Helen Lasker scholar Tulane U., 1957-58, Chaffey H.S. Dist., Internat. U., Mex., 1993. Mem. NEA, AAUW, L.A. County Mus. of Art, Smithsonian, Chaffey Cmty. Art Assn., Nat. Art Edn. Assn., Assn. Chaffey Tchrs. (mem. safety task force in union negotiations 1993, rep. to dist. safety com. 1993-99, mem. human rights com., 1997-99), Bowers Mus. Democrat. Avocations: travel, foreign language, reading, music, biking.

STOCKS, MARY LEE, social worker, social services administrator; b. Marietta, Ohio, Sept. 3, 1949; d. Graham Lee and Virginia Eleanor (Donaldson) Stocks. BA, Marietta Coll., 1971; MSW, Ohio State U., 1985. Lic. ind. social worker Ohio. Asst. supr. and social worker Franklin County Welfare Dept., Columbus, Ohio, 1972—74; social worker Ctrl. Ohio Psychiat. Hosp., Columbus, 1974-76, 1981-86; aftercare liaison Columbus Area Cmty. Mental Health Ctr., 1976-77, N. Ctrl. Mental Health Ctr., Columbus, 1977-80; aftercare specialist Worthington Cmty. Counseling Svcs., 1980-81; program specialist office of consumer svcs. Ohio Dept. Mental Health, Columbus, 1986—93, spl. projects coord. office sys. devel. and tng., 1993—97; ret., 1997. Dir. Improve(e)-Ohio Mental health Players, Columbus, 1986—97; mental health rep. Ohio Devel. Disabilities Coun., 1990—93, Ohio State use Com., 1991—94; pub. rels. chair ADA Bus. and Disability Tech. Assistance and Info. Ctr.; presenter on mental health history, mental illness and treatment, vocational accomodation and empowerment issies.; spkr. in field. Co-author: (book) Ohio's Curriculum for Case Managers, 1995; contbr. articles to self-help and profl. jours. and publs. Bd. dirs. Women's Outreach for Women, Columbus, 1991—92; mem. consumer adv. com. Ohio Rehab. Svcs. Commn.; mem. All-Ohio Youth Choir Alumni Assn. Mem.: Mental Health Assn. Ohio (chmn. statewide task froce stigma and mentall illness, bd. dir.), Mental Health Assn. Franklin County (trustee), Ohio Advocates Mental Health (life), Humane Soc. U.S., Gamma Sigma Sigma, Alpha Delta Mu. Presbyterian. Avocations: camping, fishing, gardening, crafts, music. Personal E-mail: mstocks@insight.rr.com.

STOCKWELL, MARY DIAMOND, information technology manager; b. Baton Rouge, La., Mar. 7, 1957; d. Jack Lamar and Frances Eaton Diamond; m. Julius Reginald Stockwell, Aug. 16, 1952; 1 child, Katherine Rachel. Catering asst. Prince Murat Inn, Baton Rouge, 1976; key punch operator 1 La. Dept. Health & Human Resources, 1976—77, keypunch operator 2, 1977; data entry operator 2 La. Dept. Social Services, 1977—79, info. systems data entry operator 3, 1979—84, info. systems prodn. control technician 2, 1984—93, info. systems prodn. control technician 3, 1993—96, La. Dept. Transp. & Devel., 1996—98, info. systems prodn. control supr. 1, 1998—99, info. tech. prodn. control supr., 1999—2006; ret., 2006. Troop leader, co-leader, asst. leader, religious emblems counselor Girl Scouts Am., 1997—2006. Named Green Angel, Girl Scouts Am., 2000. Mem.: Am. Red Cross (angels mem. 2001—), Cath. Dau. of Am. (parlimentarian 1989—91), Baton Rouge Village Krewe (New Eng. village dir., publicity chmn., v.p. 1992—), Bengal Belles, Beta Sigma Phi (life; pres., v.p, sec., city coun. rep. 1976, Perfect Attendance award 1976—2005, Woman of Yr. award 1977, 1985, Order of the Rose award 1995, Woman of Yr. award 1999, 2001, Silver Cir. award 2001). Roman Catholic. Avocations: travel, photography, community service, volunteer work, football. Office: La Dept Transp & Devel 1201 Capitol Access Rd Baton Rouge LA 70802 Personal E-mail: marylsu2003@aim.com.

STODDARD, ALEXANDRA, interior designer, educator, writer; b. Weston, Mass., Nov. 8, 1941; d. Robert Powell and Barbara Rutledge (Green) Johns; m. Brandon Stoddard (div.); children: Alexandra Brandon, Brooke Goodwin; m. Peter Megargee Brown, May 18, 1974. Diploma in design, N.Y. Sch. Interior Design, 1961. Designer McMillen, Inc., N.Y.C., 1963-77; pres., CEO Alexandra Stoddard Inc., N.Y.C., 1977—. Founder, pres. Design & Art Soc., Ltd., N.Y., 1987—. Author: Style for Living: How to Make Where You Live You, A Child's Place: How to Create a Living Environment for Your Child From Birth through Adolescence, Reflections on Beauty: Lectures and Notes on Interior Design, The Postcard as Art: Bring the Museum Home (Cert. of Merit award 1986), Living a Beautiful Life: 500 Ways to Add Elegance, Order, Beauty and Joy To Every Day of Your Life, 1997, Alexandra Stoddard's Living Beautifully Together, Alexandra Stoddard's Book of Color, Gift of a Letter, Daring to be Yourself, 1990, Creating a Beautiful Home, 1992, Grace Notes, Making Choices, Alexandra Stoddard's Tea Celebrations, The Art of the Possible, Mothers: A Celebration, Gracious Living in a New World, The Decoration of Houses, Open Your Eyes - 1000 Simple Ways to Bring Beauty into Your Home and Life Each Day, Feeling at Home - Defining Who You are and How You Want to Live, 1999, Choosing Happiness: Keys to a Joyful Life, 2002, Things I Want My Daughters to Know--A Small Book About the Big Issues in Life, 2004, Time Alive: Celebrate Your Life Every Day, 2005; contbg. editor Country Antiques and Collectibles, Decorating with Americana; back page columnist Design Times--The Art of Interiors; columnist McCall's mag.; contbr. articles to profl mags. and jours. Founding mem., chmn. spiritual direction com. Ch. of Heavenly Rest, 1975-77; former mem. bd. regents Cathedral St. John the Divine; dame Am. Soc. of Order of St. John Hosp. of Jerusalem. Recipient Burlington prize, 1975, award for design Greenwich Arts Coun., 1985, Interior Design award Brandeis U., 1986, cert. of spl. merit Graphic Art Inst., Designer of Yr. award Kips Bay Boys and Girls Club, 1997, Disting. Womans' award Northwood U., 1999, Lit. Lion, 100th Anniversary prize 2000 Stonington (Conn.) Libr. Mem. English Speaking Union, New Eng. Soc. Republican. Episcopalian. Home: 1125 Park Ave New York NY 10128-1243 Office: Rev John Rathbone House 87 Water St Stonington CT 06378-1432 also: 1125 Park Ave Ste 6A New York NY 10128-1243 Office Phone: 212-289-5509.

STODDARD, ERIN, actress, artist; d. Carl and Lynne Stoddard. BA, NYU, 1989—92. Actress: Evita, 1992—93; Cabaret, 1993—94; Joseph and the Amazing Technicolor Dreamcoat, 1996; Showboat, 1997—98; A Christmas Carol, 1994—95, 1999—2000; Beauty and the Beast, 2000—01; 42nd St, 2001—05; One Way Ticket to Hell, 2005—06; My One and Only, 2006; (films) That Old Song and Dance, 2004; (TV series) Common Space, 2005. Recipient White Sweater award, David Prouty H.S., 1989, Miss Dance of Conn., Dance Masters of Am., 1989; scholarship, Joffrey Ballet - NYC, 1983, Edward Villella - Cape Cod Conservatory, Overall scholarship, Dance Masters of Am., 1988. Mem.: Screen Actor's Guild, Actor's Fed. TV and Radio Assn., Actor's Equity Assn. Avocations: sculpting, writing, painting, tennis. Personal E-mail: erinstoddard@nyc.rr.com.

STODDARD, PATRICIA FLORENCE COULTER, retired psychologist; b. Detroit, Oct. 13, 1923; d. Glenn Monroe and Doris Carlyle (McDonald) Coulter; m. Charles Hatch Stoddard, June 30, 1956 (div. 1991); children: Glenn, Jeffrey. BA, U. Mich., 1945; MA, George Washington U., 1953; MA in Gerontology, Coll. of Scholastica, Duluth, Minn., 1987. Asst. to dir. personnel Dewey & Almy Chem. Co., Cambridge, Mass., 1946-48; asst. dir. mgmt. tng. program Radcliffe Coll., Cambridge, 1948-49; tng. rep. Woodward Lothrop, Washington, 1949; personnel assoc. Hot Shoppes, Inc., Washington, 1950-53; placement officer George Washington U., Washington, 1953-58; placement asst. U. Minn., Duluth, 1967; psychiat. social worker Northwood Children's Home, Duluth, 1968-80; coord. adult day svcs. Benedictine Health Ctr., Duluth, 1980-98; ret. Adv. com. on aging Regional Area Redevel. Agy., Duluth, 1992—; apptd. State Commn. on Aging, Minn., 1997. Author: Wolf Springs 100 Years: A Century of Life on One Piece of Land, 1991; contbr. articles to profl. jours. Pres. Maple Crest Village Homeowners Assn., Duluth, 1997; vol. recruiter Am. Reads Project. Mem. LWV, Area Aging Network, Algonquin Club. Avocations: tennis, elderhostels, reading, aerobics. Home: Apt 255 70 St Marie St Duluth MN 55803

STODDARD, SANDOL, freelance/self-employed writer; b. Birmingham, Ala., Dec. 16, 1927; d. Carlos French and Caroline (Harris) S.; m. Felix M. Warburg (div. 1966); children: Anthony, Peter, Gerald, Jason; m. Peter R. Goethals, May 1, 1984. BA magna cum laude, Bryn Mawr Coll., 1959. Author 26 books including: Growing Time, 1971, The Doubleday Children's Bible, 1983 (Lewis citation 1983), The Hospice Movement: Updated and Expanded Edition, 1992, Prayers, Praises and Thanksgivings, 1992. Bd. dirs., co-founder Hospice of Kona, Kailua-Kona, Hawaii, 1985; co-founder Kona Theol. Inst., 1990; bd. dirs. Choice in Dying, N.Y.C. Recipient Humanitarian Svc. award Forbes Health System, 1979, Notable Book award ALA, 1964, Founder's award Nat. Hospice and Palliative Care Orgn., 2006. Mem.: AAUW, Nat. Writer's Guild, Internat. Work Group on Death Dying and Bereavement (IWG), Cosmpolitan Club. Democrat. Episcopalian. Home and Office: 78-6646 Mamalahoa Hwy Holualoa HI 96725-9734

STODDARD-HAYES, MARLANA KAY, artist, educator; b. Ottumwa, Iowa, Nov. 5, 1957; d. Roy Keables Stoddard, Jr. and Joyce Ellen McNeight; m. Robert Lee Hayes, Sept. 25, 1993. BFA in Painting, Colo. State U., 1980; MFA in Painting, Wichita State U., 1983; MA in Interdisciplinary Studies, Maryhurst U., 2002. Artist-in-residence Kans. Arts Commn., 1983—95, Neskowin Coast Found., Cascade Head, Oreg., 1990—91; prof. art Dodge City (Kans.) CC, 1995—2000; adj. prof. drawing Clark Coll., Vancouver, W.Va., 2000—; adj. prof. art Portland (Oreg.) CC, 2001—. Exhibited in group shows at St. John's Coll., 2002, one-woman shows include Trish Higgins Gallery, 2003, RC Gallery, 2006, exhibitions include Mid-Four Biennial, Nelson-Atkins Mus., 1987, Newman U., Kans., 1987, Lawrence Lithography Workshop, 1987, exhibitions include solo Reuben Saunders Gallery, 1983, 1987, 1991. Mem.: PEO, Coll. Art Assn. Democrat. Episcopalian. Avocations: gardening, reading, walking. Home: 4424 Cedar Oak Dr West Linn OR 97068 Personal E-mail: marlana.stoddard@comcast.net.

STOENNER, JESSAMINE, music educator; b. Dalton, Ga., Aug. 12, 1908; d. John Fletcher and Johnnie Jessamine (Richardson) Tarver; m. Walter George Stoenner, June 22, 1930 (dec. July 1987); children: Jessamine Marie, June Louise, Willa Jean, James Tarver. B in Music, Mo. Valley Coll., 1928, BA, 1930; cert. piano tchr., Music Tchrs. Nat. Assn., Warrensburg, Mo., 1977. Music tchr.; ch. ogranist Presbyn. Ch., Richmond, Mo., 1945-95; dir. Girls Glee Club, Mo. Valley Coll., Marshall, Mo., 1929, tchr. asst. music dept., 1929-30. Pres. PTA, Richmond Schs., 1942; leader Girl Scouts Am., Richmond, 1942-51; literacy tchr., Richmond, 1994-97; contbr., adoptee Children's Internat., 1996-99; mem. Ray County Meml. Hosp. Aux., Richmond, 1989-99, Ray County Cmty. Arts Assn., Richmond, 1993-99, Ray County Hist. Soc. Recipient Christian Family award Richmond Presbyn. Ch., 1976, Dedicated Svc. award, 1999. Mem. AAUW, PEO, DAR (regent 1949-50, Am. Heritage Music award 1998), Music Tchrs. Nat. Assn., Mo. Music Tchrs. Assn., Warrensburg Area Music Tchrs. Assn. Republican. Presbyterian. Avocations: reading, flowers, travel, poetry, bridge. Home: 804 Wollard Blvd #531 Richmond MO 64085-2227

STOESSER, SUSAN ALICE (SUSAN ALICE LANGE), retired librarian, educator, media generalist; b. Milw., May 15, 1947; d. Louis Albert and Ethel (Freeman) Lange; m. Gregory Alan Stoesser, Oct. 17, 1969; children: Matthew Alan, Margaret Alice. BS in Elem. Edn., U. Wis., LaCrosse, 1969; postgrad., U. Wis., Whitewater, 1976-81, U. Wis., 1985-91, Hamline U.,

1993-96, Alfred Adler Inst., 1994. Cert. elem. edn. tchr. and media generalist, Minn.; cert. elem. sch. media dir., Wis. Libr. Randall Sch., Bassett, Wis., 1971-75, Trevor (Wis.) Sch., 1976-77, Brighton Elem. Sch., Kansasville, Wis., 1976-93, Lincoln Elem. Sch., Robbinsdale, Minn., 1993-94, Meadow Lake Elem. Sch., Robbinsdale, 1994—2000, Lakeview Elem. Sch., Robbinsdale, NY, 2000—06; ret. Bd. dirs. Kenosha County Libr. Bd., 1981-87. Various leadership roles Salem (Wis.) United Meth. Ch., 1975-93; mem. com., bd. dirs. Wis. Conf. United Meth. Ch., Sun Prairie, Wis., 1987-91; pres., mem. Cmty. Libr., Silver Lake, Wis., 1977-82; mem. diaconate bd. Union Ch., Elk River, Minn., Handbell Choir Befriender Min. Named Woman of Yr., Bus. and Profl. Women, 1984. Avocations: walking, reading, sewing. Personal E-mail: stoesser30@aol.com.

STOETZER, KRISTEN GOTTLEIB, music educator; b. Balt., Oct. 30, 1978; BS n Music Edn., Towson U., Md., 2000; MusM, Peabody Conservatory, Balt., 2002. Dir. instrumental music Winters Mill HS, Westminster, Md., 2002—. Mem.: Md. Band Dirs. Assn. (bd. mem. 2005—06), Md. Music Educators Assn., Condrs. Guild Inc. Home: 4801 Hillock Ln Hampstead MD 21074 Office: Winters Mill High School 560 Gorsuch Rd Westminster MD 21157 Office Phone: 410-386-1500. Office Fax: 410-386-1513. Business E-Mail: kestoet@k12.carr.org.

STOFFLE, CARLA JOY, university library dean; b. Pueblo, Colo., June 19, 1943; d. Samuel Bernard and Virginia Irene (Berry) Hayden; m. Richard William Stoffle, June 12, 1964; children: Brent William, Kami Ann. AA, So. Colo. State Coll., Pueblo, 1963; BA, U. Colo., 1965; MLS, U. Ky., 1969; postgrad., U. Wis., 1980. Head govt. publ. dept. John G. Crabbe Library, Eastern Ky. U., Richmond, 1969-72; from head pub. svcs. to asst. chancellor edn. svcs. U. Wis. Parkside Libr., Kenosha, 1972—85; dep. dir. U. Mich. Libr., Ann Arbor, 1986—91; prof. libr. sci. U. Ariz., Tucson, 1991—, dean librs. and ctr. for creative photography, 1991—, acting dir. Sch. Info. Resources and Libr. Sci., 1999—2001. Adv. bd. Bowker Librs., NY, 1985—90; bd. dirs. Trejo Foster Found., 2000—; state adv. com. Ariz. State Dept. of Libr. Archives and Pub. Records, 2000—; adv. com. U. Mich. Sch. Libr. Sci., 1986—92, OCLC Rsch. Librs., 1995—2000. Co-author: Administration of Government Documents Collection, 1974, Materials and Method for History Research, 1979, Materials and Methods for Political Science Research, 1979; mem. editl. bd. The Collection Bldg., 1978—95, The Bottom Line, 1989—95, Internet and Higher Edn., 1998—99, The Univ. Ariz. Press, 1992—. Vol. Peace Corps, Barbados, West Indies, 1965—67. Named Outstanding Alumnus, Coll. Libr. and Info. Sci., U. Ky., 1989; recipient Pres.'s award, Ariz. Ednl. Media Assn., 1993, YWCA Tucson Outstanding Woman of 1992: A Woman on the Move award, 1992, Ariz. Libr. of Yr. award, 2000. Mem.: ALA (councilor 1983—93, exec. bd. dirs. 1985—93, treas. 1988—93, endowment trustee 1988—93, endowment campaign com. 1989—93, pres. adv. com. 1993—96, legis. com. 1994—96, nominations com. 1997, Lippincott award com. 1997, spectrum scholarship com. 1998—2002, endowment trustee 2001—, chair com. accreditation 2002—03, libr. and outreach svcs. adv. com. 1997-99, chair 1997-98, Miriam Dudley Bibliographic Instrn. Libr. of Yr. award 1991, Acad. Rsch. Libr. of Yr. 1992, Elizabeth Futas Catalyst for Change award 2002, Equality award 2003, Loleta Fyan award Jury 2003—04), Ctr. Rsch. Librs. (budget and fin. com. 1994—2001, exec. com., bd. dirs. 1998—, treas. 1999—2000, vice chair. bd. dirs. 2001—03, chair. bd. dirs. 2003), Ariz. State Libr. Assn., Assn. Coll. Rsch. Librs. (bd. dirs. 1978—84, mem. exec. com. 1981—84, pres. 1982—83, Planning Com. 1993—95, chair nat. conf. planning com. 1995—97), Assn. Rsch. Librs. (com. stats. and measurement 1994—2003, bd. dirs. 1997—2001, mem. steering com. Scholarly Pub. and Acad. Resource Coalition 1998—2001, mem. govt. documents digitization project work group 2004—, bd. dirs. info. policies com. 2004—). Office: U Arizona Main Libr 1510 E University Blvd Tucson AZ 85721-0055 Office Phone: 520-621-2101. E-mail: stofflec@u.library.arizona.edu.*

STOFFLE, SARAH ELIZABETH, theater educator; b. Seymour, Tenn., May 4, 1981; d. Larry Zan and Deborah Stanley Stoffle. Student, Maryville Coll. Theater tchr. Crabapple Mid. Sch., Roswell, Ga., 2003—. Dir.: (plays) Running Upstream (Superior Rating at Internat. Competition, 2006). Mem.: Ednl. Theatre Assn. (assoc.; troupe dir. 2006, play recieved Superior rating at the Internat. Theatre Festival 2006). Democrat. Office: Crabapple Middle School 10700 Crabapple Rd Roswell GA 30075 Office Phone: 770-552-4520. Personal E-mail: stoffle@fultonschools.org.

STOIAN, CRISTINA, sales executive, real estate broker, mortgage company executive, tax specialist; b. Resita, Romania, Dec. 7, 1963; came to the U.S., 1993; d. Ion and Gina Nicu; m. Costin A. Stoian, Feb. 28, 1987; children: Andreea P., Raoul S Mech. engr., Engring. Inst. Resita, 1987; quality contr., Constrn. Machinery Corp., Resita, 1989. Lic. real estate broker; registered, lic. NASD. Engr. QQ bearings ICM, Resita, 1988—93; registered rep. Janus, 2000—; realtor, mortgage specialist Creative Real Estate and Fin., 2005—. Tax preparer Jackson Hewitt, 1999 Tennis coach Tennis Drs. Assn. Resita, 1980-83 2d Place winner Nat. Tennis Championship Costinesti-Romania, 1976-77 Mem. SEC, Nat. Assn. Realtors, Romanian Am. Freedom Alliance Colo Romanian Orthodox. Avocations: painting, crafting, hiking, tennis, rock climbing. Home: 1742 W 130 Pl Westminster CO 80234 Personal E-mail: crini@hotmail.com.

STOIANOVICH, MARCELLE SIMONE, artist; b. Paris; d. Charles Caffe and Eugenie Le Nieffe; children: Christian, Diana Revson. Student, Coll. Applied Arts, Paris, 1942-46. Book jacket designer Doubleday Edits., N.Y.C., 1954; archeol. draftsperson Smithsonian Inst., Washington, 1962; window decorator Guerlain Perfumes, Paris, 1975; film creditor Am. Films Festival, Deauville, France, 1975; assoc. editor L'Officiel de la Mode, Paris, 1976-81; jeweler Henri Bendel's, N.Y.C., 1983; free-lance artist N.Y.C. and Paris, 1983—. Permanent exhibits Venable/Neslage Galleries, Washington; Lithographs, Original Print Collectors Group, N.Y.C., Bibliotheque Nationale, Paris, Zimmerli Art Mus. NJ, Fernand Braudel, Academie Francaise. Mem. Met. Mus., Nantucket Art Assn. Studio: 9 Rue Campagne Premiere 75014 Paris France Home: 2 Allee de la Ferme 92170 Vanves France Personal E-mail: marcelle.sto@club-internet.fr.

STOIBER, SUSANNE A., health science organization administrator; BA, MPA, U. Colo.; MS, London Sch. Econs. Principal analyst for health care fin. programs Congressional Budget Office; adminstr. of clinical research Nat. Inst. of Health; dir. divsn. soc. and econ. studies NRC US Dept. HHS, 1990-94, various sr. positions, 1994—98; exec. officer Inst. Medicine, 1998—. Contbr. articles to profl. jours. Recipient NIH Directors Award, 1985, Presidential Rank Award for lifetime achievement in Senior Exec. Service. Office: Inst Medicine 500 5th St NW Washington DC 20418-0007 Fax: 908-771-8618.

STOKER, ALEXANDRA IVERSON, musician, educator; b. Logan, Utah, May 30, 1981; d. David Charles and Trudy Forsgren Iverson; m. Colby L. Stoker, Dec. 16, 2003. B of Music Edn., Weber State U., 2004. Profl. educator lic. Utah, cert. nurse's asst. Utah. Secondary music educator Davis Sch. Dist., Syracuse, Utah, 2004—. Orch. dir., string project Weber State U., Am. String Tchrs. Am., Ogden, 2000—; student pres. Am. String Tchrs. Am., 1999—2004. Mem. student coun. Weber State U., 2001—02. Recipient music scholarship, Weber State U., 1999—2004, Kenley award, 2002; grantee scholarship, 1999—2004. Mem.: Suzuki Assn. Am., Utah Music Educators Assn. Democrat. Mem. Lds Ch. Avocations: skiing, backpacking, writing, composing music. Office: West Point Jr HS 2775 W 530 N Ogden UT 84404 Home: 368 W 1500 N Ogden UT 84404 Office Phone: 801-402-8182. E-mail: chocolateviolin@yahoo.com.

STOKER, PENNY S., human resources specialist; d. Dorothy J. Schenck; m. Rick L. Stoker, May 21, 1977; children: Andreana L., Andrew W. BA in Bus., Asian Studies, U. Md., 1982; MBA, Johnson Grad. Sch. Mgmt., 1987. CPA NY. Tax assoc. Coopers & Lybrand, N.Y.C., 1987—89, bus. mgr., 1989—92, head of human resources, 1992—97; vp, human resources CIGNA, Phila., 1997—2000, Internet Capital Group, Wayne, Pa., 2000—02, Amersham (now GE Healthcare), Little Chalfont, Buckinghamshire, England, 2002—04, AstraZeneca Pharm. LP, Wilmington, Del., 2004—. Bd. dirs. Women's Way, Phila., 1996—2006, Jobs for Del. Grads., 2005—; pres. adv. coun. Ronald McDonald Ho., Wilmington, 2004—06. Mem.: Human Resource Planning Soc. (assoc.), Soc. Human Resource Mgmt. (assoc.). Avocations: reading, travel, hiking, skiing. Office: AstraZeneca Pharm LP 1800 Concord Pike A2C-522 Wilmington DE 19850 Office Phone: 302-885-6944. Business E-Mail: penny.stoker@astrazeneca.com.

STOKES, ANNE DOROTHY, retired educational association administrator; b. Elyria, Ohio, Nov. 29, 1928; d. Edgar Pier and Dorothy Anne (Day) Gates; m. Kenneth Irving Stokes, June 30, 1951 (dec.); children: Alan, Randall, Bradley, Harlan. BA, Oberlin (Ohio) Coll., 1950; MEd, U. Fla., 1970, EdS, 1974, EdD, 1977. Cert. K-12 tchr., Minn.; cert. parent educator. Kdg. tchr. Elyria Pub. Schs., 1950-51, Hamden (Conn.) Pub. Schs., 1951-53; owner, tchr. Lads N Lassies Kdg., Glen Ellyn, Ill., 1961-65; trainer, cons. Head Start, Bradford and Putnam Cty., Fla., 1968-69; instr. U. Fla., Gainesville, 1968-72, curriculum developer, 1972-73; edn. dir. Palmer King Day Care, Gainesville, 1971-72; interim prof. U. Minn., Mpls., 1977-78, Concordia Coll., St. Paul, 1986; coord. early childhood family edn. St. Louis Park (Minn.) Schs., 1979-96, ret., 1996. Sec. evaluation com. Minn. State Family Edn. Resources of Minn., Dept. Edn., 1986-99; cons., spkr. schs. and chs.; bd. dirs. Bell Nursery Sch. Project, Gainesville, 1970-73; mem. ethics com. Minn. Coun. of Family Rels., 1991-99. Author: The Thinking Parent, 1993, Career Education Manual for Teachers and Supervisors, 1976; contbr. articles to profl. jours. Informal lobbyist Early Childhood Family Edn., Minn. State Capitol; spkr., workshop leader Adult Faith Resources, 1996-2000; ind. cons. parent edn., 2000—. Career Growth fellowship Bush Found. U. Minn., 1983; fellowship U. Fla., 1969. Mem. ASCD, Assn. for Childhood Edn. Internat., Minn. Coun. on Family Rels., Nat. Assn. for Edn. of Young Children, Phi Kappa Phi, Pi Lambda Theta. Mem. United Ch. of Christ. Avocations: writing, travel, painting. Home: 787 Plymouth Rd Claremont CA 91711-4249

STOKES, BETTY, music educator; b. Knoxville, Tenn. BS in Music Edn., East Tenn. State U., 1968; MusM, So. Ill. U., 1975. Cert. early adolescent young adult music tchr. Nat. Bd. Profl. Tchg. Stds., 2005. Music tchr. Brevard County schs., Titusville, Fla., 1968—70, St. Louis schs., 1972—77, Forsyth County schs., Winston-Salem, NC, 1986—94, Catawba County schs., Hickory, NC, 1996—. Mem. bldg. leadership team Banoak Elem. Sch., Vale, NC, 2001—. Mem.: NEA, Music Educators Nat. Conf. Avocation: gardening. Address: 31 35th Ave NW Hickory NC 28601-8018

STOKES, KATHLEEN SARAH, dermatologist, educator; b. Springfield, Mass., Oct. 18, 1954; d. John Francis and Margaret Cecelia (MacDonnell) Stokes; m. William Walter Greaves; children: Ian R., Spencer W., Malcolm W. BS, U. Utah, 1978, MS, 1980; MD, Med. Coll. Wis., 1987. Diplomate Am. Bd. Dermatology. Intern in internal medicine Med. Coll. Wis., Milw., 1987-88, resident in dermatology, 1988-90, chief resident, 1990-91, asst. clin. prof. dermatology, 1991—; pvt. practice, Milw., 1991—. Contbr. articles to med. jours., including Critical Care Medicine, Jour. Pediatric Dermatology. Named A Top Physician, Milw. mag., 1996, 2000, 04 Fellow Am. Acad. Dermatology, Milw. Acad. Medicine; mem. AMA, Wis. Dermatol. Soc. (sec.-treas. 2003-04, pres. 2005-06), Women's Dermatologic Soc., Tempo, Alpha Omega Alpha. Office: Affiliated Dermatologists 2300 N Mayfair Rd Milwaukee WI 53226-1505

STOKES, LORI, newscaster; Attended, Ohio State U.; grad., Howard U. Weekend anchor, med. reporter CBS affiliate WCIA-TV, Champaign-Urbana, Ill.; weekend anchor CBS affiliate WBTC, Charlotte, NC, 1988—90; reporter Fox station WBFF, Balt., 1991—92; anchor evening news for 6pm and 11pm broadcasts WJLA-TV, Wash., DC, 1992—96; anchor MSNBC, 1996—2000; anchor, corr. NBC News, 1996—2000; anchor WABC NY, 2000—. Recipient Emmy award, 1991, Peabody award, 2001. Achievements include credited with breaking the Gianni Versace's murder story. Office: 7 Lincoln Sq New York NY 10023

STOKEY, NANCY L., economist, educator; BA in Economics, U. Pa., 1972; PhD in Economics, Harvard U., 1978. Asst. prof. Kellogg Grad. Sch. Mgmt., Northwestern U., 1978—82, assoc. prof., 1982—83, prof., 1983—87, dept. chmn., 1987—89, Harold L. Stuart prof. managerial economics, 1988—90; vis. lectr. Harvard U., 1982; vis. prof. economics U. Minn., 1983, U. Chgo., 1983—84, prof. ecnomics, 1990—96, Frederick Henry Prince prof. economics, 1997—. Vis. scholar rsch. dept. Fed. Reserve Bank, Mpls., 2000—01. Author (with Robert E. Lucas, Jr. and Edward C. Prescott): Recursive Methods in Economic Dynamics, 1989. Fellow: Am. Econ. Assn. (v.p. 1996—97, nominating com. 1998, exec. com. 2000—02), Am. Acad. Arts and Scis., Econometric Soc. (coun. mem. 1996—98, 1999—2001); mem.: NAS. Office Phone: 773-702-0915. Office Fax: 773-702-8490. Business E-Mail: n-stikey@uchicago.edu.*

STOKKE, DIANE REES, lawyer; b. Kansas City, Mo., Jan. 29, 1951; d. William James and Marybeth (Smith) Rees; m. Larry Ernst Stokke, June 9, 1973; children: Michelle, Megan, Carly. AB magna cum laude, Gonzaga U., 1972; JD with high honors, U. Wash., 1976. Bar: Wash. 1976, U.S. Dist. Ct. (ea. dist.) Wash. 1976, U.S. Dist. Ct. (we. dist.) Wash. 1976, U.S. Ct. Appeals (9th cir.) 1980. Assoc. Preston, Thorgrimson, Ellis & Holman, Seattle, 1976-83; ptnr. Preston, Gates & Ellis LLP, Seattle, 1983—. Atty. Seattle Ctr. Found., 1977-83. Trustee Seattle Infant Devel. Ctr., 1984—86, Fremont Pub. Assn., 1994—2001, 2003—05. Gonzaga U. scholar, 1968. Mem. ABA, Wash. State Bar Assn. (spl. dist. counsel 1985-88), Seattle-King County Bar Assn., Wash. Women Lawyers, Order of Coif, Wash. Women Real Estate Lawyers, Am. Coll. of Mortgage Attys., Comml. Real Estate Women. Roman Catholic. Office: Preston Gates & Ellis LLP 925 Fourth Ave Ste 2900 Seattle WA 98104-1158 Office Phone: 206-623-7580. Business E-Mail: dianes@prestongates.com.

STOLBA, SOHEIR SUKKARY, anthropologist, educator; b. Damanhour, Egypt, Apr. 24, 1945; d. Abdel Moniem Nada and Zeinab I. Osman; m. Leonard B. Stolba, Sept. 11, 1980; children: Diana N, Tamir E. Sukkary. PhD, U. Calif., Davis, 1978. Prof. Am. River Coll., Sacramento, 1987—; exec. dir. SHARE Inst., Fair Oaks, Calif., 2000—. Consulting Internat. Health and Devel. Assocs., Fair Oaks, 1980—2006; cons., rschr. in field. Exec. dir. SHARE Inst., Fair Oaks, Calif., 2000—06. Recipient Tchr. of Yr., Found. Am. River Coll., 1993. Mem.: Am. Anthrop. Assn. Avocations: reading, travel. Home: 4750 Siesta Ln Fair Oaks CA 95628 Office: American River Coll 4700 College Oak Sacramento CA Office Phone: 916-484-8388. Home Fax: 916-966-7482; Office Fax: 916-966-7482. Personal E-mail: sstolba@aol.com.

STOLBERG, SHERYL GAY, journalist; b. N.Y.C., Nov. 18, 1961; d. Irving and Marcia Dawn (Papier) S. BA, U. Va., 1983. Reporter Providence Jour. Bulletin, 1983-87, L.A. Times, 1987-97; sci. & med. corr. NY Times, Washington, 1997—2002, congl. corr., 2002—06, White House corr., 2006—. Recipient Unity award Lincoln U., 1987. Office: NY Times Wash Bur 7th Fl 1627 I St NW Washington DC 20006-4007

STOLL, BOBBI, art psychotherapist; b. Williamsport, Pa., Aug. 28, 1932; d. James Calvin and Geraldine Mae (Taylor) Foust; m. Charles Weller Stoll, June 7, 1954 (div. Dec. 1973); children: Charles Robert, Lisa. BFA, Syracuse U., 1954; MA, Immaculate Heart Coll., 1975. Lic. marriage, family, child therapist; bd. cert. art psychotherapist, group psychotherapist, trauma specialist. Social case worker Dept. Pub. Social Svcs., L.A., 1955-59; computer programmer L.A. County Assessor, L.A., 1959-62; pvt. practice psychotherapy L.A., 1975—; sr. therapist Family Counseling Svc., San Gabriel, Calif., 1976-87; staff art therapist Van Nuys (Calif.) Psychiat. Hosp., 1977-78. Contract therapist Blueshield Calif., 1982—, USA Healthnet, Phoenix, 1990—, HelpNet, Long Beach, Calif., 1985—, Holman Group, Canoga Park, Calif., 1985—, Managed Health Network, Inc., Oakland, Calif., 1988—, Medview Svcs., 1996—, Green Spring Health Svcs., Columbia, Md., 1997—, Acorn Behavioral Healthcare Mgmt. Corp., Narbeth, Pa., 1997—; trainer profl. art therapy Eng., 1985, Yugoslavia, 1986, Japan, 1987, Australia, 1989, Lithuania, 1993, Sweden, 1994, Russia, 1994, Brazil, 1996, Thailand, 1999; cons. in field. Mem. internat. adv. bd. and rev. com. Internat. Jour. Arts Medicine, 1991—; mem. internat. adv. bd. House-Tree-Person viewpoints, 1996-99; adv. bd. The Arts in Psychotherapy, 1993—; spkr. art therapy conf., 1989, 91, 92, 93, 95, 97, 99; contbr. articles to profl. jours. Vol. therapist Pacific Ctr. Counseling and Therapy, West Hollywood, Calif., 1990—; chair fundraising Fashionettes, Hollywood Presbyn. Hosp., L.A., 1969; worker disaster mental health svcs. ARC, 1997—; hon. mem. Cuban Arterapia Project, Havana, Cuba, 1994. Mem. Am. Art Therapy Assn. (hon. life mem.; bd. dirs. 1981-87, pres. 1993-95), Am. Group Psychotherapy Assn., L.A. Group Psychotherapy Soc. (bd. dirs. 1982-88, pres. 1988-90), Am. Assn. Marriage and Family Therapists, Am. Profl. Soc. on Abuse of Children, Internat. Arts Medicine Assn. (bd. dirs. 1991—, 3d Annual Bridgebuilder award 1991), Internat. Networking Group Art Therapists (founder 1989); So. Calif. Art Therapy Assn., (bd. dirs., 2004—, treas., 2004—, hon., life). Avocations: travel, sewing, poetry, painting, water sports. Home: 8020 Briar Summit Dr Los Angeles CA 90046-1127

STOLL, SHIRLEY GABRIELLA, special education educator; b. Winnapeg, Manitoba, Can., May 6, 1954; d. Hans F. and Lucy E. Stoll. BA, Western Ky. U., 1978; MA, Spalding U., 1988. Home: 5803 Holly Oak Ct Louisville KY 40291-1346

STOLLER, PATRICIA SYPHER, structural engineer, executive; b. Jackson Heights, N.Y., Dec. 16, 1947; d. Carleton Roy and Mildred Vivian (Ferron) Sypher; m. David A. Stoller, Sr.; children: Stephanie Jean, Sheri Lynn. BSCE, Washington U., St. Louis, 1975; M in Mgmt., Northwestern U., 1989. R & D engr. Amcar divsn. ACF Industries, St. Charles, Mo., 1972-79; project engr. Truck Axle divsn. Rockwell Internat., Troy, Mich., 1979-81; sr. engr. ABB Impell, Norcross, Ga., 1981-83, supervising mgr., client mgr., divsn. mgr. Lincolnshire, Ill., 1983—; dir. bus. devel., v.p. VECTRA (formerly ABB Impell), Lincolnshire, 1991-94; pres., CEO ASC Svcs. Co., LLC, Chgo., 1994-97; CEO, pres. Beaumont Svcs. Co., LLC, Royal Oak, Mich., 1997—, ReSourcing Svcs. Co., LLC, Chgo., 2003—; v.p. Greenville Operations Jacobs Engring. Inc., 1997—. Author: (computer program) Quickpipe, 1983. Mem.: NAFE, ASCE, World Pres. Orgn., Chgo. Real Estate Women, Am. Nuc. Soc. (mem. exec. bd. Chgo. sect. 1991—93), Soc. Women Engrs. Achievements include patents in field. Avocations: golf, music. Office: Jacobs Engring Inc 1041 E Butler Rd Greenville SC 29607 Office Phone: 864-676-6000. E-mail: pat.stoller@jacobs.com.

STOLLER, ROSE, think-tank executive; With N.D. Dept. Human Svcs.; exec. dir. Mental Health Assn., ND, The Consensus Coun., Bismarck, ND, 2002—. Chairperson Bismarck Human Rels. Com.; vol. Mo. Slope United Way; grad. leadership program Bismarck C. of C. Recipient Mental Health Svcs. award, N.D. Psychiat. Soc., Welcome Back award, Eli Lilly Co. Office: The Consensus Coun Inc Ste 7 1003 E Interstate Ave Bismarck ND 58503-0500

STOLOFF, CAROLYN RUTH, clinical psychologist; b. N.Y.C., June 19, 1947; d. Bernard J. and Ruth Claire (Reimer) S.; m. Ronald Dennis Judkoff, June 29, 1980; 1 child, Jennifer. BA, U. Chgo., 1969; MA, U. Mich., 1972, PhD, 1979. Lic. psychologist, Colo. Sch. psychologist Ann Arbor (Mich.) Pub. Schs., 1975-77; clin. psychologist Jewish Family and Children's Svc., Denver, 1980-82; pvt. practice, Denver, 1982—. Mem. Am. Soc. Clin. Hypnosis, Colo. Psychol. Assn. (bd. dirs. 1985-88, chmn. referral svc. 1990-91, editor Bull. 1983-94), Am.Psychol. Assn., Rocky Mountain Trauma and Dissociative Soc. Democrat. Avocations: skiing, ice skating. Office: 445 Union Blvd Lakewood CO 80228

STOMS, DONNA SUE, librarian; b. Cin., Mar. 28, 1944; d. Richard Kirker and Rose June (Liming) Stoms; m. William Bernard Monnig, July 8, 1967 (div. 1997); children: Aaron William, Thomas Richard. BA, U. Cin., 1966; MA, Rosary Coll., 1970. Tchr. Finneytown (Ohio) H.S., 1966-69; head lit. & lang. depts. Pub. Libr. of Cin. and Hamilton County, 1970—, ref. libr., 1970-83, dept. head, 1983—, chair book selection policy com., 1993-94. Pres. Hope Cottage Guild, Covington, Ky., 1978; sec. Literacy Network of Greater Cin., 1990, mem. awards com., 1992-93. Mem. Ohioana Libr. Assn., Beta Phi Mu. Republican. Roman Catholic. Office: Pub Libr Cin & Hamilton Co Lit & Lang Depts 800 Vine St Cincinnati OH 45202-2009

STONE, ANN ELIZABETH, marketing agency executive, consultant, entrepreneur, volunteer; b. Bridgeport, Conn., Aug. 9, 1952; d. Jack Reginald and Edith Pauline (Christiansen) Wesche; m. Roger J. Stone, June 15, 1974 (div. Dec. 1990). BA in History and Comm., George Washington U., 1974; postgrad., Wharton Sch. Bus., Washington, 1975—76. Mktg. mgr. Human Events, Washington, 1974—76; v.p. polit. div. The Viguerie Co., Falls Church, Va., 1976—82; chmn. Capstone Lists, Alexandria, Va., 1983—, Unique Graphics, Alexandria, 1985—; vice chmn. George Washington Nat. Bank, Alexandria, 1988—; ptnr. Weintraub-Stone Direct, Inc., Woodland Hills, Calif., 1991—; pres. The Stone Group Inc. (formerly Ann E.W. Stone & Assocs.), Alexandria, 1982—. Bd. dirs. Action Products; spkr. in field. Co-host (TV show) The Alexandria Forum, TV appearances Larry King Live, Lehrer News Hour, Good Morning Am., Politically Incorrect, others; contbr. articles to profl. jours. Pres.'s exec. global adv. bd. European/Am. Women's Coun., 2003; internat. chair Empowered Women Internat. and Women Immigrant Network; arbiter Va. Bar Assn.; trustee apptd. by gov. Va. Hist. Preservation Found.; fin. dir. Alexandria Rep. Party, 1989—92; chmn. D.C. Young Reps., Washington, 1975—77; Republican candidate for mayor Alexandria, 1991; chmn., foundr Reps. for Choice, Alexandria, 1989—; bd. dirs. Campaigns and Elections Mag., Washington, 1987—, Am. Heart Assn., 1990—, chmn., 1993—94; bd. dirs. Nat. Womens History Mus., The Washington Ctr., Response mag., Influence mag. Named one of Women Who Changed Politics in Am., Campaigns and Elections mag., 1992. Mem. Direct Mktg. Assn. Washington (bd. dirs. 1974—), Renaissance Women (bd. dirs. 1985—), Alexandria C. of C. (bd. dirs. 1982), Alexandria Soc. for Preservation of Black Heritage, Animal Welfare League, Lions Club, Alexandria Seaport Fedn. (past bd. dirs.), Direct Mktg. Club (Washington). Lutheran. Avocations: reading, travel, historical renovation, rock collecting, music. Office: 205 S Whiting St 250 Alexandria VA 22304 Office Phone: 703-329-1982, 703-370-8282. Personal E-mail: tsgrp@aol.com.

STONE, ANN E.W., marketing executive; BA in History and Comms., George Washington U.; postgrad., U. Pa. Founder, pres. The Stone Group, Inc., 1982—; chmn. Capstone Lists Inc. Spkr. in field. Bd. dirs. Nat. Women's History Mus., Assn. Direct Mktg. Agys., Washington Ctr., Rep. Liberty Caucus, Campagna Ctr., Make Women Count, others; past chmn. Alexandria br. Am. Heart Assn., Alexandria Seaport Found.; founder, chmn. Republicans for Choice, Alexandria, Va; internat. chair Empowered Women Internat.; trustee Va. Historic Preservation Found.; exec. global adv. bd. European/Am. Women's Coun. Mem.: Non-Profit Mailers Fedn., Direct Mktg. Club Washington, Nat. Women's Hall of Fame, Am. Assn. Polit. Consultants (bd. dirs.), Nat. Assn. Women Bus. Owners, Alexandria C. of C. (bd. dirs.), Animal Welfare League, Soc. for Preservation of Black Heritage, Va. Trust for Hist. Preservation. Office: The Stone Group Inc 205 S Whiting St Ste 250 Alexandria VA 22304-3632 E-mail: tsgrp@aol.com.

STONE, ANNE MARIE, elementary school educator; b. New Bedford, Mass., Dec. 15, 1943; d. Emilien Raoul and Marie Rose Pelletier; m. William R. Pelletier, Jan. 11, 1964; children: Michael Thomas, Judith Anne MacDonald, Sharyn Marie. Master's degree, Bridgewater State Coll., West Bridgewater, 2003. Tchr. elem. edn. Mass. Substitute tchr. New Bedford Sch. Dept., 1999—2003, tchr. grade 6, 2003—. Leader conversational French club New Bedford Sch. Dept., 2004—. Independent. Roman Catholic. Avocation: reading. Office: New Bedford Sch Dept 81 Felton St New Bedford MA 02740 Office Phone: 508-985-4300.

STONE, BETTY FRANCES, music educator; MusB, Queen's Coll., 1973; M in Music Edn., U. Ga., 1974. Music tchr. Charleston (S.C.) County Schs., 1974—83; choreographer Young Charleston Theatre Co., 1979—83; arts supr. City of Mississauga, Ont., Canada, 1983—93; music tchr. Florence Sch. Dist. #3, Lake City, SC, 1993—; dance tchr. Dancin On Main, Lake City, 2002—. Dir. Lake City Concert Series, 1996—; grants mgr., arts coord. Florence Dist. #3, Lake City, 1999—. Vol. Lake City C. of C., 1996—2003; mistress of cermonies Miss Lake City Beauty Pagent, 2001—04; performer Lake City Cmty. Theater, 1993—2005. Recipient Champion for Pub. Edn. award, S.C. Sch. Bds. Assn., 1999, Contbr. of Yr. award, S.C. C. of C., 2003, Friends of Lake City award, 2005; grantee, S.C. Arts Commn., 1999—2006, S.C. State Dept. Edn., 2001—06. Mem.: Music Educators Nat. Conf., Delta Kappa Gamma (Svc. award). Office: Florence School District #3 125 SBlanding St Lake City SC 29560

STONE, BONNIE MAE DOMROSE, writer; b. Chgo., Jan. 26, 1941; d. George Charles and Dorothy Lovella (Maas) Domrose; m. Leighton Frank Stone, Nov. 10, 1962; children: Douglas Brian, Gregory Alan, Paul Andrew. BA in Journalism, Marquette U., 1961. Editor family sect. Angeles Mesa News advertiser, L.A., 1961-62; editor family sect. 5 newspapers Lakeland Pubs., Grayslake, Ill., 1962-64; staff reporter, feature writer News & Courier, Charleston, S.C., 1966-68; spl. assignment writer Today, Cocoa, Fla., 1970-72; vol. publicist Boy Scouts Am., 1973-75; editor Ka Nupepa, Mililani Town Newspaper, Hawaii, 1977-80; dep. pub. affairs officer Caducean, Hawaii, 1982; editor The Shopper, Hawaii, 1984-85; freelance writer, 1985—. Freelance writer, 1985—; lectr. in field; tchr. writing Dothan (Ala.) C.C.; instr. Wallace C.C., Dothan. Author: (with Betty Alt) Uncle Sam's Brides, 1990, Campfollowing, 1991; (with Virginia Smith) Aloha Cowboy, 1988, Civil War in Paradise, 1998, San Andreas Ain't No Fault of Mine, 2005; contbr. articles to nat., regional and specialized mags. Rep., Neighborhood Bd. 25, Mililani Town, Hawaii, 1974-77. Recipient Gallery awards Internat. Assn. Bus. Communicators/Hawaii, Tad Quattlebaum award in S.C., S.C. Press Assn. awards, Nat. Fedn. Press Women awards. Mem. Calif. Writers Club, Nat. League Am. Penwomen, Antelope Valley Writers (founder). Avocation: walking.

STONE, BRENDA KERSHAW, art educator; b. Lowell, Mass., Jan. 26, 1948; d. Raymond Elliott and Mary Katherine (Blair) Kershaw; m. William G. Stone Jr., July 7, 1967; 1 child, William III. BFA in Ceramic Design, Alfred U., 1973, MS in Art Edn., 1978. Cert. art tchr., N.Y., Tex. Itinerant art tchr. B.O.C.E.S. Allegany County, Belmont, N.Y., 1973-78; art tchr. Bowman Mid. Sch., Plano (Tex.) Ind. Sch. Dist., 1978-80; art tchr., dept. team leader Schimelpfenig Mid. Sch., Plano (Tex.) Ind. Sch. Dist., 1980-84, Shepton High Sch., Plano (Ind.) Sch. Dist., 1984—. Docent Dallas Mus. Art, 1997-2000; judge Lone Star Art League, 2005; speaker in field. Ceramics exhibited in group shows in McKinney Tex., 1986—, Tex. Art Edn. Assn., 1986, 87, others; appeared in PBS pottery show, Plano, 1986. Pres.-elect, pres., rep., Plano Area Art Edn. Assn., 1985-86, 92-93; exch. tchr. Pedagogical Inst., Vilnius, Lithuania, 1991. Named Tchr. of Yr., Schimelpfenig Mid. Sch., 1983, Recognized Art Tchr. NFAA, 2006. Mem. Conroe Art League. Avocations: ceramics, travel, gardening, reading. Office Phone: 469-752-7760. Business E-Mail: bstone1@pisd.edu.

STONE, CAROLINE FLEMING, artist; b. N.Y.C., Mar. 26, 1936; d. Ralph Emerson and Elizabeth (Fleming) Stone; m. Oakleigh B. Thorne, June 1956 (div. 1969); children: Oakleigh, Henry; m. John Roderick Keating, July 2002. Student, Art Students' League, 1954-57, 71-72, Pratt Graphics, 1973-74. One-woman shows include Washington Art Assn., Conn., Ella Sharp Mus., Mich., 1980, San Diego Pub. Library, 1981, Trustman Gallery Simmons Coll., Boston, 1985, Mary Ryan Gallery, N.Y.C., 1989, Boston Pub. Libr., 1994, Messiah Coll., 1995; two-person shows include Mary Ryan Gallery, 1985, Katonah Gallery, N.Y., 1986, Davidson Gallery, Seattle, 1990, The Millbrook (N.Y.) Gallery, 1993; juried shows include Silvermine Nat. Printmaking, Conn., 1978, Print Club, Phila., 1981, Trenton State (Nat. Print Exhibn. Purchase award), 1982, Minot State Coll., N.D., 1985, Boston Printmakers (Jurors Commendation), 1986; group shows include Mus. N.Mex., 1984, De Cordova and Dana Mus., Nat. Acad. Art, N.Y.C.; Boston Pub. Library, Mus. Contemporary Hispanic Art, N.Y.C., 1987, World Print Exhbn., San Francisco, Smith Coll. Gallery, Northampton, Mass., Mary Ryan Gallery, 1988, Virginia Lynch Gallery, R.I., 1989, 91, Accent on Paper, Lintas, N.Y., 1991, Women Printmaker's Nat. Touring Show, Boston Pub. Libr. 1991, The Tenth Anniversary Show Virginia Lynch Gallery, 1993; represented in permanent collections Art Inst. Chgo., Mid-West Mus. Am. Art, Ind., Mus. N.Mex., Nat. Mus. Am. Art, Boston Pub. Library, U. Chgo., U. Mich., The Portland Art Mus. Mem.: The Kitchen (bd. dirs.). Home and Office: C Stone Press 80 Wooster St New York NY 10012-4347

STONE, CATHY JEAN, elementary school educator; b. Dowagiac, Mich., Jan. 28, 1963; d. Gorden Jerry and Elizabeth Lemke Gwilt; m. Ronald Keith Stone, Aug. 23, 1986; children: Erica Elizabeth, Chase Edward, Ethan Matthew. AA, BA, Anderson U., 1985; MS in Elem. Edn., Ind. U., 2006, cert. in sch. adminstrn. Elem. tchr. Penn-Harris-Madison Sch. Corp., Mishawaka, Ind., 1987—2002, primary reading coach, 2002—. Worship team mem. Michiana Cmty. Ch. of God, Granger, Ind. Protestant. Avocations: singing, reading, counted cross stitch. Home: 66746 Conrad Rd Edwardsburg MI 49112 Office: Penn-Harris-Madison Sch Corp 55900 Bittersweet Rd Mishawaka IN 46545 E-mail: cstone@phm.k12.in.us.

STONE, ELAINE MURRAY, writer, composer, television producer; b. NYC, Jan. 22, 1922; d. H. and Catherine Fairbanks Murray-Jacoby; m. F. Courtney Stone, May 30, 1944; children: Catherine Gustavson, Pamela Webb, Victoria Mattson. Student, Juilliard Sch., 1939—41; BA, N.Y. Coll. Music, 1943; licentiate in organ, Trinity Coll. Music, London, 1947; student, U. Miami, 1952, Fla. Inst. Tech., 1963; PhD (hon.), World U., 1985, Oxford (Eng.) U., 1998. Organist, choir dir. St. Ignatius Episc. Ch., 1940-44; accompanist Strawbridge Ballet on Tour, N.Y.C., 1944; organist All Saints Episc. Ch., Ft. Lauderdale, 1951-54, St. John's Episc. Ch., Melbourne, Fla., 1956-59, First Christian Ch., Melbourne, 1962-63, United Ch. Christ, Melbourne, 1963-65, piano studio, Melbourne, 1955-70; editor-in-chief Cass Inc., 1970-71; dir. continuity radio Sta. WTAI, AM-FM, Melbourne, 1971-74; mem. sales staff Engle Realty Inc., Indialantic, Fla., 1975-78; v.p. pub. relations Consol. Cybertronics Inc., Cocoa Beach, Fla., 1969-70; writer, producer Countdown News, Sta. KXTX-TV, Dallas, 1978-80; assoc. producer Focus News, Dallas, 1980. Host producer TV show, Focus on History, 1982-94, Episc. Digest, 1984-90; judge Writer's Contest sponsored Brevard Cmty. Coll., 1987; v.p. Judges Fla. Space Coast Writer's Conf., 1985—, chmn., 1987. Author: The Taming of the Tongue, 1954, Love One Another, 1957, Menéndez de Avilés, 1968, Bedtime Bible Stories, Travel Fun, Sleepytime Tales, Improve Your Spelling for Better Grades, Improve Your Business Spelling, Tranquility Tapes, 1970, The Melbourne Bi-Centennial Book, 1976, Uganda: Fire and Blood, 1977, Tekla and the Lion, 1981 (1st pl. Nat. League Am. Pen Women), Brevard County: From Cape of the Canes to Space Coast, 1988, Kizito, Boy Saint of Uganda, 1989 (2d pl. Nat. League Am. Pen Women 1990), Christopher Columbus: His World, His Faith., His Adventures, 1991 (1st pl. Nat. League Am. Pen Women 1992), Elizabeth Bayley Seton: An American Saint, 1993 (3d pl. Nat. League Am. Pen Women 1994), Dimples The Dolphin, 1994 (1st pl. Fla. Space Coast Writer's Guild, 1994), Brevard at The Edge of Sea and Space, 1995, The Widow's Might, 1996 (1st pl. Space Coast Writer's Contest), Carter G. Woodson Father of Black History, 1997 (1st pl. Am. Heritage Contest Nat. Soc. Daus. of Am. Revolution 1997), Maximilian Kolbe: Saint of Auschwitz, 1997 (Cath. Bestseller list 1997), Albert's Jungle Piano, 1997 (1st pl. Nat. League Am. Pen Women 1997, 2d pl., Nat. League of Am. Pen Women, 1999), Mother Teresa: A Life of Love, 1999, The Taming of the Tongue, 1999, C.S. Lewis: Creator of Narnia, 2001 (3d place Nat. League Am. Pen Women 2001), Mary and the Apparitions of Guadalupe, Lourdes and Fatima, 2003, A Saint and His Lion The Story of Tekla of Ethiopia, 2003, A New Life (1st place Fla. Assn. Univ. Women 2003), Saints of the Americas, 2004, Dorothy Day: Champion of the Poor, 2004, Courtney's Seawall (2d pl. award); composer: Christopher Columbus Suite, 1992 (1st pl. Pen Women Music Awards 1992, 2d pl. 1993), Florida Suite for cello and piano, 1993, Two Crowns of St. Maximilian, 1998 (1st pl. in music Nat. League Am. Pen Women 1997), Pastorale, 2000 (1st pl. Nat. League Am. Pen Women, Washington, 2000), Anima Christi, 2000 (hon. mention Nat. League Am. Pen Women, Washington, 2000)); contbr. articles to mags., newspapers including N.Y. Herald Tribune, Living Church, Christian Life, Episcopal Life; space corr. Religious News Service, Kennedy Space Ctr., 1962-78. Exec. bd. Women's Assn., Brevard Symphony, 1967—; heritage com. Melbourne Bicentennial Commn.; mem. Evangelism Commn. Episc. Diocese Cen. Fla., 1985-94; v.p. churchwomen group Holy Trinity Episcopal Ch., Melbourne, 1988-89, Stephen minister, 1988—, pres. churchwomen group, 1989—; bd. dirs. Fla. Space Coast Council Internat. Visitors, Fla. Space Coast Philharm., 1989—, Aid for the Arts, 1994; appointee Hist. Preservation Com., Melbourne, Fla., 2003. Recipient 1st place for piano Ashley Hall, 1935-39, S.C. State Music Contest, 1939, 1st place for piano composition Colonial Suite, Constitution Hall, Washington 1987, 88, 89, 3d place for vocal composition, 1989, honorable mention for article, 1989, 2d place for piano composition, 1989, award lit. contest Fla. AAUW, 1989, 1st place award Fla. State PEN Women, 1990, 1st Place award Nat. Black History Essay Contest, 1990, 2d place Nat. League Am. Pen Women, 1999, 2d place for music composition, 1999, named Woman of Achievement, 1999, Disting. Author of Yr. plaque Fla. Space Coast Writers Guild, 1992, 96, Woman of Achievement plaque AAUW, 1997, Martha Ingram award Excellence in Arts, Ashley Hall, Charleston, 2004; honoree Nat. Polish Alliance, 3d place award for essay "Remembering C.S. Lewis" Mount Dora Festival of Music and Literature, 2001. Mem. ASCAP, Nat. League Am. PEN Women (1st place awards Tex. 1979, 1st place award for duet, Washington, 2000, pres. Dallas br. 1978-80, organizing pres. Cape Canaveral br. 1969, pres. 1988-90, 96—), Women in Comms., DAR (Fla. state chmn. music 1962-63), Colonial Dames Am. (organizing pres. Melbourne chpt. 1994), Nat. Soc. DAR (organizing regent Rufus Fairbanks chpt. 1981-85, vice regent 1987—, historian 1989—, Fla. state chmn. Am. Heritage), Children Am. Revolution (past N.Y. state chaplain), Am. Guild Organists (organizing warden Ft. Lauderdale), Space Pioneers, Fla. Press, Aid for the Arts, Space Coast Writers Guild (past v.p.). Home: 1076 Eleuthera Dr Palm Bay FL 32905 Personal E-mail: stonebooks@mailstation.com.

STONE, ELIZABETH CECILIA, anthropology educator; b. Oxford, Eng., Feb. 4, 1949; d. Lawrence and Jeanne Cecilia (Fawtier) S.; m. Paul Edmund Zimansky, Nov. 5, 1976. BA, U. Pa., 1971; MA, Harvard U., 1973; PhD, U. Chgo., 1979. Lectr. anthropology SUNY, Stony Brook, 1977-78, asst. prof., 1978-85, assoc. prof., 1985-95, prof., 1995—2002. Participated archaeol. in Eng., Iran, Iraq, Afghanistan; dir. archaeol. projects Ain Dara, Syria, Tell Abu Duwari, Iraq, Ayanis Survey, Turkey. Author: Nippur Neighborhoods, 1987; co-author: (monograph) Old Babylonian Contracts from Nippur 1, 1976, Adoption in Old Babylonian Nippur and the Archive of Mannum-meshu-lissur, 1991, The Iron Age Settlement at Ain Dara, Syria, 1999, The Anatomy of a Masopotamian City: Survey and Soundings of Mashkan-Shapin, 2004; co-editor: The Cradle of Civilization Recent Archaeology in Iraq-Biblical Archaeologist, 1992, Velles Paraules: Ancient Near Eastern Studies in Honor of Miguel Civil on the Occasion of His 65th Birthday, 1991; mem. editl. bd. Bull. Am. Schs. Oriental Rsch., 1993-95, 99—; contbr. articles to profl. jours. Assoc. trustee Am. Schs. of Oriental Rsch., 1983-90. Recipient P.E. MacAllister Field Archaeology award Am. Sch. Oriental Rsch., 2002, SUNY Rsch. Recognition award, 2003, Am. Schs. of Oriental Rsch. Spl. Recognition award, 2004; named Woman of the Yr. in Sci., Three Village Cmty., 2004; Fulbright fellow, 1986-87; rsch. grantee Ford Found., 1974, Nat. Geog. Soc., 1983, 84, 88, 90, 97-99, 2002, 03, Am. Schs. of Oriental Rsch., 1987, 88, NSF, 1989-95, 2000—, NEH, 1989-93, Andrew Mellon Found., 2003, USAID, 2003-4. Office: SUNY Dept Anthropology Stony Brook NY 11794-0001 Office Phone: 631-632-7627. Business E-Mail: estone@notes.cc.sunysb.edu.

STONE, FLORENCE SMITH, film producer, consultant; b. Balt., June 15, 1938; d. Howard Chandler and Mary (Burnam) Smith; m. Roger David Stone; 1 child, Leslie Burnam. BA, Vassar Coll., 1960; cert. Inst. Arts Adminstrn., Harvard U., 1978. Asst. to v.p. for pub. rels. Transam. Corp., San Francisco, 1962—64; newsletter editor U.S. Embassy, Rio de Janeiro, 1964—66; coord. cmty. rels. Am. Mus. Natural History, N.Y.C., 1970—79, coord. spl. progrm, 1977—84; dir. Washington Office Earthwatch, 1985—90; ind. cons. to mus. and ednl. orgns. Washington, 1990—; artistic dir., founder Environ. Film Festival, Washington, 1993—. Co-chmn. Margaret Mead Film Festival, 1977-84. Trustee The Textile Mus., Washington, 1994—, Laura Boulton Found., N.Y.C., 1980-99, Mus. of the Hudson Highlands, Cornwall-on-Hudson, N.Y., 1974-96; mem. adv. com. Margaret Mead Film Festival, N.Y.C., 1992—; active Trees for Georgetown Com., Washington, 1996—. Mem.: Textile Soc., Women in Film and Video, Ind. Film and Video Assn., Internat. Documentary Assn., Am. Assn. Mus., Cosmos Club, Cosmopolitan Club, Georgetown Garden Club. Democrat. Avocations: textiles, films, trees, performing arts, outdoor activities. Office: Environ Film Festival 1228 1/2 31st St NW Washington DC 20007-3402 Office Phone: 202-342-2564. Business E-Mail: flostonc@igc.org.

STONE, GAYNELL, museum director, educator; d. Arthur Adrian Stone and Madelyn May Fisher; m. Gerald Stanley Levine (div.); children: Andrew, Toby. AA, Del Mar Coll., Corpus Christi, Tex., 1948; BS, Tex. Woman's U., Denton, 1951; MLS, Stony Brook U., NY, 1976, MA in Anthropology, 1978, PhD, 1987. Mus. dir. Suffolk County Archaeolog. Assn., Stony Brook, 1983—. Bd. dirs. Native Am., Hauppauge, NY; adj. prof. Suffolk County C.C., Selden, 1985—; spkr. in field. Contbr. articles to profl. jours. Pres., founder Suffolk County Childhood Assn., 1962—70. Recipient Founders award, Suffolk Early Childhood Edn. Coun., 1977, Suffolk County Heritage award, 1979; grantee, NSF, 1983. Fellow: Suffolk County Archaeolog. Assn. (pres., treas., rec. sec. 1972—); mem.: Coun. Northwest Hist. Archaeology. Avocations: reading, travel, gardening. Home: 2332 N Wading River Rd Wading River NY 11792 Office: SCAA PO Box 1542 Stony Brook NY 11790

STONE, HAZEL ANNE DECKER, artist; b. Salt Lake City, Oct. 30, 1934; d. Carl Marcellus and Hazel Sheets (Van Cott) Decker; m. William Samuel Stone, July 20, 1956; children: Cynthia Anne Stone Barkanic, Lisa Marie. BS, RN, U. Utah, 1956; postgrad. in arts and humanities, Ariz. State U., 1979-81; studied with various artists, Ariz., N.Mex., 1985—. Nurse out-patient dept. Salt Lake County Hosp., 1956-57; instr. med.-surg. nursing U. Utah Coll. Nursing, 1957-59; watercolor fine artist. Art exhbn. juror in field, 1998—; workshop instr. in field. One-woman shows include Sun Cities Mus. Art, Sun City, Ariz., 1997, Downtown Deli, Phoenix, 1999, Galerie van Friend, Scottsdale, Ariz., 2003—04, two person exhbns., Church of the Beatitudes, Phoenix, 1994—95, 2003, Gallery Nineteen, 1996, three person exhbns., Grady Gammage Meml. Auditorium, Ariz. State U., 2002, Casa Grande Art Mus., 2002, exhibitions include Ariz. Artists Guild, 1986, 1988—90, 1992—97, 2005, Tucson Mus. of Art, 1988, Ariz. Watercolor Assn., 1989 (Merchant award), 1991, 1993—95 (Award of Merit, 1998), 1997—2000, 2001—05 (Award of Merit, 2005), Vistas, 1989, 1991, 1993, Sun Cities Art Mus., Ariz., 1994, Contemporary Watercolorists of Ariz., 1994—2006 (award of Excellence, 1997, Merit award, 1998, Merchant award, 2001, Award of Excellence, 2004, Merchant award, 2006, 2003, award of Excellence, 2000), Foothills Art Ctr., Golden, Colo., 1994, Bareiss Gallery, Taos, N.Mex., 1995, 13th Ann. Women's Nat. Juried Art Exhbn., Fayetteville, Ark., 1995, Q Artists, 1995—96, 1998, 2000—02, Stables Gallery, Taos, 1996, Wenatchee Valley Coll., Wash., 1997, 1999—2000, Van Vechten-Lineberry Taos Art Mus., 1997, Chandler Ctr. for Arts, Ariz., 1997, 2000, 2005, Farmington Mus. at Gateway Pk., N.Mex., 1999, West Valley Art Mus., Surprise, Ariz., 1999, Sangre de Cristo Arts Ctr., Pueblo, Colo., 1999, Tubac Ctr. of the Arts, Ariz., 1999, 2003, Watercolors Gallery, Pitts., 1999—2000, Woodmere Art Gallery, Phila., 1999—2000, Crary Art Gallery, Warren, Pa., 2000 (Hon. Mention award, 2000), Colo. Springs Fine Arts Ctr., 2001, Bellevue Art Mus., Wash., 2001, Hiestand, Art Gallery, U. Miami, Oxford, Ohio, 2001, Showcase Gallery, San Diego, 2001 (Merchant award, 2001), 2005, Acad. of Art Gallery, Calif., 2002, Minnetrista Cultural Ctr., Muncie, Ind., 2002 (Hon. Mention award, 2002), Noyes Mus. of Art, Oceanville, NJ, 2002, Albuquerque Art Mus., 2002, City of Brea Gallery, Calif., 2002, Fine Arts Ctr., Colo. Springs, 2003, Art Ctr., Western Colo. Ctr. for Arts, Grand Junction, 2003, Beverly Arts Ctr., Chgo., 2003 (Merit award, 2003), Mill Atelier Gallery, Santa Fe, 2003, Cynon Valley Mus., Aberdare, Wales, 2004 (ISEA USA Wales medallion, 2003, 2004), John Stobart's Three Rivers Gallery, Pitts., 2003, AIS, Seattle, 2004, Plains Art Mus., Fargo, ND, 2004, Springfield Art Mus., Mo., 2004, Lee County Alliance of Arts, Ft. Myers, Fla., 2004 (Medallion, 2004), Wichita Art Mus., Kans., 2004, 2005, So. Alleghenies Mus. Art, Loretto, Pa., 2005, Showcase Gallery, San Diego, 2005, Shemer Art Ctr. and Mus., 2005, Mountain Shadow Gallery, Tucson, 2005, Internat. Soc. Expl. Artists, Cardiff, Wales, 2005, Kirsten Gallery, Seattle, 2005, So. Alleghenies Mus. Art, Loretto, Pa., 2005, Berman Mus. Art, Ursinus Coll., Collegeville, PA, 2005—06, The Continental Ctr., 2006, Kaewyn Gallery, Bothell, Wash., 2006, Sweetwater Ctr. Arts, Sewickley, 2006, Hist. Nicolai Fechin House, Taos Art Mus., 2006, galleries, Vision Gallery, Chandler, Ariz., 1997— (2d Place award, Chandler Ostrich Festival Fine Arts Print Contest, 1998), The Park Gallery, Litchfield Park, Ariz., 2003—04, Mountain Shadow Galley, Tucson, 2005—, mag., The Artist's Mag.; contbr. Docent Phoenix Art Mus., 1979-80, master docent, 1989-96; mem. Ariz. Women's Caucus Art, 1988-91. Finalist Ann. Art Competition in Exptl. Art, The Artist's Mag., 1996. Mem.: Red River Watercolor Soc., Transparent Watercolor Soc. Am., Waterworks (exhbn. chair 2003—), Q Artists, Contemporary Watercolorists Ariz. (gen. chmn. 2002—04, exhbn. chmn. 2002—04, signature), Ariz. Watercolor Assn. (assoc. 1985—88, juried 1988—, bd. mem. 1994—2001, Coatimundi Honor Soc. 1995, Nat. Watercolor Exhbn. co-chair 1999, Royal Scorpion 2000, Nat. Watercolor Exhbn. chair 2000, signature), Ariz. Artists Guild (juried 1986—), Watercolor West (juried), Watercolor Art Soc. - Houston, Taos Nat. Soc. Watercolorists (signature), Phila. Water Color Soc. (signature), Pa. Watercolor Soc. (signature), N.W. Watercolor Soc. (signature), Mo. Watercolor Soc., Internat. Soc. Exptl. Artists (signature), Calif. Watercolor Assn., San Diego Watercolor Soc. (assoc.), Nat. Watercolor Soc. (assoc.), La. Watercolor Soc. (assoc.), Am. Watercolor Soc. (assoc.). Home: 3621 E Pasadena Ave Phoenix AZ 85018-1511 Office Phone: 602-956-3783. Personal E-mail: hazelstone@earthlink.net.

STONE, JACQUELYN ELOIS, lawyer; b. Williamsburg, Va., Jan. 7, 1958; d. William Thomas and Sara Elizabeth (Cumber) Stone. BA in Am. Govt., U.Va., 1980; JD, Harvard U., 1985. Bar: Va. 1985. Legis. asst. US Ho. of Reps., Washington, 1980-82; assoc. McGuire, Woods, Battle & Boothe, LLP (now McGuireWoods LLP), Richmond, Va., 1985—94, ptnr., 1994—, mem. bd. partners, firmwide hiring ptnr. & recruiting com. chair. Bd. mem. Arts Coun. of Richmond, past pres.; bd. mem. Jr. Achievement of Ctrl. Richmond, Richmond Eye & Ear Hosp., Richmond Renaissance, asst. sec.; exec. com. mem. Va. Performing Arts Found.; mem. local adv. com. Local Initiatives Support Corp.; bd. mem. Va. Commn. for the Arts. Recipient Outstanding Woman Award, YWCA, 2000. Mem.: ABA (mem. bus. law sect. 1985—), Am. Immigration Lawyers Assn., Old Dominion Bar Assn. (mem. exec. com. 1990—92), Va. Bar Assn. (exec. com. young lawyers sect. 1988—90, chmn. membership com. 1988—90), Va. State Bar. Baptist. Avocation: travel. Office: McGuireWoods LLP One James Ctr 901 E Cary St Richmond VA 23219-4030 Office Phone: 804-775-1046. Office Fax: 804-698-2183. Business E-Mail: jstone@mcguirewoods.com.

STONE, JANE BUFFINGTON, artist, writer; b. Madison, Wis., Dec. 1, 1942; adopted d. Marshall Buffington and Alvaretta (Smith) Atkinson; 1 child, Anthony Thomas. Student pub. schs., Eau Claire, Wis. Apprentice Karl Haagedorn, St. Paul, 1960-65; art instr. Head Start Program, St. Paul, 1965-67, Walker Art Inst., Mpls., 1967-69; founding mem., instr. Southside Free Sch., Mpls., 1968-69; free-lance artist Minn. and Oreg., 1965-73; art instr. Fairview Tng. Ctr., Salem, Oreg., 1974-77; founder, dir. 3 C's Sch. of Basic Carpentry, Salem, 1978-79; founder, pres. J. Stone Cards, Inc., Silverton, Oreg., 1980—. Author: Curriculum For Basic Carpentry Instruction, 1976. Newsletter editor NAACP, St. Paul, 1965-67, crisis counselor Mpls. Free Clinic, 1968-70, produce coord. Westbank Food Co-op, Mpls., 1968-70, counselor Womanspace, Salem, Oreg., 1978-80. Recipient Louie award Greeting Card Assn., N.Y.C., 1989. Mem. Am. Watercolor Assn., Oreg. Watercolor Assn. Unitarian Universalist. Avocation: foreign travel to remote tropical regions. Office: J Stone Cards Inc One J Stone Pla Silverton OR 97381 Office Phone: 503-873-3177. Personal E-mail: jstonecards@aol.com. Business E-Mail: www@j.stonecards.com.

STONE, JOSS (JOSCELYN EVE STOKER), singer; b. Dover, Eng., Apr. 11, 1987; d. Wendy. Winning contestant Jr. Star for a Night, BBC TV talent show, 2002; former back-up singer for Britney Spears. Spokeswoman The Gap, 2005. Singer: (albums) Soul Session, 2003, Mind Body & Soul, 2004 (Capital Award, London's favourite UK album, 2005), Alfie soundtrack, 2004, Spoiled, 2005. Recipient Brit Award best British female solo artist, 2005, Brit Award best British urban act, 2005, Grammy Nomination best new artist, 2005, Grammy Nomination best female pop vocal performance, 2005, Grammy Nomination best pop vocal performance, 2005.

STONE, KAREN, opera company director; b. Horsforth, Yorkshire, England, 1952; Degree, Royal Academy of Music, 1970—73, Conservatorio di Musica "Santa Celilia", 1973—76. Asst. dir. Freiburg Opera, 1982—85; dir. English Nat. Opera, 1985—86; prod. and dir. various organizations including Maggio Musicale Fiorentino (Italy), Brighton Festival (Eng.), Royal Opera House (Covent Garden), Teatro Lirico di Parma (Italy), Glyndebourne Festival Opera (Eng.), et al, 1986—94; dep. dir. Cologne Opera, Germany, 1995; gen. mgr. Theaters of Graz, Austria, 2000—03; gen. dir. Dallas Opera, 2003—. Office: Dallas Opera Campbell Centre I 8350 N Central Expy Ste 210 Dallas TX 75206*

STONE, KAREN G., writer; b. San Francisco; BA Comms., Antioch Coll. Columnist Meeting the Challenge, Albuquerque. Office: Volcano Press PO Box 270 Volcano CA 95689

STONE, KATHERINE SMITH, science educator; b. Clinton, N.C., Oct. 4, 1961; d. Leslie Sloan and Margaret Murphy Smith; m. Brian Keith Stone, July 13, 1993; 1 child, Margaret Leslie. BA, U. N.C., Wilmington, 1989. Cert. Tchr. Academically Intellectually Gifted U. Va., 2005, Framework for Understanding Poverty N.C. Tchr. Acad., 2003, Project In-Star U. Miami, 2002, Advancement Via Individual Determination NC, 1997, cert. Foundational Approaches to Sci. Tchg.-Trainer U. Hawaii, 1993. Student tchr./tchr. Noble Sch., Wilmington, 1988—89; tchr. sci. 7th and 8th grades D.C. Virgo Mid. Sch., Wilmington, NC, 1989—93; tchr. sci. 7th, 8th, 9th grades Piedmont Open IB Mid. Sch., Charlotte, NC, 1993—. Curriculum lead tchr. Charlotte-Mecklenburg Schs., NC, 2005—; chair sci. dept. Piedmont Open IB Mid., Charlotte, 1998—99, team leader 9th grade level, 1994—95, team leader 8th grade level, 1997—98; tchr. Adult H.S. Diploma Program Cape Fear C.C., Wilmington, 1991—92. Contbr. science curriculum. Tchr. mem. N.C. chpt. Health Physics Soc., 1993—2006. Finalist Tchr. of Yr., Charlotte-Mecklenburg Schs., 2003; grantee Cmty. Svc. Urban Garden, Sam's Club, 2003, 2004. Mem.: Profl. Educators N.C., Beta Sigma Phi. Roman Catholic. Avocations: surfing, travel, scrapbooks, container gardening. Home: 1510 Scott Ave Ste 246 Charlotte NC 28203 Office: Charlotte-Mecklenburg Schs Piedmont Open IB Mid Sch Charlotte NC Office Fax: 980-343-5557. Personal E-mail: k.stone@cms.k12.nc.us.

STONE, LINDA, former computer company executive, consultant, speaker, writer; Grad., Evergreen State Coll.; M. in Edn., Cognitive Psychology, and Librarianship, U. of Washington. Primary sch. teacher; sch. librarian Seattle; systems analyst, market devel. mgr., software evangelist and asst. for special projects for CEO John Sculley Apple Computer, 1986—93; joined as dir. special projects under Nathan Myhrvold Microsoft Corp., 1993, co-founder, dir. Virtual Worlds Group / Social Computing Group, v.p. corp. and industry initiatives, 2000—02; cons., 2002—. Adj. faculty NYU Tisch Sch. Arts, 1998—99; speaker, expert online social life and virtual communities. Contbr. NY Times, Newsweek, Wired, The Economist, The Boston Globe and hundreds of blogs. Nat. bd. World Wildlife Fund, Philanthropic Collaborative for Integrative Medicine; advisory bd. Rochester Inst. Tech. Lab Social Computing; advisor hidden brain drain task force Center for Work-Life

Policy. Named Outstanding Regional Volunteer of the Year, F.I.R.S.T, 2002; named one of 100 leaders of the digital revolution, Upside mag., 1996. Achievements include coined the term continuous partial attention to describe the way people work and live with information and communication overload.*

STONE, MARILYN, foreign language educator, consultant; b. N.Y.C., Jan. 14, 1935; d. Paul Ference Moskowitz and Anna Schwartz; m. Joseph Stone, Aug. 30, 1959; children: Sara Jean, Edward, Hillary, Daniel. BA in Spanish/French, Queens Coll.; MA in Spanish Lit., Columbia U.; PhD in Spanish Lit., NYU. Cert. Spanish/English translator, medieval/modern paleography profl. Spanish/English interpreter Nassau County Ct., 1985-86; Spanish lang. cons. Fine Arts Mus. of L.I., Hempstead, NY, 1986-87; Spanish instr. Dominican Coll., Blauvelt, NY, 1987, Nassau C.C., Blauvelt, NY, 1987, 92; instr. in translation methods NYU, N.Y.C., 1990—; ind. lang. cons. Chase Manhattan Bank, Bergen Lang. Inst., Teaneck, NJ, 1991—; asst. prof. transl. NYU. Presenter papers in field; adj. asst. prof. Spanish, Kingsborough C.C., CUNY, 1987-90; lectr. in field. Author: A Handbook of Courtroom Terms in Spanish and English, 1981, Marriage and Friendship in Medieval Spain, 1990, Women at Work in Spain From the Middle Ages to Early Modern Times, 1998; contbr. articles to profl. jours.

STONE, MARILYN JOANNE, elementary school educator; b. Jamestown, ND, Oct. 11, 1947; d. Ralph Woodrow and Lillian Elizabeth (Cowin) Kraft; m. Gordon Thomas Stone, Dec. 28, 1968; children: Kristen Lynne, Michael Jason. AA in Home Econs., Ctrl. Coll., McPherson, Kans., 1967; BA in Social Scis., Spring Arbor (Mich.) Coll., 1969; MEd in Elem. Edn., Ea. Mich. U., 1975. Cert. permanent tchg. cert. Mich. Elem. and mid. sch. tchr. Beecher Cmty. Schs., Flint, Mich., 1968-88; tchr. Napoleon Schs., Mich., 1988—2006; prof. Spring Arbor U., Sch. Edn., 2006—. Vol. Goodwill Industries Ctr. Mich., Jackson, 1984—88; dir. Christian edn. Free Meth. Ch., Flint, Jackson, 1969—, dir. children's ministries, steward, sec., Sunday sch. tchr., dir. vacation Bible sch., mem. ofcl. bd., mem. various coms. Mem.: NEA, Beecher Edn. Assn. (bd. dirs.), Napoleon Edn. Assn. (bd. dirs.), Mich. Edn. Assn., Women's Missionary Fellowship Internat. (children's ednl. dir.). Republican. Avocations: reading, antiques, genealogy, quilting. Home: 4545 Springbrook Rd Jackson MI 49201-9774

STONE, MARY ANN, literature and language educator; b. Freelandville, Ind., Jan. 30, 1934; d. Ralph D. and Leona Green; m. Paul R. Stone, Dec. 27, 1953; children: Sunny, Karen, Kerry, Kevin. BS, Ind. State U., 1964, MS, 1983. Lang. arts tchr. Ganada HS, Ganada, Ariz., 1983—2002. Pres. Ganada Edn. Assn., Ganada, Ariz., chmn. lang. arts; faculty coun. Ganada HS. Chmn. bd. dirs. Ganada Presbyn. Avocations: reading, gardening, needlecrafts. Home: 586 Bay N Ct Franklin IN 46131 E-mail: magreenstone@earthlink.net.

STONE, NIKKI, motivational speaker, retired Olympic athlete; b. Princeton, N.J., Feb. 4, 1971; BS in Psychology magna cum laude, Union Coll., 1997. Motivational spkr. Podium Enterprises. Freestyle aerial skier. Winner Olympic Gold Medal in aerials, Nagano, 1998, World Championship Gold Medal, 1995, World Cup title, 1995, 1 World Cup events. Address: PO Box 680332 Park City UT 84068-0332 E-mail: nikkistone@compuserve.com.

STONE, SANDRA, writer, artist; b. Portland, Oreg., Apr. 4, 1934; Visual arts cons. to individual collectors; editor Breitenbush Books, Portland, 1977-81; artist cons. Green Tiger Press, 1985. Exhibited in group shows at Portland Art Mus., 1975-80, 95, White Bird Gallery, Cannon Beach, Oreg., 1980, White Bird Gallery, 1981, N.W. Artist's Workshop, 1981, Contemporary Crafts Gallery, Portland, 1983, Am. Inst. Architects Gallery, 1994, Ricciardi Gallery, Astoria, Oreg., 1994, Orlo Found., 1994, Marylhurst Coll., Portland, 1994, Am. Inst. Architects Gallery, Portland, 1994, Spokane Ctrl. Libr. Art Gallery, 1994, Broders Books, 1995, Old City Hall, Gresham, Oreg., 1996; commd. works by Oreg. State Archives Bldg., Salem, 1991-92, Tacoma Firehouse, 1993, Spokane Ctrl. Libr, 1993-95, Portland C.C. Libr., 1994-96, Midland Regional Libr., Portland, 1994-96, U.S. Fed. Courthouse, Portland, 1995-97, Riverfront Park, Salem, Oreg., 1996-97; author: (poems) Cocktails with Brueghel in the Museum Cafe, 1996, also essays for art catalogues. Active Young Audiences Bd., Portland Art Mus., N.W. Artist's Workshop, Portland Ctr. for Visual Arts, Contemporary Crafts Gallery, Oreg. Sch. Arts and Crafts, others. Artist's fellow Va. Ctr. for Creative Arts, 1986, Oreg. Lit. Arts, 1992; recipient Purchase award U. West Fla., 1995. Mem. N.W. Dramatist's Guild, Soc. Children's Book Writers and Illustrators, Acad. Am. Poets (assoc.).

STONE, SANDRA SMITH, sociologist, researcher, academic administrator; b. Chgo., Oct. 16, 1954; d. John Lawrence and Bernice (Pickett) Smith; m. Scott Lukens, 1973 (div. 1977); m. Charles M. Huguley, Oct. 17, 1982 (div. 1988); 1 child, Bailey Anne; m. Anthony V. Stone, Aug. 4, 1990; 1 stepchild, Adam Maraman. BA, U. West Ga., 1976, MA, 1978; PhD, Emory U., 1993. Cert. mediator. Social worker Carroll County Early Childhood Ctr., Carrollton, GA., 1977, Clayton Gen. Hosp., Riverdale, Ga., 1978-80; caseworker Fulton County Dept. Family and Children Svcs., Atlanta, 1981; caseworker prin. Cobb County Dept. Family and Children Svcs., Marietta, Ga., 1981-82; children's program supr. Coun. on Battered Women, Atlanta, 1982-83; sr. rsch. assoc. Ctrs. Disease Control/Ga. Dept. Human Resources, Atlanta, 1985-87; cons. Ctrs. Disease Control, Atlanta, 1987-88; rsch. assoc. Police Exec. Rsch. Forum, Washington, 1988-90; exec. dir. Rsch. Atlanta, 1990-91; sr. rsch. assoc. Emory U. Sch. Pub. Health, Atlanta, 1991-92; dir. planning & Rsch. Ga. Dept. Children & Youth Svcs., Atlanta, 1992-96; asst. prof. to prof. U. West Ga., Carrollton, 1996—, assoc. v.p. acad. affairs. Instr., Emory U., Atlanta, 1984-89; drug policy adviser Mayor's Office, City of Atlanta, 1989-90; grant application reviewer Nat. Ctr. Child Abuse and Neglect, Washington, Ga. Dept. Human Resources, Atlanta; cons. Coun. for Children, Atlanta, 1987. Contbr. articles, reports to profl. publs. Mem. DeKalb County Task Force on Child Care, Decatur, Ga., 1984, DeKalb County Task Force on Infant Mortality, Decatur, 1985-89, DeKalb County Task Force on AIDS, Decatur, 1987-88; assessor City of Atlanta Fire Chief Assessment Ctr., 1990; vol. United Way; mem. Criminal Justice Coord. Com., 1992-96; mem. statewide Task Force on Violence and Schs., 1993-95; profl. adv. coun. Mission New Hope, 1994-98; mem. nat. adv. bd. Juveniles Taken Into Custody Project, 1994-97; cons. family connection project Haralson County, 1997-2004; chair adv. bd. Ga. Dept. Juvenile Justice, Carroll County Ct. Svcs. Office, 1999-2001. Mem. AAUP, LWV, Ga. Coun. Child Abuse, Planned Parenthood, Am. Sociol. Assn., Am. Soc. Criminology, Ga. Sociol. Assn., Am. Pub. Health Assn., Acad. Criminal Justice Scis., Sociol. Practice Assn., So. Criminal Justice Assn., Phi Kappa Phi, Alpha Kappa Delta. Democrat. Avocations: movies, theater, concerts, crafts. Home: 2078 Amberwood Way NE Atlanta GA 30345-3904 Office: U West Ga Office VP Acad Affairs Carrollton GA 30118-0001 Office Phone: 770-839-6445. Business E-Mail: sstone@westga.edu.

STONE, SHARON, actress; b. Meadville, Pa., Mar. 10, 1958; d. Joe and Dorothy S; m. George Englund Jr. (div.); m. Michael Greenburg, Aug. 18, 1984 (div. Jan. 20, 1987); m. Phil Bronstein, Feb. 14, 1998 (div. Jan. 29, 2004); 3 adopted sons, Roan Joseph, Laird Vonne, Quinn. Diploma in Creative Writing and Fine Arts, Edinboro State U. Model Eileen Ford Modeling Agy.; owner Chaos prodn. co. Actress (films) Stardust Memories, 1980, Deadly Blessing, 1981, Irreconcilable Differences, 1984, King Solomon's Mines, 1985, Allan Quatermain and the Lost City of Gold, 1986, Cold Steel, 1987, Police Academy 4: Citizens on Patrol, 1987, Action Jackson, 1988, Above the Law, 1988, Beyond the Stars, 1989 (Personal Choice award), Total Recall, 1990, Year of the Gun, 1991, Diary of a Hitman, 1991, He Said/She Said, 1991, Scissors, 1991, Basic Instinct, 1991, Where Sleeping Dogs Lie, 1992, Last Action Hero, 1993, Sliver, 1993, Intersection, 1994, The Specialist, 1994, (also co-prodr.) The Quick and the Dead, 1995 (also co-prodr.), Casino, 1995 (Golden Globe award for best actress in film 1996, Acad. award nominee for best actress 1996), Diabolique, 1996, Last Dance, 1996, Sphere, 1998, The Mighty, 1998 (Golden Global nominee), Antz, 1998 (voice), Gloria, 1999, The Muse, 1999, Simpatico, 1999, Beautiful Joe, 2000, Picking Up the Pieces, 2000, Cold Creek Manor, 2003, Cold Creek Manor, 2003, Catwoman, 2004, Jiminy Glick in La La Wood, 2004, Broken Flowers, 2005, Alpha Dog, 2006, Basic Instinct 2, 2006; TV appearances include Not Just Another Affair, 1982, Bay City Blues, 1983, Calendar Girl Murders, 1984, The Vegas Strip Wars, 1984, War and Remembrance, 1988, Tears in the Rain, 1988, (guest) The Larry Sanders Show, 1994, Big Guns Talk: The Story of the Western (tv spl.), 1997; narrator: Harlow: The Blond Bombshell, 1993, If These Walls Could Talk 2, 2000, Harold and the Purple Crayon, 2001, Cold Creek Manor, 2003, A Different Loyalty, 2004. Office: Care Guy McElwaine PO Box 7304 North Hollywood CA 91603-7304*

STONE, SHIRLEY M., pediatrician, educator; b. Carbondale, Pa., May 27, 1926; d. Ben L. Stone and Fannye Kaufman; m. Sidney Q. Cohlan (dec.); children: Barbara Coblan Perlmutter, Deborah Cohlan, John Cohlan; m. Milton Koffman, Mar. 22, 2003. BA in PHysics with honors, Syracuse U., NY, 1945, MD, 1949. Diplomate Am. Bd. Pediats. Intern Beth Israel Hosp., NYC, 1949—50; resident in pediats. NYU/Bellevue Coll. Medicine, NYC, 1950—51, Mt. Sinai Hosp., NYC, 1951—53; from instr. to prof. pediats. NYU Sch. Medicine, NYC, 1954—97, prof. pediats., 1997—; assoc. attending physician Univ. Hosp.; assoc. vis. physician Bellevue Hosp., NYC. Cons. Bank St. Coll. Edn., 1954—65. Contbr. articles to profl. jours. Fellow, Loyal League for Philanthropies, Beth Israel Hosp., 1956—60. Mem.: County Med. Soc., Teratology Soc., Am. Acad. Pediats., Phi Beta Kappa. Home: 333 E 30th St Apt 9M New York NY 10016-6473 Home (Summer): 2100 South Ocean Blvd Palm Beach FL 33480

STONE, SUSAN A., lawyer; b. 1961; BA summa cum laude, Yale U., 1983; JD cum laude, Harvard U., 1987. Bar: Calif. 1987, U.S. Dist. Ct. (no. dist.) Calif. 1987, U.S. Ct. Appeals (9th cir.) 1987, U.S. Dist. Ct. (ctrl. dist.) Calif. 1988, Ill. 1990, U.S. Dist. Ct. (no. dist.) Ill. 1990, U.S. Ct. Appeals (7th cir.) 1990. Asst. U.S. atty. U.S. Dept. Justice, LA; law clk. to Judge William J. Orrick, U.S. Dist. Ct. for No. Dist. Calif.; ptnr. Sidley & Austin (until 2001 merger), Chgo.; ptnr. litig. Sidley Austin Brown & Wood, Chgo., 2001—, and co-chair practice devel. com. Former adj. prof. trial practice DePaul U. Coll. Law, Chgo. Named one of Top Young Litigators Under 40, Ill. Legal Times, One of 40 Attorneys Under 40, Chgo. Lawyer,. Mem. ABA, Ill. Bar Assn., Calif. State Bar, Phi Beta Kappa. Office: Sidley Austin Brown & Wood LLP Bank One Plz 10 S Dearborn St Chicago IL 60603 Fax: 312-853-7036. Office Phone: 312-853-2177. E-mail: sstone@sidley.com.

STONE, SUSAN FOSTER, mental health services professional; b. Salem, Mass., Mar. 15, 1954; d. Bruce and Carolyn (Foster) Hoitt; m. Norman Michael Stone, May 18, 1981; children: Brittany, Forrest. Student, U. York, Eng., 1974-75; BA in Psychology, Colby Coll., 1976; MS in Clin. Psychology, Abilene Christian U., 1979; PhD in Clin. Psychology, Calif. Sch. Profl. Psychology, 1985. Lic. psychologist, Calif. Mem. emergency response team Simi (Calif.) Dept. Police, 1980-81; cons. Children's Hosp. L.A., 1984-85; postdoctoral fellow Neuropsychiat. Inst. UCLA, 1985-86; clin. dir. Santa Clarita (Calif.) Child and Family Devel. Ctr., 1987-94, dir. tng., 1994-95. Cons. L.A. County Adoptions, 1985-88; expert witness L.A. Superior Ct., 1987—, State Funded Early Mental Health Initiatives, 1994; assisted in drafting congl. managed health care proposal, 1995; presenter in field. Mem. adv. coun. L.A. Foster Parent Assn., 1989-91. Office Juvenile Justice Systems grantee Spl. Children's Ctr., 1990, L.A. Regional Ctr. grantee, 1990. Mem.: APA. Office: 23504 Lyons Ave Ste 304 Newhall CA 91321-5776

STONE, THERESA M., communications executive; b. Boston, 1944; Grad., Wellesley Coll.; grad. studies Cornell U.; MS, Sloan Sch. Mgmt., Mass. Inst. Tech., 1976. With Chubb Corp., 1990—97; pres., CEO Chubb Life Ins. Co. Am., 1994—97; with Morgan Stanley & Co., 1976—90; pres. Jefferson Pilot Comm., Greensboro, NC, 1997, exec. v.p., CFO, 1997—. Mem.: Burlington Industries Bd., Fed. Res. Bd., Richmond Br., MIT Corp., Greensboro United Way 1999 Campaign (pacesetters chair), Greensboro C. of C. Office: Jefferson Pilot Corp PO Box 21008 Greensboro NC 27420

STONE, VOYE LYNNE, women's health nurse practitioner; b. Grandfield, Okla., Apr. 17, 1941; d. Clint Voy and Mattie Evelyn (Averyt) Wynn; m. Don Dale Stone, Dec. 19, 1964; children: Melinda Anne Stone Phelps, Tari Elisabeth Stone Newhouse. Student, Bapt. Hosp. Sch. Nursing, Oklahoma City, 1965; diploma in nursing, U. Okla., Oklahoma City, 1965; BS, St. Joseph's Coll., North Windham, Maine, 1985; grad. women health care nursing program, U. Tex., Dallas, 1990; MS, U. Okla., 1996. Cert. women's health nurse; cert. legal nurse cons. Dietary cons. Frederick Meml. Hosp., 1967; pub. health nurse Dept. Health, State of Okla., Frederick, 1985; insvc. educator Frederick Meml. Hosp.; women's health nurse practitioner Dept. Health, State of Okla., Oklahoma City, 1990. Vol., unit pres. Am. Cancer Soc.; vol. ARC; pres. adv. coun. 4-H Club; pres. local PTA. Named one of Outstanding Young Women of Am., 1970. Mem. AWHONN, Am. Acad. Nurse Practitioners, ANA, Okla. State Nurses Assn., Okla. Pub. Health Assn., Okla. Mental Health Assn., PEO, Beta Sigma Phi (various offices, Girl of Yr. 1976, 77, 78), Sigma Theta Tau, Phi Kappa Phi, First United Methodist Ch. Home: 21918 CR EW 184 Frederick OK 73542-9721

STONEHAM, SANDRA LEE, retired music educator; b. Chgo., Sept. 30, 1950; d. Fredrick Neill and Emilie Rowena Stoneham; m. Richard Sherman Bair, June 18, 2005; children: Alethea Bair, Julia Bair, Nina Catherine. MusB in Edn., U. Ill., Urbana, 1972; MusM in Edn., Roosevelt U., Chgo., 1977. Music tchr. Bellwood Pub. Schs., Ill., 1972—80, Homer Twp. Dist. 33C, Lockport, Ill., 1980—87, Indian Prairie Sch. Dist. 204, Aurora, Ill., 1987; ret. Workshop leader, 1976—. Condr. Young Naperville Singers, Ill., 1993—96. Recipient Most Influential Educator award, Indian Prairie Sch. Dist. 204, 1991. Mem.: Music Educators Nat. Conf. Unitarian. Avocations: reading, travel. Personal E-mail: sandymusic@msn.com.

STONESIFER, PATTY (PATRICIA Q. STONESIFER), foundation administrator; b. Indpls., 1956; m. Michael Kinsley; 2 children from previous marriage. BA, Ind. U., 1982. Editor-in-chief Que Corp., Indpls.; sr. mgr. Microsoft Press, 1988-89; gen. mgr. Microsoft Can., 1989-90; gen. mgr., then v.p. product support svcs. consumer divsn. Microsoft Corp., Redmond, Wash., 1990-93, sr. v.p. consumer divsn., 1993—96; chairwoman, pres. Gates Learning Found., 1997—99; co-chair, pres., CEO Bill & Melinda Gates Found., Seattle, 2000—. Mem. US delegation to UN Gen. Assembly Spl. Session on AIDS; mem., bd. dirs. Viacom Inc., 2000—, The Seattle Found., Amazon.com. Mem. bd. regents Smithsonian Inst. Named one of 25 Most Influential People in Am., Time mag., 1996. Fellow: Am. Acad. Arts & Sci. (founding bd. mem.). Office: Bill & Melinda Gates Found PO Box 23350 Seattle WA 98102*

STONE-STREETT, NANCY HARRINGTON, art educator, painter, printmaker; b. Helena, Mont., Oct. 8, 1948; d. Harvey Harrington and Borghild Stone; m. Douglas A. Streett, Feb. 5, 1994; m. Ben Chovanak (div.); 1 child, Harvey Harrington Chovanak. BA in Art, Mont. State U., 1985; MFA in Painting and Drawing, U. Mont., 1987. Dir. Beall Park Art Ctr., Bozeman, Mont., 1994—96; instr. Miss. Delta CC, Moorhead, Miss., 1999—. Tchr. Share-Mont. Arts Coun. Program, Helena, 1975—80. Recipient Miss. Humanities Tchr. award, Miss. Humanities Coun., 2005. Democrat. Episcopalian. Home: 2193 Carol Greenville MS 38703 Office: Miss Delta CC Art Dept Moorhead MS 38761

STOODT, BARBARA DERN, retired education educator, magazine editor; b. Columbus, Ohio, June 12, 1934; d. Millard Fissel and Helen Lucille (Taes) Dern; divorced; children: Linda Stoodt Neu, Susan Stoodt Price. BS in Edn., Ohio U., 1956; MA in Edn., Ohio State U., 1965; PhD, 1970; postgrad., U. Chgo., 1967. Tchr. North Charleston (S.C.) Schs., 1956-57, Cleveland Heights (Ohio) U., 1957-58, Mansfield (Ohio) Bd. Edn., 1958-59, 65-68; dir. reading, 1968; teaching assoc. Ohio State U., 1968-70; prof. edn. U. Akron, Ohio, 1970-77, U. N.C., Greensboro, 1977-98; ret. Vis. prof. No. Ky. U. and U. Cin. Author: Reading Instruction, 1981, 2d edit., 1989, Teaching Language Arts, 1988; co-author: Secondary School Reading Instruction, 1987, 5th edit., 1994, Children's Literature: Discovery for a Lifetime, 1996, Riverside Reading Program. U.S. Office Edn. research grantee, 1970. Mem. Nat. Conf. on Research in English, Internat. Reading Assn. (Outstanding Dissertation award), Am. Ednl. Research Assn., Nat. Council Tchrs. English (outstanding research award 1971), Assn. for Supervision and Curriculum Devel., Assn. for Childhood Edn. Internat. Methodist. Avocations: gardening, travel, golf. Address: 12537 Saint Thomas Ct Midlothian VA 23114-3264

STORANDT, MARTHA, psychologist; b. Little Rock, June 2, 1938; d. Farris and Floy (Montgomery) Mobbs; m. Duane Storandt, Dec. 15, 1962; 1 child, Eric AB, Washington U., St. Louis, 1960, PhD, 1966. Lic. psychologist, Mo. Staff psychologist VA, Jefferson Barracks, Mo., 1967-68; asst. prof. to prof. Washington U., St. Louis, 1968—. Mem. nat. adv. council on aging Nat. Inst. on Aging, 1984-87; editor-in-chief Jour. Gerontology, 1981-86 Author: Counseling and Therapy with Older Adults, 1983; co-author: Memory, Related Functions and Age, 1974; co-editor: The Clinical Psychology of Aging, 1978, The Adult Years: Continuity and Change, 1989, Neuropsychological Assessment of Dementia and Depression in Older Adults: A Clinician's Guide, 1994. Recipient Disting. Service award Mo. Assn. Homes for the Aging, 1984. Fellow APA (pres. divsn. 20 1979-80, council rep. 1983-84, 86-88, Disting. Sci. Contbn. award divsn. adult devel. and aging 1988, Master Mentor award divsn. adult devel. and aging 2000, Disting. Contbns. to Clin. Geropsychology divsn. clin. psychology 2002), Gerontol. Soc. Am. Office: Washington U Dept Psychology Saint Louis MO 63130

STORCH, SUSAN BOROWSKI, lawyer; b. Jersey City, June 23, 1961; d. Raymond Edward and Clara Mary (Stryzek) Borowski; m. Michael John Storch, Feb. 9, 1985; children: Samantha Clare, Michael John Jr. BA, Rutgers U., 1983; JD, Seton Hall U., 1990. Bar: N.J. 1991. Corp. trust adminstr. Mfrs. Hanover Trust Co., N.Y.C., 1983-86; law clk. Congressman Dean Gallo, Washington, 1988, N.J. Supreme Ct. Com. on Complementary Dispute Resolution, Trenton, N.J., 1988; law clk. to asst. atty. gen. legis. affairs U.S. Dept. Justice, Washington, 1989; assoc. Rodino & Rodino, East Hanover, NJ, 1991—92; sr. assoc. Fragomen, Del Rey & Bernsen, Iselin, NJ, 1992—98, ptnr., 1998—2000; ptnr., chair corp. immigration practice group Sills Commis Radin Tischman Epstein & Gross, Newark, 2000—. Lectr. in field. Bd. dirs. Players Forum, N.Y.C., 1993-94; coord. Corp. Giving Coun., N.J. Women's Polit. Caucus, 1995; active various polit. fundraising campaigns. Recipient Commendation award Essex County Bd. Chosen Freeholders, N.J., 1990; Lyndon B. Johnson Congl. scholar, 1988. Mem.: ABA (labor and employment law sect. 1994—95), Exec. Women N.J. (nominations com.), Ctr. Study of Presidency, Psychology Assn. Am., Inst. Cont. Legal Edn. and Info. (N.J.), Coun. Internat. Personnel, Am. Immigration Lawyer Assn. (former press sec., former sec.), N.J. Bar Assn. (exec. bd. programs ctr. 1994—95). Democrat. Avocations: writing, sailing, golf. Office: Stills Cummis Radin Tischman Epstein & Gross PA One Riverfront Plaza Newark NJ 07102-5400

STORER, MARYRUTH, law librarian; b. Portland, Oreg., 1953; d. Joseph and Carol Storer; m. David Bailey, 1981; children: Sarah, Allison. BA in History, Portland State U., 1974; JD, U. Oreg., 1977; M in Law Librarianship, U. Wash., 1978. Bar: Oreg. 1978. Assoc. law libr. U. Tenn., Knoxville, 1978-79; law libr. O'Melveny & Myers, L.A., 1979-88; dir. Orange County Pub. Law Libr., Santa Ana, Calif., 1988—. Mem. Am. Assn. Law Librs. (exec. bd. 1999-2002), So. Calif. Assn. Law Librs. (pres. 1986-87), Coun. Calif. County Law Librs. (sec./treas. 1990-94, pres. 1994-96), Arroyo Sero Libr. Network (chair 2000-03). Democrat. Episcopalian. Office: Orange County Public Law Library 515 N Flower St Santa Ana CA 92703-2304 Office Phone: 714-834-3002.

STOREY, JOYCE R., writer, actress; arrived in US, 1993; d. Edison Bryar Storey and Emma Gertrude Tweedy; m. Thomas Alan Dowden, July 6, 1985 (div. 1996); m. Jeffrey Scott Wener, June 22, 1998; stepchildren: Allison Julie Wener, Erik Scott Wener. B in Music Edn., Acadia U., 1985; Prodrs. Diploma, Hollywood Film Inst., 2000; Filmmaker Diploma, Digital Film Acad., 2003. Cert. ind. filmmaker Hollywood Film Inst., 2000. Tchr. music Westwood Elem. Sch., Thompson, Manitoba, Canada, 1985—87; tchr. music, drama R.D. Parker Collegiate, Thompson, 1987—88; tchr. drama Glenlawn Collegiate Fine Arts Sch., Winnipeg, Manitoba, 1988—92; affiliate N.Y. Divsn. Westsun Internat. Inc., NYC, 1997—2000; prodn. mgr. Food for Thought, LLC, NYC, 2000; office mgr. High End Sys. Inc., NYC, 2001; gen. mgr. Stage Call Inc., NYC, 2002—. Mgr. Actor's Connection, NYC, 1993—; casting dir. Plato Films, Inc., Istanbul, 2003; sec. Bentley Prodns. Inc., NYC, 2003, Bink Inc., NYC, 2003. Columnist: Timeless Comm., 2000—, Front of House Mag., 2002—03; contbr. PLSN Mag., 2000—03; author: (poetry) Holding On To Forever, 2001 (Editor's Choice award, 2001), Pearls of the Past, 2002 (Editor's Choice award, 2002); actor: One Life to Live; (TV series) Guiding Light, As the World Turns, All My Children, The Sopranos, Sex and the City; (films) Amazing Grace, The Adulterer, Fire Storm Rising. Recipient Humanitarian award, Terry Fox Humanitarian Award program, 1984—85, Appreciation award, Allied Youth Internat., 1992. Avocations: ice skating, rollerblading, hiking, sewing, dance. Personal E-mail: joycestorey@aol.com.

STOREY, SANDRA JEAN, emergency room nurse; b. Walhalla, N.D., May 10, 1967; d. Laura (Goulet) Storey. BSN, U. N.D., 1989. Cert. NALS instr., cert. emergency nurse, ACLS instr., TNCC, PALS, BLS. Emer. rm. nurse PHS Hosp., Belcourt, N.D., 1989—. Mem. N.D. Nurses Assn., N.D. Trauma Found. Home: PO Box 1216 Belcourt ND 58316-1216 Office: PO Box 160 Belcourt ND 58316-0160 Office Phone: 701-477-8450.

STORK, VERA LEE, retired elementary school educator; b. Galveston, Tex., Dec. 21, 1942; d. Leslie Don and Ethel F. (Wakefield) Ward; m. Jack E. Stork; children: James Ward, Melissa Gayle. BS in Edn., Southwest Tex. State U., 1965; MEd, Sam Houston State U., 1974. Counselor's cert. U. Houston Clear Lake. Tchr. Port Isable (Tex.) Sch. Dist., 1965-67, Galveston Sch. Dist., 1974—; counselor Rosenberg Elem. Sch., Galveston, Tex., Boliver Elem. Sch., Galveston, 1995—2000; ret., 2000. Life mem. Tex. State PTA; first v.p. Rosenberg Sch. PTA, Galveston; active Galveston Hist. Soc., 1986-87, Galveston Hospice Group, 1986-87; mem. Leon County Rep. Women, 2000—; chmn. Neighbors Helping Neighbors, Hilltop Lakes, 2004-06; Hilltop Lakes Beautification Com., 2000—; mem. Hilltop Lakes Auxiliary Scholarship Com., 2005—, chairperson, 2006. Mem. AAUW (treas. 1978-79), LWV, Am. Field Service (pres. 1982-84), Assn. Tex. Profl. Women (bldg. rep.), Delta Kappa Gamma (project com., ceremonies com. Omicron chpt. 1975—). Beta Sigma Phi (Beta Kappa Mu chpt., 2002—, pres., 2003-04), Red Hat Soc. (La Chapequx chpt., 2004—). Episcopalian. Home: PO Box 1158 Normangee TX 77871-1158

STORM, HANNAH, newscaster; b. Oak Pk., Ill., June 13, 1962; B in Polit. Sci. and Comm., U. of Notre Dame, 1983. Sports anchor, reporter KTXH-TV, Houston; Home Sports Entertainment; KNCN-FM Radio, Corpus Christi, Tex., WNDU-TV, South Bend, Ind., 1982—88; sports reporter, anchor WPQC-TV, Charlotte, NC, 1988—89; anchor CNN Sports Tonight, 1989—92; anchor, reporter NBC Sports, 1993—2002; anchor The Early Show, 2002—. Host NBC coverage of the NBA, 1997—2002, NBC coverage of Major League Baseball, 1995—2002, NBC coverage of Major League Baseball World Series, 1995, 97, 99. Author: (sports guide for parents) Go Girl!, 2002. Recipient Gracie Allen award, Am. Women in Radio and TV.

STORM, J. RENI, nurse, consultant; d. Edmund Francis and M. Helen (Saltzmann) Corrado; m. John A. Storm, Feb. 14, 1970 (div. Sept. 1990); 1 child, Kierston L Storm-Dubois. AAS in Nursing cum laude, Dutchess C.C., Poughkeepsie, NY, 1978; BS in Health Care Cmty., SUNY, New Paltz, 1987; workshop, Scottsdale Sch. for Artists, 2001; MA in Legal and Ethical Studies, U. Balt., 2003. RN NY. Cmty. mental health nurse Dutchess County Dept. Mental Hygiene, Millbrook, NY, 1980—84; nurse Vassar Bros. Hosp., Poughkeepsie, NY, 1984—87; health svc. cons. Empire Blue Cross & Blue Shield, NYC, Albany, Poughkeepsie, 1987—92; cons. nurse III St. Vincent Hosp., Santa Fe, 1992—. Cmty. edn., mental health players NY State Psychiat. Ctr., Poughkeepsie, 1984—86; pvt. practice consulting legal nurse,

Santa Fe, 2003—06; surveyor trainee Accreditation Assn. for Ambulatory Health Care, Inc., 2006. Contbg. editor: (novel) Seas Raging, White Horse Flying; contbg. costume designer The Jungle Book, N.Mex. Ballet, creator (coloring book); exhibitions include 1st Nat. Bank Santa Fe, Limner Gallery, NYC, Santa Fe Soc. Artists, Kiva Gallery; actor: (debut) Inherit the Wind, Agatha Christie's Spider Web (Critical acclaim reviews, 1990); polit. cartoon strip, Udo. Mem. Santa Fe Coun. on Internat. Rels., N.Mex., 2002—03; mem., educator Cmty. Mental Health Players, Poughkeepsie, NY, 1984—86; tutor for cmty. immigrants Literacy Vols., Santa Fe, 2001—02; mem. founding group Santa Fe Living Wage Network, 2003—; rehab. group leader for stroke patients Santa Fe Care Nursing Home, 1999—2000; pres., bd. dirs. Mid Hudson Kennel Club, 1986—88; sponsor World Vision, Rhinebeck, NY, 1989—99; nursing, health care advisor KSK Buddhist Ctr., Santa Fe, 2001—03; AKC judges edn. coord. Mastiff Club Am., Rhinebeck, NY, 1986—88; pres. Dutchess County SPCA, Poughkeepsie, NY, 1986—88; v.p. Santa Fe Soc. Artists, 1997—98. Recipient Cmty. Svc. award for Devel. Contbn., Dutchess County SPCA Bd. Dirs., 1988; scholar, Union Plus, 2002. Mem.: Legal Nurse Consultants (Puget Sound chpt.), Am. Assn. Legal Nurse Cons. Achievements include development of long range plan for community project/Dutchess County SPCA. Avocations: world travel and cultures, cartooning, painting, writing, public speaking. Office Fax: 360-894-0549.

STORM, JACKIE, nutritionist; b. Halifax, N.S., Can., Sept. 20, 1943; d. Jack Charles Stone and Kathleen (Clow) Devisser. BA, NYU, 1979, MA, 1982, PhD, 1995. Cert. nutrition specialist. Nutrition educator N.Y. Health and Racquet Club, N.Y.C., 1973—; tchr. New Sch. Social Rsch., N.Y.C., 1980-87. Adj. prof. Kingsborough C.C., Bklyn., 1987-2001, St. Francis Coll., Bklyn., 1987; tchr. Acad. Med. Sys., 2001-. Author: There's No Such Thing As A Fattening Food!, 1983, Nutrition in a Nutshell, 2006. Mem. Am. Coll. Nutrition, Am. Nutraceutical Assn., Soc. nutrition Edn. Avocations: gardening, weightlifting. Office: 115 E 57th St New York NY 10022-2049 Office Phone: 212-220-0773. E-mail: jackiestorm@jackiestorm.com.

STORM, SUZANNE, state representative; b. Spokane, Wash., July 17, 1941; 1 child, Carmen. BA, William Jewell Coll., 1963; MS, U. Kans., 1984. Tchr. pub. schs., 1964—78; tchr. Shawnee Mission, Kans., 1978—; mem. Kans. Ho. of Reps., 1996—. Mem.: Shawnee Mission Edn. Found., Mainstream Coalition, Kans. Nat. Edn. Assn. (bd. dirs. 1990—96), NEA (pres. 1992—96). Democrat. Baptist. Office: 272-W State Capitol 300 SW 10th Ave Topeka KS 66612 Address: 8145 Mackey Overland Park KS 66204-3121 Business E-Mail: sstorm@sbcglobal.net.

STORMER, NANCY ROSE, lawyer; b. Traverse City, Mich., Mar. 7, 1950; d. Benjamin Voice and Frances Rose (Gold) S.; m. Michael Charles Bagge, Aug. 1, 1985; children: Sean, Kiernan. AA, Harriman (N.Y.) Coll., 1973; BA magna cum laude, Marist Coll., 1977; JD, Antioch Sch. Law, 1981. Bar: N.Y. 1983, U.S. Dist. Ct. (no. dist.) N.Y. 1983, U.S. Supreme Ct. 1989. Staff atty. Legal Aid Soc. Mid N.Y., Utica, 1983-95, sr. atty., 1990-95; atty. in pvt. practice Utica, 1995—. Bd. dirs. Sister City Project, Utica, 1986-90, Salvation Army, Utica, 1988-89; mem. adv. coun. office for aging Oneida County Office for Aging, Utica, 1993-96; co-chairperson adv. coun. Hispanos Unidos, Utica, 1994. Named Profl. Woman of Yr. YWCA of Mohawk Valley, 1999. Mem. N.Y. State Bar Assn., Oneida County Bar Assn., Nat. Health Lawyers. Avocations: travel, reading, crafts. Home: 1314 Rutger St Utica NY 13501-2526 Office: 1325 Belle Ave Utica NY 13501-2615

STORRS, ELEANOR EMERETT, science administrator, consultant; b. Cheshire, Conn., May 3, 1926; d. Benjamin Porter and Alta Hyde (Moss) S.; m. Harry Phineas Burchfield, Jr., Nov. 29, 1963; children: Sarah Storrs, Benjamin Hyde. BS with distinction in Botany, U. Conn., 1948; MS in Biology, NYU, 1958; PhD in Chemistry, U. Tex., 1967. Asst. biochemist Boyce Thompson Inst. for Plant Rsch., Yonkers, NY, 1948-62; rsch. scientist Clayton Found. Biochem. Inst., U. Tex., Austin, 1962-65; biochemist Pesticides Rsch. Lab., USPHS, Perrine, Fla., 1965-67; dir. dept. biochemistry Gulf South Rsch. Inst., New Iberia, La., 1967-77; adj. prof. chemistry U. Southwestern La., Lafayette, 1974-77; rsch. prof. biology Fla. Inst. Tech., Melbourne, 1977-94, cons. on leprosy-armadillo programs, 1975-94, mem. Faculty Senate, 1979-84, prof. emeritus, 1994—. Cons. in rehab. and prevention deformities leprosy Pan Am. Health Orgn., WHO, Venezuela, Argentina, Brazil, Mex., 1972-90; dep. v.p. Coll. Hansenology in Endemic Countries, 1980-85 Author: (with H.P. Burchfield) Biochemical Applications of Gas Chromatography, 1962, (with Burchfield, D.E. Johnson) Guide to the Analysis of Pesticide Residues, 2 vols, 1965; also articles, book chpts. Grantee NIH, 1968-88, CDC, 1969-73, WHO, 1973-93, Leprosy Program, 1978-93, German Leprosy Relief Assn., 1973-78, Nat. Coun. Episc. Ch., 1975-77, Brit. Leprosy Relief Assn., 1981-88; recipient plaque La. Health Dept., 1972, Disting. Alumni award U. Conn., 1975, Gold award Am. Coll. Pathologists and Am. Soc. Clin. Pathologists, 1974, Gerard B. Lambert award for spl. recognition, 1975. Fellow AAAS; mem. AAUW, Internat. Leprosy Assn., Am. Recorder Soc., Early Music Assn., Sigma Xi. Episcopalian (vestryman). Clubs: Appalachian (Boston); Green Mountain (Bear Mountain, N.Y.). Achievements include pioneering devel. leprosy in exptl. animal (armadillo) reproduction. Home: 72 Riverview Ter Melbourne FL 32903-4640

STORRS, IMMI CASAGRANDE, sculptor; b. Aug. 2, 1945; d. Leo and Carla Maria Annie (Busch) Casagrande; m. Thomas Austin Storrs, Dec. 19, 1971 (div. 1983); 1 child, A. Maya. BA, U. Denver, 1968. Nessa Cohen grantee, 1981, 82, E.D. Found. grantee, 1989, 96; recipient Purchase award, Art Students League N.Y., Chaim Gross Found. award, 1989, Nat. Acad. Mus. Speyer prize, 1992. One-woman shows include Gallery 2, Woodstock, Vt., 1973, Fairwinds Gallery, Ferrisburg, Vt., 1974, Congress Hall, Timmendorferstrand, Germany, 1976, Amerika Haus, Hamburg, Germany, 1976, Cambridge Art Assn., Mass., 1978, Goethe Inst., Boston, 1980, 83, Sutton Gallery, N.Y.C., 1981, 82, 83, 86, Madison Gallery, 1987, Bologna-Landi Gallery, Easthampton, N.Y., 1987, 93, Vorpal Gallery, N.Y.C., 1989, 91, 92, La Posada, Santa Fe, 1989, Ruth Volid Gallery, Chgo., 1990, Bachelier-Cardonsky Gallery, Kent, Conn, 1996, Hurlbutt Gallery, Greenwich, Conn., 1997, Dillon Gallery, N.Y.C., 1997, 00; group shows include Fleming Mus., Burlington, Vt., 1973, ARtist Choice Mus., N.Y.C., 1983, Nat. Acad. Mus., N.Y.C., 1988, 92, 94, 95, 97, 99, 2001, 2003, Provincetown Art Assn. & Mus., Mass., 1988, Nat. Scultpure Soc., N.Y.C., 1989, 91, Elaine Benson Gallery, bridgehampton, N.Y., 1993, Sculptors Guild, Kyoto, Japan & Washington, 1993, N.Y.C., 1994, Cline Fine Art Gallery, Sante Fe, 1994, 95, Stamford Mus., Conn., 1996, Bachelier-Cardonsky Gallery, 1996, The White House, Washington, 1996, 97; represented in permanent collections at The Nat. Mus. Women in Arts, Washington, The Snite Mus., Nat. Acad. Mus., The Herbert Johnson Mus. at Cornell, numerous pvt. collections. Mem. NAD (academician, 1994-), Century Assn., Sculptors Guild. Avocations: skiing, tennis.

STORTI, PAMELA, elementary school educator; b. Lagrange, Ill., Feb. 11, 1974; d. Micheal P. and Barbara L. Stacey; m. Joseph R. Storti, Aug. 17, 1999; children: Joseph R., Gavin M., Carter J. B, Ill. Wesleyan U., Bloomington, 1996. Elem. tchg. cert. Ill. 5th grade tchr. Charles J. Sahs Sch., Chgo., 1996—99, jr. high math tchr., 1999—. Volleyball coach Charles J. Sahs Sch., Chgo., 1998—. Avocations: scrapbooks, dance, crafts. Home: 428 Julia Dr Romeoville IL 60446 Office: Sch Dist 110 5001 S Long Chicago IL 60638 Office Phone: 708-458-1152. Business E-Mail: pstorti@sahs.k12.il.us.

STORY, JOAN H., lawyer; b. Parsons, Kans., Feb. 7, 1944; AB, Occidental Coll., 1965; MA, UCLA, 1968; JD, U. Calif., Davis, 1977. Bar: Calif. 1977. Ptnr., mem. exec. com. Sheppard, Mullin, Richter & Hampton LLP, San Francisco. Co-chair Calif. adv. bd. Trust for Pub. Land. Volume editor U. Calif. at Davis Law Rev., 1976-77. Mem. alumni bd. govs. Occidental Coll., 1982-85. Mem.: Practicing Law Inst. (real estate law adv. com.), Am. Coll. Real Estate Lawyers, Bar Assn. San Francisco, State Bar Calif. (mem. real property law sect.), U. Calif. Davis Law Sch. Alumni Assn. (bd. dirs.), Lambda Alpha. Office: Sheppard, Mullin, Richter & Hampton LLP 17 Fl Four Embarcadero Ctr San Francisco CA 94111 Office Phone: 415-774-3211. Office Fax: 415-434-3947. E-mail: jstory@sheppardmullin.com.

STORY, JULIE ANN, language educator; b. Muncy, Pa., Aug. 6, 1959; d. Phillip Mason Story and Mary Lee Peters. BA in English, Lock Haven U., 1982; MA in English, Ind. U. Pa., 1984. Assoc. dir. undergraduate writing ctr., lectr. English Pa. State U., U. Pk., 1987—2003; English instr. Juniata Coll., Huntingdon, Pa., 1987—89; dir. writing ctr., writing specialist Lock Haven U., Pa., 1998, 2003—. Internship coord. writing ctr. Pa. State U., University Park; cons. in field; faculty advisor Dangling Modifier. Mem. Pa. State Commn. for Women, University Park. Grantee, Ctr. Excellence Learning and Tchg., 2001. Mem.: NOW, Nat. Coun. Tchrs. English, Conf. Coll. Composition Comm., Ctrl. Pa. Writing Ctrs. Assn. (bd. dirs.), Nat. Conf. Peer Tutoring in Writing (adv. bd.), Mid-Atlantic Writing Ctrs. Assn. (bd. dirs.), Internat. Writing Ctrs. Assn., Phi Kappa Phi, Sigma Tau Delta. Democrat. Avocations: gardening, walking, photography, reading, movies. Home: 33 Julia Dr Lock Haven PA 17745 Office: Lock Haven Univ Pa 19 Russell Hall Lock Haven PA 17745 Business E-Mail: jstory@lhup.edu.

STORY, MARTHA VANBEUREN, retired librarian; b. Morristown, NJ, Mar. 6, 1940; d. John Mohlman and Jane de Peyster vanB.; m. William Ferguson Story, Oct. 19, 1963; children: Jessica, Alexandra. BA, Wellesley Coll., 1962; MLS, U. Md., 1975. Libr. Dewberry & Davis, Fairfax, Va., 1976-77, 80-84, Ashley Hall, Charleston, S.C., 1977-80, 85-86; cataloger Norfolk (Va.) Pub. Libr., 1987-90; dir. Mathews (Va.) Meml. Libr., 1990-99. Lay visitors com. Kingston Parish, Mathews, Va., 1996—, scholarship com., 1996—, mem. 350th Anniversary com., 2001—02. Home: Holly Cove PO Box 117 Hudgins VA 23076-0117 Personal E-mail: marthava88@yahoo.com.

STORZ, GISELA T., research scientist; PhD in Biochemistry, U. Calif., Berkeley, 1988. Postdoctoral researcher Nat. Cancer Inst., Mass. Gen. Hosp.; head, sect. on environ. gene regulation, cell biology and metabolism branch Nat. Inst. Child Health and Human Development(NICHD)/NIH, Bethesda, Md. Recipient Eli Lilly and Co. Rsch. award, Am. Soc. for Microbiology, 2000. Office: Cell Biology & Metabolism Branch NICHD Bldg 18T Rm 101 18 Library Dr MSC 5430 Nat Inst Health Bethesda MD 20892-5430 Office Phone: 301-402-0968. Office Fax: 301-402-0078. Business E-Mail: storz@helix.nih.gov.*

STOTLER, ALICEMARIE HUBER, federal judge; b. Alhambra, Calif., May 29, 1942; d. James R. and Loretta M. Huber; m. James Allen Stotler, Sept. 11, 1971. BA, U. So. Calif., 1964, JD, 1967. Bar: Calif. 1967, U.S. Dist. Ct. (no. dist.) Calif. 1967, U.S. Dist. Ct. (ctrl. dist.) Calif. 1973, U.S. Supreme Ct. 1976; cert. criminal law specialist. Dep. Orange County Dist. Attys. Office, 1967-73; mem. Stotler & Stotler, Santa Ana, Calif., 1973-76, 83-84; judge Orange County Mcpl. Ct., 1976-78, Orange County Superior Ct., 1978-83, U.S. Dist. Ct. (ctrl. dist.) Calif., L.A., 1984—. Assoc. dean Calif. Trial Judges Coll., 1982; lectr., panelist, numerous orgns.; standing com. on rules of practice and procedure U.S. Jud. Conf., 1991-98, chair, 1993-98; chair 9th cir. Pub. Info. and Cmty. Outreach, 2000-04; mem. exec. com. 9th Cir. Jud. Conf., 1989-93, Fed. State Jud. Coun., 1989-98, jury com., 1990-92, planning com. for Nat. Conf. on Fed.-State Jud. Relationships, Orlando, 1991-92, planning com. for We. Regional Conf. on State-Fed. Jud. Relationships, Stevens, Wash., 1992-93; chair dist. ct. symposium and jury utilization Ctrl. Dist. Calif., 1985, chair atty. liaison, 1989-90, chair U.S. Constn. Bicentennial com., 1986-91, chair magistrate judge com., 1992-93; mem. State Adv. Group on Juvenile Justice and Delinquency Prevention, 1983-84, Bd. Legal Specializations Criminal Law Adv. Commn., 1983-84, victim/witness adv. com. Office Criminal Justice Planning, 1980-83, U. So. Calif. Bd. Councilors, 1993-2001; active team in tng. Leukemia Soc. Am., 1993, 95, 97, 2000; legion lex bd. dirs. U. So. Calif. Sch. Law Support Group, 1981-83. Winner Hale Moot Ct. Competition, State of Calif., 1967; named Judge of Yr., Orange County Trial Lawyers Assn., 1978, Most Outstanding Judge Orange County Bus. Litig. Sect., 1990. Mem. ABA (jud. adminstrn. divsn. and litig. sect. 1984—, nat. conf. fed. trial judges com. on legis. affairs 1990-91), Am. Law Inst., Am. Judicature Soc., Fed. Judges Assn. (bd. dirs. 1989-92), Nat. Assn. Women Judges, U.S. Supreme Ct. Hist. Soc., Ninth Cir. Dist. Judges Assn., Calif. Supreme Ct. Hist. Soc., Orange County Bar Assn. (mem. numerous coms., Franklin G. West award 1984), Calif. Judges Assn. (mem. com. on jud. coll. 1978-80, com. on civil law and procedure 1980-82, Dean's coll. curriculum commn. 1981), Calif. Judges Found. Office: Ronald Reagan Fed Bldg & Courthouse 411 W 4th St Santa Ana CA 92701-4500 Office Phone: 714-338-4730.

STOTLER, EDITH ANN, retired grain company executive; b. Champaign, Ill., Oct. 11, 1946; d. Kenneth Wagner and Mary (Odebrecht) S. Student, Mary Baldwin Coll., 1964-66; AB, U. Ill., 1968. Asst. v.p. Harris Trust and Savs. Bank, Chgo., 1969-83; mgr. Can. Imperial Bank of Commerce, Chgo., 1983, sr. mgr., 1983-85, asst. gen. mgr. group head, 1985-88, v.p., dir. utilities, 1988-90; ptnr. Stotler Grain Co., Champaign, Ill., 1990—2002; pres. Homer Grain Co., Champaign, 1990-2000; pres., bd. dirs. S&I Grain Co., 1990-2000, SEMCO Energy Inc., 1987—2004. Bd. dirs., audit com., fin. com. SEMCO Energy Inc.; compensation com. Strategic Capital Bancorp, Inc., 2002—03. Past pres. liberal arts and scis. constituent bd., mem. pres.'s coun. U. Ill.; trustee, mem. fin. com. Countryside Sch., 1997—2000; mem. dean's bus. coun. U. Ill. Bus. Coll., 1998—2005, exec. com. dean's bus. coun., 1998—2005; bd. dirs. Champaign County YMCA, 2000—03; bd. dirs., treas. bd., chair investment and fin. coms. Champaign Pub. Libr. Found.; past mem. investment com., bd. trustees 4th Presbyn. Ch.; bd. dirs. Spurlock Mus., Urbana. Mem.: U. Ill. Found., Art Club (past pres., v.p.), Krannert Art Mus. Coun., Champaign Country Club (chair house com.), U. Ill. Found., Book Club. Avocations: needlepoint, reading, tennis, golf, cooking. Home: 1010 W Clark Champaign IL 61821

STOTT, BARBARA PAXTON, volunteer; b. Greenville, Miss., July 30, 1925; d. Lawrence Lipscomb Paxton and Elizabeth Lloyd; widowed; children: Sheila Stott Gourlay, Pamela Stott Kendall, Barbara Stott McCoy. Student, Gulf Park Coll., 1943. Appeared in TV Spl. "A Day in the Life of America." Mem. Am. Women's Club, London, 1977-78, Am. Women's Assn., Singapore, 1983-85, Am. Women's Club Bermuda, 1982-83. Mem. DAR, Colonial Dames, Magna Charta Dames, Delta Debutante Club (bd. dirs.). Republican. Episcopalian. Home: Osceola Plantation RR 1 Box 351 Leland MS 38756-9801

STOTT, TERRI JEUAN, residential facility administrator; b. Fort Lee, Va., Nov. 7, 1965; d. Terry and Gwendolyn Gilliam; m. Eric Lawrence Stott, Sept. 18, 1992. BSW cum laude, Norfolk State U., 1988; MSW, Howard U., 1990. Cert. brief solution focused psychotherapy Am. Hypnosis Tng. Acad. Grad. asst. office of assoc. dean Howard U., Washington, 1988—90; intern mental health therapist Arlington Mental Health Ctr., Va., 1988—90; relief counselor Prince William County Group Home for Boys, Va., 1988—91, counselor, 1991—92, asst. mgr., 1992—97; acting asst. mgr. Judge Patrick Molinari Juvenile Shelter, Manassas, Va., 1997—98, supr. shelter home, 1998—2006, youth residential adminstr., 2006—. Cons., trainer Dept. Social Svcs., Manassas, 1992—, coun. on quality, 1999—; affiliate field instr. faculty Va. Commonwealth U., Richmond, 1996-97; field program adv. com. George Mason U., Fairfax, Va., 1998—. Recipient Dale City Multicultural Scholar Fund 18th Ann. Achievement award Outstanding Pub. Svc. 2002, Suggested Artist award, 2005; named one of Outstanding Young Women of Am., 1988; Child Welfare grantee Norfolk State U., 1987; finalist Internat. Song of Yr. contest, 2004 Mem. Greater No. Va. Nat. Alumni Assn. (Millennium Leaders Excellence award 2000), Pi Sigma Delta (sec. 1989-90), Alpha Delta Mu Avocations: songwriting, reading, music, travel, fashion.

STOTTLEMYRE, DONNA MAE, retired jewelry store executive; b. Mystic, Iowa, Nov. 11, 1928; d. Clarence William and Nina Alene (Millizer) Clark; m. Robert Arthur Stottlemyre, May 8, 1946; children: Roger Dale, Amber Anita, Tamra Collette. Owner, operator Donna's Dress Shop, Unionville, Mo., 1973-76, Donna's Jewelry Box and Bridal Boutique, Unionville, 1978—86, ret. Mem. First Baptist Ch., Sunday Sch. and Bible Sch. tchr. Unionville; 4H Club judge County Fair, Unionville. Mem. C. of C. Avocations: sewing; flower arranging. Home: Stottlemyre 1904 Adams St Unionville MO 63565-1341 Office: Donna's Jewelry and Bridal 1610 Main St Unionville MO 63565-1660

STOUDT, PATRICIA LUPI, secondary school educator; b. Scranton, Pa., Nov. 1, 1958; d. Gene Americo and Barbara Margaret Lupi; m. William Paul Stoudt, Aug. 15, 1981; children: Timothy William, Nathan Daniel. BA, Wilkes Coll., Wilkes-Barre, Pa., 1980. Cert. tchr. Fla. Choral dir., musical theatre dir. Evang. Christian Sch., Fort Myers, Fla., 1996—2003; theatre dir., drama tchr. Mariner HS, Cape Coral, Fla., 2003—, music dept. chair, choral dir., 2004—. Mem.: Fla. Thespians Soc., Internat. Thespians Soc., Music Educators Assn., Fla. Vocal Assn. Conservative. Baptist. Avocations: horseback riding, singing, painting. Home: 20037 Welborn Rd North Fort Myers FL 33917 Office: Mariner High Sch 701 Chiquita Blvd N Cape Coral FL 33993 Office Phone: 239-772-3324. Office Fax: 239-772-4880. Personal E-mail: gladsong@earthlink.net. Business E-Mail: patricials@lee.k12.fl.us.

STOUT, ELVA CAROLYN FRASER, elementary school educator; b. Independence, Mo., Oct. 20; d. Gertrude Alleen Warnke, Charles Allen Fraser; m. Forrest Eugene Stout; children: Sherri Jones, Karrie Henricks, F. Evan, Eric. BS, Appalachian State U., 1972; MEd, Augusta State U., 1978; postgrad., U. S.C., 1984—88. T-6 profl. tchg. cert. Tchr. T. A. Dugger Jr. High, Elizabethton, Tenn., 1972—74, A. C. Griggs, Augusta, Ga., 1974—75, Bel Air Elem., Evans, Ga., 1975—88, Lakeside Mid. Sch., Evans, 1988—92, Riverside Mid. Sch., Evans, 1992—2003; astronomy, earth scis. cons., 2003—. Field tester Am. Geol. Inst., 1999; evaluator Scope poster, 2000; reviewer, evaluator Astronomy Edn. Rev., 2002. Adult Sunday sch. tchr. First Bapt. Ch., Augusta, 1975—. Named Outstanding Sci. Tchr., Sigma Xi, 1994, AASTRA Tchr., Am. Astron. Soc., 1996, 1997, Rsch. Based Sci. Edn. Tchr., Nat. Optical Astronomy Observatories, 1999, Best Tchr. in Sci. and Math., 1991, Best Tchr. in Sci. and Tech., 1993—94; recipient Internat. Educator of the Yr., Internat. Biog. Centre/Cambridge, England, 2004. Mem.: Profl. Assn. Ga. Educators (membership coord. sch. 1980—91), Ga.'s Sci. Tchrs.' Assn., Nat. Earth Sci. Tchrs. Assn. (presenter), Nat. Assn. Geoscience Tchrs. (Ga.'s Outstanding Earth Sci. Tchr. 1996), Phi Delta Kappa (assoc.), Alpha Delta Kappa (assoc.; dist. chaplain 1980—82). Baptist. Avocations: fossil "hunter", amateur astronomer, painting, travel. Home: 4800 Woodbridge Pl Evans GA 30809 Personal E-mail: TeacherES@aol.com.

STOUT, LEEANN MARIE, secondary school educator; b. Jacksonville, Fla., Sept. 22, 1980; d. Candace and Kenneth Williams (Stepfather), Bruce Paul and Stella Stout (Stepmother). BS in Social Sci Edn., U. Ctrl. Fla., Orlando, 1999—2003. Cert. Tchr. Fla. Dept. Edn., 2003, ESL Tchr. Fla. Dept. Edn., 2006. Social studies tchr. Winter Springs HS, Fla., 2003—. Key club co-sponsor Winter Springs HS, 2004—06, student govt. sponsor, 2005—, winter springs writes com. mem., 2005—, world history articulation coord., 2005—. Contbr. instrnl. guide. Vol. Mission Ho. Homeless Shelter, Jacksonville Beach, 1998—2000; bd. mem. Eagle Glen Homeowners Assn., Winter Springs, 2005—06; asst. youth min. Holy Family Episcopal Ch., Orlando, Fla., 1999—2001. Mem.: Seminole County Edn. Assn. Office Phone: 320-8750.

STOUT, MARY WEBB, dean; b. Richmond, Va., Dec. 24, 1947; d. Frank Edmond Webb and Edith Diuguid (Harris) Webb Steger; m. Teddy Alvin Stout, July 8, 1972. BA, Mary Washington Coll., 1970; MEd, U. Va., Charlottesville, 1972; Edn. Specialist, Coll. William and Mary, 1991, EdD, 1995; cert. in Multimedia Devel., George Mason U., 2003. Cert. Red Cross water safety instr. Tchr. Harrisonburg City Sch., Va., 1970-71, Buckingham County Sch., Va., 1972-73; guidance counselor So. European Task Force US Army, Vicenza, Italy, 1973-78, edn. specialist Quartermaster Sch. Ft. Lee, Va., 1978-80, edn. specialist Tng. Support Ctr. Ft. Eustis, Va., 1980-82; edn. specialist Hdqs. Tng., Doctrine Command, Ft. Monroe, Va., 1982-83; edn. svc. specialist Combined Arms Ctr., Ft. Leavenworth, Kans., 1983-88; instrnl. systems specialist Hdqs. TRADOC, Ft. Monroe, 1988-98; supervisory edn. svc. specialist Hdqs. US Army Pers. Command, Alexandria, Va., 1998-2000; edn. program specialist OSD Office of Chancellor Edn. and Profl. Devel., Arlington, Va., 2000—03; online faculty U. Phoenix, 2002—; edn. program specialist OSD Civilian Pers. Mgmt. Svcs., Arlington, 2003—05; acad. dean, dep. dir. U.S. Marine Corps War Coll., Quantico, Va., 2005—. Mem. devel. bd. Sch. Edn. Coll. William and Mary, 2002—. Legis. affairs rep. Running Man Homeowners Assn., Yorktown, Va., 1996—98; treas. Massanetta Springs Alumni Assn., Harrisonburg, Va., 1988—2002, membership chmn., 1998—2002, pres., 2002—04, reunion com., 2004—06. Recipient Alumni award Massanetta Springs Alumni Assn., 1996. Mem.: ASTD, U.S. Distance Learning Assn., Assn. for Instnl. Rsch., Assn. Study Higher Edn., Mary Washington Coll. Alumni Assn., U. Va. Alumni Assn., Coll. William and Mary Alumni Assn., Kappa Delta Pi. Presbyterian. Avocation: running. Home: 6006 River Dr Mason Neck VA 22079-4127 Office: Marine War Coll Marine Corps Univ 2076 South St Quantico VA 22134 Personal E-mail: mstout8895@aol.com.

STOUT, MAYE ALMA, secondary school educator; b. Reliance, S.D., Mar. 3, 1920; d. Jesse Wilbur and Susie Maude (Fletcher) Moulton; m. Dennis William Stout, Jan. 6, 1943; children: Perry Wilbur, David Jay. BA, Dakota Wesleyan U., Mitchell, S.D., 1969. Tchr. Rural Lyman County Sch., Iona/Oacoma, S.D., 1939-42, Vivian (S.D.) Pub. Sch., 1942, Rural Lyman County Sch., Reliance, S.D., 1944-45, Reliance Cons. Dist., 1945-46, 49-51, Ft. Pierre (S.D.) Ind. Sch. Dist., 1954-67, Kadoka (S.D.) Ind. Sch., 1967-82; ret. Asst. editor: Jackson/Washabaugh County History 2, 1989; contbr. articles to publications. Vol. bingo Kadoka Care Ctr., 1982-2005, vol.Veterans and Meml. Day services, 1987-2004; pres. Kadoka Community Betterment Assn., 1987; vol. Meals for Elderly; Sunday sch. tchr. asst.; tchr. 55 Alive, 1991-93; pres. Pierre/Ft. Pierre ACEI; taughy Sunday sch. 5th grade 1st United Meth. Ch., 1953-67 Mem. Am. Legion Aux. (dist. pres. 1985-89, chmn. com. Dept. Fgn. Rels. 1990-91, dept. chmn. constitution and by-laws com. 1992-93). Republican. Methodist. Avocations: reading, crocheting, travel. Address: PO Box 231 Kadoka SD 57543-0231 E-mail: mastout@gwtc.net.

STOUT, PATRICIA A., communications educator; b. St. Louis, Jan. 21, 1950; BA in Anthropology, U. Ariz., 1979; postgrad., U. Minn., 1979-81; PhD in Comm., U. Ill., 1985. Advt. mgr. alumni publ. U. Mont., Missoula, 1978-79; acct. mgmt. Judge Advt., Pub. Rels., Helena, Mont., 1979; tchg. asst., Sch. Journalism & Mass Comm. U. Minn., Mpls., 1979-80; project asst. Minn. Cmty. Prevention Program, 1980-81; vis. lectr. dept. advt. U. Ill., Urbana, 1981-84; asst. prof. dept. advt. U. Tex., Austin, 1984-90, assoc. prof. dept. advt., 1990—, assoc. dean acad. affairs Coll. Comm., 1996—. Vis. rsch. prof. Ctrs. for Disease Control and Prevention, Atlanta, 1993-94; vis. assoc. prof. dept. mktg. and internat. bus. U Auckland, New Zealand, 1994; chmn. 5 doctoral coms., numerous masters theses, profl. reports U. Tex., Austin, mem., reader numerous others; dir. grad. studies dept. advt. U. Tex., Austin, Fall 1990, Summer 1993; ad hoc reviewer Jour. Advt., Jour. Consumer Rsch., Jour. Pub. Policy & Mktg., Journalism Quar., Critical Studies in Mass Comm., Jour. Bus. Rsch. Author: (with John D. Leckenby and Nugent Wedding) Advertising Management, (with Michael Solomon and Kim Rotzoll) The Advertising Around Us: A Consumer Perspective on Marketing Communications; editor procs. of 1990 Am. Acad. of Advt. Conf.; contbr. tech. papers, procs., articles to profl. jours.; presenter in field. Recipient cartoon caption contest first place award Olympia Beer Distbrs., Missoula, Mont., 1978-79, Jour. Advt. best article award Am. Acad. Advt., 1993, vis. rsch. prof. intergovernmental pers. act award Nat. AIDS Edn. and Info. Program, Ctrs. for Disease Control and Prevention, Atlanta, 1993-94; Pub. Health Svc. Tng. fellow Lab. Physiological Hygiene, U. Minn., 1980-81, Houston Harte Centennial Comm. fellow U. Tex., Austin, 1987-88, Am. Acad. Advt. Industry fellow Advt. Rsch. Found, N.Y., 1993-94; dissertation rsch. grantee U. Ill., 1984-85, summer rsch. grantee U. Tex., Austin, 1984-85, direct support grantee U. Tex., 1985-86, 86-87, rsch. grantee Am. Acad. Advt., 1985-86, rsch. grantee Teh Ogilvy Ctr. Rsch. and Devel., San Francisco, 1985-86, U. Rsch. Inst. spl. rsch. grantee U. Tex., 1988-89, 95-96, Columbia U. Tech. Studies Seminar grantee Freedom Forum Media Studies Ctr., 1992-93, immunization of Tex. children co-investigator grantee Tex. Dept. Health, 1995-96, an exploratory study on appropriate internet content and use standards for children co-investigator grantee Hogg Found. for Mental Health, 1996-97. Mem. Internat. Comm. Assn. (ad hoc reviewer), Am. Acad. Advt. (treas. 1989, v.p. 1990, pres. elect 1991, pres. 1992, past pres. 1993, publs. com. 1997—, ad hoc reviewer), Assn. Consumer Rsch. (ad hoc reviewer), Assn. Edn. in Journalism and Mass Comm., Soc. Consumer Psychology, Phi Kappa Phi, Kappa Tau Alpha, Alpha Delta Sigma. Avocations: photography, hiking. Home: 5508 Great Divide Dr Austin TX 78738-6123 Office: Univ Tex Dept Advt CMA 7142 Austin TX 78712

STOUT, SHARON SPARKES, elementary school educator, counselor; d. Thomas and Frances Sparkes; m. Marvin Stout (div.); children: Franchesca Stout Jorgensen, Megan Stout Farias. BS in Edn., Ga. So. U., 1971, MEd, 1973; Cert. Advanced Grad. Studies, Fitchburg State Coll., 1983. Lic. mental health counselor Mass., marriage and family therapist Mass.; ednl. psychologist Mass., rehab. therapist Mass., cert. prin., reading tchr., elem. tchr., spl. edn. tchr., sch. psychometrist Ga. Spl. edn. tchr. Bulloch County Schs., Statesboro, Ga., 1971—73; learning disability specialist Screven County Schs., Sylvania, Ga., 1973—75; spl. edn. tchr. Harwich (Mass.) Pub. Schs., 1975—77, Eastham (Mass.) Elem. Sch., 1977—78; elem. sch. tchr. Chatham (Mass.) Pub. Schools, 1978—86, counselor, 1986—, devel., coord. caring for each student and bully prevention program, 2001—. Founder, dir. Cape Cod Learning Ctr., Harwich, 1980—87. Ed. chmn. Jr. Women's Club, Harwich, 1975—77; co-president Harwich Parent, Tchr. and Friends Orgn., Harwich, 1977—78; v.p. Cape Cod chpt. Mass. Assn. for Children with Learning Disabilities. Grantee, Dept. of Justice, 2001—03, Mass. Dept. Edn., 2003—06. Office: Chatham Pub Schs 147 Depot Rd Chatham MA 02633 Office Phone: 508-945-5135. Personal E-mail: capecod2000@comcast.net. Business E-Mail: sstout@chatham.k12.ma.us.

STOUTENBERG, HERMINIA LILIA, art educator; b. Kingsville, Tex., Mar. 30, 1960; d. Pedro and Gloria Villareal; m. Mitchell Jay Stoutenberg, Jan. 9, 1982; children: Breann Marie, Melisa Jay. BFA, U. Alaska, Fairbanks, BA in Secondary Edn. with honors. Cert. secondary edn., psychology, English lit., and highly qualified Nat. Bd. Profl. Tchg. Stds. Tchr. art Eielson Jr. H.S., Eielson AFB, Alaska, Eielson H.S. Nominee BP Tchr. of Yr., 2004, 2005, 2006; named Eielson Tchr. of Yr., Eielson H.S., 2003, Scholastic Art and Writing Tchr. of Excellence, 1997. Mem.: NEA, Nat. Art Edn. Assn., Fairbanks Edn. Assn. Roman Catholic. Avocations: drawing, painting, reading, snow machining, skiing. Office: Ben Eielson Jr Sr HS 675 Ravens Way Eielson Afb AK 99702-1308 Home: 3004 Timberbrook Dr North Pole AK 99705

STOVAL, LINDA, political party official; b. Kans. m. Toby Stoval. Worked on staff campaigns Gov. Dean, Senator Kerry, former Dem. Gov. Mike Sullivan, and others; local to presdl. activist, organizer, strategist, owner Gravitas Coaching Internat., Wyo.; chairperson Wyo. Dem. Party, 2001—03; polit. leadership coach, 2005—. Former chair Make-A-Wish, Wyo.; former vice chair Habitat for Humanity, Wyo.; former chair Wyoming (Americorps). Mailing: Gravitas Coaching Internat 737 Kirk Ave Casper WY 82601-3324 Office Phone: 877-734-8624. Business E-Mail: linda@gravitascoaching.com.

STOVALL, CARLA JO, former state attorney general; b. Hardner, Kans., Mar. 18, 1957; d. Carl E. and Juanita Joe (Ford) Stovall. BA, Pittsburg State U., Kans., 1979; JD, U. Kans., 1982, MPA, 1993. Bar: Kans. 1982, U.S. Dist. Ct. Kans. 1982. Pvt. practice, Pitts., 1982—85; atty. Crawford County, Pitts., 1984—88; gov. Kans. Parole Bd., Topeka, 1988—94; atty. gen. State of Kans., Topeka, 1995—2002. Lectr. law Pittsburg State U., 1982—84. Mem. bd. govs. U. Kans. Sch. Law; Nat. Ctr. Missing and Exploited Children; Am. Legacy Found.; Nat. Crime Prevention Coun.; Coun. State Govts.; mem. bd. govs. Kans. Children's Cabinet; pres. NAAG, 2001—02, chmn. exec. com. midwest region, sexually violent predator com., 1995—96; Bd. dirs., sec. Pittsburg Family YMCA, 1983—88. Named Outstanding Atty. Gen., Nat. Assn. Attys. Gen., 2001, Topeka Fraternal Order of Police's Amb. to Law Enforcement; recipient Champion award, Campaign Tobacco Free Kids, 2002, Adam Walsh Children's Fund Rainbow award, Nat. Ctr. Missing and Exploited Children, 2001, Kelley-Wyman award, Nat. Assn. Attys. Gen., 2001, Person of the Yr., Kans. Peace Officer Assn.'s Law Enforcement, Morton Baud Allied Profl. award, Nat. Orgn. Victim Assistance, Father Ken Czillinger award, Nat. Parents Murdered Children, Disting. Svc. to Kans. Children award, Kans. Children's Svc. League, Woman of Achievement award, Miss Kans. Pageant. Mem.: NAAG (pres. 2001—02), AAUW (bd. dirs. 1983—87), ABA, Bus. and Profl. Women Assn. (Young Careerist award 1984), Nat. Coll. Dist. Attys., Kans. County and Dist. Attys. Assn., Crawford County Bar Assn. (sec. 1984—85, v.p. 1985—86, pres. 1986—87), Kans. Bar Assn., Kans. Assn. Commerce and Industry (Leadership Kans. award 1983), Pittsburg Area C. of C. (bd. dirs. 1983—85, Leadership Pitts. award 1984), Pittsburg State U. Alumni Assn. (bd. dirs. 1983—88). Republican. Methodist. Avocations: travel, photography, tennis. Home: 138 S Blue Bells Ct Garden Plain KS 67050-9225

STOVER, CAROLYN NADINE, middle school educator; b. Martinsburg, W.Va., May 30, 1950; d. Norman Robert and Garnet Agnes (Zombro) Whetzel; m. James Stenner Stover Sr., Nov. 20, 1971; children: Heather N., James S. Jr. BA in Home Econs., Shepherd Coll., 1972; cert. in advanced studies, W.Va. U., 1978; cert. in tchg. methods, Marshall U., 1973; cert. in spl. edn., Shippensburg Coll., 1972. Cert. tchr., W.Va., N.Mex.; reg. EMT. Substitute tchr. Berkeley County Schs., Martinsburg, W.Va., 1972, adult edn. instr., 1972-77, home econs. instr., 1973-83; substitute tchr. Ruidoso Mcpl. Schs., N.Mex., 1984—90, child find coord. Region 9 edn. coop., 1990, life skills and at-risk educator, 1991—, coord. coun., 1991—93, mem. budget com. N.Mex., 1993. Elder First Presbyn. Ch., Ruidoso, 1984-90, 94-96, 2002-; sponsor Acad. Booster Club, Ruidoso, 1993—; instr. CPR, 1980. Named Outstanding Young Women of Am., 1981. Mem. NEA, Nat. Middle Sch. Assn., Ruidoso Edn. Assn. (reporter, membership chair), Ruidoso Bowling Assn. (sec. 1999-2001), Rotary (youth leadership councilor 1991—), Alph Delta Kappa (pres.-elect 2006-). Democrat. Avocations: cross stitch, needlecrafts, sports. Home: Box 7837 PO Box 7837 Ruidoso NM 88355-7837 Office: Ruidoso Mid Sch 100 Reese Dr Ruidoso NM 88345-6016 Business E-Mail: stovere@ruidoso.k12.nm.us.

STOVER, ELLEN L., health scientist, psychologist; b. Bklyn., Nov. 21, 1950; d. Ralph and Charlotte (Tulchin) Simon; m. Alan B. Stover, June 3, 1973; children: Elena Randall Simon, Randall Alan Simon, Samantha Anne Simon. BA with honors, U. Wis., 1972; PhD, Catholic U., 1978. Cons. NIMH, Rockville, Md., 1972-74, exec. sec. drug abuse rsch. review com., 1974-76, spl. asst. to assoc. dir. extramural programs Rockville, Md., 1976-77, chief, small grants program, 1977-79, asst., acting & chief rsch. resources br., 1980-85, dep. dir., div. basic scis., 1985-88, dir. office AIDS, 1988-97, dir. divsn. mental disorders, behavioral rsch. and AIDS, 1997—; dir. Ctr. Mental Health Rsch. on AIDS. Dir. divsn. AIDS, health, behavior NIMH. Recipient Superior Svc. award USPHS, 1987, 92, 93, Dir.'s award NIH, 1996, Presdl. Rank award, 2001. Mem. APA, Am. Psychol. Soc. Avocations: gardening, dance. Office: NIMH 6001 Executive Blvd Rm 6217 Bethesda MD 20892-0001 Office Phone: 301-443-9700. Business E-Mail: estover@nih.gov.

STOVICH, JOY, chemistry professor; b. Lubbock, Tex., July 25, 1963; d. A.L. and Doris Dean King; m. Laurence C. Stovich, Aug. 30, 1996; children: Jacob Morehead, Rebekah Morehead. BS in Chemistry, West Tex. State U., Canyon, 1985, BS in Math. Edn., 1985. Cert. environ. trainer, hazardous waste mgmt. Tchr. math. Canyon Jr. H.S., 1986-87; math./sci. tchr. San Jacinto Christian Acad., Amarillo, Tex., 1987-91; chemistry technician Mason & Hanger-Pantex, Amarillo, 1991-92, emergency response OSHA trainer, 1992-96, sect. mgr., 1996-97; instr. Traveling Chemistry Show West Tex. A&M U., Canyon, 1997—. Mem. Am. Chem. Soc., Nat. Sci. Tchrs. Assn., Sci. Tchrs. Assn. Tex. Avocations: scuba diving, reading, swimming. Home: 6403 Ridgewood Dr Amarillo TX 79109-6544 E-mail: chem4fun@cox-internet.com.

STOWE, JYNNE R., athletic trainer; b. Anderson, SC, Aug. 2, 1979; d. Timothy E. and Gwendolyn T. Stowe. BS, Erskine Coll., Due West, SC, 2001; MS, Va. Commonwealth U., Richmond, 2003—04. Cert. athletic trainer Nat. Athletic Trainers Assn., 2002, lic. Va. Bd. Medicine, 2003. Interim head athletic trainer Belmont Abbey Coll., NC, 2002, asst. athletic trainer, 2002—03; grad. asst. athletic trainer Va. Commonwealth U., 2003—04; head athletic trainer Caroline HS, Milford, Va., 2004—06, Anderson Phys. Therapy/Westside HS, 2006—. HS youth worker Crowders Creek ARP Ch., Gastonia, NC, 2002—03; mid. sch. youth worker First Bapt. Ch., Richmond, 2003—05. Scholar Grad. Assistantship, Va. Commonwealth U., 2003—04. Mem.: SC Athletic Trainers Assn., Nat. Athletic Trainers Assn. R-Consevative. Presbyterian. Avocations: singing, piano, running, sports. Home: 142 Caleb Ct Anderson SC 29265 Office: Anderson Physical Therapy/Westside HS 100 Healthy Way Ste 1110 Anderson SC 29621 Office Phone: 864-261-3099.

STOYAN, HORTENSIA RODRÍGUEZ-SÁNCHEZ, library administrator; b. Yabucoa, P.R., June 9, 1917; d. Antonio and Juana (Sanchez) R.; m. Hector Aponte (dec.); children: Gloria, Jose. BA, U. P.R., Rio Piedras, 1943; MA, State Tchrs. Coll., 1946; MS, Columbia U., 1955. Cert. pub. librarian. Tchr. elem. and jr. H.S. Town of Juncos (P.R.) Dept. Edn., 1941-44; pub. libr. Bklyn. Pub. Library, Bklyn., 1954-58; head libr. John A. Howe Library, Albany, N.Y., 1958-65; asst. dir. Farmingdale (N.Y.) Pub. Library, 1967-77, ret., 1977. Author: History of Yabucoa, 1993; contbr. articles Cana Guarapo y Melao, 1995-98. Bd. dirs. Mentally Ill Assn., 1984-98. Mem. AAUW (bd. dirs. 1996, pres. Queens N.Y. br. 1999-2001). Avocation: poetry.

STOYK, KAY MARIE, special education educator; d. Frederick William and Olive Mae Welch Stoyk. BS in Edn., Ctrl. Mich. U., Mt. Pleasant, 1982; MA in Early Childhood, Siena Heights Coll., Adrian, Mich., 1996. Spl. edn. tchr. Hillsdale (Mich.) County Intermediate Sch. Dist., 1983—. Asst. area dist. Spl. Olympics, 1990—2026; supr. Best Buddies, Hillsdale County, 1991—2006. Avocations: sports, travel, reading. Office: HCISD 3471 Beck Rd Hillsdale MI 49242

STOYTCHEVA, LILIA STEFANOVA, concert pianist, educator; b. Sofia, Bulgaria, July 13, 1962; arrived in US, 1995; d. Stefan Sotirov Stoytchev and Liliana Georgieva Sarafova. Studied with Liuba Entcheva, Bulgarian State Conservatory, M in Piano summa cum laude, 1987; M of Music summa cum laude, Winthrop U., Rock Hill, S.C., 1997; MusD in Piano Performance, U. Iowa, Iowa City, 2005. Instr. piano Bulgarian State Conservatory, Sofia, 1988—92; asst. prof. piano Sofia's U. "Kliment Ohridski", 1988—90; prof. piano State Conservatory, Czech Republic, 1992—95; asst. prof. Ctrl. State U., Wilberforce, Ohio, 2003—06; assoc. prof. piano North Greenville U., Tigerville, SC, 2006—. Composer: 1300 Anniversary Bulgaria, 1981; musician (solo pianist): Symphony Orch. of the Bulgarian State Conservatory, 1987, Symphony Orchestra of Biel/Bienne, 1992, The Jihoceske Chamber Orchestra of South Bohemia, 1992, Academic Symphony Orch. U. Iowa; musician: (pianist) Hancher Auditorium, 2002, Harper Hall, 2001, 2002, Clapp Hall, 2001, 2002, Rudolf Steiner House and St. Cyprianus Ch. Eng., 2001, Concert Hall at the Conservatory of Stravanger, 2002, Salle Munch at Ecole Normal de Musique, 2002. Recipient award, Nat. Composition Competition, Bulgaria, 1981, Internat. Piano Competition, Italy, 1988, John Simms award, 1998, 1999, 2001, award, Maia Quartet Competition, 2001; fellow Internat. Piano Master Classes with Norma Fisher, London, UK, 2001, Internat. Piano Master Classes with Nelson Delle-Vigne, John Perry, Phillippe Entremont and Einar Nokleberg, Paris, 2002; grantee, George Soros Found. Open Soc., Sofia, 1992; scholar Internat. Piano Master Classes with Rudolf Buchbinder and Victor Merzhanov, Switzerland, 1992, 1993, Walter Hautzig Piano Master Classes, S.C., 1995, 1996, U. Iowa, 2001, Internat. Piano Workshop, Stavanger, Norway, 2002. Mem.: Studio of the Young Musician, Coll. Music Soc., Phi Kappa Phi. Avocations: travel, fine arts, languages. Personal E-mail: lstoytch@hotmail.com.

STRACHAN, DINA DAWN, dermatologist, educator; AB in Biology, Harvard Coll., Cambridge, Mass., 1988; MD, Yale Med. Sch., New Haven, Conn., 1994. Lic. Am. Bd. Dermatology, 1998. Internship medicine U. Calif., San Francisco, 1994—95, residency dermatology, 1995—98, asst. prof. LA, 1999—2000; asst. prof. dept. medicine, divsn. dermatology King/Drew Med. Ctr., LA, 1999—2000; asst. clin. prof. Columbia U. Coll. Physicians & Surgeons, NYC, 2001—. Mem. Battery Dance Co., NYC, 2003—05. Recipient 40 Under Forty Achievement award, Network Jour., 2003, Best Drs. award, 2004—06. Fellow: Am. Acad. Dermatology; mem.: Manhattan County Med. Soc., Empire State Med. Assn., Med. Soc. State NY, Nat. Med. Assn. Office: 161 Sixth Ave 13th Fl New York NY 10013 Office Fax: 212-462-4130.

STRACHAN, LINDA AVERY, federal agency administrator; BA, Greensboro Coll. Spl. asst. to asst. adminstr., Offices Pesticides & Toxic Substances EPA; spl. asst. to asst. sec, Bur. Oceans, Internat. Environ. & Scientific Affairs US Dept. State, Washington; dir. congl. affairs Monsanto Co.; asst. sec. for congl. rels. USDA, Washington, 2006—.

STRACHAN, NELL B., lawyer; b. Portland, Oreg., Feb. 1, 1941; d. Louis and Agnes (Clarke) Berelson; m. Peter D. Ward, Feb. 19, 1982; children—Sarah, Margaret, Jane; stepchildren— Anne, Amy Ward. B.A., Whitman Coll., Wash., 1962; J.D. with honors, Univ. Md., 1974. Bar: Md. 1974, DC, U.S. Dist. Ct. Md. 1974, U.S. Ct. Appeals (4th cir.) 1976. Assoc., Venable, Baetjer & Howard (now Venable LLP), Balt., 1974-81, ptnr., Comml. Litigation, Appellate Litigation practices, 1982—. Chmn. task force Balt Sch. System, 1983; chmn. Balt. City Commn. on Women, 1983—85; mem. bd. overseers Whitman Coll. 1994-; mem. Md. central com. Democratic Party, 1983. Mem. ABA (assoc. editor Litigation pub. of litigation sect. 1977-83), Md. Bar Assn. (founding mem. litigation council 1978-82, chmn. judicial eval. com. 1987-91, chair judicial adminstrn. sect., co-chair spl. com. judicial personnel issues). Club: Wranglers Law (Balt.). Office: Venable LLP 1800 Mercantile Bank & Trust Blg 2 Hopkins Plz Ste 2100 Baltimore MD 21201 Office Phone: 410-244-7464. Office Fax: 410-244-7742. Business E-Mail: nbstrachan@venable.com.

STRACK, ALISON MERWIN, neurobiologist; b. Midland, Mich., Apr. 19, 1963; d. William James and Alice (Armstrong) S. BS, U. Mich., 1985; PhD, Washington U., St. Louis, 1990. Asst. rsch. physiologist U. Calif. Sch. Medicine, San Francisco, 1990-97; rsch. fellow Merck Pharms., Rahway, NJ, 1997—2005, sr. rsch. fellow, 2005—. Contbr. articles to profl. jours. Grantee Am. Heart Assn., Calif. affiliate, 1993. Mem. Soc. Neurosci. Office: Merck Rsch Labs Dept Pharmacology R80Y-145 PO Box 2000 Rahway NJ 07065 Office Phone: 732-594-8367.

STRADA, CHRISTINA BRYSON, retired humanities educator, librarian; b. Dunoon, Argyll, Scotland; d. Alexander Paul and Margaret (Spencer) Bryson; m. Joseph Anthony Strada (dec.); children: Michael, David, Elaine, Mary Margaret. AB, SUNY, Fredonia, 1968, MS, 1970; MLS, U. Buffalo, 1973. Library media specialist. Tchr. English Dunkirk (N.Y.) H.S., 1969-70, Cardinal Mindzenty H.S., Dunkirk, 1970-71, Lake Shore Cen. H.S., Angola, N.Y., 1971-72, libr., tchr., 1973-77; libr. dir. Darwin R. Barker Libr. and Mus., Fredonia, 1977-86; tchr., libr. Cassadaga (NY) Valley Sch. Dist., Fredonia, 1990—95; ret., 1995; instr. and librarian Fredonia (N.Y.) HS and BOCES Ednl. Ctr., Fredonia, 1995—2001. Instr. English composition, English lit., libr. rsch. Empire State Coll. N.Y., State Univ. Coll., Fredonia; cons. Friends of Barker Libr. and Mus., 1986—. Author short stories. Rschr. Fredonia Hist. Preservation Soc., 1986—; v.p. Friends of Barker Libr., 2001—; active Patterson Libr. Lit. Discussion Group; sec. NY State Victorian Soc., 2001—02; bd. dirs. Chautauqua County br. Lit. Vols. of Am., Dunkirk, NY, 1998—2001; bd. dirs., v.p. D.R. Barker Friends' Libr., 1997—2003. Mem. AAUW (chmn. telephone and reservations com. 1969—), NY State Libr. Assn., N.Y. State Tchr. Assn., LWV, Fredonia Shakespeare Club (v.p. 1988-89, pres. 1997-98, treas. 2002-03). Republican. Roman Catholic. Avocations: writing, reading, gardening, walking. Home: 15 Carol Ave Fredonia NY 14063-1207

STRAHAN, JULIA CELESTINE, electronics company executive; b. Indpls., Feb. 10, 1938; d. Edgar Paul Pauley and Pauline Barbara (Myers) Shawver; m. Norman Strahan, Oct. 2, 1962 (div. 1982); children: Daniel Keven, Natalie Kay. With Bechtel Nev./Lockheed Martin Nev. Techs., Las Vegas, 1967—; sect. head EG&G Co., 1979-83, mgr. electronics dept., 1984—. Recipient award Am. Legion, 1952, Excellence award, 1986. Mem. NAFE, Am. Nuclear Soc. (models and mentors), Internat. Platform Assn. Home: 5222 Stacey Ave Las Vegas NV 89108-3078 Office: Bechtel Nevada/Lockheed Martin Tech PO Box 98521 Las Vegas NV 89193 Office Phone: 702-295-2859. Personal E-mail: jeweljcs@aol.com.

STRAHM, MARY ELLEN, music educator; d. Edward Carey and Mary Margaret McBride; m. Shaun Robert Strahm, Feb. 16, 1976. MusB in Pipe Organ, Ohio U., Athens, 1971; MA in Music Edn., Ohio State U., Columbus, 1978. Elem. vocal music specialist Licking Valley Sch. Dist., Newark, Ohio, 1972—2003, St. Nicholas Sch., Zanesville, Ohio, 2003—06, Bishop Fenwick Sch., Zanesville, 2006—. Dir. of music St. John's Luth. Ch., Evang. Luth. Ch. Am., Zanesville, 2000—. Vol. Eastside Food Pantry, Newark, 1988—98; bd. dirs. Friends and Alumni of Sch. of Music, Ohio U., Athens, 1990—99. Mem.: Friends and Alumni of Sch. of Music of Ohio U. (v.p. 1995—97, bd. dirs. 1990—99), Am. Guild Organists, Ohio Music Edn. Assn. (25-Yr. award 1998), Music Educators Nat. Conf. (assoc.). Democrat. Lutheran. Avocations: walking, reading, photography. Home: 5512 Licking Valley Rd NE Nashport OH 43830 Office: Bishop Fenwick Sch 1030 E Main St Zanesville OH 43701 Office Phone: 740-453-2637.

STRAIGHT ARROW, JANET, holistic professional, educator; b. Orange, NJ, Aug. 3, 1952; d. John Paul and Martha Ann (Gallik) Bachmann; m. Steven Scott Zwiren, Sept. 25, 1971 (div. Feb. 1986); children: Paula Marie, Lisa Michelle. AA in Home Econs., Centenary Coll., Hackettstown, N.J., 1975; BA in Psychology, Coll. St. Elizabeth, Convent Station, N.J., 1987; Reiki master, Unltd. Potential, West Orange. N.J., 1994; grad., Realtors Inst., Edison, N.J., 1994. Cert. residential specialist. Title searcher Chelsea Title, New Brusnwick, NJ, 1972, Stewart Title, Morristown, NJ, 1973—75; title searcher, officer Heritage Abstract, Morristown, 1976—84; mortgage banker Fin. Investment Resources, Morristown, 1987—88, Greater Metro, Wayne, NJ, 1988; realtor residential sales Weichert Realtors, Succasunna, NJ, 1988—91, Re/Max Renown Realty, Randolph, NJ, 1991—99; Reiki Master, Shamanic practitioner Universal Life Energy Healing Ctr., Succasunna, 1994—97; dir., Shaman, Reiki master Oasis for the Soul, 1997—2003; woman of medicine, Shaman Succasunna, 2003—06; woman of medicine, Shaman, writer, spkr. Woodstock, NY, 2006—. Pvt. cons. Bus. Mktg. and Mgmt., Succasunna, 1995—. Leader Girl Scouts U.S.A., Succasunna, 1993, 1985, 88, Denville, N.J., 1981, 84; town coun. reporter League Women Voters, Randolph, 1975. Mem. Nat. Assn. Realtors, N.J. Assn. Realtors (Million Dollar Club bronze and silver awards 1988-98, Remax Internat. Hall of Fame, 1997), Morris County Bd. Realtors, Residential Spl. Coun., Grad. Realtors Inst., Remax Internat. 100 Club. Democrat. Avocations: sailing, reading, hiking, writing, travel. Office: Oasis for the Soul PO Box 1476 Woodstock NY 12498 Office Phone: 800-427-9065, 845-679-7175. Personal E-mail: jstraightarrow@aol.com. Business E-Mail: janetoasis@aol.com.

STRAIT, VIOLA EDWINA WASHINGTON, librarian; b. El Paso, Tex., Aug. 29, 1925; d. Leroy Wentworth and Viola Edwina (Wright) Washington; m. Freeman Adams, Mar. 6, 1943; 1 child, Norma Jean (Mrs. Louis Lee James); m. Clifford Moody, Jan. 8, 1950; 1 child, Viola Edwina III (Mrs. Paul M. Cunningham); m. Amos O. Strait, Dec. 9, 1972. Bus. cert., Tillotson Coll., 1946, BA, 1948; MS in Libr. Sci., U. So. Calif., 1954. Substitute tchr. El Paso Pub. Schs., 1948; sec., bookkeeper U.S.O.-YWCA, El Paso, 1948-50; libr. asst. Spl. Svcs. Libr., Ft. Bliss, Tex., 1950-53, libr., 1954-71; equal employment opportunity officer Ft. Bliss, 1971-72; dep. equal employment opportunity officer Long Beach (Calif.) Naval Shipyard, 1972-85; with Temp. Job Mart, Torrance, Calif., 1986-87; substitute tchr. Ysleta Ind. Sch. Dist., 1988-89; profl. libr. Eastwood Hts. Elem. Sch., 1989-90; sec. Shiloh Bapt. Ch., El Paso, 1991-92; br. mgr. El Paso Pub. Libr., 1992-96, retired, 1996. Host, prodr. (gospel music video with Viola Washington Strait), Time Warner TV, Cable Channel 15, 2003—04. Sec. Sunday sch. Bapt. Ch., 1956-66, 92-96, min. music, 1958-72, supr. young adult choir, 1966-72, pres. sr. choir, 1969-71; disc jockey Sta. KELP, El Paso, 1970-72; host radio show Sta. KTEP, U. Tex., El Paso, 1994-2004; hon. chmn. for ann. observance of Nat. Libr. Week, City of El Paso, 1970. Mem. ALA, Border Region Libr. Assn. (chmn. scholarship com. 1970), NAACP (sec. 1996), Alpha Kappa Alpha. Democrat. Baptist. Avocations: piano, reading. Personal E-mail: vstrait@aol.com.

STRANC, CATHLEEN L., music educator; d. George H. and Nancy L. Stranc. MusB in Bus. in Bus., So. Ill. U., 1982, MusB in edn., 1984; MusM in edn., VanderCook Coll. Music, Chgo., 1995. Cert. edn. Ill., 1984. Choral and instrumental music educator Jersey Cmty. Sch. Dist., Jerseyville, Ill., 1985—95; instrumental music educator Edwardsville (Ill.) Sch. Dist., 1995—. Guest condr. Madison County Band Festival, 2006. Named Employee of the Month, Edwardsville Sch. Dist., 1998, 2000, 2004, 2005, 2006; recipient Outstanding Mid. Sch. Activity Sponsor award, 2005. Mem.: NEA, Madison County Band Dirs. Assn. (sec. 2002—), Ill. Grade Sch. Music Assn. (sec./treas. dist. 5 2005—), Ill. Edn. Assn. (region 45 elections com. chair 2000—), Edwardsville Edn. Assn. (sec. 1998—, Local Leadership award 2005), Ill. Music Educator Assn. (dist. 6 profl. devel. chair 2000—06), Women's Internat. Band Dirs. Assn. (life), Nat. Band Assn. (life), Phi Kappa Phi (life). Home: 1 Rosewood Dr Maryville IL 62062 Office: Edwardsville Community SchoolDistrict #7 #1 District Dr Edwardsville IL 62025 Office Phone: 618-655-6800. Personal E-mail: cstranc@sbcglobal.net.

STRAND, CHERYL MARIE, Spanish language, literature educator; b. Viborg, S.D., Aug. 27, 1944; d. Alfred Nicholi and Lillian Evelyn (Wilson) S.; m. Alan Louis Kalter, Feb. 14, 1981; 1 child, Christopher Michael Kalter-Strand. BS, S.D. State U., 1966; MA, Calif. State U., Fresno, 1969; PhD, U. Calif., L.A., 1989. Tchg. asst. Calif. State U., Fresno, 1968-69, U. Calif., L.A., 1969-72, 76; instr. Ohio State U., Columbus, 1976-77; assoc. U. Wash., Seattle, 1979-83, lectr., Spanish coord., 1983-84, 86-89; instr. Shoreline C.C., Seattle, 1985; assoc. prof. Western Oreg. U., Monmouth, 1989-97, prof., 1997—. Mem. Latin Am. Exec. Bd., Oreg. State Sys. of Higher Edn., 1989-96; chmn. dept. modern langs. Western Oreg. U., Monmouth, 1991-94; mem. Spanish Proficiency Stds. Commn., Chancellor's Office, Oreg. State Sys. Higher Edn., 1993-94; presenter rsch. papers Mid-Am. Conf., Kans., Nebr., 1989, 91, Confedn. Oreg. Fgn. Lang. Tchrs. Conf., 1996, 97. Contbr. articles, reviews to profl. publs. Panelist Office of Fgn. Study Programs, Oreg. State System of Higher Edn., Corvallis, 1992, others. Recipient scholarship for study in Spain, Fulbright, 1972-73, fellowship for doctoral rsch. Del Amo Found., Spain, 1974-75; faculty devel. grantee, 1998. Mem. MLA, Twentieth Century Spanish Assn. of Am., Confedn. of Oreg. Fgn. Lang. Tchrs., AAUW, AAUP, Phi Sigma Iota, Sigma Delta Pi, Phi Kappa Phi. Avocations: photography, travel, meditation. Office: Western Oreg U Dept Modern Langs Monmouth OR 97361

STRAND, MARGARET N., lawyer; b. White Plains, NY, Apr. 27, 1946; BA, U. Rochester, 1968; MA, U. RI, 1971; JD, Coll. William and Mary, 1976. Bar: Va. 1976, DC 1977, US Supreme Ct. Chief, environ. def. sect. environ. and natural resources divsn. U.S. Dept. Justice, Washington, 1984—91; ptnr. Oppenheimer Wolff & Donnelly, Washington, Venable LLP, Washington, 2001—. Lectr. George Washington U., 1993—2002; chair environ. law com. Transp. Rsch. Bd., Nat. Acad. Scis.; bd. dirs. Environ. Law Inst.; mem. editl. bd. Environ. Law Reporter, Nat. Wetlands News. Author: Wetlands Deskbook, 1997; contbr. chapters to books, articles to profl. jours. Named a Top

Washington Lawyer, Washingtonian Mag., 2004, 2005. Mem.: ABA. Office: Venable LLP 575 7th St NW Washington DC 20004 Office Phone: 202-344-4699. Office Fax: 202-344-8300. Business E-Mail: mnstrand@venable.com.

STRANDJORD, M. JEANNINE, telecommunications industry executive; B in Acctg. and Bus. Adminstrn., U. Kans. CPA. V.p. fin. Macy's Midwest; with Kans. city Power & Light Co., Ernst and Whinney; v.p. fin. and distrbn. AmeriSource, Inc. (subs. Sprint), 1985—90, controller, 1986—90, sr. v.p., treas., 1990—98, sr. v.p. fin. global markets group, 1998—2003; sr. v.p. fin. svcs. Sprint Corp., 2003, sr. v.p., chief integration officer, 2003—. Bd. dirs. Am. Century Mutual Funds, DST Sys., Inc., Euronet Worldwide. Trustee Rockhurst U. Office: 6200 Spring Pkwy Overland Park KS 66251

STRANG, RUTH HANCOCK, pediatrician, educator, cardiologist, priest; b. Bridgeport, Conn., Mar. 11, 1923; d. Robert H.W. and Ruth (Hancock) Strang. BA, Wellesley Coll., 1944, postgrad., 1944—45; MD, N.Y. Med. Coll., 1949; MDiv, Seabury We. Theol. Sem., 1993. Diplomate Am. Bd. Pediat.; ordained deacon Episc. Ch., 1993, priest Episc. Ch., 1994. Intern Flower and Fifth Ave. Hosp., N.Y.C., 1949—50, resident in pediat., 1950—52; mem. faculty N.Y. Med. Coll., N.Y.C., 1952—57; fellow cardiology Babies Hosp., N.Y.C., 1956—57, Harriet Lane Cardiac Clinic, Johns Hopkins Hosp., Balt., 1957—59, Children's Hosp., Boston, 1959—62; mem. faculty U. Mich. Hosp., Ann Arbor, 1962—89, prof. pediat., 1970—89, prof. emeritus, 1989—; priest-in-charge St. Johns Episcopal Ch., Howell, Mich., 1994—. Dir. pediat. Wayne County Gen. Hosp., Westland, Mich, 1965-85; mem. staff U. Mich. Hosps., 1962-89; mem. med. adv. com. Wayne County chpt. Nat. Cystic Fibrosis Rsch. Found., 1966-80, chmn. med. adv. com. nat. found., Detroit, 1971-78; cons. cardiology Plymouth (Mich.) State Home and Tng. Sch., 1970-81; diocesan coun. Diocese Mich., 2003-, mem. com. on nominations and elections Diocesan Conv., 2003, chmn. com., 2004. Author: Clinical Aspects of Operable Heart Disease, 1968; contbr. numerous articles to profl. jours. Mem. citizen's adv. coun. Juvenile Ct., Ann Arbor, 1968—76; mem. med. adv. bd. Ann Arbor Continuing Edn. Dept., 1968—77; v.p. Am. Heart Assn. Mich., 1989, pres., 1991; bd. dirs. Livingston Cmty. Hospice, 1995—99, Emrich Episcopal Conf. Ctr., 1998—; ctr. bd. Emrich Episcopal Retreat, 1998—, adv. bd., 1998—; mem. Diocesan Com. for World Relief, Detroit, 1970—72; trustee Episcopal Med. Chaplaincy, Ann Arbor, 1971—96; mem. bishop's com. St. Aidan's Episc. Ch., 1966—69, sec., 1966—68, vestry, 1973—76, 1978—80, 1984—86, 1990—91, sr. warden, 1975—76, 1978, 1986, 1990; del. Episc. Diocesan Conv., 1980, 1991; mem. Congl. Life Circle Episcopal Diocese Mich., 1995—2001, mem. loans and grants com., 1995—99, mem. com. on reference ann. diocesan conv., 1995-98, chmn., 1996; mem. Diocese Mich. Clergy Family Project, 1996—98; co-dean Huron Valley area coun. Diocese Mich., 1998—2000; bd. trustees Ecumenical Theol. Sem., 1996—, chair acad. affairs com., 2000—; mem. Congl. Devel. Commn., 2001—03; bd. dirs. Livingston County Cath. Social Svcs., 2004—; mem. diocesan coun. Episc. Diocese Mich., 2004—. Recipient Alumnae Life Achievement award, Baldwin Sch., 2005. Mem. AMA, Am. Acad. Pediat., Am. Coll. Cardiology, Mich. Med. Soc., Washtenaw County Med. Soc., N.Y. Acad. Medicine, Am. Heart Assn., Women's Rsch. Club (membership sec. 1966-67), Ambulatory Pediat. Assn., Am. Assn. Child Care in Hosps., Am. Assn. Med. Colls., Assn. Faculties of Pediat. Nurse Assn./Practitioners Programs (pres. 1978-81, exec. com. 1981-84), Episc. Clergy Assn. Mich., Northside Assn. Ministries (pres. 1975, 76, 79-80), Soc. Companions of Holy Cross. Home: 4500 E Huron River Dr Ann Arbor MI 48105-9335

STRANG, SANDRA LEE, airline official; b. Greensboro, N.C., Apr. 22, 1936; d. Charles Edward and Lobelia Mae (Squires) S. BA in English, U. N.C., 1960; MBA, U. Dallas, 1970. With Am. Airlines, Inc., 1960—, mgr. career devel. for women N.Y.C., 1972-73, dir. selection and tng., 1974-75, sr. dir. selection, tng. and affirmative action, 1975-79, sr. dir. compensation and benefits Dallas/Ft. Worth, 1979-84, dir. passenger sales tng. and devel., 1984—, regional sales mgr. Rocky Mt. region Denver, 1985—. Pres. The SLS Group, Inc., (DBAs) Sales Leadership Seminars, Inc., Sr. Leadership Svcs., Inc., Svc. Leadership Seminars, Inc., Speakers, Lectrs., and Seminars, Inc, 1988—. Mem. Am. Mgmt. Assn., Assn. Advancement of Women into Mgmt., Am. Soc. Tng. and Devel., Am. Compensation Assn., Internat. Platform Assn., AARP. Office: PO Box 7609 Horseshoe Bay TX 78657-7609 Office Phone: 830-596-1715. E-mail: slsgrp@nctv.com.

STRANGE, ALICE MARIAN, social worker; b. Schenectady, N.Y., May 29, 1935; d. Horace Manchester and Dorothy Grace French; m. Alexander T. Strange, II, Dec. 21, 1973 (dec. Oct. 7, 1993); children: Mary Gartland, Julia Pulcifer, Alexander T. III, Debra Worley, Cindra Finney, Scott McGowan. BA in Sociology, U. Wash., Seattle, 1954; MA in Comty. Orgn., Cen. Mich. U., Mt. Pleasant, 1976; MSW, Mich. State U., East Lansing, 1982. Juvenile officer Sanilac (Mich.) County Probate Ct., 1971—73, Gladwin (Mich.) County Probate Ct., 1973—74; sch. social worker Clare (Mich.) -Gladwin Ind. Sch. Dist., 1974—81, Midland (Mich.) Pub. Sch., 1982—97; liaison Grad. Sch. Social Work Mich. State U., East Lansing, 1998—2002. Mem.: Zonta Club of Midland. Avocations: singing, reading, gardening. Home: 100 Harper Ln Midland MI 48640

STRANGE, SHARON LOUISE, special education educator, musician; d. William Ralph Strange and Lizzie Mae Longware-Strange. BA in Music Edn., Andrews U., Berrien Springs, Mich., 1974—76, BA in Organ Performance, 1978, MA in Music Edn. & Organ Performance, 1979; BA in Edn., Oakwood Coll., Ala., 1977; postgrad., Trinity U., DC, 2004. Cert. elem. & secondary tchr. Md., Ind., DC. Tchr. Indpls. Pub. Sch. Sys., 1979—81; tchr., registrar Seventy-Day Adventist, Oakland, Calif., 1981—82, tchr. Allegheny E. Conf., 1982—87; music and spl. edn. & tech. resource tchr. DC Pub. Sch. Sys., 1988—. Tech. resource cons. DC Pub. Schs., 2000—04; ednl. presenter DC Music Educators Assn., 2000—. Author: (handbook) Ring Ye Into All the World, 1986, (instrl. book) Come All, Ring All-For Handbells, 1988; composer (song book) Sing for Joy, 1990. Resident harpist Providence Hosp. & Manage Care Ctrs., DC, 2000—, Md., 2000—; music therapist nursing care & rehab. ctrs., DC, 2000—, Md., 2000—; mem. Project Linus, DC, 2004—, Md., 2004—; facilitator, instr. Sr. Connection Providence Hosp., DC, 2004—; founder, dir. Children's Harp Ensemble, DC, Adult/Youth Harp Ensemble, DC. Mem.: Folk Harp Soc., Am. Guild English Handbell Ringers, Am. Guild Organist, Music Educators Nat. Conf., Am. Harp Soc., Knitters Guild Am. Avocations: knitting, crocheting, harp. Home and Office: 3704 Suitland Rd SE Washington DC 20020 Personal E-mail: docstrnge@aol.com.

STRANSKY, MARIA SOLEDAD, psychotherapist; d. Theodore Jere and Ana D. Stransky. BA, U. Notre Dame, 1996; MA, U. N.C., Charlotte, 1999. Cert. sex offender treatment provider Commonwealth of Va., 2002. Grants devel. intern Mecklenburg County Health, Mental Health, and Cmty. Svcs., Charlotte, NC, 1998—99; psychology intern Cleve. Ctr., Shelby, NC, 1997—98; psychologist Mental Health Unit, Brunswick Correctional Ctr., Lawrenceville, Va., 1999—2000; psychologist sr. Sex Offender Residential Treatment Program, Brunswick Correctional Ctr., Lawrenceville, Va., 2000—05; asst. dir. Brunswick Correctional Ctr., Sex Offender Residential Treatment Program, Lawrenceville, Va., 2005—. Counselor Behavioral Awareness Ctr., Richmond, Va., 2002—. Mem.: APA (assoc.), Va. Assn. for the Treatment of Sexual Abusers (sec.), Sex Offender Program Action Com., Am. Correctional Assn., Assn. for the Treatment of Sexual Abusers. Office: Brunswick Correctional Ctr 1147 Planters Rd Lawrenceville VA 23868 Personal E-mail: msstrans@earthlink.net. E-mail: maria.stransky@vadoc.virginia.gov.

STRANTZ, NANCY JEAN, law educator, consultant; b. Calgary, Alta., Can., 1958; 1 child. LLB, U. Alta., 1981; JD, South Tex. Coll. Law, Houston, 1990; BA in Social Scis., U. N.D., Grand Forks, 1997. Bar: Alta. 1982. Articling lawyer Carma Developers Ltd., Calgary, 1981-82; barrister and solicitor Stewart & Stewart, Barristers and Solicitors, Calgary, 1982-83; rsch. asst., author Can. Inst. Resources Law, U. Calgary, 1984-85; corp. counsel Chevron Can. Resources, 1985-90, Gulf Can. Resources, 1991-94, 98; asst. prof. U. N.D. Sch. Law, Grand Forks, 1994-97. Land and legal cons. N.J. Strantz Cons., Calgary, 1991-94; adj. faculty U. Calgary, Mt. Royal Coll., So. Alta Inst. Tech., Calgary, 1991-94; with contracts adminstrn. Long View Fibre Co., 2005-. Co-author: A Reference Guide to Hardrock Mining in Canada; contbr. articles to profl. jours. Trustee Rocky Mountain Mineral Law Found., 1994-97. Pvt. Can. Dept. Nat. Def., Naval Res., 1975. Recipient award and grants. Mem. Law Soc. Alta. Avocation: swimming.

STRAPKO, IRENE, science educator; b. New Brunswick, N.J., Feb. 15, 1953; d. Eugene and Nadia Zankovich; m. Walter Strapko, May 4, 1974; children: Matthew, Jennifer. BS in Edn., Ohio U., Athens, 1973; EdM, Cleve. State U., 1977. Tchr. math. Strongsville Bd. Edn., Ohio, 1975—80; tchr. sci. East Brunswick Bd. Edn., NJ, 1995—. Sec. Strongsville Women's League, Ohio, 1983—93, com. chair. Mem.: NEA, N.J. Edn. Assn. Office: Hammarskjold Mid Sch 200 Rues Ln East Brunswick NJ 08816-3694

STRATAS, TERESA (ANASTASIA STRATAKI), soprano; b. Toronto, Ont., Can., May 26, 1938; Studied with Irene Jessner, 1956-59; grad., U. Toronto, 1959; LLD (hon.), McMaster U., 1986, U. Toronto, 1994; degree (hon.), Juilliard Sch. Music, 1995, Eastman Sch. Music, 1998, U. Rochester, 1998. Winner Met. Opera auditions, 1959; major roles in opera houses throughout world include: Mimi in La Bohème; Tatiana in Eugene Onegin; Susanna in The Marriage of Figaro; Nedda in Pagliacci; Marenka in The Bartered Bride; Three Heroines in Il Trittico; Violetta in La Traviata; title role in Rusalka; Jennie in Mahagonny; created title role in completed version of Lulu (Alban Berg), Paris Grand Opera, 1979; film appearances Kaiser von Atlantis, Seven Deadly Sins; Zefirelli's La Traviata, Salome, Lulu, Paganini, Zarewitsch, Eugene Oregin; Broadway debut in Rags, 1986; creator the role of Marie Antoinette Ghosts of Versailles world premiere Met. Opera, 1992; sang both female leading roles Il Tabarro, Pagliacci double bill opening Met. Opera, 1994, numerous recs. including Richard Strauss' Salomé, Songs of Kurt Weill. Decorated Order of Can.; recipient 3 Grammy awards, Emmy award, Drama Desk award, 1986, 3 Grammy nominations, Tony nomination, 1986, Tiffany award, 1994, Highest Paedeia award, 1996, Gemini award, 1997; named Performer of Yr., Can. Music Council, 1979. Home: 6150 Blackjack Ct N Punta Gorda FL 33982-9606

STRATING, SHARON L., elementary school educator, professional staff developer, educational consultant; b. Jamestown, ND, Jan. 20, 1949; d. Walter and Evelyn Darlene (Lang) Remmick; m. Rick Donald Strating, Dec. 24, 1978 (presently divorced); children: Heather Dawn, Amber Nicole, Ashley Renee. BS in Secondary Edn., S.W. Mo. State U., 1971; MEd in Sci. Edn., N.W. Mo. State U., 1992. Cert. elem. tchr., Mo. Tchr. Cassville R-III Sch., 1971-76, Savannah R-III Sch. Sys., Mo., 1976-91; instr. 4th grade Horace Mann Lab. Sch., Maryville, Mo., 1991—2003; profl. staff developer Regional Profl. Devel. Ctr., N.W. Mo. State U., Maryville, 2003—. Facilitator for Environ. Edn. Pilot Project Kans. U., Lawrence; co-chair EPA Pollution Prevention Adv. Task Force; mem. biol. sci. curriculum study Elem. Tchr. Module Project, 1993; instr. for coll. practicum students; Map 2000 Sr. Leader for performance-based assessment sys., Mo., 1994—. Author: Living the Constitution Through the Eyes of the Newspaper, 1987, Tabloid Teaching Tool, 6 edits., 1986-91; tchr. guides in lit. revised editions for Sadako and the Thousand Paper Cranes, The Kid in the Red Jacket, Missing Gator of Gumbo Limbo, Owls in the Family, Where the Waves Break: Life at the Edge of the Sea, 2000-2001; author: Open the Eyes of Children to the World of Literacy Through Comprehensive Literacy, Prof. Develop. Program, 2002. Chairperson March of Dimes, 1972-76, Cystic Fibrosis, 1972-78; scout leader Brownies, 1976-77; exec. bd. dirs. PTA, 1976-82, fund raising chairperson, 1976-83; program chairperson presch. PTA, 1976-80;chairperson community environ. activities, 1976—, Adopt a Hwy. Program, 1976-91; mem. Mo. Stream Team Effort, 1976—. Recipient Nat. Pres. Environ. Youth award, 1988, 89, Presdl. award State of Mo., 1992, 93, Nat. Presdl. award, 1992-93; named Mo. State Tchr. of Yr., 1990-91, Disney Salutes the Am. Tchr. award, 1995. Mem. Nat. Hist. Soc., Internat. Reading Assn., Nat. Bd. for Profl. Tching. Standards and Mid.-Age Child in Sci., Nat. Sci. Tchrs. Assn., Nat. Assn. Lab. Schs. (sec. 1994-95), Sci. Tchrs. Mo. Lutheran. Avocations: travel, ecology, creative writing, motivational speaking, arts and crafts. Office: Northwest Mo State U McKemy Ctr for Lifelong Learning Maryville MO 64468 Home: 3A Faustiana Pl Maryville MO 64468 Office Phone: 660-562-1515.

STRATMAN, HEATHER MARIE, elementary school educator; b. Granite City, Ill., July 22, 1977; d. Carl Kenneth and Laura Ann Stratman. Degree in Ednl. Studies, St. Louis U., 1999; M in Ednl. Leadership, Webster U., St. Louis, 2004. Tchr. 4th grade Rockwood Sch. Dist., Fenton, Mo., 1999—; leadership cons. R.K. Stratman, Inc., Wentzville, 2004—. Grantee, Rockwood Schs. Found., 2003. Mem.: NEA, Internat. Reading Assn. Home: 1669 East Swan Circle Saint Louis MO 63144 Business E-Mail: stratmanheather@rockwood.k12.mo.us.

STRATMANN, GAYLE G., lawyer, consumer products company executive; b. Columbia, Mo., Sept. 13, 1956; BS, MEd, U. Mo., 1979; JD cum laude, U. Mo. Sch. of Law, 1987. Bar: Mo. 1987, Ill. 1988. Atty. Greensfelder, Hemker & Gale, St. Louis, Eveready Battery Co., Inc. (div. of Energizer Holdings), 1990—96, asst. gen. counsel, 1996—2002, v.p. legal ops., 2002—03; v.p., gen. counsel Energizer Holdings, 2003—. Author: Church Employment and the First Amendment, 1986. Mem.: ABA, Mo. Bar Assn., St. Louis Bar Assn. Office: Energizer Holdings 533 Maryville University Dr Saint Louis MO 63141

STRATOS, KIMARIE ROSE, lawyer, sports association executive; b. Miami, Fla., Aug. 24, 1960; d. Jack Sloshower and Charmaine (McDougal) S. BS with high honors, U. Fla., 1981, JD with honors, 1984. Bar: Fla. 1985, U.S. Dist. Ct. (so. and mid. dist.) Fla. 1987. Ptnr. Shutts & Bowen, Miami, 1984—85, 1986—96; chair sports law dept., law clk. to judge U.S. Dist. Ct. for So. Dist. Fla., Miami, 1985-86; prin. Kimarie R. Stratos, PA, 1996—; gen. counsel Miami Children's Hosp. Bd. dirs. Fla. Sports Found., 1992—, vice chmn., 1995, chmn., 1996-; mem. Miami's 1999 Super Bowl Com. Co-author, asst. editor: Facility Development and the Sports Authority, Law of Professional and Amateur Sports; asst. editor: Clark Boardmen, 1990; contbr. articles to profl. jours. Inducted into U. Fla. Hall of Fame. Mem. ABA, Fla. Bar (bd. govs. young lawyers sect. 1987-93, exec. coun. entertainment, arts and sports law sect. 1988—), Fla. Assn. Women Lawyers, Sports Lawyers Assn. (nat. v.p. 1988-90, 93—, bd. dirs. 1990—); Phi Delta Phi, Fla. Blue Key. Avocations: running, travel. Office: Miami Children's Hosp 3100 SW 62nd Ave Miami FL 33155-3009 E-mail: kimarie.strattos@mch.net.

STRATTON, BETTY, realtor; d. Newell and Annabelle Strang; children from previous marriage: Gregory, Karen McCullock. Attended, Mont. State U., Bozeman, 1957. Realtor Realty Assoc. P.C., Billings, Mont., 1978—. Mem. bd. Billings Symphony, 1998—2002. Named Sales Person of Yr., State of Mont., 1991; recipient, Billings Assn. Realtors, 1991. Office: Realty Assoc PC Ste 9 71 25th St W Billings MT 59102 Home: 2252 Remington Sq Billings MT 59102 Office Phone: 406-652-2211. Business E-Mail: bettys@realtyassoc.com. E-mail: bettystratton@msn.com.

STRATTON, DOROTHY E., painter, printmaker; b. Worchester, Mass., Dec. 21, 1908; d. Robert Alexander and Edith Amy Stratton; m. William Asbury King, Oct. 22, 1947 (dec. 1989); m. Michael Hicks-Beach, May 25, 1928 (dec. 1994); 1 child, Heather Hicks-Beach. Studied drawing and painting, Pratt Inst., Bklyn., 1942, Bklyn. Mus. Sch., 1943, Acad. Grande Chaumiere, Andre Lhote, Paris, 1947—48; studied with Rico Lebrun, UCLA, 1956—57; studied printmaking, U. Calif., San Diego, 1966—67. Profl. artist; adminstr. art asst. LA Mcpl. Art Commn. Gallery, 1952—61; contbr. Arts In Embassies Program, 1965—80; registrar La Jolla Mus. Sch., Calif., 1965—69. Tchr. printmaking U. Calif., San Diego, 1966—67. Represented in permanent collections Georgetown U. Fine Print Collections, Corcoran Mus. Art, Washington, DC, Nat. Mus. Women in Arts, Smithsonian Instn., Acadia U., Nova Scotia, Can., U. San Diego, Pushkin Mus. Fine Art, Moscow, Long Beach Mus. Art, Calif., LA Mcpl. Art Commn., and others, one-woman shows include Pasadena Art Mus., 1959, La Jolla Mus. Contemporary Art, Calif., 1962, Jefferson Gallery, La Jolla, 1963, Maison of Culture, Tunis, Tunisia, 1965, Athenaeum, La Jolla, 1966, 1978, Roberts Gallery, Santa Monica, Calif., 1969, U. San Diego Founders' Gallery Retrospectives, 1980, 1994, Spectrum Gallery, San Diego, 1982, San Diego Print Club Gallery, 1984—85, Washington Printmakers Gallery, Washington, DC, 1985, 1988, Marymount U., Arlington, Va., 1990, Acadia U., Nova Scotia, 1991, Washington Printmakers Gallery, Washington, DC, 1992, exhibited in group shows at Calif. Soc. Printmakers Nat. Traveling Exhibits, 1972—90, Pratt Graphics Ctr., NY, 1980—83, Washington Printmakers Gallery, 1983—94, Brighton Press Gallery, San Diego, 1986, Corcoran Gallery Art, Washington, DC, 2000, Barbican Internat. Exch. Printmakers, Great Britain, Pushkin Mus. Fine Art, Moscow, Calif. Soc. Printmakers, Internat. Graphic Arts Found., Darien, Conn., San Diego Mus. Artist's Guild, St. Michael's Printmakers Assn., St. John's, Newfoundland, Washington Print Club, Washington, DC. Recipient numerous awards, honors, achievements. Mem.: Artists Equity Assn. (life), Washington Printmakers Gallery (life; founding mem.). Home: 417 Hampton Ct Falls Church VA 22046

STRATTON, EVELYN LUNDBERG, state supreme court justice; b. Bangkok, Feb. 25, 1953; came to U.S., 1971 (parents Am. citizens); d. Elmer John and Corrine Sylvia (Henricksen) Sahlberg; children: Luke Andrew, Tyler John; m. Jack A. Lundberg. Student, LeTourneau Coll., Longview, Tex., 1971-74; AA, U. Fla., 1973; BA, U. Akron, 1976; JD, Ohio State U., 1978. Bar: Ohio 1979, U.S. Dist. Ct. (so. dist.) Ohio 1979, U.S. Ct. Appeals (6th cir.) 1983. Assoc. Hamilton, Kramer, Myers & Cheek, Columbus, 1979-85; ptnr. Wesp, Osterkamp & Stratton, 1985-88; judge Franklin County Ct. Common Pleas, 1989-96; justice Ohio Supreme Ct., 1996—. Vis. prof. Nat. Jud. Coll., 1997—; spkr. legal seminars. Contbr. articles to profl. jours. Trustee Ohio affiliate Nat. Soc. to Prevent Blindness, 1989—, bd. dirs., trustee Columbus Coun. World Affairs, 1990-99, chmn. bd. dirs., 1999—; bd. dirs., trustee Dave Thomas Adoption Found., 1996—, ArChSafe Found., 1997—; mem. women's bd. Zephyrus League Cen. Ohio Lung Assn., 1989—; mem. Alliance Women Cmty. Corrections, 1993—. Recipient Gold Key award LeTourneau Coll., Gainesville, Fla., 1974, Svc. commendation Ohio Ho. of Reps., 1984, Scholar of Life award St. Joseph's Orphanage, 1998. Mem. ABA, ATLA, Columbus Bar Assn. (bd. govs. 1984-88, 90—, lectr.), Ohio Bar Assn. (jud. adminstrv. and legal reform com., coun. dels. 1992-96, Ohio Cmty. Corrections Orgn. (trustee 1995—), Columbus Bar Found. (trustee 1986-91, officer, sec. 1986-87, v.p. 1987-88), Am. Inns of Ct., Women Lawyers Franklin County, Phi Alpha Delta (pres. 1982-83). Office: Ohio Supreme Ct 65 S Front St Columbus OH 43215*

STRATTON, MARGARET ANNE, minister; b. Concordia, Kans., Oct. 10, 1948; d. Charles Edward and Marie Teresa Kier; m. Mick Stratton, June 9, 1973; children: James, Grace. BS Home Econs., Kans. State U., 1973; M Theology, Caribbean Comty. Ministerial Acad., Orlando, Fla., 1994; MDiv, So. Meth. U., 2000. Ordained elder United Meth. Ch., 2003. Pastor United Meth. Diamond Hill Parish and Mission, Ft. Worth, 2000—06, Robinson Dr. United Meth. Ch., Waco, Tex., 2006—. Chmn. Task Force on Hunger, Ctrl. Tex. Conf.; mem. Hispanic com.; mem. Confessing Movement United Meth. Ch.; clergy leadership initiative Tex. Meth. Found.; bd. dirs. Johnson Hill Children's Program, Eutaw, Ala., 1993—95. Recipient grants in field. Mem.: Confession Movement, Battalion of Deborah, Lifewatch, Nat. Assn. United Meth. Evangelists. Avocation: wood sculpting and carving. Office: 2801 Robinson Dr Waco TX 76706 Office Phone: 254-662-3155. Business E-Mail: margaretstratton@sbcglobal.net.

STRATTON, MARGARET MARY, art educator; b. Seattle, Nov. 12, 1953; d. Harold Wesley and Veronica Margaret (Weber) S. BA in Media Studies, Evergreen State Coll., Olympia, Wash., 1977; MA in Photography, U. N.Mex., 1983, MFA in Photography, 1985. Tchr. U. N.Mex., Albuquerque, 1983-85; artist-in-residence Wash. State Arts Commn., U. Puget Sound, Tacoma, 1985, Yakima (Wash) Elem. Sch. Dist., 1985; staff adj. faculty Evergreen State Coll., Olympia, 1985-86; asst. prof. art U. Iowa, Iowa City, 1986-92, assoc. prof., 1993—. Vis. prof. Cornish Coll. Art, Seattle, 1991-92, Art Inst. Chgo., 1992-93; advisor NEA regional Intermedia Arts/Minn., Mpls., 1991; juror Women in Dirs. Chair, Chgo., 1993. Videomaker: (film festivals) Berlin Film Festival, 1995, Black Maria Film Festival (dir. award 1995); contbr.: New Feminist Photographies, 1995; one-woman shows at New Image Gallery, James Madison U., Harrisonburg, Va., 1989, Sushi Inc., San Diego, 1990, Coll. of Pacific, Stockton, Calif., 1990, Intermedia Arts Gallery, Mpls., 1991, Cornish Coll. Arts, Seattle, 1991; exhibited in group shows at Rice U., Houston, 1989, Mid-Hudson Arts and Sci. Ctr., Poughkeepsie, N.Y., 1989, Arts Ctr. Gallery, Coll. DuPage, Glen Ellyn, Ill., 1989, N.A.M.E., Gallery, Chgo., 1989, Randolph St. Gallery, Chgo., 1989, Moore Coll. Art, Phila., 1989, Union Square Gallery, N.Y.C., 1989, U. Iowa Mus. Art, Iowa City, 1990, D.C. 37 Gallery, N.Y.C., 1990, Camerawork, San Francisco, 1990, 91, 93, 94, 911 Media Arts Ctr., Seattle, 1991, Kohler Art Ctr., Wis., 1991, Rena Bransten Gallery, San Francisco, 1991, Eye Gallery, San Francisco, 1992, 93, Port Angeles (Wash.) Fine Arts Ctr., 1992, Davenport (Iowa) Art Mus., 1992, Atlanta Gallery of Photography, 1992, U. Calif., Davis, 1992, Greg Kuchera Gallery, Seattle, 1992, Henry Gallery, U. Wash., Seattle, 1992, Valparaiso (Ind.) U., 1993, Gallery N.S.W., Sydney, Australia, 1993, Allied Arts Gallery/Hanford Nuclear Complex, Richland, Wash., 1993, Mus. Contemporary Photography and State Ill. Art Gallery, Chgo., 1993, The Harvard Archive, Cambridge, Mass.,1994, Portable Works Collection, Seattle Ctr. Pavilion, 1994, Women's U. Tex., Denton, 1994, Houston Ctr. Photography, 1994, Smithsonian Instn., Washington, 1994, Nathan Cummings Found., N.Y.C., 1995, Berlin Film and Video Festival, 1995. Recipient Regional Visual Fellowship award Nat. Endowment for Arts, 1987, Interdisciplinary Arts award, Intermedia Arts Nat. Endowment for Arts/Rockefeller Found., 1988, Individual fellowship in photography Nat. Endowment fo Arts, Washington, 1990, Pub. Art awards Seattle Arts Commn., 1992, Film and Video Prodn. Regional Grant Nat. Endowment for Arts/Jerome Found., Mpls., 1993, Individual fellowship in new Genres Nat. Endowment for the Arts, Washington, 1995, fac. scholar award U. Iowa, 1996. Mem. Soc. Photographic Edn. (bd. dirs. 1991-95), Coll. Art Assn. (1st chair Gay Caucus 1990-93). Achievements include research on the effects of media on stereotypes in United States/TV/Film. Home: 1611 E Court St Iowa City IA 52245-4425 Office: U Iowa Art Dept Riverside Dr Iowa City IA 52242

STRATTON, MARIANN, retired military nursing executive; b. Houston, Apr. 6, 1945; d. Max Millard and Beatrice Agnes (Roemer) S.; m. Lawrence Mallory Stickney, nov. 15, 1977 (dec.). BSN, BA in English, Sacred Heart Dominican Coll., 1966; MA in Mgmt., Webster Coll., 1977; MSN, U. Va., 1981. Cert. adult nurse practitioner. Ensign USN, 1966, advanced through grades to rear adm., 1991; patient care coord. Naval Regional Med. Ctr., Charleston, SC, 1981-83; nurse corps plans officer Naval Med. Command, Washington, 1983-86; dir. nursing svcs. U.S. Naval Hosp., Naples, Italy, 1986-89, Naval Hosp., San Diego, 1989-91; chief pers. mgmt. Bur. Medicine & Surgery, Washington, 1991-94; dir. USN Nurse Corps, Washington, 1991-94; ret. USN, 1994. Decorated Disting. Svc. medal, Meritorious Svc. medal with two stars, Naval Achievement medal, Navy Commendation medal. Mem. Interagy. Inst. Fed. Health Care Execs., Am. Volksporting Assn., Tex. Wanders, D'Vine Women, Garden Vols. of South Tex., U. Va. Raven Soc., Fiber Artists San Antonio.

STRATTON, PAULINE A., retired elementary school educator, alderman; b. Chgo., Feb. 18, 1946; d. Sam Costa and Helene (Lazaris) Stavrakas; m. George William Stratton, June 25, 1967; children: Gina Marie, Paul Kevin. B of Edn., Nat. Coll. Edn., 1967. Cert. tchr. grades K-9. Primary tchr. Worth (Ill.) Sch. Dist. # 127, 1967-70, substitute tchr., 1970-91, North Palos Sch. Dist. # 117, Palos Hills/Hickory Hills, Ill., 1976-87; alderman 2d ward City of Palos Hills, 1987—. Mem. lay adv. bd. S.W. Coop. Spl. Edn., Ill., South Met. Assn. Mem. sch. bd. North Palos Sch. Dist. # 117, Hickory Hills, 1983-91; vol., bd. dirs. Am. Cancer Soc.; vol. Diabetes Assn. Mem. Ill. Congress Parents and Tchrs. (cert. hon. life mem.), Maids of Athena (past grand pres.). Greek Orthodox. Avocations: walking, helping people. Home: 10315 S Alta Dr Palos Hills IL 60465-1705 Office: City of Palos Hills 10335 S Roberts Rd Palos Hills IL 60465-1929

STRATTON, SALLY G. (SARA), retired school system administrator; b. Huntingdon, Pa., Feb. 19, 1937; d. E. Richeard Grove and Miriam May Strait; m. Lewis Palmer Stratton, June 18, 1960 (div. Oct. 1987); children: Laurie Beth, Stephanie Jo. BA in Elem. Edn., Juniata Coll., 1959; MS in Early Childhood Adminstrn., Southeastern Nova U., 1987; postgrad., U. Maine, Fla. State U., Furman U. 1st grade tchr. Tyrone (Pa.) Sch. Dist., 1959-60, Veazie Sch. Dist., Orono, Maine, 1960-61, Wacula County Sch. Dist., Sopchoppy, Fla., 1961-62, Leon County Sch. Dist., Tallahassee, 1962-67; substitute tchr. Greenville (SC) County Schs., 1968-69; presch. tchr. First Bapt. Ch., Travelers Rest, SC, 1971-74; dir., head tchr., co-founder Furman U. Child Devel. Ctr., Greenville, SC, 1974-98; dir. residential life SC Gov. Sch. for Arts, Greenville, 1984—98; dir. student svcs. SC Gov.'s Sch. Arts and Humanities, 1998—2002. Co-author: Student Handbook for Newly Created Gov. School for Arts and Humanities, 1999. Sec. Red Sunset Corp., Greenville, 1994—2006; founding mem. 1st Internat. Assn. for Univ. Women in Russia, 1991; bd. dirs. Greenville County Child Care Assn., 1990—2003. Mem. AAUW (chair ednl. found., treas., pres. 1989-91, recipient Named Gift award 1998, 2000), Greenville County Childcare Assn. (bd. dirs. 1988—), S.C. Assn. for Children Under Six, PTA (co-pres., treas., membership chair, adv. coun.). Baptist. Avocations: travel, interior decorating, reading, choir, sports. Home: 607 Half Mile Way Greenville SC 29609-1577

STRAUB, SUNNY L., retired elementary school educator; b. Quincy, Ill., Aug. 19, 1950; d. Leonard Emery and Billie Louise Straub. BS in Elem. Edn., So. Ill. U., Carbondale, 1972; MS, Western Ill. U., Macomb, 1979. Cert. tchr. Ill., Mo., edn. adminstr. Truman State U., 1989. Tchr. Chpt. 1 reading Quincy Pub. Schs., Ill., 1974—81, tchr. reading, 1981—85, subject area leader/reading, 1981—91; dean of students Quincy Jr. H.S., Ill., 1985—91, literacy tchr., 1991—2005, English dept. chairperson, 1991—2005; ret., 2005. Tutor Woodland Home, Quincy, Ill., 1975—76; presenter Nat. Coun. Tchrs. of English, Ill. Reading Coun.; GED tchr. Quincy Pub. Schs., Ill., 1977—78, dir. Quincy conf., 1980—81, right to read coord., 1984—85; study skills program coord. Quincy Jr. H.S., Ill., 1986—90, north ctrl. evaluation coord., 1987—89, sch. improvement team leader, 1993—2005; workshop presenter, instr., lectr.; curriculum alignment leader. Election judge, Quincy, Ill., 2006; founder Kids First Coalition. Mem.: Ill. Assn. of Ret. Tchrs., Quincy Fedn. of Ret. Tchrs. Achievements include development of Curriculum Development of Reading; Literacy Block Initiative; Integrated Content Study Skills Program. Avocations: reading, volunteer, pursuit of learning, political campaigning, mentoring. Home: 1811C S Twenty-fourth Quincy IL 62301 Personal E-mail: sunni@adams.net.

STRAUB, SUSAN MONICA, special education educator; b. Tampa, Fla., Jan. 31, 1954; d. Paul Ferdinand and Betty Hew (Wellacott) S. AA, Hillsborough Community Coll., 1975; BA, U. S. Fla., 1978. Lifeguard, swimming instr. Tampa Recreation Dept., 1970-74 summers, pool mgr., 1975-76 summers, office asst. sec., 1977-78 summers; tchr. Hillsborough Assn. Retarded Citizens, Tampa, 1978-79, Hillsborough County Sch. Bd., Tampa, 1979—, Sch. of Hope, 1979-81, Mango Elem. Sch., 1981-85, Lopez Elem Sch., Seffner, Fla., 1985-93, Wilson Elem. Sch., Plant City, Fla., 1993-98, Mann Mid. Sch., Brandon, Fla., 1998-2000, Armwood H.S., Seffner, Fla., 2000—. Coach Spl. Olympics, Tampa, 1980, 2000—, games ofcl., 1982, steering com., Hillsborough County, 1984-92. Sec., treas. Superstar Bowling League for Handicapped, Tampa, 1988-89, 1st v.p., 1989-91. Recipient Spl. Olympics award Hillsborough County, State of Fla., 1980; named Vol. of Yr. Mass. Mutual, 1982, Coach of Yr. Hillsborough County Spl. Olympics, 1982, Tchr. of Yr. U. So. Fla. Alumni Assn., 1990. Mem. Coun. Exceptional Children (hospitality chair, Dept. Exceptional Student Edn. Person of Yr. 1987-88, Chpt. Tchr. of Yr. 1990), Soroptimist Internat. (1st v.p., 2d v.p. 1990-91, Team Leader 1985-91, 92-93). Democrat. Roman Catholic. Avocations: soccer, swimming. Home: 517 Somerstone Dr Valrico FL 33594 Office: Lithia Springs Elem Lynx Paw Tr Valrico FL 33594 E-mail: straubsl@gte.net.

STRAUMANIS, JOAN, academic administrator, consultant; b. NYC, Feb. 10, 1937; d. Herbert S. and Mollie (Brandt) Cole; m. Irwin H. Pomerantz, June 25, 1956 (div. 1969); children: Rebecca, Joel; m. Eric R. Straumanis, June 7, 1969 (dec. 1996); 1 child, Andrei. BA Polit. Sci., Math., Antioch Coll., 1957; MS math., U. Colo.; PhD Philosophy, U. Md., 1974. Prof. Denison U., Granville, Ohio, 1971-82; acad. dean, prof. Kenyon Coll., Gambier, Ohio, 1982-86; dean faculty, prof. Rollins Coll., Winter Park, Fla., 1986-92; program officer Fund for Improvement of Postsecondary Edn. U.S. Dept. Edn., Washington, 1992—95; dean arts and scis. Lehigh U., Bethlehem, Pa., 1995—98; program officer Fund for Improvement of Postsecondary Edn. U.S. Dept. Edn., Washington, 1998—2002; pres. Antioch Coll., Yellow Springs, Ohio, 2002—04. Office Phone: 202-277-1937. E-mail: JoanStraumanis@earthlink.net.

STRAUS, A. SUSAN, volunteer; b. Chgo., Aug. 16, 1950; d. Herman and Ruth Krisky Straus. BA, Northeastern Ill. U., 1973; cert. paralegal, Roosevelt U., 1985. Cert. notary pub. Ill. Mail supr. Corboy and Demetrio, Chgo. Anti-war activist Peace Action, Chgo., 2000—. Mem.: NOW (v.p. Chgo. chpt. 1996, pres. Chgo. chpt. 1997—98, bd. dirs. 1997—, sec. working women history project 2000—01, mem. edn. legal fund 2002—, pres. working women history project 2002—). Office Phone: 312-346-3191. E-mail: sstraus2001@yahoo.com.

STRAUS, KATHLEEN NAGLER, academic administrator, educator; b. NYC, Dec. 3, 1923; d. Maurice and Mildred (Kohn) Nagler; m. Everet M. Straus, May 29, 1948 (dec. Nov. 1967); children: Peter R., Barbara L. BA in Econs., Hunter Coll., 1944; postgrad., Columbia U., 1944—45, Am. U., 1946—47, Wayne State U., 1976—78. Various positions, 1944—50, 1966; dep. dir. Model Neighborhood Agy., City of Detroit, 1968—70; dir. social svcs. Southeastern Mich. Coun. Govts., Detroit, 1970—74; staff coord. Edn. Task Force, Detroit, 1974—75; exec. dir. People and Responsible Orgns. for Detroit, 1975—76; staff dir. edn. com. Mich. Senate, Lansing, 1976—79; assoc. exec. dir. Mich. Assn. Sch. Bds., Lansing, 1979—86; dir. cmty. rels. and devel. Ctr. for Creative Studies, Detroit, 1986—87, pres., 1987—91; mem. Mich. Bd. Edn., 1992—, pres., 2003. Mem. Mich. Bd. for Pub. Jr. and C.C.s, Lansing, 1980-92, v.p., 1989, pres., 1991; cons. Met. Columbus (Ohio) Schs. Com., 1975-76; mem. steering com. Mich. Edn. Seminars, 1979-86; mem. Adv. Com. on Higher Edn. Needs in S.W. Mich., 1971-72, Ad Hoc Com. on Equal Access to Higher Edn., 1970-71, Citizens Action Com. on Sch. Fin. Contbr. articles to profl. jours. Active numerous civic orgns.; vice chmn. downtown br. Met. Detroit YWCA, 1970-74; bd. dirs. Citizens for Better Care, Inc., 1973-78; mem. edn. com. New Detroit, Inc., 1972—; trustee Detroit Sci. Ctr., Inc., 1975—; founder, pres. Mich. Tax Info. Coun., 1982—; v.p. bd. dirs. Univ. Cultural Ctr. Assn., 1986-91; trustee Comprehensive Health Planning Coun. Southeastern Mich., 1977-78; mem. Wayne County Art and History Commn., 1988; co-chmn. Nat. Arts Program, 1987-88; bd. dirs. North Ctrl. Regional Edn. Libr.; bd. dirs. North Ctrl. Regional Edn. Lab. Recipient Amity citation, Detroit, 1966, Disting. Cmty. Svc. award Am. Jewish Com., 1988, Common Coun., Detroit, 1976, resolution Mich. Ho. of Reps., 1986, Mich. Senate, 1988, Educator of Yr. Wayne State U., 1999, Disting. Warrior award Detroit Urban League, 2000; named to Mich. Edn. Hall of Fame, 1997; inducted into Mich. Women's Hall of Fame, 2000, Lifetime Achievement award Anti Defamation League, 2004, Multi Cultural Edn. award Nat. Conf. Cmty. and Justice, 2004. Mem.: LWV (pres. Detroit 1961—63), Alpha Chi Alpha. Democrat. Avocations: travel, theater, concerts. Home: 7431 Deep Run 210 Bloomfield Hills MI 48301 Office: State Bd Edn PO Box 30008 Lansing MI 48909-7508 Office Phone: 517-373-3900. Business E-Mail: strausk@michigan.gov.

STRAUS, LORNA PUTTKAMMER, biology professor; b. Chgo., Feb. 15, 1933; d. Ernst Wilfred and Helen Louise (Monroe) Puttkammer; m. Francis Howe Straus II, June 11, 1955; children: Francis, Helen, Christopher, Michael. BA magna cum laude, Radcliffe Coll., 1955; MS, U. Chgo., 1960, PhD, 1962. Rsch. assoc. dept. anatomy U. Chgo., 1962—64, instr., 1964—67, asst. prof., 1967—73, assoc. prof., 1973—87, prof., 1987—, asst. dean, then dean students, 1967—82, dean admissions, 1975—80, marshal, 1999—. Trustee Radcliffe Coll., Cambridge, Mass., 1973-83; chmn. Cmty. Found., Mackinac Island, Mich., 1994—. Recipient silver medal Coun. for Advancement and Support Edn., 1987. Mem.: North Ctrl. Assn. (commr. 1998—, pres.-elect 2001—02, pres. 2002—04), Harvard U. Alumni Assn. (bd. dirs. 1980—83), Phi Beta Kappa. Avocations: travel, gardening. Home: 5642 S Kimbark Ave Chicago IL 60637-1606 Office: U Chgo 5845 S Ellis Ave Chicago IL 60637-1476 Business E-Mail: hlps@uchicago.edu.

STRAUS, PATRICIA W., artist, retired educator; b. Chgo., May 11, 1923; d. Charles Wesley and Bertha Amelia (Shipman) Wenner; m. Apr. 1958 (div. Jan. 1968); m. James Porter Straus, June 21, 1980. BA in Psychology and Sociology, Northwestern U., 1953; MFA in Painting, George Wash. U., 1968. Sec. to chief radiologist U. Pa. Hosp., Phila., 1957—59; asst. sec. Philco Corp., Phila., 1959—60; with Capitol Hill Rep. Policy Commn., 1960; conf. sec. Brookings Inst., Washington, 1962—65; sec. John Hopkins Sch. Advanced Internat. Studies, 1965—68; tchr. DC Pub. Schs., 1968—88; ret., 1988; freelance artist, 1988—. Asst. treas. Columbia Women, Washington, 1977-78. Numerous painting exhbns., shows, 1995—. Vol. Arlingtonians For Better Govt., 1988—. Northwestern U. scholar, Chgo., 1949-51. Mem. LWV (environ. com.). Dem. Unitarian. Avocations: gardening, swimming. Home: 850 N Kentucky St Arlington VA 22205-1317

STRAUSER, CAROL ANN, small business owner; b. Oak Ridge, Tenn., Sept. 3, 1947; d. Wilbur Alexander and Lois Irene (Carter) S. Student, U. Md. Salesperson Hecht Co., Bethesda, Md.; sec. Bricklayers, Washington, U.S. Govt., Rockville, Md. Mem. NOW, NAFE, AAUW, DAR, Mus. Women Arts. Avocations: reading, writing, painting, drawing. Home and Office: PO Box 144 Charleroi PA 15022-0144

STRAUSS, CAROLYN, broadcast executive; b. NYC, July 13, 1963; BA, Harvard U., 1985. Temp Documentaries Dept. HBO, 1986, asst. original programming, 1986—89, mgr. original programming, 1989—90, dir. original programming, 1990—94, v.p. original programming, 1994—99, sr. v.p. original programming, 1999—2002, exec. v.p. original programming, 2002—04, pres. entertainment, 2004—. Mailing: HBO Entertainment 1100 Avenue of Americas New York NY 10036*

STRAUSS, DEBORAH, foundation administrator; AB, MA, U. Chgo. Cert. Fund Raising Exec. Dir. devel. pub. rels. Chgo. Child Care Soc.; exec. dir. IT Resource Ctr., Chgo., 1985—. Mem. mgmt. team Nat. Strategy for Nonprofit Tech.; chair Tech. Resource Consortium; bd. mem. Alliance for Nonprofit Mgmt., Donors Forum of Chgo.; mem. Mayor's Coun. of Tech. Advisors, co-chair Bridging the Digital Divide Com. Mem.: Assn. of Fundraising Profls. (mem. Chgo. Chap. Bd., Benjamin Franklin Award 1993). Office: IT Resource Ctr Ste 1005 29 E Madison St Chicago IL 60602-4529 Office Phone: 312-372-4872. Office Fax: 312-372-7962. E-mail: dstrauss@itresourcecenter.org.*

STRAUSS, DIANE JAYNE, retired elementary and secondary school educator, small business owner; b. Crawfordsville, Ind., July 6, 1940; d. Harold and Madge Virginia Wright. BS, Purdue U., 1964; MS, Butler U., 1971, postgrad., 1974—, Ind. Vocat. Tech. Coll., 1983—, Ind.-Purdue U., 1980—. With Am. United Life Ins. Co., Indpls., 1959-64; tchr. St. Matthews Elem. Sch., Indpls., 1962-63, Decatur Twp. Sch. System, Indpls., 1964-71; reading coord. Benton County Sch. System, Fowler, Ind., 1971-73; tchr. Ctr. Grove High Sch., Greenwood, Ind., 1978-79; coord. title 1 dept. corrections curriculum projects Ind. U.-Purdue U., Indpls., 1980-82; tchr. Indpls. Pub. Schs., 1986—2005, instrl. coach, 2002—06; Title I reading tchr. grades 6-8 John Marshall Middle Sch., 2004—05, Cripus Attucks Mid. Sch., 2005—06; ret., 2006. Owner, co-dir. Bus. Personal Devel. Ctr., Indpls., 1971-86, Strauss Learning Ctr., Indpls., 1971-90, Strauss Enterprises, 1991—. Pres. Decatur Twp. Tchrs. Assn., Indpls., 1970, ednl. lobbist, 1964-97. Mem.: Mem. ASCD, NEA, Ind. State Tchrs. Assn., Indpls. Edn. Assn. (life), Phi Delta Kappan. Home and Office: 7370 Lions Head Dr A Indianapolis IN 46260-3460

STRAUSS, GWEN B., writer, editor; b. Deschapelles, Haiti, May 19, 1963; d. Julian Max Strauss and Katie Cowles Nichols; m. Jody Gerard Jenkins, June 22, 1996; children: Noah Jenkins, Sophie Jenkins, Eliza Jenkins. BA in Poetry, Hampshire Coll., 1986; MA in Edn., Wheelock Coll., 1987. Tchg. asst. Park Sch., Boston, 1986—87; freelance writer France, 1990—2003; editl. asst. Frank Books, Paris, 1992; editor Design Press, Savannah, Ga., 2002—04; dir. French campus Savannah Coll. of Art and Design, Lacoste, France, 2005—. Editl. cons. So. Poetry Rev., Savannah, 2003. Author: (poetry book) Trail of Stones, 1989, (children's book) Night Shimmy, 1991; contbr. short stories and poetry to various lit. jours. Finalist Nat. Poetry Series, 1995, Allen Ginsburg Poetry prize, 2003; recipient hon. mention, Atlanta Rev., 2001. Mem.: Authors Guild, Amnesty Internat., Planned Parenthood. Democrat. Avocations: gardening, sailing. Office: SCAD Rue Basse 84480 Lacoste France Personal E-mail: gbs0885@aol.com. Business E-Mail: gstrauss@scad.edu.

STRAUSS, HARLEE SUE, environmentalist, consultant; b. New Brunswick, NJ, June 19, 1950; d. Robert Lemuel and Helene (Marcus) S. BA, Smith Coll., 1972; PhD, U. Wis., 1979. Postdoctoral fellow dept. biology MIT, Cambridge, 1979-81; congrl. sci. fellow U.S. House of Reps., Washington, 1981-83; spl. asst. Am. Chem. Soc., Washington, 1983-84; spl. cons. Environ. Corp., Washington, 1984-85; rsch. assoc. Ctr. for Tech., Policy and Indsl. Devel. MIT, Cambridge, 1985-86, rsch. affiliate, 1986-92; sr. assoc. Gradient Corp., Cambridge, 1986-88; pres. H. Strauss Assocs., Inc., Natick, Mass., 1988—. Exec. dir. Silent Spring Inst., Inc., 1994-95; adj. assoc. prof. Sch. Pub. Health, Boston U., 1990-94; lectr. Sch. Medicine, Tufts U., Boston, 1988-95; mem. steering com. Boston Risk Assessment Group, 1986-95. Co-editor, author Risk Assessment in Genetic Engineering, 1991; author: Biotechnology Regulations, 1986, book chpts. in field. Active Instl. Biosafety Com., Army Rsch. Lab., Natick, 1989—94, Army Sci. Bd., 1994—2001. Mem. AAAS, Am. Chem. Soc., Assn. for Women in Sci. (chmn. com. New England chpt. 1986-88, co-chmn. legis. com. 1985-93), Biophys. Soc. (chmn. com. 1983-84, Congl. Sci. fellow 1981-83), Soc. for Risk Analysis (pres. New England chpt. 1991-92, pres.-elect 1995-2000). Jewish. Avocations: travel, hiking. Office: H Strauss Assocs Inc 21 Bay State Rd Natick MA 01760-2942 Office Phone: 508-651-8784. Personal E-mail: hstrauss@aol.com. Business E-Mail: h.strauss@rcn.com.

STRAUSS, WENDY EISENBERG, music educator; b. St. Louis, June 9, 1959; d. Goodman and Frances Elizabeth (Hewitt) Eisenberg; m. Marc W. Strauss, Aug. 9, 1981; 2 children B Music Edn., Lindenwood Coll., St. Charles, Mo., 1981; postgrad., Bradley U., 1986. Tchr. vocal music Holy Family Sch., Peoria, Ill., 1985—86; instr. music Acad. of Our Lady-Spalding Inst.-Peoria Notre Dame, 1986—. Dir. vocal music Peoria Notre Dame, 1989—; instr. music Hines Primary Sch. Peoria Pub. Schs. Dist. 150, 1992—. Mem. Anshai Emeth Temple Choir, 1985—. Mem. Music Educators Nat. Conf., Ill. Music Assn., Alpha Sigma Tau, Mu Phi Epsilon Jewish. Avocation: piano. Office: Peoria Notre Dame 5105 N Sheridan Rd Peoria IL 61614-4855

STRAVALLE-SCHMIDT, ANN ROBERTA, lawyer; b. N.Y.C., Jan. 2, 1957; Grad. cum laude, Phillips Exeter Acad., 1975; student, Occidental Coll., 1975-78, Oxford Coll., Eng., 1976-77; BS cum laude, Boston Coll., 1980; JD, Boston U., 1987; MBA, Rensselaer Poly. Inst., 2002. Bar: Conn. 1987, U.S. Dist. Ct. Conn. 1988, U.S. Supreme Ct. 1993. Consulting staff Arthur Andersen, Boston, 1980-82; supr. CID ops. Aetna Life & Casualty, Hartford, Conn., 1982-84; summer intern US Atty.'s Office, Boston, 1985; jud. clk. Hon. Judge Thayer III NH Supreme Ct., 1987-88; trial lawyer Day, Berry & Howard, Hartford, Conn., 1988-91; sr. lawyer comml. litig. and appellate practice Berman & Sable, Hartford, Conn., 1991-96; dir. maj. case unit Travelers Property and Casualty Corp., Hartford, Conn., 1996-98; sr. atty. Robinson & Cole, Hartford, Conn., 1998-2000; dir. legal svcs., gen. counsel Conn. Resources Recovery Authority, Hartford, Conn., 2000—04; gen. counsel, in-house mgr., legal, IP, warranty and reliability Jacobs Vehicle Sys. (subs. Danaher Corp.), Bloomfield, Conn., 2005—. Brief judge Nat. Appellate Advocacy Competition, 1996; online faculty U. Phoenix, 2002—, moot court judge, U. Conn., 1992, 2004. Mem. editl. bd. Conn. Bar Jour., 1990-99; contbr. articles to profl. jours. Mem. Hebron Dem. Town Com., Hebron Bd. Fin., 1995-99, Hebron Sch. Bldg. Com., 1997-99; justice of peace, 1997-99; apptd. mem. Hebron Bldg. Com., 1997-99; bd. dirs. Lawyers Without Borders, 2004; mem. adv. bd. Discovery Ctr., 2004—; mgr. Lawyers at Risk and Neutral Observer Program. Hennessey scholar Boston U. Sch. Law, 1987. Mem. ABA, Conn. Bar Assn. (founder, chair appellate practice com. litigation sect. 1994-96, mem. exec. com. litigation sect., pro bono exec. com, 2004, chair pro bono initiative, corp. counsel sect. 2004). Home: 54 Monte Alto Rd Santa Fe NM 87508 Office: Jacobs Vehicle Sys Subsidiary Danagher Corp 22 E Dudley Tour Rd Bloomfield CT 06002 Personal E-mail: astravalle@comcast.net.

STRAVINSKA, SARAH, dance educator; b. Pitts., Nov. 12, 1940; d. Robert Edwin Williams and Alice Elizabeth Markey Hildeboldt; m. George Lawrence Denton, May 10, 1959 (div. 1973); children: Kathryn, Michael, Laura, David. BFA in Dance, Fla. State U., 1977, MFA in Dance, 1979; Cert. in Ballet, Vaganova Inst., Leningrad, Russia, 1990; Cert., Raoul Gelabert Kinesiology Ins, N.Y.C., 1980. Dancer Ballet Russe, N.Y.C., 1957-58; dance choreographer Dutchess County Ballet, Beacon, NY, 1960-65; instr. Brevard C.C., Cocoa, Fla., 1969-73; chair dept. dance Randolph/Macon Woman's Coll., Lynchburg, Va., 1979-84; asst. prof. dance U. So. Miss., Hattiesburg, 1984-86; prof. and coord. dance U. La., Lafayette, 1986—. Dir. State of La. Danse Project, Lafayette, 1991-94. Choreographer original dance works: Mama! Stop the Bombs, 1989, The Yellow Wallpaper, 1990, Spring Night, 1998, Serrano!, 2002, Feather, Stone and Light, 2003, The Littlest Angel, 2005; reconstructor of classical ballets: Les Sylphides, 1991, Giselle, 1992, Swan Lake, 1993, Raymonda, Pas de Quatre, 1994. Dir. concerns for children La Danse with Acadiana Arts Coun., Lafayette, 1987-93; mem. Arts in Edn. Program, Lafayette, 1987—, coord. The Othello Project, 2003-04. Grantee Mellon Found., 1982. Mem. Am. Coll. Dance Festival Assn. (bd. dirs., festival coord. 1989-91), Dance History Scholars, CORPS de Ballet Internat. (founder), Phi Kappa Phi. Episcopalian. Avocations: writing, music, reading, biking. Office: Univ of La PO Box 43690 Lafayette LA 70504-3690 Personal E-mail: dancepro@m.efriends.net.

STRAWN, MARTHA ANN, art educator, photographer, writer; b. Washington, Apr. 29, 1945; d. Clifford Earl and Marion Anne S. BA, Fla. State U., 1967; cert. basic tech., Brooks Inst. Photography, 1968; MFA, Ohio U., 1970. Photographer Goleta (Calif.) Gazette Newspaper, 1967-68; instr. art Fla. State U., Tallahassee, 1969-70; asst. prof. art, mem. grad. faculty N.E. La. U., Monroe, 1970-71; courtesy prof. art U. Fla., Gainesville, 1985; prof. art, mem. women studies faculty U. N.C., Charlotte, 1971—2004, prof. emeritus, 2005—. Juror Nat. Endowment Arts, 1982, 95, 98; bd. trustees Ctr. Am. Places, 1993—; co-founder, dir. The Light Factory, Charlotte, 1973—, mem. adv. bd. 1974-76, 77-78, 90—; bd. trustees Friends Photography, San Francisco, 1986-94, mem. exec. bd., 1988-90. Author: Alligators, Prehistoric Presence in the American Landscape, 1997, Across the Threshold of India, 2006; exhbns. include: N.A.M.E. Gallery, Chgo., 1983, United Nations World Conf. on Women, Nairobi, Kenya, 1985, Wadsworth Atheneum, Hartford, Conn., 1985, Minn. Coll. Art and Design, 1986, Burchfield Art Ctr., Buffalo, NY, 1986, SECCA, Winston-Salem, NC, 1987, Sol Mednick Gallery, Univ. of the Arts, 1987, Indira Gandhi Ctr. for the Arts, New Delhi, India, 1994, Halsey Gallery Coll. of Charleston, SC, 1995, Richard F. Brush Art Gallery, St. Lawrence U., NY, 1996, Mint Mus. of Art, Charlotte, NC, 1997, Discovery Place Sci. Mus., Charlotte, 1997, Samuel P. Harn Mus. of Art, U. Fla., Gainesville, 2000, Sci. Mus. of Minn., St. Paul, 2000—, When Crocodiles Ruled, The Milw. County Zoo, 2003, Carnegie Mus. Natural History, Pitts., 2001-02, San Diego Mus. Natural History, 2002, Oreg. Mus. Sci. and Industry, Portland, 2002, Nat. Geog. Soc. Mus., Washington, 2001, Peter C. Bunnell Collection Exhbn., Princeton Art Mus., N.J., 2002, The Light Factory, Charlotte, NC, 2006. Mem., contbr. Am. Alligator Cycle Protection, Dade City, Fla., 1990-99, So. Poverty Law Ctr., Montgomery, Ala., 1990-99. Recipient N.C. Govs. Bus. award N.C. Coun. Arts and Humanities, 1982, First Citizens Bank/U. N.C. Rsch. scholars medal, Charlotte, 2001; Individual Artist fellow S.E. Ctr. for Contemporary Arts, 1986-87; Photog. fellow Nat. Endowment Arts, 1980. Fellow Fulbright Alumni Assn.; mem. Internat. Visual Sociol. Assn., Soc. for Photog. Edn., Davidson Lands Conservancy. Democrat. Avocations: cooking, sea kayaking, gardening. Home: PO Box 936 Davidson NC 28036-0936 Office: U NC Charlotte Dept Art Rowe Bldg Charlotte NC 28223 Personal E-mail: mstrawn@earthlink.net.

STRAWTER, LEE ANNA, secondary school educator; b. Glenwood, Ga., Mar. 7, 1953; d. Willie T. Sr. and Emma Lou (Burns) Jackson; m. Billy J. Strawter, Dec. 17, 1972; children: Billy J., Safiya Akilah BS, Ft. Valley State U., Ga., 1975; MA, Saginaw Valley State Coll., University Center, Mich., 1991. Cert. tchr., Mich. Tchr. Midland Pub. Schs., 1976—79, Tulsa Pub. Schs., 1979—84; tchr. math. Saginaw Pub. Schs., Mich., 1985—. Supr. Sunday sch. Faith Ministries Bapt. Ch., Midland, 1989— Tchg. fellow U. Mich., 1991 Mem. Delta Sigma Theta Avocations: reading, crossword puzzles. Home: 2809 Blairmont St Midland MI 48642-6696 Office: Arthur High Sch 3115 Mackinaw St Saginaw MI 48602 Office Phone: 989-399-5800. E-mail: lstrawter@spsd.net.

STRAYHORN, CAROLE KEETON, comptroller; b. Sept. 13, 1939; d. Page Keeton; m. Barr McClellan (div. 1977); m. Jim Rylander (div. 1995); m. Ed Strayhorn, 2003; children from previous marriage: Mark, Scott, Brad, Dudley 1 stepchild. Degree (hon.), U. Tex., Austin. Pub. sch. tchr.; sch. bd. mem., pres. Austin, 1972—77; mayor, 1977—83; mem. Tex. R.R. Commn., 1994—98; state comptr. of rep. accounts Tex., 1998—. Recipient Friends of Tex. Taxpayers award, Citizens for a Sound Economy, 1999, Friend of Edn. award, Tex. Classroom Tchrs. Assn. Office: Tex Comptroller Capitol Station PO Box 13528 Austin TX 78711-3528

STRAYHORN CRUMP, JORETTA PETRICE, health educator, substance abuse consultant; b. Kinston, N.C., July 25, 1968; d. Joe Louis and Pecola Inez (Simmons) S. BS, Winston-Salem State U., 1990; MAEd, East Carolina U., 1998. Cert. substance abuse prevention cons.; registered health educator. Lab. technologist Nat. Health Lab., Winston-Salem, N.C., 1991; data coord. Bowman Gray Sch. Medicine, Winston-Salem, 1992-93; educator Winston-Salem/Forsyth County Schs., 1993-94; prevention specialist Step One, Winston-Salem, 1995-97; HIV program coord. Eastern N.C. HIV/AIDS Consortium, Greenville, 1999; substance abuse edn. cons. Tideland Mental Health Ctr., Washington, N.C., 1999—. Mem. Pitt County Health Care, Greenville, 1999—, Internat. Cert. Reciprocity Consortium, Raleigh, N.C., 1997. Substance abuse edn. cons. Weed and Seed, Winston-Salem, 1997; mem. Cmty. Outreach, Winston-Salem, 1996. Mem. Nat. Assn. Alcoholism and Drug Abuse Counselors, Addiction Profls. N.C. Democrat. Mem. African Meth. Episcopal Zion Ch. Avocations: reading, music, the beach, exercising. Office: Tideland Mental Health Ctr 1308 Highland Dr Washington NC 27889-3494

STRAZ, IRENE N., special education educator; b. Parma Heights, Ohio, Mar. 4, 1954; d. Heinrich and Margaretha Kopp; m. Gary J. Straz, Mar. 9, 1991; stepchildren: Melissa B., Michael G. BS in Elem. Edn. and Educable Mentally Handicapped, Bowling Green State U., Ohio, 1976; MEd, Aurora U., Williams Bay, Wis. Cert. learning disabilities tchr. Nat. Louis U. Learning disabilities/EMH tchr. Round Lake Schs., Ill., 1991—95, Stanton Jr. H.S., Fox Lake, Ill., 1995—96; CD tchr. Lakeland Sch. of Walworth County, Elkhorn, Wis., 1995—. Tchr. liaison Friends of Lakeland Sch. Mem.: Lioness Club. Office: Lakeland School of Walworth County 504 W Court St Elkhorn WI 53121

STREAT, KAREN GRAY, community health and geriatrics nurse, adult nurse practitioner; b. Utica, NY, May 15, 1956; d. Charles Philip and Pauline (Nelson) Gray; m. Wayne Elliott Streat; children: William Charles Pigott,

Christopher McCabe Pigott. Diploma, Albany Med. Ctr. Sch. Nursing, 1978; diploma nurse practitioner, SUNY, Syracuse, 1982. RN, N.Y.; cert. adult nurse practitioner. Staff nurse Albany (N.Y.) Med. Ctr., 1978-79, St. Elizabeth's Hosp., Utica, 1979-80, Community Meml. Hosp., Hamilton, N.Y., 1980-81; nurse practitioner pvt. office, Waterville, N.Y., 1982-87, VA Med. Ctr., Gainesville, Fla., 1987-90, Balt., 1990—; adult nurse practitioner, 1998—; facility dir., 1998—2000. Cons. in field; preceptor for grad. students U. Fla., 1988-90, U. South Fla., 1989-90, U. Md., faculty assoc. Johns Hopkins U.; preceptor Cath. U., Bowie State U. Vol. health care provider Salvation Army Homeless Clinic, Gainesville, 1989-90, Spl. Olympics Events, Gainesville, 1990. Mem. ANA, Fla. Nurses Assn. (Expert in Clin. Practice award 1990). Presbyterian. Home: 20 Forest Dr Bel Air MD 21014 Office: 9512 Harford Rd Baltimore MD 21234 Office Phone: 410-882-0600. Business E-Mail: karen.streat@medstar.net.

STRECK, MELISSA LEIGH, music educator; b. Pitts., May 25, 1979; d. Thomas Edward and Judith Ann Hartman; m. John Richard Streck Jr. BS in Music Edn., Indiana U. Pa., 2002. Gen. music tchr. Morrison (Tenn.) Elem. Sch., Warren County Sch, 2003—05, Centertown Elem. Sch., Warren County Schs., McMinnville, Tenn., 2003—05, Dibrell Elem. Sch., Warren County Sch., McMinnville, Tenn., 2003—05, Pine Ridge Elem. Sch., Harris County Schs., Ellerslie, Ga., 2005—; gen. music tchr., choir dir. New Mountain Hill Elem. Sch., Harris County Schs., Fortson, Ga., 2005—. Pvt. percussion lessons, Greensburg, 1999—2005; pvt. music tchr., Columbus, Ga., 2002—; percussionist Westmoreland Symphonic Winds, Greensburg, 2003, Hempfield Cmty. Band, Greensburg, 2002—03. Mem. women's barbershop quartet; mem. chn. handbell choir Greenburg, 1994. Mem.: NEA, Percussive Arts Soc., Music Educators Nat. Conf. Avocations: performing music, horseback riding, fitness, reading, American history. Personal E-mail: streckm@hotmail.com.

STREEP, MERYL (MARY LOUISE STREEP), actress; b. Summit, N.J., June 22, 1949; d. Harry, Jr. and Mary W. Streep; m. Donald J. Grummer, Sept. 15, 1978; children: Henry, Mary Willa, Grace, Louisa. BA, Vassar Coll., 1971; MFA, Yale U., 1975, DFA (hon.), 1983, Dartmouth Coll., 1981. Co-founder Mothers & Others for a Livable Planet. Appeared with: Green Mountain Guild; actress: (Broadway plays) Trelawny of the Wells, 1975; (plays) 27 Wagons Full of Cotton (Theatre World award); A Memory of Two Mondays; Henry V; Secret Service; The Taming of the Shrew; Measure for Measure; The Cherry Orchard; Happy End; Wonderland; Taken in Marriage; Alice in Concert (Obie award, 1981); Mother Courage, 2006; (films) Julia, 1977; The Deer Hunter, 1978 (Best Supporting Actress award nat. Soc. film Critics, Acad. award nomination, 1978); Manhattan, 1979; The Seduction of Joe Tynan, 1979; Kramer vs. Kramer, 1979 (N.Y. Film Critics' award, Los Angeles Film Critics' award, both for best actress, Golden Globe award, Acad. award for best supporting actress, 1980); The French Lieutenant's Woman, 1981 (Los Angeles Film Critics award for best actress, Brit. Acad. award, Golden Globe award for best actress, Acad. award nomination, 1982); Sophie's Choice, 1982 (Acad. award for best actress, Los Angeles Film Critics award for best actress, Golden Globe award for best actress, 1983); Still of the Night, 1982; Silkwood, 1983 (Acad. award nomination); Falling in Love, 1984; Plenty, 1985; Out of Africa, 1985 (Los Angeles Film Critics award for best actress, Golden Globe award, 1985); Heartburn, 1986; Ironweed, 1987 (Acad. award nomination); A Cry in the Dark, 1988 (named Best Actress N.Y. Film Critics' Circle, Best Actress Cannes Film Festival, 1989, Acad. award nomination); She-Devil, 1989; Postcards From the Edge, 1990; Defending Your Life, 1991; Death Becomes Her, 1992; The House of Spirits, 1993; The River Wild, 1994; The Bridges of Madison County, 1995 (Acad. award nominee for best actress, 1996); Before and After, 1996; Marvin's Room, 1996; Dancing at Lugnasa, 1998; One True Thing, 1998; Music of the Heart, 1999 (Acad. award nominee for best actress); The Hours, 2002; Adaptation, 2002 (Southeastern Film Critics Assn. award for best supporting actress, 2002, Chgo. Film Critics Assn. award for best supporting actress, 2003, Golden Globe for best supporting actress, 2003); The Manchurian Candidate, 2004; Lemony Snicket's A Series of Unfortunate Events, 2004; Prime, 2005; A Prairie Home Companion, 2006; The Devil Wears Prada, 2006; (voice only) Rabbit Ears: The Tale of Peter Rabbit, 1987; Rabbit Ears: The Tale of Jeremy Fisher, 1987; The Tailor of Gloucester, 1988; Rabbit Ears: The Fisherman and His Wife, 1989; Chrysanthemum, 1999; Artificial Intelligence: AI, 2001; The Ant Bully, 2006; actress: (TV films) Secret Service, 1977; The Deadliest Season, 1977; Uncommon Women and Others, 1979; Alice at the Palace, 1982; actress, exec. prodr. First Do No Harm, 1997; narrator The Velveteen Rabbit, 1984 (Emmy award Best Children's Rec.); A Vanishing Wilderness, 1990; actress: (TV miniseries) Holocaust, 1978 (Emmy award for Outstanding Lead Actress in a Mini-series, 1978); Angels in America, 2003 (Screen Actors Guild Award for best actress, Golden Globe for best actress, Emmy award Outstanding Lead Actress in a Mini-series or a movie, 2004). Named Officer, French Ordre des Arts et des Lettres, 2000; named one of 100 Most Influential People, Time Mag., 2006; recipient Mademoiselle award, 1976, Woman of Yr. award, B'nai Brith, 1979, Hasty Pudding Soc., Harvard U., 1980, Best Supporting Actress award, Nat. Bd. of Rev., 1979, Best Actress award, 1982, Star of Yr. award, Nat. Assn. Theater Owners, 1983, People's Choice award, 1983, 85, 86, 87, 1990, Women in Film Crystal award, 1998, Gotham award for Lifetime Achievement, 1999, Bette Davis Lifetime Achievement award, 1999, Lifetime Achievement award, Am. Film Inst., 2004, most nominated actor ever for an Academy Award. Office: Creative Artists Agy 9830 Wilshire Blvd Beverly Hills CA 90212-1825*

STREET, JEANNE, psychologist; b. Lexington, Va., Oct. 1, 1952; d. Marion Scott and Wilma Mae Street; m. Clif Dopson, Nov. 23, 1979; 1 child, Lorna Street Dopson stepchildren: Jennifer Ellen Rennix, Steven Eric Dopson. BA, U. Fla., 1973, MA, 1975, PhD, 1978. Lic. Psychologist La. State Bd. Profl. Examiners. Staff psychologist Chapel Hill Mental Health Ctr., NC; pvt. practice Shreveport, La. Assoc. prof. La. State U. Health Scis. Ctr., Shreveport; consulting psychologist Brentwood Hosp., Shreveport, DeSoto Parish Office Children's Svcs., Mansfield, La. Mem. Highland Restoration Assn., Shreveport, 1982—, Highland Area Partnership, Shreveport, 1990—; bd. mem. Noel Children's Learning Ctr., Shreveport, 2005. Recipient Best Tchr. 2003, La. State U. Health Scis. Ctr., Shreveport. Mem.: APA, Soc. Personality Assessment, Southeastern Psychol. Assn., Phi Beta Kappa. Office: 610 Herndon Ave Shreveport LA 71101 Office Phone: 318-424-3867.

STREET, LELA KATHRYN, retired secondary education educator; b. Sullivan, Ind., May 2, 1942; d. Harold Seward and Kathryn Nell (Leach) Gambill; m. Robert Wayne Street, Aug. 18, 1963; children: Erin Wynne, Heather Leigh. BS, Ind. State U., 1964, MS, 1971. Tchr. Northeast Sch. Corp., Farmersburg, Ind., 1965-66, Southwest Sch. Corp., Sullivan, Ind., 1966-99; ret., 1999. Sponsor Young Astronaut-NASA, Sullivan, 1986-94, Sci. Club, 1994-99; dir. Jr. High-Elem. Sci. Fair, 1967-99; coach Sci. Olympics, Sullivan, 1990-99, Thinking Cap Quiz Bowl, Sullivan, 1992-99, Odyssey of Mind, Sullivan, 1989-90, Sullivan High and Jr. H.S. Track, 1975-96. Treas. Friends Sullivan Libr., 2001—. Named Educator of Yr. Sullivan Jaycees, 1972; nominee Golden Apple award WTHI TV, Terre Haute, Ind., 1991, 92. Mem. NEA, Nat. Mid. Sch. Sci. Tchrs. Assn., Ind. State Tchrs. Assn., S.W. Sullivan Edn. Assn. (treas., com. mem. 1966-99), Hoosier Assn. Sci. Tchrs., Sullivan County Ret. Tchrs. Assn., Delta Kappa Gamma (past rec. sec., sec., treas. 2002—), Phi Delta Kappa. Baptist. Avocations: travel, music, antiques, reading, walking.

STREET, PATRICIA LYNN, retired secondary school educator; b. Lillington, N.C., May 3, 1940; d. William Banks and Vandalia (McLean) S.; m. Col. Robert Gest, June 2, 1962 (div. 1985); children: Robert, Roblyn Renee. BS, Livingstone Coll., 1962; MEd, Salisbury State U., 1974; postgrad., various, 1968—. Tchr. Govt. of Guam Marianas Island, Agana, Guam, 1962-64; sec., typist USAF, Glasgow AFB, Mont., 1964-65, Syracuse (N.Y.) U. AeroSpace Engring., 1966-67; tchr. Syracuse (N.Y.) City Sch. System, 1967-69; lectr. U. of Md., Eastern Shore, Princess Anne, Md., 1970-72; tchr. Prince George's County Pub. Schs., Upper Marlboro, Md., 1973—. Instr. U. Guam, Anderson AFB, 1963, U.S. Armed Forces Inst., Anderson AFB, 1963, Yorktowne Bus. Inst., Landover, Md., 1987-90, Cheseapeake Bus. Inst., Clinton, Md., 1983-89; asst. advisor student tchrs. U. Md. Ea. Shore, Princess Anne, 1972; adj. instr. Bowie State U., 1990—; conv. speaker. Mem. AAUW, NEA, ASCD, Am. Vocat. Assn., Md. Bus. Edn. Assn. (pres.-elect 1987-88, pres. 1988-89, Educator of Yr. 1989), Md. Vocat. Assn. (regional rep. 1986-89, audit chmn. 1987-89, Vocat.-Tech. Educator of Yr. 1989), Ea. Bus. Edn. Assn. (co-editor newsletter 1990-91, secondary exec. dir. 1991-94, pres.-elect 1997-98, pres. 1998-99), Md. State Tchrs. Assn., D.C. Bus. Edn. Assn., Nat. Bus. Edn. Assn., Nat. Bus. Edn. Assn. (exec. bd. dirs. 1998-99), Internat. Soc. for Bus. Edn., Md. Bus. Edn. Com., Prince George's County Edn. Assn., Delta Pi Epsilon. Democrat. Baptist. Avocations: sewing, singing, modern creative dancing. Home: 10107 Welshire Dr Upper Marlboro MD 20772-6204 Office: Prince George's Pub Sch Upper Marlboro MD 20772

STREET, PICABO, Olympic athlete; b. Triumph, Idaho, Apr. 3, 1971; Downhill skier U.S. Ski Team, 1994—. Autobiography Picabo: Nothing to Hide. Named World Cup Downhill Women's Champion, 1995, 1996; recipient Silver medal Women's Downhill Alpine Skiing, Olympic Games, Lillehammer, 1994, Bronze and Gold medals, World Championships, 1996, Gold medals (3) Women's Super Giant Slalom Alpine Skiing, Nagano, Japan, 1998, medal, Winter Olympics. Office Phone: 208-578-9880.

STREET, TERRI M., artist, educator; b. Bklyn., Dec. 11, 1929; d. William George Nappenbach and Marie Virginia Caron; m. Norman Street, Oct. 11, 1962 (dec. Sept. 1979); children: Lesa, David. Student, Chinourd Art Sch., 1948, Art Students League, 1950—53, Am. Art Sch., 1953—54, NYU Inst. Fine Art, 1953—54, Nat. Acad. Design, 1953—58, Vrijy Acad., 1956. Cert. tchr. Calif. Instr. Traphagen Sch. Design, NY, 1959, Conejo Valley Adult Sch., Thousand Oaks, Calif., 1980—93; art dir. Dwight Sch. for Girls, NJ, 1960—62, Carden Conejo Sch., Calif., 1976—93; exhibit specialist Smithsonian, Wash., 1962—63; founder, dir. Burke Sch. Art, Va., 1968—70; art cons. for occupl. therapists Pediatric Rehabilitation, Poland, Slovakia, Hungary, 1988—90; founder, dir. Hawthorne Studio, Portland, Oreg., 1993—. Instr. St. Francis Svcs., Portland, 2000—. Exhibitions include Knickerbocker Art Guild, 1955, Allied Artists Nat. Acad. Design, NY, 1956, Smithsonian Art Inst., Wash., DC, 1964, Gallery 33, Portland, Oreg., 1997—98, Hawthorne Studio; illustrator: Problem Solving in Occupational Therapy; numerous pvt. collections. Cons. park and recreation Children's Art Festival, Calif.; charter mem. Nat. Women's Mus.; coun. mem. St. Francis Ch., Portland. Fogg Mus. of Haravard U. scholar, 1954, Louis Comfort Tiffany fellow, 1956. Mem.: Allied Artists, Oriental Art Soc., Oreg. Soc. Artists, Keizer Art Assn., Watercolor Soc. Oreg., Nat. Watercolor Soc. (assoc.), Northwest Watercolor Soc. (assoc.), Art Students League (life). Home and Office: Hawthorne Studio 3436 SE Madison Portland OR 97214 E-mail: tstreetart@msn.com.

STREETEN, BARBARA WIARD, ophthalmologist, medical educator; b. Candia, N.H., Mar. 3, 1925; d. Robert Campbell Wiard and Gertrude Sarah Matheson; m. David Henry Palmer Streeten, Aug. 2, 1952; children: Robert Duncan, Elizabeth Anne, John Palmer. AB magna cum laude, Tufts U., 1945, MD cum laude, 1950. Diplomate Am. Bd. Ophthalmology. Jr. resident in gen. pathology Mallory Inst., Boston City Hosp., 1951-52; fellow in ophthalmic pathology Mass. Eye and Ear Infirmary, Boston, 1952-53; resident in ophthalmology Wayne County Gen. Hosp., Eloise, Mich., 1953-56; from jr. to sr. clin. instr. ophthalmology U. Mich. Med. Sch., Ann Arbor, 1956-60; from asst. prof. to prof. ophthalmology SUNY Health Sci. Ctr. (now called SUNY Upstate Med. U.), Syracuse, 1964—, dir. eye pathology lab., 1966—; from asst. prof. to prof. pathology SUNY Health Sci. Ctr., Syracuse, 1968—. Contbr. more than 120 articles to profl. jours., chapters to books. Mem. vision study sect. Nat. Eye Inst., NIH, Bethesda, Md., 1977-80, mem. bd. sci. counselors, 1982-86; mem. editl. bd., mem. editl. adv. com. Ophthalmology jour., 1982-94; gen. editor Investigative Ophthalmology and Visual Sci., 1979-82, mem. editl. bd., 1987-92. Grantee Nat. Eye Inst., NIH, 1975—2002. Mem. Am. Assn. Ophthalmic Pathologists (charter, past pres., bd. dirs., Zimmerman medal 1997), Am. Acad. Ophthalmology (honor award 1990), Verhoeff Ophthalmic Pathology Soc. (past pres.), Assn. for Rsch. in Vision and Ophthalmology (past sect. chmn.), Internat. Soc. Ophthalmic Pathology (co-v.p. N.Am. 1990-92), Phi Beta Kappa, Alpha Omega Alpha. Episcopalian. Achievements include establishment of elastic system nature of the suspensory ligament of the ocular lens; ultrastructural and immunopathologic contributions to diseases of the ocular connective tissue matrix, particularly those related to cataract and glaucoma. Home: 334 Berkeley Dr Syracuse NY 13210-3000 Office: SUNY Upstate Med Univ WH Rm 2107 766 Irving Ave Syracuse NY 13210-1602

STREETER, CAROL, technology marketing executive; b. Radford, Va., Apr. 11, 1963; d. John Elliott Streeter and Nancy Mabry Christenson. Degree in elec. engring., Va. Poly. Inst., 1986; MBA in Fin., Loyola Coll., Balt., 1993. Electronics engr.-trainee U.S. Army, Aberdeen, Md., 1983-87; mem. tech. staff Command Ctr., Clarksburg, Md., 1987-88; svcs. mgr. Bell Atlantic, Harrisburg, Pa., 1988-93; dir. product mktg. Newbridge Networks, Herndon, Va., 1993-98, asst. v.p. product mktg., 1998—; dir. bus. devel. Interpath Comm., Raleigh, N.C., 1998; v.p. mktg. Newbridge Networks, Chantilly, Va., 1999-2000; v.p. solutions mktg. Alcatel USA, Chantilly, 2000—. Cons. mktg. devel., Gambrills, Md., 1998; presenter in field.

STREETER, STEPHANIE ANNE, printing company executive; b. Boston, Sept. 19, 1957; d. Andrew Geoffrey Galef and Suzanne Jane (Cohen) Sidy; m. Edward Stanley Streeter, Feb. 22, 1980. BA in Polit. Sci., Stanford U., 1979. Mgr. market analysis Xerox Small Bus. System, Sunnyvale, Calif., 1980-81; regional sales mgr. Xerox Office Products Divsn., Sunnyvale, Calif., 1981-83; product mgr. Decision Data Computer Corp., Horsham, Pa., 1983-85; sr. product mgr. Avery Dennison Corp., Covina, Calif., 1985-88, bus. mgr. indexes, 1988-89, bus. mgr. computer supplies, 1989-90, dir. mktg., computer products, 1990-91, v.p. gen. mgr. label divsn. Diamond Bar, Calif., 1991-93, v.p., gen. mgr., Avery Dennison Brands, 1993—96, worldwide group v.p., 1996—2000; COO idealab!, Pasadena, Calif., 2000; pres., COO Banta Corp., Menasha, Wis., 2001—02, pres., CEO, 2002—04, chmn., pres., CEO, 2004—. Bd. dirs. Banta Corp., 2001—. Bd. dirs. Wis. Mfrs. and Commerce. Fellow Internat. Women's Forum. Democrat. Avocations: bicycling, skiing. Office: Banta Corp 225 Main St Menasha WI 54952*

STREICHER, GEORGINA RODRIGUEZ, special education educator; b. Harlingen, Tex., Oct. 7, 1970; d. Rodolfo Salinas and Maria Del Socorro Rodriguez-Zamarron; m. Craig Stephen Streicher, May 2, 1992; children: Abel Lee Rodriguez, Jacob Edward, Logan Eric. BA, U. of Tex. at Brownsville, 2003, MEd, 2005. Cert. ednl. diagnostician State Bd. for Educator Certification, 2005, tchr. English and spl. edn. State Bd. for Educator Certification, 2003. Spl. edn. tchr. Harlingen C.I.S.D., Harlingen, Tex., 2002—04, South Tex. I.S.D., Mercedes, 2004—. Recipient Pres.'s Honor Roll, U. of Tex. at Brownsville, 2004. Home: 3934 Bourbon St Apt #15 Harlingen TX 78550 Office: Science Academy 900 Med High Dr Mercedes TX 78570 Office Phone: 956-565-2454. Office Fax: 956-565-9112. Personal E-mail: pebbles89@yahoo.com. E-mail: georgina.streicher@stisd.net.

STREISAND, BARBRA JOAN, singer, actress, film director; b. Bklyn., Apr. 24, 1942; d. Emanuel and Diana (Rosen) S.; m. Elliott Gould, Mar. 1963 (div.); 1 son, Jason Emanuel; m. James Brolin, July 1, 1998. Grad. high sch., Bklyn.; student, Yeshiva of Bklyn.; Doctorate of Arts and Humanities (hon.), Brandeis U., 1995. NY theatre debut Another Evening with Harry Stoones, 1961; appeared in Broadway musicals I Can Get It for You Wholesale, 1962, Funny Girl, 1964-65; motion pictures include Funny Girl, 1968, Hello Dolly, 1969, On a Clear Day You Can See Forever, 1970, The Owl and the Pussy Cat, 1970, What's Up Doc?, 1972, Up the Sandbox, 1972, The Way We Were, 1973, For Pete's Sake, 1974, Funny Lady, 1975, The Main Event, 1979, All Night Long, 1981, Nuts, 1987, Meet the Fockers, 2004; actor, prodr. (film): A Star is Born, 1976; prodr., dir., actor: Yentl, 1983, The Prince of Tides, 1991, The Mirror Has Two Faces, 1996 (ASCAP Award for score, 1996); exec. prodr.: (TV movie) Serving in Silence: The Margarethe Cammermeyer Story, 1995; TV spls. include My Name is Barbra, 1965 (5 Emmy awards), Color Me Barbra, 1966, Barbra Streisand: The Concert, 1995 (Cable ACE award for best performance and for best direction, Two Emmy awards), Barbra Streisand: Timeless, 2001 (Emmy award); rec. artist on Columbia Records; Gold record albums include People, 1965, My Name is Barbra, 1965, Color Me Barbra, 1966, Barbra Streisand: A Happening in Central Park, 1968, Barbra Streisand: One Voice, Stoney End, 1971, Barbra Joan Streisand, 1972, The Way We Were, 1974, A Star is Born, 1976, Superman, 1977, The Stars Salute Israel at 30, 1978, Wet, 1979, (with Barry Gibb) Guilty, 1980, Emotion, 1984, The Broadway Album, 1986, Til I Loved You, 1989; other albums include: A Collection: Greatest Hits, 1989, Just for the Record, 1991, Back to Broadway, 1993, Concert at the Forum, 1993, The Concert Recorded Live at Madison Square Garden, 1994, The Concert Highlights, 1995, Higher Ground, 1997, A Love Like Ours, 1999, Christmas Memories, 2001, The Essential Barbara Streisand, 2002, The Movie Album, 2003, Guilty Pleasures, 2005, Guilty Too, 2005, Nur das Beste, 2006. Recipient Emmy award, CBS-TV spl. (My Name Is Barbra), 1964, Acad. award as best actress (Funny Girl), 1968, Golden Globe award (Funny Girl), 1969, co-recipient Acad. award for best song (Evergreen), 1976, Georgie award AGVA 1977, Grammy awards for best female pop vocalist, 1963, 64, 65, 77, 86, for best song writer (with Paul Williams), 1977, 2 Grammy nominations for Back to Broadway, 1994; Nat. Acad. of Recording Arts & Sciences Lifetime Achievement Award, 1994, Cecil B. Demille Lifetime Achievement Award, 2000, Life Achievement award, Am. Film Inst., 2001, Liberty & Justice Award, Rainbow/PUSH Coalition, 2001, Humanitarian award, Human Rights Campaign, 2004. Office: Barbra Streisand c/o Martin Erlichman Assoc Inc 5670 Wilshire Blvd Ste 2400 Los Angeles CA 90036 also: Nigro Karlin Segal 10100 Santa Monica Blvd Ste 1300 Los Angeles CA 90067

STRELAU, RENATE, historical researcher, artist; b. Berlin, Feb. 1, 1951; came to U.S., 1960; d. Werner Ernst and Gerda Gertrud (Bargel) S. BA, U. Calif., Berkeley, 1974; cert. Arabic lang. proficiency, Johns Hopkins U., 1976; MA, Am. U., 1985, MFA, 1991. Rsch. asst. Iranian Embassy, Washington, 1975—80. One-woman shows include Cafe Espresso, Berkeley, 1973, Riggs Bank, Arlington, Va., 1994-95, Bank of Am., Arlington, Va., 2004-05; exhibited in group shows at Watkins Gallery, Washington, 1999, Khoja Gallery, Arlington, 2002; represented in permanent collections C. Law Watkins Meml. Collection, Am. U. Mus. Mem. Am. Hist. Assn., Orgn. Am. Historians, Soc. for Historians Am. Fgn. Rels. (life). Office: PO Box 12655 Arlington VA 22219-2655 Office Phone: 703-862-9000. Business E-Mail: strelau@renatestrelau.com.

STREMPEL, EILEEN L., singer, educator; b. Syracuse, NY, July 13, 1967; d. Patricia Louise and Carlton John Strempel; m. Stephen C. Meyer, May 30, 1992; children: Gavin Carl Meyer, Dylan Strempel Meyer. MusB, Eastman Sch. of Music, Rochester, N.Y., 1988; MusD, Ind. U., Bloomington, 1998. Asst. prof. Syracuse U., NY, 1999—. Singer: (opera, songs by women composers) Love Lies Bleeding: Songs Of Libby Larsen. Recipient Presdl. Scholar in the Arts award, NFAA and Pres. Ronald Reagan, 1984. Mem.: Music Tchrs. Nat. Assn., Nat. Assn. Tchrs. of Singing (intern), Internat. Alliance for Women in Music. Achievements include soloist at the Boshoi Opera (Violetta in La Traviata), Avery Fisher Hall, Merkin Hall, for the New York Philharmonic Chamber Music Series. Frequently writes, records, and performs the work of women. Office: Syracuse Univ 308 Bowne Hall Syracuse NY 13210 Office Phone: 315-443-5036. E-mail: strempel@syr.edu.

STRENG, SARITA B., dancer, educator; b. Sept. 12, 1970; d. William and Louisa Streng. BA, U. N.Mex., Albuquerque, 1993; MA in Dance, UCLA, 2003. Dance tchr. Arts for City Youth, LA, 1999, Mira Costa Coll., Oceanside, Calif., 2001—04, Maple St. Dance Space, Albuquerque, 2005—, Harwood Arts Ctr., Albuquerque, 2005—. Home: 1217 6th St NW Albuquerque NM 87102

STRENGTH, CATHERINE BUSH, nursing educator; b. New Orleans, Dec. 7, 1955; d. Joseph Ernest Jr. and Patsy Ruth (Johnson) Bush; m. Steven Cole Strength, Aug. 18, 1984. BSN, Southeastern La. U., 1977; M of Nursing, La. State U., 1981. RN, La.; cert. med.-surg. nurse, clin. nurse specialist, instr. BLS; registered hypnotherapist. Nurse emergency rm. East Jefferson Gen. Hosp., Metairie, La., 1977—81; dir. edn. and tng. St. Jude Hosp., Kenner, La., 1982—85; asst. prof. Charity Hosp. Sch. Nursing/Delgado C.C., New Orleans, 1990—94; assoc. prof. Charity Hosp. Sch. Nursing, New Orleans, 1994—. Mem. Nat. League Nursing, Sigma Theta Tau (hon.), Epsilon Nu. Home: 3905 Lake Des Allemands Dr Harvey LA 70058-5502 Office: Charity Delgado Nursing Sch 450 S Claiborne Ave New Orleans LA 70112-1310 Office Phone: 504-568-6458. Business E-Mail: cstren@dcc.edu.

STRENGTH, JANIS GRACE, retired management executive, educator; b. Ozark, Ala., Jan. 31, 1934; d. James Marion and Mary Belle (Riley) Grace; m. Robert Samuel Strength, Sept. 12, 1954; children: Stewart A., James Houston (dec.), Robert David (dec.), James Steven (dec.) BS in Home Econs. and Edn., Auburn U., 1956; MA in Edn., Washington U., St. Louis, 1978, MA in Adminstrn., 1980. Home economist Gulf Power Co., Pensacola, Fla., 1956-59; tchr. sci. Northside Jr. High Sch., Greenwood, S.C., 1961-68; tchrs. home econs. Greenwood High Sch., 1968-70; chairperson dept. sci. Parkway West Jr. High Sch., Chesterfield, Mo., 1975-82; tchr. sci. Parkway West High Sch., Chesterfield, 1982-88; v.p.-sec. Product Safety Mgmt. Inc., Gulf Breeze, Fla., 1989—2001; ret., 2001. Chairperson dist. Phys. Scis. Curriculum Com., 1978-85, Sci. Fair Placement Com., 1978-82, Gifted Edn., 1983-84; leader Phys. Sci. Summer Workshops, Safety Sci. Lab. Workshop; sponsor Nat. Jr. Honor Soc., Parkway West Jr. Class. Supt. youth dept. Sunday sch. Greentrails Meth. Ch., sponsor summer camp; vol. fundraiser March of Dimes, Cerebral Palsy, Multiple Schlorosis, Cancer funds; judge Parkway/Monsanto/St. Louis Post Dispatch Sci. Fairs, 1978—; mem. citizens action com. Parkway Sch. Bd., 1980-84; v.p. United Meth. Women, 2000, pres. 2004. Mem. NEA, Nat. Sci. Tchrs. Assn., Ladies Golf Assn. (sec. 1998-99, 2003—), Santa Rosa Women's Club (pres. 1998-2000), Tiger Point Country Club (Gulf Breeze), Raintree Country Club (Hillsboro, Mo.). Republican. Methodist.

STREVIG, JANICE LEE, music educator; b. Balt., Oct. 19, 1957; BS, Towson U., Towson, Maryland, 1975—79; postgrad., U. Iowa, 1980—90, Temple U., 1980—90, Bucknell U., 1980—90, Towson U., 1980—90, Peabody Conservatory, 1980—90. Tchr. Balt. County Pub. Schools, Baltimore, Md., 1980—. Freelance pit musician, Md., 1980—; performer Sentimental Journey Big Band, Balt., 1980—; pvt. clarinet tchr., Balt., 1979—95. Girls fastpitch softball coach Lansdowne (Md.) H.S. Jayvee, 1989—97; soloist Catonsville (Md.) United Meth. Ch., 1998—, dir. vocal ensemble, 2000—. Mem.: Md. Music Educators Assn. (chm. exhibits 1987—, bd. dirs. 1987—), Music Educators Nat. Conf. (25 Yr. Svc. award 2004), Kappa Delta Pi (v.p. 1978—79). United Methodist. Avocations: playing women's baseball, crossword puzzles, reading. Office Phone: 410-887-0854. Personal E-mail: jbrahms@comcast.net.

STRIBLIN, LORI ANN, critical care nurse, insurance agent; b. Valley, Ala., Sept. 23, 1962; d. James Author and Dorothy Jane (Cole) Burt; m. Thomas Edward Striblin, Oct. 26, 1984; children: Natalie Nicole, Crystal Danielle. AAS in Nursing, So. Union State Jr. Coll., Valley, Ala., 1992. RN, Ala.; cert. ACLS, BLS, in fitness nutrition ICS. Surg. staff nurse East Ala. Med. Ctr., Opelika, 1992-93, surg. charge nurse, 1993-95, critical care ICU staff nurse, 1993-95; nurse case mgr. East Ala. Home Care, Opelika, 1995-96; staff devel. coord., medicare coord. Lanett (Ala.) Geriatric Ctr., 1996-97; case mgr. Lanier Home Health Svcs., Valley, Ala., 1996-97; med. advisor Nu Image Weight Loss Ctr., Opelika, Ala., 1996-97, nurse case mgr. weight loss ctr., counselor, diet educator, 1996-98; nurse case mgr. Chattahoochie Hospice, Valley, Ala., 1998; case mgr. Chattahoochee Hospice, 1998; critical care nurse cardiovasc. ICU and telementry unit East Ala. Med. Ctr., Opelika, 1999—2002, dialysis staff nurse renal unit, 2003—; dialysis nurse Frecinus Dialysis Corp., Valley, Ala., 2002; case mgr. Alacare Home Health/Hospice, Opelika, Ala., 2004—05; clin. nurse mgr. Hughston Orthopedic Hosp., Columbus, Ga., 2006—. Clin. instr. educator So. Union C.C., Valley,

1994-97. Mem. AACN, Ala. State Nurses Assn. Baptist. Avocations: crafts, horseback riding, hiking, swimming, reading, arts. Home: 1608 31st St Valley AL 36854-2925 Office: Hughston Orthop Hosp 100 Frist Ct Columbus GA

STRICK, SADIE ELAINE, psychologist; d. Michael and Mary (Oziemblowski) Wierzbicki; m. John Mackovjak, Dec. 31, 1947 (dec. Mar. 1972); children: Deborah, Susan; m. Ellis Strick, Aug. 11, 1974 (dec Jan. 2005). BSW, U. Pitts., 1975, MEd, 1977, PhD, 1981. Lic. psychologist; fellow, diplomate Am. Bd. Med. Psychotherapists. Psychologist I Mayview State Hosp., Bridgeville, Pa., 1984-87; owner Counseling & Behavior Specialists, P.C., Pitts., 1981—. Mem. C.G. Jung Ednl. Ctr., Pitts., 1980-99; guest speaker Compassionate Friends, Pitts., 1986—, Womens Career Conv., Pitts., 1982. Bd. dirs. OAR/Allegheny, Pitts., 1981-82. Fellow Pa. Psychol. Assn.; mem. APA. Avocations: writing, walking, travel, gourmet cooking, reading, music. Home: 4601 Fifth Ave #128 Pittsburgh PA 15213 Office: Counseling and Behavior Specialists PC 429 Forbes Ave Ste 1614 Pittsburgh PA 15219-1604 Office Phone: 412-765-1665.

STRICKER, MARY FRAN, music educator; d. Elmer George and Norma Jean Stricker; m. Robert J. Erny II. BA in Music Edn., McMurry U., 1979; degree in Med. Asst., Colo. Coll. Med. and Dental Assts., 1986. Cert. tchr. music Tex., 82, med. asst. Colo., 1986. Med. asst. Redwood Med. Lab., Rohnert Pk., Calif., 1990—95; music tchr. Stephenville (Tex.) Ind. Sch. Dist., 1996—. Bookkeeper Ross Stores, Rohnert Pk., 1993—95; sales Wal-mart, Granbury, Tex., 1994—96; substitute tchr. Granbury (Tex.) Ind. Sch. Dist., 1994—96; ind. vocalist, 1973—; pvt. voice and piano tchr., 1993—. Composer: (songs) Blue & Gold Song, 1999; performer (singer): (Operas) several companies, 1983—96. Mem. Cross Timbers Fine Arts Coun., 1999—; childrens choir dir. United Meth. Ch., Rohnert Pk., 1992—95; music dir. First Christian Disciples of Christ Ch., Stephenville, 2002—. Mem.: AAUW, Tex. Music Edn. Assn., Met. Opera Assn. (opera singer 1986—), Nat. Assn. Tchrs. Singing, Tex. Fedn. Tchrs. (campus rep. 2003—). Republican. Lutheran. Avocations: swimming, bowling, antiques. Home: 1361 N Garfield Ave Stephenville TX 76401 Office: Gilbert Intermediate School 950 N Dale Ave Stephenville TX 76401

STRICKLAND, BONNIE RUTH, psychologist, educator; b. Louisville, Nov. 24, 1936; d. Roy E. and Billie P. (Whitfield) S. BS, Ala. Coll., 1958; MS, Ohio State U., 1960, PhD (USPHS fellow), 1962. Diplomate: clin. psychology Am. Bd. Examiners in Profl. Psychology. From asst. to asso. prof. psychology Emory U., Atlanta, 1962—73, dean of women, 1964—67; prof. psychology U. Mass., Amherst, 1973—2003, prof. emeritus, 2003—, chmn. dept. psychology, 1976—77, 1978—82, assoc. to chancellor, 1983—84. Mem. adv. coun. NIMH, 1984-87; Sigma Xi nat. lectr., 1991-93. Adv. editor numerous psychology jours., acad. pub. houses; contbg. author texts personality theory.; contbr. of numerous articles on social personality and clin. psychology to profl. jours.; contbg. author of two citation classics. Recipient Outstanding Faculty award Emory U., 1968-69; Chancellor's medal disting. service U. Mass., 1983. Fellow APA (pres. divsn. clin. psychology 1983, pres. divsn. gen. psychology 2005, chmn. bd. profl. affairs 1980-83, chmn. policy and planning bd. 1983-85, pres. 1987, bd. dirs. 1986-87, Outstanding Leadership award 1992, Disting. Contbns. and Psychology in the Pub. Interest award 1999, Presdl. Citation 2001), Am. Psychol. Soc. (founder 1988, bd. dirs. 1989-93), New Eng. Psychol. Assn. (Disting. Contbns. award 2002), Am. Assn. Applied and Preventive Psychology (founder 1990, bd. dirs. 1990-94, pres. 1992-94), Acad. Clin. Psychology (chmn. 1982-83). Home: 558 Federal St Belchertown MA 01007-9754 Office: U Mass Dept Psychology Amherst MA 01003-7710

STRICKLAND, BRENDA B., music educator; b. Kansas City, Mo., Jan. 18, 1952; d. Dale Dillon and Martha Anne Bunch; m. John A.V. Strickland, Nov. 23, 1985. B Music Edn., U. Mo., Kansas City, 1974, M Music Edn., 1984. Music tchr. Shawnee Mission Schs., Overland Park, Kans., 1975-78, 79-85; sales rep. wordprocessing Xerox Corp., Overland Park, 1978-79; music tchr. Blue Valley Sch. Dist., Overland Park, 1985-92, Hanahau'oli Sch., Honolulu, 1992—2001, Arbor Montessori, Decatur, Ga., 2001—. Pres. Heart of Am. Orff Schulwerk Assn., Kansas City, 1990-91. Recipient Stanley Sch. Master Tchr. award, NEA, 1988, Dist. Master Tchr. award, 1991. Mem. Am. Orff Schulwerk Assn., Music Educators Nat. Conf. (named one of Top Ten Music Educators in Hawaii 1999), Greater Atlanta Orff Schulwerk Assn., Hawaii Orff Schulwerk Assn. (pres. 1994-96), Hawaii Music Educators Assn. (Outstanding Music Educator 2000). Mem. Unity Ch. Avocations: singing, piano, reading, church work. Home: 4581 Village Dr Atlanta GA 30338-5741 Office: Arbor Montessori Sch 2998 LaVista Rd Decatur GA 30033

STRICKLAND, DOROTHY, education educator; BS, Newark State Coll.; MA, PhD, NYU. Elem. sch. tchr. N.J. pub. sch. sys., reading cons., learning disabilities specialist; prof. edn. Rutgers U., New Brunswick, NJ, 1985—, Samuel DeWitt Proctor Prof. Edn., 2002—. Active in numerous state and nat. adv. bds. Author: Language Literacy and the Child, Process Reading and Writing: A Literature Based Approach, The Administration and Supervision of Reading Programs, Educating Black Children: America's Challenge, Family Storybook Reading, Listen Children: An Anthology of Black Literature, Families: An Anthology of Poetry for Young Children, Teaching Phonics Today, 1998, Beginning Reading and Writing, 2000, Supporting Struggling Readers and Writers, 2002, Preparing Our Teachers, 2002, Language Arts: Learning and Teaching, 2003, Learning About Print in Preschool Settings, 2004. Inducted into the Reading Hall of Fame, pres., 1997-98. Mem. Nat. Coun. Tchrs. English (Rewey Belle Inglis award for Outstanding Woman in English Education Annual Conv., rsch. award, Outstanding Educator in Lang. Arts award 1998), Internat. Reading Assn. (past pres., Outstanding Tchr. Educator of reading award). Home: 131 Coccio Dr West Orange NJ 07052-4121 Office: Rutgers U Dept Edn Grad Sch Edn New Brunswick NJ 08903

STRICKLAND, JULIA B., lawyer; b. San Francisco, Aug. 21, 1954; Student, Dartmouth Coll.; BA with honors, Univ. Calif., San Diego, 1975; JD, UCLA, 1978. Bar: Calif. 1978. Summer intern Stroock & Stroock & Lavan LLP, LA, 1977, ptnr., chair, fin. svcs. litig. practice, mem., operating exec. com, 1996—. Chair, consumer fin. svcs. litig. program Practising Law Inst., 1997—. Bd. of editors Banking Law Jour., editorial bd. Wall St. Lawyer, frequent lectr., writer in field. Named a Super Lawyer, LA Mag.; named one of Top 50 Women Litigators, LA Daily Jour., 2004. Mem.: Mortgage Bankers Assn., Assn. Bus. Trial Lawyers (bd. dir.). Office: Stroock & Stroock & Lavan LLP 2029 Century Pk E Los Angeles CA 90067-3086 Office Phone: 310-556-5806. Office Fax: 310-556-5959. Business E-Mail: jstrickland@strook.com.

STRICKLAND, SYLVIA RAYE, social worker; b. Grand Prarie, Tex., Feb. 21, 1945; d. Nathaniel and Flora Evelyn Strickland; m. Julian B. Angel, Oct. 6, 1973 (div. Apr. 1983); 1 child, Sarah Renee Angel. BSW, U. So. Colo., Pueblo, 1986; MSW, N.Mex. Highlands U., Las Vegas, N.Mex., 1987. Lic. psychotherapist 1998, cert. grief recovery specialist Grief Recovery Inst., 2005. Social worker Highland Park Nursing Home, Pueblo, 1988; social worker III El Paso County Social Svcs., Colorado Springs, Colo., 1988—89; resident svcs. coord. Villa Santa Maria, Colorado Springs, Colo., 1990—91, ballot initative circulator, 1992; social worker Medalion Health Ctr., Colorado Springs, 1993—; coord. activities Medalion Health Ctr. and Personal Care Unit, 1993—96. Vol. Hospice of Comforter, 1994—96; active St. Paul's Cath. Ch.; sec. Social Work Action Team, U. So. Colo., 1984—85. Mem.: Satellite S.W. Avocations: choir, water colors, attending concerts, quilting. Home: PO Box 38123 Colorado Springs CO 80937-8123 Office Phone: 719-381-4967.

STRIDER, MARJORIE VIRGINIA, artist, educator; b. Guthrie, Okla. d. Clifford R. and Marjorie E. (Schley) S. BFA, Kansas City Art Inst., 1962. Faculty Sch. Visual Arts, N.Y.C., 1970-2001; artist-in-residence City U. Grad. Ctr. Mall, N.Y.C., 1976, Fabric Workshop, Phila., 1978, Grassi Palace, Venice, Italy, 1978. One-woman shows include Pace Gallery, N.Y.C., 1963-64, Nancy Hoffman Gallery, N.Y.C., 1973-74, Weather Spoon Mus., U.N.C., Chapel Hill, 1974, City U. Grad. Center Mall, 1976, Clocktower, N.Y.C., 1976, Sculpture Center, N.Y.C., 1983, Steinbaum Gallery, N.Y.C., 1983, 84, Andre Zarre Gallery, 1993, 95, Outdoor Installation, N.Y.C., 1997, Selby Gallery, Ringling Sch. of Art, Sarasota, Fla., 1998, Neuberger Mus., Purchase, N.Y., 1999; exhibited in group shows at Sculpture Center, N.Y.C., 1981, Drawing Biennale, Lisbon, Portugal, 1981, Newark Mus., 1984, William Rockhill Nelson Mus., Kansas City, 1985, Danforth Mus., Framingham, Mass., 1987, Delahoyd Gallery, N.Y.C., 1992; represented in permanent collections Guggenheim Mus., N.Y.C., U. Colo., Boulder, Albright-Knox Mus., Buffalo, Des Moines Art Center, Storm King (N.Y.) Art Center, Larry Aldrich Mus., Ridgefield, Conn., City U. Grad. Center, N.Y.C., Hirschhorn Mus. and Sculpture Garden, Washington, Santa Fe (N. Mex.) Mus. of Art, also pvt. collections. Grantee Nat. Endowment for Arts, 1973, 80, Longview Found., 1974, Pollock-Krasner Found., 1990, Florsheim Art Fund, 1998, 2000; Va. Ctr. for Creative Arts fellow, 1974, 92, Millay Colony for Arts fellow, 1992, Yaddo Colony, 1996-97 Office Phone: 845-246-1301. Business E-Mail: m_strider@hvc.rr.com.

STRIEBY, B. LORRAINE, artist; b. Morgantown, W.Va., Dec. 5, 1938; d. Charles Willis Ayer and Margaret Ann Ferko; m. Michael Strieby (dec.); children: Vicki Parzyk, Lisa Magistro, Lori Constantine, Ann; m. Stanley Veerin Gunn, Nov. 22, 2003. BA in Bus. Edn., Calif. State U., Northridge, 1976, secondary tchg. credential, 1977. Tchr. L.A. Unified Sch. Dist., 1978—81. Pres. Women Painters West, L.A., 1995—97. Exhibitions include Art Concepts Gallery, Tacoma, 1997, Black Sheep Gallery, Hardwarden Castle, Wales, 1999, Westminster Gallery, London, 1999, S.E. La. U. Gallery, Hammond, 2000, Segreto Gallery, Santa Fe, 2002, Barlow Gallery, New Orleans, 2004, Mus. Making Music, Carlsbad, Calif., 2004, Williamson Art Gallery and Mus., Liverpool, Eng., 2004, Sotto South Gallery, Savannah, Ga., 2004—06, Barrie Holt Gallery, New Orleans, 2006, Charlevoix Street Gallery, Albuquerque, 2006, Adobe Ranch Gallery, Chatsworth, Calif. Various positions Rep. Women West Valley, L.A., 1990—99. Recipient Golden Products award, Nat. Acrylic Painters Assn. Home: PO Box 4928 Chatsworth CA 91311 Office Phone: 818-261-3968. E-mail: adobeart818@earthlink.net.

STRIED, JESSICA NICOLE, elementary school educator; b. Marion, Ohio, July 8, 1977; d. Philip John and Debra Kay (Popp) Stephenson; m. Keith Harold Stried, Dec. 22, 2001; 1 child, Carter. BS in Biology, Ashland U., 1999, M in Edn. and Curriculum, 2002. Tchr. sci. Olentangy Schs., Lewis Ctr., Ohio, 2001—. Chair sci. dept. Olentangy Schs., 2003—, chair sci. fair, 2003—. Tchr. Sunday sch. Delaware Christian Ch., Ohio, 2004—. Personal E-mail: jessicastried@yahoo.com.

STRIEFSKY, LINDA A(NN), lawyer; b. Carbondale, Pa., Apr. 27, 1952; d. Leo James and Antoinette Marie (Carachio) S.; m. James Richard Carlson, Nov. 3, 1984; children: David Carlson, Paul Carlson, Daniel Carlson. BA summa cum laude, Marywood Coll., 1974; JD, Georgetown U., 1977. Bar: Ohio 1977. Assoc. Thompson Hine LLP (formerly Thompson, Hine & Flory), Cleve., 1977-85, ptnr., 1985—. Loaned exec. United Way N.E. Ohio, Cleve., 1978; trustee ideastream, Mus. Theater Edn. Programming. Mem. ABA (real estate fin. com. 1980-87, vice chmn. leader liability com. 1993-97, mem. non-traditional real estate fin. com. 1987—, chair securitization and spl. financing techniques com. 2006—), Am. Bar Found., Am. Coll. Real Estate Lawyers (bd. govs. 1994-98, 06—, treas. 1999), Internat. Coun. Shopping Ctrs., Nat. Assn. Office and Indsl. Parks, Urban Land Inst. (chmn. Cleve. dist. coun. 1996-2000), Cleve. Real Estate Women, Ohio Bar Assn. (bd. govs. real property sect. 1985-97), Greater Cleve. Bar Assn. (chmn. bar applicants com. 1983-84, exec. coun. young lawyers sect. 1982-85, chmn. 1984-85, mem. exec. coun. real property sect. 1980-84, Merit Svc. award 1983, 85), Pi Gamma Mu. Democrat. Roman Catholic. Home: 2222 Delamere Dr Cleveland OH 44106-3204 Office: Thompson Hine LLP 3900 Key Ctr 127 Public Square Cleveland OH 44114-1216 Office Phone: 216-566-5733. Business E-Mail: linda.striefsky@thompsonhine.com.

STRIER, KAREN BARBARA, anthropologist, educator; b. Summit, N.J., May 22, 1959; d. Murray Paul and Arlene Strier. BA, Swarthmore Coll., 1980; MA, Harvard U., 1981, PhD, 1986. Lectr. anthropology Harvard U., Cambridge, Mass., 1986—87; asst. prof. Beloit Coll., Wis., 1987—89, U. Wis., Madison, 1989—92, assoc. prof., 1992—95, prof., 1995—, dept. chair, 1994—96. Panel mem. U.S. Dept. Edn., Washington, 1989—92. Author: (book) Faces in the Forest, 1999, Primate Behavioral Ecology, 2d edit., 2003; co-author: Planning, Purposing, and Presenting Science Effectively; mem. editl. bd.: Internat. Jour. Primatology, 1990—, Primates, 1991—, Yearbook of Phys. Anthropology. Recipient Presdl. Young Investigator award, NSF, 1989—94, NAS, 2005. Fellow: AAAS (coun. del. anthropology sect. 1998—2000), Am. Anthropol. Assn. (chair elect anthropology sect. 2005); mem.: NAS, Animal Behavior Soc., Internat. Primatological Soc., Am. Assn. Phys. Anthropologists. Office: U Wis Dept Anthropology 5403 Social Sci Bldg 1180 Observatory Dr Madison WI 53706-1320 Office Phone: 608-262-0302. E-mail: kbstrier@wisc.edu.

STRIKER, SUSAN JOAN GLASER, art educator; d. Ben and Sylvia (Mann) Glaser; m. Michael Striker, Apr. 9, 1966 (div. 1991); 1 child, Jason Scot Frederic). BA in Fine Arts, Hofstra U., 1965; MA in Fine Arts, Hunter Coll., 1968. Cert. art tchr., N.Y., sch. adminstrn. and supervision, N.Y. Art tchr., Valhalla, NY, 1964-66, Uniondale, NY, 1966-79; dept. chair, 1970—77; art tchr. Lakeland Schs., Shrub Oak, NY, 1990—91, dept. chair, 1990—91; art tchr. Newburgh City Sch. Sys., NY, Greenwich Pub. Schs., Conn., 1994—. Cooperating tchr. Hofstra U., Hempstead, NY, 1966-79, instr. art, 1971, Elizabeth Seton Coll., Yonkers, NY, 1982, Manhattanville Coll., Purchase, NY, 1994-96; designer curriculum for children Brooks Meml. Art Gallery, Memphis, 1966; tchr. workshop condr., 1982-; founder, owner, dir. Young at Art, 1984—; TV appearances. Author: The Anti-Coloring Book, 1978, The Second Anti-Coloring Book, 1979, Exploring Space on Earth, 1980, The Third Anti-Coloring Book, 1980, The Anti-Coloring Book of Red Letter Days, 1981, The Fourth Anti-Coloring Book, 1981, The Anti-Coloring Book of Masterpieces, 1982, The Fifth Anti-Coloring Book, 1982, The Anti-Coloring Calendar, 1983, The Anti-Coloring Calendar, 1983, The Inventors Anti-Coloring Book, 1983, The Anti-Coloring Book for Adults, 1983, The Sixth Anti-Coloring Book, 1983, The Superpowers Anti-Coloring Book, 1984, Please Touch, 1985, Young at Art, An Anti-Coloring Book for Preschoolers, 1985, The Mystery Anti-Coloring Book, 1991, The Newspaper Anti-Coloring Book, 1992, The Circus Anti-Coloring Book, 1994, Celebrations, An Anti-Coloring Book, 1995, Artists at Work, An Anti-Coloring Book, 1996, Nature's Wonders for the Young at Art, 1998, Young at Art, 2001, contbr. articles in field. Mem. PTA. Recipient George M. Estabrook award, Houston U., 2005. Mem. NY State Art Tchrs. Assn., Nat. Art Tchrs. Assn. Jewish. Office Phone: 203-261-4567.

STRINGER, C. VIVIAN, college basketball coach; b. Edenborn, Pa. m. William D. Stringer (dec.); children: David, Janine, Justin. Grad., Slippery Rock State Coll. Head coach Cheyney State Coll., 1971—83, U. Iowa, 1983—95, Rutgers U., 1995—. Head coach US Select Team tour China, 1980, World U. Games, Kobe, Japan, 1985, World Championship Zone Qualification Tournament, San Paulo, Brazil, 1989, US Pan-American Games, Havana, Cuba, 1991. Finalist Naismith Nat. Coach of Year award, 2000, 2001, 2003; named to Women's Basketball Hall of Fame, 2001; recipient Phila. Sportswriters' Coach of Year, 1980, Phila. Sportswriters' Coach of Year, 1981, NCAA, Wade Trophy Women's Nat. Coach of Year, 1982, Converse Women's Nat. Coach of Year, 1988, Naismith award, Converse, Sports Illustrated, USA Today, Los Angeles Times and Black Coaches Assn. Women's Coach of the Year, 1993. Mem. Amateur Basketball Assn. U.S. (bd. dirs.). Achievements include 1st person (male or female) to lead 3 different schools to the NCAA final four; recorded 750th career win, 2006.*

STRINGER, GRETCHEN ENGSTROM, consulting volunteer administrator; b. Pitts., Feb. 25, 1925; d. Birger and Gertrude Anne (Schuchman) Engstrom; m. Loren F. Stringer, Oct. 3, 1953 (dec. Sept. 1992); children: Lizbeth, Pamela, William E., Frederick E. BA, Oberlin Coll., 1946; Cert. in Teaching, U. Pitts., 1951, SUNY, Buffalo, 1964, M, 1996. Cert. vol. adminstr. Owner, founder, pres. Vol. Cons., Clarence, NY, 1979—; owner, founder, officer Non Profit Mgmt. Ctr., Buffalo, 1995-2000. Founding pres., bd. dirs. Ctrl. Referral Svc. Author: The Board Manual Workbook, 1980, rev., 2004, The Instructors Guide, 1982, A Magical Formula, 1980; co-author: Non Profit Management Education, 1998; contbr. articles to profl. jours. Exec. dir. Vol. Action Ctr., United Way Buffalo and Erie County, 1978-81; founding vice chair Erie County Commn. on Status of Women, 1989-2000; pres. Girl Scout Coun. of Buffalo and Erie County, chair, gen. mgr. cadette encampment; bd. dirs. Clarence Ctrl. Sch. Dist., 1976-86; chair, gen. mgr. Buffalo and Erie County Bicentennial Parade, 1976, Erie County Ski Swap; bd. dirs. Longview Protestant Home for Children Bd., Millard Fillmore Jr. Bd., Prevention is Primary, N.Y. Bd. State Foster Care Youth Ind. Project, others; Cmty. Hero Torch Bearer Summer Olympics, 1996; del. White House Conf. on Small Bus., 1995; vol. steering com. Martin House Restoration Corp., 1988—. Recipient Pinny Wilson Vol. award Buffalo and Erie County, 1981, Continuing Svc. award Mass. Mutual, 1987, Girl Scouts Thanks Badge, 1983, Susan Reid Greene Russell award Jr. League of Buffalo, 1994, Assoc. of Yr. award Am. Bus. Women, 1997, Women Bus. Advocate of Yr. Small Bus. Adminstrn., 1998, Prime Time award Coord. Care, 1999, Woman of Achievement award AAUW, Buffalo chpt., 2001, Woman of Achievement award Every Woman Opportunity Ctr., 2004. Mem. Nat. Assn. Women Bus. Owners (bd. pres. Buffalo chpt. 1998-2000), N.Y. Assn. Vol. Ctrs. (founding exec. bd.), Vol. Admisntrs. Western N.Y. (founding pres. 1980), Buffalo Ambassadors of C. of C. (bd. dirs.), Women's Pavilion Pan Am. Centennial 2001 (founder, pres. bd. dirs. 1999-2001), Jr. League Buffalo, Inc. (sustainer v.p. 1998-2000), Assn. Vol. Adminstrn. (chair, gen. mgr. nat. conf. 1986, nat. trainer, re-cert. chair, subcom. vol. adminstrn. higher edn.). Office: Vol Cons 9015 Cliffside Dr Clarence NY 14031-1460 Office Phone: 716-633-8264. E-mail: gestringer@adelphia.net.

STRINGER, MARY EVELYN, art historian, educator; b. Huntsville, Mo., July 31, 1921; d. William Madison and Charity (Rogers) S. AB, U. Mo., 1942; AM, U. N.C., Chapel Hill, 1955; PhD (Danforth scholar), Harvard U., 1973. From asst. prof. art to prof. Miss. State Coll. for Women (now Miss. U. for Women), Columbus, 1947-91, prof. emeritus, 1991—. Regional dir. for Miss., Census of Stained Glass Windows in Am., 1840-1940. Bd. dirs. Mississippians for Ednl. Broadcasting; mem. Miss. com. Save Outdoor Sculpture, 1992-93. Recipient Medal of Excellence award Miss. U. Women, 2003; named Honored Artist Miss. Chpt. Nat. Mus. Women in Arts, 2003; scholar Fulbright Found., 1955-56; grantee Harvard U., 1966-67, NEH, 1980. Mem. AAUW (Medal of Excellence award Miss. chpt., 2003), Coll. Art Assn., Southeastern Coll. Art Conf. (dir. 1975-80, 83-89, Disting. Svc. award 1992, Miss. Hist. Soc. (Merit award 1995), Internat. Ctr. Medieval Art, Am. Birding Assn., Audubon Soc., The Nature Conservancy, Sierra Club, Phi Beta Kappa, Phi Kappa Phi. Democrat. Episcopalian.

STRINGFIELD, SHERRY, actress; b. Colorado Springs, Colo., June 24, 1967; m. Larry Joseph, 1998; 1 child. BFA, SUNY, Purchase, 1989. Theater appearances include Goose and Tom Tom, Hurly Burly, Devil's Disciple, A Dream Play, Hotel Baltimore, The Kitchen, Tom Jones; appeared in (TV series) Guiding Light, 1989-92, NYPD Blue, 1993, ER, 1994-96, 2001- (Emmy nominee Outstanding Lead Actress in a Drama Series, 1995), Going Home, 2000; (films) Burnzy's Last Call, 1995, 54, 1998, Borderline, 1998, Autumn in New York, 2000, Viva Las Nowhere, 2001; (TV movies) Border Line, 1999, Going Home, 2000; (TV appearances) Touched by an Angel, 1999, Third Watch, 2002.

STRINGHAM, AMY, secondary school educator; d. Billy Nelson and Carolyn VanderStelt; children: Emily, Samuel. BS in Biology, U. Mich., Ann Arbor, 1996; EdM in Ednl. Tech., Grand Valley State U., Allendale, 2002. Cert. secondary tchr. Mich., 1996. Mid. sch. tchr. Grand Rapids Pub. Schs., Mich., 1996—98; h.s. tchr. Grand Haven Area Pub. Schs., Mich., 1998—. Instr. Hope Coll. Upward Bound Program, Holland, Mich., 1997—2002. Vol. Harbor Humane Soc., West Olive, Mich., 2005—06. Mem.: Grand Haven Edn. Assn.

STRINGHAM, PHYLLIS JOAN, retired music educator; b. Grand Rapids, Mich., Jan. 30, 1931; d. Wilhelmina Johanna and Harry Newton Stringham. MusB, Calvin Coll., Grand Rapids, Mich., 1952; MusM, U. Mich., Ann Arbor, Mich., 1955. Organist Chatham (Va.) Hall Girls Sch., 1955—59; prof. of music Carroll Coll., Waukesha, Wis., 1959—2001. Owner and mgr. Phylllis Stringham Concert Mgmt., Waukesha, Wis., 1964—. Musician concert organist. Mem.: Am. Guild of Organists. Avocation: reading. Home: 1101 Belmont Dr Waukesha WI 53186 Office: Phyllis Stringham concert Mgt 1101 Belmont Dr Waukesha WI 53186 Office Phone: 262-542-7197. Business E-Mail: pstringh@cc.edu.

STRINGHAM, RENÉE, physician; b. Mpls., July 16, 1940; d. Clifford Leonard and Helen Pearl (Marcineak) Heinrich; children: Lars Eric, Leif Erik, Lance Devon. BS, St. Lawrence U., 1962; MD, U. Ky., 1972. Diplomate Am. Bd. Family Practice. Intern U. Fla., Gainesville, 1972-73; physician Lee County Coop. Clinic, Marianna, Ark., 1973-74; pvt. practice Coastal Health Practitioners, Lincoln City, Oreg., 1975-84; county med. officer Lincoln County Health Dept., Newport, Oreg., 1986-90; pvt. practice, 1984-90; student health Miami U., Oxford, Ohio, 1991-93; pvt. practice Macadam Clin., Portland, 1994; cons. student health Willamette U., 1994-95; contract physician West Salem Clinic, 1995-97; med. dir. Capital Manor, 1997-99; locum tenens, 1999—; physician Oreg. State Hosp., 2001—03. Trustee Coast Home Nursing, Lincoln County, 1984-86; expert witness EPA, 1980. Facilitator Exceptional Living, 1984-86. Fellow Am. Acad. Family Practice; mem. Lincoln County Med. Soc. (pres. 1984), Oreg. Med. Assn. Avocations: spontaneous music, folk dancing, sailing.

STRIPLING, BETTY KEITH, artist, retired medical/surgical nurse; b. Stephenville, Tex., Aug. 22, 1930; d. Fred Lancaster and Myrtle Ethel (Patton) Keith; m. Warren Lee Stripling, Mar. 22, 1952 (div. 1961); children: Keith, Kelley, David(dec.). Student, John Tarleton Agrl. Coll., 1948-50, Tarleton State U., 1980-85. Clk.-typist Kimbell-Food Products Co., Ft. Worth, 1950-52; LVN Stephenville Hosp. and Clinic, 1963, LVN floor duty, 1963-64, LVN surgery, 1964-66, Ft. Worth Osteo. Hosp., 1966-68; LVN, charge nurse Sunset Nursing Home, Stephenville, 1968-80, LVN, DON, 1973-78; LVN, charge nurse Cmty. Nursing Home, Stephenville, 1980-86, 89-94, pvt. duty nurse, 1986-89, cmty. nursing home LVN, 1998-99; freelance painter, 1999—2002. Democrat. Home: 3219 Kenilworth Dr Arlington TX 76001-5207 Personal E-mail: bjstrip@ont.com.

STRIPLING, BETTYE JOHNSON, civic volunteer; b. Clarksdale, Miss., Jan. 17, 1941; d. Theo Abe and Emmie (Wilcox) Johnson; m. Wilton Dennis Stripling, Aug. 22, 1964; children: Wilton Dennis II, Susan Elaine. AA, Texarkana (Tex.) Jr. Coll., 1961; BS in Home Econ. Edn., North Tex. State U., 1963; MEd, U. Houston, 1968. Cert. home econ. and spl. edn. tchr., Tex., Calif. Asst. home demonstration agent Tex. A&M U., Bell County, Belton, 1963-64; hosp. spl. edn. tchr. Galveston (Tex.) Ind. Sch. Dist., 1964-68, 69-70; spl. edn. tchr. L.A. County Schs., 1968-69; gen. equivalency diploma tchr. U.S. Army, Korat, Thailand, 1970. Pres., various offices PTA, Richardson (Tex.) Ind. Sch. Dist., 1977-91, Band Booster Club, 1984-91, Tomorrow Bd., 2002-, Budget Review, 2000-, Religious Practice Task Force, 1999-; chmn. Dallas Citizens Safety Adv. Bd., 1982—; sec. bd. trustees Richardson Ind. Sch. Dist., 1990-91, pres. bd. trustees, 1992-98; mem. Crossing Guard Bd., Dallas, 1991—; bd. dirs. Youth Svc. Coun., Richardson, 1991-99, Neighborhood Svc. Coun., Inc., Dallas, 1992-99; mem. Leadership Tex. Assn. Sch. Bds./Class, 1993-94; mem. tri-partnership initiative peer assistance teams Tex. Edn. Agy.; mem. Leadership Richardson Class XII, 1997. Mem. North Tex. Area Assn. Sch. Bds., Dallas County Sch. Bd. Assn., Tex. Assn. Sch. Bds., Richardson C. of C., North Tex. Leaders Forum. Avocations: sewing, travel, car racing. Home: 7328 Campbell Rd Dallas TX 75248-1631 Office Phone: 214-801-7411. Personal E-mail: bettyestripling@yahoo.com.

STRIPLING, KAYE, school system administrator; BS in Health and Phys. Edn., Tex. Woman's U., 1962; EdM in Spl. Edn., U. Houston, 1967, ED in Curriculum and Instrn., 1985. Tchr. spl. edn. Houston Ind. Sch. Dist., 1964—75, prin. elem. and mid. schs., 1975—87, supt. Adminstrv. Dist. XIV, 1987—90, asst. supt. staff devel., 1990—94, supt. S.W. Adminstrv. Dist., 1995—2001, acting supt. schs., 2001, supt. schs., 2001—. Named Disting. Alumna, Tex. Woman's U., 2002. Office: Houston Ind Sch Dist 3830 Richmond Ave Houston TX 77027

STRITMATER, COLLEEN LEIGH, science educator; b. Nyack, NY, Mar. 25, 1980; d. Joseph Thomas Stritmater and Susan Elaine Krok, Raymond Joseph Krok (Stepfather). BA in Molecular Biology, Fordham U., Bronx, NY, 2002; MA in Secondary Sci. Edn., CCNY, NY, 2004. Lic. Tchg. NY State Dept. of Edn., 2002. Shipping & receiving mgr. R&S Cabinet Brokers Inc., Pearl River, 1998—2002; tchr. I.s. 98, Bronx, 2002—04, Suffern HS, Suffern, 2004—. NYC Tchg. Fellows, NYC Dept. of Edn., 2002-2004. Home: 12 Sheridan Ave Apt #8 Congers NY 10920 Office: Suffern HS 49 Viola Rd Suffern NY 10901 Office Phone: 845-357-3800. Personal E-mail: clstritmater@ramapocentral.org.

STROBEL, PAMELA B., energy executive; b. Chgo., Sept. 9, 1952; BS highest honors, U. Ill., 1974, JD cum laude, 1977. Bar: Ill. 1977, U.S. Dist. (ctrl. and no. dists.) Ill. 1977, U.S. Ct. Appeals (7th cir.) 1981, U.S. Claims Ct. 1983, U.S. Ct. Appeals (fed. cir.) 1985. Ptnr. Sidley & Austin, Chgo., 1988-93; exec. v.p., gen. counsel Commonwealth Edison Co., Chgo., 1993—2000; exec. v.p. Exelon Corp., Chgo., 2000—, exec. v.p., chief adminstrv. officer, 2003—; pres. Exelon Energy Delivery Co., Chgo., 2000—, vice-chair, 2000—01, CEO, vice-chair, 2001—02, chmn., CEO, 2002—03. Mem. Kappa Tau Alpha (staff 1975-77). Office: Exelon Corp PO Box 805398 Chicago IL 60680-5398

STROBER, MYRA HOFFENBERG, education educator, consultant; b. NYC, Mar. 28, 1941; d. Julius William Hoffenberg and Regina Scharer; m. Samuel Strober, June 23, 1963 (div. Dec. 1983); children: Jason M., Elizabeth A.; m. Jay M. Jackman, Oct. 21, 1990. BS in Indsl. Rels., Cornell U., 1962; MA in Econs., Tufts U., 1965; PhD in Econs., MIT, 1969. Lectr., asst. prof. dept. econs. U. Md., College Park, 1967-70; lectr. U. Calif., Berkeley, 1970-72; asst. prof. grad. sch. bus. Stanford (Calif.) U., 1972-86, assoc. prof. sch. edn., 1979-90, prof. edn., 1990—, assoc. dean acad. affairs, 1993-95, interim dean, 1994; program officer in higher edn. Atlantic Philanthropic Svcs., Ithaca, N.Y., 1998-2000. Organizer Stanford Bus. Conf. Women Mgmt., 1974; founding dir. ctr. rsch. women Stanford U., 1974-76, 79-84, dir. edn. policy inst., 1984-86, dean alumni coll., 1992, mem. policy and planning bd., 1992-93, chair program edn. adminstrn. and policy analysis, 1991-93, chair provost's com. recruitment and retention women faculty, 1992-93, chair faculty senate com. on coms., 1992-93; mem. adv. bd. State of Calif. Office Econ. Policy Planning and Rsch., 1978-80; mem. Coll. Bd. Com. Develop Advanced Placement Exam. Econs., 1987-88; faculty advisor Rutgers Women's Leadership Program, 1991-93. Author: (with others) Industrial Relations, 1972, 1990, Sex, Discrimination and the Division of Labor, 1975, Changing Roles of Men and Women, 1976, Women in the Labor Market, 1979, Educational Policy and Management: Sex Differentials, 1981, Women in the Workplace, 1982, Sex Segregation in the Workplace: Trends, Explanations, Remedies, 1984, The New Palgrave: A Dictionary of Economic Theory and Doctrine, 1987, Computer Chips and Paper Clips: Technology and Women's Employment, Vol. II, 1987, Gender in the Workplace, 1987, Challenge to Human Capital Theory: Implications for the HR Manager, American Economic Review, 1995, Rethinking Economics Through a Feminist Lens, Feminist Economics, 1995, Making and Correcting Errors in Economic Analyses: An Examination of Videotapes, (with Agnes M.K. Chan) the Road Winds Uphill All the Way: Gender, Work, and Family in the U.S. and Japan, 1999, (with Jay M. Jackman) Fear of Feedback, 2003, Children As a Public Good, 2004, Can Harvard Ever Play a Positive Role for Women in Higher Education?, 2005; editor (with Francine E. Gordon) Bringing Women Into Management, 1975, (with others) Women and Poverty, 1986, Industrial Relations, 1990, Challenges to Human Capital Theory: Implications for HR Managers, 1995, (with Sanford M. Dornbusch) Feminism, Children and the New Families, 1988, Rethinking Economics Through a Feminist Lens, 1995, (with Agnes M.K. Chan) The Road Winds Uphill All The Way: Gender, Work and Family in the U.S. and Japan, 1999, (with Jay M. Jackman) Fear of Feedback, 2003, Application of Mainstream Economics Constructs to Education: A Feminist Analysis, 2003, Children as a Public Good, 2004, Feminist Economics: Implications for Education, 2005, Can Harvard Ever Play a Positive Role for Women in Higher Education, 2005; mem. bd. editors Signs: Jour. Women Culture and Soc., 1975-89, assoc. editor, 1980-85; mem. bd. editors Sage Ann. Rev. Women and Work, 1984—; mem. editorial adv. bd. U.S.-Japan Women's Jour., 1991—; assoc. editor Jour. Econ. Edn., 1991—; contbr. chpt. to book, articles to profl. jours. Mem. rsch. adv. task force YWCA, 1989—; chair exec. bd. Stanford Hillel, 1990-92; bd. dirs. Resource Ctr. Women, Palo Alto, Calif., 1983-84; pres. bd. dirs. Kaider Found., Mountain View, Calif., 1990-96; bd. trustees Mills Coll., 2004—. Fellow Stanford U., 1975-77, Schiff House Resident fellow, 85-87. Mem.: NOW (bd. dirs. legal def. and edn. fund 1993—98), Ctr. Gender Equality (bd. dirs. 2000—), Internat. Assn. Feminist Econs. (assoc. editor Feminist Econs. 1994—, pres. 1997), Indsl. Rels. Rsch. Assn., Am. Ednl. Rsch. Assn., Am. Econ. Assn. (mem. com. status of women in profession 1972—75). Office: Stanford U School Edn Stanford CA 94305 Office Phone: 650-723-0387. Business E-Mail: myra.strober@stanford.edu.

STROER, ROSEMARY ANN, real estate broker; b. N.Y.C., Oct. 1, 1934; d. Joseph and Rose Ann (Maguire) McBrien; m. Charles Stroer, Dec. 6, 1961 (dec. 1976). BA in English, CUNY, 1958, MA in English, 1973; MA, NYU, 1976. Dir. pub. relations PepsiCo, Purchase, N.Y., 1960-70; dir. student services and publs. N.Y.C. Bd. Edn., 1970-82; cons. pub. relations numerous orgns. including Ford Found., Architects for Social Responsibility, Cathedral St. John the Divine, Hampton Day Sch., Local TV, Inc., N.Y.C., 1975—; real estate broker, consultant Equity Analysis Internat. Inc., IT Properties, Inc., N.Y.C., 1986—96. Author: Work as You Like It, 1979; editor: Holocaust: A Study in Genocide, 1977, Minimum Teaching Essentials, 1980. Spl. rep. Mayor's Task Force on Immunization, NYC, 1982—83; spl. Dem. asst. campaign mgr. for Ho. of Reps. NYC, 1972. Recipient Order of the Sun award govt. of Peru, 1964, numerous pub. service awards. Mem. Hunter Coll. Alumni Assn., Mus. Modern Art, UNICEF. Roman Catholic. Avocations: writing, landscaping. Home: 315 E 68th St New York NY 10021-5692

STROHL, ELIZABETH G., banker; b. Omaha, Jan. 23, 1940; d. John W. and Elizabeth M. (McColl) Corrigan; m. H.W. General, July 1967; children: Matthew, Rebecca; m. George C. Strohl, May 31, 1975. BA, San Francisco State U., 1961. Programmer, analyst Bank of Am., San Francisco, 1966—73, v.p., 1973—81, sr. v.p., 1981—. Republican. Home: 461 Castanya Ct Danville CA 94526-1851

STROIK, MARILYN L., elementary school educator; b. South Milw. d. Leo Andrew and Adalyn LeVerne Stroik. BS in Edn., U. Wis., Milw., 1977; MEd, Carthage Coll., Kenosha, Wis., 1989. Lic. reading specialist Wis. Tchr. St. Alexander Sch., Milw., 1977—81; tchr., minister edn. Grace Luth. Sch., Oak Creek, Wis., 1983—. Cons. student assistance team Grace Sch., 1998—, mem. crisis intervention team, 1998—; mem. manuscript rev. bd. Internat. Reading Assn., 2001—; presenter Wis. State Reading Assn., Luth. Edn. Assn., Wis. Geographic Alliance; mem. children's lit. com. Wis. State Reading Assn., 1999—2003. Author: (pamphlet) Learning and Literacy, 1999, (article) Luth. Edn. Jour., 2005. Coord. food and toy drive Luth. Ch. and Sch., Oak Creek, 1983—. Recipient Outstanding Wis. Educator, Wis. Dept. Pub. Instrn., 2000. Mem.: Mensa, Pi Lambda Theta, Phi Kappa Phi. Office: Grace Luth Sch 8537 S Pennsylvania Ave Oak Creek WI 53154

STROM, DORIS MARIE, music educator; b. Chgo., June 28, 1933; m. Edward R. McLaughlin. BA, U. Sioux Falls, 1953; MA, U. S.D., 1969. Tchr. music, English Sioux Falls, Philip Sch. Dist., Baltic Sch. Dist., Canton Sch. Dist., SD, 1955—73; ins. agt., exec. Prudential Ins. Co., Aberdeen, Rapid City, 1974—86; ednl. svcs. mgr., promotion mgr. Rapid City Jour., SC, 1986—92. Adj. tchr. Nat. Am. U., Rapid City, 1980—89, 1999—, S.D. State U., Brookings, 1988—92; choir dir. 1st Congl. Ch., 1999—. Author: In the Village, 1996; co-author: Reflections, 1999. Avocations: gardening, cooking, reading.

STROMAN, SUSAN, choreographer, theater director; b. Wilmington, Del., Oct. 17, 1954; d. Charles and Frances Stroman; m. Mike Ockrent, 1996 (dec. Dec. 2, 1999); stepchildren: Ben, Natasha. Grad., U. Del. Choreographer Flora Roberts Inc. Dancer Chgo., 1977—78, Whoopee!, 1979, Richard III, 1980, Peter Pan, 1983, choreographer (off-Broadway) Broadway Babylon, 1984, Sayonara, 1987, Flora, the Red Menace, 1987, Shenandoah, 1988, Slasher, 1988, Rhythm Ranch, 1989, The Roar of the Greasepaint-The Smell of the Crowd, 1990, Gypsy, 1991, And the World Goes 'Round, 1991 (Outer Critics' Cir. award for choreography, 1991), A Christmas Carol, 1994, (Broadway plays) Crazy for You, 1992 (Tony award for best choreography, 1992, Drama Desk award for choreography, 1992, Outer Critics' Cir. award, 1992, Laurence Olivier award for best choreography, 1993), Picnic, 1994, Show Boat, 1994 (Tony award for best choreography, 1995, Astaire award Theatre Devel. Fund, 1995), Big, 1996 (Tony nomination for best choreography, 1996), Oklahoma, 2002 (Laurence Olivier Award for choreography, 2002, Tony nomination for best choreography, 2002), (Operas) Don Giovanni, 1989, A Little Night Music, 1990, 100 in the Shade, 1992, (spl.) Liza Minnelli: Stepping Out at Radio City Music Hall, 1991 (Emmy nomination for choreography, 1993), (films) The Producers, 2005; choreographer, conceiver (Broadway plays) Steel Pier, 1997 (Tony nomination for best choreography, 1997), dir., choreographer The Music Man, 2000 (Tony nomination for best choreography, 2000, Tony nomination for best dir., 2000), The Producers, 2001 (Tony award for best choreography, 2001, Tony award for best dir., 2001, Drama Desk Award for best dir. musical, 2001, Touring Broadway award, best direction, League Am. Theatres and Producers, 2005), The Frogs, 2004, dir., choreographer, conceiver Contact, 2000 (Tony award for best choreography, 2000, Lucille Lortel Award for outstanding direction, 2000, Tony nomination for best dir., 2000), Thou Shalt Not, 2001, Double Feature, 2004, co-conceiver Trading Places, Equity Libr. Theatre Informals, 1983, dir., co-conceiver (off-Broadway) Living Color, 1986, co-conceiver, choreographer (TV spl.) Sondheim-A Celebration at Carnegie Hall, 1992, asst. dir., asst. choreographer (Broadway plays) Musical Chairs, 1980; dir.(TV spl.): An Evening With the Boston Pops-A Tribute to Leonard Bernstein, 1989. Recipient Disting. Achievement in Musical Theatre Award, Drama League, 2001, Elan award, 2005. Address: Flora Roberts Agy Penhouse A 157 W 57th St New York NY 10019-2210*

STROMBACK, MARY BETH, secondary school educator; d. Phillip Dale and Joan Ethel Eckblad; m. Steven Wayne Stromback, Sept. 5, 1960; children: Cara Christine, Amanda Kate. BS in Secondary Edn., U. Wis., River Falls, 1988; MS in Edn., Winona State U., Minn., 1998. Sci. tchr. Winona Alternative H.S., Winona Area Learning Ctr., 1989—99; tchr. sci. Winona Sr. H.S. - Winona Area Pub. Schs., 1999—. Grad stds. implementation team Winona Area Pub. Schs., 1997—99, rep. sci. dept., 2002—, tchr. mentor, 2003—; tchr. Winona Area Pub. Sch. - Celebrating Sucess Through Tech., 1997—99. Dare to Dream grantee, Winona Area Pub. Schs. Found., 2003. Mem.: Minn. Sci. Tchrs. Assn.

STROMBERG, PATRICIA ROBERTS, retired school librarian; b. Cin., Apr. 23, 1932; d. Richard Bickmore and Ruth Hessler Roberts; children: Mark Alan Stromberg, Ruth Ann Stromberg Batson. BS in Edn., U. Cin., Ohio, 1954; postgrad., Our Lady of the Lake Coll., San Antonio, 1973-75; MA in Edn., U. Colo., Denver, 1979. Tchr. Cin. Pub. Schs., 1954-56, 1970-71, Mt. Healthy (Ohio) Pub. Schs., 1972-73; library media specialist Jefferson County Pub. Schs., Golden, Colo., 1976—97; ret. Mem. basic list com., Jefferson County Schs., 1976-77, Pleasant View Sch., 76-90, Peiffer Sch., 1990-97; computer cons. JEFFCO Schs., 1983-88; co-chair gifted and telented com. Pleasant View Sch., Golden, Colo., 1987-90; pres. JEFFCO Ednl. Media Specialists, 1990-92. Ruling elder on session Green Mt. Presbyn. Ch., 1982-84, 88-91, 2001-03, 06—, chair worship and fellowship/evangelism coms., 1988, 89, 2003-05, ch. mission com., 2006—; mem. social justice and peacemaking commn. Presbytery of Denver, 1989-92; mem. ministry evaluation, 1992 Cmty. Green Mt. Presbyn. Ch. Title IV-C Drama grantee Pleasant View Sch., 1981-84, Jeff Found. Venture grantee, 1985, CCIRA Star grantee, 1996. Mem. AAUW, Nat. Assn. Advancement and Perpetuation of Storytelling, Spellbinders, Jefferson County Internat. Reading Assn. (sec. 1978-79, area membership rep. 1991-95), Jefferson County Ret. Sch. Employees Assn., Colo. Coun. (chair Books for Kids com. 1998—) Internat. Reading Assn. (workshop presenter), Jefferson County Spellbinders Assn., Phi Delta Kappa. Republican. Avocations: internat. study children's lit., travel, storytelling, gardening, photography. Home: 12834 W Iliff Ave Lakewood CO 80228-4334 Office Phone: 303-988-3563. Personal E-mail: pstrawberry32@aol.com.

STROMBOM, CATHY JEAN, transportation planner, consultant; b. Bremerton, Wash., Nov. 4, 1949; d. Paul D. and Carolyn (Snitman) Powers; m. David Glen Strombom, June 17, 1972; 1 child, Paul Davis. BA summa cum laude, Whitman Coll., Walla Walla, Wash., 1972; M in City and Regional Planning, Harvard U., Cambridge, Mass., 1977; postgrad., U. Wash., Seattle, 1982-84. Urban planner Harvard Inst. for Internat. Devel., Tehran, Iran, 1977; sr. transp. planner Puget Sound Coun. Govts., Seattle, 1978-84; asst. v.p., west planning mgr./prin. profl. assoc. Parsons Brinckerhoff Quade and Douglas, Inc., Seattle, 1984—; vol. U.S. Peace Corps, Islamabad, Pakistan, 1994—95. V.p. Women's Transp. Seminar, Seattle, 1988-90 (Woman of Yr. 1989). Contbr. articles to profl. jours. Vol. U.S. Peace Corps, Marrakech, Morocco, 1973—75, Ahmedabad & Pune, India, 1978, Istanbul, Turkey, 1985—86, Islamabad, Pakistan, 1995—96. Mem. Am. Inst. Cert. Planners (cert.), Am. Planning Assn., Inst. Transp. Engrs., Leadership Tomorrow (bd. mem.), Phi Beta Kappa. Home: 2580 W Viewmont Way W Seattle WA 98199-3660 Office: Parsons Brinckerhoff Quade and Douglas Inc 999 3rd Ave Ste 2200 Seattle WA 98104-4044

STROMSDORFER, DEBORAH ANN, artist, educator; b. Aurora, Ill., Dec. 18, 1961; d. Frederick George and Rita Barbara Stromsdorfer; m. Gregory Bruce Bubp, Aug. 13, 1983. BFA cum laude, No. Ill. U., 1980—84, MFA suma cum laude, 1984—89. Graphic designer No. Ill. U., 1983—87, U. Ill. Coll. Medicine, Rockford, 1987—90; adj. art instr. Rock Valley Coll., Rockford, 1990—98, 2001—02. Colored pencil workshop Art Guild of Rockford, Rockford, 2002; guest artist Sinnissippi Quilter's Guild, Rockford, 2002, Barbara Olsen Ctr. of Hope, Rockford, 2004, 05; vis. artist Stevenson HS, Lincolnshire, Ill., 2006. Prin. works include book The Best of Colored Pencil 2, 1994, Art Rockford, 2004, prin. works include nat. mag. Sew News, 1999. Recipient Best of Show, Art Centre, Elk Grove Village, Ill., 1991, Colored Pencil Soc., Chgo. Chpt., Libertyville, Ill., 1996. Mem.: Wisc. Designer Crafts Coun., Chgo. Artists' Coalition. Avocations: theater, museums, art shows, gourmet cooking. Home: 3602 Grenoble Ct Rockford IL 61114

STROMSWOLD, DOROTHY, retired secondary school educator; b. Mankato, Minn., Jan. 13, 1920; d. Andrew August and Mary Angela (Wachter) Farm; m. Stanley Andrew Stromswold, Oct. 30, 1942 (dec. Apr. 1998); 1 child, Carol. BS, Mankato State U., 1941; student, Mankato Comml. Coll., 1942. Cert. tchr., Minn. Tchr. high sch., Waldorf, Minn., 1942-43, 51-52, Worthington, Minn., 1945-46, Mankato Comml. Coll., 1942, 46-47; placement officer Sch. Journalism, U. Minn., Mpls., 1947-49; patent sec. Clark Equipment Co., Buchanan, Mich., 1952-59; book reviewer South Bend (Ind.) Tribune, 1978-93. Spkr. on travel and on the Supreme Ct. Elder, deacon Presbyn. Ch., Buchanan, 1974-81, 1998—2004. Democrat. Avocations: supreme court, reading, giving informal talks. Home: PO Box 27 Buchanan MI 49107-0027

STRONG, ANNSLEY CHAPMAN, interior designer, volunteer; b. Paterson, N.J., July 18, 1947; d. Donald John and Margaret Brawley Chapman; m. George Gordon Strong, Jr., Nov. 30, 1974; children: George Gordon III, Courtney Chapman Strong Thomas, Meredith Annsley, Alexis Palmer. BA, Wheaton Coll., Norton, Mass., 1969. Cert. N.Y. Sch. Design, 1969, Interior Designers Guild, 1975. V.p. Environs, La Canada, Calif., 1984—. Treas., commr. AYSO Region 13, Pasadena, Calif., 1993—97; co-founder La Canada Sports Coalition, 1996; mem. pres.'s commn. Wheaton Coll., Norton, Mass., 1998—2004; bd. chair Hathaway Sycamores, Pasadena, Calif., 2006—; bd. sec. Verdugo Hills Hosp., Glendale, 2002—05; bd. chmn. Verdugo Hills Hosp. Found., 2002—05. Recipient 20th Century award, Pasadena YMCA, 1990, Bill Carroll Lifetime Achievement award, Am. Youth Soccer Orgn., 2000. Republican. Avocations: painting, piano, bridge, skiing, golf. Office Phone: 818-957-0086.

STRONG, AUDREY FARONE, music educator; b. Syracuse, N.Y., Mar. 27, 1952; d. Salvatore Anthony and Agnes Josephine Farone; m. Roger William Strong, Oct. 5, 1974 (div. Jan. 3, 1997); children: Amanda M., Randal W. BA, SUNY, Brockport, 1974; M of Arts and Humanities, SUNY, Buffalo, 1996. Cert. tchr. N.Y. Tchr. St. Paul's Sch., St. Paul's Roman Cath. Ch., Kenmore, NY, 1985—90; music educator Buffalo (N.Y.) Pub. Schs., 1990—94, North Tonawanda (N.Y.) City Schs., 1994—. Cons. English Lang. Arts Tchrs. Edn., North Tonawanda, 2000—. Mem.: Friends of the Riviera Theatre Orgn., Eric-Niagara Sunrise Exch. Club, Alpha Delta Kappa (v.p. 2002—, pres. 2004). Avocations: travel, quilting. Home: 35 Sutley Ct Tonawanda NY 14150 Office: North Tonawanda Schs-Ohio Elem 625 Ohio St North Tonawanda NY 14120 Office Phone: 716-807-3800 8112.

STRONG, CHRISTINA CORDAIRE, writer, artist; b. Norfolk, Va., Aug. 21, 1932; d. Cordary Baker and Christina (Swann) Heiberger; m. Henry Hooker Strong, July 27, 1957 (dec. May 1972); children: Jonathan Hooker, Johanna Harrison. BA in French and Art, Woman's Coll./U. N.C., Greensboro, 1955; postgrad., Calif. State U., Fresno, 1976-79. Cert. tchr., Va. Designer custom kitchens Eastern Electric, Norfolk, 1950-51; tchr. Nofolk Pub. Schs., 1955-57; assoc. prof. Coll. William and Mary, Norfolk, 1956; v.p. Computron, Virginia Beach, Va., 1990; salesperson The Booke Shoppe, Elizabeth City, N.C., 1991-93; writer, 1991—. Author: (novels) Heart's Deception, 1992, Love's Triumph, 1993, Pride's Folly, 1993, Daring Illusion, 1994 (Holt medallion for Best Regency 1995). Mem. Romance Writers Am. (sec. Richmond chpt. 1990—), Chesapeake Romance Writers (treas. 1995), River City Romance Writers, Strawberry River Art Assn. (sec. 1997—), Tau Psi Omega, Theta Kappa Sigma (treas., pres. 1949-51), Nat. Soc. DAR, Daus. of the Confederacy (historian 1987, v.p. 1991—), Republican. Episcopalian. Avocations: dressage, trail riding, swimming, golf.

STRONG, JUDITH ANN, chemist, educator; b. June 19, 1941; d. Philip Furnald and Hilda Bernice (Hulbert) S. BS cum laude, SUNY, Albany, 1963; MA, Brandeis U., 1966, PhD, 1970. Asst. prof. chemistry Moorhead State U., Minn., 1969—73, assoc. prof., 1973—81, prof., 1981—, chmn. chemistry dept., 1984—86, dean social and natural scis., 1986—97, assoc. v.p. acad. affairs, 1997—. Recipient Gov.'s Acts of Kindness Vol. award, 1997; fellow, NSF, 1965—67. Mem.: Minn. Acad. Sci., Assn. Women in Sci., Am. Chem. Soc., Soroptimist Internat. (gov. North Ctrl. region 2002—04, program coun. 2004—), Sigma Xi. Home: 1209 12th St S Moorhead MN 56560-3707 Office: Minn State U Moorhead Academic Affairs Moorhead MN 56563-0001 Office Phone: 218-477-2075. Business E-Mail: strong@mnstate.edu.

STRONG, KAY ELAINE, economics professor; b. Edmore, Mich., Nov. 11, 1952; d. Donald Earl and Geraldine Frances Strong; children: Christopher Michael Simmons, Annika Marie Simmons. PhD, So. Ill. U., Carbondale, 2000. Adj. lectr. econs. Ind. U. S.E., New Albany, Ind., 1984—95; assoc. prof. econs. Bowling Green State U. Firelands, Huron, Ohio, 2000—. Supervisory economist U.S. Dept. of Labor, Bur. of Labor Stats., Cleve., 1979—83; interim chair applied sciences dept. Bowling Green State U. Firelands, Huron, 2005—06, dir. initiatives for the future. Contbr. articles to profl. jours. (22nd Ann. Friends, Authors, and Artists Reception award Friends of U. Librs., 2002). Vol. Peace Corps, Thailand, 1975—77; instr. Teach for Friendship, Wuhan, Wuhan, China, 2006. Recipient Bowling Green State U. Firelands Disting. Creative scholarship, 2006. Mem.: Midwest Econs. Assn. (assoc.), So. Econ. Assn. (assoc.), GATE: Global Assn. of Tchrs. of Econs. (assoc.), Com. on Status of Women in Econs. Profession (assoc.), Am. Econs. Assn. (assoc.), Phi Delta Kappa (v.p. chpt. 1382, Kappan of Yr. 2005). Avocation: international travel. Office: Bowling Green State U Firelands One University Dr Huron OH 44839 Office Phone: 419-433-5560. Home Fax: 419-433-9696; Office Fax: 419-433-9696. Business E-Mail: kstrong@bgsu.edu.

STRONG, (LIN) LINDA LOUISE, music educator; b. Rice Lake, Wis., Apr. 26, 1948; d. Jess Willard and Lorraine H. (Scheidecker) Knutson; m. Charles William Strong, Jan. 31, 1970; children: Kirsten Anne, Michael Allan. BA, U. Wis., 1970; MAT, Northwestern U., 1971; MusB, U. Wis., Stevens Point, 1985. Pvt. piano and violin tchr., various locations, Wis., 1973—; tchr., dir. Suzuki Talent Assn. of Eau Claire, Wis., 1989—. Dir. Suzuki Kids on Tour, Eau Claire, 1991—. 1st violinist Chippewa Valley Symphony, Eau Claire, 1988—, Red Cedar Symphony, 2001—; internat. coord. Aspect Found. fgn. exch. program, 1998—. Mem.: Suzuki Assn. of the Ams., Chippewa Valley Music Tchrs. Assn. (program chair 1993—99, newsletter editor 1999—2001, v.p.), Wis. Music Tchrs. Assn. (rec. sec. 1994—2000, co-chair Eau Claire dist. 2001—02). Democrat. Methodist. Avocations: reading murder mysteries, swimming, singing. Home and Office: 1018 Yorkshire Ave Rice Lake WI 54868-1062 Personal E-mail: v_lin@charter.net.

STRONG, LOUISE CONNALLY, geneticist; b. San Antonio, Apr. 23, 1944; d. Ben Clarkson and Sarah Nell (Allen) Connally; m. Beeman Ewell Strong III, Jan. 10, 1970; children: Beeman Connally, Larkin Louise. BA, U. Tex., 1966; MD, U. Tex. Med. Br., Galveston, 1970. Diplomate Tex. State Bd. Med. Examiners. Faculty Grad. Sch. Biomed. Scis. U. Tex. Health Sci. Ctr., Houston, 1972—, rsch. assoc. Med. Genetics Ctr., 1972-73; asst. prof. pediatrics and biology, asst. geneticist U. Tex. M.D. Anderson Cancer Ctr., 1976-79, assoc. prof. exptl. pediatrics, assoc. geneticist, 1979—, Sue and Radcliffe Killam prof., 1981—. Part-time asst. prof. U. Tex. Health Sci. Ctr., 1973-78; vis. prof. pediatrics, U. Tex. Med. Sch., U. Tex. Health Sci. Ctr., 1988-95; nat. adv. bd. Dept. Health and Human Svcs., Nat. Cancer Inst., NIH, Bethesda, Md., 1984—, bd. scientific counselors Div. Cancer Etiology, Nat. Cancer Inst., 1981-84, mem. search com. for dep. dir. Div. Extramural Activities, Nat. Cancer Inst., speaker in field, others. Contbr. articles to profl. jours., books and abstracts. Named Warren E. Wheeler Vis. Prof., Children's Hosp., Columbus, Ohio, 1989; recipient Marjorie W. Margolin Award for Outstanding Achievement in Retina Rsch., Retina Rsch. Found., Houston, 1987, Outstanding Achievement in Field of Oncology, State Pres.'s BPW award Tex. Fedn. Bus. and Profl. Women's Clubs, 1984, several scholarships; grantee NIH, 1984-92, John S. Dunn Rsch. Found., 1989-91, Retina Rsch. Found., 1982-90, Joe and Jessie Crump Fund Med. Rsch., 1982-83, Kelsey-Leary Found., others. Mem. AAAS, Am. Assn. Cancer Rsch. AMA, Am. Med. Women's Assn., Am. Men and Women in Sci., Am. Soc. Human Genetics, Am. Soc. Preventive Oncology, Environ. Health Inst., Tex. Genetics Soc., Phil. Soc. Tex.; GM Adv. Council, Cancer Rsch. Found. Avocation: tennis. Office: 1515 Holcombe Blvd HMB Box #209 Houston TX 77030

STRONG, MARCELLA LEE, music specialist, educator; b. East Liverpool, Ohio, Oct. 16, 1954; d. Carl and Ruth I. (White) Hinkle; m. David Lee Strong, Feb 19, 1977. BA magna cum laude, U. Toledo, 1976; MA in Early Childhood Edn., Kent State U., 1982. Cert. music, elem. tchr., Ohio. Music instr. Cardinal Local Schs., Parkman and Huntsburg, Ohio, 1977—. Choir dir. G.V. Nazarene Ch., Orwell, Ohio 1981-83; organist, mem. bd. deacons and stewardship com., sr. choir, jr. choir and ch. band dir. Huntsburg Congl. Ch., 1985—; mem., officer Orwell Farm Bur.; band dir. Kent State U. Coll. for Kids, 1995—. Mem. Cardinal Edn. Assn. (negotiator 1982, 84, 87, 90, 93, 96, 99, 2002, sec. 1983-84, treas. 1984-85, pres. 1985-86, 89-91, 1997-2002), Ohio Music Educators Assn., Kappa Delta Pi, Mu Phi Epsilon, Delta Kappa Gamma. Democrat. Avocations: spectator sports, travel, reading, chess, member international trivia team. Home: PO Box 370 78 Chaffee Dr Orwell OH 44076-0370 E-mail: dlsmls@yahoo.com.

STRONG, NENA L., social studies educator; b. Detroit, Mar. 28, 1952; d. Lester W. and Naomi (Meredith) Adkins; m. Michael P. Strong, July 2, 2005; children: Kimberley D., Stephanie L., Sean M.; m. Thomas M. Fuller, Aug. 7, 1976 (div.); children: Erinn C. Fuller children: Hayley J. Fuller. AA, Lake Mich. Coll., Benton Harbor, Mich., 1972; BS in Edn., Ctrl. Mich. U., Mt. Pleasant, 1975; EdnM, Ind. U., South Bend, 1992. Cert. tchr. Ind. Dept. Edn., 1976. Tchr. English and social studies Elkhart Comm. Sch. Corp., Ind., 1976—80, tchr. social studies, 1990—. Bldg. rep. Elkhart Teacher's Assn., Ind., 1995—; chpt. sponsor Nat. Honor Soc., 1996—2004; mem. sch. quality team Elkhart Ctrl. H.S., 2002—05; data team leader Social Studies Dept. Elkhart H.S., 2005—. Grantee, Kurt and Tessye Simon Fund Holocaust Remembrance, 2004. Mem.: APA, Elkhart Teacher's Assn. Independent. Lutheran. Avocations: travel, gardening, reading, wine tasting, basketry. Home: 55970 Erhart Dr Mishawaka IN 46545 Office: Elkhart Comty Sch Corp Ctrl HS 1 Blazer Blvd Elkhart IN 46516 Office Phone: 574-295-4700. E-mail: nenalf@aol.com.

STRONG, RACHEL LISA, lawyer; BA in English summa cum laude, U. Md., 1991; JD, George Washington U. Law Ctr., 1994. Bar: Md. State Bar 1994, DC Bar 1996. Ptnr., pro bono & cmty. svc. Howrey Simon Arnold & White LLP, Washington. Office: Howrey Simon Arnold & White LLP 1299 Pennsylvania Ave Washington DC 20004-2402 Office Phone: 202-383-7083. Office Fax: 202-383-6610. Business E-Mail: StrongR@howrey.com.

STRONG, SARA DOUGHERTY, psychologist, family therapist, custody mediator; b. Phila., May 30, 1927; d. Augustus Joseph and Orpha Elizabeth (Dock) Dougherty; m. David Mather Strong, Dec. 21, 1954. BA in Psychology, Pa. State U., 1949; MA in Clin. Psychology, Temple U., 1960, postgrad., 1968—72; cert. in family therapy, Family Inst. Phila., 1978. Lic. psychologist and family therapist, Pa. Med. br. psychologist Family Ct. Phila., 1960-85, asst. chief psychologist, 1985-88, chief psychologist, 1988-92; pvt. practice Phila., 1992—95. Cons. St. Joseph's Home for Girls, Phila., 1963-84, Daughters of Charity of St. Vincent De Paul, Albany, NY, 1965-90, Pa. Counseling Svcs., Carlisle, 2001-2005. Mem. APA (assoc.), Am. Assn. Marriage and Family Therapists, Pa. Psychol. Assn., Nat. Register of Health Svc. Providers in Psychology. Democrat. Avocations: reading, dramatic productions, writing, yoga, dance. Office Phone: 717-240-0632. Personal E-mail: dmstrong@pa.net.

STRONG, SUSAN CLANCEY, writer, communications executive, editor; b. Cin., Nov. 10, 1939; d. William Power and Elizabeth (Browne) Clancey; m. Oliver Swigert, 1957 (div. 1972); children: Silvia, David Mack; m. Richard Devon Strong, 1977. BA, Northwestern U., 1965; MA, U. Calif., Berkeley, 1972, PhD, 1979. Tchr. Helen Bush Parkside Sch., Seattle, 1965-66, Taipei (Taiwan) Lang. Inst., 1967-68; acting instr. U. Calif., Berkeley, 1972-78, teaching fellow, 1979, lectr., 1979-84, St. Mary's Coll., Moraga, Calif., 1982-85; pvt. practice Orinda, Calif., 1985-90, 97—; sr. rsch. assoc. Ctr. for Econ. Conversion, 1990-96. Mem. Contra Costa County Conflict Resolution Panels, Calif., 1987-90; affiliate Support Ctr./CTD, San Francisco, 1987-90; del. UN Conf. on Econ. Conversion, Moscow, 1990; co-founder "The Who's Counting?" Project, 1996; founder The Metaphor Project, 1997. Author: The GDP Myth: How It Harms Our Quality of Life, and What Communities are Doing About It, 1995; editor Deficit Delirium, 1993, Shaping A New Conversion Agenda, 1995; author poetry; columnist, book reviewer, film reviewer. Mem. Bay Area Global Tomorrow Com., 1986; co-founder Peace Economy Working Group, 1988; co-founder Peace Economy Campaign, 1988; mem. Peace Action Nat. Strategy Com., 1989-95, co-chair strategy com., 1992-93; conf. co-chmn. Nat. Sane/Freeze Congress, 1989-90, rep. nat. bd. advisors Nat. Peace Action, Washington, 1989-95; mem. bd. advisors Peace and Environ. Project, San Francisco, 1986-88; chmn. No. Calif. Sane Freeze, San Francisco, 1985-89; co-convenor The Natural Step Open Space Com. Conf., San Francisco, 1997. Mem. Phi Beta Kappa. Democrat. Episcopalian. Avocations: music, gardening. Mailing: PO Box 892 Orinda CA 94563-2124 Office Phone: 925-254-7198. Office Fax: 925-254-3304. Business E-Mail: sstrong@metaphorproject.org.

STRONG, VIRGINIA WILKERSON, freelance writer, former special education educator; b. Vernal, Utah, Mar. 19, 1935; d. Arbun C. and Mildred (Wyman) Wilkerson; m. David Smith, Oct. 6, 1950 (div. Jan. 1960); children: Anna Smith Blyton, Dorothy Smith Wolf, Wendell Lee Smith, Ava Smith Eatman, Karen Smith Ritter; m. Lawrence D. Strong, June 1961 (div. May 1973); children: Lawrence D. Jr., Jeffrey A. BA, U. Miss., 1970, MEd, 1972; PhD, Ohio U., 1985; postgrad., UCLA. Cert. elem. edn. tchr., spl. edn. K-12 tchr., ednl. adminstrn., cert screenwriter, UCLA, 1995. Rsch. asst. U. Miss., University, 1968-70, Utah State U., Logan, 1974-78; tchr. spl. edn. various schs., nr. Oxford, Miss., 1969-74; instr. spl. edn., project coord., rsch. asst. Ohio U., Athens, 1978-82; supr. spl. edn. Meigs County Bd. Edn., Pomeroy, Ohio, 1982-84; tchr. spl. edn., dept. chmn. L.A. Unified Sch. Dist., 1986-93, co-faciliator alcohol drug abuse, 1990-93; freelance writer, owner, mgr. Fenix Devel., Culver City, Calif., 1990—. Early childhood adv. Utah Bd. Edn., Salt Lake City, 1976, evaluator edn. programs, Salt Lake City and Logan, 1976-77; acting dir. edn., cons. North Miss. Retardation Ctr., Oxford, 1993-94; curriclum developer Meigs County, 1982-84; dir. gifted edn. workshop Ohio U., 1980. Author: The Role of the Special Education Supervisor, 1985, (screenplays) To See the Elephant, Dark Encounters; contbr. articles to newspapers. Elector Dem. Party, Logan, 1976; religious instr. LDS Ch., various locations, 1953-97. U.S. Dept. Edn. grantee Utah State U., 1976. Mem. ASCD, Kappa Delta Pi, Phi Delta Kappa. Avocations: genealogy, gemology, photography, history buff, travel. Business E-Mail: fenix711@sbcglobal.net.

STRONG-CUEVAS, ELIZABETH, sculptor; b. St. Germain en Laye, France, Jan. 22, 1929; Am. citizen; d. George and Margaret (Strong) de Cuevas; 1 child, Deborah Carmichael. BA, Vassar Coll., Poughkeepsie, N.Y., 1952. Instr. Arts Students' League, NYC; student John Hovannes. One-woman shows include Lee Ault Gallery, NYC, 1977-78, Tower Gallery, Southampton, NY, 1980, Iolas-Jackson Gallery, NYC, 1983, 85, Guild Hall Mus., East Hampton, NY, 1985, Benton Gallery, Southampton, NY, 1987, Kerr Gallery, NYC, 1988, Grounds for Sculpture, Hamilton, NJ, 1999, Island Weiss Gallery, NYC, 2004-05, Vassar Coll., Poughkeepsie, NY, 2006; group shows include Guild Hall, East Hampton, 1980, 84, 98, Art Students League of NY, 1982, Bruce Mus., Greenwich, Conn., 1984, 85, Tower Gallery, NYC, 1984, Kouros Gallery, Ridgefield, Conn., 1985, Andre Zarre Gallery, NYC, 1985, Susan Blanchard Gallery, NYC, 1986, Ruth Vered Gallery, East Hampton, 1986-88, Benton Gallery, Southampton, 1987, 1990, Benson Gallery, Bridgehampton, NY, 1989, 99, Koln Art Fair, Germany, 1989, 1991, Feingarten Galleries, NYC, 1990, Marisa del Re Biennale III, 1993, IV, 1994, Parrish Mus., Southampton, 1994, Grounds for Sculpture, Hamilton, NJ, 1994-96, Shidoni, Tessuque, N.Mex., 1995-98, Barnard-Biderman Fine Art, Southampton, 1997, The Tolman Collection, Singapore, 1997-98, Earl McGrath Gallery, 1998, Bulgari, NY, 2000, Grounds for Sculpture, Hamilton, 2000, 02, Russian Am. Cultural Ctr., 2001, Clark Fine Art, Southampton, 2001, 2003, The Ross Sch., East Hampton, 2003, Island Weiss Gallery, NYU, 2004-06, Kouros Gallery, NYC, 2003, UBS Bank Gallery, 2005, Ann Novton Sculpture Gardens, West Palm Beach, Fla., 2006; represented in pvt. collections at Bruce Mus., Greenwich, Grounds for Sculpture, Hamilton, NJ Guild Hall Mus., Heckscher Mus., Huntington, NY, East Hampton Garden, East Hampton, 1982, Park Ave. Ter., NY, 1997. Recipient First prize, Guild Hall, NY, 1985. Mem. Vassar Club (NY). Avocation: yoga. Personal E-mail: strongworks@sc-sculpture.com.

STRONGIN, BONNIE LYNN, language educator; b. Chgo., Sept. 27, 1943; d. Arthur Caroll and Jennie Grace (Coffler) Bondy; m. Barry Michael Woldman, Jan. 27, 1965 (div. Aug. 1979); children: Scott, Erika, Jonathan; m. Stuart Jeffrey Strongin, Jan. 26, 1992. BA, Roosevelt U., 1964; MA, Concordia U., 1990. Cert. sec. English tchr., Ill. Core tchr. Dist. 15, Rolling Meadows, Ill., 1964—65, 1979—2004; English tchr., chair freshman level Leyden Twp. H.S., Franklin Park, Ill., 1965-69. Ednl. cons. French Internat. Sch. of Chgo., 1995; spkr. in field. Contbg. editor Collage Mag., 1980-82; contbr. articles to Collage Mag., Chgo. Tribune; guest Phil Donahue Show, 1984. Recipient Golden Apple State finalist award Golden Apple Found., Chgo., 1993, Excellence in English award English Speaking Union, Chgo., 1994, Tchrs. Who Care Enough to Challenge Award Ill. Math. and Sci. Acad., 2002. Fellow: Internat. Biographical Assn.; mem.: Ill. Assn. Tchrs. English, Ill. Edn. Assn., ASCD, NOW, NEA. Avocations: theater, opera, travel, films, art. Office: Plum Grove Jr HS 2600 Plum Grove Rd Rolling Meadows IL 60008-2042

STRONG-TIDMAN, VIRGINIA ADELE, marketing professional; b. July 26, 1947; d. Alan Ballentine and Virginia Leona (Harris) Strong; m. John Fletcher Tidman, Sept. 23, 1978. BS, Albright Coll., Reading, Pa., 1969; postgrad., U. Pitts., 1970-73, U. Louisville, 1975-76. Exec. trainee Pomeroy's divsn. Allied Stores, Reading, 1969-70; mktg. rsch. analyst Heinz U.S.A., Pitts., 1970-74; new products mktg. mgr. Ky. Fried Chicken, Louisville, 1974-76; dir. Pitts. office M/A/R/C, 1976-79; assoc. rsch. dir. Henderson Advt., Inc., Greenville, SC, 1979-81; sr. v.p., dir. rsch. Bozell, Jacobs, Kenyon & Eckhardt, Inc., Dallas, 1981-86, sr. v.p., dir. rsch. and strategic planning Atlanta, 1986-88; sr. v.p., dir. mktg. svcs. Bozell, Inc., Atlanta, 1988-91; sr. v.p., mng. ptnr. Henderson Adv., Inc., 1991-95; prin. Ender-Ptnr., Inc., 1995-96; v.p. mktg. Booth Rsch. Svcs., Inc., 1996-98; COO Moore & Symons, Inc., 1998—. Cons. mktg. rsch. Greenville Zool. Soc., 1981; adj. prof. So. Meth. U., 1984-85. Mem. Am. Mktg. Assn. (Effie award N.Y. chpt. 1982). Republican. Episcopalian. Home: 146 Northshores Dr Seneca SC 29672

STROOPE, KAY, mathematician, educator; b. Odessa, Tex., Mar. 28, 1947; d. Cecil Clyde and Maurita Rosa Stroope. BS, Henderson U., 1970; MS in Edn., Delta State U., 1989; postgrad., U. Ark., 1987-88. Instr. math. Miller Jr. H.S., Helena-West Helena, Ark., 1970-79, Ctrl. H.S., Helena-West Helena, 1979-87, Benton (Ark.) Mid. Sch., 1987-89, Phillips C.C. U. Ark., Helena, 1989—. Basketball coach Miller Jr. H.S., 1977-81, Ctrl. H.S., 1981-86; math crusade trainer Dept. Higher Edn., Little Rock, 1993—, CMP trainer, 1995—. Co-author (handbook) Metrifacation for Teachers, 1975. Vol. Easter Seal, Helena, 1981-86, March of Dimes, 1987-95, Am. Cancer Soc., 1987—. Named Outstanding Young Educator Helena Jaycees, 1979. Mem. Nat. Coun. Tchrs. Ark., Ark. Coun. Tchrs. Math., Am. Assn. Two-Yr. Colls. Baptist. Home: 600 Galloway West Helena AR 72390-3223 Office: Phillips CC Univ Ark Campus Dr Helena AR 72342

STROSSEN, NADINE, legal association administrator, law educator; b. Jersey City, Aug. 18, 1950; d. Woodrow John and Sylvia (Simicich) S.; m. Eli Michael Noam, Apr. 25, 1980. AB, Harvard U., 1972, JD magna cum laude, 1975; LHD (hon.), U. Vt., 1992; LHD, U. R.I., 1992; JD (hon.), San Joaquin Coll. Law, 1996; LHD (hon.), Rpcky Mountain Coll., 1996, Mass. Sch. Law, 2000. Jud. clk. Minn. Supreme Ct., St. Paul, 1975-76; assoc. Lindquist & Vennum, Mpls., 1976-78, Sullivan & Cromwell, N.Y.C., 1978-83; prof. clin. law, supervising atty. Civil Rights Clinic, Sch. Law, NYU, 1984-88; prof. law N.Y. Law Sch., N.Y.C., 1988—; adj. prof. Columbia U., 1990—; pres. ACLU, N.Y.C., 1991—. Editor Harvard Law Rev., 1975; contbr. book chpts., articles to profl. jours.; author: In Defense of Pornography: Free Speech and the Fight for Women's Rights, 1995. Mem. Coun. Fgn. Rels., 1994—. Recipient Outstanding Young Person award Jaycees Internat., 1986; named one of Ten Outstanding Young Ams., U.S. Jaycees, 1986; adj. fellow Yale U. Calhoun Coll., 1997-. Mem. ACLU, Nat. Coalition Against Censorship (bd. dirs. 1988—), Human Rights Watch (exec. com. 1989-91), Harvard Club (N.Y.C.). Avocations: travel, skiing, singing. Office: NY Law Sch 57 Worth St New York NY 10013-2960 also: ACLU 125 Broad St 18th Fl New York NY 10004 E-mail: nstrossen@aclu.org.

STROTHER, CHERI L., secondary school educator; m. Scott Strother, Aug. 28, 1992; children: Mara R., Wren R. MA in Edn., U. Colo., Boulder, Colo., 1998. Tchr. social studies Littleton (Colo.) H.S., 1999—. Office: Littleton High School 199 E Littleton Blvd Littleton CO 80121 Office Phone: 303-347-7764. Business E-Mail: cstrother@lps.k12.co.us.

STROTHER MCKEOWN, DORA DOUGHERTY, retired aviation psychologist, pilot; b. St. Paul, Nov. 27, 1921; d. John Maynard and Esther Lucile (Wardle) Dougherty; m. Lester J. Strother, 1966 (dec. 2001), m. Harry McKeown, 2002. AA, Cottey Coll., 1941; Ph.B., Northwestern U., 1949; MS, U. Ill., 1953; PhD, NYU, 1955. Lic., cert. psychologist, Tex.; lic. pilot. Flight instr., ferry pilot airports, N.Y., Ill., 1944-49; flight instr. Inst. Aviation, U. Ill., 1949-50, rsch. pilot, rsch. assoc. Aviation Psychology Lab., 1950-56; human engring. specialist Martin Co., Balt., 1957-58; human factors engr. Bell Helicopters Co., Ft. Worth, 1958-62, chief human factors group, 1962-84, mgr. human factors engring. and cockpit arrangement, 1984-86. V.p., asst. treas. Tex. Met. Publs., Inc., 1965-77; speaker in field. Contbr. articles to tech. publs. Mem. adv. coun. Tex. Aero. Commn., 1963-64; panel mem. Coll. Town Hall Programs, 1962; mem. President's adv. com. on aviation FAA, chmn. women's adv. com. on aviation, 1966-68; judge Internat. Sci. Fair, Dallas, 1966; chmn. bd. trustees Amelia Earhart Meml. Scholarship Fund of Ninety-Nines, Inc.; mem. adv. bd. United Cerebral Palsy of Tarrant County, Tex., 1972-75; mem. women's adv. coun. Tarrant County Jr. Coll., 1976-79, chmn., 1977-79; mem., tech. cons. U.S. Army Sci. Bd., 1985-91; mem. adv. bd. Dallas-Ft. Worth Airport Assistance Ctr., 1986-93, Women in Sci. Program U. Tex. at Arlington, 1979-84; mem. Tex. Edn. Agy. Adv. Coun. on Aerospace-Aviation Edn., 1978-83, chmn., 1978-80; bd. dirs. Ft. Worth Aviation Hist. Found., 1989—. Lt. col. USAFR, 1949-77, USAFR, ret., 1977—. Recipient Achievement award NYU, 1955, Amelia Earhart award Am. Women's Assn., 1957, Alumni award Cottey Coll., 1957, Recognition cert. Ft. Worth C. of C., 1961, Lady Hay Drummond-Hay trophy Women's Internat. Assn. Aero., 1961, Aviation Woman of Yr. award Women's Nat. Aviation Assn., 1961, Achievement award AAUW, 1966, Merit award Northwestern U., 1968, cert. of commendation FAA, 1968, Recognition award Women Air Force Svc. Pilots, 1975, Disting. Achievement award AAUW, San Antonio, 1976, U. Ill. Disting. Alumna award, 1990, honor USAF Air U. Air Command & Staff Coll. Gathering of Eagles, 1990; inducted into Mil. Aviation Hall of Fame of Ill., 1991, Tex. Women's Hall of Fame, 1987; holder 2 world flight records for altitude and distance of feminine rotorcraft, 1961-66. Fellow APA, AIAA (assoc., tech. judge student papers 1961, mem. tech. com. on life scis. and systems 1970-73), Human Factors Soc. Am. (Jerome H. Ely award 1968), Am. Helicopter Soc. (crew sta. and human factors engring. tech. com. 1991—); mem. Tarrant County Psychol. Assn. (pres. 1969-70), Assn. U.S. Army, Soc. Engring. Psychologists, Soaring Soc. Am., Tex. Soaring Assn. (chief tow pilot 1961-62), 99s (chmn. Ft. Worth, Chgo., Cen. Ill.), P.E.O., Whirley-Girls Inc., Nat. Safety Coun. Home: 3616 Landy Ln Fort Worth TX 76118-5507

STROTHMAN, WENDY JO, literary agent; b. Pitts., July 29, 1950; d. Walter Richard and Mary Ann (Hodtum) S.; m. Mark Kavanaugh Metzger, Nov. 25, 1978; children: Andrew Richard, Margaret Ann. Student, U. Chgo., 1979-80; AB, Brown U., 1972. Copywriter, mktg. U. Chgo. Press, 1973-76, editor, 1977-80, gen. editor, 1980-83, asst. dir., 1983; dir. Beacon Press, Boston, 1983-95; v.p., pub. adult, trade and reference Houghton-Mifflin, Boston, 1995-96, exec. v.p. trade and reference divsn., 1996—2002, lit. agent, 2003—. Trustee Brown U., 1990-96, Deerfield Acad., 2003—. Edtl. adv. bd. Scholarly Pub., 1993-94; bd. editors Brown Alumni Monthly, 1983-89; chmn., 1986-89. Bd. dirs. Editorial Project for Edn., trustee, 1987-91, treas., 1988-90. Fellow Brown U., 1997—. Mem. Renaissance Soc. (bd. dirs. 1980-83), Assn. Am. Pubs. (Freedom to Read com.), Pubs. Lunch Club (N.Y.C.), PEN New Eng. (adv. bd.), Examiner Club, NacRe Reins. Corp. (bd. dirs.). Office: The Strothman Agy LLC One Faneuil Hall Marketplace Third Fl Boston MA 02109

STROUD, BETSY DILLARD, artist; b. Roanoke, Va., Aug. 12, 1940; d. Peter Hairston Dillard and Alice Elizabeth (Fitch) Madden; m. Ethan Beden Stroud, Dec. 29, 1979 (div. Mar. 1986); 1 child, John Hatcher Fergusson, III. BA, Radford Coll., 1968; MA, U. Va., 1970. Assoc. editor Internat. Artist mag., Scottsdale, Ariz., 1998-2001; profl. artist. Tchr. workshops throughout U.S.; judge art shows including those in Farmington, N.Mex., 1999, The Adirondacks Nat. Watermedia Exhbn., Old Forge, N.Y., 1996, Contemporary Watercolorists of Ariz., 1998, others. Contbr. articles to Am. Artist mag., 1987— and other profl. jours. Mem. S.W. Watercolor Soc. (pres. 1988-89, Edgar A. Whitney award 1989), Am. Watercolor Soc. (High Winds medal 1992, Artist Mag. award 1995), Nat. Watercolor Soc., Rocky Mountain Nat. Honor Soc. (Brass Cheque award 1992), Knickerbocker Artists, Ariz. Watercolor Soc. Avocations: piano, bridge, Scrabble, movies. E-mail: betsydillart@uswest.net.

STROUD, NANCY IREDELL, retired secondary school educator, freelance writer, editor; b. Raleigh, N.C., Apr. 10, 1943; d. John Johnson and Neffie (Mitchiner) Iredell. BA in English, Morgan State U., Balt., 1964; MEd in Adult and C.C. Edn., N.C. State U., 1976; postgrad., The Am. U., 1985. Tchr. history and English Pleasant grove Sch., Sampson County, N.C., 1964-65; social rsch. asst. N.C. State U., 1970; tchr. English Garner Consol. Sch., Wake County, N.C., 1965-67, Calumet H.S., Chgo., 1967-69, LeRoy Martin Jr. H.S., Raleigh, 1971-79, Needham B. Broughton H.S., Raleigh, 1979-84, The Chelsea Sch., Silver Spring, Md., 1984-85, Gaithersburg H.S., Montgomery County, Md., 1985-98; exec. editor Cypher mag., 1998-99. Former mem. adminstrv. bd. Trinity United Meth. Ch., mem. coun. on ministries, past chmn. ch. growth, former head liturgist worship com.; mem. United Meth. Women, Libr. Congress, Smithsonian Instn., Nat. Mus. women in the Arts, U.S. Holocaust Meml. Mus., Dem. Nat. Com., The Kennedy Ctr. Outstanding Vol. award Trinity United Meth. Ch., Germantown, Md., 1986-87. Mem. AAUW, ASCD, NEA, Md. Coun. of Tchrs. of English Lang. Arts, Md. State Tchrs. Assn., Montgomery County Debate League, Montgomery County Edn. Assn., Nat. Coun. Tchrs. English, Nat. Fedn. Interscholastic Speech and Debate Assn., Nat. Ret. Tchrs. Assn., Morgan State U. Alumni Assn., N.C. State U. Alumni Assn., Tchrs. of English in Montgomery County. Avocations: genealogy, classical and jazz music, reading, writing. Home: 217 Booth St Apt 219 Gaithersburg MD 20878-5482 Personal E-mail: eyredalen@aol.com.

STROUD, PEGGY, secondary school educator; d. James and Margret Monk; m. M. Cole Elrod (div.). BS in Edn., U. Ctrl. Ark., Conway, 1977; MEd, Tex. Wesleyan U., Ft. Worth, 2002. Cert. tchr. Ark. Sub. tchr. Conway Pub. Schs., Ark., 1978—82; buyer Old Faculty House, Oklahoma City, 1982—85; buyer, R&D, TCBY, Little Rock, 1983—86; owner Hager's Jewelry Store, Conway, Ark., 1986—88; adminstrv. asst. to dir. Ark. Pks. and Tourism, Little Rock, 1988—91; tchr. Perry-Casa H.S., 1991—93, Heber Springs H.S., 1993—. Bd. dirs. Parents with Children with Disabilities, Conway, Ark. Bd. dirs., sec. Faulkner-Cleburne Regional Water Dist., Conway, Ark., 1985—91; mem. Faulkner County Reps., Conway, Ark., 1986—87; bd. dirs. First United Meth. Ch., Conway, Ark., 1988—90. Mem.: NEA, Ark. Ednl. Assn., Conway C. of C. Methodist. Avocations: arts and crafts, water sports. Office: Heber Springs HS 800 W Moore Heber Springs AR 72543

STROUP, DOROTHY ANNE, author, educator; b. Alamosa, Colo., Apr. 14, 1927; d. Harry Beam and Abigail Leila (Corlett) S. BA in English Lit., Colo. Coll., 1949; M Journalism, U. Calif., Berkeley, 1960, MA in Asian Studies, 1968. Various positions, copywriter, elem. tchr. journalist Safeway Stores, Denver, 1949-54; sec. State Dept. and Tokyo Fgn. Svc., Washington and Tokyo, 1954-57; tchr. English, Hiroshima Jogakuin and Doshisha Coll., Japan, 1960-64; instr. English composition and ESL U. Calif., Berkeley, 1967-71; instr. English composition Skyline Coll., Daly City, Calif., 1969-71; founder, dir. English lang. program for Japanese students Berkeley Inst., 1972-74; supr., instr. ELP U. Calif.-Berkeley Extension, 1974-89. Co-author: Experiences in American Language, 1977; author: In the Autumn Wind, 1987 (NEA award 1989). Bd. dirs. Friends of Hibakusha, San Francisco, 1979-89, World Wall for Peace, Berkeley, 1989-97; mem., cons. Oakland-Nakhodka Sister City Orgn., 1992—. Grantee Ctr. for Japanese Studies, U. Calif., Berkeley, 1966-69, Masaru Kurahashi Internat. Student Advisors of Japan, 1979. Avocations: travel, writing and reading. Home: 10 Claremont Crescent Berkeley CA 94705-2324

STROUP, KALA MAYS, former education commissioner, educational alliance administrator; BA in Speech and Drama, U. Kans., 1959, MS in Psychology, 1964, PhD in Speech Comm. and Human Rels., 1974; EdD (hon.), Mo. Western State Coll., 1996; LHD (hon.), Harris-Stowe State Coll., 2000. V.p. acad. affairs Emporia (Kans.) State U., 1978-83; pres. Murray State U., Ky., 1983-90, S.E. Mo. State U., Cape Girardeau, 1990-95, Am. Humanics, Kansas City, Mo., 2002—; commr. higher edn., mem. gov.'s cabinet State of Mo., Jefferson City, 1995—2002. Pres. Mo. Coun. on Pub. Higher Edn.; mem. pres.'s commn. NCAA; cons. Edn. Commn. of States Task Force on State Policy and Ind. Higher Edn.; adv. bd. NSF Directorate for Sci. Edn. Evaluation; adv. com. Dept. Health, Edn. and Welfare, chair edn. com.; citizen's adv. coun. on state of Women U. S. Dept. Labor, 1974-76. Mem. nat. exec. bd. Boy Scouts Am., nat. exploring com., former chair profl. devel. com., mem. profl. devel. com., exploring com., Young Am. awards com., 1986-87, north ctrl. region strategic planning com., bd. trustees, nat. mus. chair; mem. Gov.'s Coun. on Workforce Quality, State of Mo.; bd. dirs. Midwestern Higher Edn. Commn.; chair ACE Leadership Commn.; mem. bd. visitors Air U.; v.p. Missourians for Higher Edn.; bd. dirs. St. Francis Med. Ctr. Found., 1990-95, Cape Girardeau C. of C., 1990-95, U. Kans. Alumni Assn.; pres. Forum on Excellence, Carnegie Found.; adv. bd. World Trade Ctr., St. Louis, Svc. Mems. Opty. Colls., 1997—; mem. Mo. Higher Edn. Loan Authority, 1995—, depts. econ. devel. & agrl. Mo. Global Partnership, 1995—, Mo. Tng. & Employment Coun., 1995-2002, Concordia U. Sys. Advancement Cabinet, State Higher Edn. Exec. Officers, 1995—, mem. com. workforce edn. and tng., 1996; bd. govs. Heartland's Alliance Minority Participation, 1995-2002; chair, mem. workforce devel. com. NPEC coun. U.S. Office of Edn., 1997—; bd. dirs. Midwestern Higher Edn. Com. Distributed Learning Workshop, 1998-2002, Dept. Natural Resources Minority Scholarship Adv. Bd.; chair Show Me Results sub-cabinet Educated Missourians; mem. Pub. Policy Initiative Stakeholder Com., 1999—; mem. Coun. Higher Edn. transfer and pub. interest com.; mem. access/diversity com. State Higher Edn. Exec. Officers; trustee, mem. adv. coun. Assn. Governing Bds. of Univs. and Colls. Ctr. for Pub. Edn., 2000—. ACE fellow; recipient Alumni Honor Citation award U. Kans., Award Distinction Profl. Black Men's Club, S.E. Mo., 1990, Dist. Svc. to Edn. award Harris-Stowe State Coll., 1996; named to U. Kans. Womans Hall of Fame, Ohio Valley Conf. Hall of Fame, 1997. Mem. Am. Assn. State Colls. and Univs. (past bd. dirs., mem. Pres.'s Commn. on Tchr. Edn., Task Force on Labor Force Issues and Implications for the Curriculum), Mortar Board, Phi Beta Kappa, Omicron Delta Kappa, Phi Kappa Phi, Rotary (found. Ednl. awards com.). Office: Am Humanics 4601 Madison Ave Kansas City MO 64112 Office Phone: 816-561-6415.

STROUP, SALLY, federal agency administrator; b. Harrisburg, Pa. Grad., Ind. U. Pa., Loyola U. From staff atty. to sr. v.p. legal svcs. and chief counsel Pa. Higher Edn. Agy.; mem. profl. staff com. on edn. and the workforce US Ho. of Reps., 1993—2001; dir. industry and govt. affairs Apollo Group Inc./U. Phoenix; asst. sec. postsecondary edn. US Dept. Edn., Washington, 2001—. Office: US Dept Edn Office Postsecondary Edn 1990 K St NW Rm 7115 Washington DC 20006 Office Phone: 202-502-7750, 202-502-7714. Office Fax: 202-502-7875.

STROUPE, ASHLEY W., engineer; BS in Physics, Harvey Mudd Coll., 1990; MS in Elec. and Computer Engring., George Mason U., 1998; MS in Robotics, Carnegie Mellon U., 2001, PhD in Robotics, 2003. Staff engr., Jet Propulsion Lab. NASA, 2003—. Mem., Lunar Ice Discovery Intiative Robotics Inst., Carnegie Mellon U., 1998—99, mem. mobile autonomous robot software project, 2000—03, mem., Minnow Project, 2000—03; robotic construction crew project tech. lead NASA, 2003—05, mem. Mars Exploration Rover flight project, 2003, mem. Mars Exploration Rovers Engring. Team, Jet Propulsion Lab, 2004—, single command approach and instrument placement, 2004—, wide area prospecting Jet Propulsion Lab. software lead, 2005—. Contbr. multiple conf. papers, book chpts. and jour. articles in robotics. Office: NASA-Jet Propulsion Lab M/S 82-105 4800 Oak Grove Dr Pasadena CA 91109 Office Phone: 818-393-7111. Office Fax: 818-393-3254. Business E-Mail: Ashley.W.Stroupe@jpl.nasa.gov.*

STROUSE, JEAN, writer; b. L.A., Sept. 10, 1945; d. Carl David and Louise (Friedberg) S. BA, Radcliffe Coll., 1967. Editl. asst. N.Y. Rev. of Books, 1967-69; freelance writer N.Y.C., 1969-72; editor Pantheon Books, N.Y.C., 1972-75; freelance writer N.Y.C., 1975-79, 1983—2003; book critic Newsweek Mag., N.Y.C., 1979-83; dir. Cullman Ctr. for Scholars and Writers N.Y. Pub. Libr., N.Y.C., 2003—. Selection com. J.S. Guggenheim Found., N.Y.C., 1995-97, trustee, 1987-94, 2001—04, fellow, 1977, 86; exec. coun. Authors Guild; Ferris prof. journalism Princeton U., 1998; John J. Rhodes chair in Am. instns. and pub. policy Barrett Honors Coll., Ariz. State U., 2003. Author: Alice James, A Biography, 1980, Morgan American Financier, 1999; editor: Women & Analysis: Dialogues on Psychoanalytic Views of Femininity, 1974. Recipient Bancroft prize, Columbia U., 1981; fellow, NEH, 1976, 1992, John D. and Catherine T. MacArthur Found., 2002—06. Fellow, Am. Acad. Arts & Sci.; mem. Soc. Am. Historians (pres. 2001-02), Am Philos Soc, The Century Assn., Phi Beta Kappa (vis. scholar 1996-97).

STROZIER, NANCY JANELLE, literature and language educator; b. Tulsa, Okla., Apr. 14, 1959; d. William Paul and Betty Zane Goforth; m. Randall Lee Strozier, June 20, 1980; children: Tara Ranelle, David Marshall. BA in Oral Comm., Ctrl. State U., 1981; M in Edn. Reading, Northeastern State U., 2003. Cert. Reading Specialist Northeastern State U. Speech, drama tchr. Broken Arrow (Okla) Pub. Schs., 1982—86; preschool coord. First Bapt. Ch., Tulsa, Okla., 1987—89; reading specialist Union Pub. Schs.ols, Tulsa, 2003—. Mem.: Tulsa Reading Coun., Okla. Reading Assn., Internat. Reading Assn. Conservative. Bapt. Avocations: travel, reading, camping. Office: Union Public Schs 6515 S Garnett Broken Arrow OK 74012 Office Phone: 918-461-4005. Personal E-mail: taradvd@valornet.com. Business E-Mail: strozier.janelle@unionps.org.

STRUBEL, ELLA DOYLE, advertising executive, public relations executive; b. Chgo., Mar. 14, 1940; d. George Floyd and Myrtle (McKnight) D.; m. Richard Craig G'sell, Apr. 26, 1969 (div. 1973); m. Richard Perry Strubel, Oct. 23, 1976; stepchildren: Douglas Arthur, Craig Tollerton. BA magna cum laude, U. Memphis, 1962; MA, U. Ill., 1963. Staff asst. Corinthian Broadcasting Co., N.Y.C., 1963-65; dir. advt. and pub. rels. WANE-TV, Ft. Wayne, Ind., 1965-66; asst. dir. advt. WBBM-TV, Chgo., 1966-67, mgr. sales promotion, 1967-69, dir. advt. sales promotion and info. svcs., 1969-70; dir. pub. rels. Waltham Watch Co., Chgo., 1973-74; mgr. advt. promotion and pub. rels. WMAQ-TV, Chgo., 1974-76; v.p. corp. rels. Kraft, Inc., Glenview, Ill., 1985-87; sr. v.p. corp. affairs Leo Burnett Co., Inc., Chgo., 1987-92, exec. v.p., 1992-98; mng. dir. EllaQuent Designs, 2002—. Pres. women's bd. Rehab. Inst. Chgo., 1982—84; chair Chgo. Network, 1994—95, Rehab. Inst. Chgo., 1998—2001; vice chair Chgo. Pub. Libr. Found.; bd. dirs. Rehab. Inst. Chgo. Named Outstanding Woman in Comms. in Chgo., YWCA, 1995, one of 100 Most Influential Women in Chgo., Crain's Chgo. Bus., 1996, Who's Who in Chgo. Bus., 2002. Mem. Casino Club, Econ. Club (bd. dirs.). Democrat. Presbyterian. Home and Office: 55 W Goethe St Chicago IL 60610-7406 Office Phone: 312-255-0235. Business E-Mail: estrubel@aol.com.

STRUBLE, PAMELA LYNN, music educator; m. Gary Steven Struble, Oct. 7, 2000; children: Joselyn Rose, Brooke Hannah. MusB, Coll. of N.J., Trenton, 1996; Master's, Walden U., 2006. Music tchr. Ea. Christian Schs., Wyckoff, NJ, 1997—99, Nutley Bd. Edn., NJ, 1999—. Musician, accompanist Jacksonville Chapel, Lincoln Park, NJ, 2003—. Home: 49 Arch St Butler NJ 07405 Office: Spring Garden School 59 South Spring Garden Ave Nutley NJ 07110 Office Phone: 973-661-8983.

STRUBLE, SUSAN C., recreational therapist; b. N.Y.C., Jan. 4, 1939; d. Calvert Horton and Catherine (Snell) Crary; m. Robert Musser Struble, Mar. 30, 1985. BA, Carleton Coll., 1960. Art therapist Skills Inc., State College, Pa., 1995—, Adult Day Activities Ctr., State College, 1995—, adv. com., 2001—. Vol. art therapist Centre County Youth Ctr., Pa., 1990-93, Laurelton State Sch. and Hosp., 1973-74. Artist: works include Reclining Figure (1st prize Art Alliance Ctrl. Pa.), 1999. Asst. English tchr. Internat. Hospitality Coun., State Coll., 1995—; bd. dirs. friends Palmer Mus. of Art, Pa. State U., 1999—, sec., 2000—. Named Vol. of Yr. Ctrl. Counties Youth Ctr., 1993, Internat. Hospitality Coun., 1999, Adult Day Activities Ctr., 1999. Mem.: State Coll. Woman's Club (sec. art dept. 1998—99), Pa. Watercolor Soc. (sig. mem.), Am. Art Therapy Assn., Antique Automobile Club Am. Republican. Presbyterian. Avocations: art, music. E-mail: rmstruble@webtv.net.

STRUBLE, SUZANNE R., educator; d. Roy L. and Vera J. Stretch; m. Michael H. Struble, Oct. 11, 1981; 1 child, Megan J. MA in Profl. Edn., Seton Hall U., West Orange, N.J., 1995. Cert. K-12 secondary art edn. N.J., 1979. Educator Vernon (N.J.) Twp. Pub. Schs., 1979—. Dir. art exhibit N.J. State Fair, Augusta, 1991—2006. Lay leader, spkr. Wantage (N.J.) United Meth. Ch., 2000—06. Mem.: Nat. Art Educators Assn., N.J. Art Educators Assn., N.J. Edn. Assn., Kappa Delta Phi. Methodist. Avocations: watercolor painting, ceramics, gardening, continuing education. Office: Glen Meadow Middle School PO Box 516 Vernon NJ 07462-0516

STRUCK, JUDY KAY, special education specialist; b. Carrington, N.D., July 10, 1950; d. Milton O. and Clara (Zitterkob) Holland; m. James L. Struck, Oct. 26, 1968 (div. 1984); children: Joni, Eric, Angi. BS in Elem. Edn., Dakota State U., 1982; MA in Spl. edn., U. S.D., 1983. Cert. elem. and spl. edn. tchr., S.D.; cert. presch. handicapped tchr., Iowa. Tchr. handicapped Sioux Falls (S.D.) Sch. System, 1983-85, tchr. spl. edn. early childhood, 1985-87; specialist pediactric edn. U. N.D., Grand Forks, 1987-88; specialist early childhood Ctr. Devel. Disabilites U. S.D., Vermillion, 1988—, assoc. dir. Ctr. Devel. Disabilites, 1989—. Bd. dirs. Early Childhood Info. Resource Svcs., S.D., Early Intervention Pers. Preparation Program, S.D., Svcs. to Indian Infants and Toddlers Program, Rosebud, S.D.; cons. in field. Author: (manual) Guide to Special Education in South Dakota, 1989. Leader, Am. Legion Jr. Aux., Montrose, S.D., 1979-80; bd. dirs. Sioux chpt. Assn. for Retarded Citizens, 1986-87, Hawthorne PTA, Sioux Falls, 1987-88; vol. Handiriders, Sioux Falls, 1988. Mem. Am. Assn. U. Affiliated Programs, S.D. Coun. for Exceptional Children, S.D. Interagy., Coordinating Coun. (pub. rels. chair 1989—), Coun. for Exceptional Children, Div. Early Childhood, Phi Delta Kappa. Avocations: swimming, bicycling, gardening. Office: Univ SD Ctr Devel Disabilit 414 E Clark St Vermillion SD 57069-2307

STRUCK, NORMA JOHANSEN, artist; b. West Englewood, NJ, Feb. 17, 1929; d. Hans Christian and Amanda (Solberg) Johansen; m. H. Walter Struck, Aug. 21, 1955; children: Steven, Laurie. Student, N.Y. Phoenix Sch. Design, 1946-50, Art Students' League, N.Y.C., 1976-77. Staff artist Norcross, Inc., N.Y.C., 1950-60, free-lance artist, 1967-75; artist portraits, prints Scafa-Tornabene, Nyack, NY, 1976—; artist portraits, paintings U.S.N., U.S. Coast Guard, Washington, 1976—. Com. bd. mem. Navy Art Coop. Liaison, N.Y.C., 1976-80, Coast Guard Art Program, N.Y.C., 1980—, Navy Hist. Mus., Washington. One-woman shows include Valley Cottage Gallery, NY, Bergen Co. Playhouse, Oradell, NJ, NY Yacht Club, 2003, Nabisco Co., Fairlawn, NJ, 1987; exhibited in group shows Navy Hist. Mus., Washington, 1976, Navy Combat Art Gallery, Washington, World Trade Ctr., 1979, USCG, New Eng. Air Mus., Windsor Locks, Conn., 1984, Fed. Hall, NYC, 1986, 93-97, Salmagundi Club, NYC, Officers Club, Governor's Island, Hudson Valley Show, White Plains, NY, Intrepid Mus., NYC, Alexander Hamilton U.S. Custom House, Newington-Cropsey Mus., NY, Bergen County Mus. Art & Sci., NJ; represented in permanent collections U.S. Pentagon, Washington, Henie-Onstad Mus., Oslo, World Figure Skating Hall of Fame and Mus., Colorado Springs, Alexander Hamilton Custom House, NYC, Nat. ARts Club, NYC. Recipient Louis E. Seley award, Navy Art Program, 1979; Grumbacher award, Catherine Lorillard Wolfe, Nat. Arts Club, N.Y.C., 1978; George Gray award Coast Guard Art Program, Governors Island, N.Y., 1983, 89. Fellow Am. Artists Profl. League (pres.'s award 1979); mem. Portrait Soc. Am., Art Students League (life), Hudson Valley Assn. (bd. dirs. 1985-88, M. Dole award 1980), Soc. Illustrators, Salmagundi Club, Portrait Soc. Am., Inc., Mus. of Women in the Arts (charter). Avocations: antiques, gourmet cooking. Home: 910 Midland Rd Oradell NJ 07649-1904 E-mail: njstruck99@cs.com.

STRUHS, RHODA JEANETTE, civic and political worker; b. Fresno, Calif., Aug. 31, 1953; d. Edward Stanley and Mary Juanita (Pate) De Vere; m. Parry Leon Struhs, July 3, 1971; children: Jason, Lanisa. Grad. high sch., Fresno. Office mgr. Gunn McKay for U.S. Congress, Ogden, Utah, 1986; saleswoman Realty World-Simplified, Ogden, 1987-89; spl. edn. aide, substitute tchr. Weber Sch. Dist., Ogden, 1989-92; human svcs. aide Weber County Mental Health, Ogden, 1991; No. Utah field dir., office mgr. Pat Shea for Gov., Ogden, 1992; office adminstr. SHARE, INC., Ogden, 1993-97; mgr. cmty. resource-vol. ctr. Your Cmty. Connection, Ogden, 1997-99; Dem. adminstrv. asst. Utah Ho. of Reps., Salt Lake City, 1999—. Block leader Am. Heart Assn., March of Dimes, Easter Sales, 1979-93; troop leader, com. mem. Boy Scouts Am., Girl Scouts U.S.A., 1982-89; bd. dirs. Riverdale Elem. Sch. PTA, 1985-89, pres., 1987-88; bd. dirs. Women's Legis. Coun., 1989-91; conv. del. Weber County. Utah and Nat. Dem. Coms., 1981—; state sec. Utah Dem. Com., 1989-93; pres. Women's Legis. Coun. Weber County, 1993-95, parliamentarian, 1999-01; bd. dirs. Women's State Legis. Coun., 1993-97; vol. ctr. adv. com. Davis County United Way, 1989-99, Nat. Conf. State Legislatures, 1999—, Coun. State Govts., 1999—. Named Weber County Young Dem. of Yr., 1984, Dem. Vol. of Yr., 1986; recipient Extra Mile award Bonneville Coun. PTA, 1986, Disting. Svc. award Utah Dem. Com., 1993. Mem. Altrusa (pres. Ogden 1995-96, dist. membership chmn. 1997-99, dir. 1998-2002, Internat. Dist. Ten dir., 2001—). Avocations: handicrafts, camping, reading, travel. Home: 4312 S 700 W Ogden UT 84405-3404 Office: Utah Ho of Reps 318 State Capitol Salt Lake City UT 84114

STRUNA, NANCY L., social historian, American studies educator; b. Painesville, Ohio, May 24, 1950; d. Edward A. and Betty J. (Hoffacker) S. BS, U. Wis., 1972; PhD, U. Md., 1979. Social studies tchr. The Andrews Sch., Willoughby, Ohio, 1972-74; grad. asst. U. Md., College Park, 1974-76; tchr. 1-8 grades St. Mark's Elem., Adelphi, Md., 1976-78; instr. U. Md., College Park, 1978-80; asst. prof. U. Minn., Mpls., 1980-82; prof. dept. Am. Studies U. Md., College Park, 1982—, acting chair, 2001, exec. dir. univ. gen. edn., 2002—03. Spl. asst. to pres. women's issues, 1998-2000, fellow Acad. Affairs, 1998-99, campus legis. liaison, 1999. Author: People of Prowess, Sport, Leisure and Labor in Early America, 1996; contbr. articles to profl. jours., chpts. to books. Chair Pres. Commn. on Women's Issues U. Md., 1996—98; mem. Omohundro Inst. for Early Am. History, Culture and Soc. Named Disting. scholar Nat. Assn. Phys. Edn. in Higher Edn., 1993. Fellow Am. Acad. Kinesiology, N.Am. Soc. Sport History (pres. 1995-97), Orgn. Am. Historians, Am. Hist. Assn., Am. Studies Assn., U.S. Capitol Hist. Assn., Md. Hist. Soc. (Lord Balt. Rsch. fellow, 2004-2005). Office: U Md Dept Am Studies 1102 Holzapfel Hall Coll College Park MD 20742-5620 Business E-Mail: nlstruna@umd.edu.

STRUNK, BETSY ANN WHITENIGHT, retired education educator; b. Bloomsburg, Pa., May 28, 1942; d. Mathias Clarence and Marianna (Naunas) Whitenight; children: Robert J. Jr., Geoffrey M. BS in Edn., Bloomsburg U., Pa., 1964; MEd, West Chester U., Pa., 1969; cert. mentally/physically handicapped, Pa. State U., Delaware County, 1981; postgrad., Wilkes U., Wilkes-Barre, Pa., St. Joseph's U., Phila., Drexel U., Western Md. Coll., Westminster. Cert. elem. edn., spl. edn. tchr., single engine pvt. pilot. Tchr. Faust Sch., Bensalem Twp., Pa., 1964, Eddystone (Pa.) Elem. Sch., 1964-66, Lima Elem. Sch., Rose Tree Media (Pa.) Sch. Dist., 1966-69, Rose Tree Media Sch. Dist., 1977—2005; ret.; adj. prof. Wilkes Coll., Wilkes-Barre, Pa., 1981-86; instr. Delaware C.C., Media, 1986; instr., dir. ground sch. edn. Brandywine Airport, West Chester, Pa., 1986-88; instr. Drexel U., Phila., 1989—2001, Performance Learning Systems, Inc., Emerson, NJ and Nevada City, Calif., 1981—2001; rep. FAA, Phila., 1986-88. Spl. edn. resource rm. specialist, tchr. cons. Media Elem. Sch.; curriculum designer pvt. pilot ground sch.; instr. and course designer introduction to flying and pilot companion course; mem. educator's adv. com. Phila. Franklin Inst., 1990—92, 1995—2005; cons. ednl. programs, 1988—2005; owner, designer Betsy's Belts, Del., NJ, Pa., 1970—74, Stitches of Love, Savannah, Ga., 2006—; mem. gov. bd. Southeastern Tchr. Leadership Ctr. West Chester U., Pa.; learning support specialist Glenwood Elem. Sch., Media, Pa., 1994—2005; educator liaison between sr. citizens and learning support students Lima Estates Retirement Home and Glenwood Elem. Sch., 1994—2005; tchr. academically gifted program Indian Ln. and Glenwood Elem. Schs., 1998—99; presenter State Pa. Lead Tchr. Conf., 1994, Ind. Sch. Tchrs. Assn., 1995; project dir. video documentary Performance Learning Sys., Calif., 1994; ptnr., owner Whitenight Homestead Partnership, Bloomsburg. Program dir. video documentaries including: Learning Through Live Events and Teaching Skills for the 21st Century, 1995; editor (chairperson): Deerfield Knoll Quar. Newsletter, 1999—2003; contbr. articles to profl. jours. Mem. Middletown Free Libr. Bd., 1977—79; officer Riddlewood Aux. to Riddle Meml. Hosp., Media, 1973—76; chairperson Lima Christian Nursery Sch., Pa., 1973, March of Dimes, Middletown, 1973; creator Parents of Students with Learning Disabilities Orgn., 1979—82; pres. Roosevelt PTG (Elem. Sch.), Media, 1982; capt. March of Dimes, Media, 1987—91, Diabetes Assn., Media, 1989—91; vol. Tyler Arboretum, Middletown Twp., 1980—82; mem. cmty. rels. com. Deerfield Knoll Homeowner's Assn., 1998—, v.p., bd. dirs., 1999—2002; mem. Wilmington Opera House, Dupont Theatre; founder cmty. orgn. Antique Study Group; chairperson Investment Group, Restaurant Dining Group, 1999—2002; reunion chairperson Ben Franklin Lab. Sch., Bloomsburg U., 2004; vol. Brandywine River Mus., 2005; com. person, v.p. Middletown Twp. Dem. Com., 1974; mem.Vietnamese refugees com. Media Presbyn. Ch., 1975; assoc. mem. Skidaway Presbyn. Ch., Savannah, Ga. Recipient 1st pl. color divsn. Photography award, Pa. Colonial Plantation, 1st pl. color divsn. in Photography, Bloomsburg State Fair, 1994; grantee Fine Arts in Spl. Edn., Pa. Dept. Edn., 1993—94. Mem.: NEA, Savannah Telfair Mus. Art and Jepson Ctr., Ga. Hist. Soc., Media Soc. Performing Arts, Aircraft Owners and Pilots Assn., Nat. Staff Devel. Coun., Pa. State Edn. Assn. (ho. of dels. 1999—2005), Rose Tree Media Edn. Assn. (profl. devel. com. rep. 1990—93, profl. devel. com. chairperson 1992—93, Exceptional Svc. award), Brandywine Valley Civil War Roundtable, Chester County Hist. Soc., Phila. Zoo, Tyler Arboretum, Longwood Gardens, Alpha Delta Kappa (program com. 2003—, chmn. pub. rels. 2004—). Democrat. Avocations: reading, writing, interior decorating, nature walking, gardening. Home: Willistown Twp 203 Cohasset Ln West Chester PA 19380-6507 also: The Landings on Skidaway Island 7 Franklin Creek Rd South Savannah GA 31411

STRUPP, DARLENE CLARA, special education educator; b. Washington, Mo., Feb. 18, 1957; d. Harold Fred and Lorene Isabel Viehland; m. Steven Ray Strupp, Mar. 12, 1977; children: Steven Nicholas, Carrie Amanda, William Adam. BS in Edn., U. Mo., St. Louis, 1999; MEd, S.W. Mo.Bapt. U., Boliver, 2001; M.Spl.Edn., U. Mo., St. Louis, 2002. Cert. tchr. elem. and spl. edn. Mo. Spl. edn. tchr. N.W. R-1 Sch., House Springs, Mo., 1999—. Mem.: MNEA, Mo. DLD (pres. 2004—06, bldg. rep. 2004), Coun. for Exceptional Children. Avocations: reading, sewing, farming. Home: 5375 Viehland Farm Rd Catawissa MO 63015

STRUTHERS, ELEANOR ANN, writer, educator; b. Terril, Iowa, Apr. 15, 1930; d. Fred A. and Anna M. (Smith) Mohr; m. Melvin Struthers Jr.; children: John, Georgia, Charity, Mary. BA magna cum laude, Morningside Coll., 1952; MA, U. Iowa, 1971, PhD, 1980. Instr. writing and composition Kirkwood C.C., Cedar Rapids, Iowa, 1973-77; asst. prof. English composition Univ. No. Iowa, Cedar Falls, 1977-82; Writer in the Schs. Iowa Arts Council, Des Moines, 1982-86; vis. prof. Am. lit., writer-in-residence Coe Coll., Cedar Rapids, 1986—; lectr. in Am. Lit. Univ. Aleppo (Syria), Syria, 1996-98. Editor Coe Rev. Press, Cedar Rapids, 1990—. Author: From Persia and Other Places, 1979, Stoneboat, 1989, The Alcott Family Arrives, 1993, What You Try To Tame, 2004; editor: Holding On and Letting Go, 1996; co-editor: Turning Up the Leaves, 2000; contbr. over 50 articles, short stories and poetry to profl. jours. Coolidge fellow, Cambridge, Mass., 1989, Yaddow Writers Colony fellow, Saratoga, N.Y., 1991, Villa Montalvo Writers Colony fellow, Saratoga, Calif., 1992, Malone fellow, Mid. East travel, 1994; Fulbright fellow, Aleppo, Syria, 1996-98, Sri Lanka, 2002-03. Dem. Meth. Avocations: hiking, reading. Office: Coe Coll English Dept 1220 1st Ave NE Cedar Rapids IA 52402-5008 Home: 190 Cottage Grv Ave SE Apt 102 Cedar Rapids IA 52403-1743 Office Phone: 319-399-8615. Business E-Mail: astruthe@coe.edu.

STRUTHERS, MARGO S., lawyer; BA, Carleton Coll., 1972; JD cum laude, U. Minn., 1976. Atty., shareholder Moss & Barnett, P.A. and predecessor firms, Mpls., 1976-93; ptnr. Oppenheimer Wolff & Donnelly, LLP, Mpls., 1993—. Mem. Am. Health Lawyers Assn., Minn. State Bar Assn (bus. law sect., former chair nonprofit com., former chair and former mem. governing coun. health law sect.). Office: Oppenheimer Wolff & Donnelly LLP Plaza VII 45 S 7th St Ste 3300 Minneapolis MN 55402-1614 Office Phone: 612-607-7427, 612-607-7000. Business E-Mail: mstruthers@oppenheimer.com.

STRYKER, JOAN COPELAND, retired obstetrician, retired gynecologist, educator; b. Swayzee, Ind., Apr. 17, 1918; d. Kenneth Bayard and Elsie Weser Copeland; m. Walter Stryker (dec.); children: Sara Gill, Peter, David; m. Dawson James Lewis. BS, U. Ill., Urbana, 1939; MD, U. Ill., Chgo., 1943. Resident U. Mich., Ann Arbor, 1943—46, fellow, 1946—47; asst. prof. Wayne State U., Detroit, 1965—85, prof., 1985—2001, prof. emeritus, 2001—. Chief menopausal clinic Hutzel Hosp., Detroit, 1992—2001. Chief investigator (book) Addicted Neonatals. Med. dir. Planned Parenthood, Detroit, 1965—70, treas., 1970; staff mem. WHO, 1958—61. Named Tchr. of Yr., Wayne State U. Sch. Medicine, 1990; recipient Disting. Svc. award, 1988, Pathfinders award in medicine, 1991, Cmty. Svc. award, Gynecologist of Yr., ACOG, 1994. Mem.: ACOG (pres., Cmty. Svc. award, Gynecologist of Yr. 1994), Am. Menopausal Soc., Alpha Omega Alpha, Sigma Xi. Avocations: sailing, skiing. Home: 9784 Hawthorne Glen Dr Grosse Ile MI 48138

STUART, ALICE MELISSA, lawyer; b. NYC, Apr. 7, 1957; d. John Marberger and Marjorie Louise (Browne) S. BA, Ohio State U., 1977; JD, U. Chgo., 1980; LLM, NYU, 1982. Bar: NY 1981, Ohio 1982, Fla. 1994, U.S. Dist. Ct. (so. dist.) Ohio, 1983, U.S. Dist. Ct. (so. and ea. dists.) NY 1985. Assoc. Schwartz, Shapiro, Kelm & Warren, Columbus, Ohio, 1982-84, Paul, Weiss, Rifkind, Wharton & Garrison, NYC, 1984-85, Kassel, Neuwirth & Geiger, NYC, 1985-86, Phillips, Nizer, Benjamin, Krim & Ballon, NYC, 1987—92; pvt. practice NYC, 1992—98; atty. LeBoeuf, Lamb, Greene & MacRae, NYC, 1998—. Adj. prof. So. Coll., Orlando, Fla., 1997-98. Surrogate Speakers' Bur. Reagan-Bush Campaign, NYC, 1984; mem. Lawyers for Bush-Quayle Campaign, NYC, 1988; bd. dirs. Mayflower Soc. in State of NY, 1998-, counsellor, 2002-. Mem. ABA, NY State Bar Assn., Women's Nat. Rep. Club (bd. dirs. 2004—), Winston Churchill Meml. Libr. Soc., Jr. League, Soc. Mayflower Descs. in State of NY (bd. dirs. 1999-, counselor 2002-), Women's Nat. Rep. Club (bd. dirs. 2004—), Phi Beta Kappa, Phi Kappa Phi, Alpha Lambda Delta. Republican. Office: LeBoeuf Lamb Greene & MacRae 125 W 55th St New York NY 10019-5369 Office Phone: 212-424-8669. Business E-Mail: astuart@llgm.com.

STUART, ANN, academic administrator, writer, educator; b. Madisonville, Ky., Dec. 22, 1935; d. Peter Frank and Laura (Hatchett) S.; m. Raymond R. Poliakoff, Aug. 22, 1980. BA in Edn., U. Fla., 1958; MA in English, U. Ky., 1962; PhD in English, So. Ill. U., 1976. Tchr. Maderia Beach Jr. High Sch., St. Petersburg, Fla., 1958-59, Bourbon County High Sch., Paris, Ky., 1959-60, Henry Clay High Sch., Lexington, Ky., 1960-62; prof. of English and tech. writing U. Evansville, Ind., 1962-89, asst. dean Coll. Arts and Scis. Ind., 1979-81, 86-87, adminstrv. coordinator writing programs Ind., 1984-86; dean Sch. Arts and Scis. East Stroudsburg (Pa.) U., 1989-90; provost, v.p. acad. affairs Alma (Mich.) Coll., 1990-93; pres. Hartford (Conn.) Grad. Ctr., 1994—. Lectr. various regional and nat. profl. orgns.; dir. computer edn. Vanderbugh Sch. Corp., U. Evansville, Ball Communications, Inc., Evansville, 1985—; adminstrv. coordinator writing programs U. Evansville, 1985—; cons. various local, nat. bus., 1982—; vis. prof. computer tech. Purdue U., West Lafayette, Ind., 1987-88. Author: Writing and Analyzing Effective Computer System Documentation, 1984, Corresponding with Customers, 1985, The Technical Writer, 1987, Communication Guide For Corresponding with Students, Parents, Alumni and Donors, 1988. Bd. dirs. Evansville Arts and Edn. Council, 1972-75, Harlaxton Soc., Evansville, 1981-85. Mem. MLA, Ind. Corp. Sci. and Industry, Nat. Council Tchrs. English, Assn. Tchrs. Tech. Writing, Am. Coun. Edn., Am. Assn. Higher Edn., Am. Assn. Univ. Adminstrs., Rotary, Phi Kappa Phi, Delta Kappa Gamma. Clubs: Musicians of Evansville (pres. 1972-78). Avocations: art museums, performing arts, architecture. Office: Hartford Grad Ctr 275 Windsor St Hartford CT 06120-2910

STUART, CAROLE, publishing executive; b. N.Y.C., Feb. 22, 1941; d. Frank and Sally (Stern) Rose; m. Lyle Stuart, Feb. 4, 1982; 1 child, Jennifer Susan Livingston. Student, Bklyn. Coll. Pub. Lyle Stuart, Inc., Secaucus, NJ; assoc. pub. Carol Pub. Group, N.Y.C.; pub. Barricade Books, Inc., N.Y.C. Author: Why Was I Adopted?, To Turn You On, 39 Sex Fantasies for Women; author: (with Claire Ciliotta) Why Am I Going to the Hospital?; author: I'll Never Be Fat Again, How To Lose 5 Pounds Fast, The Thank You Book. Mem.: Authors Guild, Women's Media Group, Wine and Food Soc. N.Y. Home: 1530 Palisade Ave Apt 6L Fort Lee NJ 07024-5402 Office: Barricade Books Ste 308A 185 Bridge Plz N Fort Lee NJ 02024

STUART, CYNTHIA HODGE, literature and language educator; b. Ft. Irwin (Barstow), Calif., Feb. 1, 1962; d. Troy Marion and Laura Jane Bozarth Hodge. BS, Ark. State U., Jonesboro, AR, 1984; BS in Edn., Ark. State U., Jonesboro, 1987, MSc in Edn., 1999. Teaching Certificate 7-12 English, journalism and drama endorsement Ark., 1987, Teaching Certificate for MSE Ark. Dept. of Edn., 2000, Teaching Certificate Ark. Dept. of Edn., 2000. English tchr. Maynard H.S., Ark., 1987—; adj. instr. Black River Tech. Coll., Pocahontas, Ark., 1999—2005. Beta club sponsor Maynard H.S., Ark., 2005—. Editor and writer Randolph County Hist. and Geneal. Soc., Pocahontas, Ark., 1996—2006. Mem.: Nat. Coun. for Teachers of English (assoc.). R-Liberal. Achievements include research in genealogical and historical research. Avocations: travel, genealogy, reading, farming. Home: 1794 Legate Rd Maynard AR 72444 Personal E-mail: cindystuart@yahoo.com.

STUART, DOROTHY MAE, artist; b. Fresno, Calif., Jan. 8, 1933; d. Robert Wesley Williams and Maria Theresa (Gad) Tressler; m. Reginald Ross Stuart, May 18, 1952; children: Doris Lynne Stuart Willis, Darlene Mae Stuart Cavalletto, Sue Anne Stuart Peters. Student, Calif. State U., Fresno, 1951-52, Fresno City Coll., 1962-64. Artist, art judge, presenter demonstrations at schs., fairs and art orgns., Calif., 1962—99; retired. Editor, art dir. Fresno High School Centennial 1889-1989, 1989; art advisor Portrait of Fresno, 1885-1985; contbg. artist Heritage Fresno, 1975; exhibited in group shows, including M.H. De Young Mus., San Francisco, 1971, Charles and Emma Frye Mus., Seattle, 1971, Calif. State U.-Fresno tour of China, 1974. Mem. adv. Ctrl. Calif. Women's Conf., 1989—, Patrons for Cultural Arts, Fresno, 1987-92, bd. dirs., 1991-92. Recipient 53 art awards, 1966-84; nominated Woman of the Yr., Bus./Profl. of Fresno, 1990. Mem. Soc. Western Artists (bd. dirs. 1968-74, v.p. 1968-70), Fresno Womens Trade Club (bd. dirs. 1986-93, pres. 1988-90), Fresno Art Mus., Fresno Met. Mus., Native Daus. Golden West Fresno. Republican. Avocations: world travel, photography, collecting art and dolls of different cultures. Home and Office: 326 S Linda Ln Fresno CA 93727-5737

STUART, FLORA TEMPLETON, prosecutor; d. Ruput Alison Stuart and Elise Talmage Lieb; m. Victor Joseph Iaanuzzi, May 27, 1985; children: Natalie, Elise, Maria. BA, Western Ky. U., Bowling Green, 1972; JD, Northern Ky. U., 1976. Bar: Ky. 1976. Atty. Flora Templeton Stuart Law Firm, Bowling Green, Ky., 1976—, Warren County Pub. Advocate, Bowling Green, Ky., 1978—83. Vol. Ask the Experts, Bowling Green, Ky., 1998—2002; co-founder Cumberland Trace Legal Aid Svcs. Recipient Winner for Women of Achievement award for Entrepreneurship, Bowling

Green Human Rights Commn., 2004. Mem.: Ky. Bar Assn., Ky. Acad. for Trial Lawyers, Am. Trial Lawyers Assn. Avocation: music. Office: Law Firm Flora Templeton Stuart 607 E 10th St Bowling Green KY 42101

STUART, JACQUELYN L., state supreme court justice; b. Atmore, Ala., Sept. 23, 1955; m. George Stuart; children: Tucker, Shepard, Kelly. BA in Sociology and Edn., Auburn U., 1977; JD, U. Ala., 1980. Asst. atty. gen. State of Ala.; exec. asst. to commr. and spl. asst. atty. gen. Ala. Dept. Corrections; asst. dist. atty. Baldwin County; dist. judge, 1989—97; judge Ala. Cir. Ct., 1997—2001; justice Ala. Supreme Ct., 2001—. Faculty advisor Nat. Judicial Coll., Reno; former pres. Ala. Council of Juvenile & Family Ct. Judges; pres. Blue Ridge Inst. for Juvenile & Family Ct. Judges, 2002. Former pres. Heritage Junior Women's Club, Bay Minette Kiwanis Club, Jubilee Woman's Club; bd. mem. Ala. Federation of Women's Clubs. Republican. Office: Ala Supreme Ct 300 Dexter Ave Rm 3-215 Montgomery AL 36104-3741 Office Phone: 334-242-4584. Business E-Mail: lstuart@appellate.state.al.us.

STUART, JILL, apparel designer; m. Ron Curtis, 1986; children: Morgan, Chloe, Sophie. Student, RI Sch. of Design. Sold jewelry and handbag designs Bloomingdales, NYC; founded accessory line Jill Stuart, NYC, founded women's wear line, 1993—, launched intimate apparel, eyewear, denim and footwear lines, 2000—. Office: Jill Stuart Offices 550 7th Ave New York NY 10018 Office Phone: 212-921-2600.*

STUART, JOAN MARTHA, fund raising executive; b. June 2, 1945; d. Ervin Wencil and Flora Janet (Applebaum) S. Student, Boston U., 1963-67. Cert. fund raising exec. Prodn. asst. Random House, N.Y.C., 1968-69; book designer Simon & Schuster, N.Y.C., 1969-71; feature writer Palm Beach (Fla.) Post, 1971-72; co-founder, comm. dir. Stuart, Gleimer & Assocs., West Palm Beach, 1973-84, pres., 1982—. Fin. devel. dir. YWCA Greater Atlanta, 1984-86, Ctr. for the Visually Impaired, Atlanta, 1986-90; ea. divsn. dir. City of Hope, 1990-94; devel. dir. Jewish Family Svcs., Atlanta, 1994-99, Ctr. for Visually Impaired, 1999-2002; dir. advancement The Epstein Sch., 2002—. Contbr. articles to profl. jours. Mem. crusade com. Am. Cancer Soc. Bd., 1981—; bd. dirs. Theatre Arts Co., 1980-81; cmty. svcs. chmn., bd. dirs. B'nai B'rith Women, 1980-82; chmn. publicity Leukemia Soc. Atlanta Polo Benefit, 1983; com. chmn. Atlanta Zool. Beastly Feast Benefit, 1984; mem. Atlanta Symphony Assocs.; chmn. Salute to Women of Achievement, 1987-90; founder, advisor Lauren's Run, 1992—; grad. Leadership Midtown, 2001. Recipient Nat. award B'nai B'rith Women, 1978, Regional award, 1979, Cert. of Merit, Big Bros./Big Sisters, 1976. Mem. Nat. Soc. Fund Raising Execs. (cert.), Diabetes Assn. (bd. dirs. 1990—), Jerusalem House (bd. dirs. 1991-94), Parent to Parent (bd. dirs. 1993-95). Democrat. Jewish. Office: 335 Colewood Way NW Atlanta GA 30328 Office Phone: 404-250-5636. E-mail: jstuart@epsteinatlanta.org.

STUART, LILLIAN MARY, writer; b. Chgo., Nov. 7, 1914; d. Ira and Katherine (Tries) Daugherty; m. Robert Graham Stuart, Aug. 7, 1936 (dec. Sept. 1969); 1 child, Mary Leone. Asst. to pres. Weisberger Bros., South Bend, 1933-42; head TWX distbn. Davis-Monthan AFB, Tucson, 1946-48; artist and music tchr., 1945-55; interviewer-counselor Ariz. State Employment Commn., Tucson, 1955-70; residence dir. YWCA, Tucson, 1970-71; tax preparer Tucson, 1971-72; U.S. census taker U.S. Govt., N.Mex., 1976, 80; mng. Luna County Rep. Party, Deming, 1976; tchr. YWCA, Tucson, 1969, El Paso Coll. Bus., 1972; tutor math, English, 1981. Travel lectr. various civic groups and clubs; radio reader Lighthouse for the Blind, El Paso, 1983—89; spkr. Internat. Women's Day Celebration, San Antonio, 1996, Lovington Rotary Internat., 1999, Kiwanis Internat., Lovington, 1999, Lovington Internat. Lions Club, 1999, Women's Club, Lovington, 2000, schs. in Lovington, 2002. Contbr. stories to The Quarterly; author: The Avestan, 1997, The Broughty Series, 2004; (series of biographies) Lighthouse for the Blind; actress Studebaker Players, South Bend, 1936-42, South Bend Theatre, 1936-42, (film) Extreme Prejudice, 1986; writer Centennial Mus. at U. Tex., El Paso, 1992-95; actress in commls., 1996-97. Counselor, vol. Crisis Ctr., Deming, 1975-77. Recipient plaques and prizes for various pieces of writing. Mem. Mensa, Rosicrucians. Avocations: travel, art. Address: 212 W Avenue A Lovington NM 88260-4120 Office Phone: 505-396-1626.

STUART, MARIE JEAN, physician, hematologist, researcher; b. Bangalore, India, Sept. 11, 1943; came to U.S., 1967; d. Norman and Dorothy (Dias) S. BS, MB, Madras (India) U. Asst. prof. pediatrics SUNY Health Sci. Ctr., Syracuse, 1972-76, assoc. prof., 1976-81, prof. pediatrics, 1981-87; prof. chief hematology and oncology div. St. Christophers Hosp. for Children and Temple U., Phila., 1987-97; prof. thrombosis rsch. Temple U., 1987-97; dir. NIH Comprehensive Sickle Cell Ctr. Thomas Jefferson U., Phila., 1998—. Mem. nat. child health com. Nat. Inst. Child Health and Human Devel., Bethesda, Md., 1982-86; mem. nat. heart, lung and blood rsch. tng. com., NIH, Bethesda, 1993-2000; mem. NIH Sickle Cell Disease Adv. Coun., 2000-04; mem. NIH Erythrocyte and Leucocyte Biology Study Sect., 2003—. Mem. editl. bd. Biology of the Neonate, 2000—; contbr. chpts. to books, articles to profl. jours. Docent Phila. Mus. Art, 2005. Recipient Rsch. award Temple U., 1997. Mem. Am. Fedn. Clin. Research. Am. Pediatric Soc., Soc. for Pediatric Research. Avocations: music, art. Home: 227 S 6th St Apt 1 NW Philadelphia PA 19106 Office Phone: 215-955-9820. Business E-Mail: marie.stuart@jefferson.edu.

STUART, MICHELLE RAE, artist; b. Borrego Springs, Calif., Feb. 10, 1940; d. Charles Cameron and Ramona (Hagenauer) S. Painter, sculptor, printmaker. Represented in numerous permanent collections including The Coll. of Wooster, Ohio, The Bklyn. Mus., Cin. Art Mus., Mus. Contemporary Art, Chgo., Mus. Modern Art, N.Y.C., Phila. Mus. Art, and others; exhibited in group shows at Denver Art Mus., New Orleans Art Mus., Pa. Acad. Art, Balt. Art Mus. and others; one-woman shows include Rose Art Mus., Brandeis U., Waltham, Mass., 1988, Galerie Ueda-Ginza, Tokyo, 1987, The Parrish Art Mus, NY, The Mus. of Contemporary Art, Los Angeles, Whitney Mus. of Am. Art, N.Y.C. and others. Recipient numerous grants including Artist-In-Residence, Art Gallery of Western Australia and Curtin U. of Tech., Perth, 1989, N.Y. Found. for the Arts Artists' Fellowship, 1987, Finnish Art Assn. Fellowship, Helsinki, Finland, 1985, Nat. Endowment Arts grants, 1974, 77, 80, 89, John Simon Guggenheim Found. Fellowship, N.Y. State Creative Artists Pub. Svc. Grant, 1975, Ford Found. Tamarind Inst. Grant, Artist-In-Residence Program, Albuquerque, 1974, MacDowell Fellowship, Am. Acad. in Rome fellowship, Academician of the Nat. Acad. fellowship Avocation: photography. Gallery: Diane Villani Gallery 285 Lafayette St New York NY 10012-3225 also: B R Kornblatt Gallery 406 7th St NW Washington DC 20004-2217 E-mail: michellestuart38@aol.com.

STUART, NANCY RUBIN (NANCY ZIMMAN STETSON), journalist, writer, television producer; b. Boston, Nov. 25, 1944; d. Stuart Wendell and Ethel (Rabinovitz) Zimman; m. William W. Stetson, Apr. 28, 2001; children: Elisabeth, Jessica. BA, Tufts U., 1966; MA in Teaching, Brown U., 1967; PhD (hon.), Mt. Vernon Coll., 1995. Playwright, dir. Equity Library Theatre, Roundabout, Joseph Jefferson and St. Clement's theaters, N.Y.C., 1971-74; freelance reporter Westchester-Gannett newspapers and mags., 1975-77, N.Y. Times, N.Y.C., 1977—. Faculty affiliate Bush Ctr. in Child Devel., Yale U., New Haven, 1981-86; mem. Westchester County Women's Adv. Bd., chair, 1988; bd. dirs. Women Writing Women's Lives Seminar; mem. faculty SUNY, Purchase, 1994-95, Fordham U., N.Y.C., 1996-99. Author: The New Suburban Women, Beyond Myth and Motherhood, 1982, The Mother Mirror: How a Generation of Women is Changing Motherhood in America, 1984, Isabella of Castile: The First Renaissance Queen, 1991, American Empress: The Life and Times of Marjorie Merriweather Post, 1995, Club Dance: The Show, The Steps, The Spirit of Country, 1998, The Reluctant Spiritualist: The Life at Maggie Fox, 2005; writer, assoc. prodr: TV series America's Castles for A&E Network, 1996—99 (Telly award, 1999, Telly award (3), 2001, Writing Communicator award, 1999), The Gold Coast for The Grand Tour A & E TV, 1997, writer prodr., prodr.: TV series Restore America, 1999; writer prodr., prodr. (TV series) Restore America, 2001 (3 Telly awards); writer/assoc. prodr.: TV series Eccentrics, 1999 (Crystal award, Telly award), The N.Y. Times, 1977—; writer/assoc. prodr. Baltimore Sun, American History Magazine; contbg. editor: Parents mag., 1987—91,: McCalls, Savvy, Travel & Leisure, Ladies Home Jour., 1980—92; theater critic: Stamford Advocate, 1994—96; co-prodr.:. Recipient Washington Irving award Westchester Libr. Assn., 1993, Telly award finalist, 2001; Am. Antiquarian Soc. fellow, 2005; Time, Inc.-Bread Loaf Writers' Colony scholar, 1979. Fellow MacDowell Colony; mem. Author's Guild, Am. Soc. Journalists and Authors (Author of Yr. award 1992, hon. mention oustanding book award, gen. nonfiction 2006), PEN, Nat. Arts Club. Avocations: skiing, sailing, ballet, classical music, dance.

STUART, PAMELA BRUCE, lawyer; b. N.Y.C., Feb. 13, 1949; d. J. Raymond and Marion Grace (Cotins) S. AB with distinction, Mt. Holyoke Coll., 1970; JD cum laude, U. Mich., 1973. Bar: N.Y. 1974, D.C. 1975, U.S. Dist. Ct. D.C. 1979, U.S. Ct. Appeals (D.C. cir.) 1980, U.S. Supreme Ct. 1980, U.S. Dist. Ct. Md. 1989, Md. 1992, Va. 1993, U.S. Ct. Appeals (4th cir.) 1993, Fla. 1994, U.S. Dist. Ct. (ea. dist.) Va. 1994, U.S. Dist. Ct. (no. dist.) N.Y. 1996, U.S. Dist. Ct. (so. dist.) Fla. 1998, U.S. Dist. Ct. (so. dist.) N.Y. 1999, U.S. Dist. Ct. (ea. dist.) N.Y. 1999, U.S. Dist. Ct. (mid. dist.) Fla. 2001. Trial atty., deputy asst. dir. Bur. of Consumer Protection, FTC, Washington, 1973-79; asst. U.S. atty. U.S. Atty's Office, Washington, 1979-85; sr. trial atty. Office of Internat. Affairs, U.S. Dept. Justice, Washington, 1985-87; atty. Ross, Dixon & Masback, Washington, 1987-89; mem. Lobel, Novins, Lamont & Flug, Washington, 1989-92; pvt. practice, Washington, 1992—. Instr. Nat. Inst. for Trial Advocacy, Atty. Gen.'s Advocacy Inst., Legal Edn. Inst., Fed. Practice Inst.; mem. Jud. Conf. D.C., 1985-88, 1991-2004; mem. Jud. Conf., D.C. Cir., 1996, 98, 2000; assoc. mem. Consular Corps Washington; legal analyst CNN, MSNBC, Fox News, other TV networks. Author: The Federal Trade Commission, 1991; contbr. articles to profl. jours. Bd. dirs. Anacostia Econ. Devel. Corp., 1993—, Anacostia Holding Co., Inc. Mem. ATLA, ABA (internat. criminal law com., chmn., 1993-96, chmn. fed. crime rules subcom. white collar crime com. sect. criminal justice 1997-99), Bar Assn. D.C. (bd. dirs. 1995-2001, 03—, sec. 2003-04, treas. 2005-06), Asst. U.S. Attys. Assn. D.C. (exec. coun. 1993-99, pres. 1998-99), Women's Bar Assn. D.C., Fla. Bar (exec. coun. real property probate and trust law sect. 1999—), Alumnae Assn. Mt. Holyoke Coll. (bd. dirs. 1986-89, 92-95, mem. art adv. bd. Art Mus. 2005—, Alumnae medal of honor 1990), Edward Bennett Williams Inn of Ct. (master of bench), Fed. City Club (bd. govs. 1992—, pres. 2005-06), Cosmos Club. Avocations: writing, interior design, investments, piano, art. Home: 5115 Yuma St NW Washington DC 20016-4336 Office: The J Raymond Stuart Bldg 1750 N Street NW Washington DC 20036 Office Phone: 202-835-2200. Personal E-mail: pamstuart@aol.com.

STUART, SANDRA JOYCE, computer information scientist; b. Wheatland, Mo., Aug. 15, 1950; d. Asa Maxville and Inez Irene (Wilson) Friedley; m. John Kendall Stuart, Apr. 17, 1971; 1 child, Whitney Renee. Student, Cen. Mo. State U., 1968-69; AA (hon.), Johnson County C.C., 1980; BSBA cum laude, Avila Coll., 1992. Cert. Info. Sys. Security Profl. Statis. asst. Fed. Crop Ins. Corp., Kansas City, Mo., 1978-83; mgr. Fed. Women's Program, Kansas City, 1979-80; mgmt. asst. Marine Corps Fin. Ctr., Kansas City, 1983-85, analyst computer systems, 1985-88; computer programmer analyst Corps. of Engrs., Kansas City, 1988-91; regional program mgr. FAA, Kansas City, 1991—. Author: The Samuel Walker History, 1983. Asst. supt. Sunday sch. Overland Park (Kans.) Christian Ch., 1979-80, supt., 1980-82. Mem. Wheatland H.S. Alumni Assn. (pres. 1990-91, 2006—, v.p. 2005-06, pres. 2006-, named to Hall of Fame), Mo-Kan High Tech. Crime Investigation Assn. (charter, 2d v.p. 1998-99, 1st v.p. 1999-2000, pres. 2000-01), Kansas City Security Coalition. Avocations: needlecrafts, genealogy, reading, travel.

STUART, SANDRA KAPLAN, public policy consultant; b. Greensboro, N.C. d. Leon and Renee (Myers) Kaplan; children: Jay Jr., Timothy; m. D. Michael Murray. BA, U. N.C., Greensboro; student, Monterey Coll. Law. Chief legis. asst. Rep. Robert Matsui, Washington, 1979-81; legis. dir., assoc. staff Appropriations and Budget Coms., Washington, 1981-87, Rep. Vic Fazio, Washington, 1987-89, chief of staff, 1989-93; asst. to sec. of def. for legis. affairs, 1993-94; asst. sec. def. legis. affairs Dept. Def., The Pentagon, Washington, 1994-99; mng. dir. Clark and Weinstock, Washington, 1999—. Office: Clark & Weinstock Ste 410 S 601 13th St NW Washington DC 20005 Office Phone: 202-261-4000.

STUART, SHERRY BLANCHARD, artist; b. Newport, Ark., Feb. 19, 1941; d. Walter Thomas Blanchard and Eathel Gladys Faulkner; m. Michael John Scholl, 1963 (div. 1970); 1 child, Aaron John Scholl; m. Roy Otto Stuart, Oct. 5, 1973; 1 child, Ross. BFA, Mpls. Coll. Art and Design, 1964. Designer logos. Exhibited in group shows at Bennington Ctr. for the Arts, 1999, Ariz. Hist. Mus./Joan Cawley Gallery, 1998, Merrill Johnson Gallery, Denver, 2001, Desert Caballeros Western Mus., 2001, Hilligoss Galleries, Chgo., 2002, Nita Stewart Haley Libr. and History Ctr./Elieb Biek Art Mus., 2002, Am. Artists Profl. League, N.Y.C., 2002, Nichols Fine Art Gallery, Taos, N.Mex., 2003, Ky. Horse Park, Lexington, 2003, Breckenridge Fine Arts Ctr., 2003, Harness Tracks of Am. 26th Ann. Art Show and Auction, Lexington, 2003, Stewart Gallery, 2004, Phoenix Civic Ctr. Plaza, 2004, Phippen Mus., 2004, Howard/Mandville Gallery, Kirkland, Wash., 2004, El Presidio Gallery, Tucson, 2005, Norby Gallery, Cave Creek, Ariz., 2004, Mus. of the S.W., 2004, one-woman shows include Gold Nugget Art Gallery, Wickenburg, Ariz., 2003, exhibited in group shows at numerous other group shows, juried and invitational. Recipient People's Choice award, Am. Acad. Women Artists, 1999, 2d Ann. Western ARt Classic, Mpls., 1985, 1st place and Best of Show, Minnetonka Ctr. Arts, 1979, Award of Excellence, Chinese Artists Assn. N.Am., 2003, numerous other 1st and 2d place awards various exhbns., juried shows. Mem.: Western Artists of Am., Am. Plains Artists (signature mem.), Oil Painters of Am. (signature mem.), Am. Acad. Women Artists (signature mem.), Creative Women of Pinnacle Peak (founding mem.). Republican. Avocations: antiques, photography, cooking, golf, horseback riding. Business E-Mail: whoswho@sherryblanchardstuart.com.

STUBBLEFIELD, JENNY REBECCA, educator; b. Rome, Ga., Oct. 22, 1968; children: Ryan Thomas, Molly. MEd, State U. of West Ga., Carrollton. Tchr. Rome City Schs., 2000—. Home: 102 Wood Valley Dr Rome GA 30165

STUBBLEFIELD, LURIA SHAW, education educator; b. Morgan City, La., Oct. 16, 1969; d. Robert Lee and Emma (Barideaux) Shaw; m. Michael Andre Stubblefield, Apr. 15, 2000; children: Alaina Rionne, Michael Andre II. BS, So. U. and A&M Coll., Baton Rouge, La., 1993; MEd, La. State U., Baton Rouge, 1995, Edn. Specialist, 1997, PhD, 2004. Outreach generalist Southeastern La. U., Hammond, 1997—98; evaluator So. U. and A&M Coll. Louis Stokes La. Alliance for Minority Participation, Baton Rouge, 1998—99; program adminstr. So. U. Louis Stokes La. Alliance for Minority Participation, Baton Rouge, 1999—2004; asst. prof. curriculum and instrn. and ligo sci. edn. specialist So. U. and A&M Coll., Baton Rouge, 2004—. Cons. Evaluative and Devel. Svcs., Inc., Baton Rouge, 2005—. Co-author: (refereed jour. article) K-12 Outreach: The Model of the Timbuktu Academy, A Significant Other for Effective Education Making Adequate Time for Teaching and Learning, Competitive Mentoring: Deploying the Model of a US Presidential Award for Excellence in Science, Mathematics, and Engineering Mentoring; author: Math Anxiety Among GED Recipients in Four Year Institutions. Sec./treas. My Brother's Keeper After-Care Ministries, Zachary, La., 1996—; reviewer Am. Assn. Colls. for Tchr. Edn. Conf., Washington, 2006, Ann. Biomedical Rsch. Conf. for Minority Students, Washington, 2004—05; session chair Am. Assn. for the Study of Higher Edn. Conf., Kans. City, Kans., 2004. Named Tchr. of Yr., So. U. and A&M Coll., 2006; fellow, So. Regional Edn. Bd., 1995; grantee Co-PI, Louis Stokes La. Alliance for Minority Participation Phase III, La. Bd. Regents, 2000—, NSF, 2005—, 2005—, Co-Project Dir., Project Modeling Inquiry Sci. Edn., La. Systemic Initiatives Program, 2005—06, 2006—; Huel D. Perkins Fellow, La. State U., 1995. Mem.: AIAA, Am. Ednl. Rsch. Assn., Assn. for the Study of Higher Edn., NSTA. Conservative. Office: So Univ and A&M Coll PO Box 9983 Baton Rouge LA 70813 Office Phone: 225-771-4483. Office Fax: 225-771-3338. Personal E-mail: lshaw8944@aol.com.

STUBBS, SUSAN CONKLIN, retired statistician; b. Washington, July 26, 1935; d. Maxwell Robertson and Marcia (Nye) Conklin; m. LeRoy Carter Hostetter, May 20, 1975 (div. 1988); m. Joel Richard Stubbs, Sept. 20, 1992. BA, Pa. State U., 1957. Economist Bur. of Census, Suitland, Md., 1973—74, Bur. of Labor Stats., Washington, 1974—79, supervisory economist, 1979—84; statistician IRS, Washington, 1984—95, chief rschr. stats. of income divsn., 1989—92, coord. for indsl. classification, 1994—95; ret., 1995. Cons. joint com. on taxation U.S. Congress, 1992-94; OPM legis. fellow, 1988. Contbr. articles to profl. jours.; editor govtl. statis. publs. Leader, del., bd. dirs., v.p., chmn. nominating com. Nation's Capital coun. Girl Scouts U.S., 1968—; sec.-treas. Middlesex Beach Assn., Bethany, Del., 1991—94; jobs. editor Caucus for Women in Stats., Washington, 1992—95; mentor Mentors Inc., Washington, 1992—94; treas. Smith Point Sea Rescue, 1997—2004; docent Reedville Fisherman's Mus., 1997—, chmn. Christmas house tour, 2000—02, mem. steering com. Christmas house tour, 2002—03, fin. chmn., Christmas on Cockrell's Creek, 2002, treas., 2003, chmn. fin., 2003, chmn. planning giving com.; active Boy Scouts Am. Campaign for Family Values; tutor and mentor People Helping People; mem. Tax Economist Forum, 1990—97; mentor Northumberland Mid. Sch. in Tobacco grant program; treas. Region II, Episc. Diocese of Va., 1999—2005; bd. dirs. Rice's Hotel/Hughlett's Tavern Found., 1998—2000, Rappahannock CC Found., treas., 2003—05. Mem.: Northumberland Assn. for Progressive Stewardship (edn. com. 1997—), St. Stephen's Episcopal Ch. ECW (v.p. 2002, treas. 2003—04, del. to coun. 2005—06, mem. com. on resolutions 2006), Bus. and Profl. Women Essex County and No. Neck (sec. 1999—2001), Va. Federated Women's Clubs (pres. Northumberland County chpt. 1996—98, pres Ea. area Lee dist. 1998—2000), Rivers Bend Assn. (bd. dirs. 1996—98, chair fin. com. 1998—2001, v.p., bd. dirs. 2001—, chair bylaws com., chair long range planning com., chair fin. com. 2003—). Avocations: sailing, swimming, gardening, reading. Home: 776 Riverview Dr Heathsville VA 22473-4011 Personal E-mail: stubbs@crosslink.net.

STUBER, IRENE ZELINSKY, writer, researcher; b. Cleve., Nov. 1, 1928; d. Joseph Frank and Marian (Kulchar) Zelinsky; m. Joseph Francis Stuber, Apr. 9, 1948 (div. Aug. 1954); children: Catherine, Geraldine, William. Student, Cleve. Coll., 1946-48. Editor Cleve. Kegler, 1954-60; publs. dir. Miami (Fla.)-Dade C. of C., 1963-65; staff writer Hollywood (Fla.) Sun-Tattler, 1966-67; urban affairs writer Ft. Lauderdale (Fla.) News, 1967-74; tech. editor Bell Aerospace, New Orleans, 1977-78; owner Kulchar's Jewelry, New Orleans, 1974-83, Hot Springs, Ark., 1983-90, Jewel Box Revs. Freelance writer. Rschr., writer (Internet newsletter) Women of Achievement and Herstory, 1994—, columnist; writer (Internet newsletter) Catt's Claws, 1995—; owner, compiler www.undelete.org, 1992—. Mem. ctrl. com. Broward County (Fla.) Dem. Party, 1973-75, Garland County (Ark.) Dem. Party, 1996—; v.p. Va. Clinton Kelley Dem. Women's Club, Hot Springs, 1995-97. Recipient Pub. Svc. award City of Hollywood, 1967, Journalistic Excellence award AP, 1967, Recognition of Svcs. award Fla. Bar Assn., 1968. Mem. NOW (Ark. chpt. pres. 1993-94, Hot Springs chpt. pres. 1992-97), Harbor House (sec., bd. dirs. 1997-98), Women's Internet and Info. Network, Inc. (pres. 1997—). Avocation: "missionary" to introduce women to internet and women's history to internet. Home: PO Box 6185 Hot Springs National Park AR 71902-6185

STUCKEY, ELLEN MAE, music educator; d. Charles Franklin and Mary Dolores Hershberger; m. Joseph Bruce Stuckey, Jr., June 9, 1979; children: Laura L., Aaron N. BS in Music Edn., West Chester U., 1977; MEd in Music Edn., Pa. State U., 1981. Cert. music tchr. Pa. Dept. Edn. Music tchr. K-5 Everett (Pa.) Area Sch. Dist., 1977—82; pvt. music tchr. Martinsburg, 1982—; tchr. jr./sr. high vocal/gen. music Hollidaysburg (Pa.) Area Sch. Dist., 1988—89; music tchr. K-5 No. Bedford County Sch. Dist., Loysburg, Pa., 1990—, now music tchr. K-5. Dir. adult choir 1st Bapt. Ch. Altoona, Pa., 1977—87, Martinsburg Grace Brethren Ch., 1989—2006. Composer, lyricist: songs Hail to You, O Northern Bedford, 1995; contbr. to profl. mags.; composer 3 songs, co-author: mus. drama The Ark of Faith, 2003. Founder Aaron N. Stuckey Meml. Found.; dir. luminary svc. Am. Cancer Soc., Martinsburg, 2002, 2003; mistress of ceremonies Little Miss pageant Roaring Spring (Pa.) Lions Club, 1996, 1997, 1998. Mem.: Pa. State Educator's Assn., Nat. Guild Piano Tchrs., Am. Choral Dirs. Assn., Pa. Music Educators Assn. Republican. Grace Brethren. Avocations: spending time with family, gardening, photography, songwriting. Office: No Bedford County Sch Dist 217 NBC Dr Loysburg PA 16659 Office Phone: 814-766-2221 x 343. Business E-Mail: estuckey@nbcsd.k12.pa.us.

STUDDARD, JOY, minister; 4 children. B, ENMU, 1990. Minister Roswell City Jail, N.Mex., Midland County Jail, Midland, Tex., Mescalero Indian Jail, N.Mex., Ruidoso City Jail, N.Mex., N. Mex. Prison for Women, Santa Fe Correction Ctr., N.Mex., others. Home: 10700 Academy Rd NE Apt 323 Albuquerque NM 87111-7329 Personal E-mail: joystuddard@yahoo.com.

STUDER, KATHY LYNN, music educator; b. Decatur, Ill., June 17, 1975; d. Stanley Lee and Renne Marie Walters; m. Daniel William Studer. BS in Music Edn., U. Ill., Urbana-Champaign, 1997; MS in Music Tech., Ind.U./Purdue U., Indpls., 2006. Cert. IL Type 12 Tchg. Cert. 1997. Musician Busch Gardens Entertainment, Williamsburg, Va., 1993—94; band tchr. Kankakee Sch. Dist., Kankakee, Ill., 1997—98, Band for Today, Naperville, Ill., 1999—2000, Rondout Sch. Dist. 72, Lake Forest, Ill., 2000—06. Mem. cultural arts com. Rondout Sch., Lake Forest, Ill., 2001—06; coord. young authors Rondout Sch. Dist., Lake Forest, 2001—05. Author: (article in mag.) Teaching Music, 2005. Musician Decatur (Ill.) Mcpl. Band, 1991—93; Vol. private instr. Univ. High Sch., Urbana, Ill., 1996—96. Mem.: NEA, Ill. Grade Sch. Music Assn., Music Educators Nat. Conf., Tech. Club (coord. 2002—06). Office Phone: 847-362-2021 626.

STUDER-RABELER, KAREN ELIZABETH, director; d. Archie Ralph and Elizabeth (Kubik) Studer; m. Richard Kevin Rabeler, Aug. 2, 1986. BS, Mich. State U., Lansing, 1985. Lab. attendant Mich. State U., Lansing, 1982—85; assoc. engr. Hughes Rsch. Labs., Malibu, Calif., 1985—87; rsch. engr. iii U. Mich., Ann Arbor, 1987—91, assoc. dir. new bus. devel., 1999—; tech. mktg. and new product devel. Coy Lab. Products, Grass Lake, Mich., 1991—94; application specialist Millipore Corp., Bedford, Mass., 1994—99. Bd. dirs. MichBio, Ann Arbor, Mich.; v.p. membership Midwest Rsch. Universities Network, Mpls., 2006—, exec. bd. dirs., founding mem.; adv. bd. TechConnect, Cambridge, Mass., 2006—. Mem. at large Grass Lake (Mich.) Hist. Soc., 1990—2006; bd. dirs., past chair garden com. Whistlestop Pk. Assn., Grass Lake, 1990—2006. Named one of Most Influential Women, Ann Arbor Bus. Direct Weekly, 2003. Mem.: Mich. U. Commercialization Initiative (intellectual property commercialization com. 2004—06), Assn. U. Tech. Mgrs. Office Phone: 734-763-0614.

STUDEVANT, LAURA, medical association administrator; Pres. Nat. Environ. Health Assn., Denver; regional health mgr. Amtrak, Chgo. Address: Regional Pub Health Mgr Amtrak 210 S Canal Chicago IL 60606 Office: National Environ Health Assn 720 S Colorado Blvd Ste 970S Denver CO 80246-1925

STUDIN, JAN, publishing executive; From acct. mgr. to v.p. Woman's Day, 1982—95, v.p., advt. dir., 1995—96; v.p., pub. Woman's Day Hachette Filipacchi Mags., Inc., NYC, 1996—2002; v.p., pub. Parents Mag., 2002—06, Better Homes & Gardens Mag., 2006—. Office: Better Homes & Gardens 125 Park Ave New York NY 10017 Office Phone: 212-557-6600.*

STUDLEY, JAMIENNE SHAYNE, lawyer, educator; b. NYC, Apr. 30, 1951; d. Jack Hill and Joy (Cosor) Studley; m. Gary J. Smith, July 14, 1984. BA magna cum laude, Barnard Coll., 1972; JD, Harvard U., 1975. Bar: DC 1975, U.S. Dist. Ct. DC 1978. Assoc. Bergson, Borkland, Margolis & Adler, Washington, 1976—80; spl. asst., sec. U.S. HHS, 1980—81; assoc. Weil, Gotshal & Manges, Washington, 1981—83; assoc. dean law sch. Yale U., New Haven, 1983—87, lectr. law, 1984—87; exec. dir. Nat. Assn. for Law Placement, Washington, 1987—90; syndicated columnist Am. Lawyer Media,

1990—91; exec. dir. Calif. Abortion Rights Action League, 1992—93; dep. gen. counsel U.S. Dept. Edn., 1993—99, acting gen. counsel, 1997—99; pres. Skidmore Coll., Saratoga Springs, NY, 1999—2003; scholar-in-residence Carnegie Found. for the Advancement of Tchg., Palo Alto, Calif., 2003—04; pres. Pub. Advocates, Inc., 2004—. Vis. scholar adj. faculty U. Calif., Berkeley Law Sch., 1992; bd. dirs. Assn. Am. Colls. & U., 2001—, treas., 2006—; bd. dirs. Adirondack Trust Co., 1999—2003; vis. com. Harvard Law Sch., 1999—2005; vice chair for program The Annapolis Group, 2001—03; chair legis. com. Commn. on Ind. Colls. and Univs. N.Y. State, 2002—03. Pres. Conn. Women's Ednl. and Legal Fund, Hartford, 1986—87; co-founder Washington Area Women's Found., 1997; founding bd. dirs. Wood Art Collectors; mem. Jacob Javits fellowship bd. U.S. Dept. Edn., 2000—03; mem. policy com. Campus Compact, 2002—; co-chmn. Calif. Coalition for Civil Rights, 2005—; bd. dirs. The Urban Sch., San Francisco, 2004—, v.p., 2005—; bd. dirs. San Francisco Mus. Craft and Design, 2004—, Am. Craft Coun., 2005—. Mem.: ABA (commn. on women in the profession 1991—94, chair editl. bd. Perspectives 1991—99, chair coord. coun. legal edn. 1996—97, com. on loan repayment and forgiveness 2001—03), Nat. Adv. Coun., First Book, Nat. Assn. for Ind. Colls. and Univs. (accountability com. 1999—2002), DC Bar Assn., Barnard in Washington (pres. 1977—78), Assn. Alumnae Barnard Coll. (bd. dirs. 1978—81), Phi Beta Kappa. Office: 131 Steuart St 300 San Francisco CA 94105-1241 Office Phone: 415-431-7430.

STUDLEY, LAVADA A., music educator; adopted d. Clarence C. and Kathryn Costa; m. Joseph Stephen Studley, June 1, 1974; 1 child, Kathryn Ruth. MEd, Cambridge Coll., Mass., 1997. Eucharistic min. St. Elizabeth Seton Parish, N. Falmouth, Mass., 1988—2006. Mem.: NEA, Mass. Music Educators' Assn. (pres. 2005—, Lowell Mason award). Office: Lawrence School 113 Lakeview Ave Falmouth MA 02540 Office Phone: 508-548-0606. Personal E-mail: lstudley@falmouth.k12.ma.us. E-mail: lstudley@famouth.k12.ma.us.

STUDLEY, MICHELLE, mathematics educator; m. Andrew Broderick, 2005. M, SUNY Stonybrook, 2004. Cert. Pub. Sch. Tchr.- Provisional N.Y., 2001. Tchr. H.S. math. West Islip H.S., NY, 2002—. Coach lacrosse West Islip H.S., 2002—06. Recipient All-Intercollegiate Assoc. award, U.S. Lacrosse, 2001. Mem.: Nat. Coun. Tchrs. Math. Achievements include I am introducing new technology into the West Islip Schools. E-mail: m.studley@wi.k12.ny.us.

STUEBE, JOANNE, secondary school educator; b. Chgo., Sept. 24, 1950; d. John Joseph and Anne Klucher; m. Fred K. Stuebe, Aug. 18, 1973; 1 child, Beth Anne. BA, N. Ctrl. Coll., Naperville, Ill., 1971; MA, Purdue U., West Lafayette, Ind., 1976; MSIR, Loyola U. Chgo., 1983. Lic. tchg. N.J., Ill. Tchr. English Midlothian Dist. 143 Schs., Ill., 1971—72; tchr. English, dept. chair Matteson Dist. 162 Schs., Ill., 1972—90; instr. English Purdue U.-Calumet, Hammond, Ind., 1976—82, Bucks County C.C., Newtown, Pa., 1991—93; coord. advanced placement, tchr. English Hamilton Twp. Schs., NJ, 1993—. Praxis grader Edn. Testing Svcs., Princeton, NJ, 1994—96; tchr. evaluator Nat. Bd. Tchg. Cert., Princeton, 1998. Named Humanities Tchr. of Yr., Hamilton Twp. Schs., 2001, Outstanding Humanities Tchr., N.J. Legis., Trenton, 2001. Mem.: NEA, N.J. Edn. Assn., LWV. Avocations: antiques, travel. Office: Nottingham HS 1055 Klockner Rd Hamilton NJ 08619 Office Phone: 609-631-4161 ext. 5632.

STUEVER, ANITA CAROL, small business owner, secondary school educator; b. Yale, Mich., Jan. 22, 1956; d. Alfred Charles and Doris Estella (Brennan) S. BS, Mich. State U., 1978, MA, 1982. Cert. tchr. secondary and vocat. edn., Mich.; cert. assn. exec. Tchr. vocat. agrl., Future Farmers Am. advisor Breckenridge HS, Lakeshore HS, Stevensville, Mich., 1978-81, Cassopolis Jr., Sr. HS, 1997-98; projects asst., found. exec. dir. Mich. Assn. Future Farmers Am., Mich. State U., East Lansing, 1981-82; dir. comm. N.E. Dairy Herd Improvement Assn., Ithaca, NY, 1983-86; editor Cornell U., Ithaca, NY, 1986-91; exec. dir. Ind. Soybean Growers Assn., Lebanon, 1991-96; CEO Communication Works, 1997—. State sec. Mich. Assn. Future Farmers Am., East Lansing, 1974-75; bd. dirs., student mem. State Career Edn. Adv. Commn., Lansing, Mich., 1977-78; instrnl. devel. com. chair Mich. Assn. Tchrs. Vocat. Agr., 1979-81; publicity com. chair US Coop. Communicators Assn., 1985-86; editorial, media cons. Nat. Future Farmers Am. Orgn., Alexandria, Va., 1986-90; computer tng. cons. Bd. Coop. Ednl. Svcs., Ithaca, 1990-91; mem. Ind. Agrl. Leadership Program, 1995-96, Youth Understanding Tchr. Exch., Germany, 1999; amb. Coll. Agr. and Natural Resources, Mich. State U., East Lansing. Author: Agriscience Laboratory Manual, 1991; editor (alumni newspaper) Human Ecology News, 1990-91; contbr. over 250 articles to publs. 4-H leader, adv. com. Tompkins County Ext., Ithaca, 1984-86; Sunday sch. supt., youth group advisor, Bible sch. tchr. Stevensville, East Lansing, 1970-74, 80-85, Sunday sch. tchr., 1999-; sec. Mich. Future Farmers Am. Alumni Coun., 1981-82; pres. Press Club, 1990. Recipient Four Writing Contest Editor's Choice awards, Calif. Geneal. Soc., 2002. Mem. Am. Soc. Assn. Execs., Ind. Soc. Assn. Execs., So. Geneal. (treas.), Calhoun County Geneal. Soc. (newsletter editor, 2000-03, pres. 2001-03, rec. sec. 2005-), Alpha Zeta. Avocations: sewing, fiber arts, paper arts, calligraphy. Home and Office: 300 Carpenter Dr Battle Creek MI 49017-9712

STUHR, ELAINE RUTH, state legislator; b. Polk County, Nebr., June 19, 1936; m. Boyd E. Stuhr, 1956; children: Cynthia (Stuhr) Zluticky, Teresa (Stuhr) Robbins, Boyd E., Jr. BS, U. Nebr. Tchr. jr. and sr. vocat. h.s. Nebr. schs.; senator Nebr. Unicameral, Lincoln, 1994—; chmn. Nebr. retirement sys. com.; vice chair natural resources com.; commr. edn. com. of states; farmer Bradshaw, Nebr. Former asst. instr. U. Nebr., Lincoln; participant farmer to farmer assignment to Russia with Winrock, Internat., 1993, to Lithuania with Vol. Overseas Coop. Asistance, 1993; former pres. Agrl. Womens Leadership Network; former mem. bd. dirs. Feed Grains Coun., Nebr. Corn Bd. Past pres., bd. dirs. Found. for Agrl. Edn. and Devel.; former mem. exec. com. and bd. dirs. Agrl. Coun. Am.; nat. pres. Women Involved in Farm Econs., state pres.; mem. adv. com. Nebr. Extension Sv.; bd. dirs. Heartland Ctr. for Leadership Devel.; past chmn. Nebr. Agrl. Leadership Coun. Republican. Office: Nebr State Capitol Dist # 24 Lincoln NE 68509 Office Phone: 402-471-2756. E-mail: estuhr@unicam.state.ne.us.

STUKES, GERALDINE HARGRO, library and information scientist, educator; m. Marshall Willis Stukes, Jr., Dec. 24, 1964 (dec. May 2001); children: Marshall III, Stephen Edward. AAS, N.Y. Tech. Coll., 1968; BA, Bklyn. Coll., 1982; MLS, Pratt Inst., 1984; MA, Columbia U., 1994. Sch. sec. N.Y.C. Dept. Edn., Bklyn., 1974—86, sch. libr., 1986—2003; owner Egami Info. Svcs. Inc., Bklyn., 1989—. Adj. prof. libr. Medgar Evers Coll., CUNY, Bklyn., 1999—. Mem.: ALA, Am. Assn. of U. Women, NY Libr.Assn., Black Librs. Assn., African Am. Hist. and Geneaol. Assn. Home and Office: Egami Info Svcs Inc 69 Schenck Ave Brooklyn NY 11207

STULL, EVALYN MARIE, artist; b. Hays, Kans., June 7, 1949; d. Harold Kenneth Gossett and Helen Marie Loreg; m. Dennis Eugene Kincaid, Dec. 4, 1967 (div. 1968); children: Pamela Sue Kincaid, Mark Allen Kincaid; m. Kenneth Eugene Stull, Dec. 4, 1973 (div. 1983); children: Daniel Eugene, Carl Andrew. A in gen. studies, Morgan C.C., Fort Morgan, Colo. Owner Stull's Kinder Day Care, Fort Morgan, Colo., 1994, Paintings by Evalyn Stull, Chase, Kans., 2001—02. Home and Office: 201 Cedar/PO Box 134 Chase KS 67524

STULPIN, CYNTHIA LOUISE, mathematics professor, real estate appraiser; b. Springfield, Mass., Mar. 10, 1955; d. William Sigourney and Jeanne Rosalie Hough; m. Brian Joseph Stulpin, Oct. 18, 1992. BS in Elem. Edn., U. Hartford, West Hartford, Conn., 1977, BA in Math., 1977; MS in Math., Trinity Coll., Hartford, Conn., 1993. Computer programmer/analyst SNET, New Haven, 1977—84, sr. systems analyst, 1984—96; tech. arch. SNET/SBC, New Haven, 1996—2000; adj. faculty mem. math. dept. Middlesex C.C., Middletown, Conn., 2001—; real estate appraiser asst. Pender Property Assocs., Guilford, Conn., 2001—. Pvt. practice web design and maintenance, 2000—. Beach capt. Internat. Coastal Clean-up, Clinton, 2006; bd. dirs. Clinton Beach Assn., 2000—. Recipient Nova award, SNET, 1988, Spot award, SBC, 2000. Avocations: kayaking, conservation, bicycling, needlecrafts.

STUMP, M. PAMELA, sculptor; b. Detroit, July 8, 1928; d. Clarence Homer S. and Gladys Greening Bogue; m. David Everet Walsh, Aug. 1950 (div. 1975); children: Kimberly Klaerr, Sara Greening Walsh Munro, John Klaerr II; m. Richard Taylor White, March, 1989. B of Design, U. Mich., 1950, M of Design, 1951. Educator Ann Arbor (Mich.) Adult Edn., 1950-51, Saginaw (Mich.) Mus. Sch., 1963-68, Birmingham (Mich.) Bloomfield Art Assn., 1969, Washtenaw C.C., Ypsilanti, Mich., 1968-69, Cranbrook Ednl. Cmty., Bloomfield Hills, Mich., 1969-90. Group and one-woman shows include Cranbrook Kingswood, Bloomfield Hills, 1969-90, Mich. Women's Hist. Ctr. & Hall of Fame, Lansing, 1994, 2005, Swann Gallery, Detroit, 1997; exhibited in group shows at Cranbrook Kingswood, 1950, 70, 87, City Art Mus., St. Louis, 1951, Terry Art Inst., Miami, Fla., 1951, Temple Israel, Detroit, 1951, 58, Ceceile Gallery, N.Y.C. (3rd prize), 1956, Pa. Acad. Fine Arts, Phila., 1958, Horace H. Rackham Sch. Grad. Studies, Detroit, 1960, Detroit Artists Market, 1961, R and R Robinson Gallery, Naples, Fla., 1962, Rubiner Gallery, West Bloomfield, Mich., 1963, Mich. Fine Arts Competition (Juror's award), 1983, 87, Slusser Gallery, U. Mich., 1989, Outdoor Sculpture II, III, Southfield, Mich., 1990, 91, N.Y. Acad. Scis., N.Y.C., 1991, Oakland U., 1991-92, Urban Park, Detroit, 1991, 92, Arc Gallery, Chgo., 1992, 1 Heritage Place, Southgate, Mich., 1993, Art Ctr., Sarasota, Fla., 2000, Downriver Coun. for the Arts, Taylor, Mich., 2002, Outside the Lines, Grosse Ile, Mich., 2003, (Artist award, Wayne County Coun. for the Arts, 2004, Keep Mich. Beautiful award), Nat. Assn. Women Artists, N.Y.C., 2005 (Cleo Hartwig award for sculpture); prin. works include courtyard sculpture Kingswood Sch., steel sculpture Sister City, Tokushima, Japan, 10 bronze sculptures for Cranbrook Schs., Bloomfield Hills, Civic Ctr., Saginaw, bronze fountain at Presbyn. Ch., Grosse Ile, Mich, bronze sculpture of history of U. of Mich. Women, Ann Arbor, Mich. Bell Telephone Co., Saginaw, bronze sculpture at Providence Hosp., Southfield, meml. for poet T. Roethke Saginaw Valley State U., bronze sculpture at First Presbyn. Ch., Pompano Beach, Fla., Rochester Hills Libr., Saginaw Mus., Western Mich. U., Kalamazoo, numerous others. Mem. Emily's List, Planned Parenthood. Recipient Artist award, Coun. for the Arts, 2004. Mem. ACLU, NOW, LWV, Nat. Assn. Women Artists (Cleo Hartwig award, 2005), Nat. Mus. Women in Arts (charter), Detroit Artist Market, Detroit Inst. Arts Founders Soc., Internat. Sculptors. Avocations: reading, writing. Home: 19629 Parke Ln Grosse Ile MI 48138-1024 E-mail: lcolntu@gatecom.com.

STUMPF, CHRISTIE KELL, retired music educator; d. Morris Hubert and Delesma Dickson Kell; children from previous marriage: Karen Parks, Kurt. B in Music Edn., Ky. Wesleyan Coll., Owensboro, 1969; M in Music Edn., Western Ky. U., Bowling Green, 1972. Tchg. cert. Ky. Music tchr. Ohio County Bd. Edn., Hartford, Ky., 1970—2000, Owensboro Cath. Schs., 2001—02; ret., 2002. Pvt. piano tchr., Hartford, 1970—; substitute tchr. Ohio County Bd. Edn., Hartford, 2000—; adv. bd. Green River Home Health, Owensboro, 1988—, chair bd. dirs., 1993—96, Owensboro, 1999—2002, Owensboro, 2005—. Dir. choral music Wayland Alexander Sch., Hartford, 1980—2000, Ohio County Youth Chorus, Hartford, 1996—2000; Class 1969 amb. Ky. Wesleyan Coll., Owensboro, 2000—; mem. Owensboro Civic Chorus; music dir. Hartford U. Meth. Ch., 1969—72, 1986—94. Mem.: Music Educators Nat. Conf. (pres., elem. chair 2000—02, 2003—), Ky. Music Educators Assn. (pres. Dist. II 2000—02), Courthouse Players. Methodist. Avocations: theater, singing. Home: 111 Southdale Dr Hartford KY 42347

STUNTZ, BILLIE WILLIAMS, pediatrician; b. Beaumont, Tex., Apr. 8, 1929; d. Floyd Hughbert Williams and Maude Guidry; m. Homer Clyde Stuntz, June 7, 1952; children: Ann, Jean, Philip. BA, Baylor U., Waco, Tex., 1949; MD, Southwestern Med. U., Dallas, 1953. Pediatrician pvt. practice, Orange, Tex., 1954—87; ret. Mem. City of Orange Well Child Clinic; bd. dirs. ARC, Orange. Avocation: doll collecting. Home: 2223 24th St Orange TX 77630

STUPAK, MARY JO, psychotherapist, educator; d. Carl Elmer Cross and Georgianna Viola Jones; children: John Jr., Joseph, Michael, Steven, Carol, Curt. BS (hon.), U. Wis., 1973, MS in Cmty. Counseling, 1985. Lic. profl. counselor State of Wis. Intermediate tchr. Cathedral Sch., Superior, Wis., 1972—73; family resource coord. Head Start, Superior, 1974—76; tchr. Douglas County Citizens, Superior, 1977—82, Rape and Incest Victim Orgn., Superior, 1983—85; psychotherapy Human Resource Ctr., Superior, 1985—95; latch key lead tchr. Cathedral Sch., Superior, 2000—. Cons. Head Start, Superior, 1982—83. Contbr. articles to profl. jours. Pres. St. Williams Altar Soc., Foxboro, Wis., 1952—; organist St. Williams Ch., Foxboro, Wis., 1952—. Democrat. Roman Catholic. Avocations: painting, folk art, music, reading.

STUPKA, RENEE C., musician, educator; d. George W. Moyer and Moyer L. Dianna; m. Mark A. Stupka, Feb. 14, 2004; children: Jared C. Marthe, Joshua A. Marthe. BA, Hiram Coll., Ohio, 1994. Cert. music tchr. Ohio. Pvt. woodwinds instr., Willowick, Ohio, 1993—; music tchr. Cleve. Mcpl. Sch. Dist., 1996—. Dir. handbell choir Mentor Plains United Meth. Ch., Ohio, 1999—, pianist Praise Team, 2005—. Scholar, Hiram Coll., 1990—94. Mem.: Ohio Music Educators Assn. Office: Clark Sch 5550 Clark Ave Cleveland OH 44102 Office Phone: 216-631-2760. Office Fax: 216-634-2217. Personal E-mail: mrsstupka@adelphia.net.

STUPPARD-BYARS, DORIS J., minister; b. El Dorado, Ark., Feb. 19, 1941; d. Jimmy D. and Mozella Massey; m. Mark Byars, July 31, 2004; m. Emanuel Stuppard, Aug. 1, 1986 (div. Sept. 1, 1995); m. Van J. Whaley, Mar. 1962 (div. June 1983); children: Stephanie A. Whaley-Jones, Ralph S. Whaley, Tiffany L. Whaley-LeConte. BA in Family Life Ed & Ministry, Spring Arbor U., Spring Arbor, Mich., 1997; BS in Psycology, Detroit Inst. of Tech., Detroit, Mich., 1978. Ma Dept. of Pub. Health, Mich., 1994; cert. Tchg. Fla. State Bd. of Edn., Fla., 1985, Child Care Adminstrn. Dade County C.C., Fla., 1987. Girl scouts leader Girl Scouts Of Am., Detroit, 1966—68; exec. dir. & founder Multi-Racial Family Study & Del. Ctr., Ypsilanti, Mich., 1979—; pres. of cloverlawn block club Cloverlawn Block Club, Detroit, 1970—71; leader Adult Deliverance Study, Detroit, 1976—78; alternative sch. tchr. Ace Sch., Detroit, 1976—78; outreach min. Old Path Temple COGIC, Detroit, 1977—83; pres. of chalmers block club Chalmers Block Club, Detroit, 1978—79; evangelist (min.) Trinity Deliverance Ch., Detroit, 1979—; asst. pastor Outer Dr. United Meth. Ch., Detroit, 1995—97; leader Children's Refuge Ho. (MRFDC), Brightmoor Cmty., Mich., 1993—95. Cons. Noble Mid. Sch., Detroit, 2000—01; youth group counselor Go Lightly Elem. & Jr. High, Detroit, 1998—99; learning for life instr. Boy Scouts Of Am., Detroit, 1997—97. Author: (religous novel) The Unction it Takes to Function, (religous instruction) Hey Churchmember! Put Your Money Where Your Mouth Is!; singer (soprano): (concert) 2nd Annual Women's Conf. of Institutional Bapt. Ch. 100 Woman Concert; speaker 2nd Annual Women's Conf. of Inst. Bapt. Ch. Candidate for city coun. Detroit City Coun., Detroit, 2001—01; candidate state rep. State of Mich., Detroit, 2002—02; candidate charter commr. City of Detroit, Detroit, 1980—80. Recipient Cert. of Appreciation, Wayne County Sherrif Dept.: Exec. Dir. Robert Ficano, 2003, Cert. of Appreciation for Children's Feeding Program, City Of Detroit, 1979. Master: Word Of Deliverance (assoc.; evangelist 2004—05); mem.: Hartford Meml. Bapt. Ch. (min. 1993—2000), Leadership To Go (corr.; exec. dir. 2004—05). Independent. Achievements include Outstanding Young Woman of the Yr. DIT: 1977; Outstanding Young Woman of Am.: 1978. Avocation: traveling evangelist. Home: 51360 Mich Ave Apt 2 Belleville MI 48111-5002 Office: Multi-Racial Family Study & Devel 2430 E Mich Ave Ste D Ypsilanti MI 48198 Office Phone: 734-483-0557. Personal E-mail: messengerd7@aol.com.

STUPPLES, KAREN, professional golfer; b. Dover, Eng., June 24, 1973; Attended, Fla. State U. Winner Women's British Open, 2004, Welch's/Fry's Championships, 2004. Second-team All-Am. Fla. State U., 1995; represented England Curtis Cup, 1996, 98. Avocations: cooking, movies, football. Office: c/o LPGA 100 International Dr Daytona Beach FL 32124-1092

STURCH, LOIS J., elementary school educator; m. John R. Sturch, Sr., Aug. 19, 1972; children: Erin, John R. Jr. BS, U. Okla., Norman, 1974. Tchr. Northmoor Elem. Sch., Moore, Okla., 1978—85, Ctrl. Elem. Sch., Moore, 1985—. Mem.: PTA (treas. 1988—91). Office: Ctrl Elem Sch 123 NW 2nd St Moore OK 73160

STURGES, SHERRY LYNN, recording industry executive; b. Long Beach, Calif., Dec. 11, 1946; d. Howard George and Alice Myrtle Fairbairn; m. Jeffery Alan Sturges, Dec. 30, 1969; children: Allisun Malinda, Jay. Grad. high sch., Las Vegas, Nev. V.p. Soultime, Inc., Las Vegas, 1968-69, Universe, Inc., Las Vegas, 1971-76; co-developer, owner Fun Trax Music Video and Audio Recording Studios, Westwood, Calif., 1986—. Creative cons. John Debella Show, 1990, M.T.V., L.A., 1990, KCET-TV, L.A., 1990,KTLA-TV, L.A., 1991. Co-writer song The Sharing of Love for TV series Murder, She Wrote, 1996, feature film The Ride, 1997; song writer (film) The Ride, 1997. Officer PTA, Woodland Hills, Calif., 1977-86, pres., 1984-86; vol. Connie Stevens Charity Orgn., Beverly Hills, Calif., 1980-84; vol. Crossroads Sch. for Arts and Sci., Westwood Meth. presch., West L.A. Bapt. Sch., Northridge United Meth. Ch., St. Vincent's Parents Coun., St. Joseph the Worker Sch., Chatsworth H.S., Sepulveda Nursery Sch., Nat. Neurofibromatosis Found., Life Steps Found., Westwood Village Assn., San Joaquin Valley Actors Repertory Co., 1997—. Recipient Outstanding Contribution award L.A. Unified Sch. Dist., Oxnard Unified Sch. Dist., 1998, 99. Mem. Am. Soc. Composers, Authors and Pubs. Republican. Avocations: collecting dolls, plates and figurines. Home: 29468 Sequoia Rd Santa Clarita CA 91387-6246

STURGULEWSKI, ARLISS, state legislator, director; b. Blaine, Wash., Sept. 27, 1927; BA, U. Wash.; LLD (hon.), U. Alaska, Anchorage, 1993. Mem. Assembly Municipality of Anchorage; interim exec. dir. Alaska Sci. and Tech. Found., 1995. Vice chmn. New Capital Site Planning Commn., mem. Capital Site Selection Com.; chmn. Greater Anchorage Area Planning and Zoning Commn.; mem. Alaska State Senate, 1978-93; Rep. nominee Office Gov. Alaska, 1986, 90. Home: 2957 Sheldon Jackson St Anchorage AK 99508-4469 Office: 3201 C St Ste 405 Anchorage AK 99503-3967 Business E-Mail: a.sturgulewski@swallingcpas.com.

STURHAN, COURTNEY, secondary school educator; d. Gene and Joan M. Miller; m. Brian Craig Sturhan, May 25, 2002; 1 child, Madison Leigh. BS, U. Houston, Houston, Tex., 2003. Tchr. Austin H.S., Sugar Land, Tex., 2002—05, Elkins H.S., Mo. City, Tex., 2005—. Mem.: Tex. Dance Educators Assn. Office: Elkins High School 7007 Knights Ct Missouri City TX 77459 Office Phone: 281-634-2641. Office Fax: 281-634-2674. Business E-Mail: courtney.sturhan@fortbend.k12.tx.us.

STURM, CONNIE ARRAU, music and music education educator; b. Jackson Heights, N.Y., Mar. 7, 1957; d. Raymond Victor and Clara (Rosenthal) Arrau; m. Ronald Lee Sturm, Dec. 10, 1990. B of Music Edn., Northwestern U., 1978; MA, Ohio State U., 1980; PhD, U. Okla., 1990. Nat. cert. tchr. music. Lectr. class piano Western Ill. U., Macomb, 1980-82; instr. class piano and pedagogy U. Minn., Mpls., 1982-85; prof. class piano and pedagogy W.Va. U., Morgantown, 1986—. Author over 75 presentations and publs. Adjudicator for more than 50 music competitions, auditions and festivals at local, state and regional levels. Phi Delta Kappa Competitive Rsch. grantee; W.Va. U. faculty travel grantee; Outstanding Tchr. of Yr. W.Va. Univ. Divsn. Music, 2002-03. Mem. Music Tchrs. Nat. Assn. (nat. chair for student chpts. 1999-2001), World Piano Pedagogy Conf. (chair hist. perspectives com. 1996-2003), Nat. Conf. on Keyboard Pedagogy (chair hist. rsch. com. 2001—). Office: WVa U Coll Creative Arts PO Box 6111 Morgantown WV 26506-6111 E-mail: u1a00906@wvnvm.wvnet.edu.

STURM, SUSAN P., law educator; BA, Brown U., 1976; JD, Yale U., 1979. Law clk. to Hon. Charles E. Stewart US Dist. Ct. (So. Dist.) NY; faculty mem. U. Pa., 1986—99, Columbia Law Sch., NYC, 2000—, George M. Jaffin Prof. of Law and Social Responsibility. Mem. Presdl. Adv. Commn. on Diversity Initiatives. Co-author: Whose Qualified? The Future of Affirmative Action, 2001; author: Equality and the Forms of Justice, 2003, Law's Role in Addressing Complex Discrimination, 2005. Office: Columbia Law Sch Rm 617 435 W 116th St New York NY 10027 Office Phone: 212-854-0062. Office Fax: 212-854-7946. E-mail: ssturm@law.columbia.edu.

STURNER, LYNDA, performing company executive; b. Buffalo, July 1, 1941; d. Samuel S. and Rachel Louise Sturner; m. Jerome S. Traum, Sept. 23, 2001 (dec.); children: Daniel Matthew Traum, Edward Hart Traum stepchildren: David A. Traum, Norman D. Traum. BFA, Boston U., 1963. Actress Broadway Oliver, N.Y.C., 1964—66; artistic dir. Playwrights Forum Inc., N.Y.C., 1982—88; co-prodr. The Juniper Tree, N.Y.C., 1982; prodr. Triangle Prodns., N.Y.C., 1981—87; artistic dir. Provincetown (Mass.) Repertory Theatre, 2004—. Bd. dirs., v.p. Music Theatre Group, N.Y.C., 1981—2001; tchr. Boston U., 1983—96; playwright Woman's Project Lab., 1989—97; bd. dirs. Castle Hill Truro Ctr. for the Arts, 1980—99, Provincetown Theatre Co., 1999—2003; artistic dir. Provincetown Repertory Theatre, 2004—05. Author: (plays) Look What You Made Me Do, 2000 (Audience Choice award, 2001), Art Brute, 2001, (on-line work) TheatreMania.com, 1999—2002; co-author: (plays) Sextet, 2001; author The Death of Huey Newton. Mem.: League of Profl. Theatre Women, Screen Actors Guild, Actors Equity Assn. Democrat. Jewish. Office: Provincetown Repertory Theatre 238 Commercial St Provincetown MA 02657 E-mail: lynda_sturner@yahoo.com.

STURTEVANT, BRERETON, retired lawyer, retired federal official; b. Washington, Nov. 24, 1921; d. Charles Lyon and Grace (Brereton) S. BA, Wellesley Coll., 1942; JD, Temple U., 1949; postgrad., U. Del., 1969-71. Bar: D.C. 1949, Del. 1950. Research chemist E.I. duPont DeNemours & Co., 1942-50; law clk. Del. Supreme Ct., 1950; gen. practice law Wilmington, Del., 1950-57; partner Connolly, Bove & Lodge, Wilmington, 1957-71; examiner-in-chief U.S. Patent and Trademark Office Bd. Appeals, Washington, 1971-88. Adj. prof. law Georgetown U., 1974-79. Trustee Holton-Arms Sch., Bethesda, Md., 1977-96, chmn. or mem. all coms., trustee emerita, 1997—. Mem. ABA, Exec. Women in Govt. (charter mem., chmn. 1978-79) Clubs: Wellesley College, Washington-Wellesley (pres. 1982-84). Episcopalian. Achievements include first woman law clerk, Delaware Supreme Court; first woman patent examiner-in-chief. Home: 1227 Morningside Ln Alexandria VA 22308-1042

STURTEVANT, KRISTEN AMY, science educator; b. Portland, Maine, July 7, 1965; d. Henry Curry and Janice Louise Wolforth; m. Thomas Allen Sturtevant, July 30, 1994; children: Robert, Matthew. BS, Gordon Coll., Wenham, Mass., 1987; MEd, Notre Dame Coll., Manchester, N.H., 2002. Cert. tchr. NH. Gen. educator Iber Holmes Gove Mid. Sch., Raymond, NH, 1987—89; grade 5 & 6 elem. sci. East Rochester Sch., East Rochester, NH, 1989—92; grade 6 & 7 gen. sci. educator Rochester Mid. Sch., Rochester, NH, 1992—. Sun. sch. tchr. First United Meth. Ch., Rochester, NH, 1991—, youth group adv., 1992—94, youth group Italian night dir., 1991—; mem. Strafford County Wind Symphony, 1991—. Recipient Rochester Tchr. of the Yr., C. of C., 2002. Mem.: ASCD, NSTA. Avocations: running, theater, trumpet. Personal E-mail: sturtevant.rms@rochesternh.net.

STURTEVANT, RUTHANN PATTERSON, anatomist, educator; b. Rockford, Ill., Feb. 7, 1927; d. Joseph Hyelmun and Virginia (Wharton) Patterson; m. Frank Milton Sturtevant Jr., Mar. 18, 1950; children: Barbara (dec.), Jill Sturtevant Rovani, Jan Sturtevant Cassidy. BS, Northwestern U., Evanston, Ill., 1949; MS, Northwestern U., 1950; PhD, U. Ark., Fayetteville, 1972. Instr. life scis. Ind. State U., Evansville, Ind., 1965—72, asst. prof., 1972—74; asst. prof. anatomy Ind. U. Sch. Medicine, Evansville, 1972—74, U. Evansville,

1972—74; lectr. anatomy Northwestern U., Chgo., 1974—75; asst. prof. anatomy and surgery Loyola U., Maywood, 1975—81; assoc. prof. Loyola U. Sch. Medicine, Maywood, 1981—88, prof., 1988—90, prof. emerita, 1990—. Contbr. articles to profl. jours.; mem. editl. bd. Chronobiology Internat., 1988-90; reviewer numerous profl. jours. Active Mayor's Task Force on High Tech. Devel., Chgo., 1983-85; exec. bd. Anatomical Gifts Assn. Ill., Chgo., 1978-89. Grantee Pott's Found., NIH, others, 1978—88. Mem. Am. Assn. Anatomists, So. Soc. Anatomists (councillor 1978-80), Internat. Soc. Chronobiologists, Am. Soc. Pharmacology and Exptl. Therapeutics, Soc. for Exptl. Biology and Medicine, Am. Assn. Clin. Anatomists, League of Underwater Photographers, Sarasota Scuba Club, Sigma Xi. Avocations: photography, scuba diving, flying, digital imaging, community volunteer service. Address: 5760 Midnight Pass Rd Unit 610-D Sarasota FL 34242 Personal E-mail: patty5760@verizon.net.

STURTS, DONNA JEAN, music educator; b. Shelby, Ohio, Feb. 11, 1940; d. Charles Gilbert Burky and Martha Mabel Schwert; m. Delmar Dean Sturts, Apr. 8, 1961; children: Erica Lynn, Erin Elizabeth, Blair Alan. Cert. music tchr. Am. Coll. Musicians, 2002. Bank teller Citizens Bank, Shelby, Ohio, 1958—64; choir dir. Ctrl. Meth. Ch., Mansfield, Ohio, 1982—2000; piano tchr. Sturts Studio of Music, Mansfield, 1974—; vocal soloist various area churches, Mansfield, 1962—. Mem. Mansfield Symphony Chorus, 2004—. Gold cup chmn. Fedn. of Music Clubs, Dist. IV, Ohio, 1999—. Recipient Service award, Centra United Meth. Ch., 1986, 1996, State Gold Cup Chairmanship award, Ohio Fedn. Music Clubs, 2004. Mem.: Am. Coll. Musicians, Ohio Music Teachers Assn. (25 Yr. award 2002), Ohio Music Teachers Assn., Music Teachers Nat. Assn. (ribbon festival chmn., Richland County 1997—), Nat. Fedn. Music Clubs, Mansfield Music Study Club. Avocations: painting, woodworking, needlecrafts, travel. Home: 92 Stewart Ave Mansfield OH 44906

STURZL, ALICE A., school library administrator; b. Marshfield, Wis., May 22, 1949; d. Aloysius F. and Lorraine R. (Wolk) Beyerl; m. Bruce R. Sturzl, Sr., June 9, 1973; stepchildren: Bruce R., Scott, Daniel, Ann, Todd, Timothy. BA, U. Wis., Oshkosh, 1971. Cert. tchr., Wis. Elem. libr. Sts. Peter and Paul Parish, Oshkosh, 1970-71; libr. Sch. Dist. of Laona, Wis., 1971-73; tchr. math. Our Lady of Perpetual Help, Glendale, Ariz., 1974-75, Most Holy Trinity Parish, Sunnyslope, Ariz., 1975-76; substitute tchr. Sch. Dists. of Laona and Wabeno, Wis., 1976-77; K-12 instructional media specialist Sch. Dist. of Laona, 1977—. Mem. Northeastern Wis. In-Sch. Telecomms. Adv. Bd., Green Bay, 1987-97, pres. 1989-97; trustee, v.p., pres. Wisconsin Valley Libr. Svc. Bd., Wausau, 1984-89, 2000—. Mem. Econ. Devel. Com., Town of Laona, 1987—; mem. parish coun. St. Leonard's Cath. Ch., Laona, intermittently 1983—; active Cmty. Soup and Homecoming/Laona Lions Club, 1983—. Mem. ALA, NEA, Wis. Libr. Assn. (sec. 1993-94, v.p. 1996, pres. 1997, past pres. 1998), Laona Edn. Assn. (sec.-treas.), Wis. Edn. Assn. (No. Tier UniServ), Wis. Ednl. Media Assn., Wis. Libr. Assn. Found. (v.p., sec.). Roman Catholic. Avocations: bowling, reading, travel, helping others, working with numbers. Home: 5170 E Silver Lake Rd Laona WI 54541-9255 Office: Sch Dist of Laona PO Box 100 5216 Forest Ave Laona WI 54541

STUTZMAN, DONNA J., minister; b. Lemoyne, Ohio, Apr. 29, 1936; d. David O. Kaser and Opal M. Stockwell; m. Darrell A. Stutzman, June 7, 1958 (dec. Sept. 1993); children: Denzel, Devon, Dawn, Dara, Desmond. BS in Child and Family Cmty. Svc., Bowling Green State U., Ohio, 1987; MA in Christian Psychology, Cornerstone U., Lake Charles, La., 1992. Ordained minister Nat. Conservative Christian Ch., 1999; lic. social worker Ohio. Pvt. piano tchr., Wauseon, Ohio, 1958—; case mgr. Fulton County Maumee Valley Guidance Ctr., Defiance, Ohio, 1987—89; assoc. pastor First Ch. of God, Wauseon, 1989—91; mental health profl. Fulton County Health Ctr., Wauseon, 1991—99; social worker, music coord. Fulton Manor Nursing Home, Wauseon, 1998—; hospice chaplain Cmty. Health Profls., Archbold, Ohio, 1999—; pastor Hope Christian Fellowship, Wauseon, 1991—. Spirituality group facilitator Fulton County Health Ctr. Psychiat. Unit, 2003—. Vol. coord. Habitat for Humanity, 2003. Mem.: AAUW, Am. Acad. Bereavement, Am. Assn. Christian Counselors, Nat. Christian Counselors Assn., Phi Upsilon Omicron. Avocations: reading, music. Home: 701 Burr Rd Unit 5 Wauseon OH 43567 E-mail: djstutzman@aol.com.

STUTZMAN, GLADYS BLANCHE, retired secondary school educator, journalist; b. Sanborn, N.D., Aug. 12, 1921; d. Charles Kershaw and Mina Blanche (Kee) Crowther; m. Newell Edwin Wood, June 13, 1943 (dec. 1990); children: Terry N., Lani, Brian R., Kevin C.; m. F.L. Stutzman, Nov. 30, 1991. BA in Journalism, U. Minn., 1943; MA in Mass Comm., San Jose State U., 1972. Cert. secondary tchr., Calif. Reporter St. Paul Pioneer-Dispatch, 1943-45; editor J.C. Penney Co., N.Y.C., 1945-46; tchr. English and journalism Willow Glen H.S., San Jose, Calif., 1968-87. Freelance writer, photographer, 1947—; cons. in field. Named Secondary Journalism Tchr. of Yr. Calif. Newpaper Pubs. Assn., 1977. Mem. AAUW, AMA Alliance, Inc., Soc. Profl. Journalists, Journalism Edn. Assn., Calif. Ret. Tchrs. Assn., Women in Comm., Friends of Libr., Santa Clara County Med. Assn. Alliance (past pres.), Saratoga Foothill Club, Delta Kappa Gamma, Theta Sigma Phi, Alpha Omicron Pi. Republican. Methodist. Avocations: music, journalism, photography, travel, flute. Home: 14161 Douglass Ln Saratoga CA 95070-5535

STUTZMAN, MISTY DAWN, music educator; b. Cannelburg, Ind., Nov. 7, 1977; d. Glen Allen and Rita Anne Stutzman. BA in Music Edn., Oakland City U., Ind., 2000, BA in Music Performance, 2000; M Art Edn. in Secondary Guidance Counseling, Western Ky. U., 2006. Praise team leader Providence Mennonite Ch., Montgomery, Ind., 1996—2006. Mem.: NEA, Music Educators Nat. Conf. (assoc.), Ind. State Tchrs. Assn.

STWALLEY, DIANE MARIE, pharmacist; b. Camp Hill, Pa., Jan. 9, 1969; d. Andrew Jackson II and Eileen Joan Green; m. Brian David Stwalley, Oct. 21, 1995; 2 children, Andrew David, Lauren Anne. BS in Pharmacy, U. of the Scis., Phila., 1992. Staff pharmacist Holy Spirit Hosp., Camp Hill, Pa., 1992—. Assoc. preceptor U. Pitts., 1996—; adj. faculty U. of the Scis., Phila., 1993—. Mem. Am. Soc. of Health System Pharmacists, Pa. Soc. of Health System Pharmacists. Avocation: cross stitching. Office: Holy Spirit Hosp 503 N 21st St Camp Hill PA 17011-2288 Home: 51 Lee Ann Ct Enola PA 17025-1937

STYCOS, MARIA NOWAKOWSKA, adult education educator; b. Lwow, Poland, June 4, 1937; arrived in U.S., 1964; d. Marian Zygmunt Nowakowski and Julia Demska Nowakowska; m. Joseph Mayone Stycos; 1 child, Marek. BA, King's Coll. U. London, London, 1958; MA, Cornell U., 1967, PhD, 1977. Part time asst. prof. Ithaca Coll., NY, 1975—81; dir. Handwerker Art Gallery, Ithaca, NY, 1981—82; asst. prof. State U. of N.Y., Cortland, NY, 1982—86; sr. lectr. Cornell U., Ithaca, NY, 1986—. Cons. Cornell U. project in Costa Rica, Costa Rica, 1986; faculty adv. com. Johnson Mus. Art, Cornell U. Co-author (with E. Sanchez-Blake): Voces Hispanas Siglo XXI Entrevistas con autores en DVD, 2005; contbr. chapters to books, articles to profl. jours. including Asociacion Internat. de Letras y Cultura Femenina Hispanica, Revista/Rev, Interamericana P.R., Dictionary of the Lit. of the Iberian Peninsula, others. Planning bd. mem. Village of Lansing, NY, 2002—. Mem.: MLA, Congreso Internat. Sobre Lit. Centroamericana. Avocations: music, art, gardening, travel, poetry. Office: Romance Studies Cornell Univ Ithaca NY 14853 Business E-Mail: mns2@cornell.edu.

STYER, DENISE MARIE, psychologist; d. Kenneth James and Mary Ellen Styer; 1 child, James Kenneth Marketti. BA, U. Wisc., 1990; MA, Alfred Adler Inst. Minn., 1995; PsyD, Adler Sch. Profl. Psychology, 2001. Lic. Profl. Counselor Ill., 2001. Therapist, intake coord. SAFE Alternatives, Naperville, Ill., 2000—01; clin. coord. Self Injury Recovery Svcs. Alexian Bros. Behavioral Hosp., Hoffman Estates, Ill., 2001—. Mem.: APA (prevention rschr. adv. bd. 2005). Office Phone: 708-638-8235. Personal E-mail: drdenisestyer@aol.com.

STYER, JOANNE LOUISE, retired dietician; b. Melin, Oreg., Nov. 23, 1931; d. Raymond Louis Hosford and Gladys Lorraine Loomis; m. Lawrence Henry Styer, Aug. 20, 1955. BS in Foods and Nutrition and Instnl. Mgmt., U. Wis., Stout, 1954; postgrad., George Washington U., U. Md., U.S. Internat. U. Lic. reg. dietitian. Intern St. Mary's Hosp., Rochester, Minn., 1955; chief therapeutic dietitian Glen Dale Hosp., Washington, 1956; chief dietitian George Washington U. Med. Ctr., Washington, 1956—68; asst. dir. food svc. Montgomery County (Md.) Pub. Schs., 1968—69, dir. food svc., 1969—92; dietetic cons. Carriage Hill Nursing Home; ret. Cons. N.Y.C. Homeless Food Svc., Montgomery County Pub. Schs., USDA Commodity Processing, N.Y.C. Prison Food Svc. Evaluation; mem. adv. bd. D.C. Dairy Coun.; mem. industry adv. bd. Nat. Frozen Food Assn. Mem. editl. review panel Sch. Food Svc. Rsch. Review. Past chmn. nutrition com. D.C. Heart Assn.; nutrition com. Am. Heart Assn.; food chmn. Montgomery County Disaster Com.; nutrition com. Montgomery County Heart Assn.; expert task force USDA, Am. Cancer Soc. Named Disting. Alumni, U. Wis., Stout, 1989. Mem.: Md. Sch. Bus. Ofcls. (sect. chmn. food svc.), Md. Sch. Food Svc. Assn. (past pres.), D.C. Dietetic Assn. (past pres.), Md. Dietetic Assn., Am. Dietetic Assn. (chmn. dietetic practice group for sch. food svc.). Home: 11342 Kings Valley Dr Damascus MD 20872 Personal E-mail: lcapthook1@aol.com.

STYLES, MARGRETTA MADDEN, nursing educator; b. Mount Union, Pa., Mar. 19, 1930; d. Russell B. and Agnes (Wilson) Madden; m. Douglas F. Styles, Sept. 4, 1954; children: Patrick, Michael, Megan. BS, Juniata Coll., 1950; M. in Nursing, Yale U., 1954; EdD, U. Fla., 1968; doctorate (hon.), Valparaiso U., 1986, U. Athens, Greece, 1991. Staff nurse VA Hosp., West Haven, Conn., 1954-55; instr. Bklyn. Hosp. Sch. Nursing, 1955-58; supr. North Dist. Hosp., Pompano Beach, Fla., 1961-63; dir. nursing edn. Broward Community Coll., Ft. Lauderdale, Fla., 1963-67; assoc. prof. Sch. Nursing Duke U., Durham, N.C., 1967-69, dir. undergrad. studies, 1967-69; prof., dean Sch. Nursing U. Tex., San Antonio, 1969-73; dean, prof. Coll. Nursing Wayne State U., Detroit; prof. nursing U. Calif., San Francisco, 1977—, dean Sch. Nursing, 1977-87; chairperson Com. for Study of Credentializing in Nursing, 1976-79; mem. adv. group div. nursing HEW, 1977. Asst. dir. nursing svcs. U. Calif. Hosps. and Clinics, 1978-87; mem. Nat. Commn. Nursing, 1980—; mem. Calif. Bd. Registered Nursing, 1985—; mem. Sec.'s Commn. on Nursing HHS, 1988—. Author: On Nursing: Toward a New Endowment (Am. Jour. Nursing Book of Yr. award 1982); co-author (with A. Affara) From Principle to Power: A Guidebook to Regulation in Nursing, 1992. Recipient Disting. Alumna award Yale U. Sch. Nursing, 1979; Am. Nurses' Found. 1st disting. scholar, 1983 Fellow Am. Acad. Nursing; mem. Nat. Acad. Scis., Am. Nurses Assn. (pres. 1986-88), Internat. Coun. Nurses (bd. dirs. 1989—), Sigma Theta Tau. Office: U Calif Sch Nursing PO Box N531C San Francisco CA 94143-0001

STYLES, TERESA JO, television producer, educator; b. Atlanta, Oct. 19; d. Julian English and Jennie Marine (Sims) S. BA, Spelman Coll., Atlanta, 1972; MA, Northwestern U., Evanston, Ill., 1973; PhD, U. NC, Chapel Hill, 1998. Rschr. CBS News, NYC, 1975-80, prodr., 1980-85; instr. mass comm., English Savannah (Ga.) State Coll., 1985-89, asst. prof. English, 1990; asst. prof. mass comm. and women studies dir. Bennett Coll., Greensboro, NC, 1990-93; assoc. prof. mass comm., chmn. journalism and mass comm. NC A&T State U., Greensboro, 1993—. Rschr. documentary CBS Reports: Teddy, 1979 (Emmy cert.); assoc. prodr. documentaries for CBS Reports: Blacks: America, 1979 (Columbia Dupont cert. 1979), What Shall We Do About Mother?, 1980 (Emmy cert.), The Defense of the U.S., 1980 (Columbia Dupont cert.). Adv. bd. Greensboro Hist. Mus., Eastern Music Festival, Women's Short Film Project. Mem. Writers Guild Am. (bd. dirs. east 1991-95), Dirs. Guild Am. (bd. dirs. east 1991-95), African Am. Atelier (Greensboro, NC bd. dirs.), Eastern Music Festival (bd. dirs.). Avocation: swimming. Home: 4400 Suffolk Trl Greensboro NC 27407-7842 Office Phone: 336-334-7900. Business E-Mail: teresaj@ncat.edu. E-mail: stylest456@bellsouth.net.

STYNES, BARBARA BILELLO, integrative health professional, educator; b. N.Y.C., Apr. 24, 1951; d. Sylvester Francis and Jacqueline Marie (Giardelli) Bilello; m. Frank Joseph Stynes, Aug. 24, 1969; children: Christopher Francis, Jeremy Scott. BA, Rutgers U., 1976; MA in Health Studies, Antioch U., 1995. Cert. reiki practitioner. Mktg. rep. McNeil Consumer Products Co., Ft. Washington, Pa., 1979-82, Met Path Inc., Des Plaines, Ill., 1982-85; mktg. coord. Life program Meml. Hosp. and YMCA, Chattanooga, 1986-91; mem. Chattanooga Area Wellness Coun., 1986-91, Chattanooga Area Healthcare Coalition, 1986-91; dir. mktg. and comm., met. YMCA, Chattanooga, 1986-91, dir. internat. program, 1989-91, wellness cons., 1992-95; intern Mind/Body Inst., Affiliate Harvard Med. Sch., Deaconess Hosp, Columbus, Ohio, 1995—. Assoc. hospice residential care, 1995; therapeutic touch and presence facilitator, 1995—; lifestyle counselor, 1995—, Reiki practitioner, 1999—; program developer Set for Life, 1996; mindfulness based stress reduction facilitator, 1994—; fiber sculptor, 1975-77; weaver, 1976-79; wellness dir. Carolina Family Medicine & Wellness, Mooresville, N.C., 2000. Vol. comm. com. Am. Heart Assn., 1972-91, Spl. Olympics, Chgo., 1982-84; spkr. Tenn. Safety Belt coalition, 1986-91; clinic leader Am. Lung Assn., Chattanooga, 1986-88, YMCA cert. fitness specialist, 1986—, weight mgmt. specialist, 1987—; chairperson fundraising, trustee Pine Grove Coop. Sch., New Brunswick, N.J., 1977-78; sustaining bd. Choices, 1993-95; bd. dirs. Signal Mountain Newcomers Assn., Tenn., 1985-86; mem. sch. bd. Notre Dame H.S., 1989-91. Mem. NAFE, Omega: Inst. Holistic Studies, Inst. Noetic Scis., Am. Bus. Woman's Network Chattanooga (chair mem.), Fiber Arts Guild, Assn. Profl. Dirs., Kiwanis (chair internat. rels. com. Chattanooga chpt. 1990-91, publicity dir.), Gen. Bd. Newcomers, North Columbus, Sustaining Bd. Choices). Roman Catholic. Avocations: walking, yoga, gardening, travel, music. Home: 2706 Trent Pines Ct Sherrills Ford NC 28673-9132

STYRON, ROSE, human rights activist, poet, journalist; b. Balt., Apr. 4, 1928; d. Benjamin Bernei and Selma (Kann) Burgunder; m. William Styron, May 4, 1953; children: Susanna, Polly, Thomas, Alexandra. BA, Wellesley Coll., 1950; MA, Johns Hopkins U., 1952; LHD (hon.), Briarcliff Coll., 1976, SUNY, Purchase, 1991, Trinity Coll., 2000. Bd. dirs. Amnesty Internat., USA, N.Y.C., 1973-83, chair nat. adv. coun., 1984-94. Author: (poems) From Summer to Summer, 1965, Thieves' Afternoon, 1973, By Vineyard Light, 1995; co-author, translator: Modern Russian Poetry, 1972; contbr. editorials, profiles, articles, book revs. and poetry to maj. newspapers and mags. Chair, judge Robert F. Kennedy Meml. Human Rights Award, 1983—; mem. adv. bd. Reebok Found. for Human Rights, 1987—; mem. exec. bd. Human Rights Watch, N.Y.C., 1975-94; bd. dirs. Acad. of Am. Poets, 1995—, Equality Now, 1993—; chmn. adv. coun. Roxbury (Conn.) Libr., 1990-92; bd. dirs. N.Y. Found. for Arts, N.Y.C., 1986-94, Lawyers Com. for Human Rights, N.Y.C., 1981—, Rainforest Found., 1989-95, Assn. to Benefit Children, 1993—, Folger Shakespeare Libr., 1994-00; bd. overseers NYU Faculty of Arts and Scis., 1994—. Mem. P.E.N. (chair freedom-to-write com. 1983-89, bd. dirs. 1983-93), Coun. Fgn. Rels., Vineyard Haven Yacht Club. Democrat. Home: 12 Rucum Rd Roxbury CT 06783-1906

SUAREZ, MARIA C., health care plan company executive; BA in math/computer sci., Queens Coll., CUNY; MBA in quantitative analysis/computer info. systems, St. John's U. Applications developer Coopers & Lybrand; tech. lead managed care project North Shore U. Hosp.; dir. internet/intranet Empire BlueCross BlueShield, privacy officer, now asst. v.p. security assurance. Named one of Premier 100 IT Leaders, Computerworld, 2005. Office: Empire BlueCross BlueShield 15 Metro Tech Pl Brooklyn NY 11201 Office Phone: 212-476-1000, 718-312-5006. Office Fax: 212-476-1281. Business E-Mail: maria.suarez@empireblue.com.

SUAREZ, SALLY ANN TEVIS, health facility administrator, nurse, consultant; b. Jersey City, Jan. 23, 1944; d. Paul John and Gertrude Marie (Clancey) Tevis; 1 child, Maria E. Diploma, St. Mary Hosp. Sch. Nursing, 1965; BA in Health Edn. and Nursing, Jersey City State Coll., 1966, MA in Health Sci., 1977. Staff nurse St. Mary Hosp., Hoboken, N.J., 1965, Bayonne (N.J.) Hosp., 1966, Jersey City Med. Ctr., 1965-66; adminstr. Hoboken Med. Arts Family Health Ctr., 1969-75; adj. faculty Jersey City State Coll., 1976-77; adminstrv. supr. St. Mary Hosp., Hoboken, 1977-80; dir. North Hudson Commn. Action Corp. Clinic, West New York, N.J., 1979-88; nursing clin. dir. St. Mary Hosp., Hoboken, 1988-89; corp. dir. nursing Francisan Health System N.J., 1989-92; dir. maternal child health svcs. St. James Hosp., Newark, 1992-93, dir. Family Care Ctr., Cathedral Healthcare Sys., 1993-97, dir. nursing, 1996, 1996; cons. quality improvement preventive health Rutherford, NJ, 1996—; QI coord. United Health Care, 1998; v.p. Med. Resource Network, 1998—2000; coord. case mgmt. U. Medicine and Dentistry N.J. Univ. Hosp., 2006—. Instr. nursing St. Mary Hosp. Sch. Nursing; cons. Creative Concepts in Counseling, Rutherford, N.J., 1979-82, Com. for Cytogenetics, Newark, 1986-88; cons. in health svcs., 1996—; v.p. Med. Resource Network, 1998-2003; case mgr. workers' compensation, critical care MCR, 2000-2003; case mgr. workers' compensation CorVel Corp., 2003-2004; health ctr. coord. North Hudson Cmty. Action Corp. Health Ctr., 2004-2006; case mgr. and coord UMDNJ, 2006—. Active Hudson County ARC, 1984-88, United Way, 1984-94; mem. Hudson County Perinatal Consortium Bd., 1987-92, Gateway Consortium, 1993-96; mem. adv. bd. Health Start, 1995-97, N.J. Assn. Women Bus. Owners, 1996-98; bd. dirs. Passaic Head Start; mem. adv. bd. Harrison Care Inst., 2005—. Mem. U.S. Assn. Women Bus. Owners, Am. Cancer Soc., N.J. Family Planning Forum (exec. com. 1980-86), Family Planning Assn. N.J. (exec. com. 1986-88). Democrat. Roman Catholic. Avocation: alternative healing. Home: 113 Wilson Ave Rutherford NJ 07070-2726 Office Phone: 973-972-4655. Personal E-mail: nursesrch@aol.com, nursescch@netzero.net.

SUAREZ-MURIAS, MARGUERITE C., retired literature and language professor; b. Havana, Cuba, Mar. 23, 1921; arrived in U.S., 1935, naturalized, 1959; d. Eduardo R. and Marguerite (Vendel) Suarez-Murias. AB, Bryn Mawr Coll., 1942; MA, Columbia U., 1953, PhD, 1957. Lectr. in Spanish Columbia U., 1954-56; pub. rels. officer med. divsn. Johns Hopkins U., 1957-58; asst. prof. Spanish and French Sweet Briar Coll., 1958-59; asst. prof. Hood Coll., 1960-61; lectr. Cath. U., 1960-63, asst. prof., summers 1960-62, assoc. prof., summers 1964-66; asst. prof. dept. langs. and linguistics Am. U., 1961-63, assoc. prof., 1963-66; prof. dept. classical and modern langs. Marquette U., Milw., 1966-68; prof. Spanish and Portuguese U. Wis., Milw., 1968—83, chmn., 1972-75; ret., 1983. Guest Milw. prof. U. South Africa, Pretoria, 1980. Author: (book) La Novela Romántica en Hispanoamérica, 1963, Antología Estilística de la Prosa Moderna Española, 1968, Essays on Hispanic Literature/Ensayos de Literatura Hispana, 1982; editor: Gironella's Los Cipreses Creen en Dios, 1969; contbr. articles to profl. jours.;. Mem.: Nat. Trust Historic Preservation. Roman Catholic. Achievements include designing, building and landscaping two homes. Home: 1315 Cold Bottom Rd Sparks MD 21152-9518

SUBER, DIANNE BOARDLEY, educational administrator; b. Tallahassee, May 22, 1949; d. John Wilkerson and Barbara Ann (Baker) Boardley; BS with honors, Hampton Inst., 1971; ME., U. Ill., 1973; postgrad. Hampton U.; MEd, Old Dominion U., doctoral studies Va. Poly. Insst. and State U.; children: Nichole Reshan, Raegan Latrese; m. Robert B. Suber. Elem. tchr. Greensboro (N.C.) Public Schs., 1971-72; tchr. Newport News (Va.) Public Schs., 1973-77, asst. prin., 1977-79, 80-82, acting prin., 1979-80; elem. prin. Williamsburg, Va., 1982-85; prin. Newport (Va.) News, 1986-89, 91—, program devel. specialist, 1989-91; owner/prin. DBS and Assocs.; adj. instr. Hampton U. grad. sch. edn., 1986—; owner Child Care Resources Inc.; guest lectr. Coll. William and Mary, Williamsburg; owner human resources devel. cons. DBS & Assoc. Mem. Coalition for Good Govt. Mem. Nat. Assn. Elem. Sch. Prins., Nat. Assn. Edn. Young Children, Assn. Supervision and Curriculum Devel., Nat. Alliance Black Sch. Educators, Hampton Crusade for Votes League, Black Child Inst.; presenter nat. conf. Am. Assn. Sch. Adminstrs. State Dept. Edn., Va. and N.C. Mem. Am. Assn. Sch. Adminstrs. Democrat. Roman Catholic.

SUBER, ROBIN HALL, former medical and surgical nurse; b. Bethlehem, Pa., Mar. 14, 1952; d. Arthur Albert and Sarah Virginia (Smith) Hall; m. David A. Suber, July 28, 1979; 1 child, Benjamin A. BSN, Ohio State U., 1974. RN, Ariz., Ohio. Formerly staff nurse Desert Samaritan Hosp., Mesa, Ariz. Lt. USN, 1974-80. Mem. ANA, Sigma Theta Tau.

SUBERRI, KEREN CHANSKY, psychologist, educator, marriage and family therapist; b. Oswego, N.Y., Sept. 3, 1957; d. Norman Morton and Elissa Ruth (Ellsas) Chansky; m. Moshe Suberri, Apr. 15, 1978; children: Gilad, Kinneret. Student, Tel Aviv U., 1975-78; BA, Temple U., 1979, MEd in Ednl. Psychology, 1981, PhD in Sch. Psychology, 1987; student, Family Therapy Inst., 1991-92, Brief Family Therapy Ctr., 1993. Nat. cert. sch. psychologist; cert. sch. psychologist, N.J., Pa.; lic. psychologist, N.J. Pvt. practice, Voorhees, NJ, 1991—98; pediat. psychologist Children's Hosp., Phila., 1998—. Adj. prof. Glassboro (N.J.) State Coll., 1989-90; cons. to Devel. Follow-Up Clinic for High Risk Infants; cons. pub. schs. spl. programs Pediatric-Adolescent Residential Treatment Ctr. for Abused and Neglected, 1991-1998. Author: (with others) Children's Needs: Psychological Perspectives, 1987, Jour. Systematic Therapies, 2004; mem. editl. bd. Jour. Systemic Therapies, 1993-2005. Chmn. Early Childhood Parents' Com., Cherry Hill, N.J., 1986-87; bd. mgrs. Jewish Cmty. Ctr. South N.J., Cherry Hill, 1988-89. Mem. APA, NASP, N.J. Psychol. Assn., Delaware Valley Presch. Psychologists, Am. Friends Peace Now.

SUBICH, LINDA MEZYDLO, counseling psychology educator; b. Milw., Jan. 27, 1956; d. Ralph Joseph and Sylvia Lucille (Schultz) Mezydlo; m. Carl Brice Subich, Aug. 23, 1980. BS in Psychology, U. Wis., Milw., 1977; MA in Counseling Psychology, Ohio State U., 1979, PhD in Counseling Psychology, 1981. Lic. psychologist, Ohio. Asst. prof. counseling psychology U. Akron, Ohio, 1981-87, assoc. prof. Ohio, 1987-95, prof. Ohio, 1995—. Ad Hoc reviewer, mem. editorial bd. Jour. Counseling Psychology; mem. editorial bd. Jour. Vocat. Behavior; assoc. editor, mem. editorial bd. Career Devel. Quar.; contbr. chpts. to books, articles to profl. jours. Grantee Nat. Acad. Scis., 1986, Ohio Dept. Mental Health, 1990, 91, 93. Mem. AAUP, ACA, APA, Am. Psychol. Soc., Assn. for Women in Psychology, Phi Beta Kappa. Democrat. Roman Catholic. Avocations: cooking, cross country skiing, jogging, reading. Home: 965 Nokomis Dr Akron OH 44313-5817

SUBKOWSKY, ELIZABETH, insurance company executive; b. New London, Conn., Feb. 17, 1949; d. Thomas and Matilda (Mastroianni) Logan; m. Robert A. Subkowsky, June 9, 1972. BA with honors and dist., U. Conn., 1971; MBA, DePaul U., Chgo., 1977. Cert. Project Mgmt. Profl. 2003, sr. advisor 2003. Asst. v.p. info. tech. CNA Ins., Chgo., 1973—2002; dir. The Tri Zetto Group, Albany, NY, 2003; v.p. info. tech. Bankers Life & Casualty, Chgo., 2003—. Recipient De Paul U. Disting. Alumni award, 1999. Mem. Soc. for Info. Mgmt., Project Mgmt. Inst. Avocations: duplicate bridge, reading, golf. Office Phone: 312-396-6218. E-mail: b.subkowsky@banklife.com.

SUBOTNICK, ALI, curator, writer; Receptionist Artforum; with editl. office Art News; host radio program WPS1.org; co-founder The Wrong Gallery, NYC. Vis. critic sch. of arts Columbia U.; spkr. in field. Curator MFA Thesis Exhibition, Columbia U. Sch. of Arts, 2004, 4th Berlin Biennial, 2006; editor: Parkett mag.; co-editor: Charley mag.; contbr. articles to profl. jours. Office: c/o Columbia Univ Sch of Arts 2960 Broadway New York NY 10027-6902*

SUBRAMANIAN, LAURA SITA, public health service officer; d. R. Shankar and Jane Subramanian. BA in Biology and Sociology summa cum laude, Brandeis U., Waltham, Mass., 2001; MS, Harvard U., Boston, 2005. Howard Hughes rsch. fellow dept. biology Brandeis U., Waltham, Mass., 1999—2000; summer rsch. tng. fellow U. Calif., San Francisco, 2000; adminstrv. coord. Hospice of Good Shepherd, Newton, Mass., 2001—03; work-study cons. Educators for Social Responsibility, Cambridge, Mass., 2003—04, Our Bodies Ourselves, Boston, 2004—05; pub. health rschr. Africa Ctr. Health and Population Studies, Mtubatuba, South Africa, 2005—. Cons. Ctrs. for Disease Control and Prevention, Atlanta, 2005. Contbr.

chapters to books. Vol. Rec. for Blind and Dyslexic, Cambridge, Mass., 2002—03. Presdl. scholar, Clarkson U., 1996—97, Justice Brandeis scholar, Brandeis U., 1997—2001, Women's Studies scholar, 2000—01, Frederick Sheldon Travelling fellow, Harvard U., 2005—06. Mem.: Phi Beta Kappa (life). Avocations: music, travel. Personal E-mail: laura.sita@post.harvard.edu.

SUCICH, DIANA CATHERINE, retired marriage, family, and child psychologist, counselor; b. NYC, Apr. 23, 1948; d. Nicholas and Mildred (Bobich) S. MEd, Springfield (Mass.) Coll., 1973, cert. counseling, 1974; PhD, U.S. Internat. U., 1975. Cert. trainer, educator and practioner in psychodrama, sociometry and group psychotherapy; cert. sch. crisis response. Dean of women Anderson Sch., Staatsburg, N.Y., 1971; cons. human devel. dept. YMCA, San Diego, 1975-77; postdoctoral resident Navy Alcohol Rehab. and Tng. Ctr., San Diego, 1975-77; instr. Chapman Coll., Orange, Calif., 1977-79; pvt. practice cons.; cons., instr. Moreno Acad. Psychodrama, Beacon, N.Y., 1982-83; cons. sch. psychologist Millbrook Ctrl. Sch. Dist., N.Y., 1983-84; sch. psychologist Rhinebeck (N.Y.) Cen. Sch. Dist., 1984-86, Beacon City Sch. Dist., 1986-87, Wappingers Cen. Sch. Dist., Wappingers Falls, N.Y., 1987-92, Orange-Ulsta BOCES, 1992-93, Wallkill Ctrl. Sch. Dist., Wappingers Falls, N.Y., 1993-94, Wappingers Ctrl. Sch. Dist., Wappingers Falls, NY, 1994—2006; ret., 2006. AIDS dist. com. and sexual abuse prevention program trainer.; naturally certified sch. psychologist, cons. N.Y. State mandated course on child abuse reporting and suicide prevention, devel. of abduction prevention program, supt. search com., dist. psychologists adv. com., Crisis Safety Team VWJHS; with Wappingers Ctrl. Sch. Dist.; forensic examiner. Fellow Am. Acad. Experts in Traumatic Stress; mem. Am. Coll. Forensic Exameriners, Psychologists in Marital and Family Therapy, Fedn. Trainers and Tng. Programs in Psychodrama, Am. Bd. Examiners Psychodrama, Homeland Security, Psi Chi. Home: Stony Brook Estate 237 Old Hopewell Rd Wappingers Falls NY 12590-4428 Office: Stony Brook Estate Wappingers Falls NY 12590 E-mail: dsucich@aol.com.

SUCKIEL, ELLEN KAPPY, philosophy educator; b. June 15, 1943; d. Jack and Lilyan Kappy; m. Joseph Suckiel, June 22, 1973 AB, Douglass Coll., 1965; MA in Philosophy, U. Wis., 1969, PhD in Philosophy, 1972. Lectr. philosophy U. Wis., Madison, 1969-71; asst. prof. philosophy Fla. State U., Tallahassee, 1972-73, U. Calif., Santa Cruz, 1973-80, assoc. prof., 1980-95, prof., 1995—, provost Kresge Coll., 1983-89, provost Stevenson Coll., 2004—. Author: The Pragmatic Philosophy of William James, 1982, Heaven's Champion: William James's Philosophy of Religion, 1996, also articles, book introductions and chpts. Mem. Am. Philos. Assn., Soc. for Advancement Am. Philosophy Office: USCS Stevenson Coll Provost's Office 101 McLaughlin Dr Santa Cruz CA 95064 Office Phone: 831-459-2328. Business E-Mail: suckiel@ucsc.edu.

SUDANOWICZ, ELAINE MARIE, government executive; d. John Anthony and Helen Mary Sudanowicz. Student, Fontbonne Acad., Milton, Mass., 1974; BA, Boston State Coll., 1978; MPA, Suffolk U., Boston, 1986; grad. Exec. Leadership Devel. Program, Dept. of Def., 1993. Cert. level 2 contractor, level 3 in program mgmt., Mass. Pub. rels. office mgr. MacDonald & Evans Inc. Litho., Dorchester, 1974-78; rsch. asst. Nat. Commn. Neighborhoods, Washington, 1978; polit. cons. various nat., state and local polit. campaigns, 1974-86; telephonist supr., cons. ARC, Boston, 1980-81; adminstrv. asst. Suffolk County Courthouse Commn., Boston, 1981-82; exec. asst. sheriff Suffolk County Sheriff's Office, 1982-86; presdl. mgmt. intern ESD/PK Air Force Systems Command, Hanscom AFB, Mass., 1986-89, advanced copper CAP Andrews AFB, Md., 1989-90; contract negotiatior Hdqrs., Electronic Systems divsn. Joint STARS Program, Hanscom AFB, Mass., 1990-92; program mgr. Hdqrs., Electronic Sys. Ctr., EN-1, Hanscom AFB, 1992-95; asst. program dir. bus. acquisition re-engring. Elec. Sys. Ctr., Hanscom AFB, 1994-95; dep. commr. for transp. City of Boston, 1995—2006; inter-agy. coord. Mayor's Office Homeland Security Emergency Mgmt., 2006—. Mayor's interagency liaison Boston Emergency Mgmt. Agy., 1995—; guest spkr. Armed Forces Comm. and Elecs. Assn., 2000-; guest lectr. Suffolk U., Sawyer Sch. Mgmt., 2001-; panelist Neighborhood Issues Forum, 2002. Author: Constitutional Vignette, Separation of Powers and Contracting in the Bureaucrat, 1987; contbr. PMInformer, 1989—; also articles; agt., cons Theatre Arts-Play 1988—. Vol., cons. City & State Pub. Agys.-Pub. Sector, Boston; literacy vol., 1988-89; task force Transp. Rsch. Bd. on Critical Transp. Infrastructure Security, 1999—. Recipient Spl. Achievement award U.S. Dept. Transp., 1989, Outstanding Alumnus award Suffolk U., 1990 Mem. Am. Soc. Pub. Adminstrn. (coun. mem. 1996—, mem. exec. bd. emergency and crisis mgmt. sect. 1999—), Nat. Contract Mgmt. Assn. (bd. dirs. 1996—, photographer No. Va. chpt. 1989-90, cert. profl. contracts mgr., nat. chair program mgmt. spl. topics com.), Presdl. Mgmt. Alumni Group (nat. bd. dirs. 1989-90, N.E. field bd. dirs. 1990—, Outstanding Alumnus award 1990), Trustees of Reservations Mass., Dept. Def. Sr. Profl. Women's Assn., Boston Network for Women in Govt. and Politics, Pi Alpha Alpha (pres. Suffolk U. chpt.). Democrat. Roman Catholic. Avocations: art, cross country and downhill skiing, hiking, outdoors, gardening.

SUDBRINK, JANE MARIE, sales and marketing executive; b. Sandusky, Ohio, Jan. 14, 1942; niece of Arthur and Lydia Sudbrink. BS, Bowling Green State U., 1964; postgrad., Kinderspital-Zurich, Switzerland, 1965. Field rep. Random House and Alfred A. Knopf Inc., Mpls., 1969-72, Ann Arbor, Mich., 1973, regional mgr. Midwest and Can., 1974-79, Can. rep., mgr., 1980-81; psychology and ednl. psychology adminstrv. editor Charles E. Merrill Pub. Co. div. Bell & Howell Corp., Columbus, Ohio, 1982-84; sales and mktg. mgr. trade products Wilson Learning Corp., Eden Prairie, Minn., 1984-85; fin. cons. Merrill Lynch Pierce Fenner & Smith, Edina, Minn., 1986-88; sr. editor Gorsuch Scarisbrick Pubs., Scottsdale, Ariz., 1988-89; regional mgr. Worth Publs., Inc. - von Holtzbrinck Pub. Grp., N.Y.C., 1988-97; mktg. assoc. Harcourt Brace Coll. Pubs., Northbrook, Ill., 1997-98, cons. Mid-Atlantic Redion, Midwest, Manitoba, Can., 1998—; mktg. assoc. W.W. Norton & Co., Northbrook, Ill., 1998—. Lutheran. Home and Office: 3801 Mission Hills Rd Northbrook IL 60062-5729 Business E-Mail: jsudbrink@wwnorton.com.

SUDMEYER, ALICE JEAN, art gallery owner; b. Goldbeach, Oreg., Feb. 17, 1946; d. Harold Leo Enz Sr. and Zoa Jane (Mercer) Enz; m. Larry Gene Orrell, Jan. 11, 1970 (div. July 1974); children: Aaron Jay, Zoa Jean Easterling; m. Larry Everett Sudmeyer, Apr. 28, 1978. A Fine Arts and Letters, Mt. Hood C.C., 1977. Adminstr. dir. Art's OK!, San Diego, 1987—93; with Margaret Harwell Art Mus., Poplar Bluff, Mo., 1999—; owner, operator, artist Alice Jean Sudmeyer Artworks Gallery and Studio, Fredericktown, 2000—. With USAR, 1970—2006, ret. USAR, 2006. Decorated Liberation of Kuwait medal, Army Commendation medal, Southwest Asia medal. Mem.: DAV (life), VFW (life), Am. Legion (life). Avocations: gardening, yoga, music. Home and Office: 715 South Wood Ave Fredericktown MO 63645 Personal E-mail: jean4me@charter.net.

SUDOR, CYNTHIA ANN, sales and marketing professional; b. Hershey, Pa., June 11, 1952; d. Milan and Mary (Strahosky) Sudor. BS in Design, Drexel U., 1974. Various mktg. positions in advt., promotion and publicity Hersheypark, Hershey, Pa., 1975—85, dir. sales and mktg., 1985—90; dir. destination mktg. Hershey Entertainment and Resort Co., 1990—91, dir. corp. sponsorship, 1991; owner Cynthia A. Sudor Enterprises, Grantville, Pa., 1992—; v.p. sales, mktg. and IMAX Whitaker Ctr. for Sci. and the Arts, Harrisburg, 1998—2001. Freelance writer, spkr., seminar presenter. Contbr. to Apprise Mag., Harrisburg, Pa., 1994-95, Funworld Mag., Alexandria, Va., 1987-90. Bd. dir., v.p., mktg. chair Profiles In Excellence, Inc., Harrisburg, 1993-99, Energy Entertainment, 1998-99. Recipient Best Seminar award, Internat. Assn. Amusement Parks and Attractions, Dallas, 1988, Harriet E. Worrell award, alumni award, Drexel U., 2005, Disting. Alumni Rankin-Epstein award, 2006. Mem.: Pa. Arabian Horse Assn., Internat. Arabian Horse Assn. Avocations: travel, writing, ukrainian egg decorating, reading, horseback riding. Office: Cynthia A Sudor Enterprises 1205 Ridge Rd Grantville PA 17028-9135 Office Phone: 717-469-7329. Personal E-mail: casudor@verizon.net.

SUESS, JENNIFER LYNN, elementary school educator; b. Montclair, N.J., Jan. 7, 1966; d. John Allan and Linda Lee Burton; m. Michael Scott Suess (div.); children: Connor Patrick, Meghan Kelsey. BS in Behavioral Sci., U. Md., College Park, 1994; MS in Edn., Johns Hopkins U., Balt., 2003. Tchr. St. Timothy's Presch., Herndon, Va., 1999—2003, St. Joseph Sch., Herndon, 2003—. Mentor & tutor. Mem.: Assn. Supervision Curriculum. Republican. Roman Catholic. Avocations: reading, singing in folk choir. Home: 12638 Fantasia Dr Herndon VA 20170 Office: St Joseph Sch 750 Peachtree St Herndon VA 20170 E-mail: jsuess1@verizon.net.

SUFFREDINI, KARA S., lawyer; b. LA; BA in Psychology with distinction, Univ. Calif., Berkeley, 1997; JD cum laude, Boston Coll., 2001. Intern ACLU, San Francisco, 2000; judicial clerk, Hon. Joette Katz Conn. Supreme Ct.; legislative lawyer Nat. Gay and Lesbian Task Force, Washington. Editor-in-chief Third World Law Jour., Boston Coll. Pro bono atty. Whitman Walker Clinic HIV/AIDS legal svcs. program; family selection com. Habitat for Humanity, Washington. Grantee James A. Champy civil rights fellowship. Mem.: Gay and Lesbian Attys. of Washington (dir.), Nat. Lesbian and Gay Law Assn. (chair law student divsn. 1999, co-vice chair, co-chair-elect, chair bd. dir.). Office: Nat Gay Lesbian Task Force Ste 600 1325 Massachusetts Ave NW Washington DC 20005 Office Phone: 202-393-5177. Office Fax: 202-393-2241. Business E-Mail: ksuffredini@thetaskforce.com.

SUGAR, SANDRA LEE, art consultant; b. Balt., May 18, 1942; d. Harry S. and Edith Sarah (Levin) Pomerantz; children: Gary Lee, Terry Lynn BS Edn. and English, Towson State U., 1965; MS Edn. and Applied Behavioral Scis., Johns Hopkins U., 1986. Chairperson arts exhibit Balt. Arts Festival, 1979; med. interviewer Johns Hopkins Sch. Hygiene, Balt., 1980—82; copy writer Concepts & Comm., Balt., 1984; instr. art history and world cultures Catonsville C.C., Balt., 1981—85; instr. English C.C. Balt., 1981—85; instr. English and math. Info. Processing Tng. Ctr., Balt., 1985; info. specialist Info. Md. New Directions for Women, Balt., 1986; trainer, job developer Working Solutions, Balt., 1987—88; dir. art gallery Renaissance Fine Arts Gallery, Bethesda, Md., 1988—93; art cons. Bethesda, 1994—. Judge nat. h.s. sci. fiction contests; editing instr. USDA One-woman shows include River Rd. Gallery, Bethesda, 1997; exhibited in group shows, Georgetown D.C. Post Office, Balt. Mus. Art Bienniales, 1979, 80, Oella Mill Gallery, Balt., Nat. Press Bldg. Gallery, Washington, 1998, Howard County Arts Coun. Juried Show, 1998, Contemporary Md. Artists Juried Show, 1999, Covington & Burling Law Firm Juried Show, 1999, Pass Gallery Juried Show, 1999, Touchstone Gallery, 2001, Rockville Art Pl., 2001, Silver Spring Artwork, 2003, 006, D.C. Arts Ctr., 2002, Air Gallery, N.Y., 2005, 2006, Anne C. Fisher Gallery Washington, 2006; editor mus. guides' newsletter Guidelines, 1978; arts editor Poet Lore, 1997; represented by Georgetown Art Gallery, 1997, Dunham Gallery, Washington; radio/TV spokesperson At Your Service, Washington Docent Balt. Mus. Art, 1973-86; coord. Internat. Brass Quintet Festival, Balt., 1986; chairperson spl. events Balt. PTA, 1978-82; bd. dirs. Citizens Planning and Housing Assn., Balt., 1980-82; mem. women's com., ctr. stage hand Balt. Ballet, 1979-84, Balt. Symphony, 1979-80 FJ. Bamberger scholar, Johns Hopkins U., 1985; recipient Mayoral Vol. of Yr. award Balt. Mus. Art, 1979

SUGGARS, CANDICE LOUISE, special education educator, consultant; b. Pitts., Jan. 16, 1949; d. Albert Abraham and Patricia Louise (Stepp) S. BS in Elem. Edn., W.Va. U., 1972; MS in Spl. Edn., Johns Hopkins U., 1979. Cert. Advanced Study Johns Hopkins U., 1986. Clin. supr./head tchr. The Kennedy Krieger Inst., Balt., 1974-80, inpatient coord., 1980-83, ednl. evaluator, 1980-85, spl. educator/pediatric rehab. team, 1985-86; spl. edn. cons. Charleston County (S.C.) Sch. Dist., 1986-90, spl. edn. pre-sch. tchr., 1990-95; pvt. tutor & cons. children with spl. needs and disabilities Charleston, 1995—; spl. needs cons. U. S.C., 1996—. Mem. adv. bd. S.C. Accelerated Schs. Project, Charleston, 1994-95; parenting instr. Internat. Network of Children and Families, 1999; part-time learning specialist in a pvt. sch., 2000-04, interim learning specialist Porter Gand Sch., 2005—Contbg. author: Disadvantaged Pre-School Child, 1979, Leisure Education for the Handicapped Curriculum, 1984. Exhibitor ann. conv. S.C. State Sch. Bd. Assn., 1994; presenter Spl. Needs Conf., 2003. Mem. Coun. for Exceptional Children (hospitality chair 1987-89, publicity chair 1989-90), Nat. Assn. for Edn. of Young Children. Avocations: singing, reading, travel. Home and Office: 64 Maple St #B Charleston SC 29403-3447 Office Phone: 843-577-0362.

SUGRA, CYNTHIA MARIEL, marketing executive; d. Michael A. and Silvia A. Sugra. Degree music, UCLA. Cert. Music Bus./Audio Engring. UCLA. CEO/owner Studio 7 Media, LLC, L.A., 2001—, Tripp Factor Music, L.A., Hotllama Media LLC, L.A. Cons. in field. Office Phone: 310-320-5555. Business E-Mail: cyndee@studio7media.com.

SUH, EUN JUNG, psychologist, researcher; PhD, McGill U., Canada, 2000. Lic. Psychologist NY. Rsch. scientist NY State Psychiat. Inst., N.Y.C., 2002—; asst. prof. clin. psychology Dept. Psychiatry, Columbia U. Coll. physicians, Surgeons, N.Y.C., 2006—. Psychotherapist Pvt. Practice, N.Y.C., 2004—. Mem.: APA.

SUHR, GERALDINE M., medical/surgical nurse; b. Sumner, Iowa, Mar. 16, 1960; d. Marvin Edward and Peggy Marie (Reiser) S. Diploma, Allen Meml. Luth. Sch. Nursing, Waterloo, Iowa, 1982; student, U. No. Iowa, Cedar Falls, 1979, U. Tenn., 1995. Cert. legal nurse cons. Sr. ship's nurse Carnival Cruise Lines, Miami, Fla.; emergency room and ICU/CCU nurse New Hampton (Iowa) Community Hosp.; charge nurse Trav Corps, Malden, Mass., Flying Nurses, Dallas, Hosp. Staffing Inc., Fla.; telemetry med./surg. charge nurse, critical care nurse So. Hills Hosp., Nashville; emergency nurse, intensive care Ft. Sanders Sevier Med. Ctr., Sevierville, Tenn.; nurse cardiovasc. unit Bapt. Hosp., Knoxville, Tenn., Caris Healthcare, Knoxville.

SUHRE, EDITH LAVONNE, adult education educator; b. North Vernon, Ind., Mar. 20, 1941; d. Raymond L. and Virginia Ruth (Yeager) S.; m. Michael Lee Commons, Aug. 12, 1963 (div. Sept. 1997); children: Ruth Ellen Commons Cherry. BA in Edn., Ball State U., 1963, MA in Edn., 1971. Cert. tchr., Ind. Tchr. Jennings County Sch. Corp., North Vernon, Ind., 1963-64, Madison-Grant Sch. Corp., Fowlerton, Ind., 1964-65, Lewisville (Ind.) Sch. Corp., 1965-66; prin., tchr. Bur. Indian Affairs, Bethel, Alaska, 1966-69; tchr. Ripley County Schs., Holton, Ind., 1970, Bartholomew Sch. Corp., Columbus, Ind., 1970-71; substitute tchr. South Knox, North Knox, Knox County Schs., Vincennes, Ind., 1976-77; pastry chef Exec. Inn, Vincennes, 1976-81; tchr., prof. Ind. Bus. Coll., Vincennes, 1985-87; tchr. Gary (Ind.) Sch. Corp., 1987-93; tchr. English, writing Lakeshore Employment and Tng., Gary, 1994-96; tchr., edn. coord. workforce devel. svcs. divsn. East Chgo., 1996—. Salesperson, trainer Avon, Vincennes, Ind., 1982-87; vol., leader Reading Is Fundamental, Vincennes and Gary, 1977-93. Leader, cons. Girl Scouts Am., Vincennes, Ind., 1979-86; co. team leader AHA, East Chgo., Gary, Crown Point and Hammond, 1997—. State scholar Ind., 1959. Mem. NAFE. Democrat. Methodist. Avocations: quilting, crocheting rag rugs, embroidery, sewing. Office: WorkOne Express Workforce Devel Svcs 740 W Chicago Ave East Chicago IN 46312-3544 E-mail: esuhre@workonenw.com.

SUITOR, DORCAS P., elementary school educator; b. Albany, Vt., Aug. 5, 1944; d. Abner Joseph and Eulalee Dorothy Poutry; m. David Douglas Suitor, Dec. 24, 1966; children: Daphne Joan Morris, Dorothea Joy Alter. BS in Edn., Johnson State Coll., 1966. Tchr. 2d grade C.P. Smith Sch., Burlington, Vt., 1966—67, Swanton Elem. Sch., 1967—71; tchr. title I Sheldon Elem. Sch., 1973—75, St. Anne's Elem. Sch., Swanton, 1974—75; tchr. 1st grade Swanton Elem. Sch., 1975—94, tchr. k-1, 1994—99, tchr. 1st grade, 1999—. Mem. adv. bd. Project Scope, Swanton, 2002—; mem. local stds. bd. Franklin Northwest Dist., 1999—; mem. tech. task force Swanton Elem. Sch., 1999—; presenter in field. Mentor new tchr. FNW Supervisory Union, Swanton, 2003—; supr. student tchrs. U. Vt. and Johnson State Coll. Swanton Elem. Sch., 2001—04; trustee Meml. United Meth. Ch., Swanton, 2006—, Swanton Town Libr., 2006—. Recipient Outstanding Vt. Tchr. award, 2006. Mem.: Franklin Northwest NEA (30 Yrs. Svc. to Children award 1999), Vt. Coun. Reading. Democrat. United Methodist. Avocations: reading, cooking, making educational games, gardening. Home: 17 Dunning St Swanton VT 05488 Office: Swanton Elem Sch 113 Grand Ave Swanton VT 05488 Personal E-mail: davdor1@aol.com.

SUJANSKY, EVA BORSKA, pediatrician, geneticist, educator; b. Bratislava, Slovak Republic, Feb. 14, 1936; d. Stefan and Terezia (Kaiserova) Borsky; m. Eduard Sujansky, Apr. 2, 1960 (dec. Sept. 1979); children: Paul, Walter. MD, Comenius U., Bratislava, Czechoslovakia, 1959. Diplomate Am. Bd. Pediats., Am. Bd. Med. Genetics. Resident in pediats. U. Iowa, Iowa City, 1969-71; fellow in human genetics Mt. Sinai Sch. Medicine, N.Y.C., 1971-73; clin. geneticist Beth Israel Hosp., N.Y.C., 1973-74; dir. clin. genetics Sch. Medicine, U. Colo., Denver, 1974-90, assoc. prof. pediats., 1981—, assoc. prof. biochemistry, biophysics and genetics, 1981—98; co-dir. divsn. genetic svcs. The Children's Hosp., U. Colo., Denver, 1990—2000. Contbr. articles to profl. jours. Fellow Am. Acad. Pediats., Am. Soc. Human Genetics, Am. Coll. Med. Genetics (founding fellow). Avocations: fine arts, reading, travel. Office: U Colo Med Ctr/TCH 1056 E 19th Ave Denver CO 80218-1007 Office Phone: 303-861-6395. Business E-Mail: sujansky.eva@tchden.org.

SUK, JEANNIE, lawyer; b. Seoul, Korea, 1973; arrived in U.S., 1979; m. Noah Feldman. BA, Yale Univ., 1995; D.Phil., Oxford Univ., 1999; JD, Harvard Univ., 2002. Law clk. U.S. Ct. Appeals (D.C. cir.), Washington, 2002—03; law clk. to Hon. David H. Souter U.S. Supreme Ct., Washington, 2003—04; asst. dist. atty N.Y. county, 2004—. Author: Postcolonial Paradoxes in French Caribbean Writing, 2001. Marshall Scholar, 1999, William Thomas & Gladys Willing Grad. Scholarship, Oxford Univ., Soros Fellow, 2001. Office: District Attorney New York County 1 Hogan Pl New York NY 10013

SUKAPDJO, WILMA IRENE, language educator; b. Indpls., Nov. 8, 1936; d. Wilson Homer and Della Irene Warren; m. Humam Sukapdjo, Apr. 12, 1960; children: Tina, Stephen, Amye. AB, Butler U., 1958, MS, 1967. Tchr. French U. Wis., Madison, Gadjah Mada U., Jakarta, Indonesia, Plainfield H.S., Ind., Columbus Jr. H.S., Ben Davis H.S., Indpls.; tchr. langs. Iupui Continuing Edn., Wilhum Acad., Carmel, Oasis, Indpls. Vol. guide Eiteljorg Indian Mus., 1999—2006. Mem.: Colonial Williamsburg Found., Indpls. (Ind.) Mus. Art, Tomodachi Japan-Am. Club (pres.), Phi Kappa Phi. Republican. Presbyterian. Avocation: travel. Office: Wilhum Acad Foreign Lang 622 S Range Line Rd Ste I Carmel IN 46032-2152 Office Phone: 317-843-2874.

SULAK, PATRICIA JANE, gynecologist, educator; b. Hillsboro, Tex., Nov. 6, 1952; m. Jeffrey Alan Waxman, Dec. 6, 1980; children: David Bartholomew Waxman, Gabriel Waxman. B in pharmacy, U. Houston, Tex., 1975; MD, U. Tex. Health Sci. Ctr., San Antonio, 1980. Cert. MD Tex. State Bd. Medicine, 1980, Am. Bd. Obstetrics and Gynecology; Pharmacist Tex., 1975. Intern Bexar County Tchg. Hosp., 1980—81; obstetrics/gynecology preceptorship DeWill Army Hosp., Ft. Belvior, 1981—82; resident, obstetrics/gynecology Walter Reed Army Med. Ctr., Washington, 1982—85; physician, maj. Darnall Army Cmty. Hosp., Ft. Hood, Tex., 1985—; obstetrician, gynecologist Scott and White Hosp., Tex. A&M U., Temple, Tex., 1987—; prof. Tex. A&M Coll. Medicine, Temple, Tex., 1987—. Dir. Scott and White Dept. of Ob/gyn, Temple, Tex., 1995—; founder, dir. Scott and White Sex Edn. Program, Temple, Tex., 1996—2004. Author: Worth The Wait (Hero For Children, Tex. State Bd. Edn., 1999, Am. Coll. Obstetricians and Gynecologists Dist. VII Presdl. award for Cmty. Svc., 2004); contbr. articles to profl. jours. Maj. U.S. Army, 1981—87, Walter Reed Army Med. Ctr. and Darnall Army Com. Hosp. Recipient Hero for Children award for establishing a sex edn. curriculum in Ctrl. Tex., Tex. State Bd. Edn., 1999. Fellow: Am. Coll. Obstetricians and Gynecologists; mem.: Am. Bd. Obstetricians and Gynecologists (assoc. examiner), Alpha Omega Alpha. Achievements include research in redesign of oral contraceptives to eliminate monthly menstruation. Office: Scott and White Hosp Tex A&M U Sys 2401 S 31st St Temple TX 76508 Office Phone: 254-724-4034. Business E-Mail: psulak@swmail.sw.org.*

SULC, JEAN LUENA (JEAN L. MESTRES), lobbyist, consultant; b. Worcester, Mass., Mar. 17, 1939; d. Emilio Beija and Julia Luena; m. Lee Gwynne Mestres, Oct. 9, 1965 (div. Dec. 1973); m. Lawrence Bradley Sulc, Nov. 4, 1983. BS in Psychology, Tufts U., 1961; M in Urban and Regional Planning, U. Colo., 1976. Lic. real estate, Va.; lic. pvt. pilot. Mem. staff U.S. fgn. svc. Dept. State, Washington, 1962-65; intern Adams County Planning Dept., Brighton, Colo., 1974-75; cons. office policy analysis City and County of Denver, 1976; program dir. Coun. Internat. Urban Liaison, Washington, 1976-79; asst., dir. internat. Cities Svc. Oil & Gas Corp., Washington, 1980-81; govt. affairs rep. Cities Svc., OXY USA Inc., Washington, 1982-89; mgr. fed. rels. OXY USA Inc., Washington, 1990-95; pres. EdgeSystem.XXI, Washington, 1996—. Chmn. govt. affairs com. L.P. Gas Clean Fuel Coalition, Irvine, Calif., 1990-92. Author, editor: (newsletter) Dayton Climate Project, 1979-80; contbr. articles to newsletters. Vol. Reagan/Bush and Bush/Quayle Presdl. Campaigns and Inaugural Coms., Washington, 1984-89; pres. Hale Found., Nathan Hale Inst., Washington, 1984-85; mem. nat. panel consumer arbitrators Better Bus. Burs., Va., 1991—. Recipient Presdl. citation Nat. Propane Gas Assn., 1992; Minority Intern grantee Denver Regional Coun. Govts., 1974-76. Mem. ASTD, ABA (assoc., arbitration sect.), Am. League Lobbyists (bd. dirs. 1994-97, 2nd v.p. 1996-97, emeritus 1999—), Assn. Image Cons. Internat. (ea. regional adv. 1998—), Greater Beaufort C. of C., Psi Chi. Episcopalian. Avocations: skiing, sports shooting.

SULLENDER, JOY SHARON, retired elementary school educator; b. Bloomington, Ind., Apr. 9, 1932; d. Fred Laymond and Edith (Parrish) Medaris. BS, Ind. U., 1959, MS, 1965; postgrad., Ind. U./Purdue U., Indpls., 1991. Cert. tchr. elem. edn. 1-8. Tchr. Monroe Sch., Salem, Ind., 1952-55, Pekin (Ind.) Sch., 1955-61, Highland Park (Ill.) Sch., 1961-62, George Julian Sch. #57, Indpls., 1962—2000; ret., 2000. Mem. prin.'s adv. coun. Indpls. Pub. Schs., 1985-95, supts. adv. coun., 1982-90; state mentor student tchrs., 1969—. Author col.: Let's Be Informed, 1993-95. Class sponsor Best Friends, Indpls., 1990—; vol. Toys for Foster Children, Indpls., 1991—; workshop presenter Alpha Epsilon State, Anderson, South Bend, 1994, 95. NSF grantee, 1971. Mem. PTA (tchr. rep. 1993-95), Ind. Sch. Women's Club (v.p. 1989-91, pres. 1992-94), Woman's Dept. Club (v.p. 2002—), Delta Kappa Gamma (pres. 1978-80, state com. 1989—, state corr. sec. 1997-99). Office: George Julian School 5435 E Washington St Indianapolis IN 46219-6411 Home: 1310 N Bazil Ave Indianapolis IN 46219-4244

SULLIVAN, ANN CATHERINE, health facility administrator; b. N.Y.C., June 8, 1947; d. Joseph Patrick and Catherine (Wolt) S. AAS, Queens Boro C.C., 1971; BBA, Bernard Baruch Sch. Bus., 1975; MBA, Dowling U., 1993. Claim rep. Met. Life Ins. Co., N.Y.C., 1965-68; mgr. nat. payroll Meyers Bros. Parking, N.Y.C., 1968-73; mgr. internat. payroll Sun Chem. Corp., Fort Lee, N.J., 1973-74; chief info. officer Elmhurst (N.Y.) Med. Ctr., 1974-83; chief fin. officer Met. Hosp. Ctr., N.Y.C., 1983-87, Jacobi Med. Ctr., Bronx, N.Y., 1987-96; sr. v.p., chief info. officer, chief fin. officer Maimonides Med. Ctr., Bklyn., 1996—. COO/CFO North Bronx Health Care Network, 1994-96; bd. dirs. Inst. Urban Family Health, N.Y.C., ABC Health Plan, N.Y.C., HANYS Ins. Co. Inc., First to Care INc., Bklyn. Cares Inc., E-HMO, Inc., Clin. Care Connectors, Inc. Contbr. articles to profl. jours. Mem. Healthcare Fin. Mgmt. Assn., Health Info. Mgmt. Sys. Soc. Avocations: reading, biking, travel. Office: Maimonides Med Ctr 1039 49th St Brooklyn NY 11219-2925

SULLIVAN, ANN-CATHERINE, physical education educator; d. Robert Paul and Jeanne Shirley Sullivan. BA, St. Michael's Coll., Winooski, Vt., 1988; tchr. cert., Plymouth State Coll., NH, 1995; MA in Adapted Phys. Edn., Ohio State U., Columbus, 1997, PhD in Tchr. Edn., 2000. Grad. asst. Ohio State U., Columbus, 1996—2000; asst. prof. Saginaw Valley State U., University Center, Mich., 2000—. Mem. adv. bd. Adapted Phys. Edn. Coun., 2001—; mem. asst. adv. bd. Saginaw Valley State U., University Center, 2005—06, coord. nat. coun. accreditation tchr. edn., 2006—. Author: (book chpt.) Innovation in Teacher Education, 2005, (book) Teaching Elementary Physical Education, 2005. Instr., trainer ARC. Mem.: AAHPERD, Mich. Assn. Health, Phys. Edn., Recreation and Dance, Phi Kappa Phi.

SULLIVAN, BARBARA JEAN, artist; b. Indpls., Jan. 7, 1935; d. Charles Arthur and Melida Mae Minnick; children: Joseph Ruggless, Pamela Ruggless-Consoli, Diana Ruggless-Larsen, Milo Ballan. Fine artist, 1978—. Author (paperback cover illustrations): Winter Rage, 1991, The Horsemen, 1992, limited edit. giclee prints, 1999—; one-woman shows include Artists' Gallery, Las Vegas, 1983; exhibited in group shows U.S. Fed. Bldg. Exhbn., Las Vegas, 1982, George Phippen Meml. Invitational We. Art Show, Prescott, Ariz., 1984, Burk Gallery, Boulder City, Nev., 1983, 6th Ann. Kalispell (Mont.) Art Show and Auction, 1983, 16th Ann. C.M. Russell Auction of Original We. Art, Great Falls, Mont., 1983 (Silver medal), 7th Ann. We. Art Show and Sale, Burk Gallery, 1984,; Represented in permanent collections Nev. Nat. Bank, Virgin River Hotel and Casino, White House, Washington; guest artist Women Artists of Am. West, Pa-Jo's Gallery, Pinedale, Wyo., 1985, C.M. Russell Mus. Artist Invitational Exhibit, 1986, 10th Ann. We. Art Show and Sale, Burk Gallery, 1987, Far We. Art Assn. Show, Caesar's Palace, Las Vegas, 1987, Braithwaite Fine Arts Gallery, Cedar City, Utah, 1999, Bosque Conservatory of Art, Clifton, Tex., 2001 (Gold medal); Navarro Gallery, Sedona, Ariz., 2002, The Artist's Alley Studio Gallery, 2003, Navarro Gallery, 2003; guest artist Providence Gallery, 2006, contbr. poem to anthology, 2001; Ostrovsky Fine Art, Scottsdale, Ariz., Inspirations Gallery, Lakeport, Calif., Vincent Sheraldi Galleries, N.Y.C., Tribal Treasures Gallery, Victorville, Calif., Providence Gallery, Scottsdale, Ariz. Bd. dirs. Charles Arthur Minnick Sunset Meml. Park Found., Las Vegas, Nev., 1992-95; adv. bd. Las Vegas, 1992-95. Recipient 1st Place award, Jaycee State Fair, 1976, 1977, 5 Painting of Month awards, Las Vegas Art Mus., 1978, Popular award, San Gabriel Fine Arts Assn. Invitational, 1978, Reserve Grand Championship, Las Vegas State Fair, 1981, 1st Place Oils, Caliente Profl. Invitational, 1982, award of Excellence, Am. Mothers State Competition, 1982, 1983, Best of Show award, Las Vegas Art Mus., 1994, Judges Choice award, 1995, juried award, Canyon Country Fine Arts Competition, Braithwaite Fine Arts Gallery, 1999, Gold medal award for Best Oil, Bosque Conservatory of Art, Tex., 2001, Quick Draw award, Mont. Gov. Ted Schwinden and C.M. Russell Auction of Original Western Art, 1983, Editor's Choice award, The Best Poems and Poets of 2002, Editor's Choice award for Outstanding Achievement in Poetry, 2002. Mem. Las Vegas Art Mus., Am. Inst. Fine Art, 1984, Oil Painters of Am. Avocations: travel, photography, horseback riding, subject research, visiting art galleries. Office Phone: 775-751-9566. Business E-Mail: art@barbarasullivan.com.

SULLIVAN, CARLEY HAYDEN, political party executive; b. Elko, Nev. m. Will Sullivan; children: Blaine Sullivan Rose, Valerie Sullivan Mitchell, Dan, Peggy Sullivan Hagen. Student, U. Oreg., 1945—47. Mgmt. asst. State of Nev., Elko, 1967—. Sec. Elko County (Nev.) Dem. Ctrl. Com., 1972—, treas., 1984—86, Nev. Dem. Com., 1980—82, co-chmn. state conv., 1980, state cons. planning com., 82. Adv. bd. Nat. Coun. Juvenile Ct. Judges, 1972—74; state hosp. adv. bd., 1964—66; adv. coun. on children and youth, 1970—80; active Gov.'s State Sch. Survey Com., 1975—77, Gov.'s Drug Abuse Adv. Bd., 1974—76, Nev. Adv. Coun. for Vocat. Tech. Edn., 1982—, Nev. State Bd. Edn.; gov.'s del. to Nev. Libr. Conf., 1981; alt. del. White House Conf. on Libraries, 1982; Nev. del. to Presdl. White House Conf. on Children and Youth, 1970; exec. sec., interim mgr. Elko C. of C., 1961—68; pres. Elko Dem. Women, 1970; chmn. Rural Nev. Mental Health Adv. Bd., 1973—78; bd. dirs. Nev. PTA, 1962—72, pres., 1972—74; v.p. Am. Lung Assn. of Nev., 1972—82, pres.-elect, 1982—84, pres., 1984—; coord. Youth Traffic Safety Confs., 1968—78; bd. mgrs. Nat. Com. Health and Welfare, PTA, 1972—74; mem. 8 state project Designing Edn. for the Future, 1965—68; Nev. conv. rep. ALA, 1981; vol. Elko Hosp. Aux.; co-chmn. Rural Nev. Women's Conf., Nev., 1980; Nev. commr./nat. coun. Future of Women In The Workplace, 1983—85; Nev. rep. to Nat. Commn. for Eleanor Roosevelt Centennial, 1984—85; apptd. to Nev. U.S. Svc. Acad. Selection Com., 1987; apptd. by Gov. of Nev. to recommendation com. Nev. Legislature; del. to Dem. Nat. Conv., 84; active Nev. State Dem. Central Com.; bd. dirs. Elko Dem. Club, 1970—82. Named Citizen of Yr., Elko County Mental Health Assn., 1985; recipient award, Am. Lung Assn. Nev., C. of C., Nev. Dept. Edn., Gov.'s Office State of Nev. Mem.: Elko Bus. and Profl. Women (state legis. chmn., scholarship award com., del. to nat. conv.), Gov.'s Youth Traffic Safety Assn. (life), Sigma Kappa.

SULLIVAN, CHRISTINE ANNE, secondary school educator; b. Albany, NY, June 18, 1956; d. Francis James and Geraldine (Patterson) S. BA summa cum laude, Albertus Magnus Coll., New Haven, Conn., 1978; MS, Ctrl. Conn. State U., New Britain, 1989. Cert. profl. educator Conn., tchr. N.Y. Tchr. Spanish Sacred Heart Acad., Hamden, Conn., 1978—79; adminstrv. asst. Julio Espada, N.Y.C., 1982—83; tchr. Spanish St. Mary's H.S., New Haven, 1983—90; fgn. and internat. rsch./reference asst. Yale U. Law Sch., New Haven, 1990—93; tchr. Spanish Notre Dame H.S., Fairfield, Conn., 1993; tchr. ESL New Haven, 1993—94; tchr. Spanish Jonathan Law H.S., Milford, Conn., 1994—. Adj. prof. Spanish U. Bridgeport (Conn.), 1993—94; dir. religious edn. St. Lawrence Parish, West Haven, Conn., 1985—92. Active Econ. Devel. Commn., West Haven, Conn., 2005—. Recipient Honor scholarships, Ctrl. Conn. State U., 1987—88; grantee St. Elizabeth Seton grant, Diocese of Hartford, 1987, 1988, 1989. Mem.: Am. Assn. Tchrs. Spanish and Portuguese (dir. adv. bd. state level 1989—90), Theodore Roosevelt Assn., Sigma Delta Pi. Roman Catholic. Avocations: travel, gardening, Russian history and culture. Home: 52 Richmond Ave West Haven CT 06516 Office: Jonathan Law High Sc 20 Lansdale Ave Milford CT 06460

SULLIVAN, CONNIE CASTLEBERRY, artist; b. Cin., Jan. 8, 1934; d. John Porter and Constance (Alf) Castleberry; m. John J. Sullivan, June 6, 1959; children: Deirdre Kelly, Margaret Graham. BA, Manhattanville Coll., 1957. Spl. lectr. Cin. Contemporary Art Ctr., 1984, Toledo Friends of Photography, 1991, U. Ky. Art Mus., 1993, Dennison U. Sch. Art, 1993, El Instituto de Estudios Norte Americanos, Barcelona, 1994, Ctr. for Photography, Bombay, India, 1997, Miami U. Art Mus., Oxford, Ohio, 1998, Alice and Harris K. Weston Gallery, Aronoff Ctr. for the Arts, Cin., 2000, Columbus Mus. Art, Ohio, 2001, Mus. Fine Arts St. Petersburg, Fla., 2002. One-woman shows include Contemporary Art Ctr. Cleve., 1982, Cin. Contemporary Arts Ctr., 1983, Fogg Art Mus., Cambridge, Mass., 1983, 90, Neikrug Gallery, N.Y.C., 1984, Camden Arts Ctr., London, 1987, Evanston Art Ctr., Chgo., 1987, Silver Image Gallery Ohio State U., Columbus, 1988, Jean-Pierre Lambert Galerie, Paris, 1988, 96, David Winton Bell Gallery, Brown U., Providence, 1989, Toni Burckhead Gallery, Cin., 1989, Rochester Inst. Tech., 1991, Fotomus. im Münchner Stadtmus., Munich, 1992, U. Ky. Art Mus., Lexington, 1993, Internat. Photography Hall, Kirkpatrick Mus. complex, Oklahoma City, 1993, Institut d'Estudios Fotografics de Catalunya, Barcelona, Spain, 1994, Cheekwood Art Mus., Nashville, 1994, Museo Damy di Fotografia Contemporanea, Brescia, Italy, 1995, Photography Gallery U. Notre Dame, Ind., 1995, Louisville Visual Art Assoc., Watertower, Louisville, KY, 1995, Jean-Pierre Lambert Galarie, 1996, Museo Damy, Milan, 1997, Ctr. for Photography, Bombay, India, 1997, Miami U. Art Mus., Oxford, Ohio, 1998, Aronoff Ctr. for the Arts, Cin., 2000, Vine St. Studios, Houston, 2000, Columbus Mus. Art, 2001, Visual Studies Worshop Gall. Rochester, NY, 2000, NuNatte Duo Centre Photography, OP Photo Gall., Hong Kong, 2000, FotoFest, 2000; exhibited in numerous group shows including Robert Klein Gallery, Boston, 1981, Cin. Art Mus., 1981, 84, 85, 93, Witkin Gallery, N.Y.C., 1984, Milw. Art Mus., 1986, Dayton (Ohio) Art Inst., 1987, J.B. Speed Art Mus., Louisville, 1988, Trisolini Gallery Ohio U., 1989, Ohio U., Athens, 1989, Centre Nat. Photographie, Paris, 1989, Cleve. Ctr. for Contemporary Art, 1991, Tampa Mus. Art, 1991, 93, Images Gallery, 1991, Dayton Art Inst./Mus. Contemporary Art Wright State U., Dayton, 1992, Bowling Green State U. Sch Art, 1992, Carnegie Arts Ctr., Covington, Ky., 1993, POLK Mus. Art, Lakeland, Fla., 1993, Tampa (Fla.) Mus. Art, 1993, Adams Landing Fine Art Ctr., Cin., 1995, Checkwood Mus. Art, Nashville, 1995, Photo Forum Gallery, 1995, 96, Jean-Pierre Galerie, 1996, Soros Ctr. Contemporary Art, Kiev, Ukraine, 1996, Dom Khudozhnikv, Kharkiv, Ukraine, 1996, Wolf Photographic Galleries, Cin., 1996, Columbus Mus. Art, 1996, Mus. fine Arts, St. Petersburg, Fla., 1997, Louisville Visual Art Assn., Water Tower, 1997, Mus. Damy di Fotografia Contemporanea, Brescia, Italy, 1998, Kharkiv Mcpl. Art Gallery, Kharkiv, Ukraine, 1999, Jean-Pierre Lambert Gallery, Paris, 1999, Huntington (W.Va.) Mus. Art, 2000, Centre Socio-Cultural Galerie Pierre Tal Coat, Hunnebont, France, 2000; represented in numerous permanent collections Tampa Mus. of Art, Mûnchner Stadt Mus., Munich, Germany, Museo Damy, Brescia, Italy, Ctr. Creative Photography, Tucson, Detroit Inst. Arts, Biblioteque National, Paris, Internat. Photography Hall of Fame and Mus., Kirkpatrick Ctr. Mus. Complex, Okla. City, Nelson Gallery-Atkins Mus., Kansas City, Ctr. for Photography, Bombay, Milw. Art Mus., Mus. Photography Arts, San Diego, Musee Nat. D'Art Modern, Cin. Art Mus., High Mus., Atlanta, Mus. Fine Arts, St. Petersburg, Fla., Centre Georges Pompidou, Paris, Denver Art Mus., Boston Mus. Fine Arts, Stanford U. Mus. Art, Palo Alto, Indpls. Art Mus., New Orleans Mus. Art, Fogg Mus., Cambridge, Mass., numerous others; also pvt. collections; author: Petroglyphs of the Heart, Photographs by Connie Sullivan, 1983; work represented in numerous publs. Trustee Images Ctr. for Fine Photography, Cin., 1986-94. Named Hyde Park Living Person of Yr., 1996; recipient Juried Show, Toledo Friends Photography, 1986, Best of show, 1988, Images Gallery, 1986, Pres.'s Coun. for Arts award, Manhattanville Coll., 1991, Treasure of the Month award, Mus. Fine Arts St. Petersburg, Fla., 1995; fellow Arts Midwest fellow, NEA, 1989—90; grantee Aid to Individual Artists grantee, Summerfair, 1987, travel grantee, Ohio Arts Coun., 1995, 1997, 2000, Artist Projects, 1999, 2000. Mem. McDowell Soc. Avocations: travel, reading, gardening, music. Home: 1950 Mount Vernon Dr Fort Wright KY 41011 Fax: 513-871-6931.

SULLIVAN, DIANE P., lawyer; b. Elizabeth, NJ; BA cum laude, Fairfield U., 1984; JD, U. Pa., 1987. Bar: NJ 1987, U.S. Dist. Ct. (NJ Dist.) 1987, U.S. Dist. Ct. (So. and ea. dist. NY) 2003. Ptnr. mass torts and product liability group Dechert LLP, Princeton, NJ, 2001—. Bd. trustees Trial Attys. NJ, 2000—04; mem. policy com. Dechert LLP; lectr. in field. Named one of Top 40 Litigators Under 40, Nat. Law Jour., 2002, Top 10 Lawyers in the Country, Lawyers Weekly USA, 2005. Mem.: ABA, Internat. Assn. Def. Counsel (mem. trial acad. faculty 2002), Def. Rsch. Inst., NJ State Bar Assn. Office: Dechert LLP Princeton Pike Corp Ctr PO Box 5218 Princeton NJ 08543-5218 Office Phone: 609-620-3232. Office Fax: 609-620-3259. E-mail: diane.sullivan@dechert.com.

SULLIVAN, DOROTHY RONA, state official; b. Jan. 7, 1941; d. Lewis Robert and Dorothy (Hopkins) Sullivan. BA, Boston U., 1963; MEd, State Coll. Boston, 1966; CAGS, Boston U., 1972; postgrad., Northeastern U., 1970—71, Boston Coll., 1974—78, U. Mass., 1980. Rsch. asst. Boston Lying-In Hosp., 1963—64; employment counselor Mass. Divsn. Employment Security, Boston, 1964—66, sr. employment counselor, 1966—67, prin. employment counselor, 1967—70, employment office mgr., 1970—75, supr., 1975—78, chief rsch. dept., 1978—88, dir. def. employment analysis, 1985—87; chief rsch. dept. Mass. Divsn. Employment and Tng., 1989—98, 1998—2002. Supr. cmty. counselor interns and rehab. adminstrn. interns Northeastern U. Grad. Sch. Edn., 1968—74; supr. pub. adminstrn. interns Suffolk U., 1976; supr. econ. interns Boston U., 1979, Regis Coll., 1984, U. Mass.-Boston, 1998; presenter in field. Author: Boston Employment Service Guide, 1969, Careers and Training in the Allied Health Field, 1989, Higher Skills, Higher Wages and Higher Achievement, 1997, Career Families and Career Paths, 1997, Massachusetts Cities and Towns, 1978—82, Outplacement Program, 1993, Presentation and Performance Portfolio, 1998; editor: Mass. Trends, 1978—82; mem. editl. bd. Memos to the Gov., Mgmt. Advice from the Commonwealth's Experts in Pub. Adminstrn., 2003; contbr. articles to profl. jours.; exhibitions include Brookline Arts Ctr., Brookline Pub. Libr., Chatham Creative Arts Ctr. Recorder Gov.'s Conf. on Rehab., 1970; mem. Gov.'s Commn. Employment of Handicapped, 1972—78, Pres.'s Com. Employment of Handicapped, 1975—78; exec. bd. Greater Boston coun. Camp Fire Girls, 1971—73; R.S.V.P. adv. bd. Boston Commn. Affairs of the Elderly, 1977—78; mem. adv. com. equal employment opportunity practices Dept. Pers. Adminstrn., 1984—85; mem. adv. group Mass. Occupl. Info. Coordinating Com., 1991—98; mem. adv. bd. Mass. Ctr. Civic Edn., 2001—; bd. dirs. Doric Dames, Mass. State Ho., 2004—; 2nd v.p. Doric Docents, 2006; bd. dirs. Ethas (Boston Sr. Svcs. Agy.), 2004—. Recipient Recognition award, Nat. Occupl. Info. Coordinating Com., 1994, Exceptional Achievement award, U.S. Sec. Labor, 2003, Pres. Vol. Svc. award, 2004. Mem.: APGA (nat. recorder conf. 1968), ASPA, AACD, ACA (recorder), Am. Bus. Women's Assn. (del. nat. conv. 1980, 1983, pres. Boston chpt. 1982, Woman of Yr., Boston chpt. 1983), Am. Econ. Assn., Am. Acad. Polit. and Social Sci., Am. Fedn. State, County and Mcpl. Employees (exec. bd. local 164 1972—73, 1974—76), Nat. Rehab. Assn. (Mass. sec. 1971—72, exec. bd. 1972—74, v.p. 1974—75, pres. 1976—77), Nat. Career Devel. Assn., Am. Soc. Pub. Adminstrn. (life; region I-II liaison, sect. women in pub. adminstrn. 1988—90, Mass. chpt. coun., officer, treas. 1997, sec. 1998, v.p. 1998—, pres.-elect 1999, pres. 2000, nat. coun. campaign for internat. rels.), Charitable Irish Soc., Rockport Art Assn. (patron), Boston Ctr. for Internat. Visitors, Chatham Swim Club. Home: 33 Morey Rd Roslindale MA 02131-1037 also: Eldredge Sq Chatham MA 02633

SULLIVAN, ELIZABETH ASMANN, counselor; b. Buffalo, Nov. 26, 1950; d. Robert B. and Josephine E. (Lee) Asmann; m. Herman W. Sullivan, July 15, 1995. BS Elem. Edn., Ea. Mich. U., 1972, MA Spl. Edn. of Emotionally Impaired, 1978, MA Guidance and Counseling, 1986, Specialist Arts in Guidance-Counseling, 1989. Tchr. elem. Ypsilanti Pub. Schs., Mich., 1972—89; counselor elem. sch. Midland Pub. Schs., Mich., 1989—. Group facilitator Growing Tree Program, Ypsilanti, 1987-89, Twelve Together, Ypsilanti, 1987-88, Upward Bound, Ypsilanti, 1989 Vol. local and nat. polit. campaigns, 1975—; group coord. Midland Pub. Schs. United Way, Midland County, 1996— Fellow Ea. Mich. U., 1987-89 Mem. Am. Sch. Counselor Assn. (del. 1987—), Mich. Sch. Counselor Assn. (past pres.), Midland City Edn. Assn. (v.p. 1993-99), Alpha Delta Kappa Avocations: cooking, bridge, physical fitness, golf.

SULLIVAN, GLENDA LEE, secondary school educator; d. Clyde Albert and Elizabeth Annis Lee; m. Randall Jay Sullivan, June 22, 1985; 1 child, Biran Wesley. BA in English, Austin Peay State U., Clarksville, Tenn., 1987, MA in Speech Comm. & Theatre, 1990. Tchr. Dickson County HS, Tenn., 1981—, Austin Peay State U., 1991—. Head coach forensic team Dickson County H.S., 1985—. Dir.: (plays) Jekyll & Hyde, 2002, Cpmplete History of America, 2003, The Ghost of Jeb Taylor, 2003. Mem.: NEA, Am. Classical League, Nat. Forensic League.

SULLIVAN, IRENE A., lawyer; b. Bklyn., 1945; AB, Mount Holyoke Coll., 1967; MA, NYU, 1970; JD cum laude, Fordham U., 1975. Bar: N.Y. 1976. Ptnr. Skadden, Arps, Slate, Meagher & Flom. Nat. adv. bd. NALP Found. Rsch. and Edn., 1998—; mem. bd. visitors Fordham Law Sch., 1993—. Mem.: ABA (Task Force on Ins. Litig. 1992—93), Assn. of Bar of City NY (com. to Enhance Diversity in Profession 1998—, com. Recruitment and Retention of Lawyers 1992—94, adv. com. on Civil Practice 1986—89), City Bar Pub. Svc. Network, Women's Bar Assn. of State NY (pres. 1984—85), Phi Beta Kappa. Office: Skadden Arps Slate Meagher & Flom 4 Times Sq Fl 24 New York NY 10036-6595 Office Phone: 212-735-2410. Office Fax: 917-777-2410. E-mail: isulliva@skadden.com.

SULLIVAN, JEAN E. See NIENSTADT, JEAN

SULLIVAN, JUDITH PATRICE, social worker; b. Texarkana, Ark., Jan. 28, 1945; d. Joseph and Agnes (Wilson) Eldridge; m. J.P. Sullivan, Apr. 4, 1966 (div. 1972). BA, U. Tex., 1966; MSW, SUNY, Buffalo, 1972; cert. legal asst., VTI Inst., Dallas, 1987. Diplomate Nat. Assn. Social Work; licensed master social work, advanced clin. practitioner. Counseling supr. Erie Med. Ctr., Buffalo, 1972-74; prog. dir. child psychiatry Buffalo Children's Hosp., 1974-80; clin. assoc. prof. psychiatry, pediat. SUNY Sch. of Medicine, Buffalo, 1974-80; pvt. practice Buffalo, 1980-86, Dallas, 1988—; social worker Adoption Advisory, Inc., Dallas, 1988-90, Dallas County Mental Health/MR, Dallas, 1990-91; pvt. practice DeSoto, Tex., 1991—. Home: 4719 Cole Ave Apt 124 Dallas TX 75205-3558

SULLIVAN, KATHERINE MCGURK, lawyer; b. Holyoke, Mass., Oct. 2, 1949; d. John Joseph and Mary Helen (Knightly) McGurk; m. Thomas Christopher Sullivan, Aug. 18, 1973; 1 child, Thomas McGurk. BA, Regis Coll., Weston, Mass., 1971; JD cum laude, Georgetown U., 1988. Aide to Rep. Silvio O. Conte, US Congress, Washington, 1973—85; chief of staff Aetna Life and Casualty Co., Hartford, Conn., 1988—94; sr. v.p., gen. counsel Conn. Mut. Life Ins. Co., Conn., 1994—96, Travelers Life Ins. Co., Hartford, 1996—; pres., COO eCite, 2000—02; exec. v.p. Category Internat., 2002—04; ret., 2004. Ind. investors com. NY Stock Exch. Mem.: ABA, Am. Alliance of Rights and Responsibilities (bd. dirs.), Coalition for Justice. Democrat. Roman Catholic. Office: Travelers Life Ins Co 1 Tower Sq Hartford CT 06156-0001

SULLIVAN, KATHLEEN M. SKARO, secondary school educator; b. New Ulm, Minn., Mar. 11, 1946; d. Stanford William and Donna Elaine (Arneson) Skaro; m. Nathan Lee Sullivan, Apr. 18, 1965 (div. Dec. 1982); children: Rachel Anne, Rebekah Jean, Scott Michael, Matthew James. BS in English, Mankato State U., 1981, BS in Spanish, 1983, BS in French, 1990, MS in English, 2000. Cert. tchr., Minn. Inventory control clk. 3M Co., New Ulm, 1968-70; distbn. clk. Kraft Foods, New Ulm, 1971-74; tchr. New Ulm Sch. Dist., 1981-83; tchr., coach Gibbon (Minn.) Sch. Dist., 1984-85, Le Sueur (Minn.) Sch. Dist., 1985-86, Sebeka (Minn.) Sch. Dist., 1986-87; tchr. Dassel-Cokato (Minn.) Sch. Dist., 1987; tchr., coach Detroit Lakes (Minn.) Sch. Dist., 1988—95, Blue Earth Area H.S., 1995—2000, Lacqui Parle Valley H.S., 2000—02, Waubun Sch., 2002—. Writer and editor Office of Grants, Mankato (Minn.) State Univ., 1983-84. Mem. Minn. Coun. Teaching Fgn. Langs., Communication and Theater Assn. Minn., Alpha Delta Kappa, Alpha Mu Gamma, Phi Kappa Phi. Avocations: travel, reading, gardening, writing. Office: 1013 Third St Waubun MN 56589 Office Phone: 218-473-6138.

SULLIVAN, KATHLEEN MARIE, lawyer, educator, former dean; BA, Cornell U., 1976, Oxford (Eng.) U., 1978; JD, Harvard U., 1981. Law clk. Hon. James L. Oakes U.S. Ct. Appeals (2d cir.), 1981-82; pvt. practice, 1982-84; asst. prof. Harvard U., Cambridge, Mass., 1984-89, prof., 1989-93, Stanford U. Law Sch., Calif., 1993—, Robert E. Paradise fellow, 1995-96, Stanley Morrison prof., 1996—, dean, Richard E. Lang prof. law, 1999—2004; of counsel Quinn Emanuel Urquhart Oliver & Hedges LLP, Redwood Shores, Calif., 2005—. Vis. prov. U. So. Calif. Law Ctr., 1991, Stanford U., 1992; lectr., commentator on constnl. law. Co-editor: (with Gerald Gunther) Constitutional Law, 15th edit., 2004. Named one of 100 Most Influential Lawyers Nat. Law Jour., 2000; recipient Albert M. Sacks-Paul A. Freund award for Teaching Excellence, Harvard, 1992, John Bingham Hurlbut award for excellence in tchg. Stanford U., 1996. Fellow Am. Acad. Arts and Scis, Am. Philosophical Soc.; bd. trustees, The Century Found. Office: Quinn Emanuel Urquhart Oliver & Hedges LLP 555 Twin Dolphin Dr Ste 560 Redwood City CA 94065 also: Stanford U Law Sch Crown Quadrangle 559 Nathan Abbott Way Stanford CA 94305-8610 Office Phone: 650-801-5000. Business E-Mail: sullivan@law.stanford.edu.

SULLIVAN, KATHRYN ANN, librarian, educator; b. Elmhurst, Ill., Jan. 22, 1954; d. Joseph Terrence and Rose Marie (Wright) S. Student, Triton Jr. Coll., 1972-73; BA, No. Ill. U., 1975, MLS, 1977; D of Sci. in Info. Sci., Nova U., 1991. Chief periodicals clk. No. Ill. U., Dekalb, 1976-77; periodicals librarian West Chgo. (Ill.) Pub. Library, 1977-78, Winona (Minn.) State U., 1978-99, distance learning libr., 2000—. Contbr. articles and short stories to profl. publs. Grantee Winona State U., 1986, 88, 92, 94. Mem.: ALA, Electronically Published Internet Connections, Minn. Libr. Assn., Broad Univerce. Avocation: writing. Home: 670 Winona St Winona MN 55987-3353 Office Phone: 507-457-5150.

SULLIVAN, KATHRYN D., geologist, former astronaut, former science association executive; b. Paterson, N.J., Oct. 3, 1951; d. Donald P. and Barbara K. Sullivan (dec.). BS in Earth Scis., U. Calif., Santa Cruz, 1973; PhD in Geology, Dalhousie U., Halifax, N.S., Can., 1978; Dr. (hon.), Halhousie, Halifax, N.S., Can., 1985, SUNY, Utica, 1990, Stevens Inst., 1992, Ohio Dominican U., 1998, Kent State U., 2002; Doctorate (hon.), St. Bonaventure U., 2005. Astronaut NASA, 1979—93, mission specialist flight STS-41G, 1984, mission specialist flight STS-31, 1990, payload comdr. flight STS-45, 1992; chief scientist NOAA, Washington, 1993—96; pres., CEO Ctr. Sci. and Industry, Columbus, Ohio, 1996—2005, sci. advisor. Adj. prof. Rice U., Houston, 1985-92, geology, Ohio State U., Columbus, Ohio; mem. Nat. Commn. on Space, 1985-86; mem. exec. panel Chief of Naval Ops., 1988-96; chair, Ohio Aerospace and Defense Adv. Coun., 2003; mem. Nat. Sci. Bd., 2005—; served on Pews Oceans Commn.; advisor, Nat. Geographic, Smithsonian Inst., Pub. TV; bd. dirs. Am. Electric Power. Oceanography officer, Capt. USNR; private pilot. Recipient Space Flight medal NASA, 1984, 90, 92, Exceptional Svc. medal, 1988, 91, Nat. Air and Space Mus. trophy Smithsonian Instn., 1985, Outstanding Leadership medal, 1992, AAS Space Flight Achievement award, 1991, AAS Prather Eva award, 1992, Lone Sailor award, US Navy Meml. Found., 1997, Juliette award for Nat. Women of Distinction, Girl Scouts U.S.A., 2002, Aviation Week & Space Tech. Aerospace Legend award, 2005; named one of Ten Outstanding Young People of the World award, Jaycees Internat., 1987, Ten Outstanding Young Americans award, US Jaycees, 1987; inductee Ohio Veteran's Hall of Fame, 2001, Ohio Women's Hall of Fame, 2002, Astronaut Hall of Fame, 2004. Fellow AAAS; mem. AIAA (Haley Space Flight award, 1991, Legends Aerospace Laureate 2005), Geol. Soc. Am., Am. Geophys. Union, Soc. Women Geographers, Nat. Sci. Bd. (Public Svc. award, 2003), Explorers Club, Woods Hole Oceanographic Institution, Assn. Space Explorers. First Am. woman to walk in space.

SULLIVAN, KATHRYN LYNN, educational association administrator; d. James Norman and Barbara Garrison Kirkland; m. Daniel William Sullivan, Apr. 5, 1980; children: Allison Jin, Ashley Jin. BA, Mich. State U., E. Lansing, 1977; MEd, Fla. Atlantic U., Boca Raton. Tchr. Dekalb County Schs., Decatur, Ga., 1977—79, Sch. Bd. Broward County, Ft. Lauderdale, Fla., 1979—97, curriculum specialist, 1997—2000, asst. prin., 2000—04, intern prin., 2004—. Chair S. Ctrl. Area Asst. Prins., Ft. Lauderdale. Mem.: NASSP, ASCD. Democrat. Episcopal. Home: 6917 NW 65th Ter Parkland FL 33067 Office: Indian Ridge Middle Sch 1334 S Nob Hill Rd Davie FL 33324

SULLIVAN, KATHRYN MEARA, telecommunications industry executive; b. Schenectady, NY, Sept. 20, 1942; d. Vincent Thomas and Agnes (Pendergast) Meara; m. Paul William Sullivan; children: Mary Margaret, Paul Hammond, Patricia Eileen. BS in Physics, Bucknell U., 1964; MBA, Fairleigh Dickinson U., 1981. Software developer GE Corp., Phila., 1964-65; account exec. Honeywell Corp., Phila., 1975-77; regional sales mgr. Nicolet Instrument Corp., Northvale, NJ, 1977-81; mktg. mgr. AT&T, Basking Ridge, NJ, 1981-83, bus. devel. mgr. Berkeley Heights, NJ, 1983-86; pres. AT&T-Pixel Machines, Somerset, NJ, 1986-90; dir. sales ops. and support AT&T Computer Sys., Morristown, NJ, 1990-91, dir. sales transition Parisppany, NJ, 1991-92; dir. info. svcs. AT&T Bus. Comm. Svcs., Parsippany, 1992-93; dir. bus. applications and info. svcs. AT&T, Bedminster, NJ, 1993-95, dir. cross market product mgmt., 1995-96, dir. bus. transformation team, 1997-98, v.p. bus. markets and alliance mgmt. Europe, Mid. East, Africa, 1998—2000. Chairperson career options for women com. YWCA, Plainfield, NJ, 1989-91; bd. dirs. Marco Island Civic Assn., 2003—, treas., 2004, 05; bd. dirs. Marco Island Police Found., 2004—, Citizens for a Better Marco, 2004-05, Marco Island Found. for the Arts, 2005—. Recipient Anthony Gervino award Fairleigh Dickinson U., 1989, Pinnacle award, 1991. Mem. Nat. Computer Graphics Assn. (treas., exec. com. bd. dirs. 1989—). Avocations: reading, travel. Personal E-mail: pandksullivan@yahoo.com.

SULLIVAN, KELLY JONES, critical care nurse, educator; b. Greenwood, S.C., Jan. 13, 1959; d. Adam Crane Jr. and Shelby (Tumblin) Jones; m. Jack Owen Sullivan, Jr., Apr. 30, 1983; children: Adam Jack, Susanna Townes. AS, Lander Coll., Greenwood, 1981, BSN, 1996. RN, S.C. Med.-surg. nurse Self Meml. Hosp., Greenwood, 1981-86; vascular nurse Humana Hosp., Cartersville, Ga., 1986-87; CCU-ICU nurse Anderson (S.C.) Meml. Hosp., 1987-89; ICU nurse Self Meml. Hosp., 1990—; inst. clin. nursing Lander U., 1997—, instr. critical care nursing, 1997—, cardiovascular resource nurse for ICU/CCU, 1997—. Nurse preceptor Self Meml. Hosp., 1997—. Chmn. sch. improvement coun. Ware Shoals (S.C.) Primary Sch., 1995-97; asst. dir. children's choir Ware Shoals First Bapt. Ch., 1996—, mem. properties com., 1993-95. Mem. AACN, Nat. League Nursing, Sigma Theta Tau. Republican. Avocations: reading, piano, sports, exercise. Home: PO Box 65 Ware Shoals SC 29692-0065

SULLIVAN, LAURA ANN, secondary school educator; d. Dwayne and Joyce Sullivan. BS in Fine Arts and Comm., So. Ill. U., Edwardsville, 1991, BS in English, 1995. Cert. secondary edn. Ill. State Bd. Edn. Newspaper adviser Granite City HS, Ill., 2000—, video journalism advisor, 2001—, yearbook adviser, 2005—. Contbr. articles to textbooks. Chairperson union reps. local 743 Ill. Fedn. Tchrs., Granite City, 2000—02, union rep., 1997—2000. Mem.: Quill And Scroll (life). Democrat. Avocations: writing, art, travel, photography. Office: Granite City H S 3101 Madison Ave Granite City IL 62040 Office Phone: 618-451-5808. Business E-Mail: laura.sullivan@gcsd9.net.

SULLIVAN, MARCIA WAITE, lawyer; b. Chgo, Nov. 30, 1950; d. Robert Macke and Jacqueline (Northrop) S.; m. Steven Donald Jansen, Dec. 20, 1975; children: Eric Spurlock, Laura Macke, Brian Northrop. BA, DePauw U., 1972; JD, Ind. U., 1975. Assoc. Arnstein, Gluck, Weitzenfeld & Minow, Chgo., 1975-76; ptnr. Greenberger and Kaufmann, Chgo., 1976-86, Katten Muchin Rosenman LLP, Chgo., 1986—. Adj. prof. Kent Coll. Law, Ill. Inst. Tech., Chgo., 1991—94; pres. Chgo. Real Estate Exec. Women, 2000—01. Mem. editl. adv. bd.: Real Estate Chgo., 2001—02. Mem. NNCREW Found. Grant Making Com, 2003—04. Mem.: ABA, Chgo. Bar Assn. Avocations: bicycling, cross country skiing, gardening, camping. Office: Katten Muchin Rosenman LLP 525 W Monroe St Chicago IL 60661-3693 Office Phone: 312-902-5538. Business E-Mail: marcia.sullivan@kattenlaw.com.

SULLIVAN, MARGARET M., editor; d. John and Elaine (Saab) Sullivan; m. Charles "Bud" Anzalone; children: Alex, Grace. BA in English, Georgetown U., 1979; MS with distinction, Medill Sch. Journalism, Northwestern U., 1980. Clk. Washington bur. Gannett News Svc., 1977—80; Buffalo-area stringer N.Y. Times, 1984—89; reporter, news-feature reporter, columnist Buffalo News, 1980—87, asst. city editor, 1987—89, asst. mng. editor, 1989—98, mng. editor, 1998—99, editor, 1999—. Instr. journalism SUNY, Buffalo, 1991—93. Named One of Buffalo's Outstanding Young Bus. Leaders, Bus. 1st newspaper, 1992; named to Medill Sch. Journalism Hall of Achievement, 2003; recipient Award for Internat. Understanding, Rotary Found., 1987, Young Leadership award, YMCA, 1987. Mem.: Kappa Tau Alpha. Office: Buffalo News The News Plaza Buffalo NY 14203

SULLIVAN, MARGARET M., biologist, educator; d. Charles Watson and Ann McGee McKay; m. Jacob Edwin Sullivan, May 17, 1974 (dec. June 14, 2003); children: Margaret-Ann, Mary-Katherine, Jacob Edwin III. BS, MS, U. Ala., 1973; MEd, Ala. State U., 1991. Cert. tchr. Ala., 1991. Adj. prof. Huntingdon Coll., Montgomery, Ala., 1975—84; tchr. Montgomery Pub. Sch., 1993—2003; adj. prof. Troy U. Montgomery, 1999—; tchr. Elmore County Sch., Millbrook, Ala., 2003—05; biologist Ala. Dept. Environ. Mgmt., 2005—. Dist. trainer Montgomery County Sch., 1997—2002; cons. Ala. Wildlife Fedn., Montgomery, Ala., 2001, Dallas County Sch., Selma, Ala., 2002. Leader Girl Scouts Am., Montgomery, Ala., 1987—97; co-chair Ala. Dance Theatre Com., Montgomery, 1990—2000; v.p. Montgomery Zoo, Ala., 1990—92. Finalist Outstanding Tchr., State Farm, 1999; named Toyota Internat. Tchr., Toyota, USA, 2002, Outstanding Svc. Team leader, Girl Scouts Am., 1992, Outstanding Svc. Team Vol., 1995; recipient Outstanding Environ. Program award, Legacy, Ptnrs. in Environ. Edn., 1998, NSTA/FDA Profl. Devel. Program participant, Nat. Sci. Tchr. Assn., 2003, edn. grant, Ala. Electric Coop., 2004, 2005; fellow Operation Pathfinder, Ala., Miss. Sea Grant, 1995; grantee, Cmty. Found. of Montgomery, 1998—2000, Legacy, Ptnrs. in Environ. Edn., 1999, 2002, America's Unsung Heroes, Star Ins., 2000, Alagasco, 2000, Ala. Power Co., 2001; Eleanor Roosevelt fellow, AAUW, 2002. Mem.: Ala. Sci. Tchr. Assn., Nat. Marine Edn. Assn., Nat. Sci. Tchr. Assn., Delta Kappa Gamma.

SULLIVAN, MARILYN BOBETTE, librarian, consultant; b. Havre, Mont., July 19, 1931; d. Charles Leslie and Alice L. (Wright) Gorman; m. James F. Sullivan, Sept. 25, 1954 (div. Jan. 1983); children: Matthew, Eileen, Andrew. BA, U. Wis., 1953, MLS, 1968. Reference and cataloging libr. med. and dental libr. Marquette U., Milw., 1969-70; head reference libr. Med. Coll. Wis. Librs., Milw., 1970-75, assoc. dir., 1975-81, acting dir., 1982-83; dir. Faculty of Medicine, Kuwait U., Kuwait City, 1981-82, U. Mo. Health Scis. Librs., Kansas City, 1983—2004; libr. dir. Ross U. Sch. Medicine, Commonwealth Dominica, West Indies, 2004—. Cons. Agy. for Internal Devel., Milw. Area Tech. Coll., 1988; cons. Kuwait U. Faculty of Medicine Med. Libr., Kuwait City, 1991—, Kilamanjaro Christian Med. Coll., Moshi, Tanzania, 2002. Author: (with others) Basic Library Management for Health Sciences Librarians, 1982; contbr. articles to profl. jours. Fulbright fellow to Cairo, Egypt, 1992-93. Mem. Med. Libr. Assn. (chair internat. cooperation sect. 1991-92), Med. Libr. Assn. (Disting. Mem. of Acad. Health Info. Profls. 1990), Am. Med. Writers Assn., Sierra Club (newsletter editor 1988-90). Avocation: photography. Home: 828 Monroe St Ne Albuquerque NM 87110-6314 Office: Ross Univ Sch Medicine Commonwealth Dominica West Indies E-mail: msull_has131@hotmail.com.

SULLIVAN, MARY ANN, retired school psychologist; b. Salina, Kans., Feb. 8, 1937; d. Alfred Vesper and Helen Margaret (Bozarth) Haerer; m. Robert Emmett Sullivan, Aug. 29, 1961. BS, U. Nebr., 1959, MEd, 1965, PhD, 1979. Nationally cert. sch. psychologist. Secondary edn. tchr. San Bernardino (Calif.) Pub. Schs., 1959-60; spl. edn. tchr. Lincoln (Nebr.) Pub. Schs., 1960-76, sch. psychologist, 1976-97. Vol. Haydon Art Gallery, Lincoln, 1994-2000, Sheldon Meml. Art Gallery gift shop, Lincoln, 1997-2002; docent, mem. docent coun. Sheldon Meml. Art Gallery and Sculpture Garden, Lincoln, 2003—. Mem. Nebr. Art Assn., Mus. Nebr. Art, Nat. Assn. Sch. Psychologists (state del. 1988-92, co-chair pub. info. com. 1991-93), Nebr. Sch. Psychologists Assn. (pres. 1985-86, outstanding sch. psychologist 1991, founders award 1994), PEO Roundtable of Lincoln (pres. 1976-77), PEO (Nebr. chpt. pres. 1968-69, 81-82, Nebr. chpt. corr. sec. 2002-04, v.p. 2005-06). Avocations: skiing, sailing, hiking, walking, art. Home: 2530 Ridge Rd Lincoln NE 68512-2418

SULLIVAN, MARY ANN, writer, marketing professional; b. Springfield, Mass., Dec. 1, 1954; d. John J. and Clara (Amaral) S. BA in English, Framingham State Coll., 1982; MFA in Writing, Norwich U./Vt. Coll., Montpelier, 1986. English prof. Springfield Tech. C.C., 1986-88; Cistercian nun Trappistines, Wrentham, Mass., 1988-90; Dominican nun Dominican Nuns of Perpetual Rosary, Fatima, Portugal, 1992-96; pub. rels. supr. Blue Army, Washington, N.J., 1996-98, mktg. mgr., 1998-2000; freelance writer nat. and internat. Cath. mags. and newspapers, 1996—; owner GetSaint.com, 2000—. Author: Child of War, 1984 (Notable Book in Social Studies 1985)l editor: Blessed Margaret of Castello, 1997; author articles. Mem. Sisters in Crime, Cath. Press Assn. (assoc.; 1st place for best headline award 1998). Republican. Avocations: reading mysteries, swimming, speaking portuguese, travel. Address: PO Box 375 New Durham NH 03855-0375 E-mail: sullivan@getsaint.com.

SULLIVAN, MARY ANN, artist; b. Columbus, Ohio, June 17, 1952; d. Thomas Joseph and Mary Jane (neeHouck) Sullivan; 1 child, Benjamin James. BFA in Illustration, Columbus Coll. Art and Design, 1974. Designer, illustrator Gibson Greeting Cards, Cin., 1974—78; freelance comml. artist Artwear, Albuquerque, 1984—90; exhibiting fine artist Fine Arts Ctr. En Taos, Taos, N.Mex., 1984—86, Spangler Cummings Gallery, Columbus, 1984—88, El Taller Gallery, Taos, N.Mex., 1984—94, Roberta Kuhn Gallery, Columbus, 1988—92, various galleries, 1992—. Songs of the Earth, 1976, one-woman shows include El Taller Gallery, N. Mex., 1988, 1990, Wilmington Coll., 2001, exhibited in group shows at Ohio State Fair, 1974—2001, Spangler Cummings Gallery, Ohio, Roberta Kuhn Gallery, Grand Ctrl. Galleries, N.Y.C., 1985, Society of Illustrators, NYC, others. Mem.: Ohio Art League. Avocations: books, interior decorating.

SULLIVAN, MARY BROSNAHAN, advocate, social services administrator; m. John Sullivan, Apr. 21, 2001. Degree in Comm., Notre Dame U., 1983. With Universal Studios; press aide 1988 Dem. Presdl. Campaign; joined Coalition for the Homeless, N.Y.C., 1989, exec. dir., 1990—. Recipient Dr. Thomas A. Dooley award, Notre Dame U., 2002. Office: Coalition for the Homeless 129 Fulton St New York NY 10038

SULLIVAN, MARY ROSE, retired English language educator; b. Boston, May 13, 1931; d. John Joseph and Elinor Mary (Crotty) Sullivan BA, Emmanuel Coll., Boston, 1952; MA, Cath. U. Am., 1957; PhD, Boston U., 1964. Tchr. Woburn Pub. Schs., Mass., 1957-60; faculty Emmanuel Coll., Boston, 1960-66; prof. English U. Colo., Denver, 1966-96; ret., 1996. Book reviewing staff San Diego Mag., 1980—90. Author: Browning's Voices in the Ring and the Book, 1969; co-editor: (3 vols.) letters of E.B. Browning to M.R. Mitford, 1836-54, 1983, Women of Letters: Selected Letters of E.B. Browning to M.R. Mitford, 1987, Crime Classics, 1990, Elizabeth Barrett Browning: Selected Poetry and Prose, 1993; editl. bd. English Lang. Notes, 1970-96. Served to capt. USNR, 1952—83. Am. Coun. Learned Socs. fellow, 1973. Mem. MLA, Boston Browning Soc., Mystery Writers of Am.

SULLIVAN, MIA, special education educator; d. Thomas and Jackie Sullivan; m. Brian Simpson. BS in Liberal Studies, Longwood Coll., Farmville, Va., 2001; MSc in Spl. Edn., Longwood U., 2003. Spl. edn. tchr. Prince William County Pub. Sch., Woodbridge, Va., 2003—. Mem. Prince William County Va. Edn. Assn., Manassas, Va., 2003—; mem. beville mid. sch. adv. coun. Prince William County Pub. Sch., Woodbridge, Va., 2004—. Sorority educator adv. Alpha Sigma Tau: Zeta Tau, Farmville, Va., 2002—03. Office: Stuart M Beville Mid Sch (PWCS) 4901 Dale Blvd Woodbridge VA 22193 Office Phone: 703-878-2593.

SULLIVAN, PATRICE M., artist, educator; b. Portland, Oreg., Aug. 25, 1953; d. John Joseph and Mryna Jean Sullivan. BFA, Mass. Coll. Art, 1983; MFA, U. Pa., Phila., 1986. Lectr. Harvard U., Cambridge, Mass., 1988; prof. Colo. State U., Ft. Collins, 1991—. Adv. bd., curriculum com. Colo. State U., Ft. Collins. Home: PO Box 974 Estes Park CO 80517 Office: Art Dept Colo State Univ Fort Collins CO 80523

SULLIVAN, PATRICIA A., academic administrator; b. S.I. m. Charles Sullivan. AB cum laude, St. John's U., 1961; MS in Biology, NYU, 1964, PhD in Biology, 1967. Tchg. fellow, NIH pre-doctoral fellow NYU; post-doctoral fellow in cell biology Upstate Med. Ctr., Syracuse, NY; vis. fellow Cornell U., 1976; tchr. Wells Coll., NY; dir. biology honors program Tex. Woman's U., 1979-81; dean Salem Coll., Winston-Salem, 1981-87; v.p. acad. affairs Tex. Woman's U., 1987-94, interim pres., 1993-94; chancellor U. N.C., Greensboro, 1995—. Pres. Assn. Tex. Colls. and Univs. Acad. Affairs Officers, Assn. So. Colls. for Women, N.C. Assn. Chief Acad. Officers; active numerous coms. Tex. Higher Edn. Coordinating Bd.; lectr. in field. Contbr. articles to profl. jours. Office: U NC at Greensboro Office of Chancellor PO Box 26170 Greensboro NC 27402-6170

SULLIVAN, PEGGY, librarian, consultant; b. Kansas City, Mo., Aug. 12, 1929; d. Michael C. and Ella (O'Donnell) Sullivan. AB, Clarke Coll., 1950; MS in Libr. Sci., Cath. U. Am., 1953; PhD, U. Chgo., 1972. Children's pub. libr., Mo., Md., Va., 1952-61; sch. libr. specialist Montgomery County (Md.) Pub. Schs., 1961-63; dir. Jr. Coll. Libr. Info. Ctr., 1968-69; asst. prof. U. Pitts., 1971-73; dir. Office for Libr. Pers. Resources, ALA, Chgo., 1973-74; dean of students, assoc. prof. Grad. Libr. Sch., U. Chgo., 1974-77; asst. commr. for ext. svcs. Chgo. Pub. Libr., 1977-81; dean Coll. Profl. Studies, No. Ill. U., DeKalb, 1981-90; dir. univ. librs. No. Ill. U., 1990-92; exec. dir. ALA, 1992-94; assoc. Tuft & Assocs., 1995-98; dean Grad. Sch. Libr. and Info. Sci. Rosary Coll., 1995-97. Instr. grad. libr. edn. programs, 1958-73, UNESCO cons. on sch. librs., Australia, 1970; trustee Clarke Coll., 1969-72; sr. ptnr. Able Cons., 1987-92; cons. in field. Author: The O'Donnells, 1956, Many Names for Eileen, 1969, Problems in School Media Management, 1971, Carl H. Milam and the American Library Association, 1976, Opportunities in Library and Information Science, 1977, Realization: The Final Report of the Knapp School Libraries Project, 1968; co-author: Public Libraries: Smart Practices in Personnel, 1982. Mem.: ALA (dir. Knapp Sch. libr. project 1963—68), Ill. Libr. Assn., Cath. Libr. Assn., Caxton Club, Chgo. Lit. Club. Roman Catholic. Home and Office: 2800 N Lake Shore Dr Apt 816 Chicago IL 60657-6266 Office Phone: 773-549-5361. Business E-Mail: pslibcon@alumni.uchicago.edu.

SULLIVAN, PENELOPE DIETZ, computer software development company executive; b. Roanoke, Va., Dec. 29, 1939; d. Joseph Budding and Katherine Dietz; m. Thomas F. Sullivan, Sept. 7, 1963 (div. Mar. 1975); children: Courtney, Todd; m. Paul B. Hill, Mar. 31, 1990. BA, Colby Coll., 1961. Claims examiner Blue Cross/Blue Shield of D.C., Washington, 1961-66; self employed maker slipcovers and upholstery Springfield, Va., 1966-75; ins. sales Met. Life Ins. Co., Arlington, Va., 1975-76, Med. Pers. Pool Inc., Alexandria, Va., 1976-77; mktg. rep. IBM Corp., Washington, 1977-88, program mgr. Advanced Workstations Somers, N.Y., 1988-92; sales cons. IBM Open Sys., Washington, 1992-93; co-founder Open Sys. Assocs., Inc., Reston, Va., 1993—2001; v.p. bus. devel., co-founder Guru Networks Inc., 2001—. Avocations: golf, skiing, gardening, renovating houses. Office: 4100 Lafayette Ctr Chantilly VA 20151 Office Phone: 703-961-1405. Business E-Mail: penny@gurunet.net.

SULLIVAN, RUTH ANNE, librarian; b. Portland, Maine, Jan. 15, 1955; d. Lawrence P. and Mary Louise (Gilman) S.; m. Charles H. Sullivan, May 1, 1982; children: Nora J., Ian J. BA, Wheaton Coll., 1979; MLS, U. Ariz., 1980. Serials ref. Mass. Bay Community Coll., Wellesley, 1980-81; asst. dir. Bristol Community Coll., Fall River, Mass., 1981-86, chief libr., 1986—. Office: Bristol Community Coll 777 Elsbree St Fall River MA 02720-7307

SULLIVAN, SISTER SHARON, education educator; b. Austin, Tex., Sept. 22, 1947; d. Jack Davis and Jane Shelby (Strickland) S. AA with honors, Columbia (Mo.) Coll., 1967; BA in History, Maryville Coll., 1969; cert. elem. edn., spl. edn., Brescia Coll., 1975; MA in Edn., Western Ky. U., 1982; postgrad., U. No. Colo., 1987-88; PhD in Spl. Edn., Purdue U., 1993. Cert. elem. tchr., spl. edn. tchr., Ky. Office mgr., bookkeeper Jerrico, Inc., Lexington, Ky., 1969-71; program and tng. dir. Pennyroyal coun. Girl Scouts U.S., Owensboro, Ky., 1971-73; village leader, program dir., asst. dir. Camp Kysoc, Ky. Easter Seal Soc., Louisville, 1974-77; tchr. learning disabilities resource rm. Daviess County Bd. Edn., Owensboro, 1975-82; pastoral care Mt. St. Joseph Ursulines, Maple Mount, Ky., 1983-84; faculty Brescia Coll., Owensboro, 1987—. Diagnostician Brescia Coll. Ednl. Testing Ctr., Owensboro, 1985—, coord. summer tutoring, 1985-90, faculty 7th grad coll. experience, 1988-90; presenter State Literacy Coun., 1986-88, Internat. Coun. for Exceptional Children, 1991, 92, Nat. Learning Disability Assn. Am., 1992; asst. to editors Learning Disabilities Rsch. and Practice, 1991-92; instr. Purdue U., 1990-91, 92-93. Participant Diocesan Choir, Owensboro, 1986-90; del. governing body Chpt. in Progress, Maple Mount, Ky., 1988—; trainer, vol. Girl Scouts U.S., Owensboro, 1973—; instr. ARC, Owensboro, 1973-85; election official County Clk., Owensboro, 1973-81. Recipient Teaching Excellence award Alpha Chi, 1989; Presvc. Learning Strategies grantee Ky. Dept. Edn., 1988; Trustee's scholar Christian Coll., 1965. Mem. Coun. for Exceptional Children (pres. 1989-90), Coun. for Learning Disabilies, Ky. Assn. of Children with Learning Disabilities. Roman Catholic. Avocations: walking, reading, photography, biking, camping.

SULLIVAN, SHIRLEY ROSS (SHIRLEY ROSS DAVIS), art appraiser; b. Berkeley, Calif. d. Edwin M. Ross; m. George Freeborn (dec.); children: George, Tita, Nelly, Mary; m. Thomas Davis (dec.); m. Charles Sullivan, Sept. 6, 1997. Interior designer, Woodside, Calif., 1963-90. Tchr., lectr., Woodside, 1965-70; art collector, Woodside and San Francisco, 1968—. Trustee San Francisco Mus. Modern Art, 1986—; pres. Collectors' Art Forum, San Francisco, 1983-85; mem. collectors' com. Nat. Gallery Art, 1998—. Office: ICMS 790 Laurel St San Carlos CA 94070-3164

SULLIVAN, TERESA ANN, law and sociology educator, academic administrator; b. Kewanee, Ill., July 9, 1949; d. Gordon Hager and Mary Elizabeth (Finnegan) S.; m. H. Douglas Laycock, June 14, 1971; children: Joseph Peter, John Patrick. BA, Mich. State U., 1970; MA, U. Chgo., 1972, PhD, 1975. Asst. prof. sociology U. Tex., Austin, 1975-76, assoc. prof. sociology, 1981-87, dir. women's studies, 1985-87, prof. sociology, 1987—, prof. law, 1988—, assoc. dean grad. sch., 1989-90, 1992-95, chair dept. sociology, 1990-92, vice provost, 1994-95, v.p., grad. dean, 1995—2002; asst. prof. sociology U. Chgo., 1977-81; exec. vice-chancellor acad. affairs U. Tex. Sys., 2002—06; provost, exec. v.p. academic affairs U. Mich., Ann Arbor, 2006—. Pres. Southwestern Sociol. Assn., 1988-89; mem. faculty adv. bd. Hogg Found. Mental Health, 1989-92; mem. sociology panel NSF, 1983-85. Author: Marginal Workers Marginal Jobs, 1978; co-author: As We Forgive Our Debtors, 1989 (Silver Gavel 1990), Social Organization of Work, 1990, 2d edit. 1995; co-author: The Fragile Middle Class, 2000; contbr. articles and chpts. to profl. jours. Bd. dirs. Calvert Found., Chgo., 1978, CARA, Inc., Washington, 1985; mem. U.S. Census Bur. Adv. Com., 1989-95, chmn., 1991-92; mem. sociology panel NSF, 1983-85; trustee St. Michael's Acad., 1996-2001. Leadership Tex. 1994. Fellow AAAS (liaison to Population Assn. Am. 1989-91, chair sect. K 1996), Sociol. Rsch. Assn., Am. Sociol. Assn. (sec. 1995—, editor Rose Monograph Series 1988-92), Philos. Soc. Tex., Soc. Study of Social Problems (chair fin. com. 1986-87), Population Assn. Am. (bd. dirs. 1989-91, chair fin. com. 1990-91), Assn. Grad. Schs. (pres. 2001-2002). Roman Catholic. Avocation: reading. Office: 503 Thompson St Ann Arbor MI 48109-1340 Home: 2197 Gray Fox Ct Ann Arbor MI 48103 Office Phone: 734-764-9292. Business E-Mail: tsull@umich.edu.

SULLIVAN, TERRI, newscaster, reporter; married. BS in Broadcast Journalism, Boston U. With Sta. WBNS-TV, Columbus, Ohio, WNBC-TV, N.Y.C.; anchor, reporter Sta. WRKL, Sta. WSYX-WTTE-TV, Columbus, 1993—; anchor Sta. QJZA-FM, 1997—. Office: WSYX/WTTE-TV 1261 Dublin Rd Columbus OH 43215

SULLIVAN, TRUDY F., apparel executive; Buyer Jordan Marsh; mgmt. positions with The Avenue, Decelle, T. Deane, Filene's; pres. J. Crew Group Inc., 1997—2001; group pres. Liz Claiborne casual & Liz Claiborne woman Liz Claiborne Inc., NYC, 2001—02, exec. v.p., 2002—06, pres., 2006—. Office: Liz Claiborne Inc 1441 Broadway New York NY 10018*

SULLIVAN-SCHWEBKE, KAREN JANE, lawyer; b. Spokane, Wash., Feb. 25, 1955; d. John and Helen (Bartlett) Sullivan; m. Ethan K. Schwebke, Apr. 18, 1987; children: Noah, Eli. BA, U. Wash., 1978, MBA, JD, 1987. Exec. asst. to corp. controller Pay'n Save Corp., Seattle, 1980-83; tchg. asst. U. Wash. Coll. Bus., Seattle, 1984-85; law clk. Bogle & Gates Law Firm, Seattle, 1985, PACCAR, Inc., Bellevue, Wash., 1986, U. Wash. Law Sch., Seattle, 1987; dir. Boys and Girls Club Puget Sound, Everett, Wash., 1988-90; legal counsel Fla. State Human Rights Commn., 1995-97; exec. dir. Benton and Franklin Counties Wash. State Family Policy Coun., Kennewick, 1997-99; exec. dir., legal coun., CFO Mid-Columbia Regional Symphony and Ballet, Richland, Wash., 1999—2003; owner Art, History, Architecture Tours of Centennial Kennewick, 2003—. Author: Guide to Centennial Kennewick, 2003. Chair Civil Svc. Commn., 1998-2003; mem. City Hist. Preservation Commn., 2003—; mem., chair City Centennial Commn., 2003-04; mem. Leadership Tri-Cities Class 2001; bd. dirs. Women Helping Women Fund, 2001, Richland Opera Co., 2001-03 Mem. NOW, Kappa Delta, U. Wash. Alumnae Assn. (dist. gov.), Rotary, DOVIA. Democrat. Avocations: reading, painting, interior decorating, gardening. Home: 2001 S Newport St Kennewick WA 99337-7811 Office Phone: 509-582-2732. E-mail: schweet4@msn.com.

SULLIVAN STEMBERG, MAUREEN, interior designer; b. Brookline, Mass., July 8, 1951; d. Loretta McDermott and Herbert Michael Sullivan; m. Thomas George Stemberg, Mar. 11, 1975 (div. Sept. 0, 1989). AA in polit. sci., Newton Jr. Coll., 1969—71; degree in art history, Boston Coll., 1972—73; Fine Arts Program, Mus. of Fine Arts Sch., 1973—75; Architecture and Design, Boston Ctr. of Architecture, 1982—85. ASID, MA, 1987. CEO, interior designer Interiors of Wellesley, Inc., Wellesley, Mass., 1977—80; CEO, head designer Maureen Sullivan Stemberg Interiors, Boston-Palm Beach, 1980—98; design and fashion editor Palm Beach Illus., Palm Beach, Fla., 1990—95; CEO BabySuites.Com, Boston, 2003—04; chief creative officer Connoisseur Pub., Inc., Boston, 2004—. Chmn. and co-chairman, ann. flower show Mass. Hort. Soc., Boston, 1990—94. Designer Mahaney Baseball Club House, U. Maine (Top 5 Design winner for Baseball Complex Devel., 1994), Various Hotel Interiors (Top 20 Hotel Designers for Holiday Inns Inc., 1991), Trump Plaza, other Club Colette, Palm Beach, Fla.; contbr. articles to mag. Fund raiser Barcelona Summer Olympics, Mass., Spain, 1990—92, Am. Cup, Boston, 1993—95; trustee Boston Opera Co., 1977—81. Mem.: United Way of Mass. Bay, Nat. Trust for Hist. Preservation, Dana Farber Cancer Inst. Pediat. (hon.; dir. 1996—97), Nat. Musuem of Women in the Arts (hon.; coun. mem. 1991—93), Am. Soc. of Interior Designers (assoc.). Home: 118 Huntington Ave Ste 1403 Boston MA 02116 Office Phone: 617-266-5664. E-mail: maureen@connoiseurpublishing.com, intdesignmss@aol.com.

SULLIVAN-SZUTS, BETTY ANNE, academic administrator, educator; b. Phila., Dec. 23, 1939; d. Rowland Thomas and Elizabeth Catherine Moriarty; m. Robert Lloyd Sullivan, Sept. 21, 1957 (div.); children: Lisa Anne Sullivan, Brent Rowland Sullivan, Jamie Alexandra Sullivan; m. Ivan Ramon Szuts, May 6, 1995. BS in Home Econs. Edn., Douglass Coll., 1975; EdM in Supervision and Adminstrn., Rutgers U., 1978, EdD in Adult and Continuing Ednl. Adminstrn., 1989. Cert. sch. adminstr. N.J., prin./supr. N.J., tchr. home econs. N.J. Tchr. home econs. Freehold Regional H.S. Dist., NJ, 1975—80; state supr. home econs. edn. N.J. State Dept. Edn., Trenton, 1980—81; dir. and tchr. in-svc. Rutgers U., New Brunswick, NJ, 1981—89; vice prin. Monmouth County Vo-Tech H.S. Dist., Middletown, NJ, 1990—91; dir. Suffolk County Respite Care Program, Patchogue, NY, 1991—94; dir. gerontology program and instr. aging courses Union County Coll., Cranford, NJ, 1994—96; supr. student tchrs. Georgian Ct. Coll., Lakewood, NJ, 1994—96; vis. prof. dept. sociology Wheaton Coll., Norton, Mass., 1996—97; dir. model Tex. safe home program N.W. Assistance Ministries, Houston, 2000—02; grant coord. N. Harris Coll., 2002—03; seminar leader Spirited Elder and Assocs. Adj. prof. profl. studies grad. program LI U., Southampton, NY, 1991—94; rschr. Aging Tex. Well Coalition, 2002—; seminar leader Spirited Elder and Assocs., 2004—; presenter in field. Author: Spiritual Elders: Women of Worth in the Third Millennium, 1999. Chair edn. Harris County Area Agy. Aging, tng. com.; chair adv. bd. Acad. Lifelong Learning, North Harris Coll.; mem. Acts 16:5 task force Presbytery New Covenant, Houston; ruling elder North Woods Presbyn. Ch., 2006—. Recipient Cmty. Svc. award, North Harris Coll., 2003; grantee The Aging Tex. Well Grant, 2002—03. Mem.: Phi Delta Kappa, Kappa Delta Pi, Omicron Nu. Avocations: tennis, ballroom dancing, writing, playing the organ. Home and Office: Spirited Elder and Assocs 14311 Champions Dr Houston TX 77069 Office Phone: 281-895-0321. Personal E-mail: bettyanne.ivan@sbcglobal.net.

SULTAN, ALTOON, artist; b. Bklyn., Sept. 29, 1948; BFA, Bklyn. Coll., 1969, MFA in Painting, 1971; student, Skowhegan Art Sch., Maine, 1970. Vis. critic Univ. Pa., Phila., 1985—88; resident faculty Skowhegan Sch. Painting & Sculpture, Maine, 1988; asst. prof. San Jose State Univ., Calif., 1991—94; vis. prof. Dartmouth Coll., NH, 1998—2001; founder Mount Ara Designs, Groton, Vt. Author: The Luminous Brush: Painting with Egg Tempera, 1999; one-woman shows include First St. Gallery, NYC, 1971, 1973, 1975, Univ. SD, Vermillion, 1975, Marlborough Gallery, NYC, 1977, 1979, 1982, 1984, 1985, 1988, 1990, 1993, 1995, 1998, Marlborough Fine Art Graphics, London, 1987, Galleria Marieschi, Monza, Italy, 1999, Tibor de Nagy Gallery, NYC, 2001, exhibited in group shows at Suffolk Mus., Stony

Brook, NY, 1971, Allan Frumkin Gallery, NYC, 1975, Davis & Long Gallery, 1977, Thorpe Intermedia Gallery, Sparkill, NY, 1980, Downtown Br., Whitney Mus., NYC, 1982, Mus. Fine Arts, Boston, 1982, One Penn Plaza, NYC, 1985, Veranneman Found., Belgium, 1986, David Adamson Gallery, Washington, 1988, Flint Inst. of Arts, Mich., 1991, Am. Acad. and Inst. of Arts & Letters, NYC, 1992, Sleeth Gallery, W. Va. Wesleyan Coll., 1996, numerous others. Recipient Prix Duc de Valverde d'Ayala Valva, Fondation Monaco, 1999, Acad. award in art for egg tempera painting, Am. Acad. Arts and Letters, 1999; grantee Nat. Endowment for Arts, 1983, 1989. Mem.: NAD (academician 1995—). Studio: PO Box 2 Groton VT 05046 Office: Tibor de Nagy Gallery 724 Fifth Ave New York NY 10019

SULTAN, WAFA, psychiatrist; b. Baniyas, Syria, 1958; arrived in US, 1989, naturalized; m. David Sultan; 3 children. MD, Aleppo Univ., Syria. Lic. CA. Named one of 100 Most Influential People in World, Time Mag., 2006. Outspoken critic of violence in Muslim world saying violence destroys Islam. Home: Los Angeles CA*

SULZBACH, CHRISTI ROCOVICH, lawyer; b. L.A. BA, U. So. Calif., 1976; JD, Loyola U., 1979. Bar: Calif., 1980. Various to assoc. gen. counsel Tenet Healthcare Corp., Santa Barbara, Calif., 1983-99, exec. v.p., gen. counsel, 1999—2002, chief corp. officer, gen. counsel, 2002—. Mem. State Bar of Calif., ABA, FBA (bd. dirs. L.A. chpt.), Fedn. Am. Health Sys. (bd. dirs.), corp. adv. bd., U.S.C. Marshall Sch. Bus.

SUMLIN, MARGARET BROWN, special education educator; b. Ann Arbor, Mich., Nov. 2, 1950; d. Willis Radcliff and Eulalie (Draughon) Brown. BS, U. Ala., 1972; MA, U. South Ala., 1976. Cert. spl. edn. tchr., Ala. Spl. edn. tchr. Morningside Elem. Sch., Tuscaloosa, Ala., 1972-73; spl. edn. tchr., community coord. A.P. Brewer Developmental Ctr., Mobile, Ala., 1973-75; spl. edn. tchr. Crichton Elem. Sch., Mobile, 1975-77, Scarborough Mid. Sch., Mobile, 1977-82, Cornerstone Group Home, Mobile, 1982; spl. edn. tchr., edn. coord. Brookwood Recovery Ctr., Mobile, 1984-90, Wilmer Hall Children's Home, Mobile, 1991, art therapy tchr., 1991—92; spl. edn. coord., tchr. The Murray Sch. at Wilmer Hall, Mobile, 1992—2002, prin., spl. edn. coord., 2003—. Ednl. cons. Parkside Recovery Ctr., Mobile, 1989-90; art therapy coord. Wilmer Hall Children's Home, 1991—; founder, organizer Friends of Wilmer Hall, 1992—. Author: (program model) Classroom Structure for Emotionally Disturbed Students, 1984. Bd. dirs. Women of Ch., St. Paul Ch., Mobile, 1991—, Mobile Pub. Libr., 1992—; vol. fundraiser Am. Cancer Soc., 1992; vol. tutor Project Hope Group Home, 1974, Rotary Rehab. Ctr., 1976; vol. coord. Vol. Mobile, 1982, Mobile County Sch. System, 1984; bd. dirs. Cornerstone Group Home (pres. 1985-86); vol. Mobile Pre-Sch. for the Deaf, 1979, Rotary Rehab. Ctr. In-Patient Svcs., 1977. Named a Point of Light by Pres. George Bush, 1991. Mem. Jr. League of Mobile (vol. fundraiser 1990-91). Episcopalian. Avocations: reading, hand sewing, beach activities. Office: Wilmer Hall Childrens Home Old Shell Rd Mobile AL 36608

SUMMAR, SHARON KAY, retired elementary school educator; b. Decatur, Ill., Jan. 27, 1948; d. Robert Dean and Leola (Warren) S. BS in Edn., Ill. State U., 1970, MS in Math., 1988. Tchr., computer coord. Green Valley Grade Sch., Ill., 1970-91; tchr. Midwest Cent. Primary Sch., 1991—2004; ret., 2004. Tchr. asst. U. Ill., Urbana, 1986. Mem. Nat. Coun. Tchr. Math., Ill. Coun. Tchr. Math. Avocations: computer programming, stamp collecting/philately, reading. E-mail: ssummar@ntslink.net.

SUMMER, DONNA (LA DONNA ADRIAN GAINES), singer, songwriter, actress; b. Boston, Dec. 31, 1948; d. Andrew and Mary Gaines; m. Helmut Sommer (div.); 1 child, Mimi; m. Bruce Sudano; children: Brooklyn, Amanda. Has sold over 20 million records. Singer, 1967—; actress: (German stage prodn.) Hair, 1967-75, (Vienna Folk Opera prodns.) Porgy and Bess, (German prodns.) The Me Nobody Knows, (cable TV spl.) Donna Summer Special, 1980; recorded albums including The Wanderer, Star Collection, Love To Love You Baby, Love Trilogy, Four Seasons of Love, I Remember Yesterday, The Deep, Shut Out, Once Upon A Time, Bad Girls, On The Radio, Walk Away, She Works Hard For The Money, Cats Without Claws, All Systems Go, 1988, Another Place and Time, 1989, Mistaken Identity, 1991, Endless Summer, 1994, Christmas Spirit, 1994, I'm a Rainbow, 1996, Live & More Encore, 1999; subject My Life VH1 Concert, 1999; recorded theme song for Hunchback of Notre Dame, Disney; forerunner of disco style. Named Best Rhythm and Blues Female Vocalist, Nat. Acad. Rec. Arts and Scis., 1978, Best Female Rock Vocalist, 1979, Favorite Female Pop Vocalist, Am. Music Awards, 1979, Favorite Female Vocalist of Soul Music, 1979, Soul Artist of Yr., Rolling Stone mag., 1979; recipient Best Favorite Pop Single award, 1979, Best-selling Black Music Album for Female Artist award Nat. Assn. Record Merchandizers, 1979, Ampex Golden Reel award for album On the Radio, 1979, Best-selling Album for Female Artist, 1980, Ampex Golden Reel award for single On the Radio, 1980, Ampex Golden Reel award for album Bad Girls, Best of Las Vegas Jimmy award for best rock performance, 1980, Grammy award for best inspirational performance, 1984. Office: 2401 Main St Santa Monica CA 90405-3515

SUMMER, SHARON, marketing professional, former publisher; Nat. ad. dir. American Baby, 1989—91, pub., 1996—97; group pub. Parents Mag., Child Mag. & The Newborn Group, N.Y.C., 1997—2001; pub. Rosie Magazine, 2001, Parents Family Network, 2001—02; sr. v.p. Moda Internat. Mktg., 2003—. Office: Moda Internat Mktg 441 Lexington Ave Ste 1408 New York NY 10017

SUMMERHILL, ELAINE, music educator; BS in Music Edn., Duquesne U., Pitts., 1977; MA in Music Edn., U. South Fla., Tampa, 1997. Cert. tchr. Fla., 1980, music/early & middle childhood NBPTS Nat. Bd. Profl. Tchg. Standards, 2004. Tchr. music Woodland Elem., Zephyrhills, Fla., 1984—. Pvt. piano tchr., Zephyrhills, 1984—. Ch. organist. Mem.: Music Educators Nat. Conf., Pi Lambda Theta, Delta Kappa Gamma, Fla. Vocal Assn., Fla. Music Educators Assn. Avocations: reading, travel, bicycling. Home: 34632 Morning Glory Glen Zephyrhills FL 33541 Office: Woodland Elem 38203 Henry Dr Zephyrhills FL 33542 Office Phone: 813-794-6400. Personal E-mail: elainehill@aol.com.

SUMMERS, ANITA ARROW, finance educator; b. NYC, Sept. 9, 1925; d. Harry I. and Lillian (Greenberg) Arrow; m. Robert Summers, Mar. 29, 1953; children: Lawrence H., Richard F., John S. BA, Hunter Coll., 1945, DHL (hon.), 1995; MA, U. Chgo., 1947. Sr. econ. analyst Standard Oil Co. N.J., N.Y.C., 1947-54; asst. in econs. Yale U., New Haven, 1956-59; lectr. dept. econs. Swarthmore (Pa.) Coll., 1965-71; sr. economist Fed. Res. Bank Phila., 1971-75, research officer, 1975-79; adj. prof. pub. policy U. Pa., Phila., 1979-82, prof. pub. policy and mgmt., 1982—, dept. chair, 1983-88, univ. ombudsman, 2001—03, co-dir Wharton Urban Decentralization Project, 1987-97, dir. rsch. Wharton Real Estate Ctr., 2003—, sr. scholar Nat. Ctr. on the Edn. Quality of the Workforce, 1991—95. Expert witness schs. fin. Md., Mass., Va., 1980-85, Md., Va., 1996, Calif., 2003, bd. dirs. William Penn Found., Phila., 1993-98; chair bd. dirs. Mathematica Policy Rsch., Inc., Princeton, N.J., 1993—. Author: Economic Report on the Philadelphia Metropolitan Area, 1985, Economic Development within the Philadelphia Metropolitan Area, 1986, Local Fiscal Issues in the Philadelphia Metropolitan Area, 1987; editor: Urban Change in the United States and Western Europe, 1992, 99; contbr. articles to profl. jours. Chair econ. subcom. Pa. Three Mile Island Commn., Harrisburg, 1979; pres. Lower Merion (Pa.) LWV, 1963-65; mem. Mayor's Econ. Roundtable, Phila., 1984-88; mem. rsch. policy coun., 1992-94, Com. for Econ. Devel. Rockefeller Found. resident scholar, Bellagio, Italy, 1986. Mem. Am. Econ. Assn., Assn. for Pub. Policy and Mgmt. (policy coun. 1986), Phi Beta Kappa. Avocations: needlepoint, cooking. Home: 1400 Waverly Rd V-11 Gladwyne PA 19035-1271 Office: U Pa Wharton Sch Dept Pub Policy and Mgmt Philadelphia PA 19104 Office Phone: 215-898-4076. Business E-Mail: summers@wharton.upenn.edu.

SUMMERS, CATHLEEN, film producer; b. Chgo. d. Paul and Elizabeth Summers; m. Patrick Crowley. BA, U. So. Calif., 1973. Film editor, comml. producer, dir.'s asst. Roman Polanski, Rome, 1972; story editor Albert S. Ruddy Prodns. Paramount Pictures, L.A., 1973-74; exec. asst. Columbia Pictures, Burbank, Calif., 1974, story editor, 1974-76; devel. exec., v.p., producer Martin Ransohoff Prodns. Columbia Pictures, 1976; sr. v.p. Tri-Star Pictures, Century City, Calif., 1984-87; motion picture producer Cathleen Summers Prodns., L.A., 1989—; ptnr. ESN, Film Prodn. Resource Co.; cons., ptnr. Estudio Network. Motion picture producer, ptnr. Summers-Kouf Prodns., Burbank, 1986-87; motion picture producer Cathleen Summers Prodns., L.A., 1987, Summers-Quaid Prodns., Century City, Culver City, Calif., 1988—. Producer: (motion picture) Stakeout, 1987, DOA, 1991, Vital Signs, 1990, Mystery Date, 1991, Dogfight, 1991, The Sandlot, 1993, Stakeout II, 1993; exec. prodr. Derivations, Who New/The Real Deal, 2003. Co-founder Diane Thomas Scholarship, UCLA, 1988—; bd. dirs. L.A. chpt. Nat. Parkinsons Found.; founding bd. dirs. U.S. Comedy Arts Festival, Aspen, Colo. Mem. Am. Film Inst. (pres. 3d Decade Coun. 1995, 96, 97). Personal E-mail: july4bu@charter.net.

SUMMERS, DEBRA S., lawyer; BS magna cum laude, West Tex. State U., 1974; JD magna cum laude, U. San Francisco, 1980. Extern for Justice Matthew O. Tobriner Calif. Supreme Ct., 1980; with Wilson Sonsini Goodrich & Rosati, Palo Alto, Calif., 1983—, ptnr., chmn. real estate/environ. law dept. Adj. prof. U. Calif. Berkeley. Co-author: Office Leasing, Drafting, & Negotiating the Lease. Mem.: Calif. State Bar Assn. Office: Wilson Sonsini Goodrich & Rosati 650 Page Mill Rd Palo Alto CA 94304-1050 Office Phone: 650-493-4343. Office Fax: 650-493-6811. Business E-Mail: debrasummers@wsgr.com.

SUMMERS, JANE PFEIFER, realtor; b. Seward, Nebr., Aug. 19, 1951; d. George Henry and Mildred (Jensen) Miller; m. Robert Charles Summers; 1 child, Anthony Pfeifer. MBA, Chadwick U., 1991. CRS, GRI. Mgr. MIS Lincoln (Nebr.) Tour & Travel, 1973-83; pers. adminstr. Mechanics Wholesale, Denver, 1984-85; v.p. Strategic Mktg. Group, Englewood, Colo., 1985-89; realtor Home Real Estate, Inc., Grand Island, Nebr., 1992-97, Home Real Estate, Lincoln, Nebr., 1998—. Field svc. ARC, Conestoga Ter., 1991-92; chmn. womens div. Lincoln C. of C., 1983. Mem.: Phi Theta Kappa. Home: 3706 S 57th St Lincoln NE 68506-4508 Office: Home Real Estate 225 N Cotner Blvd Lincoln NE 68505 E-mail: summersjanetony@hotmail.com.

SUMMERS, LORRAINE DEY SCHAEFFER, retired librarian; b. Phila., Dec. 14, 1946; d. Joseph William and Hilda Lorraine (Ritchey) Dey; m. F. William Summers, Jan. 28, 1984. BA, Fla. State U., 1968, MS, 1969. Ext. dir. Santa Fe Regional Libr., Gainesville, 1969-71; pub. libr. cons. State Libr. of Fla., Tallahassee, 1971-78, asst. state libr., 1978-84; dir. adminstrv. svcs. Nat. Assn. for Campus Activities, Columbia, SC, 1984-85; asst. state libr. State Libr. of Fla., Tallahassee, 1985—2001, ret., 2001—. Bd. dirs., sec. Southeastern Libr. Network, Inc.; cons. in field. Contbr. articles to profl. jours. Del. Pres.'s Com. on Mental Retardation Regional Forum, Atlanta, 1975; del. Fla. Gov.'s Conf. on Libr. and Info. Svcs., 1978, 90. Mem. ALA (orgn. com. 1979-83, coun. 1982-84, 93-97, resolutions com. 1983-85, mem. legislation com. 1993-95, nominating com. 1996, awards com. 1998-99, Spectrum awards jury 1999-2000), Assn. Specialized and Coop. Libr. Agys. (dir. 1976-82, chmn. planning and orgn. com. 1976-80, chmn. nominating com. 1980-81, chmn. by laws com. 1985-86, exec. bd. state libr. agy. sect. 1983-86, pres. 1987-88, chmn. stds. rev. com. 1990-92), Southeastern Libr. Assn. (exec. bd. 1976-80, v.p., pres.-elect 1994-96, pres. 1996-98, past pres. 1998-2000, nominating com. 2000-02), Fla. Libr. Assn. (sec. 1978-79, dir. 1976-80, nominating com. 1995-96), Zonta (dir. 1992-95, sec. 1999-2001). Democrat. Methodist. Personal E-mail: lorsummers@worldnet.att.net.

SUMMERS, PAMELA FRENCH, literature and language professor, consultant; b. Englewood, N.J., June 18, 1951; d. Donald and LaVerne French; m. Rodger Summers, June 3, 1972; children: Megan K.F., Jordan F. BS cum laude, U. Vt., Burlington, 1973; MS, Ind. U., Bloomington, 1978; EdD, Boston U., 1980. 6th gr. tchr. St. Albans (Vt.) Sch. Dist., 1973—76; 3d gr. tchr. Essex (Vt.) Sch. Dist., Essex, Vt., 1976—77; asst. prof. Mass. Coll. Liberal Arts, North Adams, 1981—84, West Chester (Pa.) U., 1984—91, Binghamton (N.Y.)U., 1991—95; assoc. prof. SUNY, Cartland, 2001—. Cons. in field, NY, 1995—2001; pilot dir. Windsor (N.Y.) Ctrl. Sch., 1997—2003. Contbr. articles to profl. jours. Bd. trustees N. Adams Pub. Libr., 1982—84; panel mem. N.Y. Coun. Arts, Binghamton, 2002—05; Sunday sch. supt. Main St Bapt. Ch., Binghamton, 2000—. Mem.: Nat. Coun. Tchrs. English, Internat. Reading Assn., Coll. Reading Assn. Democrat. Avocations: reading, music. Office: SUNY Cortland B-100C Van Hoesen Cortland NY 13045 Office Phone: 604-753-2461. Business E-Mail: summersp@cortland.edu.

SUMMERTREE, KATONAH See WINDSOR, PATRICIA

SUMMITT, ALIXANDRA PABLITA, art educator; b. Detroit, Mar. 11, 1943; d. Edmond Walter and Helene Marie (Zapytowski) Greniewicki; m. Hans Peter Jorgensen, July 2, 1964 (div. Mar. 1981); 1 child, Inger Nova. BA, Mich. State U., 1965, MS in Ednl. Systems Devel., 1981, PhD in Adult and Continuing Edn., 1990. Coord. art edn. Bath (Mich.) Consolidated Schs., 1967-68; instr. cmty. svcs. Northwestern Mich. Coll., Traverse City, 1975-78; tchr. art Alan Sch., Lansing, Mich., 1980-81; rsch. asst., dept. Pediat. Mich. State U., East Lansing, 1981-82, supr. media ctr., Coll. Osteo. Medicine, 1982-86; instr. Lansing C.C., 1983—, faculty curriculum rep. Ctr. for Tchg. Excellence, 1996—; CEO Options in Art, East Lansing, 1990—; pres. Alixandra Summit Cons., Inc., Okemos, Mich., 1995—. Art cons. Getty Improving Art Edn. L.A., 1991—; founder The Portwood Inst. Art and Healing; dir. Reiki Master, 1993; mem. Peace Ministry, 2006; ministre Spiritual Peacemaking. Dir. Summitry Prodns., Okemos, 1996—. Charter mem. Mich. Women's Hall Fame and Hist. Ctr., com. chair 1982—, award design 1983; charter mem. Nat. Mus. Women in Arts, 1991-96; precinct del. Nat. Dem. Party, East Lansing, 1980, commr. Lansing Women's Commn., 1984-85, taskforce on women in poverty, 1985; v.p. Mid-Mich. Assn. Woking Artists, Lansing, 1978-79. Mem. Working Women Artists, Connections Collective Women Artists (chair, founder), Phi Delta Kappa (bd. dirs. 1991—, editor 1994, Mich. chpt.) Avocations: gardening, reading, music, walking. Home: 4621 Seneca Dr Okemos MI 48864-1808 Office: Lansing C C 419 N Capitol Ave Lansing MI 48933-1207

SUMMITT, APRIL, history professor; b. Knoxville, Tenn., Apr. 2, 1964; d. Ted E. and Connie L. (Westerberg) Summitt. BA in History and in English, Newbold Coll., 1987; MA in History, Andrews U., 1993; PhD, Western Mich. U., 2002. Adj. instr. Jordan Jr. Coll., Benton Harbor, Mich., 1988-93, Andrews U., 1990-92, asst. prof., 1996—. Doctoral assoc., lectr. Western Mich. U., 1993-96. Sec., bd. dirs. Berrien County Hist. Assn., 1997—. John F. Kennedy Libr. rsch. fellow, 1998. Mem. Am. Hist. Assn., Orgn. Am. Historians, Soc. for Historians of Am. Fgn. Rels., Phi Alpha Theta. Avocations: sailing, poetry, drama, cross country skiing, piano. Office: Andrews U Dept History And Polit Sci Berrien Springs MI 49104-0001 Home: 4150 E Fountain St Mesa AZ 85205-5019

SUMMITT, PATRICIA HEAD, college basketball coach; b. Henrietta, Tenn., June 14, 1952; d. Richard and Hazel Head; m. R.B. Summitt; 1 child, Ross Tyler. BS in Phys. Edn., U. Tenn., Martin, 1974; MS in Phys. Edn., U. Tenn., Knoxville, 1975. Basketball player U. Tenn., Martin, 1970—74, head women's basketball coach Knoxville, 1974—. Head coach 1st U.S. Jr. Nat. team, 1977 (2 gold medals in internat. play), U.S. Nat. team William R. Jones Cup Games, 1979, World Championships, 1979, Pan Am. Games, 1979 (2 gold medals, 1 silver medal); asst. coach U.S. Women's Olympic Basketball team, 1980-84, head coach, 1984 (gold medal); assoc. athletics dir., U. Tenn.; past v.p. USA BASKETBALL; past Olympic rep. adv. com. to USA BASKETBALL; bd. trustees Basketball Hall of Fame; bd. dirs. Women's Basketball Hall of Fame. Active Big Bros./Big Sisters; Active spokesperson United Way, Race for the Cure, Juvenile Diabetes; hon. chair Tenn. Easter Seal Soc., 1985, 87, 88, 89; Tenn. chair Am. Heart Assn., 1994. Named Naismith Coach of Yr., 1987, 1989, 1994, 1997, Naismith Coach of Century, 2000, WBCA/Converse Coach of Yr., 1983—95; named one of Women of Yr., Women in Sports and Events, 1999; named to Women's Sports Foundation Hall of Fame, 1990, Nat. Assn. for Sport and Phys. Edn., 1996, Women's Basketball Hall of Fame, 1999, Basketball Hall of Fame, 2000; recipient silver medal, Olympic Games, 1976, gold medal, Pan Am. Games, 1975, silver medal, U.S. World Univ. Games, 1973, Wooden Award, 1997, ARETE Award for Courage in Sports, 1999. Mem. Chi Omega. Achievements include coach U. Tenn. women's basketball NCAA Championship teams, 1987, 89, 91, 96, 97, 98; coach U. Tenn. women's basketball SEC Championship teams, 1980, 85, 90, 93, 94, 95, 98, 99, 2000, 01, 02, 03; became the all-time winningest coach in NCAA basketball history, March 21, 2005; first female coach ever to win 300 games, 2006.*

SUMMORS, ALMA C., principal; b. Laurel, Miss., Aug. 7, 1948; d. Irene Hampton and Sidney Henderson; m. Glen E. Summors, Mar. 29, 1969; children: Chinwee, Kai Ayana, Obinwa, Glen Jr. MEd, Bank St. Coll., NYC, 1994. Chair, bd. dirs. Chirley Chisholm Day Care Ctr., Bklyn., 1980—94; adminstr. NYC Bd. Edn., Bklyn., 1994—. Founder, chair Sisters In The Spirit, Inc, Bklyn., 2002—; spkr. in field. Recipient Cert. of Achievement, 1994; fellow, NSF, 1992—94; grantee, NY State Dept. Health, 1994—99; scholar, NYC Mayor, 1992—94; State Tech. grant, NY State, 1994, 2002. Mem.: Coun. of Supervisors and Administrators (assoc.). Baptist. Avocations: music, singing, dance. Office Phone: 718-495-7736.

SUMTER, JONI LYNN, political science professor; d. Hershel and Georgia Qualls; m. Kevin Charles Sumter; children: Nolan Thomas, Logan Wesley. BS in Biology and Physiology, Calif. State U., Fresno, 1995. Cert. Tchr. Calif., 1997. Sci. tchr. Calif. U. San Diego, Clovis, 1997—; adj. faculty Calif. State U., Fresno, 2003—06. Office Phone: 559-327-1000.

SUN, NILAJA, playwright, actress; b. NYC; BA, Franklin and Marshall Coll., Pa. HIV educator. Creator and performer (one-woman shows) La Nubia Latina, Black and Blue (Aaron Davis Hall's Fund for New Work, 2000), Insufficient Fare, Babylon, No Child., actress (plays) Santos and Santos, On the Hills of Black America, Antigone-In-Progress, Pieces of the Throne, Time and the Conways, Due To the Tragic Events of., The Cook, 2003. Recipient Princess Grace award.*

SUNDAYO, JUDY, psychologist, educator; b. Washington, Apr. 13, 1952; d. Granville N. and Thomasia (Smith) Moore; m. Guadalupe Gallegos, Mar. 25, 1978 (div. Nov. 1981); 1 child, Jaimah Aurora. BA in Psychology, Am. U., Washington, 1975; MA in Human Behavior, Internat. U., San Diego, 1983; MA in Counseling Psychology, Profl. Sch. Psychol. Studies, San Diego, 1982, PhD in Clin. Psychology, 1987. Lic. clin. psychologist, Calif. Adj. prof., group facilitator U. Ariz., 1985-88; adj. prof. U. La Verne, San Diego, 1987-89, San Diego State U., 1989-90; adminstrv. analyst June Burnett Inst., San Diego State U., 1988-89; evaluating clinician ERM Assocs. for NFL, San Diego, 1994—; pvt. practice psychology San Diego, 1992—; prof. San Diego Mesa Coll., 1989—. Contbr. poetry to anthologies, Words of Praise, 1984, Am. Poetry Anthology, 1982, Masterpieces of Modern Verse, 1985, Collectively Creatin', 1997. Mem. AAUW, APA, Assn. of Black Psychologists (life, historian 1998—, pres. 1996-98, chmn. membership com. 1990-96), Nat. Assn. of Colored Women. Avocations: writing, swimming, reading, crafts, hiking. Office: San Diego Family Institute 3225 4th Ave San Diego CA 92103-5701

SUNDERLAND, DEBORAH P., chemist, educator; d. Donald and Kathleen Polvani; m. Nicolas Sunderland; 1 child, Michael. PhD, Pa. State U., University Park, 2000. Analytical chemist GE Plastics, Evansville, Ind., 2000—02; asst. prof. chemistry Wingate U., NC, 2003—. Vol. Charlotte Homeless Men's Shelter, NC, 2003—06. Undergraduate Rsch. grantee, Wingate U., 2005—06. Mem.: Am. Chem. Soc., Phi Lambda Upsilon, Sigma Xi. Democrat. Roman Catholic. Office: Wingate U 204 Cedar Street Wingate NC 28174 Office Phone: 704-233-8323. Office Fax: 704-233-8233. Business E-Mail: dsunderl@wingate.edu.

SUNDERLAND, JACKLYN GILES, retired writer; b. Corpus Christi, Tex., Oct. 21, 1937; d. Elbert Jackson and Mary Kathryn (Garrett) Giles; m. Joseph Alan MacInnis, Nov. 24, 1963 (div. Feb. 1982); children: Mary Kendall Brady, Jackson Alan MacInnis; m. Lane Von Sunderland, June 12, 1988. BA, U. Tex., Austin, 1960. Editor's asst. House & Garden mag., N.Y.C., 1962; reporter Corpus Christi Caller-Times, 1960, 69, Home Furnishings Daily, Fairchild Publs., N.Y.C., 1961, Houston Post, 1963; writer, rschr. Saudi Press Agy., Washington, 1980; writer/rschr. for V.P. U.S. White House, Washington, 1982-84; dir. pub. affairs President's Com. on Mental Retardation, Washington, 1984-85; dir. speakers bur. Commn. on Bicentennial U.S. Constn., Washington, 1985-87; speechwriter Sec. of HHS, Washington, 1987-88, U.S. Sec. of Labor, Washington, 1989; dir. alumni affairs Knox Coll., Galesburg, Ill., 1990-92. Campaign chmn. Am. Cancer Soc., Corpus Christi, 1961; liaison Am. Embassy, Copenhagen, 1965-68; docent, tchr. art Nat. Gallery and Smithsonian Mus., Washington, 1970-73; vestrywoman Grace Episcopal Ch., Galesburg, 1991; mem. Jr. League Washington, 1963-2003; vol. Hospice, 1996-97. Recipient Continental Marine citation for community svc., Camp Pendleton, Calif., 1977. Republican. Home: 185 Park Ln Galesburg IL 61401

SUNDHEIM, NANCY STRAUS, lawyer; b. Phila., June 25, 1951; B in History, U. Pa., 1973; JD, Harvard U., 1978. With Arnold & Porter, Washington, Ropes & Gray, Boston, Dechert Price & Rhoads, Phila.; chief acquisitions counsel Unisys Corp., Blue Bell, Pa., 1987, dep. counsel, head corp. law group, 1990, corp. v.p., corp. sec., 1999, mem. exec. com., 1999—, sr. v., gen. counsel, 2001. Office: Unisys Corp Unisys Way Blue Bell PA 19424 Office Phone: 215-986-4011. Office Fax: 215-986-2312.

SUNDICK, SHERRY SMALL, author, journalist, poet; b. Washington, July 17, 1946; d. Charles Haskell and Ruth (Behrend) Small; B.A., Am. U., 1970; m. Gary Norman Sundick, Aug. 3, 1969; children— Amy Beth, Suzanne Faye. Columnist, Today Newspapers, Rockville, Md., 1973-75; journalist The Jour. Newspapers, Chevy Chase, Md., 1975—, The Potomac Almanac, 1976-80. Recipient N.Am. Mentor Mag. Ann. Mentor Poetry award, 1973. Mem. Nat. League Am. Pen Women, Writers Center, World Poetry Soc. Jewish. Author: Celebration, 1977; (with Ruth Small) Potpourri, 1978; contbr. articles to various mags. and jours. including Md. Mag., No. Va. Mag. Design, Maine Life, Feelings, Smile, The Pen Women, Haiku Headlines, others. Address: 11809 Hunting Ridge Ct Potomac MD 20854-2152

SUNDQUIST, LEAH RENATA, military officer; b. El Paso, Tex., July 22, 1963; d. Dominic Joseph and Patricia Ann (Manley) Bernardi; m. David Curtis Sundquist, June 23, 1990. AA, N.Mex. Mil. Inst., 1983; BS, U. Tex., El Paso, 1986; MEd in Curriculum and Instrn., City U., Bellevue, Wash., 1996. Field exec. Rio Grande Girl Scout Coun., El Paso, 1983-84; customer teller M-Bank, El Paso, 1984-85; soccer coach St. Clements Sch., El Paso, 1985; substitute tchr. El Paso Sch. Dist., 1986; commd. 2nd lt. U.S. Army, 1983, advanced through grades to maj., 1997, plans/exercise officer Ft. Lewis, Wash., 1990, ops. officer, 1990-1991; comdr. hdqs. Hdqs. Co. 141st Support Bn. U.S. Army N.G., 1996-97; dir. Childrens World Learning Ctr., Federal Way, Wash., 1992-94; phys. edn. specialist, tchr. K-6 Kent (Wash.) Elem. Sch., 1994-2001; health fitness tchr. Camas (Wash.) Mid. Sch., 2001—02; ops. and tng. officer bn. U.S. Army N.G., 1997-99, exec. officer, 1999—2002, bn. comdr., 2002—; recruiting Oreg. N.G., 2004—. Coord. NCCJ, El Paso, 1979-81; v.p. Jr. Achievement, El Paso, 1980-81; adult tng. vol. Girl Scout Coun., bd. dirs. Pacific Peaks coun., 1993-99, chair nominating com., 1996, jr. troop leader Totem coun. Girl Scouts U.S., 1996, chair program policies rev. com., 1997, trainer instrn. of adults, tng. coord. team mem., 1997—; bd. dirs. Jr. League Tacoma, 1993, 94, staff devel. coun. mem., 1997-2000, design com., 1998—. 3rd Res. Officer Tng. Corps scholar, 1981-83, H.P. Saunder scholar, 1982; recipient Humanitarian Svc. medal Great Fires of Yellowstone, U.S. Army, 1988, Gold award Girl Scouts U.S.A., 1981; decorated Nat. Def.

Svc. medal Desert Storm; meritorius Svc. medal, 1991. Mem. NEA, Wash. Edn. Assn., Assn. U.S. Army, Oreg. Army Nat. Guard Assn., Assn. U.S. Army, Air Def. Artillery Assn., Zeta Tau Alpha (sec. 1983-85, house mgr. 1984-86). Republican. Roman Catholic. Avocations: soccer, fishing, hunting, skydiving, rafting. Home: 1315 SE 16th Ave Canby OR 97013 Office Phone: 503-280-8160. Business E-Mail: leah.sundquist@us.army.mil.

SUNDQUIST, M. ALEXANDRA (ALIX SUNDQUIST), diplomat, consultant; b. Buenos Aires; arrived in US, 1962; m. Erik Lindon Sundquist, Mar. 1, 1975; 1 child, Karin Alexandra. BA in Govt. cum laude, Smith Coll.; MA in Econ., N.Y. U. Entered fgn. svc. U.S. Dept. State, 1979; with Chase Manhattan Bank, NYC, Chemical Bank, NYC, 1970—75; comml. attache U.S. Embassy, Jeddah, Saudi Arabia, 1980—82, 1st sec. (energy attache) Paris, 1982—86, consul gen. Bordeaux, 1991—94, counselor econ. affairs Rabat, Morocco, 1995—98; economist Bur. Econ. and Bus. Affairs Dept. State, Washington, 1986—90, chief spl. trade activities divsn., 1998—99; ret., 1999; ind. fgn. affairs advisor, 1999—. Cons. U.S. Dept. State, Washington, 2000; chargé d'Affaires, Valletta, Malta; trade policy advisor Bill Bradley Pres. Campaign. Mem.: Am. Fgn. Svc. Assn., U.S. Assn. Energy Econ., Middle East Inst., Diplomatic and Consular Officers, Retired, Inc. (gov., trustee DACOR Bacon Ho. Found.). Address: 3016 N Florida St Arlington VA 22207-1808 Personal E-mail: masundq@aol.com.

SUNDVALL, SHEILA A., lawyer; b. Cleve., Jan. 21, 1963; BA, U. Mich., 1985, JD, 1988. Bar: Ill. 1988, U.S. Dist. Ct. (no. dist.) Ill. 1988, U.S. Ct. Appeals (7th cir.) 1989. Jud. clk. judge Richard D. Cudahy U.S. Ct. Appeals 7th Cir., Chgo., 1988-89; assoc. Sidley & Austin, Chgo., 1989-96, ptnr., 1996—. Lectr. in field. Mem. Legal Club Chgo., Phi Beta Kappa, Order of Coif.

SUNG, AUDREY L., lawyer; b. Oakland, Calif., May 21, 1963; BA with high distinction, Univ. Calif., Berkeley, 1985; certificate with mention bien, Institut d'Etudes Politiques, 1988; JD cum laude, Harvard Univ., 1989. Bar: Calif. 1989. Ptnr. Holland & Knight, San Francisco. Contbr. articles to profl. journals. Mem.: State Bar Calif., Bar Assn. San Francisco, Asian Am. Bar Assn. Greater Bay Area (pres. 1997). Fluent in French, Mandarin Chinese. Office: Holland & Knight LLP Ste 2800 50 California St San Francisco CA 94111 Office Phone: 415-743-6940. Office Fax: 415-743-6910. Business E-Mail: audrey.sung@hklaw.com.

SUNI, ELLEN Y., dean, law educator; BA magna cum laude, CCNY; JD magna cum laude, Boston U. Law clerk to Chief Justice Mass. Supreme Judicial Ct., dep. legal asst. to Justices; dir. legal writing prog. Boston U. Sch. Law, asst. dean, lectr.; faculty mem. U. Mo.-Kansas City Sch. Law, 1980—, interim assoc. dean, interim dean, prof. law, 2004—, Marvin Lewis Rich Faculty Scholar. Fed. prosecutor U.S. Atty. Office, 1987—88; mem. Eighth Cir. Criminal Jury Instrns. Sub-com.; bd. mem. Pub. Interest Litigation Clinic, Police Law Inst. Contbr. articles to law jours. Legal dir. Kansas City Youth Ct.; pres. Midwestern Innocence Project. Recipient Legal Leader of Yr. Award, 2004. Office: U Mo-Kansas City Sch Law 5100 Rockhill Rd Kansas City MO 64110 Office Phone: 816-235-2372. E-mail: sunie@umkc.edu.

SUNSHOWER, SUZANNE, freelance/self-employed journalist, poet, artist; b. Detroit, Mar. 24, 1962; d. Charles and Barbara Stewart. BA in Psychology, Wayne State U., Detroit, 1991, BA in Polit. Sci., 1991, post grad. in Sci., 1991—92; post grad. in Pub. Adminstrn., Wayne State U., 1994—95. Art dir. and feature writer Phase II, Detroit, 1983—85; feature writer Detroit Women's Voice, 1983—85; pvt. duty art therapist, 1985—90; midwest corr. New Directions for Women, NJ, 1993, Off Our Backs, Washington, 2000—01; editor and adminstr. internet jour. Quiet Mountain Essays, 2003—. Clinic defender Mich. Abortion Rights Action League, Detroit, 1987—89; organizing cons. Wayne State U. chpt. NOW, Detroit, 1990; founding mem. Nat. Info. Network Environment, 1992; bd. mem. Sioux Falls (S.D.) Poetry Coun., 2003—; essayist. Author: Bi Any Other Name, 1991; performer: (radio series) Cold Cut Review, 1979—81, (poetry) Poets Against Apartheid, 1987, Poets Against Youth Violence (Save Our Sons and Daughters), 1988, Heidelberg Project, 1996, Broadside Press Reader Series, 2001, Sioux Falls Arts Coun. Reader Series, 2003, S.D. Festival of Books, 2004; ad campaign, Walk Against Crime, Detroit, 1980—82; contbr. articles to feminist publs. Driver NAACP Operation Big Vote, Detroit, 1984; social worker Franklin-Wright Homeless Shelter, 1992; environ. health educator Detroit Pub. Schs. Partnership to End Asthsma, 1997; prodr. and organizer Concert Mozambique Flood Relief, 2000; pres. Ctrl. Mich. Gay Liberation, Mt. Pleasant, 1982—83; minority caucus leader AIDS action planning com. Act-Up Detroit, 1983—89; asst. dir. Dem. Party Election Hdqs., Ecorse, 1984; poll watcher Dem. Party, SD, 2002. Scholar, Environmental Careers Orgn., 1992. Mem.: APA (affiliate), Nat. Writers Union, Internat. Women's Writing Guild (regional rep.), Acad. Am. Poets (assoc.), Mensa (editor S.D. Mensodak). Avocations: hiking, fishing, cooking, acting. Office: Quiet Mountain Essays PO Box 261 Scotland SD 57059 E-mail: administrator@quietmountainessays.org.

SUPAK, CATHY POERNER, athletic trainer, educator; b. San Antonio, Tex. d. John and Jo Ann Poerner; m. Ray Supak; children: Amanda, Cameron. BS in Edn., Tex. State U., San Marcos, 1984. Cert. athletic trainer Bd. Certification-Nat. Athletic Trainer Assn., 1987, lic. Tex. State Bd. Athletic Trainers, 1984; cert. tchr. State Bd. Edn., Tex., 1984. Athletic trainer/tchr. La Porte H.S., Tex., 1984—87; staff athletic trainer Christus St John Sports Medicine, Nassau Bay, Tex., 1992—2004, supr. athletic tng. svcs., 2004—. Vol. Boy Scouts, Houston, 1996. Recipient Cert. of Merit, ARC, 1999, Disting. Alumnus award, Dept. Phys. Edn. and Sports Sci., 1999. Mem.: Greater Houston Athletic Trainers Assn. (pres. 1998—2001, Bobby Gunn Svc. award 1999), SW Athletic Trainers Assn. (com. chair 2004—06), Nat. Athletic Trainers Assn. (Athletic Trainer Svc. award 2004). Home: 14714 Graywood Grove Lane Houston TX 77062 Office Phone: 281-333-8806.

SUPANICH, BARBARA ANN, physician; b. Detroit, Sept. 24, 1952; d. Donald George and Mildred Mary (Stanovich) Supanich. BS in Chemistry, Mercy Coll. Detroit, 1974; MD, Mich. State U., 1980. Diplomate Am. Bd. Family Practice, lic. physician Mich., Fla.; joined Sisters of Mercy, 1973. Resident in family practice Creighton U. Affiliated Hosps., Omaha, 1980—83; pvt. practice Eaton Rapids, Mich., 1983—86, Houghton Lake, Mich., 1986—92; fellow in clin. ethics Ctr. Ethics Mich. State U., East Lansing, 1992—93, asst. prof. family practice, 1993—97, assoc. prof., 1998, assoc. chair clin. svcs., dept. family practice, 1995—99, assoc. residency dir. family practice residency Munson, 1999—; fellow palliative medicine & hospice care Mayo Clinic, Jacksonville, Fla., 2005; med. dir., palliative medicine, sr. svcs. Holy Cross Hosp., Silver Spring, Md. Cons. Mich. Dept. Cmty. Health, Lansing, 1996—99. Contbr. chapters to books, articles to profl. jours. Fellow: Am. Acad. Family Physicians (bd. dirs., regional dir. 2000—04, 2d v.p. 2004—05); mem.: Am. Med. Women's Assn., Mich. Acad. Family Physicians. Roman Catholic. Avocations: swimming, bicycling, mystery and science fiction novels. Home: 4013 Postgate Ter Apt 201 Silver Spring MD 20906 Office: Holy Cross Hosp 1500 Forest Glen Rd Silver Spring MD 20910 Office Phone: 301-754-7000. Personal E-mail: barbsupanich@comcast.net.

SUPANVANIJ, JANIKAN, finance educator; b. Bangkok, Aug. 6, 1971; arrived in U.S., 1993; d. Vitaya and Sopha Supanvanij. BBA, Thammasat U., Bangkok, 1993; MFN in Fin., St. Louis U., 1995, MBA in Fin. and Econs., 1997, PhD in Fin., 2003. Cert. tchg. skills. Internat. banking facility fgn. exch. dealer The Thai Mil. Bank, Ltd., Bangkok, 1993; instr. St. Louis U., 1997—2003; asst. prof. St. Cloud State U., Minn., 2003—06, assoc. prof., 2006—. Contbr. articles to profl. jours. Recipient Rsch. Collaboration award, St. Cloud State U., 2000—05, Disting. Rsch. award, 2000—05, Tchg. Excellence award, 2004—05. Mem.: St. Louis U. Grad. Student Assn. (webmaster 1997—2002, GSA rsch. symposium program co-chair 2001—02, pres. 2002—03), Beta Gamma Sigma, Alpha Epsilon Lambda. Office: St Cloud State U 720 4th Ave S Saint Cloud MN 56301

SUPINO, PHYLLIS GAIL, medical researcher, educator; m. Rene Patrick Supino, June 7, 1980; children: Lisa Michelle, Christopher Davies. BS in Biol. Scis., CCNY, 1964; EdD in Sci. Edn., Rutgers U., 1976. Instr. psychology, rsch. assoc. in cognitive psychology Princeton U., 1975—77; dir. rsch. and evaluation The Ednl. Improvement Ctr. divsn. NJ. State Dept. Edn., West Orange, 1977—79; adj. instr. environ. and cmty. medicine, adj. instr. family medicine Robert Wood Johnson Med. Sch./U. Medicine and Dentistry NJ, Piscataway, 1979—90; asst. prof. pub. health in medicine, dir. data mgmt. Cornell U. Med. Coll., N.Y.C., 1990—95; rsch. assoc. prof. emergency medicine, rsch. assoc. prof. med. edn., dir. rsch. in emergency medicine Mt. Sinai Sch. Medicine, N.Y.C., 1996—99; assoc. rsch. prof. pub. health in medicine, dir. data mgmt., epidemiology and ednl. programs Weill Med. Coll. of Cornell U., N.Y.C., NY, 1999—. Mem. editl. bd.: Cardiology; contbr. chapters to books, articles to profl. jours. Vol. Morocco VI US Peace Corps, Washington. Recipient Phi Delta Kappa award, Rutgers U., 1976, The Howard Gilman award, The Howard Gilman Found., 1995, Best Mentor of the Yr. award, Mt. Sinai Sch. Medicine, 1998, Best Nat. Sci. Abstract award, Am. Soc. Nuc. Cardiology and Internat. Affiliates, 2001; grantee Pilot Rsch. award, Weill Med. Coll. of Cornell U. Fellow: NY Acad. Medicine (mem. evidence based medicine working group); mem.: Heart Valve Soc. Am., Am. Soc. Nuc. Cardiology, Am. Heart Assn., Am. Statis. Assn. (editl. bd.), Am. Fedn. for Med. Rsch., Kappa Delta Pi (life). Achievements include development of first comprehensive approved course on clinical research methodology for physicians at Weill Medical College and Mount Sinai School of Medicine; Research mentor to more than 50 residents, fellows and junior faculty in medicine. Avocations: theater, vocal music. Office: Weill Medical College/Cornell University 525 E 68th Street; F467 New York NY 10021 Office Phone: 212-746-2118. Business E-Mail: phs2002@med.cornell.edu.

SUPPA-FRIEDMAN, JANICE DESTEFANO, secondary school educator, consultant; b. Morristown, NJ, Apr. 27, 1943; d. Eugene Arthur and Isabella Vienna (Bottiglia) DeS.; m. Dennis Suppa, June 28, 1964 (div. May 1994); children: Julie Ann, Chad Dennis; m. Michael Jac Friedman, Oct. 7, 1995. BS in Edn., Bowling Green State U., 1964; MA in Edn., Va. Poly. Inst. & State U., 1977, cert. advanced grad. study, 1990. Cert. secondary tchr., Va. Tchr. English and reading Northwood (Ohio) Jr. High Sch., 1964—66; tchr. English and history Canaseraga (N.Y.) Ctrl. Schs., 1966—67; tchr. English and reading Marstellar Jr. High Sch., Manassas, Va., 1967—72; tchr. English Taylor Jr. High sch., Warrenton, Va., 1973—74; tchr. English and reading, lang. arts specialist, dept. head, lead tchr. Brentsville Dist. Mid.-Sr. High Sch., Nokesville, Va., 1975—99; reading specialist Graham Park Middle Sch., Dumfries, Va., 1999—2000; ednl. cons., 2000—; co-tchr./mentor Fredericksburg City Pub. Sch., 2004. Ednl. cons. So. Region Coll. Bd., 2001—; reader for advanced placement lit. and composition exam, 1996, 1998—2003; adj. prof. Old Dominion U., 1999, No. Va. C.C., 1992—94, George Mason U., 2003—04; advanced placement English tchr. mentor Coll. Bd., 2004—05. Editor newsletter Spinning Wheel, 1991-94; contbr. articles to profl. jours. Va. English Bull. Tour guide George Washington Fredericksburg Found. at Kenmore Mansion and Plantation and George Washington's Ferry Farms, Va., 2001—04; officer of election Stafford County, 2001—04; vol. visitor use assistance Survey Adminstrn. Shenandoah Nat. Pk., 2005—. Grantee Va. Comm. of the Arts, 1994-95, 2000, Prince William Edn. Found., 1996, 2000, Greater Washington Reading Coun., 1999, 2000, Va. Opera Assn., 2000, So. States Southland Corp., 2000. Mem. NATE (pres. 1992-1994), Nat. Coun. Tchrs. English (coord. Va. state Achievement in Writing awards 1995-2001, Va. state liaison 2001, judge Va. state forensics finals 2000-03, judge Va. state excellence in lit. mags. 1998-2002), Va. Assn. Tchrs. English (exec. bd. 1992—, v.p. 2001-02, pres.-elect 2002-03, pres. 2004, 05, Svc. award 1993), Phi Delta Kappa. Avocations: reading, music, hiking, bicycling, running. Personal E-mail: suppaf@aol.com. E-mail: jdsfriedman@aol.com.

SUPPES, CHRISTINE JOHNSON, publishing executive; b. LA, Mar. 3, 1953; d. Robert and Jane Johnson; m. Patrick Suppes; children: Alexandra Christine, Michael Patrick. Copygirl/editl. asst. San Francisco Examiner, 1972—73; pres. Gravure At Home, Stanford, Calif., 1997—2001; pub., editor-in-chief www.Fashionlines.com, Stanford, Calif., 1999—; chief designer Jewels by Christine, 2002—. Advt. cons. Clarum Corp., Palo Alto, Calif., 1997—, Gravure Corp., Dallas, 1997—2000; chief designer www.jewelsbyChristine.com, Stanford, Calif., 2003—; Am. rep. Of Silk, of Gold and Silver Assn., France. Author: Amanda Prescott, 1984, Clinic, 1985; contbr. revs. to San Francisco Chronicle, articles to SF Moda. Organizer, Teacher's Fund Bing School, Stanford, 1995—2001; mem. Peninsula Chpt. NARAL, Palo Alto, 1997—2000; supporter ARC, Palo Alto, 2001. Recipient Angel of Fashion com. award, N.Y.C., 1999—. Mem.: French Heritage Soc. No. Calif. (bd. dirs. 2005), Fashion Group Internat., Camera Nazionale della Moda Italiana, Federation Francaise de la Couture. Office: Fashionlines 678 Mirada Ave Stanford CA 94305 Business E-Mail: suppes@fashionlines.com.

SURAVAJJALA, MAMATHA, information technology manager; Mgr. volume planning sys., Info. Tech. Mgmt. DaimlerChrysler, Auburn Hills, Mich. Recipient Women of Color Tech. award, 2005. Office: Chrysler Group 1000 Chrysler Dr Auburn Hills MI 48326-2766*

SURFACE, CAROL PRICE, artist, educator; b. Akron, Ohio, May 10, 1955; d. Thomas Lee and Mary Anita (Stahl) Price; m. Henry E. Surface Jr., Feb. 15, 1981. BA summa cum laude, U. Ctrl. Fla., 1986. Materiels mgr. Haris Corp., Melbourne, Fla., 1973-79; purchasing agent Fujitsu Am., Melbourne, Fla., 1980-81; artist self-employed, Venice and Redondo Beach, Calif., 1988—; art tchr. Palos Verdes (Calif.) Art Ctr., 1988-96; faculty mem. art dept. Santa Monica Coll., 2000—02; model, actress Christensen Group, Orlando, Fla., 1985-88; arts writer Orlando Sentinel, 1986-88. V.p. Women Painters West, L.A., 1995—96; artist Venice Art Walk Studio Artists' Tour, 2001—05; artistic cons. Film Industry; cons. Various painting orgs., Calif.; design cons. Recipient First Place award Henry Hopkins of UCLA Armand Hammer Mus., 1995, Mayor's award City Beverly Hills, Calif., 1996, Best of Show award Art Inst. So. Calif., Laguna Beach, Calif., 1995-96. Mem. San Diego Watercolor Soc. Avocations: sewing, interior decorating, poetry. Home: 1347 Braeridge Dr Beverly Hills CA 90210 Office Phone: 310-392-9294.

SURLES, CAROL D., academic administrator; b. Pensacola, Fla., Oct. 7, 1946; d. Elza Allen and Versy Lee Smith; divorced; children: Lisa Surles, Philip Surles. BA, Fisk U., 1968; MA, Chapman Coll., 1971; PhD, U. Mich., 1978. Personnel rep. U. Mich., Ann Arbor, 1973-78, vice-chancellor adminstrn. Flint, 1987-89; exec. asst. to pres., assoc. v.p. for human resources U. Ctrl. Fla., Orlando, 1978-87; v.p. acad. affairs Jackson State U., Miss., 1989-92; v.p. adminstrn. and bus. Calif. State U., Hayward, 1992-94; pres. Tex. Woman's U., Denton, 1994-99, Ea. Ill. U., Charleston, 1999—. Trustee Pub. Broadcasting Ch. 24, Orlando, 1985-87; bd. dirs. First State Bank, Denton, Tex., Tex.-N.Mex. Power Co., TNP-Enterprise. Recipient Outstanding Scholar's award Delta Tau Kappa, 1983. Mem. AAUW, Am. Assn. Colls. and Univs., Golden Key Honor Soc., Mortar Bd. Soc., Dallas Citizens' Coun., Dallas Women's Found., Coun. of Pres. (Austin, Tex.), Phi Kappa Phi, Alpha Kappa Alpha. Methodist. Avocation: piano. Office: Ea Ill U 600 Lincoln Ave Charleston IL 61920-3011

SURMAN, SUSAN (SUSAN KRAMER), writer, actress; b. Boston, Dec. 16, 1939; d. Frank and Rachel (Alexander) Surman. BFA, Boston U., 1960. Appeared in Company, Her Majesty's Theatre, London, 1972, Hefetz, Edinburgh, Scotland, 1974, Streetcar Named Desire, Oxford (Eng.) Playhouse, 1978, The Price, Ensemble Theatre, Sydney, Australia, 1982, Born Yesterday, Sydney Theatre Co., 1984; author: (plays) George, 1980, In Between, 1984 (Writer's Digest award, 2005), The Nightgown, 1999, Hymie Moskowitz is Back!; (novels) Max and Friends, 1999 (Writer's Digest award, 2005), Sacha: The Dog Who Made it to the Palace, 2001, You Can't Dance at All the Weddings, 2006. Recipient Porter Fleming award, Ga. Arts Coun., 2000, Short Fiction award, Davidson County Writer's Guild, 2005. Avocations: travel, movies. E-mail: susansurman@yahoo.com.

SURO-BREDIE, CARMEN CECILIA, federal official; b. Washington, Aug. 19, 1947; d. Guillermo Antonio and Piedad (Castillo) Suro; m. Joseph W.B. Bredie, Oct. 26, 1974; children: Nicholas Alexander, Christopher Anthony. BA, Manhattanville Coll., 1969; MA, Johns Hopkins U., 1972; MBA, Harvard U., 1981. Dep. asst. U.S. Trade Rep. for Investment and the Uruguay Round, Washington, 1989-92, asst. for environment and intellectual property, 1992-93, asst. for L.Am., Africa and the Caribbean, 1993-95; sr. policy advisor Bur. Interam. Affairs Dept. State, Washington, 1995-96; sr. policy advisor and exec. sec. U.S. Trade Rep., Washington, 1996-00, asst. U.S. trade rep. for policy coord., 2000—. Contbr. articles to profl. publs. Coach No. Ireland Women's Coalition. Named one of Elite Women, Hispanic Bus. mag., 2005; recipient Nat. Cuban Am. Women's Assn. award, 1992. Roman Catholic. Avocations: antiques, gourmet cooking. Office: Exec Office of the Pres US Trade Rep 600 17th St NW Washington DC 20850 Office Phone: 202-395-9541. Business E-Mail: csuro-bredie@ustr.eop.gov.

SURPRISE, JUANEE, chiropractor, nutrition consultant; b. Gary, Ind., Apr. 28, 1944; d. Glenn Mark and Willia Ross (Vasser) Surprise; m. Peter E. Coakley, Feb. 12, 1966 (div. Jan. 1976); children: Thaddeus, Mariah, Darius; m. Robert T.Howell, Feb. 24, 1984. RN, Phila. Gen. Hosp. Sch. Nursing, 1965; D of Chiropractic summa cum laude, Life Chiropractic Coll., Marietta, Ga., 1981. Diplomate Nat. Bd. Chiropractic Examiners, Am. Acad. Pain Mgmt., Am. Acad. Integrated Medicine, Internat. Acad. Clin. Nutrition; bd. cert. naturopathic med. doctor; cert. clin. nutritionist, acupuncturist, Thompson technique, Nimmo receptor tonus technique. Staff nurse Children's Hosp., Balt., 1966-67; charge nurse Melrose-Wakefield Hosp., Mass., 1967-68; hosp. adminstr. Animal Hosp. of Wakefield, Mass., 1967-79; chiropractor Chiropractic Clinic of Greenville, NC, 1982-84, Family Med.-Chiropractic Clinic, Denton, Tex., 1984—; dean Sch. Nutrition Quantum-Veritis Internat. Univ. Sys., 2003—; dir. Ctr. Clin. Sci., Parker Coll. Chiropractic, Dallas, 1996-97, dir. diplomate and certification programs, 1997-2000. Mem. postgrad. faculty Northwestern U. Health Scis. Mem., chmn. Cmty. Planning Commn., North Reading, Mass., 1976-79; chmn. bldg. com. Immaculate Conception Ch., Denton, 1987-90, parish coun., 1990-92; v.p. Property Owners Assn., 2000-02. Fellow Am. Acad. Integrated Medicine; mem. Am. Assn. Pain Mgmt., Am. Chiropractic Assn., Am. Chiropractic Bd. on Nutrition (past pres.), Tex. Chiropractic Assn. (past chair), Pi Tau Delta. Republican. Roman Catholic. Avocation: health education. Office: Family Med and Chiropractic Clinic 1100 Dallas Dr Denton TX 76205-5121 Office Phone: 940-566-0000. Personal E-mail: doctormomdc@hotmail.com. Business E-Mail: info@familymedandchiro.com.

SURYANARAYANAN, SOWMYA K., endocrinologist; b. Trichy, India, Aug. 21, 1969; arrived in U.S., 2001; d. Suryanarayanan Swaminathan and Nanikutty Sankaran Nair; m. Manoj Gopalkrishnan, May 31, 2004. MBBS, Thanjavur Med. Coll., India, 1994. Diplomate Am. Bd. Internal Medicine, Am. Bd. Endocrinology. Jr. resident in medicine RMA Hosp., India, 1993—94; jr. resident in intensive care Devaki Hosp., India, 1994—95; jr. resident in pediat. Thanjavur Med. Coll., India, 1995; jr. resident in medicine St. Thomas Hosp., Madras, India, 1995—96; resident in cardiology Royal Manchester (Eng.) Infirmary, 1996—97; resident in internal medicine Prince Charles Hosp., Cardiff, Wales, 1997, Royal Liverpool (Eng.) and Broadgreen U. Hosp. NHS Trust, 1997—99, Meml. Hosp. R.I., Pawtucket, 2001—02; sr. resident in metabolic medicine Leicester (Eng.) Royal Infirmary, 1999, John Radcliffe Hosp., Oxford, England, 1999; calman specialist registrar in endo/metabolic medicine Kings, Guys and St. Thomas Hosp., London, 2000; fellow in diabetes, endocrinology & metabolism U. Mich. Hosps., Ann Arbor, 2003—. Mem.: ACP, Am. Assn. Clin. Endocrinologists, Endocrine Soc. (Outstanding Svc. in Rsch./Clin. 2003—05), Royal Coll. Physicians. Avocations: piano, tennis, swimming. Home: 2851 S Walden St Aurora CO 80013

SUSANKA, SARAH HILLS, architect; b. Bromley, Kent, England, Mar. 21, 1957; d. Brian and Margaret (Hampson) Hills; m. Lawrence A. Susanka, July 4, 1980 (div. May 1984); m. James Robert Larson, Sept. 4, 1988 (div. Jan. 2000); m. Alfred B. Urzi, May 7, 2001. BArch, U. Oreg., 1978; MArch, U. Minn., 1983. Registered architect. Founding prin. Mulfinger, Susanka, Mahady & Ptnrs., Mpls., 1983-99; founder Susanka Studios, Raleigh, NC, 1999—. Author: The Not So Big House, 1998, Creating the Not So Big House, 2000, Not So Big Solutions for Your Home, 2002; columnist Fine Homebuilding mag. Mem. AIA. Office: 2600 Salisbury Pln Raleigh NC 27613-4331 E-mail: ssusanka@notsobighouse.com.

SUSKIND, DIANA LEE, education educator; b. Syracuse, NY, June 30, 1947; d. Philip and Ida (Landau) S.; m. Mitchell G. Roth, Aug. 5, 1979 (div. Aug. 1989). BS in Elem. Edn., SUNY, Brockport, 1969; postgrad., Syracuse U., 1970, Harvard U., 1994, Emmi Pikler Inst., Budapest, Hungary, 1992; MS in Early Childhood Edn., 1973; EdD in Early Childhood Edn., U. Ill., 1979. Tchr. Earlington Heights Elem. Sch., Miami, Fla., 1969-71; reading specialist Syracuse (N.Y.) Sch. Dist., 1971-72; English tchr., dir. Parent Coop. Nursery Sch. Am. U. Assn., Chaing Mai, Thailand, 1972; childcare giver Kibbutz Beeri, Negev, Israel, 1973; lectr. Fitchburg (Mass.) State Coll., 1973-75; grad. asst. dept. elem. and early childhood edn. U. Ill., Urbana, 1975-79; asst. prof., supr. tchr. tng. Sch. Edn. Calif. State U., L.A., 1980-81; lectr. continuing edn. dept. U. Alaska, Fairbanks, 1984-89; edn. specialist coord. Child Devel. Svcs., Ft. Wainwright Army Base, Alaska, 1985-88, edn. specialist, 1988-89; lead edn. specialist Child Devel. Svcs. Smiley Barracks, Karlsruhe, Germany, 1988-91; asst. prof. edn. Fitchburg State Coll., 1991-99, assoc. prof. edn., 1999—. Head tchr. Pacific Oaks Children's Sch., Pasadena, Calif., 1981; vis. faculty dept. psychology U. Alaska, Anchorage, 1981—82; art instr. Fine Arts Camp, 1985; coord. State Wide Early Childhood Conf., Fairbanks, 1985—86; lead preshc. tchr. New Eng. Dance Camp, Poland Spring, Maine, 1993, lead infant-toddler tchr., 1994—95; trainer European Edn. Specialists, Germany, 1991; vis. acad. Ctr. for Applied Studies, Queensland U. Tech., Brisbane, Australia, 1998; participant NEH Faculty Devel. Workshop for Infusing African and Asian Studies into the Undergrad. Curriculum, 2000, Whispering Woods Conf., Olive Branch, Miss.; guest prof. U. Udine, Italy, 2001; Fulbright sr. specialist N.Z. Child Care Assn., 2003, Tetari Puna Ora o Aotearoa, 2003; keynote spkr. Fairbanks Assn. Young Children, 2002; vis. instr. Taizhau Hosp. of Zhejiang Province, Linai City, China, 2004; spkr., presenter in field. Contbr. articles to profl. publs.; art exhibited in one woman shows at Karlsruhe, 1987-89; exhibited work at Palace, Haiti, 1994, Leominster Art Assn., 1997 (1st prize, 3d prize, 2d prize Gardner Art Assn. 1998); columnist Anchorage Times, Fairbanks Daily News Miner, 1981-87. Mem. Mayor's Task Force on Families and Children, Fairbanks, 1988-89, vocat. Adv. Coun., Fairbanks North Star Borough Sch. Dist., 1987-88, mem. alternative elem. com., 1986-87; mem. CCREE State Task Force on Early Childhood Edn., 1981-83; bd. dirs. Tanina Child Devel. Ctr., Anchorage, 1981-82. Grantee Fitchburg State Coll. Alumni Assn., 1974, State of Alaska Dept. Cmty. and Regional Affairs, 1988, Project Palms, 1993, A-Tip Alumni Assn., 1974, 93, 96, Marion and Jasper Whiting Found., 1996; fellow Resource for Infant Educarers, 1988—; Fulbright Sr. scholar specialist New Zealand Child Care Assn., 2003, U. Udine, 2005. Mem Fairbanks Assn. for Edn. Young Children (v.p. 1985), Kappa Delta Pi, Pi Delta Kappa. Home: 20 Main St 5th Fl Apt O Leominster MA 01453-5530 Office Phone: 978-665-3371. Personal E-mail: dsuskind@comcast.net.

SUSKO, CAROL LYNNE, lawyer, accountant, educator; b. Washington, Dec. 5, 1955; d. Frank and Helen Louise (Davis) S. BS in Econs. and Acctg., George Mason U., 1979; JD, Cath. U., 1982; LLM in Taxation, Georgetown U., 1992. Bar: Pa. 1989, D.C. 1990; CPA, Va., Md. Tax acct. Reznick Fedder & Silverman, P.C., Bethesda, Md., 1984-85; sr. tax acct. Pannell Kerr Forster, Alexandria, Va., 1985; tax specialist Coopers & Lybrand, Washington, 1985-87; supervisory tax sr. Frank & Co., McLean, Va., 1987-88; mem. editl. staff Tax Notes Mag., Arlington, Va., 1989-90; adj. faculty Am. U., Washington, 1989—; tax atty. Marriott Corp., Washington, 1993-94; sr. tax mgr. Host Marriott Inc., Washington, 1994-99, KPMG LLP, McLean, Va., 1999—. Mem. ABA, AICPAs, Va. Soc. CPAs, D.C. Soc. CPAs, D.C. Bar Assn. Office: IRS 11166 Fairfax Blvd Ste 500 Fairfax VA 22030 Personal E-mail: l8636@aol.com. Business E-Mail: carol.l.susko@irs.gov.

SUSSE, SANDRA SLONE, lawyer; b. Medford, Mass., June 1, 1943; d. James Robert and Georgie Coffin (Bradshaw) Slone; m. Peter Susse, May 10, 1969 (div. May 1993); 1 child, Toby. BA, U. Mass., 1981; JD, Vt. Law Sch., 1986. Bar: Mass. 1986, U.S. Dist. Ct. Mass. 1988, U.S. Ct. Appeals (1st cir.) 1995. Staff atty. Western Mass. Legal Svcs., Springfield, 1986—. Mem. ABA, Hampden County Bar Assn. Avocations: hiking, german literature, films, skating. Address: Western Mass Legal Serv 127 State St Fl 4 Springfield MA 01103-1905 Office Phone: 413-781-7826 ext. 124. Business E-Mail: ssusse@wmls.org.

SUSSKIND, TERESA GABRIEL, publishing executive; came to U.S., 1945; d. Aaron and Betty (Fox) Gabriel; m. Charles Susskind, May 1, 1945; children: Pamela Pettler, Peter Gabriel, Amanda. Student, U. London, 1938-40. Profl. libr. Calif. Inst. Tech., Pasadena, 1946-48, Yale U., New Haven, 1948-51, Stanford (Calif.) U., 1951-52, SRI Internat., Menlo Park, Calif., 1953; founder, pres. San Francisco Press, Inc., 1959—. Active in cultural affairs; bd. govs. San Francisco Symphony, 1986-89. With Women's Royal Naval Svc., 1943-45. With Women's Royal Naval Svc., 1943—45. Mem. Town and Gown Club (Berkeley, Calif.; pres. 1984-85). Office: 660 Spruce St Berkeley CA 94707-1730

SUSSMAN, JANET I., social sciences educator; b. N.Y.C., Sept. 24, 1952; d. Joseph I. and Selma H. Sussman. BA, Douglas Coll., 1974. Pub. Harcourt Brace, N.Y.C., 1974—76, Van Nostrand Reinhold, N.Y.C., 1975—77, Sky & Telescope Mag., Cambridge, Mass., 1977—80, Wholistic Edn. & Svcs., Inc., Charlotte, NC, 1984—90, No. Star Dimensions, Charlotte, 1986—; pub., cons. Time Portal Pubs., Fairfield, Iowa, 1993—. Author: Timeshift: The Experience of Dimensional Change, 1996; musician: (CD) Bridges, 2002; author: The Reality of Time, 2005. E-mail: timeport@lisco.com.

SUSSMAN, LAUREEN GLICKLIN, elementary school educator; b. NYC, Mar. 21, 1953; d. Harry and Ruth (Goldstein) G.; m. Alan Neil Sussman, May 30, 1977; children: David Efrem, Adam Jacob, Daniel Joshua. BA, Bklyn. Coll., 1974; MS, MSc, Hofstra U., 1998. Cert. tchr. nursery-6, spl. edn. tchr. all grades. Sec. McCann-Erickson, Inc., N.Y.C., 1974-75; adminstrv. asst., tour operator EasTours divsn. Fgn. Tours, N.Y.C., 1975-78; adminstrv. asst. Alan N. Sussman, CPA, Woodmere, NY, 1978-96; kindergarten tchr. Hebrew Acad. Long Beach (N.Y.), 1996-97; jr. HS tchr. Torah Acad. Girls, Far Rockaway, NY, 1997—. Participant Instrumental Enrichment/IRI Skylight, N.Y., 1995, 98, Dynamic Assessment project Touro Coll., N.Y.C., 1996; CSE parent rep., adv. Lawrence (N.Y.) Pub. Schs., 1992-97; trainer Life Tech., Cedarhurst, N.Y., 2004—05. Contbr. articles to profl. jours. Mem. Spl. Edn. PTA Lawrence Schs., 1986-2003, Sisterhood Congregation Bais Tefilah, 1990-2003; mem. Sisterhood East Meadow Jewish Ctr., chair social action, Israel affairs, 1979-81; mem. adv. bd. Kulanu of the South Shore of Nassau County, 2000—; mem. Sisterhood Kehillah Aish Kodesh, Emunah of Am. Mem.: AMIT Women (Masada chpt.), OTSAR (founder Nassau County chpt. 1987—, nat. bd. dirs., pres. Nassau chpt. 1987—2002). Democrat. Avocations: Israeli and simcha dancing, walking, reading, needlepoint. Office: Torah Acad Girls 444 Beach 6 St Far Rockaway NY 11691 Personal E-mail: lauglick@aol.com.

SUSSMAN, MONICA HILTON, lawyer; b. NYC, Apr. 2, 1952; BA cum laude, Syracuse U., 1973; JD, Hofstra U., 1977. Bar: Va. 1977, DC 1978. Legis. coun. NY State Gov's. Office, Washington, 1977-79; spl. asst. to under sec. US Dept. HUD, Washington, 1979-80, br. chief office State Agy. and Bond Fin. programs, 1980-82, office gen. counsel, 1982-83, also bd. dirs., 1988-95, v.p., 1989-93, treas. Nat. Housing Conf., 1990-93, pres. Nat. Housing Conf., 1997—2000, also programs and regulations dep. gen. counsel; ptnr. McDermott, Will & Emery, Washington, Peabody & Brown, Washington, 1996-99, Nixon Peadoby LLP, Washington, 1999—. Mem.: ABA, Mortgage Bankers Assn., Nat Leased Housing Assn., Va. State Bar, DC Bar Assn. Office: Nixon Peabody LLP 401 9th St NW Ste 900 Washington DC 20004 Office Fax: 202-585-8080. E-mail: msussman@nixonpeabody.com.

SUTA, DEBORAH, secondary school educator; b. Jersey City, Dec. 27, 1946; d. James Clifford Gregory and Dorothy Eulalia (Donnelly) Conniff; m. Robert Wendell Suta, June 7, 1975; 1 child, John Gregory. BA, Caldwell Coll., NJ, 1968; MA, Montclair State Coll., 1990. Cert. elem. and secondary edn. tchr., NJ. Tchr. St. Joseph Sch., Lincoln Park, NJ, 1968-69, Sacred Heart Sch., Lyndhurst, NJ, 1969-76, St. Joseph Sch., Lodi, NJ, 1981-82; tchr., student assistance counselor St. Mary HS, Rutherford, NJ, 1982-93; tchr. religion Immaculate Heart Acad., Washington Twp., NJ, 1995—. Adj. prof. St. Peter Coll., Jersey City, 1977. Mem. adv. bd. Alternatives to Domestic Violence, 1993, 2004. Recipient Lilli Graham Leadership award Bergen County Alternatives to Domestic Violence, 1992. Roman Catholic. Avocations: reading, knitting. Office: Immaculate Heart Acad 500 Van Emburgh Ave Township Of Washington NJ 07676 E-mail: ddebscs@aol.com.

SUTCLIFFE, MARY OGDEN, clinical social worker; b. Chgo., June 9, 1928; d. Dana Presley and Vera Marie (Gassman) Ogden; m. Herbert Alfred Sutcliffe, Oct. 30, 1963; children: Stephen, Timothy, James, Penney Stahl. AA, Colby/Sawyer Coll., 1948; BS in Journalism, Syracuse U., 1950; MSW, Howard U., 1967. Cert. clin. social worker. Asst. editor House & Garden Mag., N.Y.C., 1949-51; reporter Bay News, East Meadow, N.Y., 1956-58; chief social worker Cmty. Mental Health Clinic, Manassus, Va., 1967-72, Children & Youth Health Ctr., Exeter, N.H., 1978-82, Rockingham Child and Family Svc., 1982-88; assoc. prof. psychology Garrett Coll., Oakland, Md., 1989-93; clin. social worker pvt. practice, Bethesda, Md., 1972-78, Durham, N.H., 1978-88, Oakland, Md., 1988-98; pvt. practice Durango, Colo., 1999—. Sec. Rep. Club, Port Washington, L.I., N.Y., 1972; v.p. Garrett County Alliance for Mentally Ill. Mem. AAUW (pres. 1961), Toastmasters (v.p. 1988), Pi Beta Phi. Avocations: triathlon, skiing, computers, rv travel, senior olympics.

SUTHERLAND, MARY (MARCUS), composer, musician; d. T. Frederick Sholtis and Veronica Kuharik; m. Howard Lawrence Sutherland, Apr. 6, 1997; children: Jennifer, Nancy. MusB, DePaul U., 1967; MusM, U. Ky., 1978; postgrad., U. Memphis, 1978—80. Tchr., vocal coach, Memphis, 1978—94, St. Louis, 1994—; pianist Opera Memphis, Memphis Symphony Chorus, Regional Met. Opera, 1980—94; pianist, narrator, mgr. Sutherland Duo, St. Louis, 1992—; condr., art dir., mgr. devel. Midwest Chorale, St. Louis, 1994—2002; pianist Clayton H.S., St. Louis, 1997—; dir. music Clayton Cmty. Theater, Mo., 2004—. Composer: Exaltation: Songs of Women-Sacred Solos, 2005, Premier: The Winter's Tale, A Musical Romance, 2005; composer: (May Sarton) Franz, 2005, A Goose Soliloque: Myself to a Beguine, 2005, EineKleine Snailmusik, 2005. Participant Mentor St. Louis, 1996—2002; tutor Oasis, St. Louis, 2002—. Recipient Best Achievement in Musical Direction award, Arts for Life, 2004; grantee Pres.'s fellow, U. Memphis, 1978—80. Mem.: Am. Composters Forum, Internat. Alliance for Women in Music, Pi Kappa Lambda. Democrat. Avocations: reading, travel, theater. Home: 3104 Longfellow Blvd Saint Louis MO 63104 Office: The Sutherland Duo 3104 Longfellow Blvd Saint Louis MO 63104 Personal E-mail: msongmaker@sbcglobal.net.

SUTHERLAND, SUSAN J., lawyer; b. Canton, Ohio, 1957; m. Robert B. Opatrny. BA, Denison Coll., 1979; JD, NYU, 1982. Bar: NY 1983. Ptnr. Skadden, Arps, Slate, Meagher & Flom LLP, NYC. Office: Skadden Arps Slate Meagher & Flom LLP 4 Times Sq New York NY 10036 Office Phone: 212-735-2388. Office Fax: 917-777-2388. E-mail: ssutherl@skadden.com.

SUTLIN, VIVIAN, advertising executive; b. Chgo. d. Samuel E. and Doris (Weinberg) S. BA, Roosevelt U. V.p. creative group head Grey North Advt., Inc., Chgo.; v.p., creative dir., founder Pilot Products, Inc., Chgo.; TV writer, producer Grey Advt., Inc., N.Y.C.; sr. writer Young and Rubicam, Inc., N.Y.C.; v.p., creative dir. Dodge and Delano, N.Y.C., NY; pres. Vivian Sutlin Advt., new products and consumer packaged goods specialist with full svc. TV and print, domestic and internat. ops.; creative supr. William Douglas McAdams, Inc., NY, Grey Med. Advt., Inc., NY; pres. Vivian Sutlin Comm. Cons. Consumer and Med./Pharm. Advt.; pres. Signature Products East, N.Y.C., Internat. Packaging, Printing and Promotional Products Co. Co-author: Industry Women Speak Out. Recipient Chgo. Fedn. Advt. Clubs award, Am. TV Commls. Festival award, TV award Art Dirs. Club Chgo., Triangle award Med. Advt. Print, Internat. Broadcasting award, Best of Decade award RX Club, Guacaipuro TV award. Avocations: jogging, aerobics, tennis, art.

SUTTER, DAWN MARIE, special education educator; b. Buffalo, Aug. 7, 1975; d. Harry and Mildred Louise Sutter. BA, Canisius Coll., 1998, MS, 2000; cert., D'Youville Coll., 2003. Cert. spl. edn., elem. tchr., sch. counselor. Asst. to chmn. psychology dept. Canisius Coll., Buffalo, 1997—98; day asst. Cantalician Ctr. Workshop, Buffalo, 1998—2000, rehab. counselor, 2000—01; substitute tchr. Amhurst (NY) Pub. Sch., 2003—04; tchr.'s asst. Gateway-Longview Sch., Williamsville, NY, 2002—03; spl. edn. tchr. Buffalo Pub. Schs., 2004—. Mem.: NEA, aca, Western NY Counseling Assn.

SUTTER, ELEANOR BLY, retired diplomat; b. NYC, Oct. 21, 1945; d. Samuel M. and Sylvia Gertrude Bly; children: Deborah Nelson, Willis. BA, Swarthmore Coll., 1966; MA, Am. U., 1978; diploma in strategic studies, U.S. Army War Coll., 1997. Instr. English Thammasat U., Bangkok and Udornthani Tchr. Tng. Coll., 1967-71, Lomonosov State U., Moscow, 1973-74; rschr. Kennan Inst. for Advanced Russian Studies, 1977-79; fgn. svc. officer Office Soviet Internal Affairs Dept. of State, 1979-80, fgn. svc. officer Office of Strategic Nuc. Policy, 1986-88, fgn. svc. officer Office of Soviet Union Affairs, 1988-90, office dir. Washington, 1997-99, sr. inspector Office Inspector Gen., 1999-2001, dir. Office of Proliferation Threat Reduction, 2001—02; fgn. svc. officer U.S. Embassy, Kinshasa, 1980-82, London, 1982-85, Moscow, 1990-92, charge d'affaires ad interim Bratislava, 1993, dep. prin. officer, 1993-95, dep. chief of mission, 1995-96. Exec. dir., exec. sec., advisor U.S. Del. to Nuclear and Space Talks, Geneva, 1987-91; teaching fellow Russian lit. The Am. U., 1976-77; escort interpreter and translator Dept. of State, 1976. Co-author: Final Report of the Kennan Institute's Soviet Research Institutes Project, 1981. Founder Camp Wocsom, Moscow, 1974. Mem. Am. Fgn. Svc. Assn. Avocations: music, folk dance.

SUTTER, ELOUISE C., retired art educator; b. Jersey City, Feb. 10, 1925; d. Alfredo G. Conte and Asunta Maddalena; m. John H. Sutter, Sept. 2, 1956; children: Susan, Maria; 1 child, Sally. Art tchr., supr. Milford Sch., Milford, Del., 1947—51, Newark Sch., Del., 1951—52. Mem. World Affairs Coun., San Francisco, 1956—; pres. bd. Oakland YWCA, Calif. Mem.: Am. Humanistic Soc. Democrat. Presbyn. Avocations: archaeology, travel, reading, art. Home: 3627 Klamath St Oakland CA 94602

SUTTER, EMILY MAY GEESEMAN, retired psychologist, educator; b. St. Louis, Nov. 18, 1939; d. George Robert and Cora Hamilton (Glasgow) Geeseman; m. Gordon Frederick Sutter, Aug. 13, 1960; children: John Blaine, Steven George. BS, U. Pitts., 1960, M in Retailing, 1961; MEd, Wayne State U., 1965; PhD, U. Tex., 1967. Lic. psychologist, Tex. Chief psychologist Richmond State Sch., Houston, 1967-71; dir. Fairhill Sch., Houston, 1971-72; assoc. dir. Battin Clinic, Houston, 1972-81; from asst. to assoc. prof. U. Houston, Clear Lake, 1981-93, prof., 1993—2005, interim dean, 1990-92, 2001—02, prof. emerita, 2005—. Appointee Tex. State Bd. Examiners Psychologists, 1993-2002, chair, 1997-2000. Contbr. articles to profl. jours. Mem. APA, Tex. Psychol. Assn. (treas. 1978, liaison officer 1985-87, pres. 1990), Houston Psychol. Assn. (pres. 1976-77). Avocation: gardening. Home: 2110 Airline Dr Friendswood TX 77546-5504 Office Phone: 281-283-3511.

SUTTER, JANE ELIZABETH, conservationist, science educator; b. St. Louis, Nov. 27, 1939; d. Richard A. and Elizabeth Henby Sutter. AB in Sociology and English, Vassar Coll., 1961; MA in Health Facilities Mgmt., Webster Coll., St. Louis, 1979. Healthcare analyst, Chgo. and St. Louis, 1966-83; asst. dir. radio, TV and motion picture dept. AMA, Chgo., 1966-67; staff coord., rsch. assoc. Chgo. water quality study and environ. health study Inst. of Medicine of Chgo., 1967-69; dir. environ. health planning Comprehensive Health Planning, Inc., Chgo., 1969-73; planning assoc., spl. asst. to med. dir. Sutter Clinic, Inc., St. Louis, 1975-84; vol. activist, educator; founder, dir. for conservation and gardening for birds Wild Birds for the 21st Century (a non-profit ednl. svc.), 1994—; ednl. writer www.wildbirds.org. Author: City Approved Medical Emergency Plan of Operation O'Hare International and Midway Airports, 1971. Chmn. Opera Theatre of St. Louis Newsletter, Recitative, Vol. 1, No. 1, 1980, Vol. 1, No. 2, 1980; co-founder, com. mem. 1st Internat. Alewife Festival of Chgo., Chgo. Yacht Club, summer 1968; appointee Gov.'s Com. for Pure Air and Water, Chgo., 1968; spl. advocate N.Am. Migratory Birds particularly hummingbirds; mem. Ladue Chapel. Mem. Nat. Garden Clubs, Inc., Federated Garden Clubs of Mo., Inc., Clayton Garden Assn., Mo. Bot. Garden, St. Louis Artists' Guild (mem. artists' sect. 1992-95, portraitist), Mo. Bird Conservation Initiative, Neotropical Bird Club (UK), Univ. Club St. Louis, Vassar Club St. Louis, Bradenton C. of C. Avocations: gardening, writing. Home: 7376 Pershing Blvd Saint Louis MO 63130-4206

SUTTLE, HELEN JAYSON, retired elementary school educator; b. Plattsburgh, NY, Dec. 13, 1925; d. Harold Lincoln Jayson and Blanche Rabideau Jayson Woods; widowed, 1993; 1 child, Adolphia Helen Suttle Blanton. BA in Edn., Limestone Coll., 1961; MA in Edn., Winthrop U., 1973. Cert. tchr., S.C. Tchr. Madden Elem. Sch., Spartanburg, S.C., 1961-71, West Jr. High Sch., Gaffney, S.C., 1971-81, L.L. Vaughn Elem. Sch., Gaffney, S.C., 1981-88; substitute tchr. Gaffney Dis. 1, 1988—. Vol. SC Budget Control Bd., Upstate Carolina Med. Ctr., Meals on Wheels, Literacy Assn., local soup kitchen; chmn. Cherokee County Rep. Com.; v.p. Ch. Women's Guild, pres., 1998—; dir. religious edn. Sacred Heart Ch., 2001—; pres. Sacred Heart Sr. Citizens Club; treas. ch. com. Greenville Deanery; pres.-elect Piedmont Deanery, 2002—; Eucharistic min., lector; mem. exec. bd. SC Coun. Cath. Ch. Women, 1998—, chair family commn., 1998—; pres. Piedmont Deanery, 2002—03; trustee Limestone Coll. Named Woman of Yr., S.C. Coun. Cath. Women Greenville Deanery, 1996, Alumna of Yr., Limestone Coll., 2004. Fellow Internat. Biog. Assn. (life, dep. gov. Am. chpt.), Limestone Coll. Alumni Assn. (pres., chpt. pres.), Fountain Club (charter mem.), Kalosophia Honor Soc. Roman Catholic. Avocations: writing, art, gardening, crafts. Home: 201 Trenton Rd Gaffney SC 29340-3626

SUTTON, BEVERLY JEWELL, psychiatrist; b. Rockford, Mich., May 27, 1932; d. Beryl Dewey and Cora Belle (Potes) Jewell; m. Harry Eldon Sutton, July 7, 1962; children: Susan, Caroline. MD, U. Mich., 1957. Diplomate Am. Bd. Pediat., Am. Bd. Psychiatry and Neurology. Rotating intern St. Joseph Mercy Hosp., Ann Arbor, Mich., 1958; resident in child psychiatry Hawthorne Ctr., Northville, Mich., 1958-62; resident in pediat. U. Hosp./U. Mich. Med. Ctr., Ann Arbor, 1959-61; resident in psychiatry Austin (Tex.) State Hosp., 1962-64, dir. children's svc., 1964-89, dir. psychiat. residency program, 1989—, dir. tng. and rsch., 1993-98. Cons. in field. Contbr. articles to profl. jours. Active numerous civic orgns. Recipient Outstanding Achievement award, YWCA, 1989, Jackson Day award, Tex. Soc. Child and Adolescent Psychiatry, 1989, Showcase award, Tex. Dept. Mental Health/Mental Retardation, 1990. Fellow Am. Acad. Child and Adolescent Psychiatry (life), Am. Psychiat. Soc., Am. Pediatric Assn.; mem. Tex. Soc. Child and Adolescent Psychiatry (pres. 1979-80), Tex. Soc. Psychiat. Physicians (Disting. Svc. award 1990), AMA, Tex. Med. Soc., Am. Genetics Soc. Office: Seton Shoal Creek Hosp 3501 Mills Ave Austin TX 78731 Business E-Mail: bsutton@seton.org.

SUTTON, CECILIA (CECE SUTTON), bank executive; b. Charlotte, NC; B in Psychology, U. SC; MBA, Winthrop U. Branch manager First Union Corp., Raleigh and Cary, NC, consumer credit sales mgr. Charlotte, NC, 1984—86, consumer banking mgr. Greenville, SC, 1986—89, consumer bank training dir. Charlotte, NC, 1988—89, area exec. Rock Hill, SC, 1989—92, head SC Gen. Banking Group Greenville, SC, 1992—93, area exec. Rock Hill, SC, 1993—95, consumer banking exec. SC, exec. v.p. SC, 2001; exec. v.p., head retail Wachovia Corp. (merged with First Union Corp), Charlotte, 2001—. Office: Wachovia Corp 301 S Coll St Charlotte NC 28288-0018

SUTTON, DOLORES, actress, writer; b. N.Y.C. BA in Philosophy, NYU. Appeared in broadway plays including Man With the Golden Arm, 1956, Career, 1958, Machinal, 1960, Rhinoceros, Liliom, She Stoops to Conquer, Hedda Gabler, Anna Karenina, Eccentricities of a Nightingale, Brecht on Brecht, Young Gifted and Black, Luv, The Friends, The Web and the Rock, The Seagull, Saturday, Sunday, Monday, The Little Foxes, What's Wrong With This Picture, The Cocktail Hour, My Fair Lady (Broadway revival), 1994, My Fair Lady (nat. tour), 1993-94; films include The Trouble With Angels, Where Angels Go, Trouble Follows, Crossing Delancey, Crimes and Misdemeanors, Tales of the Darkside; TV appearances include Studio One, Hallmark Hall of Fame Prodn. An Wilderness, Theatre Guild of the Air: Danger, Suspense, Gunsmoke, Valiant Lady, General Hospital, From These Roots, As the World Turns, Edge of Night, F. Scott Fitzgerald in Hollywood, Patty Hearst Story, All in the Family, Bob Newhart Show, All My Children, others, (TV writer) Lady Somebody, 1999, The Secret Storm, Loving; playwright: Down at the Old Bull and Bush, The Web and the Rock, Born Yesterday, 1995, A Perfect Ganesh, 1995, Detail of a Larger Work, 1995, The Front Page, 1996, The Exact Center of the Universe, 1997, A Drop in the Bucket, 1997, Spring Storm (newly discovered Tennessee Williams play), 1997, Signs and Wonders, 1998, It Gives Me Great Pleasure, 2001, Company Comin', 2006, and others; prodns. Free Ascent, 2001, Burial Society, 2001, The Find, 2002. Mem. Actors Studio, League of Profl. Theatre Women (bd. dirs.), Ensemble Studio Theatre (bd. dirs.). Personal E-mail: suttonplace@webtv.net.

SUTTON, JULIA, musicologist, dance historian; b. Toronto, July 20, 1928; d. Samuel L. and Anne R. (Rubin) Sumberg. AB summa cum laude, Cornell U., 1949; MA, Colo. Coll., 1952; PhD, U. Rochester, 1962. Instr. music history New Sch. for Social Rsch., 1962-63; instr. music Queens Coll., CUNY, 1963-66; instr. music history and musicology New Eng. Conservatory Music, 1967—90, instr. and prof. musicology, 1967—90, chmn. dept. music history and musicology, 1971-90, chmn. faculty senate, 1971-73, prof. emerita, 1992. Vis. asst. prof. George Peabody Coll. for Tchrs., 1966-67; instr. NYU, summers 1963, 64; pvt. tchr. piano, 1949-65; lectr., rsch. dir. in musicology, music as related to the dance; presenter numerous workshops and summer insts. on Renaissance dance. Dance dir. N.Y. Pro Musica prodn. An Entertainment for Elizabeth, Caramoor, N.Y., Saratoga, N.Y., U. Ariz., Stanford U., UCLA, 1969, ann. nationwide tours, 1970-1973; dance dir. Descent of Rhythm and Harmony, Colorado Springs, Colo., 1970, Renaissance Revisited, Phila., 1972, An Evening of Renaissance Music and Dance, York U., Toronto, 1974; author: Jean Baptiste Besard's Novus Partus 1617, 1962; editor: Thoinot Arbeau: Orchesography 1588, 1967; translator, editor: Fabritio Caroso: Nobiltà di dame 1600, 1986, reprinted 1995; producer, co-dir. (tng. video) Il Ballarino, 1991; contbr. numerous articles to profl. jours. and Internat. Ency. of Dance, The New Grove Dictionary of Music and Musicians 1st and 2d edit., Die Musik in Geschichte und Gegenwart, 1st edit. Mem. Am. Musicological Soc., Soc. of Dance History Scholars, Phi Beta Kappa. Office Phone: 781-893-0856. E-mail: julia-sutton@rcn.com.

SUTTON, JULIA ZEIGLER, retired special education educator; b. Greenville, Ala, July 24, 1935; d. Floyd Millard and Edith Nettles Zeigler; m. William G. Sutton, June 16, 1956; children: William F., Joseph S., Julia N., John M. BS in Edn., 1958. Cert. spl. edn./mental retardation tchr., Ala. Tchr., DIAL III vol. Huntsville City Sch., Ala., 1966, spl. edn. tchr., 1973—98; tchr. Christian Women's Job Corps, Huntsville, 1999—. Mem. adv. bd. Coll. Edn., U. Ala., Tuscaloosa, 2001—. Mem. Civic Club Coun., Huntsville, 1967—68, Huntsville Hosp. Aux., 1965—73, pres., 1967—68; mem./ choir and various positions First United Meth. Ch., Huntsville, 1975—; life mem. Huntsville Hosp. Angel; chmn. Spl. Ministries FUM Ch., 1982—85; vol. DIAL III readiness testing in city and county sch., 2000—. Named one of Outstanding Young Women of Am., 1968; recipient Listed in Who's Who of Am. Women, 2002—03. Mem.: DAR (Twickenham Town chpt. 1st vice regent 2002—), Organizing mem. of Hunts./Madison Co. Panhellenic, Huntsville Alpha Gamma Delta Alumnae Club (past pres. 1962), Coll. of Edn. Capstone Soc., Camellia Soc. (organizing pres. 2001—02), Huntsville Bot. Garden and Garden Guild, Early Works Soc. (chmn. mem. event 1998—), Twickenham Hist. Preservation (bd. dir. 1975—2000, dist. assn. sec. 1985—2000). Methodist. Avocations: cooking British tea foods, heraldry-painting coats of arms, aerobics, community volunteering, collecting teapots and tea china.

SUTTON, KAREN E., museum director; b. New Brunswick, N.J., Aug. 26, 1952; d. Alfred Michael and Carmen (Collado) Sutton; children: Sloane, Brooke, Devon, Megan, Christopher. BA, Hofstra U., 1974; postgrad., NYU, 1987—89. Asst. to dir. Mus. Am. Folk Art, N.Y.C., 1975-76, acting dir., 1976-77, bd. dirs., exec. com. officer, 1980-88, gallery dir., 1989-92, dir. ops., 1992-94, dep. dir. planning and adminstrn., 1994-95; v.p. Sotheby's, N.Y.C., 1995-96, sr. v.p. adminstrn., 1996-2001, sr. v.p. worldwide mktg., 2001—. Bd. dirs. Family Dynamics, N.Y.C., 1976-80. Mem.: NY Women in Real Estate, Cosmopolitan Club (younger members chmn.). Democrat. Episcopalian. Office: Sotheby's 1334 York Ave New York NY 10021-4806 Home: 132 E 72 St New York NY 10021 Office Phone: 212-606-7410. E-mail: karen.sutton@sothebys.com.

SUTTON, LOIS GENE, elementary school educator; b. Weiser, Idaho; d. Milton William and Ellen Hilma Branch; m. Vernon Clarence Sutton, Jan. 28, 1967; children: Lodi Ellene, Toni LaGene. BA in Edn., Boise State U., 1973; MA in Curriculum and Instrn., Northest Nazarene U., 1999. Nat. cert. NBOT, 2000. Elem. tchr. Midvale Sch. Dist., Idaho, 1976—2005. Adj. prof. Treasure Valley C.C., Ontario, Okla., 2002—04. Named to Idaho 4-H Hall of Fame, Idaho 4-H Office, Moscow, 2002; recipient Tchr. of Yr., Salubria Masonic Lodge, 1997. Mem.: Idaho Edn. Assn., NEA, Idaho Reading Coun., Nat. Assn. Edn. of Young Children, Midvale Lions Club (sight chmn., treas.). Home: 3336 Farm to Market Rd Midvale ID 83645

SUTTON, LYNN SORENSEN, librarian; b. Detroit, July 31, 1953; d. Leonard Arthur Edward and Dorothy Ann (Steele) Sorensen. AB, U. Mich., 1975, MLS, 1976. Dir. Med. Libr. South Chgo. Cmty. Hosp., 1976-77; corp. dirs. librs. Detroit-Macomb Hosp. Corp., Detroit, 1977-86; dir. librs. Harper Hosp., Detroit, 1987-88; dir. Sci. and Engring. Libr. Wayne State U., Detroit, 1989-95, dir. undergrad. libr., 1996—2004; dir. Z. Smith Reynolds Libr. Wake Forest U., Winston-Salem, NC, 2004—. Cons. Catherine McAuley Health Sys., Ann Arbor, Mich., 1993. Contbr. articles to profl. jours. Mem. ALA, Assn. Coll. and Rsch. Librs. (budget and fin. com. 1995—), Mich. Health Scis. Librs. Assn. (pres. 1987-88), Met. Detroit Med. Libr. Group (pres. 1983-84), Phi Beta Kappa, Beta Phi Mu. Office: Z Smith Reynolds Libr Wake Forest U Box 7777 Reynolda Station Winston Salem NC 27109 Office Phone: 336-758-5090. Business E-Mail: suttonls@wfu.edu.*

SUTTON, NANCY THURMOND, music educator; d. A. L. Thurmond and Rosetta Irene (Posey) Thurmond-Hale; m. Geoffrey Coe Sutton, June 25, 1977 (div. 1999); 1 child, Brittany Brafford. BMus, U. Memphis, 1969, MusM, 1979; cert., Royal Sch. Ch. Music, Croydon, Eng., 1994; D of Musical Arts, U. Calif., L.A., 2000. Organist, choirmaster St. Paul's Episcopal Ch., Memphis, 1965—68; organist, dir. music St. George's Episcopal Ch., Germantown, Tenn., 1968—97; dir. choral activities U. N.C., Charlotte, NC, 2000—. Dir. St. George's Festival of Music, Germantown, 1982—97; music instr. U. Memphis, 1975—76; faculty Sewanee Music Conf., 1995; tchr., mentor Memphis City Schs., 1969—73. Conductor Andrew Lloyd Webber's Requiem, 1986, Arvo Part's Miserere, 1990, Lalo Schifren's Cantos Aztecas, American Premier, 1992, pub. Sun Splendor, 2000. Organist, choirmaster St. Christopher's Cath. Ch., Dickson, Tenn., 2003—05; dir. choral workshops Roman Cath. Dioceses, Tenn., Ky.; organist, dir. music Church of the Most Holy Trinity, Augusta, Ga., 2005—, Musician Artist Trust Fund grantee,

1980—97. Mem.: Orch. League, Assn. Anglican Musicinas (conv. chair 1982), Am. Guild Organists (dean 1980—81). Episcopalian. Avocations: horseback riding, walking, reading, water-skiing, skiing. E-mail: nants@knology.net.

SUTTON, WANDA LYNNE, language educator; b. Trenton, Mich., Mar. 1, 1961; d. Bobby Joe and Jo Ann Kilgore Sutton. BS in Secondary Edn., U. North Ala., Florence, 1983; MEd, Bob Jones U., Greenville, SC, 1991; student, U. North Ala., Florence, 2002. Tchr. Kingwood Christian Sch., Alabaster, Ala., 1984—85, Shelby Christian Acad., Pelham, 1985—87, 1989, Florence Christian Acad., 1987—88; proofreader, editor Bob Jones U., Greenville, SC, 1989—91; tchr. Harvest Christian Acad., Barrigada, Guam, 1991—2005; tchr. English Covenant Christian Sch., Tuscumbia, Ala., 2005—. Advisor yearbook Harvest Christian Acad., 1991—95, advisor sr., 2000—05, advisor beta, 2000—05; sr. sponsor Covenant Christian Sch., 2006—, advisor yearbook, 2005—, adv. nat. H.S., 2005—. Republican. Baptist. Avocations: travel, reading. Home: 600 Firestone Ave Apt 1116 Muscle Shoals AL 35661 Office: Covenant Christian Sch 1900 Covenant Dr Tuscumbia AL 35674

SUTTON-CREECH, DONNA LYNN, gifted and talented educator; b. Arcadia, La., Dec. 14, 1963; d. Jerry Lamar and Betty Muse Sutton; m. Stephen Orel Creech, July 9, 2005. BA, La. Tech. U., 1984, MA, 1985, EdD in curriculum and instruction, 2002. Compensatory edn. tchr. Bienville Parish Sch. Sys., Arcadia, La., 1985—90; parttime computer instr. Northwest La. Tech. Coll., Minden, La., 2002—04; gifted program tchr. Bienville Parish, Sch. Sys., Arcadia, 1990—. Computer workshop presenter Bienville Parish La. Libr., Arcadia, La., 2003. Publr. genealogy column, Bienville Democrat. Participant Tech Rome 1987, La. Tech. U. Named Tchr. of Yr., Ringgold Elem. Sch., 1995; recipient Daughters of Am. Revolution Outstanding Jr. Mem. award, Dorcheat-Bistineau, 1997; La. Heritage Edn. grant, La. Divsn. Archaeology and Hist., 2003. Mem.: DAR (Dorcheat-Bistineau chpt. officer, regist & historian, chpt. chair, Dorcheat-Bistineau chpt. scholarship com., Good Citizens award), Phi Delta Kappa, Krewe of Gemini, Colonial Dames Seventeenth Century (state jr. mem. chair 2001—04, Martha Randolph chpt. v.p. 2002—04, state pages chair), Nat. Soc. Magna Carta Dames and Barons, USA Order of Crown of Charlemagne. Republican. Baptist. Avocations: genealogy, reading, travel, painting.

SUVARI, MENA, actress; b. Newport, RI, Feb. 9, 1979; d. Ando and Candance Suvari; m. Robert Brinkmann, Mar. 4, 2000. Actor: (TV films) Atomic Train, 1999; (TV series) Six Feet Under, 2004—; (films) Nowhere, 1997, Snide and Prejudice, 1997, Kiss the Girls, 1997, Slums of Beverly Hills, 1998, The Rage: Carrie 2, 1999, American Pie, 1999, American Beauty, 1999, American Virgin, 2000, Loser, 2000, Sugar & Spice, 2001, American Pie 2, 2001, The Musketeer, 2001, Sonny, 2002, Spun, 2002, Trauma, 2004, Beauty Shop, 2005, Domino, 2005, Rumor Has It., 2005. Office: c/o Gersh Agy 232 N Canon Dr Beverly Hills CA 90210*

SUZUKI, WENDY A., neurology educator; BA in Physiology and Anatomy, U. Calif., Berkeley, 1987; PhD in Neurosci., U. Calif., San Diego, 1993. Postdoctoral rschr., lab. neuropsychology Nat. Inst. Mental Health, 1993—97; assoc. prof., neural sci. NYU, N.Y.C., 1998—. Contbr. articles to profl. jours. Recipient Donald B. Lindsley prize in Behavioral Neurosci., Soc. for Neurosci., 1994, Troland Rsch. award, Nat. Acad. Scis., 2004; scholar, McKnight Found., 1998. Office: NYU Meyer 2-4 Wash Pl 1061 New York NY 10003 also: Ctr for Neural Sci NYU 4 Washington Pl Rm 809 New York NY 10003

SVADLENAK, JEAN HAYDEN, museum director, consultant; b. Wilmington, Del., Mar. 4, 1955; d. Marion M. and Ida Jean (Calcagni) Hayden; m. Steven R. Svadlenak, May 26, 1979. BS in Textiles and Clothing, U. Del., 1977; MA in History Mus. Studies, SUNY, Oneonta, 1982; postgrad., U. Calif., Berkeley, 1982. Curatorial asst. The Hagley Mus., Wilmington, 1976-77; curator of costumes and textiles The Kansas City (Mo.) Mus., 1978-82, chief curator, 1982-84, assoc. exec. dir. for collection and exhibits mgmt., 1984-86, interim pres., 1986-87, pres., 1987-89. Researcher, guest curator N.Y. State Hist. Assn., Cooperstown, 1980; grant reviewer Inst. for Mus. Svcs., 1985-89; ad hoc faculty U. Kans., 1991-2001, U. Mo., Kansas City, 1992-98. Mem. Am. Assn. Mus. (surveyor mus. assessment program 1985-89, accreditation vis. com. 1990—), Am. Assn. State and Local History, Heritage League Kansas City (bd. dirs. 1987-89), Midwest Mus. Conf. (coun. 1992-94), Mo. Mus. Assocs. (pres. 1992-94), Com. on Mus. Profl. Tng. (2d v.p. 1994-96, at-large rep. 1997-2000). Avocation: cooking. Home: 624 Romany Rd Kansas City MO 64113-2037

SVEINSSON, LINDA RODGERS, engineering company executive; b. Tuscaloosa, Ala., July 1, 1938; d. Eric and Sarah Ella (Haughton) Rodgers; m. Hjalmar Sveinsson, May 29, 1971; children: Martha M. Moreno, Stephen R.M. Moreno, III. BA in Math., Birmingham-So. Coll., 1960; MS in Indsl. Engring., U. Ala., 1972. Sys. analyst U. Ala. Med. Ctr., Birmingham, 1967-69; sys. mgr. Internat. Data Sys., New Orleans, 1969-70; computer scientist Computer Scis. Corp., Silver Spring, Md., 1973-76; computer sys. specialist Sys. Devel. Corp., McLean, Va., 1976-78; mem. tech. staff Bell Labs., Holmdel, NJ, 1978—80, tech. supr. Columbus, Ohio, 1980—85; mgr. bus. devel. No. Telecom., Inc., Research Triangle Park, N.C., 1985-88; dept. mgr. network ops. and mgmt. systems GTE Fed. Systems, Ctr., 1988-94; cons. Bell Atlantic, 1994-95, AT&T Solutions, 1996-97, Mitretek Sys., 1998—. Mem. IEEE, Phi Beta Kappa, Alpha Pi Mu. Republican. Methodist. Home: 8911 Old Courthouse Rd Vienna VA 22182-2107 Office: 3150 Fairview Park Dr S Falls Church VA 22042 Business E-Mail: linda.sveinsson@mitretek.org.

SVETLOVA, MARINA, ballerina, retired choreographer; b. Paris, May 3, 1922; arrived in U.S., 1940; d. Max and Tamara (Andreieff) Hartman. Studied with Vera Trefilova, Paris, 1930-36, studied with L. Egorova and M. Kschessinska, 1936-39; studied with A. Vilzak, N.Y.C., 1940-57; D (hon.), Fedn. Francaise de Danse, 1988. Ballet dir. So. Vt. Art Ctr., 1959-64; dir. Svetlova Dance Ctr., Dorset, Vt., 1965-95; prof. ballet dept. Ind. U., Bloomington, 1969-92, prof. emeritus, 1992—, chmn. dept., 1969-78. Choreographer Dallas Civic Opera, 1964—67, (ballets) Ft. Worth Opera, 1967—83, San Antonio Opera, 1983, Seattle Opera, Houston Opera, Kansas City Performing Arts Found., The Fairy Queen, 1966, L'Histoire du Soidat, 1968, ballerina Ballet Russe de Monte Carlo, 1939—41, guest ballerina Ballet Theatre, 1942, London's Festival Ballet, Teatro dell Opera, Rome, Nat. Opera Stockholm, Suomi Opera, Helsinki, Finland, Het Nederland Ballet, Holland, Cork Irish Ballet, Paris Opera Comique, London Palladium, Teatro Colon, Buenos Aires, others, prima ballerina Met. Opera, 1943—50, N.Y.C. Opera, 1950—52; performer: (ballets) Graduation Ball; contbr. articles to profl. jours. Mem.: Nat. Soc. Arts and Letters (nat. dance chmn.), Conf. Ballet in Higher Edn., Am. Guild Mus. Artists (bd. dirs.). Office: 2100 E Maxwell Ln Bloomington IN 47401-6119 Office Phone: 812-330-0567.

SVOBODA, JANICE JUNE, nurse; d. Alfred A. and Jessie (Boor) Hinke; m. Glenn R. Svoboda, July 20, 1957; children: Melora, Kevin, Craig. Diploma, Luther Hosp., 1954; cert., U. Wis., 1955; student, U. Wis., Madison, 1955—57; BS in Health Edn. cum laude, U. Wis., Milw., 1980; student, Alverno Coll., 1991-92. Pub. health nurse Ozaukee County, Wis., 1979, 86; asst. instr. nursing Milw. Area Tech. Coll., 1979-83; instr. seminar Cardinal Stritch Coll., Milw., 1985-87; nutritional counselor Nutri-Sys., Grafton, Wis., 1987-90. Instr. seminar Milw. Area Tech. Coll., 1983, 90, coping with stress course, 1985-86, assertiveness training course, 1985, health seminars Alverno Coll., Milw., 1991-95, designed and implemented alternative health and healing seminar, Alverno Coll., 1994-97; pvt. practice holistic nurse cons., nutrition and herbal therapy, 1997—; lectr. pub. on nutrition and anti aging. Mem. Am. Holistic Nurses Assn. (cert. and recert.), Ctr. for Sci. in the Pub. Interest. Office Phone: 262-372-1242.

SVOBODA, PATRICIA HELEN, art historian; b. Washington, Dec. 22, 1950; d. Ladislav Maurice and Marie Martina (Vojta) S. BFA in Graphic Design, U. Wash., 1974, BA in Art History, 1974, MA in Art History, 1980. Graphic artist freelance, Seattle, Washington, 1971—86; art history rschr. for exhbns. Collaboration of Seattle Art Mus. & U. Wash., Seattle, 1977—78; graphic artist U. Rsch. Tech. Edn. Ctr., Rockville, Md., 1984; graphic artist, adminstrv. asst. U.S. Dept. Commerce Office Publs. Svc., Washington, 1984—88; lectr. art history Phillips Collection, Washington, 1987—; coord. rsch. Smithsonian Instn. Nat. Portrait Gallery, Washington, 1988—; lectr. art history Georgetown U., Washington, 1989—97. Rep. Art Svcs. Internat., Alexandria, Va., 1990-92; contbr. Inst. for Classical Studies, Prague, Czech Republic, 1993-94, Inst. for the Classical Tradition, Boston U., 1995, Mus. of Decorative Arts, Prague, Czech Republic, 1996. Author: Zoe Dusanne, 1980; interviewer for Northwest Traditions, 1978; prin. work includes Seattle YMCA mural Olympic Race, 1982; contbr. articles to profl. jours. Keyworker Combined Fed. Campaign, Washington, 1985-88; participant Internat. Partnerships among Mus. Programs Am. Assn. Mus., 2003-05. Recipient Nat. Pks. Svc. Purchase Prize award Soc. Illustrators, 1974, Cert. of Performance award Smithsonian Instn., 1989-2006. Mem. Am. Assn. Mus., Internat. Coun. Mus., Coll. Art Assn., Czechoslovak Soc. Arts & Scis., Internat. Soc. for Classical Tradition, U. Wash. Alumni Assn. Avocations: literature, history, langs., music, photography. Office: Smithsonian Instn Nat Portrait Gallery Victor Bldg-Ste 8300 PO Box 37012 Washington DC 20013-7012 Business E-Mail: svobodap@si.edu.

SVRAKA, PATTI A., elementary school educator; b. Rockville Ctr., N.Y., Feb. 11, 1972; d. Charles and Mary Winterfeldt; m. Samir Svraka, July 7, 2000; children: Sean Patrick, Kerry Rose. BEd, Wagner Coll., S.I., N.Y., 1994, MEd, 1996. Tchg. asst. Baldwin Sch. Dist., NY, 1997—98; tchr. elem. sch. Hicksville Sch. Dist., NY, 1998—. Mem.: PTA, NEA. Republican. Roman Cath. Avocations: reading, basketball, travel. Home: 5 Chester Ln Farmingdale NY 11735 Office: East Street Sch 50 East St Hicksville NY 11801

SWAFFAR, GLENDA JEAN, director; d. Glen Edward and Imagean Perkins; m. J.D. Swaffar, Aug. 27, 1992; children: Leeann Glynette Pratt, Mark Tillman Pratt. BA, U. Mo., Columbia, 1969; MS summa cum laude, U. Mo.-Kans. City, 1988, Edn. Specialist, 1990. Cert. tchr./media specialist Mo. Dept. Elem. and Secondary Edn., 1983. Media specialist Hickman Mills HS, Kans. City, 1985—99, instrnl. facilitator, A+ coord., 1999—. Adv. com. Tchr. Edn. U. Mo., Kans. City; elector for bishop Episcopal Ch., Kans. City, 1984—85. Mem.: Mo. Assn. Sch. Librs. (assoc.), Am. Assn. Sch. Librs. (assoc.), ASCD (assoc.), Internat. Reading Assn. (assoc.), Phi Kappa Phi. Achievements include successfully writing grant to secure funding and then led staff of 100 teachers through a three-year improvement process to prepare our school for designation by the state as an A+ high school. Avocations: reading, travel, swimming, scrapbooks, fabric arts. Office: Hickman Mills HS 9010 Old Santa Fe Rd Kansas City MO 64138 Office Phone: 816-316-7259. Office Fax: 816-316-7248. Business E-Mail: glendas@hickmanmills.org.

SWAIN, JUDITH LEA, cardiologist, educator; b. Long Beach, Calif., Sept. 24, 1948; m. Edward W. Holmes. BS in Chemistry with deptl. honors, UCLA, 1970; MD, U. Calif., San Diego, 1974. Diplomate Am. Bd. Internal Medicine, cardiovasc. disease; lic. physician Calif., Pa., N.C. Intern in medicine Duke U. Med. Ctr., 1974-75, resident in medicine, 1975-76, fellow in cardiology, 1976-80, assoc. in medicine, 1979-81, from asst. prof. medicine to assoc. prof. medicine, 1981-91, asst. prof. physiology, 1981-88, assoc. prof. microbiology & immunology, 1988-91, Herbert C. Rorer prof. med. scis., prof. genetics, 1991-92, mem. molecular biology grad. group, 1991-92, chief cardiovasc. divsn., 1991-92; chair dept. medicine Stanford (Calif.) U., 1996—; dir. Coll. Integrated Life Scis. U. Calif., San Diego, 2004—. Vis. asst. prof. dept. genetics Harvard Med. Sch., Boston, 1985-86; mem. search com. for dir. Ctr. for Aging, Duke U. Med. Ctr., 1991—, mem. exec. com. deptl. awards selection, 1992—, chmn. combined degree dir. search com., 1993, mem. clin. rsch. ctr. adv. com., 1993-94, mem. grad. student admissions com., 1993, mem. search com. for chief cardiovasc. surgery, 1992, dept. medicine intern selection com., 1992—; mem. instnl. rev. com. Pa. Muscle Inst., 1993; cardiology adv. com. Nat. Heart, Lung, & Blood Inst., 1989-93; dir. USA-Russia Cardiovasc. Rsch. Program, 1992—; mem. NIH Task Force on Heart Failure, 1992-93, dirs. standing com. on clin. rsch. NIH, 1995—; cons. Netherlands Rsch. Initiative in Molecular Cardiology, 1993; external adv. com. Ctr. for Prevention of Cardiovasc. Disease, Harvard Sch. Pub. Health, 1993—; adv. coun. NHLBI, 1995—, Friends of NHLBI com., 1996—, lectr. in field. Exec. editor: Trends in Cardiovascular Medicine, 1990-93; mem. editl. bd. Circulation Rsch., 1991—, Circulation, 1991—, Jour. Clin. Investigation, 1992—; cons. editor: Circulation, 1993—; contbr. articles to med. jours. Mem. exec. com. Coun. on Basic Sci., Am. Heart Assn., 1986-93, chmn. Katz Prize Award Com., 1989-92, rsch. rev. com., 1990-93, fellowship rsch. com., 1992—, program com., 1992—, mem. Levine Young Investigator Awards Com., Coun. on Clin. Cardiology, 1994—, mem. Basic Sci. Coun.; bd. dirs. Southeastern Pa. Heart Assn., 1992—. Recipient Bristol-Myers Squibb Cardiovasc. Achievement award, 1992, also numerous rsch. grants. Fellow Am. Coll. Cardiology (internat. edn. com. 1994—, chair cardiovasc. rsch. com. 1996—), Coll. Physicians of Phila.; mem. Assn. Univ. Cardiologists, Assn. Am. Physicians, Assn. Prof. of Cardiology, Am. Soc. Cell Biology, Am. Fedn. Clin. Rsch., Am. Soc. Clin. Investigation (pres.-elect 1994—, councilor 1991—), Internat. Soc. Heart Rsch. (councilor 1988—), Interurban Clin. Club, Clin. and Climitol. Soc., John Morgan Soc. Office: U Calif Sch Medicine 410 Pepper Canyon Hall 9500 Gilman Dr La Jolla CA 92093-0602 Office Phone: 858-534-7658. E-mail: jlswain@ucsd.edu.

SWAIN, LAURA TAYLOR, federal judge; b. Bklyn., 1958; d. Justus E. and Madeline V. (Allgood) Taylor; m. Andrew J. Swain, 1991. AB, Harvard U., 1979, JD, 1982. Bar: Mass. 1982, N.Y. 1983, U.S. Dist. Ct. (so. and ea. dists.) N.Y. 1983. Law clk to chief judge U.S. Dist. Ct. (so. dist.) N.Y., 1982-83; assoc. Debevoise & Plimpton, N.Y.C., 1983-95, counsel, 1995-96; U.S. bankruptcy judge U.S. Bankruptcy Ct., Bklyn., 1996-2000; judge U.S. Dist. Ct. (So. Dist.), NY, 2000—. Mem. N.Y. State Bd. Law Examiners, Albany, 1986-96; mem. multistate bar exam. com. Nat. Conf. Bar Examiners, 1987-99, mem. testing, R&D devel. com., 1990-94, mem. long range planning com., 1994-96; cons. N.Y. Profl. Edn. Project, 1995-96; adv. com. for fules of banruptcy procedures Judicial Conf. U.S., 2002-. Co-contbr. articles on employee benefits, employee stock ownership plans, acctg. and bankruptcy to profl. publs.; contbg. author: New York Insurance Law, 1991. Trustee Diocese of N.Y. (Episcopal), 1991-92; mem. Dessoff Choirs, N.Y.C., 1984-92; bd. dirs. Episcopal Charities, Inc., 1996-2003, Coalition Consumer Bankruptcy Debtor Edn., 1998—. Mem. ABA, Assn. of Bar of City of N.Y., Met. Black Bar Assn., N.Y. State Bar Assn., Nat. Conf. Bankruptcy Judges, Nat. Assn. Women Judges, Fed. Judges Assn. (bd. dirs. 2005-). Episcopalian. Avocation: music. Office: US Courthouse 40 Centre St Rm 1205 New York NY 10007

SWAIN, MARY ANN PRICE, university official; b. Chardon, Ohio, Apr. 20, 1941; d. A. David and Mary A. Price; m. Donald B. Swain, June 27, 1964; children: Judy, Brenda. BA in Psychology, DePauw U., 1963; MA in Psychology, U. Mich., 1964, PhD in Psychology, 1969. Dir. Sch. Nursing Doctoral Program U. Mich., Ann Arbor, 1975—76, chmn. dept. nursing rsch., 1977—82, assoc. v.p. acad. affairs, 1983—93, interim co-dir. pers., 1986—88, interim dir. affirmative action, 1988—89, interim v.p. student svcs., 1990—92; provost and v.p. acad. affairs SUNY, Binghamton, 1993—. Evaluation site visotor U. Balt. Sch. Law, 1996—97, Tes. Wesleyan U., 1998—99, U. Va. Sch. Nursing, Charlottesville, 1994—95; chmn. coun. acad. affairs Nat. Assn. State Univs. and Land Grant Colls., 1998—99. Co-author (with H. Erickson and E. Tomlim): Modeling and Role-modeling: A Theory and Paradigm for Nursing, 1983. Chmn. campaign United Way Broome COunty, Binghamton, 1998—99; pres. bd. dirs. Vis. Nurses Assn. Huron Valley, Ann Arbor, 1989—92. Fellow Woodrow Wilson fellow, 1963. Mem.: Am. Psychol. Soc., Am. Assn. Higher Edn., Am. Soc. Quality Control, Sigma Theta Tau, Phi Beta Kappa, Golden Key Hon. Soc. Office: SUNY at Binghamton Provost Office PO Box 6000 Binghamton NY 13902-6000 Office Phone: 607-777-2141. E-mail: mswain@binghamton.edu.

SWAIN, NICOLE FALVO, psychologist; d. Ronald Anthony and Carol Ann Falvo; m. James Scott Swain, Dec. 14, 2002. BSc, Otterbein Coll., 1993; MA, Xavier U., 1997, PsyD, 2001. Lic. Psychologist OH, 2003, Colo., 2004. Psychol. asst. St. Joseph Orphanage, Cin., 1998—2000; psychology intern Children's Hosp., Columbus, Ohio, 2000—01; post-doctoral psychology fellow Children's Hosp. Med. Ctr., Cin., 2001—03, elected co-chief post doctoral fellow, 2002—03; clin. psychologist Boulder Cmty. Hosp., Colo., 2004; pediatric psychologist Children's Hosp., Denver, 2004—. Contbr. articles to profl. jours. in field. Mem.: APA, OH Psychol. Assn., Am. Pain Soc. (Young Investigator's Travel award 2003), Soc. Pediatric Psychology. Roman Catholic. Avocations: tennis, sports, exercise. Office: Children's Hosp Dept Rehab 1056 E 19th Ave B285 Denver CO 80218-1088

SWAIN, SUSAN MARIE, communications executive; b. Phila., Dec. 23, 1954; d. Samuel B. Swain and Marie Paget. BA in Comms. magna cum laude, U. Scranton, Pa., 1976, Doctorate (hon.), 2000. Reporter Sta. WDAU-TV, Scranton, 1975-76; pub. rels. staff Up With People, Inc., Tucson, 1976—78; supr. Raytheon Service Co., Cambridge, Mass., 1978-80; research assoc. Nat. Counsel Assocs., Washington, 1980-82; producer C-SPAN Cable Network, Washington, 1982-83, dir. pub. relations, 1983-87, v.p. corp. communications, mem. exec. mgmt. com., 1987-89, sr. v.p., 1989—95, exec. v.p., co-chief oper. officer, 1995—; also creator & host "American Writers", C-SPAN. Officer The Nat. Cable Satellite Corp.; bd. mem. C-SPAN Ednl. Found.; bd. mem., dir. Talbot's Inc. Moderator (TV program) C-SPAN Viewer Call-In, 1982—; editl. mgr. Booknotes, 1997, Booknotes: Life Stories, 1999, Booknotes: Stories from History, 2001, Booknotes: On American Character, 2004. Trustee U. Scranton, 1992—2000. Recipient Alumni award U. Scranton, 1976, Disting. Achievement award, 1991. Mem. Cable Telecom. Adminstrn. and Mktg., Mus. TV and Radio, Cable TV Pub. Affairs Assn. (bd. dirs. 1986-90, sec. 1988-89), Washington Cable Club, Alpha Sigma Nu. Roman Catholic. Avocations: sailing, biking. Office: C-SPAN 400 N Capitol St NW Ste 650 Washington DC 20001-1550 E-mail: sswain@c-span.org.

SWALLUM, MARYANN, musician, educator; b. LA, Sept. 6, 1944; d. Robert James and Alice Agasteen S. BM, Immaculate Heart Coll., LA, 1966; MM, Northwestern U., 1972. Registered tchr., trainer Suzuki piano. Dir. piano program Our Lady of the Holy Rosary Sch., Sun City, Calif., 1964-66; music dir. N.W. Suburban Aide for Retarded Adults, Park Ridge, Ill., 1970-72; piano instr. Elmhurst (Ill.) Coll., 1972-79; founder, dir. Swallum Music Sch., Wilmette, Ill., 1974-79; music dir. Montessori sch., Park Ridge, Ill., 1975-79; music dir. Suzuki piano Dunbarton Sch., Hamilton, Bermuda, 1993-94; chair, instr. prep. dept. Coll. St. Scholastica, Duluth, Minn., 1994—. Piano instr., clinician Suzuki Inst. U. Wis., Stevens Point, 1978-82, U. We. Ont., London, 1980-82; dist. chair Am. Music Scholarship Competition, Cin., 1976-78; founder, dir. piano workshop for children; piano judge Ill. State Music Tchrs. Assn., Winnetka, 1977-78, Minn. State Music Tchrs., Duluth, 1980-92. Presdl. scholar The White House Commn., 1985; grantee to study with Daniel Pollack Steinway Recording Artist, 1989. Mem. Music Tchrs. Nat. Assn., Cecilian Soc. (sec. 1991-92, founder, dir. 1998), Suzuki Assn. Am. Avocations: hiking, skiing, snow shoeing.

SWAN, ANNALYN, writer; b. Biloxi, Miss. d. Ethelynn Swan; m. Mark Whitney Stevens, June 12, 1977; children: Emmelyn Swan, Julia Philippa. Former writer Time mag.; former music critic & sr. arts editor Newsweek; has also written for The New Republic, The Atlantic Monthly, NY Times Mag. Co-author (with Mark Stevens): de Koonig: An American Master, 2004 (Nat. Book Critics Circle Award for biography/autobiography, 2005, Pulitzer Prize for biography, 2005).

SWAN, BARBARA J., lawyer; BA in History, Macalester Coll., St. Paul, 1973; JD, William Mitchell Coll. of Law, St. Paul, 1979. Atty. Axley Brynelson Law Firm, 1981—87; assoc. gen. counsel Wisconsin Power & Light (subsidiary of Alliant Energy), 1987—93, gen. counsel, 1993—94, v.p., gen. counsel, 1994—98, pres., 1998—; exec. v.p., gen. counsel Alliant Energy, 1998—. Mem. Edison Electric Inst. Gen. Counsel Com.; vice chair electricity com. ABA Section of Public Utility, Communications and Transportation Law. Cabinet mem. Dane County United Way, 2000—02; bd. mem. Nat. Assn. of Manufacturers, Alliant Energy Found., Forward Wisconsin; corp. chair Dane County Walk To Cure Juvenile Diabetes, 2003. Office: Alliant Energy PO Box 77007 4902 N Biltmore Ln Madison WI 53707-1007

SWAN, BETH ANN, nursing administrator; b. Phila., Nov. 11, 1958; d. John H. and Elizabeth A. Jenkins; m. Eric J. Swan, Apr. 11, 1987. BSN, Holy Family Coll., Phila., 1980; MSN, U. Pa., 1983, PhD in Nursing, 1996. RN, Pa.; cert. adult nurse practitioner ANCC. Nursing adminstr. spl. project s U. Pa., Phila., 1980—. Mem.: ANA, Am. Acad. Ambulatory Nursing Care, Pa. Nurses Assn., Assn. Health Svcs. Rsch., Sigma Theta Tau.

SWAN-EAGAN, CYNTHIA J., music educator; m. Michael Eagan, May 0, 1955. MusM in Edn., VanderCook Coll. Music, Chgo., 1987. Dir. bands Manistee Area Pub. Schs., Mich., 1982—; dir. concert band Ferris State U., Big Rapids, 2000—02. Recipient Mich. Tchr. Yr., Mich. Sch. Band and Orch. Assn., 2000. Mem.: Am. Sch. Band Dirs. Assn. (state chpt. pres. 1999—2000), Mich. Sch. Band and Orch. Assn. (v.p., com. chair 1998—2006, pres. 2005—, Tchr. of the Yr. 2000). Avocations: travel, collage & mixed media art, photography. Office: Manistee Area Public Schools 525 12th Street Manistee MI 49660 Office Phone: 231-398-3677. E-mail: cseagan@manistee.org.

SWANER, PAULA MARGETTS, clinical psychologist; b. Salt Lake City, Nov. 23, 1927; d. Sumner Gray and Pauline (Moyle) Margetts; m. Leland Scowcroft, May 22, 1951; children: Leland S., Jr., Sumner Margetts, Paula June Swaner-Sargetakis. BA in Eng. Lit., U. Utah, 1949, MA in Eng. Lit., 1972, MS in Ednl. Psychol., 1978, PhD in Clin. Psychology, 1986; postgrad., Washington Sch. Psychiatry, 1991, Mill Valley Calif. Acad., 1990; MA, in Mythological Studies, Pacifica Grad. Inst., 2003. Lic. clin. psychologist, Utah. Psychotherapist Granite Mental Health Ctr., Salt Lake City, 1978-80; intern Mental Health Unit, Juvenile Ct., Salt Lake City, 1984-87; pvt. practice Salt Lake City, 1986—. CEO Evergreen Coalition, 1993—2002; faculty Internat. Psychotherapy Inst., Chevy Chase, Md., 1996—, dir., Salt Lake City, 1996, founder, 2000, Infant Observation Teleconferencing Satellite Program, 2000; established master tchrs. svcs. IPI Videoconf. Supervision and Clin. Application Program, 2001. Chair Swaner Nature Preserve Found., 1993-2002; established Rock Mountain Psychol. Ctr. for Therapy and Tng., Salt Lake City, 2003. Mem.: APA, Utah Psychol. Assn. (mem. task force 2002—06). Democrat. Avocations: hiking, cross country skiing, swimming.

SWANGO, COLLEEN JILL, science educator; b. Izmir, Turkey, Sept. 8, 1956; d. Charles Irvan Swango and Altamae Silva. BS in Edn., Ind. U., 1978; MS in Edn., Ind. U.-Purdue, 1984. Lic. tchr. Ind. Tchr. Share's Inc., Shelbyville, Ind., 1978—85, supervising tchr., 1979—85; sci. tchr. Brownsburg (Ind.) Jr. High, 1986—, chair sci. dept., 1993—. Co-prodr.: Help! I'm Teaching Middle School Science, 2003. Mem.: Nat. Sci. Tchrs. Assn., Hoosier Assn. Sci. Tchrs., Brownsburg Classroom Tchrs. Assn. (past pres., rep.). Independent. Methodist. Avocations: music, reading, theater, travel. Home: 104 Sterling Dr Pittsboro IN 46167

SWANK, ANNETTE MARIE, software designer; b. Lynn, Mass., Nov. 9, 1953; d. Roland Paterson and Rita Mary (Edwards) S. BSEE and Computer Sci., Vanderbilt U., 1975; M of Engring. Sci., Pa. State U., 2003. Lead programmer GE, Phila., 1975-80; system analyst SEI Corp., Wayne, Pa., 1980-82; mgr., designer Premier Systems, Inc., Wayne, Pa., 1982-85, dir., 1985-88, tech. advisor, 1988-90, tech. architect, 1990-92, Funds Assocs. Ltd., Wayne, 1992-99; sr. bus. analyst First Data Investor Svcs. Group, Berwyn, Pa., 1999; prin. bus. analyst PFPC Inc., King of Prussia, 1999—2000, v.p., mng. dir. SURPAS bus. unit Berwyn, Pa., 2000—. Mem. exec. coun. internat. bus. critical sys. Hewlitt Packard, 2002—. Designer: (programming lang. and data dictionary) Vision, 1985. Treas. Master Singers, Plymouth Meeting, Pa., 1987-88. Mem. Assn. Computing Machinery, Gamma Phi Beta (com. chmn. alumna Phila. 1986-87). Avocations: singing, dance, bowling, bridge, wine tasting. Home: 136 Pinecrest Ln King Of Prussia PA 19406-2368 Office: PFPC Inc 760 Moore Rd King Of Prussia PA 19406

SWANK, HILARY ANN, actress; b. Lincoln, Nebr., July 30, 1974; m. Chad Lowe, Sept. 28, 1997 (separated 2006). Actor: Buffy the Vampire Slayer, 1992, The Next Karate Kid, 1994, Sometimes They Come Back.Again, 1996, Kounterfeit, 1996, The Way We Are, 1997, Heartwood, 1998, Boys Don't Cry, 1999 (Golden Globe for Best Actress, 2000, Academy award for Best Actress, 2000), Affair of the Necklace, 2000, The Gift, 2000, The Affair of the Necklace, 2001, Insomnia, 2002, The Core, 2003, Million Dollar Baby, 2004 (best actress, Boston Film Critics award, 2004, Golden Globe award for best actress, 2005, Screen Actors Guild award, for outstanding performance by female actor in leading role, 2005, Acad. award for Best Actress, 2005), The Black Dahlia, 2006; (TV movies) Cries Unheard: The Donna Yaklich Story, 1994, Terror in the Family, 1996, Dying to Belong, 1997, The Sleepwalker Killing, 1997, Iron Jawed Angels, 2004; (TV series) Evening Shade, 1991-92, Camp Wilder, 1992, Beverly Hills, 90210, 1997-98, Leaving L.A., 1997; actor, exec. prodr. (films) 11:14, 2003; (TV appearances) Growing Pains, 1985, Harry and the Hendersons, 1991. Named one of Time Mag. 100 Most Influential People, 2005; recipient Little Screen/Big Star award, TV Land, 2006. Avocations: sky diving, river rafting, skiing, swimming. Office: William Morris Agy 151 S El Camino Dr Beverly Hills CA 90212*

SWANN, ELIZABETH, director, personal trainer; d. Thomas and Virginia Swann; m. Brian Anderson, Jan. 16, 2005. MA, U. Tex., Austin, 1999; PhD, U. So. Miss., Hattiesburg, 2001. Cert. athletic trainer Nat. Athletic Trainers Assn, Fla., 1994. Asst. prof. East Carolina U., Greenville, NC, 2001—03; program dir. Nova Southeastern U., Fort Lauderdale, Fla., 2003—. Column editor Athletic Therapy Today, 2005. Mem.: Nat. Athletic Trainers Assn. (com. mem. 2006—). Office: Nova Southeastern Univ 3301 College Ave Division MST Fort Lauderdale FL 33314 Office Phone: 954-262-8334. Business E-Mail: swann@nova.edu.

SWANN, JERILYN MITCHELL, science educator; b. Tuscaloosa, Ala., Feb. 7, 1970; d. Jerry Willoughby and Sharon Atkins Mitchell; m. William Edward Swann, Mar. 19, 1994; children: Josephine Ruth, Mitchell William, Samantha Abigail. BS in Zoology, U. Tenn., Knoxville, 1992, MS in Zoology, 1994, PhD, 1998. Biology instr. Itawamba C.C., Fulton, Miss., 1997—99; assoc. prof. biology Maryville (Tenn.) Coll., 1999—. Program coord. Rural Coll., Cmty. Summit, Maryville, 2001—02, Presdl. Scholars Enrichment Program, Maryville, 2004—. Contbr. scientific papers. Organizer Service Learning Freshman Biology, Maryville, 1999—2004. Recipient Sci. Alliance award, U. Tenn. Grad. Sch., 1993, 1996, First Pl. Sci. Poster Competition, SE Regional Soc. Toxicology, 1994; Fred M. Roddy scholarship, Roddy Coca-Cola Found., 1988-1992, Isabel Griscom scholarship, U. Tenn., 1992-1993, Faculty grant, East Tenn. Consortium Service Learning, 2000, Faculty Exploration Vocation grant, Lilly Found., 2002. Mem.: NSTA, AAAS, Am. Soc. Cell Biology, Phi Beta Kappa. Office: Maryville Coll 502 E Lamar Alexander Pwy Maryville TN 37804 Office Phone: 865-981-8068. E-mail: jerilyn.swann@maryvillecollege.edu.

SWANN, LOIS LORRAINE, writer, editor, educator; b. N.Y.C., Nov. 17, 1944; d. Peter J. and Edith M. (De Rose) Riso; m. Terrence Garth Swann, Aug. 15, 1964 (div. 1979); children: Peter Burgess, Polly Swann Coward; m. Kenneth E. Arndt, Sept. 3, 1988. BA, Marquette U., 1966. Editor Peat, Marwick, Mitchell & Co., N.Y.C., 1980-81; publs. cons. Mfrs. Hanover Trust, N.Y.C., 1981-88. Cons. bus. writing, 1988—; tchr. West H.E.L.P., Mt. Vernon, NY, 1991; tchr. nontraditonal age students writing; founder, reader Calliope's Chamber, 1995—. Author: (novels) The Mists of Manittoo, 1976 (Ohioana Libr. award for 1st novel, 1976), Torn Covenants, 1981; contbr. articles to mags. Election insp. Dem. Party, Bronxville, NY, 1990—. Mem.: Poets and Writers, Authors Guild. Avocation: interior design. Home and Office: 270 Bronxville Rd Bronxville NY 10708

SWANN, MELISSA LYNNE, psychologist; b. Albuquerque, Aug. 25, 1962; d. Jimmie Gleen and Medgie (Nix) Swann. AA, Hinds C.C., Raymond, Miss., 1986; BA, Belhaven Coll., Jackson, Miss., 1989; MEd, Miss. Coll., Clinton, 1992; PhD, Southwest U., Kenner, La., 2000. Cert. emergency med. technician; lic. psychometrist. Youth counselor Cath. Charities, Jackson, 1991-92; psychologist Miss. State Hosp., Whitfield, 1992—. With Miss. Air N.G., 1985—. Named to Outstanding Young Women of Am., 1997. Mem. VFW, Am. Legion. Office: Miss State Hosp Psychology Dept Whitfield MS 39193

SWANSEN, DONNA MALONEY, landscape designer, consultant; b. Green Bay, Wis., July 8, 1931; d. Arthur Anthony and Ella Marie Rose (Warner) Maloney; m. Samuel Theodore Swansen, June 27, 1959; children: Jessica Swansen Bonelli, Theodor Arthur Swansen, Christopher Currie Swansen. AS in Integrated Liberal Studies, U. Wis., 1956; AS in Landscape Design, Temple U., 1982. Bridal cons. Richard W. Burnham's, Green Bay, Wis., 1951-54, 57-58; asst. buyer Shreve Crump & Low, Boston, 1958-59; buyer Harry S. Manchester, Madison, Wis., 1959-62; ptnr. Corson Borie & Swansen, Ambler, Pa., 1976, Swansen & Borie, Ambler, 1977-82; owner, operator Donna Swansen/Design, Ambler, 1983—. V.p. Energy Islands Internat. Inc., East Troy, Wis., 1963-94. Editor: Internat. Directory Landscape Designers, 1993. Co-founder Friends of Rising Sun, Ambler, Ambler Area Arts Alliance, 1975—76; founder, 1st pres. Plant Ambler, 1973—83, 1997—; chair Do It, Dig It exhibit Temple U., 1987; judge Temple U., 2002, Bucks County Beautiful Flowers Show, 2002, Assn. Profl. Landscape Designers, 2002; Dem. candidate for judge elections, 1988; active Gwynedd (Pa.) Monthly Meeting of Friends, 1974—; judge Del. Valley Coll., Doylestown, Pa., 2002; search com. for chair dept. landscape arch. and horticulture Temple U., 1987, curriculum rev. com., 1993; adv. com. Green Bay Bot. Garden, 1993—, Del. Valley Coll., Doylestown, Pa., 2000—, adv. bd., 2000—. Recipient Key to the Borough, Borough of Ambler, 1972; winner urban beautification project Roadside Coun. Am., Ambler, 1975, Athena award Wissahickon Valley C. of C., 1996, Cert. Hon. award Temple U., 2006; named to Alumni Gallery of Success, Ambler Coll., Temple U., 2004. Mem. Assn. Profl. Landscape Designers (cert., co-founder, 1st pres. 1989-91, bd. dirs. 1989-95, 1st pres. Landscape Design Network Phila. 1978-85, Distinction award 1996, judge internat. design competition 2002, 03, 06), Sigma Lambda Alpha (charter mem.). Democrat. Avocations: encouraging women, travel, gardening. Home and Office: 221 Morris Rd Ambler PA 19002-5202 Business E-Mail: donna@donnaswansendesign.com.

SWANSINGER, A. JACQUELINE, history professor, academic administrator; b. Orleans, France, Apr. 10, 1954; d. Joseph and Edna Theresa Swansinger; m. Delbert L Findley, 1976; children: Katherine Elizabeth Findley, Jennifer Alexandra Findley, Renee Victoria Findley, David Maximillian Findley. BA/BS, Georgian Ct. Coll., Lakewood, N.J., 1974; MA, Rutgers U., New Brunswick, N.J., 1982; PhD, Rutgers U., 1988. V.p. Freedom Oil, Washington, NJ, 1980—81; asst. prof. SUNY, Fredonia, 1988—95, chair, history dept., 1995—96, founding chair, interdisciplinary internat. studies maj., 1997—2000, interim dean of arts and humanities, 1996—97, dir., tittle iii grant - diversity, 1998—2001, chair, faculty senate, 2000—01, interim dean of grad. studies and lifelong learning, 2006—, dir., history grad. studies, 2004—06, chair, u. senate, 2005—06; am. coun. of edn. fellow W.Va. U., Morgantown, W.Va., 2002—03. Cons. Coll. Bd. for World History, Princeton, NJ, 1996—2005, W.Va. U., Morgantown, 2003, Barker Libr., Fredonia, 1992; grant dir. World History Assn., Coll. Bd. and Nat. Endowment for the Humanities, 1999—2001; lectr. in field. Contbr. articles to profl. jours. Mem. Peace and Justice, Fredonia, NY, 1989—2002; co-leader Girl Scouts of North Brunswick, NJ, 1984—88; pres. Swim Club, North Brunswick, 1984—88, Fredonia, NY, 1988—95; treas. Fredonia Mid. Sch. PTA, 1989—91; softball coach Fredonia Little League, 1989—91; bd. dirs., publ. coord. Chautauqua Cmty. Day Care, Fredonia, 1997—2001; organizer Robotics League, Pitts., 2004—06. Recipient Chancellor's Award for Excellence in Tchg., SUNY, 2001; fellow History fellow, Rutgers U., 1985. Mem.: Mid-Atlantic World History Assn. (pres. 2000—06), World History Assn. (sec. 2000—06, treas. 2006—). Avocations: travel, politics.

SWANSON, ANN ELIZABETH, family counselor; b. Greenfield, Iowa, Dec. 5, 1938; d. John Edred and Jeanette A. (Peck) Don Carlos; m. Eric R. Swanson, June 16, 1967; children: Wendy A., Lorna K. AA, Stephens Coll., 1958; BA, Drake U., 1960; MA in Psychology, U. Iowa, 1963; postgrad., UCLA, UCB, UCSD. Cert. water safety instr. ARC, canoeing instr. ARC, Am. Canoeing Assn. Pers. specialist Rike-Kumler Co., Dayton, Ohio, 1960-61; clin. asst. Child Devel. Clinic, SUI, Iowa City, Iowa, 1961-63; counselor, asst. prof. Bakersfield (Calif.) Coll., 1963-67; counselor Grossmont Coll., El Cajon, Calif., 1967-69; pvt. practice individual and family counseling San Diego, 1976-88; individual and family counselor Pt. Loma Counseling Ctr., San Diego, 1988—. Chair Sunset Cliffs Natural Park Recreation Coun., San Diego, 1988-2000; mem. coastal area com. San Diego Parks and Recreation Dept., 1978-2003; 2d v.p. Peninsula Community Planning Bd., San Diego; active, past pres. San Diego City Schs. PTA, 1980's. Mem. Am. Assn. Marriage and Family Therapists, Calif. Assn. Marriage and Family Therapists, San Diego Assn. Marriage and Family Therapists, Internat. Assn. Marriage and Family Counselors. Avocations: backpacking, canoe trips, photography. Home: 3611 Warner St San Diego CA 92106-3244 Office: Point Loma Counseling Ctr 3725 Talbot St Ste D San Diego CA 92106-2050 Office Phone: 619-223-2165.

SWANSON, CAROLYN RAE, news reporter, counselor; b. Riverton, Wyo., Nov. 10, 1937; d. Leonard Rae Swanson and Ruby Francis Mulholland Laliberte; m. William Glenn (dec. 1959); children: Donald, Rocky, Laurel; m. Larry T. Hess, Nov. 23, 1962; children: Lance Hess, Aaron Hess. AA, West Valley Coll., Saratoga, Calif., 1970; BA, San Jose State U., 1975. Cert. substance abuse counselor. Counselor, program dir. Carson Regional Coun., Carson City, Nev., 1977-82; Women's Internat. News Gathering Svc. news reporter Radio for Peace Internat., Costa Rica, 1988-89; reporter Nevada City, Calif., 1990-97; dir. Innovative Voices, Paradise, Calif., 1990—. Mem. adv. bd. UN U. of Peace, Costa Rica, 1988-89; bd. dirs. No. Nev. Lang. Bank, 1978-80; cons. Intertribal Coun., Nev.-No. Calif., 1977-80; mem. exec. bd. Grandparent State Coun., Calif., 1992-96. Coord. shelter for battered women, Carson City, 1979; U.S. del. Soviet-Am. dialog, Washington, 1988; N.Am. del. Peace Conf., Costa Rica, 1989; leader Fellowship of Reconciliation, Chico-Paradise area, 1991-92; Butte County contact Green Party, 1991—; Humboldt County coord. Postcorporate World, 1999—; adv. com. Children's Theater, Arcata, Calif, 2003—; Docent Arcata Museum, Yosemite, 2000. Recipient Promoting Arts award Villa Montalvo Theatre, Saratoga, Calif., 1975, award Nat. Inst. on Drug Abuse, Utah, 1978. Avocations: reading, travel, hiking, theater, writing. Office: Swanson Hess Glenn PO Box 298988 Wasilla AR 99629-8988

SWANSON, CELIA, retail executive; BA in Fashion Merchandising, U. Nebr., 1977. Sr. v.p. human resources and adminstrn. PACE Membership Warehouse, Inc., Denver; dr. dir. people group Sam's Club, 1994—95, v.p. people group, 1995—97, sr. v.p. membership, mktg. and adminstrn., 1997—2000, exec. v.p. membership, mktg. adminstrn., 2000—. Bd. govs. Children's Miracle Network, 2000—. Mem.: Nebr. Alumni Assn. (bd. dirs. 1999—). Office: Wal-Mart Stores Inc 702 SW Eighth St Bentonville AR 72716

SWANSON, DOLORES, special education educator, musician; b. Omaha, Sept. 5, 1931; d. Oswald Adelord Albert Hawkins and Mary Margaret Franckewicz; m. Emory Wilkins Bridgeford (div. July 1970), children: Emory Wilkins Jr., Lenora, Joseph, Mary, Irwin, Peter, Jeannette, Patrick, Mark, Gerard; m. Conrad John Swanson, Oct. 15, 1970 (div.). B Music Edn., U. Nev., Reno, 1985. Cert. spl. edn. tchr., generalist resource, Nev. Sec. Natelson's Women's Apparel, Omaha, 1949-50; sec.-stenographer U.S. Army Chem. Corps, Denver, 1952-54; singer, entertainer in midwest and western U.S., 1964-79; co-founder, instr. adult basic edn. Truckee Meadows C.C., Reno, 1989-91, 93-95; tchr. music Washoe County Sch. Dist., Reno, 1986-87, tchr. spl. edn., 1991—. Bd. dirs. No. Nev. Bus. Inst., Reno, 1971-72; choir dir. Our Lady of Wisdom Newman Ctr., Reno, 1996—. Recipient Fred and Anna Stadtmuller Meml. award U. Nev., 1987; Command scholar U. Nev., 1983-84. Mem. NEA, Coun. for Exceptional Children, Nev. Tchrs. Assn., Washoe County Tchrs. Assn. Democrat. Roman Catholic. Avocations: sewing, crafting, ceramics, crocheting, gardening. Office: Marvin Picollo Sch 900 Foothill Rd Reno NV 89511-9427

SWANSON, JACQUELINE V., academic administrator, educator, women's health nurse practitioner; b. Houston, Feb. 12, 1944; d. Ivan Jack and Edith Wilson; m. James Swanson, Aug. 21, 1965; children: Jim, Charlotte, Robert, Guy, Danny. BS, Tex. Woman's U., 1967, MS, 1974; PhD, U. North Tex., Denton, 1989. Cert. clin. nurse specialist, in maternal-newborn health, women's health nurse practitioner Planned Parenthood of Rocky Mountains, sexual assault nurse examiner. Various clin. nursing positions, Tex. and Kans., Tex., 1967-73; supr. obstet. and nursery Harris County Hosp. Dist., Houston, 1970-73; instr. Prairie View (Tex.) A&M U., 1973-75; asst. prof. Tex. Woman's U., Denton, 1975-85; labor and delivery nurse Tarrant County Hosp. Dist., Ft. Worth, 1987-89; assoc. prof., chmn. dept. nursing Ft. Hays State U., Hays, Kans., 1989-94; dir. BS nursing program Lamar U., Beaumont, Tex., 1994-95; prof., dean Coll. Nursing, Mont. State U. No., Havre, 1995—98, prof. nursing, 1998-2000; assoc. prof. nursing Tarleton State U., 2000—03, women's health nurse practioner Student Health Clinic, 2003—04; clin. instr. Tex. Christian U., 2005; dean Sch. Nursing Bacone Coll., 2005—. Contbr. articles to profl. jours.; presenter U.S. and internat. Mem. Denton Area War on Drugs. Mem. AAUP, ANA, Nat. Assn. Nurse Practioners Women's Health, Assn. Women's Health, Obstetric and Neonatal Nurses, Kans. State Nurses Assn., Tex. Nurses Assn., Tex. Nurse Practioner's Assn., Mont. Nurses Assn., Internat. Coun. on Women's Health Issues, Internat. Soc. for Univ. Nurses, Sigma Theta Tau. Home: 416 N 16th Muskogee OK 74401

SWANSON, JOYCE EILEEN, elementary school educator; b. Massillon, Ohio, Nov. 2, 1955; d. Willis Merle and Marjorie Eileen (Day) Haughton; m. Michael Paul Swanson, July 6, 1985; children: Ryan, Scott, Craig. BS, U. Akron, 1977; MS, Kent State U., 1982. Tchr. Carrollton (Ohio) Exempted Village Schs., 1979—. Mem. NEA, Ohio Edn. Assn., Carrollton Edn. Assn. Republican. Avocations: reading, travel, family. Home: 1431 Chadford Gate SE Canton OH 44709-4818 Office Phone: 330-735-2850. Business E-Mail: swanson@carrollton.k12.oh.us.

SWANSON, JUDITH SELEEN, artist, graphics designer, advocate; b. Aug. 7, 1935; d. John and Laura Seleen; m. Stephen Olney Swanson, June 10, 1956; children: Scott, Shelley, Noel, Kim, Brian. BA, Augustana Coll., SD, 1957; student, St. Olaf Coll., Northfield, Minn., U. Oreg., Eugene, Tex. Luth. U., Seguin, Mpls. Coll. Art and Design. Art tchr. Tex. Luth. U.; book jacket designer, illustrator Augsburg Pub. House, Fortress Press, The Am. Luth. Ch., Evang. Luth. Ch. in Am., 1974—2003. Designer, illustrator logos Luth. World Relief, NY, The William Mitchell Coll. Law and Luth. Svcs. in Am., St. Paul Am. Baptist Woman's Ministries, Valley Forge, Pa., space designer Montreat Presbyn. Ctr., NC, 1974—2006, designer permanent and festival banners nationwide chs. Rockefeller Chapel, U. Chgo., 1998, designer worship and display spaces nat. ch. convs. Kansas City, Detroit, San Antonio, Washington, Orlando, Milw. and Mpls., 1978—96, designer sets St. Olaf Coll. Christmas Festival, 1991. Mem. bd. Hist. Preservation Commn. and Planning Commn., 1980—. Named Disting. Alumna, St. Olaf Coll., 1992; Travel grantee, Am. Luth. Ch. (The Holy Land), 1989, Luth. World Relief, Peru, 1999, Winds of Peace Found., Nicaragua and Honduras, 2002. Home: 910 Saint Olaf Ave Northfield MN 55057-1527

SWANSON, KARIN, hospital administrator, consultant; b. New Britain, Conn., Dec. 8, 1942; d. Oake F. and Ingrid Lauren Swanson; m. B. William Dorsey, June 26, 1965 (div. 1974); children: Matthew W., Julie I., Alison K.; m. Sanford H. Low, Oct. 14, 1989. BA in Biology, Middlebury Coll., 1964; MPH, Yale U., 1981. Biology tchr. Kents Hill (Maine) Sch., 1964-66; laboratory instr. Bates Coll., Lewiston, Maine, 1974-78; asst. to gen. dir. Mass. Eye and Ear Infirmary, Boston, 1979-80; v.p. profl. services Portsmouth (N.H.) Hosp., 1981-83; v.p. Health Strategy Assn. Ltd., Chestnut Hill, Mass., 1983-85; v.p. med. affairs Cen. Maine Med. Ctr., Lewiston, 1986-89; health care mgmt. cons. Cambridge, Mass., 1989-91; CEO Hahnemann Hosp., Brighton, Mass., 1991-94; adminstr. Vencor Hosp., Boston, 1994-95; pres., CEO The Laser Inst. New Eng., Newton, Mass., 1996-97; real estate developer Newcastle, Maine, 1997—. Mem. Phi Beta Kappa. Avocations: reading, gardening, walking. Home and Office: PO Box 1281 Damariscotta ME 04543-1281

SWANSON, LYNNETTE SUE, special olympics coordinator, special education educator; d. Carl Robert and Betty Jane Krambier; m. David John Swanson, June 2, 1984. BS cum laude, Brenau U., 2004. Cert. spl. edn. Ga., 2005. Spl. edn. paraprofl. Gwinnett County Pub. Schs., Lawrenceville, Ga., 1994—2000, coord. spl. olympics, 2000—. Coach Ga. women's volleyball team Spl. Olympics USA, Dublin, 2003. Mem.: Nat. Rlwy. Hist. Soc., Kappa Delta Pi, Phi Theta Kappa. Avocations: volunteer coaching, travel, crafts. Home: 4875 Five Forks Trickum Rd Lilburn GA 30047 Office: Gwinnett County Spl Olympics 950 McElvaney Ln Lawrenceville GA 30044 Office Phone: 678-985-3592. E-mail: lynnette_swanson@gwinnett.k12.ga.us.

SWANSON, MARTI, retired secondary educator, consultant; b. Berwyn, Ill., June 8, 1935; d. Francis M. and Irville (Miller) Baldwin; m. Kenneth A. Swanson, Mar. 27, 1954; children: Rick, Gary, Laurie Swanson Bender. Student, Ill. Wesleyan U., 1953-54; BS in Edn. with high honors, No. Ill. U., 1967, MS in Edn., 1973; student, Goddard Coll., Plainfield, Vt., Elmhurst Coll., Roosevelt U., Chgo. State U. Cert. tchr., Ill. Tchr. English, Grant Community High Sch., Fox Lake, Ill., 1967-92, chmn. dept., 1975-86. Local site coord. Am. Fedn. Tchr. ednl. rsch. and dissemination project local 504, Lake County Fedn. Tchrs., Waukegan, Ill., 1987—94; workshop presenter in field; cons. on inventory ednl. progress Ill. Bd. Edn., Springfield, 1985; mem. panel to select Chgo. Tribune's 1992 All-State Acad. Team, 1992. Editor newsletter the Grant Slant, 1986-89, Five-Oh For Retirees, 1992-98, Citizens For Ringwood Orgn., 1993—98, the Baldwin Family Bull., 2001—; author essays. Treas. Wildflower Preservation and Propagation Com., 1993—2004. Recipient Supt.'s G award Grant Community High Sch., 1989. Mem. Am. Fedn. Tchrs., Ill. Fedn. Tchrs. (co-chmn. ednl. excellence com. 1989-93), Lake County Fedn. Tchrs. (sec. 1984-95) Grant Coun. Local 504 (sec. 1975-83, pres. 1983-92, sec. retirees coun. 1992-98), Ill. Ret. Tchrs. Assn. (chair region 2 legis. com. 1994-95, chair state legis. com. 1995-99), Lake County Ret. Tchrs. Assn. (chair, legis. com., 2006—), McHenry County Ret. Tchrs. Assn. (chmn. legis. com. 1992-95, v.p. 2000-01, pres. 2002-2005), Ill. Assn. Tchrs. English (hon. life, exec. bd. 1971-89, sec. 1977-89), McHenry County (Ill.) Geneal. Soc. (treas. 2000—, pres. 2005—). Democrat. Methodist. Avocations: camping, photography, family history. Home: 5615 N Ridgeway Rd Ringwood IL 60072-9634

SWANSON, MARY CATHERINE, educational association administrator; b. Kingsburg, Calif., Sept. 3, 1944; d. Edwin Elmore and Corrine (Miller) Jacobs; m. Thomas Edward Swanson, Aug. 27, 1966; 1 child, Thomas Jacobs. BA in English and Journalism, Calif. State U., San Francisco, 1966; standard teaching credential in secondary edn., U. Calif., 1966; MA in Edn., U. Redlands, 1977; DHL (hon.), U. San Diego, 2002, U. LaVerne, 2003. Svc. adminstrv. credential, Calif.; specialist learning handicapped, Calif.; gifted cert., Calif. Tchr. English and journalism Woodland (Calif.) High Sch., 1966-67, Armijo High Sch., Fairfield, Calif., 1967-69, Moreno Valley High Sch., Sunnymead, Calif., 1969-70, Clairemont High Sch., San Diego, 1970-86; coord. San Diego County Office Edn., 1986-90, dir. AVID project, 1990-92; founder, exec. dir. AVID Ctr., 1992—. Newspaper and yearbook advisor Moreno Valley High Sch., Moreno Valley Sch. Dist., 1969-70; reading program coord. Clairemont High Sch., 1974-80, project English coord. and site plan coord., 1975-80, English dept. chairperson, 1978-86, coord. Advancement Via Individual Determination and WASC accreditation, 1980-86, in-sch. resource tchr., 1982-86; mem. numerous positions and coms. San Diego City Schs., 1974-91; mem. com. univ. and coll. opportunities commn. Calif. State Dept. Edn., 1981-82; mem. adv. com. tchr. edn. program Pt. Loma Coll., 1982-83, tchr. English methods course for tchrs. secondary edn., 1986-87; mem. accreditation vis. com. WASC, 1983, integration monitoring team Crawford High Sch., 1984, adv. com. San Diego Area Writing Project, 1987—; developer numerous curricular programs, 1967—. Community leader Olivenhain Valley 4-H Club, 1981-90; founder Olivenhain Valley Soccer Club, 1982; coord. Clairemont High Sch./Sea World Adopt-A-Sch., 1982-84. Named Headliner of Yr.-Edn./Creative Tchg., San Diego Press Club, 1991, Headline of Yr.-Cmty. Activist, 2002, Woman of Vision, LWV-San Diego, 1992, Nat. Educator of Yr., McGraw Hill, 2001, America's Best Tchr., Time Mag. and CNN, 2001; named to Pres.'s Forum on Tchg. as a Profession, Am. Assn. Higher Edn., 1991; recipient EXCEL award for excellence in tchg., 1985, Exemplary Program award, Nat. Coun. States on Insvc. Edn., 1990, Pioneering Achievement in Edn. award, Charles A. Dana Found., 1991, Lifetime Achievement award, Calif. Assn. Tchrs., 2006; grantee, BankAmerica Found., 1980, UCSD Acad. Support Svcs., 1980, San Diego Gas and Elec. Found., 1984. Mem. Nat. Coun. Tchrs. English (Nat. Ctr. Excellence award 1985-87), Calif. Coun. Tchrs. English, Calif. Assn. Gifted Edn., Golden Key Nat. Honor Soc. (hon. mem.), Phi Kappa Phi. Office: AVID Ctr 5120 Shoreham Pl Ste 120 San Diego CA 92122 Business E-Mail: mcswanson@avidcenter.org.

SWANSON, MARY F., education educator; d. Harry Eldon and Fay Katherine Francis; m. Robert Lee Swanson, Aug. 19, 1967; children: Leigh A., Mitchell P. BS, Okla. State U., Stillwater, 1964, EdD, 2004; MS, Purdue U., West Lafayette, Ind., 1969; MS in Tchg., U. Wis., Superior, 1980. Lifetime K-8 tchg. lic. Wis., Reading Specialist Degree Wis. Tchr. Jefferson County Pub. Schs., Denver, 1966—68, Dept. of Def., Frankfurt, Germany, 1967—68, Valparaiso (Ind.) Pub. Schs., 1967—68, Duneland Sch. Dist., Chesterton, Ind., 1968—70, Fox Point (Wis.)-Bayside Schs., 1970—71; title one resource tchr. Ashland (Wis.) Pub. Schs., 1977—81; resource tchr. Kenosha (Wis.) Pub. Schs., 1981—99; adj. prof. Okla. State U., Stillwater, 1999—2004; asst. prof. Northeastern State U., Broken Arrow, Okla., 2004—. Lectr. edn. Carthage Coll., Kenosha, 1996; cons. in literacy Okla. Pub. Schs., 2004—; presenter in field. Nominee Cir. of Excellence award, Northeastern State U., 2005. Mem.: Okla. Reading Assn. (bd. dirs., webmaster 2004—06), Internat. Reading Assn., Okla. Higher Edn. Reading Coun. (assoc.), Delta Kappa Gamma. Avocations: reading, cooking, travel. Home: Route One Box 478 Stroud OK 74079 Office: Northeastern State University 3100 E New Orleans St Broken Arrow OK 74014 Office Phone: 918-449-6598. Business E-Mail: swansomf@nsuok.edu.

SWANSON, PATRICIA KLICK, retired academic administrator, retired foundation administrator; b. St. Louis, May 8, 1940; d. Emil Louis and Patricia (McNair) Klick; 1 child, Ivan Clatanoff. BS in Edn., U. Mo., 1962; postgrad., Cornell U., 1963; MLS, Simmons Coll., 1967. Reference librarian Simmons Coll., Boston, 1967-68, U. Chgo., 1970-79, sr. lectr. Grad. Library Sch., 1974-83, 86-88, head reference service, 1979-83, asst. dir. for sci. libraries, 1983-93, acting asst. dir. for tech. svcs., 1987-88, assoc. provost, 1993-98; program officer MacArthur Found., 1999—2005; ret., 2005. Project dir. Office Mgmt. Svcs., Assn. Rsch. Librs., 1982-83; speaker in field; cons. on libr. mgmt., planning and space. Author: Great is the Gift that Bringeth Knowledge: Highlights from the History of the John Crerar Library, 1989; contbr. articles to profl. jours. Program officer MacArthur Found., 1999—2001.

SWANSON, VICTORIA CLARE HELDMAN, lawyer; b. Aug. 28, 1949; d. Paul F. and Anne F. (Thomas) Schmitz; m. Louis M. Heldman, Sept. 21, 1971 (div. 1973); m. John Askins, Feb. 28, 1975 (div. 1977); m. Thomas C.

Swanson, Feb. 13, 1988 (div. 2004). BA in journalism with distinction, Ohio State U., 1972; JD, U. Detroit, 1975. Bar: Mich. 1975, Colo. 1984, U.S. Dist. Ct. (ea. and we. dists.) Mich. 1975, U.S. Ct. Appeals (6th cir.) 1977, U.S. Ct. Appeals (3d cir.) 1980, U.S. Supreme Ct. 1983, U.S. Ct. Appeals (10th cir.) 1984, U.S. Ct. Appeals (5th cir.) 1989, cert.: NBTA (civil trial advocate) 1994. Assoc. Lopatin, Miller, Bindes & Freedman, Detroit, 1973—76; ptnr. Schaden, Swanson & Lampert, Detroit, 1977—90, Sears, Anderson & Swanson, P.C., Colorado Springs, Colo., 1991—96, Sears & Swanson, Colorado Springs, 1997—. Adj. prof. U. Detroit Sch. Law, 1982. Author (chpt.): (non-fiction) Anatomy of a Personal Injury Lawsuit, 1992; author, editor: handbook Colorado Auto Litigators Handbook, 1995, Colorado Courtroom Handbook, 1998, author, editor: 2nd edit., 2006, Colorado Evidence Handbook, 2005; co-author (with Richard F. Schaden): (non-fiction) Product Design Liability, 1982; co-author: (with others) Women Trial Lawyers: How They Succeed in Practice and in the Courtroom, 1986. Mem.: Mich. Trial Lawyers Assn., Colo. Trial Lawyers Assn. (past pres., Kripke Lifetime Achievement award 2005), Assn. Trial Lawyers Am., Colo. Bar Assn., Mich. Bar Assn. Office: Sears & Swanson 2 N Cascade Ave Colorado Springs CO 80903-1631 Office Phone: 719-471-1984. Business E-Mail: victoria@searsandswanson.com.

SWANSON, ZONA LUCIEL, retired elementary school educator; b. Orr, N.D., Nov. 14, 1923; d. Fred L. and Hilda Dora (Rose) Neumann; m. Lyle R. Swanson, June 23, 1943; children: Barbara Jean Swanson Serr, Daniel Raymond. AA, Mayville State Tchrs., N.D., 1941—43; BA, Mayvill State Tchrs., N.D., 1959; MEd, U. N.D., Grand Forks, 1966. Elem. tchr., rural schools, Larimore, ND, 1950—52; tchr., grades 1-8, small town sch. Kempton, 1954—59; tchr., grades 5-8, small town sch. Arvilla, 1952—54; tchr., grades 5 & 7, AFB Grand Forks, 1959—69; tchr., grade 6 Viking Grade Sch., Grand Forks, 1969—89; retired, 1989. Sec. Grand Forks Edn. Assn., 1960—61; pres. N.D. Classroom Tchr.'s Assn., Bismarck. Active Girl Scouts, U.S., Civil Air Patrol, Farmer's Union, Larimore United Luth. Ch. Mem.: VFW, NEA (life), N.D. Edn. Assn. (life), Am. Legion. Democrat. Lutheran. Avocations: stamp collecting/philately, reading, doll collecting, teddy bear collecting. Home: 2429 W Fallcreek Ct Grand Forks ND 58201 Personal E-mail: zswanson@webtv.net.

SWANTON, SUSAN IRENE, retired library director; b. Rochester, N.Y., Nov. 29, 1941; d. Walter Frederick and Irene Wray S.; m. Wayne Holman, Apr. 12, 1969 (div. June 1973); 1 child, Michael; ptnr. James Donald Lathrop; children: Kathryn, Kristin. AB, Harvard U., 1963; MLS, Columbia U., 1965. Libr. dir. Warsaw (N.Y.) Pub. Libr., 1963-64, Gates Pub. Libr., Rochester, NY, 1965—2003; ret., 2003. Pres. Drug and Alcohol Coun., Rochester, 1985-91, mem. adv. coun., 1992-94; bd. dirs., co-chair info. svcs. Rochester Freenet, 1995—; sec. Gates Hist. Preservation Commn., 2000-03, Friends of Rochester Pub. Libr., 2004—; chmn. Gates Dem. Com., 2004—; v.p., sec. Friends of Gates Pub. Libr., 2004—; newsletter editor Empire (N.Y.) Friends Roundtable, 2004—. Mem. Gates Hist. Soc. (bd. dirs., pres. 1998—2002, v.p. 2002—03), Gates-Chili C. of C. (pres. 1982, sec. 1990-94, 2004—, bd. dirs. 2003, Citizen Yr. 1994), Harvard Club of Rochester (mem. adv. bd.). Home: 284 Gatewood Ave Rochester NY 14624-1622 E-mail: sswanton@ggw.org.

SWANTON, VIRGINIA LEE, writer, publisher; b. Oak Park, Ill., Feb. 6, 1933; d. Milton Wesley and Eleanor Louise (Linnell) Swanton. BA, Lake Forest (Ill.) Coll., 1954; MA in English Lit., Northwestern U., 1955; cert. in acctg., Coll. of Lake County, Ill., 1984. Editorial asst. Publs. Office, Northwestern U., Evanston, Ill., 1955-58; reporter Lake Forester, Lake Forest, 1959; editor Scott, Foresman & Co., Glenview, Ill., 1959-84; copy editor, travel coord. McDougal Littell/Houghton Mifflin, Evanston, 1985-94; sr. bookseller B. Dalton Bookseller, Lake Forest, Ill., 1985—2004; author, pub. poetry books, reference works Gold Star Publ. Svcs., Lake Forest, 1994—. Contbr. articles to profl. jours. Former sec. bd. dirs., newsletter editor Career Resource Ctr., Inc., Lake Forest; current events discussion vol. Lake Forest/Lake Bluff Sr. Ctr.; mem. bd. deacons First Presbyn. Ch. Lake Forest. Mem.: Lake Forest/Lake Bluff Hist. Soc. (vol.), Chgo. Women in Pub. Presbyterian. Avocation: gardening. Office: Gold Star Publ Svcs PO Box 125 Lake Forest IL 60045-1333

SWARD, ANDREA JEANNE, information and computer scientist, musician; b. Hackensack, NJ, June 25, 1951; d. George Frederick and Carol Jeanne (Snoad) Lankow; m. Jeffrey Edwin Sward, June 7, 1975. Student, U. Minn., Duluth, 1969-72; BA in Psychology, Calif. State U., Fullerton, 1973, MS in Info. Sci., 1974, MS in Edn., 1976; cert. Bus. Intelligence and Data Warehousing, U. Calif. Irvine, 2003. Librarian, prof. Calif. State U., Fullerton, 1972—97; violist Anaheim Cultural Arts Ctr. Orch., Calif., 1978-80, Anaheim Civic Light Opera, 1978-80, Calif. European Tour Orch., Fullerton, 1978-79, Fullerton Cmty. Orch., Fullerton, 1978—86; computer programmer, analyst Hughes Aircraft, Fullerton, 1980-81, Smith-Kline/Beckman, Fullerton, 1981-83, ConAgra/Hunt-Wesson, Irvine, 1983—2004; librarian Downey City Library, Calif., 1985, Orange Pub. Library, Calif., 1985—90, Huntington Beach Library, Calif., 1985—; sys. analyst New Century Mortgage, Irvine, Calif., 2004—. Editor Vis À Vis; An Interdisciplinary Journal, 1972-74. Contbr. articles to profl. jours. Mem., contbr. Newport Harbor Art Mus., Newport Beach, Calif., 1975—, Los Angeles County Mus. of Art, 1975—, ACLU, 1976—, Cousteau Soc., 1978—, Audubon Soc., 1985—, Amigos de Bolsa Chica, 1985—, Spl. Olympics, 1987—; wildlife rehabilitator Wetlands and Wildlife Care Ctr., Orange County, 1999—. Fridley (Minn.) Edn. Assn. scholar, 1969, Spl. Edn. Assn. scholar, 1972; Edwin Carr fellow, 1976; Ptnrs. in Excellence grantee, 1979. Mem. ALA, Assn. for Computing Machinery, Calif. Library Assn., Calif. Reading Assn., Reading Educators Guild, Penguini Poets and Philosophers Guild of Placentia (co-founder). Democrat. Avocations: sports, reading, dance, theater, art. Home: PO Box 7019 Huntington Beach CA 92615-7019 E-mail: ajsward@yahoo.com.

SWART, BONNIE BLOUNT, artist; b. Shreveport, La., May 19, 1939; d. Jonathan Prescott and Alice Florence (Crawford) Blount; m. Carter Eaton Swart; children: Kathleen Anne, Nancy Laurie, Sherry Colleen. Student, U. Calif., Davis, Ventura Coll., 1984-88. Exhibited in group exhbns. at Am. Acad. Equine Art, 1989, 92, 93, 94, 96, 97, 2000, 01, 03, Nat. Mus. of the Horse, Lexington, Ky., Pastel Soc. of West Coast, Sacramento, 1995, 96, 97, Ann. Exhbn. on Animals in Art, La. State U., Baton Rouge, 1995, 96, Art at the Dog Show, Wichita, Kans., 1995, Harness Tracks of Am., Lexington, 1994, 96, Arabian Jockey Club Art Auction, Del. Park, Del., 1991, Equine Rsch. Benefit, Morvin Park, Leesburg, 1991, Arabian Horse Trust Art Auction, Scottsdale, 1990, 97-98, Women Artist's of the West, Biloxi, Miss., 1989, 97, 98, Internat. Arabian Horse Assn., Ky. Horse Park, Louisville, 1989, Arabian Horse Trust Mus. Exhibit, Westminster, Colo., 1987-89, Oil Painters of Am., Taos, N.Mex., 1997, Nat. Sporting Libr., Middleburg, Va., 2001; represented in pvt. collections. Mem. Am. Acad. Equine Art (assoc.), Knickerbocker Artists (signature mem.), Pastel Soc. West Coast (signature mem.). Home: 160 Lakeside Loop Crescent City CA 95531 E-mail: bbswart@earthlink.net.

SWARTZ, JULIANNE, artist; b. Phoenix, Apr. 29, 1967; BA in Photography and Creative Writing, U. Ariz., 1989; postgrad., Skowhegan Sch. for Painting and Sculpture, 1999; MFA, Bard Coll., 2002. One-woman shows include currents1: Julianne Swartz, Colby Coll. Mus. Art, Waterville, Maine, 2004, Speculative Mechanics *persistant optimism, Josee Bienvenu Gallery, NY, 2004, Partial Excavation (in pink), Angles Gallery, Santa Monica, Calif., 2005, Elevator Music 4, Frances Young Tang Mus., Skidmore Coll., Saratoga Springs, NY, 2005, exhibited in group shows at Shadow House, Ricco/Maresca Gallery, NY, 2000, Luminous, Bellevue Art Mus., Seattle, 2000, Pop Mechanics, Susquehanna Art Mus., Harrisburg, Pa., 2000, Interval: New Art for New Space, Sculpture Ctr., NY, 2001, Landing - the Bubble (with Piot Brehmer), 123 Watts, NY, 2001, Bklyn.!, Inst. Contemporary Art, Palm Beach, Fla., 2001, Periphera, Murray Guy Gallery, NY, 2002, Garden Details, Imported and Compressed, Schroeder Romero, NY, 2002, Line Drawing, Artist Space Project Rm., NY, 2003, Plastic Gardens, Cristinerose I Josee Bienvenu Gallery, NY, 2003, Breaking Away, P.S. 1 Inst. Contemporary Art, Queens, NY, 2003, Counter Culture, New Mus. Contemporary Art, NYC, 2004, Biennial, Whitney Mus. Am. Art, NY, 2004, Press Play, Green on Red Gallery, Dublin, Ireland, 2005, Sixteen:One, Santa Monica, 2005. Artist in Residence grant, NY Found. Arts, 1997, Spl. Editions grant, Lower East Side Printshop, 1998, Artist in Marketplace, Bronx Mus. Arts, 1999, Richard Kelly Found. grant, 1999, Cite Internationale des Arts, Paris, 2000, grant, P.S. 1 Mus., Nat. and Internat. Studio Program, 2002, Pub. Art Fund, NY, 2002, Art Omi Internat. Artists Colony, Ghent, NY, 2003. Mailing: c/o Josee Bienvenu Gallery 529 W 20th St New York NY 10011 E-mail: info@joseebienvenu.com.

SWARTZ, RENEE BECKER, civic volunteer; b. Newark, Feb. 25, 1935; d. Sidney David and Adeline (Kleinberg) Becker; m. Harry Mason Swartz, Mar. 8, 1931; children: Stephen, Addi-Lyn, Sidney. Student, Rutgers U., 1950-52, Bryn Mawr Coll., 1952-53; BA, Barnard Coll.-Columbia U., 1955. Planning com. N.J. White Ho. Conf. on Librs. and Info. Sci., 1975-79, del. selection com., mem. programs com., 1978-79; chair del. White Ho. Conf., 1979; re-elected permanent N.J. rep. Nat. Commn. Follow-up Activities White Ho. Conf., 1991, chairperson nat. awards com., 1984-86, chair fundraising com., 1989-90; chmn. N.J. Del. White Ho. Conf. of Librs. and Info. Svcs., 1991—. Pres. Friends of Monmouth County Libr. Assn., 1964-68; founding mem. N.J. Citizens for Better Librs., 1982; chair bldg. com. Dorothy L. Spiwak Meml. Libr., Rumson, N.J., 1971-73, trustee, 1971—; active N.J. Libr. Devel. Com., 1973-84; chair, bd. trustees Grad. Sch. of Comm., Info. and Libr. Studies, Rutgers U., 1980—, chair, 1983—; gov. appointee N.J. State Libr. Adv. Coun., 1975, chair, 1986—, Monmouth County Libr. Commn., 1965—, chair, 1976—; past trustee Barnard Coll., pres. Alumnae Assn., 1981-84, trustee, 1981-85; founder NJ Ctr. in the Book, 2001—, chair, state coord.; presdl. appointee Nat. Inst. Mus. and Libr. Svcs. Bd., 2004— Recipient Hanna G. Solomon award Greater Red Bank sect. Nat. Coun. Jewish Women, 1979, Pres. medal Barnard Coll.-Columbia U., 1984, Columbia U. medal, 1985, Woman or Achievement award Monmouth County Adv. Com., 1991; named Nat. Trustee of Yr. ALA, 1991. Mem. Nat. Citizens Com. for Pub. Libraries (steering com. 1980-84), Am. Library Trustee Assn. (pres. com. 1983, nat. intellectual freedom com. 1984—), N.J. Library Assn. (centennial com. 1986-89, chairperson N.J. Ednl. Inst. com. 1987-88, N.J. Trustee of Yr. 1980, 99), N.J. Library Trustee Assn. (exec. com. 1976-81, regional rep. 1983-86), Assn. N.J. Library Commrs. (pres. 1973-75), Capitol Hill Club, Lotus Club N.Y., Ocean Club NJ, Cosmos Club Avocations: tennis, sailing, walking. Home: 136 Rumson Rd Rumson NJ 07760-1238 Office Phone: 732-431-7235. Business E-Mail: rswartz@co.monmouth.nj.us.

SWARTZ, ROSLYN HOLT, real estate company executive; b. L.A., Dec. 9, 1940; d. Abe Jack and Helen (Canter) Holt; m. Allan Joel Swartz, June 2, 1963. AA, Santa Monica (Calif.) Coll., 1970; BA summa cum laude, UCLA, 1975; MA, Pepperdine U., 1976. Cert. CC instr., student-pers. worker Calif. Mgr. pub. rels. Leader Holdings, Inc., L.A., 1968-75, pres., 1991—, sec., treas. North Hollywood, Calif., 1975-81, pres., 1981-91; CEO Beverly Stanley Investments, L.A., 1979—. Pres. Leader Properties, Inc., Leader Fairfax, Inc., Leader 358, Inc., Leader 359, Inc., Leader Ventura, Inc., 1996—; condr. Oral History Elderly Jewish Cmty. Venice, Calif. Los Angeles County Planning Dept. Libr., 1974. Founder Pres.'s Cir. L.A. County Mus. Art, UCLA Affiliates Sch. of Medicine Scholarship Com., 2004—06; past trustee Odyssey Theatre Ensemble; mem. coun. Libr. Found.; supporting founding mem. Kirk Douglas Theatre; founder Disney Hall; hon. chmn. bus. adv. coun. Nat. Rep. Congl. Com.; bd. dirs. House Ear Inst.; hon. bd. dirs. West L.A. Symphony. Mem.: NAFE, ARCS Found., Inc. (Achiev. rewards for coll. scientists), KCET Womens Coun., Comml. Real Estate Women, Am. Pharm. Assn., First Century Soc. at UCLA, Royce Ctr. Cir., UCLA Las Donas (exec. bd.), Friends of Robinson Gardens, Town Hall (life), UCLA Alumni Assn. (life), Santa Monica Coll. Alumni Assn. (life), Nat. Mus. Women in Arts (So. Calif. coun.), Friends of Fox, UCLA Chancellor's Assocs. (mem. leadership coun. W. L.A. chpt.), Women's Guild Cedars-Sinai Med. Ctr., Fashion Cir. Costume Coun. of LACMA, UCLA Prytanean Alumnae Assn., Ctr. Dance Assn. (charter), Women and Philanthropy at UCLA (cir. level.), The Blue Ribbon Club, Club 100, Westwood Women's Bruins Club, Order Eastern Star, Phrateres Internat., Phi Beta Kappa (Bicentennial fellow), Pi Lambda Theta, Pi Gamma Mu, Phi Delta Kappa, Alpha Kappa Delta, Alpha Gamma Sigma, Phi Alpha Theta. Avocation: horticulture. Office: PO Box 241866 Los Angeles CA 90024-9666

SWARTZ, WILMA JEEANNE, music educator; b. Marshfield, Oreg., Mar. 8, 1926; d. Henry Dewey Sr. and Gladys Kathleen Wilson; m. Allan Ernest Swartz, Sept. 2, 1950 (dec. Mar. 1996); children: Ted A., Dawn K., Timothy W., Amanda Williams. BA in Music, U. Oreg., 1948; MusM in Piano, U. Mich., 1950. Nat. cert. music tchr. 1975. Pvt. practice, Muskegon, Mich., 1951—. Active Reach for Recovery Am. Cancer Soc., Muskegon, 1998-99; women's pres. Forest Park Covenant Ch., diaconate, 1996-99, ch. bd. sec.; co-founder Joseph/Wilson Fund for Music Student Study Awards. Named Music Tchr. of Yr. Greater Muskegon Music T. Assn., 1990, 97. Mem.: Pi Kappa Lambda, Music Tchrs. Nat. Assn., PEO Sisterhood (pres. 2004—05, chpt. sec., treas., chaplain, v.p., pres., 60 Yr. award), Mich. Fedn. of Music Clubs (jr. club counselor 1951—, 50 Yr. award), Mu Phi Epsilon. Republican. Avocations: sewing, photography, travel. Home: 3070 Sherwood Ct Muskegon MI 49441-1158 Office Phone: 231-755-2875.

SWARTZBAUGH, DOROTHY STOEPPELWERTH, middle school educator; b. Lawrence, Kans., Oct. 19, 1939; d. Walter William and Leona Stoltenberg Stoeppelwerth; m. Richard Grey Swartzbaugh, Oct. 27, 1962; children: Alfred Walter, Richard Andrew, Anne Elizabeth, Frederick Allen. BA in History and German, Valparaiso U., 1961; MA in German Lit., Ohio State U., 1966; PhD in German Lit. and Comparative Lit., U. Ill., 1982. Cert. tchr. Ill. Tchr. Hamilton Twp. Schs., Columbus, Ohio, 1962—64; German instr. Ea. Ky. U., Richmond, 1966—68; tchr. Mattoon (Ill.) Mid. Sch., 1979—. German instr. U. Miss., Oxford, 1968—72; presenter at confs. Recipient Key award, Phi Delta Kappa, 1988. Home: 880 7th St Charleston IL 61938 Office: Mattoon Mid Sch 1200 S 9th St Mattoon IL 61938 Office Phone: 217-238-5800.

SWATZELL, MARILYN LOUISE, nurse; b. Johnson City, Tenn., July 31, 1942; d. Dallas Fred and Minnie Thelma (Clark) S. BS cum laude, East Tenn. State U., 1966, MS, 1967; BSN, U. Tenn., 1974. Chmn. pediatric nursing Meth. Hosp. Sch. Nursing, Memphis, 1978—80; head nurse Le Bonheur Children's Med. Ctr., Memphis, 1981—83; dir. maternal child nursing Jackson (Tenn.) Madison County Gen. Hosp., 1985—88; staff nurse Vanderbilt U. Hosp., Nashville, 1988—90; supr. Meth. Hosp. Lexington, Tenn., 1990—2003; dir. case mgmt. Henderson County Cmty. Hosp., Tenn., 2003—. Contbr. articles on care plans to profl. jours. Mem. ANA, Tenn. Nurses Assn., Tenn. Orgn. Nurse Execs., N.W. Assn. Case Mgrs. Home: 231 Law Ln Lexington TN 38351-6048 Office Phone: 7909681840.

SWAZEY, JUDITH POUND, academic administrator, science educator; b. Bronxville, NY, Apr. 21, 1939; d. Robert Earl and Louise Titus (Hanson) Pound; m. Peter Woodman Swazey, Nov. 28, 1964; children: Elizabeth, Peter. AB, Wellesley Coll., 1961; PhD, Harvard U., 1966. Rsch. assoc. Harvard U., 1966-71, lectr., 1969-71, rsch. fellow, 1971-72; cons. com. brain scis. NRC, 1971-73; staff scientist neuroscis. rsch. program MIT, Cambridge, 1973-74; assoc. prof. dept. socio-med. scis. and cmty. medicine Boston U., 1974-77, prof., 1977-80, adj. prof. Schs. Medicine and Pub. Health, 1980—; exec. dir. Medicine in the Pub. Interest, Inc., Boston and Washington, 1979-82, 89-93; pres. Coll. of the Atlantic, Bar Harbor, Maine, 1982-84, Acadia Inst., Bar Harbor, 1984-2001, founding pres., sr. scholar, 2001—. Mem. Army Sci. Bd., 1987-92. Author: Reflexes and Motor Integration, the Development of Sherrington's Integrative Action Concept, 1969, (with others) Human Aspects of Biomedical Innovation, 1971, (with R.C. Fox) The Courage to Fail, a Social View of Organ Transplants and Hemodialysis, 1975, rev. edit., 1978, 02 (hon. mention Am. Med. Writers Assn., C. Wright Mills award Am. Sociol. Assn.), Chlorpromazine in Psychiatry, a Study of Therapeutic Innovation, 1974, (with K. Reeds) Today's Medicine, Tomorrow's Science, Essays on Paths of Discovery in the Biomedical Sciences, 1978; editor: (with C. Wong) Dilemmas of Dying, Policies and Procedures for Decisions Not to Treat, 1981, (with F. Worden and G. Adelman) The Neurosciences: Paths of Discovery, 1975, (with R.C. Fox) Spare Parts, Organ Replacement in American Society, 1992, Japanese transl., 1999, (with C. Messikomer and A. Glicksman) Society and Medicine. Essays in Honor of Renée Fox, 2002; assoc. editor IRB: A Jour. of Human Subjects Rsch., 1979-00; mem. editl. bd. Sci. and Engring. Ethics, 1994—; contbr. articles to profl. jours. Mem. Maine Dept. Human Svcs. Bioethics Adv. Com. (chair 1991-94); mem. Commn. on Rsch. Integrity, 1994-95; bd. dirs. Maine Bioethics Network, 1994-99. Wellesley Coll. scholar, 1961; Wellesley Coll. Alumnae fellow Harvard U., 1966, NIH predoctoral fellow, 1966, Radcliffe Coll. Coll. grad. fellow, 1966. Fellow AAAS (sci. freedom and responsibility com. 1986-89, nominations com. 2003-2004), Inst. Medicine of NAS (mem. health scis. policy bd. 1986-89), Grad. Record Exam. (bd. dirs. 1987-91), Phi Beta Kappa, Sigma Xi (mem. ethics com. 2004-). Office: PO Box 243 Bar Harbor ME 04609-0243 Business E-Mail: jswazey@verizon.net.

SWE, NI NI, psychiatrist; b. Rangoon, Burma, July 2, 1950; came to U.S., 1980; d. U. Myint and Daw Tin (Twe) S. MBBS, Inst. Medicine, Rangoon, 1975; MD, E.C.F.M.G., 1981. Intern Rangoon Gen. Hosp./Ctrl. Women's Hosp./Children's Hosp., Rangoon, 1976-77; family practice Rangoon, 1977-80; flex intern, 1982; physician asst. to plastic surgeon Calif., 1981-83; resident U. Tex. Southwestern Med. Sch., Dallas, 1984-88; pvt. practice psychiatry, Bedford, Tex., 1991—. Psychiatrist Tarrant County Mental Health Mental Retardation, Ft. Worth, 1988-91, Wise Couny Mental Health Mental Retardation, Decatur, Tex., 1989—. Named to Outstanding Young Men of Am., 1986. Mem. Am. Psychiat. Assn., Tex. Soc. Psychiat. Physicians (quality control com., fgn. med. grads. com.), Tarrant County Med. Soc., Tex. Med. Assn., Tex. Med. Found. (life). Republican. Buddhist. Office: 1901 Central Dr Ste 204 Bedford TX 76021-5824

SWEARINGEN, LAURA COLLEEN, music educator, director; b. St. Louis, Apr. 10, 1973; d. Paul Andrew and Karen Marie Hogan; m. Gary William Swearingen, Aug. 16, 1997; children: Shane Michael, Zoe Nichole. MusB, So. Ill. U., Edwardsville, 1995; MusM, Webster U., St. Louis, 1999. Choir dir. Brentwood Sch. Dist., Mo., 1993—2003; music tchr. Hillsboro Sch. Dist., 1996—98; choir dir. Festus Sch. Dist., Mo., 1998—99, Lindbergh Sch. Dist., St. Louis, 2003—. All-state choir coord. St. Louis Suburban Music Educators Assn., 2006—. Singer: (voice recital) Art Song by French Composers, (mezzo-soprano soloist) Brahm's Requiem; prodr.: (show choir competition show) Money, Gangsters; singer: St. Louis Chamber Chorus. Mem.: NEA, Mo. Music Educators Assn., Mo. State Tchrs. Assn., Mo. Choral Dirs. Assn., Am. Choral Dirs. Assn., St. Louis Irish Arts, Sigma Alpha Iota (pres. 1994—95). Conservative. Roman Catholic. Avocations: exercise, reading, geocaching, sports. Office: Lindbergh HS 4900 S Lindbergh Blvd Saint Louis MO 63126 Office Fax: 314-729-2443. Business E-Mail: lswearingen@lindberghschools.ws.

SWEARINGEN, LUCINDA ELLEN, counselor, educational adminstr.; b. Ft. Collins, Colo., May 21, 1932; d. Glen Vincent and Mary (Baccus) Swearingen; children: Nicholas Paul, Terence Philip. BS, Colo. State U., 1953, MEd, 1968; Cert., Am. Inst. Fgn. Trade, 1957. Nat. cert. counselor and career counselor. Tchr. Agana Jr. HS, Guam, 1953-54; dir. guidance svcs. Am. Cmty. Sch., Buenos Aires, Argentina, 1962-65; dir. testing svc., staff psychologist Colo. State U., Ft. Collins, 1968—2001, ret., 2001. Contbr. articles to profl. jours. Mem., chmn. Personnel bd., City of Ft. Collins, 1973-79, Larimer County Mental Health Bd., Ft. Collins, 1979-84; mem., v.p. Larimer County Women's Polit. Caucus, 1979-82. WEEA grantee, 1977-78. Mem. Am. Coll. Personnel Assn., Rocky Mountain Psychol. Assn.

SWEAT, LYNDA SUE, cooking instructor, catering company owner, deaconess; b. Phoenix, Apr. 5, 1949; d. Troy Eugene and Patricia June (Tignor) Lauchner; m. Doyle Dwayne Sweat, Feb. 7, 1976; children: Shannon Sue, Derek Dwayne. BA in Am. Studies, Ariz. State U, 2001, M in Religious Studies, 2002, Diploma Barrett Honors Coll., 2002. Leasing sec. Coldwell, Banker, Phoenix, 1968-74; exec. sec. Santa Anita Devel., Phoenix, 1974-78; prin., owner Tummy Yummy's, Phoenix, 1989—. Instr., Women's Seminars for Chs. on Christian Hospitality, 1984—; deaconess Palmcroft Bapt. Ch., Phoenix, 1989—, dir. fellowship com., editor and writer newsletter. Mem. Ariz. Bar Assn. Women's Aux., Maricopa County Bar Assn. Women's Aux., Southwestern Bible Coll. Women's Aux., Women in Food and Wine in Ariz. Club, Piecemakers (pres.). Republican. Avocations: crafting, quilting, porcelain doll making. Home: 6633 W Via Montoya Dr Glendale AZ 85310-5714

SWEAT, NORA ELLEN, home economics educator; b. Glendale, Ky., July 11, 1948; d. Joseph Francis and Juanita Gertrude (Boarman) Vaillancourt; m. Michael Francis Sweat, July 21, 1973; 1 child, Joseph William. BS, We. Ky. U., 1970, MA, 1977. Cert. tchr., Ky. Tchr. home econs. West Hardin H.S., Stephensburg, Ky., 1970—90, Ctrl. Hardin H.S., Cecilia, Ky., 1990—2000. Sec. Hardin County Schs. Performing Arts Ctr., 2001—. Mem. Am. Vocat. Assn. (Region II Vocat. Edn. Tchr. of Yr. 1992), Ky. Vocat. Assn. (v.p. 1987-91, Vocat. Edn. Tchr. of Yr. 1992), Ky. Future Homemakers (hon.), Ky. Home Econs. Tchrs. Assn. Democrat. Roman Catholic. Avocations: cooking, entertaining, piano. Home: 2862 Shepherdsville Rd Elizabethtown KY 42701-9539 Office Phone: 270-769-8837. E-mail: msweat7@alltel.net.

SWEAT, SARA J., secondary school educator; b. Monroe, Mich., May 13, 1979; d. Ronald F. and Anna Jo Sweat. BA in History and English, U. Mich., Ann Arbor, 2001. Cert. secondary tchr. Mich., 2002. Social studies tchr. Monroe (Mich.) Pub. Schs., 2002—. Youth and govt. advisor Monroe H.S., 2003—, varsity football acad. advisor, 2004—. Leader Raisinettes 4-H Club, Dundee, Mich., 1999—2005; supt. Monroe County 4-H, 2005—06; del. Dem. Nat. Conv. Mich. Dem. Party, 2004—04; vol. John Kerry Presdl. Campaign, Monroe, 2004; sec. Monroe County Dem. Com., 2004—06; vol. coord. Com. to Elect Kathy Angerer for State Rep., Temperance, Mich., 2004—04. Baptist. Avocations: travel, reading, sports. Office: Monroe High School 901 Herr Rd Monroe MI 48161 Office Phone: 734-265-3616. E-mail: ssweat@umich.edu.

SWEATMAN, WENDY LEIGH, secondary school educator; d. Diane Moulder and Winton Lyvoid Sweatman. MEd with honors, Walden U., 2006. HS math tchr. Forsyth County Bd. Edn., Cumming, Ga., 1994—96, Fulton County Bd. Edn., Alpharetta, Ga., 1999—2006, Habersham County Bd. Edn., Mount Airy, Ga., 2006—. Home: 5610 Burruss Rd Cumming GA 30040 Office: 171 Raider Cir Mount Airy GA 30563 Personal E-mail: sweatm_w@bellsouth.net.

SWEATT, ERMELINDA ESPINOLA, retired mathematics educator; d. Edmund Joseph and Mary Sylvia Espinola; m. Ronald Burnett Sweatt, Feb. 13, 1971; children: Tanya Sylvia, Jason Safford Edmund. BA in Math., Nasson Coll., Springvale, Maine, 1969; MA in Secondary Math. Edn., U. Conn., Storrs, 1974. Math. educator cert. Conn., dept. chairperson cert. Conn. Tchr. Ayer Jr.-Sr. HS, Mass., 1969—71, Plainfield HS, Conn., 1971—2005, dept. chairperson, 1987—2005; acct. Bustins Builders LLC, Bustins Island, Maine, 1980—. Cooperating & mentor tchr. Conn. Dept. Edn., Hartford, 1978—2005; advisor Plainfield Nat. Honor Soc., 1987—2005. Chairperson numerous dist. coms. Plainfield Pub. Schs., 1971—2005; coach girls field hockey Plainfield HS, 1971—73, coach girls cross country, 1974—80; officer Cottagers Assn. Bustins Island, 1979—88; exec. bd. Conn. Assn. Nat. Honor Socs. Recipient Outstanding Conn. Tchr. of Math., Conn. Dept. Edn., 1992, 2000. Mem.: NEA, Nat. Coun. Tchrs. Math., Conn. Edn. Assn., VFW Aux. Avocations: reading, writing, drawing, swimming, golf. Home: 37 Cooney Rd Pomfret Center CT 06259

SWECKER, VALERIE ANN, accountant, consultant; b. L.A., Sept. 6, 1958; d. Louis and Connie Mendoza. BS in Bus., U. Las Vegas, 1981. CPA, Nev. Acct. Fox & Co., 1981-84; ptnr., v.p. Swecker & Co., Ltd., 1985-95; owner, pres. Canyon Lake Rehab., Canyon Lake Chiropractic, 1995-97, Swecker Cons., Swecker Med. Mgmt., 1997—. Named among disting. women of Nev., 1992, 93. Avocations: water-skiing, skiing, reading, travel, tennis. Office: Box 25 849 St Heliers Auckland New Zealand

SWEED, PHYLLIS, publishing executive; b. NYC, Dec. 6, 1931; d. Paul and Frances (Spitzer) S.; m. Leonard Bogdanoff (dec. Oct. 1975); children: Patricia Romano (dec. June 1994), James Alan. BA, NYU, 1950. Asst. buyer Nat. Bellas Hess, N.Y.C., 1950; assoc. editor Fox-Shulman Pub., N.Y.C., 1951-57; significant products and components editor Product Engring. mag. McGraw-Hill Pub., N.Y.C., 1957—61; mng. editor Haire Pub., N.Y.C., 1962-66; editor Gifts & Decorative Accessories Mag., 1966-78; sr. v.p. Geyer-McAllister Pub., N.Y.C., 1978-98, editor-in-chief, co-pub., 1978—98; dir. editl. devel. Gifts & Decorative Accessories, N.Y.C., 1998-99; prin. P.S. Comms. & Mktg., 1999—; editor-in-chief, pub. Gift Executive, 1999—. Bd. dirs. Frances Hook Scholarship Fund, 1989-96. Recipient Editl. Excellence award Indsl. Mktg., 1964, Nat. Assn. Ltd. Edit. Dealers award, 1993, 96, MagWeek Excellence award, 1992, Dallas Mktg. Ctr. award, 1969, 80, 82. Mem. Nat. Assn. Ltd. Edit. Dealers (assoc.), Internat. Furnishings and Design Assn. Avocations: gardening, collecting antique Belleek. Office: 505 La-Guardia Pl Ste 17D New York NY 10012-2004 Personal E-mail: psweed505@aol.com.

SWEENEY, ANNE M., cable television company executive; b. Nov. 4, 1957; m. Philip Miller; children: Rosemary, Christopher. BA, Coll. of New Rochelle, N.Y., 1979; EdM, Harvard U., 1980. With Nickelodeon/Nick at Nite, 1981-93, sr. v.p. program enterprises; chmn., CEO Fx Networks, NYC, 1993-96; exec. v.p. Disney/ABC Cable Networks, pres. Disney Channel Walt Disney Co., 1996—98, pres. Disney/ABC Cable Networks, Disney Channel, 1998—2000, pres. ABC Cable Networks Group, Disney Channel Worldwide, 2000—04, co-chair Media Networks divsn., pres. Disney/ ABC TV, 2004—. Bd. dirs. Mus. Radio & TV; hon. chair Cable Positive. Bd. trustees Coll. of New Rochelle, Harvard U. Ptnrs. Coun.; hon. chair Cable Positive; bd. dirs. Walter Kaitz Found, Spl. Olympics Internat. Named one of 50 Most Powerful Women in Bus., Fortune mag., World's 100 Most Powerful Women, Forbes mag., 100 Most Powerful Women in Entertainment, Hollywood Reporter, 2004, 2005, 100 Most Powerful Women, Forbes mag., 2005—06, 50 Women to Watch, Wall St. Journal, 2005, 50 Most Powerful Women in Bus., Fortune mag., 2006; named to Hall of Achievement, Am. Advt. Fedn., 1996; recipient Lucy award, Women in Film, 2002, Chair Award, Caucus for TV Prodrs., Writers, and Dirs., 2003, President's award, Cable TV Pub. Affairs Assn., 2004. Mem. Nat. Acad. Cable Programming (bd. dirs.), Women in Cable NY (founding mem.), Women in Cable (Exec. of Yr. 1994, Woman of Yr. 1997, Advocate Leader award So. Calif. Chpt. 1998). Office: The Walt Disney Co 500 S Buena Vista St Burbank CA 91521

SWEENEY, COLLEEN LAUREN, elementary school educator; d. Tom and Barbara Sweeney. BS in Social Sciences Edn., Fla. State U., Tallahassee, Fla., 2002. Lic. tchr. Dept. Edn., Fla., 2002. Tchr. Westglades Mid. Sch., Parkland, Fla., 2002—, team leader, 2004. Coach cheerleading Westglades Mid. Sch., 2002—. Named Social Studies Tchr. of Yr., Westglades Mid. Sch., 2005.

SWEENEY, EILEEN MARY, librarian, director; b. Elma, Iowa, Feb. 15, 1944; d. George Joseph Frana and Cecelia Margaret Kuhn-Frana; m. Patrick Herman Sweeney, Aug. 22, 1964; children: Pauline, Susan, Sheryn, Patrick Jr. Assoc. degree, N. Iowa Area CC, 1997. Cert. libr. Iowa. Libr., asst. dir. Alta Vista Pub. Libr., Iowa, 1988—89, head libr., dir., 1990—. Cons. mem. Chickasaw Libr. Assn., Chickasaw County, New Hampton, 1990—. Mem. band & choral music booster club New Hampton Sch., 1984—94; vol. Colonial Manor Nursing Home Aux., 1990—; sec./treas. St. Patrick's Rosary Soc., 1964—; mem. Immaculate Conception Ch. Rosary Soc., 1974—; mem. parents assn. Talented and Gifted Orgn., Alta Vista, New Hampton, 1980—94. Grant award, Bill Gates Corp. & Found., Seattle, 2003. Mem.: Lee Middleton Doll Club, Red Hat Soc. Democrat. Roman Catholic. Home: 8519 185th St Elma IA 50628 Office: Alta Vista Pub Libr 203 S White Ave Alta Vista IA 50603 Office Phone: 641-364-6009.

SWEENEY, KATHLEEN P., special education educator; b. Carnedonagh, Ireland, June 28, 1959; d. Hugh Joseph and Mary Staunton McGonagle; m. George Edward Sweeney, July 18, 1981; children: Erin, Kathleen Elizabeth, George Hugh. BA, Rosar Coll., 1981; MSc in Spl. Edn., Dominican U., 2003. Fourth grade tchr. St. Williams Sch., Chgo., 1981—82; first grade tchr. St. Francis Xavier Sch., La Grange, Ill., 1995—99; resource tchr. Whittier Sch. Dist. 97, Oak Pk., Ill., 1999—. Mem.: Coun. of Exceptional Children, Kappa Delta Pi. Avocations: drawing, painting, reading.

SWEENEY, MARGARET MARY, federal judge; b. 1955; BA in History, Coll. Notre Dame, Md., 1977; JD, Del. Law Sch., 1981. Bar: Supreme Ct. Pa., DC Ct. Appeals. Master Del. Family Ct., 1981—83; atty. Fedorko, Gilbert, & Lanctot, 1983—85; law clk. to Hon. Loren A. Smith US Ct. Fed. Claims, 1985—87; trial atty. gen. litigation sect., environ. and nat. resources divsn. US Dept. Justice, 1987—99, atty. adv. office intelligence policy and rev.; spl. master US Ct. Fed. Claims, 2003—05, judge, 2005—. Mem.: US Ct. Fed. Claims Bar Assn. (mem. bd. 1990—, pres. 1999). Office: US Ct Fed Claims 717 Madison Pl NW Washington DC 20005 Office Phone: 202-219-9657.*

SWEENEY, MICKEY, literature and language professor; b. Chgo. d. Jamie and Birgit Sweeney. BA in English with honors, NYU, 1990; German cert., Goethe Inst., Munich, 1991; MA in English, U. Mich., Ann Arbor, 1992; PhD, Trinity Coll., Dublin, Ireland, 1996. Asst. lectr. in Old and Middle English Univ. Coll., Dublin, 1998—99; asst. prof. English dept. U. Mo., Rolla; prof. Dominican U., River Forest, Ill., 2002—. Gov.-apptd. bd. dirs. Mo. Humanities Coun.; vis. lectr. semester in London program Dominican U., 2004; presenter confs. in field. Author: (book) Magic in Medieval Romance: Chretien de Troyes to Geoffrey Chaucer, 2000; contbr. articles to profl. jours. Mentor Holy Family Scholarship, Chgo., 2003—06. Recipient Dominican grant for profl. workshops, 2002, rsch. assistance grant, Dominican Faculty Devel. Com., 2006; grantee, Mo. Humanities Coun., 2001, Christianity and Culture Project, 2001—02. Mem.: MLA, New Chaucer Soc., Christianity and Culture Project (bd. dirs.), Medieval Assn. Am. (councilor 2006), Societas Magica, Internat. Courtly Lit. Soc. Office: Dominican U 7900 W Division River Forest IL 60305

SWEENEY, PATRICE ELLEN, health administration executive; b. Denver, Sept. 19, 1953; d. Floyd L. and Martha Lou (Ray) S.; m. Steven Michael Wilk, June 25, 1977; children: Adam, Kristen, Ryan. AB, Princeton U., 1975; MHA, Duke U., 1977. Adminstrn. resident U. Hosp. Jacksonville, Fla., 1977-78; fellow Am. Hosp. Assn., Blue Cross Blue Shield, Chgo., 1978-79; from dir. corp. svcs. to sr. corp. planner Md. Health Care System, Balt., 1979-82; spl. asst. to pres. Am. Hosp. Assn., Chgo., 1982-85; from dir. hosp. rels. to asst. v.p. hosp. rels. Premier Hosps. Alliance, Westchester, Ill., 1985-89, v.p. hosp. rels., 1989-95; v.p., owner, affiliate svcs. Premier, Inc., Westchester, 1996-99, sr. v.p. relationship mgmt., 1999—. Contbr. articles to profl. jours. NCAA wrestling announcer Princeton (N.J.) U., 1975, 81; nursing home visitor Manor Care, Balt., 1980-81; head room mother Lane Sch., Hinsdale, Ill., 1990-98; Sunday Sch. tchr. Union Ch., Hinsdale, 1992-96; bd. dirs. Rape Crisis Ctr., Balt., 1980-82. Population Inst. fellow, 1976-77; King Edward's Hosp. Fund fellow, 1977. Avocations: gardening, piano, cooking, needlecrafts. Office: Premier Inc 700 Commerce Dr Oak Brook IL 60523

SWEENEY, SHAWNA ELIZABETH, political science professor, researcher; b. New Bedford, Mass., Aug. 9, 1967; d. John Brennan and Elizabeth Theresa Sweeney. BA magna cum laude, U. Mass., Dartmouth, 1992; MA, SUNY, Binghamton, 1997, PhD, 2006. Sr. rsch. assoc. Ctr. Policy Analysis, U. Mass. Dartmouth, 1998—; vis. asst. prof. policy studies dept. U. Mass., Dartmouth, 2005—. Rsch. asst. SUNY Human Rights Data Set funded by NSF and World Bank, Binghamton, NY, 1993—98; guest editl. asst. spl. issue Spill Sci. and Tech. Bull., 2001—02; human rights cons. World Bank, 2003—06. Grantee, NSF, 2003—06; scholar, SUNY Binghamton, 1993—98. Mem.: Internat. Studies Assn., So. Polit. Sci. Assn., Am. Polit. Sci. Assn. Avocations: travel, animal welfare, photography, kayaking, hiking. Office: U Mass Dartmouth 285 Old Westport Rd Dartmouth MA 02719 Office Phone: 508-999-8254. Business E-Mail: ssweeney@umassd.edu.

SWEENEY, SUSAN LYNN, science educator; b. Phila., Apr. 10, 1952; d. Wiulliam and Suzanne M. Sweeney; m. Dale E. McCullough, Mar. 7, 1998. BS in Zoology, Ohio State U., Columbus, 1974; MS in Biology, Shippensburg U., Pa., 1984. Cert. tchr. Pa. Tchr. biology Trinity H.S., Camp Hill, Pa., 1978—. Chair dept. sci. Trinity H.S., Camp Hill, Pa., 1982—. Office: Trinity HS 3601 Simpson Ferry Rd Camp Hill PA 17011-6475 Office Phone: 717-761-1116. Personal E-mail: ssweene2882@aol.com.

SWEENEY-ZAMBONI, EILEEN T., literature and language professor; b. Wilkes Barre, Pa., June 13, 1969; d. John D. and Maureen C. Sweeney; m. Dan Zamboni, May 24, 1996; 1 child, Madeline Claire Zamboni. BA, King's Coll., Wilkes Barre, Pa., 1996; MA, U. Scranton, Pa., 1998. Instr. King's Coll., 1996—. Mem. core project team King's Coll., 1996—, dir. faculty seminars writing across curriculum and computer tech., 2000—02; vis. lectr. Sussex County C.C., Newton, NJ, 2003—03; adj. prof. Wilkes U., 2004—06; presenter in fields of English composition and lit., popular culture. Mem. com. Holy Saviour Ch., Wilkes Barre, 1980—2005. Avocations: bicycling, writing, reading, travel. Office: King's College 133 N River Street Wilkes Barre PA 18711 Office Phone: 570-208-5900 5761. E-mail: etsweene@kings.edu.

SWEET, PORTIA ANN, retired human resources specialist; b. Charleston, W.Va., Jan. 14, 1939; BA, U. Houston, 1973. Sr. profl. in human resources. Adminstrv. mgr. Great Am. Ins. Co., Houston, Cin., Denver, 1973-81; cons., owner Sweet Encounters, Greeley, Colo., 1982-89; risk mgmt. splst. Hi/LO Auto Supply, Houston, 1991-94; human resources mgr. Chevron Products/MKTG, Houston, 1994-2000; ret., 2000. Vol. dir. Greeley Conv. Bur., 1986; bd. dirs. Women's Resource Ctr., Durango, Colo., 1988-89; vol. Houston Area Women's Ctr., 1990-91. Recipient Cert. Appreciation A Woman's Place, 1981. Mem. NAFE, NOW, Human Resources Mgmt. Assn. (bd. sec. 1995-96), Soc. Human Resources Mgmt., Houston Human Resources Mgmt. Assn., Risk and Ins. Mgmt. Soc., Ind. Ins. Agents (Big I). Episcopalian. Avocations: needlecrafts, flower gardening, classical music. Home: 5800 Lumberdale Rd Apt 80 Houston TX 77092-1512 Office: Chevron Products Co 5959 Corporate Dr Houston TX 77036-2302

SWEETMAN, BEVERLY YARROLL, physical therapist; b. Phila., Apr. 8, 1939; d. Albert Henry and Theresa (Payne) Yarroll; m. Denman John Sweetman, Apr. 1, 1961; children: Denman Eric, John Albert. BA in Biology, Hood Coll., 1961; cert. phys. therapist, Hahnemann U., 1983. Rsch. technician Mass. Gen. Hosp., Boston, 1961-62, Princeton (N.J.) U., 1965-66; co-owner, phys. therapist Pain & Stress Control Ctr., Allentown, Pa., 1983—85; pvt. practice Grants Pass, Oreg., 1985; pres. Body Ease Phys. Therapy Ctr., Staunton, Va., 1986—. Developer and co-presenter Total Body Concept Seminars, Total Body Concept Aquatic Workshops; v.p. VMG Med., Staunton, 1988—; cons., co-presenter Lossing Orthop., Mpls., 1985—95; lectr. in field. Fellow Am. Back Soc.; mem. Am. Phys. Therapy Assn. Office: Body Ease Phys Therapy Ctr 542 Walnut Hills Rd Staunton VA 24401-6936 Office Phone: 540-337-1999. Personal E-mail: bys@applelinks.net.

SWEEZY, VICKY LYNN, science educator, emergency medical technician; b. Manchester, NH, July 13, 1970; d. Leonard William and Jacqueline Marie Sweezy; life ptnr. Troy W. Andrews; children: Shayna Osicea, Chayton Galen. BS, U. New Eng., Maine, 1993. Cert. Nat Cert. EMT 2003; experienced educator cert. NH, 1999. H.s. sci. tchr. Stevens H.S., Claremont, NH, 1998—2002, Alton Ctrl. Sch., Alton, NH, 2002—04, Prospect Mountain H.S., 2004—; EMT Alton Fire and Rescue Dept., 2004—. Sci. curriculum leader Prospect Mountain H.S., Alton, NH, 2004—; youth advisor Alton Explorers, 2004—. CPR instr. Am. Red Cross, first responder instr. Avocations: swimming, reading, hiking, alternative medicine. Office: Prospect Mountain High Sch 242 Suncook Valley Rd Alton NH 03809 Office Phone: 603-875-3800. Personal E-mail: vsweezy@pmhschool.com.

SWENSEN, COLE, poet, educator; BA, MA, San Francisco State U.; PhD in Comparative Lit., U. Calif., Santa Cruz. Dir. creative writing prog. U. Denver; assoc. prof. U. Iowa Writers' Workshop. Author: It's Alive, She Says, New Math, 1988 (Nat. Poetry Series winner), Park, 1991, Numen, 1995, Noon, 1997 (New Am. Poetry Series Award), Try, 1999, Oh, 2000 (Iowa Poetry Prize), Such Rich Hour, 2001, Goest, 2004 (Nat. Book Award finalist, 2004); contbg. editor American Letters and Commentary, Shiny, translation editor How2. Office: Grad Prog Creative Writing U Iowa 102 Dey House Iowa City IA 52242-1408 Office Phone: 319-335-0416.

SWENSEN, JOAN LINDA, elementary school educator; b. Ida Grove, Iowa, Jan. 5, 1948; d. Melvin August and Virginia Ann (Lindskoog) Schmidt; m. Dwain Donald Swensen, Aug. 6, 1977; children: Jennifer Ann, Jodie Lynn. BA, U. Northern Iowa, 1970. Elem. edn. tchr. Webster City (Iowa) Cmty. Schs., 1970-72, Morrison Acad., Taichung, Taiwan, Republic of China, 1973-75, Ida Grove (Iowa) Cmty. Schs., 1976-77, Odebolt (Iowa) Cmty. Schs., 1978—. Vol. children's groups Kiron Bapt. Ch., Kiron, Iowa, 1977—. Mem. Quint-County Reading Coun. (corresponding sec. 1982-83, treas. 1985-86), Iowa Reading Assn., Internat. Reading Assn. Avocation: cooking. Home: 1231 290th St Kiron IA 51448-7502 Office: Odebolt-Arthur Cmty Sch 600 S Maple Odebolt IA 51458

SWENSON, ADA PEREZ, artist; m. Roy Swenson, Oct. 30, 1994; children: Miguel Weissman, Wendy Robin Weissman. Student, Stony Brook U., 1965—66, Indian River C.C., 2002—05, Art Student League, 1951—54; studied with, Richard Cardoff, 1965—68, John Seerey Lester, 2004. One-woman shows include Bahia Redonda Resort and Marina, Venezuela, 1999, Port de Plaisance, St. Maarten, Netherlands, 1999, Harbor Village, Bonaire, Netherlands, 1999, Vero Beach Main Libr., Fla., 2002—06, Count Down Studio, N.Y.C., 2000—06, 2006, Everglades Nat. Park Mus., Homestead, Fla., 2005, exhibitions include Vero Beach Mus., Vero Beach Main Libr., 2001—04, 2005, 2006, Meghan Candler Galley, Vero Beach, 2004, 2005, 2006, Arte Direct Galley, Naples, Fla., 2004—06, Everglades Nat. Park Visitors Ctr. Mus., 2005—06, Represented in permanent collections U. Fla. Rsch. Ctr., Ft. Pierce, S.C. State Park, Dillon, Littman Jewelers, Bonaire, Count Down Studio, Everglades Nat. Park; art coord. Indian River Main Libr., Vero Beach, 2006. Recipient Scholastic Art award, Pratt U., 1948, awards, AE Backus Mus., Ft. Pierce, 2002, Ctr. for the Arts, Vero Beach, 2002, Everglades Nat. Park, 2004. Mem.: Vero Beach Art Club, Nat. Acad. Profl. Plein Air Painters, Am. Impressionist Soc., Plein Air Painters of East Coast, Fla. Watercolor Soc. Home: 256 Marina Dr Fort Pierce FL 34949 Office Phone: 772-595-3158. Personal E-mail: apswenson@comcast.net.

SWENSON, CHRISTINE ERICA, microbiologist; b. N.Y., Apr. 27, 1953; d. Oscar Adolf and Marjorie Claire Swenson; m. James Yasinski, Sept. 6, 1980; children: Jeffrey, Emma. BA, Middlebury Coll., 1975; PhD, Cornell U., 1980. Postdoctoral fellow Rockefeller U., N.Y., 1980-82, U. Calif., San Francisco, 1982-84; scientist The Liposome Co., Inc., Princeton, N.J., 1984-88, dir. preclin. devel., 1988—. Office: Elan Pharmaceutical 7475 Lusk Blvd San Diego CA 92121-5707

SWENSON, CONSTANCE RAE, lawyer; d. Albin Linus Peterson and Lillian; m. Keith Howard Swenson, June 20, 1970; children: Jeffrey, Melissa, Stacy, Justin. BA in Zoology, Rockford Coll., Ill., 1968; diploma for law studies, East China Sch. of Law and Politics, Shanghai, 1988; JD, Northwestern Sch. Law, Portland, 1990; diploma in Spanish, El Centro de Idiomas y Estudios, Mex., 1993; BA in French (hons.), Portland State U., 1996. Bar: Oreg. 1991, Esquire Dist.: Oreg. 1991, atty., counselor: U.S. Ct. Appeals 4th Cir. 2001. Librarian asst. Rockford Pub. Libr., Ill., 1968—69; law internship internat. banking Crédit de Nord, Paris, 1989; atty. Connie Swenson, Atty., Portland, Oreg., 1991—93; art dept. asst. Portland State U. Bookstore, 1993—96, 1997; realtor Century 21, Gresham, Oreg., 1997; student asst. to adminstr. Portland State U., Oreg., 1997—98; atty. Connie Swenson, Atty., Portland, Oreg., 2000—06. Hearings officer Multnomah Animal Ctrl., 2003—. Arbitrator Better Bus. Bur., Portland, 2006; adv. council U. Oreg., Eugene, 2004—06. Mem.: Multnomah Bar Assn. (CLE com. 2000—06), Am. Trial Lawyers Assn. (advocate 2005), Oreg. Trial Lawyers Assn. Mem. Evangelical Covenant Ch. Avocations: ice skating, hiking. Office: Connie Swenson Atty 465 NE 181 Ave #149 Portland OR 97230

SWENSON, DIANE KAY, legal association administrator; b. Sioux Falls, SD, June 16, 1952; d. Clarence Donald and Mildred Ann (Meyer) S. BA magna cum laude, Augustana Coll., 1974; JD, Hamline U., 1981. Bar: Minn. 1981. Tchr. Malvern (Iowa) Pub. Schs., 1974-76, Rosemount Pub. Schs., Apple Valley, Minn., 1976-78; legis. asst. to Senator Larry Pressler, U.S. Senate, Washington, 1981-86; exec. v.p. Am. Tort Reform Assn., Washington, 1986-99, Nat. Assn. Fed. Credit Unions, Washington, 1999—. Exec. v.p. Emmanual Luth. Ch., Bethesda, Md., 1997. Mem. ABA. Republican. Lutheran. Avocation: skiing. Home: 6140 Stonehenge Place Rockville MD 20852-5807 Office: Nat Assn Fed Credit Unions 3138 10th St N Arlington VA 22201-2149 Office Phone: 703-522-4770. Business E-Mail: dswenson@nafcu.org.

SWENSON, MICHELE ANN, middle school educator; b. Hammond, Ind., July 14, 1956; d. John Edward and Marjorie Ann Hicks; children: Julia Mary, David Charles. B in Elem. Edn., Purdue U. Calumet, Hammond, Ind., 1978; EdM, Stephen F. Austin State U., Nacogdoches, Tex., 1984. Jr. h.s. math tchr. Goose Creek Consol. Ind. Sch. Dist., Baytown, Tex., 1979—88; mid. sch. math tchr. Merrillville Cmty. Schs., Ind., 1988—. Math team coach Baytown Jr. Sch., Tex., 1979—88; volleyball, basketball, track coach Merrillville Cmty. Schs., 1979—92, spell bowl coach and hoosier academic super bowl coach, 1988—2003. Mem., ret. racing greyhound adopter Greyhound Guardians, Crown Point, Ind., 2002—06. Mem.: NEA. Avocations: gift basket design, tutoring. Office Phone: 219-650-5308.

SWENSSON, EVELYN DICKENSON, conductor, composer, librettist; b. Woodstock, Va., Sept. 18, 1928; d. Glenn Gilmer and Evelyn Christine (Ring) Dickenson; m. Sigurd Simcox Swensson, June 9, 1949; children: Lisë, Karen, Erik, Jon. Cert. in piano, Ward-Belmont Coll., Nashville, 1946; BA in Piano and Voice, Hollins Coll., Roanoke, Va., 1949; MusM, West Chester U., Pa., 1972. Condr. Aldersgate Meth. Ch., Wilmington, Del., 1969—2002, Brandywiners Ltd., Kennett Sq., Pa., 1973—2004, Opera Del., Wilmington, 1974—, Bi-Centennial Chorus, Wilmington, 1976; guest condr. Del. Symphony Orch., Wilmington, 1977; condr. Ardensingers, Wilmington, 1978-80; condr. 200th Anniversary Meth. Ch. Am., Balt., 1984. V.p. Opera for Youth Inc.; dir. family opera theater Opera Del., Wilmington, 1974—. Condr.: inaugural concert for Gov. P.S. duPont IV, 1977, Sleeping Beauty (Respighi), 1977, The Zoo (Sullivan and Rowe), 1980, The Lion, the Witch and the Wardrobe (John McCabe), 1980, celebration of Swedes Landing, 1988, The Boy Who Grew Too Fast (Menotti), 1982, Charlotte's Web (Strouse), 1989, A Wrinkle in Time (Larsen), 1992, composer, condr.: The Enormous Egg, 1993, The Adventure of Beatrix Potter, 1994, The Jungle Book, 1995, Anne of Green Gables, 1996, The Homecoming, 1997, The Legend of Redwall Abbey, 1998, All Through the Night, 1999, The Trumpet of the Swan, 2000, The Mixed-Up Files of Mrs. Basil E. Frankweiler, 2002, Billy Lee's Washington, 2003, The Secret of NIMH, 2004, What Child is This?, 2005. Recipient W. W. Laird Music award, Opera Del., Wilmington, 1987, Internat. Reading Coun. Literacy award, 1989, Disting. Alumna award, West Chester U., 1989, 5 composition awards, Nat. League Am. Pen Women, 2000, Outstanding Svc. award, Nat. Opera Assn., 2004. Mem.: Am. Guild Organists (choir master). Home: 166 Heyburn Rd Chadds Ford PA 19317

SWERDLOVE, DOROTHY LOUISE, librarian, consultant; b. N.Y.C., Jan. 4, 1928; d. Louis and Belle (Cohn) S. BA, Swarthmore Coll., 1948; MLS, Columbia U., 1961. Rsch. asst. Fed. Res. Bank N.Y., N.Y.C., 1948—49; social sci. analyst Congl. Ref. Svc. Libr. Congress, Washington, 1949—53; rsch. asst. Princeton U., NJ, 1953—54, Chase Manhattan Bank, N.Y.C., 1954—55; economist Caltex Oil Corp., N.Y.C., 1955—61; libr. Theatre Collection N.Y. Pub. Libr., N.Y.C., 1961—90, 1st asst. Theatre Collection, 1967—80, curator Theatre Collection, 1980—90, ret., 1990. Cons. rev. 2d edit. Random House Unabridged Dictionary of English Language, 1987. Asst. editor: abstracts series Pub. Affairs Abstracts, 1950-51; contbr. articles to profl. jours.; author: (with Patterson and Gunn) Survey of U.S. International Finance, 1954. Bd. advisors Night 100 Stars for Actors Fund Am., 1982-90; eligibility com. Tony awards, 1983-84; nominating com. Brendan Gill Prize, Municipal Art Soc. N.Y., 1987-96. Mem. ALA, Am. Soc. Theatre Rsch. (exec. bd. 1979-81, 85-88), Spl. Libraries Assn. (rep. 1971-86), Drama Desk, New Drama Forum Assn. (treas. 1979-82), Theatre Libr. Assn. (exec. bd. 1966-86, 93-95, pres. 1983-85, Disting. Svc. award 1996), Internat. Assn. Performing Arts Libraries and Mus. (v.p. 1991-95), Outer Critics Circle (treas. 1986-96), League of Am. Theatres and Prodrs. (hist. and curators com. 1993-94), Amateur Comedy Club, Snarks. Home: 9225 E Tanque Verde Rd #19204 Tucson AZ 85749-7740

SWERDLOW, AMY, historian, educator, writer; b. N.Y.C., Jan. 20, 1923; d. Joseph and Esther (Rodner) Galstuck; m. Stanley H. Swerdlow, Nov. 27, 1949 (dec. Sept. 1991); children: Joan Swerdlow-Brandt, Ezra, Lisa, Thomas. BA, NYU, 1963; MA, Sarah Lawrence Coll., 1973; PhD, Rutgers U., 1984. Prof. emerita Sarah Lawrence Coll., Bronxville, NY, 1981-95, dir. grad. studies in women's history, 1983-95, dir. women's studies program, 1983-95. Mem. adv. bd. Feminist Press, 1973-90. Editor: Memo, Women Strike for Peace, 1969—73; editor, co-author Families in Flux, 1980, (reprint), 1989; author: Women Strike for Peace, Traditional Motherhood and Radical Politics in the 1960s, 1993; editor: Feminist Perspective on Homework and Childcare, 1978; co-editor: Class, Race, and Sex: The Dynamics of Control, 1983, Rethinking Women's Peace Studies, 1995; co-author: The Readers Companion to U.S. Women's History (anon.), 1998, Notable American Women, 2004; contbr. book reviews to jours., essays to various pubs. Peace History Soc. non-govtl. rep. to UN, 1994—2005; panelist Bronx (N.Y.) Mus. History, 1995. Rutgers U. fellow, 1977-81, Woodrow Wilson Dissertation fellow, 1980. Mem. Berkshire Conf. in Women's History (program com.). Home: 33 Wheelock Walk East Hampton NY 11937-3937 Office Phone: 212-666-7227. Personal E-mail: amnerm@aol.com.

SWERGOLD, MARCELLE MIRIAM, sculptor; b. Antwerp, Belgium, Sept. 6, 1927; Student, NYU, Arts Students League, Sculptors Workshop. Sculptor, 1965—. One woman exbhns. include: Studio 12, N.Y.C., 1980, 82, 86, Nat. Fedn. Temple Sisterhoods, 1984; group exbhns. include Farleigh Dickinson U., Teaneck, N.J., 1972, Womanart Gallery, 1977, 78, Audubon Artist Ann., N.Y.C., 1978, 86, 88, 89, 90, 91, 92, 93, Am. Friends of Hebrew U, 1978, Internat. Treasury Fine Arts, Plainview, N.Y., 1979, Studio 12, 1980, 82, 86, New Britain (Conn.) Mus., 1980, also Cork Gallery, Lincoln Ctr., N.Y.C., Allied Artists Nat. Acad. Galleries, N.Y.C., U.S. Custom House, N.Y.C., others; represented in permanent collection New Britain Mus. Am. Art, in sculpture garden of Yad Vashem-Holocaust Mus., Jerusalem, Monument in the Park of the City of Ma'aleh Adumim, Israel, Sculpture in lobby at Fairlawn (N.J.) Jewish Ctr., Holocaust Meml. in lobby of Jewish Ctr., N.Y., Shaare Zedek Med. Ctr. in Jerusalem; represented in pvt. collection of Master Moshe Castel, Israel, Norman Levy, Harts Mountain Industries, Inc., Imri Rosenthal, Rosenthal and Rosenthal, N.Y., Itzrak Devier, Tel-Aviv, Mudge, Rose, Guthrie & Alexander, N.Y., Sylvian Sternberg, Jerusalem, others. Recipient Best in Show award for Tetons, Woman's Art Gallery, N.Y.C., 1977, 1st prize for sculpture Stanley Richter Assn. Arts, 1985, Vincent Glinski Meml. award Aububon Artists, 1986. Mem. N.Y. Soc. Women Artists (pres. 1979-81, exec. v.p. 1981—), Artists Equity, Contemporary Artists Guild. Home: 450 W End Ave New York NY 10024-5307 Studio: 246 W 80th St New York NY 10024-5705

SWICKERT, RHONDA J., psychology professor; b. Staunton, Va., Mar. 25, 1967; d. Rodney James and Lois Marie Swickert; m. James Bryant Hittner, May 6, 2001; 1 child, Julie Hittner. BS, Emporia State U., Kans., 1988; MS, Calif. State U., Long Beach, 1992; PhD, U. Okla., Norman, 1996. Instr. U.

Okla., 1992—96; asst. prof. Coll. of Charleston, SC, 1996—2001, assoc. prof., 2002—. Test developer Am. Savs. Bank, Irvine, Calif., 1991. Nominee Best Article of Yr., Jour. Rsch. in Personality, 1998. Mem.: Soc. for Personality and Social Psychologists, Internat. Soc. for Study of Individual Differences. Avocations: running, piano, reading, crafts. Office: Coll of Charleston 57 Coming St Charleston SC 29424 Office Phone: 843-953-5046. Office Fax: 843-953-7151. E-mail: swickertr@cofc.edu.

SWIENER, RITA ROCHELLE, psychologist, educator; b. Pitts., July 31, 1941; d. Julius D. and Rose (Sheinbein) Swiener; 1 child, Samuel L. Schuff. BA, U. Mo., St. Louis, 1970; MA in Psychology, So. Ill. U., Edwardsville, 1973. Prof. Psychology State Cmty. Coll., East St. Louis, Ill., 1972-96; pvt. practice St. Louis, 1972—. Adj. faculty St. Louis C.C., Meramac, 1993—; pres. Ill. C.C. Faculty Assn., 1979-80; trustee State Univs. Retirement Sys., 1990; pres. local 3912 IFT-AFT, East St. Louis, 1983-92; chairperson social and behavior panel Ill. C.C. Bd. and Bd. of Higher Edn. Articulation Initiative, 1992-96. Pres. Call-for-Help, Inc., Edgemont, Ill., 1990-92, 94-97; pres. and founder Santa's Helpers, Inc., St. Louis, 1966—; mem., founder Joy E. Whitener scholarship com. U. Mo. at St. Louis, 1990—. Recipient Outstanding C.C. Faculty Mem. award Ill. C.C. Trustees Assn., 1985, David Erikson award for Outstanding Leadership Ill. C.C. Faculty Assn., 1988, Hometown Hero award KPLR-TV, Suburban Jour., Hardees, St. Louis, 1994, Christmas Spirit award KSD-TV, John Pertzborn, St. Louis, 1990. Mem. APA, U. Mo. St. Louis Psychology Alumni Assn. (treas. 1989-91, Disting. Alumni award 1992), St. Louis Women Psychologist, Mo. Psychol. Assn. Jewish. Avocations: boating, travel, reading. Home: 7832 Balson Ave Saint Louis MO 63130-3624 Business E-Mail: rswiener@stlcc.edu.

SWIFT, CONSTANCE REDMOND, special education educator; b. Cleve., Aug. 31, 1950; d. Charles Clovis and Sally McMahon Redmond; m. Robert Jeffrey Swift, Sept. 17, 1977 (div. Aug. 1, 1990); children: Robert J., Michael J., J. Patrick, Sally M., Terrence M. BS in Psychology, Loyola U., Chgo., 1972; postgrad., Sam Houston State U., Houston, 1991—93; MA in Counseling Psychology, Sam Houston State U., Huntsville, Tex., 1997. Cert. tchr., spl. edn., tchr., master reading and ESL Tex. Pre-trial coun. Harris County Criminal Ct., Houston, 1990—91; spl. edn. tchr. Houston Ind. Sch. Dist., 1991. Psychology prof. Kingwood Coll., Houston, 1998—; guided studies prof. Houston CC, 2001—03; mem. attendance com. Houston Ind. Sch. Dist., 2004—06, mem., shared decision making com., 2005—; v.p. Swift Entertainment, 2004—06. Social dir. United Way, Houston, 1990—91; active Centre Stage Theatre, Kingwood, 1995—2006. Mem.: Houston Fedn. Tchrs. Democrat. Roman Catholic. Avocations: tennis, reading, working out. Home: 40-22 60th St Woodside NY 11377 Office Phone: 713-805-5966. E-mail: constance_swift@hotmail.com.

SWIFT, JANE MARIA, former governor; b. North Adams, Mass., Feb. 24, 1965; d. John Maynard and Jean Mary (Kent) S.; m. Charles T. Hunt III, Feb. 19, 1994. BA in Am. Studies, Trinity Coll., Hartford, Conn., 1987. Exec. mgmt. trainee G. Fox. & Co., Hartford, 1987-88; adminstrv. aide Sen. Peter C. Webber, Boston, 1988-90; mem. Mass. State Senate, Boston, 1991-96, 3d asst. minority leader, 1993-96; coord. strategic devel. of regional airports Mass. Port Authority, Boston, 1997; dir. consumer affairs and bus. regulation Commonwealth of Mass., lt. gov., 1999-2001, gov., 2001—03. 3d asst. minority leader, 1993-96. Republican. Roman Catholic.

SWIFT, KATHARINE I., cytotechnologist; b. Providence, Sept. 17, 1946; d. Oscar and Mary (Polly) Bergstrom; children: James P., Suzanne. BS, Empire State Coll., 1996. Cert. cytotechnologist. Cytology supr. St. James Hosp., Hornell, NY, 1986—93, Noyes Meml. Hosp., Dansville, NY, 1988—2000, Corning (N.Y.) Hosp., 1993—. Worked with Pan Am. Med. Mission setting up lab in San Cosme, Mex. Elder, United Presbyn. Ch., Hornell, 1993—; vol. case worker Tri County Housing, Steuben County, N.Y., 1994-99; case worker Interfaith Caregivers, Steuben County, 1996—; mem. Red Cross Disaster Team, Steuben County, 1999—, outreach caseworker, Red Cross, Ground Zero, N.Y.C., 2002; literacy vol., Steuben County, 1993-97; mem. peacemaking com. Geneva Presbytery, 2000—; mem. subcom. on mission to Mex., 1999—. Mem. Am. Soc. Cytology, Upper N.Y. State Soc. Cytology, Student Alumni Assn. Empire State Coll. (v.p. 1996-99, bd. govs. 1999—). Avocations: restoring homes, cross country skiing, travel. Address: Evening Tribune Maple City Dr Hornell NY 14843 Home: 5235 Nipher Rd Bath NY 14810

SWIFT, MARY LOU, art dealer, financial consultant; b. Syracuse, N.Y., July 25, 1942; d. Andrew G. Swift and E.R. Ensle. BA, Sarah Lawrence Coll., Bronxville, N.Y., 1964; postgrad, U. Pa., 1964-66, NYU Bus. Sch., 1967-69, N.Y. Inst. Finance, 1967-69. Registered stockbroker N.Y. Stock Exch. and Nat. Assn. Securities Dealers. Adminstrv. head of syndicate dept. Drexel Harriman Ripley, N.Y.C., 1966-71; product mgr. Fieldcrest Mills, N.Y.C., 1971-74; acct. supr. advtg. Rosenfeld Sirowitz Lawson, N.Y.C., 1974-76, BBDO, N.Y.C., 1976-78, Cavalieri, Kleier, Pearlman, N.Y.C., 1978-79; bus., mktg. cons. Mary Lou Swift & Co., N.Y.C., 1979-81; instnl. stockbroker Mabon Securities, N.Y.C., 1981-91; Gerard Klauer Mattison, N.Y.C., 1992-93; pvt. art dealer internat. modern and contemporary art Mary Lou Swift Fine Arts, N.Y.C., 1994—. Cons. Miller Tabak & Co., Inc., 1994—2006. Recipient Undergraduate Fellowship (2) Am. Mus. Nat. History, 1962, 63. Avocations: golf, travel, languages. Office: Mary Lou Swift Fine Arts 161 Breese Ln PO Box 1496 Southampton NY 11969

SWIFT, PATRICIA ANNE, school psychologist; b. South Bend, Ind., Mar. 18, 1951; d. William Mac and Betty Jo Thomas; m. Michael Alan Swift (div.); children: Amy Jo, Carrie Elizabeth. BS in Social Work, Ball State U., Muncie, Ind., 1972; MA in Sch. Psychology, Ball State U., 1982. Nat. cert. sch. psychologist, ind. practice lic., spl. edn. dir.'s lic. Social worker Cass County Assn. Mentally Retarded, Logansport, Ind., 1973—75; sch. psychologist Hancock-South Madison Joint Svcs., Greenfield, Ind., 1981—2000, 2003—, RISE Spl. Svcs., Indpls., 2000—03. Mem. coordinating team Step A Head, Greenfield, 1992—95. Organizer Child Find Dinosaur Discovery, Greenfield, 1994—2000; developer Typical Peer Program, Greenfield, 1995—98, Parents of Spl. Needs Children's Meetings, Greenfield, 1995—98. Mem.: Nat. Assn. Sch. Psychologists, Ind. Assn. Sch. Psychologists (chair lending libr. 2003—). Methodist. Avocations: gardening, travel, reading, yoga. Office Phone: 317-462-9219.

SWIFT, PEGGY LYNETTE, elementary school educator; b. Forrest City, Ark., Aug. 6, 1969; d. Paul Edward Tabron and Willean Hicks; m. Leonard Terrell Swift, July 3, 1993; 1 child, Symone Sydnee. BS, U. Ark., Pine Bluff, 1992; MS in Edn., Ark. State U., Jonesboro, 2003. Cert. reading specialist Ark. 6th grade classroom tchr. Ector County Ind. Sch. Dist., Odessa, Tex., 1992—93; 4th grade classroom tchr. Marion Sch. Dist., Ark., 1993—2001; literacy coach Earle Sch. Dist., Ark., 2003—. Named Master Edcuator, Reading Renaissance /Accelerated Reading. Mem.: Memphis RAW Readers and Writers Sistaz, Alpha Kappa Alpha (life). Democrat. Baptist. Home: 601 Charles Wood Dr Marion AR 72364 Office: Earle Sch Dist PO Box 637 Earle AR 72331 Office Phone: 870-792-7816. Office Fax: 870-735-1704. Business E-Mail: leonardswift@aol.com.

SWIGART, JOAN B., artist, consultant; b. Peoria, Ill., Jan. 30, 1930; d. Claude S. and Elvera V. (Seeber) Bradley; m. Lynn S. Swigart, Mar. 30, 1952; children: Christopher, Paul Tag, Ann, Leigh. Student, Bradley U., 1948-50, 79-81, Ill. State U., Normal, 1981-84. Dir. multimedia arts inst. Bradley U., Peoria, 1973, 74, program dir. Econs. Fair, 1976, 77; artist-in-residence for several Ill. sch. dists. Ill. Arts Coun., Chgo., 1983, 84, 85. Vice pres. bd. dirs., chair cultural outreach Peoria Arts and Sci. Coun., 1986—88; chair pub. art com. Peoria City Beautiful Commn., 1986—88; bd. dirs. Peoria Art Guild, 1969—88; chair resident artist coun. Westport (Conn.) Art Ctr., 1990—92; bd. dirs. Gloucester (Mass.) Cultural Coun., chmn., 2002—04. Exhibited in numerous solo, 2-person and group exhbns., 1980—. Dir. Sch. of Art, Peoria Art Guild, 1972-76; bd. dirs. Peoria Arts Festival, 1987-88, Urban League, Peoria, 1970-76, Planned Parenthood, Peoria, 1981-86; mem. edn. com. Lakeview Mus., 1985-88. Grantee Ill. Arts Coun., 1983, 84, 85. Democrat. Home: 13 Marble Rd Gloucester MA 01930-4324 Office: Swigart Studios 97 E Main St Gloucester MA 01930-4324 Personal E-mail: lswigart@verizon.net.

SWIGER, ELINOR PORTER, lawyer; b. Cleve., Aug. 1, 1927; d. Louie Charles and Mary Isabelle (Shank) Porter; m. Quentin Gilbert Swiger, Feb. 5, 1955; children: Andrew Porter, Calvin Gilbert, Charles Robinson. BA, Ohio State U., 1949, JD, 1951. Bar: Ohio 1951, Ill. 1979. Sr. assoc., now of counsel Robbins, Schwartz, Nicholas, Lifton & Taylor, Ltd., Chgo., 1979—. Author: (book) Mexico for Kids, 1971, Europe for Young Travelers, 1972, The Law and You, 1973 (Literary Guild award), Law in Everyday Life, 1977, Careers in the Legal Professions, 1978, Women Lawyers at Work, 1978. Mem. Glenview (Ill.) Fire and Police Commn., 1976—86; chmn. Glenview Zoning Bd. Appeals, 1987—97. Mem.: Chgo. Bar Assn. (chmn. legis. exec. com. 1990—92), Women Bar Assn. Ill., Ill. Coun. Sch. Attys. (past chmn.), Ohio State U. Coll. Law Alumni Coun., Soc. Midland Authors. Republican. Home: 1933 Burr Oak Dr Glenview IL 60025 Office: Robbins Schwartz Nicholas Lifton & Taylor 20 N Clark St Ste 900 Chicago IL 60602-4115

SWIGER, ELIZABETH DAVIS, chemist, educator; b. Morgantown, W Va, June 27, 1926; d. Hannibal Albert and Tyreeca Elizabeth (Stemple) Davis; m. William Eugene Swiger, June 2, 1948 (dec.); children: Susan Elizabeth Swiger Knotts-Case, Wayne William; m. James E. Coleman, Dec. 11, 2004. BS in Chemistry, W.Va. U., 1948, MS in Chemistry, 1952, PhD in Chemistry, 1964. Instr. math. Fairmont State Coll., 1948-49, instr. math. and phys. sci., 1956-57, instr. chemistry, 1957-60, from asst. prof. to assoc. prof., 1960—66, prof., 1966-92, chmn., divsn. sci., math, and health careers, 1991-92; NSF fellow rsch. W.Va. U., Morgantown, 1963-64, prof. emerita, 1992. Advisor Am. Chem. Soc. student affiliates, 1965-88. Author: Morton Family History, 1984-2004, Davis-Winters Family History, 1994—, Civil War Letters and Diary of Joshua Winters, 1991, 2d edit., 1996; contbr. articles to profl. jour. Chmn. Blacks Chapel Meml. Found., 1993—; rep. adv. coun. to Bd. Regents Fairmont State Coll., Charleston, W.Va., 1977—78, rep. instl. bd. advisors, 1990—92. NSF grantee, 1963; named Outstanding Prof. W.Va. Legislature, Charleston, 1990. Mem.: Am. Chem. Soc. (advisor student affiliates 1965—88, sec. chmn. North W.Va. 1975—83), W.Va. Acad. Sci. (life; pres. 1978—79, exec. com. edn. chmn. 1990—93), Nature Conservancy (bd. dir. W.Va. chpt. 1970—86, chmn. 1980—82), Prickett's Fort Meml. Found. (life; bd. dir. 1988—2000, chmn. elect 1990—92, chmn. 1992—96, bd. dir 2002—), Marion County Hist. Soc. (life), Fairmont Lions Club, Morning Gardeners Garden Club (pres. 1999—2003). Republican. Methodist. Avocations: local history, genealogy, gardening, computers, quilting. Home: 1599 Hillcrest Rd Fairmont WV 26554-4807 Home (Winter): 242 Laird Dr Freeport FL 32439

SWIHART, SUSANNAH M., bank executive; AB, Harvard Coll.; MBA, Harvard U. With BankBoston, Boston, 1980—, chief of staff, vice chmn., CFO. Bd. dirs. Boys and Girls Clubs of Boston, Inc. Office: 100 Federal St Boston MA 02110-1802

SWIKARD, SANDRA J., secondary school educator; d. E.L. and Josephine Swikard; m. Patrick Ojeda. B, U. Calif., San Diego, 1988. Cert. tchr. gifted and talented edn. Calif., social sci. tchr. Calif., English tchr. Calif. Tchr. Hoover H.S., San Diego, 1992—96; tchr., dept. chair Patrick Henry H.S., San Diego, 1996—. Master, mentor tchr. San Diego State U. Recipient Ellen Harcourt award, San Diego State U., 1992, Excellence in Tchg. award, U. Calif., 1996—2006, Tchg. Excellence award, U. Chgo., 2002. Office: 6702 Wandermere Dr San Diego CA 92120 Office Phone: 619-286-7700.

SWILDENS, KARIN JOHANNA, sculptor; b. Amsterdam, The Netherlands, June 22, 1942; arrived in U.S., 1979; d. Petrus Bernardus Swildens and Ceclia Thecla Maria Vernimmen; m. Gilles Roger Basset, Mar. 25, 1963 (div. Jan. 1968); children: Eric Gilles Basset, Laurent Patrice Basset; m. Claude Maurice Gaignaire, June 28, 1972; 1 child, Gazelle Gaignaire. Diploma in art, L'Ecole des Arts Decoratifs, Paris, 1963. Exhibitions include Speak Easy Gallery, L.A., Waldo Collection, West Hollywood, Calif., Trios Gallery, Solana Beach, Calif., Tops, Malibu, Calif., Hamilton Gallery, Santa Monica, Calif., Glass Garage Gallery, West Hollywood, Calif., The Figurative Gallery, La Quinta, Calif. Vol. instr. Brentwood Unified Sci. Magnet Sch., 1979—82. Recipient Daumier Sculpture award, 1993. Home and Office: 1872 Midvale Ave Apt 303 Los Angeles CA 90025-6349 Office Phone: 310-441-0126. E-mail: karinswildens@verizon.net.

SWINBURN, CAROL DITZLER, retired state and municipal agency administrator; b. Washington, July 9, 1945; d. John Nevin and Mildred Peterman Ditzler; m. Charles Swinburn, Dec. 16, 1972; children: Ann Elizabeth, Catherine Knowles. BA, Ursinus Coll., Collegeville, Pa., 1967. Founder, dir. The Healthy Gourmet, West Chester, Va., 1990—95; campaign exec. United Way, Alexandria, 1994—95; acting dir., counselor Women's Empowerment Program, Alexandria, 1995—97; dir., coord. Alexandria Criminal Justice Svcs., Va., 1997—2004; sr. staff Alexandria Criminal Justice Bd., 1997—2004. Author: (cookbook) Recipes from the Healthy Gourmet Cooking Classes. Shelter staff vol. Domestic Violence Program, Alexandria, 1995—97; shelter staff vol. teen runaway shelter This Way House, Alexandria, 1994—95; parent edn. chair PTO, Alexandria, 1994—96, mem., fundraising chair Chadds Ford, Pa., 1986—90; bd. dirs. Delray Beach Condo Assn., 2006. Named Woman of Yr., Alexandria Commn. on Women, 1997. Mem.: NOW, Planned Parenthood, Emily's List, Boca Raton Resort & Club. Democrat. Avocations: travel, beachwalking, yoga.

SWINDELL, DOLORES HOLLAND, retired school librarian; b. Indpls., Oct. 20, 1935; d. Earle Rupert and Ada Irene (Rubush) Holland; m. Archie C. Swindell, Dec. 28, 1962; children: Randy Zidick, Matthew Earle. BS in Geology/Geography, So. Meth. U., 1957; MLS, U. N.C., 1970; 6th yr. Edn. Leadership, So. Conn. State U., 1990; M in Computer Edn., Johnson/Wales U., 1995. Cert. media specialist 1-12 Conn., edn. adminstrn. Lab. technician R & D Sun Oil Co., Richardson, Tex., 1957—62; libr. asst. rare books Cornell U. Olin Libr., Ithaca, 1962—64; lab. technician vet. sch. Cornell U. Vet. Virus Rsch. Inst., Ithaca, 1964—66; libr. K-6 Dryden Cent. Sch., 1966—67, Cortland N.Y. Pub. Sch., 1967—68; libr. asst. catalog dept. Wilson Libr., Chapel Hill, NC, 1968—69; dir. Geol./Zoology Librs., Chapel Hill, 1969—70; media specialist K-6 NE Sch. Groton Pub. Sch., Conn., 1970—77, media specialist K-6 Noank Sch. Conn., 1977—88, media specialist grades 6-8 West Side Sch. Conn., 1988—95. Independent. Avocation: reading. Home: 192 Monument St Groton CT 06340 Personal E-mail: swindelldh@aol.com.

SWINDELLS, SUSAN, HIV specialist; b. Manchester, Eng., Apr. 11, 1954; came to US, 1979; d. Charles Hubert and Nanette May S.; m. Timothy A. Galbraith, Apr. 22, 1983; children: Emily, Charles. MB, BS, U. Coll., London, 1977. Med. house officer Univ. Coll. Hosp., London, 1977-78; surg. house officer Royal No. Hosp., London, 1978-79; resident family medicine U. Wash., Seattle, 1979-80; staff physician N.W. Emergency Physicians, Seattle, 1980-81; trainee gen. practitioner U. Manchester, England, 1981-82; resident psychiatry St. Bernard's Hosp., London, 1982-83; staff physician Cmty. Physicians, Inc., St. Louis, 1983-84; primary physician Southside Family Health Ctr. Columbus Health Dept., Ohio, 1988-91; clin. asst. prof. dept. medicine Ohio State U. Hosps., Columbus, 1988—91; preceptor dept. family medicine Grant Med. Ctr., Columbus, 1988—91; HIV clinic med. dir., asst. prof. medicine dept. internal medicine U. Nebr. Med. Ctr., Omaha, 1991—96, HIV clinic med. dir., assoc. prof., 1996—2000, co-dir. Ctr. Neurovirology and Neurodegenerative Disorders, 1998—, assoc. prof., 2000—02, Terry K. Watanabe Disting. Chair HIV/AIDS Rsch. and Care, 2001—, prof., 2002—; prin. investigator AIDS Clin. Trial Grp. Subunit, 1992—; dir. Nebr. AIDS Edn. and Tng. Ctr., 1992—; asst. clin. prof. depts. med. microbiol. and medicine Creighton U. Sch. Medicine, Omaha, 1994—96. Cons. Columbus Health Dept., 1988—91, chair pharmacy rev. com., 1988—91; mem. AIDS tech. adv. com. Nebr. State Health Dept., 1991, chair drug utilization rev. com., 92, mem. care options subcommittee, 92, mem. health care workers and invasive procedures subcommittee, 92; mem. systemic mycoses pathogen study grp. AIDS Clin. Trials Grp., Rockville, Md., 1994—96. Contbr. articles to profl. jours., chapters to books; co-editor: Mountain-Plains Regional AIDS Edn. and Tng. Ctr., 5th edit., 1994, Neurology of AIDS, 1998. Vol. Columbus Free Clinic, Ohio, 1989—91; med. cons. AIDS Coalition for Empowerment, 1992; co-chair Nebr. Walk for AIDS; mem. adv. bd. Wellness Ctr., 1994; bd. dirs. Nebr. AIDS project 1996; mem. adv. com. Hospice House, 1997. Recipient Caregiver award, AIDS Interfaith Network Omaha, 1999. Mem.: Royal Coll. Gen. Practitioners, UK, Nebr. Med. Assn., Am. Acad. Family Practitioners, AMA, Internat. Soc. NeuroVirology (founding mem. 1998). Office: Dept Internal Medicine Sect Infectious Disease 985400 Nebr Med Ctr Omaha NE 68198-5400 E-mail: sswindells@unmc.edu.*

SWINEA, MELISSA BAILEY, nursing educator; b. Huntingdon, Tenn., May 1, 1963; d. Samuel David and Rebecca Sue Bailey; m. Matthew Thomas Swinea, Aug. 28, 1999; 1 child, Ashlyn Doraye. BS, David Lipscomb U., 1985; BSc in Nursing, U. Ala., 1996; MSc in Nursing, Vanderbilt U., 1999. Cert. adult nurse practitioner, Am. Nurses Credentialing Ctr., RN advanced practice, Tenn. Bd. Nursing. RN Huntsville Hosp., Ala., 1996—98; nurse practitioner Huntingdon Med. Assocs., Tenn., 1999—2002; owner/nurse practitioner Adult Health Clinic, Huntingdon, 2002—04; asst. dir. nursing/prof. nursing Bethel Coll., McKenzie, Tenn., 2004—. Mem. adv. bd. Carroll County Tech. Sch., Huntingdon, 1999—. Mem.: Am. Acad. Nurse Practitioners. Office: Bethel Coll 325 Cherry Ave Mc Kenzie TN 38201 Business E-Mail: swineam@bethel-college.edu.

SWINFORD, MARGARET LYNN WRIGHT, medical/surgical nurse, educator; b. Spencer, W.Va., June 4, 1940; d. Ernest Wilford and Eleanor Ann (Lawrence) Wright; m. Paul W. Swinford, 1961; children: Richard Wright, Stephen Paul. Diploma, Bethesda Hosp. Sch. Nursing, 1961; BSN, Edgecliff Coll., 1980; MSN, U. Ky., 1984. Instr. Bethesda Hosps. Inc., Cin., Cin. State Coll., Cin. Mem. Nat. League for Nursing, Nursing Diagnosis Assn. N.Am., Sigma Theta Tau. Home: 6773 Le Conte Ave Cincinnati OH 45230-2936

SWING, AMY EILEEN, elementary school educator; d. Neal Walden and Barbara Jackson; m. Charles Eric Swing, Apr. 5, 2002; children: Jacob, Rebecca. AS, Gainesville Coll., 1993; BS, North Ga. Coll. and State U., Dahlonega, 1996, EdM, 2002. Cert. tchr. Ga., 1996. Residence hall coord. Brenau U., Gainesville, 1996—99; tchr. Ctrl. Heights Christian Sch., Cornelia, Ga., 1999—2001, White County Mid. Sch., Cleveland, Ga., 2001—. Named Tchr. of Yr., Ctrl. Heights Christian Sch., 2000—01, STAR Tchr., PA Ga. Educators, Ga. Dept. Edn., Ga. C. of C., 2002. Mem.: PA Ga. Educators. Home: 235 Pilgrim Rd Cleveland GA 30528 Office: White County Middle School 283 Old Blairsville Rd Cleveland GA 30528 Office Phone: 706-865-4060.

SWING, ELIZABETH SHERMAN, education educator; b. Boston, June 29, 1927; d. James Beatty and Hilda (Ford) Sherman; m. Peter Gram Swing, May 27, 1948; children: Pamela, Bradford. AB cum laude, Harvard U., 1949, MA, 1952; PhD, U. Pa., 1979. Tchr. English Marple Newtown High Sch., Newtown Sq., 1966-73; rsch. asst. U. Pa., Phila., 1973-75; asst. prof. West Chester State U., Pa., 1975-77, St. Joseph's U., Phila., 1978-84, assoc. prof., 1984-89, prof. edn., 1989—99, prof. emeritus, 1999—. Coord. commn. V, World Congress of Comparative Edn. Socs., Prague, 1992. Author: Bilingualism and Linguistic Segregation in the Schools of Brussels, 1980; mem. editorial bd. European Edn., 1983—; contbr. articles to profl. jours. Mem. Collaborative Com. Phila. Schs. and Colls., 1983-90. Decorated knight Order of Crown (Belgium), 1989; recipient Legion of Honor award Chapel of Four Chaplains, 1984; grantee NEH Summer Seminar, 1981, U.S. Dept. Edn., 1984-87, Fulbright Found., 1989-90; vis. fellow U. London Inst. Edn., 1989-90. Mem. AAUP, Comparative Edn. Soc. Europe, Comparative and Internat. Edn. Soc. (bd. dirs. 1988-91, historian 1999, hon. fellow 2000). Home: 3500 West Chester Pike Newtown Square PA 19073-4101

SWING, MARCE, film producer, director, writer; b. Wichita, Kans., Dec. 3, 1943; d. Eldon Derry and Ruth (Biddle) S. Bus. mgr. Old Westport Med. Assn., Kansas City, Mo., 1972-73; dept. chmn., instr. Ft. Bragg (N.C.) Nursery and Kindergarten, 1965-66, Luth. Schs., Tex. Dist., Irving, 1966-68, Kansas City (Kans.) Sch. Dist. 500, 1973-78, Extension Dept. U. Calif., Northridge, 1979-82, Pima Coll., Tucson, 1983-84, Kinder Care, Lake Buena Vista, Fla., 1989-90; TV/motion picture exec. producer, dir., writer Swing Prodns., Orlando, Fla., 1989—; owner, pres. Swing Enterprises/Swing Prodns., Orlando, 1978—, Living for Edn., Inc., Orlando, 1994—; owner Edn. in the New Millennium, Inc., 2002; founder, pres. Digital Media Arts Incubator Lab, Inst. Ind. Filmmakers, Orlando, Fla.; projects prodr. read24-7.com. Exec. mgmt., acctg. andmktg. cons. to major internat. corps.; lectr., seminar instr., guest speaker, anchorperson, moderator, panelist. Exec. producer, dir., writer, featured talent on-air live and taped programming for networks, network affiliates and cable, feature motion pictures, on air internationally and web sites, interactive TV episodes, with mdse, 34 children's books and CD ROMS, puppets and collectables, V series, mini series, 30 celebrity profiles, 36 documentaries, 14 televents, 45 pub. svc. spots, 30 minute infomat, 12-hour entertinment Christmas Eve project; developer entertainment informational, ednl. and indsl. TV programs and videos; contbr. articles to profl. jours. Corp. adminstr., TV exec. producer, dir., fundraiser nat. hdqrs. March of Dimes, White Plains, N.Y., 1984-86, Arthritis Found., Atlanta, 1985; ofcl. hostess Seattle World's Fair; mem. Nat. Task Force for Child Care, Nat. Task Force for Youth Suicide, Nat. Task Force for Child Abuse; mem. Ariz. Commn. on Arts. Recipient local, regional and nat. art and craft awards. Mem. NEA, NAFE, AAUW, Am. Mgmt. Assn., Nat. Assn. Women Artists, Profl. Assn. Producers and Dirs., Nat. Printmaker's Assn., Nat. Thespian Soc., Thousand Oaks Art Assn., Internat. Digital Media Arts Alliance (founding mem.), Orange County, Fla. Govt. Arts and Cultural Affairs, Coun. Art Edn. and Resources, Show of Hands Gallery, Nat. Youth Camps. Lutheran. Avocations: reading, writing, photography, cooking, mural painting.

SWINSON, SARA HOPE, writer; b. Denver, Sept. 10, 1964; d. Honey Constance Harriet Shulman and Thomas Stanley Swinson. BA in Bible and Religion, Montreat, NC, 1993; MA in Exegetical Theology, Covenant Theol. Sem., Mo., 1996. Social worker MERS, Goodwill Industries, St. Louis, 1998—2005; media coord. Zip for Senate, Jefferson County, Mo., 2005; with hosp. chaplaincy, clin. pastoral edn. St. Louis U. Hosp., 2005—06; vocat. evaluator, social worker Lakes Country Resource Ctrs., St. Louis, 2005—06; hosp. chaplain, resident in clin. pastoral edn. St. Luke's Hosp., St. Louis, 2006—. Columnist St. Louis Suburban Jours., 2004—05; staff writer, music journalist Nighttimes.com, St. Louis, 2005—; freelance writer. Writer (humor columns, social critiques, revs.) Opinion Shaper's Columnist, archaeological (byzantine mosaic floor) Abila of the Decapolis; exhibit, Prophetic Self-Portrait. Staff writer New City Fellowship's Mainliner, St. Louis, 2001—. Mem.: St. Louis Writer's Guild, St. Mary's Hosp. Bioethics Com. (com. mem. representing patient's rights 2001—03), Ctr. for Culture and Bioethics. Independent. Avocations: travel, painting, acting, collecting globes and pens. Home: 10331 Oxford Hill Dr Apt 3 Saint Louis MO 63146 Personal E-mail: shswinson@yahoo.com.

SWIRE, EDITH WYPLER, music educator, violist, violinist; b. Boston, Feb. 16, 1943; d. Alfred R. Wypler Jr. and Frances (Glenn) Emery Wypler; m. James Bennett Swire, June 11, 1965; 1 child, Elizabeth Swire Falker. BA, Wellesley (Mass.) Coll., 1965; MFA, Sarah Lawrence Coll., Bronxville, N.Y., 1983; postgrad., Coll. of New Rochelle, 1984-85, Sarah Lawrence Coll., 2000—04. Tchr. instrumental music, viola, violin The Windsor Sch., Boston, 1965-66; tchr., dir. The Lenox Sch., N.Y.C., 1967-76; music curriculum devel. The Nightingale-Bamford Sch., N.Y.C., 1968-69; head of fine arts dept. The Lenox Sch., N.Y.C., 1976-78, head of instrumental music, 1978-80; founder, dir., tchr. of string sch. Serpentine String Sch., Larchmont, 1981—96. Mem. founding com. Inter Sch. Orch., N.Y.C., 1972, trustee, 1976-85; panelist Nat. Assn. Ind. Sch. Conf., N.Y.C., 1977. Mem. music and worship com., Larchmont Ave. Ch., 1978-82, 88. Mem. Westchester Musicians Guild, N.Y.

State Music Tchrs. Assn., Music Tchrs. Nat. Assn., Music Tchrs. Coun. Westchester (program com.), Violin Soc. Am., Wellesley in Westchester, Am. String Tchrs. Assn., The Viola Soc. of N.Y. Avocations: chamber music, mind/body healing, palliative care. Home and Office: 4 Mill Pond Ln New Rochelle NY 10805 Personal E-mail: edieswire@lrsoft.com.

SWIRIDOFF, CHRISTINE, literature and language professor; PhD, Temple U., Phila. Prof. English Cerro Coso C.C., Ridgecrest, Calif., 1998—. Coord. honors program Cerro Coso C.C. Office: Cerro Coso CC 3000 College Heights Blvd Ridgecrest CA 93555 Office Phone: 760-384-6312.

SWITALSKI, JOY PATRICIA, athletic trainer; b. Shelby, NC, Jan. 19, 1978; d. Ralph Palmer and Lynda Mingoia Glenn; m. Jeffrey Peter Switalski, Dec. 4, 2004. BA in Sports Medicine, U. NC, Wilmington, 2000. Cake designer Designing Joy, Concord, NC, 1992—; tchr., athletic trainer Hunter Huss HS, Gastonia, NC, 2001—02; cert. athletic trainer, lic. Sports Plus Phys. Therapy, Gastonia, 2002—03; fitness dir. Sportscenter Athletic Club, Concord, 2003—04; cert. personal trainer Strong 3, Concord, 2003—; cert. athletic trainer, lic. Mortor Racing Outreach, Concord, 2004—. Cons., coach Strong 3, 2003—. Vol. staff Mt. Sinai Bapt. Ch., Shelby, NC, 2000—03, Univ. City Fellowship, Concord, 2004—06. Mem.: NC Athletic Trainers Assn., Nat. Athletic Trainers Assn. (cert. athletic trainer), Omicron Delta Kappa. Home: 168 Pounds Ave SW Concord NC 28025

SWITTENBERG, MICHELLE MINUS, telecommunications industry executive; b. 1968; BS in Sci., Univ. Penn. Wharton Sch., 1989; MBA, Duke Univ. Fuqua Sch. Bus. Retail mktg. exec. Verizon Comm. Inc., Dallas, exec. dir. NYC. Panelist SMB Forum Yankee Group, 2003; spkr. in field. Named one of Forty Under 40, Crain's N.Y. Bus., 2004. Office: Verizon Communications Inc 1095 Ave Americas 36th Fl New York NY 10036 Office Fax: 212-921-2917.

SWITZER, CAROLYN JOAN, artist, educator; b. Petoskey, Mich., Apr. 20, 1931; d. Eugene Constant and Burnis Hazel (Lower) S. Student, Wayne State U., 1954-55, St. John's Coll., Santa Fe, N.Mex., 1993; BA, Mich. State U., 1953, MA, 1964. Cert. tchr., Mich. Art tchr. Ferndale Bd. of Edn., 1953-56, Birmingham Bd. of Edn., Mich., 1956-96; pvt. tchr. drawing and painting. Exhbns. include state and local shows, galleries and pvt. collections. Cons. Girl Scouts U.S., Birmingham, Petoskey, Mich.; mem. Crooked Tree Arts Coun., Petoskey; deacon, mem. choir First Presbyn. Ch. of Petoskey. Recipient recognition award for svc. to community, Birmingham Edn. Assn. Coun., 1967, Outstanding Sr. Woman Lantern Night MSU, 1953. Mem. AAUW (scholar, Mich. State U., 1962), Nat. Art Edn. Assn., Mich. Art Edn. Assn., Mich. Edn. Assn., Detroit Inst. Art, Nat. Mus. for Women in Arts, Mich. Coun. for Arts, Art Study Club of Petoskey, Zonta Internat., Crooked Tree Arts Ctr. Petoskey, PEO, Little Traverse Hist. Soc. Avocations: music/singing, reading, exercise class, walking, photography. Home: 805 Lindell Ave Petoskey MI 49770-3159

SWITZER, JO YOUNG, college president; b. Huntington, Ind., Mar. 4, 1948; d. John Frederick and Miriam Lucile (Kindy) Young; children: Sarah Kate Keller, John Christian Keller. BA, Manchester Coll., 1969; MA, U. Kans., 1977, PhD, 1980; postdoctoral, Ind. U., 1983, Harvard U., 1995. Asst. instr. U. Kans., Lawrence, 1977-79; asst. prof. Ind. U.-Purdue, Ft. Wayne, Ind., 1979-82; assoc. prof. Manchester Coll., North Manchester, Ind., 1982-87, Ind. U.-Purdue, Ft. Wayne, Ind., 1987-93; v.p., dean for acad. affairs and prof. comm. studies Manchester (Ind.) Coll., 1993—2004, pres., 2004—. Recipient E. C. Buehler award U. Kans., 1978; grantee NEH, 1983. Mem. Central States Comm. Assn. (Outstanding Young Educator award 1982), Coun. of Ind. Colls., Am. Coun. on Edn., Am. Assn. Colls. and Univs. Office: Manchester Coll Office of Pres 604 E College Ave North Manchester IN 46962-1276 Home: Tall Oaks 1408 East St North Manchester IN 46962 Office Phone: 260-982-5050. Office Fax: 260-982-5042. Business E-Mail: jyswitzer@manchester.edu.

SWITZER, SHARON CECILE, language educator, researcher; PhD, Lesley U., Cambridge, Mass., 2003. Dir. of ESL Martha's Vineyard Sch. Dist., Martha's Vineyard, Mass., 2000—04; asst. prof. East Stroudsburg U., Pa., 2004—. Bd. dirs. Pa. TESOL E., Phila., 2004—. Bd. dirs. Pocono Svcs.s for Family and Children, East Stroudsburg, 2005—06. Grantee Head Start Rsch. scholar, Adminstrn. Children Youth and Families, 1999—2001. Mem.: TESOL. Avocations: painting, travel, yoga. Office: East Stroudsburg University 200 Prospect St East Stroudsburg PA 18301 Office Phone: 570-422-3368.

SWITZER, TOCCOA, artist; b. Clinton, S.C., Dec. 14, 1930; d. Hercules Milledge and Mercer Bailey (Vance) Wise; m. James Layton Switzer, Feb. 20, 1954 (dec.); children: James Layton Jr., Toccoa Bailey, Paul Kent III; m. Paul Kent Switzer, Jr., Oct. 12, 1990. AA, Stephens Coll., Columbia, Mo., 1951; BFA, Ohio State U., Columbus, 1953. Chmn. Switzer/Wise Investment LP, Union, S.C., 1989—. Bd. dirs. M.S. Bailey and Son, Bankers, Clinton, Clinton Investment Co.; mem. adv. bd. Anchor Fin. Corp., Myrtle Beach, S.C. Den mother Cub Scouts Am., Union, 1962-65; vol. ARC, Union, 1968—; Sunday Sch. tchr. Grace United Meth. Ch., Union, 1954-95, chmn. bldg. com., 1976-77, bd. trustees 1985—; bd. dirs. Great Town Program, Union, 1976-82; bd. dirs. Union Main St. Program, 1983-84; mem. bldg. com. Union Carnegie Libr., 1983-85; bd. mem. Union County Health Care Found., Union, 1993—; bd. trustees Wofford Coll., Spartanburg, S.C., 1990—; bd. dir. Bailey Found., Clinton, 1989—; bd. mem. U. S.C.-Union Partnership Bd., 1989—. Recipient Founder Day award U.S.C., Union, 1999. Mem. Friends of the Libr., Union Cotillion Club (pres.), Book and Garden Club (pres. 1989-90), Union County C. of C. (pres. 1981-82). Methodist. Avocations: painting, gardening, reading.

SWOAP, KRISTIN GENTY, marriage and family therapist; d. Gordon L. and Barbara A. Genty; children: Brittany N., Ashley K. AA in Psychology, South Prairie Coll., Levelland, Tex., 2001; BA in Psychology, Tex. Tech. U., Lubbock, 2003, MEd in Counseling, 2005. NCC, LPCI Tex. Therapist Family Counseling Svcs., Lubbock, 2004—, David Allison, Lubbock, 2004—, Lubbock County Residential Treatment Ctr., 2006—. Vol. crisis team Lubbock Police Dept., 2004—. Mem.: ACA (student mem.), APA (student mem.), Internat. Assn. Marriage and Family Counselors (student mem.).

SWOFFORD, BETH, agent; Motion picture agent Creative Artists Agency (CAA), Beverly Hills. Trustee Mus. of Contemporary Art, LA. Named one of Top 200 Collectors, ARTnews Mag., 2004. Avocation: Collector of Contemporary Art. Office: Creative Artists Agency 9830 Wilshire Blvd Beverly Hills CA 90212 E-mail: bswofford@caa.com.

SWOFFORD, SHARON EHLERS, medical/surgical nurse; b. Stamford, Conn., Feb. 7, 1952; d. Robert C. and Betty Mary (Stevens) E. U. Conn., 1973; MA in Nursing, NYU, 1982. Nurse clinician NYU Med. Ctr.; clin. coordinator White Plains (N.Y.) Med. Ctr.; adminstrv. supr. Weiler Einstein Med. Ctr., Bronx; renal clin. specialist N.Y. Hosp., N.Y.C.; clin. transplant coord., transplant case mgr. Yale-New Haven Hosp. Mem. ANNA, N.Am. Transplant-Coords. Orgn., Internat. Transplant Nurses Soc., Sigma Theta Tau. Home: 147 Pheasant Ln Branford CT 06405-5926 E-mail: seehlers@sbcglobal.net.

SWOOPES, SHERYL DENISE, professional basketball player; b. Brownfield, Tex., Mar. 25, 1971; d. Louise Swoopes; m. Eric Jackson, June 7, 1995 (div. 1999); 1 child, Jordan Eric Jackson. Student, South Plains Jr. Coll., Tex.; grad., Tex. Tech. U., 1993. Basketball player South Plains Jr. Coll., 1989—91, Tex. Tech U., 1991—93; profl. basketball player Houston Comets, WNBA, 1997—. Founder Sheryl Swoopes Found. for Youth. Named Nat. Player of Yr., USA Today, Sports Illustrated, others, 1993, Most Outstanding Player, NCAA Final Four, 1993, Most Valuable Player, WNBA, 2000, 2002, Defensive Player of Yr., 2000, 2002, 2003, Female Athlete of Yr., AP, 1993; named to First Team All-WNBA, 1998—2000, 2002, WNBA All-Star Team, 1999, 2000, 2002, 2003; recipient Coll. Performer of Yr. Award, ESPY award, 1994, Women's Pro Basketball Player of Yr. Award, 2001, Best WNBA Player, 2006. Achievements include mem., Texas Tech NCAA Championship Team, 1993; mem., US Women's Basketball Gold Medal Team, World Championships, 2002; mem., US Women's Basketball Gold Medal Team, Atlanta Olympics, 1996; mem., US Women's Basketball Gold Medal Team, Sydney Olympics, 2000; mem., US Women's Basketball Team, Athens Olympics, 2004; first woman to have a Nike shoe, the Air Swoopes, named after her. Office: Houston Comets 1510 Polk St Houston TX 77002-1099*

SWOPE, FRANCES ALDERSON, retired librarian; b. Richmond, Va., Dec. 5, 1911; d. Joseph Newman and Frances (Richardson) Alderson; m. Kenneth Dabney Swope, Dec. 27, 1958; stepchildren: Jeanne Weikel, Lee Smith. BA, U. Ky., Lexington, 1933; BS in Libr. Sci., U. Ill., 1939; postgrad., U. Va., U. Mich., U. London. Tchr. Alderson (W.Va.) H.S., 1933-39; ext. libr. Circleville (Ohio) Pub. Libr., 1939-41, Kanawha County Pub. Libr., Charleston, W.Va., 1941-43; alt. custodian comdt.'s confidential and secret files 3rd Naval Dist. Hdqrs., N.Y.C., 1943-45; cataloguer Yale U. Libr., New Haven, 1946-47; chief ext. libr. Kanawha County Pub. Libr., 1947-67; archivist Greenbrier Hist. Soc., Lewisburg, W.Va., 1969-97. Named W.Va. History Hero, 1997. Mem. Nat. Trust Historic Preservation, Nat. Soc. Colonial Dames in Am., W.Va. Libr. Assn. Lt. USNR, 1943-45. Democrat. Presbyterian. Avocation: walking. Home: 1130 Highland Pl Apt 303 Harrisonburg VA 22801

SWYSTUN-RIVES, BOHDANA ALEXANDRA, dentist; b. Kopychynci, Ukraine, Jan. 31, 1925; came to U.S., 1951; d. Peter and Maria (Ottawa) Swystun; m. John Rives, June 20, 1952 (div. 1960); 1 child, Peter A. DMD, Ludwig Maximillians Universitat, Munich, 1951; DDS, NYU, 1960. Dentist Dr. Joseph Matriss, East Rutherford, N.J., 1960-61; gen. practice dentistry Clifton, N.J., 1961-99. Vol. dentist Felician Sisters Orphanage, Lodi, N.J., 1982—; mem. Presdl. Task Force, Washington. Mem. ADA (award for commitment to professionalism and health), Ukrainian Med. Assn., Ukrainian Nat. Assn., Ukrainian Inst. Am., Clifton-Pasaic (N.J.) C. of C. Republican. Ukrainian Catholic. Avocations: reading, fgn. langs., walking, gold jewelry. Home: 2350 Heartland Park Owensboro KY 42303-7621

SYDNEY, DORIS S., sports association executive, interior designer; b. N.Y.C., Feb. 18, 1934; d. Morris and Frances (Terrace) Steinman; m. Herbert P. Sydney, Oct. 20, 1957; children: Madeleine Jane, Peter Samuel. Student, Vassar Coll., 1950-52; BS, Columbia U., 1952-55; postgrad., NYU, 1956-57, N.Y. Sch. Interior Design, 1974. Cert. documentor Equitable Life Ins. Co., N.Y.C. 1955-57; rschr. Fairchild Publs., N.Y.C., 1957-58; furniture sales Steinman's Inc., N.Y.C., 1958-60; interior designer, prin. Doris S. Sydney Interiors, Armonk, N.Y., 1975; exec. asst. Tennis Europe Inc., Conn., 1984—. Pres. Coman Hill Sch. PTA, 1971-72, Byram Hills H.S. PTA, 1977-79, pres. Byram Hills Scholarship Fund, 1980-82, chair Non-partisan Nominating Com., 1982-84; coun. del. Vassar Coll. Alumni Assn., Poughkeepsie, N.Y., 1973-77; chair Fred Caruolo Meml. Fund, 1979-81; pres. bd. trustees North Castle Pub. Libr., 1981-90; v.p. Friends North Castle Pub. Libr., 1993—; treas., pres. Armonk Hadassah, 1980—. Recipient Friend of Yr. award, N. Castle Libr., 2001, Pat Bresha award for cmty. svc., Lions Club, North Castle, 2003. Republican. Jewish. Home: 65 Windmill Rd Armonk NY 10504-2833 E-mail: dorissyd@aol.com.

SYJUD, LAURA BETH, music educator; b. Phoenix, Nov. 17, 1980; d. Richard Andrew Muterspaugh, Jr. and Susan Margaret Muterspaugh; m. Ryan Raymond Syjud, Dec. 28, 2002. B in Music Edn., No. Ariz. U., Flagstaff, 2004. Cert. tchr. Ariz., 2004. Pvt. lessons tchr., Scottsdale, Ariz., 1998—; string orch. specialist Paradise Valley Unified Sch. Dist., Phoenix, 2004—. Performing violinist weddings, ch. gigs, funerals, etc., Scottsdale, 2000—. Ch. musician Moon Valley Bible Ch. and Local Chs., Phoenix, 2000—. Recipient Outstanding Sr. award, No. Ariz. U., Coll. of Arts and Letters, 2004. Mem.: Nat. Assn. for Music Edn., MENC. Conservative. Evangelical Christian. Avocations: travel, reading. Office Phone: 602-867-5100.

SYKES, DIANE S., federal judge, former state supreme court justice; b. Milw., Dec. 23, 1957; 2 children. BA, Northwestern U., 1980; JD, Marquette U., 1984. Reporter Milw. Jour.; law clk. to Hon. Terence T. Evans US Dist. Ct. (ea. dist.) WI, 1984—85; assoc. Whyte & Hirschboeck S.C., 1985—92; judge Milw. County Ct., 1992—99, Wis. Supreme Ct., Madison, 1999—2004, US Ct. Appeals (7th cir.), 2004—. Mem.: St. Thomas More Soc., Milw. Lawyers Chpt., Federalist Soc., Fairchild Inn, Am. Inns of Ct., Assn. for Women Lawyers, Seventh Cir. Bar Assn., Milw. Bar Assn., Wis. Bar Assn. Office: US Ct Appeals 7th Cir 371 US Court House 517 E Wisconsin Ave Milwaukee WI 53202 also: Dirksen Fed Bldg Rm 2742 219 S Dearborn St Chicago IL 60604 Office Phone: 414-727-6988.

SYKES, LINDA DIANE, elementary school educator, music educator; b. Indpls., Aug. 23, 1950; d. Theodore Ross and Mary Elizabeth Willits; m. Gregory Allen Sykes, Nov. 29, 1946; children: Amanda Ruth, Bryan Paul. MusB in Edn., U. Evansville, Indi., 1972; MusM, Butler U., Indpls., 1976. Tchr. elem. music Jac-Cen-Del Schs., Osgood, Ind., 1972—73; tchr. music grades k-12 NHJ United Sch. Corp., Trafalgar, 1974—86; tchr. elem. music MSD Warren Twp., Indpls., 1986—. Indpls. Alumnae chpt. pres. Sigma Alpha Iota, 1984—88, 1999—2000; vestry mem. St. Matthews Episcopal Ch., Indpls., 2006—; pres., bd. mem. Sounds Hope Alumni Assn., North Webster, Ind. Mem.: Ind. Kodaly Educators (founding pres. 1993—99), Orgn. Am. Kodaly Educators (midwest divsn. pres. 2003—05). Episcopalian. Avocations: travel, reading, needlecrafts, scrapbooks. Home: 5619 Allan Ct Indianapolis IN 46239 Office: Lowell Elementary School 2150 Hunter Rd Indianapolis IN 46239 Office Phone: 317-532-3945. Personal E-mail: lsykes4188@aol.com. E-mail: lsykes@warren.k12.in.us.

SYKES, PLUM, writer; b. London, 1969; married. BA in Modern History, Oxford U. Fashion writer Vogue (British), 1993—97; contbg. editor Vogue (Am.), 1997—. Author: (novels) Bergdorf Blondes, 2004 (Publishers Weekly Bestseller lists), The Debutante Divorcee, 2006. Office: c/o Janklow & Nesbit 445 Park Ave New York NY 10022*

SYKES, WANDA, comedienne, actress; b. Portsmouth, Va., Mar. 7, 1964; BS, Hampton U. Actor: (TV series) Best of Chris Rock, 1999, Larry David: Curb Your Enthusiasm, 1999, Crank Yankers, 2003—, Wanda Does It, 2004; (films) Tomorrow Night, 1998, Nutty Professor II: The Klumps, 2000, Down to Earth, 2001, Pootie Tang, 2001, Monster-in-Law, 2005, Clerks II, 2006, My Super Ex-Girlfriend, 2006, (voice) Over the Hedge, 2006, Barnyard: The Original Party Animals, 2006; actor, writer (TV series) The Chris Rock Show, 1997—2000 (Emmy award for outstanding writing, 1999), The Downer Channel, 2001, writer, creator, actor, prodr. Wanda at Large, 2003, writer The Keenen Ivory Wayans Show, 1997, guest appearances include The Drew Carey Show, Chappelle's Show; author: Yeah I Said It, 2004; appears on (TV series) Inside the NFL, 2002—. Recipient Am. Comedy award for Funniest Female Stand-Up Comic, 2001. Office: Creative Artists Agy 9830 Wilshire Blvd Beverly Hills CA 90212*

SYLVER, DONNA, bank executive; BS in Accounting, Wesleyan Coll., NC, 1989. With dept. budgeting Pioneer Savings Bank; with three banking firms, 1998—2004; sr. v.p., CFO Mut. Cmty. Savings Bank, Durham, NC, 2004—. Named one of 25 Most Powerful Women in Banking, USBanker Mag., 2005. Mem.: United Way African Am. Leadership Initiative. Office: Mut Cmty Savings Bank 315 E Chapel Hill St Durham NC 27701 Office Phone: 919-688-1308.

SYMENS, MAXINE BRINKERT TANNER, retired marketing professional; b. Primghar, Iowa, June 12, 1930; d. George Herman and Irene Marie (Dahnke) Brinkert; m. Jack Frederiksen Tanner, Dec. 28, 1950 (dec. Oct. 1976); m. Delbert Glenn Symens, Sept. 26, 1981. BS magna cum laude, Westmar Coll., 1970. Cert. tchr., Iowa. Elem. tchr. Rural Sch. O'Brien Co., Primghar, 1949-54, Gaza (Iowa) Com. Sch., 1954-60; secondary tchr. Primghar Com. Sch., 1960-81; fitness salon owner Slim 'N' Trim, George, Rock Rapids, Iowa, 1982-87; restaurant owner George Cafe, 1985-90, Pizza Ranch, 1988-96; with network mktg. divsn. Espial, 1997-99; dir. Coastal Vacations, 2000—03, Delmax Liquidations, 2004—, Delmax Debt Arbitration, 2004—. Advt. sales cons. Antique & Gift Shop, 1998-2000. Pres. Primghar Edn. Assn., 1970-71. Mem. George C. of C., George Kiwanis Club (sec. 1991-2005), Delta Kappa Gamma. Lutheran. Home: 307 Dell St NE George IA 51237-1030 E-mail: delmax@siebring.com.

SYMONETTE, LYS, foundation executive, musician, writer; b. Mainz, Germany, Dec. 21, 1920; came to U.S., 1936; d. Max Weinschenk and Gertrude (Metzger) Honheisser; m. Randolph Symonette, Sept. 1, 1949; 1 child, Victor. Student, Curtis Inst., Phila., 1937-39. Piano accompanist to internat. singers, 1940—. Musical asst. to Kurt Weill and L. Lenya, 1945-81; tchr. Curtis Inst., Phila., 1976—; musical exec., v.p. Kurt Weill Found., N.Y.C., 1981—. Translator operas from English to German and German to English, 1945—; co-editor Speak Low, Family Letters, 1996. Mem. Am. Fedn. Musicians, Alumni Assn. Curtis Inst. Music. Home: 160 W 73rd St New York NY 10023-3012 Office: Kurt Weill Found for Music 7 E 20th St New York NY 10003-1106

SYMONS, BARBARA ADELE SCHALK, academic administrator, counselor; b. Chgo., Jan. 16, 1939; d. Stanley Steven and Adele Mary (Maniak) Schalk; m. Frederick E. Symons, June 17, 1992. BS, Coll. of St. Catherine, St. Paul, 1960; MEd, U. Pitts., 1968. Cert. tchr.; lic. counselor. Camp dir. Mpls. Girl Scout Coun., summers 1960-67; tchr. St. Margaret's Acad., Mpls., 1960-63, Community Sch. Dist., Blue Island, Ill., 1963-67; sch. counselor Shaler Area Sch. Dist., Glenshaw, Pa., 1968-69, guidance counselor, 1970—95, chair guidance dept., 1989—95; ret., 1995. Mem. NEA, Pa. State Edn. Assn., Am. Assn. Counseling and Devel., Am. Sch. Counselors Assn., Allegheny County Counselors Assn. (sec. 1979-93, Counselor of Distinction 1988), Pa. Sch. Counselors Assn. (conf. registrar 1983-92, bd. govs. 1988-91). Avocations: hiking, reading, crossword puzzles, travel, shopping.

SYMS, HELEN MAKSYM, educational administrator; b. Wilkes Barre, Pa., Nov. 12, 1918; d. Walter and Anna (Kowalewski) Maksym; m. Louis Harold Syms, Aug. 16, 1947; children: Harold Edward, Robert Louis. BA, Hunter Coll., 1941; MS, Columbia U., 1947. Cert. tchr. Calif. State U. Northridge, 1964. Statis. clk. McGraw Hill Pub. Co., N.Y.C., 1941-42; acct. Flexpansion Corp., N.Y.C., 1943-47, Oliver Wellington & Co., N.Y.C., 1947-48, Broadcast Measurement Bur., N.Y.C., 1948-51; tchr. Calif. State U., Northridge, 1964, Burbank (Calif.) Unified Sch. Dist., 1964-79; chmn. bus. edn. dept. Burbank H.S., 1974-79; docent, acct. arts coun. Calif. State U., Northridge, 1979—; tchr. MEND-Meet Each Need with Dignity Learning Ctr., Pacoima, Calif., 1987-89; assoc. dir. M.E.N.D. (Meet Each Need with Dignity) Learning Ctr., Pacoima, Calif., 1989-96. Mem. Phi Beta Kappa, Delta Kappa Gamma (pres. 1972-74, treas. Xi chpt. 1982-90, 92-2002, treas. area IX 1975-78). Home: 9219 Whitaker Ave Northridge CA 91343-3538

SYNNESTVEDT, KIRSTIN, musician, educator; b. Bryn Athyn, Pa., Jan. 8, 1940; d. Raymond Harvey and Katherine Riefstahl Synnestvedt. Student, Tanglewood Berkshire Mus. Ctr., Lenox, Mass., 1956-59; BS, Juilliard Sch., N.Y.C., 1963; MusM, Syracuse U., N.Y., 1966; D of Musical Arts, U. Iowa, Iowa City, 1979. Coll. organist, instr. music Doane Coll., Crete, Nebr., 1966-69; ch. organist, choir dir., solo recitalist Chgo., 1973—. Organ concert broadcasts Sta. WNIB, Chgo., Sta. WDCB, Glen Ellyn, Ill., Sta. WMWA, Glenview, Ill.; adjudicator organ contests, Lincoln, Nebr., Des Moines, Iowa, Chgo. Creator, performer one-woman show of hats. Mem. Fire Buffs of Ill., Chgo., Ill. Fire Safety Alliance, Mt. Prospect, Ill. Hon. scholar, Juilliard Sch., 1961—63. Mem. Nat. Assn. Tchrs. Singing, Music Tchrs. Nat. Assn., Am. Guild Organists, Soc. for Preservation and Appreciation of Antique Motorized Fire Apparatus, 5-11 Club, Chgo. Club Women Organists (pres. 1980-82, 87-90), Pi Kappa Lambda (hon. mem.). Avocations: creative writing, cooking, gardening, modern dance, fast walking.

SYNNOTT, MARCIA GRAHAM, history professor; b. Camden, N.J., July 4, 1939; d. Thomas Whitney and Beatrice Adelaide (Colby) S.; m. Willard Edwin Sharp, June 16, 1979; children: Willard Sharp, Laurel Beth Sharp. AB, Radcliffe Coll., 1961; MA, Brown U., 1964; PhD, U. Mass., 1974. History tchr. MacDuffie Sch., Springfield, Mass., 1963-68; instr. U. S.C., Columbia, 1972-74, asst. prof., 1974-79, assoc. prof. history, 1979-97, dir. grad. studies history dept., 1990-92, prof. history, 1997—. Author: The Half-Opened Door, 1979; contbr. essays to books, articles to profl. jours. and to scholarly jours. Active university-wide cmty. svc. projects. Grantee, Am. Coun. Learned Socs., 1981; Fulbright scholar, 1988. Mem. Am. Hist. Assn., So. Hist. Assn., Orgn. Am. Historians (membership com. 1990-93), S.C. Hist. Assn. (pres. 1994-95), History of Edn. Soc. (mem. editl. bd. 1996, 97, 98, bd. dirs. 2000-02). Avocations: history, skiing, walking. Office: U SC Dept History Columbia SC 29208-0001 Office Phone: 803-777-2585. Business E-Mail: synnott@gwm.sc.edu.

SYPOLT, DIANE GILBERT, retired judge; b. Rochester, N.Y., June 14, 1947; d. Myron Birne and Doris Isabell (Robie) Gilbert; m. Dwight Douglas Sypolt; children: Andrew, David Weinstein. BA, Smith Coll., Northampton, Mass., 1969; postgrad., Stanford U., 1977-78, Georgetown U., 1978; JD, Boston U., 1979. Bar: D.C. 1979, Mass. 1979. Law clk. to judge D.C. Ct. Appeals, Washington, 1979-80; assoc. Peabody, Lambert & Meyers, Washington, 1980-83; asst. gen. counsel Office of Mgmt. and Budget, Washington, 1983-86; dep. gen. counsel U.S. Dept. Edn., Washington, 1986-88, acting gen. counsel, 1988-89; legal counselor to V.P. of U.S., White House; counsel Pres.'s Competitiveness Coun., Washington, 1989-90; judge U.S. Ct. Fed. Claims, Washington, 1990—2005; ret., 2005. Bd. dirs. Democracy Devel. Inst. Recipient Young Lawyer's award Boston U. Law Sch., 1989. Mem. Fed. Am. Inn of Ct. (Master), Federalist Soc. Personal E-mail: dgsypolt@yahoo.com.

SYPOLT, SHIRLEY RAE, elementary school educator; b. Farmville, Va., Sept. 9, 1953; d. Benifield and Ruth Bethel Burnett; m. Russell Eugene Sypolt, Jr., Sept. 1, 1974; children: Russell Eugene III, Jason Michael, Ryan Alexander. AS, Southside Va. CC, Keysville, 1973; BS in Edn., U. Nebr., Omaha, 1991; MSc in Tchg. Environ. Edn., Christopher Newport U., Newport News, Va., 2001. Lic. early childhood k-4, mid. grades 4-8 Va. Bd. Edn., cert. mid. childhood generalist Nat. Bd. Profl. Tchg. Stds., 2005. Pre-sch. tchr. Greenfield Childhood Devel. Ctr., Bossier City, La., 1986—88; sub. tchr. Bossier Parish Sch. Dist., 1988—89, Omaha Pub. Schs., Nebr., 1992; 5th grade tchr. Hampton City Schs., Va., 1992—; k-5 sci. instrnl. leader Cooper Elem. Schs., 1999—. State facilitator, project learning tree Va. Dept. Forestry, Richmond, 1999—; state facilitator, project WET Va. Dept. Environ. Quality, Richmond, 1999—; state facilitator, project WILD Va. Dept. Game, Richmond, 2000—; adj. prof. Christopher Newport U., 2002—05; edn. adv. panel Nat. Wildlife Fedn., 2002—; exec. adv. com. Gov.'s Environ. Edn., 2001; adv. com. Project Learning Tree, 2000—. Author: (poem) Earth's Rock Cycle, 2002, project WILD k-12 curriculum & activity guide. Chair Sch. Pride in Action Com., Hampton, 1998—, Hampton Clean City Commn., 2004—. Recipient Pres.' Coun. Environ. Quality Tchr. Tng. award, NEETF, 2001, Outstanding Educator award, Nat. Project Learning Tree, 2001, Presdl. award for Excellence in Math. & Sci. Tchg., Nat. Sci. Found., 2003. Mem.: NSTA (Disting. Tchg. award 2003), Nat. Wildlife Fedn. Leaders Club, Soc. Elem. Presdl. Awardees, Assn. Presdl. Awardees in Sci. Tchg. Republican. Protestant/Methodist. Avocations: gardening, reading. Home: 6 Enscore Ct Hampton VA 23666 Office: Cooper Elem Magnet Sch 200 Marcella Rd Hampton VA 23666 Office Phone: 757-825-4645. Personal E-mail: shirleysyp@aol.com.

SYVERTSON, MARGUERITE, geologist; b. Saratoga, Calif. BS in Geology, Cornell U.; postgrad, UCLA, 1991. Sys. engr. NASA Jet Propulsion Lab., Pasadena, Calif., with atmosphers and oceans sect., dep. project scientist, 1992, outreach mgr. atmospheric infrared sounder project, 1993—. Mem. adv. coun. women NASA Jet Propulsion Lab., Pasadena, 1993—95.

Avocations: working out, gardening, cooking, reading. Office: NASA Jet Propulsion Lab, MS 183-335 4800 Oak Grove Dr Pasadena CA 91109-8099 Business E-Mail: marguerite.l.syvertson@jpl.nasa.gov.

SZABLYA, HELEN MARY, writer, language educator; b. Budapest, Hungary, Sept. 6, 1934; came to U.S., 1963; d. Louis and Helen (Bartha) Kovacs; m. John Francis Szablya, June 12, 1951; children: Helen, Janos, Louis, Stephen, Alexandra, Rita, Dominique-Mary. Diploma in Sales, Mktg., U.B.C., 1962; BA in Fgn. Lang., Lit., Wash. State U., 1976. Freelance writer, translator, 1967—; columnist Cath. News, Trinidad, West Indies, 1980-91; adult educator TELOS Bellevue (Wash.) C.C., 1987-89; adult educator Pullman-Spokane (Wash.) C.C., 1976-80; faculty Christian Writers' Conf., Seattle, 1983-88, Pacific N.W. Writers' Conf., Seattle and Tacoma, 1987—92; hon. consul for Wash., Oreg., Idaho Republic of Hungary, 1993—. Lectr. Washington Commn. for Humanities, 1987-89. Author (with others): Hungary Remembered, 1986 (Guardian of Liberty award, 1986, George Washington Honor medal, Freedoms Found. award, 1988); author: 56-os Cserkészcsapat, 1986; author: (with others) The Fall of the Red Star, 1996, Hungarian transl., 1999 (1st prize Wash. Press Assn., 1st prize Nat. Fedn. Press Women); pub., editor Hungary Internat. newsletter, 1990—93, columnist Hungarian Bus. Weekly, 1994—95; translator: Emlékezünk, 1986, Mind Twisters, 1987, A vörös csillag lehull, 1999. Recipient Nat. 1st place editl. Nat. Fedn. Press Women, 1987, Senator Tom Martin Meml. award Pacific N.W. Writers Conf., 1979, Pro Auxilio Civium Hungarorum, Min. Fgn. Affairs, Republic of Hungary, 2003, Order of Merit, Republic of Hungary, 2005, Pro Communitate, City of Pecs, Hungary, 2006; grantee Hungarian Am. Assn. Wash., 1986, Wash. Com. for Humanities, 1986; named Cmty. Woman of Yr. Am. Bus. Women Assn., 1990. Mem. AAUW, Wash. Press Assn. (pres. 1987-88, 1st and 2nd place awards, several editl. and profile awards 1983, 87, 89, 90, 91, 92, 96, Communicator of Achievement award 1987), Nat. Fedn. Press Women (Affiliate Pres.' award 1988, bd. dirs. edn. fund N.W. quadrant, mem. 21st century planning com.), Authors Guild, Am. Translators Assn., Arpad Acad. (Gold medal 1987), Nat. Writers Club, Internat. PEN Club, Sigma Delta Chi (editl. award 1989). Avocations: children, reading, dance, swimming, travel. Home and Office: PO Box 578 Kirkland WA 98083-0578 Office Phone: 425-739-0631. Personal E-mail: szablyahj@aol.com.

SZAKSZTYLO, KATHEE, design technologist; b. Chgo., Nov. 19, 1969; d. Casimir and Lillian Marie Szakszytlo. Film studies internship, Moscow U., 1992; BA in cinema, photography, So. Ill. Univ., 1993; MFA in tng., edn., Roosevelt U., Schaumburg, Ill., 1998. Program dir. Vill. of Hawthorn Woods (Ill.), 1988—94; sales support mgr. Corporate Computing, Bannockburn, Ill., 1994—96; tng. coord. W.W. Grainger, Inc., Lincolnshire, Ill., 1996—98, tng. specialist Lake Forest, Ill., 1998—2001, tech. tng. specialist, 2002, design technologist, 2003—. Roman Catholic. Avocations: painting, writing, environment, filmmaking. Office: WW Grainger Inc 100 Grainger Pkwy Lake Forest IL 60045-5201 Home: 435 W PArk Ave Libertyville IL 60048

SZALKOWSKI, DEBORAH, music educator; b. Ithaca, N.Y., Nov. 25, 1956; d. Leslie Rudy and Mary Jane Worden; m. Mark James Szalkowski, July 21, 1990. MusB, Ithaca Coll., 1977; MEd, SUNY, Albany, 1982. Profl. tchg. cert. Fla., N.Y. Tchr. vocal music Marathon (N.Y.) Ctrl. Schs., 1977—78; tchr. Voorheesville (N.Y.) Sr. H.S., 1978—80, Troy (N.Y.) City Schs., 1980—85; choir dir. Guilderland (N.Y.) Ctrl. Sch., 1985—95; tchr. Pinellas County Schs., Tarpon Spring, Fla., 1995—96, choir dir. Largo, Fla., 1996—. Choral arranger:. Mem.: Pinellas County Music Educators, Fla. Vocal Assn., Fla. Music Educators Assn. (25 Yr. Svc. award 2002), Music Educators Nat. Assn. Avocations: travel, boating. Home: 10111 Tarpon Dr Treasure Island FL 33706 Office: Pinellas Pk HS 6305 118th Ave N Largo FL 33773 Personal E-mail: debchoir1@cs.com.

SZCZECHOWICZ, GRETCHEN, medical/surgical nurse; b. Middletown, Conn., Apr. 13, 1939; d. Norman and Ellen G. (Green) Wilson; m. Fred Szczechowicz, Oct. 3, 1968; 1 child, Christopher. Diploma, Salem Hosp. Sch. Nursing, 1959; student, Boston U., Emmanuel Coll., St. Joseph's Coll. Cert. coll. health nurse, ANCC. Staff nurse Salem Hosp., Mass., supr., med. surg. Mass.; health svc. coord. Salem State Coll., Mass.; telephone triage Ambulatory Care Facility. Recipient Mass. Commonwealth Citation for Outstanding Performance, Merit awards. Mem. APHA, Am. Coll. Health Assocs., New Eng. Coll. Health Assn.

SZCZESNY, MARCIA LINDA, elementary school educator; d. Ted and Virginia Szczesny. M, Nova U., Ft. Lauderdale, Fla., 1990. Cert. tchr. Fla., 1975. Tchr. sci. Lake Stevens Jr. H.S., Carol City, Fla., 1975—80, Pioneer Mid. Sch., Davie, Fla., 1981—82. Gifted sci. tchr. Jupiter Mid. Sch., Fla., 1982—. Mem.: NEA, Classroom Tchrs. Assn. Office: 15245 N Military Tr Jupiter FL 33458

SZCZUBLEWSKI, WENDY SUE, small business owner, musician, freelance/self-employed writer; b. Dunkirk, NY; d. Bernard and Rosemary Dougherty; m. Michael Szczublewski, June 26, 1999; 1 child, Preston Thomas. BA in polit. sci. cum laude, SUNY Coll. at Fredonia, 1987—91. Project mgr. Vanstar Corp., Vienna, Va., 1996—97; proposal mgr. RS Info. Systems, Inc., McLean, Va., 1997—98; writer/editor Computer Assoc. Internat., Inc., Herndon, Va., 1999—2002; pres. and ceo WoBop Music, Columbia, Md., 2002—; owner Szuzublewski Music, Columbia, Md., 2005—. Mem.: Nat. Guild of Piano Teachers, Am. Coll. of Musicians, MENSA. Avocations: baking, gardening, reading, bicycling, hiking. Office Phone: 410-772-1097. Business E-Mail: wszczub@szczublewski.com.

SZEGO, CLARA MARIAN, cell biologist, educator; b. Budapest, Hungary, Mar. 23, 1916; arrived in U.S., 1921, naturalized, 1927; d. Paul S. and Helen (Elek) S.; m. Sidney Roberts, Sept. 14, 1943. AB, Hunter Coll., 1937; MS, U. Minn., 1939, PhD, 1942. Instr. physiology U. Minn., 1942-43; Minn. Cancer Rsch. Found. fellow, 1943—44; rsch. assoc. OSRD, Nat. Bur. Stds., 1944-45, Worcester Found. Exptl. Biology, 1945-47; rsch. instr. physiol. chemistry Yale U. Sch. Medicine, 1947-48; mem. faculty UCLA, 1948—, prof. biology, 1960—. Contbr. articles to profl. jours., book chapters and revs. Garvan fellow U. Minn., 1939; Guggenheim fellow, 1956; named Woman of Year in Sci. Los Angeles Times, 1957-58; named to Hunter Coll. Hall of Fame, 1987. Fellow AAAS; mem. Am. Physiol. Soc., Am. Soc. Cell Biology, Endocrine Soc. (CIBA award 1953), Soc. for Endocrinology (Gt. Britain), Biochem. Soc. (Gt. Britain), Internat. Soc. Rsch. Reproduction, Phi Beta Kappa (pres. UCLA chpt. 1973-74), Sigma Xi (pres. UCLA chpt. 1976-77). Home: 1371 Marinette Rd Pacific Palisades CA 90272-2627 Office: U Calif Dept Molecular Cell & Devel Biology Los Angeles CA 90095-1606 Business E-Mail: cmszego@ucla.edu.

SZELIGA, VICTORIA I., social studies educator; b. Williamsport, Pa., Nov. 29, 1950; d. George E. Mayer and Dorothy M. Thomas; m. Martin A. Szeliga, Jan. 24, 1972; children: Christopher M., Bryan J. MA, U. No. Colo., Greeley, 1975. Tchr. Dist. #11, Colorado Springs, Colo., 1973—83, Acad. Dist. #20, 1983—2006. Author: (educational materials) Book Bridges #1. +80 gallon blood donor Penrose Hosp., Colorado Springs, Colo., 1976—. Named Tchr. of Yr., Rockrimmon Elem., 1986; grantee, Pikes Peak Coalition Ctr., 1985, 1987, Colo. Endowment Humanities, 1991, Colo. Geog. Alliance, 1992, Acad. Dist. #20, 2001; scholar, Ctr. Tchg. Internat. Rels. U. Colo., 1988, Nat. Geog. Soc., 1997, Econ. Tchr. award, Found. Tchg. Econ., 2001. Achievements include development of science, social studies and technology curricula. Avocations: reading, hunting, fishing, hiking. Office Phone: 719-234-3400. E-mail: vszelig@d20.co.edu.

SZENTIRANYI, JUDITH, physician, educator; b. Miskolc, Borsod, Hungary, Apr. 4, 1928; arrived in US, 1957; d. Charles Szasz and Magda Rosenberg; m. Andor Szentivanyi, July 14, 1948; children: Peter Szentivanyi, Eddie Szentivanyi. MD, Med. Sch. Debrecen, Hungary, 1952. Basic sci. cert. Intern Med. Sch. Drebrecen, 1951—52; resident Internal Medicine Med. Sch., Budapest, Hungary, 1952—56; asst. prof. U. Budapest, 1954—56, U. Colo., Denver, 1962—66; rotating intern Woodlawn Hosp., Chgo., 1957—58; fellow, resident Asthmatic Children's Hosp., Denver, 1960—61; instr. dermatology Creighton Med. Sch., Omaha, 1970—71; clin. asst. prof. U. S.Fla., Tampa, 1972—, assoc. prof., 1985—87. Pvt. practice, Aurora, Colo., 1966—67, Tampa, 1972—80. Contbr. articles to profl. jours.

SZEREMETA-BROWAR, TAISA LYDIA, endodontist; b. Geneva, N.Y., Mar. 21, 1957; d. Swiatoslaw Bohdan and Stefania (Melnyk) Szeremeta; m. Andrew Wolodymyr Browar, Sept. 19, 1981. BS in Dentistry, Case Western Res. U., 1978, DDS, 1980; cert. specialty endodontics magna cum laude, U. Ill., Chgo., 1982. Pvt. practice Hinsdale (Ill.) Periodontics and Endodontics, 1982—; asst. clin. prof. Northwestern U. Dental Sch., Chgo., 1986—. Adminstr. Werahian Sch. Dance, 2001—. Counselor, mem. Plast-Ukrainian Scouting, 1963—; presenting team Worldwide Marriage Encounter, Chgo., 1985-94; mem. parish coun. Sts. Volodymyr and Olha, Chgo., 1985-94. E. Wach rsch. grantee U. Ill., Chgo., 1980. Mem. ADA, Am. Assn. Endodontists, Am. Coll. Stomatologic Surgeons, Ukrainian Med. Assn. (chair membership 1983-88), Ill. Assn. Endodontists (pres. 1990-91), Ill. State Dental Soc., Chgo. Dental Soc. (sec. table clinic 1990, vice chair 1991, chair 1992, sec. dental benefits com. 2002, 05, 06, vice chmn., 2003, chmn. 2004), Hinsdale C. of C. Ukrainian Catholic. Avocations: embroidery, marriage enrichment, marriage preparation, theology. Office: Hinsdale Periodontics & Endodontics 40 S Clay St Ste 111W Hinsdale IL 60521-3280 Office Phone: 630-655-3737.

SZETO, YVONNE, architectural firm executive; b. Hong Kong, July 4, 1956; naturalized; BArch, U. Minn., 1977; MArch, Harvard U., 1979. Registered N.Y., cert. Nat. Coun. Archtl. Registration Bds. With I.M. Pei & Ptnrs., 1977—89, Pei Cobb Freed & Ptnrs., 1989—99; ptnr. Pei Cob Freed & Ptnrs., N.Y.C., 1999—. Guest critic Yale U.; panel mem. Bilbao: The Transformation of the City Art Inst. Chgo.; jury Bus. Week/Archtl. Record Awards, 2000. Mem.: AIA (medal and Cert. of Merit 1977). Office: Pei Cobb Freed & Ptnrs LLP 88 Pine St New York NY 10005

SZILAGYI-HAWKINS, ELIZABETH MARIA, social services administrator; b. Chgo., Dec. 28, 1949; d. Bernard and Elizabeth (Szombathy) Szilagyi; m. Robert Lee Hawkins. BS in Social Welfare, Olivet Nazarene U., 1973. Lic. social worker, Ill. Social worker Proviso Council on Aging, Bellwood, Ill., 1980-84, dir. sr. citizen services, 1984—. Mem. Older Adults Job Fair com. Operation Able, Oak Park, Ill., 1983-86, Gottlieb Hosp. Home Health Adv. Bd., 1988—. Mem. Proviso Coord. Com. (sr. com., pres. 1986-87, 959-96), Family Care Sr. Companion Adv. Coun. (v.p. 1985-86, pres. 1986-87). Avocations: bicycling, swimming, sewing. Office: Proviso Coun on Aging 439 Bohland Ave Bellwood IL 60104-1833

SZKODY, PAULA, astronomy educator, researcher; b. Detroit, July 17, 1948; d. Julian and Pauline (Wolski) S.; m. Donald E. Brownlee, Mar. 19, 1976; children: Allison, Carson. BS in Astrophysics, Mich. State U., 1970; MS in Astronomy, U. Wash., 1972, PhD in Astronomy, 1975. Rsch. asst. Observatoire de Geneve, 1969, Kitt Peak Nat. Obs., 1970; rsch., teaching asst. U. Wash., Seattle, 1970-75, rsch. assoc., lectr., 1975-82, sr. rsch. assoc., 1982-83, rsch. assoc. prof., 1983-91, rsch. prof., 1991-93, prof., 1993—. Part-time mem. faculty Seattle U., 1974-75, 82, Bellevue Coll., 1975-77; vis. scientist Kitt Peak Nat. Obs., 1976; vis. instr. UCLA, 1977, adj. asst. prof., 1980, 81; vis. asst. prof. U. Hawaii, 1978; vis. assoc. prof. Calif. Inst. Tech., 1978-79, 80, mem. XTE users com., 1996-99; mem. users com. Internat. Ultraviolet Explorer, 1983-85, 93-97; mem. A.J. Cannon adv. com. AAUW, 1986-91, chmn. 1988-90; mem. mgmt. ops. working group on Ultraviolet/Visual/Relativity, NASA, 1988-91; mem. rep. Assocs. U. Rsch. Astronomy, 2000—. Scientific editor ApJ, 2002—; contbr. numerous articles to profl. jours. Recipient Annie J. Cannon award, 1978. Fellow AAAS (mem. nominating com. 1990-93, chairperson 1993, mem.-at-large 1995-99); mem. Am. Assn. Variable Star Observers (coun. mem. 2004—), Am. Astron. Soc. (councilor 1996-99), Internat. Astron. Union; mem. commn. 42 organizing com. 1991—, v.p. 1997-00, pres. 2000—03), Astron. Soc. Pacific (bd. dirs. 1988-92), Phi Beta Kappa. Office: U Wash Dept Astronomy PO Box 351580 Seattle WA 98195-1580 Business E-Mail: szkody@astro.washington.edu.

SZWABO, PEGGY ANN, social worker, educator, nurse, psychotherapist; RN, Jewish Hosp. of St. Louis; BSN, St. Louis U.; MSW, Washington U., St. Louis; PhD, St. Louis U. Cert. advanced practice nurse. Staff nurse surg. svc. fl. Jewish Hosp. of St. Louis; head nurse, drug study coord. Mo. Inst. of Psychiatry; nurse Kinloch Mental Health Ctr.; coord. Kinloch Mental Health Ctr./St. Louis State Hosp. Clinic; instr. Barnes Hosp.; dir. out-patient svcs., geriatric psychiatry clinician St. Louis U. Dir. Psychiatry Edn. Ctr., 1995-97; psychiatry clinician St. Louis U.; assoc. prof. St. Louis U. Med. Sch., 1984-2001, asst. prof. Sch. Social Svc., asst. in nursing Sch. Nursing, 1976-99, assoc. prof., 1999—; practicum instr. St. Louis U. Sch. Social Work/Washington U. George Warren Brown Sch. Social Work. Bd. dirs. Kinloch Mental Health Ctr.; vol. YWCA Leader Lunch, 1985; mem. Arts Coun. Lafayette Sq., 1986-88. Mem. NASW (diplomate), ANA, Am. Nurse's Coun. Nurse Clin Specialists, Acad. Cert. Social Workers, Assn. for Aging with Devel. Disabilities (bd. dirs.). Avocations: music, dance, gourmet cooking. Home: 6318 Washington Ave Saint Louis MO 63130-4705 E-mail: szwabop@aol.com.

SZYMANSKI, EDNA MORA, dean; b. Caracas, Venezuela, Mar. 19, 1952; came to U.S., 1952; d. José Angel and Helen Adele (McHugh) Mora; m. Michael Bernard, Mar. 30, 1973. BS, Rensselaer Poly. Inst., 1972; MS, U. Scranton, 1974; PhD, U. Tex., 1988. Cert. rehab. counselor. Vocat. evaluator Mohawk Valley Workshop, Utica, N.Y., 1974-75; vocat. rehab. counselor N.Y. State Office Vocat. Rehab., Utica, 1975-80, sr. vocat. rehab. counselor, 1980-87; rsch. assoc. U. Tex., Austin, 1988-89; asst. prof. U. Wis., Madison, 1989-91, assoc. prof., 1991-93, assoc. dean sch. edn., 1993—99, dir. rehab. rsch. and tng. ctr., 1993-96, prof. rehab. psychology and spl. edn., 1997—99, chair dept. rehab. psychology and spl. edn., 1997-99, fellow tchg. acad., 1997; dean Coll. Edn. U. Md., College Park, 1999—2006; sr. v.p. acad. affairs, provost U. Maine, Orono, 2006—. Cons. Rsch. Assocs. Syracuse, N.Y., 1988-90. Co-author various book chpts.; co-editor: Rehabilitation Counseling Basics and Beyond, 1992, 98, 2005; co-editor Work and Disability, 1996, 2003, Rehabilitation Counseling Bull., 1994-2000; contbr. articles to profl. jours. Mem. Pres.'s Com. on Employment of People with Disabilities, Washington, 1987-97. Recipient Rsch. award Am. Assn. Counselor Edn. and Supr., 1991. Mem. ACA (chair rsch. com. 1992-94, Rsch. awards 1990, 93, 95), Am. Rehab. Counseling Assn. (pres. 1985-86, rsch. award 1989, 94, Disting. Profl. award 1997, James F. Garrett award for disting. career in rehab. rsch. 1999), Coun. Rehab. Edn. (chair rsch. com. 1990-95, v.p. 1993-95, 97), Nat. Coun. Rehab. Edn. (chair rsch. com. 1992-99, Rehab. Edn. Rschr. of Yr. 1993, New Career in Rehab. Edn. award 1990). Office: U Maine Office of Provost 201 Alumni Hall Orono ME 04469 Personal E-mail: emsqy@aol.com.

SZYMECZEK, PEGGY LEE, contract specialist; b. Piqua, Ohio, Jan. 31, 1953; d. Titus Taft and Veda Eura (Carpenter) Hooley; m. Fredrick Jones, Oct. 5, 1978 (div. Nov. 1985); 1 child, Fredrika; m. Larry D. Szymeczek, Jr., June 12, 1994. BA, Judson Coll., 1976; MPA, Golden Gate U., 1987. Telephone operator Dept. of the Army, Ft. Huachuca, Ariz., 1984-87; mgmt. asst., 1987-89; maint. svcs. asst., 1989-92; contract splst., 1992—. Adj. prof. German Cochise Coll., Sierra Vista, Ariz., 1983-84. Fin. chair Advance Planning Briefing for Industry, Ft. Huachuca, 1999. Splst. 4 U.S. Army, 1976-78. Recipient Army Achievement Medal; named Hon. mem. 54th Signa Bn., 1995. Mem. AAUW, Nat. Contract Mgmt. Assn. (sec. Coronado chpt. 1994-96, Robert Drew meml. award 1996, treas. 1998, officer S.W. region, functional dir. membership 1996-97). Avocations: reading, music. Office: USACECOM Acquisition Ctr AMSEL-AC-CC-S-RT-C Bldg 61801 Rm 3413 Fort Huachuca AZ 85613-5000 Home: 132 Kingsbridge Dr Goose Creek SC 29445-6645

SZYMONIAK, ELAINE EISFELDER, retired state senator; b. Boscobel, Wis., May 24, 1920; d. Hugo Adolph and Pauline (Vig) Eisfelder; Casimir Donald Szymoniak, Dec. 7, 1943; children: Kathryn, Peter, John, Mary, Thomas. BS, U. Wis., 1941; MS, Iowa State U., 1977. Speech clinician Waukesha (Wis.) Pub. Sch., 1941-43, Rochester (N.Y.) Pub. Sch., 1943-44; rehab. aide U.S. Army, Chickasha, Okla., 1944-46; audiologist U. Wis., Madison, 1946-48; speech clinician Buffalo Pub. Sch., 1948-49, Sch. for Handicapped, Salina, Kans., 1951-52; speech pathologist, audiologist, counselor, resource mgr. Vocat. Rehab. State Iowa, Des Moines, 1956-85; mem. Iowa Senate, Des Moines, 1989—2000; ret., 2000. Bd. dir. On With Life, Terrace Hill Found. Adv. bd. Iowa State Inst. for Social and Behavioral Health; mem. Child Care Resource and Referral Cmty. Empowerment Bd., Greater Des Moines Coun. for Internat. Understanding, United Way, 1987—88, Urban Dreams, Iowa Maternal and Child Health com.; pres. Chrysalis Found., 1997; mem. City-County Study Commn.; Mem. Des Moines City coun., 1978—88; bd. dirs. Nat. League Cities, Washington, 1982—84, Civic Ctr., House of Mercy, Westminster House, Iowa Leadership Consortium, Iowa Comprehensive Health Assn. Named Woman of Achievement, YWCA, 1982, Visionary Woman, 1993, Young Women's Resource Ctr., 1989; named to Iowa Women's Hall of Fame, 1999; named Des Moines Woman of Influence, Bus. Record, 2000. Mem. Am. Speech Lang. and Hearing Assn., Iowa Speech Lang. and Hearing Assn. (pres. 1977-78), Nat. Coun. State Legislators (fed. state com. on health, adv. com. on child protection), Women's Polit. Caucus, Nexus (pres. 1981-82, mem. Supreme Ct. Select Com.), Wellmark Found. (adv. bd.), Des Moines (Iowa) Women's Club (bd. dir. 2003—), Prairie Club. Avocations: reading, travel, swimming, whitewater rafting. Home: 2909 Woodland Ave Apt 1011 Des Moines IA 50312-3877 Personal E-mail: ElaineSzy@aol.com.

TABAKA, SANDRA LEE, retired medical/surgical nurse; d. Elmer William and Elaine Verba Viehmann; m. John Lawrence Tabaka, Oct. 8, 1960 (div. Nov. 1985); children: James Lawrence, Anthony Michael, Theresa Lynn. ADN, St. Mary's Coll., O'Fallon, Mo., 1978; BSN, Webster U., 1993. RN Mo. Staff nurse St. Luke's Hosp., Chesterfield, Mo., 1978—82, assoc. head nurse, 1982—94, staff nurse, 1994—2004, ret., 2004. Founding mem. St. Charles Countians Against Hazardous Waste, 1982—84; bd. mem. Cedar Groves Townhomes Assn., St. Charles, 1999—2002. Mem.: Oncology Nursing Soc. (oncology cert. nurse). Home: 244 Cedar Grove Dr Saint Charles MO 63304

TABAKA, SHEILA MARIE, theater educator; b. Merrill, Wis., Sept. 16, 1967; d. Burnell Fred Leo and Louise Marie (Kriehn) Pyan; m. James Alan Tabaka, Nov. 7, 1964; children: Eukariah James, Sally Sue, Margaret Elizabeth, Lillian Rose. MFA, Minn. State U., Mankato, 1998. Grad. asst. Minn. State U., Mankato, 1996—98; assoc. prof. theatre SW Minn. State U., Marshall, 1998—. Costume designer, costumer SW Minn. State U., 1998—. Costume designer/costumer (theatrical production) Costumer of many productions over the last 18 years, director To KIll A Mockingbird, The Lion, the Witch and the Wardrobe, Antigone, Godspell, West Side Story. Guest dir. Marshall Area Stage Co., Minn., 2002—03; tchr., lectr. Marshall Talents Acad., 2003—; chmn. bd. christian edn. Good Shepherd Luth. Ch., 2005, bd. Evangelism, 2001—05. Grantee, SW Minn. State U., 1998—2006, SW Minn. Arts and Humanities Coun., 1999, 2003. Mem.: US Inst. Theatre Tech. (no. boundary sect.-mem.-at-large sw 2003), Am. Coll. Theatre Festival (costume parade coord. 2003—), Costume Soc. Am. Lutheran. Avocations: bicycling, travel, tennis, art. Home: 1003 Poplar Avenue Marshall MN 56258 Office: Southwest Minnesota State University 1501 State Street Marshall MN 56258 Office Phone: 507-537-6273. Home Fax: 507-537-7014; Office Fax: 507-537-7014. Business E-Mail: stabaka@southwestmsu.edu.

TABANDERA, KATHLYNN ROSEMARY, secondary school educator; b. Honolulu, Aug. 6, 1960; d. William Fernandez and Sakae Sandra (Shibata) Rosa; m. Russell Takao Tabandera, Dec. 24, 1979 (div. 2000); children: Tiffany Nohelani, Christine Lei, Angela Nani, Nicole Ku'ulei, Ricky William Kanaina. BA in Psychology, U. Hawaii, Hilo, 1988, BA in Econs., 1988, BBA in Bus. Adminstrn., 1988, Tchr. Edn. Program, 1988, Profl. Edn. Program, 1989, Natural Sci. Certificate Program, 1994; MEd, Almeda Coll. and U., 2002. Profl. cert. secondary educator, Hawaii; cert. paralegal, driver's educator, 2005. Adminstr. Tabandera Fishing Co., Hilo, Hawaii, 1980-85; tchr. Kohala High Sch. Alternative Learning Ctr., 1989-91; social studies tchr. Honoka'a High Sch., 1991-92; real estate appraiser Hilo, 1992; realtor assoc. Ala Kai Realty Inc., Hilo, Hawaii, 1985—; owner Tracks Enterprises, Hilo, Hawaii, 1985—. Tchr. Hilo H.S. Alt. Learning Ctr., 1992-94, Waiakea H.S., 1994-2001, social studies tchr. Kea'au H.S., 2001—; mentor, tutor Kamehameha Schs. Talent Search, 1993-94; commr. on mayor's com. on people with disabilities, 1993-96; sales dir. Amerivox, 1995-97; adminstrv. asst. Newmans Nursery, 1995-97; coach Lifesmarts Hawaii State Champions, 2005; coll. connections tutor, 2005. Named to Dean's List, U. Hawaii, 1985-88. Mem. AAUW, NEA, NAFE, ASCD, Am. Soc. Profl. Appraisers, Hawaii Island Bd. Realtors, Hawaii Assn. Realtors, Nat. Assn. Realtors, Hawaii State Tchrs. Assn., Adminstrn. of Justice. Avocations: animal breeding and raising, ornamental horticulture, reading.

TABAZADEH, AZADEH, environmental scientist, researcher; b. Tehran, Iran, Feb. 17, 1965; came to U.S., 1982; d. Modjtaba and Fatema (Beigi) T.; m. Mark Z. Jacobson, Aug. 30, 1993; children: Dionna Shelly Jacobson, Daniel Forest Jacobson. BS in Chemistry, UCLA, 1988, MS in Chemistry, 1990, PhD, 1994. Rsch., tchg. asst. UCLA, 1989-94; postdoctoral NASA, Moffett Field, Calif., 1994-97, rsch. sci., 1997—. Lectr. in field. Contbr. articles to profl. jours. including Jour. Geophys. Rsch., Geophys. Rsch. Letters, Sci. NASA fellow, 1991-94, 94-97; recipient Presdl. Early Career award for Scientist and Engrs., 1998; named to Brilliant 10, Popular Science Mag., 2002. Mem. Am. Chem. Soc., Am. Geophysical Union (James B. Macelwane medal, 2001), Am. Assn. Aerosol Rsch., Air and Waste Mgmt. Assn., UCLA Chemist Assn. Achievements include discovery of narrow rings of cold air over the Earth's poles that help to form clouds which contribute to the destruction of the ozone layer. Fax: 650-604-3625. Business E-Mail: azadeh.tabazadeh-1@nasa.gov.

TABBUT, LOREEN M., power industry executive; Dir. projects and applications services Calif. Ind. Sys. Operator (Cal ISO); v.p. info. services Calpine Corp., San Jose, Calif., 2001—. Named one of Premier 100 IT Leaders, Computerworld, 2005. Office: Calpine Corp 50 W San Fernando St San Jose CA 95113 Office Phone: 408-995-5115. Office Fax: 408-995-0505.

TABER, MARGARET RUTH, retired engineering technology educator; b. St. Louis, Apr. 29, 1935; d. Wynn Orr and Margaret Ruth (Feldman) Gould Stevens; m. William James Taber, Sept. 6, 1958 B of Engring. Sci., Cleve. State U., 1958, BEE, 1958; MS in Engring., U. Akron, 1967; EdD, Nova Southeastern U., 1976; postgrad., Western Res. U., 1959-64. Registered profl. engr., Ohio; cert. engring. technologist. From engring. trainee to tng. dir. TOCCO divsn. Ohio Crankshaft Co., Cleve., 1954-64; from instr. elec.-electronic engring. tech. to prof. Cuyahoga C.C., Cleve., 1964-79, chmn. engring. tech., 1977-79; assoc. prof. elec. engring. tech. Purdue U., West Lafayette, Ind., 1979-83, prof., 1983-2000, prof. emeritus, 2000—. Lectr. Cleve. State U., 1963-64; mem. acad. adv. bd. Cleve. Inst. Electronics, 1981—; cons. in field. Author: (with Frank P. Tedeschi) Solid State Electronics, 1976; (with Eugene M. Silgalis) Electric Circuit Analysis, 1980; (with Jerry L. Casebeer) Registers, 1980; (with Kenneth Rosenow) Arithmetic Logic Units, 1980, Timing and Control, 1980, Memory Units, 1980; 6809 Architecture and Operation, 1984, Programming I: Straight Line, 1984; contbr. articles to profl. jours. Bd. dirs. West Blvd. Christian Ch., deaconess, 1974-77, elder, 1977-79; deacon Federated Ch., 1981-84, 86-89, Stephen Leader, 1988—2002; mem. Cancer Support Group; vol. Lafayette Adult Resource Acad., 1992—; ednl. resource vol., vol. tchr. Sunburst Farm Rainbow Acres, Ariz., 1988—. Recipient Helen B. Schleman Gold Medallion award Purdue U., 1991, The Greater Lafayette Cmty. Survivorship award, 1994, Outstanding Alumni award U. Akron Coll. Engring., 1994, Disting. Alumni award, Cleve. State U., 2002; Margaret R. Taber Microcomputer Lab. named in her honor Purdue U., 1991; NSF grant, 1970-73, 78; Rainbow Acres Computer Lab named The Marge Taber Computer Lab., 2002. Fellow Soc. Women Engrs. (counselor Purdue chpt. 1983-94, Disting. Engring. Educator award 1987); mem. IEEE (life sr.), Am. Cancer Soc. (co-chair svc. and rehab com. 1992-94, vol. coord. CanSurmount 1993-98, chair Cmty. Connections, mem. Resource, Info. and Guidance CoreTeam, 1994-98, v.p. Tippecanoe bd. dirs. 1996-98, relay for life hon. chair 1999), Am. Bus. Women's Assn. (edn1. chmn. 1964-66), Am. Soc. Engring. Edn., Am. Tech. Edn. Assn., Tau Beta Pi (hon.), Phi Kappa Phi. Avocations: robotics, computers. Home: 3036 State Rd 26 W West Lafayette IN 47906-4743 Office: Purdue U Elec Engring Tech Dept Knoy Hall Tech West Lafayette IN 47907

TABET, RENEE' B., voice educator, director; b. Belen, N.Mex., May 9, 1958; d. Gilbert R. Tabetr and Sylvia Tabet Griego; m. Greg J. Halverson, July 27, 1991; children: Cameron J. Halverson, Bryce P. Halverson, Haley E. Halverson. B of Music Edn., N.Mex State U., Las Cruces, 1981; AA, U. Colo., Colorado Springs, 1998, Colo. State U., Ft. Collins, 2003, Alamosa State U., Colo., 2006. Vocal music dir. Alameda Jr. H.S., Las Cruces, 1981—84; vocal music, drama dir. Horace Mann Jr. High, Coloado Springs, 1984—96; vocal music dir. Wasson H.S., Colorado Springs, 1996—. Dept. chair Wasson H.S., Colorado Springs, 1991—2003. Religious educator St. Patrick's Cath. Ch., Colorado Springs, 2004—06. Recipient Superior & Excellent plaque, Colo. HS Activities Assn., 1984—2005, First pl. State Show, Jazz Choir award, 1998—2004, Gold 1st pl. and Silver 2d pl. trophy, Heritage Music Festivals, 1999—2001, 2006, First pl. Show & Jazz trophy, Winter Pk. Ski/Music Festival, 1991—92, 1994—97, 2001—05, First & Second pl. trophy, Breckenridge Music Festival, 1993, Music Educator award, Sch. Dist. 11, 1994. Mem.: Colo. Music Educators Assn. Avocations: swimming, skiing, piano, dance. Home: 2115 Afton Way Colorado Springs CO 80918 Home Fax: 719-328-2001. Personal E-mail: tabetr@d11.org.

TABOR, LINDA J., performing arts educator; b. Bridgeport, Conn., May 10, 1965; d. James Atwood Tabor and Ruth Paula Sykes. BFA magna cum laude, U. Bridgeport, 1999. Tchr. drama and dance Music and Arts Ctr. for the Handicapped, Bridgeport, 1987-2000, co-coord. new visions dance project, 1989-91; tchr. drama and dance Charles D. Smith Jr. Found., Bridgeport, 1993-94. Tutor Literacy Vols. of Am., Bridgeport, 1995-96. Mem.: Phi Kappa Phi. Avocations: music, reading, t'ai chi, writing children's books.

TABOR, LISA ANN, theater educator; b. Dallas, Oct. 4, 1966; d. Charles Remy and Barbara Joe Tabor. BFA in Acting, Baylor U., Waco, Tex., 1985—89. Cert. Secondary Tchr. Tex. Dept. Edn., 1999. Asst. to fine arts dir. Calvary Temple Ch., Irving, Tex., 1992—2001; theater tchr. Coppell HS, 1999—. Sponsor Internat. Thespian Soc., Coppell, 2001—; sponsor, drama club Coppell HS, 2001—. Office: Coppell HS 185 W Parkway Blvd Coppell TX 75019 Office Phone: 214-496-6100.

TABRIZI, LILI H., electrical engineer, educator; d. Hedayat Tabrizi and Alieh Amid; m. Iraj B. Nejad, Oct. 29, 2000; 1 child, Laila B. Nejad. PhD, Mich. State U., East Lansing. Full prof. elec. engring. Calif. State U., L.A., 1988—. Coord. NASA SHARP program Calif. State U., L.A., 1995—2005. Office: Calif State Univ Dept Elec Engring 5151 State University Dr Los Angeles CA 90032 Office Phone: 323-343-4529.

TABUENCA-CORDOBA, MARIA-SOCORRO, academic administrator; b. El Paso, Tex., Dec. 9, 1955; d. Manuel Tabuenca-Gutierrez and Socorro Cordoba De Tabuenca. BA, U Tex., El Paso, 1976; MA, U. Tex., El Paso, 1979; PhD, SUNY, Stony Brook, 1997. Instr. El Paso CC, 1992—98; lectr. U. Tex., El Paso, 1993—, tchr. asst., 1996—98; regional dir. El Colegio de la Frontera Norte, Ciudad Juarez, Chihuahua, Mexico, 1995—99, dean NW region, 1999—. Vis. prof. N.Mex. State U., Las Cruces, 1998. Regional dir. Hunger Project Mex., Ciudad Juarez, 1984—85; adv. bd. Techo Comunitario Found., Ciudad Juarez, 1993—2006; mem. Immigration Mus., U. Tex., El Paso, 2002—04; bd. advisors folklife festival Rio Bravo/Rio Grande exhibit Smithsonian Instn., Washington/Ciudad Juarez, 1999—2003; student rep. Turner Fellows, SUNY, Stony Brook, 1990—92. Recipient Pres. Selection Com. for Nat. Poetry award, Instituto Sonorense De Cultura, 1995; W.B Turner fellow, Suny, Stony Brook, 1990—94, Transl. Of Chicana Authors grantee, Fideicomiso Para La Cultura Mexico-estados Unidos, 1996—97, Nat. Rsch. scholar, Consejo Nacional De Ciencia Y Tecnologia, 1998—, Cooperation US/Spain Latinos in Spain fellow, Instituto De Cooperacion Iberoamericana, Paso Del Norte Region Bldg. Project grantee, William and Flora Hewlett, 2001—03, Student Mobility Project grantee, Secretaria De Educacion Publica, 2004—. Mem.: MLA (assoc.), Latin Am. Studies Assn. (assoc.), Raza Assn. (assoc.). Roman Catholic. Achievements include research in methodology for study of borders' literatures between the US and Mexico. Avocations: reading, swimming, walking, travel, movies. Office: El Colegio de la Frontera Norte Ave Insurgentes # 3708 Chihuahua Ciudad Juarez Mexico Business E-Mail: tabuenca@colef.mx.

TACATA, FELISA PADUA, psychiatrist, researcher; d. Felix and Valentina Tacata. BS in Biology and Chemistry, Calif. State U., Sacramento, 1993; MD, Am. U. Caribbean, St. Maarten, Netherland Antilles, 2001; postgrad., Maricopa Integrated Health Systems, Mesa, Ariz., 2002—06. Clin. lab. sci. Am. Soc. Clin. Pathologists and Nat. Credentialing Agy. Lab. Pers., Sacramento, 1994—; psychiatrist Maricopa Integrated Health Systems, Mesa, Ariz., 2002—. Mem.: AMA, Am. Soc. Clin. Pathologists, Am. Psychiatric Assn. Avocations: photography, hiking. Office: Maricopa IHS Desert Vista BH 570 Brown Rd Mesa AZ 85201 Office Phone: 480-344-2049.

TACHA, ATHENA, sculptor, artist, educator; b. Larissa, Greece, Apr. 23, 1936; arrived in U.S., 1963; MA, Nat. Acad. Fine Arts, Athens, Greece, 1959; MA in Art History, Oberlin Coll., 1961; PhD, U. Paris, 1963. Curator modern art Allen Art Mus., Oberlin, Ohio, 1963-73; prof. art Oberlin Coll., 1973-2000; adj. prof. art U. Md., College Park, 1999—. One-woman shows include Zabriskie Gallery, NY, 1979, 81, Max Hutchinson Gallery, NY, 1984, High Mus. Art, Atlanta, 1989, Franklin Furnace, NY, 1994, Beck Ctr., Cleve., 1998-99, Found. for Hellenic Culture, NY, 2001, Marsha Mateyka Gallery, Washington, 2004, Am. Univ. Mus., Washington, 2006, others; prin. pub. commns. include sculptures at Am. Airlines Ctr., Dallas., City of Phila., Dept. Environ. Protection, Trenton, NJ, Case-Western Res. U., Cleve., Low Water Dam Riverfront Pk., Tulsa, Dept. of Transp., Hartford, Conn., Metrorail, Miami, Fla., Ecology Dept. U. Minn., St. Paul, Strathmore Music Ctr., Bethesda, Md., Metro Morgan Sta., Washington, Light Rail Sta., Newark, NY, Light Rail Stas., Newark; collections include Hirshhorn Mus., Washington, Albright-Knox Art Gallery, Buffalo, Mus. Fine Arts, Houston, Nat. Coll. Fine Arts, Washington, Cleve. Mus. Art, Munson-Williams-Proctor Inst., Uttica, Nelson-Atkins Mus. Art, Kansas City, Allen Art Mus., Oberlin, Speed Art Mus., Louisville; author: (as A. T. Spear) Rodin Sculpture in the Cleveland Museum of Art, 1967, Brancusi's Birds, 1969; contbr. articles to profl. jours.; subject of book Cosmic Rhythms: Athena Tacha's Public Sculpture (E. McClelland), 1998, Dancing in the Landscape: The Sculpture of Athena Tacha, 2000. Recipient 1st prize May Show, Cleve. Mus. Art, 1968, 71, 79; NEA grantee, 1975; Bogliasco Found./Liguria Study Ctr. fellow, 2003. Home: 3721 Huntington St NW Washington DC 20015-1817 E-mail: atacha@umd.edu.

TACHA, DEANELL REECE, federal judge; b. Goodland, Kans., Jan. 26, 1946; m. John Allen Tacha; children: John Reece, David Andrew, Sarah Nell, Leah Beth. BA, U. Kans., 1968; JD, U. Mich., 1971. Spl. asst. to U.S. Sec. of Labor, Washington, 1971—72; assoc. Hogan & Hartson, Washington, 1973, Thomas J. Pitner, Concordia, Kans., 1973—74; dir. Douglas County Legal Aid Clinic, Lawrence, Kans., 1974—77; assoc. prof. law U. Kans., Lawrence, 1974—77, prof., 1977—85, assoc. dean, 1977—79, assoc. vice chancellor, 1979—81, vice chancellor, 1981—85; judge U.S. Ct. Appeals (10th cir.), Denver, 1985—, chief judge, 2001—; mem. U.S. Sentencing Commn., 1994—98; nat. pres. Am. Inns. of Ct., 2004—. Office: US Ct Appeals 643 Massachusetts St Ste 301 Lawrence KS 66044

TACHNA, RUTH C., retired lawyer; b. NYC; d. Max and Rose (Rosenblatt) T.; m. Paul Bauman (dec.); children: Leslie Levy, Lionel Bauman. BA, Cornell U., 1935; LLB cum laude, Bklyn. Law Sch., 1937. Bar: N.Y. 1938, Calif. 1978, U.S. Dist. Ct. (so. dist.) N.Y. 1966, U.S. Ct. Appeals (2d cir.) 1966, U.S. Supreme Ct. 1956. Founding atty. Legal Aid, Westchester, N.Y., 1960-64; sr. ptnr., of counsel Tachna & Krassner, White Plains, NY, 1964—2001; ret. Prof. law Northrop U. Sch. Law, L.A., 1977-85; speechwriter for many office holders including Franklin D. Roosevelt. Group mng. editor Matthew Bender, N.Y.C., 1968-77; editor law rev. Bklyn. Law Sch. Staff atty., founder Legal Aid for Srs., Santa Monica, Calif., 1980-83. Mem. Calif. Bar Assn., L.A. County Bar Assn. Home: 5400 Eagles Point Cir Apt 106 Sarasota FL 34231-9154

TACKE, ELEANOR, archivist; b. Highland Park, Mich., Feb. 13, 1939; d. Harold Starr and Margaret Eleanor (Gillett) Atherton; m. Carl Ewald Tacke, Nov. 24, 1961; children: Lisa Kathleen, Paul Christopher. B Gen. Studies, Wayne State U., 1991, M of Libr. Info. Sci., 1998. Sec. Gen. Motors Corp., 1961—65, exec. sec., 1979—95; tng. archivist Wayne State U., Detroit, 1996—97, grad. rsch. asst., 1997—98; photog. archivist Schroeder Info. Sys., Inc., Detroit, 1998—2000; archivist papers of James Beardsley Hendryx Leelanau Hist. Mus., Leland, Mich., 2003. Pres., Warren Coop. Nursery, 1971-72, Friends of Interlochen Pub. Libr.; trustee Interlochen Pub. Libr., 2002—; pres., 2000-04; dir. Women's History Project N.W. Mich., Traverse City. Mem. AAUW (pres. Traverse City area chpt. 2004—), LWV of Grosse Pointe (v.p. 1995-2000), Mich. Archival Assn., Soc. Am. Archivists. Avocations: swimming, reading, travel, going to concerts and plays. Home: 5713 Bush Rd Interlochen MI 49643-9592 Personal E-mail: etacke@charter.net. E-mail: etacke@traverse.net.

TACKETT, GAYLE ENSLOW, medical/surgical nurse; b. Lakin, Kans., May 17, 1956; BSN, Ft. Hays State U., Hays, Kans., 1979. RN, Kans.; cert. med.-surg. nursing ANCC. Staff nurse Hutchinson (Kans.) Hosp. Corp., 1979-80, Hadley Reg. Med. Ctr., Hays, Kans., 1980-81; charge nurse St. Catherine Hosp., Garden City, Kans., 1981-2000, case mgr. Wound Care Ctr., 2000—. Named Nurse of the Yr., 1987. Mem. AAUW. Home: PO Box 46 Deerfield KS 67838-0046

TACKETT, MARESA D., medical technician; b. Bogalusa, La., July 23, 1975; Cert. surgical technician Tenn. Tech. Ctr. of Memphis, 2000, laproscopic specialist. Surgical technologist Baptist Hosp., Collerville, Tenn., 2000—01; cert. surg. technologist O.R., Inc., Memphis, 2001—. Home: 180 Stonewall Rd Byhalia MS 38611

TACKETT, NATALIE JANE, state administrator; b. Wausau, Wis. d. Roland Elsworth and Natalie (Zanon) Kannenberg; m. William Marshall Tackett, July 1975 (dec.); children: Roland, Scott, Renee, William. BA in English with highest honors, N.W. Mo. State U., 1966, MA in English, 1968. Instr. English Tarkio (Mo.) Coll., 1968-70, N.W. Mo. State U., Maryville, 1970-78; rsch. dir. Mo. Dept. Revenue, Jefferson City, Mo., 1978-81; rsch. analyst Mo. Ho. of Reps., Jefferson City, 1981-84; dir. oversight div. Mo. Gen. Assembly, Jefferson City, 1984—. Contbr. articles to profl. jours. Councilman N.W. Mo. Subarea Coun. Area II Health Sys. Agy., 1976-77; bd. dirs. Nodaway County Nursing Svcs. and Health Ctr., pres., 1974-76; gov.'s adv. coun. Comprehensive Health Planning, 1976; chmn. Nodaway County Citizen's Com. for a County Health Ctr., 1972-74; pres. Cole County Hist. Soc., 1996-1998, 2004—. Recipient Outstanding Woman award Maryville chpt. Soroptimist Internat. 1975, Joy of Achievement award 1975. Mem. AAUW (legis. com. 1985-87, pres. Mo. div. 1983-85, Woman of Distinction award 1984, Outstanding Contbn. in the Area of Legis., Mo. div. 1987), Legis. Program Evaluation Soc. Office: Mo Gen Assembly Oversight divsn State Capitol Rm 132 Jefferson City MO 65101

TACKETT, SUSAN J., language educator; b. Ft. Worth, 1949; d. Charles A. Tackett. BA English, Okla. Bapt. U., Shawnee, 1971, MusB Edn. Voice, 1973; MA Lit., U. Tex. San Antonio, 1990. Tchr. English and music Macomb Sch., Okla., 1973—75; min. music and youth Salem United Ch. of Christ, Louisville, 1975—76; tchr. English South San Antonio H.S., 1976—. Chairperson English dept. South San Antonio H.S., 1998—. Mem. Human Rights Campaign, San Antonio; choir mem. St. Mark's Episcopal Ch., San Antonio, 2003—06. Named Tchr. of Yr., South San Antonio Ind. Sch. Dist., 2002, Faculty - South San Antonio H.S., 1987, 2002; recipient Finalist - Trinity Prize for Excellence in Tchg., Trinity U. and HEB, 2002. Mem.: Tex. Coun. Tchrs. English and Lang. Arts, Tex. Assn. for Gifted and Talented, Am. Fedn. Tchrs. D-Liberal. Avocations: travel, reading, music. Office: South San Antonio High School 2515 Navajo San Antonio TX 78224 Personal E-mail: eurotrek@mac.com. E-mail: stackett@southsanisd.net.

TACKITT, KAREN ANN, social sciences educator; b. Carlsbad, N.Mex., July 27, 1953; d. James Norman and Mattie Lee Stanley; m. Ronald Lee Tackitt, June 21, 1974; children: Elba Christina Rodgers, Ronald Michael. AA, N.Mex State U., Carlsbad, 1974; BS, Coll. SW, Hobbs, N.Mex., 1996; MA, N.Mex State U., Las Cruces, 2001. Tchr. Carlsbad H.S., 1996—. Tchr. Sunday sch. First Assembly God, Carlsbad, 1974—2006. Assembly Of God. Avocations: reading, hiking, baking. Home: 403 N 2nd Carlsbad NM 88220 Office: Carlsbad High School 3000 W Church Carlsbad NM 88220 Office Phone: 505-234-3319.

TADDEI, LOIS ANNETTE MAGOWAN, artist, interior designer; b. Phila., Sept. 17, 1935; d. Frank Rue Magowan and Grace Gloria (Valentino) Weinstein; m. Robert Matthew Taddei, May 21, 1960; 1 child, Robyn Grace. Degree, Pierce Coll. Represented by Phila. Mus. of Art. Watercolor botanicals shown at Phila. Mus. Art; one-woman shows include Pa. Hort. Soc., Phila, La Grande Gallery, Moorestown, N.J., Camden County Libr.; group shows include Art at Armory, Phila, Great Galleries, New Hope, Pa., Hardcastle Gallery, Wilmington, Del., Hockessin, Del., Gallery I, Chadds Ford, Pa., Rhoads Gallery, Gwynedd Valley, Pa., Festival Arts, Cape May, N.J., Ocean City (N.J.) Arts Festival; designer Vassar Designers Showcase House, 1991-92, Haddonfield Design Showcase House, 1992, Barry Decorators Haddonfield & Cherry Hill, Interiors by Marilouise, West Chester, Pa., Rocco Marianni & Assoc. Interior Design, Haddonfield. Mem. Graphic Artist Guild, United Visual Artists, Burlington Country Art Guild. Avocations: gardening, needlepoint, ballet, museums.

TADDEO, LEXI-ANNE, special education educator; b. Chgo., Apr. 22, 1951; d. Bette Florence and Alex A. Brown; 1 child, Justen Haynes. M, Colo. Christian U., Denver, 1996. Residential sch. counselor Calif. Sch. for Deaf, Riverside, Calif., 1968—70; tchr.'s asst. San Bernardino County Schs., Redlands, Calif., 1973—79; tchr. Riverside County Office Edn., 1980—89, Corona/Norco Sch. Dist., Calif., 1989—93, Mesa Valley County Sch. Dist., Grand Junction, Colo., 1999—. Mem. Christian edn. bd. First Congl. Ch., Grand Junction, 2001—06, mem. handbell choir, 1994—2006. Mem.: Assn. Am. Educators, Internat. Reading Assn. (Colo. chpt.). Office: Mount Garfield Middle School 3475 Front Street Clifton CO 81520

TADEO, ELVIA, artist; b. Ensenada, B.C., Mex., Nov. 21, 1970; d. Austreberto and Consuelo (Tadeo) T. Student art, Rafael Contreras, Ensenada, 1986-89, Lorraine M. Rowley, San Diego, 1990-96, Silvia Moonier, 1997-98, Edward Mores, 1998-99. Represented by The Gallery on Broadway, San Diego. Juror La Jolla Art Assn., 1999-2001, Del Mar Fair, Calif., 2001—. Contbg. artist pastel painting: Baja 4 You, 1999; poetry pub. in Art Venues Mag., Newsletter of Pastel Soc. San Diego, Pastel Soc. West Coast; exhibited at LaJolla (Calif.) Art Assn. Gallery, 1997-2001, Galerias Internacionales of Hotel Hyatt Regency, Guadalajara, Mex., 1996-98, Gallery of Pastel Soc. of West Coast, Camino, Calif., 1997, Ceudonium de la Mujer, Ensenada, 1999-2001, Galeria de la Ciudad de Ensenada, B.C., Mex., 2000, Giorgio Santini's Gallery of Fine Arts, Rosarito, Mex., 2000-2001, El Centro Cultural San Angel, Mexico City, 2000, Centro Cultural Riviera, Ensenada, 2000, Centro Cultural Siglo 21, Mexico City, 2001, Hosp. Tembre, Mexico, 2001, Teatro la Cjuda-deia, Mexico, 2001, Hosp. of Pemex City, 2002, House of Reps., Mexico City, 2002, The Gallery on Broadway, San Diego; rep. Gallery on Broadway, San Diego, Gallery Giorgio Santini, Rosarito, San Diego Mus. of Art, Artist Guild, 2002-03. Art cons. Cultural Ctr. of Ensenada, 2000—; nat dir. Mexican Rep. in the Art Miles project, United Nations U.S.A. rep., 2002-03. Recipient 1st place Del Mar Fair, 1996, Spl. award, 1996. Mem. LaJolla Art Assn. (publicity chair 1999-2001), Pastel Soc. of West Coast, Degas Pastel Soc., Pastel Soc. San Diego, Carlsbad and Oceanside Art League, Internat. Assn. Pastels, Directorio Enciclopedico de las Artes Plasticas, Directorio of Artistas Plasticos de la Cordinacion Nacional de Artes Plasticas de Bellas Artes. Roman Catholic. Avocations: horseback riding, hiking. Office: PO Box 2229 Vista CA 92085 E-mail: elviatadeo@aol.com.

TADLOCK, ANITA CONNER, volunteer; b. New Orleans, Sept. 11, 1944; d. Marion and Lorena (Dobyns) Conner; m. Norman Edward Tadlock, June 25, 1966; children: Edward Scott, Stephanie Lee, Elizabeth Conner, Stephen Dobyns. BMusic, Queens Coll., Charlotte, N.C., 1966; student, U. Vienna, 1964, Colegio de Espana, Salamanca, Spain, 1993. Social worker Bur. Children's Svcs., Morristown, N.J., 1966-67, 69-70; pvt. piano tchr. N.J., 1966-82. Donations chair Am. Women's Assn. Singapore, 1992, chair cmty. svcs. com., 1993, 1st v.p., 1994, pres., 1994-95; bd. dir. Am. Assn. of Singapore, 1994-95; chair in charge of food George Washington Ball com., 1996-97; bd. dirs. Am. Club of Singapore, 1994-96, membership chair, 1996-97; docent Singapore Nat. History Mus., 1995-97; mem. fin. com. Trinity United Meth. Ch., Hackettstown, N.J., 1998-2000; mem. Jr. League of London, 1984-91; active Boy Scouts Am., Girl Scouts U.S.; pres. PTA, 1982-84. Recipient Outstanding Vol. award Am. Assn., Singapore, 1996, Am. Women's Assn., Singapore, 1996. Mem. DAR (Cobbs Hall chpt. chmn. cmty. svcs. award com.), Delta Omicron, Kappa Delta. Methodist. Avocations: travel, reading, antiques. E-mail: Nandatadlock@aol.com.

TAETZSCH, LYNNE, writer, artist, educator; b. East Orange, N.J., Sept. 24, 1941; d. William Kilpatrick and Ella (Kroupa) T.; m. John Stoessel (div.); 1 child, Blixy Taetzsch; m. Adrian Stanley Epstein, July 4, 1981. BA, Rutgers U., 1971; MA, San Diego State U., 1988; PhD, Fla. State U., 1992. Freelance writer, artist, 1965—; sr. trainer Blue Cross-Blue Shield, Newark, 1969-71; editor The Econ. Press, Fairfield, N.J., 1976-81; asst. editor Fiction Internat. San Diego State U., 1988-89; instr. English George Washington U., 1992-94, asst. prof., 1994—95, Morehead State U., 1995—98, assoc. prof., 1998—2000. Lectr. Grossmont-Cuyamaca Community Colls., El Cajon, Calif., 1988-89, San Diego State U., 1988-89. Author: Opening Your Own Retail Store, 1977, The Bipolar Dementia Art Chronicles: A Memoir, 2006, others; co-author: Practical Accounting for Small Business, 1977, Taking Charge on the Job, 1978; contbr. critical articles, poetry, creative non-fiction and fiction to lit. jours.; contbg. author: Minding the Body (by Patricia Foster) 1994; solo exhnbs. include Paula Insel Gallery, N.Y.C., 1964, Hartley Gallery, Winter Park, Fla., 1990, Pres.'s Gallery Fla. State U., Tallahassee, 1990, Astraea Gallery, Washington, 1991, Mt. Sterling Gallery Arts, Ky, 1998, Tumpkins Cortland C.C., Dryden, NY, 2000, Cmty Sch. Music & Art, Ithaca, 2000, Clinton House Art Space, Ithaca, NY, 2001, Gallery Hawthorne Plz, Overland Park, Kans., 2004. Recipient 1st Pl. award for painting Foothills Festival of Arts, 1989. Office Phone: 607-276-0266. E-mail: lynne@artbyct.com.

TAFOYA, MICHELE, sports reporter; Talk show host Minn. Vikings Talk Radio, KFAN, 1993—94; reporter CBS Sports, 1994—2000, ESPN, 2000—, NBA on ABC, 2003; sideline reporter Sunday Night NFL, ESPN, 2002—04, Monday Night Football, ABC, 2004—.

TAGGART, BARBARA ANN, retired language educator; b. Richmond, Va., Jan. 23, 1930; d. Harry Lee and Ann Lee (Shutter) Taggart. BA in Spanish & Music, U. Richmond, Va., 1950; attended, Middlebury Coll., Vt., 1952, Presbyn. Sch. Christian Edn., Richmond, 1959—60; postgrad., Va. Commonwealth U., 1954, U. Richmond, Va., 1958; MA in Spanish Letters, U. Nat. Atuonoma Mex., Mexico City, 1957. Cert. tchr. Va. Tchr. English and Spanish New Castle HS, Craig County, Va., 1950—51; English tchr. Poguozon HS, York County, Va., 1951—52; tchr. English and civics Washington-Henry HS, Hanover County, Va., 1954; English tchr. Highland Springs Jr. HS, Henrico County, Va., 1958; asst. prof. Spanish U. Richmond, 1959; educator, evangelist Presbyn. Ch., Mexico, 1960—65; educator, facilitator Mexico, 1966—86; ret., 1986. Escort, interpreter US Dept. of State. Contbr. articles to various periodicals. Counselor summer youth camp Ginter Pk. Bapt. Ch., Richmond, 1945—; vol. work camp Am. Friends Svc. Com., Mexico, 1952—58; vol. Cruz Rosa, Mexico, 1961—86, Red Cross, Richmond, 1987—; mem. Bellevue Civic Assn., 1986—; participant Hope in the Cities, 1990—, History, Healing and Hope, 2000—. Grantee World Coun. Chs., 1959; scholar U. Richmond, 1946—50, U. Nat. Autonoma Mex., 1954—55. Avocations: music, reading, researching, writing, hiking. Home: 1621 Pope Ave Richmond VA 23227-3725

TAGGART, LINDA DIANE, retired women's health nurse; b. Balt., June 14, 1940; d. Louis and Annie Helena (Heertje) Glick; divorced; 1 child, Keri Anne. AS in Nursing, Pensacola Jr. Coll., 1967; BA, U. West Fla., 1970; postgrad., St. Joseph's Coll., 1976-78. RN, Fla., Ala. Staff nurse Bapt. Hosp., Pensacola, Fla., 1967-70, head nurse, 1970-72; dir. in-svc. edn. Baycrest, Inc. Extended Care Facility, Pensacola, 1973, DON, 1973-74, Medica Media, Pensacola, 1974; clinic adminstr. Cmty. Healthcare Ctr. (formerly Medica Media), Pensacola, 1974—2006. Dir. sex and health edn. Cmty. Healthcare Ctr., Pensacola, 1974—; regional dir. Medica Media, ea. U.S., 1990; testified before Jud. com. U.S. Ho. of Reps., 1994. Contbr. project The Gideon Project, 1993, project Wrath of Angels, 1998, articles to profl. jours.; appeared on (documentaries) Dateline NBC, 48 Hours, Nightline, Turning Point, ABC, CNN, (HBO documentaries) Soldiers in the Army of God, 2000, Keeping It Real, Program of RCRC, South Africa, 2002; contbr. documentary I, Witness, 1998, documentary AGB "I Witness" Addy & Goldwater, 1999. Bd. dirs. Rape Crisis Ctr., Pensacola, 1976-91, chair, 1980, 84, 89 (Addie Brooks award 1984); mem. exec. com. Lakeview Community Mental Health Ctr., Pensacola, 1989 (Expression of Appreciation award 1980-91). Recipient Pioneer/Heroe award Fla. Abortion Coun., 1989, Woman of Yr. award NOW, 1995, Women's Equity Day award 1986. Mem.: ACLU, Am. Assn. Sex Educators, Counselors and Therapists (cert. sex educator), Planned Parenthood Fedn. Am., So. Poverty Law Ctr., People for Am. Way, Religious Coalition for Reproductive Choice (bd. dirs. 2000—), Feminist Majority Found. Democrat. Presbyterian. Avocations: skiing, jewelry design, cross-stitch, reading, ballroom dancing. Office Phone: 850-478-9660. Personal E-mail: ldtagg@aol.com.

TAGGETT, LAURA KIMBERLY, literature educator; d. John D. and Charlene Winter; m. Matthew Turner, May 21, 2005. BA, Saginaw Valley State U., Mich., 1996; MA, Iowa State U., 1999. Assoc. prof. english Ellsworth Coll., Iowa Falls, Iowa, 2000—03, Cy-Fair Coll., Cypress, Tex., 2003—. Faculty advisor Phi Theta Kappa Cy-Fair Coll. Actor: (plays) Cy-Fair Coll. Mem.: Am. Cancer Soc. Office Phone: 281-290-3293.

TAGGETTE, DEBORAH JEAN, special education educator; b. Dover Foxcroft, Maine, Sept. 24, 1952; d. Ernest Lyford and Arlene Elizabeth (Dority) Fairbrother; m. Berton Louis Taggette, July 19, 1975; children: Angela Beth, Chad Berton. BS in Edn., U. Maine, Fort Kent, 1975. Asst. tchr. spl. edn. Cmty. HS, Fort Kent, 1978—79, substitute tchr. spl. edn., 1980, tchr. severely handicapped, 1984—92, resource rm. tchr., 1992—94, self contained tchr., 1994—, leadership team, 2003—, grade II team leader, 2003—04, 2006. Transistion team of disabled students Community High Sch., 1993. Tchr. religious edn. St. Charles Parish; foster parent. Mem. DAV (life mem.), Order of Ea. Star (Miriam 140), Order of Rainbow for Girls (worthy advisor chpt. 17 1970-71), Grand Assembly (Grand Cross of Colors 1970), Vet. Meml. Fund of St. Francis. Avocations: reading, sewing, snowmobiling, boating, camping. Home: 1033 Main St Saint Francis ME 04774-9701 Office: SAD 27 Community High Sch Pleasant St Fort Kent ME 04743-1240 E-mail: detagga@yahoo.com.

TAGHIZADEH, GEORGEANNE MARIE, medical/surgical nurse; b. Cleve., July 14, 1969; d. George Dennis Hancsak, Ellyn Marie (Liedtke) Hancsak; m. Touraj Taghizadeh, Sept. 19, 2000; children: Alex children: Darius. AAS, Cuyahoga C.C., Cleve., 1993, AS, 1995; nursing diploma,

Fairview Gen. Hosp. Sch. Nursing, 1995. RN Ohio, registered diagnostic cardiac sonagrapher. Cardiac sonagrapher U. Hosps. Cleve., 1993—96, staff nurse, clin. nurse sonagrapher, 1997—98, advanced practice nurse/cardiac sonagrapher, 1998—. Mem.: Soc. Diagnostic Med. Sonagraphers, Am. Coll. Cardiovasc. Nursing, Ohio Nurses Assn., Am. Soc. Echocardiography. Roman Catholic. Avocations: jogging, travel. Home: 22184 Horseshoe Ln Strongsville OH 44149 Personal E-mail: Georgetouraj@ameritech.net.

TAGIURI, CONSUELO KELLER, child psychiatrist, educator; b. San Francisco; d. Cornelius H. and Adela (Rios) Keller; m. Renato Tagiuri; children: Robert, Peter, John. BA, U. Calif.-Berkeley; MD, U. Calif.-San Francisco. Diplomate Am. Bd. Psychiatry and Neurology. Resident psychiatry Mass. Gen. Hosp., Boston; staff psychiatrist Children's Hosp., Boston, 1951-59; med. dir. Gifford Sch., Weston, Mass., 1965-85; chief psychiatrist Cambridge (Mass.) Guidance Ctr., 1961-84; mem. faculty dept. psychiatry Harvard Med. Sch., 1965—2002; cons. early childhood program Children's Hosp., 1985—. Contbr. articles in field to books. Fellow Am. Orth. Psychiat. Assn., Mass. Med. Soc., New Eng. Coun. Child Psychiatry.

TAGLIAFERRI, REBECCA ANNE, mathematics educator; d. Lester L. and Patricia J. Clark; m. Cary D. Tagliaferri, Aug. 14, 1976; children: Karen L., David A., Krista A. BS in Elec. Engring., Tri-State U., Angola, Ind., 1972—77. Cert. Tchr. Ind. Dept. Edn., 2003. Co-op elec. engr. Burroughs Corp., Plymouth, Mich., 1975—77; math tchr. Penn HS, Mishawaka, 1999—. Coach, future problem solving academic competition team Penn HS, 2003—. Leader Girl Scouts Am., Singing Sands Coun., South Bend, 1987—2006, svc. unit mgr., 1992—95, assn. registrar, 1995—2000; religious edn. tchr. St. Monica's Cath. Ch., Mishawaka, 1991—2000. Recipient Outstanding Leader award, Girl Scouts Am., Singing Sands Coun., 1989, 1993, Coun. Oak award, 1995, Coun. Appreciation Pin, 2000. Republican. Mem. Christian Ch. Avocations: camping, hiking. Office Phone: 574-259-7961 2664.

TAGLIENTE, JOSEPHINE MARLENE, artist; b. Chisholm, Minn., Nov. 23, 1939; d. Joseph and Carmela (DeLuca) T.; m. Wayne W. Brown, May 28, 1960 (div. 1972); children: Michael Anthony, Troy Tagliente, Roben Tagliente, Angela Monique, Ninon Terese, Anina Maria (dec.). Student, Mpls. Coll. Art and Design, 1957-59, Mankato State Coll., 1966, Kansas City Art Inst., 1972; MFA, U. Guanajuato, Mex., 1974. Artist-in-residence Jewish Cmty. Ctr., Wilmington, 1969; illustration chairperson, mem. faculty Ray Coll. of Design, Chgo., 1980-87; adj. faculty Paradise Valley C.C., Phoenix; spkr. in field. One-woman exhbn. Natalini Gallery, Chgo., 1986; group exhbns. include Windbell Gallery, Wilmington, Del., Newark (Del.) Gallery, Galeria San Miguel, Mex., Galeria Osman, Mex., Galeria Condor, Mex., Torres Gallery, Albuquerque, Dartmouth Gallery, Albuquerque, Edith Lampert Gallery, Santa Fe, La Luna Nueva, Santa Fe, Herberger Theatre, Phoenix Little Theatre, Artesimo Gallery, Scottsdale, Ariz., Del. Art Mus., Wilmington, Sky Harbor Airport, 1994, Westaff, UK-Ariz., Canticles: Sight and Sound, 2002, others; represented in corp. collections Collins, Miller & Hutchins, Chgo., Mt. Sinai Hosp., N.Y.C.; also pvt. and pub. permanent collections; represented by Artisimo Gallery, Scottsdale; illustrations published in books; poetry published in anthologies; inventor garden products, office implements. Vol. art educator St. Anne's Intercity, Wilmington, 1967-68, Recreation Intercity, Chgo., 1978-79; cultural advocate for homeless Cultural Labor Party, Chgo., 1980-87, cultural advocate for minority concerns, 1985-88. Recipient Fine Art award Artist's Guild of Chgo., 1977, Print Drawing award, 1978, Educator/Svcs. award Sauk Area Career Ctr., 1984. Mem. Nat. Mus. Women in Arts, The Drawing Soc., Soc. Children's Book Writers and Illustrators, Statue of Liberty-Ellis Island Found. Social Democrat. Avocations: writing, digital painting, raising turtles and studying their habitat. E-mail: joyfulsunrise@qwest.net.

TAGUE, VICKIE, music educator; d. Dick V. and Yvonne Eddleman; m. Vern B. Tague, June 29; children: April C. Forgue, Aundrea R. Waltz, Laurie A. Bronniman, Jonathan B. BA, Regis U., Colo., 2002. Cert. Music Tchr. K-12 Colo. Dept. of Edn., 1996. Music, band tchr. McClave Sch., Colo., 1996—2001; music tchr. Wash. Elem. Sch., Lamar, Colo., 2001—. Mem.: CMEA. Home: 206 E Parkway Dr Lamar CO 81052 Home Fax: none. Personal E-mail: vickie.tague@lamar.k12.co.us.

TAHIR, MARY ELIZABETH (LIZ TAHIR), marketing professional, consultant, writer; b. Greenwood, Miss., Dec. 14, 1933; d. Mahmoud Ibrahim and Mary Constance Tahir. Student, U. Miss., 1951-53. Cert. Profl. Cons., Acad. Profl. Cons. and Advisors. Mgmt. trainee Neiman-Marcus Co., Dallas, 1954-56; asst. buyer D.H. Holmes Co. Ltd., New Orleans, 1956-58, buyer, 1958-65, assoc. divisional mdse. mgr., 1965-67, divisional v.p., 1969-79, corp. v.p., gen. mdse. mgr., 1979-89; pres. Liz Tahir & Assocs., New Orleans, 1990—. Author: Mexico's Cosmetic and Fragrance Market: Past, Present and Future Opportunities, 1991, The Changing World of Mexican Retail Opportunities, 1991, Mexico: Window of Opportunity, 1991, Art of Negotiating, 1993, Negotiating More Profitable with Your Suppliers, Customers and Employees, 1994, Sizzling Customer Service, 1998. Bd. dirs. Vieux Carre Property Owners Assn., New Orleans, 1990, 2002, YWCA, 1996-2002. Recipient Role Model award, YWCA, 1990, Woman Bus. Owner of Yr. award, 1996, Women of the Yr., City Bus. Pub. New Orleans, 2004, New Orleans Woman of Yr. award, 2001. Mem. Women's Profl. Coun. (pres. 1998, chmn. New Choices 1989), Fashion Group Internat. (Alpha award 1987-88, Lifetime Achievement award 1993), Nat. Spkrs. Assn., Am. Mktg. Assn. (bd. dirs. 1996—, pres. 1997), Am. Assn. Profl. Cons., Am. Mgmt. Assn., Fgn. Rels. Assn. (bd. dirs. 1992-2001, pres. bd. dirs. 1994-96), Nat. Retail Fedn. Avocations: art collecting, textiles collecting. Office: Liz Tahir & Assocs 201 Saint Charles Ave Ste 2500 New Orleans LA 70170-2500 Office Phone: 504-569-1670. Personal E-mail: liz@liztahir.com.

TAI, ELIZABETH SHI-JUE LEE, library director; b. Si-Ann, China, Aug. 12, 1942; arrived in U.S., 1965; d. Jun-Yee Lee and Fang-Yee Liu; m. Hsiang Tai, Dec. 29, 1969; children: Alan C., Victoria C., Brian C. BA in English Lang. and Lit., Nat. Cheng Kung U., Taiwan, 1965; M in Libr. and Info. Sci., Tex. Woman's U., 1967. Sr. libr. Queens (N.Y.) Borough Pub. Libr., 1967-73; asst. regional libr. Cin. Pub. Libr., Libr. for Blind and Physically Handicapped, 1973-75; libr. Ga. State Libr., Atlanta, 1975-78; dir. Poquoson (Va.) Pub. Libr., 1979—. Vol. ARC York County chpt., Va., 1980—; mem. York County Sch. Sys. Extend Program Coun., 1997; mem. Va. social svcs. bd. York County/City of Poquoson, 2002—; vice chmn. Peninsula Ret. Sr. Vol. Program Coun., Newport News, Va., 1994—99, chmn., 2000; bd. dir. Peninsula Ret. Sr. Vol. Program, 2001—, sec., 2002—. Named City Employee of Yr., City of Poquoson, Va., 1989; recipient Letter of Commendation, Va. Gov. James Gilmore III, 2001, Unsung Hero/Heroine award Nat. Cheng Kung U. N.Am. Alumni and Found., 2003. Mem. ALA, Va. Libr. Assn., Va. Pub. Libr. Dirs. Assn. (region 3 rep. 2003-05, treas., 2004—, Outstanding Pub. Rels. award 1998, 2001, 02, 04, 06, Outstanding Facility award 1998, Outstanding Young Adult Program award 1999, Outstanding Children's Program award 1999, Outstanding Libr. Staff award 2003, Outstanding Va. Pub. Libr. Dir. award 2004), Va. Peninsula Chinese Am. Assn. (bd. mem. 2004—, pres. 2006—), Tidewater Area Libr. Dirs. Coun., Peninsula Chinese Am. Assn. (bd. dir. 2004—), Kiwanis Club (charter mem. Tabb chpt., chmn. youth program 2005—). Avocations: reading, gardening, swimming, tennis. Home: 129 Loblolly Dr Yorktown VA 23692-4254 Office: 500 City Hall Ave Poquoson VA 23662-1996 Office Phone: 757-868-3066. Business E-Mail: etai@ci.poquoson.va.us.

TAICHERT, LOUISE CECILE, retired psychiatrist; b. Las Vegas, N.Mex., May 16, 1925; d. Joseph A. Taichert and Annie Sophie Stein; m. Sanford E. Feldman; children: David, Wendy, Laurie; 1 child from previous marriage, John. BA, U. Calif., Berkley, 1947; MS, U. Denver, 1950; MD, U. Colo., 1954. Cert. Am. Bd. Pediats., diplomate Am. Bd. Pediatrics, 1961, registered DEA. Pediatrician pvt. practice, 1960—67; assoc. clinical prof. U. Calif., San Francisco, 1967—2000; behavioral pediatrician pvt. practice, 1967—77, psychiatrist, 1977—2000; ret., 2000. Author: (jour. articles) Pediatric and Psychiatric Jours. Mem. mental health com. San Francisco Med. Soc., 1954—2005. Mem.: Soc. for Behavioral Pediatrics, Calif. Med. Assn. (sch. and coll. health com. 1970—81, sch. and coll. health chmn. 1979—81), San Francisco Med. Soc. (chmn. sch. and health com. 1973—74), Museo Italo Americana (bd. mem. 2004), No. Calif. Psychiatric Soc. Child and Adolescent Com. (assoc.), APA (assoc.), Am. Acad. Child Psychiatry (assoc.). Avocations: tennis, travel, opera, Italian language study. Personal E-mail: louise.taichert@ucsf.edu.

TAKANISHI, RUBY, foundation administrator, researcher; d. Kazuo and Misae Takanishi; 1 child. AB in Psychology, Stanford U., 1968; AM, U. Mich., 1969; postgrad., U. Chgo., 1969-70; PhD, Stanford U., 1973; postgrad., Harvard U., 1978-79. Teaching asst. Bing Nursery Sch. Stanford U., 1968, teaching asst. Sch. Edn., 1972, 73; asst. prof. dept. edn. Grad. Sch. Edn. UCLA, 1973-80, acting head early childhood devel. specialization, 1974, faculty Bush Tng. Program in Child Devel. and Social Policy, 1978-80, assoc. prof., 1980-86; exec. dir. Carnegie Coun on Adolescent Devel Carnegie Corp., N.Y., 1986—. Vis. asst. prof. dept. psychology Yale U., 1980; adj. assoc. prof. Tchrs. Coll., Columbia U., 1981-82; exec. dir. Fedn. Behavioral, Psychol. and Cognitive Scis., Washington, 1982; co-investigator Asian-Am. Edn. Project, 1973-76; bd. dirs. Grantmakers for Children, Coun. Founds.; rsch. assoc. Stanford Ctr. for Rsch. and Devel. in Teaching, Stanford U., 1973; adv. bd. Ms. Found. for Women, 1992, divsn. biobehavioral scis. and mental disorders Inst. Medicine, 1992; U.S. rep. UNESCO Mexico Conf., 1972; Harvard-Henry A Murray Ctr., Cambrige, Mass., 1997, Agy. Health Care Rsch. and Quality/U.S. Dept. Health and Human Svcs., Washington, 1997—; cons. to numerous insts. Assoc. editor: Am. Psychologist; consulting editor: Rehab. Psychology, Young Children; mem. editorial bd. Early Childhood Rsch. Quar.; mem. bd. reviewing editors: Ednl. Researcher; reviewer Am. Ednl. Rsch. Journ., Child Devel., Health Psychology, Psychology of Women Quar., Rev. Ednl. Rsch.; contbr. articles to profl. jours., chpts. to books; co-author: Preparing Adolescents for the 21st Century, 1997. Bd. trustees St. Augustine-by-the-Sea Sch., Santa Monica, Calif., 1976-77; mem. child care com. Calif. LWV, 1975-77; legis. asst. Office of Senator Daniel K. Inouye, Washington, 1980-81. Named one of Outstanding Young Women of Am., 1978. Mem. AAAS, APA (fellow, dir. office sci. affairs 1984-86, adminstrv. officer for children, youth and family policy office of nat. policy studies 1982-83, pub. interest, ethnic minority), APHA, Am. Ednl. Rsch. Assn. (program chair learning and devel. 1978, program chair spl. interest group in early edn. 1980), Nat. Assn. Edn. Young Children (chair com. orgnl. history and archives 1976-78), Soc. Rsch. in Child Devel. (program com. 1985-89, governing coun. 1989-95), Soc. Rsch. in Adolescence, Phi Beta Kappa. Avocation: volunteering for community service. Business E-Mail: ruby@fcd-us.org.

TAKENAGA, DIANA YAYOI, elementary school educator; b. Whittier, Calif., Mar. 31, 1948; d. Tsutomu Ben and Kimiko (Saito) Takenaga; m. Hiroyuki Christopher Taga (div.); m. David Harold Wendt, July 18, 2004. BA, UCLA, 1971; MS in Edn., U. So. Calif., L.A., 1996; cert. in Early Childhood, Calif. State U., Long Beach, 1976, cert. in Multiple Subjects, 1985. Tchr. Compton Youth Devel. Agy., Head Start, L.A., 0192—1975; elem. tchr. L.A. Unified Sch. Dist., 1979—2003, advisor elem. sci., 2003—. Elem. tchr. entomology Nat. History Mus. L.A. County, 1990—91; adj. prof. U. So. Calif., L.A., 2004—. Active Ctr. Future Tchg. and Learning, Santa Cruz, Calif., 1998—99, 2002; lead tchr. MetLife Nat. Tchr. Policy Inst., N.Y.C.; mem. instrnl. materials assessment panel com. Calif. Dept. Edn., Sacramento, 2006; mem. expert panel rev. math. and sci. edn. U.S. Dept. Edn., Boston, 1999. Recipient Earthwatch Scholarship award to study Mex. Megafauna, 1996, Earthwatch Scholarship award to study Mallocca's Copper Age, 1999, Presdl. award for excellence in sci. tchg. in Calif., NSF, 1998, award, U. So. Calif. Trojan League, 1999; L.A. Riordan grantee, Riordan Found., 2000. Mem.: Nat. Sci. Tchrs. Assn., Calif. Sci. Tchrs. Assn. (primary dir. 1994—, bd. dirs.), Greater L.A. Tchrs. Sci. Assn. (pres. 1995, bd. dirs.). Office Phone: 818-759-5310. Fax: 818-765-4101. E-mail: dianataga@yahoo.com.

TAKENAKA, TOSHIKO, lawyer, educator; b. Tokyo, July 10, 1958; LLB, Seikei Univ., Tokyo, 1981; LLM, Univ. Wash., 1990, PhD, 1992. Bar: N.Y. 1993. Patent preparation analyst Texas Instruments Japan, 1981—86; assoc. Yamasaki Law & Patent Office, Tokyo, 1987—89; vis. rsch. assoc. Univ. Tokyo, 1999; adj. prof. George Washington Univ., 1998; vis. scholar U.S. Ct. Appeals Fed cir., 1998; assoc. prof. Univ. Washington Sch. Law, 1993—2003, W. Hunter Simpson prof., 2003—; dir. Ctr. Advanced Study & Rsch. Intellectual Property, Univ. Washington; vis. scholar Max Planck Inst., Munich; vis. prof. Wasenda Univ., Tokyo, 2003—. Contbr. articles to prof. jour. Mem.: Internat. Assn. for Advancement of Tchg. & Rsch. in Intellectual Property, Am. Intellectual Property Law Assn. (mem. exec. com., Intellectual Property sect.), N.Y. State Bar Assn., Assn. Am. Law Sch. Office: University of Washington Law School 1100 NE Campus Pky Seattle WA 98118

TAKIS, STEPHANIE, retired state senator; Dem. rep. dist. 36 Colo. Ho. of Reps., 1996-2000; Dem. senator dist. 25 Colo. State Senate, 2000—; fin. specialist FEMA, Denver, 1992—94; rep. AtLarge City Coun., Aurora, Colo., 1989—93; mgmt. analyst U.S. Army, Aurora, Colo., 1983—92; congl. rels. Dept. Commerce, Washington, 1980—82; asst. to sen. Housing & Urban Devel. Com., Washington, 1979—80; ret. Mem. bus. affairs and labor and fin. coms. Colo. Ho. of Reps.; mem. legis. audit coms. Colo. State Senate, bus., labor com.; chair Trans com. Office: Colo State Senate State Capitol 200 E Colfax Denver CO 80203 Business E-Mail: stephanie.takis.senate@state.co.us.

TAKKE, KARYN COPPOCK, social worker, educator; b. Sacramento, June 13, 1961; d. Arthur Clifton Coppock and June Marie Betz; m. Vince Takke, Sept. 15, 1991; children: Jake Taylor, Kyle Hunter, Chad Brigham, Joshua Spencer. BS in Social Work, Brigham Young U., 1982; MSW, U. Tex., Austin, 1989. LCSW Utah. Dir. The Adoption Ctr., Orem, Utah, 2001—; med. social worker Intermountain Health Care-Home Care, Orem, 2002—05; pediat. continuum care mgr. Primary Children's Med. Ctr., Salt Lake City, 2005—. Adj. faculty Brigham Young U., Provo, Utah, 2003—, Utah Valley State Coll., Orem, 2003—. Mem., tchr. The Relief Soc., 1979—; vol. Sun Porch Group Home, Palo Alto, Calif., 1983—86; Sunday sch. tchr. LDS Ch., Calif. and Utah, 1990—; bd. dirs. LDS Family Svcs., Fresno, Calif., 1999. Republican. Avocations: reading, gardening, needlework, baking. Office: Utah Valley State Coll Behavioral Sci Dept 800W University Pky #MC Orem UT 84058 Office Phone: 801-718-4375. Fax: 801-302-7301. E-mail: karyn.takke@intermountainmail.org.

TALAG, TRINIDAD SANTOS, educator; b. Manila, Philippines, June 12, 1932; came to the U.S., 1954; d. Telesforo and Felisa A. Santos Talag. BS in Edn., U. Philippines, Quezon City, 1953; BS in Physical Edn., U. Oreg., 1955, MS in Physical Edn., 1956; PhD, U. Md., 1972. Instr. Centro Escolar U., Manila, Philippines, 1957-60; asst. prof. Northeastern U., Boston, 1962-66, Slippery Rock State Coll., Pa., 1966—73; assoc. prof. Elizabeth City State U., NC, 1989—90, prof., 1990—. NIH rsch. fellow, 1976-78. Mem. Bus. Profl. Women's Club, Am. Coll. Sports Medicine, Am. Alliance for Health, Phys. Edn., Recreation and Dance. Avocations: reading, plays, concerts, dance. Home: 4632 Broad St Virginia Beach VA 23462

TALAMANTES, CLAUDIA LILIANA, secondary school educator; d. Jose and Petra Diaz. BS in Math., U. Tex., El Paso, 1995, MA in Tchg., 2005. Master tutor U. Tex., El Paso, 1993—95; math. tchr. Del Valle HS, El Paso, 1995—. Lectr. math. U. Tex., El Paso, 1998—2005; instr. math. Cmty. Coll., El Paso, 2005—. Model Laura's Prodn., El Paso, 2006. Named one of Top Ten Tchrs., Nat. Honor Soc. Del Valle HS, El Paso, 1998. Avocations: exercise, languages. Office: Del Valle High Sch 950 Bordeaux El Paso TX 79907

TALBERT, DEBRA KAISER, elementary school educator, artist; b. Louisville, May 14, 1970; d. John Richard and Gwen Richter Kaiser, Rochelle Weaver Kaiser (Stepmother); m. John Matthew Talbert, June 20, 1992; 1 child, Alyssa Rose. BFA, Murray State U., Ky., 1994, MA in Edn., 2001. Cert. tchr. Ky. Itinerant art tchr. Massac County Schs. Unit #1, Metropolis, Ill., 1994—97; art tchr. Reidland Elem. Sch., Paducah, Ky., 1997—. Webmaster, tech. leader Reidland Elem. Sch., 2001—, coord. sch. tech., 2006—; mem. Sch. Based Decision Making Coun., Paducah, 2000—03; mem. dist. decision making coun. McCracken County Schs., Paducah, 2002. Mem. Kentuckiana Girl Scouts, Louisville, 1976—87, unit mgr. Paducah, 1994—96; youth leader First Presbyn. Ch., Paducah, 2001—04. Named Outstanding Young Am., 1997. Mem.: McCracken County Edn. Assn., Ky. Edn. Assn. Office: Reidland Elem Sch 5741 Benton Rd Paducah KY 42003 Office Phone: 270-538-4180. Personal E-mail: jtalbert0001@comcast.net. E-mail: debra.talbert@mccracken.kyschools.us.

TALBERT, DOROTHY GEORGIE BURKETT, social worker; b. Rison, Ark.; d. Booker T. and Dorothy (Ragan) Burkett; m. Ernest Talbert, May 14, 1949; children— Ernest George, Dorothy Ernette. A.B., Ark. State A. M. and N. Coll., 1946; M.S.W., Atlanta U., 1948; postgrad. U. Pa., 1962, Tulane U., 1965. Caseworker child welfare services Miss. Dept. Pub. Welfare, 1948-49, Ill. Pub. Aid Commn., Chgo., 1951-53; probation counselor Family Ct. Del., 1956-58; with Del. State Dept. Pub. Welfare, Dover, 1958-71, unit supr., 1962-64, supr. licensing and day care services, 1964-67, chief program devel. Child Welfare Services, 1967-68, chief services to families and children, 1968-71; asst. dir. family services, div. social services Del. Dept. Health and Social Services, 1971-78, dep. dir. adult and spl. services, 1978-82, adult crisis intervention coordinator, Newark, 1982—, staff tng./resource developer, 1985—; instr. continuing edn. program U. Del., part time 1968—, ret. 1989—; mem. social services adv. com. Del. Adolescent Program, 1969-75, bd. dirs., 1969-75; mem. State Adv. Council on Alcoholism, 1972-76; mem. Del. Devel. Disabilities Planning Council, Del. Adv. Council for Coordination of Services to Handicapped; social work edn. adv. com. Del. State Coll., 1978—. Bd. dirs. United Way of Del., 1979. Mem. Nat. Assn. Social Workers, Am. Pub. Welfare Assn., Nat. Council Pub. Welfare Adminstrs., Black Profl. Forum (sec. 1979), Nat. Caucus Black Aged, NAACP, Delta Sigma Theta. Home: 3007 W 3rd St Wilmington DE 19805-1703 Office: Div State Service Ctrs 501 Ogletown Rd Newark DE 19711-5403

TALBOT, CARLA RENEE, elementary school educator, veterinarian technician; b. Paducah, Ky., May 30, 1956; d. David William and Barbara Lindell Howard; m. Joseph Clarence Talbot, June 28, 1978; children: Brandon Joseph, Jodi Beth. BS in Edn., U. Mo., Columbia, 1978; MS in Edn., SW Mo. U., Bolivar, 2000. Tchr. Lincoln Co. R-II Sch., Elsberry, Mo., 1978—; vet. asst. Elsberry Animal Hosp., 2000—. Coach Elsberry R-II Schs., 1985—2004. Tchr. Ch. of Christ, Troy, Mo., 1990—2006. Mem.: Daughters of New Century Club (pres. 1984—86). Democrat. Mem. Church Of Christ. Avocations: reading, travel. Home: 1478 Fox Run Rd Elsberry MO 63343 Office: Lincoln Co R-II School 188 Tomahawk Dr Elsberry MO 63343 Personal E-mail: ctalbot@elsberry.k12.mo.us.

TALBOT, MARY LEE, minister; b. Cleve., Apr. 18, 1953; d. Richard William and Mary Helen (Jacobs) T. BA, Coll. Wooster, 1975; MDiv, Andover-Newton Theol. Sch., 1979; MPhil, Tchrs. Coll. Columbia U., 1990; PhD, Columbia U., 1997. Ordained to ministry Presbyterian Ch. (U.S.A.), 1981. Asst. in ministry Grace Congl. Ch., Framingham, Mass., 1975-78; resources coord. Women's Theol. Coalition, Boston, 1977-79; assoc. editor Youth Mag., Phila., 1979-80; co-dir. youth and young adult program Presbyn. Ch. U.S.A., N.Y.C., 1981-88; cons. in religious edn. N.Y.C., 1988-90; dir. continuing edn. Pitts. Theol. Sem., Pitts., 1990—2001; interim pastor Hebron U.P. Ch., Clinton, 2002—03, supply pastor, 2004—. Bd. dirs. Christian Assn., U. Pa., 1979-81; mem. religion com. Chautauqua Inst., 1988-91. Author, editor Suicide and Youth, 1981, (newsletter) Trackings, 1986—88; editor: Racism and Anti-Racism, 1982, One Fantastic Book, 1982, My Identity: A Gift from God, 1987, A Guidebook for Presbyterian Youth Ministry, 1988, God's Gift of Sexuality, 1989, Celebrate Bible Study, 1990, The C.L.S.C. Banner Book, 2004; contbr. articles to popular mags., profl. jours. Bd. dirs. Christian Assn., U. Pa., 1979-81. Recipient English award Bus. and Profl. Women, 1971. Mem. Assn. Presbyn. Ch. Educators, Assn. Presbyn. Clergywomen, Religious Edn. Assn. (bd. dirs. 1986-91), History of Edn. Soc., Kappa Delta Pi. Democrat. Office: 1767 Rte 30 Clinton PA 15026 Office Phone: 724-899-2620. Personal E-mail: mltalbot@aol.com.

TALBOT, NYNA LUCILLE, psychologist, writer; b. Warrington, Eng., May 24, 1954; d. John Robert Talbot and Lois June Snow. MA, Calif. Inst. Integral Studies, 1997, PhD, 2000; BA, Elmhurst Coll., 1976. Sr. tech. writer Hitachi Data Sys., Santa Clara, Calif., 1986—2006. Clin. psychology intern San Mateo County Emergency Response Team, 1990—91, San Mateo County Mental Health Svcs., Half Moon Bay, 2000—01. Clin. psychology intern mem. Red Cross, San Mateo, 1990—91. Mem.: Internat. Coun. Psychologists, Assn. Transpersonal Psychology, APA. Achievements include research in the relationship of companionship coupling in two significant populations. Avocations: painting, poetry. Office: Hitachi Data Sys 750 Central Expressway MS3288 Santa Clara CA 95050-2627 Personal E-mail: drnyna@yahoo.com. Business E-Mail: nyna.talbot@hds.com.

TALBOT, PAMELA, public relations executive; b. Chgo., Aug. 10, 1946; BA in English, Vassar Coll., 1968. Reporter Worcester, Mass. Telegram and Gazette, 1970—72; account exec. Daniel J. Edelman, Inc., Chgo., 1972—74, account supr., 1974—76, v.p., 1976—78, sr. v.p., 1978—84, exec. v.p., gen. mgr., 1984—90; pres. Edelman West, Chgo., 1990—95; pres., CEO Edelman U.S., 1995—. Office: Edelman Pub Rels 200 E Randolph Dr Ste 6300 Chicago IL 60601-6436 E-mail: pam.talbot@edelman.com.

TALBOT, PHYLLIS MARY, reading educator; b. Chgo., Mar. 14, 1949; d. James Joseph Watson and Sylvia (Slyk) Parker; m. Laurel Curtis Talbot, Oct. 6, 1967; children: Bill, Dennis, Mary, Anna, Tim. BS, Northwest Mo. State U., 1991, MEd, 1993, EdS, 1994. Cert. early childhood, elem., reading K-12, supt., adult basic edn. Literacy coord. N.W. Mo. Literacy Coun., Maryville, 1994-95; Title I reading tchr. St. Clair Sch. Dist., Appleton City, Mo., 1995—99, prin. Montrose, Mo., 1999—2002; supt., Title I reading tchr., spl. edn. tchr. Ballard Sch. Dist., Mo., 2003—; tchr. St. Mary's Catholic Sch., Montrose, Mo., 2005—06. Mem. AAUW, Mo. State Tchrs. Assn., Internat. Reading Assn. Roman Catholic. Home: 409 W Miller St Appleton City MO 64724-1523 Office: St Mary Cath Sch Montrose MO

TALBOT, PRUE, biology professor; b. Mass. BA, Wilson Coll., 1966; MA, Wellesley Coll., 1968; PhD, U. Houston, 1972. Postdoctoral fellow U. Houston; from asst. prof. to assoc. prof. U. Calif., Riverside, 1977-85, prof., 1986—. Assoc. editor several profl. jours.; contbr. articles to profl. jours. Mem. Am. Soc. Cell Biology, AAAS, Crustacean Soc., Sigma Xi. Office: U Calif Riverside Dept Biology Riverside CA 92521-0001

TALBOT-ELLIOTT, SUSAN, artist; b. Budapest, Hungary, July 12, 1954; arrived in US, 1969; d. Louis and Victoria (Talbot) Kovacs; m. James W. Elliott, Dec. 22, 1979; children: Shawn, Christopher. BA magna cum laude, Marymount Manhattan Coll., N.Y.C., 1977; MSBA cum laude, Boston U. Italy ext., Vicenza, Italy, 1983. Represented by Cudahy's, Richmond, Va., 1994—2004, Studios on the Square Gallery, Roanoke, Va., 1996—2001, The Little Gallery, Moneta, Va., 2000—, Fisher Galleries, Washington, 1994—99, White Canvas Gallery, Richmond, 2005—. Solo exhibns. include Lynchburg (Va.) Fine Art Ctr., 1996, Studios on the Square Gallery, Roanoke, 1997, Nat. Arts Club, N.Y.C., 1995, Knickerbocker Artists Signature, Scottsdale, Ariz., 1997, Frazer Gallery, Washington, 1999, commd. portraits. Recipient Award of Excellence, Arts Coun. Blue Ridge, 1994. Mem.: Oil Painters of Am., Knickerbocker Artists USA, Portrait Soc. Am., Allied Artists Am. E-mail: talbotelliott@earthlink.net.

TALBOT-KELLY, SAMANTHA RACHEL, artist; b. Royal Leamington Spa, England, Jan. 15, 1969; arrived in U.S., 2001; d. Giles Richard and Maeve Philomena Talbot-Kelly; m. Alfred Slade Mills; children: Tobias Quinn Slade Mills, Sienna-Piper Mills. BFA in Studio Arts, Concordia U., Montreal, Canada, 1995, M Art Edn., 2000; M Printmaking, Santa Reparata Sch. Art and Design, Florence, Italy, 2000; MFA, U. Tex., San Antonio, 2001.

Mgr., coord. art edn. Art Therapy Resource Ctr., 1990—2000; drama and English tchr. Yeungham U., Taegu, Republic of Korea, 1997; art instr. Royal Vale Math. and Sci. Alternative Sch., Montreal, Canada, 1998—99; artist, tchr. Chaffee Ctr. Visual Arts, Rutland, Vt., 2003—; artist Artist Resource Assn., Montpelier, Vt., 2004—. Landscape gardener, designer Designing Gardens, Ottawa, Canada, 1990—96; gardening supr. Quintessence & Dynamic Gardens, Vancouver, Canada, 1994—96. One-woman shows include Kellog-Hubbard Libr., Montpelier, 2006, exhibitions include T.W. Good Gallery, 2005, Chaffee Ctr. Visual Arts, 2005, T. Wood Gallery, Montpelier, 2004, 2005, Satellite Space, San Antonio, 2004, Chaffee Ctr. Visual Arts, Rutland, Vt., 2005, Barre Opera House, Vt., 2006, Salaam, Montpelier, 2006, numerous others; set designer: Yeungham U. English Sch.; Theatre Works, 1997; contbr. articles to profl. publs. Mem. art edn. com. Blue Star Art Space, San Antonio, 2000, edn. coord., 2000—01; cmty. rels. grad. studio rep. GAS, U. Tex., San Antonio, 2001—02; vol. Firehouse Ctr. for Visual Arts, Burlington, Vt., 2004; stage mgr. Theatre Works, Montreal, 1999. Recipient Art Edn. Coord. award, Blue Star Art Space, 2001, Tchg. award, Yeungnam U., 1998. Fellow: Nat. Mus. Women in Arts, Artist Resource Assn.; mem.: Washington Art Assn. Home: 527 North St Montpelier VT 05602 E-mail: artod3@yahoo.com.

TALBOT-ROSS, TIFFANY LYN, secondary school educator; d. Lloyd C. Talbot and Lynda M. Weinstein, Neal Weinstein (Stepfather); m. Dennis M. Ross, July 31, 1993; children: Bailey V. Ross, Chloe I. Ross. BA, Calif. State U., Fresno, 1991. Tchr. Porterville Unified Sch. Dist., Calif., 1991—. Office Phone: 559-782-7075.

TALBOTT, JANET K., information technology executive; d. Ernest Leon and Juanita Sullivant Dunning; children: Frank Robert, Ernest Lee. MBA in Mgmt., Webster U., 1982, D in Mgmt. Work, 1990. Cert. enterprise integrator Soc. Mfg. Engrs., 1999; in small bus. State of Ill., woman owned bus. State of Mo., female bus. enterprise Ill., disadvantaged bus. enterprise Mo. Dept. Transp., Dept. Transp. Tex. Adj. faculty Lindenwood U., St. Charles, Mo., 1983—84, So. Ill. U. at Carbondale, 1983—2000; staff mgr., acctg. and info. systems Southwestern Bell Tel. Co., St. Louis, 1979—80; engr. Combustion Engring., St. Louis, 1980—82, GM, Wentzville, Mo., 1982—85; mfg. systems engring. mgr. McDonnell Douglas (Boeing), Wentzville, Mo., 1985—91; advanced mgmt. cons. A. T. Kearney / Electronic Data Systems (EDS), Chgo., 1991—98; acting dir. BAAN, Herndon, Va., 1998—2000; key oper. exec., info. tech. Woods Equipment Co., Oregon, Ill., 2000—00; CEO Janet K. Talbott, Bethalto, Ill., 2001—. Commr. Accreditation Bd. for Engring. and Tech., N.Y.C., NY, 1984—89; U.S. Congl. appointee NRC, Washington, 1999—2001; bd. of assessment - panel mem., NIST, Gaithersburg, Md.; industry bd. advisors, Coll. Engring. U. of Mo., Columbia, Mo., 1983—90, Rolla, Mo., 1982—89; chair, computer logistics edn. industry subcom. U.S. Dept. Def., 1989—90. Author: Managing Your Growth Oriented Development, 1995; editor: Automating Die Management Systems, 1998, Manufacturing Engineering Wheel (Soc. of Mfg. Engring. - Blue Book Award, 1998). Elder New Wine Ch.; active Jesus Food Pantry Ministries. Recipient Meet the Competition award, Instn. of Indsl. Engrs., 1989. Mem.: NAFE, ASME (hon.; subcom. chair, product data exch. std. 1987—89), Conf. Minority Transp. Ofcls., Internat. Orgn. of Stds. (chair subcom. 1985—89), Assn. Integrated Mfg. Tech. (chair 1985—85, numerous), Inst. Indsl. Engineers (chair 1985—86, numerous), Soc. Mfg. Engrs. (chair, Computer and Automated Sys. Assn. 1997—98, Young Engr. of the Yr. Nominee 1984), Nat. Assn. Women Bus. Owners. Achievements include development of Product Data Exchange Specification (PDES) Commitee Chair; research in United States Air Force Letter of Achievement for work in Computer Aided Logistics Support. Office: 3 Cypress St Bethalto IL 62010-1020 E-mail: consulting@ijanet.com.

TALESE, NAN AHEARN, freelance/self-employed publishing executive; b. NYC, Dec. 19, 1933; d. Thomas James and Suzanne Sherman (Russell) Ahearn; m. Gay Talese, June 10, 1959; children: Pamela Frances, Catherine Gay. BA, Manhattanville Coll. of Sacred Heart, 1955; LHD (hon.), Manhattanville, 2003. Fgn. exchange student 1st Nat. City Bank, London and Paris, 1956; editorial asst. Am. Eugenics Soc., NYC, 1957-58, Vogue mag., NYC, 1958-59; copy editor Random House Pub., NYC, 1959-64, assoc. editor, 1964-67, sr. editor, 1967-73, Simon & Schuster Pubs., NYC, 1974-81, v.p., 1979-81; exec. editor, v.p. Houghton Mifflin Co., NYC, 1981-83, v.p., editor-in-chief, 1984-86, v.p., pub., editor-in-chief, 1986-88; sr. v.p. Doubleday & Co., NYC, 1988—; pres., pub., editorial dir. Nan A. Talese Books, 1990—.*

TALIAFERRO, ELIZABETH W., manufacturing executive; BA, Smith Coll.; MBA, Harvard Univ. Sr. analyst, corp. devel. Penn Ctrl. Corp., dir., fin. controls, 1986—91; v.p., ops analysis and inventory mgmt. Carol Cable, 1991—92; controller, consumer products group General Cable, Highland Heights, Ky., 1992—94, dir., sys. analysis, 1994—98, sr. v.p., customer integration, supply chain, 1998—2002, sr. v.p., gen. mgr., indl., specialty products, 2002—04, sr, v.p., corp. devel. and info., 2004—05, sr. v.p., chief info. officer, 2005—. Office: General Cable 4 Tesseneer Dr Newport KY 41076*

TALIK (LOGAN), REBECCA LYN, chemistry professor; b. Flint, Mich., May 12, 1981; d. Arthur Paul and Lynda Lou Logan; m. Andrew Gregory Talik, July 9, 2005. BS, Alma Coll., 2003. Secondary Education Certification Mich., 2004. Chemistry and phys. sci. tchr. Carrollton H.S., Mich., 2004—. Sci. club adv. Carrollton H.S., Mich., 2005—. Mem.: Am. Chem. Soc., Mich. Sci. Teacher's Assn., Nat. Sci. Teacher's Assn., Nat. Mole Day Found (sec. 2005—). Office: Carrollton HS 1235 Mapleridge Rd Carrollton MI 48724 Home: 3896 Leaman Ct Freeland MI 48623 Office Phone: 989-753-3433. Personal E-mail: rebeccalyn12@hotmail.com.

TALL, SUSAN PORTER, music educator; b. NYC, Apr. 16, 1942; m. Alan R. Tall, July 27, 1979; 1 child, Alexander A.; m. Burton F. Porter (div.); 1 child from previous marriage, Anastasia Porter. BA, Montclair State U., 1965; MA in Musicology, NYU, 1973; postgrad., U. Ill., 1978—80. Instr. music Am. Sch. London, 1966—68; instr. music, dir. inst. music Russell Sage Coll., Troy, NY, 1971—74; grad. asst. in conducting U. Ill., Champagne-Urbana, 1978—79; mem. faculty music Tenafly Sch. Sys., NJ, 1980—. Dir. music, condr. Presbyn. Ch., Tenafly, 1980—90, 1995—2005, North Jersey Symphony Orch., Tenafly, 1984—89, Concerto Orch. N.J., Tenafly, 1986—88; guest condr. in field. Organizer, dir. Fanfare for Humanity, Tenafly, 2001, 2005, THS Chorus and Orch. Benefit, Tenafly, 2005. Nominee Disting. Secondary Sch. Tchg. award, Princeton U., 1990; named Tchr. of Yr., Tenafly Sch. Dist., 2002; recipient Disting. Tchg. award, Tenafly H.S., 2002, Tchr. Recognition award, Gov., N.J., 2002, Disting. Leadership in Arts Edn. award, Gov. of N.J., 1997. Mem.: N.J. Music Educators Assn. (Master Tchr. award 1997). Avocation: classical guitar. Home: PO Box 104 Cresskill NJ 07626 Office: Tenafly Sch Dist Dept Music 19 Columbus Dr Tenafly NJ 07626 Office Phone: 201-816-6621. Business E-Mail: stall@tenafly.k12.nj.us.

TALLANT, CAROLE E., communications educator; b. Richmond, Va., Oct. 15, 1951; d. William Ellsworth and Rebecca Ellsworth Armstrong; m. James Tallant, Aug. 12, 1978; 1 child, Ryan. BA, U. NC, Chapel Hill, 1974, MA, 1976; PhD, La. State U., Baton Rouge, 1980. Prof. comm. studies U. NC, Wilmington, 1980—. Contbr. chapters to books. Storyteller and tutor for elem. schs. Forest Hills Elem. Sch., Wilmington, 1996—2006. Named NC Prof. of Yr., Carnegie Found. for the Advancement Tchg., 2004; recipient Disting. Tchg. Professorship award, 2006. Mem.: Nat. Storytelling Assn., NC Storytelling Guild. Episcopalian. Avocations: reading, cooking, travel, hiking. Office: Univ NC Wilmington 601 S College Rd Wilmington NC 29403-5933 Office Phone: 910-962-3443. Business E-Mail: tallantc@uncw.edu.

TALLENT, BRENDA COLENE, social worker, psychotherapist; b. Albany, Ky., Nov. 29, 1939; d. Hubert Lesco Denney and Roxie Mae Cowan-Denney; m. Norman Kenneth Tallent, Feb. 27, 1958 (dec. June 1975); children: Norma Houch, Delores, Sheila Weaver, Terry. BA Social Work, Ea. Ky. U., 1973; MPS, Western Ky. U., 1980; MSSW, U. Louisville, 1991. LCSW. Food stamp eligibility worker Cabinet for Human Resources, Frankfort, Ky., 1973—75, care home inspector, 1975—78, family svcs. clinician, 1978—88; mental health therapist Lake Cumberland Clinician Svcs., Somerset, 1988—90; county mgr. mental health svc. Adanta Clinical Svcs., 1990—94, site supr. mental health, 1994—96; CEO Expanding Horizons Counseling Ctr., 1996—. Cons. in field. Author poems. Mem.: NASW, Am. Fedn. Women, Nat. Acad. Social Workers, Albany Lions Club. Republican. Baptist. Avocations: writing, interior decorating, gardening, cooking, travel. Home: 1006 Ravenway PO Box 412 Albany KY 42602 Office: Expanding Horizons Counseling Ctr 1006 Allen St Albany KY 42602

TALLETT, ELIZABETH EDITH, biopharmaceutical company executive; b. London, Apr. 2, 1949; d. Edward and Edith May (Vickers) Symons; m. James Edward Wavle Jr.; children: James Edward Tallett, Alexander Martin Tallett, Christopher Andrew Wavle. BS with honors, U. Nottingham (Eng.), 1970. Ops. rsch. analyst So. Gas Bd., 1970-73; mgmt. svcs. mgr. Warner-Lamber (UK), Eastleigh, England, 1973-77, strategic planning mgr., 1977-81; internat. dir. strategic planning Warner-Lambert, Morris Plains, NJ, 1981-82, corp. dir. strategic planning, 1982-84; dir. mktg. ops. Parke-Davis, Morris Plains, 1984-87; exec. v.p. therapeutic products Centocor, Malvern, Pa., 1987-89, pres. pharms. div., 1989-92; pres., CEO Transcell Techs., Inc., Monmouth Junction, NJ, 1992-96, Dioscor, Inc., Stockton, 1996—2003; prin. Hunter Ptnrs. LLC, 2002—. Bd. dirs. Prin. Fin. Group, Inc., Varian, Inc., Coventry Health Care, Inc., IntegraMed Am. Inc., Immunicon Inc., Varian Semi Conductor Equipment Assoc. Inc.; dir. Biotech. Coun. N.J., NJ Ctr. Life Sci. Contbr. articles to profl. jours. Avocations: acting, badminton, travel, skiing. Personal E-mail: dioscor@comcast.net.

TALLEY, BRENDA S., performing arts center director, theatrical light designer; b. Las Vegas, Nev., Jan. 17, 1955; d. Wanda Marie and Milton Rex Linn; m. Donald P. Kennedy, June 7, 1975 (div. Nov. 19, 2001); m. Douglas L. Talley, Nov. 29, 2003; children: Ryan Rex Kennedy, Krista Marie Kennedy, Dawnie Rose Kennedy, Breanna (Annie) Linn Kennedy. AA in Gen. Studies, C.C. So. Nev., 1989; BA in Bus. Mgmt., St. Regis U., 2002. Ho. mgr. C.C. So. Nev. Performing Arts Ctr., 1996—2000; performing arts ctr. asst. dir. C.C. So. Nev., 2000—02, performing arts ctr. dir., 2002—. Mem. C.C. So. Nev. Lecture Com., 2000—; chmn. C.C. So. Nev. Honors Com., 2000—02, Campus Environment Coun., North Las Vegas, 2000—02; mem. Nev. C.C. Conf., 2001—02. V.p. Tule Springs Preservation Com., Las Vegas, 1998—2003; vice chair Congress of States Nat. Parent Tchr. Assn., Chgo., 1999—2001; pres. Nev. Parent Teachers Assn., Las Vegas, 1999—2001. Recipient Hon. Life Membership, Nat. PTA, 1994, Nev. PTA, 1996, Parent Hall of Fame, Clark County Sch. Dist., 1996, High Honors, Phi Theta Kappa, 1989. Mem.: AAUP (assoc.), Nev. Faculty Alliance (assoc.). Democrat. Latter Day Saint. Avocations: theater, rapelling, hiking, camping, music. Office: Community College Southern Nevada 3200 East Cheyenne Ave North Las Vegas NV 89030

TALLEY, DANA SMITH, principal; b. Monroe, La., June 29, 1972; d. Audrey Ross and Dennis Wayne Smith; m. Shawn Day Talley, Sept. 1, 1991. BS, La. Tech U., Ruston; MS, La. Tech. U., Ruston, 2004. Tchr. Ruston H.S., La., 1997—2005; disting. educator La. Dept. Edn., Baton Rouge, 2005; prin. Simsboro Sch., La., 2006—. Named Young Educator of Yr., Ruston Jaycees, Tchr. of Yr., Ruston H.S.; recipient, Lincoln Parish. Mem.: La. Assn. Tchs. of Math. (assoc.), Nat. Coun. Tchrs. of Math. (assoc.), Delta Kappa Gamma (assoc.). Home: 348 Liberty Hill Rd Arcadia LA 71001 Office: Simsboro Sch # 1 Tiger Dr Simsboro LA 71275 Office Phone: 318-247-6265. Personal E-mail: shawnanddana@hughes.net. E-mail: dtalley@lincolnschools.org.

TALLEY, DIANE YVONNE, special education educator; b. Sault Saint Marie, Mich, May 8, 1950; d. Floyd E. and Helen Doris (Taylor) Brown; m. Dewey Edward Talley, Mar. 28, 1975 (div. Sept. 23, 1981); 1 child, Dilena Lee Talley; m. Kenneth Leo Strike, Mar. 25, 1993 (div. 1997). AA in Computer Programming and Keypunch, Davis Jr. Coll., 1969; BFA, U. Houston, 1986; MS in Tech., Nova Southeastern U., 2000, EdS Curriculum Instrn. and Tech., 2003. Cert. spl. educator, art educator, Fla. Computer analyst Gordon Jewelers, Houston, 1971—80; tchr. spl. edn. Lake County Sch., Leesburg, Fla., 1988—91, Volusia County Sch., Daytona Beach, Fla., 1991—. Adj. instr. Daytona Beach (Fla.) C.C., 1992-2001; bd. dirs. Guardian Ad Litem, Daytona Beach. Author: (book) Introduction to Computers, 1997; (mag.) HAAUG Beginners Corners, 1985-89; grantee in field. Mem. Am. Chippewa Nat. of Sault, Sault St. Marie, 1986-; Union Stewart Volusia County Tchr. Organ., Daytona Beach, 1988—, Fla. Coun. Social Studies, 2001-. Ormand Beach, Fla. Rotary Club grant, 1997, Target Donations grantee, 1998, Fla. Coun. Exceptional Children mini grant, 1999; recipient Jr. League grant, Daytona Beach, 1996 Mem. Houston Area Apple Users Group, Ceramic Assn., Coun. Exceptional Children (membership chair chpt. 260, Rookie of Yr. nomination 1991, grantee Fla. Edn. 1996, 97, 98), Native Am. Indian Assn. (bd. dir., pres. 1997-2000), Rep. Assoc. with Pub. Schs. Club (sponsor 1993-98, 3d Pl. award 1996), Koi Club (v.p. 2005-). Native American. Avocations: computer, technology, edn., arts and crafts, Native Am. art. Home: 155 N Lanvale Ave Daytona Beach FL 32114-3429 Office: Mainland H S 1255 W Internat Speedway Blvd Daytona Beach FL 32114 E-mail: dsmemories@hotmail.com.

TALLMAN, ANN MARIE, lawyer; b. Iowa; BS in Psychology and Polit. Sci., with distinction and spl. honors, U. Iowa; JD, U. Calif. Berkeley, Boalt Hall Sch. Law. Atty. Kutak Rock, Denver; dep. dir. & head Planning and Community Develop. Agy. City and County of Denver; with Fannie Mae, Pasadena, Calif., 1994—2004; pres., CEO Fannie Mae Found., Washington, 1998—99; pres., gen. counsel MALDEF (Mexican Am. Legal Def. and Edn. Fund), LA, 2004—06. Bd. mem. MALDEF (Mexican Am. Legal Def. and Edn. Fund), 1998—2006; bd. dirs. J. C. Penney Company, Inc., 2006—. Founding bd. mem. Hispanic PAC USA; exec. dir. Colo. Hispanic League, 1990.

TALLMER, MARGOT SALLOP, psychologist, gerontologist, psychoanalyst; b. N.Y.C., NY, Sept. 8, 1925; d. Harry and Mildred (Schifrin) Sallop; m. Jonathan Tallmer, Apr. 12, 1949 (dec.); children: Mary, Megan, Jill, Andrew. MS, NYU, 1948; MA, Yeshiva U., 1962, PhD, 1967; cert. in psychotherapy and psychoanalysis, NYU, 1976. Faculty dept. psychol. founds. Hunter Coll., NYC, 1969-76, assoc. prof., 1976-79, prof., 1979—94, prof. emeritus; staff psychologist Mt. Sinai Hosp., NY, 1967-68; pvt. practice NYC, 1979—; faculty NY Ctr. for Psychoanalytic Tng., NY. Lectr. N.Y. Ctr. Psychoanalytic Tng. Author: Sex in Later Life, 1996; editor: Sex and Life Threatening Illness, HIV Testing Positive, The Child and Death, Sexuality and the Older Adult; co-author: Suicide in the Elderly; mem. edtl. bd. Current Issues in Psychoanalysis, Psychoanalytic Rev.; contbr. chpts. to textbooks, articles to profl jours. Mem. APA, Boston Soc. Gerontologic Psychiatry, N.Y. State Psychol. Assn. (past pres. divsn. adult devel. and aging), Nat. Psychol. Assn. for Psychoanalysis (trustee 1972-2005, bd. dir. 1972—). Address: 515 E 85th St New York NY 10028-0246 Personal E-mail: mamadoc4@n.y.c.rr.om. E-mail: mamadoc4@gmail.com.

TALLON, BECKY JO, computer scientist, educator; b. Nashville, N.C., Jan. 15, 1946; d. Miles Jeffererson and Pattie Ruth Joyner; m. William Alexander Tallon, Dec. 21, 1969; children: William Alexander Jr., Patricia Louise. BS in Math., U. N.C., Greensboro, 1968; MS, Clemson U., S.C., 1970; MS in Computer Sci. Edn., U. Evansville, Ind., 1989. Tchr. math. grades 9-12 Interlachen H.S., Fla., 1970—71; libr. asst. Maury County Pub. Libr., Columbia, Tenn., 1971—76; occassional adj. math. Columbia State C.C., Columbia, Tenn., 1975—79; tchr. math Santa Fe H.S., 1979—90; adj. in computing Columbia State C.C., 1988—90; instr. math. and computing Lipscomb U., Nashville, 1989—95, asst. prof computing and info. sci., 1995—. Dir. info. tech. program Lipscomb U., Nashville, 2005—; presenter to profl. grups; grant and jour. reviewer. Contbr. articles to profl. jours. Vol. hurricane relief campaign McNair Found., Nashville, 2005; tchr. pre-school childern Woodmont Hills Ch. of Christ, 1989, nursery worker, 1989—2006, ministry leader Servant Hands Servant Heart, 1993. Grantee, Eisenhower Program, 1991, 1992, 1993, 1994, 1995, No Child Left Behind U.S. Dept. Edn., 2005. Mem.: Consortium Computing in Small Colls. (life; sec. southeastern sect. 1999—2006, web contest dir. 2001—05), Spl. Interest Group in Computer Edn. (life). Achievements include development of current program (ITP) to have all freshman pass the Information Technology Requirement. Home: 4708 Richmar Ct Nashville TN 37211 Office: Lipscomb Univ 3901 Granny White Pike Nashville TN 37204 Office Phone: 615-279-5824.

TALLY, LURA SELF, state legislator; b. Statesville, NC, Dec. 9, 1921; d. Robert Ottis and Sara (Cowles) Self; m. J.O. Tally Jr., Jan. 30, 1943 (div. 1970); children: Robert Taylor, John Cowles. AB, Duke U., 1942; MA, NC State U., 1970. Tchr., former guidance counselor Fayetteville (NC) city schs.; mem. NC Ho. of Reps. from 20th Dist., 1971—83, chmn. com. higher edn., 1975, 1980—83, vice-chmn. com. appropriations for edn., 1973—86; state senator from 12th Dist. NC, 1983—95; chmn. NC Senate Com. of Natural Resources, Cmty. Devel. and Wildlife, 1987, Environment and Natural Resources, 1989—94. Past pres. Cumberland County Mental Health Assn., NC Historic Preservation Soc.; trustee Fayetteville Tech. Inst., 1981—94; active Legis. Rsch. Com. Mem.: Am. Pers. and Guidance Assn., Fayetteville Woman's Club (past pres.), Fayetteville Bus. and Profl. Women's Club, Kappa Delta, Delta Kappa Gamma. Methodist. Office: W Jones St Raleigh NC 27601

TALLY, PAULA SINIARD, counselor; b. Gadsden, Ala., Oct. 4, 1945; d. Thomas Clifford and Viva Gwendolyn (Blackwood) Siniard. BS, U. Ala., 1967, MA, 1971. Tchr. Muscogee County Bd. Edn., Columbus, Ga., 1967-68; tech. writer Regional Curriculum Project, Atlanta, 1968-69; employment counselor Ga. Dept. Labor, Atlanta, 1968-69, unit supr., 1969-70, supr. counselors, 1971-72; advisor residence hall U. Ala., Tuscaloosa, 1970-71; planner Ga. Manpower Planning Council, Atlanta, 1972-73; mgr. office Kimbrough and Assocs., Auburn, Ala., 1973-74; guidance counselor Lee County Schs., Jackson County Schs., Opelika and Scottsboro, Ala., 1974-86; exec. dir. Jackson County Rural Health Project, Scottsboro, 1986-87; guidance counselor Scottsboro City Schs., 1987—91, Huntsville City Schs., Ala., 1991—99; adminstrn. asst. Siniard, Timberlake & League, PC, 1999—. Chmn. bd. Stevenson (Ala.) Pub. Library, 1981-86; bd. dirs. Scottsboro-Jackson Heritage Ctr., 1982-86; mem. adv. bd. Jackson County Juvenile Ct., Scottsboro, 1982—; mem. organizational com., life mem. Friends of Stevenson Depot Mus.; mem. women's com. Jackson County Farm Bur.; charter mem. Friends of Lee County Jail; life mem. Friends of Library; bd. dirs., sec. Marshall Jackson Mental Health Bd. Recipient Woman of Achievement award Stevenson Bus. and Profl. Women's Club, 1982, Community Service award Stevenson Civic Club, 1984. Mem. AAUW, Ala. Assn. for Counseling and Devel. (treas. dist. II 1982-84, sec. 1988—), Ala. Primary Health Care Assn. (bd. dirs. 1986-87), Orgn. Active Women (pres. Stevenson chpt. 1982-84), Scottsboro-Jackson County C. of C. (bd. dirs. 1987—, v.p., Athena award 1987), Delta Kappa Gamma (2d v.p. Rho chpt. 1982-84, 1st v.p. 1984-86, pres. 1986-1988, Kappa chpt., 1991—, Achievement award 1986), Ala. Counseling Assn. (Counseling Yr., 1990), Ala. Sch. Counselors Assn., Kappa Delta Pi. Democrat. Methodist.

TALTON, KAREN BRYANT, nurse; b. St. Louis, Aug. 6, 1955; d. Albert Lee and Loretta (Hadley) B.; m. Robert L. Talton, 1990. Diploma, Ga. Bapt. Hosp. Sch. Nursing, 1978; BS in Nursing, Med. Coll. Ga., 1982; MS in Nursing, U. Ala., Birmingham, 1984. RN; CEN, CCRN; cert. nursing adminstr., cert. clin. specialist in med.-surg. nursing; cert. ACLS instr., paramedic instr., regional faculty Am. Heart Assn. Staff nurse intensive care unit Houston County Hosp., Warner Robins, Ga., 1978-79, charge nurse intensive care unit, 1979-81; staff nurse neuro intensive care unit Univ. Hosp., Augusta, Ga., 1981-82; staff nurse emergency dept. Med. Ctr. Cen. Ga., Macon, 1981-82, clin. nurse emergency ctr., 1986-87, clin. specialist critical care, 1987-88; staff nurse intensive care Med. Ctr. Houston County, 1982-84; clin. edn. dir. Houston Med. Ctr., 1988-94; clin. supr. intensive care unit and critical care unit Charter Northside Hosp., Macon, 1984-86; clin. dir. Houston Heart Inst., 1995-96; asst. nurse mgr. Med. Intensive Care Unit, Robins, Ga., 1996—. Mem. advanced cardiac life support subcom. State of Ga., 1992—; mem. NCLEX-RN panel content experts Nat. Assn. State Bd. Nursing, 1992. Mem. ANA, Ga. Nurses Assn., AACN (pres. Ga. chpt. 1986-87), Emergency Nurses Assn., Am. Soc. Healthcare Edn. and Tng., Nat. Nurses in Bus. Assn., Inc., Ga. Soc. Healthcare Edn. and Tng., Sigma Theta Tau. Baptist. Avocations: travel, reading, antiques, collectibles. Home: 219 Blue Meadow Cir Kathleen GA 31047-2815

TALTY, LORRAINE CAGUIOA, accountant; b. Makati, Manila, The Philippines, July 3, 1957; arrived in U.S., 1973, naturalized, 1983; d. Leon Perez and Asuncion (Rodriguez) Caguioa; m. Kevin Michael Talty, Jan. 23, 1982; 1 child, Leah Marie. BBA in Acctg. magna cum laude, Chaminade U., Honolulu, 1979. Office mgr., comptr. Caro of Honolulu, 1976-82; acct. David Schenkein, CPA, Latham, NY, 1984-86; sales rep. Caromat Corp., Torrance, Calif., 1985-86; owner Kevlor Internat., Fairport, NY, 1985—; acct. Cortland L. Brovitz & Co., CPA's, Rochester, NY, 1986-87; pvt. practice Fairport, 1986—2000. Comptr. Tal-Tee Assocs., Inc., Webster, NY, 1995—. Newsletter editor Country Knolls West Civic Assn., Clifton Park, 1984—85, civic com. rep., 1985—86; bd. dirs., vol. coord. Rochester Children's Theatre, 1994—96; treas. adv. com. St. Joseph's Sch., Penfield, NY, 1995—99, chair, 1999—2000; treas. Fil-Am. Assn., Rochester, 1998—99; Class of 2006 parents' bd. rep. Our Lady Mercy HS, 2000—06, treas. parents assn., 2002—06. Home: 8 Silver Fox Dr Fairport NY 14450-8665 Office Phone: 585-872-1981. Business E-Mail: ktalty1@rochester.rr.com.

TAMAREN, MICHELE CAROL, spiritual director, writer, retired special education educator, personal coach, presenter; b. Hartford, Conn., Aug. 2, 1947; d. Herman Harold and Betty (Leavitt) Liss; m. David Stephen Tamaren, June 8, 1968; 1 child, Scott. BS in Elem. Edn., U. Conn., 1969; MA in Spl. Edn., St. Joseph Coll., West Hartford, Conn., 1976; student, Claritas Inst. for Interspiritual Inquiry, Boulder, Colo., 2005—. Cert. elem. and spl. edn. tchr. Conn., Mass. Tchr. N.Y. Inst. Spl. Edn., Bronx, 1971-74; ednl. cons. Renbrook Sch., West Hartford, 1975-78; grad. instr. St. Joseph Coll., 1978; elem. tchr. Acton (Mass.) Pub. Schs., 1969-70, tchr. spl. edn., 1978-94, inclusion and behavioral specialist, 1996-2000; learning specialist and writer Educators Pub. Svc., Cambridge, Mass., 1994-96. Personal coach; cons., presenter in field. Author: (book) I Make a Difference, 1992; contbr. articles to profl. jours. Bd. dirs. United Way, Acton-Boxborough, 1996—99. Grantee, Mass. Gov.'s Alliance Against Drugs, 1992; Horace Mann grantee, Mass. Dept. Edn., 1987, 1988. Mem.: Kappa Delta Pi, Phi Kappa Phi. Avocations: travel, writing, reading, yoga, swimming. Home and Office: 34 Constitution Way Apt D Marblehead MA 01945-4652 Personal E-mail: to_life@earthlink.net.

TAMBARO, MARIE GRACE, health specialist, nursing educator; b. N.Y.C., June 28, 1946; d. Louis Vincent and Jeanette (Motto) Nunziato; m. Arthur Michael Tambaro, Sept. 20, 1964; children: Celeste, Joseph, Arthur Michael Jr., Louis Derek. BSN with honors, CUNY, 1981; postgrad., Seton Hall U., 1985. CCRN, ACLS. Critical care staff nurse Richmond Meml. Hosp., S.I., N.Y., 1980-83; nursing insgr. Brookdale C.C., Lincroft, N.J., 1983—; health specialist Holmdel (N.J.) Bd. Edn., 1990—. Apptd. to Holmdel Twp. Bd. of Health, 1989—, Holmdel Bd. of Edn. Dist. Instrnl. Coun., 1994; chair Holmdel Drug and Alcohol Commn., 1986-88; rep. to N.J. State Drug and Alcohol Commn., 1987. Mem. AAUW. Republican. Roman Catholic. Avocations: reading, gourmet cooking, exercise. Home: 15 Seven Oaks Dr Holmdel NJ 07733-1924 Office: Holmdel Twp Bd Edn 4 Crawfords Corner Rd Holmdel NJ 07733-1908

TAMBLYN, AMBER ROSE, actress; b. Santa Monica, Calif., May 14, 1983; d. Russ and Bonnie Tamblyn. Actor: (TV series) General Hospital, 1995—2001, Joan of Arcadia, 2003—05; (films) Live Nude Girls, 1995, Rebellious, 1995, Johnny Mysto: Boy Wizard, 1996, The Ring, 2002, The Sisterhood of the Traveling Pants, 2005, Stephanie Daley, 2006, The Grudge

2, 2006, (guest appearances): Buffy the Vampire Slayer, 2001, Boston Public, 2002, Twilight Zone, 2002, CSI: Miami, 2002, Without a Trace, 2003, Punk'd, 2003. Office: 8383 Wilshire Blvd Ste 530 Beverly Hills CA 90211*

TAMEN, HARRIET, lawyer; b. Yonkers, NY, May 17, 1947; d. Saul and Lily (Balglau) T. AB, Bryn Mawr Coll., 1969; JD, George Washington U., Washington, 1973. Bar: N.Y. 1974, U.S. Dist. Ct. (so. dist.) N.Y. 1975. Atty. W.T. Grant, N.Y.C., 1974-76, City of N.Y. Office Econ. Devel., divsn. Real Property, N.Y.C., 1977-81, Credit Lyonnais Bank, N.Y.C., 1981-86, Chase Manhattan Bank, 1986-89; v.p., counsel internat. corp. fin. Citibank, 1989-92; ptnr. Claugus Tamen & Orenstein, 1992-93; pvt. practice N.Y.C., 1994—. Bd. dirs. Dromenon Theatre, N.Y., 1980-86, Nat. Dance Inst., N.Y., 1982, chmn. bd. dirs., 1984-87; chmn. bd. dirs. Theatre & Dance Alliance, 1989-90; del. exch. program Women in Law, South Am., 1987—; mem. campaign staff Ed Koch for Mayor, N.Y.C., 1977; mem. steering com. Soviet Am. Banking Law Working Group, 1991—; guest lectr. Moscow Conf. on Banking, 1992, Ulaan Baatar, Mongolia, 1993-94, 96, Harriman Inst. of Columbia U., 1994; co-chair N.Y. Lawyers Com. for Clinton-Gore; mem. adv. coun. U.S. Export Import Bank, 2000. Mem. ABA, Assn. of Bar of City of N.Y.

TAMSETT, SUSAN O., architect, artist; b. Balt., Oct. 29, 1948; d. John Fredrick and Evelyn Imogene (White) Ott; m. Stephen James Tamsett, July 8, 1967 (div. Aug. 28, 1998); children: Anne Marie, Stephen James Jr., Alison Marie. Student, U. Ga., 1966—69; BFA in Architecture, R.I. Sch. Design, 1986, BArch, 1987. Asst. to prin. Architects Design Group II, Wellesley, Mass., 1988—89; assoc. Ann Beha Assocs., Boston, 1989—90; freelance design cons., freelance illustrator Ridgefield, Conn., 1990—95; sr. designer, project mgr. Shope Reno Wharton, Greenwich, Conn., 1995—96; prin. Studio 584, LLC, Ridgefield, 1996—. Exhibited in group shows at Art Students League, N.Y. (Best of contemporary Printmakers of N.Y.C., 02), Cork Gallery, Lincoln Ctr., N.Y., 2002—05, Silvermine Guild Arts Ctr., Ctr. Contemporary Printmaking, Norwalk, Conn., 2005, Hunterdon Mus., Clinton, N.J. Nat. membership chair Interfaith Forum on Religious Art and Architecture, Washington, 1992—94; mem. Archtl. Adv. Com., Ridgefield, 1999—; founding mem. Sexual Assault Recovery and Healing, St. Barts of N.Y.C., 2000—; project coord. Documentation and Conservation Modern Movement Modern House Survey, New Canaan, Conn., 2001—. Mem.: AIA (assoc.; bd. dirs. profl. interest area on religious architecture 1994—98), Silvermine Guild, Alpha Lambda Delta. Congregationalist. Avocations: rowing, kayaking, painting, bicycling, printmaking. Office: Studio 584, LLC PO Box 675 Ridgefield CT 06877

TAN, AMY RUTH, writer; b. Oakland, Calif., Feb. 19, 1952; d. John Yueh-han and Daisy Ching (Tu) T.; m. Louis M. DeMattei, Apr. 6, 1974. Student, Linfield Coll., McMinnville, Oreg., San Jose (Calif.) City Coll.; BA in Linguistics and English with honors, San Jose (Calif.) State U., 1973, MA in Linguistics, 1974; LHD (hon.), Dominican Coll. San Rafael, 1991. Specialist lang. devel. Alameda County Assn. for Mentally Retarded, Oakland, 1976-80; project dir. M.O.R.E. Project, San Francisco, 1980-81; mng. editor Emergency Medicine Reports newsletter, San Francisco; freelance writer, 1981-88; literary editor West mag. LA Times. Author: (novels) The Joy Luck Club, 1989 (Nat. Book Critics Cir. award for best novel nomination 1989, LA Times Book award nomination 1989, Gold award for fiction Commonwealth Club 1990, Bay Area Book Reviewers award for best fiction 1990), The Kitchen God's Wife, 1991, The Hundred Secret Senses, 1995, The Bonesetter's Daughter, 2001, The Opposite of Fate: A Book of Musing, 2003, Saving Fish from Drowning, 2005; (children's books) The Moon Lady, 1992, The Chinese Siamese Cat, 1994; also numerous short stories and essays; screenwriter, prodr.: (film) The Joy Luck Club, 1993. Recipient Best Am. Essays award, 1991. Office: c/o Putnam Publicity 375 Hudson Street New York NY 10014*

TAN, COLLEEN WOO, communications educator; b. San Francisco, May 6, 1923; d. Mr. and Mrs. S.H. Nq Quinn; m. Lawrence K.J. Tan; children: Lawrence L., Lance C. BA in English/Am. Lit., Ind. U., 1950, MA in English, 1952; MA in Speech Arts, Whittier Coll., 1972; postgrad., U. Calif. Berkeley, 1952-53. Cert. secondary edn. tchr., K-12, community coll., Calif. Tchng. aide English U. Calif., Berkeley, 1952-53; tchr. English and Social Studies Whittier (Calif.) High Sch., 1957-60; prof. speech comms. Mt. San Antonio Coll., Walnut, Calif., 1960-94; dir. forensics, 1969-80; sen. acad. senate Mt. San Antonio Coll., Walnut, Calif., 1982-90, faculty rep., 1990—. Recipient Woman of Achievement Edn. award San Gabriel Valley, Calif. YWCA, 1995; named Outstanding Prof. Emeritus, Mt. San Antonio Coll. Found., 1994, Oustanding Alumnae, Mary Knoll Sisters Sch., 1997. Mem. AAUW (pres. Whittier Br. 1982, cultural interests chair Calif. state divsn. 1985-87, Fellowship award 1973-74, Las Distinguidas award 1992, Found. honoree Whittier br. 2004-05), Calif. Asian-Am. Faculty Assn., Delta Kappa Gamma, Phi Beta Kappa (Outstanding Educator of Am. award 1972), Alpha Delta Kappa (interim pres. 2003-04) Roman Catholic. Avocations: creative writing, reading fiction, attending theater, music, dance. Home: 13724 Sunrise Dr Whittier CA 90602-2547 Office: Mt San Antonio 1100 N Grand Ave Walnut CA 91789-1341

TAN, LI-SU LIN, accountant, insurance company executive, consultant; b. Keelung, Taiwan, Republic of China, Mar. 7, 1956; arrived in US, 1985; d. I-Chang and Sung-Mei (Chen) Lin; m. Bert T. Tan, Aug. 19, 1985; children: Patricia Tan, Peter Puwen Tan, Lotus Tan. BBA, Nat. Taiwan U., 1978; MBA, Ill. Inst. Tech., Chgo., 1991. CPA, Ill., Taiwan; lic. ins. agt., Ill.; registered investment advisor. Asst. mgr. T.N. Soong & Co. (mem. firm Arthur Anderson & Co., SC), Taipei, 1978—85; practitioner Li-Su Lin, CPA, Taipei, 1981—85, Li-Su Lin Tan, CPA, Naperville, Ill., 1988—90; pres. Lisu L. Tan & Co., Ltd., CPAs, Naperville, 1990—; agt. Mut. Omaha Co., Lombard, Ill., 1991—94, Met. Life and Affiliated Cos., Bloomingdale, Ill., 1993—98, GE Fin. Assurance, Schaumburg, Ill., 1999—. Chair family Naperville Chinese Assn., 1990. Mem.: AICPA (tax divsn., quality control program), Ill. Soc. CPA, Amitabha Buddhist Libr. Chgo. (pres. 2003—, bd. dirs.), Buddha's Light Internat. Assn. (pres. Chgo. chpt. 2002—04, bd. dirs.), Chinese Am. Culture Found. (pres. 2001—, bd. dirs.), Nat. Taiwan U. Alumni Assn. Greater Chgo. (bd. dirs. 1999—2003), World Taiwanese C. of C. (dep. treas. 1998—99), Taiwanese C. of C. N.Am. (treas. 1998—99, bd. dirs.), Greater Chgo. Area Taiwanese Am. C. of C. (bd. dirs. 1995—2006), Taipei First Girls High Alumni Assn. (treas. 1990—94). Buddhist. Avocations: travel, art, photography. Office: Lisu L Tan & Co Ltd CPAs 6S235 Steeple Run Dr #200 Naperville IL 60540-3754 Office Phone: 630-416-9422. Business E-Mail: lisu@lisutancpas.com.

TANAKA, PATRICE AIKO, public relations executive; b. Hawaii; BA, U. Hawaii, 1974. Editor Hawaii Press Newspapers, 1974-77; dir. pub. rels. Hotel Inter-Continental Maui, 1977-79; acct. exec. to sr. v.p. and creative dir. Jessica Dee Comm., NYC, 1979-87, exec. v.p., gen. mgr., 1987-90; CEO, creative dir. PT&Co., NYC, 1990—2005, CRT/tanaka, 2005—. Featured in books: American Dreamers, Visionaries and Entrepreneurs, 1995, The Art of Public Relations, 2002. Bd. dirs. Greater NY coun. Girl Scouts US, US Fund for UNICEF, Family Violence Prevention Fund, Asian Pacific Am. Women's Leadership Inst. Named one of nation's 500 Most Influential Asian Ams., Avenue mag., 1996; recipient Mothering That Works award, Working Mother mag., 1994, Women Mean Bus. award, Bus. and Profl. Women U.S.A., 1999, Paul M. Lund award for pub. svc., Pub. Rels. Soc. Am., 2002. Mem.: Asian Women in Bus. (bd. dirs.), Coun. Pub. Rels. Firms (founding bd. dirs.), Women Execs. in Pub. Rels., NY Women in Comm. (pres. 2001—02, 2002—03, Matrix award for pub. rels. 1996), Asian Pacific Am. Women's Leadership Inst. (founding bd. dirs.), Women's Forum NY, U. Hawaii Alumni Assn. (bd. dirs. NY chpt.). Office: CRT/tanaka 320 W 13th St Fl 7 New York NY 10014-1200

TANDY, JEAN CONKEY, clay artist, potter, painter, retired educator; b. Reese, Mich., May 17, 1931; d. Samuel Hall and Christine Margaret Conkey; m. Norman Edward Tandy, Jan. 25, 1952; children: Michelle Tandy Ryan, Kristen, Peter Spence. BA, Mich. State U., 1962, MFA, 1965. Instr. French Bath Cmty. Schs., Mich., 1961, instr., designer program art curriculum, 1962—67; instr. art Mahar Regional Schs., Orange, Mass., 1966—67, Athol-Royalston Regional Schs., Mass., 1967—68; invited designer, developer art curriculum Mt. Wachusett C.C., Gardner, Mass., 1968, chair art dept., 1968—97, prof. art, 1968—97, prof. emerita, 1997—. Pres. Richmond Cmty. Newsletter, NH, 1972—80. Watercolors and clay exhibited on regular basis Greentrees Gallery, Northfield, Mass., 1968—. Mt. Wachusett C.C. grantee, 1970-96, Fed. Govt. grantee, 1978; chosen for subject of Mount Wachusett C.C. Most Valuable Faculty Series Film; recipient honor for clay and painting Welkinwind Studios, Richmond, N.H. Mem. Women's Caucus for Art, Mass. CC Coun., Women in Arts, Tchg. Faculty Assn. (v.p. 1979-80, pres. 1980-81, grievance officer 1981-82, honored with a cast bronze for contbn. to art dept. as ongoing importance to coll.) Avocations: gardening, writing poetry and children's stories, reading, political activism. Address: Welkinwind Studios PO Box 2 Winchester NH 03470-0002

TANDY, KISHA RENEE, curator; b. Indpls., July 21, 1975; d. Floyd Allen Tandy, Shirley Ann Tandy. BA in Am. History, Ind. Purdue U., 1997, postgrad., 1997—. Summer asst. Ind. Hist. Soc., Indpls., 1997—97, 1998—98, 1999—99; exhbns. asst., 1998—98, edn. and pub. programming intern, 2000—01; collections intern Ruth Lilly Spl. Collections and Archives, Indpls., 1998—99, Morris-Butler House Mus., Indpls., 1999—2000; summer intern Riley Old Home Soc., Greencastle, Ind., 2000—00; asst. curator Ind. State Mus., Indpls., 2001—. Contbr. articles to profl. jours. Scholar, Indpls. Found., 1993—97, Minority Achievement scholar, Ind. U. Purdue U. Indpls., 1996—97, Zora Neale Hurstson-Mari Evans scholar, Ind. U. Purdue U. Sch. Liberal Arts, 1997—2000. Mem.: FIESTA Indianapolis, Inc., Ind. State Mus. Found., Ind. Hist. Soc., Ind. Freedom Trails, Ind. African Am. Genealogy Group, Hist. Landmarks Found. Ind., Am. Assn. for State and Local History. Avocation: reading. Office: Ind State Mus 650 W Washington St Indianapolis IN 46204 Business E-Mail: ktandy@dnr.state.in.us.

TANE, SUSAN JAFFE, retired manufacturing company executive; b. NYC; d. Irving and Beatrice (Albert) J.; m. Irwin R. Tane; children by previous marriage: Robert Wayne, Stephen Mark. BS, Boston U., 1964; postgrad., Hofstra U., C.W. Post U. Elem. sch. tchr., Long Beach, NY, 1964-67; pres. Fashions by Appointment, Glen Cove, NY, 1967-71; adminstrv. asst. Peerless Sales Corp., Elmont, NY, 1967-71; from sales mgr. to mktg. dir. United Utensils Co., Inc., Port Washington, NY, 1973-78; v.p. ops. and control United Molded Products divsn. United Utensils Co., Inc., Port Washington, 1978-80; v.p. mktg. Utensco, Port Washington, 1980-88. Bd. dirs. Peerless Aerospace Corp. Co-inventor plastic container and handling assembly. Life mem. Ronald McDonald House; friend N.Y. Pub. Libr.; pres. Susan Jaffe Tane Found., Am. Jewish Congress, sr. v.p.; life mem. Hadassah; chair Commn. for Women's Equality/Am. Jewish Congress; bd. dirs. Poe Found. Mem. Boston U. Alumni Assn., Cornell Weil Med. Coll., Ptnrs. in Leadership, Shareholder ASsn. Rsch. and Edn. Leadership Coun., Poe Studies Assn. (sponsor), Boston U. (sponsor poetry workshop), Lotos Club.

TANENBAUM, JUDITH HERTZ, psychiatrist; b. Denver, Sept. 27, 1958; d. Sanford B. Hertz and Phyllis M. Kippur; m. William A. Tanenbaum, June 15, 1986. BS, U. Colo., 1980, MS, 1981; cert. in Gen. Studies, Columbia U., 1984; MD, Cornell U., 1988. Diplomate Am. Bd. Psychiatry and Neurology, 1993. Intern NY Presbyn., NYC, 1988—92; pvt. practice psychiatrist NYC, 1992—. Recipient Spl. Achievement as Resident award, NIMH, 1992. Mem.: Am. Psychiat. Assn. Office: 930 Park Ave 1C New York NY 10028 Office Phone: 212-744-4818.

TANG, ESTHER DON, real estate developer, consultant, social worker; b. Tucson, Mar. 5, 1917; d. Don Wah and Yut (Gnan) Fok; m. David W. Tang, June 14, 1942; children: Patricia Karen Tang Crowley, Diana Cheryl Tang Simoes, David. Jr., Elizabeth Carol. Student, Draughn's Bus. Sch., San Antonio, 1936, U. Ariz., 1938-41. DHL, LHD, U. Ariz., 1992. Owner, operator supermarket, Tucson, 1940-66; exec. dir. Pio Decimo Ctr., Cath. Diocese, Tucson, 1966-85; cons., ptnr., vice chmn. bd. Netwest Devel. Corp., Tucson, 1985—. Prodr.: (video) Tapestry of Tucson (award winning). Mem. Tucson Airport Authority, 1975—, Pima County Crime and Pub. Safety Coun., 1999; chmn. Tucson-Taichung Sister Cities, 1979-91; chmn. Tucson Sister Cities Steering Com., 1984—, Sister Cities Assn. Tucson, 1990, Ariz. Pers. Bd.; chmn. bd. dirs. Pima Community Coll., 1975-85; pres. bd. dirs. Pima Coun. on Aging, 1986-90; coord. US Bicentennial, Tucson; mem. adv. bd. Ariz. Dept. Econ. Security; master of ceremonies to welcome Pres. Clinton, City of Tucson, 1999. Named Woman of Yr., City of Tucson, 1955, Woman of Yr. in Adminstrn., 1968, Lady Comdr. the Holy Sepluchre Jerusalem; recipient Disting. Friend of the Humanities award Nat. Adv. Bd., 1989, Jefferson award Ariz. Daily Star, 1987, Svc. award Pima Coun. on Aging, 1987-89, Disting. Svc. award U. Pima CC Found., 1988, Roots and Wings Cmty. award, 1988, Rosie award So. Ariz. Ctr. Against Sexual Assault, 1990, Lifetime Achievement award YWCA, 1992, 93, La Doña de los Descendientes del Precido de Tucson, 1997-98, centennial alumni award U. Ariz., 1998, Pan-Asian Cmty. Leadership award, 1999, Arthritis Humanitarian award, 1999, Altrusa Women in Svc. award, 2000, Asia Am. Times Devel. Mgmt. Excellence award, 2000, Voices into the Millennium award Ariz. Border Patrol, Dynamic Duo—Pointing Lives in New Directions award Compass Health Care, Congl. Recognition, 2002, Lulac Nat. Presdl. citation, 2002, award Agave Ariz. Hist. Tape TV, 2002, Lifetime award U. Ariz. Coll. Agr. and Life Sci., 2002; Learning Svc. Bldg. and Gallery named in her honor, U. Ariz., 2001; named Ariz. History Maker State of Ariz. Hist. League, 2003, 15th annual Cath. Found. Honoring Esther Don Tang, 2004; featured as an active activist Foothills Publ., 2005; named to Hall of Fame Tucson H.S. Badger Found., 2006. Mem. Soroptimist (hon., Women Who Helped Build Tucson award), Rotary Club Tucson (4 way test award 1998) Cath. Found. Diocese of Tucson (honorable mention, honoree Corner Stone Gala, 2004). Roman Catholic. Avocations: travel, cooking, golf. Home: 701 E Camino De Los Padres Tucson AZ 85718-1921

TANGUAY, JANET, recreational therapist, writer, filmmaker; b. Newport, Vt., Oct. 27, 1964; d. Marcel Maurice and Nancy Carol Tanguay. BA, u. Vt., 1986. Talk show prodr. WKXE-FM, White River Junction, Vt., 1986; asst. prodr. Northland Video Prodn., Lebanon, Vt., 1987-89, Mount View Prodns., Schenectady, N.Y., 1989-91; owner, pres. Studio J, Schenectady, 1991-94; mktg. rep. Adirondack Scenic, Glens Falls, N.Y., 1994; br. mgr. Manpower, Troy, N.Y., 1994—. Author: (children's book) Dustbunnies Don't Eat Carrots, 1998; screenwriter: Phoenix, 1999; prodr. promotional video. Mem., tutor Literacy Vols. Am., Schenectady, 1998—; mem. Sch.-to-Work Com., Troy, 1998—; mem. Voluntary Simplicity, Troy, 1998—. Mem. Rensselaer C. of C. (membership com. 1997-99), Upstate Inds. Avocations: tennis, film tai chi, yoga, weightlifting. Home: 13 Northampton Rd Amsterdam NY 12010-2401

TANIS, BARBARA ANN, science educator; b. Paterson, NJ, Sept. 4, 1945; d. Ralph Gerard and Irene (Stockinger) Marcantonio; children: Michael Stracco, Scott Stracco. BA in Sci. Edn., Jersey City State Coll., 1966; MEd, William Paterson U., 1992; postgrad., NJ City U., 2005. Sci. tchr. Dover (NJ) Pub. Schs., NJ, 1966—69, Caldwell (NJ)/West Caldwell Schs., 1971—74, Paterson Pub. Schs., 1984—; grant writer City of Paterson, 1974—84. Vice chmn. bd. trustees Passaic County CC, Paterson, Jerry Speziate Cmty. Outreach Fund., Wayne, NJ; Congressman William Pascrell Assemblywoman Alfred Steele, Paterson, 1987—96; mem. liaison com. Assemblywoman Nellie Pow, Paterson, 1997—2002, Assemblywoman Alfred Steele, Paterson, 1997—2002; vice chmn. Passaic County Dem. Commn. Recipient Harvey Nutter Humanitarian award, Interfaith Performance Art Ctr. Internat. Mem.: Passaic County Edn. Assn., Paterson Edn. Assn., NJ Edn. Assn., NEA. Roman Catholic. Avocations: reading, dance, travel. Home: 162 Katz Ave Paterson NJ 07502 Office Phone: 973-321-2390.

TANKARD, ELAINE F., editor, writing consultant; b. Cleve., Sept. 9, 1947; d. Robert Wynn Fuller and Antonette (Antonia) Breitschwerdt; m. James William Tankard, Jr., July 21, 1973; children: Amy Elizabeth Tankard Hill, Jessica Hope, Margaret Elaine. BS in Journalism, U. Fla., Gainesville, 1969; MA in Journalism, U. Tex., Austin, 1975. Tchr. ESL Head Start Program, Peace Corps, Palau, Babeldaup, Palau, 1969; editl. page writer Fla. Times-Union, Jacksonville, 1970—71; copywriter Lewis Advt. Agy., Mobile, Ala., 1971—72; tchg. asst. editing, dept. journalism U. Tex., Austin, 1972—74; prodn. editor Contemporary Psychology, Am. Psychol. Assn., Austin, 1975—79; instr. Journalism Southwest Tex. State U., San Marcos, 1980; editl. dir. Tankard Prodns., Austin, 1980—. Vis. co-editor Lampasas Dispatch-Record, Tex., 1974; freelance book editor Inst. Humanities, Salado, Tex., 1987—97. Contbr. articles to mag. and jour. Tutor Laubach Literacy, Jacksonville, 1970; vol. Alzheimer's Assn., Austin, 1992—2002; leader Girl Scouts, 1993—99; parent rep. AISD Gifted and Talented Com., Austin, 1994—99; v.p. Austin Assn. Gifted and Talented, 1996—97; apptd. mem. AISD Textbook Selection Com. on Spelling, Austin, 1997—98; vol. Bldg. Bridges com. Am. Cancer Soc.; elder Westminster Presbyn. Ch., 1992—; chair bd. dirs. Westminster Presbyn. Day Sch., Austin, 1986—87; bd. dirs. West Austin Caregivers, 2004—05. Mem.: Soc. Scholarly Pub. (charter mem.), Word Guild (founding mem.), Tex. Assn. Gifted and Talented, Writers' League Tex., Faculty Wives Club, U. Ladies Club, Savant U. Fla. (founding mem.), Phi Kappa Phi, Zeta Phi Eta, Theta Sigma Phi. Democrat. Presbyterian. Avocations: reading, travel, hiking, needlecrafts, watercolor. Office: Tankard Prodns 3300 Jamesborough St Austin TX 78703-1132 Office Phone: 512-453-6885.

TANKERSLEY, SARAH, lawyer; b. Radford, Va., Feb. 5, 1969; d. Ben Davis Jr. and Allie Gray Keen Eichelberger; m. Howard Litton Tankersley; children: Elizabeth Gray, Rachel Sue. BA, No. Ky. U., Highland Heights, 1993; JD, U. Ky., Lexington, 1997. Bar: Ohio 1997, Ky. 1998. Law clk. to Hon. Robert Kraft Hamilton County Ct. of Common Pleas, Cin., 1997—98; ptnr. Santen & Hughes, LPA, Cin., 1998—. Mem. svc. team Girl Scouts, Boone County, Ky., 1995. Mem.: Hamilton County Trial Lawyers Assn., Ohio Acad. Trial Lawyers, No. Ky. Bar Assn., Cin. Bar Assn. Office: Santen & Hughes LPA 312 Walnut St Ste 3100 Cincinnati OH 45202 Office Phone: 513-721-4450. Office Fax: 513-721-0109. E-mail: sbt@santen-hughes.com.

TANNEN, DEBORAH FRANCES, writer; b. Bklyn., June 7, 1945; d. Eli S. and Dorothy (Rosen) T. BA, SUNY, Binghamton, 1966; MA, Wayne State U., 1970, U. Calif., Berkeley, 1976; PhD, U. Calif., 1979. English instr. Mercer County C.C., Trenton, NJ, 1970-71; lectr. in acad. skills CUNY, Bronx, NY, 1971-74; asst. prof. Georgetown U., Washington, 1979-85, assoc. prof. linguistics, 1985-90, prof. linguistics, 1989-91, univ. prof., 1991—. McGraw disting. lectr. in writing Coun. for Humanities and dept. anthropology Princeton U., fall 1991; visitor Inst. for Advanced Study, Princeton, spring 1992; fellow Ctr. for Advanced Study in Behavioral Scis., Stanford, Calif., 1992-93. Author: Lilika Nakos, 1983, Conversational Style: Analyzing Talk Among Friends, 1984, That's Not What I Meant!: How Conversational Style Makes or Breaks Your Relations With Others, 1986, Talking Voices: Repetition, Dialogue and Imagery in Conversational Discourse, 1989, You Just Don't Understand: Women and Men in Conversation, 1990, Gender and Discourse, 1994, Talking From 9 to 5: Women and Men in the Workplace: Language, Sex and Power, 1994, The Argument Culture: Moving from Debate to Dialogue, 1998, The Argument Culture: Stopping America's War of Words, 1999, You're Wearing That? Understanding Mothers and Daughters in Conversation, 2006; editor: Analyzing Discourse: Text and Talk, 1982, Spoken and Written Language: Exploring Orality and Literacy, 1982, Coherence in Spoken and Written Discourse, 1984, Perspectives on Silence, 1985, Linguistics in Context: Connecting Observation and Understanding, 1988, Gender and Conversational Interaction, 1993, Framing In Discourse, 1993, (play) An Act of Devotion, 1994. Rockefeller Humanities fellow, 1982-83; grantee NEH, 1980, 85, 86; recipient Elizabeth Mills Crothers prize U. Calif., 1976, Dorothy Rosenberg Meml. prize U. Calif., 1977, Joan Lee Yang Meml. Poetry prize U. Calif., 1977, Shrout Short Story prize, 1978, Emily Chamberlain Cook prize, 1978. Office: Georgetown U Lang & Linguistics ICC Bldg Rm 471 37th & O St NW Washington DC 20057-0001 Office Phone: 202-687-5910. Business E-Mail: tannend@georgetown.edu.*

TANNEN, RICKI LEWIS, lawyer, psychologist, educator; b. N.Y.C., Apr. 29, 1952; d. Paul and Lillian (Singer) Lewis; m. Marc Jay Tannen, Aug. 25, 1972; children: Laine Amy, Adam Jesse. BA in Social Scis., U. Fla., 1975, MEd in Psycholinguistics, 1981, JD with honors, 1981; LLM, Harvard U., 1991; PhD, Pacifica Grad. Inst., 2002. Bar: Fla. 1982. Tchr., guidance counselor Oak Hall Pvt. Sch., Gainesville, Fla., 1976-79; atty., jud. clk. U.S. Dist. Cts., Miami, Fla., 1981-82; rep. assoc. Ft. Lauderdale (Fla.) News, Sun-Sentinel newspaper, Ferrero, Middlebrooks, Strickland & Fischer, 1982-88; of counsel Klein & Tannen, Hollywood, Fla., 1990-91; mem., 1992—. Mem. gender bias study commn. Fla. Supreme Ct., 1986, apptd. commr., reporter, 1987—; adj. prof. women and the law, media law, rhetoric, comm. law Fla. Atlantic U., 1984-88, 1995-2002; mem. faculty Chautauqua Instn., 1995-98; co-chmn. Fla. Bar Media Law Conf., 1996; rsch. coord. Ctr. for Govtl. Responsibility, Gainesville, 1979-81; bd. dirs. smashhitmusicco.com. Editor: Elderly Law in Florida, 1982; author: Report of the Florida Supreme Court Gender Bias Commn.; contbr. articles to profl. jours. Pres. Ctr. for Jungian Studies, 2002—; dir. Inner Work Studies Program, 1995—; dir. Communitas. Mem. APA, ABA, AAUW, NOW, Nat. Coun. Jewish Women, Fla. Bar Assn. (com. on equal opportunity 1988—), Fla. Assn. Women Lawyers, Assn. Psychol. Type, Assn. Transpersonal Psychology. Address: 9610 Conchshell Manor Plantation FL 33324 E-mail: rtannen@gate.net.

TANNENBAUM, BERNICE SALPETER, national religious organization executive; b. NYC; d. Isidore and May Franklin; 1 child, Richard Salpeter. BA, Bklyn. coll. Chmn. Commn. on the Status of Women of the World Jewish Congress; mem. exec. bd. Am. sect. World Jewish Congress; chmn. internat. affairs com.; mem. Zionist Gen. Coun.; active Exec. World Zionist Orgn. Bd. dirs., mem. gen. assembly Jewish Agy.; bd. dirs., v.p. United Israel Appeal; mem. exec. com. Am. Zionist Movement; former chair Hadassah mag.; nat. pres. Hadassah, 1976-80; nat. chmn. Hadassah Internat., 1984-95; liaison Hadassah Found.; sec. Jewish Telegraphic Agy.; bd. govs. Hebrew U. Office: Hadassah 50 W 58th St New York NY 10019-2590

TANNENBAUM, JUDITH NETTIE, writer, educator; b. Chgo., Feb. 13, 1947; d. Robert and Edith (Lazaroff) Tannenbaum; 1 child, Sara Rachel Press. BA, U. Calif., Berkeley, 1968; MA, Sonoma State U., 1979. Cert. c.c. tchr. Calif. Artist-in-residence San Quentin State Prison, Tamal, Calif., 1986—89, Calif. Arts Coun., Albany, 1993—96; tng. coord. WritersCorps, San Francisco, 1993—; artist-in-residence Albany Schs., 1996—. Author: Disguised as a Poem: My Years Teaching Poetry at San Quentin, 2000, Teeth Wiggly as Earthquakes: Writing Poetry in the Primary Grades, 2000. Mem.: PEN West, Calif. Poets in the Schs. Home: 3120 Yosemite El Cerrito CA 94530

TANNENBAUM, KAREN JEAN, library services supervisor; b. Evansville, Ind., Mar. 5, 1962; d. William J. and Mary Katherine Doom. MLS, Ind. U., 1995. Dir. youth svcs. Knox County Pub. Libr., Vincennes, Ind., 1996—98; supr. youth svcs. Evansville(Ind.) Vanderburgh Pub. Libr., Ind., 1998—. Reviewer: Sch. Libr. Jour., 2001. Mem. edn. com. Evansville Philharm. Guild; part-time cantorial soloist Temple Adath B'nai, Evansville, 2001—. Mem.: ALA-Young Adult Libr. Svcs. Assn. (mem. young adult outreach com.), ALA-Assn. Libr. Svcs. for Children (mem. presch. and parent edn. com. 2000—03, best books for young adults com. 2003—, mem. best books for young adults com.), AAUW (Evansville br., pres. 2000—02), Goodwill Ladies Aux., Hadassah (life; bd. dirs. 2001—, pres. 2002, Evansville chpt.). Jewish. Avocations: cantoring, travel, creative writing, reading. Office: 55 SE 5th St Evansville IN 47708-1603

TANNENBAUM, REBECCA JO, historian, writer; d. Theodore and Shirley Ann Tannenbaum; m. Charles David Bailyn, Dec. 18, 1993; 1 child, Jane Swope Bailyn. BA, Wesleyan U., Middletown, Conn., 1984; MPhil, PhD, Yale U., New Haven, 1997. Asst. prof. U. Ill., Chgo., 1997—2000; lectr. Yale U., New Haven, 2001—. Cons. Old North Ch., Boston, 2005—. Mem. editl. bd.: Commonplace: An Interactive Jour. Am. Life, 1998—2002; contbr. articles to profl. jours. Mem.: Am. Hist. Assn., Orgn. Am. Historians. Avocations: travel, birdwatching, poetry. Office: Yale University Dept History PO Box 208324 New Haven CT 06520 Office Phone: 203-432-1662. Personal E-mail: rebecca.tannenbaum@yale.edu.

TANNENWALD, LESLIE KEITER, rabbi, justice of peace, educational association administrator, chaplain; b. Boston, May 5, 1949; d. Irving Jules and Barbara June (Caplan) Keiter; m. Robert Tannenwald. BA, Brandeis U., 1971, MA, 1976; MA in Edn. and Counseling, Simmons Coll., Boston, 1972. Cert. social worker, tchr., Mass.; justice of the peace. Sr. assoc. Combined Jewish Philanthropies of Greater Boston, 1977-84; ednl. cons. Bur. Jewish Edn., Boston, 1985-87; ednl. dir. Congregation Shalom Emeth, Burlington, Mass., 1987-92; religious sch. dir. Falmouth (Mass.) Jewish Congregation, 1993-99; pres. Jewish Life Svcs., Newton, Mass., 1993—; rabbi, religious leader Sherborn Congregation, 1995—97, Congregation Agudath Achim, Medway, 1999—2001, Temple Emmanuel, Chelsea, 2001—. Cons. Selected Ednl. Orgns., Boston, 1972; chaplain, rabbi to local nursing home facilities. Author: Curriculum, Male and Female, 1979 (Honors award 1971), Understanding the Holocaust, 1990, Awakening: Alternative Creative Learning Techniques, 1995. Officer, bd. dirs. Combined Jewish Philanthropies of Greater Boston, 1972—; title of damsel Imperial Order St. John Ecumenical Found. Recipient Leadership award Inst. Leadership Devel. and Fund Raising Mem. Nat. Alliance Profl. and Exec. Women, Alumni Assn. Benjamin S. Hornstein Program Jewish Communal Svc., Assn. Jewish Cmty. Pers., Am. Jewish Congress. Democrat. Avocations: swimming, watercolor painting, music. Home: 6 Clifton Rd Newton MA 02459-3147 Office Phone: 617-559-9746. E-mail: rabbiles18@aol.com.

TANNER, HELEN HORNBECK, historian, consultant; b. Northfield, Minn., July 5, 1916; d. John Wesley and Frances Cornelia (Wolfe) Hornbeck; m. Wilson P. Tanner, Jr., Nov. 22, 1940 (dec. 1977); children: Frances, Margaret Tanner Tewson, Wilson P., Robert (dec. 1983) AB with honors, Swarthmore Coll., 1937; MA, U. Fla., 1949; PhD, U. Mich., 1961. Asst. to dir. pub. rels. Kalamazoo Pub. Schs., 1937-39; with sales dept. Am. Airlines Inc., N.Y.C., 1940-43; tchg. fellow, then tchg. asst. U. Mich., Ann Arbor, 1949-53, 57-60, lectr. ext. svc., 1961-74, asst. dir. Ctr. Continuing Edn. for Women, 1964-68; project dir. Newberry Libr., Chgo., 1976-81, rsch. assoc., 1981-95, sr. rsch. fellow, 1995—. Expert witness in Indian treaty litig., 1963—; dir. D'Arcy McNickle Ctr. for Indian History, 1984-85; mem. Mich. Commn. Indian Affairs, 1966-70; cons. in field Author: Zespedes in East Florida 1784-1790, 1963, 89, General Green Visits St. Augustine, 1964, The Greeneville Treaty, 1974, The Territory of the Caddo Tribe of Oklahoma, 1974, The Ojibwas, 1992; editor: Atlas of Great Lakes Indian History, 1987, The Settling of North America: An Atlas, 1995. Named to Mich. Women's Hall of Fame, 2006; NEH grantee, 1976, fellow, 1989; ACLS grantee, 1990. Mem. Am. Soc. Ethnohistory (pres. 1982-83), St. Augustine Hist. Soc., Conf. L.Am. History, Soc. History Discoveries, Chgo. Map Soc., Hist. Soc. Mich. Home: 5178 Crystal Dr Beulah MI 49617-9618 Personal E-mail: hhtanner@charter.net.

TANNER, JOANNE ELIZABETH, psychologist, researcher; b. Tulsa, Apr. 27, 1944; d. Eugene Simpson T. and Ada Charlotte (Thomas) Jaquet; m. Clarence Cooper, June 14, 1965 (div. 1976); 1 child, Duncan; m. Charles Ernest, Apr. 24, 1987. MusB, Oberlin Coll., 1965; postgrad., U. Calif., Santa Cruz, 1989-91; PhD, U. St. Andrews, Scotland, 1998. Rsch. asst. Gorilla Found., Woodside, Calif., 1981-92; postgrad. teaching asst. in anthropology U. Calif., Santa Cruz, 1989-92. Lectr. Gorilla Found., 1984-92; symphony violinst, various cities, 1965-89; pvt. violin tchr., Cupertino, Calif., 1980-92; instr. violin Met. State Coll., Denver, 1967-72. Contbr. articles to profl. jours. Achievements include research in gestural communication of zoo gorillas. Home: 3071 Dover Dr Santa Cruz CA 95065-2014 Office: U Saint Andrews Scottish Primate Rsch Group Saint Andrews KY169JU Scotland

TANNER, LAUREL NAN, education educator; b. Detroit, Feb. 16, 1929; d. Howard Nicholas and Celia (Solovich) Jacobson; m. Daniel Tanner, July 11, 1948; m. Kenneth J. Rehage, Nov. 25, 1989. BS in Social Sci, Mich. State U., 1949, MA in Edn., 1953; EdD, Columbia U., 1967. Pub. sch. tchr., 1950-64; instr. tchr. edn. Hunter Coll., 1964-66, asst. prof., 1967-69; supr. Milw. Pub. Schs., 1966-67; mem. faculty Temple U., Phila., 1969—, prof. edn., 1974-89, prof. emerita, 1993—; prof. edn. U. Houston, 1989-96. Vis. professorial scholar U. London Inst. Edn., 1974—75; vis. scholar Stanford U., 1984—85, U. Chgo., 1988—89; curriculum cons., 1969—; disting. vis. prof. San Francisco State U., 1987. Author: Classroom Discipline for Effective Teaching and Learning, 1978, La Disciplina en la enseñanza y el Aprendizaje, 1980, Dewey's Laboratory School: Lessons for Today, 1997; co-author: Classroom Teaching and Learning, 1971, Curriculum Development: Theory into Practice, 1975, 4th edit., 2006, Supervision in Education: Problems and Practices, 1987, (with Daniel Tanner) History of the School Curriculum, 1990; editor Nat. Soc. Study Edn. Critical Issues in Curriculum, 87th yearbook, part 1, 1988. Faculty rsch. fellow Temple U., 1970, 80, 81; recipient John Dewey Rsch. award, 1981-82, Rsch. Excellence award U. Houston, 1992, Outstanding Writing award Am. Assn. Colls. Tchr. Edn., 1998; Spencer Found. rsch. grantee, 1992. Mem. ASCD (dir. 1982-84), Soc. Study Curriculum History (founder, 1st pres. 1978-79), Am. Edn. Rsch. Assn. (com. on role and status of women in ednl. R & D 1994-97), Profs. Curriculum Assn. (Factotum 1983-84, chair membership com. 1994-95), Am. Ednl. Studies Assn., John Dewey Soc. (bd. dirs. 1989-91, pres. 2000-01), Alumni Coun. Tchrs. Coll. Columbia U.

TANNER, LYNN, actress; b. NYC, Mar. 22, 1953; d. Harry J. and Barbara Sylvia (Hirschman) Maurer; m. Allen Barry Witz, Aug. 31, 1975. BS, NYU, 1975; JD, DePaul U., 1980. Bar: Ill. 1980. Actress, various, 1980—; chair, pres., CEO, Artists Funding Group, Inc. Actor: (films) Human Error, 1987, Another Time, Another Place, 1988, Twisted, 1995; (TV series, pilot) Hollywood Flat; (plays) Pack of Lies, Back at the Blue Dolphin Saloon, Toyer, Burying Rose, Dolores and Her Loved Ones, Final Placement, Facing the Dragon, The Workroom, Sign in Sidney Brusteins Window, Summer and Smoke, The Maids, Under Milkwood, Dark at the Top of the Stairs, Rosa; co-author: (screenplays) Wrong Turn, Tessa Deare, Reasons; co-prodr.: Hollywood Flat; dir.: (plays) Dickens, A Christmas Story, 2003. Pres./CEO Artists Funding Group Inc.; pres., CEO The Gambian Bridge to Hope. Mem. SAG, AFTRA, Actors Equity Assn., Women in Film, Women in Theatre, Ill. Bar Assn. Office Phone: 310-785-9079. E-mail: lynnjettstar@gmail.com.

TANNER-OLIPHANT, KAREN M., family and consumer science educator; children: Christopher Oliphant, Michael Oliphant. BS mgana cum laude, Hampton U., 1977; MA in Edn. Adminstrn, Seton Hall U., South Orange, N.J., 2006; postgrad., Kean U., Union, N.J. Cert. home econ. edn. NJ. Tchr. family and consumer sci. Paterson Bd. Edn., NJ, 1977—82; mktg. specialist IBM Corp, Dallas, 1983—93; tchr. family and consumer sci. Roselle Bd. Edn., NJ, 1993—. Coord. character edn. ACHS. Named Tchr. of Yr., N.J. Assn. Family and Consumer Scis., 2000, ACHS Tchr. of Yr., Gov. N.J., 2002; recipient Role Model award, NAACP, 2004. Mem.: Family, Cmty. Career, Leaders of Am. (advisor, ACHS chpt. advisor, Advisor Recognition award), Am. Assn. Family and Consumer Scis. (bd. trustees 1995—), The Links, Inc. (past chpt. pres., past chmn. com.), Alpha Kappa Mu, Alpha Kappa Alpha (past officer, chmn. com.). Avocations: event planning, cooking, mentoring culinary career graduates. Office: Roselle Bd Edn 710 Locust St Roselle NJ 07203

TANNERY, GINGER, art educator; b. Dallas, May 15, 1956; d. William Adam McCommas and Lenora (Bothwell) Vilbig; m. Myron Kent Tannery, Oct. 13, 1986 (div. May 1999); children: Heather Elizabeth, Kyle Adam, Clayton. BS in Horticulture, Stephen F. Austin State U., 1988, MEd, 2000, mid mgmt. cert., 2000. Cert. tchr. Stephen F. Austin State U. Art tchr. Diboll (Tex.) Ind. Sch. Dist., 1994—. Strategic planning bd. Diboll Ind. Sch. Dist., 1997-98, tech. com., 1997—, lead tchr., 1999-2000. Recipient scholarship Houston Livestock and Rodeo, Tex., 1987-88, scholarship Delta Tau Alpha Agr. Honor Soc., 1986-88. Mem. Tex. State Tchrs. Assn., Assn. for Supervision and Curriculum Devel., Tex. Computer Edn. Assn., Bus. and Profl. Women's Assn., Phi Delta Kappa. Roman Catholic. Avocations: watercoloring, jewelry, teaching sunday school, working out, extra-curricular school activities. Home: 3906 Maid Marion Ln Nacogdoches TX 75965-2324 Office: Diboll Jr HS 403 Dennis St Diboll TX 75941-2123 E-mail: gtannery@diboll.esc7.net.

TANOUE, DONNA A., bank executive, former federal agency administrator; BA, U. Hawaii, 1977; JD, Georgetown U., 1981. Spl. dep. atty. gen. Dept. Commerce and Consumer Affairs, Hawaii, 1981-83; commr. financial inst. State of Hawaii, 1983-87; ptnr. Goodsill Anderson Quinn & Stifel, Hawaii, 1987-98; chmn. FDIC, Washington, 1998—2002; vice chmn. Bank of Hawaii, 2002—. Office: PO Box 2900 Honolulu HI 96846-6000

TANOUS, MELISSA LYNN, science educator; b. Olean, N.Y., Jan. 25, 1974; d. Michael David and Cathy Lee Tanous. BS in Biochemistry, Tex. A&M U., 1996; MS in Biochemistry, Case Western Res. U., 2000. Chemistry instr. Cuyahoga C.C., Cleve., 2000—02; tchr. Hockaday Sch., Dallas, 2002—, level coord., 2005—, load and compensation com., 2005—. Instrnl. design New Ho. Comm. and Freelance, Cleveland Heights, Ohio, 2000—02; presenter nat. indep. sch. conf. Prayer com. veritas calss Pk. Cities Presbyn. Ch., Dallas, 2004—06, bible study leader, 2005—06, ch. liason internat. student ministry, 2006. Grantee, NSF, 2003. Mem.: NSTA (assoc.). Office: Hockaday Sch 11600 Welch Rd Dallas TX 75229 Office Phone: 214-360-6431.

TANTILLO, MARY DARLENE, nurse; b. Rochester, N.Y., July 28, 1960; d. Salvatore Augustus and Constance Tantillo; m. Odysseus Adamides, Oct. 2, 1993; 1 child, Odysseus Alexander Adamides. AAS in Nursing, Monroe C.C., Rochester, NY, 1980; BS in Nursing, Nazareth Coll. Rochester, NY, 1982; MS in Psychiat. Mental Health Nursing, U. Rochester Sch. Nursing, NY, 1986; PhD, Adelphi U., Garden City, N.Y., 1992. Profl. RN, N.Y., 1980. Nurse mgr. behavioral medicine unit U. Rochester/Strong Meml. Hosp., 1985—86, clinician II clin. nurse specialist cons., 1986—90, assoc. dir. adult ambulatory svcs.-psychiatry, 1990—94, adminstrv. dir. ambulatory svcs.-psychiatry, 1994—98, dir. eating disorder treatment svc., 1997—2000; dir. eating disorders program Unity Health Sys. Dept. Psychiatry and Behavioral Health, Rochester, 2000—, dir. We. N.Y. Comprehensive Care Ctr. for Eating Disorders, 2005—. Chair legis. com. Rochester Area Psychiat. Mental Health Nurse Clin. Specialist Group, 1986—94; chairperson Rochester Consortium on Eating Disorders, 1990—93; coord. Jean Baker Miller Tng. Inst. Rsch. Network, Wellesley, Mass., 1996—; pres., bd. dirs. Mental Health Assn., Rochester, 2002—05; bd. dirs. Acad. Eating Disorders, Northbrook, Ill., 2002—05, chairperson credentialing task force, 2004—; clin. assoc. prof. psychiatry U. Rochester Med. Ctr., 2004—; co-chair Rochester Eating Disorders Cmty. Adv. Bd., 2004—. Mem. mental health outreach Spiritus Christi Ch., Rochester, 2000—. Recipient Ann. Outstanding Nurse award for Excellence in Patient and Family Nursing, U. Rochester Dept. Psychiat. Nursing, 1984, Rsch. award, Sigma Theta Tau Internat. Inc. Epsilon xi Chpt., 1996, Gottschalk Mental Heatlh Rsch. award, Mental Health Assn., 1996, Excellence in the Treatment of Eating Disorders, Excellus, Blue Cross/Blue Shield of Rochester, 2002—, Woman of Influence in Health Care, Girl Scouts Genesee Valley, Inc., 2005; fellow, Acad. Eating Disorders, 2003. Fellow: Acad. Eating Disorders; mem.: Nat. Ctr. Addictions and Substance Abuse, Nat. Alliance for the Mentally Ill, Nat. Eating Disorders Assn., AAUW, Sigma Theta Tau Internat., Wellesley Centers for Women, Nat. Registry Cert. Group Psychotherapists, Jean Baker Miller Tng. Inst., Am. Group Psychotherapy Assn., Rochester Area Group Psychotherapy Soc., Genesee Valley Nurses Assn. Democrat-Npl. Catholic. Avocations: bicycling, hiking, dance, swimming, crafts. Office: Unity Health System Dept of Psychiatry 835 W Main St Rochester NY 14611 Office Phone: 585-368-6550 8590. Office Fax: 585-368-6540. Business E-Mail: mtantillo@unityhealth.org.

TANUR, JUDITH MARK, sociologist, educator; b. Jersey City, Aug. 12, 1935; d. Edward Mark and Libbie (Berman) Mark; m. Michael Isaac Tanur, June 2, 1957; children: Rachel Dorothy, Marcia Valerie. BS, Columbia U., 1957, MA, 1963; PhD, SUNY, Stony Brook, 1972. Analyst Biometrics Rsch., N.Y.C., 1955-67; lectr. SUNY, Stony Brook, 1967-71, from asst. prof. to prof. sociology, 1971-94, disting. teaching prof., 1994—2006. Cons. NBC, N.Y.C., 1976—89, Lang. of Data Project, Los Altos, Calif., 1980—89, Inst. for Rsch. on Learning, 1994—95; mem. com. on nat. stats. NAS, 1980—87, com. on applied and theoretical stats., 1997—2000; trustee NORC, U. Chgo., 1987—; bd. dirs. Social Sci. Rsch. Coun., 2000—06; mem. adv. com. SBE, NSF, 2000—06. Author: The Subjectivity of Scientists and the Bayesian Approach, 2001; editor: Statistics: A Guide to the Unknown, 1972, Internat. Encyclopedia of Statistics, 1978, Cognitive Aspects of Survey Methodology, 1984, Questions About Questions, 1991, Cognition and Survey Research, 1999, Internat. Ency. of Social Scis., 1963—67; contbr. articles to sci., stats., and social sci. jours. Bd. dirs. Vis. Nurse Svc., Great Neck, N.Y., 1970-2000; bd. govs. Gen. Soc. Survey, Chgo., 1989-92. Sr. rsch. fellow, Am. Statis. Assn./NSF/Bur. Labor Stats., 1988—89. Fellow AAAS, Am. Statis. Assn. (Founders award 1997); mem. Internat. Statis. Inst., Phi Beta Kappa. Home: PO Box 280 Montauk NY 11954 Office: SUNY Dept Sociology Stony Brook NY 11794-4356 Office Phone: 631-632-7738. Business E-Mail: jtanur@notes.cc.sunysb.edu.

TANZI, ELIZABETH LYN, dermatologist; b. West Islip, N.Y., Jan. 1, 1970; d. Joseph and Lyn Tanzi; m. Peter A. Pinto, Aug. 25; 1 child, Peter Joseph Pinto. BS, Hartnick Coll., Oneonta, N.Y., 1992; MD, Syracuse Med. Sch., N.Y., 1996. Diplomate Am. Bd. Dermatology. Resident in dermatology Columbia U., N.Y.C., 2001; co-dir. laser surgery Washington Inst. Dermatologic Laser Surgery, 2001—. Home: 5503 Alta Vista Rd Bethesda MD 20814-1612

TANZMAN, MARY, social worker; b. Bialystok, Poland, Sept. 29, 1915; came to U.S., 1920; d. Jacob and Bertha (Cohen) Grodman; m. Jack Tanzman, Feb. 22, 1942; children: Elaine, Edward. BA in Social Work, Wayne State U., 1939; MSW, U. Chgo., 1964. Social worker, dist. supr. Jewish Family and Community Services, Chgo., 1942-49; dir. social work marital dept. Forest Hosp., Des Plaines, Ill., 1959-64; pvt. practice social work Evanston, Ill., 1955—. Cons. in field. Fellow Am. Orthopsychiat. Assn. (life); mem. NASW, Am. Assn. Marital and Family Therapists (clin.). Home: 2960 N Lake Shore Dr Apt 3203 Chicago IL 60657-5664

TAPIA, JO-DI LYNN, secondary school educator; b. Kans. City, Mo., May 19, 1956; d. Alvin Joseph and Diane Grace (Rossi) Johnson; m. Leslie Franklin Tapia, June 22, 1985; children: Christina Marie, Brian Joseph. BA, U. Colo., Boulder, 1978; M in Health, U. No. Colo., Greeley, 1988. Cert. tchr. Colo. Tchr. Mountain Range HS, Northglenn, Colo., 1982—. H.S. gymnastics official, Denver, 1982—. Mem.: Am. Alliance for Health, Phys. Edn., Recreation and Dance. Business E-Mail: jo-di.tapia@adams12.org.

TAPIA PARKER, CARRIE-ANNE, massage therapist, healthcare educator; d. Gregory Allen and Christine Johnson (Stepmother); m. Jon E Parker, May 14, 2004; children: Isaac S Tapia, Corrina N Tapia, Daniel A Tapia. Lic. massage therapist Calif., 2002, cert. nutritional cons. Calif., 2006. Med. massage therapist in pvt. practice, Redlands, Calif., 2000—; holistic healthcare practitioner, 2000—; nutrition cons., 2005—; clin. aromatherapy practitioner, 2000—; herbal grower and product formulator Calif. Essentials, Redlands, Calif., 2005—; life coach. Adv. bd. mem. Concorde Career Inst., San Bernardino, Calif., 2003—04. Author: (on line health journal) Holistic Life & Times. Contbg mem. United Ch., L.A., 2001—06; elem. sch. site coun. Franklin Elem., Redlands, 2003—06. Independent. Achievements include development of Therapeutic herbal skin care; research in effects of essential oil therapy on stroke patients; effects of essential oil therapy on female depressive disorders; therapeutic nutrition's impact on immunity of children under 15; the health impact of a holistic lifestyle on adolescent development . Avocations: gardening, reading, writing, cuisine, dance. Office: Ca Essentials 466 N Orange St # 324 Redlands CA 92374 Office Phone: 909-534-3656. Personal E-mail: carrieannetapia@hotmail.com.

TAPKEN, MICHELLE G., prosecutor; BA in Edn., U. SD, 1967, MA in Ednl. Psychology, 1970, JD, 1989. Bar: South Dakota; lic. Psychologist. Fed. law clerk, Lincoln, Nebr., 1989—90; prosecutor US Atty. Office, Sioux Falls, SD, 1990—2001; interim US atty. Dist. SD US Dept. Justice, 2001, 2002, 1st asst. US atty. Dist. SD, 2005—. Recipient Director's award, US Dept. Justice, 1996, 2006. Office: 325 S 1st Ave Sioux Falls SD 57104

TAPP, MAMIE PEARL, educational association administrator; b. Aiken, SC, July 20, 1955; d. Willie Lee and Nancy (Madison) Garrett; m. Anthony Karl Tapp, Aug. 13, 1983; children: Anthony K. II, Barry Garrett, Myles Jarvis. BA, CUNY, 1977; MA, New Sch. for Social Rsch., 1984; student, Nova Southeastern U., 1994—2000. Flight attendant Capitol Airlines, Jamaica, N.Y., 1976-81; pers. assoc. Cmty. Svc. Soc., N.Y.C., 1982-83; pers. specialist Marriott Hotel, Tampa, Fla., 1983-84; dir. placement Tampa Coll., 1984-86, facility coord., 1986-87, compliance officer, 1987-88; career counselor Alpha House, Tampa, 1988-91; career specialist U. Tampa, 1991-96, adj. prof., 1992-93; career specialist Jr. Achievement Greater Tampa, Inc., Tampa, 1996—, tchr. asst. program adv. com. mem., 1996-98; area mgr. BBBS, Belcamp, Md., 2004—05. Tchr. asst. program adv. com. Hillsborough H.S., 1996-97; sr. edn. svc. mgr. Jr. Achievement, 1997-2004; faculty U. Phoenix, 2005. Author: (novels) Resumes, 1992, Cover Letters, 1991, Thank You Letters, 1992, (poetry) Inner Peace, 1999; co-editor: I Cried, 2001, Life, 2002. Bd. dirs. Children's Mus. Tampa, 1992-94; com. mem. United Way, Tampa, 1994-95; mem. bd. St. Peter Claver Cath. Sch., Tampa, 1995-99, exec. com. Glee Club, 1995; vol. Scout troop leader, 1997-98. Recipient Outstanding Bus. Woman award Am. Bus. Women's Assn., Tampa, 1987, Cmty. Svc. award Tampa Connections, 1993, Editor's Choice award Internat. Libr. of Poetry, 1999. Mem.: AAUW, Fla. Assn. Women in Edn., Am. Vocat. Assn. Roman Catholic. Avocations: reading, sewing. Office: Appollo Group Inc 4324 Marigold Ln Belcamp MD 21017 Personal E-mail: tapptbjpt@earthlink.net.

TARAKI, SHIRLEE, librarian; b. Chgo., Apr. 25, 1922; d. Frank and Leah (Simon) Heda; m. Mohamed Rasul Taraki, June 3, 1944 (dec. Aug. 1972); children: Lisa, Yosuf. BA in Psychology, U. Chgo., 1943, MA in Edn., 1947. Instr. English, Ministry of Edn., Kabul, Afghanistan, 1947-65, materials technician, 1965-72; libr. asst. Northwestern U., Evanston, Ill., 1973-90; libr. Ctr. for Women's Health St. Francis Hosp., Evanston, 1990-95. Producer slide presentation An American Woman in Afghanistan, 1974—. Vol. Mather Pavilion at Wagner, Evanston, 1993—; mem. Evanston Comm. on Aging, 1999-2003. Mem. NOW (Evanston-North Shore chpt., founder), Circle Pines Ctr., Afghanistan Reconstrn. Support Com. (co-chair), Afghan Women's Task Force (founder, chair), Amnesty Internat., Phi Beta Kappa. Avocations: music, needlecrafts.

TARANTO, MARIA ANTOINETTE, psychology researcher, educator; b. Framingham, Mass., Dec. 28, 1941; d. Gaetano (Tom) Peter and Rose Marie (Busceme) T.; m. John Curtis Mahon, June 5, 1988. BA in Psychology, Bennington Coll., 1965; MA in Psychology, George Peabody Coll., 1968; M Philosophy in Psychology, Columbia U., 1981, PhD, 1985. Tchr. Head Start Pub Sch. System, Pitts., 1966-67; rsch. assoc. Hofstra U., Hempstead, NY, 1968-69, instr., 1969-72; co-dir. Inst. for Piagetian Studies, Hempstead, 1972-76; instr. Nassau C.C., Garden City, NY, 1976-78, asst prof., 1978-85, assoc. prof. psychology, 1985-95, prof. emeritus, 1996—. Jour. reviewer Baywood Pub. Co., Long Island, N.Y., 1989, Karger, Basel, Switzerland, 1989. Contbr. articles to profl. jours. Mem. Union of Concerned Scientists, 1981—, Amnesty Internat., 1987—; sponsor Pearl S. Buck Found., 1984—; hon. pres. Eoliano Mus. Emigrazione, Salina, Italy. Recipient Mellon fellowship CUNY, N.Y.C., 1987, Woman of Yr. award Sicilia Mondo Soc., 2004. Mem. APA, Jean Piaget Soc., Gerontol. Soc., New Eng. Psychol. Assn., Filicudi Assn. (pres. 2002—) Avocations: hiking, gardening, picniking, cooking. Personal E-mail: minervasowl2@earthlink.net.

TARASENKO, OLGA, biologist, educator; d. Elizaveta Grebenyuk; m. Pierre Alusta. MD, Kyrgyz State Med. Acad., Kyrgyzstan, 0190, PhD, 1998. Postoctoral rsch. assoc. Poly. U., N.Y., 2001—05; asst. prof. U. Ark., Little Rock, 2005—. Mentor biology club U. Ark., 2005—06. Named Exceptional Inventions award, Govt. of Kyrgyz Republic, State Agy. of Sci. and Intellectual Properties, 2004; recipient Med. Student Conf. First prize, Kyrgyz State Med. Acad., 1990, Appreciation cert., Polytechnic U., 2002; fellow, Union Hematological Ctr., Moscow, Russia, 1991, Rsch. Inst. Hematology and Blood Transfusion, St. Petersburg, Russia, 1991, 1992; grantee, European Sch. Transfusion Medicine, 1993; scholar, Asian Devel. Bank, 1999—2001. Mem.: Am. Soc. Biology and Biochemistry, Kyrgyz Soc. Allergy and Immunology (assoc.), MidSouth Computational Biology and Bioinformatics Soc. (assoc. grantee 2006), Am. Soc. Microbiology (assoc.), Sigma Xi Sci. Rsch. Soc. (assoc.). Achievements include research in detection and inhibition of bacterial spores; patents for protective immunogenetics factors against tuberculosis; patents pending for glycoconjugate sensors; inhibitors of spore-forming pathogens; destruction of spores through glycoconjugate enhanced phagocytosis. Office: University of Arkansas at Little Rock 2801 South University Little Rock AR 72204 Office Phone: 501-569-3504.

TARASIEWICZ, TAMARA, painter; b. Hajnowka, Poland, Feb. 23, 1950; arrived in US, 1996; d. Wlodzimierz and Anastazja Rygorowicz; m. Sergiusz Tarasiewicz, Aug. 28, 1976; children: Radek, Anna. ADN, Med. Sch., Poland, 1970; B, Tchrs. Med. Sch., Poland, 1976; M, Med. Academy, Poland, 1982. Nurse ZOZ, Hajnowka, Poland, 1982—88; painter Bialowieza, Poland, 1988—96; art gallery dir. Forest Mus. and Gallery, 1994—96; painter Chgo., 1997—; art gallery dir. Tammy's Gallery, 1998—2001. Contbg. artist New Art International, 2002—05; one-woman shows include, Poland, Russia, France, Germany, US, 1991—, Tamara Tarasiewicz Art, Byelorussian TV, 1992—; contbr. art to popular mags., chapters to books. Recipient Cert. Recognition, George H. Ryan Office Gov., Chgo., 2001—02, Cook County Treas. Maria Pappas, Chgo., 2005, First prize of Art of Hajnowaka Region, Poland, 1992—93, Bialowieza Mayor award, Dist. Bialowieza, Poland, 1993. Mem.: Art Inst. Chgo., Nat. Mus. Women in Arts, Oil Painters of America, No. Ind. Arts Assn., Tall Grass Arts Assn. Personal E-mail: anix@netzero.net.

TARASUK, PENELOPE ANTOINETTE, psychoanalyst, artist; b. Washington, Oct. 21, 1947; d. Francis Joseph Tarasuk and Patricia Ann (Maher) Donohoe; children: Jesse Alexander, Gabriel. BA, U. Md., 1972, MA, 1973; PhD in psychoanalysis, Internation U., 2002. Jungian psychoanalyst Internat. Assn. of Analyst Psychology, Santa Fe, 1994—2005. Pro bono cons. Santa Fe Animal Shelter Humane Soc., 1998—2005. Mem.: Internat. Assn. of Analytical Psychoanalysts. Avocations: writing, poetry, photography, art, nature. Home: 8 Mountain Rd South Deerfield MA 01373 Personal E-mail: life4dream@gmail.com.

TARBUCK, BARBARA JOAN, actress; b. Detroit, Jan. 15, 1942; d. George and Ruth Erma (Fillmore) T.; m. James Denis Connolly, May 17, 1980; 1 child, Jennifer Lane. B of Philosophy, Wayne State U., 1963; MA, U. Mich., 1965; postgrad., Ind. U., 1965-66. Author: (children's play) Who Am I?, 1972; Author/actor: They Call Me Dr. Greer, 1994; Actress:(TV movies) The Cracker Factory, 1979, Mrs. R's Daughter, 1979, A Christmas Without Snow, 1980, Between Two Loves, 1982, Victims for Victims: The Theresa Saldana Story, 1984, Out of Time, 1988, David, 1988, I Know My First Name is Steven, 1989, Death of the Incredible Hulk, 1990, A House of Secrets and Lies, 1992, A Child Lost Forever: The Jerry Sherwood Story, 1992, Jack Reed: Badge of Honor, 1993, Moment of Truth: Eye of the Stalker, 1995, Seduced by Madness: The Diane Borchardt Story, 1996, Before He Wakes, 1998, Mr. Murder, 1998, Just Ask My Children, 2001; (films) Short Circuit, 1986, Big Trouble, 1986, Curly Sue, 1991, Midnight Witness, 1993, Scanner Cop II, 1995, Tie That Binds, 1995, Legend of Razorback, 2002, Tulse Luper Suitcases: The Moab Story, 2003, Walking Tall, 2004; guest appearances: (TV shows) include M*A*S*H*, 1982, Cagney & Lacey, 1983-84, Falcon Crest, 1986-87, The Golden Girls, 1997, Knots Landing, 1979, Quantum Leap, 1992, Picket Fences, 1992, The Practice, 1997 ER, 1999, CSI, 2000, Judging Amy, 2001, Crossing Jordan, 2001, Six Feet Under, 2002, Without a Trace, 2003, Cold Case, 2003; Broadway shows include Brighton Beach Memoirs, Water Engine, Landscape and Silence; nat. tours: Broadway Bound, America Hurrah!. Fulbright grantee, 1966-67; recipient L.A. Drama Critics award, 1985. Mem. Zeta Phi Eta. Democrat. E-mail: btarbuck@futurewest.ca.

TARDIFF, JILL ALEXANDRIA, publishing executive, photographer; b. Morristown, N.J., Apr. 8, 1953; d. Howard James Tardiff and Jean Elizabeth Cook; m. Paul Edward Kozlowski, Feb. 11, 1984. BA in liberal arts, Coll. St. Elizabeth, 1975. Cert. teacher, K-12 NJ, 1975. Mgr. retail Hallmark Cards Inc./Flagship, N.Y.C., 1976—81; mgr./gen. mgr. Doubleday Book Shops/Flagship, N.Y.C., 1981—91; sales mgr./dir. of sales Tiffany & Co., N.Y.C., 1991—93; entrepreneur, self-propr. Bamboo River Assocs., Hoboken, NJ, 1993—; mng. editor/sr. rschr. Lintel Press, N.Y.C., 1993—94; assoc. editor BookWire Online, N.Y.C., 1995—98; contbg. editor/project mgr. Pubs. Weekly, N.Y.C., 1996—; mgr. advt. Persimmon, Asian Lit., Arts, and Culture Mag., N.Y.C., 1999—2002. Profl. spkr./tour facilitator Bamboo River Associates, Hoboken, 1991—; sec./bd. dirs. Contemporary Asian Culture Inc., N.Y.C., 1999—; adv. bd. mem. Women's Ink., N.Y.C., 1999—2004. Contbr. book Bob Vila's Guide to Historic Homes Series; reporter Shinbunka Weekly, Tokyo, 1995—2000. Mem.: AAUW (assoc.), Internat. Women's Writing Guild (hon.), N.Y. Women in Comm. (assoc.), Women's Nat. Book Assn. (assoc.; main rep. UN DPI/NGO 2000—, nat. v.p., pres. elect 2002—04, nat. pres. 2004—06), Women's Nat. Book Assn. (assoc.; newsletter editor/v.p. N.Y.C. chpt. 1997—2000, pres. N.Y.C. chpt. 2000—, immediate past nat. pres. 2006—), Editl. Freelancers Assn. (assoc.), Diev Donné Papermill (assoc.), Japan Soc. (assoc.), Asia Soc. N.Y. (assoc.). Avocations: travel, photography, gardening, architecture, paper making. Office: Bamboo River Associates 625 Madison StSte 2 Hoboken NJ 07030-6305 Personal E-mail: jat-bambooriver@worldnet.att.net.

TARDOS, ANNE, artist, writer, composer; b. Cannes, France, Dec. 1, 1943; arrived in U.S., 1966; d. Tibor and Berthe (Steinmetz) T.; m. Oded Halahmy, Nov. 6, 1976 (div. Dec. 1979); m. Jackson Mac Low, Jan. 20, 1990; step-children: Mordecai-Mark Mac Low, Clarinda Mac Low. Student, Acad. für Musik und Darstellende Kunst, Vienna, Austria, 1961—63, Art Students League NY, 1966—69. Guest tchr. Sch. Visual Arts, NYC, 1974, 87, SUNY, Albany, 1986, U. Calif., San Diego, 1990, Schule für Dichtung in Wien, Vienna, Austria, 1992-96. Author: Cat Licked the Garlic, 1992, Mayg-shem Fish, 1995, Uxudo, 1999, The Dik-dik's Solitude: New & Selected Works, 2002, A Noisy Nightingale Understands the Tiger's Camouflage Totally, 2003; composer: (CD) Museum Inside the Telephone Network, 1991, Chance Operation: Tribute to John Cage, 1993, Open Secrets, 1993, (cassette) Gatherings, 1980, Songs and Simultaneities, 1985; exhibitions include Jack Tilton Gallery, N.Y.C., 1989, Mus. Modern Art, Bolzano, Italy, 1989, Venice Biennale, 1990, Galerie 1900-2000, Paris, 1990, Mus. Modern Art, N.Y.C., 1993; author: (radio plays) Stimmen, 1986, Phoneme Dance for John Cage, 1986, Among Men, 1996. Personal E-mail: annetardos@att.net. E-mail: info@annetardos.com.

TARGOVNIK, SELMA E. KAPLAN, retired dermatologist; b. NYC, Apr. 22, 1936; d. Harry A. and Helen (Goodstein) Kaplan; m. Jerome H. Targovnik, Dec. 2, 1961; children: Nina Rebecca, Labe Eric (dec.), Diane Michelle. BA, NYU, 1957; MD, Albert Einstein Col. Medicine, 1961. Diplomate Am. Bd. Dermatology. Intern Kaiser Found. Hosp., San Francisco, 1961-62; resident in internal medicine Bellevue Hosp., NYU Med. Ctr., 1962-63, U. Colo. Med. Ctr., Denver, 1963-64; rsch. fellow, resident in dermatology Boston U. Med. Ctr., 1964-66, mem. staff, 1968-69, NYU Med. Ctr., 1966-68, St. Joseph's Hosp., Phoenix, 1969—98, Good Samaritan Hosp., Phoenix, 1969—98; ret. Staff Carl Hayden VA Hosp., Phoenix, 1998—; mem. staff St. Joseph's Hosp., Phoenix, St. Luke's Hosp., Phoenix; chief divsn. dermatology Good Samaritan Hosp., Phoenix, 1985-90; adj. assoc. prof. Midwestern U. Coll. Medicine, Glendale, Ariz., 1998—; clin. assoc. prof. dermatology Kirksville Coll. Osteopathic Medicine, 2000—, clin. assoc. prof. dermatology, 1998. Bd. dirs. ACLU, Ariz., 1973-78, 83-94, Congregation Beth El, Phoenix, 1971-75, Flagstaff Festival of the Arts, 1984-86; active Jewish Nat. Fund. Fellow Am. Acad. Dermatology, Assocs. for the Weizmann Inst. Sci., Assocs. for the Technion Inst.; mem. Am. Technion Soc. (bd. dirs. 1988-92, pres. Ariz. divsn. 1990-92), Dermatology Found., Sonoran Dermatologic Soc., Southwestern Dermatologic Soc., Pacific Dermatological Soc., Noah Worcester Dermatol. Soc., Phi Beta Kappa, Mu Chi Sigma, Pi Delta Phi, Beta Lambda Sigma. Democrat. Jewish. Home: 3706 E Rancho Dr Paradise Valley AZ 85253 Office Phone: 602-954-8335. Personal E-mail: selmaderm@cox.net.

TARITAS, KAREN JOYCE, customer service administrator; b. Ft. Wayne, Ind., June 5, 1957; d. George and Patricia Louise (Smith) T. BS, Purdue U., 1988; AAS, Ind. U., 1980. Cert. managed healthcare profl. Billing rep., experience analyst Lincoln Nat. Life Ins. Co., Ft. Wayne, 1974-82; customer svc. rep., underwriting asst. K&K Ins. Co., Ft. Wayne, 1984-86; telemarketing mgr. Stanley Steemer Carpet Cleaner, Ft. Wayne, 1990-98; svc. cons. AETNA U.S. Healthcare, Ft. Wayne, 1998—2002; with Ins. & Risk Mgmt., 2002, customer svc. rep., 2002—03; data conversion operator U.S. Postal Svc., 2004; ctrl. sta. operator Cert. Burglar and Fire Alarm Sys., Inc., 2006. Mem. Nat. Geographic Soc., Am. Mus. Nat. History, Smithsonian Instn., Nat. Women's History Mus., Purdue U. Alumni Club, Ind. U. Alumni Club, Delta Sigma Pi. Avocations: collecting music boxes, cross stitch/needlepoint. Home: 4414 Hanna St Fort Wayne IN 46806-4744 E-mail: taritaskj@yahoo.com.

TARNOFSKY-OSTROFF, DAWN, broadcast executive; BA in Journalism, Fla. Internat. U. Reporter WINZ (CBS affiliate), Miami; v.p. dev. Kushner-Locke Co., 1984-89; pres. Michael Jacobs Prodns.; sr. v.p. creative affairs 20th Century Fox TV, 1989-96; sr. v.p. programming, prodn. Lifetime TV, NYC, 1996-99, exec. v.p. entertainment, 1999—2002; pres. UPN Entertainment, LA, 2002—. Office: Lifetime TV 309 W 49th St Fl 16 New York NY 10019-7316

TARNOSKI, LORI M., apparel executive; b. 1940; From staff to sec. V F Corp., Wyomissing, Pa., 1961—79, v.p., 1979—. Office: VF Corp 1047 N Park Rd Wyomissing PA 19610-1339

TARNOVE, LORRAINE, medical association executive; b. Atlantic City, July 26, 1947; d. Leonard Robert Tarnove and Jeanne Tarnove Yudkin; m. Steven B. Friedman, June 1, 1969; children: K. Brooke, Ari-Benjamin. BA, U. Md., 1969. Pres. Lorraine Tarnove Consulting, Columbia, Md., 1985-93; exec. dir. Am. Med. Dirs. Assn., Columbia. Contbr. chpt. to book. Office: AMDA 10840 Little Patuxent #760 Columbia MO 21044*

TAROY-VALDEZ, LOLITA B., nursing educator, nurse; b. Cogon, Mindanao, Philippines, Sept. 3, 1951; d. Horonio Taroy and Florentina Lucagbo Bequiso; married, May 28, 1990. BSN, Mountain View Coll., Philippines; MN, U. Philippines, Diliman, Quezon City, 1981. Cert. AACN, 1994. Dir. Hongkong Adventist Sch. Nursing, 1985—88; asst. prof. Southwestern Adventist U., Keene, Tex., 1991—. Dean Mountain View Coll. Sch. Nursing, Valencia, Bukidnon, Philippines, 1982—85. Coord. mission trips to Philippines Healing Outreach Profl. Endeavor, Keene, 2004—05, sec., 2000—06. Named one of Gt. 100 Nurses, Dallas /Ft. Worth Hosp. Council-Nurse Exec. Forum and Tex. Nurses Assn., 2002; recipient President's award for svc., Mountain View Coll. Sch. Nursing Alumni Assn., 1997, Leadership award, 1997. Home: 2725 Hill Ln Cleburne TX 76031 Office: Southwestern Adventist U Hillcrest Keene TX 07659 Home Fax: 817-641-9988. Personal E-mail: valdezl@swau.edu.

TARPEH-DOE, LINDA DIANE, controller; b. Laramie, Wyo., Mar. 19, 1957; d. Leland Dean and Marilyn Lee (McClurg) Wheeler; m. Nyenpan Tarpeh-Doe, Jan. 16, 1982 (div. Nov. 1985); 1 child, Nyenpan Tarpeh-Doe II. BS in Acctg., U. Colo., 1979. CPA, Cert. Govt. Fin. Mgr. Asst. auditor First Bank Holding Co., Lakewood, Colo., 1979-80; internat. devel. intern USAID, Monrovia, Liberia, 1981-82, sys. acct. Washington, 1982-84, fin. analyst Kingston, Jamaica, 1984-88, macs coord. Washington, 1988-93, contr. Colombo, Sri Lanka, 1993-97, REDSO, Nairobi, Kenya, 1997-2000, USAID/Ethiopia, Addis Ababa, 2000—02, USAID, Jakarta, Indonesia, 2002—. Mem.: AICPA, Assn. Govt. Accts. Democrat. Methodist. Avocations: music, reading. Home: 3851 Paseo Del Prado Boulder CO 80301-1527 Office: Am Embassy Jakarta Unit 8135 USAID Fpo AP 96520-8135 Office Phone: 62-21-3435-9445. Business E-Mail: ltarpeh-doe@usaid.gov.

TARPENNING, EMILY, music educator; b. Portsmouth, N.H., Dec. 9, 1942; d. Alvie Earl and Alta Bernice (Crenshaw) Ryan; m. Bobby Gene Tarpenning, Sept. 1, 1961 (div. Apr. 1983); children: Virginia Lynn Richards, Michael Darrin. BA, Tex. Wesleyan U., Ft. Worth, 1993; MMus, U. North Tex., Denton, 1997. Tchr. piano, music theory, Bethany, Okla., 1969-72, Keller, Tex., 1972-86; tchr. piano Ft. Worth, 1986—, Tarrant County Coll., Hurst, Tex., 1993—2000, Fossil Ridge High Sch., Ft. Worth, 1998. Adjudicator Am. Coll. Musicians, 1994—; owner Treasures from Tex. Author: Fanny Mendelssohn Hensel: A Bridge Between, 1997; composer many piano and choral compositions. Music dir., pianist Haslet United Meth. Ch., Tex., 1997-2003, chmn. worship com., 1999; choir dir., pianist Light World Lutheran Ch., Ft. Worth, Tex., 2000-04; charter mem. mental health task force First United Meth. Ch., Ft. Worth, 1993-97; state theory test designer, Tex. Music Tchrs. Assn., 2001-2004; knitting instr. Michaels, Keller, Tex., 2005—; pianist Haslet Cmty. Ch., 2005-. Mem. Am. Coll. Musicians, Nat. Guild Piano Tchrs. (adjudicator 1997—), Music Tchrs. Nat. Assn., Tex. Music Tchrs. Assn. (state theory test designer 2000-02), Mid-Cities Music Tchrs. Assn., Ft. Worth Music Tchrs. Assn. (cert. chmn. 1997-98). Democrat. Avocations: cross-stitch, knitting, reading, crafts, painting. Home: 9048 Magnolia Blossom Trail Fort Worth TX 76131-4126

TARR, LINDA HAAS, psychologist; b. Chgo., Feb. 24, 1948; d. Francis and Sonia (Bogin) Haas; m. David Gerald Tarr, June 17, 1971; children: Michael, Adam. BA, U. Pa., 1970; PhD, Ohio State U., 1973. Lic. psychologist, Va., D.C. Cons. sch. psychologist Montgomery (Md.) and Fairfax (Va.) County Pub. Schs., 1979-80; cons. NIH, Bethesda, Md., 1980-90; psychologist Potomac Ctr., Alexandria, Va., 1985—, Kaiser Permanent, Fairfax, Va., 1994—98. Fellow NDEA, 1970-71, NSF, 1971-73. Mem. APA. Office: Potomac Ctr 5276 Dawes Ave Alexandria VA 22311-1482

TARR-WHELAN, LINDA, policy center executive; b. Springfield, Mass., May 24, 1940; d. Albert and Jane Zack; m. Keith Tarr-Whelan; children: Scott, Melinda. BSN, Johns Hopkins U., 1963; MS, U. Md., 1967; PhD in Public Svc. (hon.), Chatham Coll. Program dir. AFSCME AFL-CIO, Washington, 1968-74, union area dir., 1974-76; adminstrn. dir. N.Y. State Labor Dept., Albany, N.Y., 1976-79; dep. asst. to pres. Carter White House, Washington, 1979-80; dir. govt. rels. NEA, Washington, 1980-86; CEO, pres. Ctr. for Policy Alternatives, Washington, 1986—2000, bd. dirs., 1985—; mng. dir. Tarr-Whelan Assoc. Inc., St. Helena Island, SC, 2000—. Apptd. U.S. rep. UN Commn. on Status of Women, 1996—. Bd. dirs. Benton Found., Adv. Inst., Ind. Sector; pres. State Issues Forum; mem. Freddie Mac Affordable Housing Adv. Bd. Recipient Disting. Grad. award Johns Hopkins U., 1981, Breaking the Glass Ceiling award, 1996; leadership fellow Japan Soc., 1987-88; named one of 50 Most Powerful Women in Washington, Ladies Home Journal. Democrat. Avocations: walking, travel. Home: Tarr-Whelan Assoc Inc PO Box 1012 Saint Helena Island SC 29920

TARSES, JAMIE, television producer, former television network executive; b. Pitts., Pa., 1964; d. Jay and Rachel Tarses; m. Dan McDermott (div.). BA in Theater, Williams Coll., 1985. Casting dir. Lorimar Prodns.; mgr. creative affairs NBC, 1987, mgr. current comedy programs, 1987-88, mgr. comedy devel., 1988-89, dir. comedy devel., 1989-94, supr. programming team, 1994-95, sr. v.p. primetime series, 1995-96; pres. ABC Entertainment, 1996—99; founder, owner Untitled Burke-Tarses Project, 2003—05; ptnr. Pariah, 2005—. Consulting prodr. (TV films) Imagine That, 2002; exec. prodr.: (TV films) Crazy Love, 2003.

TARTER, JILL CORNELL, science foundation director, astronomer, researcher; BEP, Cornell U. Sch. of Engring., 1966; attended, Cornell U. Grad. Sch. Theoretical Physics, 1965—67; MA in Astronomy, U. Calif., Berkeley, 1971, PhD in Astronomy, 1975. Teaching & rsch. asst. U. Calif., Berkeley, Calif., 1965—75; NRC resident rsch. assoc. postdoctoral fellow NASA Ames Rsch. Ctr., Moffett Field, Calif., 1975—77; asst. rsch. astronomer II-IV U. Calif. Space Sciences Lab, Berkeley, Calif., 1977—83, assoc. rsch. astronomer I, 1983—85; assoc. rsch. astronomer dept. of astronomy U. Calif., Berkeley, Calif., 1983—93; co-founder SETI Inst., Mountain View, Calif., 1984—, principal investigator, 1984—89, project scientist NASA SETI Microwave Observing Project & High Resolution Microwave Survey, 1989—93, dir. Project Phoenix, 1993—99, Bernard M. Oliver chair, 1997—; dir. SETI Research, Mountain View, Calif., 1999—2000, Ctr. for SETI Research, Mountain View, Calif., 2000—. Chair Internat. Acad. of Astronautics SETI Com., 1997—, Internat. Square Kilometer Arry Steering Com., 2002—; adv. bd. mem. Odyssey Mag., 1997—, Space.com, 2000—. Recipient Public Service medals, NASA, 1993, HRMS Group Achievement award, 1993, Chabot Observatory Person of Yr. award, 1997, Women's Fund Women of Achievement award, San Jose Mercury News, 1998. Fellow: Com. for Scientific Investigation of Claims of the Paranormal, Calif. Acad. Sci., Explorer's Club; mem.: AAAS (fellow 2002), World Tech. Network, Women in Aerospace (Lifetime Achievement award 1989), Internat. Soc. for Study of Origin of Life, Internat. Acad. of Astronautics, Internat. Radio Sci. Union (URSI Commn.), Internat. Astronomical Union, Am. Astronomical Soc. Office: Seti Institute 515 N Whisman Rd Mountain View CA 94043-2172

TARVER, BETTY GAIL, music educator; d. Garland E. and Evelyn J. Schiller; m. Robert D. Tarver, July 20, 1991. AA, Temple Jr. Coll., 1978; B of Music Edn., Sam Houston State U., Huntsville, Tex., 1980. Cert. Kodaly Sam Houston State U. Music tchr. Magnolia Elem. Sch., Tex., 1980—83, Bear Br. Elem. Sch., Magnolia, 1983—. Mem.: Assn. Tex. Profl. Educators (assoc.), Tex. Music Educators Assn. (assoc.). Avocations: travel, piano. Office: Bear Branch Elem Sch 8909 FM 1488 Magnolia TX 77354 Office Phone: 281-356-4771.

TASMAN, ALICE LEA MAST, not-for-profit fundraiser; d. Clarence Kurtz Mast and Florence Larue Barkley; m. William S. Tasman, Nov. 8, 1962; children: James B., W. Graham, Alice. BA, Barnard Coll., 1956; postgrad., U. Pa. Tchr. Am. Cathedral, Paris, 1953—54; asst. dir. pub. rels. Phila. Art Mus., 1956—61; pub. rels. exec. WUHY-FM, 1976—77; cons. Franklin Mint, 1991—94. Author: Wedding Album: Customs & Lore Through the Ages, 1981, Adam, A Three Island Cat, 1984. Women's bd. Thomas Jefferson U. Hosp., 1983—; chmn. Art in City Hall, 1995—2003; fundraising com., spl. events Recording for Blind, 1993—95; devel. com., trustee Woodmere Art Mus., 1994—2003; mem. Associated Svcs. for Blind; originator, chmn. annual exhibit Form in Art, 1987—; vol. Phila. Mus. Art, 1984—; annual concert and ball com. Phila. Orch., 1972—75; libr. Chestnut Hill Acad. and Springside Sch., 1977—78; antiques show com. U. Pa., 1972—75; coord. long-term patient care Chestnut Hill Hosp., 1981; fundraising and publicity chair Project Orbis, 1982; fundraiser Am. Diabetes Assn., 1984; vol. Chestnut Hill Hosp., 1978—87; hon. chair fundraising Overbrook Sch. for Blind, 1989; fundraiser Am. Indian Fund, 1989; hon. chair symposium, fundraiser 1st Nat. Inst. Blind Artists, 1990; internat. ambassador City of Phila., 1993; assoc. trustee Sulgrave Manor, London; fundraising, corp. devel. exec. Wills Eye Hosp., 1996—, chair 17th ann. forum art exhbn.; co-organizer Haitian Arts Exhbn. Friends of Hosp. Albert Schweitzer, Haiti; bd. dirs. Chestnut Hill Presbyn. Ch., 1989—93, Nat. Exhibits by Blind Artists, 1987—, Chestnut Hill Women's Com. Phila. Orch., 1965—, Chestnut Hill Cmty. Ctr. and Women's Exchange, 1978—; bd. dirs. coun. visual arts Chestnut Hill Acad., 1997—; bd. dirs. Art in City Hall, 1993—2003, Hitchcock Found., 1982—83. Recipient Cert. of Appreciation, Phila. Arts Fest., 1959, Wills Eye Hosp., 1994, Overbrook Sch. for Blind award, 1989, Louis Braille award, Associated Svcs. for Blind, 1993, Founder's award, Nat. Exhibits by Blind Artists, Disting. Daughters of Pa. award, Gov. and Mrs. Tom Ridge, 1997, Lady of Dumbarton award, Nat. Soc. Colonial Dames, 1999, Lifetime Achievement award, Little Rock Found., 2001. Mem.: Friends Vielles Maisons Francaises, Am. Ophthalmology Soc. (chair pres. dinner 1989—), Am. Bd. Ophthalmology (chair 75th anniversary dinner 1992), Am. Acad. Ophthalmology (chair Christian med. dental luncheon 1991—92, organizer 2nd Ann. Orbital Gala), French Huguenot Soc., Chestnut Hill Hist. Soc. (pres. 1972—74, program chair 1974—75, fundraising and spl. events chair 1981—), Nat. Soc. Colonial Dames Commonwealth Pa. (house com. 1980—89, garden com. 1987, house com. 1993—94, chair program com. 1993—96, first v.p. 1998—2002, co-chair capital campaign fund 1999—2001, pres. 2002—05, Alice Lea Mast Tasman ednl. chair), Rotary, Jr. League. Avocations: travel, skiing, painting, crafts, gardening.

TASSE, MARIE JEANNE, retired art educator; b. Worcester, Mass., Mar. 25, 1925; d. Paul Charles and Marie Antoinette (DesRosiers) T. AB, Anna Maria Coll., 1955; MA, U. Notre Dame, 1962; PhD, Boston U., 1972. Tchr. music., dir. choir St. John's Sch., Newton, Mass., 1945-50, Notre Dame High Sch., Central Falls, R.I., 1950-53; instr. to prof. Anna Maria Coll., Paxton, Mass., 1955-75; from assoc. prof. to prof. Marietta (Ohio) Coll., 1975-92, chmn. art dept., 1977-82, cons. to faculty, 1981-85, dir., instr. Inst. for Learning in Retirement, 1992—. Founder Marietta Calligraphy Soc., 1981—; dir. Letters at an Exhbn., Marietta, 1984, 86, 88, 92, 99, 2003, 2005, By Women's Hands Exhbn., Marietta, 1989-91. Calligrapher wall hangings, handmade books, broadsides (Merit award 1991). Pres., v.p. bd. The Marietta Chorale, 1978-88; dir. St. Mary's Ch. Choir, Marietta, 1978-88; bd. dirs. Artsbridge, Marietta/Parkersburg, 1981-94, Blennerhasset Hist. Found., 2000—, River Cities Symphony, 2006—. Recipient Art Educator award Artsbridge, 1991, Alumni award for profl. achievement, 2001; named Zonta Woman of Yr., 2006. Mem. Nat. Soc. Arts and Letters (local pres., v.p. bd. 1982—, nat. resolutions chair 1988-90, nat. career liaison 1992-94, nat. editor membership directory 1994-2000, nat. historian 1996-98, nat. pres., 2000-2002, organizer A Showcase of the Arts 1992—, editor Career Award Winners). Roman Catholic. Avocations: music, needlecrafts, reading, travel.

TASSINARI, MELISSA SHERMAN, reproductive toxicologist; b. Lawrence, Mass., Sept. 26, 1953; m. R. Peter Tassinari; children: Michael, Emily, Sara. AB, Mt. Holyoke Coll., 1975; postgrad., U. St. Andrews, Scotland, 1973-74; PhD, Med. Coll. Wis., 1979. Diplomate Am. Bd. Toxicology. Rsch. asst. in orthopedic surgery., Lab. Human Biochemistry Children's Hosp. Med. Ctr., Boston, 1981-83; rsch. affiliate in toxicology Forsyth Dental Ctr., Boston, 1983-86, staff assoc. dept. toxicology, 1986-89; asst. prof. cell biology U. Mass. Med. Ctr., Worcester, 1989-91; head reproductive and developmental toxicology Pfizer Global R&D, Groton/New London, Conn., 1991—99, group dir. worldwide safety scis., 2001—04, sr. dir. regulatory policy and intelligence, 2004—. Rsch. fellow oral biology Harvard Sch. Dental Medicine, Boston, 1978-81, instr. oral biology and pathophysiology, 1981-83; asst. prof. biol. scis. Wellesley Coll., Mass., 1985-91, biology Simmons Coll., Boston, 1986-87. Contbr. abstracts, articles to profl. jours. Mem. Teratology Soc. (coun. 2000—, v.p. 2004, pres. 2005-06), Neurobehavioral Teratology Soc., Mid. Atlantic Reprodn. and Teratology Assn. (steering com. 1994), Midwest Teratology Assn., Soc. Toxicology. Office: Pfizer Inc 50 Pequot Ave New London CT 06320

TASSLER, NINA, broadcast executive; Pres. CBS Entertainment, 2004—. Mailing: CBS Entertainment CBS Television City 7800 Beverly Blvd Los Angeles CA 90036*

TASSONE, GELSOMINA (GESSIE TASSONE), metal products executive; b. NYC, July 8, 1944; d. Enrico and A. Cira (Petriccione) Gargiulo; children: Ann Marie, Margaret, Theresa, Christine; m. Armando Tassone, Mar. 20, 1978. Student, Orange County Community Coll., 1975-79, Iona Coll., 1980—. Head bookkeeper Gargiulo Bros. Builders, N.Y.C., 1968-72; pres., owner A&T Iron Works, Inc., New Rochelle, N.Y., 1973—. Recipient Profl. Image award Contractors Coun. Greater N.Y.C., 1986; named Businesswoman of Yr., Contractors Coun. Greater N.Y.C., 1985, N.Y. State Small Bus. Person of Yr., 1988, Entrepreneur of Yr. Inc. mag., 1990; company named a Successful Small Bus. Co. Westchester County C. of C./BSBA, 1986-88. Mem. Nat. Ornamental and Miscellaneous Metal Assn., Builders Inst. Westchester and Putnam County, Westchester Assn. Women Bus. Owners, Profl. Women in Constrn., New Rochelle C. of C. Office: A&T Iron Works Inc 25 Cliff St New Rochelle NY 10801-6803 Office Phone: 914-632-8992. Personal E-mail: gesjames@aol.com. Business E-mail: info@atironworks.com.

TASSOS, ALICE CROWLEY, writer; b. Dallas, June 19, 1925; d. Thomas Francis and Geneiva Edna (Lee) Crowley; m. John Tassos, Mar. 4, 1950 (div. June 1960); 1 child, Penelope Geneiva Tassos Grima. BA in English, French, BS in Journalism, So. Meth. U., 1945, BA in Psychology, 1960; MA in French, Columbia U., 1947. Solo pilot cert. Sec. to fashion editor Vogue Mag., N.Y.C., 1945-46; airline stewardess Trans-Caribbean Airline, N.Y.C., 1946; embassy libr. U.S. Info. Svc. Fgn. Svc. Dept. State, Athens, Greece, 1947-49; jr. exec. J. Walter Thompson Co., N.Y.C., 1950-51; city side reporter Miami Daily News, 1952; pub. rels. exec. Boca Raton (Fla.) Hotel & Club, 1953; pvt. practice writer, linguist Dallas, 1960—. Author poems. Canvasser Am. Heart Assn., New Canaan, Conn., 1959; office sec. Easter Seals, Dallas, 1960-61; vol. recreational therapy asst. Timberlawn Psychiat. Hosp., Dallas, 1961-64; vol. March of Dimes, Dallas, 1997. Sr. scholar So. Meth. U., Dallas Woman's Club, 1944-45; consumer price index pub. svc. commendation Dept. Commerce, Dallas, 1999. Mem. AAUW, NAFE, Cmty. of the Holy Spirit (assoc.), Daus. of the King, Alpha Theta Phi, Theta Sigma Phi, Psi Chi. Episcopalian. Avocations: skin diving, swimming, bicycling, walking.

TATÁR, ANNA, library director; Grad., DePauw U.; MLS, U. Mich. Dir. San Diego Pub. Libr. Named one of 50 People to Watch in 2003, San Diego Mag. Mem.: ALA. Office: San Diego Pub Libr Ctrl Div 820 E St San Diego CA 92101-6478 Office Phone: 619-236-5870. E-mail: atatar@sandiego.gov.*

TATE, DEBORAH TAYLOR, commissioner; b. Murfreesboro, Tenn. d. Louis Carlton Taylor; m. William H. Tate; children: Will, Taylor, Carlton. BA, JD, U. Tenn.; attended, Vanderbilt U. Cert.: Tenn. Supreme Ct. (Rule 31 Mediator). Atty., sr. policy advisor to Gov. Lamar Alexander and Gov. Don Sundquist, Tenn.; dir. Tenn. Regulatory Authority, 2000—06, chmn., 2003—04; commr. FCC, Washington, 2006—. Former dir. state and local policy ctr. Vanderbilt Inst. for Pub. Policy Studies; guest lectr. Vanderbilt U. Fellow: Nashville Bar Found.; mem.: Lawyer's Assn. for Women, Nashville Bar Assn. Office: FCC 445 12th St SW Washington DC 20554

TATE, SHEILA BURKE, public relations executive; b. Washington, Mar. 3, 1942; d. Eugene L. and Mary J. (Doherty) Burke; m. William J. Tate, May 2, 1981 (dec. Aug. 1998); children: Hager Burke Patton, Courtney Paige Patton Manzel; m. John K. Yovel, Nov. 26, 2005. BA in Journalism, Duquesne U., 1964; postgrad. in mass comm., U. Denver, 1975—76. Rsch. asst. Westinghouse Air Brake Co.; asst. account exec. Fahlgren and Assocs.; copywriter Ketchum, MacLeod and Grove, 1964—66; account exec. Burson-Marsteller Assocs., Pitts., 1967, sr. v.p. Washington, 1985—87; pub. rels. mgr. Colo. Nat. Bank, Denver, 1967—70; account exec. Hill and Knowlton, Inc., Houston, 1977—78, v.p. Washington, 1978—81; dep. to the chmn. Hill and Knowlton Inc., Washington, 1987—88; press sec. to First Lady White House, Washington, 1981—85; press sec. George Bush for Pres. Campaign, 1988; press sec. to Pres.-elect George Bush, 1988—89; vice chmn. Cassidy and Assocs. Pub. Affairs, Washington, 1989—91; pres. Powell Tate, Washington, 1991—99, vice-chmn., 1999—. Bd. dirs., former mem. Corp. for Pub. Broadcasting, vice chmn., 1990—92, chmn., 1992—94; bd. dirs. Ethics Resource Ctr., Washington, Guest Svcs. Corp., Fairfax, Va. Mem. nat. adv. bd. The Salvation Army; adv. bd. Am. Acad. Family Physicians, Kansas City, Kans. Mem.: Nat. Press Club, Belfair Club, Farmington Country Club, Washington Golf and Country Club, Duquesne U. Century Club. Office: Powell Tate 700 13th St NW Ste 1000 Washington DC 20005-5926 Business E-Mail: state@webershandwick.com.

TATELBAUM, LINDA, literature educator, writer; b. Rochester, NY, Feb. 28, 1947; d. Milton and Harriet Frank Tatelbaum; m. Kalman Aaron Winer, Feb. 2, 1975; 1 child, Noah Tatelbaum Winer. BA, Cornell U., Ithaca, NY, 1968, MA, 1969, PhD, 1972. Prof. English Colby Coll., Waterville, Maine,

1982—. Humanist Maine Humanities Coun., Portland, 1985—93. Author, pub.: novels Yes & No (Paris 1969), 2004 (Maine Lit. award for Best Self-Published Book, 2006), Writer on the Rocks: Moving the Impossible, 2000 (Writers' Jour. Best, 2002), memoir Carrying Water as a Way of Life: A Homesteader's History, 1997. Jewish. Avocations: gardening for family food production, stone work, swimming, herbal medicine, tai chi chuan. Office Phone: 207-859-5288.

TATLOCK, ANN, writer; married. Author: (novels) A Room of My Own, 1998 (Silver Angel award, Excellence in Media, 1999), A Place Called Morning, 1998, All the Way Home, 2002 (First Place Adult Fiction, Midwest Ind. Publ. Assn., 2002, Christy award Contemporary Fiction, 2003), I'll Watch the Moon, 2003 (First Place Gen. Fiction, Midwest Ind. Publ. Assn., 2003, Best of Genre Christian Fiction, Libr. Jour., 2003), Things We Once Held Dear, 2006. Mailing: Bethany House Publ 11400 Hampshire Ave Minneapolis MN 55438 E-mail: anntatlock@yahoo.com.*

TATLOCK, ANNE M., trust company executive; b. White Plains, NY, July 1, 1939; d. John and Kathleen (McGrath) McNiff; m. William Tatlock, Apr. 29, 1967; children: Julina, Kerry, Christopher. BA, Vassar Coll., 1961; MA in Econs., NYU, 1968. 1st v.p. Smith Barney Harris Upham, NYC, 1962-84; exec. v.p. Fiduciary Trust Internat., NYC, 1984-94, pres., 1994—99, pres., CEO, 1999—2000, chmn., CEO, 2000—. Bd. dirs. Fortune Brands, Deerfield, Ill., 1996—, Franklin Resources, San Mateo, Calif., 2001—, Merck, NJ, 2000—. Trustee Am. Ballet Theatre, N.Y.C., 1994-, pres., 1998-2001; trustee Vassar Coll., 1994-2006, The Teagle Found., N.Y.C., 1995-2006; trustee Andrew W. Mellon Found., NYC, 1995—, chmn., 2003—; trustee Cultural Instns. Retirement Sys., NYC, 1989-2005, chmn., 1996-2001; trustee Howard Hughes Med. Inst., Md., 2000—, The Conf. Bd., NYC, 2001—, Mayo Found., Minn., 2002—, World Trade Ctr. Meml. Found., 2005—. Fellow: Am. Acad. Arts and Scis. (elected 2004); mem.: Coun. on Fgn. Rels.

TATMAN, SANDRA L., design educator; m. Johnathan W. Ericson, July 2, 1979; children: Rebekka W. Ericson, Brita T. Ericson. PhD, U. Del., Newark, 1994. Archtl. libr./curator Athenaeum of Phila., 1978—86; assoc. prof. dept. art Towson U., Md., 1999—. Principal investigator (website databank) Phila. Architects and Buildings Project. Office: Art Department Towson University 8000 York Rd Towson MD 21252 Office Phone: 410-704-4693.

TATNALL, ANN WESLAGER, reading educator; b. Uniontown, Pa., June 1, 1935; d. Clinton Alfred and Ruth Georgia (Hurst) Weslager; m. George Gress Tatnall, Oct. 8, 1954; children: Peggy Ann, George Richardson. BS in Edn., U. Del., 1967; MA in Edn., Glassboro State Coll., 1979. Cert. reading specialist, cert. supr., cert. elem. tchr., N.J. Tchr. reading Oldmans Twp. Bd. of Edn., Pedricktown, NJ, 1972—78, reading specialist, 1978—95, reading supr., 1981—95. Mem. N.J. Dept. of Edn. Minimum Basic Skills Test Devel. Com., Trenton, 1981-82; mem. Quad-Dist. Reading Coordination Com., Salem County, N.J., 1987-95; chairperson Adminstrv. Com. of Oldmans Twp. Schs., Pedricktown, 1993-95. Chair Woodstown (N.J.) Candlelight House Tour, 1983-99, homes chair, 2000—; pres. Pilesgrove-Woodstown Hist. Soc., 1994-99, v.p., 1999-2001, pres. 2002-03, trustee, 2003—; v.p. Pilesgrove Libr. Assn., 1994-2002, pres., 2003, sec., 2005—; sec. Hist. Preservation Commn., Woodstown, 1989-2004, chairperson, 2005—; mem. jr. bd. Wilmington (Del.) Med. Ctr., 1969—, treas. Thrift Shop, 1970-75; trustee United Way of Salem County, 1997-99; mem. Salem County Cultural and Heritage Commn., 1997-2004. Recipient Gov.'s Tchr. Recognition Program award Gov. of N.J., 1988; selected Hands Across the Water, Russian/USA Tchr. Exch., 1990-91; named Salem County Woman of Achievement, 1998. Mem. AAUW, Internat. Reading Assn., N.J. Reading Assn., Woman's Club Woodstown. Avocations: travel, reading, historic preservation, gardening. Home: 209 N Main St Woodstown NJ 08098-1227

TATREAU, (DOLORES) MAXINE, artist; b. Minden, Iowa, Sept. 6, 1929; d. Charles Ross Teninty and Hester Evaline Peterson Teninty Hadfield; m. Donald Max Tatreau, Aug. 18, 1949; children: Douglas M., Dean M., Kevin L. Student, U. No. Iowa, 1947, Iowa State Tchrs. Coll, U. Nebr., Omaha. Receptionist, typesetter Neola (Iowa) Gazette Newspaper, 1946—47; rural sch. tchr. Neola, 1947—48; office worker Orchard and Wilhelm Furniture Co., Omaha, 1948—50; comptometer operator Western Elec., Omaha, 1950—53; office worker Western Elec. (AT&T Tech.), Omaha, 1969—86; artist Tatreau Studio, 1972—; represented by Wickwire Gallery, Hendersonville, NC, Carolina Gallery Art, Spartenburg, SC. Pres. Art League Henderson County, 2004. Exhibitions include Kans. Watercolor Soc. Competition (Purchase award), Rocky Mountain Nat. Watercolor Soc., Phi Theta Kappa Six State Regional Competition, Brand Libr. and Art Gallery, Glendale, Calif., Passageway Gallery, Omaha, Asheville Gallery of Art, 2000—04, Aberdale, Wales, 2004, many others, invitational exhibitions, Edina Art Ctr., Mpls., Conn Gallery, Landrum, SC, Wichita Art Gallery, Kans., Statehouse Gallery, Lincoln, Nebr., many others, numerous corp. and pvt. collections in US and Europe. Den mother Boys Scouts Am., Omaha; wedding coord. 1st Luth. Ch., Omaha, Sunday sch. tchr., children's summer bible sch. leader, circle leader. Mem.: Kans. Watercolor Soc. (signature), So. Watercolor Soc., Upstate Visual Arts Greenville, SC, Watercolor Soc. NC (Purchase award), Tryon Painters and Sculptors, Nat. Watercolor Soc., Art League Henderson County, Internat. Soc. Exptl. Artists (signature), Nat. Mus. Women (charter). Lutheran. Avocations: golf, bridge, jewelry making, quilting, church choir. Home and Studio: 2701 Kalmia Ln Hendersonville NC 28791-1838

TATSCH, JACKI LYNN, music educator, diversified financial services company executive; b. Willimantic, Conn., Mar. 11, 1971; d. Jack Adrian and Ellen Ann Wallis; m. Clinton Edward Tatsch, Aug. 7, 1993; 1 child, Bryan Edward. BS in Music Edn., Ea. Nazarene Coll., 1993. Cert. tchr. K-9 and 5-12 Mass., 1993. Pvt. music instr., Lynchburg, Va., 1994—99; music tchr. Nazarene Christian Sch., Asheville, NC, 1999—2001, Biltmore Bapt. Sch. Music, Arden, NC, 2000—03; pvt. music instr. Arden, 1999—2001, Asheville, 2001—03, Hendersonville, NC, 2003—; prin., owner Hart Lane Enterprises Inc., 2005—. Music tchr. AIMA Ctrl., Va., 1994—96; saxophonist Land Sky Concert Band, Asheville, 2002—03; saxophonist and clarinetist Bathtub Gin, Little Switzerland, 2002—03, Nouveau-Passe Orch., Hendersonville, 2004—; clarinetist Hendersonville Cmty. Band, 2004—05; freelance musician. Mem.: Internat. Clarinet Assn., Nat. Assn. Music Educators, U.S. Amateur Ballroom Dance Assn. Home: 28 Hart Ln Hendersonville NC 28792 Personal E-mail: jackitatsch@hotmail.com.

TATUM, BETTY JOYCE, secondary school educator; b. Oklahoma City, Dec. 19, 1949; d. Howard and Elaine (Easley) Lisby; m. Frank Dennis Tatum, Dec. 27, 1980. BA, Okla. State U., 1972, MS, 1984. Cert. secondary tchr., Okla. 9th grade English tchr. Ponca City (Okla.) Pub. Schs., 1972-80, 7th grade English tchr., 1985-87, H.S. English tchr., 1988—; tchr. learning disabilities students Calcasieu Sch. Sys., Lake Charles, La., 1981-83. Mem profl. devel. task force com. Ponca City Schs., 2000-01. Named Tch. of Yr., Ponca City HS, 2006; recipient Citation of Tchr. Appreciation, Okla. Sch. Sci. and Math., 1997, Olka. Found. for Excellance, Ponca City's Acad. All-State Scholars, 2003. Mem. NEA, Okla. Edn. Assn., Ponca City Panhellenic, Alpha Delta Pi, Okla. State U. Alumni Assn. (bd. dirs. 1993-96), Delta Kappa Gamma. Avocations: bridge, reading, travel, crafts, writing. Home: 621 Greenbriar Rd Ponca City OK 74601-1622 Office: Ponca High HS 927 N 5th St Ponca City OK 74601-3302

TATUM, BEVERLY DANIEL, psychology and education educator; b. Tallahaassee, Sept. 27, 1954; d. Robert Alphonse and Catherine Faith (Maxwell) Daniel; m. Travis James Tatum, July 28, 1979; children: Travis Jonathan Daniel, David Alexander Daniel. BA, Wesleyan U., Middletown, Conn., 1975; MA in Psychology, U. Mich., 1976, PhD, 1984. Lic. clin. psychologist. From asst. prof. to assoc. prof. dept. psychology Westfield (Mass.) State Coll., 1983-89; assoc. prof. dept. psychology and edn. Mt. Holyoke Coll., South Hadley, Mass., 1989—; pvt. practice Northampton, Mass., 1989—. Lectr. dept. black studies U. Calif., Santa Barbara, 1980-83, counseling psychologist, 1979-83; vis. scholar Stone Ctr., Wellesley (Mass.) Coll., 1991-92; chair, bd. dirs. Equity Inst., Emeryville, Calif., 1987-89. Author: Assimilation Blues, 1987. Predoctoral fellow APA Minority Program, 1976-79, dissertation fellow U. Calif., 1980-81, postdoctoral fellow Ford Found., 1991. Mem. APA, Am. Psychol. Soc., Ea. Psychol. Assn., Mass. Psychol. Assn., Assn. Women in Psychology, Assn. Black Psychologists. Office: Mount Holyoke College Dept Psychology And Ed South Hadley MA 01075

TAUBER, MICHELE ANN, actress; d. Arthur and Jean Pearl Tauber. BFA, Montclair State U., Upper Montclair, N.J., 1986; MFA, U. Del., Newark, Del., 1999. Actress Running Rabbit Family Prodns., Upper Montclair, NJ, 2003—, Syracuse Stage, NY, 2005—. Actor: (plays) Women of Lockerbie, The Tempest, A Christmas Carol, House of Blue Leaves, The Importance of Being Earnest, Man of the Moment (Am. premiere), Arsenic and Old Lace, Sophie, Totie and Belle, Kiss The Bride, Pierrot Le Quin, Jasper Lake, O, Pioneers!, Macbeth, Food Fright (musical revue), The Merry Wives of Windsor, Anthony & Cleopatra, The Miser, Fiddler on the Roof, Rumors, A Comedy of Errors (musical), Romeo and Juliet, The Charity That Began at Home, The Heiress, A Perfect Analysis Given by a Parrot; (films) Funny Money; (TV series) Kate and Allie, The Street. Com. mem. Vincent Borelli Meml. Com., Long Branch, NJ, 2005—06. Finalist Gemini award, Am. Coll. Theatre Festival, 1987; recipient Excellence in Acting award, 1980; Dennis K. MacDonald Meml. scholar, Dept. Theatre Montclair State U., 1979. Mem.: Actor's Equity Assn. (life). E-mail: micheletauber@comcast.net.

TAUBER, SONYA LYNN, nurse; b. Harford County, Md., Apr. 22, 1963; d. Daniel Raymond and Helen Tauber. AA, Harford Community Coll., 1987; student, Frostburg State Coll., 1981-83; BSN, Notre Dame Nursing Coll., 1997. Cert. geriatric aide, intravenous therapy. Nurse Bel Air (Md.) Convalescent Ctr.; staff nurse orthopedic fl., developer policies and procedure Greater Balt. Med. Ctr., 1987-95; hospice home care Stella Maris Hospice Home Care, Balt., 1995-97; nurse Blakehurst Retirement Cmty. Health Care Ctr., Balt., 1997-98; program dir./nurse adult med. day program United Cerebral palsy of Ctrl. Md., Essex, 1998—.

TAUBIN, DAWN, film company executive; Staff prodr., cable television programming Warner Amex Cable Comms., Ohio; dir., publicity and promotion Nat. Amusements Inc., Boston, 1983—85; west coast regional publicity/promotion rep. to v.p., publicity MGM, 1985—89; v.p., publicity Warner Bros. Pictures, 1989—93, v.p., advt. and publicity, 1993—96, sr. v.p., advt. and publicity, 1996—99, exec. v.p., mktg., 1999—2001, pres., domestic mktg., 2001—. Named an 100 Most Powerful Women in Entertainment, Hollywood Reporter, 2005; named one of, 2004. Office: Warner Bros Pictures 4000 Warner Blvd Burbank CA 91522-0001*

TAUBMAN, JANE ANDELMAN, literature and language professor; b. Boston, Oct. 23, 1942; d. Hyman M. and Esther (Rosenthal) Andelman; m. William Chase Taubman; children: Alexander, Phoebe. BA, Radcliffe Coll., 1964; MA, Yale U., 1968, PhD, 1972. Instr. Russian Smith Coll., Northampton, Mass., 1968-72; asst. prof. Russian Amherst (Mass.) Coll., 1973-83, assoc. prof. Russian, 1983-89, prof. Russian, 1989—. Author: A Life Through Poetry: Marina Tsvetaeva's Lyric Diary, 1989, Russian transl., 2000, Cinetek: Asthenic Syndrome, 2000, Kira Muratova, 2004; co-author: Moscow Spring, 1989; co-editor: Marina Tsvetaeva: One Hundred Years, 1994. Woodrow Wilson Found. fellow, 1964—, Am. Coun. Learned Socs.-SSRC, 1974, trustee-faculty fellow Amherst Coll., 1978, fellow Nat. Def. Title VI, 1965-68; grantee Am. Philos. Soc., 1975, Amherst Coll., 1991, 94, IREX grantee USSR, 1988. Mem. AAUP, Am. Assn. Tchrs. Slavic and East European Langs., Am. Assn. Slavic Studies, Am. Coun. Tchrs. of Russian. Office: Amherst Coll Dept Russian Amherst MA 01002 Office Phone: 413-542-2047. Business E-Mail: jataubman@amherst.edu.

TAULBEE, DIANNE R., special education administrator; b. Macomb, Ill., Aug. 17, 1942; d. Gaylord James and Lorene (Putman) Jackson; m. Jack L. Taulbee, Feb. 14, 1981; children: Brent, Janyse, Cheryl, Richard. BS, We. Ill. U., 1967; M, Ill. State U., 1970. Cert. adminstrn., Ill., 1980. Speech therapist Peoria (Ill.) State Hosp., 1970-72; sch. psychologist Schaumburg (Ill.) Sch. Dist., 1972-75, dir. early childhood, 1975-79; tchr. Nat. Coll., Evanston, Ill., 1975; dir. pupil personnel West Aurora (Ill.) Sch. Dist., 1979-81; supr. spl. edn. Jackson (Mich.) County Intermediate Sch. Dist., 1981—2002; grant writer United Way, 2002—. Grant writer for underprivileged children after-sch. programs, 2000-2003; hearing officer State of Ill., Springfield, 1978-81. Author: Curriculum for Emotionally Impaired, Curriculum for Early Childhood, Intellectual Milestones. Chmn. speakers bur. Jackson County Spl. Edn. Dept., 1989-90. Demonstration Project grantee, Fed. Govt., Schaumburg, 1975-79. Mem. Emotionally Impaired Students (coord. donations 1990-91), Interfaith Shelter (coord. donations 1991), Goldwing Assn. (pub. rels. 1990-91). Avocations: walking, reading, writing, painting, travel. Personal E-mail: ladydirae@cablespeed.com.

TAURASI, DIANA, college basketball player; Grad, U. Conn., 2004—. Guard women's basketball U. Conn., 2000—04; profl. basketball player Phoenix Mercury, WNBA, 2004—. Player USA Senior Nat. Team, 2004. Named Big East Preseason Rookie of the Yr., 2000—01, Most Outstanding Player of the NCAA East Region, 2000—01, Big East Championship Most Outstanding Player, 2000—01, Kodak All-Am. and AP Second Team All Am., 2001—02, Naismith Player of the Yr., 2001—02, 2003, NCAA Final Four and East Regional Most Outstanding Player, 2003, USBWA Nat. Player of the Yr., 2003, Big East First Team Performer, 2002—03, Preseason All-Am., 2003, WNBA Rookie of the Yr., 2004; named to Big East All-Rookie Team, 2000—01, NCAA Mideast Region All-Tournament Team, 2001—02, All Big-East First Team, 2002, Big East All Tournament Team, 2002, Big East All-Tournament Team, 2003; recipient Honda award for Women's Basketball Finalist, 2001—02, Honda Trophy Award, 2003, Wade Trophy, 2003, Espy Award for Best Female College Athlete, ESPN, 2003, 2004, Espy Award for Best Female Athlete, 2004. Office: c/o Phoenix Mercury 201 East Jefferson St Phoenix AZ 85004

TAUSCHER, ELLEN O., congresswoman; b. Newark, 1951; 1 child, Katherine. BS in early Childhood Edn., Seton Hall U., 1974. With Bache Securities, NYC, NY Stock Exch.; dir. Tauscher Found.; mem. US Congress from 10th Calif. dist., 1997—; mem. ho. armed svcs. com., ho. transp. com. US Ho. Reps. Founder The ChildCare Registry; bd. regents Seton Hall U.; co-chair Dianne Feinstein, US Senate Campaign, 1994; transp. and infrastructure com., surface transp. and water resources and environ. Author: The ChildCare Sourcebook, 1996. Chair New Dem. Coalition, Bipartisan Freshman Campaign Fin. Reform Task Force, House Cancer Awareness Working Group, Congl. Caucus on the Arts; co-chair Congl. Iraqi Women's Caucus; vice-chair Calif. Dem. Del., Dem. Leadership Coun. Democrat. Roman Catholic.

TAUZIAT, NATHALIE, professional tennis player; b. Bangui, Central African Republic, Oct. 17, 1967; d. Bernard and Regine Tauziat. Profl. tennis player. Established tennis acad., Cabreton, France, 1994. Winner Wimbledon, 1989, Birmingham, 1997, Eastbourne 1995, Quebec City 1993, Futures/Val d Oise-FRA, 1990, 92, Bayonne 1990, Futures/Limoges-FRA, 1987, Wimbledon, 1989; placed 2nd Australian Open; 3 time champion U.S. Open; winner 4 singles titles, 14 doubles titles. Mem. WTA Tour Players Assn. (bd. dirs. 1997-98). Avocations: music, playing golf, watching soccer. Office: care USTA 70 W Red Oak Ln White Plains NY 10604-3602 also: Sanex Wta Womens Tennis 1 Progress Plz Ste 1500 Saint Petersburg FL 33701-4335

TAVAKOLI, SIRPA AULIKKI, physician; b. Helsinki, Finland, May 7, 1958; d. Irja Tytti Kyllikki Kuvaja; m. Bruce Tavakoli, July 29, 1985; children: Emilia, Samin. Cert. in med. lab. tech., Stockholm Lab. Asst. Sch., 1982; MD, Karolinska Inst., Stockholm, 1992. Lab. technician Karolinska Inst., 1982—84; lab. physician Ryhov County Hosp., Jonkoping, Sweden, 1992—93, clin. intern, 1993—95; ward physician Karolinska Hosp., Stockholm, 1995; family dr. Rinkeby Family Dr.'s Surgery, Stockholm, 1995—96; ward physician NWPHD Psychiatric Unit, Stockholm, 1996—97; psychiatry resident Okla. U. Coll. Medicine, Tulsa, 1999—. Avocations: reading, family, yoga, downhill skiing.

TAVARES, MARCIA LYNN, mental health services professional; b. Fall River, Mass., Jan. 15, 1979; d. Jorge M. and Joana M. Tavares. Bachelor's, U. Mass., Dartmouth, 2002; Master's, U. Mass., Boston, 2006. Clinician S. Bay Mental Health Ctr., Fall River, 2005—. Mem.: Am. Counseling Assn., Psi Chi, Phi Beta Lambda. Office Phone: 508-324-1060. E-mail: marciatavares@msn.com.

TAVARES, SAMANTHA, psychologist, educator; b. Bahia, Brazil, Oct. 23, 1968; arrived in U.S., 1984; d. Jose and Clarice Maria Tavares; 1 adopted child, Satyana Lua 1 child, Titus Sol. BA in Chinese Lang. Studies, Taipei, 1988; BA in Asian Studies, UCLA, 1990; M in Psychology, Forest Inst. Profl. Psychology, 1993; MA in Ea. Religion, U. Hawaii, 2000; PhD in Clin. Psychology, Am. Schs. Profl. Psychology, 1995. Lic. psychologist Hawaii, 1996, cert. hypnotherapist 1994, level II cert. Eye Movement Desensitization and Reprocessing. 1998, cert. holistic therapist 2000. Sch. counselor Han Guan Inst., China, 1986—88; pvt. practice clin. psychology Honolulu, Kailua, Hawaii, 1995—; clin. psychologist Dept. Health, Honolulu, 1996—98; clin. supr. Alaka'I Na Keiki, Inc., 1996—; clin. psychologist evaluator Dept. Edn. Dist. Hawaii, 1997—2000; assoc. prof. Holos U. Grad. Seminary, 2000—; faculty staff Inst. for Sci. Med. Intuition, 2000—04. Co-founder Samba Axe Hawaii, 1993—; dance instr., performer, 1993—; project dir. Support Adoption Hawaii, 2005—; exec. dir. Hawaii Hearts Helping Adoptions, 2005. Author: (compact disk, cassette tape) Transformative Liberation, 2005. Avocations: dance, yoga, meditation, running, surfing. Office: 43 Oneawa St Kailua HI Office Phone: 808-261-3731. E-mail: dr.tavaressam@yahoo.com.

TAWEEL, JANICE M., artist, educator; b. Ennis, Tex., Nov. 24, 1950; d. Josh H. and Evelyn M. Rivers; m. George M. Taweel, Nov. 24, 1973 (dec. Aug. 21, 1996); 1 child, Lorie M. BS, Lamar U., Beaumont, Tex., 1976. Cert. Tchg. Tex. Edn. Agy./Austin, Tex., 1976, Elem. Edn. Tex. Edn. Agy./Austin, Tex., 1990, All Level Art Tex. Edn. Agy./ Austin, Tex., 1976. Florist Designs by Delle Florist, Houston, 1968—69; credit/ billing lead Rogers Enterprises, Beaumont, Tex., 1976—90; owner Jan's Art, Beaumont, Tex., 1980—90; co-owner George's Boot and Shoe Repair, Beaumont, Tex., 1980—90; art educator Dallas Ind. Sch. Dist., Dallas, 1991—; owner The Artist Paper Trail, Dallas, 2004—. Sch. site coord. ArtsPartners, Dallas, 1999—, Crayola Dream-Makers, Dallas, 1999—; academic art sponsor Adamson H.S. Academic Fair, Dallas, 1999—; sch. site coord. Dallas Mus. of Art/ Go Van Gogh, Dallas, 1999—. Prin. works include Mushrooms, Iris, The Villiage, Nature on the Lake, White Whooping Crane, Orchid. Sponsor Future Educators, Dallas, 2005. Grantee, Hispanic Salute North Tex. Ford Dealers, 2001, Jr. League of Dallas, 2002, 2003. Mem.: Dallas Art Educator Assn. (assoc.). Independent. Bapt. Avocations: painting, travel, photography, art, crafts. Office: The Artist Paper Trail 8229 Cr 3823 Murchison TX 75778 Office Phone: 214-207-1293. Business E-Mail: jrserendipity@aol.com.

TAYLER, IRENE, English literature educator; b. Abilene, Tex., July 13, 1934; d. B. Brown Smith and Madeline (Bowron); m. Edward W. Tayler, June 3, 1961 (div. 1971); children: Edward Jr., Jesse; m. Saul Touster, Jan. 14, 1978. BA in Philosophy, Stanford U., 1956, MA in Am. Lit., 1961, PhD in English Lit., 1968. Tchr. Breadloaf Sch. of Eng., Middlebury, Vt., 1970, 71, 75, 76; teaching asst. Stanford U., Calif., 1958-60; lectr. Columbia U., N.Y., 1961-71; asst. prof. CUNY, 1971-73, assoc. prof., 1973-76, MIT, Cambridge, 1976-82, prof., 1982-96, sec. of the faculty, 1993-95, retired, 1996. Chair gov. com. The English Inst., 1981. Author: Blake's Illustrations to the Poems of Gray, 1971, Holy Ghosts: The Male Muses of Emily and Charlotte Bronte, 1990; editor: Samuel Bak: Between Worlds, Paintings and Drawings from 1946 to 2001, 2002; contbr. articles to profl. jours. Internat. Inst. Edn. fellow U. Munich, 1957-58; Wilson fellow Stanford U., 1961-62; NEH sr. scholar fellow, 1980; Mac Vicar faculty fellow MIT, 1993-2003; ACLS study grantee, 1968-69; Faculty Rsch. Found. grantee CUNY, 1972-73; first occupant Thomas Meloy chair rhetoric MIT, 1979-83. Mem.: St. Botolph Club (Boston) (pres. 2000—03). Business E-Mail: itayler@mit.edu.

TAYLOR, ALICIA, art educator; b. Detroit; d. Orange and Beverly Taylor. BS in art edn., Wayne State U., Detroit, 1997; MA in humanities, Ctrl. Mich. U., Mt. Pleasant, 2006. Cert. tchr. Mich. Art tchr. Office: Southfield-Lathrup HS 19301 W 12 Mile Rd Lathrup Village MI 48076-2557

TAYLOR, ANDREA REED, elementary school educator; b. Evansville, Ind., Feb. 19, 1979; d. Barry and Donna Logsdon Reed; m. John Carter Taylor, IV, Mar. 27, 2004 (dec. May 12, 2006); children: Carter William, Gabrielle McKenna. BS in Justice Adminstrn., U. Louisville, 2000, MAT in Middle Sch. Sci., 2004, postgrad., 2006—. Cert. sci. tchr. grades 5-9 Ky. Classroom tchr. Jefferson County Bd. Edn., Louisville, 2000—. Mem.: Jefferson County Tchrs. Assn. Democrat. Methodist. Home: 407 E Charlestown Ave Jeffersonville IN 47130

TAYLOR, ANGELA DAWN, primary school educator; d. Oscar Lee and Verna Irene Moore; m. Grover Durwood Taylor, Jr., Jan. 12, 1982; children: Tres, Mason, Nathaniel, Michael, Nicholas. BA, U. Ky., Lexington, 1992, MA, 1998, Edn. Specialist, 2005. Adminstrv. asst. Custom Cylinders Internat., Inc., Winchester, Ky., 1995—98; primary tchr. Fayette County Schs., Lexington, 1999—2001, intermediate tchr., 2003—05; K-1 tchr. Fayette County Schs./Rosa Parks Elem. Sch., 2005—; 3d grade tchr. Nelson County Schs., Bardstown, Ky., 2001—03. Bd. chair Victory Christian Ch., Lexington. Mem.: ASCD, Kappa Delta Pi. Christian Ch. Home: 2144 Roswell Dr Lexington KY 40513

TAYLOR, ANN, human resources specialist, educator; b. Gordonville, Pa., Feb. 28, 1940; d. Gideon S. and Elizabeth L. Stoltzfus; m. James R. Taylor III, Feb. 18, 1983 (dec. Sept. 1995). BA, Ea. Mennonite U., 1966; MEd, Millersville (Pa.) U., 1979; EdD, Temple U., 1995. Caseworker Lancaster (Pa.) Welfare Dept., 1969-72, Rockingham County Welfare Dept., 1966—67, Lancaster County Probation Parole Dept., 1967-69; parole agent Pa. Bd. Probation, Parole, Harrisburg, 1972-85; human resource cons., trainer Taylor Assocs., Lancaster, 1985—. Adj. prof. bus. mgmt. Pa. State U., Lancaster, 1979-2000; spkr. in field; free lance trainer Hamilton Bank, Lancaster, 1985-91, Armstrong World Industries, Lancaster, 1987, 91; adv. com. staff trainer Vantage Drug and Alcohol Facility, Lancaster, 1983-85. Co-author: Fire Up Your Brilliance; co-author articles to profl. jours. Vol. Lancaster County Mental Health Ctr., 1983-94; seminar leader Fulton County (Pa.) C. of C., 1985-86, York County (Pa.) C. of C., 1985-86, Lancaster County C. of C., 1985-88. Mem.: Am. Counseling Assn. Democrat. Episcopalian. Avocations: travel, reading, gardening, hiking. Office: 214 E King St Lancaster PA 17602 Office Phone: 717-394-6859. Personal E-mail: brilliance@comcast.net.

TAYLOR, ANNA DIGGS, federal judge; b. Washington, Dec. 9, 1932; d. Virginius Douglass and Hazel (Bramlette) Johnston; m. S. Martin Taylor, May 22, 1976; children: Douglass Johnston Diggs, Carla Cecile Diggs. BA, Barnard Coll., 1954; LLB, Yale U., 1957. Bar: D.C. 1957, Mich. 1961. Atty. Office Solicitor Gen. US Dept. Labor, 1957-60; asst. prosecutor Wayne County, Mich., 1961-62; asst. US atty. (ea. dist.) Mich. US Dept. Justice, 1966; ptnr. Zwerdling, Maurer, Diggs & Papp, Detroit, 1970-75; asst. corp. counsel City of Detroit, 1975-79; judge US Dist. Ct. (ea. dist.) Mich., Detroit, 1979—. Hon. chair United Way, Cmty. Found., S.E. Mich.; trustee emeritus Detroit Inst. Arts; co-chair, vol. Leadership Coun.; vice-chair Henry Ford Health Sys. Mem. Fed. Bar Assn., State Bar Mich., Wolverine Bar Assn. (v.p.), Yale Law Assn. Episcopalian. Office: US Dist Ct 740 US Courthouse 231 W Lafayette Blvd Detroit MI 48226-2700

TAYLOR, ANNE WILKERSON, elementary school educator; b. DeFuniack Springs, Fla., Oct. 10, 1950; d. Coston Ingram Wilkerson and Lelan Irene Blair; m. William Henry Taylor, Nov. 9, 1968; children: Matthew Allen, Randall Henry, William Jason. BS in Elem. Ed., Troy U., Ala., 1979; M in Elem. Ed., U. South Ala., 1991, adminstrv. degree, 2001. Cert. Project CRISS trainer. 6th grade tchr. Escatawpa (Miss.) Elem. Sch., 1985—88; 5th and 6th grade tchr. Castlen Elem. Sch., Grand Bay, Ala., 1988—98; 6th and 8th grade tchr. Grand Bay Mid. Sch., 1998—; 4th grade tchr. Dauphin Island Elem., Ala., 2005—. Title I parenting coord., staff dev. coord. Grand Bay Mid. Sch., 2003—. Named Tchr. of Yr., Castlen Elem. Sch. and Grand Bay Mid. Sch., 1997, 2004. Home: 10428 Knoke Ave Grand Bay AL 36541 Office Phone: 251-861-3864. Personal E-mail: wmhbilltaylor@aol.com.

TAYLOR, ARDIS, science educator; b. Lisbon, N.D., July 16, 1934; d. Oscar A. and Magnhild (Johnson) Ringdahl; m. Harvey A. Taylor, Apr. 2, 1962 (dec., 2005); 1 child, Miles. BS, Colo. State U., 1958; M, N.D. State U., 1980. Tchr. sci. Lisbon (N.D.) Pub. Schs., 1958-63, Sheldon (N.D.) Pub. Schs., 1969-76, Sargent Ctrl. Sch., Forman, N.D., 1976-94; ret., 1994. Author The Skanings of Aliceton, 1967, The Skanings Revisited 1882-1982, 1994, White Stone Hill, 1981, On The Taylor Trail, 1980, Taylor Legends, 1991, William Taylor Sr., 1999, A Few More Taylors, 2003, books on pioneer and area history; contbr. articles to profl. jours. and newspapers. Recipient Seim-Forred Soil Stewardship award, 1977, Sargent County Educator of Yr. award, 1994, Friend 4-H award, Ransom County, 1991, Sargent County, 1999. Mem. Quarter Horse Assn. (co-founder N.D. chpt., 1960, Founders award 1985). Home: 13532 77th St SE Lisbon ND 58054-9473

TAYLOR, BARBARA ANN OLIN, writer, educational consultant; b. St. Louis, Feb. 8, 1933; d. Spencer Truman and Ann Amelia (Whitney) Olin; m. F. Morgan Taylor Jr., Apr. 5, 1954; children: Spencer O., James W., John F., Frederick Morgan. AB, Smith Coll., 1954; MBA, Northwestern U., 1978, PhD, 1984; LHD, U. New Haven, 1995. Mem. faculty Hamden (Conn.) Hall Country Day Sch., 1972-74; cons. Booz, Allen & Hamilton, Inc., Chgo., 1979; program assoc. Northwestern U., Evanston, Ill., 1982; co-founder, exec. dir. Nat. Ctr. Effective Schs. R&D, Okemos, Mich., 1986-89, rsch. assoc., 1987; chmn. Nat. Ctr. for Effective Schs. Resource and Devel. Found., 2002—03; cons. on effective schs. rsch. and reform Nat. Ctr. Effective Schs. R&D U. Wis., Madison, 1990-96; pres. Excelsior! Found., Chgo., 1994—. Mem. exec. com. Hudson Inst. New Am. Schs. Devel. Corp. Design Team, 1990—94; Danforth Disting. lectr. U. Nebr., Omaha, 1993. Co-author: (book) Making School Reform Happen, 1993, Keepers of the Dream, 1994, The Revolution Revisited: Effective Schools and Systemic Reform, 1995; editor: Case Studies in Effective Schools Research, 1990; contbr. articles to profl. jours. Co-chair Coalition Housing and Human Resources, Hartford-New Haven, 1970—73; co-chair steering com. Day Care Conn., Hartford, 1971—73; trustee U. New Haven, 1961—71, Smith Coll., Northampton, Mass., 1984—90, Choate Rosemary Hall Sch., 1973—78, Lake Forest Coll., 1996—, Hudson Inst., 1989—97, Northwestern U., 1998—2002; pres. Jr. League New Haven, 1967—69, NCCJ, New Haven, 1971—73. Recipient Humanitarian award, Mt. Calvary Bapt. Ch., 1988, Oustanding Alumna award, John Burroughs Sch., 1994, Pres.'s award, U. New Haven, Alumni Merit award, Northwestern U., 2004. Mem.: ASCD, Nat. Staff Devel. Coun., Nat. Commn. Citizens Edn. (bd. dirs. 1980—86), Phi Delta Kappa (Internat. award Outstanding Svc. 2000). Episcopalian. Office: Nat Ctr Effective Schs Rsch & Devel 1124 Lake Rd Lake Forest IL 60045-1723

TAYLOR, BARBARA MAE HELM, artist, educator; b. Salina, Kans., Aug. 4, 1940; d. Wilber John and Mildred Mae (Walters) Helm; m. Walter Luther Taylor, II, Feb. 11, 1957; children: Walter Luther III, Natalie Sue Taylor Estes, Laura Marie, Toby Clark. AA, East Ark. C.C., Forrest City, 1990; BFA, Ark. State U., Jonesboro, 1992, MA, 1994. Portrait painter Barbara Taylor Art Studio, Palestine, Ark., 1992—. Adj. prof. Mid South C.C., West Memphis, Ark., 1996—98, East Ark. C.C., Forrest City, Ark., 1998—2006. Author: Every One and Me; numerous shows. Country fiddle player Ark. Gospel Assn., Forrest City, 1994—; violin player Midway Bapt. Ch., Palestine, 1988—. Mem.: Smithsonian Soc., Audubon Soc., Little Rock Art Links, Am. Soc. Portrait Artists (assoc.), Ark. Artist Registry (life), Delta Art Soc. (v.p. 1999—2000), Memphis Art Links, St. Francis Art Club (life; founder, pres. 2000—), Gamma Beta Phi (life). Avocation: birdwatching. Home: 523 Saint Francis 867 Palestine AR 72372 Office: Barbara Taylor Art Studio 493 St Francis Co 867 Palestine AR 72372-8936 Office Phone: 870-581-3890. Business E-Mail: barbhelmtaylor@arkansas.net.

TAYLOR, BRANDY MILLER, music educator; b. Decatur, Ala., Nov. 15, 1973; d. Patricia N. Miller; m. T. Brian Taylor, June 9, 2001. B in Music Edn., U. Montevallo, 1997, MusM, 1999. Cert. Orff-Schulwerk level 1, level 2 Nat. Orff-Schulwerk Assn., prevention and management of aggressive behavior specialist Ala. Reading Initiative. Tchr. music, dir. choir John E. Bryan Elem. Sch., Morris, Ala., 1997—. Grantee multiple grants, Ednl. Found. Mem.: Jefferson County Edn. Assn. (assoc. rep. 2002—), Ala. Edn. Assn., Ala. Orff-Schulwerk Assn., Ala. Music Educators' Assn. (publicity mgr. 2003—), Music Educators Nat. Conf. Office: John E Bryan Elementary School 600 Kimberly Cut-Off Road Morris AL 35116 Personal E-mail: muscmaker@yahoo.com.

TAYLOR, CAROLYN KAY, music educator; b. Protection, Kans., Mar. 30, 1938; d. Thomas George and Ruby D. Boone; m. Joseph Taylor; children: Corinne K. Maloch, Holly D. Peter, Daren K. Degree in Liberal Studies, Calif. State U., Chico, 1981. Life credential in music Calif. C.C., 1976, cert. multiple subject K-8 Calif., 1991. Instr. Butte C.C., Oroville, Calif., 1976—98; fine arts and music specialist Chico Unified Sch. Dist., Calif., 1985—. Handbell choir dir. First Christian Ch., Chico, 1976—94; choir and handbell choir dir. Bidwell Meml. Presbyn. Ch., Chico, 1979—81; choir dir. Aldersgate United Meth. Ch., 1998—. Musician: Touring Handbell Choir, 1980. Grantee, Kappa Delta Pi, Calif. State U., Chico, 1981. Mem.: Calif. Music Educators' Assn. (treas. exec. bd. 1994—98, sec. exec. bd. 1998—2001), Am. Orff-Schulwerk Assn. (pres. 1987—89, sec. 1999—2001), Mt. Lassen Chapter, American Orff-Schulwerk Association, California Music Educators' Association, Northern Section. Methodist. Avocation: music. Office: Chapman Sch 1071 E 16th St Chico CA 95928 Office Fax: 530-891-3294.

TAYLOR, CAROLYN ROBERTS, small business owner, chef; b. Washington, Feb. 10, 1946; d. Thomas Edward and Mary Splawn Taylor; m. James Joseph Maranville, June 25, 1994; m. David R. Williams (div.); children: Nathan J. Williams, Samuel T. Williams. At, Guilford Coll., Greensboro, N.C., 1964—67; BS, Ill. Inst. Tech., Chgo., 1969; cert., Cordon Bleu Sch. Cooking, London, 1974. Summer chef Mt. Desert Biol. Lab., Maine, 1981—83; pastry chef Al Forno Restaurant, Providence, 1983; sous chef Jordan's Restaurant, Leesburg, Va., 1984; chef Middleburg Tennis Club and Catering, 1985—88; chef and co-owner Taylor & Fuog Catering, Hamilton, 1988—91; pastry chef ARA at Xerox Tng. Ctr., Leesburg, 1991—93; chef Morningside Ho., 1993—96; owner and operator Taylor Made Cakes, Hamilton, 1997—. Baking instr. Boston Adult Edn., 1976; pvt. cooking instr., Providence, 1976—79; guest tchr. Chef's Co. Sch., Barrington, 1983; cons. Battletown Inn, Berryville, Va., 1985; adv. bd. culinary program Monroe Va. Tech. Sch., Leesburg, 1998—. Tutor and coord. non-tutoring vols. Loudoun Literacy Coun., Leesburg, Va., 1997—98; vol. Loudoun Hosp., 1985. Mem.: Cake and Sugar Artists No. Va., Internat. Cake Exploration Soc., Shenendoah Wedding Profls. Democrat. Mem. Soc. Of Friends. Avocations: scuba diving, snorkeling, country dancing, hiking. Office: Taylor Made Cakes PO Box 523 Purcellville VA 20132 Office Phone: 540-338-2324. Personal E-mail: crtbake@aol.com.

TAYLOR, CELIANNA ISLEY, information systems specialist; b. Youngstown, Ohio; d. Paul Thornton and Florence (Jacobs) Isley; divorced; children: Polly, Jerry, Jim. BA in Philosophy, Denison U., 1939; MLS, Western Res. U., 1942. Worked in several pub. libns. and univ. librs., 1939-50; head Libr. Cataloging Dept. Battelle Mem. Inst., Columbus, Ohio, 1951-53; head pers. office, assoc. prof. libr. adminstrn. Ohio State U. Librs., Columbus, 1954-65; coord. info. svcs., assoc. prof. libr. adminstrn. Nat. Ctr. for Rsch. in Vocat. Edn., Ohio State U., Columbus, 1966-70; sr. rsch. assoc., adminstrv. assoc., assoc. prof. libr. adminstrn. dept. computer and info. sci. Ohio State U., Columbus, 1970-86, assoc. prof. emeritus Univ. Librs., 1986—. Mem. Task Force on a Spl. Collections Database, Ohio State U. Librs., Columbus, 1988-89, comm. systems and recs. coord. Ohio State U. Retirees Assn., Columbus, 1992-93, info. specialist, MacForum, Ohio State U., Columbus, 2001-2004; cons. profl. orgns. including Ernst & Ernst CPA's and Oreg. State Sys. of Higher Edn., 1961-82. Author: (with J. Magisos) Guide for State Voc-Tech Edn. Dissemination Systems 1971; editor: (with A.E. Petrarca, and R.S. Kohn) Info. Interaction 1982; Highlights-Coun. for Ethics in Econs., 1997—; contbr. several articles to profl. jours.; designer info. sys.: CALL Sys., 1977-82, Channel 2000 Proj. Home Info. Svc., 1980-81, Continuing Education Info. Ctr., 1989-90, Human Resources (HUR) Sys., 1976-77,1979-82, DECOS, 1975-86, Computer-asst. libr. Sys., Optical Scan Sys., 1972-73, ERIC Clearinghouse for vocat. edn., 1966-70. Chmn. subcom. on design, info. and ref. com. Columbus United Cmty. Coun., 1972-73; bd. dirs. Columbus Reg. Info. Svc., 1974-78, Cmty. Info. Referral Svc., Inc. 1975-81; dir. Computer Utility for Pub. Info. Columbus, 1975-81; acct. coord. Greater Columbus Free-net, 1994-98; info. specialist, coord. LWV Met. Columbus Website Com., 2001-02; judge Laws of Life Ohio Statewide H.S. Essay Contest, 2005—; interprofessional pub. policy panel on tech. and ethics, Interprofessional Commn. Ohio, 2006—. Mem. ALA, Assn. Computing Machinery (Ctrl. Ohio chpt.), Am. Soc. Info. Sci. and Tech., Assn. Faculty and Profl. Women Ohio State U., Columbus Metro Club, Coun. for Ethics in Econs., World Future Soc., Olympic Indoor Tennis Club. Avocations: bird watching, gourmet cooking, tennis, water aerobics. Home and Office: 3471 Greenbank Ct Columbus OH 43221-4724 Office Phone: 614-876-0069.

TAYLOR, CHARLOTTE NICOLE, literature and language educator; b. Atlanta, Apr. 16, 1981; d. Ronnie Lee and Robin Basham Taylor. Degree in secondary edn., Carson-Newman Coll., Jefferson City, Tenn., 2004. Lang. arts tchr. Maury Mid. Sch., Dandridge, Tenn., 2004—. Coach dance team, Dandridge, 2005—06. Dir.: (play) Bugsy Malone, Hollywood Hillbillies. Constrn. work Habitat for Humanity, Knoxville, Tenn., 2005—06. Mem.: NEA, Jefferson County Educators Assn.

TAYLOR, CHRISTINE, actress; b. Allentown, Pa., July 30, 1971; d. Skip and Joan Taylor; m. Ben Stiller, May 13, 2000; children: Ella Olivia, Quinlin Dempsey. Actor: (films) Calendar Girl, 1993, Showdown, 1993, The Brady Bunch Movie, 1995, Breaking Free, 1995, The Craft, 1996, A Very Brady Sequel, 1996, Cat Swallows Parakeet and Speaks, 1996, Campfire Tales, 1997, The Wedding Singer, 1998, Overnight Delivery, 1998, Denial, 1998, Kiss Toledo Goodbye, 1999, Desperate But Not Serious, 1999, Zoolander, 2001, Dodgeball: A True Underdog Story, 2004; (TV films) Here Come the Munsters, 1995, To the Ends of Time, 1996, Heat Vision and Jack, 1999. Office: United Talent Agy 9560 Wilshire Blvd Ste 500 Beverly Hills CA 90212

TAYLOR, CORA HODGE, social worker; b. Fayetteville, N.C., Nov. 25, 1942; d. John Marlin and Cora Louise (Mitchell) Hodge; m. Charles L. Taylor, June 26, 1965; children: Charles L., John M. BS, N.C. Coll., Durham, 1963; MSW, U. N.C., Chapel Hill, 1965. Clin. social worker VA Hosp., Bedford, Mass., 1965-68, 73-79; chief social worker Regional Health Center, Wilmington, Mass., 1978-79; clin. social worker VA Hosp., Bedford, Mass., 1979-91, supervisory social worker geriatrics and long term care, 1991—2000, coord. contract programs, 1993—. Field instr. Boston U. Sch. Social Work, 1979-87, Smith Coll. Sch. of Social Work, 1986-89; instr., cons. primary care residents Tufts U. Med. Sch., Regional Health Center, Wilmington, Mass., 1978-79. Mem. Town Meeting, Billerica, Mass., 1981-2000; precinct clk., 1981, 82, 89, precinct chmn., 1984, 85, 86; deacon first Congl. Ch., 1986—; women vets. coord. VA Bedford; Social Work Leadership Tng. program, 1998; mem. bd. commrs. Housing Authority Atlantic Beach, SC, 2003-04. Mem. LWC (dir. 1970-73), Acad. Cert. Social Workers, Nat. Assn. Social Workers.

TAYLOR, DIANA LANCASTER, state official; b. Summit, N.J., Feb. 6, 1955; d. Edwin Douglas and Lois Johnston (O'Neill) T. AB, Dartmouth Coll., 1977; MBA, Columbia U., 1979-81. Analyst N.Y. State Dept. Soc. Service, N.Y.C., 1977-79; assoc. Smith, Barney, Harris, Upham, N.Y.C., 1981-82, Lehman Brothers Kuhn Loeb, N.Y.C., 1982-83, v.p., 1983-84, Donaldson, Lufkin & Jenrette, N.Y.C., 1984-86, sr. v.p., mgr. short-term banking, 1987-88, sr. v.p., mgr. edn. fin. group, 1987-88; founding ptnr. M.R. Beal & Co., 1988—90, pres., 1990—93; exec. v.p., head capital markets Muriel Siebert & Co., 1993—95; sr. v.p. pub. fin. Smith Mitchell Investment Group Inc., 1996—99; asst. sec. for pub. authorities State of NY, 1999; v.p. governmental and regulatory affairs KeySpan Energy, N.Y.C., 2000—; CFO LI Power Authority, NY, 2001—02; dep. sec. for state authorities State of NY, 2002—03, dep. sec. for fin. & housing, 2003, supt. banks, 2003—. Bd. dirs. YMCA Greater NYC, Hudson River Park Trust, The After Sch. Corp., NYC Transit Mus., Bklyn. Acad. Music. Office: Supt Banks NY State Banking Dept One State St New York NY 10004-1417 Office Phone: 212-709-3501.

TAYLOR, DONNA LEONA, advocate, writer; b. Staunton, Va., Nov. 7, 1971; d. George and Leona Ellis Taylor. BA in Polit. Sci., Mary Baldwin Coll., Staunton, 2006. Editl. asst., prodn. coord., sr. prodn. coord. Procs. of the NAS, Washington, 2001—04; shelter mgr., supr. New Directions Ctr., Staunton, 2004—. Literacy mentor In2Books, Inc., Washington, 2003—04. Avocations: horseback riding, music. Home: PO Box 472 Fishersville VA 22939 Office Phone: 540-885-7273. Office Fax: 540-885-0686. Personal E-mail: donna.taylor@gmail.com.

TAYLOR, E. JANE, lawyer; b. Niagra Falls, N.Y., Dec. 16, 1954; BA cum laude, Kent State U., 1977; JD, U. Akron, 1980. Bar: Ohio 1981, U.S. Dist. Ct. No. Dist. Ohio 1981, U.S. Ct. Appeals (6th cir.) 1985, U.S. Dist. Ct. So. Dist. Ohio 2002. Assoc. atty. Guy Lemmert & Towne, Akron, Ohio, 1981—90, ptnr., 1990—. Mem. Akron Law Rev., 1979—80. Mem. bd. trustees United Way Summit County, 1995—2002, past chair svc. rev. team, mem. cmty. investment coun., chair portfolio coun. improving health and wellness, past mem. planning and allocations com., co-chair task force multi-yr. funding. Named one of 100 Women of Distinction, Akron Area YWCA, 2001. Mem.: ABA, Comml. Law League Am., Ohio Women's Bar Assn., Nat. Conf. Bar Presidents, Ohio State Bar Assn. (mem. bd. govs. 2000—03, mem. coun. delegates 1996—2003, pres.-elect 2004—), Akron Bar Assn. (pres. 1994—95, v.p. 1993—94, bd. trustees 1990—93, chair bar applicants and students com. 1988—90, mem. bankruptcy and comml. law sect. 1989—, outstanding com. chairperson 1997—98). Office: Guy Lammert & Towne 2210 First Nat Twr 106 S Main St Akron OH 44308 Office Phone: 330-535-2151. Office Fax: 330-535-9048. E-mail: guylaw2210@aol.com.

TAYLOR, EDNA JANE, retired employment program counselor; b. Flint, Mich., May 16, 1934; d. Leonard Lee and Wynona Ruth (Davis) Harvey; children: Wynona Jane MacDonald, Cynthia Lee Zellmer. BS, No. Ariz. U., 1963; MEd, U. Ariz., 1967. Tchr. h.s. Sunnyside Sch. Dist., Tucson, 1963—68; employment program counselor employment devel. State of Calif., Canoga Park, 1968—98; ret., 1998. Mem. adv. coun. Van Nuys Cmty. Adult Sch., Calif., 1983-96, steering com., 1989-91, leadership coun., 1991-92; mem. adv. coun. Pierce C.C., Woodland Hills, Calif., 1979-81; first aid instr., recreational leader ARC. Mem. NAFE, Internat. Assn. of Pers. in Employment Security, Calif. Employment Counselors Assn. (state treas. 1978-79, state sec. 1980), Delta Psi Kappa (life). Avocations: writing, tennis, health and fitness, gardening. Personal E-mail: tauchi2@mindspring.com.

TAYLOR, ELEANOR ROSS, writer; b. Norwood, N.C., June 30, 1920; d. Fred Elbert and Jennie Catherine (Lilly) Ross; m. Peter Hillsman Taylor, June 4, 1943; children: Katherine Baird, Peter Ross. BA, U. N.C., 1940. Author: (poetry) Wilderness Of Ladies, 1960; Welcome Eumenides, 1972, Selected, 1983 Days Going/Days Coming Back, 1992, Late Leisure, 1999. Recipient Shelley Meml. award Poetry Soc. Am., 1998, Libr. of Va. Poetry prize, 2000, Aiken-Taylor award Sewanee Review, 2001, literary award Am Acad. of Arts and Letters, 1967

TAYLOR, ELIZABETH (DAME ELIZABETH ROSEMOND TAYLOR), actress; b. London, Feb. 27, 1932; d. Francis Lenn and Sara Viola (Warmbrodt) Taylor; m. Conrad Nicholas Hilton Jr., May 6, 1950 (div. Feb. 1, 1951); m. Michael Wilding, Feb. 21, 1952 (div. Jan. 30, 1957); children: Christopher Edward, Michael Howard; m. Michael Todd, Feb. 2, 1957 (dec. Mar. 22, 1958); 1 child, Elizabeth Frances; m. Eddie Fisher, May 12, 1959 (div. Mar. 6, 1964); m. Richard Burton, Mar. 15, 1964 (div. June 26, 1974); 1 adopted child, Maria; m. Richard Burton, Oct. 10, 1975 (div. Aug. 1, 1976); m. John W. Warner, Dec. 4, 1976 (div. Nov. 7, 1982); m. Larry Fortensky, Oct. 6, 1991 (div. Oct. 31, 1996). Student, Byron House, Hawthorne Sch., Metro-Goldwyn-Mayer Sch. Ptnr., cons. House of Taylor Jewelry, Inc, 2005—. Actress: (films) There's One Born Every Minute, 1942; Lassie Come Home, 1943; The White Cliffs of Dover, 1944; Jane Eyre, 1944; National Velvet, 1944; Courage of Lassie, 1946; Cynthia, 1947; Life with Father, 1947; A Date with Judy, 1948; Julia Misbehaves, 1948; Little Women, 1950; Conspirator, 1950; The Big Hangover, 1950; Father of the Bride, 1950; Quo Vadis, 1951; Father's Little Dividend, 1951; A Place in the Sun, 1951; Callaway Went Thataway, 1951; Lover is Better Than Ever, 1952; Ivanhoe, 1952; The Girl Who Had Everything, 1953; Elephant Walk, 1954; Rhapsody, 1954; Beau Brummel, 1954; The Last Time I Saw Paris, 1954; Giant, 1956; Raintree County, 1957; Cat on a Hot Tin Roof, 1958; Suddenly, Last Summer, 1959; Scent of Mystery, 1960; Butterfield 8, 1960 (Acad. award for Best Actress, 1960); Cleopatra, 1963; The V.I.P.'s, 1963; The Sandpiper, 1965; Who's Afraid of Virginia Woolf?, 1966 (Acad. award for Best Actress, 1966); The Comedians, 1967; Reflections in a Golden Eye, 1967; Dr. Faustus, 1967; Boom!, 1968; Secret Ceremony, 1968; Anne of the Thousand Days, 1969; The Only Game in Town, 1970; Under Milkwood, 1971; X, Y and Zee, 1972; Hammersmith is Out, 1972; Night Watch, 1973; Ash Wednesday, 1973; That's Entertainment, 1974; The Driver's Seat, 1974; Blue Bird, 1975; Winter Kills, 1977; A Little Night Music, 1977; The Mirror Crack'd, 1980; Young Toscanini, 1988; The Flintstones, 1994; Actress, prodr. The Taming of the Shrew, 1967; Actress: (TV films) Divorce His-Divorce Hers, 1973; Victory at Entebbe, 1977; Return Engagement, 1979; Between Friends, 1982; Malice in Wonderland, 1986; There Must Be a Pony, 1986; Poker Alice, 1987; Sweet Bird of Youth, 1989; These Old Broads, 2001; (TV miniseries) North and South, 1985; (TV series) General Hospital, 1981; All My Children, 1984; Hotel, 1984; The Simpsons, 1993; The Nanny, 1996; Murphy Brown, 1996; High Society, 1996; theatre appearances include: (Broadway plays) The Little Foxes, 1981; Private Lives, 1983; narrator: (documentaries) Genocide, 1981; exec. prodr.: (films) Number 13, 1962; exec. prodr.: (films) Oz, 1967; assoc. prodr.: (films) The Caretaker, 1963; author: (autobiography) Elizabeth Taylor, 1965, Elizabeth Taylor Takes Off: On Weight Gain, Weight Loss, Self Esteem and Self Image, 1988, Elizabeth Taylor: My Love Affair with Jewelry, 2002; co-author (with Richard Burton): (novels) World Enough and Time, 1964; lic. (fragrances) Elizabeth Taylor's Passion, Passion for Men, White Diamonds/Elizabeth Taylor, Elizabeth Taylor's Diamonds & Emeralds, Diamonds and Rubies, Diamonds & Sapphires, Elizabeth Taylor Black Pearls. Active philanthropic, relief, charitable causes internationally, including Israeli War Victims Fund for the Chaim Sheba Hosp., 1976, UNICEF, various children's hosps., med. clinics, Botswana; initiated Ben Gurion U. - Elizabeth Taylor Fund for Children of the Negev, 1982; supporter AIDS Project, L.A., 1985; founder, nat. chmn. Am. Found. for AIDS Rsch. (AmFAR), 1985—, internat. fund, 1985—; founder Elizabeth Taylor AIDS Found., 1991—. Named a Kennedy Ctr. Honoree, John F. Kennedy Ctr. for the Performing Arts, 2002; named Comdr. Arts Letters, France, 1985, an honoree with dedication of Elizabeth Taylor Med. Ctr. Whitman - Walker Clinic, Washington, 1993, Dame Comdr. of Order of British Empire, 1999; recipient Legion of Honor (for work with AmFAR), France, 1987, Aristotle S. Onassis Found., 1988, Jean Hersholt Humanitarian Acad. award (for work as AIDS advocate), 1993, Life Achievement award, Am. Film Inst., 1993, BAFTA Fellowship Award, British Acad. Film and Television Arts, 1999, Presdl. Citizen's Medal, 2001. Address: Elizabeth Taylor AIDS Found PO Box 55995 Sherman Oaks CA 91413

TAYLOR, ESTELLE WORMLEY, language educator, dean; b. Washington, Jan. 12, 1924; d. Luther Charles and Wilhelmina Wormley; m. Ivan Earle Taylor, Dec. 26, 1953. BS magna cum laude, Miner Tchrs. Coll., 1945; MA, Howard U., 1947; PhD, Cath. U. Am., 1969. Instr. English Howard U., 1947-52; tchr. Langley Jr. H.S., Washington, 1952-55, Eastern Sr. H.S., Washington, 1955-63; from instr. to prof. D.C. Tchrs. Coll., 1963—76; assoc. provost Fed. City Coll., Washington, 1974-75; prof. Howard U., 1976-91, chmn. dept. English, 1976-85, assoc. dean Coll. Liberal Arts, 1985-86, dir. expository writing program Grad. Sch. Arts and Scis., 1988-91, prof. emeritus, 1991. Mem., sec. Edn. Licensure Commn. of D.C., 1993—; mem. Commn. on Higher Edn., Mid. States Assn. Colls. and Schs., 1984-87, 88-90, co-chair steering com. to revise Characteristics of Excellence, 1992-93; mem. ctrl. exec. com. Folger Inst. Renaissance and 18th Century Studies, 1982-91; adv. bd. Humanities Inst. Montgomery Coll., 1997—. Contbg. editor A Howard Reader, 1997. 1st v.p. Order Daus. of King Episc. Ch. Diocese, Washington, 1994-98; commr. Edn. Licensure Com. of D.C., 1993—, also sec., vice chmn., 1995—; trustee U. D.C., 1979-83, vice chmn., 1983; mem. D.C. Cmty. Humanities Coun., 1990-91; co-chmn. planning com. Centennial Celebration of the Andrew Rankin Chapel Howard U., 1994; adv. bd. Coll. Arts and Svcs., Howard U., 2002—; mem. selection bd. Fgn. Agrl. Svc., 2002. Named Disting. Alumni, Howard U., 1995, Alumni award for Disting. Postgrad. Achievement in Edn. and Lit., 1997; So. fellow, 1968-69; Rockefeller/Aspen Inst. fellow, 1978-79. Mem. MLA (del. assembly 1994—), Nat. Assn. for Equal Opportunity in Higher Edn., Coll. Lang. Assn., Shakespeare Assn. Am., Pub. Mems. Assn. Fgn. Svc. Dept. of State, Links (v.p. Capital City chpt. 1979-81, corr. sec. 1989, rec. sec. 1991-93, 95—). Democrat. Home: 3221 20th St NE Washington DC 20018-2421

TAYLOR, FANNIE TURNBULL, art association administrator, educator; b. Kansas City, Mo., Sept. 11, 1913; d. Henry King and Fannie Elizabeth (Sills) Turnbull; m. Robert Taylor, Dec. 2, 1938 (div. 1974); children: Kathleen Muir Taylor Isaacs, Anne Kingston Taylor Wadsack. BA, U. Wis., 1938; LHD (hon.), Buena Vista Coll., Storm Lake, Iowa, 1975. Mem. faculty U. Wis., Madison, 1941—, prof. social edn., 1949—, emerita, 1979—. Dir. Wis. Union Theater, 1946-66, coord. univ. systems arts coun., 1967-70, assoc. dir. Ctr. Arts Adminstrn., 1970-72, coord. Consortium for Arts, 1976-84; cons. in field. Author: The Arts at a New Frontier: The National Endowment for the Arts, Wisconsin Union Theater: Fifty Golden Years (Book award of Merit, State Hist. Soc. Wis. 1990); contbr. articles to profl. jours. Program dir. music Nat. Endowment Arts, 1966-67, program info. dir., 1972-76; bd. dirs. Wis. Arts Coun., 1964-72, Wis. Found. Arts, 1976-91, Madison Civic Music Assn., 1976-84, Madison Children's Mus., 1983-96, Chazen Art Coun., 1976—, chair 1983-86; Madison Civic Ctr. Found., 1981-94; hon. chair Wis. Union Theater Program Endowment Fund, 1985—; bd. dirs. Wis. chpt. Nature Conservancy, 1963-84, chmn. 1976-77; bd. dirs. Shorewood Hills Found., 1976-2002, pres., 1976-81. Recipient Oak Leaf award Nature Conservancy, 1981, Wis. Gov.'s award in Support of the Arts, 1992, Madison Cmty. Found. Asset Builders Leadership award, 2002, Madison Children's Mus. Star Soc. award, 2005; named Woman of Distinction, Madison YWCA, 1994. Fellow Wis. Acad. Scis., Arts and Letters; mem. Assn. Performing Arts Presenters (founder, exec. dir. 1957-72, 1st recipient Fannie Taylor Disting. Svc. award 1972), Am. Assn. Dance Cos. (bd. dirs. 1967-72), Nat. Assn. Regional Ballet (bd. dirs. 1975-77), Nat. Guild Cmty. Music Schs. Arts (bd. dirs. 1977-80), Women in Comm. (Writers' Cup 1980), U. Wis. Found., U. Wis. Alumni Assn. (Disting. Svc. award 1979), Bach Dancing and Dynamite Soc. (bd. dirs. 1993-2004, Big Band award), Madison Civics Club (pres. 1969-70), Univ. Club (pres. 1982-85), Blackhawk Club. Home: 8301 Old Sauk Rd Apt 303 Middleton WI 53562-4393 Business E-Mail: ftaylor@facstaff.wisc.edu.

TAYLOR, GINA ADELE, dermatologist; d. Earle Spencer Taylor and Elaine Joy Bogle-Taylor. BA, Johns Hopkins U., Balt., 1995; MD, U. Pa., Phila., 2000. Lic. physician NY, diplomate Am. Bd. Dermatology. Attending dermatologist Downstate Med. Ctr., Bklyn., 2005—, Kings County Hosp. Ctr., Bklyn., 2005—. Dir. of svc. dermatology Kings County Hosp. Ctr., 2005—. Recipient Nancy C. Bell, MD Meml. prize, Dept. Dermatology, U. Pa. Sch. Medicine, 2000, The Residents and Fellows Alumni Soc. award, Dept. Dermatology, SUNY Downstate Med. Ctr., 2004. Fellow: Am. Acad. Dermatology. Office Phone: 718-270-1229.

TAYLOR, GLORIA A., minister, educator; d. Walter Hedland and Margaret Rose Atkinson; m. Frederic Edward Taylor, Feb. 23, 1947; children: Greg Eugene, Lance Norman, Brett Jack, Scott Frederic, Penny Gay. Ordination, Diocesan Sch. Faith & Ministry, 1989. Ordained Diocese No. Ind., 1989. Chairperson Episcopal AIDS Ministry, South Bend, Ind., 1989—99; deacon St. Paul Episcopal Ch., Munster, Ind., 1989—93, Trinity Ch., Mich. City, Ind., 1993—. Support groups for people with HIV/AIDS and mothers, South Bend, 1988—99; provider pastoral care for women in all walks of life. Conservative. Episcopal. Achievements include being the first woman ordained in the 100 year old diocese in 1989. Avocations: travel, watercolor. Home: 1809 Holly Lane Munster IN 46321 Office Phone: 219-874-4355. Personal E-mail: gataylor89@aol.com.

TAYLOR, GRACE ELIZABETH WOODALL (BETTY TAYLOR), law educator, library administrator; b. Butler, N.J., June 14, 1926; d. Frank E. and Grace (Carlyon) Woodall; m. Edwin S. Taylor, Feb. 4, 1951 (dec.); children: Carol Lynn Taylor Crespo, Nancy Ann Filer. AB, Fla. State U., 1949, MA, 1950; JD, U. Fla., 1962. Instr. asst. librarian U. Fla., 1950-56, asst. law libr. Coll. Law, 1956-62; dir. Legal Info. Ctr., 1962—2003, prof. law, 1976—2003; Clarence J. TeSelle prof. of law U. Fla., 1994—2003, historian, archivist Call-Law, 2003—. Trustee Nat. Ctr. for Automated Rsch., N.Y.C., 1978-96; past chmn. joint com. on LAWNET, Am. Assn. Law Librs., Am. Assn. Law Schs. and ABA, 1978—; cons. to law librs., 1975—; mem. adv. com. N.E. Regional Data Ctr., U. Fla., 1990—. Co-author: American Law Publications, 1986, 21st Century: Technology's Impact, 1988, Law in the Digital Age: The Challenge of Research in Legal Information Centers, 1996, also articles. Recipient 1st Disting. Alumni award Fla. State U. Libr. Sch., 1983, 2d Marya Lange/C.Q. award law and polit. sci. sect. ACRL and Congl. Quar., 1997; Lewis Scholar Fla. Legislature, 1947-50; grantee NEH, 1981-82, Coun. Libr. Resources, 1984-86; Dist. Svc. award, Florida Library Assn., 2000. Mem.: ABA (Law Libr. Congress facilities com. 1991—97), Am. Assn. Law Schs. (accreditation com. 1978—81), Am. Assn. Law Librs. (exec. bd. 1981—84, Marian Gould Gallagher Disting. Svc. award 1997, Aspen Law and Bus. Rsch. grant 1997), OCLC Users Coun. (pres. 1983—86), Beta Phi Mu, Phi Beta Kappa (v.p. U. Fla. chpt. 1994—95, pres. 1995—96). Democrat. Methodist. Avocations: computers, genealogy, crafts, gardening. Office: U Fla Legal Info Ctr Gainesville FL 32611 E-mail: Taylor@law.ufl.edu.

TAYLOR, HEATHER MARIE, director; b. Park Ridge, Ill., May 21, 1974; d. Kent Emil and Rebecca Jo Buchholz; m. Christopher Lee Taylor, Jan. 13, 2001. BA in English and Secondary Edn., No. Ill. U., 1996; MS in Integrated Mktg. Comm. summa cum laude, Roosevelt U., 2000. Writer corp. comm. 360 Comm., Chgo., 1995—96; tchg. asst. No. Ill. U., DeKalb, 1995—96; tchr. Streamwood (Ill.) H.S., 1996—97; sr. mktg. mgr. Hanley-Wood, LLC, Addison, Ill., 1997—2002; owner, pres. Pro Writer Ltd., Portage, Ind., 2000—; dir. comms. for admissions, fin. aid and mktg. Valparaiso (Ind.) U., 2002—, adj. prof., 2006—. Adj. prof. Roosevelt U., Chgo., 2001—. Contbr. Of Diamonds and Rust, 1989, Great Poems of the Western World Vol. 2, 1990, articles to profl. jours. Mem.: NEA, Am. Mktg. Assn., Roosevelt Adj. Faculty Orgn., Sigma Tau Delta, Phi Kappa Phi, Golden Key. Lutheran. Avocations: photography, writing, travel. Home: 5683 Dovedale Ave Portage IN 46368 Office: Valparaiso U 1700 Chapel Dr Valparaiso IN 46383 Office Phone: 219-464-5011. Business E-Mail: heather.taylor@valpo.edu.

TAYLOR, HELEN SHIELDS, civic worker; b. Bloomington, Ind., Nov. 27, 1922; d. Lester Howard Shields and Mary Margaret (Galyan) Shields-Fleener; m. Richard R. Hurst, July 29, 1945 (div. Feb. 1959); children: Pamela Hurst Hayes, Richard S.; m. Clyde Leon Taylor, Dec. 2, 1961 (dec. Aug. 2, 2006); 1 child, John P. AA, Coll. Sequoias, 1975; BA, Calif. State U., Fresno, 1979. Active Bd. Edn. Pipeline Program; bd. dirs. Taylor Machinery, Inc., Visalia, Calif. Author: Japanese Invasion of the Philippines, 1977, Russia Today, 1979 Active in registration of legal immigrants with County; bd. dirs. Town Hall, Inc., Fresno, 1990-96; past pres. Tulare County Symphony, Visalia, Meth. Women, Visalia, 1952-96; mem. Ice House Theatre, Visalia, 1980-96; mem. justice and edn. Tulare County Grand Jury, 2000-01 Recipient Award of Recognition, Veva Blunt Sch. Mem. AAUW (grantee 1979), U.S. Fgn. Policy Assn. (co-chair 1986-96), Alpha Gamma Sigma Democrat. Avocations: investing, travel, book reviewing, public speaking. Home: 1545 S Chinowth St Visalia CA 93277-3909 Office: Taylor Machinery Inc 6988 Avenue 304 Visalia CA 93291-9510

TAYLOR, HOLLY ANN, music educator; b. Midland, Tex., Oct. 11, 1978; d. Thomas Woods and Donna Louise Hughston; m. Mark Alan Taylor, July 22, 2006. MusB in Music Edn., George Mason U., Fairfax, Va., 2003, M in Music Performance, 2006. Cert. tchr. Va., 2003. Music/strings tchr. Fairfax County Pub. Schs., 2003—. Freelance performer Haase Quartet, Fairfax, 1999—. Mem.: Music Educators Nat. Conf. Office Phone: 703-715-3800. Personal E-mail: holly.taylor@fcps.edu.

TAYLOR, J. MARY (JOCELYN MARY TAYLOR), museum director, educator, zoologist; b. Portland, Oreg., May 30, 1931; d. Arnold Llewellyn and Kathleen Mary (Yorke) T.; m. Joseph William Kamp, Mar. 18, 1972 (dec.); m. Wesley Kingston Whitten, Mar. 20, 2001. BA, Smith Coll., 1952; MA, U. Calif., Berkeley, 1953, PhD, 1959. Instr. zoology Wellesley Coll., 1959-61, asst. prof. zoology, 1961-65; assoc. prof. zoology U. B.C., 1965-74; dir. Cowan Vertebrate Mus., 1965-82, prof. dept. zoology, 1974-82; collaborative scientist Oreg. Regional Primate Research Ctr., 1983-87; prof. (courtesy) dept. fisheries and wildlife Oreg. State U., 1984-95; dir. Cleve. Mus. Nat. History, 1987-96, dir. emerita, 1996—. Adj. prof. dept. biology Case Western Res. U., 1987-96. Assoc. editor Jour. Mammalogy, 1981-82. Contbr. numerous articles to sci. jours. Trustee Benjamin Rose Inst., 1988-93, Western Res. Acad., 1989-94, U. Circle, Inc., 1987-96, The Cleve. Aquarium, 1990-93, Cleve. Access to the Arts, 1992-96; corp. bd. Holden Arboretum, 1988-98, The Cleve. Mus. Natural History, 1996—, The Catlin Gabel Sch., 1998-2000, The Inst. for the Northwest, 1999—2001. Recipient Lake County Environ. award, Lake county metro parks.; Fulbright scholar, 1954-55; Lalor Found. grantee, 1962-63; NSF grantee, 1963-71; NRC Can. grantee, 1966-84; Killam Sr. Rsch. fellow, 1978-79 Mem.: Rodent Specialist Group of Species Survival Commn. (chmn. 1989—93), Assn. Sci. Mus. Dirs. (v.p. 1990—93), Cooper Ornithol., Australian Mammal Soc. (hon. life), Am. Soc. Mammalogists (1st v.p. 1978—82, pres. 1982—84, hon. life, Hartley T. Jackson award 1993), Soc. Women Geographers, Sigma Xi. Home: 2718 SW Old Orchard Rd Portland OR 97201-1637 E-mail: taylorjm@teleport.com.

TAYLOR, JANE BARTLETT, biology professor, educational consultant; d. James Holly and Vera Bartlett; m. David Leroy Taylor (div.); 1 child, Maria Siobhan Chi. BS in Zoology, U. Ill., Urbana, 1960; MS in Zoology, U. Hawaii, Honolulu, 1967, PhD in Zoology, 1975. Mid. sch. biology tchr. Ankara Koleji, Turkey, 1961—62; med. technician Hacettepe Children's Hosp., Ankara, 1962—63; HS tchr., biology & chemistry Am. Sch. in Japan, Tamabochimae, Chofu-shi, 1963—65; tchg. asst. dept. zoology U. Hawaii, Honolulu, 1966—67; instr., marine ecology Hawaii Loa Coll., Kaneohe, 1970; asst. prof., biology Prescott Coll., Ariz., 1971—75; prof., biology Northern Va. CC, Woodbridge, 1975—. Faculty co-chairperson Prescott Coll., 1973—74. Author: Study Guide and Workbook to accompany Biology: The Unity and Diversity of Life, by Cecie Starr and Ralph Taggart, 3d through 9th edits., 1980—90; co-author (with John Jackson): Study Guide and Workbook to accompany Biology: The Unity and Diversity of Life, by Cecie Starr and Ralph Taggart. Ind. del. Va. State Dem. Party, 1992. Acad. Yr. Inst. fellow, U. Hawaii, 1965—66, NDEA fellow, HEW, 1967—70. Mem.: Am. Malacological Soc., The Sierra Club, The Nature Conservancy. Independent. Unitarian. Avocations: gardening, singing, piano, guitar, folk dancing. Office: No Va CC Natural Scis & Math Dept 15200 Neabsco Mills Rd Woodbridge VA 22191-4099

TAYLOR, JANET DROKE, judicial assistant; b. Bristol, Tenn., Feb. 26, 1961; d. Jimmie D. and Nancy Bell (Sluder) Droke; m. Terry E. Taylor; children: Leslie Ann, Laurie Elizabeth. AA, East Tenn. State U., 1980; student, Milligan Coll., Johnson City, Tenn., 1988-89. With Sullivan County Election Commn., Blountville, Tenn., 1978; legal sec. Boarman & Vaughn, Johnson City, 1980-84; legal asst. Bob McD. Green and Assocs., Johnson City, 1985-89; fed. jud. sec. to U.S. cir. judge U.S. Ct. Appeals (4th cir.), Abingdon, Va., 1989—2003; jud. asst. to U.S. dist. judge U.S. Dist. Ct. (we. dist.) Va., Roanoke, 2003—. Adv. bd. legal asst. program Milligan Coll., Johnson City, 1988—89. Mem.: Fed. Jud. Secs. Assn. (4th cir. rep. 1992—), Appalachian Paralegal Assn., Tenn. Paralegal Assn. (treas. 1989, pub. rels. dir. 1990). Republican. Avocations: reading, piano, travel. Office: care Hon Glen E Conrad US Dist Judge PO Box 2822 Roanoke VA 24001

TAYLOR, JANICE KEITH, elementary school educator; b. Vicksburg, Miss., Dec. 27, 1945; d. John Franklin and Venie (Cannon) Keith; m. James Ronald Taylor, July 16, 1967; 1 child, James Lloyd. BSE, Delta State U., Cleveland, Miss., 1967; MLS, U. Miss., 1980. Tchr. Senatobia (Miss.) Jr. High Sch., 1967-70; libr. media specialist Coldwater (Miss.) High Sch., 1970-78, Senatobia Mid. Sch., 1978—2000; tchr. Magnolia Hts. Sch., Senatobia, 2000—. Dir. Friends of Senatobia Pub. Libr., 1993-95, treas., 1995—. Mem. Miss. Libr. Assn., Coterie Club (v.p. 1993-95). Baptist. Avocations: reading, cross stitch, sewing. Office: Magnolia Hts Sch 1 Chiefs Dr Senatobia MS 38668

TAYLOR, JANIE, ballerina; b. Houston; Student, Giacobbe Acad. Dance, New Orleans, Sch. Am. Ballet, 1994—95. Apprentice N.Y.C. Ballet, 1998, mem. corps de ballet, 1998—2001, soloist, 2001—. Dancer (films) Center Stage, (ballets) Divertimento No. 15, A Midsummer Night's Dream, The Nutcracker, Scotch Symphony, Western Symphony, Swan Lake, The Four Seasons, Harmonielehre, Burleske, Them Twos, Viva Verdi, many others. Office: NYC Ballet NY State Theatre 20 Lincoln Ctr Plz New York NY 10023-6913

TAYLOR, JEAN ELLEN, mathematics professor, researcher; d. Richard and Donna Taylor; m. John Mark Guckenheimer, Apr. 18, 1969 (div.); m. Frederick J. Almgren, Oct. 6, 1973 (dec. 1997); 1 child, Karen Taylor Almgren stepchildren: Ann Almgren, Robert Almgren; m. William T. Golden, July 8, 2001 (div.). AB summa cum laude, Mt. Holyoke Coll., 1966, DSc (hon.), 2001; MS in Chemistry, U. Calif., Berkeley, 1968; MS in Math., U. Warwick, Coventry, Eng., 1971; PhD, Princeton U., 1973. Instr. MIT, Cambridge, Mass., 1972-73; asst. prof. Rutgers U., New Brunswick, N.J., 1973-77, assoc. prof., 1977-82, prof., 1982-87, prof. II, 1987—2002, prof. emeritus, 2002—; vis. scholar Courant Inst., NYU, 2002—. Mem. Inst. for Advanced Study, Princeton, N.J., 1974-75, 77-78, 85, 95-96; Miller vis. prof. U. Calif., Berkeley, 1999; vis. scholar Stanford (Calif.) U., 1989; visitor Princeton U., 1980-81; mem. Geometry Computing Group (permanent faculty of the Nat. Sci. and Tech. Ctr. for Computational and Visualization of Geometric Structures); cons. Nat. Bur. Standards, Gaithersburg, Md.; guest expert 3-2-1 Contact program Children's TV Workshop, 1978; mem. exec. com. Conf. Bd. of the Math. Scis., 2000-2002; lectr. in field. Contbr. articles in math., physics and materials sci. to profl. jours. Recipient Presdl. Pub. Svc. award Rutgers Coll. Class of 1962, 1999; Sloan Found. fellow, 1976-78; NSF grad. fellow, 1966-72, hon. fellow Woodrow Wilson Found.; rsch. grantee NSF, 1973—97, Air Force Office Sci. Rsch., 1987-94; vis. scholar Phi Beta Kappa, 2006—. Fellow: AAAS (bd. dir. 1995—99, chair sect. 2004—05), Assn. for Women in Sci., Am. Acad. Arts and Scis.; mem.: Soc. for Indsl. and Applied Math., Assn. for Women in Math. (pres. 1999—2001, nominating com. chair 2003—04), Math Assn. Am., Materials Rsch. Soc., Am. Math. Soc. (nominating com. 1977—78, coun. 1984—89, exec. com. 1985—88, v.p. 1994—97, trustee 2003—, chair bd. trustees 2006—), Assn. Princeton Grad. Alumni (governing bd. 1999—2003), Phi Beta Kappa. Democrat. Achievements include proof, in the context of Geometric Measure Theory, that the singular set in a mathematical model for soap bubble clusters and soap films on wire frames is what is physcally observed, thereby solving a 100 year old problem; development of mathematical models for treating shapes of surfaces and interfaces for crystalline materials and use of them to model crystal growth. Office: Courant Inst 251 Mercer St New York NY 10012 Business E-Mail: jtaylor@cims.nyu.edu.

TAYLOR, JEAN MULL, secondary school educator; b. Clover, Va., Feb. 18, 1953; d. Albert Herman and Helen (Jones) Mull; m. Derek Lester, June 28, 1975; children: Jennifer, Brian. BS, Longwood Coll., 1975; postgrad., Clemson U., 1984, U. S.C., 1986, U. Va., 1991; MS, Va. Poly. and Tech. U., Blacksburg, 1995; EdD, Cambridge Coll., Mass., 2006. Cert. tchr., nutritionist, Va., S.C. Tchr. home econs. Bluestone Sr. HS, Skipwith, Va., 1975, Whitlock Jr. HS, Spartanburg, SC, 1976-80, McCracken Jr. HS, 1984-85, James F. Byrnes HS, 1985-87; tchr. occupl. home econs. Park View Sr. HS, South Hill, Va., 1987—96; tchr. home econs. Cape Hatteras Sch. Career Devel. Ctr., Buxton, NC, 1996—; asst. prin. Cape Hatteras Secondary Sch., Buxton, NC, 1996—. State officer advisor, master advisor FHA/HERO, Va., 1990-94, advisor mentor, 1992-93; cons. home econs.; mem. adv. bd. Va. Assn. Future Homemakers Am.-Home Econs. Related Occupations, Richmond, Va., 1989—; journalist cmty. newspaper, Spartanburg, 1983-87. Pres. Upsy Daisy Garden Club, Spartanburg, 1980; moderator Presbyn. Women, Chase City, Va., 1989-91; enabler Presbyn. Women, Presbytery of the James, 1991-95; lead tchr., coord. Cmty. of Caring. Student Body Nutrition Edn. grantee Va. Dept. Edn., 1991-92. Mem. Va. Home Econs. Tchr. Assn. (pres. elect 1992-93, South Ctrl. Tchr. of Yr. 1991, pres. 1993-94, Tchr. of Yr. 1993), Am. Vocat. Assn., Va. Vocat. Assn., Am. Home Econs. Assn., Va. Home Econs. Assn., N.C. Spl. Needs Assn., N.C. Assn. for Career and Tech. Edn. (tchr., mentor Dare County Schs.), N.C. Vocat. Assn. (spl. pops and guidance divsn.), Garden Clubs S.C. (life), Nat. Fedn. of Garden Clubs, Kiwanis Club (pres. 2002—). Avocations: boating, gardening, collecting books and antiques, cooking. Home: PO Box 283 Frisco NC 27936-0283 Office: Park View Sr High Sch RR 1 Box 118 South Hill VA 23970-9506 also: Cape Hatteras Sch Career Devel Ctr PO Box 948 Buxton NC 27920-0948 Office Phone: 252-995-5730 X 3036.

TAYLOR, JUDITH CAROLINE, entrepreneur; b. Quincy, Ill., June 23, 1948; d. Earl George and Caroline Clara (Knuffman) Schenk; m. Richard Odell Taylor, Nov. 28, 1970; children: Alexander James and Nicholas James (twins). BA, Quincy (Ill.) U., 1985; grad., Unity Sch. Religious Studies, 1997. Ordained Unity minister, 1997. Resident mgr. Landing Heights Apts., Brighton, N.Y., 1973-75; facilitator adult student program Quincy U., 1983-85; dist. mgr. Creative Expressions, 1981-85; mgr. mem. svcs. Quincy Conv. and Visitors Bur., 1985; sales dir. Motor Inn Hotel, Quincy, 1986; entrepreneur Taylor Enterprises, Quincy, 1985—; exec. dir. The Kensington, Quincy, 1987-90; sales mgr., co-owner Taylor's Fine Furniture & Gifts, Quincy, 1990-95; pastor, minister Unity Ch. Quincy, 1997-99; founding minister Christ Ch. Unity, 1999—. Cons., freelance designer. Designed, marketed series I and II Quincy Postcards, 1987, 90; photo show John Wood C.C., 1993. House tour chair Quincy Perserves Bd., 1989; pres. Quincy Newcomers Club, 1980; pres. Great Rivers Mothers of Twins, Quincy, 1979; student min. Unity Ch., Quincy, 1996-97; vol. chaplain Blessing Hosp., Quincy, 1998-02, 05-06, 06-, emergency rm. weekend chaplain, 2006-; br. mgr. Quincy Alzheimer's Assn., 1999-02; min. Fairfield Unity Ch., Iowa, 2002-04; dir. Life Enrichment Ctr., 2004—. Recipient Americanism award VFW, Quincy, 1966. Mem. AAUW (pres. 2003-04), Older Womens League (pres. 1988), Altrusa Club, League of Women Voters, Quincy Area Ministerial Assn. (v.p. 1999-01). Avocations: photography, gardening, dollhouses. Home: 1461 Maine St Quincy IL 62301-4260

TAYLOR, JUNE RUTH, retired minister; b. Annapolis, Md., June 27, 1932; d. Benjamin and Naomi Medora (Dill) Michaelson; m. Thomas Wayne Taylor, Mar. 20, 1954; children: Rebecca Susan Taylor DeLameter, Michael Steven. AB, Goucher Coll., 1952; MRE, Presbyn. Sch. of Christian Edn., Richmond, Va., 1954; MDiv., McCormick Theol. Sem., 1978. Ordained to ministry Presbyn. Ch. (U.S.A.), 1976. Min. Christian Edn. Congl. United Ch. of Christ, Arlington Heights, Ill., 1974-79; dir. pastoral svcs. Presbyn. U. Hosp., Pitts., 1979-89; dir. chaplaincy svcs. Ephrata (Pa.) Community Hosp., 1991-96; ret., 1996; interim pastor Kreutz Creek Presbyn. Ch., Hellam, Pa., 2001; interim parish vis. Highland Presbyn. Ch., Lancaster, Pa., 2004. Chaplain Rush-Presbyn. St. Luke's Med. Ctr., Chgo., 1976-78; chair exec. com. Presbyn. Assn. Specialized Pastoral Ministries, Louisville, 1987-89; bd. dirs. Cocalico Place. Book reviewer in field. Fellow Coll. Chaplains (sec. exec. com. 1985-87); mem. Soc. Chaplains, Hosp. Assn. Pa. (pres. 1983), Assn. Profl. Chaplains (cert.), Assn. Mental Health Clergy, Assn. for Clin. Pastoral Edn. (clin.), Rotary (liaison to Boys and Girls Club S.W. Pitts. chpt. 1990-91, v.p., program chair Denver-Adamstown club 1996-97, pres.-elect 1997-98), York North Rotary Club (chmn. vocation svc. 2003-2005), Mental Health Assn. York County (bd. dirs. 1999—2005), Gamma Phi Beta Alumnae Club (pres. 1990-91).

TAYLOR, KAREN ANNETTE, mental health nurse; b. Kinston, N.C., Oct. 7, 1952; d. Emmett Green and Polly Ann (Taylor) Tyndall; m. Paul Othell Taylor Jr, June 24, 1979 (div. 1996); 1 child, Clarissa Anne. AA, Lenoir C.C., Kinston, 1972; Diploma, Lenoir Meml. Hosp. Sch. of, Nursing, 1984; student, St. Joseph's Coll., Windham, Maine, 1993-94. RN NC. Staff nurse Lenoir Meml. Hosp., 1984-86; staff nurse, relief patient care dir. Brynn Marr Hosp., Jacksonville, N.C., 1987-90; staff nurse, quality assurance Naval Hosp., Camp Lejeune, N.C., 1990-92. Recipient Meritorious Unit Commendation, Am Fedn Govt Employees, 1992. Baptist. Avocations: reading, crocheting. Personal E-mail: karenttaylor@peoplepc.com.

TAYLOR, KAREN MARIE, education educator; b. Batavia, NY, June 15, 1961; d. Francis Edward and Barbara (Kearney) Dyrbala; m. Kenneth Douglas Taylor, July 3, 1992; 1 child, Kyle. AS, Genesee Community Coll., 1982; BS, Utah State U., 1984; MS, Nazareth Coll., 1991. Cert. tchr., N.Y., Ark. Reading coord. Genesee-Wyoming BOCES, Batavia, N.Y., 1985; secondary English educator Penn Yan (N.Y.) Acad., 1985-92; instr. TESOL Hobart Coll., Geneva, N.Y., 1991; adj. instr. English Genesee Cmty. Coll., Batavia, N.Y., 1993-97, assoc. prof. English/TESOL, 1997—. Class advisor Penn Yan Acad., 1986-89, drug free schs. mem., 1989-90, student coun. advisor, 1989-92, coord. natural helpers, 1990-92; vis. lectr. English Ark. Tech. U., Russellville, Ark., 1992-93; TESOL instr. Genesee Valley BOCES, 1993-97. Author: (poetry) A Child's World, 1985, Always: A Vilanelle, 1985, You, 1985, The American Flag, 1986 Democrat. Roman Catholic. Avocations: creative writing, canoeing, fishing, hiking. Home: 206 North St Batavia NY 14020-1610 Office Phone: 585-343-0055 ext 6288. Business E-Mail: kdtaylor@genesee.edu.

TAYLOR, KATHERINE, social services administrator; b. Milw., Feb. 26, 1958; d. James Albert Sr. and Cordelia Taylor; 1 child, Alyssa K. Degree in correctional adminstrn, U. Wis., 1979, degree in sociology, 1979. Coord. summer youth program Milw. County Econ. Devel., Milw., 1981—82, sr. compliance monitor, 1982—83; asst. dir. planning Opportunities Industrialization Ctr. Greater Milw., 1983—84, dir. planning, 1985—88, asst. to sr. v.p., 1989—90, mgr. transp. programs, placement and employee svcs., 1991—93; asst. adminstr. Family House, Inc., Milw., 1994—. Bd. dirs., sec. African World Festivals, Milw., Family House, Inc., Family House Med. Assesment Referral Ctr., Milw. Recipient Love in Action award, Cmty. Youth Devel. Milw., 2001. Mem.: African Am. Coalition Empowerment. Avocations: reading, cooking. Office: Family House Inc 3269 N 11th St Milwaukee WI 53206 E-mail: familyhouseinc@cs.com.

TAYLOR, KATHLEEN (CHRISTINE TAYLOR), physical chemist, researcher; b. Cambridge, Mass., Mar. 16, 1942; d. John F. and Anna M. T. BA in Chemistry, Douglass Coll., New Brunswick, N.J., 1964; PhD in Phys. Chemistry, Northwestern U., 1968. Postdoctoral fellow U. Edinburgh, Scotland, 1968-70; assoc. sr. rsch. chemist Gen. Motors Rsch. Labs., Warren, Mich., 1970-74, sr. rsch. chemist, 1974-75, asst. phys. chemistry dept. head, 1975-83, environ. sci. dept. head, 1983-85, phys. chemistry dept. head, 1985-96; physics and phys. chemistry dept. head Gen. Motors Global Rsch. & Devel. Operations, Warren, Mich., 1995-98, materials and processes dir., 1998—2002. Recipient Mich. Sci. Trailblazer award Detroit Sci. Ctr., 1986. Fellow AAAS, Soc. Automotive Engrs. Internat., mem. NAE, Am. Chem. Soc. (Garvan medal 1989), Materials Rsch. Soc. (treas. 1984, 2d v.p. 1985, 1st v.p. 1986, pres. 1987), N.Am. Catalysis Soc., Am. Acad. Arts Sci, Sigma Xi.

TAYLOR, KATHLEEN P., hotel executive; married; 3 children. BA, U. Toronto, 1980; MBA, York U., 1984; JD, Osgoode Law Sch. Atty. Goodmans law firm; with Four Seasons Hotels and Resorts, 1989—, v.p., gen. counsel, 1992—93, sec., bd. dirs., 1993, sr. v.p., 1993—95, sr. v.p. corp. planning and devel., 1995—97, exec. v.p., 1997—98, exec. v.p., chief corp. officer, 1998—99, pres. worldwide bus. ops., 1999—. Dir. Royal Bank Canada, mem. audit com., human resources com. Cabinet mem. United Way of Greater Toronto; chair Endowment Giving portfolio; bd. dirs. The Hosp. for Sick Children Found. Mem.: Schulich Sch. Bus. (mem. internat. adv. coun.), Am. Hotel and Motel Assn. (mem. industry real estate financing adv. coun.), World Travel and Tourism Coun. Office: Four Seasons Hotels and Resorts 1165 Leslie St Toronto ON M3C 2K8 Canada*

TAYLOR, KATHRYN DENISE, music educator; b. Waynesboro, Va., Aug. 9, 1980; d. David Allen and Velma Kathryn Harner; married, Apr. 23, 2005. BA, Bridgewater Coll., 2002. Lic. tchr. Va. Music dir. Guy K. Stump Elem. Sch., Stuarts Draft, Va., 2002—05; music tchr. Sunset Beach Elem. Sch., Haleiwa, Hawaii, 2005—. Pvt. piano instr., Lyndhurst, Va., 2001—05. Mem.: Music Educators Nat. Conf. Republican. Mem. Mennonite Church. Avocations: reading, cooking, crossword puzzles. Home: 5209 Fuqua Lane Honolulu HI 96818 Office: Sunset Beach Elem Sch 59-360 Kamehameha Hwy Haleiwa HI 96712 Office Phone: 808-638-8777. Personal E-mail: koolkat2697@yahoo.com.

TAYLOR, KATHY, mayor; d. Jim and Lola Taylor; m. Bill Lobeck; 1 child. BA in Journalism, Okla. U., JD, 1981. Atty. pvt. practice; v.p., gen. counsel Thrifty Car Rental, 1988—2003; sec. Dept. Commerce State of Okla., 2003—05; mayor City of Tulsa, 2006—. Office: Office of Mayor City Hall 200 Civic Ctr 11th Fl Tulsa OK 74103 Office Phone: 918-596-7411. Office Fax: 918-596-9010.*

TAYLOR, KATHY LYNN, elementary school educator; b. Artesia, N.Mex., Feb. 9, 1953; d. Owen Cranfill Jr. and Iris June (Winner) T. BS in Elem. Edn., Baylor U., 1975; M in Elem. Edn., Ea. N.Mex. U., 1985. Med. receptionist Byron D. Braly MD, Irving, Tex., 1975-79; office mgr. Linz Jewelers-Northpark, Dallas, 1979-80; tchr. Artesia Pub. Schs., 1980—. Contact person Systemic Initiative in Math. and Sci. Edn., Yeso Elem. Sch., Artesia, 1995-97. Bldg. rep. Artesia Edn. Assn., 1988-96; dir., Sunday sch. tchr. First Bapt. Ch., Artesia, 1982—. Mem.: Delta Kappa Gamma. Republican. Baptist. Home: 1403 W Mahone Dr Apt 8 Artesia NM 88210-1758 Office: Artesia Pub Schs 1106 W Quay Ave Artesia NM 88210-1826 Office Phone: 505-748-2755. Business E-Mail: kltaylor@bulldogs.org.

TAYLOR, LANEY W., mathematics educator; b. Columbia, S.C., May 10, 1970; d. Wayne Carnes and Donna Jo Walsh; m. Kevin Taylor, June 12, 1993; children: Brody Logan, Landon David. BS Secondary Math Edn., U. S.C., 1993. Tchr. algebra & geometry Dorchester Acad., St. George, SC, 1994—. Coach math team Dorchester Acad., St. George, 1994—. Tchr. Sun. sch. First Bapt. Ch., Harleyville, SC, 2005—06, tchr. vacation Bible sch., 1993—2006, mem. social com., 1995—2006. Named to Who's Who Among H.S. Tchrs.,

Who's Who, Dean's List, U. S.C., 1988—92. Mem.: S.C. Edn. Assn., Nat. Coun. Tchrs. Math. Home: 580 Taylor Pond Rd Dorchester SC 29437 Personal E-mail: laney.taylor@dorchesteracademy.org.

TAYLOR, LESLI ANN, pediatric surgeon, educator; b. NYC, Mar. 2, 1953; d. Charles Vincent Taylor and Valene Patricia (Blake) Garfield. BFA, Boston U., 1975; MD, Johns Hopkins U., 1981. Diplomate Am. Bd. Surgery. Surg. resident Beth Israel Hosp., Boston, 1981—88; rsch. fellow Pediat. Rsch. Lab. Mass. Gen. Hosp., Boston, 1984—86; fellow pediat. surgery Children's Hosp. Phila., 1988—90; asst. prof. pediat. surgery U. N.C., Chapel Hill, 1990—97, assoc. prof. pediat. surgery, 1997—2005; prof., chief pediat. surgery East Tenn. State U., Johnson City, 2005—. Author: (booklet) Think Twice: The Medical Effects of Physical Punishment, 1985. Recipient Nat. Rsch. Svc. award NIH, 1984-86. Fellow ACS; mem. AMA, Am. Acad. Pediat., Am. Pediat. Surg. Assn. Achievements include research on organ preservation for pediatric liver transplantation and short bowel syndrome. Office: East Tenn State Univ Dept Surgery Box 70575 Johnson City TN 37614 Office Phone: 423-439-6165. Business E-Mail: taylorla@etsu.edu.

TAYLOR, LILI, actress; b. Chgo., Feb. 20, 1967; Appeared in films Mystic Pizza, Say Anything, Born on the Fourth of July, Bright Angel, Dogfight, Watch It, Household Saints, Short Cuts, Rudy, Arizona Dream, Mrs. Parker and the Vicious Circle, Ready to Wear, The Addiction, Cold Fever, I Shot Andy Warthol, Girls Town, Ransom, Cosas Que Nunca te Deve, 1996, Letters Not About Love, 1997, Kicked in the Head, 1997, O.K. Garage, 1998, Pecker, 1998, The Impostors, 1998, Spring Forward, 1999, A Life Slipping Down, 1999, Janis, 1999, The Haunting, 1999, High Fidelity, 2000, Julie Johnson, 2001, Gaudi Afternoon, 2001, Casa de los Babys, 2003, Factotum, 2005; broadway plays include What Did He See, Aven U Boys; regional plays include Mud, The Love Talker, Fun.; TV appearance in (films) Subway Stories: Tales from the Underground, 1997, Deadline, 2000, Anne Frank: The Whole Story, 2001, Live From Baghdad, 2002, (TV series) Six Feet Under, 2002-2005. Office: c/o William Morris Agy 151 S El Camino Dr Beverly Hills CA 90212-2704

TAYLOR, LINDA JANELLE LAYNE, secondary school educator; b. Winchester, Tenn., Jan. 6, 1947; d. Joseph Elbert and Mary Elsie (Payne) Layne; children: Mary Megan.; David R. Taylor, Dec. 15, 2002. BS, Mid. Tenn. State U., 1968, MEd, 1971, EdS, 1988. Tchr. Westwood Jr. High Sch. Manchester City Schs., Tenn., 1969—2000; tchr. Pelham Elem. Sch. Grundy County Schs., Pelham, Tenn., 1974-75, 80-85; tchr. Motlow C.C., 1995. Author: History of Grundy County Schools, 1988; co-author: Homecoming 86 History of the Elk River Valley, 1986 (award Tenn. Hist. Soc. 1986); editor: Grundy County TN Heritage Book 1844-2004. Pres. Grundy County Hist. Soc., 2002—; active Leadership Grundy Alumni and Bd., 2003—06; participant Leadership Grundy, 2004. Mem. Tenn. Edn. Assn., Manchester Edn. Assn. (pres. 1993-94, Tchr. of Yr. 1978). Methodist. Avocations: genealogy, local history. Office: Westwood Jr High Sch 515 Taylor St Manchester TN 37355 Home: 2973 State Route 50 Pelham TN 37366-9710

TAYLOR, LINDA RATHBUN, investment manager; b. Rochester, N.Y., May 25, 1946; d. Lewis Standish and Elizabeth Florence (Hunt) Rathbun; m. Donald Gordon Taylor, Mar. 1, 1975; children: Alexander Standish, Abigail Elizabeth, Elizabeth Downing. BA, Vassar Coll., 1968; MBA, Harvard U., 1973. Cert. CFA Cert. Fin. Analyst Inst., 1981. Assoc. corp. fin. Donaldson, Lufkin & Jenrette, N.Y.C., 1973-75; cons. IBRD, Washington, 1975; fin. analyst U.S. Treas. Dept., Washington, 1976-78; chief investment officer United Mine Workers Fund, 1978-85; investment mgr. Cen. Pension Fund Internat. Union Oper. Engrs., Washington, 1985-86; investment banker Saranow Co., 1986-89; pvt. investor, 1990—; mng. ptnr. Sakonnet Mgmt., LLC, 1998-2000. Pres. Boundary Farm Inc.; CEO CMAC, LLC, 2001—03, New Hope Pharms., Inc., 2004—; dir. Legg Mason Instnl. Funds, 1999—2002; bd. dirs. J.P. Morgan Venture Capital Investors, J.P. Morgan Corp. Fin. Investors, Fauquier Hosp. Found. Devel. Coun. Contbr. articles to profl. jours. Trustee Montgomery County (Md.) Employees' Retirement Sys., 1987-93; bd. dirs. Washington Internat. Horse Show, 1995-2003; com. mem. Vassar Coll. Endowment Fund, 1992—; elder Bradley Hills Presbyn. Ch., 1992-95; dir. bd. pensions Presbyn. Ch. U.S.A., 1996-99; dir. Va. Horse Shows Assn. Found., 1998—. Recipient Disting. Alumni award Carolina Day Sch., 1996. Mem. Jr. League Washington, Washington Soc. Investment Analysts (bd. dirs. 1984-85), Cert. Fin. Analyst Inst. Republican. E-mail: lrtaylorcfa@aol.com.

TAYLOR, LULA YVONNE, music educator; b. Houston, Dec. 21, 1936; d. George Blackman and Alice Myrtle ing; m. Ulysses Taylor, Jan. 31, 1975; children: John, Cedric, Carlos, Pamela. MusB, Tex. Southern U., Houston, 1960. Cert. elem.-secondary tchr. Calif. Tchr. Beauregard Parish Sch. Bd., De Ridder, La., 1960—61, Langston (Okla.) Elem., Jr. HS, 1962—64; English, music tchr. Carver Elem., Jr. HS, De Ridder, 1964—65; music specialist spl. svcs. Ft. Polk La. Armed Forces, 1966—68; tchr. Monterey (Calif.) Peninsula Unified Sch. Dist., 1969—70; vocal music tchr. Monterey Peninsula Unified Sch. Dist., 1970—74, Monterey Peninsula Unified Sch. Dist., 1998—2005; substitute tchr. Monterey Peninsula Unified Sch. Dist., 1992—98; continuation HS tchr. Pacific Grove (Calif.) Unified Sch. Dist., 1975—81; elem. vocal music tchr. Alisal Union Elem. Sch. Dist., Salinas, Calif., 1981—83; student Monterey Acad. Hair Design Sch., 1983—85; salon owner Lulu's Glamorama, Seaside, 1986—89; vocal music, math tchr. Ravenswood Elem. Sch. Dist., E. Palo Alto, Calif., 1989—91; alternative sch. tcrh. Eastside Union HS, San Jose, Calif., 1991—92; substitute tchr. North County Unified, Salinas, 1992—98; ret., 2005. Author: (tchg. music tutorial on DVD) Learn to Play Lulu's Way, 2005. Gospel organist various ch. Mem.: NAACP, Nat. Educators Assn., Calif. Music Educators Assn., Elks I.B.P.D.E.W. Kismet Temple #966 (Pacific states organist, songbird, vice daughter ruler 1975—). Democrat. Bapt. Avocations: singing, dance, Bingo, movies. Home and Office: Lulu Maes Music Bus 1580 Ancon St Seaside CA 93955 Business E-Mail: lulutaylor@sbcglobal.net.

TAYLOR, LYDA REVOIRE WING, artist, gallery owner; b. Oakland, Calif., Jan. 25, 1952; d. Clinton Harold and Lettie Chaffey Wing; m. Kevin Bradford Taylor, June 22, 1985; children: Jeffrey, Heather, Jessica. BA, U. Calif., Davis, 1974. Founder, owner, artist Valley Arts Faire Gallery, Los Olivos, Calif., 1978-92; owner, artist The Taylor Collection, Angels Camp, Calif., 1999. Asst. dir. Peppertree Ranch Western Art Show, Santa Ynez, Calif., 1976-85; official artist Easter at the White House, 1986. Represented in White House collection; exhbns. include Valley Arts Gallery, 1978-89, Bill Dodge Gallery, Carmel, 1985-90, Donlee/Lee Yougman Gallery, Calistoga and Los Olivos, 1985-99, Taylor Collection Gallery, Angels Camp, 1999-2001; Winters Gallery, Carmel, 2001-2003; Main St. Gallerey, Murphys, 2001-. Set designer, painter Summer Funner Children's Theatre, San Diego, 1992-94, Michelson Drama Club-Childrens Theatre, Murphys, Calif., 1995-99; sec., treas., girls divsn. organizer Ebbetts Pass Youth Soccer, Murphys, 1995-2001. Mem. Calaveras County Arts Coun. (grantee 1998), Angels Camp Bus. Assn. Republican. Avocations: walking, gardening, children's sports.

TAYLOR, MARGARET TURNER, clothing designer, architectural designer, economist, writer, planner; b. Wilmington, N.C., May 7, 1944. A.B. in Econs., Smith Coll., 1966; M.A. in Econ. History, U. Pa., 1970, now Ph.D. candidate in City and Regional Planning. Tchr. Jefferson Jr. High Sch., New Orleans, 1966-69; instr. econs. U. Tex.-El Paso, 1974-75; adj. prof. econs., Salisbury State U., Md., 1976-78; prin. mgr., designer Margaret Norriss, women's clothing, Salisbury, Md., 1980-95; owner Functional Design Ideas, Inc., 1995—; planner at Wharton Ctr. Applied Research, Phila., 1985-86; planning cons., writer.

TAYLOR, MARGARET UHRICH, educational association administrator; b. Lebanon, Pa., Nov. 27, 1952; d. William Murray and Anne (Schultz) Uhrich; m. Timothy Norman Taylor, Sept. 29, 1979; 1 child, Walter Marshall. BA, Shippensburg U., 1974. Adminstrv. asst. Patriot-News Co., Harrisburg, Pa., 1974; reporter Pub. Opinion sect., Chambersburg, Pa., 1975-78; assoc. editor, Miami bur. chief OAG, Inc., N.Y.C., 1978-79; dir. mktg., pub. affairs Wilson Coll., Chambersburg, 1980-90, co-founder women in transition program, 1985; pres. Margaret Taylor's Mktg. Comms., 1989; sr. rschr. Brizius & Foster, McConnellsburg, Pa., 1990, pvt. practice cons., 1990—; exec. dir. Fulton County Econ. Devel. Corp., 1993-96, Fulton Indsl. Devel. Assn., McConnellsburg, 1997-2000; comm. chair Pa. Econ. Devel. Assn., 1997-2000; owner McConnellsburg Inn, 1992-2000; dir. instnl. advancement Pa. State U. Mont Alto Campus, 2000—04; dir. devel. and univ. rels. Pa. State U. The Behrend Coll., 2004—. Adj. faculty Shippensburg U., Pa., 1981-90; lectr. comms. Wilson Coll. Founding mem. Commonwealth Assn. Students, 1972; charter mem. Friends of Fulton County Libr., McConnellsburg, 1975; founder Unforgettable Charity Ball, Chambersburg, 1983-86; active Gotemba Sister-City Com., Borough of Chambersburg, 1981-90; pub. rels. counsel Greater Chambersburg Area United Way, 1985-90; cons. dir. Straight Love Franklin County, Chambersburg, 1982-83; founder Women's Network Franklin County, 1982-90; bd. dirs. Fulton County Med. Ctr. Corp., 1987-93, sec. 1989-90, vice-chmn. 1990-91, chmn. 1992-93; bd. dirs. Pa. Downtown Ctr. Assn., 1998-2000, Fulton County Tourist Promotion Agy., 1995-2000, Pa. Rural Devel. Coun., 1999-2001; bd. dirs. Inst. for Caregiver Edn., 2003—. Mem. Soc. Profl. Journalists (treas. Central Pa. chpt. 1981-82, v.p. 1982-83, pres. 1983-84, chmn. freedom of info. com. 1980-81, chpt. del. nat. conv. 1977). Rotary (chair ambassaborial scholarship com.). Kittochtinny Hist. Soc. (bd. dirs. 2002-04), Erie County Hist. Soc. (bd. dirs., 2005—). Home: 110 Fischer DR Erie PA 16511

TAYLOR, MARGARET WISCHMEYER, retired language educator; b. Terre Haute, Ind., Aug. 5, 1920; d. Carl and Grace (Riehle) Wischmeyer; m. John Edward Taylor, Sept. 5, 1942 (dec. 1988); children: Deborah Ann, Tobin Edward (dec. 2002), Mary Leesa. BA magna cum laude, Duke U., 1941; MA, John Carroll U., Cleve., 1973. Feature writer Dayton (Ohio) Daily News, 1945-53; freelance writer Cleve., 1953—; asst. to Dr. Joseph B. Rhine Duke U. Parapsychology Lab., Durham, NC, 1941; asst. prof. English and journalism Ea. Campus, Cuyahoga CC, Cleve., 1973-92, prof. emeritus, 1992—, advisor campus newspaper, 1973-84, dir. Writers Conf., 1975-90. Writing cons., editor various co. and pubs., Cleve., 1973—; founder, operator Grammar Hot Line, 1987-92. Author: Crystal Lake Reflections, 1985, English 101 Can Be Fun, 1991, The Basic English Handbook, 1995. Recipient top state honors Ohio Newspaper Women's Assn., 1947, award for best ednl., best overall stories Am. Heart Assn., 1970, Besse award for tchg. excellence, 1980, Profl. Excellence award, 1985, Provost's Pride award, 1987, Nat. Tchg. Excellence award Coun. for Advancement and Support of Edn., 1989; named Ohio Outstanding Citizen, Ohio Ho. Reps., 1987, 89, Innovator of Yr., League for Innovations in C.C.s, 1988, Pres.'s award Cuyahoga C.C., 1992. Mem. Mensa, Phi Beta Kappa, Pi Beta Phi. Presbyterian. Avocations: grammar consulting, reading, writing. Home: 27900 Fairmount Blvd Cleveland OH 44124-4616 Personal E-mail: taylorstock@gmail.com.

TAYLOR, MARILYN JORDAN, architectural firm executive; m. Brainerd O. Taylor; children: Brainerd I., Alexis. Degree in govt. and urban affairs, Harvard Coll., 1969; MArch, U. Calif., Berkeley; postgrad., MIT. Joined Skidmore, Owings and Merrill LLP, Washington, 1971, urban designer, dir. design stations program of N.E. Corridor Improvement Project, 1978—85, chief urban design and planning practice NYC, 1985—2001, ptnr., 1987—, chmn., 2001—04. Past pres. N.Y.C. chpt. AIA; chmn. Nat. AIA Regional and Urban Design Com.; vis. prof. Harvard Grad. Sch. Design; David Rockefeller fellow N.Y.C. Partnership, fellows adv. com. Key projects include N.J. Performing Arts Ctr., Newark, Riverside South, Manhattan, NYNEX Hdqs., Battery Park City, Penn Sta. Redevelopment Project, various airports, many others. Chmn. Urban Land Inst., 2005—; bd. dirs. NYC Bldg. Congress (chmn. 2002-04), Comml. Real Estate Women N.Y., Inst. for Urban Design. Named Woman of Yr., Comml. Real Estate Women N.Y., 1998; named one of Most Influential Women in Am. Real Estate, GRID mag., 2001; named to List of Most Influential Women, Crain's N.Y., 1996, 2000; recipient Profl. Leadership award, Profl. Women in Constrn., 2001. Office: Skidmore Owings and Merrill LLP 14 Wall St New York NY 10005*

TAYLOR, MARJORIE, psychology professor; m. Bill Harbaugh; children: Sarah, Amber, Anna. BS, Acadia U., NS, Can., 1979, MS, 1981. Prof. and head Dept. Psychology U. Ore. Author: Imaginary Companions and the Children Who Create Them, 1999; contbr. articles to profl. jours. Office: Dept Psychology 1227 University of Oregon 395 Straub Hall Eugene OR 97403-1227 Office Phone: 541-346-4933. E-mail: mtaylor@uoregon.edu.*

TAYLOR, MARTHA SUE, librarian; b. Sweetwater, Tex., Aug. 16, 1947; d. John Neville Shipley and Erma Hall Shipley Neeper; m. Linn Bryant Taylor, May 22, 1981; children: Mark Bryant, Melissa Anne. BA in English and Govt., Tex. Tech U., 1969, MA in English, 1971; postgrad. in Libr. Sci., U. Tex., 1973. Tchr. English Sweetwater Ind. Sch. Dist., 1971-73, supr. elem. libr., 1973-78, tchr. govt. and English, 1978-83, libr. high sch., 1983—. Mem. dist. improvement coun. Sweetwater Ind. Sch. Dist., 1991-94, 95—, sec., 1993-94, v.p., 1995-96, mem. H.S. campus improvement com., 1991—; instr. govt. Western Tex. Coll., Snyder, 1983-88; com. to draw up new state libr. standards, 2001-03. Sec. adminstrv. bd. 1st United Meth. Ch., 1978-83, organist, 1979—. Mem. AAUW (pres. 1971-73, 1st v.p. 1985-87, treas. 1989-90), Tex. State Tchrs. Assn. (pres. 1987-88), Tex. Libr. Assn. Methodist. Avocations: organ, piano. Home: 1632 Morris Ave Sweetwater TX 79556-2646 Office: Sweetwater High Sch 1205 Ragland St Sweetwater TX 79556-2438

TAYLOR, MARY, state representative; M in Taxation, U. Akron. CPA. Sr. mgr. Bober, Markey, Fedorovich & Co.; state rep. dist. 43 Ohio Ho. of Reps., Columbus, 2002—, mem. edn., econ. devel. & environ. ways and means. Councilwoman, fin. com. chair, mem. rules & pers. and intergovtl. and utilities coms. Green (Ohio) City Coun., 2001—. Republican. Office: 77 High St llth fl Columbus OH 43215-6111 Office Phone: 614-466-1790.

TAYLOR, MARY JANE, artist, educator; b. Schenectady, N.Y., May 30, 1953; d. Robert Richard and Mary Jane (Thomson) Bender; m. George Richter Taylor, June 21, 1975; children: George Ryan, Rachel Marie. BFA, Valdosta (Ga.) State U., 1975; MEd, U. Ga., 1980, EdD, 1995. Cert. tchr., Ga. Tchr. art grades 9-12 Colquitt County Schs., Moultrie, Ga., 1975-76, Valdosta (Ga.) City Schs., 1976-78; tchr. art grades K-6 Clark County Schs., Athens, Ga., 1978-79; mem. faculty visual arts Brenau U., Gainesville, Ga., 1979—2004. Mem. adj. faculty Ga. Mil. Coll., Valdosta, 1977-78; dir. visual arts Brenau U., 1980-97, dir. gallery, 1979-90, acting chair fine arts, 1990-92, chair fine arts, 1993-94, dir. visual arts 1995-98, prof., 1998, dir. art edn., 1998—; mem. faculty art Elderhostel/Brenau U., Gainesville, 1980, 85; mem. adv. bd. Brenau Galleries, Interior Design, Gainesville, 1990-2004; mem. faculty visual arts Forsyth Ctrl. H.S., 2004—; tchr. ceramics and sculpture Forsyth County Schs., Camming, Ga., 2005. One-woman show at Brenau U., 1988; exhibited in group show at Phila. Rug & Carpets, 1975 (1st place), Nat. Invitational Art Exhbn., 1992 (1st prize clay), Sautee Nacoochee Arts Ctr., 1994. Bd. dirs. Ga. Mountains Mus., Gainesville, 1995-98, Quinlan Art Ctr., 1991-93; co-chair state conf. Nat. Art Honor Soc., 1992; mem. stds. com., juror 502 Gallery, Gainesville, 1993-94; coord. visual art Ga. Mountains Jubilee, Gainesville, 1983. Art and mus. program grantee Coca Cola Found., 1993-96, 97-2000; recipient Faculty Recogniton Award, 1997-98, Vulcan Matericals Co. Teaching Excellence and Campus Leadership award, 1998; Target-Brenau U. Cmty. art program grantee, 2002-04. Mem. AAUP, Nat. Art Edn. Assn., Ga. Art Edn. Assn. (pres. Pioneer Dist. 1987-90, dir. spl. activities 1990-95, dir. higher edn. divsn. 1995-97, mem.-at-large 1998-99), Omicron Delta Kappa, Sigma Alpha Iota. Republican. Presbyterian. Avocations: hiking, antiques. Home: 6300 Brady Rd Murrayville GA 30564-1102 Office: Brenau U 1 Centennial Cir Gainesville GA 30501-3697 Personal E-mail: 1taylor@bellsouth.net.

TAYLOR, MARY KAY, medical, surgical nurse; b. Knoxville, Iowa, Jan. 26, 1954; d. Wendell Shawver and Margery Ethel (Beebe) Kubli; m. Gregory Taylor, Sept. 4, 1993. ADN, Indian Hills Community Coll., 1979; BSN, Teikyo Marycrest U., 1993. RN, Iowa. Staff nurse Mercy Hosp., Des Moines, 1979-81, Knoxville Area Community Hosp., 1981-83, VA Med. Ctr., Knoxville, 1983-98, Iowa Meth. Med. Ctr., Des Moines, 1998—2005, Va. Med. Ctr., Knoxville, 2005—. Home: PO Box 646 Knoxville IA 50138-0646 Personal E-mail: mtaylor@lisco.com. Business E-Mail: mtaylor@iowatelecom.net.

TAYLOR, MARY LEE, retired college administrator; b. Amarillo, Tex., Nov. 13, 1931; d. David Kelly and Bessie F. (Peck) McGehee; m. Lindsey Taylor, Sept. 13, 1950 (dec. Aug. 1985); children: Gary, Kent, Ronald. BS, W. Tex. State U., 1959; MEd, Tex. Tech U., 1975. Tchr. Mesquite (Tex.) Pub. Schs., 1961-63; resource tchr. Amarillo Pub. Schs., 1971-79, supr., 1979-80; reading instr. Amarillo Coll., 1981-88, asst. prof. reading, 1988-93, assoc. prof., 1994-95; ret., 1995. Project dir. Tex. Edn. Agy., Austin, 1984-85, 85-86, Amarillo Coll., 1988-89. Instr. GED Ctr. for Neighborhood Ministries, Phoenix, 2001—02. Mem. Tex. Assn. for Children with Learning Disabilities (meritorious svc. award 1985), Coll. Reading and Learning Assn. (spl. interest group leader 1987-89, cert. 1988, editor newsletter 1987-89), Am. Assn. Cmty. and Jr. Colls., North Plains Assn. for Learning Disabilities (pres. 1987-88, coord. accessibility svcs. 1993—), Tex. Assn. Developmental Educators (membership chmn. 1992-93), Assn. of Higher Edn. and Disabled Students. Avocations: camping, hiking. Personal E-mail: mlltaylor@aol.com.

TAYLOR, MICHELLE Y., human resources consultant; b. L.A., Aug. 23, 1965; d. Lucille S. Taylor, Rodney A. Taylor. B in Comm., U. San Diego, 1987; M in Orgnl. Mgmt., U. Phoenix, San Diego, 1994. Asst. program dir. Partnerships With Industry, San Diego, 1987—88; placement dir. Eldorado Coll., Escondido, Calif., 1988—89; supr. Kelly Staffing Svcs., San Diego, 1989—91; office mgr. Scripps Hosp., La Jolla, Calif., 1991—93; supr. Remedy Staffing Svcs., San Diego, 1993—94; corp. edn. mgr. U. Phoenix, San Jose, Calif., 1994—95; staffing mgr. Superior Design, San Jose, 1995—96; dir. human resources SV Probe, Inc., San Jose, 1996—98; v.p. human resources San Jose Nat. Bank, 1998—2000; cons. Michelle Y. Taylor Consulting, San Diego, 2000—01; sr. human resources cons. Paychex, Inc., San Diego, 2001—. Mem. Employment Advisory Coun., San Jose, 1998—2000. Scholar, U. San Diego, 1983. Mem.: Soc. for Human Resources Mgmt. Avocations: books on tape, exercise, collecting modern art, travel.

TAYLOR, MILDRED D., author; b. Jackson, Miss., Sept. 13, 1943; d. Wilbert Lee and Deletha Marie (Davis) Taylor. BA in Edn., U Toledo, 1965; MA, U Colo., 1969. Vol., tchr. English and history Peace Corps, Ethiopia, 1965-67, then recruiter U.S., 1967-68; study skills coord. black edn. program U. Colo., 1969-71. Author: (children's fiction) Song of the Trees, 1975 (Coun. on Interracial Books for Children award 1975), Roll of Thunder, Hear My Cry, 1976 (Newbery medal, 1977), Let the Circle Be Unbroken, 1981, The Gold Cadillac, 1987 (Christopher award), The Friendship and Other Stories, 1987, Mississippi Bridge, 1990 (Christopher award), The Road to Memphis, 1990, The Well, 1995 (winner Jane Addams book award, 1996), The Land, 2001 (Coretta Scott King award, L.A. Times Book award, Scott O'Dell award, Pen USA award). Address: care Dial Books For Young Readers 375 Hudson St New York NY 10014-3658

TAYLOR, MILLICENT RUTH, elementary school educator; b. Kingston, Jamaica, Nov. 18, 1944; came to U.S., 1981; m. Henry Taylor; children: T'ousant, Howard, Annette, Kerry-Ann. BE, U. West Indies, 1981; MS, U. Miami, 1991. Cert. elem. edn. tchr., secondary social sci. tchr., Fla.; nat. bd. cert. tchr., 2004. Chairperson dept. history Mays Middle Sch., Miami, Fla., 1987—, peer tchr., 1987—; clin. tchr., 1990—; seminar presenter Mays Middle Sch., Miami, Fla., 1987-88, clin. tchr., 1990—. Leader, trainer Global Edn., Miami, Fla. 1989, sponsor History Bee, Miami, 1988-90, Geography Bee, 1988-90, 2003. Recipient State award for tchg. econs. Dade County Sch., 1992, Nat. award for tchg. econs. Joint Coun. Econ. Edn., 1991, State award for Gov. Awards for Excellence, 1995, Nat. award for tchg. econs. Nat. Coun. Econ. Edn., 1995. Mem. ASCD, Seventh Day Adventist. Avocations: reading, travel, sewing, photography. Home: 19834 SW 118th Ave Miami FL 33177-4435 Office: Mays Middle Sch Goulds FL 33170

TAYLOR, NANCY ALICE, mechandiser, buyer; b. Sept. 25, 1956; AA, Santa Fe C.C., Gainesville, Fla., 1977; BS, Fla. State U., Tallahassee, 1979. Asst. to dir. of mdse. and design Nanlien Internat. Corp., L.A., 1980; fashion designer LV Industries, L.A., 1981-86; ptnr., mgr., designer Benz The Sun Society, Venice, Calif., 1982-85; fashion designer, mdse. mgr. Asics, Santa Ana, Calif., 1986-88, Ocean Pacific Lifestyles, Tustin, Calif., 1988-89; owner, mgr., buyer Century West Car Wash, Inc., L.A., 1989-99; owner, mgr. Nantex Recycling LLC, Cocoa Beach, Fla., 1999; merchandiser, clothing buyer Cocoa Beach Surf Co., 2000—. Mem. Solid Waste Assn. N.Am. Office: 2210 S Atlantic Ave Cocoa Beach FL 32931 E-mail: taylor.n.a@att.net.

TAYLOR, NANCY ELIZABETH, lawyer; b. Salt Lake City, Apr. 6, 1956; d. Calvin Walker and Dorothy (Cope) Taylor; m. Christopher Robbins Bowen, Jan. 22, 1978; children: Elizabeth Grant Bowen, Alexandra Taylor Bowen. BS, U. Utah, 1978; JD, Cath. U., 1988. Health policy dir. Senate Com. on Labor and Human Resources, Washington, 1981-91; ptnr. Law Offices of Deborah Steelman, Washington, 1991-93; prin. shareholder, nat. co-chair health law dept. Greenberg Traurig LLP, Washington, 1993—. Testimony presentor Rep. Nat. Conf., 1992. Recipient Commr. award FDA, 1989. Mem. Nat. Health Lawyers, Women & Gov. Rels., Food and Drug Law Inst. Republican. Mem. Lds Ch. Office: Greenberg Traurig LLP Ste 500 800 Connecticut Ave NW Washington DC 20006 Office Phone: 202-331-3100. Office Fax: 202-331-3101. Business E-Mail: taylorn@gtlaw.com.

TAYLOR, NATHALEE BRITTON, retired nutritionist, freelance/self-employed writer; b. Lubbock, Tex., June 8, 1941; d. Nathaniel E. and Dessie Pauline (Moss) Britton; children by previous marriage: Clay H., Bret N. Courtney. BS in Home Econs., Tex. Tech U., 1963. Home economist Pioneer Gas, Lubbock, Tex., 1963-65; dietitian Tex. Tech U., Lubbock, 1966-71; home economist South Plains Electric Co-op., Lubbock, 1986; mgr. quality control Rip Griffins Enterprises, Lubbock, Tex., 1987; sales rep. Time Chem., Lubbock, 1987—2003; with Sentry, Lubbock; mktg. rep. Dodson Group Ins., Lubbock, Farmers Ins., Lubbock, Southwestern Bell Wireless; ret., 2003. Ranch Historian. Co-author: (cookbook) From Our House to Yours, 1975; columnist: Lubbock Lights mag., Ranch Record; presenter TV show Southwestern Cooking Sta. KTXT; contbr. articles to profl. publs. Bd. dirs. Am. Heart Assn., Lubbock, 1985-87; mem. Home Economist in Bus., pres. Lubbock chpt., 1985; culinary co-chmn. Lubbock C. of C. Arts Festival, 1982, 83, 84. Named Lincoln County Fair Queen. Mem. Tech. Home Econs. Alums (sec./treas.), Am. Home Econs. Assn. (v.p., sec./treas.), Bd.-Cove, Soroptomist (v.p. Lubbock club). Democrat. Avocations: gardening, writing, cooking, horseback riding. Personal E-mail: nathaleet@door.net.

TAYLOR, NICOLE RENÉE (NIKI TAYLOR), model, shop owner; b. Miami, Fla., Mar. 5, 1975; d. Ken and Barbara Taylor; m. Matt Martinez (div.); 2 children. With Tri Star Sports and Entertainment Group, Brentwood, 2006—; owner Abbie and Jesse's, Cool Springs, Tenn., 2006—, Franklin, Tenn., 2006—. Contracts with L'Oreal, 1990-92, Cover Girl Makeup; appeared in Seventeen (cover girl) 1989, Vogue, Elle, Mademoiselle, Harper's Bazaar; modeled for Yves Saint Laurent, Karl Lagerfeld; modeled swimsuit Sports Illus., 1997, cover Sports Illus. Calendar, 1998. Founder Begin Found. Achievements include appearing on over 320 magazine covers worldwide; youngest model to appear on the cover of Vogue; holds the world record for being the youngest model to receive a six figure deal. Office: TriStar Entertainment Group Suite 200 215 Ward Circle Brentwood TN 37027 Office Phone: 615-309-0969. Business E-Mail: tristar@tristarse.com.

TAYLOR, PATRICIA NAIL, mathematics and science educator; b. Birmingham, Ala., Apr. 13, 1973; d. Cecil Thomas Nail and Mickie Kelley Sullivan; m. John Lynwood Taylor, May 4, 1996; 1 child, Levi Thomas. B in Elem. Edn. cum laude, U. Ala., 1996, M, 2000. Fourth grade tchr. Jefferson County Bd. Edn. Fultondale Elem., 1996—. Grade level chair Fultondale

Elem., Ala., 2004—06, discipline com. chair, 2004—06, mem. textbook com., 2005—06, mem. scheduling com., 2003—06. Mem.: Ala. Edn. Assn. Avocations: horseback riding, softball. Office: Fultondale Elem 1500 Walkers Chapel Rd Fultondale AL 35068

TAYLOR, PATTI ANN, psychologist, educator; b. Chickasha, Okla., Apr. 22, 1949; d. Thomas Elias Novotny and Marguerite Bonita Wampler Novotny; m. Neal Cavin Taylor, Aug. 8, 1987; children from previous marriage: Jennifer Lenora Magers Juric, Jessica Maritte Juric 1 stepchild, Travis Lee. BSN with honors, U. of Ctrl. Okla., Edmond, 1976; MA summa cum laude, No. Ariz. U., Flagstaff, 1993, EdD, 2001. Lic. psychologist Ariz.; RN Okla., Alaska, Ariz., Tex.; cert. sch. psychologist Ariz. Nurse Santa Rosa Med. Ctr., San Antonio, 1980—81; charge nurse Okla. Children's Med. Ctr., Oklahoma City, 1976—77; mem. staff Fairbanks Meml. Hosp., Alaska, 1981—82; clin. nurse leader, asst. mgr. Tucson Med. Ctr., 1982—87; mem. staff Chandler Regional Hosp., Ariz., 1987—91; counselor owner pvt. practice Northland Hypnotherapy, Flagstaff, Ariz., 1991—94; sch. psychometrist Kyrene Sch. Dist., Tempe, Ariz., 1996—97, sch. psychologist intern, 1997—98; sch. psychologist Chandler Unified Sch. Dist., Chandler, 1998—2004, Dr. Patti Novotny Taylor & Assocs., Mesa, Ariz., 2004—05; psychologist Kyrene Sch. Dist., Tempe, Ariz., 2005—. Cert. instr. Nat. Safety Coun., Juvenile Offender Diversion Program, Flagstaff, Ariz., 1992—93; facilitator (counselor) Tucson Med. Ctr., 1983—87; cert. peri-natal grief counselor Chandler Regional Hosp., Chandler, Ariz., 1989—91; guest lectr. No. Ariz. Inst. of Tech., Flagstaff, Ariz., 1991—93; crisis counselor Coconino County Juvenile Ct., Flagstaff, Ariz., 1992—93; counseling workshops leader Northland Hypnotherapy, Flagstaff, Ariz., 1991—94; spl. guest KVNA Radio, Flagstaff, Ariz., 1993—93; lectr. in field; condr. workshops in field. Author (co-author): (professional article) Reaching the Jury: A Case for Multimodal Presentation; lecturer (seminars and video tapes) Transporting Critical Infants to Tertiary Care Centers, Care of the Newborn Infant. Vol. Paz De Cristo, Mesa, Ariz., 1997—98; counselor educator Gilbert Presbyn. Ch., Gilbert, Ariz., 1996—98; vol. counselor educator Tucson Med. Ctr., 1983—87. Capt. U.S. Army, 1977—80. Mem.: APA, ACA. Avocations: reading, writing, travel, dance. Office: Dr Patti Novotny Taylor & Associates 2156 South Longwood Cir Mesa AZ 85208-6610 Business E-Mail: patti_taylor1@yahoo.com.

TAYLOR, PAULETTE ANN, special education educator, educational consultant; b. Plainfield, N.J., June 8, 1948; d. Arthur John and Bess Ealy Taylor. AA, Centenary Coll. for Women, Hackettstown, N.J., 1966—68; BS in Edn., U. Tenn., Knoxville, 1968—70; MEd, Memphis State U., Tenn., 1972—73. Cert. English tchr. (7-12) N.J. Bd. Edn., 1970, English/Psychology tchr. (7-12) Tenn. Bd. Edn., 1970, Spl Edn. tchr. (with endorsements) Tenn. Bd. Edn., 1970, English tchr. (9-12) Minn. Bd. Edn., 1976, Spl. Edn. tchr. (k-12) Minn. Bd. Edn., 1976, Secondary tchr. (with approvals in English, Mental Disabilities Resouce) Iowa Bd. Edn., 1977, Spl. Edn. tchr. (k-12) Iowa Bd. Edn., 1977, Ednl. Cons. Iowa Bd. Edn., 1977. Para-educator Willis Sch. of Ednl. Therapy, Bound Brook, NJ, 1971; English tchr. Marshall County Sr. HS, Lewisburg, Tenn., 1971—72; spl. edn. tchr. Coro Lake Elem. Sch., Memphis, 1973—76, Inver Grove Heights Jr. High, Minn., 1976—77, Black Hawk Jr. HS, Pleasant Valley, Iowa, 1977—88; spl edn./ednl. cons. Miss. Bend Area Edn. Agy., Bettendorf, 1988—. Mem. negotiations team Pleasant Valley Edn. Assn., 1979—85, pres. elect, 1981—82, pres., 1982—84, past pres., 1984—85; pres. elect Miss. Bend UniServ Unit, 1985—86, pres., 1986—87, past pres., 1987—88; exec. bd. mem., profl. staff orgn. Miss. Bend Area Edn. Agy., 1989—, membership co-chair, profl. staff orgn., 1993—, mentor for new cons., 1995; vol. practicum supr. St. Ambrose U., Bettendorf/Davenport. Vol. Homework Hotline, Betttendorf, 1986—96; exec. bd. mem./grant reader Riverboat Devel. Authority, Davenport, 1989—99; bd. dirs. Scott. Co. Hist. Preservation Soc., Davenport, 1980—85, 1991—96, awards com., 1980—85, 1992, 1994, 1996, hist. homes tour organ. com. mem., 1984—95; bd. dirs. Neighborhood Housing Svc., Davenport, 1987—89; mem. organizing/steering com. East Bluff Neighborhood Dist., Davenport, 2004—06. Mem.: NEA (del. to 3 conventions 1982—86), Coun. for Exceptional Children, Iowa State Edn. Assn. (del. to 7 conventions 1981—87), Cornbelt Running Club (vol.), Delta Kappa Gamma (mem. program com., mem. membership com.). Democrat. Meth. Avocations: reading, gardening, exercise, computers. Office: Miss Bend Area Edn Agy 729 21st St Bettendorf IA 52722

TAYLOR, PHYLLIS MILLER, energy executive; m. Patrick F. Taylor (dec. 2004). Grad., U. S.W. La.; LLB, Tulane U. Law clerk for Supreme Ct. La., Orleans Parish Civil Dist. Ct.; in-house counsel for John W. Mecom, Sr., 1972; exec. v.p., bd. mem. Taylor Energy Co. LLC, New Orleans, 1979—2004, chmn., CEO, 2004—. Chmn., pres. Patrick F. Taylor Found. Named an Forbes' Richest Americans, 2006. Office: Taylor Energy Co LLC 1615 Poydras St New Orleans LA 70112 Office Phone: 504-581-5491.*

TAYLOR, REGINA, actress; b. Dallas, Aug. 22, 1960; d. Nell Taylor. Student, So. Meth. U. TV appearances include (movies) Crisis at Central High, 1981, Howard Beach: Making the Case for Murder, 1989, Children of the Dust, 1995, Hostile Waters, 1997, The Third Twin, 1997, Strange Justice, 1999, Cora Unashamed, 2000, In from the Night, 2006, (TV series) I'll Fly Away, 1991-93 (Emmy award nominee best actress in a drama 1993, Golden Globe award), Feds, 1997, The Education of Max Bickford, 2001-02, The Unit, 2006-; films include Lean on Me, 1989, Losing Isaiah, 1995, Clockers, 1995, The Keeper, 1995, Spirit Lost, 1996, A Family Thing, 1996, Courage Under Fire, 1996, The Negotiator, 1998; stage appearances include Romeo and Juliet, 1986, King Lear, 1987, The Tempest, 1988, one-woman show Escape From Paradise, 1994. Office: c/o William Morris Agency 1350 Avenue Of The Americas New York NY 10019-4702*

TAYLOR, RENEE, actress, writer; b. NYC, Mar. 19, 1933; m. Joseph Bologna, 1965; 1 child, Gabriel. Grad., Acad. Dramatic Arts; doctorate (hon.), Hofstra U. Actress (films) The Errand Boy, 1961, The Detective, 1968, A New Leaf, 1971, Last of the Red Hot Lovers, 1972, Lovesick, 1983, White Palace, 1990, Delirious, 1991, End of Innocence, 1990, All I Want for Christmas, 1991, Forever, 1992, Love Is All There Is, 1996, Dying on the Edge, 2001, 61*, 2001, Dr. Dolittle 2 (voice), 2001, Returning Mickey Stern, 2002, Lady Killers, 2003, Alfie, 2004, Kalamazoo?, 2005, A-List, 2005, Boynton Beach Club, 2006, Ice Age: The Meltdown, 2006, Kalamazoo?, 2006, (TV series) Dream On, 1992-94, Daddy Dearest, 1993, The Nanny, 1993-99, (stage) Three Sisters, Machinal, Annie Get Your Gun, Li'l Abner, Wish Your Were Here; writer (film) Lovers and Other Strangers (Academy award nomination), (TV) Paradise, (HBO spl.) Bedrooms (Writers Guild award); author: My Life On A Diet. Address: 16830 Ventura Blvd Ste 326 Encino CA 91436-1725*

TAYLOR, ROSE PERRIN, social worker; b. Lander, Wyo., Feb. 11, 1916; d. Wilbur Rexford Perrin and Agatha Catherine (Hartman) Perrin DeMars; m. Louis Kempf Kugland, Sept. 1942 (div. 1951); children: Mary Louise, Carolyn Kugland McElhany; m. Wilfred Taylor, Oct. 13, 1962 (dec. 1991). AB, U. Mich., 1937; MSW, U. Denver, 1956; student, Columbia U., N.Y.C., 1936, Santa Rosa Jr. Coll., Calif., 1974-93, Coll. of Marin, Kentfield, Calif., 1995-98. Group worker Dodge Cmty. House, Detroit, 1937-38; case worker Detroit Welfare Dept., Detroit, 1938-40; child welfare worker Fremont County Welfare Dept., Lander, Wyo., 1940-42; worker children's svcs. Laramie County Welfare Dept., Cheyenne, Wyo., 1951-57, dir., 1957-58; supr. San Mateo (Calif.) County Health & Welfare, 1958-74; dir. Fed. Day Care Project, San Mateo, 1964—74. Tchr. Sch. Pub. Health Nursing, U. Wyo., 1951-55, Sch. Social Work, U. Calif., San Jose, 1962-63; workshop leader NIMH, Prescott, Ariz., 1961, Ariz. State U., Phoenix, 1962, Oreg. State Welfare Dept., Otter Crest, 1973; cons. in field Author: (memoir) In the Shadow of the Rimrocks, 2005; contbr. articles to profl. jours Adminstrv. vol. Buck Ctr. for Rsch. in Aging, Marin County, 1994-95, vol. epidemiol. rschr. nutrition validation study for people in their 80's and 90's, 1995; bd. dirs. Friends of Redwoods, 2000-03, United Ch. of Christ, 2002-03; task force on programs and svcs. Redwood Bd., 2002-03; vol. aux. bd. Redwoods, 2003-05, leader low vision program, 2003 Recipient Resolution of Commendation, Calif. State Senate, 1974; Annual Rose Taylor award San Mateo Child Care Coordinating Coun., 1982, Founder's Recognition award, 1997. Mem. NASW. Democrat. Mem. United Ch. of Christ. Avocations: artist, creative writing, poetry. Home: The Redwoods # 10105 40 Camino Alto Mill Valley CA 94941-2943 Personal E-mail: rose@kugland.net.

TAYLOR, ROSEMARY, artist; b. Joseph, Oreg. d. Theodore and Sarah A. (Lambright) Resch; m. Robert Hull Taylor; children: Barbara Taylor Ryalls, Robert H. Student, Cleve. Inst. Art, 1937—40, NYU, 1947. Tchr. pottery Rahway (N.J.) Art Ctr., 1950-55. Pottery cons. McCalls Mag., 1962-72. One woman shows include Paterson (N.J.) Coll., 1964, Westchester (Pa.) Coll., 1970, Gallery 100, Princeton, N.J., 1967, George Jensen's, N.Y.C., 1972, Artisan Gallery, Princeton, 1974, Am. Crafts (Ohio), 1979-99, Guild Gallery, 1986-91, Little Art Gallery, N.C., 1985-99, Olde Queens Gallery (N.J.), 1987, N.J. Designer Craftsmen, 1990, 97, 98, 99 (bd. dirs. 1986-87, std. chmn. 1994), Creative Hands, 1995, 97, 98, 99, Princeton, 1994; group shows include Mus. Natural History, N.Y.C., Newark Mus., Trenton (N.J.) Mus., Montclair (N.J.) Mus., Phila. Art Alliance, Pa. Horticulture Soc., 1988, Nat. Design Center, N.Y.C., Michener Mus., Pa., 1996; represented in permanent collection Westchester Coll. Bd. dirs. Solebury Cmty. Sch.; mem. Fulbright award com., 1982, 83. Mem. LWV (pres. Plainfield, N.J. chpt.), Am. Craft Coun., N.J. Designer-Craftsmen, Phila. Craft Group, Bucks County (Pa.) C. of C., Visual Artists and Galleries Assn., Nat. Assn. Am. Penwoman, Michener Mus., Doylestown, Pa., Women in the Arts (charter). Democrat. Unitarian Universalist. Home: 10 Beech Cluster Doylestown PA 18901-2134 E-mail: romy282@nni.com.

TAYLOR, RUTH ARLEEN LESHER, marketing educator; b. Riverton, Iowa, Mar. 7, 1941; d. Clyde Almond and Bernice Emogene (Graves) Lesher; m. Leslie (Milburn) Taylor, Aug. 10, 1963; children: Treg Anthony, John Leslie II. BS in Home Econs. Edn. magna cum laude, U. Houston, 1975; MEd, Tex. Christian U., 1977; PhD, U. N. Tex., 1981; PhD (hon.), U. Nat. Mayor de San Marcos, Lima, Peru, 2006. Prof. mktg. Tarrant County C.C., Ft. Worth, 1977-78, North Tex. State U., Denton, 1978-81, Southwestern U., Georgetown, Tex., 1982-87, S.W. Tex. State U., San Marcos, 1981-82, 87—; hon. prof. mktg. U. Nat. Mayor de San Marcos, Lima, Peru, 2006—. Dir. travel to China, Japan, Hong Kong, Costa Rica, Morocco, Europe, Eng., Mex., Dominican Republic, Venezuela, Chile, Peru; faculty intern Tex. Dept. Econ. Devel. and Tex. Sec. of State Office; collaborator STAT-USA and Internat. Catalog Exhbn. U.S. Dept. Commerce; dir. study program, Washington. Author: Text Maps Study Guides, 1994—; contbg. author: The Psychology of Fashion, 1985, Ethics in Accounting, 1994; contbr. articles to profl. jours. Mem. Lost Creek Garden Club, Austin, Tex., 1985—, v.p.; vol. Bob Bullock State Hist. Mus. Recipient Tchg. award McCoy Coll. Bus., 2005, N.Am. Small Bus. Trade Educators award 2005; nominated Gary Woods Rsch. award 2005; grantee Merrick Found., 1991; Fulbright sr. specialist, Peru, 2006. Mem.: DAR, Am. Soc. for Competitiveness, Winthrop Soc., French Huguenot Soc., Colonial Dames, Internat. Hospitality Coun. (bd. dirs.), Mayflower Soc., Mktg. Mgmt. Assn., Western Mktg. Educators Assn., Am. Mktg. Assn., Alpha Mu Alpha, Alpha Kappa Psi, Phi Delta Kappa, Phi Epsilon Omicron, Beta Gamma Sigma. Avocations: travel, gardening, reading, entertaining. Office: Texas State University 601 University Dr San Marcos TX 78666-4685 E-mail: rt01@txstate.edu.

TAYLOR, SHELLEY E., psychology researcher, educator; b. Mt. Kisco, NY, Sept. 10, 1946; d. Charles Fox and Pearl May (Harvey) T.; m. Mervyn Francis Fernandes, May 1, 1972; children: Sara F., Charles F. AB magna cum laude in Psychology, Conn. Coll., 1968; PhD in Social Psychology, Yale U., 1972. Asst. prof. psychology and social rels. Harvard U., Cambridge, Mass., 1972-77, assoc. prof., 1977-79; assoc. prof. psychology UCLA, 1979-81, prof., 1981—. Mem. vis. faculty dept. adminstrv. scis. Yale U., New Haven, 1971-72, vis. Sloane fellow, 1978; mem. basic sociocultural rsch. rev. com. NIH, 1979-83; Katz-Newcomb lectr. U. Mich., 1982; cons. to pub. houses and TV producers. Author: Social Cognition, 1986, 2d edit., 1991, Health Psychology, 1986, 3d edit., 1995, 5th edit., 2002. Positive Illusions: Creative Self-Deception and the Healthy Mind, 1989, The Tending Instinct: How Nurturing is Essential to Who We Are and How We Live, 2002; contbr. numerous articles to sci. publs. Active numerous charitable and fund-raising orgns. including Curtis Sch. PTA and U. So. Calif./Norris Cancer Ctr. Recipient Rsch. Scientist Devel. award NIMH, 1981-86, 86-91, MERIT award, 1987, Donald Campbell award for disting. sci. contbn. to sociology, 1995; numerous rsch. grants in field; Winthrop scholar, 1967; Woodrow Wilson fellow, 1968, NIMH fellow, 1968-72. Fellow APA (Sci. Weekend lectr. 1988, Disting. Sci. award 1980, Outstanding Sci.Contbn. award Divsn. 38, 1994), Brit. Psychol. Soc. (flying fellow), Acad. Behavioral Medicine Rsch., Soc. Psychol. Study Social Issues, Soc. Behavioral Medicine; mem. AAAS, Soc. Exptl. Social Psychology, Western Psychol. Assn. (pres. 1993-94), Inst. Medicine. Office: UCLA Dept Psychology Franz 4611 Box 951563 Los Angeles CA 90095-1563

TAYLOR, SUE ANN, film and television producer; b. Sanford, Maine, Sept. 29, 1954; d. Sidney M. Hall Jr.; m. Roy H. Taylor III, May 27, 1984; children: Michael, Katharine, Jessica. Student, U. Maine, 1972-74, Vt. Coll. Creative dir. Ad Lib Graphics, Mt. Laurel, N.J., 1976-80; pres. Hall-Yusem Advt., Phila., 1980-86, Hollyberry Post and Prodns., Allentown, Pa., 1986-93; ptnr. Finestkind Film & Video, Wells, Maine, 1993-94; pres. Natural Resources.A Wealth of Wellness, Canton, Ga., 1994—, Tapestry Prodn. Ga., Canton, 1996-2000; exec. dir. WILD Weekend, Canton, 1996—, Blue Heron Films, 2000. Mem. adv. bd. WILD Found., 1998—. Pub. Back to One Mag., 1999—. Founder Consumer Choice in Dental Care Project, Washington, 1996—. Recipient 7 Videographer awards, 2000, 9 Telly awards, 5 Communicators awards, 2000, 1 Emmy nomination, 2000. Mem. NATAS, Soc. Profl. Journalists (pres.). Avocations: biking, conservation activities, reading, travel. Home: 360 E Marietta St Canton GA 30114-3017

TAYLOR, SUSAN GARRETT, academic administrator, school psychologist; b. Jamaica, N.Y., May 9, 1937; d. Elmer Ellsworth and Florence Marjorie (Rome) Garrett; m. Alva Melbourne Taylor; children: Anne Carol McAuliffe, Stephen Andrew Morgan. AB, Boston U., 1959; MA, Assumption Coll., 1972, Cert. of Advanced Grad. Study, 1976; EdD, U. Mass., Amherst, 1995. Cert. sch. supt., Mass. Tchr. Sudbury (Mass.) Jr. High Sch., 1959-60, Wahconah Reg. High Sch., Dalton, Mass., 1962—63; sch. adjustment counselor Milford (Mass.) Pub. Schs., 1972-74, sch. psychologist, 1974-88, dir. spl. edn., 1988-90; dir. curriculum, instr., spl. svcs. Scituate (Mass.) Pub. Schs., 1990—96; asst. supt. Randolph (Mass.) Pub. Schs., 1996—2003; ret., 2003. Founder Sch. Psychologists for Licensure and Legis. Action, Boston, 1986-88. Mem. Mass. Sch. Psychologists Assn. (pres. 1990-92). Avocations: gardening, classical music, travel. Home: 7 Greenleaf Rd Natick MA 01760-3115 E-mail: alvasue@rcn.com.

TAYLOR, SUSAN L., magazine editor; b. N.Y.C., Jan. 23, 1946; d. Lawrency and Violet (Weekes) T.; m. William Bowles (div.); 1 child, Shana-Nequai; m. Khephra Burns, 1989-. BA in Sociology, Fordham U., 1991, postgrad.; doctorate (hon.), Spelman Coll., Bennett Coll., Del. State, Fisk U., Lincoln U. Founder, rschr. and developer of a line of customized cosmetics and natural skin care line Nequai Cosmetics, 1970—81; freelance beauty editor to fashion Essence Mag., NYC, 1971-81; editor-in-chief Essence Comm., Inc., NYC, 1981—2000, v.p, 1986—93, sr. v.p., 1993, editl. dir., 2000—, also bd. dir. Host, exec. prodr. weekly tv show Essence, 1983-87; exec. prodr. and driving force behind Essence Awards and Essence Music Festival; served on Comm. on Rsch. in Black Edn. through the Assn. Ednl. Rsch. Assn; spkr. in field. Author: In the Spirit: The Inspirational Writings of Susan L. Taylor, 1993, Lessons in Living, 1995; co-author with husband Confirmation: The Spiritual Wisdom That Has Shaped Our Lives, 1997; co-editor of several books. Co-chair Danny Glover for Shared Interest (to raise money to build housing in rural areas of S. Africa); bd. dir. Joint Ctr. for Polit. and Econ. Studies, Washington; mem. adv. bd. Black Adminstr. in Child Welfare; mem. La. Recovery Authority; committed to serving and empowering the poor and work with disadvantaged women and teenagers to encourage them take charge of their lives. Recipient Henry Johnson Fisher award, 1998, President's award, NAACP Image award, 2006. Mem.: Women in Communications, Am. Soc. Mag. Editors (inducted into Hall of Fame 2002), Nat. Assn. Black Journalists. Office: Essence Comm Inc 135 W 50th St 4th Fl New York NY 10020*

TAYLOR, SUSAN M., museum director; Dir. Davis Mus. and Cultural Ctr., Wellesley Coll., Mass., Princeton U. Art Mus., NJ, 2000—. Office: Princeton U Art Mus Mc Cormick Hall Princeton NJ 08544 Office Phone: 609-258-3788.

TAYLOR, SUSAN S., performance consultant; b. Minneapolis, Oct. 17, 1945; d. Lucius O. and Mary Elizabeth (McNaughton) T. BS in Edn., U. Minn., 1967; MS in Ednl. Rsch. & Testing, Fla. State U., Tallahassee, 1971, PhD in Instl. Sys., 1974. Cert. tchr., Minn., Mo. Tchr. Minnetonka (Minn.) Pub. Schs., 1967—68; tchr./author CAI Lab.-Kansas City Pub. Schs., 1968-70; grad. asst. Fla. State U., Tallhassee, 1970-74; cons./mgr. Control Data Corp., 1974-88; tech. dir. WICAT Sys., Orem, Ut., 1989-90; owner/cons. SST Enterprises, Bloomington, Minn., 1990—. Presenter in field. Author: (book chpt.) CREATE: A Computer-Based Authorizing Curriculum, 1979. Sec. Minn. Episcopal Cursillo Coun., Minn., 1998—2001. Mem. Internat. Soc. Performance Improvement (co-chair independent cons., past pres., treas. Minn. chpt.), Am. Soc. Tng. & Devel. Avocations: gardening, genealogy, reading, walking, crafts. Office: SST Enterprises 7430 Autumn Chace Dr Ste 203 Bloomington MN 55438-1115

TAYLOR, SUSAN SEROTA, biochemist, researcher; b. Racine, Wis., June 20, 1942; d. Rudolph M. and Helen L. (Vohs) S.; m. Palmer William Taylor, July 3, 1965; children: Tasha Katherine, Ashton David, Palmer Andrew. BS, U. Wis., 1964; PhD, Johns Hopkins U., 1968. Postdoctoral fellow MRC Lab. Molecular Biology, Cambridge, England, 1969—71, U. Calif. San Diego, La Jolla, 1971-72, asst. prof. chemistry, 1972-79, assoc. prof., 1979-85, prof. chemistry, biochemistry, 1985—, prof. pharmacology dept. chemistry. biochemistry, 2004. Investigator Howard Hughes Med. Inst., 1997—; mem. adv. coun. GM Cancer Rsch. Found. Recipient Career Devel. award NIH; postdoctoral fellow NIH 1969-72, Fogarty Internat. Fellow NIH, 1981-82. Mem. Am. Chem. Soc., AAAS, NAS, Inst. Medicine, Am. Soc. Biochemistry and Molecular Biology (mem. coun. 1989-92, pres. 1995-96). Office: U Calif San Diego Dept Chemistry MC 0654 La Jolla CA 92093-0654 Business E-Mail: staylor@ucsd.edu.

TAYLOR, SUZONNE BERRY STEWART, real estate broker; b. Memphis, Sept. 27, 1926; d. Andrew Cleveland and Sue Hodge (Berry) Stewart; m. Robert Allen Taylor, Sr., June 15, 1946; children: Robert A. Jr., Suzonne Stewart Taylor Davids. Student, Rhodes Coll., Memphis, 1948, U. S.C., Columbia, 1969. Cert. residential specialist CRS Coun., 1996; grad. Realtors Inst.; cert. real estate broker; accredited buyer's rep. Am. Bd. Realtors. Sales agt. E. Roy Stone Realtors, Greenville, SC, 1967—69; real estate broker Aven Assoc. Realtors, Dover, Del., 1970—80, Emerson & Co. Realtors, Dover, 1980—2000; realtor ERA Harrington Realty, 1998—. Active Cresent Music Club, Greenville, 1955, Wildwood Garden Club, Greenville, 1960; mem., costume chmn. Greenville Little Theater, Jr. League Greenville, 1956-66, sustaining mem., 1966—, Jr. League Wilmington, Del., 1999—, dir., 1999. Recipient Beyond Excellence award, ERA, 2004, 2005. Mem. Nat. Bd. Realtors, Del. Bd. Realtors, Kent County Bd. Realtors, Del. Hist. Soc., Biggs Mus., Alpha Omicron Pi. Republican. Episcopalian. Home: 517 Greenhill Rd Dover DE 19901-3766 Office: ERA Harrington Realty 1404 Forest Ave Dover DE 19904 Office Phone: 302-674-4663. Business E-Mail: staylor@harringtonera.com.

TAYLOR, SYLVIA DAWN, music educator; b. Elizabethtown, N.C., Sept. 1, 1954; d. Byron Shaw and Kate Gustava Taylor. MusB in Applied Clarinet, Mars Hill Coll., NC, 1976; MusM in Edn., Mich. State U., 1978. Assoc. dir. bands Burns Jr. and Sr. H.S., Lawndale, NC, 1978—84; dir. bands N.E. Jr. H.S., Charlotte, NC, 1984—95, Elem. Band Program, Charlotte, 1995—97, J.M. Alexander Mid. Sch., Huntersville, NC, 1997—. Singer: Charlotte (N.C.) Oratorio Singers, 1984—86, Charlotte (N.C.) Oratorio Chamber Singers, 1984—86, Cavata, 1979, Ritual and Capriccio, 1980, Images of Aura Lee, 1981, Celebration for Band, 1982. Named Outstanding Educator, J.M. Alexander Mid. Sch., 1998. Mem.: South-Ctrl. Band Dirs. Assn., Music Educators Nat. Conf., Am. Sch. Bandmasters Assn. (NC Stanbury award 1985, S.E. United States Stanbury award 1986). Avocation: music. Home: PO Box 812 Harrisburg NC 28075 Office: JM Alexander Middle Sch 12201 Hambright Rd Huntersville NC 28078-7670 Office Phone: 980-343-3830 ext. 253.

TAYLOR, TERESA, communications executive; BS, U. Wis., LaCrosse. Joined US West (now Qwest), 1988; exec. v.p. wholesale markets group Qwest Comm. Internat., Inc., 2003—, exec. v.p. products and pricing group, 2000—03. Bd. dirs. Colo. Inst. Tech., Colo. Children's Campaign. Office: Qwest Comm Internat Inc 1801 California St Denver CO 80202

TAYLOR, TERESA MARIE, realtor; b. San Antonio, Nov. 21, 1949; d. Willie G. and Theresa (Page) Murillo; m. Ralph W. Taylor, June 30, 1972 (div. 1979); children: Lisa, Phillip; m. Michael Brock Toon, Nov. 29, 1997. Grad., Exec. Sectl. Sch., 1969; student, Richland Coll., 1989, Brookhaven Coll., 1990. Lic. real estate agt., Tex. Sec. to controller Steak and Ale Restaurants, 1969-73; sec. Henry S. Miller Co., 1974—76; exec. sec. to sr. v.p. of fin. Jet Fleet Corp., 1976-78; exec. sec. to exec. v.p. and sr. v.p. J.L. Williams & Co., Inc., 1978-80; exec. sec. U.S. Lend Lease Inc., 1980-82; exec. sec. to gen. mgr. Melrose Hotel, 1982-83; exec. sec. to dir. North Tex. sales MCI Telecommunications, 1986-91; leasing agt. Lou Smith Realtors, Dallas, 1988; sales assoc. Christensen Realtors, Dallas, 1988-97; adminstrv. asst. to info. tech. group, ptnr. Kenneth Leventhal & Co., Dallas, 1991-95; adminstrv. asst. to regional v.p. Bristol Hotel Co., 1995-98; sales assoc. Henry S. Miller Realtors, 1997—2001, Coldwell Banker, 2001—05; founding assoc. Keller Williams Elite, Dallas, 2005—. Active Profl. Members League, Dallas Mus. Art, 1993-95; bd. dirs., v.p. fund raising Am. Kidney Fund, 1989-93, chmn. for ann. fund raiser; bd. dirs. Restart Orgn., 1990-93; fundraiser Nat. Marrow Donor Program, 1995-97; vol. KERA Channel 13, 1994—. Mem.: Metro Tex. Assn. Realtors (Paint the Town participant 1989—92, Leadership alumni 2000—, Multi-Million Dollar Prodr.), Tex. Assn. Realtors, Nat. Assn. Realtors, Am. Bus. Women's Assn. (bull. editor 1987—88, publicity editor 1988—90, program chmn. 1989—90, hostess chmn. Dallas area coun. 1988—90, chn. pub. rels. com. 1990—92, Woman of the Yr. 1990). Republican. Roman Catholic. Avocations: tennis, skiing, cooking, needlepoint. Home: 4149 Republic Dr Frisco TX 75034-6327 Office Phone: 214-808-4673. E-mail: teri@teritaylor.com.

TAYLOR, TERRY R., editor, educator; b. Valley Forge, Pa., Oct. 4, 1952; d. Thomas R. and Anna P. (Bystrek) T. BA in Journalism, Temple U., 1974. Reporter gen. assignments, sch. news Charlotte (N.C.) News, 1974-77; supr., writer AP, Phila., 1977-81, supr., writer sports desk N.Y.C., 1981-85, asst. editor sports, 1985-87, dep. editor sports, 1987-91, asst. chief bur., 1991-92, editor sports, 1992—; asst. editor sports N.Y. Times, 1991. Assoc. in journalism Columbia U., N.Y.C., 1991-95; adv. bd. Honda Awards, 1996—. Recipient John A. Domino Meml. award St. Bonaventure U., 1996, Founder's award Temple U., 1999; inductee Delaware County Sports Hall of Fame, 1998. Roman Catholic. Achievements include first woman sports editor at the AP. Office: AP Sports 50 Rockefeller Plz New York NY 10020-1605

TAYLOR, WINNIFRED JANE, psychologist; b. Akron, Ohio, Aug. 27, 1925; d. Edwin Dain and Jessie Pearl (Keeran) Fletcher; B.S., U. Akron, 1962, M.S., 1965, Ph.D., 1971; m. John Idris Taylor, June 22, 1943; children— John Frederick Taylor, Timothy David Taylor, Kathryn Sue Taylor Cline. Tchr., Akron and Barberton, Ohio, 1959-65; sch. psychologist Akron Pub. Sch., 1965-74; pvt. practice family counseling and psychology, Clinton, Ohio, 1969-74; assoc. prof. and coordinator counseling programs U. Wis., Superior, 1974-93, prof. emeritus, 1993—; pvt. practice counseling psychology and family therapy, 1982—; lectr. Sun Am. Seminars, 1993-95. Author:

AMP Therapy: Strategies for Anger Management and Violence Prevention, 1996; syndicated columnist; contbr. articles to profl. jours. Recipient Freedom Found. award for Teaching, 1965-66. Mem. Nat. Assn. Sch. Psychologists, Am., Wis. personnel and guidance assns., Am. Soc. Adlerian Psychology, Am. Edn. Research Assn., Am. Sch. Counselors Assn., Assn. Humanistic Psychology, Douglas County Mental Health Assn., Am. Soc. Indiviual Psychology. Home: 1421 E 6th St Superior WI 54880-3315

TAYLOR-BROWN, CAMERON ANN, artist, educator, consultant; b. L.A., Oct. 2, 1953; d. James Hutton and Ann Rossner (Hinsdale) Taylor; m. Charles Albert Brown, July 8, 1978; children: Julia, Peter. Student, Vassar Coll., 1970—71; BA, U. Calif., Berkeley, 1975; BS, Phila. Coll. Textiles, 1977. Fabric stylist Cheney Bros., N.Y.C., 1977—79; instr. design Phila. Coll. Textiles, 1979—83; rsch. assoc., curator Goldie Paley Design Ctr., Phila., 1980—83; artist, educator Phila. and L.A., 1979—; regional rep. fibers L.A., 1983—; ednl. cons. ACCESS Cmty. Arts and Edn., L.A., 1997—. Mem. com. Getty Edn. Inst./Fairfax Family Sch., L.A., 1997; lectr., workshop presenter Bobbinwinders, Creative Weavers Guild, the Shepherdess, South Coast Spinners and Weavers, So. Calif. Guild Handweavers Convergence. Artist, contbr. Fiberarts mag., 1985, 87, Fiberarts Design Book 4, 1991, Design Book 5, 1995, Design Book 6, 1999, Design Book 7, 2004, Shuttle, Spindle & Dyepot, 1997; exhbns. include Artspace Gallery, Woodland Hills, Calif., 1992, Del Mano Gallery, 1994, Downey Mus. Arts, 1995, Riverside Mus. Art, 1997, Wignall Gallery, 1999, La Jolla Fiber Arts, 2003, Gallery Contemporary Art, Colo. Springs, 2004, Woven Fiber House, West Chester, Pa., 2005 Mem. program devel. com., fundraiser, cmty. outreach com., grant writer Friends of Third St. Sch., L.A., 1989-99, co-pres., 1997-99—. Recipient Woman of Larchmont Cmty. Svc. award Larchmont Chronicle, 1997. Mem. Textile Group L.A. (bd. dirs. 1984-90), Designing Weavers (bd. dirs.), Calif. Fibers (regional liaison 1993—) Avocations: reading, gardening, travel, skiing.

TAYLOR-DUNN, CORLISS LESLIE, marriage and family therapist; d. Hilary Oliver and Sally Wilkins Taylor; m. David Charles Dunn, Aug. 2, 1975 (dec. Apr. 6, 2001). BA in Performing Arts, classically trained dramatic soprano, Ctrl. State U., 1971; MA in Marriage & Family Therapy, Azusa Pacific U., Calif., 1995; student in Counseling for the Ministry, Biola U., 1991—93; DS in Psychology, Calif. Coast Coll., 2006. Lic. marriage & family therapist Bd. of Behavioral Scis., Calif., 2000. Psychotherapist Helicon Youth Ctr., Riverside, Calif., 1998—2001, Genesis Counseling Svcs., San Bernardino, Calif., 2002—02; pvt. practice Fort Garland, Colo., 2003—; pres., CEO, tchr. The Dunn Ctr. of Ft. Garland, Fort Garland, 2002—. Pres., CEO, nationwide safe ho. planter, tchr. www.freudsfunstuff.com, Fort Garland, 2002—; tchr. music, drama and dance Cmty. Ctr.; presenter in field. Author: (plays) (with Sandra Reaves-Phillips) Musical, Opening Night, 1981—82 (nominated for 3 off-Broadway Audelco awards, 1983); composer; dir.: Musical, Opening Night; author: (plays) Sojourner; The Story of an Ex-Slave (The Brody Art award Calif.Commn. Nat. Edn. Arts Assn., 1987); actor: (plays, Broadway) Ella, Bubbling Brown Sugar, 1977, Rockette Spectacular, Pin 'N Needles, Don't Bother Me I Can't Cope, (Broadway tour) Ruth in Raisin, 1976, 1988—89; prodr.: (TV films) Safehouse. Mem. Friends of the Fort support com. Fort Garland (Colo.) Mus.; founder Buffalo Soldiers Essay Contest Colorado Schs.; established David Charles Dunn scholarship Bilola U., 2002; mem. steering com. Rural Philanthropy Days; bd. dirs. Cmty. Revitalization Com., Neighborhood Action Group, Marketing Com. Friends of the Fort. Mem.: Am. Assn. Marriage and Family Therapists (licentiate), Calif. Assn. Marriage and Family Therapists (licentiate), Internat. Fellowship Christians and Jews, Costilla County C. of C. (mktg. com. 2003). Republican. Avocations: gardening, travel, acting, interior decorating, performing. Office: The David Charles Dunn Foundation 611 Macdonald Place Fort Garland CO 81133 Personal E-mail: ctaylordunn@aol.com.

TAYLOR-HALL, MARY ANN, writer; b. Chgo., Ill., Oct. 17, 1937; d. Edmund Haynes and Mildred Dubina Taylor; m. James Baker Hall, Sept. 30, 1982; children: Lawrence Russell Pemble, Matthew Russell Hall, Michael Walker Hall, William Alexander Henry. BA, U. Fla., 1959; MA, Columbia U., NY, 1961. English instr. Auburn U., La., 1962—64, U. Ky., Lexington, 1965—68, U. PR, Rio Pedras, 1968—71, Miami U., Oxford, Ohio, 1971—77. Author: (short stories) How She Knows What She Knows About Yo-Yos, 2001, (novels) Come and Go Molly Snow, 1995. Tutor, literacy program Cynthiana, Ky., 1998—2000. Mem.: Ky. Arts Coun., Nat. Endowment for the Arts. Home: 617 Dividing Ridge Rd South Sadieville KY 40370

TAYMOR, JULIE, theater, film and opera director and designer; b. Newton, Mass., 1952; d. Melvin L. and Betty Taymor. BA in folklore and mythology, Oberlin Coll., 1974; attended, L'Ecole Mimet Theatre in Paris, France, Herbert Berghof Studio, N.Y.C. Founder Teatr Loh. Dir. Way of Snow, The Transposed Heads, 1984, The Tempest, 1986, Liberty's Taken, 1985, Juan Darién, 1988, Fool's Fire, 1992, Titus Andronicus, 1994, Oedipus Rex, 1992, The Magic Flute, Salomé, The Flying Dutchman, The Lion King, 1997, (Tony awards for best director and costume design 1998), operas, classical plays and exptl. theater projects; prodr. Shakespeare plays and operas; designer puppets, masks, imaginative costumes and other visual elements. MacArthur grantee, Watson fellow, 1974-79, Obie awards, 1988.

TAZBIR, JANICE ELAINE, nursing educator; b. Chgo., Aug. 6, 1965; d. William John and Deanna Faye Stasiuk; m. Johnny Bernard Tazbir, Jan. 27, 1995; children: Jade Nicole, Joule Evon. MSN, Purdue U. Calumet, Hammond, Ind. RN Ill., Ind. Nurse U. Chgo., 1988—; assoc. prof. nursing Purdue U. Calumet, 1997—. Contbr. articles to profl. jours., chapters to books. Mem.: AACN, Am. Assn. Neurosci. Nurses. Home: PO Box 227 Saint John IN 46373 Office: Purdue Univerisity Calumet 2200 169th Street Hammond IN 46423 Office Phone: 219-989-2857. Personal E-mail: jtazbir@calumet.purdue.edu. E-mail: tazbir@calumet.purdue.edu.

TCHOUMAK, ADELINA, corporate financial executive; b. Chishinau, Moldovia, Feb. 16, 1974; arrived in U.S., 1990; d. Mercuriu and Olga Ciumac. BBA in Econs. summa cum laude, U. Anchorage, 1995. Performance analyst Clay Finlay Inc., NYC, 1996—2000; asst. v.p. Oppenheimer Capital, 2000—02; sr. performance analyst Citigroup N.A., 2002—. Sponsor Children Internat., Honduras, 2002—. Atheist. Avocations: reading, yoga. Home: 223 Dean St #2 Brooklyn NY 11217 Office: Citigroup NA 111 Wall St 14th Fl New York NY 10005 Office Phone: 212-657-7924. Personal E-mail: tadelina@hotmail.com.

TEAGUE, CAROLYN LOUISE, daycare administrator; b. Cin., Dec. 26, 1943; d. Leroy and Gladys Brockwell (Reed) Nooks; m. Will Teague, Nov. 24, 1976; children: Lauren Nicole, Will Ryan. BA, U. Cin., 1966; MEd, Coll. Mt. St. Joseph, 1993; EdD, U. Cin., 2006. Cert. permanent elem. tchr. Ohio. Ednl. cons. Chgo. Ctr. Inner City Studies; tchr. Chgo. Pub. Schs.; ednl. cons. Harcourt Brace Pub., Skokie, Ill.; tchr. Winton Woods Schs., Cin., Cin. Hills Christian Acad.; dir. Kinder Care Learning Ctrs., Cin. Co-author: Psycholinguistic Approach to Learning, 1970. Mem.: Assn. Supr. and Curriculum Devel., Nat. Sci. Tchrs. Assn., Jack and Jill Am., Phi Delta Kappa. Bapt. Avocations: music, dance, travel. Home: 6555 Lewis Clark Trail Cincinnati OH 45241 Business E-Mail: carolyn.teague@chca-oh.org.

TEAGUE, DEBORAH GANT, elementary school educator; b. Mankato, Minn., Jan. 23, 1952; d. Dorsett H. and Gwynlyn (Himmelman) Gant; m. William Lial Teague, June 7, 1991. AA, Meramec C.C., Kirkwood, Mo., 1972; BS, U. Mo., 1974, Edn. Specialist, 1989; MS, U. Minn., 1982. Tchr. Mexico (Mo.) Pub. Sch., 1977—. Recipient Presdl. Award in Excellence in Math. and Sci., NSF and Nat. Sci. Tchr. Assn., 1993; Fulbright Exch. fellow, 1985; Mo. State Incentive grantee Mo. State Dept. Edn., 1987, 88. Mem. Nat. Sci. Tchrs. Assn., Coun. of Elem. Sci. Teaching Internat., Assn. Presdl. Awardee Sci. Tchrs., Mo. Sci. Tchrs. Assn., N.E. Mo. State Tchrs. Assn. (exec. com. 1992-94), Phi Delta Kappa. Avocations: walking, swimming, travel. Home: 701 Ringo St Mexico MO 65265-1220 Office: Mexico Public Sch 1250 W Curtis St Mexico MO 65265-1855

TEAHON, JEAN ANN, county official; b. Dunning, Nebr., June 19, 1936; d. Norman Arthur and Margaret Elsa (Terwilliger) Linder; m. Charles Gerald Teahon, Aug. 31, 1958; children: Geri Ann, Peggy Lynn, Tedd Norman. AA, Kearney State Coll., 1958. Cert. assessor Nebr. Elementary tchr. Compton Sch., Valentine, Nebr., 1956, Calamus Valley Sch., Ainsworth, Nebr., 1956-57, Willow Lake Sch., Elsmere, Nebr., 1957-59, German Valley Sch., Brewster, Nebr., 1968-72; dep. county clk. Blaine County, Brewster, 1980-90, county clk./assessor, 1995—; office mgr. Ctrl. Sandhills Area Ext., Thedford, Nebr., 1992-94. Author: Blaine County History, 1988. Active Dunning United Ch. of Christ, 1949—, memorial chair, 1992—. Mem. Nat. Assn. County Ofcls., Nebr. Assn. County Ofcls. Democrat. Office: Blaine County # 1 Lincoln Ave Brewster NE 68821 E-mail: jteahon@yahoo.com.

TEAL, ARABELLA W., lawyer, former state attorney general; b. NYC, Jan. 1961; m. Gary Teal; 2 children. BA, Harvard Coll., 1984; JD, Georgetown U. Law Ctr., 1987. Law clerk for sr. judges D.C. Superior Court, 1987—88; section chief General Litigation Section I, 1996—99; acting prin. dep. corp. counsel D.C., 1999—2000, prin. dep. corp. counsel, 2000—02, interim corp. counsel, 2002—03; atty. McCabe & Mack LLP, Poughkeepsie, 2003—. Office: McCabe & Mack LLP 63 Washington St PO Box 509 Poughkeepsie NY 12602-0509

TEARNEY, MELISSA BAYER, lawyer; BA magna cum laude, Harvard Coll., 1988, JD cum laude, 1991. Bar: Mass. 1991. Ptnr. Nixon Peabody LLP, Boston. Chair United Way Allocations Com.; bd. dirs. Women's Auxiliary, Hebrew Rehab. Ctr. for Aged. Mem.: Women's Bar Assn., Mass. Bar Assn., Phi Beta Kappa. Office: Nixon Peabody LLP 100 Summer St Boston MA 02110 Office Phone: 617-345-1323. Office Fax: 866-947-1808. E-mail: mtearney@nixonpeabody.com.

TEATER, DOROTHY SEATH, retired county official; b. Manhattan, Kans., Feb. 11, 1931; d. Dwight Moody and Martha (Stahnke) Seath; m. Robert Woodson Teater, May 24, 1952; children: David Dwight, James Stanley, Donald Robert, Andrew Scott. BS, U. Ky., 1951; MS, Ohio State U., 1954. Home econs. tchr. Georgetown (Ky.) City Schs., 1951-53; extension specialist Ohio Coop. Extension, Columbus, 1967-73; consumer affairs adminstr. City of Columbus, 1974-79, Bank One Columbus NA, 1980-85; councilmember Columbus City Coun., 1980-85; commr. Franklin County, Columbus, Ohio, 1985-2000; ret. Mem. Columbus Met. Area Cmty. Action Orgn.; mem. adv. bd. Ohio Housing Trust; chairwoman Franklin County Children's Cabinet; pub. mem. Ohio Bd. Pharmacy, 2000—. Bd. dirs. BBB;, Silesian Boys and Girls Club, Rickenbacker-Woods Mus.; mem. hon. adv. bd. Girl Scouts. Recipient Outstanding Alumnus award U. Ky., 1989, Women of Achievement award YWCA, 1995, Disting. Svc. award Ohio State U., 1997; named Disting. Alumni, Ohio State U., 1977. Mem. County Commrs. Assn. Ohio (pres. 1994), Columbus Met. Club, Greater Columbus C. of C. (Columbus award 1997). Republican. Methodist. Avocations: gardening, sewing.

TEATER, TRICIA L., human resources specialist; b. Des Moines, Iowa, Dec. 3, 1956; d. Harold Lord and Patricia Mae Teater. BA in Journalism, Drake U., 1982; MPA, Roosevelt U., 1991. Legis. asst. Alderman David Orr, Chgo., 1984-85; exec. asst. to commr. City of Chgo., Dept. Human Svcs., 1985-89; dir. human resources Cook County Clk.'s Office, Chgo., 1990—. Vol. chaplain Ind. Dept. Corrections, Michigan City, Ill. Dept. Corrections; vol. ethics com. Horizon Hospice, Chgo.; bd. dirs. Prologue Alternative H.S., Chgo. Mem. ASPA, Soc. for Human Resources Mgmt. Democrat. Buddhist.

TEBBS, CAROL ANN, secondary school educator, academic administrator; b. Columbus, Ohio, Sept. 9, 1939; d. John Arthur and Ann Laurie (Wickham) Williams; m. Ronald Daniel Tebbs, Mar. 31, 1957; children: Kimberly Ann, Ronald Dan. BA in English, Whittier Coll., 1963, MA in English and Edn., 1972. Cert. tchr. K-adult Calif. Tchr. art and English Hacienda La Puente Unified Sch. Dist., Hacienda Heights, Calif., 1963-84; tchr. advanced placement English, acad. decathlon advisor, yearbook advisor Glen A. Wilson H.S., Hacienda Heights, 1984—2000. Mentor tchr. Hacienda La Puente Sch. Dist., Hacienda Heights, 1988—2000; reader, tchr. trainer advanced placement English Coll. Bd., 2000—; bd. dirs. Kepler Coll., Lynnwood, Wash., pres., 2003—; bd. dirs., tchr. Online Coll., 2000—. Contbr. articles to profl. jours. Named Tchr. of the Yr., Nat. Walmart Stores Found., 1998; recipient D. Fedderson Cmty. Svc. award, PTA, 1970, Teacher of the Year, 1971, Glen A. Wilson Faculty Tchr. of Yr. award, 1999—2000. Mem.: United Astrology Congress (program chair 1986, 1989, 1992, coord. 1995, bd. chmn. 1995—99, co-founder), Internat. Soc. Astrol. Rsch. (pres. 1988—95, bd. dirs. 1995—2004), Delta Kappa Gamma. Methodist. Home: 56870 Jack Nicklaus Blvd La Quinta CA 92253-5074 Office: 4630 200th St SW Ste A-1 Lynnwood WA 98036 Office Phone: 425-673-4292. Personal E-mail: caroltebbs@aol.com.

TEBEDO, MARYANNE, state legislator; b. Denver, Oct. 30, 1936; m. Don Tebedo; children: Kevin, Ronald, Linda, Thomas, Christine. Profl. registered parliamentarian. Mem. Colo. Ho. of Reps., Denver, 1982-88, Colo. Senate, Denver, 1988—2001; owner, pres. Colo. Mediation and Parliamentary Profls., Colorado Springs. Mediator 4th Jud. Dist. Colo. Mem.: Nat. Assn. Parliamentarians, Colo. Assn. Parliamentarians (pres.). Republican. Office Phone: 719-471-2561. E-mail: matebedo@isp.com.

TEBOH, BRIDGET A., history professor, researcher; d. Samuel Kanda and Esther Acha Teboh. BA with honors, U. Cameroon, Yaounde, 1986; Diplome U. Etudes Francais, U. Jean-Moulin, Lyon III, France, 1986; MAAS, UCLA, 1994, PhD, 2002. Adj. prof. African history UCLA, 1999—2003, Woodbury U., Burbank, Calif., 1999—2003, U. Calif., Long Beach, 1999—2003; asst. prof. (history) U. of Wis., La Crosse, Wis., 2003—05; asst. prof. African history U. Mass., North Dartmouth, 2005—. Sec., comm. asst. Pacific Inst. Women's Health, LA, 1999—2002; cons., African expert Revolutions Studio, Hollywood Films, Santa Monica, Calif., 2000—03; translator, exec. sec. U.S. African Devel. Found., Yaounde, 1988—92. Mem. Westwood Hills Christian Ch. Internat. Women's Group, LA, 1996—2002; initial contact counselor Office of Internat. Students and Scholars, LA, 1995—98; mem. Internat. Women's Group, La Crosse, Wis., 2003—05. Fellow, UCLA, 1996—98, 2000, 2002; grantee, U. Mass., Dartmouth, 2005—06; rsch. grantee, U. Wis., La Crosse, 2004—05. Mem.: Assn. African Women Scholars (corr.), African Studies Assn. (assoc.). Presbyterian. Avocations: reading, cooking, travel, dance, women's issues. Office: U Mass Dartmouth History Dept 285 Old Westport Rd North Dartmouth MA 02747 Office Phone: 1 508-999-8172. Office Fax: 1-508-999-8809. Business E-Mail: bteboh@umassd.edu.

TEBOH-EWUNGKEM, MIRANDA IJANG, education educator; d. Aaron Bagen and Christiana Enih Teboh; m. Julius Ewungwo Ewungkem, July 31, 1998; 1 child, Julius Jr. Ewungwo Ewungkem. BS in Math., U. Buea, 1996, MS in Math., 1998; PhD in Math., Lehigh U., 2003, MS in Stats, 2003. Tchg. asst. U. Of Buea, Cameroon, 1997—98; dean's fellow Lehigh U., Bethlehem, Pa., 1998—99, tchg. asst., 1999—2003, hsiung vis. asst. prof., 2003—04; vis. post doc U. Mich., 2004—04; vis. asst. prof. Lafayette Coll., Easton, Pa., 2004—. Author: (conference book of abstracts) International Conference for Mathematics in Biology and Medicine, International Conference on Applied Math, International Conference on Mathematical Biology; contbr. articles to jours. Landahl student travel grant, Soc. of Math. Biology, 2002, Travel grant, AWM, 2004, Reidler grant, Lehigh U., 2003, SMB Travel grant, SMB, 2004, Commonwealth scholarship, Commonwealth group, 1998. Mem.: Soc. of Indsl. and Applied Mathematicians, Soc. for Math. Biology, Am. Math. Soc., Assn. for Women in Math. Christian. Avocations: reading, tennis. Office: Lafayette Coll Pardee Hall 225A Easton PA 18042 Office Phone: 610 330 5328. Office Fax: 610 330 5721. Business E-Mail: tebohewm@lafayette.edu.

TEBOUT, WYNTA BARBARA, elementary school educator; d. Ray Allen Tebout and Loretta Ramona Ritter-Tebout, Betty Addie Ritter. BA in English, Shaw U., Raleigh, N.C., 1998. Cert. early childhood tchr. N.C., elem. tchr. N.C. Tchr. Wake County Sch. Sys., Raleigh, NC, 2000—02; tchr. 7th grade lang. arts Durham Pub. Sch. Sys., NC, 2003—. Mem.: N.C. Assn. of Educators (assoc.; del. and tutor). Office Phone: 919-560-3955.

TECCA, KIMBERLY ANN, physician assistant; b. Detroit, Nov. 20, 1947; d. George Leonard and Jeanne (Austin) Wilkie; m. Joseph P. Tecca; 1 child, Aaron Thomas Kunkel. AA, Pensacola Jr. Coll., 1971; BS in Medicine, physician's asst. cert. in medicine, U. Ala., Birmingham, 1976; cert. in mgmt., Am. Mgmt. Assn., 1989; postgrad., U. West Fla., 1995—. Cert. physician's asst. Asst. mgr. Christo's, Gulf Breeze, Fla., 1966-67; teller, bookkeeper loan dept. Bank Gulf Breeze, 1967-72; med. tech. aide USN Hosp., Pensacola, 1972, physician's asst., 1972-73, John Kingsley, MD, Pensacola, 1976, Mountain Comprehensive Health Corp., Whitesburg, Ky., 1976-78, N.W. Fla. Nephrology, Pensacola, 1978-87, med. adminstr., 1987-95, Nephrology Ctr. of Pensacola, Fla., 1987-95; COO Nephrology Ctr. Inc., Crestview, Pensacola, 1995—, Nephrology Ctr., Inc., Crestview, Pensacola, 1995-96, Nephrology Ctr. Assocs., Pensacola, 1995-96; regional COO, Renal Care Group Inc., Pensacola, Fla., 1996-98; COO Nephrology Ctr. Assoc. PA, 1998-99; area administr. Renal Care Group Inc., Houston, 1999—2002, clin. ops. cons., 2002, dir. clin. ops., 2002, 2002—; dir. regulation affairs Fresenius Med. Care, 2006—. Fellow Am. Acad. Physician's Assts. (del. nat. meeting 1978—), Nat. Commn. on Cert. Physician's Assts., Nat. Renal Adminstrs., Fla. Acad. Physician's Assts. (jud. com. 1979-80), National Wildlife Assn., Assn. Practioners Infection Control, Nat. REnal Adminstrn. Assn. Republican. Roman Catholic. Avocations: photography, antiques, reading, wildlife preservation. Office: Fresesnius Med Care 95 Navden Ave Lexington MA 02420

TEDD, MONIQUE MICHELINE, artist; b. Sotteville-les-Rouen, France, Jan. 25, 1943; came to U.S., 1968; d. Maurice Joseph and Dolly Jeanne (Carpentier) T.; m. Asiat A. Ali, Dec. 23, 1967; 1 child, Asiat Allum Ali. MFA in Painting, Beaux-Arts Sch. of Rouen, Seine Rouen Maritime, France, 1967. Art tchr. Vernon, France, 1967-68; advt. Hahn J. Shoes, Washington, 1968-69, Magrams, Burlington, Vt., 1974—. Set decorator Lyric Theater, Burlington, Vt., 1975. One-woman shows include St. Michael's Coll., Winooski, Vt., 1972, 91, Peel's Gallery, Danby, Vt., 1978-79, Gov.'s Corridor, State Capital, Montpelier, Vt., 1980, The Living and Learning Ctr., U. Vt., Burlington, 1982, Passepartout Gallery, Winooski, 1983, Gallery Two, Woodstock, 1984; exhibited in group shows at The Gallery, Washington, 1969, N.Y. First Internat. Art Show, 1970, Galerie des Trois Arts, Burlington, Vt., 1970-71, Fleming Mus., Burlington, 1972, Frog Hollow, Middlebury, 1973, The Four Winds Gallery, North Ferrisburg, Vt., 1975, Norwich U. Armory Show, Hanover, N.H., 1976, Old Bergen Art Guild Touring Exhibit, 1978-80, Stratton Art Festival, Stratton, Vt., 1979, Women's Ednl. Ctr., Essex Junction, Vt., 1981-82, Pocketbook Wood Gallery, Montpelier, 1981-82, Window, a Women's View, Burlington, 1981-82, Passepartout Gallery, 1985, Smith Coll., 1985, Wood Art Gallery, Montpelier, 1985, 86, 87, Helen Day Ctr., Stowe, Vt., 1986-87, Gallery Two, 1991, Shelburne Mus., 1996, Beaux Arts Studio, Essex Junction, Vt., 1998—; selected for exhibit and calendars Paysage de France, a 12-city exhibit, 1965. Recipient 1st prize Rouen C. of C., 1964, 3rd prize Grand Prix Internat. of Deauville, 1987, open studio 7th Vt. Craft Coun., 2000. Home: 9 Seneca Ave Essex Junction VT 05452-3521 E-mail: teddali@verizon.net.

TEDESCO, KRISTI, newscaster; married; 1 child. Degree in Comms., U. Ariz. Reporter, Topeka; anchor, reporter Sta. KWCH-TV, Wichita, Kans., Sta. WRTV-TV, Indpls., 2000—. Recipient First Pl. award, Kans. Assn. Broadcasters, 1995. Office: WRTV TV 1330 N Meridian St Indianapolis IN 46202

TEE, VIRGINIA, lawyer; b. Damariscotta, Maine, Aug. 7, 1956; d. Lawrence Edward and Rosamond (Stetson) Tee; m. David A. Danaee, Oct. 29, 1982; children: Christina Nicole Danaee, Erica Michelle Danaee. BA in English, Fla. State U., 1978; JD, U. Puget Sound, 1992. Bar: Fla. 1992, Wash. 1994. Corp. counsel AT&T Wireless Svcs., Inc., Redmond, Wash., 1993-99; asst. gen. counsel drugstore.com,inc., Bellevue, Wash., 1999—. Mem. editl. adv. bd. Wash. State Bar News, 1996-98; mem. MCLE Bd., 1998—, chair, 2000-01. Mem. Wash. State Bar Assn., Fla. State Bar Assn. Office: drugstore dot com 13920 SE Eastgate Way Bellevue WA 98005-4440 Home: 16586 Haynie Ln Jupiter FL 33478-8209

TEEGARDEN, NICOLEE, artist, consultant, retired educator; d. Charles Whitney and Mary Lucille (Neiman) Webster; m. Ernest Allen Teegarden, Sept. 2, 1962 (div. May 1970); m. Joseph John Rozman, Jr., Dec. 26, 1973 (div. July 1986); m. Clark Love, Aug. 1986 (div. Dec. 1989). BFA in Art Edn., Drake U., 1967; MS in Painting, U. Wis., 1972, MFA in Painting, 1980. Relief house parent Evang. Children's Home, St. Louis, 1962; ward clk., male neurosurg. ward U. Ill., Neuropsych Inst. Rsch. and Edn. Hosp., Chgo., 1963; dental asst., office mgr. Des Moines, Iowa, 1963; tissue technician, INH sponsored arteriosclerosis rsch. lab. Coll. of Osteopathy, Des Moines, Iowa, 1963; med. records clk. Broadlawns County Hosp., Des Moines, 1963—66; elem. art specialist Kenosha (Wis.) Unified Sch. Dist., 1969—71; tchr. Tremper H.S., 1971—2000, chair dept. art, 1978—79; sabbatical leave, 1979—80; chair dept. art Tremper H.S., Kenosha, Wis., 1984—99; instr. drawing Advanced Placement Studio Art, 1992—2000; instr. advanced drawing Kenosha Inst. Arts, 2002—03; pres. N.Am. Sintered Metal Corp., Kenosha, 2003—, Havencrest Garden Studio, Racine, Wis., 2005—. Instr. Coll. Lake County, Grayslake, Ill., 1970; mem. steering com. Nat. Scholastic Art Awards, Washington, 1993—94; artist in residence Havencrest Studio Gardens, Racine, Wis., 2005—. One-woman shows include Carthage Coll. Art Gallery, Kenosha, 1971, Daken Gallery, Waukegan, Ill., 1971, David Barnett Gallery, Milw., 1972, U. Wis. Fine Arts Gallery, 1972, Marine Bank Gallery, 1980, Upstairs/Downstairs Gallery, Kenosha, 1980, Ctr. City Espresso, Racine, Wis., 1991, Racine St. Visitors and Conv. Bur., 1996, Hist. 6th St. Art Walk, Christian Sci. Reading Room, 2006. Regional Scholastic Art Awards adv. com. Milw. Art Mus., 1980—94, com. chair, 1990—94. Named Scholastic Art Awards Disting. Alumni, Milw. Art Mus., 1993; recipient Lakefront Festival Arts award of excellence, 1981; Nat. Art Inst. scholar, Alliance Ind. Colls. Art and Design Studio, N.Y.C., 1988. Home: 1701 Wisconsin Ave Racine WI 53403 Office Phone: 262-634-8256.

TEEL, GINA A., language educator; d. Gene A. and Jaunita M. Teel. BA, Okla. City U., 1985; MDiv, So. Meth. U., Dallas, 1989; MA, U. Ark., Little Rock, 1991. Instr. of English and speech SE Ark. Coll., Pine Bluff, 1998—. Co-sponsor Phi Theta Kappa chpt. at SE Ark. Coll., Pine Bluff, 1998—2002, Alpha Mu Gamma chpt. at SEARK Coll., Pine Bluff, Ark., 2003—. Mem. of vestry Grace Episcopal Ch., Pine Bluff, Ark., 2005; lic. preacher Episcopal Diocese of Ark., Little Rock, 2006—; bd. mem. and vice chair of bd. Ark. Coordinated Child Effort in State Svcs., Pine Bluff, 2000—03. Achievements include participant in NEH Summer Inst.-A Literature of Their Own?, U. N.C., Chapel Hill, 2003. Office: SE Ark Coll 1900 Hazel Pine Bluff AR 71603 Office Phone: 870-543-5961.

TEEL, JOYCE RALEY, retail executive; b. 1930; m. James Teel. Dir. Raley's, West Sacramento, 1950—; co-chmn. bd. dirs. Raley's, Bel Air Markets, Food Source, Nob Hill Foods, No. Calif., Nev., NMex., 1991—. Dir. non-profit Food for Families. Named one of Forbes' Richest Americans, 2006. Office: Raleys & Belaire 500 W Capitol Ave West Sacramento CA 95605-2696*

TEETER, LORNA MADSEN, art educator; b. Salt Lake City, Dec. 10, 1948; d. Orrin Andersen and Marie Eliza (Hunter) Madsen; m. Steven Church Teeter, June 9, 1971; children: Heather, Michael Patrick, Michelle, Russell Scott, Kurt Andrew, Ryan Anthony, Sean Douglas. BS, U. Utah, 1971; MOE, Keene (N.H.) State Coll., 1978; postgrad., Novosibirsk (Russia) State U. Cert. tchr. secondary edn. and mid. sch. in art, home econs., geography and bus., Utah. Instr. Keene State Coll., 1975-77; ptnr. The Tack and Hammer/Mobile Decorator Showroom, Nelson, N.H., 1976-84; tchr. Provo (Utah) Sch. Dist., 1984—. Presenter Getty Ctr. for Arts Conf., L.A., 1989; dist. art curriculum leader Provo Sch. Dist., 1989-91; gifted and talented specialist Farrer Mid.

Sch., Provo, 1991—. Leader 4-H, Nelson, 1973-76; den mother Cub Scouts, Provo, 1984-86. Mem. NEA, Nat. Art Edn. Assn., Utah Edn. Assn., Utah Art Edn. Assn., Provo Edn. Assn. (instrnl. and profl. devel. 1989-91). Mem. Ch. of Jesus Christ of Latter-day Saints. Avocations: outdoors, travel. Home: 1152 W 400 N Provo UT 84601-2410 Office: 750W 200N Provo UT 84601

TEETER, RAE JEAN, music educator; b. Troy, Ohio, Mar. 4, 1966; d. William Monroe and Margaret Marie Hartley; m. Patrick Joseph Teeter, Apr. 15, 1990; children: Sean Patrick, Katherine Margaret, Michael William Frederick. MusB, Eastman Sch. Music, 1988; MusS, Coll. St. Rose, 1994. Cert. tchr. NY. Music tchr. Farnsworth Mid. Sch., Guilderland, NY, 1988—95; choral dir. New England Music Camp, Oakland, Maine, 1995—96, Skidmore Coll., Saratoga Springs, NY, 2004; dir. vocal music Guilderland HS, 1995—. Pvt. vocal tchr., 1988—; music cons. Christ's Ch., Albany, NY, 2005; clinician, guest condr. Contbg. author: Teaching Music through Performance in Choir Vol. II, 2006. Recipient tchrs. award, Guilderland Ctrl. Schs., 2003. Mem.: Am. Choral Dirs. Assn. (HS repertoire and stds. chmn. NY chpt. 2005—), Music Educators Nat. Conf. Avocations: motorcycling, camping, theater, hiking. Office: Guilderland HS 8 School Rd Guilderland Center NY 12085

TEETERS, LINDA MARIE, retired educator; b. Cin., Aug. 22, 1945; d. Irvin Louis and Shirley H. (Huenefeld) T. Cert. dental asst. U. N.C., 1973. Pharmacy intern Edward W. Wolff Pharmacy, 1963-67; dental asst. to various dentists, 1967-73; coordinator dental asst. clinics Hamilton County (Ohio) Bd. Health, 1973-76; dental coordinator Western Hills Vocat. High Sch., Cin., 1976-94, chmn. adv. bd. for dental program, 1976-94; mem. Ohio Commn. Dental Assisting Certs., 1981-93. Mem. Delhi Civic Assn., 1988—. Mem. Am. Dental Assts. Assn. (3d dist. trustee 1984-86), Ohio Dental Assts. Assn. (pres. 1982-83, editor newsletter 1979-84), Cin. Dental Assts. Assn. (pres. 1971-72, 77-78). Democrat. Roman Catholic. Club: Internationally Yours (pres. local chpt. 1985-89, 93-97, historian internat. chpt. 1986-93, 1st v.p. internat. bd. 1987-89, internat. pres. 1989-93, 95-2001). Home: 267 Anderson Ferry Rd Cincinnati OH 45238-5632

TEETERS, NANCY HAYS, economist, director; b. Marion, Ind., July 29, 1930; d. S. Edgar and Mabel (Drake) Hays; m. Robert Duane Teeters, June 7, 1952; children: Ann, James, John. AB in Econs., Oberlin Coll., 1952, LLD, 1979; MA in Econs., U. Mich., 1954, postgrad., 1956—57, LLD (hon.), 1983, Bates Coll., 1981, Mt. Holyoke Coll., 1983. Tchg. fellow U. Mich., Ann Arbor, 1954—55, instr., 1956—57, U. Md. Overseas, Germany, 1955—56; staff economist govt. fin. sect. Bd. Govs. of FRS, Washington, 1957—66, mem. bd., 1979—84; economist (on loan) Coun. Econ. Advs., 1962—63; economist Bur. Budget, 1966—70; sr. fellow Brookings Instn., 1970—73; sr. specialist Congl. Rsch. Svc., Library Congress, Washington, 1973—74; asst. dir., chief economist Ho. of Reps. Com. on Budget, 1974—78; v.p., chief economist IBM, Armonk, NY, 1984—90. Author: (with others) Setting National Priorities: The 1972 Budget, 1971, Setting National Priorities: The 1973 Budget, 1972, Setting National Priorities: The 1974 Budget, 1973; contbr. articles to profl. publs. Recipient Comfort Starr award in econs. Oberlin Coll., 1952; Disting. Alumnus award U. Mich., 1980 Mem. Nat. Economists Club (v.p. 1973-74, pres. 1974-75, chmn. bd. 1975-76, gov. 1976-79), Am. Econ. Assn. (com. on status of women 1975-78), Am. Fin. Assn. (dir. 1969-71) Democrat. Home: 77 3rd St C-8 Stamford CT 06905

TEETSELL, JANICE MARIE NEWMAN, business owner, lawyer; b. NYC, Aug. 11, 1951; d. Robert and Clara (White) Swindler; m. Roger Kevin Newman, Jan. 20, 1972 (div. 1980); 1 child, Germaine M. Swindler-Newman (dec.); m. Robert Charles Teetsell, Dec. 29, 1998. BA, Smith Coll., 1973; JD, Rutgers U., 1980. Bar: N.J. 1983, U.S. Supreme Ct. 1987. Adminstrv. asst. Corp. Ann. Reports, N.Y.C., 1972-73; pub. rels. asst. Lippincott & Margulies, N.Y.C., 1973; journalist Essex Forum Newspaper, East Orange, N.J., 1973; pub. info. officer City of Newark, 1974-82; producer, host Newark and Reality TV show, Newark, 1974-85; asst. communications dir. Mayor's Office, Newark, 1982-86; legis. liaison, publ. info. officer N.J. Div. on Women, Trenton, 1988-90, acting dir., 1990, women svcs. coord., 1990-91; environ. issues specialist N.J. Dept. Environ. Protection and Energy, Trenton, 1991-92; comm. specialist Dept. Environ. Protection, Lawrenceville, N.J., 1992-95; pvt. practice South Orange, N.J., 1994—; host, prodr. New Jersey Issues TV Show, 1995-98; adj. prof. Fairleigh Dickinson U., 2005. Mem. working group N.J. Supreme Ct. Domestic Violence, 1994-96; pres. JM Newman & Assocs.; chair Interest on Lawyers Trust Accounts, 1995-96, mem., 1986-96; dir. Legal Consultation Svc. Resource Ctr. Women, 1997-99. Mem. editl. bd. N.J. Lawyer mag., 1987-96, The Voice, Episcopal Diocese of Newark, 1999—; design editor: The Voice, 1993-94; contbr. articles to mags. Bd. dirs. Instrns. Exposures Experiences, 1983-87, Greater Newark Conservancy; 2d v.p. Women's Polit. Caucus, N.J., 1991-92, 1st v.p., 1992-93; appt. to N.J. Supreme Ct. Com. on Women in the Cts., 1990-94, Com. on Character, 1992—, N.J. Women Vets. Adv. Com., 1993-94; lay reader, Episc. Diocese of Newark, 1980—, eucharistic lay min., 1993—, parliamentarian, 1992-94; sr. warden, House of Prayer Episc. Ch., Newark, 1992; vestry clk. St. Andrew Holy Communion Episcopal Ch., 1997-99, warden, 2001-02, sr. warden, 2002-04 Recipient Pub. Svc. award N.J. Voice Newspaper, 1977, Achievement award Minority Contractors and Craftsmen Trade Assn., 1982, award Nat. Council Negro Bus. and Profl. Women Legal Achievement, 1987, award N.J. Unit Nat. Assn. Negro Bus. and Profl. Women's Clubs, 1987; named to Outstanding Young Women Am. U.S. Jaycees, 1984. Mem. Nat. Assn. Media Women (rec. sec. 1985-87, Media Woman of Yr. award 1985, pres. N.J. chpt. 1986-88), N.J. Bar Assn. (pub. rels. com. 1987—, 2d vice chmn. women's rights sect., 1990-92, 1st vice chmn. women's rights sect., 1992-93, chmn., 1993-95, trustee minorities in the profession sect., Cmty. Svc. award young lawyers divsn. 1989), N.J. State Bar Found. (trustee 1994-95), N.J. Women Lawyers Assn. (pres. 1986-88, trustee pub. rels. com., entertainment and arts com., Essex County Bar Assn. (mem. exec. bd. family law sect. 2006—), Nat. Coun. Negro Women, Garden State Bar Assn., Essex County Women Lawyers (trustee 1991-94, v.p. 1997-99), Rotary (pres. South Orange 1999-2000, 06—, dist. gov. nominee 2006—, Paul Harris fellow 2000, asst. gov. 2001-02, 04-05, dist. pub. rels. chair 2003-04, dist. youth exch. program chair 2005—). Democrat. Episcopalian. Home: 40 Woodland Ave East Orange NJ 07017 also: 76 S Orange Ave Ste 308 South Orange NJ 07079-1923 Office Phone: 973-378-3700. Personal E-mail: Jteetsell@aol.com.

TEFANI, NANCY ANN, music educator; d. Roscoe Harvey and Helen Monimia (Rockwell) Smyth; children: Michael, Mary Anne Novello, Peter, Richard, Barbara Parent. BBA, U. Mich., 1948; MA in Music, U. Nev., 1972. Sec. Union Carbide, NYC, 1949—51, various employers, Reno, 1951—55; tchr. music Washoe County Schs., Sparks, 1971—74; orch. performer various hotel showrooms, Tahoe, 1971—80, Las Vegas, 1971—80; realtor Red Carpet Realty, Reno, 1974—84; ins. agt. various employers, 1984—97. Mem.: Am. String Tchrs. Assn., Music Educators Nat. Conf. Home: 4704 Newton Dr Las Vegas NV 89121 Office: Family Music Ctrs 2714 N Green Valley Pky Henderson NV 89012

TEGARDEN, LORETTA TUDOR, retired counselor; b. Chico, Mont., Aug. 10, 1940; d. Lewis and Florence Ina (Kenyon) Tudor; m. Bill Delmer Tegarden, July 5, 1965. BS in Edn., Abilene (Tex.) Christian U., 1962; MA, U. of South Fla., 1979. Tchr. Milam Sch., Odessa, Tex., 1962-63, Morningside Sch., Great Falls, Mont., 1963-66, Highland Sch., Billings, Mont., 1966-69, Williams Sch., Tampa, Fla., 1971-80; guidance counselor Twin Lakes Sch., Tampa, Fla., 1980—2001, Shaw Elem. Sch., Tampa, Fla., 1983—2001; ret., 2001. Bd. dirs. Shaw Sch. PTA, Tampa, 1988-89; co-chmn. Elem. Counselors Adv. Coun., Hillsborough County, Fla., 1989-90. Pres. Civic Assn., Lake Padgett Estates, Fla., 1979; chmn. Mcpl. Svcs. Tax Unit, Lake Padgett Estates, 1979. Fellow NEA, Classroom Tchrs. Assn., AACD. Republican. Mem. Ch. of Christ. Avocations: reading, gardening. Office: Shaw Sch 11311 N 15th St Tampa FL 33612-5935

TEGELER, REBECCA SUE, elementary school educator; b. Lincoln, Nebr., Apr. 10, 1977; d. Phillip Mark and Nancy Sue Tegeler. BA in Elem. and Mid. Grades Edn., U. Nebr., Kearney, 2000. Sch. cmty. intervention coord. Culler Mid. Sch., Lincoln, 2004—. Named Rrookie Tchr. of Yr., Nebr. State Edn. Assn., 2001. Mem.: Lincoln Edn. Assn. (com. mem.). Lutheran. Home: 5201 Vine St Lincoln NE 68504 Office: Culler Middle School 5201 Vine St Lincoln NE 68504 Office Phone: 402-436-1210. Business E-Mail: rtegel@lps.org.

TEGETHOFF, ALLECE D., elementary school educator, pharmacy technician; b. Goodland, Kans., May 17, 1947; d. Gordon A. and Pearl M. Erickson; m. Frosty Tegethoff, June 21, 1969; children: Mindy L. Schooling, Jami D., Brandi L. BA in Edn. and Music, Kans. Wesleyan U., Salina, 1969. Cert. tchr. Kans., 1969. Tchr. grade 4 Hageman Elem., Salina, Kans., 1969—70; tchr. grades 4-6 Mahaska Grade Sch., Kans., 1970—71; music tchr. Morland Elem. and H.S., Kans., 1971—75; tchr. music grades k-6 Valley Ctr. Elem. Sch., Kans., 1975—76; tchr. grades 1-3 Kanorado Elem., Kans., 1976—77; tchr. music grades k-6 West Elem. Sch., Goodland, Kans., 1977—79; music tchr. k-8 Nickerson Elem., Kans., 1979—87; music tchr. grades 6-8 McPherson Mid. Sch., Kans., 1987—; pharmacy tech The Medicine Shoppe, McPherson, 2003—; elem. tchr. 1st grade USD, Goodland, Kans. Dir./co-dir. McPherson Arts Coun. Children's Choir, 1988—2004; coord. music festival USD 418 and area schs., McPherson, 2003—05; curriculum coordinating coun. USD 418, McPherson, 2004—, music mentor, 2005—. Youth choir dir. & chancel choir First United Meth. Ch., McPherson, 1988—2006. Recipient Master Tchr. Candidate, Nickerson Sch. Dist., 1986, McPherson Sch. Dist., 2002. Methodist. Avocations: volleyball, travel, sewing, sports, gardening. Home: 1511 Trail W Mcpherson KS 67460 Office: USD 418 700 E Elizabeth Mcpherson KS 67460 Office Phone: 620-241-9450. Office Fax: 620-241-9456. Business E-Mail: allece.tegethoff@mcpherson.com.

TEGGE, PATRICIA ANN, retired administrative assistant; b. Milw., Oct. 25, 1922; d. Edmund Finegan and Norma Berthe (Kussel) Jones; m. Lloyd Frederick Tegge, Oct. 23, 1946 (dec. 1994); 1 child, Mark. B in Philosophy and Journalism, Marquette U., 1945. Adminstrv. sec. Family Svc. of Waukesha, Wis., 1966-91; ret., 1991. Mem. adv. bd. Salvation Army, past chmn. Recipient Outstanding Svcs. award Salvation Army 1983-85. Mem. DAR, Women in Communications (Southeastern Wis. chpt.), Nat. Assn. Parliamentarians (past pres. Wis. chpt.), Wis. Regional Writer's Assn. (chmn.), Wis. Soc. (recording sec. 1989—), Altrusa Club of Waukesha, Waukesha Women's Club (past pres.), Wis. Fedn. Women's Clubs (dist. pres. 1990—), Waukesha County Geneal. Soc. (newsletter editor 1997-2000). Republican. Lutheran.

TEHRANI, FLEUR TAHER, electrical engineer, educator, researcher; b. Tehran, Iran, Feb. 16, 1956; came to U.S., 1984; d. Hassan and Pourandokht (Monfared) T.; m. Akbar E. Torbat, June 16, 1997. BS in Elec. Engring., Arya-Mehr U. of Tech., Tehran, 1975; DIC in Comm. Engring., Imperial Coll. Sci. and Tech., London, 1977; MSc in Comm. Engring., U. London, 1977, PhD in Elec. Engring., 1981. Registered profl. engr., Calif. Comm. engr. Planning Orgn. of Iran, Tehran, 1977-78; lectr. A elec. engring. Robert Gordon's Inst. Tech., Aberdeen, U.K., 1982-83; lectr. II elec. engring. South Bank U., London, England, 1983—84; asst. prof. elec. engring. Calif. State U., Fullerton, 1985-91, assoc. prof. elec. engring., 1991-94, prof. elec. engring., 1994—, dir. pharm. engring. program, 1999-2001. Vis. assoc. prof. elec. engring. Drexel U., Phila., 1987-88; sys. cons. Telebit Corp., Cupertino, Calif., 1985; engring. cons. PRD, Inc., Dresher, Pa., 1989-92; mem. NASA/Am. Soc. Engring. Edn. summer faculty Jet Propulsion Lab., Calif. Inst. Tech., Pasadena, 1995, 96. Contbr. articles to profl. jours.; patentee in field. Recipient Best Rsch. Manuscript award Assn. for the Advancement of Med. Instrumentation, 1993, NASA/Am. Soc. Engring. Edn. Recognition award for rsch. contbns., 1995, 96. Fellow: Grad. Women in Sci. Sigma Delta Epsilon (nat. life mem.), Inst. Advancement of Engring.; mem.: IEE, IEEE, Assn. Profs. and Scholars Iranian Heritage (pres. 1991—92), Women in Sci. and Engring. (chair Calif. State U. chpt. 1990—91). Avocations: music, literature, poetry, stamp collecting/philately. Office: Calif State U Coll Engring & Computer Sci 800 N State College Blvd Fullerton CA 92831-3547 Business E-Mail: ftehrani@fullerton.edu.

TEICH, THERESA MARIE, educator; b. Duluth, Minn., May 14, 1948; d. Kenneth William Teich and Charlotte Marie (Kouba) Hughes; m. Mark R. Walters, March 1, 2006. BS in Home Econs., U. Minn., Duluth, 1971, BS in English, 1975; MS in Reading, U. Wis., Superior, 1979. Tchr. home econs. and English Ordean Jr. High Sch., Duluth, 1972-75, tchr. English and media, 1976-78; tchr. home econs. and English West Jr. High Sch., Duluth, 1975-76, tchr. remedial reading, 1978-80; tchr. devel. reading, English Lincoln Jr. HS, Duluth, 1980-82; tchr. English, journalism Washington Jr. HS, Duluth, 1982-92, coach, judge Odyssey of Mind; tchr. English Ctrl. HS, 1992—96; tchr. English, reading Lincoln Park Mid. Sch., 1996—2003; ret., 2003. Mem. reading com. Ind. Sch. Dist. 709, Duluth, 1983-87, elected mem. relicensure com., 1991-94. Author: Lake Superior Mag., 1980-83. Com. chmn. for tng. and community rsch., vol. Jr. League of Duluth, 1980-89; program com. Leadership Duluth, 1986-87, participant, 1991-92; vol. Publ. Libr. Found. Bd., 1996-, Speak Your Peace, 2003-. Mem. AAUW (publicity and arrangements chmn. Duluth chpt. 1976-79, 89—), Duluth Pub. Libr. Minn. (trustee, bd. dirs., pres. 1980-95), Minn. Home Econs. Assn. (dist. pres. 1977), Internat. Reading Assn., Nat. Coun. Tchrs. English, Keel Club (editor), Alpha Delta Kappa, Phi Delta Kappa (rsch. chair 1994). Home: 508 N 12th Ave W Duluth MN 55806-2300

TEIGLAND, BRITTANY PAIGE, music educator; d. Marvin Gene and Tonya Ann Pember; m. Nathan Andrew Teigland, July 5, 2005. B in music edn., Evangel U., Mo., 2001. Cert. tchr. Colo. Minister of music Charity Bapt. Ch., Springfield, Mo., 1997—2001; elem. music specialist, choral dir. Pinnacle Charter Sch., Federal Heights, Colo., 2002—. Pvt. voice and piano lessons, Broomfield, Colo., 2002—06; mentor tchr. Pinnacle Charter Sch., Federal Heights, Colo., 2005—06, specials dept. chair, 2005—06. Prodr.(dir.): (choir musicals and concerts), 2002—06, (HS musical) Princess and the Pea, 2005, Give My Regrets to Broadway, 2006. Minister of music Broomfield Assembly of God, Colo., 2002—05, youth dir. asst., 2002—05. Music and Acad. Scholarship, Evangel U., 1997—2001, Wanda Shows Meml. Scholarship, 2000. Mem.: Colo. Music Educators Assn. Republican. Assembly Of God. Avocations: singing, piano, reading, rock climbing. Home: 1031 East 1st Ave Apt 934 Broomfield CO 80020 Office: Pinnacle Charter Sch 1001 W 84th Ave Federal Heights CO 80260 Personal E-mail: brittany.teigland@adams12.org.

TEITSWORTH, MARGARET YVONNE, nursing educator; b. Farmersville, Ill., Apr. 19, 1922; d. Paul Irving and Nona Olive (Dawson) Best; m. William Reed Teitsworth, Nov. 22, 1945 (dec.); 1 child, Sharon Lou Payne; 1 child, Richard Lee. RN, Passavant Hosp. Sch. Nursing, Jacksonville, Ill., 1943; cert. in psychiatric nursing, Highland Hosp., Asheville, N.C., 1944; postgrad., DaKa U. Nurse Barnes Hosp., St. Louis, 1943—44, head nurse psychiatric unit, 1944—46; head nurse women's admission Wernersville State Hosp., Pa., 1964—65, nurse edn. dept., 1965—76, clin. staff edn., 1976—83; ret., 1983. Vol. Berks County Mental Health Assn., Reading, Pa., 1972—79; vol. tchr. West Reading Fire Co. #1, Pa., 1975—81. Recipient Deaconess award, Phoebe Ministries, Allentown, Pa., 2001. Mem. United Ch. Of Christ. Avocations: reading, exercise, tai chi, walking. Home: 1940 W Turner St Apt 310 Allentown PA 18104

TEITZ, BETTY BEATRICE GOLDSTEIN, retired interior designer; b. Mar. 10, 1914; d. Albert Stanley and Dora (Finestone) Gould; m. Milton A. Nusbaum, Apr. 10, 1943 (dec. Nov. 1956); 1 child, Alberta Joyce Nusbaum Duckman; m. Harry Teitz, Dec. 28, 1959. Student, Rochester Bus. Inst., 1932—34, Rochester Inst. Tech., 1950—51, Columbia U., 1957—58. Owner design studio, Rochester, 1957; trainee W.J. Sloane, 1958; head design dept. Mason Furniture Co., Fall River, Mass., 1959; pvt. practice Providence, 1961—65; pres. Indesign Inc., Newport, RI, 1974—2003. Designer guest house The White House, Washington, U.S. War Coll., Newport, 1969—70; redesigned R.I. Corp. Rooney Plotkin & Willey, Newport, 1992, Providence, 92; designed the beginning restoration of Touro Synagogue, Newport, 94; interior designer Bryant Coll., Smithfield, RI, 2001—02; lectr. Navy Wives U.S.A.; designer renovations Bryant Coll., Smithfield, RI, 2001—02. Staff asst. Motor Corps Grey Lady Rochester chpt. ARC Rochester, 1941—46, active Newport chpt.; Gray Lady vol. Genesee Hosp., Rochester, 1945—55; mem. Rochester Planned Parenthood, 1945—48; active Mental Health Clinic Citizens Adv. Com., Newport, 1967—78; yachting com. Am.'s Cup Race, 1950. Recipient Centennial Pageant Scenic award, Rochester, 1948, ARC awards, 1943—53, 10 yr. svc. pin, Genesee Hosp., 1955, Blue Ribbon award for flower show arrangements, 1950, 1952, 1955. Mem.: Preservation Soc. Newport R.I. (ednl. reproduction com. 1990—2000), Constrn. Specifications Inst. R.I. (sec.), Am. Inst. Interior Designers, Flower City Garden Club (past v.p. Rochester), Newport C. of C. (bldg. com.). Home: Apt 73 24 Tabor Xing Longmeadow MA 01106-1756 Office Phone: 413-567-3616.

TEJEDA-BROWN, MARY LOUISE, artist; b. L.A., Jan. 11, 1921; d. Francisco Tejeda and Elizabeth (Kramis) Tejeda; m. William Reynold Brown, Oct. 26, 1946 (dec. 1991); children: Marie, Reynold, Franz, Elisa, Cristina, Regina, Marta, Mariane. Student, Frank Wiggens Trade Sch., L.A. Artist Raymond Advt. Co., L.A., 1938-40, No. Am. Aviation, Inglewood, Calif., 1941-46; freelance artist Whitney, Nebr., 1989—. Represented by Elaine's Art Gallery, Alliance, Nebr., Shamon Gallery, Hot Spring, S.D. One-woman shows include Mus. of Nebr. Arts, Kearney, 1998-99, Lee Dam Art Ctr., Kans., 1998, West Nebr. Arts Ctr., Scottsbluff, 1998, Chase County Art Ctr., Imperial, Nebr., 2000, U. Place Art Ctr., Lincoln, Nebr., 2001, Elaine's Fine Art Gallery, Aliance, Nebr., 2001; exhibited in shows at Gallery East, Loveland, Colo., 1991, Chadron (Nebr.) State Coll., 1989, 91, 93, 2003, West Nebr. Arts Ctr., 1992, 94, 95, Ft. Robinson Art Show, Nebr., 1991, 92, 93, Dakota Art Gallery, 1994, Agate Beds Nat. Monument, Nebr., 1994, Pastel Soc. Am., N.Y.C., 1994, Univ. Pl. Art Gallery, 1995, Gov.'s Mansion, Lincoln, Nebr., 1995, 2003, Mus. of Nebr., 1995, Colo. History Mus., Denver, 1998, Dakota Art Gallery, Rapid City, S.D., 2001, Mid-Am. Pastel Soc., 2002, Carnegie Arts Ctr., Alliance, Nebr., 2003 (Best of Show award), Dunedin (Fla.) Fine Art Ctr., 2004, Wichita Ctr. for Arts (hon. mention), 2004, Mus. Nebr. Art, Kearney, 2004, Gov.'s Mansion, Lincoln, Nebr., 1995, Carnegie Arts Ctr., Alliance, Nebr., 2004 (Best of Show, Dir.'s Choice award, 1st pl. award, Hon. Mention award Carnegie Art Ctr., Alliance, Nebr.); featured in Pastel Artist Internat. Mag., 2000; contbr. articles to profl. jours. Avocations: reading, travel. Home: 379 Bethel Loop Rd Whitney NE 69367-1730

TEJKL, PAMELA MARIE, secondary school educator; d. Joseph J. Tejkl and Sandra K. Tejkl-Homola. BS in Biology, Mich. State U., East Lansing, 1983, degree in tchg., 1987, M, 1996. Cert. tchr. Mich. Biology, chemistry & physics tchr. Shelby (Mich.) Pub. Schs., 1987—91; chemistry & biology tchr. Math and Sci. Ctr., Battle Creek, Mich., 1993—96; anatomy/physiology & chemistry tchr. Traverse City (Mich.) Ctrl. HS, 1996—. Sci. cons., tutor, 504 cons., rsch. mentor. Mem.: Am. Chem. Soc., Human Anatomy/Physiology Soc. Office: Tcaps 1150 Milliken Traverse City MI 49686 Office Phone: 231-933-5837.

TELBAN, ETHEL, retired librarian; b. Renton, Wash., Mar. 31, 1914; d. Blase and Amelia (Podbregar) T. BA, Ctrl. Wash. U., Ellensburg, 1938; M Librarianship, Denver U., 1950. Cert. educator, libr. Elem. tchr. Thorp (Wash.) Sch. Dist., 1935-36, Renton (Wash.) Sch. Dist., 1937-50, libr. supr., 1950-74; libr. Western Wash. U., Bellingham, 1965. Instr. libr. U. Wash., Seattle, summers 1955, 58, 59, 60; libr. Ctrl. Wash. U., Ellensburg, summers 1941, 51, 53, 57; mem. Curriculum Commn., State Dept. Edn., Olympia, Wash., 1954-55. Editor: (history book) From Coal to Jets, 1976. Mem. Mcpl. Arts Commn., Renton, 1973-75; mem. bicentennial com. City of Renton, 1975-76. Named Renton Citizen of Yr., Elks, Renton, 1977, Vol of Yr., Assoc. King County Hist. Assn., Seattle, 1994; recipient Individual Excellence award Wash. Mus. Assn., Richland, 1994, Cert. of Commendation, Am. Assn. State and Local History, Nashville, 1995. Mem. ALA (mem. Newbery-Caldecott com. 1960-61), Sch. Librs. Assn. Wash. State (state pres. 1962-63), Renton Hist. Soc. (pres. 1966-96, editor newsletter 1970-94), Renton Retired Tchrs. (sec. 1950-96), PEO Sisterhood (sec. 1959-96), Soroptimist Internat. (pres. 1951-96), Delta Kappa Gamma. Avocations: local history, travel, reading, gardening, crafts. Home: 17406 N Escalante Lane Surprise AZ 85374

TELFER, MARGARET CLARE, internist, hematologist, oncologist; b. Manila, Apr. 9, 1939; came to U.S., 1941; d. James Gavin and Margaret Adele (Baldwin) T. BA, Stanford U., 1961; MD, Washington U., St. Louis, 1965. Diplomate Am. Bd. Internal Medicine, Am. Bd. Hematology, Am. Bd. Oncology; lic. Ill., Mo. Resident in medicine Michael Reese Hosp., Chgo., 1968, fellow in hematology and oncology, 1970, assoc. attending physician, 1970-72, dir. Hemophilia Ctr., 1971—, interim dir. div. hematology and oncology, 1971-74, 81-84, 89—, attending physician, 1972—, Rush-Presbyn. St. Luke's Hosp., 1999—, Olympia Fields (Ill.) Hosp., 1999—, Cook County Hosp., Chgo., 2000—, dir. hematology/oncology fellowship, 2002—; asst. prof. medicine U. Chgo., 1975-80, assoc. prof. medicine, 1980-85, assoc. prof. clin. medicine, 1985-89; assoc. prof. medicine U. Ill., Chgo., 1990-2001, Rush U., Chgo., 2001—. Mem. med. adv. bd. Hemophilia Found. Ill., 1971, chmn., 1972—83, lectr. annual symposium, 1978—84; mem. med. adv. bd. State of Ill. Hemophilia Program; dir. hematology-oncology fellowship program Michael Reese Hosp., 1971—75, 1981—84, 1989—2000, dir. Cook County Fellowship Program, 2004—, mem. numerous coms.; lectr. in field. Contbr. articles to profl. jours. Fellow ACP; mem. Am. Soc. Clin. Oncology, Am. Assn. Med. Colls., Am. Soc. Hematology, World Fedn. Hemophilia, Blood Club (Chgo.), Thrombosis Club (Chgo.). Office: Stroger Cook County Hosp Rm 750 Adminstrn Bldg 1900 W Polk Chicago IL 60612 Office Phone: 312-864-7250. Business E-Mail: mtelfer@ccbhs.org.

TELLEEN, JUDY, counselor; b. Chgo., Dec. 13, 1942; d. Kurt Theodore and Gertrude Lillian Lockwood Johnson; m. David Roger Telleen, June 15, 1964; children: Karin, Kirstin, Erik. BA, Lawrence U., 1964; MA, U. Mich., 1967, PhD, 1970. Program dir. counseling svcs. Asian Human Svcs., Chgo., 1994-95, coord. of counseling svcs., 1995-96, coord. of case mgmt., 1997-98; adj. prof. Gov.'s State Univ., University Park, Ill., 1995-99; counselor Arlington Heights, Ill., 1999—. Adv. com. mem. Bd. Suprs. and Sch. Bd., Va., 1993; mem. Pub. Policy and Legis. com. Ill. Counseling Assn., 1994, mem. governing coun., 2000—. Author: (book) A Predictive Model of the Cumulative Academic Achievement of Indian Students, 1970, (monograph) Guidance Factors Influencing Indian Students to Attend the University of Michigan, 1971; mem. editl. bd. (periodical) Ill. Counseling Assn. Quarterly, 1995—98. Youth adv. Bridge Youth & Family Svcs., Palatine, Ill., 1994—96; chairperson learning com. All Saints Luth. Ch., Palatine, 1993—2001. Mem. Am. Counselor's Assn., Ill. Counselor's Assn., Ill. Assn. of Couples & Family Couns. (pres.), Ill. Assn. for Multicultural Counseling, Ill. Assn. Mental Health Counselors, Assn. for Multicultural Counseling Develop., Internat. Assn. Marriage & Family Counselors, Internat. Assn. Addictions & Offender Counselors, Pi Lambda Theta, Phi Kappa Phi. Lutheran. Office: Ste 102 1040 S Arlington Heights Rd Arlington Heights IL 60005-3162

TELLEM, NANCY REISS, broadcast executive; b. Danville, Calif., Dec. 13, 1953; m. Arn Tellem; children: Michael, Matthew, Eric. BA in Polit. Sci., U. Calif., Berkeley, 1975; JD, Hastings Coll. Law, 1979. Intern to Congressman Ron Dullums, Washington, 1974; with legal affairs dept. Lorimar TV; joined Warner Bros. TV, 1987, exec. v.p. bus. and fin. affairs; exec. v.p. bus. affairs CBS Entertainment, exec. v.p. CBS Prodns. CBS, 1997—98, pres. CBS Entertainment, 1998—2004; pres. CBS Paramount Network TV Entertainment Group, 2004—. Bd. dirs. ThirdAge Media. Named one of 100 Most Powerful Women in Entertainment, Hollywood Reporter, 2005—06. Avocations: tennis, yoga, hiking, photography. Office: CBS Entertainment 7800 Beverly Blvd Los Angeles CA 90036*

TELLEM, SUSAN MARY, public relations executive; b. NYC, May 23, 1945; d. John F. and Rita C. (Lietz) Cain; m. Marshall R.B. Thompson; children: Tori, John, Daniel. BS, Mt. St. Mary's Coll., L.A., 1967. Cert. pub. health nurse; RN. Pres. Tellem Pub. Rels. Agy., Marina del Rey, Calif., 1977-80, Rowland Grody Tellem, L.A., 1980-90; chmn. The Rowland Co., L.A., 1990—; pres., CEO Tellem, Inc., L.A., 1992-93. Instr. UCLA Extension, 1983-97; adj. prof. Pepperdine U., 1999—; speaker numerous seminars and confs. on pub. rels. Editor: Sports Medicine for the '80's, Sports Medicine Digest, 1982-84. Bd. dirs. Marymount High Sch., 1984-87, pres., 1984-86; bd. dirs. L.A. Police Dept. Booster Assn., 1984-87; mem. Cath. Press Coun.; mem. pres.'s coun. Mus. Sci. and Industry. Mem. Am. Soc. Hosp. Mktg. and Pub. Rels., Healthcare Mktg. and Pub. Rels. Assn., Pub. Rels. Soc. Am. (bd. dirs. 1994—), L.A. Counselors, PETA, Am. Lung Assn. (chair comm. com. L.A. chpt.) Soc. for Prevention of Cruelty to Animals (chair PetSet), Sports Club (L.A.). Roman Catholic. Avocations: reading, tennis, aerobics. Office: 23852 Pacific Coast Hwy # 928 Malibu CA 90265-4879 Fax: 310-589-6101. Office Phone: 310-479-6111. Business E-Mail: stellem@tellem.com.

TELLER, DAVIDA YOUNG, psychology, physiology and biophysics educator; b. Yonkers, N.Y., July 25, 1938; d. David Aidan and Jean Marvin (Sturges) Young; m. David Chambers Teller, June 18, 1960 (div. May 1986); children: Stephen, Sara; m. Anthony William Young, July 28, 1990. BA, Swarthmore Coll., 1960; PhD, U. Calif., Berkeley, 1965. Lectr., research prof. U. Wash., Seattle, 1965-69, asst. prof. psychology, physiology and biophysics, 1969-71, assoc. prof., 1971-74, prof., 1973—. Researcher visual sci. and devel.; rsch. affiliate Regional Primate Rsch. Ctr., Child Devel. & Mental Retardation Ctr.; mem. com. on vision Nat. Acad. Scis.-Nat. Rsch. Coun., 1971-80, vision rsch. program com. Nat. Eye Inst. and NIH, 1973-76, visual scis. B study sect. NIH, 1981-85, chmn. 1983-85; U. Wash. appointments include chmn. Univ. Com. on Vision, 1971; mem. Univ. Coun. Women, 1971-76, Faculty Senate Spl. Com. Faculty Women, 1972-75, ad hoc com. Evaluation Dir. Black Studies Program, 1976, faculty adv. bd. Women Studies, 1980-82, ad hoc com. to search for Chmn. Psychology, 1981, standing com. Women Studies, 1982—, faculty senate coun. Grants & Contract Rsch., 1985-86, Univ. Acad. Coun., 1986—; dept. psychology appoints include Exec. Com., 1973-75, 77-79; chmn. Budget and Facilities Com., 1979-81; mem. ad hoc com. Staff Employment, 1982-83; honors advisor and dir. Honors Program, 1982—; mem. planning com. 1984-87, 90—. Mem. editorial bd. Infant Behavior and Development, 1981-85, Behavioral Brain Research, 1984-87, Vision Research, 1985—, Clinical Vision Sciences, 1986-87; contbr. numerous articles to profl. jours.; patentee in field. Recipient Sabbatical award James McKeen Cattell Fund, 1981-82. Fellow AAAS, Optical Soc. Am. (program com. vision 1986-88, vice chmn. vision tech. group 1986-87, chmn. 1988-89, tech. coun. 1988-89, Tillyer award 1987—); mem. Assn. Rsch. Vision & Ophthalmology, Assn. Women Sci., Am. Acad. Ophthalmology (Glenn Fry award 1982). Office: U Wash Dept Psychology Ni 25 Seattle WA 98195-0001

TELLER, SUSAN ELAINE, lawyer; b. San Diego, Calif., May 27, 1953; d. Jack and Joan (Mayer) T.; m. Donald F. Austin, July 6, 1980; children: Greg Austin, Cary Austin, Jack Austin. BA, Calif. State U., Sonoma, 1975; JD, Hastings Coll. of Law, 1979. Bar: Calif. 1980, Oreg. 1994, Wash. 1994. Assoc. Shapiro and Thorn, San Francisco, 1981—83; ptnr. Silverman and Teller, Alameda, Calif., 1983—93; assoc. Gevurtz, Menashe, et. al., Portland, Oreg., 1993—95; ptnr. Demary & Teller, Portland, 1995—2002; pvt. practice Portland, 2002—. Bd. dirs. Bus. and Profl. Women, Alameda; pres. PTA, Alameda. Named Woman of the Yr. Bus. Owner, Alameda Bus. and Profl. Women, 1988. Mem. Soroptimist Internat., AAUW, Oreg. Women's Lawyers, Queen's Bench, Soroptimist Internat. (bd. dirs. 1989). Office: 1123 SW Yamhill St Portland OR 97205-2106 Office Phone: 503-241-4171.

TELLERS, CHERYL LEE, art association administrator, consultant; b. Knoxville, Iowa, Nov. 4, 1954; d. William Wallace Blair and Joyce Vivan Humphries; children: Blair Elizabeth, Molly Anne. BA, Calvin Coll., Grand Rapids, 1976. Art edn. dir. Donald H.S., Vicotria, Australia, 1976—79; world explore many countries, 1979—81; arts edn. tchr. Leffingwell Christian, Norwalk, Calif., 1981—83, Valley Christian H.S., Bellflower, Calif., 1983—94; nat. arts cons. Davies Publ., Worchester, Mass., 1985—95, McGraw Hill Co., N.Y., 1996—. Presenter and speaker in field. Contbr. articles pub. to profl. jour. Adoptive parent World Vision. Mem.: Nat. Arts Edn. Assn., Calif. Arts Edn. Assn., Nat. Women inthe Arts Mus. Christian. Avocations: walking, gardening, pottery, painting.

TELLES, CYNTHIA ANN, psychologist; b. El Paso, Tex., Aug. 10, 1952; d. Raymond Lawrence and Delfina Telles; m. David Jimenez (div. Aug. 1991); 1 child, Raymond Jimenez. BA, Smith Coll., Northampton, Mass., 1974; PhD, Boston U., 1982. Cert. psychologist, Calif. Psychologist U. Hosp. Boston U. Med. Ctr., 1977-78; rsch. fellow psychology dept. Spanish Speaking Mental Health Rsch. Ctr. UCLA, 1978-79, co-investigator, rsch. diagnostician dept. psychiatry, 1982-84, investigator and mgr. Spanish instrument tng. Dept. Psychiatry, 1981-87; clin. project dir., co-investigator NIMH, 1984-86, investigator, 1986-90; project dir., co-prin. investigator Calif. State Dept. Mental Health, 1986—; psychologist adult outpatient dept. UCLA Neuropsychiat. Inst., 1979-80; co-dir. UCLA Spanish Speaking Psychosocial Clinic, 1980-87, dir., 1988—. Media psychologist for TV and radio; cons. Boston City Police, 1975, Boulder County Community Mental Health Ctr., 1978, Spl. Svc. for Groups, L.A., 1982, Ministry of Health, Lima, Peru, 1982, NIMH, 1984—, L.A. County Dept. Mental Health, 1985—, Calif. Sch. Profl. Psychology, 1986—; presenter in field; teaching fellow Boston U. Sch. Medicine, 1975-78; lectr. dept. psychiatry UCLA, 1980-85, asst. clin. prof., 1986-96, assoc. clin. prof., 1996-, mem. faculty adv. com. Chicano Studies Rsch. Ctr., 1988—. Author: (with others) Psychiatric Epidemiology and Prevention: The Possibilities, 1985, Violence and Homicide in Hispanic Communities, 1988; contbr. articles to profl. jours.; mem. editorial bd. Hispanic Jour. Behavioral Scis., 1978-79; ad hoc reviewer Psychology of Women Quar., 1986-87. Bd. dirs. Coalition Pro-Salud Hispana, Boston, 1977-78, Nat. Hispanic Psychol. Assn., 1984-86, Ctr. for Study of Youth in Groups/Teen Line, Dept. of Psychiatry, Cedars-Sinai Med. Ctr., 1986-88, NCCJ, Southern Calif., 1990—, El Centro Human Svcs. Corp., 1988-90, Calif. Endowment, 2001-, bd. chair, 2004-; mem. Nat. Adv. Com. on Hispanic Women and AIDS, Ctrs. for Disease Control and Hispanic Designers Inc., 1989—; pres., founder Hispanic Health Found., 1988-98. Boston U. Grad. scholar, 1975-79, APA Minority fellow, 1975-79; recipient Humanitarian award East L.A. Coll., 1988, Civic and Community Leadership award Nat. Network of Hispanic Women, 1989, First Annual Achievement award for mental health pub. svc. APA Minority Fellowship Program, 1989. Mem. Nat. Hispanic Psychol. Assn. (charter), APA. Roman Catholic. Office: UCLA Dept Psychiatry 300 Ucla Medical Plz Los Angeles CA 90095-8346

TELLEZ, LAURA LYNN, elementary school educator; b. L.A., Aug. 14, 1978; d. Anthony William and Regina Ann Migler; m. Julio Cuauhtemoc Tellez, Nov. 4, 2000. BA, U. Calif., Santa Barbara, 2001; MS, Grand Canyon U., Phoenix, 2004; postgrad., Loyola Marymount U., L.A., 2004—. Jr. h.s. math and sci. tchr. St. Anthony's Sch., Oxnard, Calif., 2000—02; jr. h.s. history tchr. St. Mary Magdalen Sch., Camarillo, Calif., 2002—; site coord., educator Sci. Adventures, Ventura, Calif., 2002—. Visitation team mem. Western Assn. of Sci. Colls., 2003; adminstr. small bus. Telco, Camarillo, 2005—; founder, moderator NJHS Student Coun., Camarillo, 2003—. Mem.: ASCD, Nat. Cath. Edn. Assn., Golden Key, Alpha Lambda Delta. Roman Catholic. Avocation: archaeology.

TELNAES, ANN, cartoonist; b. Stockholm, 1960; m. David Lloyd. BFA, Calif. Inst. Arts. Animator and layout designer for various animation studios in London, L.A., Taiwan and N.Y.C., Warner Bros., Walt Disney Imagineering; editorial cartoonist. Bd. dirs. Cartoonists Rights Network. Named Best Cartoonist, Population Inst. XVIIth Global Media awards, 1996, Best Editl. Cartoonist, 6th Ann. Environ. Media Awards, 1996; recipient Nat. Headliner award for Editl. Cartoons, 1997, Pulitzer prize, 2001, Berryman award, Nat. Press. Found., 2003. Mem.: Assn. Am. Editl. Cartoonists (past v.p.).

TELOWITZ, MARILYN MARIE, English and social studies educator; b. St. Louis, Oct. 31, 1952; d. Nicholas John and Audrey Mulhern Telowitz. BA, U. Mo., Columbia, 1972; cert. 7-12 in English and social studies, U. Mo., St. Louis, 1975. Tchr. English and social studies Rosary H.S., St. Louis, 1977—2003, chairperson English dept., 1982—2003; tchr. English and social studies Trinity Cath. H.S., St. Louis, 2003—, dean humanities, 2003—04, chairperson English dept., 2004—. Mem. Spanish Lake (Mo.) Comty. Assn., 2005—. Mem.: Nat. Coun. for Social Studies, Nat. Coun. Tchrs. English. Democrat. Roman Catholic. Avocation: travel. Home: 804 Vista Pointe Saint Louis MO 63138 Office: Trinity Cath H S 1720 Redman Rd Saint Louis MO 63138

TEMA-LYN, LAURIE, management consultant; b. Bklyn., Mar. 25, 1951; d. Morton and Jeanne (Lite) Carlin. BA, Bklyn. Coll., 1972. Mgmt. supr. Rapp & Collins, Inc., N.Y.C., 1972-78, v.p., 1978-80; assoc. Synectics, Cambridge, Mass., 1980-83; founder, gen. ptnr. IdeaScope Assocs., Cambridge, 1983-95; prin. Practical Imagination Enterprises, Carlisle, Mass., 1995—. Presenter European Conf. on Innovation and Creativity, 1987, 94. Performer: VOICES Chorale; contbr. articles to profl. jours. Bd. dirs. Arica Inst., N.Y.C., 1979-80; pres. bd. dirs. Savoyand Light Opera Co.; bd. mem., performer Voices Chorale; mem. Heartland Cir., Hunterdon Radio Theater. Mem. Creative Problem Solving Inst. (presenter, leader), Am. Mktg. Assn., Direct Mktg. Assn. (presenter), Product Devel. Mgmt. Assn., Creative Edn. Found., New Eng. Bus. Assn. for Social Responsibility, Qualitative Rsch. Cons. Assn., Boston Womens Network, Mgmt. Roundtable, Sharing a New Song, Heartland Cir., Hunterdon Radio Theater. Office: Practical Imagination Enterprises 18 Losey Rd Ringoes NJ 08551-1206 Office Phone: 908-237-2246. E-mail: laurie@practical-imagination.com.

TEMME, MARCIA E. See HARDCASTLE, MARCIA E.

TEMPEL, JEAN CURTIN, venture capitalist; b. Hartford, Conn., Mar. 23, 1943; d. John J. and Sally (Miller) Curtin Jr.; m. Louis J. Tempel, Nov. 23, 1968 (div. 1978); m. Peter A. Wilson, May 10, 1980. BA in Math., Conn. Coll., 1965; MS in Computer Sci., Rensselaer Poly. Inst., 1972; advanced mgmt. program cert., Harvard U., 1979. Various sr. mgmt. positions Conn. Bank and Trust Co., 1965-80; mgr. strategic planning and mktg. Bank New Eng., 1980-82; sr. v.p., mgr. of custody The Boston Co., 1983, pres. Boston Safe Clearing Corp., 1984-90, exec. v.p., chief ops., info. officer, 1985, exec. v.p., COO, 1988-90; prin. Tempel Ptnrs. Inc., Boston, 1991; pres., COO Safeguard Scientifics Inc., Wayne, 1992-93, bd. dirs.; gen. ptnr. TL Ventures LP, Boston, 1994-96, spl. ltd. ptnr., 1997-99; founder, mng. ptnr. First Light Capital Inc., 2000—. Bd. dirs. Cambridge (Mass.) Tech. Ptnrs., Cambridge, Mass., 1991-98, Centocor, Malvern, Pa., Sonesta Internat. Hotels, Inc., Boston; trustee Scudder Funds, Boston, Northeastern U., Conn. Coll. Trustee Northeastern U., Conn. Coll. Mem. Internat. Women's Forum (dir.). Avocations: skiing, bicycling, sailing.

TEMPLETON, ANN, artist, educator; b. Houston, July 2, 1936; d. Lawrence L. and Marie L. (Bergeron) St. Pe'; m. James D. Templeton, Nov. 19, 1955; children: Pamela A., Donna M., James D. II, Donald L. Student, Massey Bus. Coll. Sec. A.M. Lockett Inc., Houston; owner Studio I and Gallery II, Houston; self-employed artist, instr. Ann Templeton Arts Inc., Houston, Ruidoso Downs, N.Mex. Instr. workshops and seminars, 1983—; juror at numerous art shows; instr. Okla. Christian Coll., Norman, 1997, Grayson County Coll., Tex., 1986, Jackson Jr. Coll., Tenn., 1983, 86, Lufkin Jr. Coll., Tex., 1986, San Juan Coll., Farmington, N.Mex., 1988, 90, 92, Ea. N.Mex. U., Ruidoso, 1994; artist-in-residence Fairmont (W.Va.) State Coll., 1998; represented by Brazier Fine Arts, Richmond, Va., Mahon Fine Arts, Ruidoso, Total Arts Gallery, Taos, N.Mex., Rich Designs, Colorado Springs, Colo Author: The Art of Ann Templeton: A Step Beyond, 2005; exhibited in group shows at Colony Show, Ruidoso, 1990-91, Tex. Arts Festival, Lubbock, 1990, 96, N.Mex. State Arts Fair, 1990-91, Knickerbocker N.Y., 1990, Mus. of the Horse, Ruidoso, 1992-95, 97, Shasta County Western Invitational, 1993, Tres Amigoes, Ruidoso, 1993-97, N.Mex. State Capitol, 1994, Roby Mills Exhbn., Colorado Springs, Colo., 1995, Permian Basin Art Inst., Odessa, Tex., 1995-96, Lafayette Art Assn., 1996, N.Mex. Pastel Soc., 1996, N.W. Pastel Soc., Washington, 1996, Pratt Gallery, San Diego, 1996, 98-99, Bardean Gallery, Albuquerque, 1997-98, Allied Artists Am., 1997, Brazier Fine Arts, Richmond, Va., 1998, Carlsbad (N.Mex.) Mus., 1998, Fairmont State Coll., W.Va., 1998, Heart Inst., Magnolia, Ark., 1998, Quinlan Art Ctr., Gainsville, Ga., 1999; represented in permanent collections at San Juan C.C., Farmington, N.Mex., Brownsville (Tex.) Art Mus., Hill Country Arts Found., Ingram, Tex., Coupeville (Wash.) Arts Ctr., Ellen Noe'l Art inst. of Permian Basin, Odessa, Carlsbad Art Mus., also corp. and pvt. collections Recipient Best and Brightest award Scottsdale Artists Sch., 1989, awards N.Mex. Art League, 1993, Franklin Sq., N.C., Merit award J.R. Mooney Debut, 1994, Harbor County competition, 1995, Grumbacher Gold medal Lafayette Art Assn., 1996, 2d pl. award Mus. of the Horse, 1997, Slide Registry award Internat. Assn. Pastel Socs., 1998, 2d pl. award EuroFare Internat. Art Competition. others. Mem. N.Mex. Art Guild (life, hon.), Gulf Coast Art Guild (pres.), Pasadena Gulf Coast Art Soc. (hon., past pres.), Women in Arts, N.Mex. State Arts Assn., N.Mex. Art League (hon., award 1993), Oil Painters Am. (assoc.), Allied Artists Am. (assoc.), Pastel Soc. Am. (signature), Knickerbocker Artists USA (signature), Kans. Soc. Oil Painters (signature, award 1987). Roman Catholic. Avocations: music, books. Home: PO Box 651 Ruidoso Downs NM 88346-0651

TEMPLETON, HOLLY JAYNE, elementary school educator; b. Hamilton, Ohio, Nov. 8, 1973; d. Betty Sue Owen; m. Joseph Ronald Templeton, Aug. 21, 1974. B in Edn., Miami U., Oxford, Ohio, M in Edn., 1997. Tchr. Fairfield City Schs., Ohio, 1997—. Author science curriculum. Recipient Sch. Bell award, 2005. Home: 932 North Lawn Ave Hamilton OH 45013 Office: Fairfield Intermediate School 255 Donald Drive Fairfield OH 45014 Office Phone: 513-829-4504.

TENANTY, JANE ELIZABETH, secondary school educator; b. Knoxville, May 23, 1956; d. Evan Philip and Mary Adelia (Blanc) Comer; m. Bruce Allen Beckner (div. 1985); m. Robert Michael Tenanty, Mar. 6, 1997; 1 stepchild, Robert Michael Jr. BS in Edn., Bloomsburg U., 1979; student, William Mitchell Coll. Law, 1986—87. Cert. K-12 reading tchr. State of Md. Bd. Edn., K-8 regular tchr. State of Md. Bd. Edn. Legal sec. various pvt. law firms, 1979—93; legal asst. Office of Atty. Gen., Annapolis, Md., 1993—96; substitute tchr. several counties in Md., 1996—2001; reading and math. tchr. Sylvan Learning Ctr., Easton, Md., 2003—04; facilitator distance learning Chesapeake Coll., Cambridge, Md., 2004—. Tutor Laubach Literacy, Red Wing, Minn., 1982—84, Project READ Md., Cambridge, 2000—01. Contbr. poems to lit. mags. and anthologies. Vol. ARC, Red Wing, Minn., 1982—84, Hosp. Aux., Red Wing, Minn., 1982—84. Democrat. Avocations: writing, reading, outdoor activities, singing. Home: 714 Glasgow St Cambridge MD 21613-1738

TENENBAUM, ANN G., art association administrator; b. Savannah, Ga., June 1961; m. Thomas H. Lee; children: Stephen Zachary, Robert Schiff. Grad., Sarah Lawrence Coll. Mem. vis. com. dept. photogs. Met. Mus. Art, 1996—2005, trustee, 2005—; vice chmn. bd. trustees Dia Art Found., NYC, 1994—2006. Co-pres. bd. trustees Film Soc. Lincoln Ctr. for Performing Arts; founding mem. bd. govs. Bard Coll. Ctr. Curatorial Studies; bd. dirs. Sarah Lawrence Coll., Channel 13/WNET, Studio Mus., Harlem, Second Stage Theatre, Guild Hall East Hampton; mem. chmn.'s coun. Mus. Modern Art. Named one of Top 200 Collectors, ARTnews mag., 2003—06; recipient Leo award, Ind. Curators Internat., 2003, Child Advocacy award, NYU Child Study Ctr., 2003. Avocation: Collector of Modern and contemporary art; Egyptian art. Office: c/o Met Mus Art 1000 5th Ave New York NY 10028*

TENENBAUM, INEZ MOORE, school system administrator; b. Hawkinsville, GA; m. Samuel J. Tenenbaum. Bsc, U. Ga., 1972, MEd, 1974; JD, U. S.C., 1986. Tchr. Elementary Sch.; dir. rsch. S.C. House Reps., 1977-83; attorney Sinkler & Boye, P.A., 1986-92; supt. edn. S.C. Dept. Edn., Columbia, 1999—. Founder S.C. Ctr. Family Policy. Office: South Carolina Dept Edn Rutledge Bldg 1429 Senate St Columbia SC 29201-3730

TENER, CAROL JOAN, retired secondary school educator, consultant; b. Cleve., Feb. 10, 1935; d. Peter Paul and Mamie Christine (Dombrowski) Manusack; m. Dale Keith Tener, Feb. 13, 1958 (div. Aug. 1991); children: Dean Robert, Susan Dawn Tener Belair. Student, Cleve. Mus. Art, 1948-53, Cleve. Art Inst., 1953-54; BS in Edn. cum laude, Kent State U., 1957; MS in Supervision, Akron U., 1974; postgrad., Kent State U., 1964, 81, 88-90, Akron U., 1975, 79, John Carroll U., 1982, 83, 85-86, Ohio U., 1987, Baldwin Wallace Coll., 1989. Cert. permanent K-12 tchr., Ohio; cert. vol. counselor for Ohio sr. health ins. Ohio Dept. Ins. Stenographer Equitable Life Iowa, Cleve., 1953-54; tchr. elem. art Cuyahoga Falls (Ohio) Bd. Edn., 1957-58, 62-63, 65-68, tchr. jr. high sch., 1968-69; tchr. high sch. Brecksville (Ohio)-Broadview Heights Sch. Dist., 1969-94; chmn. dept. art Brecksville-Broadview Heights (Ohio) HS, 1979—94, chmn. curriculum devel., 1982, 1989, quality deployment team employee recognition district- wide bd. level, 1993—94; ret., 1994. Instr. for children Kent State U., 1956; advisor, prodr. cmty. svc. in art Brecksville Broadview Heights Bd. of Edn., 1969-94; former tchr. recreation and adult art edn. City of Cuyahoga Falls, 1967-68; com. mem. North Ctrl. evaluation com. Nordonia H.S., Nordonia City, Ohio, 1978, Solon H.S., Solon City, Ohio, 1989; chmn. north ctrl. evaluation com. Garfield Heights H.S., 1991; chair pilot program curriculum devel. com. in art/econs. Brecksville-Broadview Heights H.S., 1985-86, 86-87; spkr. in field. Contbr. articles to newspapers, brochures, mags.; commd. artist for mural Brecksville City's Kids Quarters, 1994, Christopher Columbus/John Glen portraits in relief commemorating Columbus Day, 1961, Wooster (Ohio) Products Co.; editor Greater Cleve. chpt. Ohio Ret. Tchrs. Assn., 1998-2002; contbr. to Resources for You, 2003, Ohio Sr. Health Ins. Info. Program, Ohio Dept. Ins., 2001—. Chmn. Artmart Invitational Exhibit PTA, 1982-94; active Meals on Wheels program in Brecksville and Broadview Hts., 1995-98, Heart Disease collection, 1995, Stow-Glen Assisted Living Visitations, 1994-95, NCR Assisted Living transp. provision to hosps. and dr. in neighboring county; trustee, sec. Gettysburg Devel. Block Group Parma, 1995-96, Kids Quarters, 1994; Med Save fraud vol. Cuyahoga County Dept. Sr. and Adult Svcs., 2000-2002, spkrs. bur.; sr. health ins. info. program, cert. vol. counselor of OSHIIP under the Dept. of Insurance, Ohio Dept. Ins., 2001-04—, vol. of OSHIIP, 2004-05. Recipient Ohio Coun. on coord. spkr. and healthfair mktg., OSHIIP, 2004-05. Recipient Ohio Coun. on Econ. Edn. award, 1985-86, award for significant svc. to cmty. Ret. and Sr. Vol. Program of USA, 1996, Svc. award Greater Cleve. Chpt./Ohio Ret. Tchrs. Assn., 1998, Outstanding Svc. award Sr. Medicare Patrol Projects, Cert. of Appreciation, U.S. Dept. Health and Human Svcs. Adminstrn. on Aging, 2002; Pres.'s scholar Kent State U., 1954-57; Resolution to thank a Med-Save Project Vol. signed by Cuyahoga County Commrs. Tim McCormack, pres., Jimmy Dimora, v.p., and Peter Lawson Jones, commr. Mem.: NAFE, ASCD, NEA (life), AAUW, S.W. Area Ret. Educators (co-chair 1996—98, program chair 1996—98, program coord. 1999—2000), Nat. Mus. Women in Arts, Cleve. Mus. Art, Acad. Econ. Edn., Brecksville Edn. Assn., Internat. Platform Assn., Nat. Art Edn. Assn., Ohio Ret. Tchrs. Assn. (life; registration chair 1997—98, pres.-elect Cleve. chpt. 1998, program chair 1998, interim editor 1998, circulation mgr. 1998—2002, chpt. pres. 1999, editor 1999—2002, trustee 2000, guest spkr. on newsletter writing and pub. 2000, nominating chair 2000—01, by-law chair 2000—01, Pub. Rels. awards 1999—2002), Phi Delta Kappa Pi. Roman Catholic. Avocations: photography, collecting books on architecture, painting. Home: 7301 Sagamore Rd Parma OH 44134-5732 Office Phone: 440-885-2231.

TEN EYCK, DOROTHEA FARISS, real estate agent; b. Pulaski County, Va., Dec. 2, 1923; d. Orel Cronk and Esther Mildred (Rexrode) Fariss; m. George Ten Eyck, Jan. 4, 1949 (dec.); m. John S. Kreeger, Aug. 27, 1965 (dec.); m. Robert L. Ten Eyck, Oct. 30, 1994; 4 children Student, Ind. U. Market rsch. Proctor & Gamble, Cin., 1944-47; ptnr. Santee Builders, 1960—63; sales real estate Lockwood Doeuch, Cin., 1963-65. Pres. women's com. Cin. Art Mus., mem. adv. com., docent emeritus; mem. Elder Indian Hill Ch. Independent. Presbyterian. Avocations: golf, gardening, travel, volunteerism. Home: 3032 Alpine Ter Cincinnati OH 45208-2925

TENNANT, BONNIE W., retired music educator; b. Meadvile, Pa., Apr. 17, 1945; d. Joseph Elah and Ida Fay (Perry) Williams; m. Theodore Harold Tennant, Aug. 18, 2001; stepchildren: Brenda Genant, Peggy Lattimore; m. Willard C. Lawton (dec.). BS in Music Edn., Mansfield State Coll., 1967; MEd in Music Edn., Mansfield State Coll. (now Mansfield U.), 1974. Cert. pub. sch. tchr. U. State N.Y., 1968, State Edn. Dept., 1978, music hist. and violin Mozarteum, Salzburg, Austria, 1970. Music tchr. string & orch. Corning Painted Post Sch. Dist., N.Y., 1967—86; children's choir dir. First United Meth. Ch., Corning, 1968—70; chancel choir dir. Corning First United Meth. Ch., 1975—86; music tchr. strings & orch. Auburn Enlarged City Sch. Dist., N.Y., 1986—2001; chancel choir dir. (adult) First United Meth. Ch., Auburn, 1991—. Violinist/violist Corning Philharm. Orch., 1967—86; violinist/concertmaster (part-time co-concertmaster) Auburn Chamber Orch., 1986—. Composer: (string sextet/string orch.) Cayuga Legends, 2004, (recital pieces (5) Sisters, Strings & Songs. Vol. Faith in Action, Auburn, 2002—03, Retired Sr. Vol. Program, Auburn, 2004—. Mem.: N.Y. State Sch. Music Assn. (adjudicator 1968—), Music Educator's Nat. Conf. Methodist. Avocations: golf, playing handbells, reading, exercise. Home: Southfield Apt I-33 Auburn NY 13021

TENNANT, DONNA KAY, writer; b. Waynesburg, Pa., Nov. 28, 1949; d. Daniel Clay and Mary Aliff (Cole) T. BA in Philosophy, U. Rochester, 1971; MA in Art History, U. N.Mex., 1978. Art critic Houston Chronicle, 1979-81; assoc. editor Mus. Fine Arts, Houston, 1985-86; gallery mgr. Jeremy Stone Gallery, San Francisco, 1982-84, 89-91; adminstr. Houston Art Dealers Assn., 1987-89, 91-98; editor Mus. and Arts Mag., Houston, 1993-94, POLO Mag., 1998—99, 2004; mng. editor Houston Life Mag., 1994-95; sr. editor S.W. Art mag., Houston, 1996—98. Adj. lectr. U. Houston Downtown, 2001—06. Freelance writer, editor, photographer various local and nat. publs., 1978—. Personal E-mail: donna@donnatennant.com.

TENNANT-SNYDER, NANCY, appliance company executive; BA in Sociology, West Va. U., 1980, MS in Indsl. Rels., 1981; Doctorate degree in orgn. behavior, George Washington U., 1996. Various mgmt. positions in orgn. development Kaiser Aluminum; with Whirlpool Corp., 1986—, corp. dir., organizational leadership development, 1994—99, corp. dir., strategic process, 1999—2000, v.p., strategic innovation and knowledge mgmt., 2000—01, corp. v.p. strategic competencies and leadership, 2001—. Spkr. in field; adj. prof. in exec. edn. U. Notre Dame. Author of numerous publs.; co-author: Mastering Virtual Teams and Strategiv Innovation. Bd. dir. First Tee, Benton Harbor, Mich. Named one of 25 Masters of Innovation, BusinessWeek. Office: Whirlpool Corp 2000 N M-63 Benton Harbor MI 49022-2692 Business E-Mail: nancy_t_snyder@whirlpool.com.

TENNEY, SARAH G., music educator; b. N.Y.C., Apr. 30, 1948; d. John Wool Griswold and Margaret Brett Tenney. BA, Bennington Coll., 1971; MusM, New Eng. Conservatory, 1976. Founder Spectrum Young Audiences Trio, Boston, 1976-80; marimba, percussion tchr. Rivers Music Sch., Weston, Mass., 1976-80, 85—, St. Ann's Sch., Bklyn., 1980-85; founder, dir. Marimba Magic, Weston, 1987—; tchr. improvisation Northeastern U., Boston, 1991-95. Percussionist on 6 Revel records; percussionist/timpanist in Christmas Revels, 1980—; presenter in field. Composer: (composition/musical) Gamelon Dream, 1989, Mysterious Waltz, 1991, Whole Tone Dream, 1996, Adventures, 1999, Machines, 2000, Jaja Mani Dreams, 2001, Drum Circle, 2002, 3 Canons, 2003, Moving Music, 2004, More Moving Music, 2005. Concert performer Concerts for Children, 1976-80, Cambridge World's Fair, 1997, 98, Clarimba Duo, 2002—03, WCRB Cartoonfest, Symphony Hall, 2005. Recipient Am. Composers Forum grant. Mem. Music Tchrs. Nat. Assn. (conf. presenter 1991), Musicians Union, Music Educators Nat. Conf. (presenter ea. conf. 1992, 96), Percussive Arts Soc. (presenter internat. conv. 1989, 97), Orff Schulwerk Assn. (presenter nat. conf. 1996) presenter European Piano Tchrs. Assn., Internat. Conf., Budapest, 2000, Internat. Marimba Conf., Belgium, 1992. Office: The Rivers Music Sch 337 Winter St Weston MA 02493-1072 Office Phone: 781-235-6840.

TENNIHILL, SALLY KAY, writer, music educator; b. Columbus, Feb. 14, 1941; d. Wayne Harris and Ruth Anne Downs; m. Jack Tennihill (dec.), Oct. 17, 1961; children: John, Ralph, Myrtle, Joe. Student, Ohio State U., 1959—61; BA in English, Northwest Mo. State U., 1985, MA in English,

1987. Tchr. piano, Maryville, Mo., 1970—; cert. nurse asst. Nodaway Nursing Home, Maryville, Mo., 1982-84; grad. asst. Northwest Mo. State U., Maryville, Mo., 1985-86, tchg. asst., 1986-87; substitute tchr. St. Joseph (Mo.) Sch. Bd., 1988-93; stringer St. Joseph News-Press, 1988-92. Contbr. poems, short stories to books, anthologies; editor: (creative mag.) Envy's Sting, 1985-86; dir., actor Nodaway County Theatre Co., Maryville, 1991-96. Mem. Coalition Against Domestic Violence, Maryville, Mo., 1987-96, Prison Fellowship, Maryville, 1996, Willa Cather Found., Maryville, 1993-96; head Women's Resource Ctr. Northwest Mo. U., Maryville, 1984-87; pres. M.S. Support Group, Maryville, 1995-96; v.p. Nodaway County Civil War Roundtable, pres. 1996-2002. Recipient Mattie Dykes Creative Writer scholarship, Presdl. Scholar's scholarship. Mem. AAUW, Retired Tchrs. Maryville, Sons and Daus. of the Civil War, N.W. Mo. Multiple Sclerosis Support Group. Home: 123 Park Ave Maryville MO 64468-1347

TENTSCHERT, CHERYL ANN, middle school educator; b. St. Louis, Sept. 9, 1970; d. Edwin Peter and Suzanne Marie Berger; m. Kent Francis Tentschert, Apr. 22, 1995; children: Paige Elizabeth, Colin Patrick. A in Gen. Edn., St. Louis C.C.-Meramec, 1990; BS in Elem. Edn. magna cum laude, U. Mo., St. Louis, 1995, MA in Spl. Edn., 1999. Zone mgr., St. Louis, 1988—90; cashier, hostess Olive Garden, St. Louis, 1990—92; assoc. mgr. Lerner NY, St. Louis, 1992—96; tchr. Miriam Sch., Webster Groves, Mo., 1995—97; tchr. Am. history Buerkle Mid. Sch., Mehlville, Mo., 1996—. Advisor, editor Buerkle Bobcat Cry, Mehlville, 1996—2001; trainee Mo. Assessment Program, St. Louis, 1998—2001; mentor Mehville R-IX Sch. Dist., St. Louis, 2005—. Contbr. articles and case studies to profl. jours. Finalist Mo. State Tchr. of Yr., Mo. Dept. Elem. and Secondary Edn., 2003; named Mehlville Tchr. of Yr., Mehlville R-IX Sch. Dist., 2003-2004. Mem.: Mo. NEA, Girl Scout Coun. Greater St. Louis (cookie mgr. 2005—06). Avocations: reading, swimming, travel. Home: 873 Wycliffe Ct Saint Louis MO 63125 Office: Buerkle Mid Sch 623 Buckley Rd Saint Louis MO 63125 Office Phone: 314-467-6941. Office Fax: 314-467-6899. E-mail: tentschertc@mehlville.k12.mo.us.

TENUTA, LUIGIA, lawyer; b. Madison, Wis., June 4, 1954; d. Eugene P. and Nancy (Gardner) T. AB in Internat. Studies with honors, Miami U., Oxford, Ohio, 1976; JD, Capital U., 1981; postgrad., Pontifical Coll. Josephinum, 1987-88. Bar: Ohio 1981. With internat. mktg. dept. Dresser Industries, Columbus, Ohio, 1976-80, analyst strategic planning, 1980, mgr. internat bus. planning Stratford, Conn., 1981; pvt. practice law Columbus, 1981—. Former mem. devel. com. Miami U. Mem. Ohio Bar Assn., Columbus Bar Assn. Roman Catholic. Office: 6400 Riverside Dr Dublin OH 43017-5197

TEPE, JUDITH MILDRED, vocal music teacher, choral director; b. Merrill, Wis. d. Herbert August and Mildred Lorna (Utech) Zamzow; m. Roger Charles Tepe, Aug. 7, 1976; children: Elizabeth, Jonathan, Rachel. BA in Music Edn., Concordia Coll., Moorhead, Minn., 1972; ME in Curriculum and Instrn., Lesley Coll., Cambridge, Mass., 1993. Choral and gen. music tchr. Shawano (Wis.) Sch. Dist., 1972-74, Howard-Suamico Schs., Green Bay, Wis., 1974-77; dir. music Pilgrim Luth. Ch., Green Bay, 1975-80; choral and band tchr. NEW Luth. H.S., Green Bay, 1977-78; dir. music Faith Luth. ch., Green Bay, 1982-91; artistic dir. Green Bay Boy Choir, Wis., 1990—2002, DePere, Wis., 2005—; vocal music specialist Green Bay Pub. Schs., 1991—. Recipient Golden Apple Tchr. of Distinction award Green Bay C. of C., 1997. Tchr. of Distinction, 2003. Mem. Am. Choral Dirs. Assn., Music Educators Nat. Conf., Voice Care Network. Democrat. Avocations: reading, golf, cooking, travel, the outdoors. Home: 5050 Scottie Ct New Franken WI 54229-9600 E-mail: beasinger50@hotmail.com.

TEPE, VICTORIA, research psychologist, women's health care advocate; b. Chgo., May 5, 1961; d. Donald James and Lillian Gloria (Hagberg) T.; m. Erik Torgny Nasman, Sept. 27, 1984 (div. Mar. 1994). BA in Psychology, Saginaw Valley State U., 1983; Grad. Diploma in Social Sci., U. Stockholm, 1984; MS in Psychology, Northwestern U., 1987, PhD in Psychology, 1988. Rsch. assoc., grad. student summer rsch. program Air Force Office Sci. Rsch., Brooks AFB, Tex., 1986, 87; instr. psychology univ. coll. Northwestern U., Evanston, Ill., 1987-88; rsch. assoc. Chgo. Inst. Neurosurgery & Neuroresearch, 1989-90, Nat. Rsch. Coun./NAS, Washington and Wright-Patterson AFB, Ohio, 1990-92; coord. vol. svcs. Dayton (Ohio) Women's Ctr., 1991—99; sr. human factors engr. Logicon Tech. Svcs., Inc., Dayton, 1992—97; rsch. psychologist, cons. ProActive Rsch., Kettering, Ohio, 1994—99; tech. program mgr. ASE Inc., 2001—. With cmty. outreach/rsch./media Dayton Women's Ctr., 1991-99; adminstrv. & rsch. asst. Artemis Ctr. Alts. Domestic Violence, 1996-98. Author, editor Choice Mail Internet Newsletter, 1992-2002; contbr. articles to profl. jours. and newspapers. Pres. Miami Valley Voters Legal Abortion, Dayton, 1994. Benton J. Underwood Grad. fellow Northwestern U., 1988; Univ. scholar Northwestern U., 1984. Mem. APA, Nat. Abortion Fedn., Soc. Psychophysiological Rsch. Democrat. Avocations: writing, tennis.

TEPPER, MARCY ELIZABETH, drug education director; b. Salt Lake City, Aug. 22, 1949; d. Warren Roswell and Rosemary Tepper. PhD, U. Ariz., Tucson, Ariz., 1983; MEd, U. Utah, Salt Lake City, Utah, 1972; Filosfia Y Letras, U. Valencia, Valencia, Spain, 1971; BA, San Francisco Coll. for Women, San Francisco, Calif., 1971. Cert. principal, mathematics, spanish tchr. 1990. Adjunct asst. prof. U. Arizona, Tucson, 1983—86; dir., owner 1.2.1 Tutoring, Tucson, 1984—90; counselor Teton County Sch. Dist., Jackson, Wyo., 1990—94; lectr. Ariz. State U., Tempe, Ariz., 1995—98; tchr. Santa Fe Public Schools, Santa Fe, 1998—99; coun. Safe Sch. Healthy Students Grant, Ethete, Wyo., 1999—2001; mid. sch. coord. Fremont County Schools #14, Ethete, Wyo., 2001—. Bd. mem. Ariz. Women Mathematics Sci., Tempe, 1997—98. Recipient Nat. Outdoor Leadership Sch. (NOLS) scholarship, 2003. Mem.: Interagy. Coord. Coalition (v.p. 2000—01, pres. 2001—03), Teton County Task Force (bd. 1992—94). Office: Wyoming Indian Sch 638 Blue Sky Highway Ethete WY 82520 Personal E-mail: marcyet@mail.trib.com. Business E-Mail: marcyt@fremont14.k12.wy.us.

TEPPER MADOVER, ARIELLE, theater producer; d. Martin Tepper and Susan Levin. BFA, Syracuse U., 1996. Bd. govs. League Am. Theaters and Producers; founder Summer Play Festival, 2004; panelist Coll. Visual and Performing Arts Drama Dept. Prodr.: (Broadway plays) Harlem Song, A Class Act (5 Tony award nominations), James Joyce's The Dead (Tony award), Freak (2 Tony award nominations), Sandra Bernhard's I'm Still Here.Damn It, A Raisin in The Sun (4 Tony nominations), Jumpers (4 Tony award nominations), Hollywood Arms (Tony award), Monty Python's SPAMALOT, The Pillowman, West End: Guys and Dolls, (off-Broadway plays) The Last Five Years (2 Drama Desk awards), De La Guarda Villa Villa, Goodnight Children Everywhere (Olivier award for best play, 2000), Trainspotting; (films) 30 Days, 2000, (off-Broadway) Bounce, The Moonlight Room. Bd. trustees Syracuse U.; mem. adv. bd. Coll. Visual and Performing Arts; bd. trustees The Dalton Sch. Office: 1501 Broadway Ste 1301 New York NY 10036

TERADA, ALICE MASAE, retired elementary school educator; b. Hilo, Hawaii, Nov. 13, 1928; d. David Matsuo and Mitsuko (Sekido) Marutani; m. Harry T. Terada, Aug. 25, 1951; children: Suzanne T. Henderson, Keith Y., Lance S. Diploma, Queen's Hosp. Sch. Nursing, 1950; BS, We. Res. U., 1953; MEd, U. Hawaii, 1971. Cert. tchr., Hawaii. Registered nurse County Meml. Hosp., Hilo, Hawaii, 1950-51, U. Hosps., Cleve., 1952-53; lang. arts tchr. Dept. Edn., Honolulu, 1967-68; reading tchr. Reading Ctr., Honolulu, Hawaii, 1968-82; ret. Author: Under the Starfruit Tree, 1989, The Magic Crocodile, 1994. Mem. AAUW, Internat. Reading Assn., Zonta Club Internat., Zonta Club Honolulu (bd. dirs. 1996-97). Avocations: art, art history, porcelain antiques, yoga, swimming.

TERAKEDIS, KATHRYN DELEE, mathematics educator; b. Indpls., Nov. 2, 1980; d. Kirby Lee and Marjorie McNaul Terakedis. BA in Math. Edn., Western Mich. U., Kalamazoo, 2003; postgrad., Grand Canyon U. Cert. secondary math. tchr. Colo. and Mich., 2003. Mid. sch. math. tchr. River Valley Sch. Dist., Three Oaks, Mich., 2004—05; h.s. math. tchr. Englewood (Colo.) Schs., 2005—. Asst. coach cheerleading Englewood H.S., 2005—. Named KYGO Tchr. of Week, KYGO Radio Sta., 2005. Mem.: Nat. Coun. for Tchrs. Math. Avocations: travel, exercise, hiking, skiing, soccer. Home: Apt M 207 901 Englewood Pkwy Englewood CO 80110 Office: Englewood School District 3800 S Logan Englewood CO 80113 Office Phone: 303-806-2383. Personal E-mail: kdterakedis@hotmail.com. Business E-Mail: kathryn_terakedis@englewood.k12.co.us.

TERBORG-PENN, ROSALYN MARIAN, historian, educator; b. Bklyn., Oct. 22, 1941; d. Jacques Arnold Sr. and Jeanne (Van Horn) Terborg; 1 dau., Jeanna Carolyn Terborg Penn. BA in History, Queens Coll. CUNY, 1963; MA in History, George Washington U., 1967; PhD in Afro-Am. History, Howard U., 1978. Daycare tchr. Friendship House Assn., Washington, 1964-66; program dir. Southwest House Assn., Washington, 1966-69; adj. prof. U. Md.-Balt. County, Catonsville, 1977-78, Howard C.C., Columbia, Md., 1970-74; prof. history Morgan State U., Balt., 1969—, project dir. oral history project, 1978-79, coord. grad. programs in history, 1986—. Project dir. Assn. Black Women Hist. Rsch. Conf., Washington, 1982-83. Author: (with Thomas Holt and Cassandra Smith-Parker) A Special Mission: the Story of Freedman's Hospital, 1862-1962, 1975, African American Women in the Struggle for the Vote, 1850-1920, 1998; editor: (with Sharon Harley) The Afro-American Woman: Struggles and Images, 1978, 81, 97, (with Darlene Clark Hine and Elsa Barkley Brown) Black Women in America: An Historical Encyclopedia, 1993, 94, (with Sharon Harley and Andrea Benton Rushing) Women in Africa, 1987, (with Andrea Benton Rushing) Women in Africa and the African Diaspora: A Reader, 1996, (with Janice Sumler-Edmond) Black Women's History at the Intersection of Knowledge and Power, 2000; history editor Feminist Studies, 1984-89; mem. editl. bd. Md. Hist. Mag., 1988-94. Founding mem. Howard County Commn. for Women. Ford Found. fellow, 1980-81, Smithsonian Instn. fellow, 1982, 94-95; Howard U. grad. fellow in history, 1973-74, recipient Rayford W. Logan Grad. Essay award Howard U., 1973, Letitia Woods Brown Meml. prize for best article, 1988, Anna Julia Cooper award for disting. scholarship Sage Women's Ednl. Press, 1993, Letitia Woods Brown Meml. Book prize, 1998, Disting. Black Marylander in Edn. award, Towson Univ., 2003. Mem. Assn. Black Women Historians (co-founder, 1st nat. dir. 1979-83, nat. treas. 1982-84, cert. outstanding achievement 1981, Lorraine A. Williams Leadership award 1998), Am. Hist. Assn. (mem. com. on women historians 1978-81, Joan Kelly Prize com. 1984-86, chair com. on women historians 1990-94), Orgn. Am. Historians (mem. black women's history project adv. com. 1980-81, nominations com. 2005—), Alpha Kappa Alpha (mem. Internat. Archives and Heritage com. 1994-96). Office: Morgan State U 1700 E Cold Spring Ln Baltimore MD 21251-0002

TERCERO, STEPHANIE TAVAREZ, biology educator; b. Odessa, Tex., June 16, 1982; d. Jose Steve and Aurora Tavarez Tercero. BS in Biology, Tex. Tech U., 2004. Cert. State Bd. Educator Cert., Tex. Biology tchr. Odessa (Tex.) H.S., 2004—. Advisor student coun., 2004—; advisor students in philantropy, 2004—. Grantee, Meadows Found., 2005. Mem.: Assn. Tex. Profl. Educators, Nat. Sci. Tchr.'s Assn., Kappa Delta Chi (treas. 2003—04, Penguin Pride award 2003). Roman Catholic.

TERKEL, SUSAN NEIBURG, author; b. Lansdale, Pa., Apr. 7, 1948; d. Sidney Aaron and Deborah (Burstein) Neiburg; m. Lawrence Arthur Terkel, Oct. 25, 1970; children: Ari Garth, Marni Anne, David Samuel. BS, Cornell U., 1970. Freelance writer, 1978—. Author: Ethics, 1992, Finding Your Way, 1995, People Power, 1996, Drug Laws: Time for a Change?, 1997. Co-founder, bd. dirs. Spiritual Life Soc., Hudson, Ohio, 1978—, Ohio State Freeze Campaign, Columbus, 1987, Soviet-Am. Youth Ambs., 1988. Charles Rieley Armington Found. grantee Case Western Res. U., 1988. Mem. P.E.N., Author's Guild, Soc. Children's Writers. Democrat. Jewish. Avocation: painting.

TERNBERG, JESSIE LAMOIN, pediatric surgeon, educator; b. Corning, Calif., May 28, 1924; d. Eric G. and Alta M. (Jones) T. AB, Grinnell Coll., Iowa, 1946, ScD (hon.), 1970; PhD, U. Tex., Austin, 1950; MD, Washington U., St. Louis, 1953; ScD (hon.), U. Mo., St. Louis, 1981. Diplomate: Am. Bd. Surgery. Intern Boston City Hosp., 1953—54; asst. resident in surgery Barnes Hosp., St. Louis, 1954-57, resident in surgery, 1958-59; rsch. fellow Washington U. Sch. Medicine, 1957-58; practice medicine specializing in pediatric surgery St. Louis, 1966—; instr., DGMS trainee in surgery Washington U., 1959-62, asst. prof. surgery, 1962-65, assoc. prof. surgery, prof., 1965-71, prof. surgery, 1971-96, chief divsn. pediatric surgery, 1972-90, prof. emeritus, 1996—; mem. staff Barnes Hosp., 1959—90; gen. surgeon in chief Children's Hosp. of St. Louis, 1974-90. Mem. staff Children's Hosp., dir. pediatric surgery, 1972-90. Contbr. numerous articles on pediatric surgery to profl. jours. Trustee Grinnell Coll., 1984—. Recipient Alumni award Grinnell Coll., 1966, Faculty/Alumni award Washington U. Sch. Medicine, 1991, 2nd Century award 2006, 1st Aphrodite Jannopaulo Hofsommer award, 1993, Local Legend Changing the Face of Medicine award AMWA. Fellow AAAS; mem. SIOP, Am. Pediatric Surg. Assn., We. Surg. Assn. (2d v.p. 1984-85), St. Louis Med. Soc., Soc. Surgery of the Alimentary Tract, Am. Acad. Pediatrics, Soc. Pelvic Surgeons (v.p. 1991-92), Brit. Assn. Paediatric Surgeons, Assn. Women Surgeons (disting. mem. 1995), Mo. State Surg. Soc., St. Louis Surg. Soc. (pres. 1980-81), St. Louis Pediatric Soc., Soc. Surg. Oncology, Pediatric Oncology Group (chmn. surg. discipline 1983-96), St. Louis Childrens Hosp. Soc. (pres. 1979-80), Acad. Sci. St. Louis (Trustees award 2002), St. Louis Met. Med. Soc. (hon., councilor, trustee), Barnes Hosp. Soc., Phi Beta Kappa, Sigma Xi, Iota Sigma Pi, Alpha Omega Alpha. Office: St Louis Childrens Hosp 1 Childrens Pl Saint Louis MO 63110-1002 Business E-Mail: ternbergj@wudosis.wustl.edu.

TERNOVITZ, RUTH, mathematics and computer educator; b. Podmokly, Czechoslovakia, 1947; came to U.S., 1959; d. Moses and Nellie (Farkas) T. BA in Psychology, Bklyn. Coll., 1967, MA in Edn., 1970, MA in English Lit., 1978; postgrad., CUNY, 1978-83. Elem. sch. tchr. Pub. Sch. 115, Bklyn., 1968-85; computer documenter Malam Inc., Jerusalem, 1986-88; computer tchr. Pub. Sch. 219, Bklyn., 1989-96; math. tchr. Pub. Sch. 104, Bklyn., 1996—. Jewish. Avocations: oil and watercolor painting, drawing, travel, photography. E-mail: rternovitz@aol.com.

TERNUS, MARSHA K., state supreme court chief justice; b. Vinton, Iowa, May 30, 1951; married; 3 children. BA, U. Iowa, 1972; JD, Drake U., 1977. Bar: Iowa 1977, Ariz. 1984. With Bradshaw, Fowler, Proctor & Fairgrave, Des Moines, 1977—93; justice Iowa Supreme Ct., Des Moines, 1993—, chief justice, 2006—. Former mem. Iowa Jury Instructions Com.; former bd. mem. Polk County Legal Aid Soc.; pres. bd. of counselors Drake U. Law Sch.; former mem. Iowa Supreme Ct. Commn. on Planning for the 21st Century, MultiState Perf. Test Policy Com., Nat. Conf. of Bar Examiners. Editor-in-chief: Drake Law Rev., 1976—77. Mem.: Iowa State Bar Assn. (bd. governors), Polk County Bar Assn. (pres. 1984—85), Order of Coif, Phi Beta Kappa. Office: Iowa Supreme Ct Jud Branch Bldg 1111 E Ct Ave Des Moines IA 50319-0001*

TERPENING, VIRGINIA ANN, artist; b. Lewistown, Mo., July 17, 1917; d. Floyd Raymond and Bertha Edda (Rodifer) Shoup; m. Charles W. Terpening, July 5, 1951; 1 child by previous marriage, V'Ann Baltzelle Deatrick. Student, William Woods Coll., Fulton, Mo., 1936-37, Washington U. Sch. Fine Arts, St. Louis, 1937-40. Lectr. on art; jurist for selection of art for exhibits Labelle (Mo.) Centennial, 1972; chmn. Centennial Art Show, Lewistown, 1971, Bicentennial, 1976; dir. exhibit high sch. student for N.E. Mo. State U., 1974; supt. ann. art show Lewis County (Mo.) Fair, 1975-90. One-woman shows include Culver-Stockton Coll., Canton, Mo., 1956, Creative Gallery, N.Y.C., 1968, The Breakers, Palm Beach, Fla., 1976, others; group shows include Mo. Ann. Show, City Art Mus., St. Louis, 1956, 65, Madison Gallery, N.Y.C., 1960, Ligoa Duncan Gallery, N.Y.C., 1964, 78, Two Flags Festival of Art, Douglas, Ariz., 1975, 78-79, Internat. Art Exhibit, El Centro, Calif., 1977, 78, Salon des Nations, Paris, 1985, UN World Conf. of Women, Narobi, Kenya, 1985, William Woods Coll., Fulton, Mo., 1992-95, La Junta Coll. Art League Internat., 1992, 94, Coffret Musée, Paris, 1995; represented in permanent collection Nat. Mus. of Women in Art, 1990; executed Mississippi RiverBoat oil painting presented to Pres. Carter by Lewis County Dem. Com., Canton, 1979. Mem. Lewistown Bicentennial Hist. Soc.; charter mem. Canton Area Arts Coun. of N.E. Mo. Recipient Cert. of Merit Latham Found., 1960-63, Mo. Women's Festival of Art, 1974, Bertrand Russell Peace Found., 1973, Gold Medallion award Two flags Festival of Art, 1975, Safeco purchase award El Centro (Calif.) Internat. Art Exhibit, 1977, 1st Pl. award LaJunta (Colo.) Fine Arts League, 1981, diploma Univ. Delle Arti, Parma, Italy, 1981, Purchase award Two Flags Art Festival, 1981, award Assn. Conservation and Mo. Dept. Conservation Art Exhibit, 1982, Purchase award Canton Area Arts Coun., 1988, Colorado Springs Art Festival, 1989; paintings selected for Competition '84 Guide by Nat. Art Appreciation Soc., 1984, 1st Pl. award New Orleans Internat. Art Exhibit, 1984, Two Flags Festival of Art, 1986, Sunflower Judges award Harlin Mus., West Plains, Mo., 1994, Key to City, Lifetime award, 1998; named artist laureate, Nepenthe Mondi Soc., 1984. Mem. Artist Equity Assn., Internat. Soc. Artists, Internat. Platform Assn., Nat. Mus. Women in Art (charter), Animal Protection Inst. Mem. Christian Ch. (Disciples Of Christ). Address: 105 S Vine St PO Box 117 Lewistown MO 63452-0117

TERR, LENORE CAGEN, psychiatrist, writer; b. NYC, Mar. 27, 1936; d. Samuel Lawrence and Esther (Hirsch) Cagen; m. Abba I. Terr; children: David, Julia. AB magna cum laude, Case Western Res. U., 1957; MD with honors, U. Mich., 1961. Diplomate Am. Bd. Psychiatry and Neurology (subspecialty bd. child and adolescent psychiatry). Intern U. Mich. Med. Ctr., Ann Arbor, 1961-62; resident Neuropsychiat. Inst. U. Mich., Ann Arbor, 1962-64, fellow Children's Psychiat. Hosp., 1964-66; from instr. to asst. prof. Case Western Res. U. Med. Sch., Cleve., 1966-71; pvt. practice Terr Med. Corp., San Francisco, 1971—; from asst. clin. prof. to clin. prof. psychiatry Sch. Medicine U. Calif., San Francisco, 1971—. Lectr. law, psychiatry U. Calif., Berkeley, 1971—90, Davis, 1974—88; dir. Am. Bd. Psychiatry and Neurology, 1988—96, chair psychiatry coun., 1996. Author: Too Scared to Cry, 1990, Unchained Memories, 1994, Beyond Love and Work, 1999; contbr. articles to profl. jours.; exhibited works in art show at Canessa Gallery, San Francisco, 2002. Named to Cleveland Heights H.S. Disting Alumni Hall of Fame, 2003; recipient Career Tchr. award, NIMH, 1967—69, Child Advocacy award, APA, 1994; grantee project, Rosenberg Found., 1977, William T. Grant Found., 1986—87, Leon Lowenstein Found., 2002; scholar-in-residence, Rockefeller Found., Italy, 1981, 1988. Fellow: Am. Acad. Child and Adolescent Psychiatry (coun. 1984—87), Am. Coll. Psychiatrists (program chair 1991—92, Bowis award 1993), Am. Psychiat. Assn. (Child Psychiatry Rsch. award 1984, Clin. Rsch. award 1987, Marmor Sci. award 2002); mem.: Phi Bet Kappa, Alpha Omega Alpha. Avocations: piano, walking, travel, gardening, needlepoint. Office Phone: 415-433-7800.

TERRADAS, SHIRLEY ARNOLD, clinical psychologist; b. Great Bend, Kans., Apr. 12, 1963; d. Bobby Gene and Bettie Lou (Johnson) Arnold; married, June 5, 1993; children: Will, Mary Charlotte. AA, Mo. So. State Coll., 1984, BS, 1985; MS, Fla. Inst. Tech., 1987, Psychology D., 1989. Counselor various orgns., Mo., Fla., 1979-88; psychologist U.S. Army, Ft. Gordon, Ft. Stewart, Ga., 1988-90, chief div. mental health Ft. Stewart, 1990-91; staff psychologist Fed. Bur. of Prisons, Jesup, Ga., 1991-92, chief psychologist, 1993—. Psychologist suicide prevention team U.S. Army, 1989-91; mental health cons. hostage negotiation team Fed. Bur. Prisons, Jesup, 1991-2004, crisis support team, 2004—. Capt. U.S. Army, 1989-91. Decorated Bronze Svc. Star (2), Appreciation Award. Mem. APA. Avocations: swimming, hiking, travel. Office: Fed Bur of Prisons Fci Hwy # 301 S Jesup GA 31599-0001

TERRANOVA, ELIZABETH (ELISA) JO, artist; b. Monrovia, Liberia, Jan. 15, 1954; (parents Am. citizens); d. Joseph and Joy Alice Terranova; life ptnr. Mark Gerard Domzalski, Oct. 19, 1996; life ptnr. Russell James Sether (div.); m. John Kenneth Mayes (div.). BFA in Art Edn., Ariz. State U., Tempe, 1987, MFA in Painting, 1993. Fine artist, 1980—; founder / pres. Sacred Heart Studios, Folsom, Calif., 1995—. Art film maker Twenty-three Degrees, Sacramento, 2001—; lectr. / guest spkr. colls., univs., fine art galleries. Short animated film, Trompe L'oeil, exhibitions include Orlando (Fla.) Mus. Art, Florence (Italy) Internat. Biennale, 2003, one-woman shows include U. Club Gallery, Winter Park, Fla., Women Image Now Gallery, Ariz. State U., Tempe, 1986, 1987, Harry Wood Gallery, Ariz. State U., Tempe, 1989, Student Union Art Gallery, San Francisco State U., 1993, James Kaneko Galler, Am. River Coll., Sacramento, 1994, Sheppard Fine Arts Gallery, U. Nev., Reno, Ridley Gallery, Sierra Coll., Rocklin, Calif., 2001; artist (invitational group shows) Ctr. Contemporary Art, Sacramento, (internat. juried group shows) Sacramento Fine Arts Ctr. (Excellence award, Merit award), (group shows) Crest Theater, Sacramento, 2002, (video group shows) Gallery Horse Cow, (group shows) Fortezza da Basso, Florence, 2003, Toyroom Gallery, Sacramento, 2004; Exhibited in group shows at Sacramento French Film Festival, 2003, 2004. Phelps Dodge scholar, 1990—91. Achievements include In collaberation with the United Nations and Italy, I have been nominated and accepted as one of the US representatives to display my artwork at the Florence International Biennale 2003, Italy; I was selected to participate in a juried exhibition at the Orlando Museum of art. The exhibit traveled to the Rotunda Building at the US capitol in Washington, D.C; development of my art serves as a visual diary that describes the human condition as told from the perspective of a quadriplegic. Like the works of Frida Kahlo and The Diary of Anne Frank; I hope to inspire this message that great things can be achieved against all odds. Avocations: art history, digital animation, computer animation, gardening. Office: Sacred Heart Studios Folsom CA 95763-6566 E-mail: elisa@elisat.com.

TERRAS, AUDREY ANNE, mathematics professor; b. Washington, Sept. 10, 1942; d. Stephen Decatur and Maude Mae Bowdoin. BS with high honors in Math., U. Md., 1964; MA, Yale U., 1966, PhD, 1970. Instr. U. Ill., Urbana, 1968-70; asst. prof. U. P.R., Mayaguez, 1970-71, Bklyn. Coll., CUNY, 1971-72; asst. prof. math. U. Calif.-San Diego, La Jolla, 1972-76, assoc. prof., 1976-83, prof., 1983—. Prin. investigator NSF, 1974-88; vis. positions MIT, fall 1977, 83, U. Bonn West Germany, spring 1977, Inst. Mittag-Leffler, Stockholm, winter, 1978, Inst. Advanced Study, spring 1984, Math. Scis. Rsch. Inst., Berkeley, Calif., winter 1992, spring 1995, U. Aachen, Germany, 1998, Tsuda Coll., Tokyo, 1999, CRM, U. Montreal, 1999, U. Colo., Boulder, 2006, others; dir. West Coast Number Theory Conf., U. Calif.-San Diego, 1976, AMS joint summer rsch. conf., 1984; lectr. in field. Author: Harmonic Analysis on Symmetric Spaces and Applications, Vol. 1, 1985, Vol. II, 1988, Fourier Analysis on Finite Groups and Applications, 1999; editor: The Selberg Trace Formula and Related Topics, 1986; contbr. chapters to books, articles to profl. jours. Woodrow Wilson fellow, 1964, NSF fellow, 1964-68; NSF grantee Summer Inst. in Number Theory, Ann Arbor, Mich., 1973. Fellow: AAAS (nominating com. math. sect. project 2061); mem.: Assn. for Women in Sci., Assn. for Women in Math. (travel grants com. 1996), Soc. Indsl. and Applied Math., Math. Assn. Am. (program com. for nat. meeting 1988—90, chair joint program com. Am. Math. Soc. and Math. Assn. Am. 1991), Am. Math. Soc. (com. employment and ednl. policy com. on coms., coun., trans. editor, com. for the yr. 2000, western sect. program com., assoc. editor book revs. Bull., assoc. editor Notices). Achievements include research in harmonic analysis on symmetric spaces; number theory; graph theory. Office: U Calif San Diego Dept Math La Jolla CA 92093-0112

TERRASSA, JACQUELINE, museum director; MFA, U. Chgo., 1994. Staff mem. Columbia Coll., Chgo.; edn. dir. Hyde Park Art Ctr., David and Alfred Smart Mus. Art, U. Chgo., 1998—, interim dir., 2004—05, established SmART Explorers sch. program, dep. dir. collections, programs, & interpretation, 2005—. Office: Smart Mus Art U Chgo 5550 S Greenwood Ave Chicago IL 60637*

TERRELL, KARENANN, information technology executive; BSEE, Gen. Motors Inst., 1986; MSEE, Purdue Univ., 1988. Dir. eConnect platform, Chrysler Group DaimlerChrysler Corp., Auburn Hills, Mich., dir. managed services & internat. process systems, v.p., CIO Chrysler Group & Mercedes Benz No. Am., 2005—. Mem. adv. bd. Women in Tech. Internat. Named one of 100 Influential Women in Automotive Bus., Automotive News; recipient Women's Corp. Tech. award, Women in Tech. Internat., 2005, Office Depot Bus. Woman of the Yr.*

TERRIQUEZ-KASEY, LAURA MARIE, emergency nurse; b. Bronx, N.Y., May 12, 1950; d. Gilbert Manuel and Elizabeth (Arevena) Terriquez; m. William Kasey, July 23, 1988 (dec. May 1995). AAS, SUNY, Morrisville, 1971; BSN, Long Island U., 1980; MSN, CUNY, 1985. RN, N.Y., Tex. Commd. 2d lt. AUS, 1974, advanced through grades to maj., 1993; staff nurse emergency svc. Bellevue Hosp. Ctr., N.Y.C., 1971-73, head nurse emergency svc., 1973-81, nursing supr., 1981-84; clin. nurse coord. South Nassau Cmty. Hosp., Oceanside, N.Y., 1984-85; staff nurse Brooke Army Med.Ctr., San Antonio, 1985-86; head nurse vascular surg. ward Brooke Army Med. Ctr., San Antonio, 1987-89, charge nurse, EMT, head nurse PACU, 1987-89; staff nurse med. ICU William Beaumont Army Med. Ctr., Ft. Bliss/El Paso, Tex., 1985-90, staff nurse trauma unit, 1990-91, head nurse trauma unit, 1991-92, asst. chief nurse, 1992-93; nurse mgr. emergency/trauma svcs. Bassett Health Care Sys., Cooperstown, N.Y., 1993-2000, adminstr. emergency and svc. tng. program, 1997-98, co-chair network adv. group, nurse advisor emergency svcs.; clin. lectr. SUNY Sch Nursing, Binghamton, 2000; now clin. lectr. Sch. Nursing, Binghamton U. Instr. U. El Paso, Tex., 1991-92; mem. com. nursing adv. Southwest Organbank, El Paso, 1992—; adj. instr. U. Tex. Dept. Nursing, El Paso, 1992; Advanced Emergency Med. Technic Critical Care, N.Y. State Dept. Health sponsor for EMS programs, 2000-02; lectr. in field. With disaster med. assistance team Team Houston, Tex., 2001; with disaster med. assistance team team response Anthrax Postal Response, N.Y.C., 2001; mem. disaster med. assistance team NY Dept. Health and Human Svcs., NY, 2001; Ground Zero med. team World Trade Ctr., 2001; mem. hurricane disaster med. assistance team N.Y. Disaster Med. Assistance Team, FEMA, Fla., 2004. Decorated Army Commendation medal with 3 oak leaf clusters, Army Achievement award; recipient Meritorious Svc. award San Antonio Police Dept., 1988, Svc. award ARC, 1980, Cert. Appreciation N.Y. Emergency Med. Svcs., 1984, Chancellors award for internat. edn. program on cmty. health in Dominican Republic. Mem.: Emergency Nurses Assn. (pres. rural nursing orgn. 2006), Am. Legion, Sigma Theta Tau. Avocations: swimming, biking. Home: 125 Park Dr Angel Heights Oneonta NY 13820 Office: Decker Sch Nursing Box 6000 SUNY Binghamton Binghamton NY 13902 Office Phone: 607-777-6033. Personal E-mail: LKasey@STNY.rr.com. Business E-Mail: kasey@binghamton.edu.

TERRIS, KATHLEEN ELIZABETH, social studies educator; b. Cin., May 25, 1972; d. Robert John and Judith Ann Terris; m. Carlos H. Miranda, June 17, 2005; 1 child, Carlos Antonio Miranda Terris. BEd, U. Dayton, Ohio, 1994; MEd, U. Dayton, 2000. Social studies tchr. Milford H.S., Cin., 1995—2003, Baldwin Sch., San Juan, PR, 2003—, girls soccer coach, 2005, class advisor, 2005—06. Avocations: soccer, travel, beaches.

TERRIS, LILLIAN DICK, psychologist, health facility administrator; b. Bloomfield, N.J., May 5, 1914; d. Alexander Blaikie and Herminia (Doscher) Dick; m. Louis Long, Apr. 22, 1935 (dec. Sept. 1968); 1 son, Alexander Blaikie Long; m. Milton Terris, Feb. 6, 1971 (dec. Oct. 2002). BA, Barnard Coll., 1935; PhD, Columbia U., 1941. Diplomate Am. Bd. Examiners in Profl. Psychology. Instr. psychology Sarah Lawrence Coll., Bronxville, NY, 1937-40; jr. pers. tech. SSA, Washington, 1941; sr. pers. clk. OWI, N.Y.C., 1941-43; dir. profl. examination svc. Am. Pub. Health assn., N.Y.C., 1943-70; pres., 1970-79; pres. emeritus, 1979—. Assoc. editor: Jour. Pub. Health Policy, 1979—; contbr. articles to profl. jours. Recipient Nat. Environ. Health assn. award, 1976, Cert. Svc. award Bd. Preventive Medicine, 1979. Fellow Am. Psychol. Assn., Am. Coll. Hosp. Adminstrs. (hon.); mem. Am. Pub. Health Assn., N.Y. State Psychol. Assn., Phi Beta Kappa, Sigma Xi. Home: 1450 Post St 506 San Francisco CA 94109 Office: 475 Riverside Dr New York NY 10115-0122 E-mail: jphpterris@aol.com.

TERRIS, SUSAN, physician, cardiologist, researcher; b. Morristown, N.J., Sept. 5, 1944; d. Albert and Virginia Terris. BA in History, U. Chgo., 1967, PhD in Biochemistry, 1975, MD, 1976. Diplomate in internal medicine, endocrinology and metabolism, cardiovasc. disease Am. Bd. Internal Medicine. Resident in internal medicine Washington U., Barnes Hosp., St. Louis, 1976-78; fellow in endocrinology and metabolism U. Chgo., 1978-80, fellow cardiology, 1980-83, U. Mich., Ann Arbor, 1983-85, instr. cardiology, 1985-86; head cardiac catheterization lab., head cardiology Westland (Mich.) Med. Ctr., 1985. Contbr. articles to Jour. Biol. Chemistry, Am. Jour. Physiology, Am. Jour. Cardiology, Jour. Clin. Investigation, other profl. publs. Grantee Juvenile Diabetes Found., 1978-80, NIH, 1978-79. Mem. AAAS, Am. Heart Assn., N.Y. Acad. Sci. Achievements include rsch. demonstrating dependence of intracellular degradation of insulin upon its prior adsorptive pinocytotic uptake by liver; studies on the electrophysiologic effect of cathecholamimes on sheep Parkinje fibers and on the hemodynamic effects of various drugs on the human circulatory system.

TERRITO, MARY C., health facility administrator, hematologist, educator; BS in Biology, Wayne State U., 1965, MD, 1968. Intern/resident in internal medicine Parkland Hosp., Dallas, 1971-73; fellow in hematology/oncology Harbor-U. Calif., L.A., 1973-74, UCLA, 1974-75; rsch. assoc. Wadsworth VA Hosp., L.A., 1975-81; asst. prof. dept. medicine UCLA, 1975-81, assoc. prof., 1981-96, prof., 1996—, dir. bone marrow transplant program Ctr. Health Scis., 1981—. Contbr. articles to profl. jours. Office: UCLA Bone Marrow Transplantation Program Ctr 42-121 CHS 10833 Le Conte Ave Los Angeles CA 90095-3075

TERRY, APRIL LYNNE, physical education educator; b. Salt Lake City, Utah, Apr. 4, 1975; d. Edward J. and Shelby Marie Box; m. Benjamin D. Terry, Nov. 29; 1 child, Madison Grace. BS, U. Utah, Salt Lake City, 1998, MS, 2000; tchg. cert., U. Great Falls, Mont., 2006. Cert. ATC Nat. Athletic Tng. Assn., health and edn. specialist. Asst. athletic trainer Utah Starzz, Salt Lake City, 1998—2000; head athletic trainer, prof. sports medicine Ea. Oreg. U., La Grande, 2000—03; head athletic trainer Flathead H.S., Kalispell, Mont., 2003—, educator health enhancement, 2003—; prof. health and phys. edn. U. Great Falls, 2006—.

TERRY, BARBARA L., human services administrator; b. Cin., Mar. 17, 1955; d. Robert H. and Elizabeth (Addison) Akers; m. Dennis P. Terry. BA, Bowling Green State U., 1977; MS, Mich. State U., 1987. Registered social worker 1979, credentialed substance abuse counselor 1988. Program dir. Jackson-Hillsdale Mental Health, Jackson, Mich., 1977—84; program adminstr. Damar Homes, Indpls., 1984—85; exec. dir. Student Assistance Programs, Jackson, Mich., 1988—90; divsn. dir. Kent County Health Dept., Grand Rapids, Mich., 1990—97, dep. health dir., 1997—2001; v.p. Heart of West Mich. United Way, Grand Rapids, Mich., 2001—. Vol. mentor Grand Rapids Pub. Schs., 2001—. Recipient Profl. Svc. to Children award, Kent County Coun. for the Prevention of Child Abuse and Neglect, 1994, Outstanding Contbn. to Student Assistance award, South Ctrl. Mich. Substance Abuse Commn., 1990, Exceptional Svc. to Children award, Wood County Children's Services Assn., 1977. Mem.: Healthy Kent, Kent County Emergency Needs Task Force (Health Subcommittee Chair; Funding Chair 2000—01), Kent County Child & Family Coordinating Coun. (Executive Committee Member 1998—99). Avocations: travel, reading.

TERRY, DORIS D., music educator; b. Forrest City, Ark., Aug. 23, 1936; d. Samuel and Elizabeth Phillips; m. Ronald E. Terry; 5 children. BA, Adams State Coll., Alamosa, Colo., 1960; EdM, N. Tex. State U., Denton, 1970; postgrad. studies, Ga. Coll., Milledgeville, 1985; Honorary (hon.), Trinity Coll., Birmingham, Ala., 1985. Tchr. Mary Holmes Coll., West Point, Miss., Sims H.S., Holly Springs, Miss.; choral dir. LaVega H.S., Waco, Tex.; music tchr. Sheridan Middle Sch., Mpls.; choral dir. Southwest H.S., Macon, Ga.; dir. music Bibb County Schs, Macon, Ga. Mus. dir. Cherry Blossom Concert, Macon, Ga.; mem. Arts Alliance, Macon. Mem.: Ga. Music Educators (25 Yr. Svc. Plaque), Am. Choral Dirs. Assn., Music Educators Nat. Conf. Home: 1490 New Castle Dr Macon GA 31204

TERRY, ELIZABETH HUDSON, personal care industry executive, realtor; d. Otis Hudson and (Russell) Evelena; m. Lester Terry; 1 child, Darric. Student, Clark Coll., Atlanta, 1966; BA business, Atlanta Sch. Bus., 1968; student, Dekalb Perimeter Coll., Decatur, Ga., 1978—83; cert. enterpreneurship program, U. Ga., 1993; cert., Speak Easy Sch., Atlanta, 1993. Lic. real estate salesperson Ga., 1996. Asst. dir. Count Jackson Studio, Atlanta, 1968—72; mgr. BellSouth Corp., Atlanta, 1970—97, Bank of Am., Atlanta, 1999—; wedding dir., cons. Weddings by Liz, Decatur, Ga., 1980—; realtor, sales assoc. Coldwell Banker Buckhead Brokers, Tucker, 1996—2000, Quest Realty Inc., Decatur, 2000—. Notary, Decatur; featured in numerous newspapers and mags.; guest appearances on several t.v. and radio shows. Author: Just Think About It, 1993. Mem. planning bd. sch. in Haiti; mem. Veracruz Homeowners Assn., Decatur, 2001—, Nat. Coalition of 100 Black Women's Assn., NAACP, United Negro Coll. Fund; pub. rels. advisor Uptown Social Club, Decatur; vol. Habitat for Humanity, Atlanta; asst. dir. The Colored People Prodn., Atlanta; program dir. Azusa St. Revival Prodn., 1995; asst. dir., program dir. Fix Me Jesus Prodn., Atlanta; mem. Jr. Achievement Mentoring Program, 1990—96; founding mem. Nat. Campaign Tolerance, 2005; mem. Beulah Bapt. Ch., Decatur; adv. bd., bd. dirs. Suncrest Resources, Inc., Stone Mountain, Ga., 1986. Recipient Pearl award, Diamond award, Ruby award, Emerald award, Gold award. Mem.: Midnight Expression Orgn., Chamber of Commerce, Rainbow Internat. chpt. (Am. Bus. Women's Assn.) (founder 1985—86, v.p. 1985—86, pres. 1986—87, chmn. Program Com., Woman of the Year 1985—86), Sphnix chpt. (Am. Bus. Women's Assn.) (exec. bd. secy. 1984, chmn. Extension Com., Woman of the Year 1984—85, Woman of Quarter 1985, Hand of Friendship award), St. Peter and Paul Parent-Teacher Assn., United Coun. for Negro Women Assn., Am. Bus. Women's Assn. (chpt. chmn. adminstrv. bd. 1986—88, chmn. mem. com., chmn. bus. assn. com., chmn. edn./scholarship com.), Starwood Vistana Vacation Assn., Toastmasters (v.p. edn. 2003—04, pres. Bank of Am. 2004—, A.T.M. Bronze award 2006, Competent Toastmaster award 2004, Competent Leadership award). Avocation: writing. Home: 3941 Veracruz Dr Decatur GA 30034 Office Phone: 770-374-4900.

TERRY, FRANCES JEFFERSON, retired psychiatric nurse practitioner; d. Walter Louis and Ruth Williams Jefferson; m. Robert Terry, Sept. 29, 1926; children: Deborah Ella Terry-Hays, Robert David, Michael Duane, William Brian, Walter Louis. BSN, Seattle U., 1951; MSN, U. Wash., Seattle, 1981. Lic. Advanced RN Practitioner, ANCC. Health enhancement-program nurse Ctrl. Area Sr. Ctr., Seattle; staff nurse Providence Hosp., Seattle; prescribing and consulting nurse Cmty. Ho. Mental Health Agy., Seattle; psychiat. mental health practitioner U. of Wash.-Harborview Med. Ctr., Seattle; nursing instr. Shoreline C.C., Seattle; nurse case mgr.-mental health U. of Wash.; nursing instr. Seattle U.; dir. of health svcs. NW Ctr. for Disabled, Seattle; sch. nurse Seattle Pub. Schs.; pub. health nurse Seattle King County Health Dept., Seattle. Diabetes support group facilitator Joslin Diabetes Ctr., Seattle. Auditor/ch. coun. ImmaculateConception Ch., Seattle; mem. Seattle Ctrl. Cmty. Coll. Found.; planning com. Susan G. Komen Breast Cancer Found./Puget Sound, Seattle. Named Outstanding Nurse, U. of Wash.-Harborview Med. Ctr., 1993; named to Hall of Fame, Wash. State Nurses Assn., 2000; recipient Cmty. Svc. Award, Seattle U., 2004. Mem.: Mary Mahoney Profl. Nurses Assn., Am. Nurses' Assn. (life), Alpha Kappa Alpha Sorority (life). Office Phone: 206-325-3944. Personal E-mail: bobfrater@comcast.net.

TERRY, MITZI H., secondary school educator; d. Zandora Fulmer Hanback; m. Michael A. Terry, June 27, 1987; children: Morgan Anthony, Emma Marie. BS in Secondary Edn., U. Tenn., Martin, 1984. Educator/gifted edn. cons. Franklin (Tenn.) H.S., 1986—. Leader Girl Scouts Am., Nashville, 2003—06. Named Williamson County Secondary Tchr. of Yr., 1994. Avocation: volunteering for activities involving my children. Office Phone: 615-472-4451 3407.

TERRY, RACHEL MARIE, music educator; b. Kingston, NY, July 17, 1980; d. David R. Terry and Kathleen J. Haas-Terry. BM in Music Edn., Marywood U., 2003. Cert. instrnl. I Pa. Dept. oEdn., 2003. Music tchr. Christopher Columbus Charter Sch., Phila., 2003—04, Holy Rosary Sch., Scranton, Pa., 2004—. Singer: (choral performances) Mendelssohn Club Phila., The Robert Dale Chorale; featured soloist (CD) With One Voice, 2004. Mem.: Pa. Music Educators Assn., Music Educators Nat. Conf. Roman Catholic.

TERRY, ROBIN, museum director; b. 1969; Degree in Telecom. and Film, Eastern Mich. U., 1992. Dir., Pub. Rels. Motown Hist. Mus., Detroit, 1992—95, dep. dir., 2002—04, exec. dir., 2004—; worked for D'Arcy Masius Benton & Bowles Inc., Troy, Mich., 1995, Gable Grp.; dir., Pub. Rels. Coll. for Creative Studies; devel. officer Focus: HOPE, 1998—2002. Named one of 40 Under 40, Crain's Detroit Bus., 2006. Office: Motown Historical Museum 2648 W Grand Blvd Detroit MI 48208 Office Phone: 313-875-2264.*

TERRY, SANDRA ELEANOR, visual artist; b. Clifton Forge, Va., May 23, 1947; d. Robert B. and Grace J. (Amante) T. BA, Mary Baldwin Coll., 1990; MFA, Ind. State U., 1994; MA in Liberal Studies, New Sch. for Social Rsch., N.Y., 1998. Cert. tchr., Ind. Substitute tchr. Seymour (Ind.) Pub. Sch. Sys., 1990; tchg. asst., instr. Ind. State U., Terre Haute, 1991-94, tutor humanities Student Acad. Svcs., 1992-95. Baker, pastry chef, Different Drummer Restaurant, Staunton, Va., White Star Mills Restaurant, Staunton, McCormicks Restaurant, Staunton, Rising Sun Bakery, Charlottesville, Va., Claire's Restaurant, Charlottesville, South Street Restaurant, Charlottesville, Toast Restaurant, Broadway, N.Y., 2001-02; gallery docent Anderson Gallery, Seattle, 1967-70, Manolides Gallery, Seattle, 1967-70, Polly Friedlander, Seattle; lectr. in field. One-woman shows include Arts Illiana Exhbn. Space, Terre Haute, 1993, Turman Gallery, Ind. State U., 1994; exhibited in group shows at Turman Gallery, 1991-92, 94, Sheldon Swope Art Mus., Terre Haute, 1991-93, Bare-Montgomery Meml. Gallery, Ind. State U., 1992, Broad St. Gallery, New Castle, Ind., 1992, Coffee Grounds Gallery, Terre Haute, 1993, Saint Mary-of-the-Woods Coll., Ind., 1993, Shircliff Gallery of Art, Vincennes (Ind.) U., 1993, Soc. Am. Graphic Artists, 2002, 05, The Old Print Shop, 2004, Art Students League, NY, 2002-04, U. Miami, 2005, 90th Anniversary Show, Soc. Am. Graphics, 2005; permanent collections include Bratislava Sch. Art, Slovakia, U. Man., Winnipeg, Can., Mary Baldwin Coll., Staunton, Va., Ind. State U., Terre Haute; prodr., host Bluegrass music WTJU-FM, Charlottesville, 1983-87, WMRA-FM, Harrisonburg, Va., 1983-87; bassist Ham & Eggs Bluegrass Band, 1978-88, Blue Horizon, 1978-88; graphic designer KRAB-FM program guide, 1968-70 Apr. Artists' fellowship, 2005, 2006. Mem.: Artist's Fellowship, Soc. Am. Graphic Artists (newsletter graphic designer, newsletter mng. dir., exhbn. catalogue graphic designer).

TERSINE, BRENDA L., funeral director; b. Punxsutawney, Pa., June 2, 1948; d. G.J. and Mary V. tersine; m. Bill Goichberg, Feb. 20, 1993. BS in Edn., Indiana U. Pa., 1970; Diploma, Pitts. Inst. Mortuary Sci., 1971; MA, SUNY, Albany, 1985. Lic. funeral dir., N.Y., Pa. Embalmer, funeral dir., Punxsutawney, 1971-75; embalmer, funderal dir. Oliver H Bair, Phila., 1976-80; per diem substitute Phila. Bd. Edn., 1978-80; embalmer, anatomical gifts Albany Med. Coll., 1980-90; asst. prof. mortuary sci. Hudson Valley C.C., Troy, N.Y., 1980-90; funeral dir., embalmer Salisbury Mills, N.Y., 1990—. Contbg. author: Embalming History, Theory and Practice, 1990. Vice pres. adv. bd. Continental Chess, Salisbury Mills, 1991—; supportive counseling/crisis intervention YWCA, Troy, 1989-91. Mem. Acad. Profl. Funeral Svc. Practice (life), Funeral Svc. Ednl. Found., Nat. Funeral Dirs. Assn., Cath. daus. of Am. Democrat. Roman Catholic. Avocation: organizing chess tournaments.

TERTELING-PAYNE, CAROLYN ANN, city official; b. Buhl, Idaho, Dec. 20, 1936; d. Carl Treva and Ann Christine (Witt) Edwards; m. Joseph Loyd Terteling, June 20, 1959 (div. Sept. 1991); children: Joseph Nixon, Steven Loyd, Thomas Edward, Andrew James; m. Frank Adrian Payne, May 13, 1995. BA with highest honors, U. Idaho, Moscow, 1959. Grad. tchg. asst. Ariz. State U., Phoenix, 1959-60; mem. Boise City Coun., 1993—, pres., 1996—2003; mayor City of Boise, Idaho, 2003—. Sustainer Boise Jr. League; mem. Collector's Forum, Boise Art Mus.; trustee, mem. exec. com., mem. bldg. and planning com. St. Lukes Regional Med. Ctr.; pres. Boise Pub. Libr. Found.; dir., past pres. U. Idaho Found.; dir. Fundsy Charitable Found., Boise River Festival; mem. adv. bd. Lit. Lab, Warm Springs Counseling Ctr.; hon. bd. Idaho Zool. Soc.; emeritus dir. Boise Philharmonic; past dir. Boise Mus. Art, Boise Bicentennial Commn., Boise Sch. Vols., Idaho Hist. Preservation Coun., Morriso Ctr. for Ars. Endowment Dr., Women's Life at St. Lukes, Idaho Law Found.; mem. adv. bd. Children at Risk Evaluative Svcs.; past dir. area coun. 11 Western states, Assn. Jr. Leagues Am.; past pres. St. Lukes Hosp. Aux., U. Idaho Found., Boise Jr. League; past chair symposium Albertson Coll. Idaho, Grand Opening of Morrison Ctr. for Arts, Sun valley, Arts and Humanities Benefit, Alternate Mobility Adventure Seekers, Boise State U. Named Idaho Statesman Disting. Citizen, 1979, Woman of Yr., C. of C., 1986; recipient Woman of Today and Tomorrow award Girl Scouts, 1992, Disting. Svc. award Idaho State Bar, 1992, Cultural Heritage award Coll. Letters and Sci. U. Idaho, 1994. Mem. U. Idaho Alumni Assn., Hillcrest Country Club (past dir.), PEO, Phi Beta Kappa, Gamma Phi Beta. Avocations: golf, tennis, gardening, reading. Home: 2050 Table Rock Rd Boise ID 83712-6663 Office: City Hall 150 N Capitol Blvd Boise ID 83702-5920

TERVALON, JOSEPHINE M., psychotherapist, social worker; b. Pender County, N.C., Oct. 9, 1939; d. Joseph Samuel and Dorothy Ann (Messick) Merritt; m. William F. Cunningham Jr. (div.); children: Charles F. Cunningham, Steven Troy Cunningham; m. Albert T. Tervalon, Mar. 20, 1999; stepchildren: Albert L. III, Mark, Brett, Tasha. BS, Tuskegee Inst., 1961; MSW, Smith Coll., 1963. Diplomate Am. Bd. Examiners in Clin. Social Work; LCSW Tex. State Bd. Examiners, cert. Registry of Cert. Group Psychotherapists N.Y., profl. coach Grow Tng. Inst. Sr. psychiatric social worker Cmty. Guidance Ctr., San Antonio; dir. outpatient svc., chief social worker San Antonio Children's Ctr.; program coord. adolescent ctr. Houston Internat. Hosp.; dir. social svcs., coord. adolescent unit W.Oaks Hosp., Houston; dir. unit programs Psychiatric Inst. Houston; pvt. practice Houston. Cons., Houston; practicum asst. prof. Worden Sch. Social Svcs., Our Lady of Lake U., 1975—80; clin. instr. Baylor Coll. Medicine, 1981—2000; adj. asst. prof. Smith Coll. Sch. Social Work, 1985—. Mem.: Nat. Assn. Female Exec. (workshop presenter 1990—92), Tex. Soc. Clin. Social Work (keynote spkr. 2001). Office: Cunningham Tervalon Assoc 4801 Woodway Dr Ste 350W Houston TX 77056

TERZIAN, GRACE PAINE, communications executive; b. Boston, Oct. 19, 1952; d. Thomas Fite and Grace Hillman (Benedict) Paine; m. Philip Henry Terzian, Oct. 20, 1979; children: William Thomas Hillman, Grace Benedict Paine. BA in Art History, Williams Coll., Williamstown, Mass., 1974. Art dir. The New Republic, Washington, 1976-78; asst. editor The Chronicle of Higher Edn., Washington, 1978-79; rsch. editor Archtl. Digest, L.A., 1982-85; pub. The Women's Quar., Arlington, Va., 1994—2004; exec. dir. Allergy and Asthma Network Mothers of Asthmatics, 2004—06; v.p. comm. Hudson Inst., Washington, 2006—. Editor Ex Femina, 1996—2004; sr. v.p. Ind. Women's Forum, 1998-2004. Mem. Soc. Colonial Dames in Am., Phi Beta Kappa. Episcopalian. Home: 10505 Adel Rd Oakton VA 22124-1605 Office Phone: 202-974-2417. Personal E-mail: gterzian@cox.net. Business E-Mail: gracet@hudson.org.

TERZIS, JULIA KALLIPOLITOU, plastic surgeon; b. Salonica, Greece, Feb. 28, 1943; MD, Thomas Jefferson U., Phila., 1970; PhD in Neurophysiology, McGill U., Montreal. Cert. plastic surgery 1983, hand surgery 1990. Intern Royal Victoria Hosp., Montreal, Canada, 1970—71, resident, surgery, 1971—74; resident, plastic surgery Dalhousie U., Halifax, Canada, 1974—76, rsch. fellow, 1976—77; staff mem. Royal Victoria Hosp., Montreal, Canada; prof., dept. surgery, divsn. plastic surgery Ea. Va. Med. Sch., Norfolk, dir., microsurg. program. Contbr. articles to profl. jours.; author: 4 textbooks. Recipient James Barrett Brown award, Am. Assn. Plastic Surgeons, 1976, 2000, Gold medal, Royal Coll. Physicians and Surgeons of Can., 1981, Achievement in the field of Natural Scis., AHEPA Ednl. Found., 1987. Mem.: Internat. Soc. for Reconstructive Microsurgery, Plastic Surgery Rsch. Coun. (past chmn.), Internat. Microsurg. Soc. (past pres.), Am. Soc. Peripheral Nerve (founding pres.), World Soc. for Reconstructive Microsurgery (bd. mem., New Orleans, pres.-elect), Am. Soc. Reconstructive Microsurgery (founding mem., past pres.). Office: Eastern Va Med Sch PO Box 1980 Norfolk VA 23501-1980

TESAR, PATRICIA MARIE, academic coordinator; b. Cleve., Oct. 7, 1955; d. John Joseph and Florence Louise Tesar. BA in Interpersonal Comm., Cleve. State U., 1982; MA in Rehab. Counseling, Gallaudet Coll., 1986; PhD in Spl. Edn. Adminstrn., Gallaudet U., 2002. Ind. living counselor ind. living program Health Hill Hosp., Cleve., 1982-83; practicum rehab. counselor for the deaf Va. Dept. Rehabilitative Svcs., Springfield, 1985; career counselor student spl. svcs./career ctr. Gallaudet U., Washington, 1984-90, coord. spl. svcs. Office for Students with Disabilities, 1990—. Co-chair subcom. adult employment Devel. Disabilities State Planning Coun. DC, 1997—. Recipient Mima Bravo Counseling award, 1986, U.S. Congl. award of achievement, 1986, 92, Nat. Disting. Svc. Registry Counseling award, 1990; Quota Internat. fellow, 1986; Mary Pickford scholar, 1985; Gallaudet U. Pres.'s scholar, various yrs. Mem. ASCD, Am. Deafness and Rehab. Assn. (sec. met. Washington chpt. 1986-88, pres. 1988-90, 90-92), Am. Assn. Counseling and Devel., Nat. Rehab. Assn., Nat. Assn. for Deaf, Am. Assn. for Deaf-Blind, Md. Career Devel. Assn., Md. Rehab. Counseling Assn., Washington Consortium of Univs. Career Devel. Group, Washington Consortium of Univs. Student Support Svcs. Coalition (regional conf. coord.), Met. Washington Assn. Deaf-Blind, Coll. Placement Coun., Registry of Interpreters for the Deaf, Assn. Higher Edn., Coun. Exceptional Children, Kappa Delta Pi. Baptist. Avocations: reading, sign language interpreting. Home: 6500 Alexis Dr Bowie MD 20720-4755 Office Phone: 202-651-5256. E-mail: Patricia.Tesar@gallaudet.edu.

TESCHER, JENNIFER, bank executive; b. 1971; Grad., Northwestern U.; MA in pub. policy, U. Chgo. With ShoreBank Corp., Chgo., 1996—, ShoreBank Adv. Services, Chgo., 2002—04; dir. Ctr. Fin. Services Innovation, Chgo., 2004—. Pres. bd. Ctr. Econ. Progress, Chgo.; monthly columnist Am. Banker. Named one of 40 Under 40, Crain's Chgo. Bus., 2006. Office: Ctr Fin Services Innovation Ste 200 2230 S Michigan Ave Chicago IL 60616 Office Phone: 312-881-5856. Office Fax: 312-881-5801. E-mail: cfsi@cfsinnovation.com.*

TESKA, JANE E., science educator; b. Detroit; d. Wilfred Louis and Mary Ellen Teska. BA in Chemistry, Wayne State U., Detroit, 1972, MAT, 1974; MS in Adminstrn., Madonna State U., Livonia, Mich., 1991; EdD in Ednl. Leadership, Ea. Mich. U., Ypsilanti, 2003. Cert. tchr. Mich., 1979. Curriculum dir. Nat. Inst. Tech., East Pointe, Mich., 1982—84; tchr. and coord. advanced placement Southfield Pub. Schs., 1985—. Adj. instr. electronics Schoolcroft CC, Livonia, Mich., 1985—2000; uniserve dir. Mich. Edn. Assn., Lansing, 2000—01; com. mem. Mich. Dept. Edn., 2000—02; presenter to profl. confs., 1998—2006. Vol. coach Southfield Pub. Schs., Southfield, Mich., 1978—85, support group mentor, 1994—98; vol. probation supr. 36th Dist. Ct., Detroit, 1992—93. Named to Nat. Dean's List, 1993—96. Mem.: Mich. Edn. Assn. (sec. 1993—96), Alpha Delta Kappa (pres. and sec. 2002—, Mich. state pres. 2006—), Phi Delta Kappa (pres. and treas. 2000—03). Office: Southfield Pub Schs 24675 Lahser Rd Southfield MI 48034 Office Fax: 248-746-8916. Business E-Mail: teskaje@southfield.k12.mi.us.

TESKE, RACHEL, professional golfer; b. Port Macquarie, Australia, Apr. 23, 1972; m. Teske Dean Teske, May 22, 1998. Attended, Fla. State U. Winner First Union Betsy King Classic, 1998, Chick-fil-A Charity Championship,

1999, City of Hope Myrtle Beach Classic, 1999, Evian Masters, 2001, PING Banner Health, 2002, Jamie Farr Kroger Classic, 2002, Giant Eagle LPGA Classic, 2003, Wegmans Rochester LPGA, 2003; second place finish British Open, 2004, Australian Open, 2004. Winner New South Wales Jr. Championships, 1989, 90, 91, 92; mem. Australian Tasman Cup Team, 1989, 91, 93; winner NSW Amateur Open, 1992. Avocations: music, movies, hiking. Office: c/o LPGA 100 International Golf Dr Daytona Beach FL 32124-1092

TESMAN, LAURA LYNN, education educator; b. Englewood, Colo., Nov. 20, 1968; d. Robert Martin and Sharon Lynn Tesman. BA, Colo. State U., 1987—91; MA, U. of Warwick, 1993—94; D, U. of Colo., 1997—2001. Asst. prof., theatre dir. U. of Colo., 2001; assoc. co. mem. Curious Theatre Co., Denver, 2003. Dir.: (theatre) Vinegar Tom; actor: Streetcar Named Desire; dir.: Petticoats & Pistols, Bloody Poetry; actor: The Cherry Orchard; dir.: The Dispute by Marivaux, Italian American Reconciliation by John Patrick Shanley; actor: The Good Woman of Szechuan by Bertoldt Brecht (Best Actress, 2002); dir.: Doctor Faustus Lights the Lights by Gertrude Stein. Adv. bd. TheatreWorks, Colorado Springs, Colo., 2001. President's Fund for the Humanities, U. of Colo., 2004—05, Rsch. and Creative Works grant for rsch. on Petticoats & Pistols, 2002—03, Devel. Grant for Petticoats & Pistols, Ctr. for Women's Studies & Women's Faculty Com., Thomas Edwin Devaney Dissertation fellowship, Ctr. for Humanities and the Arts, UC Boulder, 2000—01. Mem.: Lit. Managers and Dramaturgs of the Americas (assoc.), Nat. New Play Network (assoc.), Am. Theatre in Higher Edn. (assoc.; acting focus group mem. at large 1999—2001). Democrat-Npl. Avocations: travel, yoga, hiking, writing, snowboarding. Office: Univ of Colo 1420 Austin Bluffs Pkwy PO Box 7150 Colorado Springs CO 80933 Office Phone: 719-262-4083. Business E-Mail: ltesman@uccs.edu.

TESORI, JEANINE, composer; b. 1961; m. Michael Rafter; 1 child. Composer: (Broadway plays) How to Succeed in Business Without Really Trying, 1995, Violet, 1997, Dream, 1997, Twelfth Night, 1998 (Tony nom. best original musical score, 1999), Swing!, 1999, Thoroughly Modern Millie, 2002 (Tony nom. best original musical score, 2002), Caroline, or Change, 2004 (Tony nom. best original musical score, 2004, Drama Desk award best musical score, 2004, Obie award, 2004). Office: Eugene O'Neill Theatre 230 W 49th St New York NY 10019

TESREAU, CYNTHIA LYNN, elementary school educator; b. Jackson, Tenn., Apr. 29, 1960; d. Dewitt Talmadge and Brenda Lynn Coppedge; m. Kevin Paul Tesreau, Mar. 29, 1997; children: Kristen Lynn Burrage, Nick Lee Burrage. BS in Elem. Edn., U. of Houston, 1983; MA in Tchg., Cumberland U., Lebanon, Tenn., 2001. Cert. tchr., adminstr. Tenn., Administration Tenn., 2005. Tchr. Spring Br. Ind. Sch. Dist., Houston, 1984—87, Shelby County Schs., Memphis, 1987—. Women's ensemble leader Trinity Bapt. Ch., Memphis, 2003—06, women's mininstry team mem., 2003—06. Named Tchr. of Yr., Chimneyrock Elem. Sch., 2005, Bailey Station Elem. Sch., 2006, Shelby County Schs., 2006; recipient, Patricia Ashcraft award for outstanding tchg., 2005. Mem.: NEA (assoc.), Tenn. Ednl. Assn. (assoc.), Shelby County Ednl. Assn. (assoc.), Pi Delta Kappa (assoc.), Pi Lambda Theta (life). Baptist. Avocations: needlepoint, quilting, water sports, travel. Office: Bailey Station Elementary 3435 Bailey Station Elementary Collierville TN 38017 Office Phone: 901-853-6380. E-mail: ctesreau@scsk12.org.

TESSENEER-STREET, SUSAN, photographer, artist, writer; b. Murray, Ky., Dec. 14, 1939; d. Ralph Athen and Susan Geneva (Kirkland) Tesseneer; m. Robert Beni Street Sr., Jan. 16, 1939 (div.); children: Robert Beni II, Ralph Calvin Sr. Student, Blue Mountain Coll. for Women, 1959—61, Memphis State U., 1963—66; BA, S.E. Mo. U., 1974; student, Harvard U., 2002. Tchr., 1974-79; bus. owner, 1977-85; writer, 1984-86; photographer, 1990—; artist, 1998—. Author: (book) Gift in Celebration of Women. Mem. Sikeston Art League, 1980—, pres., 1990-94; sec., treas., organizer Cmty. Concert, Sikeston, 1989. Mem. AAUW (charter), Profl. Photographers Am., Am. Soc. Portrait Artists, Hemingway Soc., Nat. Writers Club, Women in the Arts (charter), Am. Soc. Portrait Painters, Impressionist Soc., Nat. Writers Assn., Hemingway Soc., Nat. Assn. Women Writers, Nat. Women's History Mus. (charter).

TESTER-LAMAR, CYNTHIA COREYN, lawyer; b. San Gabriel, Calif., May 6, 1962; d. Robert Louis Tester and Rosalind Karen Lentz; m. Stephen C. LaMar, Oct. 11, 2005; children: Lucas Hunter Goettle, Hannah Collier Goettle, Mackenzie Taylor Goettle, Sarah Aileen Motsenbocker. BS in Internat. Fgn. Policy and Polit. Sci. magna cum laude, UCLA, 1989; JD, U. Denver, 1993. Bar: Colo. 1993, U.S. Dist. Ct. Colo. 1993, U.S. Ct. Appeals (10th cir.) 1993. Assoc. White & Steele, Denver, 1990—92, Greengard, Senter, Goldfarb & Rice, 1992—94, Nicholas McGrath PC, Aspen, Colo., 1994—95, Beattie & Chadwick, Glenwood Springs, 2000—04; ptnr. Leavenworth & Tester, Glenwood Springs, 1994—2000; sr. assoc. Garfield & Hecht, Glenwood Springs, 2005—06; mng. ptnr. Tester & Assocs., Snowmass Village, Colo., 2006—. Mem.: ATLA, Colo. Bar Assn. (litig. sect., mcpl. sect., real estate sect.), Colo. Trial Lawyers Assn. (award 1993), Pitkin County Bar Assn., Garfield County Bar Assn., Order St. Ives. Republican. Episcopalian. Avocations: skiing, hiking, motorcycling. Home: 233 Stellar Ln PO Box 5998 Snowmass Village CO 81615 Office: 25 Lower Woodbridge Rd Ste 201 PO Box 5998 Snowmass Village CO 81615 Office Phone: 970-923-0215. Business E-Mail: ctester@testerlawfirm.com.

TESTY, KELLYE, dean; BA cum laude, Ind. U., 1982; JD grad. minor in Women's Studies, Ind. U. Sch. Law, 1991. Clk. to Hon. Jesse E. Eschbach US Ct. Appeals (7th Cir.); prof. Seattle U. Sch. Law, 1992—, Patricia Wismer prof., 2001—03, dean, 2005—. Lectr. in field; co-founder Access to Justice Inst.; founding adv. Seattle Jour. Social Justice. Editor-in-chief Ind. Law Jour. John H. Edwards Fellow, Chancellor's Scholar. Mem.: Order Coif. Office: Seattle U Sch Law Office of Dean 901 12th Ave PO Box 222000 Seattle WA 98122-1090 Office Phone: 206-398-4309. E-mail: ktesty@seattleu.edu.

TESVICH, LISA KAY, industrial and organizational psychologist; b. New Orleans, July 21, 1965; d. Peter J. and Ann S. Tesvich; m. Rich Bonora. BA in Pers. Psychology, U. Calif., Santa Barbara, 1987; MS, Tulane U., 1992, PhD, 1994. Tchg. asst. Tulane U., New Orleans, 1989-94; assoc. Drake, Beam, Morin, New Orleans, 1992-94, Coopers & Lybrand, Chgo., 1994-95, cons., 1995-97; sr. cons. PricewaterhouseCoopers, Chgo., 1997—2002; assoc. prin. Buck Cons., 2002—. Mem. APA, Soc. for Human Resource Mgmt., Soc. Indsl./Orgnl. Psychology, Golden Key Honor Soc., Phi Beta Kappa. Avocations: travel, shopping, football, volleyball. Home: 2432 Oriole St New Orleans LA 70122-4338 E-mail: ltesvich@san.rr.com.

TETELMAN, ALICE FRAN, small business owner; b. NYC, Apr. 15, 1941; d. Harry and Leah (Markovitz) T.; m. Martin A. Wenick, Dec. 7, 1980. BA, Mt. Holyoke Coll., South Hadley, Mass., 1962. Rsch. and info. asst. Edn. and World Affairs, N.Y.C., 1963-67; legis. asst. U.S. Sen. Charles Goodell, Washington, 1968-70; land use and energy specialist Citizens Adv. Com. on Environ. Quality, Washington, 1973-74; sr. assoc. prog. mgr. Linton & Co., Washington, 1971-73, 75-76; pub policy cons. Washington, 1977-78; adminstrv. asst. U.S. Congressman Bill Green (N.Y.), Washington, 1978-81; cons. The Precious Legacy Project, Prague, Czechoslovakia, 1982-83; Rep. staff dir. Select Com. on Hunger, U.S. Ho. of Reps., Washington, 1984-85; dir. State of N.J. Washington Office, 1986-90; exec. dir. Coun. of Gov.'s Policy Advisors, Washington, 1991-94; dir. Washington Office, The City of N.Y., 1994-98. Pres. Italian Vacation Villas, Washington. Bd. dirs. Republican Women's Task Force, Nat. Women's Polit. Caucus, 1976-80, Women in Senate and House (WISH) List, 1998-2001. European Community grantee, 1975. Mem. Ripon Soc. (nat. exec. com. 1971-73). Office: Italian Vacation Villas PO Box 9586 Washington DC 20016-9586

TETER, PATRICIA ANN, librarian; b. Brookfield, Mo., Aug. 6, 1942; d. Marvin T. and Thelma L. Christy; m. Thomas Lee Teter, Apr. 21, 1962; children: Michelle Reiter, Shawn. BS in Edn., Truman State U., Kirksville, Mo., 1964; MLS, U. Mo., 1985. H.S. English tchr. Macon County R-1 Schs., Mo., 1964—66, Callao C-8 Sch., Mo., 1972—75; elem. sch. libr. Macon County R-1 Schs., Mo., 1979—82; cataloger Truman State U., Kirksville, Mo., 1982—87, head bibliographic control, 1988—98, head tech. svcs. and systems, 1999—. Faculty senate Truman State U., Kirksville, Mo., 1992—96, North Ctrl. Assn. self-study steering com., 1994—96, planning workshop group leader, 1995, higher learning commn. self-study com. cons., 2003—04; chair Mo. Libr. Network Corp./OCLC Users Group, 1994—95; chair catalog design adv com. MOBIUS, Mo., 2000, users conf. planning com., Mo., 2003—05. Com. mem. Callao Harvest Fiesta, Mo., 1970—72; adult leader Callao Shamrock 4-H Club, 1979—82; Sunday sch. tchr., vacation Bible sch. leader, Bible bowl sponsor Callao Christian Ch., 1972—78; worthy matron Callao Chpt. No. 44, Order of Ea. Star, 1969. Mem.: Beta Phi Mu. Avocations: travel, genealogy. Home: 19581 Tamarack Tr Kirksville MO 63501 Office: Truman State Univ 100 E Normal Kirksville MO 63501

TETTEGAH, SHARON YVONNE, secondary school educator; b. Wichita Falls, Tex., Jan. 14, 1956; d. Lawrence Guice and Doris Jean (Leak) Oliver; 1 child, Tandra Ainsworth; m. Joseph Miller Zangai, Dec. 22, 1978 (div. 1983); 1 child, Tonia Monjay Zangai; m. George Tettegah, Apr. 28, 1989 (div. Sept. 2004); children: Nicole Jennifer, Michael Scott. AA, Coll. Alameda, 1985; BA, U. Calif., Davis, 1988, teaching cert., 1989, MA, 1991; PhD in Ednl. Psychology, U. Calif., Santa Barbara, 1997. Cert. elem. tchr., Calif., Online web-based tchg. and learning, Calif. State U., Hayward. Clk. II Alameda County Mcpl. Ct., Oakland, Calif., 1976-77; acct. clk. Alameda County Social Svcs., Oakland, 1977-78, eligibility technician, 1978-82; supervising clk. Alameda County Health Care Svcs., Oakland, 1982-84; tchr. Davis (Calif.) Joint Unified Sch. Dist., 1988-89, L.A. Unified Schs., L.A., 1990-92, Oakland Unified Sch. Dist., Oakland, 1992—, tchr. sci. mentor, 1993—; teaching asst. U. Calif., Santa Barbara, 1993-94; adminstrv. intern Oxnard Unified Sch. Dist., 1994, U. Calif. Cultural Awareness Program, Santa Barbara, 1994; rsch. cons. to vice chancellor students affairs, cons. tchr. edn. program, facilitor registrar's office U. Calif., Santa Barbara, 1995-96, rsch. asst. Grad. Sch. Edn., 1996—; asst. prof. tchr. edn. Calif. State U., Hayward, 1998—, cons. Cal Teach, Office of the Chancellor, 1999; asst. prof. U. Ill., Math, Sci. and Tech., Urbana Champaign, 2001—; faculty fellow Nt. Ctr. for Super Computing Applications, 2003—04, Bur. Ednl. Rsch, Coll. of Edn., U. Ill., Urbana Champaign, 2002—03, 2005—; mem. faculty ednl. psychology, divsn. cognitive sci. tchg. and learning and culture U. Ill., Urbana Champaign, 2005—, faculty affiliate Beckman Inst., 2005—. Cons. U. Calif., Davis, 1988-89, Montessori Ctr. Sch., Santa Barbara, Calif., 1996, Oakland-Hayward Sch. Partnership, Oakland, 1998-99, Cal Teach, Office of the Chancellor, 1999; multicultural cons. Davis Unified Sch. Dist., 1988-89; edn. cons. Ednl. Testing Svc., Emeryville, Calif., 1994; cons., dir., 2000—; chair diversity com. of Santa Barbara Village Charter Sch.; mem. academic senate com. undergrad enrollment and admissions U. Calif. Santa Barbara, 1995, tchr. cross-cultural interactions course, summer, 1995; mem. academic affairs affirmative action com. U. Calif. Santa Barbara, 1995-96, grad. sch. of edn., grad. affairs and affirmative action comms. U. Calif. Santa Barbara, 1995-96; rsch. cons. Oakland Unified Sch. Dist., 1998-99, African Am. Literacy and Culture Project, Oakland Pub. Schs., Oakland, 1998—; gubernatorial appointee to State Interagy. Coord. Coun., 1999—; chmn. Com. on Rsch., Calif. State U., 2000-01, mem. Academic Senate, Hayward; faculty Univ. Ill., Urbana-Champaign, 2001, v.p. Distance Edn. Soc. of Info. Tech. and Tchr. Edn., 2003-2004, mem. chancellor's ad hoc cybersecurity com., 2003—; faculty fellow Nat. Ctr. Supercomputing Applications, 2005—, Buf. Ednl. Rsch., 2005—; panel reviewer NSF, 2005-06; mem. editl. bd. Urban Edn. Sage Press, 2005—. Contbr. articles to profl. jours. Mem. U. Calif. Santa Barbara Acad. Senate Bd. Undergraduate Admissions and Records; co-chair Diversity Com. Montecito-Santa Barbara Charter Sch.; pres. African-Am. Grad. and Profl. Students Orgn., Davis, 1988-89; gubernatorial appointee State Interagy. Coordinating Coun., Calif., 1999; commissioned Calif. Policy Makers Inst. Health & Poverty, Lt. Gov., 2001; bd. dirs. YMCA, 2004—. Recipient Charlene Richardson Acad. Honors award Coll. Alameda, 1985, Faculty Rsch. Bd. award U. Ill., 2004, Rsch. Bd. award, 2003-2004, 2005-2006; Calif. State Acad. fellow, 1989-91, Grad. Opportunity Acad. Excellence fellow, 1994-95, Vice Chancellors Acad. Achievement fellowship U. Calif. Santa Barbara, 1995-96, Vice Chancellors Acad. Fellowship Grad. Divsn., 1995-96, 96-97. Mem. APA, Am. Ednl. Researchers Assn., Calif. Sci. Tchrs. Assn., Calif. Advocacy for Math and Sci., Calif. Tchrs. Assn., Calif. Media Libr. Educators Assn., PTA, Multicultural Curriculum Assn., Supervision and Curriculum Leadership Assn., Bay Area Sci. and Tech. Educators Corsortium, Pan-African Students Assn., U. Ill. Urbana Champaign Acad. Senate, Media Psychology Am. Psychological Assn., Assn. of Computing Machinery, Am. Sociological Assn., Info. and Communications, Inernat. Soc. for Tech. in Edn., Spl. Interest Group, Kappa Delta Pi. Avocations: travel, reading, preparing gourmet foods, tennis. Office: U Calif Santa Barbara Sch Edn/Ednl Psychology Santa Barbara CA 93106 Office Phone: 217-265-6206. Business E-Mail: stettega@uiuc.edu.

TEZANOS-PINTO, ROSA, Hispanic American literature educator; d. Alfredo Tezanos Pinto and Enriqueta Otiniano Tezanos Pinto; m. Jose L. Vargas Vila, Aug. 6, 1993; children: Sebastian Martin Valverde, Isabel Maria Valverde. BA, U. Miami, 1979, MA, 1994, PhD, 2002. Cons. and test evaluator U. Fla., Tampa, 1985—99; pres. Sigma Delta Pi, Miami, 1988—91; coord. symposia Michel de Certeau Ctr. for Critical Studies, Coral Gables, Fla., 1990—92; lectr. U. Miami, Coral Gables, 1992—99; dir. John Adams Pub. Co., Coral Gables, 1994—97; prof. of hispanic Am. lit. Lebanon Valley Coll., Annville, Pa., 1999—; dir. Alroquema Pub., Miami, 1999—; coord. youth scholars program in Spanish Lebanon Valley Coll., Annville, 2000—, advisor Spanish club, 2001—, advisor Spanish majors and minors, open majors, 2001—; dir. Asociación de Poetas de América, Buenos Aires, 2000—; coord., meeting hispanic authors program Lebanon Valley Coll., Annville, 2001—; advisor Nat. Assn. of Fellowships Advisors, 2002—. Rschr. Alroquema Pub. Co., Miami, 2003—. Editor: Redimiendo la Infancia en la estructura poética, 2004, Nation and Narration in The LUSO - Hispanic World, 2005. Recipient Jayanca Disting. Visitor Diploma, Chiclayo, Peru, 2002, Comodoro Rivadavia Book Fair Plaque, Comodoro Rivadavia Book Fair (Argentina), 2001; Profl. grant, Lebanon Valley Coll., 2001—03. Mem.: Latin Am. Inst. Pa. (pres.), Assn. Cervantistas, Colloquium Com., Diversity Adv. Com., Círculo Panamericano, Instituto Literario y Cultural Hispánico, Casa del Poeta del Perú, Am. Assn. of Teachers of Spanish and Portuguese, Nat. Assn. of Fellowships Advisors, Grad. Fellowship Com., Sigma Delta Pi, Phi Sigma Iota. Achievements include research in the relationship in form and practice of poetic language and the Freudian psychoanalytic language; the hidden text of Infancy in the Poetic works of Ester de Izaguirre and Loreina Santos Silva and testimonial literature; publications in the USA, France, Spain, Argentina, Peru, Paraguay, Brazil, Puerto Rico, India, etc; presented papers at USA, Chile, Venezuela, Guatemala, Puerto Rico, Australia, Peru, Colombia, Paraguay, Argentina, Spain, France, India, Mexico and Brazil. Office: Lebanon Valley College 101 North College Ave Annville PA 17003 Office Phone: 717-867-6257. E-mail: tezanos@lvc.edu.

THACHER, BARBARA BURRALL, psychologist, educator; b. N.Y.C., May 17, 1943; d. Thomas and Barbara (Auchincloss) T.; m. David Lewis Plimpton, Sept. 17, 1977; children: Sarah Thacher, Elizabeth Anne. AB magna cum laude, Bryn Mawr Coll., 1965; postgrad., Bank State Coll. Edn., 1967; PhD in Clin. Psychology, CUNY, 1981. Lic. psychologist, N.Y. Tchr. Fieldston Lower Sch., Bronx, N.Y., 1967-74; psychology intern Bronx Mcpl. Hosp. Ctr.-Albert Einstein Coll. Medicine, 1977-79; supervising psychologist dept. child and adolescent psychiatry St. Lukes-Roosevelt Hosp., N.Y.C., 1981-88; pvt. practice Bklyn., 1982—; instr. dept. psychiatry Sch. Medicine Columbia U., N.Y.C., 1984-93; adj. supr. doctoral program in clin. psychology CUNY, 1988—. Fulbright fellow (Rome), 1965-66. Mem. APA, Orton Dyslexia Soc. Democrat. Office: 26 Court St Ste 2700 Brooklyn NY 11242-1127

THACHER, MARY MCGRATH, historian, genealogist; b. N.Y.C., Dec. 20, 1933; d. Raymond Dyer McGrath and Anne Creveling Serre; m. Peter Shaw Thacher, Mar. 4, 1957 (dec.); children: Anne Creveling Thacher Tate, Linda Shaw Thacher Visscher, Peter Shaw Thacher Jr. BA, Bryn Mawr Coll., 1954; diploma, Ecole Superieure des Arts Visuels, Geneva, 1978. Avocations: photography, printmaking. Home: 54 Gold St Stonington CT 06378

THACKER, STACY LEIGH, psychologist; b. Chicopee Falls, Oct. 4, 1967; BA, U. Calif., Irvine, 1989; MS, Colo. State U., Ft. Collins, 1995, PhD, 1997. Lic. psychologist State of Calif. Staff psychologist Atascadero (Calif.) State Hosp., 1997—2001, sr. psychologist, 2001—. Vol. Amigos de las Americas, Dominican Republic, 1984—85; bd. dirs. Habitat for Humanity, Orange County, Calif., 1989—92. Mem.: APA, Calif. Psychol. Assn. Avocations: water-skiing, swimming, bicycling, running, snow skiing. Office: Atascadero State Hosp PO Box 7001 Atascadero CA 93423

THACKER-ESTRADA, ELIZABETH LORELEI, librarian, historian; b. Burbank, Calif., Nov. 29, 1957; d. Ernest Wichman and Mariam Lorelei (Ihrig) Thacker; m. Hedwing José Estrada, Nov. 29, 1997. BA summa cum laude, U. Calif., Santa Barbara, 1979; M in Libr. and Info. Studies, U. Calif., Berkeley, 1986. Part-time reference libr. Advanced Info. Mgmt., Mountain View, Calif., 1987—93; head libr. Inst. Transpersonal Psychology, Menlo Park, Calif., 1988—90; part-time faculty Foothill Coll., Los Altos Hills, Calif., 1990; interim campus libr. San Jose (Calif.) State U., Salinas, 1991, part-time reference libr. San Jose, 1994; reference libr. San Francisco (Calif.) Pub. Libr., 1993—95, collection devel. libr., 1995—2000, unit mgr., 2000—02, spl. projects mgr., 2002—04, govt. info. ctr. dir., 2004—. Editl. bd. mem., cons. Nat. First Ladies Libr., Canton, Ohio, 2003—. Mem. editl. bd.: White House Studies; contbr. chpts. to books, encycs., articles to profl. jours. Chair missions and social outreach team Burlingame (Calif.) United Meth. Ch., 2003—. H. W. Wilson Found. scholar, U. Calif., Berkeley, 1985. Mem.: ALA, Inst. Hist. Study, Western Social Sci. Assn. (conf. panelist 2000—02), Govt. Docs. Round Table, Libr. History Round Table, Am. Hist. Assn., Sch. Info. Mgmt. and Systems Alumni Assn. (life), Calif. Alumni Assn. (life), Sierra Club (life), Mortar Bd. / Pi Sigma Alpha (life). Democrat. Methodist. Office: San Francisco Public Library 100 Larkin St San Francisco CA 94102-4733 Office Phone: 415-557-4201. Office Fax: 415-557-4475. Business E-Mail: ethacker@sfpl.org.

THALER, LINDA KAPLAN, advertising executive; m. Fred Thaler; children: Michael, Emily. BA magna cum laude, CCNY, MA in music. Former music instr. CCNY; with J. Walter Thompson, most recently as exec. v.p., exec. group creative dir.; exec. v.p., exec. creative dir. Wells Rich Greene BDDP, 1994—97; founder, CEO, chief creative officer Kaplan Thaler Group Ltd., NYC, 1997—. Former mem. comedy improv troupe. Author: (jingle) I Don't Want to Grow Up, I'm a Toys 'R' Us Kid, Eastman Kodak-Because Time Goes By, (book) BANG! Getting Your Message Head in a Noisy World, 2003. Named Advertising Women of Yr., Advertising Women of NY, 2001; recipient 13 Clio awards. Office: Kaplan Thaler Group Ltd 825 Eighth Ave - 34Fl New York NY 10019-7498 Office Phone: 212-474-5000. Office Fax: 212-474-5702. E-mail: kaplanthalergroup@kaplanthaler.com.

THALER-DEMERS, DEBRA, clinical nurse; b. Glen Ridge, N.J., Oct. 12, 1954; d. Aaron and Ida (Bederman) Thaler; children: Joshua DeMers, Gabrielle DeMers. AB, U. Calif., Berkeley, 1976; BSN magna cum laude, San Jose State U., 1991. RN; cert. oncology nurse, pain resource nurse; bd. registered pub. health nurse, Calif. Staff nurse oncology Good Samaritan Regional Cancer Ctr., San Jose, Calif., 1992—2001; staff nurse hematology-oncology Peterson Cancer Ctr., Stanford Hosp. and Clinics, 2001—; lectr. San Jose State U., 1996—2002. Pres. Cancer ACCESS, San Jose, 1996—, instr. Oncology Nursing Soc., 1995—. Co-Author: The Cancer Survival Toolbox (audio tape set, resource book), 1997; contbg author: Oncology Nursing Secrets, 1998, Building a Legacy: Voices of Oncology Nurses, 1996, Imperatives for Qualtity Care: Access, Advocacy, Action and Accountability, 1996, Teamwork, 1998, Men's Cancers, 2000. Consumer rep. Nat. Cancer Inst., 1999-. Named Cert. Nurse of 2005, Oncology Nursing Cert. Corp. Mem. Nat. Coalition for Cancer for Cancer Survivorship (bd. dirs., 1991-97; v.p., 1997—), Oncolgy Nursing Soc., Nat. Hospice Orgn., Nat. Cancer Inst., Cure for Lymphoma Found., Sigma Theta Tau. Avocations: opera, theater. Home: 2866 Sweetleaf Ct San Jose CA 95148 Business E-Mail: dthalerdemers@stanfordmed.org.

THALL, LETTY DERMAN, social services administrator; b. New Orleans, Jan. 6, 1947; d. Herbert and Mary Virginia (Coughlin) Derman; m. Bruce Louis Thall, June 23, 1968; children: Gregory Coughlin, Mary Courtney. BA, Skidmore Coll., 1968; M.S.S., Bryn Mawr Coll., 1974. Trainer, cons. Bell Telephone Co., Phila., 1968-71; policewoman Phila. Police Dept., 1971; planning cons. Health and Welfare Coun., Phila., 1974-75; dir. WOAR, Phila., 1975-77; program coordinator Hall-Mercer Ctr., Phila., 1978-80; divsn. dir. and planner Community Services Planning Council, Phila., 1980-85; exec. dir. Delaware Valley Child Care Council, 1986—95; cons. Social Svcs. Agys., 1996-99; exec. dir. Children, Youth and Family Coun. Edn. Consortium, 1999-2002, regional dir. Pa. Coun., 1999-2002; v.p. Devel. Edn. Children for Parenting, 2003-04; dir. pub. policy Maternity Care Coalition, 2004—; pres. bd. CHOICE, 1977-80; alumni com. mem. Community Leadership Seminars, Phila., 1978-83. Coord. Shirley Chisholm for Pres., Miami, Fla., 1972; fin. dir. Bill Gray for Congress Com., Phila., 1978; co-chair Marion Tasco for City Commr., Phila., 1983; mem. Phila. Mayor's Commn. for Women, 1980-85, vice-chair., 1983-85; bd. dirs. City Parks Assn., 1986-89, Ctr. for Responsible Funding, 1987-2004; treas. Friends Phila. (Pa.) Free Libr., 2004—; sec., treas., 1990-92; bd. mem. Friends of Phila Free Libr., 2000–, Pa. Women's Campaign Fund, 2003--, v.p. S.E. chpt., 2005—. Mem. NASW, Mid Atlantic Assn. for Tng. and Counseling (trainer, group facilitator 1979-89), Women's Way (co-founder; bd. dirs. 1975-81), Assn. for Creative Change. Democrat. Office: 2000 Hamilton St Ste 205 Philadelphia PA 19130

THARNISH, ROSE MARIES LEHMAN, veterinarian; b. Greenville, Miss., Sept. 23, 1942; d. Isadore Hyman Lehman and Leatha Josephine Haynes; m. Robert Earley (div.); m. Larry Leslie Tharnish, Feb. 3, 1981. Student, N.W. Jr. Coll., Delta State U.; B, Memphis State U. N.Y.; JD, U. Tenn. Pres., owner Faith Ministry, Walls, Miss. Chmn. adv. bd. Rep. Nat. Com.; pres., bd. dirs. ACLU. Mem. Gardening Club, Audio Club, Book Club, Sierra Club, VFW, NAPCA. Avocation: scuba diving. Home: 5491 Adams Cir Walls MS 38680-8935

THARP, KAREN ANN, insurance agent; b. Montpelier, Ohio, Sept. 24, 1944; d. Howard Wesley and Thelma (Myers) Skiles; children: Pamela Lyn Tharp Grasso, James Alan, Jennifer Ann Tharp McCue. Grad. high sch., Edon, Ohio. Sales agt. Equitable Life, Delray Beach, Fla., 1978-79; owner, pres. Fin. Profiles, Inc., Coral Springs, Fla., 1980—. Mem. Nat. Assn. Life Underwriters, Million Dollar Round Table. Republican. Avocations: sewing, art, spa. Home: 7306 NW 127th Way Parkland FL 33076-1980 Address: 12472 W Atlantic Blvd Coral Springs FL 33071 Office Phone: 800-848-0222. Business E-Mail: karen@financialprofilesinc.com.

THARP, MARY THERESE, middle school educator; b. Englewood, NJ, Sept. 11, 1970; d. John J. Campbell and Eileen A. Kelly; m. Jade Vincent Tharp, May 26, 1996; children: Bailey Douglas, Bradey Colleen. BA, Curry Coll., 1992; MEd, Brenau U., 2002; EdS, Lincoln Meml. U., 2003. Tchr. St. John the Bapt. Sch., Hillsdale, NJ, 1992—93, East Hall Mid. Sch., Gainesville, Ga., 1999—2004; instructional lead tchr. South Hall Mid. Sch., 2004—. Mem.: Kappa Delta Pi. Avocations: dance, swimming, mothering. Office Phone: 770-532-4416. E-mail: mttharp@lycos.com.

THARP, TWYLA, dancer; b. Portland, Ind., July 1, 1941; m. Peter Young (div.); m. Robert Huot (div.); 1 child, Jesse Huot. Student, Pomona Coll.; BA in Art History, Barnard Coll., 1963; D of Performing Arts (hon.), Calif. Inst. Arts, 1978, Brown U., 1981, Bard Coll., 1981; LHD, Ind. U., 1987; DFA, Pomona Coll., 1987; studied with Richard Thomas, Merce Cunningham, Igor Schwezoff, Louis Mattox, Paul Taylor, Margaet Craske, Erick Hawkins. Dancer Paul Taylor Dance Co., 1963-65; freelance choreographer with own modern dance troupe and various other cos. including Joffrey Ballet and Am.

Ballet Theatre, 1965-87; founder, choreographer Twyla Tharp Dance Found., N.Y.C., 1965-87; artistic assoc., resident choreographer Am. Ballet Theatre, N.Y.C., 1987-91; teaching residencies various colls. and univs. including U. Mass., Oberlin Coll., Walker Art Ctr., Boston U. Choreographer White Oak Dance Project. Choreographer Tank Dive, 1965, Re-Moves, 1966, One Two Three, 1966, Forevermore, 1967, Generation, 1968, Medley, 1969, After Suite, 1969, Dancing in the Streets of London and Paris, 1969, The One Hundreds, 1970, The Fugue, 1970, The Bix Pieces, 1971, Eight Jelly Rolls, 1971, The Raggedy Dances, 1972, Deuce Coupe, 1973, As Time Goes By, 1974, Sue's Leg, 1975, Ocean's Motion, 1975, Push Comes to Shove, 1976, Once More Frank, 1976, Mud, 1977, Baker's Dozen, 1979, When We Were Very Young, 1980, Nine Sinatra Songs, 1982, The Catherine Wheel, 1982, Bach Partita, 1984, The Little Ballet, 1984, with Jerome Robbins Brahms Handel, 1988, At the Supermarket, 1984, In the Upper Room, 1987, Ballare, 1987, Stations of the Crossed, 1988, Everlast, 1989, Quartet, 1989, Bum's Rush, 1989, The Rules of the Game, 1990, Brief Fling, 1990, Grand Pas: Rhythm of the Saints, 1991, Deuce Coupe II, 1992, The Men's Piece, 1992, with Mikhail Baryshnikov Cutting Up, 1992—93, Demeter and Persephone, 1993, Waterbaby Bagatelles, 1994, Demeter and Persephone, 1994, Red, White & Blues, 1995, How Near Heaven, 1995, I Remember Clifford, 1995, Jump Start, 1995, Americans We, 1995, Movin' Out, 1998 (Touring Broadway awards, best choreography, 2005), The Times They Are A-Changin', 2006, (films) Hair, 1979, Ragtime, 1981, Amadeus, 1984, White Nights, 1985, Valmont, 1989, I'll Do Anything, 1994, video spls. Making Television Dance, 1977, CBS Cable Confessions of a Corner Maker, 1980, (Broadway plays) Sorrow Floats, 1985, Singin' in the Rain, 1985, TV Baryshnikov by Tharp, 1985 (Emmy award for Outstanding Choreography, 1985, Emmy award for Outstanding Writing of Classical Music/Dance Programming, 1985), The Catherine Wheel, 1982 (Emmy award nomination for Outstanding Choreography, 1982); author (autobiography): When Push Comes to Shove, 1982. Recipient Creative Arts award, Brandeis U., 1972, Dance Mag. award, 1981, Univ. Excellence medal, Columbia U., 1987, Lions of the Performing Arts award, N.Y. Pub. Libr., 1989, Samuel M. Scripps award, Am. Dance Festival, 1990; MacArthur Found. fellow, 1992.

THAXTON, JESSIE J., elementary school educator; d. Jesse Edwin and Rebecca Hutto Jordan; children: Kyle Rawls, Jordan Adams. BA, Coker Coll., 1974; M of Elem. Edn., U. S.C., 1990. Tchr. Timmerman Sch., Columbia, SC, 1974—78, 1982—86, Satchel Ford Elem. Sch., 1986—; cooperating tchr. Columbia Coll., 1995—. Mem.: NEA. Republican.

THAYER, CHRISTINA SIA, music educator; b. Indpls., Sept. 30, 1981; d. Thomas Lee and Aspasia Chris Thayer. MusB, Oberlin Coll., Ohio, 2003; MusM, U. Mich., Ann Arbor, 2005. Grad. student instr. U. Mich., Ann Arbor, 2003—05. Pres. Oberlin Music Coalition, 2002—03; presenter in field. Recipient Carol Nott Piano Pedagogy prize, Oberlin Conservatory, 2003, Young Performing Artist award, Yamaha Corp. Am., Bloomington, Normal, Ill., 2003; grantee scholarship, U. Mich., 2003—05. Mem.: Music Tchr.'s Nat. Assn. Home: 51 Canterbury Ln Belle Mead NJ 08502

THAYER, CYNTHIA A., farmer, writer; b. N.Y.C., Apr. 11, 1944; d. Charles Coll and Margaret M. (Mac Willie) Underwood; m. William H. Thayer, Feb. 23, 1937; children: Thomas, Robin. BA, Bridgewater (Mass.) State Coll., 1972. Cert. secondary English tchr. Owner, operator Darthia Farm, Gouldsboro, Maine; owner, operator weaving bus. Tch. Bridgewater and Raynhanm, Mass., 1972-76, Sumner Adult Edn., Sullivan, Maine. Tchr. Summer Adult Edn., Sullivan, Maine; author: Strong for Potatoes, 1998, A Certain Slant of Light, 2000, A Brief Lunacy, 2005. Pres. Schoodic Futures, Prospect Harbor, Maine, 1997-98. Author: Starong for Potatoes, 1998 (Discover award 1998). Mem. Maine Organic Farmers and Gardeners Assn. (bd. dirs.), Schoodic Pen C. of C. (pres. 1995-97), Maine Won't Discriminate, Directions-Crafts Orgn. (pres. 1990—). Avocations: bagpiping, spinning, reading, swimming, bookeeping. Home and Office: Box 520 Gouldsboro ME 04607

THAYER, EDNA LOUISE, health facility administrator; b. Madelia, Minn., May 21, 1936; d. Walter William Arthur and Hilda Engel Emily Ann (Geistfeld) Wilke; m. David LeRoy Thayer, Aug. 30, 1958; children: Scott, Tamara, Brenda. Diploma in nursing, Bethesda Luth., 1956; BS in Nursing Edn., U. Minn., 1960; MSN, Washington U., St. Louis, 1966; MS in Counseling, Mankato (Minn.) State U., 1972. Cert. nursing adminstr. advanced ANA. Nurse Bethesda Luth. Hosp., St. Paul, 1956-58, U. Minn. Hosp., Mpls., 1958; from nurse to asst. head nurse supr., edn. dir. Fairmont (Minn.) Community Hosp., 1959-63; instr. Alton (Ill.) Meml. Hosp., 1963-66; from nursing instr. to assoc. prof. and dean Sch. Nursing Mankato State U., 1966-77; asst. adminstr. Rice County Dist. One Hosp., Faribault, Minn., 1977-89; RN, adminstrv. supr. St. Peter (Minn.) Regional Treatment Ctr., 1990-96; spkr., 1996—. Nurse surveyor Minn. Dept. Tech. Edn., St. Paul, 1980-93; mem. adv. co. LPN and MA programs Tech. Inst., Faribault, 1977-2001. Co-author (with Mary Huntley and Linda Beer): Celebrating the First Fifty Years, 2003; co-author: (with Mary Huntley) A Mirthful Spirit: Embracing Laughter for Wellness, 2006. Mem. Rice County Ext. Bd., Faribault, 1986-91, adult leader 4-H Club, Rice County and St. Paul, 1971-97; advisor Med. Explorers, Faribault, 1977-89; mem. Rep. Rodosovich Health Com., Faribault, 1984-94; coun. mem. Our Savior's Luth. Ch., Faribault, 1984-87; mem. Rep. Boudreau Health Care Adv. Com., 1996-2001. Recipient alumni award Nat. 4-H Club, 1983, Disting. Friend of Nursing award Mankato State U., 1995. Mem. Minn. Orgn. Nurse Execs. (bd. dirs. 1987-89), Dist. F Nursing Svc. Adminstrs. (pres. 1980-82), Minn. Nurses Assn. (bd. dirs. 1982-87, Pres.'s award 1983, pres. 5th dist. 1974, 75, pres. 13th dist. 1984-86), AAUW, Sigma Theta Tau, Delta Kappa Gamma (pres. Pi chptr. 1982-84, Woman of Achievement award 1985), Hosp. Aux., Legion Aux. Republican. Avocations: crafts, volunteer work, theater, plays. Home: 7 Roots Beach Ln Elysian MN 56028-9731 Office Phone: 507-267-4588. Personal E-mail: dethayer@myclearwave.net.

THAYER, JANE HILLIS, psychologist; b. N.Y.C., June 17, 1930; d. Harold Lee and Ruth Evelyn (Caldwell) Hillis; m. Roger Eugene Thayer, June 16, 1951; children: Peggy, David, Cynthia. BA in Psychology, Cornell U., 1952; MA in Clin. Psychology, George Washington U., 1956, PhD in Clin. Psychology, 1969. Lic. psychologist, D.C. Intern in psychology St. Elizabeth's Hosp., Washington, 1965-66, intern in rsch., 1966-68; staff psychologist Alexandria Cmty. Mental Health Ctr., 1968-71, acting chief psychologist, 1969-70; pvt. practice Washington, 1971—96, Martha's Vineyard, 1999—. Cons. in field; pres. Gestalt Inst., Washington, 1973. Mem. APA, Sigma Xi, Psi Chi. Democrat.

THAYER, JOAN PEREGOY, ancient language educator; b. Bklyn., Mar. 7, 1938; d. Robert Elmer and Helen Bruce Peregoy; m. Edwin Cabot Thayer, June 24, 1961; children: Bruce, Laura, Richard, Will. BA in English and Latin cum laude, Bucknell U., Lewisburg, Pa., 1959; MA in English Lit., U. Pa., Phila., 1961. Cert. tchr. Va. Latin tchr. Thomas Williams Jr.H.S., Wyncote, Pa., 1960—61; Latin and English tchr. Hughes Mid. Sch., Reston, 1983—87; Latin tchr. South Lakes H.S., Reston, Va., 1987—92, Herndon H.S., Va., 2000—03, Fairfax County Pub. Sch., Herndon, 2003—06, Briar Woods H.S., Loudoun County, Va., 2006. Home: 11902 Triple Crown Rd Reston VA 20191-3016

THAYER, MARTHA ANN, small business owner; b. Santa Fe, N.Mex., May 8, 1936; d. Duren Howard and Lena Odessa (Fox) Shields; m. Norman S. Thayer Jr., Jan. 30, 1960; children: Murray Norman, Tanya Noelle. BS, U. N.Mex., 1960. Child welfare worker State of N.Mex., Farmington and Santa Fe, 1961-64; owner Baskets by Thayer, Albuquerque, 1975-83, Noelle's, Albuquerque, 1985-89; ptnr., co-owner Indian Originals, Albuquerque, 1989-94, Native Design, 1995-96; owner Martha A. Thayer, 1996-98; treas. DHS Properties, Inc., 1994—; agt. for Elizabeth Abeyta, Adrian Quintana, Alexandria Rohrscheib, Albuquerque, 1995—2001; owner Martha A. Thayer Enterprises L.L.P., 1998—2001; co-owner Shields Investments Enterprises L.L.P., 1998—2000; treas. DHS Property Inc., 1995—. Crafts instr. Village Wool, Continuing Edn., Albuquerque, 1975-78. Contbr. articles, revs. to craft publs.; juried show, Mus. of Internat. Folk Arts, 1975; baskets exhibited in group shows at N.Mex. State Fair, 1980 (1st place award), Women's Show, 1983 (1st place award). Campaign mgr. Dem. Candidate for State Supreme Ct., Bernalillo County, N.Mex., 1970; founding mem. Women's Polit. Caucus, Bernalillo County; chmn. Mother's March of Dimes, Bernalilto County, 1974; trustee Shields Trust, 1994-2005. Mem. Hist. Preservation Soc., Petroleum Club, Mus. Albuquerque (assoc.). Avocations: genealogy, gardening, anthropology, politics, antiques, native american art collector.

THAYER, NANCY J., artist, educator; BA with honors, Mich. State U., 1966, MA, 1971; MFA, Instituto Allende, Mexico, 1977. Instr. Coll. Creative Studies, Detroit, 1979—. Artist, CEO Archiforms, Franklin, Mich., 1978—; adj. asst. prof. U. Mich., Ann Arbor, 1994—2005. One-woman shows include Sch. Art Inst., Chgo., Saginaw Art Mus., Flint Inst. Arts, St. Peters Ch., NYC, 2003, exhibitions include Nancy Thayer New Work, Ruth Volid Gallery, Chgo., Detroit Inst. Arts, Belgian Cultural Ctr., Duren, Germany, Bergstrom-Mahler Mus., Neenah, Wis., Leopold-Hoesch Mus., Duren, Royal Palace Nat. Libr., Budapest, Birmingham Bloomfield Art Assn. (1st award, 1993), Galeria La Princesa, San Miguel, Mex., Sarasota Art Assn., Fla., Detroit Inst. Arts, Freeman Gallery, East Lansing, Mich., Novo Gallery, NYC. Bd. dirs. Interfaith Ptnrs. Nat. Conf. Cmty. and Justice, Detroit, 2006, First Ch. Christ, 1999—2001, chmn. bd. dirs., 2001; exec. bd. Internat. Assn. Hand Papermakers and Paper Artists, Germany, 1988—90; bd. dirs., adv., cons. Birmingham Cmty. Ho. Our Town Exhbn., Mich., 1998—2002; chmn. com. Detroit Artists Market, 1984—87; alumni bd. U. Mich. Sch. Art & Design, Ann Arbor, 1990—96; bd. rep. Cranbrook Mus. Art, Bloomfield Hills, 2003—06; bd. dirs. Saginaw Art Mus., 1974—76; artist in residence U. Southampton, NY, 1986—86. Grantee, Mich. Coun. Arts and Cultural Affairs, 1982—83, 1996—97. Office: Coll Creative Studies 201 E Kirby St Detroit MI 48202 Office Phone: 313-872-3118.

THEE, CYNTHIA URBAN, psychotherapist; b. Phila., Feb. 12, 1960; d. Francis Joseph Jr. and Barbara (Fierro) Urban; m. Michael Gerard Thee, Oct. 26, 1991; children: Michael, Chelsea, Julia, Janelle, Eric. BA in Econs., Georgetown U., 1982; MSW, Syracuse U., 1985. Lic. social worker, Pa. Asst. coord. recreation/socialization pilot program Sussex County (N.J.) Welfare Bd., 1984; family-based social worker Youth Svcs., Inc., Phila., 1985-87; family therapist Family Preservation Svcs., Hudson and Camden County, N.J., 1987-89; individual and family therapist CORA Svcs., Inc., Phila., 1989-90; asst. mgr. for EAP ACORN Psychol. Mgmt. Corp., Phila., 1990-91; pvt. practice psychotherapist Feasterville, Pa., 1991—. Pvt. clin. cons. Penn Valley Cons. Assn., Lansdale, Pa., 1991-92, Main Line Health Psychiat. Group, Ardmore, Pa., 1991-92, Starting Point of N.J., Westmont, 1991-92, ACORN Psychol. Mgmt. Corp., 1989-92. Counselor Mother Teresa's Home for the Destitute and Dying, Calcutta, India, 1982-83, Damien Leprosy Social Welfare Ctr., Bihar, India, 1982-83. Named to Citizen Ambassador Program, 1994, 98; recipient Commendation for Leadership, ARC, 1982, Outstanding Citizen award Twp. of Ogdensburg, 1974. Mem. NASW, Acad. Cert. Social Workers. Democrat. Roman Catholic. Avocations: gardening, painting, photography, music, biking. Home and Office: 1841 Buck Rd Feasterville Trevose PA 19053

THEISS, PATRICIA KELLEY, public health researcher, educator; b. Atlanta, Dec. 12, 1934; d. Charles Henry and Susie Carlota (Tate) Kelley; m. Erich Albert Theiss (div. Aug. 1996). BA, Wellesley Coll., 1956; MS, Howard U., 1958, Cert. in Secondary Edn., 1959. Rsch. asst. Armed Forces Inst. Pathology, Washington, 1959-61; heath edn. phone coord. Howard U. Cancer Ctr., Washington, 1977-81; program assoc. D.C. Lung Assn., Washington, 1981-85; co-project dir. Know Your Body Evaluation Project Georgetown U. Sch. Medicine, Washington, 1985-87; coord. minority health grant for cancer coalition Commn. Pub. Health, Washington, 1988-89, coord. data-based intervention rsch., 1989-93, protocol coord. immunization protocol NIH-DC initiative, 1994-97; pub. health advisor Dept. Health State Ctr. Health Stats. Inst. Minority Health Statistics Initiative, Washington, 1997—; coord. D.C. Healthy People 2010 Plan Initiative, 1998—; state contact U.S. Office Minority Health, Washington, 1999—. Mem. task force for substance abuse use Abuse Edn. for D.C. Pub. Schs., 1984-85; mem. Health Mothers/Health Babies Coalition, 1985-89. Contbr. articles to profl. jours. Chair health and welfare com. D.C. PTA, 1986-89; coord. AIDS awareness edn. State PTA, D.C., 1987-89. Recipient Cmty. Svc. award D.C. Assn. Health, Recreation and Dance, 1987. Mem. APHA, Met. Washington Pub. Health Assn. (pres. 1987-88). Democrat. Congregationalist. Avocations: painting, horseback riding. Home: 2501 Calvert St NW #902 Washington DC 20008 Office: DC Dept Health SCHS 825 N Capitol St NE Washington DC 20002-4210 E-mail: patricia.theiss@dc.gov.

THELEN, PHYLLIS B., artist; b. July 28, 1926; d. William James and Mildred Emison (Bonnell) Barnhill; m. Max, Jr. Thelen, Mar. 8, 1952; children: Nancy Rehkopf, Jane Greene, Max, William. BFA, Stephens Coll., Mo., 1946; BA, Conn. Coll., 1948; PhD (hon.), Dominican U., Calif., 2000. Student dir. Calif. state United World Federalists, San Francisco, 1948—50, nat. student dir. N.Y.C., 1950—51; fgn. travel agt. Calif. State Auto (AAA), San Francisco, 1951—52. Dir., pres. Marin Ballet, San Rafael, Calif., 1975—95, Artisan's, Mill Valley, Calif., 1993—95, Art Works Downtown, San Rafael, Calif., 1997—2006. Pres. Cultural Affairs Commn., San Rafael, Calif., 1995—99; gen. plan steering com. City of San Rafael, Calif., 2000—02; mem. Renaissance com. Marin County, Calif. Recipient Hall of Fame award, Woman's Comm., 2000. Avocations: events planner, art. Home: 200 Deer Valley Rd San Rafael CA 94901

THENHAUS, PAULETTE A., artist, writer; b. St. Louis, Mo., Nov. 8, 1948; d. Clarence Thenhaus. BA, Webster U., St. Louis, 1971; MFA, Southern Ill., Carbondale, 1987. Educator Branson Sch., Marin, Calif., 1979—83; writer Zephyr, Galesburg, Ill., 1993—; owner/sole proprietor Art Naturally, Galesburg, 1994—98; edcuator Carl Sandburg Coll., Galesburg, 2000—03; owner/artist Studio T, Galesburg, 2003—. Mem.: Galesburg Civic Art Ctr., Chgo. Artists Coalition. Avocation: photography. Office: Studio T 251 E Main St Galesburg IL 61401 Office Phone: 309-342-3547. Personal E-mail: plette1431@yahoo.com.

THEODORE, CRYSTAL, artist, retired educator; b. Greenville, S.C., July 27, 1917; d. James Voutsas and Florence Gertrude (Bell) T. AB magna cum laude, Winthrop Coll., 1938; MA, Columbia U., 1942, EdD, 1953; postgrad., U. Ga., 1947. Instr. art Winthrop Coll., 1938-43; prof. art, head dept. Huntingdon (Ala.) Coll., 1946-52, E. Tenn. State U., 1953-57, Madison Coll., 1967—68; vis. prof. art World Campus Afloat Chapman Coll., Calif., 1967; prof. art James Madison U., Harrisonburg, Va., 1968-83, prof. emeritus, 1983—. Contbr. articles to profl. jours.; paintings in regional and nat. art exhbns. Bd. dirs. Rockingham Fine Arts Assn., 1980—85, 1989, Citizens for the Downtown, 1989, Women's Coop. Coun. Harrisonburg and Rockingham County, 1976—79, Valley Coun. of the Arts, 1998—99, Shenandoah Coun. of the Arts, 1996—, pres., 1996—2002; founder OASIS Co-op Gallery, 2000. With USMC, 1944—46. Gen. Edn. Bd. of Rockefeller Found. fellow, 1952-53; recipient award Carnegie Found. Advancement of Tchg., 1947, 48, 49, 50; Ednl. Found. Program grantee AAUW, 1981-82; rsch. grantee Ednl. Radio and TV Ctr., 1956. Mem.: AAUW (cultural interests rep., nat. dir. 1980—82), Va. Mus., Va. Watercolor Soc., Mensa, Pi Lambda Theta, Eta Sigma Phi, Kappa Pi. Democrat. Lutheran. Home: 150 Bear Wallow Ln Harrisonburg VA 22802-0153

THEODOROPOULOS, CHRISTINE O., architecture educator; BS in Civil Engrng., Princeton U., 1979; MArch, Yale U., 1982. Registered arch., Calif., 1997; civil engr., Calif. Assoc. prof., dept. head dept. arch. U. Oreg., Eugene. Office: Dept Arch 210 Lawrence Hall 1206 Univ Oreg Eugene OR 97403-1206

THERIOT, JULIE, microbiologist, medical educator; BS, MIT, 1988; PhD in Cell Biology, U. Calif. San Francisco, 1993; predoctoral fellow, Howard Hughes Med. Inst., 1988—93; fellow, Whitehead Inst.for Biomedical Rsch., 1993—97. Asst. prof., biochemistry, microbiology and immunology Stanford U. Sch. Medicine, Calif., 1997—. Author: of numerous articles pub. in such acad. jour. as Nature, Proceedings of the Nat.l Acad. of Sci. USA, and Jour. of Cell Biology. Office: Theriot Lab Beckman Ctr Dept Biochemistry Stanford Univ Med Sch Stanford CA 94305*

THERIOT, LISA MARIE, social worker; b. St. Martinville, La., Apr. 18, 1964; d. Harry Pierre Theriot, Sr. and Jeanette Marie Theriot. BA in Psychology, U. Southwestern La., 1988; MSW, La. State U., 1991. LCSW. Psychotherapist Philip Rowden, M.D., Baton Rouge, 1991—92; home health med. social worker Capital Home Health, Baton Rouge, 1992—96; psychotherapist Leinweber & Assoc., Baton Rouge, 1995—97; home health med. social worker Profl. Healthcare Svcs., Baton Rouge, 1997—99; social svcs. dir. and recreational dir. St. James Pl., Baton Rouge, 1999—2000; med. social worker Our Lady of the Lake, Baton Rouge, 2000—01; clin. mgr. Profl. Healthcare Svcs., Hammond, La., 2001—. Mem.: NASW. Avocations: writing songs, playing guitar, gospel singing, woodworking, home theater. Office: Professional Healthcare Service PO Box 1336 Brusly LA 70719-1336

THERNSTROM, ABIGAIL, federal agency administrator, writer; b. NYC, Sept. 14, 1936; d. Ferdinand and Helen Mann; m. Stephan Thernstrom, Jan. 3, 1959; children: Melanie, Samuel. BA, Barnard Coll., N.Y.C., 1958; MA, Harvard U., 1961; PhD, 1975. Lectr. Harvard U., Cambridge, Mass., 1975-78; project dir. The Twentieth Century Fund, N.Y.C., 1981-86; vis. lectr. Harvard U., Cambridge, Mass., 1988-89, Boston Coll., 1990; stringer The Economist, London, 1988-92; adj. prof. Sch. Edn. Boston U., 1991—93; sr. fellow The Manhattan Inst., N.Y.C., 1993—. Domestic strategy group Aspen (Colo.) Inst., 1992-97; edn. policy com. Hudson Inst., 1994-97; bd. dirs. Inst. for Justice, Washington; adv. bd. Am. Friends the Inst. for Justice, London, 1993-2003; mem. Mass. State Bd. Edn., 1995—; commr. US Commn. on Civil Rights, 2001—, vice-chair, 2004—. Author: Whose Votes Count?: Affirmative Action and Minority Voting Rights, 1987, School Choice in Massachusetts, 1991; co-author: (with Stephan Thernstrom) America in Black and White: One Nation Indivisible, 1997, No Excuses: Closing the Racial Gap in Learning, 2003; editor: A Democracy Reader, 1992; co-editor: Beyond the Color Line: New Perspectives on Race and Ethnicity in America, 2002; contbr. articles to profl. jours. Mem. Citizen's Initiative on Race and Ethnicity, 1998—2002; vice chair U.S. Commn. on Civil Rights, 2004—; mem. bd. advisors U.S. Election Assistance Commn., 2006—. Recipient Anisfield Wolf Book award, 1987, Am. Bar Assn. cert. merit, 1988, Best Policy Book award Polit. Studies Orgn., 1987, Benchmark Book award Ctr. for Judicial Studies, 1987. Am. Polit. Sci. Assn. Home and Office: 1445 Massachusetts Ave Lexington MA 02420-3810 Office Phone: 781-861-7634. Business E-Mail: thernstr@fas.harvard.edu.

THERON, CHARLIZE, actress; b. Benoni, South Africa, Aug. 7, 1975; d. Charles and Gerda Theron. Studied dance, Joffrey Ballet, N.Y.C. TV and print ad representative for J'Adore perfume Christian Dior, 2004—. Actor: (films) Children of the Corn III, 1995, 2 Days in the Valley, 1996, That Thing You Do!, 1996, The Devil's Advocate, 1997, Trial and Error, 1997, Celebrity, 1998, Mighty Joe Young, 1998, The Astronaut's Wife, 1999, The Cider House Rules, 1999, Reindeer Games, 2000, The Yards, 2000, Men of Honor, 2000, The Legend of Bagger Vance, 2000, Sweet November, 2001, 15 Minutes, 2001, The Curse of the Jade Scorpion, 2001, Trapped, 2002, Waking Up in Reno, 2002, The Italian Job, 2003, (also prodr.) Monster, 2003 (Golden Globe for best dramatic actress, 2004, Screen Actors Guild Award for best actress, 2004, Acad. Award for best actress, 2004), Head in the Clouds, 2004, North Country, 2005, Aeon Flux, 2005; (TV films) The Life and Death of Peter Sellers, 2004, Hollywood Confidential, 1997, (guest appearance): (TV series) Arrested Development, 2005—. Named one of 50 Most Beautiful People, People Mag., 2000; recipient Best Performance by a Human-Female (In Aeon Flux), Spike TV Video Game awards, 2005, Spirit of Independence award, LA Film Festival, 2006. Address: United Talent Agy Ste 500 9560 Wilshire Blvd Beverly Hills CA 90212*

THEVENET, PATRICIA CONFREY, social studies educator; b. Norwich, Conn., Apr. 16, 1924; d. John George and Gertrude Pauline (Doolittle) Confrey; m. Rubén Thevenet, Dec. 15, 1945 (dec. Mar. 1983); chldren: Susanne, Gregory, Richard, R. James. BS, U. Conn., 1944; AM, U. Chgo., 1945; EdM, Columbia U., 1992, EdD, 1994. Cert. elem. tchr., N.J. Counselor testing and guidance U. Chgo., 1945; home economist Western Mass. Electric Co., Pittsfield, 1946; tchr. Unquowa Sch., Fairfield, Conn., 1950-53, Alpine (N.J.) Sch., 1968-86; program asst. soc. studies Tchrs. Coll. Columbia U., N.Y.C., 1987-93; ret., 1993. Historian Borough Northvale, N.J., 1987-94; participant summer seminar Smithsonian Instn., Washington, 1984. Del. 2d dist. rep. Town Mtg., Trumbull, Conn., 1954-56; pres., trustee Northvale Pub. Libr. Assn., 1957-63; trustee Northvale Bd. Edn., 1963-72, pres. Northvale Bd. Edn., 1969-70; exec. bd. dirs. Bergen County (N.J.) County Bds. Edn., 1965-72; mem. Evening Sch. Comm. No. Valley Regional Dist., Bergen County, 1976-83; trustee Voluntown Libr., 1997-2001. Mem. Voluntown Hist. Soc., Friends of Slater Mus., DAR. Home: 88 N Shore Rd # B Voluntown CT 06384-1719

THIBAUDEAU, MARY FRANCES, cultural organization administrator; b. Anaconda, Mont., Dec. 6, 1943; d. Frank Albert and Mary (May) T.; m. Alex W. Wells, Jr.; 1 child, Christopher. BA magna cum laude, U. Wash., Seattle, 1969. Therapist, counselor Thibaudeau and Assocs., Atlanta, 1976-88; chmn. Vietnam Reconciliation Bus. Group, Atlanta, 1988—. Cons. Ga. Vets. Leadership Program, Atlanta, 1994. Exec. prodr. (documentaries) Vietnam: POWs Return—The Final Healing, 2000, TET '68: Healing Wounds of War.30 Years After, 1998, TET Vietnam Reconciliation Documentary; co-author, editor (feature film screenplay) Perfume River, 2002. Exch. dir. Friendship Force Internat., Atlanta, 1993-94; co-founder, chmn. Tet Vietnam Reconciliation Found. for Internat. Healing/Friendship Ctr., 2002. Named Ga. Outstanding Citizen, Ga. Sec. State, 1994. Mem. Atlanta Vets. Assn. (hon.). Avocations: travel, reading, languages, hiking, photography. Home and Office: 800 Marshview Close Roswell GA 30076-3285

THIBIDEAU, CAROLYN C., musician, educator; d. Emery Spencer and Elizabeth Anne Cartwright; m. Robert James Thibideau, Dec. 28, 1958; children: Stephen Robert, Michael Charles, Richard Dayton, Peter John. BS, Oakland U., 1974; MusM, U. Mich., 1980. Cert. tchr. Mich., registered music educator Music Educators Nat. Conf. Music tchr. West Bloomfield (Mich.) Schs., 1975—2003. Organizing dir. Cmty. Music Series, Orchard Lake, Mich.; composer, arranger, conductor, performer organ, piano, trumpet. Music dir., organist 1st Presbyn. Ch., Pontiac, Mich., 1994—. Finalist Tchr. of the Yr., Mich. Dept. of Edn., 1992. Mem.: Am. Guild English Handbell Ringers (past Mich. chairperson, clinician, conductor, past Mich. chair, clinician, conductor, Nat. Exemplary Handbells in Edn. award 1992), Am. Guild Organists (assoc.; nat. conv. program com. 1980—86, bd. dirs. 1986—89, performer, mem. nat. conv. com. 1982—86). Avocations: music, opera. Office: Antioch Pub 8593 Cooley Lake Rd Commerce Township MI 48382 Personal E-mail: Carolynct1@Yahoo.com.

THIBIDEAU, REGINA, retail executive, social worker; b. Quincy, Mass., Sept. 18, 1943; d. Roy John Joseph Robicheau and Cora Drew Cross; m. Bruce Edward Maranda, Aug. 27, 1966 (div. June 1980); children: Hathaway Jakobsen, Kenseth Thibideau; m. Ronald William Joseph Thibideau, Sept. 24, 1984. BA, U. Vt., 1965; MEd, No. Ariz. U., 1998. Sec. clin. psychology office U. Mass., Amherst, 1966-67; social worker Mass. Dept. of Welfare, Amherst, 1967-69, East Boston, 1969-70, Quincy, Mass., 1971-73; CPR coord. Am. Heart Assn., Hyannis, Mass., 1978-80; child advocate Office for Children, Hyannis, 1980; owner, retailer Maggie O'Shaughnessy's, Sun City West, Ariz., 1983—2002. Facilitator Mercy Otis Warren Women's Ctr., Hyannis, 1980-81. Contbg. writer T.J. Reid's Newsletter, Amite, La., 1999; writer Maggie's Newsletter, Sun City West, 1996—2002. Organizer Mother's Day Celebration, 1999, 2000; mem. Litchfield Park Libr. Assn., 1985-98; vol. French tutor, Barnstable Middle Sch.; vol. Save Our Sound in Hyannis; cmty.

liaison vol. Elder Svcs. Cape Cod. Named Top 10 Boutiques in Ariz., Ariz. Woman mag., 1999, 2000, 2001, 02, One of Top Bus. in Ariz., 2000, 01, 02. Mem. AAUW, Sundome Merchants Assn. Avocations: travel, painting, computers, reading, walking.

THIBODEAU, VIRGINIA DURBIN, artist; b. Toledo, Ohio, Dec. 12, 1912; d. Charles Cleophas and May Gertrude (Stoeckle) Durbin; m. Robert E. Thibodeau, Aug. 10, 1935 (dec. Aug. 1983); children: Bernadette Judith, Joseph Henry. Student, Wayne State U., Detroit, Coll. Creative Studies, Cranbrook Acad. Arts, Bloomfield Hills, Mich., 1950. Comml. artist Toledo and Detroit Dept. Stores, 1930's and 40's; head art dept. Convents of the Sacred Heart, Grosse Pointe, Mich., 1950-69; artist in residence Grosse Pointe Acad., 1979—. Artist solo exhbns. including Toledo Mus. Art, 1945. Recipient art awards, Cannes, France, Nat. Miniature Show, Washington, Toledo Mus. Art, 1945-56, award Internat. Ecclesiastical Art Show, Detroit. Mem. Nat. Miniature Painters and Sculptors, Scarab Club, Women in the Arts, Grosse Pointe Artist Assn. (pres., awards 1949-92), Toledo Area Artists (juror 1956), Hilliard Soc. Roman Catholic. Home: 1729 Broadstone Rd Grosse Pointe Farms MI 48236-1948

THIBODEAUX, DARLA FAUL, gifted and talented educator; b. Crowley, La., July 29, 1963; m. Adam Paul Thibodeaux, Aug. 3, 1990; children: Victoria, Adam, Gavin. B in Gen. Studies, U. Southwestern La., Lafayette, 1988, BA in Elem. Edn., 1990; MEd, U. La., Lafayette, 2001. Elem. tchr. Acadia Parish Sch. Bd., Crowley, La., 1990—2000, tchr. gifted and talented, 2000—. Vol. Crowley Christian Care Ctr., La., 1995—96, Christmas in Apr., 2002; Bible sch. tchr. Immaculate Heart of Mary Ch., 2003. Grantee, Bell South, 1995, 2006. Mem.: La. Assn. Educators. Office: Acadia Parish Sch Bd 1102 S Parkerson Ave Crowley LA 70526 Office Phone: 337-783-1300. E-mail: dthibodeaux@acadia.k12.la.us.

THIBODEAUX, RUBY See PRIVAT, RUBY

THIEDE, ELENA M., elementary school educator; b. Staples, Minn., June 11, 1958; d. Alphonse P. and Elayne A. Welle; m. Robert D. Thiede, Sept. 2001; children: Nicholas P., Nathan E. AA, Ctrl. Lakes Coll., Brainerd, Minn., 1992; BS, St. Cloud State U., Minn., 1995; EdM, Graceland U., Lamoni, Iowa, 2005. Admissions sec. Brainerd Area Tech. Coll., 1977—78; sec. Morey Fish Co., Motley, Minn., 1978—80; math tchr. Staples Motley Mid. Sch., 1995—. Chmn. tech. com. Ind. Sch. Dist. 2170, Staples, 2005—, chmn. math curriculum com., 2002—04; jr. high knowledge bowl coach Staples Motley Mid. Sch., 1996—2002.

THIELE, GLORIA DAY, librarian, small business owner; b. L.A., Sept. 4, 1931; d. Russell Day Plummer and Dorothy Ruby (Day) Plummer Thi; m. Donald Edward Cools, June 13, 1953 (div.); children: Michael, Ramona, Naomi, Lawrence, Nancy, Rebecca, Eugene, Maria, Charles. MusB, Mt. St. Mary's Coll., L.A., 1953. Libr. asst. Anaheim (Calif.) Pub. Libr., 1970-73, head Biblioteca de la Comunidad, 1973-74, children's libr. asst., 1974-76, childre's br. specialist, 1976-78, children's libr., 1978-81; head children's svcs. SantaM Maria (Calif.) Pub. Libr., 1981-85; cons. Organizationsl Ch.-Sch. Libr., L.A., 1980; owner, founder Discovery Garden, Grass Valley, Calif., 1989-93. Guest lectr. children's lit. Allan Hancock Coll., Santa Maria, 1981-85; cons. children's libr. programs, 1986—; profl. storyteller, 1989—. Contbr. poems to Amherst Soc.'s Am. Poetry Ann., 1988. Libr. liaison Casa Amistad Cmty. Svc. Group, Anaheim, 1973-74; mem. outreach com. Santiago Libr. System, Orange County, 1973-74, mem. children's svcs. com., 1971-81; mem. Cmty. Svcs. Coord. Coun., Santa Maria, 1982-85; chair children's svcs. com. Black Gold Libr. System, 1983-84; Allegro Alliance vol. for music in mountains, 1994-98; vol. Oasis Sr. Ctr., 1998-2002; mem. steering com. Cmty. Svcs. Dist. Status, Orcutt, 1999-2002; rep. 4th supervisorial dist. adv. com. Santa Barbara County Libr., 1999-2002. Mem. So. Calif. Coun. Lit. for Children and Young People, Kiwanis (sec., publicity chair, newsletter editor 1996-98, sec. Orcutt 1999-2000, Central Coast Winds & Waves, 2000—, bd. dirs. 2000-2001), Orcutt Friends of Libr. (v.p. 1999-2000, pres. 2000), P.E.O. Sisterhood (rec. sec. chpt. VZ 2002-03), Delta Epsilon Sigma. Republican. Roman Catholic.

THIELE, MICHELLE RENEE, special education educator; b. New Haven, Ind., May 8, 1967; d. Larry Lee and Linda Louise (Heller) T. BS, St. Francis Coll., Ft. Wayne, Ind., 1990; M in Counselor Edn., Ind. U.-Purdue U. Ind., 1998. Cert. tchr., Ind. Tchr. Indpls. Pub. Schs., 1990—2000, Cen. Noble Mid. Sch., Albion, Ind., 2000—. Tutor Chpt. 1, Indpls., 1991-2000. Club sponsor Just Say No, Indpls., 1990-2000; leader Best Friends Program, Indpls., 1990-91. Mem. ASCD, Coun. for Exceptional Children. Lutheran. Avocation: sports. Office: Cen Noble Mid Sch 401 E Highland Indianapolis IN 46201 Home: 140 S 400 E Lagrange IN 46761-9507

THIEME, JEAN LOUISE, art association administrator; b. Greenville, Ohio, May 9, 1926; d. William Edward and Dorothy Coppock Hole; m. Walter Irving Thieme, June 18, 1948; foster children: Ilona Jekabsons Reif, Gracie Hill Ratliff children: Michael Alan, Rebecca Louise, Susan Kathleen. AB in Chemistry, U. Mich., Ann Arbor, 1947; cert. in mgmt., Radcliffe Coll., Cambridge, Mass., 1948; postgrad., Earlham Coll., Richmond, Ind. Trustee Migrant Health Bd., Greenville Ministerial Assn., Ohio, 1970—73; exec. dir. Migrant Health Clinic (later Family Health Svcs.), Greenville, 1973—81, Darke County Ctr. for the Arts, Greenville, 1982—90; trustee Ctr. for the Arts Bd., Jackson, Wyo., 1997—. Editor: This is Darke County, 1982. Organizer FISH emergency phone svc., 1975—; trustee The Brethren's Home, Greenville, 1982—90, H.O.P.E. Found. of Darke County, 1990—2002; bd. internat. studies U. Wyo., 2001—05; mem. design com. Downtown Greenville, Inc., 2001—06; trustee Offsquare Theatre Co., Jackson, 2006—. Recipient Citizenship award, VFW, Greenville, 1981, Svc. to Mankind award, Greenville Sertoma Club, 1984. Episcopalian. Avocations: family reunions, gardening, reading, travel, performing arts. Home: 3565 Hollansburg Sampson Rd Greenville OH 45331 also: PO Box 3858 Jackson WY 83001 E-mail: thieme@blissnet.com, thieme@wesnet.com.

THIES, JULIE ANN, music educator; b. Janesville, Wis., Apr. 28, 1960; d. Allen Junior and Marion Luella (Hoeft) Pudleiner; m. Thomas Earl Thies, Aug. 28, 1982. MusB cum laude, U. Wis., 1982. Instr. piano Suzuki Music Acad. Chgo., 1983-84, Suzuki Piano Studio, Hazel Crest, Ill., 1985—. Mem. Music Tchrs. Nat. Assn. (nat. cert.), Suzuki Assn. of Ams., Ill. State Music Tchrs. Assn. (2nd v.p. membership 1995-99, rec. sec. 1993-95), South Suburban Music Tchrs. Assn. (pres. 1992-94, v.p. 1990-92, treas. 1988-90, Mem. of Yr. 1999). Avocations: bicycling, hiking, in-line skating. Home: 1825 Olive Rd Homewood IL 60430-2316 Office: Suzuki Piano Studio 3000 W 170th Pl Hazel Crest IL 60429-1174 E-mail: julie.thies@comcast.net.

THIES, LYNN WAPINSKI, elementary school educator; b. Pottsville, Pa., Aug. 11, 1946; d. Stanley Walter and Mary Etta (Stevens) Wapinski; m. Wynn Gerrard, June 14, 1969; children: Heather Anne, Kevin Leonard. BA in Edn., Assoc. Libr. Sci., U. S.C., 1968; MS in Curriculum and Instrn., Portland State U., 2000. Tchr. 5th grade Ft. Jackson Elem. Sch., SC, 1968-70; tchr. 4th and 5th grades Groner Elem. Sch., Scholls, Oreg., 1970-72; tchr. 1st grade Welches Elem., Oreg., 1980; tchr. 6th grade Sandy Elem. Sch. Dist. 46, Oreg., 1983-87, tchr. 3rd grade, 1987-94, tchr. mixed-age class, ages 7 and 8, 1994-96, 2nd grade tchr., 1996—98, 3rd grade tchr., 1998—2000; adj. prof. Concordia U., Portland, 2000—02. Mem. lang. arts curriculum com. Firwood Elem. Sch., Sandy Elem. Sch. Dist. 46, 1986-87, mem. 21st Century S.I.T.E. com., 1994-97, sci. curriculum com., 1995—; active Oreg. Consortium Quality Sci., Portland, 1985-87, Oreg. Cadre Quality Sci. Edn., Sandy, 1987-89, Sci. Curriculum Consortium, Sandy, 1989-92; Eisenhower chair Oreg. Trail Sch. Dist., 1997-1999. Leader, mem. Day Camp core staff Girl Scouts U.S., mem. hist. re-enactment group, vol. Columbia River Girl Scout coun., Portland, 1972-92; mem. Oreg. Dept. Edn. Eisenhower grantee, 1994, 95, 96, 97, Oregon Dept. Edn. Primary Math Project grantee, 1996-97. Mem. NEA, ASCD, Internat. Reading Assn., Oreg. State Tchrs. Assn., Oreg. Consortium for Quality in Sci. Edn., Oreg. Cadre for Assistance to Tchrs. Sci., Oreg. Sci. Tchrs. Assn., Clackamas County Sci. Tchrs. Assn., Barlow Trail Long Rifles. Democrat. Roman Catholic. Avocations: historical reinactment, percussion rifle competitions, historical memorabilia, research into american history. Home: 51956 E Terra Fern Dr Sandy OR 97055-6478

THIESFELDT, SHEILA M., artist, educator, small business owner; b. San Juan, San Juan, Puerto Rico, Aug. 14, 1973; d. Edmund Thiesfeldt and Margarita Gonzalez. BFA, Jersey City State Coll., Jersey City, New Jersey, 1998. Art tchr. Art Ctr. No. Nj, New Milford, NJ, 1998—2001; camp art dir. Overpeck Riding Acad., Leonia, NJ, 1998—2001, camp dir., 2002—, bus. owner after sch. art sch., 2001—. Exhibited in group shows, N.J., P.R. Established Equine Art program, Leonia, NJ. Avocations: skiing, horseback riding. Office: Overpeck Fine Art 40 Fort Lee Road Leonia NJ 07605 E-mail: start125@aol.com.

THILL, LINDA SUSAN, secondary school educator; b. Waukegan, Ill., Sept. 25, 1950; d. John Herbert Roos and Dorothy A. Hartwick; m. Keith Ronald Thill, June 28, 1975. BS in Music Edn. with distinction, U. Minn., 1972; MA in Music Edn., U. St. Thomas, 1996. Music specialist Moundsview Schs., New Brighton, Minn., 1972—75, Howard-Suamico Schs., Green Bay, Wis., 1976—89, Einstein Jr. High, Appleton, Wis., 1989—97, Ferber Elem., Appleton, 1990—2004; choral dir. East H.S., Appleton, 2004—. Handbell choir dir. Pilgrim Congl., Green Bay, 1985—2006; artistic dir. Green Bay Girl Choir, 1999—. Big sister Big Bro./Big Sister, Mpls., 1971—72. Tech. grantee, Mielke Found., 1992. Mem.: Am. Choral Dirs. Assn., Brown County Civic Music (exec. bd. 1988—2005, v.p. campaign 1990—2002, talent com. 1990—2005). Avocations: travel, decorating, collecting antique glass and ornaments. Home: 422 Silver Spring Dr Green Bay WI 54303 Office: Green Bay Girl Choir 1678 E Mason St Green Bay WI 54302

THILTGEN, CHRISTINE, law educator; ADN, San Joaquin Delta Coll., Stockton, Calif., 1970; JD, U. Pacific, Sacramento, 1984. Bar: Calif. 1985; RN Calif. Program coord., prof., legal assisting Am. River Coll., Sacramento, 1997—. Mem. Resource Rev. Bd., Stocklton, 1980; elected mem. San Joaquin Delta Coll., Stockton, 1992—96; mem., pres. San Joaquin Meml. Hosp.-Delta Coll. Nurses Alumni, Stockton, 1980—97. Office: American River Coll 4700 College Oak Dr Sacramento CA 95841 Office Phone: 916-484-8619. Business E-Mail: thiltgc@arc.losrios.edu.

THIMMIG, DIANA MARIE, lawyer; b. Germany, May 5, 1959; BA cum laude, John Carroll U., 1980; JD, Cleve. State U., 1982. Bar: Ohio 1983, U.S. Dist. Ct. (no. dist.) Ohio 1983, U.S. Ct. Appeals (6th cir.) 1983, U.S. Supreme Ct. 1983, U.S. Ct. Appeals (3d cir. 1996); cert. Am. Bankruptcy Bd. for Consumer and Bus. Bankruptcy. Ptnr. Roetzel & Andress, Cleve. Contbr. articles to profl. jours. Hon. consul of Germany, 1988—; trustee Geauga United Way Svcs. Coun., 1992-96, Altenheim, 1992-97, Internat. Svcs. Ctr., 1998-04; trustee Cuyahoga County Bar Assn., 1995-05, pres., 2005-06; trustee Legal Aid Soc., 1998-2006, pres., 2003-05. Mem. Women's City Club Cleve. (pres. 1995-97). Office: Roetzel & Andress 1375 East Ninth St One Cleveland Ctr Ninth Floor Cleveland OH 44114 Office Phone: 216-696-7078. Business E-Mail: dthimmig@ralaw.com.

THISTLETHWAITE, SUSAN BROOKS, religious organization administrator; BA, Smith Coll.; MDiv summa cum laude, Duke Div. Sch.; PhD, Duke Univ. Ordained minister United Ch. Christ, 1974—; former prof. theol. Chgo. Theol. Sem., former dir., PhD ctr., pres., 1999—. Translator two translations of Bible; leadership adv. com. Assn. of Theol. Schools, 2000—; adv. com. Lilly Endowment, 2000—; bd. dir. Medill Ctr. for Religion and the News Media, Northwestern Univ., 2001—. Author: Metaphors for the Contemporary Church, 1983, Sex, Race, and God: Christian Feminism in Black and White, 1989; co-author (with Rita Nakashima Brock): Casting Stones: Prostitution and Liberation in Asia and the US, 1996; co-author: (with Mary Potter Engel) Lift Every Voice: Constructing Christian Theologies from the Underside, 1998; contbg. editor: Adam, Eve and the Genome: The Human Genome Project and Theology, 2003; editorial bd.: Theology Today, 1993—. Named one of Chicago's Most Influential Women, Crain's Chicago Business mag., 2004. Office: Office of President Chgo Theol Seminary 5757 S Univ Ave Chicago IL 60637

THOMAS, AELICIA, lawyer; d. George Cannon and Grozielia Thomas. BA, Alcorn State U., Lorman, Miss; JD, U. Miss., Oxford; M Biblical Studies, Exodus Sch. Bible, Cleveland, Miss. Assoc. atty. Turnage Law Office, Cleveland, Pittman & Hopson, Clarksdale, Miss.; staff atty. North Miss. Rural Legal Svcs., Greenville; owner, mng. atty. Thomas Law Office, Cleveland. Bd. atty. Town of Gunnison, Gunnison, Miss., Town of Beulah, Miss., Town of Pace, Miss. Address: PO Box 912 Rosedale MS 38769

THOMAS, ANDREA B., food products executive; B, U. Utah; MBA, Brigham Young U., Provo, Utah. Dir., new product mktg. Pizza Hut, Inc.; v.p., retail mktg. and promotions, Fritos and Tostitos brands Frito-Lay, Inc., v.p., innovation; v.p. global chocolate Hershey Co., 2006—. Named one of 25 Masters of Innovation, BusinessWeek. Office: Hershey Co 100 Crystal A Dr Hershey PA 17033-0810*

THOMAS, ANGELA M., marketing professional; b. Quincy, Mass., Oct. 19; d. Robert and Beverly Thomas. BS in Comm., Suffolk U., Boston, 1985. Music dir. WCOZ Radio, Boston, 1981, WILD Radio, Boston, 1982—86; N.E. regional promotion mgr. MCA Records, N.Y.C., 1986—89; assoc. dir. product mktg. Columbia Records, N.Y.C., 1989—90, dir. product mktg./Def Jam Venture, 1990—92, sr. dir. product mktg., 1992—93; v.p. artist devel. Columbia Records, Sony Music, 1993—95; v.p. urban music Capitol Records, EMI Music Group, N.Y.C., 1995—96; sr. v.p. mktg. and artist devel. Island Records, Polygram, N.Y.C., 1996—99; v.p. mktg., artist devel. RCA Records, BMG, N.Y.C., 2000—01; pres. Prana Mktg., Englewood, NJ, 2001—. Expert witness Universal Music, N.Y.C., 2003—, Proskauer Rose, N.Y.C., 2003—. Bd. dirs. Seeking Harmony in Neighborhoods Every Day (SHINE), N.Y.C.

THOMAS, ANN VAN WYNEN, retired law educator; b. The Netherlands, May 27, 1919; arrived in U.S., 1921, naturalized, 1926; d. Cornelius and Cora Jacoba (Daansen) Van Wynen; m. A. J. Thomas, Jr., Sept. 10, 1948. AB with distinction, U. Rochester, 1940; JD, U. Tex., 1943; degree, So. Meth. U., 1952. U.S. fgn. svc. officer, Johannesburg, London, The Hague, The Netherlands, 1943-47; rsch. atty. Southwestern Legal Found. So. Meth. U. Sch. Law, Dallas, 1952-67, asst. prof. polit. sci., 1968-73, assoc. prof., 1973-76, prof., 1976-85, prof. emeritus, 1985—. Author: Communism versus International Law, 1953, Non-Intervention - The Law and Its Import in the Americas, 1956, OAS: The Organization of American States, 1962, International Legal Aspects of Civil War in Spain, 1936-1939, 1967, Legal Limitations on Chemical and Biological Weapons, 1970, The Concept of Aggression, 1972, An International Rule of Law - Problems and Prospects, 1974, Presidential War Making Power: Constitutional and International Law Aspects, 1981; author: (with A. J. Thomas, Jr.) International Treaties, 1950. Chmn. time capsule com. Grayson County Commn. Tex. Sesquicentennial, 1986—88; co-chmn. Grayson County Commn. Bicentennail U.S. Constn., 1988—93, Grayson County Commn. Millenium, 1997—; co-chmn. com. Grayson County Sesquicentennial, 1994—97. Recipient Am. medal, Nat. DAR, 1992. Mem.: Grayson County Bar Assn., Am. Soc. Internat. Law, Tex. Bar Assn. Home: Spaniel Hall 374 Coffee Cir Pottsboro TX 75076-3164

THOMAS, AUDREY CORBIN, music educator; b. Jacksonville, Fla., July 8, 1982; d. Alice Harding and Robert Boyce Thomas. Degree in music edn., James Madison U., Harrisonburg, Va., 2004. Choral dir. Va. Beach City Pub. Sch., Viriginia Beach, 2004—. Core soprano Va. Symphony Orch. Chorus, Norfolk, 2004—; chamber singer dir. Va. Children's Chorus, Norfolk, 2005—. Soprano sect. leader Freemason St. Bapt. Ch., Norfolk, 2006—. Mem.: MENC. Office Phone: 757-474-8555.

THOMAS, BARBARA L., not-for-profit executive; 2 children. With CBS. Named one of Most Influential Black Americans, Ebony mag., 2006. Mem.: Nat. Black MBA Assn. (life; pres. Boston Chpt., v.p. fin. and administrn., CFO, interim pres., CEO 2003—04, pres., CEO 2004—). Office: NBMBAA Ste 1400 180 N Michigan Ave Chicago IL 60601 Office Phone: 312-236-2622. Office Fax: 312-236-0990.*

THOMAS, BETTY, director, actress; b. St. Louis, July 24, 1948; BFA, Ohio U., 1969. Former sch. tchr.; co-star Hill St. Blues, from 1981. Joined Second City Workshop, Chgo.; appeared on Second City TV, 1984; appeared in after sch. spl. The Gift of Love, 1985, Prison of Children, 1986. Appeared in The Fun Factory game show, 1976; (TV films) Outside Chance, 1978, Nashville Grab, 1981, When Your Lover Leaves, 1983, The Late Shift, 1996 (Dirs. Guild Am. dramatic spl. award 1996); star TV series Hill Street Blues, 1981-87 (Emmy nominations 1981, 82, 83), (Emmy award, 1985); dir.: (TV) Hooperman, 1987, Doogie Howser, M.D., 1989, Mancuso, FBI, 1989, Shannon's Deal, 1990, Dream On: "For Peter's Sake" (Emmy award, Outstanding Individual Achievement in Directing in a Comedy Series, 1993), 1993, Parenthood, 1990, Sons and Daughters, 1991, On the Air, 1992, My Breast, 1994, Couples, 1994, The Late Shift, 1996, The Loop, 2006-; (films) Troop Beverly Hills, 1989, The Brady Bunch Movie, 1995, Private Parts, 1997, Doctor Dolittle, 1998, 28 Days, 2000, I Spy, 2002, R3, 2003, John Tucker Must Die, 2006; prodr.: Can't Hardly Wait, 1998, Surviving Christmas, 2004; exec. prodr. (films) Charlie's Angels, 2000, Guess Who, 2005, (TV films) Silicon Follies, 2001. Recipient Women in Film Crystal award, 2001.*

THOMAS, BEVERLY IRENE, special education educator, counseling administrator, educational diagnostician; b. Del Rio, Tex., Nov. 12, 1939; d. Clyde and Eve Whistler; m. James Thomas, Jan. 28, 1972; children: Kenneth (dec.), Wade, Robert, Darcy, Betty Kay, James III, Debra, Brenda, Michael. BM summa cum laude, Sul Ross State U., 1972, MEd, 1976, MEd in Counseling, 1992, MEd in Mid. Mgmt., 1996. Cert. music, elem. edn., music edn., learning disabilities, spl. edn. generic, ednl. diagnosis, ednl. counseling, spl. edn. counseling and mid. mgmt., anger resolution therapist; cert. correctional justice addictions profl. Tchr. Pecos-Barstow-Toyah Ind. Sch. Dist., 1974—92, 1999—2000; edn. diagnostician West Tex. State Sch., Tex. Youth Commn.; tchr. spl. edn. and enhanced 5th grade Pecos-Barstow-Toyah Ind. Sch. Dist., 1999-2000; youth counselor Tex. Workforce Ctr., Pecos, 2000; substance abuse counselor Reeves County Detention Ctr., 2001—. Gifted-talented coordinator 5th grade, Pecos-Barstow-Toyah Ind. Sch. Dist., 1999-2000. Mem. AAUW, ASCD, NEA, MENSA, Assn. for Children with Learning Disabilities (local sec. 1974), Tex. State Tchrs. Assn. (treas. 1991-94), Tex. Ednl. Diagnosticians Assn., Tex. Profl. Ednl. Diagnosticians, Reeves County Assn. of Children with Learning Disabilities, Nat. Coun. Tchrs. of Maths., Nat. Coun. Tchrs. English, Learning Disabilities Assn., Nat. Coun. for Geog. Edn., Learning Disabilities Assn., Tex., Coun. for Exceptional Children, Tex. Counseling Assn., Am. Correctional Assn., Alpha Chi, Kappa Delta Pi, Chi Sigma Iota. E-mail: beverlythomas@valornet.com.

THOMAS, BEVERLY T., education educator; d. James E. and Georgetta V. Taylor; 1 child, Matthew Thomas-Ives. MA in Human Resource Tng. and Devel., Webster U., Charleston, S.C., 1989. Lic. profl. counselor SC, 1999. Adj. instr. Trident Tech. Coll., Charleston, SC, 1995—, Charleston So. U., 2003—. Vol. Berkeley County Schs., Moncks Corner, SC, 2000—06; group facilitor Berkeley Bapt. Ch., Moncks Corner, 2006. Mem.: ARC (assoc.). Avocations: golf, camping, reading. Office Phone: 8438637900. Business E-Mail: bthomas@csuniv.edu.

THOMAS, CAROLE LESNIAK, retired music educator; d. Stanley Joseph and Mae Ann Lesniak; m. Dennis Michael Thomas, Sept. 9, 1978; 1 child, Barbara Anne Kopp. BS in Edn., No. Ill. U., 1964; MusM, U. Ill., 1966, MS in Music Edn., 1968. Cert. music tchr. Music Tchrs. Nat. Assn. Music edn. specialist Kenwood Elem. Sch., Champaign, Ill., 1967—68; music instr. U. Ill., Urbana, 1968—70; piano instr. U. Iowa, Iowa City, 1970—72, asst. prof. piano, 1972—77, assoc. prof. piano, 1977—2002, emerita assoc. prof., 2002—. Head piano Sch. Music U. Iowa, 1992—2000; performer, presenter Nat. Conventions Music Tchrs. Nat. Assn., Denver, NYC, Little Rock, Ark., DC, 1975—94. Grantee Iowa Arts Coun. Grant, 1986—87, 1991—94. Mem.: Music Tchrs. Nat. Assn. (chmn. West Ctrl. Divsn. Collegiate Artist Auditions 1975—77), Iowa Music Tchrs. Assn. (state group piano chmn. 1978—91, pres. East Ctrl. Assn. 1991—93, chair state convs.), Iowa Fedn. Music Clubs (adv. bd. 2003—), Pi Kappa Lambda (chpt. pres. 1977—79), Sigma Alpha Iota (chpt. advisor 1972—, pres. Iowa City alumnae chpt. 2005—). Republican. Roman Catholic. Achievements include being active in the establishment of the Zeta Epsilon Chapter of Sigma Alpha Iota; participated in chartering the Iowa City Alumnae Chapter of Sigma Alpha in 1980. Avocations: reading, sewing, knitting. Home: 1614 13th St Coralville IA 52241 Business E-Mail: carole-thomas@uiowa.edu.

THOMAS, CHERRYL T., former federal agency administrator; b. Oct. 31, 1946; BS Biology & Chem., Marquette U.; MS Physiology, U. Illinois, Chicago. Dir., mgmt. services Dept. Aviation, 1983—89; dir., personnel policy & utilization Dept. Water, 1989—92; deputy chief of staff Mayor Richard M. Daley City of Chgo., 1992—94, commr. Dept. Bldgs., 1994-98, chmn. U.S. Railroad Retirement Bd., 1998—2003. Mem., bd. trustees U. Chgo., 2000—. Home: 5020 S Lake Shore Dr Apt 2716N Chicago IL 60615-3220

THOMAS, CLARA MCCANDLESS, retired literature educator; b. Strathroy, Ont., Can., May 22, 1919; d. Basil and Mabel (Sullivan) McCandless; m. Morley Keith Thomas, May 23, 1942; children: Stephen, John. BA, U. Western Ont., London, 1941, MA, 1944; PhD, U. Toronto, 1962; DLitt (hon.), York U., 1986, Trent U., 1991; LLD (hon.), Brock U., 1992. Instr. English U. Western Ont., London, 1947-61, U. Toronto, 1958-61; asst. prof. English York U., Toronto, 1961-68, prof., 1969-84, prof. emeritus, Librs. Can. Studies Rsch. fellow, 1984—; acad. adv. panel Social Scis. and Humanities Research Council, 1981-84; mem. Killam Awards Selection Bd., 1978-81; rsch. fellow York U. Librs. Can. Studies, 1984—. Author biography of Anna Jameson, 1967, of Egerton Ryerson, 1969, of Margaret Laurence, 1969, 75, (with John Lennox) of William Arthur Deacon, 1982; Literary criticism (Can.), 1946, 72, 94, Memoir, 1999; mem. editl. bd. Literary History of Can., 1980—, Collected Works of Northrop Frye, 1993—. Recipient Internat. Coun. of Can. Studies prize No. Telecom, 1989; grantee Can. Coun., 1967, 73, Social Sci. and Humanities Rsch. Coun. Can., 1978-80, Clara Thomas Archives and Spl. Collections, York U., 2005. Fellow Royal Soc. Can.; mem. Assn. Can. Univs., Tchrs. English (pres. 1971-72), Assn. Can. and Que. Lit., Bus. and Profl. Women's Club, Assn. for Can. Studies. New Democratic. Office: York U 305 Scott Libr 4700 Keele St North York ON Canada M3J 1P3 Office Phone: 416-736-2100 22374.

THOMAS, CLAUDIA LYNN, orthopedic surgeon; b. N.Y.C., Feb. 28, 1950; d. Charles Mitchell and Daisy Mae T; m. Maxwell Delaine Carty, Aug. 24, 1985. BA, Vassar Coll., 1971; MD, Johns Hopkins U., 1975. Diplomate Am. Bd. Orthopedic Surgery. Intern Yale-New Haven Hosp., 1975-76, resident in surgery, 1976-77, resident in orthopaedic surgery, 1977-80; orthopaedic trauma fellow Md. Inst. Emergency Med. Services Systems, Balt., 1980; asst. prof. orthopaedic surgery Johns Hopkins Hosp., 1981-85, Balt. City Hosp., 1981-85; mem. staff Children's Hosp., Provident Hosp. (both Balt.). Mem. AMA, Eastern Orthopaedic Assn., Yale Orthopaedic Assn., Newington Alumni Assn., Nat. Med. Assn., Monumental Med. Assn. (v.p. 1983-85), Johns Hopkins Minority Faculty Assn. (pres. 1983-85). Author: (with A.A. White, M.M. Panjabi) Clinical Biomechanics of the Spine, 1978; (with P. Leppert, E. Siff, C. Thomas) Being a Woman: Your Body and Birth Control, 1979. First black female orthopedic surgeon; contbr. articles to profl. jours. Democrat.

THOMAS, DEBI (DEBRA J. THOMAS), ice skater; b. Poughkeepsie, N.Y., Mar. 25, 1967; d. McKinley and Janice Thomas; m. Christopher Bequette, Nov. 1996; children: Christopher Jules II, Luc. BS, Stanford U.; MD, Northwestern U., 1997; grad., Charles R. Drew U., 2005. Competitive figure skater, 1976-88. Winner U.S. Figure Skating Championship, 1986, 88, World Figure Skating Championship, 1986, World Profl. Figure Skating Championship, 1988, 89, 91. Recipient Am. Black Achievement Award, Ebony mag., named Women Athlete of Yr., 1986; winner Bronze medal Olympic Games, 1988; named to U.S. Figure Skating Hall of Fame, San Jose Sports Hall of Fame. Address: Mentor Mgmt 5610 Town Center Dr # 5 Granger IN 46530-

THOMAS, DENISE M., chemistry educator, director; b. Lodi, Calif., Feb. 20, 1978; d. Ken and Eileen Nakawatase; m. Colin A. Thomas, June 18, 2005; 1 child, Phil. BS in Chemistry, U. Calif., Davis, 2000; M in Tchg., Johns Hopkins U., Balt., 2002. Sci. tchr. Carver Vo-Tech H.S., Balt., 2000—02; dir. edn. Sylvan Learning Ctr., Atlanta, 2002—03; sci. tchr. Chamlee Charter H.S., Atlanta, 2003—05; grant coord. Wichita State U., Kans., 2006—. Mem.: Nat. Sci. Tchrs. Assn. Avocation: scrapbooks.

THOMAS, DEONA LEE, music educator; b. Nashville, Dec. 15, 1955; d. Joseph Benjamin and Frances Lee (Gwaltney) Thomas. BMus in Edn., Belmont Coll., Nashville, 1978; MusM in Edn., Peabody Coll. Vanderbilt U., Nashville, 1980. Cert. tchr. Tenn., 1978. Pvt. practice tchr. music, Carthage, Tenn., 1982—2001. Dir. Women's Missionary Union, 1980—; coord. North Ctrl. Region Children's Bible Drill, 2000—. Mem.: DAR (historian Carey Fork chpt.), Am. Orff Schulwerk Assn., Am. Guild Organists, Am. Coll. Musicians, Hist. and Geneological Soc., Sigma Alpha Iota, Beta Sigma Phi. Baptist. Avocations: sewing, church activities. Home: 220 Jenkins Hill Rd Alexandria TN 37012

THOMAS, DORIS AMELIA, family practice nurse practitioner; b. Somerville, N.J., Sept. 6, 1933; RN, Martland Med. Ctr., 1954; AA, Thomas Edison State Coll., 1992. Pub. health nurse Ocean Co. Health Dept., Toms River, 1976—94; RN staff nurse Camp Tapanemus, Freehold, 2001; RN supr. Kensington Manor, Toms River, 2002—03. Founder and pastor St. Thomas AME Ch., 1980—2001. Author: Points of Excellence, 2002. Home: 1724 Fairfield St Toms River NJ 08757 Office: St Thomas AME Ch 285 Whitesville Rd Jackson NJ 08527

THOMAS, DOROTHY, indexing consultant, writer; b. N.Y.C., Mar. 3, 1923; d. Hyman and Clara (Lond) Fisch; student Hunter Coll., 1940-43; cert. N.Y. U. Sch. Bus., 1944; m. Sidney Thomashower, Sept. 2, 1944; children—William Jay, James Evan. Personnel troubleshooter W.P.B., 1943; employment mgr. Emerson Radio & Phonograph Corp., 1943-47; editor, author, 1947—; indexer, cons., N.Y.C., 1960—; biographer, lectr., radio producer and moderator; specialist in history of women in legal profession; dir. spl. projects Found. Continuing Legal Edn.; dir. Documentation Abstracts Inc., lectr. colls., clubs, orgns. Active legis. reform and women's movement; mem. Nat. Women's Polit. Caucus, NOW. Mem. AFTRA, Am. Soc. Indexers (pres. elect 1982-83, pres. 1983-84, dir.), Coalition of Labor Union Women, Friends of Columbia Libraries, Friends of Schlesinger Library of Harvard U., N.Y. Hist. Soc. Ind. Democrat. Club: Women's City (N.Y.C.). Author: Women Lawyers in the U.S., 1957; Women, The Bench and The Bar, in preparation; contbr. articles and biographies to Notable American Women, 1607-1950, 1971, Law Book Indexing, 1983; author: Wigmore on Evidence, Vol. XI, 1985, also other indexes and tables. Home and Office: 123 W 74th St New York NY 10023-2209

THOMAS, DYNDA A., lawyer; b. Springfield, Ill., 1959; BA magna cum laude, Miami U., 1982; JD, U. Cin., 1986. Bar: Ohio 1986. Ptnr. Squire, Sanders & Dempsey LLP, Cleve., co-chmn., Project Fin. Practice Group. Mem.: ABA (global infrastructure com., Pub. Utility, Comm. & Transp. Law Sect.), Cleve. Bar Assn. (Real Property, Probate & Trust Law Sect.). Office: Squire Sanders & Dempsey LLP 4900 Key Tower 127 Public Sq Cleveland OH 44114-1304 Office Phone: 216-479-8583. Office Fax: 216-479-8780. Business E-Mail: dthomas@ssd.com.

THOMAS, ELAINE FREEMAN, artist, educator; b. Cleve., July 21, 1923; d. Daniel Edquard and Ellen Douglas (Wilson) Freeman; m. Frederick Lindel Thomas, June 28, 1943 (dec. May 1969); children: Janet Thomas Sullen, Frederick L. III. BS, Tuskegee (Ala.) U., 1945; MA, NYU, 1949; postgrad., U. Paris, 1966, U. Poona, India, 1973, Columbia U., 1970. Fellow Northwestern U., Evanston, Ill., 1944; Rosenwald fellow Black Mountain (N.C.) Coll., 1945; faculty, art dept. chair Tuskegee U., 1945-89. Fellow Berea (Ky.) Coll., 1956, U. of Ams., Mexico City, 1956; curator George Washington Carver Mus., Tuskegee Inst., 1962-77; mem. Fulbright-Hays Faculty Rsch., Senegal and LaGambia, Africa, 1989; panelist expansion arts Nat. Endowment of Arts, Washington, 1977-79; fgn. svc. officer evaluator U.S. Dept. State, Washington, 1979; mem. exec. com. Ala. Coun. Arts, Montgomery, 1986-91; numerous TV appearances. One-woman exhbn. Hallmark Greeting Cards, Crown Ctr., Kansas City, Mo.; participant TV documentary, 1974, 77, 82, 85, 87, 91, 94; set up George Washington Carver Exhbn., White House. Chmn. nat. screening com. Fulbright Grad. Fellows in Design, Inst. Internat. Edn., N.Y.C. Named A Woman of Distinction, Auburn (Ala.) U., Ms. Sr. Am. of Ala., 1994, 1st runner up Ms. Sr. Am., 1994; recipient Disting. Svc. award U.S. Dept. Interior, Nat. Park Svc., Bicentennial award Pres. Gerald Ford, Resolution HR 274 award State of Ala. Ho. of Reps., Ms. Sr. Ala. award, 1994; named to 1995 Ala. Sr. Citizens Hall of Fame. Mem. Nat. Mus. of Women Artists, Optimists, Tau Beta Sigma, Delta Sigma Theta, Zeta Phi Beta (Woman of Yr. award 1978). Avocations: music, fashion, cross cultural consulting, retired senior volunteer. Home: 202 Rush Dr Tuskegee AL 36083-2707

THOMAS, ELIZABETH MARSHALL, writer; b. Boston, Sept. 13, 1931; d. Laurence K. and Lorna (McLean) Marshall; m. Stephen Thomas, 1956; children: Stephanie, Ramsay. Student, Smith Coll.; BA in English, Radliffe Coll., 1954. Writer, 1954—. Author: The Harmless People, 1959, Warrior Herdsmen, 1965, Reindeer Moon, 1987, The Animal Wife, 1990, The Hidden Life of Dogs, 1993, The Tribe of Tiger, 1994, Certain Poor Shepherds, 1998, The Social Lives of Dogs, 2000. Office: 80 E Mountain Rd Peterborough NH 03458-2318

THOMAS, ELLEN LOUISE, school system administrator; b. Doylestown, Pa., Nov. 30, 1940; d. Edward Martin and Evelyn Graham (Axenroth) Happ; m. Eugene Greene Leffever, June 30, 1963 (dec. Nov. 1978); children: Eugene Greene II, Jeanette Ellen Dellaripa; m. William Dewey Thomas, Sept. 15, 1981; 1 child, Jeremiah David. BA in Edn., Immaculata (Pa.) Coll., 1962; postgrad., Pa. State U., 1962-67. Pvt. practice tutor, Doylestown, 1958-65; tchr. Cen. Bucks Sch. System, Doylestown, 1962-65; adminstr. The Curiosity Shoppe, Doylestown, 1965—, The Toddler Ctr., Doylestown, 1979—; exec. dir. Camp Curiosity, Doylestown, 1984—, Thomas Lea Equestrian Ctr., Doylestown, 1988—. Tchr. trainer Confortunity of Christian Doctrine, Doylestown, 1965-78; cons. early childhood Am. Sch. in Hong Kong, 1981-84; lectr. in early childhood Bucks County Community Ctr., Newtown, Pa., 1978-90; workshop facilitator Head Start, Phila., 1990; cons. day care Cen. Bucks C. of C., Doylestown, 1989-90; ednl. coord. Forest Grove Presbyn. Ch., 1984-90. Mem. U.S. C. of C., Washington, Bucks County C. of C., Doylestown, Nat. Fedn. of Ind. Bus., Washington; children's ministry coord. Jesus Focus Ministry, 1995—; trainer Pa. Child Care, 1995—; past pres. Pa. Day Camp Assn., 1998-2001; Sunday sch. tchr. Hilltown Bapt. Ch., 1995-2000; mem. Am. Camping Assn., 1994-, Plumstead Christian Sch. Bd., 1995-2001; varsity tennis coach, Plumstead Christian Sch.-boys, 1998-, girls, 2001-; children's chmn. Central Bucks Village Fair, 2001-03; mem. Quality Child Care Coun., Pa. Keystone Stars; bd. dirs., ednl. chair Plumstead Christian Sch., 2002-05. Mem. ASCD, Assn. for Childhood Edn. Internat., United Pvt. Acad. Schs. Assn., Bucks County Assn. Edn. Young Children (pres. 1974-78). Office: The Curiosity Shoppe 4425 Landisville Rd Doylestown PA 18901-1134 E-mail: FaxThomdew@aol.com.

THOMAS, ENOLIA, nutritionist, educator; b. Little Rock, June 1, 1938; d. Calvin - and Bernice Thomas. BS, Lincoln U., Jefferson City, Mo., 1960. Hosp. dietician Dept. Health, Christiansted, Saint Croix, Virgin Islands, 1969—72; chief nutritionist Dept. Social Welfare, St Croix, Virgin Islands, 1972—83; hosp. dietician Vets Administrn., Kerrville, Tex., 1984—85; rsch. dietician King Fasial Specialist Hosp. and Rsch. Ctr., Riyadh, Saudi Arabia, 1985—96; nutritionist Denver Dept. Human Svcs., 1996—; host CC1 exchange student program; mgr. family properties. Contbr. articles to profl. jours. Vol. libr. docent Denver Pub. Libr., 1997—. Major USAF, 1960—69. Recipient Title 7 Older Americans Act/ Virgin Islands Elderly Nutrition Program, Commission On Aging, 1973 - 1983. Mem.: Nat. Assn. Commodity Supplemental Food Program (bd. dirs. 1999—2001), Am. Dietetic Assn., Stiles African Am. Heritage Ctr. (bd. dirs. 2001—04), Girl Scouts of Am. (life; troop leader 1962—83), Toastmasters Internat. (Toastmaster of the Yr. 1995), Alpha Kappa Alpha, Inc. (life; pres. 1978—82, Outstanding Woman in the Field of Nutrition). Home: 2298 S Kenton Way Aurora CO 80014 Office: Denver Food Assistance 1200 Federal Blvd Denver CO 80204-3221

THOMAS, ESTHER MERLENE, elementary and adult education educator; b. San Diego, Oct. 16, 1945; d. Merton Alfred and Nellie Lida (Von Pilz) T. AA with honors, Grossmont Coll., 1966; BA with honors, San Diego State U., 1969; MA, U. Redlands, 1977. Cert. elem. and adult edn. tchr.; cert. in crosscultural lang. and acad. devel., English lang. devel. Tchr. Cajon Valley Union Sch. Dist., El Cajon, 1969—; sci. fair coord. Flying Hills Sch. Tchr. Hopi and Navajo Native Americans, Ariz., Utah, 1964-74, Goose and Gander Nursery Sch., Lakeside, Calif., 1964-66; dir., supt. Bible and Sunday schs. various chs., Lakeside, 1961-87; mem. sci. com., math. coun. Cajon Valley Union Sch. Dist., 1990-91, libr. com., 1997-98. Author: Individualized Curriculum in the Affective Domain; co-author: Campbell County, The Treasured Years, 1990, Legends of the Lakeside; songwriter: songs Never Trouble Trouble, Old Glory, Jesus Is Our Lord, Daniel's Prayer, There Lay Jesus, God's Hands, Washing Machine Charlie, Playmates, The Kid in the Hall, Spring Time on the Blue Ridge, Christ's DNA, If You Need Me, Chances (Four Star award, 2003), Blame, The Star of Bethlehem, Where the Eagle Flies, Born to Win, Happy Birthday Dear Jesus, Christmas Lights, Walk the Line, You Don't Know What Repentance Is, I'm Asking You, Clear the Path Lord, Aqua Forte, In the Volume of the Book, Home is Where the Heart Is, You Don't Even Know Who I Am, No Place to Cry, To Walk With God, Ixnay, If You Never Loved Me, for Columbine Records Corp., Life of A Single Woman, Take This Pain Away, We Can Keep In Touch, Let Me Know, A Letter Is A Letter, The Battle, 2004; contbr. articles to profl. jours., newspapers, chpts. to books. Tem. U.S. Senatorial Club, Washington, 1984—, Conservative Caucus, Inc., Washington, 1988—, Ronald Reagan Presdl. Found., Ronald Reagan Rep. Ctr., 1988, Rep. Presdl. Citizen's Adv. Commn., 1989—, Rep. Platform Planning Com., Calif., 1992, at-large del. representing dist. #45, Lakeside, Calif., 1992, 1995—, Am. Security Coun., Washington, 1994, Congressman Hunter's Off Road Adv. Coun., El Cajon, Calif., 1994, Century Club, San Diego Rep. Century Club, 1995; mem. health articulation com. project AIDS, Cajon Valley Union Sch. Dist., 1988—, Recruit Depot Hist. Mus., San Diego, 1989, Citizen's Drug Free Am., Calif., 1989—, The Heritage Found., 1988—; charter mem. Marine Corps Mus.; life mem. San Diego Aerospace Mus.; mem. Lakeside Centennial Com., 1985-86; hon. mem. Rep. Presdl. Task Force, Washington, 1986; del. Calif. Rep. Senatorial Mid-Term Conv., Washington, 1994; mus. curator Lakeside Hist. Soc., 1992-93, life mem.; mem. Rep. Nat. Com., Washington, 2003 Recipient Outstanding Svc. award PTA, 1972-74, Outstanding Tchr. award KYXY Radio, San Diego, 1999, Dream Classroom award KSWB-TV, San Diego, 2005; recognized for various contbns. including Hats Off to Tchr. recognition for music Comdg. Post Gen., San Diego Bd. Edn., 1989. Mem. NRA, Tchrs. Assn., Calif. Tchrs. Assn., Cajon Valley Educators Assn. (faculty advisor, rep. 1980-82, 84-86, 87-88), Nat. Trust for Hist. Preservation, Christian Bus. and Profl. Women, Trust for Hist. Preservation, Nat. WWII Memml. (life, charter), Ridgecrest Golden Terrace Park Assn. (pres. 1998-99), Nashville Songwriters Assn., Capitol Hill Women's Club, Am. Ctr. for Law and Justice, Internat. Christian Women's Club (Christian amb. to Taiwan, Korea, 1974), Paul Revere Soc. Republican. Avocations: travel, vocal music, piano, guitar. Home: 13594 Hwy 8 # 3 Lakeside CA 92040-5235 Office: Flying Hills Elem Sch 1251 Finch St El Cajon CA 92020-1433

THOMAS, EVELYN B., agricultural products supplier; Sec., treas., bookkeeper Brandt Fertilizer, Pleasant Plains, Ill., 1953—; co-owner Har Brand, 1963-67, Brandt Chemical, 1967; sec./treas. Brandt Consolidated, Pleasant Plains, Ill. Office: Brandt Consolidated PO Box 350 Pleasant Plains IL 62677-0277 Fax: 217-626-1927. E-mail: bcadmin@brandtconsolidated.com.

THOMAS, HANNAH H., retired elementary school educator; b. Florence, Ala. d. Everett Napoleon and Evernee Hawkins; m. Monroe Thomas, June 11, 1945. BS, A&M U., Huntsville, Ala., 1951; MEd, U. Cin., 1964. Tchr. 4th, 5th and 6th grades Lauderdale Sch. Sys., Florence, 1948-55, tchr. sci. and biology, 1955-57, tchr. 4th and 5th grades, 1957-58; tchr. 4th, 5th and 6th grades Cin. Sch. Sys., 1958-74, remedial tchr. 4th, 5th and 6th grades, 1974-80; ret., 1980. Organizer, dir. Sojourner Truth Theater, Cin., 1985—, African-Am. Heritage Day, Cin., 1988—. Named Woman of Yr., Cin. Enquirer, 1992, Tchr. of Yr. Lauderdale County Tchr., 1956, Woman of Yr., Zeta Phi Beta, 1998, one of 200 Great Cincinnatians, Cin. Bicentennial, 1988. Mem. Harriet Beecher Stowe Hist.-Cultural Assn. (pres. 1980—), NAACP, AARP, CH Forum. Baptist. Avocation: reading writing poetry and songs. Home: 1059 Loiska Ln Cincinnati OH 45224-2731

THOMAS, HAZEL BEATRICE, state official; b. Franklin, Tenn. d. William Henry Fuller and Mattie Betty (Covington) Fuller Young; m. Charles B. Thomas (dec. 1969); children; Charles Bradford Jr., Deborah Carlotta (dec.). BA, Fisk U., 1946; MA, Tenn. State U., 1972. Cert. elem. and secondary tchr., Tenn. Tchr. elem. Met.-Nashville Sch., 1954—87; rsch. assoc. Johns Hopkins U., Balt., 1978—79, Marquette U., Milw., 1979—86; exec. asst. to commr. edn. Tenn. Dept. Edn., Nashville, 1987—. Cons. Peer Mediated Learning System, Nashville, 1980-82; instr. Met. Sch. Tchr. Ctr., Nasvhville, 1985-87; mem. tech. assistance team for high sch. that work, So. Regional Edn. Bd., 1998-99; nat. disseminator student team learning rsch. project, Johns Hopkins U., 1978-1979. Author training modules Substitute Teaching, Tchr. Aides. Pres. Davidson County Dem. Women, Nashville, 1985-87; v.p. Tenn. Fedn. Dem. Women, 1989-91, pres., 2001—; pres. elect Nashville Women's Polit. Caucus, 1991—; pres. Tenn. Women's Polit. Caucus, 1994-95; mem. adminstrv. com. of bd. Nat. Women's Polit. Caucus, 1993-95, v.p., 1995—, v.p. edn. and tng., 2001—; mem. Tenn. Leadership, Inc., 1992—; spkr., polit. trainer U.S. Info. Agy., Nairobi, Kenya, 1997; mem. exec. bd. Citizen's Com. for Ann. Gov.'s Prayer Breakfast, 1992—; mem. exec. com. Tenn. Dem. Party, 2001—; chmn. edn. com. Bellevue C. of C.; pres. Tenn. Fedn. Dem. Women, 2001-03; v.p. Nat. Fedn. Dem. Women, 2002-05, 3d v.p., 2005—; mem. pub. edn. and govt. com. Metro. Govt. Nashville, Tenn., 2002-03; apptd. to pub. ednl. and govtl. access oversight com. Nashville Mayor Purcell, 2003—; apptd. to pub. edn. govt. com. Metro Nashville City Coun., 2002 Recipient Svc. to Edn. and Teaching Profession award Nat. Coun. Negro Women, 1988; Nat. Def. Edn. Act scholar, 1965, 67. Mem. Am. Bus. Womens Assn. (charter), Tenn. Edn. Assn. (pres. dept. classroom tchr. 1974-75, state dept. affiliate, pres. 1988-Ed. c90), Bellevue C. of C. (bd. govs. 1990-91, edn. chair 2002-03), Assn. Classroom Tchrs. (pres. S.E. region 1975-76), Met. Nashville Edn. Assn. (exec. bd. 1971-77), Bellevue Sertoma Club (life, pres. 1990-91), Nat. Women's Polit. Caucus (v.p. 1995—), Nat. Assn. Dem. Women (v.p., 2003-05, named Woman of Distinction for Tenn., 2002, 03), Nat. Fedn. Dem. Women (v.p. 2003). Baptist. Avocations: reading, bridge. Office: Tenn Dept Edn Andrew Johnson Tower 710 James Robertson Pkwy Nashville TN 37243-1219 Office Phone: 615-532-5740. E-mail: hazel.thomas@state.tn.us.

THOMAS, HEIDI JANET KRUEGER, social studies educator; b. Davenport, Iowa, Mar. 19, 1972; d. L.J. Louis and Janet K Krueger; m. Brian Matthew Thomas, Aug. 23, 1997; children: Elizabeth J., Grace M., Marcella A. BS, Iowa State U., Ames, 1995; MS, St. Mary's U., Minn., 2002. Social studies tchr. Minnetonka H.S., Minn., 1996—. Bldg. leadership team Minnetonka H.S., 1997—99, mock trial coach, 1997—2003; social studies dist. chair Minnetonka Sch. Dist., 2003—05. Recipient Tchr. Who Made A Difference, Who's Who Among America's Tchr., 2000; grantee Tchr. Initiated Enrichment grantee, The Minnetonka Pub. Schs. Found., 2006—, 2005—06, Nick and Ann Duff Multicultural Fund grantee, 2004—05. Mem.: Nat. Coun. for Social Studies (assoc.), Am. Sociol. Assn. (assoc.), APA (assoc.). Office: Minnetonka High School 18301 Hwy 7 Minnetonka MN 55345 Office Phone: 952-401-5858. E-mail: hthomas@minnetonka.k12.mn.us.

THOMAS, HELEN AMELIA (MRS. DOUGLAS B. CORNELL), editor-in-chief, former White House correspondent; b. Winchester, Ky., Aug. 4, 1920; d. George and Mary (Thomas) T.; m. Douglas B. Cornell. BA, Wayne State U., 1942; BA in Law, Mount Vernon Coll., 1999; LHD, Wayne State U., 1974, U. Detroit, 1979; LLD, Ea. Mich. State U., 1972, Ferris State Coll., 1978; LLD (hon.), Brown U., 1986, St. Bonaventure U., 1988, Franklin Marshall U., 1989, No. Mich. U., 1989, Northeastern U., 1990, Skidmore Coll., 1992, Susquehanna U., 1993, Sage Coll., 1994, U. Mo., 1994, Franklin Coll., 1995, Mich. State U., 1996, Potsdam U., 1998, A. Willenberg Univ., 1999, Milliken U., 2002, Am. U. Beirut, 2003, Western Ky. U., 2005, Cabrini Coll., 2005; LittD, Ohio Dominican U., 2004. With United Press Radio, UPI, 1943-2000, wire svc. reporter Washington, 1943-74; White House corr. Washington, 1970; White House bur. chief UPI, Washington, 1974-2000; columnist Hearst Newspapers, 2000—. Author: Dateline White House, Front Row at the White House: My Life and Times, 1999, Thanks for the Memories Mr. President: Wit and Wisdom from the Front Row at the White House, 2002, Watchdogs of Democracy?: The Waning Washington Press Corps and How It Has Failed the Public, 2006; columnist Hearst Newspapers. Named one of the 25 Most Influential Women in Am., World Almanac; recipient Woman of Yr. in Comm. award, Ladies Home Jour., 1975, 4th Estate award, Nat. Press Club, 1984, Journalism award, U. Mo., Al Newharth award, 1990, Ralph McGill award, 1995, Lifetime award, Internat. Media Found., Internat. Women's Press Found., 1996, Lowell Thomas award, Marist Coll., 2001, Kahlil Gibran award, 2003, NOW award, 2003, Torch Bearer award, Planned Parenthood award, Physician Social Responsibility award, Utah Am. Women of Yr., 2004, Eleanor Roosevelt Legacy award, 2004, Lifetime Achievement award, Glamour mag. Mem. Women's Nat. Press Club (pres. 1959-60, William Allen White Journalism award), Am. Newspaper Women's Club (past v.p.), White House Corrs. Assn. (pres. 1976, Helen Thomas Lifetime Achievement award 1998), Nat. Newspaper Assn. (Lifetime award 2002), Gridiron Club (pres. 1993), Sigma Delta Chi (fellow, Hall of Fame), Delta Sigma Phi (hon.). Achievements include fighting hard for women's representation in the fields of journalism and politics, and in clubs and organizations where they had been excluded; the first women officer of the National Press Club, the White House Correspondents Association, and first women member of the Gridiron Club; entered into political reporting in 1961, when she began filing stories about the Kennedy administration. She has covered nine presidents; only woman print journalist to go on President Nixon's historic trip to China and traveled with presidents Ford, Carter, Reagan, Bush, Sr., Clinton, & Bush; first female White House chief of a wire service in 1974; considered the "dean of Washington press corps" and she was allowed to ask the first question at the presdl. conferences; referred to as "The First Lady of the Press"; at the end of her first presidential press conference in 1961, she said "Thank you, Mr. President", following a tradition, which recently ended in 2003; covered every presdl. econ. summit until 1999. Office: Hearst Corp 959 8th Ave New York NY 10019 Office Phone: 202-263-6437. Business E-Mail: helent@hearstdc.com.

THOMAS, JACQUELYN MAY, librarian; b. Mechanicsburg, Pa., Jan. 26, 1932; d. William John and Gladys Elizabeth (Warren) Harvey; m. David Edward Thomas, Aug. 28, 1954; children: Lesley J., Courtenay J., Hilary A. BA summa cum laude, Gettysburg Coll., 1954; student, U. N.C., 1969; MEd, U. N.H., 1971. Libr. Phillips Exeter Acad., Exeter, NH, 1971-77, acad. libr., 1977—. Chair governing bd. Child Care Ctr., 1987-91; chair Com. to Enhance Status of Women, Exeter, 1981-84; chair Loewenstein Com., Exeter, 1982—; pres. Cum Laude Soc., Exeter, 1984-86; James H. Ottaway Jr. prof., 1990—; mem. bldg. com. Exeter Pub. Libr., 1986-88; chair No. New Eng., Coun. for Women in Ind. Schs., 1985-87; chmn. Lamont Poetry Program, Exeter, 1984-86. Editor: The Design of the Library: A Guide to Sources of Information, 1981, Rarities of Our Time: The Special Collections of the Phillips Exeter Academy Library; pub.: Memorial Minutes, Phillips Exeter Academy, 1936-2002, Friends of the Academy Library, Collected Letters Book, Class of 1945 special collections brochure, other Phillips Exeter materials. Libr. trustee, treas. Exeter Day Sch., 1965-69; bd. Exeter Hosp. Vols., 1954-59; mem. Exeter Hosp. Corp., 1978—; bd. dirs. Greater Portsmouth Cmty. Found., 1990—; active AAC&U, On Campus with Women, Wellesley Coll. Ctr. for Rsch. on Women; mem. People to People Amb. Program, sch. and youth svcs. libr. del. to People's Rep. China, 1998. Grantee N.H. Coun. for Humanties, 1981-82, NEH, 1982; recipient Lillian Radford trust award, 1989. Mem. ALA, Internat. Assn. Sch. Librs., New Eng. Libr. Assn., N.J., Ednl. Media Assn., New Eng. Assn. Ind. Sch. Librs., Am. Assn. Sch. Librs. (chmn. non-pub. sch. sect.), Phi Beta Kappa. Home: 17 Eagle Dr Newmarket NH 03857 Office: Class of 1945 Libr Phillips Exeter Acad 20 Main St Exeter NH 03833-2460 Office Phone: 603-777-3328. Office Fax: 603-777-4389. Business E-Mail: jthomas@exeter.edu.

THOMAS, JANE ELLEN, elementary school educator; b. New Brighton, Pa., Jan. 30, 1950; d. Frederick Glynn and Wilma (Fogel) T.; m. Avin L. Brown. BS, Clarion U., 1971; MEd, Coll. of Mt. St. Joseph, 1988. Cert. tchr., Ohio. Tchr. Warren (Ohio) City Schs., 1971—, adult basic edn. tchr., 1988-90. V.p., bd. dirs. Contact Internat., Warren, 1974-81; vol. Am. Cancer Soc., Warren, 1985-92, Rape Crisis Ctr., Warren, 1973-76; founder Heritage Gallery, Jefferson Sch., 1989—; sec. local PTO, 1973-74. Martha Holden Jennings Found. scholar Kent State U., 1977-78, 2006-. Mem. NEA, Ohio Edn. Assn., Warren Edn. Assn. (mem. governing bd., bldg. rep. 1972-92). Avocations: travel, reading. Home: 1967 Parkwood Dr NW Warren OH 44485-2324 Office: Emerson Sch 1619 Drexel Ave Warren OH 44485 Office Phone: 330-841-2396.

THOMAS, JANET Y., political science professor, researcher; d. Ehoch Thornton and Florence Rose Thomas. BA, Norfolk State U., 1991; EdM, Widener U., 1997; PhD, U. Ill., 2000. Rsch. assoc. Hahnemann U., Phila., 1995—97; assoc. rsch. scientist Johns Hopkins U., Balt., 2000—03; with dept. academic support programs Office of Dep Provost, U. Pa., Phila., 2003—. Author: Educating Drug-Exposed Children, 2004. Mem.: Am. Edn. Assn., Am. Edn. Rsch. Assn., Kappa Delta Pi, Phi Delta Kappa. Office: 220 S 40th St Ste 240 Philadelphia PA 19106 Business E-Mail: janety@pobox.upenn.edu.

THOMAS, JEANETTE MAE, public accountant; b. Minn., Dec. 19, 1946; d. Herbert and Arline Harmon; m. Gerald F. Thomas, Aug. 9, 1969; children: Bradley, Christopher. BS, Winona State U., 1968; postgrad., Colo. State U.; CFP, Coll. for Fin. Planning, Denver, 1985. Enrolled agt.; cert. fin. planner; registered rep. NASD; registered investment advisor; accredited tax advisor. Tchr. pub. schs. systems, Colo., N.Mex., Mich., 1968-72; adminstrv. asst. Bus. Men's Svcs., Ft. Collins, Colo., 1974-75; tax cons. Tax Corp. Am., Ft. Collins, Colo., 1972-80; chief acct. Jayland Enterprises, La Porte, Colo., 1981—2003; pres., CEO Thomas Fin. Svcs. Inc., Ft. Collins, 1980—2003. Contbr. articles to newspapers and profl. newsletters. Bd. dirs. local PTO, 1984-85; treas. Boy Scouts Am., 1985-88; master food safety advisor coop. ext. Colo. State U., 1988-2002; spkr., steering com. AARP Women's Fin. Info. Program, 1988-98; past chair adv. bd. Larimer County Coop. Ext., Colo. State U.; quality rev. com., sch. to career adv. bd. Poudre R-1 Schs.; judge county fairs. Mem. Internat. Assn. Fin. Planning (past officer), Am. Soc. Women Accts. (bd. dirs. 1984-86, 96-98), Workforce Investment Bd. (chair 1994-95), Nat. Soc. Accts., Colo. Soc. Pub. Accts., Inst. CFPs, Am. Notary Assn., Ft. Collins C. of C. (red carpet com. bus. assistance coun. 1989-96). Avocations: sewing, bread baking, food preservation, fly fishing, golf. Office: 400 S Howes St Ste 2 Fort Collins CO 80521-2802 Home: PO Box 559 Hale MI 48739-0559

THOMAS, JENNIE **See ORR, JENNIE**

THOMAS, JO, journalist, educator; b. Long Beach, Calif., Dec. 7, 1943; d. Guy O'Neil DeYoung, Jr. and Josephine (Bradley) DeYoung; m. William L. Thomas III, June 12, 1965 (div. Sept. 1969); m. William F. Kelleher Jr., Dec. 19, 1985; children: Susan Elizabeth Kelleher, Kathleen DeYoung Kelleher. BA summa cum laude, Wake Forest U., 1965; MA, U. N.C., 1967. Reporter Cin. Post and Times-Star, 1966—70, Detroit Free Press, 1971—77; from Washington corr. to writer N.Y. Times, 1977—2001, writer, 2001—02; assoc. prof. U. Ill., Urbana, 1987—94, asst. chancellor, 2003—04; assoc. chancellor Syracuse U., NY, 2004—, prof. journalism, 2004—. Contbr. articles to newspapers and mags. Bd. dirs. Ctr. Cmty. Alternatives. Recipient Outstanding Reporting award Detroit Press Club, 1974-75, Robert F. Kennedy award, 1973; Nieman fellow Harvard U., 1970-71; mem NY Times staff team winning Pulitzer prize, 2002. Mem. Phi Beta Kappa, Kappa Tau Alpha. Office Phone: 315-443-3793. Personal E-mail: jothom@gmail.com.

THOMAS, JOAN E., music educator; MusM, Columbus State U., Ga.; MS n Edn., Troy Stat U., Phenix City, Ala., 1998—2000. Cert. tchr. State of Ga. Dir. of choral activities Upson-Lee H.S. and Upson-Lee Mid. Sch., Thomaston, Ga., 1982—2002; min. of music First Presbyn. Ch., Thomaston, Ga., 1996—2000; grad. asst. Columbus State U., 2002—04; min. of music First United Meth. Ch., Thomaston, 2004—; dir. of choral activities Pike County Schs., Zebulon, Ga., 2004—. Home: 2 Thomas Way Thomaston GA 30286 Office: Pike Middle School PO Box 405 Zebulon GA 30295 Office Phone: 770-468-9425. Personal E-mail: jethomas@alltel.net. E-mail: thomasj@pike.k12.ga.us.

THOMAS, JOI J., personal trainer; d. Robert and Regina Thomas. BS, U. of Wyo., Laramie, 1999; MS, U. of Wyo., 2006. Cert. athletic trainer Nat. Athletic Trainers' Assn., 2000. Head athletic trainer Carroll Coll., Helena, Mont., 1999—2004; grad. asst. athletic trainer U. of Wyo., Laramie, 2004—05, asst. athletic trainer, 2005—. Instr. U. of Wyo., 2004—. Founding mem. Helena Area Disordered Eating Task Force, Mont., 2000—04; cert. athletic trainer Nat. Safe Kids Campaign, Helena, 2001—03. Grantee Get Into the Game grantee, Nat. Safe Kids Campaign, 2002. Mem.: Wyo. Athletic Trainers' Assn., Rocky Mountain Athletic Trainers' Assn., Nat. Athletic Trainers' Assn., Elks. Catholic. Avocations: reading, travel. Office: University of Wyoming Dept 3414 1000 E University Ave Laramie WY 82070

THOMAS, JULIE ELIZABETH, clinical psychologist, educator; b. Ernakulam, Kerala, India; came to U.S., 1988; d. George and Mary Thomas. BA, Sophia Coll., Bombay, India, 1986-88; MA, U. Bombay, 1986-88; PhD, U. Tenn., 1993; postdoc., Dartmouth Med. Sch., 1993-95. Lic. psychologist, Ohio. Asst. prof. dept. of child psychiatry Dartmouth Med. Sch., Lebanon, N.H., 1995-96; asst. prof. dept. of psychology Youngstown (Ohio) State U., 1996—. Recipient Outstanding Svc. award YSU-NAACP, 1999. Mem. AAUW, Am. Psychol. Assn., Ohio Psychol. Assn. Avocation: karate (1st degree black belt). Office: Youngstown State U One University Plaza Youngstown OH 44555 E-mail: jethomas@cc.ysu.edu.

THOMAS, KAREN E., elementary school educator; d. James and Susan Thomas. MS, Nova Southeastern U., Orlando, Fla., 2005. Cert. tchr. Fla. ESE instr. Orange County Pub. Schools, Orlando, Fla., 1998—. Office: Olympia HS 4301 S Apopka-Vineland Rd Orlando FL 32835 Office Phone: 407-905-6400 3199. Business E-Mail: thomask@ocps.net.

THOMAS, KAREN P., composer, conductor; b. Seattle, Sept. 17, 1957; BA in Composition, Cornish Inst., 1979; MusM in Composition and Conducting, U. Wash., 1985. Condr. The Contemporary Group, 1981-85; condr., music dir. Wash. Composers Forum, 1984-86; artistic dir., condr. Seattle Pro Musica, 1987—. Conducting debut Seattle, 1987; composer: Four Delineations of Curtmantle for Trombone or Cello, 1982, Metamorphoses on a Machaut Kyrie for Strong Orch. or Quartet, 1983, Cowboy Songs for Voice and Piano, 1985, There Must Be a Lone Range for Soprano and Chamber Ensemble, 1987, Brass Quintet, 1987, Four Lewis Carroll Songs for Choir, 1989, (music/dance/theater) Boxiana, 1990, Elementi for Clarinet and Percussion, 1991, (one-act children's opera) Coyote's Tail, 1991, Clarion Dances for Brass Ensemble, 1993, Roundup for Sax Quartet, 1993, Three Medieval Lyrics for Choir, 1992, Sopravvento for Wind Quartet and Percussion, 1994, When Night Came for Clarinet and Chamber Orch. or Clarinet and Piano, 1994, Over the City for Choir, 1995, also numerous others. Recipient Composers Forum award N.W. Chamber Orch., 1984, King County Arts Commn., 1987, 90, Artist Trust, 1988, 93, 96, Seattle Arts Commn., 1988, 91, 93, New Langton Arts, 1988, Delius Festival, 1993, Melodious Accord award 1993; fellow Wash. State Arts Commn., 1991; Charles E. Ives scholar AAAI. Mem. Am. Choral Dirs. Assn., Broadcast Music, Am. Music Ctr., Internat. Alliance for Women in Music, Soc. Composers, Chorus Am., Conductors Guild. Office: 4426 1st Ave NW Seattle WA 98107-4306 E-mail: kpthomas1@aol.com.

THOMAS, KATHERINE CAROL, special education educator; b. Alice, Tex., June 15, 1943; d. Charles Anthony Sr. and elvira (Garcia) Rogers; m. Richard Harold Jr. Thomas, Aug. 9, 1980; 1 child, Rhonda Crystal. BS in Edn., Tex. A&I U., 1965; MS in Edn., Anticoch U., 1975. Tchr. Salazar Elem. Sch., Alice, Tex., 1965-73; supr. Alice Identification and Referral System, 1975-78; supr. bilingual edn. Alice (Tex.) Sch. Dist., 1978-80, tchr., supr. migrant edn., 1980-83, tchr. spl. edn., 1983—. Sec.-treas. Slazar PTA, 1965-75; mem. com. Water Authority Commn., Alice, 1981. Mem. Tex. Tchrs. Assn., NEA, Am. Tchrs. Prins. Assn., Childhood Edn. Assn. (treas. 1968-74), AAUP, Spl. Edn. Assn. Democratic. Roman Catholic. Home: PO Box 3132 Alice TX 78333-3132

THOMAS, KATHERINE M., humanities educator, department chairman; d. Dorothy McDaniel; m. James Thomas, Jan. 28, 1961; children: D. Michael, Michele Comana. AB, St. Louis U.; MA, Fordham U.; DEd, Pa. State U., State College, 1976. Instr. Ga. Coll. & State U., Milledgeville, 1988—93; prof. humanities Southeast Ky. CTC, Cumberland, 1994—. Editor: Ky. Jour. Excellence, 2003—; reviews editor: Jour. Caribbean Studies, 2004—. Mem.: Nat. Assn. Devel. Educators, Ky. Assn. Devel. Educators, Ky. Philol. Assn. (past pres.), Assn. Caribbean Studies (v.p. 2005). Office: Southeast Ky CTC 700 College Rd Cumberland KY 40823 Office Phone: 606-589-2145. Business E-Mail: katherine.thomas@kctcs.edu.

THOMAS, LEONA MARLENE, healthcare educator; b. Rock Springs, Wyo., Jan. 15, 1933; d. Leonard H. and Opal (Wright) Francis; children: Peter, Paul, Patrick, Alexis. BA, Govs. State U., University Park, Ill., 1982, MHS, 1986; cert. med. records adminstrn., U. Colo., 1954. Asst. prof. Chgo. State U., 1984—, acting dir. health info. adminstrn. program, 1991-92; acting dir. health info. Internat. Coll., Naples, Fla., 1994; dir. Chgo. State U., 1994—. Chairperson dept. health info. adminstrn. Chgo. State U., 1994—. Mem. adv. com. Wellness Ctr., mem. adv. com. occupl. therapy program Chgo. State U. Mem. Assembly on Edn., Am. Health Info. Mgmt. Assn., APHA, Chgo. and Vicinity Med. Records Assn., Ill. Assn. Allied Health Profls., Gov.'s State Alumni Assn. Democrat. Methodist. Home: 6340 Americana Dr Apt 1101 Willowbrook IL 60527 Office: Chgo State U Coll Health Scis 95th at King Dr Chicago IL 60628 Personal E-mail: lthomas@msn.com.

THOMAS, LESTENE, nurse; b. Hampton, Ark., May 1, 1956; d. James Earnest Moore and Alma Lee Moore-Penny; m. Emile Garth Thomas; children: Learie D., Stephen J.R. AAS in Nursing, U. Ark. Little Rock, 1978. RN; notary public, Ark. Nurse U. Hosp., Little Rock, 1978-82, Vets. Hosp., Little Rock, 1982-86, Ctrl. Ark. Home Health Agy., Little Rock, 1986-89, St. Vincent Infirmary, Little Rock, 1989-90, Jefferson Regional Med. Ctr., Pine Bluff, Ark., 1990-94, Ark. Convalescent Nursing Home, Pine Bluff, 1996-97, Pulaski County Regional Detention Facility, Little Rock, 1998—2002, Maxim Health Svcs., 2002—, Parkview Rehab. and Health Care, 2003—. Mem. Angel Flight, UAM, Monticello, Ark., 1975—76. 2d lt. Ark. NG, 1984—86. Mem.: Nat. Alliance for Mentally Ill, Zeta Phi Beta. Baptist. Avocations: calligraphy, photography, music, international pen-friends. Home: 8501 Dreher Ln Apt 25 Little Rock AR 72209

THOMAS, LISE-MARIE, actress; b. Dallas, June 16, 1963; d. Robet Harold and Camilla Delores (Wicks) T.; m. Dietmar Rudolf Wertanzl, Aug. 1, 1992; 1 child, Sterling Alexa. BA in Liberal Studies, San Francisco State U., 1997. Actress/singer Beach Blanket Babylon, San Francisco, 1983-84, So. Az. Light Opera Co., Tucson, Az., 1991-95, Crystal Cruises, Inc., L.A., 1991-95; actress Soap Operas, L.A., 1988-99; asst. dir. Crystal Cruises, Inc., L.A., 1995-99; dir. various cabaret artists, L.A., 1999-2000. Principal Sterling Cons. Co., L.A., 1999; original cast mem. Tune the Grand Up (cabaret gold award), 1985. Mem. Phi Beta Kappa. Avocations: reading, skiing, travel, motherhood.

THOMAS, LIZANNE, lawyer; BA, Furman U, 1979; JD, Washington & Lee, 1982. Bar: Ga. 1982. Ptnr. bus. practice group Jones Day, Atlanta, firmwide adminstrv. ptnr., 2003—. Lectr. corp. fin. U. Calif., Berkeley and Davis; pres. Law Alumni Assn. Washington and Lee U., 2001—02; bd. dirs. Krispy Kreme Doughnuts, 2004—. Recurring panelist Directors' Inst. of the Conf. Bd. Mem. adv. bd. Salvation Army Metro Atlanta; former bd. dirs. Ga. C. of C. Mem.: State Bar of Ga. Office: Jones Day 1420 Peachtree St NE Atlanta GA 30309-3053 Office Phone: 404-581-8411. Office Fax: 404-581-8330. Business E-Mail: lthomas@jonesday.com.

THOMAS, LOIS C., musician, educator, religious organization administrator, composer; b. Ft. Worth, Oct. 15, 1932; d. Walter Scott and Margaret Alice Dawn Cook; m. Richard Wallace Thomas, Nov. 5, 1988. BA in Organ Performance, Tex. Christian U., 1966; postgrad., SWBT Sem. Organist Western Hills Bapt. Ch., Ft. Worth, 1959-69, 1st Ch. of Christ, Scientist, Ft. Worth, 1969-84, First Congl. Ch., Ft. Worth, 1985-87; organist, dir. Anglican Ch. St. Charles the Martyr, Grand Prairie, Tex., 1989—99; organist, dir., assoc. rector Anglican Ch. St. Raphael, the Archangel, Grand Prairie, 2002—04. Deacon United Cath. Ch., 1996; priest Communion Evang. Episcopal Chs., 1997; fin. officer USCG Aux., Grapevine, Tex., 1989—95, sec., Grand Prairie, Tex., 1995. Commd.: hymnal Diocese St. Paul, the Apostle, 2000. Mem.: Music Tchr.'s Nat. Assn., Tex. Music Tchr.'s Assn., Arlington Music Tchr.'s Assn. (phone com.), Am. Guild Organists (phone com., svc. playing cert.). Home: 1501 Connally Ter Arlington TX 76010-4514

THOMAS, LORELLE OTIS, graphics designer, educator; b. Ann Arbor, Mich., July 13, 1947; d. Erwin James Otis, Jr. and Nedra Smith Otis; m. Leon Michael Korzenowski, Oct. 20, 1990; 1 child, Kristin Anne. BA in Art Edn., Ea. Mich. U., Ypsilanti, 1968—70; MFA, Syracuse U., NY, 1988—90. Cert. Montessori tchr. St. Nicholas Acad., London, 1972. Sr. graphic designer Sea World, Inc., San Diego, 1980—83; supr. graphic svcs. Ea. Mich. U., 1985—90; assoc. prof. Grand Valley State U., Allendale, Mich., 1990—. Freelance illustrator & designer Lorelle Otis Thomas Illustration/Design, Allendale, Mich., 1974—. Educational game, Math Animals, society of illustrators exhibition, Favorite Flix, First Wheels, illustration, An Old Time Christmas by Helen Steiner Rice, commd. painting, GVSU Health Scis. Bldg., Timeless Voices, GVSU Water Resources Bldg., graphic design for brochure, Dutch Collection of Contemporary Prints (Mich. Mus. Assn. Quest for Excellence award, 2003), graphic design brochure, Tjukurrpa: Australian Aboriginal Art of the Dreaming (Heritage Paper award, 2002). Mem.: Soc. Children's Book Writers & Illustrators, Soc. Illustrators. Independent. Office: Grand Valley State Univ Calder Art Ctr 1 Campus Dr Allendale MI 49401 Business E-Mail: thomasl@gvsu.edu.

THOMAS, LUCILLE COLE, librarian; b. Dunn, NC, Oct. 1, 1921; d. Collie and Minnie (Lee) Cole; m. George Browne Thomas, May 24, 1943; children: Ronald C., Beverly G. BA, Bennett Coll., 1941; DHL (hon.), Benentt Coll., 1996; MA, NYU, 1955; MS, Columbia U., 1957. Tchr. Bibb County Bd. Edn., Macon, Ga., 1947—55; libr. Bklyn. Pub. Libr., 1955—56, NYC Bd. Edn., Bklyn., 1956—68, supr. librs., 1968—77, dir. elem. sch. librs., 1977—83; program dir. Weston Woods Inst., Weston, Conn., 1984—85; adj. prof. libr. sci. Queens Coll., CUNY, 1986—89; libr. cons., 1989—. Prof. libr. sci. St. John's U., 1986, Pratt Inst., 1989; founder Sch. Libr. Media Day, NY State, 1973, Nat. Sch. Libr. Media Month, 1985; cons. Putnam Pub. Group, NYC, 1983; bd. examiners NY City Bd. Edn., 1983—91; adv. bd. Regents' Adv. Council on Learning Tech., Albany, NY, 1982—88; reviewer U.S. Office Ednl. Rsch. & Improvement, 1988—90; coord. UNESCO/Internat. Assn. Sch. Librarianship Book Program for devel. countries, 1980—89; chair seminar for librs. from devel. countries, Spain, 1993; trustee NY Met. Ref. and Rsch. Libr. Agy., NYC, 1979—83; liaison Freedom to Read Found., 1986—88; 1st v.p. Shomburg Corp., 1983—85. Contbr. articles to profl. jours.; editor: Insight, 1974, Cultural Heritage Through Literature, 1993. Del. White House Conf. Libr. and Info. Svcs., 1979, World Conf. on Edn. for all in Jamtien, Thailand, 1990; hon. del. White House Conf. Libr. and Info. Svcs., 1991; treas. Bklyn. Home for Aged Commn., 1967—; del. NY Gov's. Conf. on Librs., 1978, 1990; adv. bd. Books Kids, 1989—; mem. libr. sect. Nat. Martin Luther King, Jr. Commn., 1990—95; trustee Bklyn. Pub. Libr., 1993—, v.p., 2000—03, pres., 2003—06, chair audit com., 2006—; pres. bd. trustees St. Mark's Day Sch., 2001—; trustee Trustee of Leroy Merritt Humanitarian Award, 2005—; vestry mem. St. John's Episcopal Ch., Bklyn., 1988—90, chair stewardship com., 1987—90; active St. Mark's Ch., Bklyn., 1969—85, 1990—; bd. dirs. NY is Book Country, 1991—96. Named Woman on the Move, State Sen. Carl Andrews, 2003; recipient Disting. Alumna award, Bennett Coll., 1981, Edn. award, Bus. and Profl. Women's Club, 1983, Achievement award, Columbia U. Sch. Libr. Svcs., 1987, Grolier Found. award, 1988, Disting. Pub. Svc. award, SUNY, Albany, 1989, Cmty. Svc. award, North Queens, NY, 1993, Disting. Svc. award, St. Mark's Ch., 2003, Achievement award, Consortium of Doctors, 2004, NY Black Librs., 2004, citation, Bklyn. Borough Pres., 2005, Letter of Commendation, First Lady Laura Bush, 2005, Faithful Servant award, Concord Bapt. Ch., 2006. Mem.: ALA (hon.; councilor 1980—91, exec. bd. 1984—91, direction and rev. com. 1985—91, chair nominations and spl. assignments com. 1987—88, chair Hqtrs. Libr. Rev. Accountability Com. 1987—88, exec. bd. found. 1987—89, pers. com. 1988—89, chair ALA/AASL disting. svc. award com. 1989—90, disaster relief com. 1989—91, chair rev. com. of office for rsch. 1990—91, AASL/SIRS Disting. Libr. Svc. award sch. adminstrs. com. 1990—91, chair rsch. rev. com. 1990—91, AASL internat. rels. com. 1990—94, internat. com. 1991—95, councilor 1993—2002, Disting. Svc. award Black Librs. Caucus 1992, Trailblazer's award Libr. Black Caucus 1995), NY Libr. Assn. (pres. sch. libr. media sect. 1973—74, pres. 1977—78, v.p. 1976—77, appreciation cert. 1983, oustanding achievement award 1984, achievement award 1988), Internat. Assn. Sch. Librarianship (pres. 1989—95), Internat. Fedn. Libr. Assn. (sec. 1985—96, chair sch. librs. sect. 1989—93, ofcl. rep. UN and UNICEF 1991—94, chair planning and implementation com.), NYC Sch. Librs. Assn. (pres. 1970—72, chair sch. librs. sect. 1989—93), Bklyn. Hist. Soc. (named one of outstanding women of Bklyn. 1985), Schomburg Commn. (1st v.p. 1986—90), Women's City of NYC Club (bd. dirs. 1986—2000, vice chmn. 1987—89, chair edn. com. 1989—92, v.p. 1992—93), NY Libr. Club (v.p. 1976—77, pres. 1977—78), Alpha Kappa Alpha (Pi Phi Omega chpt. parliamentarian 1990—92, v.p. 1990—94, pres. 1994—2000, mem.-at-large 2004—, v.p. 1992—94, co-coord. 1996—2000). Democrat. Home: 1184 Union St Brooklyn NY 11225-1512 Personal E-mail: lucillecthomas@aol.com.

THOMAS, M. ANN, bank executive; m. Tony Singer, Aug. 31, 2001. JD, Ohio No. U., 1985. Atty. Bracewell & Patterson; exec. v.p. Woodforest Nat. Bank, Houston, 1995—99, COO, 1999—2001, pres., COO, 2001—. Named one of 25 Women to Watch, US Banker Mag., 2003. Office: Woodforest Nat Bank 13301 E Fwy Houston TX 77015

THOMAS, MARGARET ANN, principal; b. Waukesha, Wis., June 19, 1951; d. Melvin Michael and Elizabeth (Brewer) Thomas; m. Bruce Fiedler; 1 child, James. BA in Art Edn., Beloit Coll., 1974; MA in Edn., U. Wis., Whitewater, 1985; MS in Ednl. Adminstrn., U. Wis., 1995, PhD in Ednl. Adminstrn., Ednl. Psychology. Cert. K-12 art tchr., Wis., elem. and H.S. prin., curriculum dir. K-12, supt. Tchr. art Beloit (Wis.) Pub. Schs., 1974—; adj. prof. Beloit Coll., 1992—; prin. Mclenegan Elem. Sch., Beloit, 1999—2001, adminstr. grants, 2001—02, adminstr. acad. reporting sys., 2002—; prin. Synectics Mid. Charter Schs., 2003—. Muralist instr. Beloit Coll., summers, 1985-91, adj. prof., 1993—; adj. prof. Nat. Louis U., 1994—; adminstr. Charter Schs., 2003. Author: Effective Teachers; Effective Schools, 1989; contbr. articles to profl. jours. Bd. dirs. Wis.-Gate Found., 1985-87, Wis. Racquetball Assn., 1986-87, Wis. Future Problem Solving, 1986-87; pres. bd. dirs. YWCA, 1987-91; dir. Beloit and Vicinity Art Show, Beloit Coll., 1982-84, Rock Prairie Showcase Festival; founder Summer Explorers Beloit Coll. Mem. Wis. Coun. for Gifted and Talented (bd. dirs. 1984-87, v.p. 1985-86, pres. 1986-87). Home: 4421 Ruger Ave Janesville WI 53546-9780 Office Phone: 608-361-3632. Business E-Mail: mathomas@sdb.k12.wi.us.

THOMAS, MARGARET ANN, not-for-profit developer; b. Milw., Sept. 12, 1946; m. John Thomas. Bachelor's Degree, U. Wis., 1973; Master's Degree, DePaul U., 1979. Pers. dir. Goodwill Rehab. Ctr., Milw., 1974—80; exec. dir. Hagerstown Goodwill Industries, 1980—84; pres. Goodwill Industries of Southeastern Pa., Inc., 1984—91, Goodwill Industries of the Gulf Coast, Inc., 1991—94, Goodwill Industries of the Chesapeake, Inc., 1994—. Chair leadership devel. task team Goodwill Industries Internat., mem. exec. coun., bd. mem., 1998—2001, chair, pub. policy com. bd., 2002—; mem. workforce investment bd. City of Balt., 1998—; mem. adv. bd. Schaefer Ctr., U. Balt., 1998—2001; vice chair Md. Assn. Non-profits. Treas. Anne Arundel County Cultural Art Found., 2001—, trustee, chair planning com., 1999—2001; co-chair Opera Gala Annapolis Opera Co., 1998, 1999; bd. mem. Scholarships for Scholars, 2000—; apptd. mem. Md. Coun. on Mgmt. and Productivity, 1999, 2000. Finalist Young Entrepreneur of Yr., Ernst & Young, 2000, 2001; named Kenneth K. King award for CEO of Yr., Goodwill Industries Internat., 1999; named one of Md. Top 100 Women, Daily Record, 2001, 2005; recipient Mayor's Bus. Recognition award, Office of Mayor and Greater Baltimore Com., 1998, Bus. 2000 award, Network 2000 and The Daily Record, 1999, Svc. Above Self award/Outstanding Non-Profit Agy., Rotary Club Woodlawn-Westview, 1999. Mem.: Md. Works (sec. 1999—2000), Md. Assn. Non-Profits (treas. 2001, 2002, current vice-chmn.). Office: Goodwill Industries Chesapeake Inc 222 E Redwood St Baltimore MD 21202-3312

THOMAS, MARIANNA, volunteer community activist, writer, speaker; b. Greenville, Ohio, Dec. 9, 1927; d. John Darl and Eva Jane (Hill) Munn; m. Harold D. Krickenbarger, Aug. 31, 1947 (div.); children: Harold Krickenbarger Jr., Jane Krickenbarger, Maryln Krickenbarger, John Krickenbarger; m. Lowell J. Thomas, Jan. 5, 1977 (dec.); 1 stepchild, Lowell J. Student, Dayton (Ohio) Art Inst.; MA (hon.), Union (Ky.) Coll., 1978. Farmer Holstein Show Herd, Arcanum, Ohio, 1947-68; advt., broadcasting sta. work and writing positions Arcanum Times; sales and decorating positions Lowe Bros., Greenville, Ohio; exec. dir./fundraising Help for Children in the Holy Land/Spafford Children's Ctr., NYC, 1969-76. Author: Catitudes, 1987, The Second Mrs. Lowell Thomas, 2000; mem. bd. contbrs. Dayton Daily News. Founder Citizens for Moral War peace orgn., 1967—70; mem. coun. Freedoms Found. Valley Forge, 1982—84; founder, chmn. US Civil Responsibilities, Dayton, 1988—93; nat. bd. dirs. Family Svc. Assocs. Am., NYC, 1979—85, Am. Judicature Soc., 1978—80. Mem.: Dayton Engrs. Club (hon.). Avocations: painting, poetry, swimming, cooking. Home: PO Box 626 Dayton OH 45405-0626

THOMAS, MARIANNE GREGORY, school psychologist; b. N.Y.C., Dec. 10, 1945; BS, U. Conn., 1985; MS, So. Conn. State U., 1987; cert. advanced studies, ednl. adminstrn., NYU, 1998. Cert. sch psychologist Conn, NY. Sch. psychology intern Greenwich (Conn.) Pub. Schs., 1986-87; sch. psychologist Hawthorne (N.Y.)-Cedar Knolls, U.F.S.D., 1987-88, Darien (Conn.) Pub. Schs., 1988—. Adj. instr. Coll. New Rochelle, 2002. Mem.: APA, NASP (cert), Conn Asn Sch Psychologists, Kappa Delta Pi, Phi Delta Kappa. Home: 154 Indian Rock Rd New Canaan CT 06840-3117

THOMAS, MARLO (MARGARET JULIA THOMAS), actress; b. Detroit, Nov. 21, 1943; d. Danny and Rose Marie (Cassanti) T.; m. Phil Donahue, May 21, 1980. Ed., U. So. Calif. Theatrical appearances in Thieves, Broadway, 1974, Barefoot in the Park, London, Social Security, Broadway, 1986, The Shadow Box, Broadway, 1994, Two Goldsteins on Acid, 1999; star: TV series That Girl, 1966-71 (Golden Globe award Best TV actress, 1967); appeared in TV films: The Body Human: Facts for Girls (Emmy award Best Performer Children's Program), 1981, The Last Honor of Kathryn Beck, 1984 (also exec. prodr.), Consenting Adults, 1985, Nobody's Child, 1986 (Emmy Best Dramatic Actress), Held Hostage: The Sis and Jerry Levin Story, 1991, Ultimate Betrayal, 1994, Reunion, 1994, A Century of Women, 1994, Playing Mona Lisa, 2000; TV movies: Two Against Time, 2002, Our Heroes, Ourselves, 2002, Deceit, 2004; TV appearances include Friends, 1996, 2002, Roseanne, 1996, Ally McBeal, 2000, Law & Order: Special Victims Unit, 2004; conceived book and record, starred in TV spl. Free to Be.You and Me, 1974 (Emmy for best children's show); films include Jenny, 1963, Thieves, 1977, In the Spirit, 1991, The Real Blonde, 1997, Startucker, 1998; conceived book, record and TV spl. Free to Be A Family (Emmy Best Children's Show). Recipient 4 Emmys, Golden Globe award, George Foster Peabody award, Tom Paine award Nat. Emergency Civil Liberties Com.; inducted into Broadcasting & Cable Hall of Fame. Mem. Ms. Found., Nat. Women's Polit. Caucus. Address: William Morris Agy 151 El Camino Dr Beverly Hills CA 90212 also: Creative Artists Agy 9830 Wilshire Blvd Beverly Hills CA 90211 Office: Kerner Entertainment 8522 National Blvd Ste 109 Culver City CA 90232-2454

THOMAS, MARTHA S., secondary school educator; b. Charleston, W.Va. BA. in Edn., U. Ky., Lexington, 1971, MSLS, 1974; MS Instrnl. Systems Design, Fla. State U., Tallahassee, 2006. Cert. tchr. Nat. Bd. for Profl. Tchg. Standards, 2003. Tchr. Fayette County Sch., Lexington, Ky.; media specialist Bowie County Sch., Simms, Tex.; pub. libr. Texarkana Pub. Libr., Tex.; tchr. Seminole County Schs., Sanford, Fla., 1985—. Cons./adj. instr. Stetson U. Virtual Sch., Celebration, Fla., 2004—, mem. of adv. bd., 2005—. Mem.: Nat. Coun. of the Social Studies (assoc.), Phi Lambda Theta (assoc.).

THOMAS, MARY ANN MCCRARY, counselor, school system administrator; b. Washington, Feb. 11, 1935; d. Frank Robert and Mary (Davison) McCrary; m. John Ralph Thomas, Sept. 30, 1961; children: Robert Davison, John Shannon, Kristen Aldridge. BA, U. Calif., Berkeley, 1956; MA, UCLA, 1959. Cert. tchr., Calif. Supr. Pacific Bell, San Francisco, 1962-67; advisor gifted, talented San Rafael (Calif.) City Schs., 1973—, counselor, 1973—, dir. student affairs, 1982—. Pres. San Rafael PTA Coun., 1981-84, outstanding svc. award, 1983, 86, 89, San Rafael High Sch. Site Coun., 1985; pres. bd. dirs. Marin Wildlife Ctr., 1979-85. Recipient Golden Bell award, Marin Community Found., 1987, Outstanding Student Activities program state award, 1992; named Pub. Schoolmaster of Yr., 1993. Mem. Calif. Assn. Gifted, Calif. Assn. Tchrs. English. Republican. Episcopalian. Avocations: reading, gardening. Home: 70 Windsor Ave San Rafael CA 94901-1068 Office: Davidson Mid Sch 280 Woodland Ave San Rafael CA 94901-5097

THOMAS, MARY LEE, property manager; d. Louis and Virgie Mae Bedford; children: Tamara Simone Times, Bobbi Makeda. A in Liberal Arts, S.W. Ill. Coll., 2003; B in Bus. Adminstrn., Lindenwood U., 2005. Mgmt. intern program East St. Louis Housing Authority, 1992, cert. earned income dissallowance specialist Nan Mckay And Assoc., 2003, pub. housing rent calculation specialist Nan Mckay And Assoc., 2004, universal phys. condition stds. specialist Nan McKay & Assocs., 2005. Property mgr. East St. Louis (Ill.) Housing Authority, 1990—2004, asset mgr., 2004—. Mem.: Nat. Assn. Housing Redevelopment Orgn. (cert. pub. housing mgr. 1992). Democrat. Baptist. Achievements include received award for providing inspiration to co-workers and residents by singing at various functions within the housing authority and the community. Avocations: singing, cycling, walking, tae-bo, skating. Home: 718 Country Meadow Ln Belleville IL 62221 Office: E St Louis Housing Authority 700 N 20th St East Saint Louis IL 62205 Office Phone: 618-646-7321. Business E-Mail: mthomas@elsha.org.

THOMAS, MARYELLEN, public relations executive; b. Chgo., Mar. 31, 1943; d. Thomas Ward and Lillian (Henton) Ward/Vesely; m. Kenneth Thomas, Apr. 20, 1963; children: Maria, Crystal. Diploma in nursing, Ill. Rsch. Coll., 1959; BA, Columbia Coll., Chgo., 1962. Nurse Chgo. Bd. Health, 1965—69; copywriter N.W. Ayer, Chgo., 1969—70; with pub. affairs dept. Blue Cross/Blue Shield, Chgo., 1970—75; pub. rels. rep. Proctor and Gardner Co., Chgo., 1975—. Chmn. com. Pvt. Industry Coun., Chgo. Mem.: Women in Comm., Publicity Club of Chgo., League of Black Women (asst. to pres. 1979—81). Democrat. Roman Catholic.

THOMAS, MATILDA ANN, art educator; b. Cuba, Mo., Oct. 8, 1950; d. James Albert and Rose Mary (King) Ousley; m. James Michael Thomas; children: Jeremy Michael, Jacob Michael. BA, Coll. of Ozarks, 1973. Cert. K-12 art edn., Mo. Art tchr. Kickapoo/Springfield (Mo.) Pub. Schs., 1974-77, Forsyth (Mo.) Pub. Sch., 1977—81, Taneyville (Mo.) RIII Sch., 1977-81; office mgr. Taney County Reassessment, Forsyth, 1982-83; art tchr. Cedar Creek (Mo.) Sch., Forsyth (Mo.) Pub. Sch., 1989—97; art tchr. jr. high Branson Pub. Schs., 1998—. Former pres. Taneyville (Mo.) RIII Sch. Bd., mem. 1985-1997. Mem. Forsyth Art Guild, S.W. Dist. Art Tchrs. Assn., Nat. Art Edn. Assn. Baptist. Avocations: painting, crafts, sewing, tennis, golf.

THOMAS, NANCY HINCKLEY, special education educator; b. L.A., Mar. 7, 1939; d. Barton Armin and Helen (Ferguson) Hinckley; children: Gregory Dean, Garold Daniel, Deanna Nancy, Barton William, Deborah Hinckley, Bryan Joseph. AB, Stanford U., Calif., 1959. Resource Specialist Calif. Dept. head K-Mart Corp., Petaluma, Calif., 1982—89; spl. edn. tchr. R-House, Santa Rosa, Calif., 1994—2005, resource specialist, 1998—. St. Rose Sch., 2005—. Resource specialist St. Rose Sch., Santa Rosa, Calif., 2005—06. Mem.: AAUW (treas. 1965—67), Commonwealth Club, Nat. Trust Hist. Preservation. Avocations: reading, gardening. Home: 724 Bassett St Petaluma CA 94952

THOMAS, NINA K., psychologist; b. N.Y.C., Dec. 13, 1945; BA, Wellesley Coll., 1966; MPhil, Columbia U., 1979, PhD, 1980. Lic. psychologist, N.Y., N.J.; diplomate in psychoanalysis Am. Bd. Profl. Psychology. Pvt. practice psychology N.Y.C., Morristown, N.J., 1981—. Adj. assoc. prof. social scis. NYU Sch. Profl. & Continuing Studies, 1995-2002; founder, pres. Nat. Mental Health Forum, N.Y.C., 1995-2002; co-chair relational orientation postdoctoral program psychotherapy and psychoanalysis NYU, 2004— . Honoree, Eastern Group Psychotherapy Assn., 2003. Fellow APA; mem. N.J. Psychology Assn. (pres. 1993, psychologist of yr. 1995). Avocations: tennis, skiing, biking. Office: 51 South St Morristown NJ 07960-4137 Office Phone: 212-877-7282, 973-540-9894.

THOMAS, PAMELA ADRIENNE, special education educator; b. St. Louis, Oct. 28, 1940; d. Charles Seraphin Fernandez and Adrienne Louise (O'Brien) Fernandez Reeg; divorced, 1977; m. Alvertis T. Thomas, July 22, 1981. BA in Spanish and EdS, Maryville U., 1962; Cert. EdS, U. Ky., 1966-67; MA in Edn., St. Louis U., 1974. Cert. learning disabilities, behavior disorders, educable mentally retarded, Spanish, Mo. Tchr. Pawnee Rock Kans. Sch., 1963-64; diagnostic tchr. Frankfort State Hosp. Sch., Ky., 1964-67; spl. edn. tchr. St. Louis City Pub. Schs., 1968-71, itinerant tchr., 1971-73, endl. strategist, 1973-74, elem. level resource tchr., 1974-78, secondary resource tchr., dept. head, 1978—, head dept. spl. edn., 1978—, resource tchr., 1998—, dept. head, 1998; ret., 2000. Co-author: Sophomore English Resource for Credit Curriculum Handbook, 1991. Co-author: Teaching Foreign Language to Handicapped Secondary Students, 1990. Pres. Council for Exceptional Children, local chpt. #103, 1982-83, Mo. Division of Mentally Retarded, 1985-87. Mem. Alpha Delta Kappa (St. Louis chpt. pres. 1982-84). Avocations: travel, reading, swimming, theater, crafts. Home: 4534 Ohio Ave Saint Louis MO 63111-1324

THOMAS, PATRICIA AGNES, school system administrator; b. Hagerstown, Md., Oct. 11, 1931; d. Herbert Martin and Sarah Esther Schlotterbeck; m. Harry Walker Thomas (dec.); children: Steven Walker, David Martin. B, Towson State Tchrs. Coll., Balt.; EdM, Westminster Coll., Md. Cert. spl. edn. Md., reading tchr. Md. Tchr. Hagerstown Sch. Sys., Md.; vice prin. Washington County Bd. Edn., prin.; admistr. Hagerstown Sch. Sys. Coord. Title I program Hagerstown Sch. Sys., Md., math tutor, spl. edn. tutor. Mem.: Delta Kappa Gamma. Democrat. Lutheran. Home: 110 Rosedale Hershey PA 17033

THOMAS, PATRICIA ANNE, retired law librarian; b. Cleve., Aug. 21, 1927; d. Richard Joseph and Marietta Bernadette (Teevans) T. BA, Case Western Res. U., 1949, JD, 1951. Bar: Ohio 1951, U.S. Supreme Ct. 1980. Libr. Arter & Hadden, Cleve., 1951-62; asst. libr., libr. IRS, Washington, 1962-78; libr. dir. Adminstrv. Office U.S. Cts., 1978-93; ret., 1993. Mem. Am. Assn. Law Librs., Soc. D.C. (pres. 1967-69), Soc. Benchers (Case Western Res. Law Sch.)

THOMAS, REGENA L., former state official; b. Clinton, Ky., Oct. 31, 1957; BA in U. Studies, Morehead State U. Cons. Dem. Gov.'s Assn.; legislative analyst Legislative Research Commn., KY State Legislature, 1980—85; ptnr. IEM Mesage mgmt., Inc.; served Torricelli for Senate, 1996, McGreevey for Gov., 1997, Corzine for Senate, 2000; sec. state State of N.J., Trenton, 2002—06. Prin. liaison non-govtl. orgns., key Dem. constituencies; dep., dir. Constituent Svcs. Govt. Dist. Columbia; legis. analyst Legis. Rsch. Commn. Ky. State Legislature; with Nat. Rainbow Coalition and its founder, Rev. Jesse L. Jackson.*

THOMAS, ROMAINE B., principal, consultant; d. Edmond Lee and Mamie Artisst (Pinkett) Bell; m. Harry Lester Thomas; children: Debra Lyneer Truhart, Harry L. Jr. BS, Miner Tchrs. Coll., 1951; MA, Vanderbilt U., 1965, cert., 1989, Prin. Inst. Quality Leadership, 1999. Tchr. elem. sch. D.C. Pub. Schs., Washington, 1952—65; instr., supr. D.C. Tchrs. Lab. Sch. Miner Tchrs. Coll., Washington, 1966—68; asst. prin. D.C. Pub. Schs., 1968—71, prin., 1971—2003. Intern in edn. Nat. Assn. Elem. Prins., Arlington, Va., 1986—87; coord. summer headstart D.C. Pub. Schs., Washington, 1965—68; adv. bd. Experience Corps., Washington; bd. dirs. Healthy Babies, Washington. Mem. D.C. Hist. Preservation Bd., Arts and Humanities Bd. Mem.: NAUW, Nat. Assn. Elem. Sch. (pres. local chpt.), D.C. Congress Parents and Tchrs. (life; 3d v.p.), Phi Delta Kappa. Democrat. Avocations: travel, reading, baseball, football. Home: 4003 21st St NE Washington DC 20018

THOMAS, SARA ALICE FOLGER, school librarian, curator; b. Crossville, Tenn., June 23, 1935; d. Dagnall Frank and Genevieve Morrow Folger; m. Bruce Lorrey Thomas, Mar. 18, 1961; children: Richard Folger, Alice Lorrey Thomas Cervantes. Student, Ga. State Coll. Women, Milledgeville, 1952—54; BA in Sociology, U. NC, Chapel Hill, 1956; cert. tchr., Youngstown State U., Ohio, 1983, MEd, 1992. Dir. teenage program YWCA, Providence, 1958, program Pitts., 1958—63; founder, pres. Children's Sch. Washington, Pa., 1970—76; ednl. aide Warren City Schs., Ohio, 1978—82; outreach organizer Campfire Assn., Warren, 1979; elem. sch. libr. Niles City Schs., Ohio, 1983—2000; asst. curator Sutliff Mus., Warren, 2006—. Editor TELMA Tattler, Trumball Ednl. Libr. Media Assn., Warren, 1996. Docent Butler Inst. Am. Art, Youngstown, 2001—04; mem. cmty. adv. panel Warren City Schs., 2004—06; libr. 1st Presbyn. Ch. Warren, 2000—; bd. dirs. Friends of McKinley Meml. Libr., Niles, 1990—2000, Warren Chamber Orch., 1980—82. Mem.: YWCA (pres. Washington chpt. 1974—76), AAUW (officer Warren chpt. 1992—), Ch. and Synagogue Libr. Assn. NE Ohio, Monday Afternoon Study Club (sec. 2005—), Warren Book Club, Lit. Club. Avocations: art, gardening, travel, reading, storytelling.

THOMAS, SARAH E., librarian; AB, Smith Coll., 1970; MS in Libr. Sci., Simmons Coll., 1973; PhD in German, Johns Hopkins U., 1982; student, Universität Hamburg, Germany, 1968—69, Albert-Ludwigs Universität, 1971, Johann Wolfgang Goethe Universität, 1977—78. Preliminary cataloger Widener Libr., Harvard U., Cambridge, Mass., 1970—71, catalog intern & reference libr., 1971—73, original cataloger Germanic languages, 1973, head departmental libr. cataloging sect., 1974, head computer-based cataloging, 1974—75; instr. elem. German Johns Hopkins U., Balt., 1976—77, instr. intermediate German, 1978—79, sr. cataloger Eisenhower Libr., 1978—79; libr. coord. Rsch. Libraries Group, Stanford, Calif., 1979—80, mgr. libr. coordination, 1980—83; Coun. Libr. Resources academic libr. mgmt. intern U. Ga., Athens, 1983—84; assoc. dir. tech. services Nat. Agrl. Libr., Beltsville, Md., 1984—92; dir. cataloging Libr. Congress, Washington, 1992—94, acting dir. pub. services and collection mgmt., 1995, acting dir. public svc. collections, 1995—96; Carl A. Korch U. Libr. Cornell U., Ithaca, NY, 1996—, adj. prof. German dept. modern languages, 1996—. Faculty adv. bd. on info. tech. Cornell U., 1996—; corp. vis. com. for the libraries of MIT, 1997—; bd. governors Cornell Inst. for Social and Econ. Rsch., 1997—; vis. com. Carnegie Mellon Libr., 1999—; overseers' com. to visit the libr. Harvard U., 1999—; chair exec. com. Smith Coll. Libraries, 2002—; chair adv. bd. Project Euclid, 2002—; ctrl. adv. bd. PubMed, 2003—; adminstrv. bd. Cornell U. Coun. Named Online Computer Libr. Ctr. Disting. Scholar, 2000; recipient Cert. Merit, Nat. Agrl. Libr., 1989, Superior Svc. Award, USDA, 1990; Deutscher Akademischer Austauschdienst Fellowship, 1977—78. Mem.: ALA (life), Assn. Libr. Collections and Tech. Services, Assn. Coll. & Rsch. Libraries, Assn. Rsch. Libraries (bd. mem. 1999—, pres. 2003—04, membership com. 2003—, chair nominating com. 2003—), Grolier Club. Office: Cornell U 201 Olin Libr Ithaca NY 14853 Office Phone: 607-255-3689. Office Fax: 607-255-6788. Business E-Mail: set9@cornell.edu.*

THOMAS, SARAH ELAINE, music educator; b. Little Rock, Aug. 8, 1947; d. William and Madie Murle (Stout) Collins; m. Gary Wayne Thomas Aug. 8, 1970 (dec. Nov. 1991). MusB in Edn., U. N. Tex., 1970; M in Ednl. Adminstrn., Dallas Bapt. U., 1997. Cert. tchr.-all-levels, Tex., prin. Music tchr. Winnetka Elem., Dallas, 1970-82, L. K. Hall Elem., Dallas, 1982-94, Kleberg Elem., Dallas, 1994—2001, Pleasant Grove Elem., 2001—05; supr. elem. fine arts Lincoln Instrnl. Ctr., 2005—. Staff. devel. presenter Dallas Ind. Sch. Dist., 1977-97, 97-2005; workshop presenter Tex. Arts Coun., Austin, 1990-94. Bd. dirs. Dallas PTA, 1980-82; bd. dirs. Dallas All-City Elem. Choir, chair, 1991—, dir., 1999-2004. Named Class Act Teacher, Sta. KDFW-TV, Dallas, 1992. Mem. PTA (life), Am. Fedn. Tchrs., Tex. Music Educators Assn., Dallas Music Educators Assn. (v.p. 1992), Am. Orff-Schulwerk Assn., Music Educators Nat. Conf., Rotary (Svc. Above Self award 2003). Avocations: cooking, sewing, gardening, travel. Home: 2407 Norwich Ct Arlington TX 76015-3262 Office: Lincoln Instrnl Ctr 5000 S Malcom X Blvd Rm 104 Dallas TX 75215 Office Phone: 972-749-2545. Personal E-mail: elainethomas3@comcast.net. Business E-Mail: elthomas@dallasisd.org.

THOMAS, SHARON M., city official; b. New Bedford, Mass., June 23, 1969; d. Tony C. and Rosemary F. (Couto) Teixeira; m. David Alan Thomas, July 25, 1992; 1 child, David A. Thomas II. Grad. h.s. Asst. coun. sec. New Bedford City Coun., 1987-89, city coun. sec., 1989-96, asst. coun. clk., office mgr., 1996—. Home: 64 Snow St New Bedford MA 02740-1431 Office: New Bedford City Coun 133 William St New Bedford MA 02740-6132

THOMAS, SHERASA MALONE, secondary school educator; b. Lubbock, Tex., Oct. 25, 1973; d. Herman L. and Anita S. Malone; m. Eric Tramell Thomas, Aug. 31, 1996; children: Zharia Yulon, Miles Jai. Degree in history, Grambling State U., La., 1996. Cert. tchr. Tex. Edn. Assn. Tchr. Dallas Ind. Sch. Dist., Dallas, 1997—2001, Garland Ind. Sch. Dist., Garland, Tex., 2001—. Mentor, creator Just Us Girls, Garland, 2001—; 7th grade team leader Garland Ind. Sch. Dist., 2002—04, mem. campus improvement team, 2002—04; ESL lead trainer Delta Tng. Group, Garland, Afghanistan, 2002—04; chairperson multural com. Garland Ind. Sch. Dist., Brandenburg Mid. Sch., 2001—; rep. dist. ednl. improvement com. Garland Ind. Sch. Dist., 2004—05. Campaign mgr. DISD Sch. Bd. Election, Dallas, 2006. Named Tex. History Tchr. of Yr., Daus. of Republic of Tex., 2003—04. Mem.: Tex. Coun. for Social Studies (assoc.; historian 2002—05). Independent. Avocation: writing.

THOMAS, SPRING URSULA, not-for-profit developer, educator, photographer; b. N.Y.C., Apr. 20, 1946; d. Everett John and Ursula (Reich) Voeglie; m. Raymond Tillman Gibson, July 4, 1972 (dec. Apr. 15, 1975); 1 child, Rick Tillman; m. Michael Alan Thomas, June 15, 1991; stepchildren: Cheryl Ritzel, Jennifer Adams. Degree in tchg., Seattle U., 1976, BA Magna Cum Laude, 1977. Cert. ESL tchr. Cons. Seattle U., 1977—84, Kodiak (Alaska) Childcare Ctr., 1977; co-owner Convention Photographers N.W., Seattle, 1985—92; program dir. Earth Corps (formerly Cascadia Quest), Seattle, 1992—94; co-founder The IronStraw Group, Ellensburg, Wash., 1994—, also. pres. bd. dirs. Contbg. photographer (book) Seattle Tashkent Internat. Sister Cities, 1990. Citizen diplomat Seattle Tashkent Peace Park, 1988; developer Seattle Tashkent Children's Art Exch., 1989; com. mem. Ellensburg C. of C., 2003. Recipient Ptnrs. Participating Edn. award, 1987, World Citizen's Award, Physicians for Social Responsibility, 1988, Founders of a New Northwest, Pioneering Achievement award, Sustainable N.W., 2000. Avocations: philanthropy, the arts, nature. Business E-Mail: spring@ironstraw.org.

THOMAS, SUE ANN APPLETON, librarian, reading consultant; b. Washington, May 27, 1942; d. George Frederick and Opal Ann (Roberts) Appleton; m. Francis Bruce Thomas, Aug. 19, 1977 (div. Jan. 1988). BA, Coll. William and Mary, 1963; student, George Mason U., 1969-70; MEd, U. Va., 1992. Cert. tchr., librarian, Va. Libr. asst. Arlington County Pub. Libr., Arlington, Va., 1964-69; elem. sch. tchr. Prince William County Sch. Bd., Manassas, Va., 1970-84; high sch. librarian, media specialist Spotsylvania County Sch. Bd., Spotsylvania, Va., 1984—, ret., 1999. Mem. social studies curriculum com. Prince William County Schs., 1979; parttime libr. asst. Ctrl. Rappahannock Regional Libr., 2000-. Mem. NEA, Va. Edn. Assn., Va. Ednl. Media Assn., Va. Reading Assn., Spotsylvania Edn. Assn. (rep. 1992, pres. 1993-96), Beta Sigma Phi (pres. 1993—), Alpha Delta Kappa Honoarary Edn. Sorority for Women (pres. 2002-04), Christ Episc. Ch. (edn. comm. chair 2003-, vestry 2004-2006). Republican. Episcopalian. Avocations: gardening, walking, aerobics, reading, travel. Home: 5800 Queens Mill Cir Fredericksburg VA 22407-7606 Office: Spotsylvania High Sch 6975 Courthouse Rd Spotsylvania VA 22553-3322

THOMAS, SUSAN BETH, writer; b. N.Y.C., Jan. 8, 1946; d. William Thomas and Charlotte Rodney; m. Joel Gregory Goldman, June 5, 1966 (div. Feb. 1974); m. Peter Jay Sills, June 18, 1978; children: Daniel Joshua, Noah Simeon. BA, Sarah Lawrence Coll., 1969, MFA, 1980. Contbr. numerous short stories and poetry to anthologies and other publs., including Nimrod, 1999, numerous short stories New Delta Rev., 1999, numerous short stories Feminist Studies, 1999, numerous short stories So. Peotry Rev., 1998, numerous short stories Columbia, 1998, numerous short stories The Midwest Quar., 1998, numerous short stories Kalliope, 2000, numerous short stories others. Recipient 1st prize, Tenn. Writer Alliance, 1999, Spoon River Poetry Rev., 1999; grantee, Va. Arts Coun., 1999, 2001. Avocations: mythology, nature, gardening. Home: 1010 Ennis Hill Rd Marshfield VT 05658-8241

THOMAS, TERESA ANN, microbiologist, educator; d. Sam Charles and Edna Thomas. BS cum laude, Coll. Misericordia, 1961; MS in Biology, Am. U., Beirut, 1965; MS in Microbiology, U. So. Calif., 1973; cert. in ednl. tech., U. Calif., San Diego, 1998. Tchr., sci. supr., curriculum coord. Meyers H.S., Wilkes-Barre, 1962-64, Wilkes-Barre Area Pub. Schs., 1961-66; rsch. assoc. Proctor Found. Rsch. in Ophthalmology U. Calif. Med. Ctr., San Francisco, 1966-68; instr. Robert Coll. of Istanbul, Turkey, 1968-71, Am. Edn. in Luxembourg, 1971-72, Bosco Tech. Inst., Rosemead, Calif., 1973-74, San Diego C.C. Dist., 1974-80; prof. microbiology and ecology Sch. Math Sci. and Engring. Southwestern Coll., Chula Vista, Calif., 1980—2005, prof. emeritus, 2005—; mem. Vecinos Baja Studies EcoMundo team internat. program Southwestern Coll. Pres. acad. senate, 1984-85, del., 1986-89; chmn., coord., steering com. project Cultural Rsch. Ednl. and Trade Exch., 1991-2000, Southwestern Coll.-Shanghai Inst. Fgn. Trade; coord. Southwestern Coll. Great Tchg. Seminar, 1987, 88, 89, coord. scholars program, 1988-90; steering com. Southwestern Coll.; exec. com. Acad. Senate for Calif. C.C.s, 1985-86, Chancellor of Calif. C.C.s Adv. and Rev. Coun. Fund for Instrnl. Improvement, 1984-86; co-project dir. statewide, coord. So. Calif. Biotech. Edn. Consortium, 1993-95, steering com., 1993-98; adj. asst. prof. Chapman Coll., San Diego, 1974-83, San Diego State U., 1977-79; chmn. Am. Colls. Istanbul Sci. Week, 1969-71; adv. bd. Chapman Coll. Cmty. Ctr., 1978-81; cons. sci. curriculum Calif. Dept. Edn., 1986-89; pres. Internat. Rels. Club, 1959-61; mem. San Francisco World Affairs Coun., 1966-68, San Diego World Affairs Coun., 1992—; v.p. Palomar Palace Estates Home Owners Assn., 1983-85, pres., 1994-99, 2003-2004, v.p., 1999—; mem. Rsch. Conf. on Undergrad. Microbiology Edn., Conn. Coll., 1999; bd. dirs. US Orgn. Med. Ednl. Needs, US Internat. Boundary and Water Commn. Citizens Forum Bd.; mem. South Bay Networking Group, 2006—; presenter in field. Emeritus mem. edilt. rev. bd.: Jour. of Coll. Sci. Tchg. Life mem. Chula Vista Nature Ctr.; mem. Internat. Friendship Commn., Chula Vista, 1985-95, vice chmn., 1989-90, chmn., 1990-92; mem. US-Mex. Sister Cities Assn., nat. bd. dirs., 1992-94, gen. chair 30th nat. conv., 1993; founding pres. Chula Vista-Odawara Sister Cities Assn., 1993—; mem. City of Chula Vista Resource Conservation Commn., 1996-05, chmn. 2002-04; mem. Chula Vista Bd. Ethics, 1999-2000, County San Diego Solid Waste Hearing Panel, 2000-05; co-organizer Chula Vista People-to-People Sister City Dels. to Odawara City, Japan, 1991, 94, 99; cmty. adv. com. San Diego Mus. Man, 2000-03; citizens forum bd. U.S. Internat. Boundary and Water Commn., 2001—; steering com. Chula Vista Gen. Plan Update, 2002-05; com. mem. Chula Vista Environ., Open Space and Sustainable Devel., 2002-05; alt. del. citizens adv. com. Port of San Diego and City Chula Vista Bayfront Master Plan, 2003-06; assoc. mem. Calif. Local Govts. Commn., 2005—; mem. Sister Cities Internat. 50th Anniversary Cir. of Distinction. Vols., 2006; docent Bonita Mus. and Cultural Ctr., 2006—. Grantee Pa. Heart Assn., 1962; fellow NSF, 1965, USPHS, 1972-73; recipient Nat. Tchg. Excellence award Nat. Inst. Staff and Orgnl. Devel., 1989; named Southwestern Coll. Woman of Distinction, 1987, Hon. Coach Southwestern Coll. Ladies Basketball Apaches, 2001, Jaguars Basketball Team, 2003, Chula Vista Environmentalist of Yr., 2005, 50th Anniversary Cir. Dist. Vol. award Sister Cities Internat., 2006. Mem.: NIH (mentor Bridges to the Future program Southwestern Coll. and San Diego 1993—98, steering com.), NSTA (life; coord. internat. honors exch. lectr. competition 1986, internat. com.), NEA (life), Marty Altbaum S.W. San Diego Country Club (Marty Altbaum Lion of Yr. 2006), Faculty Assn. Calif. C.C.s (state policy com. 2003—05), Am. Assn. Cmty. and Jr. Colls., Am. Soc. Microbiology (So. Calif. MicrobeDiscovery Team 1995—99), San Diego Yokohama Sister City Soc. (life), Calif. Sci. Tchrs. Assn. (life), Calif. Tchrs. Assn. (life), Nat. Assn. Biology Tchrs. (life), Chula Vista N.W. Civic Assn., Am.-Lebanese Assn. San Diego (1st v.p. 1984—91, pres. 1988—93, chmn. scholarship com., hon. life mem. 2006), Chula Vista Nature Ctr. (life), Japan Soc. San Diego and Tijuana (life), Japanese Am. Hist. Soc. (life), San Diego Zool. Soc., Am. U. Beirut Alumni and Friends of San Diego (1st v.p. 1984—91), Chula Vista C. of C., Chula Vista-Odawara (Japan) Sister Cities Assn. (founding pres. 1993—), Lions Club (Lion of the Yr. 2006), Am. Lebanese Syrian Ladies Club (pres. 1982—83), Lions Internat. (bull. editor 1991—93, 2d v.p. 1992—93, 1st v.p. 1993—94, editor Roaring Times Newsletter 1993—94, chmn. dist. internat. rels. and cooperations com. 1993—95, pub. rels. 1997—98, S.W. San Diego County v.p. 2006—, Best Bull. award 1992—93, S.W. San Diego County Lion of Yr. 2000, 2006), Delta Kappa Gamma (Gamma Omicron chpt. corr. sec. 2006—, Outstanding Pub. Svc. award Gamma Omicron chpt. 2003), Phi Theta Kappa, Sigma Phi Sigma, Kappa Gamma Pi (pres. Wilkes-Barre chpt. 1963—64, pres. San Francisco chpt. 1967—68), Alpha Pi Epsilon (life; advisor Southwestern Coll. chpt. 1989—90, founder). Office Phone: 619-427-3181. Personal E-mail: terrytom@ix.netcom.com.

THOMAS, VICKI WEBB, theater educator; b. Wilson, N.C., June 25, 1961; d. Jimmie and Anne Harrell Webb; 1 child, Jonathon Hunt. BA in English, Elizabeth City State U., N.C., 1990; M of Performing Arts, Oklahoma City U., Okla., 1994. Instr. drama Edmond North H.S., Okla., 1998—; tech. dir. Lyric Theatre of Okla., Oklahoma City, 1999—2001. Adj. faculty Oklahoma City U., 1995—99. Author: (play) Trapped For Life!. Avocations: writing historical novels, genealogy. Office: Edmond N HS 215 W Danforth Rd Edmond OK 73003 Office Phone: 405-715-6386. E-mail: vicki.thomas@edmondschools.net.

THOMAS-BEVINGTON, VERA ELLEN BALL, retired physical education educator; b. Kingsport, Tenn., Apr. 7, 1941; d. Fred Edison and Alma Josephine (Lane) Ball; m. Roger Evan Thomas, Sept. 6, 1966 (dec. 1995); 1 child, Heather Brooke Thomas; m. Richard E. Bevington, July 8, 2000. BS, Carson-Newman Coll., 1963; MS, U. Tenn., 1964; postgrad., Appalachian State U., 1972-73. Asst. prof. Appalachian State U., Boone, NC, 1964—2000. Womens golf coach Appalachian State U., Boone, 1975-85, clogging coach, 1975-99; golf chair N.C. Assn. Intercollegiate Athletics for Women, 1976-79. Co-founder, pres. Dance Assn. N.C. Educators, 1976. Mem. AAHPERD, Nat. Dance Assn., N.C. Alliance Health, Phys. Edn., Recreation and Dance, N.C. Dance Assn., N.C. Women's Golf Assn. (bd. dir. 1991—). Presbyterian. Avocations: golf, gardening. Home: PO Box 507 Blowing Rock NC 28605-0507

THOMAS-CAPPELLO, ELIZABETH, performing arts association administrator; b. Bridgeport, Conn., Apr. 12, 1970; d. Leon Evan Thomas III and Mary Guccione Olson; 1 child, Chandler John Hunt; m. John Christopher Cappello, Jan. 2, 1999; 1 child, Camille Cappello. BS, So. Ill. U., Carbondale, 1993; MS, U. Ill., Springfield, 1996. Asst. to the dir. Univ. Mus., Carbondale, 1994; asst. dir. Peoria (Ill.) Art Guild, 1995; devel. Springfield Art Assn., 1995; exec. dir. Arts Coun. Orange County, Middletown, N.Y., 1996-97; cons. Dutchess County Arts Coun., Poughkeepsie, N.Y., 1997—; substiture art tchr. Valley Ctrl. Sch. Dist., Montgomery, N.Y., 1999—. Bd. dirs. Newburgh Ctr. for the Arts, chair, 1998—; bd. dirs. Museum Village, 1997-99; mem. Leadership Orange, 1998—. Home: 78 Ulster Ave Walden NY 12586-1442

THOMAS-GRAHAM, PAMELA, apparel executive; b. Detroit, 1963; d. Albert and Marian Thomas; m. Lawrence Otis Graham; 3 children. Grad., AB, Harvard Coll.; MBA, Harvard Bus. Sch.; JD, Harvard Law Sch. With McKinsey & Co., 1989—99, ptnr., 1995—99; pres., CEO CNBC.com, 1999—2001, CNBC, Ft. Lee, NJ, 2001—05, chmn., 2005; group pres. Liz Claiborne, Inc., NYC, 2005—. Editor: Harvard Law Rev.; author: Ivy League Mystery Series, (novels) A Darker Shade of Crimson, 1998, Blue Blood, 1999, Orange Crushed, 2004. Bd. dirs. Clorox, Idenix Pharms., NYC Opera. Named Woman of Yr., Finl. Women's Assn.; named one of Forty Under Forty Rising Young Bus. Leaders, Crain's N.Y. Bus., Top 20 Women in Fin., Global Fin. Mag., Top 10 Cons. in Am., Cons. Mag.; recipient Matrix award, N.Y. Women Comm., 2001. Mem.: Phi Beta Kappa.

THOMAS-HARRIS, YVONNE ANITA, writer, poet; b. Millington, Tenn., Aug. 27, 1964; d. William Albert and Romelia Louise (Rich) Thomas; m. Gregory Harris; children: Antonio Dewayne James, Trishanna Renea, Chantell S. Harris, Ashley K. Harris, Gregory Juwan Harris. Cert., Morris & McDaniel Sch., Memphis, 1987, ITT Career Tng. Ctr., 1991; diploma, Jefferson Bus. Coll., Memphis, 1988; attended, Southwest Tenn. C.C., 2005; attneded, World Harvest Bible Coll., 2006. Security guard Ringling Bros. and Barnum Bailey, Washington, 1986; mental health tech. S.E. Mental Health Ctr., Memphis, 1987; nursing asst. St. Peters Villa, Memphis, 1987; profl. model Memphis, 1990; housekeeper Econo Inn, Millington, 1990; med. asst. Primary Med. Care, Inc., Memphis, 1991; receptionist, supr. H & R Block, Memphis, 1991—; adminstrv. asst. Perea Presch., Memphis, 2006; prin., sec. UT Health Sci. Ctr., Coll. of Dentistry, 2006. Med. office asst./receptionist psychiatry dept. U. Tenn. Med. Group, 1996. Contbr. poems to World Treasury of Golden Poems, 1990, Poetic Voices of America, 1992, Shadows and Light, 1996; songwriter Cream High Records, Blue Time Blues, 1986, A Surrender to the Moon, 2005. Sec. Project Amos, Memphis, 1989; vol. Dept. Human Svcs., Memphis, 1988. Mem.: ADEA. Democrat. Avocations: quilting, photography, drawing, crafts. Home: 3815 Kerr Rd Millington TN 38083 Office Phone: 901-527-8344. Personal E-mail: yvonneharris64@yahoo.com. Business E-Mail: yvonhrr5@aol.com.

THOMASHOW, LINDA SUZANNE, microbiologist; b. Norwood, Mass. d. John Michael and E. Jean (Cole) Ravinski. BS, U. Mass., 1968; PhD, UCLA, 1979. Asst. prof. Wash. State U., Pullman, 1983-84; rsch. geneticist USDA Agrl. Rsch. Svc., Pullman, 1985—. Adj. prof. dept. plant pathology Wash. State U. Editorial bd. Applied & Environ. Microbiology, Washington, 1990-98; contbr. articles to profl. jours. Mem. Am. Soc. Microbiology, Am. Phytopathol. Soc. (Ruth Allen award 1997), Internat. Soc. for Molecular Plant-Microbe Interactions. Achievements include research in production of antibiotics by beneficial bacteria that live in association with the roots of plants, structure, function and regulation of genes involved in antibiotic synthesis by bacteria, the ecological significance of antibiotic production in natural environments. Office: Wash State Univ PO Box 646430 Dept Plant Pathology Pullman WA 99164-6430

THOMAS-JOHN, YVONNE MAREE, artist, interior designer; b. Leeton, NSW, Australia, Sept. 8, 1944; came to U.S., 1966; d. Percy Edward and Gladys May (Markham) Thomas; m. Michael Peter John, Aug. 20, 1966; children: Michael Christian, Stephen Edwin Dennis. Student, Buenaventura Coll., 1969, U. Calif., Santa Barbara, 1975; cert., United Design Guild, 1975; AA, Interior Design Guild, 1976. Designer Percy Thomas Real Estate, Leeton, 1960-66; cosmetologist, artist Bernard's Hair Stylists, Ventura, Calif., 1966-67, 74-73; cosmetologist Banks Beauty Salon, Chgo., 1968-69; owner, mgr. Yvonne Maree Designs, Ventura and Olympia, Wash., 1978—. Owner, cosmetologist Mayfair Salon, Leeton, 1962-66; owner, mgr. Y.M. Boutique, Griffith, Australia, 1965-66. Author short stories, numerous poems; one-woman shows include Royal Mus. Sydney, Australia, 1954, exhibited in group shows at Ventura County Courthouse, 1970, Wash. Women in Art, Olympia, 1990, Timberland Libr., 1990, Maska Internat. Gallery, Seattle, 1991, Nat. Hdqrs. of Am. Soc. Interior Designers, Washington, 1992, Michael Stone Collection, 1992, Funding Ctr., Alexandria, Va., 1992, Mus. Modern Art, Bordeaux, France, 1993, Abney Galleries, NYC, 1993, NE Trade Ctr. & Exposition Ctr., Mass., 1993, Mus. Modern Art, Miami, 1993, Hargus Unique Gallery, Pomona, Calif., 1994, Gallery Brindabella, Oakville, Ont., Can., 1996, Art Comm. Internat., Phila., 1996, World Bank, Washington, 1996—97, UN Fourth World Conf. on Women, Beijing, China, 1995, others, exhibitions include Hargus Unique Gallery, Pomona, Calif., 1994, Represented in permanent collections Royal Mus. Sydney, O'Toole Collection, Melbourne, Nat. Mus. Women in Arts, Washington, Patterson Collection, Mich., Witherow Collection, Washington, Samaniego Collection, Calif., Ronald Reagan Collection, Calif. Artist Ventura County Gen. HOsp. Recipient award, Sydney newspapers, 1950, Ribbons, County Fairs, Australia, 1950, 1st round winner painting, Hathaway Competition, 1970. Mem. Am. Platform Assn. Republican. Roman Catholic. Avocations: swimming, tennis, walking, books, music. Office: PO Box1036 Shelton WA 98584 Office Phone: 360-426-8794. Fax: 360-426-3509. Office Phone: 360-426-3509. E-mail: ymaree@ix.netcom.com.

THOMAS-LÖWE, CHRISTINE L., small business owner; d. Alfred Joseph Thomas and Loyce Mae Argo-Thomas; m. Scott H. Lowe, Feb. 8, 1997. BA Edn., Western Ky. U., Bowling Green, 1972; MPS in Pub. Adminstrn., Western Ky. U., 1982; MS in Data Processing & Mgmt. & Info. Sys., Amber U., Garland, Tex., 1985. Bus. analyst and ISO internal auditor ADP, Coppell, Tex., 2000—03; prin., owner CLL Consulting & Documentation Svcs., Owensboro, Ky., 2003—. Software tester and documentation specialist IBM, Dallas, 1997—2000. Composer (and lyrics): (opera) Soldato Del Destino (Soldier of Destiny), 2003—06; author: (screenplay) Soldato Del Destino; performer: (opera excerpts) Batesville Symphony, 2004, Owensboro Youth Symphony, 2006, Batesville Symphony Orch. Mem.: Am. Mensa (assoc.). Roman Catholic. Home: 2020 York Dr Owensboro KY 42301-3436 Office: CLL Consulting & Documentation Services 2020 York Dr Owensboro KY 42301-3436 Office Phone: 270-926-5336. Personal E-mail: lowes@bellsouth.net.

THOMASON, AMY LYNN, history educator; b. Miami, Mar. 15, 1975; d. Joseph and Suzanne Cianflone; m. Chris Thomason, Nov. 16, 2002. BS in Social Sci. Edn., Kennesaw State U., Ga., 1998. Tchr. history North Cobb Christian Sch., Kennesaw, Ga., 1998—2006. Conservative. Baptist. Avocations: travel, reading. Personal E-mail: thomasonamy@yahoo.com.

THOMASON, LYNNE, councilman, medical technician; b. St. Paul, Aug. 2, 1953; d. Glenn O. and Helen M. Thomason. Laser electro-optics diploma, Hennepin Tech. Coll., 1996, laser marking cert., 1996, laser engraving cert., 1996. Cert. direct endorsement underwriter U.S. Dept. HUD. Sr. closer Knutson Mortgage, Mpls., 1991-94; sr. med. laser technician Latis, Inc., Mpls., 1997—. Cons. Illumenex Corp., Mpls., 1998—; auditor, underwriter RMS, Mpls., 1998—. Vol. counselor North Heights Counseling Clinic, St. Paul, 1994-98; coun. mem. City of Mounds View, Minn., 1998—; commr. Mounds View Econ. Devel. Authority, 1999; coun. liaison Mounds View Econ. Devel. Commn., 1999; bd. dirs. N.W. Youth and Family Svcs. Mem. North Suburban C. of C. (assoc.). Lutheran. Avocations: reading, interior design, volunteer counseling.

THOMASON, SANDRA LEE, elementary school educator; d. Eugene LeRoy Ducat and Jean Frances Miller-Ducat; 1 child, Eric Christopher. EdB, U. Toledo, 1968, MEd, 1974. Permanent Tchg. Cert. Ohio State Dept. Edn., 1993, Reading Cert. K-12 Ohio State Dept. of Edn., 1993. Primary edn. tchr. Wash. Local Schs., Toledo, 1968—75, Sylvania (Ohio) schs., 1985—2000; vis. prof. U. Toledo, 1999—2003; reading instr. Ohio State Dept. of Edn., Perrysburg, Ohio, 1999—2003, Sylvania, 1999—2003, Toledo, 1999—2003; guest tchr. Lourdes Coll., Sylvania, Ohio, 2000; literacy specialist Sylvania Schs., 2000—03; reading cons., tchr., trainer NW Ohio Regional Profl. Devel. Ctr., Toledo, 2000—03; literacy support tchr., mid. sch. Olentangy Local Schs., Powell, Ohio, 2003—. Program adminstr. Summer Fun Summer Play Sch., Toledo, 1979; literacy specialist Ohio State Dept. of Edn., 1999—2003; counseling support group leader U. Toledo Counseling Ctr., 1982—84; youth enrichment seminar tchr. Sylvania Schs., Sylvania, 1996—97, 1996—97; spkr. Lourdes Coll., 1997—98; presenter, integrated curriculum with a lit. base, k-4 Patrick-Henry Local Schs., Deshler, Ohio, 1995—96; cons. in field. Dir.: (exhbn.) Developmentally Appropriate and Integrated Activities Across the Curriculum; contbr. articles to popular mags. Sect. leader Toledo 20/20 City Initiative. Mem.: ASCD, Ohio Coun. of the Tchrs. Lang. Arts, Internat. Reading Assn., Pi Lambda Theta (hon.), Phi Delta Kappa (hon.). Achievements include development of curriculum for primary grade children, balanced literacy curriculum for elementary and middle school students; design of edn. programs for summer sch. students in presch. and primary grades. Office: Olentangy Local Schs 814 Shanahan Rd Ste 300 Lewis Center OH 43035 Office Phone: 740-657-4050. Business E-Mail: sandra_thomason@olentangy.k12.oh.us.

THOMASON-MUSSEN, JANIS FAYE, human services administrator; b. Rome, N.Y., Oct. 6, 1946; d. Howard Irving and Marjorie Ellen (Thomason) Mussen; children: John Kennedy Pratt, Wendy Jo Pratt Bowen, Amara Jo Pratt. BA in Journalism, Syracuse U., 1983. Reporter, columnist Oneida (N.Y.) Daily Dispatch, 1983-85; editor Coll. Graphic Arts and Photography Rochester (N.Y.) Inst. Tech., 1985-87; freelance writer, editor, photographer Rochester, 1987-88; exec. dir. Come-Unity Ctr., Inc. Wayne County Rural Ministry/Come-Unity Ctr., Inc., Williamson, N.Y., 1988—. Founder Wayne County (N.Y.) Coalition of Migrant Farmworker Svcs., 1991—; mem. Wayne County Task Force on In-Home Svcs. for Elderly, 1989—. Scholarship Gannett News Svc., 1982, 83; named Woman of Excellence Seven Lakes Girl Scout Coun., 1995. Mem. Sigma Delta Chi. Home: PO Box 698 Williamson NY 14589-0698 Office: Wayne County Rural Ministry PO Box 73 Williamson NY 14589-0073

THOMAS-ROOTS, PAMELA M., writer, educator; b. New Haven, May 3, 1965; BA in Biology, Am. U., 1989. Author: You Have One Body. Take Care of It!, 1999, PTR's Educational Fun Booklets, Collection One, 1999, PTR's Educational Fun Booklets, Collection Two, 2000, More Fun with Pamma Lamma, 2002, Pages in the Library, 2003, East Entry Log of Books Read, 2004, Easy Entry Log of Movies Seen, 2005, Easy Entry Log of Places Traveled, 2005, Easy Entry Log of Favorite Television Shows, 2006, A Whole Lot Of Fun With Pamma Lamma and Pummy Wammy Activity Coloring Fun Book, Amazing More Fun With Pamma Lamma and Pammy Wammy Activity Coloring Fun Book, Justified Revenge, 2005. Avocations: exercise, reading, mystery shows, travel.

THOMASSON, AMIE LYNN, philosopher, educator; b. Gainesville, Fla., July 4, 1968; d. Walter Neill and Clarissa Camfield Thomasson; m. Peter John Lewis, June 6, 1996. BA, Duke U., Durham, N.C., 1989; MA, U. Calif., Irvine, Calif., 1992; PhD, U.Calif., Irvine, N.C., 1995. Asst. prof. Tex. Tech U., Lubbock, Tex., 1995—98; rsch. asst. prof. U. Hong Kong, China, 1999—2000; asst. prof. U. Miami, Coral Gables, Fla., 2000—03, assoc. prof., 2003—. Co-editor (with David W. Smith): Phenomenology and Philosophy of Mind; contbr. over 30 articles to profl. jours. Fellow, NEH, 2003, Summer Stipend, Australian Nat. U., Ctr. Consciousness, 2005; grantee, NEH, 2002. Mem.: Am. Soc. Aesthetics (trustee 2005—), Am. Philos. Assn. (life). Avocations: travel, photography, kayaking. Office: Department of Philosophy University of Miami Box 248054 Coral Gables FL 33124-4670 Office Phone: 305-284-5315. Office Fax: 305-284-5594.

THOMAS-WRIGHT, LISA ANN, elementary school educator; b. Rochester, Pa., Apr. 13, 1974; d. James and Cathy Thomas; m. Carl J. Wright, June 27, 1998; children: Grayson, Maura, Elizabeth. MusB in Music Edn., Westminster Coll., New Wilmington, Pa., 1996; MEd in Ednl. Adminstrn. and Supervision, U. Pitts., 2004. Cert. prin. Pa. Dir. music Highland Presbyn. Ch., New Castle, Pa., 1996—97; music specialist Aliquippa (Pa.) Sch. Dist., 1997—98, Blackhawk Sch. Dist., Beaver Falls, Pa., 1998—. Pvt. music instr., Pa., 1994—. Author: numerous poems. Children's music dir. Meth. Ch., Beaver County, Pa., 1996—2000. Western Pa. Writing Project fellow. Mem.: Phi Mu (life). Methodist. Avocations: art, reading. Office: Blackhawk Sch Dist 500 Blackhawk Rd Beaver Falls PA 15010 Office Phone: 724-827-2116. Personal E-mail: lisatw@adelphia.net. Business E-Mail: thomas-wrightl@bsd.k12.pa.us.

THOMPKINS, JENNIFER ELEY, physician assistant, consultant; b. Barstow, Calif., Apr. 24, 1952; d. Thomas Jefferson Eley and Charlotte Anne (Whittington) Moore; m. Tommy Ray Thompkins, Jan. 7, 1978; 1 child, Benjamin Ellis. BS in Microbiology, U. So. Calif., 1974; B in Med. Sci., Emory U., 1977. Physician asst. div. plastic surgery Emory U., Atlanta, 1978-80; physician asst. dept. offender rehab. State of Ga., Stone Mountain, 1981-82; sr. physician asst. dept. neurology Tex. Tech. U., Lubbock, 1982-84; clin. trials coord. Baylor Coll. Medicine, Houston, 1984-85; sr. physician asst. VA Med. Ctr., Bay Pine, Fla., 1985-87; dir. clin. ops. Porton Med. Group, Sherman Oaks, Calif., 1987-89; chmn. T & J Tompkins Assoc. Ic., Woodland Hills, Calif., 1989—. Cons. to pharm. industry, 1989—. Contbr. chpt.: Manual of Clinical Oncology, 1988. First aid/CPR instr. ARC, Van Nuys, Calif., 1991—. Fellow Am. Acad. Physician Assts.; mem. Assocs. Clin. Rsch. Profls. Avocations: hiking, scuba diving, conservation. Office: T & J Thompkins Assocs Inc 24007 Ventura Blvd Ste 102 Calabasas CA 91302-2549

THOMPSON, ABIGAIL, mathematics professor; PhD, Rutgers U., 1986. Prof., dept. math. U. Calif., Davis, 1988—. Dir., COSMOS program U. Calif., Davis. Contbr. articles to profl. jours. Recipient Ruth Lyttle Satter prize in Math., Am. Math. Soc., 2003. Office: Math Sciences Bldg U Calif One Shields Ave Davis CA 95616 Office Phone: 530-752-8236. Office Fax: 530-752-6635. Business E-Mail: thompson@math.ucdavis.edu.*

THOMPSON, ANNE, music educator; MusB, Western Mich. U., Kalamazoo, 1993; MusM, U. Notre Dame, Ind., 1995. Cert. music tchr. Mich. Orch. dir. Kentwood Pub. Schs., Mich., 1997—; pvt. cello instr. Grand Rapids, Mich., 1997—. Sect. cello West Shore Symphony Orch., Muskegon, Mich., 1999—; performer Mich. Music Concert. Sec. Mich. Sch. Band and Orch., Grand Rapids, 2001—03. Mem.: Am. Fedn. Musicians, Music Edn. Nat. Conf., Am. String Tchr. Assn., Suzuki Assn. Am., Phi Kappa Phi. Avocations: running, travel, golf, bicycling. Office: Kentwood Public Schs 5820 Eastern Ave SE Kentwood MI 49508 Office Phone: 616-455-4400.

THOMPSON, ANNE ELISE, federal judge; b. Phila., July 8, 1934; d. Leroy Henry and Mary Elise (Jackson) Jenkins; m. William H. Thompson, June 19, 1965; children: William H., Sharon A. BA, Howard U., 1955, LLB, 1964; MA, Temple U., 1957. Bar: D.C. bar 1964, N.J. bar 1966. Staff atty. Office of Solicitor, Dept. Labor, Chgo., 1964-65; asst. dep. public defender Trenton, N.J., 1967-70; mcpl. prosecutor Lawrence Twp., Lawrenceville, N.J., 1970-72; mcpl. ct. judge Trenton, 1972-75; prosecutor Mercer County, Mercer County, Trenton, 1975-79; judge U.S. Dist. Ct. N.J., Trenton, 1979—. Vice chmn. Mercer County Criminal Justice Planning Com., 1972; mem. com. criminal practice N.J. Supreme Ct., 1975-79, mem. com. mcpl. cts., 1972-75; v.p. N.J. County Prosecutors Assn., 1978-79; chmn. juvenile justice com. Nat. Dist. Attys. Assn., 1978-79 Del. Democratic Nat. Conv., 1972. Recipient Assn. Black Women Lawyers award, 1976, Disting. Service award Nat. Dist. Attys. Assn., 1979, Gene Carte Meml. award Am. Criminal Justice Assn., 1980, Outstanding Leadership award N.J. County Prosecutors Assn., 1980, John Mercer Langston Outstanding Alumnus award Howard U. Law Sch., 1981; also various service awards; certs. of appreciation. Mem. Am. Bar Assn., Fed. Bar Assn., N.J. Bar Assn., Mercer County Bar Assn. Democrat. Office: US Dist Ct US Courthouse-4000 402 E State St Trenton NJ 08608-1507

THOMPSON, ANNE KATHLEEN, entertainment journalist; b. NYC, Aug. 10, 1954; d. Charles Torrington Thompson and Eleanor Josephine (Callahan) Dekins; m. David Christopher Chute, Oct. 23, 1983; 1 child, Nora Thompson Chute. BA in Cinema Studies, NYU, 1976. Asst. mgr. Bleecker St. Cinema, NYC, 1975—76; publicist United Artists, NYC, 1976—79; account exec. P/M/K Pub. Rels., NYC, 1979—81; assoc. editor Film Comment Mag., NYC, 1981-82, west coast editor, 1982-96; publicity dir. Twentieth Century Fox Pictures, 1983-85; wrote column Risky Bus. LA Weekly, LA Times Syndicate, 1985-93; columnist Inside Film, 1988-90; U.S. editor Empire Mag., London, 1989-91; sr. writer Entertainment Weekly, 1993-96; west coast editor Premier Mag., 1996—2002; contbr. Premiere, Filmmaker, Wired, NY Times, Washington Post, NY mag., London Observer; dep. film editor The Hollywood Reporter, LA, 2005—. Mem. Nat. Writer's Union, Women in Film. Office: The Hollywood Reporter 5055 Wilshire Blvd Los Angeles CA 90036-4396

THOMPSON, ANNIE FIGUEROA, retired academic administrator; b. Río Piedras, P.R., June 7, 1941; d. Antonio Figueroa-Colón and Ana Isabel Laugier; m. Donald P. Thompson, Jan. 23, 1972; 1 child, John Anthony. BA, Baylor U., 1962; MSLS, U. So. Calif., 1965; AMD, Fla. State U., 1978, PhD, 1980. Educator Mayan Sch., Guatemala City, Guatemala, 1962-63; cataloger libr. sys. U. P.R., Río Piedras, 1965-67, head music libr., 1967-81, assoc. prof. librarianship, 1981-85, dir. grad. sch. libr. info. sci. Rio Piedras, 1986-93, prof., 1986-96; ret., 1996. Author: An Annotated Bibliography About Music in Puerto Rico, 1975; co-author: Music and Dance in Puerto Rico from the Age of Columbus to Modern Times, An Annotated Bibliography, 1991; contbr. articles to profl. jours.; performed song recitals Inst. of P.R. Culture and U. P.R. Artist Series, 1974-78; soloist with P.R. Symphony Orch., San Juan, 1978; performed in opera, on radio and TV, San Juan, 1968-81. Sec. P.R. Symphony Orch League, San Juan, 1982-84; mem. pub. libr. adv. com. Adminstrn. for Devel. of Arts and Culture, P.R., 1982-84, Pub. Libr. Adv. Bd., 1989-94. Recipient Lauro a la Instrucción Bibliotecaria Sociedad de Bibliotecarios de P.R., 1985, Lauro a la Bibliografía Puertorriqueña, 1993. Mem. Sarasota Rotary (bd. dirs. 2000-02), Sociedad de Bibliotecarios de P.R. (pres. 1994-96), Music Libr. Assn. (bd. dirs. 1982-84, asst. conv. mgr. 2002-04, conv. mgr. 2004-06), Sarasota Rotary Found. (bd. dirs.), Sigma Delta Kappa, Mu Phi Epsilon, Beta Phi Mu. Episcopalian. Home: 435 S Gulfstream Ave Sarasota FL 34236-6736 Personal E-mail: annietmla@aol.com.

THOMPSON, BARBARA STORCK, state official; b. McFarland, Wis., Oct. 15, 1924; d. John Casper and Marie Ann (Kassabaum) Storck; m. Glenn T. Thompson, July 1, 1944; children— David C., James T. BS, Wis. State U., 1956; MS, U. Wis., 1959, PhD, 1969; L.H.D. (hon.), Carroll Coll., 1974. Tchr. pub. schs., West Dane County, Mt. Horeb, Wis., 1944-56; instr. Green County Tchrs. Coll., Monroe, Wis., 1956-57; coordinator curriculum Monroe Pub. Schs., 1957-60; instr. U. Wis., Platteville, 1960; supr. schs. Waukesha County Schs., Wis., 1960-63, supt. schs., 1963-65; prin. Fairview Elem. Schs., Brookfield, Wis., 1962-64; adminstrv. cons. Wis. Dept. Pub. Instrn., Madison, 1964-72, state coordinator, 1971-72; instr. U. Wis., Madison and Green Bay, 1972; supt. pub. instrn. Madison, Wis., 1973—81. Mem. Wis. State Bd. Vocat. Edn., 1973-81, Wis. Edn. Comm. Bd., 1973-81, Univ. Wis. Sys. Bd. Regents, 1973-1981. Author: A Candid Discussion of Critical Issues, 1975; mem. editorial bd.: The Education Digest, 1975—; contbr. articles to profl. jours. Mem. White House Conf. Children, 1970, Gov.'s Com. State Conf. Children and Youth, 1969-70, Manpower Council, 1973-81; bd. dirs. Vocational, Tech. and Adult Edn., 1973-81, Ednl. Communications, 1973-81, Higher Edn. Aids, 1973-81, Agy. Instructional TV, 1975-81; mem. nat. panel on SAT score decline; bd. regents U. Wis., 1973-81, U.S. office f Edn. Visiting Sch. Team - England, GErmany, Sweden, Poland, Iran, Syria, India, and Japan. Recipient State Conservation award Madison Lions CLub, 1956; Waukesha Freeman award, 1961 Mem. Nat. Coun. Adminstrv. Women in Edn. (named Woman of Year 1974), Nat. Coun. State Cons. in Elem. Edn. (pres. 1974-75), Wis. Assn. Sch. Dist. Adminstrs., Assn. Supervision and Curriculum Devel., Wis. Assn. Supervision and Curriculum Devel., Southwestern Wis. Assn. Supervision and Curriculum Devel., Southeastern Wis. Assn. Supervision and Curriculum Devel. (mem. exec. council 1972-73), Dept. Elem. Sch. Prins., Wis. Elementary Sch. Prins. Assn., NEA, Wis. Edn. Assn. (pres. local chpt. 1970-71); life mem. So. Wis. Edn. Assn., Wis. Ednl. Rsch. Assn., Dept. Elem.-Kindergarten-Nursery Edn., Assn. Childhood Edn. Internat., Assn. Childhood Edn., Coun. Chief State Sch. Officers, Edn. Commn. of States, Nat. Coun. State Cons. in Elem. Edn. (pres. 1974-75), Am. Assn. Sch. Dist. Adminstrs. (chmn. policy com. 1963-81), Madison Ctrl. Internat. Lions Club, U. Wis. Alumni Orgn. (Sarasota, Fla. and Madison), U. Wis. League (Madison chpt.), Delta Kappa Gamma, Pi Lambda Theta. Office: Apt 123 325 S Yellowstone Dr Madison WI 53705-4301

THOMPSON, BECKY LOUISE, English educator; b. Balt., Mar. 2, 1969; d. Richard Dale and Barbara Elaine Thompson. EdD, Bob Jones U., Greenville, S.C., 2006. Head of English dept. Northland Bapt. Bible Coll., Dunbar, Wis., 1993—2002; asst. prof. of English North Greenville U., Tigerville, SC, 2002—. Writing ctr. dir. North Greenville U., Tigerville, SC, 2003—. Recipient Christian Svc. award, Bapt. Student Union, 2005—06, Recognition award, Student Govt. Assn., 2005—06. Mem.: Nat. Coun. Tchrs. English. Office: North Greenville University 7801 N Tigerville Rd Tigerville SC 29688 Office Phone: 864-977-7065. E-mail: bthompson@ngc.edu.

THOMPSON, BERNIDA LAMERLE, principal, consultant, educator; b. Tuskeegee, Ala., July 5, 1946; d. Berry James Sr. and Doris LaMerle (Askey) T.; m. Rolando Amerson, June 15, 1968 (div. Aug. 1988); children: Afriye Amerson, Mwando Amerson. BS in Elem. Edn., Cen. State U., 1968; MEd in Adminstrn. and Curriculum, Miami U., Oxford, Ohio, 1971; EdD in Early and Mid. Childhood Edn., Nova U., 1992. Classroom elem. sch. tchr. Dayton Pub. Schs.; asst. prin., intern St. James Cath. Sch., Dayton, Ohio; tchr. St. Augustine Cath. Sch., Washington; sci. resource tchr. D.C. Pub. Schs., Washington; founding tchr., prin. Roots Activity Learning Ctr., Washington, 1977—, Roots Pub. Charter Sch., 1999—. Multicultural advisor HBJ 1992 Reading Textbook. Author: Black Madonnas and Young Lions a Rite of Passage for African American Adolescents, 1992, rev. edit., 1998, Africentric Interdisciplinary Multi-Level Hands On Science, 1994, rev. edit., 2001; contbr. articles to profl. jours. Mem. Nat. Assn. Edn. Young Children, World Coun. Curriculum Instrn., Coun. Ind. Black Inst., Inst. Ind. Edn., Nat. Black Child Devel. Inst. Office: Roots Pub Charter Sch 15 Kennedy St NW Washington DC 20011-5201 Office Phone: 202-882-8073. Business E-Mail: bthompson@rootspcs.org.

THOMPSON, BERTHA BOYA, retired education educator; b. New Castle, Pa., Jan. 31, 1917; d. Frank L. and Kathryn Belle (Park) Boya; m. John L. Thompson, Mar. 27, 1942; children: Kay Lynn Thompson Koolage, Scott McClain. BS in Elem. & Secondary Edn., Slippery Rock State Coll., 1940; MA in Geography and History, Miami U., 1954; EdD, Ind. U., 1961. Cert. elem. and secondary edn. tchr. Elem. tchr., reading specialist New Castle (Pa.) Sch. System, 1940-45; tchr., chmn. social studies Talawanda Sch. System, Oxford, Ohio, 1954-63; assoc. prof. psychology and geography, chair edn. dept. Western Coll. for Women, Oxford, 1963-74; assoc. prof. edn., reading clinic Miami U., Oxford, 1974-78, prof. emeritus, 1978—. Contbr. articles to profl. jours. Folk art com. Miami U. Art Mus., Oxford, 1974—76; adv. com. Smith libr., Oxford Pub. Libr., 1978—81. Mem. AAUP, Nat. Coun. Geographic Edn. (exec. bd. dirs. 1966-69), Nat. Soc. for Study Edn., Assn. Am. Geographers, Soc. Women Geographers, Nat. Coun. for the Social Studies, Pi Lambda Theta, Zeta Tau Alpha, Pi Gamma Mu, Gamma Theta Upsilon, Kappa Delta Pi. Avocations: antiques, reading, travel, tennis. Home: 6073 Contreras Rd Oxford OH 45056-9708

THOMPSON, BETTY JANE, retired small business owner; b. Ladysmith, Wis., Nov. 18, 1923; d. Edward Thomas and Mayme Selma (Kratwell) Potter; m. Frederick Sturdee Thompson, Apr. 19, 1945 (div. Apr. 1973); children: Denise Alana, Kent Marshall; m. J.R. Critchfield, Feb. 14, 1977 (div. 1989). Student, Jamestown (N.D.) Coll., 1946-47, U. Calif., Long Beach, 1964-69; AA, Orange Coast Coll., 1976; postgrad., Monterey Peninsula Coll., 1979-80; SBA Cert., Hartnell Coll., 1982. Cert. fashion cons. Owner, mgr., buyer Goodview (Minn.) Food Mart, 1947-50; dist. mgr. Beauty Counselor of Minn., Winona County, 1951-61; Boy Scout liaison J.C. Penney Co., Newport Beach, Calif., 1969-72; dept. mgr. and buyer boyswear At Ease, Newport Beach, 1972-77; mgr. Top Notch Boys Wear, Carmel, Calif., 1977-83, buyer, 1984-88; owner, mgr. Top Notch Watch, Sun City, Ariz., 1989-95; editor H&R Block, 1995-98; employee Wells Fargo and Co., 1998—2004; ret., 2004. V.p., chmn. Don Loper Fashion Show, 1967, pres., 1968, bd. dirs., 1969. Co-editor Aux. Antics mag., 1965. Vol. fundraising leadership Family Svc. Assn., Orange County, Calif., 1962-68, other orgns.; chmn. publicity, study group, Sunday sch. tchr., Congl. Ch., Winona, Minn., 1956-58, fellowship pres., Santa Ana, Calif., 1963-65; pres. Goodview Civic Club, 1948; mem. Wells Fargo and Co. Bank Silver Bullets, Sr. Citizens of the Sun Cities, Phoenix, 1998-2000; counselor AARP Tax Aide, 1997—; moderator Congrl. Christian Fellowship, 1999-2001; sec. Tont Ct. Condominium, 1998-2004. Recipient Athena award Panhellenic Assn. Orange City, Calif., 1968, El Camino Real Dist. Svc. award Orange Empire coun. Boy Scouts Am., Baden-Powell award, Outstanding Leadership award, El Camino Real Dist., Calif., 1972. Ringling North award, 1949; named Outstanding Svc. Vol. Family Svc. Assn., 1969. Mem. Carmel Bus. Assn. Avocations: genealogy, photography, ballroom dance, bicycling, skiing. Home and Office: 10048 W Hawthorn Dr Sun City AZ 85351-2829 E-mail: tbjtonto@aol.com.

THOMPSON, BIRGIT DOLORES, civic worker, writer; b. Jamestown, N.Y., Apr. 7, 1930; d. Oscar Einar and Karin Johanna (Videll) Wolff; m. William Andrew Thompson, Jan. 26, 1952 (div. June 1978); children: William A., Christina A., Michael J., Timothy A., Kathleen S., Jeffrey B. AB summa cum laude, SUNY, Fredonia, 1974. Exec. dir. Fenton Hist. Ctr., Jamestown, 1975-82; fin. dir. Amicae, Inc., Fredonia, 1983-90; office mgr. JEM Counseling Ctr., Jamestown, 1990-93; resource/info. person Audubon Nature Ctr., Jamestown, 1993—. Author: Illustrated History of Jamestown and Chautauqua County, 1983, Jamestown Audubon Society 50th Year History; musician Jamestown String Quartet, violist local orchestras, 1970-2000; contbr. articles to newspapers. Historian City of Jamestown, 1978—; bd. dirs., chair scholarship com. Mozart Club, 2001—05; play selection com. Lucille Ball Little Theatre of Jamestown, 1976—, pit orch.; mem. steering and fin. coms. Underground Railroad Tableau Project; v.p., bd. trustees Unitarian Universalist Congregation Jamestown; bd. dirs. Jamestown YWCA, Chautauqua Regional Youth Symphony, pres., 1996—2001; com. mem. Jamestown Audubon Soc., newsletter editor, 1982—98. Recipient Women of Achievement award in civic category, YWCA, 2004. Mem. AAUW (chmn. What's New Fair Jamestown 1988-94, legislative breakfast 1995—, bd. dirs., pres. 1988-92, co-pres. 2000-06, v.p. membership 2006—, named gift award 1987), Interclub Coun. Jamestown (treas. 1998—, Woman of Yr. award 1992). Avocations: museums, concerts, reading, gardening. Home: 13 Lamont St Jamestown NY 14701-2021 E-mail: musicat@netsync.net.

THOMPSON, CARLA ANNE, literature and language educator; m. Douglas Marshall Thompson, Aug. 14, 1971; children: Matthew Scott, Dawn Elizabeth. BA in Secondary Edn. and English, SUNY, Fredonia, 1973, MA in ESL, 1975. Cert. N.Y. State Edn. Dept., 1973, Nat. Bd. Profl. Tchg. Stds., 2002. Tchr. Lake Shore Sr. H.S., Angola, NY, 1975—, ELA dept. chairperson, 2003—. Tchr. Shakespeare Lives-Buffalo Niagara-Kenan Ctr., Lockport, NY, 2004—; tchr. in-svc. provider Western N.Y. Writing Project, Buffalo, 1997—, outreach coord., 2003—. Organizer Lorinda-2004 Olympic Pursuit, Angola, NY, 1999—2001; organizer fantasy fair Town of Evans, Angola, NY, 2004; singer St. Anthony's Folk Group, Farnham, NY. Mem.: Am. Fedn. Tchrs., N.Y. State Tchrs. Assn. (corr.; nat. presenter). D-Liberal. Roman Catholic. Avocations: dance, theater, travel. Office Phone: 716-549-2128.

THOMPSON, CARRIE LORRAINE, volunteer; b. Portsmouth, Va., Sept. 1, 1953; d. Gordon Howard and Marjorie Lorraine Hausenfluck; m. Rickie Lee Thompson, Oct. 13, 1972; children: Katynia Lorraine Speight, Vicktrie Leighanne Tucker, Brandon Lee, Mariah Lynnette. AA, Eastfield Jr. Coll., Mesquite, Tex., 1973. With Meals on Wheels; dir. vols. Conn. Food Bank at Norwich Worship Ctr., Norwich, 1992—. Home: 21 Winchester St Norwich CT 06360 Office: Conn Food Bank Lawler Ln Norwich CT 06360

THOMPSON, CATHERINE LILA, retired medical center nurse; b. East Saint Louis, Ill., July 29, 1925; d. Guy Vincent and Beatrice (Wayne) T. Diploma, St. Joseph's Sch. Nursing, 1948; BSNED, DePaul U., Chgo., 1952; MEd, Loyola U., 1970. Cert. in nursing adminstrn. Supr. med. ward Charity Hosp., New Orleans; asst. exec. sec. La. State Bd. Practical Nurses, New Orleans; dir. inservice edn. Touro Infirmary, New Orleans; asst. chief nurse ambulatory care svc. VAMC, New Orleans, to 1999; ret. Mem.-at-large Am. Lung Assn.; mem. ARC; mem. adv. bd. practical nurse program Sidney Area Vocat. Sch. Named Great 100 Nurse NODNA, 1988. Home: 9 George Wells Rd Carriere MS 39426

THOMPSON, CHARLOTTE ELLIS, pediatrician, educator, writer; d. Robert and Ann Ellis; divorced; children: Jennifer Ann, Geoffrey Graeme. BA, Stanford U., 1950, MD, 1954. Diplomate Am. Bd. Pediat. Intern Children's Hosp., San Francisco, 1953-54; resident UCLA, 1960-61, L.A. Children's Hosp., 1962-63; pvt. practice La Jolla, Calif., 1963-75; dir. Muscle Disease Clinic Univ. Hosp.-U. Calif. Sch. Medicine, San Diego, 1969-80, asst. clin. prof. pediat., 1969—; founder, dir. Ctr. for Handicapped Children and Teenagers, San Francisco, 1981—2004. Cons. U.S. Naval Hosp., San Diego, 1970-91; dep. dir. Santa Clara County Child Health and Disability, Santa Clara, Calif., 1974-75; dir. Ctr. for Multiple Handicaps, Oakland, Calif., 1976-81; co-dir. Muscle Clinic Children's Hosp., San Diego, 1963-69; dir. muscle program U. Rochester, 1957-60. Author: Raising a Handicapped Child: A Helpful Guide for Parents of the Physically Disabled, 1986, 4th edit., 1991, rev., expanded edit., 2000, Allein leben: Ein umfassendes Handbuch für Frauen, 1993, Making Wise Choices: A Guide for Women, 1993, Raising a Child with a Neuromuscular Disorder, 1999, Raising A Handicapped Child, 1999, 101 Ways To The Best Medical Care, 2006; contbr. articles to med. jours., including Clin. Pediat., New Eng. Jour. Medicine, Neurology, Jour. Family Practice, Mothering, Jour. Pediatric Orthopedics, Pediatrician, Am. Baby, Pediatric News, also chpts. to books. Mem. Calif. Children's Svc. Com., 1977—. Fellow: Am. Acad. Pediat. Avocations: tennis, ice skating, opera. Office: 8070 La Jolla Shores Dr # 514 La Jolla CA 92037-3296 Personal E-mail: cetmd@earthlink.net.

THOMPSON, DAYLE ANN, small business owner, consultant; b. Grand Forks, N.D., Jan. 6, 1954; d. Duane Theodore and Anna Mae (Desautel) T.; m. Michael Gary Sciulla, Aug. 6, 1977 (div. Sept. 1980); m. Manfred Hans von Ehrenfried II, June 11, 1982. Secretarial degree, Aaker's Bus. Coll., Grand Forks, 1973; Masters Cert. in Project Mgmt., George Washington U., 1995. Receptionist U.S. Rep. Norman F. Lent U.S. Ho. of Reps., Washington, 1973-74; office mgr., personal sec. U.S. Rep. Les AuCoin, U.S. Ho. of Reps., Washington, 1975-78; bus. mgr., bookkeeper Virgin Islands POST, St.Thomas, USVI, 1978; office and pers. mgr. Internat. Energy Assocs. Ltd., Washington, 1978-82; program support mgr. MSI Svcs. Inc., Washington, 1982-84; pres., treas., chief exec. officer Tech. and Adminstrv. Svcs. Corp., Washington, 1984-2000; acctg. mgr. Carolyn Kinder, Inc., Clearwater, Fla., 1997—2002; mgmt. and acctg. sys. cons. St. Petersburg, Fla., 2000—04; pres. Get Taxes Back, Inc., St. Petersburg, Fla., 2004—. Hosp. vol. ARC, Arlington, Va., 1987. Recipient Group Achievement award NASA, 1984, 93, Commendation Letter, NASA, 1985, 87, 88, 91, 93, 94, Small Bus. Prime Contractor of Yr. award Small Bus. Adminstrn. Region 5, 1994, Adminstr. award for Excellence. Mem. Washington Space Bus. Roundtable (sponsor-benefactor 1990-92). Republican. Roman Catholic. Avocations: boating, fishing, reading. Home and Office: 4250 42d Ave S Saint Petersburg FL 33711-4231 Business E-Mail: dthompson@gettaxesback.com.

THOMPSON, DEBORAH G., secondary school educator; d. Gallagher; children: James, Amy L Thomas, Michael A. BA, U. of Ala.-Birmingham, 1977; MEd, U. Montevallo, Ala., 1988; Edn. Specialist, U. Montevallo, 1990—91. Cert. tchr. Ala., 2005, Ga., 2005. Tchr. Shelby County Bd. of Edn., Columbiana, Ala., 1977—. English instr. Jefferson State C.C., Birmingham, 2000—03. Named Nat. Tchr. of the Yr., Chadwick's of Boston, 2001, Tchr. of the Yr., Thompson H.S., 2001. Mem.: Ala. Edn. Assn. (assoc.; assn. rep. 1995—2003). Office Phone: 205-682-5700.

THOMPSON, DEBORAH K., elementary school educator; b. Spirit Lake, Iowa, Mar. 8, 1955; d. Alfred Libby and Sheila Klein; m. Kenneth Wayne Thompson, Aug. 9, 1975; children: Seth(dec.), Tyler J. BA in Elem. Edn., U. No. Iowa, Cedar Falls, 1978. Tchr. 1st grade Green Mountain Elem. Sch. Green Mountain Ind. Sch. Dist., Iowa, 1978—87; tchr. 2d grade Rogers Elem. Sch. Marshalltown Comty. Schs., Iowa, 1987—91; tchr. 1st, 2d, and 5th grades Mary Herbert Elem. Sch. Emporia Unified Sch. Dist., Kans., 1992—2003, tchr. 2d grade Timmerman Elem. Sch., 2003—. Contbr. articles to profl. jours. Vol. March of Dimes, Emporia. Recipient Golden Apple award nomination, Presdl. Award for Excellence in Math. and Sci. Tchg. nomination. Mem.: NEA, Emporia H.S. Thespian Boosters (treas. 2005—07), Nat. Sci. Tchrs. Assn. (presenter nat. confs.). Avocations: piano, singing. Office: Grant F Timmerman Elem 2901 Timmerman Dr Emporia KS 66801

THOMPSON, DIANA ROSEBUD, poet, educator, history exhibit coordinator, marketing consultant, playwright; b. NYC, Dec. 25, 1957; d. Samuel Joseph Daniels and Anna Louise Thompson. BA in Psychology, Columbia U., 1979; AAS in cosmetics mktg., Fashion Inst. Tech., 1979—81; MS in early childhood edn., Bklyn Coll., CUNY, 1987—89; JD, Fordham U. Sch. Law, 1990—93. Cert. victim relief training NY Evang. Sem., 2001. Prin. coll. instr. D.R. Thompson Enterprises, NYC, 1980; mktg. cons. 127th Street Repertory Ensemble, 1982—83, 20 West Theatre, NYC, 1983, Art Against Apartheid, NYC, 1984; guest curator, Visual Art of Bill Miller Am. Indian Cmty. Ho. Gallery, 2006. Judge math. NAACP Acad., Cultural, Technol. and Sci. Olympics Competition II, Queens, NY, 1980; adj. prof. Touro Coll., NYC, 2002—; curator The Visual Art of Bill Miller, AICH Gallery, N.Y.C., 2006. Author: (plays) Who Needs Earthlings?; co-host: Educators of Digital Media Network; host Writers, Actors and Artists Forum of Digital Media Network (www.dmnforums.com), 2003; group show, Am. Indian Cmty. House Gallery, 2005. House builder Habitat for Humanity, 2000; vol. Ctrl. Pk. Conservancy, NYC, 1998—2003; chair Am. Culture Assn., 2006; soloist and song leader NYC Marathon Worship Svc., 2001—. Recipient cert. merit, Nat. Council Negro Women, N.Y.C., 1981, Centrum Creative Residency, Centrum Creative Edn., Port Townsend, WA, 2003, Ann. Poetry Slam, Exoterica, 1995, NY Regional Winner of Singing/Songwriting Contest, Lever Bros., 1996, Cert. Appreciation, FDIC - NY, 1998, 1999. Mem.: NARAS, AAUW (publicity chmn. Queens br. 1980—81), MLA, Am. Soc. Composers, Authors and Publs., Metamorphosis Writers Collective, Dramatists Guild Am., Am. Indian Comty. House, NY Rd. Runners, Zeta Phi Beta (fin. sec. L.I. br. 1980—81). Achievements include finished N.Y.C. Marathon, 1998-2005. Personal E-mail: dianapoet@aol.com.

THOMPSON, ELEANOR DUMONT, nurse; b. Derry, N.H., May 26, 1935; d. Louis Arthur and Florence Berthae (Gendreau) D.; m. Carl Hugh Thompson, Aug. 22, 1959; children: Justine, Julie. Student, Dartmouth Hitchcock Nur. Sch., 1956; BA, New Eng. Coll., 1977; MS, Drake U., 1984. Registered art therapist. Pediatric instr. Hanover (N.H.) Sch. Practical Nursing, 1958-61; pub. W.B. Sanders Co., Phila., 1962-95; pediatric instr. St. Joseph Hosp., Nashua, N.H., 1978-81; cert. clin. nurse specialist Mercy Hosp. Med. Ctr., Des Moines, 1987-90; clin. nurse specialist Portsmouth (N.H.) Regional Hosp., 1991-2000; pvt. practice Silverman & Assoc., Inc., 1991-93. Puppeteer St. Joseph's Hosp. Sch. Nursing, Nashua, 1981-82; created and conducted shows on hospitalization for children; nursing cons. Hospice Cen. Iowa, Des Moines, 1982-89; cons. art therapy N.H. Hosp., 2001-04. Author: Pediatric Nursing An Introductory Text, 1965, 6th edit., 1992, (translations in Spanish, Italian and Portuguese), Introduction to Maternity and Pediatric Nursing, 1990, 2d edit., 1995. Vol. nurse Vietnam Vets. Ctr., Des Moines, 1985-87, Camp Apanda Childrens Cancer Camp Boone, Iowa, 1984-86; pipe organist Philips Ch., Exeter, N.H., 2006. Democrat. Roman Catholic. Avocations: playing piano and organ, travel. Home: 13 Sherman Ave Brentwood NH 03833-6225

THOMPSON, ELIZABETH, bank executive; Comptroller First Regional Bancorp, 1998—2003, CFO, 2003—. Office: First Regional Bancorp 1801 Century Park East Los Angeles CA 90067

THOMPSON, ELLEN ANN, elementary school educator; b. Newton, Mass., Mar. 23, 1955; d. Arthur Malachi and Eva Louise (Harris) T.; m. John A. Rasys, Nov. 30, 1980 (div. Apr. 1987); 1 child, Christopher Michael Rasys; m. James E. Holzschuh, July 1, 1995. BS in Edn., U. Vt., 1977, MEd, 1986, postgrad. Cert. elem. tchr., spl. edn. tchr., Vt.; nat. bd. cert. tchr. early childhood generalist. Title I tchr. remedial reading grades 1-3 Colchester (Vt.) Sch. Dist., 1977-78; title I readiness rm. tchr. Union Meml Sch., Colchester, 1978-79, tchr. grade 2 transitional grade, 1979-81, classroom tchr. grades 1-3 multiage, 1981-99; adj. instr. dept. grad. edn. U. Vt., Burlington, 1987—; adj. instr. undergrad. edn. program Trinity Coll., Burlington, 1992-94. Presenter N.E. Whole Lang. Conf., Johnson (Vt.) State Coll., 1987-97, resource agt. tchr. insvc. programs Vt. Dept. Edn., 1988—, resource cons. Vt. Writing Portfolio Assessment Program, 1990—, network leader # 16, 1991-95; conf. presenter, adj. instr. Am. Inst. for Creative Edn., Augusta, Maine, 1988-92; art cons. Within the Forest, Sci. Rsch. Assocs., 1991—; ednl. cons., presenter Soc. for Devel. Edn., Peterborough, N.H.; teaching fellow regional lab. Rural Small Sch. Network, 1991-92; pres. Ellen A. Thompson, Inc., 1999—; reading lang. arts cons., Vt. Dept. End., 1999-2000; adj. prof. U. Vt., Undergrad. Sch. Edn., literacy cons. Reading Excellence Award Grant Program, Winooski, Vt., Gloucester, Mass., 2000—. Author: (videos) The Nuts and Bolts of Multiage Classrooms, 1994, How to Teach in a Multiage Classroom, 1994, (book) I Teach First Grade!, 2001. Recipient State Teacher of the Yr. awd., Vermont, Coun. of Chief State School Offices, 1993. Mem. ASCD, Nat. Coun. Tchrs. English (presenter 1991, 92), Internat. Reading Assn. (presenter annual conf. 1991, Leaders of Readers award 1990), Vt. Coun. on Reading (newsletter editor and conf. presenter 1988—, pres. 1991-92), Vt. Tchrs. Applying Whole Lang., Colchester Edn. Assn. (internal newsletter 1987-89, newsletter editor 1988-89, 96-98), Phi Delta Kappa. Mailing: Univ Vermont Education Dept Waterman Bldg Burlington VT 05405 Office Phone: 802-656-3356. E-mail: Ellen.Thompson@uvm.edu.

THOMPSON, EMILY, historian; b. Pitts., Feb. 20, 1962; d. George John and Majorie Haseman Thompson. BS in Physics, Rochester Inst. of Tech., 1980—84; PhD in History, Princeton U, 1986—92. Sr. tech. assoc. Bell Lab., Holmdel, NJ, 1985—86; vis. asst. prof. Rensselaer Poly. Inst., Troy, NY, 1992—93; post doctoral fellow Harvard U, Cambridge, Mass., 1993—94; asst. prof. Iowa State U, Ames, Iowa, 1994—95, U Pa., Philadelphia, Pa., 1995—2002; sr. fellow Dibner Inst. for History of Sci. and Tech., Cambridge, Mass., 2002—03; assoc. prof. history U. Calif., San Diego, 2005—. Asst. prodr. (albums) Carl Arter, Songs From Afar, 1984; co-editor: The Architecture of Sci., 1999; author: The Soundscape of Modernity, 2002. Recipient Derek Price Prize, History of Sci. Soc., 2000, John Hope Franklin prize, Am. Studies Assn., 2003, Sci. Writing prize, Acoustical Soc. Am., 2002; John Slater Fellow, Am. Philos. Soc., 1989—90, Rsch. Fellow, NSF, 1998—2001, NEH, 2004, MacArthur Fellow, John D. and Catherine T. MacArthur Found., 2005. Mem.: Am., Studies Assn., Soc. For the History of Tech., History of Sci. Soc. Office: Univ Calif San Diego History 0104 9500 Gilman Dr La Jolla CA 92093-0104 Office Phone: 858-822-1532. Office Fax: 858-534-7283. E-mail: emilyt@ucsd.edu.*

THOMPSON, EMMA, actress; b. London, Apr. 15, 1959; d. Eric Thompson and Phyllida Law; m. Kenneth Branaugh, Aug. 20, 1989 (div. Oct. 1995); m. Greg Wise, July 29, 2003, 1 child Gaia Romilly Wise Student of English, Cambridge U., Eng. Performances include: (films) Henry V, 1989, The Tall Guy, 1989, Dead Again, 1991, Impromptu, 1991, Howard's End, 1992 (Acad. award for best actress 1993), Peter's Friends, 1992, Much Ado About Nothing, 1993, The Remains of the Day, 1993 (Acad. award nominee for best actress 1993), In the Name of the Father, 1993 (Acad. award nominee for best supporting actress 1993), My Father, the Hero, 1994, Junior, 1994, Carrington, 1995 (Best Actress award Nat. Bd. Rev. 1995), Sense and Sensibility, 1995 (Golden Globe award nominee for best actress in film 1996, Acad. award nominee for best actress 1996), Winter Guest, 1996, Primary Colors, 1998, Judas Kiss, 1998, Maybe Baby, 2000, Treasure Planet (voice), 2002, Love Actually, 2003, Imagining Argentina, 2003, Harry Potter and the Prisoner of Azbakan, 2004, Nanny McPhee, 2005; (TV films) Al Fresco, Up For Grabs (a.k.a. Sexually Transmitted), Tutti Frutti, Fortunes of War, 1987, Cheers, 1991, Wit, 2001; (miniseries) Angels in America, 2003; (London stage) Me and My Girl, Look Back in Anger; also writer screen adaptation: Sense and Sensibility (Jane Austin), 1995 (Best Screenplay award N.Y. Film Critics 1995, L.A. Film Critics 1995, Boston Film Critics 1995, Golden Globe award for best adapted screenplay 1996, Acad. award for best adapted screenplay 1996, BAFTA Best Actress award 1996), Nanny McPhee, 2005. Active in Footlights Theatrical Group, Cambridge, Eng. Office: William Morris Agy 151 S El Camino Dr Beverly Hills CA 90212-2775*

THOMPSON, EWA M., foreign language educator; b. Kaunas, Lithuania; came to U.S., 1963; d. Jozef and Maria Majewski; m. James R. Thompson. BA in English and Russian, U. Warsaw, Poland, 1963; MFA in Piano, Sopot Conservatory Music, 1963; MA in English, Ohio U., 1964; PhD in Comparative Lit., Vanderbilt U., 1967. Instr. Vanderbilt U., Nashville, Tenn., 1964-67; asst. prof. Ind. State U., Terre Haute, 1967-68, Ind. U., 1968-70, Rice U., Houston, 1967-73, assoc. prof., 1974-79, prof., 1979—, chair, 1987-90; assoc. prof. U. Va., Charlottesville, 1973-74. Cons. NEH, 1973—, The John D. and Catherine T. MacArthur Found., The John Simon Guggenheim Found., U.S. Dept. Edn.; vis. cons. Tex. A&M U.; seminar dir. NEH Summer Inst., Southeastern La. U., 1990; chair Russian lit. conf. Rice U., 1989; lectr. various colls. and univs. Author: Russian Formalism and Anglo-American New Criticism: A Comparative Study, 1971, Witold Gombrowicz, 1979, Polish transl., 2002, Understanding Russia: The Holy Fool in Russian Culture, 1987 (Chinese transl. 1995, 2nd Chinese edit. 1998), The Search for Self-Definition in Russian Literature, 1991, Imperial Knowledge: Russian Literature and Colonialism, 2000, Polish transl., 2000; editor the Sarmatian Rev., 1988—; contbr. articles to profl. jours., chpts. to books. Recipient Silver Thistle award Houston's Scottish Heritage Found, 1988; Mellon grantee, 1990, Rice U. grantee, 1990, Internat. Rsch. and Exchanges Sr. Scholar grantee, 1991; Hoover Inst. fellow, 1988; Vanderbilt U. scholar, 1964-67, Will Herberg award, ISI, 2003. Roman Catholic. Office: Sarmatian Rev PO Box 73119 Houston TX 77279-9119 Office Phone: 713-467-5836.

THOMPSON, FRANCES MCBROOM, mathematics professor, writer; BS in Edn., Abilene Christi1n U., Tex., 1963; MA, U. Tex., Austin, 1967; EdD, U. Ga., Athens, 1973. Math. cons., tchr., 1963—84; math. prof. Tex. Woman's U., Denton, 1984—. Author: (tchr. resource books) Hands on Math for Grades 4-8, 1994, Hands on Algebra for Grades 7-12, 1998, Math Proficiency Lessons and Activities, Fourth Grade, 2003, Math Essentials, Middle School Level, 2005, Math Essentials, High School Level, 2005. Bible class coord.; tchr., 1982—95. Recipient Mary Mason Lyon Jr. Faculty award, Tex. Woman's U., 1992, Alumni Citation for achievement, Abilene Christian U., 1998, Grover C. Morlan Outstanding Educator award, 2005, Distinction in Svc. award, Tex. Woman's U., 2006. Mem.: Rsch. Coun. for Math. Learning, Tex. Coun. Tchrs. Math., Tex. Assn. Suprs. Math., Math. Assn. Am., Nat. Coun. Tchrs. Math. Office: Tex Woman's U PO Box 425886 Denton TX 76204-5886 Office Phone: 940-898-2157. Business E-Mail: fthompson@twu.edu.

THOMPSON, GERALDINE KELLEHER RICHTER, retired orthopedist; b. Tokyo, Aug. 22, 1948; (parents Am. citizens); d. Edward Elkins and Marguerite Geraldine Kelleher; m. Wayne Wray Thompson, Dec. 30, 2000; m. Paul S. Richter (div.); children: Karl Kelleher Richter, Brian Kelleher Richter, Kelly Kelleher Richter. BA with high honors, Wellesley Coll., Mass., 1969; MD, Georgetown U., Washington, 1973. Intern internal medicine Georgetown U. Hosp., Washington, 1973—74, residency orthop. surgery, 1974—78; pvt. practice orthop. surgery Fairfax and Manassas, Va., 1978—2002; assoc. prof. orthop. surgery Georgetown U., Washington, 1978—2002; fellow Am. Acad. Orthop. Surgery, 1981—2001. Pres. Prince William Med. Soc., 1999—2000. Parent leader Boy Scouts Am., 1990—99; mem. parents assn. St. Albans Sch., Washington, Nat. Cathedral Sch. Girls. Fellow: Am. Acad. Orthop. Surgeons; mem.: Wellesley Literary Cir., AOA, Sigma Xi, Phi Beta Kappa. Avocations: art history, literature, cultural history, history of medicine. Home: 2720 N Quincy St Arlington VA 22207-5055

THOMPSON, GLORIA MATTHEWS, marketing and statistics educator; b. Havre De Grace, Md., Apr. 22, 1947; d. Henry and Elsie Matthews; children: Christina Laureen, Michael Gene. BA in music edn., Cath. U. Am., 1969; MBA, York Coll. Pa., 1999; D in bus. adminstrn., Nova S.E. U., 2004; MA in edn., U. Phoenix, 2003. Dept. chair, grad. bus. and mgmt. U. Phoenix, Phila. campus, Wayne, Pa., 2000—; owner/mgr. Country Fabrications, York, Pa., 1984—99; music tchr. Prince George's County Schools, Upper Marlboro, Md., 1969—78. Mktg. rsch. project dir. York Coll. Pa, 1999; academic program coun. U. Phoenix, 2001—02, curriculum devel., 2002, assessment devel., 02; adj. faculty Harrisburg Area CC, Pa., 1999—2000; adj. prof. Ctrl. Pa. Coll., Summerdale, 1999—2000. Mem.: SHRM (Soc. Human Resource Mgmt.), Mktg. Mgmt. Assn., Am. Mktg. Association. Office: U Phoenix Phil 170 S Warner Rd Ste 200 Wayne PA 19087 E-mail: gloria.thompson@phoenix.edu.

THOMPSON, HOLLEY MARKER, lawyer, consultant, marketing professional; b. Jamestown, NY, Jan. 30, 1947; d. Burdette James and Mary (Novitske) Marker; m. Lawrence D. Thompson; children: Jennifer Kristen Simos, Kendra Elise Blair, Jennifer Lynn, Stephanie Lynn. AAS, Jamestown C.C., 1966; BS, Ohio U., 1969; MA, W.Va. U., 1974, JD, 1980. Bar: W.Va. 1980, U.S. Dist. Ct. (so. dist.) W.Va. 1980, Pa. 1982, U.S. Dist. Ct. (we. dist.) Pa. 1982. Tchr. math. various pub. schs., Santa Ana (Calif.), Lakewood (N.Y.) and Morgantown (W.Va.), 1970-77; atty. for students W.Va. U., Morgantown, 1980; assoc. libr., lectr. W.Va. U. Coll. Law, Morgantown, 1980-83; assoc. libr. Jackson, Kelly, Holt & O'Farrell, Charleston, W.Va., 1983-86; cons. Hildebrandt, Inc., Somerville, NJ, 1986-94; sr. v.p. mktg. and preference markets LexisNexis, Dayton, Ohio, 1994—2006; ptnr. The Sterling Group 925, Springboro, Ohio, 2006—. Spkr. in field. Contbr. articles to profl. jours. Mem.: Am. Assn. Law Librs., Phi Delta Phi. Personal E-mail: holleymthompson@aol.com.

THOMPSON, JACQUELINE, retired military officer; b. Racine, Wis., Apr. 22, 1936; d. Edward Joseph and Gwenneth Ione (Wells) Sack; m. Claude Edward Osbourn, Dec. 17, 1955 (div. 1967); children: Jaime Edward, Rochelle Ione, Shannon Gaye, Desiree Patrice, Forest Kendall; m. George Wiley Glenn, Nov. 7, 1967; children: Brent Landry, Breanna Laura, Zane Aaron. AA, Gainesville Jr. Coll., Oakwood, Ga., 1982; DARB, USAF, Marietta, Ga., 1996. Joined USAF, 1972; supt. 94th Mobility Squadron, 1993-96; ret., 1996. Mem. NARFE (sec.-treas.), C. of C., Villa Rica Hist. and Mineral. Soc. (sec. 1997-99). Libertarian. Roman Catholic. Avocation: tracing ancestry. Office: 1637 County Road 34 Ranburne AL 36273-4017

THOMPSON, JAIME LYNN, social studies educator; b. Frederick, Md., June 28, 1979; d. Daryl and Diane Rowe; m. Stephen Garnett Thompson, Aug. 9, 2003. BA, Hood Coll., Frederick, Md. Tchr., dept. chair Frederick County Pub. Schs., Md., 2001—. Mentor tchr. Hood Coll. Mem., vol. The Salvation Army, Frederick. Fellow, James Madison Meml. Fellowship Found. Mem.: Nat. Coun. Social Studies. Office: Windsor Knolls Middle School 11150 Windsor Road Ijamsville MD 21754 Office Phone: 240-236-5000. Personal E-mail: jaime.thompson@fcps.org.

THOMPSON, JAN NEWSTROM, art historian, educator; b. Buffalo, Mar. 19, 1947; d. Marvin William and Nadene (Newstrom) T.; m. Paul L. Goldstein, Aug. 28, 1977; 1 child, Elizabeth Esther Thompson Goldstein. BFA, SUNY, Buffalo, 1968, MA, 1971, Rutgers U., New Brunswick, N.J., 1974, PhD, 1980. Instr. art history Canisius Coll., Buffalo, 1973-74; instr. art history, studio art Union Coll., Cranford, N.J., 1974-77; instr. art history Santa Clara (Calif.) U., 1977-94, San Jose (Calif.) U., 1988—, San Francisco Museum of Modern Art, 1987. Author: Frank Duveneck: Lost Paintings Found, 1987, Theodore Wores: An American Artist in Meiji, Japan, 1993. Mem. adv. bd. No. Calif. Coun. of Nat. Museum of Women in the Arts, 1995—; trustee Triton Museum of Art, Santa Clara, 1980-90. Mem. Coll. Art Assn. Am. Avocations: equestrian sports, dressage. Office: San Jose Stat U Dept of Art and Design 1 Washington Sq San Jose CA 95192-0001

THOMPSON, JANE ANN, elementary school educator, researcher; b. Dallas, Tex., Oct. 22, 1940; d. Mary Helen Hazelwood and Bert Cooper; m. Bob Joe Thompson, Oct. 16, 1959; children: Caryn Jones, Dana Finch, Perri Lawrence. EdB, U. North Tex., Denton, Tex., 1985, Med Reading Specialist, 1989. Cert. Elem. Self-Contained Tex., 1985, Learning Resource Endorsement Grades PK-12 Tex., 1998, Reading Specialist PK-12 Tex., 1989, Elem. English Grades 1-8 Tex., 1985, Elem. Reading Grades 1-8 Tex., 1986, Secondary English Grades 1-8 Tex., 1991. Tchr./curriculum developer Lewisville Ind. Sch. Dist., Lewisville, Tex., 1973—92; tchr. Carroll Ind. Sch. Dist., Southlake, Tex., 1992—94; instr. Dallas County C.C., Farmers Br., Tex., 1988—92, Tex. A&M at Commerce, Commerce, Tex., 2001—; cons. Region 10 Edn. Svc. Ctr., Richardson, Tex., 1994—2003; instr. Dallas County C.C. Sys., Dallas, 1989—92. Organizer and pres. Lewisville Area Reading Coun., Lewisville, Tex., 1989—90, founder and pres., 1988—92; chairperson of student media com. Tex. State Libr. Assn., Statewide, Tex., 1998—99; chairperson intellectual freedom com. Tex. State Reading Assn., Statewide, Tex., 1988—89; chmn. of intellectual freedom com. Tex. Reading Assn., Tex.; chairperson of student media com. Tex. State Libr. Assn., Tex.; trainer N.J. Writing Project of Tex. Mem.: ALA, Nat. Coun. of Teachers of English, Tex. Assn. for Gifted & Talented, Internat. Reading Assn., Tex. State Reading Assn., Tex. Computers Educators Assn., Tex. State Assn. of Sch. Librarians, Am. Assn. of Sch. Librarians, Tex. State Libr. Assn. (assoc.). R-Liberal. Bapt. Office: TAMU-Commerce Sowers Bldg Elementary Edu Commerce TX 75428 Office Phone: 903-886-5537.

THOMPSON, JANIS GROCOCK, biology professor; BA in Vet. Medicine, Mich. State U., East Lansing, 1979, DVM, 1981. Pathologist's asst. Dr. Robert Peterson, Gaylord, Mich., 1976—79; tchg. asst. histology Mich. State U., East Lansing, 1980—81; staff veterinarian Benson Animal Hosp., Lansing, 1981—82, Lorain County Vet. Clinic, Grafton, Ohio, 1983—89; assoc. prof. biology Lorain County C.C., Elyria, Ohio, 1983—. Mem. learning assessment team Lorain County C.C., Elyria, Ohio, 2001—, program rev.

chmn., 2004—. Author: Anatomy and Physiology I Manual, 2002, Anatomy and Physiology II Manual, 2002, Human Biology Lab Manual, 1999. Mem. bell and sr. choirs First Ch. in Oberlin United Ch. Christ, Ohio, 1982—. Nominee Tchr. of the Yr., Ohio Assn. Two Yr. Colls., 2005; recipient Faculty Excellence award, Lorain County C.C. Found., 2005, Tchg. award, Northeast Ohio Coun. on Higher Edn., 2005. Mem.: Nat. Tech Prep Network, Ohio Acad. Sci., Sci. Edn. Coun. Ohio, Nat. Assn. Biology Tchrs., Am. Assn. Anatomists, Human Anatomy and Physiology Soc. (chair testing com. 2002—05). Office: Lorain County CC 1005 N Abbe Rd Elyria OH 44035 Office Phone: 440-366-7245.

THOMPSON, JAYNE CARR, public relations and communications executive, lawyer; b. Oak Park, Ill., Apr. 7, 1946; d. Robert Edward and Laurette (Rentner) Carr; m. James R. Thompson, June 19, 1976; 1 child, Samantha Jayne. BA, U. Ill., Chgo., 1967; JD, Northwestern U., 1970; degree (hon.), Lincoln (Ill.) Coll., 1990, St. Xavier U., Chgo., 1995, Ill. Coll., 1995. Assoc. in litigation McDermott, Will & Emery, Chgo., 1970; asst. atty. gen. State of Ill., Chgo., 1970-77, chief of criminal appeals divsn., 1972-77, dep. chief prosecution assistance bur., 1975-76, dep. chief criminal divsn., 1976-77, acting chief criminal divsn., 1977; of counsel Brown, Hay & Stephens, Springfield, Ill., 1977-78, Silets & Martin, Chgo., 1983-84; house counsel and v.p. devel. Nat. Coll. Edn., Evanston, Ill., 1984-85; atty. Lydon & Griffin, Chgo., 1989-91; prin. Didenschneider Group Inc., Chgo., 1999-2000, mng. prin., 2000—02; CEO, pres. Jayne Thompson and Assocs. Ltd., 2002—. Contbr. chpt. to book, articles to profl. jours. First Lady of Ill., Springfield, 1977-91; mem. Ill. Commn. on Status of Women, 1997-2001; pres. bd. dirs. Chgo. Pub. Libr., 1998—; mem. women's bd. Northwestern U., 1978—; bd. dirs. Chgo. Pub. Libr. Found., 1998—; mem. adv. bd. for Ill. Treas. for Women's Issues, 2002—; mem. chmn.'s adv. coun. Lincoln Pk. Zoo, 2002—; mem. Met. Planning Coun., 2002--. Mem. Ill. State Bar Assn., Execs. Club (Chgo.), Coun. on Fgn. Rels. (Chgo. com.), Econ. Club (Chgo.). Avocations: reading, cooking, tennis. Office: Jayne Thompson & Assocs Ltd 33 N Dearborn St Ste 2200 Chicago IL 60602 E-mail: jthompson@jaynethompson.com.

THOMPSON, JEAN TANNER, retired librarian; b. San Luis Obispo, Calif., June 15, 1929; d. Chester Corey and Mildred (Orr) T.; 1 child, Anne Marie Miller Student, Whitworth Coll., Spokane, Wash., 1946-49; AB, Boston U., 1951; postgrad., U. Wis., Eau Claire, 1964-67; MSL.S., Columbia U., 1973; Ed.M., U. Va., Charlottesville, 1978. Asst. social sci. librarian Univ. Libraries Va. Polytechnic Inst. and State U., Blacksburg, 1973-77, head social sci. dept. Univ. Libraries, 1977-83; head reference dept. Meml. Library U. Wis., Madison, 1983-86, asst. dir. reference and info. svcs., 1986-91, ret. Contbg. editor: ALA Guide to Information Access, 1994; mem. editorial bd. RQ, 1984-89. Mem. ALA, Assn. Coll. and Research Libraries (edn. and behavioral sci. sect. vice chmn. 1985-86, chmn. 1986-87), Wis. Library Assn., Wis. Assn. of Acad. Librarians. Presbyterian. Home: 4929 High Grove Rd Tallahassee FL 32309-2957

THOMPSON, JEWEL TAYLOR, music educator; b. Kinsale, Va., Oct. 27, 1935; d. Waverly Edward and Ella Joyce (Holman) Taylor; m. Leon Everette Thompson, June 10, 1961 (dec. June 1983); children: Sonca Patrice, Miya Kateri. BS, Va. State U., 1956; MA, Eastman Sch. of Music, 1960, PhD, 1982. Asst. prof. Va. State U., Petersburg, 1960-62, W.Va. State Coll., Institute, 1967-68, W.Va. Inst. Tech., Montgomery, 1968-72; adj. asst. prof. Hunter Coll., CUNY, 1972-85, asst. prof., 1985-90, assoc. prof., 1990-96, prof., 1997—. Organist Abyssinian Bapt. Ch., N.Y.C., 1978-83, minister of music, choirmaster, 1983—; ea. area music dir. Links, Inc., 1995-2003, nat. music dir., 2004—. Author: Samuel Coleridge-Taylor, 1994; composer and arranger numerous compositions; contbr. Internat. Dictionary of Black Composers, 1999. Scholarship selection com. United Negro Coll. Fund; chair art program Links, Inc., 1989-93; music dir. at area and nat. levels; mem. Am. Music Ctr., Inc. Named Dame of Honour, Knights of Malta, 1982; recipient Hunter Coll. Presdl. award for excellence in svc., 1998, Outstanding Ministry award, Coun. Chs. of NYC, 2005; Hattie M. Strong Found. fellow, 1959—60, Ford Found. fellow, 1974—77, Prince Hall Masons grantee, 1977—78. Mem. ASCAP, Am. Women Composers, Inc., Music Theory Soc. N.Y. State. Avocations: travel, art. Home: 1425 Lozier Pl Teaneck NJ 07666-5106 Office: CUNY Hunter Coll 695 Park Ave New York NY 10021-5024 Office Phone: 212-650-3608.

THOMPSON, JOAN (JO), anthropologist; b. Colo. B in Psychology and Sociology, Wittenberg Univ., Ohio, 1978; M in Anthropology, Univ. Colo., 1992; PhD in Biological Anthropology and Primatology, Univ. Oxford, Eng., 1997. Founder, dir. Lukuru Wildlife Research Project, Democratic Republic of Congo, 1992—98; fund-raiser LWRP, Colo. (due to unrest in DRC). Named an assoc. laureate, Rolex award for Enterprise, 2004. Achievements include 13 years of conducting biological field rsch., community-based conservation and wildlife edn. in the Dem. Republic of the Congo on behalf of human and primate populations, particularly bonobos. Office: Lukuru Wildlife Rsch Found PO Box 1284 La Grande OR 97850-6284 Business E-Mail: jat434@aol.com.

THOMPSON, JOSIE, nurse; b. Ark., Apr. 16, 1949; d. James Andrew and Oneda Fay (Watson) Rhoads; m. Mark O. Thompson, Feb. 14, 1980. Diploma, Lake View Sch. Nursing, 1970; student, Danville C.C., 1974-75, St. Petersburg Jr. Coll., 1979. RN Ill., Wyo., cert. Devel. Disabilities Divsn., N.Y. Staff nurse St. Elizabeth Hosp., Danville, Ill., 1970-78, Osteo. Hosp., St. Petersburg, Fla., 1980-81, Wyo. State Hosp., Evanston, 1981-83, Wyo. Home Health Care, Rock Springs, 1984—, adminstr., 1986-95; pres. Home Health Care Alliance Wyo., 1991-92; staff nurse home health Interim Health Care, Cheyenne, Wyo., 1996-97; staff nurse Rocky Mountain Home Health Care, Green River, Wyo., 1997—, dir. nursing, 2000-01; staff nurse Sageview Care Ctr., 2001, S.W. Wyo. Rehab. Ctr. for Mentally and Physically Handicapped Persons, Rock Springs, Wyo., 2001—03; pvt. practice Wyo., 2004—. Mem. nursing program adv. bd. Western Wyo. C.C.; mem. Coalition for the Elderly, Spl. Needs Com. Sweetwater County, 1992-93. Home: PO Box 1154 Rock Springs WY 82902-1154 Office Phone: 307-350-7827.

THOMPSON, JOYCE LURINE, retired information systems specialist; b. White Oak Twp., Mich., Mar. 5, 1931; d. Orla Jacob and Ethel Inita (Thayer) Sheathelm; m. Robert E. Thompson, Dec. 10, 1949 (div. 1972); children: Wendy, Robin, Kristen (dec.). Student, Mich. State U., 1973—78, Lansing C.C., Mich., 1976—77. Programmer, analyst Mich. State U., East Lansing, 1966-73; database coord. Mich. Dept. Treasury, Lansing, 1977-79; sys. engr. 4-Phase Sys., Grand Rapids, Mich., 1979—81; mktg. rep. Motorola, Grand Rapids, 1981—84; data analyst Whirlpool Corp., Benton Harbor, Mich., 1984—88, data adminstr., 1989—; owner, propr. Thompson House, South Haven, Mich., 1994—. Activity chmn. Girl Scouts U.S.A., East Lansing; leader 4-H Clubs, East Lansing; vol. Stepping Stones South Haven, ADA Com., Lake Mich. Maritime Mus., Scott Club South Haven, 2000—, treas., 2001-2004. Mildred Erickson fellow Mich. State U., East Lansing, 1974-78. Mem. Assn. Sys. Mgmt. (sec. 1984), Data Adminstrn. Mgmt. Assn. Avocations: photography, music, beach combing, antiques.

THOMPSON, JUDITH GEOFFRIAU, psychometrician, consultant; b. Ann Arbor, Jan. 3, 1976; d. Jean-Michel and Sandra Lynn Geoffriau; m. Gregory Mark Thompson, Dec. 19, 1997; 1 child, John Gordon. BS in Edn., Belhaven Coll., Jackson, Miss., 1998; MEd in Psychometry cum laude, Miss. Coll., Clinton, 2001. Lic. psychometry Miss. State Dept. Edn. Tchr. Jackson (Miss.) Pub. Schs., 1998—2000, Hinds CC, Raymond, 2004; cons. psychometrician Morris and Assoc., Jackson, 2000—04, Thompson Consulting, 2002—. Spl. projects coord. Morris and Assoc., Jackson, Miss., 2004—. Named to Nat. Dean's List, Belhaven Coll., 1998; Presdl. scholar, 1993—98. Mem.: APA, Miss. Assn. Gifted Children, Miss. Rep. Women. Presbyterian. Avocations: reading, cooking, gardening, entertaining. Office: Thompson Consulting PO Box 5071 Jackson MS 39296

THOMPSON, JUDITH KASTRUP, nursing researcher; b. Marstal, Denmark, Oct. 1, 1933; came to the U.S., 1951; d. Edward Kastrup and Anna Hansa (Knudsen) Pedersen; m. Richard Frederick Thompson, May 22, 1960; children: Kathryn Marr, Elizabeth Kastrup, Virginia St. Claire. BS, RN, U. Oreg., Corvallis, 1958; MSN, U. Oreg., 1963. RN Calif., Oreg. Staff nurse U. Oreg. Med. Sch., Eugene, 1957-58, Portland, 1958-61, head staff nurse, 1960-61; instr. psychiat. nursing U. Oreg. Sch. Nursing, Portland, 1963-64; rsch. asst. U. Oreg. Med. Sch., Portland, 1964-65, U. Calif., Irvine, 1971-72; rsch. assoc. Stanford (Calif.) U., 1982-87; rsch. asst. Harvard U., Cambridge, Mass., 1973-74; rsch. assoc. U. So. Calif., L.A., 1987—. Contbg. author: Behavioral Control and Role of Sensory Biofeedback, 1976; contbr. articles to profl. jours. Treas. LWV, Newport Beach, Calif., 1970-74; scout leader Girl Scouts Am., Newport Beach, 1970-78. Named Citizen of Yr. State of Oreg., 1966. Mem. Soc. for Neurosci., Am. Psychol. Soc. (charter), ANA, Oreg. Nurses Assn. Republican. Lutheran. Avocations: art collecting, travel, tennis. Home: 28 Sky Sail Dr Corona Del Mar CA 92625-1436 Office: U So Calif University Park Los Angeles CA 90089-0001 Office Phone: 213-740-7350. Business E-Mail: judith@usc.edu.

THOMPSON, JUDY ELLEN, elementary school educator; b. Bristol, Tenn., May 13, 1940; d. Hal Henry McNutt and Lucy Georgia Mahady; children from previous marriage: Robin Buchanan, Glen Roger II, Stacy Hilliard. Attended, U. Tenn., Knoxville Coll.; BS in Elem. Edn., E. Tenn. State U., Johnson City, 1964. Tchr. Knox County Sch., Knoxville, 1965—2002, career leader III. Mem. altar guild Ch. Ascencion, 1998—2006, mem. FISH, 2000—06, chmn. wedding guild, 2000—06. Mem.: NEA, Knox County Edn. Assn., Tenn. Edn. Assn. Republican. Episcopalian. Avocations: travel, hiking, reading, gardening. Home: Gate House 5709 Lyons View Pike Knoxville TN 37919

THOMPSON, KAREN MARIE, art educator; d. Carl Henry and Bernice Pearson Pohle; m. Stanley Wendell Thompson, May 1, 1957 (dec. Nov. 11, 2001); children: Jay Scott, Karilyn Lee Thompson-Starks. MA in Art History, U. Hawaii, 1984. Assoc. dir. U. Hawaii Art Gallery, Honolulu, 1984—91; curator of edn. Honolulu Acad. Arts, 1991—. Bd. dirs., adv. com. Applied History of Art and Architecture Ednl. Found., Honolulu, 2001—; advisor U. of Hawaii Coll. of Edn., Tchr. Edn. Com. for Art, Honolulu, 1995—2000. Author: (exhbn. booklet for children) First Emperor of China: A Search for Immortality, 1995, Art All Around, 1998, Discovering the Art of Ancient Egypt, 2000, A Visit to Grandfather's House, 2003, Faces and Figures: Pacific Islands Art; co-author: (exhbn. catalogue) Jean Charlot: Artist and Scholar, 1991; contbr. exhbn. catalogue: A Hawaii Treasury: Masterpieces from the Honolulu Academy of Arts, exhbn. catalogue: The Art of Asian Costume, exhbn. catalogue: Greek and Russian Icons; curator (art exhibition) Tales from The Tomb, 2000, Dream Worlds/Real Worlds of William Joyce, 2002, (art exhbn.) Russia Through the Eyes of Children, 2003, Wisdom and Wonder: Children's Book Ullustrations by Paul Zelinsky, 2004, co-curator Paris and the Countryside: Impressionism/Postimpressionism, Honolulu Acad. Arts, 2004, The Pacific Islands. Mem.: Hawaii Mus. Assn., Hawaii Alliance for Arts Edn., Nat. Art Edn. Assn. (Hawaii Art Educator of Yr. 2003). Office: Honolulu Acad Arts 900 South Beretania St Honolulu HI 96814 Office Phone: 808-532-8727. Personal E-mail: kthompson@honoluluacademy.org.

THOMPSON, KATE ELAINE, school librarian, educator; b. Gloversville, NY, June 11, 1958; d. John Lucius Goodrich and Marilyn Joan Walrath; m. Michael William Thompson, May 31, 1988; children: Max Michael, Sam John. BS in Edn., U. Kans., Lawrence, 1980; MS in Secondary Edn., Kans. State U., Manhattan, 1993; M Liberal Arts, Baker U., Baldwin, Kans., 1986. Cert. tchr. Nat. Bd. Profl. Tchg. Stds., 2002. Speech, drama tchr. Olathe Unified Sch. Dist., Kans., 1981—88, libr. media specialist, 1996—, Shawnee Mission Sch. Dist., Kans., 1993—96. Named Master Tchr., Faculty Pioneer Trail Jr. HS, 2002. Mem.: NEA (exec. bd. mem. 2003—06), ALA, Am. Assn. Sch. Librs., Kans. Assn. Sch. Librs. Republican. Home: 18945 W 116th St Olathe KS 66061 Office: Olathe NW HS 21300 College Blvd Olathe KS 66061 Office Phone: 913-780-7150. Business E-Mail: kthompsonnw@olatheschools.com.

THOMPSON, KATHLEEN SHAMBAUGH, marriage and family counselor; b. Bakersfield, Calif., Oct. 22, 1945; d. Stephen W. and Marilyn L. Shambaugh; m. John W. Thompson, June 10, 1967 (dec. Mar. 1971); children: Stephen, Charles. Student, Colo. Women's Coll., 1964; BA in English, U. Colo., 1968; MA in Counseling, U. Denver, 1976. Tchg. credential U. Colo., 1971, lic. marriage and family counselor Denver, Colo., Calif., 1978. Tchr., Denver, 1971—78; marriage, family and child counselor, 1982—. Editor, proofreader, 1977—80. Author: An American Girl in Canada, 2002, Going Through Life-Poems and Short Works, 2004, Coping with Grief and the Death of Loved Ones, 2004, A Life Filled With Poetry, 2004, Professional Guides: The Case Study, Human Sexuality in Marriage, Crime and Rehabilitation, Introducing the Gap Theory, 2004, Counseling Helps, 2005, The Surgery Experience, 2005, Writers and Writing, 2005, Landscaping Any Small Lot, 2005, Gina's Rehabilitation, 2006, The Equal Personage of the Child, 2005, Going Through Life, 2005, Brown Flowers in Gloucester, 2006, I Care For My Cats, 2006, Charlie and Mom Cat, 2006, Travellers, 2006, Getting Through Life--Other Poems and Short Works, 2006, Funeral Planning, Memorial Services, and Coping with Death, 2006. Named one of Best Poets of 2000, Internat. Libr. Poetry, 2001, 2005. Mem.: Internat. Soc. Poets (Internat. Poet Merit 2000), Delta Delta Delta. Presbyterian/Swedenborgian. Avocations: stamp collecting/philately, doll collecting, art, literature, gardening. Home and Office: 1655 W Ajo Way # 170 Tucson AZ 85713

THOMPSON, KATHY C., bank executive; From. sr. v.p. to exec. v.p. Stock Yards Bancorp Inc, Louisville, 1992—96, exec. v.p., 1996—. Named No. 3 Fast Tracker in the Industry, U.S. Bankers Mag., 2003. Office: Stock Yards Bancorp Inc 1040 East Main St Louisville KY 40206

THOMPSON, KATHY SELF, secondary school educator; b. Birmingham, Ala., Nov. 3, 1961; d. Lawrence Thomas and Paula June (Adams) Self; m. Mark Thomas Thompson, July 14, 1994; children: Jacob Thomas, Sarah Kathryn. BA in English and Music, U. Montevallo, 1984; MA in Tchg., U. Louisville, 1995. Cert. tchr. Ky., nat. bd. cert. in young adult/late adolescent English/lang. arts 2003. Tchr. Central Hardin HS, Cecilia, Ky., 1991—. Home: 1921 Mud Splash Rd Glendale KY 42740 Office: Central Hardin HS 3040 Leitchfield Rd Cecilia KY 42724 Office Phone: 270-737-6800. Business E-Mail: kathy.thompson@hardin.kyschools.us.

THOMPSON, LEA, actress; b. Rochester, Minn., May 31, 1961; m. Howard Deutch. Actress: (films) Jaws 3-D, 1983, All the Right Moves, 1983, The Wild Life, 1984, Red Dawn, 1984, Back to the Future, 1985, Howard the Duck, 1986, Space Camp, 1986, Some Kind of Wonderful, 1987, Casual Sex, 1988, The Wizard of Loneliness, 1988, Going Undercover, 1988, Back to the Future II, 1989, Back to the Future III, 1990, Article 99, 1991, Dennis the Menace, 1993, The Beverly Hillbillies, 1993, The Little Rascals, 1994, The Right to Remain Silent, 1996 (TV movies) Nightbreaker, 1989, Montana, 1990, Stolen Babies, 1993, The Substitute Wife, 1994, The Unspoken Truth, 1995, The Unknown Ciclist, 1997, (TV series) Tales from the Crypt, 1989, Robert Wuhl's World Tour, 1990, Caroline in the City, 1995—, (TV miniseries) A Will of Their Own, 1998. Pa. Ballet Co. scholar, Am. Ballet Theatre scholar, San Francisco Ballet scholar.

THOMPSON, LEIGH LASSITER, psychologist, educator; b. Houston, Jan. 13, 1960; d. Don Raines and Ann Janet (Visintin) Thompson; m. Robert Warner Weeks, June 20, 1992. BS, Northwestern U., 1982, PhD, 1988; MA, U. Calif., Santa Barbara, 1984. Asst. prof. psychology U. Wash., Seattle, 1988-92, assoc. prof., 1992-95; prof. J.L. Kellogg Disting. chair organ. behavior NorthWestern U., Evanston, Ill., 1995—. Fellow Ctr. for Advanced Study in the Behavioral Scis., 1994-95. Edtl. bd. Orgnl. Behavior & Human Decision Processes, Internat. Jour. Conflict Mgt., Jour. Exptl. Social Psychology, 1990—; assoc. editor Group Decision Making and Negotiations; contbr. articles to profl. jours. Recipient Presdl. Young Investigator award NSF, 1991, Grad. Rsch. award Sigma Xi Found., 1987; grantee NSF, 1991, 89—, Nat. Inst. Dispute Resolution, 1987, APA, 1989. Fellow Am. Psychol. Soc.; mem. APA (S. Rains Wallace Dissertation award 1989), Acad. Mgmt. Achievements include discovery of lose-lose outcomes in negotiation; theory of socially-shared cognition in group decision making and negotiation. Office: Northwestern U Kellog Sch Orgn Bevavior Kellogg Sch Evanston IL 60208-0001

THOMPSON, LINDA A., art educator; m. W. Lawrence Thompson IV; children: Lars, W. L. V, Brody, Devin. BS Secondary Edn. Earth and Gen Sci., SUNY Oneonta, 1973; MLA, Empire State Coll., Utica, N.Y., 1991. Tchr. sci. 7-12 Albany City Schools, 1973—84; tchr. sci. 7-8 Goff Mid. Sch., East Greenbush, NY, 1988—2004, tchr. art, 2004—. Mentor Goff Mid. Sch., East Greenbush, 2003—. Office Phone: 518-477-2731.

THOMPSON, LINDA RUTH, psychology educator, university administrator; b. Wichita, Kans., Mar. 7, 1949; d. Earl Edmond and Ada Jean (Hatfield) Minor; m. Wesley Travis Thompson, Aug. 29, 1968; 1 child, Travis John. BA in Music, Harding Coll., 1972; MEd in Counselor Edn., U. Ark., 1976; EdD in Higher Edn., Memphis State U., 1993. Adj. instr. psychology/sociology Mich. Christian Coll., Rochester, 1977-78; counselor La. State U., Eunice, 1981-83, N.E. La. U., Monroe, 1983-85; dir. program for acad. success Harding U., Searcy, Ark., 1986-87, instr. psychology, 1986-88, dir. learning assistance programs, 1987-90, asst. prof., dir. student support svcs., 1990—2003, assoc. prof., 1996—; dir. Ronald E. McNair Post Baccalaureate Achievement Program, 2003—. Counselor, cons. Acad. Enhancement for Gifted and Talented in Summer programs Harding U., 1986-2001, mem. various coms., sponsor Dactylology Club, 1987—; field reader Upward Bound proposals U.S. Dept. Edn., 1992, 95, 98; field reader talent search proposals U.S. Dept. Edn., 2001; participant many ednl. seminars, insts. and workshops, 1986—; presenter profl. confs. Mem. editl. review bd.: The Ctr. for Rsch. in Developmental Edn. and Urban Literacy, 2001—05. Program chairperson Operation Stormwater, Pine Bluff, Ark., 1979-80; vol. MADD DAsh, Searcy, 1992; mem. Associated Women for Harding, 1986—, pres., 1989-90; active Coll. Ch. of Christ, tchr. kindergarten, 1986-89, interpreter for deaf, 1987—. Recipient Cert. of Merit, Am. Coll. Testing/Nat. Acad. Advising Assn. Recognition, 1988; named one of Outstanding Young Women of Am., 1982. Mem. Nat. Assn. for Devel. Edn. (co-chair nat. conf. 1996, mem. awards com. 1987-88, mem. publs. com. 1991-92, pres. elect 1992-2000, pres. 2000-01, emeritus council 2002—, cert. council review coord. 2003—), Ark. Assn. for Devel. Edn. (sec. 1987-88, pres.-elect 1989-91, pres. 1991-93, chair conf. 1990-91, editor newsletter 1988-90, jour. editor 1996-99). Republican. Avocations: reading, swimming, sign language. Home: 1 Harding Dr Searcy AR 72143-5704 Office: Harding Univ McNair Scholars Program HU Box 12235 Searcy AR 72149-2235 Office Phone: 501-279-4416. E-mail: LThompson@Harding.edu.

THOMPSON, LOIS JEAN HEIDKE ORE, psychologist; b. Chgo., Feb. 22, 1933; d. Harold William and Ethel Rose (Neumann) Heidke; m. Henry Thomas Ore, Aug. 28, 1954 (div. May 1972); children: Christopher, Douglas; m. Joseph Lippard Thompson, Aug. 3, 1972; children: Scott, Les, Melanie. BA, Cornell Coll., Mt. Vernon, Iowa, 1955; MA, Idaho State U., 1964, EdD, 1981. Lic. psychologist, N.Mex. Tchr. pub. schs. various locations, 1956—67; tchr., instr. Idaho State U., Pocatello, 1967—72; employee/orgn. devel. specialist Los Alamos Nat. Lab., N.Mex., 1981—84, tng. specialist N.Mex., 1984—89, sect. leader N.Mex., 1989—93; pvt. practice indsl. psychology and healthcare, Los Alamos, 1988—. Sec. Cornell Coll. Alumni Office, 1954-55, also other orgns.; bd. dirs. Parent Edn. Ctr., Idaho State U., 1980; counselor, Los Alamos, 1981-88. Editor newsletter LWV, Laramie, Wyo., 1957; contbr. articles to profl. jours. Pres. Newcomers Club, Pocatello, 1967, Faculty Womens Club, Pocatello, 1968; chmn. edn. com. AAUW, Pocatello, 1969. Mem.: APA, N.Mex. Soc. Adlerian Psychology (pres. 1990, treas. 1991—97, bd. dirs. 1996—), N.Mex. Psychol. Assn. (bd. dirs. divsn. II 1990, 1999, sec. 1988—90, chmn. 1990, 1999—2000). Mem. Lds Ch. Avocations: racewalking, backpacking, skiing, tennis, biking. Home and Office: 340 Aragon Ave Los Alamos NM 87544-3505

THOMPSON, MARGARET M., physical education educator; b. Merrifield, Va., Aug. 1, 1921; d. Lesley L. and Madeline (Shawen) T. BS, Mary Washington Coll., 1941; MA, George Washington U., 1947; PhD, U. Iowa, 1961. Tchr., supr. phys. edn. Staunton (Va.) City Schs., 1941-44; tchr. jr. high sch. phys. edn. Arlington County, Va., 1944-47; instr. women's phys. edn. Fla. State U., Tallahassee, 1947-51; instr., asst. prof., assoc. prof. phys. edn. Purdue U., Lafayette, Ind., 1951-65, dir. gross motor therapy lab., 1963-65; assoc. prof. phys. edn. U. Mo., Columbia, 1965-68, prof., 1968-71, dir. Cinematography and Motor Learning Lab. Dept. Health and Phys. Edn., 1965-71; prof. phys. edn. U. Ill., Champaign-Urbana, 1971-87, prof. emeritus, 1987—. Vis. prof. Escola de Educacão Fisica, U. de Saõ Paulo, Brazil, 1985; vis. prof. phy. edn. Inst. Bioscis. de Rio Claro, U. Estadual Paulista, Brazil, 1991. Author: (with Barbara B. Godfrey) Movement Pattern Checklists, 1966, (with Chappelle Arnett) Perceptual Motor and Motor Test Battery for Children, 1968, (with Barbara Mann) An Holistic Approach to Physical Education Curriculum: Objectives Classification System for Elementary Schools, 1977, Gross Motor Inventory, 1976, revised edit., 1980, Developing the Curriculum, 1980, Setting the Learning Environment, 1980, Sex Stereotyping and Human Development, 1980; also film strips, articles. Mem.: AAHPER. Home and Office: 1311 Wildwood Ln Mahomet IL 61853-9770

THOMPSON, MARGIE ANN, artist; b. L.A., Nov. 5, 1934; d. John William Jr. and Odessa Addie Meek; m. Donald Leroy Thompson, June 29, 1956; children: Mark(dec.), Laurie, Donna, Lee. Grad. high. sch. Various office positions, Calif., 1952—80; freelance graphic designer Saugus, Calif., 1980—88; advt. designer The Signal, Saugus, 1988—89; watercolor artist Quartz Hill, Calif., 1990—. Mem.: Antelope Valley Allied Arts Assn. (various positions 1990—97). Republican. Personal E-mail: donandmargie@adelphia.net.

THOMPSON, MARGUERITE MYRTLE GRAMING (MRS. RALPH B. THOMPSON), librarian; b. Orangeburg, S.C., Apr. 23, 1912; d. Thomas Laurie and Rosa Lee (Stroman) Graming; m. Ralph B. Thompson, Sept. 17, 1949 (dec. Oct. 1960). BA in English cum laude, U. S.C., 1932, postgrad., 1937; BLS, Emory U., 1943. Tchr. English pub. high schs., S.C., 1932-43; libr. Rockingham (N.C.) High Sch., 1943-45, Randolph County (N.C.) Libr., Asheboro, 1945-48, Colleton County (S.C.) Libr., Walterboro, 1948-61; dir. Florence (S.C.) County Libr., 1961-78. Sec. com. community facilities, svcs. and instns. Florence County Resources Devel. Com., 1964-67; vice chmn. Florence County Coun. on Aging, 1968-70, exec. bd. 1968-82, bd. treas., 1973-75, bd. sec., 1976-77, bd. v.p., 1979; mem. Florence County Bicentennial Planning Com., 1975-76; mem. rels. and allocations com. United Way, 1979-80. Named Boss of Yr. Nat. Secs. Assn., 1971. Mem. ALA (coun. 1964-72), Southeastern Libr. Assn., S.C. Libr. Assn. (pres. 1960, chmn. assn. handbook revision com. 1967-69, 80, sect. co-chmn. com. standards for S.C. pub. librs. 1966-75, fed. rels. coord. 1972-73, planning com. 1976-78), Greater Florence C. of C. (women's div. chmn. 1969-70, bd. dirs. 1975-77), S.E. Regional Conf. Women in C. of C. (bd. dir. 1970-71), Florence Bus. and Profl. Women's Club (2d v.p. 1975-76, Career Woman of Yr. 1974, parliamentarian 1980-81, chmn. scholarship com. 1981-82), Delta Kappa Gamma (county chpt. charter pres. 1963-65, treas. 1966-70, chmn. com. on expansion 1977-80, 82-84, state chpt. chmn. state scholarship com. 1967-73, state 2d v.p. 1971-73, state 1st v.p. 1973-75, state pres. 1975-77, chmn. policy manual 1977-81, chmn. adv. coun. 1978-85, chmn. fin. com. 1981-83, parliamentarian 1987-91, adminstrv. bd. 1987—, chmn. nominations com. 1989-91, dir. S.E. Region 1978-80, coord. S.E. Regional Golden Anniversary Conf. 1979, internat. scholarship com. 1970-74, internat. exec. bd. 1975-77, 78-80, internat. adminstrv. bd. 1978-80, internat. constn. com. 1980-82, internat. achievement award com., 1986-88), Florence Literary Club (sec. 1964-66, 79-82, pres. 1970-72). Methodist (chmn. ch. libr. com. 1965-71, chmn. com. ch. history, 1968-69, sec. adminstrv. bd. 1979-82). Home: 1000 Live Oaks Dr SW # 8B Orangeburg SC 29115-9600

THOMPSON, MARI HILDENBRAND, medico-legal and administrative consultant; b. Washington, Apr. 26, 1951; d. Emil John Christopher Hildenbrand and Ada Lythe (Conklin) Hildenbrand-Kammer; m. R. Marshall Thompson, Sept. 27, 1970 (div. June 1981); 1 child, Jeremy Marshall. BA in Secondary Edn., Am. U., 1976, BA in Performing Arts, 1976. Cert. med. staff coord.; cert. profl. credentialing specialist. Employment interviewer Scripps Meml. Hosp., La Jolla, Calif., 1977-81; office mgr. Jacksina & Freedman Press Office, N.Y.C., 1982-83; staffing coord., med. staff asst. Am. Med. Internat. Clairemont Hosp., San Diego, 1983-85; adminstrv. asst. Am. Med. Internat. Valley Med. Ctr., El Cajon, Calif., 1985-88; med. staff coord. Sharp Meml. Hosp., San Diego, 1988-92; adminstrv. asst. Grossmont Hosp., La Mesa, Calif., 1992-93, coord. Sharp family practice residency program, 1993-94; mgr. Sharp Meml. Hosp. med. staff svcs., San Diego, 1994-96; cons. med. staff svcs. San Diego Rehab. Inst., 1997. Cons. and adminstrv. support for Legal Support, Inc., 1989—, St. Charles Med. Ctr., 1998—2004; cons. Legal Support N.W., LLC, 1999—; coord. Deschutes Ct. Defenders, 1999-2005; wardrobe mistress various cmty. theatres, San Diego, 1978-79, actress, San Diego, 1979-81. Co-founder N.Y.C. Playreaders Group, 1981-83, N.J. Shakespeare Theatre, Madison, 1982, Good Humor Improv Co., N.Y.C., 1982-83; contbg. writer to Poetry Revival: An Anthology, 1994. Bd. dirs. Estates of Sebring Park Home Owners Assn., 2006—; active Dem. Nat. Com., 1996—; vol. Cascades Theatre Co., 1997-2005. Named one of Outstanding Young Women of Am., 1986. Mem. AFTRA. Democrat. Buddhist. Avocations: poetry, swimming, gardening, fishing.

THOMPSON, MARIE ANGELA, computer engineer, consultant; b. Sheffield, Yorkshire, Eng., Aug. 8, 1951; came to U.S., 1979. d. Leslie Arthur and Gloria Mabel (Sheldon) Findley; m. Stephen J. Thompson, Feb. 10, 1990. BS with honors, U. Leeds, 1973; MS, U. Reading, 1975. Software engr. ITT, London, 1975-79, GTE, Northlake, Ill., 1979-80, St. Petersburg, Fla., 1980-82, Reston, Va., 1982-83; dir. rsch. Northcor, Hamden, Conn., 1985-90; mgr. spl. projects SAC of Am., Ridgefield, Conn., 1990-98; cons. Universal Solutions 2000, Ridgefield, Conn., 1998, Thompson, Findley & Co., Hampton Bays, NY, 1998—. Cons. Ivy League Corp., Ridgefield, Conn., 1995—98, Digital Network 1, Ridgefield, 1995—98. Dir. concessions Pop Warner Football, Ridgefield, 1993, 94, dir. registration, 1994, 95, 96, 97, dir. fundraising, 1996-98. Recipient Bob Scalzo Meml. award Ridgefield Pop Warner Football, 1997. Mem. AAUW, AAAS, Am. Inst. Chem. Engrs., Conn. Assn. for the Gifted, N.Y. Acad. Scis., Conn. Business and Industry Assn., Ridgefield C. of C., Mensa. Avocations: tennis, Go, computing, skiing, reading. Office: Thompson Findley & Co 14 Rutland Plz 301 Rutland VT 05701

THOMPSON, MARIE KATHLYN, middle school educator; d. Fred and Delores Thompson. BS in Mass Comm. TV/Radio, So. Ill. U., Edwardsville, 1991; cert. mid. sch. comm. arts and social studies 5th-9th grades, U. Mo., 2000. Educator Langston Mid. Sch., St. Louis, 1992—. Office: Langston Mid Sch 5511 Wabada Saint Louis MO 63112 Office Phone: 314-383-2908. Personal E-mail: marie.thompson@slps.org.

THOMPSON, MARY B., writer, illustrator; b. Corpus Christi, Tex., Dec. 11, 1929; d. Henry Charles and Marjorie Murray Keller. BA in Psychology, So. Meth. U., 1957; MA in Secondary Edn., NYU, 1961, MA in Creative Writing, 1961, ABD in Higher Edn. Adminstrn., 1969. Cert. secondary edn. English N.Y. Rschr. Ruder & Finn Inc., N.Y.C., 1958—60; TV script writer Philco Corp., N.Y.C., 1961, Phila., 1961; faculty The New Lincoln Sch., N.Y.C., 1961—64, So. Meth. U., Dallas, 1964—68; freelance writer, 1968—81; freelance writer pub. rels. Albany, NY, 1981—85; real estate developer, 1985—90; author, pub. Melior Press, Leesburg, Fla., 1997—2000; author, illustrator The Lighthouse Press, Deerfield Beach, Fla., 2000—. Mem. curriculum com. So. Meth. U., Dallas, 1966; vol. tchr. advanced English classes Leesburg H.S. Author: (novella) Closed Circuit, 1961, (book) B.S. Detecting, 1999, illustrator: B.S. Detecting: Success Possible Communicating, 2000, 2d edit., 2004. Mem.: LWV, Nat. Writers Union, Defenders of Wildlife, South Lake Animal League, Sierra Club, Kappa Delta Pi. Avocations: gardening, recreational vehicle travel. Home: 6623 Hopi Trail Leesburg FL 34748

THOMPSON, MARY CECILIA, nurse midwife; b. Georgetown, Guyana; came to the U.S., 1977; d. John Alexander and Monica Eileen (Thorne) T. RN, Southend-on-Sea Sch. Nursing, Essex, Eng., 1973; cert. midwife, Basildon & Thurrock Sch., Essex, Eng., 1975; perinatal nurse practitioner, Cmty. Gen. Hosp., Syracuse, N.Y., 1986; cert. nurse midwife, Frontier Sch. Midwifery, Hyden, Ky., 1990. Cert. nurse midwife. Staff nurse pediatric unit Rochford Hosp., Essex, 1973-74; staff midwife Basildon & Orsett Maternity Units, Essex, 1975-76, St. Peter's Hosp. Chertsey, Surrey, Eng., 1976-78; staff nurse pediatric critical care SUNY Health Sci. Ctr., Syracuse, 1978-82; staff nurse pvt. duty nursing Med. Pers. Pool, Syracuse, 1982-83; staff nurse labor and delivery Cmty. Gen. Hosp., Syracuse, 1983-86, perinatal nurse practitioner, 1986-90; pvt. practice cert. nurse midwife Syracuse, 1990—. Mem. AWHONN, Am. Assn. Nurse Practitioners, Am. Coll. Nurse Midwives. Roman Catholic. Avocations: embroidery, reading, tennis, music, travel. Home: 4904 Razorback Run Syracuse NY 13215-1347 Office: Choices West Med Ctr West W Genesee St Camillus NY 13031-2238

THOMPSON, MARY EILEEN, chemistry professor; b. Mpls., Dec. 21, 1928; d. Albert C. and Blanche (McAvoy) T. BA, Coll. St. Catherine, 1953; MS, U. Minn., 1958; PhD, U. Calif., Berkeley, 1964. Tchr. math. and sci. Derham Hall H.S., St. Paul, 1953-58; mem. faculty Coll. of St. Catherine, St. Paul, 1964-69, prof. chemistry, 1969-2000, chmn. dept., 1969-90, prof. emeritus, 2000—. Project dir. Women in Chemistry, 1984-98. Contbr. articles to profl. jours. Named one of 100 persons honored, Coll. St. Catherine's 100th Anniversary. Mem. AAAS, Am. Chem. Soc. (chmn. women chemists com. 1992-94, award for encouraging women into chem. scis. careers 1997), Coun. Undergrad. Rsch. (councillor 1991-96), N.Y. Acad. Scis., Chem. Soc. London, Sigma Xi, Phi Beta Kappa (senator 1997-2003). Democrat. Roman Catholic. Achievements include research interests in Cr(III) hydrolytic polymers, kinetics of inorganic complexes, Co(III) peroxo/superoxo complexes. E-mail: MTHOM17349@aol.com.

THOMPSON, MARY ELIZABETH, application developer; d. William Reid Jones and Mildred Faye King; 1 child, Barbara Chancee Craig. MA, St. Mary Coll., 1995; BFA, U. of Kans., 1963. Cert. Computer Programming and Operations Ga., 1980; supr. devel. program for higher edn. Art dir. Quantico Va. Dependents Sch. Sys., Quantico, Va., 1964—65, Camp LeJeune NC Dependents Sch. Sys., Camp Lejeune, NC, 1965—67; computer programmer analyst Bank of the South, Atlanta, 1980—82, Hanes Corp., Atlanta, 1982—82; computer programming instr. Cobb County Cmty. Sch. Sys., Marietta, Ga., 1983—83; computer info. sys. instr. Johnson County C.C., Overland Park, Kans., 1987—88; computer info. sys. sr. prof. DeVry U., Kansas City, Mo., 1988—, suprv. devel. program, 2005—. Kansas designer craftsman show, (Charles Rombold Art Award, 1963), philharmonic showhouse book. Mem. Jr. Women's Philharm. Assn., Kansas City, Mo., 1970—73; chairperson Alpha Phi Help Lick Heart Disease, Kansas City, Mo., 1974; mem. Jr. League of Johnson County, Overland Park, Kans., 1998—99. Recipient New Prof. Prime Addition award, DeVry U., 1988, Mo. Governor's award for Excellence in Tchg. and Performance Excellence in Edn., The State of Mo., 2004. Mem.: Kans. City Profl. Devel. Coun., Micro Focus User Group, Assn. of Info. Tech. Profls., Alpha Phi Sorority (life; alumni rep. 1963—63). Achievements include development of faculty adv. for portfolio devel; exploring teamwork in the classroom seminar; textbook selection chairperson; assessment faculty adv. com; development of mentor to new faculty. Home: 10801 W 115th St Overland Park KS 66210 Office: DeVry U 11224 Holmes Rd Kansas City MO 64131 Office Phone: 816-941-0430. E-mail: mbthompson@kc.devry.edu.

THOMPSON, MARY KOLETA, small business owner, not-for-profit developer; b. Portsmouth, Va., Dec. 27, 1938; m. James Burton Thompson, May 5, 1957; children: Burt, Suzan, Kate, Jon. BFA, U. Tex., 1982; postgrad., Boston U.; MA in Philanthropy and Devel., St. Mary's U. Minn., 1999. Cert. non-profit mgmt. Pres., CEO The Planning Resource People, Burnet, Tex., 1990—; Tex. fin. devel. specialist ARC Tex., 1994-98; devel. dir. Very Spl. Arts Tex., 1991-92; dir. devel. ARC, Austin, 1992-94; pub. affairs adminstr. Pink Palace Mus. and Memphis Mus. Inc., Memphis, 1998; CEO Lamapasas C. of C., Lampasas, TX, 1998-99; pres., CEO Assn. Non-Profit Orgns., 1998—, Tex. Assn. Bed and Breakfast Innkeepers, 1998; pres. A Little Cottage B&B, 1999—2004; owner Heritage Sta. Antiques, 1999—. Dir. Tex. Children's Mus., Fredericksburg, 1987-88, Internat. Hdqrs. SHAPE Command Arts and Crafts Ctr., 1985-86; com. chmn. Symposium for Encouragement Women in Math. and Natural Sci., U. Tex., Austin, 1990; instr. nonprofit mgmt., fin. devel., bd. leadership, grant proposal writing Ctrl. Tex. Coll., 2002—. Sculptor portrait busts. Bd. dirs. Teenage Parent Coun., Austin, 1990-92, ARC. Named U.S. Vol. of Yr., NATO-Shape Belgium Cmty. Svcs., 1986; grantee, NEA, 1988. Mem.: AAUW (life; pres. 1990—92), Women in Comm. (co-chmn. SW regional conf.), Lometa Lions Club (pub. rels. com. 1999—), Heritage Station Antique Vehicle Show (founder), Heritage Station Antiques Show and Sale (founder), Leadership Tex. (life), U. Tex. Ex-Student Assn. (life), Heritage Station Antiques Forum (founder), Raleigh Tavern Soc. (founder), Leadership Tex. Alumnae Assn. (bd. dir.), Tex. Hist. Found (life). Avocations: writing, lecturing, meeting and strategic planning.

THOMPSON, MARY LOU, elementary school educator; b. Cambridge, Mass., Dec. 29, 1933; BS in Edn., Framingham State Tchrs. Coll., Mass., 1956; MEd, Boston U., 1962; postgrad., Simmons Coll., Boston, Lesley Coll., Cambridge, Mass., Fitchburg State Coll., Mass. Elem. tchr. Burlington (Mass.) Pub. Sch., 1956—61, Sudbury (Mass.) Pub. Sch., 1961—2001; substitute tchr. Maynard Pub. Schs. Tutored learning disabled adult, 1997—99. Author curr. materials. Edn. liaison state senate campaign, Sudbury, Mass., 2002. Recipient sculpture placed in Sudbury Libr. in honor, by staff and parents of Israel Loring Sch., 2001. Mem.: NEA, Mass. Tchr. Assn. Avocations: art hist., reading, gardening, home maintenance, photography. Home: 4 DeMarco Rd Sudbury MA 01776-2036

THOMPSON, NANCY, art director; b. Mobile, Ala., Apr. 19, 1953; d. leon and Roas C Wiggins; m. John Michael Thompson, Mar. 14, 1956; 1 child, Laine Michael. BS in music edn., U. Ala., 1975; MEd, U. S. Ala., 1985. Cert. admin. U. S. Ala., 1998. Band dir. Mobile County Sch. Sys., Ala., 1976—2001, asst. prin., 2001, fine arts supr., 2002—. Presenter, cons. Mobile County Sch. Sys., 2001—03. Contbr. articles various profl. jours. Pres. Mobile County Pub. Sch. Bands, 2001. Named Worthy Maton, Order of Easton Star. Mem.: Music Edn. Nat. Conf., US Sports Acad., Vol. of Am., Order of LaShe's (pres. 1998), Kappa Kappa Iota (pres. 1985). Meth. Avocations: music, fishing, painting. Home: 1016 Orepoll Blvd Mobile AL 36695 Office: Mobile County Pub Sch Sys 504 Governor St Mobile AL 36602 Office Phone: 251-221-4087. E-mail: nthompson@mcpss.org.

THOMPSON, PAMELA A., nurse administrator; b. Silsbee, Tex., Apr. 7, 1949; d. John David and Peggy Gean (Gholson) Austin; m. Robert Laurence Thompson, May 26, 1979; children: Garrett Austin, Durete Abdella. BSN, U. Conn., 1971; MSN, U. Rochester, 1979. RN. Dir. maternal and child health Copley Meml. Hosp., Aurora, Ill., 1980-82; dir. emergency svcs. and pediatrics LaGrange (Ill.) Cmty. Hosp., 1982-86; v.p. Dartmouth Hitchcock Med. Ctr., Lebanon, N.H., 1986—. Pres. bd. Behavioral Health Network, Concord, N.H., 1997-99; chair Ctrl. and Eastern Europe Nursing Task Force, Washington, 1994-98. Sec., Andover (N.H.) After Sch. Program, 1994-96. Mem. ANA, Am. Coll. Healthcare Execs., Am. Orgn. Nurse Execs. (bd. dirs. 1997-98), N.H. Orgn. Nurse Execs. (pres. 1992-96), N.H. Hosp. Assn. (pres. bd. 1997-98), Ctr. for Nursing Leadership (mem. coun. 1998—). Democrat. Roman Catholic. Avocations: cooking, horseback riding, reading, sewing. Office: Dartmouth Hitchcock Med Ctr One Medical Center Dr Lebanon NH 03756 Home: 10524 Knollwood Dr Manassas VA 20111-2834

THOMPSON, PAMELA PADWICK, public relations executive; b. Columbus, Ohio, June 13, 1943; d. Frank John and Tiami Judith (Padwick) T.; stepfather, James William Bampton; m. Fairman Rogers Thompson, Jan. 10, 1942; children: Ryder McNeal, Darby McNeal. BA, U. Louisville, 1994; MA, U. Dayton, 1998. Ptnr. Crutcher, Kelly and Assocs., Louisville, 1979-83; owner Transl. Co., Louisville, 1981-83, Technigraphics, Louisville, 1984-87; v.p. dir. individual support Grtr. Louisville Fund for the Arts, Louisville, 1989-92; v.p. comms. John Templeton Found., Radnor, Pa., 1997—. Adj. prof. U. Louisville, 1997. Contbr. articles to profl. jours. including Small Group Behavior. Chair pub. rels. com. Keene Valley Libr., 2000-01; bd. dirs. Louisville Nature Ctr., 1996-97; mem. ad hoc com. State Ky. Biodiversity Coun., Louisville, 1996-97; city commr. City of Rolling Fields, Louisville, 1991-94; alliance bd. dirs. J.B. Speed Art Mus., Louisville, 1986-92. Mem. APA, Soc. for Consumer Psychology, Pub. Rels. Soc. Am., Jr. League Phila., Cosmo. Club Phila., Ausable Club. Episcopalian. Avocations: hiking, gardening, tennis, travel. Home: 4 Porter Ln Rose Valley PA 19086 Office: John Templeton Foundation 300 Conshohocken State Rd Ste 500 Conshohocken PA 19428-3801 Fax: (610) 687-8961. Office Phone: 610-941-5194. Business E-Mail: pthompson@templeton.org.

THOMPSON, PATRICIA DUBOIS, elementary school educator; b. Swainsboro, Ga., Dec. 18, 1954; d. Clarence Hazel and Phyllis June (Prior) DuBois; m. Johnny Darrell Thompson, July 24, 1976; children: Alison Ashley, Austin Antony AS, S.W. Va. C.C., 1975; BS, Concord Coll., 1976; MS, Radford U., 1981. Cert. elem. tchr., Va. Tchr. nursery Sunday Sch., pianist Adria Advent Christian Ch., North Tazewell, Va., 1968—78; tchr. 1st grade McDowell County Schs., Bradshaw, W.Va., 1976—77; tchr. kindergarten Cove Primary Sch., Tazewell, Va., 1977—90; tchr. 3d grade Tazewell Elem. Sch., 1990—94, tchr. 1st grade, 1994—. Tchr. rep. Tazewell Com. Rural Devel., 1992— Gen. Appalachian youth sec. Appalachian A.C. Youth, Blowing Rock, N.C., 1969-70; sponsor Children's Garden Clubs, 2000-06. Mem. Nat. Coun. Tchrs. Math., Va. Edn. Assn., NEA, Tazewell Edn. Assn., Kappa Delta Pi Avocations: needlecrafts, music, poetry. Home: 624 Hurst St North Tazewell VA 24630-9535 Office: Tazewell Elem Sch 110 Maplewood Dr Tazewell VA 24651-1299

THOMPSON, PATRICIA RATHER, literature educator, department chairman; b. Houston, Nov. 27, 1939; d. Daniel Irvin and Veda Byrl (Page) R.; m. Bobby Dean Thompson, Sept. 3, 1960; children: Troy, Byron, Mark. BA, Sam Houston State U., 1962, MA, 1980. Tchr. Houston Ind. Sch. Dist., 1962-65; tchr., dept. chair Klein (Tex.) Ind. Sch. Dist., 1980—. Tchr. North Harris Montgomery County C.C., Conroe, Tex., 1993-96, 2001--; writing cons., Spring, Tex., 1990—; online communication cons., 1997--. Contbr. poetry and articles to profl. jours. Mem. ASCD, Tex. Gifted and Talented, Tex. State Tchrs. English. Home: 210 Shannondale Ln Spring TX 77388-5965 Office: Klein High Sch 16715 Stuebner Airline Rd Klein TX 77379-7394

THOMPSON, PHYLLIS D., judge, lawyer; b. Washington, Oct. 1, 1952; BA in Anthropology, with distinction, George Washington U., 1974; MA in Religion (focus in Ethics), Princeton U., 1976; JD with high honors, George Washington U., 1981. Bar: DC 1981. Instr., lectr. Georgetown U., Washington, 1977-81; joined Covington & Burling, Washington, 1982—, now ptnr., fed. benefits programs practice group; assoc. judge DC Ct. Appeals, Washington, 2006—. Instr. & lectr. - Theology Dept. Georgetown U., Washington, 1977—81. Co-author (with Susan L. Burke): Analysis Has Its Privileges: Compliance Rev. May Be Protected From Discovery, 1999. Mem.: Am. Health Lawyers Assn., DC Bar Assn. (steering com. affairs divsn.). Office: Covington & Burling 1201 Pennsylvania Ave NW PO Box 7566 Washington DC 20044-7566 also: DC Ct of Appeals Moultrie Courthouse 500 Indiana Ave NW Washington DC 20001 Office Phone: 202-662-5668. Office Fax: 202-662-6291. Business E-Mail: pthompson@cov.com.*

THOMPSON, PHYLLIS DARLENE, retired elementary school educator; b. West Milton, Ohio, May 21, 1934; d. Howard Luther and Dorothy Mae (Heisey) Yount; m. Joel Kent Thompson, Aug. 22, 1954 (div. Feb. 1981); children: George Kevin, Jolanna Renee, Howard Kraig. BS in Edn., Manchester Coll., 1956; MEd, LaVerne U., 1977. Cert. tchr., Ill. Tchr. Dist. 83, North Lake, Ill., 1956—59; missionary, tchr. Ambon U., Indonesia, 1961—62; tchr. Dist. Unit 46, Elgin, Ill., 1969—2000; ret., 2000. Organizer Mother Goose Day Care Ctr., Elgin, 1970s. Choir mem. Highland Ave Ch. of the Brethren, Elgin, 1964—, bd. chair, 1980-83, ch. bd., 1997-98, 2004—. Recipient Ednl. Excellence award State of Ill., 1978, Disting. Educator award Kane County, 1978. Mem. NEA, Ill. Edn. Assn., Elgin Tchrs. Assn. (bldg. rep. 1994-96), Alpha Delta Kappa (pres., v.p., sec. 1972—), Elgin Area Retired Tchrs. Assn. (bd. 2002-2003), Ill. Retired Tchrs. Assn. Democrat. Avocations: letter writing, reading, cross stitching, walking. Home: 11 Kensington Loop Elgin IL 60123-2720

THOMPSON, RAMONA KAY, special education educator; b. Dodge City, Kans., Jan. 17, 1945; d. William Andrew and Mary Emma (Cadman) Bell; m. Richard Edward Thompson, May 29, 1971; Frances Michelle, Stacy Kay. BA in German and Edn., Friends U., Wichita, Kans., 1968; MS in Spl. Edn., Ctrl. State U., Edmond, Okla., 1973; postgrad., North Tex. State U., 1978-80; student, Carthage Coll., Kenosha, Wis., 1990. Cert. tchr., Ill.; cert. paralegal, Wis. Tchr. 8th grade English and teenage mothers Kansas City (Kans.) Bd. Edn., 1968-70; tchr. TMH-self-contained Wichita Pub. Schs., 1971; tchr. grades 6 to 8 learning disabled Stillwater (Okla.) Pub. Schs., 1971-74; tchr. behavioral disordered, emotionally disabled Cin. Pub. Schs., 1974-76; tchr. high sch. generic spl. edn., diagnostician N.W. Ind. Schs., Justin, Tex., 1982-86; tchr. Libertyville (Ill.) High Sch. Spl. Edn. Dist. Lake County, Gurnee, Ill., 1986—2001; lead tchr. spl. edn. Bossier Parish Schs., La., 2001—. Bd. dirs. Ch. Pre-Sch., Denton, Tex., 1985-86. Server, Soup Kitchen, Waukegan, Ill., 1990-91; worker for the homeless, PADS, Mundelein, Ill., 1990-92; assigned to state monitoring team Special Edn. IEP's, 2004-05. Named Mid. Sch. Tchr. of Yr., Bossier Parish Schs., 2006. Mem. Coun. for Exceptional Children. Avocations: gardening, needlecrafts. Office Phone: 318-549-5427.

THOMPSON, RONELLE KAY HILDEBRANDT, library director; b. Brookings, S.D., Apr. 21, 1954; d. Earl E. and Maxine R. (Taplin) Hildebrandt; m. Harry Floyd Thompson II, Dec. 24, 1976; children: Clarissa, Harry III. BA in Humanities magna cum laude, Houghton Coll., 1976; MLS, Syracuse U., 1976; postgrad., U. Rochester, 1980, 81; cert., Miami U., 1990. Libr. asst. Norwalk (Conn.) Pub. Libr., 1977; elem. libr. Moriah Ctrl. Schs., Port Henry, NY, 1977—78; divsn. coord. pediat. gastroenterology and nutrition U. Rochester (N.Y.) Med. Ctr., 1978—81, cons., pediat. housestaff libr. com., 1980—81; dir. Medford Libr. U. S.C., Lancaster, 1981—83; dir. Mikkelsen Libr., Libr. Assocs., Ctr. for Western Studies, mem. libr. com. Augustana Coll., Sioux Falls, SD, 1983—, adminstrv. pers. coun., 1989—94, 1997—2004. Presenter in field. Contbr. articles to profl. jours. Mem. S.D. Symphony; advisor pers. dept. City of Sioux Falls. Recipient leader award YWCA, 1991; Gaylord Co. scholar Syracuse U., 1976; named S.D. Libr. of Yr., 1998. Mem. ALA, AAUW, Assn. Coll. and Rsch. Librs. (nat. adv. coun. coll. librs. sect. 1987—), Mountain Plains Libr. Assn. (chair acad. sect., nominating com. 1988, pres. 1993-94), S.D. Libr. Assn. (chair interlibr. coop. task force 1986-87, pres. 1987-88, chair recommended minimum salary task force 1988, chair local arrangements com. 1989-90, 2002-03), S.D. Libr. Network (adv. coun. 1986—, exec. com. 1992-96, 1998-2000, chair adv. coun. 1994-96, 98-2000). Office: Augustana Coll Mikkelsen Libr 29th & Smt Sioux Falls SD 57197-0001 Office Phone: 605-274-4921. Business E-Mail: ronelle.thompson@augie.edu.

THOMPSON, SADA CAROLYN, actress; b. Des Moines, Sept. 27, 1927; d. Hugh Woodruff and Corlyss Elizabeth (Gibson) T.; m. Donald E. Stewart, 1949; 1 dau., Liza. BFA, Carnegie Inst. Tech., 1949; DFA, Carnegie Mellon, late 1970's. Speech tchr. 92d St YMHA, N.Y.C. Stage debut in The Time of Your Life at Carnegie Inst. Tech. Drama Sch., 1945; co-founder Univ. Playhouse, Mashpee, Mass., 1947, appeared at Pitts. Playhouse, The Playhouse, Erie, Pa., summer stock prodns. at Henrietta Hayloft Theatre, Rochester, N.Y., Cambridge, Mass.; New York debut in Under Milk Wood, at YMHA, 1953; appeared in Off-Broadway revival at Circle in the Sq. Theatre, 1961, and Nat. Edn. Television presentation, 1966; appeared in plays The Clandestine Marriage, Provincetown Playhouse, N.Y.C., 1954, The White Devil and, The Carefree Tree at, Phoenix Theatre, N.Y.C., 1955, The Misanthrope, Off Broadways Theatre East, 1956, The River Line, Carnegie Hall Playhouse, 1957; joined Am. Shakespeare Festival, Stratford, Conn., 1957 appearing in Othello, Much Ado About Nothing, 1957-58, The Merry Wives of Windsor, Alls Well That Ends Well, 1959, Twelfth Night, The Tempest and, Antony and Cleopatra, 1960; appeared in Off Broadway prodn. of Chekhov's Ivanov, 1958, Broadway prodn. of Juno and the Paycock, 1959, Tartuffe at Lincoln Center Repertory Theatre, 1965, Johnny No-Trump, 1967, The American Dream, 1968, The Effect of Gamma Rays on Man-in-the-Moon Marigolds, 1970, Twigs, 1971, Mourning Becomes Electra, 1971, Sat.Sun-.Mon early 1980's, Any Given Day 1995; motion pictures include You Are Not Alone, 1961, Desperate Characters, 1971, The Pursuit of Happiness, 1971; starred in TV series: Sandburg's Lincoln, 1974-76, Family, 1976-79 (Emmy award for outstanding actress in a dramatic series); TV spl. The Entertainer, 1976; appeared in TV mini-series Marco Polo, 1982, Princess Daisy, 1983, Queen, 1993, (TV movies) Adventures of Huckleberry Finn, 1985, My Love, 1986, Fatal Confession: A Father Dowling Mystery, 1987, Home Fires Burning, 1987, Fear Stalk, 1989, The Skin of Our Teeth, 1980's, Painting Churches, 1980's, Andre's Mother, 1990, Indictment: The McMartin Trial, 1995. Recipient Tony award 1972, New York Drama Critics award for best actress of year Variety 1971-72, 2 Obie awards, Atlanta Drama Critics Mask award as best actress for performance in The Vinegar Tree 1978; Any Mother's Son, 1997; The Patron Saint of Liars, 1998, tv.; Pollock, 1999, film. Named to Theater Hall of Fame, 2005. Office: Richard Bauman & Assocs 5757 Wilshire Blvd Ste 473 Los Angeles CA 90036-3635 Address: PO Box 490 Southbury CT 06488-0490*

THOMPSON, SANDRA GUERRA, lawyer, educator; BA, Yale Univ., 1985, JD, 1988. Asst. dist. atty. N.Y. County, 1988—90; prof. Univ. Houston Law Ctr., 1990—; dir. Criminal Justice Inst., Univ. Houston. Co-author: The Law of Asset Forfeiture; contbr. articles to prof. jour. Mem.: Assn. Am. Law Sch. (chair, Criminal Justice sect. 2001), Hispanic Bar Assn. (mem. bd. dir.), Houston Bar Assn., Am. Law Inst. (mem. bd. adv. Model Penal Code: Sentencing project). Office: Criminal Justice Institute 100 Law Ctr 4800 Calhoun Rd Houston TX 77204

THOMPSON, SANDRA LEE, library administrator; b. Dover, Ohio, Jan. 23, 1968; d. Robert Leonard and Gwendolyn Ruth Stewart; m. Alan McKinney Thompson, Sept. 9, 1990; children: LeeAnna, Alisha, James. BS in Edn., Ohio U., 1989; M of Libr. Info. Sci., U. S.C., 2001. Tchr. Harrison Hills City Sch. Dist., Hopedale, Ohio, 1989-90; asst. dir. Puskarich Pub. Libr., Cadiz, Ohio, 1990-97, dir., 1998—. Mem. Ohio Libr. Coun., Columbus, 1994—; bd. dirs. Southeastern Ohio Libr. Orgn., Caldwell, 1997—, Ohio Pub. Libr. Info. Network. Mem.: Cadiz Rotary Assocs. (trustee), Am. Libr. Assn. Office: Puskarich Pub Libr 200 E Market St Cadiz OH 43907-1200 E-mail: sthompson@oplin.org.

THOMPSON, SHARON HOWELL, health educator; b. Greenwood, S.C., Oct. 8, 1958; d. Alfred Wayne and Dolores Antley Howell; m. Frank Austin Thompson, July 24, 1982; children: Leslie Allison, Austin Howell. BS in Plant Sci., Clemson U., S.C., 1980; MEd in Cmty. Edn., U. S.C., Columbia, 1982, EdS in Ednl. Adminstrn., 1993. Cert. health edn. specialist Nat. Commn. for Health Edn. Credentialing, Inc. Tchr. Horry County Schs., Myrtle Beach, SC, 1982—90; prof. Coastal Carolina U., Conway, 1999—2006. Contbr. articles to profl. jours. Chmn. Waccamaw Youth Ctr., Conway, SC, 1994—2006, Horry County Schs. Comprehensive Health Com., Conway, 1994—2006; mem. adv. bd. StepUp!, Conway, 2005—06. Named Health Edn. Profl. of Yr., SC Assn. for Advancement of Health Edn., 1997, Vol. of Yr., The Sun News, 2003, Disting. Teacher-Scholar Lectr., Coastal Carolina U., 2004; recipient Student Affairs award, 1998, Excellence in Cmty. Nutrition award, Dannon Inst., 2003; grantee, SC. Commn. Higher Edn., 2003. Methodist. Avocations: cycling, travel. Office: Coastal Carolina U PO Box 261954 Conway SC 29528 Office Phone: 843-349-2635. Business E-Mail: thompson@coastal.edu.

THOMPSON, SHARON RUTH, special education educator; d. Arthur Louis and Dorothy Ruth Knudtson; m. William John Thompson, Sept. 8, 1984; children: Hannah Ruth, Matthew John, Rachel Marie. BS in Edn., Ea. Mont. Coll., Billings, 1984. Resource spl. edn. tchr. Sheridan (Wyo.) Sch. Dist., 1984—94; spl. edn. tchr. Annette Island Sch. Dist., Metlakatla, Alaska, 1994—96, Kenai Peninsula Borough Sch. Dist., Soldotna, Alaska; with Nikiski Mid. H.S. Recipient Tchr. of Excellance award, BP Com., 2005. Office: Nikiski Mid High Sch PO Box 7112 Nikiski AK 99635 Office Phone: 907-776-3456.

THOMPSON, SUE WANDA, small business owner; b. Azle, Tex., Nov. 26, 1935; d. Weldon W. Beasley and Eula Mae Hardee; m. William Henry Clark, Feb. 20, 1952 (div. 1959); children: Gloria, Russ, Bonnie; m. Robert L. Thompson Jr., Sept. 20, 1963; stepchildren: Christene, Lee. Nurse Harris Hosp., Ft. Worth, 1960-62, Denton State Sch., 1962-63; owner, v.p. Dalworth Med. Labs., Ft. Worth, 1963-68; sales leader, trainer Home Interior and Gifts, Dallas, 1970-80; owner, pres. Thompson Enterprises, 1980—; mgr., trainer Jafra Cosmetics, West Lake Village, Calif., 1981-84, Jewels by Park Lane, Chgo., 1984-89, Just Am., Rutlerfordton, N.C., 1989-91; with sales Dyna Tech Nutritionals, Willston Park, N.Y., 1993-94. Dir. parks and recreation City Forest Hills, Tex., 1970. Mem. Beta Sigma Phi (treas. Eta Lambda chpt. 1971-72, pres. 1972-73, Girl of Yr. 1974). Republican. Mem. Ch. Nazarene. Avocations: sports, singing, crafts. Home: 4717 Applewood Rd Fort Worth TX 76133-7435 Office Phone: 817-294-7576.

THOMPSON, TARA D., illustrator, writer, career planning administrator; b. Borger, Tex., June 7, 1962; d. Sammy Jo and Jeannean (Johansen) T. AA, Tex. State Tech. Inst., 1982; AAS, Richland Coll., 1991; BA, U. Tex., Dallas, 1993; MA in Counseling, Amber U., 1995. Art dir. Dalco Athletic Lettering, Garland, Tex., 1983-85; office mgr. Jean West Enterprises, Dallas, 1985-86; dept. adminstr. Dean Witter Reynolds, Inc., Dallas, 1986-87; info. specialist, pub. relations asst. Anderson Fischel Thompson Advt., Dallas, 1986-87, office mgr., 1987-89, traffic mgr., 1989-90; writer, illustrator Garland, Tex., 1990—; intern Richland Coll., Dallas, 1994-95; career cons. Career Dimensions, Dallas, 1995—97. Adj. faculty mem. Richland Coll., Dallas, 1995—2003; facilitator Career Fitness Workout, 1996-97; lead acad. career advisor Richland Coll., 1997-. Vol. listener Dallas Ind. Sch. Dist., 1991-92. Mem. NACADA, Nat. Career Devel. Assn., Undergrad. Psychology Assn. U. Tex. (treas. 1992), Toastmasters (pres. 1992-93, v.p. pub. rels. and membership Speaking Scholars, CTM 1993, Thunderducks,2003-04), People for the Ethical Treatment of Animals. Avocations: roller skating, motorcycling, bicycling, hiking, motocross. Office: 12800 Abrams Rd Dallas TX 75243-2199 Office Phone: 972-238-6328. Business E-Mail: tarat@dcccd.edu.

THOMPSON, TERESA ACKERMAN, special education educator; b. Elkhart, Ind., June 11, 1971; d. Robert Lee and Mary Marie Ackerman; m. Tedd Bennett Thompson, Sept. 20, 1996. BA in Social Scis., Mich. State U., 1995; tchg. cert., Olivet Coll., 1996; M in Edn., Grand Valley State U., 2001. Tchr. Mich. State U., E. Lansing, 1994-96, Okemos H.S., Mich., 1996-97, Holt H.S., Mich., 1997—. Presenter in field. Vol. Mich. Rschrs. Assn., Spl. Olympics, Holt, Mich., 1999—. Democrat. Roman Catholic. Avocations: reading, hiking, travel, boating, walking. Home: 12463 Cherry Leaf Ln Brighton MI 48114-8150 Office: Holt High School 5885 Holt Rd Holt MI 48842-8677 E-mail: ttbytwo@aol.com.

THOMPSON, TERRIE LEE, graphic designer; b. Myrtle Creek, Oreg., Apr. 22, 1960; d. Claud Willie and Blanche Bernice Thompson. Student, Umpqua C.C., 1983-84; BFA, Pacific N.W. Coll. Art, 1988. Freelance graphic designer Terrie Thompson Design, Portland, 1987-90; graphic designer Promotion Products Inc., Portland, 1989-90, L. Grafix Inc., Portland, 1990-91, Warn Industries, Milwaukie, Oreg., 1991-92; pres. Thompson Typographics Inc., Portland, 1990—; typography contractor Nike Inc., Beaverton, Oreg., 1992—. Typography trainer for various design firms and agys., Portland, 1992-98, pres. Seeing Spots, Inc., 1998—. Work published in various design publs., including The Best in Catalogue Design, Comm. Arts Design Ann., How Mag. Computer Art and Design Ann.; creator cartoon character "Spot", 1989. Vol. graphic designer Washington Park Zoo, Portland, 1990; vol. art dir. Portland Mac Users Group, Portland, 1995; vol. beach clean-up crew Stop Oreg. Litter and Vandalism, 1990—. Recipient Bronze award Optima Design Awards, 1995, Digital Art and Design Ann. award Print Mag., 1997, Regional Design Ann. award Print Mag., 1997, 2004, Applied Arts Annual, 1997, 98, Good Neighbor award Forest Park Neighborhood Assn., 1999. Avocations: hiking, travel, camping, photography, music. Home and Office: Thompson Typographics Inc PO Box 83327 Portland OR 97283-0327

THOMPSON, THELMA BARNABY, university president, classical languages educator; b. Balaclava, Jamaica, West Indies, July 22, 1940; d. Claude Noel and Elaine Jordan (Robertson) Barnaby; m. Winston Lloyd Thompson, June 15, 1976; 1 child, Lisa Valdeen. BA, Howard U., Washington, D.C., 1970; MA, Howard U., 1972, PhD, 1978; diploma, Bethlehem Tchrs. Coll., Malvern, Jamaica, West Indies, 1960. Lectr. CUNY, 1972—74; asst. prof. Bowie (Md.) State Coll., 1974—76; assoc. prof., asst. chmn. English dept. U. DC, Washington, 1976—88, assoc. dean, 1988—90; dean Sch. Arts and Letters Norfolk State U., 1990—98, v.p. acad. affairs, 1998—2002; pres. U. Md. Ea. Shore, Princess Anne, 2002—. Author: The Seventeenth Century English Hymn; also articles. Named one of Md.'s 100 Outstanding Women, 2004, Women Shaping the World, Essence Mag., 2005; recipient Bethlehem Coll. Medal of Distinction, scholarship and grad. fellowship, award for outstanding accomplishment in field of edn., Howard U., 2005, Best of St. Bess award, Jamaica, West Indies, 2003. Mem. MLA, Coll. Lang. Assn., South Atlantic MLA, Middle Atlantic Writers, Phi Beta Kappa, Phi Delta Kappa (award for disting. svc. and commitment to excellence in edn. 1991). Achievements include extensive outreach work in Africa and the Caribbean. Office: U Md Eastern Shore JT Williams Hall Rm 2107 Princess Anne MD 21853 Office Phone: 410-651-6101. Business E-Mail: tbthompson@umes.edu.

THOMPSON, TINA MARIE, professional basketball player; b. LA, Feb. 10, 1975; B in sociology, U. So. Calif., 1997. Basketball player U. So. Calif., 1993—97; profl. basketball player Houston Comets, WNBA, 1997—. Named All-Star Game MVP, WNBA, 2000; named to First Team All-WNBA, 1997, 1998, WNBA All-Star Team, 1999, 2000, 2001, 2002, 2004. Achievements include No. 1 draft pick in 1997, the first WNBA draftee in the history of the league; mem. Houston Comets WNBA Championship Teams, 1997, 98, 99, 2000; mem. US Women's Basketball Team, Athens Olympics, 2004.

THOMPSON, TRACY ANN, mathematics educator; d. David Thompson and Jean Eno, Virginia Thompson (Stepmother); 1 child, Miranda Chesna Carlyn Mead. BA in Black Studies, U. Calif., Santa Barbara; BA in Math., U.Calif., Santa Barbara; MA in Edn., U. Calif., Santa Barbara; Clear SST Math., UCSB, Santa Barbara. Math. tchr. Santa Barbara HS Dist., 1990—.

THOMPSON, VETTA LYNN SANDERS, psychologist, educator; b. Birmingham, Ala., Sept. 7, 1959; d. Grover and Vera Lee (King) S.; m. Cavelli Andre Thompson, May 27, 1990; children: Olajuwon, Malik Rashad, Kimberlyn, Assata Iyana. BA, Harvard U., 1981; MA, Duke U., 1984, PhD, 1988. Cert. psychologist and health svc. provider, State of Mo. Com. Psychologists. Psychology intern Malcolm Bliss Mental Health Ctr., St. Louis, 1985-86; psychotherapist, testing coord. Washington U. Child Guidance Clinic, St. Louis, 1986-87; psychologist, treatment team coord. Hawthorn Children's Psychiatric Hosp., St. Louis, 1987-89; asst. prof. U. Mo., St. Louis, 1989-95, assoc. prof., coord. black studies, 1995—. Tchg. asst. Duke U., Durham, N.C., 1982-84, rsch. asst., 1984-85; chair monitoring com. crisis access sys. Ea. Regional Adv. Coun. Dept. Mental Health, St. Louis, 1995-97; chair African Am. Task Force on Mental Health, Jefferson City, Mo., 1995-97; chair budget and planning com. Ea. Regional Adv. Coun., Dept. Mental Health, St. Louis, 1996-97, pres. Ea. Regional Adv. Coun., 1997-99; mem. children's mental health planning group St. Louis Mental Health Bd., 1996-97. Mem. editl. adv. bd. A Turbulent Voyage: Readings in African American Studies, 1995-96; mem. bd. editl. advisors Gt. Plains Rsch.; contbr. articles to profl. jours. Mem. adv. com. on violence prevention and investment in youth Mo. House, Jefferson City, 1995; mem. managed care steering com. Dept. Mental Health, Jefferson City, 1995—96, mem. strategic planning adv. coun., 1997; mem. Mo. Bd. for Respiratory Care, 1997; mem. state com. for psychologists Mo., 1997—; chair Mo., 2000—02; sec., chair discipline com. Mo., 1999—2000; bd. dirs. St. Louis Mental Health Assn., sec., 2000—02, chair planning com., 2002, 2d v.p., 2002, pres., 2003. Kellogg Found.-Mo. Youth Initiative fellow, 1991-93; Ctr. for Great Plains Studies fellow U. Nebr., 1995—; recipient Disting. Svc. award Mental Health Assn. St. Louis, 1998, 99. Mem. APA (divsns. 1, 45), Assn. Black Psychologists, Am. Orthopsychiat. Assn. Methodist. Avocations: aerobics, walking, jazz.

THOMPSON, VICKI LEWIS, writer; Author:Promise Me Sunshine, 1984 (Rita finalist, 1985), When Angels Dance, 1985 (Rita finalist, 1986), Butterflies in the Sun, 1986 (Rita finalist, 1987), Be Mine, Valentine, 1989 (Rita finalist, 1990), It Happened One Weekend, 1991 (Rita finalist, 1992), Loverboy, 1994 (Affaire de Coeur Mag. Silver Cert., 1994), Holding Out for a Hero, 1996 (Romantic Times Mag. Reviewers' Choice award, 1996), Mr. Valentine, 1997 (Rita finalist, 1998), Operation Gigolo, 1998 (Desert Rose Romance Writers of Am. Chpt. Golden Quill award, 1999), Pure Temptation, 1999 (Rita finalist, 2000, Romantic Times Mag. Reviewers' Choice award, 1999), Bringing Up Baby New Year, 1999 (Heart and Scroll, Romance Writers Am. Chpt. Madcap award, 2000), Notorious, 2001 (Rita finalist, 2002, Heart of Denver Aspen Gold award, 2001), The Nights Before Christmas, 2001 (Tara Scarlett Letter award, 2002, Tara Virginia Henley award, 2002), Double Exposure, 2002 (Desert Rose Romance Writers Am. Chpt. Golden Quill award, 2002), Drive Me Wild, 2003 (Wordweaving award for Excellence, 2003), After Hours, 2003 (Romantic Times Mag. Reviewers' Choice award, 2003), (anthology) Mystery Lover, Midnight Fantasies, 2001 (Tara Scarlett Letter award, 2002), (Nerd Series) Nerd in Shining Armor, 2003, The Nerd Who Loved Me, 2004, Nerd Gone Wild, 2005, Gone with the Nerd, 2005, others. Mailing: Publicity Dept St Martin's Press 175 Fifth Ave New York NY 10010 E-mail: VLTauthor@aol.com.

THOMPSON, WANDA DAWSON, music educator; b. Lakeland, Fla., Apr. 13, 1948; d. Fuller Leon and Nell Davis Dawson; m. Richard Louis Jackson, June 5, 1970 (div. 1980); 1 child, Lea Jackson Poole; m. Glenn Edward Thompson, Sept. 1, 1984; children: Ashley Carol, Cline Davis. BS in Music Edn., U. Ala., 1970; MA in Music Edn., U. N.Ala., 1977. Musical dir. Morgan County High, Hartselle, Ala., 1970—80; choral dir. Hartselle High, 1980—95, choral dir. and tchr. gen. music, 1999—; tchr. gen. music grades K-5 Barkley Bridge Elem., Hartselle, 1995—99. Choral dir. Hartselle Jr. High, 1970—74; tchr. gen. music grades K-5 Burleson Elem., Hartselle, 1979—81; choral dir. Calhoan C.C., Decatur, Ala., 1994—2001. Named Ala. Outstanding Young Educator, Ala. Jaycees, 1981. Mem.: Music Educators Nat. Conf., Ala. Edn. Assn., Am. Choral Dirs. Assn. Democrat. Avocation: sewing. Home: 709 Celia Dr SE Hartselle AL 35640 Office Phone: 256-773-5427. Business E-Mail: wldthompson@charter.net.

THOMPSON-DRAPER, CHERYL L., electronics executive, real estate executive; b. Houston, Dec. 11, 1950; d. J. R. and Mary Claude Thompson; m. John T. Draper, Aug. 17, 1991; children: Mary-Catherine, John M., Tom. Student, Houston C.C., Massey Bus. Coll. Various positions Warren Electric Group hdqrs., 1970-85; mgr. Warren Electric Co., 1985-89, v.p., bd. dirs., sec., 1990-92; chmn. bd., CEO, owner Warren Electric Co., 1992—, Warren Electric Del Caribe, 1992—, Warren Electric of La., 1992—, Warren-Dominican Republic, 1992—, Warren Electric of Tex., 1992—; mgr., CEO, owner Warren Electric Telecomms.-Utility Co., 1995—; chmn., pres., CEO, owner Warren Electric Group Ltd.; chmn. bd., CEO, pres., owner Thompson Real Estate Ltd., 1995—. Cons. in field. Contbr. articles to profl. jours. Bd. dirs., v.p. San Jacinto coun. Girl Scouts U.S., chmn. fundraiser Urban Campout 1995-96, Houston Sports Found.; vice chmn. Theatre Under the Stars, 1997-2001, chmn. bd., 2001—; bd. dirs. Houston Livestock Show and Rodeo, 1994—; mem. spkrs. and internat. com. All Those Texans, pres., 1997; bd. dirs., mem. exec. com. Greater Houston Partnership, 1996—; mem. Tex Fedn. of Rep., Montgomery County Fair Adv. Bd., 1996—; bd. dirs. Nat. Edn. Found.; mem. med. adv. coun. and vet. med. adv. coun. Tex. A&M U., mem. tech. adv. coun. Coll. Engring.; chmn. indsl. distbn. adv. coun. U. Houston Coll. Engring.; mem. Am. Leadership Forum-Houston, 2000. Recipient Texan of Yr. award All Those Texans, 1994, Mktg. Excellence award-Indsl. Sales, Affiliated Distbrs., 1994, Woman on the Move award City of Houston, 1995, Outstanding Family Owned Bus. award State of Tex., 1995, 1st Largest Woman-Owned Bus. award Houston Bus. Jour., 1998, 99, 2000, 01, Warner Cable's Hometown Hero award, 1996, 3rd Largest Woman-Owned Bus. award State of Tex, Woman Enterprise Mag., 1996, 1997, Disting. Svc. award Houson Elec. League, 1996, Leadership Tex 1997 Class, Cora Bacon Foster award, 1997, 1998, Cmty. Svc. award Houston Bus. Jour., 1997, Indsl. Distbn. award of Distinction, Texas A&M U., 1997, Honeywell's Supplier of Yr. award, 1998. Fellow Paul Harris Rotary Club of Houston (bd. dirs.); mem. Nat. Assn. Elec. Distbrs. (bd. dirs., v.p. 1999-00); mem. NAFE, U.S. C. of C. (internat. com.), Am. Alliance of Family Bus., Nat. Assn. Corp. Dirs., Tex. Exec. Women, Exec. Women Internat., DAR, Petroleum Club of Houston, Pasadena C. of C., Women's C. of C. of Tex., Women's Contractor Assn. Republican. Methodist. Office: Warren Electric Group PO Box 67 Houston TX 77001-0067 Fax: 713-236-2188. E-mail: cheryltd@warrenelectric.com.

THOMS, JANNET, rapid transit executive; BBA in Mgmt. Info. Systems, U. Memphis; MS in Bus., Ctrl. Mich. U.; PhD in Info. Systems, pending dissertation, Nova Southeastern U. Sr. v.p. info. tech. Tech. Plus Corp.; dir. info. tech. dept. BellSouth Corp., assoc. dir. E-Directory; dir. info. tech. dept. Halo Solutions; dir. info. tech. mgmt. and planning Met. Atlanta Rapid Transit Authority (MARTA), 2002—05, asst. gen. mgr. tech. and customer svc. delivery, 2005—, chief information officer, 2005—, mem. smart card automated fare collection exec. steering com., chair info. tech. working group., Bus. Transformation Program. Mem. leadership program Am. Pub. Transp. Assn., 2004—05. Named Woman of Yr. Tech. (not for profit/public sector), (WIT) Women in Tech., 2006; named one of Next Generation of Bus. Leaders Under 40, Minority MBA, 2004. Mem.: Nat. Black MBA Assn., Inc. (Atlanta chpt. pres. 2004, Atlanta chpt. dir. econ. devel.), Am. Profl. Transit Assn., Conference Minority Transp. Officials, Women's Transp. Seminar, Coalition of 100 Black Women (Metro Atlanta chpt.). Office: MARTA Attn: CIO 2424 Piedmont Rd NE Atlanta GA 30324-3311*

THOMS, JEANNINE AUMOND, lawyer; b. Chgo. d. Emmett Patrick and Margaret (Gallet) Aumond; m. Richard W. Thoms; children: Catherine Thoms, Alison Thoms. AA, McHenry County Coll., 1979; BA, No. Ill. U., 1981; JD, Ill. Inst. Tech., 1984. Bar: Ill. 1984, U.S. Dist. Ct. (no. dist.) Ill. 1984, U.S. Ct. Appeals (7th cir.) 1985; cert. mediator 19th Jud. Cir. Ill. Assoc. Foss Schuman Drake & Barnard, Chgo., 1984-86, Zukowski Rogers Flood & McArdle, Crystal Lake and Chgo., 1986-92, ptnr., 1992—. Arbitrator 19th Jud. Ct. Ill., 1991—. Mem. women's addv. coun. to Gov. State of Ill.; mem. adv. coun. McHenry County Mental Health Bd., 1991—98, v.p., 1993—94, pres., 1995—98; mem. governing coun. Advocate Good Shepherd Hosp., Barrington, Ill., 2001—; mem. adv. com. Adv. Found., 2003—, McHenry County Cmty. Found., 2004—. Named one of Ill. Super Lawyers, 2005. Mem.: LWV, ABA, Acad. Family Mediators (cert.), Am. Trial Lawyers Assn., McHenry County Bar Assn., Chgo. Bar Assn., Ill. State Bar Assn. (coun. trust and estates sect. 2000—01, Ill. legis. dist. scholarship com. 2001, 2002—05), Phi Alpha Delta. Office: Zukowski Rogers Flood & McArdle 50 N Virginia St Crystal Lake IL 60014-4126 Office Phone: 815-459-2050.

THOMS, JOSEPHINE BOWERS, artist; b. Lansing, Mich., Sept. 14, 1922; d. Raymon Lyon and Adele (Hammond) Bowers; m. Bert Thoms, June 4, 1945 (dec.); 1 child, Adele Lucile Thoms; m. Peter Blackford Lauck, May 10, 1983. BA, Hillsdale Coll., 1944; MA, Md. Inst. Coll. Art, 1977. Instr. modern dance Hillsdale (Mich.) Coll., 1943-44; artist-in-residence St. John's Coll., Annapolis, Md., 1953-55, 68-70; instr. art Washington and Jefferson Coll., Washington, Pa., 1956, Bethany (W.Va.) Coll., 1963-65; illustrator Md. Dept. Natural Resources, Annapolis, 1977-95. Joint owner Onset Bay Gallery and Studio, Onset, Mass., portrait artist, colorist; instr. Washington Art Assn., 1958-69; art dir. Md. Fedn. Art, Annapolis, 1970-72, pres., 1972-74. Illustrator: Federal Prose, 1947; executed murals: History of Electricity, Hillsdale, 1942, The Harbor at Annapolis, Crownsville, Md., 1989. Mem. Caritas Soc. at St. John's Coll., 1969—, Md. Peace Action, Annapolis, 1983—. Recipient 1st prize for Exhbn. of Nature-Related Art, Adkins Arboretum, Tuckahoe State Pk., Denton, Md., 1995. Mem. Md. Soc. Portrait Painters (cert., exhibits chairperson 1995—), Annapolis Watercolor Club (1st prize 1993). Democrat. Episcopalian. Avocations: swimming, aerobics, piano, needlepoint design. Home: 61 Southgate Ave Annapolis MD 21401-2829

THOMS, SUSAN STUCKEY, ophthalmologist; b. Detroit, June 20, 1948; d. James E. and Joyce C. Stuckey; m. David M. Thoms, Dec. 16, 1972. BA, Kalamazoo Coll., 1970; MD, Wayne State U., Detroit, 1974. Diplomate Am. Bd. of Ophthalmology. Physician/owner Consultants in Ophthalmology, P.C., Detroit, 1978—95; clin. asst. prof. dept. ophthalmology and vis. scis. U. Mich., Ann Arbor, 1995—. Vol. laser tchr. S.E.E. Internat., Ulaan Baatar, Mongolia, 1997; vol. surgery tchr. ORBIS, Ulaan Baatar, Mongolia, 2004; internat. task force on diabetic retinopathy Am. Acad. of Ophthalmology, San Francisco, 2001—02; med. dir. U. Mich. Ctr. for Splty. Care Clinics, Livonia, 2004—; lectr. in field. Contbr. articles to profl. jours. Ann. presenter at H.S. career workshop for women in scis. Explorathon, AAUW, Birmingham, Mich., 1991—2005; vol./cons. Program for Vision Impaired Adults Salvation Army, Detroit; mentor to H.S. girls Edumentor, Bloomfield Hills, Mich., 1991—2004; bd. mem. Greater Detroit Agy. for Blind and Visually Impaired. Recipient Appreciation Award for svc. to visually impaired, Mich. Ophthal. Soc., 1999. Fellow: Am. Acad. of Ophthalmology; mem.: Detroit Ophthal. Club, Mich. Ophthal. Soc. Avocations: world travel, masters swimming, German language study, cooking. Office: Univ Mich Specialty Care 19900 Haggerty Ste 111 Livonia MI 48152 Office Phone: 734-432-7811. Office Fax: 734-432-7822. Business E-Mail: sthoms@umich.edu.

THOMSEN, LINDA CHATMAN, federal agency administrator; d. William C. Chatman; m. Steuart Hill Thomsen, Oct. 16, 1982. BA, Smith Coll., 1976; JD, Harvard U. Atty. Davis Polk & Wardwell, Washington, NYC; asst. U.S. atty. Dist. Md. US Dept. Justice; asst. chief litigation counsel SEC, Washington, 1995—97; asst. dir. Divsn. Enforcement, SEC, Washington, 1997—2000, assoc. dir., 2000—02, dep. dir., 2002—05, dir., 2005—. Named one of 50 Women to Watch, Wall St. Journal, 2005. Office: SEC 450 Fifth St NW Washington DC 20549*

THOMSEN, MARY JOAN MARGARET, psychology educator; b. St. Paul, Sept. 10, 1934; d. Samuel Wade and Margaret Lois (View) T.; 1 child, Cynthia Louise Leuba. BA, UCLA, 1955, MA, 1960. Info. oper. Pacific Telephone Co., Hawthorne, Calif., 1951; libr. clk. L.A. County Libt. System, Lennox, Calif., 1951-53; rsch. asst. UCLA Psychology Dept., L.A., 1955-57, reader, 1957-58; social psychology intern VA, West Los Angeles, Calif., 1959; human factors analyst Boeing Airplane Co., Seattle, 1960; evening sch. clk. L.A. Adult Schs., 1962-64; prof. psychology L.A. Community Colls., 1964—. Mem. LWV, L.A., 1988. Mem. Am. Psychol. Assn. (assoc.), Assn. Consumer Educators, Western Psychol. Assn., UCLA Design for Sharing. Avocations: travel, art, music, reading, gardening. Office: LA Pierce Coll 6201 Winnetka Ave Woodland Hills CA 91371-0001 Home: 10341 Canoga Ave #12 Chatsworth CA 91311 Personal E-mail: zeromaryl@netzero.com.

THOMSEN, PEGGY JEAN, mayor, educator; b. St. Louis, Feb. 28, 1940; d. Harold Herman and Crystal Mary (Margolf) Levora; m. John Henry Thomsen, Dec. 1, 1961; children: Dianna, James, Robert. BA, Calif. State U., Fresno, 1961, MA with honors, 1968; PhD, U. Calif., Berkeley, 1997. Gen. secondary credential, Calif. Instr. Ctrl. Tex. Coll., 1980-83, City Colls. Chgo., 1983-86, Heald Colls., San Francisco, 1987; mayor, coun. mem. City of Albany, 1997—. Mem. East Bay Econ. Alliance, 1997—, Nat. Mayors Conf., 1998-99, Alameda County Mayor's Conf., 1998-99; bd. alt. Waste Mgmt. Authority, 1999—; bd. dirs. Alameda County Congestion Mgmt. Agy., 1997—. Editor City of Albany (Calif.) Newsletter, 1987. Mem. sch. bd. Albany Unified Sch. Dist., 1978-97, pres. sch. bd., 1980-81, 85-86, chmn. bond oversight com., 2004—; pres. PTA, Albany, 1976-78, 69-71; leader Girl Scouts U.S.A., Albany, 1970-82; mem. fund-raising team YMCA, Albany, 1981-88; bd. dirs., sec. Bay Area chpt. March of Dimes, San Francisco, 1979-88, chmn., 1985-86, chmn. Alameda County chpt., 1985-88; mem. adminstrv. code Rev. com. Calif. Dept. Edn., 1981-83, chmn. sch. improvement program selection panel, 1981, mem. fin. com., 1982, state budget com., 1982; Acorn Br. Assoc. Children's Hosp., Oakland; coun. mem. City of Albany, 1997-2004, chmn. social and econ. justice commn., 2005—; bd. dirs. Waste Mgmt. Auth., 1999-2004, Alameda County Congestion Mgmt. Agy., 1997-2004. Recipient Svc. award Jaycees, Albany, 1970, Svc. awards Calif. PTA, 1971, 78, Vol. of Yr. award March of Dimes, Alameda County, 1984; named Sta. KABL Citizen of Day, 1984. Mem. NEA, LWV, Nat. Sch. Bds. Assn., Calif. Sch. Bds. Assn., Calif. Elected Women's Edn. Asn., League Calif. Cities (pres.-bd. mem. East Bay divsn. 1997—), Calif. Elected Women's Assn. for Edn. and Rsch., Congestion Mgmt. Agy. (bd. mem. 1997—), Pi Gamma Mu. Democrat. Avocations: needlecrafts, editing, reading. Home: 757 Pierce St Albany CA 94706-1033 Office: City of Albany 1000 San Pablo Ave Albany CA 94706-2226

THOMSON, AUDREY SHIRE, volunteer; b. Paterson, NJ, Nov. 21, 1929; d. Gerald John Shire, Maybelle Conover; m. Norman B. Thomson, Oct. 17, 1954 (div. May 1985); children: Norman B., Christine de Armas, Scott B. BA, Coll. of St. Elizabeth, Morristown, N.J., 1950; MPA, NYU, 1990. Jr. pharmacologist Hoffman LaRoche, Nutley, NJ, 1950—55; exec. asst. Am. Cancer Soc. Nat. Office, N.Y.C., 1983—86; exec. asst. to pres. United Fedn. Tchrs., N.Y.C., 1986—89; asst. to pres. Grand Ctrl. Partnership, N.Y.C., 1990—93, 34th St. Bus. Improvement Dist., N.Y.C., 1990—93, Bryant Park Restoration Corp., N.Y.C., 1990—93; asst. to founding ptnr. Edison Project, N.Y.C., 1992—93. Mgr. first night events Pierpont Morgan Libr., NYC, 1992—93. Editor: (newsletter) Mus. Pieces, 1978—81; contbr. articles to profl. jours. Fundraiser Coll. of St. Elizabeth, 1995—2000, capital campaign com., steering com., 2003—, class chmn., 2003—; vol. Ga. Radio Reading Svc., 2004—. Mem.: AAUW (program organizer 1994—2004, bd. dirs., ednl. equity chmn., fundraising chmn. 1994—2004, fundraiser task force 2002—04, Eleanor Roosevelt Ednl. Found. award 1999, Platinum award 1997—2001, Rosborough Meml. award, Silver award 2002). Roman Catholic. Avocations: reading, sewing, walking Civil War battlefields. Home: 7600 Central Ave Savannah GA 31406

THOMSON, HELEN LOUISE, retired artist; b. Lewiston, Ill., Nov. 28, 1928; d. Clyde Arthur Pomeroy and Myrtle Lynch Cluney; m. William Edward Thomson, 1950; children: Persephone Ann, Lucinda Renee, Cynthia Louise. Student, Western Ill. U., 1972, 78, 85, U. Ill., 1972; diploma, North Light Art Sch. Artist, Table Grove, Ill., 1970—. Adj. prof. Western Ill. U., Macomb, 1985-94; mem. spkrs. roster Spoon River Coll., Canton, Ill., 1986-94; exec. dir. Two Rivers Arts Coun., Macomb, 1985-94. Exhibited in numerous one woman and group exhbns.; contbr. art to calendars United Fed. Savs. & Loan, 1980, 86. Pres. Spoon River Coll. Found., Canton, Ill., 1979-85, Fulton County Arts Coun., Canton, 1973-83; bd. dirs. Regional Arts Adv. Coun., Western Ill. U., 1978-85; mem. adv. panel Ill. Arts Coun., Chgo., 1980-83; officer PTA, Table Grove, 1957-85. Recipient Ruth Watts Svc. award Performing Arts Soc., Western Ill. U., 1994, award Two Rivers Arts Coun., 1994; selected for feature stories on pub. TV stas. WMEC, 1997, Canton Daily Ledger, Macomb Jour., Peoria (Ill.) Jour. Mem.: Chgo. Art Inst., Galesburg Civic Art Ctr. (exhbn. awards), Ill. Watercolor Soc., Ill. Art League (exhbn. awards), PEO Sisterhood (pres., sec., chaplain, v.p.). Avocations: antiques, antique dolls, family history, travel. Home: 404 S Broadway St PO Box 163 Table Grove IL 61482-0163

THOMSON, JANE H., elementary school educator; b. Warrenton, Va., Aug. 12, 1950; d. Robert Presley and Ruby Embrey Hudson; m. Larry Elwood Thomson, June 18, 1993; children: Clay, Neil, Ford, Hudson Martin, David A. Martin. BS in Elem. Edn., Stratford Coll., Danville, Va., 1972. 4th/5th grade tchr. A.G. Richardson Sch., Culpeper, Va., 1973—77; Title I reading tchr.

Pearl Sample Elem. Sch., 1998—. Deacon, elder Culpeper Presbyn. Ch., 1993—97; bd. dirs. Culpeper Town and County Libr., 1977. Avocations: walking, tennis. Home: 1816 Fairway Ct Culpeper VA 22701

THOMSON, KATHLEEN KEPNER, retired state agency administrator; b. Raton, N.Mex., Mar. 30, 1929; d. John C. Kepner and Ruth Edna Whitford; m. George William Thomson, June 23, 1979 (dec. Nov. 17, 1996). BA in Social Studies, U. N.Mex., 1951; MS in Polit. Sci., U. Wis., 1955. Cert. tchr. N.Mex. Rschr. budget Office of Gov., Madison, Wis., 1954; rsch. assoc. Wis. Legis. Reference Bur., Madison, 1954—64, Wis. Taxpayers Alliance, Madison, 1964—66; sr. rsch. assoc. Citizens Rsch. Coun. Mich., Detroit, 1966—86, ret., 1986. Chair Mich. Natural Resources Coun., 1990—94. Recipient Disting. Svc. award, Mich. Botanical Club, 1999. Mem.: Govt. Rsch. Assn. (hon.), Mich. Bot. Club (pres. S.E. chpt. 1995—2001), Mich. Cactus and Succulent Soc., Archaeology Conservancy. Unitarian Universalist. Avocations: music, conservation, reading. Home: 5066 Elmhurst Ave Royal Oak MI 48073-1102 Personal E-mail: tkatkep@aol.com.

THOMSON, SONDRA K., secondary school educator; b. Audubon, Iowa, Aug. 24, 1940; d. Merlyn Franklin and Leona Marie Peterson; m. Alan Richard Thomson, Sept. 3, 1989; children from previous marriage: Paul Spiegel, Joni Spiegel, Steve Spiegel. BA magna cum laude, Calif. State U., Hayward, 1988; MA in Spl. Edn., Chapman U., 2000. Cert. resource specialist Calif., learning handicapped credential Calif., social sci. credential Calif., English lang. devel./specially designed acadmeic instrn. in English Calif., 2006. Co-founder, assoc. editor Am. Remnant Mission, Pleasant Hill, Calif., 1977—84; substitute tchr. Mt. Diablo Sch. Dist., Concord, Calif., 1985—90; spl. day class tchr. Antioch (Calif.) Sch. Dist., 1997—99; resource specialist Deer Valley HS, Antioch, 1999—. Mem. adv. coun. Deer Valley HS, 2002—. Contbr. articles to mags. Office: Deer Valley HS 4700 Lone Tree Way Antioch CA 94509

THOMSON, THYRA GODFREY, former state official; b. Florence, Colo., July 30, 1916; d. John and Rosalie (Altman) Godfrey; m. Keith Thomson, Aug. 6, 1939 (dec. Dec. 1960); children— William John, Bruce Godfrey, Keith Coffey. BA cum laude, U. Wyo., 1939. With dept. agronomy and agrl. econs. U. Wyo., 1938-39; writer weekly column Watching Washington pub. in 14 papers, Wyo., 1955-60; planning chmn. Nat. Fedn. Republican Women, Washington, 1961; sec. state Wyo. Cheyenne, 1962-86. Mem. Marshall Scholarships Com. for Pacific region, 1964-68; del. 72d Wilton Park Conf., Eng., 1965; mem. youth commn. UNESCO, 1970-71, Allied Health Professions Council HEW, 1971-72; del. U.S.-Republic of China Trade Conf., Taipei, Taiwan, 1983; mem. lt. gov.'s trade and fact-finding mission to Saudi Arabia, Jordan, and Egypt, 1985 Bd. dirs. Buffalo Bill Mus., Cody, Wyo., 1987—; adv. bd. Coll. Arts and Scis., U. Wyo., 1989, Cheyenne Symphony Orch. Found., 1990—. Recipient Disting. Alumni award U. Wyo., 1969, Disting. U. Wyo. Arts and Scis. Alumna award, 1987, citation Omicron Delta Epsilon, 1965, citation Beta Gamma Sigma, 1968, citation Delta Kappa Gamma, 1973, citation Wyo. Commn. Women, 1986; named Internat. Woman of Distinction, Alpha Delta Kappa, Keith and Thyra Honors Convocation in her honor Coll. of Arts and Scis. U. Wyo., 1997. Mem. N.Am. Securities Adminstrs. (pres. 1973-74), Nat. Assn. Secs. of State, Council State Govts. (chmn. natural resources com. Western states 1966-68), Nat. Conf. Lt. Govs. (exec. com. 1976-79) Republican. Home: 3102 Sunrise Rd Cheyenne WY 82001-6136

THOMSON, VIRGINIA WINBOURN, humanities educator, writer; b. Oakland, Calif., Aug. 6, 1930; d. Harry Linn and Jennie Cook (Vineyard) Thomson. AA, San Mateo Coll., 1949; BA, San Jose State Coll., 1951; MA, U. Calif., Berkeley, 1952. Cert. secondary tchr. Calif. Tchr. social sci. Capuchino H.S., San Bruno, Calif., 1952—54, Watsonville H.S., Calif., 1954—87. Saleswoman, storyteller Home Interiors, San Mateo, 1963—64. Author: The Lion Desk, 1965, Short Talks Around the Lord's Table, 1985, Lawson's Castle, 2001, numerous poems. Mem.: AAUW (life), Nat. Geog. Soc. (life), Calif. Alumni Assn. (life), Calif. Writer's Club (life), Homer Honor Soc., Internat. Poets, Phi Alpha Theta. Republican.

THON, MELANIE RAE, writer; b. Kalispell, Mont., Aug. 23, 1957; d. Raymond Albert and Lois Ann (Lockwood) T. BA, U. Mich., Ann Arbor; MA, Boston U., 1982. Instr. U. Mass., Boston, 1988-91, Emerson Coll., Boston, 1988-93, Harvard U., Cambridge, Mass., 1989-93; prof. Syracuse (N.Y.) U., 1993-96, Ohio State U., 1996—2000, U. Utah, 2000—. Author: Meteors in August, 1990, Girls in the Grass, 1991, Iona Moon, 1993, First, Body, 1997, Sweet Hearts, 2000. Avocations: hiking, swimming, snow shoeing, skiing, photography.

THOR, LINDA M., college president; BA, Pepperdine U., 1971, EdD, 1986; MPA, Calif. State U., L.A., 1980. Dir. pub. info. Pepperdine U., Los Angeles, 1971-73; pub. info. officer L.A. C.C. Dist., 1974-75, dir. comm., 1975-81, dir. edn. svcs., 1981-82, dir. high tech., 1982-83, sr. dir. occupl. and tech. edn., 1983-86; pres. West Los Angeles Coll., Culver City, Calif., 1986-90, Rio Salado Coll., Phoenix, 1990—. Contbr. articles to profl. jours. Active Continuous Quality Improvement Network for Cmty. Colls., 1991—; mem. Ariz. Gov.'s Adv. Coun. on Quality, 1992—97; pres. Ariz. Cmty. Coll. Pres.'s Coun., 1995—96; bd. dirs. Coun. for Adult and Experiential Learning, 1990—2005, C.C. Baccalaureate Assn., 2000—, Ariz. Town Hall, 2005—, Nana's Children Mental Health Found., 2003—, Friends of Pub. Radio Ariz. Named Woman of the Yr., Culver City Bus. and Profl. Women, 1988, Pacesetter of Yr., Nat. Coun. Mktg. and Pub. Rels., 1998; recipient Delores award, Pepperdine U., 1986, Alumni Medal of Honor, 1987, Outstanding Achievement award Women's Bus. Network, 1989, Shirley B. Gordon award of distinction, Phi Theta Kappa Internat. Honor Soc., 2000, Paul A. Elsner Excellence in Leadership award, Chair Acad., 2003. Office: 2323 W 14th St Tempe AZ 85281-6950 Business E-Mail: linda.thor@riomail.maricopa.edu.

THORELLI, SARAH V., economist, researcher; b. Atlanta, Dec. 30, 1922; m. Hans B. Thorelli; children: Irene, Tom. AB, U. Ga., 1944; MA, U. Ala., 1945; Ph.Lic., U. Stockholm, 1954. Free-lance researcher and scholar; v.p. Intopia, Inc. Cons. FTC, NSF, Sears, Roebuck and Co.; ofcl. translator legal documents Swedish Fgn. Office, Stockholm; intelligence rsch. analyst U.S. Dept. State; overseas rep. Equifax Co.; account exec. J. Walter Thompson Advt. Agy., N.Y.C. Co-author: Consumer Information Handbook: Europe and North America, Consumer Information Systems and Consumer Policy; contbr. articles to profl. jours. Mem. Ind. U. Women's Club, AAUW, Network Career Women, Local Coun. Women, Psi Iota Xi. Home and Office: 2604 E 2nd St Apt F Bloomington IN 47401-5351 Office Phone: 812-333-3174.

THORIN, SUZANNE E., dean, university librarian; BA in music edn., N. Park Coll., Chgo., 1963; MA in music history, lit., Univ. Mich., 1964, MLS, 1968. With Libr. Cong., Washington, 1980—96, chief of staff, 1992—96; Ruth Lilly univ. dean of univ. libr. and assoc. v.p. digital libr. devel. Ind. Univ., 1996—2005; univ. libr., dean of libr. Syracuse Univ., 2005—. Office: Dean of Libr Syracuse Univ 221 E S Bird Libr 2573 Syracuse NY 13244 Office Phone: 315-443-2573. Business E-Mail: sethorin@syr.edu.*

THORMODSGARD, DIANE, bank executive; Controller, asst. treas. First Bank System (now US Bancorp), 1978, sr. v.p. Regional Cmty. Banking, 1985—89, sr. v.p. ops., 1989—93, sr. v.p., treas., chief adminstr. officer, 1993—95, sr. v.p., chief adminstr. officer Corp. Trust, 1995—99, pres. Corp. Trust., Inst. Trust and Custody Svcs., 1999—. Office: US Bancorp US Bancorp Ctr 800 Nicollet Mall Minneapolis MN 55402 Office Phone: 612-303-7936. E-mail: diane.thormodsgard@usbank.com.

THORN, SUSAN HOWE, interior designer; b. Washington, Apr. 22, 1941; d. James Bennett Cowdin and Lois (Fiesinger) Howe; m. William D. Thorn, June 22, 1963; children: Melissa Ann, William David. Lighting design, Parsons Sch. Design, 1975—77; BA, Syracuse U., 1962; AB, N.Y. Sch. Interior Design, 1995. Owner, designer Susan Thorn Interiors, Inc., Cross River, NY, 1965—. Designer total bldg. Cooper Labs, Bedford Hills, N.Y., 1973, total redesign Nycrest Corp., Cold Spring, N.Y., 1973-75, showrooms, model rooms stylist and coordinator France Voiles Co. Inc., N.Y.C., 1976, total design new corp. hdqrs. in Gen. Dynamics Bldg. (with Marjorie Borradaile Helsel), Robert E. Eastman Co., N.Y.C., 1967, Cummin & Friedland Capital Corp., 1982; designer offices, stores, employee areas comml., public, residential clients, including Waccabuc (N.Y.) Country Club, 1969, S. Salem (N.Y.) Library, St. Vincent's Hosp., N.Y.C., 1996; instr. adult edn. dept. John Jay High Sch.; spkr. civic orgns. Mem. Am. Soc. Interior Designers (profl.), Internat. Assn. Lighting Designers (assoc.), Decorators Club, Club of N.Y., Waccabuc Country Club. Episcopalian. Home: 88 N Salem Rd Cross River NY 10518 Office Phone: 914-763-1210. Business E-Mail: thorninteriors@earthlink.net.

THORNBURG, LINDA A., writer; b. Denver, Aug. 8, 1949; d. William J.R. Thornburg and Marjory Smith. BA, U. Colo., 1973. Pres., prin. Word Wizards, Fredericksburg, Va., 1990—. Author: (book series) Cool Careers for Girls, 1999—2004; editor: iLinx, Society for Human Resource Management, 2000—03, Staffing Management, Society for Human Resource Management, 2004—05, ADA Compliance Guide, 2006, Section 504 Compliance Handbook, 2006. Mem.: AAUW (br. sec. 2000—02, br. program chair 2004), Washington Ind. Writers. Personal E-mail: wordwzrds@aol.com.

THORNE, ANN LARAYNE, secondary school educator; b. Salt Lake City, Mar. 13, 1945; d. Ellvert Hiram and Mildred Anna (Harter) Himes; m. Conrad H. Thorne, Dec. 15, 1966 (div. 1986); children: Nathan, Jon Paul, Jason, Janna. BA, Utah State U., 1967; MA, U. Phoenix, 1997. Cert. K-12 secondary tchr. Ariz. Tchr. York Cmty. HS, Elmhurst, Ill., 1967—68, Shadow Mountain HS, Phoenix, 1984—, adviser newspaper journalism, 1994—2002, adviser lit. mag., 1996—99. Author: (novels) Somewhere in My Heart, 1996, Next Time My Love: Echoes of the Heart, 1997. Mem.: Ariz. Interscholastic Press Assn. (bd. dirs. 2001—, rec. sec. 2002—), Journalism Edn. Assn. Mem. Lds Ch. Avocations: writing, poetry, reading. Home: 3016 E Yucca St Phoenix AZ 85028 Office: Shadow Mountain HS 2902 E Shea Blvd Phoenix AZ 85028

THORNE, EVA TRENEICE, political science professor; d. Elliott Harcourt and Hazeltyne Holland Thorne; m. Andre James Norman, May 29, 2004; 1 child, Brooks Elliott Norman. B, Harvard Coll., Cambridge, Mass., 1989; D, MIT, Cambridge, Mass., 1998. Asst. prof. politics Brandeis U., Waltham, Mass., 2001—04, Meyer and Walter Jaffe asst. prof. politics, 2002—. Bd. dirs. Caribbean Ctrl. Am. Rsch. Coun., Austin, Tex. Grantee, Ford Found., 2002. Mem.: Latin Am. Studies Assn., New Eng. Coun. L.Am. Studies. Office: Brandeis U 415 South St Waltham MA 02454 Office Phone: 781-736-3496. Office Fax: 781-736-2755. Personal E-mail: ethorne@brandeis.edu.

THORNE, REBECCA CLAIRE, ballet director, choreographer; b. Little Rock, Dec. 28, 1976; d. George and Martha Elaine Antolik; m. Bradley Allen Thorne, Aug. 5, 2000. BFA in Ballet Performance, U. Okla., 1999. Ballet dancer Ballet Ark., Little Rock, 1997—2001, Los Angeles Contemporary Ballet, Calif., 2001—02; dancer Various TV shows and Films, 2002—05; choreographer Pasadena Jr. Theatre and JK's Dance Co., Calif., 2003—; ballet dir. The Vibe Dance Studio, Montrose, Calif., 2002—06, Revolution Dance Ctr., Tujunga, Calif., 2006—; master tchr. Spotlight Prodns., 2006—. Asst. dir. of dance performances City of Hope Cancer Hosp., Calif., 2004, 2006; dancer tchr. for children with autism, 2006—. Recipient Critic's Choice award, Encore Performing Arts, 2006. Avocations: movies, hiking, beach.

THORNTON, ANN MURPHY, retired military officer; b. Fargo, N.D., Sept. 8, 1920; d. Matthew William and Ethel Geneva (Brink) Murphy; m. William Aloysius Curtin Jr., Nov. 20, 1948 (div. Apr. 1958); m. Clarke Wayne Thornton Jr., Aug. 21, 1961 (dec.). BS, N.D. State U., 1942. Reporter Fargo Forum, 1942-43; commd. 2d lt. U.S. Army, 1944, advanced through grades to maj., 1959; served as feature writer pub. rels. office 9th Svc. Command, Ft. Douglas, Utah; conf. officer, officer in charge overseas conf. rm. Office of Chief of Staff, U.S. Army, The Pentagon, 1944-49; asst. dir. advt. Army Navy Air Force Jour., Washington, 1949—50; security officer USAREUR, Frankfurt, Germany, pub. info. officer Siene area commd. Paris, Ala., 1955-56; exec. officer, officer tng. co. 1st WAC Tng. Ctr., Ft. McClellan, Ala., 1955-56; asst. sec. XIIth Conf. Mil. Advisors to SEATO, Washington (D.C.); asst. exec. officer U.S. Army Recruiting Hdqs. 6th U.S. Army, San Francisco, 1961; ret. U.S. Army, 1961; asst. dir. advt. Army Navy Air Force Jour., 1956—57. Wife of press attache, Pretoria, South Africa, Cultural Counselor, Cape Town, South Africa. Mem. Res. Officer Assn. U.S., Ret. Officers Assn., Century Club Calif., Kappa Kappa Gamma. Episcopalian. Home: 1499 Sutter St San Francisco CA 94109-5417

THORNTON, DEBRA ANN, special education educator; b. Valparaiso, Ind., July 15, 1953; d. Daniel Edward and Marlene Joan (Harrington) Darner; m. Richard Michael Thornton, Oct. 20, 1979; 1 child, Sarah Marlene. BS, Ind. State U., 1976, MS, 1979. Lic. edn., Ind. Spl. edn. tchr. Kankakee Valley Sch. Corp., Wheatfield, Ind., 1976—. Bd. directions Oak Grove Christian Ret. vill. Mem. Coun. for Exceptional Children, Internat. Reading Assn., KanKaKee Valley Reading Assn., Ind. State Tchrs. Assn. (del. to rep. assembly 1991-93, 99—, mem. grievence com. 2003—, mem. dist. coun., 1993—), KanKaKee Valley Tchrs. Assn. (corr. sec. 1986, negotiation team 1988-93, discussion team 1983, second v.p. 1994—, mem. ins. com.), Qualified Mental Retardation Profls. Democrat. Roman Catholic. Avocations: painting, reading, cross stitch. Home: 219 Carnation St NE Demotte IN 46310-9406 Office: Wheatfield Elem Sch PO Box 158 Wheatfield IN 46392-0158

THORNTON, FELICIA D., food service company executive; BSc Econs., Santa Clara U.; MBA Corp. Fin., Mktg., U. So. Calif. V.p., corp. planning and acctg. Ralphs Grocery Co., v.p., admin., 1998, group v.p., fin. and adminstrn., 1999—2001; group v.p. retail ops. Kroger Co., 2000—01; exec. v.p., CFO Albertson's, Inc., 2001—. Office: Albertson's Inc 250 Parkcenter Blvd Boise ID 83706*

THORNTON, NANCY FREEBAIRN, psychotherapist, consultant, military officer; b. Mexico, Mo., Feb. 9, 1949; d. John Arthur Black Sr. and Pauline Cearley Black; children: Marinda Jane, William Thomas IV, Ann Elizabeth. BS, Ariz. State U., 1971; MA, U. Okla., 1978; PhD in Clin. Psychology, Forest Inst., 1990. Lic. Psychotherapist Ala., 1988. Commd. U.S. Army, 1971—85, advanced through grades to major, 1983, company cmdr. engr. basic tng., 1976—77; tactical officer U.S. Mil. Acad., West Point, NY, 1978—81; ret. U.S. Army, 1983; pvt. practice Cullman, 1988—. Cons. in field. Vol. Girl Scouts Am., 1957—. Named Subject of Paul Harvey Rest of Story radio show, 1983; named one of Top 35 Adults Under 35, U.S. Mag., 1980; named to featured story in, Esquire Mag., 1983; recipient Unsung Hero award, Cullman Times, 1998. Mem.: Cullman Women's League (officer). Achievements include first female engineer officer in the U.S. Army. Home: 1809 Loch Ave Cullman AL 35055

THORNTON, PAULINE CECILIA EVE MARIE SUZANNE, special education educator; b. LA, July 1, 1951; d. John Woodrow Thornton and Pauline Lucia DeWolfe; children: Patrick Ellis Hooker-Wafford, Damien Charles Wafford. Student, L.A. City Coll., 1969—71; BA in English, UCLA, 1975; postgrad. in Spl. Edn., Calif. State U., L.A. and Bakersfield, 2004. Profl. clear multiple-subjects credential/profl. clear learning Calif. State Dept. Edn., 1999. Reading tutor L.A. Unified Sch. Dist., 1970—71, instrnl. asst., 1975, tchrs. asst., 1975—78; childcare worker Children's Home Soc. Bakersfield, 1981—84; instnl. technician Nat. Assn. for People with Disabilities, 1981—85; instrnl. aide I Bakersfield City Sch. Dist., 1981—85, substitute tchr., 1985—94, cert. spl. edn. tchr., 1994—. Author: (poetry) Internat. Soc. Poetry Anthologies, 2000—05, (anthology) Theatre of the Mind, 2003, Noble House Anthologies, 2003—05. Mem.: NEA, Elem. Tchrs. Assn., Calif. Tchrs. Assn., Folgers Shakespeare Libr., Am. Acad. Poets, Internat. Soc. Poets, English Scholars Soc., Nuc. Peace Orgn., ACLU Alumni, Amnesty Internat., The Wisdom Fund, Peace and Freedom Party, Internat. Soc. for Krishna Consciousness, Muslim Peace Fellowship, United Lodge Theosophists, Sigma Tau Delta. Roman Catholic. Avocations: science fiction, jazz, philosophy, beaches. Office Phone: 661-631-5370. E-mail: thorntonp@bcsd.com.

THORNTON, RITA LOUISE, environmental scientist, lawyer; b. Long Branch, N.J., May 28, 1952; d. Donald Everett Thornton and Itasker Frances Edmonds-Thornton. BS, Monmouth U., 1973; JD, Seton Hall U., 1993; PhD, N.J. Inst. Tech., 2006. Toxicologist Johnson & Johnson Ethicon, Somerville, NJ, 1973—81; distributor ednl. film MGM/United Artists Entertainment, N.Y., 1981—83; chmn. Dept. Sci. Vail-Deane Sch., Mountainside, NJ, 1983—88; rschr. Reheis Chem. Co., Berkeley Heights, NJ, 1988—90; specialist hazardous site mitigation N.J. Dept. Environ. Protection, Trenton, 1990—97, rule mgr., 1997—99, supr. environ. specialization, 1999—, sect. chief, 2005—. Adj. prof. N.J. Inst. Tech., Newark, 2003; exec. dir. Environ. Justice and Equity Cmty. Based Teamwork, Inc, Atlantic Highlands, 1999—. Co-author: A Suitcase Full of Dreams, 1996; author (editor): New Jersey Solid and Hazardous Waste Transporter Quick Access Guide Book, 2000—05. Founder, CEO Thronton Sisters Found., Inc., Atlantic Highlands, 1991—. Nominee Nat. Minority Role Model in Sci., Nat. Sci. Inst. and Minority Access, Inc., 2006; fellow, Alliance Grad. Edn. and Professorale, 2001—06; grantee, U.S. Environ. Protection Agy., 1998, 2000. Mem.: Soc. Women Environ. Profls., Nat. Honor Soc., Alpha Epsilon Lambda. Business E-Mail: rita.thornton@dep.state.nj.us.

THORNTON, YVONNE SHIRLEY, obstetrician, writer, musician; b. N.Y.C., Nov. 21, 1947; d. Donald E. and Itasker F. (Edmonds) T.; m. Shearwood McClelland, June 8, 1974; children: Shearwood III, Kimberly Itaska. BS in Biology, Monmouth Coll., 1969; MD, Columbia U., 1973, MPH, 1996; DSc (hon.), Tuskegee U., 2003. Diplomate Am. Bd. Ob-gyn. Resident in ob-gyn Roosevelt Hosp., N.Y.C., 1973-77; fellow maternal-fetal medicine Columbia-Presbyn. Med. Center, N.Y.C., 1977-79; commd. lt. comdr. M.C. USN, 1979; asst. prof. ob-gyn Uniformed Svcs. U. Health Scis., 1979-82; assoc. prof. Cornell U. Med. Coll., N.Y.C., 1989-92; dir. clin. svcs. dept. ob-gyn N.Y. Hosp.-Cornell Med. Center, 1982-88; asst. attending N.Y. Lying-In Hosp., 1982-89; assoc. clin. prof. ob-gyn. Columbia P&S, 1995-98, assoc. clin. prof., 2001—02; clin. prof. ob-gyn. U. Medicine and Dentistry N.J., 1998-2000; prof. clin. ob-gyn. Med. Coll. Cornell U., 2003—05. Dir. Chorionic Villus Sampling Program, 1984-92; dir. perinatal diagnostic testing ctr. Morristown Meml. Hosp., 1992-2000, divsn. maternal-fetal medicine St. Luke's Roosevelt Hosp. Ctr., 2000-02; vice chair ob-gyn, dir. maternal-fetal medicine, Jamaica Hosp. Med. Ctr., 2002-05; staff Nat. Naval Med. Ctr., Bethesda, Md.; saxophonist Thornton Sisters ensemble, 1955-76; vis. assoc. physician The Rockefeller U. Hosp., 1986-96; prof. clinical OB/GYN Cornell U. Med. Coll., 2003-05; examiner Am. Bd. Ob-Gyn, 1997—; vice chmn. Dept. Ob-Gyn. Jamaica Hosp. Med. Ctr.; bd. dirs. Integra Med Am., 2006. Author: The Ditchdigger's Daughters, 1995, (named best books for young adults ALA, Excellence in Lit. award, N.J. Edn. Assn., One Book N.J., N.j. Libr. Assn., 2006, nominated Pulitzer Prize 1995) Primary Care for the Obstetrician and Gynecologist, 1997, Woman to Woman, 1997. Recipient Excellence in Literature award, N.J. Edn. Assn., 1996, winner Daniel Webster Oratorical Competition, Internat. Platform Assn., 1996; nominated Pulitzer Prize, 1995. Fellow: ACOG, ACS; mem.: AMA, Am. Fedn. Musicians, Soc. Maternal-Fetal Medicine, Assn. Women Surgeons, N.Y. Acad. Medicine. Democrat. Baptist. Office Phone: 201-570-8181. Business E-Mail: thornton@carroll.com.

THORNTON-ARTSON, LINDA ELIZABETH, psychiatric nurse; b. Balt., Dec. 27, 1956; d. Herbert and Helen (Thornton) Powell; m. Michael C. Artson, Oct. 28, 1983; children: Michelle Cherise, Mia Charmain. AA in Psychology, Community Coll. of Balt.; BSN, Coppin State Coll. Cert. gerontol. nurse; cert. psychiat. nurse; cert. nurse cons. in case mgmt.; cert. med.-legal cons. Charge nurse Melchor Nursing Home, 1973-83; med./surg. nurse North Charles Gen. Hosp., Balt., 1975-80; psychiat. nurse Wyman Park Psychiat. Hosp., Balt., 1980-84; dir. nurses Lebran Nursing Home, Cin., 1984-85, George A. Martin Gerontology Ctr., Cin., 1983-84; staff nurse Walter P. Carter Psychiat. Hosp., Balt., 1986-90; pvt. cons. Woodbridge, Va., 1999. Expert witness in elderly abuse, head injury, and myofacial pain syndrome; instr. for med. tech. nursing assistance course in cert. nursing assts. for Va.; med.-legal cons. for Suder & Suder Lar Firm; lectr. in field psychiat. nursing and gerontology nursing; cons. long-term care; cons. for law firms, nursing students, case mgmt. for ins. cos.; mem., supporter AIDS Fuond., Whitman-Walker Clinic Inc., Washington; v.p. Artson Ent., 1985—. Co-author: Warehouse of the Living Dead, 1989; appeared on nat. TV as expert on elderly abuse; contbr. articles to profl. jours. Mem. NAFE, ANA, ABA, Nat. League for Nursing, Am. Heart Assn., Md. Nurses Assn., WHO, Nat. Found. for Depressive Illness Inc., Nat. Headache Found., Nat. Cleft Palate Soc., Psychiat. Nurse Soc., Back Pain Assn. Am., Am. Pain Soc., Am. Acad. Pain Mgmt., Am. Chronic Pain Assn., Pain Found., Arthritis Found., Head Injury Found., Va. Nursing Assn., Head Injury Svc. Partnership, Fibromyalgia Assn. Washington, Coppin State Coll. Alumni Assn., Brain Injury Assn. of Va., Am. Chronic Pain Assn. (leader Woodbridge Va. chpt.), Head Injury Partnership Va., Am. Bd. Forensic Nursing (diplomate), Am. Coll. of Forensic Examiners, Am. Assn. Legal Nurse Consultants, Nat. Assn. Legal Assistants, Am. Assn. Nurse Attys., Internat. Assn. Forensic Nurses, Va. Inst. Forensic Sci. Med. Avocations: reading, cooking, art, travel, head injury advocacy.

THORPE, DEVORIA D., real estate agent; d. Tyler and Gertrude Thorpe; children: Lekia, Kelin. BS in Mgmt. in Human Resources, Bluefield Coll., 1995; MA with hon. in Career and Tech. Edn., Va. Tech., Blacksburg, 2006. Lic. real estate agt. Va. Sales rep. Outdoor East Advt., Dublin, Va.; dir. innovative programs Girl Scouts of Va. Skyline Coun., Roanoke; instr. New River C.C., Dublin, Va.; realtor McNeil Real Estate, Christiansburg, Va. Advisor Alpha Phi Omega, Blacksburg; dir. Christiansburg Cmty. Ctr.; active Upward Youth League, New River Valley, Va.; bd. dirs., advisor Cmty. Found., New River Valley. Recipient Women's Leadership award, AAUW and YMCA, New River Valley, 2005. Baptist. Avocations: sports, community projects, technology. Office: McNeil Real Estate 17N Franklin St Christiansburg VA 24073 Business E-Mail: soldbydd@thorpeandturner.com.

THORPE, JANE FUGATE, lawyer; b. Hazard, Ky., 1954; BA, Univ. Ga., 1976, JD, 1979. Bar: Ga. 1979. Ptnr., food, drug, device products liability group Alston & Bird LLP, Atlanta. Frequent contbr. to profl. journals, frequent lectr. on scientific evidence; co-author: Court-Appointed Experts and Technical Advisors, 2000, Science and Expert Opinion: A Response to the Attack Upon Judge Jones and the Hall Opinion. Mem.: Internat. Assn. Defense Counsel. Office: Alston & Bird LLP One Atlantic Ctr 1201 W Peachtree St NW Atlanta GA 30309-3424 Office Phone: 404-881-7822. Office Fax: 404-881-7777. Business E-Mail: jthorpe@alston.com.

THORPE, JANET CLAIRE, judge; b. Bklyn., Dec. 8, 1953; d. Burton Walter and Phyllis Claire (Read) T.; m. David Frank Palmer, Aug. 26, 1978 (div. Aug. 1988); children: Katherine Elaine, Jennifer Claire; m. James Francis Box, June 29, 1991; children: Melissa Richelle, Maergrethe Cashel. Student, Boston U., 1972-74; BA in Polit. Sci. & History with honors, Union Coll., 1975; postgrad., Western New Eng. Sch. Law, 1975-76; JD, Emory U., 1978. Bar: Ga. 1978, U.S. Ct. Appeals (5th and 11th cirs.) 1978, 80, Fla. 1987, U.S. Dist. Ct. (mid. dist.) Fla. 1987. Law clk. to judge U.S. Dist. Ct., Atlanta, 1978; regional atty. Comptroller of Curency, Atlanta, 1978-80; assoc. corp. counsel Trust Co. Ga., Atlanta, 1980-86; dir. Trusco Properties, Inc., Atlanta, 1981-86; gen. counsel, corp. sec. SunTrust Banks Fla., Inc., Orlando, 1986-2000; gen. counsel SunTrust Bank N.A., Orlando, 1986-2000; group v.p. SunTrust Banks, Inc., 1995-2000; cir. ct. judge State of Fla. (9th cir.), Orlando, Fla., 2000—. Mem. Coun. Battered Women, Atlanta, 1983-86, bd. dirs., 1986; bd. visitors Cornell Mus. Fine Art, Rollins Coll., 1990-96; mem. bd. zoning variances City of Orlando, 1996-99; bd. dirs. Orange County Cmty. Alliance, 2000-03. Mem. Ga. Bar Assn., Fla. Bar Assn., Assn. Bank Holdings Cos (lawyers com. 1983-90), Am. Corp. Counsel Assn. (bd. dirs.

ctrl. Fla. chpt. 1991-99), Am. Diabetes Assn. (bd. dirs. Fla. chpt. 1989-97), Leadership Orlando. Episcopalian. Avocations: gardening, child rearing, house renovation, photography. Office: Orange County Courthouse 425 N Orange Ave Orlando FL 32801

THORSEN, MARIE KRISTIN, radiologist, educator; b. Milw., Aug. 1, 1947; d. Charles Christian and Margaret Josephine (Little) T.; m. James Lawrence Troy, Jan. 7, 1978; children: Katherine Marie, Megan Elizabeth. BA, U. Wis., 1969; MBA, George Washington U., 1971; MD, Columbia Coll. Physicians and Surgeons, 1977. Diplomate Am. Bd. Radiology. Intern. Columbia-Presbyn. Med. Ctr., NYC, 1977-78, resident dept. radiology, 1978-81; asst. prof. radiology Med. Coll. Wis., 1982-84, assoc. prof., 1984-89, prof., 1989-94; dir. computed tomography Waukesha Meml. Hosp., 1994—, Oconomowoc Meml. Hosp., 1994—. Contbr. articles to profl. jours. Fellow computed body tomography Med. Coll. Wisc., Milw, 1981-82; Am. Coll. Radiology, Radiol. Soc. N. Am., Wis. Radiologic Assn. (v.p., 2005, pres.-elect, 2006). Office Phone: 262-928-2400. Personal E-mail: mkthorsen@aol.com.

THORSEN, NANCY DAIN, real estate broker; b. Edwardsville, Ill., 1944; d. Clifford Earl and Suzanne Eleanor (Kribs) Dain; m. David Massie, 1968 (div. 1975); 1 child, Suzanne Dain Massie; m. James Hugh Thorsen, May 30, 1980. BSc in Mktg., So. Ill. U., 1968, MSc in Bus. Edn., 1975; grad., Realtor Inst., Idaho, 1983. Cert. residential and investment specialist, fin. instr., luxury home mktg. specialist, 2004; designated real estate instr. State of Idaho; accredited buyer rep. Personnel officer J.H. Little & Co. Ltd., London, 1969-72; instr. in bus. edn. Spl. Sch. Dist. St. Louis, 1974-77; mgr. mktg./ops. Isis Foods, Inc., St. Louis, 1978-80; asst. mgr. store Stix, Baer & Fuller, St. Louis, 1980; assoc. broker Century 21 Sayer Realty, Inc., Idaho Falls, Idaho, 1981-88, RE/MAX Homestead Realty, 1989—. Spkr. in field; real estate fin. instr. State of Idaho Real Estate Commn., 1994; founder Nancy Thorsen Seminars, 1995; pres. S.E. Idaho Women's Coun. of Realtors, 2006 Bd. dirs. Idaho Vol., Boise, 1981-84, Idaho Falls Symphony, 1982; pres. Friends of Idaho Falls Libr., 1981-83; chmn. Idaho Falls Mayor's Com. for Vol. Coordination, 1981-84; power leader Power Program, 1995; mem. Mtn. River Valley Red Cross, chair capital campaign, cmty. gifts chair ARC. Recipient Idaho Gov.'s award, 1982, cert. appreciation City of Idaho Falls/Mayor Campbell, 1982, 87, Civilian Disting. Pres. award, 1990, Bus. Women of the Yr. award C. of C., 1998; named to Two Million Dollar Club, 1987, 88, Four Million Dollar Club, 1989, 90, Top Investment Sales Person for Eastern Idaho, 1985, Realtor of Yr. Idaho Falls Bd. Realtors, 1990, Outstanding Realtors Active in Politics, Women of Yr. Am. Biog. Inst., 1991, Profiles of Top Prodrs. award Real Estate Edn. Assn., Above the Crowd award 1997; named Western Region Power Leader, Darryl Davis Seminars. Mem. Nat. Spkrs. Assn., Idaho Falls Bd. Realtors (chmn. Orientation 1982-83, chmn. edn. 1983, chmn. legis. com. 1989, 95—, chmn. program com. 1990, 91), Idaho Assn. Realtors (pres. Million Dollar Club 1988-2001, edn. com. 1990-93, Mem. of Yr. 1991), Women's Coun. Realtors, Am. Bus. Women's Assn., So. Ill. U. Alumni Assn., Idaho Falls C. of C. (Bus. Woman of the Yr.-Professions, 1997), newcomers Club, Civitan (pres. Idaho Falls chpt. 1988-89, Civitan of Yr. 1986, 97, Outstanding Pres. award 1990, Hall of Fame 1998), Real Estate Educators Assn. Office: RE/MAX Homestead Inc 1301 E 17th St Ste 1 Idaho Falls ID 83404-6273 E-mail: thorsen@srv.net.

THORSEN, PHYLLIS LORANE, middle school educator; b. Manistee, Mich., Feb. 26, 1942; d. LaVerne Marshall and Jeanette Mildred Thorsen. BS, Ferris State U., Big Rapids, Mich., 1969. Tchr. Durand (Mich.) Mid. Sch. Owner Resort Cottages, Manistee, 1962—2006. Com. mem. Manistee City Coun., 1961—62; leader cadets Girl Scout Am., Manistee, 1961—83. Named Tchr. of Month award, Durand Mid. Sch., 2003. Mem.: NEA, Durand Educators Assn., Mich. Educators Assn. Avocations: coin collecting/numismatics, watch collecting. Office: Durand Mid Sch 9550 E Lansing Rd Durand MI 48429

THORSON, CONNIE CAPERS, library educator; b. Dallas, July 25, 1940; d. Ewing Ashby and Constance (Romberg) Capers; m. James Llewellyn, June 6, 1970. BA, U. Ark., 1962, MA, 1964; PhD, U. N.Mex., 1970; MS in Library Sci., U. Ill., 1977. Instr. English S.E. Mo. State U., Cape Girardeau, 1963-67; with U. N.Mex., Albuquerque, 1970-71, 79-95, acquisitions libr., 1980-94, head reference, 1994-95, assoc. prof. libr., 1984-90, prof., 1990-95, prof. emerita, 1995—; prof., libr. dir. Allegheny Coll., Meadville, Pa., 1995—2000, ret., 2000—; fulbright, sr. scholar Belarus, 2005—. Author: The RFP Process: Effective Management of the Acquisition of Library Materials, 1998; editor: A Million Stars, 1981, Pocket Companion for Oxford, 1989. Scholar, Fulbright Found., 2005—. Mem. South Cen. Soc. for 18th Century Studies (pres. elect 1988-89, pres. 1989-90, 2002-2003), Modern Lang. Assn. Am., Am. Soc. for 18th Century Studies, ALA. Avocations: travel, reading, walking.

THORSTED, V. DARLEENE, neonatal/perinatal nurse, community health nurse; b. Albuquerque, Dec. 4, 1944; d. Charles F. and Violet J. (Keefe) Perry; m. Lawrence H. Thorsted, Nov. 1, 1974; children: Melanie, Dennis, Deidra. ADN, Coll. So. Idaho, 1973; BSN, Boise State U., 1987. RN Idaho. Staff nurse Magic Valley Regional Med. Ctr., Twin Falls, Idaho, 1973; coord. med. care Intracorp, Missoula, Mont., 1987; case mgr. home care, primary nurse St. Luke's Regional Med. Ctr., Boise, Idaho, 1977-90, staff nurse neonatal ICU, 1977-90; exec. dir. Idaho Bd. Medicine, 1994—2000; RN Medicare coord. Boise Samaritan Village, 2000—. Mem.: Idaho Nurses Assn., Sigma Theta Tau. Home: 1881 Hendricks Ct Meridian ID 83642-1337 Office Phone: 208-343-7726.

THOYER, JUDITH REINHARDT, lawyer; b. Mt. Vernon, NY, July 29, 1940; d. Edgar Allen and Florence (Mayer) Reinhardt; m. Michael E. Thoyer, June 30, 1963; children: Erinn Thoyer Rhodes, Michael John. AB with honors, U. Mich., 1961; LLB summa cum laude, Columbia U., 1965. Bar: N.Y. 1966, D.C. 1984. Law libr. U. Ghana, Accra, Africa, 1963-64; assoc. Paul, Weiss, Rifkind, Wharton & Garrison, N.Y.C., 1966-75, ptnr., 1975—. Mem. TriBar Opinion Com., 1995—. Bd. visitors Law Sch. Columbia U., N.Y.C., 1991—; bd. dirs. Women's Action Alliance, N.Y.C., 1975-89, pro bono counsel, 1975-97; mem. Women's Coun. Dem. Senatorial, campaign com., 1993-97; organizing com. Alumnae Columbia Law Sch., 1996—. Recipient medal for excellence, Columbia Law Sch., 2003. Mem. N.Y. County Lawyers Assn. (mem. securities and exchs. com. 1976-98), Assn. of Bar of City of N.Y. (mem. securities regulation com. 1976-79, mem. recruitment of lawyers com. 1980-82, mem. com. on mergers, acquisitions and corp. control contests 1996—). Home: 1115 5th Ave Apt 3B New York NY 10128-0100 Office: Paul Weiss Rifkind Et Al 1285 Ave of Americas New York NY 10019-6028

THRALL, EILEEN FOWLER, real estate broker; b. Washington, July 20, 1943; d. Edward Earl and Violet Wells (Ashford) Fowler; m. William Anthony Thrall, Feb. 2, 1963; children: James Edward, Jennifer Dianne, John Joseph. AS in Bus. Adminstrn., Am. U., 1964; BSBA, George Mason U., 1985. Cert. real estate broker. Girl Friday property mgmt. rental cashier The Carey Winston, Co., Washington, 1964-65; adminstrv. asst., asst. rental mgr. Reston, Va., Inc., 1965-67; cmty. columnist Potomac News, Woodbridge, Va., 1981-85; realtor, salesperson Old Mill Properties ERA Tatum, Inc., Prince William, Va., 1985-92; realtor, assoc. broker ERA Tatum, Inc., Better Homes Realty, Prince William, 1992—; asst. to chmn. bd., county supr. Prince William County Govt., Prince William, 1992-99. Bd. dirs. Prince William County Pub. Schs., 1991-92; mem. magisterial dist. chair Prince William County Dem. Com., 1975-2001; mem. steering com. No. Va. C.C. Tech. Consortium, Woodbridge, Va., 1991-98; mem. various offices Dumfries Meth. Ch., 1977-2003; mem. Bd. Zoning Appeals, Prince William, 2002—. Mem. Nat. Assn. Realtors, Va. Assn. Realtors, Prince William Assn. Realtors. Democrat. Methodist. Avocations: reading, bicycling, boating, camping, cooking. Office: Better Homes Realty Inc 16150 Country Club Dr Dumfries VA 22026-1633

THRASH, PATRICIA ANN, retired educational association administrator; b. Grenada, Miss., May 4, 1929; d. Lewis Edgar and Weaver (Betts) T. BS, Delta State Coll., 1950; MA, Northwestern U., 1953, PhD, 1959; cert. Inst. Edn. Mgmt., Harvard U., 1983; EdD (hon.), Vincennes U., 1997; DHL, Drake U., 1997, Adrian Coll., 1998. Tchr. high sch. English, Clarksdale, Miss., 1950-52; head resident Northwestern U., 1953-55, asst. to dean women, 1955-58, asst. dean women, 1958-60, lectr. edn., 1959-65, dean women, 1960-69, assoc. prof. edn., 1965-72, assoc. dean students, 1969-71; asst. exec. sec. Commn. on Instns. Higher Edn., North Central Assn. Colls. and Schs., 1972-73, assoc. exec. dir., 1973-76, assoc. dir., 1976-87, exec. dir., 1988-96; exec. dir. emeritus, 1997—. Mem. adv. panel Am. Coun. on Edn., MIVER program evaluation mil. base program, 1991-94; mem. nat. adv. panel Nat. Ctr. Postsecondary Tchg., Learning & Assessment, 1991-95. Author (with others): Handbook of College and University Administration, 1970; editor Jour. Northwestern U. Inst. for Learning in Retirement, 2000-02, course coord., 2000—; contbr. articles to ednl. jours. Bd. dirs. Delta State U. Found., 2000-02. Mem. Nat. Assn. Women Deans and Counselors (v.p. 1967-69, pres. 1972-73), Ill. Assn. Women Deans and Counselors (sec. 1961-63, pres. 1964-66), Am. Coll. Pers. Assn. (editl. bd. jour. 1971-74), Coun. Student Pers. Assns. in Higher Edn. (program nominations com. 1974-75, adv. panel Am. Coll. Testing Coll. Outcome Measures project 1977-78, staff Coun. on Postsecondary Accreditation project for evaluation nontraditional edn. 1977-78, mem. editl. bd. Jour. Higher Edn. 1975-80, guest editor Mar.-Apr. 1979, co-editor NCA Quar. 1988-96, vice-chair regional accrediting dirs. group 1993, exec. com. Nat. Policy Bd. for Higher Edn. Inst. 1993-95), Mortar Bd. (hon.), Phi Delta Theta, Pi Lambda Theta, Alpha Psi Omega, Alpha Lambda Delta. Methodist. Home: 2337 Hartrey Ave Evanston IL 60201-2552 Personal E-mail: patsy1941@comcast.net.

THRASHER, ALLISON, elementary school educator; b. Burkesville, Ky., Apr. 23, 1972; d. Raymond and Ruby Sue Parrigin; m. Mark Thrasher, Dec. 17, 1993; children: Ashton, Raegan. BA in Edn., We. Ky. U., Bowling Green, 1994, MA in Elem. Counseling, 1998, degree in Rank I Elem. Counseling, 2000. Cert. reading specialist Ky., reading first Ky. Tchr. Albany Elem. Sch., Ky., 1995—. Coord. family literacy Albany Elem. Sch., 2004—, chmn. literacy team, 2004—. Mem.: Arts Coun., Ky. Reading Assn., Parent Tchr. Orgn. (officer 2003). Home: 505 Bristow St Albany KY 42602 Office: Albany Elem 819 Third St Albany KY 42602

THRASHER, DIANNE ELIZABETH, mathematics educator, computer scientist, consultant; b. Brockton, Mass., July 11, 1945; m. George Thomas Thrasher, Jan. 28, 1967; children: Kimberly Elizabeth, Noelle Elizabeth. BA in Math., Bridgewater State Coll., 1967, post grad in computer sci., 1987. Cert. secondary math., history tchr. Tchr. math. Plymouth/Carver Regional Schs., Plymouth, Mass., 1976-78, Alden Sch., Duxbury, Mass., 1980-82, Marshfield (Mass.) H.S., 1982-84; computer cons. TC2I-Thrasher Computer Cons. and Instrn., Duxbury, Mass., 1988—; dir., owner Internat. Ednl. Franchise, 1991-95; owner Duxbury Math. Ctr. K-Adult, 1995—. Owner New Eng. Regional Kumon Ednl. Franchise, 1991-95, 2000—; Mass. State approved profl. point devel. provider for tchr. cert., 1996. Active U.S. Figure Skating Assn., Colorado Springs, 1978-85; 2d reader First Ch. Christ Scientist, Plymouth, 1971-73; bd. govs. Skating Club of Hingham, Mass., 1978-85, pres., 1983-85, dir. Learn to Skate program, 1983-85; active First Ch. Christ Scientist, Boston, 1964—; with New Eng. Regional Kumon Franchise Owners, 1991-95; charter mem. Nat. Adv. Coun. of the U.S. Navy Meml. Found., 1992, Mary Baker Eddy Libr. for the Betterment of Humanity, Boston, 2002. Recipient Presdl. Nomination for Excellence in Tng. Math., NSF, 1992, Ed Taylor Meml. Vol. Svc. award Skating Club Hingham, 1995, Amateur Photo award Internat. Libr. Photography, 1999. Mem. NAFE, AAUW, Math. Assn. Am., Am. Math. Soc., Am. Nat. Coun. Tchrs. Math, Nat. Hist. Trust and Preservation Soc., Smithsonian, Internat. Soc. Photographers (Amateur Photo award 1999). Avocations: antiques, bicycling, skating, sailing. Home: 140 Toby Garden St Duxbury MA 02332-4945 Personal E-mail: sumizumi@aol.com.

THRASHER, JACQUELINE F., elementary school educator; b. Detroit, Sept. 23, 1957; d. Homer E. Premil and Frances H. Litchford; m. John A. Thrasher, Jan. 5, 1980; children: Jason, Jessica. BMus in Instrumental Music Edn., Ariz. State U., 1979. Instrumental music tchr. Alhambra H.S., Phoenix, 1980, Washington Elem. Sch. Dist., Phoenix, 1980—. Flutist Ariz. Winds Concert Band, Glendale, Ariz., 1980—2004. Candidate Ariz. legis. dist. 10 State Ho. of Reps., Phoenix, 2002, 2004; elected precinct committeeperson Ariz. Dem. Party D-10, Phoenix, 2002—; mem. exec. com., state committeeperson Ariz. Dem. Party, 2005. Mem.: Washington Dist. Edn. Assn. (bargaining chair 1998—2004, v.p., bargaining chair 2005—), Music Educators Nat. Conf. Democrat. Lutheran. Avocation: reading. Home: 4537 W Park Pl Glendale AZ 85306 Personal E-mail: jackiethrasher@cox.net.

THRASHER, MARY AHLF MARCROFT, educator, social worker; b. St. Louis, Apr. 25, 1923; d. Gustave and Florence Regina (Froelich) Ahlf; m. Keith R. Marcroft, Mar. 23, 1946 (div. 1969); children: Joanne Marcroft Williamson, Karen A. Marcroft; m. Hugh Riley Thrasher, June 28, 1989 (dec. Jan. 2006). BS, Ind. U., 1944; postgrad., U. Md., 1968-69, U. Evansville, 1971-72. Lic. tchr., Ind., Ky. Office mgr. U. Utah, Salt Lake City, 1946-48; sec. Brown Shoe Co., St. Louis, 1948-52; sch. tchr. Prince George's County Schs., Bowie, Md., 1965-70, Troy Twp. Sch. Corp., Tell City, Ind., 1970-73; sec. Perry County Extension Svc., Cannelton, Ind., 1973-75; caseworker Perry County Dept. Pub. Welfare, Cannelton, 1975—86. Composer, lyricist (musical play) ON MAIN STREET, 1988. Pres. Am. Legion Aux., 1986-87, Tell City Hist. Soc., 1987-89. Mem. AAUW, Order of Eastern Star. Mem. United Ch. of Christ. Avocations: choir member, church organist, accompanist to vocal and instrumental soloists, painter, gardener. Home: 225 11th St Tell City IN 47586-1907 E-mail: humathra@sbcglobal.net.

THRASHER, ROSE MARIE, critical care and community health nurse; b. Urbana, Ohio, Jan. 19, 1948; d. Jesse and Anna Frances (Clark) T. Student, Mercy Med. Ctr. Sch. Med. Tech., 1966—67, Wittenberg U., 1969—70; BSN, Ohio State U., 1974, BA in Anthropology, 1994, BA in Art History, 1997, BA in Geography, 2002, postgrad., 2005—. RN, Ohio; bd. cert. cmty. health nurse ANA; cert. provider BCLS and ACLS, Am. Heart Assn., CCRN, AACN; cert. asthma mgmt. edn. Am. Lung Assn. Ohio. Critical care nurse Staff Builders Health Care Svc., Oakland, Calif., 1975—76, 1981—85; supr., case mgr. and home health nurse passport and intermittent care programs Interim Health Care, Columbus, Ohio, 1976—77, 1985—2004; pub. health nurse Columbus Health Dept., 1977—78; critical care nurse VA Med. Ctr., San Francisco, 1981; chart reviewer Interim Health Care Support Svc., Columbus, 1996—98; IRP nurse Ohio State U. Hosps. East, 1999—2003; ind. home health nurse, provider med. svcs. State of Ohio Dept. Human Svcs., 1999—2005; home health nurse Interim Health Care, Newark and Pataskala, Ohio, 2004—. Acad. scholar Wittenberg U., Ohio State U. Mem. AACN, ANA (coun. cmty. health nursing), AAUW, AAAS, Internat. Union Anthrop. and Ethnol. Scis., N.Y. Acad. Scis., Ohio Nurses Assn., Intravenous Nurses Soc., Ohio State U. Alumni Assn., Am. Anthrop. Assn., Midwest Art History Soc., Coll. Art Assn., Nat. Mus. Women in Arts, Nat. Women's Hall of Fame, Ohio Acad. Sci., Ohio State U. Coll. of Nursing Alumni Soc. Office: 112 International Dr Pataskala OH 43062 Business E-mail: thrasher.2@osu.edu.

THREEDY, DEBORA LYNN, law educator; b. Chgo., June 10, 1951; d. Edward Clarence and Irene Frances (Palenik) T. BA, Beloit Coll., 1973; JD, Loyola U., 1980. Bar: Ill. Law clk. to Hon. Getzendanner U.S. Dist. Ct. (no. dist.) Ill., Chgo., 1980-82; assoc. Mayer Brown & Platt, Chgo., 1982-86; assoc. prof. law U. Utah, Salt Lake City, 1986—, prof. law, assoc. dean academic affairs, acting dean, 2004—. Contbr. articles to profl. jours. Bd. dirs. ACLU, Salt Lake City, 1990; trustee Theater Works West, Salt Lake City, 1990. McCormick Scholar Loyola U., 1980, Owens Scholar, 1980. Mem. Phi Beta Kappa. Office: U Utah Coll Law 332 South 1400 East Salt Lake City UT 84112-1107

THRIFT, JULIANNE STILL, academic administrator; b. Barnwell, S.C. m. Ashley Ormand Thrift; children: Lindsay, Laura. BA, MEd, U. S.C.; PhD in Pub. Policy, George Washington U. Formerly asst. exec. dir. Nat. Assn. Coll. and Univ. Attys.; ombudsman U. SC; exec. dir. Nat. Inst. Ind. Colls. and Univs., 1982-88; exec. v.p. Nat. Assn. Ind. Colls. and Univs., Washington, 1988-91; pres. Salem Acad. and Coll., Winston-Salem, NC, 1991—2006. Recipient Order of the Long Leaf Pine, State of NC, 2006. Achievements include becoming first female president of Salem Academy & College.

THUM, D. MAUREEN, language educator; d. Harold and Dora Wright; m. Reinhard Thum, Oct. 26, 1967 (dec.); children: Johanna Esther Krishnan, Angela Maureen. BA, Queen's U., Kingston, Canada, 1966, MA, 1970; PhD, Mich. State U., East Lansing, 1996. Lectr. in English U. Mich., Flint, 1980—, asst. dir. honors program, 1997—2001, dir. honors program, 2001—. Presenter in field. Contbr. articles to profl. jours. Chmn. orgnl. com. Holy Redeemer Ch., Burton, Mich., 1984—92. Summer fellow, NEH, 1986, 1989. Mem.: Popular Culture Assn. (chmn. Brit. popular culture 1995—), Mich. Acad. Sci., Arts and Letters (chmn. lang. and lit. 1990—2006, mem.-at-large exec. com. 2001—05, sec. exec. com. 2005—), Soc. Reformation Rsch. (program sec. 1996—). Office: U Mich Flint Dept English 326 French Hall Flint MI 48502 Office Phone: 810-762-3285.

THUMPSTON, KATHLEEN MARIE, music educator; b. Erie, Pa., Oct. 28, 1961; d. Eleanor and Ronald Thumpston. BS in Music Edn., Ind. U., Pa., 1979—83; MEQ Edn., Various colleges. Instrumental music tchr. Otto-Eldred Sch. Dist., Duke Center, Pa., 1983—2000, Bradford Area HS, 2000—. Mem.: Pa. State Educators Assn., Pa. Music Educators Assn., Phi Beta Mu, Delta Omicron (life; chpt. pres. 1982—83). Office: Bradford Area HS 81 Interstate Pkwy Bradford PA 16701 Office Phone: 814-362-3845. Office Fax: 814-362-1765. Business E-Mail: kthumpston@bradfordareaschools.org.

THURBER, KIRSTEN NORA, music educator; b. Providence, R.I., Mar. 21, 1982; d. Earle Emery and Margaret Nora (McLoughlin) Thurber. BS in Music Edn., R.I. Coll., Providence, 2004. Pvt. piano instr., R.I. and Mass., 1998—; tchr. music/choral dir. Mendon-Upton Regional Sch. Dist., Mendon, Mass., 2004—. Mem. Character Edn. Com., Mendon, 2005—06; music minister, vol. choir dir. St. Paul's Ch., Foster, RI, 1998—. Recipient Outstanding Grad. Sr. award, R.I. Coll., 2004, Honoring Gift for Dedicated Educator, Mendon-Upton Edn. Found., 2005, Alia K. Pelligrino Music Edn. award, R.I. Coll. Found., Providence, 2004—05. Mem.: Am. Choral Dir.'s Assn., Music Educators Nat. Conf., Kappa Delta Phi. Avocations: bicycling, dance, skiing, volleyball, travel. Home: 26 1/2 Brook St Whitinsville MA 01588 Office: Miscoe HS 140 N Ave Mendon MA 01756 Business E-Mail: kthurber@mu-regional.k12.ma.us.

THURBER, SHARON LEE, elementary resource educator; d. Donald Lee and Alka Mae Shears; m. Donald Lee Thurber, Mar. 30, 1983. BE, Ind. State U., Terre Haute, 1971; MEd, Ind. U., Bloomington, 1976. Cert. in tchg. Alaska, Ind., Tex., Fla. Elem. tchr. grade 3 Martinsville Ind. Sch. Dist., 1971—81; elem. tchr. grade 6 Galena Pk. Sch. Dist., Houston, 1981—82; elem. tchr. grades 1 and 2 Burton Ind. Sch. Dist., Tex., 1982—84; elem. tchr. grades 4-6 Archer City Ind. Sch. Dist., Tex., 1984—88; elem. resource tchr. South Elem. Sch., Okeechobee, Fla., 1988—89, Ocala Springs Elem. Sch., Fla., 1989—90, Russian Jack Elem. Sch., Anchorage, 1991—. Named Highly Qualified Tchr., Anchorage Sch. Dist., 2004; named to Career Ladder Excellent Tchrs. Tex., 1984—88. Mem.: NEA, Educators Social Responsibility, Anchorage Edn. Assn. (bldg. rep. 1994—96). Office: Russian Jack Elem Sch 4420 E 20th Ave Anchorage AK 99508 Office Phone: 907-742-1300. Business E-Mail: thurb2r_sharon@asdk12.org.

THURMAIER, MARY JEAN, educational association administrator; b. Delavan, Ill., Dec. 14, 1931; d. Emil Edward Pech and Grace May Creager; m. Roland J. Thurmaier, Oct. 22, 1955 (dec.); children: Kurt, Barbara, John, Matthew. B in edn., U. Iowa, 1960; M in Reading, U. Wis., Stevens Point, 1971. Mgr. City Bus. Sys., Stevens Point, 1974—78; office mgr. Carter/Mondale Campaign, Milw., 1980; exec. dir. Stevens Point Conv. and Vis. Bur., 1986—89; with NSBA Fed. Rels. Network, Washington, 1987—; chair bd. trustees Ins. Plan State, Madison, Wis., 1997—. Mem. bd. rev. City of Stevens Point; mem. Stevens Point Bd. Edn.; statutory chair Portage County Dem. Party, Stevens Point. Methodist.

THURMAN, CYNTHIA DENISE, human services administrator; b. Ft. Myers, Fla., Mar. 14, 1970; children: Asia Naikee Garcia, Jai'ya Ja'V-ae Armani. Grad. high sch. Residential care coord. Sandy Pk. Redevelopment Ctr., North Fort Myers, Fla., 2001—; human services worker Gulf Coast Ctr., Ft. Myers, 2003—. Author: (poems) Soon. Recipient Shakespare Trophy of Excellence, Famous Poets Soc., 2004. Home: 4926 Gary Dr Fort Myers FL 33905 Office: Gulf Coast Center 5820 Buckingham Rd Fort Myers FL 33905 Office Phone: 239-694-2151 226. Personal E-mail: cind33905@aol.com.

THURMAN, KAREN L., former congresswoman, lobbyist; b. Rapid City, S.D., Jan. 12, 1951; d. Lee Searle and Donna (Altfillisch) Loveland; m. John Patrick Thurman, 1973; children: McLin Searl and Liberty Lee. BA, U. Fla., 1973. Mem. Dunnellon City Coun. (Fla.), 1975—83; mayor of Dunnellon Dunnellon, 1979-81; mem. Monroe Regional Med. Ctr. Governancy Com., Comprehensive Plan Tech. Adv. Com., Fla. State Senate, 1983—93, U.S. Congress from 5th Fla. dist., 1993—2002, ways and means com., 1996—2002, House agrl. comm., comm. on gov. reform and oversight; lobbyist eAppeals, Miami, 2004—, Freedom Healthcare, Hollywood, 2004—. Del. Fla. Dem. Conv., Dem. Nat. Conv., 1980; mem. Regional Energy Action com. Recipient Svc. Above Self award Dunnellon C. of C., 1980, Regional Coun. Appreciation for Svc. award. Mem. Dunnellon C. of C. (dir.), Fla. Horseman's Children's Soc. (charter). Democrat. Episcopalian.

THURMAN, UMA KARUNA, actress; b. Boston, Apr. 29, 1970; d. Robert and Nena (von Schlebrugge) T.; m. Gary Oldman, Oct. 1990 (div. 1992); m. Ethan Hawke, May 1, 1998 (div. July 20, 2004); children: Maya Ray, Roan. Spokesperson Lancome cosmetics, 2000. Appeared in films Kaze no tani no Naushika, 1984, Kiss Daddy Good Night, 1988, Johnny Be Good, 1988, Dangerous Liaisons, 1988, The Adventures of Baron Munchausen, 1988, Where the Heart Is, 1990, Henry and June, 1990, Final Analysis, 1992, Jennifer Eight, 1992, Mad Dog and Glory, 1993, Even Cowgirls Get the Blues, 1993, Pulp Fiction, 1994 (Acad. award nom. Best Supporting Actress), A Month By the Lake, 1995, The Truth About Cats and Dogs, 1996, Beautiful Girls, 1996, Batman & Robin, 1997, Gattaca, 1997, Avengers, 1998, Les Miserables, 1998, Vatel, 1999, Sweet and Lowdown, 1999, Vatel, 2000, Tape, 2001, Chelsea Walls, 2001, Kill Bill: Volume 1, 2003, Paycheck, 2003, Kill Bill: Volume 2, 2004, Be Cool, 2005, Prime, 2005, The Producers, 2005, My Super Ex-Girlfriend, 2006; TV movies include Robin Hood, 1991, Duke of Groove, 1996, The Golden Bowl, 2000, Hysterical Blindness, 2002 (also exec. prodr., Golden Globe for Best Performance by an Actress). Bd. dirs. Room to Grow. Named a knight in the Order of Arts & Letters, France, 2006. Office: Creative Artists Agy care Brian Lourd 9830 Wilshire Blvd Beverly Hills CA 90212-1804*

THURNER, AGNES H., retired administrative secretary; b. Manistique, Mich., July 21, 1934; d. Joseph and Elise Kaulfuerst; m. James C. Wegner, June 5, 1954 (div. 1969); children: Robin, Leonard; m. Maximilian Franz Joseph Thurner, May 29, 1993. Dir. Statesman's Club of First Federal Savings, 1969—79; pres. Sq. Dance Assn., Milw., 1987-2000; ret., 2000. Author: Square Dancing in Wisconsin, 1998. Pollworker Ozaukee County, Mequon, Wis., 1995—. Named to, Wis. S.E.A. Square Dance Hall of Fame, 2004. Mem. Wis. Regional Writers Assn., Children's Book Writers and Illustrators. Lutheran. Avocations: reading, music, crafts, dance, composer/lyricist.

THURSTON, ALICE JANET, former college president; b. Milw., Mar. 20, 1916; d. Karl J. and Nellie Ann (Smith) Stouffer; children: Anne, Robert. BA, Denison U., 1937; MA, Northwestern U., 1938; PhD, George Washington U.,

1960. Mem. faculty dept. psychology, counselor, dean students Montgomery Coll., Takoma Park, Md., 1950-65; dir. counseling Met. Campus, Cuyahoga Community Coll., Cleve., 1965-66; dean of students Western Campus, Cuyahoga Community Coll., 1966-67; vis. lectr. U. Ill., 1968-69; dir. Inst. Research and Student Services Met. Jr. Coll. Dist., Kansas City, Mo., 1969-71; pres. Garland Jr. Coll., Boston, 1971-75, Los Angeles Valley Coll., Van Nuys, Calif., 1975-81. Lectr. Pepperdine U., L.A., 1978-81, Calif. State U., Worthridge, 1984-95; mem. adv. com. grad. program student affairs Calif. State U., Northridge. Author works in field. Bd. dirs. New Dir. for Youth, Van Nuys, Calif.; mem. ministerial search com. Unitarian Ch., Studio City, Calif., 1991-92, chair caring com., 1994—. Recipient Disting. Alumnae award Denison U., 1987, Humanitarian award Juvenile Justice Connection Project, 1987. Mem. Kappa Alpha Theta, Mortar Bd. Democrat. Unitarian Universalist. Home: 211 N Ridge Dr Oxford OH 45056-8868

THURSTON, BONNIE BOWMAN, religious studies educator, minister, poet; b. Bluefield, W.Va., Oct. 5, 1952; d. Ernest Venoy and Eleanor Sabina (King) Bowman; m. Burton Bradford Thurston, May 29, 1980 (dec. Nov. 1990). BA summa cum laude, Bethany Coll., 1974; MA, U. Va., 1975, PhD, 1979; postgrad., Harvard Div. Sch., 1983, Eberhard Karls U., Germany, 1983—84, Ecole Biblique, Jerusalem, 1993. Ordained to ministry Disciples of Christ Ch., 1984. Instr., asst. dean U. Va., Charlottesville, 1979—80; adj. prof. Wheeling Coll. (now Wheeling Jesuit U.), W.Va., 1980—81, assoc. prof., chair dept. theology, 1985—95; asst. prof. Bethany Coll., W.Va., 1981—83; assoc. prof. N.T. Pitts. Theol. Sem., 1995—99, William F. Orr prof., chair, 1999—2002. Vis. scholar Harvard U. Div. Sch., Cambridge, Mass., 1983; tutor Inst. Study of Christian Origins, Tubingen, Germany, 1983—85. Author: (books) The Widows, 1989, Wait Here and Watch, 1989, Spiritual Life in the Early Church, 1993, Women in the NT, 1998, To Everything a Season, 1999, Preaching Mark, 2002, Philippians and Philemon, 2004, (books of poetry) The Heart's Land, 2001, Hints and Glimpses, 2004; contbr. articles to profl. jours., poetry to jours. Mem.: Soc. for the Study of Christian Spirituality, Disciples Hist. Soc., Soc. for Buddhist-Christian Studies, Internat. Thomas Merton Soc., Soc. Bibl. Lit., Cath. Bibl. Assn. Avocations: gardening, music, cooking. Office: PO Box 2258 Wheeling WV 26003

THURSTON, KATHY LYNN, paralegal; b. Indpls., Dec. 3, 1957; d. G. Weldon and Juanita J. (Trotter) Johnson; m. Harold O. Thurston, Jr., June 21, 1997; 1 child, Jonathan Grant Much; 3 stepchildren: Kate Elizabeth Thurston, Jennifer Leigh Thurston, Abigail Ann Thurston. BA, Ind. U., 1980. Paralegal, office mgr. Johnson, Lawhead, Buth & Pope, P.C., Indpls., 1983-99, G. Weldon Johnson, Atty. at Law, 2000—04; paralegal Hall, Render, Killian, Heath & Lyman PC, 2004—. Mem. Ind. Paralegal Assn. (chmn. continuing legal edn. 1990-92, chmn. probate and tax sect. 1990—2005, pres. 1992-93, Para-Potential award 1991, Paralegal of Yr. award 1995, Lifetime Achievement award 2000), Indpls. Bar Assn. (charter paralegal com., chmn. 1993, 94, mem. exec. com. 1993-2005, Paralegal of Yr. award 2000). Office: Hall Render Killian Heath & Lyman PC One American Sq Ste 2000 Indianapolis IN 46282 E-mail: kthurston@hallrender.com.

THURSTON, SALLY A., lawyer; b. Glens Falls, N.Y., 1961; BS, Cornell U., 1983; JD, Harvard U., 1986. Bar: N.Y. 1987. Ptnr. Skadden, Arps, Slate, Meagher & Flom, N.Y.C.; v.p., tax counsel NBC, Inc., N.Y.C., 1994—. Office: Skadden Arps Slate Meagher & Flom LLP 4 Times Sq New York NY 10036-6595 Business E-Mail: sthursto@skadden.com.

TIANO, LINDA V., lawyer; b. 1957; BA summa cum laude, U. Cin.; JD cum laude, Boston U. Assoc. Epstein Becker and Green, P.C., 1981—90, ptnr., stockholder, 1990—92; v.p. for legal and govt. affairs, gen counsel MVP Health Plan, 1992—95; sr. v.p., gen. counsel Empire BlueCross BlueShield, 1995—, WellChoice, Inc., N.Y.C., 2002—. Office: WellChoice Inc 11 W 42nd St New York NY 10036

TIBBITTS, BARBARA J., music educator; d. Donald R. and Elsie K. Craig; m. Christopher Michael Tibbitts, July 31, 1981; children: Jack Craig, Dean Michael, Chad Christopher. B in Music Edn., Kent State U., Ohio, 1978; MA in Tchg., Marygrove Coll., Mich., 1997. Music tchr. Parma City Sch. Dist., Ohio, 1978—. Profl. musician/worship leader St. Paul Luth. Ch., Berea, Ohio, 2005—. Dir.: student choral/vocal concerts; musician: profl. accompanist. Mem.: MENC, Parma Edn. Assn., Ohio Music Educators Assn. Office: Parma City Sch Dist 5401 W 54 St Parma OH 44129 Office Phone: 440-885-2351.

TIBBS, KAY, director; d. Vic and Joyce Litchfield; m. Mark Tibbs, June 17, 1989; children: Jordan, Donovan. MEd, Southwestern Coll., 1995. Cert. tchr. Kans., 2005. Tchr. Unified Sch. Dist. 353, Wellington, Kans., 1995—2005; dir. edn. Challenger Learning Ctr. Kans., Wellington, 2005—, lead flight dir., 2005—. Mem.: Lions Club (webmaster 2005—06). Methodist. Avocations: drawing, web site development, scrapbooks, digital video. Office: Challenger Learning Center of Kansas 316 N Washington Wellington KS 67152 Office Phone: 620-326-3727. Office Fax: 620-326-5334.

TIBBS, MARTHA JANE PULLEN, civic worker, retired social worker; b. Memphis, Feb. 12, 1932; d. John Thomas Jr. and Martha Frances (Gragg) Pullen; m. Eugene Edward Tibbs; children: Martha Katherine, Eugene Edward Jr. BSBA, U. Tenn., 1953; MA Edn., U. Memphis, 1958. Cert. tchr., social worker, Tenn. Tchr. Lausanne Sch., Memphis, 1954-55, Millington H.S., Memphis, 1955-56, Presbyn. Day Sch., Memphis, 1956-57, St. Mary's Episcopal Sch., Memphis, 1958-60; social worker Tenn. Dept. Pub. Welfare, Memphis, 1962-63. Author geneal. works. Mem. Memphis Vol. Svc. Bd., 1963-64; mem. Shelby County Hist. Comm., 1983-97, commr., 1983—; block worker Cancer, Kidney and Heart Fund, Memphis, 1984—; sec., treas. Eastland Presbyterian Ch. Mem.: DAR (past chpt. regent, sec.-treas. regents coun.), AAUW, NEA, Tenn. Geneal. Soc., Tenn. Tchrs. Assn., Colonial Dames of Am., Memphis Scottish Soc., Sovereign Colonial Soc. Ams. Royal Descent, Tenn. State Dames of Ct. of Honor (pres. 2003—05, historian, 1st v.p., nat. def. chmn.), Cleve. Med. Aux. (sec./treas.), West Tenn. Hist. Soc., Chicasaw Dist. DAR Sch. (Tenn. state vice chmn. DAR schs., parliamentarian Zachariah Davies chpt., chmn. Zachariah Davies chpt.), Nat. Registrar Daus. of Founders and Patriots Am. (past Tenn. state registrar 2006—, v.p. Tenn. chpt.), Tenn. State Registrar Founders and Patriots (pres. 2003—), Nat. Soc. Colonial Dames XVII Century (1st v.p., pres. 2003—, 2d v.p. past treas. Chucaqua chpt.), Nat. Soc. So. Dames Am. (historian 2001—02, sec. 2002—, past pres. Memphis chpt., past state pres.), Colonial Dames Am., Tenn. State DAR (transp. chmn. 2001—), Cleve. Jr. Aux., Colonial Order of Crown, Soc. Descendants of Knights Most Noble Order of Garter, Family of Bruce Soc., Planetgenet Soc., Am. Clan Donald Soc., Am. Clan Gregor Soc., Tenn. Soc. Pres. Founders and Patriots of Am., Nat. Soc. Magna Charta Dames and Barons (past state sec. 2000—02, past Magna Carta sec. West Tenn. chpt. 2001—02, treas. West Tenn. chpt. 2002—04), Cleve. Garden Club (past pres.), U. Club Memphis, Early Settlers Shelby County (registrar 1988, bd. dirs. 1992—, sec. 1998—, pres. 2002—), Nineteenth Century Club (newsletter editor 1985—88, sec. 1993—95, corr. sec. 1999—), Racquet Club, Cleve. Women's Club, Alpha Omega Pi. Republican. Presbyterian. Avocations: art, genealogy, computers, dance, tennis. Home: 2008 Massey Rd Memphis TN 38119-6404 Personal E-mail: mtptmem@aol.com.

TICE, CAROL HOFF, intergenerational specialist, consultant; b. Ashville, N.C., Oct. 6, 1931; d. Amos H. and Fern (Irvin) Hoff; m. (div.); children: Karin E., Jonathan H. BS, Manchester Coll., North Manchester, Ind., 1954; MEd, Cornell U., 1955. Cert. tchr., Mich., N.Y., N.J. Tchr. Princeton (N.J.) Schs., 1955-60, Ann Arbor (Mich.) Schs., 1964—; dir. intergenerational programs Inst. for Study Children and Families Eastern Mich. U., Ypsilanti, 1985-96. Founder, pres. Lifespan Resources, Inc., Ann Arbor, 1979—; presdl. appointee to U.S. Nat. Commn. Internat. Yr. of the Child, Washington, 1979-81; del. to White House Conf. on Aging, Washington, 1995; founder, bd, mem. Tchg.-Learning Community. Innovator, program, Tch. Learning Intergenerational Communities, 1971; author: Guide Books and articles, Community of Caring, 1980; co-producer, Film, What We Have, 1976 (award, Milan, Italy Film Festival 1982). Trustee Blue Lake Fine Arts Camp, Twin Lake, Mich., 1975—; dir. Visual Arts Colony, 1990—. Recipient Program Innovation award, Mich. Dept. Edn., 1974—80, C.S. Mott Found. award, 1982, Nat. Found. Improvement in Edn. award, Washington, 1986, Disting. Alumni award, Manchester Coll., 1979, A+ Break the Mold award, U.S. Sec. of Edn., 1992, Ann Arbor Sch. Supts. Golden Apple award, 1999, Disting. Svc. award, Mich. Art Edn. Assn., 2001; fellow Ford Found. fellow, Ithaca, N.Y., 1955. Mem. AAUW (agt. 1979, Agent of Change award), Generations United (hon. com. for Margaret Mead Centennial 2001, 1998—, Pioneer award 1989), Mich. Edn. Assn. (hon. mention Program Innovation 2000), Optimist Club (Humanitarian award). Democrat. Presbyterian. Office: Scarlett MS 3300 Lorraine St Ann Arbor MI 48108-1970

TICE, DIANNE LISA, social services administrator; d. Amos Leon Tice and Annie Mae Mobley; 1 child, Daivd J. AA, N.Fla. Jr. Coll., Madison, 1975; BS in Family & Consumer Sci. Edn., Fla. State U., Tallahassee, 1978; MPA, Fla. Internat. U., Miami, 1996. Cert. tchr. Fla., 1978. Social worker State of Fla., Miami, 1985—87; substitute tchr. Hillsbouorgh County Pub. Schs., Tampa, Fla., 1988—89; recreational leader Miami Dade County Parks and Recreation, 1989—91; job developer Miami Dade County Cmty. Action Agy., 1991—. Vol. Inter-City Youth Coun., Miami, 1998—2001. Recipient Centennial Laureate, Fla. State U., 2005; Delores Auzene fellow, Fla. Internat. U., 1995. Mem.: NAACP, Fla. Assn. Cmty. Action (assoc.), Nat. Assn. Family and Consumer Scis. (assoc.), Nat. Coun. Negro Women, Fla. Internat. U. Alumni Asssn. (assoc.), Fla. State U. Alumni & Boosters Assns. (assoc.), Zeta Phi Beta. Democrat. Avocations: walking, bicycling, board games, jazz, card games. Home: 7905 East Dr #11A North Bay Village FL 33141 Office: Miami Dade County Cmty Action Agy 17801 Homestead Ave Miami FL 33157 Office Phone: 305-254-5804. Office Fax: 786-293-4598. Business E-Mail: dtice@miamidade.gov.

TICER, TERRI JEAN, sales executive; b. Childress, Tex., Apr. 15, 1955; d. Jerry H. and J. Colene (Eudey) T. AA, Clarendon Jr. Coll., 1977; BS, W. Tex. State U., 1979. Human svcs. dir. S. Plains Coll., Plainview, Tex., 1979-81; sales rep. Avon Products, NYC, 1981—2001, 2004—. Contbr. articles to profl. jours. Vol. Hospice of Plains, Plainview, 1985—2002, Meals on Wheels, 1997—98, 2003—, Hale County Crisis Ctr., 2002; mem. Faith in Sharing House, 1985—89, 1995, Friends of Libr., Plainview, 1986—91, Humane Soc., Plainview, 1987—92; chmn. Youth Group Reunion, 1990—91; mem. disaster team ARC, 1997—2000; vol. Muscular Dystrophy Jailathon, 1997—2002; mem. adult choir College Heights Bapt. Ch.; bd. dirs. Big Bros./Big Sisters, 1986—88, 2002—, City of Plainview Blue Eyes, 2002—. Mem.: AAUW (membership v.p. 1987—89, chmn. edn. found. 1989—92, hosp. aux. 1992—98), Plainview Writers Guild (treas. 1993—96), Austin Writers League (mem. 1993—96), Nat. Womens Book Assn., W. Tex. State U. Alumni Assn., Toastmasters (v.p. 2002—03, sgt.-at-arms 2004—, v.p. membership 2005—), Plainview Lions Breakfast Club (treas. 1995—97, newsletter ed. 1995—98, bd. dirs. 1998—), Plainview/Hale County In Safe Hands Program (co-dir. 2002—), Plainview C. of C. (mem. 2002—). Avocations: reading, writing short stories, photography, weights. Home: 2503 W 13th St Apt 5 Plainview TX 79072-4869 E-mail: territicer@yahoo.com.

TICK, JUDITH, music historian, educator; Matthews Distinguished U. prof., dept. music Northeastern U., Boston, 1999—. Author: Women Making Music: The Western Art Tradition 1150-1950, 1986 (ASCAP Deems Taylor award (co-edited with Jane Bowers), 1987), Ruth Crawford Seeger: A Composer's Search for American Music, 1997 (Outstanding Academic Book, 1998, Named Best Book, Soc. Am. Music, 1998, ASCAP Deems Taylor award, 1998), articles on Charles Ives; assoc. editor for the Am. Music sect. Musical Quarterly, 1991—. Recipient Hon. Citation award for Svc., Am. Women Composer, Inc. (NY Chpt.), 1993. Mem.: Am. Acad. Arts and Scis. Office: Dept Music Northeastern U 351 Ryder Hall Boston MA 02115 Office Phone: 617-373-8537. Office Fax: 617-373-4129. Business E-Mail: j.tick@neu.edu.

TICKNER, JUDITH ANN, political science educator; b. London, Mar. 1, 1937; d. Frederick James and Lucy Winifred (James) T.; m. Hayward R. Alker Jr., June 3, 1961; children: Joan Christina, Heather Jane, Gwendolyn Ann. BA, London U., 1959; MA, Yale U., 1960; PhD, Brandeis U., 1983. Lectr. Boston U., 1979-82; asst. prof. polit. sci. Coll. of the Holy Cross, Worcester, Mass., 1984-90, assoc. prof. polit. sci., 1990—. Rsch. assoc. Wellesley Coll., 1990-91; acad. visitor London Sch. Econs., 1989; vis. scholar Ctr. for Women Scholars, Uppsala U., Sweden, 1989. Author: Gender in International Relations, 1992, Self-Reliance Vs Power Politics, 1987. Mem. Am. Polit. Sci. Assn., Internat. Studies Assn. Home: 1746 Sunset Ave Santa Monica CA 90405-5920 Office: Internat Rel U So Calif VKC 330 Los Angeles CA 90089-0043

TICOTIN, RACHEL, actress; b. Bronx, NY, Nov. 1, 1958; m. David Caruso, 1983 (div. 1989); 1 child; m. Peter Strauss, Dec. 31, 1998. Actor: (films) King of the Gypsies, 1978, Fort Apache the Bronx, 1981, Critical Condition, 1987, Total Recall, 1990, One Good Cop, 1991, F/X2, 1991, Where the Day Takes You, 1992, Falling Down, 1993, Criminal Passion, 1994, Don Juan DeMarco, 1995, Steal Big Steal Little, 1995, Turbulence, 1997, Con Air, 1997, Civility, 2000, Can't Be Heaven, 2000, Desert Saints, 2002, Something's Gotta Give, 2003, Man on Fire, 2004, Sisterhood of the Traveling Pants, 2005, (TV films) Love, Mary, 1985, When the Bough Breaks, 1986, Rockabye, 1986, Spies, Lies & Naked Thighs, 1988, Prison Stories: Women on the Inside, 1991, Keep the Change, 1992, From the Files of Joseph Wambaugh: A Jury of One, 1992, Thicker Than Blood: The Larry McLinden Story, 1994, Deconstructing Sarah, 1994, The Wharf Rat, 1995, First Time Felon, 1997, Aftershock: Earthquake in New York, 1999, Warden of Red Rock, 2001, (TV series) For Love and Honor, 1983, Ohara, 1987-88, Crime and Punishment, 1993, (voice) Gargoyles, 1994-96, American Family, 2002-04, Skin, 2003.

TIDBALL, M. ELIZABETH PETERS, physiologist, educator; b. Anderson, Ind., Oct. 15, 1929; d. John Winton and Beatrice (Ryan) Peters; m. Charles S. Tidball, Oct. 25, 1952. BA, Mt. Holyoke Coll., 1951, LHD, 1976; MS, U. Wis., 1955, PhD, 1959; MTS summa cum laude, Wesley Theol. Sem., 1990; DSc (hon.), Wilson Coll., 1973, Trinity Coll., 1974, Cedar Crest Coll., 1977, U. of South, 1978, Goucher Coll., 1979, St. Mary-of-The-Woods Coll., 1986; LittD (hon.), Regis Coll., 1980, Coll. St. Catherine, 1980, Alverno Coll., 1989; HHD (hon.), St. Mary's Coll., 1977, Hood Coll., 1982; LLD (hon.), St. Joseph Coll., 1983; LHD (hon.), Skidmore Coll., 1984, Marymount Coll., 1985, Converse Coll., 1985, Mt. Vernon Coll., 1986. Tchg. asst. physiology dept. U. Wis., 1952—55, rsch. asst. physiology dept., 1958—59; rsch. asst. anatomy dept. U. Chgo., 1955-56, rsch. asst. physiology dept., 1956-58; USPHS postdoctoral fellow NIH, Bethesda, Md., 1959-61; staff pharmacologist Hazleton Labs., Falls Church, Va., 1961, cons., 1962; assoc. in physiology George Washington U. Med. Ctr., 1960-62, asst. rsch. prof. dept. pharmacology, 1962-64, assoc. rsch. prof. dept. physiology, 1964-70, rsch. prof., 1970-71, prof., 1971-94, prof. emeritus, 1994—; asst. dir. M of Theol. Studies program Wesley Theol Sem., 1993-94; disting. rsch. scholar Hood Coll., Frederick, Md., 1994—, co-dir. Tidball Ctr. for Study of Ednl. Environments, 1994—. Lucie Stern Disting. vis. prof. natural scis. Mills Coll., 1980; scholar in residence Coll. Preachers, 1984, Salem Coll., 1985, Wesley Theol. Sem., 1992; Disting. scholar in residence So. Meth. U., 1985; vis. trustee prof. Skidmore Coll., 1995; cons. FDA, 1966-67, assoc. sci. coord. sci. assocs. tng. programs, 1966-67; com. on NIH tng. programs and fellowships NAS, 1972-75; faculty summer confs. Am. Youth Found., 1967-78; founder, dir. Summer Seminars Women Am. Youth Found., 1987-95; cons. for instl. rsch. Wellesley Coll., 1974-75; exec. sec. com. on edn. and employment women in sci. and engring. Commn. on Human Resources, NRC/NAS, 1974-75, vice-chmn., 1977-82; cons., staff officer NRC/NAS, 1974-75; cons. Woodrow Wilson Nat. Fellowship Found., 1975-99, NSF, 1974-91; bd. mentor Assn. Governing Bds. Univs. and Colls., 1991-2000, Gale Fund for the Study of Trusteeship Adv. Comm., 1992-98; cons. Women's Coll. Coalition Rsch. Adv. Com., 1992-2000; Single Gender Schooling Working Group, US Dept. Edn., 1992-94, Women's Colls. Roundtable, 1998; rep. to DC Commn. on Status of Women, 1972-75; nat. panelist Am. Coun. on Edn., 1983-90; panel mem. Congl. Office Tech. Assessment, 1986-87; fellows selection com., fellows mentor Coll. Preachers, 1992-05. Lead author: Taking Women Seriously: Lessons and Legacies for Educating the Majority, American Council on Education Higher Education Series, 1999; columnist Trusteeship, 1993-95; mem. editl. bd. Jour. Higher Edn., 1979-84, cons. editor, 1984—; mem. editl. bd. Religion and Intellectual Life, 1983—; contbr. articles to profl. jours. Trustee Mt. Holyoke Coll., 1968-73, vice chmn., 1972-73, trustee fellow, 1988—; trustee Hood Coll., 1972-84, 86-92, exec. com., 1974-84, 89-92, trustee emerita, 1997—; overseer Sweet Briar Coll., 1978-85, dir. emerita, 2003—; trustee Cathedral Choral Soc., 1976-90, pres. bd. trustees, 1982-84, hon. trustee, 1991—; trustee Skidmore Coll., 1988—, mem. exec. com., 1993—, trustee Bishop Claggett Ctr., 2003—; mem. governing bd. Cathedral Coll. of Preachers, 1979-85, chmn., 1983-85; mem. governing bd. Protestant Episcopal Cathedral Found., 1983-85, mem. exec. com., 1983-85; bd. vis. Salem Coll., 1986-93; ctr. assoc. Nat. Resource Ctr., Girls Club Am., 1983-90; mem. governing bd. Buckinham's Choice Residents' Assn., 1999-2002; mem. cathedral vol. coun. Washington Nat. Cathedral, 2006. Named Outstanding Grad., The Penn Hall Sch., 1988; recipient Alumnae medal Honor, Mt. Holyoke Coll., 1971, Outstanding Svc. award, Am. Youth Found., 1975, Valuable Contbns. Gen. Alumni Assn. award, George Washington U., 1982, 1987, Pres.'s medal, 1999, Chestnut Hill medal Outstanding Achievement, Chestnut Hill Coll., Phila., 1987, Lifetime Svc. and Scholarship award, Bd. Women's Coll. Coalition and Nation's Women's Coll. Presidents, 1998, Order of Merit, Cathedral Choral Soc., 2000, Shattuk fellowship, 1955—56, Mary E. Woolley fellowship, Mt. Holyoke Coll., 1958—59, postdoctoral fellowship, USPHS, 1959—61. Mem. AAAS, Am. Physiol. Soc. (chmn. task force on women in physiology 1973-80, com. on coms. 1977-80, mem. emeritus 1994—), Am. Assn. Higher Edn., Mt. Holyoke Alumnae Assn. (dir. 1966-70, 76-77), Histamine Club, Sigma Delta Epsilon, Sigma Xi. Episcopalian. Home: 4100 Cathedral Ave NW Washington DC 20016-3584 also: 3200 Baker Cir # I-235 Adamstown MD 21710 Personal E-mail: ctidball@gwu.edu.

TIDD, JOYCE CARTER, etiquette educator; b. Chipley, FL, May 29, 1932; d. Brown Carter and Gussie Gurtrude Tiller; m. Matthew Heywood Tidd, Jan. 27, 1951; 1 child, Michael Heywood. Diploma, U. Ext. Conservatory, Chgo., 1971. Ch. choir dir. Hamp Stevens Meth. Ch., Columbus, Ga., 1949—50; co-chmn. of music Morningside Presbyn., Columbus, Ga., 1965—72; founder, owner Joyce Tidd Music Studio, Columbus, Ga., 1956—2001; founder, tchr. Sherwood Etiquette Sch., Columbus, Ga., 1996—2001. Home: 5846 Eula Ave Columbus GA 31909

TIDWELL, BETTY DAVENPORT, special education educator; b. Birmingham, Ala., Feb. 15, 1953; d. William Harry and Edna Earl (Staggs) Davenport; m. Michael J. Tidwell; children: David, Daniel. Dental technician, Carrer Acad., Atlanta, 1973; BS in Spl. Edn. with honors, Auburn U., 1992, M in Mild Learning Handicapped, 1994. Cert. spl. edn. tchr., Ala. Dental technician Clanton Dental Lab., Ala., 1973—86; tchr. asst. Clanton Elem. Sch., 1988—92, tchr. spl. edn., 1992—; tchr. emotionally conflicted Children's Harbor Sch., Ala.; edn. coord. Cmty. Intensive Treatment for Youth, Clanton, 1994—. Sec. Thorsby (Ala.) Band Boosters, 1989-91; parade organizer Thorsby Swedish Heritage Com., 1992-93. Mem. NEA, Ala. Edn. Assn., Coun. for Exceptional Children, Kappa Delta Phi, Phi Kappa Phi. Baptist. Avocations: crafts, playing piano, singing, special olympics. Home: PO Box 1 Jones AL 36749-0001 Office Phone: 205-755-2779.

TIDWELL, KATHY, literature and language educator; BS, U. of North Tex., Denton, 1979. Cert. Tchr. Tex., 1982. Tchr. North Mesquite H.S., Mesquite, Tex., 1984—89, A.C. New Mid. Sch., Mesquite, Tex., 1989—90, Dr. Ralph H. Poteet H.S., Mesquite, Tex., 1990—94, Crandal H.S., Crandall, Tex., 1994—. Auction item scheduler KERA, Dallas, 1985—86. Fellow Tchg. fellow, North Tex. State U., 1979—80. Mem.: Assn. of Tex. Profl. Educators (assoc.).

TIDWELL, TRISHA MCINTOSH, elementary school educator, department chairman; b. Nurnberg, Germany, Oct. 11, 1955; d. James and Lois McIntosh; m. Gerald Tidwell, Apr. 4, 1998 (div. Oct. 5, 2001); children: Jenny Robinson, Jason. BS, Baylor U., Waco, Tex., 1973—77; MEd, Tex. A&M U., College Station, Tex., 1976—78. Gifted & Talented Endorsement Tex. Dept. Edn., 2004. Reservation flagship sales Am. Airlines, Honolulu, 1978—88; exec. dir. United Travel Schs., Dallas, 1989—90. Recipient VIP award, Carrollton Farmers Br. Ind. Sch. Dist., 2005. Mem.: NEA, Sci. Tchrs. Tex., TSTA, Assn. Former Students (life), Baylor Alumni Assn. (life). Office: Dan F Long Mid Sch 2525 Frankford Rd Dallas TX 75287 Office Phone: 972-968-4100. Business E-Mail: tidwellp@cfbisd.edu.

TIEDGE-LAFRANIER, JEANNE MARIE, editor; b. N.Y.C., July 24, 1960; d. Richard Frederick and Joan Jean (Gerardo) Tiedge; m. John Daniel Lewis Lafranier, Oct. 8, 1989; children: Katelyn Ellen, John Richard. BA, Drew U., 1982. Asst. Denise Marcil Lit. Agy., N.Y.C., 1982-84; sr. editor New Am. Libr., N.Y.C., 1984-87, Warner Books, N.Y.C., 1987-95; editor corp. comm. Disticor, Ajax, Ont., Can., 1995—. Avocations: marathoner, equestrian.

TIEDT, IRIS MCCLELLAN, emeritus university dean; b. Dayton, Ohio, Feb. 3, 1928; d. Raymond Hill and Ermalene (Swartzel) McClellan; m. Sidney W. Tiedt, 1949; children: Pamela, Ryan; m. John Allan, 2005. BS in English Edn., Northwestern U., 1950; MA in Curriculum and Instrn., U. Oreg., 1961; PhD in Curriculum and Instrn., Stanford U., 1972. Cert. life K-12 adminstrn. and supervision, life secondary English and Spanish tchr., elem. English, Spanish and reading tchr., Calif. Tchr. pub. schs., Chgo., 1950-51, Anchorage, 1952-57, Eugene, Oreg., 1959-61; prof., dir. tchr. edn. Santa Clara U., Calif., 1968-75; prof., dir. South Bay Writing Project San Jose State U., Calif., 1975-87; supr. student teaching U. Oreg., Eugene, 1959-61; vis. prof. U. Wash., Seattle, 1964-65; dean edn. No. Ky. U., Highland Heights, 1987-89; dean edn. and regional svcs. Minn. State U. (Moorhead), 1989-94. Author: Exploring Books with Children, 1979, Multicultural teaching, 1979, 7th edit., 2005, The Writing Process: Composition and Applied Grammar, 1981, Teaching Writing in K-8 Classrooms, 1983, The Language Arts Handbook, 1983, Lessons from a Writing Project, 3 vols., 1987, Teaching Thinking in K-12 Classrooms, 1989, Writing: From Topic to Evaluation, 1989, Reading, Thinking, and Writing: A Holistic Language and Literacy Program, 1989, Teaching with Picture Books in the Middle School, 2000, Toadstools, Tiger Lilies, and Thunderbolts: Engaging Students with Poetry, 2002; also articles. Mem. ASCD, AAUW (life), Nat. Coun. Tchrs. English (editor Lang. Arts 1972-76), Am. Assn. Colls. Tchr. Edn., Am. Ednl. Rsch. Assn., Coun. Rsch. in English, Sierra Club (life), Stanford Alumni Assn. (life), Phi Delta Kappa. Democrat. Home: 6566 Lincoln St Petaluma CA 94952-9721

TIEFEL, VIRGINIA MAY, librarian; b. Detroit, May 20, 1926; d. Karl and June Garland (Young) Brenkert; m. Paul Martin Tiefel, Jan. 25, 1947; children: Paul Martin Jr., Mark Gregory. BA in Elem. Edn., Wayne State U., 1962; MA in Library Sci., U. Mich., 1968. Librarian Birmingham Schs., Mich., 1967-68; librarian S. Euclid-Lyndhurst Schs., Cleve., 1968-69; acquisitions-reference librarian Hiram Coll., Ohio, 1969-77; head undergrad. libraries Ohio State U., Columbus, 1977-84, dir. library user edn., 1978-95, faculty outreach coord., 1995-98. Contbr. articles to profl. jours. Recipient Disting. Alumnus award, U. Mich. Sch. Info. and Libr. Studies, 1993. Mem. ALA (v.p. Ohio sect. 1973-74, pres. 1974-75, Miriam Dudley Bibliographic Instrn. Librarian of Yr. 1986), Acad. Library Assn. Ohio (Outstanding Ohio Acad. Librarian 1984), Assn. Coll. and Research Libraries (chmn. bibliographic instrn. sect. com. on research 1983-84, chmn. com. on performance measures 1984-90). Lutheran. Achievements include Excellence in Teaching award at Ohio State University Libraries established in her honor in 2004. Home: 4711 Oak Bluff Ct Eau Claire WI 54701 E-mail: vtiefel1@aol.com.

TIEFENTHAL, MARGUERITE AURAND, school social worker; b. Battle Creek, Mich., July 23, 1919; d. Charles Henry and Elisabeth Dirk (Hoekstra) Aurand; m. Harlan E. Tiefenthal, Nov. 26, 1942; children: Susan Ann, Daniel E., Elisabeth Amber, Carol Aurand. BS, Western Mich. U., 1941; MSW, U. Mich., 1950; postgrad., Coll. of DuPage, Ill., 1988-90. Tchr. No. High Sch., Flint, Mich., 1941-44, Cen. High Sch., Kalamazoo, 1944-45; acct. Upjohn Co., Kalamazoo, 1945-48; social worker Family Svc. Agy., Lansing, Mich., 1948-50, Pitts., 1950-55; sch. social worker Gower Sch. Dist., Hinsdale, Ill., 1962-70, Hinsdale (Ill.) Dist. 181, 1970-89, cons., 1989—; sch. social worker Villa Park (Ill.) Sch. Dist. 45, 1989; addictions counselor Mercy Hosp., 1990-92; asst. prof. sch. social work, liaison to pub. schs. Loyola U., Chgo., 1990-98, ret., 1998. Field instr. social work interns U. Ill., 1979-88; impartial due process hearing officer; mem. adv. com. sch. social work Ill. State Bd. Edn. approved programs U. Ill. and George Williams Coll.; speaker Nat. Conf. Sch. Social Work, Denver, U. Tex. Joint Conf. Sch. Social Work in Ill.; founder Marguerite Tiefenthal Symposium for Ill. Sch. Social Work Interns. Co-editor The School Social Worker and the Handicapped Child: Making P.L. 94-142 Work; sect. editor: Sch. Social Work Quarterly, 1979. Sec. All Village Caucus Village of Western Springs, Ill., mem. village disaster com.; deacon Presbyn. Ch. Western Springs, Sunday sch. tchr., mem. choir; instr. Parent Effectiveness, Teacher Effectiveness, STEP; trainer Widowed Persons Service Tng. Program for Vol. Aides AARP. Recipient Ill. Sch. Social Worker of Yr., 1982. Mem. Nat. Assn. Social Workers (chmn. exec. council on social work in schs.), Ill. Assn. Sch. Social Workers (past pres., past conf. chmn., conf. program chmn.), Ladies Libr. Assn., Sch. Social Workers Supervisors Group (del. to Ill. Commn. on Children), Programs. for Licensure of Social Work Practice in Ill., Ladies Libr. Assn. (Kalamazoo), LWV, DKG, PEO. Avocation: sewing. also: 3151 West B Ave Plainwell MI 49080

TIEKEN, LISA MARIE, science educator; b. Hondo, Tex., May 10, 1964; d. Jimmy Joe and Doris Fey Jefferies; m. Richard Vaughn Tieken, Mar. 19, 1992; children: Kelsey Noel, Richard Travis, Kasey Michelle, Ryan Vaughn. BS in Edn., SW Tex. State U., San Marcos, 1987; MEd, Our Lady of the Lake U., San Antonio, Tex., 2002. Cert. tchr. Tex. Edn. Agy., 1991. Tchr. sci./coach Eagle Pass H.S., Tex., 1987—89; tchr. sci. Floresville Mid. Sch., Tex., 1990—. Chair sci. dept. Floresville Mid. Sch., 1998—; dist. technology trainer Floresville Ind. Sch. Dist., 1998—, loti trainer, 2005—. Mem. Delta Psi Kappa, San Marcos, Tex., 1985—97. Recipient LoTi Tchr. of Week, Floresville Ind. Sch. Dist., 2006; grantee CoMet, Our Lady of the Lake U., 1999-2002. Mem.: Tex. Sci. Tchrs. Orgn. (assoc.), ATPE (assoc.), Floresville FFA Boosters (assoc.). Avocations: softball, stockshow animals, fishing, hunting, NASCAR racing. Home: 2075 County Rd 132 Floresville TX 78114 Office: Floresville Mid Sch 2601 B St Floresville TX 78114 Office Phone: 830-393-5350. Business E-Mail: ltieken@fisd.us.

TIEMANN, BARBARA JEAN, special education educator; b. Gothenberg, Nebr., Jan. 22, 1955; d. Thurl L. Rogge and Betty R. (Kent) Van Eperen; m. Robert L. Tiemann, June 3, 1977; children: Erich, Hans, Robin (dec.) BS in Elem. Edn., U. Nebr., 1987, MEd, 2000, MEd with severe/profound endorsement. Cert. tchr. Nebr., Fla. Kindergarten tchr. Ft. Pierce (Fla.) Elem. Sch., 1988-89, devel. kindergarten tchr., 1989; psychol. svcs. asst. Beatrice State Devel. Ctr., 1993—2000; resource tchr. Lincoln (Nebr.) Schs., 2000—. Mem. Creighton Parents Assn., Humanities Coun. Mem. NEA, Eastern Star, Lincoln Edn. Assn., Nebraska Edn. Assn., After 5, U. Nebraska Alumni, Compassionate Friends.

TIEMANN, JEANNINE E., music educator; b. Florissant, Mo., Nov. 24, 1970; d. Lambert Owen and Janet Evelyn T. BA in Music Edn., So. Ill. U. Edwardsville, 1994, MA in Music Edn., 1996. Cert. special tchr. K-12. Pvt. piano/voice instr. So. Ill. U., Edwardsville, 1991-99; choral dir. Edward A. Fulton Jr. High, O'Fallon, Ill., 1996—. Mem. Am. Choral Dirs. Assn., Music Educators Nat. Conf., Ill. State Music Tchrs. Assn., Ill. Music Educators Assn. (chmn. dist. 6 1999—), Sigma Alpha Iota (mem. award 1994, sword of honor 1994, sec. 1992-93, treas. 1993-94, v.p. mem. 1998-2000, sec. 2000-). Republican. Luth. Avocations: bowling, counted cross stitch. Office: Edward A Fulton Jr High 307 Kyle Rd O Fallon IL 62269-6611 E-mail: jtiemann@ofallon90.net.

TIEMANN, KAREN, elementary school educator; d. Al and Adeline Ferry; m. James Tiemann (dec.). BS, U. Ill., 1989, MA, 1995. Tchr. Grayslake Mid. Sch., Ill., 1989—2001; dir. West 40 Safe Sch. West 40, Lyons, Ill., 2001—. Office Phone: 708-447-2515.

TIEMANN, KATHLEEN ANNE, sociologist, educator; BA, Grand Valley State U., 1978; MA, Western Mich. U., 1980, PhD, 1984. Prof. U. Md. European Divsn., Heidelberg, Germany, 1984-85, Mercer U., Macon, Ga., 1985-88, U. N.D., Grand Forks, 1988—. Co-editor: Intersections: Readings in Sociology, 4th edit.; editor: Crossroads: Readings in Social Problems, 4th edit. Pres., exec. officer Red River Valley Habitat for Humanity, Grand Forks, 1989-99; steering com. Flood Oral History Project, Grand Forks, 1997-98; vol. Friendship Pl. Psychosocial Rehab. Ctr., Grand Forks, 1989-92. Recipient Outstanding Achievement award, Western Mich. U. Coll. Arts and Scis., 2004, Svc. award, Great Plains Sociol. Assn., 1992. Mem. Assn. Humanist Sociology (pres. 1988-89), Great Plains Sociol. Assn. (pres. 1989-90), Am. Sociol. Assn. (rep. of yr. 1992, svc. award 1990), Soc. Study Social Problems, Midwest Sociol. Soc., Alpha Kappa Delta Internat. Sociology Honor Soc. Office: Gillette Hall Rm 202 225 Centennial Dr Srlop 7136 Grand Forks ND 58202

TIEMANN, MARGARET ANN, health educator; b. St. Louis, June 24, 1956; d. Herman T. and Margaret Ellen (Drury) Volkerding; m. Mark G. Tiemann, Nov. 4, 1978; children: Michelle, Jeffrey. Diploma in nursing, DePaul Hosp Sch. Nursing, St. Louis, 1978; BS in Bus. Adminstrn., Fontbonne Coll., 1991. RN, Mo. Staff nurse Christain Hosp. N.E., St. Louis, 1975-79; staff nurse ICU St. Joseph's Health Ctr., St. Charles, Mo., 1979-91; instr. St. Mary's Coll. of O'Fallon, Mo., 1987-88; asst. prof. St. Charles County C.C., St. Peters, Mo., 1988-96. Adv. bd. mem. St. Charles County C.C. Health Info. Tech. Adv. Com., St. Peters, 1988—, faculty advisor, 1993-96; mem. self-evaluation com. St. Charles County C.C., St. Peters, 1988—; cons. Serenity Mgmt. and Cons., St. Louis, 1990. Mem. Ea. Mo. Health Info. Mgmt. Assn. (assoc.), St. Louis Met. Critical Care Soc., DePaul Hosp. Sch. Nursing Alumni. Roman Catholic. Avocations: reading, travel.

TIENDA, MARTA, demographer, educator; b. Tex. BA in Spanish magna cum laude, Mich. State U., 1972; MA in Sociology, U. Tex., Austin, 1975, PhD in Sociology, 1977. From asst. prof. to prof. rural sociology U. Wis., Madison, 1976—87; vis. prof. Stanford U., 1987; Ralph Lewis prof. sociology U. Chgo., 1994—97, chmn. dept. sociology, 1994—96; prof. sociology and pub. affairs Princeton U., NJ, 1997—, dir. office population rsch., 1998—2002, Maruice P. During prof. demographic studies, 1999—. Rsch. assoc. office population rsch. Princeton U., 1997—; bd. dirs. Fed. Res. Bank N.Y. Co-author: Hispanics in the U.S. Economy, 1985, Hispanic Population of the United States, 1987, Divided Opportunities, 1988, The Color of Opportunity, 2001, Youth in Cities, 2002; editor: Ethnicity and Causal Mechanisms, 2005, Hispanics and the Furure of America, 2005, Multiple Origins, Uncertain Destinies: Hispanics and the American Future, 2005; contbr. articles to profl. jours. Trustee Corp. of Brown U., Jacobs Found. of Switzerland, Sloan Found.; bd. dirs. Princeton Med. Ctr. Named one of 80 Elite Hispanic Women, Hispanic Bus. Mag., 2003, Top 100 Influential Hispanics, 2003; recipient Lifetime Achievement award, Hispanic Bus. Inc., 2004; Guggenheim fellow. Fellow: AAAS, Am. Acad. Political Social Sci., Ctr. Advanced Study Behavioral Scis.; mem.: Internat. Union for Sci. Study of Population, Population Assn. Am. (past pres.), Am. Econ. Assn., Am. Sociol. Assn. Office: Office Population Rsch Princeton U 247 Wallace Hall Princeton NJ 08544-2091*

TIERNEY, MAURA, actress; b. Boston, Feb. 3, 1965; m. Billy Morrissette, 1994. Student, NYU, Cir. in the Sq. Theatre Sch. Actor: (TV series) 704 Hauser St., —, News Radio, 1995—2000, ER, 2000—; (TV films) Flying Blind, 1990—, Out of Darkness, —, Student Exchange, —, Crossing the Mob, —, (guest appearance): (TV series) Growing Pains; (TV films) Family Ties; (TV series) Law & Order, The Van Dyke Show,: (films) Dead Women in Lingerie, 1991, The Linguini Incident, 1991, White Sands, 1992, Fly By Night, 1993, The Temp, 1993, Primal Fear, 1996, Primary Colors, 1997, Liar, Liar, 1997, Primary Colors, 1998, Forces of Nature, 1999, Instinct, 1999, Welcome to Mooseport, 2004, Danny Roane: First Time Director, 2006; (plays) Some Girl(s), 2006. Office: c/o Creative Artists Agy 9830 Wilshire Blvd Beverly Hills CA 90212*

TIETJEN, MILDRED CAMPBELL, librarian, college official; b. Rome, Ga., May 26, 1940; d. William Franklin and Willie (Bohannon) Campbell; m. William Leighton Tietjen, Dec. 15, 1968; 1 child, William Campbell. AB, Berry Coll., Mt. Berry, Ga., 1961; M.A in L.S., Peabody Coll., Nashville, 1962. Librarian Gordon Lee High Sch., Chickamauga, Ga., 1962-64; dir. library Ga. Southwestern Coll., Americus, 1964-83, assoc. dean for acad. affairs, 1984—. Contbr. articles to profl. publs. Mem. Sumter Hist. Preservation Soc., Americus, 1985 Council on Library Resources fellow, 1975 Mem. ALA, Southeastern Library Assn., Ga. Library Assn. (scholarship chmn. 1982—), Bus. and Profl. Women (sec. Americus and Sumter County 1984, parliamentarian 1985, Woman of Achievement award 1982), DAR (historian Council of Safety chpt. 1984-85), Beta Phi Mu, Kappa Delta Pi, Alpha Epsilon, Delta Kappa Gamma (pres. 1976), Alpha Chi Clubs: Ga. Southwestern Coll. Faculty Women (pres. 1982-83). Presbyterian. Home: Rte 2 RR 2 Box 192 Plains GA 31780-9802 Office: Georgia Southwestern College Wheatley St Americus GA 31709-3700

TIETZE, MARTHA KATHERINE, secondary school educator; b. Nevada, Mo., Sept. 14, 1946; d. Clinton Mynatt and Ella Corene (Gillogly) Goss; m. Thomas Charles Tietze, Nov. 26, 1981. BS, U. Kans., Lawrence, 1968, MA, 1978. Tchr. Shawnee Mission (Kans.) Sch. Dist., 1968—. Named Secondary Math Tchr. of Yr., Pitts. State U., 2005; recipient Honorable Mention Tandy award, No. Ariz. U., 1995; grantee NSF, U. Ill., 1969, No. Ariz. U., 1989. Mem.: Kans. Assn. Math. Tchrs. (Presdl. award for tchg. excellence in secondary math. 1992, Woodrow Wilson fellow 1990), Nat. Coun. Tchrs. Math.

TIFT, MARY LOUISE, artist; b. Seattle, Jan. 2, 1913; d. John Howard and Wilhelmina (Pressler) Dreher; m. William Raymond Tift, Dec. 4, 1948. BFA cum laude, U. Wash., 1933; postgrad., Art Ctr. Coll., L.A., 1945-48, U. Calif., San Francisco, 1962-63. Art dir. Vaughn Shedd Advt., L.A., 1948; asst. prof. design Calif. Coll. Arts & Crafts, Oakland, Calif., 1949-59; coord. design dept. San Francisco Art Inst., 1959-62. Subject of cover story, Am. Artist mag., 1980, studio article, 1987; one-woman shows, Gumps Gallery, San Francisco, 1977, 1986, 90, Diane Gilson Gallery, Seattle, 1978, Oreg. State U., 1981, Univ. House, Seattle, Frye Art Mus., Seattle, 2000; exhibited in group shows including Brit. Biennale, Yorkshire, Eng., 1970, Grenchen Triennale, Switzerland, 1970, Polish Biennale, Crakow, 1972, Nat. Gallery, Washington, 1973, Madrid Biennale, 1980, U.S.-U.K. Impressions, Eng., 1988; represented in permanent collections, Phila. Mus. Art, Bklyn. Mus., Seattle Art Mus., Library Congress, Achenbach Print Collection, San Francisco Palace Legion of Honor, San Diego Mus. Art, U.S. Art in Embassies. Served to lt. USNR, 1943-45. Mem. Print Club Phila., World Print Council, Calif. Soc. Printmakers, Phi Beta Kappa, Lambda Rho. Christian Scientist. Studio: 4400 Stone Way N Apt 521 Seattle WA 98103-7487

TIGETT-PARKS, ELIZABETH, arts administrator; b. Houston, Apr. 29, 1971; d. Joel Ray and Zane Ann Tigett; m. Christopher Dylan Parks, July 10, 1999. BA in Art History magna cum laude, Rollins Coll., 1993; MA in Visual Arts Admin. summa cum laude, NYU, 1999. Property contr. Christie's East, N.Y.C., 1993-95; adminstr. contemporary art Christie's Inc., N.Y.C., 1995-97; asst. to the dir. Diane Upright Fine Arts, N.Y.C., 1997-99; dir. Bronwyn Keenan Gallery, N.Y.C., 1998-99; contemporary art specialist eArtGroup-.com, N.Y.C., 1999-2000; sr. account exec. artnet.com, 2000—. Contbr. articles to profl. jours. Mem. MOMA (jr. assoc.). Democrat. Christian. Avocations: painting, in-line skating, hiking, scuba diving, writing.

TIGHE, MARY ANN, real estate company executive; m. David Hidalgo; 1 child from previous marriage, Aaron. BA in art history, Cath. U.; MA in art history, U. Md. Staff mem. Smithsonian Instn.; arts adv. to v.p. Walter Mondale; dep. chmn. Nat. Endowment Arts; v.p. Am. Broadcasting Co.; sales assoc. Edward S. Gordon Inc. (name changed to Insignia/ESG Inc. 1997), 1984; exec. mng. dir. Insignia/ESG Inc., NYC, 1993—99, vice chmn., 1999—2002; pres., CEO NY Tri-State Region CB Richard Ellis, NYC, 2002—. Dir. Imperial Parking Corp. bd. dirs. NYC Ballet, Parrish Art Mus., The New 42nd St., Joan's Legacy: The Joan Scarangello Found. to Conquer Lung Cancer. Recipient Woman Yr., Comml. Real Estate Women NY, 2001. Mem.: Real Estate Bd. NY (exec. com. bd. govs. 2001—, Henry Hart Rice award 1997, 2002, Robert T. Lawrence award 1992, 1998). Office: CB Richard Ellis Group Inc 200 Park Ave New York NY 10166

TIGHE-MOORE, BARBARA JEANNE, electronics executive; b. Wadsworth, Ohio, Jan. 12, 1961; d. Norton Raymond and Laura Alida (Frank) Tighe; m. Derek William Moore, June 26, 1982. Student summa cum laude, Hocking Tech. Coll., 1981; student, Sinclair Coll., 1986; BBA magna cum laude, Kent State U., 1988. Lic. amateur radio operator. Tech. writer computer dept. Sinclair Coll., Dayton, Ohio, 1983; project mgr. O'Neil & Assocs., Dayton, 1983-84; biomed., bio-acoustic real-time flight simulation tempest developer Systems Rsch. Labs., Dayton, 1984-86; computer specialist Kent State U. Press, 1987-88; mgmt. analyst Electronic Warfare Frontier Engring. Inc., 1988-89; supr. computer tech. svcs. Frontier Engring., Inc., 1989-90, project engr., 1990-92; ptnr., bd. dirs. MKCC, Dayton, 1990—, SDCC, Dayton, 1992—; regional mgr. User Tech. Assocs., Dayton, 1993-96; pres., owner Lida Ray Techs., Dayton, 1978—; prof. dept. computer sci. Nat. Coll. Bus. and Tech. Graphics steering com., mem. sanctioned UNIX software adv. team Aero. Sys. Divsn.; program chair IEEE Internat. Wireless LAN Conf.; pres. Engring. Application Support Environ. Security Working Group, 2000; proceedings chmn. Nat. Aerospace & Electronics Conf., 1995—97, pres., 2000; bd. dirs. MKCC, Dayton, Cin. Digital Women; spkr. in field. Author: Job Search Strategies for the 90's, 1993, Through the Glass Ceiling, 1997, Riding the 5:15, 2000, Convergence of Socio-Economic and Technology Factors, 2001; co-author: Women on a Wire, 1996, vol. 2, 2001; editor: Graphics Directions, 1990—91; pub.: Team Advisor, SDCC Cleaning Times, IEEE Update; author: numerous poems; contbr. articles to profl. jours. Counselor Kwam's Kinder Kamp; tchr. Bible Sch.; cook Meals on Wheels; organizer/cook funeral Svcs. Dinners. Recipient Vol. Citizen award Wadsworth C. of C. 1979, Ohio Essayist award, 1979, Virginia Perryman award, 1979, Disting. Leadership award, 1990-91 Mem.: IEEE (former treas., sec. Dayton sect., bd. dirs. 1995—97, chmn. bd. dirs. Dayton sect. 1999, region 2 chpt. coord. 2000—), Equestrian Team (point rider 1977—87), Armed Forces Comms. and Electronics Assn. (judge sci. fair western dist. 1992—), Internat. Film Soc. (pres. 1986—88), Assn. Internat. Students Econs. & Commerce (pres. 1986—87), Def. Planning Analysis Soc. (exec. bd.), Assn. Computer Machinery, Data Processing Mgmt. Assn., Tech. and Soc. of IEEE, Engring. Mgmt. Soc. of IEEE, Computer Soc. of IEEE (sec. 1991—92, vice chmn. 1992—93, chmn. 1994—95), Mortar Bd., Fencing Club, Beta Gamma Sigma, Omicron Delta Kappa, Phi Theta Kappa. Avocations: travel, investing, equestrian show jumping, soccer, painting. Home: 729 Kyle Dr Tipp City OH 45371-1435 Office Phone: 937-667-4972. Business E-Mail: bjmoore@lidaray.com.

TIGUE, VIRGINIA BETH (GINNY TIGUE), volunteer; b. Owosso, Mich., Sept. 10, 1945; d. Joseph Frederick and Florence Marion Sahlmark; m. Joseph James Tigue Jr., Aug. 12, 1967; children: James Christopher, Molly Elizabeth. BS, cert. in phys. therapy, U. Mich., 1967. Registered phys. therapist, Mich., Calif. Phys. therapist at hosps., rehab. ctrs. and pvt. practice. Co-owner Tigue Property Co.; former co-owner Tex. Toyota of Grapevine. Councilman Pl. 5 City of Colleyville, 1998—2004, mayor pro tem, 2000—04, bond steering com., 1991, master plan revision com., 1997-98, chmn. cmty. ctr. adv. com. 1998; mem. Art Coun. Ft. Worth and Tarrant County Bd., Ft. Worth, 1997-2005, Tarrant County College Found. Bd., 2001-; founding bd. dirs. Grapevine-Colleyville Ind. Sch. Dist. Edn. Found., 1998-2004; bd. dirs. Colleyville C. of C., 1991—, chmn., 1994; founding chmn. women's adv. bd. Harris Meth. HEB Hosp. 1992, 93, bd. trustees, 1999-, vice chmn., 2005; bd. Meth. Health Harris Found. 2001-; bd. dirs. Arts Coun. N.E. Tarrant, 1991-98, chmn., 1995-96; bd. dirs. Origins Mus., 1998—, v.p. 2000-2001; bd. dirs. Vol. Ctr. of Tarrant County, 1998-2002, chmn. 2000; bd. dirs. Dallas Mus. Art League, 1999-2000, United Way of Met. Tarrant County, 2000-, exec. bd. dir., 2002-; bd. dirs. N.E Leadership Forum, 1999—, chmn., 2004; sustaining mem. Dallas Jr. League, 1991—; founding bd. dirs. Tarrant County Coll. Found., 2001—; sr. advisor Nat. Charity League, 1994,; bd. dirs. N.E. Tarrant County divsn. Am. Heart Assn., 1993-94, co-chmn. gala 1997; fund raising chmn. Friends of Colleyville Libr., 1992—; home tour com. Colleyville Women's Club, 1990, 93, 96, fashion show chmn., 1996; mem. adv. bd. Women's Shelter, 1996-98; mem. Women Leader's Summit, Washington, 1995, 96, 98, 99, 05; mem. Women's Policy Forum, 1999—, Women's Found. of Tarrant County, 2000—. Named Most Influential Bus. Woman, The Bus. Press, 1997, Vol. of Yr., City of Colleyville, 1997, Colleyville Citizen of Yr., 2001, Colleyville Rotary Citizen of Yr., 2002; recipient Legacy of Women award The Women's Shelter, 1995, Herman J. Smith Leadership award Colleyville C. of C., 1994, Proclamation as Outstanding Citizen of Colleyville, 1995. Mem. Colleyville Area C. of C. (bd. dirs. 1990-98, pres.-elect 1993, pres. 1994, vice-chmn. membership devel. 1997, vice-chmn. cmty. devel. 1998, 2003, 2005, vice chmn. bus. devel. 2004, Citizen of Yr. 2001, exec. bd. 2003-), Tex. Congress Parents and Tchrs. (hon. life mem.). Republican. Methodist. Avocations: golf, travel, reading, the arts. Home: 4415 Meandering Way Colleyville TX 76034-4513

TILESTON, JACKIE, artist, educator; b. Manila, Philippines, Dec. 11, 1960; arrived in U.S., 1979; d. Peter Ayer and Margaret Doreen Tileston. BA in fine arts (painting) summa cum laude, Yale U., New Haven, Conn., 1983; MFA in painting, Ind. U., Bloomington, 1988. Faculty Glassell Sch. Art Mus. Fine Arts, Houston, 1990—98; asst. prof. painting U. N.Mex., Albuquerque, 1998—2000; asst. prof. fine arts U. Pa., Phila., 2000—. Adj. faculty mem. U. Houston, 1993—98; adj. faculty Rice U., 1997; faculty Glassell Sch. of Art, Mus. of Fine Arts, Houston, 1990—98. One-woman shows include W.A. Graham Gallery, Houston, 1990, 1992, Mus. Art, Longview, Tex., 1994, Lawing Gallery, Houston, 1997, Satellite Space, U. Tex., San Antonio, 1998, U. N.Mex., Albuquerque, 2000, Barbara Davis Gallery, Houston, 2003, 2006, Phila. Art Alliance, 2003, Zg Gallery, Chgo., 2005, Holly Johnson Gallery, Dallas, 2005, Not Always So, Barbara Davis Gallery, Houston, 2006, Chromatopia, Rowan U. Gallery, Glassboro, NJ, 2006, numerous group shows, Represented in permanent collections JP Morgan Chase, Mus. Fine Arts, Houston (Catalog). Named Bellagio resident, Rockefeller Found., 2005; recipient Fellowship Award in Painting, Mid-Am. Arts Alliance/Nat. Endowment for the Arts, 1994; fellow, John S. Guggenheim Meml. Found., 2006; Academic fellow, Ind. U., Bloomington, 1986—88, Core Fellowship resident, Mus. Fine Arts, Houston, 1988—90, PEW Found. fellow, Phila., 2004. Mem.: Coll. Art Assn., Phi Beta Kappa. Office: Fine Arts Univ Pa 100 Morgan Bldg 205 S 34th St Philadelphia PA 19104 Business E-Mail: tiletson@design.upenn.edu.

TILGHMAN, ELIZABETH W., retired medical/surgical nurse; b. Hazleton, Pa., Sept. 17, 1931; d. Edward John and Mildred Mae (Ringlaben) Wiegand; m. Henry W. Tilghman, Apr. 7, 1956; children: Michelle Lynn, Victoria Renee. Diploma in nursing, U. Pa., Phila., 1952. RN, Fla.; cert. emergency nurse, ACLS. Staff nurse Plantation Gen. Hosp., Fla.; nurse mgr. emergency dept. Humana Hosp. Biscayne, Miami, Fla., head nurse outpatient surg.; ret. Mem. Dade/Broward Emergency Nurses Assn. (treas. 1982-83, pres. 1985).

TILGHMAN, SHIRLEY MARIE, academic administrator, biology professor; b. Toronto, Can., Sept. 17, 1946; 2 children. BSc in Chemistry with honors, Queen's U., Kingston, Ont., 1968, DSc (hon.), 2002; PhD in Biochemistry, Temple U., Phila., 1975; DSc (hon.), Oxford U., 2002, NYU, 2005; postgrad., NIH. Secondary sch. tchr., West Africa, Sierra Leone, 1968—70; Fogarty internat. fellow NIH, Bethesda, Md., 1975—77; investigator Inst. Cancer Rsch., Phila., 1979—86, Howard Hughes Med. Inst., Chevy Chase, 1988—2001; asst. prof., Fels Rsch Inst. Temple U., Phila., 1978—79; prof. molecular biology Princeton U., NJ, 1986—, Howard A. Prior prof. life scis., 1986—2001, chair Coun. Sci. and Tech., 1993—2000, pres., 2001—. Founding dir. Lewis-Sigler Inst. Integrative Genomics, 1998—2003; adj. assoc. prof. human genetics and biochemistry and biophysics U. Pa., 1980—86; adj. prof. Robert Wood Johnson Medical Sch., 1988—2001; mem. sci. adv. bd. Whitehead Inst. for Biomedical Scis., MIT, 1995—2001; founding mem. Nat. Adv. Coun. Human Genome Project Initiative NIH; founder Princeton Postdoctoral Tchg. fellow. Trustee The Jackson Lab., 1994—, Carnegie Endowment Internat. Peace, 2005—, Google Inc., Rockefeller U., Cold Spring Harbor Lab.; mem. Pew Charitable Trusts Scholars Prog., Biomedical Scis. Selection Com., Lucille P. Markey Charitable Trust Scholar Selection Com. Recipient Pres.'s award disting. tchg., Princeton U., 1996, L'Oréal-UNESCO Internat. Women in Sci. award, 2002, Lifetime Achievement award, Soc. Devel. Biology, 2003, Radcliffe Inst. medal, Harvard U., 2004, Presdl. Medal of Honor, Dillard U., 2006. Mem.: NAS, Am. Acad. Arts and Scis., Royal Soc. London, Inst. Medicine, Am. Philos. Soc. Achievements include first to identify the H19 gene in mice, an early example of parental imprinting; research in cloning the first mammalian gene. Office: Princeton U Office of Pres One Nassau Hall Princeton NJ 08544-0001 Office Phone: 609-258-6101.

TILLER, ANNA FRANCES, music educator; b. Dorhan, Ala., Apr. 8, 1945; d. Woodrow Wilson Jackson and Helen Elizabeth Erwin; m. Ira Quincy Tiller, Jr., June 8, 1968; children: Quincy, Keith. AA in Edn., Young Harris Jr. Coll., Ga., 1965; EdB, Woman's Coll. Ga., Milledgeville, 1967; MEd, U. Ga. Tchr. Lake Park Elem. Sch., Ga., 1967—68, Clark County Bd. Edn., Athens, Ga., 1968—71, Hazlehurst Mid. Sch., Ga., 1968, 1971—72, Wilkes County Bd. Edn., Washington, Ga., 1972—73, 1988—2006, Wilkes Acad., Washington, 1973—78, Washington 1st Bapt. Ch., 1986—88. Mem.: Ga. Music Educators Assn., Profl. Assn. Ga. Educators, Greater Augusta Arts Coun., Alpha Theta chpt. Delta Kappa Gamma (pres. 2002—04). Baptist. Avocations: piano, singing, cooking, gardening, reading. Office: WW Primary Sch 910 E Robert Toombs Ave Washington GA 30673

TILLER, OLIVE MARIE, retired church worker; b. St. Paul, Dec. 13, 1920; d. Otto William and Myrtle Alice (Brougham) Foerster; m. Carl William Tiller, June 21, 1940; children: Robert W., Jeanne L. Peterson; m. Edward J. Alo, Dec. 15, 2001. BS, U. Minn., 1940. Spl. edn. tchr., Prince Georges County, Md., 1955-63; spl. asst. for profl. svcs. Kendall Demonstration Elem. Sch., Gallaudet Coll., Washington, 1971-78; spl. asst. for program Ch. Women United, N.Y.C., 1979-80; exec. asst. to gen. sec. Nat. Coun. Chs. of Christ in U.S.A., N.Y.C., 1981-87; dep. gen. sec. for coop. Christianity Am. Bapt. Chs. of U.S.A., Valley Forge, Pa., 1987-88. Author (with Carl W. Tiller): At Calvary, 1994. Mem. Human Rels. Commn. Prince George's County, 1967—73; bd. dirs. Am. Leprosy Missions, Greenville, SC, 1981—95, Bapt. Peace Fellowship of N.Am., Charlotte, NC, 1984—95; mem. Nat. Interreligious Svc. Bd. for Conscientious Objectors, 1991—98, treas., 1994—98, sec., 1997—98; mem. nat. coun. Fellowship of Reconciliation, 1985—88, 1996—97; mem. Study Commn. on Human Rights Bapt. World Alliance, 1995—2000, mem. Study Commn. on Freedom and Justice, 2000—05, mem. World Aid com., 2000—05; v.p. Am. Bapt. Chs. U.S.A., Valley Forge, 1976—77. Named to Hall of Fame, St. Paul Ctrl. H.S., 1993; recipient Dahlberg Peace award, Am. Bapt. Chs., 1991, Valiant Woman award, Ch. Women United, 1978, Meeker award, Ottawa U., 1995, Luke Mowbray Ecumenical award, Am. Bapt. Chs., 1999, Girls Dormitory at Ulaya Secondary Sch. in Tanzania named for Olive Marie Tiller. Baptist. Home: 283 Norman Dr Cranberry Township PA 16066-4235 Personal E-mail: olivet@zoominternet.net.

TILLEY, CAROLYN BITTNER, information scientist; b. Washington, July 29, 1947; d. Klaud Kay and Margaret Louise (Hanson) Bittner; m. Frederick Edwin Dudley, June 18, 1985 BS, Am. U., 1975; M.L.S., U. Md., 1976. With

NIH, 1965-71; statis. research asst. Health Manpower Edn., Bethesda, Md., 1971-72; tech. info. specialist Nat. Libr. Medicine, Bethesda, Md., 1972-81, head medlars (med. lit. analysis and retrieval sys.) mgmt. sect., 1981—2002, advisor for UMLS support, 2002. Mem. editl. bd. Med. Reference Svcs. Quar. Recipient Merit award NIH, 1984, Rogers award Nat. Libr. Medicine, 1991. Mem. Med. Libr. Assn., IEEE Libr. Adv. Coun. Presbyterian. Avocation: horseback riding. Office: Nat Libr Medicine 8600 Rockville Pike Bethesda MD 20894-0002

TILLEY, CHRISTINE LYNN, secondary school educator; b. St. Louis, La., Aug. 6, 1972; d. Carrel Dean and Pansy Joyce Dover; m. Lee John Tilley, Nov. 18, 2000; 1 child, Makenna Leigh. BS in Edn., Harris Stowe U., St. Louis, 1998; MBA, Lindenwood U., St. Charles, Mo., 2002. Tchr. Hazelwood Sch. Dist., Florissant, Mo., 1998—2005; quality assurance trainer MCI WorldCom, Weldon Spring, Mo., 2000—02; drama dir. Troy Buchanan H.S., Mo., 2005—. Speech and Drama scholar, Haris Stowe U., 1998. Office Phone: 636-699-5470. Business E-Mail: tilleyc@troy.k12.mo.us.

TILLEY, DIANE, elementary school educator; b. Pawnee City, Nebr., Jan. 27, 1955; d. Raymond and Kathleen Mitchell; m. Keith E. Tilley, June 12, 1976; children: Amy, Stacey, Brian. AA, Cloud County C.C., Concordia, Kans., 1975; BS, Kans. State U., Manhattan, 1988. Elem. tchr. St. Gregory's Sch., Marysville, Kans., 1988—95, Unified Sch. Dist. 380/Vermillion, Frankfort, Kans., 1995—. Treas. Frankfort Janes, 1980—; mem. Annunciation Altar Soc., Frankfort, 1978—. Mem.: Oreg. Trail Reading Assn., Kans. Reading Assn. Roman Catholic. Avocations: reading, walking, travel. Home: 114 W 9th Frankfort KS 66427 Office: Frankfort Schs 604 N Kansas Frankfort KS 66427

TILLEY, TANA MARIE, pharmaceutical executive; b. Athens, Ga., Dec. 28, 1955; d. Harry Sanford Pierce and Shirley Joanne Webster; m. Scott David Tilley, Aug. 28, 1977; children: Christopher Scott, Lauren Brooke. AD in Nursing, U. S.C., 1980, BS in Nursing cum laude, 1990. Asst. mgr. Brook's Fashions, 1975-78; staff nurse labor and delivery Spartanburg Regional Hosp., 1980-84, head nurse labor and delivery, 1984-89, staff nurse emergency rm., 1989-90; profl. sales rep. L'Nard & Assocs., 1989-90, TAP Pharm., 1990-92, regional hosp. liaison, 1992-95, dist. mgr., hosp. acct. execs., 1995-96, dist. mgr., 1996, 1997-2000, regional sales mgr., 2000—. Methodist. Home: 605 Shade Lake Ct Alpharetta GA 30004 Office: TAP Pharmaceuticals 1050 Crown Point Ste 1445 Atlanta GA 30338 E-mail: tanatilley@tap.com.

TILLMAN, DAISHA A., athletic trainer; d. Jennene C. Tillman. BS in Edn., U. Tenn., Knoxville, 2001; MS, U. Tenn., Chattanooga, 2004. Cert. athletic trainer Nat. Athletic Trainers' Assn., 2002. Athletic trainer Foxcroft Sch., Middleburg, Va., 2004—05; athletic trainer and asst. athletic dir. Empire H.S., Tucson, 2005—. Vol. worker Avon Walk for Breast Cancer, Washington, 2005. Mem.: Nat. Athletic Trainers Assn. Office: Empire HS 10701 E Mary Ann Cleveland Way Tucson AZ 85747 Office Phone: 520-762-3056. E-mail: tillmand@vail.k12.az.us.

TILLMAN, MERCIA V., musician; b. Chatham, Eng. Singer Sid Mills Band, London, 1932—39; club hostess, catering mgr. U.S. Mil. Officer Clubs, 1955—69; owner Mercia Tillman Wedding Cons. & Catering, Manassas, Va., 1972—73; dir. svcs. Innisbrook Resort, Tarpon Springs, Fla., 1975—76; columnist West Coast Publs., Largo, Fla., 1977—78; owner Mercia Tillman Prodns., 1996—. Author: (songs) Florida, My State of Dreams, 1996, Walk Around the Mall, 1996, Goodbye Little Princess, 1998, Hello, My Love, Hello, 2000; author and pub.: Little Gems, 2004. Named Ms. Fla. Sr. Am., 1996; recipient Vol. Woman of Yr., Soroptimist Internat., Fla., 1997, Blue Cross/Blue Shield Ageless Hero award, State of Fla., 1999, 2000, Inductee Sr. Hall of Fame, City of St. Petersburg, Fla., 2000, KFC Col.'s Way award, State of Fla., 2000. Mem.: WWII Meml. Soc. (charter), Ms. Sr. Am. Fla. Cameo Club. Personal E-mail: merciav.tillman@att.com.

TILLMAN, SHIRLEY, retired military officer; b. Poplarville, Miss., Mar. 23, 1950; d. L. S. Collins and Pairlee (Goines) Flowers. AB, Jones County Jr. Coll., 1970; BSc in Mgmt., Park Coll., 1990. Desert 300 Runner cert. U.S. Army, 1991. Enlisted US Army, 1972, advanced through grades to sgt. major, 1993; personnel records specialist Fitzsimmons Gen. Hosp., Denver, 1972—73; unit clk. Fitzsimmons Army Med. Ctr., Denver, 1973—79, 10th Co., Ft. Benning, Ga., 1979—80; various personnel positions US Army, various, 1980—94; divsn. sgt. major FORSCOM, Ft. McPherson, Ga., 1995—97; pers. sgt. major Ft. Rucker, Ala., 1997—2000; ret. US Army, 2000. Youth vol. various, 1972—. Avocations: painting, ceramics, fishing, hunting, sewing.

TILLMAN, VICKIE A., financial information company executive; BA in comm., U. Pitts., MPA in fin. With Standard & Poor's, 1977—, exec. mng. dir. pub. fin. ratings dept., exec. v.p. structured fin. ratings, 1994—99, exec. v.p., 1999—, mem. exec. com. Office: Standard & Poor's 55 Water St New York NY 10041

TILLOTSON, ELLEN KNIEBERG, communications educator; b. Bronx, N.Y., May 24, 1948; d. Fred H. Knieberg and Annette Ruth Schmier-Knieberg; m. Robert John Knieberg, Aug. 4, 1974; children: Lara Michole Tillotson-Joyal, Joshua Klinton. BS in Edn., U. Tex., Austin, 1970; MS in Comm., U. N.Tex., Denton, 1981. Cert. edn. State of Tex., 1970. Tchr. pub. speaking and theater arts Dallas Ind. Sch. Dist., 1970—75; tchr. U.S. history, pub. speaking and debate Lewisville Ind. Sch. Dist., Marcus H. S., Flower Mound, Tex., 1978—2006. Diversity trainer Lewisville Ind. Sch. dist., Tex., 1988—2001. V.p. in charge of mem. Congregation Kol ami, Flower Mound, Tex., 2000—03. Mem.: Nat. Forensic League (life Diamond coach 1992). Home: 2225 Pendleton Ln Flower Mound TX 75028 Office: Marcus High Sch 5707 Morriss Rd Flower Mound TX 75028 Office Phone: 972-539-1591 11109. Personal E-mail: lnt48@aol.com.

TILLOTSON, MARY, cable television host; BA in Journalism, U. Ala. Anchor WSB-Radio, Atlanta; news anchor WMAL-Radio, Washington; reporter, anchor WTTG-TV, Washington; congl. reporter Ind. TV News Assn., Washington; news anchor Mutual Radio Network, Washington; reporter CNN, 1981-85, White House corr., 1985-88, Capitol Hill corr., 1988-91; TV talk show host CNN & Co. Atlanta, 1991—. Nominee CableACE award for best talk show interviewer, 1996.

TILLY, JENNIFER, actress; b. Harbor City, Calif., Sept. 16, 1958; m. Sam Simon, 1984 (div., 1991). Grad., Stephens Coll., 1979. TV series include: Shaping Up, 1984, Key West, 1993, Out of Practice, 2005-; TV movies include: Heads, 1994; films include: No Small Affair, 1984, Moving Violations, 1985, He's My Girl, 1987, Inside Out, 1987, Rented Lips, 1988, High Spirits, 1988, Johnny Be Good, 1988, Remote Control, 1988, The Fabulous Baker Boys, 1989, Let It Ride, 1989, Far From Home, 1989, Scorchers, 1991, Shadow of the Wolf, 1992, Made in America, 1993, At Home With the Webbers, 1993, Double Cross, 1994, Bullets Over Broadway, 1994 (Academy award nomination best supporting actress 1994), The Getaway, 1994, The Pompatus of Love, 1996, Liar, Liar, 1996, House Arrest, 1996, Edie & Pen, 1996, Bound, 1996, American Strays, 1996, Bride of Chucky, 1998, Music From Another Room, 1998, The Muse, 1999, Goosed, 1999, Do Not Disturb, 1999, (voice) Bartok the Magnificent, 1999, (voice) Stuart Little, 1999, Play It to the Bone, 1999, Bruno, 2000, Cord, 2000, The Crew, 2000, The Cat's Meow, 2001, Monsters, Inc. (voice), 2001, Jericho Mansions, 2003, The Haunted Mansion, 2003, Home on the Range (voice), 2004, El Padrino, 2004, St. Ralph, 2004, Deluxe Combo Platter, 2004, Seed of Chucky, 2004, Bailey's Billion$, 2005, Lil' Pimp (voice), 2005, The Civilization of Maxwell Bright, 2005, Tideland, 2005. Achievements include won Ladies No-Limit Texas Hold'Em World Series of Poker Tournament, Las Vegas, 2005, World Poker Tour Ladies Night III, 2005. Home: Care Carrol Gettko 118 S Beverly Dr Beverly Hills CA 90212-3003

TIMCENKO, LYDIA TEODORA, secondary school educator, biochemist; b. Beograd, Yugoslavia, July 4, 1951; arrived in U.S., 1975; d. Teodor Pavle and Branislava (Spasojevic) Timcenko; m. Ghazi Youssef, June 16, 1980 (div. Oct. 1989); children: Ali Alexander Youssef, Kareem Misha Youssef; m. Peter Porzio, Mar. 11, 1996. BS in Chemistry, U. Belgrade, Yugoslavia, 1975; MS, Wayne State U., 1977, PhD, 1984. Grad. asst. Wayne State U., Detroit, 1976-78, 81-84, rsch. assoc., 1986—88, lectr. in chemistry, 1989; postdoctoral fellow Mich. Cancer Found., Detroit, 1985; postdoctoral fellow Sch. Medicine Wayne State U., 1986—88; lectr. in chemistry Lawrence Tech. U., Southfield, Mich., 1989, 90-91; biochemist Strohtech, Inc., Detroit, 1990—91; prof. chemistry Sussex County Coll., Newton, NJ, 1997—99; asst. prof. chemistry N.Y. Techol. Coll., City U. Bklyn., 1999—; sci. tchr. New Milford (NJ) H.S., 2002, Newton (N.J.) H.S., 2002—; adj. assoc. prof. organic chemistry Pace U., N.Y.C., 2004—05; tchr. chemistry, physics, biology Dwight Morrow H.S., Englewood, NJ, 2004—; sci. tchr. Jonathon Dayton H.S., Springfield, NJ, 2005—. Prin. investigator, rsch. scientist ICN Galenika Inst., Clin. Ctr. Serbia, Belgrade, 1991—96; rsch. scientist, mktg. cons. Huet Biol., Birmingham, Mich., 1987—91; adj. prof. chemistry Kean Coll.; adj. prof. dept. chemistry and chem. biology Stevens Inst. Tech., Castle Point on Hudson, Hoboken, NJ; adj. assoc. prof. organic chemistry Pace U., N.Y.C., 2002—04; adj. prof. in organic and biochemistry CUNY, 2004. Contbr. articles to profl. jours. Mem.: Am. Chem. Soc., Am. Soc. Microbiology, Phi Lambda Upsilon. Achievements include research in shigella toxin in shigella and E. coli; mitoch GPO in advenal cortex; liberation of labile sufur from ferredoxins; adhesion shigella to HCTH and HELA; localization of GST and GP in adrenal. Home: 306 State Route 94 Columbia NJ 07832-2771 Personal E-mail: ltim51@cs.com. Business E-Mail: pjp@eclipse.net.

TIMCO, MELANIE SUZANNE, science educator; b. Akron, Ohio, Mar. 22, 1979; d. Jack S. and Carol S. King; m. Joseph Justin King, July 15, 2000; children: Joseph Andrew, Jonathon James. BS in Edn., U. Akron, Ohio, 2000; MA in Edn., Baldwin Wallace Coll., Berea, Ohio, 2004. Tchr. Brunswick City Schs., Ohio, 2000—. Dist. curriculum adv. com. Bruncswick City Schs., Ohio, 2001, sci. curriculum adv. com., gade level assessment writing team, intervention assistance team; tchr. internship Cleve. Mus. of Natural History, 2005—05. Dir. Christian edn. Living Word Luth. Ch., Medina, Ohio, 2003—03. Recipient Tchr. of the Week award, WGAR radio sta., 2005; grant, Martha Holden Jennings Found., 2003. Home: 7347 Meadowhaven Dr Chippewa Lake OH 44215 Office: Willetts Mid Sch 1045 Hadcock Rd Brunswick OH 44212 Office Phone: 330-273-0489.

TIMKO, KATHLEEN, communications executive; BS in Mech. Engring., Viginia Poly. Inst.; MS in Computer Sci., Boston Univ. V.p. engring., COO, InterExchange Divsn. of IDT, 1998—2001; dir., telecom divsn., Chief Tech. Officer IDT, 2001—. Office: IDT 520 Broad St Newark NJ 07102 Office Fax: 973-482-3971.*

TIMLIN-SCALERA, REBECCA MARY, neuropsychologist; b. Hartford, Conn., Aug. 20, 1972; d. Thomas Francis and Rosalie Marie Timlin; m. Thomas Michael Scalera, June 11, 1999. BA in Psychology, Fairfield U., 1994; MS in Edn., Fordham U., 1997, profl. diploma in sch. psychology, 2001, PhD in counseling Psychology, 2001. Lic. psychologist Conn., NY, cert. neurofeedback provider. Bilingual vocat. counselor Easter Seals Rehab. Ctr., Hartford, Conn., 1994—95; extern psychologist Bellevue Hosp. Ctr., N.Y.C., 1998—99; intern psychologist NYU Med. Ctr.-Risk Inst., N.Y.C., 2000—01, fellow psychologist, 2001—02; neuropsychologist Neuropsychology Cons., LLC, Norwalk, Conn., 2002—. Cons. neuropsychologist Norwalk (Conn.) Hosp., 2002—, St. Joseph's Manor, Trumbull, Conn., 2002—; adj. prof. U. Conn., Stamford, 1999—2002, Fairfield (Conn.) U., Fairfield, 2000. Author: articles in field; contbr. articles to numerous mags., including Cosmopolitan. Vol. vocat. counselor Pacific House Men's Shelter, Stamford, 1999—2001. Mem.: APA, Conn. Psychol. Assn., Psi Chi (Regional Rsch. award 1997). Avocations: tennis, acting, travel, yoga, piano. Office: Neuropsychology Cons LLC 111 East Ave Ste 313 Norwalk CT 06851 Office Phone: 203-855-9691.

TIMM, NICOLETTE DEE, special education educator; b. West Allis, Wis., Feb. 1, 1969; d. Nicholas Tennis and Darlene Apalsch; m. Andrew P Timm, Aug. 15, 1992; children: Amanda Rae, Christian Micah. BS in Edn., U. of WI-Whitewater, 1991; MS in Edn., U. of Wi- Whitewater, 2004. Tchr. of students with severe emotional disturbance Milw. Pub. Schs., 1992—96; tchr. of students with emotional disabilities Greenfield Sch. Dist., Greenfield, Wis., 1997—2001; alternative sch. site leader CESA # 1, Wauwatosa, Wis., 2001—02; tchr. of students with emotional and learning disabilites Greendale Sch. Dist., Greendale, Wis., 2002—. Mentor for new tchrs. Greendale Sch. Dist., Greendale, Wis., 2005—. Sunday sch. tchr. St. Jacobi Ch., Greenfield, Wis. Mem.: Wis. Reading Assn. (assoc.). Right To Life Party. Lutheran. Avocations: tennis, volleyball, camping, travel. Office Phone: 414-423-2750. Personal E-mail: detimm@sbcglobal.net.

TIMMER, BARBARA, state agency administrator; b. Holland, Mich., Dec. 13, 1946; d. John Norman and Barbara Dee (Folensbee) T. BA, Hope Coll., Holland, Mich., 1969; JD, U. Mich., 1975. Bar: Mich. 1975, U.S. Supreme Ct. 1995. Assoc. McCrosky, Libner, VanLeuven, Muskegon, Mich., 1975-78; apptd. to Mich. Women Commn. by Gov., 1976-79; staff counsel subcom. commerce, consumer & monetary affairs Ho. Govt. Ops. Com., U.S. Ho. of Reps., 1979-82, 85-86; exec. v.p. NOW, 1982-84; legis. asst. to Rep. Geraldine Ferraro, 1984; atty. Office Gen. Counsel Fed. Home Loan Bank Bd., 1986-89; gen. counsel Com. on Banking, Fin. and Urban affairs U.S. Ho. of Reps., Washington, 1989-92; asst. gen. counsel, dir. govt. affairs ITT Corp., Washington, 1992-96; sr. v.p., dir. govt. rels. Home Savs. of Am., Irwindale, Calif., 1996-99; ptnr. Manatt, Phelps & Phillips, Washington, 1999—; gen. counsel MyPrimeTime, Inc., San Francisco, 2000-01; asst. sec. U.S. Senate, 2001—02, asst. sgt. at arms, 2003; chief info. officer Calif. Dept. Transp., Sacramento, 2003—. Mem. info. tech. coun. Women's Transp. Seminar, Calif., 2004—. Editor: Compliance With Lobbying Laws and Gift Rule Guide, 1996. Mem. Calif. State CIO Coun., 2004—05; bd. dirs. Women's High Tech Coalition. Named to Acad. of Women Achievers, YWCA, 1993; recipient Affordable Housing award, Nat. Assn. Real Estate Brokers, 1990, Disting. Alumni award, Hope Coll., 2003. Mem.: FBA (chair exec. coun. banking law com.), ABA (bus. law sect., electronic fin. svcs. subcom.), Bar of D.C., Mich. Bar Assn., Supreme Ct. Hist. Soc., Supreme Ct. Bar Assn., Women in Housing and Fin. (bd. dirs. 1992—94, gen. counsel 1994—98), Exchequer Club. Episcopalian. Office: 2629 Main St PMB 115 Santa Monica CA 90405 E-mail: btimmerdc@earthlink.net.

TIMMER, MARGARET LOUISE (PEG TIMMER), art educator; b. Osmond, Nebr., July 4, 1942; d. John Henry and Julia Adeline (Schilling) Borgmann; m. Charles B. Timmer, May 23, 1964 (div. June 1990); children: Jill Marie, Mark Jon. AA, N.E. Community Coll., Norfolk, Nebr., 1987; BA in Edn., K-12 art endorsement, Wayne (Nebr.) State U., 1988; MEd, Bank Street Coll./Parsons Sch. Design, N.Y.C., 1992. Cert. tchr., Nebr. Bookkeeper Goeres Electric, Osmond, 1960-61; tel. operator Northwestern Bell, Norfolk, 1961-64; with want advt. dept. Washington Post, 1964-65; saleswoman Jeannes Fashion Fabrics, Norfolk, 1970-72, Tripps, Norfolk, 1986-87; office and fin. mgr. Tim's Plumbing & Heating Inc., Norfolk, 1972-86; tchr. art Norfolk Cath. Schs., 1988—, mem. bd., 1985-88. Instr. art history N.E. Community Coll., 1992—; mem. youth art bd. Norfolk Art Ctr., 1988—, visual arts com.; del. Oxford (Eng.) Round Table, 2006. One-woman show Uptown Restaurant, Norfolk, 1993, Norfolk Art Ctr., 1996; exhibited in group shows Sioux City (Iowa) Art Ctr., 1988, Columbus (Nebr.) Art Ctr., 1993, Noyes Gallery, Lincoln Norfolk Art Ctr, Reeder Original Norfolk, 2003, 04; artist (novel) West With the Moon, 2006. Mem. choir St. Mary's Cath. Ch., Norfolk, 1991—; mem. Norfolk Community Choir, 1991; bd. dirs. Norfolk Community Concerts Assn., 1984-87; treas. Norfolk Cath. Booster Club, 1985-86; leader 4-H, Madison County, 1973-78; judge art show Laurel (Nebr.) Women's Club, 1988; presenter Oxofrd Roundtable, Eng., 2006. Named outstanding profl. vol. Norfolk Art Ctr., 1996; recipient Crystal Apple award Norfolk (Nebr.) C. of C., 1999. Mem. N.E. Nebr. Art Assn., Nebr. Art Edn. Assn. (3d place award 1988). Avocations: painting, gardening, reading, gourmet cooking, sewing. Home: Rte 2 Box 239 55380 Warnerville Dr Norfolk NE 68701-9758 Office: Norfolk Cath Schs 2300 Madison Ave Norfolk NE 68701-4456 Personal E-mail: ptimmer@yahoo.com.

TIMMERMAN, ANNE N., retired public relations executive; b. Evanston, Ill., May 10, 1910; d. Charles Edward and Agnes (Bateman) N.; m. John C. Timmerman, Sept. 30, 1933; 1 child, Jan LaTrobe. AB, U. S.C., 1930; postgrad., Hunter Coll., 1930-31, NYU, 1932-33. APR (Accredited Pub. Relations Practitioner). Editl. asst. Pictorial Rev. Mag., N.Y.C., 1930—32; copy asst. J. Walter Thompson Co., N.Y.C., 1932—33; sub editor Cosmopolitan Mag., N.Y.C., 1933—37; with Girl Scouts of U.S., N.Y.C., 1937—57, chief pub. rels. officer, 1945—57; dir. pub. info. edn. Nat. Recreation and Park Assn., 1957—66; spl. asst. gen. dir. Internat. Social Svc. Am. Br., N.Y.C., 1966—68; dir. devel. Nat. Accreditation Coun. for Agys. Serving Blind and Visually Handicapped, N.Y.C., 1969—78; pres. Timmerman & New Inc., Mamaroneck, NY, 1980—2001; ret., 2001. Cons. dept. pub. adminstrn. Baruch Coll., CUNY, 1987-94, Sch. Pub. Affairs, 1994-99. Author: Service For Givers, The Story of the National Information Bureau, 1983, Raise More Money for Your Nonprofit Organization, 1991; contbr. articles to profl. jours. Bd. dirs. Mamaroneck (N.Y.) United Fund, 1963-64; chair nominating com. LWV, Mamaroneck, 1988; warden emerita St. Thomas' Episc. Ch., Mamaroneck. Recipient Marzella Garland award for outstanding achievement in promotion of improved housing conditions in Mamaroneck Village, 1995. Mem. Pub. Rels. Soc. Am. (bd. dirs. N.Y. chpt. 1958-72), Women Execs. Pub. Rels. (sec. 1962-63), Assn. Fundraising Profls. (bd. dirs. Greater N.Y. chpt. 1978-84), Phi Beta Kappa. Democrat.

TIMMERMAN, DORA MAE, community volunteer, art advocate; b. Wichita, Mar. 28, 1931; d. George M. and Effie (Stevens) Branham; m. Lewin E. Timmerman, Oct. 30, 1949 (dec. 1990); children: Curt E., Kyle A Student, Wichita State U., Kans., 1948—50, student, 1973—75. Legal sec., Wichita, 1948—55; mgr. Wichita Art Mus. Shop, 1977—81; owner, mgr. Rubbing Renaissance, Wichita, 1981—. Co-chair Greater Wichita Save Outdoor Sculpture Project Smithsonian Instn.'s Nat. Mus. Am. Art, Nat. Inst. Conservation Cultural Property, 1992-97, chair, 1997—; presenter workshops on brass and stone rubbing, lectr. and program presenter mus., coll., libr. and sch. orgns.; lectr. and tour guide for Wichita's outdoor sculpture and pub. art; dir. Unified Sch. Dist. 259 Interactive Sculpture Project Wichita, 1995— Pres., bd. dirs. Wichita Bar Assn. Aux., 1961-62, Kos Harris PTA, 1963-64, Twentieth Century Cornelias, 1966-68, Met. Arts Bd., 1980, Lands and Peoples Club, 1982-83; bd. dirs. Wichita Arts Coun., Wichita State U. Fine Arts Alliance, Project Beauty, Inc., 1968-99, women's divsn. Inst. Logopedics, YWCA, UNICEF adv. coun., 1985; founding mem. Wichita Pub. Arts Task Force, 1988-90, Wichita Pub. Art Adv. Bd., 1990-2000, chmn. 1992; chmn. Friends Soldiers & Sailors Civil War Monument; charter and exec. bd. mem. Friends Campbell Castle, 1993-95; exec. bd. mem. Sedgwick County Cmty. Image Task Force, 1993-2000; pres., vol. svcs. bd. Wichita Art Mus., 1975-77, travel chair, trustee, 1999-2000; active Wichita Sculptors Guild, 2000—, Wichita Ctr. for Arts, Wichita-Sedgwick County Arts and Humanities Coun.; mem. outdoor sculpture com. Edwin A. Ulrich Mus. Wichita State U., 2001—; Wichita-Sedgwick County Hist. Mus., Project Concern Internat., 1978-85, various youth and charitable orgns.; chair Friends Wichita Art Mus., 1999-2000; bd. dirs. Wichita Greyhound Charities, Inc.; mem. mus. policy com. Mid-Am. All-Indian Ctr., 2000, chmn. plane crazy artists support team, street sculptures 100th Anniversary Celebrations, 2002, 06; bd. dirs. Wichita Arts Coun., 2005-. Recipient many awards from: Project Beauty, Inc., Kans. State Hist. Soc., City of Wichita Pub. Art Adv. Bd., Smithsonian SOS! Achievement award, Recognition award Sedgwick County Bd. Commrs., Arts Advocate award Wichita Sedgwick County Arts and Humanities Coun., 2003, Friend Edn. award United Tchrs. Wichita, 2003 Mem. Friends Botanica (charter), Stock Markettes Investment Club, Present Day Club, PEO Presbyterian. Avocations: calligraphy, reading, bridge, travel, art. Home: 6606 Magill St Wichita KS 67206-1344

TIMMINS, MARYANNE, real estate accountant, educator; b. Hackensack, N.J., Feb. 15, 1975; d. Paul Langerfeld and Loretta Timmins. BS, Rutgers U., 1997. CPA Am. Inst. CPA's. Personal banking rep. PNC Bank, Hackensack, 1996-97, personal banking rep. supr. Lyndhurst, N.J., 1997-98; auditor Valley Nat. Bank, Wayne, N.J., 1998-99, Summit Bancorp, Ridgefield Park, N.J., 1999-2000; fin. instr. Ctr. Fin. Tng., Clifton, N.J., 1999—; sr. acctg. assoc. Prudential Real Estate Investors, Parsippanny, NJ, 2000—. Religious instr. Queen of Peace Ch., North Arlington, N.J., 1997—. Samuel and Marcella S. Geltman scholar Rutgers U., 1997. Mem. AICPA, N.J. Soc. CPAs. Avocations: computers, step aerobics, reading, gardening. Home: 74 Birchwood Dr North Arlington NJ 07031-5130 Office: Prudential Investment Mgmt 8 Campus Dr 4th Fl Parsippany NJ 07054-4409 E-mail: maryanne.timmins@prudential.com.

TIMMONS, EVELYN DEERING, pharmacist; b. Durango, Colo., Sept. 29, 1926; d. Claude Elliot and Evelyn Allen (Gooch) Deering; m. Richard Palmer Timmons, Oct. 4, 1952 (div. 1968); children: Roderick Deering, Steven Palmer. BS in Chemistry and Pharmacy cum laude, U. Colo., 1948. Chief pharmacist Meml. Hosp., Phoenix, 1950—54; libr. med. lit. rsch. Hoffman-LaRoche, Inc., Nutley, NJ, 1956—57; staff pharmacist St. Joseph's Hosp., Phoenix, 1958—60; relief mgr. various ind. apothecaries, Phoenix, 1960—68; asst. then mgr., dir. compounding Proff. Pharmacies, Inc., Phoenix, 1968—72; mgr. Mt. View Pharmacy, 1972—76, owner/mgr., 1976—; pres. Ariz. Apothecaries, Ltd., 1976—. Mem. profl. adv. bd., bereavement counselor Hospice of Valley, 1983-96; mem. profl. adv. bd. Upjohn Health Care and Svcs., Phoenix, 1984-86; bd. dirs. Am. coun. on Pharm. Edn., Chgo., 1986-92, v.p., 1988, 89, treas., 1990-91; mem. expert adv. bd. compounding pharms. U.S. Pharmacoepial Conv., 1992—; preceptor U. Ariz., 1965—, Midwestern Coll. Pharmacy, Ariz. Campus, 1998—; chief cons. bioidentical hormone replacement therapy and safety; disease mgmt. specialist; lectr. on NHRT and BHRT. Mem. edit. adv. bd. Internat. Jour. Pharm. Compounding, 1997-2000; author poetry; contbr. articles to profl. jours. Mem. Scottsdale (Ariz.) Fedn. Rep. Women, 1963-68; various other offices Rep. Fedn.; mem. platform com. State of Ariz., Nat. Rep. Conv., 1964; asst. sec. Young Rep. Nat. Fedn., 1963-65; active county and state Rep. coms.; adv. bd. Internat. Jour. of Pharm. Compounding, 1996-2001; fin. chmn. Internat. Leadership Symposium: Women in Pharmacy, London, 1987; treas. Leadership Internat. Women Pharmacy, 1991-2001; mem. founders circle Gladys Taylor McGarey Med. Found., 1996—. Named Outstanding Young Rep. of Yr., Nat. Fedn. Young Reps., 1965, Preceptor of Yr., U. Ariz./Syntex, 1984; recipient Disting. Pub. Svc. award Maricopa County Med. Soc., 1962, Disting. Alumni award Wasatch Acad., 1982, Career Achievement award Kappa Epsilon, 1983, Leadership and Achievement award Upjohn Labs., 1985-86, Outstanding Achievement in Profession award Merck, Sharp & Dohme, 1986, award of Merit Kappa Epsilon, 1988, Disting. Coloradoan award U. Colo., 1989, Vanguard award Kappa Epsilon, 1991, Unicorn award Kappa Epsilon, 1993, Compounding Pharmacist of the Yr. award Profl. Compounding Corp. of Am., 1994, 96, Healing Heart award Gladys Taylor McGarey Found., 1998, 50 Yr. Certificate U. Colo., 2000. Fellow Am. Coll. of Apothecaries (v.p. 1982-83, pres. elect 1983-84, pres. 1984-85, chmn. bd. dirs. 1985-86, adv. coun. 1986-92, Chmn. of Yr. 1980-81, Victor H. Morganroth award 1985, J. Leon Lascoff award 1990), Internat. Acad. of Compounding Pharmacists (bd. dirs. 1993-2000, hon. life fellow 2005); mem. Ariz. Soc. of Hosp. Pharmacists, Am. Pharm. Assn. (Daniel B. Smith award 1990), Ariz. Pharmacy Assn. (Svc. to Pharmacy award 1976, Pharmacist of Yr. 1981, Bowl of Hygeia 1989, 1st Innovative Pharmacy award 1994, 50 Yr. Practice and Membership award 2001), Maricopa County Pharmacy Assn. (pres. 1977, Svc. to Pharmacy award 1977), Am. Soc. of Hosp. Pharmacists, Am. Aircraft Owners and Pilots Assn., Air Safety Found., Nat. Assn. of Registered Parliamentarians, Civinettes (pres. Scottsdale chpt. 1960-61), Kappa Epsilon (recipient Career Achievement award 1986, Vanguard award 1991, Unicorn award 1993). Avocations: flying, skiing, swimming, hiking, writing. Office: Mt View Pharmacy 10565 N Tatum Blvd Ste B-118 Scottsdale AZ 85253-1095 Office Phone: 480-948-7065. Personal E-mail: evelyntimmons@cox.net.

TIMMONS, ROBBIE, news anchor; m. Jim Brandstatter. Grad., Ohio State U. Anchor WILX-TV, Lansing, Mich., 1972—76, WJBK-TV, Detroit, 1976—82, WXYZ-TV, Detroit, 1982—. Recipient numerous Emmy awards, Silver Cir. award, Nat. Acad. TV Arts and Scis., 1998, Most Powerful Woman in Mich., 2002. Achievements include being the first woman in the US to anchor TV news at 6 & 11pm. Office: WXYZ-TV 20777 W Ten Mile Rd Southfield MI 48037 E-mail: rtimmons@wxyz.com.

TIMMONS, SHARON L., retired elementary school educator; b. South Kansas City, Mo., July 25, 1949; d. Clyde George and Sarah Ethyl (Thrift) Manley; m. Joseph D. Timmons, June 6, 1970; children: Stacia, Matt. BSE, U. Kans., 1972; MA, U. Mo., Kansas City, 1980. Cert. elem., jr. high tchr., Mo; elem. tchr., Kans. Team tchr. elem. Loretto Acad., Kansas City, Mo., 1976—80; team tchr. lead med. sch. and block schedule programs, 8th grade, Ctr. Sch. Dist. 58, Kansas City, Mo., 1980—94; ret., 1994. Author: (Title II grants) For Indivdualized Math Program, Kansas City Rep. for Scientific Literacy. Mem. Sigma Kappa.

TIMMS, MICHELE, retired professional basketball player; b. Australia, June 28, 1965; Guard Australia's Women's Nat. Basketball League - Bulleen Boomers, 1984-85, Nunawading Spectres, 1985, Lotus Munchen, Germany, 1989-90, Perth Breakers, Australia, 1991-92, Basket Firenze, Italy, 1993-94, Sydney Flames, Australia, 1995, WTV Wuppertal, Germany, 1995-96, Phoenix Mercury, 1997—2001. Named WNBL Player of Yr., 1995, 96. Avocations: tennis, golf.

TIMPA, VICKI ANN, government health program administrator; b. Houston, Aug. 20, 1955; d. Edmund Burke and Helen Kanosky Huber; m. John Gerrard Fewel, May 27, 2000; children: Julie Marie Fecht, Anthony Alan. BSN, U. Tex., 1977; MSN in Edn. Adminstrn. and Rsch., Tex. Woman's U., 1990, advanced nurse practitioner degree, 1993. Cert. ACLS, domestic prepardness for biol.-radiol.-chem. VA, neurosurg. cert., cert. prevention inst. instr.; critical care nurse; cert. Covey trainer, appraiser. Team leader cardiopulmonary shock trauma emergency ctr., nurse Ben Taub Emergency Ctr., Harris County Hosp. Dist., Houston, 1977; emergency rm. and GI lab staff nurse Mesquite Hosp., Tex., 1978—80; nurse Baylor U. Med. Ctr. Hosp. Sys., Dallas, 1980—90; rsch. nurse coord. VA, Dallas, 1990—93; dept. of edn. mgr. Meth. Hosps. of Dallas, 1993; patient health edn. coord. VA North Tex. Health Care Sys., Dallas, 1993—; peritoneal dialysis nurse Parkland Meml. Hosp., Dallas County Hosp. Dist. Coord. nat. rsch. studies VA, Dallas, 1990—92, nat. liaison for Nat. Ctr. for Health Promotion and Disease Prevention, Durham, NC, 2002—05, congl. legis. cons., Washington, 2000—; ICU mock code creator and trainer Baylor U. Hosp. Sys., Dallas, 1980—90; cardiopulmonary resuscitation instr. Am. Heart Assn., Dallas, 1989—94; Plain Lang. Act cons. Exec. Br., Washington, 1995—. Contbr. articles to profl. jours. V.p. Miracle Wish Found., 2006. Named Most Valuable Person, VA Rsch., 1992; named one of Great 100 Nurses award, 1997; recipient Unsung Hero award, VA, 1993. Mem.: Sigma Theta Tau (fin. and fund raising com. 1993—2001, Academic Excellence and Rsch. Excellence awards 1993, 2001, Nat. Plank Owner award 2005). Roman Catholic. Avocations: travel, antiques and collectibles appraising. Home: 1307 High Ridge Dr Duncanville TX 75137 Office: VA 4500 S Lancaster Rd (141P) Dallas TX 75216 Office Phone: 972-572-5525. Home Fax: 972-572-5525. Personal E-mail: vickiern7@netzero.net. Business E-Mail: vicki.timpa@med.va.gov.

TIMPANO, ANNE, museum director, art historian; b. Osaka, Japan, June 17, 1950; d. A.J. and Margaret (Smith) T. BA, Coll. William and Mary, 1972; MA, George Washington U., 1983. Program mgmt. asst. Nat. Mus. Am. Art, Washington, 1977-86; dir. The Columbus (Ga.) Mus., 1986-93, DAAP Galleries, U. Cin., 1993—. Grant reviewer Inst. Mus. Svcs., Washington, 1988—, Ga. Coun. for Arts, Atlanta, 1988-91. Mem. 1992 Quincentenary Commn., Columbus, 1987-92. Recipient David Lloyd Kreeger award George Washington U., 1980. Mem. Am. Assn. Mus. (surveyor mus. assessment program), Assn. of Coll. and Univ. Mus. and Galleries, Coll. Art Assn., Midwest Mus. Conf. Roman Catholic. Home: 85 Pleasant Ridge Ave Fort Mitchell KY 41017-2861 Office: U Cin PO Box 210016 Cincinnati OH 45221-0016 E-mail: anne.timpano@uc.edu.

TIMS, JANE MOORE, art educator; b. Millington, Tenn., July 4, 1955; d. Robert Dent Moore and Nancy Blake Ponder; m. Robert Austin Tims, June 6, 1980; children: Chelsea, Shana. BSE, Ark. State U., 1976. Art tchr. Trumann Pub. Schs., Ark., 1977—. Ednl. officer CAP, Jonesboro, Ark., 1986—93. Mem.: Nat. Edn. Assn., Ark. Edn. Assn. Avocations: gardening, reading. Home: 1616 Alonzo St Jonesboro AR 72401 Personal E-mail: jtims@abslogic.com.

TINCHER, ANNE HARRIS, elementary school educator; d. H. Hoyt and Marlyn Harris; m. Stephen Scott Tincher, July 26, 1980; children: Michael, Christopher. BA, U. Ala., 1978, MA, 1979. Cert. tchr. elem. sch. Ala. Dept. Edn., 1979. Tchr. elem. sch. Huntsville (Ala.) City Schs., 1978—2004, reading coach, 2004—. Tutor in field; mem. textbook adoption com. State of Ala.; acad. coach Ala. Reading Initiative, 2005—06. Mem.: Kappa Delta Pi. Home: 1401 Owens Drive Huntsville AL 35801 Office Phone: 256-428-7020.

TINER, KATHY ANN, special education educator; b. Valley City, N.D., May 18, 1949; d. James Frederick and Karen (Knecht) Abrahamson. BS, Moorhead State U., 1971; MA, Adams State U., 1986; postgrad., Fielding Inst. Spl. edn. tchr. Sch. Dist. 90, Melrose, Minn., 1971-73, Sch. Dist. 60, Pueblo, Colo., 1973—. Cons. Curriculum Writing Team, Pueblo, 1980; co-chairperson Spl. Edn. Art Fair, Pueblo, 1987; mem. Colo. State Adv. Bd. Spl. Edn., 1980-81. Author: A Guide to Local Resources for People with Developmental Disabilities and their Families, 1990, Guide for Professionals, 1990. Coach Spl. Olympics, 1974-89; chairperson St. Jude Bike-A-Thon, Beulah, Colo., 1983. Named Tchr. of Yr. Pueblo Assn. Retarded Citizens, 1984; recipient tchr. recognition Am. Assn. Mental Deficiency, 1985. Mem. NEA, Coun. Exceptional Children, Assn. Devel. Disabilities (v.p. 1991, Tchr. of Yr. 1989), Colo. Edn. Assn. Avocations: snow and water skiing, bicycling. Home: 1029 E 8th Ave Apt 702 Denver CO 80218-3345

TINGEY, JOANNA, secondary school educator, mathematician; d. Nolland and Betty Tingey. BA, Brigham Young U., Provo, Utah, 2004. Cert. tchr. math Utah State Office Edn., 2004. Office specialist Dept. Chemistry and Biochemistry Brigham Young U., Provo, Utah, 2001—04; tchr. math. San Juan H.S., Blanding, Utah, 2004—. Inst. pres. LDS Ch., Blanding, Utah, 2005—06. Mem.: Utah Edn. Assn. Avocations: fly fishing, travel.

TINGLER, MARLENE JOHANNSEN, music educator, insurance agent; b. St. Louis, Aug. 22, 1948; d. Otto August and Charlotte (Sachse) Johannsen; m. Charles E. Tingler, June 19, 1971; 1 child, Matthew Johannsen. BS in Edn., William Jewell Coll., 1970; studied with Max Rabinovitsj, 1970—73; postgrad., Ctrl. Mo. State U., U. Mo., Kansas City. Cert. ins. Mo.; tchr. Mo. Pvt. violin tchr., St. Louis, Kansas City, 1971—; orch. dir., head dept. Berkeley (Mo.) Sch. Dist., 1971—73, Luth. Sch. Sys., Kansas City, 1989—2002; orch. dir. Parkway Schs., St. Louis, 1974—75; office mgr. Pa. Life Ins., Kansas City, 1976—84; mgr. Liberty (Mo.) Symphony Orch., 1977—85, BTI Ins. Co., Kansas City, 1985—88; v.p. Harry Loves Bess, Kansas City, 1999—. Instr. William Jewell Coll., Liberty, 1978—79; world judge, coach State Bd. Odyssey of the Mind. Musician: Jacksonville (Ill.) Symphony, St. Joseph (Mo.) Symphony, St. Louis Philharm. Recipient Outstanding Svc. award, Liberty Symphony, Hickman Mills, Mo. Sch. Dist. Mem.: Music Educators Nat. Conf., Delta Zeta (music dir. 1968—71), Sigma Alpha Iota (sec. 1968—71). Lutheran. Avocations: computers, travel. Personal E-mail: tingler207@aol.com.

TINGSTRUM, NANCY ASH, dietitian; d. Howard Wesley and Ruth Hamilton Ash; m. James Frederick Tingstrum, Oct. 22, 1988; 1 child, Michelle Martin Monts; m. Ralph K Martin (div.); 1 child, Noelle Lisa Vail. BS, Penn State U., 1964; MBA, George Mason U., 1988. Registered Dietitian Am. Dietitic Assn., 1972. Hosp. dietician RI Hosp., 1965—66; budget analyst Dept. of Def. Pentagon, Wash., DC, 1982—84, program analyst, 1995—2001, dept. team chief, program analyst, 2001—02; ret., 2002. Recipient Civilian Superior Svc. award, Dept. Army, Pentagon, Achievement medal for Commander's Award. Avocations: reading, exercise, gardening, quilting.

TINKELMAN, JOAN, lawyer; b. St. Louis, Apr. 25, 1952; d. Philip and Elizabeth (Cohen) I.; m. David Tinkelman, Jan. 24, 1999. Student, Fleming Coll., Lugano, Switzerland, 1969-70, U. Colo., 1970-71; BS, RN, U. Mo., 1974; BS/RN, St. Louis U., 1976, JD cum laude, 1980. Bar: Mo. 1981, U.S. Dist. Ct. (ea. dist.) Mo. 1981, U.S. Ct. Appeals 1981, Ill. 1981, Colo. 1984, U.S. Dist. Ct. Colo. 1984. RN St. Louis Children's Hosp., 1976-77; assoc. Shepherd, Sandberg & Phoenix, St. Louis, 1980-82; risk mgr. Luth. Med. Ctr., Wheat Ridge, Colo., 1983-91; v.p. risk mgmt. Rose Health Care Systems, Denver, 1991—96; dir. risk mgmt. Denver Health and Hosp. Authority, 1997—99; ind. practice, 1999—. Named Outstanding Young Woman Am., 1984. Mem. ABA, Mo. Bar Assn., Colo. Bar Assn., Denver Bar Assn., Am. Acad. Hosp. Attys., Am. Soc. Healthcare Risk Mgmt., Colo. Health Lawyers Assn. (bd. dirs. 1984-85), Colo. Hosp. Assn. Risk Mgrs. (founder, pres. 1985). Jewish. Office Phone: 303-466-6744.

TINKLEPAUGH, VALERIE MARIE, physical education educator; b. Reading, Pa., Jan. 20, 1981; d. Terrel Alden Tinklepaugh and Susan Beth Fisher. BS, Tex. Tech U., Lubbock, 2003; MS, Bloomsburg U., Pa., 2004; postgrad., Villanova U., Pa., 2004—. Asst. athletic trainer Bloomsburg U., 2003—04, Villanova U., 2004—; adj. prof. Ea. U., St. Davids, Pa., 2005—. Summer camp mgr. Gatorade, Villanova, 2005—. Mem.: Nat. Strength and Conditioning Assn., Nat. Athletic Trainers Assn. Office: Villanova U 800 Lancaster Nevin Fieldhouse Villanova PA 19085

TINNER, FRANZISKA PAULA, social worker, artist, apparel designer, educator, entrepreneur; b. Zurich, Switzerland, Sept. 18, 1944; arrived in U.S., 1968; d. Siegfried Albin and Gertrude Emilie (Sigg) Maier; m. Rolf Christian Tinner, Dec. 19, 1976; 1 child, Eric Francis. Student, U. Del., 1973-74, Va. Commonwealth U., 1974; BFA, U. Tenn., 1984; BA of Arts, U. Ark., Little Rock, 1991, postgrad. Lic. real estate broker. Dominican nun, Ilanz, Switzerland, 1961-67; waitress London, 1967-68; governess Bryn Mawr, Pa., 1969; saleswoman, 1970-90; model, 1983; artist, designer Made For You, Kerrville, Tex. and Milw., 1984-90; realtor Century 21, Milw., 1987-91; owner, entrepreneur Exquisite Treasures by Swiss Miss, 1998—. Intern Birch Community Ctr., 1992-93. Designer softsculptor doll Texas Cactus Blossom, 1984; author: (poems) The Gang (recorded by Nat. Libr. of Poetry), 1996, Cry Out for Help, 1998 (pres. choice award 1999), Springtime, 2000 (contest finalist). Ombudsman Action 10 Consumerline, Knoxville, Tenn., 1983—84; foster mother Powhatan, Va., 1976—81; vol. ARC, Knoxville, 1979; Va. Home for Permanently Disabled, 1975; vol., counselor Youth ofr Understanding-Fgn. Exch., Powhatan, 1975—77; tchr. pager/archiving host, mentor, area expert on Am. On Line, 1992—98; vol. Interactive Ednl. Svcs., Ark., 1999—; vol. infant intensive care Ark. Children's Hosp., 1999—; vol. Online Internet Emotional/Psych Support BB (WWW), 1999—. Recipient Art Display award U. Knoxville, 1983, Prof. Choice of Yr. award, 1983, Outstanding Achievemnt award TV Channel 10, Knoxville, 1984, 1st place award for paintings and crafts State Fair Va., Tenn., 1st place award Nat. Dollmakers, 1985, finalist Best of Coll. Photography, 1991, Achievement award Coll. Scholar af Am., 1991, Achievement cert. in technique of anger therapy, 1993, Achievement cert. in crisis response team tng., 1994, Achievement cert. vol. work tchg. AOL. Mem. NASW, NAFE, Milw. Bd. Realtors, Homemakers Club (pres. 1979-80), Newcomers Club, Bowlers Club (v.p.), Internat. Platform Assn. Avocations: art, cooking, teaching, writing, helping disabled and mentally ill. E-mail: elfqueenz@aol.com.

TINNEY, HARLE HOPE HANSON, museum administrator; b. Providence, Apr. 15, 1941; d. Frederick Charles and Grace Alma (Williamson) Hanson; m. Donald Harold Tinney, Dec. 2, 1960. Student, Albion Coll., 1959—60, Brown U., 1960. Tour guide Belcourt Castle, Newport, RI, 1959-60, mus. ptnr., owner, 1972—; stained glass crafter St. Luke Studio, Providence, 1961-89; exec. dir. Royal Arts Found. at Belcourt Castle, Newport, 2000—. Sec. founder Royal Arts Found., Newport, 1969—, events planner, 1984—, treas., 1996—; donor svcs. Mosaic Club, Newport, 1984-2000, Shake-A-Leg, Newport, 1980-1989, Newport Music Festival, 1964—; ch. organist St. Declan Chapel, 1998-2001. Mem. Sovereign Order Knights Hospitaller St. John Jerusalem (asst. editor newsletter 1998—), Royal Arts Found. (exec. dir. 2002-). Avocations: music, cello, church organ, antique restoration. Home: Belcourt Castle 657 Bellevue Ave Newport RI 02840-4280 Office Phone: 401-846-0669. E-mail: royalarts@aol.com.

TINSLEY, ADRIAN, former college president; b. NYC, July 6, 1937; d. Theodore A. and Mary Ethel (White) Tinsley. AB, Bryn Mawr Coll., 1958; MA, U. Wash., 1962; PhD, Cornell U., 1969. Asst. prof. English U. Md., College Park, 1968-72; dean William James Coll., Grand Valley State, Allendale, Mich., 1972-80; assoc. vice chancellor acad. affairs Minn. State U., St. Paul, 1982-85; exec. v.p., provost Glassboro (N.J.) State Coll., 1985-89; pres. Bridgewater (Mass.) State Coll., 1989—2002, pres. emerita, 2002—. Coord. women higher edn. adminstrn. Bryn Mawr & Hers Summer Inst., Bryn Mawr, Pa., 1977—. Editor: Women in Higher Education Administration, 1984. Office: Boyden Hall Bridgewater State Coll Bridgewater MA 02325-0001 Office Phone: 508-697-9656. Business E-Mail: atinsley@bridgew.edu.

TINSLEY, BARBARA SHER, historian, educator, writer; b. Gloversville, N.Y., Apr. 29, 1938; d. Max and Ruth Ida (Shpritzer) Sher; m. William Earl Tinsley, Dec. 30, 1959; children: Claire Jennifer, Yve Hillary. BA, U. Wis., Milw., 1959; MA, U. Calif., Berkeley, 1960; PhD, Stanford U., 1983. Instr. English and French Stephens Coll., Columbia, Mo., 1963-64; asst. prof. European history San Jose (Calif.) State U., 1969-71; prof. European history Foothill Coll., Los Altos Hills, Calif., 1974—; lectr. in history Santa Clara (Calif.) U., 1977-79. Lectr. in western culture Stanford (Calif.) U., 1985, vis. scholar, 1989—. Author: History and Polemics in the French Reformation: Florimond de Raemond Defender of the Church, 1992, Reconstructing Western Civilization: Irreverent Essays on Antiquity, 2005; co-author (with Lewis W. Spitz) Johann Sturm on Education, 1995, Pierre Bayle's Reformation Conscience and Criticism on the Eve of the Enlightenment, 2001; contbr. articles to profl. jours. Woodrow Wilson fellow U. Calif.-Berkeley, 1959-60; NDEA fellow Mich. State U. and Emory U., 1961, 63; Jessie Speyer fellow Stanford U., 1965-67; Fulbright fellow U. Strasbourg, 1983-84; NEH fellow Duke U., 1988, Princeton, 1995, U. N.C., 2001. Mem. Am. Hist. Assn., Sixteenth Century Studies Conf., YMCA. Democrat. Avocations: sewing, piano, gardening, swimming, painting. Home: 15550 Glen Una Dr Los Gatos CA 95030-2936 Office Phone: 408-354-0917.

TINSLEY, JENNIFER, ballerina; b. Dallas; Student, Brookhaven CC, Nancy Schoeffenburg Ballet Sch., Dallas Ballet, Dallas Met. Ballet; student (summer), Sch. Am. Ballet, 1983—88, student, 1988—90. Apprentice N.Y.C. Ballet, 1990—91, mem. corps de ballet, 1991—99, soloist, 1999—. Guest tchr. N.Y., Tex.; guest performer Vt., Portugal, Argentina, Eng. Featured dancer (CD-ROM) Ballet is Fun by Bill Atkinson, dancer (PBS broadcast) Balanchine Celebration, Live from Lincoln Ctr: Swan Lake, (films) The Nutcracker, 1993, Accent on the Offbeat, (ballets) Jewels, Ballo Della Regina, Chaconne, La Sonnambula, Fearful Symmetries, Jeu De Cartes, Slavonic Dances, Polyphonia, many others. Office: NYC Ballet NY State Theatre 20 Lincoln Ctr Plz New York NY 10023-6913

TINSLEY, KAREN MCCOY, psychology professor; b. Cleve., Ohio, Feb. 18, 1963; d. Hester Pendleton Mccoy; children: Kianna Jeanne, Michael Alexander, Matthew Christopher. PhD, U. Va., Charlottesville, 1991. Psychology prof. Southeastern La. U., Hammond, 1991—92, Pa. State U. Beaver, Monaca, 1993—94, Geneva Coll., Beaver Falls, Pa., Ferrum Coll., Va., 1995—98; chair dept. psychology Guilford Coll., Greensboro, NC, 1998—. Chair cultural pluralism com. Guilford Coll., Greensboro, 1999—2000, chair African Am. studies, 2000—04; dir., founder St. Paul After Sch. Acad., Greensboro; spkr. in field. Mentor, tutor St. Paul After Sch. Acad., Greensboro, 2001—02; com. mem. Ea. Star Scholarship Com., Greensboro. Named Club Adv. of Yr., Ferrum Coll., 1998; recipient Faculty Empowerment award, Guilford Coll., 2003. Baptist. Avocations: travel, music, bicycling. Home: 6309 Rye Mill Ct Greensboro NC 27410 Office: Guilford Coll 5800 W Friendly Ave Greensboro NC 27410 Office Phone: 336-316-2318. Business E-Mail: ktinsley@guilford.edu.

TINSLEY, NIKKI LEE RUSH, federal agency administrator; b. Apr. 23, 1948; BS in Bus. Admistrn., Ohio State U./Va. Commonwealth U., 1970; MS in Bus. Admistrn., U. Colo./U. No. Colo., 1981. Ednl. program asst. Office of Edn., Wash., 1971; bookstore mgr. U.S. Govt. Printing Office, Denver, 1971-76; auditor U.S. GAO, Denver, 1976-82; supervisory auditor Dept. of Interior, Minerals Mgmt. Svc., Lakewood, Colo., 1982-90; divsnl. insp. gen. EPA, Kansas City, Kans., 1990—95, dep. insp. gen. Washington, 1995-96, acting insp. gen., 1997-98, insp. gen., 1998—. Chair human resources com. Pres.'s Coun. on Integrity and Efficiency, 2002—04; mem. Adv. Coun. on Govt. Auditing Stds., Comptroller Gen.'s Domestic Working Group. Recipient Bronze medal for commendable svc. EPA, 1995. Mem.: Colo. Soc. CPAs, Inst. Internal Auditors, Assn. Govt. Accts. (Disting. Fed. Leadership award 2004). Office: EPA MC 2410 1200 Pennsylvania Ave NW Washington DC 20460-0001 Office Phone: 202-566-0847. E-mail: tinsley.nikki@epa.gov.

TINSLEY, SHELIA C., nurse; b. Roanoke, Va., Nov. 8, 1955; d. Irvin Daniel and Mary Davis (Flippen) Childress; m. Carl Terrie Tinsley, Sept. 4, 1976; children: Carl, De Anthony. ADN, CHRV Coll. Health Sci., Roanoke, 1989; BSN, Va. Commonwealth U., 1993; MEdn. in Health Edn. RN, Va., 2000; cert. CPR instr; cert. Health Edn. Specialist. Staff nurse Friendship Manor Nursing Home, Roanoke, Meml. Hosp., Roanoke, Lewis Gale Clinic, Salem, Va.; coord. maternal infant care Roanoke City Health Dept., 1989-92; with Roanoke Meml. Hospice, 1992-93; nurse pediat. Va. Dept. Health Roanoke City Health Dept., Pub. Health Nurse Svc. Public Health Sr., 1994—. Recipient Award for Nursing Excellence, 1989; Med. Found. scholar. Mem. ANA, Roanoke Valley Black Nursing Assn. Home: 6622 Hartman Ct Roanoke VA 24019-3186

TINSMAN-SCHAFFER, PATRICIA JOAN, secondary school educator, artist; b. Lower Merion Twp., Pa., May 27, 1959; d. James Herbert and Joan Cummings (Grimes) Tinsman; m. Wayne Kenneth Schaffer, Mar. 26, 1988; children: Lynley, Olivia; stepchildren: Tyler, Christina, Nathan. BFA, U. Pa., Kutztown, 1984, cert. in art edn., 1985, MA in Edn., 1993. Sign painter Kutztown Folk Festival, 1979-88, craftsman, 1980-95; mid. sch. art tchr. Allentown Sch. Dist., Pa., 1985—, mid. sch. conflict mgmt. coord. Pa., 1991—, student conflict mgr., tng. specialist, 1993—, conflict mgmt. coord. Frances D. Raub Mid. Sch., 1985—2003, adult conflict mgmt. tng. specialist, 1994—, conflict mgmt. coord. L.E. Dieruff HS, 2003—. Dir., supr. children's art area Mayfair, Allentown, 1987-92; spkr. in field. Chmn. evangelism com. Pennsburg (Pa.) UCC, 1993-95; dir. Project Sch. Link, Allentown, 1994-96. Mem. Pa. State Edn. Assn., Pa. Art Edn. Assn. (Outstanding Mid. Level Art Educator of Yr. 1996), Allentown Edn. Assn. (v.p. mid. schs. 1995—, Outstanding Tchr. award 1996). Office: Allentown Sch Dist 31 S Penn St Allentown PA 18102-5489

TIPPING, SHARON RUTLEDGE, elementary school educator; b. Odessa, Tex., Jan. 24, 1948; d. L.D. Rutledge and Hazel (Simpson) Smithee; m. Eldon Tipping Jr., Dec. 21, 1968; 1 child, Teresa Lynn. BA magna cum laude, Baylor U., 1969; MEd, Tex. A&M U., 1973. Cert. provisional elem. tchr., profl. counselor, provisional lang. and learning disabilities. Tchr. Oakdale Elem. Sch., Springlake, N.C., 1969-70, Hamilton Park Elem. Sch., Richardson Ind. Sch. Dist., Dallas, 1979-90, Brentfield Elem. Sch., Richardson Ind. Sch. Dist., Dallas, 1990-92; ednl. cons. Jostens Learning, 1992-94, nat. curriculum and instrn. specialist, 1994-97, regional mktg. mgr., 1997—2000; acct. exec. Compass Learning, 2000—03, Istation, 2003—04, regional v.p. sales, 2005—. Cons. REgion X Svc. Ctr., 1988-90. Chmn. Mother's March of Dimes, Richardson, Tex., 1976, 77, 78; vol. caseworker Family Outreach, Richardson, 1975-79; pres. Hamilton Park Elem. PTA. Mem. ASCD, Nat. Staff Devel. Coun., Nat. Coun. Tchrs. Math., Assn. Tex. Profl. Educators, N. Tex. Reading Coun., Richardson Edn. Assn., Phi Delta Kappa. Home and Office: 3700 Nightingale Ct Plano TX 75093-7525 Office: 800 E Campbell Rd Richardson TX 75080 Office Phone: 972-643-3458.

TIPPITT, RHONDA CLEMENT, library director; b. Chgo., Aug. 18, 1967; d. Thomas Earl and Lucindia McCoy Clement; children: Logan Heath, Caroline Lucindia. AAS, Phillips Jr. Coll., Huntsville, Ala., 1992; B in Sci. Family and Consumer Sciences Edn. summa cum laude, U. Tenn., Martin, 2001; M in Edn. Libr. Sci., Union U., 2004. Houseparent Bapt. Children's Home, Brentwood, Tenn., 1987—89, United Meth. Children's Home, Huntsville, Ala., 1989—92; ins. data entry clk. The Doctor's Office, Huntsville, 1992—94; office mgr. Benton County Cable, Camden, Tenn., 1995—97; libr. dir., head libr. Benton County Pub. Libr., Camden, 2002—. Presenter in field. Mem. Bus. and Profl. Women, Camden, Tenn., 1995—2004, Ret. Sr. Vol. Program, Camden, 2002—05. Grantee, Tenn. State Libr., 2003—04; scholar, U. Tenn., Martin, 1998—2001. Mem.: Tenn. Libr. Assn. Republican. Baptist. Avocations: travel, interior decorating, antiques, hiking. Home: 1490 Natchez Trace Rd Camden TN 38320 Office: Benton County Pub Libr 121 S Forrest Ave Camden TN 38320 Office Phone: 731-584-4772. Office Fax: 731-584-1098. Personal E-mail: rhoctipp@yahoo.com. Business E-Mail: rhondatippitt@bellsouth.net.

TIPTON, JENNIFER, lighting designer; b. Columbus, Ohio, Sept. 11, 1937; d. Samuel Ridley and Isabel (Hanson) T. BA, Cornell U., 1958. Artist in residence Nat. Theater Artist Residency Program at Wooster Group funded by the PEW Charitable Trusts, 1994; assoc. prof. lighting Yale U. Sch. of Drama. Work includes: Paul Taylor Dance Co., Twyla Tharp and Dancers, Am. Ballet Theater, Jerome Robbins, Dana Reitz, Guthrie Theater, Hartford Stage Co., Murder Among Friends, 1975, Rex, For Colored Girls Who Consider Suicide When the Rainbow is Enuf (Drama Desk award), The Landscape of the Body, Newman Theatre, The Cherry Orchard (Drama Desk award, Tony award 1977), Agamemnon, Beaumont Theatre, Happy End, Martin Beck Theatre, Agamemnon, Delacorte Theatre, 1977, Museum, Public Theatre, Runaways, Public Theatre and Plymouth Theatre, All's Well That Ends Well, Taming of the Shrew, Delacorte Theatre, After the Season, Academy Festival Theatre, A Month in the Country, Williamstown Theatre Festival, Mikhail Baryshnikov's Don Quixote, Am. Ballet Theatre, Drinks Before Dinner, Public Theatre, The Pirates of Penzance, Public Theatre, 1978, Lunch Hour, 1980, Billy Bishop Goes to War, 1980, The Sea Gull, 1980, Sophisticated Ladies, 1981, The Wake of Jamie Foster, 1982, Uncle Vanya, 1983, Orgasmo Adulto Escapes from the Zoo, 1983, Baby with the Bathwater, 1984, Hurlyburly, 1984, Whoopi Goldberg, 1984, Endgame, 1984, Jerome Robbins' Broadway (Tony award 1989), A Moon for the Misbegotten, 2005 (Conn. Critic Cir. award, outstanding lighting design, 2005). Recipient Chgo.'s Joseph Jefferson award, 1976-77, Obie award 1979, Brandeis U. Creative Arts medal in dance, 1982, Mpls. Kudos award 1983, N.Y. Bessie award 1984, (with Dana Reitz), 1987, Guggenheim fellowship, 1986-87, Am. Theater Wing award 1989, Commonwealth award in dramatic arts, 1989, Lawrence Olivier award, 1991, Dance Mag. award, 1991, NEA Disting. Theater Artist award 1991. Home: 11 W 18th St New York NY 10011-4603

TIPTON, MELANIE CAROL, music educator; b. Jacksonville, Ark., May 13, 1972; d. John David and M. Carol Odell; m. Adam Robert Tipton, June 11, 1994. B of Vocal Music, Ouachita Bapt. U., 1996; postgrad., So. Bapt. Theol. Sem., 1996, postgrad., 2000—01. Piano/vocal coach Bader Music Village, Louisville, 1996—2000; music min. Midlane Park Bapt. Ch., Louisville, 1999—2001; music tchr. Graceland Bapt. Sch., New Albany, Ind., 2000—01, Christian Acad. Louisville, 2002—. Owner Melanie's Melodies, Louisville, 2001—03. Composer: (songs) David's Song, 2002. Recipient Tchr. award, Star Sys., 2002. Mem.: Ky. Music Educators Assn. (superior/excellent ratings 2003), Music Educators Nat. Corp. Southern Baptist. Avocations: scrapbooks, walking, gardening.

TIRABASSI, LINDA SUE, secondary school educator; b. Niagara Falls, N.Y., Aug. 31, 1950; d. Alfred Angelo and Carmela Dolores T. AA, Niagara County Cmty. Coll., Niagara Falls, 1970; BS, SUNY (Brockport), 1972; MS, Calif. State U. (Fullerton), 1992. Tchr. St. Edward's Sch., Corona, Calif., 1977-81; tchr., pub. rels. Notre Dame H.S., Riverside, Calif., 1981-88; tchr. Ramona H.S., Riverside, Calif., 1988—. Conflict resolution coord. Ramona H.S., 1994—. Recipient Tchr. Yr., YWCA, 2002. Mem. Calif. Assn. Peer Programs. Office: Ramona HS 7675 Magnolia Ave Riverside CA 92504-3627 Office Phone: 951-352-8429.

TIRELLI, MARIA DEL CARMEN S., retired realtor; b. Rio Grande, PR, Apr. 8, 1919; d. Carmelo Siaca Pacheco and Luisa Guzman Berrios; m. Francesco Tirelli, Dec. 20, 1947 (dec. Oct. 2002); children: Rosina, Frank, Marie, Angelo. BS, U. P.R., 1941; MS, U. Chgo., 1944; JD, InterAm. U., 1978. Cert. home econs. tchr., N.Y., Spanish tchr., N.Y.C.; registered dietitian/nutritionist; cert. realtor, counselor. Home econs. tchr. Dept. Edn., San Juan, PR, 1941-43; nutritionist USDA, San Juan, 1944-45, Dept. Health, San Juan, 1946-47; sch. lunch supr. III & IV Dept. Edn., San Juan, 1948-55; dietitian Good Samaritan Hosp., West Islip, NY, 1961-62; food svc. dir. N.Y. Dept. Mental Hygiene, Islip, NY, 1964-74; sch. lunch dir. North Babylon (N.Y.) Schs., 1964-74; realtor C-21, Watson, Coldwell Banker, Brandon, Fla., 1982-00; realtor, assoc. Coldwell Banker, Brandon, 1985—95; ret., 2000. Pres. P.R. Dietetic Assn., San Juan, 1951-52, L.I. (N.Y.) Dietetic Assn., 1973; cons. dietitian various nursing homes, L.I., 1973-75; ad honorem lectr. U. P.R., Rio Piedras, 1955. Contbr. articles to profl. jours. Mem. Nativity Ch. Chorale, 1982-00. Recipient scholarship U. P.R., San Juan, 1943, grant U. Chgo., 1943. Mem. Nat. Assn. Realtors, Fla. Assn. Realtors., Tampa Board of Realtors (realtor assoc., mem. legis. title com. 1983), Legion of Mary (Brandon, sec. 1983-91). Republican. Roman Catholic. Avocations: music, piano, chorale, gardening. Home: 2130 Durant Rd Valrico FL 33594

TIRELLO, MARIA EUGENIA DUKE, artist; b. San Salvador, El Salvador, Sept. 27, 1947; arrived in U.S., 1980, permanent resident, 1993, naturalized, U.S., 2000; d. Carlos Alberto Duke Tomasino and Ana Maria (Ruiz-Flores) Duke; m. Mario Ernesto Tirello Hill, Nov. 7, 1970; 1 child, Juan Antonio Tirello Duke. Diploma in computer programming, Charron Williams Coll., 1983; diploma exec. sec., Elinor Smith, 1986; studied art with Victor Manuel Rodriguez Preza, El Salvador; studied with some of the finest nat. and internat. artists, U.S. Lic. real estate 1992. Lectr. in field. Artist (one-woman shows) Common Market, Miami, 1990, Sky Gallery, 1996, Nicaragua C. of C. Gala, Miami, 2002; Exhibited in group shows at Met. Mus., Coral Gables, 1989, Wirtz Gallery, South Miami, 1989, 1993, 1996, 2001, One Brickell Sq. Lobby Gallery, Miami, 1989, 1992, 1993, 1994, 1996, 1997, 1998, 2000, 2001, 2003, Pioneer Mus. Depot, Fla. City, 1990, 1991, 1992, Coral Gables Fed., 1993, Am. Assn. Salvadorenos Profls., Miami, 1994, 1996, 1997, Am. Arts Profl. League, Miami, 1994, 1996, 1999, Heim Am. Gallery, Fisher Island, 1995, Galeria 1-2-3, El Salvador, 1995, Coconut Grove Conv. Ctr., 1995, Mus. Sci. and Space Transit Planetarium, Miami, 1995—2001, Fla. Mus. Hispanics and Latin Am. Art, Miami, 1995 (Honorable Mention, 1997), 1997, SunTrust Bank Lobby Gallery, Miami, 1996, 1997, 1999, 2000, Art Expo N.Y., 1996, Astoria Fine Art Gallery, Coral Gables, Fla., 1996, One Datra Ctr. Lobby Gallery, Miami, 1996, Royal Poncian Fiesta, Miami, 1996 (Honorable Mention, 1996), Union Planters Bank Lobb Gallery, Miami, 1996, Ctr. Art Gallery Alvaro Gomez Hurtado, Miami, 1997, IV Congreso Continental de la Mujer Americana, Miami, 1997, Salon de Pintoras Latinoamericanas, Miami, 1997, Europe Gallery, Miami, 1998—99, South Dade Regional Libr., Miami, 1998, Brickell Key Day, Miami, 2000 (3d pl., 2000), Lift Ctr. Gallery, Miami, 2000 (Honorable Mention, 2000), Bet Breira Gallery, Miami, 2000 (Honorable Mention, 2000, 2002), 2001, 2002, Ann Kolb Nature Ctr., Hollywood, Fla., Represented in permanent collections SunTrust Bank, Miami, Merrill Lynch, Miami, Arimar Corp., Fla., BANCORP, El Salvador, BanCo, El Salvador, Industrias Cristal, El Salvador, M.A. Lima Assoc. S.A. de C.V., El Salvador. Mem.: Waterworks, Gold Coast Watercolor Soc., Fla. Profl. Artists Guild (Merit award 2000, SunTrust Bank Purchase award 2001, hon. mention Amerkan award 2003, Honorable Mention 2003), Fla. Watercolor Soc., Miami Watercolor Soc. (3d place 1995, Merrill Lynch Purchase award 1995, Salis Internat. award 1998, Color Q, Inc. award 1999, Best in Show 2001, Outstanding award 2001, Merit award 2002). Roman Catholic. Avocations: art, music, movies. E-mail: MTirello@aol.com.

TIRONE, BARBARA JEAN, retired health insurance administrator; b. Celina, Ohio, Nov. 19, 1943; d. Vincent James and Theresa Barbara (Goettermoeller) G. BA, Miami U., 1965; MBA, U. Chgo., 1977. Asst. dir. for internat. trade State of Ill., Chgo., Brussels, Hongkong and Sao Paulo, Brazil, 1973-76; dir. office of mgmt. and planning Office Human Devel. Svcs., Chgo., 1976-79; dep. regional adminstr. Health Care Financing Adminstrn., Chgo., 1979-82, regional adminstr., 1982-87, dir. bur. of prog. ops. Balt., 1987-92; dir. health stds. and quality bur. Health Care Fin. Adminstrn., Balt., 1992-96; pres., CEO AdminaStar, Inc., Indpls., 1996-2001; ret., 2002. Recipient Presdl. Disting. Rank award 1988, 94, Presdl. Meritorious Rank award 1987, 92; named Fed. Exec. of Yr., 1987. Home: 11212 Appaloosa Dr Reisterstown MD 21136 Office Phone: 410-833-5570. Personal E-mail: bgagel@comcast.net.

TIRSCHWELL-NEWBY, KATHY ANN, events production company executive; b. Hudson, Wis., Jan. 8, 1961; d. Walter Haskell and Doris Hilda (Dornfeld) T. DDS (hon.), Roth/Williams Ctr., 1993. Traffic dir. Sta. KRKC, King City, Calif., 1978-79; office mgr. Cable TV of King City/Greenfield, 1979-82; lead cashier Del Webb's High Sierra Hotel & Casino, Lake Tahoe, Nev., 1982-84; acctg. analyst Hyatt Hotels, Burlinghame, Calif., 1984-87; v.p., owner Computer Diagnostic Info Inc., Burlingame, 1987-93; exec. dir. Roth/Williams Ctr., Burlingame, 1990-93; event support mgr. Stuart Rental Co., Sunnyvale, Calif., 1994-96, Cheskin & Masten/ImageNet, Redwood Shores, Calif., 1996; adminstr. Bayshore Animal Hosp., San Mateo, Calif., 1996-97; event sales mgr. Stuart Rental Co., Sunnyvale, 1997-2000; prodr. sports and corp. events E2k/Olmstead Prodns., Palo Alto, Calif., 2000—04; event cons. Classic Party Rentals, Burlingame, Calif., 2004—. Pres. Jr. Fairboard, Salinas Valley Fair, King City, Calif., 1979-80; adv. bd. San Francisco State U. Dept. Recreation and Leisure Studies. Mem.: Internat. Spl. Events Soc. (pres. 2003—05, Attitude award 2005). Office: Classic Party Rentals 1635 Rollins Rd Burlingame CA 94010 Office Phone: 650-652-0300. Business E-Mail: knewby@classicpartyrentals.com.

TISCH, WILMA STEIN, foundation administrator; b. Asbury Park, N.J., June 25, 1927; d. Joseph F. and Rose E. (Liebesman) Stein; m. Laurence A. Tisch (dec. 2003); children: Andrew H., Daniel R., James S., Thomas J. BS, Skidmore Coll., Saratoga Springs, N.Y., 1948, LHD (hon.), 1990, Mt. Sinai Med. Sch., 1990, CUNY, 1990, NYU, 2006. Trustee Blythedal Children's Hosp., Valhalla, N.Y., 1964-71, Fedn. of Jewish Philanthropies, N.Y.C., 1971—, pres., 1980-83. Trustee Coun. Jewish Fedns., N.Y.C., 1980-87, Jewish Communal Fund, N.Y.C., Am. Jewish Joint Distribution Com., N.Y., 1986-94, United Way N.Y.C., 1986—, Skidmore Coll., 1994—, Carnegie Corp., N.Y.C., 1994-98, WNYC Radio, N.Y.C., 1984—, pres., 1988-93; trustee coun. advisors Hunter Coll. Sch. Social Work, N.Y.C., 1986-97. Mem. N.Y. State Gov.'s Select Com. on Capital Health Care Needs, N.Y.C., 1983, Mayor's Transition Coun., N.Y.C., 1993, Carnegie Coun. on Adolescent Devel., N.Y.C., 1987—97; co-chmn. Task Force on Youth Devel. and Cmty. Programs, N.Y.C., 1990—94; chmn. transition adv. team Parks and Recreation Cultural Affairs, N.Y.C., 1993; mem. policy bd. Sept. 11th Fund, 2001—04. Recipient Louis D. Marshall medal Jewish Theol. Sem., 1980; Milender fellow Brandeis U., 1982; named one of Forbes Richest Americans, 2006. Fellow: Am. Acad. Arts & Sciences. Jewish.

TISCHHAUSER, KATHERINE JETTER, music educator, cellist; b. Raleigh, NC, May 25, 1968; d. Frederick Robert and Glenda Bagwell Jetter; m. Andreas P. Tischhauser, Oct. 13, 1996. BM in Cello Performance, E. Carolina U., 1991, BA in Applied Math., 1991; M in Cello Performance, Fla. State U., 1993, D in Cello Performance, 2002. Tchg. asst. Fla. State U., Tallahassee, 1991—96; assoc. prof. cello & music theory Ft. Lewis Coll., Durango, Colo., 1996—. Dir. student honors orch. Ft. Lewis Coll., 2002, 05. Musician: (prin. cellist) Showcase Chamber Orch., 1996—, San Juan Symphony, 1996—, (recital soloist) Ft. Lewis Coll., 1996—2003, (ensemble) Amical, 2001—, (performer) Formula 151 Band. Mem.: ISB, ASTA (state sec. 1999—2005), Phi Kappa Phi (life). Avocations: gardening, sewing, cooking, bicycling. Office: Ft Lewis Coll Music Dept 1000 Rim Dr Durango CO 81301 Business E-Mail: jetter_k@fortlewis.edu.

TISCHLER, JUDITH BLANCHE, retired publishing executive; b. N.Y.C., May 14, 1933; d. Max and Anna (Drescher) Zucker; m. Alfred Tischler, Dec. 14, 1958; children: Marva, Mira, Gary. MA, CCNY, 1975; PhD, Jewish Theol. Sem., 1989. Editor, dir. Transcontinental Music Publs., N.Y.C., 1981—2000. Prof. music Jewish Theol. Sem., H.L. Miller Cantorial Sch. French hornist various concerts worldwide, 1952-71. Office: HL Miller Cantonal Sch Jewish Theol Sem of Am 3080 Broadway New York NY 10027 E-mail: tisch33@netvision.net.il, judithtischler@hotmail.com.

TISCH SUSSMAN, LAURIE, art gallery director; d. Preston Robert Tisch; 2 children from previous marriage. B, Duke U.; MFA, Catholic U. Chmn. Ctr. Arts Edn. Inc., Children's Mus. Manhattan; pres. Laurie Tisch Found.; cmmnr. NY City Dept. Cultural Affairs. Sec. Whitney Mus. Am. Art, bd. dir.; dir. Mattel Entertainment, FAO Schwartz. Mem.: NY State Coun. Arts. Mailing: c/o Whitney Mus Am Art 945 Madison Ave New York NY 10021

TISCORNIA, ANA MARIA, artist, educator, writer; b. Montevideo, Uruguay, Nov. 24, 1951; arrived in U.S., 1991; d. Carlos Tiscornia and Hilda Gascue. BArch, Inst. Vazquez-Acevedo, Montevideo, 1971. Prof. visual art Sch. Printmaking, Montevideo, 1984—87; prof. graphic expression Sch. Arch. U. de la Republica, Montevideo, 1985—89; prof. art U. de los Andes, Bogota, Colombia, 1992; adj. prof. SUNY, New Paltz, 1996—98, Jersey City U., 2000—02, SUNY, Old Westbury, 2000—03, asst. prof., 2003—06; dir. Amelie A. Wallace Gallery, 2005—06. Dir. Club de Grabado de Montevideo, 1985—87; art editor Point of Contact, A Publication on Visual and Verbal Arts, Syracuse, NY, 2002—06. Contbr. articles to profl. jours. Recipient 1st prize, Fellowship Paul Cezanne, France/Uruguay, 1986, Hon. prize, II Havana (Cuba) Biennial, 1986; grantee, Pollock-Krasner Found., N.Y.C., 2000; fellowship, N.Y. Found. for the Arts, 2004. Home: 720 Greenwich St Apt 10G New York NY 10014 Office: SUNY Old Westbury Campus Ctr F-101 Old Westbury NY 11568 Office Phone: 516-876-3056. E-mail: anatiscornia@earthlink.net.

TISHMAN, LYNN P., psychoanalyst, psychologist; b. Yonkers, NY, Apr. 3, 1951; d. Neal and Olga Petrucci; m. Peter V. Tishman, May 31, 1992; stepchildren: Steven, Linda, Anita. AAS in Acctg., Westchester CC, 1971; BA summa cum laude in Psychology, Hunter Coll., 1993; MSW, LCSW with honors, Hunter Sch. Social Work, 1995; student in Clin. Psychology, Columbia U. Cert. massage therapist Swedish Inst., NY, 1980, biofeedback therapist BCIA, 1985, adult and child cert. psychoanalyst Psychoanalytic Inst. Postgrad. Ctr., NYC, 2002, cert. psychoanalyst, psychotherapist, and researcher. Child devel. specialist and rschr. Pacella Parent Child Ctr., NY Psychoanalytic Inst. Mem.: NASW, APA, Assn. Applied Psychophysiology and Biofeedback, Postgrad. Psychoanalytic Soc. Avocations: running, weightlifting, bicycling, sailing.

TISINGER, CATHERINE ANNE, retired history professor; b. Winchester, Va., Apr. 6, 1936; d. Richard Martin and Irma Regina (Ohl) T. BA, Coll. Wooster, 1958; MA, U. Pa., 1962, PhD, 1970; LLD (hon.), Coll. of Elms, 1985. Provost Callison Coll., U. of Pacific, Stockton, Calif., 1971—72; v.p. Met. State U., St. Paul, 1972—75; v.p. academic affairs Southwest State U., Minn., 1975—77, interim pres., 1976—77; mem. gov.'s office staff State of Minn., 1979; dir. Ctr. for Econ. Edn., R.I. Coll., Providence, 1979—80; v.p. acad. affairs Ctrl. Mo. State U., Warrensburg, 1980—84; pres. North Adams State Coll., Mass., 1984—91; dean arts and scis. Shenandoah U., Winchester, Va., 1991—2001, prof. history and econs., 2001—04, disting. prof., 2001—, prof. emerita, 2004—, acting dean continuing edn., 2006. Cons. North Cen. Assn. Colls. and Schs., 1980-84, New Eng. Assn. Schs. and Colls., 1978-79, 85-91, Minn. Acad. Family Physicians, 1973-77; mem. adv. bd. First Agrl. Bank, North Adams, 1985-91; pres. No. Berkshire Cooperating Colls., 1986-91; v.p. Coll. Consortium for Internat. Studies, 1989-90; cons. Inst. for Experiential Learning, 2002—; dean arts and scis. Zayed U., UAE, 2001-02. V.p. Med. Simulation Found., 1986-88; cons. historian, curator Shenandoah Ctr. for Heritage and Environment, 2002—, bd. dirs. 2004—; bd. dirs. Williamstown Concerts, 1988-91, Shawnee coun. Girl Scouts U.S.A., 1992-93, Parents' Choice, 1997-98, Parents Guide to Children's Media, Inc., 1998-2004, pres. 2004—. Mem. No. Berkshire C. of C. (bd. dirs. 1984-89, v.p. 1986-89). Avocations: fiber and textile arts, photography. Office: Shenandoah U 1460 University Dr Winchester VA 22601-5195 E-mail: ctisinge@su.edu.

TISON-BRAUN, MICHELINE LUCIE, French language educator; b. Arras, France, Apr. 7, 1913; came to U.S., 1947, naturalized, 1964; d. Eugène and Lucie (Duchat) T.; m. Lev Braun, Apr. 1, 1948. Agregée ès lettres, 1937, Docteur ès lettres, 1972. Prof. French Education Nationale, London, 1938-47; translator BBC, London, 1941-45; translator, précis writer UN, N.Y.C., 1947-54; prof. French Lycée N.Y., City U. N.Y. Grad. Ctr. and Hunter Coll., 1961-81. Author: La Crise de l'Humanisme, vol. I, 1957, rev. edit., 1963, vol. II, 1968, Nathalie Sarraute la Recherche de l'Authenticitè, 1971, Dada et le Surréalisme, 1975, Tristan Tzara, 1977, Poetique du Paysage, 1980, L'Introvable Origine, 1981, Ce Monstre Incomparable, A. Malraux et le Probleme de la Personnalite (Prix Jouvenel), 1982, Marquerite Duras, 1983, Le Moi dècapitè Lang, 1989, L'Esprit Createur, 1995. Decorated Palmes Academiques; Guggenheim fellow, 1978-79 Mem. MLA, Am. Assn. Tchrs. French, Pen Club, Gens de Lettres, Société d'Histoire littéraire de la France.

TITLE, GAIL MIGDAL, lawyer; b. Waldenberg, Germany; AB, Wellesley Coll.; JD, U. Calif., Berkeley. Bar: Calif. Mng. ptnr. Katten Muchin Rosenman, LLP, LA. Adj. prof. law Loyola U.; head Nat. Entertainment Litigation Practice; former trustee Ctr. for Law in the Pub. Interest, 1976-96; exec. com., bd. Pub. Counsel Law Ctr. & Constl. Rights Found; co-chair USDC Magistrate Selection Com., ctrl. Calif. Named a Woman of Distinction, Women's Lawyer's Assn. LA. Mem. ABA (litigation sect., forum com. entertainment), Assn. Bus. Trial Lawyers, State Bar Calif. (standing com. pub. interest law 1976—), Beverly Hills Bar Assn., LA Copyright Soc. (trustee). Office: Katten Muchin Rosenman LLP 2029 Century Park E Los Angeles CA 90067 Office Phone: 310-788-4727. Office Fax: 310-712-8427. Business E-Mail: gail.title@kattenlaw.com.

TITUS, ALBERTA CHRISTINE, secondary school educator; b. Pecos, Tex., Jan. 16, 1951; d. Grady Ralph and Cora Christine Poe; children: Beverly Christine Tomek, Bruce Earl Scull, Brenda Cathleen Hermes. BS in Edn., Sul Ross State U., Alpine Tex., 1974. Cert. tchr. math., English and spl. edn. Tex. Edn. Agy., 1974. Math tchr. Balmorhea Ind. Sch. Dist., Tex., Pecos-Barstow Ind. Sch. Dist., Bloomington Ind. Sch. Dist., Aransas Counry Ind. Sch. Dist., Sacred Heart Cath. Sch., Victoria Ind. Sch. Dist., 1974—99; math. tchr. Del Valle Ind. Sch. Dist., Tex., 2000—. Mem.: Alpha Chi. Home: 1392 Hwy 71 E #19 Bastrop TX 78602 Office: Del Valle ISD 5201 Ross Rd Del Valle TX 78617 Office Phone: 512-386-3200. Office Fax: 512-386-3275. Personal E-mail: albertat@ev1.net. E-mail: atitus@del-valle.k12.tx.us.

TITUS, DONNA G., psychologist; b. Louisville, Oct. 27, 1945; d. Edward John Gnadinger and Helen Elizabeth Pitan; m. Thomas George Titus; children: Meredith E., Lauren K. BA, Ky. So. Coll., 1967; MA, U. Louisville, 1973; PsyD, Spalding U., 1991. Lic. clin. psychologist Ky. Bd. Psychology, 1991. Psychologist Psychological & Edn. Ctr., Clemson, SC, 1972—73; staff psychologist Forensic Psychiatry, Louisville, 1973—75; sr. therapist Seven Counties Svcs., Louisville, 1979—89, clin. supr., 1989—91; licensed psychologist Ctr. State Hosp., Louisville, 1991—2000; pvt. practice Louisville, 1991—. Cons. St. Matthew's Assoc. Ministries, Louisville, 1991—92, Options for Individuals, Louisville, 1993—97; contract forensic cons. Ctr. State Hosp., Louisville, 2000—03; registrant Coun. for the Nat. Register of Health Svc. Providers in Psychology, 1996—. Contbr. articles to profl. jours. Recipient Departmental Psychology award, Ky. So. Coll., 1967, Sr. Ann Horrigan Disting. Grad. Psychology award, Spalding U., 1991. Mem.: APA, Ky. Psychology Assn., Nat. Mus. Women in Arts (charter mem. 1992). United Ch. Christ. Achievements include being one of three clinicians whom developed a system-wide treatment program in family violence for Seven Counties Centers Community Mental Health Services beginning in 1984. Avocations: book collecting, travel. Office: Donna G Titus PsyD 3906A Dupont Square S Louisville KY 40207 Office Phone: 502-896-1850.

TITUS, JULIA YEREMINA, Slavic languages educator, translator; b. Moscow, Apr. 12, 1968; came to U.S., 1992; d. Oleg Georgievich and Galina Alexandrovna (Gorbatych) Yeremin; m. Donald Webster Titus, Dec. 28, 1991. BA, Moscow State U., 1992, MFA, 1990; MA, Yale U., 1999. Translator, interpreter Am.-Soviet Theatre Initiative, Moscow, 1989-90, Soyuzmultfilm animation studio, Moscow, 1990-91; freelance translator Random House, N.Y.C., spring 1992, Yale U. Press, New Haven, summer 1992; lectr. Slavic langs., sr. lectr. Yale U., New Haven, 1992—. Mem. lang. com. dept. Slavic langs. Yale U., New Haven, 1992—. Contbr. papers to profl. jours. Mem. Am. Assn. Tchrs. of Slavic and Ea. European Langs., Am. Coun. Teaching Fgn. Langs. Avocations: reading, travel, gardening. Home: 131 George St East Haven CT 06512-4727 Office: Yale Univ Dept Slavic Langs 2710 Hall of Grad Studies PO Box 208236 New Haven CT 06520-8236 E-mail: julia.titus@yale.edu.*

TITUS, KAREN J., small business owner; b. Sharon, Pa., Mar. 7, 1947; d. Cordino and Loretta Longiotti; m. Michael J. Titus, June 10, 1960; children: Lisa C., Marci M. Titus Hall, Ethan M., Adam C. Computer specilist Bellview Elem. Sch., Ashland, Oreg., 1987—2003; prin., owner Electric Beach, Ashland, Oreg., 2003—. Home: 2319 Ranch Rd Ashland OR 97520 Office: Electric Beach 1253 Siskiyou Blvd Ashland OR 97520 Office Phone: 541-552-0857. Business E-Mail: mktitus@charter.net.

TITUS-DILLON, PAULINE YVONNE, associate dean academic affairs, medical educator; b. Petersfield, Jamaica, Jan. 1, 1938; came to U.S., 1954; d. Ernest H. Titus and Vera I. (Tate) Harvey; m. Owen C. Dillon, Nov. 29, 1963. Student, Pratt Inst., 1954-57; BS in Chemistry summa cum laude, Howard U., 1960, MD, 1964. Diplomate Nat. Bd. Med. Examiners, Am. Bd. Internal Medicine. Intern Freedmen's Hosp. (name now Howard U. Hosp.), Washington, 1964-65, asst. resident, 1965-67, resident, chief resident, 1967-68, family practice physician, 1971, attending, 1971—; fellow in endocrinology and metabolism Georgetown U. Hosp., Washington, 1968-69; postdoctoral fellow NIH, Bethesda, Md., 1975-77; outpatient clinic physician Vets.' Adminstrn. Hosp., Columbia, S.C., 1969-71; from asst. prof. to assoc. prof. dept. medicine Howard U. Coll. Medicine, Washington, 1971-81, prof. internal medicine, 1981—, assoc. dean acad. affairs, 1980—2000; chief med. officer, residency prog. dir. Howard U. Med. Svc. D.C. Gen. Hosp., Washington, 1977-80, attending, 1977-80; sr. assoc. dean Howard U. Coll. Medicine, Washington, 2000—. Cons. Malawi, Africa project of Dept. Cmty. Health and Family Practice, 1989, Nat. Bd. Med. Examiners, 1995, Ednl. Commn. for Fgn. Med. Grads., 1997; Howard U. Coll. Medicine rep. Am. Assn. Med. Colls., 1980—, coord. activities, presenter, 1982-83, exec. devel. seminar for women, 1983, mem. Nat. Identification Prog. for Advancement of Women in Higher Edn., 1985, others; exec. chief proctor Nat. Bd. Med. Examiners, 1983—, liaison rep. for Howard U. Coll. Medicine, 1987—, mem. steering com. for liaison rep., 1989—, prin. investigator for Computer Based Exams. project, 1989—, mem. bd., 1997—; mem. numerous hosp., coll. coms., subcoms., reviews; lectr., presenter confs., workshops, symposiums. Contbr. articles to profl. jours. Recipient Joseph L. Johnson physiology award, 1961-62, Jacobi Soc. cert. of merit for proficiency in pediatrics, 1964, James E. Simpson Meml. prize Howard U., 1964, psychiatry prize, 1964, dept. surgery prize, 1964, Matilda Davis-Cunningham award, 1964, Am. Acad. Dental Medicine award, 1964, Daniel Hale Williams internship award, 1966, Daniel Hale Williams residency award, 1968, Nat. Rsch. Svc. award, 1975-77, inspirational leadership award Student Coun. Coll. of Medicine, 1979, superior performance as Chief Med. Officer award Howard U. Med. Svc., D.C. Gen. Hosp., 1980, student coun. award Howard U. Coll. Medicine, 1995, Pearl A. Watson award for excellence in delivery of health care Caribbean Am. Intercultural Orgn., 1996;; named Doctor of Year, D.C. Gen. Hosp., 1980; Alma Wells Givens scholar, 1962-63. Fellow ACP; mem. AMA, Nat. Med. Assn., Am. Med. Women's Assn. (liaison officer Howard U. Coll. Medicine, v.p. br. 1 Washington chpt. 1991-92, pres. 1992-93, Janet M. Glasgow Meml. award 1964), Nat. Bd. Med. Examiners, N.Y. Acad. Scis., D.C. Med. Soc., Phi Beta Kappa, Sigma Xi, Beta Kappa Chi, Alpha Omega Alpha (sec., treas. 1977-98, Gamma chpt. of Washington, councillor 1998—). Avocations: sewing, crochet, aerobics. Office: Howard Univ Coll Medicine 520 W St NW Washington DC 20059-0001 Fax: 202-806-7934.

TITZMAN, DONNA M., energy executive; BBA in Acctg., U. Tex. CPA. Acct. natural gas liquids Valero Energy Corp., San Antonio, 1986—89, various positions with fin. dept., 1989, v.p., treas., 1999—. Office: Valero Energy Corpn PO Box 696000 San Antonio TX 78269-6000

TJANDRASWITA, MARIA C. INAWATI, lawyer; b. Malang, Indonesia, Dec. 22, 1964; arrived in US, 1983; d. Paulus Agus Tjandraswita and Maria Atikah Susetya. BA, Barnard Coll., NYC, 1987; JD, UCLA, 1990. Bar: Calif. 1990. Assoc. atty. Russell & Mirkovich, Long Beach, Calif., 1990—95; pvt. practice Laguna Niguel, Calif., 1996—. Vice-chair State Bar Ethnic Minority Lawyers Com., 1993—94. Active Long Beach/Bacolod Sity City, 1993—95; bd. dirs. Long Beach Bar Assn., 1994—95. Mem.: LA Bar Assn., Juvenile Bar Assn. Democrat. Roman Catholic. Avocations: dance, swimming, travel, dining, movies. Home: 25 S Peak Dr Laguna Niguel CA 92677 Office: PO Box 7358 Laguna Niguel CA 92607

TJERSLAND, TRINA J., performing arts educator; b. Wilmington, Del., Mar. 18, 1957; d. Charles Sentz and Joanne (Smith) Tjersland. BA in English Lit., U. Del., 1984. Freelance actress, LA, 1978—80; English and drama tchr. Ursuline Acad., Wilmington, 1985—87; English tchr. Tower Hill Sch., 1987—96, head drama dept., 1987—. Bd. dirs. Del. Theatre Co., Wilmington, 1990—2004. Mem.: Am. Alliance Theatre & Edn. (co-chair HS Network 1999—2005). Avocations: reading, travel. Home: 1410 Ashland Rd Hockessin DE 19707 Office: Tower Hill Sch 2813 W 17t St Wilmington DE 19806

TLSTY, THEA DOROTHY, research scientist, educator; b. Mobile, Ala., Jan. 28, 1952; d. Theodore H. and Josepine M. Tlsty. BS in zoology, U. South Fla., 1973; PhD in molecular biology, Washington U., 1980. Asst. prof. pathology U. NC, Chapel Hill, 1985-92, mem. Lineberger Comprehensive Cancer Ctr., 1985—95, assoc. prof. pathology, 1992—95, U. Calif., San Francisco, 1995—96, dir. molecular pathology, 1995—96, mem. Cancer Rsch. Inst., 1995—96, prof. pathology, 1996—, dir. Ctr. for Translational Rsch. in the Molecular Genetics of Cancer, 1996—, dir. program cell cycling and signaling, Comprehensive Cancer Ctr., 1996—. Predoctoral fellow cellular and molecular biology program, Wash. U., St. Louis, 1976-80, postdoctoral fellow dept. microbiology and immunology, 1980-81; postdoctoral fellow/sr. rsch. assoc. dept. biological sciences, Stanford U., 1981-85; vis. scientist U. Geneva, 1982; vis. scholar U. Zimbabwe, 1992; cons. Bristol-Meyers Co., 1987, Glaxo, 1990—94, Geron, 1993—95, Oncormed, 1995-97, Onyx, 1997-98, Day Casebeer, 1999-2000, Pennie and Edmonds, 2001-02; mem. editl. bd. Molecular Carcinogenesis, 1992-, Carcinogenesis, 1993-, Cancer Rsch., 1995-, Environ. Health Perspectives, 1996-, Am. Jour. Pathology, 1997-; mem. adv. coun., GM Cancer Rsch. Found. Contbr. numerous articles to sci. jours. Recipient Gold Key Honor Soc. Award; Starter Grant Award, Pharmaceutical Mfrs. Assn.; Avon Scholar, 2001-. Mem. AAAS, Am. Soc. Microbiology, Am. Assn. Cancer Rsch., Am. Soc. Biological Chemists and Molecular Biologists, Assn. for Women in Sci., Women in Cancer Rsch., Women in Cell Biology, Calif. Soc. Pathologists, Assn. Molecular Pathologists, Am. Soc. Investigative Pathology, Am. Soc. Cell Biology, Am. Soc. Biochemistry and Molecular Biology. Avocations: bicycling, sculpting, swimming. Office: U Calif Box 0506 San Francisco CA 94143-0506

TOAL, JEAN HOEFER, state supreme court chief justice; b. Columbia, S.C., Aug. 11, 1943; d. Herbert W. and Lilla (Farrell) Hoefer; m. William Thomas Toal; children: Jean Toal Eisen, Lilla Patrick. BA in Philosophy, Agnes Scott Coll., 1965; JD, U. S.C., 1968; LHD (hon.), Coll. Charleston, 1990; LLD (hon.), Columbia Coll., 1992, The Citadel, 1999, Francis Marion U., 1999, U. S.C., 2000. Bar: S.C. Assoc. Haynsworth, Perry, Bryant, Marion & Johnstone, 1968—70; ptnr. Belser, Baker, Barwick, Ravenel, Toal & Bender, Columbia, 1970—88; assoc. justice S.C. Supreme Ct., Columbia, 1988—2000, chief justice, 2000—. Mem. S.C. Human Affairs Commn., 1972-74; mem. S.C. Ho. of Reps., 1975-88, chmn. house rules com., constitutional laws subcom. house judiciary com.; mem. parish coun. and lector St. Joseph's Cath. Ch.; chair S.C. Juvenile Justice Task Force, 1992-94; chair S.C. Rhodes Scholar Selection Com., 1994; bd. dirs. Nat. Ctr. State Cts., 2005-; pres.-elect Conf. Chief Justices, 2006-. Mng. editor S.C. Law Rev., 1967—68. Bd. visitors Clemson U., 1978; trustee Columbia Mus. Art, 1980-85; bd. trustees Agnes Scott Coll., 1996—. Named Outstanding Legislator of Yr., Greenville News, 1976, Woman of Yr., U. S.C. Mortar Bd., 1989; named one of Top 25 Doers, Dreamers & Drivers, Govt. Tech. Mag., 2002; recipient Disting. Svc. award, S.C. Mcpl. Assn., 1980, U. Notre Dame award, 1991, Algernon Sydney Sullivan award, U. S.C., 1991, Agnes Scott Coll. Outstanding Alumna award, 1991, John W. Williams award, Richland County Bar Assn., 1995, Jean Galloway Bissell award, S.C. Women Lawyers Assn., 1995, Margaret Brent Women Lawyers of Achievement award, 2004. Mem. ABA, S.C. Women Lawyers Assn., S.C. Bar Assn., John Belton O'Neall Inn of Ct., Phi Beta Kappa, Mortar Bd., Order of the Coif Office: Supreme Ct SC PO Box 11330 Columbia SC 29211-2456 Business E-Mail: jtoal@sccourts.org.

TOAY, THELMA M., columnist, poet; b. Anamosa, Iowa, Feb. 22, 1915; d. Frank Leroy and Edna May Stoughton; m. John S. Toay; 3 children. Student, St. Lukes Sch. Nursing, Davenport, IA, 1933, Highland Coll., 1966—67; AA in Journalism, N.E. Iowa C.C., Peosta, 1995—97; student, U. Iowa, 2001—03. Contbr. newspapers, Freeport, Ill., 1962—; contbr. Julien's Jour., Dubuque, Iowa, 1995—. Author: Bittersweet, 1979, Places for the Heart - Profiles of Life, 2001. Avocations: theater, music, reading, flower gardening.

TOBACH, ETHEL, retired curator; b. Miaskovka, USSR, Nov. 7, 1921; arrived in U.S., 1923; d. Ralph Wiener and Fanny (Schechterman) Wiener Idels; m. Charles Tobach, 1947 (dec. 1969). BA, Hunter Coll., 1949; MA, NYU, 1952, PhD, 1957; DSc (hon.), LI U., 1975. Lic. psychologist N.Y. Rsch. fellow Am. Mus. Natural History, N.Y.C., 1958-61, assoc. curator, 1964-69, curator, 1969-90, emerita curator; rsch. fellow NYU, N.Y.C., 1961-64, ret., 1990. Adj. prof. psychology and biology CUNY, N.Y.C., 1964—; disting. cons. faculty Saybrook Inst., San Francisco, 1998—. Co-editor: (series) T. C. Schneirta Conference Series, 1981, Genes & Gender Series, 1975; editor: Internat. Jour. Comparative Psychology, 1987—93; assoc. editor: Peace and Conflict: Jour. Peace Psychology, 1994—. Recipient NIHH Career Devel. award, 1964—74, Disting. Sci. Career, Assn. Women in Sci., 1974, Disting. Sci. Publ., Assn. Women in Psychology, 1982, Kurt Lewin award, Soc. Psychol. Study Social Issues, 1993, Gustavus Myers award for Outstanding Pub. Human Rights in N.Am., 1996, Lifetime Achievement Psychology in Pub. Interest Gold Medal award, Am. Psychol. Found., 2003. Fellow: APA (pres. comparative psychology divsn. 1985, peace psychology divsn. 2003, Leadership award Com. in Women in Psychology 2005); mem.: Soc. Study Peace, Conflict and Violence (pres. 2003, Lifetime Peace Activity award 1999), Psychologists for Social Responsibility, N.Y. Acad. Scis. (v.p. behavioral scis. 1973—76), Eastern Psychol. Assn. (pres. 1987, bd. dirs. 2001—, mem. exec. com. 2002—), Internat. Soc. Comparative Psychology (hon.; sec. 1988—92, pres.). Office: Am Mus Natural History Central Pkwy 79th St New York NY 10024-5192 Business E-Mail: tobach@amnh.org.

TOBEN, DOREEN A., telecommunications industry executive; b. Curacao; m. Ed Toben; 2 children. AB Polit. Sci., Rosemount Coll.; MBA Fin. and Mktg., Fairleigh Dickinson Univ. Dir. corp. planning AT&T, 1972; exec. dir. mktg. Bell Atlantic Enterprises Internat., Inc., 1989; various positions equipment engring., ops., and small bus. and consumer market mgmt. Bell Atlantic Inc., Pa., dir. fin., 1983, divsn. mgr. strat. planning, 1984, asst. v.p.-comptroller, 1992, CFO, 1993, v.p. corp. fin., mem. com., v.p., CFO telecom. network, 1997—99; v.p., controller Verizon Communications Inc., 1999—2000; sr. v.p., CFO telecom. group Verizon Communications, Inc., 2000—02, exec. v.p., CFO, 2002—. Bd. dirs. NY Times Co., 2004—. Named one of 50 Most Powerful Women in Bus., Fortune mag., 2005, 2006, 10 Most Powerful Women in NJ Bus., Star-Ledger, 2006. Office: Verizon 1095 Avenue of Americas New York NY 10036*

TOBER, BARBARA D. (MRS. DONALD GIBBS TOBER), editor; b. Summit, NJ, Aug. 19, 1934; d. Rodney Fielding and Maude Starkey; m. Donald Gibbs Tober, Apr. 5, 1973. Student, Traphagen Sch. Fashion, 1954-56, Fashion Inst. Tech., 1956-58, N.Y. Sch. Interior Design, 1964. Copy editor Vogue Pattern Book, 1958-60; beauty editor Vogue mag., 1961; dir. women's services Bartell Media Corp., 1961-66; editor-in-chief Bride's mag., N.Y.C., 1966-94; chmn. Mus. Arts and Design; pres. Acronym, Inc., N.Y.C., 1995—, The Barbara Tober Found., 1995—. Sec.-treas., dir. Sugar Foods Corp.; adv. bd. Traphagen Sch.; coord. SBA awards; Am. Craft Coun., 1983—, benefit food com. chmn., 1984-87. Author: The ABC's of Beauty, 1963, China: A Cognizant Guide, 1980, The Wedding.The Marriage.And the Role of the Retailer, 1980, The Bride: A Celebration, 1984 Mem. Nat. Council on Family Relations, 1966; nat. council Lincoln Center Performing Arts, Met. Opera Guild; mem. NYU adv. bd. Women in Food Service, 1983; NYU Women's Health Symposium: Steering Com., 1983—. Recipient Alma award, 1968, Penney-Mo. award, 1972, Traphagen Alumni award, 1975, Diamond Jubilee award, 1983, Disting. Women award Northwood U., 1997. Mem. Fashion Group, Internat. Furnishings and Design Assn. (v.p., program chmn.), Am. Soc. Mag. Editors, Am. Soc. Interior Designers (press mem.), Intercorporate Group, Women in Communications (60 yrs. of success award N.Y. chpt. 1984), Nat. Assn. Underwater Instrs., Pan Pacific and S.E. Asia Women's Assn., Asia Soc., Japan Soc., China Inst., Internat. Side Saddle Orgn., Millbrook Hounds, Golden's Bridge Hounds, Wine and Food Soc., Chaines des Rotisseurs (chargée de press) (bd. dirs.), Dames d'Escoffier, Culinary Inst. Am. Home and Office: 620 Park Ave New York NY 10021-6591 Office Phone: 212-879-2785.

TOBIAS, DOROTHY BURTON, retired music educator, consultant; b. Columbia, S.C., Jan. 6, 1936; d. Joseph Nathaniel Burton and Dorothy Simons Bryan; m. William Raymond Tobias, Aug. 16, 1957 (dec. Nov. 25, 1994); children: William Raymond Jr., Dorothy Burton Tobias Yeley, Lawerence Hodge. BS Vocal performance and Music Edn., Winthrop Univ., Rock Hill, S.C., 1957; MHDL, Univ. N.C., Charlotte, 1981. Music specialist Orff Schulwerk master classes levels I, II and II Charlotte City Sch., 1957—58; elem. music specialist Charlotte-Mecklenburg Sch., 1975—80; devel. dir. WFAE Pub. Radio, Univ. N.C., Charlotte, 1980—81; elem. gen. music specialist Charlotte-Mecklenburg Sch., 1981—2001. Ch. choirs, childrens choir various orgn.; conf. presenter various workshops. Contbr. chapters to books. Precinct chair Dem. Party, Charlotte, 1970; mem., arts chair Jr. Women's league, Charlotte, 1965—72; bd. mem. Friends of the Arts Davidson Coll. Found., Davidson, NC, 1989—91, Friends of Music Queens Univ., Charlotte, 1994—, Golden Cir. Theatre, Charlotte, 1978—82; pres. of aux. Theatre Charlotte, 1974—75. Recipient Tchr. of the Yr., Charlotte-Meck Sch. Spl. Area, 1989; grantee N.C. Music Edn. Grant Winner, 1994, Charlotte-Mecklenburg Arts & Sci. Grant Winner, 1993, 1994, 1995; fellowship to study with Royal Shakespeare Co., Stratford, London, Eng., 1984. Mem.: Am. Orff Schulwerk Assn. (Piedmont chpt. sec., v.p. 1982, 1983, 2001, pres. 1984, nat. adv. bd. 1984), Music Educators Nat. Conf., N.C. Music Edn. Assn. (bd. chair elem. sect. 1994). Democrat. Meth. Avocations: antiques, cooking, travel, reading. Home: 2248 Colony Rd Charlotte NC 28209-1712 Office Phone: 704-375-3510.

TOBIAS, JUDY, university development executive; b. Pitts. d. Saul Albert Landau and Bess (Previn) Kurzman; m. Seth Tobias (dec. May 1983); children: Stephen Frederic, Andrew Previn; m. Lewis F. Davis, 1990. Student, Silvermine Artists Guild, 1951-55; BA (hon.) (hon.), New Coll. of Calif., 1989. Art cons. Westchester Mental Health Asn., White Plains, NY, 1968-69; cons. sch. social work NYU, 1973-74, devel. exec., 1976—. Conf. coord. Today's Family: Implications for the Future, N.Y.C., 1974-75; cons. Playschools, Inc., N.Y.C., 1975; majority counsel mem. Emily's List, 1991—. Mem. Gov.'s Commn. on Continuing Edn., Albany, N.Y., 1968-70, Nat. Coun. on Children and Youth, Washington, 1974-75, Manhattan Inter-Hosp. Group on Child Abuse, 1975-76; chmn. N.Y. met. com. for UNICEF, 1976-77; mem. exec. com. Town Hall Found., N.Y.C., 1979—, vice chmn., 1986-90; founder, bd. dirs. N.Y. chpt. WAIF, Inc., 1961-99, nat. pres., 1978-82, nat. bd. dirs., 1978-2000; pres. emeritus, 1993-99; bd. dirs. Citizen's Com. for Children, City of N.Y., 1975—, v.p., 1983-90, 97-99; bd. dirs. Am. br. Internat. Social Svc., 1965-80; bd. dirs. Andrew Glover Youth Program, 1986-89, mem. adv. coun., 1989—; bd. dirs. Goddard Riverside Cmty. Ctr., 1985—. Dance Mag. Found., 1986-92, St. John's Place Family Ctr., 1987-93, Capitol Hall Preservation Corp., 1989-93, Inst. for Cultural Diversity; steering com. The Leadership Connection, 1992—. Recipient Nat. Humanitarian award, WAIF, 1990, Millennium Honoree award, NYU Sch. Social Work, 2000. Mem. Child Study Assn. Am. (bd. dirs. 1963-71, pres. 1969-71, bd. dirs. Wel-Met Inc. 1972-85), Brookings Instn. (coun. mem. 1998—), Emily's List (majority coun. 1990—), Women Matter (bd. chmn. 2003—). E-mail: ajtdavis@aol.com.

TOBIAS, SHEILA, writer, educator; d. Paul Jay and Rose (Steinberger) Tobias; m. Carlos Stern, Oct. 11, 1970 (div. 1982); m. Carl T. Tomizuka, Dec. 16, 1987. BA, Harvard Radcliffe U., 1957; MA, Columbia U., 1961, MPhil, 1974; PhD (hon.), Drury Coll., 1994, Wheelock Coll., 1995; PhD (hon.), SUNY, Potsdam, 1996, Mich. State U., 2000, Worcester Polytech, 2002. Journalist, Germany, 1957-65; lect. in history CCNY, NYC; univ. adminstr. Cornell U., Wesleyan U., 1967-78; lect. in women's studies U. Calif., San Diego, 1985-92; lect. in war, peace studies U. So. Calif., 1985—88. Vis. prof. U. Amsterdam, U. Leiden, 1994—97; cons. sci. and bus. U. Amsterdam, Leiden, Netherlands, 1995—98, pres. Outreach coord. sci. master's initiative, 1997—2006, pres., sr. cons. to coun. of grad. schs., 2006—. Author: Overcoming Math Anxiety, 1978, rev. edit., 1994, Succeed with Math, 1987, Revitalizing Undergraduate Science: Why Some Things Work and Most Don't, 1992, Science as a Career: Perceptions and Realities, 1995; co-author: The People's Guide to National Defense, 1982, Women, Militarism and War, 1987, They're Not Dumb, They're Different, 1990, (with Carl T. Tomizuka) Breaking the Science Barrier, 1992, Rethinking Science as a Career, 1995, (with Jacqueline Raphael) The Hidden Curriculum, 1997, Faces of Feminism, 1997. Exec. v.p. Vet. Feminists of Am., 2002—. Fellow AAAS; mem. Am. Assn. Higher Edn. (bd. dirs. 1993-97), Mentornet (bd. dirs., 2005-). Avocations: outdoor hiking, skiing.

TOBIASSEN, BARBARA SUE, systems analyst, consultant, volunteer; b. Bklyn., Feb. 22, 1950; d. Vincent and Esther Alice (Hansen) M. BA in Math Edn., Rider Coll., 1972; postgrad., Montclair State U., 1973. Cert. secondary tchr., NJ. Math tchr. Westwood (NJ) H.S., 1973-80; programmer Prudential Ins. Co., Roseland, NJ, 1980-81; programmer, analyst Grand Union, Paramus, NJ, 1981-82; cons. Five Techs., Montvale, NJ, 1987-90; project mgr. Info. Sci., Inc., Montvale, 1982-84, cons., project mgr., 1987-90; pres. B. Maxwell Assoc., Inc., Westwood, 1990—; vol. Peace Corps; mem. Peace Corps., 2001—02; tchr. St. Paul's Luth., Accra, Ghana, 2002—03. Guest spkr. Info. Sci., Best of Am., Computer Assocs. B.A.C.; educator, Ghana W. Africa, 2002-. Contbr. articles to profl. jours. Vol. Peace Corps, 2001—02. Mem.: APA (v.p. N.J. chpt. 1996), NAFE, Am. Payroll Assn., N.J. Info. Republican. Lutheran. Avocations: travel, reading, gardening, hiking. E-mail: btobiassen2003@yahoo.com.

TOBIN, BARBARA KAY, minister; b. Davenport, Iowa, Oct. 9, 1943; d. Robert Thomas Myers and Frances Louella Davis; m. Richard James Tobin, Feb. 12, 1966; 1 child, Mary Beth Tobin Peter. B.Humanities, Social Sci. and Edn., Purdue U., 1966; BEd, Ball State U., 1968; MDiv, Colgate Rochester Div. Sch., 1994. Cert. tchr. N.Y., ordained to ministry Presbyn. Ch., 1994. Fgn. lang. tchr. West Irondequoit Schs., Rochester, NY, 1968—93; chaplain Strong Meml. Hosp., Rochester, 1993—94; pastor of visitation First Presbyn. Ch., Pittsford, NY, 1994—96; assoc. pastor Perinton Presbyn. Ch., Fairport, NY, 1995—2000; pastor Irondequoit Presbyn. Ch., Rochester, 2000—. Sec., bd. dirs. Irondequoit Sr. Transp. Ministry, Rochester, 2002—; mem. com. on prep. ministry Genesee Valley Presbytery, 2001—05; leader internat. study tours West Irondequoit Schs., 1983—88; leader student mission trips Perinton Presbyn. Ch., 1991—99. Mem. Irondequoit Youth Bureau Adv. Bd., 2004—; leader,youth mission trips, 1992—99. Mem.: N.Y. State Ret. Tchrs. Assn., Purdue U. Alumni Assn. (life; pres.'s coun. 1993—). Presbyterian. Avocations: reading, travel, sailing. Office: Irondequoit Presbyn Ch 2881 Culver Rd Rochester NY 14622 Office Phone: 585-266-3370. Personal E-mail: pastorbobbi@rochester.rr.com.

TOBIN, MARGARET ANN, clinical educator; b. Oakland, Calif., Dec. 10, 1959; d. William Leroy Jones Sr. and Barbara Kay (Rains) Carter; m. Wesley Vernon Keene, June 21, 1977 (div. June 1984); m. James Edward Tobin, Aug. 15, 1985; 1 child, Nicholas William. ADN, Ctrl. Tex. Coll., 1983; BSN, U. Mary Harden Baylor, 1994; MSN, Tex. A&M U., Corpus Christi, 1997. RN, Tex.; cert. med.-surg. nurse, edn. nurse ANCC; cert. BCLS, BCLS instr., ACLS, ACLS instr.; cert. trainer prevention and mgmt. of disturbed behavior. Grad. nurse surg. fl. Olin E. Teague VA Ctr., Temple, Tex., 1983-84, staff nurse cardiac med. ICU, 1984-95, nurse mgr. surg. ICU, 1995-96, nurse mgr. cardiac med. ICU, 1996, clin. instr., 1996—. Mem. Tar Wars Kids Against Tobacco, Temple, 1993—. Mem.: AACN (pres.-elect 1993—94, pres. 1994—95), Sigma Theta Tau. Baptist. Home: 4307 Sunflower Ln Temple TX 76502 Office Phone: 254-743-2909. E-mail: jim_tobin@sbcglobal.net, margaret.tobin@med.va.gov.

TOD, MARTHA ANN, retired small business owner; b. Nogales, Ariz., Dec. 20, 1927; d. R.T. and Beatrice Martha (Jones) Frazier; m. James William Tod, April 18, 1952; children: James, Bill, Bob, John, Gerry. BA, U. Ariz., Tucson, 1952; postgrad., Ariz. State U., Tempe, 1977. Cert. elem. and spl. edn. tchr. Spl. edn. tchr. Paradise Valley. Schs., Phoenix, 1976-77, Round Valley Schs., Springerville, 1977-88; resort owner Tod's Antler Ridge, Greer, Ariz., 1977—98, ret., 1998. Mem. Title XX Bd., Town Hall; treas. WMC Hosp. Bd. Springerville, 1980; pres. Cocopah PTA Paradise Valley, 1967; former touring docent Phoenix Art Mus.; touring docent Butterfly Lodge Mus., Greer, Ariz. Named Tchr. of Yr. Springerville Rotary, 1985. Mem. Assn. for Children and Adults with Learning Disabilities, Greer Civic Club, Ariz. Archaeology Soc. Avocation: acting. Home: 450 Raven Hill Rd Clarkdale AZ 86324-3111 Address: Box 182 592 County Rd 1122 Greer AZ 85927

TODARO, MOLLY ANN, secondary school educator; b. Conneaut, Ohio, Aug. 13, 1977; d. James M. and Cheryl A. Poff; m. Anthony August Todaro, July 30, 2005. Bachelors, Mt. Union Coll., 2000; Attended, Northwestern U., 2004—05. Cert. Profl. Tchng. Ill. Tchr. Cleve. Mcpl. Schs., 2000—01, Sch. St. Mary, Lake Forest, Ill., 2001—05, Chgo. Pub. Schs., 2005—. Summer edn. dir. Good Shepherd Luth. Ch., Conneaut, 2006—06. Recipient Five Yr. Membership award, Kappa Delta Pi, 2005. Mem.: NSTA, Kappa Delta Pi (hon.), Alpha Xi Delta (life). Luth. Office Phone: 773-535-4565.

TODD, CATHERINE JACKSON, writer; b. L.A., Jan. 31, 1947; d. Hubert Edward and Carolyn Arden (Laws) Jackson; m. Timothy Gordon Todd, Aug. 24, 1968. AB cum laude, Occidental Coll., 1968; MA, Stanford U., 1969. Cert. tchr., Calif. Tchr. English, French Sequoia Union H.S., Redwood City, Calif., 1968-73, Country Day Sch., San José, Costa Rica, 1970-72; tchr. English Grossmont Union H.S., La Mesa, Calif., 1991-93; bus. svcs. writer San Diego, 1993—. Author: Bond of Honor, 1981, Marian, 1991, (as Elizabeth Jackson) A Brilliant Alliance, 1993, (as Elizabeth Jackson) Galatea's Revenge, 1993, (as Elizabeth Jackson) Rogue's Delight, 1995, Making Waves, 1997, Staying Cool, 1997, Exit Strategies, 2002, Secret Lives of Second Wives, 2003; contbr. articles to profl. jours. Mem. Authors Guild, Romance Writers Am., Phi Beta Kappa. E-mail: cathetoddbooks@aol.com.

TODD, CHERIE CLEMONS, elementary school educator; b. Paducah, Ky., Apr. 25, 1950; d. William Francis and Faye (Polk) Clemons; m. John William Todd, Jan. 8, 1972; 1 child, John William Jr. BA, U. Ky., 1973; MA, U. Louisville, 1986. Cert. tchr., Ky. Resource tchr. Louisville Pub. Schs.-Jefferson County Pub. Schs., 1973-79; lead tchr. U. Louisville Child Care Ctr., 1982-86; elem. sch. tchr. Jefferson County Pub. Schs., Louisville, 1986—; team leader Jefferson County Pub. Schs., Lowe Elem. Sch., Louisville, 1990-94; cluster leader written portfolio assessment Jefferson County Pub. Schs., Louisville, 1991-94; primary tchr. The Brown Sch., 1994—. Solicitor Tchrs. for Books-Friends of Pub. Libr., Louisville, 1986. Tchr. Bible sch. Watson Meml. Bapt. Ch., Louisville, 1984-86. Fellow Nat. Edn. Assn., Jefferson County Tchrs. Assn. (grievance rep. 1975-76), Ky. Edn. Assn.; mem. Louisville Assn. for Children Under Six (pres. 1986-87), Ky. Assn. for Children Under Six (rec. sec. 1984-86), So. Assn. Children Under Six (state multicultural rep. 1984-85), Internat. Reading Assn., Nat. Coun. Tchrs. English (nat. writing project). Democrat. Avocations: reading, travel. Home: 209 Ash Run Rd Louisville KY 40245-6112 Office: Jefferson County Pub Schs PO Box 34020 Louisville KY 40232-4020

TODD, CHERYL, art educator; b. Winston-Salem, N.C., Nov. 9, 1947; d. Dwight Lionel and Betsy Ann Gordon; m. David Gary Todd, June 27, 1970; children: Kevin, Tate. BS, East Carolina U., 1970; MEd, U. S.C., 1989. Chairperson fine arts dept., art and English tchr. Myrtle Beach (S.C.) H.S., 1972-99. Sponsor Interact, sr. class sponsor, cheerleeding Myrtle Beach H.S.; shag dance instr. Myrtle Beach Recreation Dept. Avocations: watercolor painting, snorkeling, biking. Home: 3900 Oak Cir Myrtle Beach SC 29577-0870 E-mail: ctodd@mbh.sccoast.net.

TODD, DEBORAH KATHLEEN, library media specialist; b. Arlington, Va., June 5, 1954; d. William Walton and Edna Mae (Saul) T. BA in Libr. Sci., Madison Coll., Harrisonburg, Va., 1976; MEd Sch. Libr. Media Svcs., James Madison U., 1985. Libr. Spotsylvania (Va.) Jr. H.S., 1976-79; libr. media specialist Spotsylvania H.S., 1979—. Editor: Resource Guide to Intellectual Freedom. Life mem. Va. PTA., 1997. Recipient Margaret Morfit svc. award Spotsylvania H.S. Parent Tchr. Student Assn. Mem. NEA, Va. Ednl. Media Assn. (Meritorious Svc. award 1992, Intellectual Freedom award 1997), Hist. Fredericksburg Found., Spotsylvania Edn. Assn., Va. Edn. Assn., Am. Libr. Assn. Methodist. Avocations: photography, needlecrafts, travel. Home: 423 Greenbrier Ct Fredericksburg VA 22401-5562 Office: Spotsylvania HS 6975 Courthouse Rd Spotsylvania VA 22553-3322

TODD, JAN THERESA, counselor; b. Mobile, Ala., Mar. 20, 1961; d. Joseph Thomas and Lessie Grey (Sullivan) T. BA, U. Tex., San Antonio, 1983, MA, 1992. Cert. profl. counselor; cert. provisional tchr. English tchr. Bandera HS-Bandera Ind. Sch. Dist., Tex., 1987-91; counselor Yorktown HS-Yorktown Ind. Sch. Dist., Tex., 1992-93, John F. Kennedy HS-Edgewood Ind. Sch. Dist., San Antonio, 1993-95, Lackland Jr./Sr. HS, San Antonio, 1995-97, Comfort HS, Comfort Ind. Sch. Dist., Tex., 1997—98, North East ISD, 1998—. Mem. Assn. Tex. Profl. Educators. Home: 6401 Red Jacket Dr San Antonio TX 78238-1529 Office: Macarthur HS 2923 Bitters Rd San Antonio TX 78217

TODD, KATHERINE LAWS, filmmaker, retired writer, human resources specialist; d. Richard Franklin and Winifred Howell Laws; m. H. Schuyler Todd, Oct. 23, 1976; m. Richard Wellington Rossignol, Dec. 7, 1957 (div. June 30, 1967); stepchildren: Mark Schuyler, Kristen Hollis Gonzalez children: Deborah Lynne Rossignol, Richard Thomas Rossignol, Lara Rossignol, Alan Theodore Rossignol. BS, U. San Francisco, L.A., 1983. Area labor rels. mgr. Carnation Co., L.A., Calif., 1975—79, dir. eeo affairs, 1979—83. Asst. dir. of pers., corp. offices Carnation Co., L.A., Calif., 1972—74; pres. Burnt Meringue, Prodn. Co., L.A., Calif., 1993—97. Prodr.: (films) The Celebration (Gold Medal, NY Film & TV Festival, 1990). Grand juror County, Civil Grand Jury 2002-2003, L.A., 2002—03; ct. apptd. spl. adv. for children Superior Ct. of Calif., County of LA, L.A., 1995; past pres. Ctr. Theatre Group Affiliates, L.A., 1988; bd. mem. Founding Assocs. of John Douglas French Alzheier's Found., L.A., Calif., 2003; pres. So. Calif. Coun. of the Nat. Mus. of Women in the Arts, L.A., 2004. Recipient Best Student Film, Youth in Film Awards, 1990. Mem.: So. Calif. Coun. of Nat. Mus. of Women in Art (pres. 2004—). R-Liberal. Episcopal. Avocations: building miniature houses, scrapbooks, collecting art, and dolls. Home: 7301 Easthaven Lane West Hills CA 91307 Personal E-mail: rosstodd@aol.com.

TODD, LINDA MARIE, nutrition researcher, circulation manager, financial consultant, pilot; b. LA, Mar. 30, 1948; d. Ithel Everette and Janet Marie Fredricks; m. William MacKenzie Cook, Jan. 11, 1982 (div. Oct. 1989); m. Robert Oswald Todd, Apr. 8, 1990; 1 child, Jesse MacKenzie Todd. BA in Psychology and Sociology, U. Colo., 1969; student in Psychology, U. No. Colo., 1970; ins. and estate planning courses, 1990—, mgmt. tng. programs, 2001—. Pilot lic., weather cert., FCC lic., Calif. life ins. lic., coll. teaching credential; registered with Nat. Assn. Securities Dealers. Counselor Jeffco Juvenile Detention Ctr., Golden, Colo., 1969-71; communications Elan Vital, Denver, 1971-81; legal sec. Fredman, Silverberg & Lewis, San Diego, 1980-82; escrow supr. Performance Mktg. Concepts, Olympic Valley, Calif., 1982-85; mgmt. commn. instr. Sierra Coll., Truckee, Calif., 1986-87; regional mgr. Primerica Fin. Svcs., Reno, 1987-91; air traffic, weather advisor Truckee Tahoe Airport Dist., Calif., 1986-96; circulation mgr. Tahoe World Newspaper, 2001—03, Sierra Sun, 2001—. Student tour leader, air show organizer Truckee (Calif.) Tahoe Airport, 1986-96; fin. cons. Primerica Fin. Svcs., Truckee, 1987-91; gen. agt. TTS Fin., 1992—; co-founder Todd Nutrition, 1995—; co-owner Todd Aero, 1990—; bd. dirs. Pacific Crest Fin. Corp., 1996—. Editor: (newsletter) Communications, 1975. Chorus mem. operas and musicals, 1960s-70s; prodn. crew Lake Tahoe Summer Music Festivals, 2000-03; sec. gen. Arapahoe H.S. Model UN, Littleton, Colo., 1965; del. State Model UN, Colo., 1966; conv. del. Elan Vital, The Ninety-Nines, Inc.; pub. affairs officer CAP. Univ. scholar Littleton (Colo.) Edn. Assn., 1966, flight scholar The Ninety-Nines Inc., Reno, 1990; named Recruiter of Month, Al Williams Primerica, Reno, 1987. Mem. CAP, Elan Vital, Plane Talkers, The Ninety Nines, Planetary Soc. Avocations: hiking, skiing, swimming, flying, soaring. Home and Office: PO Box 1303 Truckee CA 96160-1303 Personal E-mail: toddaero@sbcglobal.net.

TODD, MARGARET DONNELLAN, librarian, director; MLS, U. So. Calif.; MBA, Pepperdine U. Sr. libr. mgr. Orange Pub. Libr., Calif.; dir. Whittier Pub. Libr., Calif., 1989—2001; county libr. County of LA Pub. Libr., Calif., 2001—. Mem.: Calif. Libr. Assn. Office: County of LA Pub Libr 7400 East Imperial Highway Downey CA 90241-7011 Office Phone: 562-940-8400. E-mail: mdtodd@gw.colapl.org.*

TODD, MARY BETH, oncologist, researcher; b. Tulsa, Okla., June 10, 1951; d. Earl K. and Edith (Beaty) T. BA, Okla. City U., 1972; postgrad., U. Tulsa, 1973-74; DO, Okla. State U., 1978. Assoc. rsch. scientist Yale Sch. Medicine, New Haven, 1984-86; dir. outpatient svc. Yale Medical Sch., New Haven, 1986-93; asst. prof. Sch. Medicine Yale U., New Haven, 1986-91, assoc. prof., 1991-93; assoc. prof. medicine UMDNJ-RWJMS, New Brunswick, 1993—2002, prof. medicine, 2002—; deputy dir. The Cancer Inst. N.J., New Brunswick, NJ, 1993—, COO, chief med. officer, 2005—. Scientific adv. panel for immunology svcs. Food & Drug Adminstrn., Washington, 1991-95; scientific adv. bd. HEM Pharmeceuticals Corp., 1991-93; external medical adv. bd. Conn. Hospice, 1990-92; co-chair N.J. Working Group to Improve Outcomes in Cancer Patients. Recipient grants Nat. Inst. Health, 1989-98. Mem. Am. Coll. Physicians, Am. Fedn. Clinical Rsch., Am. Soc. Clinical Oncology, Am. Assn. Cancer Rsch., Am. Soc. Hemetology. Internat. Soc. Interferon and Cytokine Rsch. Office: The Cancer Inst NJ 195 Little Albany St New Brunswick NJ 08903-2681

TODD, NORMA ROSS, retired government official; b. Butler, Pa., Oct. 3, 1920; d. William Bryson and Doris Mae (Ferguson) Ross; m. Alden Frank Miller, Jr., Apr. 16, 1940 (dec. Feb. 1975); 1 child, Alden Frank III; m. Jack R. Todd, Dec. 23, 1977 (dec. Sept. 1990). Student, Pa. State U., Donora,

1944—46, Yale U., New Haven, Conn., 1954-57. Exec. mgr. Donora C. of C., Pa., 1950-57, pres. Pa., 1972; exec. mgr. Donora Cmty. Chest, 1950-57; office mgr. Donora Golden Jubilee, 1951; staff writer Donora Herald-American, 1957, city editor, 1957-70; assoc. editor Daily Herald, Donora and Monongahela, 1970-73; svc. rep. Pitts. Telesvc. Ctr., Social Security Adminstrn., HHS, 1977-83. Mem. Mayor's Adv. Coun., Donora, 1965-69, Citizens' Adv. Coun., Donora, 1965-69; mem. Donora Bd. Edn., 1954-60, pres., 1960; mem. Donora Borough Coun., 1970-72; bd. dirs. Mon Valley chpt. ARC, 1964-99, sec. bd., 1964-97, chmn. bd. dirs., 1997-99, mem. lifetime adv. bd., 2000; bd. dirs. Washington County Tourism Agy., 1970-90, sec., 1972-90; bd. dirs. Washington County History and Landmarks Found., 1971-80, 91-92, sec., 1975-80, 91-93, hon. life mem., 1996; bd. dirs. Mon Valley YMCA, 1960-66, Mon Valley coun. Camp Fire Girls, 1965-79, Mon Valley Drug and Alcoholism Coun., 1971-78; hon. life mem. Pa. Congress PTAs; bd. dirs. United Way Mon Valley, 1973-82, chmn. pub. rels., 1973-74; rep. nat. com. Eisenhower Commn., 2005; Platinum mem. Presdl. Task Force, 2004-06; commr. Rep. Sen. Inner Cir., 2005. Recipient Fine Arts Festival of Pa. Poetry first prize award Fedn. Women's Clubs, 1987, 1st and 2d pl. awards for photography Washington County Fine Arts Festival, County Fedn. Women's Clubs, 1990, Disting. Svc. award Donora Rotary Club, 1997, Millenium Peace award, India, 2001, Two World Poets awards J. Mark Press, 2002, U.S. Rep. Senatorial Medal of Freedom, 2003, 2006, Congl. Order Merit, 2003, Cert of Recognition U.S. Justice Found, 2004, cert. appreciation Ronald Reagan Presdl. Found., 2006; pub. in Best Poems of 1995 Nat. Libr. of Poetry, Best Poems of 1996, Best Poems of 1997, Outstanding Poets of 1998, Am. at the Millennium The Best Poets of the 20th Century, The Best Poems and Poets of 2001, The Best Poems and Poets of 2002, of 2003, 04, 05 and numerous anthologies in U.S., Italy, Great Britain and India. Mem. Svc. Corps Ret. Execs. (sec. 1998-2005), Pa. Soc. Newspaper Editors, Pitts. Press Club, Donora C. of C. (pres. 1971-72), DAR (regent Monongahela Valley chpt. 1974-77, treas. 1992-2001), Internat. Platform Assn. (finalist Acad. of Poets Competition, 2001), World Poetry Soc. Internat., Internat. Poets Acad., Famous Poet Soc., U.S. Poets, Metverse Muse (hon. life, India), Washington County Poetry Soc. (pres. 1967-69), Donora Hist. Soc. (curator 1990—), Family of Bruce Internat. Descs. of King Robert the Bruce of Scotland, Clan Ross Assn., Mt. Vernon Ladies Assn., Washington County Fedn. Women's Clubs (rec. sec. 1964-66, pub. rels chmn. 1990-92), Order Ea. Star (worthy matron 1966-67, treas. 1986-94, 98—2003, bd. dirs. Western Pa. Eastern Star Home 1997-98, adv. bd. Masonic Eastern Star Home-West 1998-2000), White Shrine of Jerusalem (high priestess 1973-74, treas. 1995-2001), Order of Amaranth (royal matron 1966, dist. dep. 3 times, grand rep. W.Va. 1979-80), Donora Forecast (pres. 1957-59), Donora Unidon (pres. 1965-66, 56-57). Avocation: genealogy. Home: Overlook Ter Donora PA 15033 also: 1310 Mckean Ave Donora PA 15033-2200

TODD, SHIRLEY ANN, school system administrator; b. May 23, 1935; d. William Leonard and Margaret Judy (Simmons) Brown; m. Thomas Byron Todd, July 7, 1962 (dec. July 1977). BS in Edn., Madison Coll., 1956; MEd, U. Va., 1971. Cert. tchr. Va. Elem. sch. tchr. Fairfax County Sch. Bd., Fairfax, Va., 1956—66, mid. sch. tchr., 1966—71; guidance counselor James F. Cooper Mid. Sch., McLean, Va., 1971—88, dir. guidance, 1988—96; chmn. mktg. Lake Anne Joint Venture, Falls Church, Va., 1979—81, mng. ptnr., 1980—82. Del. Fairfax County Rep. Conv., 1985. Fellow: Fairfax Edn. Assn. (bd. dirs. 1968—70, profl. rights and responsibilities commn. 1970—72); mem.: ASCD, NEA, Va. Sch. Counselors Assn., Va. Counselors Assn., Va. Counselors Assn. (exec. com. 1987), No. Va. Counselors Assn. (exec. bd. 1982—83, hospitality and social chmn.), Va. Edn. Assn. (state com. on local assns. and urban affairs 1969—70), Vintage Ladies of No. Va. (newsletter editor 2002—03), Women's Golf Assn. (pres. 1997—98), Welcome Club of No. Va. (pres. 2003—04), Chantilly Nat. Golf and Country Club (v.p. social 1981—82). Baptist. Avocations: golf, tennis. Home: 6543 Bay Tree Ct Falls Church VA 22041-1001

TODD, SUZANNE MARIE, film producer; b. Las Vegas, Nev., June 1, 1965; d. James Patrick Bailey and Leslie Todd; m. Doug Aarniokoski July 1999; children: Hunter, Dashiell. BA in Film and TV Prodn., U. So. Calif., L.A., 1986. V.p. prodn. Silver Pictures, Burbank, Calif., 1988—. Assoc. prodr. (TV series) Tales From the Crypt, 1989; exec. prodr. (TV films) If These Walls Could Talk, 1996, If These Walls Could Talk 2, 2000; co-producer (film) Ricochet, 1990; prodr. (films) The Adventures of Ford Fairlane, 1990, Die Hard 2, 1990, Predator 2, 1990, Hudson Hawk, 1991, Live Wire, 1992, Loaded Weapon 1, 1993, Mighty Morphin Power Rangers: The Movie, 1995, Now and Then, 1995, Austin Powers: International Man of Mystery, 1997, G.I. Jane, 1997, Idle Hands, 1999, Austin Powers: The Spy Who Shagged Me, 1999, Boiler Room, 2000, Momento, 2000, Austin Powers in Goldmember, 2002, Must Love Dogs, 2005, Prime, 2005, Zoom, 2006; exec. prodr. (films) Christmas with the Kranks, 2004. Mem. Young Artists Guild.*

TODD, VICTORIA L., chlid psychoanalyst; b. Warren, Ohio, Oct. 29, 1954; d. Martin August and Marguerite Virginia (Campsey) T. BA, Kent State U., Ohio, 1976; M in Social Service Adminstrn. summa cum laude, Case Western Res. U., 1987. Social worker Children and Family Services, Youngstown, Ohio, 1977-78, Summit County Children Services Bd., Akron, Ohio, 1978-89, Family Recovery Ctr., Akron, 1988-89, Children's Aid Soc., Cleve., 1989—2000, Hanna Perkins, 2000—. Mem. Ohio Child Sexual Abuse Grant Treatment Com., Akron, 1985-86; mem. adv. bd. guardian ad litem program Summit County Juvenile Ct., 1988-89. Vol. Akron Art Mus., 1983-85; chmn. pub. relations Akron Art Fest, 1984. Mem. Nat. Assn. Social Workers, Jr. League (Akron chpt. bd. dirs. 1984-85, chmn. community research 1984-85). Republican. Roman Catholic. Home: 23812 Russell Rd Bay Village OH 44140-2839 Office: 35000 Ctr ridge Ste 6 Westlake OH 44145 Office Phone: 440-835-5770.

TODD COPLEY, JUDITH A., engineering educator; b. Wakefield, West Yorkshire, Eng., Dec. 13, 1950; arrived in US, 1978; d. Marley and Joan Mary (Birkinshaw) Booth; m. David Michael Todd, June 17, 1972 (div. June 1981); m. Stephen Michael Copley, Aug. 3, 1984; 1 child, Amy Elizabeth. BA in Materials Sci., Cambridge U., Eng., 1972, MA, PhD in Metall./Materials Sci., 1976. Rsch. asst. Imperial Coll. Sci. and Tech., London, 1976-78; rsch. assoc. SUNY, Stonybrook, 1978; rsch. engr. U. Calif., Berkeley, 1979-81; asst. prof. materials sci. and mech. engring. U. So. Calif., L.A., 1982—90; assoc. prof. metall. and materials engring. Ill. Inst. Tech., Chgo., 1990-97, assoc. chair mech. materials and aerospace engring., 1995—2001, prof. materials and mech. engring., 1997—2002, assoc. dean rsch. Armour Coll. Engring. and Sci., 2001—02; P.B. Breneman dept. head chair chair dept. engring. sci. and mechanics Pa. State U., University Park, 2002—. Mem. task force Materials Property Coun., N.Y.C., 1979—89; prof. Iron and Steel Soc., 1996—2002; mem. editl. bds. Contbr. articles to profl. jours.; patentee in field. Recipient Brit. Univs. Student Travel award, 1972, Brit. Fedn. Univ. Women award, 1972, Faculty Rsch. award Oak Ridge (Tenn.) Nat. Lab., 1986, Vanadium award British Inst. Materials, 1990; Kathryn Kingswell Meml. scholar, 1972, Julia Beveridge Award, IIT, 1998, Cert. Appreciation Am. Soc. Mech. Engrs., 1995, 97, Forging Industry Ednl. Rsch. Found., 1993, Booz-Allen and Hamilton Award for Tchg. and Svc., Ill. Inst. Tech., 1996, Mary Ewart Traveling Scholarship, Cambridge Univ., 1972, Sci. Rsch. Coun. Fellowship and Overseas Travel Award, 1972. Fellow ASM Internat., ASME Internat. (chmn. materials and fabrication com. 1993-97, pressure vessel and piping divsn. membership chair PVP divsn., 1997-2001, assoc. editor Jour. Pressure Vessel and Piping Tech. 1994-2001, exec. com. and publs. chair PVP divsn. 2001-05, v.p. mfg. group 2002-05, tech. program chair, 2004-05, tech. conf. chair 2005—, bd. on women and miniorites award 1997), Soc. Engring. Sci. (bd. dirs. 2006—), Assn. Women in Sci., ASM Internat. (chmn. LA chpt. 1986-87, coun. mem. materials sci. divsn. 1984-89); mem. AIME (Rsch. award 1983), ASTM, AAUW, Soc. Women Engrs. (sr.), Electron Microscopy Soc., Electrochem. Soc., Hist. Metallurgy Soc., Nat. Soc. Corrosion Engrs. (Seed grant award 1983), Microbeam Analysis Soc., Soc. Mfg. Engrs. (sr.), Instn. Materials, Chartered (sr.) Engr. Status, Minerals, Metals, Materials Soc. of the Am. Inst. Mining, Metall. Petroleum Engrs., Am. Ceramics Soc., Ill. Microscopical Soc., Soc. Engring. Sci. (mem. bd. dirs.). Avocation: archaeology. Office: Pennsylvania State Univ Dept Engring Sci and Mechanics 212 Earth-Engring Sci Bldg University Park PA 16802-6812 Office Phone: 814-863-0771. E-mail: jtodd@psu.edu.

TODEBUSH, PATRICIA METTHE, chemistry professor; BA, Smith Coll., Northampton, Mass., 1996; PhD, U. of Ga., Athens, 2000. Lectr. Northwestern U., Evanston, Ill., 2001—04; asst. prof. of chemistry Clayton State U., Morrow, Ga., 2004—. Achievements include research in Chemical Education and Computational Chemistry. Office: Clayton State Univ 2000 Clayton State Blvd Morrow GA 30260 Office Phone: 678-466-4788.

TODOROVA-MORENO, ILINA, psychologist, educator; arrived in U.S., 1996; children: Barbara Cvejik, Simonida Cvejic. PhD, U. Belgrade, 1987. Lic. psychologist Mo. Prof. U. Chyril and Methodius, Skopje, 1975—96, St. Louis U., 2000—. Exec. dir., psychotherapist, founder CARE MHS, St. Louis, 2002—; pres., founder Harmony in Life, St. Louis, 2002—. Author: (book) My Drawings-My Truth: Psychology of Children's drawings, 1997, Wake Up Your Creative Mind: Psychology of Creative Thinking, 1994, Psychology, 1996. Mem.: APA. Office: Ilina Todorova Moreno 3615 Morganford Rd Saint Louis MO 63116-1612 Personal E-mail: ilinam@aol.com.

TOENSING, VICTORIA, lawyer; b. Colon, Panama, Oct. 16, 1941; d. Philip William and Victoria (Brady) Long; m. Trent David Toensing, Oct. 29, 1962 (div. 1976); children: Todd Robert, Brady Cronon, Amy Victoriana; m. Joseph E. diGenova, June 27, 1981. BS in Edn., Ind. U., 1962; JD cum laude, U. Detroit, 1975. Bar: Mich. 1976, D.C. 1978. Tchr. English, Milw., 1965-66; law clk. to presiding justice U.S. Ct. Appeals, Detroit, 1975-76; asst. U.S. atty. U.S. Atty.'s Office, Detroit, 1976-81; chief counsel U.S. Senate Intelligence Com., Washington, 1981-84; dep. asst. atty. gen. criminal div. Dept. Justice, Washington, 1984-88; spl. counsel Hughes Hubbard & Reed, Washington, 1988-90; ptnr. Cooter and Gell, Washington, 1990-91; ptnr., co-chmn. nat. white collar group Manatt, Phelps and Phillips, Washington, 1991-95; founding ptnr. diGenova & Toensing, Wasington, 1996—. Mem. working group on corp. sanctions U.S. Sentencing Commn., 1988-89; co-chairperson Coalition for Women's Appts. Justice Judiciary Task Force, 1988-92; spl. counsel for Teamsters investigation, U.S. Ho. of Reps., Subcom. on Oversight and Investigations of com. on Edn. and the Workforce, 1997-98. Author: Bringing Sanity to the Insanity Defense, 1983, Mens Rea: Insanity by Another Name, 1984; contbg. author: Fighting Back: Winning The War Against Terrorism, Desk Book on White Collar Crime, 1991; contbr. articles to profl. jours. Founder, chmn. Women's Orgn. To Meet Existing Needs, Mich., 1975-79; chmn. Republican Women's Task Force, 1979-81; bd. dirs. Project on Equal Edn. Rights, Mich., 1980-81, Nat. Hist. Intelligence Mus., 1987-95, America's Talking Legal Analyst, 1995; MSNBC legal analyst, 1998-99. Recipient spl. commendation Office U.S. Atty. Gen., 1980, agy. seal medallion CIA, 1986, award of achievement Alpha Chi Omega, 1992; featured on cover N.Y. Time Mag. for anti-terrorism work, April 1991. Mem. ABA (mem. standing com. on law and nat. security, mem. coun. criminal justice sect., mem. adv. com. complex crimes and litigation, vice chmn. white collar crime com., chmn. subcom. on corp. criminal liability). Office Phone: 202-289-7701.

TOEPFER, SUSAN JILL, editor-in-chief; b. Rochester, Minn., Mar. 9, 1948; d. John Bernard and Helen Esther (Chapple) Toepfer; m. Lorenzo Gabriel Carcaterra, May 16, 1981; children: Katherine Marie, Nicholas Gabriel. BA, Bennington Coll., 1970. Mng. editor Photoplay Mag., N.Y.C., 1971-72; freelance writer N.Y.C., 1972-78; TV week editor N.Y. Daily News, N.Y.C., 1978-79, leisure editor, 1979-82, features editor, 1982-84, arts and entertainment editor, 1984-86, exec. mag. editor, 1986-87; sr. writer People Mag., N.Y.C., 1987-89, sr. editor, 1989-91, asst. mng. editor, 1991-94, exec. editor, 1994—2000, dep. mng. editor, 2000—02; editor-in-chief Rosie Mag., 2002, Devel. G+J USA, N.Y.C., 2003—04, Quick & Simple, N.Y.C., 2005—. Home: 225 7th Ave #10X New York NY 10001

TOERGE, LYNN, athletic trainer; b. Pitts., Nov. 11, 1955; d. John Elmer and Mary Ruth Toerge. BS, Ind. State U., Terre Haute, 1981. Athletic trainer, phys. ed. tchr. Hampton Sch. Dist., Allison Park, Pa., 1983—87, cert. athletic trainer, 1983—. EMT, paramedic Ross/West View EMS, Pitts., 1987—97. Mem.: Nat. Athletic Trainers Assn. (licentiate athletic trainer cert.). R-Conservative. Avocations: golf, drawing, weightlifting. Home: 203 Monroe Dr Pittsburgh PA 15229 Office: Hampton Sch Dist 2929 McCully Rd Allison Park PA 15101 Office Phone: 412-486-6000. Office Fax: 412-486-7050. Personal E-mail: ltoerge@comcast.net.

TOFFLER, HEIDI, author, futurist; b. N.Y.C., Aug. 1, 1929; d. William and Elizabeth A. (Kraayer) Farrell; m. Alvin Toffler April 29, 1950; 1 daughter, Karen. AB, Long Island U., 1949; Doctor of Laws (hon.), Manhattan Coll.; Doctor of Letters (hon.), Dowling Coll. Pres., exec. prod. Triwave Prodns., inc., Dover, Del., 1981—; Adjunct prof. National Defense U., D.C, 1994—. Author (with Alvin Toffler) The Culture Consumers, 1964, Future Shock, 1970, The Eco-Spasm Report, 1975, The Third Wave, 1980, Previews and Premises, 1983, The Adaptive Corporation, 1986, Powershift, 1990, War and Anti-War, 1983, Creating a New Civilization, 1995; editor, Schoolhouse in the City, 1968, The Futurists, 1972, Learning for Tomorrow, 1974; contbr. articles to national and internat. journals. Mem. adv. bd. Democracy Inst. D.C. 1994—. Hon. Co-chair Unifem USA (UN Development Fund for Women) N.Y.C. 1988—, Sci. Adv. Comm. Piu Manzu Found. Italy, 1987—, Bd. Govs. Intern Inst. Stress, 1983. Recipient Prix du Meilleur Livre Etrange, France 1971, Medal for Distinguished Contribution to Management Literature, McKinsey Foundation, 1971, Golden Key Award, China, 1987, Medal of the President of the Italian Republic, Government of Italy, 1987; National Book Award (nominee) 1970. Address: C/O Linda Paul 1015 Gayley Ave Ste 1204 Los Angeles CA 90024-3424

TOFT, MONICA DUFFY, economics professor; d. William John Jude and Joan Marie (Clancy) Duffy; m. Ivan Michael Arreguin-Toft, May 1, 1961; children: Samuel Lawton, Sophia Eleanor. AA, U. Md., Augsburg, 1987; BA, U. Calif., Santa Barbara, 1990; MA, U. Chgo., 1992, PhD, 1998. Asst. prof. Harvard U., Cambridge, Mass., 1999—2004, asst. dir. John M. Olin Inst. Strategic Studies, 1999—, assoc. prof., 2004—. Sgt. U.S. Army, 1983—87. Office: Harvard U 79 JFK St Cambridge MA 02138

TÖGEL, CORNELIA (CONNI) D., artist; b. Winfield, Ill., July 24, 1965; d. Heinrich and Lisa Scherz; m. Peter Horst Tögel, Apr. 1, 1989; children: Jamie-Lee, Holly, Annie-Mae. Grad. Kolping Coll. Applied Graphics, Stuttgart, Germany, 1993. With Charisma Art, Colorado Springs, Colo. Author: Briefe die das Leben schrieb; exhibitions include Magnum Opus XIV, Sacramento Fine Arts Ctr., Pandora's Box, Manitou Springs Bus. Art Ctr., Colo. Artist Show, Denver, Charisma Art Gallery, Colo. Springs, Colo., Earth Works Art Gallery & Studio, NY, DK Galleries, Germany, Galeria Columbretes, Spain, Represented in permanent collections George W. Bush, Quincy Jones, Kevin Michaels, prin. works include various mags. Founder Artbus.com. Mem.: Am. Watercolor Soc., Nat. Watercolor Soc., Watercolor West, Pikes Peak Watercolor Soc. (assoc.), Askart.com, 5 Graces, AskART.com. Business E-Mail: conni@charisma-art.com.

TOGNOLI, ERA M., performing company executive, artistic director; b. Italy; Gen. mgr., artistic dir., founder Metro Lyric Opera, Allenhurst, NJ, 1959—. Office: Metro Lyric Opera PO Box 35 Allenhurst NJ 07711-0035*

TOKER, KAREN HARKAVY, physician; b. New Haven, Oct. 23, 1942; d. Victor M. and Nedra (Israel) Harkavy; m. Cyril Toker, Sept. 1, 1968; children: David Edward, Rachel Lee. BS in Chemistry, Coll. William and Mary, 1963; MD, Yale U., 1967. Diplomate Am. Bd. Pediat. Intern dept. pediat. Bronx Mcpl. Hosp. Ctr., Albert Einstein Coll. Medicine, N.Y., 1967-68, asst. resident dept. pediat., 1968-69, sr. resident dept. pediat., 1969, 70-71, attending pediatrician, 1971-72, 73-76; pediatrician Montgomery Health Dept., Silver Springs, Md., 1976-83; pediatric cons. Head Start Program Montgomery County Pub. Schs., Rockville, Md., 1976-83; pvt. practice gen. pediat. Rockville, 1983-89; pediatrician Nemours Children's Clinic, Jacksonville, Fla., 1991-95; med. dir. Pearl Plaza Pediatrics, Duval County Pub. Health Unit, 1995-97; instr. pediat. Albert Einstein Coll. Medicine, N.Y., 1971-74, asst. prof. pediat., 1974-76; clin. asst. prof. U. Fla., 1995—2003; med. dir. Ctr. for Women and Children, Duval County Health Dept., 1997—2003; pediatric cons. Urban Child Health, 2003—. Exec. bd. sec. Congregation Har Shalom, Potomac, 1989-91. Fellow Am. Acad. Pediat.; mem. Fla. Med. Assn., Duval County Med. Soc., Ambulatory Pediatric Assn. Democrat. Jewish. Avocations: piano, opera, ballet, swimming. Home and Office: 6030 Oakbrook Ct Ponte Vedra Beach FL 32082 Office Phone: 904-285-6851.

TOKHEIM, SARA ANN, writer, information technology professional; b. Cedar Rapids, Iowa, Dec. 15, 1941; d. George Elmer and Helen Clay (Blessing) Tokheim. Programmer Westinghouse Learning Corp., Iowa City, Iowa, 1969-75; cons. U. Iowa, 1976-81, Davis Thomas & Assocs., Mpls., 1982-86, IBM, Mpls., 1986-92. Ind. cons., 1992-96, State of N.Mex., 1996—. Author: (play) The Hand, 1998. Pres., SCORE, Santa Fe, 1997-98. Mem City Different Bus. and Profl. Orgn. (treas.). Avocations: softball, writing screenplays and poetry. Office: 4491 Cerrillos Rd Santa Fe NM 87507-9721

TOKUNAGA, YASUKO, performing company executive; b. Salt Lake City, Utah, July 17, 1948; d. Shigao and Utako Seiki Tokunaga. BFA, The Juliard Sch., 1970. Co-founder, artistic dir. Tokunaga Dan Ko, N.Y.C., NY, 1967—; dir. The Boston Coservatory, Dance Divsn., Boston, 1989—. Bd. dirs. Boston Dance Alliance, Boston, 1992; profl. adv. Dance Notation Bur., N.Y.C., NY, 2001—05; panelist Mass. Culture Coun., Boston, 1987—88, 2004—05. Choreographer The Stream Flows, Harvard U., 2004, NEC, 2005. Recipient Meritous Svc. award, SC State Coll., 1984, Lincoln U., 1983, Keys to City, Japan, 1987. Mem.: Nat. Dance Alliance, Internat. Assn. of Dance Medicine, Nat. Assn.Schs. Dance (pres. 1989). Home: PO Box 1008 Boston MA 02123 Office: The Boston Conservatory 8 The Fenway Boston MA 02215 Office Phone: 617-912-9137. E-mail: ytokunaga@bostonconservatory.edu.

TOLAR, ANNE MELTON, minister, music educator; b. Geneva, Ala., Jan. 17, 1937; d. Ernest Lester and Lovie Hewett Melton; m. Robert F. Tolar, Apr. 21, 1966; children: Robert Jr., William, Sharon Tolar Stone, Ginny Tolar Knight. BA in English & Psychology, U. Ala., 1959; BA in Music/Piano, U. W. Fla., 1960. Teller/bookkeeper 1st Bank & Trust, Pensacola, Fla., 1952—56, collections & loan officer Atlanta; br. office asst. mgr. 1st Fed. Savings & Loan Assn., Atlanta, 1970—73; evangelist, musician, tchr. Fountain of Praise Ministries, St. Pauls, NC, 1972—; presbyter, min. Missionary Ch. Internat., Columbia, SC, 1985—; music tchr. St. Pauls; tchr., musician, pastor Fountain of Praise Ch., Lumberton, NC, 2001—. Judge Mountain Gospel Music; v.p. Fountain of Praise Ministries, Missionary Ch. Internat., Lumberton, NC, 2001—; spkr. in field. Author: (book) Wilt Thou Be Made Whole?, 1988; songwriter: 106 songs and cantatas. Named Internat. Savings & Loan Speech Contest, Atla., 1972; recipient Mother of Yr. award, Fountain of Praise Ch., St. Pauls, N.C., 1998. Republican. Mem. Christian Ch. Office: Fountain of Praise Ministries Cedar St Lumberton NC 28358

TOLBERT, BETH WILLDEN, real estate company executive, broker; b. Delta, Utah, Apr. 7, 1935; d. Delbert B. and Mildred (Twitchell) Willden; m. Stanley Tolbert, May 12, 1955; children: Keven, Tracy, Troy. Student, Brigham Young U., 1953-54. Cert. residential specialist. Realtor Harding Realty, Am. Fork, Utah, 1976-82; associate broker Pine Valley Realty, Alpine, Utah, 1982-97; prin., owner Beth Tolbert Realty Group, St. George, Utah, 1997—; ptnr., prin. broker Tolbert & Nielsen Realty Group, LLC, St. George, Utah, 2003—. Apptd. Utah Real Estate Commn., Salt Lake City, 1993—, chair 1993-94; bd. trustees Utah Valley State Coll., Orem, 1991—, chair 1996-97; pres. Nat. Womens Coun. Realtors, 1994; bd. trustees Leadership Dixie, 2000-01. Recipient Realtor of Yr. award Utah Assoc. Realtors, 1984, Distinguished Svc. award 1994, 97, Realtor of Yr. award Utah County Bd. Realtors, 1984. Home: 656 Country Ln Santa Clara UT 84765-5471

TOLBERT, CORNELIA EMMA, music educator; b. St. Louis, Mo., Sept. 15, 1954; d. Cornelius and Morzell Tolbert. BA, St. Louis U., 1977. Cert. instrumental and vocal music tchr. grades K-12 Mo., 1982. Substitute tchr. St. Louis Pub. Schs., 1975—83, piano and voice tchr., 1976—78, vocal music tchr., 1985—95, asst. music tchr., 1997—2001, instrumental music asst. tchr., 2001—; pvt. piano and organ tchr. Ludwig Aeolian Music Store, 1982—85. Music choral dir. Meth. Ch., St. Louis, 1972—, asst. orgn., 1977—2003, pianist, 2003—. Vol. phone bank St. Louis Tchrs. Union, 2004; coord. for United Way St. Louis Pub. Schs., 2004, coord. William L. Clay Scholarship fund, 2004. Recipient Editor's Choice award, Internat. Soc. Poets, 2001. Mem.: St. Louis Univ. Alumni Assn., Internat. Soc. Poets, Am. Fedn. Tchrs., St. Louis Tchrs. Union Local 420, Nat. Music Educators Assn., Mo. Music Tchrs. Assn. Democrat. Methodist. Avocations: bowling, tennis, ping pong/table tennis, writing songs, gardening.

TOLBERT, NINA DIANNE, library and information scientist; b. Washington, July 20, 1964; d. Alvin Joseph and Cleora Demetrice (Cato) T. BA cum laude, Marymount Coll., 1986; Diploma, Strayer U., Washington, 2003. Libr. page Folger Shakespeare Libr., Washington, 1986-87; tech. editor Vitro Corp., Silver Spring, Md., 1987; sec. HAY Systems, Inc., Washington, 1988; proofreader ASCI Corp., Washington, 1989; sec. USAF, Washington, 1991-94; libr. technician Telesec, Gaithersburg, Md., 1995, Libr. Systems & Svcs., Washington, 1995-99; proofreader, intellectual property specialist trainee Oblon, Spivak, McClelland, Maier and Neustadt, P.C., Alexandria, Va., 2000—. D.C. Sch. Librs. scholar, 1982, Marymount Coll. scholar, 1983-84. Democrat. Baptist. Avocations: stamp collecting/philately, piano, reading. Office Phone: 703-412-1438. E-mail: ninit71964@earthlink.net.

TOLCHIN, JOAN GUBIN, psychiatrist, educator; b. NYC, Mar. 10, 1944; d. Harold and Bella (Newman) Gubin; m. Matthew Armin Tolchin, Sept. 1, 1966; 1 child, Benjamin. AB, Vassar Coll., 1964; MD, NYU, 1972. Diplomate Am. Bd. Gen. Psychiatry, Am. Bd. Child Psychiatry. Rsch. asst. Albert Einstein Coll. Medicine, N.Y.C., 1964-68; instr. psychiatry med. coll. Cornell U., N.Y.C., 1977-78, clin. instr., 1978-86, clin. asst. prof., 1986—2004, clin. assoc. prof., 2004—. Contbr. articles to profl. jours., chapters to books. Fellow: Am. Acad. Child and Adolescent Psychiatry; mem.: N.Y. Coun. Child and Adolescent Psychiatry (bd. dirs. 1992—96, pres. 1994—95, bd. advisors 2001—), Am. Acad. Psychoanalysis and Dynamic Psychiatry (sec. 1998—2001), Alpha Omega Alpha. Office: 35 E 84th St New York NY 10028-0871

TOLCHIN, SUSAN JANE, political science professor, writer; b. N.Y.C., Jan. 14, 1941; d. Jacob Nathan and Dorothy Ann (Markowitz) Goldsmith; m. Martin Tolchin, Dec. 23, 1965; 1 child, Karen Rebecca. BA, Bryn Mawr Coll., 1961; MA, U. Chgo., 1962; PhD, NYU, 1968. Lectr. in polit. sci. CCNY, N.Y.C., 1963-65, Bklyn. Coll., 1965-71; adj. asst. prof. polit. sci. Seton Hall U., South Orange, NJ, 1971-73; assoc. prof. polit. sci., dir. Inst. for Women and Politics, Mt. Vernon Coll., Washington, 1975-78; prof. pub. adminstrn. George Washington U., Washington, 1978-98; prof. pub. policy Sch. Pub. Policy George Mason U., Fairfax, Va., 1998—. Disting. lectr. Indsl. Coll. Armed Forces, 1994. Author: The Angry American: How Voter Rage is Changing the Nation, 1996, 2d edit., 1998; author: (with Martin Tolchin) To the Victor: Political Patronage from the Clubhouse to the White House, 1971, Clout--Womanpower and Politics, 1974, Dismantling America--The Rush to Deregulate, 1983, Buying Into America--How Foreign Money Is Changing the Face of Our Nation, 1988, Selling Our Securit--The Erosion of America's Assets, 1992, Glass Houses--Congressional Ethics and the Politics of Venom, 2001, A World Ignited: How Apostles of Ethnic, Religions and Racial Hatred Torch the Globe, 2006. Bd. dirs. Cystic Fibrosis Found., 1982-98; county committeewoman Dem. Party, Montclair, N.J., 1969-73. Recipient Founder's Day award NYU, 1968, Trachtenberg award for rsch. George Washington U., 1998; named Tchr. of Yr., Mt. Vernon Coll., 1978; Dilthey fellow George Washington U., 1983, Aspen Inst. fellow, 1979. Fellow Nat. Acad. Pub. Adminstrn.; mem. Am. Polit. Sci. Assn. (pres. Women's Caucus for Polit. Sci.

1977-78), Am. Soc. Pub. Adminstrn. (chair sect. natural resources and environ. adminstrn. 1982-83, Marshall Dimock award 1997). Democrat. Office: Sch Pub Policy George Mason U Fairfax VA 22030 Business E-Mail: tolchin@gmu.edu.

TOLEDO, BRIDGET MARIE, librarian; b. Pitts., Aug. 26, 1959; d. Vincent and Teresa (Palumbo) Gazzo; m. Luis Jorge Toledo, Nov. 7, 1981. BA, Westminster Coll., 1981; MLS, U. Md., 1984. Tech. svcs. libr. Am. Coun. Life Ins., Washington, 1984; libr. fellow USIA, Quito, Ecuador, 1985-86; libr. Pre-Columbian Studies Dumbarton Oaks Rsch. Libr., Washington, 1987—. Mem. ALA. Home: 319 E Clifford Ave Alexandria VA 22305-2708 Office: Pre-Columbian Studies Dumbarton Oaks Rsch Libr 1703 32nd St NW Washington DC 20007-2934

TOLER, PENNY, former professional basketball player, sports team executive; b. Mar. 24, 1966; B in Psychology, Long Beach State U., 1989. Guard, Montecchio, Italy, 1989—91, Pescara, Italy, 1991—94, Sporting Flash, Greece, 1994—96, Ramat HaSharon, Israel, 1996—97, Los Angeles Sparks, (WNBA), 1997—99; gen. mgr. L.A. Sparks, 1999—. Mem. U.S. Basketball Olympic Com., 1999—. Founder Points from Penny Program, 1998. Named All-Am. & Co-Player of Yr./Big West, 1988, 1989. Achievements include scored first ever basket in WNBA history. Avocations: ping pong/table tennis, tennis, craps. Office: LA Sparks Great Western Forum 555 N Nash St El Segundo CA 90245-2818

TOLIA, VASUNDHARA K., pediatric gastroenterologist, educator; b. Calcutta, India; came to U.S., 1975; d. Rasiklal and Saroj (Kothari) Doshi; m. Kirit Tolia, May 30, 1975; children: Vinay, Sanjay. MBBS, Calcutta U., 1968-75. Intern, resident Children's Hosp. Mich., Detroit, 1976-79, fellow, 1979-81, dir. pediat. endoscopy unit, 1984-90, dir. pediat. gastroenterology and nutrition, 1990—2005. Instr. Wayne State U., Detroit, 1981—83, asst. prof., 1983—91, assoc. prof., 1991—97, prof., 1997—2005. Mem. editl. bd. Inflammatory Bowel Diseases, 1999— Am. Jour. Gastroenterology, 1999, Rev. of World Lit. in Pediatrics, 1999—, AAP Grand Rounds and Therapy, 2006—; contbr. articles to profl. jours. Named Woman of Distinction, Mich. chpt. Crohn's and Colitis Found. Am., 1991. Fellow Am. Coll. Gastroenterology (chair ad-hoc com. pediat. gastroenterology 1998-2000), Am. Acad. Pediats.; mem. Am. Gastroenterology Assn., N.Am. Soc. Pediat. Gastroenterology and Nutrition, Soc. Pediat. Rsch. Office Phone: 248-737-8793. Personal E-mail: vasu.tolia@gmail.com.

TOLL, BARBARA ELIZABETH, art gallery director; b. Phila., June 8, 1945; d. Joseph M. and Evelyn Toll BA, Goucher Coll., 1967; MFA, Pratt Inst., 1969. Asst. dir. jr. coun. Mus. Modern Art, N.Y.C., 1969-70; dir. Hundred Acres Gallery, N.Y.C., 1971-76; curator David Rockefeller Collection, N.Y.C., 1975-81; pres., dir. Barbara Toll Fine Arts, N.Y.C., 1981-94, dir., 1994—. Bd. dirs. Corp. Yaddo; curator Focus: Donald Judd Furniture, Parrish Art Mus., Southampton, NY, 1996, Friendships in Arcadia: Writers and Artists at Yaddo in the 90s, 2000, Follies: Fantasy in the Landscape, Parrish Art Mus., 2001, Reconfiguring Space: Blueprints for Art in Gen., 2003. Trustee Ind. Curators Internat.; nat. bd. dirs. ArtTable, 2001—04. Avocation: gardening. Office: 138 Prince St New York NY 10012-3135

TOLLE, MELINDA EDITH, engineer, researcher; b. N.Y., Aug. 8, 1964; d. Robert Dale and Mildred Elva Tolle. BS in Physics, U. Utah, 1986, BS in Geophysics, 1986, MS in Mech. Engring., 1988. Cert. quality engr. Am. Soc. for Quality; cert. quality mgr. Am. Soc. for Quality. Engr. assoc. Thiokol, Brigham City, Utah, 1987-88, sr. engr. assoc., 1988-90, engr., 1990-92, sr. scientist, sr. engr., 1992-98, prin. scientist, prin. engr., 1998-2000; sr. prin. scientist, sr. prin. engr. Alcoa, Brigham City, Utah, 2000—. Adj. instr. Weber State U., Ogden, Utah, 1996—. Mem. AIAA (regional dep. dir. Meb 2000—, Utah sect. chair-elect 1998-99, chair 1999—), Am. Soc. for Quality (sect. chair 1997-98, mem. chair 1995-96, vice chair 1996-97, strategic mgmt. plan chair 2000—), Am. Nuc. Soc., Utah Engring. Coun. (bd. dirs. 1998—), Alpha Nu Sigma (pres. 1988). Office: Thiokol PO Box 707 Brigham City UT 84302-0707

TOLLEY, MICHELLE RENEE, secondary school educator; b. Borger, Tex., Feb. 12, 1962; d. Johnny and Dianna Lee Sursa; m. David Lee Tolley, June 9, 1984; children: Kristen, Katrina, Karlye. BS in Home Econs., Tex. Tech. U., Lubbock, 1989. Cert. tchr. Tex. Tchr. elem. edn. Houston Ind. Sch. Dist., 1989—92; tchr. secondary edn. Bay Area Christian Sch., League City, Tex., 1997—. Club sponsor Tex. Jr. Beta, Tex., 1996—, Tex. sponsor-elect, 2003—05, Tex. state sponsor, 2005—07. Mem.: Amateur Softball Assn. (cert. coach 2003—06). Republican. Bapt. Avocations: coaching softball, crafts. Home: 10347 Sagegate Houston TX 77089 Business E-Mail: mtolley@bacschool.org.

TOLLISON, COURTNEY L., history professor; b. Greenville, SC, Aug. 26, 1977; d. Charles David and Linda Surett Tollison. BA, Furman U., 1999; MA, U. SC., 2001, PhD, 2003. Rsch. asst. Smithsonian Instn., Nat. Mus. of Am. History, Washington, 1998—98; instr. history Columbia Coll., SC, 2001—01, Dalton State Coll., Ga., 2003—03; vis. adj. asst. prof. history Furman U., Greenville, SC, 2004—; dir. oral history project Office of Pres. David E. Shi, Furman U., Greenville, SC, 2004—. Advanced placement reader for us history advanced placement exam Ednl. Testing Svc., Princeton, NJ, 2004—05. Author: Furman University, 2004 (Matrix award Nat. Assn. Women in Comms., 2005); contbr. chapters to books. Head agt. class of 1999 Furman U. Devel. Office, Greenville, SC, 2004—05, class agt., coll. graduating class, 1999—2004; reunion com. co-chair Furman U., 2004. Named Communicator of Yr. award, Assn. Women in Comm., 2005; named one of 35 and Under Best and Brightest, Greenville Mag.; recipient Young Profl. Yr., Greenville, SC C. of C., 2006, Head Agy Yr. award, Furman U., 1999, 2005—06. Mem.: So. Assn. of Women Historians, SC. Hist. Assn., Orgn. of Am. Historians, Am. Hist. Assn., Phi Alpha Theta, Alpha Delta Pi (life; stds. chair 1997—98). Avocations: reading, swimming, travel, ballet. Office Phone: 864-294-2377. Personal E-mail: courtneytollison@yahoo.com. Business E-Mail: courtney.tollison@furman.edu.

TOLLIVER, DOROTHY, librarian; b. N.Y.C., Apr. 10, 1937; d. Morris and Rose (Poliner) Lamm; m. Robert F. Tolliver, Sept. 3, 1956; children: Craig Lee, Marc Alan. BA, Ind. U., 1958; MSLS, U. Ill., Champaign-Urbana, 1973. Inter-libr., reference libr. L.A. County Libr., 1958-59; dir. libr. Temple City (Calif.) Pub. Libr., 1959-60; reference, young adult libr. Burbank (Calif.) Pub. Libr., 1960-62; PTA libr. Roselawn Elem. Sch., Danville, Ill., 1970-72; reference libr. Danville Area C.C., 1970—72, head libr., 1973—88; libr. dir. Kahului Pub. Libr., 1988—89; head libr. UH Maui C.C., Kahului, 1989—, unit head for outreach and acad. support, 2004—. Cons. Ill. Office Edn., 1980-88, Hawaii Dept. Edn., 1992—. Mem. Commn. Status of Women, 1992—98; sec. Maui County Com. Status of Women, 1991—96; dir. Jewish Arts and Edn. Coun. Maui, 1996—99; mem. Hawaii Book Acad., judge Ka Pala Pala Po'okela awards, 2002—; chair Maui County Women's Conf., 1993; vice chair Maui County Commn. Persons with Disabilities, 1996—2001; pres. S&M Katz Jewish Libr. of Maui, 1996—, Hawaii Ctr. for the Book, 2002—; bd. dirs. Congregation Gan Eden, 1990—, pres., 1991—95; bd. dirs. Congregation Israel, pres., 1983—87; bd. dirs. Maui Cmty. Theater, 1997—; actor, dir. Voices on the Wind Readers' Theater, 1992—. Recipient Little Red Schoolhouse award Danville Schs. Citizens Com., 1972, Hawaii State award for leadership in promoting postive soc. change, edu. and womens equity, 1997. Mem.: AAUW (pres. Maui chpt. 1993—97, state bd. dirs. 1993, Hawaii State award), ALA, Am. Coll. and Rsch. Librs., Maui County Libr. Assn. (pres. 1990—96), Hawaii Libr. Assn. (bd. dirs.), Phi Beta Mu (alpha chpt.). Jewish. Avocations: reading, theater, travel. Office: Maui Community Coll 310 W Kaahumanu Ave Kahului HI 96732-1617 Office Phone: 808-984-3583. E-mail: tolliver@hawaii.edu.

TOLLIVER, LORRAINE, language educator, writer; d. Elbert and Maggie Tolliver; m. Gerald Levin, 1974 (div. 1986); 1 child from previous marriage, Roger Anthony Regensburg (dec.). BA, Calif. State U., Northridge, 1963; MA, U. Calif. L.A., 1966. Radio and TV writer WHIO, Dayton, Ohio, 1954—57, WCPO, Cin., 1953—54; reporter and editl. writer Advertiser - Press Newspapers, Hawthorne, Calif., 1971; instr. English upper divsn. Chapman Coll. Residence Ctr., Riverside, Calif., 1968—69; instr. English Long. Beach (Calif.) City Coll., 1969—89; prof. English Compton Coll., Calif., 1971—2000; instr. English West L.A. Coll., Culver City, Calif., 1974—. Instr. and coord. Compton Coll. Work Experience Program, 1974—75; pub. reader, presenter. Author: (books) Sibelius, 2002 (Dance of the Sun Pubs. award); poet: poem Feelings of the Heart, 2001 (2d pl., 2001), front cover poem Scroll Original Artist mag., 2002, Freshwater Poetry mag., 2003 (Spl. Recognition award, 2003). Mem.: AFT. Achievements include over two hundred poems published in literary jours. in approximately thirty states, mostly on the east and west coasts. A few have been published in Can. Avocations: hiking, travel, hosting cultural groups, theater, creative writing workshops. Home: 3873 Woodside Dr Richmond IN 47374

TOLLIVER, SHEILA MAUREEN, county administrator; b. Washington, Oct. 16, 1946; d. Wallace Charles and Marcella June (Strampe) Young; m. Larry Wayne Tolliver, June 12, 1966; children— Perry Todd, Danielle Rebecca. B.A., U. Md., 1968, M.A., 1972, Ph.D., 1984. Tchr. English, Annapolis Schs. (Md.), 1968-70, Prince George's County Schs., Bowie, Md., 1970-72; grad. asst. U. Md., College Park, 1975-77, lectr. 1976; exec. aide for edn. Office of Gov. Md., Annapolis, 1977-87; administrv. intern to dir., 1976—; asst. v.p. policy and planning system adminstrn. U. Md., 1987-88, asst. dep. chancellor system adminstrn., 1988-1993; adminstr. Howard County Coun., 1993-94, 98—; alderman Annapolis City Coun., 1997-2005; cons. Spl. Edn. Task Force, Md. State Dept. Edn., 1977; coordinator Md. State Edn. Policy Seminars Program, 1982—86; mem. Johns Hopkins U. Ctr. for Met. Planning and Research, Task Force Urban Edn. and Met. Labor Force, 1983; adv. com. U. Md. Vocat. Rehab., 1978-83, State Occupational Info. Coordinating Com., 1980; mem. State Coordinating Com. Edn. of Handicapped Children, 1978-83, Task Force on Gifted and Talented, U. Md., 1980, State Adv. Council on Reading, State Dept. Edn., 1978, State Coun. on Vocat. Tech. Edn.; alderman Annapolis City Coun., Md., 1997-2005; staff dir. Comm. on Excellence in Higher Edn., Task Force on Flexibility in Higher Edn. Bd. dirs. Interstate Conf. State Employment Security Adminstrs.; Howard County Coun., 1993-95, 1998—; employmeny security State of Md. 1993-97. HEW fellow Bur. of Edn. for Handicapped, 1974-75; toll fellow council of State Govts., 1986—. Mem. spl. Am. Edn. Fin. Assn., Council for Exceptional Children. Democrat. Lutheran. Office: Howard County Coun 3430 Court House Dr Ellicott City MD 21043-4300

TOLMACH, JANE LOUISE, community activist, municipal official; b. Havre, Mont., Nov. 12, 1921; d. Robert Francis and Veronica (Tracy) McCormick; m. Daniel Michael Tolmach (Dec.), Sept. 9, 1946; children: James, Richard, Eve Alice, Adam, Jonathan. AB, UCLA, 1943; M in Social Scis., Smith Coll., 1945; JD, S. We. U., L.A., 1981. Social worker ARC Field Svcs. Corona Naval Hosp., Norco, Calif., 1945-46; chmn. bd. dirs. Camarillo (Calif.) State Hosp., 1959-68; trustee Oxnard (Calif.) Union High Sch. Dist., 1965-72; mem. state reclamation bd. Calif., 1981-82; mem. bd. govs. Calif. C.C., 1982-87; mem. bd. St. John's Regional Hosp., Oxnard, 1986-89; mem. bd. of assessment appeals County of Ventura, Ventura, Calif., 1992—2002, transp. commr., 2002—05, mem. campaign fin. ethics commn., 2005—, mem. fin. ethics commn., 2006—. Chmn. fin. com. Ventura County Grand Jury, 1958; mem. Oxnard (Calif.) Planning Commn., 1957-62; exec. mem. So. Calif. Assn. Govts., L.A., 1975-76. Author: Smith Studies, 1945. Chmn. dem. com., Ventura County, 1959-62, mem. campaign fin. ethics commn., 2006—; alternate or del. Dem. Nat. Convs., 1960, 68, 76, 88, 92, alt. 1956, 64; Women'schm. S. Calif. Dem. Com., 1966-70; nominee state assembly, 36th dist., Ventura, Calif., 1976; elected Oxnard City Coun. 1970-78, mayor, 1973-74. Home: 656 Douglas Ave Oxnard CA 93030-4614 Personal E-mail: jane.tolmach@adelphia.net.

TOLMACHOFF, WILLADENE, accountant, auditor; b. Mt. Vernon, Ky., July 13, 1945; d. Willie and Wanda Thacker; m. Innokenty Tolmachoff, July 27, 1968. MS, George Washington U., 1978; M. in Gen. Adminstrn., U. Md., 1994. Cert. fin. mgr. Audit mgr. USDA, Washington, 1987-97; dir. performance audits Office of Inspector Gen., Washington, 1998-2000; cash mgmt. dep. project mgr. Office of Fin. and Sys., Washington, 2000—01, internal audit/internal security audit mgr., 2001—. Adj. prof. Strayer U., 1997—. Mem.: Assn. Govt. Accts. Avocations: walking, bicycling, reading. Home: 1010 Rhode Island Ave NE Washington DC 20018 Office: Rm 367 810 1st St NE Washington DC 20002 E-mail: tolmachev@aol.com.

TOLMICH, ANDREA J., music educator, department chairman; d. Andrew John and Jane (Kolka) Podraskie; m. Leslie Alan Tolmich, Jan. 27, 1980; 1 child, Jennifer. MusB (with distinction), U. Rochester, NY, 1969; MS in Edn., Queens Coll. of CUNY, 1974. Cert. highly qualified instrumental music-orch. Mich. & NY, K-12 music Mich., gen. edn. K-6 Mich. Orchestra, gen. music tchr. W. Babylon Jr. High, NY, 1969—70; elem. and jr. high orch. tchr. Plainedge Pub. Schs., NY, 1970—72; elem. and mid. orch. tchr. Walled Lake Consolidated Schs., Mich., 1972—, elem. instrumental music dept. chairman, 1974—94. Solo ensemble festival adjudicator Mich. Sch. Br. and Orch. Assn., Okemos, 2006—. Violist Birmingham Bloomfield Symphony Orch., 1974—86. Mem.: Nat. Edn. Assn., Mich. Edn. Assn., Mich. Am. String Tchrs. Assn., Am. Viola Soc., Mich. Bd. and Orch. Assn. (solo and ensemble adjudicator 2006), Am. String Tchrs. Assn. Avocations: reading, travel, kayaking. Office: Walnut Creek Mid Sch 7601 Walnut Lake Rd Bloomfield MI 48323 Home: 31176 Country Way Farmington Hills MI 48331 Business E-Mail: tolmica@walledlake.k12.mi.us.

TOLSTEDT, CARRIE L., bank executive; BS in Bus. Adminstrn., U. Nebr.; degree in Banking, U. Wash. From credit tng. program to corp. banking officer United Bank Denver, corp. banking officer; from v.p. corp. banking to sr. v.p. downtown Omaha (Nebr) retail banking Norwest Bank Nebr., Omaha, 1986—95; sr. v.p. corp. retail FirstMerit Corp., Akron, Ohio, 1995—96, pres., CEO Citizens Nat. Bank and Peoples Nat. Bank, 1996—98, exec. v.p., 1996—98; with Norwest Corp., 1998; regional pres. Ctrl. Calif. Wells Fargo & Co., San Francisco, 1998—2001, exec. v.p. regional banking, 2001—. Bd. dirs. The Cmty. Coll. Found. Mem.: Consumer Bankers Assn. (bd. dirs.), U. Nebr. Alumni Assn. (bd. dirs.), Calif. C. of C. (bd. dirs.). Office: Wells Fargo & Co 420 Montgomery St San Francisco CA 94163

TOM, CYNTHIA, sales executive, consultant; d. Richard Tom and Sue Homshee. BA, San Francisco State U., 1983. Exec. cardiology splty. rep. outside sales Merck, San Francisco, 1988—. Cons. Rolston and Rolston Consulting, Sacramento, 1994—2002. Artist-in-Residence grantee, San Francisco (Calif.) Fine Arts Mus., 2002, 2004. Mem.: Nat. Mus. Women in Arts, Planned Parenthood, San Francisco (Calif.) Conv. and Visitors Bur. (assoc.), Asian Am. Women Artist's Assn. (v.p. 2004—06). Office: Cynthia Tom Fine Art Studios 1890 Bryant St 302 San Francisco CA 94110 Office Phone: 415-722-4296. Business E-Mail: cynthiatom@mindspring.com.

TOM, LAUREN, actress, singer; b. Chgo., Aug. 4, 1959; d. Chan and Nancy (Dare) T.; m. Curt Kaplan, Oct. 1999; 1 child. Student, Northwestern U., 1977; BA, NYU. Actress (Broadway plays) A Chorus Line, 1978—79, Doonesbury, 1983—84, Hurlyburly, 1985, (plays) The Music Lessons, 1980, Family Devotions, 1981, (one woman show) 25 Psychics (Dramalogue awards, best performance), (films) Nothing Lasts Forever, 1982, Joy Luck Club, 1993, Mr. Jones, 1993, When a Man Loves a Woman, 1994, With Friends Like These, 1998, Catfish in Black Bean Sauce, 1999, Manhood, 2003, Bad Santa, 2003, God's Waiting List, 2006, (TV series) The Facts of Life, 1982, Grace Under Fire, 1993, DAG, 2000, Max Steel, 2001—02, Men in Trees, 2006, actress (voice) Superman, 1996—99, King of the Hill, 1997—2006, Batman, 1999, Futurama, 1999—2003, Rocket Power, 1999—2004, Samurai Jack, 2001—04, Codename: Kids Next Door, 2002, Fillmore, 2002—04, Clifford's Puppy Days, 2003—, Teacher's Pet, 2004, W.I.T.C.H., 2004—06, Kim Possible, 2005, American Dragon, 2005. Supporter Asia Inst., Washington. Mem. Actors' Equity Assn., Screen Actors Guild, AFTRA. Office: c/o Kelly Garner Pop Art Films and Mgmt 9615 Brighton Way Ste 426 Beverly Hills CA 90210*

TOMAJKO, KIMBERLY ANN, mathematics and science educator; b. Greensburg, Pa., Jan. 12, 1969; d. George Edward and Shirley Ann Tobias; m. Kenneth Michael Tomajko, May 24, 1991; children: Zachary Michael, Brian Edward, Melissa Ann. BS in Secondary Math. Edn., Ind. U. Pa., Indiana, 1991; cert. in Secondary Gen. Sci., Calif. U. of Pa., 1996. Tchr. Sylvan Learning Ctr., Greensburg, Pa., 1992—93; math and sci. instr. CWCTC, New Stanton, Pa., 1992—. Kidwatch instr. Hempfied Parks and Recreation, Greensburg, Pa., 1987—92; sec., baseball softball coach, recreation bd. vol. New Stanton (Pa.) Recreation, 1998—. Recipient Paul Harris award, New Stanton Youngwood Rotary, 2004. Mem.: PSEA (life). Home: RD 1 Box 519 New Stanton PA 15672

TOMAN, BARBARA KATHERINE, renal, cardiac, vascular nurse; b. Omaha, Oct. 7, 1941; d. Albert Joseph and Rosemary (Cloidt) Ulrich; m. Gary David Toman, Oct. 7, 1961 (div. 1988); children: Cindy Penke, Bob Toman, Kim Volwiler, Vicki Toman; m. Gary Morris, Nov. 7, 1992. Nursing diploma, Creighton Meml. Hosp., 1961. RN, Nebr. Staff nurse St. Joseph Hosp., Omaha, 1961-70, Am. Med. Inst., Omaha, 1975-88, 90—; night supr. Nebr. Masonic Home, Omaha, 1988-90; staff RN step-down telemetry unit, 1992—94; pre-op, post recover staff RN. Bd. dirs. Am. Diabetic Assn.; Retainment, Recruitment Com., Omaha, 1990-92; critical care teelmetry unit Critical Care Edn. Com., 1992. Bd. mem. Cass County 4-H Coun., Weeping Water, N.C., 1976-86; leadership club mem., Plattsmouth, N.C., 1976-86; spl. events. chmn. Cass County Dem., Plattsmouth, 1986—. Roman Catholic. Avocations: volleyball, sewing, grandchildren. Home: 2104 Hedgeapple Rd Plattsmouth NE 68048

TOMAN, MARY ANN, federal official; b. Pasadena, Calif., Mar. 31, 1954; d. John James and Mary Ann Zajec T.; m. Milton Allen Miller, Sept. 10, 1988; 1 child, Mary Ann III. BA with honors, Stanford U., Calif., 1976; MBA, Harvard U., 1981. Mgmt. cons. Bain and Co., Boston, 1976—77; mgr. brand Procter & Gamble Co., Cin., 1977—79; summer assoc. E.F. Hutton, N.Y.C., 1980; head corp. planning Burton Group, PLC, London, 1981—84; pres., founder Glenclair Ltd., London, 1984—86; pres. London Cons. Group, London, Beverly Hills, Calif., 1987—88; mem. U.S. Presdl. Transition Team, Bus. and Fin., 1988—89; dep. asst. sec. commerce, automotive affairs, consumer goods U.S. Dept. Commerce, Washington, 1989—93; commr., chmn. L.A. Indsl. Devel. Authority, 1993—95; dep. treas. State of Calif., Sacramento, 1995—99. Bd. dirs. U.S. Coun. of Devel. Fin. Agencies, 1994-97. Founder, chair Stanford U. Fundraising, London, 1983-88; chair Reps. Abroad Absentee Voter Registration, London, 1983-88; bd. dirs. Harvard Bus. Sch. Assn., London, 1984-87; vol. Bush-Quayle Campaign, 1988; trustee Bath Univ., Eng., 1988—; apptd. by Gov. Wilson to State of Calif. Econ. Devel. Adv. Coun., 1994-97, Jobs Tng. Coordinating Coun., 1998-2000; first vice chmn. Rep. Party L.A. County, 1996-99, chmn., 1999—; mem. exec. bd. Coun. Calif. County Chairmen, 1999—; mem. U.S. Presdl. Transition Team, 2000-2001; Rep. candidate for Calif. State Treas., 2002. Named Calif. Mother of Yr., 1997. Mem. Stanford Club U.K. (pres. 1983-88), Harvard Club N.Y., Harvard Club Washington, Harvard Club Boston, Nat. Assn. of Urban Rep. County Chmn. Roman Catholic. Home: 604 N Elm Dr Beverly Hills CA 90210-3421 Office: PO Box 71483 Los Angeles CA 90071-0483 Office Phone: 310-274-4822. Business E-Mail: tomanmail@aol.com.

TOMASKY, SUSAN, electric power industry executive; b. Morgantown, W.Va., Mar. 29, 1953; m. Ron Ungvarsky; 1 child, Victoria. BA cum laude, Univ. Ky., 1974; JD (hons.), George Washington Univ., 1979. Staff mem. House Com. Interstate and Fgn. Commerce, Washington, 1974—76; with Office Gen. Counsel Fed. Energy Regulatory Commn., Washington, 1979—81; assoc. Van Ness, Feldman & Curtin, Washington, 1981—86; ptnr. Van Ness, Feldman & Curtis, Washington, 1986—93; gen. coun. Fed. Energy Regulatory Commn., Washington, 1993—97; ptnr. Hogan & Harts, Washington, 1997-98; sr. v.p., gen. coun. & sec. Am. Electric Power Co., Columbus, Ohio, 1998—2000, exec. v.p., gen. counsel, sec., 2000—01, exec. v.p., CFO, 2001—06, exec. v.p. Shared Services, 2006—. Staff mem. George Washington U. Law Rev., 1979. Trustee Columbus Symphony Orch., Columbus Sch. for Girls; co-chair Keystone Energy Bd. Mem. Greater Columbus C. of C., Phi Beta Kappa. Office: American Electric Power 1 Riverside Plz Fl 30 Columbus OH 43215-2355*

TOMASULO, VIRGINIA MERRILLS, retired lawyer; b. Belleville, Ill., Feb. 10, 1919; d. Frederick Emerson and Mary Eckert (Turner) Merrills; m. Nicholas Angelo Tomasulo, Sept. 30, 1952 (dec. May 3, 1986); m. Harrison I. Anthes, Mar. 5, 1988. BA, Wellesley Coll., 1940; LLB (now JD), Washington U., St. Louis, 1943. Bar: Mo. 1942, U.S. Ct. Appeals (D.C. cir.) 1958, Mich. 1974, U.S. Dist. Ct. (ea. dist) Mo. 1943, U.S. Supreme Ct. 1954, U.S. Tax Ct. 1974, U.S. Ct. Appeals (6th cir.) 1976. Atty. Dept. of Agr., Office of Solicitor, St. Louis and Washington, 1943-48; chief counsel's office IRS, Washington and Detroit, 1949-75; assoc. Baker & Hostetler, Washington, 1977-82, ptnr., 1982-89, of counsel, 1989, ret., 1989. Sec. S.W. Day Care Assn., Washington, 1971—73; state bd. mem., dir. region IV Fla. Life Care Residents Assn., 2002—04; mem. adv. bd. Brede-Wilkins Scholarship Found., 2002—. Mem.: ABA, Mo. Bar, Village on the Green Residents Assn. (mem. coun. 1998—2000, chair health care com. 1999—2001, chair fin. com. 2004—05, mem. fin. com.), Wellesley Club (Ctrl. Fla.). Episcopalian. Home: 570 Village Pl Apt 300 Longwood FL 32779-6037

TOMASZEWSKI, KATHLEEN BERNADETTE, social worker, educator; b. Detroit, Jan. 31, 1945; d. Thomas Joseph and Margaret Rice Gilmore; m. Kenneth Patrick Tomaszewski, July 30, 1966; children: Kenneth Kara, Kristyn, Kraig. BS, Wayne State U., 1981; MEd, U. Toledo, 1983; MSW, U. Mich., 1984. Cert. social worker, Mich. Social worker hemophilia-obstetrics, child abuse and neglect N.W. Ohio Ctr. for Women & Children, Toledo, 1984-87; social worker nephrology Hosp. for Sick Children, Toronto, Ont., Can., 1987-90; social worker cystic fibrosis and craniofacial Childrens Hosp., Phila., 1990-91; dir. placement svcs. Childrens Bur. of Del., Wilmington, 1991-92; pvt. practice in adoption and counseling Beijing, 1993-94; social worker Crittenton Hosp., Rochester Hills, Mich., 1995-97; therapist Cath. Social Svc., Flint, Mich., 1998—, ret., 2003. Pvt. cons. adoptions, home studies, counseling, 2000—; tchr. NYU, Toronto, 1991; bd. dirs. Nat. Hemophilia Assn., Toledo. Contbr. to profl. publs. Rsch. grantee Can. Kidney Assn., 1991. Mem. NASW (cert.), Am. Assn. Marriage and Family Therapists (cert., clin. assoc.), Am. Assn. Play Therapists. Avocations: writing, photography, gardening, travel. Home: 4184 Neal Ct Linden MI 48451-9095 E-mail: kathiken18@charter.net.

TOMB, CAROL E., retail executive; b. Balt., Nov. 3, 1952; d. Richard John and Doris Elaine Tomb; children: Kurt M., Kristen E., Kevin R. AS, Harcum Coll., 1973; cert., Inst. Cert. Fin. Planners, 1988; BA, Simpson Coll., 2001. Various retail mgmt. positions, N.Y. and Iowa, 1973-78; pres. Nouveau Riche, Ltd., Des Moines, 1986-95; dist. mgr. bookstore ops. Des Moines Area C.C., Knowledge Knook Bookstore, Ankeny, Iowa, 1998—. Mem. Des Moines Civic Ctr., People to People Internat. Avocation: international travel. Office: Knowledge Knook Bookstore Des Moines Area CC 2006 S Ankeny Blvd Ankeny IA 50021-8995 Business E-Mail: cetomb@dmacc.edu.

TOMB, DIANE LENEGAN, former federal agency administrator; Grad., Mt. St. Mary's, Md. Assoc. dir. Office Bus. Liaison U.S. Dept. Commerce, 1991—93, dir. pub. affairs for Internat. Trade Adminstrn.; dir. pub. affairs practice, mktg. dir. Washington regional office Burson-Marsteller, 1994—97; dep. dir. comm. for Senator Bob Dole US Senate, Washington, 1996; sr. v.p. for comm. Fannie Mae Found., 1997—2002; asst. sec. for pub. affairs US

Dept. Housing & Urban Devel., Washington, 2002—04; sr. advisor "Mel Martinez for Senate" Campaign, 2004; founder Tomb & Associates, LLC, Washington, 2005—. Office: Tomb & Associates LLC 1455 Pennsylvania Ave NW Ste 100 Washington DC 20004

TOMBERS, EVELYN CHARLOTTE, lawyer, educator; b. Phila., Nov. 7, 1956; d. Gerold G. and Margot (Ort) Knauerhase; m. Peter C. Tombers. AS, Temple U., 1976, BA, 1977; JD, Thomas M. Cooley Law Sch., 1991. Bar: Mich. 1991. Dist. intake counselor Fla. Dept. Health Rehab. Svc., Naples, 1985-87; satellite dir. Youth Shelter S.W. Fla., Naples, 1987-88; adj. prof. Thomas M. Cooley Law Sch., Lansing, Mich., 1991-92; jud. law clk. to Justice Patricia J. Boyle Mich. Supreme Ct., Detroit, 1992-94; assoc. Harvey, Kruse, Westen and Milan, Troy, Mich., 1994-95, Bowen, Radabaugh, Milton & Brown, Troy, Mich., 1995-99, Morrison Mahoney & Miller LLP, Southfield, Mich., 1999—2000. Chmn. State Bar Mich. Appellate Practice Sect., 2001-2002. Named one of Outstanding Women Grads., Women Lawyers Am., 1991. Avocation: golf. Home: 1289 Tracilee Dr Howell MI 48843 Office: Thomas M Cooley Law Sch 300 S Capitol Ave Lansing MI 48901

TOME, CAROL B., consumer home products company executive; b. Jackson, Wyo., Jan. 8, 1957; BS in Comm., U. Wyo.; MBA in Fin., U. Denver. Comml. lender United Bank Denver (now Wells Fargo); dir. banking Johns-Manville Corp.; v.p., treas. Riverwood Internat. Corp., 1992—95, Home Depot, 1995—2000, sr. v.p. fin., 2000—01, exec. v.p., CFO Atlanta, 2001—. Bd. dirs. United Parcel Svc., 2003—. Bd. dirs. Girls Inc.; trustee Ga. Substance Abuse Adv. Coun., Home Fund; chair adv. bd. Met. Atlanta Arts Fund. Office: Home Depot Inc 2455 Paces Ferry Rd Atlanta GA 30339-4029

TOMEI, CAROLYN, state representative; m. Gary Michael. BS in Psychology, Portland State U., MSW. State rep., dist. 41 Oreg. House Rep., Salem, 2001—; mayor City of Milwaukie, Oreg.; child devel. specialist Portland Pub. Schs. Vice-chair Health and Human Svcs. Com.; mem. Water Com.; instr. Portland C.C. Democrat. Office: 900 Court St NE H-388 Salem OR 97301 Office Phone: 503-986-1441. E-mail: rep.carolyntomei@state.or.us.

TOMEI, MARISA, actress; b. Bklyn., Dec. 4, 1964; d. Gary and Patricia Tomei. TV appearances include (series) As the World Turns, 1983-88, A Different World, 1987, Only Love, 1998, My Own Country, 1998, Since You've Been Gone, 1998, (films) The Flamingo Kid, 1984, Playing for Keeps, 1986, Parker Kane, 1990, Oscar, 1991, Zandalee, 1991, My Cousin Vinny, 1992 (Acad. award best supporting actress 1993), Chaplin, 1992, Untamed Heart, 1993, Equinox, 1993, The Paper, 1994, Only You, 1994, The Perez Family, 1994, Four Rooms, 1995, Unhook the Stars, 1996, What Women Want, 2000, Dirk and Betty, 2000, Driven, 2000, King of the Jungle, 2000, In the Bedroom, 2001 (ShoWest award best supporting actress, 2002), Someone Like You, 2001, The Guru, 2002, The Wild Thornberrys Movie (voice), 2002, Anger Management, 2003, Loverboy, 2004, Alfie, 2004; theatre appearances include Slavs! Thinking About the Longstanding Problems of Virtue and Happiness, 1994, Welcome to Sarajevo, 1997, This Is How It Goes, 2005. Office: United Talent Agy 9560 Wilshire Blvd Ste 500 Beverly Hills CA 90212

TOMICH-BOLOGNESI, VERA, education educator; b. L.A. d. Peter S. and Yovanka (Ivanovich) T.; m. Gino Bolognesi, July 12, 1969. AA, John Muir Jr. Coll., Pasadena, Calif., 1951; BA in Polit. Sci., UCLA, 1953, MEd, 1955, EdD, 1960. Cert. secondary tchr., Calif.; cert. secondary sch. adminstrn., Calif.; cert. jr. coll. tchr., Calif. Tchg. asst. dept. edn. UCLA, 1956; tchr., dept. chmn. Culver City (Calif.) Unified Sch. Dist., 1956-91; rschr., writer U.S. Dept. Edn., Washington, 1961, del. to Yugoslavia, 1965; co-owner, exec. Metrocolor Engring., San Gabriel, Calif., 1973—. Cons., Continental Culture Specialists, Inc., Glendale, Calif., 1985-92; rsch. asst. Law Firm of Driscoll & Tomich, San Marino, Calif., 1989—. Author: Education in Yugoslavia and the New Reform, 1963, Higher Education and Teacher Training in Yugoslavia, 1967; screenplay editor 1996—. Bd. trustees St. Sava Serbian Orthodox Ch., San Gabriel, 1975—, mem., 1960—. Named an Outstanding Young Women of Am., 1966; recipient Episcopal Gramata, Serbian Orthodox Ch. of Western Am., 1996, 2002. Mem. NEA (life), Calif. Tchrs. Assn., UCLA Alumni Assn., Alpha Gamma Sigma, Pi Lambda Theta. Home: 100 E Roses Rd San Gabriel CA 91775-2343 Office: Metrocolor Engring 5110 Walnut Grove Ave San Gabriel CA 91776-2026

TOMINACK, DEBRA DILLARD, science educator; d. Marion Robley Dillard and Jane Juanita Dick; m. Ivan Louis, Jr. Tominack, June 1, 1979; children: Ivan Louis III, Bonnie Jane. BS in Biology, Western Ky. U., Bowling Green, 1974; Tchr. Edn. Program, Christopher Newport U., Newport News, Va., 1992. Cert. Mid. Sch. Tchr. Va., 1992, Nat. Bd. Cert. Early Adolescence/Sci. U.S., 2004. Serologist FBI Crime Lab., Washington, 1974—79; lab. technician Urology Clinic, Rapid City, SD, 1979—81; docent Va. Living Mus., Newport News, 1991; math./sci. 6th grade educator SP Morton Mid. Sch., Franklin, Va., 1992—93; life sci. educator Lindsay Mid. Sch., Hampton, Va., 1994—98; life sci./phys. sci. educator Jones Magnet Mid. Sch., Hampton, Va., 1998—. Judge Odyssey of the Mind, Hampton, Va., 1992—98; odyssey of the mind coach Jones Magnet Mid. Sch., Hampton, Va., 1998—, sci. instrnl. leader, 2002—04, 2006—; life and phys. sci. curriculum writer Hampton City Schs., Va., 1999—2005, master tchr., 2003—; end-of-course sci. content area bias rev. com. Dept. of Edn., Richmond, 2004. Del. U.S./China Joint Edn. Conf. to People's Rep. of China, Bejing, China, 2005. Named Ky. Col. Mem.: Va. Assn. Sci. Tchrs., Va. Forum for Va. Nat. Bd. Cert. Tchrs., Nat. Sci. Tchr. Assn. Conservative. Mem. Lds Ch. Avocations: travel, sewing, knitting. Office: Jones Magnet Mid Sch 1819 Nickerson Blvd Hampton VA 23663 Office Phone: 757-848-2363.

TOMKOW, GWEN ADELLE, artist; b. Detroit, May 16, 1932; d. Galen A. and Edythe Christine (Barr) Roberts; m. Michael Tomkow, Nov. 14, 1953; children: Eric Michael, Thomas Edward, Nikola Christine, Kit Adair. A of Bus., Detroit Bus. Inst., 1952; student, Birmingham Bloomfield Art Assn., Mich., 1985—87, Visual Art Assn., Livonia, Mich., 1984—89. Tchr. watercolor Visual Art Assn., Livonia, 1989—; tchr. watercolor workshop Village Fine Art Assn., Milford, Mich., 1996; tchr. workshop Ella Sharp Mus. Jackson Civic Art, Mich., 1996—2003; slide lectr. Livonia Artist Club, 1995, Palette and Brush Club, Southfield, Mich., 1995, Pontiac Oakland Artists, Mich., 1995, Ea. Mich. U. Watercolor Soc., 1994; tchr. watercolor workshop Ann Arbor Women Painters U. Mich. Art Sch., 1997; slide lectr. We. Ohio Water Color Soc., 1999; tchr. watercolor workshop Awakening Artist Inside Art Emporium, 2004, Crystal Lake Art Ctr., Frankfort, Mich., 2005. Artist-in-residence Farmington Art Commn., Farmington Hills, 1988; slide lectr. Springfield (Ohio) Art Mus; mem. Framington Hills Art Commn., 2002-05; tchr. cultural arts Farmington Heritage Studios, 2003-04; juror Livonia Fine Arts Exhibit, 2004. One-woman shows include Cary Gallery, 1997—2003, exhibitions include Joppich's Bay St. of Northport, 1988—98, 2000—03, Cary Gallery, 1995—, Art Corridor, 1998, Cary Gallery, 2003, Sherrus Gallery, Northville, Mich., 2005, Represented in permanent collections E. Carothers Dunnegan Gallery of Art Mus., Bolivar, Mo., Sherrus Gallery, Northville, Oakland C.C. Recipient Purchase awards U.S.A. Springfield (Mo.) Art Mus., 1990, 93, 94, Watercolor U.S.A., 1999, 1st prize Helen de Roy Competition, Oakland C.C., Farmington, Mich., 1988, 92, Grumbacher Gold medal Farmington Artists Club, 1992, 2001, Farmington Hills, Mich., 1995, 98. Mem. Nat. Watercolor Soc. (signature, Alex Nepote Meml. award 1998), Mich. Watercolor Soc. (Meml. award 1992), Farmington Art Assn. (pres. 1987-89), Detroit Soc. Women Painters Sculptors (sec. 1994-95, award 1999), Palette and Brush (v.p. 1982-83), Founders Soc. Detroit Inst. Arts, Nat. Mus. Women in the Arts, Birmingham Soc. Women Painters (Juror's award 2005). Presbyterian. Avocations: tennis, golf, choir singer, theater.

TOMLIN, CLAIRE J., aeronautical engineer, educator; b. Southampton, Eng., 1969; BASc in Elec. Engring., U. Waterloo, 1992; MSEE, Imperial Coll., London, 1993; PhD in Elec. Engring. and Computer Sci., U. Calif., Berkeley, 1998. Assoc. prof. dept. aeronautics and astronautics Stanford U., Calif. Courtesy assoc. prof. elec. engring. Stanford U.; assoc. prof. dept. elec. engring. and computer sci. U. Calif., Berkeley. Contbr. articles to sci. jours., chapters to books; co-editor: Hybrid Systems: Computation and Control, 2002. Named one of Top 100 Innovators, MIT Tech. Rev., 2003; recipient Zonta Amelia Earhart awards for Aeronautics Rsch., 1996—98, Career award, NSF, 2000—03, Donald P. Eckman award, Am. Automatic Control Coun., 2003; MacArthur Fellow, John D. and Catherine T. MacArthur Found., 2006. Office: Stanford U Dept Aeronautics and Astronautics Durand Bldg 496 Lomita Mall Stanford CA 94305-4035 E-mail: tomlin@stanford.edu.*

TOMLIN, JEANNE BRANNON, real estate broker, small business owner; b. Carroll, Iowa; d. James Leonard and Mary Agnes (Cavenaugh) Brannon; widowed; children: David, Elizabeth; m. James W. Tomlin; stepchildren: Angela, Julie, Lori, Fran. A in Archtl. Tech., Ind. U. Purdue U., Indpls., 1970, student. Lic. real estate broker. Salesperson F.C. Tucker, Indpls.; mgr. Dan Nichols Builder, Greenwood, Ind.; asst. mgr. Carpenter Better Homes and Gardens, Carmel, Ind., sales broker, 1989-92, Tomlin Realtors, Greenwood, 1992-97, pres., CEO, 1997—. Mem. com. Nat. Handicapped Sports, Indpls., 1986-88; mem tech. task force Met. Indpls. Bd. Realtors, 1993-94, mem. comm. com., 1998—. Mem. Indpls. C. of C., Greenwood C. of C., Golden Key Nat. Honor Soc., Alpha Sigma Lambda. Avocations: scuba diving, skiing. Office: Tomlin Realtors 306 Madison Ave Ste 204 Greenwood IN 46142-3123 Office Phone: 317-882-1044. Personal E-mail: jbtomlin@insightbb.com.

TOMLIN, LILY, actress; b. Detroit, Sept. 1, 1939; Student, Wayne State U.; studied mime with Paul Curtis, studied acting with Peggy Feury. Co-founder Lily Tomlin Jane Wagner Cultural Arts Ctr., LA. Appearances in concerts and colls. throughout U.S.; TV appearances include The Music Scene, 1969-70, Laugh In, 1970-73, Lily Tomlin, CBS Spls., 1973, 81, 82; 2 ABC Spls., 1974, 75, Edith Ann Animated Specials, ABC, 1994, The Magic School Bus, 1994 (voice), Murphy Brown, 1996-98, The West Wing, 2002-06; motion picture debut in Nashville, 1975 (N.Y. Film Critics award); also appeared in The Late Show, 1977, Moment by Moment, 1978, The Incredible Shrinking Woman, 1981, Nine to Five, 1980, All of Me, 1984, Big Business, 1987, Shadows and Fog, 1992, The Player, 1992, Short Cuts, 1993, The Beverly Hillbillies, 1993, And the Band Played On, HBO, 1993 (Best Supporting Actress Emmy nominee - Special, 1994, Emmy nominations guest appearance Homicide, 1996), Getting Away with Murder, 1995, The Celluloid Closet, 1995, Blue in the Face, 1995, Flirting With Disaster, 1996, Reno Finds Her Mom, 1997, Get Bruce, 1999, Krippendorf's Tribe, 1998, Tea with Mussolini, 1999, Picking Up the Pieces, 2000, The Kid, 2000, Orange County, 2002, I Heart Huckabees, 2004, A Prairie Home Companion, 2006, (voice) The Ant Bully, 2006; exec. prodr. TV series Citizen Reno, 2001; one-woman Broadway show Appearing Nitely, 1977 (Spl. Tony award), The Search for Signs of Intelligent Life in the Universe, 1985 (Drama Desk award, Outer Critics Circle award, Tony award 1986, Cable Ace award); recs. include This is a Recording, And That's The Truth, Modern Scream, On Stage. Recipient Grammy award 1971, 5 Emmy awards for CBS Spl. 1973, 81, Emmy award for ABC Spl. 1975, Emmy award Magic Sch. Bus, 1995, Peabody award Celluloid Closet, 1997, Peabody Edith Ann's Christmas, 1997, Mark Twain Prize for Am. Humor, Kennedy Center, 2003. Office: Lily Tomlin Jane Wagner Cultural Arts Ctr Village at Ed Gould Plz 1125 N McCadden Pl Los Angeles CA 90038-1212*

TOMLIN-HOUSTON, LISA, higher education administrator, director; b. Bklyn., Apr. 6, 1965; d. George L. and Joan J. (Hill) Tomlin; m. Anthony D. Houston, Feb. 2, 1991. BA in Psychology, Oberlin Coll., Ohio, 1987; MEd in Counseling Psychology, Rutgers U., 1990. Career counselor U. Pa., Phila., 1990-93; dir. career svcs. H. John Heinz III Sch. of Public Policy and Mgmt., Carnegie Mellon U., Pitts., 1993-95; mgmt. cons. Ford Found., 1995—97; mgr. undergrad. and MBA recruitment Barclays Capital, 1998—2000; pres. Creative Solutions Strategies, LLC, 2000—02; dir. career svcs. Baldwin-Wallace Coll., Berea, Ohio, 2002—. Mem. Nat. Assn. Coll. and Employers, Pub. Rels. Soc. Am., Soc. Human Resources Profls., Cleve. Soc. Venture Ptnrs. Avocations: reading, travel, woman's issues. Office: Baldwin-Wallace Coll 275 Eastland Rd Berea OH 44017

TOMLINSON, SUSAN K., elementary school educator; 1 child, Chris. Degree Mid. Sch. Edn., U. N.C.-Wilmington, 1991. 7th/8th. arts/soc.studies tchr. Washington County Union Sch., Roper, NC, 1992—98; 8th grade math tchr. Mattamuskeet Mid. Sch., Swan Quarter, NC, 1998—99; 7th/8th math/ss/l.arts tchr. Elizabeth City Mid. Sch., NC, 1999—. 21st CCLC site coord. Elizabeth City Mid. Sch., Elizabeth City, NC, 2005—. Scholar N.C. Tchg. fellow, N.C. Gen. Assembly/Tchg. Fellows Commn., 1997. Mem.: NCAE. Office: Elizabeth City Middle School 306 North Road St Elizabeth City NC 27909 Office Phone: 252-335-2974. E-mail: stomlinson@ecpps.k12.nc.us.

TOMLINSON-KEASEY, CAROL ANN, academic administrator; b. Washington, Oct. 15, 1942; d. Robert Bruce and Geraldine (Howe) Tomlinson; m. Charles Blake Keasey, June 13, 1964; children: Kai Linson, Amber Lynn. BS, Pa. State U., University Park, 1964; MS, Iowa State U., Ames, 1966; PhD, U. Calif., Berkeley, 1970. Lic. psychologist, Calif. Asst. prof. psychology Trenton (NJ) State Coll., 1969-70, Rutgers U., New Brunswick, NJ, 1970-72; prof. U. Nebr., Lincoln, 1972-77, U. Calif., Riverside, 1977-92, acting dean Coll. Humanities and Social Scis., 1986-88, chmn. dept. psychology, 1989-92, vice provost for acad. planning and pers. Davis, 1992-97, vice provost for acad. initiatives, 1997-99, chancellor, 1996—2006. Author: Child's Eye View, 1980, Child Development, 1985, numerous chpts. to books; contbr. articles to profl. jours. Recipient Disting. Tchr. award U. Calif., 1986. Mem. APA, Soc. Rsch. in Child Devel., Riverside Aquatics Assn. (pres.). Office: PO Box 2039 Merced CA 95344 Office Phone: 209-228-4400. Personal E-mail: caroltk@yahoo.com.

TOMLJANOVICH, ESTHER M., retired judge; b. Galt, Iowa, Nov. 1, 1931; d. Chester William and Thelma L. (Brooks) Moellering; m. William S. Tomljanovich, Dec. 26, 1957; 1 child, William Brooks Tomljanovich. AA, Itasca C.C., 1951; BSL, St. Paul Coll. Law, 1953, LLB, 1955. Bar: Minn. 1955, U.S. Dist. Ct. Minn. 1958. Asst. revisor of statutes State of Minn., St. Paul, 1957-66, revisor of statutes, 1974-77, dist. ct. judge Stillwater, 1977-90; assoc. justice Minn. Supreme Ct., St. Paul, 1990—98, ret., 1998. Adv. bd. women offenders Minn. Dept. Corrections, 1999—; leadership com. So. Minn. Legal Svcs. Corp., 1999—. Former mem. North St. Paul Bd. Edn., Maplewood Bd. Edn., Lake Elmo Planning Commn.; trustee William Mitchell Coll. Law, 1995—2004, Legal Rights Ctr., 1995—2004, pres., 1999; bd. dirs. Itasca C.C. Found., 1996—, Medica Health Ins. Co., 2001—, vice chair, 2003—. Recipient Centennial 2000 award William Mitchell Coll., Disting. Alumna award, First Ann. Esther Tomljanovich Lifetime Achievement award, 2005; named one of One Hundred Who Made a Difference William Mitchell Coll. Law. Mem. Minn. State Bar Assn., Bus. and Profl. Women's Assn. St. Paul (former pres.), Minn. Women Lawyers (founding mem.). Office: 8533 Hidden Bay Trail Lake Elmo MN 55042 Office Phone: 612-777-5970.

TOMPKINS, ELIZABETH J., secondary school educator; b. Yonkers, N.Y., June 16, 1949; d. William M. and Elizabeth (Coles) Whelan; m. Clifford C. Tompkins, Jr., Aug. 23, 1969; children: Ryan, Tyler. BA in English and Spanish, U Dubuque, 1971; MSEd, Western Conn. State U., 1981. Tchr. Spanish, English Cuba City (Wis.) High Sch., 1971-74, North Salem (N.Y.) High Sch., 1974—; tchr. Nat. Sch. Excellence, 1988-89. Speaker in field; cons. N.Y. Stated Edn. Dept., 1998—, chair subject area com., 2002—. Contbr. articles to popular mags, rsch. to profl. jours. Named Tchr. of Excellence in Drama, N.Y., 1983. Mem. Pi Lambda Theta, Phi Delta Kappa. Office: North Salem High Sch RR 24 North Salem NY 10560

TOMPKINS, JULIE LYNBERG, market research consultant; b. Monterey Park, Calif., Mar. 14, 1953; d. Leland Dwayne and Vivian Joanne (Share) Lynberg; m. Terry Cady Tompkins, Mar. 11, 1978; children: Jeffrey, Devon, Christopher. BA in Human Biology, Stanford U., 1974; MBA in Mktg., U. Santa Clara, 1979. Chemist Syntex Corp., Palo Alto, Calif., 1974-78; market rsch. analyst Syntex Labs., Palo Alto, 1978-80, mgr. new product planning, 1980-85, mgr. market analysis, 1985-86; pres., founder Medsearch Inc., Cupertino, Calif., 1986—. Mem. Med. Mktg. Assn., Pharm. Market Rsch. Group. Avocations: stained glass, needlecrafts.

TOMPSETT, LESLEY ANN, elementary school educator; b. Mishawaka, Ind., June 5, 1975; d. Nikki Allen and Betty Jo (Hagye) Tompsett, Betty Diane Klosinski (Stepmother). BS in Exercise Sci. Fitness/Wellness, Ball State U., 1996; BS in Elem. Edn., Ind. U., South Bend, 2000, MS in Elem. Edn., 2003; D in Ednl. Leadership, U. Phoenix, 2004. Cert. tchr. Ind. 6th grade tchr. South Bend Cmty. Sch. Corp., Ind., 2000—03, 5-8th health and phys. edn. tchr., 2003—. 7th and 8th grade softball coach Brown Intermediate Ctr., South Bend, Ind., 2003—05, 5th and 6th grade basketball coach, 2004—05; H.S. pom-pon coach Adams H.S., South Bend, Ind., 2003—04. Mem.: NEA, Ind. State Tchrs. Assn. Methodist. Avocations: photography, scrapbooking, reading, outdoor activities. Home: 51199 Hollyhock Rd South Bend IN 46637 Office: Brown Intermediate Ctr 737 W Beale St South Bend IN 46616 Office Phone: 574-287-9680. Personal E-mail: ltompsett@comcast.net. E-mail: ltompsett@sbcsc.k12.in.us.

TOMPSON, MARIAN LEONARD, professional society administrator; b. Chgo., Dec. 5, 1929; d. Charles Clark and Marie Christine (Bernardini) Leonard; m. Clement R. Tompson, May 7, 1949 (dec. 1981); children: Melanie Tompson Kandler, Deborah Tompson Frueh, Allison Tompson Fagerholm, Laurel Tompson Davies, Sheila Tompson Doucet, Brian, Philip. Student public and parochial schs., Chgo. and Franklin Park, Ill. Co-founder La Leche League (Internat.), Franklin Park, 1956, pres., 1956-80, dir., 1956—, pres. emeritus, 1990—; exec. dir. Alternative Birth Crisis Coalition, 1981-85; founder, pres., CEO AnotherLook, Inc., 2001—. Cons. WHO; bd. dirs. N.Am. Soc. Psychosomatic Ob-Gyn, Natural Birth and Natural Parenting, 1981-83; mem. adv. bd. Nat. Assn. Parents and Profls. for Safe Alternatives in Childbirth, Am. Acad. Husband-Coached Childbirth; mem. adv. bd. Fellowship of Christian Midwives; mem. profl. adv. bd. Home Oriented Maternity Experience; guest lectr. Harvard U. Med. Sch., UCLA Sch. Pub. Health, U. Antioquia Med. Sch., Medellín, Columbia, U. Ill. Sch. Medicine, Chgo., U. W.I., Jamaica, U. N.C., Nat. Coll. of Chiropractic, Am. Coll. Nurse Midwives, U. Parma, Italy, Inst. Psychology, Rome, Rockford (Ill.) Sch. Medicine, Northwestern U. Sch. Medicine, NGO Forum/4th World Conf. on Women, Beijing; mem. family com. Ill. Commn. on Status of Women, 1976-85; mem. perinatal adv. com. Ill. Dept. Pub. Health, 1980-83; mem. adv. bd. Internat. Nutrition Comm. Svc., 1980—; bd. cons. We Can, 1984—; exec. adv. bd. United Resources for Family Health and Support, 1985-86; mem. internat. adv. coun. World Alliance of Breast Feeding Action, 1996. Author: (with others) Safe Alternatives in Childbirth, 1976, 21st Century Obstetrics Now!, 1977, The Womanly Art of Breastfeeding, 6th edit., 1997, Five Standards for Safe Childbearing, 1981, But Doctor, About That Shot., 1988, The Childbirth Activists Handbook, 1983; author prefaces and forwards in 11 books; columnist La Leche League News, 1958-80; columnist People's Doctor Newsletter, 1977-88, mem. adv. bd., cons., 1988-92; assoc. editor Child and Family Quar., 1967—; mem. med. adv. bd. East West Jour., 1980—; also articles. Mem. adv. bd. Shelters for Healthy Environments, 1998—2002, The Beginning Project, 2000. Recipient Gold medal of honor Centro de Rehabilitacao Nossa Senhora da Gloria, 1975, Night of 100 Stars III Achiever award Actors Fund Am., 1990, N.Y. Soc. Ethical Culture Ethical Humanist award, 1999, 100 Women Making a Difference Today's Chgo. Woman. Mem. Nat. Assn. Postpartum Care Svcs. (adv. bd.), Chgo. Cmty. Midwives (adv. bd.), World Alliance for Breast Feeding Action (mem. internat. adv. coun. 1997). Office: 1400 N Meacham Rd Schaumburg IL 60173-4808 Office Phone: 847-869-1278. Personal E-mail: m.tompson@comcast.net. E-mail: mt@anotherlook.org.

TOMS, KATHLEEN MOORE, nurse; b. San Francisco, Dec. 31, 1943; d. William Moore and Phyllis Josephine (Barry) Stewart; m. Benjamin Peskoff (dec. Aug. 2002); children from previous marriage: Kathleen Marie Toms Myers, Kelly Terese Toms Shaver. AA, City Coll., San Francisco, 1963; BPS in Nursing Edn., Elizabethtown Coll., Pa., 1973; MS in Edn., Temple U., 1977; MS in Nursing, Gwynedd Mercy Coll., 1988; grad., US Army War Coll., 1999. RN, Calif. Med.-surg. nurse St. Joseph Hosp., Fairbanks, Alaska, 1963-65, emergency rm. nurse Lancaster, Pa., 1965-69, blood, plasma and components nurse, 1969-71; pres. F.E. Barry Co., Lancaster, 1971—; dir. insvc. edn. Lancaster Osteo. Hosp., 1971-75; coord. practical nursing program Vocat. Tech. Sch., Coatesville, Pa., 1976-77; dir. nursing Pocopson Home, West Chester, Pa., 1978-80, Riverside Hosp., Wilmington, Del., 1980-83; assoc. Coatesville VA Hosp., 1983-89, chief nurse, 1984-89; with VA Ctrl. Office; supr. psychiat. nursing Martinez (Calif.) VA Med. Ctr., 1989-94; assoc. chief nursing svc. edn. VA Ho. Calif. Sys. Clinics, Pleasant Hill, 1994—; nurse mgr. VA Ctr. Rehab. and Extended Care, Martinez, 1996—; patient health edn. coord. VA No. Calif. Health Care Sys., Martinez, 2000—. Trainee assoc. chief Nursing Home Care Unit, Washington; mem. Pa. Gov.'s Coun. on Alcoholism and Drug Abuse, 1974-76; mem. Del. Health Coun. Med.-Surg. Task Force, 1981-83; dir. Lancaster Cmty. Health Ctr., 1973-76; lectr. in field. Col. Nurse Corps, USAR. Decorated Army Commendation medals (6), Meritorious Svc. medals (2); recipient Cmty. Svc. award Citizens United for Better Pub. Rels., 1974; award Sertoma, Lancaster, 1974; Outstanding Citizen award Sta. WGAL-TV, 1975; U.S. Army Achievement award, 1983. Mem. Elizabethtown U. Alumni Assn., Temple U. Alumni Assn., Pa. Nurses Assn. (bd. dirs. 1972-76), Sigma Theta Tau, Beta Gamma. Achievements include invention of auto-infuser for blood or blood components. Home: 208 Sea Mist Dr Vallejo CA 94591-7748 E-mail: ktoms007@aol.com.

TONELLO-STUART, ENRICA MARIA, political scientist, economist; b. Monza, Italy; d. Alessandro P. and Maddalena M. (Marangoni) Tonello; m. Albert E. Smith; m. Charles L. Stuart. BA in Internat. Affairs, Econs., U. Colo., 1961; MA, Claremont Grad. Sch., 1966, PhD, 1971. Sales mgr. Met. Life Ins. Co., 1974-79; pres., CEO, ETS R&D, Inc., Palos Verdes Peninsula, Calif., 1977—2004; ret. Pub., editor Tomorrow Outline Jour., 1963—, The Monitor, 1988; pub. World Regionalism-An Ecological Analysis, 1971, A Proposal for the Reorganization of the United Nations, 1966, The Persuasion Technocracy, Its Forms, Techniques and Potentials, 1966, The Role of the Multinationals in the Emerging Globalism, 1978; developed the theory of social ecology and econsociometry. Organizer 1st family assistance program Langley FB Tractical Air Command, 1956-58. Recipient vol. svc. award VA, 1956-58, ARC svc. award, 1950-58. Mem. Corp. Planners Assn. (treas. 1974-79), Investigative Reporters and Editors, World Future Soc. (pres. 1974-75), Soc. Environ. Journalists, Chinese Am. Assn. (life), Palos Verdes C. of C., L.A. Press Club (bd. dirs.), Zonta (chmn. internat. com. South Bay), Pi Sigma Alpha. Avocations: writing, collecting old books and maps, community service, travel. Office Phone: 310-377-7608. Personal E-mail: stuarteeix@netcom.com.

TONEY, BRENDA SUE, special education educator; m. George Marvin Toney, Jan. 19, 1996; children: Jerrard, Lindsay Collins, Katie, Kathy. B in Spl. Edn., Ball State U., Muncie, Ind., 1982; M in Spl. Edn., BallState U., Muncie, Ind., 1991. Home visitor, home-based supr., disabilities coord. Madison County Head Start, Anderson, Ind., 1985—96; resource tchr., life skills tchr. Madison Grant United Sch. Corp., Fairmount, Ind., 1996—2004; elem. spl. edn. tchr. Elwood Cmty. Sch. Corp., Ind., 2004—. Volleyball coach Elwood Mid. Sch., Ind., 1985—90; varsity volleyball coach Elwood H.S., Ind., 2005—. Vol. Girls City Softball League, Ind., 1990—2006. Mem.: NEA (assoc.), Ind. Girls Coaches Assn. (assoc.), Ind. State Teacher's Assn. (assoc.). Office: Oakland Elem Sch 2100 So P St Elwood IN 46036 Office Phone: 765-552-9823. Business E-Mail: brendatoney@elwood.k12.in.us.

TONG, KAITY, anchor; m. Patrick Callahan; 1 child. BA, Bryn Mawr Coll.; MA, Stanford U. Street reporter various West Coast radio/tv networks; anchor KCRA, Sacramento, WABC Eyewitness News, WB-11 News at 10/WPIX-TV, N.Y.C. Recipient Exceptional Achievement award, Disting. Woman award, Star award, Edward R. Murrow award, 3 Emmy awards Acitve United

Cerebral Palsy, Children's Mus. of Manhattan, Juvenile Diabetes Found., Friends for Life, League for the Hard of Hearing. Office: WPIX-TV/Tribune Co 220 E 42d St New York NY 10017 Business E-Mail: ktong@tribune.com.

TONG, ROSEMARIE, humanities educator, philosopher; b. Chgo., July 19, 1947; d. Joseph John and Lillian (Nedued) Behensky; m. Paul Ki-King Tong, Aug. 15, 1971 (dec. Apr. 1988); children: Paul Shih-Mien Tong, John Joseph Tong; m. Jeremiah Putnam, Aug. 1, 1992. BA, Marygrove Coll., 1970; MA, Cath. U., 1971; PhD, Temple U., 1978; LLD (hon.), Marygrove Coll., 1987; LHD (hon.), SUNY, Oneonta, 1993. Asst. and assoc. prof. philosophy Williams Coll., Williamstown, Mass., 1978-88; vis. disting. prof. humanities Davidson (N.C.) Coll., 1988-89, Thatcher Prof. in med. humanities and philosophy, 1989-99; prof. humanities and philosophy U. N.C., Charlotte, 1999—; dir. Ctr. for Profl. and Applied Ethics, Charlotte, 2002—. L. Stacy Davidson vis. chair in liberal arts U. Miss., Oxford, 1998; Louise M. Olmstead vis. prof. philosophy and women's studies, Lafayette Coll., Easton, Pa., 1993; disting. prof. health care ethics U. N.C., Charlotte, 1999—; manuscript reviewer Wadsworth Pub. Co., 1985-92; curriculum reviewer philosophy dept. Carlton and Bowdoin Colls., 1986; honors examiner Hobart and William Smith Colls., 1990; dissertation dir., adj. faculty The Union Inst., 1992-93; cons., judge, panelist, organizer and speaker in field; mem. numerous U. coms. Author: Women, Sex and the Law, 1984, Ethics in Policy Analysis, 1985, Feminist Thought: A Comprehensive Introduction, 1989, Feminist Philosophies: Problems, Theories, and Applications, 1991, Feminine and Feminist Ethics, 1993, Feminist Thought: A More Comprehensive Introduction, 1998, (with Larry Kaplan) Controlling Our Reproductive Destiny, 1994, Feminist Philosophy: Essential Readings in Theory, Reinterpretation and Application, 1994, Feminist Bioethics, 1997, Feminist Thought: A More Comprehensive Ethics, 1998, Globalizing Feminist Bioethics: Crosscultural Perspectives, 2000; editor: (with Anne Donchin and Susan Dodds) Linking Visions: Feminist Bioethics, Human Rights, and the Developing World, 2004; contbr. numerous articles to profl. jours.; mem. various editl. bds. Project reviewer Annenberg/CPB Project, Washington, 1986; policy writer dvsn. health svcs. rsch. and policy U. Minn., 1988, Frank Graham Porter Early Childhood Ctr., U. N.C. Chapel Hill, 1988; mem. Charlotte task force Congl. Task Force Health Care, Congressman Alex McMillan, 1991, standards and ethics com. Hospice N.C., 1991, resource and ethics coms. McMillan-Spratt Task Force Health Care Policy, 1992, pastoral care com. Carolinas Med. Ctr., 1990—, ethics com. Presbyn. Hosp., 1990—, N.E. Regional Hosp., 1991, Nat. Adv. Bd. Ethics in Reproduction, Washington, 1993; active Hastings Ctr. Project Undergrad. Values Edn., Briarcliff Manor, N.Y., 1993, N.C. Found. Humanities and Pub. Policy; mem. bioethics Resource Group, 1992—; mem. feminist approaches to bioethics network, 1996—; dir. med. humanities program Davidson Coll., 1988-98. Named Prof. of Yr., Carnegie Found. and Coun. Advancement and Support of Edn., 1986. Mem. Internat. Assn. for Feminist Approaches to Bioethics Network (coord. 1999—), Internat. Assn. Bioethics (chair 2003—), Am. Assn. for Bioethics and Humanities, Am. Cath. Philos. Assn., Am. Philos. Assn. (ad hoc com. computers, pub. and role of Am. Philos. Assn. 1984, adv. com. to program com. 1986-88, nomination com. 1989-91, nat. com. on status of women 1989-93, 2003—), Am. Legal Studies and Assn., Am. Soc. Pol. and Legal Philosophy, Am. Soc. Law and Medicine, Nat. Coun. Rsch. on Women, Nat. Women Studies Assn., Internat. Assn. Philosophy Law and Social Philosophy, Assn. Practical and Profl. Ethics, Society Christian Ethics, Soc. Women in Philosophy, Soc. Philosophy and Tech., Soc. Philosophy and Pub. Affairs, Soc. Study of Women Philosophers, Network Feminist Approaches to Bioethics, The Hastings Ctr., Triangle Bioethics Group, So. Soc. Philosophy and Psychology. Avocations: aerobics, boating, hiking. Office Phone: 704-687-2850. Business E-Mail: rotong@email.uncc.edu.

TONICK, ILLENE, clinical psychologist; b. Bronx, N.Y.; d. Benjamin and Mollie (Airov) T.; m. Michael S. Levine, May 30, 1984. BA, SUNY-Stony Brook, 1973; MS, U. Utah, 1979, PhD, 1981. Staff psychologist Neuropsychiat. Inst., UCLA, 1980-82, asst. clin. prof. dept. psychiatry, 1984—; clin. supr. Ctr. Legal Psychiatry, L.A., 1982-83; pvt. practice psychology, L.A., 1982—. Dir. Acad. Rev. Psychol. Lic. Workshops., L.A., 1983—. Contbr. articles to profl. jours. NIMH fellow, 1973-76, Solomon Baker fellow 1979-80. Mem. Am. Psychol. Assn., Nat. Register Health Providers in Psychology, So. Calif. Psychotherapy Affiliation, Phi Kappa Phi. Office: 941 Westwood Blvd Ste 221 Los Angeles CA 90024-2940

TONIETTE, SALLYE JEAN, physician; b. Sulphur, La., 1929; d. Eugene Augusta and Sallye (Tanner) T. Student, John McNeese Jr. Coll., 1946-47; BS, La. State U., 1949, tchrs. cert., 1950, MD, 1955. Intern Crawford W. Long Meml. Hosp., Emory U., Atlanta, 1955-56, resident in ob-gyn., jr., sr., chief residencies, 1956-59; practice in ob-gyn. Sulphur, La., 1959—. Mem. med. staff West Calcasieu Cameron Hosp., 1959—. Dir. Calcasieu Parish Cancer Soc., 1963-67. Named Woman of Distinction, Calcasieu Parish Police Jurors, also Bus. and Profl. Women's Club of West Calcasieu, 1969; Queen of Krewe of Cosmos, 1963, Mardi Gras. Fellow Am. Coll. Ob-Gyn.; mem. La. Med. Assn., Calcasieu Parish Med. Soc., La. Wildlife Fedn., Am. Quarter Horse Assn., Assn. Am. Physicians and Surgeons, Bayou Oaks Country Club (v.p., bd. dirs. 1974—), Krewe de Bon Coer, Krewe of Cosmos, Alpha Chi Omega, Beta Tau Mu, Iota Sigma Pi, Phi Theta Kappa, Beta Sigma Phi. Republican. Methodist. Home: 4917 La Paix Dr Sulphur LA 70665 Office: 521 Cypress St Sulphur LA 70663-5049 Personal E-mail: sassy29@xspedius.net.

TONJES, MARIAN JEANNETTE BENTON, education educator; b. Rockville Center, NY, Feb. 16, 1929; d. Millard Warren and Felicia E. (Tyler) Benton; m. Charles F. Tonjes (div. 1965, dec.); children: Jeffrey Charles, Kenneth Warren. BA, U. N.Mex., 1951, cert., 1966, MA, 1969; EdD, U. Miami, 1975. Dir. recreation Stuyvesant Town Housing Project, N.Y.C., 1951—53; tchr. music., phys. edn. Sunset Mesa Day Sch., Albuquerque, 1963—64; tchr. remedial reading Zia Elem. Sch., 1965—67; tchr. secondary devel. reading Rio Grande H.S., 1967—69; rsch. asst. reading Southwestern Coop. Ednl. Lab., 1969—71; assoc. dir., vis. instr. Fla. Ctr. Tchr. Tng. Materials U. Miami, 1971—72; asst. prof. U.S. Internat. U., San Diego, 1972—75; prof. edn. Western Wash. U., Bellingham, 1975—94, prof. emerita, 1994—; dir. summer study at Oriel Coll. Oxford U., England, 1976—93; adj. prof. U. N.Mex., 2005—. Reading supr. Manzanita Ctr., 1968; vis. prof. adult edn. Palomar (Calif.) Jr. Coll., 1974; vis. prof. U. Guam, Mangilao, 1989-90; invited guest Russian Reading Assn., Moscow, 1992; internat. travel adv. Vantage Deluxe Travel, 2002-05; spkr. European Conf. reading, Tallinn, Estonia, 2003, symposium chair World Congress, Manila, 2004; cons. in field. Author: (with Miles V. Zintz) Teaching Reading/Thinking Study Skills in Content Classroom, 3rd edit., Secondary Reading, Writing and Learning, 1991, Integrated Content Literacy, 1999, (with Ray Wolpow) Integrated Content Literacy, 5th edit., 2006. Trustee White Mountain Sch., 2000—06; tour dir. In the Footsteps of Dickens, England, 2001; hon. trustee Lomonosov Sch., Moscow; read by three com. Albuquerque Bus. and Edn. Compact, 1999—2002. Tng. Tchr. Trainers grantee, 1975; NDEA fellow Okla. State U., 1969; nominated Profl. Outstanding Alumna McDaniel Coll., 2005. Mem.: Am. Reading Forum, Internat. Reading Assn., PEO (past chpt. pres.), World Congress in Reading Buenos Aires, European Coun. Internat. Schs., European Conf. in Reading, UK Reading Assn., Internat. Reading Assn. (non-print media and reading com. 1980—83, workshop dir. S.W. regional confs. 1982, travel, interchange and study tours com. 1984—86, com. internat. devel. N.Am. 1991—96, Outstanding Tchr. Educator award 1981), Am. Reading Forum (chmn. bd. dirs. 1983—85), Oxonian and Friend of Oriel Coll. (Oxford) (hon.), Circumnavigators, Internat. Soc. Rwy. Travelers, Albuquerque Tennis Club, Delta Delta Delta. Presbyterian. Avocations: miniatures, tennis, bridge, art, travel. Business E-Mail: mtonjes@unm.edu.

TONN, ANKE, library and information scientist, researcher; b. Hamburg, Germany, Feb. 3, 1944; arrived in U.S., 1964, naturalized, 1972; d. Albert Theodor Tonn and Annemarie Christa Herzog; children: Deszoe Tibor Vaghy, Tuende Lilla Vaghy Forrest. BA in German Lit. and Art History, Queen's U., Kingston, Ontario, Can., 1988; MLIS, Dalhousie U., Halifax, Nova Scotia, Can., 1988—2000. Cataloger Ellender Meml. Libr. Nicholls State U., Thibodaux, La., 1996—2000, head interlibrary loan, 2000—. Serials and theses cataloger Howard-Tilton Meml. Libr. Tulane U., New Orleans, 1994—96; grant writer and program dir. 10th Ann. Cajun/Zydeco Music and Dance Exhibit, Thibodaux, 2005—06. Contbr. scientific papers, articles to profl. jours. Mem.: ALA, La. Libr. Assn. Achievements include research in history of Louisiana dance halls. Home: 504B Parkside Dr Thibodaux LA 70301 Office: Nicholls State Univ Ellender Meml Library Thibodaux LA 70310 Office Phone: 985-448-4633. Office Fax: 985-448-4925.

TONSFELDT, LORI ANN, secondary school educator; b. Iowa City, Iowa, June 26, 1955; d. Clifford Harvey Bennett and Rosetta Maxine Bennett (Blankenhorn); m. David James Tonsfeldt, Nov. 11, 1955; children: Jill Nicole Anderson, Sara Cathryn Olmstead, Kate Elizabeth. BS, Iowa State U., Ames, 1973—76. Substitute tchr. West Del. Sch. Dist., Manchester, Iowa, 1978—79, Mt. Pleasant Sch. Dist., Iowa, 1979—81; substitue tchr. Wash. Sch. Dist., Iowa, 1981—85; substitute tchr. Omaha Pub. Schs., Nebr., 1985—86, Cedar Rapids Schs., 1986—88; 7th grade tchr. Taft Mid. Sch., Cedar Rapids, 1988—. Mem. AAUW, Washington, 1981—85. Mem. Ref. Women in Am., Cedar Rapids, 1987—2006. Recipient Top of Class, Cedar Rapids Gazette, 2000, Tchr. of Yr., Walt Disney Co., 2001, Wal-Mart, 2005, Tchr. of Week, KDAT, 2005. Republican. Mem. Christian Ch. Avocations: singing, flutist, travel, gardening, walking. Home: 508 Stone Hedge Dr NW Cedar Rapids IA 52405 Office: Taft Mid Sc 5200 E Ave NW Cedar Rapids IA 52405 Office Phone: 319-558-2243. Personal E-mail: ltonsfeldt@hotmail.com. Business E-Mail: ltonsfeldt@crk12.ia.us.

TOOKER, MICHELLE, secondary school educator; d. John and Vivian Tooker. Bachelor's, Western Conn. State U., Danbury, 1995, Master's, 2006. Tchr. Danbury H.S., 2001—. Coach girls track & field team Danbury H.S., 2001—. Named Asst. Track Coach of Yr., CHSCA, 2004. Mem.: NEA, Conn. Edn. Assn.

TOOLE, CHRISTINE R., science educator; m. Michael Toole; children: Ian, Ryan. BS in Environ. Cons., Cornell U., N.Y., 1978; BS in Sci. Edn., Clarion U., Pa., 1994. Cert. tchr. Pa., 1995. Gymnastics team coach YMCA, Warren, Pa., 1985—91; sci. tchr. Warren (Pa.) County Sch. Dist., 1995—. Recipient Educator of Yr., Warren County Conservation Dist., 2005. Mem.: Pa. Edn. Assn., NEA. Avocations: hiking, snowboarding, gardening, embroidery. Office Phone: 814-723-3370.

TOOLE, JOAN TRIMBLE, financial consultant; b. Ipswich, Mass., Apr. 3, 1923; d. Dana Newcomb and Barbara (Campbell) T.; m. John R. Marchi, Dec. 28, 1943 (div. Aug. 1959); children: Jon, Jael, Charis, Peter; m. Kenneth Ross Toole, Apr. 22, 1960 (dec. Aug. 1981); children: Dana O'Keefe, David Campbell. BA, Antioch Coll., Yellow Springs, Ohio, 1946; MS in Fin., U. Mont., 1976; MPA, Harvard U., 1985. Rancher J/J and KJ Ranches, 1955-82; Mont. legis. asst., researcher, 1981-83; cons. Mont. Dept. Revenue, 1985-87, U. Mont. Biol. Sta., 1987-89; pvt. practice, 1987—. State coord. Cranston for Pres., 1983-84; lobbyist Office Pub. Instrn., 1989-90; tax appeals bd. Ravalli County, 1981-84; active Mont. Bd. Natural Resources and Conservation, 1986-90, LWV, Mont. Environ. Info. Ctr., No. Plains Resource Coun.; bd. dirs. Mont. Conservation Voters, 1992—; mem. Lewis & Clark City/County Health Bd., 1994-98, treas. Montanans for Coal Trust, 1999-2005, Montanans for Common Sense Mining, 1998-; bd. dirs. Forever Wild Endowment Mem. AARP (vol. income tax preparer 1993—), Harvard Club (bd. dirs. ch. schs. and scholarships), Mont. Dem. Womens Club (regional dir.) Democrat. Episcopalian. Home and Office: 104 S Cooke St Helena MT 59601-5235

TOOMEY, JEANNE ELIZABETH, animal activist; b. N.Y.C., Aug. 22, 1921; d. Edward Aloysius and Anna Margaret (O'Grady) Toomey; m. Peter Terranova, Sept. 28, 1951 (dec. 1968); children: Peter Terranova (dec.), Sheila Terranova Beasley. Student, Hofstra U., 1938-40; student law sch., Fordham U., 1940-41; BA, Southampton Coll., 1976; postgrad., Monmouth Coll., 1978-79. Reporter, columnist Bklyn. Daily Eagle, 1943-52; with The Fitzgeralds, NBC Radio, N.Y.C., 1952-53; reporter, writer King Features Syndicate, N.Y.C., 1953-55; reporter, columnist N.Y. Jour.-Am., N.Y.C., 1955-61; newsman AP, N.Y.C., 1963-64; stringer; columnist News Tribune, Woodbridge, NJ, 1976-86; editor Calexico (Calif.) Chronicle, 1987-88; editor community sect. Asbury Park (N.J.) Press, 1988; pres., dir. Last Post Animal Sanctuary, Falls Village, Conn., 1989—. Author: Murder in the Hamptons, 1994, Assignment Homicide, 1998. Chmn. com. to establish Wildlife Preserve Hackensack Meadows, NJ, 1968—69. Named Woman of the Yr. N.Y. Women's Press Club, 1960. Mem. Newswomen's Club of N.Y., Overseas Press Club, N.Y. Press Club, Silurians. Roman Catholic. Address: PO Box 259 Falls Village CT 06031-0259 Office: 95 Belden St Falls Village CT 06031 Office Phone: 860-824-0831. Office Fax: 860-824-5460.

TOOMEY, LAURA CAROLYN, psychologist; b. Manchester, Conn., Mar. 29, 1929; d. David Clark and Olive (Hutchinson) T. BS, Bates Coll., 1950; MA, U. Conn., 1954, PhD, 1961. Lic. psychologist, Conn. Psychologist Community Child Guidance Clinic, Manchester, 1959-64; from psychologist to chief psychologist Springfield Hosp., Mass., 1964-73; with Conn. Valley Hosp., Middletown, 1973—92, acting dir. psychol. svcs., 1986-87, dir. clin. internship tng., 1974-92, asst. chief of psychol. svcs., 1987-91. Co-author: Evaluation of Changes Associated with Psychiatric Treatment, 1959; contbr. chpts. in books and articles to profl. jours. Justice of the peace Town of Bolton, Conn., 1954-89; mem. Bolton Town Commn. on Aging, 1972-76, Bolton Bd. Health, 1993-2006, sec., 1995-2006; sec. Bolton Property Owners Assn., 1964-76. Mem. Am. Psychol. Assn. (treas. div. clin. psychology 1982-90), Conn. Psychol. Assn. (coun. bd. dirs. 1975-86). Republican. Avocations: reading, travel. Home: PO Box 9486 40 Steel Crossing Rd Bolton CT 06043-7623

TOOMEY, PAULA KATHLEEN, special education educator, educational technologist, consultant; b. Framingham, Mass., July 15, 1959; d. Paul Joseph and Mary Theresa (Coronella) T. AB in Econs., Boston Coll., 1984; postgrad., Harvard U., 1993—; MS in Edn., Simmons Coll., 1998. Office supr. ADIA, Cambridge, Mass., 1985-87; accounts receivable coord. WGBH Ednl. Found., Boston, 1987-88; fin. analyst Sta. WGBH-TV, Boston, 1988-91; unit mgr. Descriptive Video Svc. WGBH Ednl. Found., Boston, 1991-96; tchr. Franciscan's Children's Hosp.--Kennedy Day Sch., 2000—04; special educator Westford, N.Mex., 2004—05, Lit. Exentsion Applicatiion Practice program, 2005—. Cons. accessible technologies specialist. Vol. cons. Grow Golphybhangyang, Nepal, 1993-95; vol. tchr. Jr. Achievement, Boston, 1987; vol. master's swim coach YMCA, Brighton, Mass., 1990-93; vol. Franciscan Children's Hosp., Brighton, 1991-93; active NOW. Mem. AAUW. Roman Catholic. Avocations: creative writing, photography, trekking, swimming, bicycling.

TOOTHE, KAREN LEE, elementary and secondary school educator; b. Seattle, Dec. 13, 1957; d. Russell Minor and Donna Jean (Drolet) McGraw; m. Edward Frank Toothe, Aug. 6, 1983; 1 child, Kendall Erin. BA in Psychology with high honors, U. Fla., 1977, MEd in Emotional Handicaps and Learning Disabilities, 1979. Cert. behavior analysis Fla. Dept. Profl. Regulation, behavior analyst Nat. Behavior Analyst Bd. Alternative edn. self-contained tchr. grades 2 and 3 Gainesville Acad., Micanopy, Fla., 1979; emotional handicaps self-contained tchr. Ctr. Sch. Alternative Sch., Gainesville, Fla., 1979-80; learning disabilities resource tchr. grades 2 and 3 Galaxy Elem. Sch., Boynton Beach, Fla., 1980-81, learning disabilities self-contained tchr. grades 1-3, 1981, varying exceptionalities self-contained tchr. grades 3-5, 1981-83, chpt. one remedial reading tchr. grades 3 and 4, 1982-83; sec. and visual display unit operator Manpower, London, 1983-84; dir. sci./geography/social studies program Fairley House Sch., London, 1984-86, specific learning difficulties self-contained tchr. ages 8-12, dir. computing program, 1984-89; specific learning difficulties resource tchr. ages 8-16 Dyslexia Inst., Sutton Coldfield, Eng., 1990; behavior specialist, head Exceptional Student Edn. dept. Gateway High Sch., Kissimmee, Fla., 1990, behavior specialist, head ESE dept., 1991, resource compliance specialist, head ESE dept., 1991-93, tchr. summer youth tng. and enrichment program, 1993, Osceola High Sch., Kissimmee, 1992; resource compliance specialist, program specialist for mentally handicapped, physically impaired, occupational and phys. therapy programs St. Cloud (Fla.) Mid. Sch., 1993-96, local augmentative/assistive tech. specialist, 1995—; resource compliance specialist, program specialist physically impaired occupl./phys. therapy programs, local augmentative/assistive tech. specialist Hickory Tree Elem. Sch., 1996-97, program specialist assistive tech., occpl., and phys. therapy, physically impaired programs, 1997-99, program specialist assistive tech., 1999—. Sch. rep. CREATE, Alachua County, Fla., 1979-80, Palm Beach County South Area Tchr. Edn. Ctr. Coun., 1980-83, chmn., 1982-83; mem. writing team Title IV-C Ednl. Improvement Grant, Palm Beach County, Fla., 1981; mem. math. curriculum writing team Palm Beach County (Fla.) Schs., 1983; mem., co-dir. Fairley House Rsch. Com., 1984-90; co-founder, dir. Rsch. Database, London, 1984-89; co-chmn. computer and behavior/social aspects writing teams Dyslexia Inst. Math., Staines, Eng., 1990; lectr., course tutor Brit. Dyslexia Assn., Crewe, Eng., 1990; mem. Vocat.-Exceptional Com., 1991-93; mem. Osceola Reading Coun., 1991-98; mem. sch. adv. com. Gateway High Sch., 1991-93, St. Cloud Mid. Sch., 1993-96; mem. sch. adv. com. Hickory Tree Elem. Sch., 1999-2000, Ctr. for Ind. Living Assitance for Tech. Divsn.; presenter in field. Mem. bd. assistive tech. divsn. Ctr. for Ind. Living. Named Mid. Sch. Profl. of Yr. Osceola chpt. Coun. Exceptional Children, 1995, 96, Profl. Recognized Spl. Educator, 1997; winner Disney's Teacherific Spl. Judges award, 1997; recipient Outstanding Svcs. to Coun. for Exceptional Children award, 2002, 2003, Outstanding Related Svcs. Tchr. of Yr., 2003, Outstanding Support Svcs. award, 2003. Mem. CEC (named local chpt. Mid. Sch. Profl. of Yr. 1995, 96, exec. com. 1997-2002, C.A.N. rep. 1997-99, pres.-elect 1999-2000, pres. 2000-01, Outstanding Svcs. to CEC award 2002, 03, Outstanding Related Svcs. Tchr. of Yr. 2003, Outstanding Support Svcs. award 2003), Fla. Soc. for Augmentative and Alt. Comm., Phi Beta Kappa. Avocations: travel, reading, exercise, scuba diving, crafts. Home: 2175 James Dr Saint Cloud FL 34771-8830 Office: Osceola Dist Schs ESE Adminstrv Annex 805 Bill Beck Blvd Kissimmee FL 34744-4492 Office Phone: 407-518-8147. Business E-Mail: toothek@osceola.k12.fl.us.

TOPACIO, ANGELA, marketing executive; b. Germany, 1968; m. Matt DiDio. Brand mgr. Saks Inc.; project mgr. Gyro Creative Grp., Detroit, 1999, majority owner. Named one of 40 Under 40, Crain's Detroit Bus., 2006. Office: Gyro Creative Group 400 Grand River Ave Ste 200 Detroit MI 48226 Office Phone: 313-964-0100. Office Fax: 313-964-0101.*

TOPALIAN, NAOMI GETSOYAN, writer; b. Beirut, Jan. 26, 1928; came to the U.S., 1953; d. Avedis S. and Zarouhi T. (Yezegelian) G.; m. Paul G. Topalian, Sept. 18, 1954; children: Andrew P., Janet Z. Topalian Moffatt. Diploma, Am. U. Hosp. Sch. Nursing, Beirut, 1952; BS, Boston U., 1967. RN, Mass. Pediat. nurse Children Med. Ctr., Boston, 1954-55; inservice edn. supr. Winchester (Mass.) Hosp., 1967-70; tchr. nursing Northeastern Vocat. H.S., Wakefield, Mass., 1970-72; med. and surg. nurse various tchg. hosps., Boston, 1973-87. Author: Dust to Destiny, 1986, People, Places and Moultonborough, 1989, Legacy of Honor, 1995; contbr. Personality and Presidency: A Scientific Inquirey, 1998, Breaking the Rock of Tradition, 2000; contbr. articles to profl. jours. Supt. primary divsn., Sunday sch. tchr., mem. pulpit com., co-pres. couples club Armenian Meml. Ch., Watertown, Mass.; Armenian lang. tchr. First Armenian Ch. of Belmont; active Belmont Coun. Chs., chair religious edn. com.; pres. Armenian Women's Edn. Club. Mem. Armenian Internat. Womens Assn. Avocations: needle work, knitting, counseling the bereaved. Home: 46 Circle Rd Lexington MA 02420-2926

TOPCIK, DEBORAH FAY, marketing executive; b. Louisville, Ky., Nov. 12, 1975; d. Charles Melvin and Evelyn Lou Topcik. BA in Econ., Hollins U., 1998. Mktg. analyst Papa John's Internat., Louisville, 1998—2001; dir. mktg. JBC Entertainment, Louisville, 2001—. Vol. Big Bros. Big Sisters, Louisville, 2002—06; sec. Keneseth Israel, Louisville, 2002—05; chair holocaust remembrance day Jewish Cmty. Fedn., Louisville, 2001—05. Recipient Young Leadership award, Jewish Fedn. Louisville, 2003, Vol. of Yr. award, Keneseth Israel, 2002. Jewish. Avocation: volunteering. Home: 3411 Ingle Ave Louisville KY 40207 Office: JBC Entertainment 11851 Commonwealth Dr Louisville KY 40299 Office Phone: 502-213-9272. Personal E-mail: debfay@aol.com.

TOPELIUS, KATHLEEN ELLIS, lawyer; b. July 15, 1948; BA, U. Conn., 1970; postgrad., U. Md., 1971-74; JD, Cath. U. Am., 1978. Bar: D.C. 1978, U.S. Supreme Ct. 1988. Atty. office of gen. counsel Fed. Home Loan Bank Bd., 1978-80; ptnr. Morgan, Lewis & Bockius, Washington, 1985-93, Bryan Cave, Washington, 1993—. Recipient Alpha award Fed. Home Loan Bank Bds., 1979. Office: Bryan Cave 700 13th St NW Fl 7 Washington DC 20005-5921 Office Phone: 202-508-6140. Business E-Mail: ketopelius@bryancave.com.

TOPETZES, FAY KALAFAT, retired school guidance counselor; b. Auburn, Ind., July 13, 1923; d. Alexander Christ and Andromache Basiliou Kalafat; m. Nick John Topetzes, Jan. 31, 1953; children: Andrea Topetzes Mann, John Nick, Sophia Angela Strelka BS in Acctg. and English, Ind. U., 1945; cert. tchr., Marquette U., 1969, MS in Guidance and Counseling, 1973. Cert. tchr., Wis. Acct. Dana Corp., Auburn, Ind., 1945-47; mgr. theaters Kalafat Bros., Ind., 1947-53; tchr. Univ. Sch. of Milw., 1962-64, Spencerian Bus. Coll., Milw., 1959-62, Milw. Pub. Schs., 1962-69; counselor, dir. guidance West Allis (Wis.) Ctrl. H.S., 1969-86; ret., 1986. Charter pres., mem. Ind. U. Greek Am. Student Assn., 1942-45; bd. dir. Gov.'s Tourism Milw., 1990—, FLW Heritage Bd., Madison, Wis., 1990—; vol. for charitable orgns.; mem. parish coun. Annunciation Greek Orthodox Ch. Mem. AAUW (past pres., pub. policy chair, other CTE chmn. Nat. award 1994-95), Wis. Pers. and Guidance Assn., Wis. Assn. Sch. Counselors, Milw. Found. Women, Daus. of Penelope (dist. gov. dists. 12 and 13, nat. chmn. coms. 1994-96, Penelope of Yr. award) Suburban Guidance Counselors Assn. (past pres.). Home: 9119 N White Oak Ln Ste 216 Bayside WI 53217-6203

TOPHAM, SALLY JANE, performing arts educator; b. N.Y.C., June 2, 1933; d. William Holroyd Topham and Marian Phyllis (Thomas) Topham Halligan; m. Joseph Vincent Ferrara, Dec. 27, 1958 (div. 1977); children: Gregory Paul Ferrara, Mark Edward Ferrara. Student Ballet Theatre Sch., Royal Acad. Dance, London; trained in Europe. Freelance profl. dancer ballet, opera ballet, summer stock, 1956-59; founder, dir. Monmouth Sch. Ballet, N.J., 1963-83; dir. Shore Ballet Theatre Sch., 1986-95; freelance tchr., choreographer, 1996—. Tchr., dir. Mount Allison U. Summer Sch., New Brunswick, Canada, 1973—77; dir. Westfield Sch. Ballet, NJ, 1976—77; artistic dir. Shore Ballet Co., 1977—; prof. ballet Monmouth Coll., West Long Branch, NJ, 1981—83; founder Ctrl. Jersey Acad. Ballet, Red Bank, NJ, 1983—85; dir. Acad. Shore Ballet, 1995—2000; cons. formulation dance curriculum for N.J. pub. schs. State Bd. Edn., 1997; tchr. Colts Neck Dance Acad., 2000—03, Middletown Dance Acad., 2003—, Spring Lake Sch. Dance, 2003—. Choreographer (ballets) Nutcracker, 1985, Homage to Bournonville, 1977, Shubert Songs, 1980, Coppelia, 1981, 1990, 1996, Cinderella, 1988; staged numerous ballets and opera ballets. Bd. dirs. Monmouth Arts Found., Red Bank, 1972—85, Shore Ballet Co., Red Bank, 1976—2000; founder, bd. dirs. Monmouth Civic Ballet, Red Bank, 1972—75. Mem.: English Speaking Union (bd. dirs., treas. 2004), Am. Acad. Ballet (assoc.), Royal Acad. Dance (assoc.; reg. tchr., advanced tchg. diploma 1979). Avocations: theater, music, books, travel. Office: Shore Ballet Co 8 Hunt St Rumson NJ 07760-1428

TOPHAM, SUZANNE CASTON, journalist; b. Kansas City, May 12, 1948; d. Charles and Jeanne McCaughey Caston; m. Ralph E. Topham, June 20, 1970 (div. Jan. 1990); children: Roger Elliott, Elizabeth Jeanne; BJ, U. Mo., Columbia, 1970. Wire editor Minot Daily News, ND, 1970—72; news copy editor St. Louis Globe Dem., 1974—76; freelance editor, 1976—88; features copy editor St. Louis Post Dispatch, 1988—97, features copy desk chief, 1997—2001, nat., fgn. copy desk chief, 2001—03, asst. editor, nat. and fgn. desk, 2003—06, editor, 2006—. Editor, pub. LWV, St. Louis, 1977—79. Mem.: AAUW, Am. Copy Editors Soc. Avocations: travel, gardening, art, interior decorating, walking. Home: 634 Carman Forest Ln Manchester MO 63021 Office: St Louis Post-Dispatch 900 N Tucker Blvd Saint Louis MO 63101 Office Phone: 314-340-8240. Personal E-mail: suzanne818@charter.net.

TOPINKA, JUDY BAAR, state official, political organization worker; b. Riverside, Ill., Jan. 16, 1944; d. William Daniel and Lillian Mary (Shuss) Baar; 1 child, Joseph Baar. BS, Northwestern U., 1966. Features editor, reporter, columnist Life Newspapers, Berwyn and LaGrange, Ill., 1966-77; with Forest Park (Ill.) Rev. and Westchester News, 1976-77; coord. spl. events dept. fedn. comm. AMA, 1978-80; rsch. analyst Senator Leonard Becker, 1978-79; mem. Ill. Ho. of Reps., 1981-84, Ill. Senate, 1985-94; treas. State of Ill., Springfield, 1995—; chmn. State Rep. Party, 2002—. Former mem. judiciary com., former chmn. senate health and welfare com.; former mem. fin. instn. com.; former co-chmn. Citizens Coun. on Econ. Devel.; former co-chmn. U.S. Commn. for Preservation of Am.'s Heritage Abroad, serves on legis. ref. bur.; former mem. minority bus. resource ctr. adv. com. U.S. Dept. Transp.; former mem. adv. bd. Nat. Inst. Justice. Founder, pres., bd. dirs. West Suburban Exec. Breakfast Club, from 1976; chmn. Ill. Ethnics for Reagan-Bush, 1984, Bush-Quayle 1988; spokesman Nat. Coun. State Legislatures Health Com.; former mem. nat. adv. coun. health professions edn. HHS; mem., GOP chairwoman Legis. Audit Commn. of Cook County; chmn. Riverside Twp. Regular Republican Orgn., 1994—. Recipient Outstanding Civilian Svc. medal, Molly Pitcher award, Abraham Lincoln award, Silver Eagle award U.S. Army and N.G. Office: Office of Ill State Treasurer 100 W Randolph St Ste 15-600 Chicago IL 60601-3232

TOPLITT, GLORIA H., music educator, actress, vocalist; b. St. Louis, May 22, 1925; d. Wade Fitzgerald Hamilton and Neyneen Farrell Pires; m. James Parnell, 1942 (div. July 1949); 1 child, Dennis James Parnell; m. Abraham Toplitt, Aug. 19, 1968. Student, Guy Bates Post Acad. Dramatic Arts, L.A., 1941-43. Stage performer, N.Y.C., 1944-59; dir. entertainment Holland Am. Lines, 1959-61; tchr. voice North Hollywood (Calif.) Conservatory, 1965-67; pvt. voice tchr. North Hollywood, 1968-95; music specialist outreach program NASA Space Sci. and Tech., Inc., Springfield, Va., 1997—. Dir. Workshop Theatre Program, North Hollywood, 1968—78; coach for impaired voices, North Hollywood, 1968—. Author, composer: Parade of Planets, 1998, Space Challenge, 1999; actor: (plays, N.Y. stage prodns.) appeared as leading lady Oklahoma, Chocolate Soldier, Lend an Ear, Courtin' Time, Showboat, Take Me Along, Auld Lang Syne, Three Musketeers, Carousel, Oh! Captain, Brigadoon, Guys and Dolls, Hit the Deck, Finian's Rainbow, others; voice rec. Songs of Harriet Ware Meml., Smithsonian Instn. Mem. election bd. Office of Voter Registrar, North Hollywood, 1996—98. Avocations: poetry, travel, theater, elderhostel classes, reading. Home: 4405 Carpenter Ave North Hollywood CA 91607-4110

TOPOLEWSKI, NANCY ELEANOR, minister; b. Kingston, Pa., Sept. 7, 1953; d. Paul Mott and Eleanor (Kandler) Rodda; m. John Leo Topolewski, June 14, 1975. BA summa cum laude, Wilkes Coll., 1975; MDiv summa cum laude, Princeton Theol. Sem., 1978; MPhil, Drew U., 1990, PhD with distinction, 1993. Recognition of ordination/probationary membership Wyo. Ann. Conf., The United Meth. Ch., N.Y., 1989, ordained elder Presbytery of Lackawanna, Pa., 1978. Min. Ashley Presbyn. Ch., Pa., 1978—85, Welsh Presbyn. Ch., Warrior Run, Pa., 1978—85, Flemingville United Meth. Ch., Owego, N.Y., 1987—88, First United Meth. Ch., Kirkwood, N.Y., 1988—96; adminstrv. asst./office mgr. Oneonta Dist., Wyo. Ann. Conf., United Meth. Ch., Sidney, N.Y., 1988—96; min. Vestal Ctr. United Meth. Ch. Author: (doctoral dissertation) Under the Mercy: The Doctrine of the Atonement in the Novels and Theological Works of Charles Walter Stansby Williams (1886-1945) (Helen LePage and William Hale Chamberlain Prize, Drew U., 1993); editor (contbr.): Where Rivers Run and Mountains Rise: Essays in Celebration of the Sesquicentennial of the Wyoming Annual Conference; author: (scholarly article) Under the Mercy: An Introduction to the Life and Work of Charles Williams, (sermons) The Minister's Annual Manual for Preaching and Worship Leadership, Church Management: The Clergy Journal; editor: (conf. jour.) Jour. and Yearbook Wyo. Annual Conf., United Meth. Ch. Mem.: Binghamton Downtown Singers.

TOPOLEWSKI-GREEN, MARY JO THERESE, small business owner; b. Toledo, Ohio, June 29, 1969; d. Leonard Martin and Carol Ann Topolewski; m. Robert Wendell, Jr. Green, Oct. 12, 2000. Student, Davenport U., 2002, Bowling Green State U., Ohio, 1987—90. Office adminstr. Mich. Dept. Transp., 1993—95; adminstrv. asst. Schrader Ent., Fairview, Mich., 1997—2001, Reliance Heating and Cooling, Mio, Mich., 1998—99; co-owner Sunfish Studios, Fairview, 1999—; adminstrv. asst. Otsego Meml. Hosp., Gaylord, Mich., 2002—. Freelance profl. dance instr.; web-site designer and cons.; audio/video prodn. and sound recording cons. Mem.: Internat. Thespian Soc. (life; chpt. pres. 1986—87). Avocations: dance, singing, computers.

TOPOLSKI, CATHERINE, science educator; b. Bridgeport, Conn., Feb. 23, 1948; d. Edward Joseph and Jean (Skierski) Topolski; m. Richard A. Hoffman, Feb. 1970 (div. June 1981); children: Alan Hoffman, Alexandria Hoffman, Aaron Hoffman. BS, Sacred Heart U., Fairfield, Conn., 1984; MS, So. Conn. State U., 1993. Sci. tchr. Emmett O'Brien Vocat. Tech. H.S., Ansonia, Conn., 1985—2002, Bullard Havens Vocat. Tech. H.S., Bridgeport, Conn., 2002—. Class advisor, ski club advisor, student assistance team peer mediator Emmett O'Brien Vocat. Tech. H.S., 1987—. Organizer Emmett O'Brien River Cleanup Naugatuck River Watershed Assn., Conn., 1994—. Mem.: Conn. Sci. Tchrs. Assn., New Eng. Sci. Tchrs. Assn., Sacred Heart Alumni Assn. Roman Catholic. Avocations: reading, exploring nature, volleyball.

TOPPER, BARBARA MACNEAL BLAKE, secondary school educator; b. Wilmington, Del., July 18, 1942; d. George Mitchell and Jean (Strickland) Blake; m. George Lee Topper, Aug. 7, 1964; children: Gordon Lee, Geoffrey Logan. MusB, Peabody Conservatory, 1964; MusM, Peabody Conservatory, Balt., 1968. Tchr. Prince George's County Schs., Upper Marlboro, Md., 1964-67; piano tchr. Peabody Prep. Sch., Balt., 1964-67; vocal music specialist Harford County Pub. Schs., Bel Air, Md., 1968-76; piano tchr., coord. continuing edn. Cecil Community Coll., North East, Md., 1977-82; vocal music specialist Cecil County Pub. Schs., Elkton, Md., 1981-86; 2001vocal music specialist Balt. County Pub. Schs., Towson, Md., 1986—2001; staff Md. State Boychoir, Balt., 2001—04. Spl. lectr. music and music edn. Washington Coll., Chestertown, Md., 1970-74; choral adjudicator, guest conductor, clinician, supr. student tchrs., 1973; accompanist Md. Ctr. for the Arts. Developer ednl. curriculum; contbr. articles to profl. jours. Music libr. Men and Boys Choir, Ch. of Nativity, Timonium, Md., 2000—05. Mem. NEA, Md. Music Educators Assn. (exec. bd., sec. 1974-88), Music Educators Nat. Conf., Johns Hopkins Alumni Assn. (steering com. 1987-96), Phi Delta Kappa. Roman Catholic. Avocations: reading, concerts, theater. Home: 111 Hamlet Hill Rd Unit 609 Baltimore MD 21210-1510

TOPPER, PATRICIA MARGARET, music educator; b. Phila., Apr. 29, 1951; d. Vito Joseph Parisi and Margaret Mary Adelsberger; m. Dennis John Topper, Nov. 29, 1975 (div. Apr. 29, 1996); children: Kristin Marie, Joseph Stephen, Joan Catherine. BS in Music Edn., Quincy U., Ill., 1973. Cert. K-12, music, instrumental and vocal tchr. Pa., 1975. Gen., vocal music tchr. Cheltenham Sch. Dist., Elkins Park, Pa., 1989—. Recipient Judith Wand Meml. award, Quincy U., 1972, Joseph Fisher Performance award, 1973; scholarship, 1969, 1970, 1971, 1972, Music scholarship, 1969, 1970, 1971, 1972. Mem.: NEA, PSEA, CEA. D-Conservative. Avocations: listening to classical music, walking, reading, swimming, hiking. Office: Cheltenham Sch Dist 1000 Ashbourne Rd Elkins Park PA 19027

TOPPING, AUDREY RONNING, photojournalist; b. Camrose, Alta., Can., May 21, 1928; arrived in U.S., 1967; d. Chester Alvin and Inga Marie (Horte) Ronning; m. Seymour Topping, Nov. 10, 1949; children: Susan, Karen, Lesley, Robin, Joanna. Student, Augustana Univ., Camrose, 1943-46, Nanking (China) U., 1947-48, Berlin Art Sch., 1956-58, U. B.C., 1949-50; D of Arts (hon.), Rider Coll., N.J., 1983. Freelance journalist N.Y. Times Mag., N.Y.C., 1966—2001; writer, photographer Nat. Geographic, Washington, 1971-79; columnist Earth Times, N.Y.C., 1996—; spl. corr. Houston Chronicle, 1997—2001; photjournalist-at-large Earthuman Mag., 2002—. Advisor U.S.-China Arts Exch., 1997—; commentator, writer Great Wall Across The Yangtze (PBS), Homecoming (Chinese TV), 2002; TV scriptwriter China Mission, 1975. Author: Dawn Wakes In the East, 1972, The Splendors of Tibet, 1981, Charlie's World, 2000; A Day in the Life of Can., 1986, two children's books, N.Y. Times, Nat. Geographic, Readers Digest, Time, Life, Geo, Sci. Digest, Earth Times, others, exhibitions include Royal Ont. Mus., Toronto, 1980, Hallmark Gallery, NYC, 1973, Overseas Press Cub, 1975, Westchester C.C., 1989, 2004, Libby Gallery, Purchase, NY, 2004, Bhutan UN Embassy, NY, 2004, Hammond Mus., North Salem, 2005, CUNY Grad. Ctr. Gallery, 2006. Recipient Alumni award Augustana Univ. Coll., 1989, Medallion award Westchester C.C., 1989, Greenway Winship award Internat. Ctr. Journalists, 2000. Mem.: Coun. of Fgn. Relations, Soc. Woman Geographers, Asia Soc., Fgn. Policy Assn., Fox Meadow Tennis Club, Jr. Fortnightly. Avocations: sculpture, painting, tennis, skiing, exploring. Home and Office: 5 Heathcote Rd Scarsdale NY 10583-4413 E-mail: topaud@aol.com.

TORGERSON, JENNIFER ANN, athletic trainer; b. Bremerton, Wash., Dec. 9, 1976; d. Gary M. and Bonnie L. Torgerson. BA in Psychology, Pepperdine U., Malibu,Calif., 1999; MS, Western Wash. U., 2001. Cert. Trainer Nat. Athletic Training Assn., 2002. Student athletic trainer Pepperdine U., Malibu, Calif., 1996—99; asst. supr. Western Wash. U., 1999—2001; healthy lifestyle counselor YMCA, Vancouver, Wash., 2002; physical therapy aide Rebound Rehabilitation, Vancouver, 2002—03; asst. athletic trainer Southern Utah U., 2003—05, Jacksonville State U., Ala., 2006. Athletic trainer Bellingham Bells Semi Pro Baseball, 1999—2001. Vol. student athletic trainer Portland State U., Oreg., 2001—03; mem. Am. Humanics, Malibu, 1995—99, treas. Mem.: Nat. Athletic Trainers Assn. Democrat. Christian. Avocations: sports, travel. Home: 625 Gadsen Rd NW Apt 21C Jacksonville AL 36265 Office: Jacksonville State U 700 Pelham Rd Gamecock Fieldhouse Jacksonville AL 36265

TORGERSON, KATHERINE P., media consultant, corporate communications specialist; Now v.p. human resources and exec. adminstrn. Penton Media, Inc., Cleve., with.

TORGERSON, LINDA BELLE, music educator; b. Sioux City, Iowa, Dec. 16, 1951; d. Fredric William and Clara Jeanette Wilson; m. Peter Kinsey Torgerson; children: Christopher, Patricia. Diploma, Ctrl. H.S., 1971; MusB Edn., Morningside Coll., 1976; MEd, City U., 1999. Cert. Iowa tchr., tchr. Mont., Washington. Choral dir. First United Meth. Ch., Sioux City, Iowa, 1974—76, First Presbyn. Ch., Kalispell, Mont., 1976—80; pvt. music instr. Self-employed, Kalispell, Mont., 1976—80; music tchr. St. Matthews Sch., Kalispell, Mont., 1976—77; music dir., coord. Flathead County Rural Schools, Kalispell, Mont., 1979—85; music dir. Clarkston Sch. Dist., Clarkston, Wash., 1985—. Treas. Clarkston Edn. Assn., Clarkston, Wash., 1988—90, v.p., 1990—92, Clarkston, 2001—03, pres., 1991—92; sec. Wash. uniserv polit. action com. Wash. Edn. Assn., Olympia, Wash., 1992—93; bldg. rep. Clarkston Edn. Assn., Clarkston, Wash., 1993—94; jazz band dir. Lincoln Mid. Sch., Clarkston, Wash., 1996—; bldg. rep. Clarkston Edn. Assn., Clarkston, Wash., 2000—01, v.p., 2001—03; co-director for asotin county teens against smoking Asotin County Devel. Services, Clarkston, Wash., 2001—02. Singer (composer): (commercial) Flathead County Milk Music Ad for the Radio, 1978; contbr. articles to profl. jours. Mem. U-Pac bd. for SE Wash. Edn. Assn., Kennewick, Wash., 1992—93. Grantee Dist., Clarkston Sch. Dist., 1994, 1995. Mem.: NEA, Clarkston Edn. Assn. (v.p. 2001), Clarkston Edn. Assn. (bldg. rep. 1992—94), Clarkston Edn. Assn. (pres./past pres. 1991—92), Clarkston Edn. Assn. (v.p. 1989—91), Clarkston Edn. Assn. (treas. 1987—89), SE Wash. Music Educators Assn. (pres. 2002—), Wash. Music Educators Assn., Music Educators Nat. Conf. Home: 1505 8th St Clarkston WA 99403 Office: Lincoln Mid Sch 1945 4th Ave Clarkston WA 99403 Office Phone: 509-758-5506 x5245. Personal E-mail: torgersons@cableone.net. Business E-Mail: torgersonl@csdk12.org.

TORIANI, DENISE MARIA, hospital residency coordinator; b. Oakland, Calif., Dec. 30, 1954; d. David and Doris Elizabeth (Cantrell) Eirich; m. Robert Joseph Turocy, Dec. 30, 1972 (div. 1976); children: Robert Justin, Shannon James; m. Oscar Quiroga DeLaRosa, May 1, 1983 (div. 1992); m. Dennis James Toriani, June 22, 1996. AAS, Truman Coll, Chgo., 1983; BABA, De Paul U., Chgo., 1987. Legal adminstr. Taylor, Miller, Sprowl, Hoffnagle & Merletti, Chgo., 1985-91, Leonard M. Ring & Assocs., Chgo., 1991-93, Boehm, Pearlstein & Bright, Ltd., Chgo., 1994-95, Purcell & Wardrope Chartered, Chgo., 1995-99; coord. emergency medicine residency dept. Resurrection Med. Ctr., 2000—. Mem. Germans from Russia Heritage Soc., Am. Hist. Soc. Germans from Russia, Alliance of Grandparents Against SIDS Tragedy, Emergency Medicine Assn. Residency Coords. Democrat. Roman Catholic. Office: 7435 W Talcott Ave Chicago IL 60631-3717

TORIBARA, MASAKO ONO, voice educator; b. Fresno, Calif., Sept. 8, 1925; d. Mataichi Harry and Sawo Ono; m. Taft Y. Toribara, Aug. 28, 1948; children: Lynne Suzanne, Neil Willard. B Music Edn. magna cum laude, U. Mich., 1946, MusM in Voice, 1949. Instr. Bowling Green State U., Ohio, 1946—48, Hochstein Music Sch., Rochester, NY, 1965—66; instr. to lectr. Eastman Sch. Music, Rochester, 1965—, prof. emerita, 1999—. Mem. Opera Under the Stars, Rochester, 1954-56; judging panel Rochester Philharmonic Young Artist Audition, 1986, 98, 99; adjudicators various competitions. Soprano soloist Dewey Ave. Presbyn. Ch., Rochester, 1953-59, 1st Bapt. Ch. Rochester, 1961-77, Ars Antiqua, Rochester, 1961-65. Den mother Brownie Scouts, Rochester, 1959; co-pres. Jr. High Family Faculty Forum in Mid. Sch. in Gates Sch., Rochester, 1964-66. Mem. Music Tchrs. Nat. Assn. (state and nat. cert.), Nat. Assn. Tchrs. Singing, Pi Kappa Lambda, Phi Beta Kappa, Phi Kappa Phi, Mu Phi Epsilon, Pi Lambda Theta. Avocations: reading, travel, attending musical events, cooking. Home: 54 Timpat Dr Rochester NY 14624-2928 Office: Eastman Sch Music 26 Gibbs St Rochester NY 14604-2599

TORKZADEH, RITA, health information scientist; BS in Biology, U. Mich., 1997; MS in Health Informatics, U. Tex. Health Sci. Ctr., 2001. Grad. rsch. asst. U. Tex. Health Sci. Ctr., Houston, 2000—01; product mgr. WorldDoc, Inc., Las Vegas, 2002—04; med. systems specialist Nev. Cancer Inst., 2005—. Exec. sec. Nev. Healthcare Exec. Forum chpt. Am. Coll. Healthcare Execs., Las Vegas, 2004—05; presenter in field. Recipient Mich. Scholar award, U. Mich., 1993-1997, NIH Fogarty Internat. Ctr. Minority Intramural Rsch. Tng. award, U. Mich. Ctr. Human Growth and Devel., 1996; Adelia Cheever Ho. scholar, U. Mich. Cheever Ho. Coop., 1995-1996, Competitive Acad. scholar, Univ. Tex. Health Sci. Ctr. Sch. Health Info. Scis., 2000, NIH Intramural Rsch. Tng. award fellow, Bethesda, Md., 1997—99. Mem.: Am. Med. Informatics Assn., Nev. Health Exec. Forum (sec. 2003—05), Healthcare Info. Mgmt. Sys. Soc. Achievements include work on conceptualization, design, development and implementation of information systems solutions that streamline healthcare business processes and promote patient-centered care delivery.

TORLEY, MARGARET JEAN, elementary school educator; b. Denver, Oct. 21, 1947; d. Henry Waller and Josephine H. (McDonnell) Bradley; m. Michael N. Torley, Aug. 8, 1981; children: Sara M., Patrick M. BA in Elem. Edn., U. No. Colo., Greeley, 1971, MA in Spl. Edn., 1977. Lic. tchr. elem. and K-12 educationally handicapped. Switchboard operator Mountain Bell Telephone, Denver, 1965-71; 4th grade tchr. Ouray (Colo.) Schs., 1971-72; 3rd, 4th and 6th grade tchr. Strasburg (Colo.) Elem. Sch., 1973-77; 5th grade tchr. Northeast Elem., Parker, Colo., 1977-84; 4th grade tchr. Northridge Elem., Highlands Ranch, Colo., 1984—. Cons. elem. math. classrooms Pub. Edn. Bus. Coalition, Denver, 1997-99; math. resource tchr. Douglas City Schs., Highland Ranch, Colo., 1993-97; mem. Goals 2000 Math Project for Douglas County, Colo., 1992-96, Douglas County Math Trainers Team, 1992-96. Mem. spl. com. on focus issues Denver Found., 1996-97. Mem. Colo. Coun. Tchrs. Math. (Outstanding Elem. Math. Tchr. 1996, nat. bd. cert. mid. childhood generalist, 2000), Internat. Readng Assn., PTA. Roman Catholic. Avocations: power walking, singing, teenagers. Office: Northridge Elem Sch 555 Southpark Rd Highlands Ranch CO 80126-3107

TORME, MARGARET ANNE, public relations executive, management consultant; b. Indpls., Apr. 5, 1943; d. Ira G. and Margaret Joy (Wright) Barker; children: Karen Anne, Leah Vanessa. Student, Coll. San Mateo, 1961—65. Pub. rels. mgr. Hoefer, Dieterich & Brown (now Chiat-Day), San Francisco, 1964-73; v.p., co-founder, creative dir. Lowry & Ptnrs., San Francisco, 1975-83; pres., founder Torme and Lauricella Comm., San Francisco, 1983—. Cons. in comm. Mem. Coun. Pub. Rels. Firms, Jr. League (adv. bd.), Pub. Rels. Orgn. Internat. Office: 847 Sansome St San Francisco CA 94111-2908 Office Phone: 415-956-1791. Business E-Mail: margaret@torme.com.

TORNEDEN, CONNIE JEAN, banker; b. Tonganoxie, Kans., Sept. 14, 1955; d. Byron Calvin and Edna Jeannette (Keck) Swain; m. Lawrence Dale Torneden, Sept. 18, 1976; 1 child, James Milton. Bus. cert., Kansas City (Kans.) C.C., 1974; student, Nat. Compliance Sch., Norman, Okla., 1984; Mortgage Lending Diploma, ABA Am. Inst. Banking, 1997. Adminstrv. sec. to chmn. of bd., pres. First State Bank and Trust, Tonganoxie, 1974-80, asst. cashier, 1981-83, asst. v.p. and compliance officer, 1984-97, bank security officer, 1989-95, loan ops. officer, 1998, loan prodn. specialist, 1999—2002, loan asst., 2002—. Lobbyist, treas. 24-40 Hwy. Task Force, Leavenworth, Kans., 1989-91; bd. dirs. sec. Reno Cemetery Assn., Tonganoxie, 1986—; co-founder Tonganoxie Days, chmn., 1986, 88-93, 95—; grad. So. Leavenworth County Leadership Devel., 1991; sec.-treas. Maple Grove Cemetery Assn., 1995—, Reno Twp. Fire Dept., 1996—. Mem. Am. Bus. Women's Assn. (treas. 1986-87, sec. 1997-98, 2001-03, Woman of Yr. award Twilight chpt. 1994, nominee Top Ten Bus. Women, 2005), Mid-Am. Dairymen Assn. (sec. 1978-80), Nat. Assn. Old West Gunfighter Teams (nat. champions 1989, 90), Linwood Grange (5th and 6th degrees 1978), Tonganoxie C. of C. (sec. 1983-86, 92-94, pres. 1986, 88, 89, 96, v.p. 1995, treas. 1997, Mem. of Yr. award 1990, 92, Citizen of Yr. award 2001), Tonganoxie Jaycees (sec. 1991). Democrat. Mem. Soc. Of Friends. Avocations: music, fossil collecting, stamp collecting/philately, coin collecting/numismatics, writing poetry and short stories. Office: First State Bank and Trust PO Box 219 Tonganoxie KS 66086-0219

TORNEY-PURTA, JUDITH VOLLMAR, developmental psychologist; b. Oakland, Calif., Oct. 2, 1937; d. Ralph C. and Anne (Flournoy) Vollmar; m. E. Keith Torney, Sept. 10, 1960 (div. 1978); children: Elizabeth A., Katherine D.; m. Paul P. Purta, Oct. 18, 1980. AB in Psychology, Stanford U., 1959; postgrad., Harvard U., 1959-60; MA in Human Devel., U. Chgo., 1962, PhD in Human Devel., 1965. Asst. prof. psychology Ill. Inst. Tech., Chgo., 1967-69; asst. prof. edn. U. Ill., Chgo., 1969-70, assoc. prof. psychology and edn., 1970-77, prof., vice chmn. psychology dept., 1977-81; prof. human devel. U. Md., Coll. Pk., 1981—95, affiliate prof. psychology dept., 1981—. Vis. prof. Stanford (Calif.) U. Sch. Edn., 1988, 91; evaluator Internat. Communication Negotiations Simulation, College Park, 1983—; mem. bd. on internat. studies in edn. NRC, NAS, Washington, 1988-95, mem. U.S. Nat. com. for Psychology 2003—; mem. task force on youth devel. Carnegie Corp., N.Y.C., 1990-92; Carnegie Found. for the Advancment of Tchg., Stanford, Calif. Co-author: Development of Political Attitudes, 1967, (award NEA 1967), reissued 2006, Civic Education in Ten Countries, 1975, Development of Political Understanding, 1992, Citizenship and Education in Twenty Eight Countries, 2001 Strengthening Democracy in the Americas, 2004; contbr. chpts. to books, articles to profl. jours. Mem. U.S. Nat. Commn. for UNESCO, Washington, 1976-82, 83-85. Recipient career rsch. award, Nat. Coun. for Social Studies, 1977, Global Apple award, Am. Forum for Edn., 1988, Decade of Behavior Rsch. award in Democracy, 2005, Internat. Landmark Rsch. award, U. Md., 2005. Fellow APA, Am. Psychol. Soc.; mem. Am. Ednl. Rsch. assn. (chmn. book award com. 1991-92), Soc. for Rsch. in Child Devel. (chmn. internat. com. 1991-93), Comparative and Internat. Edn. Soc. (editorial bd. 1990-92), Internat. Assn. Evaluation Ednl. Achievement (chmn. civic edn. com. 1971-80, 93-05, Internat. Soc. for Polit. Psychology (Nevitt Sanford award, 2001), Phi Beta Kappa, Sigma Xi. Avocations: cooking, singing.

TORNOW, BARBARA, academic administrator; b. Buffalo, Feb. 17, 1943; d. Elmer Henry and Elizabeth Jane S. Tornow; m. Charles Jack Sheehan, Sept. 1987 (dec. 1992); stepchildren: Charles, Jacquelyn. BA summa cum laude, William Smith Coll., 1965; MA in Polit. Sci., U. Pa., 1966, postgrad., 1966-70. Residence dir. Phila. Coll. Art, 1969-72, asst. dir. fin. aid./housing, 1972-77; dir. fin. aid Clark U., Worcester, Mass., 1977-79, Brandeis U., Waltham, Mass., 1979-86; dir. fin. assistance Boston U., 1986-96, exec. dir. fin. assistance, 1996—2002, sr. advisor, v.p. enrollment and student affairs, 2002—. Trustee, admissions com. chair Hobart and William Smith Colls., Geneva, 1994—2006; mem., bd. dirs. TERI, Boston, 1985—, chmn., 1985—88. Chair Action Ctr. Ednl. Svcs. & Scholarships, Boston, 1998-99, mem., 1986-99; participant U.S. Dept. Edn. Negotiated Rulemaking, Washington, 1999, Project EASI, 1996-98. Mem.: Student Loan Mktg. Assn. (adv. com. 1995—2004), Mass. Assn. Student Fin. Aid Adminstrs. (pres. 1982—83, Svc. to Profession 1991), Nat. Assn. Student Fin. Aid Adminstrs. (bd. dirs. 1994—97), Phi Beta Kappa. Democrat. Avocations: horseback riding, travel, classical music. Office: Boston U 881 Commonwealth Ave Boston MA 02215-1300 Office Phone: 617-353-4176. E-mail: btornow@bu.edu.

TORO-GABRYS, PATRICIA, secondary education educator, artist; b. St. Paul, Dec. 20, 1953; d. Ivor Mitchell and Doreen Evelyn Margaret Hunt; m. Reneé José Toro, Sept. 20, 1974 (div. June 1981); m. William Lawrence Gabrys, July 31, 1998. Grad. in cosmetology, Horst Edn. Ctr., Mpls., 1977; BA, Hamline U., 1989; MEd, U. Minn., 1993. Cert. tchr., Minn.; cert. cosmetologist, Minn. Cosmetologist T & G Hair Design, Mpls., 1980-91; tchr. Rosemont Sch. Dist., Apple Valley, Minn., 1989-90; tchr. Spanish, Osseo (Minn.) Sch. Dist., 1990—. Rep. Task Force for Lang., Maple Grove, Minn., 1990—. Exhibited in group shows at Robbin Gallery, Robbinsdale, 1997-99 (Best of Show award, hon. mention), Theatre in the Round, 2000, Elk River Govt. Ctr., 1998 (Merit award); one-woman shows include Robbin Gallery, 1998, Theatre in the Round, 1999-2000, Luth. Brotherhood, Mpls., 2002. Mem. Elk River Arts Coun. 1998—. Mem. Maple Grove Tchrs. Union (union rep. 1994-98), Mpls. Inst. Arts. Democrat. Lutheran. Avocations: art, music. E-mail: toroart@att.com.

TOROK, MARGARET LOUISE, insurance company executive; b. Detroit, June 22, 1922; d. Perl Edward Ensor and Mary (Seggie) Armstrong; m. Leslie A. Torok, Aug. 14, 1952; 1 child, Margaret Mary Ryan. Lic. Ins. Agy. From ins. agt. to corp. officer Grendel-Wittbold Ins., Southgate, Mich., 1961-72, pres. of corp., 1972—2001. Bd. dirs. Ind. Ins. Agts. of Mich., Lansing, 1984-92, Ind. Ins. Agts. of Wayne County, Dearborn, 1967—, pres. 1978. Bd. dirs. So. Wayne County C. of C., Taylor, 1975-2005, CEO, chmn. bd. dirs., 1997-98; bd. dirs. City of Southgate Tax. Increment Fin. Authority Dist. and Econ. Devel. Commn., 1987—, YMCA, mem. endowment coun., Southgate, 1978—, chmn. Leadership, 1980-88; bd. dirs. Downriver Cmty. Alliance, 1990-94; lay chmn. Cath. Svc. Appeal for Archdiocese of Detroit, 1989; co-chair fundraiser Sacred Heart Ch.; com. mem., bd. dirs. New Workforce Devel. Com., gov. appt., charter mem.; hon. chmn. Art Ambience, 2002; mem. Downriver Coun. of the Arts, Island Animal League Shelter, Friends of Detroit River, Grosse Isle Land Conservancy, Grosse Isle Hist. Soc.; bd. dirs. MESC Employers Com., 1991-95, chmn., 1991-95. Recipient Capital award Ind. Ins. Agts. of Mich., 1988, Lifetime Achievement award, Amb. award, 1994, Woman of Yr. AAUW, 1994, Salute to Excellence award Downriver Coun. of Arts, 1993-94, Chmn. of Yr. award MESC Job. Svc. Employers Com., 1991, Robert Stewart award Wyandotte Svc. Club Coun., 1994, Partnership award The Info. Ctr., 1996, W.O. Hildebrand award Mich. Assn. Ins. Agts., 1997; named to Ins. Hall of Fame, Olivet Coll., 1998. Mem.: Mich. Assn. Ins. Agts., Grosse Ile Hist. Soc., Down River Coun. Arts, Arts Alliance, U.S. Power Squadron, Am. Legion Aux., Soroptimist Club of Wyandotte

Southgate Taylor (pres. 1984—86, Advancing Status Women award 1988, Soroptimist of Yr. award 1993—94), Wyandotte Yacht Club. Roman Catholic. Office: Grendel Wittbold Agy Inc 12850 Eureka Rd Southgate MI 48195-1344 Office Phone: 734-284-4740.

TOROK, SARAH E., psychology professor; b. Erie, Pa., Aug. 10, 1978; d. Frank A. and Pamela J. Torok. BA in Psychology, Mercyhurst Coll., 2000; MS in Ednl. Psychology, PhD in Ednl. Psychology, SUNY, Albany, 2006. Vis. asst. prof. psychology Skidmore Coll., Saratoga Springs, NY, 2004—06; asst. prof. psychology Mt. Union Coll., Alliance, Ohio, 2006—; vis. scientisti BOCES, 2005—06. Vis. scientist Bd. Coop. Ednl. Svcs., NY, 2005—. Mem.: Ea. Psychol. Assn., Assn. Psychol. Sci., New Eng. Ednl. Rsch. Orgn., Soc. Rsch. Child Devel., Psi Chi. Independent. Business E-Mail: torokse@muc.edu.

TOROK, TAMMY, mathematics educator; b. Canton, Ohio, Sept. 26, 1957; d. James Paul and Dorothy Ann (Mazeall) Warren; m. John Martin Torok, Feb. 14, 1987; children: John Martin Torok II, James Stephen. BS in Edn., Bowling Green State U., Ohio, 1975—79; MA in Curriculum & Instrn., Malone Coll., Canton, Ohio, 1990—92. Cert. Tchr., math. & sci. grades 7-12 Ohio Dept. Edn. Math./sci. tchr. Alliance City Schs., Ohio, 1979—84; math. tchr. Canton City Schs., 1984—. Avocations: bowling, golf, china painting. Office: Timken Sr HS 521 Tuscarawas St W Canton OH 44702 Business E-Mail: torok_t@ccsdistrict.org.

TOROSIAN, SONA, secondary school educator; b. Chgo., Aug. 11, 1971; d. John and Emma Bedenian; m. Sevon Torosian, Oct. 28, 1995; children: Talia, Armen, Raffi. Bachelor's, Aurora U., Ill., 1993; Master's, Chgo. State U., 2001. Cert. tchr. Ill., 1997. With sales dept. Charmilles Tech., Lincolnshire, Ill., 1994—99; tchr. phys. edn. Maine South H.S., Park Ridge, Ill., 1999—. Sponsor Varsity Club Maine South H.S., Park Ridge, 2001—, mem. JKB leadership com., 2002—, mem. NHS com., 2005—. CPR and lifeguard instr. Am. Red Cross, Chgo., 1999—; mem. Homenetmen of Chgo., Glenview, Ill., 1991—. Mem.: Am. Alliance Health, Phys. Edn., Recreation and Dance, Ill. Assn. Health, Phys. Edn., Recreation and Dance, Armenian Youth Fedn. Alumni. Home: 811 Spring Cove Dr Schaumburg IL 60193 Office: Maine S HS 1111 S Dee Rd Park Ridge IL 60068 Office Phone: 847-692-8573. Business E-Mail: storosian@maine207.org.

TORRACO, PAMELA LOUISE, psychotherapist; b. Mineola, NY, Feb. 22, 1944; d. Peter and Willamy King Torraco. BA, Wittenberg U., Springfield, Ohio, 1965; MSW, U. Mich., Ann Arbor, 1967. Psychiatric social worker Henry Ford Hosp., Detroit, 1967—69; prin. social caseworker Detroit Health Dept., 1969—72; group & individual psychotherapist Dr. Reuven Bar-Levav & Assoc., PC, Southfield, Mich., 1971—; social worker Kingswood Hosp., Ferndale, Mich., 1972—75. Presenter, panelist in field, 1975—; pres., faculty mem. The Inst. Individual & Group Psychotherapy, Southfield, 1978—; program chair Mich. Group Psychotherapy Soc., Detroit, 1982—84, pres., Southfield, 1984—86. Contbr. articles to profl. jours. Sec. Bar-Levav Family Found., Southfield, 1999—. Mem.: Mich. Group Psychotherapy Soc., Am. Group Psychotherapy Assn., Nat. Assn. Social Workers. Independent. Jewish. Avocations: hiking, music, travel, languages. Office: Dr Reuven Bar-Levav and Assocs PC 29600 Northwestern Hwy Ste 100 Southfield MI 48034 Office Phone: 248-353-0050. E-mail: pamtor@sbcglobal.net.

TORRENCE, MARGARET ANN JOHNSON, data processing executive, writer; b. Memphis, Apr. 25, 1946; d. Simon Robert and Earline Juanita (Parker) Johnson; m. Tony Horace Robinson, Oct. 16, 1965 (div. 1968); 1 child, Veronica Antoinette; m. David Torrence, Feb. 16, 1968 (div. Jan. 1997); 1 child, Erika Joyce. BSBA, Pacific Western U., L.A., 1989, MS in Counseling and Human Svcs., 1991; PhD, Kensington U., Glendale, Calif., 1993. Paralegal Torrence Lawn Care, Rialto, 1985—91, contract adminstr., 1985—91; pres. Torrence Scholarship Svc., 1986—89; CEO Torrence Group Home, Inc., San Bernardino, Calif., 1990—95; tng. specialist, data conversion operator, notary pub., group leader U.S. Postal Svc., 1995—; notary pub., 2005—. Author: Abuses in Am. Soc., 1991, Children of Abuse-A Continuing Cycle-Past, Present, Future, 1993. With USAF, 1964-65. Mem. NAFE, Am. Acad. Profl. Coders, Women in Mil. Svc. Am. Meml. Found., Inc., Nat. Mgmt. Assn. Avocations: reading, tennis, swimming, travel.

TORRENCE-THOMPSON, JUANITA LEE, editor, public relations executive; b. Brockton, Mass., Nov. 08; d. James Lee Torrence and Zylpha Odyselle Mapp-Robinson; m. Hugh Warren Thompson, Dec. 19, 1965; 1 child, Derek Rush. BS in Bus. & Comm., Empire State Coll., Old Westbury, N.Y., 1983; MA in Comm., Fordham U., 1989. Newsletter editor UN Internat. Sch., 1976-77; pub. rels., editl. asst. Nat. Assn. Theatre Owners, 1979-80; asst. acct. exec. Richard Weiner, Inc., 1984; newsletter editor SUNY Empire State Coll., 1985-87; editor Dorf & Stanton Comm., Inc., 1987-88; pub. rels. exec. pvt. practice, 1988—2006; editor, pub., owner Mobius, The Poetry Mag., 2006—. Adj. prof. pub. rels. Coll. New Rochelle, N.Y., 1997. Author: Spanning The Years, Wings Span to Eternity, Celebrating a Tapestry of Life; poetry columnist, 2004—; contbr. articles, poems, short stories, essays to mags., newspapers, newsletters and children's poetry (as Micki Caldwell Nixon, Jr.). Bd. dirs So. Queens Park Assn., Jamaica, N.Y., 1988-91; mem. parent faculty soc. UN Internat. Sch., N.Y.C., 1976-80; pub. rels. cons. UN Coll. Fund, N.Y.C., 1994; mem. Queens Coun. on the Arts. Recipient Feature Article award Writers Digest, 1985, Meritorious Svc. award United Negro Coll. Fund, 1994, Editors Choice award Nashville Newsletter, 1994, 2004, Robins Nest Mag., 1996, First prize N.Y. Pub. Libr. Contest, 1996, Outstanding Achievement award SUNY, Empire State Coll., Old Westbury, honoree, Margaret A. Walker Short Story Competition award 1999, 2000, 2d prize in 3 categories Internat. Poetry award, Poetry Soc. Mich., HM award in short story competition. Mem. AAUW, Nat. Assn. Black Journalists, Poetry Soc. Am., Acad. Am. Poets, Black Ams. in Pub., Poets and Writers, Queens Coun. on the Arts, Fresh Meadows Poets. Avocations: travel, theater, films, opera, concerts. Office: PO Box 671058 Flushing NY 11367-1058 E-mail: poetrytown@earthlink.net.

TORRES, ARELIS, elementary school educator; arrived in U.S., 1988; d. José Luis Torres and Elizabeth Gómez. B in Psychology, U. P.R., 1988; EdM, Adelphi U., 1991. Tchr. Pub. Sch. 143, Queens, NY, 1988—99, Pub. Sch. 16, Corona, NY, 1999—. Activist, educator SHARE, NYC, 1996—, translator, 1998—; active SHARE-Latina SHARE, NYC, 1998—; vol. Learning Leaders, NYC, 2000—01. Named Most Valuable Vol., SHARE, 2000; recipient Citizenship award, N.Y.C. Coun., 2000, The Best of Our Cmty. Svc. award, Comité Noviembre, 2004, Citation in Edn., N.Y.C. Coun., 2004. Mem.: NSTA, United Fedn. Tchrs. Avocations: poetry, painting, music, bicycling. Office Phone: 718-505-0140.

TORRES, BARBARA WOOD, technical services professional; b. Coudersport, Pa., Sept. 18, 1945; d. Ken and Myrna Wood; m. James Torres, July 3, 1965; children: James C, William D. BS in Physics, U. N.Mex., 1969, MS in Physics, 1972. Mem. staff Quantum Systems, Inc., Albuquerque, 1967-72, EG&G, Albuquerque, 1972-76, Mission Rsch. Corp., Albuquerque, 1977-78; from staff mem. to v.p. test engring. BDM, Albuquerque, 1978-97; dir. test engring. Northrop Grumman Mission Sys. (formerly TRW), Albuquerque, 1998—2000, divsn. dir. ethics and bus. conduct, 2001—. Mem. N.Mex. State Sci. and Tech. Commn., 1983—86; mem. com. NEWTEC Joint Venture, N.Mex., 1998—2004. Mem. adv. bd. N.Mex. Comprehensive Regional Ctr. Minorities, 1993—96; judge N.Mex. Regional and State Sci. Fair, 1986—; bd. dirs. N.Mex. Network for Women in Sci., 1988—92, 2003—. Named Outstanding Grad., Rio Grande H.S., 1995; recipient Gov. Award for Outstanding N.Mex. Women, 1988. Mem.: IEEE, Soc. Internat. Affairs, Ethics Officers Assn., Inst. Test and Evaluation Assn., Am. Bus. Women's Assn. (dist. v.p. 1995—96, nat. sec. 1996—97), Am. Phys. Soc. Avocations: travel, mystery and spy novels, walking. Office: Northrop Grumman Mission Sys 100 Sun Pl NE Ste 300 Albuquerque NM 87109

TORRES, CYNTHIA ANN, marketing professional; b. Glendale, Calif., Sept. 24, 1958; d. Adolph and Ruth Ann (Smith) T.; m. Michael Victor Gisser, Mar. 11, 1989; children: Spencer Williams Gisser, David Westfall Torres Gisser. AB, Harvard U./Radcliffe Coll., 1980; MBA, Harvard U., 1984. Rsch. assoc. Bain & Co., Boston, 1980-82; assoc. Goldman, Sachs & Co., NYC, 1984-88, v.p., 1988, First Interstate Bancorp, LA, 1989—92; dir. Fidelity Investments Mgmt. Ltd., Hong Kong, 1993-96; pres. Integrity Investments Consultants, Ltd., 1996—99; dir. mktg. Diamond Portfolio Advisors LLC, Santa Monica, Calif., 2000—. Mem. judiciary rev. bd. Bus. Sch. Harvard U., Boston, 1983—84; mem. fin. oversight com. Santa Monica-Malibu Unified Sch. Dist.; chair site governance coun. Franklin Sch. Santa Monica. Rockefeller Found. scholar, 1976; Harvard U. Ctr. for Internat. Affairs fellow, 1979-80; recipient Leadership award Johnson and Johnson, 1980; by Council for Opportunity in Grad. Mgmt. Edn. fellow, 1982-84. Mem.: Fin. Women's Assn. Hong Kong (past pres.), Asia Soc., Acad. Polit. Sci., Harvard Alumni Assn. (regional dir.), Harvard-Radcliffe Club So. Calif. (pres.). Office: Diamond Portfolio Advisors LLC 10940 Wilshire Blvd Ste 600 Los Angeles CA 90024 Personal E-mail: cynthiatorres@earthlink.net.

TORRES, DARA, Olympic athlete; b. Beverly Hills, Calif., Apr. 15, 1967; Degree in broadcasting, U. Fla. Intern CNN and NBC Sports; commentator TV sports NBC, ESPN, TNT, Fox News, Fox Sports; ret. swimmer TV reporter: Good Morning America, Inside Edition; host Oxygen Sports. Olympic team capt., 1992; spokesperson Tae Bo workout tapes. Host sci. and tech. show Discovery Channel. Recipient Gold medal (2) 4 x 100-meter freestyle, 4 x 100-meter medley (team), Bronze medal (3) 50 and 100-meter freestyle, 100-meter fly Sydney Olympics, 2000, Gold medal 100-meter freestyle, 4 x 100-meter freestyle, 4 x 100-meter relay (team) Pan Pacific Championships, 1987, Gold medal 4 x 100-meter freestyle relay (team) L.A. Games, 1984, Bronze medal 4 x 100-meter freestyle relay (team), Silver medal 4 x 100-meter medley (team), 1988, Gold medal 4 x 100-meter free relay (team) Barcelona Olympics, 1992; 12-time nat. champion; former world-record holder 50-meter freestyle, Am.-record holder 50-meter freestyle and 100-meter fly, 1991 Summer Nationals Kiphuth award, 1991, Summer Nationals Comeback award Achievements include first American female to swim in four Olympics, five time US Open champion, seven time National A team member, two time All Star team. Office: USA Swimming 1 Olympic Plz Colorado Springs CO 80909-5746

TORRES, SUSIE APURON, special education educator; b. Dededo, Guam, Apr. 25, 1955; d. Jesus Nededog and Francisca (Apuron) Torres; children: Victor, Brian, Simon. BA, U. Guam, 1989; MEd, Portland U., 1992. Tchrs. aide Brodie Meml. Sch., Tumon, Guam, 1982-87, speech and lang. asst., 1987-89; basic life skills instr. Guam C.C., Mangilalo, 1989-90; community base educator George Washington High Sch., Mangilalo, 1991-92; resource instr. Dededo Middle Sch., 1992—, Astumbo Elem. Sch., 1997—, spl. edn. tchr., 1998—. Presenter in field; rental mgr., 1990—. Adviser 4-H Club, 2002—, del. to Washington nat. conf., 2003. Roman Catholic. Home: 118 Gloria Cir Dededo GU 96929-5300 Office: Astumbo Elem Sch DOE PO Box Agana Heights GU 96910

TORRES-DICKSON, TERESITA SANCHO, elementary school educator; b. Manila, Oct. 22, 1955; came to the U.S., 1960; d. Ramon F. and Teresita (Sancho) Torres; m. Johnny Dickson, May 14, 1983. Assoc. Degree, Lansing (Mich.) C.C., 1977; BA, Mich. State U., 1980, MA, 1986. Substitute tchr. various schs., Mich., 1980-83; tchr.-aide hearing impaired East Lansing (Mich.) Schs., 1982-83; tchr. 4th grade Lansing (Mich.) Pub. Schs., 1983-84, sci. tchr. K-5, 1984—. Chairperson sci. steering com., 1994—, Lansing, Mich. Pub. Schs., 1994—, sci. presenter, 1993—; Mich. Edn. Assessment Program test item writer, Mich. Dept. Edn., 1994-95, sci. presenter. Recipient Presdl. awards for excellence in sci. tchg. NSF, Arlington, Va., 1993. Avocations: fishing, biking, travel, tennis, reading. Office: Lansing Pub Schs 4200 Wainwright Ave Lansing MI 48911-2248

TORRES-MABASA, VIRGINIA MARIA, physician assistant; b. Red Bluff, Calif., Sept. 16, 1969; d. Ben Alvarado Torres, Maria Beatriz Velez-Topete; m. Rodrigo Icawalo Mabasa, July 29, 1991; 1 child, Kiara Marie Mabasa. AA in Biology cum laude, Miracosta Coll., 1998; BS in Physician Asst. Practice with honors, U. So. Calif., L.A., 2001. Cert. surg. technologist Liaison Coun. for Certification for Surg. Tech., 1994, physician asst. Med. Bd. Calif., 2002, Nat. Comm. Certification for Physician Assts., 2002. Surg. technologist Scripps Meml. Hosp. Surgery Ctr., La Jolla, Calif., 1995—98, Virginia Beach (Va.) Ambulatory Surgery Ctr., Va., 1998—99; physician asst. primary care program Keck Sch. Medicine U. So. Calif., 1999—2001; physician asst. Pasadena Rehab. Inst., Pasadena, Calif., 2002—. Asst. instr. Spanish Primary Care Physician Asst. Program U. So. Calif. Keck Sch. Medicine, L.A., 2000—00. V.p. Future Physician Assts. Am., Miracosta Coll., Oceanside, 1997—98. E-4 USN, 1989—94. Decorated Navy Achievement medal USN. Mem.: Assn. Surg. Technologists, Calif. Acad. Physician Assts., Am. Acad. Physician Assts., Phi Theta Kappa (life), Gamma Beta Phi (life; sec. 2000—01). Avocations: travel, reading, skating. Personal E-mail: tutvikia@aol.com.

TORRESYAP, PEARL MARIE, surgical nurse; b. Cleve., Oct. 1, 1930; d. Clyde E. and Pearl C. (Flanagan) Callender; m. Fortunato Torresyap, Oct. 30, 1953; children: Joy, Gay, Fay. Diploma, Luth. Hosp. Sch. Nursing, 1951. Cert. nurse in oper. rm. Staff nurse Lakewood (Ohio) Hosp., 1951-54, Choate Hosp., Woburn, Mass., 1976-78; thoracic charge nurse Boston VA Med. Ctr., 1979-94, orthopedic charge nurse in oper. rm., 1994-96, ret., 1996. Contbr. articles to jours. in field. Vol. Mus. Sci. Human Body Connection, 1996—; bd. dirs. Vol. Svc. League, 2002–, Mus. of Sci., 2002—. Mem. ANA, Assn. Oper. Rm. Nurses (pres. Mass. chpt. I 1988-89, book reviewer for jour.), Mass. Coun. Nursing Orgns. (rep. 1989-93), Mass. Nurses Assn., Internat. Toastmasters (treas. 1989-90). Personal E-mail: beanblossom@aol.com.

TORREY, BARBARA BOYLE, research council administrator; b. Pensacola, Fla., Nov. 27, 1941; d. Peter F. and Elsie (Hansen) Boyle; m. E. Fuller Torrey, Mar. 23, 1968; children: Michael, Martha. BA, Stanford U., 1963, MS, 1970. Vol. Peace Corps, Tanzania, 1963-65; fiscal economist Office Mgmt. and Budget, Washington, 1970-80; dept. asst. sec. HHS, Washington, 1980-81; dir. Ctr. for Internat. Rsch. Census Bur., Washington, 1984-92; pres. Population Reference Bur., Washington, 1992-93; exec. dir. Commn. on Behavioral and Social Scis. and Edn. NRC, NAS, Washington, 1993—. Bd. dirs. Luxembourg Income Study. Co-editor: The Vulnerable, 1987, Population and Land Use, 1992; contbr. articles to profl. jours. Fellow AAAS; mem. Population Assn. Am. (bd. dirs. 1993—). Office: Population Ref Bur 1875 Connecticut Ave NW Ste 520 Washington DC 20009-5728 Office Phone: 202-939-5455.

TORREZ, CAROLINE HERMINIA, human resources specialist, director, actress, musician, singer, dancer; d. Philip Hernandez and Lucy Mercedes Rivera; m. Robert Pierre Torrez, June 10, 1995. BA, Calif. State U., Fullerton, 1975. Sec. to exec. dir. Pinto program CSUF, 1972—73, oral history interpreter, 1973—75; asst. Spanish tchr. Cerritos Coll., Calif., 1974—75; export parts specialist export dept. C.B.S. Musical Instruments/Fender, Rogers & Rhodes, Fullerton, 1975—77; bilingual interviewer Orange County Housing Authority, Santa Ana, Calif., 1977—79, field rep., 1979—83, mktg. rep., 1983—87; recreation dir. City of Anaheim (Calif.) Parks and Recreation/Let's Play to Grow program/Joseph P. Kennedy Found., 1983—87; Home Investment Partnership Act coord. Urban County Housing and Cmty. Devel. Orange County, Santa Ana, 1987—99; v.p. internal ops. CHAMP, Inc., Santa Ana, 2000—06; dir. Champ Steel, Santa Ana, 2006—. Musician (actress): Yorba Linda Symphony Orch.; singer: So. Calif. Chamber Singers. Charter mem. Brea (Calif.) Jaycee Women, 1980; coach Spl. Olympics City of Anaheim, Calif., 1982—87; coord. Hands Across Am., Orange County, 1986; dist. dir. Region 8 Orange County Jaycees, 1987; pres. Fountain Valley (Calif.) Jaycees, 1989; mem. Men-On-A-Missions-Eastside Christian Ch.; mem. bd. dirs. Alliance/Mentally Ill, Orange County, 1988—89. Mem.: SAG, Nat. Assn. Exec. Women, Southern Calif. Chamber Singers. Avocations: acting, viola, dance, singing, opera. Office: CHAMP Inc 633 Young St Santa Ana CA 92705

TORREZ, MICHELLE MARIE, artist, educator; b. Denver, Feb. 3, 1956; d. John Thomas and Geri Anne Chestor; children: Gwenevieve Louise, Nicole Michelle. Assocs. Visual Comm. and Advt. Design, Art Inst. Colo., Denver, 1986. Art dir. Mentler and Co., Dallas, 1986—87, Hamilton Sweeney Advt., Denver, 1987—94; owner Studio M, Denver, 1994—98; workshop instr. Art in the Aspens, Colo., 2005—, Taos Painters Workshop, N.Mex., 2005—. Adj. instr. painting Met. State Coll. Denver, 2004—; traveling lectr. U.S. State Dept.-Art in Embassies, Sofia, Bulgaria, 2003; invited participant Coors Invitational We. Art Exhibit, 2002—05. S.W. Art Mag., one-woman shows include Michelle Torrez: One Woman Show, Metaphor - Art in Embassies Calendar, 2003, exhibitions include Colo. Gov.'s Office, 2002—05. Named to Hall of Fame, Art Inst. of Colo., 2004; recipient Colo. ALFIE award for art direction of pub. svc. comml., Denver Advt. Agy., 1991, CLEO award for art direction of pub. svc. TV comml., City of Denver, 1991; Travel grant, Christian Solidarity Internat., 2005. Mem.: Denver Art Students League (assoc.), Denver Art Mus. (assoc.), Nat. Mus. of Women in the Arts (assoc.).

TORRIANI-GORINI, ANNAMARIA, microbiologist, educator; b. Milan, Dec. 19, 1918; came to U.S., 1955, naturalized, 1962; d. Carlo and Ada (Forti) Torriani; m. Luigi Gorini (dec. Aug. 1976); 1 child, Daniel. PhD, U. Milan, Italy, 1942. Research assoc. Istituto Ronzoni Chimica-Biochimica, Milan, 1942-48; charge de recherche Institut Pasteur, Paris, 1948-56; research assoc. NYU, 1956-58, Harvard U., Cambridge, Mass., 1958-60, MIT, Cambridge, 1960-71, assoc. prof. microbiology, 1971-76, prof., 1976—; prof. emerita, 1989. Recipient NIH Career award, 1962-72; Fulbright fellow, 1956-58. Mem.: Am. Soc. Microbiology, Soc. Française de Microbiologie (hon.). Home: 115 Longwood Ave Brookline MA 02446-6625 Office: MIT Dept of Biology 68-371 Cambridge MA 02139 Business E-Mail: pho@mit.edu.

TORRIE, JANE MARIE, chiropractor, secondary school educator; d. Douglas Edward and Carolyn Cooper Torrie; children: Cecilio Eduardo, Benjamin Lucas. BS in Human Biology, Cleve. Chiropractic Coll., L.A., 1985, Dr. in Chiropractic, 1985. Lic. chiropractor Calif., Ariz., N.Mex; cert. tchr. Tex. Pvt. practice as chiropractor, Espanola, N.Mex., 1987—94; tchr. Northwest H.S., Justin, Tex., 1999—. Adj. instr. Tarrant County Coll., Ft. Worth, 2003—. Mem. missions coun. 1st Ch. Nazarene, Denton, Tex., 2001—06. Conservative. Nazarene. Avocation: reading.

TORSEN, MARILYN JOANNE, counselor, retired; b. Portland, Oreg., Feb. 26, 1937; d. Leighton Eugene and Dorris Mary (Scott) Roy; m. Richard Morris Torsen, June 22, 1958; children: Michelle, Danielle, Chantelle. BS in Home Econs., Oreg. State U., 1964; MS in Counseling, Calif. State U., Hayward, 1989. Crisis intervention counselor Contact-Care, Lafayette, Calif., 1982-84; pregnancy counselor Planned Parenthood, Walnut Creek, Calif., 1984-87; counselor Family Counseling Svc., Walnut Creek, 1986-87; hospice team mem. Farmington Valley Hospice, Simsbury, Conn., 1988-90; youth svcs. coord. Town of East Granby, Conn., 1990-91; vol. coord. City of Oregon City, Oreg., 1993-94; ret., 1994. Co-chair Clackamas County Youth Issues and Planning Com., Oregon City, 1991-97; steering com. Youth Gangs Task Force, Oregon City, 1992-94. Editor (newsletter) Focal Point, 1993-94 (2nd place 1994); author of poetry. Chair Status on Women, Concord, Calif., 1986; mem. pub. facilities task force, West Linn, Oreg., 1992, recycling/solid waste com., West Linn, 1996; group leader, mem. vision com., West Linn, 1992-93. Mem. AAUW (state diversity task force 1994-96, libr. bd. 2002-, chmn. 2006, mem. police adv. com. 2003-05). Home: 2010 Conestoga Ln West Linn OR 97068-2536

TORYKIAN, JOAN MARIE, archivist; b. NYC, Sept. 13, 1936; BA in Polit. sci., U. Calif. Berkeley, 1958; cert. de français usuel, U. Paris, 1961; postgrad., U. Oslo, 1963—67; MA in Pub. Adminstrn., U. Calif. Berkeley, 1970; postgrad., U. Calif. Davis, 1970—73; cert., We. Archives Inst., 1992. Secretariat 1st Peacekeeping Conf. Nobel Inst., Oslo, 1964; libr. Norwegian Inst. Internat. Affairs, Oslo, 1963; exec. dir. Svc. Civil Internat., Oslo, 1965; rschr. Internat. Population and Urban Rsch. Inst. U. Calif. Berkeley, 1967—68, rschr. Sch. Law, 1976; career cons. Berkeley, 1977—95. Conf. coord., writing group chair Sociologists for Women in Soc., San Francisco, 1980—86; adv. to bd. dirs. Easy Bay Women in Sci., San Francisco, 1993—2003; founder, adv. Armenian Women's Archives, 1988—. Author: Dialogues with the Gods: Poems for John, 1980, The Wounding Animus: Its Socio-Archetypal Influences on Intellectual Integrity, 2000; co-author (booklet): The A B Cs of Rent Control for Tenants. Friend Bancroft Libr. U. Calif. Berkeley, 2001—. Mem.: U. Calif. Berkeley Women's Faculty Club, Women's Classical Caucus, Soc. Calif. Archivists. Home and Office: North Berkeley Sta PO Box 9267 Berkeley CA 94709-0267

TOSCANO, MARGARET MERRILL, humanities educator, writer; b. Mesa, Ariz., Feb. 12, 1949; d. Lenna (Petersen) and John Arthur Merrill; m. Paul James Toscano, Sept. 23, 1978; children: Angela Rose, Elizabeth Ann, Mary Katherine, Sarah Teresa. PhD, U. Utah, Salt Lake City, 2002. Asst. prof. Classics U. Utah, Salt Lake City, 2002—. Author: (book theol. essays) Strangers in Paradox: Explorations in Mormon Theology, (feminist jour. essays) Dialogue: Journal of Mormon Thought, (book essay) Transforming the Faiths of Our Fathers: Women Who Changed American Religion, Women and Authority: Re-emerging Mormon Feminism. Organizer Mormon Women's Forum, Salt Lake City, 1989—2006. Recipient Woman of Courageous Action award, Utah Chpt. NOW, 1993. Office: University of Utah 255 S Central Campus Dr Rm 1400 Salt Lake City UT 84112 Office Fax: 801-581-7581. E-mail: margaret.toscano@utah.edu.

TOSHACH, CLARICE OVERSBY, real estate developer, retired computer company executive; b. Firbank, Westmoreland, Eng., Nov. 21, 1928; came to U.S., 1955; d. Oliver and Nora (Brown) Oversby; m. Daniel Wilkie Toshach, July 30, 1965 (dec. Aug. 1992); 1 child, Duncan Oversby Toshach; 1 child from previous marriage, Paul Anthony Beard. Textile designer Storeys of Lancaster, Eng., 1949-55; owner, operator Broadway Lane, Saginaw, Mich., 1956-70; pres., owner Clarissa Jane Inc., Saginaw, 1962-70, Over-Tosh Computers, Inc. dba Computerland, Saginaw and Flint, Mich., 1983-95; mgr., ptnr. Mich. Comml. Devel. L.L.C., Saginaw, 1995—. Trustee Saginaw Gen. Hosp., 1977-83, Home for the Aged, 1978-80; bd. dirs. Vis. Nurse Assn., pres., 1981-83; bd. dirs. Hospice of Saginaw, Inc., v.p., 1981-83; mem. long range planning com. United Way of Saginaw, 1982-83; cmty. advisor Jr. League of Saginaw, 1982-83; pres. Saginaw Gen. Hosp. Aux., 1972-82, pres., 1976-77.

TOSI, GLORIA C., labor union administrator; Adminstrv. asst. Fed. Maritime Commn., 1969; dir. govtl. affairs Internat. Longshoremen's Assn.; from dir. corp. affairs to pres. Am. Maritime Congress, Washington, 1981—2000, pres., 2000—. Office: American Maritime Congress 1300 I St NW Ste 250 West Washington DC 20005

TOSSI, ALICE LOUISE, special education educator; b. St. Augustine, Fla., Feb. 25, 1941; d. Hubert Parker and Marie Francis (Mecca) Hahn; m. Donald Joseph Tossi, Feb. 19, 1966; children: Kevin, Craig, Raymond. BA, Rollins Coll., 1978. Cert. elem. tchr., Fla. Sec. Diocese of St. Augustine, Fla., 1958-59, Fla. East Coast Ry., St. Augustine, 1959-60; legal sec. Mahon & Stratford, Jacksonville, Fla., 1960-61; sec. comptroller's dept. Esso Standard Oil S. A., Ltd., Coral Gables, Fla., 1962-63; sec. Kelly Temporary, Maitland, Fla., 1976-78; tchr. All Souls Elem., Sanford, Fla., 1979-81, Harbor Elem., Maitland, 1981-82; sec., tech. asst. physically impaired Seminole County Sch. Bd., Sanford, 1983—; chorus pars profl. Sweet Adelines show Lakeview Mid. Sch., 1957—2003; asst. Highlands Elem. Sch., Winter Springs, Fla. Bd. dirs. Seminole County Dem. Assn., 1983. Mem. Coun. of Exceptional Edn. (sec. 1986-90, Placque 1987), Seminole County Sch. Bd. Assn. (sec. polit. action com.). Roman Catholic. Home: 114 W Woodland Dr Sanford FL 32773-5706

TOSTI, ANNETTE BREWER, artist; b. Indpls., June 20, 1958; d. William Marion and Patricia Davis Brewer; m. Donald Thomas Tosti, Dec. 29, 1989; children: Tabitha Szary, Todd, Rene Foppe, Alicia Anderson, Roxanna LaValley, Brett. BA, U. Montevallo, 1979; BS, U. Ala., 1985; MA, U. of Pacific, 1989; MFA, Calif. Coll. Arts, 1992. One-woman shows include San Francisco Art Commission Gallery, Carnegie Art Ctr. Art Commission Gallery, Turlock, Calif., exhibitions include San Diego Museum Art, Center for Visual Arts, Oakland, Calif., Sonoma Valley Mus. Art, SITE, LA, Claudia Chapline Gallery, Stinson Beach, Calif., California College of Arts, Oakland, AXIS Gallery, Sacramento, Calif., Matrix Gallery, Sacramento, California Crafts Mus., San Francisco, Kellogg Gallery, California State Poly. U., Pomona, Di Rosa Preserve, Napa, Calif., San Francisco Art Inst., Sebastapol (Calif.) Ctr. Arts. Recipient Straw Into Gold award, Coll. of Marin, 1991, Discovery award, Art of Calif. Mag., 1992; grantee, Marin Cmty. Found., 1992; Grad. Rsch. scholar, Western Psychol. Soc., 1988, grad. scholar, Calif. Coll. Arts, 1992. Mem.: Coll. Art Assn. Libertarian. Office: Prime Performance 41 Marinita Ave San Rafael CA 94901 Office Phone: 415-457-8700. Personal E-mail: annette101@aol.com.

TOSTI, SUSAN MARIE, reading specialist, educator; b. Fort Dix, NJ, Nov. 10, 1959; m. Louis Joseph Tosti, Aug. 6, 1994; children: Christina Lee Brightbill, Keri Lynn Painter, Jennifer Sue Mulhern, Kevin Daniel Mulhern, Nicholas Louis. EdD, Widener U., Chester, Pa., 2006. Cert. reading specialist NJ, 2000, Pa., 1996, spl. edn. NJ, 2000, Pa., 1986. Spl. educator Chichester Sch. Dist., Boothwyn, Pa., 1986—2000; reading specialist Cinnaminson Sch. Dist., NJ, 2000—. Mem.: Internat. Reading Assn. (assoc.). Home: 815 Witherspoon Way Mullica Hill NJ 08062 Office: Cinnaminson School District 1197 Riverton Rd Cinnaminson NJ 08077 Office Phone: 856-829-7770. Business E-Mail: tostis@cinnaminson.com.

TOTENBERG, NINA, journalist; b. NYC, Jan. 14, 1944; d. Roman and Melanie (Shroder) T.; m. Floyd Haskell, Feb. 3, 1979 (dec.); m. H. David Reines, 2000. Student, Boston U.; LLD (hon.), Haverford Coll.; LLD, Mt. Holyoke Coll.; LLD (hon.), Chatham Coll., Gonzaga U., Northeastern U., Mt. Holyoke Coll., St. Mary's, SUNY; LHD, Lebanon Valley Coll., Westfield State Coll., Pa. State U., Pine Manor Coll., De Paul U., Simmons Coll. Reporter Boston Record Am., 1965, Peabody Times, 1967, Nat. Observer, 1968-71, Newtimes, 1973, Nat. Pub. Radio, Washington, 1974—, Inside Washington, 1992—; reporter Nightline ABC, 1993-98. Contbr. articles to N.Y. Times Mag., Harvard Law Rev., Christian Sci. Monitor, N.Y. Mag., Parade. Recipient Sidney Hillman award, 1983, Alfred I. Dupont award Columbia U., 1988, 91, George Foster Peabody award, 1991, George Polk award, 1991, Joan Barone award, 1991, Silver Gavel award ABA, 1968-98, Woman of Courage award Women in Film, 1991, Athena award, 1994, Presdl. Commendation, Radcliffe Coll., 1998, Ohio U. Carr van Anda award Outstanding Journalists, 2005; named outstanding broadcast journalist of yr. Nat. Press Found., 1999. Mem. Sigma Delta Chi (award 1991). Office: NPR 635 Massachusetts Ave NW Washington DC 20001-3740

TOTER, KIMBERLY MROWIEC, nurse; b. Chgo., Apr. 22, 1956; d. A. Kenneth and Megan Dawson (Schiefer) Mrowiec; m. William Frank Toter, Dec. 16, 1978; children: William Kenneth, Kimberly Helen, Tod Frank, Matthew Jonathan, Haley Victoria, Toria Megan. BS in Biology, Millikin U., 1978; cert. sch. nursing, Decatur (Ill.) Meml. Hosp., 1978. RN operating room nurse., Ill. Oper. room nurse Riddle Meml. Hosp., Media, Pa., 1979-89; pres., chief exec. officer Towic Med., Inc., Park Ridge, Ill., 1986—; staff nurse oper. room Luth. Gen. Hosp., Park Ridge, 1991; perioperative nurse, 1991—. Instr. Delaware Community Coll., Media, 1986; reviewer, cons. Perioperative Nursing Care Planning; speaker laparoscopy seminar Luth. Gen. Hosp., 1992, 93; cheerleading coach St. Paul of the Cross, 1993-96, volleyball coach, 1997—. Contbg. author: Decision Making in Perioperative Nursing, 1987; also articles; patentee gastric drainage system. Cheerleading coach St. Paul of the Cross, 1993-96, volleyball coach, 2000—. Recipient Young Alumnus of Yr. award Millikin U., 1991. Mem. Assn. Operat. Rm. Nurses (v.p. Southeast Pa. chpt. 1983-85, pres.-elect 1985-86, pres. 1986-87, ednl. chmn. 1983-85, chmn. bylaw and policy com. 1987—89, bd. dirs. 1983-89, chmn. 1987-88, bd. dirs. NW suburban chpt. 1995—), Pa. Coun. Oper. Rm. Nurses, Am. Tech Mgmt. (bd. dirs. 1989), Pi Beta Phi. Roman Catholic. Avocations: jogging, swimming, aerobic dance, photography, volleyball. Personal E-mail: ktoter22@comcast.net.

TOTH, SUSAN HELEN, government agency administrator; b. N.Y.C., Dec. 30, 1964; d. John Brewster and Ida (Hawa) Smith. BA in English, Tex. A&M U., 1986; MA in Journalism, Ind. U., 1988; MBA, U. N.C., Wilmington, 1997. Parachutist and broadcast journalist 1st Special Ops. Command, Ft. Bragg, N.C., 1989-91; media rels. journalist U.S. Army Parachute Team - Golden Knights, Ft. Bragg, N.C., 1991-92; TV reporter Sta. WLTX-TV, Columbia, S.C., 1992; bus. writer The Herald, Rock Hill, S.C., 1992-94; plant comms. specialist Brunswick Nuclear Plant Carolina Power & Light, Southport, 1994-97; fin. advisor Morgan Stanley Dean Witter, Wilmington, NC, 1997—2001; investment exec. Ferris, Baker, Watts, Inc., Wilmington, 2001—02; pub. affairs supr. Operation Iraqi Freedom, 2003—04; outreach specialist Dept. Vet. Affairs, 2004—. With U.S. Army, 1988-92, Panama, Persian Gulf, Operation Iraqi Freedom. Recipient South Korean Jump Wings Republic of Korea Spl. Warfare Ctr., 1989. Mem. VFW. Baptist. Avocations: running, the outdoors, bodybuilding. Office: Dept Vets Affairs 1513 Pickens St Columbia SC 29201-1623 Office Phone: 803-765-4944. Business E-Mail: Susan.Toth@va.gov.

TOTMAN, SHARON TAYLOR, special education educator; b. Arlington, Va., Jan. 17, 1948; d. Francis Taylor III and Genevieve Toner; m. Stephen Wayne Totman, July 28, 1973 (dec.); children: Stephanie Faye, Lynne Marie, Shannon Rachel. BA, Mary Wash. Coll., Fredericksburg, Va., 1969. Tchr. grades 4, 5, 6 Dahlgren Elem Sch., Dahlgren, Va., 1968—70; tchr. special needs grade 6 Oak Grove Elem. Sch., Oak Grove, Va., 1970—73; tchr. grade 5 Falmouth Elem. Sch., Falmouth, Va., 1973—74; tchr. special edn. grades 3-5 Durham Elem. Sch., Durham, Maine, 1985—2005; tchr. itnerrelated spl. edn. Futral Rd. Elem. Sch., Griffin, Ga., 2005—. Pres. Durham Tchrs. Assn., Durham, Maine, 1992, sec., 2000—02. Bd. dirs. Pathways Inc., Auburn, Maine, 1997—2003, program com., 1997—2003. Mem.: NEA, Ga. Assn. Educators, Maine Tchrs. Assn., Coun. of Excep̈tional Children. Democrat. Protestant. Avocations: reading, knitting, cross stitch. Office: Futral Elem Sch 180 Futral Rd Griffin GA 30224 Home: 106 Pony Pl Griffin GA 30224 Office Phone: 770-229-3735.

TOTTEN, GLORIA JEAN (DOLLY TOTTEN), real estate company executive, financial consultant; b. Port Huron, Mich., Sept. 23, 1943; d. Lewis Elmer and Inez Eugenia (Houston) King; m. Donald Ray Totten, Feb. 5, 1961 (div. Apr. 1981); children: D. Erik, Angela J. Totten Sales, Kymberly D. Totten DiVita. Student, instr., Patricia Stevens Modeling Sch., Detroit, 1976-79; student, Gold Coast Sch., West Palm Beach, Fla., 1988; degree in mktg., St. Clair County Coll., Port Huron, Mich., 1979. Lic. real estate saleswoman, Fla., Mich.; registered real estate appraiser, Fla. Demonstrator, saleswoman Hoover Co., 1969-75; instr., promoter Port Huron Sch. Bus., 1973-75; real estate broker Select Realty, Port Huron, 1979-81, Earn Keim Realty, Port Huron, 1981-83, Schweitzer's Better Homes and Gardens, Marysville, Mich., 1983-86, Coldwell Banker Property Concepts Corp., North Palm Beach, Fla., 1986-94; pres., broker, owner Dolly Totten Real Estate Inc., West Palm Beach, Fla., 1994—; travel agt. Global Access, Lake Park, Fla., 1997—; registered real estate appraiser State of Fla., Fla., 2001—. Model, instr. Patricia Stevens Modeling Sch., Troy, Mich., 1972-75; beauty cons. Mary Kay Cosmetics, 1982—; ind. travel agt. Global Access Internat., 1997; owner Gloria Totten Vending. Grantee Mich. State U., 1972. Mem. Nat. Assn. Realtors, North Palm Beach Bd. Realtors, Million Dollar Club, Women's Coun. Realtors (co-founder Port Huron chpt.). Avocations: tap dancing, singing, acting, horticulture, music. Home and Office: 118 E 24th St Riviera Beach FL 33404-4555 Office Phone: 561-863-5527. Personal E-mail: gjtotten@bellsouth.net.

TOTTON, GAYLE, professional sports team executive; Owner, CEO Sacramento Sirens (IWFL), Calif. Mailing: Sacramento Sirens 4500 73rd St Sacramento CA 95820 Office Phone: 916-456-8649. E-mail: ceo@sacramentosirens.com.

TOTZ, SUE ROSENE, secondary school educator; b. Rockford, Ill., June 13, 1954; d. Wendell O. and Irene Rose (Suski) Rosene; m. Ronald R. Totz, June 28, 1975. BSEd, Rockford Coll., 1980; MSEd, No. Ill. U., 1987; student, Nat. Coll. of Edn., Lombard, Ill.; cert. in Libr. Media, U. Moscow, Idaho, 1995. Cert. tchr. reading, k-12, Ill. Instr. Rockford (Ill.) Coll., Rock Valley Coll., Rockford; tchr. 4th grade Christian Life Ctr. Sch., Rockford; tchr. middle sch. reading Woodstock (Ill.) Sch. Dist., 1987-97, dir. Learning Resource Ctr., 1997—. Regional rep. to state bd. Ill. Assn. Mld. Schs., 1989-2004; presenter Assn. Ill. Mid. Sch. Conf., 1988, 91-97, Ill. Sch. Libr. Media Assn., 2004, 05, Ill. Computer Educators, 2004, 05. Recipient award Those Who Excel award of merit Ill. State Bd. Edn.; named Sch. Dist. Tchr. of Yr., 1990--. Mem. ALA, Ill. Sch. Libr. Media Assn., Internat. Reading Assn., Ill. Reading Coun., No. Ill. Reading Coun., Nat. Mid. Sch. Assn. (presenter 1994, 95, 98), Alpha Delta Kappa (pres. Alpha Psi chpt. 2004-06) Office: 2121 N Seminary Ave Woodstock IL 60098-2641 Business E-Mail: stotz@d200.mchenry.k12.il.us.

TOUBES, JUDITH ESTHER, retired writer; b. Chgo., May 13, 1930; d. Benjamin and Lena Levine Toubes. Bachelors, Stanford U., 1951. Statistical writer County of LA, 1962—87. Mem. Amnesty Internat. (Broward County), 1990—2000. Mem.: Am. Contract Bridge League, LACERA, Sierra Club. Democrat. Jewish. Home: 4980 Sa Bal Palm Blvd Apt 223 Tamarac FL 33319

TOUBY, KATHLEEN ANITA, lawyer; b. Miami Beach, Feb. 20, 1943; d. Harry and Kathleen Rebecca (Hamper) T.; m. Joseph Thomas Woodward; children: Mark Andrew, Judson David Touby. BS in Nursing, U. Fla., 1965, MRC in Rehab. Counseling, 1967; JD with honors, Nova U., 1977. Bar: Fla. 1978, D.C. 1978. Counselor Jewish Vocat. Svc., Chgo., 1967-68; rehab. counselor Fla. Dept. Vocat. Rehab., Miami, 1968-70; spl. asst., asst. U.S. atty. U.S. Dept. Justice, Miami, 1978-80; assoc. Pyszka & Kessler, P.A., Miami, 1980-83; ptnr. Touby & Smith, P.A., Miami, 1983-89, Touby, Smith, DeMahy & Drake, P.A., Miami, 1989-94, Touby & Woodward, P.A., Miami, 1994—. Chmn. adv. exec. bd. Paralegal Edn. program Barry U., 1986-87; lectr. Food and Drug Law Inst., 1987-89, 91; lectr. environ. law Exec. Enterprises, 1987-88; lectr. trial techniques, Hispanic Nat. Bar Assn., St. Thomas Law Sch.; adj. prof. product liability Can. Govt., U.S. Trade and Mktg. Dept., 1989-95. Co-author: The Environmental Litigation Deskbook, 1989; contbr. chpts. to books, articles to profl. jours. Mem. ABA, Am. Inns of Ct. (pres. 1998-99, pres.-elect St. Thomas Law Sch. chpt. 1997-98, pres. 1998-99), Dade County Bar Assn. (legal aid, pub. svcs. com. 1988), Fed. Bar Assn. (bd. dirs. 1989—, v.p. 1991-92, pres.-elect So. Fla. chpt. 1992-93, pres. 1993-94), Cuban-Am. Bar Assn., Phi Delta Phi (province pres. 1982-85, bd. dirs. 1985-87). Roman Catholic. Home: 4150 Bay Point Rd Miami FL 33137-3352 Office: Touby & Woodward PA 2030 Douglas Rd Ste 217 Coral Gables FL 33134 Office Phone: 305-442-2318.

TOUBY, LINDA, artist; b. Bklyn. d. Nat and Cele Touby; 1 child, Jaqueline. BFA, Pratt Inst., 1964; postgrad., Nat. Acad., N.Y.C., 1976, Art Students League, 1990. Pvt. tchr. Art, N.Y.C., 1990—. Author, illustrator: Sasaphras, 1974, Up, Up and Away, 1980; illustrator: Glimmerings (Zack Ragow), 1978; solo exhibitions: Mus. Realism and Atheism, Lvov, Ukraine, 1990, Alex Gallery, 1991-2006, Provincetown (Mass.) Art Assn. and Mus., 1992-2006, Tribeca Gallery, 1992-93, Rice/Polak Gallery, Provincetown, 1992-2006, Gallerie Roseg, St. Moritz, Switzerland, 1993, Eva Cohon Gallery Ltd., Chgo., 1993-94, Mus. Gallery, Boca Raton, Fla., 1993, La Mama La Galleria, NYC, 1993, 95, Novart Gallery, Madrid, 1996, Albert-Knox Art Gallery, Buffalo, 1995, Goya Art Gallery, NYC, 1995, Kouros Gallery, NYC, 1995, 98, 2005, Gallery de Arte Novart, Madrid, 1996, Blanvar Gallery de Arte, Majorca, Spain, 1996, Casa de Agua, Polencia, Spain, 1997, Bill Hodges Gallery, NYC, 1998-2006, Rieder, Munich, Germany, 2000-01, Artspace/Virginia Miller Galleries, Coral Gables, Fla., 2000, 02, 04-05, 06, Iandor Fine Art, Newark, 2002-06, Timothy Yarger Fine Art, Bangkok, Thailand, 2003-06, Madelyn Jordon Gallery, Scarsdale, NYC, 2003-06, Beverly Hills, Calif., 2004-06; permanent collections: Gen. Motors Corp., Phillips, Corp., Profl. Indemnity Agy., Inc., Bertholon-Rowland Corp., U.S. State Dept., Washington, Antonio Morales, Correo del Arte Publisher, Spain, Danforth Mus. Fine Arts, Framingham, Mass., and numerous pvt. collections. Grantee Change, Inc., 1995. Avocations: photography, writing. Studio: 500 W 52nd St New York NY 10019-5060 Office Phone: 212-245-6521. Personal E-mail: ltouby@rcn.com.

TOUCHETTE, COLLETTE W., mathematics professor; MEd, U. N.C., Greensboro, 1976. Quality mgr. Polaroid, Waltham, NC, 1978—84, Digital Equipment Corp., Andover, Mass., 1988—2001, Compaq Computers, Houston, 2001—02; prof. math. Catawba Valley C.C., Hickory, NC, 2002—. Office: Catawba Valley Community College 2550 Hwy 70 SE Hickory NC 28601 Office Phone: 828-327-777 X 4253. E-mail: ctouchette@cvcc.edu.

TOUHILL, BLANCHE MARIE, retired academic administrator, historian, educator; b. St. Louis, Mo., July 1, 1931; d. Robert and Margaret (Walsh) Van Dillen; m. Joseph M. Touhill, Aug. 29, 1959. BA in History, St. Louis U., 1953, MA in Geography, 1954, PhD in History, 1962. Prof. history and edn. U. Mo., St. Louis, 1965-73, assoc. dean faculties, 1974-76, assoc. vice chancellor for acad. affairs, 1976-87, vice chancellor, 1987-90, chancellor, 1991—2002, chancellor emeritus, 2002—. Bd. dirs. Peabody Energy, Inc. Author: William Smith O'Brien and His Irish Revolutionary Companions in Penal Exile, 1981, The Emerging University UM-St. Louis, 1963-83, 1985; editor: Readings in American History, 1970, Varieties of Ireland, 1976. Named Outstanding Educator St. Louis chpt. Urban League, 1976; recipient Leadership award St. Louis YWCA, 1986. Mem. Nat. Assn. State Univs. and Land Grant Colls. (exec. com. 1988—), Am. Com. on Irish Studies (pres. 1991—), Phi Kappa Phi, Alpha Sigma Lambda. E-mail: j_touhill@hotmail.com.

TOULANTIS, MARIE J., retail executive; BBA in Mktg., Pace Univ. V.p. The Chase Manhattan Bank, NYC, 1987-96, sr. v.p., 1996-97; exec. v.p. fin. Barnes & Noble Inc., NYC, 1997-99, CFO barnesandnoble.com Inc., 1995—2001, pres., COO, barnesandnoble.com, 2001, now CEO, barnesandnoble.com. Bd. dir. Hershey Foods Corp. Adv. bd. Lubin Sch. Bus., Pace University. Office: Barnes & Noble dot com Barnes & Noble Inc 2nd fl 122 Fifth Ave New York NY 10011

TOUSSIENG, YOLANDA, make-up artist; Television work includes: (movies) Fallen Angel, 1981, 1981, Blue de Ville, 1986, (series) Pee-wee's Playhouse, 1986, (mini-series) North and South, Book II, 1986, films include Blue City, 1986, No Man's Land, 1987, Beetlejuice, 1988, Gross Anatomy, 1989, Three Fugitives, 1989, Farewell to the King, 1989, Edward Scissorhands, 1990, Flatliners, 1990, Everybody Wins, 1990, Hoffa, 1992, Batman Returns, 1992, Mrs. Doubtfire, 1993, Rising Sun, 1993, Ed Wood, 1994 (Acad. award for Best Make-up, 1994), Being Human, 1994, Junior, 1994. Office: IATSE Local 706 11519 Chandler Blvd North Hollywood CA 91601-2618

TOUTLOFF, BETTY JANE, retired social worker; b. Sheboygan, Wis., Jan. 9, 1940; d. Herman Frederick William and Hazel Marie (Ackeret) Boehm; m. John Lloyd Toutloff, Sept. 7, 1963; children: Michelle, Catherine. BA, Lakeland Coll., 1963; MA, No. Mich. U., 1977. Caseworker Dept. Social Services, Wis., 1963-67; sch. social worker Delta/Schoolcraft Intermediate Sch., Mich., 1974-76; family assessment specialist Child and Family Svcs., Delta County, 1978-79; sch. social worker Escanaba Area Pub. Schs., Mich., 1979; caseworker Juvenile div. Probate Ct., Escanaba, 1980—2001; ret., 2001. Active Girl Scouts U.S., Escanaba, 1976-88; past area chmn. United Way, Escanaba. Mem. LWV (active various coms., pres. 1971—). Roman Catholic. Avocation: travel. Home: 710 N Bluff Dr Gladstone MI 49837-2039

TOVORNIK, MARY ROSE, physical education educator; d. Darlene G. (Gross) and Albert John Tovornik. MA, U. Conn., Storrs, 1997—2004, ABD, 2002. Cert. athletic trainer Nat. Athletic Trainers Assn., 1997, profl. rescuer in CPR and automated external defibrillator ARC. Grad. asst. athletic trainer football, women's soccer, baseball U. Conn., 1997, asst. athletic trainer football, 2002—04; asst. athletic trainer, asst. prof. Lock Haven U., Pa., 2004—. Site host athletic trainer Big East women's basketball tournament Hartford, Conn. U. Conn., 2004, site host athletic trainer NCAA women's basketball tournament, 04; faculty adv., huddle leader Fellowship of Christian Athletes, Lock Haven, 2005—; clin. instr. Bd. Cert. Athletic Tng.; spkr. in field. Active Susquenhanna Pacers Running Club, Lock Haven, 2005. Fellow, U. Conn., 2000; grantee Grad. Athletic Tng. award, Conn. Athletic Trainer's Assn., Larry Sutton Post Grad. scholarship, Mid-Atlantic Athletic Trainers' Assn., 1996; scholar, Nat. Athletic Trainers' Assn. Rsch. & Edn. Found., 1997. Mem.: ARC (instr.), Nat. Athletic Trainer's Assn. Avocations: running, writing, weightlifting.

TOWE, A. RUTH, retired museum director; b. Circle, Mont., Mar. 4, 1938; d. David and Anna Marie (Pedersen) James; m. Thomas E. Towe, Aug. 21, 1960; children: James Thomas, Kristofer Edward. BA, U. Mont., 1960, MA, 1970; postgrad., Am. U., 1964. Cert. master gardener 2005. Bookkeeper, copywriter Sta. KGVO, Missoula, Mont., 1960-61; grad. asst. Sch. of Journalism U. Mont., Missoula, 1961-62; editl. asst. Phi Gamma Delta mag., Washington, 1964; reporter The Chelsea (Mich.) Standard, 1965-66; dir. Mont. Nat. Bank, Plentywood, 1966-73; bookkeeper, legal sec. Thomas E. Towe, Atty. of Law, Billings, Mont., 1967-68; dir. Mont. Nat. Bank, Browning, 1972-73; mus. exec. dir. The Moss Mansion Mus., Billings, 1988—2003; ret., 2003. Bd. dirs. Billings Depot, Inc., sec., 1999-2003. Mem. Mont. Coun. of Family Rels. & Devel., 1970, Mont. Com. Humanities, 2005—; pres. Mont. Assn. of Symphony Orchs., 1987-88; sheriff Yellowstone Corral of Westerners, Billings, 1993; pres. Yellowstone Hist. Soc., 1998-2000; vice-chmn. Yellowstone Dem. Ctrl. Com., Billings, 1983-84; mem. Billings Friends Mtg., 1986—. Mem. AAUW, PEO, Mus. Assn. Mont. (pres. 1990-92, bd. dirs. 1989-96), Jr. League, Theta Sigma Phi (hon.). Avocation: gardening. E-mail: r.towe@bresnan.net.

TOWER, JOAN PEABODY, composer, educator; b. New Rochelle, N.Y., Sept. 6, 1938. B.A., Bennington Coll., 1961; M.A., Columbia U., 1964, D.M.A., 1978. Pianist, Da Capo Chamber Players, 1969-84; compositions include: Sequoia (premiered by Am. Composers Orch.), Silver Ladders, 1985 (premiered by St. Louis Symphony, Grawemeyer award, U. Louisville, 1990), Breakfast Rhythms, Black Topaz, Amazon, Wings (solo clarinet), Fantasy (clarinet and piano), Cello Concerto, Piano Concerto, Clarinet Concerto, Flute Concerto, Violin Concerto, "Music for Cello and Orchestra", "Island Prelude" for oboe and strings by Cleveland, Philadelphia, and Seattle Symphony Orchestras and "Fanfare for the Uncommon Woman" by more than 200 ensembles; works recorded; Compact Discs have been released on Koch International, Delos, and d'Note Records; commns.: Contemporary Music Soc., Jerome Found., Mass. State Arts Council, Schubert Club St. Paul, Richard Stoltzman, St. Louis Symphony, Pitts. Symphony, Houston Symphony, Elmar Oliveira, N.Y. Philharm., Chgo. Symphony, Sharon Isbin, Carol Wincenc, Fromm Found., NEA, Carnegie Hall, Milw. Ballet, Lincoln Ctr. Chamber Soc., Aspen Festival, Cleve. Muir Quartets, L.A. Chamber Orch.; assoc. prof. Bard Coll., Annandale On Hudson, N.Y., from 1972, currently Asher B. Edelman prof. music (composition); composer-in-residence St. Louis Symphony Orchestra, 1985-88, 1999-2002. Recipient N.Y. State Council for Arts award, 1980, Alfred Dupont award for disting. composers and conductors; Guggenheim fellow, 1976, Nat. Endowment Arts fellow, 1974, 75, 80, 84, Koussevitzky Found. grantee, 1982, Meet the Composer Consortium grantee, 1989, 91, 92, Nat. Endowment Rec. grantee, 1993. Fellow Am. Acad. Arts and Sciences; mem. Am. Acad. of Arts and Letters (award in music Am. Acad. and Inst. Arts and Letters, 1983). Office: Bard Coll Conservatory of Music PO Box 5000 Annandale On Hudson NY 12504-5000 Office Phone: 845-758-7196. Business E-Mail: tower@bard.edu.

TOWER, MOLLIE GREGORY, writer, educator, consultant; b. San Antonio, Tex., July 17, 1945; d. Malcolm Russell and Margaret Halm Gregory; children: Debbie Tower Tannert, Sheryl Tower Maklary. MusB, U. Tex., Austin, 1967; MEd, U. Tex., Austin, Tex., 1981. Cert. Texas Music K-12 Tex. Edn. Agy., 1967, Texas Supr. Tex. Edn. Agy., 1981. Elem. music tchr., k - 6 Austin Ind. Sch. Dist., Tex., 1967—78, elem. music coord., 1978—92, coord. of choral and gen. music, k-12, 1992—98; author Glencoe/McGraw-Hill, Woodland Hills, Calif., 1995—, Macmillan/McGraw-Hill Pub. Co., N.Y.C., NY, 1982—96, Silver-Burdett Pub. Co., N.Y.C., NY, 2004—; sr. author arts edn. IDEAS Pub. Co., Norwalk, Conn., 1998—. Cons. Various sch. dist., 1975—2006; pres. Tex. Music Educators Conf., Tex., 1993—96, Tex. Music Admintrs. Conf., Tex., 1996—97, Tex. Coalition for Music Edn., Tex., 1992—93. Author: (ann. elem. curriculum program) Music Memory Bulletin, 1981—2005, (textbook) Music Reading Charts, Grade One & Grade Two, 1988, Songs in Spanish, Primary and Intermediate, 1989, Musica para todas, primary and intermediate, 1995, Choral Connections, 1997, Experiencing Choral Music, 2005. V.p., commr. Austin Arts Commn., Austin, Tex., 1985—89. Mem.: Sigma Alpha Iota, Delta Kappa Gamma. Achievements include Ann. Host of Riverside Symphony Music Memory Contest, Lincoln Ctr., N.Y.C., 1999-2006; Ann. Host of Kansas State Univ. Music Memory Contest, Manhattan, Kan., 2003-2006. Personal E-mail: mtower@realtime.net.

TOWER, RONI BETH, psychologist; b. Akron, Ohio, Dec. 11, 1943; d. Arnold Edward Weinstein and Elva Hermoine (Gross) MacRae; children: Jennifer, Daniel. BA, Barnard Coll., N.Y.C., 1964; MS, Yale U., 1977, M in Philosphy, 1979, PhD, 1980. Lic. in clin. psychology, Conn., N.Y.; diplomate Clin. Psychology Am. Bd. Profl. Psychology. Psychologist Silver Hill Found., New Canaan, Conn., 1979—81; pvt. practice Westport, Conn., 1981—97; rsch. affiliate dept. epidemiology Yale U., New Haven, 1995—; pvt. practice Tarrytown, NY, 2004—. Lectr. in psychology Yale U., New Haven, 1981-89, Am. Bd. Profl. Psychology seminar, Washington, 1990; adj. assoc. prof. Tchrs. Coll., Columbia U., N.Y.C., 2002-06; cons. in field. Cons. editor Jour. of Imagination Cognition and Personality, 1983—; contbr. numerous articles to profl. jours. Active Yale Alumni Fund Bd. Recipient Traineeship award USPHS, 1979-80; postdoctoral fellow Yale Sch. Epidemiology and Pub. Health, 1992-95. Mem.: APA, Internat. Assn. for Relationship Rsch. Avocations: dance, travel. Office: 25 Wyldwood Dr Tarrytown NY 10591-5057 Office Phone: 914-366-6644. Personal E-mail: ronibtower@aol.com.

TOWER, SUE WARNCKE, artist; b. Seattle, Mar. 25, 1940; d. Edgar Dean and Ione Althea (Smith) T.; m. Donald Frank Speyer, Dec. 31, 1958 (div. June 1968); children: Stacy, Monte. BFA, Pacific N.W. Coll. Art, 1982. Vis. artist So. Oreg. State Coll., 1996; performing artist (slide presentation) Oreg. Arts Commn. Arts-in-Edn. Program, Salem region, 1996-98; featured artist Oreg. Symphony's Composer Program Cover Art Project, 1997. One woman exhibits include Jacobs Gallery Hult Ctr. Performing Arts, Eugene, Oreg., 1993, Littman Gallery, Portland (Oreg.) State U., 1994, BICC Libr., Oreg. Health Scis. U., 1994, City of Las Vegas Reed Whipple Cultural Ctr., 1996; group exhibits inlcude Bellvue Art Mus., 1992, Galerie Bratri Capku and The Okresni Mus., Prague and Jicin, Czech Republic, 1995, State Capital, Salem, Oreg., 1995, Maryhill Mus. of Art, Goldendale, Wash., 1998, Blackfish Gallery, 1998, Orange County Art Ctr., 1998, Beaverton Arts Commn., 1998, Wheeler (Oreg.) Gallery, 1999, 20th anniversary catalog and exhbn. Blackfish Gallery, 1999. Fundraiser, donor Blackfish Gallery, Pacific N.W. Coll. Art, 1994; donor Cascade AIDS Project Benefit Art Auction, 1996. Avocation: ballet. Home: 3659 NE Wasco St Portland OR 97232 Personal E-mail: towjptr@aol.com.

TOWERS, KAREN R., education educator; d. Carleton W. and Mabel Faye Lauridsen; m. James Towers, Aug. 18, 1973; children: Devon Charles, Jaimee Faye Elizabeth. PhD, U. Iowa, Iowa City, 1990. Dir. internat. edn. and off-campus programs St. Mary's U., Winona, Minn., 1988—98, asst. prof.

edn., 2000—. Asst. dean students Knox Coll., Galesburg, Ill., 1985—88. Office: Saint Mary's University of MN 700 Terrace Heights #23 Winona MN 55987-1399 Office Phone: 507-457-6637. Office Fax: 507-457-1992. Business E-Mail: ktowers@smumn.edu.

TOWERY, SARAH CARLISLE, artist, retired educator; b. Alexander City, Ala., Oct. 4, 1911; d. Washington Homer Carlisle and Artimisha Motley; children: Carlisle, Misha Sampson, Sarah Wade. Attended, Huntington Coll., 1930—32, U. Montevallo, 1940—45, Black Mountain Coll., 1944, Pen State U., 1951. Instr. U. Montevallo, Ala., 1945, So. Union Jr. Coll., Wadley, Ala., 1953—56; docent, team leader pvt. studio, Alexander City, 1948—2000; owner, tchr. pvt. kindergarten sch., Alexander City, 1951—53; organizer, session planner World Art Workshop, San Miguel, Mexico, 1972—94. Tchr., mentor Alexander City Pub. Schs., 1959—61; charter mem. World Art Workshop, San Miguel, 1972—94; found., continuing bd. mem. Sarah Carlisle Towery Art Colony-Lake Martin, Alexander City, 1991—. Wall mural, First Meth. Ch., Alexander City, 1952; executor, designer (wall mural) Town History: Racial Segregation, 1978; wall mural, Alexander City Elem. Sch., 1978; contbr. paintings Operation Downtown, Alexander City, 2001, 2002. Recipient Govs. award, Ala. State Coun. Arts, 1999, Artist Select Exhibit award, Comer Mus. Arts Ctr., 1999. Mem.: Ala. Art League, Birmingham Art Assn., Montgomery Art Guild. Republican. Protestant. Avocation: travel. Home: 273 Glenhaven Dr Alexander City AL 35010

TOWLE, MELISSA MANCHESTER, music educator; b. Quincy, Mass., May 18, 1975; d. Richard Milton and Carolyn Manchester Hover; m. Christopher Eldon Towle, July 15, 1995; children: Bailey Christopher, Bodey Richard, Braeden Eldon. B in Music Edn., Johnson State Coll., Vt., 1997. Gen. music tchr. Orchard Elem. Sch., South Burlington, Vt., 1997—2000; choral tchr. Lamoille Union Mid./HS, Hyde Park, Vt., 2000—01; music tchr. Hyde Pk. Elem. Sch., 2000—. Piano tchr., Johnson, 1994—. Music dir. Lamoille Valley Ch. of Nazarene, Johnson, 1994—. Office: Hyde Park Elem Sch Main St Hyde Park VT 05655 Office Phone: 802-888-2237. Business E-Mail: mtowle@hpes.org.

TOWLER, KATHERINE, writer; b. Pontiac, Mich., Sept. 1, 1956; d. Lewis W. Towler and Jane B. Kellogg; m. James A. Sparrell, Sept. 14, 1991. BA in English lit., U. of Mich., Ann Arbor, Michigan, 1974—78; MA in English lit., Middlebury Coll., Middlebury, Vermont, 1980—84; MA in fiction writing, Johns Hopkins U., Baltimore, Maryland, 1981—82. Freelance writer, publications cons. self-employed, Portsmouth, NH, 1987—; mem. faculty MFA Program in Writing, So. NH U., 2006—. Author: (novels) Snow Island, 2002 (Barnes and Noble Discover Great New Writers title, Borders Original Voices title, Booksense selection), Evening Ferry, 2005 (Booksense selection). Fellow George Bennett Fellowship, Phillips Exeter Acad., 1989-1990, Individual Artist Fellowship, NH. State Coun. on the Arts, 2003, Fellowship, Yaddo Artists Colony, 1985, 1983, Va. Ctr. for the Creative Arts, 1987, Working Scholarship, Bread Loaf Writers Conf., 1983. Mem.: Authors Guild, NH Writers Project (assoc.; bd. of trustees 1994—97), PEN New Eng. (assoc.). Avocations: bicycling, gardening, bird watching.

TOWN, CHARLOTTE, artist, small business owner; b. Vancouver, Wash., Mar. 26, 1951; d. Joseph Donald Kurth and Genevieve Northrop, Gail Kurth (Stepmother); m. Kevin G. Town, Aug. 13, 1993; children: Debbie K. Mills, Michael S. Mills, Robert J Mills. BA, U. Alaska, 2006. Quality control asst. Delmonte Corp., Vancouver, Wash., 1974—81; janitorial Am. Bldg. Maintenance, 1981—82; taxi driver Anchorage, 1983—93; dispatch/phone answerer Alaska Cab, 1993—95; disability support asst. U. Alaska, 1995—2000; free lance artist, 2000—; graphic artist, multimedia specialist U.S. Army, Fort Richardson, 2000—; prin., owner Alaska Sex Stones Studio. Exhibitions include Anchorage Fur Rendezvous (Divsn. Champion, 1999), U. Alaska Galleries, Northwest Art Assn. (Hon. Mention, 1977), Alaska State Fair (1st Pl., 1999, 2d Pl., 1999), Working Benifitaction, 2006. Second v.p. AMVETS Post 2, Anchorage, 1992—99; vol. as costume creatures; vol./Mrs. Santa Claus. Mem.: Women in Arts (assoc.). Achievements include Moose Nugget Incense. Avocations: boating, fishing, gardening, darts, travel. Office Phone: 907-337-7514.

TOWNE, MONICA NOELLE, music educator; b. Syracuse, N.Y., Dec. 26, 1979; d. George Frank and Eva May Gigon; m. Mark A. Towne, July 10, 2004. B in Music Edn., SUNY, Potsdam, 2002. 6-12 music tchr. Elmira Heights (N.Y.) Sch. Dist., 2002—03; k-5 music tchr. Ctrl. Sqaure (N.Y.) Sch. Dist., 2003—. Disc jockey Generations, Constantia, NY, 2005—. Actor: (musical) Alice In Wonderland. Mem.: VFW (sec. 2004—05). Office Phone: 315-668-4229.

TOWNER, MARGARET ELLEN, retired minister; b. Columbia, Mo., Mar. 19, 1925; d. Milton Carsley and Dorothy Marie (Schloeman) Towner. BA, Carleton Coll., 1948; MDiv, Union/Auburn Theol. Sem., 1954; MA in Guidance and Counseling, Western Mich. U., 1967; DDiv (hon.), Carroll Coll., 1989. Ordained to ministry Presbyn. Ch., 1956. Dir. Christian edn. Takoma Park (Md.) Presbyn. Ch., 1954-55; min. of edn. 1st Presbyn. Ch., Allentown, Pa., 1955-58, assoc. pastor Kalamazoo, 1958-69, Northminster Presbyn. Ch., Indpls., 1970-72; exec. dir. Kalamazoo YWCA, 1969-70; co-pastor Kettle Moraine Parish, Waukesha County, Wis., 1973-90; pastor emerita Delafield Presbyn. Ch., Wis., 2006—. Mem. Christian edn. and youth coms. Western Mich. Presbytery, So. Mich. Presbytery; chair synod sch. com. Synod of Mich.; mem. nominating com. Whitewater Presbytery, Ind.; mem. adv. com. discipleship and worship Gen. Assembly Mission Coun., commr., 1965—81, vice moderator, 1981—82, boundries com., 1983; chair Synod of Lakes and Prairies Comprehensive Rev. Com.; mem. coun. advisors Dubuque Theol. Sem.; vice moderator gen. assembly Presbyn. Ch., 1982; records and overtures Peace River Presbyn. Ch.; parish assoc. Siesta Key Chapel, Sarasota, Fla. Contbr. articles, photographs to profl. publs. Pres. Timberlake Homeowners Assn., Sarasota, 1992—95, Lakes Maintenance Bd., Sarasota, 1994—96; chair bd. trustees Camp Brainerd, Pa., 1955—56; mem. Sch. Faith Com., Faculty Greater Washington Coun. Chs., radio-TV, C.E. and youth coms., pub sch. com.; mem. cmty. com. UNICEF; bd. dirs. Planned Parenthood; mem. inter-agy. exec. com. HEW, Kalamazoo; vol. chaplain emergency rm. Waukesha Meml. Hosp., Meml. Hosp. Oconomowoc, Wis.; dean, dir. Coun. Chs. Leadership Schs., Kalamazoo; mem. Japan Internat. Christian U. Indpls. Com. Recipient Disting. Alumnus award, Carleton Coll., 1983. Mem.: PEO (guard, historian 1972—), Nat. Assn. Presbyn. Clergywomen. Avocations: golf, photography, travel, environmental studies. Home and Office: 7333 Scotland Way # 2120 Sarasota FL 34238-9852

TOWNER, NAOMI WHITING, fiber artist, educator; b. Providence, May 8, 1940; d. Basil J. and Nellie (Woolhouse) Whiting; B.F.A. in Textile Design, R.I. Sch. Design, 1962; postgrad. (Textron fellow) Foreningen Handarbetets Vanner, Stockholm, 1962-63; M.F.A. in Textile Design, Rochester Inst. Tech., 1965. Internat. studies with faculty Ill. State U., People's Republic of China and Thailand, 1986; Teaching grad. asst. Sch. Am. Craftsmen, Rochester (N.Y.) Inst. Tech., 1963-65, instr. textile design, summer 1964; instr. Ill. State U., Normal, 1965-68, asst. prof., 1968-72, assoc. prof., 1972-76, prof. art, 1976—; lectr. various art guilds and schs., 1967—; pres., ptnr. Smiling Camel Choklits, Ltd., Bloomington; dir. workshops on weaving and textile design, 1964—. One person shows art fabrics include: Fox Valley Art League, St. Charles, Ill., 1968, Fine Arts Ctr. Clinton (Ill.), 1971, Old Town Gallery, St. Charles, Mo., 1973, Lincoln Coll., Lincoln, Ill., 1974, Craft Alliance Gallery, St. Louis, 1974, Unitarian Ch., Bloomington, Ill., 1975, The Art-In, Riverton, Wyo., 1975, Xavier U., Cin., 1992; numerous group shows including: Mus. Contemporary Crafts Fabrics Internat. travelling exhibit, 1961-62, Security Trust Co., Rochester, N.Y., 1965, Ill. State U., Normal, 1965-68, 71, 73-86, Old Town Art Ctr., Chgo., 1967, Brooks Meml. Art Gallery, Memphis, 1967, Lakeview Ctr. for Arts, Peoria, Ill., 1967-68, Ill. State Mus., 1968, Wis. State U., Oshkosh, 1969, Art Inst. Chgo., 1971, No. Ill. U., DeKalb, 1971, U. Mass. Art Gallery, Amherst, 1972, Evansville (Ind.) Mus. Arts and Scis., 1973, 88, Eureka Coll. (Ill.), 1973, Mills Coll., Oakland, Calif., 1974, Columbus (Ga.) Mus. Arts and Crafts, 1974, Wright Art Center, Beloit (Wis.) Coll., 1975, Lowe Art Mus., U. Miami (Fla.) Goldstein Gallery, 1976, U. Minn., St. Paul, 1977, Paul Sargent Gallery, Eastern Ill. U., Charlestown, 1977, Boise (Idaho) State U., 1978, Cin. Art Mus., 1978, Kearney (Nebr.) State Coll. Art Gallery, 1979, Coll. Art Gallery, 1979, Rahr-West Mus., Manitowoc, Wis., 1979, Ill. State Mus., Springfield, 1979, No. Calif. Handweavers, Inc., San Mateo, 1979, Ill. Arts Council Gallery, Chgo., 1979, Tex. Tech U., Lubbock, 1980, Caterpillar Internat., Peoria, Ill., 1980, No. Ill. U., Midwest Constructed Fibers, 1940-80, travelling exhibit, 1980-82, Loveland (Colo.) Mus., 1981, Ft. Collins (Colo.) Mus., 1981, Fiber Art Trends, 1982, Pyramid Arts Ctr., Rochester, 1983, U. Wis.-Green Bay travelling exhibit, 1984-85, Ariel Gallery, Naperville, Ill., 1984, Premonitions, Nashville, 1985, Ill. State Fair Profl. Art Exhbn., Springfield, 1986 (1st place award craft media, merit award 1987), 7th ann. Cen. Ill. Arts Consortium Visual Arts Touring Exhbn., 1984-86 (merit award), Juror's Exhbn.: New Dimensions in Fiber II, Coll. Du Page, Ill., 1986, U. Galleries Ill. State U., Normal, 1987, Creative Arts Guild, Dalton, Ga., 1988, No. Ill. U. Art Gallery, Chgo., 1988, Merchandise Mart, Chgo., 1988, Evansville (Ind.) Mus. Arts & Scis., 1988, Midwest Weavers Assn. Conf., Cin., 1989, Malton Gallery, Cin., 1989, U. Art Gallery/Mus. Western Ill. U., Macomb, 1989, Upper Gallery, Milw., 1990, Henderson Gallery, Yellow Springs, Ohio, 1990, Butler Inst. Am. Art, Youngstown, Ohio, 1991, Xavier U. Art Galleries, Cin., 1992, Springfield (Ill.) Art Assn., 1992, Craft Alliance Gallery, St. Louis, 1992; represented in permanent collections Ill. State Mus., Springfield, Washington U., St. Louis, Eureka (Ill.) Coll., corp. and pvt. collections; juror exhbns. Recipient numerous awards including Silver Shuttle award U. Rochester, 1964, Owens-Corning Fiberglas competition, 1964, award of excellence Ill. Craftsmen's Council Invitational, 1967, Merit award Springfield Art Assn., 1976, Hon. mention Tchr. of Yr. awards, 1986; grantee Handweavers Guild Am. and Ill. Arts Council, 1975-78. Mem. Am. Crafts Council, Midwest Weavers Conf., Am. Fedn. Tchrs., AFL-CIO, Handweavers Guild Am. (rep. 1973-77, bd. dirs. 1978-80), ACLU, Surface Design Assn. Contbr. articles on textile design and weaving to profl. publs.; editor Fiber News, 1975-85; mem. editorial bd. Ars Textrina, 1985—. Home: 1505 Sweetbriar Dr Bloomington IL 61701-8326

TOWNES, SANDRA L., federal judge; BA, Johnson C. Smith, 1966; JD, Syracuse U., 1976. Tchr. English Carver H.S., 1966—67, Dunbar H.S., 1967—70, D.C. Evening Adult Edn. Prog., 1967—70, Corcoran H.S., 1971—73, P.E.A.C.E. Learning Ctr., 1971—73; asst. D.A. County Onondaga, N.Y., 1977—85, sr. asst. D.A., 1983—86, chief asst. D.A., 1986—87; adj. prof. Syracuse U. Coll. Law, 1987—95; judge Syracuse City Ct., 1988—99; adj. prof. Onondaga C.C., 1992—99; justice N.Y. Supreme Ct. (5th jud. dist.), 2000—01; assoc. justice N.Y. Supreme Ct. (Appellate divsn., 2d dept.), 2001—04; judge U.S. Dist. Ct. (ea. dist.) N.Y., 2004—. Mem.: Onondaga County Bar Assn., N.Y. State Women's Bar Assn., N.Y. State Bar Assn. Office: 225 Cadman Plaza E Brooklyn NY 11201 Office Phone: 718-613-2160.

TOWNSEND, ALAIR ANE, publishing executive; b. Rochester, N.Y., Feb. 15, 1942; d. Harold Eugene and Dorothy (Sharpe) T.; m. Robert Harris, Dec. 31, 1970 (div. 1994). BS, Elmira Coll., 1962; MS, U. Wis., 1964; postgrad., Columbia U., 1970-71. Assoc. dir. budget priorities Com. on Budget, U.S. Ho. of Reps., Washington, 1975-79, dep. asst. sec. for budget HEW, 1979-80, asst. sec. for mgmt. and budget, 1980-81; dir. Office Mgmt. & Budget NYC, 1981-85, dep. mayor for fin. & econ. devel., 1985-89; pub. Crain's N.Y. Bus., NYC, 1989—2006, v.p., 1993—, pub. dir., 2006—. Bd. overseers Tchrs. Ins. and Annuity Assn.-Coll. Retirement Equities Fund; former mem. adv. bd. Ford Motor Credit Corp.; former bd. mem. Armor Holdings Inc. Former vice-chmn., trustee Elmira Coll.; former mem. Coun. Fgn. Rels.; former bd. govs. Am. Stock Exch.; former chmn. Am. Woman's Econ. Devel. Corp.; former chmn. N.Y.C. Sports Commn.; former chmn. Consol. Corp. Fund of Lincoln Ctr.; bd. dirs. Lincoln Ctr.; vice-chmn. Buffalo Fiscal Stability Auth. Mem. Women's Forum, Partnership for NYC (bd. dirs.), N.Y. State Bus. Coun. (bd. dirs.), Econ. Club N.Y. (bd. dirs.). Office: Crain's NY Bus 711 3d Ave New York NY 10017

TOWNSEND, ANN VAN DEVANTER, foundation administrator, art historian; b. Washington, June 20, 1936; d. John Ward and Ellen Keys (Ramsey) Cutler; m. Willis Van Devanter, Dec. 27, 1958 (div. May 1974); 1 child, Susan Earling Van Devanter (Mrs. John Philip Newell); m. Lewis Raynham Townsend, Dec. 10, 1983. BA, Brown U., Providence, R.I., 1958; MA, George Washington U., Washington, DC, 1975. Grantsmanship ctr. cert. Guest curator Balt. Mus. Art, 1971-77; dir. cultural affairs Chevy Chase Savs. & Loan, Inc., Md., 1978-81; dir. spl. partnership projects NEA, Washington, 1982-83; founding pres. The Trust for Mus. Exhbns., Washington, 1984—. Organizer over 60 nat. and internat. mus. exhbns. for more than 240 mus. Co-author: Self-Portraits of American Artists, 1670-1973, 1974; author: Anywhere So Long As There Be Freedom, 1975, Two Hundred Years of American Painting, 1976; contbr. articles to mags. U.S. commr. Cagnes-Sur-Mer Internat. Afts Festival, France, 1977, 78; mem. women's com. Washington Opera, 1993—; bd. dirs. Friends of Corcoran Gallery of Art, Washington, 1975-76, Strathmore Hall Arts Ctr., Rockville, Md., 1978-80, Am. Swedish Hist. Mus., Phila., 1987-89, U.S. World Fedn. Friends of Mus., 1995—. Acad. grad. fellow Johns Hopkins Sch. Advanced Internat. Studies, 1958. Mem. Nat. Soc. Arts and Letters, Soc. Women Geographers, Am. Assn. Mus., Internat. Coun. Mus., Am. Assn. Royal Acad. Trust, Am. Friends of the Hermitage Mus., Am. Friends of French Heritage, Cir. of the Nat. Gallery of Art, Sulgrave Club, Cosmos Club. Episcopalian. Avocations: backgammon, gourmet cooking, ballroom dancing, bridge. Office: The Trust for Mus Exhbns 2121 K St NW Ste 800 Washington DC 20037 Office Phone: 202-745-2566. Business E-Mail: atownsend@tme.org.

TOWNSEND, ELIZABETH KATHLEEN, performing arts educator; b. Galveston, Tex., Apr. 4, 1980; d. Joseph Emmett and Irene Eileen Townsend. BA Theatre and Dance, BS Radio, TV, Film, U. Tex., Austin, 2003. Cert. Tchr. State Tex., 2005. Tchr. speech, theatre, dance H.S. LaMarque Ind. Sch. Dist., Tex., 2004—05; tchr. theatre H.S. Clear Creek Ind. Sch. Dist., Houston, 2005—. Instr. hip-hop, tap, jazz dance Broadway Bound, Galveston, Tex., 2004—. Actor: (regional/profl. theatre) Acting. Parishioner St. Mary's Cath. Ch., League City, Tex. Mem.: Beta Sigma Phi (life; Beta Kappa Nu sister 2005). Roman Catholic. Avocations: reading, films, singing, exercise. Office: Clear Lake High School 2929 Bay Area Blvd Houston TX 77058 Office Fax: 281-284-2405.

TOWNSEND, FRAN (FRANCES FRAGOS TOWNSEND), federal official; b. Mineola, NY, Dec. 28, 1961; m. John M. Townsend; 2 children. BA in Polit. Sci., BS in Psychology, Am. U., 1982; JD, San Diego U., 1984; student, Inst. on Internat. & Comparative Law, London, 1986. Asst. dist. atty., Bklyn., 1985—88; atty., US Atty. Office (so. dist.) NY US Dept. Justice, 1988—91, chief to staff to asst. atty. gen. criminal divsn., 1993—95, dir. internat. affairs criminal divsn., 1995—97, acting dep. asst. atty. gen., 1997—98, counsel Office of Intelligence Policy and Rev., 1998—2001; asst. comdt. for intelligence USCG, US Dept. Homeland Security, 2001—03; dep. asst. to Pres., dep. nat. security adv. for combating terrorism The White House, 2003—04, asst. to Pres for homeland security & counterterrorism, 2004—; chair Homeland Security Coun., 2004—. Office: Eisenhower Exec Office Bldg Rm 313 17th St & Pennsylvania Ave NW Washington DC 20504

TOWNSEND, JANE KALTENBACH, biologist, educator; b. Chgo., Dec. 21, 1922; BS, Beloit Coll., 1944; MA, U. Wis., 1946; PhD, U. Iowa, 1950. Asst. in zoology U. Wis., 1944-47, asst., project assoc. in pathology, 1950—53; asst., instr. U. Iowa, 1948-50; rsch. fellow Wenner-Grens Inst. Am. Cancer Soc., Stockholm, 1953—56; asst. prof. zoology Northwestern U., 1956-58; asst. prof. to assoc. prof. zoology Mt. Holyoke Coll., South Hadley, Mass., 1958-70, prof., 1970-93, chmn. biol. scis., 1980-86, prof. emeritus, 1993—; summer investigator Marine Biol. Lab., Woods Hole, Mass., 1993—. Contbr. articles to profl. sci. jours. Fellow AAAS (sec. sect. biol. sci. 1974-78); mem. Am. Assn. Anatomists, Am. Inst. Biol. Scis., Soc. Integrated Comparative Biology, Soc. Exptl. Biology and Medicine, Soc. Devel. Biology, Corp. of Marine Biol. Lab., Sigma Xi, Phi Beta Kappa. Achievements include research in amphibian metamorphosis and immune responses in marine sponges. Office: Mount Holyoke Coll Dept Bio Scis South Hadley MA 01075 Office Phone: 413-538-2124. Business E-Mail: jtownsen@mtholyoke.edu.

TOWNSEND, JULIE RAE, artist, educator; b. Davenport, Iowa, Oct. 26, 1964; d. Richard Earl and Gladys Imogene Crow; m. Kelvin Leroy Townsend, Sept. 26, 1989; children: Stephanie Allisson, Elliott Russell. BFA, St. Ambrose U., Davenport, Iowa, 1983—87, BA in Art Edn. K-12, 2001—02. Cert. tchr. Iowa, 2003. Tchr. Davenport Mus. Art, 2002, Lincoln Fundamental Elem., Davenport, Iowa, 2003; tchr. Kaleidoscope program Augustana Coll., Rock Island, Ill. Presenter Ea. Iowa Writing Project workshop. Commissions, exhibitions include 700 sq. ft. mural 1st Presbyn. Ch., Davenport, exhibitions include Dubusque Mus. Art, Tri-Ann. Tri-City Exhbn., Moline's Reher Gallery, Ill., prin. works include charcoal Rapunzel's Bad Hair Day (Hon. Mention, 1995), prin. works include drawing Still Life (Scholastic Achievement Award, 1982); contbr. articles to profl. jours. Vol. Midcoast Fine Arts, Rock I., Ill., 1995—2003; vol. Friends of Catich St. Ambrose U., Davenport, Iowa, 2003—; leader Girl Scouts (Miss. Valley coun.), Davenport, Iowa, 1997—2003; vol. First Presbyn. Ch., Davenport, Iowa. Named 1st Best 2D Artist Quad Cities, River Cities Reader, 2003; recipient 3d Best 2D Artist Quad Cities, 2001, 2d Best 2D Artist Quad Cities, 2002. Mem.: Ea. Iowa Writing Project Adv. Com., Nat. Art Edn. Assn. (assoc.), Davenort Mus. of Art (assoc.), Nat. Oil Painter's Soc. (assoc.), Midcoast Fine Arts (life; vol. various jobs 1996—2003). Home: 1131 E Columbia Ave Davenport IA 52803 Personal E-mail: julesart@netexpress.net.

TOWNSEND, KATHERYN ESTELLE, chemistry professor; b. Brownfield, Tex., Mar. 25, 1980; d. Nathan Craig and Carol Ann Gilbreth; m. Jonathan Michael Townsend, Aug. 9, 2003; 1 child, Katelynn Anne. AS, South Plains Coll., Levelland, Tex., 2000; BS in Math., Howard Payne U., 2002; BS in Chemistry, Howard Payne U., Brownwood, Tex., 2002; Med, Tex. Tech U., Lubbock, 2005. Chemistry instr. South Plains Coll., Levelland, Tex., 2002—; chemistry rsch. asst. Tex. Tech U., Lubbock, 2002—03. Adv. Am. Chem. Soc., Levelland, Tex., 2004—; stockroom adv. South Plains Coll., Levelland, Tex., 2006—. Recipient Chancellor's List, Ednl. Comm., 2005. Mem.: NSTA, Tex. C.C. Teachers Assn., Am. Chem. Soc. Independent. Bapt. Avocations: general crafts, camping, scrapbooks. Office Phone: 806-894-9611 2310.

TOWNSEND, KATHLEEN KENNEDY, former lieutenant governor; b. Greenwich, Connecticut, July 4, 1951; d. Robert F. and Ethel S. Kennedy; m. David Townsend; children: Meaghan, Maeve, Kate, and Kerry. BA cum laude, Harvard Univ., 1974; JD, U. N.Mex., 1978. Instr. Dundalk Cmty. Coll., 1985-86, Essex Cmty. Coll., 1986-87, U. Pa., 1987-88; exec. dir. Md. Student Svc. Alliance, State dept. of Edn., 1987—93; dep. asst. atty. gen. U.S. Dept. Justice, Washington, 1993-94; lt. gov. State of Md., 1995—2003; pres. Operation Respect, 2003; adj. prof. Georgetown's Sch. of Pub. Policy, 2003. Chair so. region Nat. Conf. Lt. Gov., chair oversight com. Johns Hopkins U., Peabody Inst., 1995-96; nat. adv. bd. Export-Import Bank U.S.; bd. adv. Johns Hopkins U. Sch. Advanced Internat. Studies, Inst. Human Virology U. Md; chair, State House Trust, 1995-2003, Adv. Bd., After-School Opportunity Programs, 1999-, co-chair, Safe Schools Interagency Steering Com., 1999-2003; Delegate, Dem. Party Nat. Conv., 1988, 1996, 2000; chair, Dem. Caucus of Lt. Gov. Editor U. N.Mex. Law Rev.; contbg. articles to profl. jour. and newspapers. Founder Robert F. Kennedy Human Rights Award; chair Cabinet Coun. Criminal and Juvenile Justice, 1995-2003; chair Cabinet Coun. for Bus. and Econ. Devel.; chair Md. del. Pres. Summit Am. Future, 1997; chair State Sys. Reform Task Force for Children and Youth Reform, 1996, Task Force to study increasing availability of substance abuse programs, 1998-2001, Gov.of the Yr. 2000 Pub. Info.; chair adv. bd. after sch. opportunity programs; co-chair Md. Family Violence Coun.; bd. dir. John F. Kennedy Libr. Found., Nat. Inst. Women's Policy Rsch.; chair external adv. bd. Kennedy Krieger Inst. Early Infant Transition Ctr.; sr. advisor, Appropriations Com., House of Delegates, 1984-85; asst. Atty. Gen., Md., 1985-86; bd. ptnr. Radcliffe Coll. Recipient 4 hon. degrees; Visionary Leadership Award, Healthy Families Am., 2000, Clinton Ctr. Award for Leadership, Dem. Leadership Coun., 2002. Mem., Econ. Devel. Commn., Baltimore County, 1987, Gov. Exec. Coun., Gov. Commn. on Svc. and Volunteerism, 1998-. Democrat.

TOWNSEND, LINDA LADD, mental health nurse; b. Louisville, Apr. 26, 1948; d. Samuel Clyde and Mary Elizabeth Ladd; m. Stanley Allen Oliver, June 7, 1970 (div. 1978); 1 child, Aaron; m. Warren Terry Townsend Jr., Jan. 1, 1979; children: Mark, Amy, Sarah. Student, Catherine Spalding Coll., 1966-67; BSN, Murray State U., 1970; MS in Psychiat./Mental Health Nursing, Tex. Woman's U., 1976. RN, Tex., Ky.; lic. advanced practice RN, profl. counselor, marriage and family therapist, Tex.; cert. group psychotherapist. Charge nurse med. and pediatric units Murray (Ky.)-Calloway County Hosp., 1970-71; team leader surg./renal transplant unit VA Hosp., Nashville, 1971-73; team leader, charge nurse gen. med.-surg. unit Providence Hosp., Waco, Tex., 1973-74; outpatient therapist Mental Hygiene Clinic, Ft. Hood, Tex., 1975-76; outpatient nurse therapist Ctrl. Counties Ctr. for Mental Health/Mental Retardation, Copperas Cove & Lampasas, Tex., 1977-80; psychiat. nurse clin. specialist, marriage/family therapist Profl. Counseling Svc., Copperas Cove, 1979—. Cons. Metroplex Hosp. and Pavilion, Killeen, Tex., 1980—. Founding mem. Family Outreach of Coryell County, 1986—, past pres. and past sec.; founding memd. Partnership for a Drug and Violence-Free Copperas Cove; advocate Tex. Peer Assistance Program for Nurses, Walk to Emmaus, 1993; disaster mental health svc. counselor ARC, 1998. Recipient Mary M. Roberts Writing award Am. Jour. of Nursing, 1970; named Mem. of Yr.-Vol., Family Outreach of Coryell County. Mem. ANA (cert. clin. specialist in adult psychiat. and mental health nursing, cert. clin. specialist in child and adolescent psychiat. and mental health nursing), Tex. Nurses Assn., Am. Group Psychotherapy Assn. (cert.), Inst. for Humanities at Salado, Sigma Theta Tau. Democrat. Methodist. Avocations: genealogy, camping, nature activities, music, sports. Office: Profl Counseling Svc 806 E Avenue D Ste F Copperas Cove TX 76522-2231

TOWNSEND, MARJORIE RHODES, aerospace engineer, engineering executive; b. Washington, Mar. 12, 1930; d. Lewis Boling and Marjorie Olive (Trees) Rhodes; m. Charles Eby Townsend, June 7, 1948; children: Charles Eby Jr., Lewis Rhodes, John Cunningham, Richard Leo. BEE, George Washington U., 1951. Electronic scientist Naval Rsch. Lab., Washington, 1951-59; rsch. engr. to sect. head Goddard Space Flight Ctr.-NASA, Greenbelt, Md., 1959-65, tech. asst. to chief systems divsn., 1965-66, project mgr. small astronomy satellites, 1966-75, project mgr. applications explorer missions, 1975-76, mgr. preliminary systems design group, 1976-80; aerospace and electronics cons. Washington, 1980-83; v.p. systems devel. Space Am., 1983-84; aerospace cons. Washington, 1984-90; dir. space systems engring. BDM Internat., Inc., Washington, 1990-91; dir. space applications BDM ESC, Washington, 1991-92; sr. prin. staff mem. BDM Fed., Inc., Washington, 1992-93. Aerospace cons., Washington, 1993—. Patentee digital telemetry system. Decorated Knight Italian Republic Order, 1972; recipient Fed. Women's award, 1973, EUR award for Culture, 1974, Engr. Alumni Achievement award George Washington U., 1975, Gen. Alumni Achievement award George Washington U., 1976, Exceptional Svc. medal NASA, 1971, Outstanding Leadership medal NASA, 1980, Eye-of-the-Needle award NASA, 1991. Fellow IEEE (chmn. Washington sect. 1974-75), AIAA (chmn. nat. capitol sect. 1985), AAAS (coun. del. 1985-88), Washington Acad. Sci. (pres. 1980-81); mem. Internat. Acad. Astronautics, Am. Geophys. Union, Soc. Women Engrs., Wing of Aerospace Med. Assn., Inc. (hon.), DAR, Daus. Colonial Wars, Mensa, Sigma Kappa, Sigma Delta Epsilon (hon.). Republican. Episcopalian. Home and Office: 3529 Tilden St NW Washington DC 20008-3122 Office Phone: 202-966-2330. E-mail: mrtownsend@aol.com.

TOWNSEND, SUE JOYCE, retired air traffic controller; b. Delhi, N.Y., June 1, 1941; d. John and Ida Frances (Turner) Mostert; m. Burdette David Townsend, June 28, 1986 (dec. Nov. 1997). BGS, George Washington U., 1977. Cert. paralegal; lic. real estate salesperson, N.Y., Fla.; lic. real estate broker, Fla. Air traffic controller, instrument instr. Ross Aviation Inc., Ft. Rucker, Ala., 1966-68; air traffic controller Eastern region FAA, 1968-91. Flow controller N.Y. TRACON, Westbury, 1982-83, tng. instr., 1983-84; FAA supr. Binghamton (N.Y.) Tower, 1984-88. Chair Town of Delhi Zoning Bd., 1991-93; mem. Delaware County Planning Bd., Delhi, 1992—; pres. Delhi Beautification Com., 1999—. Served with U.S. Army, 1959-66. Recipient Legis. Resolution, N.Y. state Senate, 1999. Mem. Am. Legion (post 190 Delhi), Profl. Women Controllers (co-founder, 1st pres.), Kiwanis (pres. Delhi). Avocations: golf, bicycling, swimming, travel, camping. Office: Harry W Hawley Realty 4 Court St Delhi NY 13753-1082 also: ERA Mt Vernon Sarasota FL 34234 Home: 4997 Stonecastle Dr Venice FL 34293-8203 E-mail: susiet@Catskill.net.

TOWNSEND, TERRY, publishing executive; b. Camden, N.J., Dec. 14, 1920; d. Anthony and Rose DeMarco; m. Paul Brorstrom Townsend, Dec. 8, 1961; 1 child, Kim. BA, Duke U., 1942; LHD (hon.), Dowling Coll., 1991. Dir. pub. rels. North Shore U. Hosp., Manhasset, NY, 1953—68; pres. Theatre Soc., L.I., 1967—70, Townsend Comm. Bur., L.I., 1970—98; ptnr. L.I. Communicating Svc., Bellport, 1977—. Pub. L.I. Bus. News, 1979-98, pub. emeritus, 1998—; v.p. ParrMeadows Racetrack, Yaphank, N.Y., 1977; mem. Bellport Archtl. Rev. Bd., 1997—. Columnist, writer L.I./Bus., Ronkonkoma, 1970-75. Assoc. trustee North Shore U. Hosp., 1968—; bd. govs. Adelphi U. Friends Fin. Edn., 1978-85; chmn. ann. archtl. awards competition N.Y. Inst. Tech., 1970-83; trustee Dowling Coll., 1984—; trustee L.I. Fine Arts Mus., 1984-85; pub. broadcasting PBS Sta. WLIW TV, Garden City, L.I., N.Y., 1990-93; bd. dirs. Family Svc. Assn. Nassau County, 1982-92; dinner chmn. L.I. 400 Ball, 1987; trustee L.I. Mus. Art, 1994-2003. Recipient Media award 110 Ctr. Bus. and Profl. Women, 1977, Enterprise award Friends of Fin. Edn., 1981, L.I. Loves Bus. Showcase Salute, 1982, Cmty. Svc. award N.Y. Diabetes Assn., 1983, Disting. Long Islander in Comm. award L.I. United Epilepsy Assn., 1984, Spl. award Dowling Coll. Spring Tribute, 1989, Disting. Svc. award Episcopal Health Svcs., 1989, Disting. Citizen award Dowling Coll., 1991, Gilbert Tilles award Nat. Assn. Fundraising Execs., 1994, Hadassah Cmty. Svc. award, 1996, Golden rule award Little Village Sch., 1997, Lifetime Achievement award L.I. Assn., 1998, Promote L.I. Achievement award, 1998, Lifetime Achievement award Advancement for Commerce & Industry, 1999; named 1st Lady of L.I., L.I. Pub. Rels. Assn., 1973, L.I. Woman of Yr. L.I. Assn. Action Com., 1989; Paul and Terry Townsend Sch. of Bus., Dowling Coll., designated in her honor, 2004. Mem.: Bellport Women's Golf Club (pres. 2003—04), Deepdale Golf Club (assoc.). Office: LI Communicating Svcs PO Box 915 Bellport NY 11713-0915 E-mail: terytowns@aol.com.

TOWNSEND, WENDY, retired marketing executive; b. N.Y.C., Nov. 28, 1942; d. Paul Brorstrom Townsend and Ruth Grace (Moerchen) Burgess; m. Robert Joe Baker, Aug. 2, 1970; children: Lynn Baker, Robert Baker, Michelle Townsend. BS, Boston U., 1965; MA, Antioch U., Seattle, 1993. Comm. specialist GE Co., Lynn, Mass., 1964-67; pub. rels. dir. Unitarian-Universalist Svc. Com., Boston, 1967-70; comm. specialist Gen. Foods Co., Sydney, Australia, 1974-75; pub. rels. devel. dir. Seattle-King County Coun. of Camp Fire, 1976-83; east reg. pub. rels. mgr. Group Health Coop., Seattle, 1983-85; v.p. mktg. Wash. Credit Union, Lynnwood, 1986-96; prin. Townsend Assocs. West, Seattle, 1996—2000; v.p. mktg. Washington's Credit Union, Mountlake Terrace, Wash., 2000—04; ret., 2004. Nat. tng. staff Camp Fire, 1979-80; bd. dirs. Victory Hts. Cmty. Coun., Seattle, 1992-94; cons. strategic planning EarthSave, Seattle, 1994-97; mem. mktg. com. Youth Care, Seattle, 1997. Mem. AAUW (pres. 1971), Pub. Rels. Soc. Am. (accredited, chpt. pres. and bd. dirs. 1996, assembly del. 2000—, Totem award 1980), Mktg. Comm. Execs. Internat. (bd. dirs. 1992-96), Women in Comm. (chpt. pres. 1981-82, bd. dirs. 1980-86). Episcopalian. Avocations: hiking, yoga, creative writing. Home: 10312 17th Ave NE Seattle WA 98125-7661

TOWNSEND-BUTTERWORTH, DIANA BARNARD, educational consultant, educator; b. Albany, N.Y., Dec. 12; d. Barnard and Marjorie (Bradley) Townsend; m. J. Warner Butterworth, Jan. 23, 1969; children: James, Diana. AB, Harvard-Radcliffe Coll., 1960; MA, Tchrs. Coll., Columbia U., 1971. Tchr. St. Bernard's Sch., N.Y.C., 1963-78, head of lower sch. English, 1965-71, head of jr. sch., 1971-78; assoc. dir. Early Care Ctr., N.Y.C., 1984-87; acad. advisor Columbia Coll., N.Y.C., 1987-88; ednl. cons., lectr. N.Y.C., 1988—. Dir. parent involvement initiative Ctr. Ednl. Outreach & Innovation, Tchrs. Coll., Columbia U., 1996, chmn. devel. com. alumni coun. Tchrs. Coll., 1994-98; chmn. sub-com. Harvard schs. com. Harvard Coll., Cambridge, Mass., 1975—. Author: Preschool and Your Child: What You Should Know, 1995, Your Child's First School, 1992 (Parent's Choice award 1992), (book chpt.) Handbook of Clinical Assessment of Children and Adolescents; contbr. articles to ednl. publs. and jours. Mem. women's health symposium steering com. N.Y. Hosp., N.Y.C., 1988—. Mem. Assn. Lower Sch. Heads (co-founder 1975), Alumni Coun. Tchrs. Coll. (com. chair 1993-98), Harvard Faculty Club. Avocations: skiing, hiking, swimming, theater, reading. Home: 1170 5th Ave New York NY 10029-6527

TOWSLEE, JANET L., special education educator; b. Louisville, Apr. 4, 1942; d. James and Juanita (Flowers) T.; m. Donald Collier, Aug. 28, 1964; children: Richard Louis, Rebecca Elizabeth. BS in Russian Studies, Fla. State U., 1963; MA in Spl. Edn., U. Louisville, 1967; EdD in Spl. Edn., Ind. U., 1974. Cert. tchr. spl. edn. Tchr. Jefferson County Schs., Louisville, 1963-69; teaching asst. Ind. U., Bloomington, 1969-72; with dept. spl. edn. Ga. State U., Atlanta, 1972—, assoc. dean, dir. ednl. field svcs. dean's office, 1978-91; faculty dept. spl. edn. Clayton State Coll., 1992—. Instr. edn. U. Louisville, 1966-67, 69; tchr. basic adult edn. Jefferson County Bd. Edn., 1963-69. Author: Future Educator of America Handbook, 1989, 91, 93; editorial cons. Profl. Educator, 1986—; contbr. articles, book revs. to profl. jours. Bd. dirs. Tommy Nobis Ctr., 1987—, also twice pres. Recipient Outstanding Svc. award Tommy Nobis Ctr., 1987; named Disting. Adminstr. of Yr. Mortar Bd. Ga. State U., 1983. Mem. Assn. Tchr. Educators (one of 70 Leaders Tchr. Edn. 1990, pres. 1987-88, Pres. award for Svc. 1983, 86, Honor Roll 1984), Comparative and Internat. Edn. Soc., Nat. Coun. States Insvc. Edn., U.S.-China Tchr. Edn. Consortium, Assn. Spl. Edn. Tech., Coun. Exceptional Children Internat. (divs. mental retardation, tchr. edn., career devel. internat. edn. and svcs.), Am. Assn. Colls. Tchr. Edn. (NCATE exec. bd.), S.E. Regional Assn. Tchr. Educators, Ga. Assn. Tchr. Educators, Ga. Staff Devel. Coun., Ga. Coun. Exceptional Children, Met. Atlanta Tchr. Edn. Group. Home: 1194 W Nancy Creek Dr NE Atlanta GA 30319-1644

TOWSNER, CYNTHIA MERLE, academic administrator, educator; b. Washington, Apr. 23, 1939; d. Philip and Edith Towsner; married, 1963; 1 child, Scott David Garrison. BS, U. Md., 1961, postgrad., 1964-65, Am. U., 1987. cert. contracting officer's rep., U.S. Dept. Edn. Tchr. Montgomery County Pub. Schs., Rockville, Md., 1961-66, 72-80; spl. asst. to commr. rehab. svcs. adminstrn. U.S. Dept. Edn., Washington, 1981—85, spl. asst. to the dir. Office Intergovtl. & Interagy. Affairs, 1985—87, acting dir. intergovtl. affairs office, 1987, ednl. program specialist Office Bilingual Edn. & Minority Languages Affairs, 1987—93, edn. program specialist Bilingual Vocat. Tng., 1993—96, nat. coord. health literacy and literacy vols. for adults, 1996—2002, coord lit. vols., 1996—, coord. lit. vols., health literacy, 2005—. Pres. Office Vocat. Adult Edn., U.S. Dept. Edn., Educare Programs, Inc., Chevy Chase, Md., 1988—; cons. R.J. Comer Comm., Inc., Jacksonville, Fla., 1995-97; v.p. Dalmahoy Group Internat., Chevy Chase, 1997-99. Photographer Project Education Reform: Time for Results, vol. 1, 1987. Vol. Holy Cross Hosp., Silver Spring, Md., 1969-74; asst. to pres. for edn. issues, chair nominating com., chair cmty. directory Rock Creek Hills Civic Assn., Kensington, 1968-85; v.p. D.C., Md. and Va. region, chair youth rally, chair radiothon publicity St. Jude's Children's Rsch. Hosp., Aiding Leukemia Stricken Am. Children, Memphis, 1969-81; chair internat. festival Larchmont Elem. Sch. PTA, Montgomery County, MD, 1976-78; bd. dirs., mem., chair Citizens for Edn., Montgomery County, Md., 1977-82; active Renaissance Women, Washington, 1983-87; chair corp. and bus. contbns. Hosp. Relief Fund for the Caribbean, Chevy Chase, 1989-91, annual ball com., 1989-94; vol. tutor Laubach Literacy Action and Literacy Vols. Am., Chevy Chase, 1989-93. Recipient Meritorious Svc. medal Am. Automobile Assn., Washington, Honors award Rock Creek Hills Civic Assn., Kensington, Md., 1979, Pres. award Combined Fed. Campaign, Washington, 1987, Hammer award V.P. of the U.S., Washington, 1996, 1st place ribbon in photography Montgomery County Agrl. Fair, Gaithersburg, Md., 1998, 1st, 2d and 3d place ribbons in photography Montgomery County Agrl. Fair, Gaithersburg, 1999, 1st and 2d place ribbons in photography Md. State Fair, Timonium, 1999, 1st pl. award Md. State Fair, 2000, Achievement in Amateur Photography award, Internat. Libr. Photographs, 2004. Mem. AAUW, Internat. Freelance Photographers Orgn. (life, Master Photographer 2002), Assn. for Career and Tech. Edn., Soc. Govt. Meeting Profls., Nat. Trust for Scotland, Nat. Mus. Women in the Arts (founding mem.), Nat. Women's History Mus. (charter mem.). Avocations: photography, reading, travel. Home: 4620 N Park Ave Apt 1404E Chevy Chase MD 20815-4563 Personal E-mail: cindy.towsner@verizon.net.

TOZZI, DEBORAH FRANCES, elementary school educator; d. J. and A. Poland; m. Russell Tozzi, Aug. 0, 1971; children: Douglas, Roberta. BS in Edn. with honors, Ga. State U., 1988; MEd, U. Ga., 1996, EdS, 2000. Cert. Reading Recovery Coun. N.Am. Tchr. Norcross (Ga.) Elem. Sch., 1988—. Mem.: Kappa Delta Pi (classroom tchr. grantee 2003, 2005). Office Phone: 770-448-2188.

TRACHUK, LILLIAN ELIZABETH, music educator; b. Monroe, Wis., July 28, 1921; d. William John Blair and Stella Mae Harness-Blair; m. Max A. Trachuk, Dec. 21, 1949 (dec. Sept. 1983); children: Thomas Max, William Anton. Piano tchr., Newport News, Va., 1964—. Home: 101 Burnham Pl Newport News VA 23606 Office Phone: 757-595-3588. Personal E-mail: gaeltrachuk@verizion.net.

TRACY, ANN ANDERSON, pediatrician; b. Buffalo, Oct. 13, 1918; d. Ernest David and Anna Veronica; m. Charles Klall Tracy, Sept. 6, 1947 (dec. Nov. 2003); children: Charles Anderson, Donald Anderson. BA, Trinity U., Wash., DC, 1940; MD, SUNY, Buffalo, 1958. Pediatric resident Buffalo Children's Hosp., NY, 1958—61; pvt. practice in pediatrics Buffalo, 1961—64; resident psychiatry Buffalo State Hosp., 1964—68, psychiatrist, 1968—72; psychiatrics West Seneca State Sch., NY, 1972—77. Home: 2200N Lakeside Dr Lake Worth FL 33460

TRACY, JANET RUTH, law educator, law librarian, director; b. Denison, Iowa, July 16, 1941; d. L. M. and Grace (Harvey) T.; m. Rodd Mc Cormick Reynolds, Feb. 15, 1975 (dec. June 1993); children: Alexander, Lee. BA, U. Oreg., 1963; ML, U. Wash., 1964; JD, Harvard U., 1969. Bar: N.Y. 1970. Reference libr. Harvard Coll. Librs., Cambridge, Mass., 1964-66; assoc. Kelley Drye & Warren, N.Y.C., 1969-71; dir. data base design Mead Data Ctrl., Inc., N.Y.C., 1971-75; dir. rsch. Mvpl. Employees Legal Svc. Fund, N.Y.C., 1975-76; from asst. to assoc. prof. N.Y. Law Sch., N.Y.C., 1976-82; asst. libr. dir. Law Libr. Columbia U., N.Y.C., 1982-86; prof., law libr. dir. Fordham U., N.Y.C., 1986—2004; ret., 2004. Chmn. Conf. Law Librs. Jesuit Univs., 1988-89. Co-author: Professional Staffing and Job Security in Academic Law Libraries, 1989. Recipient Catalog Automation award Winston Found., 1990, 91, 92. Home: 285 Riverside Dr New York NY 10025-5276 Office: Fordham U Sch of Law 140 W 62nd St New York NY 10023-7407 E-mail: jtracy@law.fordham.edu.

TRACY, NADINE RUTH, secondary school educator; b. Sandimas, Calif., July 20, 1973; d. Terry and Clifford Curtis; m. Gerald Tracy, Feb. 18, 1994; 1 child, Dean. BS in Theatre Arts, Weber State U., Utah, 1996; MEd (hon.), U. Phoenix, Utah. Lic. Profl. Educators Bd. Edn., Utah, 2005, cert. Career and Technical Edn. Utah State Bd. of Edn., 2005, American Sign Lang. Utah State Bd. of Edn., 2005, Theatre Arts 6-12 Utah State Bd. of Edn., 2005, ESL Endorsement Davis Sch. Dist., Utah State Bd., 2005. Theatre tech. Weber State U., Ogden, Utah, 1991—95; asst. mgr. Mullboons, Ogden, Utah, 1993—95; tchrs. aide Utah Sch. for Deaf and Blind, Ogden, Utah, 1995—97; drama tchr. Roy Jr. High, Utah, 1999—2000; Am. sign lang. and drama tchr. Roy HS, Utah, 1997—. Adv. bd. co-chair HOSA, Salt Lake City, 2005—06. Mem.: Health Occupations Students of Am. (licentiate; adv. bd. co-chair 2005—06, One Yr. Svc. award 2005). Home: 8154 Shepherd Ogden UT 84408 Office: Roy HS 2150 W 4800 South Roy UT 84067 Office Phone: 801-476-3600.

TRACY, SAUNDRA J., academic administrator; m. Doug Tracy; children: Steve, Elaine. BA in Spanish, Carroll Coll., Waukesha, Wis., 1968; M Ed in Fgn. Lang. Instrn., U. Pitts., 1971; PhD in Edn. Adminstrn., Purdue U., West Lafayette, Ind., 1981. Dir. Greater Cleve. Adminstr. Assessment Ctr., 1968—88; asst. to assoc. prof. edn. Cleve. State U., 1981—88; exec. dir. sch. study coun. Lehigh U., 1989—91, dir. ednl. programs Lee Iacocca Inst., 1990—92, assoc. prof. to prof. edn., 1988—94; dean of coll. of edn. Butler U., 1994—98; v.p. acad. affairs Mt. Union Coll., 1998—2001; pres. Alma Coll., 2001—. Fellow, Am. Coun. of Edn., 1992—93. Office: Alma Coll 614 West Superior St Alma MI 48801-1599 Office Phone: 989-463-7146.

TRADER, PATRICIA ANNETTE, music educator; b. Royal Oak, Mich., June 23, 1964; d. William Richard and Janet Arlene Lee; m. Kevin Patrick Trader, Aug. 14, 1987. BME, Grand Valley State U., Mich., 1986. Tchr. Franklin Schs., NH, 1991—; organist, choir dir. United Meth. Ch. of Sunapee, NH, 1995—. Mem.: MENC. Home: PO Box 356 North Sutton NH 03260 Office: Franklin Mid Sch 200 Sanborne St Franklin NH 03235 Office Phone: 603-934-5828. Office Fax: 603-934-2432. Business E-Mail: ptrader@franklin.k12.nh.us.

TRAFFORD, ABIGAIL, columnist, editor, writer; b. NYC, July 14, 1940; d. William Bradford and Abigail (Sard) T.; children: Abigail Brett Miller, Victoria Brett. BA cum laude, Bryn Mawr Coll., 1962. Researcher Nat. Geog. Soc., Washington, 1964-67; tchr. Hermansberg Mission, Northern Ter., Australia, 1967-68; spl. corr. Time mag., The Washington Post, Houston, 1969-74; writer, asst. mng. editor U.S. News & World Report, Washington, 1975-86; health editor The Washington Post, 1986-00, columnist, 2000—. Author: Crazy Time: Surviving Divorce and Building a New Life, 1982, revised edit., 1992, My Time: Making the Most of the Rest of Your Life, 2004. Journalism fellow Harvard Sch. Pub. Health, 1980, 2000; sr. fellow Civic Ventures. Mem. Washington Press Club Found. (bd. mem. 1989—, pres. 1993-95). Home: 2600 Upton St NW Washington DC 20008-3826 Office Phone: 202-966-3516. Business E-Mail: trafforda@washpost.com.

TRAHAN, ELLEN VAUNEIL, retired foundation administrator, public information officer; b. Rosie, Ark., June 30, 1941; d. Jess James Ross and Ellen Alabama (Spears) Massey; m. Terrance Dale Trahan, June 9, 1961; children: Ginny-Marie, Anthony Scott, Julie Jeanette. BA in Home Econs., Magic Valley Christian Coll., Albion, Idaho, 1962; BA in Psychology, Pepperdine U., 1966; postgrad., Willamette U., 1983-84; MBA, Chaminade U., Honolulu, 1985. Social worker Los Angeles Dept. Social Service, 1966-70; adminstr. Socialization Ctr. Marion County Mental Health Clinic, Salem, Oreg., 1973; social service worker Fairview Hosp. and Tng. Ctr., Salem, 1973-85; exec. dir. Autistic Vocat. Edn. Ctr., Honolulu, 1986-89; supr. adult clin. svcs. community mental health Cen. Oahu Community Mental Health, Mental Health Div. Hawaii, Pearl City, 1989—2004; social work supr. Hawaii State Hosp., 1999—2004; ret., 2004. Supr. practicum Sch. Social Work U. Hawaii. Mem. bus. adv. com. Supported Employment Task Force, Goodwill Corp, 1986-87; orgn. cons. Fairview Parents Club, Salem, 1977-85; advisor Honolulu Dept. Health Community Service to Developmentally Disabled, 1986-91. Mem. NAFE, ACLU, NOW, Nat. Soc. Autistic Citizens, Assn. Retarded Citizens, Nat. Alliance for the Mentally Ill. Home: 250 Ohua Ave Apt 8D Honolulu HI 96815-3634 E-mail: trahane001@hawaii.rr.com.

TRAHAN, GRACE, newscaster; m. Joe Rodecap; 1 child. BA in Mass Comms., Okla. City U., 1987. Anchor KFDM-TV, Beaumont, Tex.; reporter Sta. WRTV-TV, Indpls., 1994, anchor, 1994—. Recipient Tex. Sch. Bell award. Office: WRTV TV 1330 N Meridian St Indianapolis IN 46202

TRAICOFF, SANDRA M., lawyer; b. O'Neill, Nebr., Aug. 31, 1944; d. Theodore Edwin and Ella Pauline (Fuhrer) Rustemeyer; m. Chris J. Traicoff, Feb. 17, 1973. BA in Polit. sci. and Asian studies, U. Kans., 1967; MA in L.S, U. Ill., 1970; JD, DePaul U., 1978. Bar: Ill. 1978, Mich. 1990. Asst. reference and documents libr. U. Ill. Law Libr., Urbana, 1970—73; assoc. libr. head pub. svcs. DePaul U. Law Libr., Chgo., 1973—77; loan rev. officer Comml. Nat. Bank of Peoria, Ill., 1978—82; corp. sec. Midwest Fin. Group, Inc., Peoria, 1982—86, v.p., sec. and gen. counsel, 1986—89; atty. Howard & Howard Attys. P.C., Peoria, 1989—. Lectr. Grad. Sch. Libr. Scis., U. Chgo., 1975—77; lectr., cons. Comml. Nat. Mgmt. Cons. Co., Peoria, 1979—82. Bd. dirs. Heart of Ill. Big Bros./Big Sisters, Peoria, 1981—86, pres. bd., 1981—82; bd. dirs., mem. coms. YWCA, Peoria, 1981—92, bd. dirs., 1986—92, v.p., 1987—89, pres. bd., 1989—91. Fellow Univ. Fellow, U. Ill., Urbana, 1968; scholar Regents scholar, U. Colo., Boulder, 1962. Mem.: Peoria County Bar Assn., Mich. Bar Assn., Ill. Bar Assn., ABA, Beta Phi Mu. Home: 912 W Shoreline Ct Dunlap IL 61525-9541

TRAIL, MARGARET ANN, retired employee benefits company executive, rancher; b. Bryan, Tex., July 17, 1941; d. Louis Milton and Margaret (Stromberg) Thompson; m. Robert A. Rosemier, Aug. 25, 1962 (div. Feb. 1973); 1 child: Gretchen Elisabeth Jolly; m. Newt Shands Trail, Dec. 4, 1989. BSN, U. Iowa, 1963; MS, No. Ill. U., 1971. Instr. Cooley Dickinson Hosp., Northampton, Mass., 1964-65; dir. nursing De Kalb (Ill.) Pub. Hosp., Kishwaukee Cmty. Hosp., 1972—76, Terre Haute (Ind.) Regional Hosp., 1976—78; from mgr. clin. systems to dir. spl. projects Hosp. Corp. Am., Nashville, 1978-86; from dir. med. mgmt. to v.p. Equicor, Nashville, 1986-90; divsn. v.p. The Travelers Ins. Co., Hartford, Conn., 1990-93; asst. v.p. health svcs. quality mgmt. Aetna, Hartford, 1993—2003, ret., 2003. Mem. LWV (pres. DeKalb chpt. 1970-72) Avocations: gardening, beekeeping, genealogy.

TRAILLE, JOY MYRA, microbiologist, eldercare service provider; arrived in U.S., 1971; d. Randolph and Leanorah Williams; m. Winston Traille, June 6, 1981; children: Nichola Davis, Kevin. MS, L.I. U., 1981; PhD, Union Inst., Cin., 1991; MBA, Iona, New Rochelle, N.Y., 2002. Cert. Am. Soc. Clin. Pathologist, 1981. Med. technologist Gouverneur Hosp./NYU, N.Y.C., 1978—83; microbiology clin. scientist Kingsbrook Jewish Med. Ctr., Blkyn., 1983—87; microbiologist Mary Immaculate Hosp., Jamaica, NY, 1987—91; adminstrv. dir. Manhattan Eye Ear & Throat Hosp, N.Y.C., 1991—98; dir. Cryobank for Oncology & Reproduction, Middletown, NY, 1998—; owner/pres. Comfort Keepers, Cortlandt Manor, NY, 2003—. Infectious disease bd. mem. Manhattan Eye Ear & Throat Hosp., N.Y.C., 1991—98; adv. bd. mem. Cryobank for Oncology & Reproduction, Middletown, NY, 1998—. Author, pub.: magazine Caribbean Heritage, 1999—2003; author: (a handbook for caregivers) You Are Not Alone, 1991. Adv. bd. coun. eldercare United Way, Westchester, NY, 2004—05. Mem.: Soc. For Cert. Sr. Advisors, Am. Soc. Microbiology. Avocations: writing, reading, travel, drama/musicals, dance. Office: Comfort Keepers Ste 104B 2127 Crompond Rd Cortlandt Manor NY 10566 Office Phone: 914-734-2616. Business E-Mail: peekskill@comfortkeepers.com.

TRAIMAN, HELEN, school nurse practitioner; d. David Resnick and Rebecca Gertz; m. Samuel Traiman, June 14, 1949 (dec. 1986); children: Susan, Elliot, Leonard. Degree in Nursing, Kings County Hosp., 1945; BS, Jersey City State Coll., 1971. RN N.Y., 1946. Pub. health nurse N.Y.C. (N.Y.) Dept. Health, Bklyn., 1946—51; pvt. duty nurse North Jersey, 1957—60; sch. nurse substitute West Paterson (N.J.) Schs., 1959—64; sch. nurse West Paterson (N.J.) Mid. Sch., 1964—90, ret., 1990. Camp nurse various camps, NY, 1964—68. Mem.: Jewish Cmty. Ctr. Greater Washington (vol. meal server 1997—99). Avocation: singing.

TRAINER, KARIN A., librarian; BA in English, Rutgers U., 1970; grad. work in English, Bryn Mawr Coll.; MLIS, Drexel U., 1972; M in liberal studies, NYU, 1983. Descriptive catalogue Libraries of Princeton U., 1972—74, catalogue maintenance libr., 1974—78; dir. tech. and automated services NYU Libraries, 1978—83; assoc. univ. libr. Yale U., 1983—96, fellow and freshman advisor Ezra Stiles Coll.; univ. libr. Princeton U., 1996—. Office: Princeton U Libr One Washington Rd Princeton NJ 08544 Office Phone: 609-258-3170. Business E-Mail: ktrainer@princeton.edu.*

TRAINES, ROSE WUNDERBAUM, sculptor, educator; b. Monroeville, Ind., Sept. 13, 1928; d. Louis and Leah (Fogel) Wunderbaum; m. Robert Jacob Traines, June 25, 1949; children: Claudia Denise Traines Lang, Monica Rae Traines Martin Student, Ind. State Tchr.'s Coll., 1946—48, Mich. State U., 1948—49; BS, Ctrl. Mich. U., 1951. Lectr. in field. One person shows include Ctrl. Mich. U., Mt. Pleasant, 1964, Alma Artmobile, Mich., 1972, Ctrl. Mich. Homecoming, Mount Pleasant, 1982, Internat. Inst. Scrap Iron and Steel, Inc., Washington, 1983, Fontainebleau Hotel, Miami Beach, Fla., 1983, Elliott Mus. Art Gallery, Stuart, Fla., 1988, 98, Walt Kuhn Gallery, Cape Neddick, Maine, 1988, Coll. Club Boston, 1990, Brass Latch Gallery, Montpelier, Ind., 1991, 96, 98, Vero Beach Ctr. Arts, Fla., 1992, Maritime and Yachting Mus., Stuart, 1997, Mid-Mich. Regional Med. Ctr., Healing Arts Gallery, Midland, 1997, Northwood Gallery, Midland, Commerca Bank Art Series, Palm Beach Gardens, 2002, Gallery Five, Tequesta, Fla., 2002, Mich. U. Park Libr. Gallery, 2002, Art Reach Mid. Mich., Mt. Pleasant, 2002, Arthur Glick Jewish Cmty. Ctr., Indpls., 2004, Art Reach Ctr. Mid-Mich., Mt. Pleasant, Elliott Mus. Gallery, Stuart, Fla., 2006; two-person shows include Gallery One, North Palm Beach, 1973, Midland Ctr. Arts, 1976, Springfield Art Mart, Ohio, 1977, Hillel Student Ctr. Gallery-U. Cin., 1993; exhibited in group shows including Saginaw Mus. Art, Mich., 1965, Grand Rapids Mus., Mich., 1966, Kalamazoo Mus., Mich., 1967, Kellogg/Kresge Art Ctr., Mich. State U., East Lansing, 1967, Art Reach Mid-Mich., 1987, Salmagundi Club, N.Y.C., 1988, 91-92, 96, Copley Soc., Boston, 1990, 95, Allied Artists Am., Inc., N.Y.C., 1995-96, Self Family Arts Ctr., Hilton Head Island, S.C., 1996-97, Palm Beach Gardens Fla. City Hall, 2003, Palm Beach Gardens Cmty. Ctr., 2003, Art Reach Mid Mich., 2006, Elliott Mus., Stuart, Fla., 2006; represented in permanent collections at Dow-Corning Corp. Collection, Midland Ctr. Arts, Elliott Mus., Walt Kuhn Gallery, Coll. Club Boston, Pullen Elem. Sch., Isabella Bank and Trust Co., Ctrl. Mich. U., Blake Libr, Stuart, La Belle Mgmt. Corp., Morey Bandit Industries, Mich., Ctrl. Mich. Cmty. Hosp., Northwood U., Vets. Meml. Libr., Mt. Pleasant, Pub. Libr., Clare, Mich., Brass Latch Gallery, Northville (Mich.) Pub. Libr, Norman Cousins, Carl Gerstacker Found., Fannie Traines, Doctor Tom Keating, Olga and Rollie Denison, Claudia and Yaroh Lang, Marjorie Fishbain, Kitti Pyne, Don Hersee, pvt. collections. Tchr. Jewish Sunday Sch., Mt. Pleasant, 1955-70; officer Child and Youth Study Clubs, Mt. Pleasant, 1963-73; mem. City Recreation Commn., Mt. Pleasant, 1963-73, Area Health Planning Coun., Mt. Pleasant, 1974-80; pres., vol. Hosp. Aux. Med. Care, Red Cross Blood Bank, United Fund Cancer Dr., Mt. Pleasant, 1960-80; storyteller pub. libr., Mt. Pleasant, 1957-79 Recipient Northwood U. Artist award, Midland Ctr. for Arts, Mich., 2002. Mem.: Brass Latch Gallery, Art Reach Mid-Mich., Hilton Head Art League S.C. (Lifetime of Creative Excellence award 1998), Copley Soc. Boston (signature), Allied Artists Am. (Merit award 1996, Raymond H. Brumer Meml. award 1999), Nat. Mus. Women in Arts (charter), Salmagundi Club (Philip Isenberg award 1993, Pamela Singleton award 1997, Elliot Liskin Meml. award 1998, Anonymous award 1998, Peters Sculpture Materials award 2001, Alphaeus P. Cole Meml. award 2001, Meml. award 2003). Jewish. Avocations: lecturing, community work, tennis, presenting humorous programs, drums. Home: 1217 North Dr Mount Pleasant MI 48858-3226 Office Phone: 989-773-3873. Personal E-mail: fundametal2@webtv.net.

TRAINOR, SHEENA MARIE, music educator; d. Joseph Edward and Kathy Ann Trainor. BSc in Music Edn., Chestnut Hill Coll., Phila., 2004. Music dir. Bishop McDevitt H.S., Wyncote, Pa., 2004—; gen. music tchr. Queen of Peace Cath. Sch., Ardsley, Pa., 2004—; choral dir. Archbishop Ryan H.S., Phila., 2004—. Mem.: Music Educators Nat. Conf.

TRALIS-LEVY, DESPI, writer, painter; b. Ansonia, Conn., Mar. 11, 1918; d. Peter and Anna (Pappas) Tralis. Student, Wash. U., St. Louis, 1944—45, Am. Acad. Art, N.Y.C., 1946, Art Students League, 1947—49. Asst. NYU, 1950—53. Exhibitions include Borgenicht Gallery, N.Y.C., 1952—56, Poindexter Gallery, 1957—58, Coliseum Gallery, 1957, UN Gallery, 1960; author: (novels) Mariquita, 1965, The Candidate From Hotchkiss Corners, 1968, The Geritol Baracudas Dixieland Murder Mystery, 1973, Deisidemonia, 1980, (plays) The Pawn's Queening, 1967, The Elderdown Quilt, 1969. Widow Harris Levy scholar, Am. Acad. Art, 1946. Mem.: Dramatists Guild. Greek Orthodox. Avocations: violin, flamenco guitar.

TRAMMEL, DENISE, science educator; b. Cin., Ohio, Oct. 28, 1952; d. Benjamin Thomas and Imogene Gilbert; m. James L. Trammel, June 17, 1972; children: Mindy Rae Trammel Moore, James Thomas. BS in Edn., Miami U., Oxford, Ohio, 1980; MEd, Wright State U., Dayton, Ohio, 1987. Cert. tchr. kindergarten - elem. Ohio, lic. gifted and talented grades 1-12 Ohio. Clk. Goodyear, Sharonville, Ohio, 1971; inventory Wickes Furniture, Sharonville, 1971; sec. order svc. GE, Blue Ash, Ohio, 1971—76; substitute tchr. Kings Mills Sch. Dist. Mason City Schs., Mason, Kings Mills, West Chester, Ohio, 1981—83; tchr. Little Miami Sch. Dist., Morrow, Ohio, 1983—88, Mason City Schs., 1988—. 4th grade sci. chairperson Mason City Schs., 1994—2006, ednl. enrichment for kids in sci., 1996—2006. Named Warren County Conservation Tchr. of Yr., 1998; grantee, Western Row Sch. Mem.: Nat. Sci. Tchr. Assn. Republican. Baptist. Avocations: camping, boating, taking cruises, playing piano.

TRAN, ALICE, automotive executive; b. Aurora, Colo., Apr. 12, 1982; d. Hoanh Van and Hanh Ho Tran. BSBA in Mktg., U. Colo., 2004. Regional consumer affairs specialist Nissan N.Am., Inc., Gardena, Calif., 2004—. Avocation: snowboarding.

TRAN, JUDITH THUHA, psychiatrist; arrived in US, 1975; d. Phuong Nguyen and Ailien Huynh; children: Christopher Baoquoc, STephen Anhkhoa. BS in Biology, Tex. U., San Antonio, 1990; MD, Temple U., Phila., 1994. Intern Pa. Hosp., Phila., 1995—96, resident, 1996—99, chief resident, 1998—99; asst. dir. Friends Hosp. Crisis Response Ctr., 1999—2000; med. dir. Friends Hosp., 2000—03, Mercy Hosp. Phila. Crisis Response Ctr., 2003—. Recipient Merit award, Pa. Hosp., 1998—99. Mem.: Phila. Psychiat. Soc. (com. mem. 1999), Am. Psychiat. Assn. Avocations: reading, dance, swimming. Office: Mercy Hosp Phila 501 S 54th St Philadelphia PA 19143

TRANE, LESLIE, science educator; b. Provo, Utah, Dec. 13, 1977; d. Blake and Barbara Trane. BS in Biology, So. Utah U., Cedar City, 2000. Mid. sch. sci. tchr. Jordan Sch. Dist., Riverton, Utah, 2000—. Mem.: NSTA (assoc.).

TRANQUILLO, MARY DORA, organization development consultant, educator; b. Pitts., Apr. 14, 1943; d. Guy and Dora (Grossi) Caranfa; m. Joseph Anthony Tranquillo. BFA, Pratt Inst., 1965; MA, NYU, 1971; PhD, Union Grad. Sch., 1987. Program coord. St. Petersburg Jr. Coll., Clearwater, Fla., 1974—98; prof. Ctrl. Mich. U., 2004—; assoc. campus dean Strayer U., Charlotte, NC. Pres. Productivity Improvement, Safety Harbor, Fla., 1987—. Author: Styles of Fashion, 1984, A New Look at Management Development, 1994, Leading a Diverse Workforce, 1994. Recipient Outstanding Svc. award Distributive Edn. Clubs Am., 1980, award for contbn. to Women's Equality Day, Fed. Women's Program, 1989. Mem. Am. Soc. Tng., Orgn. Devel. Inst., Orgn. Devel. Network, Am. Psychol. Assn., Soc. Psychologists in Mgmt., Married Couples Club (host), NC Indsl. Orgnl. Psychologists So. Mgmt. Assn. Avocations: sewing, crafts, reading, aerobic dancing. Office: Strayer Univ 2430 Whitehall Park Dr Charlotte NC 28273 Home: 9003 Davis Crossing Ct Charlotte NC 28269-3304 Office Phone: 704-587-5449. Business E-Mail: mtr@strayer.edu.

TRANSCHEL, KATE, social sciences educator; b. Concord, Calif., May 13, 1954; d. Bill and Kathryn Transchel; m. Dee Randolph, Sept. 14, 2004. BA, U. Hawaii, Honolulu, 1988; MA, U. NC, Chapel Hill, 1990, PhD, 1996. Prof. Calif. State U., Chico, 1996—. Chairperson Coordinative Coun. on Alcoholism, Moscow, 1992—94. Author: Under the Influence: Working Class Drinking Temperance and Cultural revolution in Russia, 1895-1932, The Breakup of Yugoslavia: Conflict in the Balkans; translator: Our Daily Bread: Socialist Distribution and the Art of Survival. Long-term Rsch. grantee, Internat. Rsch. and Exch. Bd., 1992—93, Summer Rsch. grantee, NEH, 1997, Post Doctoral fellow, Nat. Coun. for Eurasian and East European Rsch., 1999, Academic fellow, Found. for the Def. of Democracies, 2006. Mem.: Am. Assn. for the Advancement Slavic Studies. Buddhist. Avocations: travel, writing, backpacking, scuba diving. Office: California State University Trinity Hall Chico CA 95926-0735 Office Phone: 530-898-6417. Business E-Mail: ktranschel@csuchico.edu.

TRANSOU, LYNDA LOU, advertising art administrator; b. Atlanta, Dec. 11, 1949; d. Lewis Cole Transou and Ann Lynette (Taylor) Putnam; m. Lue Gregg Loso, Oct. 25, 1991. BFA cum laude, U. Tex., 1971. Art dir. The Pitluk Group, San Antonio, 1971, Campbell, McQuien & Lawson, Dallas, 1973-74, Bozell & Jacobs, Dallas, 1974-75; art dir., ptnr. The Assocs., Dallas, 1975-77; art dir. Belo Broadcasting, Dallas, 1977-80; creative dir., v.p. Allday & Assocs., Dallas, 1980-85; owner Lynda Transou Advt. & Design, 1986—. Recipient Merit award, N.Y. Art Dirs. Show, 1980, Gold award, Dallas Ad League, 1980, Silver award, 1980, 1981, 1982, 2 Merit awards, Houston Art Dirs. Club, 1978, Dallas Ad League, 1986, Merit award, Broadcast Designers Assn., 1980, Merit awards, Dallas Ad League, 1978, 1987, Silver award, Houston Art Dirs. Show, 1982, Gold award, Tex. Pub. Rels. Assn., 1985, N.Y. One Show, 1982, Creativity awrd, Art Direction mag., 1986, Print award, Regional Design Annual, 1988, 2 Gold Adrian awards, 1997, Katy award, Dallas Press Club, 2001. Dallas Soc. Visual Comm. (Bronze award 1980, Merit award 1978-86), Delta Gamma (historian 1969-70).

TRANZOR, TINA, elementary school educator; b. Great Lakes, Ill. BA in English, U. Calif., Berkeley, 1989; JD, U. Iowa, Iowa City, 1993; Edn. Specialist Degree, Union U., Germantown, Tenn., 2006. Multiple subject profl. clear lic. Calif. Dept. Edn., 2001. 6th grade tchr. Oakland Unified Sch. Dist., Calif., 2000—02, Memphis City Schs., 2003—. Office Phone: 901-416-3092. Office Fax: 901-416-3093.

TRAPANE, RUTH, educator, artist; b. Danville, Pa., July 18, 1945; d. Richard L. and Oda M. (Sager) Day; m. Mar. 21, 1965 (div. 1983); children: Michael W., Timothy R.; m. Philip B. Trapane, Aug. 23, 1985; stepchildren: Sean, Philip. BS, Bloomsburg U., Pa., 1967, MS, 1975, MA, 1990. Grad. asst. Bloomsburg U., 1989; tchr. Berwick Elem. Sch., Pa., 1967-88, 90—. Speaker 1st European Space Art Symposium & Exhibitor, Montrieux, Switzerland, 1992, tour India 6 wks., 1994; space art exhibitor Spaceweek Internat., 1994, Art on Mir Space Station, First Exhibit in Space, 1995-96, Art to the Stars (Ars Ad Astra) 1996-98, Nova Southeastern U. Author curriculum guides; exhibited in Internat. Encaustic Art Show, Nebr., 1989, Selinsgrove, Pa., 1990 (People's Choice award 1990), Cheney, Wash., 1991, Gagarin Collaboration, Moscow, 1990. Mem. NEA, Pa. Edn. Assn., Internat. Assn. Astron. Artists, Hazelton Art League, Susquehanna Art League, North Mt. Art League. Independent. Avocations: scuba diving, online and mystery games, interior design, video authoring. Home: 511 Hickory Dr Bloomsburg PA 17815-8902

TRAPANI, GINA, web programmer, writer; Spkr. in field. Editor: (weblog on software and productivity) Lifehacker.com, 2005— (PC Mag. lists in its Top 101 Websites, 2005, Time Mag. lists as one of its 50 Coolist Websites, 2005, Editors' award for Online Excellence, The Morning News, 2005, nominee, Bloggie award: Weblog of Yr., Best Group Weblog and Best Computers or Tech. Weblog, 2006, WIRED Rave award-Blogs, 2006); contbr. writings to Popular Science; work mentioned in Time Mag., NY Times, and PC Mag.; prodr.: (monthly online mag. for visual journalism) The Digital Journalist; publisher (web developers notebook) Spun, mng. guest editor Afar, 2005, publisher (column) Ask the Geek, Laptop Mag., 2005.*

TRAPHAGAN, HELEN MARIE, voice educator; b. Orange, Calif., Jan. 17, 1965; d. Robert and Clarissa Hamilton, Walter Barnhart (Stepfather) and Gail Barnekow (Stepmother); m. Russ Traphagan, July 10, 1999; children: Trevor Williams, Robert, Peyton. BS in Edn., Mo. State U., Springfield, 1991. Vocal music tchr. Campbell Elem. Sch., Springfield, 1992—2005, Carver Mid. Sch., Springfield, 2005—. Music dir. Selmore Christian Ch., Ozark, Mo., 2000—. Singer: (performer) Springfield Little Theater and Springfield Regional Opera. Mem.: Mo. Music Educators Assn. Office: Carver Mid Sch 3325 W Battlefield Springfield MO 65807 Office Phone: 417-523-6880. Personal E-mail: htraphagan@spsmail.org.

TRAPP, ANGELA MICHELE, counselor; b. Murfreesboro, Tenn., Jan. 29, 1978; d. Larry Wayne and Sandra Gail Moffitt; m. Steve Donald Trapp, Aug. 2, 2002; 1 child, Dylan. BA in Psychology, Mid. Tenn. State U., Murfreesboro, 2001; MA in Profl. Counseling, Argosy U., Nashville, 2005. Family counselor Youth Villages, Cookeville, Tenn., 2002—04; aid counselor Centerstone, McMinnville, Tenn., 2004—05; counselor Warren County Schs., McMinnville, 2005—. Mem.: Am. Counseling Assn. Avocations: reading, running, sports.

TRASK, PAULA ELIZABETH, mathematics educator; d. Alvin Pierce and Beatrice Louise Trask; life ptnr. Larry Edward Bowden. BS, U. Maine, Orono, Maine, 1978. Math tchr. Bangor Sch. Dept., Bangor, Maine, 1978—. Mem.: NEA, Maine Edn. Assn. D-Conservative. Avocations: reading, cooking. Home: POBox 57 Holden ME 04429 Office: Bangor School Dept/JFDoughty School 143 Fifth St Bangor ME 04401

TRATTNER, LAURA V., middle school eductor; b. East Cleve., Ohio, Oct. 26, 1955; d. Harold and Carol Elaine Trattner. BS in Edn., Bowling Green State U., Ohio, 1977; MA in Edn., Baldwin-Wallace U., Berea, Ohio, 1981. Math. tchr. Parma City Schs., Ohio, 1978—. Grantee 3 mini grants, Parma City Schs., 1995—96. Democrat. Jewish. Avocations: contra, swing and ballroom dancing, gardening, aquacise. Office: Greenbriar Mid Sch 11810 Huftman Rd Cleveland OH 44130 E-mail: trattnerl@parmacityschools.org.

TRAUGER, ALETA ARTHUR, judge; BA in English magna cum laude, Cornell Coll., Iowa, 1968; MAT, Vanderbilt U., 1972, JD, 1976. Tchr., Tenn., Eng., 1970-73; assoc., law clk. Barrett, Brandt & Barrett, P.C., Nashville, 1974-77; asst. U.S. atty., first asst., chief of criminal divsn. Mid. Dist. Tenn., 1977-82, No. Dist. Ill., 1979-80; assoc. Hollins, Wagster & Yarbrough, P.C., Nashville, 1983-84; legal counsel Coll. of Charleston, SC, 1984-85; counsel, ptnr. Wyatt, Tarrant, Combs, Gilbert & Milom, Nashville, 1985-91; judge Tenn. Ct. of the Judiciary, 1987-93; chief of staff Mayor's Office, Nashville, 1991-92; bankruptcy judge U.S. Bankruptcy Ct. (mid. dist.) Tenn., Nashville, 1993-98; dist. judge U.S. Dist. Ct. (mid. dist.) Tenn., Nashville, 1998—. Mem. hearing panel bd. profl. responsibility Tenn. Supreme Ct., 1983-84, mem. adv. com. on rules of civil and appellate procedure, 1989-96; lectr. Vanderbilt U. Sch. Law, 1986-88, mem. Law Sch. alumni bd., 1989-92; master of bench Harry Phillips Am. Inn of Ct., 1990-94; mem. Internat. Women's Forum, 1993—, v.p. Tenn. chpt., 1996-97; mem. Nat. Conf. Bankruptcy Judges, 1994-98, chmn. ethics com., 1994-98; trustee Cornell Coll., 1998—. Bd. dirs. Nashville Inst. for Arts, 1992-99, Miriam's Promise (adoption agy.), 1995-98, Renewal House, 1996-98, trustee Cornell Coll, 1998—2006, mem. Vanderbilt Law Sch. Nat. Coun., 2004—. Fellow: Nashville Bar Found., Tenn. Bar Found. (life), Am. Bar Found. (life); mem.: FBA (v.p. 1983—84, 1985—86), ABA, Fed. Judges Assn., Nat. Assn. Women Judges (liaison to ABA commn. on the status of women in the profession 2000—01), Tenn. Lawyers Assn. for Women (v.p. 1988—89, pres. 1989—90, bd. dirs. 1990—91), Lawyers Assn. for Women (pres. 1982—83, bd. dirs. 1983—84, 1986—88), Nashville Bar Assn. (bd. dirs. 1984, 1989—91). Office: 825 US Courthouse 801 Broadway Nashville TN 37203-3816

TRAUGOTT, ELIZABETH CLOSS, linguist, educator, researcher; b. Bristol, Eng., Apr. 9, 1939; d. August and Hannah M. M. (Priebsch) Closs; m. John L. Traugott, Sept. 26, 1967; 1 child, Isabel. BA in English, Oxford U., Eng., 1960; PhD in English lang., U. Calif., Berkeley, 1964. Asst. prof. English U. Calif., Berkeley, 1964-70; lectr. U. East Africa, Tanzania, 1965-66, U. York, Eng., 1966-67; lectr., then assoc. prof. linguistics and English Stanford (Calif.) U., 1970-77, prof., 1977—2003, chmn. linguistics dept., 1980-85, vice provost, dean grad. studies, 1985-91, mem. grad. record examinations bd., 1989-93, mem. test of English as a fgn. lang. bd., 1990—92, chmn. test of English as a fgn. lang. bd., 1991—92. Mem. higher edn. funding coun. Eng. Assessment Panel, 1996, 2001. Author: (book) A History of English Syntax, 1972; author: (with Mary Pratt) Linguistics for Students of Literature, 1980; author: (with Paul Hopper) Grammaticalization, 1993, rev. edit., 2003; author: (with Richard Dasher) Regularity in Semantic Change, 2002; author: (with Laurel J. Brinton) Lexicalization and Language Change, 2005; editor (with ter Meulen, Reilly, Ferguson): (book) On Conditionals, 1986; editor: (with Heine) Approaches to Grammaticalization, 2 vols., 1991; series co-editor: Topics in English Linguistics; contbr. articles to profl. jours. Am. Coun. Learned Socs. fellow, 1975—76, Guggenheim fellow, 1983—84, Ctr. Advanced Study Behavioral Scis. fellow, 1983—84. Fellow: AAAS; mem.: AAUW, AAUP, MLA, Internat. Pragmatics Assn. (bd. dirs. 2000—), Internat. Soc. Hist. Linguistic (pres. 1979—81), Linguistic Soc. Am. (pres. 1987, sec.-treas. 1994—98). Office: Stanford Univ Dept Linguistics Bldg 460 Stanford CA 94305-2150 Business E-Mail: traugott@stanford.edu.

TRAUTMAN-KUZMA, ALTA LOUISE, nurse, funeral director, writer; b. McKeesport, Pa., Oct. 30, 1954; d. Ernest Bernhardt and Eleanor Jeannette (Runge) Trautman; m. Dennis M. Kuzma. AAS in Nursing, Cmty. Coll. Allegheny County, West Mifflin, Pa., 1974; Diploma Grad. Funeral Dir., Pitts. Inst. Mortuary Sci., 1989. RN Pa.; lic. funeral dir. Pa. Staff nurse U. Pitts. Med. Ctr., McKeesport, 1974-80, emergency room nurse, 1981-2001; flight nurse Allegheny Gen. Hosp., Pitts., 1980-81; arranger, embalmer D.J. Heatherington Funeral Home, 1990-91; funeral dir. Teichart-Gracan Funeral Home, 1999; quality assurance and process improvement coord. Three Rivers Family Hospice, White Oak, Pa., 2000—01; staff nurse, emergency dept. and indsl. nursing Nurse Finders, 2001—03; asst. recovery of flight 93 Shanksville, Pa., 2001; infusion specialist Integrated Health Care Advantage, North Huntington, Pa., 2002—; emergency dept. nurse Jefferson Regional Med. Ctr., 2003—. Cons. in emergency and forensic nursing. Co-compiler, author: Grandma's Favorite Recipes, 1997, co-compiler: Grandma's Lost Recipes, 2002, Hey Good Lookin What's Cooking.Anything Your Heart Desires, Honey!. Lutheran. Avocations: cooking, needlecrafts, altar designs. Office Phone: 412-403-0175. Business E-Mail: rnfd@libcom.com.

TRAUTMANN, PATRICIA ANN, communications educator, storyteller, art educator; b. Hot Springs, SD, Jan. 6, 1932; d. Forest Houston and Clara Ruth (Allen) Doling; m. Robert D. Trautmann, Aug. 11, 1954; children: Kurt, Elaine, Sarah, Cynthia, Gretchen. BA, Jamestown Coll., 1954; MA, U. No. Colo., 1962; PhD, Vanderbilt U., 1984; post grad., Ga. So. U., 1992-93. Tchr. various sch., Colo., ND, Mich., 1954-67; part-time instr. English Kans. State Coll., Pitts., 1967-70; part-time instr. English, children's lit. Baldwin-Wallace Coll., Berea, Parma, Ohio, 1970-73; part-time instr. children's lit., reading, lang. arts U. Tenn., Nashville, 1973-78; English instr. Valdosta H.S., Ga., 1978-82; assoc. prof. English, Speech, Lang., asst. dir. programs Ga. Mil. Coll., Milledgeville, 1982-86; assoc. prof. English, art, humanities, lang. South Ga. Coll., Douglas, 1986-94, chair humanities and art history, 1988-94, prof. art history, 1989; assoc. prof. English, comm. skills Isothermal C.C., Spindale, NC, 1995—, prof. art appreciation and history, 1996—. Cons. for reading, children's books in schs. and other instns., Kans., Ohio, Tenn., Ga., N.C., 1964—. Storyteller, spkr., internat. lore, poetry, children's lit., world mythology, 1967—. Recipient Humanities award, South Ga. Coll., 1993. Mem. AAUW, Music Club. Democrat. Avocations: drawing, painting, singing, gardening, hiking. Home: 257 N Washington St Rutherfordton NC 28139-2405 Office: Isothermal C C Dept English nd Comm Skills Spindale NC 28139 Office Phone: 828-286-3636 x446. Business E-Mail: ptrautma@isothermal.edu.

TRAVAILLE, MADELAINE, science educator; b. Paterson, N.J., Feb. 4, 1974; d. Jesus I. and Surina Cepero; m. Jason M. Travaille, June 28, 1998; children: Abigail Marie, Lily Anna. BS in Environ. Sci., Rutgers U., 1998; MS in Biology, Montclair State U., 2003. Cert. biol. sci., phys. sci. tchr. N.J. Sci. tchr. Montville Twp. HS, NJ, 1998—2004; master tchr. dept. molecular biology Princeton U., NJ, 2002—; sci. tchr. High Point Regional HS, Sussex, NJ, 2004—06; adj. faculty biology Sussex County CC, Newton, NJ, 2005—. Advisor Sci. Rsch. Club, Sussex, NJ, 2005—06. Mem.: Biology Tchrs. Assn. of NJ, NJ Sci. Tchr. Assn. Roman Catholic. Office Phone: 973 875 3101 x 705.

TRAVER, SUE MONTGOMERY, secondary school educator; b. Dallas, Nov. 9, 1959; d. Charles David and Mary Elizabeth Montgomery; m. David Robert Traver, May 30, 1981; children: Patricia, Melissa. BFA in Crafts, U. North Tex., Denton, 1982. Cert. tchr. Tex., 1985. Instr. Ctrl. Jr. H.S., Euless, Tex., 1985—86; instr. art Trinity H.S., Euless, 1986—. Mem.: Tex. State Tchrs. Assn. Meth. Avocations: sculpting, swimming, reading, bicycling. Office: Trinity High Sch 500 N Industrial Blvd Euless TX 76039

TRAVERSE, LYN D., not-for-profit fundraiser, communications executive; b. Kalamazoo, Mich., May 7, 1952; d. Robert Clinton Traverse and Betty Larue Kemp; m. Jonathan G. Tidd (div.); 1 child, Emily. Student, NYU, 1970—74; BA, U. Conn., 1996. Devel. officer NYU, NYC, 1974—80, U. Hartford, Conn., 1980—83; dir. devel. and comms. Forman Sch., Litchfield, Conn., 1983—88, Ethel Walker Sch., Simsbury, Conn., 1988—96, The Nature Conservancy, Middletown, Conn., 1996—2000, Long Wharf Theatre, New Haven, 2000—03, Haskins Labs., New Haven, 2003—06; campaign dir. Friends Sem., NYC, 2006—. Trustee U. Hartford Art, West Hartford, Conn., 1999—; trustee, treas. Endangered Lang. Fund, New Haven, 2004—. Actor: (films) Plainsong, 1983. Mem. patrons bd. New Haven Free Pub. Libr., 2004—; mem. steering com. Simsbury (Conn.) Land Trust, 1999—2002. Mem.: Alpha Sigma Lamda. Office: Friends Seminary 222 E 16th St New York NY 10003

TRAVIS, GERALDINE WASHINGTON, political organization worker; d. Joseph Thomas and Dorothy Marshall Washington; m. William Travis, June 30, 1949; children: William A. Jr., Michael B., Annemarie, Gerald S., Gwendolyn D. Student, Xavier U., 1947—49. Del. Dem. Nat. Conv., 1972, alt. del., 1976; coord. Nat. Women's Polit. Caucus, 1973—75; mem. Nat. Conf. on Observance of INT Women's Yr., Mont. Bd. Crime Control, 1975—79; Dem. presdl. elector, 1980; precinct committeewoman Ariz. State Com. Mem. Mont. U.S. Civil Rights Com., 1973—79. Mont. state rep. Dem. Party, 1975—77; Ariz. Dem. Precinct com. Person Leg Dist. #12; bd. dirs. YMCA, Great Falls, Mont., 1978—80. Mem.: DAV, ACLU, Am. Contract Bridge League, NAACP. Avocation: bridge. Home: 7421 W Denton Ln Glendale AZ 85303

TRAVIS, KAREN S., clinical social worker; b. Magnolia, Miss., Dec. 9, 1957; d. Otis B. and Lena Opal (Williams) T. BA, Southeastern La. U., 1978; MSW, La. State U., 1980. Diplomate in clin. social work; cert. group psychotherapist. Mem. mental health team La. State Penitentiary, 1980-82; social worker La. Tng. Inst. Dept. Corrections, Baton Rouge, 1982-84; clin. social worker, program coord. for treatment Parkland Hosp., Baton Rouge, 1984-86, Gestalt contract social worker; clin. social worker Navin Patel, M.D., Baton Rouge, 1986-92, pvt. practice, Baton Rouge, 1992—. Adj. faculty La. State U., 2004—. Mem. NASW (chairperson Baton Rouge chpt. 1989-90, bd. dirs., rep. 1990-92, fundraising chairperson 1990-92), Am. Group Psychotherapy Assn., La. Group Psychotherapy Assn. (pres. 1994-96). Avocations: biking, camping, travel, gardening, reading. Office: 7936A Wrenwood Blvd Baton Rouge LA 70809-7701

TRAVIS, NANCY, actress; b. New York, NY, Sept. 21, 1961; m. Robert N. Fried, 1994; 2 children. BA, NYU. Actor: (films) Three Men and a Baby, 1987, Eight Men Out, 1988, Married to the Mob, 1988, Air America, 1990, Internal Affairs, 1990, Loose Cannons, 1990, Three Men and a Little Lady, 1990, Passed Away, 1992, Chaplin, 1992, The Vanishing, 1993, So I Married an Ax Murderer, 1993, Greedy, 1994, Fluke, 1995, Destiny Turns On the Radio, 1995, Lieberman in Love, 1995, Bogus, 1996, Auggie Rose, 2000, The Sisterhood of the Traveling Pants, 2005, (TV films) Malice in Wonderland, 1985, Harem, 1986, I'll Be Home for Christmas, 1988, Body Language, 1995, My Last Love, 1999, Running Mates, 2000, (TV miniseries) Rose Red, 2002, (TV series) (voice) Duckman, 1994-97, Almost Perfect, 1995-96, Work with Me, 1999, Becker, 2002-04; Stage appearances include: Brighton Beach Memoirs (touring prodn.), It's Hard to Be a Jew, 1984, I'm Not Rappaport, 1986, The Signal Season of Dummy Hoy, 1987-88. Office: Creative Artists Agy c/o Rick Kurtzman 9830 Wilshire Blvd Beverly Hills CA 90212-1804

TRAVIS, SARAH, orchestrator; Trained at City U.; trained at Guildhall Sch. Music and Drama, UK. Orchestrator, musical supervisor Mack & Mabel, Pinafore Swing, Fiddler on the Roof, Gondoliers, Ten Cents a Dance, Piaf and Carmen, Sweeney Todd, 2005 (Tony award, best orchestrations, 2006, Drama Desk award, outstanding orchestrations, 2006); composer: Peter Pan, A Star Danced, The Last Fattybottypuss in the World, Tales My Lover Told Me, A Womb With A View; pianist Fascinating Aida, Drop Dead Divas. Office: Eugene O'Neill Theatre 230 W 49th St New York NY 10036

TRAVIS, TRACY LEIGH, emergency physician; b. Lynchburg, Va., Aug. 27, 1957; d. Charles C. Jr. and Mildred (Lindsay) T.; m. David Stephens; children: Jennifer Koecke, Travis Stephens. BS in Biology, Lynchburg Coll., 1979; MD, Eastern Va. Med. Sch., 1982. Diplomate Am. Bd. Emergency Medicine. Resident Butterworth Hosp., Grand Rapids, Mich., 1987; emergency physician Mary Washington Hosp., Fredericksburg, Va., 1988-93, ExpressCare, Stafford, Va., 1992-96, Inova Emergency Care, Fairfax, Va., 1996—2002, Inova Fairfax Hosp., 1998—2002; med. dir. DEA Training Acad., Quantico, Va., 2002—. Fellow Am. Coll. Emergency Physicians; mem. Phi Kappa Phi. Home: 10856 Meadow Pond Ln Oakton VA 22124-1446 Office Phone: 703-632-5084. Personal E-mail: tltmd@aol.com.

TRAVITZKY MCBRIDE, VIRGINIA ANNE, administrator; b. Norristown, Pa., June 2, 1958; d. Thomas James and Mary Ann (Gleason) T.; m. Andrew J. McBride. Diploma, Lankenau Hosp., 1979; BS, Coll. of St. Francis, 1997. RN; cert. procurement transplant coord. Staff nurse Phoenixville (Pa.) Hosp., 1979-82; staff nurse, charge nurse Lankenau Hosp., Phila., 1982-86; transplant coord. Delaware Valley Transplant Program, Phila., 1987-90; dir. recovery svcs. La. Organ Procurement Agy., Metairie, 1990—. Cons. in field. Recipient Disting. Svc. award, Nat. Kidney Found., 1990. Mem. North Am. Transplant Coord. Orgn. (chmn. edn. com. 1990-92, bd. dirs. 1992-93), Am. Bd. Transport Coords., Am. Assn. Organ Procurement Orgns. (chmn. program com. 1997—), United Network for Organ Sharing (profl. stds. com. 1995-96, patient affairs com. 1997—). Roman Catholic. Avocations: travel, reading, music. Office: La Organ Procurement Agy 3501 N Causeway Blvd Ste 940 Metairie LA 70002-3626

TRAYLOR, ANGELIKA, stained glass artist; b. Munich, Bavaria, Germany, Aug. 24, 1942; Came to U.S., 1959; d. Walther Artur Ferdinand and Berta Kreszentia (Boeck) Klau; m. Lindsay Montgomery Donaldson, June 10, 1959 (div. 1970); 1 child, Cameron Maria Greta; m. Samuel William Traylor III, June 12, 1970. Student, Pvt. Handelsschule Morawetz Jr. Coll., Munich, 1958. Freelance artist, 1980—. Works featured in profl. jours. including the Daylily Jour., 1987, Design Jour., South Korea, 1989, The Traveler's Guide to American Crafts, 1990, Florida Mag., 1991, Florida Today, 1993, Adventures in Art, vol. 3, 1993, Melbourne Times, 1994, The Orbiter, 1996, The Glass Collector's Digest, 1996, (TV) Focus on History, 1993, Focus, 1998, Space Coast Press, 1999, Weekend Decorating Projects-Women's Day, 1999, Pen Women, 1999, Stained Glass for the First Time, 2000, Creative Stained Glass, 2004; represented in permanent collections White House Christmas Ornament Collection, Holmes Regional Med. Ctr., Melbourne, Fla., Williams Childs Hospice House, Palm Bay, Fla., others Recipient Fragile Art award Glass Art mag., 1982, 1st Yr. Exhibitor award Stained Glass Assn. Am., 1984, 2d pl. Non-figurative Composition award Vitraux des USA, 1985, Best of Show Stained Glass Assn. Am., 1989, 3d pl., 1989, Merit award George Plimpton All-Star Space Coast Art Open, 1994; named Hist. Woman of

Brevard, Brevard Cultural Alliance, 1991, one of 200 Best Am. Craftsmen Early Am. Life mag., 1994-95, 97-98, 2000. Home and Office: 100 Poinciana Dr Indian Harbor Beach FL 32937-4437 Office Phone: 321-773-7640.

TRAYLOR, JESSICA STEPHENS, psychologist; b. Clayton, Ga., Nov. 13, 1979; d. Timothy Earl and Angela Irene Stephens; m. Ryran Reshard Traylor, Aug. 7, 2004; 1 child, Ryla. AS in Psychology, Gordon Coll., 2000; BS in Psychology, Ga. State U., 2000; MEd in Sch. Psychology, Ga. So. U., 2003, postgrad., 2003—. Pvt. practice svc. coord., Savannah, Ga., 2003—05; psychology intern Chatham County Schs., Savannah, 2004—05. Mem.: APA. Avocations: yodelling, photography, drawing. Home: 1406 E 50th St Savannah GA 31404

TRAYLOR, SHARON ELAIN, writer, school food service staff member; b. Whiteville, Tenn., Nov. 27, 1957; d. J.B. and Rosie G.; m. Ricky R. Traylor, Oct. 26, 1998; children: Nickie Brown, Keisha Gibbs. Grad. h.S., Bolivar, Tenn.; food service student, Whiteville (Tenn.) Vocat. Sch. Mem. food svc. staff Whiteville (Tenn.) Vocat. Sch., 1977-78; cashier Whiteville Elem. Sch. Cafeteria, 1985-99; teller Merchants and Planters Bank, 1999; asst. mgr. Family Check Advance, 1999—. Author: (poetry) Inspiring Poems. With U.S. Army, 1975-76. Home: 728 Blue Bonnett Ln Bolivar TN 38008-1049

TRAYNHAM, LURENE JONES, retired secondary school educator; b. Yazoo City, Miss., July 11, 1925; d. Thomas McKinley and Olivia Purvis Jones; m. Young Robinson (dec.); m. William H. Traynham (dec.); 1 child, Thomas Jefferson Jones. BS, Miss. State U., 1947; MEd, U. Ill., Urbana, 1958. Tchr. pub. schs., Canton, Miss., 1947—48, West Point, Miss., 1949—71, Columbus, Miss., 1971—87; ret., 1987. Mem. dist. adv. bd. NHA, Columbus, 1952—72; mem. internat. bd. fgn. students MUW, Columbus, 1978—82; mem. state adv. bd. FHA Hero, Jackson, Miss., 1972—87. Organizer Columbus Head Start, 1965. Recipient Cmty. Svc. award, Miss. Union Bapt. Ch., Columbus, 1987, Nat. Bapt. Women's Aux. award, So. Regional Conf., Columbus, 2004, cert. of leadership, Nat. Bapt. Conv., Balt., 2006. Mem.: Columbus Ret. Tchrs. Assn., Gamma Gamma Zeta (chaplain 1994—2006, organizer Amicae 1994, Disting. Dove award 2005). Democrat. Avocations: cooking, sewing, singing, travel, piano. Home: 1602 Martin Luther King Dr Columbus MS 39701

TRAYNOR, TAMI LEE, lawyer; b. Ann Arbor, Mich., Sept. 30, 1966; d. David A. and Pamela L. Traynor; m. David M. Wible, Mar. 21, 2003; children: Dillen M. Wible children: Hannah S. Wible. BA, U. Mich., 1988; JD, Temple U., 1992. Bar: Pa. 1992, N.J. 1992. Assoc. Miller, Alfano & Raspanti, P.C., Phila., 1992—2002, shareholder, 2002—. Bd. dirs. Phila. (Pa.) Com. End Homelessness, 2005—. Named Pa. Super Lawyer, Law and Politics and Phila. (Pa.) Mag., 2006. Mem.: Profl. Women's Roundtable, Temple Am. Inn Ct., Young Friends Phila. (Pa.) Mus. of Art (exec. com. 1998—2004, co-chmn. exec. com. 2000—03). Office: Miller Alfano & Raspanti PC 1818 Market Street Suite 3402 Philadelphia PA 19103 Office Phone: 215-972-6400. Office Fax: 215-981-0082.

TREA, MELISSA ANN, mathematics educator; b. Nurenburg, Germany, June 15, 1975; d. Robert Allen and Deborah Rose Green; m. Jason Michael Trea, Apr. 21, 2001; 1 child, Ariel Nicole Hicks. BS cum laude, Tenn. State U., Nashville, 2004. Office mgr., bookkeeper A+ Carpet Cleaning Co., Nashville, 1999—2002; math tchr. Smyrna (Tenn.) H.S., 2004—. Office: Smyrna High School 100 Bulldog Dr Smyrna TN 37167 Office Phone: 615-904-3865. Personal E-mail: tream@rcs.k12.tn.us.

TREACY, SANDRA JOANNE PRATT, artist, educator; b. New Haven, Conn., Aug. 5, 1934; d. Willis Hadley Jr. and Gladys May (Gell) P.; m. Gillette van Nuyse, Aug. 27, 1955; 1 child, Jonathan Todd. BFA, R.I. Sch. Design, 1956; student, William Paterson Coll., 1973-74. Cert. elem. and secondary tchr., N.J. Tchr. art and music Pkwy. Christian Ch., Ft. Lauderdale, Fla., 1964-66; developer Pequannock Twp. Bd. of Edn., Pompton Plains, NJ, 1970-72, tchr. art, 1972-76; vol. art tchr. Person County Bd. of Edn., Roxboro, NC, 1978-80, tchr. art, 1980-91, So. Jr. High Sch., Roxboro, 1989-91, Woodland Elem. Sch., Roxboro, 1989-93; tchr. Helena Elem. Sch., Timberlake, NC, 1991-93. Tchr. elem. art Bethel Hill Sch., Roxboro, 1974-79, vol. art tchr., 1979-80; tchr. basic art, vol. all elem. schs. Person County, Roxboro, 1977-80; tchr. arts and crafts, summers 1981-882; tchr. art home sch. So. Mid. Sch., 1981-2005, Person H.S., 1993-94 Artist, illustrator. Mem. Roxboro EMTs, 1979-81; bd. dirs. Person County Arts Coun., 1980-81, 93-95, pres., 1981-82; piano and organ choir accompanist Concord United Meth. Ch., 1981—; leader Morgan Trotters, 1992-94, asst. dir., 1993-96, bd. dirs.; coach, horseback riding for handicapped. Mem. NEA, Nat. Mus. of Women in the Arts (continuing charter), Smithsonian Assocs., N.C. Assn. Arts Edn., N.C. Assn. Educators, N.C. Art Soc. Mus. of Art, Internat. Platform Assn., Womans Club (tchr. Pompton Plains chpt. 1974-79), Person County Saddle Club (rec. sec. 1981-84), Puddingston Pony Club (dist. sec. 1974-75 Montville Twp. chpt.), Roxboro Garden Club (continuing, commr. 1980-82, pres. 1982-84, 2004—, sec. 1993-94, 97-98, v.p. 1993-95), Roxboro Woman's Club (arts dept.) Republican. Avocations: horseback riding, swimming, sailing, reading, playing piano and organ. Home: 1345 Kelly Brewer Rd Leasburg NC 27291-9622 Office Phone: 336-599-6995 2404. Personal E-mail: SJPTreacy@esinc.net.

TREADWAY, JESSICA, writer, educator; b. Albany, N.Y., Mar. 21, 1961; d. Ralph Stephen and Ann Olivia (Olson) T. BA, SUNY, Albany, 1982; MA, Boston U., 1985. Lectr. Ext. Sch. Harvard U., Cambridge, Mass., 1994-98; lectr. Tufts U., Medford, Mass., 1994-98; dir. MFA program, asst. prof. Emerson Coll., Boston, 1998—. Author: Absent Without Leave, 1993 (John C. Zacharias award 1993). Fellow Radcliffe Coll., 1993, Mass. Cultural Coun., 1996, NEA, 1998. Mem. AAUW, PEN/New Eng. (coun. 1998—). Office: Emerson Coll 120 Boylston St Boston MA 02116-4624

TREADWAY-DILLMON, LINDA LEE, actress, stuntwoman, dancer, dispatcher, athletic trainer; b. Woodbury, NJ, June 4, 1950; d. Leo Elmer and Ona Lee (Wyckoff) Treadway; m. Randall Kenneth Dillmon, June 19, 1982. BS in Health, Phys. Edn. & Recreation, West Chester State Coll., 1972, MS in Health and Phys. Edn., 1975; postgrad., Ctrl. Mich. U., 1978; Police Officer Stds. Tng. cert. complaint dispatcher, Goldenwest Coll., 1982. Cert. EMT Am. Acad. Orthopaedic Surgeons; in safety edn. West Chester State Coll. Grad. asst., instr., asst. athletic trainer West Chester (Pa.) State Coll., 1972-76; asst. prof., program dir., asst. athletic trainer Ctrl. Mich. U., Mt. Pleasant, 1976-80; police dispatcher City of Westminster, Calif., 1980-89; oncology unit sect. Children's Hosp. Orange County, Calif., 1989-96; control clk. food and beverage Marriott Hotel, Anaheim, 1996—2005. Stuntwoman, actress United Stunt Artists, SAG, L.A., 1982—; dancer Disneyland, Anaheim, Calif., 1988—; contbr. articles to profl. jours. Athletic trainer U.S. Olympic Women's Track and Field Trials, Frederick, Md., 1972, AAU Jr. World Wrestling Championships, Mt. Pleasant, Mich., 1977, Mich. Spl. Olympics, Mt. Pleasant, 1977, 78, 79. Recipient bronze and gold Spirit of Disneyland Resort awards, 1997; named Outstanding Phys. Educator, Delta Psi Kappa, Ctrl. Mich. U., 1980, Outstanding Young Woman of Am., 1984; named to Disneyland Entertainment Hall of Fame, 1995. Mem. SAG, Nat. Athletic Trainers Assn. (cert., women and athletic tng. ad hoc com. 1974-75, placement com. 1974-79, program dirs. coun. 1976-80, ethics com. 1977-80, visitation team 1978-80, 25 Yr. award 1997), U.S. Field Hockey Assn. (player), Pacific S.W. Field Hockey Assn. (player, Nat. Champion 1980, 81, 82), L.A. Field Hockey Assn. (player), Swing Shift Dance Team (dancer). Presbyterian. Avocations: flying, piano, athletics, stitchery, travel. Home: 18073 Scanlan Ct Fountain Valley CA 92708-5865

TREADWELL-RUBIN, PAMELA A., lawyer; b. Arlington, Tex., Dec. 15, 1960; BA in Polit. sci., U. Ariz., 1982, JD, 1985. Bar: Ariz. 1985. Prosecutor, Tucson City, 1985—87; dep. atty. Pima County, 1987—93; atty. Goering, Roberts, Rubin, Brogna, Enos & Treadwell-Rubin, PC, Tucson. Mem. Ariz. Juvenile Justice Adv. Coun., 1993—96. Fellow: Ariz. Bar Found. (bd. dirs. 1991—94, chair victims' rights pro bono panel 1992—93); mem.: Pima County Bar Assn. (bd. dirs. 1989—90, pres. Young Lawyers divsn. 1989—90, bd. dirs. 1996—2005), Ariz. Women Lawyers Assn., State Bar Ariz. (pres. Young Lawyers divns. 1994—95, cert. specialist worker's compensation 1995—, bd. govs. 1996—2005, pres. 2003—04, Outstanding Young Lawyer 1997). Office: Goering Roberts Rubin Brogna Enos & Treadwell-Rubin PC Ste 200 3320 N Campbell Ave Tucson AZ 85719 Office Phone: 520-577-9300.

TREANOR, BETTY MCKEE, interior design educator; b. Tooele, Utah, Oct. 2, 1938; d. Oscar Hart and Mable Genevieve (Smith) McK.; m. James Treanor, Dec. 27, 1978. BA, Brigham Young U., 1966; MA, Iowa State U., 1970. Instr. Brigham Young U., Provo, Utah, 1966-68; grad. teaching asst. Iowa State U., Ames, 1968-70; instr. Ariz. State U., Tempe, 1972-74; asst. prof. U. Tex., Austin, 1974-80; assoc. prof. S.W. Tex. State U., San Marcos, 1980—, coord. interior design program, 1999—2002. Freelance designer, artist craftsman, 1972—; comml. interior designer, Phoenix, 1970-72; interior design program coord., S.W. Tex. State U., 1999-2002. Editor: Comprehensive Bibliography for Interior Design, 1984, 87. Fellow Interior Design Educators Coun. (southwest regional chair 1977-88), Internat. Interior Design Assn., Am. Soc. Interior Designers, Found. for Interior Design Edn. Rsch. (chmn. bd. 1990, 92, trustee 1986-94, accreditation com. 1979-86), Irish Georgian Soc., Tex. Assn. for Interior Design (edn. rep. 1985-90). Home: 10806B Pinehurst Dr Austin TX 78747-1621 Office: SW Tex State U FCS 601 University Dr San Marcos TX 78666-4685

TREAS, JUDITH KAY, sociology educator; b. Phoenix, Jan. 2, 1947; d. John Joseph and Hope Catherine (Thomas) Jennings; m. Benjamin C. Treas II, May 14, 1969; children: Stella, Evan. BA, Pitzer Coll., Claremont, Calif., 1969; MA, UCLA, 1972, PhD, 1976. Instr. U. So. Calif., L.A., 1974-75, asst. prof., 1975-81, assoc. prof., 1981-87, dept. chair, 1984-89, prof., 1987-89, U. Calif., Irvine, 1989, dept. chair, 1989-94. Bd. overseers Gen. Social Survey, 1986-88; cons. social sci. and population study sect. NIH, 1989-92. Contbr. articles to profl. jours. Trustee Pitzer Coll., 1977-79. Recipient Rsch. award NSF, 1978-81, 84-91, NIH, 1979-81; Univ. scholar U. So. Calif., 1982-83. Fellow Gerontological Assn. Am.; mem. Golden Key (hon.), Am. Sociol. Assn., Population Assn. Am. Office: U Calif Dept Sociology Irvine CA 92697-0001

TRECHSEL, GAIL ANDREWS, museum director; b. Calif. children: Julia, Andrew. MA, Cooperstown. Curator decorative arts, adminstr. Birmingham Mus. Art, 1976—96, R. Hugh Daniel dir., 1996—. Peer rev. panelist NEA, Inst. Mus. Services; mem. Birmingham Arts Commn., U. Ala. at Birmingham Leadership Cabinet; former co-chair Region 20/20 Arts and Culture Task Force. Named to Ala. Acad. of Honor, 2005; fellowship, NEA. Mem.: Ala. State Arts Coun., Am. Assn. Mus. (reviewer, accreditation com.), Assn. Art Mus. Directors (mem. bd., treas.). Office: Birmingham Mus Art 2000 8th Ave North Birmingham AL 35203-2278

TREFTS, JOAN LANDENBERGER, retired principal; b. Pitts., Jan. 31, 1930; d. William Henry III and Eleanore (Campbell) Landenberger; m. Albert Sharpe Trefts Sr., June 20, 1952 (dec.); children: Dorothy, Albert Jr., William, Deborah, Elizabeth. AB, Western Coll. for Women, 1952; M, John Carroll U., 1982, M, 1984. Lic. and cert. home economist, cert. prin., N.Y., Ohio, supr., biol. sci., econs., voact. edn., pre-kindergarten edn. Summer sch. prin. John Adams H.S., Collinwood and South High, Cleve., 1972—95; ret., 1995. Cons. Cleve. Partnership Program. Trustee Chautauqua Literacy and Sci. Cir., Presbyn. Assn. Chautauqua, NY. Named Tchr. of Yr., Cleve., 1994. Mem.: DAR (state officer 2000—), Ohio Vocat. Assn. (bd. dirs.), Am. Vocat. Assn. (nat. com.), Am. Home Econs. Assn., Presbyn. Assn. (trustee), Dames of Ct. of Honor (pres. gen. 2001—), Colonial Daus. of 17th Century (nat. officer), Daus. Am. Colonists (state officer), Nat. Officers Colonial Clergy (nat. officer, chancellor), Colonial Dames Am. (pres. chpt. 18, nat. officer ct. honor), U.S. Daus. of 1912, Colonial Dames of XVII Century, New Eng. Soc. of Western Res. (pres.), Clearwater Country Club, Cleve. Skating Club, Union Club. Republican. Presbyterian. Avocations: curling, rug hooking, needlepoint. Home: 20101 Malvern Rd Shaker Heights OH 44122-2825 Address: 219 Park Cir Dunedin FL 34698 also: PO Box 761 Chautauqua NY 14722

TREIBER, SUSAN, music educator; MusB, Kans. State U., 1979, MusM, 1981; diploma in Music Performance, St. Louis Conservatory of Music, 1988. Principal's Certificate State of Mo., 2002, Teacher's Certificate State of Mo., 1988. Instrumental music tchr. Stilwell Pub. Schools, Okla., 1981—82, Sapulpa Pub. Schools, Okla.; vocal music tchr. St. Louis Pub. Schools, 1989—95; instr. Lindbergh Sch. Dist., St. Louis, 1995—99, Pky. Sch. Dist., Chesterfield, Mo., 2000—. Musician St. Louis Wind Symphony, 1998—2003, Tulsa Cmty. Orch., Okla., 1981—87, Tulsa Cmty. Band, 1984—85, U. Ark. Early Music Group, Fayetteville, 1981—82, Vaughn Bolton Dance Band, Manhattan, Kans., 1981—82, Manhattan City Band, Kans., 1980—82, Marshall's Civic Band, Topeka, 1979, Manhattan Chamber Orch., Kans., 1977—78, Atchison Symphony, Kans., 1974—75, St. Joseph Symphony, Mo., 1974—75, Merawood Orch., St. Louis, 1998—2003, Flo-Valley Orch., St. Louis, 1989—90, Compton Heights Band, St. Louis, 1988—89, Brentwood Orch., St. Louis, 1988—99, Okla. Sinfonia Orch., Tulsa, Okla., 1985—87, Quintessence Wind Quintet, Tulsa, Okla., 1985—87, Tulsa Starlight Band, 1984—87, Tulsa Recorder Consort, Okla., 1982—87. Grant, Pky. Edn. Found., 2005. Mem.: NEA (assoc.), ASCD (assoc.), Internat. Clarinet Soc. (assoc.), Am. Fedn. of Musicians (assoc.), Mu Phi Epsilon (assoc.), Kappa Delta Pi (assoc.).

TREICHEL, MONICA ZIMMERMAN, accountant, educator; b. Ephrata, Pa., Mar. 17, 1964; d. Leroy M. and Bonita J. Z.; m. Rudolph J. Treichel, March 8, 2003. BS, Messiah Coll., 1986; MBA, Pa. State U., 1988; PhD, Temple U., 1998. CPA, 1988. Acct. Miller & Miller CPAs, Lititz, Pa., 1988-90; pvt. practice, East Earl, Pa., 1990-93; from rsch. asst. to asst. prof. Temple U., Phila., 1993—. Judge sm. bus. awards SBA. Rev.: Jour. Small Bus. Strategy; contbr. articles to profl. jours. Bd. dirs. Beth Shalom, Lancaster, Pa., 1988-93; mem., reporting sec. Young Reps., Montgomery County, Pa., 1995-97; chmn. Leroy Zimmerman legis. dist. re-election campaign, 2002; vol. Interfaith Hospitality Network of Mainline, 2000—; mem. coll. retention com., Phila., Pa., 2000; judge Pa. 50 Best Women in Bus., Pa. Dept. Cmty. and Devel., 2001-03. Sam Walton fellow Students in Free Enterprise, 1998-2000, Irwin L. Gross Bus. Inst. Rsch. fellow, 2000—, Tchg. fellow 2000—, Temple U. Mem. Acad. Mgmt., AICPA, Pa. Inst. CPA, Temple U. League for Entrepreneurial Women (co-chmn.), U.S. Assn. Small Bus. and Entrepreneurship (project dir. C.R.E.A.T.E. program, 2000-03), Acad. Mgmt., Women's Investment Network (adv. bd.), Nat. Assn. Women Bus. Owners, Jr. League Phila., Friends of the Am. Red Cross. Presbyterian. Avocations: walking, swimming, golf. Office: Temple U 1810 N 13th St 380 Speakman Hall 006-100 Philadelphia PA 19122 E-mail: monica.treichel@temple.edu.

TREITLER, RHODA CHAPRACK, artist; b. N.Y.C., Apr. 18, 1937; d. Arthur A. and Lillian Chaprack; m. Byron M. Treitler, May 15, 1960; children— Michael Eric, Betsy Dale. A.B., Bennington Coll., 1958; studied with Paul Feeley, 1954-58; student Artists in Am., 1973-78. Editorial asst. McCalls mag., N.Y.C., 1958-60; artist, N.Y., 1970—; pres. Aquarelle, Port Washington, N.Y., 1984;—86 Exhibitions include Coe Hall, Locust Valley, N.Y., 1976, Firehouse Gallery, Nassau Community Coll., Garden City, N.Y., 1977, 78, 80, 81, Plandome Gallery, Manhasset, N.Y., 1980, 85, Bryant Library, Roslyn, N.Y., 1981, Seamans Bank, Manhasset, 1981, Adelphi U., Garden City, N.Y., 1983-87, Fed. Bldg. N.Y.C., 1982-94, Hempstead Harbor Gallery, Glen Cove, N.Y., 1983, Post Coll., Brookville, N.Y., 1983-84, 87, Nassau County Mus. Fine Art, Roslyn, 1982, 83, Veridian Gallery, N.Y., 1987, Upstairs Art Gallery, N.Y., 1988, Locust Valley Lib., N.Y., 1989, 91, 97-98, New World Art Ctr., N.Y.C., 1998-99, The Banana Factory, Bethlehem, Pa., 2002. Pres. Parents Assn., Roslyn Elem. Sch., 1970-72, Parents Assn. Roslyn High Sch. 1977-79, budget advisor, 1974-76; mem. coordinating council Parents Assn. liaison with Sch. Bd., 1970-82. Mem. Aquarelle, Nat. Assn. Women Artists (exec.bd., v.p. 2000), Huntington Twp. Art League, Nassau County Fine Art Mus. (council for celebration of arts). Clubs: Racquet at Old Westbury (N.Y.); Hunters Run Racquet (Boynton Beach, Fla.). Avocations: tennis; music; travel.

TREJOS, CHARLOTTE MARIE, humanities educator, consultant; b. Trout Lake, Mich., July 5, 1920; d. Charles Floyd and Lula May (Force) Draper; m. J. Mario Trejos, Jan. 8, 1961; 1 child, J. Mario Jr. Tchg. credentials, State of Calif., 1989; MA, Hawthorne Coll., 1975; DD, Min. Salvation Ch., 1986. Tchr. English El Colegio Anglo-Am., Cochabamba, Bolivia, 1965-66; tchr. Hawthorne (Calif.) Christian Sch., 1966-75; owner Trejos Literary Cons., Carson, Calif., 1976—. Author: My Carson, Your Carson, 1987, Variegated Verse, 1973, Yesterday Was Sunday, 1994; Artist: Am Legion Post Number 6, Nat. Mus. Women Arts, Mus. Latin Am. Art; contbr. articles to profl. jours. Voter registerer Democrats. With U.S. Army, 1942-43. Named Poet of Yr. Nat. Poetry Pub. Assn., 1974; recipient Golden Poet award World of Poetry, 1993. Mem. Soc. Ibero-Am. Escritores de Los Estados Unidos Am. (pres. 1985—, Cert. Recognition 1986). Avocations: music, tap dancing, art, gardening.

TREMBLAY, GAIL ELIZABETH, art educator; b. Buffalo, N.Y., Dec. 15, 1945; d. Roland Gilbert and Leela Mae Tremblay. BA in Drama, U. N.H., 1967; MFA in English, U. Oreg., 1969. Lectr. Nathaniel Hawthorne Coll., Antrim, NH, 1969—70, U. N.H., Durham, NH, 1971, Keene State Coll., Keene, NH, 1971—77; asst. prof. U. Nebr., Omaha, 1977—80; mem. faculty The Evergreen State Coll., Olympia, Wash., 1981—. Author: Annex 21 #3 Talking to the Grandfathers, 1979, Indian Singing in 20th Century America, 1991, Indian Singing, 2000. Bd. dir. Women's Caucas for Art, N.Y.C., 1988—2000, pres. bd., 1999—2000; pres. bd. dir. Indian Youth Am., Sioux City, Iowa, 1980—; bd. dir. Wash. Commn. for Humanities, Seattle, 1998—2003. Recipient Alfred E. Richards Poetry prize, U. N.H., 1966, Kathe Kollowitz award, Seattle Women's Caucus for Art, 2000, Gov.'s Art award, Wash. State, 2001, Pres. award of achievement in the Arts, Nat. WCA, 1993. Mem.: Coll. Art Assn. Avocations: gardening, Scrabble, flower arranging. Office: The Evergreen State Coll Lab 2 3250 Olympia WA 98505

TREMBLY, CRISTY, television executive; b. Oakland, Md., July 11, 1958; d. Charles Dee and Mary Louise (Cassidy) T.; m. Roman Ziombra. BA in Russian, German and Linguistics cum laude, W.Va. U., 1978, BS in Journalism, 1978, MS in Broadcast Journalism, 1979; advanced cert. travel, West L.A. Coll., 1982; advanced cert. rec. engring., Soundmaster Schs., North Hollywood, Calif., 1985. Engr. videotape Sta. WWVU-TV, Morgantown, W.Va., 1976—80; announcer, engr. Sta. WVVW Radio, Grafton, W.Va., 1979; tech. dir., videotape supr. Sta. KMEX-TV, L.A., 1980—85; broadcast supr. Sta. KADY-TV, Oxnard, Calif., 1988—89; dir. news tech. Sta. KVEA-TV, Glendale, Calif., 1985—89; asst. editor, videotape technician CBS TV Network, Hollywood, Calif., 1989—90; supr. videotape Sta. KCBS-TV, Hollywood, 1990—91, mgr. electronic news gathering ops., 1991—92; studio mgr., engr.-in-charge CBS TV Network, Hollywood, 1992—2001, mgr. transmission and satellite, 1994—, mgr. videotape, 2001, mgr. syndication, 2001, mgr. prodn., 2001—. Radio operator KJ6BX Malibu Disaster Comm., 1987—; coun. mem. L.A. World Affairs 2000—. Prodr. (TV show) The Mountain Scene, 1976-78. Vol. Ch. Coun., L.A. Riot Rebldg., Homeless shelter work, VA Hosps., Mus. docent; sponsor 3 overseas foster children; fundraiser La Mision Orphanage Ensenada Libr. Flying Samaritans, 2000—; L.A. Dist. rep. Calif.-Pacific conf.comm. commn. United Meth. Ch., 2002—; chmn. adminstrv. coun. Malibu United Meth. Ch., 1993—, choir, 1995—, comm. commn. rep., 2002—; sec., mem. adv. com. Tamassee (S.C.) Sch., 1992—; sr. orgn. pres. Children of the Am. Revolution, Malibu, Calif., 1992—; mem. internat. vis. coun. Outstanding Program Resource; mem. L.A. World Affairs Coun., 2000—. Named one of Outstanding Young Women of Am., 1988, Internat. Vis. Coun. Outstanding Pvt. Resource, L.A. County; recipient Asst. editor Emmy award Young and the Restless, 1989-90, Golden Mike award Radio/TV News Assn., 1991, 92, Pub. Svc. commendation, County of L.A., 1999, cert. leadership, USIA, cert. commendation, City of L.A., 1999. Mem.: DAR (state chair motion pictures, radio and TV, Calif. 1988—90, Mex. 1990—, nat. vice-chair units overseas Mex. 1998—, organizing regent Baja Calif. chpt. 1999—, state conf. chair 2001, state sec. 2001—04, 2001—, nat. vice-chair media awards 2001—, nat. vice-chair chpt. devel. 2004—, state conf. chair 2004—, vice regent Mex. 2004—, Nat. Outstanding Jr. 1993), ATAS (judge local and nat. Emmy awards 1991—, exec. com. on electronic prodn. 1992—, membership com. 1994—96, awards com. 1994—, engring. awards com. 1997—, gov. 2000—, daytime awards com. 2000—, awards com. 2000—, chair tech. com. 2001—, activites com. 2002—, theatre stds. com. 2002—, diversity com. 2004—), Nat. Broadcasting Soc. (conf. spkr. 2001), Women in Comm., Soc. Profl. Journalists, Women in Film Internat. (com. 1999—), Am. Women in Radio and TV (bd. dirs. So. Calif. chpt. 1984—85, 1993—2000, pres. 1996—97), Travelers Century Club (life; program chair 1987—), Mensa (life), Travelers Century Club (life), Beta Sigma Phi. Democrat. Methodist. Avocations: singing, cooking, travel, genealogy, languages. Home: 2901 Searidge St Malibu CA 90265-2969 Office: CBS TV City 7800 Beverly Blvd Los Angeles CA 90036-2188

TRENDLER, TERESA ANN, science educator; b. Escondido, Calif., Jan. 16, 1969; BS in Biology, Biola U., 1990; MS in Biology, San Diego State U., 1994; EdD, U. La Verne, 2006. Prof. Pasadena (Calif.) City Coll., 1997—. Office: Pasadena City Coll 1570 E Colo Blvd Pasadena CA 91106 Office Phone: 626-585-7675. Business E-Mail: tatrendler@pasadena.edu.

TRENT, GRACE CHEN, communications executive; Sr. v.p. pub. rels., chief of staff MCI, Inc., Ashburn, Va., 2003—. Named Pub. Rels. Profl. of Yr., Pub. Rels. Soc. Am., 2004. Office: MCI Inc 22001 Loudoun County Pkwy Ashburn VA 20147

TRENT, JUDITH SWANLUND, communications educator; b. Grand Rapids, Aug. 29, 1940; d. Vincent George Swanlund and Evelyn Barrows; m. Jimmie Douglas Trent, Dec. 19, 1969; 1 child, Lawrence Andrew. BS, Western Mich. U., Kalamazoo, 1962; MA, U. Mich., Ann Arbor, 1968; PhD, U. Mich., 1970. Dir. of debate U. Mich., Ann Arbor, 1967—69; asst. prof. Youngston (Ohio) State U., 1970—71; prof. U. Dayton, Ohio, 1971—84; Am. coun. on edn. fellow U. Cin., 1983—84, assoc. v.p., 1984—2000, prof. dept. comm., 1984—. Author (with Jimmie D. Trent and Daniel J. O'Neill): Concepts in Communication, 1973; author: (with Jimmie D. Trent) Instructor's Guide to Accompany Concepts in Communication, 1973; author: (with Robert V. Friedenberg) Political Campaign Communication: Principles and Practices, 1983, 5th edit., 2004; editor: Communication: Views From The Helm For The Twenty First Century, 1998, Included in Communication: Learning Climates That Cultivate Racial and Ethnic Diversity, 2002; contbr. chapters to books, articles various profl. jours. and book reviews. Mem.: Eastern Comm. Assn., Ctrl. States Comm. Assn. (pres. 1982, Hall of Fame 2006), Nat. Comm. Assn. (pres. 1997, Disting. Svcs. award 2004). Avocations: travel, gardening. Home: 101 Country Club Oxford OH 45056 Office: U Cin Dept Comm Cincinnati OH 45221 Office Phone: 513-556-4493. Business E-Mail: judith.trent@uc.edu.

TRENTON, PATRICIA JEAN, art historian; m. Norman B. Trenton; children: James Davis, Jeffrey Norman. PhD, U. Calif., 1980. Curator of Am. art Denver Art Mus., 1969—74; Editor Am. Personality Drawing Exhibition Catalog, UCLA, 1976; curator of art Union League Club Chgo., 1981; guest curator Western Am. Art, Palm Spring Desert Mus., 1981—82, Bowers Mus., Santa Ana, Calif., 1984, Southwest Mus., Los Angeles, Calif., 1984, Laguna Art Mus., Laguna Beach, Calif., 1987—91, Autry Mus. Western Heritage, Los Angeles, Calif., 1993—97; art curator Los Angeles Athletic Club, 1982—2001; guest curator San Jose Mus. Art, San Jose, Calif., 2003, Irvine Mus., Irvine, Calif., 2005. Lectr. various profl. conf. Contbr. articles various profl. jours.; Crocker Art Mus., Sacramento, Calif., 1990, Laguna Art Mus., Laguna Beach, Calif., 1990, Dixon Gallery and Gardens, Memphis, Tenn., 1991, Montclair Art Mus., Montclair, NJ, 1991, Gene Autry Western Heritage Mus., 1990, Bowers Mus., 1984, Buffalo Bill Hist. Ctr., Wy., 1983, Palm Springs Desert Mus., 1982. Art adv. bd. Yosemite Exhibition, Autry Mus.,

2002—. Recipient Susan Koppleman award, 1995, Caroline Bancroft Hist. prize, Indep. Spirits, 1995, Western Heritage Wrangler award, Nat. Cowboy Hall of Fame and Western Heritage Ctr., 1995, Nat. Am. Publisher's award, U. Okla. Press's Publication, 1983; Rockefeller Fellowship award, UCLA, 1977. Mem.: Mus. Western Art (dir, adv. bd. 1985—87), Am. Mus. Assn., Am. Social Studies, Coll. Art Assn., Los Angeles County Mus. of Art, Am. Art Coun. Steering Com., KCET Women's Coun. Home: 10112 Empyrean Way 303 Los Angeles CA 90067 Personal E-mail: pdtrenton@aol.com.

TREPPLER, IRENE ESTHER, retired state senator; b. St. Louis County, Mo., Oct. 13, 1926; d. Martin H. and Julia C. (Bender) Hagemann; student Meramec Community Coll., 1972; m. Walter J. Treppler, Aug. 18, 1950; children: John M., Steven A., Diane V. Anderson, Walter W. Payroll chief USAF Aero. Chart Plant, 1943-51; enumerator U.S. Census Bur., St. Louis, 1960, crew leader, 1970; mem. Mo. Ho. of Reps., Jefferson City, 1972-84; mem. Mo. Senate, Jefferson City, 1985-96; chmn. minority caucus, 1991-92. Alt. del. Rep. Nat. Conv., 1976, 84. Recipient Spirit of Enterprise award Mo. C. of C., 1992, appreciation award Mo. Med. Assn., Nat. Otto Nuttli Earthquake Hazard Mitigation award, 1993, Disting. Legislator award Cmty. Colls. Mo., 1995; named Concord Twp. Rep. of Yr., 1992. Mem. Nat. Order Women Legislators (rec. sec. 1981-82, pres. 1985), Nat. Fedn. Rep. Women, Tesson Ferry Twp. Rep. Club. Mem. Evangelical Ch.

TRESSLAR, NOLA V., artist, retired marketing professional, retired foundation administrator; b. Tacoma, Mar. 10, 1942; d. Arthur and Viola Mafalda (Sirianni Di Carlo) De Caro; m. Lloyd E. Montgomery, Dec. 8, 1961 (div. 1971); children: Gina N. Montgomery, Melissa R. Montgomery; m. Walter B. Swain, Mar. 11, 1977 (div. 1994); m. Guy E. Tresslar, May 16, 1997. Student, U. Puget Sound, 1959-62. Cert. real estate appraiser. Real estate appraiser Wash. Appraiser/assessor Pierce County Assessors Office, Tacoma, 1971-77; chief appraiser Otero Savs. & Loan, Colorado Springs, 1977-78; pvt. fee appraiser, co-owner N.W.S. & Assocs., Colorado Springs, 1978—. Pres., designer N.V.S. Enterprises, Colorado Springs, 1980—89; dir. mktg. U.S. West Edn. Found., Seattle, 1990—92; exec. dir. N.W. Baby Talk, 1993—95; designer numerous gift items. Fund devel., pub. rels. mgr. Child Abuse Prevention Resources, 1995—97; mem. cmty. cultural enrichment adv. coun. MetroParks of Tacoma/Pierce County, 1997—. Recipient Women at Work award, Coun. Working Women, 1985, Pub. Svc. award, Colorado Springs Assn. Life Underwriters, 1985, Booster of the Yr. award, Salesman With a Purpose, 1986. Mem.: NOW, NAFE, Sumi Collage Mixed Media Painting, Soc. Real Estate Appraisers (candidate, treas. 1978, bd. dirs. 1982—84), Nat. Coll. Soc., Tacoma Jr. League (cmty. adv. bd.), Urban League, Cmty. and Cultural Arts Adv. Coun. Met. Parks, Pacific Gallery Artists, Puget Sound Sumi Artists, Chi Omega Alumnae. Democrat. Avocations: travel, sumi painting, crafts, photography, volunteering. Personal E-mail: nvtresslar@aol.com.

TRESTON, SHERRY S., lawyer; BA, Dominican U., 1972; MS, Purdue U., 1973; MBA, U. Chgo., 1979; JD with honors, DePaul U., 1983. Bar: Ill. 1983. With planning dept. Fed. Res. Bank, Chgo., 1973—77; with sys. dept. Sears Bank & Trust Co., Chgo., 1977—78; with trust dept. 1st Nat. Bank Chgo., 1978—83; assoc. Sidley Austin LLP, Chgo., 1983—91, ptnr., 1991—. Trustee Dominican U. Office: Sidley Austin LLP 1 S Dearborn Chicago IL 60603-2000 Fax: 312-853-7036.

TRETTIN, ROSEMARY ELIZABETH, secondary school educator; b. Appleton, Wis. d. August W. and Elizabeth C. (Etten) T. BA, Mt. Mary Coll., Milw., 1945. Tchr., forensic coach Pulaski (Wis.) High Sch., 1947-51, Freedom (Wis.) High Sch., 1951-60, St. Mary Cen. High Sch., Menasha, Wis., 1960-79; forensic coach Xavier High Sch., Appleton, 1979-86; pres. St. Mary Ct. Nat. Catholic Soc. Foresters, Appleton, 1953-86, 91—, nat. dir., 1974-78, nat. v.p., 1978-86, nat. pres., CEO, 1986-90; sec. Green Bay (Wis.) Diocesan Assn., 1974-78, pres., 1978-86. Mem. Nat. Cath. Comms. Found., N.Y.C., nat. dir., 1986-89, exec. v.p., 1989-90; dir. Wis. Fraternal Congress, 1982-83, Ill. Fraternal Congress, 1989-90; co-leader Fish Cmty. Svc., Civic Leaders Am., Nat. Cath. Soc. Foresters (Fraternalist of Yr. 2002). Eucharistic min. St. Mary Ch., coord. leisure club, 1993—. Named to Hall of Fame, Wis. Forensic Coaches Assn., 1994, Nat. Cath. Soc. Foresters fraternalist, 2002. Mem. Nat. Cath. Forensic League (sec., pres.), Nat. Forensic League (Double Diamond Key award 1983), Cath. Daus. Am., Outagamie County Hist. Soc., Monté Alverno Retreat Guild (treas. and pres.), Optimist (Neenah-Menasha Breakfast Club), St. Joseph Fraternity of Secular Franciscans (sec.), Christ Child Soc., Monte Alverno Retreat Guild (v.p., 2003-04, pres. 2005). Roman Catholic. Avocations: gardening, travel.

TREUTING, EDNA GANNON, retired nursing administrator, educator; b. New Orleans, Dec. 16, 1925; d. Alphonse Joseph and Clara Josephine (David) Gannon; m. August Raymond Treuting, Sept. 4, 1948 (dec.); children: Keith, Karen Treuting Stein, Madeline Treuting LeBlanc, Jaime Treuting Gonzales, Jay (dec.). Diploma, Charity Hosp. Sch. Nursing, New Orleans, 1946; BS in Nursing Edn., La. State U., 1953; MPH, Tulane U., 1972, DPH, 1978. RN, La.; cert. family nurse practitioner Tulane U. Head nurse premature nursery Charity Hosp., New Orleans, 1946-47, head nurse pediatrics, 1947-49; instr. pediatrics Charity Hosp. Sch. Nursing, New Orleans, 1949-52, 54, instr., LPN, 1953; pvt. duty Touro, Hotel Dieu, New Orleans, 1957-59; instr. maternal and child health La. State U. Sch. Nursing, New Orleans, 1960, 65, 69-71; from instr. to prof., sect. head Tulane Sch. Pub. Health and Tropical Medicine, New Orleans, 1972-83; dean, prof. Our Lady Holy Cross Coll. Nursing Div., New Orleans, 1983-84; chief nurse Dept. Health and Hosp., New Orleans, 1987-94, Region IV nurse practitioner Baylor U., Health Edn. and Welfare, 1974-76; citizen amb. to South Am. People to People, 1979; presentor U. Hawaii Pub. Health and Nursing, 1977; planner, advisor, reviewer continuing edn. U. Tenn., Memphis, 1990-95. Author, editor: Occupation Health Nursing, 1979; sect. head, prin. investigator Practitioner Programs Family and Pediatric, 1973-83; item writer Nurse Practitioners, Community Health and Occupational Nursing, 1974-80; mem. editl. bd. to sci. jours. and Nurse Practitioner Jour., 1974-2005. Pres. Oti-Mrs. Internat., New Orleans, 1955-68; sponsor bd. dirs. Holy Cross H.S. Treuting Scholarship, New Orleans, 1966—; hurricane and disaster nurse ARC, New Orleans, 1966-77; v.p. Pandora Carnival Club, New Orleans, 1968-78; alternate state health dept. Commn. Nursing Supply and Demand by Legislation, 1991-94; planner, presentor La. State Rsch. Day, 1990-92. Named outstanding woman in the mainstream world's fair women of achievement, 1984. Mem. AARP (chpt. 3086 pres. 2000—, sr. mem., chpt. pres. 2001, Mandeville chpt. pres. 2001-, Cmty. Svc. award 2006), New Orleans Dist. Nurses Assn. (First J.B. Hickey Meml. Cmty. award 1985, Great 100 Nurse-First Yr. 1987), La. Pub. Health Assn. (Dr. C.B. White Merritorious Diligent Svc. 1990), La. Nurse Practitioners Assn.(Edna Treuting scholarship named in her honor), Tulane U. Alumni Assn. (past pres.), Tulane Med. Alumni Assn. (past pres.), New Image Club of Mandeville (chmn. 1986-2003), Mandeville Rep. Women, Mandeville Srs., New Image Club (chmn. line dance, co-chmn. trips and travel 1995-2004, Young at Heart, New Image Club (chmn. trips and travel, vice chmn.), Delta Omega (nat. and chpt. past pres.), Sigma Theta Tau Republican. Roman Catholic. Avocations: travel, dance, swimming, photography, reading. Home: 1914 Marlin Dr Mandeville LA 70448-1069

TREVINO, KATHERINE ANN, elementary school educator; b. Pearsall, Tex., Jan. 11, 1966; d. Frank Gallardo and Anna Lois Trevino; m. Fabian Salazar Ledesma, July 3, 1994; children: David Trevino Ledesma, Danielle Marie Ledesma. Bachelor, U. Tex., Austin, 1993. Tchr. phys. edn. Huggins Elem., Fulshear, Tex., 1993—97, A.W. Jackson Elem., Rosenberg, Tex., 1997—. Religious edn. tchr. Cath. Ch., Richmond, Tex., 2000—05, lector, 2002—05. Recipient Tchr. of Yr. award, Lamar Consol. Sch. Dist., 1998. Mem.: Tex. Assn. for Phys. Edn., Recreation and Dance. Roman Catholic. Avocations: reading, exercising. Office: Lamar Consolidated Sch Dist 301 Third St Rosenberg TX 77471 Office Phone: 832-223-1800.

TREYBIG, EDWINA HALL, sales executive; b. Ft. Worth, Dec. 12, 1949; d. George Edward and Lillian Wanita (Herring) Hall; m. Jerry Kenneth Treybig, Sept. 20, 1980; children: Allison Lindsey, Gifford Carl, Brick Edward. BS in Home Econs., Tex. Tech U., 1972. Office mgr. Am. Internat. Rent-A-Car, Dallas, 1973, gen. mgr., 1973-74; sales rep. Martinez Mud Co., Denver, 1977-80, Am. Mud Co., Denver, 1980-83, Robinson Construction Co., Denver, 1983-87, Dig-It, Inc., N.Y.C., 1987-88; sales rep., corp. sec. Treybig Enterprises, Littleton, Colo., 1984—. Organizer Mile High Golf Tournament, Denver, 1980-84; mem. subcom. Colo. Devel. Disabilities Planning coun., Denver, 1989-90; mem. Coalition to Insure the Uninsurable, Denver, 1989-90; founder Littleton Acad., 1996-97: founder, pres. governing bd. Littleton Prep. Charter Sch., 1998-2001. Mem. Soc. Petroleum Engrs. (organizer golf tournament), Internat. Assn. Drilling Contractors, Ind. Producers Assn. Mountain States, Assn. Retarded Citizens, Denver Petroleum Club (organizer golf tournament), Alpha Chi Omega (social chmn. 1970-72). Republican. Mem. Ch. of Christ. Avocations: doll and bear collecting, down-hill skiing. Home and Office: 7397 S Fillmore Cir Littleton CO 80122-1942

TRIANA, GLADYS, artist; b. Camaguey, Cuba, Nov. 17, 1937; came to U.S., 1974; d. Jose Daniel Triana and Francisca Maria Perez; m. Manuel Angel Malleiro, Apr. 11, 1974. Student, Oriente U., Santiago de Cuba, 1957; B in Art summa cum laude, Mercy Coll., 1976; MEd, L.I. U., 1977. Art educator N.Y.C. Bd. Edn., 1978—. Exhbn. cons.; created and implemented Children Expressions Mural Program at Cmty. Sch. Bd. Dist. #2, N.Y.C., 1987—. One women shows include Lyceum Gallery, Havana, Cuba, 1962, 63, Tramontana Gallery, 1971, Intar Gallery, 1975, Cuban Mus. Art and Culture, Miami, Fla., 1988, Mus. Contemporary Hispanic Art, N.Y., 1990, Mus. Modern Art, Santo Domingo, 1991, Nader Gallery Fine Arts, Santo Domingo, Bronx Mus. Arts, 1995, Jeux De Memoire, Espace Nesle, Paris, Trapecio Gallery, Lima, Peru, 1997; exhibited in group shows at Palacio de Bellas Artes Mus., 1962, 91, Sala de Arte Gallery, Madrid, 1971, Mus. Sci., Chgo., 1975, Inst. de Cultura Puertoriquena, Museo de Ponce, P.R., 1976, 92, Queens Coll., 1979, Meeting Point Gallery, Miami, 1982, Todd Capp Gallery, N.Y., 1986, Mus. Contemporary Hispanic Art, N.Y., 1988, Warehouse Gallery, N.Y.C., 1989, Stratus Gallery, N.Y.C., 1989, L.I. U., 1989, Mus. Contemporary Art, Caracas, Venezuela, 1990, Discovery Mus., Bridgeport, Conn., 1990, Modern Art Latin Am., Washington, 1990, Humphrey Gallery, N.Y.C., 1992, Paine Weber Art Gallery, N.Y.C., 1992, Artspace, New Haven, Conn., 1992, Adriana Landon Gallery, N.Y.C., 1993, Sotavento Gallery, Caracas, 1995, Nat. Libr. Can., Ottawa, Ont., 1996, Mexic-Art Mus., Austin, Tex., 1997, Espace Nesle, Paris, Trapecio Gallery, Lima, 1998, Tampa Mus. Art. Mem. Mus. of Women, Washington, 1990—, Women of Caucus, N.Y.C., 1992—, Ctr. for Books of Art, N.Y.C., 1993—. Cintas fellow, 1993. Avocations: music, ballet, opera, tennis, bicycling.

TRIBBLE, JOAN LUCILLE (JOAN FARNSLEY TRIBBLE), retired literature and language professor, writer; b. New Albany, Ind., Oct. 8, 1928; d. William Newland and Elsie Lenora Farnsley; m. Robert Samuel Tribble, Oct. 6, 1950; children: Robert Samuel Jr., David Michael, Linda Joyce. BA with honors in English, U. Louisville, 1950, MA in English, 1968. H.s. tchr. Ky. Substitute tchr. Jefferson County Pub. Sch. Sys., Louisville, 1963—66; grad. asst. in English U. Louisville, 1966—67, adj. instr. in English, 1968—68, U. Ky./Jefferson CC, Louisville, 1968—71, from instr. to assoc. prof. English, 1972—88. Author: The Farnsleys of Kentuckiana; contbr. articles to profl. jours. Mem.: The Soc. Ky. Pioneers, Ky. Hist. Soc., So. Ind. Genealogy Soc., Ky. Genealogy Soc., U. Louisville Golden Alumni Soc., The Hon. Order Ky. Colonels, Woodcock Soc. Achievements include development of Diagnostic Placement Test for Students of English as a Second Language; design of Computer Tutorial Programs on English Grammar for Developmental Students. Avocations: genealogy, writing, needlecrafts, water sports. Home: 429 Tandywood Dr Pendleton KY 40055-8923

TRIBIÉ, AMY KATHLEEN, music educator; b. Manassas, Va., Feb. 17, 1981; d. Noreen Margaret and William Daniel McCafferty; m. Christopher Michael Tribié, June 26, 2004. Music Edn. Dual Licensure, Shenandoah U., Winchester, Va., 1999—2003. Music educator Loudoun County Pub. Schs., Ashburn, Va., 2004—. Singer The Wash. Chorus, Washington, 2000. Grantee Steve Morris Meml. scholarship, Laurie Nelson, 1999, Harry C. Rickard scholarship, Shenandoah U., 2001. Mem.: Music Educators Nat. Conf. (pres. of shenandoah u. chpt. 2002—03, Va. collegiate state sec./treas. 2001—02, Outstanding New Mem. award 2000), Sigma Alpha Iota (life; sgt. at arms 2001—03). Home: 43970 Choptank Ter Ashburn VA 20147 Office: Loudoun County Pub Schs 21000 Education Ct Ashburn VA 20148 Office Phone: 571-252-1000. Personal E-mail: atribie@gmail.com. Business E-Mail: atribie@loudoun.gov.

TRIBLE, MARTHA GREGORY, secondary school educator; b. Nassawadox, Va., Apr. 30, 1949; d. Levin Melson and Shirley Grace Gregory; m. Robert Waring Trible, Aug. 18, 1979; children: C. Morgan, M. Meredith, G. Waring. BS, James Madison Univ., Harrisonburg, Va., 1971; MEd, Univ. Va., Charlettesville, Va., 1973. Reading learning ctr. coord. Henrico County Sch., Richmond, Va., 1973—78; instr.-English J. Sargeant Reynolds, Richmond, Va., 1976—79, Rappahannock CC, Glenns, Va., 1982—2000; tchr. English King and Queen Cmty. Sch., King and Queen, 0000—2002, Charleston County Schools, King William County Schs., 2005—. Sch. bd. mem. W. Point Sch., W. Point, Va., 1997—2001; tchr. altar guild St. Johns Episc., W. Point, Va., 1980—2002. Mem.: King and Queen Edn. Assn., Nat. Coun. Tchrs. English. Avocations: reading, tour guide. Home: 4270 Mockingbird West Point VA 23181

TRICASE, ELIZABETH, gymnast; b. Elmhurst, Ill., July 26, 1986; d. Pino and Sheila. Gymnast Ill. Gymnastics Inst./U.S. Natl. Team, 2001—; competed in U.S. Gymnastics Championships, Cleve., 2001, 2002, 2003, Spring Cup, Burlington, Ontario, Canada, 2002, Pacific Alliance Championships, Vancouver, Canada, 2002, U.S. Classic, Pomona, Calif., 2001, Virginia Beach, Va., 2002, San Antonio, 2003, FL Gym Open, Luxembourg City, Luxembourg, 2004, Am. Classic, Ontario, Calif., 2004, Nat. Elite Podium Meet, NYC, 2004. Named U.S. Nat. Vault Champion, 2002; recipient 1st place vault, U.S. Gymnastics Championships, 2002, FL Gym Open, 2004. Avocations: soccer, basketball, running track. Office: 145 Plaza Dr Westmont IL 60559

TRICE, DOROTHY LOUISE, physician; b. Bklyn., Jan. 12, 1924; d. George Cooper and C. Rosella Trice. RN, Lincoln Sch. Nurses, Bronx, 1945; BS Edn., Hunter Coll., N.Y., 1947; MD, Med. Coll. Pa., Phila., 1956; MPH, Columbia U., N.Y.C., 1959. Health officer N.Y.C. Health Dept., 1959—72, dep. commr., 1972—74, regional dir., 1974—77; dir. ambulatory care and cmty. medicine L.I. Jewish Hosp., Queens Gen. Hosp., 1977—79; ret., 1979. Mem.: APHA, Kings County Med. Soc., Internat. Soroptimists. Home: 105 Ashland Pl 3E Brooklyn NY 11201

TRICHE, JANE M., lawyer; b. Napoleonville, La., Mar. 2, 1957; d. Eisley Claiborne Charles and Clara Caballero Triche; m. John W. Nilazzo, Jr., Sept. 25, 1999; stepchildren: John W. III, Jennifer S.; m. Kurt J. Perque (div.); children: Richard G., Anne Louise, Jerome F., K. Joseph Jr. BA, Nicholls State U., Thibodaux, La., 1977; JD, La. State U., Baton Rouge, 1992. Bar: La. Assoc. Law Office Risley Triche, Napoleonville, 1992—98, ptnr., 1998—. Mem., del. Dem. State Cen. Com., 2000—04, 2004—. Mem.: ABA, La. Trial Lawyers Assn., Assumption Parish Bar Assn. (pres.), JDC Bar Assn. (v.p. 23d dist., pres. 23d dist. 2004—05), La. State Bar Assn. (mem. ho. of dels. 1992—). Democrat. Roman Catholic. Avocations: reading, cooking. Home: 5184 Hwy 308 Napoleonville LA 70390 Office: Law Office Risley Triche 4759 Hwy 1 Napoleonville LA 70390

TRICHEL, MARY LYDIA, middle school educator; b. Rosenberg, Tex., Feb. 2, 1957; d. Henry John and Henrietta (Jurek) Pavlicek; m. Keith Trichel, Aug. 8, 1981; children: Daniel, Nicholas. BS cum laude, Tex. A & M U., 1980. Cert. tchr., Tex. Social studies tchr. grades 6, 7 and 8 St. Francis de Sales, Houston, 1980-81; English tchr. grades 7 and 8 Dean Morgan Jr. High, Casper, Wyo., 1983-86; English and journalism tchr. grades 9 and 11 Tecumseh (Okla.) High Sch., 1987; English tchr. grade 6 Christa McAuliffe Middle Sch., Houston, 1988-92; tchr. Tex. history grade 7, journalism grade 8 Lake Olympia Middle Sch., Missouri City, Tex., 1991-92; tchr. social studies 6th grade Lake Olympia Mid. Sch. Ft. Bend Ind. Sch. Dist., 1993-96; tchr. social studies 6th grade Atascocita Mid. Sch. Humble Ind. Sch. Dist., 1997—. Recipient teaching awards. Mem. Nat. Coun. Tchrs. English, Nat. Coun. Tchrs. Social Studies, Am. Fedn. Tchrs. Avocations: desktop publishing, scuba diving, travel. Home: 14711 Kings Head Dr Houston TX 77044 Personal E-mail: theaggies4@entouch.net.

TRICKLER, SALLY JO, illustrator; b. Burlington, Iowa, Jan. 7, 1948; d. Frank Joseph and Florence Christina (Hein) Koehler; m. James Edward Trickler, Nov. 4, 1967 (div.); 1 child, Brenda Jo. AA, Southeastern C.C., West Burlington, Iowa, 1976; BA, Western Ill. U., 1988. Draftsman Iowa Army Ammunition Plant, Middletown, 1967-73; sr. tech. illustrator J.I. Case Co., Burlington, 1973—. Rep. tech. illustrating Burlington Cmty. H.S. Career Day ann. event, 1985-91. Pub. History of Saints John and Paul Church (1839-2000), 2000. Mem. pub. rels. com. United Way, Burlington, 1975, chmn. pub. rels. 1976-77, art designer, 1987. Mem. Burlington Engrs. Club (v.p. 1974-75, pres. 1975-76, chmn. H.S. counseling com. on career days, 1977-80), Allegro Motor Home Club Iowa, Phi Kappa Phi. Clubs: Good Sam (Big River Sams, Iowa) (sec./treas. 1985-87). Roman Catholic. Avocations: creative writing-poetry, fiction, landscape design, photography. Home: 11904 44th St Burlington IA 52601-8966 Office: Case New Holland 1930 Des Moines Ave Burlington IA 52601-4441

TRIECE, ANNE GALLAGHER, magazine publisher; b. Bklyn., July 1, 1955; d. Anthony J. and Mary Ann (Clines) Gallagher; m. David Mark Triece, Nov. 3, 1990; 1 child, Elizabeth Renee. BBA cum laude, CUNY, 1978. Media planner Isidore Lefkowitz Elgort, N.Y.C., 1978-80; sr. media supr. Ted Bates Advt., N.Y.C., 1980-83; account mgr. Prevention mag., N.Y.C., 1983-85; N.Y. mgr. Home mag., N.Y.C., 1985-92; assoc. pub. Met. Home mag., N.Y.C., 1992—. Coord. Arts Program for Homeless, N.Y.C., 1994. Recipient advt. excellence award Knapp Comm., 1985. Mem. Advt. Women N.Y. (commendation 1985). Roman Catholic. Avocations: scuba diving, tennis, skiing. Office Phone: 212-767-5516.

TRIESCHMANN, ELIZABETH SUZANNE, elementary school educator; b. Hot Springs, Ark., Mar. 16, 1960; d. Willian Douglas II and Anna Sue (Looper) McCoy; m. John Cypert Treischmann, Dec. 20, 1980; children: John Benjamin, Ashley Rebekah. BS in Edn., Henderson State U., 1982, Masters in Spl. Edn., 1998. Cert. tchr. Ark. Substitute tchr. Hot Springs (Ark.) City Schs., 1982; tchr. Greehouse Pre-Sch., Yuma, Ariz., 1983-84, Stone St. Elem. Sch., Camp LeJeune, N.C., 1985-86, Hot Springs City Schs., 1990-91, 1993—, St. Francis of Assisi Sch., Jacksonville, N.C., 1986-90, 91-93. Mem. Internat. Reading Assn. (Onslow county), Beta Sigma Phi (Gamma Theta chpt., sec. 1992-93), Alpha Delta Kappa. Methodist. Avocations: reading, swimming, cross stitch. Home: 840 Red Wings Rd Bismarck AR 71929

TRIFOLI-CUNNIFF, LAURA CATHERINE, psychologist, consultant; b. L.I., N.Y., June 8, 1958; d. Peter Nicholas and Susan Maria (Graziano) T.; m. John Kevin Cunniff, June 6, 1992; children: James Peter, Capri Susan. BA, Hofstra U., Uniondale, N.Y., 1980, MA, 1982, PhD, 1986. Founder, prin. Quality Cons., West Islip, N.Y., 1980-87; sr. tng. officer Norstar Bank, Garden City, N.Y., 1985-87; asst. v.p. mgmt. devel. First Boston Corp., N.Y.C., 1986-90; mgr. exec. devel. Merrill Lynch, N.Y.C., 1990-91; pres. The Exec. Process, 1991—. Cons. Am. Mgmt. Assn., N.Y.C., 1981-83, AT&T, Basking Ridge, N.H., 1982-83, The First Boston Corp., 1991—, Goldman Sachs, 1991—, Merrill Lynch & Co., 1991—, Union Bank of Switzerland, 1991—, Sanford C. Bernstein & Co., 1992—, Alexander & Alexander, 1993—, S.G. Warburg, 1994; instr. dept. psychology Hofstra U., 1983-85. Author: Vietnam Veterans: Post Traumatic Stress and its Effects, 1986; contbr. articles to profl. publs. Shift coord. Islip Hotline, 1976-78; eucharistic min. Hofstra U. Cath. Soc., 1980-85, Good Samaritan Hosp., West Islip, N.Y., 1988—. Scholar, Hofstra U., 1978-81, fellow, 1980, 81. Mem. Am. Psychol. Assn., Am. Soc. Tng. and Devel., Nat. Psychol. Honor Soc., Internat. Platform Soc. Roman Catholic. Avocations: equestrian sports, art, music. Office: 2906 Bree Hill Rd Oakton VA 22124-1212

TRIGOBOFF, SYBELLE, artist, educator; b. Bklyn., Feb. 20, 1932; d. Sol and Esther Devorah (Novack) Rosenberg; m. Harold Trigoboff, 1950; children: Norman Jed, Sharon Malva, Hinda Leah. Curator, artist Amontri-gallery, N. Bellmore, NY, 1964-66; lectr., critique Greenbriar Art Workshops, N. Bellmore, NY, 1970—, Drawing From Life Model Workshops, N. Bellmore, NY, 1975—. Vis. lectr. B.O.C.E.S. Cultural Arts Ctr., Syosset, NY, 1990-91; Alice Sawyer lectr. Hofstra U., 2005; art adv. com. N. Bellmore Pub. Libr., 1972-77; owner, cons. Atrigart, LI, NY, 1980—; curator Good Deed Link, Nat. Com. Furtherance of Jewish Edn., 1997; lectr. in field. Designer artist 18 ft. menorah commd. by Nat. Com. for Furtherance of Jewish Edn., Nassau County, 1984; contbg. artist: World's Women, 1995-96; contbg. author: Total Immersion, 1995; curated and exhibited: SUNY, Stony Brook, 1999; exhibited: Phoenix Gallery, NYC, 2000, Graphic Eye Gallery, Port Washington, NY, 2003. Pres. LWV, Town of Hempstead, NY, 1965-67; adv., LI rep., Bais Chana Women Internat., 1994—. Spl. Opportunity grant NY Found. Arts and East End Arts Coun., 1997; Sarah Domb Jewish Ed. award NCFJE, NYC, 1999. Avocation: gardening. Home: 1272 Greenbriar Ln North Bellmore NY 11710-2306

TRIIPAN, MAIVE, library director; b. Virumaa County, Estonia, Jan. 4, 1942; d. Osvald and Minna (Olesk) Triipan; m. Kalle Dobkevich, Mar. 6, 1971 (div. June 4, 1974); 1 child, Raul. B. of Libr., Tartu U., Tartu, Estonia, 1967. Rsch. mgmt. asst. Libr. of Estonian Acad. Sci., Tallinn, Estonia, 1967-74, asst. dir. rsch. work, 1974-84, dir., 1984—; head PR Astangu Vocat. Rehab. Ctr., Tallinn, 2003. Mem. State Libr. Coun., Tallinn, 1974-87, State Libr. Coun. at Dept. of Culture and Edn., Tallinn, 1989—, Tech. U. Coun., Tallinn, 1993—, Estonian Nat. Libr. Coun., Tallinn, 1994—; fin. mgr. Merelaug, 1998-99; project mgmt. Scs. Dept. Estonian Inst. Pub. Adminstrn.; project mgmr. Style Wear, Tallinn, 2000-01; specialist further edn. Astangu Vocat. Rehab. Ctr., Tallinn, 2000, head dept. IT and staff tng., 2002-, head dept. pub. relationship, 2003. Editl. bd. Estonian Retrospective, 1975; mng. pub. National Bibliography 1525-1940, 1993. Mem. Estonian Librs. Assn. Avocations: literature, music, art. Business E-Mail: maive.triipan@astangu.ee.

TRIMBLE, CELIA DENISE, lawyer; b. Clovis, N.Mex., Mar. 3, 1953; d. George Harold and Barbara Ruth (Foster) T.; m. Billy W. Boone, Apr. 21, 1990. BS, Ea. N.Mex. U., 1976, MA, 1977; JD, St. Mary's U., San Antonio, 1982. Bar: Tex. 1982, U.S. Ct. Appeals (5th cir.) 1985, U.S. Supreme Ct. 1986; cert. family law Tex. Bd. Legal Specialization, 1987, Family Law Exam. Commn., 2002. Instr. English Ea. N.Mex. U., Portales, 1977-78; editor Curry County Times, Clovis, 1978-79; assoc. Schultz & Robertson, Abilene, Tex., 1982-85, Scarborough, Black, Tarpley & Scarborough, Abilene, Tex., 1985-87; ptnr. Scarborough, Black, Tarpley & Trimble, Abilene, Tex., 1988-90, Scarborough, Black, Tarpley & Boone, Abilene, Tex., 1990-94; of counsel Scarborough, Tarpley, Boone & Fouts, Abilene, Tex., 1994-96; prin. Law Office of Celia D. Trimble Boone, Abilene, Tex., 1996—. Instr. legal rsch. and writing St. Mary's Sch. Law, 1981-82; mem. family law exam. com. Tex. Bd. Legal Specialization, 2002—, vice chair, 2005—. Legal adv. bd. to bd. dirs. Abilene Kennel Club, 1983-85; landmarks commn. City of Abilene, 1989-90. Mem. ABA, State Bar Tex. (disciplinary rev. com. 1989-93), Am. Trial Lawyers Assn., Tex. Trial Lawyers Assn., Tex. Criminal Def. Lawyers Assn., Tex. Acad. Family Law Specialists, Abilene Bar Assn. (bd. dirs. 1985-88, sec.-treas. 1985-86), Abilene Young Lawyers Assn. (bd. dirs. 1985-89, treas. 1985-86, pres.-elect 1987-88, pres. 1988-89). Avocations: needlecrafts, gardening. Office: 104 Pine St Ste 316 Abilene TX 79601-5930 E-mail: mail@celia.net.

TRIMNAL, WANDA LEE, secondary school educator; b. Balt., Apr. 7, 1950; d. Lyde Haston and Lena Gertrude (Mangum) T. BA in English and French, Frostburg State U., Md., 1972; MLA, Johns Hopkins U., Balt., 1976. Adv. profl. cert. in secondary edn. Tchr. English and journalism Arundel H.S.,

Gambrills, Md., 1972—. Graphic artist The Md. Pennysaver, Hanover, part-time, 1988-92; leader Weight Watchers, Balt., part-time, 1978—; layout and design tchr. Md. Scholastic Press Assn., College Park, summers 1992-94; advisor/sponsor Spectrum (sch. newspaper), 1985—, Panorama (sch. yearbook), 2000—. Organist Randall St. Christian Ch., Balt., 1968; organist, part-time choir dir. Cmty. Ch. of God, Glen Burnie, Md., 1972-82, Sunday sch. tchr., 1972-82, pianist, 1998—; mem. Arundel Singers, Brooklyn, Md., 1982-87, 96—, v.p., 1984, pres., 1985-87, bd. dirs., 1983-87. Mem. NEA, Journalism Edn. Assn., Md. State Tchrs. Assn., Tchrs. Assn. Anne Arundel County, Md. Scholastic Press Assn. (bd. dirs. 1992—), Columbia Sch. Press Assn. (medalist award 8 times, gold medal 1996, 97), Quill and Scroll (internat. 1st place 8 times), Sigma Tau Delta Hon. English Frat. (pres. 1971-72). Avocations: singing, playing organ and piano, sewing, needlecrafts, gardening. Office: Arundel High School 1001 Annapolis Rd Gambrills MD 21054-1099 E-mail: wtrimnal@aacps.org.

TRIPLETT, ARLENE ANN, management consultant; b. Portland, Oreg., Jan. 21, 1942; d. Vincent Michael and Lorraine Catherine (Starr) Jakovich; m. William Karrol Triplett, Jan. 27, 1962; children: Stephen Michael, Patricia Ann. BA, U. Calif., Berkeley, 1963. Budgets and reports analyst Cutter Labs., Berkeley, 1963-66; controller Citizens for Reagan, 1975-76; dir. adminstrn. Republican. Nat. Com., 1977-80; asst. sec. Dept. Commerce, Washington, 1981-83; assoc. dir. mgmt. Office Mgmt. and Budget, Exec. Office of Pres., Washington, 1983-85; prin. assoc. McManis Assocs., Inc., 1985-87, v.p., 1987-89, sr. v.p., 1989-93; from v.p. to exec. v.p. Am. Tours Internat., Inc., L.A., 1993-97; prin. McManis Assoc., Manhattan Beach, Calif., 1997-98, IBM, Manhattan Beach, Calif., 1999—2002; fin. mgmt. cons., 2002—. Roman Catholic. Office Phone: 310-650-2822.

TRIPP, AILI MARI, political scientist, educator; b. Market Harborough, UK, May 24, 1958; came to US, 1974; d. Lloyd William Frederick and Marja-Liisa (Aro) Swantz; m. Warren Earl Tripp, Aug. 28, 1976; children: Lloyd Max, Leila Mari. BA, U. Chgo., 1983, MA, 1985; PhD, Northwestern U., Evanston, Ill., 1990. Prof. dept. polit. sci. and womens studies program U. Wis., Madison, 1992—; dir. Women's Studies Rsch. Ctr., 2000—; assoc. dean Internat. studies Northwestern U, Evanston, Ill., 2003—. Author: Changing the Rules: The Politics of Liberalization and the Urban Informal Economy in Tanzania, 2001, Women and Politics in Uganda, 2001. Am. Coun. of Learned Soc. fellow, 1991; grantee Inst. for the Study of World Politics, 1988, John D. and Catherine T. MacArthur Found., 1993, AAUW, 1993, Social Sci. Rsch. Coun., 1995, UN World Inst. for the Study of Devel. Econ. Rsch., 1987, Am. Scandinavian Found., 1999. Mem. Am. Polit. Sci. Assn. (Victoria Schuck award 2001), African Studies Assn.

TRIPP, KAREN BRYANT, lawyer; b. Rocky Mount, NC, Sept. 2, 1955; d. Bryant and Katherine Rebecca (Watkins) Tripp; m. Robert Mark Burleson, June 25, 1977 (div. 1997); 1 child, Hamilton Chase Tripp Barnett. BA, U. NC, 1976; JD, U. Ala., 1981. Bar: Tex. 1981, US Dist. Ct. (so. dist.) Tex. 1982, US, Ct. Appeals (fed. cir.) 1983, US Dist. Ct. (ea. dist.) Tex. 1991, US Dist. Ct. (we. dist.), 2005, US Supreme Ct. 1994, US Dist. Ct. (no. dist.) Tex. 1998, US Ct. Appeals (5th and 9th cirs.) 2000, US Ct. Appeals (3d cir.) 2001. Law clk. Tucker, Gray & Espy, Tuscaloosa, Ala., 1978-81; law clk. to presiding justice Ala. Supreme Ct., Montgomery, Ala., summer 1980; atty. Exxon Prodn. Rsch. Co., Houston, 1981-86, coord. tech. transfer, 1986-87; assoc. Arnold, White and Durkee, Houston, 1988-93, shareholder, 1994-98; shareholder, head intellectual property sect. for Houston office Winstead, Sechrest & Minick, Attys. at Law, Houston, 1998; pres. Blake Barnett & Co., 1996—2003; pvt. practice Houston, 1999—. Creator, program planner, master of ceremonies 1st and 2d intellectual property law confs. for women corp. counsels; adj. prof. of intellectual property law Inst. for Advanced Legal Studies, Houston, 2005—. Editor: Intellectual Property Law Rev., 1995—2006; contbr. articles to profl. jour. Chair U. Houston and Houston intellectual Property Law Assoc. Fall CLE Inst. on Intellectual Property, 2000. Mem. ABA (intellectual property law sect., ethics com. 1992-96), Houston Bar Assn. (interprofl. rels. com. 1988-90), Houston Intellectual Property Law Assn. (outstanding inventor com. 1982-84, chmn. 1994-95, sec. 1987-88, treas. 1991-92, bd. dir. 1992-94, 98-2000, nominations com. 1993, 96, chmn. fall CLE Inst. 2000), Houston Bar Found. (fellow), Tex. Bar Assn. (antitrust law com. 1984-85, chmn. internat. law com. intellectual property law sect. 1987-88, internat. transfer tech. com. 1983-84, planning com. continuing legal edn. conf. on intellectual property 2003), planning comm. for 2003 CLE Inst. on Intellectual property Law, Tex. Exec. Women, Women's Fin. Exch., Am. Intellectual Property Lawyers Assn. (patent law com. 1995), Intellectual Property Owners Assn. (copyright com.), Women in Tech. (founder), Lil Eli's Club (founder), Phi Alpha Delta. Republican. Episcopalian. Office: PO Box 1301 Houston TX 77251-1301 Office Phone: 713-658-9323. Business E-Mail: ktripp@tripplaw.com.

TRIPP, LINDA A. LYNN, small business owner; b. Patterson, Ga., Nov. 11, 1946; d. Bert L. and Jelain (Crews) Lynn; m. J. Randolph Tripp, Sept. 25, 1977. Student, South Ga. Coll., 1964-67, Pitt Community Coll., Greenville, N.C., 1977-78; cert. real estate broker, East Carolina U., 1979, BS, 1980, MA, 1981. Adminstr. State of N.C., Greenville, 1968-79; co-owner, dir. AmeriCom Prodn. Group, Inc., 1989—; CEO Carolina Ct. Reporters, Inc., 1999—. Charter mem. Greenville Aquatics and Fitness Ctr.; chmn. bd. Am. Prodn. Group, Inc., Carolina Ct. Reporters. Contbr. articles to profl. jours. Vol., adv. bd. Pitt C.C., Greenville, 1984; vol. Greenville Parks and Recreation, 1987; active St. Timothy's Episc. Ch., Greenville, Greenville Mus. Art; pres. Performing Arts and Friends of the Theater, 2002-; dirs. cir. summer theater, art enthusiast East Carolina U.; co-chair Pitt County Heart Gala, 2002; chair Performing Arts Valentines Gala, 2002; mem. airport authority bd. Pitt-Greenville Counties Named to East Carolina U. Hall of Fame, 2006; recipient Citizen of Yr., Greenville Pitt County, 2005, Disting. Alumni award, East Carolina U., 2006. Mem. Nat. Steno Verbatin Reporters Assn., N.C. Verbatim Reporters Assn., Am. Pers. and Guidance Assn., N.C. Real Estate Commn., Ayden (N.C.) Country Club, Pirate Club of East Carolina U. (dir.), Ironwood Golf and Country Club, Chancellor's Soc., Jockey Club (adv. bd.), Pi Omega Pi. Republican. Avocations: golf, tennis, swimming. Office: Carolina Ct Reporters Inc 105 Oakmont Profl Plz Greenville NC 27858

TRIPP, MARIAN BARLOW LOOFE, retired public relations executive; b. Lodgepole, Nebr., July 26; d. Lewis Rockwell and Cora Dee (Davis) Barlow; m. James Edward Tripp, Feb. 9, 1957; children: Brendan Michael, Kevin Mark. BS, Iowa State U., 1944. Writer Dairy Record, St. Paul, 1944-45; head product promotion divsn., pub. rels. dept. Swift & Co., Chgo., 1945-55; mgmt. supr. pub. rels. J. Walter Thompson Co., N.Y.C. and Chgo., 1956-76, v.p. consumer affairs Chgo., 1974-76; pres. Marian Tripp Communications Inc., Chgo., 1976-94. Mem. Am. Inst. Wine and Food, Confriere de la Chaine des Rotisseriers (officer Chgo. chpt.), Mayflower Soc., Daughters of the Am. Revolution, Les Dames D'Escoffier. Episcopalian.*

TRIPP, SUSAN GERWE, museum director; b. Balt., Dec. 28, 1945; d. Earl Joseph and Maria Elizabeth (Wise) Gerwe; m. David Enders Tripp, June 9, 1977. BS, U. Md., 1967. Home econs. tchr. Balt. County Pub. Sch. Sys., 1967-74; curator of art Johns Hopkins U., Balt., 1974-76, curator of art, archivist, 1976-78, instr. evening coll., 1978-84, dir. univ. collections, 1979-91; supr., instr. art history Goucher Coll., Notre Dame U., Balt., 1977-86; dir. docent tng. Homewood Mus., Balt., 1987-89; exec. dir. Old Westbury Gardens, NY, 1992-96; writer Stuyvesant, NY, 1996—. Dir. Homewood Restoration Adv. Com., 1983-92, Evergreen Restoration Adv. Com., 1988-92, Advancement Basilica Hist. Trust, Inc., 2000-2001; lectr. in field. Co-author: The Garrett Collection of Japanese Art, 1993 (NEA Grant 1980), Contbr. articles to profl. jours. Bd. dirs. Columbia County Hist. Soc., 1996-2002, 2003—, pres. bd. dirs., 1997-2002, chmn. Vanderpoel house restoration, 2002-03, sec., 2003—, interim exec. dir., 2006-; trustee Regional and Cmty. Hist. Preservation Benefit Plan, 2002—; judge Hist. Hudson Preservation Awards, 2000—; bd. trustees Am. Numismatic Soc., 2003—. Recipient Hist. Preservation award Balt. Heritage, Inc., 1988, 91, Rsch. award Am. Soc. Interior Designers, 1991. Fellow Am. Numismatic Soc. (standing com., libr., trustee 2003—); mem. Oriental Ceramic Soc., Balt. Mus. Art, Furniture History Soc., Columbia County Hist. Soc. (bd. dirs. 2003—, sec. bd. dirs. 2003—), Omicron Nu. Avocations: architecture, archaeology, chinese ceramics, historical restoration. Office: PO Box G Stuyvesant NY 12173-0009

TRIPPLE, AMY COLLEEN, elementary school educator; d. Gary and Jacquelyn Sinclair; m. David Tripple, Aug. 7, 2004. BS cum laude in Elem. Edn., Taylor U., 2005. Kindergarten tchr. Westlake Elem., Indpls., 2004—. Scholarship, Ballinger and Hansen Endowed, 2005-2006. Mem.: Internat. Reading Assn.

TRITCH, TERESA, editor, writer; b. LA; BA in German, UCLA, 1984; MA in Journalism, Columbia Univ., 2001. Joined Money Mag., 1988, bur. chief Washington, 1993—97, sr. editor NYC, 1997—2000; contributing editor Gallup Mgmt. Jour., 2001—03, Stanford Social Innovation Rev., 2003; editl. bd. mem. NY Times, 2004—. Co-editor: America at War: The Battle for Iraq in Words, 2003. Knight-Bagehot Fellow in Bus. and Econ. Journalism, Columbia Univ., 2000—01. Office: Editl Bd NY Times 229 W 43rd St New York NY 10036 Office Phone: 212-556-1876. Office Fax: 212-556-3815.*

TRITTEL, REBECCA B., art historian, educator; d. William A. and Mildred P. Blass; m. Edward Charles Trittel Jr., May 31, 2003. PhD, U. Essex, Colchester, Eng., 2005. Prof. art history Savannah Coll. Art and Design, Ga., 2001—, chair dept. art history, 2005—. Mem.: Coll. Art Assn. Office: Savannah Coll Art and Design PO Box 3146 Savannah GA 31402 Office Phone: 912-525-6099. Office Fax: 912-525-6064. E-mail: rtrittel@scad.edu.

TROBAUGH, TARA MICHELLE, music educator; d. Mike D. and D. Ann Turnmire; m. Kevin Craig Trobaugh, Nov. 6, 1999. MusB in Edn., Jacksonville State U., Alabama, 2000; M of Music Edn., U. Ga., 2005. Music tchr. Rossville Elem., Ga., 1998—. Choir mem. Silverdale Bapt. Ch., Chattanooga, 2005, Choral Arts Chattanooga. Finalist Tchr. of Yr., Walkers County, 2005; recipient Tchr. of Yr. award, Rossville Elem., 2005. Mem.: Delta Kappa Gamma (assoc.), Sigma Alpha Iota (life; corr. sec. 1994—98). Baptist. Avocations: knitting, cello, scrapbooks, piano.

TROGANI, MONICA, ballet dancer; b. Newark, Sept. 2, 1963; m. Jay Brooker, July 3, 1993. Grad. high sch., 1980. Ballet dancer N.J. Ballet, West Orange, 1980-83; field asst., coder Reichman Rsch., Inc., NYC, 1984-86; ballet mistress, prin. dancer Dance Theatre of L.I., Port Washington, N.Y., 1984-88; exec. sec. programming dept. The First N.Y. Internat. Festival of the Arts, NYC, 1987-89; guest regisseur Alta. Ballet, Edmonton, Can., 1988-89, ballet mistress, asst. to artistic dir., 1989-93; guest regisseur Ballet du Nord, Roubaix, France, 1991, Dance Theatre of Harlem, NYC, 1993-94; ballet mistress Les Grands Ballets Canadiens, Montreal, 1994—2003; rehearsal dir. Hubbard Street Dance Chicago, 2003—. Avocation: singing. Office: Hubbard St Dance Chicago 1147 W Jackson Blvd Chicago IL 60607

TROIANI, MARYANN VICTORIA, psychologist; b. Chgo., Jan. 23, 1958; d. Edward and Josephine (Gall) T. BA, Northeastern Ill. U., 1980; MA, Forest Inst., 1986, PsyD, 1987. Lic. clin. psychologist, Ill. Psychotherapist Seven Springs HRC, Des Plaines, Ill., 1985-87; staff psychologist Psychotherapy Assocs., Chgo., 1987-90; psychologist Forest Hosp., Des Plaines, 1990—97; pvt. practice clin. psychology, 1990—; clin. psychologist in eating disorders program Forest Hosp., Des Plaines, 1990—96; mental health dir. Delphia Group, Cary, Ill., 1992—97; psychologist Mercer Group Inc, Barrington, Ill. Cons. Norridge (Ill.) Nursing Home, 1986-88; speaker in field. Co-author: Spontaneous Optimsin: Stratgies for Health, Prosperity and Happiness; contbr. articles to profl. publs. Mem. Am. Psychol. Assn., Ill. Psychol. Assn., Internat. Assoc. Eating Disorders Profls. E-mail: damacy@mercersystems.com.

TROIANO, MARIE, music educator; d. Anthony Paul and Rebecca Troiano; m. James Olden. MusB, Coll. NJ, Ewing, 1998; EdM, So. Conn. State U., New Haven, 2002. Music tchr. Race Brook Elem. Sch., Orange, Conn., 1999—. Pvt. piano instr., 1996—2006. Mem.: Music Educators Nat. Conf. Office Phone: 203-891-8030.

TROLL, KITTY, actress, writer; b. N.Y.C., Dec. 18, 1950; d. Hans and Lillian Holland (Ellman) T.; m. Douglas Getchell (div.); 1 child, Wyatt Theodore. Student, Cambridge Sch. of Weston; studied with Lee Strasberg, Michael Howard, N.Y.C. Instr. drama Pacific (Calif.) High Sch.; founder Mixed-Media Theatre, Dallas. Appeared in (stage prodns.) A Grape for Seeing, The Night of the Iguana, Blues for Mr. Charlie, A Midsummer Night's Dream, Spoon River Anthology, The Moon is Blue, Day of the Races, Old Wives Tale, Bandits, Survivors, Beggar's Choice, Much Ado About Nothing, (films) Stardust Memories, 1980, The Last to Know, 1981, Sun and Moon, Permanent Wave, 1986, (TV) As the World Turns, All My Children, For Richer, for Poorer, Texas; author (screenplay) Holding the Bag, (teleplay) Malpractice, (book) The Party Book. Mem. Actors' Equity Assn., Screen Actors Guild, AFTRA.

TROLL, LILLIAN ELLMAN, psychologist, educator; b. Chgo., Sept. 24, 1915; d. Morris C. and Bertha H. (Holland) Ellman; divorced; children: Kathren, Jeanne, Gregory. BS in Psychology, U. Chgo., 1937, MA in Human Devel., 1966, PhD in Human Devel., 1967. Pers. technician U.S. War Dept., Washington, 1941-45; sch. psychologist Newton (Mass.) Pub. Schs., 1957-63; cons. State Calif., San Francisco, 1964-65; sr. rsch. assoc. Merrill-Palmer Inst., Detroit, 1967-70; assoc. prof. psychology Wayne State U., Detroit, 1970-75; prof. Rutgers U., New Brunswick, 1975—87; adj. prof. human devel. and aging, med. anthropology U. Calif., San Francisco, 1986—98; ret. Vis. prof.; lectr. in field 47 convs. and invited talks. Author: Family Issues in Current Gerontology, 1986, Continuations: Development After 20, 1982, Development in Early and Middle Adulthood, 1975, rev. edit., 1985, 32 chpts. in other books; co-author: (with Joan and Kenneth Israel) Looking Ahead: A Woman's Guide to the Problems and Joys of Growing Older, 1977, (with Nancy Schlossberg) Perspectives on Counseling Adults, 1978, (with Sheila Miller and Robert Atchley) Families of Later Life, 1979, (with Barbara Turner) Women Growing Older, 1994; contbr. over 30 articles to profl. jours. Recipient Eminent Women in Psychology award, 1988, Disting. Contbn. Div. Adult Devel. and Aging award APA, 1989, Women's Heritage Inst. award, 1992, Disting. Creative Contbn. to Gerontology award, 1993. Fellow APA (sec.-treas. 1973-76, 84-87, pres. 1986-87), Gerontol. Soc. Am. (sec.-treas. behavioral and soc. scis. sect. 1981-87). Home: 1001 Shoreline Dr Apt 302 Alameda CA 94501-5925 E-mail: l.troll@comcast.net.

TROMBETTA, ANNAMARIE, artist; b. Bklyn., Aug. 5, 1963; d. Philip and Maryann (Lepere) T. Student, Bklyn. Mus. Sch. Fine Arts, 1980-83, Parsons Sch. Design, N.Y.C., 1983-86, Nat. Acad. Sch. Fine Arts, 1989-93; cert., N.Y. Acad. Art, N.Y.C., 1986-89. One-woman show Liederkrantz Club, NYC, 1993, Hist. Richmondtown Mus., 2001, Garibaldi-Meucci Mus., 2002, Wagner Coll., 2003, The Dana Discovery Ctr., 2003, Staten Island Inst. Arts & Sciences, 2004, Citibank, SI, NY, 2005 (Junefest award 2005); exhibited in group shows Bklyn. Mus., 1983, Parsons Sch. Design Art Gallery, 1985, Salamagundi Club, NYC, 1988, 92, 93, 94, 95, 96, NAD, 1990, 93, Columbia U., 1990, Lincoln Ctr., 1991, 92, Union League Club, NYC, 1991, Atlantic Gallery, NYC, 1993, 95, 97, First Street Gallery, NYC, 1994, Nat. Arts Club, NYC, 1994, Pakistan Mission, NYC, 1997, 98, Nat. Arts Club Grand Gallery, Godwin-Ternbach Mus., 2001, also others; group exhbns. include Arnot Art Mus., Bendheim Gallery, Greenwich, Conn., Yellow Gallery, Cross River NY, 64th Annual Audubon Artists, NY; art provided for Prasad Art Auction,Manhattan Studios, 1998; represented in pvt. collections, mural executed SI Ctr., 1981. Recipient Philip Isenberg Meml. award, 1991, 1992, Frank Dumond Meml. award, 1991, John and Anna Lee Stacey award, 1992, Valerie Delacorte Scholarship award, 1992, Arthur and Melville Philips award, 1993, Frank Duveneck Meml. award, 1994, Julius Allen award, 1996, Jacqueline Fowler award, 1996, Inga Denton award, 1997, Award-winning photo-feature, Manhattan Arts Internat. mag., 1997; grantee Coun. Art and Humanities, 2005, Pollack-Krasner Found., 2004, Richmond County Found., 2004, 2005, India Traveling grant, Richmond County Saving Found., 2006; Premier grantee, Coun. Arts & Humanities Staten Island, 2001, Encore grantee, 2004, Edwin Austin Abbey Mural Workshop scholar, 2002. Mem. William Butler Yeats Soc. N.Y. (bd. dirs. 1991—, scholarship to W.B. Yeats Summer Sch., Sligo, Ireland 1990), Salmagundi Art Club N.Y. (com. 1996), Theosophical Soc., Painting Group in Soho, Pastel Soc. of Am. Avocations: poetry, running, cooking, biking. Home and Office: 175 E 96th St Apt 14P New York NY 10128-6207 Office Phone: 212-427-5990. Personal E-mail: trombettaart@yahoo.com.

TRONVOLD, LINDA JEAN, occupational therapist; b. Yankton, S.D., Dec. 8, 1950; m. Marvis D. Tronvold, July 7, 1976; children: Marcie, Tami, Kristi, Bradley, Cindy. Student, Mt. Marty Coll., 1989; AS, Kirkwood Community Coll., Cedar Rapids, Iowa, 1989; BS, Creighton U., 1991. Registered occupl. therapist, S.D., Neb., Iowa. Psychiatric aide S.D. Human Svcs. Ctr., Yankton, 1969-74, mental health technician, 1974-85, occpul. therapist asst., 1985-91, occupl. therapist, 1991-92; mem. edn. svc. unit Human Svcs. Ctr., Yankton, 1991-93; program dir. occupl. therapy asst. Western Iowa Tech. C.C., Sioux City, Iowa, 1993—2002; registered occupl. therapist Nova Care, Inc., 1992-96; occupl. therapist Human Svcs. Cmty., 2001—. Guest speaker Creighton U., Omaha, U. S.D., Vermillion; mem. student staff Upward Bound, Omaha, 1989-91, Scout leader Boy Scouts Am., Hartington, Nebr., 1977-80, Girl Scouts USA, Yankton, 1986-89; Sunday sch. tchr. United Ch. of Christ, Yankton, 1984-88; mem. spl. populations staff YWCA, Cedar Rapids, Iowa, 1987-88. Mem. Am. Occupl. Therapy Assn., S.D. Occupl. Therapy Assn., Nebr. Occupl. Therapy Assn., Iowa Occupl. Therapy Assn., Creighton U. Student Occupl. Therapy Assn., VFW Aux., Sq. Dance Club (pres. 1979-81, 96-97, v.p. 1995-96), Alpha Tri Ota Club. Avocations: camping, cake decorating, swimming, dance, sewing. Home: 705 Broadway St Yankton SD 57078-3923 E-mail: tronvol@witcc.com.

TROP, SANDRA, museum director; b. Bklyn. BS, NYU; cert. in arts adminstrn., Harvard U. Dir. Everson Mus. Art, Syracuse, NY, 1995—. Advt. copy writer; adj. prof. Syracuse U. Mem. founding bd. dirs. Lowe Art Ctr., Syracuse U., Salt City Playhouse, Folk Art Gallery, Syracuse Landmark Theatre; mem. Internat. Com. for Museums and Collections of Modern Art; mem. Literacy Vols. Am.; appointed to Mayor's Commn. on Fin. Planning for City of Syracuse. Mem. Am. Arts Alliance, Am. Assn. Museums, N.E. Regional Mus. Conf. Office: Everson Museum Art 401 Harrison St Syracuse NY 13202-3091

TROST, EILEEN BANNON, lawyer; b. Teaneck, N.J., Jan. 9, 1951; d. William Eugene and Marie Thelma (Finlayson) Bannon; m. Lawrence Peter Trost Jr., Aug. 27, 1977; children: Lawrence Peter III, William Patrick, Timothy Alexander. BA with great distinction, Shimer Coll., 1972; JD cum laude, U. Minn., 1976. Bar: Ill. 1976, U.S. Dist. Ct. (no. dist.) Ill. 1976, Minn. 1978, U.S. Tax Ct. 1978, U.S. Supreme Ct. 1981. Assoc. McDermott, Will & Emery, Chgo., 1976-82, ptnr., 1982-93; v.p. No. Trust Bank Ariz. N.A., Phoenix, 1993-95; ptnr. Sonnenschein Nath & Rosenthal, Chgo., 1995—. Mem. Am. Coll. Trust and Estate Coun., Minn. Bar Assn., Internat. Acad. Estate and Trust Law, Chgo. Estate Planning Coun. Roman Catholic. Office: Sonnenschein Nath & Rosenthal 7800 Sears Tower Chicago IL 60606 Office Phone: 312-876-8149. E-mail: etrost@sonnenschein.com.

TROTT, MENA, application developer; b. 1977; m. Ben Trott. Co-founder, pres. Six Apart, Inc., 2004—. Named one of Top 100 Young Innovators, MIT Tech. Review, 2004. Achievements include creator of TypePad and Moveable Type, software tools for publishing weblogs. Office: Six Apart 548 4th St San Francisco CA 94107-1621

TROTT, NANCY ROBERTS, editor; b. New Britain, Conn., 1968; BA, U. NH. Supervising editor AP, Concord, NH, 1993—96; with Seattle Post-Intelligencer, 1996, ABC News, Seattle, 1997—99; news editor AP, Seattle, 1999—2002, regional news editor Washington, 2002—03, Wash. & Idaho bur. chief Seattle, 2003—06, regional news dir. Western burs., 2006—. Office: AP Seattle Bur Ste 750 3131 Elliot Ave Seattle WA 98121-1095 Office Phone: 206-682-1812. Office Fax: 206-621-1948. E-mail: ntrott@ap.org.*

TROTTA, MARCIA MARIE, librarian, consultant, education educator; b. Meriden, Conn., Nov. 12, 1949; d. Salvatore Dominic and Teresa Stella (Fuda) Marando; m. Carmine Joseph Trotta, Oct. 23, 1971; 1 child, Christopher Michael. AB, Albertus Magnus Coll., 1971; MLS, So. Conn. State U., 1979. Tchr. St. Mary's Sch., Meriden, 1971-73; circulation libr. Meriden Pub. Libr., 1973-74, asst. children's libr., 1974-76, reference libr., 1976-81, dir. children's libr., 1981-91, asst. dir., 1992—, dir., 1994—2005; ret., 2005. Adj. prof. So. Conn. State U., New Haven, 1987—, Albertus Magnus Coll., 1996—; cons. Pfzier Metall. Libr., Wallingford, Conn., 1987, Woodbridge Town Libr., 1987-89, Conn. Assocs. for Counseling, Wilton, 1988—, Conn. Humanities Coun. Author: (books) Managing Outreach Programs, 1992, Successful Staff Development, 1995, Special Events Program, 1997; editor: CDA Manual, Outreach Services for Children and Youth, 1992, Librarian's Facilities Management Handbook, 2000, Supervisor's Handbook, 2006. Mem. coun. Day Care Adv. Com. Meriden, 1990-95, coun. Student Drug and Alcohol Abuse Prevention, Meriden, 1990-94; pres. Conn. Jaycee Women, 1984-85. Named one of Outstanding Women of Am., U.S. Jaycees Women, 1983; Outstanding Alumna Nat. Cath. Edn. Assn., 1997; Paul Harris fellow Rotary, 1997; recipient Steve Little award, 1986, YWCA Outstanding Profl. Woman award, 1995, Greater Meriden C. of C. Cmty. Partnership award, 1996, Faith Hecktoen award, Conn. Libr. Assn., Woman of Yr., Girls Inc., 2002. Mem. ALA, Conn. Libr. Assn. (pres. 1991-92, Outstanding Libr. 1986, 93), New Eng. Libr. Assn., Rotary Internat. (Rotarian of Yr. 1994, Disting. Svc. award 1998, pres. Meriden Rotary 2000-01). Democrat. Roman Catholic. Avocations: writing, gourmet cooking, puppetry, children's book collector. Office: Meriden Pub Libr 105 Miller St Meriden CT 06450-4213

TROUSDALE, MARGARET MARY, science educator; d. Charles Eastman and Mary Margaret Trousdale; children: Joseph I. Lombrozo, Aaron C. Lombrozo, Leon J. Lombrozo. BS in Health Sci., Calif. State U., Long Beach, 1980, MA, 2003. Profl. Clear Credential Commn. on Tchr. Credentialing, Calif., 2001, cert. Clear Crosscultural, Lang. and Acad. Devel. Commn. on Tchr. Credentialing, Calif., 2001. Tchr., life sci., 7th grade, English lang. learners Lynwood Unified Sch. Dist., Calif., 1998—. Contbr. articles to profl. jours. Candidate bd. edn. Anaheim Union H.S., Calif., 2005. Grantee Tuition, Tchr. Edn., Calif. State U. Long Beach, 1998—2000. Mem.: Orange County Beekeepers Assn., Calif. (assoc.; editor, monthly newsletter, Little Stinger 2006). Office: Lynwood Middle School 12124 Bullis Road Lynwood CA 90262 Office Phone: 310-603-1466. Personal E-mail: mmtrousdale@yahoo.com.

TROUT, DEBORAH LEE, clinical psychologist, healthcare executive, consultant, director; b. Manistee, Mich., May 8, 1953; d. Paul Eugene and Rosemary Ruth (Beebe) T.; m. Curtis Lee Harris, June 5, 1982; 1 child, Sarah Elizabeth. AB cum laude, Bucknell U., 1975; MA in Clin. Psychology, U. Kans., 1978, PhD in Clin. Psychology, 1980. Lic. psychologist, Minn. Intern Minn. Mgmt. Inst. U. Minn., Mpls., 1979-80, 95; psychotherapist, dept. psychiatry Ramsey Clinic, St. Paul, 1980-82, psychologist, 1983-86, dir. prepaid psychiatry, 1986-88, dir. managed care and off campus ops., 1988-90; dir. utilization review and network programs United Behavioral Systems, Inc., 1990-91; ops. dir., 1991-92; v.p. clin. systems, 1992-94; v.p. ops., 1994-95; COO, 1995—96; sr. v.p. managed care United Behavioral Health, 1996—97; gen. mgr. behavioral health divsn. Kapi'olani Med. Specialists, Honolulu, 1997—99; gen. mgr., internal auditor Kapi'olani Health, 1999—2001; exec. v.p., chief clin. officer Magellan Behavioral Health, 2001—03; pvt. practice, 2004—05; dir. office behavioral health and housing Colo. Dept. Human Svcs., Colo., 2005—. Psychotherapist Washington Co. Human Svcs., Inc., Oakdale, Minn., 1981-83. Mem. Nat. Register Health Svc. Providers in Psychology, So. Poverty Law Ctr., Phi Beta Kappa, Alpha Lambda Delta, Psi Chi. Avocations: drawing, sculpture, travel, hiking. Office: United Behavioral Systems Inc PO Box Mn06-0210 Minneapolis MN 55440-1459

TROUT, LINDA COPPLE, state supreme court justice; b. Tokyo, Sept. 1, 1951; BA, U. Idaho, 1973, JD, 1977; LLD (hon.), Albertson Coll. Idaho, 1999. Bar: Idaho 1977. Atty. Blake, Feeney & Clark, 1978—83; judge magistrate divsn. Idaho Dist. Ct. (2d jud. divsn.), 1983-90, dist. judge Lewiston, 1991-92, acting trial ct. adminstr., 1987-91; justice Idaho Supreme Ct., 1992—, chief justice, 1997—2004. Instr. coll. law U. Idaho, 1983, 88; chair Idaho State Supreme Ct. Judicial Education Com. Mem. bd. directors Lewiston City Library, Northwest Children's Home, Lewiston YWCA. Mem. Idaho State Bar Assn., Clearwater Bar Assn. (pres. 1980-81). Office: Idaho Supreme Court PO Box 83720 Boise ID 83720-3720*

TROUT, MARGIE MARIE MUELLER, civic worker; b. Apr. 27, 1923; d. Albert Sylvester and Pearl Elizabeth (Jose) Mueller; m. Maurice Elmore Trout, Aug. 24, 1943; children: Richard Willis, Babette Yvonne. Student, Webster Coll., 1944-45. Cert. genealogist Bd. Cert. Genealogy. Sec. offices Robertson Aircraft Corp., St. Louis, 1942; speed lathe and drill press operator Busch-Selzer Diesel Engine Co., St. Louis, 1942-43; Cub Scout den mother Vienna, Austria, 1953-55, Mt. Pleasant, Mich., 1955, London, 1956-57; leader Nat. Capitol coun. Girl Scouts U.S.A., Bethesda, Md., 1963-65; co-chmn. Am. Booth YWCA and Red Cross Ann. Bazaars, Bangkok, 1970-72; worker ARC, Vientiane, Laos, 1959-60, Bangkok, 1970-72; activities co-chmn., exec. bd. mem. Women's Club Armed Forces Staff Coll., Norfolk, Va., 1975-77. Mem. Am. Women's Clubs, Embassy Clubs, Internat. Women's Clubs Vienna, 1952-55, London, 1956-59, Vientiane, 1959-61, Munich, Germany, 1965-69, Bangkok, 1969-72, Norfolk, 1975-77. Crochet articles exhibited Exhbn. of Works of Art by the Corps Diplomatique, London, 1958. Home: 6203 Hardy Dr Mc Lean VA 22101-3114

TROUTMAN, VIRGINIA E., elementary school educator; b. Cin., Mar. 17, 1952; d. Earl F. and Maryanne Ragland Roades; m. David L. Troutman, July 31, 1976; children: Mary E., Benjamin D. BA in Elem. Edn., Oral Roberts U., Tulsa, Okla., 1974, MA in Reading & Adult Literacy, 1984. Tchr. Anderson Elem. Sch., Sand Springs, Okla., 1970—74; tchr. English Chengdu U. Sci. & Tech., Chengdu, Sichwan, China, 1985—88; tchr. mid. sch. sci. Evangelistic Temple Sch., Tulsa, Okla., 1988—2005. Named Tchr. of Yr., Walmart, Tulsa, Christian Sch., 2005. Office: Evangelistic Temple Sch 1339 E 55th St Tulsa OK 74105

TROUTWINE, GAYLE LEONE, lawyer; b. Kansas City, Mo., Feb. 26, 1952; BS, N.W. Mo. U., 1973; JD with honors, U. Mo., 1978, postgrad., 2003—. Bar: Mo. 1978, Oreg. 1983, U.S. Dist. Ct. (we. dist.) Mo., Wash. 1984, U.S. Ct. Appeals (9th cir.), U.S. Dist. Ct. (we. dist.) Wash., U.S. Supreme Ct., Hawaii 1995. Ptnr. Williams & Troutwine, P.C., Portland, Oreg., 1986—99, Troutwine Law Offices, Maui, Columbia, Osage Beach, Mo., 1999—; pres., CEO Hula Moons Farm, Maui, Hawaii, 1999—2002, Apricot Rose, Kahului, Hawaii, 1999—2003; CEO Aloha Enterprises, 2004—. Spkr. in field; mem. Maui Bd. Realtors. Contbr. articles to profl. jours. Mem. Jud. Steering Com., 1994, Made in Hawaii Coun., 2000—02, pres., 2004—; bd. mem. Portland Area Women's Polit. Caucus, 1992—95, Oreg. Women's Polit. Caucus, 1996—99; candidate Columbia City Coun., 2005; steering com. mem. Breast Implant Litig., 1992—, Tobacco Litig. Named Queen of Torts, Wall St. Jour., 1996. Mem.: ATLA (bd. govs.), Cmty. Assn. Inst., Maui Bd. Realtors, Western Trial Lawyers Assn. (bd. govs. 1992—), Greater Kansas City (sec. 1981—82), Women Lawyers Assn., Wash. Trial Lawyers Assn., Hawaii Trial Lawyers Assn., Calif. Trial Lawyers Assn., Oreg. Trial Lawyers Assn. (bd. govs. 1987—91), Wash. State Bar, Oreg. State Bar (exec. bd. litig. sect. 1984—88, chmn. 1987—88, procedure and practice com. 1985—88, bd. govs. 1990—93), Mo. Bar, Hawaii State Bar. Democrat. Office: 1218 Hwy KK Osage Beach MO 65065 Office Phone: 573-348-2434. Office Fax: 573-348-4204. Business E-Mail: gtroutwine@troutwinelaw.com.

TROW, JO ANNE JOHNSON, retired university official; b. Youngstown, Ohio, Feb. 10, 1931; d. Raymond Leonard Johnson and Mary Belle Beede; m. Clifford W. Trow, Oct. 10, 1969. BA, Denison U., 1953; MA, Ind. U., 1956; PhD, Mich. State U., 1965. Case worker Office Pub. Assistance, Cleve., 1953-54; asst. dean women Denison U., Granville, Ohio, 1956-59, Wash. State U., Pullman, 1959-63; asst. dir. resident program Mich. State U., East Lansing, 1964; dean women Oreg. State U., Corvallis, 1965-69, assoc. dean students, 1969-83, v.p. student affairs, 1983-95, program dir., 1983-95. Presenter, speaker in field. Contbr. articles to profl. jours. Bd. dirs. Benton County Mental Health Assn., 1975-79, United Way Benton County, 1977—, United Way Oreg., 1977-80; mem. adv. bd. Old Mill Sch., 1979-95, chmn., 1983, 94-95; mem. Oreg. Cmty. Corrections Adv. Bd., 1988-95; moderator 1st Congl. Ch., 1977, trustee, 1979-83, 91-95; mem. Oreg. Gov.'s Com. on Status of Women, 1972-78, vice chmn., 1976-77; mem. fund campaign Good Samaritan Hosp. Found. Cancer Care Ctr., 1982-83. Recipient Corvallis Woman of Achievement award, 1974, Boss of Yr. award Oreg. State U. Office Personnel Assn., 1979, White Rose award March of Dimes, 1987, Elizabeth A Greenleaf Disting. Alumna award Ind. U., 1987, Scott Goodnight award, 1989, Disting. Alumni Citation, Denison U., 1993, Coun. Woman of Distinction award Oreg. State U. Meml. Union Program, 1993; named Sr. First Citizen Corvallis, 1999. Mem. Nat. Assn. Women Deans, Adminstrs. and Counselors (pres. 1981-82), Am. Coll. Personnel Assn. (sec. 1969-70), Nat. Assn. Student Personnel Adminstrs., Am. Coun. on Edn., N.W. Assn. Schs. and Colls. (comn. on colls. 1989-95), Am. Assn. for Higher Edn., N.W. Coll. Personnel Assn. (life, pres. 1969-70), Assn. Oreg. Faculties, AAUW (state and local bd. dirs.), LWV (bd. dirs., v.p. Corvallis 1966-69, 79-80), Corvallis Area C. of C. (bd. dirs. 1972-74, 78-80), Mortar Bd., Phi Delta Kappa, Phi Kappa Phi, Alpha Lambda Delta. Democrat.

TROXELL, LUCY DAVIS, management consultant; b. Cambridge, Mass., Apr. 25, 1932; d. Ellsworth and Mildred (Enneking) Davis; m. Charles DeGroat Bader, June 13, 1952 (div. Aug. 1974); children: Christie P. Walker, Mary Bader Montgomery, Charles D. Bader Jr., David Bradford Bader; m. Victor Daniel Shirer Troxell, Aug. 1974. BA, Smith Coll., Northampton, Mass., 1952; grad., Inst. Paralegal Training, Phila. Cert. employee benefit specialist, assoc. in risk mgmt. Paralegal O'Melveny & Myers, L.A., 1976-77; acct. exec. Olanie Hurst & Hemrich, L.A., 1977-78; asst. to trustee Oxford Ins. Mgmt., L.A., 1978-80; dir. corp. svcs., asst. corp. sec. Consolidated Elec. Distbrs., Inc., Westlake Village, Calif., 1980-93; pres. MONMAK LDT, Westlake Village, 1993—. Vol. Friends of the Westlake Village Libr., 2000—, ARC; bd.dirs. Friends of the West Lake Village, 2004—, v.p., 2006; clk. St. Mathew's Parish Vestry, Pacific Palisades, Calif., 1988, sr. warden, 1989—90; lic. lay eucharistic min. Episcopal Ch.; sustaining bd. dirs. Jr. League, Hartford, Conn., 1952—58, L.A., 1952—60; bd. dirs. Smith Coll. Club, Hartford, 1952—58, Nat. Charity League, L.A., 1964—68, Theatre Palisades, 1960—74; bd. dirs., treas. HOA Lakeshore Cmty. Assn., 1999—2002, v.p., 2005—. Sophia Smith scholar. Fellow: Risk and Ins. Mgmt. Soc. (program chmn. L.A. chpt. 1985—86), Internat. Soc. Cert. Employee Benefit Specialists (bd. dirs., sec., treas. 1988—89, pres. 1989—90, edn. chmn. L.A. chpt. 1986—88). Republican. Avocations: finance, acting, music, art. Home: 450 Puerto Del Mar Pacific Palisades CA 90272-4233 Office: MONMAK LDT 32001 Viewlake Ln Westlake Village CA 91361

TROXLER, WILLIE THOMASENE, retired elementary school educator; b. Raleigh, N.C., Sept. 3, 1925; d. Charles Gilmer Cates and Addie Gaye Long; m. Roger Vernon Troxler, Mar. 18, 1950; children: Bonnie Lynn, Teri. BA, St. Mary's Jr. Coll., Raleigh, 1945; BA Journalism, U. N.C., Chapel Hill, 1947; MA Lang. Arts, U. N.C., Charlotte, 1976. Reporter State Advt. Divsn., NC, 1947—48; assoc. editor Carolina Road Builders Trade Mag., NC, 1948—50; tchr. elem. sch. Salisbury City Schs., NC, 1961—78. Exhibited in group shows at Page Walker Arts and History Ctr., Cary, NC, 1999, Rowan Regional Hosp., Salisbury, 1999, Davidson County Mus. Art, Lexington, NC, 1999, one-woman shows include Depot Visual Arts Ctr., Mooresville, NC, 1997, Rowan Pub. Libr., Salisbury, 1982, Chatham County Hosp., Asheboro, NC, 1982, Salisbury Pub. Sch. Supplementary Ctr. Art Gallery, 1982. Active Salisbury Symphony Guild; 2d v.p. Rep. Women, Salisbury. Recipient 1st pl. Collage, Rowan County Silver Arts, 2005, 2d pl., Rowan County Art Group, 2005, 1st Pl. Mem. Choice award, Rowan County Art Show, 2005. Mem.: Stanley County Art Guild, Davidson County Art Guild (Judges Commendation 1986, Pres. Choice Stuffer Myer's Meml. award 1995, Third pl. 1998, First pl. 2002), Mooresville Art Guild, Waterworks Visual Art Works, Watercolor Soc. N.C. (Fifth pl. Fall Show 1997, Merit award Spring Show 1999), Carolina Artist (past pres.). Home: 131 Richmond Rd Salisbury NC 28144-2847 E-mail: ttroxler@salisbury.net.

TROYANSKAYA, OLGA, biomedical researcher, computer scientist; BS in biology and computer sci. summa cum laude, Richmond U., 1999; PhD in biomedical informatics, Stanford U. Asst. prof. dept. computer sci. Princeton U. Contbr. articles to profl. jour. Named one of Top 100 Young Innovators, MIT Tech. Review, 2004; Predoctoral Fellow, Howard Hughes Med. Inst., 1999. Office: Princeton U Dept Computer Sci 35 Olden St Princeton NJ 08544 Business E-Mail: ogt@cs.princeton.edu.

TRUBOW, SUSAN ELIZABETH, visual artist, educator; b. San Francisco, Aug. 19, 1949; d. William Gordon and Thelma (Schneider) Johnson; m. George Trubow, Aug. 12, 1972. AA, City Coll. San Francisco, 1970; BA, standard elem. teaching credential, San Francisco State U., 1972; BFA, Calif. Coll. Arts and Crafts, 1989. Tchr. San Mateo (Calif.) City Sch. Dist., 1973—; artist San Mateo, 1975—. One-woman shows include 1870 Gallery and Studios, Belmont, Calif., 1986, 89, 91, 2004-06, Twin Pine Art Ctr., San Mateo, Calif., 1983, Montalvo Ctr. for the Arts, Saratoga, Calif., 1982, Dolphin Gallery, Gualala, Calif., 1979, Belmont Arts Coun., Calif., 2005; two-person shows include Valley Art Gallery, Calif., 1982, San Mateo Arts Coun., 1980; exhibited in group shows at Kaiser Ctr., Oakland, 1990, Metro Gallery, Foster City, Calif., 1988, L.A. Printmaking Soc., 1985, Calif. Soc. Printmakers, Montalvo, 1985, 91, Mission Cultural Ctr., San Francisco, 2006, Syaopsis, San Jose, 2005; drawings pub. in Serious Drawing, 1989, Bitter Fruit, 1992; also many nat.-internat. exhbns. Democrat. Avocations: music, philosophy. Home: 116 Chestnut Ln San Mateo CA 94403-3317

TRUBY, BETSY KIRBY, artist, illustrator, photographer; b. Winchester, Va., Nov. 8, 1926; d. Thomas Gomery and Nellie Gray Kirby; m. Frank Keeler Truby, Sept. 4, 1948; children: Thomas Lee, Scott R., Susan Alida. Student, Hiram Coll., 1946—48, Cleve. Sch. Art, 1949, N.Mex. Tech., 1951—54, U. N.Mex., 1960. Asst. dir. Yucca Art Gallery, Old Town Albuquerque, 1970—71. Exhibitions include N.Mex. State Mus., 1964—68, Nat. Art Show, Lawton, Okla., 1974, commd. by, Congressman Albert G Simms, 1964, Christmas card, Easter Seal Soc., 1969, Cystic Fibrosis Found., N.Mex., 1976—77, one-woman shows include Hiram Coll., 1987, exhibitions include Bardean Gallery, N.Mex., 2004 (2d pl., 2004), PBS TV show, The Creative Process, 1983. Mem.: Pastel Soc. N.Mex. (charter mem.), Nat. League Am. Pen Women (v.p. Yucca br. 1978—79, photographer Yucca br. 1992—2005, 1st pl. painting 1974, Best of Show 2003, 1st pl. 2003, 2d pl. in pastel State Show, Socorro, N.Mex. 2005), Yucca Art Gallery (charter mem.). Presbytertian. Avocations: boating, swimming. Home and Office: 6609 Loftus Ave NE Albuquerque NM 87109 Office Phone: 505-884-8459.

TRUCHOT, JANICE ELAINE, elementary school educator; b. Casper, Wyo., Sept. 6, 1953; d. John F. Jr. and Violet I. (Sword) T.; m. Bernie R. Schnorenberg, Mar. 19, 1977; 1 child, Megan Diane Schnorenberg. BA, Macalester Coll., 1975; MST, U. Wyo., 1977. Cert. elem. tchr., spl. edn. tchr. Tchr. elem. Moorcroft (Wyo.) Elem. Sch., 1977-79, 4 Oaks Rural Sch., Aladdin, Wyo., 1979-81; tchr. spl. edn. Sundance (Wyo.) Elem. Sch., 1981-87, tchr. grade 5, 1987-90, tchr. grade 6, 1990—. Recipient Presdl. award NSF, 1994; named Wyo. State Tchr. of Yr., 1988. Mem. NSTA, Nat. Coun. Tchrs. Math., Coun. Presdl. Awardees Math., Soc. Elem. Presdl. Awardees, Phi Delta Kappa, Delta Kappa Gamma. Home: PO Box 742 237 Canyon Rd Sundance WY 82729 Office: Sundance Elem Sch PO Box 870 Sundance WY 82729-0870

TRUCKENBRODT, YOLANDA BERNABE, retired air force officer, consultant; b. Manila, June 17, 1952; d. Nestor Leynes and Zenaida Bernabe Javier; m. Edmund Phillip Truckenbrodt, July 27, 1972. BA, Far Ea. U., Manila, 1971; AAS, C.C. of Air Force, 1979; MBA, Angelo State U., 1980; MPA, U. West Fla., 1987; D of Pub. Adminstrn., Nova Southeastern U., 2000; diploma, Air Command and Staff Coll., 1995. Cert. Dept. of Def.'s Acquisition Profl. in Program Mgmt., USAF Software Quality Assurance. Enlisted USAF, 1974, advanced through grades to maj., 1992, ret., 1998; program mgr. KC-135 Reengine Dep. for Airlift and Trainer Sys., Wright-Patterson AFB, Ohio, 1980—84; mgr. electronic warfare program Tactical Sys. Divsn., Eglin AFB, Fla., 1985—89; program mgr. Airborne Warning and Control Sys. Elec. Sys. Ctr., Hanscom AFB, Mass., 1989—92; program analyst ballistic missile def. hdqs. Air Force Materiel Command, Wright-Patterson AFB, 1992—94; congl. liaison staff officer Plans and Programs Divsn., Wright-Patterson AFB, 1995—98. Flight comdr. detachment 847 Res. Officers Tng. Corps, San Angelo, Tex., 1978—80; chairperson Asian-Am. Pacific Islander Heritage Com., Eglin AFB, 1986—87; officer-in-charge Air Force Assn. Nat. Acquisition Symposium, Wright-Patterson AFB, 1993—94; student-in-residence Def. Sys. Mgmt. Coll., Ft. Belvoir, Va., 1994; staff officer Directorate of Plans and Programs, Wright-Patterson AFB, 1995—98; guest spkr. Nat. Bus. and Profl. Assn., San Angelo, 1993. Contbr. articles to profl. jours. Pres. Filipino-Am. Assn., Fort Walton Beach, Fla., 1987; vol. Air Force Mus., Dayton, Ohio, 1995—96; vol. reading tutor Ohio Reads Program, 2002—; vol. Nightingale Ho., Wright-Patterson AFB, 1996—98; vol. income tax preparer Ret. Officers Assn., Wright-Patterson AFB, 1999—; vol. social worker United Way, Dayton, 1982—84; bd. dirs. Filipino-Am. Assn., Ft. Walton Beach, Fla., 1987, Filipino-Am. Coun. N.W. Fla. Nominee Lt. Robert Sullivan Meml. award, Eglin AFB, 1985; named Airman of the Quarter, Air Weather Svc. Comm. Squadron, 1975, Career Woman of Yr., Gayfers Career Club of Okaloosa County, Fla., 1987, Jr. Officer of the Quarter, Airlift and Trainer Sys., Wright-Patterson AFB, 1983, Airborne Warning and Control Systems, Hanscom AFB, 1991, winner, State of Ohio Summer Biathlon Series Championship Cup, 2002, 2d Pl. Overall winner for half-marathon, 4th Internat. Marathon on Great Wall, China, 1999, winner numerous race awards in track and field and Summer Biathlons; named one of Outstanding Young Women of Am., 1983, 20 Outstanding Filipino-Ams. in U.S. and Can., 2004; recipient Appreciation and Recognition award, Dyess AFB Human Rels. Coun., 1976, 1977, Air Force Res. Tng. Corps (ROTC) Leadership award, 1979, Arnold Air Soc. Outstanding Pledge award, 1979, Drill Commandant of Yr. award, 1978; Robert G. Carr scholar, Detachment 847 ROTC, Angelo State U., 1978, 1980. Mem. Women in Mil. Svc. Am. Meml. (charter), Air Force Women Officers Assoc., Air Force Meml. Found. (charter), Angelo State U. Alumni Assn. (Disting. ROTC Alumnae of Yr. 2002), Air Force Meml. Found. (charter), Ohio River Rd. Runners Club, Sigma Beta Delta. Avocations: travel, arts and music, summer biathlons, marathons, photography.

TRUCKSIS, THERESA A., retired library director; b. Hubbard, Ohio, Sept. 1, 1924; d. Peter and Carmella (DiSilverio) Pagliasotti; m. Robert C. Trucksis, May 29, 1948 (dec. May 1980); children: M. Laura, Anne, Michele, Patricia, David, Robert, Claire, Peter; m. Philip P. Hickey, Oct. 19, 1985 (dec. May 1993). BS in Edn., Youngstown Coll., 1945; postgrad., Youngstown State U., 1968-71; MLS, Kent State U., 1972. Psychometrist Youngstown (Ohio) Coll., 1946-49; instr. ltd. svc. Youngstown State U., 1968-71; libr. Pub. Libr. Youngstown & Mahoning County, Youngstown, 1972-73, asst. dept. head, 1973-74, asst. dir., 1985-89, dir., 1989-97, NOLA Regional Libr. System, Youngstown, 1974-85. Contbr. articles to profl. jours. Mem. bd. Hubbard Sch. Dist., 1980-85. Mem. ALA, Ohio Libr. Assn. (bd. dirs. 1979-81), Pub. Libr. Assn. Address: 133 Viola Ave Hubbard OH 44425-2062

TRUDEL, JANICE CUEVAS, music educator; b. Odenton, Md., July 16, 1964; d. Alberta Hartz and Clemence August Cuevas; m. Paul Alan Trudel, June 7, 1986; children: Kristin Elizabeth, Laura Marie, Jenna Lynne. B, Pembroke State U., NC, 1986. Lic. music edn. K-12 N.C., 1986. Music tchr. Ponderosa Elem. Sch., Fayetteville, NC, 1996—. Dir.: Ponderosa Show Choir. Grantee, Jr. League of Fayetteville, 1998—2001. Office Phone: 910-864-1048.

TRUE, ALISON COCHRAN, newspaper editor; b. Detroit, Aug. 10, 1961; d. Thomas Perry and Valery (Martin) T.; m. Frederick Mosher, June 12, 1993; children: Henry Arthur True Mosher. BA, Vassar Coll., 1984. Various positions including mailroom clk., asst. to editor, asst. editor Chgo. Reader, 1984—94, editor, 1994—. Named one of Chgos. 100 Most Influential Women, Crain's Chgo. Bus., 2004. Office: Chgo Reader 11 E Illinois St Chicago IL 60611-5652

TRUE, JEAN DURLAND, entrepreneur, oil industry executive, gas industry executive; b. Nov. 27, 1915; d. Clyde Earl and Harriet Louise (Brayton) Durland; m. Henry Alfonso True Jr., Mar. 20, 1938; children: Tamma Jean (Mrs. Donald G. Hatten), Henry Alfonso III, Diemer Durland, David Lanmon. Student, Mont. State U., 1935-36. Ptnr. True Drilling Co., Casper, Wyo., 1951—94, True Oil Co., Casper, 1951-94, Eighty-Eight Oil LLC, 1955-94, True Geothermal Energy Co., 1980—, True Ranches, 1981-94. Officer, dir. White Stallion Ranch, Inc., Tucson, Smokey Oil Co., Casper. Mem. steering com. YMCA, Casper, 1954-55, bd. dirs., 1956-68; mem. bd. dirs. Gottsche Rehab. Ctr., Thermopolis, Wyo., 1966-93, mem. exec. bd., 1966-93, v.p., 1983-90; mem. adv. bd. for adult edn. U. Wyo., 1966-68; mem. Ft. Casper Commn., Casper, 1973-79; bd. dirs. Mus. of Rockies, Bozeman, Mont., 1983-87, mem. Nat. Adv. Bd., 1997-2000; bd. dirs. Nicolaysen Art Mus., 1989-93, Nat. Cowboy and We. Heritage Mus., 1997-2002, dir. emeritus, 2002--; mem. Nat. Fedn. Rep. Women's Clubs; dep. Rep. Nat. Conv., 1972; trustee Trooper Found., 1995—. Mem.: Casper Area C. of C., Casper Country Club, Petroleum Club, Alpha Gamma Delta. Episcopalian. Office: PO Box 2360 Casper WY 82602-2360

TRUEBLOOD, SUSAN ANN, music educator; b. Logansport, Ind., Nov. 24, 1951; d. James Parks and Joan Wise Scott; m. Ronald Eugene Allread, Dec. 22, 1973 (div. Sept. 1992); 1 child, John Edward Allread; m. William Ray Trueblood, June 15, 2002. BS in Music K-12 and English 7-12, BS in Instrumental Music, Ball State U., Muncie, Ind., 1973; MS in Edn., Ind. U.-Purdue U., Indpls., 1977. Life profl. tchg. lic. Ind. Music tchr. Pioneer Regional Schs., Royal Center, Ind., 1973—78; pvt. tchr. piano and woodwinds Camden, Ind., 1978—; substitute tchr. Logansport, Carroll Consol. and Delphi Cmty. Schs., 1986—88; music tchr. Hillcrest Elem. Sch., Delphi Cmty. Sch. Corp., Ind., 1988—. Accompanist Delphi Cmty. Schs., 1988—, mem. tech. com., 1999—2003, mem. policy com., 2003—; accompanist Missoula Children's Theater, Delphi, 2003—; coord. area elem. academic spell bowl competition Ind. Assn. Sch. Prins., Delphi, 2003—; clinician for non-competitive choral festival Ind. Music Educators Assn., Muncie, Ind., 2004—06. Contbg. friend Carroll County Cmty. Found., Delphi, 2006—. Named Outstanding Elem. Sch. Music Educator of Yr., State of Ind., 2004; grantee, Ind. Arts Commn., 1993, Tippecanoe Arts Fedn., 1998, 1999, EDS, 2004, Ind. Dept. Edn., 2005—06. Mem.: Music Educators Nat. Conf. (licentiate), Ind. Music Educators Assn. (life), Delphi Classroom Tchrs. Assn. (life), Delta Kappa Gamma (life; state music rep. 2000—02), Order Ea. Star, Kappa Kappa Kappa (life; corr. sec., rec. sec., v.p. 2003—04). Avocations: reading, travel, gardening. Home: 9175 N 150 East Camden IN 46917 Office: Hillcrest Elem Sch 300 W Vine St Delphi IN 46923 Office Phone: 765-564-3895. Business E-Mail: truebloods@delphi.k12.in.us.

TRUESDALE, CAROL A., music educator; b. Rochester, N.Y., June 24, 1949; d. Ralph Edward and Bernice Elizabeth Truesdale. BA in English/Edn., SUNY, Geneseo, 1972, MA in English, 1977. Cert. tchr., N.Y. Tchr. Churchville-Chili Ctrl. Schs., North Chili, N.Y. Author: The Ancient Ones, 1998; lyricist Maybe We Can, 1988, Ted E. Bear, 1981, New Shoes Blues, 1989. Mem. Rep. Com., City of Rochester; mem. edn. com. Martin L. King Found., Rochester, 1995—. Fellow Robert W. MacVittie Soc.; mem. ASCAP. Avocations: travel, history, reading, volunteering. Home: 2470 East Ave Rochester NY 14610-2509

TRUEX, BRENDA, music educator; d. George Richard Wells and Sarah Irene Shimer-Wells; m. Duane P. Truex IV (div.); children: Phillip, Sarah. MusB, SUNY, Potsdam, 1977; MusM, Ithaca Coll., 1982; cert. Kodaly tchr., Kodaly Mus. Tng. Inst. Band dir. Selmer Music - Music for America, Elizabeth, NJ, 1977—78, Maine (NY)-Endwell Schs., 1978—. Clarinetist So. Tier Concert Band, Endwell, NY, 1999—. Active PTA, 1978—; bd. dirs. Binghamton (NY) Figure Skating Club, 2004—. Recipient Founders Day award, PTA, Endwell, 1995. Mem.: NEA, NY State Sch. Music Assn., Broome County Music Educators Assn. (adjudicator, orgnl. chmn. 1978—), Music Educators Nat. Conf. Methodist. Avocations: skiing, swimming, camping. Office: Maine Meml Sch 2693 Main St Maine NY 13802 E-mail: bee2002true@yahoo.com.

TRUEX, DOROTHY ADINE, retired university administrator; b. Sedalia, Mo., Oct. 6, 1915; d. Chester Morrison and Madge (Nicholson) T AB, William Jewell Coll., 1936; MA, U. Mo., 1937; EdD, Columbia U., 1956. Asst. dean women N.W. Mo. State U., Maryville, 1939-43, dean women, 1943-45, Mercer U., Macon, Ga., 1945-47, U. Okla., Norman, 1947-69, assoc. prof., 1969-72, dir. rsch. and program devel., 1969-74, prof. edn., 1972-74, dir. grad. program in student pers. svcs., 1969-74; vice chancellor for student affairs U. Ark., Little Rock, 1974-83, alumni specialist, 1983-84, acad. adviser, 1984-87. Exec. bd. N. Cen. Assn. Schs. and Colls., 1977—83. Author: Rich Choices, 1994, A Visit to Spitesville, 1999, The 13th Bridesmaid, 1999, Carved in Stone, 2000, Full Circle, 2002, The Twenty Million Dollar Giveaway, 2001, A Left Handed Chord, 2003, Life with Cheryl, 2005. Mem. Nat. Assn. Women Deans, Adminstrs. and Counselors (pres. 1973-74), So. Coll. Pers. Assn. (pres. 1970), Okla. Coll. Pers. Assn. (pres. 1972-73), William Jewell Coll. Alumni Assn. (pres. 1970-73), Woman's City Club (pres. 2000-2001), Pi Beta Phi, Alpha Lambda Delta, Mortar Bd., Sigma Tau Delta, Cardinal Key, Gamma Alpha Chi, Kappa Delta Pi, Pi Lambda Theta, Alpha Psi Omega, Pi Gamma Mu, Delta Kappa Gamma, Phi Delta Kappa, Phi Kappa Phi. (nat. v.p. 1986-89) Avocations: writing, aerobics. Home: 14300 Chenal Pkwy Apt 7422 Little Rock AR 72211-5819

TRUFANT, CAROL ANN, psychologist, consultant; b. Berkeley, Calif., Dec. 17, 1941; d. Ralph Homer and Doris Vivian Trufant. AB, U. Calif., Berkeley, 1969; MA, Mich. State U., 1972, PhD, 1977. Psychologist Calif., Wis., lic. marriage and family therapist. Pre-doctoral intern Neuropsychiat. Inst., UCLA, 1974—75; staff psychologist, cmty. cons. Des Moines Child and Adolescent Guidance Ctr., 1978—81; lectr. Calif. State U. Bay Area, Hayward, 1989; civilian clin. psychologist USAF, Naples, Italy, 1992; emergency substitute tchr. Novato Unified Schs., 2001—; cons. pvt. practice, 2006—. Cons.-in-tng. Mich. State U., Lansing, 1973—74; panelist Pre-Law Conf. Drake U. Law Sch., DesMoines, 1981; panelist People Are Talking KPIX-TV, San Francisco, 1989; facilitator Metro Women's Network, Des-Moines, 1982. Fellow, Nat. Inst. Mental Health, 1970, 1971; dissertation fellow, Black Analysis Inc., Adminstrn. for Children, Youth and Families, 1976. Mem.: APA, Am. Group Psychotherapy Assn. (clin. mem.), Family Firm Inst. Inc., Am. Assn. Marriage and Family Therapists (clin. mem.), Nat. Assn. Cognitive-Behavioral Therapists. Achievements include patents pending for Design and Utility; patents in field; invention of Surface Pattern for an Intergroup Working Model for Social Conflict Resolution to a Setting or Room for Adults; Design patent. Avocations: movies, jazz, salsa dancing, sailing. Mailing: PO Box 4008 Alameda CA 94501-0408

TRUJILLO, ANNA, food company administrator, city official; b. Brownsville, Tex., Mar. 5, 1945; d. Santos S. and Minerva C. Saldivar; m. Jose Antonio Trujillo, June 5, 1964 (div. 1971); children: Michael A., Joeanna K., David A., Sandra A. AA in Sociology, N.Mex. Jr. Coll. Notary pub., State of N.Mex., 1990-94. Office mgr., osner La Poblanita Foods, Lovington, N.Mex., 1964-96; officer mgr. N.Mex. Trujillo Foods, 1995—2001; city commr. City of Lovington, 1988—2003. Bd. dirs. Lea County Extraterritorial, Lovington, 1992-2003, Lea County Registration, Lovington, 1985-87; bd. mem. Brownsville Cmty. Health Clinic, 2004-; sec. Preservation Brownsville, 2004-. Vice chair Lovington Dem. Party, Hobbs, N.Mex., 1983; mem. com. N.Mex. State Ctrl. Com., 1984. Named Outstanding Lea County Woman, 1991, Lea County Pioneer, 1994; recipient Leadership award Dem. Com. N.Mex., 1996. Mem.

Lovington Women's Club (sec. 1981-82), Altar Soc., Rebecca Lodge. Democrat. Roman Catholic. Avocations: reading, painting, bike riding, gardening. Home: 1657 McKinley Brownsville TX 78521 Personal E-mail: annacommissioner@aol.com.

TRUJILLO, STEPHANIE N., social sciences educator; M, N.Mex State U. Tchr. Santa Teresa H.S., N.Mex., 1995—, social studies chair. Sgt. USMC. Decorated Navy Good Conduct Achievement medal USMC. Mem.: Rio Grande Women Educators Assn., USTA. Office Phone: 505-589-5300.

TRUMAN, MARGARET, writer; b. Independence, Mo., Feb. 17, 1924; d. Harry S (32nd Pres. U.S.) and Bess (Wallace) T.; m. E. Clifton Daniel Jr., Apr. 21, 1956; children: Clifton T., William, Harrison, Thomas. LHD, Wake Forest U., 1972; HHD, Rockhurst Coll., 1976. Concert singer, 1947-54, actress, broadcaster, author, 1954—; author: Souvenir, 1956, White House Pets, 1969, Harry S. Truman, 1973, Women of Courage, 1976, Murder in the White House, 1980, Murder on Capitol Hill, 1981, Letters from Father, 1981, Murder in the Supreme Court, 1982, Murder in the Smithsonian, 1983, Murder on Embassy Row, 1985, Murder at the FBI, 1985, Murder in Georgetown, 1986, Bess W. Truman, 1986, Murder in the CIA, 1987, Murder at the Kennedy Center, 1989, Murder in the National Cathedral, 1990, Murder at the Pentagon, 1992, Murder on the Potomac, 1994, First Ladies, 1995, Murder in the National Gallery, 1996, Murder in the House, 1997, Murder at the Watergate, 1998, Murder in the Library of Congress, 1999, Murder at Foggy Bottom, 2000, Murder in Havana, 2001, Murder at Ford's Theatre, 2002, The President's House, 2003, Murder at Union Station, 2004, Murder at the Washington Tribune, 2005; editor: Where the Buck Stops: The Personal and Private Writings of Harry S. Truman, 1989. Trustee and v.p. Harry S. Truman Inst.; sec. bd. trustees Harry S. Truman Found.

TRUMAN, RUTH, administrator, writer, lecturer, consultant; b. Ashland, Ky., Oct. 5, 1931; d. Rexford Maitland and Allene G. (Barber) Dixon; BS, Taylor U., 1952; MS, Calif. State U., 1967; PhD in Higher Edn., UCLA, 1978; m. Wallace Lee Truman, June 5, 1952; children— Mark, Rebecca, Timothy, Nathan. Tchr. Atco (N.J.) Elem. Sch., 1954; tchr. home econs. Chatham (NJ) HS, 1955; counselor, instr. Citrus Coll., Azusa, Calif., 1967-70; dir. counseling Calif. Luth. Coll., Thousand Oaks, Calif., 1971-74; cons. Women's Ednl. Improvement Program, L.A., 1978-80; women's center facilitator Mt. San Antonio Coll., Walnut, Calif., 1981-82; free-lance writer, lectr., cons., 1982-83; coord. Cancer Mgmt. Network, U. So. Calif., 1983, assoc. dir. office cancer comm. Norris Comprehensive Cancer Ctr., 1984-85; dir. Cancer Info. Svc. Calif., U. So. Calif., 1985-86; dir. cert. programs Calif. State U., Fullerton, 1986-88, dir. extended edn., program svcs., 1988-90, acting v.p. extended edn., rsch., 1990-91, dir. program svcs, 1991-92, ret., 1992. Trustee Baker Home for Ret. Ministers, Rowland Heights, Calif., 1982-88; chmn. Com. Status and Role of Women, Pacific and Southwest Conf., United Meth. Ch., 1980-82, mem. Bd. Higher Edn., 1983-84; mem. exec. com. Ventura County Council Drug Abuse, 1972-73. Mem. UCLA Doctoral Assn., Phi Delta Kappa. Democrat. Methodist. Author: How To Be A Liberated Christian, 1981; Spaghetti From the Chandelier, 1984; Mission of the Church College, 1978; Underground Manual for Ministers' Wives and Other Bewildered Women, 1974, Not Of This Fold, 2001. Home: 2259 Barbara Dr Camarillo CA 93012-9379

TRUMP, BLAINE (MARTHA LINDLEY BLAINE BEARD TRUMP), philanthropist; m. Robert Trump, 1984; 1 child, Christopher. Student, U. Tokyo. Clothing line creator Am. Classics by Blaine Trump, QVC, 1999. Fundraiser Am. Ballet Theatre, Meml. Sloan-Kettering Cancer Ctr.; vice-chair God's Love We Deliver. Named one of 50 Most Beautiful People World, People mag., 1998; recipient Marietta Tree award for pub. svc., Citizen's Com. for NYC, 1998. Achievements include all proceeds from clothing line Am. Classics by Blaine Trump go to God's Love We Deliver. Office: God's Love We Deliver 166 Ave of the Americas New York NY 10013

TRUPE, MARY-ANN, secondary school educator; b. Trenton, NJ, Jan. 6, 1939; d. Norman Louis Green and Jean Hortense Lurvey; m. Robert Arthur Barclay, Nov. 28, 1955 (dec. July 2, 1965); children: Mary Ann, Alison Jean; m. Titus Weidman Trupe, Dec. 30, 1966; children: Amy Suzanne, Sara Diana. BA, Houghton Coll., 1960; French cert., Millersville U., 1981, Spanish cert., 1985; Sign lang. cert., Deaf & Hearing Sch., Lancaster, Pa., 2001. Pvt. elem. reading tchr., 1955—59; tchr. Erlton Elem. Sch., NJ, 1955—59; tchr. French and Spanish lang. St. Joseph Acad., Columbia, Pa., 1981—91; tchr. English Lancaster Cath. H.S., Lancaster, 1991—, chair English dept., 1993—2005. Troop leader Girl Scouts Am., Horseheads, NY, 1967—73; Sunday Sch. tchr. Horseheads Presby. Ch., 1974—77, youth leader, 1975—77. Recipient Nat. Gold Apple Tchr. award, Scholastic, 2001. Mem.: AAUW (pres. 1973—75), Lancaster Lit. Guild. Republican. Presbyterian. Avocations: gardening, painting, reading, travel, piano. Home: 105 Green St Canton MA 02021

TRUSDELL, MARY LOUISE CANTRELL, retired state educational administrator; b. Chandler, Okla., Oct. 24, 1921; d. George Herbert and Lois Elizabeth (Bruce) Cantrell; m. Robert William Trusdell, Jan. 7, 1943; children— Timothy Lee, Laurence Michael. BA, Ga. So. Coll., 1965; MEd, U. Va., 1974. Dir. specific learning disabilities program Savannah Country Day Sch., Ga., 1960-65; learning disabilities tchr. Richmond pub. schs., Va., 1966-73; dir. New Community Sch., Richmond, 1974-75; dir. Fed. Learning Disabilities Project, Dept HEW, Mid. Peninsula, Va., 1975-76; supr. programs for learning disabled Va. Dept. Edn., Richmond, 1976-86; bd. dirs. Learning Disabilities Council, Richmond, Very Spl. Arts- Va., 1986-91; mem. adv. com. Learning Disabilities Research and Devel. Project, Woodrow Wilson Rehab. Ctr., Fisherville, Va., 1983. Co-editor: Understanding Learning Disabilities: A Parent Guide and Workbook, 1989, 3d edit., 2002. Bd. dirs. Savannah Assn. Retarded Children, 1957-60, Meml. Guidance Clinic, Richmond, 1966-69. Named Tchr. of Yr., Learning Disabilities Ctr., Richmond, 1972. Mem. Orton Dyslexia Soc. (pres. capital area br. 1968-70, nat. bd. dirs. 1970-72, Va. br. 1986-91), Alliance for the Mentally Ill. Cen. Va. (pres. 1991-93). Presbyterian. Avocations: travel, theater, reading.

TRUTOR, GENEVIEVE WILLIAMSON, museum director; b. Benson, Vt., Aug. 26, 1923; d. Clayton John and Caroline Aileen (Walker) Williamson; m. John Trutor, May 4, 1946 (dec.); children: Barry, John W., Elizabeth, William C. Diploma, Rutland Bus. Coll., 1942. Sec. War Prodn. Bd., Washington, 1942—45, Soc. Am. Foresters, Washington, 1945—47; adminstrv. asst. Benson Village Sch., Benson, Vt., 1971—89; dir. Benson Lumbar Yard Inc., Benson, 1963—2002; founder, curator Benson Mus., Benson, 1980—. Lib. commr. Town of Benson, 1959—61; dir. Lower Champlain Housing Corp., 1977—82; mem. Benson's Cmty. Hall Restoration project, 1975—80; chmn. Nat. Bicentennial Celebration, Benson, Vt., 1976, State Bicentennial Celebration, Vt., 1977, Benson Bicentennial Celebration, 1980; sec., treas. Benson Health Com., 1961—70; trustee Pub. Funds, 1981—87, 1996—, Bertha R. Franke Scholarship Fund, 1971—79. Republican.

TRYLOFF, ROBIN S., food products executive; BS, U. Mich.; MS, U. Chgo. Exec. dir., cmty. rels. Sara Lee Corp.; exec. dir. Sara Lee Found., pres., 2002—. Chair, bd. dirs. Donors Forum of Chgo., 2004. Office: Sara Lee Found 3 First Nat Plz Chicago IL 60602-4260

TRYON, ELIZABETH ANNE, educational association administrator; b. Columbus, Ohio, May 1, 1957; d. Anne Colwell Tryon; m. Ted M. Petith, Sept. 9, 1989; children: Charmaine Elizabeth Tryon-Petith, Clayton Colwell Tryon-Petith, Miles William Tryon-Petith. B of music, U. of Ill., 1987—91. Touring performer/rec. artist Cowboy Jazz, Balt., 1977—81; bassist/vocalist freelance, Champaign, Ill., 1983—92, jazz educator/performer Carbondale, Ill., 1992—99; v.p. of mktg. smartgroove.com, Madison, Wis., 1999—; asst. to dir. of human issues program Edgewood Coll., Madison, Wis., 2004—. Event planner Carbondale Cmty. Arts; WDBX radio, Carbondale, Ill., 1992—98; v.p. for edn. Champaign-Urbana Symphony, Ill., 1990—92; v.p. of edn., exec. bd. Krannert Art Mus. Coun., Champaign, Ill., 1990—92. Composer (performer, producer): (audio recording) Chaos Theory, (audio cd) Mr. Fix-It (hon. mention, 1997); editor: (booklet/cd) The Groove Project; musician: (jazz concert) Whitaker Jazz Festival, St. Louis, Groove Merchants. Cultural arts com. mem. Randall PTO, Madison, Wis., 2003—05; fundraising chair Sinfonia da Camera, Urbana, Ill., 1991—92; campaign worker Feingold for Senate, Madison, Wis., 2004. Recipient Vocalist of the Yr., So. Ill. Music Assn., 1997, Outstanding Vocalist, Elmhurst Coll. Jazz Festival, 1989; Music Edn. Residencies, Dane County Cultural Affairs Commn., 2000—03. Mem.: Wis. Music Educators Assn. Achievements include development of music education method for improvisation. Avocations: ceramics, sailing, swimming, knitting, bicycling. Office Phone: 608-633-2889. Personal E-mail: beth@smartgroove.com.

TSACOUMIS, STEPHANIE, lawyer; b. Aug. 31, 1956; BA magna cum laude, Coll. of William & Mary, 1978; JD, Univ. Va., 1981. Bar: DC 1981, Md. 1982. Of counsel Morrison & Foerster, Washington, 1988—91, ptnr., 1991—96; of counsel, corp. fin. Gibson Dunn & Crutcher LLP, Washington, 1996—2000, ptnr. corp. transactions and securities, 2000—, and co-ptnr.-in-charge DC office. Adj. faculty Georgetown Univ. Law Ctr., 2001—. Sr. editor Va. Jour. of Internat. Law, contributing author Corporate Communications and the Federal Antifraud Rules, 1992, Securities in the Electronic Age, 2001. Mem.: ABA, Md. State Bar Assn., DC Bar, Phi Beta Kappa. Office: Gibson Dunn & Crutcher LLP 1050 Connecticut Ave NW Washington DC 20036 Office Phone: 202-955-8277. Office Fax: 202-530-9613. Business E-Mail: stsacoumis@gibsondunn.com.

TSAI, RUTH MAN-KAM, nurse; b. China, Aug. 9, 1942; came to U.S., 1963; d. William Y.S. and Dorris (Young) T.; m. James Migaki, Aug. 19, 1967 (div. Aug. 1975); children: Grace, Paul; m. Patrick Joseph McFaden, July 24, 1982 (div. June 1997). BSN, Biola U., 1979. RN Calif. Vis. nurse Vis. Nurses Assn., Long Beach, Calif., 1987-88; mental health nurse VA Med. Ctr., Loma Linda, Calif., 1988-89, 92-93, W. Los Angeles, 92-93; home health care nurse Interhealth, Inc., Whittier, Calif., 1990-91; vocat. nurse instr. Pacific Coast Coll., Santa Ana, Calif., 1991-92; nurse evaluator II Dept. Health Svcs., L.A., 1994-95; home health nurse Procel Internat. Corp., Hermosa, Calif., 1995-96; mental health nurse Premiere Nursing Svcs., Long Beach, 1995—2005; vocat. nurse instr. Concorde Career Inst., Garden Grove, 1999—2001; charge nurse Harbor View Adolescent Ctr., Long Beach, Calif., 2001—, Del Amo Hosp., Torrance, Calif., 2004—, Little Co. of Mary, San Pedro, Calif., 2005—. Quality rev. coord. Calif. Med. Audit, Arcadia, 1997; disability analyst, mem. Am. Bd. Disability Analysts, 1998. Lions & Kiwanis Clubs scholar, 1964, Blue Cross scholar, L.A., 1975. Republican. Evangelical. Avocations: crafts, movies, ping-pong, walking, reading.

TSALIKIAN, EVA, physician, educator; b. Piraeus, Greece, June 22, 1949; came to U.S., 1974; d. Vartan and Arousiak (Kasparian) T.; m. Arthur Bonfield, Apr. 8, 2000. MD, U. Athens, 1973. Rsch. fellow U. Calif., San Francisco, 1974-76; resident in pediats. Children's Hosp., Pitts., 1976-78, fellow in endocrinology, 1978-80; rsch. fellow Mayo Clinic, Rochester, Minn., 1980-83; from asst. prof. to prof. pediats. U. Iowa, 1983—2004, prof. pediats., 2004—, dir. pediat. endocrinology hosps. and clinics, 1988—, vice chmn. clin. affairs Dept. Pediats., 2005—, chief staff hosp., 2006—. Recipient Young Physician award, AMA, 1977; fellow, Juvenile Diabetes Found., 1978—80, Heinz Nutrition Found., 1980—81. Mem. Am. Diabetes Assn. (bd. dirs. Mid-Am. sect.), Endocrine Soc., Soc. Pediat. Rsch., Am. Pediat. Soc., Lawson Wilkins Soc. for Pediat. Endocrinology, Internat. Soc. Pediat. and Adolescent Diabetes Home: 206 Mahaska Dr Iowa City IA 52246-1606 Office: U Iowa Dept Pediatrics 2856 JPP Iowa City IA 52242

TSAO, JANIE, information technology executive; m. Victor Tsao. BA, U. Tamkang, Taiwan. Programmer Carter Hawley Hale, Calif.; co-founder Linksys, Irvine, Calif., 1988; v.p. worldwide sales, mktg. & bus. devel. Linksys divn. Cisco Systems Inc., Irvine, Calif., 1988—. Named Entrepreneur of Yr., Orange County (Calif.) Bus. Assn., 2000, Inc. mag., 2004; recipient BridgeGate 20 award, 2002, Women of Vision award for Leadership, Anita Borg Inst., 2005. Office: Linksys 121 Theory Dr Irvine CA 92612 Office Phone: 949-823-3000. Office Fax: 949-823-3002.*

TSCHOEPE, DEBORAH E., special education educator; b. Beaumont, Tex., Feb. 3, 1951; d. Woodrow Wilson Davis, Sr. and Willie Etta Marie Russell; m. Vernon K. Tschoepe, Jan. 16, 1987; children: Jay Woodrow, Stephen Michael. BA, U. Houston, Tex., 1971, MEd, 1975; studied, U. Tex., San Antonio, 1992. Speech lang. therapist Caldwell Ind. Sch. Dist., Tex., 1971—72; tchr. Inter-Agy. for M.H. Children, Houston, 1972—74, program devel. trainer, 1974—77, cons., 1976—77; spl. edn. tchr. Cypress Fairbanks Ind. Sch. Dist., Houston, 1978—83, North East Ind. Sch. Dist., San Antonio, 1983—92, campus coord., spl. edn., 1993—. Coach Tex. Spl. Olympics, San Antonio, 1984—92; min. Lutheran Ch., San Antonio, 1992, youth dir., 1992—98. Mem.: Assn. for Tex. Profl. Educators, Assn. for Secondary Curriculum & Devel. Avocations: reading, boating. Home: 13846 Brook Hollow San Antonio TX 78232

TSE, MARIAN A., lawyer; AB, Vassar Coll., 1976; JD, Columbia Univ., 1979. Bar: Mass. 1979. Ptnr., chair, ERISA/employment benefits practice Goodwin Procter LLP, Boston, mem., diversity com. Bd. dir. Greater Boston Legal Services. Mem.: ABA, Asian Am. Lawyers Assn. Mass., New England Employee Benefits Coun., Boston Bar Assn. Office: Goodwin Procter LLP Exchange Pl 53 State St Boston MA 02109 Office Phone: 617-570-1169. Office Fax: 617-523-1231. Business E-Mail: mtse@goodwinprocter.com.

TSENG, ROSE, academic administrator; BS, Kansas State U.; MS, U. Calif., Berkeley, PhD Nutrition. Registered dietician. Prof., chair, dir., assoc. dean San Jose State U., 1970—86, dean Coll. Applied Scis. and Arts, 1986—93; chancellor, CEO West Valley-Mission C.C., Calif., 1993—98; chancellor U. Hawaii-Hilo, 1998—. Office: U Hawaii-Hilo 200 W Kawili Hilo HI 96720-4091

TSIANG, GRACE RENJUEI, economist, educator; b. Washington, July 12, 1958; d. Sho-Chieh Tsiang and Hsi-Tsin Ma; m. Lars Peter Hansen, Aug. 25, 1984; 1 child, Peter Hansen. BA, Yale U., New Haven, 1979; MA in Econs., U. Chgo., 1983, PhD, 1991. Vis. instr. Stanford U., Palo Alto, Calif., 1990—91; rsch. assoc. Nat. Opinion Rsch. Ctr., Chgo., 1991—92; sr. lectr. U. Chgo., 1992—. Asst. dir. undergrad. econs. program U. Chgo., 1994—98, co-dir., undergrad. econs. program, 1998—2003, D. Gale Johnson dir. undergrad. econ. studies, 2004—. Mem.: Am. Econs. Assn. Avocation: piano. Office: Univ Chicago Dept Econs 1126 E 59th St Chicago IL 60637 Office Phone: 773-702-3410.

TSOH, JANICE YUSZE, clinical psychologist, researcher; b. Hong Kong, May 26, 1968; d. Ka Kuk Tsoh and Chung Mei Lee; m. Dave Lee, July 26, 1997. BA, SUNY, Binghamton, 1990; MA, U. R.I., 1993, PhD, 1995. Rsch. asst. Cancer Prevention Rsch. Consortium, U. R.I., Kingston, 1990-94; psychology resident U. Miss., VA Med. Ctrs., Jackson, 1994-95; postdoctoral fellow U. Tex, MD Anderson Cancer Ctr., Houston, 1995-97, U. Calif., San Francisco, 1997-99, asst. rsch. psychologist, 1999-2000, asst. adj. prof., 2000—; attending med. staff Langley Porter Psyc. Inst., 2001—. Cons. Lifescan Inc., Milpitas, Calif., 1999-2001, Am. Cancer Soc., 2001, nat. Asian Women's Health Orgn., 2000—. Mem. rev. bd. Am. Jour. Health Behaviors, 1996—99, reviewer Addiction Jour. Drug and Alcohol Dependence, Jour. Consulting and Clin. Psychology, Health Psychology, CNS Drugs, Jour. Abnormal Psychology, Jour. Substance Abuse Treatment; contbr. articles. Recipient Travel award Nat. Inst. on Drug Abuse, 1998, New Investigator award Tobacco-Related Rsch. Program, 1999—2003, Pilot Study Fund U. Calif. Treatment Rsch. Ctr., San Francisco, 1999, Career Devel. award Nat. Inst. Drug Abuse, 2000—; fellow Univ. Found. U. Tex. MD Anderson Cancer Ctr., Houston, 1996-97, Rsch. Scholar grant, Am. Cancer Soc., 2003—. Mem. APA, Soc. Behavioral Medicine, Soc. for Rsch. on Nicotine and Tobacco, Nat. Asian Women's Health Orgn., Phi Beta Kappa, Psi Chi. Office: U Calif Dept Psychiatry LPP I 401 Parnassus Ave 0984-TRC San Francisco CA 94143-0984

TSOODLE-MARCUS, CHARLENE, education educator, school system administrator; b. May 8, 1947; d. Charles and Patrita (Lujan) Tsoodle; m. Joe David Marcus, July 29, 1976; 1 child, Keith Eagle Marcus. AA in Police Sci., Monterey Peninsula Coll., 1968; BA in Criminal Justice, N. Mex. State Univ., 1971. Indian justice specialist planner Gov. Coun. on Criminal Justice, Santa Fe, 1972-80; records adminstr. N. Mex. Corrections Dept., Santa Fe, 1980-93; govs. asst. Taos Pueblo Govs. Office, N.Mex., 1993-94; coord. Taos County Gov. Planning Dept., 1994-95, Northern Pueblos Inst., Northern N. Mex. C. C., Esponola, N.Mex., 1995—2001; jail adminstrn. Taos County Detention Ctr., 2001—. Chmn., housing commr. No. Pueblos Housing Authority, Santa Fe, 1993—; bd. mem. Rocky Mountain Youth, Taos, 1998—; steering com. mem. Rio Arriba Environ. Health, Espanola, 1999—. Photo feature Nat. Geog., 1994. Vice chair, com. mem. Taos County Tax Adv., 1993—95; vol. Indian Culture Clubs, Santa Fe, 1980—93, Taos Indian Bapt. Ch., Taos, 1980—93. Mem.: Am. Indian Sci. & Engring. Soc. (adv. 1999—), Nat. Congress Am. Indians (life), Phi Theta Kappa, Alpha Iota Sigma. Avocations: jewelry making, Indian pottery, arts and crafts.

TSU, SUSAN, costume designer, educator; d. Tsung-Chi and Wan-pei Chang Tsu; m. Scott Nelson Kiser, Jan. 7, 2006; children: Christian Tsu-Raun, Morgan Tsu-Raun. MFA, BFA, Carnegie Mellon U., Pitts., 1974. Head of costume design Boston U., 1986—91; head of costume program U. Tex., Austin, 1991—2002; full prof. of design Carnegie Mellon U., Pitts., 2002—. Costume designer nat. and internat., 1967—. Designs for theatre, opera, television, Godspell, Joy Luck Club, The Balcony, The Greeks, classics to premieres (NY Drama Desk, NY Drama Critics, NY Young Film Critics, LA Disting. Designer, Austin Cir. of Critics, Richmond Phoebe Awards). Dirs. Theatre Comm. Group, N.Y.C., NY, 2000—06; mem. United Scenic Artists, N.Y.C., NY, 1976—2006; evaluator Nat. Endowment for the Arts, Washington; curator nat. & student exhibits USITT-Prague Quadrennial-2007, Prague, Czech Republic, 2005—06; task force mem. Am. Theatre Mag.TCG, N.Y.C., NY, 2003—06. Recipient Kennedy Ctr. medallion, US Inst. for Theatre Tech., 2005. Mem.: Nat. Theatre Conf., United Scenic Artists-local 829, Phi Kappa Phi. Office: Carnegie Mellon Univ- School of Drama 349 Purnell Center for the Arts Pittsburgh PA 15213 Office Phone: 412-268-3130. E-mail: stsu@andrew.cmu.edu.

TSUI, SOO HING, educational research consultant; b. Hong Kong, Aug. 2, 1959; came to U.S., 1985; d. Sik Tin and Yuk Kam (Cheung) T. BSW cum laude, Nat. Taiwan U., 1983; MSW cum laude, Columbua U., 1987, postgrad., 1992—. Cert. social worker, N.Y. Dir. cmty. handicapped ctr., Taipei, Taiwan, 1983-85; dir. youth recreational program N.Y., 1986; social work dept. supr. St. Margaret's House, N.Y.C., 1987-89; chief bilingual sch. social work N.Y.C. Bd. Edn., 1990—, rsch. cons., 1993—; rschr. Columbia U., N.Y.C., 1991-95; chief rsch. cons. N.Y.C. Dept. Transp., 1993-96; cheif rschr. immigrant social svcs. N.Y.C. Bd. Edn., 1996—. Bilingual social worker Nat. Assn. Asian/Am. Edn., 1989—; union social work regional rep. N.Y.C. Bd. Edn., 1990-93, citywide bilingual social work rep., 1991-93, citywide social work budget allocation comms. rep., 1992-93; mem. conf. planning com. bd. Amb. For Christ, Boston, 1991-93; coord. doctoral colloquial com. bd., 1991-93, Scholarships Coun. Social Work Edn., Columbia U., N.Y.C., 1992-94; mem. planning com. social work bd. Asian Am. Comms., N.Y.C., 1991-95; exec. dir. alumni bd. Columbia U. Sch. Social Work, 1995—, exec. dir. bd. Columbia newsletters Columbia U. Sch. Social Work, 1996—; exec. bd. dirs. Chinese for Christ, 1993-95. Recipient Nat. Acad. award, 1979-83; Nat. Acad. scholar, 1987-88; Nat. Rsch. fellow Sch. Coun. on Social Work Edn., 1992-94. Home: 65-38 Booth St Apt 2B Rego Park NY 11374 E-mail: sc99001@yahoo.com.

TUAN, DEBBIE FU-TAI, chemist, educator; b. Kiangsu, China, Feb. 2, 1930; arrived in U.S., 1958; d. Shiau-gien and Chen (Lee) T.; m. John W. Reed, Aug. 15, 1987. BS in Chemistry, Nat. Taiwan U., Taipei, 1954, MS in Chemistry, 1958, Yale U., New Haven, Conn., 1960, PhD in Chemistry, 1961. Rsch. fellow Yale U., New Haven, 1961-64; rsch. assoc. U. Wis., Madison, 1964-65; asst. prof. Kent (Ohio) State U., 1965-70, assoc. prof., 1970-73, prof., 1973—; vis. scientist Yeshiva U., N.Y.C., summer 1966; rsch. fellow Harvard U., Cambridge, 1969-70; vis. scientist SRI Internat., Menlo Park, Calif., 1981; rsch. assoc. Cornell U., Ithica, N.Y., 1983. Vis. prof. Acad. Sinica of China, Nat. Taiwan U. and Nat. Tsing-Hwa U., summer 1967, Ohio State U., 1993, 95. Contbr. articles to profl. jours. Recipient NSF Career Advanced award, 1994—; U. Grad. fellow Nat. Taiwan U., 1955-58, F.W. Heyl-Anon F fellow Yale U., 1960-61, U. Faculty Rsch. fellow Kent State U., 1966, 68, 71, 85; Pres. Chiang's scholar Chinese Women Assn., 1954, 58, Grad. scholar in humanity and scis. China Found., 1955. Mem.: Am. Chem. Soc., Am. Phys. Soc., Sigma Xi. Office: Kent State U Chemistry Dept Williams Hl Kent OH 44242-0001

TUBB, BETTY FREEZE, music educator; b. Oklahoma City, Oct. 6, 1932; d. Eugene Woodrow Freeze and Otha Merle Perkins; m. Boyd Junior Bryce, Aug. 6, 1948 (dec. June 1965); children: Donna Bryce Lacquement, DiAnn Bryce Neff; m. Curtis O'Connor Tubb, Dec. 30, 1969; 1 child, Tara Elizabeth Tubb Foster. BMus in Piano, Oklahoma City U., 1966. Cert. piano tchr. Ala. Pvt. music tchr., Oklahoma City, 1960—70; faculty Tonsmeire Sch. Music, Mobile, Ala., 1970—71, Mobile Christian Sch., 1971—73; pvt. music tchr. Cross City, Fla., 1980—85; faculty Wrights Girls Sch., Mobile, 1986—87; pvt. music tchr., ind. piano tchr. Mobile, 1988—. Adjudicator Nat. Guild Piano Tchrs., 1962—91. Mem.: Music Tchrs. Nat. Assn., Ala. Music Tchrs. Assn., Nat. Guild Piano Tchrs. (adjudicator 1962—99, treas., chair scholarship com.), Mobile Music Tchr. Assn. (pres. 1972—74, treas. 2001—02, scholarship chmn.), Sigma Alpha Iota. Republican. Mem. Church Of Christ. Avocation: heritage. E-mail: bettyt10063@cs.com.

TUBB, ELAINE ANN, secondary school educator; b. Cheverly, Md., Apr. 26, 1955; d. Robert Allen and Barbara Ann Clark; m. Donald Allen Tubb, June 7, 1975; children: Laura Elaine, Stephen Matthew, Jennifer Diane. AA, Prince Georges CC, Largo, Md., 1974; BA, U. Md., 1976; MA, George Wash. U., 1983. Cert. tchr. Md., in history Nat. Bd. Profl. Tchg. Stds. Tchr. Charles County Pub. Schs., La Plata, Md., 1977—; chmn. dept. Milton Somers Mid. Sch., La Plata, 1990—2006, govt. resource tchr., 2006—. Dept. chairperson Milton Somers Mid. Sch., La Plata, Md., 1990—2006. Named Tchr. of the Yr., Charles County Pub. Schs., 2003, Md. History Day Tchr. of Yr., Md. Coun. for Humanities, 2002, Alumni Tchr. of Yr., U. Md. Coll. Edn., 2003; recipient Disting. Cmty. Svc. award, Greater Waldorf Jaycees, 2006. Mem.: Nat. Coun. History Edn., Nat. Coun. Social Studies. Avocations: travel, reading. Office: Milton Somers Mid Sch 300 Willow Ln La Plata MD 20646 Home Fax: 410-257-9482. Business E-Mail: etubb@ccboe.com.

TUBBS, CECILIA SAULTERS, academic administrator, educator; b. Birmingham, Ala., Jan. 7, 1959; d. Gene Tunney and Emily Louise Saulters; m. William Ray Tubbs, June 30, 1989; children: Gena Rae, Sarah Marie. MS in Criminal Justice, U. Ala., Birmingham. Rschr., site dir. Nat. Inst. Justice/Police Found., 1987—90; probation officer US Probation, Birmingham, 1991—96; adj. prof. UAB, Birmingham, 1991—, Samford U., Birmingham, 1991—; criminal justice program coord. Jefferson State CC, Birmingham, 1996—. Pres. Ala. Coun. Crime & Delinquency, Ala., 2000—01; mem., presenter Acad. Criminal Justice Scis. Contbr. articles. Judge Ala. Ctr. Law & Civic Edn., Birmingham, 1992—2006; bd. mem. A Family Pl., Birmingham, 1995—98; adv. bd. McAdory HS, Bessemer, Ala., 2000—03, Hoover HS, Ala., 2004—06; pres. Blount County Children's Ctr., Oneonta, Ala., 1990—94. Nominee Chancellor's award, State Ala. Dept. Edn., 2002, 2005; recipient Spl. Svc. award, US Ct., No. Dist. Ala., 1992, US Ct., No. Dist Ala., 1995, Pres. award, Ala. Coun. Crime & Delinquency, 1996, 2000, 2005, Outstanding Faculty award, Jefferson State CC, 2003; grantee Ann. Conf. Tng. Scholarship, Am. Correctional Assn., 2001. Mem.: So. States Correctional Assn. (multiple com. chair 1998—). Office: Jefferson State CC 2601 Carson Rd Birmingham AL 35215 Office Fax: 205-856-8572. Business E-Mail: ctubbs@jeffstateonline.com.

TUBBS, MARY S., curriculum coordinator; m. Ronald James Tubbs, Jr., Mar. 25, 2000. AA in Humanities with honors, Chabot Coll., 1975; BA in Psychology, U. Calif-Berkeley, 1978; MEd with honors, San Francisco State U., 1982. Cert. K-8 tchr., reading K-12 tchr. Calif., Hawaii. Head tchr. Jack & Jill Nursery Kindergarten, San Francisco, 1979—80; kindergarten tchr. St. James Early Childhood Devel. Ctr., San Francisco, 1980—81; substitute tchr. San Francisco Unified Sch. Dist., 1981—82; clin. psychol. asst. State Hawaii, 1982; owner Akamai Tutoring, Kailua, Hawaii, 1988—89; psychol. examiner State Hawaii, Dept. Edn., Windward Oahu, 1983—88, spl. edn. tchr. Waianae, 1989—90, Title I reading coord., 1999—2001, tchr. Kailua, 2001—02, curriculum and standards coord., 2002—; dist. resource, diagnostic prescriptive tchr. State Hawaii, Dept. Edn. Spl. Svcs., Honolulu, 1991—99, title I math. coord., 2005—. Chair Windward Oahu Dist. Sch. Climate Task Force, Kailua, 1986—88; facilitator Tchr. Assistance Team, Nanaikapono E., Hawaii, 1989—90. Recipient Summer Tchg. Trning. scholarship, Whittier Coll., 1971, Am. Bus. Women's scholarship, Alameda Bus. Women, 1978. Mem.: NEA, Hawaii State Tchr. Assn. (dist. rep. 1998), Nat. Assn. Sch. Psychologists, Hawaii Humane Soc., Susan G. Komen Breast Cancer Assn. (sec. 2003—), Reading Club (program creator, facilitator 1995—96, grant 1995). Avocations: reading, German shepherds, remodeling. Office: Mokapu Elem Sch 1193 Mokapu Rd Kailua HI 96734 Home (Summer): PO Box 1434 Kailua HI 96734-1434 Office Phone: 808-254-7964.

TUBBS, PENNY L., art educator; b. Alexandria, La., Mar. 23, 1955; d. Jerry L. and Nellouise S. Sherman; children: Shauna, Jessica, Haylee. B of Art Edn., U. Kans., Lawrence, 2000. Tchr., dir. T&T Am. Career Coll., Topeka, 1983—90; children's dir., pastor 1st Christian Ch., Lawrence, Kans., 1993—98; tchr. Unified Sch. Dist. 434, Carbondale, Kans., 2002—06, Unified Sch. Dist. 497, Lawrence, 2002—. Guest spkr. Rotary Club, Overbrook, Kans., 2005, Leavenworth Sch. Dist., Leavenworth, Kans., 2005. Named Honored Tchr., Channel 49, 2004; named one of Tchrs. Who Make a Difference; recipient Fulbright fellowship, Govt. Japan, 2005. Mem.: NEA, Kans. Art Edn. Assn. (presenter 2006), Nat. Art Edn. Assn. (presenter 2005). Home: 718 N 1532 RD Lawrence KS 66049 Office: Unified Sch Dist 434 Santa Fe Trail 315 N 4th St Carbondale KS 66414 Personal E-mail: dtravelinggirl@yahoo.com.

TUBLISKY, MARCY, association administrator; m. Mark Tublisky; children: Ilyse, Beth. M, Queen's Coll. Exec. dir. Hauppauge (N.Y.) Indsl. Assn., Hauppauge, NY, 1989—. Apptd. by Suffolk County Legis. to Small Bus. Adv. Coun.; mem. Suffolk County Police Res. Recipient Dist. Bus. Leaders award, March of Dimes, 1996. Office: Hauppauge Industrial Assn 225 Wireless Blvd Hauppauge NY 11788-3914 E-mail: mtublisky@hia-li.org.

TUCCERI, CLIVE KNOWLES, writer, science educator, consultant; b. Bryn Mawr, Pa., Apr. 20, 1953; d. William Henry and Clive Ellis (Knowles) Hulick; m. Eugene Angelo Tucceri, Sept. 1, 1984 (div. Nov. 1991); 1 child, Clive Edna. BA in Geology, Williams Coll., 1975; MS in Coastal Geology, Boston Coll., 1982. Head sci. dept. Stuart Hall Sch., Staunton, Va., 1975-77; mem. sci. faculty William Penn Charter Sch., Phila., 1977-79, Tower Sch., Marblehead, Mass., 1982-86, Bentley Coll., Waltham, Mass., 1986-88; adminstrv. dir., co-founder Stout Aquatic Libr. Nat. Marine and Aquatic Edn. Resource Ctr., Wakefield, R.I., 1982-89; sci. faculty Mabelle B. Avery Sch., Somers, Conn., 1989—90; faculty, head sci. dept. MacDuffie Sch., Springfield, Mass., 1992—93; sci. faculty East Hampton (Conn.) Middle Sch., 1993—, sci. team leader, 1994—95, sci. chmn. grades K-12, 1995—. Cons. Addison-Wesley Pub. Co., Menlo Park, Calif., 1986—94, Longmeadow (Mass.) Pub. Schs., 1989—94; cons. and freelance writer Prentice-Hall Inc., Needham, 1991; cons. web content devel. Conn. Sci. Ctr., 2005—. Co-head class agt. Williams Coll. Alumni Fund, 2000—, vice chair, 2003—06; admissions rep. Williams Coll., 2001—; vol. The Bushnell Ctr. for Performing Arts, 2001—; mem. search com. Christ Ch., Middle Haddam, Conn., 2000—01, mem. vestry, 2002—05; bd. dir. People Against Rape, Staunton, 1976—77. Mem.: AAUW (bd. dirs., br. pres.-elect 1975—77, v.p. 1985—86, sec. 1986—87), NEA, NSTA, Cousteau Soc., Conn. Edn. Assn., Conn. Sci Tchrs. Assn., Conn. Sci. Suprs. Assn., Mass. Environ. Edn. Soc. (bd. dirs. 1985—88), Mass. Marine Educators (pres. 1987—89, bd. dirs. 1983—91, editor Flotsam and Jetsam MA Marine Educators newsletter 1991—97), Southeastern New Eng. Marine Educators (publs. chair Nat. Conf. com.), Nat. Mid. Level Sci. Tchrs. Assn., Nat. Marine Edn. Assn. (sec. 1986—87, chpt. rep. 1987 1989), Sigma Xi. Episcopalian. Avocations: renovating old homes, sailing, gardening, reading. Home: 12 Birchwood Dr East Hampton CT 06424-1312 Personal E-mail: ctucceri@aol.com.

TUCCILLO, ELAINE, psychologist, educator; b. Mt. Vernon, N.Y., Aug. 17, 1946; d. Charles and Victoria (Castiglia) Tuccillo; m. Scott Baum, Dec. 19, 1981; children: Jonathan Baum-Tuccillo, Micaella Baum-Tuccillo. BA in Math./Psychology, SUNY, Albany, 1968; MA in Psychology, City Coll., NYC, 1974; PhD in Clin. Psychology, City U. NY, 1977. Lic. psychology N.Y. State Edn. Dept. Staff psychologist Nassau County Med. Ctr., East Meadow, NY, 1974—78; psychologist supervising faculty Brookdale Med. Ctr., Bklyn., 1978—85; psychologist N.Y. Soc. Bioenergetic Analysis, N.Y.C., 1983—, Internat. Inst. Bioenergetic Analysis, N.Y.C. and Switzerland, 2005—, Am. Group Psychotherapy Assn., 1985—. Mem.: APA, U.S. Assn. Body-Oriented Psychotherapy, Ea. Group Psychotherapy Assn. Avocations: jazz, piano. Office: 711 W End Ave #1A N New York NY 10025 Office Phone: 212-665-3907.

TUCHOLKE, CHRISTEL-ANTHONY, artist, educator; b. Leczyca, Poland, Mar. 2, 1941; arrived in U.S., 1952; d. Alfred and Eleonore Marie (Mundt) T.; m. Anthony C. Stoeveken, June 9, 1967; children: Jennifer, Joshua. BS in Art Edn., U. Wis., Milw., 1964, MS in Fine Arts Drawing and Painting, 1965. Grad. tchg. asst. U. Wis., Milw., 1964-65; art instr. Milw. Pub. Schs., 1965-66; univ. instr. Western Carolina U., Cullowhee, N.C., 1966-67; print curator Tamarind Lithography WK, L.A., 1968; artist, 1970—. Vis. artist, designer Artists Ltd. Edits., Kohler (Wis.) Co., 1989. Exhibited in 98 shows; commns. include Wis. Arts Bd., Miller Brewing Co., Northwestern Mut. Life. Mem. Profl. Dimensions (hon. mem.). Home: 8535 W Mequon Rd Mequon WI 53097-3101 Office Phone: 262-242-0475.

TUCK, AMY, lieutenant governor; b. Starkville, Miss., July 8, 1963; d. Grady William and Mary (Boykin) Tuck. BA in Polit. Sci., Miss. State U., Starkville, 1985; postgrad., Miss. State U., Miss. State U., Starkville, 1992—; JD, Miss. Coll., 1989. Legal asst. Ben. F. Hilburn Jr., Atty. at Law, Starkville, Miss., 1984-85; grad. asst. dept. polit. sci. Miss. State U., Starkville, 1986-87; law clk. Minor Buchanan, Jackson, Miss., 1987-88, Deposit Guaranty Nat. Bank, Jackson, 1988-89; state senator dist. 15 State of Miss., Jackson, 1990-99, lt. gov., 2000—. Adj. prof. Wood Jr. Coll., Mathiston, Miss., 1990-95. Mem. Oktibbeha County Voter Re-Registration Com., Oktibbeha County Fedn. Dem. Women; bd. dirs. Oktibbeha County Am. Cancer Soc., 1991-92; mem. local rels. com. Children and Family Svcs.; assoc. mem. Nat. Mus. Women in the Arts, 1992-93. Mem. NAFE, Am. Legis. Exch. Com., Am. Soc. Pub. Adminstrs., Nat. Conf. State Legislature, Nat. Order Women Legislators, Miss. State U. Alumni Assn., Starkville Area Bus. and Profl. Women's Club, Oktibbeha County C. of C., Gamma Beta Phi, Pi Sigma Alpha, Omicron Delta Kappa, Phi Delta Phi (vice-magister 1988, historian 1988-89). Democrat. Methodist. Office: Office of the Lt Gov PO Box 1018 Jackson MS 39215-1018 Office Phone: 601-359-3200. Office Fax: 601-359-4054. E-mail: ltgov@mail.senate.state.ms.us.*

TUCK, CAROLYN WEAVER, middle school educator; b. Petersburg, Va., Nov. 18, 1947; d. Fred William Weaver and Virginia Evelyn (Fick) Lang; m. Michael Lewis Jones, Dec. 27, 1969 (div. 1991); children: Kristen Michelle Jones, Kara Denise Jones; m. Richard Harper Tuck, July 30, 1994. BS, Radford U., 1970, MS, 1971; adminstrv. cert., William and Mary Coll., 1991, George Washington U., 1991; libr. media specialist cert., Old Dominion U., 2005. Cert. secondary sch. prin., English and history tchr., Va. English tchr. Galax (Va.) City Schs., 1971-72, Waynesville (N.C.) Schs., 1973-75; circulation libr. Western Carolina U., Cullowhee, N.C., 1972-73; English and history tchr. Poquoson (Va.) City Schs., 1975—81, 1985—2002; acting asst. prin. Poquoson (Va.) Mid. Schs., 1989; libr. media specialist Poquoson (Va.) Mid. Sch., 2002—. Rep. to state MS conf. Va. Bd. Edn., Poquoson, 1991. Writer advanced social studies/English curriculum; contbr. articles to profl. jours. Solicitor Am. Cancer Soc., Poquoson, 1992-98, Mother's March of Dimes, 1996-2000; bible sch. tchr. Tabernacle Meth. Ch., Poquoson, 1994. Mem. NEA, Va. Edn. Assn., Poquoson Edn. Assn. (v.p. 2000—), Nat. Mid. Sch. Assn., Pi Gamma Mu, Sigma Tau Delta. Avocations: bridge, travel, doll collecting, genealogy. Home: 105 Shallow Lagoon Yorktown VA 23693-4111 Office: Poquoson Mid Sch 985 Poquoson Ave Poquoson VA 23662-1799

TUCK, LILY, writer; b. Paris, 1938; Author: Interviewing Matisse; Or the Women Who Died Standing Up, 1991, The Women who Walked on Water, 1996, Siam; Or the Women Who Shot a Man, 1999 (nominated PEN/Faulkner Award, 2000), The News from Paraguay, 2004 (Nat. Book Award for Fiction, 2004), (collection) Limbo: And Other Places I Have Lived, 2002. Address: c/o Georges Borchardt 136 E 57th St New York NY 10022

TUCKER, AMANDA YEATES, history educator; b. Houston, Tex., Oct. 13, 1979; d. Jack Wilson Tucker, Jr. and Diane Principe Tucker; m. Vino Delmar Underwood, June 10, 2006. Student, Yunnan Normal U., Kunming, Yunnan, China, 2001; BA in Anthropology, The U. Tex., Austin, Tex., 2002. Cert. tchr. secondary sch. N.Mex, 2006. Instr. art Tohatchi Mid. Sch., N.Mex., 2003—04; instr. history Tohatchi H.S., 2004—. Coach softball Tohatchi H.S., 2004—06, creator, coach cheerleading squad, 2005—06, creator, sponsor, and editor Tobatchi Prowler Newspaper, 2004—05. Vol. in Ecuador Amigos de las Americas, Houston, 1997—97; vol. Meals on Wheels, Lufkin, Tex., 1997—97, The Sanctuary, Austin, 1998—99, Corn Pollen Pathway Program, Tohatchi, 2006—06, Houston Downtown Cmty. Garden, 1996—97, Grenias for Mayor, Houston, 1998—98; mem. John McCain for Pres., Austin, Tex., 1999—99. Grantee, Gallup-Mckinley County Schs., 2004—06. Mem.: U. Tex. Anthropology Soc., Lambda Alpha. Republican. Avocations: travel, Tae Kwon Do, writing, jewelry design, bicycling. Home: PO Box 1649 Tohatchi NM 87325 Office: Tohatchi High School 1 Cougar Ln Tohatchi NM 87325 Office Phone: 505-733-2206. Personal E-mail: atucker@gmcs.k12.nm.us.

TUCKER, ANN, secondary school educator; b. Bonham, Tex., Aug. 5, 1947; d. Rex Maurice and Athelia Ladell Jackson; m. Gary Thomas Tucker, Dec. 20, 1969; 1 child, Stacy Ann Taylor. BS in Edn., U. North Tex., Denton, 1969; MLA, So. Meth. U., Dallas, 1985. Tchr. Richardson North Jr. H.S., Tex., 1969, Inst. Logopedics, Wichita, Kans., 1970—72, Classic Sch., Dallas, 1972—74, Haggard Mid. Sch., Plano, 1976—. Mem.: Assn. Tex. Profl. Educators, Tex. Coun. Social Studies, Nat. Coun. Social Studies. Avocations: travel, reading, shopping. Home: 3920 Wyeth Dr Plano TX 75023-5907 Office Phone: 469-752-5463. Business E-Mail: atucker@pisd.edu.

TUCKER, ANNE WILKES, curator, historian, photographer, critic; b. Baton Rouge, Oct. 18, 1945; BA in Art History, Randolph-Macon Women's Coll., Lynchburg, Va., 1967; AAS in Photographic Illustration, Rochester Inst. Tech., 1968; MFA in Photographic History, SUNY, Buffalo, 1972. Rsch. asst. Internat. Mus. Photography at the George Eastman House, Rochester, NY, 1968—70; rsch. assoc. Gernsheim Collection U. Tex., Austin, 1969, 1970; curatorial intern dept. photography Mus. Modern Art, NYC, 1970—71; photography cons. Creative Artists Pub. Svc. Program, NYC, 1971—72; vis. lectr. New Sch. for Social Rsch., NY, 1973; dir. photography lecture series Cooper Unionn Forum, NYC, 1972—75; lectr. Cooper Union for Advancement of Arts and Sci., NY, 1972—75; vis. lectr. Phila. Coll. Art, 1973—75; affiliate artist U. Houston, 1976—80; curator photography Mus. Fine Arts, Houston, 1976—; Gus and Lyndall Wortham cur., photographic historian and critic, lectr., 1984—. Trustee Visual Studies Workshop, 1980—, Houston Ctr. Photography, 1991—96, Houston Foto Fest, 1988—, art adv. bd., 1987—, bd. dirs., 1990—; visual arts panel The Houston Festival, 1981—83; adv. bd. Randolph-Macon Woman's Coll. Art Gallery, 1982—84; bd. trustees Am. Leadership Forum, 1992—94, co-chair selection com., 1993—94; dir. numerous exhbns. and workshops; lectr. in field; mem. numerous juries and panels. Author: (books and catalogues) Walker Evans: Photographs, 1971, The Woman's Eye, 1973; author: (with Lee Witkin) Rare Books and Photographs, Catalogue 1, The Witkin Gallery, 1973; author: (with William C. Agee) The Target Collection of American Photography, 1977; author: Target II: 5 American Photographers, 1981, Target III: In Sequence, 1982; author: (with Philip Brookman) Robert Frank: New York to Nova Scotia, 1986; author: A Photographic Portrait, Vol. 1: Historic Texas; Vol. II: Contemporary Texas, 1986; author: (with Maggie Olvey) The Sonia and Kaye Marvins Portrait Collection, 1986; author: Photo Notes & Filmfront, 1977; author: (with other curators) The Museum of Fine Arts, Houston: A Guide to the Collection, 1981; author: Unknown Territory: Photography by Ray K. Metzker, 1957-83, 1984, Fifth Annual International Fine Art Photography Exposition, 1984; author: (with Andy Grundberg) American Prospects: The Photographs of Joel Sternfeld, 1987, 2d edit., 1994; author: (with Willie Morris) American Classroom: The Photographs of Catherine Wagner, 1988; author: Five Jerome Artists, 1988; author: (with Pamela Allara) Crosscurrents/Crosscountry, 1988; author: The Art of Photography 1839-1989, 1989, A Permanent Legacy: 150 Masterpieces From the Museum of Fine Arts, Houston, 1989; author: (with other authors) Money Matters: A Critical Look at Bank Architecture, 1990; author: The Blue Man: Photographs by Keith Carter, 1990; author: (with Pete Daniel) Carry Me Home: Photographs by Debbie Fleming Caffery, 1990; author: George Krauze, 1991, Ansel Adams: American Icons, 1992, Tradition and the Unpredictable: The Allan Chasanoff Photographic Collection, 1994, Quest for the Moon and other stories: Three Decades of Astronauts in Space, 1994, Toshio Shibata: Landscape, 1996 (Photo-Eye Best Contemporary Monograph award, 1996), Crimes and Splendors: The Desert Cantos of Richard Misrach, 1996 (Golden Light award, 1996), Charles Schorre, 1997, Myths, Dreams and Realities: Contemporary Argentine Photographs, 1997, Irving Penn, 1999, Mario Carvo Neto, 1999, Amy Blakemore, 1999, Irving Penn Dancer: Photographs of Alexandra Bellar, 2001, Heart and Soul: The Photographs of Ray Carrington III 1993-2002, 2002, Joe Mills: Inner City, 2003, History of Japanese Photography 1853-2000, 2003 (Golden Light award), First Down Houston, Birth of An NFL Franchise, 2003, La Oscura Piel De La Luz; La Obra Fotografica De Mario Cravo Neto, 2003, David Carol: 40 Miles of Bad Road, 2004, Alec Soth: Sleeping by the Mississippi, 2004, Documenting Poetry Contemporary Latin American Photography, 2005, Icons of Photography, 2005, On Assignment, 2005, Mark Cohen: Grim Street, 2005, David Maisel: Terminal Mirage, 2005, (exhbns. and catalogues) A Fotographia Na Arte Contemporanea, 1995;: The Sonia and Kaye Marvins Portrait Collection, 1995, Keith Carter: Reinventing the World, 1995, Illuminations: Women writing on Photography from the 1850's to the present, 1996, Brassai: The Eye of Paris, 1999, Louis Faurer, 2001 (Mus. Pub. Design Competition First prize, 2002), This Was the Photo League: Compassion and the Camera from the Depression to the Cold War, 2001 (Photo-Eye runner-up Best Visual Anthology, 2001), History of Japanese Photography, 2003 (named to Top 12 Photo Books of 2003, Spl. Commendations from Kraszna-Krausz Photography Book Awards, 2005); co-prodr. (video) Fire in the East: The Portrait of Robert Frank, 1986; editor: (books and catalogues) The Anthony G. Cronin Memorial Collection, 1979, (manual) Suzanne Bloom and Ed Hill, 1980, (exhbns. and catalogues) Reframings, New American Feminist Photographies, 1995, The Photo League, 1987, Czech Modernism 1900-1945, 1990, Paul Strand: Essays on His Life and Work, 1990, George Krause, 1992; co-editor: Building a Photographic Library, 2001; singer (photographer): Caught in Act: Lou Stoumen Vintage Photographs, 1995; contbr. articles to numerous profl. jours. and mags., essays to books; subject of numerous interviews and articles. Named Best Curator, TIME Mag., 2001; named to The 100 Most Important People in Photography, American Photo Mag., 2005; recipient Third Ann. Publ. award, Internat. Ctr. Photography, 1987, Bronze Apple award, Am. Film and Video Festival, 1987, John Simon Guggenheim Meml. Alumna Achievement award, Randolph-Macon Woman's Coll., 1993, Alumnae Achievement award, 1993, Lifetime Achievement award, Griffin Mus., 2006; grantee Nat. Endowment Arts grantee, 1976, 1986, 1989; fellowship for mus. profls., Nat. Endowment Arts, 1990, John Simon Guggenheim Meml. Found. fellowship award, 1983—84, Rsch. Support grant, The Getty Ctr. for the History of Art and the Humanities Resource Collections, 1995. Mem.: Houston Ctr. for Photography (adv. bd 1980—90, bd. trustees 1990—93, sec. 1990—93, adv. bd. 1994—95, exhbn. com. pres. 1999—), Art Table, Inc., Coll. Art Assn., Soc. Photographic Edn. (nat. bd. dirs. 1976—80, sec. nat. bd. 1977—79). Office: Mus Fine Arts PO Box 6826 Houston TX 77265 Office Phone: 713-639-7347. Business E-Mail: atucker@mfah.org.

TUCKER, BERNADINE, patient registrar; b. Feb. 27, 1945; d. Erie Wendell and Ethel M. Tucker; children: Andrew Edwards II, Alicia Edwards. Student, U. Md., Madrid, 1970—71, U. Mass., 1976—77; Cert. in Mgmt., Hampshire Coll. Med. transcriptionist Glens Falls (N.Y.) Hosp., 1965—66, Physicians Hosp., Plattsburgh, NY, 1966—67; outreach worker Ednl. Opportunity Ctr., Chicapee, Mass., 1975; asst. dir. fin. aid U. Mass., Amherst, 1975—79; patient registrar Glens Falls Hosp., 2001—. Outreach YWCA, Springfield, Mass., 1975; facilitator Coll. Fair, Springfield, Mass., 1975. Recipient award, Internat. Yr. of Women, 1975. Democrat. Avocations: poetry, needlecrafts, sketching, painting, journals. Home: 196 Ridge St Glens Falls NY 12801

TUCKER, BEVERLY SOWERS, library and information scientist; b. Trenton, N.J., Dec. 1, 1936; d. Eldon Jones and Verbeda Eleanor (Roberts) Sowers; m. Harvey Richard Tucker, Dec. 27, 1958 (div. Nov. 1983); children: Randall Richard, Brian Alan. BS in Chemistry with distinction, Purdue U., 1958; MS in Geology, No. Ill. U., 1985; MA in Library and Info. Sci., Rosary Coll., 1989. Asst. rsch. librarian CPC Internat., Argo, Ill., 1958-62; chem. patent searcher Chgo., 1962-66; info. specialist C. Berger & Co., Wheaton, Ill., 1986, Amoco Corp., Naperville, Ill., 1987-99; faculty Coll. Du Page, Glen Ellyn, Ill., 1989—; libr. cons. Baxter Healthcare, Round Lake, Ill., 1999—2003; libr. Seyfarth and Shaw, Chgo., 2005—. Mem. Spl. Libraries Assn., Ill. Fedn. Women's Club (treas. 5th dist. 1979-81, Outstanding Jr. Clubwoman award 1979-80), Garden Club Council Wheaton (pres. 1981-82), Wheaton Jr. Woman's Club (pres. 1977-78, Single Parent scholar 1984), Gardens Etc. Club (pres. 1978-79), Alpha Lambda Delta, Delta Rho Kappa, Theta Sigma Phi, Alpha Chi Omega (grantee 1985). Republican. Presbyterian. Avocations: bridge, needlecrafts, gourmet cooking. Home: 1507 Paula Ave Wheaton IL 60187-6135

TUCKER, BRENDA BRUNETTE, elementary school educator; b. Corinth, Miss., Nov. 1, 1958; d. Willie Bishop and Maggie Belle Graham; m. Ralph O. Tucker, Dec. 24, 1980; children: Orion, Jonathan, Cameron. BS, Kust Coll., 1980; MEd, We. Ky. U., 1993, cert. in Prin. Supr., 2002. Lic. tchr. Ky. Dept. Profl. Bds. Tchr. spl. edn. Corinth (Miss.) H.S., 1981; instr. Dept. Def., Wurzburg, Germany, 1981—87; tchr. Hardin County Schs., Radcliff, Ky., 1987—98, Ft. Knox (Ky.) Schs., 1998—, guidance counselor, 1999—. Prof. McKendree Coll., Radcliff, 2000—. Chmn. publicity NAACP, Radcliff, 2004. Mem.: Counselors Assn., Optimist Club Radcliff (pres. 1998, chmn. programs 1998—99, named Optimist Educator of Yr.), Delta Sigma Theta (pres. 1995, chaplain 1997—2003). Avocations: reading, g, community service, walking, watching sunrise and sunsets. Office: Kingsolver Elementary Sch 1488 3rd Ave Fort Knox KY 40121-2287

TUCKER, CYNTHIA ANNE, journalist; b. Monroeville, Ala., Mar. 13, 1955; d. John Abney and Mary Louise (Marshall) Tucker; m. Michael Pierce, Dec. 26, 1987 (div. 1989). BA, Auburn U., 1976. Reporter The Atlanta Jour., 1976-80, editorial writer, columnist, 1983-86; reporter The Phila. Inquirer, 1980-82; assoc. editorial page editor The Atlanta Constitution, 1986-91, editorial page editor, 1992—. Bd. dirs. ARC, 1989-93, Families First, 1988—, Internat. Women's Media Found., 1994—. Nieman fellow Harvard U., 1988-89; Pullitzer Prize finalist for commentary, 2004. Mem.: Coun. Fgn. Rels., Nat. Assn. Minority Media Execs., Nat. Assn. Black Journalists, Am. Soc. Newspaper Editors (Disting. Writing award 2000). Mem. United Ch. Christ. Office: Atlanta Constitution 72 Marietta St NW Atlanta GA 30303-2804

TUCKER, HELEN WELCH, writer; b. Raleigh, N.C., Nov. 1, 1926; d. William Blair and Helen (Welch) Tucker; m. William T. Beckwith, Jan. 9, 1971. BA, Wake Forest Coll., 1946; postgrad., Columbia U., N.Y.C., 1957—58. Reporter Burlington Times-News, NC, 1946—47, Times-News, Twin Falls, Idaho, 1948—49, Idaho Statesman, Boise, 1950—51; copy writer Sta. KDYL, Salt Lake City, 1952—53; copy supr. Sta. WPTF, Raleigh, NC, 1953—55; reporter Raleigh Times, NC, 1955—57; editl. asst. Columbia U. Press, N.Y.C., 1959—60; dir. publicity and publs. N.C. Mus. Art, Raleigh, NC, 1967—70. Author: The Sound of Summer Voices, 1969, The Guilt of August Fielding, 1971, No Need of Glory, 1972, The Virgin of Lontano, 1973, A Strange and Ill-Starred Marriage, 1978, A Reason for Rivalry, 1979, A Mistress to the Regent, 1980, An Infamous Attachment, 1980, The Halverton Scandal, 1980, A Wedding Day Deception, 1981, The Double Dealers, 1982, Season of Dishonor, 1982, Ardent Vows, 1983, Bound by Honor, 1984, The Lady's Fancy, 1991, Bold Impostor, 1991; contbr. (to nat. mags. short stories). Named Artist of Yr., Arts Coun. Frankling Co. (N.C.), 1992; recipient Disting. Alumni Award in Journalism, Wake Forest U., 1971. Anglican. Home: 2930 Hostetler St Raleigh NC 27609-7702

TUCKER, KAREN SUE, association executive; b. Booneville, Mo., Feb. 1, 1949; d. William Russell and Viola Maxine (McCoy) Ault; m. Joseph G. Wansing, Oct. 18,1969 (div. May 1979); children: Tambria Jo Cussimanio, Kara Dawn; m. Lee Gary Tucker, Aug. 1, 1981; 1 stepchild, Karen Marie Tucker Herrera. BBA, U. Mo., 1989. Cert. assn. exec. Adminstrv. and tech. positions ANA, Kansas City, Mo., 1972-83, coord. governance, 1983-85; dir. adminstrv. svcs. Oreg. Nurses Assn., Portland, Oreg., 1985-88; sr. staff specialist fin. planning and analysis ANA, Kansas City, Mo., 1988-92, mgr. governance Washington, 1992-94, dir. governance, 1994-95, dep. exec. dir., membership, 1995-97; pres., CEO, Am. Coll. Health Care Adminstrs., Alexandria, Va., 1997—. Spkr., facilitator Washington Area State Health Regional Group, 1994, Pub. Risk Mgmt. Assn., Washington, 1994, Nat. Rural Health Assn., Kansas City, Mo., 1992, Kansas City Soc. of Assn. Execs., 1991. Mem. Greater Washington Area Soc. of Assn. Execs. (spkr., facilitator 1994, 95, law and legis. com. 1994-95, sr. edn. task force 1994-95), Am. Soc. of Assn. Execs. (edn. com. 1993-95, mktg. sect. coun. 1995-99, vice-chair mktg. sect. coun. 1997-98, chair mktg. sect. coun. 1998-99). Avocations: writer, reader, health. Office: Am Coll Health Care Adminstrs 325 S Patrick St Alexandria VA 22314-3580 Home: 8525 Avonlea Ln Port Tobacco MD 20677-2015

TUCKER, KIMBERLY JOAN, music educator; b. Racine, Wis., May 4, 1977; d. Joan Marie and Robert Edward Griswold (Stepfather), Joseph Zoltan and Lilac Kriston (Stepmother); m. Christopher Michael Tucker, Aug. 14, 2004. B Music Edn., U. North Tex., 2000; postgrad., Tex. A&M U., Commerce, 2005—. Asst. band dir. DeSoto West Jr. H.S. and Amber Ter. Intermediate Sch., Tex., 2000—02, dir. bands, 2002—05; band tchr. Rockwall ISD, 2005—. Sch. rep. DeSoto Dist. Advocacy Com., 2000—02. Recipient Sweepstakes award, U. Interscholastic League Region 20, 2002—04, Beach Within Reach Contest, 2002—04, Sandy Lake Music Festival, 2002—04. Fellow: Alpha Lambda Delta (life); mem.: Nat. Flute Assn. (corr.), Internat. Clarinet Assn. (corr.), Music Educators Nat. Conf. (corr.), Tex. Bandmasters Assn. (corr.), Tex. Music Educators Assn. (corr.), Sigma Alpha Iota (life; rec. sec. 1998—2000, Sword of Honor 1999). Roman Catholic. Avocations: practicing instruments, singing, sketching. Home: 684 Danielle Ct Rockwall TX 75087 Office Phone: 972-768-4784. Office Fax: 214-771-0026. Personal E-mail: kimberkris1@aol.com.

TUCKER, MARNA S., lawyer; b. Phila., Mar. 5, 1941; BS, U. Tex., 1962; LLB, Georgetown U. Law Ctr., 1965; JD (hon.), U. DC Sch. Law, 1995. Bar: D.C. 1966, Calif. 1969, U.S. Supreme Ct. 1970. Deputy dir. legal svcs. program western region Office Of Econ. Opportunity, 1967-69; spl. asst. to Allard K. Lowenstein, Pa. congressman, 1969-70; dir. ABA Pro Bono Project, 1971—73; ptnr. Feldesman, Tucker, Leifer, Fidell and Bank (now Feldesman Tucker Leifer Fidell LLP), Washington; sr. ptnr., family law Feldesman Tucker Leifer Fidell LLP, Washington. Adj. prof. of law georgetown U. Law Ctr., 1972; lectr. of law Cath. U., Columbus Sch. Law, 1972-74. Apptd. Bd. Prof. Responsibility, D.C. Ct. Appeals, 1977-83; mem. U.S. Cir. Ct. Com. on

Admissions and Grievances, 1979-89, U.S. Jud. Nominating Com. for D.C., 1977-80; bd. regents Georgetown U., 1986-89; bd. visitors, Georgetown Law Ctr., 1994-2000; trustee Ctr. for Law and Social Policy, 1977-99, Pub. Defender Svc. D.C., 1986-92; founding bd. mem., sec./treas., bd. trustee, Nat. Women's Law Ctr., 1981-; mem. exec. com. Washington Lawyers Com. for Civil Rights Under Law, 1973—; chair Mayor's Commn. on Violence Against Women, 1996-2002; commr., U.S. Comm. of Child and Family Welfare, 1994. Named Women Lawyer of Yr. Women's Bar Assn. of D.C., 1985; recipient Annual Alumni Achievement award Georgetown Alumni Club, 1986, Alumni Achievement award, Georgetown Law Ctr., 1998, Exceptional Achievement award NAACP Legal Def. and Ednl. Fund, Inc., Washington Com., 1985; named one of 75 Best Lawyers in Washington, Washingtonian Mag., 2002, (several times) Top Divorce Lawyer. Fellow Am. Bar Found. (chair, 1995), Am. Acad. Matrimonial Lawyers, Am. Coll. Trial Lawyers; mem. ABA (chmn. sect. individual rights and responsibilities 1982-83, chmn. commn. on pub. understanding about law 1979-82, chmn. standing com. profl. discipline 1987-90, house of del. bar del., 1974-80, 1988-, co-chmn. Commn. on Domestic Violence, 1995-97, Margaret Brent Women Lawyers of Achievement award, Robert Drinan Disting. Svc. award), ACLU Nat. Capital Area (bd. dirs. 1973-76), Nat. Legal Aid and Defender Assn. (v.p. 1973-77, Nat. Legal Aid and Defender Assn. Annual award, 1993), D.C. Bar (pres. 1984-85, legal ethics com. 1974-76, del. ABA ho. of dels. 1974-91), Nat. Conf. Bar Pres. (pres.-elect, pres. 1991), Women's Forum Washington; chair Fellows Am. Bar Found., 1995-96; bd. mem. Fed. Jud. Ctr. Found. Bd., 1997-, chair, 2000. Office: Feldesman Tucker Leifer Fidell LLP 2001 L St NW 2nd Fl Washington DC 20036 Office Phone: 202-466-8960. Office Fax: 202-293-8103. Business E-Mail: mtucker@feldesmantucker.com.

TUCKER, MAUREEN ANN, musician; b. Jackson Heights, N.Y., Aug. 26, 1944; d. James Thomas and Margaret Mary (Daly) T.; divorced; children: Kerry, Keith, Austen, Kate, Richard. Grad., Levittown (N.Y.) Meml. H.S., 1962. Drummer Velvet Underground, 1965-71; guitarist, songwriter, singer Moe Tucker Band, 1989—. Recordings include (singer, guitarist, songwriter) Playin Possum, 1981, Life in Exile After Abdication, 1986, (prodr., arranger) I Spent a Week There The Other Night, 1990, Dogs Under Stress, 1993; drummer Lou Reed Band, Japan, 1990, European tours with Velvet Underground, 1993, Moe Tucker Band, 1989—. Tchr. English St. Pauls Hispanic Ministry, Douglas, Ga., 1990—. Inducted into Rock & Roll Hall of Fame, 1996. Roman Catholic. Office: Maureen Tucker PO Box 2357 Douglas GA 31534-2357

TUCKER, REBECCA DENISE, science educator; b. Ft. Oglethorpe, Ga., Nov. 22, 1970; m. Casey Edward Tucker, Apr. 3, 2004; 1 child, Colton. BS in Secondary Edn., Sci. and Biology, Kennesaw State U., 1999. Cert. tchr. secondary edn., gen. sci. 1998. Sci. tchr. Sprayberry H.S., Marietta, Ga., 1999. Home: 18 Etowah Ridge Dr Cartersville GA Office: Sprayberry High School 2525 Sandy Plains Rd Marietta GA 30066 Personal E-mail: rebecca.tucker@cobbk12.org.

TUCKER, RHONDA RENEÉ, music educator; b. Gallapolis, Ohio, Apr. 11, 1959; d. Jimmy Gene and Margaret June Tucker. BME, Birmingham-So. Coll., 1981; MusM in Edn., Samford U., 1990. Cert. tchr. Ala., nat. bd. cert. tchr. Music tchr. Southside Baptist Ch. Early Childhood Ctr., Birmingham, Ala., 1981—82, Shades Cahaba Elem. Sch., Homewood, Ala., 1982—. Author: Words to Play By, 2001. Nominee Disting. Tchr., Birmingham Post Herald, 1998—99. Mem.: NEA, Ala. Music Educator's Assn. (pres. elect 2001—03, pres. 2003—05), Am. Orff-Schulwerk Assn. (pres. 1993—95). Republican. Methodist. Avocations: musical theatre, singing, playing piano, playing flute, tap dancing. Office: Shades Cahaba Elementary School 3001 Montgomery Hwy Homewood AL 35209

TUCKER, ROCHELLE, special education educator; m. Charles Tucker, Aug. 6, 1994; children: Abigail, Charles. BS, Tex. Woman's U., Denton, 1997. Cert. spl. edn., elem. edn. tchr. State Bd. of Edn., Tex., 1997. Spl. edn. - life skills Hurst-Euless-Bedford ISD - Meadowcreek Elem., Tex., 1997—2000; spl. edn. tchr. - lead tchr. Marshall ISD - Crockett Elem., Tex., 2000—01; spl. edn. - resource/inclusion Wylie ISD - Wylie H.S., Tex., 2001—. Recipient Bronze and Silver Level Achievement awards, Wylie ISD, 2005. Office Phone: 972-429-3100.

TUCKER, SHIRLEY LOIS COTTER, botanist, educator; b. St. Paul, Apr. 4, 1927; d. Ralph U. and Myra C. (Knutson) Cotter; m. Kenneth W. Tucker, Aug. 22, 1953. BA, U. Minn., 1949, MS, 1951; PhD, U. Calif., Davis, 1956. Asst. prof. botany La. State U., Baton Rouge, 1967-71, assoc. prof., 1971-76, prof., 1976-82, Boyd prof., 1982-95, prof. emerita, 1995—. Adj. prof. dept. biology U. Calif., Santa Barbara, 1995—. Co-editor: Aspects of Floral Development, 1988, Advances in Legume Systematics, Vol. 6, 1994; contbr. numerous articles on plant devel. to profl. jours. Recipient, Outstanding Alumni Achievement award U. Minn., 1999; fellow Linnean Soc., London, 1975—, Fulbright fellow Eng., 1952-53; named to Hall of Distinction La. State U., Baton Rouge, 2006. Mem. Bot. Soc. Am. (v.p. 1979, program chmn. 1975-78, pres.-elect 1986-87, pres. 1987-88, Merit award 1989, Centennial award, 2006), Am. Bryological and Lichenological Soc., Brit. Lichenological Soc., Am. Inst. Biol. Scis., Am. Soc. Plant Taxonomists (pres.-elect 1994-95, pres. 1995-96), Phi Beta Kappa, Sigma Xi. Home: 3987 Primavera Rd Santa Barbara CA 93110-1467 Office: U Calif Dept Biology EEMB Santa Barbara CA 93106 Business E-Mail: tucker@lifesci.ucsb.edu.

TUCKER, TANYA DENISE, singer; b. Seminole, Tex., Oct. 10, 1958; d. Beau and Juanita Tucker; children: Presley Tanita, Beau Grayson, Layla LaCosta. Singer Tanya Tucker Inc., 1959—. Regular on Lew King Show; rec. artist formerly with Columbia Records, MCA Records, Capital Records; albums include The Sound of Tanya Tucker, 1972, Tear Me Apart, Chagnes, Delta Dawn, 1972, What's Your Mamma's Name, 1973, Would You Lay With Me (In a Field of Stone), 1974, Girls Like Me, Tanya Tucker's Greatest Hits, 1975, Greatest Hits, 1975, Tanya Tucker, 1975, Greatest Hits Encore, 1976, Here's Some Love, 1976, Lovin' and Learnin', 1976, You Are So Beautiful, 1977, Greatest Hits, 1978, T.N.T., 1978, Ridin' Rainbows, 1979, Tear Me Apart, 1979, Should I Do It, 1981, Dream Lovers, 1981, Live, 1982, The Best of Tanya Tucker, 1982, Changes, 1983, Love Me Like You Used To, 1987, Strong Enough to Bend, 1988, Greatest Hits, 1989, Tennessee Women, 1990, Ridin Rainbows/Here's Some Love, 1990, Lovin' and Learnin'/Tanya Tucker, 1990, Greatest Country Hits, 1991, What Do I Do With Me, 1991, Collection, 1992, The Best of Tanya Tucker, 1992, (with Delbert McClinton) Can't Run From Youself, 1992, Greatest Hits, 1993, Lizzie & the Rain Man, 1993, Greatest Hits (CEMA), 1993, Greatest Hits (Capitol), 1993, Country Queen, 1993, Greatest Hits 1990-1992, 1993, Soon, 1993, Girls Like Me, 1994, Fire to Fire, 1995, (with T. Graham Brown, Delbert McClinton) Tanya, 1995, Christmas with Tanya Tucker and Suzy Bogguss, 1995, The Best of My Love, 1995, Love Songs, 1996, Complicated, 1997, Little Things, 1997, Super Hits, 1998, What's Your Mama's Name/Would You Lay With Me (In a Field of Stone), 1999, Best of My Love, 2000, Sisters: An Anthology, 2000, Country Classics, Vol. 2, 2000, 20 Greatest Hits, 2000, 20th Century Masters-The Millennium Collection: The Best of Tanya Tucker, 2000, The Dresden Dolls, 2001, Tanya Tucker Country Classics, 2001, Tanya, 2002, The Upper 48 Hits 1972-1997, 2002, Country Classics, 2002, Very Best Of, 2004, Country Greatest: EMI Years, 2004, Live at Billy Bob's Texas, 2005; TV appearances include A Country Christmas, 1979, The Georgia Peaches, 1980, The Love Boat, 1982, Delta, 1992; actress: (mini-series) The Rebels, 1979, (film) Jeremiah Johnson, 1972, Amateur Night At the Dixie Bar & Grill, 1978, When I Was A Girl, 2003, (TV series) Tuckerville, 2005-; published (autobiography) Nickel Dreams, 1997; author: 100 Ways to Beat the Blues, 2005. Nat. amb. Nat. Multiple Sclerosis Soc.; philanthropist March of Dimes, St. Jude's Children's Hosp., Doris Kupferle Breast Centers, Coors Literacy Project, Recording Artists Against Drunk Driving, Planet Hope, Boys and Girls Clubs, charitable events for T.J. Martell Found. Named Top New Female Vocalist, Acad. Country Music, 1972, Most Promising Female Artist of Yr., Music City News Country, 1973, Female Vocalist of Yr., Country Music Assn., 1991, Female Video Artist of Yr., Country Music TV, 1993, Showcase Artist of Month, Country Music TV, 1997; recipient Music Video of Yr., Country Music Assn., 1992, Video of Yr. for Two Sparrows in a Hurricane, Acad. Country Music, 1993; nominee for two Grammy awards, 1994. Avocations: avid competitor in cutting horse contests, motorcycling. Office: Tanya Tucker Inc c/o Curtis & Co Plc 109 Westpark Dr Ste 400 Brentwood TN 37027-5032

TUCKER-KETO, CLAUDIA A., academic administrator; b. Phila., Jan. 24, 1948; d. Arthur and Erma (Miller) Tucker; children: Victor Lefa, James Lefanyana (twins). BA, Temple U., 1982. With adminstrv. office Pa. Supreme Ct., Phila.; coll. adminstr., family resource specialist Camden County Coll., Blackwood, N.J. Coord. women's programs Camden County Dept. Health and Human Svcs., Camden, N.J. mem. ethics com. Dist. IV Supreme Ct., 1993-95. Legis. chairwoman N.J. Fed. Dem. Women, Trenton, N.J.; mem. planning com. U.S. Dept. Labor Women's Bur. Region II, N.Y.; commr. N.J. Martin Luther King Jr. Organization, Trenton; bd. dir. N.J. Women's Summit, Sicklerville, N.J.; chairwomen Camden County Commn. on Women, N.J. Recipient Women in Bus. award Nat. Hookup of Black Women, 1992, Outstanding Svc. to Women award African Am. Women's Network, 1994 Mem. AAUW. Baptist.

TUCKNESS, AMBER VICTORIA, music educator; b. Salt Lake City, July 31, 1975; d. Mark and Victoria Theresa Woolley; m. Robert Corey Tuckness, Oct. 27, 2000; 1 child, Abriel Victoria. MusB in Edn., U. Utah, Salt Lake City, 1997. Dir. instrumental music Cottonwood H.S., Salt Lake City, 1997—. Dir. music Granite Youth Symphony Orch., Salt Lake City, 2002—. Office Phone: 801-646-5264. E-mail: amber.tuckness@granite.k12.ut.us.

TUDMAN, CATHI GRAVES, elementary school educator; b. Fresno, Calif., June 24, 1953; d. Robert Eugene and Bettyelou (Seagraves) Graves; divorced; children: Colleen Melissa, Andrew James. BA in Music cum laude, Calif. State U., Fresno, 1978, MA in Communication, 1991. Gen. elem., English, music and gen. sci. teaching credentials, Calif. Founder, coord. Lake Sequoia Symphonic Music Camp, Miramonte, Calif., 1985—; asst. lectr. communications speech dept. Calif. State U., 1988-91, instr. reading ednl. opportunity program summer bridge, 1990, instr. writing ednl. opportunity program summer bridge, 1991, coach, judge Peach Blossom Festival, 1988-91; band dir. Yosemite Mid. Sch., 1991—2004, Mayfair Elem. Sch., 1991—2000, Hidalgo Elem. Sch., 1991-92, 94-96, Balderas Elem., 1992-93, Turner Elem., 1993-96, Burroughs Annex Elem. Sch., 1993-95; art dir. Yosemite Mid. Sch., 2000—04, Ft. Miller Med. Careers Magnet Sch., SC, 2004—; physical sci. instr. Ft. Miller Med. Careers Ctr., 2004—. Instr. comms. dynamics Phillips Coll., Fresno, 1989-90; rsch. assoc. Renshaw Assocs., Fresno, 1989-91; flutist, piccoloist Fresno Philharm. Orch., 1981—, libr., 1985, pers. mgr., 1984-85; flute clinician Selmer Corp., Ind., 1988-93; festivals chmn. cen. sect. Calif. Music Educators, 1972-82, publicity chmn., 1992-93; pvt. tutor in math., music and social studies; chmn. Fresno Unified Showcase Mid. Sch. Massed Band, 1991, 93. Flute clinician Fresno County Schs., 1980—; founder San Joaquin Valley Instrument Fund, 1984; bd. dirs. Community Concert Series, Fresno County, 1986-88; liaison com. bd. dirs. Fresno Philharm. Orch., 1992-94, mem. bd., 2002-04, edn. com., 2003-05; asst. chair FMCMEA Hon. Band, 1992-93; bd. dirs. Cen. Valley YMCA, 1994-95; music chair Fresno Met. Mus., 1996-97; mem. Yosemite Mid. Sch. Site Coun. 2000-2003, pres., sec., by-laws chair Fresno Arts Coun., bd. dirs. 2002-04, Tree Fresno-Rails to Trails Project, 2000; Great TV auction vol. Valley Pub. TV, 2005. Rsch. grantee Calif. State U., 1991, Cmty. Enrichment grant, 1999-2002; recipient Outstanding Teaching award Internat. Communication Assn., 1991. Mem. Western States Communication Assn., Fresno-Madera Music Educators Assn., Fresno Tchrs. Assn. (dir.-at-large, 2002-05), Calif. Tchrs. Assn. (rep. coun. 2000-2005), Fresno Mus. Club (social chmn. 1992-95) Calif. Music Educators (festival chmn. cen. sect. 1972-82), Sci. & Math. Educators Consortium, Calif. State U.-Fresno Alumnae Assn. (sec. 1982-83, nat. friendship chmn. 1979-81), Blue Key (Tokalon alumni 1978), Phi Kappa Phi, Mu Phi Epsilon (pres., v.p. Phi Chi chpt.). Avocations: quilting, kite making, church musician. Home: 5467 E Saginaw Way Fresno CA 93727-7536 Office: Fort Miller Mid Sch 1302 E Dakota Fresno CA 93704 Office Phone: 559-248-7100. E-mail: cgtudman@att.net.

TUDOR, BRENDA S., retail company executive; CPA. Acct. Strand, Skees, Jones & Co., Asheville, N.C.; gen. acctg. mgr. Ingles Markets, Inc., Black Mountain, N.C., 1984-88; controller, sec., 1988-98; v.p., CFO, 1998—; also bd. dirs.

TUENGEL, LISA MARIE, elementary school educator; b. Port Townsend, Wash., July 26, 1959; d. Konrad Willi Karl and Jane Marie Schwencke; m. Bradley Marcus Tuengel, Aug. 23, 1987; children: Marcus, Martin, Marie. BA in Elem. Edn., Concordia Coll., Portland, Oreg., 1981; MA in Am. Studies, Pepperdine U., Malibu, Calif., 1992. Profl. edn. cert. continuing tchr. Wash. Tchr., coach Evansville Luth. Sch., Ind., 1981—85, Zion Luth. Sch., Snohomish, Wash., 1985—90; tchr., phys. edn. specialist Snohomish Sch. Dist., 2000—. Sunday sch. tchr., mem. choir Zion Luth. Ch., Snohomish, 2004—. Recipient Athlete of Yr. award, Concordia Coll., 1981; Am. studies fellow, Pepperdine U., 1986—89. Mem.: AAHPERD, Washington Alliance for Health, Phys. Edn., Recreation and Dance (award phys. edn. divsn. 2005). Avocations: sports, photography, knitting. Home: 1610 S Machias Rd Snohomish WA 98290 Office: Machias Elem Sch 231 147th Ave SE Snohomish WA 98290 Office Phone: 360-563-4871. Office Fax: 360-563-4828. E-mail: lisa.tuengel@sno.wednet.edu.

TUETING, SARAH, professional hockey player; b. Winnetka, Ill., Apr. 26, 1976; Student, Dartmouth Coll., 1994—96. Goaltender U.S. Nat. Women's Hockey Team, 1996—. Recipient ice hockey Gold medal Olympic Games, Nagano, Japan, 1998. Avocations: soccer, tennis, playing piano and cello. Office: c/o USA Hockey 1775 Bob Johnson Dr Colorado Springs CO 80906

TUFANO, SYLVIA HOPE, obstetrician, gynecologist; b. Bklyn., June 21, 1972; d. Pascal and Rosa Tufano; m. Jacques Lucien LeClaire, June 24, 2005. BS, Cornell U., Ithaca, NY, 1994; MD, U. Buffalo, NY, 1999. Diplomate Am. Bd. Ob-Gyn, 2005. Physician Suffolk Ob-Gyn, Port Jefferson, NY, 2004—. Fellow: ACOG. Office Phone: 631-473-7171.

TUFO JARNAGIN, KELLI, social studies educator; b. LaGrange, Ill., Apr. 1, 1971; d. Daniel and Carol Tufo; m. Dayton T. Jarnagin, June 27, 2001. BA in Polit. Sci., U. Iowa, Iowa City, 1993; MS in Ednl. Leadership, No. Ill. U., DeKalb, 2000. Social studies tchr. Waubonsie Valley HS, Aurora, Ill., 1995—97, Neuqua Valley HS, Naperville, 1997—. Head sponsor Youth & Govt., Naperville, 1999—. Mem. Wheatland Twp. Parks Com., Naperville, 2004—. Recipient Dist. 204 Most Influential Educator award, Indian Prairie Edn. Found., 2000, 2001, 2006. Mem.: NEA, Nat. Coun. Social Studies.

TUFT, MARY ANN, executive search firm executive; b. Easton, Pa., Oct. 11, 1934; d. Ben and Elizabeth (Reibman) T. BS, West Chester State Coll., Pa., 1956; MA, Lehigh U., 1960. Cert. assn. exec. Nat. trainer Girl Scouts U.S.A., N.Y.C., 1965-68; cons. Nat. League for Nursing, N.Y.C., 1968-69; exec. dir. Nat. Student Nurses Assn., N.Y.C., 1970-85; mem. Commn. on Dietetic Registration, Am. Dietetic Assn., 1981-85; pres. Specialized Cons. Ltd., 1983-85; exec. dir. Radiol. Soc. N.Am., Oak Brook, Ill., 1985-88; pres. Tuft & Assocs., Inc., 1989—. Trustee, Found. of the Nat. Student Nurses Assn., 2001—; adv. bd. Cognitive Neurology and Alzheimer's Disease Ctr. of Northwestern Univ./Feinberg Sch. of Medicine; mem. pres.'s adv. coun. Sch. Nursing, Saint Xavier U., 2006—. Bd. dirs. Nurses House, Inc., 1981-85, nat. bd. Am. Friends of Hebrew U., 2000-06; mem. exec. com. Chgo. Sinai Cong., 1987-91, v.p., 1988. Recipient Disting. Alumnus award West Chester State Coll., 1979; Mary Ann Tuft Scholarship Fund named in her honor Found. Nat. Student Nurses Assn.; Kepner-Tregoe scholar, 1966. Mem. ALA (pub. mem. com. on accreditation 1993-95), Am. Soc. Assn. Execs. (bd. dirs. 1980-83, trustee for cert. 1980-83, vice chmn. 1983-84), N.Y. Soc. Assn. Execs. (pres. 1978-79, bd. dirs. 1975-78, 1st Outstanding Exec. award 1982), Continuing Care Accreditation Assn. (bd. dirs. 1983-85), Specialized Cons. in Nursing (faculty), Am. Dietetic Assn. (pub. mem. commn. on accreditation for dietetics edn.), Sigma Theta Tau (hon.). Office Phone: 312-642-8889. Business E-Mail: matuft@tuftassoc.com.

TUFTON, JANIE LEE (JANE TUFTON), dental hygienist, lobbyist; b. Allentown, Pa., Jan. 6, 1949; d. Robert Harry and Jean Lorraine (Seng) T. BS in Edn., Indiana U. Pa., 1979; postgrad. in English, 1979—82. Registered dental hygienist, Pa., N.J., Calif.; cert. tchr., Pa. Dental hygientist pvt. dental practices, Pa., N.J., Calif., 1976-90. Author bd. game for dental health edn., 1974. Lobbyist, activist for animal rights; bd. dirs. and pub. rels. Lehigh Valley Animal Rights Coalition, 1984-93; active civil rights movement, cultural events, literacy programs, detoxification units for drug and alcohol abuse, venereal disease clinics, practical-life workshops for the cognitively impaired, suicide hotlines, YWCA, Girl Scouts U.S. Recipient recognition Pa. Dental Hygienists Assn., 1974 Mem. Am. Anti-Vivisect. Soc., Nat. Humane Edn. Soc., The Fund for Animals, The Humane Soc. of the U.S., Nat. Alliance for Animals, Internat. Soc. for Animal Rights, Physicians Com. for Responsible Medicine, Culture and Animals Found., Animal Legal Def. Fund, People for the Ethical Treatment of Animals, Farm Animal Reform Movement, Farm Sanctuary, Com. to Abolish Sport Hunting, Animal Rights Mobilization, In Def. of Animals, United Animal Nations, Internat. Platform Assn., Internat. Network for Religion and Animals, Humane Religion, Performing Animal Welfare Socs., Disabled and Incurably Ill for Alternatives to Animal Rsch., United Poultry Concerns, Am. Soc. for Prevention of Cruelty to Animals. Avocations: photography, tennis, reading, environmental issues, women's studies. Home: 2102 S Lehigh Ave Whitehall PA 18052-5532

TUGGLE, CONNIE KERSEY, biology educator, department chairman; d. Boyd Dewitt and Dorthy June Kersey; m. Dennis Wayne Kersey, Aug. 9, 1980; 1 child, Joshua Wallace. BSE, Henderson State U., Arkadelphia, Ark., 1977. Cert. tchr. in sci., health, art and phys. edn. Ark. Sci. dept. chmn. Glen Rose H.S., Malvern, Ark., 1980—, Poyen H.S., Ark. Sch. dist. sci. facillitator Dawson Ednl. Coop., Arkadelphia, 1980—; state bd. mem. Ark. State Sci. Fair Bd., Conway, Ark., 1980—; tchr. mem. INTEL Internat. Sci. and Engrng. Fair, 1988—; tchr. Internat. Sci. and Engring. Fair, 1998—. Recipient Sch. Champions award, Ark. State Sci. Fair, 2003—04. Mem.: Ark. Sci. Tchrs. Assn., Nat. Sci. Tchrs. Assn., Alpha Delta Kappa.

TUISKU, MARY JOAN, volunteer, advocate; b. Laurium, Mich., May 30, 1946; d. Allwin Eugene Dina Joseph and Gladys Muriel Prideaux; m. Richard H. Tuisku, June 24, 1967; children: Tammy Ann Bricker, Jason Christian, Jodi Marie. Assoc. Deg., No. Mich. U., 1966. Customer svc. Sears, Houghton, Mich., 1966—68, D&N Bank, Hancock, Mich., 1982—91. Active Hancock Recreation Commn., 1980—94, Sister Cities Com., 1988—2003, Hancock Finnish Theme Com., 1990—2003, Hancock Planning Commn., 1990—95, Hancock Hist. Preservation Commn., 1992—95, Quincy Area Adv. Coun., Hancock, 1992—95, Mich. Tech. U. Multi-cultural Com., Houghton, Hancock Pub. Schools Libr. Adv. Com.; chairperson Hancock Ordinance Revision Com., 1990—93; commr. We. Upper Peninsula Planning & Devel. Region, Houghton, 1990—95, Keweenaw Nat. Hist. Pk. Adv. Commn., Calumet, Mich., 1993—97; bd. mem. BHK Child Devel. Found.; city councilor City of Hancock, 1982—2006, mayor, 1990—95; chairperson new ch. bldg. com. Glad Tidings, Hancock; chairperson Mich. Technol. U. Cmty. Adv. Coun., Houghton, 1992—95; panelist Mich. Coun. Arts and Cultural Affairs, Lansing. Named Civic Leader of the Yr., Keweenaw Peninsula C. of C., 1994, Citizen of the Yr., Salvation Army. Mem.: Omicron Delta Kappa. Independent. Avocations: reading, travel, music, sports, art. Home: 939 Lynn St Hancock MI 49930 Office: MJET Consulting 939 Lynn St Hancock MI 49930 Office Phone: 906-482-7368. E-mail: mtuisku@charter.net.

TULBERT, CARRIE ANN, literature and language educator, gifted and talented educator; b. Cin., Jan. 8, 1979; d. William Carl and Ruth Ann Swart; m. William Barton Tulbert, Apr. 27, 2002. BA in English, Meredith Coll., Raleigh, N.C., 2001. Tchr. English Lakeshore Mid. Sch., Mooresville, NC, 2001. Specialist academically and intellectually gifted edn. Iredell- Statesville Sch. Sys., NC, 2001—. Named Tchr. of Yr., Lakeshore Mid. Sch., 2005—06. Mem.: ASCD.

TULIN, MARNA, psychotherapist; b. N.Y.C., Feb. 23, 1930; d. Irving Bernsohn and Gloria Bernsohn Turner; m. Harold Klingbeil, Feb. 14, 1948 (dec. May 1952); 1 child, Deborah Klingbeil Tulin-Donnell; m. Stephen Wise Tulin, Jan. 31, 1959; children: Douglas Wise, Andrea Wise, Houlihan. BA, NYU, 1960; MSW, Columbia U., 1962; PhD in Psychology, Tulane-Pacific Western U., 1988. LCSW N.Y., Vt., diplomate social work. Caseworker Cmty. Svc. Soc., N.Y.C., 1962-63, Jewish Child Care Assn., N.Y.C., 1964-67; psychotherapist Jewish Child Care Psychiat. Clinic, N.Y.C., 1967-70; cons. pre-K, spl. needs program, home learning Mamaroneck (N.Y.) Sch. Sys., 1976-80; pvt. practice psychotherapist N.Y.C., Westchester, 1980-92, North Ferrisburg, Vt., 1993—; cons. parents place Mamaroneck (N.Y.) Sch. Sys., 1980-81; cons. Stamford (Conn.) Sch. Sys., 1981, Bank St. Coll. Edn., 1980-81; cons. Stamford (Conn.) Sch. Sys., 1981, Bank St. Coll. Edn., N.Y.C., 1987; pvt. practice North Ferrisburg, 1993—. Chmn. bd. Louise Wise Svc., N.Y.C., 1991—93, dir. emeritus; trustee Howard Ctr. for Human Svcs., Burlington, Vt., 1997—; mem. profl. adv. com. Mental Health Assn. N.Y., 1993—2000. Mem. AAUW, Internat. Conf. for Advancement Pvt. Practice Social Workers, Pi Sigma Alpha. Democrat. Jewish. Avocation: antique dealing. Home and Office: 100 Champlin Hill Rd North Ferrisburg VT 05473-4076 Fax: 802-425-3384.

TULL, THERESA ANNE, retired diplomat; b. Runnemede, N.J., Oct. 2, 1936; d. John James and Anna Cecelia (Paull) T. BA, U. Md., 1972; MA, U. Mich., 1973; postgrad., Nat. War Coll., Washington, 1980. Fgn. svc. officer Dept. State, Washington, 1963, Brussels, 1965-67, Saigon, 1968-70; dep. prin. officer Am. Consulate General, Danang, Vietnam, 1973-75; prin. officer Cebu, Philippines, 1977-79; dir. office human rights, 1980-83; charge d'affaires Am. Embassy, Vientiane, Laos, 1983-86; Dept. State Senior Seminar, 1986-87; ambassador to Guyana, 1987-90; diplomat-in-residence Lincoln U., Pa., 1990-91; dir. office regional affairs, bur. East Asian & Pacific affairs Dept. State, Washington, 1991-93; amb. to Brunei Bandar Seri Begawan, 1993-96. Recipient Civilian Service award Dept. of State, 1970, Superior Honor award, 1977 Mem. Am. Fgn. Svc. Assn., Women's Civic Club. Address: 3500 Boardwalk Apt 726N Sea Isle City NJ 08243

TULLO, BARBARA ANN, performing company executive; d. Roland Gaston LaPointe and Mary Ann Pastorello; m. Duke Joseph Tullo, Aug. 2, 1975; 1 child, Heather Marie. BA, Wagner Coll., Staten Island, NY, 1973; MA in Music Edn., Bklyn. Coll., 1975; profl. diploma in Ednl. Adminstrn., C.W. Post, 1981. Music tchr. choral St. Brendan's HS, Bklyn., 1973—77; music tchr. orch. H. Frank Carey Jr./Sr. HS, Franklin Square, NY, 1979—83; dist. strings. dir. East Rockaway Pub. Sch., East Rockaway, NY, 1989—. Violinist South Shore Philermonic, West Hemstead, NY, 1999—2002, CW Post Orchestra, Brookdale, NY, 2003—06. Mem.: Music Educators Nat. Conf., NY State Sch. Music Assn. Roman Catholic. Personal E-mail: btullo@hotmail.com.

TULLY, CATHERINE L., physical educator instructor; b. Oak Park, Ill., Feb. 22, 1968; d. Joseph T. and Dolores P. Tully; m. Scott B. Wahlen, Oct. 11, 2002. BA in Exercise Sci. and Fitness Mgmt., Concordia U., River Forest, Ill., 2001. Faculty/dance instr./phys. edn. instr. Trinity H.S., River Forest, 2002—05; adj. faculty/dept. of human performance Concordia U., River Forest, Ill., 2005—; pub. rels., mktg. coord. Oak Pk. Arts Dist., Oak Park, Ill., 2006—. Outside Europe rep. Nat. Dance Tchrs. Assn./UK, 2004—. Contbr. articles to profl. jours. Mem.: Psi Chi. Roman Catholic. Avocation: travel. Office Phone: 708-771-8300. Personal E-mail: ctu@earthlink.net.

TULLY, SUSAN BALSLEY, pediatrician, educator; b. San Francisco, July 12, 1941; d. Gerard E. Balsley Sr. and Norma Lilla (Hand) Carey; m. William P. Tully, June 19, 1965; children: Michael William, Stephen Gerard. BA in Premed. Studies, UCLA, 1963, MD, 1966. Diplomate Am. Bd. Pediat. with subsplty. in pediatric emergency medicine. Intern L.A. County-U. So. Calif. Med. Ctr., 1966-67, jr. resident pediat., 1967-68; staff pediatrician, part-time Permanente Med. Group, Oakland, Calif., 1968; sr. resident pediat. Kaiser Found. Hosp., Oakland, 1968-69, Bernalillo County Med. Ctr., Albuquerque, 1969-70, chief resident pediatric outpatient dept., 1970; instr. pediat., asst. dir. outpatient dept. U. N.Mex. Sch. Medicine, Albuquerque, 1971-72; asst. prof. pediat., dir. ambulatory pediat. U. Calif., Irvine, 1972-76, asst. prof. clin. pediat., vice chair med. edn., 1977-79; staff pediatrician Ross-Loos Med. Group, Buena Park, Calif., 1976-77; assoc. prof. clin. pediat. and emergency medicine U. So. Calif. Sch. Medicine, 1979-86; dir. pediatric emergency dept. L.A. County/U. So. Calif. Med. Ctr., 1979-87; prof. clin. pediat. and emergency medicine U. So. Calif. Sch. Medicine, 1986-89; dir. ambulatory pediat. L.A. County/U. So. Calif. Med. Ctr., 1987-89; clin. prof. pediat. UCLA, 1989-93, vice chair pediat., 1996-97, prof. clin. pediat., 1993-97, prof. emeritus, 1997—; dir. ambulatory pediat. Olive View-UCLA Med. Ctr., 1989-96, chief pediat., 1996-97, cons. pediatrician, 1997—. Mem. survey team pediatric emergency svcs. L.A. Pediatric Soc., 1984—86; mem. adv. bd. preventive health project univ. affiliated program Children's Hosp. L.A., 1981—83; lectr. nursing pediat. nurse practitioner program Calif. State U., L.A., 1997—; pediat. toxicology cons. L.A. County Regional Poison Control Ctr. Med. Adv. Bd., 1981—97; clin. faculty rep. pediatric advancement and promotion com. UCLA Sch. Medicine, 1992—93; pediatric liaison dept. emergency medicine Olive View/UCLA Med. Ctr., 1989—96, dir. lead poisoning clinic, 1993—99; mem. quality assurance com. Los Angeles County Cmty. Health Plan, 1986—89. Author: (with K.E. Zenk) Pediatric Nurse Practitioner Formulary, 1979; (book chpt. with W.A. Wingert) Pediatric Emergency Medicine: Concepts and Clinical Practice, 1992, 2d edit., 1997; (with others) Educational Guidelines for Ambulatory/General Pediatrics Fellowship Training, 1992, Physician's Resource Guide for Water Safety Education, 1994; reviewer Pediatrics, 1985-89; editl. cons. Advanced Pediatric Life Support Course and Manual, 1988-89, Archives of Pediatrics and Adolescent Medicine, 1996-2001; dept. editor Pediatric Pearls Jour. Am. Acad. Physician Assts., 1989-94; tech. cons., reviewer Healthlink TV Am. Acad. Pediatrics, 1991; reviewer Pediatric Emergency Care, 1992—; question writer sub-bd. pediatric emergency medicine Am. Bd. Pediatrics, 1993-98; assoc. editor: Curriculum for the Training of General Pediatricians, 1996; cons. to lay media NBC Nightly News, Woman's Day, Sesame Street Parents, Parenting, Los Angeles Times; author numerous abstracts; contbr. articles to profl. jours. Cons. spl. edn. programs Orange County Bd. Edn., 1972-79; mem. Orange County Health Planning Coun., 1973-79; co-chairperson Orange County Child Health and Disability Prevention Program Bd., 1975-76; mem. Orange County Child Abuse Consultation Team, 1977-79; mem. project adv. bd. Family Focussed "Buckle Up" Project, Safety Belt Safe, U.S.A., 1989-96. Fellow Am. Acad. Pediat. (life, active numerous sects. and coms., active Calif. chpt.); mem. Ambulatory Pediatric Assn., L.A. Pediatric Soc. (life). Democrat. Avocations: art needlework, reading. Office: Olive View UCLA Med Ctr Pediatrics 3A108 14445 Olive View Dr Sylmar CA 91342-1495 Personal E-mail: SBTully@aol.com.

TULO, KELLIE J., think-tank executive, director; d. William C. and Maureen E. Myers; m. Steve J. Tulo III, Nov. 18, 2000. Student, Johnson & Wales U., Providence, R.I. Sponosrships and events manger Washingtonpost-.Newsweek Interactive, Arlington, Va., 2000—04; dir., spl. events & corp. sponsorships Wash. Hosp. Ctr. Found., Washington, 2004—. Bd. mem. DC Ad Club, Washington, 2003—. Recipient Am. Advt. Fedn. Dist. 2 Governors Award, 2004. Mem.: AMP, AAF, AAAA, DC Ad Club. Office: Wash Hosp Ctr Found 110 Irving St NW EB 1001 Washington DC 20010 Office Phone: 202-877-3028. Office Fax: 202-877-5148. Personal E-mail: ktulo@aol.com. Business E-Mail: kellie.tulo@medstar.net.

TUMA, MICHELE, music educator; b. Mount Holly, NJ, May 20, 1958; d. Marvin and Jan Weisbrot; m. Kerry Tuma, June 28, 1981; children: Casey, Max. BS in Music Edn., West Chetser U., Pa., 1980. Cert. music edn. tchr. Pa., NJ, 1980. Music tchr. Florence Twp Sch. Dist., NJ, 1980—89; music tchr. grades k- 5 Evesham Twp. Sch. Dist., Marlton, NJ, 1989—. Mem.: SJ Choral Dirs. Home: 8 Pickwick Dr Marlton NJ 08053 Office: Rice Elementary School 50 Crown Royal Pkwy Marlton NJ 08053 Office Phone: 856-988-0685. Office Fax: 856-988-7799. Personal E-mail: bdwaymom@comcast.net.

TUMIO, VERA ANN, Reiki master priest; b. Manhattan, N.Y., Apr. 10, 1951; d. Anthony T. Tumio and Ermina L. Russo. BA in Sociology and History magna cum laude, CUNY, Bronx, 1977; student, Birmingham U., Eng., 1975—76; MA in American History with distinction, CUNY, Queens, 1991; postgrad., Grad. Sch. Univ. Ctr., Manhattan, N.Y., 1994—99. Cert. Reiki Master, ordained priest Reunification Ch. in the Order of Melchizedek, 2004. Reading, study skills tchr. Baldridge Reading Program, Greenwich, Conn., 1978—79; with Cigna Property and Casualty Co., L.I., 1980—89, br. mgr., 1987—89; home office examiner Am. Internat. Underwriters, Manhattan, 1991—92; ins. cons. Ins. Overload Systems, L.I., 1997—2001; worker's compensation specialist Riskco Svcs./CNA, Manhattan, 2001—02; ins. cons. Ins. Overload Systems, L.I., 2002—04; Reiki master V.A. Tumio, LLC, Monroe/Brookfield, Conn., 2004—05. Reiki master Healing Arts Cmty. of Conn., Brookfield, 2004—05; Reiki master practitioner/tchr. in pvt. practice, 1999—; condr. workshops in field. Vol. Dem. Polit. campaigns, 1974—92; co-founder, pres. Morningside House N.H. Family Coun., Bronx, 1999—2001. Fellow NSF fellow, 1975; scholar Mary Neil White scholar, Herbert H. Lehman Coll., 1977. Mem.: Internat. Assn. of Reiki Profls., Alpha Kappa Delta. Democrat. Avocations: walking, singing, jogging, writing, dancing. Office Phone: 203-261-1214.

TUNISON, DAWN M. R., music educator; b. Baldwin, Wis., Dec. 6, 1963; d. Paul C. and Barb A. Ramberg; m. William C. Tunison, Oct. 3, 1987; children: Emily M., Alexander P. MusB in Edn., U. Wis., River Falls, 1986. Cert. instrumental, choral, and gen. music tchr. Wis. Dept. of Pub. Instrn. Music tchr. Glidden Sch., Wis., 2002—. Office: Glidden School 370 S Grant St Glidden WI 54527 Office Phone: 715-264-2141.

TUNNELL, CLIDA DIANE, air transportation specialist; b. Durham, N.C., Nov. 20, 1946; d. Kermit Wilbur and Roberta (Brantley) T.; m. Michael A. Murphy, May 24, 1997. BS cum laude, Atlantic Christian Coll., 1968; pvt. pilot rating, instr. rating, Air Care, Inc., 1971, pvt. pilot rating, instr. rating, 1983. Cert. tchr. Tchr. Colegio Karl C. Parrish, Barranquilla, Colombia, 1968—69, Nash County Schs., Nashville, NC, 1969—86; instr. ground sch. Nash. Tech. Coll., Nashville, 1984—85; specialist Am. Airlines, Dallas-Ft. Worth Airport, 1987—, A300 lead developer in flight tng. program devel., 1988—89, with flight ops. procedures flight ops. tech., 1990—, F100-fleet specialist, flight ops. tech., 1990—98, 737 fleet specialist, 1998—2002, mgr. flight ops. procedures, 2003—05; specialist product support tech. Boeing, 2005—. Ednl. cons., Euless, Tex., 1989—; profl. artist. State Tchrs. Scholar N.C., 1964-68, Bus. and Profl. Women Scholar, 1980-81. Mem. 99, Internat. Orgn. Women Pilots (various offices), AMR Mgmt. Club. Avocations: flying, painting, writing, travel. Office: Boeing PO Box 68126 Seattle WA 98168 Home: 24122 145th Ave Kent WA 98042

TUNSTALL, DOROTHY FIEBRICH, retired pre-school administrator; b. Elizabeth City, Va., Sept. 18, 1939; d. Louie Ludwig and Nancy Julia (Drafts) Fiebrich; m. Frank S. Clark Jr., June 11, 1961 (div. 1970); children: Sherri Ann D'Alessio, Debra Sue Pate, Frank S. Clark III; m. Jim Tunstall, June 1987 (div. 1995). BA in Elem. Edn., Stetson U., 1961, MA in Edn., 1963; Ed. Spec. in Edn. Adminstrn., U. S.C., 1991, PhD in Early Childhood, 1993. Cert. tchr. Fla., S.C. Substitute tchr. Broward County Schs., Ft. Lauderdale, Fla., 1963-70, EABE tchr., 1972-80; title I, tchr. for fed. govt. South Fla. State Hosp., Pembroke Pines, Fla., 1970-72; tchr. spl. edn. Richland Sch. Dist. #2, Columbia, S.C., 1980-81; COBOL programmer Comptr. Gen.'s Office, Columbia, 1982-85; tchr. spl. edn. Calhoun County Schs., St. Matthews, S.C., 1985-88; tchr. kindergarten Fairfield County Schs., Winnsboro, S.C., 1989-92; dir. St. Paul's Child Care Ministry, Columbia, SC, 1997—2000, Good Shepherd Day Sch., Columbia, 2001—05; ret., 2005. Adj. prof. U. S.C., Columbia, 1994—99. Active Lexington County Adolescent Pregnancy Prevention Bd., 1999—, Lexington County First Steps Bd., 2001—03; v.p. unit 7 Am. Legion Aux., 2000—02, pres. unit 7, 2002—04, pres. dist. 10, 2004—05, jr. v.p. S.C., 2005—06, sr. v.p. S.C., 2006—. Mem.: DAR, AAUW (pres. 1998—2002), Herb Bunch, Mental Health Assn. in Mid-Carolina (v.p. 1992—93, bd. dirs., Pres. award 1993), Lexington County Arts Assn. (pres. 1992—93, Newcomer's award 1981), Wildlife Action Inc. (pres. 1991—93), Beta Sigma Phi (Girl of Yr. 1967). Avocations: reading, gardening, dance. Home: 159 Corley Mill Rd Lexington SC 29072-7600 E-mail: dottun57@peoplepc.com.

TUPPER, BECKY JEAN, registrar; d. Leonard Martin Roe and Violet Fern Opdahl; m. Loren Gregory Tupper, June 5, 1976; children: Jessica, Kristina, Roberta. BS, SD State U., Brookings, 1975; MS, Okla. State U., Stillwater, 1977. Adminstrv. asst. Okla. Wesleyan U., Bartlesville, 1991—97, ann. fund dir., 1997—2000, dir. assoc.'s program, 2000—02, registrar, 2002—. Office: Okla Wesleyan U 2201 Silver Lake Rd Bartlesville OK 74006-6233 Business E-Mail: btupper@okwu.edu.

TURA, CAROL ANN, medical/surgical and intravenous therapy nurse; b. Plymouth, Mass., Sept. 21, 1939; d. Elisha D. and Delia Pattison (Washburn) Lacey; m. Francis V. Tura, May 23, 1964; children: Philip, Elizabeth, Linda, Jennifer. Diploma in nursing, Brockton (Mass.) Hosp., 1960. RN, Mass. Supr. Jordan Hosp., Plymouth, 1961-65, nurse med.-surg. unit, 1972-81, nurse mgr. intravenous therapy unit, 1991-95, clin. leader intravenous therapy unit, 1995—2004. Affiliate faculty in CPR, bd. dirs. CPR/Emergency Cardiac Care program, Am. Heart Assn., S.E. and Cape Islands, 1989-91; adv. bd. trustees Jordan Hosp., Inc. Recipient Peter A. Chapman award, Jordan Hosp., 2002. Mem. Intravenous Nurses Soc. (treas. New Eng. chpt., past dist. leader), Brockton Hosp. Sch. Nursing Alumni Assn., Nat. Intravenous Nurses Soc. Home: 59-3 South Meadow Vlg Carver MA 02330-1860

TURCHETTI, CELINE MARIE, elementary school educator; d. Edward and Alice Christen Lorang; m. Thomas Paul Turchetti, Apr. 14, 1973; children: Victoria Ann, Yvonne Marie. AA, Cazenovia Coll., N.Y., 1969; BS, Russell Sage Coll., Troy, N.Y., 1971, MS, 1975. Cert. tchr. N.Y., 1974. Elem. tchr. Stillwater Ctrl. Sch., 1971—73, Red Hook Ctrl. Sch., NY, 1973—. Bldg. level team Red Hook Ctrl. Sch., 1994—, dist. level team, 2004—. Pres. Red Hook Student Aid Assn.; past mem. Red Hook Rec Pk., Inc.; pres. Red Hook Alumni Assn., 2005—06; past v.p. Raiders Sports Club, Red Hook. Recipient Booster of Yr., Raiders Sports Club, 2006. Mem.: Red Hook Faculty Assn. (bldg. rep 2004—). Roman Catholic. Home: 77 Pitcher Lane Red Hook NY 12571

TURCOT, MARGUERITE HOGAN, medical researcher; b. White Plains, N.Y., May 19, 1934; d. Joseph William (dec.) and Marguerite Alice (dec.) Barrett) Hogan; children: Michael J., Susan A. Turcot, William R. Student, Syracuse U., 1951-54; BSN, U. Bridgeport, 1968. RN, Conn., N.C. Nurse Park City Hosp., Bridgeport, Conn., 1968-69, Meml. Mission Hosp., Asheville, N.C., 1969-70; instr. St. Joseph's Hosp., Asheville, 1970-71, oper. rm. nurse, 1973-77, charge nurse urology-cystoscopy, 1977-85; tchr. Asheville-Buncombe Tech. Coll., Asheville, 1971-72, Buncombe County Child Devel., Asheville, 1972-73; rschr. VA Med. Ctr., Asheville, 1988—; owner Reed House Bed & Breakfast, Asheville, 1985—2001. Bd. dirs. RiverLink, Quality Foreward. Charter mem. French Broad River Planning Com., Asheville, 1987—, Biltmore Village Hist. Mus.; mem. Asheville Bicentennial Commn., 1990-93; exec. dir. Preservation Soc. Asheville and Buncombe County. Recipient Griffin award, 1994, Friend of the River award, Land of Sky Regional Coun., 1995, Sondley award, Hist. Resources Commn. Asheville and Buncombe County, 1996, Vol. of Yr. award, RiverLink, 2001, Critical Link award, 2003; grantee U. Bridgeport, 1967—68; scholar Syracuse U. Faculty, 1951—54. Mem. Am. Urology Assn. (presenter VA urology workshop Asheville chpt. 1981, nat. meeting allied), Am. Bd. Urologic Allied Health Profls., Nat. Trust for Hist. Preservation, Preservation Found. N.C., Blue Ridge Pkwy. Assn., Preservation Soc. Asheville and Buncombe County (bd. dirs., past pres.), Asheville Newcomers Club (founder, 1st pres.), Earthwatch, Friends of Blue Ridge Pkwy. Inc. Republican. Roman Catholic. Avocations: preservation, history, architecture, sewing, hiking. Office: Preservation Soc Asheville & Buncombe County PO Box 2806 Asheville NC 28802

TURCZYN, CHRISTINE LILIAN, English literature and writing educator; d. Paul and Bohdanna (Felker) Turczyn. BA, Cornell U., Ithaca, N.Y., 1982; MA, U. Wis., Milw., 1989; PhD, Binghamton U., N.Y., 1995. Cert. in grant writing SUNY Tng. Ctr. Asst. editor Scholastic, Inc., N.Y.C., 1985—86; assoc. editor Holt, Rinehart & Winston, N.Y.C., 1987—97; asst. prof. William Peterson U., Wayne, NJ, 1997—2001, Passaic County C.C., NJ, 2002—03; instr. Dutchess C.C., Poughkeepsie, NY, 2004—. Mem. scholarship com. Dutchess C.C., 2005, 06; grad. asst. U. Wis. Milw., 1988—89; instr. creative writing Binghamton U., 1992—95; adj. prof. composition Montclair State U., NJ, 1995—96. Contbr. articles to profl. jours. Recipient Ednl. Opportunity Program Appreciation cert., Dutchess C.C., 2005, 1st prize, Allen Ginsberg Poetry, 1999; grantee, Fulbright Commn., 1982—83; scholar, Harvard U., 1984; Instrn. Improvement grant, Dutchess C.C., 2006, Writers grant, Vt. Studio Ctr., 2003, Geraldine R. Dodge fellow, 2002, Vt. Studio Ctr., 2000. Mem.: Nat. Coun. Tchrs. English, Cornell Club N.Y., Fulbright Assn. Avocations: swimming, painting.

TURCZYN-TOLES, DOREEN MARIE, pharmaceutical consultant; b. Chelsea, Mass., Aug. 5, 1958; d. Francis Henry and Rosalie (Lomba) Turczyn. BA cum laude, Boston U., 1981; MA, U. Chgo., 1984. Programming subcontr. Abbott Labs., Abbott Park, Ill., 1983-84; programmer, analyst Nat. Opinion Rsch. Ctr., Chgo., 1984-88; statis. computing analyst G.D. Searle & Co., Skokie, Ill., 1988-90; supr. Parke-Davis Pharms., Ann Arbor, Mich., 1990-92; mgr. applications programming Univax Biologics, Inc., Rockville, Md., 1993-95; asst. project dir. Apache Med. Sys., Inc., McLean, Va., 1995-96; group mgr. Westat, Inc., Rockville, Md., 1996—2002. Mem. NAFE, NOW, Am. Psychol. Assn. (exec. assoc. 2003—). Democrat. Presbyterian.

TUREK, SONIA FAY, journalist; b. NYC, Aug. 2, 1949; d. Louis and Julia (Liebson) Turek; m. Gilbert Curtis, June 18, 1995. BA in English, CCNY, 1970; MSLS, Drexel U., 1972; MS in Journalism, Boston U., 1979. Children's libr. Wissahickon Valley Pub. Libr., Ambler, Pa., 1973; supr. children's svcs. Somerville Pub. Libr., Somerville, Mass., 1973-78; stringer The Watertown (Mass.) Sun, 1979, The Bedford (Mass.) Minuteman, 1979; reporter The Middlesex News, Framingham, Mass., 1979-83, The Boston Herald, 1983, asst. city editor, city editor, 1983-86, asst. mng. editor features, 1986-89, asst. mng. editor Sunday, 1989-93, dep. mng. editor, arts and features, 1993-99, wine columnist, 1984—. Tchr. Cambridge (Mass.) Ctr. for Adult Edn., 1982, 83; adj. prof. Boston U., 1986; travel writer The Boston Herald, 1984-2003. Avocations: wine and food, travel, sailing. Personal E-mail: sfturek@aol.com.

TURETSKY, JUDITH, librarian, researcher; b. Bklyn., Jan. 19, 1944; d. Samuel and Ruth (Moskowitz) Turetsky. BS, Boston U., 1965; MS, Long Island U., 1969. Tchr. Trumbull (Conn.) Bd. Edn., 1965-66; libr. Darien (Conn.) Bd. Edn., 1968-69, Albert Einstein Coll., Bronx, 1969-74; researcher Koskoff, Koskoff & Bieder, Bridgeport, Conn., 1977-86. Author:(book and micro film), The History and Development of the D. Samuel Gottesman Library of Albert Einstein College of Medicine. Mem.: AMIT (life), Med. Libr. Assn., Yeshiva U. Women's Orgn. (life), Hadassah U. Women's Orgn. (life). Democrat. Avocations: reading, classical music, crocheting, doll collecting. Home and Office: 62 Gate Ridge Rd Fairfield CT 06825- Business E-Mail: judyturet@sbcglobal.net.

TURK, ELEANOR LOUISE, history professor; b. Charlottesville, Va., Sept. 9, 1935; d. Alan P. and Louise H. (Goodman) Fort; divorced; 1 child, Andrew Kittridge. BA, Ohio Wesleyan U., 1957; MA, U. Ill., 1970; PhD, U. Wis., 1975. Asst. dean Coll. Arts and Scis. U. Kans., Lawrence, 1976—78; asst. dean Sch. Humanities and Social Scis. Ithaca (N.Y.) Coll., 1978-83; from assoc. prof. to prof. history Ind. U. East, Richmond, 1983—2003, prof. history emerita, 2003—, chmn. divsn. Humanities and Social Scis., 1983-87, asst. vice chancellor for assessment, 1993-97, faculty colloquim on excellence in teaching, 1991—, chmn. instnl. self-study com., 1990-92. Author: The History of Germany, 1999 (Choice Outstanding Acad. Title award, 1999), Issues in Germany, Austria and Switzerland, 2003. Bd. dirs., dep. chair Inst. for Advanced Studies, Ind. U., Bloomington, 1991-92, chair, 1992-94; mem. pres.'s coun. for internat. programs, 1984-2003; pres. Sister Cities of Richmond, Inc., 1987-90, bd. dirs., 1987-92, 95-98; del., panel chair USSR/USA Sister Cities Conf., Tashkent, 1989; bd. dirs., treas. Wayne County Arts Consortium, Richmond, 1986-89. Recipient Excellence in Writing award Kans. State Hist. Soc., 1983, Cmty. Leadership award Richmond YWCA, 1989, John W. Ryan award for Disting. Contbns. to Internat. Programs and Studies Ind. U., 1995; Fulbright scholar Kiel U., Germany, 1957-58, German Landeskunde, 1992. Mem. Soc. for German-Am. Studies, Kans. State Hist. Soc. (life), Phi Beta Kappa, Phi Alpha Theta, Pi Sigma Alpha. Democrat. Unitarian Universalist. Business E-Mail: eturk@indiana.edu.

TURK, ELIZABETH ANN, music educator; b. N.Y.C., July 10, 1957; d. William Robert Turk, Elizabeth Ann Brittingham. BA in Music and History, Dowling Coll.; MA in German Lang. and Lit., Hofstra U.; MA in European History, SUNY Stony Brook; MA in Music Libr. Sci., Columbia U. Tchg. asst SUNY, Stony Brook, 1986—88; lectr. music Dowling Coll., Oakdale, NY, 1988—91; choral tchr. music Amityville (NY) Pub. Schs., 1991—; dir. theater arts, dir. choral music Miller Pl. HS; theater dir. Amityville HS; music dir. theater prodns. Commack HS South, Carriage House Players, Kids for Kids Theater, Inc.; music dir. theater Syosset Mid. Sch., Conn., Jericho H.S. Tchr. vocal music Miller Place Middle Sch., Miller Place, NY, Hewlett Woodmere HS, NY; pvt. tchr. and vocal coach, Massapequa, NY. Singer (soloist): (lead rolls) Rome Opera Festival, 1989, 1990; performer: Tchaikovsky Competition, 1978, 1982, 1986, Minn. Opera, 1979, 1980, 1981, L.I. Youth Orch. Summer Tours; dir.: Sleeping Beauty, Sound of Music, Fiddler on the Roof, Little Shop of Horrors, Cinderella, Oliver, numerous others; choreographer Fiddler on the Roof, Sound of Music, Little Shop of Horrors, Oliver, Grease; dir.: 42nd Street, West Side Story, Guys & Dolls, Mikado, HMS Pinafore & Pirates of Penzance, King and I, Best of Broadway. Recipient award for further study, Met. Opera, 1981—90, Herald award for choreography and music dir. Mem.: Suffolk County Music Educators Assn., Music Educators Nat. Assn., Suffolk County Wrestling Assn. (tournament dir. league V 1974—, numerous awards), White Star Triangle (Beloved Queen 1973—74), Order Ea. Star (various offices, assoc. condr.). Home: 90 Clock Blvd Massapequa NY 11758

TURK, JANE SKOUGE, education educator; b. Sioux City, Iowa, July 3, 1951; d. Bernard Forseth and Virginia Dahl Skouge; m. Lawrence Harvey Turk, June 21, 1971; children: Adam Forseth, Jeremy Lawrence. Tchr. White Plains Schools, NY; adj. prof. Pace U., Pleasantville, NY; instr. NYSUT, Albany. Mem. Rye Neck Bd. Edn., Mamaroneck, 1981—88. Home: 133 Woodbrook Rd White Plains NY 10605

TURK, ROSEMARY EILEEN, mathematics educator; d. Mary Alyce Kielp; m. James Francis Turk, June 23, 1979; children: Steven James, Angela Marie, Jonathan Joseph. BS in Edn., No. Ill. U., DeKalb, Ill., 1972; MS in Edn., DePaul U., Chgo., 1979. Tchr. math. 5th-8th grade Holy Family Sch., North Chgo., 1972—74; tchr. math. Parkland Mid. Sch., McHenry, Ill., 1974—86; tchr. math. 6th-8th grade Huntertown Sch., Ind., 1979—80, St. Anastasia Sch., Waukegan, Ill., 1996—2001; tchr. Ninth Grade Ctr. Waukegan H.S., Ill., 2001—. Mem.: AAUW.

TURKA, VOLEEN CLAIRE, surgeon; b. Fayetteville, NC, Nov. 5, 1961; d. Michael and Charlotte Turka; m. Jason Stephenson, 1998. BS in Chemistry, Fayetteville State U., NC, 1983; MD, U. NC Chapel Hill, 1987. Intern UNC, Chapel Hill, 1987—87, surgical resident, 1987—92; staff surgeon Grand Forks Grace Hosp., ND, 1992—99, Meriks Med. Ctr., Fargo, ND, 1999—. Contbr. articles to profl. jours. Mem.: Assn. Women Surgeons, Am. Coll. Surgeons. Avocations: cooking, Scrabble, theater. Office: Mericks Med Ctr 1009 19th St S Fargo ND 58103-2931 Business E-Mail: drturka@meriksmedicalcenter.org.

TURKOVÁ, HELGA, librarian; b. Prague, Czech, Apr. 20, 1942; d. Johann Turek and Anna (Kusbachová) Turková. Grad., Charles U., Prague, Czech, 1964, PhD, 1969. Diploma in librarianship. Libr. Czechoslovak Acad. of Scis., Prague, 1964—65, Prague Info. Svc., 1965—65; ind. specialist. libr. Nat. Mus. Libr., Prague, 1967—90, dir., 1990—2005; dir. dept. hist. Castles Libr., Prague, 2005—. Co-author: (book) Rilke and Kraus and Vrchotovy J., 1985, (catalogue) Catalog incunabula in Castle Libraries, 1992, 2001; editor: Sborník Národního muzea-rada C-literární historie, 1990—. Mem coun Friends Old Prague, 1963—, Soc R M Rilke, 1992—. Mem.: Literary Sci Soc Sci Acad Czech Republic, Spolecnost Národního muzea, Asn Librarians. Roman Catholic. Avocations: history of Prague, art. Office: Knihovna Národni muzeum Václavské námĕstí 68 115 79 Prague 1 Czech Republic Office Phone: 00420 224 497 368. Business E-Mail: helga_turkova@nm.cz.

TURLEY, LINDA, lawyer; b. Altus, Okla., July 16, 1958; d. Windle and Shirley (Lacey) Turley; 1 child, Lacey. BS, Georgetown U., 1980; JD with honors, U. Tex., 1983. Bar: Tex. 1983; bd. cert. in personal injury trial law. Atty., head product liability dept. Law Offices of Windle Turley, P.C., Dallas, 1986-95; personal injury trial lawyer Turley Law Firm, 2001—05; ptnr. Turley & Stutz, P.C., Dallas, 1997—2001; with Turley Law Firm, 2006—. Mem. task force on Tex. rules of civil procedure Tex. Supreme Ct., 1992-93. Mem. ATLA (bd. govs. 1993-96, chair women trial lawyers' caucus 1989-90, chair product liability sect. 1996-97), Am. Bd. Trial Advocates, Tex. Trial Lawyers Assn. (bd. dirs. 1989—). Office: 1000 Turley Law Ctr 6440 N Central Expy Dallas TX 75206 Office Phone: 214-691-4025. Business E-Mail: lindat@wturley.com.

TURLEY, SUSAN GWEN, minister; b. Boston, June 19, 1952; d. Calvin Earl and Marilyn (Anderson) Turley; m. Clifford Jesse Moore, Jr., Jan. 7, 1978; 1 child, Keith Jesse. BA in Sociology, Urbana (Ohio) U.; MEd, Suffolk U. Lic. cert. social worker, Mass.; ordained to ministry Swedenborgian Ch. Pvt. practice as pastoral psychotherapist Turley and Assocs., Newton, Mass., 1979-81; pastor Swedenborgian Ch., Portland, Maine, 1981-84; pastor on ministerial team Wayfarer's Chapel, L.A., 1984-87; founder, dir. Swedenborgian Social Action Concerns Com., 1987-92; guidance counselor Fairbanks Elem. Sch., Sacramento, 1987-89; interim assoc. pastor Swedenborgian Ch., San Francisco, 1989-90; chaplain and pastoral staff New Ch. Youth League West Coast, 1990-92; founding exec. dir. of living waters HIV ministry Swedenborgian Ch., San Francisco, 1992—, pastor. Hosp. chaplain St. Mary's Med. Ctr., San Francisco; dir. clin. pastoral edn. St. Francis Meml. Hosp., San Francisco; supr. Assn. Clin. Pastoral Edn. Mem. ACA, Nat. Coun. of Chs. (counseling com. 1977—),

TURLINGTON, PATRICIA RENFREW, artist, educator; b. Washington, Sept. 14, 1939; d. Henry Wilson and Anne Ruth (Bright) Renfrew; m. William Troy Turlington III, June 3, 1963 (div. Oct. 1971); children: William Troy IV, David Yelverton; m. William Archie Dees, Jr., June 4, 1994. Student, Meredith Coll., 1957, Washburn U., 1965-66, N.C. State UY., 1969-72. Comml. artist Adlers Inc. & McJoseph's, Raleigh, N.C., 1959-62; exec. dir. Goldsboro (N.C.) Art Ctr., 1973-78; elem. art tchr. Wayne Country Day Sch., Goldsboro, 1979-86; art prof. Wayne C.C., Goldsboro, 1986—2005. Artist-in-residence Edward Laredo Inst. of the Humanities, Cochabamba, Bolivia, summer 1988; vis. artist Va. Western C.C., Roanoke, Va., 1986, Wake Forest U., Winston Salem, 1987, Catawba Valley C.C., Hickory, N.C., 1989, Salem Coll., Winston Salem, N.C., 1992. Works represented in permanent collections Blue Cross-Blue Shield, Durham, N.C., Duke Med. Ctr., Mint Mus., Charlotte, U. N.C., Chapel Hill, Wachovia Bank and Trust Co., Winston-Salem; corp. and pub. brick sculpture commissions Brick Assn. N.C., Greensboro, Cohn Enterprises, Lenoir, N.C., Cordova Elem. Sch., Rockingham, N.C., Wilkes C.C., Wilkesboro, N.C., Hocker Bros. Brick and Tile Co.,

Inc., Green Bay, Wis., Kincaid Brick Co., Tampa, Fla., Koontz Masonry, Lexington, N.C., McDonald's Restaurants, Knoxville, Tenn., Jonesville, N.C., Cary, N.C., Gastonia, N.C., Knightdale, N.C., Fayetteville, N.C, N.Y.C. Transit Authority, N.Y.C., North Dr. Elem. Sch., Goldsboro, N.C., Rowan Meml. Hosp., Salisbury, N.C. Atlantic Ctr. for the Arts fellow, New Smyrna Beach, Fla., 1986; Pntrs. of the Ams. grantee, U.S. Info. Agy., Washington, 1988. Home: 709 Park Ave Goldsboro NC 27530-3834 Office Phone: 919-734-3459. E-mail: turlingtondees@nc.rr.com.

TURNAGE, KAREN L., medical technician; b. Bethel, N.C., Oct. 19, 1957; d. Lionel Anderson and Lula Jane Turnage; m. Frederick Zeno Mills, Dec. 24, 1982 (div. 1992); 1 child, Travis Colby Mills. BS, Fairleigh Dickinson U., 1980. Med. technologist Duke U. Med. Ctr., Durham, N.C., 1980-81; sr. med. technologist Univ. Health Sys. Eastern N.C., Greenville, 1981-87; displayer/decorator Home Interiors, Dallas, 1987-89; med. technologist supervisor Univ. Health Sys. Eastern N.C., 1987—. Pres. PTA E.B. Aycock Sch., 1998-99; women's day pres. Mt. Calvary Bapt. Ch., Greenville, 1994-95. Mem. Am. Soc. Clin. Pathologists. Democrat. Avocations: acting, gardening, weightlifting, skiing, decorating. Home: 107 Fox Run Cir Greenville NC 27858-9730

TURNAGE, MARTHA ALLEN, academic administrator; b. Wake County, NC, May 23, 1922; d. Charles Nicholas and Lona (Williams) Allen; widowed; children: Sherrod, Barbara, Russell, Charles. BA, Wake Forest U., 1944; MA, Coll. of William and Mary, 1970; EdD, Va. Inst. Tech., 1978. Dir. learning resources Va. Highlands C.C., Abingdon, 1970—71; dean students and cmty. svc. Mountain Empire C.C., Big Stone Gap, Va., 1971-73; dean cmty. devel. J. Sargeant Reynolds CC, Richmond, Va., 1974-76; exec. asst. to pres. Bluefield State Coll., W.Va., 1976-77; lifelong learning project dir. Am. Assn. Cmty. & Jr. Colls., Washington, 1978; v.p. external affairs and govt. rels. George Mason U., Fairfax, Va., 1978-84; v.p. for univ. rels. Ohio U., Athens, 1984-92; ret., 1992. Author: Company Town Shutdown, 1994. Founder Job Preparedness Ctr., Saltville, Va., 1970—71; vol. Colonial Nat. Pk., Yorktown, Va., 2003—; mem. Northwest Ordinance Bicentennial Commn., Ohio, 1987. Mem. Phi Beta Kappa, Phi Kappa Phi. Democrat. Methodist. Home: 3800 Treyburn Dr Apt B122 Williamsburg VA 23185-6410

TURNAU, VIVIAN WILLIAMSON, retired literature and language educator; b. N.Y.C., N.Y., Apr. 16, 1957; d. Albin Creo and Elizabeth Chaffers Williamson; m. Roger William Turnau, Apr. 1 (dec.); children: Theodore Arthur III, Roger Williamson. BA in French Edn., Russell Sage Coll., Troy, N.Y., 1958; cert. French studies, U. Lausanne, Switzerland, 1959; MA in Spanish, State U. Pa., Millersville, 1995; postgrad., U. N.C., Greensboro, 2003. Adminstrv. asst. United Way Berks County, Reading, Pa., 1988—90; tchr. Spanish and ESL Reading Area C.C., 1991—93; tchr. French and Spanish Wyomissing Sch. Dist., Pa., 1990—94, Bishop Wood H.S., Warminster, Pa., 1994; tchr. Spanish Salem Acad., Winston-Salem, NC, 1995—96; ret., 1997; tutor YMCA, Winston-Salem, 1999—2006; substitute tchr. Summit Sch., Winston-Salem, 2004—05. Exch. fellow, Inst. Internat. Edn., 1958—59.

TURNBACH, ANN, publishing executive; Joined Houston Chronicle, 1983—, v.p. human resources, 1995—; and diversity dir. Hearst Newspapers, 1997—. Bd. dir. Avondale House. Named Best Human Resources Exec., HR.com, 2005. Mem.: Media Human Resources Assn. (John D. Blodger Diversity award 2002), Newspaper Assn.Am. (diveristy com.). Office: Houston Chronicle 801 Texas Ave PO Box 4260 Houston TX 77210-4260 Office Phone: 713-220-7171. Office Fax: 713-362-7870. E-mail: ann.turnbach@chron.com.*

TURNBULL, ANN PATTERSON, special education educator, consultant, research director; b. Tuscaloosa, Ala., Oct. 19, 1947; d. H. F. and Mary (Boone) Patterson; m. H. Rutherford Turnbull III, Mar. 23, 1974; children: Jay, Amy, Kate. BS in Edn., U. Ga., 1968; MEd, Auburn U., 1971; EdD, U. Ala., 1972. Asst. prof. U. N.C., Chapel Hill, 1972-80; prof., co-dir. Beach Ctr. U. Kans., Lawrence, 1980—. Author: Free Appropriate Public Education, 2000, Exceptional Lives: Special Education in Today's Schools, 2004, Families, Professionals and Exceptionality, 2006. Recipient Rose Kennedy Internat. Leadership award, Kennedy Found., 1990, 20th Century award in Mental Retardation, 1999; Joseph P. Kennedy Jr. Found. fellow, 1987-88. Mem.: The Arc-U.S. (named Educator of Yr. 1982), Am. Assn. on Mental Retardation (bd. dirs. 1986—88, v.p. 2001, pres.-elect 2002, pres. 2003—04, Rsch. award 2004). Democrat. Avocations: travel, exercise. Office: Univ Kans Beach Ctr 3136 1200 Sunnyside Dr Lawrence KS 66045-7534 Home: 730 New Hampshire St Ste 3K Lawrence KS 66044 Office Phone: 785-864-7608. E-mail: turnbull@ku.edu.

TURNBULL, CHERYL LANKARD, investment company executive; b. Chicago Heights, Ill., Aug. 21, 1960; d. David Reid and Bettina Anne (Priamvera) L.; m. Michael Lambo Turnbull. BBA, Miami U., 1982; Masters of Mgmt. in Fin. & Internat. Bus., Northwestern U., 1987. Analyst corp. fin. divsn. Continental Ill. Nat. Bank & Trust Co.; assoc., Mergers & Acquisitions dept. Prudential Securities, 1987—90; v.p. Prudential Bache Interfunding, 1990—91; mng. dir. Aston Ltd. Partners, LP, 1992—95; with Bank One Corp., 1996—2003; spl. limited ptnr. Phronesis Partners LP, Columbus, Ohio, 2005—. Bd. dirs. Quick-Med Technologies Inc., 2006—. Mem. Kellogg Alumni Assn. Office: Phronesis Partners LP 180 E Broad St Ste 1704 Columbus OH 43215

TURNBULL, MARGARET COOMBS, librarian; b. Manitowoc, Wis., June 28, 1953; d. Leonard Alden and Margaret Mary (Carlton) C.; m. Bruce Robert Turnbull, June 16, 1984; 1 child, Andrew Stuart. BA, U. Wis., 1975; M Libr. and Info. Scis., U. Tex., 1981; postgrad., W.Va. Inst. Grad. Coll., 1993, Concord U., 1995-96. Libr. asst. Austin (Tex.) C.C., 1976-81, Tex. State Libr., Austin, 1981-82; staff libr. W.Va. Grad. Coll., Beckley, 1982-83; instr. libr. sci. Concord Coll., Athens, W.Va., 1983-86, adj. asst. prof. social scis., 1989-93, reference libr., 1994-96; staff libr., archivist Bluefield (W.Va.) State Coll., 1996—. Sec.-treas. ARCS, Inc., 1997-1999. Treas. Mercer County Peace Coalition, Athens, 1986-88; sec. Bluefield Dist. United Meth. Women, 1990-94, treas., 1995-96; sec.-treas. Citizens Against the High Voltage Power Line, Athens, 1991-1998; treas. Concord United Meth. Ch., 2005—. Mem.: Bluefield State Coll. Classified Staff Coun. (sec. 2000—02, chair 2002—05), W.Va. Libr. Assn. (chair social responsibility 1999, chair acad. libr. sect. 2000, chair intellectual freedom 2001, chmn. govt. documents 2005—06). Home: PO Box 222 Athens WV 24712-0222 Office: Bluefield State Coll Libr Bluefield WV 24701 Office Phone: 304-327-4053.

TURNBULL, MARY REGINA, secondary school educator; b. Phila., Aug. 27, 1935; d. Thomas Lawrence and Mary Catherine (Shaughnessy) T. BA in Humanities, Villanova U., 1965; MA in Theology/Adolescent Psychology, LaSalle U., Phila., 1969. Cert. tchr., Pa. Tchr. elem. sch., suburban Phila., 1953-64, secondary sch., Warminster, Pa., 1964-69; supr. State Farm Ins., Springfield, Pa., 1969-73; optometric asst. Dr. Ellis S. Edelman, Newtowne Square, Pa., 1973-76; tchr. vocat. h.s., Phila., 1976-80, secondary sch., Drexel Hill, Pa., 1980—2005. Tutor special need young adults; vol. Surry Svcs. for Srs.; instr., catechist St. Pius X. Roman Catholic. Office: Msgr Bonner HS 263 Lansdowne Ave Drexel Hill PA 19026 Personal E-mail: jeant19008@msn.com.

TURNBULL, SUSAN, political organization worker; m. Bruce Turnbull; 2 children. BS in Community Svc. magna cum laude, U. Cincinnati; BS in Interior Design, Marymount U.; MS in Urban Studies, U. Md. Principal Interior Space Planning bus.; various positions working in both House and Senate; vice chair Montgomery County Dem. Party, 1990—93, chair, 1993—94; mem. Dem. Nat. Com., 1992—, mem. exec. com., 1997—, mem. leadership team, women's leadership forum, 1995—, chair women's caucus, 1997—2003, founding co-chair, women's vote ctr., 2001—, dep. chair, 2003—05, vice chair, 2005—. Appearances include FOX News Channel, MSNBC. Named Montgomery County Dem. Party Dem. of the Yr., 2000; recipient Md. Dem. Party Disting. Svc. award, 2003. Office: Dem Nat Com 430 S Capitol St SE Washington DC 20003

TURNER, ALICE KENNEDY, editor; b. Mukden, Manchuria; d. William Taylor and Florence Bell (Green) T. BA, Bryn Mawr Coll., 1962. Sr. editor Holiday mag., N.Y.C., 1969-70; assoc. editor Publishers Weekly, N.Y.C., 1972-74; sr. editor Ballantine Books, N.Y.C., 1974-76, New York mag., N.Y.C., 1976-80; fiction editor Playboy mag., Chgo., N.Y.C., 1980—2001. Author: Yoga for Beginners, 1973, The History of Hell, 1993; co-author: The New York Woman's Guide, 1975; editor: Playboy Stories, 1993, The Playboy Book of Science Fiction, 1996; contbg. editor: Playboy Mag., 2001—; co-editor: Snake's-hands: The Fiction of John Crowley, 2002. Home: 2 Charlton St New York NY 10014-4909 Personal E-mail: aktnyc@gmail.com

TURNER, ANN MARIE, art therapist; d. William Elias Turner III and Marie Therese Keane; m. John Wood-Taylor, May 1990; children: Silas DuRand, Tiernan Keane. AAS, Fashion Inst. Tech., N.Y.C., 1974; BS, SUNY, New Paltz, 1977, MA in Edn., 1995. Cert. tchr.K-12 fine arts N.Y. State Dept. Edn. Leather designer Hernando, N.Y.C., 1969—71; design asst. Best of Three Worlds, N.Y.C., 1971—72; instr. fashion design Bklyn. Sch. Dressmaking & Design, 1973—75; photographer Resort Photogr態py Inc., Greenfield Park, NY, 1977—81; mental health counselor Ulster County Mental Health Svcs., Kingston, NY, 1985—89; replacement art tchr. various pub. sch. dists., Ulster and Sullivan Counties, NY, 1989—97; therapeutic art tchr. Ives Sch. - Lincoln Hall, Lincolndale, NY, 1997—. Cons. A Smile Jeans, N.Y.C., 1974; mental health counselor, advisor Backwoods Basics, Ellenville, NY, 1985—; jewelry designer Backwoods Beadery, Kerhonkson, NY, 2003—. Author: (instrnl. manual) Handbuilding in Clay, 2000, Basic Scratchboard Technique, 2001, Embossed Metalwork, 2002. Mem.: Wise Women, Mac Women. Avocations: travel, beading and jewelry making, glass and clay art, digital art, photography. Personal E-mail: annmturner@gmail.com. E-mail: aturner@lincolnhall.org.

TURNER, BELINDA ENGRAM, physical education educator, athletics coordintaor; d. Willie Milford and Johnnie Grace Engram; m. Fred, Jr. Turner; children: Shuntil, Michael, Fred Anthony. AS, So. Ill. U., Carbondale, 1974, MS, 1977. Physical edn. tchr. Dist. 60 Sch., Waukegun, Ill., 1976—. Vol. Lake County Health Dept., 2004—06, Ill. Prison Ministry Assn., Waukegun; leader Shalem Ch. Health Ministry, Waukegun, Ill., 2004—05, asst. leader, 2006—. Recipient Prison Ministry award, Ill. Prison Ministry Assn. Mem.: Ill. Assn. Health, Physical Edn., Recreation and Dance, Ill. Fedn. Tchrs. Avocations: reading, walking, exercise. Personal E-mail: beebuzz4@aol.com.

TURNER, BERNICE HILBURN, recording industry executive; b. Black Rock, Ark., Jan. 13, 1937; d. Floyd W. and Clementime (Higgins) Hilburn; m. Doyle Turner, Feb. 28, 1957 (div. Jan. 1980); children: Johnny, P.J., Danny, Jill, Robby. PhD in Applied Psychology, 1974. Musician Hank Williams Sr., Nashville and Montgomery, Ala., 1950-52, 1952-76; owner Onyx Recording Studio, Memphis, 1985—, Turner Limousine Svc., Memphis, 1988—. Named Pioneer in Country Music, United Music Heritage of Tenn., 1989. Mem. Unity Ch. Home: 1646 Bonnie Dr Memphis TN 38116-5732

TURNER, BONESE COLLINS, artist, educator; b. Abilene, Kans. d. Paul Edwin and Ruby (Seybold) Collins; m. Glenn E. Turner; 1 child, Craig Collins. BS in Edn., MEd, U. Idaho, Moscow; MA, Calif. State U., Northridge, 1974. Adj. prof. L.A. Pierce Coll., Woodland Hills, Calif., 1964—. Prof. art Calif. State U., Northridge, 1986-89; adj. prof. L.A. Valley Coll., Van Nuys, 1987-89, Moorpark (Calif.) Coll., 1988-98, Arrowmont Coll. Arts and Crafts, Gatlinburg, Tenn., 1995-96; advisor Coll. Art and Arch. U. Idaho, 1988—; juror for art exhbns. including Nat. Watercolor Soc., 1980, 91, San Diego Art Inst., Brand Nat. Watermedia Exhbn., 1980, 96-97, prin. gallery Orlando Gallery, Tarzana, Calif.; with U. Idaho Hartung Performing Arts Ctr., Moscow Idaho Installation, 1994; juror Montrose Verdugo Juried Art Exhibit, 2005; tchr. watercolor seminar Dale Chihuly Found., WEst Hills, Calif., 2005. Represented in permanent collections Smithsonian Inst., Olympic Arts Festival, L.A.; one-woman shows include Angel's Gate Gallery, San Pedro, Calif., 1989, Art Store Gallery, Studio City, Calif., 1988, L.A. Pierce Coll. Gallery, 1988, Brand Art Gallery, Glendale, Calif., 1988, 93, 2000, Coos (Oreg.) Art Mus., 1988, U. Nev., 1987, Orlando Gallery, Sherman Oaks, Calif., 1993, 98, 2002, 05, Burbank (Calif.) Creative Arts Ctr., 2000, Village Sq. Gallery, Montrose, Calif., 2002, 05, Pierce Art Gallery, 2005; prin. works in pub. collections include The Smithsonian Inst., Hartung Performing Arts Ctr., Moscow, Idaho, Robert V. Fulton Mus. Art, Calif. State U., San Bernardino, Calif., Springfield (Mo.) Art Mus, Home Savs. and Loan, San Bernardino Sun Telegram Newspapers, Oreg. Coun. for the Arts, Newport, Oreg. Pub. Librs., Brand Libr., Glendale, Calif., Lincoln (Nebr.) Pub. Lib., Indsl. Tile Corp., Lincoln. Recipient Springfield (Mo.) Art Mus. award, 1989, 2002, 1st prize Brand XXVIII, 1998, Glendale, Calif., Butler Art Inst. award, 1989, 1st award in graphics Diamond Jubilee Exhibit/Pasadena Soc. Artists, 2002, Nat. award Acrylic Painters Assn. Eng. and U.S.A., 1996, Ruth Kain award, LA Brewery, 2003. Mem. Nat. Acrylic Painters Assn. of Eng. (award 1996), Nat. Mortar Bd. Soc., Nat. Watercolor Soc. (life, past pres., Purchase prize 1979), Watercolor U.S.A. Honor Soc. (awards), Watercolor West. Avocations: bicycling, music, singing.

TURNER, BRACHA, painter; b. Jerusalem; Exhbns. include 55 solo exhbns. and numerous juried exhbns.: J.F. Kennedy Art Gallery, Montreal, New Eng. Fine Arts Inst., Boston, Internat. Women in the Arts Conf., Beijing, Galerie Everarts, Paris; permanent display of paintings include Hadassah Hdqrs., N.Y., ZOA House, Tel-Aviv, Nat. Coun. of Jewish Women, N.Y., Ichilov Hosp., Tel-Aviv, Office of the Mayor of Jerusalem, Israel, The Bible Mus. Tel Aviv, Office of the Mayor N.Y.C., Rambam Hosp., Haifa, Israel, others; painting reproduced on cards by Hadassah; contbr. drawings to Sara's Daughters Sing, 1989.

TURNER, BRENDA GAIL, elementary school educator; b. Littlefield, Tex., Sept. 4, 1951; d. Raymond Lewis and Doris Jean Scott; m. John Scott Turner, Mar. 26, 1983; 1 child, Dusty Scott. BS, Tex. Tech U., 1974. Cert. elem. edn. tchr. Tex. Tchr. Muleshoe (Tex.) Ind. Sch. Dist., 1975—83, Hereford (Tex.) Ind. Sch. Dist., 1983—94, Portales (N.Mex.) Sch. Dist., 1994—96, Center Point (Tex.) Ind. Sch. Dist., 1996—. Founder, organizer mil. Christmas project Vol. Orgn., Center Point, 2004—05. Mem.: Assn. Tex. Profl. Educators (treas./sec. 2002—06, Outstanding Mem. 2004). Democrat. Baptist. Avocations: gardening, crafts. Home: Box 412 Center Point TX 78010 Office Phone: 830-634-2257.

TURNER, BRENDA LORRAINE, social worker; b. Salisbury, N.C., Feb. 23, 1947; d. Limuel Jerome and Willie Bernice (Lynn) Grasty; m. Charles Augustus Turner, June 5, 1971; children: Toni Lorraine, Terri Loretta-Bernice. BA, Johnson C. Smith U., 1969; MSW, Howard U., 1979. Acad. Cert. Soc. Workers. Group worker Friendship House, Washington, 1969-71; coordinator job corp. program YWCA Greater Washington, 1971-73; dir. Vista Project Boys Clubs Greater Washington, 1977-78, dir. aging program, 1978-79; dir. aging services Washington Urban League Inc., 1979—. Chmn. Adv. Com. Literacy Project Nat. Council Aging, 6 St. Regional Steering Com. Region 3 Administn. Aging, Phila., 1987; v.p. bd. dirs. Rosedale Estates-Condominum, Ft. Washington, MD. 1985; bd. dirs. Henson Valley Montessori Sch., Temple Hills, Md., 1983; mem. parents club Queen Anne Coll. Prep. Sch., Upper Marlboro, Md., 1986. Mem. Acad. Cert. Social Worker, Nat. Assn. Social Workers. Clubs: Delta Sigma Theta Sorority, Tots & Teens Parents. Democrat. Baptist. Avocations: oil and acrylic painting. Office: Washington Urban League Inc 2900 Newton St NE Washington DC 20018-2961

TURNER, CAMILLA ANN, music educator; b. Maysville, Ky., July 23, 1978; d. Larry Donald and Melanie Jane Roberson; m. Jonathan Stewart Turner, Oct. 27, 1976. B in Music Edn., U. Ky., Lexington, 2001. Music specialist Ashland Elem., Lexington, 2002—06, Glenn R. Marshall Elem., Richmond, Ky., 2006—. Children's choir dir. Maxwell St. Presbyn. Ch., Lexington, 1999—.

TURNER, CYNTHIA M., science educator; b. Delavan, Ill., Oct. 18, 1973; d. Stephen L. and Georgann E. Turner. EdB, Millikin U., Decatur, Ill., 1995; postgrad., Eastern Ill. U., Charelston, 2005—. 3rd grade tchr. Durfee Magnet Sch., Decatur, Ill., 1995—96; 4th grade tchr. Pks. Elem., Pasadena, Tex., 1996—98; 5th grade tchr. Williamsville Mid. Sch., Ill., 1998—99; 8th grade sci. tchr. Tayorville Jr. High, Ill., 1999—. Delegation leader People to People Student Ambs., Springfield, Ill. Vol. counselor Camp Care-A-Lot, Jacksonville, Ill.; eucharistic minister St. Mary's Cath. Ch., Taylorville, Ill. Mem.: Am. Sch. Counselor Assn. (student), Nat. Sci. Tchrs. Assn., Taylorville edn. Assn. Avocations: walking, camping. Office: Taylorville Jr High 120 E Bidwell Taylorville IL 62568

TURNER, DORIS SEWELL, counselor, educator; b. Memphis, Mar. 18, 1925; d. Oscar James and Lois Marie (Parke) Sewell; m. Max Wesley Turner, June 23, 1950 (dec. 1979). AB, U. Ill., 1946; MS, So. Ill. U., 1949. Counselor Stephen's Coll., Columbia, Mo., 1946-47; dean women So. Ill. U., Carbondale, Ill., 1947-49; staff, dean women U. Ill., Champaign, Ill., 1949-50; tchr., student tchr. supr. Pub. Schs., Carbondale, Ill., 1950-55; from lectr., psychology dept. to acad. adv. So. Ill. U., Carbondale, Ill., 1956-83. Chmn. curriculum com./So. Ill. U. Women's Studies Com., 1981-83; bd. dirs. Nat. Women's Conf. Com., 1986-91; mem. Ariz. Gov.'s Task Force on Juv. Corrections, 1990-95, steering com. Ariz. Gov.'s Leadership Confs., 1989-90, statewide com. on Ill. Legislative Reform, 1975-80, Ill. Curriculum Com., 1973-75; workshop presenter Decade for Women Conf. Nairobi; Ariz. Judicial Performance Review Com., 2000-. Bd. dirs. ERA Ill., 1981-83; com. Phoenix Women's Commn., 1985, Ariz. Women's Partnership; organizer, chair So. Ill. U. Women's Caucus, 1975-83; mem. So. Ill. U. Adminstrn. and Profl. Staff Coun; deacon, 2002-2006, mission com., 1995—, Northminster Presbyn. Ch., Phoenix. Named Regional Woman of So. Ill., Women's History Assn., Carbondale, 1983. Mem. AAUW (chmn. nat. nominating com. 1991-93, state pres., Ariz., 1987-89, state bd. dirs. Ill., 1969-81, Ariz., 1984-89, pres. Carbondale br. 1967-69 (AAUW named, gift honoree Carbondale br., 1975, Phoenix br., 1991, Doris Sewell Am. fellowship), Ariz. LWV (bd. dirs. 1991-93), Nat. Acad. Advising Assn. (prog. com. 1979-83), Carbondale Edn. Assn. (pres. 1954-55), others. Democrat. Presbyn. Avocations: travel, horseback riding, swimming, music. Home: 3417 W Saint Moritz Ln Phoenix AZ 85053-4744 Personal E-mail: dturner18@aol.com.

TURNER, ELIZABETH ADAMS NOBLE (BETTY TURNER), real estate company executive; b. Yonkers, NY, May 18, 1931; d. James Kendrick and Orrel (Baldwin) Noble; m. Jack Rice Turner, July 11, 1953; children: Jay Kendrick, Randall Ray. BA, Vassar Coll., 1953; MA, Tex. A&I U., 1964. Ednl. cons., Tex. sales mgr. Noble & Noble Pub. Co., N.Y.C., 1956-67; psychometrist Corpus Christi Guidance Ctr., 1967-70; psychologist Corpus Christi State Sch., 1970-72, dir. programs, asst. supt., 1972, dir. devel. and vol. svc., 1972-76, dir. rsch. and tng., 1977-79; psychologist Tex. Mental Health and Mental Retardation, 1970-79, program cons., 1979-85; pres. Turner Co., 1975-82; mayor pro tem Corpus Christi, 1981-85; mayor, 1987-91; CEO, pres. Corpus Christi C. of C., 1991-94; pres. Betty Turner Real Estate, 1999—. V.p. bus. and govt. rels. ctrl. and south Tex. divsns. Columbia Healthcare Corp., 1994—99. Author: The Noble Legacy. Dir. alumni Corpus Christi State U., 1976-77; coord. vols. Summer Head Start Program, Corpus Christi, 1967; chmn. spl. gifts com. United Way, Corpus Christi, 1970; mem. Corpus Christi City Coun., 1979-91; family co-founded Barnes and Noble, N.Y.C.; founder Com. of 100 and Goals for Corpus Christi; pres. USO; bd. dirs. Coastal Bend Coun. Govts., Corpus Christi Mus., Harbor Playhouse, Cmtys. in Schs., YWCA, Y-Teen Sponsor, Del Mar Coll. Found., Tex. A&M at Corpus Christi Pres.' Coun., Food Bank, Hispanic C. of C., TAMACC Corp. Ptnrs., Salvation Army, Jr. League, Coun. Deaf Silent Found.; bd. Southside Cmty. Hosp., 1987-93, Gulfway Nat. Bank, 1985-92, bd. dirs.; strategic planning com. Meml. Hosp., 1992, Tex. Capital Network Bd., 1992-95, Humana Hosp., Physician Relocation and Condo Sales, Rehab. Hosp., dir. of vols., South Tex., Admiral Tex. Navy; bd. dirs. Pacific Southwest Bank, 1997-2000, St. David's/Austin and Medth. Healthcare Sys., San Antonio, 1997-99; apptd. Gov.'s Commn. for Women, 1984-85, Leadership Tex. Class I, Corpus Christi, Class II; founder Goals for Corpus Christi, Bay Area Sports Assn., Assn. Coastal Bend Mayor's Alliance; founder Mayor's Commn. on the Disabled, Mayor's Task Force on the Homeless; active Port Aransas Cmty. Ch., U. Tex. Sch. Nursing Adv. Coun., 1998-99; bd. dirs. Del Mar Coll. Found., 1998-2005, Am. Heart Assn., 1999-2000, Bethune Day Care Nursery, 1999-2004, Jr. League Cmty. Adv. Coun., 1999-2000, Strategic Planning Com., 2000—, Silent Found., 2001—, 21st Century Charter Sch., 2001-02, Boys and Girls Club of Corpus Christi, 2002-05, Nat. AARP, 2002-04; pres. Food Bank, 2004-05; elder Cmty. Presbyn. Ch. Named Corpus Christi Newsmaker of Yr., 1987; recipient Love award, YWCA, 1970, Y's Women and Men in Careers award, 1988, Recognition award, Rotary, 1991, Comdr.'s award for pub. svc., U.S. Army, Scroll of Honor award, Navy League, award, Tex. Hwy Dept., Road Hand award, Tex. Hwy. Commn., Women of Distinction award, Girl Scouts Tex. Mem. NAACP (life), Tex. Psychol. Assn. (pres., mem. exec. bd.), Psychol. Assn. (pres., founder), Tex. Mcpl. League (bd. dirs.), Jr. League Corpus Christi, Tex. Bookman's Assn., Tex. Assn. Realtors, Corpus Christi Town Club, Corpus Christi Yacht Club, Jr. Cotillion Club, hon. Delta Kappa Gamma, Kappa Kappa Gamma. Home: 403 Blue Heron Dr Port Aransas TX 78373 Office Phone: 361-749-5712. Business E-Mail: bettyturner@centurytel.net.

TURNER, FLORENCE FRANCES, ceramist; b. Detroit, Mar. 9, 1926; d. Paul Pokrywka and Catherine Gagal; m. Dwight Robert Turner, Oct. 23, 1948; children: Thomas Michael, Nancy Louise, Richard Scott, Garry Robert. Student, Oakland C.C., Royal Oak, Mich., 1975-85, U. Ariz., Yuma, 1985, U. Las Vegas, 1989—. Pres., founder Nev. Clay Guild, Henderson, 1990-94, mem. adv. bd., 1994-2000, v.p., 2000—02. Workshop leader Greenfield Village, Dearborn, Mich., 1977-78, Plymouth (Mich.) Hist. Soc., 1979, Las Vegas Sch. System, 1989-90, Detroit Met. area, 1977-85. Bd. dirs. Las Vegas Art Mus., 1987-91; corr. sec. So. Nev. Creative Art Ctr., Las Vegas, 1990-94. Mem.: Nev. Camera Club, Las Vegas Gem Club, Phi Kappa Phi. Avocations: photography, collecting gems, travel.

TURNER, GLADYS TRESSIA, retired social worker; b. Tamo, Ark., Sept. 16, 1935; d. Willis J. and Mary (Bluford) T.; m. Frederick M. Finney, July 1, 1972. BA, U. Ark., 1957; MSW, Atlanta U., 1959. Lic. social worker, Ohio. Social worker Childrens' Med. Ctr., Dayton, Ohio, 1965-66, dir. social work, 1966-75; social worker Day Mont West Community Mental Health Ctr., Dayton, 1975-77, coord. outpatient and cons. and edn svcs., mgr. quality assurance, 1977-82; social worker VA Med. Ctr., Dayton, 1982—97; ret. Bd. dirs. Daybreak, Inc.; bd. mem. West Dayton Neighbors for Edn., Inc., 1999—. Author: The Autobiography of Tammy, 1978, Papa Babe's Stamp Collection, 1982; contbr. articles to profl. jours. Bd. dirs. Daybreak Inc., 1991—; mem. citizens adv. bd. Dayton Mental Health Ctr., 1983-89. Recipient Disting. Alumni, Nat. Assn. for Equal Opportunity in Higher Edn., 1985, Outstanding Svc. award, Ohio NASW, 2001, Mary Scott Legacy award, 2006; Scholar State of Ohio Dept. of Mental Hygiene, 1964. Mem. Nat. Assn. Social Workers (pres. Miami Valley chpt. 1975-76, Social Worker of Yr. Miami Chpt. 1978), Am. Hosp. Assn., Soc. for Hosp. Social Work Dirs., Delta Sigma Theta, Read and Chat Literary Club. Democrat. Presbyterian. Avocations: writing, travel, stamp collecting/philately. Home: 3955 Denlinger Rd Dayton OH 45426-2329

TURNER, JANET SULLIVAN, painter, sculptor; b. Gardiner, Maine, Nov. 15, 1935; d. Clayton Jefferson and Frances (Leighton) Sullivan; m. Terry Turner, Oct. 6, 1956; children: Lisa Turner Reid, Michael Ross, Jonathan Brett. BA cum laude, Mich. State U., 1956. Rep. Am. Women in Art, UN World Conf. on Women, Nairobi, Kenya, 1985. One-woman shows include

San Diego Art Inst., 1971, St. Joseph U., Phila., 1981, Villanova (Pa.) U. Gallery, 1982, Pa. State U., Middletown (Pa.), 1985, Temple U. (Pa.), 1986, Widener U. Art Mus., Chester, Pa., 1987, 94, Rosemont Coll., Pa., 1995, Sande Webster Gallery, Phila., 1998, 2000, retrospective Widener U. Art Gallery, 2005; exhibited in group shows at Del. Art Mus., Wilmington, 1978, Woodmere Art Mus., Phila., 1980, 2000, Port of History Mus., Phila., 1984, Allentown Art Mus., 1984, Trenton (NJ) City Mus. Ellarslie Open VIII, 1989, Ammo Gallery, Bklyn., 1989, Pa. State Mus., Harrisburg, 1990-94, Galeria Mesa, Ariz., 1991, Del. Ctr. for Contemporary Arts, Wilmington, 1992, Holter Mus., Helena, Mont., 1992, S.W. Tex. State U., San Marcos, 1993, Fla. State U. Mus., Tallahassee, 1993, Newark Mus., 1993, U. Del., 1994, 1st St. Gallery, NYC, 1994, Noyes Mus., NJ, 1995, Sande Webster Gallery, Phila. 1995-2006, Phila. Art Mus., 1997, Krasdale Gallery, White Plains, NY, 2001, Moore Coll. of Art, Phila. Sculptors, Phila. Pa., 2002, Philips Mus, Franklin Marshall Coll., 2004, Sumner Sch. Art Mus., Washington, otheres; represented in permanent collections Nat. Mus. Women in Arts, "American Album", Wash. D.C., Kresge Art Mus., East Lansing, Mich, ARA Svc. Inc., Phila., Blue Cross/Blue Shield, Phila., Am. Nat. Bank and Trust Co., Rockford, Ill., Burroughs Corp., Lisle, Ill., State Mus. Pa., Harrisburg, Bryn Mawr (Pa.) Coll., Rosemont Coll., Villanova (Pa.) Coll., LaSalle U. Art Mus., Phila., Noyes Mus., NJ, Nat. Liberty Mus., Phila., Kimmel Ctr., Phila. Bd. dirs. Rittenhouse Sq. Fine Arts Ann., Phila., 1984—86. Recipient 2d pl. award San Diego Art Inst. 19th Ann. Exhbn., 1971, award of merit Pavilion Gallery, Mt. Holly, N.J., 1991, 3d pl. Katonah Mus. of Art, N.Y., 1992, purchase award State Mus. of Pa., Harrisburg, 1992. Mem. Artists Equity (pres. 1987-88), Nat. League of Am. Pen Woman, Phila. Watercolor Club, Delta Phi Delta. Republican. Roman Catholic. Home: 88 Cambridge Dr Glen Mills PA 19342-1545 Office Phone: 610-358-2094.

TURNER, JANINE, actress; b. Lincoln, Nebr., Dec. 6, 1963; d. Janice Gaunt.; 1 child. Appearences include (TV) Behind the Screen, 1981-82, General Hospital, 1982-83, Northern Exposure, 1990-95 (Hollywood Fgn. Press Assn. award 1992, Emmy award nominee 1993), Stolen Women, Captured Hearts, 1997, Circle of Deceit, 1998, Beauty, 1998, Fatal Error, 1999, A Secret Affair, 1999, Strong Medicine, 2000-02, (films) Young Doctors in Love, 1982, Knights of the City, 1985, Tai-Pan, 1986, Monkey Shines: An Experiment in Fear, 1988, Steel Magnolias, 1988, The Ambulance, 1990, Cliffhanger, 1993, Leave It to Beaver, 1997, The Curse of the Inferno, 1997, Dr. T and the Women, 2000, Birdie and Bogey, 2004, No Regrets, 2004, Trip in a Summer Dress, 2004. Office: Creative Artists Agy 9830 Wilshire Blvd Beverly Hills CA 90212-1804

TURNER, JEAN ISABEL, musician, educator; b. Postville, Iowa, Aug. 28, 1941; d. William Richard Belschner and Clara P. (Nelson) Blessum; m. James Robert Turner, May 27, 1962; 1 child, Drew R. BA in Music Edn., U. Northern Iowa, 1962; cert., Sacramento State U., 1963, U. Nebr., 1976, cert., 1983. Substitute tchr. Mills Jr. H.S., Rancho Cordove, Calif., 1963-68; sky lark dir. Grand Forks (N.D.) AFB, 1969-71, Plattsburg (N.Y.) AFB, 1971-74; substitute tchr. Beckmantown (N.Y.) Pub. Sch., 1971-74, Bellevue (Nebr.) Sch. System, 1974-77, tchr., 1978; pvt. music tchr. Bellevue, 1981-89, Arlington, Iowa, 1990—. Substitute music tchr. Starmout Sch., Arlington, 1990-95. Contbr. articles on auctions. Music dir., organist St. John Luth. Ch., Arlington, 1990—. Mem. Upper Iowa Music Tchrs. Assn. (sec. 1995-96, v.p. 1996-97). Republican. Lutheran. Avocations: flower show judge, antique collector, music, legion auxilary, church. Home: 2281 Bell Rd Arlington IA 50606-8103

TURNER, JUDY C., research scientist; d. John W. and Alma Turner; m. Timothy Fritz Turner, Jan. 26, 1976. BA in Sociology, U. Tenn., Knoxville, 1972; MA in Sociology, Middle Tenn. State U., Murfreesboro, 1975; PhD, Tex. A&M U., Coll. Sta., 1986; grad., Command & Gen. Staff Coll., 1986. Rsch. psychologist USAF, San Antonio, 1986—99; psychometrician Harcourt Edn. Measurement, San Antonio, 2000—03; chief scientist Space and Info. Divsn. L-3Com Titan Corp., San Antonio, 2004—. Officer personnel divsn. U.S. Army, 1973—96, Korea, Germany, Hawaii. Mem.: Reserve Officer Assn. (life; sec., v.p., pres. 1990, state historian 1982, Scabbard and Blade award 1982, Sec. News Editor award 1992). Avocations: photography, bicycling, hiking, reading, writing. Office: L-3Com Tital Corp Space & Info Divsn 6100 Bandera Rd San Antonio TX 78238

TURNER, KATHLEEN, actress; b. Springfield, Mo., June 19, 1954; m. David Guc, 1977 (div. 1982); m. Jay Weiss, 1984; 1 child, Rachel Ann. Student, Cen. Sch. of Speech and Drama, London, Southwest Mo. State U.; BFA, U. Md., 1977. Various theater roles, Broadway debut: Gemini, 1978, Cat on a Hot Tin Roof, 1990, Indiscretions, 1995, Who's Afraid of Virginia Woolf?, 2005; appeared in TV series The Doctors, 1977, Style and Substance, 1996; TV movies inlcude Friends At Last, 1995, Moonlight and Valentino, 1995; films include Body Heat, 1981, A Breed Apart, 1982, The Man With Two Brains, 1983, Crimes of Passion, 1984, Romancing the Stone, 1984, Prizzi's Honor (Golden Globe award for best actress), 1985, The Jewel of the Nile, 1985, Peggy Sue Got Married, (D.W. Griffith award for best actress, Oscar nomination for best actress) 1986, Julia and Julia, 1988, Switching Channels, 1988, Who Framed Roger Rabbit, 1988, Accidental Tourist, 1988, The War of the Roses, 1989, V.I. Warshawski, 1991, Undercover Blues, 1993, House of Cards, 1993, Serial Mom, 1994, Naked in New York, 1994, A Simple Wish, 1997, The Real Blonde, 1998, Baby Geniuses, 1999, The Virgin Suicides, 1999, Prince of Central Park, 2000, Beautiful, 2000, Without Love, 2004, (voice) Monster House, 2006, (TV films) Love in the Ancient World, 1997, Legalese, 1998, Cinderella, 2000; dir. (Showtime cable movie) Leslie's Folly, 1994; also performed in radio shows with the BBC, 1992, 93; voice: Bad Baby, 1997, Beautiful, 2000. Office: ICM care Chris Andrews 8942 Wilshire Blvd Beverly Hills CA 90211-1934*

TURNER, KATHLEEN KALIN, musician, art director; b. Elmira, N.Y., Feb. 21, 1964; d. Edris Kalin; m. Roy Clyde Turner, III, Jan. 18, 1949; children: Christopher Michael Griffin, Alan, Brendan. MusB, Eastman Sch. Music, Rochester, N.Y., 1986; M of Sacred Music, Westminster Choir Coll., Princeton, N.J., 1988. Cert. Orff Schulwerk Am. Orff Schulwerk Assn., 2000, in organ performance Eastman Sch. Music, 1986, in oboe performance Eastman Sch. Music, 1986. Organist/choirmaster Trinity Cathedral, Little Rock, 1992—96, Christ Ch. Frederica, St. Simons Island, Ga., 1997—2000; artistic dir. Austin Children's Choir, Austin, Tex., 2002—. Recipient Winner, Nat. MTNA-Wurlitzer Collegiate Artist Competition in Organ, 1988. Mem.: Orgn. Kodaly Educators (assoc.), Am. Choral Dir.'s Assn. (assoc.), Anglican Assn. Musicians (assoc.), Am. Guild Organists (assoc.), Am. Orff Schulwerk Assn. (assoc.), Mu Phi Epsilon (assoc.). Episcopalian. Achievements include being one of few graduates of the Eastman School of Music to be awarded the distinguished Performer's Certificate in two disciplines, in Organ and Oboe. Avocations: swimming, baking. Office: Austin Children's Choir 3400 IH 35 North Austin TX 78705 Office Phone: 512-486-1221. Business E-Mail: office@austinchildrenschoir.com.

TURNER, KATHY ANN, special education educator; b. Cinn., May 16, 1962; d. James Robert and Alice Louise Taylor; m. Michael Arcia Turner, Jr., June 1, 1985; children: Joseph Paul, Christopher James, Sarah Alyse. AA, Riverside C.C., 1998; BS in Edn., Lewis Clark State Coll., 2002. Spl. edn. asst. Corona-Norco Unified Sch. Dist., Norco, Calif., 1996—98; direct care provider devel. disabilities Inclusion North, Inc., Grangeville, Idaho, 1998—2000; tech. for tchrs. asst. Lewis Clark State Coll., Lewiston, Idaho, 2000—01; sub. tchr. Prairie Sch., Idaho, 2001—03; psychol. social rehab. provider Frontier Journeys, Grangeville, Idaho, 2002—05; specialist devel. disabilities Opportunities Unltd., Inc., 2003—05; psycho social rehab provider Camas Profl. Counseling, 2005—06; spl. edn. tchr. lower Kuskokwim sch. dist. Bethel Regional HS, Ark., 2006—. Counselor Hope Pregnancy Ctr., Grangeville, 2003—06. Portrait, Liz (2nd pl. award Idaho County Art Competition, 1998). Daffodil days chmn. Am. Cancer Soc., Corona, Calif., 1995—98; com. mem. Relay for Life, 2005. Named Life Woman of the Yr., Norco C. of C., 1995. Mem.: Coun. for Exceptional Children, Grangeville Elks, Kappa Delta Pi (pres. 2001—03). R-Consevative. Avocations: baking, canning, fishing, card playing. Home: PO Box 1901 Bethel AK 99559 Office Phone: 907-543-3957. Personal E-mail: imspcl2002@yahoo.com.

TURNER, LANELL DAPHENE, physical education educator; b. Ft. Worth, Mar. 1, 1965; d. Walter Lee and Elnora Turner; 1 child, DeUntae Rashad Richardson. AS, Kilgore Coll., Tex., 1985; BS, Tex. Woman's U., Denton, 1990. Cert. all-level phys. edn. Tex., 1990, grades K-8 elem. edn. Tex., 1992. Phys. edn. tchr. Amber Terrance Intermediate, Desoto, Tex., 1985—86; sci. tchr., coach Vanston Mid. Sch., Mesquite, Tex., 1987—2005, phys. edn. tchr., coach, 2005—. Mem.: TAHPERD, Tex. Girls Coaches Assn., Delta Sigma Theta. Home: 7513 Bryn Mawr Rowlett TX 75089 Office: Vanston Middle School 3230 Karla Dr Mesquite TX 75150 Office Phone: 972-882-5801. Home Fax: 972-882-5848; Office Fax: 972-882-5848. Business E-Mail: nturner@mesquiteisd.org.

TURNER, LAWALTA DEAN, educator; b. Clarksdale, Mo., July 31, 1941; d. Harry Delmar and Helen Norine (West) Heyde; 1 child, Heyde Faye Class; m. Kenneth Turner, Aug. 28, 1982. BS in Edn., U. Kans., 1964. Educator Detroit Pub. Sch., 1964-66, Palatine (Ill.) Rolling Meadows Pub. Sch., 1966-71, Dodge City (Kans.) Pub. Sch., 1971-73, Enid Pub. Sch., Okla., 1974—2001. Author: Gifted and Talented Curriculum Guide Kindergarten to 3rd Grade, 1984, Outdoor Education, 1976. Mem. LWV; mem. Ctrl. Christian Ch., 1982—; trustee Garfield County/Enid Libr., 2001—; mem. Chautagua in the Park Bd., 2001-06. Recipient Outstanding Conservation Svc. award USDA Soil Conservation Svc., 1991, grantee, 1975-78, 90. Mem. NEA (life), AAUW, Okla. Edn. Assn. (life), Enid Edn. Assn., Okla. Sci. Tchrs. Assn., Delta Kappa Gamma (pres. Alpha Upsilon chpt. 1992-94, World Fellowship chmn. 1993-95, U.S. forum chmn. 1995—), Garfield Ret. Tchrs. Assn., Okla. Libr. Assn. (legis. com., 2003—, legis. day com., 2004—), Beta Sigma Phi (pres. Laureate Gamma chpt. 1992-93, pres. Delta Masters chpt., 2003-04, Woman Yr. award 2003-04), Delta Kappa Gamma (internat. pres. Okla. 2005—). Democrat. Avocations: antiques, travel. Home: 3608 East Keowee Rd Kremlin OK 73753

TURNER, LETITIA RHODES, artist; b. Media, Pa., Aug. 17, 1923; d. Samuel Noblit and Letitia (Eves) Rhodes; m. Ellwood Jackson Turner Jr., Aug. 1, 1942; children: Rue Baronsky, Letitia Mayo, Elizabeth Rorke. Diploma, Cowanova Sch. Dancing, 1941. Dance instr. Cowanova Sch. Dancing, 1939—41; sec., treas. Rose Tree Realty Inc., Media, Pa., 1961-81. Dance tchr., 1939, 40, 41. Portrait painter (Portrait of Mary 3d pl. 1990, Portrait of Brett 2d pl. 1987); painter portrait commns., 1977-95. Mem. Optimisses 1956-1958, pres Am. Legion Aux., Media, 1991-2002, photographer, 1992, sec., 1993—; sec. Del. County Am. Legion Aux., 1994, historian, 1995; 1st v.p. Woman's Aux. Media Presbyn. Ch., Media, 1963; mem. D.A.R.E., Media, 1983-91, 92, 93—. Mem. Artist Guild Delaware County, Art League Delaware County, Artist Guild of Riddle Village, Am. Legion Aux. (sec. Del. County 1993, historian 1994). Republican. Avocation: needlepoint. Home and Office: Riddle Village L-302 Media PA 19063

TURNER, LISA PHILLIPS, human resources executive; b. Waltham, Mass., Apr. 10, 1951; d. James Sinclair and Virginia Turner. BA in Edn. and Philosophy magna cum laude, Washington Coll., Chestertown, Md., 1974; AS in Electronics Tech., AA in Engring., Palm Beach Jr. Coll., 1982; MBA, Nova U., 1986, DSc, 1989; PhD, Kennedy Western U., 1990. Cert. sr. profl. in human resources; cert. quality engr.; lic. USCG capt.; lic. pvt. pilot FAA, IFAA lic. airframe and powerplant mechanic, 2004. Founder, pres. Turner's Bicycle Svc., Inc., Delray Beach, Fla., 1975-80; electronics engr., quality engr. Audio Engring. and Video Arts, Boca Raton, Fla., 1980-81; tech. writing instr. Palm Beach Jr. Coll., Lake Worth, Fla., 1981-82; adminstr. tng. and devel. Mitel Inc., Boca Raton, 1982-88; mgr. comm. and employee rels. Modular Computer Systems, Inc., Ft. Lauderdale, Fla., 1988-89; U.S. mktg. project mgr. Mitel, Inc., Boca Raton, 1990-91; v.p. human resources Connectronics, Inc., Ft. Lauderdale, 1991-93; sr. mgr. human resources Sensormatic Electronics Corp., Boca Raton, 1993-98, dir. human resources, 1998—2001; chief tng. officer and dir. human resources Tyco Fire and Security Svcs., Inc., Boca Raton, 2001—05, Six Sigma black belt, 2005—. Contbg. author Kitplanes Mag. With USCG Aux. Recipient Human Resources Profl. Excellence award, Soc. Human Resource Mgmt., 1999. Mem. Soc. for Human Resource Mgmt., Internat. Assn. Quality Cirs., Am. Soc. Quality Control, Fla. Employment Mgmt. Assn., Am. Acad. Mgmt., Employment Assn. Fla., Am. Capts. Assn., Citizens Police Acad., Aircraft Owners and Pilot's Assn., Exptl. Aircraft Assn., Fla. Aero. Club. Achievements include being the first female to construct, complete and fly a pulsar XP aircraft. Home: 1358 Fairfax Cir E Boynton Beach FL 33436-8612 Office: Tyco 1 Town Center Rd Boca Raton FL 33436-1010 Office Phone: 561-989-7979. Personal E-mail: lisaturner@prodigy.net. Business E-Mail: lisaturner@tycoint.com.

TURNER, LOUISE (LEE) KREHER, retired dance educator; b. New Orleans, July 30, 1914; d. Charles William Kreher and Hazel Hilliary Brennan; m. Frank Allen Turner, Sept. 5, 1954. BA, Southwestern La. Inst., 1933; MA, La. State U., 1936; MS, La State U., 1937; PhD, NYU, 1970; Assoc. Prof. Emerita (hon.), Auburn U., 1975. Dance instr. La. State Normal Coll., Natchitoches, 1934; tchg. fellow La. State U., Baton Rouge, 1935—37; dance instr. Stuart Hall, Staunton, Va., 1937; assoc. prof. Auburn U., Ala., 1938—76. Playground and teenage ctr. dir. City of St. Petersburg, Fla., 1948—49; recreation dir. City of Opelika, Ala., 1950; recreation broadcaster Sta. WJHO, Auburn, 1952; in-sch. ednl. telecaster PBS Channel 7, Auburn, 1953; dir./coord. Forest Ecology Preserve, Sch. of Forestry, Auburn U., 1997—2000. (choreography) Choreography; author: (genealogy/historical novel) Margaretha's Trunk. Recipient Assoc. Health, Phys. Edn. and Recreation award, State of Ala., 1956, Auburn Citizen of Yr., Auburn Civitan Club, 1954, 2000, Outstanding Alumnus, U. of SW La., 1979, W. Kelly Mosley Environ. award, Auburn U., 2000, Martha Wayles Jefferson Cmty. Svc. award, DAR, 2004, Environ. Awareness award, 2004. Mem.: Am. Assn. Health Phys. Edn. Recreation and Dance, Delta Zeta, Delta Kappa Gamma. Achievements include donated land and established Forest Ecology Preserve, Auburn University, 1993; established F. Allen and Louise K. Turner Charitable Foundation, 2000; development of cultural exchange program with Guatemala, Partners in America with Auburn, 1974; historic preservation of Pre-Civil War dwelling, 1980-1985. Home: P O Box 1407 Auburn AL 36831 Personal E-mail: turnelo@mindspring.com.

TURNER, MADELINE, elementary school educator; b. Mobile, Ala., May 28, 1946; d. Melvin and Cora Thomas; m. Ladonal Turner (div.). BSc, Ala. State U., Montgomery, Ala., 1968; MEd, Olivet Nazaeene U., Bourbonnis, Ills., 2000. Tchr. Donalsonville Elem., Donalsonville, Ill., 1968—70, Clark County HS, Grove Hill, Ala., 1970—71, Selma Elem. Sch., Selma, Ala., 1971—72, Goldblatt Elem. Sch., Chgo., 1981—87, Depriest Elem. Sch., Chgo., 1987—96, Nash Elem. Sch., Chgo., 1996—. Cons. tchr. Nash Elem., 1998—2001, local sch. coun., 1999—2003. Recipient Tchr. of the Yr., Goldbatt Elem., 1986, Depriest Elem. Sch., 1999, Nash Elem., 2000. Mem.: Assn. for Suprvision, Cirriculm Devel., Nat. Sci. Tchrs. Assn., Delta Kappa Pi.

TURNER, MARY ALICE, curriculum specialist; b. Birmingham, Ala., Aug. 8, 1946; d. Henry and Elzona (Griffin) Johnson; m. Raymond Carver Turner, July 6, 1968; 1 child, Taunya Nicole. BS in Edn., Ala. A&M U., 1968, MEd, 1992. Cert. tchr. home econs. edn., elem. edn., early childhood edn., adminstrn. and supervision 1994. Title I curriculum specialist Huntsville City Schs., Ala., 1969—. Mem. Parent/Sch./Tchr. adv. bd. Ridgecrest Elem. Sch., Huntsville, 1978; tchr. rep. PTA, Rolling Hills Elem. Sch., Huntsville, 1988-93. Recipient Award for Dedicated Svc. Rolling Hills PTA, 1988. Mem. ASCD, NEA, Ala. Edn. Assn., Huntsville Edn. Assn. (sch. rep. 1969-96, mem. budget com., rule and regulations com. review), Ala. Reading Assn., Alpha Kappa Alpha. Democrat. Baptist. Avocations: needlepoint, sewing, reading, public speaking. Home: 213 Lake Carmel Ct Huntsville AL 35811-8005 Office: Terry Heights Elem Sch 2820 Barbara Dr Huntsville AL 35816 Business E-Mail: mturner@hsv.k12.al.us.

TURNER, MEGAN WHALEN, author; b. Fort Sill, Okla., Nov. 21, 1965; d. Donald Peyton and Nora Courtenay (Green) Whalen; m. Mark Bernard Turner. BA in English Lang. and Lit. with honors, U. Chgo., 1987. Buyer children's books Harper Court Bookstore, Chgo., 1988-89, Bick's Books, Washington, 1991-92. Author: Instead of Three Wishes, 1995, The Thief, 1996 (Newbery Honor award 1997), The Queen of Attolia, 2000. Mem. Authors' Guild. Address: care Greenwillow Books 1350 Ave of the Ams New York NY 10019

TURNER, MONICA GOIGEL, ecologist; b. N.Y.C., Dec. 9, 1958; d. Peter Joseph and Dorothy Ann (Burger) Goigel; m. Michael G. Turner, Aug. 28, 1982. BS in biology summa cum laude, Fordham U., 1980; PhD in ecology, U. Ga., 1985. Environ. specialist US Nat. Park Svc., Washington, 1981; grad. non-teaching asst. U. Ga., Athens, 1980-83, rsch. asst. Inst. Ecology, 1983-85, postdoctoral rsch. assoc. Inst. Ecology, 1985-87; Hollaender fellow Oak Ridge Nat. Lab., Tenn., 1987-89, rsch. staff scientist environ. scis. divsn., 1989—94; asst. prof. zoology U. Wis., 1994—95, assoc. prof. zoology, 1995—99, prof. zoology, 1999—. Adj. asst. prof. ecology U. Tenn., 1990—94. Editor: Landscape Heterogeneity and Disturbance, 1987; co-editor-in-chief: Ecosystems; mem. editl. bd.: BioScience, Conservation Ecology, Ecological Applications. Mem. Internat. Assn. Ecology, Internat. Assn. Landscape Ecology (program chair U.S. chpt. 1986—), AAAS, Am. Inst. Biol. Scis., Ecol. Soc. Am., NAS, Phi Beta Kappa, Phi Kappa Phi. Roman Catholic. Office: Univ Wis Dept Zoology 432 Birge Hall 430 Lincoln Dr Madison WI 53706 Office Phone: 608-262-2592. E-mail: turnermg@wisc.edu.*

TURNER, NANCY ELIZABETH, artist, designer; b. Cumberland Mountains, Ky. d. Earl K. and Mary Lee (Jones) T.; m. Peter Alvet, Mar. 31, 1989. BA in Liberal Arts, U. Southwestern La.; Master Painter and Restorer, Yelland Acad. Fine Art, Calif.; cert. completion, Interior Decorators Inst. of L.A., 1990. Owner, chmn. The Turner Studio, Los Angeles; head artist/designer The Art Connection, Beverly Hills, Calif. Work includes fine paintings, artwork and decorative svcs. for residential and comml. interiors, trompe l'oeil murals, huge comml. fine art murals and signs, The Creator of "Fine Art Naturalism", A Method of Painting very Realistic Lifesize Flowers and Foliage in Large Scale Setting, hand painted furniture and standing screens; creator bestselling collector's plates Michael's Miracle, 1982, Susan's World, 1983, illustrations appearing in the L.A. Times, and Sunset Mag. Leader nat. multi-ch. religious freedom crusade, 1985-86. Winner Lithograph of Yr. award, 1982. Mem. Am. Inst. Fine Arts, Am. Soc. Interior Designers (accessorizing cons.), The Calif. Arboretum Found. and The Nat. Mus. of Women in Arts. Address: 3240 Mccarthy Dr Los Angeles CA 90065-4915

TURNER, NATALIE A., retired consultant; b. Vancouver, B.C., Can. d. Walter P. and Jenny (Ferley) Koohtow; m. George M. Turner, Jr. BS, McGill U., 1949. Rsch. asst. in neurophysiology Allen Meml. Inst., Montreal, 1949—51; rsch. asst. Harvard Med. Sch., Boston, 1951—54; chem. program mgr. in r&d, tech. svc. mgr. to Internat. Ops., clearance officer for Latin-Am. and Asia-Pacific comapnies Gillette Co., Boston, 1954—88; ret., 1989. Technician Red Cross Blood Transfusion Svc., Montreal, 1949; tech. cons. Damon Biotech, Boston, 1988-89, rsch. asst., Harvard Sch. of Pub. Health Co-author rsch. publs. in field. Bd. dirs. Children's Mus. in Easton, Mass., 1989—. Mem. NAFE, Internat. Congress Physiology, Am. Chem. Soc., Soc. Cosmetic Chemists (life, pres. New Eng. chpt., dir. US Nat. Bd., US rep. to Internat. Fedn. Exec. Bd.), New Eng. Women Bus. Owners, Kappa Alpha Theta (life). Avocations: sewing, golf, portraits in fabric and oils.

TURNER, PAMELA JAYNE, federal agency administrator; b. Newport, R.I., Oct. 29, 1944; d. Fontaine S. and Irene L. T. BA, Ind. U., 1966. Legis. asst. to Sen. Edward Gurney US Senate, Washington, 1967-75, chief legis. asst. to Sen. John Tower, 1975-80; dep. asst. for legis. affairs (Senate) to Pres. The White House, Washington, 1981—89; sr. v.p. govt. affairs Nat. Cable & Telecommunications Assn., 1989—2003; asst. sec. for legis. affairs US Dept. Homeland Security, Washington, 2003—. Office: US Dept Homeland Security 7th & D Sts SW Washington DC 20024

TURNER, RUTH, academic administrator; b. Gibsland, La., Aug. 3, 1926; married; children: George R., William P. BA in Elem. Edn., U. Southwestern La., 1947; MEd in Supervision, Tex. Woman's U., 1970; EdD in Adminstrn., Nova U., 1974. Tchr., Mansfield, La., 1947-48, New Iberia, La., 1948-50; tchr. spl. edn. Shreveport, La., 1954-57; tchr. visually impaired Dallas Ind. Sch. Dist., 1961-64, tchr. State Pilot Program Emotionally Disturbed, 1964-68, cons. spl. edn., 1968-71, cons., prin., 1971-73, program facilitator learning disabilities, 1973-74, asst. dir. spl. edn., 1974-81, dir., 1981-84, adminstr. spl. edn., project dir. Sch. of Future, 1984-91, edn. cons., 1991—. Presenter state and nat. confs., 1968-90. Contbr. articles to profl. jours. Office: 6909 Heatherknoll Dr Dallas TX 75248-5533

TURNER, SHARON P., dean, dentist, educator; b. Charleston, W.Va., Aug. 8, 1950; d. George Brock and Anna Hopkins Pullen; m. Aubrey Williams Turner, Jr., Feb. 26, 1972; children: Brock Leslie Turner, Martin Gresham Turner, Karen Anna Turner. BA in Biology, Winthrop U., 1971; DDS, U. N.C., 1979; JD, N.C. Ctrl U., 1995. Bar: NC; lic. dentist NC, Oreg., Ky., diplomate Am. Acad. Pain Mgmt. Pvt. dental practitioner Dengler & Turner, Raleigh, NC, 1985-86; asst. prof. of diagnostic scis. U. N.C. Sch. of Dentistry, Chapel Hill, 1986-94, assoc. prof. of diagnostic scis., 1994-98, dir. patient admissions and emergency svcs., 1986-94, dir. dental faculty practice, 1989-98, assoc. dean for adminstrn. planning, 1994-98; dean, prof. dentistry Oreg. Health and Sci. U. Sch. Dentistry, Portland, 1998—2003; dean U. Ky. Coll. Dentistry, Lexington, 2003—. Cons. VA Hosp., Durham, N.C., 1999. Contbg. author: Oral Surgery, 1999. Youth group leader Eno River Unitarian Universalist, Durham, 1996-97, Sunday Sch. tchr., 1997-98; girl scout leader Pines of Carolina Coun., Girl Scouts U.S., Durham, N.C., 1990-94. Named one of Top 25 Visionary Leaders in Dentistry, Am. Student Dental Assn., 1999. Fellow Internat. Coll. Dentists, Am. Coll. Dentists, Am. Coll. Legal Medicine, Piere Fourchard Acad.; mem. ADA, Am. Dental Edn. Assn., Am. Acad. Pain Mgmt., Internat. Assn. Dental Rsch., Intenat. Assn. for Study of Pain, Soc. for Exec. Leadership in Academic Medicine (v.p. 1999-2000, pres. 2000-01), Acad. General Dentistry. Avocations: swimming, hiking, singing, reading. Office: U Ky Coll Dentistry Chandler Med Ctr D136 800 Rose St Lexington KY 40536-9707 Office Phone: 859-323-5786. Business E-Mail: turnersp@uky.edu.

TURNER, TINA (ANNA MAE BULLOCK), singer; b. Brownsville, Tenn., Nov. 26, 1939; m. Ike Turner, 1956 (div. 1978); children: Craig, Ike Jr., Michael, Ronald. Singer (with): Ike Turner Kings of Rhythm, and Ike and Tina Turner Revue; appeared in (films) Gimme Shelter, 1970, Soul to Soul, 1971, Tommy, 1975, Sgt. Pepper's Lonely Hearts Club Band, 1978, Mad Max Beyond Thunderdome, 1985, Break Every Rule, 1986, Last Action Hero, 1993, concert tours of Europe, 1966, Japan and Africa, 1971, Showtime TV concert Wildest Dreams, albums with Ike Turner Hunter, 1970, Ike and Tina Show II, Ike and Tina Show, 1966, Ike and Tina Turner, Bad Dreams, 1973, Ike and Tina Turner Greatest Hits, vol. 1.2 and 3, 1989, Greatest Hits, 1990, Proud Mary, 1991, The Ike and Tina Turner Collection, 1993, solo albums Let Me Touch Your Mind, 1972, Tina Turns the Country On, 1974, Acid Queen, 1975, Love Explosion, 1977, Rough, 1978, Airwaves, 1979, Private Dancer, 1984, Break Every Rule, 1986, Tina Live In Europe, 1988, Foreign Affair, 1989, Simply the Best, 1991, What's Love Got to Do With It? (soundtrack), 1993, All the Best, 2005, recordings Sixties to Nineties, with others, 1994, Wildest Dreams, 1996, Twenty Four Seven, 2000; performer (with USA): for Africa on song We are The World, 1985; author: (autobiography) I, Tina, 1985; (film of autobiography) What's Love Got To Do With It?, 1993. Nominee Grammy (Best Pop Female Vocal) for "I Don't Wanna Fight", 1994; named to Rock and Roll Hall of Fame, 1991; recipient Grammy award, 1972, 1985, 1986, Kennedy Ctr. Honor, John F. Kennedy Ctr. for Performing Arts, 2005.*

TURNER, VALARIE ENGLISH, electronics company administrator; b. Chgo., June 15, 1957; d. Benjamin and LaVelma (Gaddis) English; m. John D. Turner, Aug. 23, 1986. BA, Northwestern U., 1979; MBA, Western Ill. U., 1981. Acct. exec. AT&T, Oakbrook, Ill., 1981-83; buyer Westinghouse Electric Corp., Pitts., 1983-84, sr. buyer Hunt Valley, Md., 1984-89, subcontracts buyer, 1989. Mem. Smithsonian Institute, Washington, 1987. Mem. Nat. Assn. Black MBA's. Clubs: Toastmasters. Avocations: aerobic dancing, music. Home: 9854 S Walden Pky Apt 2 Chicago IL 60643-1707 Office: Westinghouse Electric Corp 7267 Park Circle Dr Hanover MD 21076-1325

TURNER, VICKY JO, music educator; b. Kansas City, Mo., Mar. 17, 1968; d. James Phillip and Virginia Joan Turner. BS in Music Edn., N.W. Mo. State U., 1992. Lic. tchr. Mo., 1993. Music tchr. Linn County Sch. Dist., Purdin, Mo., 1994—96, McDonald County Sch. Dist., Jane and Rocky Comfort, Mo., 1999—2002, Kennett Sch. Dist., Mo., 2002—06, Adrian R-III Sch. Dist., 2006—. Mem. first bapt. choir First Bapt. Ch., Kennett, 2002, Sunday sch. sec. 1st and 2d grade students, 2003. Recipient Cert. of Appreciation, Am. Legion, 1999. Mem.: Mo. Band Dir.'s Assn. (licentiate), Am. Choral Dir.'s Assn. (licentiate), Music Educator's Nat. Conf. (licentiate), Mo. State Tchr.'s Assn. (licentiate). Baptist. Avocations: exercise, singing, birdwatching, hiking, music. Office: Adrian R III Sch Dist Butler MO 64730 Office Phone: 816-287-2158. Office Fax: 816-297-2980. E-mail: vjturner@netection.net.

TURNER-REID, MARSHA MARIE, science educator; b. Chgo., Jan. 10, 1960; d. Theodore Roosevelt Turner, Jr. and Betty Jean Smitherman; m. Peter Earl Reid (div.); 1 child, Melia Dyan Reid. BA, Jackson State U., Miss., 1984; MEd, Nat. Louis U., Chgo., 2002. Sci. tchr. Gwendolyn Brookes Mid. Sch., Oak Pk., Ill., 2002—. Co-chair, tchr. Leadership Team, Oak Pk., 2004.

TURNER-WARWICK, MARGARET, physician, educator; b. Nov. 19, 1924; d. William Harvey and Maud Kirkdale (Baden-Powell) Moore; m. Richard Trevor Turner-Warwick, Jan. 21, 1950; children: Gillian, Lynne. MA, BM, BCh, Oxford (Eng.) U., 1950, DM, 1956; PhD, London U., 1961; DSc (hon.), NYU, 1985, Exeter U., 1990, U. London, 1990, Hull U., 1991, U. Sussex, 1992, U. Oxford, 1992, U. Cambridge, 1993, U. Leicester, 1997. Clin. tng. U. Coll. Hosp., Brompton Hosp., 1950-61; cons. physician Elizabeth Garrett Anderson Hosp., 1961-67, Brompton and London Chest Hosps., 1967-72; prof. medicine Brompton and Cardio Thoracic Inst., London, 1972-87; dean Cardiothoracic Inst., London, 1984-87; pres. Royal Coll. Physicians, London, 1989-92. Chmn. UKCCCR, London. Author: (book) Immunology of Lung, 1979. Non-exec. mem. Royal Brompton Governing Body, London; chmn. Royal Devon Exeter Healthcare Trust, 1992-95. Decorated dame comdr. Brit. Empire; recipient Osler medal Oxford, 1996, Pres. award European Respiratory Soc., 1997. Fellow: ACP (hon.), Royal Coll. Radiology, Acad. Med. Sci. (founder fellow 1998), Royal Coll. Physicians Ireland, Royal Coll. Physicians and Surgeons Glasgow, U. Coll. London, Faculty Pub. Health Medicine, Faculty Occupl. Medicine, Royal Australian Coll. Physicians, Imperial Coll. London (hon.), Royal Coll. Physicians and Surgeons Can. (hon.), Royal Coll. Anaesthetists (hon.), Coll. Medicine South Africa (hon.), Royal Coll. Pathologists (hon.), Bencher Mid. Temple (hon.), Royal Coll. Surgeons England (hon.), Royal Coll. Gen. Practitioners (ad enundum), Royal Coll. Physicians Edinburgh, Royal Coll. Gen. Practitioners, Green Coll. Oxford (hon.), Lady Margaret Hall Oxford (hon.), Girton Coll. Cambridge (hon.); mem.: Brit. Thoracic Soc. (pres. 1982, President's medal 1999), Acad. Malaysia, South German and Australasian Thoracic Socs. (hon.), Assn. Physicians Gt. Britain and Ireland (hon.), Alpha Omega Alpha. Avocations: gardening, violin, country life, watercolor painting. Home: Pynes House Thorverton Nr Exeter Devon EX5 5LT England

TURNEY, SHARON JESTER, retail executive; b. 1958; BA in Bus. Edn., U. Okla. With Foley's, 1979—88, Neiman Marcus, 1989—2000, sr. v.p. gen., mgr. gen. merchandise, 1997—98, exec. v.p. merchandising, creative prodn., advt. and pub. rels., 1998; pres., CEO Neiman Marcus Direct, 1999—2000; CEO, pres. Victoria's Secret Catalogue, 2000—. Office: Victorias Secret Direct LLC 3425 Morse Crossing Columbus OH 43219

TURNEY, VIRGINIA, writer; b. Raton, N.Mex., Oct. 14, 1929; d. Otto and Lillian G. Olson; m. Eugene T. Turney Jr., July 17, 1962 (dec. Oct. 1979); children: Dianne Bohannan, Djinee Turney Jeffrey, Tore Nils and Nils Tore (twins); m. William M. Adams. BA, UCLA, 1950; DPsy, U. Miami, Fla., 1966. V.p. Anodyne, Inc., 1967-78; founder, pres., chmn. Ginni Lee All Sports, 1973—; chmn., pres. E.T. Turney, Inc., 1978—; pres. ToysCrafts-Games, Islamorada, Fla., 1985—. Psychologist People's Ct. for Handicapped Teens. Author: Cuban Spy for Freedom, 1981, Operation Truth, 1988. Mem. Save-A-Turtle Found., Whale Protection Assn., Gorilla Found. Mem. Miami Jockey Club, Palm Bay Rolls Royce Owners Club, Rolls Royce Enthusiasts, Key West Garden Club, Island Fishing, Club, Internat. Women's Fishing Club, Catskill Fly Fishing Club, West Palm Beach Fishing Club.

TURNLUND, JUDITH RAE, nutritionist; b. St. Paul, Sept. 28, 1936; d. Victor Emanuel and Vida Mae (Priddy) Hanson; m. Richard Wayne Turnlund, Nov. 9, 1957; children: Michael Wayne, Mark Richard, Todd Hanson. BS in Chemistry and Psychology, Gustavus Adolphus Coll., 1958; PhD in Nutrition, U. Calif., Berkeley, 1978. Registered dietitian. Postdoctoral fellow U. Calif., Berkeley, 1978-80, lectr., 1982-92, adj. assoc. prof., 1989-97; rsch. nutrition scientist Western Regional Rsch. Ctr./Western Human Nutrition Ctr., USDA, San Francisco, Albany, and Davis, Calif., 1980—; rsch. leader Western Human Nutrition Ctr. USDA, San Francisco, 1993-96; adj. prof. nutrition U. Calif., Davis, 2000—. Vis. asst. prof. Am. U. Beirut, Lebanon, 1979, 80. Editor: Stable Isotopes in Nutrition, 1984; contbr. articles to profl. jours. Recipient Cert. of Merit, USDA/ARS, 1984, 93, 98, Disting. Alumni citation Gustavus Adolphus Coll., 1988, Am. Inst. Nutrition's Lederle award in Human Nutrition, 1996; USDA grantee, Nat. Dairy Coun. grantee. Fellow Am. Soc. Nutritional Scis.; mem. Am. Soc. Clin. Nutrition, Am. Dietetic Assn. Home: 2276 Great Hwy San Francisco CA 94116-1555 Office: U Calif USDA/ARS Western Human Nutrition Rsch One Shields Ave Davis CA 95616 E-mail: jturnlun@whnrc.usda.gov.

TURO, JOANN K., psychoanalyst, psychotherapist, consultant; b. Westerly, R.I., Feb. 13, 1938; d. Angelo and Anna Josephine (Drew) T. BS in Biology and Chemistry, U. R.I., 1959; MA in Human Rels. and Psychology, Ohio U., 1964; postgrad., NYU, 1966-71, N.Y. Freudian Inst., N.Y.C., 1977-85, Mental Health Inst., 1977-80. Rsch. asst. biochemistry studies on schizophrenia Harvard U. Med. Sch., Boston, 1959-60; indsl. psychology asst. studies on managerial success N.Y. Telephone Co., N.Y.C., 1964-66; staff psychologist Testing and Advisement Ctr. NYU, 1966-70; psychology intern Kings County Hosp., Bklyn., 1970-71; staff psychologist M.D.C. Psychol. Svcs., N.Y.C., 1971-72; clin. dir. Greenwich House Substance Abuse Clinic, N.Y.C., 1973-76; cons. psychotherapist Mental Health Consultation Ctr., N.Y.C., 1977-82; pvt. practice N.Y.C., 1981—. Mental health cons. Bklyn. Ctr. for Psychotherapy, 1976-78; with Psychoanalytic Consultation Svcs., 1994—; presenter in field. Mem. Internat. Psychoanalytic Assn. (cert.), Soc. for Personality Assessment (cert.), N.Y. Freudian Soc. (cert., co-chmn. grad. com. 1985-86, mem. continuing edn. com. 1986—, pub. rels. com. 1992-93, psychoanalytic consult svc. 1994—, tng. and supr. psychoanalyst 1995—, ethics com. 1999—, tng. analyst panel 2000—, chair 2002-2003, presenter 2002, bd. dirs. 2003-06, v.p. 2005-2006), N.Y. Coun. Psychoanalytic Psychotherapists (cert.), Met. Assn. for Coll. Mental Health Practitioners (cert.). Office: 175 W 12th St Apt 15A New York NY 10011-8211 Office Phone: 212-691-2041. Personal E-mail: jturo@nyc.rr.com.

TUROCK, BETTY JANE, library and information science professor; b. Scranton, Pa., June 12; d. David and Ruth Carolyn (Sweetser) Argust; m. Frank M. Turock, June 16, 1956; children: David L., B. Drew. BA magna cum laude (Charles Weston scholar), Syracuse U., 1955; postgrad. (scholar), U. Pa., 1956; MLS, Rutgers U., 1970, PhD, 1981. Library and materials coordinator Holmdel (N.J.) Public Schs., 1963—65; story-teller Wheaton (Ill.) Public Library, 1965—67; ednl. media specialist Alhambra Public Sch., Phoenix, 1967—70; br. librarian, area librarian, head extension service Forsyth County Public Library System, Winston-Salem, NC, 1970—73; asst. dir., dir. Montclair (N.J.) Public Library, 1973—76; asst. dir. Monroe County Library System, Rochester, NY, 1978—81; asst. prof. Rutgers U. Sch. Comms., Info. and Libr. Studies, 1981—87, assoc. prof., 1987—93, prof., 1994—, dept. chair, 1989—95, 2002—03, dir. MLS program, 1990—95, 2002—03, assoc. dean, 2002—04, Rutgers U. Sch. Comm. Info and Libr. Studies, 2004—06; prof. emeritus, assoc. dean emeritus; pres. Rock Info. Assocs., 2004—. Vis. prof. Rutgers U. Grad. Sch. Library and Info. Studies, 1980-81; adviser U.S. Dept. Edn. Office of Libr. Programs, 1988-89. Author: Serving Older Adults, 1983, Creating a Financial Plan, 1992; editor: The Bottom Line, 1984-90; contbr. articles to profl. jours. Trustee Raritan Twp. (N.J.) Pub. Libr., 1961—62, Keystone Coll., 1991—, Freedom to Read Found., 1994—97, Librs. for the Future, 1994—97, Fund for Am.'s Librs., 1995, Trejo Found., 1995—, Bd. Am. Libr., Paris, 1999—; mem. Bd. Edn. Raritan Twp., 1962—66; ALA coord. Task Force on Women, 1978—80; mem. action coun.; treas. Social Responsibilities Round Table, 1978—82; mem. bd. visitors Johns Hopkins Sch. Medicine, 2005—. Charles Weston scholar Syracuse U., 1955; recipient N.J. Libr. Leadership award, 1994; named Woman of Yr. Raritan-Holmdel Woman's Club, 1975. Mem. AAUP, Am. Soc. Info. Sci., Assn. Libr. and Info. Sci Edn., ALA (pres. 1995-96, pres.-elect 1994-95, exec. bd. 1991-97, coun. 1988-97, Equality award 1998, Lippincott award 2006), Rutgers U. Grad. Sch. Library and Info. Studies Alumni Assn. (pres. 1977-78, Disting. Alumni award 1994), Phi Theta Kappa, Psi Chi, Beta Phi Mu, Pi Beta Phi. Unitarian Universalist. Office: Rutgers Univ 4 Huntington St New Brunswick NJ 08901-1071 Home: The Colony House 1050 George St 12-D E New Brunswick NJ 08901 Office Phone: 732-846-4406. Business E-Mail: bturock@scils.rutgers.edu.

TUROCK, JANE PARSICK, nutritionist; b. Peckville, Pa., Apr. 15, 1947; d. Paul Charles and Elizabeth Dorothy (Mistysyn) Parsick; m. Michael John, July 12, 1968; children: Eric Matthew, Nathan Andrew, J. Seth, Melanie Kay. BS, Marywood Coll., Scranton, Pa., 1969, MS, 1982. Registered dietitian; cert. nutrition specialist. Registered dietitian Jane P. Turock, Scranton, Pa., 1985—; founder and chief dietitian Gastric Bubble, Scranton, Pa., 1986—; prof. Penn State Coll., Scranton, Pa., 1987—; dietitian & presenter WNEP TV Healthwatch, Avoca, Pa., 1988—; dir. & chief dietitian Vascular Inst. of Northeast Pa., Pa., 1989—; owner Terrace Profl. Plaza, Olyphant, Pa.; owner, mgr. Nutrition.Plus/Fitness Unlimited, Scranton, Pa., 1991—; owner Pauliz Profl. Plz., Olyphant, Pa., 2006—. Cons. Home Health Care Assn., Clarks Summit, 1985—; dietitian Clarks Summit, 1985—; founder Nat. Nutrition Month Bakeoff; dir. Camp Jane. Treas. Lackawanna County Med. Soc. Aux., 1974-76, pres., 1979-80, bd. dirs., 1980-81; allocations com. United Way Lackawanna County, 1990—; mem. bd. dirs. Lupus Found., 1995, St. Francis of Assissi Kitchen, 1995; coord. Gary DiBileo For Mayor 07 Scranton Campaign, 2005. Mem. Am. Dietic Assn., Northeast Dist. Pa. Dietic Diet Therapy, Consulting Nutritionists in Pvt. Practice, Am. Diabetic Assn., Northeast Womens Network, Allied Wedding Firm. Republican. Roman Catholic. Avocations: skiing, tennis, gourmet cooking, jogging, swimming. also: Jane P Turock MSRD 397 N 9th Ave Scranton PA 18504-2005 Office: Pauliz Plaza Profl Offices Terrace Dr Olyphant PA 18447 E-mail: janeturock@excite.com.

TURÓN, MERCEDES, emeritus language professor; b. Madrid, Aug. 12, 1930; d. Vicente Turón-Bendicho and Mercedes Castells Cabezón. PhD, Mich. State U., 1970. Vice dir. Instituto de Cultura Hispánica, Brasilia, Brazil, 1972-77; prof. U. Montevallo, Ala., 1984-95, prof. emeritus Ala., 1995—. Lectr. in field. Contbr. articles to profl. publs.; contbr. poetry to jours Home: 630 Riverchase Pkwy W Birmingham AL 35244-1128

TURQUETTE, FRANCES BOND, editor; b. Atlanta, Sept. 25, 1931; d. Sewell Hinton and Lavonia DeLay Dixon; m. Charles Eugene Bond, Sept. 12, 1952 (div. Jan. 1969); children: Turner D., Laura S., L. Irene, Cynthia D., Nelson K.; m. Atwell Rufus Turquette, Dec. 27, 1998. Student, Wesleyan Coll., 1948—50; BA in Journalism, U. Ga., 1952; MA in Art History, U. Ill., 1971. Editl. asst. Meth. Pub. Ho., Nashville, 1952-53, Rsch. Press, Champaign, Ill., 1972-73; editing supr. McGraw-Hill Book Co., N.Y.C., 1974-80; publs. editor pub. affairs U. Ill., Urbana, 1974, 80-88; editor Nat. Ctr. for Supercomputing Applications, Champaign, 1988-96. Vis. faculty, editor Coll. of Commerce, U. Ill. Urbana, 1972-74; ref. com., Editorial and Composition Standards McGraw Hill Book Co., N.Y.C., 1975-77; editor, writer access, 1988-96. Mem. program chair, liaison, bd. govs. Channing Murray Found., Urbana, 1982-92; mem. adv. bd. to freeze nuclear weapons 15th Congrl. Dist., 1982-87; co-pres. SANE/Freeze, Champaign County, 1992-94. Mem. Nat. Assn. Sci. Writers, Art Inst. Chgo. (family mem.), Lyric Opera Chgo., Oriental Inst., U. Chgo., Champaign-Ubana League Women Voters, Channing-Murray Found., Am. Assn. U. Women, Theta Sigma Phi. Unitarian Universalist. Avocations: travel, writing, gardening, photography. Home: 914 W Clark St Champaign IL 61821-3328 Personal E-mail: turquette@sbcglobal.net.

TURTURRO, AIDA, actress; b. NYC, Sept. 25, 1962; Grad., State U. NY, New Paltz, 1984. Actor: (films) Life with Mikey, 1993, Money Train, 1995, Sleepers, 1996, Fallen, 1998, Celebrity, 1998, Deep Blue Sea, 1999, Mickey Blue Eyes, 1999, Bringing Out the Dead, 1999, Play It to the Bone, 1999, Crocodile Dundee in Los Angeles, 2001; (TV series) As the World Turns, 1998, The Soprano's, 2000—; (Broadway plays) A Streetcar Named Desire, 1992, (guest appearance): (TV series) Law and Order, 1990.

TUSKEY, LAURA JEANNE, music educator, pharmacologist; b. Virginia Beach, Va., May 7, 1966; d. Cromer Lee Ishmael and Annabell E. Eschbach; m. John Phillip Tuskey, June 26, 1998. Student, Old Dominion U., Norfolk, Va., 1984—86. Cert. pharmacy technician Pharmacy Technician Certification Bd., 2003. Pianist Cath. Ch. of St. Mark, Virginia Beach, Va., 1991—; office mgr. CompuGeek, L.L.C., Chesapeake, Va., 2002—03; pharmacy technician Farm Fresh, Inc., Virginia Beach, Va., 2002—, Phar Mor, Inc., Norfolk and Virginia Beach, Va., 1991—98; music therapist Our Lady of Perpetual Health, Virginia Beach, Va., 1999—2000. Aromatherapy educator, Hampton Roads, Va., 2000—. Contbr. articles to profl. jours. Mem.: Alzheimer's Assn. (chmn. memory walk com. 2001), Nat. Pastoral Musicians Assn. R-Liberal. Roman Catholic. Avocations: aromatherapy, musical events, reading, travel. Office: Catholic Church of St Mark 1505 Kempsville Rd Virginia Beach VA 23464

TUSSING, MARILEE APPLEBY, music educator; b. Decatur, Ill., Feb. 6, 1953; d. Robert William and Dorothymaie (Mallory) Appleby; m. Donald Tussing, April 17, 1976; 1 child, Torrance Ashley. B in Music Edn., Ill. State U., 1975; M in Music Edn., U. Okla., 1985. Nat. bd. cert. early and mid. childhood music 2004. Music tchr. Shannon Elem., Shannon, Ill., 1976-80, Thompson Schs., Thompson, Ill., 1980-82; Kodaly music specialist Southgate Elem., Moore, Okla., 1982—. Riding instr. Shenandoah Riding Ctr., Galena, Ill. 1977-81, freelance Norman, Okla., 1982—; creator Sooner Pony Club Worksheet Program; founder Southgate String Players; clinician Orgn. Am. Kodaly Educators Conf., 2006. Musician: (band) Traditions, 1999—. Dist. Commr. Sooner Pony Club, 1985—; judge Okla. Kids Talent Search, 1993-96; mem. Moore Assn. Classroom Tchrs. 1982—; pres. Moore Elem. Music Orgn., 1990-91; founder Southgate Entertainer's Club; dir. Am. Kids Celebrity Chorus, 1996-97; mem. Irish Arts Project, 2002—; mem. Comhaltas Ceoltiori Eirhann, 2004— Recipient Equestrian Event Silver medal Sooner (Okla.) State Games, 1989.; grantee Okla. Found. for excellence in edn., 2006. Mem. Midwest Kodaly Music Educators (bd. dirs. 1983-85), U.S. Pony Club (knowdown judge, 1990-98, tech. del.), U.S. Combined Tng. Assn. (cert. of achievement, 1985, 89, area V adult team mem. award, 1993), Nat. Edn. Assn., Okla. Edn. Assn., Am. Quarter Horse Assn., Orgn. Am. Kodaly Educators, Okla. City Traditional Music Assn., Am. Connemera Pony Soc Republican. Mem. Christian Ch. (Disciples Of Christ). Avocations: skiing, needlepoint, violin, guitar, collecting and reading horse books. Home: 11850 E Rock Creek Rd Norman OK 73026-8155

TUSTIN, KAREN GAIL, mathematics educator; d. Milton Ray and Della Jo Hennig; m. Jimmy Doyle Tustin; children: Travis Nicholas, Chase Morgan. BS, East Tex. State U., 1990; MSc, Tex. A&M-Commerce, 1999. Mid. sch. math tchr. McDonald Mid. Sch., Mesquite, Tex., 1990—93; h.s. math tchr. North Mesquite H.S., 1993—2001; h.s. math tchr./dept. chair Dr. John Horn H.S., Mesquite, 2001—. H.s. swim coach Mesquite Ind. Sch. Dist., 1990—93; student coun. sponsor North Mesquite H.S., 2000—01, Dr. John Horn H.S., Mesquite, 2001—05. Mem.: Assn. of Tex. Profl. Educators (assoc.). Christian. Avocations: swimming, scuba diving, travel, camping. Office: Dr John Horn HS 3300 Cartwright Rd Mesquite TX 75181 Office Phone: 972-882-5200. Home Fax: 972-882-5291; Office Fax: 972-882-5291. E-mail: ktustin@mesquiteisd.org.

TUTCHTONE, SHARON SABRINA, secondary school educator; b. Greenville, Ala., Dec. 12, 1969; d. Smith, Jr. and Jean N. Tutchtone. M in Edn. History, Auburn U., Montgomery, 1993. Cert. tchr. Ala. Tchr., coach Abbeville Christian Acad., Ala., 1994—96, Prattville HS, Ala., 1996—. Republican. Roman Catholic. Office: Prattville High Sch 1315 Upper Kingston Rd Prattville AL 36067 Office Phone: 334-365-8804. Office Fax: 334-358-0111.

TUTINO, ROSALIE JACQUELINE, college administrator; b. Bklyn., Dec. 28, 1937; d. Peter Rocco and Rose (Oliva) T. BA, St. Joseph's Coll., 1959; MA, NYU, 1964. Licensed ins. broker, N.Y. Publ., annuity mgr. Equitable Life Assurance, N.Y.C., 1959-62; instr., dept. chmn. Our Lady Perpetual Help High Sch., Bklyn., 1962-70; dir. coll. relations St. Joseph's Coll., Bklyn., 1970-75, devel. and coll. rels. dirs., 1975-77, v.p. devel. and coll. rels., 1977—. Pres. Rosalie Tutino Assocs., Hampton Bays, N.Y., 1980. Bd. dirs. Suffolk coun. Boy Scouts Am., 1988—, Suffolk Coun., 1988, Archtl. Review Bd., Town of Southampton. Mem. L.I. Coalition for Fair Broadcasting, Nat. Soc. Fundraising Execs., Pub. Rels. Soc. Am., L.I. Assn., CASE. Republican. Roman Catholic. Avocations: painting, sailing, photography, golf. Home: 49 Romana Dr Hampton Bays NY 11946-3718 Office: Saint Josephs Coll 155 W Roe Blvd Patchogue NY 11772-2325

TUTTLE, ANNE PALMER, artist, education educator; b. Phila., Pa., May 28, 1922; d. Edward Lionel and Anna Margaret Palmer; m. Herbert Robert Pfister, Dec. 11, 1976 (dec.); m. Bruce Nelson Tuttle (div.); children: William, Patricia, David, Stephen, Amy. BA, Long Isl. Univ, N.Y., 1944; MA, SUNY, Stony Brook, N.Y., 1977; student, Madison Art Sch., 1966—73, Pratt Graphics Ctr., N.Y., 1975. Tng. supr. Fredrick Loeser & Co., Bklyn., 1944—46; proprietor Anne Tuttle Studios, Setauket, NY, 1973—; printmaker Bermond Art Ltd., Lake Success, NY, 1975—86; instr. Empire State Coll., Old Westaury, NY, 1980—2004; master instr. Islip Art Mus., East Islip, NY, 1982—. Vis. artist Pima County Cultural, Tucson, 1994; judge art exhibits, Long Island, NY, 1978—; lectr. in field, Long Island, NY, 1980—. Prin. works include portrait Arthur Tuttle v.p. treas. RCA, 1976, pres. Patricia Designs, 1980, pres. Elec. workers union, 1981, prin. works include in numerous galleries, U.S., Can., Eng., France, Germany, Holland, South Africa. Pro bono mentor to artists, Long Island, NY. Recipient 1st prize portraits, Awixa Art League, 1969, Felician Art League, 1973, 2nd prize etching, Krishna Reddy, 1978. Republican. Avocations: reading, sailing, camping. Home: 239 Sheep Pasture Rd PO Box 142 East Setauket NY 11733 Office: Ann Tuttle Studios 239 Sheep Pasture Rd PO Box 142 East Setauket NY 11733-0142 Office Phone: 631-751-0111. Personal E-mail: annetuttle@hotmail.com.

TUTTLE, KAREN ANN, violist, educator; b. Lewiston, Idaho, Mar. 28, 1920; d. Ray and Eunice Valborg (Nelson) T.; m. Morton Herskowitz; 1 child, Robin Ray Heald. MusB, Curtis Inst. Music, 1944, MusD (hon.), 2005. Ind. violist, 1944—; tchr. viola Curtis Inst. Music, Phila., 1945—. Mem. The Schneider Quartet, Philomusica chamber group; instr. Mannes Coll. Music, Manhattan Sch. Music, Peabody Conservatory Music; faculty Juilliard Sch. Music, ret., 2005, Banff Sch. Arts. Carnegie Hall debut, N.Y.C., 1960. Home: 2132 Pine St Philadelphia PA 19103-6535

TUTTLE, MARCIA, retired elementary school educator, music educator; b. Spirit Lake, Iowa, Dec. 30, 1945; d. Frank Ewing and Ann Parsons Tuttle; 1 child, Amy Beth Gould. BA in English, Elem. Edn., U. Iowa, 1969, MA in Reading Disabilities, 1975; BA in Piano Pedagogy summa cum laude, Mt. Mercy Coll., 1985. Cert. tchr. Iowa. Elem. tchr. Cedar Rapids (Iowa) Cmty. Schs., 1969—2001; piano tchr. Cedar Rapids, 1981—2001, Salmon Creek Piano Studio, Vancouver, Wash., 2002—. Composer, performer Iowa Composers Concerts, Cedar Rapids, 1983—85; adjudicator Pvt. Music Teachers Assn. Competition, Cedar Rapids, 1994—95, Kalina Piano Studio Competition, Cedar Rapids, 1996—2000. Composer: Tempus Suite, Sibelius Publication. Coord. Cedar Rapids Cmty. Sch. Dist. Music Contest, 1987—92; big sister Big Bros./Big Sisters Assn., Cedar Rapids, 1986—; vol. HOSTS Reading Readiness, Vancouver, Wash., 2002—; music dir., pianist Living Branch Luth. Ch., Woodland, Wash., 2002—. Named honoree, Belin-Blank Ctr. for Gifted Edn., U. Iowa, 1996, 1998; recipient Outstanding Music Grad. award, Mt. Mercy Coll., 1985, Hero award, Big Bros./Big Sisters, Cedar Rapids, 2000. Mem.: Music Tchrs. Nat. Assn., Wash. Music Tchrs. Assn., Clark County Music Tchrs. Assn. (2d v.p. 2003—), S.W. Wash. Watercolor Soc., Beethoven Club. Avocations: watercolor painting, music, travel. Home: 2202 NW 143d Cir Vancouver WA 98685

TUTTLE, MARTHA BENEDICT, artist; b. Cin., Feb. 4, 1916; d. Harris Miller and Florence Stevens (McCrea) Benedict; m. Richard Salway Tuttle, June 3, 1939; children: Richard, Jr., McCrea Benedict (dec.), Martha (dec.), Elisabeth Hall. Grad. high sch., Cin.; student, Art Acad. Cin., 1934-38. V.p. Barq Bottling Co., Inc., Cin., 1948-80. One-woman shows include KKAE Gallery, 1963, Univ. Club, 1967, Miller Gallery, 1971, St. Clements, N.Y., 1973, Livingston Lodge, 1974, Holly Hill Antiques, 1979, Peterson Gallery, 1983, Art Acad. Cin., 1984, Closson Gallery, 1986, Camargo Gallery, 1992; represented in permanent collection Cin. Art Mus. Tchr. Sunday sch. Grace Episcopal Ch. and Indian Hill Ch., Cin., 1953-75; shareholder Cin. Art Mus.; founder partnership to save the William and Phebe Betts House; donor with partnership to The Nat. Soc. Colonial Dames of Am. the William and Phebe Betts House for establishing a Rsch. Ctr. Mem. Soc. Colonial Dames Am. (bd. dirs. 1976-89), Camargo Club, Univ. Club. Republican.

TUTTLE, MARY CELIA PUTNAM, retired social worker; b. Brookings, S.D., Jan. 7, 1927; d. Henry Oakes and Hazel Una (Bacon) Putnam; m. Lewis Potter Tuttle, May 9, 1953; children: Amy Lucinda, Brian Paul, Rebecca Susan. Student, Cottey Coll., 1944-45; BA, U. Minn., 1948; MSW, Mich. State U., 1984. Lic. Master's Social Worker Clin. and Macro Mich. Dir. YWCA Teen-Age Program, Santa Monica, Calif., 1948-50, Lansing, Mich., 1950-53; vol. coord. CPCAN Family Growth Ctr., Lansing, 1980-81; drug educator project parent Tri-County Cmty. Mental Health Bd., Lansing, 1981, 82-83; med. social worker Sparrow Hosp., Lansing, 1984, nephrology social worker dialysis unit, 1984-95, ret., 1995. Active Edgewood United Ch. of Christ. Mem. NASW, LWV (v.p. Dearborn 1966-67, pres. 1967-69, Mich. bd. dirs. 1971-73), Physicians for Nat. Health Program, Universal Health Care Action Network, Mich. Universal Health Care Access Network (bd. dirs.), P.E.O. (pres. Mich. chpt. CJ 1969-71, chpt. AG 1974-76, 97-99, corresponding sec., 2001-2003, treas., 2003-05), Acad. Cert. Social Workers, Phi Alpha. Democrat. Avocations: travel, photography.

TUTTLE, TARA MARIE, literature and language educator; d. Kenneth Avery and Carol Elaine Tuttle. BS in Premedicine, Ball State U., Muncie, Ind., 2000; MA in Humanities, Ind. State U., Terre Haute, 2002; postgrad. in Humanities, U. Louisville, 2003—. Cert. Grad. Women's and Gender Studies U. Louisville, 2005. Grad. asst. to dir. u. honors program and coord. office nat. scholarships Ind. State U., Terre Haute, 2000—02; instr. English Vincennes U., Vincennes, 2000; ACT test prep instr. Sylvan Learning Ctr., Nashville, 2002—03; grad. tchg. asst. Humanities dept. U. Louisville, Louisville, 2003, instr. humanities, 2004—. Faculty mentor U. Louisville, Louisville, 2006—, faculty rep. Disney alumni program, 2006—; part-time instr. English Ivy Tech. CC, Madison, Wis., 2006. Sec. Jefferson County NOW, Louisville, 2004—06, young feminism coord., 2006—; activist tng. NOW, Washington, 2005—05. Recipient William Ashbrook Award for Disting. Work in the

Humanities, Ind. State U., 2002. Mem.: NAACP, AAUW, UNICEF, Amnesty Internat. USA. Home: 2233 Arthur Ford Ct Apt 3 Louisville KY 40217 Office: U Louisville Bingham Humanities Bldg 212 Louisville KY 40292 Office Phone: 502-852-3924. Personal E-mail: taratuttle@yahoo.com.

TUTWILER, MARGARET DEBARDELEBEN, stock exchange executive, former federal agency administrator; b. Birmingham, Ala., Dec. 28, 1950; d. Temple Wilson and Margaret (DeBardeleben) Tutwiler, II. Student, Finch Coll., 1969-71; BA, U. Ala., 1973. Sec. Ala. Rep. Party, Birmingham, 1974; scheduler Pres. Ford Com., Birmingham, 1975-78; exec. dir. Pres. Ford Com. Ala., Birmingham, 1976; pub. rels. rep. Nat. Assn. Mfrs. for Ala. and Miss., Birmingham and Washington, 1977-78; dir. scheduling George Bush for Pres. Com., Houston and Washington, 1978-80; spl. asst. to Pres. Reagan and exec. to Chief of Staff The White House, Washington, 1981-85; asst. sec., pub. affairs & public liaison U.S. Dept. Treasury, 1985-88; sr. advisor transition team U.S. Dept. State, Washington, 1988-89, asst. sec. pub. affairs, spokesman, 1989-92, U.S. amb. to Morocco Rabat, 2001—03, under sec., pub. diplomacy & pub. affairs Washington, 2003—04; ptnr. Fitzwater & Tutwiler, Inc., Washington, 1993—2001; exec. v.p., comm. & govt. relations NY Stock Exchange Inc., NYC, 2004—. Dep. chmn. Bush-Quayle '88, Washington, 1988. Recipient Woman of Yr. award Wake Forest U., 1986, Alexander Hamilton award, 1988, Am. Ctr. for Internat. Leadership's Marshall award for outstanding leadership Birmingham Sothern's GALA 10, 1991. Republican. Episcopalian. Office: NY Stock Exchange 11 Wall St New York NY 10005

TUZEL, SUZANNE L., psychiatrist; b. Jacksonville, Fla., Aug. 12, 1960; children: Haldun, Kenan. MD, U. Istanbul Med. Sch., 1986. Diplomate bd. cert. in psychiatry and neurology 1992. Chief resident Creedmoor Psychiatric Ctr., Queens Village, NY, 1992—95, chief psychiatrist, 1995—96; chief of psychiatry Pilgrim Psychiatric Ctr., Brentwood, 1997—99, acting clin. dir., 1999—2000, asst. clin. dir., 2000—02; pvt. practice North Shore Psychiatric Cons., Smithtown, 2002—; attending psychiatrist St. Catherine of Siena Med. Ctr., 2002—; med. dir. Huntington Drug and Alcohol Project, 2006—. Addiction fellow North Shore U. Hosp., Smithtown, 2000. Mem.: Am. Psychiatric Assn. Office: 222 Mid Country Rd Smithtown NY 11787 Office Phone: 631-265-6868.

TVELIA, CAROL ANN, principal, elementary school educator; b. Flushing, N.Y., Aug. 21, 1947; d. Calogero Frank and Mary Elizabeth (D'Alessio) Vitanza; m. Richard Anthony Tvelia, July 12, 1969 (div. Mar. 1984); children: Tracy Ann, Richard A. Jr.; m. Theodore William Polson, Aug. 22, 1986 (div. Aug. 1994). BA in Elem. Edn., Queens Coll., 1969; MA, SUNY, Stony Brook, 1974; cert. in advanced study supervision, Hofstra U., 1993. Cert. tchr., N.Y. Elem. tchr. Bayshore (N.Y.) Ctrl. Sch. Dist., 1969, Mid. Country Ctrl. Sch. Dist., Centereach, N.Y., 1969-70, Longwood Ctrl. Sch. Dist., Middle Island, N.Y., 1976—; house capt. Longwood Mid. Sch., Middle Island, N.Y., 1992—. Sci. mentor K-8 N.Y. State Dept. Edn., Albany, 1991—, N.Y. Sci. and Tech. Project resource agt., 1993—. Author (newsletter) Nat. Mid. Level Sci. Level Line, 1992-93. Mem. ASCD, NSTA, N.Y. Sci. Tchrs. Assn. (Mid. Level Sci. Tchr. award 1991), Nat. Sci. Suprs. Assn., N.Y. State Sci. Suprs. Assn. (exec. bd. mem.), Nat. Soc. Studies Assn., N.Y. State Social Studies Assn., Suffolk County Social Studies Assn., Suffolk County Sci. Tchrs. Assn. Democrat. Avocations: reading, sewing, gardening, travel. Home: 25 Stephani Ave East Patchogue NY 11772-5523 Office: Joseph A Edgar Sch 525 Rte 25A Rocky Point NY 11778 Office Phone: 631-744-1600 2400. E-mail: sciencecat@optonline.net.

TWADDELL, KAREN GRACE, elementary school educator; b. Newark, Apr. 24, 1950; d. Miles Edmiston and Grace Rita (Rodgers) T.; children: Colleen Michel Anderson, Christopher Matthew Anderson. BS in Spl. Edn., Cen. Mich. U., 1971; MA in Spl. Edn., Calif. State U., Turlock, 1990; postgrad., U. Pacific, 1998—. Tchr. Mojave (Calif.) Elem. Sch., 1972-74, All Hallows Sch., Sacramento, 1977-79, Crowell Sch., Turlock, Calif., 1981-85; resource specialist Julien Elem. Sch., Turlock, 1986-87; tchr. Hempstead (Tex.) Elem. Sch., 1987—; resource specialist Crowell Sch., 1988—2002, reading recovery tchr., 1994—; resource specialist Rancho Sandusto Mid. Sch., Hollister, Calif., 2002—03, ap, 2003—04; summer sch. prin. Sunnslope Elem. Sch., Hollister, Calif., 2003; v.p. spl. assignments, program specialist Hollister Sch. Dist., 2004—05, dir. student svcs., 2005—. Advisor, spl. edn., Calif. State U., Stanislaus, 1990—. Recipient Young Educators award, Turlock Jaycees, 1989. Mem. Nat. Tchrs. Assn., Calif. Tchrs. Assn., Turlock Tchrs. Assn., Coun. for Exceptional Children. Democrat. Roman Catholic. Home: 902 Suiter St Hollister CA 95023-4630 Office: 2690 Cienega Rd Hollister CA 95023 Office Phone: 831-630-6356. Business E-Mail: ktwaddell@hsd.k12.ca.us.

TWAIN, SHANIA (EILLEEN REGINA EDWARDS), musician; b. Windsor, Ontario, Can., Aug. 28, 1965; d. Sharon and Jerry Twain (Stepfather), Clarence Edwards; m. Robert John Lange, Dec. 28, 1993; 1 child, Eja. Recs. Beginnings, 1989—90, 1999, Shania Twain, 1993, The Woman in Me, 1995 (Acad. Country Music Assn. Award for Album of Yr., 1995, ABC Radio Networks Country Music Award for Female Video Artist of Yr., 1995, Billboard Music Award for Country Album of Yr., 1996, Grammy award for Best Country Album, 1996), These Blues are Mine, 1996, Come on Over, 1997, Star Profile, 1999, Maximum Shania, 2000, Complete Limelight Sessions, 2001, Up!, 2002 (Can. Country Music Assn. Award for Album of Yr., 2003, Billboard Music Award for Country Album of Yr., 2003), Greatest Hits, 2004. Recipient Country Music TV (Europe) Rising Star award, 1993, Am. Music Award for Favorite New Country Artist, 1995, Can. Country Music Assn. Award for female vocalist of yr., 1995, Acad. of Country Music Award for Top New Female Vocalist, 1995, Best Country Album Grammy award, 1995, Blockbuster Entertainment Award for Favorite New Country Artist, 1996, Country Music TV (Europe) award for Female Artist of Yr., 1996, Juno Award for Country Female Vocalist of Yr., 1996, Juno Award for Entertainer of Yr., 1996, World Music Award for World's Best Selling Country Artist, 1996, Favorite New Artist award, Am. Music Awards, 1996, Am. Music Award for Best Female Country Artist, 1997, Juno Award for Country Female Vocalist of Yr., 1997, Juno Award for Internat. Achievement, 1997, Am. Music Award for Favorite Female Country Artist, 1998, Billboard Music Award for Female Artist of Yr., 1998, Country Music Assn. Award for Entertainer of Yr., 1999, Acad. Country Music Award for Entertainer of Yr., 1999, Am. Music Award for Favorite Female Country Artist, 1999, Am. Music Award for Favorite Female Pop/Rock Artist, 1999, Blockbuster Entertainment Award for Favorite Overall Single, 1999, Juno Award for Country Female Vocalist of Yr., 1999, Grammy Award for Best Female Country Vocal Performance (You're Still The One), 1999, Grammy Award for Best Country Song (You're Still The One), 1999, Juno Award for Best Songwriter, 2000, Juno Award for Best Country Female Artist, 2000, Grammy Award for Best Female Vocal Country Performance (Man!I Feel Like A Woman), 2000, Grammy Award for Best Country Song (Come On Over), 2000, Acad. Country Music Award for Entertainer of Yr., 2000, Billboard Music Award for Top Country Artist of Yr., 2003, Billboard Music Award for Country Album Artist of Yr., 2003, Juno Fan Choice Award, 2003, Juno Award for Artist of Yr., 2003, Juno Award for Country Rec. Yr. (I'm Gonna Getcha Good), 2003, Can. Country Music Assn. Award for Video of Yr. (I'm Gonna Getcha Good), 2003, Can. Country Music Assn. Award for Female Artist of Yr., 2003, Order of Canada, 2005. Office: Mercury Records 66 Music Sq W Nashville TN 37203-4315 Address: Shore Fire Media c/o Georgette Pascale 32 Court St Fl 16 Brooklyn NY 11201-4404 Office: c/o Q Prime 131 S 11th St Nashville TN 37206

TWALE, DARLA JEAN, education educator; b. McKeesport, Pa., Sept. 23, 1951; d. Franklin Louis and LaVerne (Morgenstern) T. BA, Geneva Coll., 1973; MA, DuQuesne U., 1976, U. Pitts., 1980, PhD, 1985. H.S. tchr. Elizabeth (Pa.)-Forward H.S., 1973-74; sociology instr. C.C. of Allegheny County, West Mifflin, Pa., 1976-77, Pa. State U., McKeesport, 1979-80, Geneva Coll., Beaver Falls, Pa., 1982; vis. prof. edn. U. Pitts., 1986-87; edn. prof. Auburn (Ala.) U., 1987-98; prof. edn. U. Dayton, Ohio, 1998—. Contbr. articles to profl. jours. Mem. Mon-Yough Trail Coun., Ea. Ednl. Rsch. Assn., Assn. for Study of Higher Edn. Methodist. Avocations: trail biking, gardening, flying. Office: Univ Dayton 300 College Park Dayton OH 45469-0530 Business E-Mail: darla.twale@notes.udayton.edu.

TWARDOWSKI, KRISTEN M., special education educator; b. North Kingstown, RI, July 12; d. David Michael and Linda Ann (Vadenais) Twardowski. BS, R.I. Coll., 2003; MEd in Spl. Edn. and Spl. Edn. Adminstrn., Providence Coll., 2005. Tchg. certificates elem. edn. and spl. edn. Case mgr. Spurwink, Cranston, R.I., 2001—; spl. edn. tchr. HS East Greenwich Pub. Schs., R.I., 2003—. Religious educator St. Mary's Ch., West Warwick, 2004—. Mem.: Pi Lambda Theta Honor Soc., Kappa Delta Pi Honor Soc. (v.p. 2003—04). Roman Catholic. Avocations: home decorating, volleyball. Office: E Greenwich HS 300 Avenger Dr East Greenwich RI 02818

TWICHELL, CHASE, poet; b. New Haven, Conn., Aug. 20, 1950; d. Charles P. and Ann (Chase) T. BA, Trinity Coll., Hartford, 1973; MFA, U. Iowa, 1976. Editor Pennyroyal Pr., W. Hatfield, Mass., 1976-84; assoc. prof. English U. Ala., 1984-88; mem. MFA Program in Creative Writing, Warren Wilson Coll., 1999—; editor Ausable Press, 1999—. Asst. prof. Hampshire Coll., 1983-84; co-editor Alabama Poetry Series, 1984-88; lectr. Princeton U., 1990-98; faculty MFA program in creative writing Goddard Coll., 1997-99. Author: (poetry) Northern Spy, 1981, The Odds, 1986, Perdido, 1991, The Ghost of Eden, 1995, (book) Dog Language, 2005; editor: The Practice of Poetry, 1992, The Snow Watcher, 1998, Ausable Press, 1999—; translator The Lover of God, 2003. Recipient Acad. award in lit. Am. Acad. Arts and Letters, 1994; Nat. Endowment for Arts fellow, 1987, 93, Guggenheim fellow, 1990.

TWINING, LYNNE DIANNE, psychotherapist, professional society administrator, writer; b. Midland, Mich., Aug. 14, 1951; d. James and Dorothy Twining; m. Alan Howard Mass; 1 child, Allegra Liliane Twining-Mass. BA in Psychology, Oakland U., 1974; MSW, Wayne State U., 1977; MA in Psychology, Yeshiva U., 1993, D in Psychology, 1995. Cert. Bklyn. Inst. Psychotherapy and Psychoanalysis. Social work supr. non-profit orgn., Detroit, 1977-83; co-founder, co-dir. Women Psychotherapists Bklyn., 1986-95, dir., 1995—; co-dir. Affiliated Psychotherapists of Greater N.Y.C. and Phila., 1996—; pvt. practice Bklyn., N.Y.C., 1987—; psychotherapy rschr. Beth Israel Med. Ctr., N.Y.C., 1992-94; fac. Bklyn. Inst. Psychotherapy and Psychoanalysis, 2003—. Author: (with other) Metro Detroit Guide, 1975; contbg. editor: Detroit Guide, 1983; asst. prodr. docudrama Home; columnist Bklyn. Woman; contbr. articles to profl. jours. Bd. dirs. Progressive Artists and Educators Coalition, Detroit, 1977-79. Fellow Am. Orthopsychiat. Assn.; ACLU (sec. exec. bd. Mich. chpt. 1982-83), APA, Am. Mental Health Alliance (charter), Internat. Fedn. Psychoanalytical Edn., N.Y. State Psychol. Assn., N.Y. Acad. Scis., Soc. for Psychotherapy Rsch., Nat. Trust for Hist. Preservation, Tng. Inst. Nat. Assn. Advancement Psychoanalysis (affiliate), Women Psychotherapists Bklyn. (founding mem.), Amnesty Internat. (freedom writer), Bklyn. Inst. Psychotherapy and Psychoanalysis Soc. (bd. dirs. 2003-), Families With Children From China. Avocations: jazz, travel, piano, reading, contemporary art. Office: 55 Eastern Pky Ste 3H Brooklyn NY 11238-5913 also: 5 E 22nd St New York NY 10010

TWISS, PAMELA, social worker, educator; d. Herbert and Ena Casey; m. Thomas Twiss, Oct. 4, 1991; 1 child, Noah. MSW, U. Pitts., 1987, PhD, 1993. Asst. prof. Marywood U., Scranton, Pa., 1994—97, West Chester U. Pa., 1997—99; assoc. prof. California U. Pa., 1999—. Senator faculty senate California U. Pa., 2000—03, bd. dirs. instl. rev. bd., 2001—, sec. univ.-wide promotion com., 2005—, adv. bd. mem. honors program, 2005—; presenter in field. Consulting editor: Jour. Baccalaureate Social Work Edn., 2003—, reviewer: Jour. Cmty. Practice, 2003—04; contbr. articles to profl. jours. Task force mem. Fayette County Partnership Housing and Homelessness, Uniontown, Pa., 2001—05; recruiter Ch. World Svc. CROP Walk, Pitts., 2004—. Recipient Student Club Advisor of the Yr., SAI Inc. California U. Pa., 2006; grantee, Marywood U., 1996—97, Ctr. Rural Pa., 2002—04; Faculty Profl. Devel. Rsch. grantee, California U. Pa., 2000—01, FPD Ann. grantee, 2003—04. Mem.: NASW, Baccalaureate Program Dirs. Assn., Appalachian Studies Assn., Coun. Social Work Edn. Presbyterian. Avocations: dance, tang soo do karate. Office: California U Pa 250 University Ave California PA 15419 Office Phone: 724-938-4053.

TWIST-RUDOLPH, DONNA JOY, neurophysiology and neuropsychology researcher; b. Cape May, N.J., Dec. 3, 1955; d. Donald and Mary Ann (Johnson) Twist; m. Daniel Jay Rudolph, Jan. 10, 1981; children: Andrew, Adam, Matthew. BS, Boston U., 1978; MA, SUNY, Stony Brook, 1984; PhD, SUNY, 1986. Licensed phys. therapist, N.Y., Conn. Postdoctoral fellow, rsch. scientist N.Y. U. Med. Ctr., Rusk Inst. Rehab. Medicine, N.Y.C., 1986-87; dir. rsch. and edn. Norwalk (Conn.) Hosp., 1987-98, dir. rsch., dir. rehab. svcs., 1994—; dir. devel. Bridgeport Hosp. Found., Yale New Haven Health, Bridgeport, Conn., 2002—. State bd. examiner N.Y. State Phys. Therapy Licensing Exam. Profl. Svcs., Albany, 1986—; adj. asst. prof. Mt. Sinai Sch. Med., N.Y.C., 1990—. Exec. prodr.: All the King's Horses, All the King's Men: How to Prevent Head Injury in Our Children (Gold award Houston Internat. Film Festival, 1992, 1997), Save Me a Dance (Silver award Charleston Internat. Film Festival, 1997). Named one of Outstanding Young Woman Am., 1981, 83; grantee Easter Seal Rsch. Found., 1985-87, Rehab. Svcs. Adminstr. Dept. Edn., 1991, U.S. Dept. Edn., Pfizer Inc.; recipient Therapeutic Techs. Ins. award, 1989, Sci. Rsch. award Sigma Xi. Mem. Am. Phys. Therapy Assn., Am. Congress Rehab. Medicine, N.Y. Acad. Scis. Home: 371 Midlock Rd Fairfield CT 06430-1857 Office: Bridgeport Hosp 267 Grant St Bridgeport CT 06611

TWYMAN, NITA (VENITA TWYMAN), music educator; b. Beloit, Wis., July 14, 1948; d. W.R. and Geneva L. (Goodman) Corvin; m. Dennis D. Twyman, Aug. 16, 1969; children: Christopher Grant, Kevin Scott. AA with honors, Southwestern Coll., Oklahoma City, 1968; B Music Edn. cum laude, So. Nazarene U., 1971; postgrad., U. Okla., 1970-71, 91-94; MMus, Okla. City U., 1975. Piano instr. Oklahoma City Southwestern Coll., 1968-70; pvt. music instr. Twyman Piano Studio, Oklahoma City, 1968—. Adj. faculty mem. Redlands C.C., El Reno, Okla., 1995—, Rose State Coll., Oklahoma City, 2003—; creative cons. Great Start in Music ednl. music video; choir dir. Ctrl. Ch., Oklahoma City, 1989; staff accompanist Oklahoma City First Pentecostal Holiness Ch., 1966-68. Solo performances at local churches. Mem. Nat. Guild Piano Tchrs. (nat. tchr. cert., nat. adjudicator), Music Tchrs. Nat. Assn. (nat. cert. in piano and music theory, Piano Technicians Guild grantee 1991), Okla. Music Tchrs. Assn. (adjudicator), Ctrl. Okla. Music Tchrs. Assn. (sec., parliamentarian, treas., mem. various coms.), Okla. Fedn. Music Clubs (adjudicator), Oklahoma City Pianists Club (performer), Phi Kappa Lambda. Avocations: scuba diving, bicycling, water-skiing, skiing. Office: Nita Twyman Piano Studio 5915 NW 23rd St Ste 107 Oklahoma City OK 73127-1254

TYDINGCO-GATEWOOD, FRANCES MARIE, judge; b. Oahu, Hawaii, Jan. 21, 1958; d. Daniel J. and Francesca S. Tydingco; m. Robert Gatewood; children: Daniel Gatewood, Michael Gatewood, Stephen Gatewood. BA in Polit. Sci., Marquette U., 1980; JD, U. Mo., Kansas City, 1983. Law clk. to Hon. Forest W. Hanna Jackson County Cir. Ct., Kansas City, 1983—84; asst. atty. gen. Govt. of Guam, 1984—88, chief prosecutor, 1990—94; asst. prosecutor Jackson County Prosecutor's Office, Mo., 1988—90; trial judge Superior Ct. Guam, 1994—2002; assoc. judge Supreme Ct. Guam, 2002—. Profl. Tech. scholar, Govt. of Guam. Office: Supreme Ct Guam Guam Jud Ctr Ste 300 120 W O'Brien Dr Hagatna GU 96910 Home: 222 Chalan Santo Papa Ste 222 Hagatna GU 96910 Business E-Mail: ftgate@guamsupremecourt.com.*

TYDLACKA, PATRICIA ANN, retired elementary school educator; m. Donald Charles Tydlacka; children: Bridget Folse, Douglas. BS Elem. Edn., Lamar State Coll. Tech., Beaumont, 1964; MA in Counseling, Prarie View A & M, Tex., 1999. Tchr. math. Vidor Ind. Sch. Dist., Tex.; tchr. math., English Beaumont Ind. Sch. Dist., 1972—77; tchr. math., art Hamshire-Fannett Ind. Sch. Dist., 1977—84, Mayde Creek Jr. High, Katy Ind. Sch. Dist., Houston, 1985—2006; ret., 2006. Sponsor MCJH Nat. Jr. Honor Soc., Houston, 2004—06. Dir. ladies guild St. Bartholomew's Cath. Ch., Katy, Tex. Recipient Tchr. Yr., Mayde Creek Jr. High, 1997, Katy Ind. Sch. Dist., 1997, Nat. and So. Regional Tchr. Yr., Chadwick's Boston, 2000, Lifetime Achievement award, Nat. PTA, 2006; grantee, Katy Ind. Sch. Dist., 2001, 2003; scholar, Rice U., 1998, 2002, Target Stores, 1999. Mem.: Assn. Tchr. & Profl. Educators (rep. 2003—06), Parent Tchr. Assn. (life Lifetime Membership 1997).

TYL, JENNIFER AMANDA, special education educator; b. Victorville, Calif., May 4, 1976; BS in Spl. Edn., Tenn. Technol. U., 1999, MA in Spl. Edn., 2000; Ednl. Specialist in Instrnl. Leadership, Tenn. Technol. U., 2001; postgrad., Argosy U., 2004. Spl. edn. tchr. Park Creek Elem. Sch., Dalton, Ga., 2001—. Mem.: Coun. Exceptional Children (presenter nat. conf. 2002), Kappa Delta Pi. Roman Catholic. Avocations: walking, travel. Home: 411 College Dr Apt C7 Dalton GA 30720-3723 Personal E-mail: jtyl@juno.com.

TYLER, ANNE (MRS. TAGHI M. MODARRESSI), writer; b. Mpls., Oct. 25, 1941; d. Lloyd Parry and Phyllis (Mahon) T.; m. Taghi M. Modarressi, May 3, 1963 (dec. Apr. 1997); children: Tezh, Mitra. BA, Duke U., 1961; postgrad., Columbia U., 1962. Author: If Morning Ever Comes, 1964, The Tin Can Tree, 1965, A Slipping-Down Life, 1970, The Clock Winder, 1972, Celestial Navigation, 1974, Searching for Caleb, 1976, Earthly Possessions, 1977, Morgan's Passing, 1980, Dinner at the Homesick Restaurant, 1982, The Accidental Tourist, 1985, Breathing Lessons, 1988 (Pulitzer Prize for fiction 1989), Saint Maybe, 1991, (juvenile) Tumble Tower, 1993, Ladder of Years, 1995, A Patchwork Planet, 1998, Back When We Were Grownups, 2001, The Amateur Marriage, 2004, (juvenile) Timothy Tugbohom Says No, 2005, Digging to America, 2006; contbr. short stories to nat. mags. Home: 222 Tunbridge Rd Baltimore MD 21212-3422

TYLER, BEVERLY OTT, medical/surgical nurse; b. Bridgeton, N.J., Jan. 15, 1947; d. William M. and Mary Belle (Williams) Ott; m. Jack D. Tyler, Jr., Oct. 4, 1981; 1 child, Lindsey Tyler. Diploma, Hosp. of the U. of Pa., Phila., 1968. Cert. perioperative nurse, CNOR, Cert. Bd. Peripentive Nursing, 2001. Staff nurse, oper. room U. Pa. Hosp., Phila.; staff nurse to head nurse Elmer (N.J.) Community Hosp.; staff nurse, oper. room Burdette Tomlin Meml. Hosp., Cape May Court House, N.J., head nurse. Med. explorer leader Boy Scouts Am., 9 yrs. Recipient Award of Merit, Boy Scouts Am. Mem. AORN (past pres., bd. dirs., treas./adv., item writer for cert. exam). E-mail: jtyler605@comcast.net.

TYLER, CECILIA KAY, retired military officer; b. McCall, Idaho, May 18, 1956; d. Cecil Edward and Ruby Ilene (Wine) Oatney; m. Nelvin Eugene (Gene) Tyler Jr., Dec. 24, 1991. BBA in Acctg., Idaho State U., 1978; MS in Econs. and Ops. Research, Colo. Sch. Mines, 1987; MS in Nat. Resourcing Strategy, Nat. Def. U., 2000; student, Command and Gen. Staff Coll., Leavenworth, Kans., 1989—90, Indsl. Coll. Armed Forces Nat. Def. U., Ft. McNair, Washington, 1999—2000. Commd. 2d lt. U.S. Army, 1978, advanced through grades to col., 2000, platoon leader A, B and C Cos. 8th Signal Battalion Bad Kreuznach, Fed. Republic of Germany, 1978-81, logistics officer, 1981; promoted to capt., 1982; divsn. radio officer 2AD U.S. Army, Ft. Hood, Tex., 1982—83, comdr. C co. 142d Signal Battalion, 1983—85, chief market analysis 6th Recruiting Brigade Ft. Baker, Calif., 1987-89; promoted to maj., 1990; chief strategic systems plans br. 5th Signal Command U.S. Army, Fed. Republc of Germany, 1990-91, chief plans & programs div., 1991, exec. officer 509th Signal Battalion Camp Darby Italy Camp Darby, Italy, 1991-92, exec. officer office dep. chief staff, info. mgmt. Heidelberg, Germany, 1992-94, promoted to lt. col., 1994; dep. brigade comdr. 2d Sig BDE, Mannheim, Germany, 1994—96; comdr. 504th Signal Battalion, Fort Huachuca, Ariz., 1996-98; chief current ops. divsn. Army Signal Command, Fort Huachua, Ariz., 1998-99; dep. dir. Coalition Warfare, Internat. Cooper. Office of Under Sec. of Def. Acquisition, Tech. & Logistics Pentagon, Washington, Va., 2000—04; sr. sys. analyst B2C, Inc., 2005—06, NWSS task lead for def. threat reduction agy., 2006—. Pres. 4-H Club, Valley County, Idaho, 1973-74. Mem. Armed Forces Communication-Electronics Assn., Assn. U.S. Army. Avocations: skiing, sewing, fishing. Home: 8661 Pohick Forest Ct Springfield VA 22153 Office: B2C Inc 200 Daingerfield Rd Ste 101 Alexandria VA 22314 Office Phone: 703-822-8806. Personal E-mail: tylercg@cox.net. Business E-Mail: tylerc@saic-trsc.com.

TYLER, DANA, anchor; b. Columbus, Ohio; BA in Mktg. and Broadcast Journalism, Boston U. Intern WBNS-TV, Columbus, gen. assignment reporter, 1981—83, co-anchor weekday newscasts, 1983—90; weekend co-anchor/corr. WCBS-TV, N.Y.C., 1990—. Lectr. in field. Vol. N.Y.C. Sch. Vol. Programs. Honored by Harlem YMCA, Y of Greater N.Y.; recipient Emmy award for outstanding anchor, 1987, Emmy award for outstanding newscast, 1996, Emmy award for coverage of NYC Blackout, 2004. Office: WCBS-TV/CBS Corp 524 W 57th St New York NY 10019-2924

TYLER, EIKO NAKAYAMA, mathematician, educator; arrived in U.S., 1968; d. Motouemon and Otome Nakayama; m. William Anthony Tyler, Feb. 2, 1970; children: Lea Andrea Darrah, Stacy Alicia, Erica Adrian. BS in Math., U. Calif., Davis, 1990, MA in Math., 1992, PhD in Math., 2001. Assoc. instr. math. U. Calif., Davis, 1996—98, lectr. math., 2001—02; adj. prof. math. Am. River Coll., Sacramento, 2002, Cosumnes Coll., Sacramento, 2002—03, Sierra Coll., Rocklin, Calif., 2002—03; lectr. math. Chaminade U., Honolulu, 2003—04, asst. prof. math., 2004—, program advisor math., 2004—, advisor to math club, 2003—. Author: Manifolds on Which Analysis Meets Topology, 2001; translator: A Mathematical Gift I, II, 2004, A Mathematical Gift III, 2005. Mem. Svc. Learning FAcility/Chaminade U., 2003; chair Kyoto Now Chaminade, 2003. Grantee Kyoto Now Chaminade, The Marianist Sharing Fund, 2006. Mem.: Japan Math. Biology Assn., Am. Math. Soc., Math. Assn. Am.

TYLER, GAIL MADELEINE, nurse; b. Dhahran, Saudi Arabia, Nov. 21, 1953; (parents Am. citizens); d. Louis Rogers and Nona Jean (Henderson) T.; m. Alan J. Moore, Sept. 29, 1990; 1 child, Sean James. AS, Front Range C.C., Westminster, Colo., 1979; BSN, U. Wyo., 1989. RN, Colo. Ward sec. Valley View Hosp., Thornton, Colo., 1975-79; nurse Scott and White Hosp., Temple, Tex., 1979-83, Meml. Hosp. Laramie County, Cheyenne, Who., 1983-89; dir. DePaul Home Health, 1989-91; field staff nurse Poudre Valley Hosp. Home Care/Poudre Care Connection, 1991-98, Rehab. and Vis. Nurses Assn., Fort Collins, Colo., 1999—2003; resource pool nurse Poudre Valley Hosp., Fort Collins, Colo., 2003—. Parish nurse Rocky Mountain Parish Health Ministry Orgn., pres., 2004—05, past. pres., 2005—06. Avocations: doll collecting, sewing, reading, travel. Office: Poudre Valley Hosp 1024 S Lemay Ave Fort Collins CO 80524

TYLER, HELENE RENÉE, mathematics professor; b. N.Y.C., Mar. 20, 1970; d. Irwin and Gail Iris Tyler; m. Ronald Zwerdling. BA, Purchase Coll., 1993; MA, Syracuse U., 1996, PhD, 2002. Asst. prof. Manhattan Coll., Riverdale, NY, 2002—. Mem.: Math. Assn. Am., Am. Math. Soc. Office: Manhattan College Manhattan College Pkwy Bronx NY 10471

TYLER, JANET IRENE, music educator; b. Topeka, June 30, 1965; d. John Thomas and Norma Jean Robinson; m. Michael Ray Tyler, Oct. 3, 1997. MusB, MusM, U. Kans., 1992. Grad. tchg. asst. U. Kans., Lawrence, 1990—92; dir. choir Garside Mid. Sch., Las Vegas, Nev., 1993—95, Eldorado H.S., Las Vegas, 1995—. Composer (vocal composition): Just Look at Us Now, 2002. Mem.: Music Educators Nat. Conf., Am. Choral Dirs. Assn. (chair vocal jazz 1993—), Internat. Assn. Jazz Edn. (pres. 2002—05). Democrat. Avocations: dog breeding, organist, interior design. Office: Eldorado H S Choral Music Dept 1139 N Linn Ln Las Vegas NV 89110 Office Phone: 702-799-7200 4050.

TYLER, LIV, actress; b. Portland, Maine, Jan. 7, 1977; d. Steven Tyler (lead singer: Aerosmith) and Bebe Buell; m. Royston Langdon, Mar. 25, 2003; 1 child. Motion picture actress and print model. Actress (films): Silent Fall, 1994, Heavy, 1995, Empire Records, 1995, Stealing Beauty, 1996, That Thing You Do!, 1996, Inventing the Abbotts, 1997, U-Turn, 1997, Armageddon, 1998, Onegin, 1999, The Little Black Book, 1999, Cookie's Fortune, 1999, Plunkett & MacLeane, 1999, Dr. T & the Women, 2001, One Night at McCool's, 2001, Lord of the Rings: The Fellowship of the Ring, 2001, The Lord of the Rings: The Two Towers, 2002, The Lord of the Rings: The Return of the King, 2003, Jersey Girl, 2004.; appeared in Aerosmith's music video, Crazy, 1994. Office: c/o Creative Artists Agy 9830 Wilshire Blvd Beverly Hills CA 90212-1804*

TYLER, PEGGY LYNNE BAILEY, lawyer; b. Seattle, Oct. 15, 1948; d. John Thomas and Doris Mae (Lindgren) Bailey; m. Tom Kenneth Newton, May 25, 1975 (div. 1980); m. Allan Gregory Lambert, Aug. 3, 1980 (div. May 1996); m. Charles Kevin Tyler, Sept. 12, 1997; children: Eli Raven, Joshua Alec. BA in Psychology, Beloit Coll., 1970; MS in Counseling Psychology, Ill. Inst. Tech., 1973; JD, Syracuse U., NY, 1978. Bar: D.C. 1983. Mental health specialist Ill. Dept. Mental Health, Chgo., 1971-72; mem. rsch. faculty Cornell U., Ithaca, N.Y., 1973-75; assoc. O'Connor, Sovocool, Pfann and Greenburg, Ithaca, 1978, Dacy, Richin & Meyers, Silver Springs, Md., 1979-81; ins. adminstr. Nat. Assn. Broadcasters, Washington, 1981-86, dir. ins. programs, 1986-90; assoc. gen. counsel Architect of the Capitol, Washington, 1990—. Co-author, editor: Broadcaster's Property and Liability Insurance Buying Guide, 1989. Bd. dirs. Hartford-Thayer Condominium Assn., 1994-2006, pres., 1995-96, sec., 1996-2000, treas., 2000-05. Mem. D.C. Bar Assn. (mem. steering com. of arts entertainment, sports law sect. 1989-90, sect. editor newsletter 1989-90). Independent. Jewish. Avocations: antiques, gourmet cooking, ballet. Office: Architect of the Capitol Office General Counsel Rm H2-265A Ford House Office Bldg Washington DC 20515-0001 Office Phone: 202-225-1210. Business E-Mail: ptyler@aoc.gov.

TYLER, WAKENDA KACHINA, orthopedist, surgeon, researcher; b. Phila., June 9, 1975; d. Page L. and Barbara L. Tyler. BA, Millersville U., Millersville, Pa., 1997; MA in Pub. Health, Johns Hopkins Sch. of Pub. Health, Balt., 2001; MD, Johns Hopkins Sch. of Medicine, Balt., 2002. Orthopaedic surg. resident Hosp. for Spl. Surgery, NY, 2002—. Scholar Deborah J Joyner High Achievement Award, Monumental City Med. Soc., 2001, Watt-Hansel Scholarship, Johns Hopkins Sch. of Pub. Health, 2000. Mem.: Am. Acad. Orthopaedic Surgeons (life), Phi Beta Kappa, Alpha Omega Alpha. Liberal. Avocations: running, rock climbing, scuba diving, poetry. Office: Hosp for Spl Surgery 535 East 70th St New York NY 10021

TYNDALL, KRYSTAL GWEN, secondary school educator; b. Jacksonville, N.C., July 20, 1979; d. Wilfred Travis and Margie Gwen Tyndall. BA, Meredith Coll., Raleigh, N.C., 2001. Tchr. dance Broughton H.S., Raleigh, NC, 2001—. Mem.: Dance Assn. N.C. Educators (pres. exec. bd. 2003—05, bd. dirs. 2001—06, named N.C. Dance Educator of Yr. 2004), N.C. Alliance for Athletics, Health, Phys. Edn. and Dance (exec. bd. 2003—05). Democrat. Home: 3050-202 Trailwood Pines Lane Raleigh NC 27603 Office: Broughton High School 723 St Mary's Street Raleigh NC 27605 Office Phone: 919-856-7810. Personal E-mail: ktyndall@wcpss.net.

TYNER, BARBARA JANE, art historian, writer; b. Los Angeles, Calif., June 20, 1962; d. James Grant and Doreen Margaret Tyner; m. Richard Michael Plunkett, July 8, 2001. BA, U. Calif., Los Angeles, 1987; MA in Art Edn., U. N.Mex, Albuquerque, 1998. English editor, writer ArtSpace Publications, Seoul, Republic of Korea, 1988—89; arts and women's issues writer Various Publications, 1990—; archeologist Southwestern United States, N.Mex., 1991—94; dir., instr. Art Fundamentals, Albuquerque, 1999—; instr., art history, women's studies Albuquerque TVI Coll., 2001—; guest lectr. Feminist Rsch. Inst., U. of N.Mex, 2005. Exhibitions include U. of N. Mex. Dept. of Art Edn., N. Mex. Art League, Crashing Thunder Studio Gallery, N. Mex., Galeria Gecko, Oaxaca, Mex. Vol. fund-raiser Lance Armstrong Found., Austin, Tex., 2002—06; vol. art instr. Palo Duro Sr. Ctr., Albuquerque, 1999—2006. Nominee Governor's award, Gov. of N.Mex, 2006; recipient Five N.Mex State Championship Rd. Cycling medals, Am. Cycling Assn., 2004; Grad. fellowship, U. of N.Mex, 1995—96. Mem.: AAUW, Nat. Mus. of Women in the Arts. Achievements include creator and director of Sunshine Spin Productions, a fundraising body for the Lance Armstrong Foundation supporting cancer survivorship. Avocations: painting, road cycling, gardening, travel, birdwatching. Home: 317 Vassar Dr SE Albuquerque NM 87106 Office Phone: 224-363-0983.

TYNER, LEE REICHELDERFER, lawyer; b. Annapolis, Md., Mar. 12, 1946; d. Thomas Elmer and Eleanor Frances (Leland) Reichelderfer; m. Carl Frederick Tyner, Aug. 31, 1968; children: Michael Frederick, Rachel Christine, Elizabeth Frances. BA, St. John's Coll., 1968; MS, U. Wash., 1970; JD, George Washington U., 1975. Bar: DC, US Dist. Ct. (DC), US Ct. Appeals (4th cir., 1st cir., 9th cir., DC cir., 5th cir., 8th cir., 11th cir., 10th cir.), US Ct. Claims, US Supreme Ct. Profl. staff US Senate Commerce Com., Washington, 1970-72; trial atty. Land and Natural Resources div. US Dept. Justice, Washington, 1975-85; atty. Office of Gen. Counsel US EPA, Washington, 1985—. Bd. dirs. Grace Episcopal Day Sch., Silver Spring, Md., 1987-89, vestry Grace Episcopal Ch., 1997-2003, 2004—, sec., 2004-; den leader, cubmaster Boy Scouts Am., Silver Spring, 1987-91. Recipient Bronze medals, US EPA, 1988, 1992, 2002, 2003, 2006. Mem.: Order of the Coif. Episcopalian. Home: 1401 Geranium St NW Washington DC 20012-1401 Office: US EPA 2366A 1200 Pennsylvania Ave NW Washington DC 20460 Personal E-mail: skildpadde@aol.com. Business E-Mail: tyner.lee@epa.gov.

TYNG, ANNE GRISWOLD, architect; b. Kuling, Kiangsi, China, July 14, 1920; d. Walworth and Ethel Atkinson (Arens) T.; 1 child, Alexandra Stevens. AB, Radcliffe Coll., 1942; M of Architecture, Harvard U., 1944; PhD, U. Pa., 1975. Assoc. Stonorov & Kahn, Architects, 1945-47; assoc. Louis I. Kahn Architect, 1947-73; pvt. practice architecture Phila., 1973—; adj. assoc. prof. architecture U. Pa. Grad. Sch. Fine Arts, 1968-96. Assoc. cons. architect Phila. Planning Commn. and Phila. Redevel. Plan, 1954; vis. disting. prof. Pratt Inst., 1979-81, vis. critic architecture, 1969; vis. critic architecture Rensselaer Poly. Inst., 1969, 78, Carnegie Mellon U., 1970, Drexel U., 1972-73, Cooper Union, 1974-75, U. Tex., Austin, 1976; lectr. Archtl. Assn., London, Xian U., China, Bath U., Eng., Mexico City, Hong Kong U., 1989, Baltic Summer Sch., Architecture and Planning, Tallinn, Estonia, Parnu, Estonia, 1993, Alicante U., Spain, 1997, Barcelona U., Spain, 1997; panel spkr. Nat. Conv. Am. Inst. Architects, N.Y.C., 1988, also numerous univs., throughout U.S. and Can.; asst. leader People to People Archtl. del. to China, 1983; vis. artist Am. Acad., Rome, 1995. Subject of films Anne G. Tyng at Parsons Sch. of Design, 1972, Anne G. Tyng at U. of Minn., 1974, Connecting, 1976, Forming the Future, 1977; interview by Robert Kirkbride, Form is Number and Number is Form, 2005; work included in Smithsonian Travelling Exhbn., 1979-81, 82, Louis I. Kahn: In the Realm of Architecture, 1990-94, Mus. Contemporary Art Travelling Exhbn., L.A., 1998—; author, editor: Louis Kahn to Anne Tyng, The Rome Letters 1953-1954, 1997; contbr. articles to profl. publs.; prin. works include Walworth Tyng Farmhouse (Hon. mention award Phila. chpt. AIA 1953); builder (with G. Yanchenko) Probability Pyramid, 1984. Fellow, Graham Found. for Advanced Study in Fine Arts, 1965, 1979—81. Fellow AIA (Brunner grantee N.Y. chpt. 1964, 83, dir., mem. exec. bd. dirs. Phila. chpt. 1976-78, John Harbeson Disting. Svc. award Phila. chpt. 1991); mem. Nat. Acad. Design (nat. academician), C.G. Jung Ctr. Phila. (planning com. 1979-97), Form Forum (co-founder, planning com. 1978-85). Democrat. Episcopalian. Office Phone: 415-464-1424.

TYO BOSCOE, DENISE MARIE, art educator; b. Gouveneur, N.Y., Aug. 25, 1957; d. James Robert and Patricia Boscoe; children: Ian Michael Tyo, Erin Marie Tyo, Hayden James Tyo. BS, SUNY, Potsdam, 1991; MA, SUNY and St. Lawrence U., Potsdam and Canton, N.Y., 2003. Workshop facilitator Robert Moses Park State, Massena, NY, Massena Pub. Libr.; art instr. Lisbon (N.Y.) Ctrl. Sch., Malone (N.Y.) Ctrl. Sch. Pres., facilitator art club Lisbon Cen. Sch., 1998—, pres., facilitator dance club, 2006; vol. vis. artist-in-residence pub. schs., Trinidad and Tobago, 03; guest lectr. SUNY, Potsdam, 2004. Exhibitions include Gibson Gallery, Potsdam, SUNY, 1988—91. Recipient departmental art scholarship, SUNY, Potsdam, 1991. Mem.: Dance Club. Office: Lisbon Cen Sch 6866 County Rte 10 Lisbon NY 13658

TYRRELL-MEIER, CASSANDRA B., banker; b. Compton, Calif., May 15, 1942; d. Edwin Rudolph and Katherine Jahn; m. Harlan Meier, May 27, 2000; children: Dennis, Debra, Cassandra, Daniel, Michael; stepchildren: Jeffrey L. Meier, Chris H. Meier, Julie F. Moser, Vickie K. Hess. Degree in banking, Am. Inst. Banking, Denver, 1958; certificate, Dale Carnegie, 1979. Proof operator Internat. Bank & Trust, Denver, 1958-89, First Nat. Bank, Denver, 1959-61; motor bank supr. Jefferson Bank & Trust, Lakewood, Colo., 1972-76; head teller United Bank of Broomfield, Colo., 1976-79; auditor Western Nat. Bank, Denver, 1980-82; sr. v.p., cashier North Valley Bank, Thornton, Colo., 1982—. Asset/liability mgmt. North Valley Bank, 1988—, 401(K) trustee, 1988—, also mem. investment com. Mem. North Metro C. of C., Fin. Mgmt. Soc., Fin. Women Internat., Western Ind. Bankers and CFOs, Colo. Disaster Back-up Assn., Am. Mgmt. Assn., Ind. Banker Network. Roman Catholic. Home: 14850 E 120th Ave Brighton CO 80603-6905 E-mail: ctyrrell@nvbank.com.

TYSON, CHARLOTTE ROSE, software development manager; b. San Mateo, Calif., Aug. 14, 1954; d. Herbert Parry and Rose (Goldner) T.; m. Edward Phillip Sejud, Aug. 11, 1979; children: Laura Rose, Elizabeth Ann. AA in Physics, DeAnza Coll., 1974; BS in Elec. Engring., U. Calif.-Berkeley, 1976; MS in Computer Info. Systems, U. Denver, 1992. From engr. to engr. to mgr. software mfg. ops. IBM, Boulder, Colo., 1976—93; systems devel. and program mgr. Storage Tek, Louisville, Colo., 1993—, mgr. software solutions integrated svcs., 1996-97, mgr. multiplatform solns devel., 1997-98, mgr. client server tape software, 1999-2000, dir. storage solutions integration ctr., 2000—02, dir. storage solutions ops., 2002—. V.p. corp. adv. bd. women in engring. program U. Colo., 2000—; women in tech. com. 2001 Women's Summit, 2001—; corp. rep. to bd. dirs. Colo. Software and Internet Assocs., 2002—. Leader Mountain Prairie Coun. Girl Scouts U.S., 1992-94; fund raiser Longmont Symphony Guild, 1994; team mgr., treas. girls competitive soccer St. Vrain Express, 1995-96; dir. Longmont Lightning Girls Competitive Basketball League, 1997-99; host gardener Longmont Garden Tour, 1999; gen. mgr. girls basketball Longmont H.S., 2000— Mem.: IEEE (chmn. Denver sect. 1982—83, Debt of Gratitude award 1981, 1982, 1983), AAUW, Electromagnetic Compatability Soc. (chmn. Boulder chpt. 1979—91, registration chmn. EMC internat. symposium 1981, bd. dirs. 1985—90, awards and membership chmn. 1986—90, treas. 1998, EMC symposium 1996—99), Soc. Women Engrs. (sr.; life), St. Vrain Hist. Soc. Office: Storage Tek One StorageTek Dr Louisville CO 80028-0001 E-mail: charlotte_tyson@storagetek.com.

TYSON, CICELY, actress; b. NYC, Dec. 19, 1933; d. William and Theodosia Tyson; m. Miles Davis, 1981 (div. 1988). Student, NYU, Actors Studio; doctorate (hon.), Atlanta U., Loyola U., Lincoln U. Former sec., model. Co-founder Dance Theatre of Harlem; bd. dirs. Urban Gateways Actor: (off-Broadway plays) The Blacks, 1961-63, Moon on a Rainbow Shawl, 1962-63, Tiger, Tiger, Burning Bright, Broadway; (films) Odds Against Tomorrow, 1959, The Last Angry Man, 1959, A Man Called Adam, 1966, The Comedians, 1967, The Heart is a Lonely Hunter, 1968, Sounder, 1972 (Best Actress, Atlanta Film Festival, Nat. Soc. Film Critics, Acad. award nominee, Best Actress, Emmy award, Best Actress in a spl., 1973), The Blue Bird, 1976, The River Niger, 1976, A Hero Ain't Nothin' but a Sandwich, 1978, The Concorde-Airport 79, 1979, Bustin' Loose, 1981, Fried Green Tomatoes, 1991, Hoodlum, 1997, Because of Winn-Dixie, 2005, Diary of a Mad Black Woman, 2005 (Outstanding Supporting Actress in a Motion Picture, NAACP Image award, 2006), Madea's Family Reunion, 2006, Fat Rose and Squeaky, 2006, Idlewild, 2006; (TV series) East Side, West Side, 1963-64, The Guiding Light, 1966, Sweet Justice, 1994-95; (TV films) Marriage: Year One, 1971, The Autobiography of Miss Pittman, 1974 (Emmy award Actress of the Year, 1974, Emmy award Best Lead Actress in a Drama, 1974), Just an Old Sweet Song, 1976, Wilma, 1977, A Woman Called Moses, 1978, The Marva Collins Story, 1981, Benny's Place, 1982, Playing With Fire, 1985, Samaritan: The Mitch Snyder Story, 1986, Acceptable Risks, 1986, Intimate Encounters, 1986, The Women of Brewster Place, 1989, Heat Wave, 1990 (Cable Ace award 1991), The Kid Who Loved Christmas, 1990, When No One Would Listen, 1992, Duplicates, 1992, House of Secrets, 1993, Oldest Living Confederate Widow Tells All, 1994 (Emmy award Best Supporting Actress), Road to Galveston, 1996, Bridge of Time, 1997, The Prince of Heaven, 1997, Riot, 1997, Ms. Scrooge, 1997, Mama's Flora Family, 1998 (Image award 1999), Always Outnumbered, 1998, A Lesson Before Dying, 1999, Aftershock: Earthquake in NY, 1999, Jewel, 2001, The Rosa Parks Story, 2002; (TV miniseries) Roots, 1977, King, 1978,; TV appearances include: Frontiers of Faith, 1961, The Nurses, 1962, Naked City, 1963, I Spy, 1965, 66, Cowboy in Africa, 1967, The FBI, 1968, 69, Here Comes the Brides, 1970, Mission Impossible, 1970, Gunsmoke, 1970, Emergency!, 1972, B.L. Stryker, 1990, Touched by an Angel, 2000, The Outer Limits, 2000. Trustee Human Family Inst.; trustee Am. Film Inst. Recipient Vernon Price award, 1962; also awards NAACP Nat. Council Negro Women; Capitol Press award. Mem.: Delta Sigma Theta (hon.).*

TYSON, CYNTHIA HALDENBY, academic administrator; b. Scunthorpe, Lincolnshire, Eng., July 2, 1937; came to U.S., 1959; d. Frederick and Florence Edna (Stacey) Haldenby; children: Marcus James, Alexandra Elizabeth. BA, U. Leeds, Eng., 1958, MA, 1959, PhD, 1971; DHL (hon.), Mary Baldwin Coll., 2003, Queens U., Charlotte, 2006. Lectr. Brit. Council, Leeds, 1959; faculty U. Tenn., Knoxville, 1959-60, Seton Hall U., South Orange, NJ, 1963-69; faculty, v.p. Queens Coll., Charlotte, NC, 1969-85; pres. Mary Baldwin Coll., Staunton, Va., 1985—2003, pres. emerita, 2003—; pres. Robert Haywood Morrison Found., 2002—. Pres. adv. cir. Queens U., Charlotte, NC, 2005—; WDAV radio adv. bd. Davidson (NC) Coll., 2005—. Contbr. articles to profl. jours. Mem. Va. Internat. Trade Comm., Richmond, 1987; trustee Am. Frontier Culture Mus., Va.; mem. Va. Lottery Bd., 1987-94; chair selection com. State of Va. Rhodes Scholarship Competition, 1993-97; bd. dirs. Cmty. Found. Staunton, Augusta County and Waynesboro, 1993-98; mem. adv. bd. WDAV Radio of Davidson Coll., 2005—; mem. pres.'s adv. cir. Queens U. of Charlotte, NC, 2005—. Fulbright scholar, 1959; Ford Found. grantee Harvard U., 1981; Shell Oil scholar Harvard U., 1982. Mem.: Assn. Presbyn. Colls. and Univs. (bd. dirs. 1998), So. Assn. Colls. and Schs. (vice chair 1998, pres.-elect 2001, pres. 2002), Assn. Va. Colls. and Univs. (pres. 1997—98), So. Assn. Colls. for Women (pres. 1980—81), Mary Baldwin Coll. (hon.), Phi Beta Kappa. Republican. Office: Robert Haywood Morrison Found 1373 East Morehead St Ste 2 Charlotte NC 28204-2979

TYSON, KATHLEEN HAYHURST, educational association administrator; b. Oakland, Calif., Mar. 6, 1947; d. Amos Ira and Marie Gertrude (Sanchez) Hayhurst; 1 child, Kathryn Elena. BA, San Jose State U., Calif., 1971; MA, St. Mary's Coll., Moraga, Calif., 1995. Cert. tchr. Calif., tchr. learning handicapped Calif., resource specialist Calif., in addiction studies. Tchr. elem. Richmond Sch. Dist., Calif., 1972—79; tchr. learning handicapped Richmond Elem. Sch. Dist., Calif., 1979—81; resource specialist West Contra Costa Sch. Dist., Pinole and Hercules, Calif., 1992—. Software designer Beck Tech., Berkeley, Calif., 1991—92; coord. At Risk Program Dept. Drug and Alcohol, Hercules, Calif., 1994—97; dir. Reading Intervention Program Elem. Schs., Hercules; instr. lang. arts Calif. State U., Hayward San Pablo; ednl. cons., intervention tutor, Orinda; supr. student tchrs. San Francisco State U., Hercules, 2005. Author: (Intervention Program) Star Trak, 1989—92, (Reading Intervention program) Firebear, 1995—2003; editor: (book) Habitats, 1998. Organizer, fund raiser Tsunami Toy Drive Orinda Sch., Hercules, 2005; facilitator, instr. Parent Workshop for At Risk Students, Hercules, 1996—97; literacy trainer staff training workshops Hercules, 1998—99; min. Unity Ch., 1999—, spiritual mentor, 1997—99; amb. People to People, Spokane, Wash., 2000. Recipient You Make a Difference award, Contra Costa County, 1991, Cert. Excellence in Svc., Contra Cost. County, 1992. Mem.: Calif. Reading Assn., Coun. for Exceptional Children, Calif. Tchrs. Assn. Avocations: gardening, reading, travel, tennis. Office: West Contra Costa Sch Dist 1616 Pheasant Dr Hercules CA 94563

TYSON, LAURA D'ANDREA, dean, finance educator; b. Bayonne, NJ, June 28, 1947; BA, Smith Coll., 1969; PhD, MIT, 1974. Prof. econ. and bus. adminstrn. U. Calif., Berkeley, 1978-98, BankAmerica dean Haas Sch. Bus., 1998—2001; chmn. Coun. Econ. Advisors Exec. Office of the Pres., Washington, 1993-95; nat. econ. advisor to Pres. U.S. Nat. Econ. Coun., Washington, 1995-96; dean London Sch. Bus., 2002—. Bd. dirs. S&C Comm., Inc., Eastman Kodak Co., Morgan Stanley, BRUEGEL, Brookings Instn., Coun. Fgn. Rels. Editor: (with John Zysman) American Industry in International Competition, 1983, (with Ellen Comisso) Power, Purpose and Collective Choice: Economic Strategy in Socialist States, 1986, (with William Dickens and John Zysman) The Dynamics of Trade and Employment, 1988, (with Chalmers Johnson and John Zysman) Politics and Productivity: The Real Story of How Japan Works, 1989, Who's Bashing Whom? Trade Conflict in High Technology Industries, 1992; econ. viewpoint columnist: Bus. Week mag. Mem. Nat. Bipartisan Commn. Future Medicare, 1997—99. Office: London Business Sch Regent's Park London NW1 4SA England Office Phone: 020 7262 5050. Office Fax: 020 7724 7875.

TYSON, LISA N., food products executive; Assoc. atty. corp. securities group Winstead, Sechrest & Minick, 1991—98; v.p., asst. gen. counsel Suiza Foods, 1998—2002; sr. v.p., dep. gen. counsel, asst. sec. Dean Foods, 2002—. Office: Dean Foods 2515 McKinney Ave Ste 1200 Dallas TX 75201-1945

TYSON, LUCILLE R., health facility administrator, geriatrics nurse; b. North Wales, Pa., Feb. 14, 1939; d. Edwin Shelly and Marion (Wenhold) Rosenberger; m. Ronald Saylor Tyson, June 29, 1963; children: Bryan, Bruce. AS, Middlesex County Coll.; BA, Wheaton Coll.; MSW, Rutgers U. Cert. gerontol. nurse; lic. social worker; RN. Dir. N.J. Parkinson Info. & Referral Ctr. Robert Wood Johnson U. Hosp., New Brunswick, NJ; human svcs. planner Middlesex County Dept. Human Svcs., New Brunswick; dir., right to know regulations Roosevelt Hosp., Edison, NJ; dir., quality assurance Cen. N.J. Jewish Home for Aged, Somerset, NJ. Mem. Piscataway (N.J.) Twp. Coun., 1990—; mem. rev./appeals com. Middlesex County Dept. Human Svcs., 1992—; bd. dirs. Metlar Ho. Found.; mcpl. dir. Piscataway Rep. Orgn., 1995—; county committeewoman Middlesex County Rep. Orgn., 1995—2001; rep. exec. committeewoman Greenville County, SC, 2001-. Mem. ANA, NASW, Nat. Soc. DAR, N.J. Nurses Assn., Assn. Quality Assurance Profls. N.J., Geriatric Inst. N.J., Rep. Exec. Comm.

TYSZKA, CORTNEY MARIE, athletic trainer, educator; b. Bridgeport, Conn., Sept. 9, 1980; d. Frank Jon and Shirley Tyszka. BS in Sports Medicine, Merrimack Coll., North Andover, Mass., 2002; MS in Sch. Health Edn., So. Conn. State U., New Haven, 2005. Cert. health tchr. K-12 Conn. Athletic trainer HealthSouth Phys. Therapy and Sports Medicine, Trumbull, Conn., 2002—05; head athletic trainer, educator St. Luke's Sch., New Canaan, Conn., 2005—. Clin. instr., lectr. Sacred Heart U., Fairfield, Conn., 2003—. Mem.: Nat. Athletic Trainers Assn. (life; cert. athletic trainer). Personal E-mail: tisk101@hotmail.com.

TYTLER, LINDA JEAN, science administrator, retired state legislator; b. Rochester, NY, Aug. 31, 1947; d. Frederick Easton and Marian Elizabeth (Allen) Tytler; m. George Stephen Dragnich, May 2, 1970 (div. July 1976); m. James Douglas Fisher, Oct. 7, 1994. AS, So. Va. Coll., Buena Vista, Va., 1967. Spl. asst. to Congressman John Buchanan, Washington, 1971-75; legis. analyst US Senator Robert Griffin, Washington, 1975-77; ops. supr. Pres. Ford Com., Washington, 1976; office mgr. US Senator Pete Domenici Re-election, Albuquerque, 1977; pub. info. officer S.W. Cmty. Health Svc., Albuquerque, 1978-83; cons. pub. rels. and mktg. Albuquerque, 1983-84; account exec. Rick Johnson & Co., Inc., Albuquerque, 1983-84; dir. mktg. and comm. St. Joseph Healthcare Corp., 1984-88; mktg. and bus. devel. cons., 1987-90; dir. comm. and pub. affairs Def. Avionics Systems Honeywell Inc., 1990-2000, dir. comms., 2000—01; dep. dir. pub. affairs Los Alamos Nat. Lab., 2001—05, group leader emergency response instl. svcs., 2006—. Capt. N.Mex. Mounted Patrol, 1998—2002; bd. dirs. Jobs for N.Mex., N.Mex chpt. ARC, Albuquerque, 1984; chmn. legis. campaign com. Rep. Com.; co-chair del. to China Am. Coun. Young Polit. Leaders, 1988; mem. N.Mex. Ho. of Reps., Santa Fe, 1983—95, vice chmn. appropriations and fin. com., 1985—86, chmn. Rep. Caucus, 1985—88. Recipient award, N.Mex. Advt. Fedn., Albuquerque, 1981, 1982, 1985, 1986, 1987, Honeywell Cmty. Svc. award, 1997. Mem.: N.Mex. Assn. Commerce and Industry (bd. dirs., exec. com. 1996—2002), Am. Mktg. Assn., Soc. Hosp. Planning and Mktg., Nat. Advt. Fedn., Am. Soc. Hosp. Pub. Rels. (cert.). Republican.

TZITSIKAS, HELENE, retired literature educator; b. Athens, Greece, Apr. 2, 1926; came to U.S., 1944; d. Christos Jean and Evangelia (Chouases) T. BA, Lake Forest (Ill.) Coll., 1952; MA, Northwestern U., 1954, PhD, 1963. Instr. Rockford (Ill.) Coll., 1962-63, asst. prof., 1963-65; assoc. prof. Hispanic lit. Mich. State U., East Lansing, 1965-71, prof., 1971-91, prof. emerita, 1991—. Author: Santiago Ramón y Cajal-Obra Literaria, 1965, El Pensamiento Español 1898-1899, 1967, Fernando Santiván - Humanista y Literato, 1971, 2d edit., 1985, Dos Revistas Chilenas: Los Diez y Artes y Letras, 1973, El sentimiento Ecológico, 1977, La supervivencia existencial de la mujer, 1982, El Quijotismo y la raza en la Generacion de 1898, 1988, Los exiliados argentinos en Montevideo durante la éoca de Rosas, 1991. Recipient Diana award YWCA, Lansing, Mich., 1988, cert. of employee recognition, 1988. Mem. MLA, AAUP, MLA Am., Am. Assn. Tchrs. Spanish and Portuguese, Univ. Club Mich. State U., Daus. Penelope. Greek Orthodox. Avocations: theater, music, painting, gardening. Office: Mich State U Dept Romance and Classical Langs East Lansing MI 48824 Office Phone: 517-355-8350.

UBEL, OLIVE JANE, retired secondary school educator; b. Newton, Kans., June 20, 1932; d. Arnold Jantz and Emma Decker; m. Jake Ralph Ubel, Dec. 20, 1953 (dec. Dec. 1995); children: Mary Colleen, Douglas Ralph. BS, Kans. State U., 1953, MS, 1975. Tchr. home econs. and sci. Westmoreland (Kans.) H.S., 1954—56; tchr. art Highland Park Jr. High, Topeka, 1956—58; sec. U.S. Borax and Chem. Corp., Topeka, 1958—70; tchr. art and home econs. Shawnee Heights Unified Sch. Dist. 450, Tecumseh, Kans., 1970—93; cons./ret. Kans. Assn. Family and Consumer Scis. Trustee Human Ecology Found. Bd. Kans. State U., Manhattan, 1995—2003; trustee Kans. State U. Found. Bd., Manhattan, 2002—. Mem. woman's bd. Mulvane Art Mus., Washburn U., Topeka, 1993—; elder Trinity Presbyn. Ch., Topeka, 1967—69, 1980—82, 1994—96; bd. dirs. Presbyn. Manor, Topeka, 1996—2002, Aux. League Topeka Symphony, 1998—. Mem.: PEO Internat. (chaplain, v.p. 2002—03, pres. 2003—), AAUW, Topeka Assn. Family and Consumer Sci., Kans. Assn. Family and Consumer Sci., Am. Assn. Family and Consumer Sci. (cert. family and consumer scis., programs chair), Am. Legion Aux. (Topeka chpt.), Women of the Moose, Phi Kappa Phi, Phi Delta Kappa, Kappa Omicron Nu, Delta Delta Delta, Alpha Delta Kappa. Avocations: sewing, dance, gardening, drawing and painting, design.

UCHIDA, JANICE YUKIKO, plant pathologist/mycologist, researcher; b. Kealakekua, Hawaii, Jan. 17, 1949; d. Tamotsu Tom and Misao (Oshima) Kadooka; m. Raymond Sueyoshi Uchida; children: Duane, Janelle. BA in Botany, U. Hawaii, 1970, MS in Bot. Sci., 1972, D in Bot. Sci. in Plant Pathology, 1984. Instr. dept. gen. sci. U. Hawaii, Honolulu, 1972-76, rsch. assoc. dept. plant pathology, 1976-87, asst. plant pathologist dept. plant pathology, 1987-94, assoc. plant pathologist dept. plant and environmental protection scis., 1994—. Mem. exec. com. U. Hawaii Manoa Faculty Senate, 2003—05. Assoc. editor: jour. Plant Disease, 2001, sr. editor: jour., 2003—05; contbr. rsch. articles and papers to sci. jours. Coord. Urata Music, Honolulu, 1995—. Ednl. Challenge grantee USDA, 1997-99; grantee State of Hawaii, 19800172, USDA, 1999-2004; Mentor NSF scholar, 1995-96. Mem. Am. Phytopathol. Soc., Mycol. Soc. Am., Phi Kappa Phi, Gamma Sigma Delta (assoc. editor Plant Disease 2001-2003, sr. editor 2004—, uniov. faculty senate excellence com. 2003—, Excellence in Rsch. award 2000). Office: U Hawaii Dept Plant and Eviron Protection Scis 3190 Maile Way Honolulu HI 96822-2232 Fax: 808-956-2832. E-mail: juchida@hawaii.edu.

UCHIDA, MITSUKO, pianist; b. Dec. 20, 1948; d. Fujio and Yasuko Uchida. Student, Hochschule für Musik, Vienna, Austria. Artist-in-residence Cleve. Orch., 2001—. Performer: performs with Berlin Philharm., Vienna Philharm., Cleve. Orch., LA Philharm., Chgo. Symphony Orch., London Symphony, NY Philharm., others, recs. include complete piano sonatas and concertos of Mozart, Beethoven's piano concertos, Debussy's Etudes, Schubert Sonatas and Impromptus, Schoenberg Piano Concerto, Carnegie Hall recital series Mitsuko Uchida: Vienna Revisited, 2002—. Recipient Gramophone award, 2001, Instrumental Award, Royal Philharm. Soc., 2004. Avocation: music. Address: Victoria Rowsell Artist Mgmt Ltd 34 Addington Sq London SE5 7LB England E-mail: management@victoriarowsell.co.uk.

UCKO, BARBARA CLARK, writer; b. Cambridge, Mass., Mar. 27, 1945; d. Hugh Kidder and Marie (Folsom) Clark; m. David Alan Ucko, Aug. 13, 1972; 1 child, Aaron Mark. BA in Art History, Oberlin Coll., 1967; MA in English, U. Mo., Kansas City, 1992. Copywriter Bantam Books, N.Y.C., 1974—76; promotion dir. Pocket Books, N.Y.C., 1976—77, Antioch Bookplate, Yellow Springs, Ohio, 1977; instr. composition Sch. of Chgo. Art Inst., Chgo., 1986; mgr. corp. comm. Sprint, Westwood, Kans., 1992—98; pvt. piano tchr. Kansas City, Mo., 1998—2001. Author: (novels) Family Trappings, 1985, Scarlett Greene, 1987, (short stories) Laurel Review, Nit and Wit, Open, Artful Dodge and Chatelaine. Various libr. bds., sch. vol. and hosp. bds. Calif., Mo., Washington D.C. Recipient 1st pl. award, Barbara Storck Short Fiction Competion, U. Mo., 1991, 2d pl., 1992. Mem.: Soc. Midland Authors. Democrat. Avocations: crafts, crossword puzzles, piano, walking, reading. E-mail: Barbara.Ucko@verizon.net.

UCMAKLI, NACIYE GUNGER, oncologist; b. Istanbul, Turkey, Feb. 2, 1929; arrived in U.S., 1956; d. Aziz and Vedia Isbilen; m. Alptekin Ucmakli; children: Aziz, Ahmet. MD, Istanbul U., 1956. Intern Graslands Hosp., 1956; resident Valhalla Hosp., N.Y.C., 1957—60; oncologist Roswell Park Meml. Inst., Buffalo, 1960—62, Ont. Cancer Inst., Toronto, 1962—64; radiologist Am. Mil. Hosp., Aneheim, Germany, 1965—67, Phila., 1967—69, Boston, 1969—79, San Clemente, Calif., 1979—2001, Las Vegas, Nev., 2001—06, Winchester, Calif., 2006—. Avocations: painting, gardening, swimming. Home: 32146 Spun Cotton Dr Winchester CA 92596

UDALL, VESTA HAMMOND, special education educator; b. Jacksonville, Fla., Dec. 8, 1942; d. Vesta Shields and Gladys Wilcox Hammond; m. John Scriven Udall, July 18, 1964 (div. Feb. 27, 1973); children: Adrien Evelyn, Peter John. BA, Winthrop U., 1964; MEd, U. Phoenix, 1997; postgrad., U. Fla., No. Ariz. U., Ariz. State U. Cert. tchr. Ariz. Various elem. and H.S. tchg. positions Duval County Schs., Jacksonville, 1964—68; tchr. Flagstaff (Ariz.) Jr. H.S., 1974—76, Fickett Jr. H.S., Tucson, 1976—78, Devereux Sch., Scottsdale, Ariz., 1978—80, East Valley H.S., Maricopa County Regional Sch. Dist., Phoenix, 1989—97, Madison Jail and Maricopa County Sheriff's Office, Phoenix, 1997—2000; prof. Phoenix Coll., 1998—; spl. edn. tchr. Westwood H.S., Mesa (Ariz.) Sch. Dist., 2000—. Presenter in field; developer spl. edn. programs. Precinct committeeman Rep. Party, Mesa, 1985—. Named Educator of Yr., Phoenix Sun, 1995. Mem.: Nat. Edn. Assn., Mesa Edn. Assn. Ariz. Republican. Mem. Lds Ch. Avocations: hiking, river running, birdwatching, biking. Home: 2264 E Fairfield St Mesa AZ 85213 Office: Phoenix Coll 1100 W Thomas Rd Phoenix AZ 85013 Personal E-mail: vhudall@aol.com.

UDARBE, CHRISTINE, registrar; BA in Zoology, U. Hawaii at Manoa, 1995, EdM in Tchg., 1998. Lic. tchr. Hawaii, 1998. AP biology/biology/zoology tchr. Castle H.S., Kaneohe, Hawaii, 1997—98; biology/environ. sci. tchr. Kaimuki H.S., Honolulu, 1998—2000; chemistry/biology tchr. Kalaheo H.S., Kailua, Hawaii, 2000—01; AP chemistry/gen. chemistry tchr. Kaimuki H.S., Honolulu, 2001—03, registrar, 2003—. Office: Kaimuki High School 2705 Kaimuki Ave Honolulu HI 96816 Office Phone: 808-733-4900 230.

UDY, RAE, columnist, writer; b. Ogden, Utah, Mar. 24, 1950; d. Verl Nish Udy and Elizabeth Jones White; m. Steven James Weese, Apr. 9, 1971; children: Nation Verl Weese, Luke Ray Weese. Student, Weber State U., 1968. Columnist Longview News-Jour., Longview, Tex., 1989—; lifestyle editor Marshall News Messenger, Marshall, Tex., 1999—2000. Mem. and past v.p. East Tex. Writers Assn., 1987—; former contbr. Idaho Enterprise, Harleton Happenings. Author: (book) Countdown Cooking, 1993. Mem.: Ladies Aux. of Frat. of Eagles. Democrat. Christian. Avocations: gardening, travel, camping. Office: PO Box 5965 Longview TX 75608 Office Phone: 903-777-2723. Personal E-mail: raeudy@gmail.com.

UEHLING, BARBARA STANER, academic administrator; b. Wichita, Kans., June 12, 1932; d. Roy W. and Mary Elizabeth (Hilt) Staner; children: Jeffrey Steven, David Edward. BA, U. Wichita, 1954; MA, Northwestern U., 1956, PhD, 1958; degree (hon.), Drury Coll., 1978; LLD (hon.), Ohio State U., 1980. Mem. psychology faculty Oglethorpe U., Atlanta, 1959-64, Emory U., Atlanta, 1966-69; adj. prof. U. R.I., Kingston, 1970-72; dean Roger Williams Coll., Bristol, RI, 1972-74; dean arts scis. Ill. State U., Normal, 1974-76; provost U. Okla., Norman, 1976-78; chancellor U. Mo.-Columbia, 1978-86, U. Calif., Santa Barbara, 1987-94; mem. Pacific Rim Pub. U. Pres. Conf., 1990-92; exec. dir. Bus. and Higher Edn. Forum, Washington, 1995-97. Cons. North Ctr. Accreditation Assn., 1974-86; mem. nat. educator adv. com. to Comptr. Gen. of U.S., 1978-79; mem. Commn. on Mil.-Higher Edn. Rels., 1978-79, Am. Coun. on Edn., bd. dirs. 1979-83, treas., 1982-83, mem. Bus.-Higher Edn. Forum, 1980-94, exec. com. 1991-94; sr. vis. fellow Am. Coun. Edn., 1987; mem. Commn. on Internat. Edn., 1992-94, vice chair 1993; bd. dirs. Coun. of Postsecondary Edn., 1986-87, 90-93, Meredith Corp., 1980-99; mem. Transatlantic Dialogue, PEW Found., 1991-93; mem. West Coast adv. bd. Inst. Internat. Edn., 2004—. Author: Women in Academe: Steps to Greater Equality, 1979; mem. editl. bd. Jour. Higher Edn. Mgmt., 1986-95; contbr. articles to profl. jours. Bd. dirs., chmn. Nat. Ctr. Higher Edn. Mgmt. Sys., 1977-80; trustee Carnegie Found. for Advancement of Tchg., 1980-86, Santa Barbara Med. Found. Clinic, 1989-94; bd. dirs. Resources for the Future, 1985-94; mem. select com. on athletics NCAA, 1983-84, also mem. presdl. commn.; mem. Nat. Coun. on Edn. Rsch., 1980-82. Social Sci. Rsch. Coun. fellow, 1954-55; NSF fellow, 1956-57; NIMH postdoctoral rsch. fellow, 1964-67; named one of 100 Young Leaders of Acad. Change Mag. and ACE, 1978; recipient Alumni Achievement award Wichita State U., 1978, Alumnae award Northwestern U., 1985, Excellence in Edn. award Pi Lambda Theta, 1989. Mem. Am. Assn. Higher Edn. (bd. dirs. 1974-77, pres. 1977-78), Western Coll. Assn. (pres.-elect 1988-89, pres. 1990-92), West Coast Adv. Bd., Inst. Internat. Edn., Golden Key, Sigma Xi.

UEJO, COLLEEN MISAYE, elementary school educator; b. Honolulu, Oct. 18, 1953; d. Masaichi and Esther Itoyo Uejo. EdB, U. Hawaii, Manoa, 1976, M in Spl. Edn., 1983. Tchr. Liholiho Elem., Honolulu, 1979, Tenrikiyo Preschool, Honolulu, 1976—84, Queen Emma Preschool, Honolulu, 1984—88, Kaimuki Mid. Sch., Honolulu, 1988—99, Linapuni Elem., Honolulu, 1999—. After sch. care staff Waiolani Judd Sch., Honolulu, 1971—76; big sister Big Bros./Big Sisters Hawaii, Honolulu, 1984—88; coach Spl. Olympics, Honolulu, 1988—99. Yonashiro Chojin Kai v.p. Hawaii United Okinawan Assn., Honolulu, 1994. Named Uchinanchu of Yr., Hawaii United Okinawan Assn., 1998, Honolulu Dist. Tchr. of Yr., State Hawaii Dept. Edn., 2006. Mem.: ASCD, Nat. Coun. Tchrs. for Math., Nat. Assn. for the Edn. Young Children, Coun. for Exceptional Children, Phi Delta Kappa Internat. Office: Linapuni Elementary School 1434 Linapuni St Honolulu HI 96819 Office Phone: 808-832-3303.

UGGAMS, LESLIE, entertainer; b. N.Y.C., May 25, 1943; d. Harolde Coyden and Juanita Ernestine (Smith) Uggams; m. Grahame John Kelvin-Pratt, Oct. 16, 1965; children: Danielle Nicole Pratt, Justice Harolde John Kelvin-Pratt. Student, Juillard Sch. Music, 1961-63; degree (hon.), Jarvis Coll., Tyler, Tex., Wilberforce U., Ohio. Appeared on (TV series) Beulah, 1949, featured on Sing Along with Mitch, 1961—64, starred in (Broadway plays) Hallelujah Baby, 1967 (Tony award, 1968), Her First Roman Broadway Musical, 1968, On Golden Pond, 2005 (nominated Helen Hayes award for best actress, 2005), star of (weekly TV variety show) The Leslie Uggams Show, 1969, appearances in nightclubs top TV mus. variety shows, appeared in films Two Weeks in Another Town, Black Girl, 1962, Skyjacked, 1972, Poor Pretty Eddie, 1973, appeared in (TV miniseries) Roots, ABC-TV, 1977 (Critics Choice award as best supporting actress, 1977), (TV films) Sizzle, 1981, Harlem, 1993, star (Broadway musicals) Blues in the Night, 1982, (Broadway musical) Jerry's Girls, 1985, Anything Goes, 1987, (off-Broadway) The Old Settler, 1999 (Audelco award as best actress), (dramatic play), 1999; apeared in: Thoroughly Modern Millie, 2004; star (musical play) King Hedley II, 2001 (nominated Tony award best actress, 2001), Thunder Knocking on the Door, 2002 (Audelco award best actress, 2002), (TV miniseries) Backstairs at the White House, 1979, co-host (TV series) Fantasy TV, 1982—83 (Emmy award 1983, 1983); author: The Leslie Uggams Beauty Book, 1966. Founding mem. BRAVO chpt. City of Hope, Los Angeles, 1969, treas., 1969—79. Named best singer on TV, 1962—63; recipient Drama Critics award, Newspaper and TV critics, 1968, Tony award, 1968, Emmy award, 1993. Mem.: SAG, NARAS, AFTRA, Actors' Equity Assn. Democrat. Presbyterian. Avocations: needlepoint, knitting, tennis, squash, exercising. Office: The Gage Group Inc care Phillip Adelman 315 W 57th St Frnt 4H New York NY 10019-3158 Business E-Mail: leslie@leslieuggams.com.

UHL, KATHLEEN, federal agency administrator; b. May 12, 1962; BA in Chemistry, Temple U.; MD, Med. Coll. Pa. Intern, resident Fort Benning, Ga.; fellow Uniformed Svcs. U. Health Scis.; physician Walter Reed Army Med. Ctr., Washington; with FDA, Rockville, Md., 1998—, reviewer office clin. pharmacology and biopharmaceutics, dep. divsn. dir. office post-mktg. drug risk assesment, acting divsn. dir., supervisory med. officer ctr. drug eval. and rsch., dir. Office Women's Health, 2005—. Capt. USPHS. Contbr. articles to profl. jours. Recipient Meritorious Svc. Medal. Office: FDA 5600 Fishers Ln Rockville MD 20857*

UHLMANN, JAMIE A., secondary school educator; b. Flint, Mich., Sept. 22, 1957; m. Mark A. Uhlmann, Aug. 4, 1979; children: Erika A., Nikolas A. BS, U. of Mich., Ann Arbor, 1981; MA, Wayne State U., Detroit, 1993; Edn. Specialist, Wayne State U., 1997. Tchr. Lamphere Schs., Madison Heights, Mich., 1990—, chair, 1998—. Mem.: Mich. H.S. Athletic Assn., Mich. Social Studies Assn. Roman Catholic. Avocations: coaching, kayaking, antiques. Home: 51 Devonshire Rd Pleasant Ridge MI 48069 Office: Lamphere Schools 610 W 13 mile Rd Madison Heights MI 48071 E-mail: uhlmannj@lamphere.k12.mi.us.

UHRICH, TABATHA A., education educator; b. Lebanon, Pa., Jan. 10, 1967; d. Richard J. Uhrich, Jr. and Reta J. Bingmer. BS, Va. Commonwealth U., Richmond, 1989; MEd, Pa. State U., Harrisburg, 1998; PhD, Temple U., Phila., 2005. Phys. edn. tchr. Union Canal Elem. Sch., Lebanon, Pa., 1990—2001; prof. Towson U., Md., 2001—. Co-author: (book) Simon Says.Reading is Fun, 2002. Mem.: Internat. Reading Assn., Am. Alliance Health, Phys. Edn., Recreation & Dance. Avocations: reading, surfing, mountain biking. Office: Towson U Dept Kinesiology Rm 315 8000 York Rd Towson MD 21252

UKEN, MARCILE RENA, music educator; b. Avon, SD, Sept. 16, 1931; d. Martin Andrew and Helen (Janssen) Bertus; m. Emil Jaden Uken, Dec. 8, 1953 (dec. 1990). BS, Southern State Coll., 1952. Cert. secondary sch. tchr., Nebr. Tchr. pub. sch., Delmont, S.D., 1952-53, Carroll (Nebr.) Pub. Sch., 1954-56; spl. edn. tchr. State of Nebr., Wayne, 1953-60; piano tchr. pvt. studio, Wayne, 1955. Co-chairperson Am. Cancer Soc., Wayne, 1964-76; mem. Federated Women's Club, Wayne. Fellow Nat. Fedn. Music Clubs, Music Tchrs. Nat. Assn., Nebr. Music Tchrs., Siouxland Music Tchrs.; mem. Bus. and Profl. Women. Avocations: concerts, working with youth groups, exercise, bible studies.

ULEN, GENE ELDRIDGE, elementary school educator; b. Detroit, June 13, 1939; d. James Swan and Dorothy Benson Eldridge; m. Ian Paul Ulen, Aug. 10, 1933; children: Heather Jean, Lori Dorothy. BA in Edn., Mich. State U., 1960, MA in Edn., 1961; adminstrv. credential, Point Loma U., 1987. 2nd grade tchr. San Diego Unified Schs., San Diego, 1962—70; 6th grade tchr. Crown Pointe Elem. Sch., San Diego, 1971—86; 4th-5th gifted class tchr. Cadman Elem. Sch., San Diego, 1987—2000; substitute tchr. All Saints Sch., San Diego, 2000—. Active San Diego Nat. Women Polit. Group, 1995—2000; sec. LaJolla (Calif.) Dem. Club, 2000—02. Mem.: LWV, LaJolla Book Club, Phi Delta Kappa (bd. mem. 1986—2000). Episcopalian. Avocations: roses, sailing, bridge, tennis.

ULGEN, AYSE, statistical geneticist, educator; d. Mehmet and Pervin Ulgen. BSc in Computer Sci. and Stats., U. London, 1993; PhD, SUNY, Stony Brook, 2001. Rsch. scientist Rockefeller U., N.Y.C., 2001—02; rsch. fellow Columbia U., N.Y.C., 2002—04, assoc. rsch. scientist, 2004—. Fellow Inserm, 2005—. Contbr. articles to profl. jours. Fellow, INSERM, 2005—; scholar, Fulbright, 1990, 1995; William Wilberforce scholar, Brit. Coun., 1990. Mem.: N.Y. Acad. Sci., Internat. Genetic Epidemiology Soc. Achievements include research in genetic epidemioloy and statistical genetics. Office Phone: 212-305-4344.

ULLERY, PATRICIA ANNE, marketing professional; b. Casper, Wyo., July 13, 1949; d. Warren James and Nella Marie (Hammack) U.; m. Royce Edward Gilpatric, Apr. 1, 1968 (div. 1992); children: Royce Edward Gilpatric II, Eric Wynn Gilpatric. AA, Oakland C.C., Auburn Hills, Mich., 1978; student, Oakland U., 1979; BS in Internat. Bus. and Econs., Regis U., 1992; postgrad., U. Colo., 1994—. Divsn. editor Richardson Vick, Inc., Phila., 1979-81; dir. mktg. Rocky Mountain region Flack & Kurtz, Denver, 1982-86; dir. mktg. western region M.A. Mortenson Co, Denver, 1986-88; dir. mktg. Associated Gen. Contractors Colo., Denver, 1990-91; mgr. comml. devel. Cybercon Corp., Denver, 1992—. Mem. real estate coun. U. Colo.; bd. dirs. Lower Downtown Dist., Inc., mktg. com., 1993-94. Mem. steering com. Great City Symposium '84, Urban Design Forum, Met. Denver's Great Neighborhoods, 1985, Parks and Pub. Spaces, 1986, bd. dirs. 1986-89; chair New Denver Airport design conf., 1987; mem. mktg. and mgmt. com. lower downtown task force Downtown Plan, 1986; mem. comprehensive plan land use/urban design task force City of Denver, 1987-88; bd. dirs. Community Housing Svcs., 1994; mem. Downtown Denver, Inc., 1982—. Recipient Outstanding Bus. Comm. Merit award Internat. Assn. Bus. Communicators, 1982, Fifty for Colo. award Colo. Assn. for Commerce and Industry, 1988, Ace Constrn. Excellence award Associated Gen. Contractors Colo., 1988, 91, Bus. in Arts award COlo. Bus. Com. for Arts, 1991. Mem. Soc. for Mktg. Profl. Svcs. (publicity chair Colo. chpt. 1984, v.p. 1985, pres. 1986, chair editorial com. Marketer, 1986-87, nat. bd. dirs. 1987-90, Leonardo award 1986), Ctrl. City Opera House Assn. (bd. dirs., pres. OperaPros 1993-94). Republican. Methodist. Avocations: skiing, golf, hiking, gardening, piano/. Home: 7880 W Woodard Dr Denver CO 80227-2438

ULLMAN, JOAN CONNELLY, history professor, researcher; b. N.Y.C., July 8, 1929; d. Charles James and Gladys (Mullen) Connelly; m. Edward Louis Ullman, June 14, 1967 (dec. Apr. 1976); m. Donald Elliot Spickard, Mar. 19, 1982. Student, UCLA, 1947-48; BA, U. Calif-Berkeley, 1951; MA, Bryn Mawr Coll., 1953, PhD, 1963. Commd. fgn. service officer Dept. State, 1953, served in fgn. service Washington, 1953, Guatemala, 1954-55, Madrid, 1955-58; dir. Internat. Inst., Madrid, 1958-62, 78-79; dean of students Elbert Covell Coll., U. Pacific, Stockton, Calif., 1963-66; asst. prof. history U. Wash., Seattle, 1966-68, assoc. prof., 1968-73, prof., 1973—. Vis. prof. U. Mich., Ann Arbor, 1977; guest scholar Woodrow Wilson Ctr., 1985. Author: The Tragic Week, 1968, Spanish rev. edit., 1972; contbr. articles to profl. jours.; editor, translator: Approaches To The History of Spain (Vicens), 1968. Mem. adv. bd. Seattle Psychoanalytic Assn., 1969-78; bd. dirs. Madison Park Community Council, Seattle, 1975-79; trustee Bryn Mawr Coll., 1984-90. Fellow AAUW, 1962-63; Guggenheim fellow, 1972-73; transl. grantee NEH, 1982-83, AHA Nat. Nominations com., 1976-79 Mem. Am. Hist. Assn. (Pacific Coast exec.1983-86, nominations 1974-77), Soc. for Spanish and Portuguese Hist. Studies (nominating com. 1976-79, editor bull. 1973-76), Internat. Inst. (bd. dirs. 1979-83), Real Academia de la Historia Madrid (corr.), Wash. State Jewish Hist. Soc. (bd. dirs. 1980—), Phi Beta Kappa Roman Catholic. Home: 1620 43rd Ave E # 12B Seattle WA 98112-3222

ULLMAN, NELLY SZABO, statistician, educator; b. Vienna, Aug. 11, 1925; came to U.S., 1939; d. Viktor and Elizabeth (Rosenberg) Szabo; m. Robert Ullman, Mar. 20, 1947 (dec.); children: Buddy, Wiliiam John, Martha Ann, Daniel Howard. BA, Hunter Coll., 1945; MA, Columbia U., 1948; PhD, U. Mich., 1969. Rsch. assoc. MIT Radiation Lab, Cambridge, Mass., 1945; instr. Polytechnic Inst. of Bklyn., 1945-63; from asst. prof. to prof. Ea. Mich. U., Ypsilanti, 1963—2002, prof., 2002; ret., 2002. Author: Study Guide To Actuarial Exam, 1978; contbr. articles to profl. jours. Mem. Am. Math. Assn., Am. Assn. Univ. Profs. E-mail: nullman@emich.edu.

ULLMAN, TRACEY, actress, singer; b. Slough, Eng., Dec. 30, 1959; m. Allan McKeown, 1983; children: Mabel Ellen, John Albert Victor. Student, Itaia Conti Stage Sch., London. Appeared in plays Gigi, Elvis, Grease, The Rocky Horror Show, Four in a Million, 1981 (London Theatre Critics award), The Taming of the Shrew, 1990, The Big Love, (one-woman stage show) 1991; films include Give My Regards to Broad Street, 1984, Plenty, 1985, Jumpin' Jack Flash, 1986, I Love You To Death, 1990, Household Saints, 1993, Robin Hood: Men in Tights, 1993, I'll Do Anything, 1994, Bullets over Broadway, 1994, Ready to Wear (Prêt-à-Porter), 1994, Everybody Says I Love You, 1996, Panic, 2000, Small Time Crooks, 2000, A Dirty Shame, 2004, (voice) Corpse Bride, 2005, (TV films) Women of the Night IV, 1995, Once Upon a Mattress, 2004; Brit. TV shows include Three of a Kind, A Kick Up the Eighties, Girls on Top; actress TV series: The Tracey Ullman Show, from 1987-90 (Emmy award Best Performance, Outstanding Writing, 1990, Golden Globe award Best Actress, 1987), Tracey Takes On, 1996—99 (four Emmys including Outstanding Music, Comedy and Variety Show 1997, Cable Ace award for best comedy variety series 1996), Visible Panty Lines, 2001-; albums You Broke My Heart in Seventeen Places (Gold album), You Caught Me Out, 1984, Takes on the Hits, 2002. Recipient Brit. Acad. award, 1983, Am. Comedy award, 1988, 90, 91, Emmy award for Best Performance in a Variety/Music Series for "Tracey Ullman Takes on New York", 1994. Office: IFA Talent Agy 8730 W Sunset Blvd Ste 490 Los Angeles CA 90069-2248

ULLRICH, LINDA J., medical technologist; b. Rockford, Ill., May 10, 1944; d. Glenn H. and R. Catherine (Mathews) Person; m. John R. Brody, June 11, 1966 (div. July 1978); children: Kevin R. Brody, Keith A. Brody; m. Sterling O. Ullrich Sr., Mar. 10, 1979 (dec. Oct. 1999); stepchildren: Sterling O. Jr., Eugene, Lee Anna, Michelle. BA, Thiel Coll., 1966; MPA, Kent State U., 1993, postgrad., 1996—2003. Cert. med. tech. Am. Soc. Clin. Pathologists, specialist in hematology. Staff med. tech. Sharon Gen. Hosp., Pa., 1966—76; supr. hematology, coagulation, urinalysis sects. Sharon Regional Health Sys. (formerly Sharon Gen. Hosp.), 1976—96, lab. mgr., 1996—2003; lab cons. Condell Med. Ctr., Chgo., 2003—. Edn. coord. Beaver County C.C., Pa., 1976-80; tech. supr. lab. Cancer Care Ctr., Hermitage, Pa., 1993-2003; adj. prof. Thiel Coll., Greenville, Pa., 1994-95, 97-99,; com. mem. Sharon Regional Health Sys., 1990-2003. Merit badge counselor, com. mem. Troop 67 Boy Scouts Am., Newton Falls, Ohio, 1982-95; hospice vol., 2002-03. Lutheran. Avocations: bicycling, hiking, knitting, reading. Office: Condell Acute Care 6440 Grand Ave Gurnee IL 60031 E-mail: ljullrich@netscape.com.

ULLRICH, POLLY, art critic; BA in Journalism, MA in Journalism, U. Wis., Madison; MA in Art History, Theory and Criticism, Sch. Art Inst. Chgo. Lectr. in field; served on panels and juried and curated exhbns. Independent art critic, freelance journalist for New York Times, Newsweek, Chicago Magazine, Chicago Sun-Times and the Milwaukee Journal, written analyses and reviews on contemporary art for Sculpture Magazine, frieze, American Craft, KeramikMagazin, Bridge, Metalsmith, Fiberarts, Surface Design Journal, New Art Examiner, Ceramics Art and Perception. Mem.: Chgo. Art Critics Assn. Address: 852 W Wolfram St Chicago IL 60657 E-mail: PUllr1234@aol.com.

ULLRICH, ROXIE ANN, special education educator; b. Ft. Dodge, Iowa, Nov. 10, 1951; d. Rocco William and Mary Veronica (Casady) Jackowell; m. Thomas Earl Ullrich, Aug. 10, 1974; children: Holly Ann, Anthony Joseph BA, Creighton U., 1973; MA in Teaching, Morningside Coll., 1991. Cert. tchr. Iowa, cons. in spl. edn. Iowa. Tchr. Corpus Christi Sch., Ft. Dodge, Iowa, 1973—74, Westwood Cmty. Schs., Sloan, Iowa, 1974—80, Sioux City Cmty. Schs., 1987—. Cert. judge Iowa High Sch. Speech Assn., Des Moines, 1975—; supt. Woodbury County Fair; leader 4H Club; mem. Westwood Cmty. Sch. Bd., Sloan, Iowa. Mem.: Sioux City Art Ctr., Sioux City Hist. Assn., Am. Paint Horse Assn., Am. Quarter Horse Assn., Red Hat Soc., M.I. Hummel Club, Phi Delta Kappa. Avocations: doll collector, plate collector, horse-back riding. Home: PO Box W 819 Brown St Sloan IA 51055

ULMEN, KATHRYN T., neuroscience clinical nurse specialist; b. Green Bay, Wis., Dec. 23, 1952; d. Joseph H. and Dorothy M. (Gavronski) Ulmen. RN, Holy Family Hosp. Sch. Nursing, Manitowoc, Wis., 1976; BSN, U. Wis., 1980; MS, Tex. Woman's U., Dallas, 1981. CNRN. Staff nurse U. Wis. Hosp., Madison; neurosci. clin. nurse specialist St. Vincent Hosp., Green Bay. Mem.: ANA, Am. Heart/Stroke Assn., Nat. Stroke Assn., Am. Assn. Neurosci. Nurses, Am. Brain Tumor Assn., Am. Assn. Neurol. Surgeons, Sigma Theta Tau.

ULMER, DONNA K., business educator, writer; b. Highland, Ill. d. Willard Aloysius Hartzheim and Catherine Ruth Parkes; 1 child, Angela. BSBA, MBA, So. Ill. U., Edwardsville; PhD, St. Louis U., 1999. CPA Ill. Assoc. prof. bus. Webster U., St. Louis, 2005—. Pres. Soaring Corp., Lake St. Louis, Mo., 1995—. Author: (text) Computer Accounting with QuickBooks Pro, (novel) The Creator Report. Cons. SFK, LA, 2005—06. Mem.: Mo. Soc. CPAs, AICPA (cert. info. tech. profl.). Office: Webster U 470 E Lockwood Saint Louis MO 63119 Office Phone: 314-968-6800. Business E-Mail: dulmer@webster.edu.

ULMER, EVONNE GAIL, health science association administrator; b. Bagley, Minn., Sept. 12, 1947; d. John Ferdinand and Elsie Mabel (McCollum) Lundmark; m. G. Bryan Ulmer, Jan. 11, 1969; 1 child, G. Bryan. Diploma, St. Luke's Hosp., Duluth, Minn., 1968; BS, St. Joseph's Coll., N. Windam, Maine, 1981; MHA, U. Minn., 1984; JD, T.M. Cooley Law Sch., Lansing, Mich., 1997. Bar: Mich. 1997. Staff nurse Baton Rouge Gen., 1969—70, St. Luke's Hosp., Duluth, Minn., 1968—69, 1971—72; asst. adminstr. Hickory Heights Care Ctr., Metarie, La., 1972—73; asst. head nurse Eisenhower Hosp., Colorado Springs, Colo., 1973—74; dir. patient care svcs. St. Vincent's Gen. Hosp., Leadville, Colo., 1974—78; dir. insvc., quality assurance Watsatch Hosp., Heber City, Utah, 1979; adminstr. Prospect Park Living Ctr., Estes Park, Colo., 1982—84; asst. adminstr. Estes Park Med. Ctr., 1979—84; CEO Weston County Hosp. and Manor, Newcastle, Wyo., 1984—92, Ionia County Meml. Hosp., Mich., 1992—; pres. Ionia County Health Sys., 1995—, Ulmer Law Firm Evonne G. Ulmer, PLC, 2006—. Mem. Am. Hosp. Assn. Chgo. (trustee 1998-01, past tech. small and rural governing coun., past del. region and policy bd., past chair small and rural governing com., leadership com.), Am. Soc. Healthcare Risk Mgmt. (editl. adv. bd.), Medicare Geog. Reclassification Rev. Bd., Mich. Health and Hosp. Assn. (past bd. dirs., vice-chair smaller hops. coun.). Republican. Lutheran. Home: 536 Skyview Dr Ionia MI 48846-9776 Office Phone: 616-523-1000. Personal E-mail: evonneulmer@hotmail.com. Business E-Mail: eulmer@ioniahospital.org.

ULMER, FRANCES ANN, retired state official; b. Madison, Wis., Feb. 1, 1947; m. Bill Council; children: Amy, Louis. BA in Econs. and Polit. Sci., U. Wis.; JD with honors, Wis. Sch. Law. Polit. advisor Gov. Jay Hammond, Alaska, 1975-81; former mayor City of Juneau, Alaska; mem. Alaska Ho. of Reps., 1986-94, minority leader, 1992-94; lt. gov. State of Alaska, 1995—2002; U.S. rep. to North Pacific Anadramous Fish Commn., 1994—; disting. prof. U. Alaska, Anchorage, 2003—, dir. Inst. Social and Econ. Rsch., 2004—. Office Phone: 907-786-7710. E-mail: fran.ulmer@uaa.alaska.edu.

ULRICH, JOANN D., elementary school educator; b. Mishawaka, Ind., Dec. 4, 1941; d. Thomas R. and Leona Mary Demark; m. Robert G. Ulrich, July 3, 1965; children: Jill Elizabeth, Jane Ashley Mehringer. BA, William Jewell Coll., Liberty, Mo., 1965; MA, U. Mo., Kans. City, 1970. Second grade title ii tchr. Maplewood-Richmond Heights Sch. Dist., Richmond Heights, Mo., 1965—66; elem. sch. tchr. Liberty Pub. Schools, Mo., 1966—67; elem. french tchr. Consol. Dist. #2, Raytown, Mo., 1967—73; mid. sch. history, fgn. lang. tchr. Pembroke Hill Sch., Kans. City, Mo., 1981—. Tchr. bibl. studies First Family Ch., Lenexa, Kans., 1999—. Contbr. collection of stories about love. Dir. FLOCK ministry to women First Family Ch., 2005; mentor, spkr. Moms 'n Mentors, Lenexa, 2001—04; alumni bd. of governors: chair, cmty. mentoring program William Jewell Coll., Liberty, Mo., 1999—2002; open arms ministry First Family Ch., Lenexa, Kans., 2000—06. Recipient Woman of Yr., First Family Ch., 2000; Faculty Summer grant, Pembroke Hill Alumni Assn., 1984, 1996. Mem.: Nat. Coun. Social Studies. Avocations: Bible studies, reading, foreign travel. Home: 303 Northwest Locust St Lees Summit MO 64064 Office: Pembroke Hill Sch 5121 State Line Rd Kansas City MO 64112 Office Phone: 816-936-1200. Office Fax: 816-936-1509.

ULRICH, LAUREL THATCHER, historian, educator; b. Sugar City, Idaho, July 11, 1938; d. John Kenneth and Alice (Siddoway) Thatcher; m. Gael Dennis Ulrich, Sept. 22, 1958; children: Karl, Melinda, Nathan, Thatcher, Amy. BA in English, U. Utah, 1960; MA in English, Simmons Coll., 1971; PhD in History, U. N.H., 1980. Asst. prof. humanities U. N.H., Durham, 1980-84, asst. prof. history, 1985-88, assoc. prof., 1988-91, prof., 1991-95; prof. history and women's studies Harvard U., Cambridge, Mass., 1995—, James Duncan Phillips prof. early Am. history, 1997—, dir. Charles Warren Ctr., 1997—. Audiocourse cons. Annenberg Found.; cons., participating humanist numerous exhibits, pub. programs, other projects; project humanist Warner (N.H.) Women's Oral History Project; bd. editors William & Mary Quar., 1989-91, Winterthur Portfolio, 1991—. Author: Good Wives: Image and Reality in the Lives of Women in Northern New England, 1650-1750, 1982, A Midwife's Tale: The Life of Martha Ballard Based on Her Diary, 1785-1812, 1990 (Pulitzer Prize for history 1991), The Age of Homespun: Objects and Stories in the creation of an American Myth, 2001; contbr. articles, abstracts, essays and revs. to profl. publs. Coun. mem. Inst. Early Am. History and Culture, 1989-91; trustee Strawberry Banke Mus., 1987-93. NEH fellow, 1982, 84-85, MacArthur Fellowship award, 1992-97, John Simon Guggenheim fellow, 1991-92; women's studies rsch. grantee Woodrow Wilson Fellowship Found., 1979; co-recipient Best Book award Berkshire Conf. Women's Historians, 1990; recipient Best Book award Soc. for History of Early Republic, 1990, John S. Dunning prize and Joan Kelly Meml. prize Am. Hist. Assn., 1990, Bancroft Prize for Am. History, 1991. Mem. Orgn. Am. Historians (nominating com. 1992—, ABC-Clio award com. 1989), Am. Hist. Assn. (rsch. coun. 1993-96). Office: Harvard U Charles Warren Ctr Emerson Hall 4th Fl Cambridge MA 02138

ULRICKSON, CHERYL J., elementary school educator; b. Aberdeen, SD, Apr. 24, 1950; d. Jacob J. and Rose Weber; m. John K. Ulrickson, June 24, 1974; children: Sara Ulrickson Owen, Sonja Ulrickson Butenhoff. BE, No. State U., Aberdeen, 1972; M, Minn. State U., Moorhead, 1994. Tchr. Lincoln Elem. Sch., Yankton, SD, 1972—74, Howard Hedger Elem. Sch., Aberdeen, 1975—82, West Fargo Sch. Dist., ND, 1983—91, reading specialist, 1992—. Mem.: NEA, ND Edn. Assn., West Fargo Edn. Assn., Internat. Reading Assn., Assn. Tchr. Educators, Valley Reading Coun., Beta Sigma Phi. Avocations: reading, golf, gardening. Home: 1614 15th Ave E West Fargo ND 58078 Office: West Fargo Sch Dist 631 4th Ave E West Fargo ND 58078

ULTRA VIOLET, artist; b. France, July 6, 1935; arrived in U.S., 1955; d. Pierre Collin-Dufresne and Paule Clement. BA in Art, Le Sacre Coeur, Grenoble, France, 1953; student, studio asst., Salvador Dali, 1955. Founder workshop for emerging artists, Nice, France, 1980. Author: (plays) You Are Who You Eat, 1980; musical comedy, Tabernacle of Clay, 1980; author: Fanous for Fifteen Minutes, My Years with Andy Warhol, 1988 (Frankfurt Libr. award); series of artworks, Super Sonic Angels, 1991; author: Celebration of Light, 1993, (films) The Secret Collection of Salvado Dali, 1994, Message to Andy Warhol, 2002; one-woman shows include galerie du Cirque, Paris, 1998, Gallery Hans Kostenberger, Obdach, Austria, 1998, Internat. Art Junction, Nice, 1999, Ctr. de la Terre Gallery, Alain Vagh Ramatuelle, France, 1999, Gallery Sabine Watchers, Knokke-le-Zoute, Belgijm, 1999, Winsdor Hotel, Nice, 2000, Lilo Marti Gallery, St. Paul de Vence, France, 2000, Lesbian, Gay, Bisexual and Transgender Cmty. Ctr., NYC, 2001, le Galerie Sainte-Reparate, nice, 2001, NJ City U., Jersey City, 2003, exhibited in group shows at Palais Carnoles, Menton, France, 1999, Modern Art Couture, Monte Carlo, Monaco, 1999, Musee de Prehistore regionale, Menton, 2000, Washington County Mus. Fine Arts, Hagerstown, Md., 01, Woodard Gallery, NYC, 2001, Gallery 911, Phila., 2001, 2003, numerous others. Home: 19 E 88th St New York NY 10128 Studio: Ultra Violet Studio 525 W 26th St New York NY 10001

UMAN, SARAH DUNGEY, editor; b. Dayton, Ohio, July 22, 1942; d. Arthur Bertram and Lucretia M. (Nash) Dungey; children: Michael Uman, Sebastian Rosset. Student, New Sch. for Social Rsch., 1962-64. Editl. assoc., publicity dir. Grove Press, Inc., N.Y.C., 1970—79; sr. editor Playboy Paperbacks, N.Y.C., 1979—81, Berkley Pub., N.Y.C., 1982—85; exec. editor Consumer Reports Books, Yonkers, NY, 1985—94; dir. Red Bear Editl. Svcs., N.Y.C., 1996—.

UMANSKY, DIANE, editor-in-chief; B in journalism, U. RI. Corr. Bergen Record; writer various teen publs. including Scholastic; mng. editor Nickelodeon; sr. editor First for Women; editor-in-chief MediZine Guidebook, 1995—. Freelance writer First for Women, SELF, Family Circle, American, Harper's Bazaar, Working Mother, Good Housekeeping, Weight Watchers. Office: Medizine Inc Fl 2 298 5th Ave New York NY 10110-0002 Office Phone: 212-695-2223.*

UMEH, MARIE ARLENE, language educator; b. Bklyn., Aug. 29, 1947; d. Rudolph Vasper and Erma Eunice (Hinds) Linton; m. Davidson C. Umeh, Jan. 7, 1976; children: Ikechukwu, Uchenna, Chizoba, Ugochukwu. BA, St. John's U., Jamaica, N.Y., 1970; MS, Syracuse U., 1972; MPS, Cornell U., 1977; MA, U. Wis., 1980, PhD, 1981. Instr. SUNY, Brockport, 1972-74, Oneonta, 1974-75; asst. instr. Cornell U., Ithaca, N.Y., 1976-77; prin. lectr. Anambra State Coll., Awka, Nigeria, 1982-89; substitute assoc. prof. Medgar Evers Coll., CUNY, Bklyn., 1989; adj. prof. Hostos C.C., CUNY, Bronx, 1990—2003, Queens Coll., CUNY, Flushing, N.Y., 1990; assoc. prof. English John Jay Coll., CUNY, 1990—2006, faculty advisor, 1989—. Adj. prof. SUNY, Stony Brook, 2000—. Editor: Flora Nwapa, 1998, Buchi Emecheta, 1996; editor Rsch. in African Lit., 1995, Who's Who Among American Teachers, 1998; contbg. editor: Who's Who in Contemporary Women's Writing, 2001; editor-in-chief The Flora Nwapa Soc. Newsletter, 2004-06. Recipient Africademic award, John Jay Coll. African Students Assn., 1996, Dominican Students award, 1993, PSC-CUNY award, 1998, 1999, Gender Studies award, John Jay Coll.,CUNY, 2001, Social Promotions Incorp. award, 2006; fellow Summer Tchrs. Workshop, NEH, 2003. Mem.: AAUW, MLA (African Lit. Divsn. exec. 1999—2001), Virginia Woolf Soc., N.Y. African Studies Assn., African Lit. Assn., The Flora Nwapa Soc. (pres.). Avocations: reading, writing, aerobics, jazz. Office: CUNY John Jay Coll Criminal Justice Dept English 445 W 59th St New York NY 10019-1104 Office Phone: 212-237-8726. E-mail: Msumeh@aol.com.

UMLAUF, LYNN CHARLOTTE, art educator, sculptor; b. Austin, Tex., Jan. 8, 1942; d. Charles Julius and Angeline Allen Umlauf; m. Michael Sylvan Goldberg. BFA, U. Tex., Austin, 1960—65, MFA, 1966—68. Prof. art history Rockland CC, Suffern, NY; prof. art Fairleigh Dickenson U., Teaneck, NJ, Phila. Coll. Art; prof. art & art history Kutztown State Art Coll., Pa.; prof. art history Quinnipiac Coll., Hamden, Conn.; prof. art Ohio State U., Columbus; prof. fine art Sch. Visual Arts, N.Y.C. Prof. sculpture Acad. Architecture, Wismar, Germany; prof. art Vt. Studio Ctr., Johnson; artist residency Villa Waldberta, Munich, 2002. Exhibitions include Penine Hart Gallery, N.Y.C., 1990—94, Galleria Peccolo, Livorno, Italy, 1983—2001, Galerie Biedermann, Munich, 1988—2003, Valentino Turchetto Gallery, Milan & Udine, Italy, 1982—2004, installation, Project Room, Stark Gallery, N.Y.C., 2002, Medusa Gallery, Slovenia, 2005, installation & book, Transparent Installation and Book, Sopra Tutto Libri, Prato, Italy, 2005—06. Home: 222 Bowery #6 New York NY 10012

UNDERDOWN, JOY, retired elementary school educator; b. Boston, Feb. 21, 1935; d. Nathaniel Ridley and Eleanor Johnston (Abbe) U. AA, Stephens Coll., 1954, BA, 1972; MEd, U. Mo., 1974. Cert. tchr., Mo. Tchr. kindergarten Buckley Sch., Sherman Oaks, Calif., 1955-57; tchr. nursery and kindergarten John Thomas Dye Sch., L.A., 1959-63; tchr. kindergarten Palm Valley Sch., Palm Springs, Calif., 1963-66; tchr. Buckley Sch., Sherman Oaks, Calif., 1966-70, Fairview Elem. Sch., Columbia, Mo., 1974-91; curriculum cons. Mo. Edn. Ctr., Columbia, 1991—2002; ret. Mem. NSTA (com., presenter), AAUW, Coun. Elem. Sci. Internat. (treas. 1982-86, 1998—, presenter), Mo. Tchrs. Assn. (chmn. dist. com. 1982-83), Mo. Ret. Tchrs. Assn., Delta Kappa Gamma, Pi Lambda Theta (pres. 1974-76). Avocations: travel, animals, children's literature. Home: 2900 Hal Ct Columbia MO 65203-0147 Personal E-mail: joy2cats@aol.com.

UNDERNEHR, LAURA LEE, elementary school educator; b. Tulsa, Apr. 22, 1947; d. James Marion and Opal Lee (Bradford) Garman; m. Donnie Ray Undernehr, Aug. 12, 1971. BS, Northeastern State U., 1969, MEd, 1973; postgrad., Okla. State U., 1973-85, cert., 1988. Cert. elem. edn. and reading tchr., Okla. Tchr., team leader Tulsa Pub. Schs., 1969-88, tchr., 1988—, dean of students, 1998—, asst. prin., 1998-99, prin., 1999—. Treas. Tulsa Daniel Webster Alumni Found., 1991—. Mem. NEA, Okla. Edn. Assn., Tulsa Classroom Tchrs. Assn., Tulsa County Reading Coun., Civitans (v.p. 1997—, pres.-elect Tulsa 1987-88, pres. 1989-90), Delta Zeta (pres. Tulsa chpt. 1989—). Home: 8125 S 40th West Ave Tulsa OK 74132-3042 Office: Clinton Mid Sch 2224 W 41st St Tulsa OK 74107-6706 Office Phone: 918-746-8640. E-mail: underla@tulsaschools.org, whitecoach@aol.com.

UNDERWOOD, BRENDA S., information specialist, microbiologist, grants administrator; b. Oak Ridge, Tenn., Mar. 19, 1948; d. William Henry Hensley and Maudell Townsend; m. Thomas L. Janiszewski, Feb. 14, 1984; 1 child, Thomas Zachary Janiszewski. BS, U. Tenn., 1970; MS, Hood Coll., 1980; MBA, Mt. St. Mary's Coll., 1993. Scientist I chem. carcinogenesis Frederick (Md.) Cancer Rsch. Ctr., 1977-84; microbiologist NCI/NIH, Bethesda, Md., 1984-86; sci. tech. writer Engring. and Econs. Rsch., Germantown, Md., 1987-88; spl. asst. to dir., program dir. grants div. Cancer Biology Diagnosis Ctrs., NCI/NIH, Bethesda, 1988-91; indexer, divsn. extramural activities Rsch. Analysis and Evaluation br. NCI/NIH, Bethesda, 1991—, sect. chief for rsch. documentation sect., supr. tech. info. specialist, 1991—2002; br. chief, referral and program analysis br. NICHD/NIH, 2002—. Vol. Riding for the Handicapped, Frederick, 1990-96; mem., recreational sec. Capital Hill Equestrian Soc., Washington, 1988. Mem. AAAS, Am. Soc. for Microbiology, Am. Assn. for Cancer Rsch., Women in Cancer Rsch., Federally Employed Women. Avocations: english riding, hiking, swimming, biking, gardening. Office: NICHD NIH RPAB Divsn Extramural Activ Bethesda MD 20892-0001

UNDERWOOD, CARRIE MARIE, singer; b. Muskogee, Okla., Mar. 10, 1983; d. Stephen and Carol Underwood. BA magna cum laude, Northeastern State U., 2006. Recording artist RCA Music Group, NYC, 2005—. Singer: (albums) Some Hearts, 2005, (songs) Inside Your Heaven, 2005, Jesus, Take the Wheel, 2005 (Single Record of Yr., Acad. Country Music, 2006), Some Hearts, 2005. Named Country Single Sales Artist of Yr., Billboard Music Awards, 2005, New Female Vocalist, Acad. Country Music award, 2006; recipient Top-Selling Hot 100 Song of Yr. for song Inside Your Heaven/Independence Day, Billboard Music Awards, 2005, Top-Selling Country Single of Yr., 2005, Female Video of Yr. and Breakthrough Video of Yr. for Jesus Take the Wheel, CMT Awards (Country Music TV), 2006. Baptist. Achievements include winning the fourth season of American Idol on May 25, 2005. Avocations: guitar, piano. Office: RCA Music Group 1540 Broadway New York NY 10036*

UNDERWOOD, DEANNA KAY, librarian; b. Medicine Lodge, Kans., Oct. 2, 1962; d. Kenneth Edward and Janet Sue (Hammond) Winters; m. Roger Alan Underwood, Aug. 2, 1986; children: Lane Alan, Lindsey Kay. BS in Elem. Edn., Sterling (Kans.) Coll., 1984. Tchr. 4th grade White Rock Elem. Sch., Burr Oak, Kans., 1984-86, tchr. kindergarten Esbon, Kans., 1986-87; libr. aide mid. and high schs. White Rock Schs., Esbon and Burr Oak, 1987-91, K-12 libr., 1992—. Chmn. reading com., mem. edn1. leadership team com. Unified Sch. Dist. 104, Esbon and Burr Oak, 1993—. Chmn. adminstrv. coun. United Meth. Ch., Esbon, 1989—, trustee coun., 1993—. Mem.: Kans. Assn. Sch. Librs. Republican. Avocations: reading, cooking, cross-stitch. Home: RR 1 Box 14 Esbon KS 66941-9703 Office: White Rock HS PO Box 345 633 Main St Burr Oak KS 66936-9738 Business E-Mail: dunderwood@usd.104.com.

UNDERWOOD, JANE HAINLINE HAMMONS, anthropologist, educator; b. Ft. Bliss, Tex., Oct. 30, 1931; d. Frank and Lydia (Williams) Hammons; m. Van K. Hainline, Oct. 20, 1947 (div. 1966); children: Michael K., Susan J.; m. John W. Underwood, July 4, 1968; 1 dau., Anne K. AA, Imperial Valley Coll., 1957; BA, U. Calif., Riverside, 1960; MA, UCLA, 1962, PhD, 1964. Asst. prof. U. Calif., Riverside, 1963-68; research anthropology Yap Islands, 1964, 65-66; prof. anthropology U. Ariz., Tucson, 1968-99, prof. emeritus, 1999—, assoc. dean Grad. Coll., 1979-80, asst. provost for grad. studies, 1980-82, acting dir. Sch. Health Related Professions, 1980-82, asst. v.p. research, assoc. dean Grad. Coll., 1982-87; assoc. Micronesian Area Rsch. Ctr., 1987—. Contbr. articles to profl. jours. Woodrow Wilson fellow, 1960-61; UCR Jr. Faculty fellow, 1968 Fellow AAAS; mem. Am. Assns. Phys. Anthropologists (v.p. 1980-82), Assn. Study Human Biology, Pacific Sci. Assn. (life), Assn. for Study Social Biology (bd. dirs. 1996-99), Sigma Xi (pres. U. Ariz. chpt. 1991-92). Home: 2228 E 4th St Tucson AZ 85719-5118 E-mail: kammagar@prodigy.net.

UNDERWOOD, JOANNA DEHAVEN, environmental services administrator; b. N.Y.C., May 25, 1940; d. Louis Ivan and Helen (Guiterman) U.; m. Saul Lambert, July 31, 1982; stepchildren: Jonathan Whitty, Katherine Aviva. BA, Bryn Mawr Coll., 1962; Diplome d'etudes de Civilisation francaise with honors, Sorbonne U., Paris, 1965; DS (hon.), Wheaton Coll., 1999. Co-dir. Council on Econ. Priorities, N.Y.C., 1970-73; founder, pres. INFORM, Inc., N.Y.C., 1974—. Bd. dirs. Robert Sterling Clark Found., N.Y.C., Washington, Clean Vehicle Edn. Found.; mem. Dow Environ. Adv. Coun., 1992-96; awards com. Pres.'s Coun. on Environ. Quality, 1991; mem. eco-efficiency task force Pres.'s Coun. on Sustainable Devel., 1995-96. Author (with others) Voices from the Environmental Movement: Perspectives for a New Era, 1991; co-author: Paper Profits, 1971; editor: The Price of Power, 1972; contbr. articles to profl. jours. Former circle of dirs. Planned Parenthood of N.Y.C. Recipient Region II Environ. Achievement award U.S. EPA, 1992, Adminstrs. award, 1992, Recognition award, 1987. Home: 138 E 13th St New York NY 10003-5306 Office: INFORM Inc 120 Wall St Fl 14 New York NY 10005-3904

UNDERWOOD, JULIE K., dean, former law educator; b. 1954; d. Kenneth and Shirley Underwood; m. William Young, July 4, 1991; children: David, Chris, Kate, Maggie. BA in Polit. Sci. and Sociology, DePauw U., 1976; JD, Ind. U., 1979; PhD, U. Fla., 1984. Clk. Ind. Ct. Appeals, 1979-81; instr. sch. law U. Fla., Gainesville, 1981-82, rsch. assoc. Inst. Ednl. Fin., 1981-82; asst. prof. ednl. adminstrn. U. N.D., 1982-85, assoc. prof., 1982-86, asst. dean Ctr. Teaching and Learning, 1986; asst. prof. dept. ednl. adminstrn. U. Wis., Madison, 1986-89, prof., edn. adminstrn., 1990-93, chair, dept. edn. adminstrn., 1993—94, assoc. prof. sch. law, 1992—95, dean, Sch. Edn., 2005—; interim counsel Wis. Dept. Pub. Instrn., Madison, 1990; dean, Sch. Edn. & Allied Professions Miami Univ., Ohio, 1995—98; assoc. exec. dir. gen. counsel Coun. Sch. Attys, Nat. Sch. Bds. Assn., Alexandria, Va., 1998—2005. 2d level spl. edn. reviewing officer State Wis., 1988; hearing officer Wis. Tchr. Cert., 1993. Author: Legal Aspects of Special Education and Pupil Services, 1994; editor: (with D. Monk) Microlevel School Finance: Issues and Implications for Policy, 1988, (with W. Camp and M. Connelly) Principals' Handbook: Current Issues in School law, 1989, (with D. Verstegen) The Impact of Litigation and Legislation on Public School Finance, 1989, (with W. Camp, M. Connelly and K. Lane) The Principal's Legal Handbook, 1993; asst. editor Jour. Edn. Fin., 1981-83, legis. editor, 1985-88, legal editor, 1988—; mem. author's com. Edn. Law Reporter, 1982—; editor The Sch. and the Cts.; contbr. articles to profl. jours., chpts. to books. Grantee U. Wis., 1988, 89, 90-93. Mem. Am. Edn. Fin. Assn. (bd. dirs. 1984-88, chair Outstanding Svc. award 1987-88), Nat. Orgn. Legal Problems of Edn. (chair membership com. 1987-88, bd. dirs. 1987-91, chair ann. conf. program com. 1988-89, chair publs. com. 1989-91, constl. review com. 1990-92). Office: Dean Sch Edn 123 Edn Bld Univ Wisconsin 1000 Bascom Mall Madison WI 53706-1398 Office Phone: 608-262-6137.

UNDERWOOD, KIRSTEN FEDJE, musician, educator; MusB, Willamette U., 1978; MusM, Boston U., 1981; postgrad., U. Okla., 1998—. Cellist Okla. City Philharm., 1990—96; asst. prof. Cameron U., Lawton, Okla., 1997—. Founder Lawton Cello Club, Okla. Mem.: AAUW, Am. String Tchrs. Assn., Am. Fedn. Musicians, Hardanger Fiddle Assn. Am., Lawton Bus. & Profl. Women, Gamma Beta Phi, Phi Kappa Phi, Mu Phi Epsilon, Pi Kappa Lambda (pres., Theta Sigma chpt. 1999—2004). Office: Cameron Univ Dept of Music & Theatre 2800 W Gore Blvd Lawton OK 73507 Office Phone: 580-581-2445. E-mail: kirstenu@cameron.edu.

UNDERWOOD, KRISTIN DANA, elementary school educator; b. Casper, Wyo., May 22, 1971; d. Michael Dean and Leslyn Ann Lewallen; m. Carey Dean Underwood, Mar. 1, 1997; children: Deanna, Timothy, Emily. BS, U. Wyo., Laramie, 1997, MS, 2005. Phys. edn. tchr. Natrona County Sch. Dist., Casper, 1997—, phys. edn. program coord., 2005—. Mem. phys. edn. adv. bd. Natrona County Sch. Dist. #1, 2005—, student wellness facilitator, 2005—; active Wyo. Action for Healthy Kids, 2005—. Coord. Coll. Heights Bapt. Vacation Bible Sch., Casper, 2002—, dir., 2003—. Recipient Wyo. Phys. Edn. Elem. Tchr. of Yr., 2005; Phys. Edn. Program Grant, Fed. Dept. Edn., 2004. Mem.: Nat. Assn. Sport and Phys. Edn. (Best Trainer), Wyo. Assn. Health, Phys. Edn., Recreation Dance (v.p. recreation, pres. elect), Am. Alliance Health, Phys. Edn., Recreation Dance. Office: Natrona County Sch Dist 539 Payne #4 Casper WY 82609 Business E-Mail: kristin_underwood@ncsd.k12.wy.us.

UNDERWOOD, LORI J., philosophy educator; d. Clyde L. and Linda Murray; m. David Underwood; children: Andrew, Hannah. BA in Philosophy and History, Memphis State U., 1992; MA in Philosophy, U. Memphis, 1994; PhD in Philosophy, U. Mo., Columbia, 1999. Asst. prof. philosophy Christopher Newport U., Newport News, Va., 1999—2005, assoc. prof. philosophy, 2005—. Lector St. Jerome Cath. Ch., Newport News, 2002—06. Mem.: Am. Philos. Assn. (assoc.). Office: Christopher Newport U 1 University Place Newport News VA 23606 Office Phone: 757-594-8828. Office Fax: 757-594-7349. Business E-Mail: underwo@cnu.edu.

UNDERWOOD, LUCINDA JEAN, poet, playwright, small business owner, researcher; b. Troy, Mich., Aug. 1, 1964; d. Harold L. and Betty Jo (Arms) U. Grad. high sch., Livingston, Tenn., 1982. With Dawn Wells, Nashville, 1976-80; owner, mgr. Cindy's Critter Care, Cookeville, Tenn., 1986—. Author: (poetry) The Mystic, 1996; songwriter. Mem. Nat. Pony Express Assn. Office: Cindy's Critter Care 836 Bray St Apt B Cookeville TN 38501-3733

UNDERWOOD, PATRICIA FORD, elementary school educator; b. Boise, Idaho, Dec. 22, 1957; d. Hugh Francis and Julia Grace Ford; m. Charles Arthur Underwood, June 24, 1984; children: Lindsay Frances, Hadley Moran. BA in Elem. Edn., Boise State U., Idaho, 1981. Cert. tchr. Dept. Edn. and Early Devel./Alaska, 1982, elem. tchr. K-8 State Bd. Edn. Idaho, 1982. Tchr. 2d grade Anchorage Sch. Dist., Anchorage, 1983—86, tchr. 1st grade, 1986—89, tchr. kindergarten, 1989—. Tchr. adv. bd. Nat. Energy Edn. Devel. Project, Manassas, Va., 2001—. Recipient Presdl. award for Excellence in Tchg. Math and Sci., Pres. U.S., 2004. Mem.: Anchorage Edn. Assn., NEA, Nat. Assn. for the Edn. of Young Children, NSTA, Soc. Elem. Presdl. Awardees (life). Avocations: reading, gardening, cooking, walking, sewing, quilting. Office: Inlet View Elem Sch 1219 N St Anchorage AK 99501 Office Phone: 907-277-7681. Office Fax: 907-277-7674. Business E-Mail: underwood_patty@asdk12.org.

UNGAR, ROSELVA MAY, primary and elementary school educator; b. Detroit, Oct. 31, 1926; d. John and Elva Rushton; m. Kenneth Sawyer Goodman, Dec. 26, 1946 (div. 1950); m. Fred Ungar, June 22, 1952 (div. 1977); children: Daniel Brian, Carol Leslie, Lisa Maya. Student, U. Mich., 1946—48; BA, UCLA; MA, Pacific Oaks Coll. Cert. elem. tchr.; cert. early childhood; bilingual cert. of competency in Spanish. Recreation dir. Detroit City Parks and Recreation, 1946-50, L.A. Unified Sch. Dist., 1950-52, tchr., 1984—2001, mentor tchr. elem. edn. L.A., 1988-94, ret., 2001; tchr. head start Found. Early Childhood Edn., L.A., 1965-73; staff organizer Early Childhood Fedn. Local 1475 AFT, L.A., 1973-79; staff rep. Calif. Fedn. Tchrs., L.A., 1979-83. Site supr. UCLA, 2001—02. Contbr. articles to profl. jours. Mem. Gov.'s Adv. Com. Child Care, L.A., 1980-83; mem. Sierra Club, 1978—; mem. So. Calif. Libr. Social Studies, L.A., 1989—; charter mem. Mus. Am. Indian Smithsonian Inst., Womens Internat. League for Peace and Freedom, ACLU, So. Poverty Law Ctr., Food First, Meiklejohn Civil Liberties Inst.; bd. dir., pres. Found. for Early Childhood Edn. Mem. So. Calif. Assn., Edn. Young Children, Early Childhood Fedn. (pres. emeritus 1979—), United Tchrs. L.A. (chpt. chair 1984-96, east area dir. and UTLA bd. dirs. 1996-99), L.A. Coalition Labor Union Women (charter; bd. dirs. 1980-86, UTLA-R officer 2001—), L.A. Coun. Aging, Found. Early Childhood Edn. (pres. 1997—). Avocations: guitar, folk songs, hiking. Personal E-mail: roselvau@yahoo.com.

UNGARO, SUSAN KELLIHER, foundation administrator, former magazine editor; married; 3 children. BA, MA, William Patterson Coll., Wayne, NJ. From editl. asst. to editor-in-chief Family Circle mag., NYC, 1976—94, editor-in-chief, 1994—2005; pres. James Beard Found., NYC, 2006—. Bd. dirs. Brazelton Found., Nat. Marrow Found., H.E.L.P. (Housing Enterprise for the Less Privileged). Named named Top Businessperson of Yr., Irish America magazine; recipient President's-Award, New Jersey Press Women's Assn., 1995, William Paterson University Legacy Award, 1998, Muriel Fox communications award for professional excellence and commitment to advocacy journalism, NOW Legal Defense Fund, 1998. Mem.: Am. Soc. Mag. Editors (bd. dir. 1998—, pres. 2003—). Office: James Beard Foundation 167 West 12th St New York NY 10011 Office Phone: 212-499-1986, 212-675-4984.*

UNGER, BARBARA, poet, retired educator; b. NYC, Oct. 2, 1932; d. David and Florence (Schuchalter) Frankel; m. Bernard Unger, 1954 (div. 1976); m. Theodore Sakano, 1987; children: Deborah, Suzanne. BA, CCNY, 1955, MA, 1957; advanced cert., NYU, 1970. Grad. asst. Yeshiva U., 1962-63; edn. editor County Citizen, Rockland County, NY, 1960-63; tchr. English N.Y.C. Pub. Schs., 1955-58, Nyack (N.Y.) H.S., 1963-67; guidance counselor Ardsley (N.Y.) H.S., 1967-69; prof. English Rockland C.C., Suffern, NY, 1969—95, ret., 1995. Adj. prof. Rockland C.C., 1995-2003, Rockland Sr. Citizen Coll., 2001-2003; poetry fellow Squaw Valley Cmty. of Writers, 1980;

writer-in-residence Rockland Ctr. for Arts, 1986. Author: (poetry) Basement, 1975, Learning to Fox Trot, 1989, The Man Who Burned Money, 1980, Inside the Wind, 1986, Blue Depression Glass in Troika One, 1991, (fiction) Dying for Uncle Ray, 1990; co-author (with Lloyd Ultan): (non-fiction) Bronx Accent: A Literary and Pictorial History of the Borough, 2001 (N.Y. Soc. Libr. Book award, 2001, J.M. Kaplan Furthermore grantee, Hermalyn Family Urban History award, 05); contbr. Anthology Mag. Verse, Yearbook Am. Poetry, 1984, Anthology Mag. Verse, Yearbook Am. Poetry, 1989, poetry and fiction to more than 75 lit. mags. Ragdale Found. fellow, 1985, 86, 89, SUNY Creative Writing fellow, 1981-82, Edna St. Vincent Millay Colony fellow, 1984, Djerassi Found. fellow, 1991, Hambidge Ctr. for Creative Arts and Scis. fellow, 1988, Dorset Colony fellow, 2005; NEH grantee, 1975; recipient Goodman Poetry award, 1989, Anna Davidson Rosenberg award Judah Magnes Mus., 1989, Roberts Writing award, 1990, New Letters Lit. awards, 1990; finalist Am. Fiction Competition, 1982, John Williams Narrative Poetry Competition, 1992; honorable mention Chester Jones Nat. Poetry Contest. Mem.: PEN, Assn. Writers and Writing Programs, Poets and Writers.

UNGER, JANE ELLEN, performing company executive; b. Bay Shore, N.Y., Feb. 11, 1949; d. Robert Samuel and Beverly Shirley Unger; m. Douglas John Baldwin, Feb. 12, 1983; children: Julia Ruby Unger Baldwin, Stella Amelia Unger Baldwin. BA, U. Wash., 1971; MA, Hofstra U., 1976. Cert. tchr. N.Y. Equity actress Hartford Stage Co., 1977—84; freelance dir.; artistic dir. Profile Theatre Project, Portland, Oreg., 1998—. Mem.: Portland Oreg. Visitors Assn., Portland Area Theatre Assn. (Best Dir. award 1998). Avocations: swimming, cross country skiing, reading. Office: Profile Theatre Project PO Box 14845 Portland OR 97293

UNGER, LAURA SIMONE, lawyer, commissioner; b. NYC, Jan. 8, 1961; d. Raymond and Susan Marie (Vopata) Simone; m. Peter Van Buren Unger, June 29, 1991. BA in Rhetoric, U. Calif., Berkeley, 1983; JD, N.Y. Law Sch., 1987. Bar: Conn. 1987, N.Y. 1988. Staff atty. divsn. enforcement SEC, 1988-90; legis. counsel to Sen. Alfonse M. D'Amato, 1990-91; minority counsel Senate com. banking, housing and urban affairs, 1991-95, counsel, 1995-97; commr. U.S. SEC, Washington, 1997—, acting chmn., 2001. Bd. dirs. MBNA Corp., 2004—. Recipient Performance award SEC, N.Y., 1988, D.C., 1989. Mem. ABA (subcom. on civil litigation and SEC enforcement matters and subcom. on SEC adminstrn., budget and legislation of the ABA bus. law sect. com. on federal regulation of securities), Fed. Bar Assn., Jr. League Washington, Decade Soc., Women in Housing and Fin. Roman Catholic. Avocations: tennis, jogging, movies, concerts, music. Office: US SEC 450 5th St NW Ms 6/8 Washington DC 20549-0001

UNGER, RHODA KESLER, psychology educator; b. Bklyn., Feb. 22, 1939; d. Gustav and Ellen (Samuels) Kesler; m. Burton M. Unger, Apr. 11, 1966; children: Laurel, Rachel BS, Bklyn. Coll., 1960; AM, Radcliffe Coll., 1964; PhD, Harvard U., 1966. Asst. prof. Hofstra U., Hempstead, NY, 1966—72; asst. prof., assoc. prof. psychology Montclair State Coll., Upper Montclair, NJ, 1972—81, prof., 1981—96, prof. emeritus, 1999—. Vis. prof. U. Haifa, Israel, 1988-89, Ochanemizu U., Tokyo, 2005; dir. honors Montclair State Coll., 1985-96 Author: Female and Male, 1979, Resisting Gender, 1998; co-author: Women and Gender, 1992, 96, 2000; editor: Representations, 1989, Handbook of the Psychology of Women and Gender, 2001, Analyses of Social Issues and Public Policy, 1998-2005; co-editor: Women, Gender and Social Psychology, 1985, In our own Words, 1997, 2000 Fulbright sr. prof., 1988-89; resident scholar women's studies rsch. ctr. Brandeis U., 1998— Fellow APA (pres. divsn. psychology of women 1980-81, disting. leadership award com. for women in psychology 1991, 1st Carolyn Wood Sherif Meml. award 1985), Am. Psychol. Soc., Soc. for Psychol. Study Social Issues (exec. com. 1980-86, pres. 1998-99); mem. Assn. Women in Psychology (Disting. Publ. award 1984, 86, Disting. Career award 1990) Jewish. Avocations: travel, cooking, reading, speculative fiction. Home: 3 Newport Rd Apt 4 Cambridge MA 02140-1587 Office: Brandeis U Womens Studies Rsch Ctr Waltham MA 02454-9110 Office Phone: 781-736-8107.

UNGER, SUSAN J., automotive executive; b. Detroit, Apr. 8, 1950; BA in Economics, Mich. State U., 1972; MBA in Fin., Wayne State U., 1976. Fin. analyst, sales and mktg. DaimlerChrysler AG, 1972, various financial positions, fin. dir. product devel. and Jeep/Truck Ops., exec. dir. mgmt. info. sys., 1993, sr. v.p., 1998—, chief info. officer, 1998—. Mem., past pres., Eli Broad Bd., Coll. Bus. Mich. State U.; bd. dir. Cyberstate.org; nat. adv. com. Coll. of Engring. U. Mich.; adv. tech. bd. Oakland U. Named 100 Leading Women in N.Am. Auto Industry, Automotive News, 2002, CIO of Yr., Automation Alley, 2002, Salomon Smith Barney, 2002, Disting. Alumnus of Yr., Wayne State U. Sch. Bus. Adminstrn., 2002; named one of Detroit's Most Influential Women, Crain's Detroit Bus., 2002; recipient Top Am. Woman award, Assn. Woman in Computing, 2003, Pioneer award, Phoenix Hill Women's Mus., 2004, Disting. Svc. Citation, Automotive Hall of Fame, 2006. Mem.: Automotive Womens Alliance, Kleiner Perkins CIO Strategy Exch. Forum. Office: Daimler-Chrysler Corp 1000 Chrysler Dr Auburn Hills MI 48326-2766*

UNGER, SUZANNE EVERETT, musician, educator; b. Valdosta, Ga., Oct. 19, 1959; d. Robert Wayne and Susan Pendleton Everett; m. Gary Phillip Unger; children: Andrew, Sara. BA in Music Edn., Tift Coll., 1981; MEd in Instrnl. Tech., Valdosta State U., 2004. Cert. Orff Schulwerk level 1, Performance Based Tchg.-5 level tchr. Music educator Dougherty County Schs., Albany, Ga., 1981—84, Lee County Elem. Sch., Leesburg, Ga., 1984—89, 1994—99, Lee County Primary Sch., Leesburg, 1986—; Pianist/Organist 1st United Meth. Ch., Albany, Ga., 1991—; accompanist Albany (Ga.) Chorale, 1999—. Accompanist All State Choir, 1997. Recipient Creation Station grant, LeeFocus, 2001, enhanced comm. through multimedia grant, Sumter Electric Corp., 2003. Mem.: Music Educators Nat. Conf. (gen. music chair dist. 2 1996—98). Methodist. Avocations: cross stitch, computer use, collecting Precious Moments figurines. Home: 309 Northampton Rd Leesburg GA 31763 Office: Lee County Primary Sch 282 Magnolia St Leesburg GA 31763 Personal E-mail: gsunger@earthlink.net. Business E-Mail: ungersu@lee.k12.ga.us.

UNGERLEIDER, DOROTHY FINK, recreational therapist; b. Chgo., Apr. 22, 1934; d. Theodore I. and Florence R. (Jacobson) Fink; m. J. Thomas Ungerleider, Dec. 19, 1954; children: John, Margot Ellen. BSEd in Spl. Edn. with honors, U. Mich., 1955; MA in Spl. Edn. with honors, Calif. State U., Northridge, 1975. Cert. ednl. therapist; cert. elem. and spl. edn. tchr., Calif. Edn. therapist in pvt. practice, Encino, Calif., 1968—. Lectr. in field; mentor schs. attuned program L.A. Unified Schs., 1999—. Author: Reading, Writing and Rage, 1985, 2d edit., 1996; contbr. articles to profl. jours. Pro bono cons., ednl. therapist Juvenile Justice Connection Project, New Directions for Youth, Van Nuys H.S. Tech. Program. Fellow Assn. Ednl. Therapists (founding pres. 1979-82, chair adv. bd. 1983—, honoree Ann. Conf. 1994). Avocations: hiking, speed walking, skiing, travel. Office: Association Of Educational Therapists 210 N Glenoaks Blvd Ste C Burbank CA 91502-1255 E-mail: dotrwr@earthlink.net.

UNGERLEIDER, LESLIE G., neuroscientist; b. NYC, Apr. 17, 1946; d. Albert and Frieda (Mandel) Cohen; m. Robert Desimone, Sept. 6, 1982; 1 child, Matthew David. BA magna cum laude, SUNY, Binghamton, 1966; PhD, NYU, 1970. Asst. prof. psychology Okla. State U., Oklahoma City, 1970-72; postdoctoral fellow Dept. Psychology Stanford (Calif.) U., 1972-75, Neuropsychology Lab. NIMH, Bethesda, Md., 1975-78, staff fellow, 1978-80, sr. staff fellow, 1980-85, rsch. psychologist, 1985-91, chief sect. neurocircuitry, 1992—95, chief lab brain and congnition, 1995—. Mem. editorial bd. Neuropsychologia, 1990—, J. Neurosci, 1996—, Cerebrol Cortex, 1998—, Human Brain Mapping, 1993—; contbr. articles to profl. jours. Fellow AAAS, APA, Am. Psychol. Soc.; mem. Soc. Neurosci., NAS Inst. Medicine. Achievements include basic research on nonhuman primates revealing neural mechanisms and cortical circuitry underlying visual perception and memory. Office: NIH Bldg 10 / Rm 4C104 10 Center Dr Bethesda MD 20892-0001

UNGER YOUNG, ELIZABETH (BETTY), hospital chaplain; b. Manitoba, Can., Mar. 4, 1936; came to U.S. 1962; d. Johann Cornelius and Ottillie (Hirsch) U.; m. Alvin Young, 1993. BA, Andrews U., 1967, MA in Teaching, 1972. Office clk. Overland Express, St. Catherines, Ont., Can., 1954-55; bookkeeper G.A. Moggridge Printing Co., St. Catherines, Ont., Can., 1955-56; sec., receptionist, asst. to cost acct. Anthes-Imperial, St. Catherines, Ont., Can., 1956-60; ins. claims dir. North York Branson Hosp., Toronto, Ont., Can., 1960-62; teacher, registrar Mt. Pisgah Acad., Chandler, N.C., 1967-69; spiritual counselor, chaplain Portland (Oreg.) Adventist Med. Ctr., 1971-83; chaplain Hinsdale (Ill.) Hosp., 1984-90, Porter Hospice, 1991—92; ret., 1992. Fellow Coll. of Chaplains, 1987. Seventh-day Adventist. Avocations: decorating, cooking, painting. Home: 1103 S County Road 137 Bennett CO 80102-8508

UNIKEL, EVA TAYLOR, interior designer; b. Hungary; arrived in Can., 1956; came to U.S., 1967; d. Istvan Domolky and Lea Maria (Koszegi) Coan; m. Alan L. Unikel; 1 child, Renee Christine; m. June 26, 1993. BS, So. Ill. U., 1972. Dir. mktg. Lococo Design, St. Louis, 1982-83; project mgr., nat. dir. mktg. hosp. div. Hotel Restaurant Planners div. Profl. Interiors, St. Louis, 1983-87; founder Interior Solutions Inc., Hinsdale, Ill., 1987—. Mem. AIA (assoc.), Nat. Assn. Women Bus. Owners, Am. Soc. Interior Design (chairperson 1984-86), Nat. Assn. Indsl. Office Pks., Bldg. Owners and Mgrs. Assn., Internat. Interior Design Assn. Roman Catholic. Office: 500 E Ravine Rd Hinsdale IL 60521-2449 Office Phone: 630-986-0166.

UNITAS ROOS, CAROLYN ELLEN, music educator, voice instructor, classical singer; b. Flushing, NY, Sept. 23, 1969; d. James Shepherd and Kathleen Maree (McDaid) Unitas; m. John Paul Roos, Apr. 17, 1993; children: Ciara Danielle Roos, Colton Matthew Roos. MusB in Vocal Performance, SUNY, Buffalo, 1987—91, MusM in Vocal Performance, 2000—03. Cert. pub. sch. tchr. U. State NY Edn. Dept., 2003. Music min., cantor, soloist Roman Cath. Diocese Buffalo, 1988—; mktg. agt. Buffalo Philharm. Orch., 1991—92; pvt. voice instr. Cmty. Music Sch. Buffalo, 1993—95, Studio Carolyn Unitas, Pendleton, NY, 1993—; elem. music tchr. St. Mary's Elem. Sch., Swormville, NY, 1994—98, Wilson Ctrl. Sch. Dist., NY, 1998—2000; v.p. Steelhead Tool & Die, Inc., Pendleton, NY, 1998—; HS music instr. Buffalo Acad. Sacred Heart, Eggertsville, 2004—. Soprano soloist various performances in NY, So. Ontario, Calif., and Ireland, 1987—; coord. music ministry Buffalo Acad. Sacred Heart, 2004—, music dept. pub. rels. assoc., 2006—. Singer: (operatic production) Mozart in the Middle, Dido and Aeneas, (operetta production) Utopia Limited, (operatic production) La Traviata, (soloist) Buffalo Philharmonic, 1991, 1992. Moderator Buffalo Acad. Sacred Heart Respect Life Club, 2005—; liturgy com. mem. St. Mary's Roman Cath. Ch., Swormville, NY, 1994—2005; organizer benefit concert Christian Children's Fund Tsunami Relief, Buffalo, 2004; singer,vol. various non-profit orgns., Buffalo, 1987—2006; mem., parent vol. Starpoint Parent Tchr. Assn., Pendleton, NY, 2000—06; bldg. team mem. Starpoint Fricano Elem. Sch., Pendleton, 2002—05; co-dir. Starpoint Ctrl. Schs. Talent Show, Pendleton, 2005. Mem.: NYS Sch. Music Assn. (assoc.), Erie County Music Educators Assn. (assoc.), US C. of C. (assoc.), Arts Coun. Buffalo & Erie County (assoc.), Ch. Musician's Guild (assoc.). Republican. Roman Catholic. Avocations: piano, reading, viola, violin, tennis. Personal E-mail: carolynunitas@adelphia.net.

UNITHAN, DOLLY, visual artist; b. Kelantan, Malaysia; arrived in US, 1976; Postgrad., Brit. Coun. Fine Arts Exch., 1974, Ecole Nationale des Beaux Arts de Nancy, France, 1974; BFA, Hornsey Coll. Art, 1975; MFA, Pratt Inst., 1978. Summer intern Guggenheim Mus, NYC, 1976; panelist, artist in residence Asian Am. Arts Ctr., 1993; lectr. in field. One-woman shows include Internat. Art Ctr., London, 1975, Am. Assn. State Colls., Univ., Orlando, Fla., 1977, Sloan Gallery, Lock Haven State Coll., Pa., 1978, Permanent Mission Malaysia, UN, NYC, 1987, Kerr Gallery, 1987, Lyman Allyn Art Mus., New London, Conn., 1990, UN Secretariat, NYC, 1991, Gracie Mansion, 1994, Angel Orensanz Found., 1995, Cathedral of St. John the Divine, St. Boniface Chapel Gallery, 1996, exhibited in group shows at Palace of Westminster, Hos. of Parliament, London, 1978, City Mus. Art Gallery, Gloucester, Eng., 1978, Contemporary Gallery, Warsaw, Poland, 1978, BWA Gallery, Wroclaw, Poland, 1978, Szczecin, Poland, 1978, Arts Coun. Gallery, Belfast, No. Ireland, 1978, Parrish Art Mus., Southampton, NY, 1979, Modern Art Ctr., Guadalajara, Mex., 1979, Alternative Mus., NYC, 1981, Nat. Mus. Fine Arts, Havana, Cuba, 1986, Hillwood Art Mus., Brookville, NY, 1988, PS 1 Mus., NYC, 1990, Nat. Art Gallery, Kuala Lumpur, 1991—92, League of Nations Archives, Palais des Nations, Geneva, 1993, Jewish Mus., Vienna, Austria, 1993, Peace Mus., Remagen, Germany, Westbeth Galleries, NYC, Tweed Courthouse Gallery, 1994, China Art Mus., Beijing, 1995, Raiffeisenkasse, Ulrich bei Steyr, Peace parish, Austria, 1996, Ctrl. Children's & Youth Arts Palace, Samarkand, Uzbekistan, 1997, Palais des Nations, UN Office, Geneva, 1998, Firehouse, NYC, 1999, Cathedral of St. John the Divine Synod Hall, 2002, Asian Am. Arts Ctr., 2002, Represented in permanent collections Lock Haven State Coll., Pa., Am. Assn. State Colls., Univ., Washington, Permanent Mission of Malaysia to UN, Wilfredo Lam Ctr., Havana, Malaysian Embassy, Washington, Spirit Found., NYC, Asian Am. Arts Ctr., World Bank, Washington, Lib. Congress, artwork included in jours., Multicultural Edn., 1994, Artspiral, 1994, books, Imagine Strawberry Fields, Sculpture, Technique, Form, Content. Named grad. scholar, Mara, Malaysia, 1976—78, Archives of Contemporary Arts, Venice Biennale, 1990; recipient Artist award, Rainbow Art Found., NYC, 1985, Art award ArtQuest '88, Internat. Art Competition, Calif., 1988; grantee, Lee Found., Singapore, 1972, 1976, Pollock-Krasner Found., 1991—92. Avocation: collecting antiques. Office Phone: 212-583-1946. Personal E-mail: dollyunithan@yahoo.com.

UNKENHOLZ, KARLA J., elementary school educator; b. Dickinson, N.D., Jan. 23, 1954; d. Karleton Ringsrud and Dolores Jean Johnson; m. Mark W. Unkenholz, June 7, 1974; children: Matthew Mark, Patrick Mark. AA, Bismarck State U., N.D.; BS, MA, U. N.D., Grand Forks. Tchr. Minot Pub. Schs., ND, Dallas Ind. Sch. Dist., Highland Park Day Care, Dallas, Richardson Ind. Sch. Dist., Tex. Home: 13675 Peyton Dr Dallas TX 75240 Office: Richardson Ind Sch Dist 1600 E Spring Valley Richardson TX 75081

UNSAL-TUNAY, NURAN, geological engineer, researcher; b. Igdir, Turkey, Dec. 26, 1956; came to U.S., 1995; d. Kamil and Feride (Gunay) Tunay; m. Ilhan Unsal, Oct. 28, 1979; 1 child, Volkan. Diploma in Geol. Engring., Earth Sci. Geol. Engring. Turkey, 1982; cert. in Civil Engring., Min. Pub. Works Turkey, 1985. Geol. engr. Gen. Directorate of Bank of Provinces, Konya-Ankara, Turkey, 1982—84, Gen. Directorate of Hwy., Kayseri-Ankara, Turkey, 1984—89, Adminstrn. Pub. Works, Manisa, Turkey, 1989—95. Cons. Pub. Works, Manisa, Turkey, 1989-95; adv. bds. Pub. Works, Municipality, Civil Cts., Manisa, Turkey, 1992-95. Inventor: Adaptation of Stabilized Hydrated Lime, Publication of the Chamber of Geol. Engring. of Turkey, 1993. Recipient of presentations 46th Congress of Geology of Turkey, Ankara, 1993. Fellow Geol. Assn. Can.; mem. Geol. Soc. Am., Chamber of Geol. Engrs. of Turkey. Achievements include the soil improvement with hydrated lime stabilization; applied in the area of Manisa Teachers House Buildings, was one of the first applications in Turkey. Home: 23-13 28th Ave Apt 2F Astoria NY 11102 Personal E-mail: nuranunsal@hotmail.com.

UNTERBERGER, BETTY MILLER, history professor, writer; b. Glasgow, Scotland, Dec. 27, 1923; d. Joseph C. and Leah Miller; m. Robert Ruppe, July 29, 1944; children: Glen, Gail, Gregg. BA, Syracuse U., N.Y., 1943; MA, Harvard U., 1946; PhD, Duke U., 1950. Asst. prof. E. Carolina U., Greenville, 1948-50; assoc. prof., dir. liberal arts ctr. Whittier Coll., Calif., 1954-61; assoc. prof. Calif. State U.-Fullerton, 1961-65, prof., chmn. grad. studies, 1965-68; prof. history Tex. A&M U., College Station, 1968—. Vis. prof. U. Hawaii, Honolulu, 1967, Peking U., Beijing, 1988; vis. disting. prof. U. Calif., Irvine, 1987—, Patricia and Bookman Peters prof. history, 1991-2005; vis. prof. Charles U., Prague, Czechoslovakia, 1992, Regents prof., 2000—; adv. com. fgn. rels. U.S. Dept. State, 1977-81, chair, 1981; hist. adv. com. U.S. Dept. Army, 1980-82, USN, 1991—; mem. Nat. Hist. Publs. and Records Commn., 1980-84; history rev. panel to Dir. of CIA, 1999—. Author: America's Siberian Expedition 1918-1920: A Study of National Policy, 1956, 69 (Pacific Coast award Am. Hist. Assn. 1956); editor: American Intervention in the Russian Civil War, 1969, Intervention Against Communism: Did the U.S. Try to Overthrow the Soviet Government, 1918-20, 1986, The United States, Revolutionary Russia and the Rise of Czechoslovakia, 1989, paperback edit. with a 2000 yr. perspective, 2000; contbr.: Woodrow Wilson and Revolutionary World, 1982, The Liberal Persuasion, 1997, The United States and the Russian Civil War, microfilm edit., 25 reels, 2001; mem. editl. adv. bd. The Papers of Woodrow Wilson, Princeton U., 1982-92, Internt. History, 1999—; bd. editors: Diplomatic History, 1981-84, Red River Valley Hist. Rev., 1975-84. Trustee Am. Inst. Pakistan Studies, Villanova U., Pa., 1981—, sec., 1989-92; mem. League of Women Voters. Woodrow Wilson Found. fellow, 1979; recipient Disting. Univ. Tchr. award State of Calif. Legislature, 1966; Betty Miller Unterberger dissertation prize, Soc. Historians Am. Fgn. Rels., 2004. Mem. LWV, NOW, AAUW, Am. Hist. Assn. (chair 1982-83, nominating com. 1980-83), Orgn. Am. Historians (govt. relations com.), Soc. Historians of Am. Fgn. Relations (exec. council 1978-81, 86-89, govt. relations com. 1982-84, v.p. 1985, pres. 1986, co-winner Myrna F. Bernath prize 1991), Am. Soc. for Advancement Slavic Studies, Coordinating Com. on Women in Hist. Profession, Rocky Mountain Assn. Slavic Studies (program chair 1973, v.p. 1973-74), So. Hist. Assn., Asian Studies Assn., Assn. Third World Studies, Czechoslovak Soc. Arts and Scis., Czechoslovak History Conf., Women in Nat. Security, Women's Fgn. Policy Coun., Beyond War, Peace History Soc., Sierra Club, Phi Beta Kappa, Phi Beta Delta. Office: Tex A&M U Dept History College Station TX 77843-0001 Business E-Mail: bettymu@tamu.edu.

UNVERFERTH, BARBARA PATTEN, small business owner; b. Hartford, Conn., Sept. 27, 1945; d. Leslie A. and Mildred B. (Owen) Patten; m. Robert L. Gerbig, June 1968 (div. 1977); children: Patricia G. Toohey, R. Braden Gerbig, Jo Ann Gerbig; m. Donald Unverferth, Dec. 29, 1978 (deceased); children: Katherine J. Unverferth, Megan M. Unverferth. BA cum laude, Ohio Wesleyan U., 1967; MS in Zoology, Ohio U., 1969; MS in Pathology, Ohio State U., 1980. Rsch. asst. Scripts Inst., LaJolla, Calif., 1969-70; tchr. biology Mariemont H.S., Cin., 1970-71; rschr. dept. cardiology Ohio State U., Columbus, 1980-84; gen. ptnr. Art Access, Columbus, 1993—. Founder, pres. Unverferth House Inc., Columbus, 1988—; mem. dirs. cir. Wexner Ctr., Columbus, 1995—. Author (book chpt.) Dilated Cardiomyopathy, 1985. Corr. sec. Jr. League, Columbus, 1974; corr. sec., mem. exec. bd. Childhood League, Columbus, 1980-85; sec. womens bd. Mus. of Art, Columbus, 1992-93; mem. Columbus AIDS Task Force, 1998. NSF grantee, 1966, NSF fellow, 1968; named Woman of Yr. Rotary Club Upper Arlington, Ohio, 1993. Mem. Kappa Alpha Theta (pres. alumni club 1976). Avocations: tennis, skiing. Office: Art Access 540 S Drexel Ave Bexley OH 43209 E-mail: unvi@aol.com.

UPBIN, SHARI, agent; b. NYC; children: Edward, Elyse, Danielle. Master tap instr. Talent mgr. Goldstar Talent Mgmt., Inc., N.Y.C., 1989-91. Faculty Nat. Shakespeare Conservatory, N.Y. Asst. dir.: (plays, 1st Black-Hispanic Shakespeare prodn.) Julius Caesar, 1979; dir.(choreographer): (plays) Matter of Opinion, 1980, Side by Side, 1981; prodr.(dir.): Vincent, The Passions of Van Gogh, 1981,: (Broadway plays) Bojangles, The Life of Bill Robinson, 1984; dir.: Captain America, 1996; dir., choreographer (plays) Fiddler of the Roof, Cabaret, Life with Father, Roar of the Grease Paint, 1979—82; dir.: (plays) Feminist Movements, 1997, Danny Kaye and Sylvia, 2005; co-prodr.: One Mo' Time; prodr., dir.: Flypaper, 1991—92; Women on Their Own, Things My Mother Never Told Me; How Could Cupid Be So Stupid!, 1999; Timeless Divas, 2003, 2005; prodr.: Vintage 2001, Timeless Divas! Salute to Women in Cabaret, Broadway Over 40, Timeless Divas! Musical Stars of The Silver Screen, 2004. Founder Queens Playhouse, N.Y., Children's Theatre, Flushing, N.Y.; mem. Willy Mays' Found. Drug Abused Children. Recipient Jaycees Svc. award Jr. Miss Pageants Franklin Twp., N.J., 1976. Mem. League Profl. Theatre Women (past pres.), Soc. Stage Dirs. and Choreographers, Coalition of Women in Arts & Media (bd. dirs.), Actors Equity Assn., Villagers Barn Theatre (1st woman pres.), N.Y. Womens Agenda (bd. dirs.). Personal E-mail: sharivpbin@aol.com.

UPCHURCH, CAROL J., elementary school educator; b. Seminole, Okla., Jan. 3, 1948; d. William Thomas and Mildred Jewel (Ellison) Wages; m. Stanley R. Upchurch, May 2, 1969; 1 child, Kimberly Noel. BS in Edn., U. Okla., 1969, MS in Edn., 1981. Tchr. Norman (Okla.) Pub. Schs. Head tchr. Jefferson Elem. Sch., Norman, 1987-89. Mem. Jefferson Elem. PTA, Norman, 1971-95, Friends of the Okla. Zoo, Oklahoma City, 1992-95. Recipient grant Norman Sch. Found., 1987-90, Barbara Spriestersback award Okla. Libr. Assn., 1992, Presdl. award of Excellence in Math. and Sci. Teaching, NSF, 1994; Tchr. of Yr. finalist Norman Pub. Schs., 1993. Mem. NSTA, NEA, Okla. Edn. Assn., Okla. Sci. Tchrs. Assn., Profl. Educators of Norman. Avocation: camping. Home: 617 Leaning Elm Dr Norman OK 73071-7057 Office: Jefferson Elem Sch 250 N Cockrel Ave Norman OK 73071-6012

UPDIKE, HELEN HILL, financial advisor; b. NYC, Mar. 27, 1941; d. Benjamin Harvey and Helen (Gray) Hill; m. Charles Bruce Updike, Sept. 7, 1963 (div. 1989); m. Asa Rountree, Oct. 10, 1998. BA, Hood Coll., 1962; PhD, SUNY, Stony Brook, 1978; postgrad., Harvard U., 1986. Lectr. SUNY, Stony Brook, 1969-75; asst. prof. U. Mass., Boston, 1975-77, Hofstra U., Hempstead, NY, 1978-85, assoc. prof., 1985-90, chmn. dept. econs. and geography, 1981-84, assoc. dean Hofstra Coll., 1984-87; pres. Interfid Capital Corp., 1987—2001; prin. Bridgewater Advisors, N.Y.C., 2001—. Cons. econ. policy, 1973—; vis. asst. prof. SUNY, Stony Brook, 1977—78; commentator WNYC Radio, 1997—; bd. dirs. Faberge, McCrory Corp. Author: (book) The National Banks and American Economic Development, 1870-1900, 1985. Trustee Madeira Sch., Greenway, Va., 1984—88, Literacy, Inc., 1998—2001; mem. nat. adv. bd. Outward Bound, 1986—92; trustee, v.p. L.I. Forum Tech., 1979—85; trustee NY Outward Bound, 1988—97. Mem.: AAAS. Office: Bridgewater Advisors 489 Fifth Ave New York NY 10017

UPDYKE, ROSEMARY KATHRYN, writer; b. Corcicana, Tex., Apr. 12, 1924; d. C.C. and Polly Ann Durbin; m. Herbert D. Johnston, Sept. 14, 1945 (dec. Feb. 1985); children: Jon Michael, Peggy; m. Henry Kissinger; m. Delbert N. Updyke, June 16, 1994. Grad., Tyler (Tex.) C.C., 1943. Sr. sec. Am. Nickeloid Co., Garden City, L.I., N.Y., 1943-63. Author: Quanah Parker Comanche Chief, 1991, Jim Thorpe: The Legend Remembered, 1997. Med. sec. Camp Fannin (Tex.) Hosp., 1943-45. Mem. Pocono Writers. Avocations: writing, knitting for community poor. Home: 950 Morgan Hwy Rm 222 Clarks Summit PA 18411-8728

UPRIGHT, DIANE WARNER, art dealer; b. Cleve. d. Rodney Upright and Shirley (Warner) Lavine. Student, Wellesley Coll., 1965-67; BA, U. Pitts., 1969; MA, U. Mich., 1973, PhD, 1976. Asst. prof. U. Va., Charlottesville, 1976-78; assoc. prof. Harvard U., Cambridge, Mass., 1978-83; sr. curator Ft. Worth Art Mus., 1984-86; dir. Jan Krugier Gallery, N.Y.C., 1986-90; sr. v.p., head contemporary art dept. Christie's, N.Y.C., 1990-95; pres. Diane Upright Fine Arts, N.Y.C., 1995—. Author: Morris Louis: The Complete Paintings, 1979, Ellsworth Kelly: Works on Paper, 1987, various exhbn. catalogues; contbr. articles to art jours. Mem.: Art Table, Inc. Office: Diane Upright Fine Arts 188 E 76th St New York NY 10021-2826

UPSHUR, CAROLE CHRISTOF, psychologist, educator; b. Des Moines, Oct. 18, 1948; d. Robert Richard and Margaret (Davis) Chistofk; 1 child, Emily. AB, U. So. Calif., 1969; EdM, Harvard U., 1970, EdD, 1975. Lic. psychologist, Mass. Planner Mass. Com. on Criminal Justice, Boston, 1970-73; licensing specialist, planner, policy specialist Mass. Office for Children, Boston, 1973-76; asst. prof. Coll. Pub. and Cmty. Svc. U. Mass., Boston, 1976-81, assoc. prof., 1982-93, prof., 1993-2001, chmn. Ctr. for Cmty. Planning, 1979—81, 1984—86, 1995—96; prof. family medicine and cmty. health U. Mass. Med. Sch., Worcester, 2004—. Sr. rsch. fellow Maurice Gaston Inst. Latino Pub. Policy, 1993—2004, Ctr. Social Devel. & Edn., 1991-2001, Gerontology Inst., 1996-2001, McCormack Inst. for Pub. Affairs, dir. PhD in Pub. Policy program, 1995-2001; cons. to govt. and cmty. agys.; assoc. in pediat., sr. rsch. assoc. U. Mass. Med. Sch., 1983-94; adj. prof.

Heller Sch. Social Welfare, Brandeis U., 1985-98; prof. family medicine and cmty. health U. Mass. Med. Sch. and Meml. Health Care, 2004—; assoc. dean, Clin. and Population Health Rsch. Grad. Sch., U. Mass. Med. Sch., 2004—; Zuckerbert Endowed Leadership chair U. Mass., 2006-2007. Contbr. articles to profl. jours. Mem. Brookline Human Rels.-Youth Resources Commn., 1988-91, Gov.'s Commn. on Facility Consolidation, 1991-92, Mass. Healthcare Adv. Com., 1993—. Fellow Mass. Psychol. Assn.; mem. APA, APHA, Soc. Tchrs. of Family Medicine. Office: U Mass Med Sch Dept Family Med 55 Lake Ave N Worcester MA 01655

UPSON, HELEN RENA, retired history educator; b. Southington, Conn., Aug. 18, 1912; BA, Grinnell (Iowa) Coll., 1958; MA, U. Iowa, 1960, PhD, 1969. Commd. USN, 1943, advanced through grades to lt. comdr., ret., 1958; adminstrv. officer math., scis. divsn. Office of Naval Rsch., Washington, 1949-50; instr. Armed Forces Info. Sch., Carlysle, Pa., Ft. Slocum, N.Y., 1950-53; tng. officer Naval Air Sta., Hutchinson, Kans., 1953-55; pub. info. officer 17th Naval Dist., Kodiak, Alaska, 1955-57, Office of Chief of Info., Office of Sec. Navy, Washington, 1957-58; grad. asst. instr. U. Iowa, 1958-65; assoc. prof. Am. and European history Calif. Western U./U.S. Internat. U., San Diego, 1965-76, adj. prof. Am. econ. history and internat. European problems, 1976-81. Author: Order and System: Charles Frances Adams Jr. and the Railroad Problem, 1970, The western Odyssey of Nin Connecticut Brothers: An Intimate History of American Enterprise, 1989. Mem. Tierrasanta Cmty. Coun., San Diego and chmn. lit. com., 1982-83. Mem. AAUW, Nat. Ind. Scholars, Am. Hist. Soc. Unitarian Universalist. Avocations: swimming, hiking, skiing, photography, travel.

UPSON, JEANNINE MARTIN, retired academic administrator; b. Woonsocket, R.I., Aug. 11, 1942; d. Leo Herve and Irene Florence (Dubois) Martin; m. Dean Blanchard Upson, Apr. 29, 1967; children: Ben Andrew and Jed Miles (twins). BA in History cum laude, Eastern Conn. State U., 1986; MA, U. Conn., 1993. Asst. to v.p. for fin. and adminstrn. U. Conn., Storrs, 1979-87, asst. to pres. for adminstrn. affairs, 1987-92, interim dir. devel., 1992-94, dir. advancement systems, 1994—97, ret., 1997. Editor: (book) Union Lands: A People's History, 1984-89, As Time Goes by: Images of Union, 2002; cons. (book) Lebanon, CT Town History, 1985. Founder, organizer, pres. Union (Conn.) Hist. Soc., Inc., 1974—; mcpl. historian Town of Union, 1990—; clk., historian, mem. prudential com., deacon, mem. parish project group Congl. Ch. of Union, Inc. Grantee George Dudley Seymour Trust, 1984. Avocations: history, photography, travel.

UPTON, SHELLY ANN VOSBURG, elementary school educator; b. New Roads, La., Jan. 22, 1961; d. Sheldon Isadore Vosburg, Jr. and Peggy Ann (Hebert) Vosburg; children: Taylor Ann, Austin Reid. BA cum laude, La. State U., Baton Rouge, 1983. Tchr. phys. edn. Broadmoor H.S., Baton Rouge, 1983; tchr. adapted phys. edn. East Baton Rough Parish, 1984—91; tchr. sci. St. Joseph Jr. H.S., Jackson, Miss., 1991—92; tchr. phys. edn. Leander Sch. Dist., Tex., 1992—93, Elm Grove Elem. Sch., Buda, Tex., 2001—. Tchr. religious edn. St. Joan of Arc, Danville, 1997—2002. Coach, dir. events Spl. Olympics, Baton Rouge, 1987; Cub Scouts coord. John Baldwin Elem. Sch., Danville, 1998—2002; coord. Hays Wellness Com., Buda, 2004—05. Nominee Mortar Bd., La. State U., Baton Rouge, 1982, Tchr. of Yr., Elm Grove Elem. Sch., 2005—06; named to Dean's List, La. State U., Baton Rouge, 1979—83. Mem.: AAHPERD, Assn. Tchrs. Phys. Edn., Tex. Assn. Health, Phys. Edn., Recreation and Dance. Avocations: travel, hiking, bicycling, skiing, camping. Office: Elm Grove Elem Sch 801 S Fm 1626 Buda TX 78610 Business E-Mail: uptons@hayscisd.net.

URATO, BARBRA CASALE, entrepreneur; b. Newark, Oct. 10, 1941; d. Dominick Anthony and Concetta (Castrichini) Casale; m. John Joseph Urato, June 20, 1965; children: Concetta U. Graves, Gina E., Joseph D. Student, Seton Hall U., 1961-63. File clk. Martin Gelber Esquire, Newark, 1956-58; policy typist Aetna Casualty Ins., Newark, 1959-61; sec. to dean Seton Hall U., South Orange, N.J., 1961-63; paralegal sec. Judge Robert A. McKinley, Newark, 1963-65, Joseph Garrubbo, Esquire, Newark, 1965-66; office mgr. Valiant I.M.C., Hackensack, N.J., 1971-73; asst. pers. mgr. Degussa Inc., Teterboro, N.J., 1975-78; night mgr. The Ferryboat Restaurant, River Edge, N.J., 1976-78; mgr. Fratello's and Ventilini's, Hilton Head, S.C., 1978-80; day mgr. Ramada Inn Restaurant, Paramus, N.J., 1980-81; mgr. Gottlieb's Bakery, Hilton Head, 1982-83; asst. mgr. closing dept. Hilton Head Mortgage Co., 1983-84; owner, mgr. All Cleaning Svc., Hilton Head, 1984—; owner Hilton Head Investigations, 1990-93, Hilton Head Island, 1990-92, Aaction Investigators, 1992-94; owner, ptnr. Sisters Hair & More, 2006—. Mem. NAFE, Profl. Women of Hilton Head, Assn. for Rsch. and Enlightenment, Rosicrucian Order. Roman Catholic. Avocations: metaphysics, music, gardening, learning.

URBAN, AMANDA (BINKY URBAN), literary agent; m. Ken Auletta, 1977; 1 child. BA in English, Wheaton Coll., Mass. Gen. mgr. N.Y. mag.; editl. mgr. Esquire mag.; literary agent Internat. Creative Mgmt., N.Y.C., v.p., co-dir. lit. dept., 1988—98, co-head, 1999—. Office: Internat Creative Mgmt 40 W 57th St New York NY 10019 E-mail: aurban@icmtalent.com.*

URBAN, CARRIE, computer specialist; b. Summit, N.J., Nov. 30, 1969; BS in Fin., U. Colo., Colorado Springs, 1994, MBA in Info. Systems, 1996; grad. child psychology, Stratford Career Inst., Washington, 1999, grad. sewing and dressmaking, 2000. Sys. operator Celestial Light BBS, Colorado Springs, 1984-98, Country Estate BBS, Casa Grande, Ariz., 1999; freelance computer cons. Casa Grande, 1998—. Intern Interactive Mgmt. Systems, Colorado Springs, 1997; tech. support profl. Gateway Computers, Colorado Springs, 1998; computer tutor Judith Crawford, Colorado Springs, 1998-99; computer troubleshooter Summit Home Health Care, Colorado Springs, 1999, Millie Forbush, Casa Grande, 2000. Writer newsletter column Transgender Connection, 1996-97, Transgender Jour., 1998-99; writer Ground Zero, Colorado Springs, 1996-97. Mem. adv. coun. Equality Colo., Colorado Springs, 1998-99. Mem. Nat. Rifle Assn. (cert. personal protection course), Christian Broadcasting Network, Concerned Women of Am., Humane Soc. U.S. Republican. Baptist. Avocations: reading, bowling, singing, writing.

URBAN, CATHLEEN ANDREA, graphics designer; b. Elizabeth, N.J., June 7, 1947; d. Emil Martin and Susan (Rahoche) Cupec; m. Walter Robert Urban, Nov. 5, 1966; children: Karen Louise, Kimberly Ann. Student, Rutgers U., 1965-66, 91-94; AS in Bus. Adminstrn., Raritan Valley C.C., North Branch, N.J., 1990, AAS in Computer Programming, 1990. Office mgr. K-Mart Corp., Somerville, N.J., 1987-90; software developer Bellcore, Piscataway, N.J., 1990-93, sys. tech. support cons., 1993-94, software developer, 1994-96, software quality assurance tester, 1996-97, project mgr., 1997—; graphic designer, owner CathiCards, Inc., Neshanic Station, N.J., 1995—. Leader Somerset County 4-H Program, Bridgewater, 1978-87. Mem. NAFE, AAUW, Nat. Space Soc., Internat. Platform Assn., Project Mgmt. Inst., Internat. Guild Candle Artisans, Golden Key Honor Soc., Mensa, Phi Theta Kappa. Roman Catholic. Avocations: science fiction, reading, dog shows, candle making. Office: Bell Comm Rsch 444 Hoes Ln Piscataway NJ 08854-4104

URBAN, DIANE, psychologist, educator; b. Queens, N.Y., June 27, 1954; d. Jerome and Carmela Chiappise; m. Walter Urban, Dec. 29, 1979; children: Nicholas, Amanda. BA, Queens Coll., 1976; MA, St. John's U., Queens, N.Y., 1979; PhD, New Sch. U., N.Y.C., 1987. Lic. psychologist N.Y. Asst. prof. Westchester C.C., Valhalla, NY, 1980—; instr. Manhattan Coll., Riverdale, NY, 2004—. Active Westchester Emergency Vol. Res., Med. Res. Corps. Mem.: APA. Home: 106 Eastview Dr Valhalla NY 10595

URBAN, NINA B.L., psychiatrist, psychotherapist, researcher; b. Offenbach, Hessen, Germany, Oct. 10, 1975; arrived in U.S., 2003; d. Richard and Siegrun Urban. MD, Humboldt U., Berlin, 2001; MS, U. Oxford, Eng., 2003. Cert. ECFMG. Ho. staff U. Rochester, NY, 2003—04, Mt. Sinai-Cabrini Med. Ctr., NYC, 2004—, chief resident dept. psychiatry, 2006—. Local activist Worldwide Fund for Nature, Frankfurt and Berlin, 1993—2002; healthcare vol. Missionaries Charity/Motehr Teresa, Calcutta, India, 1994; fundraiser Leukemia and Lymphoma Soc., NYC, 2005. Named studentship, McDonnell Inst. for Neurosci., Oxford, Eng., 2002—03; grantee, ERASMUS Program, 1998. Mem.: Med. Soc. N.Y. State, Am. Psychiat. Assn. (vice chair NY county dist. br. com. 2005—), Oxford Alumni Soc. N.Y. Avocations: opera, equestrian, art, travel. Office: Cabrini Med Ctr 227 E 19th St New York NY 10003

URBANSKI, JANE F., retired microbiologist; b. Buffalo, N.Y., Aug. 21, 1943; d. Francis C. and Jane J. Urbanski. BS in Med. Tech. cum laude, Rosary Hill Coll., 1965. Registered med. tech. Am. Soc. Clin. Pathology. Med. tech. Millard Fillmore Hosp., Buffalo, 1965—68, microbiology supr., 1968—72; lab. supr. Physician's Diagnostic Lab., Buffalo, 1972—73; microbiology supr. Sister's of Charity Hosp., Buffalo, 1973—74; chief bacteriologist Erie County Pub. Health Lab. Health Dept., Buffalo, 1974—2002; ret., 2002. Clin. instr. SUNY, Buffalo, 1975—2002. Vol. Haven House, Buffalo, 1985, City Mission, Buffalo, 2004. Mem.: Am. Soc. for Clin. Lab. Sci. (ret.), Empire State Assn. for Med. Tech. (ret.), Am. Soc. Clin. Pathologists (ret.), English First, Am. Immigration Control, Second Amendment Found., Mensa. Conservative. Roman Catholic. Avocations: travel, growing orchids, reading, logic puzzles. Home: 185 Bridle Path Orchard Park NY 14127

URDA KASSIS, CYNTHIA E., lawyer; b. Stamford, Conn., 1958; BA, U. Va., 1980; MA, U. Notre Dame, 1981; JD, Am. U., 1984. Bar: NY 1985. Assoc. Shearman & Sterling LLP, NYC, 1984—92, ptnr., 1992—, co-head firm project devel. and fin. group. Mem.: ABA. Office: Shearman & Sterling LLP 599 Lexington Ave New York NY 10022-6069 Office Phone: 212-848-7969. Office Fax: 646-848-7969. E-mail: curdakassis@shearman.com.

URDANG, NICOLE SEVERYNA, psychotherapist; b. N.Y.C., May 16, 1953; d. Laurence and Irena Urdang; BA in Psychology, U. Conn., 1974; MS in Marriage and Family Counseling, So. Conn. State Coll., 1980; Doctorate in Homeopathic Medicine British Inst. of Homeopathy, 1994; Cert. counselor; m. Mark Alan Criden, Mar. 1, 1980; children: Madelaine, Maxwell. Co-mng. editor CBS Almanac, Essex, Conn., 1975; psychiat. aide Inst. of Living, Hartford, Conn., 1975-76; supr. Alcohol Aftercare Ctr., Middletown, Conn., 1977-78; interim dir. Alcoholism Svcs. Orgn., New Haven, 1978; alcoholism program coord. Yale-New Haven Hosp., 1978-80; pvt. practice psychotherapy, New Haven, 1980-81, Buffalo, 1981—; radio psychotherapist Sta. WKBW, Buffalo, 1982-84; vol. counselor Norwich State Hosp., 1973-74, Planned Parenthood, 1975, Wesleyan U. Women's Ctr., 1977-78, New Haven Women's Ctr., 1979; lectr. in field. Author poems, short fiction, essays; columnist Met. Community News, 1985. Mem. Am. Counseling Assn., Planned Parenthood, Nat. League Am. Pen Women, NOW, Albert Ellis Inst. (assoc. fellow, supr.). Home and Office: 650 Lafayette Ave Buffalo NY 14222-1436 Office Phone: 716-882-0848. Personal E-mail: urdang@buffalo.com.

URIA, ADRIANA C. OCAMPO, geologist; b. Columbia; U.S. BS in Geology, Calif. State U., L.A.; MS in Geology, Calif. State U., Northridge. Rsch. scientist NASA Jet Propulsion Lab., 1973—98; program exec. NASA, Washington, 1998—. Prin. organizer Space Conf for the Americas: Prospects in Cooperation, Costa Rica, 1990; lectr. Stanford U., 1995, Caltech, 1995, U. Calif., Berkeley, 1995, U. Reno, 1996, Nat. Inst. Std. and Tech., 1997, Santa Monica City Coll., 1997, U. Oreg., 1998; mem. adv. coun. women NASA Jet Propulsion Lab., participant Spkrs. Bur.; rep. internat. adv. bd. Embrace Space. Named Woman of the Yr., Comision Femenil, 1994; recipient Tech. award, Chicano Fedn., 1997; grantee, NASA, 1991. Mem.: AIAA, Awwn. Women Geoscience, Soc. Hispanic Profl. Engrs. (nat. sec. bd. dirs., nat. v.p. bd. dirs., chair internat. affairs com.), Planetary Soc. (grantee 1995, 1996, 1998). Office: NASA Bldg HQ Rm 5V86 Washington DC 20546-0001 Business E-Mail: aocampo@mail.hq.nasa.gov.

URIBE, JENNIE ANN, elementary school educator; b. National City, Calif., Apr. 17, 1958; d. Robert and Alice (Packard) U. BA, San Diego State U., 1981, cert. teacher, 1982; MB, Nat. Univ., 2000. Tchr. Langdon Ave. Sch., L.A. Unified Sch. Dist., Sepulveda, Calif., 1984-94, tchr. potentally gifted students class, 1987-94; tchr. Spreckels Elem. Sch., San Diego City Schs., 1994—97, Rosa Elem., 1997—. Tchr./advisor for student govt., 1987-93; guide tchr., 1997—; prof. deve. advisor, 1997—. Mem. adv. coun. Sch. Site, 1992-1997. Avocations: tennis, music, movies, reading. Home: 2259 Peach Tree Ln Spring Valley CA 91977-7046 Office: Rosa Parks Elem Sch 4510 Landis St San Diego CA 92103

URIBE, LAURA BETH, elementary school educator; d. Debra Lynn Moretto. BS, Ill. State U., Normal, 2002. Tchr. history grade 7 Crete-Monee Mid. Sch., University Park, Ill., 2003—04; tchr. history grade 8 Saline Mid. Sch., Mich., 2004—. Office Phone: 734-429-8070.

URSO, IDA, psychologist; arrived in U.S., 1954; BA, Kent State U., 1969; MA, UCLA, 1974, PhD, 1983; cert., N.Y. Open Ctr., 1997. Sr. staff assoc. Ctr. for Human Interdependence, Orange, Calif., 1986—90; lectr. Chapman Coll., Orange, 1984—90; dir. World Goodwill, N.Y.C., 1990—96; integrative spiritual psychologist Chaitanya, Hoboken, NJ, 1997—; pres., founder Aquarian Age Cmty., Jersey City, 1998—. Elem. sch. cons. St. Pedro St. Sch., L.A., 1976—77; bd. mem. Calif. Coun. for UN U., L.A., 1982—84; lectr. Immaculate Heart Coll. Ctr., L.A., 1985, L.A., 98. Writer, editor: newsletter Diamond Light, 1997—; contbr. chapters to books. Bd. mem. Orange County chpt. UN Assn./USA, 1988—90, edn. chairperson Orange County, 1989—90; UN Dept. Publ. Info., Non Govtl. Orgn. World Goodwill, N.Y.C., 1990—96, Children of Earth Lifebridge, N.Y.C., 1998—2000, Aquarian Age Cmty., N.Y.C., 2003—. Mem.: Nicholas Roerich Mus., Am. Mus. Natural History. Avocations: community service, reading, music, meditation. Office: Aquarian Age Cmty 233 Bay St #206 Jersey City NJ 07302 Office Phone: 201-659-3060 ext. 145. Business E-Mail: un@aquaac.org.

USHENKO, AUDREY ANDREYEVNA, artist, educator; b. Princeton, July 28, 1945; d. Andrew Pavlevitch and Fay (Hampton) U.; m. S.M. Harcaj; 1 child, Emily. Student, Sch. of Art Inst., 1963-64; BA, Ind. U., 1965; MA, Northwestern U., Evanston, Ill., 1967, PhD, 1979. Instr. Valparaiso (Ind.) U., 1968-73, asst. prof., 1978-79; instr. Alan R. Hite Inst. U. Louisville, 1973-74; asst. prof. Northwestern U., Evanston, Ill., 1974-75; vis. faculty Columbia Coll., 1980-88; assoc. prof. Ind.-Purdue U., Ft. Wayne, Ind., 1988—. Gallery artist Gruen Gallery, Chgo., 1983—, Denise Bibro Gallery, N.Y.C., 1993—, Yvonne Rapp Gallery, Louisville, 1989—; artist oil paintings Bacchus & Ariadne III, 1987 (NAD Clark prize), Social Security, 1987 (Purchase prize 1989), Chgo. Art Expo, 1996, Marriage Project-Travelling Exhbn., 1996, Conviviality, 1997 (NAD Isidor Medal 1997), Fort Wayne Mus. of Art, 1998; curator exhbn., N.Y.C., 1998-99. Mem. AAUP (sec. local chpt. 1990—), NAD. Democrat. Orthodox. Avocations: reading, music. Home: 2519 East Dr Fort Wayne IN 46805-3612

USHER, ANN L., music educator; d. Richard D. and Margaret L. Miller; m. Thomas E. Usher, Aug. 12, 1989; children: Kelsey M., Adam T., Logan R. MusM, Kent State U., Ohio, 1993, PhD, 2005. Permanent tchg. cert. Ohio. Music educator Parma (Ohio) City Schs., 1990—92, Solon (Ohio) City Schs., 1992—2000; asst. prof. to assoc. prof. music U. Akron, Ohio, 2000—. Dir. Cleve. Orch. Children's Chorus. Office: U Akron Guzzetta Hall 366 Akron OH 44325-1002 Office Phone: 330-972-6923. Business E-Mail: ausher@uakron.edu.

USHER, ELIZABETH REUTER (MRS. WILLIAM A. SCAR), retired librarian; b. Seward, Nebr. d. Paul and Elizabeth (Meyer) Reuter; m. Harry Thomas Usher, Feb. 25, 1950; m. William Arthur Scar, Mar. 28, 1992. Diploma, Concordia Tchrs. Coll., Seward, Litt.D. (hon.), 1981; BS in Edn., U. Nebr., 1942; BS in library Sci., U. Ill., 1944. Tchr. Zion Luth. Sch., Platte Center, Nebr. and; St. Paul's Luth. Sch., Paterson, N.J.; library asst. charge res. book reading room U. Nebr., 1942-43; asst. circulation librarian Mich. State U., 1944-45; librarian Cranbrook Acad. Art, Bloomfield Hills, Mich., 1945-48; catalog and reference librarian Met. Mus. Art, N.Y.C., 1948-53, head cataloger and reference librarian, 1953-54, asst. librarian, 1954-61, chief of art reference library, 1961-68, chief librarian, Thomas J. Watson Library, 1968-80, chief librarian emeritus, 1980—, acting librarian, 1954-57. Contbr. articles to profl. periodicals, library publs. Trustee N.Y. Met. Reference and Research Library Agy., 1968-80, sec. to bd., 1971-77, v.p., 1977-80; 1st v.p. Heritage Village Library, 1982-88, 91-92, pres., 1988-91, 95-2000. Mem. Spl. Libraries Assn. (pres. 1967-68, dir. 1960-63, 66-69, Hall of Fame 1980—), Coll. Art Assn. (chmn. libraries session 1972-73), N.Y. Library Club, Archons of Colophon (convener 1980-82), Heritage Village Rep. Club (pres. 1992-95, 97-99), Philanthropic Ednl. Orgn. (v.p. chpt. Q 1994-97, pres. 1997-98). Lutheran. Home: 517 NW Hope Ln Lees Summit MO 64081-1301 E-mail: usherscar@aol.com.

USHER, NANCY SPEAR, retired language arts educator; b. Malden, Mass., Mar. 13, 1938; d. George Alonzo and Mary Elizabeth (York) Spear; m. Walter Lansley Whitlock, June 13, 1959 (div. Oct. 1961); m. Frederic Laurence Usher, Apr. 19, 1970 (dec. April 1998). BS in Edn., U. So. Maine, 1960; postgrad., Boston U., Salem State Coll., 1964-68. 5th grade tchr. Melrose (Mass.) Sch. Dept., 1961-63, 7th grade English tchr., 1963-65, 71-97, 7th grade spl. needs tchr., 1965-70; ret., 1997. Freshman girls' basketball coach Melrose High Athletic Dept., 1973-77. Mem. U. So. Maine Alumni Assn. Avocations: golf, boating, reading.

USHER, PHYLLIS LAND, state official; b. Winona, Miss., Aug. 29, 1944; d. Sandy Kenneth and Ruth (Cottingham) Land; m. William A. Usher (dec. Dec. 1993). BS, U. So. Miss., 1967; MS, U. Tenn., 1969; postgrad., Purdue U., Ind. U., Utah State U. Libr. Natchez (Miss.) - Adams County Schs., 1967-68; materials specialist Fulton County Bd. Edn., Atlanta, 1969-71; cons. divsn. instructional media Ind. Dept. Pub. Instrn., Indpls., 1971-74, dir. divsn., 1974-82, dir. fed. resources and sch. improvement, 1982-85; acting assoc. supt. Ind. Dept. Edn., 1985, sr. officer Ctr. Sch. Improvement, 1985-96, asst. supt., 1996—. Pres. bd. dirs. INCOLSA, mcpl. corp., 1980-82; pres., owner Usher Funeral Home, Inc.; pres. NU Realty Corp.; mem. task force sch. Libraries Nat. Commn. Libraries and Info. Sci.; cons. in field. Bd. dirs. Hawthorne Cmty. Ctr.; mem. Gov. Inst. Conf. Children and Youth Task Force. Recipient citation Internat. Reading Assn., 1975; Title II-B fellow, U. Tenn., 1968-69. Mem. ALA, Nat. Assn. State Ednl. Media Profls., West Deanery Bd. Edn., Indpls. Archdiocese, Delta Kappa Gamma. Office: State House Rm 229 Indianapolis IN 46204-2728

USHRY, ROSELYN, minister; b. Balt., Dec. 23, 1943; d. Lawrence and Dorothy Louise (White) Blake; m. Wyman Ushry, Jr., Dec. 23, 1970; m. Charles C. Jones (div. Sept. 1970). AA, Balt. C.C., 1977; BS, Morgan State U., 1980; postgrad. in M Theology program, St. Mary's Sem. U., Balt. Ordained evangelist United Coun. Christian Cmty. Chs. of Md., 1977. Caseworker assoc. I-II Dept. Social Svcs., Balt., 1972—80; adminstrv. asst. Dept. Child Support Enforcement, Balt., 1980—83; asst. dir. Child Support Adminstrn., Balt., 1983—89, dir., 1989—97, Customer Svc. Child Support, Balt., 1997—99; pastor Wilson Park Christian Cmty. Ch., Balt., 1989—. Exec. sec. Christian Cmty. Coun., Balt., 2000—. Featured Lift Every Voice and Sing, WMAR TV, 2000—01. Dir. summer camp, Balt., 1999—2001; instr. GED classes, Balt., 1999—; mem. bd. neighborhood assn., Balt., 1989—; ordained elder United Coun. Christian Cmty. Chs. of Md. and Vicinity, 1985—. Recipient Outstanding Pastor award, WWIN Spirit 1400, 2001—02, Most Inspirational Person award, Balt. City Pub. Schs., 2001. Avocation: missionary work in foreign countries. Home: 1515 Winston Ave Baltimore MD 21212

USINGER, MARTHA PUTNAM, counselor, educator, dean; b. Pitts., Dec. 10, 1912; d. Milo Boone and Christiana (Haberstroh) Putnam; m. Robert Leslie Usinger, June 24, 1938 (dec Oct. 1968); children: Roberta Christine (dec.), Richard Putnam. AB cum laude, U. Calif., Berkeley, 1934, postgrad., 1935—36, Oreg. State U., 1935—37, U. Ghana, 1970, Coll. Nairobi, 1970. Tchr. Oakland (Calif.) Pub. Schs., 1936-38, Berkeley (Calif.) Pub. Schs., 1954-57, dean West Campus, counselor, 1957-78. Lectr., photographer in field. Author: Ration Books and Christmas Crackers, 1989, Threading My Way, 3 vols., 2003; contbg. author: Robert Leslie Usinger, Autobiography of an Entomologist, 1972. Mem. DAR, Berkeley Ret. Tchrs., U. Calif. Emeriti Assn., U. Calif. Alumnae Assn., Prytanean Alumnae Assn. (alumnae pres. 1952-54), Berkeley Camera Club, Mortar Bd., Am. Friends of Puttenham, P.E.O., Delta Kappa Gamma. Avocations: photography, slide shows and lectures, ethnic textiles, travel, geneology.

USMAN, MARION WILMA, retired medical/surgical and mental health nurse; b. Phila., Nov. 16, 1941; d. Einar Wangan and Luellar Johanna (Jones) Larsen; m. Ahmed Usman, Mar. 10, 1961; children: Mahmood A., Saleem A. Diploma, Stamford (Conn.) Hosp., 1967; BSN, Fairfield (Conn.) U., 1986; MS, Wright State U., 1998. Cert. gerontology nurse. Staff nurse Stamford Hosp., 1967-69, 86-87, St. Joseph Med. Ctr., Stamford, 1987-89, health care coord. Liberation Programs, 1989-91; asst. nurse mgr. Ohio State U. Hosps., Columbus, 1991-95; nurse mgr. VA Med. Ctr., Chillicothe, Ohio, 1995—2001; ret.

USSERY, LUANNE, retired communications consultant; b. Kershaw, S.C., Feb. 20, 1938; d. Ralph Thurston and Mary Elizabeth (Haile) U. BA, Winthrop Coll., 1959. Assoc. editor Kershaw (S.C.) News-Era, 1959-61; advtsg. saleswoman Nonpareil newspaper, Coun. Bluffs, Iowa, 1961-67; mag. editor Mutual of Omaha-United of Omaha Ins. Co., 1968-87; asst. v.p., 1978-82; 2nd v.p., 1982-87. Editor: The Presbyterian, Presbytery of Missori River Valley, Omaha, 1984-88, Presbyterian Times, Providence Presbytery, Rock Hill, S.C., 1990-93, 96-98, co-ed itor, 1993-96; weekly columnist Kershaw News Era, 1988-92. Elder, clk. session First Presbyn. Ch. U.S.A., Coun. Bluffs, 1974-88, Beaver Creek Presbyn. Ch., Kershaw, 1990-92, 97—; chair comms. com. Presbytery of Mo. River Valley, 1985-87, moderator, 1988; trustee Christian Home Assn./Children's Squ. U.S.A., Coun. Bluffs, 1985-88,Internat. Assn. Bus. Communicators (pres. Omaha chpt. 1972, Communicator of Yr. award Omaha chpt. 1973).

UTAY, CAROL MITNICK, special education educator, computer consultant; b. Pitts., Sept. 25, 1955; d. Leonard and Helen (Danovitz) Mitnick; m. Joe Martin Utay, Aug. 15, 1976; 1 child, Andrea. BS, U. Pitts., 1976; MEd, East Tex. State U., 1981, EdD in Spl. Edn., 1992. Prin. North Hills Community Sch., Pitts., 1974-76; tchr. Community Day Sch., Pitts., 1976-79, Dallas Ind. Sch. Dist., 1979-81, Shelton Sch., Dallas, 1981-86, dir. mid. sch., 1986-89, dir. computer lab., 1989-93; dir. tech. Jessamine County Schs., Nicholasville, Ky., 1993—99; exec. dir. Total Learning Ctrs., 1999—. Author: Term Paper Guide, 1986, Homonyms A, 1987, Hononyms B, 1987, Social Skills for the Real World, 1988, Test Taking Tips, 1993, Success with Keyboarding, 1994, 95, 97, 98; columnist No. Connections, North Hills Monthly. Mem. ISTE Leadership Acad., Am. Coun. on Learning Disabilities (speaker 1987—), Orton Dyslexia Soc., Tex. Computer Educators Assn. (steering com. 1991-92), Ky. ASsn. Tech. (exec. bd. 1993—). Home: 130 Ashley Hill Dr Wexford PA 15090-9457 Office: Learning Ctrs 12045 Perry Hwy Wexford PA 15090

UTECHT, ANDREA E., lawyer; b. Olean, NY, Nov. 30, 1948; BA magna cum laude, Elmira Coll., 1970; MS, U. Pa., 1972, MBA, JD, U. Pa., 1975. Bar: Pa. 1975, NY 1976. Assoc. corp. counsel Colonial Penn Group, Inc., 1975—81; sr. v.p., gen. counsel, sec. AtoFina Chemicals, Inc., 1996—2001; v.p., gen. counsel, sec. FMC Corp., Chgo., 2001—. Mem.: Am. Corp. Counsel Assn., Phila. Bar Assn., Assn. Corp. Counsel (bd. mem.), Am. Arbitration Assn. (bd. mem.), Phi Beta Kappa. Fluent in French. Office: FMC Corp 200 E Randolph Dr Chicago IL 60601 Office Phone: 312-861-6000. Office Fax: 312-861-7127.

UTGOFF, KATHLEEN PLATT, economist, pension fund administrator; b. Trenton, N.J., Feb. 5, 1948; d. Francis J. and Helen Platt; m. Victor Utgoff; children: Anna, Margaret. Student, Rutgers U., 1966-68; BA in Econs., Calif. State U., Northridge, 1971; PhD in Econs., UCLA, 1978. Employment counselor Dept. Human Resources, Van Nuys, Calif., 1971-72; economist Ctr. for Naval Analysis, Alexandria, Va., 1974-83; sr. staff economist Council Econ. Advisors, White House, Washington, 1983-85; exec. dir. Pension Benefit Guaranty Corp., Washington, 1985—. Mem. Women in Govt. Relations, Am. Econ. Assn., Women in Employee Benefits. Republican. Office: Pension Benefit Guaranty Corp 1200 K St NW Fl 4 Washington DC 20005-4026

UTLEY, EBONY A., communications educator; m. William Moses Summerville, June 5, 2004. BA in Speech Comm., Ind. U., Bloomington, 2001; MA in Comm. Studies, Northwestern U., Evanston, Ill., 2002, PhD in Comm. Studies, 2006. Arnold L. Mitchem fellow Marquette U., Milw., 2005—06; asst. prof. Calif. State U., Long Beach, 2006—. Contbr. chpt. to book. Recipient Indpls. PA award, City of Indpls., 2004; Ronald E. McNair Postbaccalaureate achievement program scholar, Ind. U., 1996—2001, Herman B. Wells scholar, 1997—2001, Jacob K. Javits fellow, Dept. of Edn., 2001—05, summer doctoral fellow, Wash. State U., 2005. Mem.: Nat. Communication Assn., Phi Beta Kappa Soc. Avocation: tennis. Personal E-mail: utley@hotmail.com.

UTLEY, JANE BESON, poet; b. Houston, Dec. 14, 1954; d. John Mark and Frances Ester (Rupert) Beson; m. Ronald Gene Utley, June 29, 1985. Asst. mgr. McCoy Devel. Corp., Houston, 1978-81; with accounts receivable dept. Arpco Office Supply, Houston, 1981; payroll analyst Toshiba Internat., Houston, 1981-86. Songwriter Jeff Roberts Pub., 1996-97. Contbr. poems to Best Poems of the 90's, 1996, American Poetry Annual, 1997, Word Weaver, 1997, Treasure the Moment, vol. X, 1997, A Celebration of Poets, 1997, (audio tape) Internat. Libr.'s The Sound of Poetry, anthologies; pub. comml. song Majestic Records and Countrywine Pubs. Mem. Top RecordsSongwriters Assn. Avocations: writing, fishing, gardening, reading. Office: Flooring Cons PO Box 1610 Brookshire TX 77423-1610 E-mail: jutley3169@aol.com.

UTLEY, NANCY, film company executive; Exec. v.p. mktg., media, and rsch. 20th Century Fox, Beverly Hills, Calif.; pres. mktg. Fox Searchlight Pictures. Office: 20th Century Fox PO Box 900 Beverly Hills CA 90213-0900*

UTSEY, GLENDA FRAVEL, architecture educator; BArch, U. Oreg., 1971, MLA, 1977. Assoc. head for student affairs dept. arch. U. Oreg., Eugene. Office: Dept Arch 210 Lawrence Hall 1206 Univ Oreg Eugene OR 97403-1206

UTZ, SARAH WINIFRED, nursing educator; b. San Diego; d. Frederick R. and Margaret M. (Gibbons) U.; BS, U. Portland, 1943, EdM, 1958; MS, UCLA, 1970; PhD, U. So. Calif., 1979. Clin. instr. Providence Sch. Nursing, Portland, Oreg., 1946-50, edn. dir., 1950-62; edn. dir. Sacred Heart Sch. Nursing, Eugene, Oreg., 1963-67; asst. prof. nursing Calif. State U., L.A., 1969-74, assoc. prof., 1974-81, prof., 1981—, assoc. chmn. dept. nursing, 1982—; cons. in nursing curriculum, 1978—; healthcare cons., 1991—; past chmn. edn1. adminstrs., cons., tchrs. sect. Oreg. Nurses Assn., past pres. Oreg. State Bd. Nursing; mem. rsch. program Western Interstate Commn. on Higher Edn. in Nursing; chmn. liaison com. nursing edn. Articulation Coun. Calif. Author articles and lab manuals. Served with Nurse Corps, USN, 1944-46. HEW grantee, 1970-74, Kellogg Found. grantee, 1974-76, USDHHS grantee, 1987—; R.N., Calif., Oreg. Mem. Am. Nurses Assn., Calif. Nurses Assn. (edn. commr. region 6 1987—, chair edn. interest group region 6, 1987—), Am. Ednl. Rsch. Assn., AAUP, Phi Delta Kappa, Sigma Theta Tau. Formerly editor Oreg. Nurse; reviewer Western Jour. Nursing Rsch. Office: 5151 State University Dr Los Angeles CA 90032-4226

UZAROWSKI, LAURA HELEN, physical therapist; b. Balt., Dec. 8, 1979; d. Leonard Alfred and Dorothy Anne Uzarowski. Cert. in Afro-Am. studies, U. Md., College Park, 2002, BS, 2002; PhD of Phys. Therapy, U. Md., Balt., 2005. Lic. phys. therapist Md. Athletic trainer Cardinal Gibbons HS, Balt., 2003—05; phys. therapist Good Samaritan Hosp., Balt., 2005—. Sec. Md. Athletic Trainers' Assn.; supporter Adopt-a-Platoon, 2002—06. Recipient Recognition award, Cardinal Gibbons Sch., 2005; Max Crowder Meml. Student Atheltic Trainer scholar, Atlantic Coast Conf. Athletic Trainers, 2002. Mem.: Armed Forces Athletic Trainers' Soc., Am. Phys. Therapy Assn. (cert.), Nat. Strength and Conditioning Assn. (cert.), Nat. Athletic Trainers Assn. Achievements include research in biomechanics of baseball pitching and injury prevalance. Office: Good Samaritan Hosp Baltimore MD

UZMAN, BETTY BEN GEREN, retired pathologist; b. Ft. Smith, Ark., Nov. 17, 1922; d. Benton Asbury and Myra Estelle (Petty) Geren; m. L. Lahut Uzman, Dec. 17, 1955 (dec.); 1 dau., Betty Tuba. Student, Ft. Smith Jr. Coll., 1939—40; BS, U. Ark., 1942; MD, Washington U., 1945; postgrad., MIT, 1948—50; MA (hon.), Harvard U., 1968. Intern Childrens Hosp., Boston, 1945—46; resident pathology Barnes Hosp., St. Louis, 1946—48; Am. Cancer Soc. rsrch. fellow MIT, Cambridge, 1948—50; chief biol. ultra structure and exptl. pathology Children's Cancer Rsch. Found., Boston, 1950—71; instr. Harvard Med. Sch., Boston, 1949—53, assoc., 1953—56, rsch. assoc., 1956—67, assoc. prof., 1967—71, prof., 1971-72; head rsch. dept. Sparks Regional Med. Ctr., Ft. Smith, 1972—74; prof. pathology La. State U., Shreveport, 1974—77, U. Tenn., Memphis, 1978—89, ret., 1989. Assoc. chief staff rsch. VA, Shreveport, 1974-77; staff pathologist VA, Memphis, 1978-89, chief lab. svc., 1986-87; chief field ops., spl. asst. to dir. VA Ctrl. Office, Washington, 1978-79, dir. med. rsch. svcs., 1979-80; chmn. pathology A Study sect. NIH, 1973-76; cons. to sci. dir. Children's Cancer Rsch. Found., Boston, 1971-73; mem. adv. com. on prevention, diagnosis and treatment Am. Cancer Soc., 1970-73, 77-80; mem. adv. bd. Office Regeneration Rsch., VA, 1985-89; disting. vis. investigator Inst. Venezolano Investigation Cientificas, Caracas, 1972-74 Decorated Order Andres Bello 1st class Venezuela; recipient Weinstein award United Cerebral Palsy, 1964 Mem. AAAS, Am. Soc. Cell Biology (emerita), Microscopy Soc. Am. (emerita, Diatome poster award 1985), Internat. Acad. Pathology (emerita), Am. Assn. Neuropathology (emerita, assoc.), Soc. Neurosci. (emerita), Am. Assn. Cancer Rsch. (emerita). Home and Office: Geren Farm 16048 E State Hwy 197 Scranton AR 72863-0048 Personal E-mail: bettyguzman@wildblue.net, bguzman@aol.com.

UZODINMA, MINTA LAVERNE SMITH, retired nursing administrator, nurse midwife; b. Des Moines, Mar. 29, 1935; d. Gerald Stanley and Dorothy LaVerne (Miles) Smith; m. John E. Uzodinma, Aug. 8, 1957 (dec. June 1994); children: Chinwe Uzodinma Thomas, Chika Uzodinma Hunter, Eze A., Amechi J. BSN, U. Iowa, 1957; cert nurse-midwifery, U. Miss., Jackson, 1970, MSN, 1975. Staff-head nurse pediatrics unit, supr. insvc. edn. Univ. Hosp., Iowa City, 1957-58, 61-64; clin. instr. med.-surg. nursing Iowa Meth. Sch. Nursing, Des Moines, 1958-59, 60; staff nurse, instr., assoc. dept. ob-gyn-dir. midwifery svc. U. Miss. Med. Ctr., Jackson, 1966-74, instr. nurse-midwifery edn., 1974-77, asst. prof., 1979-85, module coord. nurse-midwifery edn., 1977-81; staff nurse VA Med. Ctr., Jackson, 1985-87; nurse-midwife Coastal Family Health Ctr., Gulfport, Miss., 1987-89; asst. dir. nursing Miss. Dept. Health, Jackson, 1989-95, chief nurse cons., 1995—2001; clin. instr. nursing U. Miss. Med. Ctr., Jackson, 1992—2005, ret., 2001. Acting dir. nursing area Rust Coll., Holly Springs, Miss., 1975; mem. Miss. Bd. Nursing, 1979-84, treas., 1980-82, pres., 1983-84. Asst. editor region 3 Jour. Nurse-Midwifery, 1986-94; contbr. article to nursing jour. Bd. dirs. Hinds County unit Am. Cancer Soc., 1976-83; v.p. Poindexter Elem. Sch. PTA, 1966, pres., 1974-75. Recipient Alton B. Cobb Lifetime Achievement award Miss. Pub. Health Assn., 1996, Thelma Worksman award LWV Miss., 1998, Nursing Alumni of Decade award U. Miss., 1998; U. Iowa scholar, 1953-56; named Maternal-Child Health Cmty. Nurse of Yr., Miss. March of Dimes, 1995,98. Fellow Am. Coll. Nurse-Midwives (chpt. sec.-treas. 1985-86, treas. 1978-80, proctor divsn. examiners 1975-85, nat. chmn. nominating com. 1978-79, mem. task force on refresher programs 1984-88, chpt. chair 1991-94, bd. rev. 1987-90, sec. region III chpt. 4 1984-86, bd. govs. regional gov. 1997—, award for excellence 1997); mem. ANA, Miss. Nurses Assn. (chmn. affirmative action com. 1977-78, continuing edn. approval unit 1990-95, nurse practitioner spl. interest group 1984—, dir. edn. 1995-97, Pub./Cmty. Health Nurse of Yr. 1998, named Nurse of Yr. 2001), Eliza Pillars RN Assn., AAUW, U. Miss. Alumni Assn. (Nursing Alumni of Decade award 1971-80, 1998), Sigma Theta Tau. Home: 2832 Gretna Green St Jackson MS 39209-6907 Personal E-mail: muzocnm@aol.com.

UZZELL-BAGGETT, KARON LYNETTE, career officer; b. Goldsboro, N.C., Apr. 28, 1964; d. Jesse Lee and Ernestine Smith Uzzell; m. Ronald Walter Baggett, July 26, 1990; 1 child, Kathleen; stepchildren: Christina, Brian, Adam. BS, U. N.C., Chapel Hill, 1986; postgrad., U. Md., College Park, 1993—96. Commd. 2nd lt. USAF, 1986, advanced through grades to lt. col., 1990, exec. officer 6ACCS Langley AFB, Va., 1986—88, ops. tng. officer 7393MUNSS Murted AFD, Turkey, 1988—89, command and control officer 52FW Spangdahlem AB, Germany, 1989—92, SENEX mission dir. 89AW Andrews AFB, Md., 1995—95, dep. chief classified control Office Sec. Def., 1995—97, chief classified control Office Sec. Def., 1998—99, flight comdr., dir. ops. 82TRSS Sheppard AFB, Tex., 1999—2001; detachment comdr. USAFE MSS, Vicenza, Italy, 2001—02; comdr. 78MSS, Robins AFB, Ga., 2002—04, 416EMSS, Karshi-Khanabad, Uzbekistan, 2003—04; dir. pers. OSC-A, Kabul, Afghanistan, 2005, plans officer, 2005; dir. pers. Air U., Maxwell AFB, Ala., 2004—. Emergency med. technician Orange County Rescue Squad, Hillsborough, N.C., 1985-86; treas. Melwood PTA, Upper Marlboro, Md., 1994-97; meml. vol. Women in Mil. Svc., Washington, 1993—; entitlements vol. Whitman Walker Clinic, Washington, 1993-98. Mem. So. Poverty Law Ctr. Democrat. Baptist. Avocations: running, weightlifting, sewing, cross stitching, gardening. Home: 2319 Walbash Dr Montgomery AL 36116

VAAS, LORI RHODES, music educator; b. Upper Sandusky, Ohio, Oct. 3, 1954; d. Herschel Almar and Jeannette N. Rhodes; m. Mark J. Vaas, Mar. 22, 2005; children: Karina, Jonathan, Natalie. MusB summa cum laude, Ohio State U., 1977, MA, 1992. Music instr. Northland Acad., Westerville, Ohio, 1978—82; gen. music instr. Gahanna Mid. Sch. Ea., Ohio, 1984—88, Brookside Elem. Sch., Worthington, Ohio, 1988—. Prin. oboe player Grace Bethran Orch., Westerville, Ohio, 1988—; music dir. Worthington Cmty. Theatre, Ohio, 1993; choir dir. Brookside 5th/6th Choir, Worthington, 1988—. Sunday sch. tchr. Christ the King Luth., Westerville, 1980—84, choir dir., 1984—88. Recipient Innovation award, Worthington Friends of Edn., 1997. Mem.: Worthington Educator's Assn., Music Educators Nat. Conf., Ohio Music Educators Assn. Avocations: camping, hiking, exercise, reading, photography. Home: 7015 Hatherly Pl Columbus OH 43235 Office: Worthington Schools 6700 McVey Blvd Newark OH 43055

VACANTI, MARY PARISI, director, consultant; b. Buffalo, Oct. 28, 1947; d. Joseph Anthony and Marjorie Ronan Parisi; children: Michael Charles, David Joseph. BS Edn., SUNY Buffalo, 1969, MSEd, 1972. Cert. sch. adminstr. NY. Reading specialist Tonawanda Bd. Edn., NY, 1987—2004; dir. Tonawanda/Grand Island Tchr. Ctr., 2001—. Instr. Canisius Coll., Buffalo, 2000—01. Recipient Outstanding Achievement award, Regional Reading Conf., 1989; Spl. Legis. grantee, NY State Legislature, 2001—05. Mem.: Assn. Supervision Curriculum and Devel., Niagara Frontier Reading Coun. (bd. dirs. 1987—98, Outstanding Achievement 1989), Phi Delta Kappa (assoc.). Avocations: travel, reading, piano. Home: 450 Berryman Dr Amherst NY 14226 Office: Tonawanda/Grand Island Tchr Ctr 80 Clinton St Tonawanda NY 14150 Office Phone: 716-695-6172. Office Fax: 716-694-7394. Personal E-mail: mvacanti@localnet.com.

VACCARIELLO, LIZ, editor-in-chief; b. 1968; m. Steve Vaccariello; 2 children. BA, U. Mich. Editor-in-chief, v.p. editorial Cleve. mag.; articles editor, dep. editor Fitness mag., 1999, exec. editor, 2000—06; editor-in-chief Prevention mag., 2006—. Office: Rodale Inc 33 E Minor St Emmaus PA 18098-0099 Office Phone: 610-967-5171. Office Fax: 610-967-7726.*

VACCARO, ANNETTE ANDRÉA, music educator; b. Port Chester, N.Y., June 12, 1957; BS in Music Edn., Mercy Coll., 1980; cert. in Tchg., Manhattanville Coll., 1980; MS in Music Edn., We. Conn. State U., 1984; PhD in Adminstrn. and Supervision, Fordham U., 1990. Music tchr. Lakeland Ctrl. Schs., Shrub Oak, NY, 1980—, theatre dir., 1980—2002, with adminstrn. support Lakeland H.S., 2005—06. Adj. prof. Mercy Coll., Yorktown Heights, NY, 1993—95; advisor Wig 'n' Whiskers Drama Club Lakeland HS, Shrub Oak, 1986—, mem. AIDS Awareness Com., 1990—93, adminstrv. support, 2005—06; guest condr. Dutchess County (N.Y.) Music Festival, 1991, Westchester Broadway Theatre, Elmsford, NY, 2006; adminstrn. mentoring com. Lakeland Sch. Dist., Shrub Oak, 2002—03. Named Alumni of Yr., Lakeland (N.Y.) Edn. Found., 1999, Tchr. of Yr., Walmart Corp., 2001; recipient Nat. Theatre award, BRAVO Channel, 1999, Am. Tchr. award, The Walt Disney Corp., 2001, Cab Calloway Lifetime Achievement award, 2005; grantee, Lakeland (N.Y.) Edn. Found., 1999. Home: 129 Fields Lane Peekskill NY 10566 Office: Lakeland High School 1349E Main St Shrub Oak NY 10588

VACCARO, BRENDA, actress; b. Bklyn., Nov. 18, 1939; d. Mario and Christine (Pavia) V. Student, Neighborhood Playhouse, 1958-60. Appeared in Broadway plays: Everybody Loves Opal, 1961, The Affair, 1962, Tunnel of Love, 1962, Children from Their Games, 1963, Cactus Flower, 1965 (Tony award best supporting actress), The Natural Look, 1967, How Now Dow Jones, 1968 (Tony nomination best actress in mus. comedy), The Goodbye People, 1968 (Tony nomination for best actress in drama), Father's Day, 1971, California Suite with Neil Simon, The Odd Couple, 1985 with Sally Struthers, Jake's Women, 1992 with Alan Alda-A Neil Simon Play, Full Gallop (one woman show), 1998; motion pictures include: House by the Lake, 1977, Midnite Cowboy, 1969, Where It's At, 1969, I Love My Wife, 1970, Summer Tree, 1971, Going Home, 1971, Once Is Not Enough, 1975, Airport '77, 1977, Fast Charlie, 1977, Capricorn One, 1978, First Deadly Sin, 1980, Zorro, The Gay Blade, Supergirl, 1984, Water, 1986, Heart of Midnight, 1988, Cookie, 1988, Ten Little Indians, 1988, Masque of the Red Death, 1989, Love Affair, 1994, The Mirror Has Two Faces, 1996, Sonny, 2002, The Boyton Beach Bereavement Club, 2005; TV appearances in The Greatest Show on Earth, 1963, Fugitive, 1963, Defenders, 1965, Doctors and Nurses, 1965, Coronet Blue, 1967, Naked City, The FBI, 1969, The Psychiatrist, 1971, Name of the Game, 1971, Marcus Welby, M.D, 1972, Banacek, 1972, McCloud, 1972, McCoy, Streets of San Francisco, Sara, 1976 (Emmy nomination for best dramatic actress), Paper Dolls, Dear Detective, 1979, The Pride of Jesse Hallam, 1980, A Long Way Home, 1981, Star Maker, 1981, The Love Boat, 1984, Deceptions, 1985, St. Elsewhere, Murder She Wrote, 1990, Trials of Rosie O'Neil, 1991, Civil Wars, 1991, Flesh and Blood, 1991, Friends, 1995, The King of Queens, 1998, Ally McBeal, 1998, Becker, 2001, American Dad!, 2005, The War at Home, 2006; TV movie appearances in Travis Logan, D.A, 1971, What's A Nice Girl Like You, 1971, Honor Thy Father, 1973, Sunshine, 1973, The Big Ripoff, 1975, Julius and Ethel Rosenberg, 1978, Guyana Tragedy: The Story of Jim Jones, 1980, Paper Dolls, Dear Detective, 1989, Stolen: One Husband, Columbo, 1990, Once Is Not Enough (Academy award, Golden Globe award, People's Choice award), The Shape of Things (Emmy award for supporting actress), Golden Girls Ebbs Tide Revenge (Emmy award 1991), Red Shoe Diaries, 1991, Following Her Heart, 1994, Sing Me the Blues Lena, 1995, Touched by an Angel, 1996, Stolen One Husband, 1997, Johnny Bravo Show (voice over series animation), 1993-2000, When Husbands Cheat, 1998, Fat Girl (voice over series animation), 2001, Just A Walk in the Park, 2002, Just Desserts, 2004; TV Series (voice) Spawn, 1997. Recipient Theatre World award, 1961-62, 3 Tony nominations, 2 Hollywood Fgn. Press Assn. nominations.*

VACCARO, LUELLA G., painter, ceramist; b. Miles City, Mont. d. David O. and Gladys A. Ray; m. Nick D. Vaccaro (dec. 2002); 1 child, Nick D. Jr. Student, U. Wash., 1959, U. Calif. Berkeley, 1959—61. Represented in permanent collections. Corp. USAF, 1952—55. Avocations: dance, gardening, collecting. Personal E-mail: luvaccaro@sunflower.com.

VACCINO, ALYCE KING, artist; b. Bklyn., July 20, 1924; d. Dario F. Vaccino and Alice Salmon King; m. Dario Frances Vaccino (dec.); children: Daria Francine, Donald Frances, Peter King. Student, Fordham U., 1946—47, St. Johns U., 1947—48. Founder Atelier 778 Graphic Workshop, Great Neck, NY. One-woman shows include Donell Art Libr., NYC, 1970, Palazzo Strozzi, Florence, 1974, Adelphi U., Garden City, NY, 1976, Gustafson and Andersson Corp. Offices, Stockholm, Romano Gallery, Long Beach Island, NJ, Internat. Graphics, Stockholm, exhibited in group shows at Gallery Soho 7, Great Neck, NY, Assoc. Am. Artists, NYC, 1968, Bklyn. Mus., NY, 1969, Heckscher Mus., Huntington, NY, 1980, Art Expo, NYC, 1985, Nassau County Mus. Fine Arts, Roslyn, NY, 1985, Terrain Gallery, NYC, Arte Per L'Arte, Florence, Am. Russian Women's Artists Gallery Ctr., Boca Raton, 2002, Brentano's Gallery, Manhasset, NY, 1977, Boca Raton Mus., 2004, 2006, Represented in permanent collections NY Pub. Libr., NYC, Columbia U., Adelphi U., Queensboro CC, NY, A&G Corp. Offices, Stockholm, Marchesa Antinori, Florence. Mem. Cadet Nurse Corps, 1942—45. Recipient 1st prize photography, Women in Visual Arts, Boca Raton, Mixed Media award, Boca Mus. Artists Guild, 1st prize graphics, Bklyn. Mus., Emily Lowe award, numerous others. Mem.: Soc. Am. Graphic Artists, Nat. Assn. Women Artists, Boca Mus. Artists, Women in Visual Arts. Home: 750 NE Spanish River Blvd #102 Boca Raton FL 33431 Studio: 2960 NW Boca Raton Blvd #6 Boca Raton FL 33431 Personal E-mail: akingvaccino@aol.com.

VACHÉ, MARTHA JO, retired special education educator; b. Joliet, Ill., Mar. 14, 1945; d. Max M. and Phyllis Ann (Goodwin) Summers; m. C. Louis Vaché, Nov. 23, 1967; children: Steven, William. BA, Ill. Coll., 1967. Tchr. English New Berlin (Ill.) Jr. HS, 1967-72; dir. alumni affairs Ill. Coll., Jacksonville, 1978-81; tchr. spl. edn. Pathway Sch., Jacksonville, 1986-87, Winchester (Ill.) HS, 1987—2005; ret., 2005. Pre-vocat. counselor STEP progam, Winchester, 1987-2005; chmn. Franklin HS, Vocat. Adv. Com., 1983-85. Mem. human rights com. Jacksonville Area Assn. for Retarded Citizens, 1987-; leader 4-H Club Ill. Sch. for Visually Impaired, Morgan County, 1968-2004; pres. Morgan County Fair Aux., Jacksonville, 1984-87, 2006, mem., 1983—; pres. Franklin-Alexander PTO, 1983-84; bd. dirs. Ill. Coll. Alumni, 1983, 2004; pres. United Meth. Women, 1968-72; missions chair Centenary United Meth. Ch., 1987-, stewardship chair, 1995-97, tchr. Sunday sch., 1977—, ch. staff parish com., 2006, mem. choir, 1969—; pres. South Scott Fedn. Tchrs., 1995-98. Recipient 4-H Alumni award Morgan County 4-H, Jacksonville, 1994. Mem. Coun. for Exceptional Children (publicity chair 1991-97, pres., 2004-, ICEC region VII dir., 2002-, Pub. Rels. award 1994, 95, 96, 98, 99, Tchr. of Yr. chpt. 99, 1998, Clarissa Hug Tchr. of Yr. Ill. CEC, 2004). Avocations: flower arranging, gardening, computers, choir. Home: 2462 Loami Rd Jacksonville IL 62650

VACHUDOVA, MILADA ANNA, political science professor; d. Jaroslav Vachuda and Milada Junova Vachudova; m. Chad Carl Bryant, Apr. 30, 2005. BA in Internat. Rels., Stanford U., California, 1991; PhD in Politics, U. Oxford, Eng., 1991, MPhil in Internat. Rels., 1993. Postdoctoral fellow Ctr. for Internat. Studies, Princeton U., NJ, 1998—99, Ctr. for European Studies, Harvard U., Cambridge, Mass., 1999—2000; Jean Monnet fellow European U. Inst., San Domenico Di Fiesole, Tuscany, Italy, 2000—01; asst. prof. U. NC, Chapel Hill, 2001—. Author: Europe Undivided: Democracy, Leverage and Integration After Communism, 2005. Marshall scholar, Brit. Govt., 1991—94, Faculty Rsch. Abroad grantee, Fulbright-Hayes, U.S. Dept. of Edn., 2004—05, Rsch. grantee, Nat. Coun. Eurasian and East European Rsch., 2004—06. Office: U NC Chapel Hill Campus Box 3265 Hamilton Hall Chapel Hill NC 27599-3265 Office Phone: 919-962-0415. Office Fax: 919-962-0432.

VADLAMANI, SUCHITA, newscaster; Degree, U. Chgo. Overnight anchor KSDK-TV, St. Louis; bus. anchor, corr. CNBC India, Mumbai, India, CNBC Today; anchor, co-prodr. Asian Working Woman CNBC Asia, Singapore; anchor Sta. WAGA-TV, Atlanta, 2002—. Recipient award, Indian Profl. Network, 2003. Office: WAGA TV 1551 Briarcliff Rd NE Atlanta GA 30306

VADUS, GLORIA A., scientific document examiner; b. Forrestville, Pa. Diploma, Cole Sch. Graphology, Calif., 1978; BA in Psychology Counseling, Columbia Pacific U., 1981, MA in Psychology, 1982; diploma handwriting expert, Edith Eisenberg, Bethesda, Md., 1991. Diplomate Am. Bd. Forensic Examiners (founding mem.); cert. Am. Acad. Graphology, Washington, 1978, ct. qualified sci. document examiner, registered graphologist 1978, cert. behavioral profiling and cert. questioned documents Am. Bd. Forensic Examiners, CHS Am. Bd. Homeland Security, 2004, cert. Am. Handwriting Analysis Found. Pres., owner Graphinc, Inc., 1985—. Accredited instr. graphology Montgomery County Schs., Md., 1978—79; cert. instr. Psychogram Centre, 1978—85; instr. Coun. Graphol. Socs., 1980; testifier superior and probate cts.; pub. forum panelist, lectr., rschr., script therapist pers. selection specialist; writer in field; cons. graphologist; developed Trilogy base for rsch. Am. Handwriting Analysis Found. Author: numerous studies and papers in field, also environ. papers. Chmn. Letter of Hope for POWs; vol. Montgomery County, 1985—87; bd. dirs. East Gate I Civic Assn., Potomac, Md., 1985—87, cmty. affairs chair, 1985—87; sovereign amb. Order Am. Ambs. USA, 2006. Named Outstanding Women of the 20th Century, 2000; named to Am. Hall of Fame U.S.A. for outstanding commitment, dedication and inspirational leadership, 2005; recipient Spl. award, US, Japan Marine Facilities Panel Valuable Contbr. Japanese Panel UJNR, MFP, 1978—94, Gold Nib Analyst of Yr. award, Am. Handwriting Analysis Found., 1982, Dancing Fan award, Marine Tech. Soc., Tokyo chpt., 1991, Profound Contbr. to Soc. to the Yr., 2000, Am. Bronze Medal of Hon., 2001, Internat. Peace prize, United Cultural Conv. of USA, 2003, Legion of Honor Gold medal, United Cultural Conf., 2005, Lifetime Achievement award, World Congress of Arts, Scis. and Comm., 2005, World Freedom medal, United Cultural Ctr., 2006, Excellence medal, Congress, 2006, Svcs. and Achievement Gold medal, ABI, 2006. Fellow: Am. Coll. Forensic Examiners Internat. (life; awards chair 1993—94, Meritorious award 1994, Outstanding Contbn. cert.); mem.: Coun. Graphical Socs. (bd. dirs. 1982—84), Soc. Francaise de Graphologie for Am. Handwriting Analysis Found., Nat. Assn Document Examiners (bd. dirs. 1985—92, ethics hearing bd. 1986, chmn. nominations com. 1987—88, elections chmn. 1988, parliamentarian 1988—92), Nat. Forensic Ctr., Am. Handwriting Analysis Found. (life; chmn. rsch. com., chmn. adv. bd. 1981—87, bd. dirs. 1981—91, pres. 1982—84, chmn. nominations com. 1985—86, officiator 1986, policy planning and ethics com. 1986—91, ethics chmn. 1989—91, chmn., past pres. adv. bd. 1989—91, hon. profl. women's adv. bd. 1999, cert.), Nature Conservancy, Charles F. Menninger Soc., IEEE-Distaff (internat. chmn. bd. dirs. 1969—72, fashion show chair 1969—72), Internat. Platform Assn., Nat. Wildlife Fedn., Nat. Capitol Jaguar Owners Club (judge 1975—78), Sierra Club, Henry Hicks Garden Club of the Westburys, NY (v.p., pres. elect, judge, chair flower shows, bd. dirs. 1967—71), Soroptimist Internat. (internat. chair, regional del., v.p. chpt., bd. dirs. 1987—92, regional dir. 1987—92), Nat. Writers Club. Home: 8500 Timber Hill Ln Potomac MD 20854-4237 Office Phone: 301-299-5477. Personal E-mail: jvadus@ieee.org.

VAERST, WENDY KAREN, secondary school educator; d. Edward A. and Irene L. Olson; m. Richard R Vaerst, Sept. 13, 1940; children: Lindsey K., Celia A. MEd, St. Mary's Coll., Minn., 1993. Tchr. Sanford Jr. High, Mpls., 1974—75, Ctrl. Mid. Sch., Columbia Heights, Minn., 1975—76, Simley HS, Inver Grove Heights, Minn., 1976—. Counselor Incarnation, St. James, North Oaks, Minn., 1980—2006. Mem.: Akita Fanciers Minn., Northstar Working Dog Club. Independent. Office Phone: 651-306-7907.

VAHLKAMP, MARIANNE HILL, retired elementary school educator; b. Enid, Okla., Oct. 5, 1930; d. Andrew Mantz and Grace Hott Hill; 1 child, Anne Hill Vahlkamp Hampton. BSEd, U. Mo., Columbia, 1980. Nursery sch. tchr. Ladue Chapel, St. Louis, 1960—67; co-owner Whichcraft? Inc., Creve Coeur, Mo., 1967—78; exec. dir. Talking Tapes for Blind, St. Louis, 1980—95; tchr., evaluator Sci. Ctr., St. Louis, 1996—2003. Sec. Creve Coeur Days, 1965—68; sec., bd. dirs. Manor Condo, Kirkwood, Mo., 2002—06; bd. dirs. Vol. Dirs. Coun., St. Louis, 1990—95. Mem.: Brentwood Alumni Assn. (pres. 2003—06).

VAHRADIAN, MELINDA, fine artist; b. Ridgecrest, Calif., Nov. 20, 1956; d. Judson Calkins and Susan Frances (Huffaker) Smith; m. Scott Kendall Vahradian, July 11, 1987; children: Daniel Judson, Michael Joseph, Dylan Robert. BS in Social Ecology, U. Calif., Irvine, 1978. Cert. tchr. multiple subjects, cert. learning handicapped specialist, Calif. Learning handicapped specialist San Lorenzo Valley Unified Sch. Dist., Felton, Calif., 1984-91; artist, owner Not So Still Lifes, Santa Cruz, Calif., 1996—. Bd. dirs., leader Nursing Mothers Coun., Santa Cruz, 1990-99; leader Diabetes Support Group, Santa Cruz, 1999; participant Open Studios Cultural Coun., 1999-2003. Democrat.

VAIL, ELIZABETH FORBUS, volunteer; b. July 25, 1918; d. Sample Bouvard and Elizabeth J. (Buchtenkirk) Forbus; children: Judith Ashforth, Suzanne E. Vail Lander. Student, jr. coll., Washington, 1937—39. Copywriter, asst. to Pres. Kastor Chesley, Clifford & Atherton, Inc., N.Y.C.; 1st female airport mgr. Lebanon (N.H.) Airport, 1972. Mem. tourism and devel. com. Marathon (Fla.) City Coun., apptd. to City Code Enforcement Bd., apptd. to Marathon Aviation com.; vol. Monroe County Hurricane Ctr.; former mem. Monroe County Tourist Devel. Coun.; vol. Literacy Vols. of Am. Mem.: LWV, Am. Assn. Airport Execs., Internat. Platform Assn., Friends of Marathon Libr., Marathon Yacht Club. Avocation: reading. Home: 61 Sombrero Beach Rd Marathon FL 33050

VAIL, IRIS JENNINGS, civic worker; b. NYC, July 2, 1928; d. Lawrence K. and Beatrice (Black) Jennings; grad. Miss Porters Sch., Farmington, Conn.; m. Thomas V.H. Vail, Sept. 15, 1951; children: Siri J., Thomas V.H. Jr., Lawrence J.W. Mem. exec. com. Garden Club Cleve., 1962—83; mem. women's coun. Western Res. Hist. Soc., 1960—, Cleve. Mus. Art, 1953—. Chmn. Childrens Garden Fair, 1966-75, Public Square Dinner, 1975; bd. dirs. Garden Center Greater Cleve., 1963-77; trustee Cleve. Zool. Soc., 1971-98, life trustee 1998—; mem. Ohio Arts Coun., 1974-76, pub. sq. com. Greater Cleve. Growth Assn., 1976-93, pub. sq. preservation and maintenance com. Cleve. Found., 1989-93, chmn. pub. sq. planting com., 1993. Hon. trustee Cleve. Bot. Garden, 2001. Recipient Amy Angell Collier Montague medal Garden Club Am., 1976, Ohio Gov.'s award, 1977. Mem. Chagrin Valley Hunt Club, Cypress Point Club, Kirtland Country Club, Colony Club, Women's City of Cleve. Club (Margaret A. Ireland award). Home: 14950 County Line Rd Chagrin Falls OH 44022-6800 Office Phone: 216-360-0505.

VAIL, MARY BETH, retired secondary school educator; d. Robert Link and Jane Waldbillig Fowler; m. David Clinton Vail, Feb. 19, 1972; 1 child, Susan Jane. AA in Liberal Arts, Concordia Coll., Bronxville, N.Y., 1968; BA in English, Hartwick Coll., Oneonta, N.Y., 1970; MA in Edn., U. Albany, 1975. Tchr. English Guilderland (N.Y.) H.S., 1970—2003. Yearbook advisor Guilderland H.S., 1983—2003, Key Club advisor, 1985—2003; bd. mem. Families in Need of Assistance, Albany, 1995—97; advisor H.S. Christian Youth Group. Bd. dir. Son Rise Luth. Ministries, Pottersville, NY, 2005—. Mem.: Glen Meadows Pk. Assn. (bd. dirs. 2003—), NY Key Club, Kiwanis (bd. mem 1985—, v.p. Latham chpt. 1995, pres. 1996, lt. gov. NY State Kiwanis Internat. 1998). Republican. Lutheran. Avocations: real estate investment, crafts.

VAIL, NANCY L. SCOTT, retired elementary school educator, artist; d. Mitchell Clark and Mollie Lee (Turner) Savage; m. Jackie C. Scott (dec. 1999); 1 child, Jeff Michael Scott; m. Joseph L. Vail, Sr., Nov. 4, 2000; stepchildren: Joseph L. Vail, Jr., Chris, Jennifer Allison. BE with summa cum laude, Abilene Christian Coll., Tex., 1962, MEd with summa cum laude, 1965. Cert. in Tchg. Tex., 1962, Tex., 1985. Tchr. Jane Long Elem., Abilene, Tex., 1962—65, Canyon Creek Elem., Richardson, Tex., 1965—71, Prestonwood Elem., Richardson, 1971—78, Rountree Elem., Allen, Tex., 1978—89, Vaughan Elem., Allen, 1989—98; ret., 1998. Display, Anthurium Gallery, McKinney, Tex. Nominee Tchr. of Yr., Allen Ind. Sch. Dist., 1988, 1989. Mem.: Rountree Retirees Assn., Women's Mus. Art, Scarlet O'Hatters, Richardson Civic Art (Ribbon award 2000, 2001), Allen Retired Educators Assn. (officer, com. chmn. 2001—, Outstanding Vol. of Yr. 2003, 2004, 2006), Alpha Delta Kappa Internat. Honorary Educators Sorority (pres., v.p., historian, corresponding sec., Silver Sister award 2003). Republican. Ch. Of Christ. Achievements include starting the Epsilon Lambda Chpt. of Alpha Delta Kappa in Allen, Texas. Avocations: piano, reading, exercise, travel, painting.

VAITUKAITIS, JUDITH LOUISE, medical researcher; b. Hartford, Conn., Aug. 29, 1940; d. Albert George and Julia Joan (Vaznikaitis) V. BS, Tufts U., 1962; MD, Boston U., 1966. Investigator, med. officer reproductive rsch. Nat. Inst. Child Health and Human Devel., NIH, Bethesda, Md., 1971-74; assoc. dir. clin. rsch. Nat. Ctr. Rsch. Resources NIH, 1986-91, dir. gen. clin. rsch. ctr., 1986-91, dep. dir. extramural rsch., 1991, acting dir., 1991-92, dir., 1993—2005; sr. advisor on sci. infrastructure and resources to dir. of NIH, 2005—; from assoc. prof. to prof. medicine Sch. Medicine Boston U., 1974-86, assoc. prof. physiology, 1975-80, assoc. prof. ob-gyn., 1977-80, program. dir. gen. clin. rsch. ctr., 1977-86, prof. physiology, 1980-86; head sect. endocrinology and metabolism Boston City Hosp., 1974-86. Mem. internat. sci. adv. bd. Wellcome Trust-UIC. Author: Clinical Reproductive Neuroendocrinology, 1982; mem. editl. bd. Jour. Clin. Endocrin. and Metabolism, 1973-80, Proc. Soc. Exptl. Biol. and Medicine, 1978-87, Endocrine Rsch., 1984-88; contbr. articles to profl. jours. Chair rev. com. Nat. Space Biomedical Rsch. Inst. Strategic Rsch. Plan Office of Biol. and Phys. Rsch., NASA, Washington, 2002; mem. NIH Stem Cell Task Force, 2002; bd. trustees Tufts U., 1998—. Recipient Disting. Alumna award Sch. Medicine, Boston U., 1983, Mallincrodt award for Inv. Rsch. Clin. Radiossay Soc., 1980, Alumni award Boston U., 2003; named to Nat. Inst. for Child Health and Human Devel. Hall of Honor, 2003. Mem. Am. Fedn. Clin. Rsch., Endocrine Soc., Am. Soc. Clin. Rsch., Inst. Medicine-NAS. Office: Sr Advisor Sci Infrastructure & Resources NIH Dir Elias A Zerhouni MD Bldg 1 Rm 25 1 Center Dr MSC 0162 Bethesda MD 20892-0162 Office Phone: 301-435-6721, 301-435-6721. Personal E-mail: vaitukai@verizon.net. Business E-Mail: vaitukai@mail.nih.gov.

VAJK, FIONA, psychologist, educator; d. J. Peter Vajk and Helen T. O'Keeffe Vajk. AB summa cum laude, Princeton U., 1994; PhD, U. Colo., 2001. Lic. clin. psychologist Calif. Bd. Psychology, 2003. Psychology intern U. Calif., Psychol. and Counseling Svcs., San Diego, 2000—01; vol. US Peace Corps, Dapaong, Togo, 2001—02; staff psychologist Claremont U. Consortium, Monsour Counseling Ctr., Claremont, Calif., 2003—, dir. tng., 2004—; psychologist pvt. practice, Pasadena and Claremont, 2004—. Adj. asst. prof. psychology Pitzer Coll., Claremont, Calif., 2005—06; adj. prof. behavioral scis. Yorkville U., Fredericton, New Brunswick, Canada, 2005—; vis. asst. prof. psychology Claremont McKenna Coll., Calif., 2006. Co-author: (book chapter) A Guide to Treatments that Work, Behavioral Medicine and Women: A Comprehensive Handbook. Soprano I Coventry Choir, Pasadena, 2004—. Recipient Howard Crosby Warren Jr. prize, Princeton U., Dept. Psychology, 1993, Howard Crosby Warren Sr. prize, 1994; fellow, U. San Diego Counseling Ctr., 2002—03; grantee, U. Colo. Grad. Sch., 1996, Internat. and Interdisciplinary Devel. Com., U. San Diego, 2003; Chancellor's fellow, U. Colo. Grad. Sch., 1995—97. Mem.: APA, Princeton Club So. Calif., Nat. Peace Corps Assn., Phi Beta Kappa. Avocations: singing, travel, dance, French language, writing. Office: Ste 242 250 W First St Claremont CA 91711 Office Phone: 909-621-8202. Office Fax: 909-621-8482. E-mail: fionav@cuc.claremont.edu.

VALAKIS, M. LOIS, retired elementary school educator; b. Phila., Jan. 25, 1939; d. John Demosthenes and Blanche Antoinette Marquis Valakis. BS in Edn., Framingham (Mass.) State Tchrs. Coll., 1959. Elem. edn. tchr. Town of Framingham, 1959—98. Mem. ESEA Title III project, Framingham, 1969—70. Avocations: reading, music, photography. Home: 2 Concord Ter Framingham MA 01702

VALDES, JACQUELINE CHEHEBAR, psychologist, consultant, researcher; b. Bklyn., Sept. 17, 1962; d. Gabriel and Rosy (Mosseri) Chehebar; m. Manuel Valdes, June 3, 1990; children: Raquel Elena Valdes, Michael Aaron Valdes BA, U. Conn., 1983; cert. in substance abuse studies, Nova U., Ft. Lauderdale, 1987; MS, Nova U., 1988, PhD, 1992. Diplomate Am. Coll. Forensic Examiners, Am. Coll. Psychol. Specialties in Neuropsychology. Coord. children's outpatient Jewish Family Svc., Miami Beach, Fla., 1988—89; apprentice neuropsychology Robert A. Levitt, PhD, PA, Fla., 1989—90; intern Columbia Presbyn. Med. Ctr., N.Y.C., 1990—91; fellow and resident Robert A. Levitt, PhD, PA, Ft. Lauderdale, 1991—93; pvt. practice Hollywood, Fla., 1993—; dir. neuropsychology svcs. Meml. Regional Hosp., Hollywood, 1995-99; cons. neuropsychology Devel. and Early Intervention Clinic Joe DiMaggio Children's Hosp., 2000—. Psychology supr., educator Sunrise (Fla.) Rehab. Hosp., 1992-93, neuropsychologist cons.,1992-94; rschr. North Broward Med. Ctr., 1992-93, asst. dir. internship, 1993-94, Memory Disorders Ctr. Neurolog. Inst., Pompano, Fla., 1992-98, dir., 1994-98; neuropsychologist Neurologic Cons., Fort Lauderdale, 1992-98, Neurol. Cons., Hollywood, 1992-97; chairperson minority affairs Broward County Psychol. Assn., 1997-98; dir. neuropsychology svcs. Meml. Regional Hosp., Hollywood, 1995-99; cons. neuropsychology Devel. and Early Intervention Clinic Joe DiMaggio Children's Hosp., 2000— Contbr. articles to profl. jours Sec. Spanish Speaking Neuropsychology Interest Group, L.A., 1993-94; apptd. Child Sexual Abuse Svc. Provider Task Force, 1989 Mem. APA, Internat. Neuropsychol. Soc., Nat. Acad. Neuropsychologists, Am. Acad. Neurology, Brain Injury Assn., Fla. Psychol. Assn. (pres.-elect neuropsychology sect. 2006—), Broward County Psychol. Assn. (treas.2006—). Democrat. Jewish. Home: 520 E Mt Vernon Dr Plantation FL 33325-3600 Office: 2214 Hollywood Blvd Hollywood FL 33020-6605 Office Phone: 954-927-9555. Personal E-mail: jcvaldesphd@aol.com.

VALDEZ, DENISE, newscaster; BA in TV Broadcasting, Pepperdine U. Reporter KMIR-TV, Palm Springs, 1992; weekend anchor, reporter KCCN-TV, Monterey, Calif., 1992—93; co-anchor, reporter KSAT-TV, San Antonio, 1994—2001; weekend anchor, reporter KXAS-TV (NBC), Dallas/Ft. Worth, 2001—02; co-anchor, Channel 4 News with Furnell Chatman NBC4, Los Angeles, 2002—05; noon and 4pm anchor KLAS-TV, Las Vegas, Nev., 2005—. Mem.: Nat. Assn. of Hispanic Journalists. Address: PO Box 921295 Sylmar CA 91392

VALDEZ, DIANNA MARIE, language educator, consultant; b. Santa Fe, N.Mex., July 13, 1949; d. Delfino Julian and Margaret Erlinda Valdez. BSc, U. N.Mex., 1971, MA, 1981. Cert. Reading Tchr. N.Mex., 76, English as Second Lang. & Bilingual Tchr. N.Mex., 96. From classroom tchr. to instl. coach Albuquerque Pub. Sch., Albuquerque, 1971—2002, instl. coach, 2002—. Adj. instr. Lesley Coll., Cambridge, Mass., 1986—90; writing cons. San Felipe Elem. Sch., San Felipe Pueblo, N.Mex., 1998. Author, editor: Curriculum Integration Guide, 1984. Mem. ctrl. coord. coun. Title I Homeless Project, Albuquerque, 1998—2001; active supporter All Faith's Receiving Home, Albuquerque, 1995—2001. Recipient Achievement award, Theta State, 2001. Fellow: Nat. Writing Project-Rio Grande; mem.: Internat. Reading Assn. (pres. Camino Real coun. 1999—2000, Mem. of Yr. award 2001), Delta Kappa Gamma (state 1st v.p. 1982—2002, State Achievement award 2001). Republican. Roman Catholic. Avocations: needlecrafts, reading, writing, multimedia technology, trout fishing. Home: PO Box 1071 Corrales NM 87048 Office: Albuquerque Pub Schs Griegos Elem 4040 San Isidro NW Albuquerque NM 87107

VALDEZ, MICHELLE LIANE, educator; b. Las Cruces, N.Mex., Mar. 3, 1974; d. Jimmy Dale and Linda Jean Wolfe; m. Joseph Eric Valdez, Feb. 14, 2002; children: Kaley Marie, Nathan Eric, Leah Michelle. BS in Edn., N.Mex State U., Las Cruces, 1999. Tchr. Sierra Mid. Sch., Las Cruces, 1999—. Choreographer Colorguard/Winterguard Mayfield, Las Cruces, Onate High Schools and N.Mex State U. Pride Band, Las Cruces, 1992—2001. Choreographer (exhbn. and competition) Mosaic Winterguard (Rio Grande Valley Colorguard Circuit Champions and Judges Choice award, 1999). Mem.: NEA (corr.). Office: Sierra Mid Sch 1700 E Spruce Las Cruces NM 88001 Office Phone: 505-527-9640.

VALDEZ, WANDA DANIEL, county official; b. Yuma, Ariz., May 11, 1958; d. Jose Pedro and Gloria Diaz (Otero) D.; m. Joe R. Valdez, June 26, 1976 (div. Nov. 1999); children: Kevin Lance, Kimberly Jo. Student, Pima Coll., 1978-96, Pepperdine U., Irvine, Calif, 1976-78. Office mgr. James K. Wilson Produce Co., Nogales, Ariz., 1977-96; chief dep. treas. Santa Cruz County, Nogales, 1997—. Alderwoman City of Nogales, 1996—, city coun. woman, 1997-2000; sec.-treas. Dem. Party, Nogales, 1990-96, vice chair, 1999; PTC pres. A.J. Mitchell Sch., 1986-90, Little Red Sch., 1991-96, Lourdes H.S., 1993-94. Mem. Am. Bus. Women's Assn. (sec. 1992-95). Roman Catholic. Office: Santa Cruz County Treasurers 2150 N Congress Dr Nogales AZ 85621 Home: PO Box 6322 Nogales AZ 85628-6322

VALDRINI, RITA, prosecutor; Bar: Pa. 1988. Acting US atty. (no. dist.) W. Va. US Dept. Justice, Wheeling, W.Va., 2006—. Del. Nat. Assn. Asst. US Attorneys. Office: US Attys Office PO Box 591 Wheeling WV 26003-0011*

VALE, ELEANOR P., lawyer; b. NYC; d. Alexander and Miriam Pavlo; m. Peter R. Vale, Oct. 4, 1968; children: Anthony Quincy, Nicholas Lance. BA, Vassar Coll., Poughkeepsie, N.Y.; JD, N.Y. Law Sch., N.Y.C. Bar: N.Y. State. Pvt. practice Law Firm of Eleanor Vale, N.Y.C., 2001—. Presenter on real estate Sci. Industry and Bus. Libr., N.Y.C., NY. Co-chair class fund Vassar Coll., Poughkeepsie, NY, 1998—; pro bono rep. 9-11 victims N.Y. Trial Lawyers Assn., N.Y.C., 2001—02; bd. mgrs. Internat. YMCA, 2005—. Mem.: N.Y. Women's Bar Assn. (mem. tech. and internet com. 2003—06), Assn. Bar of City of N.Y. (mem. product liability com. 2003—04, mem. real estate com. 2006—), Assn. Women in Real Estate (mem. program com. N.Y. chpt. 2005—). Avocations: skiing, tennis. Office: Law Offices Eleanor P Vale 60 E 42d St New York NY 10165

VALE, JANIE RHEA, physician; b. Springfield, Mo., June 26, 1950; d. Virgil C. and Norma O. (Spain) Rhea; m. Joe D. Vale, Jr., Dec. 20, 1972; children: Whitley W., Rhea Megan, Spencer Maxwell. BS cum laude, S.W. Mo. State Coll., Springfield, 1974; MSPH magna cum laude, U. Mo., Columbia, 1975, MD cum laude, 1977. Occupl. medicine resident Midwest Ctr. for Occupl. Safety and Health, St. Paul, Minn., 1982-84; med. dir. Health Works, Mpls., 1984-85, Smith-Glynn-Callaway Clinic, Springfield, 1985-91; dir. occup. medicine Columbia Orthopaedic Group, 1991-93; clin. dir., asst. prof. Inst. for Occup. and Environ. Mental Health, Morgantown, W.Va., 1993-94; physician, cons. Columbia Occup. Medicine, 1995—. Prin. investigator Preventive Care Inc., Jefferson City, Mo., 1992—; cons. StayWell Health Mgmt., Eagan, Minn., 1980—; chair Occup. Safety and Health Adv. Coun., Springfield, 1988-89; bd. dirs. Safety Coun. of the Ozarks, Springfield. Contbr. articles to profl. jours. Bd. dirs. YWCA, St. Paul, 1981-82, Greenwood Lab. Sch. Alumni Assn., Springfield, 1990-91; mem. profl. and pub. edn. com. Am. Heart Assn., Mpls., 1985-86. Recipient Outstanding Achievement in Pub. Edn. award Minn. divsn. Am. Cancer Soc., 1983-84; Regents scholar, 1968-70. Mem. AMA, Am. Coll. Occup. and Environ. Medicine, Boone County Med. Soc. (v.p. and pres. bus. and medicine coalition 1987-89), Mo. State Med. Soc., Gt. Plains Occup. Medicine Soc. (treas. 1987-88, 3d v.p. 1988-89). Avocations: children's activities, biking, cooking. Home: 1012 Bourn Ave Columbia MO 65203-1455 Office: Columbia Occup Medicine 1601 E Broadway Ste Ll Columbia MO 65201-5821

VALE, PATRICE J., musician, consultant; d. Maurice Bob and June Gwendolyn (Olsen) Mizzell; m. L. Kenneth Vale, June 29, 1968; 1 child, Michelle Patrice Baggett. BS, Tex. Woman's U., 1962; MA in Sociology, U. Mo., 1998. Cert. cons. in workplace mediation Mediation Tng. Inst. Internat., Mo., 2003, ABE tchr. ABE State of Mo., 2000, paralegal diploma Paralegal Studies, Mo., 1983. Music therapist State Hosp., Fulton, Mo., 1962—64; music and dance therapist DePaul Hosp., New Orleans, 1964—66; exec. dir. lions eye tissue bank U. Mo., Columbia, 1967—73; harpist self-employed, Columbia, Mo., 1982—; paralegal and legal sec. Petri, Shurtleff, Froeschner & Smith Law Firm, Columbia, 1982—84; tchg. asst. U. oMo., Columbia, 1996—98; staff devel. trainer Mo. AEL Resource Ctr., Moberly and Fulton, 1998—2000; libr. cons. for continuing edn. Mo. State Libr., Jefferson City, 2000—04. Contbr. textbook. Recipient Nat. Honor, Nat. Music Fedn. Festivals, Tex., 1952, gold certificate for yrs. of superior rating in piano, Nat. Fedn. Music Clubs, 1952, winner piano contest judged by Liberace, Las Vegas, Nev. Mem.: TOPS, INTERTEL, Mensa, Alpha Kappa Delta. Home and Office: 908 Lynnwood Court Columbia MO 65203 Personal E-mail: patrice.vale@mchsi.com.

VALEN, NANINE ELISABETH, psychotherapist, poet; b. N.Y.C., Nov. 7, 1950; d. Herbert and Felice Holman Valen; m. Gerald Charles Levinson, Nov. 17, 1978; children: Aaron Valen Levinson, Adam Valen Levinson; m. Herbert Valen Valen, 1978. BA magna cum laude, Bryn Mawr Coll., 1971, MSS, 1985. LCSW; diplomate. Writer, producer Children's Television Workshop, N.Y.C., 1974—76; writer, prodr. KQED-TV, San Francisco, 1977; writer, producer WITF-TV, Harrisburg, Pa., 1981—82; child therapist Irving Schwartz Inst. Children and Youth, Phila., 1983—84; psychotherapist Pa. Friends Behavioral Health, 1996—, pvt. practice, Swarthmore, 1989—. Author: The Devil's Tail, 1978; co-author: The Drac: French Tales of Dragons and Demons, 1995, author of poems. Fellow, Va. Ctr. Creative Arts, 1978. Mem.: NASW, Greater Phila. Soc. Clin. Therapists. Avocations: singing, travel, hiking. Home and Office: 307 Maple Ave Swarthmore PA 19081

VALENCIA, MELANIE LAINE, music educator, performer; b. Oneonta, N.Y., Dec. 5, 1962; d. Jose Lardizabal and Marcell Jewell (Wiseman) V.; m. Frederick John Kelly, Mar. 18, 1990; children: Laine Valencia, Kelly, Frederick Alexander. Student, Ithaca Coll., N.Y., 1981—85; BS in Music, Wells Coll., Aurora, NY, 1985; MFA, Carnegie Mellon U., Pitts., 1988. Tchr. flute, staff mem. various music stores, Johnson City & N.Y.C., 1981—99; conc. bookings and adminstrv. various non-profit agys., N.Y.C., 1988—94; flutist, founder Keeping Co. Ensemble, N.Y.C., 1989—2002; flutist, dir. Valencia Duo, N.Y.C. & Binghamton, 1993—; flutist, founder, dir. Contemporary Collaborative Ensemble, N.Y.C., 1993—; instr. toddler music class Vestal Recreation Dept., NY, 1995—2000; flutist Quintessence Woodwind Quintet, Binghamton, 1995—2000; piccoloist So. Tier Concert Band, Binghamton, 1995—2001; dir. elem. band Windsor Sch. Dist., NY, 1996—98; dir. small ensembles Binghamton H.S., 1998—2002; dir. West Mid. Sch., 6th grade Concert Band, 7th and 8th grade Symphonic Band, Stage Band, Clarinet Choirs, Flute Choirs, Sax Quartets, Trios, Duos Binghamton City Sch. Dist., 1998—. Mem. NEA, Nat. Flute Assn., N.Y. State United Tchrs., Broome County Music Educators Assn., N.Y. State Sch. Music Assn., N.Y. State Sch. Band Dirs. Assn., Internat. Assn. Jazz Educators, Music Educators Nat. Conf., Phi Beta Kappa. Avocations: cooking, travel, music collaborations, cross country skiing, gardening. Home: 45 Lincoln Ave Binghamton NY 13905-4242 Office: West Mid Sch West Middle Ave Binghamton NY 13905-4242 Office Phone: 607-763-8400.

VALENSTEIN, SUZANNE GEBHART, art historian; b. Balt., July 17, 1928; d. Jerome J. and Lonnie Cooper Gebhart; m. Murray A. Valenstein, Mar. 31, 1951. With dept. Asian Art Met. Mus. Art, N.Y.C., 1965—. Rsch. curator Asian Art. Author: Ming Porcelains: A Retrospective, 1970, A Handbook of Chinese Ceramics, 1975, rev. and enlarged, 1989, Highlights of Chinese Ceramics, 1975, (with others) Oriental Ceramics: The World's Great Collections: The Metropolitan Museum, 1977, rev., 1983, The Herzman Collection of Chinese Ceramics, 1992. Mem. Oriental Ceramic Soc. (London), Oriental Ceramic Soc. (Hong Kong). Office: Met Mus Art Dept Asian Art Fifth Ave at 82nd St New York NY 10028

VALENTI, LAURIE M., elementary school educator; b. Buffalo, Nov. 18, 1959; d. George A. Jr. and Doris P. Knab; m. Stephen Valenti, July 7, 1984; 1 child, Joseph Michael. BS in Music Edn., Nazareth Coll., Rochester, NY, 1981; MA in Elem. Edn., Adelphi U., Garden City, NY, 1990. Cert. tchr. N.Y., Tex., Nat. Bd. Profl. Tchg. Stds., 2004. Substitute tchr. Aldine Ind. Sch. Dist., Houston, 1981—83; jr. acct. exec. Johnson & Higgins of Tex. (now Marsh & McLennan), Houston, 1983—86; elem. music tchr. Aldine Ind. Sch. Dist., Houston; elem. music tchr./choral dir. Hicksville (NY) Unified Sch. Dist., 1988—89; elem. music tchr., choral dir. Port Wash. Unified Sch. Dist., Port Washington, NY, 1989—91, Shenendehowa Cen. Sch. Dist., Clfton Park, NY, 1993—. Sponsor tchr. for student tchr. Crane Sch. Music, Pottsdam, NY, 2005. Recipient Supt. Recognition award, Shenendehowa Cen. Sch. Dist., 2002, 2005. Mem.: Music Educators Nat. Conf. (assoc.). Home: 68 Algonquin Rd Clifton Park NY 12065 Office: Arongen Elem Sch 489 Clifton Park Ctr Rd Clifton Park NY 12065 Office Phone: 518-881-0510. Business E-Mail: valelaur@shenet.org.

VALENTINE, ANNA MAE, retired nurse; b. Owosso, Mich., July 26, 1926; d. Robert Harry and Della Jane (Gander) Thompson; m. Manley Lavern Nixon, Aug. 3, 1946 (div. 1961); children: Terry Lee, Douglas Kent, LaVerna Ann, Norma Jean; m. Donald F. Clewley, Aug. 27, 1961 (dec. 1973); m. Heinz Weidenbruch, 1984 (dec. 1999); m. Roland J. Valentine, Nov. 1, 2003. ADN, Lansing C.C., Mich., 1983; BS in Health Studies, We. Mich. U., 1993. RN, Mich. Staff nurse Sparrow Hosp., Lansing, 1958—62, Ingham Med. Hosp., Lansing, 1962—64, Lansing Gen. Hosp., 1964—66, 1977—88, Hazel I. Findlay Country Manor, St. Johns, Mich., 1987—89, Staff Builders, Okemos, Mich., 1990—96; ret., 1996. Democrat. Avocations: knitting, crocheting, embroidery, travel, dance. Home: 108 Barbara Ln Harrison MI 48625 Personal E-mail: aweidenbruch@msn.com.

VALENTINE, APRIL SUE, elementary school educator, department chairman; d. Frederick E. Krenz; m. Mark S. Valentine, June 29, 1985; 1 child, Rebecca M. B, U. Md. Balt. County, Catonsville, 1978—82; M, Loyola Coll., Balt., 1982—84. Gen. educator Anne Arundel County Pub. Sch., Annapolis, 1983—. Dept. chairperson (sci.) Anne Arundel Co Pub. Sch., 2000—; interdiscplinary leader Anne Arundel Co Pub. Schools, 1987—. Mem.: Nat. Sci. Assn. Office: Brooklyn Park Mid Sch 200 Hammonds Ln Baltimore MD 21225 Office Phone: 410-636-2967. Office Fax: 410-636-1774. Personal E-mail: avalentine@aacps.org.

VALENTINE, CHERYL ANN WHITNEY, music educator; b. Newllton, La., June 25, 1956; d. Samuel Leon and Hazel Octavia (LeBlanc) Whitney; 1 child, Andante Latrese Valentine-Burton. BA, Va. Union U., 1981; MA, Marygrove Coll., 2005. Cert. tchr. Mich. Vocal music tchr. Detroit (Mich.) Pub. Schs., 1981—. Dir. music Sanctuary Fellowship Ch., Detroit, 1996—; validator Nat. Bd. Profl. Tchg. Stds., San Antonio, 2000—. Mem.: Detroit (Mich.) Assn. Negro Musicians, Am. Choral Dirs. Assn., Music Educators Nat. Conf., Mich. Vocal Music Assn. (dist. mgr. 2002—), Zeta Phi Beta. Democrat. Baptist. Home: 19453 Whitcomb Ave Detroit MI 48235 Office: Detroit High Sch of Arts 123 Selden Ave Detroit MI 48201 Office Phone: 313-494-6000. Office Fax: 313-494-1506.

VALENTINE, DEBRA A., lawyer; b. Cleve., Apr. 16, 1953; AB magna cum laude in History, Princeton U., 1976; JD, Yale U. Law Sch., 1980. Bar: D.C., U.S. Dist. Ct. D.C., U.S. Ct. Appeals (D.C. Cir., 3d Cir., 11th Cir.), U.S. Supreme Ct. Law clk. Judge Arlin M. Adams, U.S. Ct. Appeals, 3d Cir., Phila., 1980-81; atty./advisor Office of Legal Counsel, Dept. of Justice, Washington, 1981-85; assoc. O'Melveny & Myers, Washington, 1985-91, ptnr., 1991-95; dep. dir. policy planning FTC, Washington, 1995-96, asst. dir. for internat. antitrust, 1996-97, gen. counsel, 1997-2001; ptnr., co-chair antitrust practice group O'Melveny & Myers, Washington, 2001—04; v.p., sec., assoc. gen. counsel United Technologies Corp., 2004—. Cons. Sec. of State's Adv. Com. South Africa. Bd. editors BNA Antitrust & Trade Regulation Reporter; contbr. articles to profl. jours. Bd. dirs. The Hartford Symphony; bd. electors Wadsworth Athenaeum. Fulbright scholar, 1976-77. Mem. ABA, Internat. Bar Assn., Am. Law Inst., D.C. Bar, Coun. on Fgn. Rels., Phi Beta Kappa. Office: United Technologies Corp United Technologies Bldg Hartford CT 06101

VALENTINE, JEAN, poet, educator, writer; b. Chgo., 1934; BA, Radcliffe Coll. Poetry workshop tchr. Swarthmore Coll., 1968—70, Hunter Coll., 1970—75, Sarah Lawrence Coll., NYU, Grad. Writing Prog., Columbia U., 92nd St Y, New York, NY. Author: Dream Barker, 1965, Pilgrims, 1969, Ordinary Things, 1974, The Messenger, 1979, Home Deep Blue: New and Selected Poems, 1989, The River at Wolf, 1992, The Under Voice: Selected Poems, 1995, Growing Darkness, Growing Light, 1997, The Cradle of the Real Life, 2000, Door in the Mountain: New and Collected Poems 1965-2003, 2004 (Nat. Book Award for Poetry, 2004). Recipient awards, NEA, Bunting Inst., Rockefeller Found., NY Coun. for Arts, NY Found. for Arts, Maurice English Prize, Teasdale Poetry Prize, Shelley Mem. Prize, Poetry Soc. Am., 2000; grantee Guggenheim Fellowship.

VALENTINE, MARY ANN, graphics designer; b. Balt., Jan. 27, 1935; d. Joseph Russo and Josephine Cifala; m. Joseph Paul Valentine, July 27, 1962; children: Michael, Dominic. Degree in comml. bus., St. James Coll., Balt.; degree in bus. & mgmt. applied arts, Cantonsville C.C., Balt. Graphics artist Phenix Corp., Balt., 1972—74; devel. facilitator Md. State Personal Dept., 1975—80; coord., developer Challertown Retirement Cons., 1985—90; owner, developer Frances Clair Assisted Living, 1990—2000; dir., founder St. Michael Inst., Mystic, Conn., 2002. Home: PO Box 402 Shepherdstown WV 25443

VALENTINE, NANCY MARIE, nursing administrator, educator; b. Phila. BSN, Rutgers State U., 1969; MSN, U. Pa., 1972; MPH, Harvard U., 1978; PhD in Econs. and Health Policy, Brandeis U., 1991. Child care worker Ea. State Sch. and Hosp. for Emotionally Disturbed Children, Trevose, Pa., 1968; staff nurse Abington (Pa.) Meml. Hosp., 1969-70; pub. health nurse Cmty. Nursing Svcs., Phila., 1970; camp nurse Camp Spruce Hill, Tolland, Mass., 1971; staff nurse student health ctr. Temple U., Phila., 1970-72; group co-therapist McLean Hosp., Belmont, Mass., 1974-76, 1970-72, clin. nursing supr., 1973-78; nurse therapist Expansion, Inc., Bedford, Mass., 1977-78; project dir. Boston State Coll., Mass., 1978-80; fellow HHS, Washington, 1980-81; DON Boston City Hosp., 1981-83; co-founder, cons. Nightingale, 1982-89; adminstr. for nursing McLean Hosp., Belmont, Mass., 1983-93; asst. chief med. dir. nursing programs Dept. VA, Washington, 1993—. Mem. implementation com. Inst. Mass. Gen. Hosp., Boston, 1989, assoc. prof., 1991-94; adj. instr. U. Mass., Boston, 1991—; adj. prof. Northea. U., Boston, 1990—, Cath. U., 1993—, Georgetown U., 1995; assoc. in psychiatry Med. Sch. Harvard U., 1992—; instr. psychiat. nursing Newton Jr. Coll., Newtonville, Mass., 1975; project coord. NIMH, 1974-76; clin. instr. Boston Coll., Chestnut Hill, 1979-80; lectr. Mass. Nurses Assn., 1984, 86, 91; editl. referee Jour. Studies on Alcohol; cons. N.E. Ga. Med. Ctr., 1991, 92, 93, Charter Hosp. Long Beach, Calif., 1989; mem. nursing practice adv. com. Mass. Bd. Registration in Nursing, 1991; mem. adv. bd. dept. nursing Middlesex C.C., Bedford, Mass., 1983-88; mem. interdisciplinary med. adv. com. Blue Cross/Blue Shield Mass., 1989; mem. coordinating com. house staff monitoring and clin. tng. conditions Boston U. Med. Ctr., 1989-90; cons., presenter in field. Mem. editl. bd. Nat. Nurses Soc. on Addictions, Jour. Psychosocial Nursing and Mental Health Svcs., Am. Psychiat. Nurses Assn.; mem. editl. adv. bd. Adminstrn. and Policy in Mental Health; field editor Jour. Mental Health Adminstrn.; contbr. articles to profl. jours. Mem. adv. bd. Project Task Force to Determine Feasibility of Continuing LPN Tng. Program, Youville Hosp., Cambridge, Mass., 1985-86; mem. orgn. health profls. U. Calif. San Francisco Med. Ctr., 1980-81. Capt. U.S. Army Nurse Corp Res. Grantee Robert Wood Johnson Found., 1988, McLean Hosp., 1988, Mass. State Coll. System, 1979; recipient Brandeis U., 1983-85, Phila. Bd. Edn. scholarship, 1965; Harvard U. fellow, 1977-78; recipient Outstanding Alumni award Rutgers U. Coll. Nursing, 1987, Malcolm Alderfer Schweiker award, Outstanding Alumni award U. Pa., 1987, Minkoff prize Brandeis U., 1991. Fellow Am. Acad. Nursing; mem. ANA (task force on assistive personnel 1991), Am. Orgn. Nurse Execs., Soc. for the Edn. and Rsch. of Psychiatric Nurses, Am. Coll. Mental Health Adminstrn., APHA, Nat. Nurses Soc. Addictions, Mass. Nurses Assn. (task force on nurses with substance abuse problems, chairperson task force on nurses' aides, coun. on nursing svc. adminstrn., rep. task force on nursing assts. Mass. Bd. Registration in Nursing 1989-90, liaison with Mass. Med. Soc. 1988-92, Human Need Svcs. award 1985), Mass. Orgn. Nurse Execs., Nursing Honor Soc., Mass. Pub. Health Assn., Nurses United for Reimbursement Svcs., New Eng. Orgn. for Nurses, Am. Psychiatric Nurses Assn., Brandeis U. Florence Heller Sch. of Social Welfare Policy Alumni Assn., Harvard U. Sch. of Pub. Health Alumni Assn., U. Pa. Sch. Nursing Alumni Assn., Rutgers U. Coll. Nursing Alumni Assn., Sigma Theta Tau. Office: Dept VA Nursing Program 810 Vermont Ave NW # 18 Washington DC 20420-0001

VALENTINE, PHYLLIS LOUISE, counseling administrator; d. Harold Gray and Velma Eura Long; m. Samuel L. Valentine, Dec. 30, 1995. BA, St. Augustine's Coll., 1970; MEd, Bowie State U., 1992; student, Trinity Coll., 1974—77, Georgetown U., 1989, U. D.C., 1974—88. Cert. sch. counselor K-12, reading tchr. K-12. Evening reading reacher Loton Reformatory Youth Ctr. II PSI Assocs., Washington, 1984—86; chpt. 1 reading/math. lab tchr. D.C. Pub. Schs., 1986—92, chpt. 1 resource asst., 1992—93; chpt. 1 CAI lab tchr./team coord. C.W. Harris Elem. Sch., Washington, 1992—95; sch. counselor J.C. Nalle Elem. Sch., Washington, 1995—. Mem. tchr. adv. bd. Ctr. for Artistry in Tchg., Washington, 1999—; dir., presenter J.C. Nalle Sch. Extended Day, 1998. V.p. Brandywine Sta. Townhouse Assn., Upper Marlboro, Md., 1990—97. Recipient Letter of Commendation, Exec. Dir. Chpt. 1 program, 1987, AIMs Pilot, Bryan Elem. Sch., 1984, HOST Corp., 1994, DCPS Parent Ctr. Incentive, 1997. Mem.: D.C. Sch. Counseling Assn. (newsletter editor 2004—05, corr. sec.), Am. Sch. Counseling Assn., Am. Counseling Assn., Tots & Teens Inc. (pres. 1985—93, corr. sec. 1985—93, youth leader 1987—91, D.C. chpt., award 1990—91), D.C. Counseling Assn. (pres.-elect 2001—02, pres. 2002, dedicated svc. plaque 1993), Phi Delta Kappa (mem. Beta chpt., grammateus 2003—), Nat. Sorority Phi Delta Kappa (Beta chpt.), Sigma Gamma Rho (recording sec., anti-basilus 1971—78). Avocations: gardening, listening to jazz music, dance. Business E-Mail: phyllis.valentine@k12.us.

VALENTINE, TERRI L., secondary school educator, activities director; d. Gene and Eloise Bennett; m. Scott Valentine, Nov. 5, 1982; children: Tiffany, Braye. BS in Edn., U. Ctrl. Ark., Conway, 1998. Cert. tchr. Ark. Tchr. Cabot Jr. HS South, Ark., 1998—2000, North Little Rock High E, Ark., 2000—. Costume/makeup dir., drama dept. North Little Rock HS E, 2000—, asst. parent involvement coord., 2005—, activities dir., 2005—, 2006—. Dir. Lynchview Bapt. Ch., North Little Rock, 2001—. Mem.: Ark. Speech Communication Assn. (assoc.; scholarship com. chair, Demo Day chair 1999—, theater scholar 1995—98). Avocations: swimming, running, travel. Office: North Little Rock HS E Campus 4200 Lakeview North Little Rock AR 72116 Office Phone: 501-771-8200. Office Fax: 501-771-8213. E-mail: valentinet@nlrhs.k12.ar.us.

VALENTINI, VIRGINIA REDD, audio-visual specialist, educator; b. Birmingham, Ala., May 3, 1974; d. Harold Douglas and Judith Greek Redd; m. Thomas Edward Valentini, Nov. 12, 2005. BS in Early Childhood and Elem. Edn., U. Ala., 1997; MA in Spl. Edn. of Visually Impaired, U. Ala., Birmingham, 2004. Cert. tchr. Ala. Tchr. grade 3 Tarrant City Schs., Ala., 1998—2000, Fairfield City Schs., Ala., 2000—03; grad. asst. U. Ala., Birmingham, 2003—04; tchr. visually impaired Ala. Inst. for Deaf and Blind, Talladega, 2004—. Mem.: Coun. Exceptional Children, Ala. Edn. Assn., NEA. Avocations: reading, walking. Personal E-mail: gredd2@bellsouth.net.

VALERO, MARIA TERESA, photographer, art educator; b. Venezuela; BFA in graphic design & art history, U. Kans., M art history. Dir. Sch. Art, U. Tulsa, prof., Gallery Dir., Alexandre Hogue Gallery; founder & dir. Third Floor Designs (a student run design studio). Exhibitions include, Kans., Mo., Okla., Ariz., Tex., Ark., Venezuela, Beauty of the Levant (Images of Lebanon & Syria Through Western Eyes), Syria. Recipient Graphex Award, Tulsa Addy, Creativity Today Award. Office: University of Tulsa Phillips Hall 104 600 South College Ave Tulsa OK 74104 Office Phone: 918-631-2740. Office Fax: 918-631-3423. E-mail: maria-valero@utulsa.com.

VALETTE, REBECCA MARIANNE, Romance languages educator; b. NYC, Dec. 21, 1938; d. Gerhard and Ruth Adelgunde (Bischoff) Loose; m. Jean-Paul Valette, Aug. 6, 1959; children: Jean-Michel, Nathalie, Pierre. BA, Mt. Holyoke Coll., 1959, LHD (hon.), 1974; PhD, U. Colo., 1963. Instr., examiner in French and German U. So. Fla., 1961-63; instr. NATO Def. Coll., Paris, 1963-64, Wellesley Coll., 1964-65; asst. prof. Romance Langs. Boston Coll., 1965-68, assoc., 1968-73, prof., 1973—2003, prof. emeritus, 2003—. Lectr., cons. fgn. lang. pedagogy; Fulbright sr. lectr., Germany, 1974; Am. Coun. on Edn. fellow in acad. adminstrn., 1976-77. Author: Modern Language Testing, 1967, rev. edit., 1977, French for Mastery, 1975, rev. edit., 1988, Contacts, 1976, rev. edit., 1993, 97, 2001, C'est Comme Ça, 1978, rev. edit., 1986, Spanish for Mastery, 1980, rev. edit., 1989, 94, Album: Cuentos del Mundo Hispanico, 1984, 3d edit., 2005, French for Fluency, 1985, Situaciones, 1988, rev. edit., 1994, Discovering French, 1994, 97, 2001, A votre tour, 1995, 2nd edit., 2007, Ventanas Uno, 1998, Images 1, 2, 3, 1999, Reflections on the Connolly Book of Hours, 1999, Weaving the Dance, 2000, Discovering French Nouveau, 2004, 2d edit., 2007, Federation of Alliances Francaises USA Edn. Handbook, 2005; contbr. articles to fgn. lang. pedagogy and Native Am. art publs. Decorated comdr. Palmes Académiques, chevalier Ordre Nat. du Mérite (France). Mem. MLA (chmn. divsn. on tchg. of lang. 1980-81), Am. Coun. on Tchg. Fgn. Langs., Am. Assn. Tchrs. French (v.p. 1980-86, pres. 1992-94), Alliance Francaise of Boston and Cambridge (pres. 2002—), Fedn. Alliances Francaises USA (v.p. 2003—06), Phi Beta Kappa, Alpha Sigma Nu, Pi Delta Phi. Home: 16 Mount Alvernia Rd Chestnut Hill MA 02467-1019 Office: Boston Coll Lyons 304 Chestnut Hill MA 02467-3804 Business E-Mail: valette@bc.edu.

VALFRE, MICHELLE WILLIAMS, nursing educator, administrator, writer; b. Reno, Feb. 12, 1947; d. Robert James and Dolores Jane (Barnard) Williams; m. Adolph A. Valfre, Nov. 7, 1998. BSN, U. Nev., Reno, 1973; M Health Svc., U. Calif., Davis, 1977. RN, Oreg., Ariz. Staff nurse VA Hosp., Reno, 1973—77; family nurse practitioner Tri-County Indian Health Svc., Bishop, Calif., 1977—81; instr. nursing Rogue C.C., Grants Pass, Oreg., 1981—82; psychiat. nurse VA Hosp., Roseburg, Oreg., 1982; dir. edn. Josephine Meml. Hosp., Grants Pass, 1983—84; geriat. nurse practitioner Hearthstone Manor, Medford, Oreg., 1984—86; chmn. nursing dept. Rogue C.C., Grants Pass, 1986—89; prin. Health and Ednl. Cons. Inc., Forest Grove, Oreg., 1989—. Instr. social scis. Rogue C.C., 1997-98; DON Highland House Nursing Ctr., Grants Pass, 1990; bd. dirs. Tri-County Indian Health Svc.; cons. for nursing svcs. in long-term care facilities Author: Professional Skills for Leadership, Foundations of Mental Health Care, 3d edit., 2005; contbr.: Fundamental Health Care: Concepts and Skills. Mem. Josephine County Coalition for AIDS, Grants Pass, 1990. With USN, 1965-69 Mem. NAFE, Nat. League Nursing, Oreg. Ednl. Assn., Oreg. State Bd. Nursing (re-entry nursing com. 1992-93) Office: PO Box 807 Forest Grove OR 97116 Office Phone: 503-357-2215. E-mail: avalfre@mindspring.com.

VALLA, BREE BUTLER, agricultural studies educator; b. Ventura, Calif., Dec. 31, 1977; d. Allan Clifford and Carole Jean Butler; m. Chad Fredrick Valla, Aug. 7, 2004; 1 child, Corbin John. M, Calif. Poly., San Luis Obispo, 1995—2001. Cert. Tchr. Calif. Dept. Edn., 2001. Tchr. Mupu Sch. Dist., Santa Paula, Calif., 2001, Lompoc Unified Sch. Dist., 2001—. Adv. Future Farmer's Am. Assn., Lompoc, 2001—05. Recipient Hon. State Degree, Calif. Future Farmer's Am. Assn., 2005. Mem.: Calif. Agrl. Tchrs. Assn. (v.p. 2004—05). Office: Lompoc Unified Sch Dist 320 North J St Lompoc CA 93436

VALLBONA, RIMA-GRETEL ROTHE, retired foreign language educator, writer; b. San Jose, Costa Rica, Mar. 15, 1931; arrived in U.S., 1956, naturalized, 1997; d. Ferdinand Hermann and Emilia (Strassburger) Rothe; m. Carlos Vallbona, Dec. 26, 1956; children: Rima-Nuri, Carlos-Fernando, Maria-Teresa, Maria-Luisa. BA/BS, Colegio Superior de Senoritas, San Jose, Costa Rica, 1948; diploma, U. Paris, 1953; diploma in Spanish Philology, U. Salamanca, Spain, 1954; MA, U. Costa Rica, 1962; D in Modern Langs., Middlebury Coll., 1981. Tchr. Liceo J.J. Vargas Calvo, Costa Rica, 1955—56; faculty U. St. Thomas, Houston, 1964—95, prof. Spanish, 1978—95, Cullen Found. prof. Spanish, 1989, head Spanish dept., 1966—71, chmn. dept. modern fgn. lang., 1978—80, prof. emeritus, 1995—. Vis. prof. U. Houston, 1975—76, Rice U., 1974, 1980—83, 1995, U. St. Thomas, Argentina, 1972, U. St. Thomas, Merida program, 1987—95. Author: Noche en Vela, 1968, Yolanda Oreamuno, 1972, La Obra en Prosa de Eunice Odio, 1981, Baraja de Soledades, Las Sombras que Perseguimos, 1983, Polvo del Camino, 1972, La Salamandra Rosada, 1979, Mujeres y Agonias, 1982, Cosecha de Pecadores, 1988, El arcangel del perdon, 1990, Mundo, demonio y mujer, 1991, Los infiernos de la mujer y algo mas, 1992, (crit. edit.) Vida i sucesos de la Monja Alferez, 1992, Flowering Inferno-Tales of Sinking Hearts, 1994, La narrativa de Yolanda Oreamuno, 1996, Tormy, la Prodigiosa Gata de Donaldito, 1997, Tejedoras de sueños versus realidad, 2003; mem. (editl. bd.) Letras Femeninas, 1984—98, Alba de America, U.S., sec. (culture) Inst. Literario y Cultural Hispanico; co-dir.: Foro Literario, 1987—89; contbg. editor: The Americas Rev., 1989—95; contbr. numerous articles and short stories to lit. mags. Mem. scholarship com. Inst. Hispanic Culture, 1978, 1979, 1988, 1991, chmn., 1979, bd. dirs., 1974—76, 1988—89, 1991—92, chmn. cultural activities, 1979, 1980, 1985, 1988—89; bd. dirs. Houston Pub. Libr., 1984—86, Cultural Arts Coun. Houston, 1991—92. Recipient Aquileo J. Echeverria Novel prize, 1968, Jorge Luis Borges Short Story prize, Argentina, 1977, Agripina Montes del Valle Novel prize, 1978, Constantin Found. grant for rsch., U. St. Thomas, 1981, Lit. award, S.W. Conf. Latin Am. Studies, 1982, Ancora Lit. award, Costa Rica, 1984, Civil Merit award, King Juan Carlos I of Spain, 1989, Children's Book award, Bay Area Writers League, 2003. Mem.: Soc. Children's Book Writers and Illustrators, Nat. Writers Assn., Inst. Lit. y Cultural Hispanico, Casa Argentina de Houston, Inst. Hispanic Culture Houston, Latin Am. Writers Assn. Costa Rica, Inst. Internat. de Lit. Iberoam., Latin Am. Studies Assn., Academia Norteamericana de la Lengua Espanola (elected), S.W. Conf. Orgn. Latin Am Studies, South Ctrl. MLA, Houston Area Tchrs. Fgn. Lang., Houston Area Tchrs. Spanish and Portuguese, Am. Assn. Tchrs. Spanish and Portuguese, Sigma Delta Pi, Phi Sigma Iota. Roman Catholic. Home: 3706 Lake St Houston TX 77098-5522 E-mail: rvallbona@aol.com.

VALLEE, JUDITH DELANEY, environmentalist, writer, not-for-profit fundraiser; b. N.Y.C., Mar. 14, 1948; d. Victor and Sally Hammer; m. John Delaney, Apr. 9, 1974 (div. 1978); m. Henry Richard Vallee, May 15, 1987. BA, CUNY, 1976. Exec. dir. Save the Manatee Club, Maitland, Fla., 1985—. Apptd. U.S. Manatee Recovery Plan Team, Jacksonville, Fla., 1988-97, Fla. Manatee Tech. Adv. Coun., Tallahassee, 1989-2002, Save the Manatee Com., Orlando, Fla., 1985-92, World Conservation Union/Sirenia Specialist Group, Switzerland, 1996; advisor Save the Wildlife Inc., Chuluota, Fla., 1992-93; bd. dirs. Environ. Fund for Fla. Lobbyist Save the Manatee Club, 1989; vol. Broward County Audubon Soc., Ft. Lauderdale, 1983-84, Wild Bird Care Ctr., Ft. Lauderdale, 1984. Recipient Refuge Support award Chassahowitzka Nat. Wildlife Refuge, 1989. Democrat. Avocations: creative writing, antiques, wildlife observation, canoeing. Office: Save the Manatee Club Inc 500 N Maitland Ave Ste 210 Maitland FL 32751-4458 Office Phone: 407-539-0990. E-mail: jvallee100@aol.com.

VALLEE, MICHELLE LINDA, pre-school educator; b. Passaic, NJ, Dec. 18, 1973; d. Rudolph Herman Vallee Jr. and Linda Marguerite Lombardi. Cert. in Child-Related Careers, Morris County Sch. of Tech., Denville, NJ, 1991—93; AS, County Coll. of Morris, Randolph, NJ, 2002. Cert. child devel. assoc. Washington, 1999. Presch. tchr. Page Sch., Morris Plains, NJ, 1999—2003, PACE Presch., Lake Hiawatha, NJ, 2003—05; dance tchr. Mary Lou Hale's Sch. of Dance, Lake Hiawatha, NJ, 1998—; presch. tchr. Sunnyfields, Whippany, NJ, 2005—. 3rd grade ccd tchr. St. Peter the Apostle Ch., Parsippany, NJ, 1999—. (dance solo) Dinner Party Tap Solo. 3rd grade CCD tchr. St. Peter the Apostle Ch., Parsippany, NJ, 1999—2006. Mem.: MCSSA (assoc.). Independent. Roman Catholic. Avocations: bowling, soccer, volleyball, softball, travel. Home: 4 Oak Ln Lake Hiawatha NJ 07034 Office: Sunnyfields Learning Center 494 Rte 10 W Whippany NJ 07981 Office Phone: 973-887-8522. Personal E-mail: wrightgrl05@aol.com.

VALLES, JUDITH V., former mayor, retired academic administrator; b. San Bernardino, Calif., Dec. 14, 1933; d. Gonzalo and Jovita (Lopez-Torices) V.; m. Chad Bradbury, Sept. 30, 1956 (dec. Sept. 1969); children: Edith Renella, Nohemi Renella, Chad; m. Harry Carl Smith, Oct. 13, 1985. BA in English, Redlands (Calif.) U., 1956; MA in Spanish Lit., U. Calif., Riverside, 1966; doctorate (hon.), U. Redlands, 2000. Instr. Spanish San Bernardino Valley Coll., Calif., 1963-84, head dept. fgn. lang., 1971-76, chair div. humanities, 1976-81, dean extended day, 1981-83, adminstrv. dean acad. affairs, 1983-87, exec. v.p. acad. and student affairs, 1987-88; pres. Golden West CC, Huntington Beach, Calif., 1988—95; mayor City of San Bernardino, 1998—2006. Mem. adv. com. Police Officers Standards and Tng. Commn., Sacramento, 1991—. Author fgn. lang. annals and sociol. abstracts. Speaker statewide edn. and community orgns., 1988—; bd. dirs. exec. coun. and chief exec. officers Calif. Community Colls., 1990—. Recipient Bishops award for diocese, Outstanding Pub. Svc. award NALEO, 2001; named One of Outstanding Women Orange County YWCA, 1990, Citizen of Achievement LWV, 1989, Woman of Distinction Bus. Press, 1998, Influential Latina of the Yr. Hispanic Lifestyle, 1998, State of Calif. Woman of the Yr., 1999, Humanitarian Yr. Cath. charities, 1999, Citizen Yr. Boy Scouts Am., 1999, Empire Woman Yr. State Assembly, 1999, Outstanding Cmty. Leader, Cmty. Found., 2002, Woman of Yr., State Senate, 2003; inducted into Hall of Fame, San Bernardino Valley Coll. Mem. Women's Roundtable Orange County, Conf. and Visitors Bur., C. of C. (Vanguard), Kiwanis, Charter 100. Avocations: opera, theater, reading, running.

VALLETTA, AMBER, actress, model; b. Phoenix, Feb. 9, 1974; m. Herve Le Bhihan, 1994 (div. 1996); m. Christian McCaw, Sept. 2003; 1 child, Auden. With Boss Models, N.Y.C.; Elite Models, N.Y.C., 1996—. Exec. prodr.: (films) Ticks, 1999; actor: Drop Back Ten, 2000, What Lies Beneath, 2000, The Family Man, 2000, Perfume, 2001, Max Keeble's Big Move, 2001, Duplex, 2003, Raising Helen, 2004, Hitch, 2005, Transporter 2, 2005; (TV films) Hysteria: The Def Leppard Story, 2001. Office: Fl 2 300 Park Ave S New York NY 10010-5313

VALLIANOS, CAROLE WAGNER, lawyer; b. Phila., Aug. 19, 1946; d. F. Leonard Wagner and Helen Rose Pikunas; m. Peter Denis Vallianos, June 22, 1963; children: Kelly, Denis, Jamie Vallianos-Healy. BA, Calif. State U., Fullerton, 1981; JD, Southwestern U., 1995. Bar: Calif. 1997. Nonprofit cons., Manhattan Beach, Calif., 1982—; atty. in pvt. practice, 1997—. Non-profit cons. USIA, Turkey, 1997, Cyprus, 97, Bosnia-Herzegovina, 98, India, 99. Pres. LWV Calif., 1989—91; mem. com. on pvt. judging Calif. Jud. Coun., 1989—91, mem. com. on race and ethic bias in the cts., 1991—96, mem. com. on access and fairness in the cts., 1994—97, 2002—, mem. task force on jury sys. improvements, 1998—2003; mem. Women Lawyers L.A. Jail Project; mem. adv. bd. U. Fla. Marion Brechner Citizen Access Project, 2000—02; bd. dirs. LWV U.S., 1992—98, LWV Edn. Fund U.S., 1992—98, L.A. Biomed. Rsch. and Edn. Inst., Harbor UCLA, 2002—, treas., 2003—06, chair bd. dirs., 2006—. Mem. LWV Beach Cities (former pres.), Am. Judicature Soc. (bd. dirs. 1996—, exec. com. 2001—, sec. 2003-2005, vice chair, 2005—), Calif. First Amendment Coalition, (bd. dirs. 1995-2005), Coalition for Justice (v.p. 1993-2005), Pacific Coun. Internat. Policy, Benjamin Aranda Inn of Ct. (exec. com. 2002-03). Avocations: travel, political memorabilia, literature.

VALVERDE, CHERYL LYNN, secondary school educator; b. Kans. City, Mo., Oct. 8, 1963; d. Arthur Ray and Margarette Jayne Morton; m. Clinton Daniel Valverde, Nov. 10, 1994; children: Brianna Patricia, Bryce Morton. BA in Math., St. Mary's U., San Antonio, Tex., 1985; MA in Secondary Edn., U. N.Mex, Albuquerque, N.Mex., 1999, degree in Edn. Specialty, 2000. Lic. tchr. secondary edn. Fla., 2005. Tchr. math. St. Pius X H.S., Albuquerque, 2001—03, Space Coast Jr./Sr. H.S., Cocoa, Fla., 2004—. Lt. U.S. Army, 1985—89, Germany. Grantee, Rio Rancho Sch. Bd., 1999. Office: Space Coast Jr/Sr High School 6150 Banyan Street Cocoa FL 32927 Office Phone: 321-638-0750.

VALVO, BARBARA-ANN, lawyer, surgeon; b. Elizabeth, NJ, June 7, 1949; d. Robert Richad and Vera (Kovach) V. BA in Biology, Hofsta U., 1971; MD, Pa. State U., 1975; JD, Loyola Sch. Law, 1993. Bar: La. 1993; diplomate Am. Bd. Surgery. Surg. intern Nassau County Med. Ctr., East Meadow, NY, 1975-76; resident gen. surgery Allentown-Sacred Heart Med. Ctr., Pa., 1976-80; asst. chief surgery USPHS, New Orleans, 1980-81; pvt. practice gen. surgery New Orleans, 1981-89; pvt. practice med. malpractice law, 1995—. Upjohn scholar, 1975. Fellow ACS; mem. ABA, Fed. Bar Assn., La. Bar Assn., La. Trial Lawyers Assn. Republican. Avocations: computers, raising animals. Office: 41 Harley Pl Willow Spring NC 27592 Personal E-mail: bavalvo@nc.rr.com.

VAN ALLEN, BARBARA MARTZ, marketing professional; d. Walter Atlee and Barbara Jean (Winebrenner) Martz; m. Peter Cushing Van Allen, Sept. 3, 1983; children: Caroline Kent, Peter Cushing Jr. BA with honors, U. N.C., 1976; MA, George Washington U., 1983; MBA, NYU, 1993. Legis. asst. U.S. Ho. of Reps., Washington, 1976-81, legis. dir., 1981-83; dir. ITT Corp., N.Y.C., 1984-90; pres. Van Allen Assocs., N.Y.C., 1990-93, 2000—; mng. dir. Cushman & Wakefield, Inc., N.Y.C., 1994-2000. Bd. dirs. Washington Nat. Cathedral Coll., 2000—. Mem. N.Y.C. Jr. League, 1986—; mem. econ. devel. task force N.Y.C. Mayoral Campaign and Transition Team, 1994—95; bd. dirs. 801 West End Avenue Corp., N.Y.C., 1995—99. Recipient Star awards for print campaign and internal comm. Bus. Mktg. Assn., 1996, nat. pro-comm. profl. excellence award for radio, 1996, Pro Com. award, 1997, Impact award, 1998. Mem. NAFE, Internat. Assn. Bus. Communicators (Iris Merit award 1996, Ace Merit award 1996, Ace award of excellence for pub. 1997, Ace award of merit for Reporter's Handguide 1997, N.Y. Fest. award, BMA Pro Comm. award for Direct Mail: Soup to Nuts, 1998, APEX award for Real Estatements publ., 1998), Bus. and Profl. Women's Club, YWCA Acad. Women Achievers. Home: 4407 Hadfield Ln NW Washington DC 20007-2034

VAN ALSTYNE, JUDITH STURGES, retired language educator; b. Columbus, Ohio, June 9, 1934; d. Rexford Leland and Wilma Irene (Styan) Van Alstyne; m. Dan C. Duckham (div. 1964); children: Kenton Leland, Jeffrey Clarke. BA, Miami U., Oxford, Ohio, 1956; MEd, Fla. Atlantic U., 1967. Sr. prof. Broward CC, Ft. Lauderdale, Fla., 1967-88, spl. asst. women's affairs, 1972—88, dir. cmty. svcs., 1973—74, dir. cultural affairs, 1974—75; ret., 1988. Spkr., cons. Malaysian Coll., 1984; ednl. travel group tour guide, 1984—88; v.p., ptnr. Downtown Travel Ctr., Ft. Lauderdale, 1993—. Author: (book) Write It Right, 1980, Professional and Technical Writing Strategies, 6th edit., 2004; contbr. articles and poetry to profl. jours. Bd. dirs. Broward CC Found., Inc., Fla., 1973—, Broward Friends of Libr., Fla., 1994—98, Broward Friends Miami (Fla.) City Ballet, 1994—98, 2001—03; active Sister cities/People to People, Ft. Lauderdale, 1988—99; docent Ft. Lauderdale Mus. Art, 1988—, docent coun., 1999—2002, docent pres., 2001—03; officer, mem. Friends Mus., Ft. Lauderdale, 1992—, Broward Pub. Libr. Found., Fla., 1998; v.p. Downtown Travel Ctr., Ft. Lauderdale, 1991—; bd. govs. Mus. of Art, 2003—05. Recipient Award of Achievement, Soc. Tech. Comm., 1986, Award of Distinction, Fla. Soc. Tech. Comm., 1986. Mem.: English-Speaking Union (bd. dirs. 1984—89), Travelers Century Club. Democrat. Episcopalian. Home and Office: # 265 1688 S Ocean Ln Fort Lauderdale FL 33316-3346 Office Phone: 954-524-3166. E-mail: ladyvanj@aol.com, judithvanalstyne@aol.com.

VAN ALSTYNE, RUTH BEATTIE, elementary school educator; b. Pittsfield, Mass., May 12, 1964; d. Ralph William Beattie and Nancy Laderach Christopher; m. Douglas Roger Van Alstyne, Dec. 24, 1985; children: Deryck Roger, Skylar Wells. BA in Psychology, Russell Sage Coll., 1987, BS in Elem. and Spl. Edn., 1987; MS, SUNY, Albany, 1993. Cert. permanent tchg. N.Y., 1993. Tchr. grade 6 East Greenbush Ctrl. Sch. Dist., NY, 1988—. Home: PO Box 252 East Schodack NY 12063 Office: Goff Mid Sc 35 Gilligan Rd East Greenbush NY 12061 Office Phone: 518-477-2731.

VANALTENBURG, BETTY MARIE, lumber company executive; b. Tulsa, Dec. 27, 1963; d. Floyd Albert and Charolette Virginia (Quinton) V. BA in Comm., U. Tulsa, 1986. Adminstrv. supr. All Wood Products Co., Tulsa, 1986—. Bd. dirs. Tulsa Oklahomans for Human Rights, 1987—89, interim pres., 1989; host com. Names Project, 1990, 1993, 1995, 1997, 2000, regional rep., 1999—2004, co-dir. mdse. exec. bd. dirs. Tulsa, 1988—99, 2004—05, exec. dir., 1999—, co-chair ctrl. region logistics Washington, 1996, quilt display coord., 1997—, quad leader Washington display, 2004; vol. acctg. Children's Med. Ctr.-Children's Miracle Network Telethon, 1994—2002; bd. dirs. Follies Revue, Inc., Tulsa, 1993—97, v.p., 1994—97. Mem.: Honorable Order Ky. Cols., Daus. of the Nile Zibiah Temple # 102 (Princess Tirzah 1995—96, Princess Royal 1996—97, Queen 1997—98, Supreme Appt. 2002—03, Princess Royal 2004—05, Queen 2005—06, Princess Recorder 2006—), Order of Ea. Star (worthy matron Tulsa chpt. # 133 1995—96, 1998—99). Republican. Presbyterian. Avocations: model trains, reading, travel, fundraising, native american beadwork. Personal E-mail: vancan@worldnet.att.net.

VAN ARENDONK, SUSAN CAROLE, elementary school educator; b. Marshalltown, Iowa, Feb. 16, 1954; d. Ernest Jerome and Alice Marjorie (Harmon) Groff; m. Wayne Alan Van Arendonk, Aug. 14, 1994. BS, Iowa State U., Ames, 1976; MS in Edn., U. Kans., Lawrence, 1981; EdS, U. Iowa, Iowa City, 2001. Professionally recognized spl. educator Coun. for Exception Children, 1999; nat. bd. cert. tchr. exceptional needs. Resource rm. aide Pinckney Elem., Lawrence, Kans., 1976-77; tchr. spl. edn. Booth Elem. Sch., Wichita, Kans., 1977-78; tchr. resource rm. Clinton (Iowa) Cmty. Schs., 1978-80; tchr. spl. edn. Henry Sabin Elem. Sch., Clinton, 1980-83; edn. specialist U. Iowa, 1984; cons. No. Trails Area Edn. Agy., Clear Lake, Iowa, 1984-86; tchr. resource rm. Tomiyasu Elem. Sch., Las Vegas, 1986-88, 90-92, tchr. 3d grade, 1988-90, 92-94; tchr. lang. arts, spl. edn. Haysville (Kans.) Mid. Sch., 1996-97; tchr. behavior disorders Heartspring, Wichita, Kans., 1997-98; tchr. spl. edn. Gammon Elem., Wichita, 1998-2000, Curtis Mid. Sch., Wichita, 2000—04, Maize High Sch., 2004—. Edn. specialist, student tchr. supr. U. Iowa, 1983, grad. asst. 1984; cons. Heartland Area Edn. Agy., Johnston, Iowa, 1994-96. Treas. State Rep. Campaign, Iowa, 1974, publicity chmn., 1974. Mem. Coun. Exceptional Children, Iowa State Alumni Assn. (life), U. Iowa Alumni Assn. (life), Humane Soc. Am., U. Kans. Alumni Assn., Phi Lambda Theta. Democrat. Jewish. Home: 2359 N Parkridge Ct Wichita KS 67205-2002 Office: Maize HS 11600 W 45th S Maize KS 67101 Office Phone: 316-722-0441. Personal E-mail: wvanarendonk@cox.net.

VAN ARK, JOAN, actress; d. Carroll and Dorothy Jean (Hemenway) Van A.; m. John Marshall, Feb. 1, 1966; 1 child, Vanessa Jeanne. Student, Yale Sch. Drama. Appeared at Tyrone Guthrie Theatre, Washington Arena Stage, in London, on Broadway; performances include: (stage) Barefoot in the Park, 1965, School for Wives, 1971, Rules of the Game, 1974, Cyrano de Bergerac, Ring Round the Moon, A Little Night Music, 1994, Three Tall Women, 1995, Vagina Monologues, L.A., Denver, Colo., San Diego, Calif. 2001-2002, The Exonerated, N.Y.C. 2002, (TV series) Temperatures Rising, 1972-73, We've Got Each Other, 1977-78, Dallas, 1978-81, Knots Landing, 1979-92 (also dir. episodes Letting Go, Hints and Evasions), (voice) Santa Bogito, 1995; (TV movies) The Judge and Jake Wyler, 1972, Big Rose, 1974, Shell Game, 1975, The Last Dinosaur, 1977, Red Flag, 1981, Shakedown on the Sunset Strip, 1988, My First Love, 1989, Murder at the PTA, 1990, To Cast a Shadow, 1990, Always Remember I Love You, 1990, Grand Central Murders, 1992, Tainted Blood, 1992, Someone's Watching, 1993, When the Darkman Calls, 1994, Loyal Opposition: Terror in the White House, 1998, Intimate Portrait: Michele Lee, 1999, Intimate Portrait, Joan Van Ark, 2002. Tornado Warning, 2002; (TV miniseries) Testimony of Two Men, 1978, Knots Landing: Back to the Cul-de-Sac, 1997; dir., star ABC-TV Afterschool Spl. Boys Will Be Boys, 1993; films, Frogs, 1970 Held for Ransom, 2000, UP Michigan,2001, The Icemakers, 2002. Recipient Theatre World award, 1970-71, L.A. Drama Critics Cir. award, 1973, Outstanding Actress award Soap Opera Digest, 1986, 89. Mem. AFTRA, SAG, Actors Equity Assn., Dir. Guild of Am. Address: care William Morris Agy Inc c/o Sam Haskell 151 S El Camino Dr Beverly Hills CA 90212-2704

VANARSDALE, DIANA CORT, social worker; b. N.Y.C., Oct. 27, 1934; d. Arthur and Augusta Deutsch; m. Leonard VanArsdale, Sept. 17, 1978; children by previous marriage: Hayley, Daniel. BS, NYU, 1955; MSW, Colmbia U., 1957. Clinician Payne Whitney Clinic, N.Y. Hosp., N.Y.C., 1957-59; clinician psychiat. clinic Jewish Bd. Guardians, N.Y.C., 1959-61; founder, pres. Bix Six Towers Nursery Sch., N.Y.C., 1962-67; dir. intake and social svc. L.I. Consultation Ctr., Forest Hills, N.Y., 1966-84, clin. dir., coord. clin. svcs., 1984-86; supr. faculty mem. L.I. Inst. Mental Health, 1981-87; dir. Srs. Option Svc., Allendale, NJ, 1980—90. Author: Transitions: A Woman's Guide To successful Retirement, 1991. Mem. NASW, N.Y. Soc. Clin. Social Workers. Home: 47-30 61st St 18C Woodside NY 11377-5763

VAN ARSDALE, MARIE DELVECHIO, artist; b. New Orleans, May 25, 1943; d. James and Mavis (Willoughby) Delvechio; m. Walton Starkes, Apr. 13, 1965; 1 child, James Walton Van Arsdale. BFA, U. N. Tex., 1991. Exhibited in group shows at Lost and Found: Nat. Open Exhbn., 1997, 5th annual Govs. Exhbn., 1997, Dallas Visual Art Ctr. Membership Exhbn., 1997, Tex. Visual Arts Assn. Membership Exhbn., 1998, Diverse Works Art By Women, Dallas City Hall, 1999, Sixteenth Annual Nat. Juried Art Exhbn., 1999, New Tex. Talent, 2000, Visions Reflected, Agora Gallery, Soho, N.Y., 2001, Outside the Lines Bath House Cultural Ctr., Dallas, 2002, Long Beach Arts, 2005, 2006, Rio Brazos Exhbn., one-woman shows include The Right Combination, U. Arlington, 1993, Golden Acres, Dallas, 1993, Kathleen's Art Cafe, 1997, Natural Magic, Northlake C.C., one-woman shows include painting and photography Northlake C.C., Irving, Tex., 2002. Trainer Boy Scouts Am., Richardson, Tex., 1978—. Recipient Silver Beaver, Circle Ten Coun., Dallas, 1992, disting. commr. award of merit, Boy Scouts, Richardson, Tex., 1983; recipient scholarship S.W. Watercolor Soc., 1985, Cecil Wallace Fordham award, 1989, Moss/Chumley Award, 2000. Mem.: Tex. Photographic Soc., Dallas Ctr. for Contemporary Arts, Tex. Visual Arts Assn. (photographer). Home: 24 Ole Cedar Ln Gordonville TX 76245

VANARSDEL, ROSEMARY THORSTENSON, English studies educator; b. Seattle, Sept. 1, 1926; d. Odin and Helen Catherine (McGregor) Thorstenson; m. Paul P. VanArsdel Jr., July 7, 1950 (dec. Jan. 1994); children: Mary M., Andrew P. BA, U. Wash., 1947, MA, 1948; PhD, Columbia U., 1961. Grad. tchg. asst. Columbia U., N.Y.C., 1948—50; acting instr. U. Wash., Seattle, 1961—63; asst. prof. U. Puget Sound, Tacoma, 1967—69, assoc. prof., 1970—77, prof. English, 1977—87, dir. Writing Inst., 1976—86, dir. semester abroad, 1977, dir. Legal English program Sch. Law, 1973—77, disting. prof. emeritus, 1987—. Vis. prof. Gonzaga U., Pacific Luth. U., Whitman Coll., Willamette U., 1977. Author: Victorian Periodicals: A Guide to Research, Vol. I, 1978, Vol. II, 1989, George Eliot: A Centenary Tribute, 1982, Victorian Periodicals and Victorian Society, 1994, Periodicals of Queen Victoria's Empire, An Exploration, 1996, Florence Fenwick Miller: Victorian Feminist, Journalist, Educator, 2001, Victorian Periodicals, Aids to Research: A Selected Bibliography on the Internet (updated annually); mem. editl. bd. Wellesley Index to Victorian Periodicals, 1824-1900, 1968-88, A Union List of Victorian Serials, 1979-85, Victorian Rev., 1990—; contbr. articles to profl. jours. Recipient Doris Bronson Morrill award Kappa Kappa Gamma, 1982, Disting. Alumnae award Broadway H.S., Seattle, 1991. Fellow Royal Soc. Lit.; mem. MLA, Oxford Bibliog. Soc., Nat. Coun. Tchrs. English (Achievement awards, dir. 1974-77), Rsch. Soc. for Victorian Periodicals (pres. 1981-83). Home: 5051 50th Ave NE Apt 48 Seattle WA 98105-2863

VAN ASSENDELFT, LAURA ANNE, political science professor; b. Portsmouth, Va., Aug. 10, 1967; d. John Allen McColley and Beverly Alice Foote; m. Diederik Andreas Arthur van Assendelft, Oct. 10, 1992; children: Elizabeth Cady, Emily Caroline. BA, U. of the South, Sewanee, Tenn., 1989; PhD, Emory U., Atlanta, 1994. Asst. prof. of polit. sci. Mary Baldwin Coll., Staunton, Va., 1994—2000, assoc. prof. of polit. sci., 2001—. Author: (book) Women, Politics, and American Society, Governors, Agenda Setting, and Divided Government; contbr. articles to profl. jours., chapters to books. Sunday sch. tchr. Covenant Presbyn. Ch., Staunton, 1999—2006. Recipient The Lewis Edward Moore, Sr. Meml. award, Tenn. Polit. Sci. Assn., 1989; grantee Centennial Rsch. grantee, Am. Polit. Sci. Assn., 2001. Mem.: Am. Polit. Sci. Assn. (com. on status of women), Women's Caucus for Polit. Sci. South (pres. 1996—97), So. Polit. Sci. Assn. (exec. coun. mem. 2002—06).

VAN ATTA, MARY CARTER, secondary school educator; b. Lynchburg, Va., Nov. 12, 1963; d. Franklin Hardwell and Harriet Murrell (Jones) Whitten; m. Matthew E. Van Atta. BA in History, Agnes Scott Coll., Decatur, Ga., 1986; MEd in Social Scis., U. Ga., Athens, 1994. Cert. social sci. tchr., Ga., 1994. Edn. coord. Joel Chandler Harris Assn., Atlanta, 1986-87; edn. adminstr. Atlanta Hist. Soc., Inc., 1987-92; grad. asst. U. Ga. at Athens Edn. Initiative, 1992-94; secondary social sci. tchr. Atlanta Pub. Schs., 1994—. Cons. Columbus (Ga.) Mus., 1988, co-chair North Ga. Mus. Educators, Atlanta, 1990-92. Vol. Ga. Spl. Olympics, Atlanta, 1990, 92, Athens Tutorial Program, 1994, Habitat for Humanity, 1995—, Atlanta Com. for the Olympic Games, 1996. Gov.'s intern, Ga. Mus. Art, 1993. Mem. Ga. Coun. for Social Scis., So. Ctr. for Internat. Studies, PAGE. Office: Henry W Grady High School 929 Charles Allen Dr NE Atlanta GA 30309-4204

VANAUKER, LANA, recreational therapist, educator; b. Youngstown, Ohio, Sept. 19, 1949; d. William Marshall and Joanne Norma (Kimmel) Speece; m. Dwight Edward VanAuker, Mar. 16, 1969 (div. 1976); 1 child, Heidi. BS in Edn. cum laude, Kent (Ohio) State U., 1974; MS in Edn., Youngstown U., 1989. Cert. tchr., Ohio; nat. cert. activity cons. Phys. edn. instr. St. Joseph Sch., Campbell, Ohio, 1973—75; program dir. YWCA, Youngstown, 1975—85; exercise technician Youngstown State U., 1985—86; health educator Park Vista Retirement Ctr., Youngstown, 1986—87; tchr. Salem (Ohio) City Sch., 1987—88; recreational therapist Trumbull Meml. Hosp., Warren, Ohio, 1988—. Activity cons. Mahoning/Trumbull Nursing Homes, Warren, 1990-92; adv. bd. rep. Ohio State Bur. Health Promotion Phys. Fitness, 1996—; adv. bd. Ohio State Exec. Phys. Fitness Dept. Health, 1996; tchr. Mohican Youth Ctr., Loudonville, Ohio, 1998-99; dance instr., 2004—; owner, instr. Lanas Dance Studio, 2005—; bd. dirs. USA Dance. Prodr.: Exercise is the Fountain of Youth, 1993; photographer, choreographer; cover photography feature Mahoning County Med. Soc. Bull., 2000; exhibited in group show Forum Health, 1999. Vol. Am. Cancer Soc., 1980—, Am. Heart Assn., 1986—, Dance for Heart, 1980-86; mem. State of Ohio Phys. Fitness Adv. Bd., 1996-97. Youngstown State U. scholar, 1986-89; recipient 1st pl. Kodak Internat. Newspaper Snapshot award, 1998-99, 1st Place Internat. Libr. Photography, 2000, Ballroom Dance Gold medal Sr. Olympics, 2006. Mem.: AAHPERD, U.S. Amateur Ballroom Dance Assn. (v.p. 2002—03), Pa. Activity Profl. Assn. (pres., spkr. 2001), Resident Activity Profl. Assn. (pres. 1994—96, 2001—03), Youngstown Photography Club (treas. 2006—), Youngstown Camera Club (social chair 1989—90, pres. 1993—95, treas. 2004—), Kappa Delta Pi. Democrat. Presbyterian. Avocations: photography, dance, volleyball, aerobics, travel. Home: 4133 S Turner Rd Canfield OH 44406-8737 Office: 4N Unit Forum Health 1350 E Market St Warren OH 44483-6608 Office Phone: 330-219-0008. Business E-Mail: lvanauker@fitnesstoyouth.net.

VAN AUSDAL, VIVIAN GARRISON, retired language educator; b. Palestine, Ohio, Apr. 23, 1914; d. Jesse E. Garrison and Mabel Lois Hawes; m. Gerald Francis Van Ausdal, May 29, 1938 (dec.); children: Karl H., Ray G., Paul F. BA, Miami U., Oxford, Ohio, 1937. English tchr. Ansonia HS, Ohio, 1937—38, Martinsville HS, Ohio, 1939—40, Beavercreek HS, Ohio, 1960—77; ret., 1977. Trustee Greene County Pub. Libr., Ohio, 1984—2000; chmn. Beavercreek Charter Commn., 1980—81; pres. Greene County Coun. Aging, 1998—99; candidate Ohio Ho. Reps., Greene County, 1968; mem. consistory, tchr. adult Sunday sch. class Hawker United Ch. of Christ; bd. dirs. Greene County Ednl. Svc. Com., 1984—86. Named Woman of Yr., Greene County Women's Hall of Fame, 1985, Sr. Citizen of Yr., Coun. on Aging, 2006. Mem.: AAUW, Beavercreek Women's League. Democrat. Avocations: reading, piano, volunteering.

VAN BAAREN, MARGARET MIRIAM, learning disabilities educator; b. N.Y.C., June 16, 1964; d. George Edmund and Carole Rennick (Johnson) Silver; m. Harry van Baaren, July 11, 1992; children: Ben (dec.), Simon, Max, Lily. BA in Psychology, Kenyon Coll., 1986; MS in Learning Disabilities/Spl. Edn., CUNY, 1992. Cert. tchr., N.Y., Mass. Tchr. N.Y. League Early Learning, N.Y.C., NY, 1986—92; head tchr. Astoria Blue Feather-Assn. Help of Retarded Children, N.Y.C., NY, 1992—94; dir. learning skills program Northfield (Mass.) Mt. Hermon Sch., 1994—. Mem. ASCD, NOW, Internat. Dyslexia Assn., Coun. Exceptional Children, Children and Adults with Attention Deficit Disorders, Planned Parenthood, Nat. Assn. Reproductive and Abortion Freedom, Amnesty Internat., Nature Conservancy. Avocations: hiking, swimming, reading, volleyball, movies, miniatures. Home and Office: 206 Main St Apt 4963 Northfield MA 01360-1050 Office Phone: 413-498-3591. E-mail: mvanb@nmhschool.org.

VANBROCKLIN, VICKI M., secondary school educator; d. Jon Vanbrocklin and Peggy Graw; m. Stuart Murray, Sept. 7, 1999. BS in Secondary Edn., Ctrl. Mich. U., Mt. Pleasant, Mich., 1999; MA in Eng. Lit., Middlebury Coll., Vt., 2005. Lic. tchr. Mich., Ill. Tchr. Canton (Mich.) H.S., 1999—2000, Rockford (Ill.) Pub. Schs., 2000—01, Yorkville (Ill.) H.S., 2001—. Named Influential Educator, Students Yorkville (Ill.) H.S., 2005. Avocations: writing, poetry, reading, travel.

VAN BRUGGEN, COOSJE, artist, writer; b. Groningen, The Netherlands, June 6, 1942; came to U.S., 1978, naturalized, 1993; d. J.A.R. Van Bruggen and A.M. Andriessen; m. Claes Oldenburg, July 22, 1977. DRS in Art History, Rijks U. Groningen, 1967; DFA (hon.), Calif. Coll. Art and Craft, 1996, Nova Scotia Coll. Art and Design, Halifax, 2005, Coll. Creative Studies, Detroit, 2005; DLitt (hon.), U. Teesside, Middlesbrough, Eng., 1999. Asst. curator Stedelijk Mus., Amsterdam, The Netherlands, 1967-71; prof. Acad. Fine Arts, Enschede, The Netherlands, 1971-76; sr. critic landscape arch. Harvard U., Cambridge, Mass., 1993; sr. critic dept. sculpture Yale U., New Haven, 1996-97. Co-editor Catalogue Sonsbeek, 1971; mem. selection com. Documenta 7, Kassel, Germany, 1982; curator (with Dieter Koepplin) Bruce Nauman: Drawings, 1965-1986, Basel, Switzerland, 1986-88. Author: Bruce Nauman, 1989, John Baldessari, 1990, Frank O. Gehry: Guggenheim Museum Bilbao, 1997; co-author (with Claes Oldenburg): Claes Oldenburg: Sketches and Blottings Toward the European Desk Top, 1990, Large-Scale Projects, 1994, Claes Oldenburg Coosje van Bruggen, 1999, Down Liquidambar Lane: Sculpture in the Park, 2001; co-author: (with Claes Oldenburg and Frank O. Gehry) Il Corso del Coltello, 1985; two-person shows (with Claes Oldenburg), No. Ctr. Contemporary Art, Sunderland, 1988, Leeds City Art Gallery, 1988, Palais des Beaux-Arts, Brussels, 1988, IVAM Ctr. Julio González, Valencia, 1988, Galleria Christian Stein, Milan, 1990, Leo Castelli Gallery, NYC, 1990, Pace Gallery, 1994, Museo Correr, Venice, 1999, Museu Serralves, Porto, 2001, Met. Mus. Art, NYC, 2002, PaceWildenstein, 2002, Frederik Meijer Gardens and Sculpture Park, Grand Rapids, Mich., 2002, Paula Cooper Gallery, 2004, Pace Wildenstein Gallery, 2005, Konrad Fischer Galerie, Düsseldorf, 2005, group shows with Claes Oldenburg, Guggenheim Mus., NYC, 1993, Venice Biennale, 1997, Nat. Gallery, London, 2000, others; contbr. Artforum, 1983—88; numerous pub. sculptures including, Nollen Plz., Civic Ctr., Des Moines, Mpls. Sculpture Garden, Walker Art Ctr., Mpls., Parc de la Villette, Paris, Ctrl. Gardens, Middlesborough, Eng., Guggenheim Found., Neumarkt Galerie, Cologne, Cheonguyeon Stream, Seoul, Korea, and many others. Co-recipient (with Claes Oldenburg) Distinction in Sculpture, Sculpture Ctr., N.Y.C., 1984, (with Claes Oldenburg) Nathaniel S. Saltonstall award, ICA, Boston, 1996, (with Claes Oldenburg) Ptnrs. in Edn. award, Guggenheim, N.Y., 2002, (with Claes Oldenburg) Nat. Medal award, Sch. Mus. Fine Arts, Boston, 2004.

VANBRUNT-KRAMER, KAREN, business administration educator; b. Milw., May 1, 1934; D. Roy Charles and Viola Marguerita (Yerges) VanBrunt; m. Allen Lloyd Weitermann (div. 1963); 1 child, Tera Lee Johnson; m. Keith Kramer (div. 1979); children: Holden Jon, Stafford James. BS, U. Wis., 1956; MA, NYU, 1976; PhD, Ohio State U., 1992. Owner Design By Karen Lee, Larchmont, NY, 1975—82; interior designer Maurice Vallency Design, N.Y.C., 1976—79; grad. rsch. assoc. Ctr. on Edn. and Tng. for Employment, Columbus, Ohio, 1987—92; assoc. prof. bus. adminstrn. St. Joseph Coll., West Hartford, Conn., 1992—99. Lectr. and curriculum developer entrepreneurship state vocat. schs., high schs., colls., and univs. throughout U.S. and Ea. Europe, 1987-92; instr. Berkeley Sch., White Plains, N.Y., 1968-82; adj. prof. N.Y.C. C.C., 1979-83, Milw. Area Tech. Coll., 1983-85, Columbus State C.C., 1986-90, Capital U., Columbus, 1998, U. Wis. Milw., Mt. Mary Coll., Milw.; participant Women in Soc. Citizen Amb. Program to China, 1997, leader Women in Exec. Mgmt. Bus., 1998; mem. Inst. World Affairs, U. Wis., Milw., 1999—. Mem. Wadsworth Atheneum, Hartford, 1992—99, West Hartford Art League, 1993—99; vol. U. Conn. Health Ctr., Farmington, Little Sisters of the Poor, St. Joseph Residence, Enfield, Conn., 1989—92, Milw. Art Mus.; docent Columbus Symphony Orch., 1986—92; mem. women's guild First Cmty. Ch., Columbus, 1985—92. Mem.: NAFE, AAUW (past social chair Wis. br.), AAUP (membership chair 1993—97), Svc. Corp. of Ret. Exec., Omicron Tau Theta, World Federalist Assn., Nat. Edn. Ctr. for Women in Bus. (Milw. sec./treas. 2001—03), Am. Mgmt. Assn., Am. Mktg. Assn., Coalition for Effective Orgns., Ohio Vocat. Assn., Am. Vocat. Assn., World Affairs Coun., Mil. Intercity Congregations Allied for Hope (bd. dirs. 2005—), Peace Seekers (Peace Action and Steering com. 2004—), Citizens for Global Solutions (treas. 2004—), Delta Pi Epsilon, Phi Delta Kappa, Phi Lambda Theta, Phi Kappa Phi, Phi Beta Kappa. Avocations: theater, art, music, photography, ice dancing. Home: 125 N University Dr Unit 322S West Bend WI 53095-2954

VAN BULCK, MARGARET WEST, accountant, financial planner, educator; b. Chgo., Nov. 25, 1955; d. Lee Allen and Margaret Ellen (Sauls) West; m. Hendrikus E.J.M.L. van Bulck, Aug. 7, 1976; children: Marcel Allen, Sydney Josette. BS in Mktg., U. S.C., 1978; MA in Econs., Clemson U., 1981. CPA, S.C. Econs. instr. St. Andrews Presbyn. Coll., Laurinburg, NC, 1980-82; staff acct. L. Allen West, CPA, Sumter, SC, 1982-84; ptnr. West & Van Bulck, CPAs, Sumter, 1984-88, Van Bulck & Co., CPA's, Sumter, 1989—. Part time instr. U. S.C., Sumter, 1985-87, mem. full time faculty, 1989-92. Contbr. articles to profl. jours. Treas. Make-A-Wish Found., Sumter, 1985-87, wish granting chmn. 1987-88; edn. found. chmn. Laurinburg/Scotland County chpt. AAUW, 1981-83; treas. Friends Sumter County Library, 1986-88, Sumter Gallery of Art, 1989-91; mem. Jr. Welfare League, Sumter; Circle Bible leader, Sunday Sch. tchr., hospice vol., 1990-92; deacon First Presbyn. Ch., 1994-97; den leader pack 86 Boy Scouts of Am., 1992-95, troop com. mem., advancement chair, 1998-2001, troop com. treas., 2000-. Recipient Sirrine Found. award, Clemson U., 1978, 79; grantee U.S. Dept. Labor, 1979-80. Mem. AICPA, S.C. Assn. CPAs, Internat. Assn. Fin. Planning, Sumter Estate Planning Coun. (past treas.), Trian Club (treas. 1998—), Carolinian Club, Omicron Delta Epsilon. Presbyterian. Home: 234 Haynsworth St PO Box 1327 Sumter SC 29151-1327 Office: Van Bulck & Co CPAs PO Box 1327 Sumter SC 29151-1327 Office Phone: 803-775-3000. E-mail: margaretvb@sc.rr.com, margaret@vanbulckCPAs.com.

VAN BUREN, ABIGAIL (JEANNE PHILLIPS), columnist, educator; b. Mpls., Apr. 10, 1942; d. Morton and Pauline (Friedman) Phillips, (the founder of the Dear Abby advice column in 1956). Student, U. Colo., 1960—62. Writer Dear Abby Radio Show, CBS, 1965—71; columnist Dear Abby, 1987—. Bd. mem. Planned Parenthood of Los Angeles, 1989—90; life-time cons. Group for Advancement of Psychiatry, 1995—; bd. adv. Alzheimers Assn. of Los Angeles, 1996—; bd. mem. Rose and Jay Phillips Found., 1991—, ACLU of So. Calif. Found., 1998—; adv. bd. L.A. Internat. Women's Media Found. Courage in Journalism, 2000—; bd. adv. UCLA Med. Ctr., Ctr. for Rsch. and Training in Humane and Ethical Med. Care (CHEC), 2000—. Bd. advs. Planned Parenthood Fedn. Am., 2004; bd. judges Talbot's Charitable Found. Women's Scholarship Fund, 2006—; mem. White House Commn. Rememberance; bd. dirs. Planned Parenthood of LA, 1989—90, MADD, 2003—, Children's Rights Coun., 2003—; mem. Leadership Coun. Aids Project, LA, 2004; bd. dirs. Nat. Kidney Found., 2004. Recipient Generations of Choice award, Planned Parenthood of L.A., 1999, Minority Organ/Tissue Transplant Edn. Program (MOTTEP) Key of Life award, Howard U., Wash. D.C., 2000, Award of Appreciation, U.S. Gen. Svcs. Adminstrn. Fed. Consumer Info. Ctr., 2000, Star on Hollywood Walk of Fame for Dear Abby Radio Show, 2001, Recognition by the Office of Nat. Drug Control Policy (ONDCP), award from the White House and Substance Abuse and Mental Health Svcs. Adminstrn. for help in launching Nat. Inhalants and Poisons Awareness Week, 2001, Erasing the Stigma Leadership award, Didi Hirsch Mental Health Ctr., 2001, MOTTEP Award of Excellence, 2001, Commendation for Operation Dear Abby and OperationDearAbby.net, Dept. Navy and USMC, 2002, Appreciation for support of the military svc. mems. of the U.S. for Operation Dear Abby and OperationDearAbby.net, Space and Naval Warfare Sys. Ctr. (SPAWAR), 2002, Alzheimer's Assn. Maureen Reagan Advocacy Award, 2003, Appreciation award, Overeaters Anonymous, 2003, Advocacy award, Alzheimer's Assn. L.A., 2003, award of Appreciation, U.S. GSA Fed. Citizen Info. Ctr., 2004. Mem.: Nat. Adv. Coun. of Alzheimers Assn. Syndicated in the U.S., Brazil, Mex., Japan, Philippines, Fed. Republic Germany, India, Holland, Denmark, Can., Korea, Thailand, Italy, Hong Kong, Taiwan, Ireland, Saudi Arabia, Greece, France, Dominican Republic, P.R., Costa Rica, U.S. Virgin Islands, Bermuda, China, Kuwait and Guam; published on the Internet at DearAbby.com and OperationDearAbby.net for messages to the military. Office: Philips-Van Buren Inc Ste 2710 1900 Ave of the Stars Los Angeles CA 90067

VANBUREN, CAROLYN JEAN, special education educator; d. Joseph A. and Hannah Caroline Meyers; m. Robert Mathew Simons, Sept. 1, 2001; children: Garrick Rhett, Kari Jane. BS magna cum laude, Bemidji State U., 1972; MS with honors in Edn., U. Wis., 1987. Cert. mentally retarded tchr. Wis. Dept. Pub. Instrn., 1978, early childhood-exceptional needs tchr. Wis. Dept. Pub. Instrn., 1978, 1st-8th grade tchr. Wis. Dept. Pub. Instrn., 1978. Spl. edn. tchr. Anoka Sch. Dist., Minn., 1972—74, Rice Lake Sch. Dist., Wis., 1980—; spl. edn. cons. Coop. Ednl. Svc. Agy., Cumberland, 1975—76; exceptional edn. early childhood tchr. Turtle Lake Sch. Dist., 1976—78. Ednl. cons. Countryway Group Home, Cameron, Wis., 1984—87; home health care worker Gemini, Richfield, Wis., 2004, Indianhead, Barron, Wis., 2000—00; group home house parent Ag-Ri-Cove, Cameron, 2000—01. Vol. Spl. Olympics, Barron County, 2000—01; pub. rels. rep. First Luth. Ch., Barron, 2001—05. Mem.: NEA (assoc.), Wis. Edn. Assn. (assoc.). Democrat-Npl. Lutheran. Avocations: travel, interior design, walking, yoga, gardening. Personal E-mail: carolyn@rrmsimons.com.

VANBUREN, DEBORAH ANN, health educator; b. Bronx, N.Y., Mar. 28, 1967; d. Valentino and Barbara Marie D'Andrea; m. Donald Joseph Van Buren, Sr., Oct. 27; children: Brandon, Rachel. Assoc.'s degree, Dutchess C.C., Poughkeepsie, N.Y., 1991; Bachelor's degree, SUNY, New Paltz, N.Y., 1993, Master's degree, 1995, Calif. Coll. Health Scis., 2006. Mem. faculty Dutchess C.C., Poughkeepsie, 1993—. Office Phone: 845-431-8475. Business E-Mail: vanburen@sunydutchess.edu.

VANBUREN, DENISE DORING, corporate communications executive; b. Troy, N.Y., May 15, 1961; d. James L. and Eunice A. (Myers) Doring; m. Steven Paul VanBuren, Apr. 1, 1989; children: Schuyler Paul, Troy James Doring, Brett Steven VanBuren. BA in Mass Comm. magna cum laude, St. Bonaventure U., 1983; MBA, Mount St. Mary Coll., 1997. Reporter, news anchor Sta. WGNY-AM-FM, Newburgh, NY, 1984; news dir., anchor NewsCtr. 6, Dutchess County, NY, 1985-90; dir. media rels. Ctrl. Hudson Gas & Electric, Poughkeepsie, NY, 1993—, mgr. corp. comms., 1998-99, asst. v.p. corp. comm., 1999-2000, v.p. corp. comm. and cmty. rels., 2000—. Adj. prof. Marist Coll., Poughkeepsie, NY. Co-author: Historic Beacon, 1998, Beacon Revisited, 2003. Councilwoman City of Beacon, 1992-93, chmn. 85th anniversary celebration; pres. Beacon Hist. Soc., 1989-94; bd. dirs. Locust Grove Hist. Site, Stony Kill Found., Inc.; chmn. Dutchess County United Way Campaign, 2005. Recipient Salute to Women in Bus. & Industry award D.C. YWCA, 1990, 97, Outstanding Chpt. Regent award N.Y. State orgn. DAR, 1999, Dutchess award, Dutchess County Hist. Soc., 2005; named Vol. of Yr. award, City of Beacon, 1999. Mem.: DAR (vice regent Melzingah chpt.

1990—98, regent 1998—2001, chmn. state historian com. NY state 1998—2001, nat. chmn. PR 1999—2004, editor-in-chief, Am. Spirit mag.), Greater So. Dutchess C. of C. (bd. dirs.), Nat. Soc. Daus. of Union Vets. of the Civil War, Exch. Club of So. Dutchess (bd. dirs.). Republican. Roman Catholic. Avocations: genealogy, needlecrafts. Office: CH Energy Group Inc 284 South Ave Poughkeepsie NY 12601-4838

VAN BUREN, KARI, museum director; b. Kinderhook, N.Y., Sept. 28, 1979; d. John Edward and Karen Anne Van Buren. BA, Salve Regina U., Newport, R.I., 2001; MS, U. Pa., Phila., 2004. Resident dir. Smith's Castle, North Kingstown, RI, 2004—. Mem.: Nat. Trust Hist. Preservation.

VAN CAMP, DIANA J., music educator; b. Washington, Oct. 24, 1946; d. Gordon Ashley and Gabrielle Marie-Anne Van Camp. B in Music Edn., Ind. U., 1969; MusM, Fla. State U., 1976; PhD in Music Edn., Ohio State U., 1989. Cert. tchr. music K-12 Ohio. Orch. tchr. Gainesville (Fla.) City Schs., 1969—72; orch. tchr., profl. violinist Memphis Symphony and Schs., 1975—79; music edn. and orch. tchr. Otterbein Coll., Westerville, Ohio, 1979—82; tchg. assoc. music edn. Ohio State U., Columbus, 1982—85; orch. dir. Bexley (Ohio) City Schs., 1985—86, Newark (Ohio) City Schs., 1987—. Pvt. violin studio, Newark, 1990—. Musician (violinist): Welsh Hills Symphony, 1990—2005, Southea. Ohio Symphony, 1992—, Land of Legend Philharmonic, 1995—2004, Ctrl. Ohio Symphony, 2000—04, Newark-Granville Orch., 2005—. Grantee, Nat. Endowment for the Arts, 1975—79. Mem.: Ohio Music Educators Assn., Music Educators Nat. Conf., Sigma Alpha Iota. Avocations: walking, hiking, swimming, church work. Office Phone: 740-345-4440. Personal E-mail: dvancamp0004@wowway.com.

VANCE, CYNTHIA LYNN, psychology educator; b. Norwalk, Calif., Mar. 31, 1960; d. Dennis Keith and Donna Kay (Harryman) V. BS, U. Oreg., 1982; MS, U. Wis., Milw., 1987, PhD, 1991. Tchg. asst. U. Wis., Milw., 1983-89; computer graphics mgr. Montgomery Media, Inc., Milw., 1987-92; asst. prof. Cardinal Stritch Coll., Milw., 1992-93, Piedmont Coll., Demorest, Ga., 1993-99, assoc. prof., 1999—2006, prof., 2006—. Contbr. articles to profl. jours. Mem. bd. advisors North Ga. Tech. Inst., 1997-99; vol. Dunwoody (Ga.)-DeKalb Kiwanis Club, 1993-97. Ga. Gov.'s Tchr. fellow, 2000-01. Mem. AAUP, APA, Assn. Women in Psychology, S.E. Psychol. Assn., Am. Psychol. Soc., Am. Assn. Higher Edn. Office: Piedmont Coll PO Box 10 Demorest GA 30535-0010 E-mail: cvance@piedmont.edu.

VANCE, DIANNE SANCHEZ, mathematician, educator; d. Thomas Clarence and Jean Rose Sanchez; 1 child, Jeney Michelle Sanchez. BA, Calif. State U., Fullerton, 1977; MEd, U. Utah, Salt Lake City, 1993. Tchr. Tahoe Truckee Sch. Dist., Calif., 1971—76, Wasatch Sch. Dist., Heber City, Utah, 1980—90; tennis coach Park City High Sch., 1993—98, tchr., 1990—2002; tchr., coord. English as 2d lang. Phillips Acad., Andover, Mass., 1991—2003; tchr. math. TED Kolej, Ankara, Turkey, 2002—03, Fulbright Exch. Park City Sch. Dist., 2003—. Vol. Sundance, Park City, 1995—2006; gate judge Olympics, 2002. Mem.: ASCD, Park City Edn. Assn. Avocations: travel, skiing, tennis, golf. Office: Park City Sch Dist 2700 Kearns Blvd Park City UT 84060

VANCE, KIM, lawyer; BA with highest honors, U. Ctrl. Ark.; JD with honors, U. Ark. Ptnr., supr. employment discrimination law sect. King & Ballow, Nashville; gen. counsel, corp. sec. Tractor Supply Co., Brentwood, Tenn., 2003—. Spkr. in field. Bd. dirs. Ctr. Nonprofit Mgmt. Mem.: ABA (mem. labor sect., employment law sect.), Lawyers' Assn. for Women. Office: Tractor Supply Co 200 Powell Pl Brentwood TN 37027 Office Phone: 615-366-4600.

VANCE, PATRICIA H., state senator; b. Williamsport, Pa., Mar. 19, 1936; RN, Harrisburg Hosp. Sch. Nursing, 1957. Former mem. Pa. Ho. of Reps., Harrisburg, 1990—2004; mem. Pa. Senate, Harrisburg, 2004—. Home: 3806 Market St Camp Hill PA 17011-4327 Office: Pa Senate Rm 187 Main Capitol PO Box 203031 Harrisburg PA 17120-3031

VANCE, SANDRA JOHNSON, secondary school educator; b. Parkersburg, W.Va., Oct. 23, 1945; d. Maurice Aubrey and Louise Mindwell (Price) Johnson; m. Larry Wayne Vance, June 24, 1970; children: Edward Maurice, James Allen. BS in Phys. Edn., W.Va. U., 1969; MEd, Ga. State U., 1972, EdS, 1985. Cert. mental retardation, career, phys. edn. and health, gen. sci., vocat. edn., instrnl. supervision. Tchr. interrelated resource Birney Elem. Sch., Cobb, Ga., 1969-80; tchr. MIMH Tapp Mid. Sch., Cobb, Ga., 1980-85; related vocat. instruct. specialist Pebblebrook HS, Cobb, Ga., 1980-83; related vocat. instrn. specialist Douglas County HS, Douglasville, Ga., 1983—2002, advisor for related vocat. instrn., head dept. spl. edn., 1999—2002. Treas. Related Vocat. Instrn. Enrichment Camp, 1985-93; advisor related vocat. instrn. Douglas County H.S. Club, Douglas County Student Coun. for Exceptional Children, 1988-95; instr. for staff devel. on computers, 1995—; mem. spl. edn. adv. panel Ga. Dept. Edn., 1997-99. Mem. Tech. Com.; instr. ARC; com. treas. Troop 749 Boy Scouts Am., Mableton, 1993-95. Mem. Douglas County Ret. Tchrs. Assn. (mem. chair 2006-), Ga. Ret. Tchrs. Assn., Ga. State U. Alumni Assn. (vol.), AARP Found. (tax aide counselor 2004—) Home: 4636 Rodney Pl Austell GA 30106-1938 E-mail: L-vance@bellsouth.net.

VANCE, SUE ANN, musician, educator; b. Medicine Lodge, Kans., Aug. 16, 1937; d. Trice Hubert and Catherine O. (Stone) Newsom; m. Jerry Wayne Vance, Aug. 15, 1962 (dec.); children: Todd, Kayla Vance Ginnings. B Music Edn., Wichita State U., Kans., 1959, M Music Edn., 1962. Piano instr. Labette County Cmty. HS, Altamont, Kans., 1959—61; accompanist U. La., Monroe, 1967—88; K-12 music instr. Deer Pub. Sch. Dist., Ark., 1991—2002; adj. piano instr., accompanist Ark. Tech. U., Russellville, 2002—. Part-time instr. piano U. La., Monroe, 1978—86; organist various chs., Monroe, 1976—88; organist 1st Presbyn. Ch., Harrison, Ark., 1993—2003; piano adjudicator Federated Music Clubs, Monroe, 1970—88; mem. Vance-White Duo piano team, Monroe, 1978—90. Pres. NW Ark. Concert Assn., Harrison, 1995—99. Recipient Naftzager Judges award, Wichita Symphony, 1958. Mem.: Am. Choir Dirs. Assn., Music Educators Nat. Conf., Nat. Guild Piano Tchrs. (piano adjudicator 1999—). Avocations: knitting, reading, sewing, crossword puzzles. Home: HC31 Box 393 Deer AR 72628 Office: Ark Tech U Music Dept Q St Russellville AR 72802

VANCE, TANYA LEE, music educator, director; b. Moorefield, W.Va., Jan. 6, 1970; d. Douglas Allen Vance and Donna Lynn Garrett-Vance. MusB in Edn., Shenandoah U., Winchester, Va., 1998, MusM in Edn., 1999. Dir. choir Riverton Meth. Ch., Front Royal, Va., 1991—93; dir. choral H.S. Mineral County Schs., Keyser, W.Va., 1993—96; tchr. music Prince William County Schs., Woodbridge, Va., 1996—; dir. choir Cokesbury Meth. Ch., Woodbridge, 2001—. Author: (musical CD) Unconditional Love, 1999, All of My Life, 2005. Avocations: gardening, studying Civil War history. Office: Marshall Elem Sch 12505 Kuhns Rd Manassas VA 20112

VANCE, VANESSA L., lawyer; b. Beaumont, Tex., Aug. 21, 1968; BA in Biology, Tex. A&M U., Coll. Sta., 1989; JD, South Tex. Coll. Law, Houston, 1994. Bar: Tex. 1994, US Dist. Ct. (all dists. Tex.). Atty. Connelly, Baker, Maston, Wotring & Jackson, L.L.P., Houston. Bd. dirs. Vance-Sandovel Enterprises, L.L.P., 1998—, Slaney Designs, 2003—. Named a Rising Star, Tex. Super Lawyers mag., 2006. Fellow: Houston Bar Found.; mem.: Tex. Assn. Def. Counsel, Houston Bar Assn. Office: Connelly Baker Maston Wotring & Jackson LLP 700 Louisiana St Ste 1800 Houston TX 77002 Office Phone: 713-980-6517. E-mail: vvance@connellybaker.com.*

VAN CLEAVE, MICHELLE KIM, former federal official; b. 1953; BA, MA, JD, U. So. Calif. Assoc. Hervitz and Greines, LA; asst. for def. and foreign policy to Congressman Jack Kemp, 1981—87; nat. security asst. Ho. Rep. Conf., 1981—87; staff mem. Ho. Appropriations subcom. on Fgn. Ops., 1981—87; gen. counsel, asst. dir. nat. security affairs White House Office of Sci. and Tech. Policy, 1987—93; minority counsel to com. on sci., space, and tech., 1989; of counsel Feith & Zell, P.C., 1993—97; co-founder, pres. Nat. Security Concepts, Inc., 1997—2001; spl. asst. to under sec. for policy, sr. advisor for homeland def. US Dept. Def., Washington, 2001—03; nat. counterintelligence exec. Office Nat. Counterintelligence Exec., Washington, 2003—05. Mem.: DC Bar Assn., Calif. Bar Assn.

VAN CLEVE, BARBARA PAGE, photographer; d. Paul L. and Barbara K. BA in English and Social Sci., Duchesne Coll., 1958; MA in English Lit., Northwestern U., 1963, post MA Counseling and English Lit., 1970. English and history tchr. Sacred Heart Acad., St. Charles, Mo.; language arts tchr. St. Mary Sch., Lake Forest, Ill., 1959—61; language tchr. Northbrook Jr. High, Ill., 1961—62; English inst. Loyola U., Chgo., 1965—69, Mundelein Coll., Chgo., 1969—71, comm. English asst. prof., 1971—79; pres. Van Cleve Photography, Inc., Chgo., 1969—79. Exhibitions include 46 solo exhibitions, 1985—, exhibitions include 73 selected group exhibitions, Roughstock Sonnets, The Lowell Press, 1989, Images of Montana, Mus. of the Rockies, 1989, Hard Twist: Western Ranch Women, Mus. New Mex. Press, 1995, All this Way for the Short Ride, 1996, Holding the Reins: A ride Through Cowgirl Life, Harper Collins, 2003; videographer: Barbara Van Cleve: Capturing Grace, 1993; Rooted in the Earth, 2000; Represented in permanent collections Embassies Program, U.S. Dept. State, Beijing, Moscow, Ecuador, Mus. Fine Art, Federal Reserve Bank Minn. Judge Chgo. Film Festival, 1974. Named Featured Artist, Coors Western Art Exhibit, 2005; named to Nat. Cowgirl Mus. and Hall of Fame, Chgo. Film Festival; recipient Disting. Artist of Year, Santa Fe Rotary Found., 2000, Mary Belle Grant award, Coors Western Art Found., 2001; grantee Lilly Faculty Develop. Grant, 1977. Mem.: Kappa Gamma Pi, Delta Epsilon Sigma.

VAN CLEVE, RUTH GILL, retired lawyer; b. Mpls., July 28, 1925; d. Raymond S. and Ruth (Sevon) Gill; m. Harry R. Van Cleve, Jr., May 16, 1952 (dec. Oct. 2001); children: John Gill, Elizabeth Webster, David Hamilton Livingston. Student, U. Minn., 1943; AB magna cum laude, Mt. Holyoke Coll., 1946, LLD, 1976; LLB, Yale U., 1950. Bar: D.C. 1950, Minn. 1950. Intern Nat. Inst. Pub. Affairs, 1946-47; atty. Dept. Interior, 1950-54, asst. solicitor, 1954-64; dir. Office Territorial Affairs, 1964-69, 1977-80, dep. asst. sec., 1980-81, acting asst. sec., 1993; atty. Solicitor's Office, 1981-93, FPC, 1969-75, asst. gen. counsel, 1975-77. Author: The Office of Territorial Affairs, 1974, The Application of Federal Laws to the Territories, 1993. Mem. Guam War Claims Rev. Commn., 2003—04. Recipient Fed. Woman's award, 1966, Disting. Svc. award Dept. Interior, 1968, Presdl. Rank award, Pres. U.S., 1989. Mem.: Phi Beta Kappa. Unitarian. Home: 3440 S Jefferson St Apt 1015 Falls Church VA 22041

VAN CURA, JOYCE BENNETT, librarian; b. Madison, Wis., Mar. 25, 1944; d. Ralph Eugene and Florence Marie (Cramer) Bennett; m. E. Jay Van Cura, July 5, 1986. BA in Liberal Arts (scholar), Bradley U., Peoria, Ill., 1966; MLS, U. Ill., Champaign-Urbana, 1971. Libr. asst. Rsch. Libr. Caterpillar Tractor Co., Peoria, Ill., 1966-67; ref. libr., instr. libr. tech. Ill. Ctrl. Coll., East Peoria, Ill., 1967-73; asst. prof. Sangamon State U. (U. Ill.-Springfield), Springfield, Ill., 1973-80, assoc. prof., 1980-86; head libr. ref. and info. svcs. dept. Ill. Inst. Tech., 1987-90; dir. Learning Resources Ctr. Morton Coll., 1990—2003. Reviewer Libr. Jour., Am. Ref. Books Ann.; convenor Coun. II, Ill. Clearinghouse for Acad. Libr. Instrn., 1978; presentor 7th Ann. Conf. Acad. Libr. Instrn., 1977, Nat. Women's Studies Assn., 1983, others; participant Gt. Lakes Women's Studies Summer Inst., 1981, Nat. Inst. Leadership Devel. seminar, 1995. Contbr. articles to profl. jours. Pres. Springfield chpt. NOW, 1978—79; invited Susan B. Anthony luncheon, 1978, 1979; mem. adv. bd. Suburban Libr. Sys., 1992—94, Nat. Commn. Learning Resources; v.p. membership Riverside chpt. Lyric Opera Chgo., 1994—96, 1999—, exec. bd., 2006—; active Riverside Arts Ctr.; Dem. precinct Committeewoman, 1982—85; vice-moderator Fourth Presbyn. Women, 1989—90; elder Riverside (Ill.) Presbyn. Ch., 1992—, mem. session, 1993—96, 2000—01, mem. adminstrn. com., 1993—2003, chmn. adminstrn. com., 1993—96, 1999, 2000—01, mem. endowment com., 1996—98, treas. bd. trustees, 2004—, bd. trustees, 2005—, sec. bd. trustees, 2005—; bd. dirs. Berwyn-Cicero Coun. on Aging, 2000—03. Ill. state scholar, 1962-66; recipient Citizenship award Am. Legion, 1962, Cert. of Recognition Ill. Bicentennial Commn., 1974. Mem.: AAUW (bd. dirs. Riverside br. 1992—94, 1997—99, chmn. standing com. on women Springfield br., com. on women Ill. state divsn.), ALA, Ill. Libr. Assn. (presenter 1984), Nat. Assn. Women in C.C., Springfield Art Assn., No. Ill. Learning Resources Consortium (del. 1990—2003, steering com. West Suburban postsecondary consortium 1996—2000), Nat. Women's Studies Assn. (presenter 1983, 1984, 1995), Women in Mgmt., Am. Mgmt. Assn., No. Ill. Learning Resources Consortium Bd. (del. 2006—), Spl. Librs. Assn., Ill. Assn. Coll. and Rsch. Librs. (bibliog. instrn. com.), Libr. Info. and Tech. Assn., Libr. Adminstr. and Mgmt. Assn. (ref. and adult svcs. divsn.), Assn. Coll. and Rsch. Librs., Riverside Presbyn. Ch. Women, Nat. Trust Hist. Preservation, Am. Opera Soc., Riverside Dancing Club, Riverside Garden Club, Musicians Club of Women Chgo., Beta Phi Mu. Home: 181 Scottswood Rd Riverside IL 60546-2221

VAN DE BOGART, DEBRA SCHERWERTS, medical/surgical nurse, researcher; b. Claremont, N.H., Aug. 6, 1954; d. William Earl and Barbara Louise (Hadley White) Scherwerts. RN, Sacred Heart Sch. Nursing, Manchester, NH, 1975; student, Cypress Coll., Calif., 1976, U. Calif., Riverside, 1978. RN Calif., 1975, cert. home health nurse, Calif., 1997. Charge nurse, med.-surg. pediat. West Anaheim Cmty. Hosp., Anaheim, Calif., 1975—84; charge nurse, med.-surg. geriat. Humana West Anaheim, Anaheim, Calif., 1984—87; home health nurse, obstet. Physician's Care, Brea, Calif., 1988—90, Am. Home Health, Santa Ana, Calif., 1988—92; staff nurse, rsch. clin. studies ctr. Harbor-UCLA Med. Ctr., Torrance, Calif., 1993—94; nurse rschr. various profit and non-profit orgns., Anaheim, Calif., 1994—, RN coord., cons., 1994—. Contbr. workshop Focus on Health, 1982; mem. citizens adv. com., health Calif. State Assembly, 1982—; cons., home care for MD's Am. Home Health We. Med. Ctr., Santa Ana, 1991—; RN clin. advisor, staff devel. Cmty. Svcs. Projects, Orange and LA Counties, 2000—. Recipient cert. of recognition, Calif. State Legis., 1982. Mem.: ANA, Assn. Am. Acad. Bereavement, Sigma Theta Tau. Democrat. Roman Catholic. Avocations: violin, travel.

VAN DE BOVENKAMP, SUE ERPF, charitable organization executive; b. N.Y.C.; d. George Norton and Bettina Lions (Hearst) Mortimore; student Gardner Sch., Art Students League, Cooper Union; m. Armand Grover Erpf, 1965 (dec.); children: Cornelia Aurelia, Armand Bartholomew; m. Gerrit Pieter Van de Bovenkamp, Aug. 11, 1973 (div.). Pres. Armand G. Erpf Fund, N.Y.C., 1971—; founder, hon. chmn. Erpf Catskill Cultural Ctr., 1972—. Bd. advisors, founder N.Y. Zool. Soc., 1971—, 1001 Nature Trust, 1973, William Beebe fellow, 1983—; fellow in perpetuity Met. Mus. Art, 1977; life fellow Pierpont Morgan Libr., 1974—; mem. coun.of friends Whitney Mus. Am. Art, 1971-77; mem. Whitney Circle, 1978-93; bd. dirs. Catskill Ctr. for Conservation and Devel., 1983-86; mem. adv. coun., dept. art history and archaeology Columbia U., 1972—, established univ. seminar on uses of oceans, 1977, mem. adv. coun. Translation Ctr., 1986; life conservator N.Y. Pub. Libr., 1980; fellow Frick Collection; 1971—, Whitney fellow, 2994—; mem. coun. Agribus. Coun., Inc., 1979-87; founder, life mem. World Wildlife Fund, 1973—, bd. dirs., 1984-89; mem. pres.'s coun. Columbia U., 1973-78; life mem. Mus. City N.Y., 1972—, mem. pres.'s coun., 1971—. Mem. N.Y. Acad. Scis., The Planetary Soc., Mus. Natural History (life), Asia Soc. (pres.'s coun.), Wildlife Fedn. (adv.), African Wildlife Found. (pres.'s cir.). mem. Mus. of Natural Hist. pres., coun. of the Asia Soc. Office: The Armand G Erpf Fund 640 Park Ave New York NY 10021-6126

VANDEBROEK, SOPHIE VERDONCKT, printing company executive; b. Leuven, Belgium, Feb. 17, 1962; came to U.S., 1986; d. Norbert and Jeanine (Ringoir) V.; m. Bart Vandebroek, Aug. 2, 1986 (dec. Aug. 1996); children: Elena, Arno, Jonas. B in Engring. magna cum laude, Katholieke U., 1982, MS in Electro-Mech. Engring. magna cum laude, 1985; PhDEE in Microelectronics, Cornell U., 1990. Devel. staff mem. IBM T.J. Watson Rsch. Ctr., Yorktown Heights, NY, 1990-92; competency leader J.C. Wilson Ctr. for Rsch. and Tech., Xerox, Webster, NY, 1992-95, lab. mgr., 1995-96; platform mgr. Ink-Jet Supplies Bus. Unit Xerox Corp., Webster, 1996-97, mgr. document systems coherence program, 1997-98, tech. advisor Office of the Chmn., 1998-99, chief engineer Stamford, Conn., 2002—06, chief tech. officer, 2006—, corp. v.p., 2006—; v.p. Xerox Rsch. Ctr. Can., 1999—2000, Xerox Engring. Ctr., 2002—06; pres. Xerox Innovation Group, 2006—; chief tech. officer Carrier Corp., 2000—02. Contbr. articles to profl. jours. Fulbright fellow, 1986; hon. grad. fellowship Belgian-Am. Ednl. Found., 1986; internat. travel grant Belgium Nat. Sci. Found., 1986-87; recipient Monsanto award 1986, Kieckhefer Adirondack award 1986. Mem. IEEE (sr. mem.), IEEE Electron Devices Soc. (adminstrv. com. 1995-97, internat. electron device meeting 1994-98, tech. program com. 1994-95, chair solid state devices com. 1996, publicity chair 1998, chair Rochester chpt. IEEE/EDS 1994, disting. lectr. 1994). Avocations: reading, skiing, kayaking, rollerblading. Office: Xerox Corp 800 Long Ridge Rd Stamford CT 06904*

VANDE KAPPELLE, SUSAN ELIZABETH, minister; b. Buffalo, Feb. 9, 1949; d. Walter Pandrich Hutton and Barbara Tiger Murphy; m. Robert Peter Vande Kappelle, Nov. 30, 1974; children: Robert Peter Jr., Sara Elizabeth. BA, St. Lawrence U., 1970; MDiv, Princeton Theol. Sem., 1975; DD (hon.), Waynesburg Coll., 1988; D in Ministry, Pitts. Theol. Sem., 1995. Campus chaplain Trenton State Coll., NJ, 1974—75; pastor Mt. Chestnut Presbyn. Ch., Butler, Pa., 1975—80, Fourth Presbyn. Ch., Washington, 1982—; dir. Washington Presbytery Acad., Eighty-Four, 1980—82. Moderator Synod of Trinity, Camp Hill, Pa., 1987—88; bd. pres. Presbyn. Media Mission, Pitts., 1998—2000; dir. Pitts. Theol. Sem., 2003—. Instl. rev. bd. Washington Hosp., 1998—; chairperson Washington County Health Ptnrs., 1999—2001, bd. dirs., 1999—2001. Recipient Profl. of Yr., Mental Health Assn. Washington County, Pa., 1991, Richard J. Rapp Meml. award, Pitts. Theol. Sem., 1995. Presbyterian. Avocations: tennis, photography, gardening. Home: 573 Franklin Farms Rd Washington PA 15301

VANDEL, DIANA GEIS, management consultant; b. San Antonio, Apr. 2, 1947; d. John George and Elma Ruth (Triplett) Geis; m. Jerry Dean Vandel, Apr. 17, 1976; 1 child, Jeremy Kyle. MusB, U. Tex., 1969. Cert. tchr., Tex. Tchr. music Zilker Elem. Pub. Sch., Austin, Tex., 1969-70, Isely Sch., Austin, 1986; asst. adminstr. Hillside Manor Nursing Home, Inc., San Antonio, 1970-76, 78-79, mgmt. cons., 1979-89, adminstr., 1988; mgmt. cons. Promoting Excellence Consultation, Austin, 1991-95, Winning Solutions, Austin, 1995—; owner Your Biggest Fan, 1999—2004. Owner, facilitator creative music and relaxation in motion classes, San Antonio, 1982-84; fine arts facilitator Cedar Creek Elem. Sch., Austin, 1988-91; seminar leader Movement Spiritual Inner Awareness, Austin, 1986—2003, min., 1989-2003. Austin rep. Peace Theol. Sem., L.A., 1988-93; exec. bd. Cedar Creek Booster Club, 1989-91. Avocations: photography, yoga, meditation, gardening, reading. Office: Winning Solutions 916 Calithea Rd Austin TX 78746-2716 E-mail: dvandel@earthlink.net.

VANDELL, DEBORAH LOWE, educational psychology educator; b. Bryan, Tex., June 5, 1949; d. Charles Ray and Janice (Durrett) Lowe; m. Kerry Dean Vandell, May 16, 1970; children: Colin Buckner, Ashley Elizabeth. AB, Rice U., 1971; EdM, Harvard U., 1972; PhD, Boston U., 1977. Tchr. Walpole (Mass.) Pub. Schs., 1972-73; rschr. Ralph Nader Congress Project, Washington, 1972; asst. prof. U. Tex., Dallas, 1976-81, assoc. prof., 1981-89; prof. ednl. psychology U. Wis., Madison, 1989—. Vis. scholar MacArthur Rsch. Network, Cambridge, Mass., 1985-86, U. Calif., Berkeley, 1988-89; mem. steering com. NICHD Study of Early Child Care. Assoc. editor Child Devel., 1993-95; mem. editl. bd. Child Devel., 1980-93, Jour. Family Issues, 1983-89, Devel. Psychology, 1989-93; co-author books; contbr. articles to profl. jours. Bd. dirs. Infant Mental Health Assn., 1988-89; bd. dirs. Cmty. Coord. Child Care, Madison, Wis., chair, 1991-93; mem. Day Care Adv. Bd., State of Wis.; mem. altar guild and vestry St. Andrew's Ch., 1992-95. Named Outstanding Young Scholar, Found. for Child Devel., 1982. Mem. Am. Psychol. Assn. (exec. com. div. 7 1985-88), Southwestern Soc. Rsch. in Human Devel. (pres. 1988-90), Am. Psychol. Soc., Soc. for Rsch. in Child Devel., Phi Beta Kappa. Episcopalian. Office: U Wis Dept Ednl Psychology 1025 W Johnson St Madison WI 53706-1706

VAN DEMARK, RUTH ELAINE, lawyer; b. Santa Fe, May 16, 1944; d. Robert Eugene and Bertha Marie (Thompson) Van D.; m. Leland Wilkinson, June 23, 1967; children: Anne Marie, Caroline Cook. AB, Vassar Coll., 1966; MTS, Harvard U., 1969; JD with honors, U. Conn., 1976; MDiv, Luth. Sch. Theology, Chgo., 1999. Bar: Conn. 1976, Ill. 1977, U.S. Dist. Ct. Conn. 1976, U.S. Dist. Ct. (no. dist.) Ill., U.S. Ct. Appeals (7th cir.) 1984, U.S. Supreme Ct. 1983; ordained to ministry, Luth. Ch., 1999. Instr. legal rsch. and writing Loyola U. Sch. Law, Chgo., 1976-79; assoc. Wildman, Harrold, Allen & Dixon, Chgo., 1977-84, ptnr., 1985-94; prin. Law Offices of Ruth E. Van Demark, Chgo., 1995—2003; pastor Wicker Park Luth. Ch., Chgo., 1999—. Mem. rules com. Ill. Supreme Ct., 1999-2002, chair appellate rules subcom., 1996-2002; mem. dist. ct. fund adv. com. U.S. Dist. Ct. (no. dist.) Ill., 1997—. Assoc. editor Conn. Law Rev., 1975-76. Bd. dirs. Lutheran Soc. Svcs. Ill., 1998—, sec., 2000—02, chmn., 2002-; mem. adv. bd. Horizon Hospice, Chgo., 1978—, YWCA Battered Women's Shelter, Evanston, Ill., 1982-86; del.-at-large White House Conf. on Families, L.A., 1980; mem. alumni coun. Harvard Divinity Sch., 1988-91; vol. atty. Pro Bono Advs. Chgo., 1982-92, bd. dirs., 1993-99, chair devel. com., 1993; bd. dirs. Friends of Pro Bono Advs. Orgn., 1987-89, New Voice Prodns., 1984-86, Byrne Piven Theater Workshop, 1987-90, Luth. Social Svcs. Ill. (sec., 2000—), 1998—; founder, bd. dirs. Friends of Battered Women and Their Children, 1986-87; chair 175th Reunion Fund Harvard U. Div. Sch., 1992; dean Ctrl. Conf. Met. Chgo. Synod ELCA. Mem. ABA, Ill. Bar Assn., Conn. Bar Assn., Chgo. Bar Assn., Appellate Lawyers Assn. Ill. (bd. dirs. 1985-87, treas. 1989-90, sec. 1990-91, v.p. 1991-92, pres. 1992-93), Women's Bar Assn. Ill., Jr. League Evanston (chair State Pub. Affairs Com. 1987-88, Vol. of Yr. 1983-84), Chgo. Vassar Club (pres. 1979-81), Cosmopolitan Club (N.Y.C.). Home: 2046 W Pierce Ave Chicago IL 60622-1946 E-mail: revwplc@earthlink.net.

VAN DEN BERG, ELIZABETH, actress, educator; d. Johannes and Barbara Eleanor van den Berg; m. Frank Michael Toperzer, III, Oct. 15, 1984; children: Barbara Jensen Toperzer, Frank Michael Toperzer IV. BA in Theatre Arts, San Francisco State U., 1978; MFA in Acting, NYU, 1983. Instr. acting Kennedy Ctr. Edn. Dept., Washington, 1987—90, Bethesda (Md.) Acad. Performing Arts, 1987—93; instr. voice Nat. Conservatory Dramatic Arts, Washington, 1987—89; adj. prof. U. Md., Balt., 1993—96; asst. prof. theatre arts McDaniel Coll., Westminster, 1992—. Actor, Washington, 1984—; dialect coach, Washington, 1987—; workshop coord. Kennedy Ctr. Am. Coll. Theatre Festival, Region II, Washington, 2002—06, leadership task force, 2005—. Actor: Follies - Solange, Quilters, ensemble (Helen Hayes award Best Musical, 1987). Bd. mem. New Playhouse, Frederick, Md., 2004—. Named Tchg. Artist, 2006. Mem.: AFTRA, SAG, Actors Equity Assn. (dep. 1990—92), Voice and Speech Trainers Assn. Office: Theatre Arts McDaniel Coll 2 College Hill Olney MD 20832 Office Phone: 410-857-2591. Office Fax: 410-857-2447. Business E-Mail: evandenb@mcdaniel.edu.

VANDEN BOSCH, LINDA KAE KRULL, elementary school educator; d. Albertus and Lois Krull; m. Larry D. Vanden Bosch, Aug. 8, 1998; children: Faith McCollum, Shey Krull. Diploma - Office Mgmt., NW Iowa Tech. Coll., Sheldon, 1979; BEd, Westmar Coll., LeMars, Iowa, 1986; MEd, Viterbo U., LaCrosse, Wis., 2005. Cert. Project Charlie HISD/Tex., 1988, Batterer's Edn. Program facilitator Iowa, 1997; cert. master tchr. Iowa, 1986, coach Iowa, 1986, public libr. Iowa, 1996. Tchr. Houston Ind. Sch. Dist., 1988—89; pub. libr. dir. City of Larchwood, Iowa, 1992—96; mid. sch. tchr. Clarinda Cmty. Schs., Iowa, 1997—, at-risk tutor advisor. Adv. mem. Clarinda Cmty. Sch., 1999—. Dir.: (student books) Explorer Book Exhibit. Mem. Nat. Coun. Social Studies, We the People Civic Studies, 2000—06, Iowa Edn. Assn., Des Moines, 1997—, Clarinda Edn. Assn., 1997—. Nominee Disney Tchr. of Yr.; named Lyon County Dairy Princess; grantee Big Yellow Sch. Bus, Iowa Fine Arts Coun., 2005. Mem.: NEA (corr.). Office: Clarinda Cmty Schs 305 E Glenn Miller Dr Clarinda IA 51632 Office Phone: 712-542-2132.

VANDENBURG, KATHY HELEN, small business owner; b. Clifton, N.J., Feb. 6, 1969; d. Milan and Helen (Derco) Suchanek; m. James Joseph Vandenburg III, Aug. 31, 1996 BA Psychology, Montclair State U., 1991; MA Edn., Seton Hall U., 1995; postgrad., Rider U., 1997—98. Cert. job and career transition coach Career Planning and Adult Devel. Network. Admissions counselor William Paterson U., Wayne, NJ, 1995—96; career counselor New Brunswick Pub. Schs., NJ, 1996—2000, Cornerstone Relocation Group, Warren, NJ, 2000—01; career tng. advisor Transitions Ctr. for Women, Warren County C.C., Washington, NJ, 2001—02, Transitions Ctr. for Women, NORWESCAP, Washington, NJ, 2002—. Mem.: Profl. Assn. Resume Writers and Career Coaches, Career Masters Inst. Avocations: swimming, travel, classical music, theater, cooking. Office Phone: 908-995-2193.

VANDENBURG, MARY LOU, psychologist; b. Passaic, N.J., Dec. 18, 1943; d. Nicholas and Louise (Rosiello) Yacono; m. James Joseph Vandenburg, Jr., July 2, 1966; 1 child, James Joseph III. BA, William Paterson, 1965; MA, Montclair Coll., 1982; MS, Pace U., 1986, D of Psychology, 1988. Cert. tchr., sch. guidance counselor; lic. psychologist; diplomate Am. Coll. Forensic Examiners. Elem. tchr. various, 1966-67, 76-80; therapist Pequannock Valley Mental Health Ctr., 1985-90; sch. psychologist Andover Schs., 1988—; pvt. practice Butler, N.J., 1989—. Lectr. ednl. enrichment programs, 1980—. Author children's books; contbr. articles to profl. jours. Recipient honor cert. Freedom Found., Valley Forge, Pa., Merit Scholarship, Pace U. Mem. N.J. Assn. Sch. Psychologists, Nat. Assn. Sch. Psychologists, Am. Psychol. Assn., Sussex County Assn. Sch. Psychologists, Morris County Assn. Psychologists, NJ Psychol. Assn., Nat. Register of Health Svc. Providers in Psychology, N.J. Assn. of Cognitive Behavioral Therapists. Avocations: tae kwon do karate (black belt), painting (reily league of artists). Home: 404 E Lakeshore Dr Highland Lakes NJ 07422-2212 Office: PO Box 547 3713 Rt 235 Ste 8A Newfoundland NJ 07435

VANDEN HEUVEL, KATRINA, publishing executive; b. NYC, Oct. 7, 1959; d. William Jacobus and Jean Babette (Stein) Vanden H.; m. Stephen F. Cohen, Dec. 4, 1988; 1 child, Nicola Anna. BA summa cum laude in Politics, Princeton U., 1982. Prodn. assoc. ABC Closeup Documentaries, 1982-83; asst. editor The Nation, N.Y.C., 1984-89, editor-at-large, 1989-93, acting editor-in-chief, 1994-95, editor-in-chief, 1995—, and pub., gen. ptnr., 2005—. Vis. journalist Moscow News, 1989; Moscow coord. Conf. Investigative Journalism After the Cold War, 1992; co-founder, co-editor Vyi i Myi, 1990—. Editor: The Nation, 1865-1990; The Best of the Nation, 1990-2000: Selections from the Independent Magazine of Politics and Culture, 2001, A Just Response: The Nation on Terrorism, Democracy and September 11, 2001, 2002, The Dictionary of Republicanisms, 2005; co-editor: Voices of Glasnost: Interviews with Gorbachev's Reformers, 1989, Taking Back America-And Taking Down the Radical Right, 2004; contbr. articles to newspapers. Recipient Maggie award Planned Parenthood Fedn. Am., 1994. Mem. Correctional Assn. N.Y. (dir.), Inst. for Women's Policy Rsch. (bd. dirs.), Coun. Fgn. Rels., Inst. Policy Studies (trustee), Network of East-West Women (bd. advisors), Franklin and Eleanor Roosevelt Inst. (trustee), Moscow Ctr. for Gender Studies (mem. adv. com.), World Policy Inst., Century Assn. Office: The Nation 33 Irving Pl Fl 8 New York NY 10003-2332 Personal E-mail: kat@thenation.com.

VANDERBEKE, PATRICIA K., architect; b. Detroit, Apr. 3, 1963; d. B. H. and Dolores I. VanderBeke. BS in Architecture, U. Mich., 1985, MArch, 1987. Registered arch., Ill. Archtl. intern Hobbs & Black, Assocs., Ann Arbor, Mich., 1984-86, Fry Assocs., Ann Arbor, 1988; arch. Decker & Kemp Architecture/Urban Design, Chgo., 1989-92; prin., founder P. K. VanderBeke, Arch., Chgo., 1992—. Mem. adv. com. dept. arch., Triton Coll. Contbr. photographs and articles to Inland Arch. mag.; contbr. photographs to AIA calendar. Chair recycling com. Lake Point Tower Condo. Assn., Chgo., 1990-05, chair. ops. com., 1993; mem. benefit com. The Renaissance Soc., U. Chgo., Redmoon Theater, Chgo. George S. Booth travelling fellow, 1992. Mem. AIA (participant 1st ann. leadership inst. 1997, 1st place nat. photog. contest award 1992, hon. mention 1994, Chgo. chpt. membership com., bd. dirs. 2006—), Chgo. Archl. Club, hon. mention 2000 Burnham Prize Competition, The Cliff Dwellers (mem. arts com.). Office: 155 W Burton Pl Apt 16 Chicago IL 60610-1326

VANDER HEYDEN, MARSHA ANN, business owner; b. Milw., Sept. 15, 1942; d. Bernard Aloysius and Leona Adeline (Zimpel) Vander Heyden. BA, Alverno Coll., 1964; postgrad., Layton Sch. Art, 1966; MFA, Cornell U., 1969; diploma in carpentry and cabinetmaking, Manhattan Trade Sch., 1975. Rschr. The Nigerian Mus., Lagos, 1970; tchr. The Cloisters/The Met. Mus. Art, N.Y.C., 1973-74; woodshop instr. The New Lincoln Sch., N.Y.C., 1973-75; tchr. Grand Street Settlement, N.Y.C., 1974-76; mgr., head tchr. The Woodsmith's Studio, N.Y.C., 1976-77; founder, pres. Trade Links, Inc. (runs Me Too Kids program), N.Y.C.; owner, operator Vander Heyden Woodworking, Inc., N.Y.C., 1977—, Tapestries etc. dba Vander Heyden Woodworking Inc., N.Y.C. Designer pet products under name Doggone Purrrty; patentee frame assembly. Recipient award of excellence The Archtl. Woodwork Inst., Washington, 1989. Mem.: Am. Soc. of Interior Designers. Avocations: gardening, dogs and cats, hiking, reading. Office: 151 W 25th St 8th Fl New York NY 10001-7204 Office Phone: 212-242-0525.

VANDERHOST, LEONETTE LOUISE, psychologist; b. Phila., June 11, 1924; d. Charles and Pauline (McGhaney) V. BA, CUNY, 1945; MA, NYU, 1949, PhD, 1966. Lic. psychologist, N.Y. Intern staff Lincoln (Ill.) State Sch., 1951-52; staff Evansville (Ind.) State Hosp., 1953-54, Children's Guidance Ctr., Dayton, Ohio, 1954-56; psychotherapist Hempstead (N.Y.) Consultation Services, 1963-66; staff, sr. psychologist Hillside Hosp., Glen Oaks, N.Y., 1957-64; sr. psychologist, chief West Nassau Mental Health Ctr., Franklin Sq., N.Y., 1959-63; pvt. practice psychologist N.Y.C., 1959—. Cons. Big Sisters, N.Y., 1960-62, Health Ins. Planning, N.Y., 1962-64, Head Start, N.Y., 1967-73. Mem. Am. Psychol. Assn., N.Y. State Psych. Assn.

VANDERKOLK, MARIA ELIZABETH, city official; b. Mpls., Dec. 20, 1964; d. Clarence Michael and Louise Elizabeth (Kurtzman) Lederhos; m. Michael James Vanderkolk, Nov. 28, 1987; children: Kaitlin, Nicholas. BS, BA, U. Colo., 1986; MPA, Calif. Lutheran U., 1995. Mktg. coord. MiniScribe Corp., Longmont, Colo., 1985-87; sr. mktg. coord. EeSof, Inc., Westlake Village, Calif., 1988-89; mktg. mgr. Applause, Inc., Woodland Hills, Calif., 1989-91; county supr. Ventura County, Calif., 1991-95; asst. city mgr. City of Arvada, Colo., 1996—. Mem. Ventura County Bd. Suprs., 1991—; mem. Ventura County Med. Ctr. Bd. Trustees; mem. bd. dirs. Santa Monica Mtns. Cons. Mem. Nat. Assn. Telecom. Officers and Advisors, Pub Rels. Soc. Am., City County Comm. and Mktg. Asn., Metro Mayors Commrs. Youth Awards, Kids Voting Jefferson County, Arvada Jefferson Kiwanis, Beta Gamma Sigma. Republican. Roman Catholic. Office: City of Arvada 8101 Ralston Rd Arvada CO 80002-2400 also: PO Box 8101 Arvada CO 80001-8101

VANDERLAAN, G. ANNE, artist, educator; b. LA, Mar. 1, 1953; d. Daniel Ray McDonald and Herlinda Ellen Fierro, Dale Allen Boone (Stepfather); m. Rudy J. Vanderlaan, May 21, 1988; children: Albert Max James, Antonia Marie Watkins, Linda Delaine, Kia Kristy Suddarth, Poeina Yvonne Suddarth, Niya Heavenor, Rutger Jan, Vinter Jan. AA, Seattle Ctrl. CC, 1986—88; attended, U. Wash., Seattle, 1988—93; BS, So. Utah U., Cedar City, 1999—2000; MFA, Goddard Coll., Plainfield, Vt., 2002—05. Cert. master jeweler Stewarts Sch., Fla., 2003. Tchr. Hancock Fabrics, Seattle, 1985—87; out reach tchr. Idaho State U., Pocatello, 1997—98; tchr. Acad. Lakes, Land O' Lakes, 2000—02; gallery dir. Beck Gallery, Lutz, Fla., 2000—03; tchr. VSA Am. Cancer Soc., Tampa, Fla., 2003. Painting, Joy, mural project, Wheels in Motion the Rhodes Park Project; artist, tchr. (murals, workshops) Noahs Ark and Houses, Mexican orphanage, Cmty. Sharing Project, Mexican Outreach dot-to-dot orgn., 2003. Mem.: 4Art (assoc.). Achievements include paintings shown on The Food Network and The Oprah Winfrey Show. Home: 1870 E Fireside Ct Meridian ID 83642 Personal E-mail: mail.annevanderlaan.com.

VANDERLINDEN, CAMILLA DENICE DUNN, telecommunications industry executive; b. Dayton, July 21, 1950; d. Joseph Stanley and Virginia Danley (Martin) Dunn; m. David Henry VanderLinden; Oct. 10, 1980; 1 child, Michael Christopher. Student, U. de Valencia, Spain, 1969; BA in Spanish and Secondary Edn. cum laude, U. Utah, 1972, MS in Human Resource Econs., 1985. Asst. dir. Davis County Community Action Program, Farmington, Utah, 1973-76; dir. South County Community Action, Midvale, Utah, 1976-79; supr. customer service Ideal Nat. Life Ins. Co., Salt Lake City, 1979-80; mgr. customer service Utah Farm Bur. Mutual Ins., Salt Lake City, 1980-82; quality assurance analyst Am. Express Co., Salt Lake City, 1983-86, quality assurance and human resource specialist, 1986-88, mgr. quality assurance and engring. Denver, 1988-91; mgr. customer svc. Tel. Express Co., Colorado Springs, Colo., 1991-97; dir. Call Ctr. United Membership Mktg. Group, Lakewood, Colo., 1997-98; telesvcs. industry mgr. Piton Found., Denver, 1998—; customer care and tng. dir. SafeRent, 2000—; dir. quality assurance Tele-Servicing Innovations, 2000—02; ops. mgr. Bayaud Industries, 2002—05. Adj. faculty Westminster Coll., Salt Lake City, 1987-88. adj. faculty, quality adv. bd. Red Rocks C.C., 1990-91; cons. in field. Vol. translator Latin Am. community; vol. naturalist Roxborough State Park; internat. exch. coord. EF Fgn. Exch. Program. Mem. Internat. Customer Svc. Orgn. (officer call ctr. chpt.), Colo. Springs Customer Svc. Assn. (officer). Christian. Avocation: swimming. Home: 44 Lake Lea Rd Rochester NY 14617 Personal E-mail: camillavan@usa.net.

VANDERLIP, ELIN BREKKE, professional society administrator, volunteer; b. Oslo, June 7, 1919; came to the U.S., 1934; m. Kelvin Cox, Nov., 1946 (dec. 1956); children: Kelvin Jr., Narcissa, Henrik and Katrina (twins). With Norwegian Embassy, Washington, Norwegian Fgn. Ministry, London, 1941-44, Red Cross, Calcutta, India; pres. Friends of French Art, Portuguese Bend, Calif. Sponsor of charity art conservation fundraising events Friends of French Art; tour leader Ile de France, Anjou, Bordelais, Provence-Cote d'Azur, Alsace, Dordogne, Lyonnais-Isere, Brittany, Burgundy, Normandy, Languedoc, Loire, Gascony, Le Nord, Charente, Champagne, Eure et Loir, 1978-96, Route de Berry, Auvergne and Toulouse. Decorated Comdr. Order of Arts and Letters (France) Chevalier of the Legion of Honor. Home and Office: Villa Narcissa 100 Vanderlip Dr Rancho Palos Verdes CA 90275-5920 Fax: (310) 377-4584. E-mail: VillaCissa@aol.com.

VANDER NAALD EGENES, JOAN ELIZABETH, retired small business owner, educator; b. Des Moines, Feb. 13, 1936; d. Bert and Cathryn Alice (Bunger) Vander Naald; m. David Iddings Grant, July 25, 1959 (div. Oct. 1984); children: Jeffrey, Pamela, Elizabeth, Jennifer. BA, U. Iowa, 1958. Cert. profl. in edn., Iowa, Colo.; cert. travel agt., Iowa. Instr. St. Katherine's Sch., Davenport, Iowa, 1958-59, Iowa Ctrl. C.C., Fort Dodge, 1959-61; city councilwoman Boone, Iowa, 1980-86; instr. Des Moines Area C.C., Boone Campus, 1983; founder, owner, importer Global Ednl. Svcs., Des Moines, 1992-97; receptionist, sec. Automobile Club of So. Calif., West Los Angeles, 1997-2001; ret. Bd. mem. Iowa Psychology Bd. Examiners, Des Moines, 1984-93; rsch. interviewer Iowa State U., Ames, 1984; resource tchr., workshop presenter about Russia, 1988-94; freelance photographer, 1988—. Lifetime mem. Rep. Senatorial Inner Circle, Washington, 1987—; pres. Iowa 4th Dist. Rep. Women, 1990-91, Polk County (Iowa) Rep. Women, 1994; precinct chair 12, ward 01, Des Moines, 1995-97; pres. Des Moines Metro Opera Guild, 1995-97, coun. sec., 1995-97; extensive vol. activities, including various fundraising chairs. Recipient 1st prize Youth Projects, Iowa Devel. Commn., 1983, Women Helping Women award for volunteerism, Boone, 1983; named Entrepreneur of Yr. in Iowa award GE, 1995. Republican. Avocation: swimming.

VAN DER PAARDT, TAMARA ANN, music educator; d. Glenn Elmer and Darlene Margaret Schultz; m. Peter van der Paardt, June 27, 1987; children: Nicole Marie, Melissa Krystine, Andrew Scott. BA in Music Edn., Calif. State U., Fresno, 1985. Cert. clear credential music edn. Calif., 1987. Profl. musician Fresno Philharm. Orch., Calif., 1979—; music tchr. Clovis Unified Sch. Dist., 1987—. Dir. Winter Drumline Ensemble, Jazz Ensemble. Named Outstanding Jazz Ensemble, Downbeat Internat. Music Awards, 1995, Class A World Champions, WGI Drumline Competition, 2003. Mem.: CBDA (assoc.), FMCMEA (assoc.), IAJE (assoc.), Internat. Assn. Jazz Educators, Calif. Band Dirs. Assn., Fresno-Madera (Calif.) County Music Educators Assn., Music Educators Nat. Conf. (assoc.), Calif. Music Edn. Assn. (assoc.; pres. ctrl. Calif. sect. 2003—), Winter Guard Internat. Avocations: travel, gardening, softball. Home: 1692 Richert Ave Clovis CA 93611 Office: Reyburn Intermediate Sch 4300 N DeWolf Clovis CA 93611 Office Phone: 559-327-4731.

VANDERPAN, NORMA, retired elementary school educator; b. Starkweather, N.D. m. Leslie Vanderpan; 7 children. BA, Concordia Coll.; MA, U. S.D. Mem. negotiation team West Lyon Tchr. Assn., Inwood, Iowa, 1967—69, Brookings Edn. Assn., 1973—74; organizer, rep. Ea. S.D. Uniserv, Sioux Falls, SD, 1974—75. Named Brookings Tchr. of Yr., Brookings Pub. Schs., 1976; Nat. Def. Edn. grant, U. S.D., 1965. Mem.: PEO (chaplain Chpt. P 2004—05), BARTA, Saturday Literary Club (pres. 2005—), Phi Delta Kappa, Alpha Delta Kappa (Eta chpt. sec., Eta chpt. treas., state treas. 1976—78, state chaplain 1990—92, Fidelis Gamma chpt. pres. 1992—94, Fidelis Gamma chpt. chaplain 1995—2005). Republican. Lutheran. Avocations: reading, writing, quilting, antiques, needlepoint. Home: 2009 Derdall Dr Brookings SD 57006

VANDERPOOL, SHAWNEE D., elementary school educator; b. Hayward, Calif., May 11, 1981; d. Pedro Santana Brambila and Shari D. Vanderpool. MusB in Music Edn., U. Pacific, Stockton, Calif., 2003. Cert. cross-cultural lang. and academic devel. Calif. Commn. Tchr. Credentialing, 2006. Music dir. Armona Elem. Sch. Dist., Calif., 2003—. Musician: Tigerphones Saxophone Quartet. Mem.: Sigma Alpha Iota (life; grad. advisor 2003—, v.p. ritual 2000—, v.p. membership 2000—, Sword of Honor 2003). Office: Armona Elem Sch Dist 11175 C St Armona CA 93202 Office Phone: 559-583-5000.

VANDERSLICE, ELLEN, architect, composer; b. Ann Arbor, Mich., Oct. 8, 1953; d. Ralph L. Vanderslice, Carolyn G. Vanderslice; married. BS, U. Mich., Ann Arbor, 1981, MArch, 1983. Lic. Architect, Oreg., 1996. Project mgr. Office of Transp., City of Portland, 1994—99, 2003—; project designer David Giulietti and Assocs., Portland, 1990—94; pres. America Walks, Portland, Oreg., 1996—2003. Pres. Willamette Pedestrian Coalition, Portland, 2001—03; mem. com. on pedestrians Transp. Rsch. Bd., Washington, 2001—04; mem. adv. com. Pub. Rights-of-Way Access, Washington, 1999—; co-treas. Portland chpt. Women's Transp. Seminar, 1997—98; prin. Ellen Vanderslice AIA, Portland, 1999—2003. Composer (CD): Once in a Blue Moon, 2000, The Standard Vanderslice, 2001, Don't Look Before You Sing, 2003. Sec. Northwest Dist. Assn., Portland, 1986—88. Recipient Pl. Planning award for Portland Pedestrian Master Plan and Pedestrian Design Guide, Environ. Design and Rsch. Assn., 2000, Exemplary Svc. to Pedestrian Transp. Program and Unwavering Commitment to Advocacy of Walking award, Portland Office of Transp. Engring. and Devel., 1999, Outstanding Project award for Portland Pedestrian Design Guide, Inst. Transp. Engrs. Oreg. Sect., 1999, Reclaiming Our Streets All-Star award, City Commr. Earl Blumenauer, 1991, Northwest Traffic Circulation Project Leadership award, Neighbor Newspaper, 1987, 1st prize jazz, USA Songwriting Competition, 2002, Golden Sole award, Willamette Pedestrian Coalition, 2005. Mem.: AIA (sec. Portland chpt. 1998—99, Nehemiah Housing Project award of excellence Portland chpt. 1993), Assn. Pedestrian and Bicycle Profls., Women's Transp. Seminar (co-treas. Portland chpt. 1997, Woman of Yr. Portland chpt. 2000), Nat. Assn. Watch and Clock Collectors, Jazz Soc. Oreg., Portland Songwriters Assn. (1st pl. Blues/Jazz/R&B Category 1999, 2000, 2001, 2003). Avocations: restoring eight-day clocks, canoeing, hiking. Office: 1120 SW 5th Ave Rm 800 Portland OR 97204 Office Phone: 503-823-4638. Business E-Mail: ellen.vanderslice@pdxtrans.org.

VANDERSLICE, RONNA JEAN, education educator; b. Woodward, Okla., Apr. 22, 1965; d. Ronnie Leroy and Norma Jean (Semmel) V. BA, Southwestern Okla. State U., 1986; MEd, Tex. Tech U., 1990, EdD, 1995. Cert. tchr., reading specialist, counselor spl. edn., learning disabilities, psychometry, early childhood, Tex.; mid-mgmt. cert., gifted and talented endorsement; sch. psychologist. Tchr. Highland Elem. Sch., Plainview, Tex., 1986—91; counselor 6th grade learning ctr. Ash Sch., Plainview, 1991—93; prof. Southwestern Okla. State U., Weatherford, 1993—. Mem. Higher Edn. Alumni Coun. Okla., Weatherford Kiwanis, Phi Delta Kappa, Delta Kappa Gamma, Kappa Kappa Iota. Lutheran. Avocations: sports, reading, crafts. Home: 416 Texas St Weatherford OK 73096-5632 Office: SW Okla State U 100 Campus Dr Weatherford OK 73096-3098 Office Phone: 580-774-3145. Business E-Mail: ronna.vanderslice@swosu.edu.

VANDERSYPEN, RITA DEBONA, counseling and academic administrator; d. Sam S. and Myrtle (Genova) DeBona; m. Robert Louis Vandersypen, Aug. 17, 1974; children: Regina Marie, Ryan Matthew. BA summa cum laude, La. Coll., 1975; MEd, La. State U., 1980, postgrad., 1982; EdS, Northwestern State U., Natchitoches, La., 1993. Eligibility worker Rapides Parish Office Family Svcs., Alexandria, 1975—78; welfare social worker Rapides Parish Foster Care Svcs., Alexandria, 1978—79; tchr. A. Wettermark H.S., Boyce, La., 1979—84; tchr. English Alexandria Sr. H.S., 1984—92, guidance counselor, 1992—2000; asst. prin., curriculum coord. Brame Jr. H.S., Alexandria, 2000—. Pres. Andersen Fire Protection Inc. Contbr. chapters to books. Sponsor Future Voters Am. Club, 1984-89, 4-H Club, 1988-97. Mem. Rapides Assn. Principals, Rapides Fedn. Tchrs., La. Assn. Principals, La. Vocat. Assn., La. Mid. Sch. Assn., Belgian-Am. Club, Am. Quarter Horse Assn., Phi Kappa Phi, Kappa Delta Pi, Amicus Club Roman Catholic.

VANDERTUUK-PERKINS, JENNIFER ELIZABETH, counselor, psychologist; d. Rodney Roy Perkins and Jill Ellen VanDerTuuk-Perkins; m. Joe Allen Behun II, Aug. 22, 1997; children: Lucile Elizabeth Perkins-Wagel, Gabriel Theodore Perkins-Behun, Madeline Emilie Joy Perkins-Behun; m. Ashley Allen Wagel, Dec. 26, 1993 (div. Aug. 20, 1997). MA in Ednl. and Devel. Psychology, Andrews U., Berrien Springs, MI, 1996, MA in Cmty. Counseling, 1999; PhD in Counseling Psychology, Cambridge State U., Honolulu, Hawaii, 2000; Grad. Cert. in Forensic Clin. Psychology, Capella U., Mpls., Minn., 2003. Diplomate of the Bd.- Clinical Forensic Counseling Am. Coll. of Forensic Counselors, 2003, cert. counselor Nat. Bd. for Cert. Counselors, 1999, lic. profl. counselor Mich., 2001. Counselor/legal adv. Safe Shelter, Inc., Benton Harbor, Mich., 1996—97; teen pregnancy dir. Women In Renewal, Niles, Mich., 1997—2000; dir., cons. Theragogy.com, Land O Lakes, Fla., 1997—; clin. program supr., early impact Bethany Christian Svcs., 2001—04; prof. Spring Arbor U., 2002—04, Fla. Met. U., 2004—. Autism cons. Bethany Christian Svcs., Grand Rapids, Mich., 2001—04; joint planning com. mem. Family Independence Agy., Grand Rapids, Mich., 2001—04; child disability specialist, military divsn. Ceridian Corp., St. Petersburg, Fla., 2004—. Author: (book) The Religious Experience of Asperger's Syndrome, (children's book) Life With Gabriel (A Sibling's Perspective of Autism), (volume of poetry) When You Were Young; contbr. scientific papers. Mem. P21! Family Independence Agy. - Kent County, Grand Rapids, Mich., 2001—03. Mem.: ACA (licentiate), APA (assoc.). D-Liberal. Non-Denominational. Achievements include research in choroid plexus cysts and autism; development of online counseling resource library for therapists; research in workplace effectiveness as related to environmental multiple intelligence learning styles; multiple intelligence learning sytles. Avocations: painting, writing, photography.

VANDER VEER, SUZANNE, aupair business executive; b. Phila., Sept. 21, 1936; d. Joseph Bedford Vander Veer and Ethel K. Short; m. James Robb Ledwith, Nov. 29, 1958 (div. Sept. 1978); children: Cheryl Day, James Robb Jr., Scott Wiley; m. Herbert Keyser Zearfoss, Nov. 14, 1992. AA, Colby Sawyer Coll., 1957; postgrad., State U. Iowa, 1957-58. Tchr. Booth Sch., Bryn Mawr, Pa., 1958; profl. tour guide Cities of Phila., N.Y.C. and Washington, D.C., 1976-89; regional dir. Transdesigns, Woodstock, Ga., 1979-87; area rep. Welcome Wagon Internat., Tenn., 1987-93, mem. local bd., 1987-93; condo. complex mgr. St. Davids, Pa., 1990-93; area dir. Cultural Care Aupair, Cambridge, Mass., 1993—2004. Art cons., 1979—. Chair host family program Internat. House of Phila., 1966-74; mem. women's com. Pa. Hosp., 1966-71; mem. com. Phila. Antique Show, 1995—; docent Phila. Mus. of Art, 1974-80; bd. dirs. Plays for Living, Phila., 1966-84, Kynett Found., 2002-05; chair congl. care coun. Office of Deacon Bryn Mawr Presbyn. Ch., 1997-2002. Mem. PEO (past pres.), Jr. League of Phila. (bd. dirs., sustainer chair 1993-95, Pres.' Cup 1995, sustainer bd. 1985—. Sustainer of the Yr. award 2001), Merion Cricket Club, Cosmopolitan Club of Phila. (bd. dirs.). Home: 532 Candace Ln Villanova PA 19085-1702

VANDER VLIET, VALERIE JEANNE, biology educator; b. Chgo., June 6, 1951; d. Ralph Robert and Virginia Rose Marie Ruppert; m. Steven Jay Vander Vliet, Sept. 29, 1979; children: Erin, Jackie, Steven Jr. BA, Blackburn Coll., 1973; MS, So. Ill. U., 1974, U. Mich., 1978; PhD in Sci. Edn., U. Ill., 2003. Adj. instr. biology Mundelein Coll., Chgo., 1979-80; instr. Coll. St. Francis, Joliet, Ill., 1980-81, adj. asst. prof., 1981-90, Trinity Christian Coll., Palos Heights, Ill., 1984-90, Wheaton Coll., Ill., 1987-89; prof., chair biology dept. Lewis U., Romeoville, Ill., 1991—. Presenter Am. Forum for Global Edn. and UN Assn. US, NYC, 1995; mem. Women in Sci. del. to Cairo, People to People Amb. Program, 2000. Active area sch. bd., Tinley Park, Ill., 1994-98, chair curriculum and assessment task force, 1992-94, mem. sch. bd., 1994-98, v.p. sch. bd., 1997-98; mem. steering com. Edn. 2000 Task Force, Tinley Park, 1990-97. Recipient Those Who Excel Parent Vol. award Ill. State Bd. Edn., 1992-93. Mem. Am. Edn. Rsch. Assn., Nat. Sci. Tchrs. Assn., Nat. Assn. Rsch. in Sci. Tchg., Assn. Coll. and Univ. Biology Educators, Nat. Assn. Biology Tchrs., Am. Soc. Microbiology, Ill. State Acad. Sci. Office: Lewis Univ 1 University Pky Romeoville IL 60446 Office Fax: 815-836-5955. E-mail: vanderva@lewisu.edu.

VANDERWERKEN, SHARON LYNN, nurse; b. Oneida, N.Y., Nov. 19, 1957; d. George F. and June M. (Lindroth) V. Diploma in nursing, Piedmont Hosp. Sch. Nursing, Atlanta, 1978; student, U. Cen. Fla., 1984; BSN suma cum laude, Excelsior Coll., 2005. Cert. ACLS, PALS. Staff nurse Orlando (Fla.) Regional Med. Ctr., 1978-79; nurse Camp Challenge, Easter Seals, Sorrento, Fla., 1979; staff nurse family practice unit Fla. Hosp., Orlando, 1979-81, asst. head nurse oncology-med. unit, 1981-84, staff nurse intensive care unit, 1984-86, staff nurse PACU, 1986-88, staff nurse kidneystone ctr., 1988—; PRN Winter Park Plastic Surgery, 1998—2000. CPR instr. Am. Heart Assn., 1984-86. Drama/choir First Bapt. Ch., Orlando, 1982—; camp nurse-vol. Easter Seals Camp Challenge, Sorento, 1979—; fgn. vol. missions So. Bapt. Fgn. Mission Bd., 1984—. Mem. Am. Lithotripsy Soc. (cert. renal lithotripsy specialist), Bapt. Nursing Fellowship, Nurses for Christ, Am. Urol. Assn.-Allied, Sima Theta Tau. Republican. Avocations: travel, bicycling, camping, hiking, scuba diving. Home: 212 W Orlando St Orlando FL 32804-5428 Office: Fla Hosp 601 E Rollins St Orlando FL 32803-1273

VANDERWIST, KATHRYN K., lawyer; Litig. atty. Nestle USA, 1998—99; corp. counsel Agilysys, Inc., Mayfield Heights, Ohio, 1999—2000, gen. counsel, asst. sec., 2000—01, v.p., gen. counsel, asst. sec., 2001—. Office: Agilysys, Inc 6065 Parkland Blvd Mayfield Heights OH 44124 Office Phone: 440-720-8500.

VANDER ZANDEN, MARIANNE, music educator; b. Chgo., Mar. 17, 1939; d. Martin and Mary (Evanco) Sadd; m. Cornelius Leo Vander Zanden, July 6, 1957; children: Sandra, Linda, William, Mark AA, Joliet Jr. Coll., 1978; MusB, Am. Conservatory Music, Chgo., 1982; MusM, Am. Conservatory Music, 1993, D Music, 2006; BA, Govs. State U., 1985; MA, U. Chgo., 1985. Cert. elem. tchr., Ill. Tchr. music, Mokena, Ill., 1965—2006. Mem. Children's Book Coun., Joliet Amateur Radio Soc. (pres. 1981) Republican. Roman Catholic. Avocations: astronomy, antiques, amateur radio. Home: 18830 Sara Rd Mokena IL 60448-8488

VAN DEUSEN, JENIFER, educational consultant; b. Rockville Centre, N.Y., Feb. 24, 1952; d. James A. and Gladys E. (Rinderman) V.D.; m. John A. Henkel, June 21, 1980 (div. 1991); children: Marissa Jane, Monica Rose. BS in Edn., Lesley Coll., 1975; postgrad., Sonoma State U., 1983; MEd in Ednl. Adminstrn., U. South Maine, 1992. Cert. prin., curriculum coord., tchr., Maine; cert. tchr., Mass. Therapeutic caregiver Creative Playmates, Inc., Arlington, Mass., 1971-73; with Mus. Transp., Brookline, Mass., 1974-75; tchr. Beginning Sch., Marin City, Calif., 1975-77; ungraded primary tchr. West Marin Sch., Pt. Reyes Station, Calif., 1977-84, chair sch. site coun., 1981-83; early edn. specialist Maine Dept. Edn., Augusta, 1985-93, mgr. divsn. curriculum, 1986-93; coord. Project SEED Maine Ctr. for Ednl. Svcs., Auburn, 1993—. Mem. restructuring cadre Maine Ctr. for Ednl. Svcs., 1991—; founding dir. Maine Child & Family Enterprise, Augusta, 1992—; cons. Waterville (Maine) Regional Vocat. Ctr., 1993—; mem. Spl. Commn. Early Edn. & Care, Augusta, 1988-89; chair delegation Surgeon Gen.'s Conf. on Healthy Children, Augusta, 1992; dir. legacy Me. Ctr. Edn. Svcs., 1995—. Co-author: Beyond Tinkering to Transformation, 1992, Big Book for Educators, 1988. Organizer children's programs Peace Action Nat. Congress, Portland, 1994—; bd. dirs. New Beginnings, Inc., Lewiston, Maine, 1994—, Trout Found., 1994—; active Puente de Amor, Durham, Maine, 1994—. Mem. New England Coun. Ednl. Leaders, Maine Assn. Supervision and Curriculum Devel., Nat. Assn. for Edn. Young Children, Durham Monthly Meeting. Democrat. Mem. Soc. Of Friends. Avocations: hiking, films, canoeing, reading. Home: RR 2 Box 4650 Bowdoinham ME 04008-9631 Office: Maine Ctr Ednl Svcs 223 Main St Auburn ME 04210-5833

VAN DEUSEN, LOIS M., lawyer; married. BA summa cum laude, Cedar Crest Coll., 1961; JD, Rutgers Univ., Newark, 1977. Bar: NJ, US Dist. Ct. NJ. Assoc. McCarter & English, Newark, 1977—86, ptnr. real estate law, 1986—2002, mem. exec. com., 1991—, mng. ptnr., 2002—. Twp. atty., Livingston, NJ, 1989—2002; bd. dir. CIT Group Inc., 2003—; lectr. NYU Sch. Law. Bd. mem. Habitat for Humanity Newark. Named one of NJ Women of Influence, NJBiz mag., 2002, 10 Most Powerful Women in NJ Bus., Star-Ledger, 2006; recipient Woman of Substance award, Seton Hall Law Sch., 2003, Lifetime Achievement award, Ctr. for Italian & Italian-Am. Culture, 2002, Disting. Alumna award, Rutgers Newark Law Sch., 2004. Mem.: ABA, NJ Bar Assn. Office: McCarter & English 4 Gateway Ctr 100 Mulberry St Newark NJ 07102 Office Phone: 973-639-2017. Office Fax: 973-624-7070. Business E-Mail: lvandeusen@mccarter.com.*

VAN DE WATER, READ, federal official; b. Charlotte, NC; m. Mark Van de Water; 3 children. Degree, U. South, 1986; M, George Washington U.; JD, Georgetown U. Appropriations assoc., legis. asst. Congressman Tom DeLay, Tex., 1987—91; legis. coun., dir. govt. affairs Northwest Airlines, 1991—97; legis. coun. internat. trade and investment Bus. Roundtable, 1997—99; founder Carson King Cons., 2000; asst. sec. aviation & internat. affairs U.S. Dept. Transp., Washington, 2001—03. Mem. Nat. Mediation Bd., Washington, 2003—, chmn., 2005—. Republican. Office: Nat Mediation Bd 1301 K St NW Ste 250 E Washington DC 20005-7011 E-mail: vandewater@nmb.gov.

VANDIEGRIFF, VICKI ALVINDA, realtor; b. South Bend, Ind., Nov. 16, 1945; d. Alvin Lee Atkins and Mildred Josephine Taylor-Atkins; children: Marvin L., Becky L. Student, Ind. U., South Bend, 1977—80. Property mgmt. various cos., Atlanta; realtor Remax Greater Atlanta, 2001—05, Solid Source Realty, Roswell, 2005—. Bd. sec. Learn To Grow, Inc., Atlanta. Fellow: Nat. Assn. Realtors, Atlanta Bd. Realtors (Mktg. Specialist of Yr. award 1999). Avocations: golf, travel. Office: Solid Source Realty Roswell GA Personal E-mail: vandiegriff@bellsouth.net.

VANDIVER, BETTY J., protective services professional; b. Harrodsburg, Ky., Sept. 27, 1950; d. Cecil Raymond and Ruby Marie (Hawkins) VanD. AA, Ea. Ky. U., 1971, BS, 1993—. Juvenile counselor, juvenile correctional officer Cabinet for Human Resources, Waddy, Ky., 1981—91; dir. admissions, adminstrv. asst. dept. mental health Ky. Correctional Psychiat. Ctr., LaGrange, Ky., 1991—94; ct. designated worker Cabinet of Justice-53rd Jud. Dist., various cities, Ky., 1994—98; living instr. Best House Group; telecom. officer Unit 194 Harrodsburg Police Dept., Harrodsburg, Ky., 1998—2006; telecom. officer Unit 404 Lawrenceburg Police Dept., 2006—. Bd. mem. Local Interagy. Coun., Shelbyville, Ky., Youth Adv. Coun., Shelbyville, Taylorsville, Drug and Alcohol Adv. Coun., Shelbyville.Private Childcare, Christian Children's Homes of Kentucky; supr. Christian Children's Homes Ky., Danville, Ky. Mem. NAFE, NRA, Ea. Star (Hamilton chpt. 293). Avocations: sky diving, horseback riding, fishing, rifle/handgun competition. Address: PO Box 79 Burgin KY 40310-0079 Home: 102 W Court St Burgin KY 40310 Office: 201 E Court St Louisville KY 40232 Office Phone: 859-734-3311, 502-839-5125.

VANDIVER, KATHLEEN MEAD, science educator; b. Baroda, India, Mar. 10, 1949; arrived in U.S., 1959; d. Lester Jr. and Ada Thayer Finley; m. Jonathan Taylor Mead (dec.); m. J. Kim Vandiver, Aug. 23, 1986; children: Amy, Benjamin, Alexander. BA in Zoology, Drew U., 1971; MA in Physiology, Boston U., 1974; PhD in Immunology, Tufts U., 1982; MA in Sci. Tchg., Harvard U., 1990. Cert. tchr. Mass. Rsch. technician Block Engring., Inc., Cambridge, Mass., 1973—77; biomed. rsch. scientist Optra, Inc., Topsfield, Mass., 1982—89; sci. tchr. Lexington (Mass.) Pub. Schs., 1990—2005; dir. cmty. outreach and edn. program Ctr. for Environ. Health Scis., MIT, 2005—. Sci. cons. Magic Sch. Bus. TV episode Scholasic Inc., NYC, 1992; sci. cons. Sci. Ct., Tom Snyder Prodns., Watertown, Mass., 1997—98; prin. investigator multimedia cell biology Sensimetrics Corp., Somerville, Mass., 1999—2000; on-camera classroom tchr. profl. devel. series Essential Sci. Annenberg, Harvard Smithsonian Ctr. Astrophysics, 2002. Developer LEGO Life Sci. Sets, 2002—; co-developer: 6th grade curriculumn Horace's Fridays, 1994. Recipient Best Paper award, Am. Soc. Zoologists, 1981; grantee, NIH, 1982—89. Mem.: AAAS. Achievements include research in naturally abundant basophils in the snapping turtle posses cytophilic surface antibody with reaginic function. Avocations: hiking, nature observation. Office: MIT 56-211 77 Massachusetts Ave Cambridge MA 02139 Office Phone: 617-324-0252. Business E-Mail: kathymv@mit.edu.

VANDIVER, PAMELA BOWREN, science educator; b. Santa Monica, Calif., Jan. 12, 1946; d. Roy King and Patricia (Woolard) Evans; m. J. Kim Vandiver, Aug., 1968 (div. 1984); 1 child, Amy. BA in Humanities and Asian Studies, Scripps Coll., 1967; postgrad., U. Calif., Berkeley, 1968; MA in Art, Pacific Luth. U., 1971; MS in Ceramic Sci., MIT, 1983, PhD in Materials Sci. and Near Eastern Archeology, 1985. Instr. in glass and ceramics Mass. Coll. of Art, Boston, 1972; lectr. MIT, Cambridge, 1973-78, rsch. assoc., 1978-85; rsch. phys. scientist Conservation Analytical Lab., Smithsonian Instn., Washington, 1985-89; sr. scientist in ceramics and glass Smithsonian Ctr. for Materials Rsch. and Edn., Washington, 1989—2002, dir., 2003; prof. materials sci. and engring. joint appointment in anthropology/ archaeology U. Ariz., Tucson, 2004—, co-dir. program in heritage conservation sci. Instr. semester-at-sea U. Pitts., spring 1995; prof. Northwest U. of Sci. & Tech., Xianyang, China, 1996; guest rschr. Nat. Inst. Stds. and Tech., Gaithersburg, Md., 1989-91; adj. prof. material sci. and engring. Johns Hopkins U., Balt., 2001-2003; vis. prof. dept. art history U. Del., 2000 Co-author: Ceramic Masterpieces, 1986; co-editor: Materials Issues in Art and Archaeology, vol. 1-7, 1988-2005; bd. editors Archeomaterials, 1986-93; contbr. over 100 articles to profl. jours. Sponsor mentorship program Thomas Jefferson H.S. of Sci. and Tech., Alexandria, 1992. Recipient Disting. Alumna Achievement award, Scripps Coll., 1993. Fellow Am. Anthrop. Assn.; mem. AAAS, Archeol. Inst. Am., Soc. Am. Archeol., Internat. Inst. of Conservation, Am. Inst. Conservation, Internat. Com. on Mus., Soc. for History of Tech., Am. Ceramics Soc. (ancient ceramics com. 1978-2000), Materials Rsch. Soc. (guest editor MRS Bull. 1992, 2001), Archeol. Inst. Am. (Pomerance Sci. Achievement medal 2006), Am. Chem. Soc., Cosmos Club, Sigma Xi. Avocations: sailing, diving, photography. Office: U Ariz Dept Materials Sci and Engring Mines Bldg 304 1325 E James Rogers Dr Tucson AZ 85721 Office Phone: 520-400-2270. Business E-Mail: vandiver@mse.arizona.edu.

VANDIVER, RENEE LILLIAN AUBRY, interior designer, architectural preserver; b. New Iberia, La., Nov. 7, 1929; d. Harold George and Josephine Fortier (Brown) Aubry; m. Arthur Roderick Carmody, Jr., Jan. 1952 (div. 1979); children: Helen Bragg Carmody Stroud, Renee Josephine Carmody Mathews, Arthur Roderick III, Patrick Gerard, Timothy H.A., Mary Joellyn, Virginia Caroline, Joseph Barry; m. Frank Everson Vandiver, Mar. 21, 1980. BFA, Sophie Newcomb Coll. Tulane U., 1951; postgrad., U. Paris, 1951-52, Centinary Coll., 1966-68, La. State U., Shreveport, 1978. Designer, supt. art New Iberia Parish Elementary Schs., 1951; archtl. drafter and designer Perry L. Brown, Inc., Baton Rouge, 1950-52; tchr. art St. Joseph's Elem. Sch., Shreveport, 1960-69; designer, illustrator, saleswoman Stierwalt Interiors, Shreveport, 1974-78; design cons. for president's homes and gardens North Tex. State U., Tex. A&M U., Denton, College Station, 1980-88; design cons., planner, saleswoman, pres. Renee Aubry Vandiver Interiors, College Station, Tex., 1980—; design cons. Am. U. in Cairo, 1997—; proofreader, editor, rschr., asst. Office of Frank E. Vandiver, College Station, 1998—. Interior design and house constrn. cons. Heritage Antiques and Interiors, New Iberia, 1972—; interior design cons., Tenn., La., S.C., 1980—; invited student Middle Eastern master painter Sabri Raghab; involved with consultations and contruction large new campus, pres.'s home grounds Am. U., Cairo. Editl. and illustrations collaborator works on gen. mil. history with Frank E. Vandiver, 1990—; works include design constrn. of new Pres.'s Home on campus of Am. U. of Cairo, 2004. Mem. NAFE, DAR, Constrn. Specifications Inst., Dallas Market Ctr., Houston Market Ctr., Jr. League, Textile Mus., Mus. Women in Arts, Tex. A&M U. Women's Club (hon. pres. 1981—), Fedn. Tex. A&M U. Mother's Club. Avocations: painting, playing piano, gardening, travel, reading. Home: PO Box 10600 College Station TX 77842-0600

VANDIVER, SARA ELIZABETH SHARP RANKIN, retired postmaster; d. James Earl and Celeste Heskett Sharp; m. William Doyle Vandiver, Aug. 18, 1978 (dec. Feb. 27, 1997); m. James Dorothy Rankin, Sr., Aug. 25, 1934 (dec. Aug. 3, 1971); children: James Dorothy Rankin Jr., William Earl Rankin, Carolyn Vandiver Pollan. Postmaster US Postal Svc., Driver, Ark., 1954—80; ret. Sec. St. Louis Region Postmaster Tng. Conf., 1962—73; v.p. Ark. Chpt., Nat. Assn. Postmasters, 1976—78; columnist Ark. Postmaster. Charter mem. Nat. Mus. Women in the Arts, Washington, 1990—2006; contbg. mem. Smithsonian Instn., Washington, 2000—06; pres. Wilson PTA, Ark., 1950—52, Wilson Co-Operative Club, 1952—54, Gen. Fedn. of Women's Clubs Prog. Club, Osceola, 1985—90; organizer Adopt-a-Teacher Program, Osceola Pub. Schs., 1985, Gt. Am. Family Recognition and Awards Program, Osceola, Ark., 1987; pres., state advisor Gen. Fedn. Women's Clubs, Dist. II, Ark., 1990—92, state chmn. cmty. improvement program, 1994—96; mem. Miss. County Geneal. and Hist. Soc., 1993—2006; bd. mem. Interfaith Neighbors, Osceola, 1996—2006; leader Miss. County Explorers Bible Study, Ark., 1983—96; pres. Wilson Women's Missionary Union, 1953—55; Sunday sch. tchr., 1963—. Mem.: Riverlawn Country Club.

VAN DOREN, HENRIETTA LAMBERT, nurse anesthetists; b. Birmingham, Ala., Sept. 21, 1946; d. Martin Lee and Maude Elizabeth (Land) Lambert; m. Terry Lee Van Doren, Oct. 14, 1969; children: Terry Lee Jr., Timothy Wayne. AA in Nursing, Meridian Jr. Coll., Miss., 1968; cert., Charity Hosp. Sch. Anesthesia, New Orleans, 1971; PhD in Health Svcs./Nursing Adminstrn., Columbia Pacific U., 1982. RN, cert. registered nurse anesthetist; hypnotherapist Am. Bd. Hypnotherapy. Registered hypnotherapist, chief nurse anesthetist Riley Meml. Hosp. HMA, Meridian, Miss., 1972—2000; self-employed, 2000—. Mem.: Am. Assn. Hypnotherapy, Am. Assn. Nurse Anesthetists. Republican. Baptist. Home: 2551 Campground Rd Lauderdale MS 39335-9621

VAN DOVER, KAREN, elementary school educator, consultant; b. Astoria, NY; d. Frederick A. and Frances L. Van Dover. BA, CUNY; MALS, SUNY, Stony Brook; postgrad., St. John's U., Jamaica, N.Y. Cert. permanent N-6 tchr., art tchr. K-12, sch. supr., adminstr., N.Y. Tchr., sch. dist. adminstr. St. James (N.Y.) Elem. Sch.; tchr. Nesaquake Intermediate Sch., St. James, lead tchr. English, 1984—92, Smithtown Mid Sch., St. James, 1992—93, curriculum specialist, 1993—2005; instructional specialist, staff developer Nesaquake Mid. Sch., St. James, 2004—. Leader staff devel. and curriculum devel. workshops Smithtown Sch. Dist., 1984—, mem. supt.'s adv. com. for gifted and talented, mem. supt. adv. com. for lang. arts assessment, mem. textbook selection coms. site-based mgmt. team, 1994-2004, chair 1996-99, master tchr. bd. Prentice Hall, Englewood Cliffs, N.J., 1990—, chair ELA com. for curriculum and the stds., 2000. Contbg. author: Prentice Hall Literature Copper, 1991, 94. Mem. Nesaquake Sch. PTA, 1977-92, 2004—, corresponding sec., 1990-1991; Nesaquake Sch. Improvement Team, 2005; mem. Smithtown Mid. Sch. PTA, 1992-2004. Mem. ASCD, Am. Ednl. Rsch. Assn., Nat. Assn. Secondary Sch. Prins., Nat. Assn. Elem. Sch. Prins., L.I. Lang. Arts Coun., Nat. Coun. Tchrs. English, Internat. Reading Assn., Nat. Middle Schs. Assn., N.Y. State English Coun., Internat. Platform Assn., Phi Delta Kappa. E-mail: kvandover@smithtown.k12.ny.us.

VANDREE, ELIZABETH, secondary school educator; b. St. Joseph, Mo., Dec. 27, 1979; d. Susan and James Schurman (Stepfather), Mike and Carol Jackson (Stepmother); m. Matt Vandree, June 11, 2006. B in Edn., U. of Kans., Lawrence, 2003. Cert. tchr. math. and sci. Kans., Mo. Dir. maiden unit Camp of the Rising Son, French Camp, Miss., 1996—2003; barista Starbucks, Overland Park, Kans., 2003—04; mid. sch. tchr. math. and sci. Pleasant Ridge Mid. Sch., Overland Park, 2004—06; mid. sch. sci. tchr. Sedalia Mid. Sch., 2006—. Recipient ednl. grant, Pleasant Ridge Mid. Sch. Parent Tchr. Orgn., 2004—06. Home: 10225 Bond St Overland Park KS 66214 Personal E-mail: lvandree@gmail.com.

VAN DRESAR, VICKIE JANETTE, mathematician, educator; d. David Andrew and Barbara Janet Corgnell; m. Neil Thomas Van Dresar, Aug. 11, 1984. BS in Math., Shenandoah U., 1981; MS in Math., U. Akron, Ohio, 1993; PhD in Ednl. Math., U. No. Colo., Greeley, 1996. Asst. prof. Ashland (Ohio) U., 1996—2002, assoc. prof., 2002—, co-dir. Intro. U. Life, 2004—06, asst. provost undergrad. academic affairs, 2006—. Mem.: Nat. Coun. Tchrs. Math., Ohio Coun. Tchrs. Math., Math. Assn. Am. (faculty advisor student chpt. 1998—, program chmn. Ohio chpt. 2004—05). Avocations: bicycling, backpacking, hiking. Office: Ashland Univ 401 College Ave Ashland OH 44805 Office Phone: 419-289-5265.

VAN DUSEN, DONNA BAYNE, communications consultant, educator, researcher; b. Phila., Apr. 21, 1949; d. John Culbertson and Evelyn Gertrude Bayne; m. David William Van Dusen, Nov. 30, 1968 (div. Dec. 1989); children: Heather, James. BA, Temple U., 1984, MA, 1986, PhD, 1993. Instr. Kutztown (Pa.) U., 1986—87, Ursinus Coll., Collegeville, Pa., 1987—96; cons., rschr. Comm. Rsch. Assoc., Valley Forge, Pa., 1993—96; assoc. prof. and MS in Mgmt. degree chair Regis U., Denver, 1998—, degree chair, 2005—. Rschr. Fox Chase Cancer Ctr., Phila., 1985-86; adj. faculty Temple U. Law Sch., 1994-97, LaSalle U., 1994-96, Wharton Sch., U. Pa., 1994-95; asst. prof. Beaver Coll., Glenside, Pa., 1995-96; faculty Jones Internat. U., 1996-99, Metro State U., Denver, 1997-99; cons. Human Comm. Resources and Solutions, 1997—, acad. coun. chair, 2002-04. Writer Mountain Connection, 1998-2000. Vol. Friends in Transition; vol. mediator Victim Offender Reconciliation Program. Recipient Excellence in Tchg. award, 2003. Mem.: Nat. Comm. Assn. Avocations: painting, creative writing, sailing, gardening, reading. Home: 2589 Alkire St Golden CO 80401 Business E-Mail: dvanduse@regis.edu.

VAN DUSEN, LANI MARIE, psychologist; b. Alexandria, Va., July 23, 1960; d. Arthur Ellsworth and Ann Marie (Brennan) Van D. BS magna cum laude, U. Ga., 1982, MS, 1985, PhD, 1988. Cert. secondary tchr., Ga. Tchr. Henry County Sch. Sys., McDonough, Ga., 1982-83; rsch. psychologist Metrica Inc., Bryan, Tex., 1988; asst. prof. psychology U. Ga., Athens, 1988-89, chmn. Conf. for Behavioral Scis., 1987; asst. prof. psychology Utah State U., Logan, 1989—. Cons. Western Inst. for rsch. and Evaluation, Logan, 1990—; bd. dirs. Human Learrning Clinic, Logan, 1990—, Ctr. for Sch. of Future; reviewer William C. Brown Pubs., 1990, Dushkin Pub. Group Inc., 1990-91. Contbr. articles to profl. jours. Fellow Menninger Found.; mem. APA, Psychonomic Soc., Am. Ednl. Rsch. Assn., AAUP, ASCD. Republican. Avocations: hiking, tennis, skiing, knitting, swimming. Home: 1633 N 1200 E North Logan UT 84341-2102 Office: Vandusen Consulting Ste 210 550 North Main Logan UT 84321

VAN DUZER, DORY A., translator; b. Cleve., Ohio, Oct. 11, 1949; d. Ashley Van Duzer and Virginia Hosford Jones; 1 child, Marta Elena Van Duzer-Snow. BA, Northwestern U., Evanston, Ill., 1971; MA in Bilingual Edn., Antioch Coll., Keene, N.H., 1974. Cert. tchg. bilingual, social studies and secondary edn. Commonwealth Mass., lic. riding instr. Commonwealth Mass. Curriculum writer Boston Pub. Schs., 1974—78; evaluator curriculum development Hispanic Office Planning & Evaluation, Boston, 1978—79; parent organizer Alianza Hispana, Boston, 1979—80; instr. ESL Oficina Hispana, Boston, 1981—82, Mass. Rehab. Commn., Boston, 1982—84, Roxbury C.C., Boston, 1985—90; translator/tutor Durham Pub. Schs., Durham, NC, 2002—. Pet therapist Umstead State Hosp., Butner, NC, 2002—03, Croaside Assisted Living, Durham, 2003—, Sacine Arbor Assisted Living, Durham, 2003—, Heartland Hospice, Chapel Hill, NC, 2004—. Major donor St. Luke's Ch., 1984—89, Iglesia San Juan, 1998, W6BH Edn. Found., 1999, UNC TV, 2002, Eno River Assn., 2004, El Pueblo, 2005. Mem.: Am. Quarter Horse Assn., Bay State Trail Riders, Therapy Dog Internat., Assn. Ind. Investors. Democrat. Episcopalian. Avocations: gardening, breeding/training dogs, prison ministry. Office: EK Powe Elem 913 Ninth St Durham NC 27705 Personal E-mail: dory19@aol.com.

VAN DYCK, WENDY, dancer; b. Tokyo; Student, San Francisco Ballet Sch.; BA in performing Arts, St. Mary's Coll., 2003. With San Francisco Ballet, 1979—96, prin. dancer, 1987—96, instr., tchr., 1996; co-dir. Lawrence Pech Dance, San Francisco, 1996—. Performances include Forgotten Land, The Sons of Horus, The Wanderer Fantasy, Romeo and Juliet, The Sleeping Beauty, Swan Lake, Concerto in d: Poulenc, Handel-a Celebration, Menuetto, Intimate Voices, Hamlet and Ophelia pas de deux, Connotations, Sunset, Rodin, In the Night, The Dream: pas de deux, La Sylphide, Beauty and the Beast, Variations de Ballet, Nutcracker, The Comfort Zone, Dreams of Harmony, Rodeo, Duo Concertant, Who Cares; performed at Reykjavik Arts Festival, Iceland, 1990, The 88th Conf. of the Internat. Olympic Com., LA, 1984, with Kozlov and Co. Concord Pavilion; guest artist performing role Swan Lake (Act II), San Antonio Ballet, 1985, Giselle, Shreveport (La.) Met. Ballet, 1994; featured in the TV broadcast of Suite by Smuin. Mailing: PO Box 29190 San Francisco CA 94129 Office Phone: 415-308-5881. E-mail: wvandyck7@earthlink.net.

VAN DYK, SUZANNE B., lawyer; b. 1950; BS, Univ. Wis., 1971, JD, 1975. Bar: Wis. 1975, Minn. 1975. Ptnr., banking and comml. law, firm gen. counsel Dorsey & Whitney LLP, Mpls., and mem. mgmt. com., assoc., 1975—82, ptnr., 1983—. Office: Dorsey & Whitney LLP Ste 1500 50 S Sixth St Minneapolis MN 55402-1498 Office Phone: 612-340-5631. Office Fax: 613-340-2868. Business E-Mail: van.dyk.suzanne@dorsey.com.

VAN DYKE, ANNETTE JOY, university educator; b. Sacramento, Nov. 9, 1943; d. Wallace Ford and Joy Maurine (Allen) Van D.; children: Lisa Hargrave Smith, Amy Hargrave. BA in English, Whitworth Coll., 1970; MA in English, Ea. Wash. U., 1972; PhD in Am. Studies, U. Minn., 1987. Cert. tchr., Wash. Tchr. English Coeur d'Alene (Idaho) High Sch., 1972-75, The New Sch., Spokane, Wash., 1975-76; instr. adult basic edn. Spokane C.C., 1976-78; instr. English Bemidji (Minn.) State U., 1978-81; grad. assoc. U. Minn., Mpls., 1981-87; instr. English Normandale C.C., Bloomington, Minn., 1987-88; assoc. dir. Ctr. for Women's Studies U. Cin., 1988-90; dir. women's studies Denison U., Granville, Ohio, 1990-93; prof. interdisciplinary studies U. Ill., Springfield, 1993—. Spkr. NOW, Cin., 1990, Native Am. Tchg. Workshop, Kenyon Coll., Gambier, Ohio, 1991, lit. meeting YWCA, Columbus, 1991, Crazy Ladies Bookstore, Inc., 1991, Native Am. Experience Conf. Ohio Wesleyan, Delaware, 1992, U. Minn. Am. Studies 50-Yr. Celebration, 1994, Nat. Women's Studies Assn., 2001, 02, 05, Midwest Mystery Writers Conf., 1997, Ill. Coalition Against Domestic Violence, 1999, 2006; chair grad. coun. U. Ill., Springfield, 2002—, dept. chair, 1997-888, 2002—; exec. com. U. Ill. Coll. Lib. Arts and Scis., 1997-1999, 2002—, chair status women com., 1996-1997. Author: Poems for a Revolution, 1978, The Search for a Woman-Centered Spirituality, 1992, Hooded Murder, 1996; editor The Forum, 1988-90; contbr. articles to lit. jours. Mem. gender equity adv. com. Ill. Office Ednl. Svcs., 2003—04. Grantee Denison U., 1991-92, U. Ill. Springfield, 1995, 98, 99, 2000, 06. Mem. MLA, Nat. Women's Studies Assn. (nat. bd. dirs. 1990-93, 95-2001, pres. 2000-01, editor caucus newsletter 1989-92), Midwest MLA (chair Native Am. lit. 1985-86), Western Lit. Assn., Soc. for Study of Am. Women Writers, Multi-Ethnic Lit. Assn., Assn. Native Am. Lit. Office: Univ Ill Springfield Springfield IL 62794

VAN DYKE, DEBBIE K., special education services professional; d. Charles A. and Helen M. Wallace; m. Mike H. Van Dyke, Aug. 9; 1 child, Jason Michael. BS, Henderson State U., 1976, MS in Edn., 1976. Spl. edn. tchr. Pulaski County Sch. Dist., Little Rock, 1975; spl. edn. tchr. supr. Gosnell (Ark.) Sch. Dist., 1975—82; spl. edn. tchr. Greene County Tech, Paragould, Ark., 1982—85; spl. edn. supr. Arch Ford Ednl. Svc. Coop., Plumerville, Ark., 1986—92; dir. spl. svcs. Russellville (Ark.) Sch. Dist., 1992—96; area spl. edn. supr. Ark. Dept. Edn., Little Rock, 1996—2003; spl. svcs. supr. Benton County Sch. of the Arts, Rogers, Ark., 2004—. Ednl. cons. Spl. Solutions Ark., Pea Ridge, 2003—. Mem. chair Ark. Assn. Spl. Edn. Adminstrn., Little Rock, 1988—93, Ark. Coun. for Exceptional Children, Little Rock, 1988—96. Recipient Ark. Spl. Edn. Adminstr. of Yr. award, Ark. Assn. Spl. Edn. Adminstrn., 1994, Area I Beverly Benham Spl. Edn. Adminstr. of Yr. award, Area I Ark. Assn. Spl. Edn. Adminstrn., 2000. Mem.: Coun. Exceptional Children.

VAN DYKE, MICHELLE, bank executive; BA in Bus. Econ., Calvin Coll., 1985. Joined Old Kent Bank, 1985; former sr. v.p., regional mgr. of Ill. mortgage region Old Kent Mortgage Co., pres., central region, 1997—98; exec. v.p., mgr. of retail distribution for Mich., Ind. and Ill. Old Kent Bank, 1998—2004, pres., Ill. div., 2000—04; pres., CEO, western Mich. Fifth Third Bank, Grand Rapids, Mich., 2004—. Bd. dirs. ICCF, Porter Hills Retirement Village. Named one of 25 Women to Watch, US Banker mag., 2005. Office: Fifth Third Bank 3785 Plainfield Ave NE Grand Rapids MI 49525*

VAN DYKE, WENDY JOHANNA, artist; b. Moline, Ill., July 22, 1955; d. Kreger D. and Sara K. (Weeks) Emry; m. Mikel P. Van Dyke, Feb. 11, 1978; children: Benjamin, Jonathan. BS in Bus. Adminstrn with highest honors, U. Ill., 1977. Mgr. Stringer Art Factory and Gallery, Davenport, IA, 1977-78, Warren L. Langwith, Inc., Davenport, IA, 1977-78. V. chmn. visual arts com. Quad Cities Arts Coun., Rock Island, Ill., 1979-80. Exhibited in group shows at Davenport Mus. of Art, 1977, 84, 88, 95, Muscatine (Iowa) Art Ctr., 1980, 83, 88, 90, Blanden Mem. Art Gallery, Ft. Dodge, Iowa, 1980, Graceland Coll., Lamoni, Iowa, 1980, Waterloo (Iowa) Mcpl. Art Galleries, 1980, Carrol (Iowa) Arts Coun., 1981, Clinton (Iowa) C.C., 1981, Algona (Iowa) H.S., 1981, Art Guild of Burlington, Iowa, 1981, 96, 2003, Woodbine Comm. Schs., Iowa, 1981, Cen. Coll., Pella, Iowa, 1981, Augustana Coll. Art Gallery, Rock Island, Ill., 1996, 98, 2001, Quad City Arts, Rock Island, Ill., 2003, 04, Galesburg Civic Art Ctr., Ill., 2006. Mem. fine arts com. Buchanan Sch. PTA, Davenport, 1983-92; mem. arts adv. com. Davenport Cmty. Schs., 1986-89; active devel. State of Iowa Art Curriculum, Des Moines, 1991-92; bd. dir. Quad Cities Arts Coun., Rock Island, Ill., 1979-80; mem. artist adv. coun., exhbns. and acquisitions com Davenport Mus. Art, Figge Art Mus., 2003-06. Mem. Quad City Arts, Figge Art Mus., Friends of Davenport Pub. Libr., Art Inst. Chgo. (nat. assoc.), U. Ill. Alumni Assn. (life), Phi Kappa Phi, Beta Gamma Sigma, Alpha Lambda Delta, Phi Gamma Nu. Avocations: reading, writing, bicycling, yoga. Home: 2517 W 43rd St Davenport IA 52806-4913

VAN DYKEN, AMY, Olympic athlete; b. Engelwood, Colo., Feb. 15, 1973; d. Don and Becky Van Dyken; m. Alan McDaniel, Oct. 1995. Student, Colo. State U. Swimmer U.S. Nat. Resident Team, Colorado Springs, Colo., 1994,

U.S. Olympic Team, Atlanta, 1996, Sydney, 2000; ret. Named Female NCAA Swimmer of Yr., 1994, Assoc. Press Female Athlete of the Yr., 1996, USOC Sports Woman of the Yr., 1996, Woman's Sports Found. Woman of the Yr., 1996, USA Swimming Swimmer of the Yr., 1996, Phillips Performance of the Yr. award, 1996, Female Athlete of Yr., AP, 1996; named one of Glamour's Top Ten Women of the Yr., 1996; recipient Bronze medal, World Championships, 1994, Triple Gold medals, Pan Am. Games, 1995, Silver medal, 1995, Gold medal 50 meter freestyle, Atlanta Olympic Games, 1996, Gold medal 100 meter butterfly, 1996, Gold medal 4x400 meter freestyle relay, 1996, Gold medal 4x100 meter medley relay, 1996, Gold medal 4x400 freestyle, Sydney Olympic Games, 2000, ESPY award, best female athlete, 1997. Achievements include 1st American women to win 4 gold medals in any event during a single Olympic game.

VANDYKEN, NANCY A., information technology executive, web site designer; d. Frank C. and Carol J. Radice; m. Kenneth E. VanDyken, Aug. 8, 1954; 1 child, Shera K. BS in Bus./Mktg., Mont. State U., Bozeman, 1977; MA, Trinity Theol. Sem., Newburgh, Ind., 1993. Statistician/programmer analyst Mont. Gov.'s Office - Budget & Program Planning, Helena, 1979—81; dir. computer ctr. Carroll Coll., Helena, 1981—82; sr. systems analyst IFG Leasing, Great Falls, Mont., 1982—85; pastoral asst. Bozeman Christian Ref. Ch., Mont., 1995—2000; exec. dir. Gallatin County Love Inc., Bozeman, 2001—; nat. advisor/trainer Love Inc. Nat. Hdqs., Mpls., 2005—. Website designer Ind. Consulting, Bozeman, 1998—. Editor: Tri-Cities CRC Newsletter, (newsletter) Pearl of Great Price. Co-facilitator Gallatin Violence Prevention Team, Bozeman, 2004—06; co-organizer #1 Gallatin Dad Contest, Bozeman, 2006; treas. & coun. mem. St. Anthony Orthodox Ch., Bozeman, 2003—06; mem. Gallatin Valley Christian Ministerial Assn., Bozeman, 2005—06, United Way - Emergency Food & Shelter Program, Bozeman, 2004—06. Recipient Faculty award for Academic Achievement, Mont. State U. Sch. Bus., 1977, Women's Fencing Champion, Boise State Fencing Tournament, 1976, Nat. Dean's List, 1978—79. Mem.: Mensa (life). Office: Gallatin County Love Inc PO Box 7117 Bozeman MT 59771 Office Phone: 406-587-3008.

VAN DYNE, MICHELE MILEY, information engineer; b. Harrisburg, Pa., Sept. 8, 1959; d. Joseph Lawrence Miley and Tina Theresa (Dudash) Smollack; m. David Franklin Buck, Aug. 8, 1981 (div. July 1984); m. David George Van Dyne, Sept. 9, 1989 (div. July 2005). BA in Psychology, U. Mont., 1981, MS in Computer Sci., 1985; PhD in elec. engring., U. Kans., 2003. Div. sr. tech. programmer, analyst Allied-Signal Aerospace, Kansas City, Mo., 1985-89; knowledge engr. United Data Svcs., Inc., United Telecom, Overland Park, Kans., 1989-90; pres. IntelliDyne, Inc., Kansas City, Mo., 1990—, MT Tech., U. Mont., Bulte, 2006—. Cons. Comprehensive Devel. Ctr., Missoula, Mont., 1984; spkr. Sigart, Kansas City, Mo., 1988; chmn. Expert-Sys.-Kans. and Mo. (ESKaMo), 1990—92; asst. prof. Mont. Tech. of U. Mont., Missoula, 2006—. Vol. Planned Parenthood Greater Kansas City, 1986. United Bldg. Ctrs. scholar, 1976. Mem. IEEE Computer Soc., Am. Assn. for Artificial Intelligence, Internat. Neural Network Soc., Instrnl. Tech. Network (steering com. 1990-92), Women in Tech. Network (steering com. 1990-91, chmn. pub. rels. com. 1991-92), Alpha Lambda Delta. Democrat. Episcopalian. Avocations: reading, decorating, kayaking, sewing, home remodeling. Home and Office: 852 W Granite Butte MT 59701 E-mail: mvandyne@msn.com.

VAN EKEREN, YBI, artist; b. Zwolle, Overysel, The Netherlands, Aug. 2, 1927; arrived in Can., 1951; came to U.S., 1960; AA, Riverside City Coll., 1968; BA, Fullerton State U., 1977. Exhibited in group shows at Riverside (Calif.) Art Mus., 1969 (1st award for graphics, 3rd award for sculpture), Arlington (Calif.) Art Guild, 1970 (2nd Place award for graphics), Nat. Orange Show, San Bernardino, 1994 (2nd Place award), Calif. Mid-State Fair, Paso Robles, 1996 (2nd Place award), Printmaker Show, San Luis Obispo, 1996 (Merchant's award), Fine Arts Inst., San Bern, Calif., 1999, 34st Internat. Exhibit (hon. mention), Fine Arts Inst. San Bern, 2001 (2d award). Mem. Cayucos Art Assn., San Luis Obispo Art Assn., San Luis Obispo Printmakers, Nat. Mus. of Women in the Arts (Washington). Office: Studio Art Gallery 731B Santa Ysabel Ave Los Osos CA 93402-1137

VAN ELLA, KATHLEEN E., fine art consultant; b. Flint, Mich., Apr. 16, 1943; d. Wallace Joseph Weirich and Helen Catherine Gutenkauf; m. James Eugene Van Ella, Aug. 8, 1964 (div. Apr. 1975); children: Aleen Janette Malloy, Erica Kathleen Krzyszkowski. BS in History and English Lit., Loyola U., Chgo., 1967; postgrad., Ray-Vogue Sch. Design, 1977—80. Founder, pres., dir. Portraits/Chgo. Inc.-Fine Portrait Painting and Sculpture, Lake Forest, Ill., 1980—. First program coord. Common Ground, Deerfield, Ill., 1975—77; dir. sales, mktg., pub. rels. for Chinese artists East-West Contemporary Art Gallery, Chgo., 1986—92. Mem. Chgo. Loop Alliance. Recipient award of spl. merit for pub. art, Young Lawyers Group of Chgo. Bar Assn., 1995. Mem.: Wedgwood Soc., Lake Forest C. of C. Roman Catholic. Avocations: writing, travel, nature walking, swimming, reflecting. Home: 780 Greenview Pl Lake Forest IL 60045 Office: Portraits/Chgo Inc 780 Greenview Pl Lake Forest IL 60045 Office Phone: 847-234-3030.

VAN ELSACKER, TULSA, health facility administrator; b. Kathmandu, Nepal, May 15, 1953; arrived in U.S., 1990; d. Mohan and Chandra Khapangi; m. Dilip Kumar Adhikari (dec.); children: Bimay Adhikari, Bijay Adhikari. BEd, U. Tribhuvan, Kathmandu, 1986; BS, Met. State Coll., Denver, 2001. Tchr. St. Xaviers HS, Kathmandu, 1983—90; instr Nepali lang. U. Colo., Boulder, 1992—95; asst. tchr. Montessori Sch., Louisville, Colo., 1992—95; intern Ridgepoint Assisted, The Acad., Boulder, 2001; life enrichment coord. Brookdale Sr. Living, Sterling Ho., Longmont, Colo., 2002—. Ct. interpreter Nepali lang. Vol. Alterra Ind. Living. Mem.: AAUW, Boulder Profl. Women (scholar 2000), Am. Legion Aux. Avocations: reading, gardening, travel. Home: 3240 Iris Ave # 102 Boulder CO 80301 Office: Brookdale Sr Living Sterling Ho 2240 Pratt Longmont CO 80501

VAN ENGELEN, DEBRA LYNN, chemistry educator; b. Burley, Idaho, Dec. 31, 1952; d. W. Dean and Eyvonne (Campbell) Van Engelen; 1 child, Aaron C. Coghlan. BA, Washington U., 1974; PhD, Oreg. State U., 1987. Grad. fellow Oreg. State U., Corvallis, 1982-86; asst. prof. U. N.C., Asheville, 1986-92, assoc. prof. chemistry, 1992—, dir. women's studies, 1994-97. Vis. prof. Emory U., Atlanta, summer 1992, U. Tenn., Knoxville, 1998. Contbr. articles to profl. jours. NSF rsch. awardee, 1992, 93-96, 98; grantee N.C. Bd. Sci. Tech., 1988-89, Blue Ridge Health Ctr., 1989. Mem. Am. Chem. Soc. (sec.-treas. 1991, chpt. chair 1993, fin. co-chair regional meeting 1996), Coun. on Undergrad. Rsch., Sigma Xi, Phi Kappa Phi, Phi Lambda Upsilon. Achievements include research in phytoremediation of heavy metals in soil and water and post-column derivatization for capillary electrophoresis. Office: U Redlands Dept Chemistry Redlands CA 92373

VAN ETTEN, NANCY KAY, medical/surgical nurse, consultant; b. Burlington, Colo., June 27, 1955; d. Wayne R. and Hildur E. (Walsh) Schiffner; m. Kerry W. Van Etten, Feb. 17, 1979; children: Megan L., Brian W., Gwen E. BSN, U. No. Colo., 1977; MS in Nursing, U. Kans., 1987. Cert. clin. specialist med.-surg. nursing, nurse case mgr. Staff and charge nurse St. Catherine's Hosp., Garden City, Kans.; nursing instr. Fort Scott, Kans., Ft. Scott, Pueblo, Colo.; dir. home health agency Mercy Hosp., Ft. Scott, Kans.; clinical nurse specialist St. Mary-Corwin Hosp., Pueblo, Colo.; owner Q-Aide Systems, Inc.; instr. assoc. degree program Pueblo C.C.; nurse case mgr. injured workers Concentra Integrated Svcs., 1994—. Mem. Am. Cancer Soc. Recipient Am. Cancer Soc. award, 1989. Mem. ANA, Colo. Nurses Assn. (dist. bd. dir.), Kans. State Nurses Assn. (treas.), Sigma Theta Tau. Home: 2003 Overton Rd Pueblo CO 81008-9619

VAN FLEET, LISA A., lawyer; BSW, Valparaiso U., 1982, JD, 1985. Bar: Ind. 1985, US Tax Ct. 1987, US Claims Ct. 1988, Mo. 1989, Ill. 1990. Ptnr., group leader Employee Benifits Bryan Cave LLP, St. Louis. Office: Bryan Cave LLP One Metropolitan Square 211 N Broadway, Ste 3600 Saint Louis MO 63102 Office Phone: 314-259-2326. Business E-Mail: lavanfleet@bryancave.com.

VAN GALDER, VALERIE, marketing executive; b. Chgo. Grad., UCLA. Asst. Rogers & Cowen, 1985—90; v.p. mktg. & publicity Hard Rock Am., 1990—94; head mktg. Fox Searchlight Pictures, 1994—99; exec. v.p. mktg. Sony Screen Gems, 1999—2004; pres. TriStar Pictures, 2004—05; pres. domestic mktg. Columbia TriStar Motion Picture Group, 2005—. Internat. adv. bd. Bermuda Internat. Film Festival, 2005—. Mailing: Sony Pres TriStar Pictures 9050 West Washington Blvd Culver City CA 90232*

VANGELDER, KIM E., information technology executive; BS, Rochester Inst. Tech. With Eastman Kodak Co., Rochester, NY, 1984—, dir. global ERP competency ctr., 1996—2000, dir. info. tech. for R&D org., 2000—03, dir. info. tech. digital & film imaging systems, 2003, v.p. chief info. officer, 2004—. Mem. dean's council Golisano Coll. Computing & Info. Office: Eastman Kodak Co 343 State St Rochester NY 14650*

VAN GELDER, LYDIA M., artist, educator; d. Henry Harrison and Lydia Ester McClain; m. Homer Whitney Van Gelder, July 6, 1936 (dec.); children: Peter, Dirk, Roger. Student, Calif. Sch. Fine Art, 1930—32. Instr. Santa Rosa (Calif.) Jr. Coll., 1969—85. Instr. Christ Ch., Italy. Author: IKAT, 1980, IKAT II, 1992; Represented in permanent collections Smithsonian, N.Y.C. Named Textile Legend, Textile Soc., 2004. Mem.: Sacramento Weavers and Spinners Guild (founding pres.), Spindles and Dyers Guild (hon.), Redwood Empire Hand-weavers and Spinners Guild (hon.). Republican. Episcopalian. Avocations: spinning, weaving, knitting.

VAN GINKEL, BLANCHE LEMCO, architect, educator; b. London, 1923; d. Myer and Claire Lemco; m. H. P. Daniel van Ginkel, 1956; children: Brenda, Marc. B.Arch., McGill U., 1945; M.C.P., Harvard U., 1950; PhD (hon.), U. Aix-Marseille, France, 2005. Tech. asst. Nat. Film Bd. Can., 1943-44; mgr. City Planning Office, Regina, Sask., Canada, 1946; architect Atelier Le Corbusier, Paris, 1948; asst. prof. architecture U. Pa., 1951-57; ptnr. van Ginkel Assocs., Montreal, Que., Canada, also Toronto, Ont., Canada, 1957—; prof. architecture U. Toronto, 1977—92, dir. Sch. Architecture, 1977-80, dean faculty architecture and landscape architecture, 1980-82. Vis. critic Harvard U., 1958, 70; adj. prof. U. Montreal, McGill U., others; curator exhbns. RCA, U. Toronto, others. Contbr. articles to profl. jours. Mem. Nat. Capital Planning Com., Ottawa, Art Adv. Com., Ottawa; mem. adv. com. Nat. Mus.'s Corp.; mem. Que. Provincial Planning Commn.; founder, v.p. Corp. of Urbanists of Que., 1963-65; bd. dirs. Montreal Internat. Film Festival, 1961-66. Decorated Order of Can., 2000; recipient Internat. Fedn. Housing and Planning Grand Prix award, 1956, Massey medal for arch., 1962, Mademoiselle Mag. award, 1957, Queen's Silver Jubilee medal, 1977, Citizenship citation Can. Govt., 1991, Queen's Golden Jubilee medal, 2002, award Order of Urbanists of Que., 2003. Fellow AIA (hon.), Royal Archtl. Inst. Can. (exec. com. 1971-74), Toronto Soc. Arch.; mem. Can. Inst. Planners (bd. dirs. 1961-64), Assn. Collegiate Schs. Architecture (bd. dirs. 1981-84, v.p. 1985-86, pres. 1986-87, Disting. Prof. award 1989), Royal Can. Acad. Art (bd. dirs. 1992—2000), Internat. Archive of Women Architects (bd. dirs. 1985-2001), Ont. Assn. Arch. (life), Order of Can. Office: 38 Summerhill Gardens Toronto ON Canada M4T 1B4

VAN GINKEL, MARCI LOU, education educator; b. Des Moines, May 2, 1952; d. Donald Paul and Ardath Phyllis (McCombs) Cohron; m. James Carol Van Ginkel, May 22, 1982; children: James Cohron, John Cohron. AA, Riverside City Coll., 1974; BA, U. Calif., 1976; MS, Creighton U., 1982. Counselor River Bluffs Community Mental Health Ctr., Council Bluffs, Iowa, 1977-80; coord. family program Mercy Hosp., Council Bluffs, 1980-81; grad. asst. Creighton U., Omaha, 1981-82; instr. Iowa Western Community Coll., Council Bluffs, 1982—98; ret. Bd. dirs. Exch. State Bank, Exira, Iowa, Cohron Investment Co. Bd. dirs. Alcohol and Drug Abuse Prevention Com., Atlantic, 1982-83, Cass County Arts Coun., 1982-88, Cass County unit Am. Cancer Soc., 1987—; sec., bd. dirs. Cass County unit Am. Heart Assn., 1990-95; bd. dirs. Cass County Unit Am. Cancer Soc., 1987—, bd. sec., 1996—; chmn. ACS Festival Trees Fundraiser, 1996—. Recipient Governor's Vol. award State Iowa, 1985. Mem. Newcomer's Club (v.p. 1983-84), Jr. Federated Women's Club (pres., treas., v.p. 1982-88), PEO (chpt. Mu 1993—), Beta Sigma Phi (chpt. sec. 1991-92, 2000, chpt. pres. 1992-93, 2001-2002). Republican. Presbyterian. Avocations: crafts, reading, gardening, walking, fitness classes. Home: 2806 Country Club Dr Atlantic IA 50022-2537

VAN GOETHEM, NANCY ANN, painter, educator; b. Detroit, June 27, 1950; d. Walter and Margaret E. (Cook) Van G.; m. Lawrence M. Joseph, Apr. 10, 1976. BFA, Pratt Inst., Bklyn., 1983. Artist Detroit Free Press, Detroit, 1972-81; ind. artist, 1983-92; instr. Parsons Sch. of Design, N.Y.C., 1992—. Artist in various jours. including Ontario Review, fall 1995, 2003, The Male Body U. Mich., 1994, Poetry East, fall 1993; exhbn.: History of Women in Am. Schlesinger Libr., 1994-95, Marygrove Coll., 2001. Grantee, Santa Fe Art Inst., 2002. Mem. Women's Caucus for Art, Coll. Art Assn. Home: Apt 33N 355 S End Ave New York NY 10280-1005

VAN HEMERT, PHYLLIS BROWN, counselor; d. W. Ray and Jessye Brown; m. James Mark Van Hemert, Nov. 23, 1968; 1 child, Jess. B.Mus.Edn., U. Tex., El Paso, 1972; MEd in Counseling, U. Ctrl. Okla., Edmond, 1992. Cert. profl. counselor Okla.; equine therapist. Music tchr. Yselita Schs., El Paso, 1972—74, Oklahoma City Pub. Schs., 1975—77, Heritage Hall Pvt. Sch., Oklahoma City, 1978; music, humanities tchr. Deer Creek Pub. Sch., Emond, Okla., 1979—80; music tchr. Edmond Schs., 1986—89, sch. counselor, 1990—95; pvt. practice counseling Edmond, 1995—. Equine therapist Equine Therapy Ctr., Edmond, 2003—; spkr. Words for Wellness Book Club Women's Renaissance Hosp., Edmond, 2000—05. Mem. Cmty. Edn. Orgn., Edmond, 2000—05; Sunday sch. tchr. First Presbyn. Ch., Edmond, 2000—. Mem.: Alumni U. Ctrl. Okla., Okla. Counseling Assn., Am. Counseling Assn. Office: 3855 S Boulevard Edmond OK 73013

VAN HOESEN, BETH MARIE, artist, printmaker; b. Boise, Idaho, June 27, 1926; d. Enderse G. and Freda Marie (Soulen) Van H.; m. Mark Adams, Sept. 12, 1953. Student, Escuela Esmaralda, Mexico City, 1945, San Francisco Art Inst., 1946, 47, 51, 52, Fontainbleau Ecole Arts, France, Acad. Julian and Acad., 5Grande Chaumier, Paris, 1948-51; BA, Stanford U., 1948; postgrad., San Francisco State U., 1957-58. One-Woman shows include, De Young Mus., San Francisco, 1959, Achenbach Found., Calif. Palace Legion of Honor, San Francisco, 1961, 74, Santa Barbara (Calif.) Mus., 1963, 74, 76, Oakland (Calif.) Mus., 1980, John Berggruen Gallery, San Francisco, 1981, 83, 85, 88, 91; traveling exhibit Am. Mus. Assn., 1983-85; group shows include, Calif. State Fair, Sacramento, 1951 (award), Library of Congress, Washington, 1956, 57, San Francisco Mus. Modern Art, 70 (award), Boston Mus. Fine Arts, 1959, 60, 62, Pa. Acad. Fine Arts, Phila., 1959, 61, 63, 65, Achenbach Found., 1961 (award), Bklyn. Mus., 1962, 66, 68, 77, Continuing Am. Graphics, Osaka, Japan, 1970, Hawaii Nat. Print. Exhbn., Honolulu, 1980 (award), Oakland Mus., 1975 (award); represented in permanent collections, including, Achenbach Found., San Francisco, Fine Arts Mus., Bklyn. Mus., Mus. Modern Art, N.Y.C., Oakland Mus., San Francisco Mus. Modern Art, Victoria and Albert Mus., (London), Chgo. Art Inst., Cin. Mus., Portland (Oreg.) Art Mus. (Recipient award of Honor, San Francisco Art Commn. 1981); author: Collection of Wonderful Things, 1972, Beth Van Hoesen Creatures, 1987, Beth Van Hoesen: Works on Paper, 1995, Beth Van Hoesen Teddy Bears, 2000. Mem. Calif. Soc. Printmakers (award 1993), San Francisco Women Artists. Home: 1400 Geary Blvd Apt 7F San Francisco CA 94109 Office: c/o John Berggruen 228 Grant Ave Fl 3D San Francisco CA 94108-4612

VAN HOOSER, PATRICIA LOU SCOTT, art educator; b. Springfield, Mo., Oct. 4, 1934; d. Arthur Irving and Isoline Elizabeth (Jones) Scott; m. Buckley Blaine Van Hooser, Mar. 28, 1956 (div.); children: Buckley Blaine II, Craig Alan. BA, Drury U., 1956; MS in Art, Pittsburg State U., Kans., 1968. Society writer Springfield News & Leader & Press, 1955—56; hostess radio program Sta. KSEK, Pittsburg, Kans., 1962—63; tchr. art and home econs. Hurley (Mo.) HS, 1956—57; art supr. elem. sch. Mountain Grove, Mo., 1960; tchr. art Hickory Hills Sch., Springfield, 1960—61; tchr art and English jr. and sr. schs., Baxter Springs, Kans., 1965—75; art coord. Joplin (Mo.) Elem. Sch. Dist., 1975—. Lectr. in field; chmn. for S.W. Mo., Nat. Youth Art Month. Bd. dirs. Spiva Art Ctr.; sec. Parents without Ptnrs., CV & FE Credit Union; bd. recorder S.W. Mo. Credit Unions. Mem.: ASCD, NEA, AAUW (2d v.p. Joplin br.), Epsilon Sigma Alpha, Pittsburg State U. Alumni Assn. (sec., pres. Joplin br.), Joplin Cmty. Concert Assn., S.W. Mo. Mus. Assn., Mo. Edn. Assn., S.W. Mo. Dist. Art Tchrs., Mo. Art Edn. Assn., Nat. Art Edn. Assn., Assn. Childhood Edn. Internat. (pres. Joplin br., pres. Mo. state), Writers of Six Bulls, Joplin Writer's Guild, Cafe au Lait Club. Methodist. E-mail: Pvanhooser6@cs.com.

VAN HOUTEN, ELIZABETH ANN, corporate communications executive, painter; b. Washington, Feb. 22, 1945; d. Raymond R. and Marian Edna (Hovemann) Van H. BA, Mary Washington Coll., 1966. Analyst U.S. Gov., Washington, 1966-68; dep. chief of publs. Found. for Coop. Housing, Washington, 1968-72; editor Nat. League of Savs. Inst., Washington, 1972-76; dir. pub. relations Fed. Nat. Mortgage Assn., Washington, 1976-83; v.p. communications & investor relations Sallie Mae (Student Loan Mktg. Assn.), Washington, 1983-93; v.p. corp. and investor rels. Sallie Mae, Washington, 1993-95; ret., 1995; curator Monhegan (Maine) Hist. and Cultural Mus., 1995-98; painter. Apptd. by city coun. to Master Plan Task Force, Alexandria, Va., 1987—92; sec. Monhegan Assocs., 1995—97, trustee, 1998—2001, mem. nominating com., 1999—2002; mem. campaing com. for Del Pepper, Alexandria, 1987; bd. dirs. Washington Studio Sch., 1995—99; mem. bd. dirs. Watergate of Alexandria, 1985—93, pres., 1988—89, chmn., 1991—93; chmn. emeritus Liz Lerman Dance Exch. Mem.: Women Artists of Monhegan Island, Monhegan Artists Open Studio List. Avocations: walking, music, visual arts, reading.

VANI, ANITA H., music and voice educator; b. Lapua, Finland, Sept. 6, 1963; arrived in U.S., 1965; d. Aimo K. and Mirja M. Riihiaho; children: Eric M., Alissa H. BA Music Edn., Palm Beach Atlantic Univ., W. Palm Beach, Fla., 1988. Nat. Bd. Cert. EMC/Music 2002. Music specialist Haverhill Elem., W. Palm Beach, Fla., 1988—89; instr. pvt. voice Jimmy Ferraro's Performing Arts Sch., New Port Richey, Fla., 1989—92; elem. music specialist Lee Elem./Carrollwood Elem. and Mitchell Elem., Tampa, Fla., 1989—92; owner pvt. voice studio New Port Richey, Ill., 1992—; elem. music specialist Citrus Pk. Elem., Tampa, Fla., 1992—. Composer: (CD recordings) Songs of Immigrant Finns, 2001, (CD recording) Muuttolinnun Lauhi, 2005; singer: Säteet Auringon, 1989 (top 10 listing in Finland). Founding bd. mem. Juanita Haines Charitable Found., New Port Richey, Fla. Mem.: Nat. Educators Assn., Fla. Educators Assn., Fla. Elem. Music Educators Conf., Hillsborough Elem. Music Coun., Music Educators Nat. Conf.

VANICA, KRISTENA L., principal; d. Richard H. and Hazel B. Gum; m. Ray E. Vanica, June 30, 1990; children: Jason, Aimee, Danielle, Jonathan. BS in Elem. Edn., Ea. Mont. Coll., Billings, 1987; MA in Edn. Adminstrn. Curriculum and Supervision, Ariz. State U., Phoenix, 1995. Elem. tchr. Cartwright Sch. Dist., Phoenix, 1988—95, asst. prin., 1995—2003; prin. Litchfield Sch. Dist., Litchfield Park, Ariz., 2003—. Tchr. pregnant program L.A. County Office Edn., 1991—92. Recipient Tchr. of Yr., 1995, 1996, Silver Apple award, 1996. Mem.: Ariz. Sch. Adminstrs., Nat. Assn. Elem. Sch. Prin., Internat. Reading Assn. (Internat. Reading award 1996). Office Fax: 623-547-1200. Business E-Mail: vanica@lesd.k12.az.us.

VANIER, JERRE LYNN, art director; b. Phoenix, June 11, 1957; i. Jerry Dale Barber and Betty Jane (Brady) Barber Hughes; m. Kent Douglas Wick, May 4, 1979 (div. June 1994); 1 child, Jared Kent Wick; m. Jay David Vanier, June 6, 1994; 1 child, Jolie Jacqueline. BA in Art History magna cum laude, Ariz. State U., 1978, MA in Humanities. Chmn., vice chmn. Internat. Friends of Art, Scottsdale, Ariz., 1990-96; dir. 19th and 20th century art Joy Tash Gallery, Scottsdale, 1996-97; dir. estate art Vanier Fine Art, Ltd., Scottsdale, 1997-98, dir., 1998—, Vanier Galleries on Marshall, Scottsdale, 1999—. Mem. pub. art collection adv. bd. Scottsdale Cultural Coun., 1990—, Phoenix Jr. League, Art Renaissance Initiative Faces of Ariz. Mem. DAR (Ariz. page continental congress 1993, Ariz. vice chmn. Jr. Am. Citizen com. 1998, 3d vice regent Camelback chpt. 1993), Colonial Dames Am., Daus. Republic of Tex. (non-resident), Nat. Soc. Arts and Letters (Valley of Sun chpt. bd. dirs. 1988-92, art chmn. 1988-90, membership chmn. 1990-92), Jr. League Phoenix, Alpha Delta Pi, Phi Kappa Phi. Republican. Avocations: genealogy, collecting contemporary art. Office: 7106 E Main St Scottsdale AZ 85251-4316

VANIMAN, VICKI, lawyer; BS, Okla. State U.; JD, U. Okla.; attended, Advanced Mgmt. Prog., U. Pa. Wharton Sch. Assoc. Jones, Givens, Gotcher and Bogan, P.C., Tulsa; with Pentastar Services, Inc.; v.p., gen. counsel Dollar Rent A Car, 1994; exec. v.p., gen. counsel Dollar Thrifty Automotive Group, Inc., 2003—. Bd. mem. Domestic Violence Intervention Svcs., Okla. Soc. to Prevent Blindness. Office: Dollar Thrifty Automotive Group 5330 E 31st St PO Box 35985 Tulsa OK 74135

VANISON, DENISE A., lawyer; b. Washington, Feb. 11, 1966; BA, Univ. Va., 1988; JD, Georgetown Univ., 1991. Bar: Pa. 1992, DC 1994, Supreme Ct. Pa., DC Ct. Appeals, US Dist. Ct. (DC dist.). Ptnr., Immigration & Nationality, Public Policy practices, co-chmn. pro bono com. Patton Boggs LLP, Washington. Bd. dir. Washington Lawyers' Com. Civil Rights & Urban Affairs; vol. Human Rights First, Internat. Human Rights Law Group, Whitman Warner Clinic Legal Svc. Office: Patton Boggs LLP 2550 M St NW Washington DC 20037-1350 Office Phone: 202-457-6427. Office Fax: 202-457-6315. Business E-Mail: dvanison@pattonboggs.com.

VAN LANDINGHAM, MARIAN AMELIA, retired state legislator, artist; b. Albany, Ga., Sept. 10, 1937; d. Strauder Leroy and Myrtle (Taylor) Van L. BA in Polit. Sci., Emory U., 1959, MA in Polit. Sci., 1960. Asst. dir. news bur. Emory U., Atlanta, 1960-64; sci. news editor Ga. Tech, Atlanta, 1964-66; info. generalist Nat. Communicable Disease Ctr., Atlanta, 1966-67; info. specialist Nat. Ctr. Air Pollution Control, Washington, 1968; press aide, speech writer Congressman Phil Landrum, Washington, 1968-72; program dir. Alexandria (Va.) Bicentennial Com., 1972-74; dir., founder Torpedo Factory Art Ctr., Alxandria, 1974-79; mem. Va. Ho. of Dels., Richmond, 1982—; profl. artist Torpedo Factory Art Ctr., 1974—2006; ret., 2006. Dir. Alexandria Vol. Bur., 1979-81; chair arts, tourism and cultural com. Nat. Conf. State Legislators, Denver, 1988, fed. budget taxation com., Washington, 1994. Co-editor: To Wit, Intentional and Unintentional, 1974, Composite History of Alexandria, vol. 1, 1975; author: On Target, A History of the First 25 Years of the Torpedo Factory Art Center, 1999. Mem. Alexandria Dem. Com., 1976—. Recipient Washingtonian of Yr. award Washingtonian Mag., 1974, Gov.'s award for arts Gov. Va., 1979, George Washington award for cmty. svc., 1986, Alex award for arts Alexandria C. of C., 1990, Artistic Founder award Cultural Alliance Greater Washington, 1992, Gov.'s award anti-drug efforst, 1992, Legislator of Yr. award Action for Prevention, 1992, Cmty. Care award No. Va. Cmty. Found., 1993, Legislator Adv. of Yr. award Va. Interfaith Ctr. Pub. Policy, 1992, Disting. Consumer Svc. award Va. Citizens Consumer Coun., 1996, Warren Stambaugh award for mental health work, 1996, Pub. Svc. award Whitman-Walker Clinic No. Va., 1996; named one of 10 Builders of Communities and Dreams, Nat. Women's History Project, 2006. Mem. Pen Women, Arts and Letters, Jamestown/Yorktown Found. (bd. dirs.), Delta Kappa Gamma (hon.). Methodist. Avocations: reading, walking.

VAN LEEUWEN, JEAN See GAVRIL, JEAN

VAN LEISHOUT, LESLIE ANN, theater educator, director; b. LA, Oct. 14, 1956; d. Leslie Lee Moon and Fronia (Mac) Virginia McGaha; m. James Anthony Van Leishout, June 28, 1980; children: Lillie Ann, Carli Virginia, James (J.B.) Byron, Adrian John, Henry Talbot, William Alexander. BA, Brigham Young U., Provo, Utah, 1979. Cert. tchr. Wash., Utah, Calif., 1980, theatre Wash., 1997, tech. theatre and set design Wash., 1999, English/lang. arts Wash., 1997, history/social studies Wash., 1997. Tchr., dir. Provo H.S., 1980—83; edn. dir. Wash. Shakespeare Festival, Olympia, 1988—2000; tchr., dir. River Ridge H.S. Theatre, Lacey, Wash., 1998—. River Ridge theatre facility mgr. North Thurston Pub. Schs., Lacey, 1998—, theatre arts facilitator, 2000—, sch. improvement program coord., 2004—06; v.p. bldg. learning improvement team River Ridge H.S., Lacey, 1999—2001, program leader, 2000—; arts curriculum project coord. Wash. State Arts Commn., Olympia, 2000—03; arts assessment leadership team Office Supt. Pub. Instrn. for Wash. State, Olympia, 2002—; adj. faculty South Puget Sound C.C., Olympia, 2001—02; guest artist Vancouver Film Sch., BC, Canada, 2003—04. Chpt. leader Wash. State Thespians, 2006—. Named Outstanding Theatre Program, South Puget Sound C.C., 2001, 2002, 2004. Mem.: Wash. Assn. Theatre Educators (regional rep. 2000—). Office: River Ridge High School 350 River Ridge Dr SE Lacey WA 98513 Office Phone: 360-412-4837. Office Fax: 360-412-4839. Business E-Mail: lvanleishout@nthurston.k12.wa.us.

VAN MARTER, LINDA JOANNE, pediatrician, educator, neonatologist, researcher; d. Neal Dahl and Martha Erickson Van Marter. BS, U. Pitts., 1976, MD, 1980; MPH, Harvard U., 1985. Resident in pediatrics Children's Hosp. Med. Ctr., Boston, 1980—83; fellow in neonatal perinatal medicine Joint Program in Neonatology Harvard, 1983—86; from instr. pediat. to asst. prof. pediat. Harvard Med. Sch., Boston, 1986—2002, assoc. prof. pediatrics, 2002—. Reviewer Pediat., Jour. of Pediat., Am. Jour. Pub. Health, New Eng. Jour. Medicine. Recipient Richard L. Day award in pediat. U. Pitts. Sch. Medicine, 1980, Merton S. Bernfield Mentoring award Harvard U., 2005. Fellow Am. Acad. Pediats. (perinatal sect. exec. com. 1999, chair-elect, 2004—, neoprep working group 1996—, chair 2001-03); mem. Am. Pediat. Soc., Perinatal Rsch. Soc., Ea. Soc. for Pediat. Rsch. (coun. 1998-2003), Soc. for Pediat. Epidemiol. Rsch. (sec., treas. 1987-91, pres. 1992-93), Soc. for Pediat. Rsch., Alpha Omega Alpha. Office: Children's Hosp Newborn Medicine 300 Longwood Ave Boston MA 02115-5737

VANMEER, MARY ANN, publishing executive, writer, webmaster; b. Mt. Clemens, Mich., Nov. 22, 1947; d. Leo Harold and Rose Emma (Gulden) VanM. Student, Micha. State U., 1965-66, 67-68, U. Sorbonne, Paris, summer 1968; BA in Edn., U. Fla., 1968-70. Pres. VanMeer Tutoring and Translating, N.Y.C., 1970-72; freelance writer, 1973-79; pres. VanMeer Publs., Inc., Clearwater, Fla., 1980-88, VanMeer Media Advt., Inc., Clearwater, 1987-88; exec. dir., founder Nat. Ctrs. for Health and Med. Info., Inc., Palm Beach, Fla., 1990-93; pres., CEO ThriftyTraveling.com, Inc. (formerly Traveling Free Pubs.,), 1993—. Author: Traveling with Your Dog, U.S.A., 1976, How to Set Up a Home Typing Business, 1978, Freelance Photographer's Handbook, 1979, See America Free, 1981, Free Campgrounds, U.S.A., 1982, Free Attractions, U.S.A., 1982, VanMeer's Guide to Free Attractions U.S.A., 1984, VanMeer's Guide to Free Campgrounds, 1984, The How to Get Publicity for Your Business Handbook, 1987, Asthma: The Ultimate Treatment Guide, 1991, Allergies: The Ultimate Treatment Guide, 1992, Thrifty Traveling, 1995, 2d edit., 1996; pub. Nat. Health and Med. Trends Mag., 1986-88, ThriftyTraveling.com Newsletter and website, 1993—, online and hard-copy edits., 1999—, Over 50 Thrifty Traveler Newsletter, 1997-98, Net News for the Thrifty Traveler Newsletter, 1997-98, LuxuryTraveling.com newsletter and website, 2001—; webmaster ThriftyTraveling.com, ThriftyTravelPortal-.com, 2003—, LuxuryTraveling.com and VanMeer.com websites. Pub. info. chairperson, bd. dirs. Pinellas County chpt. Am. Cancer Soc., Clearwater, 1983-84, 86-88; mem. fin. devel. com. ARC, Palm Beach County, 1990-92. Mem. Am. Booksellers Assn., Soc. Am. Travel Writers. Office: ThriftyTraveling.com Inc PO Box 8168 Clearwater FL 33758-8168 E-mail: editor@thriftytraveling.com.

VANMETER, VANDELIA L., retired library director; b. Seibert, Colo., July 17, 1934; d. G.W. and A. Pearl Klockenteger; m. Victor M. VanMeter, Jan. 21, 1954; children: Allison C., Kristopher C. BA, Kansas Wesleyan U., 1957; MLS, Emporia State U., 1970; PhD, Tex. Woman's U., 1986. Cert. libr. media specialist. Tchr. Ottawa County Rural Sch., Kans., 1954-55; social scis. tchr. McClave (Colo.) High Sch., 1957-58, Ellsworth (Kans.) Jr. High Sch., 1959-68; libr., media specialist Ellsworth (Kans.) High Sch., 1968-84; asst. prof. libr. sci. U. So. Miss., Hattiesburg, 1986-90; chair dept. libr./info. sci. Spalding U., Louisville, 1990-96, libr. dir., 1991-99, prof., 1991—99. Cons. to sch., pub. and spl. librs., Kans., Miss., Ky., 1970-99; mem. Ky. NCATE Bd. Examiners. Author: American History for Children and Young Adults, 1990, World History for Children and Young Adults, 1992, America in Historical Fiction, 1997; editor: Mississippi Library Media Specialist Staff Development Modules, 1988, Library Lane Newsletter, 1991-99; contbr. chpts. to books; contbr. articles to profl. jours. Active City Coun., Ellsworth, Kans., 1975-79, Park Bd., Ellsworth, 1975-79; bd. dirs. Robbins Meml. Libr., 1977-79. Grantee Kans. Demonstration Sch. Libr., 1970-72, Miss. Power Found., 1989, Project Technology Enhances Curriculur Instrn., 1996-97; named Women of Yr. Bus. and Profl. Women of Ellsworth, Kans., 1976. Mem. ALA, Assn. Coll. and Rsch. Librs., Ky. Libr. Assn., Assn. for Libr. and Info. Sci. Educators.

VAN METRE, MARGARET CHERYL, performing company executive, dancer, educator; b. Maryville, Tenn., Nov. 24, 1938; d. Robert Fillers and Margaret Elizabeth (Goddard) Raulston; m. Mitchell Robert Van Metre II, Aug. 25, 1956; 1 child, Mitchell Robert. Elem., intermediate and advanced tchg. certs. Dir. Van Metre Sch. of Dance, Maryville, 1958-96; artistic dir. Appalachian Ballet Co., Maryville Coll., 1972-96; founding dir. Appalachian Ballet Co., 1972; dir. Van Metre Arts Mgmt., SC, 1996—. Chmn. dance panel Tenn. Arts Commn., 1973-74; chmn. Bicentennial Ballet Project, Tenn., 1975-76; mem. Nat. Bd. Regional Dance Am., 1997—; owner Van Metre Arts Mgmt., Edisto Island, S.C., 1996—. Choreographer ballets: Delusion, 1965, Hill Heritage Suite, 1972, Dancing Princesses, 1983. Mem. Tenn. Assn. of Dance (pres. 1972), Southeast Regional Ballet Assn. (pres. 1996, 97, 98, 99, 2003—). Democrat. Episcopalian. Home: 2103 Myrtle St Edisto Island SC 29438-3437

VANN, ESTHER MARTINEZ, science educator; d. Gabriel Narvaez and Cecilia Wolfe Martinez; m. Raymundo Vann, June 10, 1973; children: Raymundo Jr., Joseph Noel, Michael Steven, Daniel Christopher. BA, St. Mary's U., San Antonio, Tex., 1975; MA, U. Tex., San Antonio, 1990. Sci. dept. head Wrenn Jr. H.S.-Edgewood Ind. Sch. Dist., San Antonio, 1978—83, Jordan Mid. Sch.-Northside Ind. Sch. Dist., San Antonio, 1992—93, Somerset Jr. H.S.-Somerset Ind. Sch. Dist., Tex., 1998—2004, Terrell Wells Mid. Sch.-Harlandale Ind. Sch. Dist., San Antonio, 2004—. Adminstrv. asst. Nurses At Home - Home Health Agy., San Antonio, 1993—98. Named one of Outstanding Young Women of Am., 1987; recipient Trinity Prize for Tchg. Excellence award, Trinity U., 2002, Tchr. of the Month award, Somerset Jr. H.S.-Somerset Ind. Sch. Dist., 2003, 2004; Tex. Aerospace scholar, NASA Johnson Space Ctr., 2002. Office Phone: 210-921-4774.

VANN, LORA JANE, retired reading educator; b. Chgo. d. Amos Alva and Mary Prudie (Ellery) V. BA, Marian Coll., Indpls., 1958; MA, Ball State U., 1963, EdD, 1985. Cert. life tchr., reading specialist, supr., Ind. Elem. tchr., asst. prin. Indpls. Pub. Schs., 1959-71; instr. dept. edn. William Woods Coll., Fulton, Mo., 1972-73; tchr. reading, supr. Washington Twp. Schs., Indpls., 1973—2002; ret., 2002. Teaching fellow Ball State U., Muncie, Ind., 1980-81; cons. Advanced Tech., Inc., Indpls., 1987; vis. cons. North Cen. Assn., Bloomington, Ind., 1988, Peace Pole Project Ideas, 2001. Author: Self-Concept and Parochial School Children, 1985, Sigma's Outstanding Women of the 20th Century, 3 vols., 1986, 88, 25th Anniversary (1965-90) History of the Life Membership (NAACP) Committee, 1990; co-author: Multi-Cultural Global Awareness African-American Resources, 1992; editor newsletters Reading Timely Topics, 1974-80, AS News, 1985-2002. Pres. St. Rita Bd. Edn., Indpls., 1987-89; founder Afro-Am. Children's Theatre, 1987. Cath. Interracial Coun. scholar, 1954; NDEA grantee, 1964, 65, Fulbright grantee, Birmingham, Eng., 1967-68, Ball State U. grantee, 1980-81. Mem. Internat. Reading Assn., Nat. Coun. Negro Women (charter, sec. Cen. Ind. sect. 1981-84), Washington Twp. Edn. Assn. (chmn. polit. action com. 1987-88, co-chmn. 1988-89), AAUW, Fulbright Assn., Kappa Delta Pi, Phi Delta Kappa, Sigma Gamma Rho (treas. cen. region 1981-86, chpt. pres. 1986-90, 96-2000, trustee nat. edn. found.). Roman Catholic. Avocations: reading, walking, playing piano. Home: 2801 Hillside Ave Indianapolis IN 46218

VANNAIS, RENAE MICHELE, elementary school educator; b. Marlton, N.J., Jan. 8, 1976; d. Thomas Raymond and Constance Ruth Wiseley; m. Ryan Ian Vannais, July 5, 2003. BA, Rowan U., Glassboro, N.J., 2000. Tchr. sci. Woodlynne (N.J.) Pub. Sch., 2000—. Mem.: Woodlynne (N.J.) Edn. Assn. (sec. 2006—), N.J. Edn. Assn. Office: Woodlynne Pub Sch 131 Elm Ave Woodlyne NJ 08107

VAN NATTER, GAYL PRICE, residential construction company administrator; b. Gothenburg, Sweden, Mar. 1, 1949; arrived in U.S., 1951; d. Harold Edgar Anderson and Jeanette Helen (Hallberg) Akeson; m. Daniel J. Baader, Nov. 27, 1971 (div. Sept. 1980); m. Leigh C. Price, Feb. 28, 1983 (dec. Aug. 2000); children: Heidi, Heather; m. Marc A. Van Natter, Sept. 4, 2005. BA in Fgn. Lang., U. Ill., 1971. Asst. buyer The Denver, 1971-73, buyer, 1973-75; from escrow sec. to br. mgr. Transam. Title, Evergreen, Colo., 1975—84, from sr. account mgr. to v.p. Denver, 1984—94; cmty. mgr. Village Homes of Colo., Littleton, Colo., 1994-2000, mgr. mktg. ops., 2000, v.p. mktg. ops., 2001—03, v.p. sales and mktg., 2003—05, Bennett Homes Inc., 2005—. Vol. Safehouse for Battered Women, Denver, 1986—, Spl. Olympics, 1986—, Adult Learning Source, 1993—, Kids Cure for Cancer, 1994—. Mem. Nat. Assn. Homebuilders (Most Profl. award 1997), Home Builders Assn. Met. Denver (bd. dirs. 1989-93, exec. com. 1991, assoc. mem. coun. 1988-93, co-chair 1990, chair 1991, Arthur Gaeth Assoc. of Yr. 1989), Sales and Mktg. Coun. Met. Denver (bd. 1986-92, 95—, Major Achievement in Merchandising Excellence chair 1989-90, Most Profl. award 1989, 97, Sales Master award 1995, Silver MAME award 1996, Gold MAME award 1997), Zonta (charter Denver II chpt., pres. 1990, Zontian of Yr. award 1988), Colo. Assn. Homebuilders (Assoc. of Yr. award 1992), Master Builders Assn. King/Snohomish County, Million Dollar Cir. (Platinum award 1996-2000). Avocations: cooking, volunteer work, travel. Home: 15021 NE 198th St Woodinville WA 98072 Office: Bennett Homes 12011 NE 1st St Ste 201 Bellevue WA 98005 Business E-Mail: gayl@bennetthomes.com.

VAN NESS, GRETCHEN, lawyer; b. Cedar Rapids, Iowa, June 23, 1958; BA in history & English magna cum laude, Wilson Coll., 1980; JD cum laude, Boston Coll., 1988. Bar: Mass. 1988, U.S. Dist. Ct. Mass. 1989, U.S. Ct. Appeals First Cir. 1992, U.S. Supreme Ct. 1995. Law clk. to Hon. Andrew A Caffrey U.S. Dist. Ct. Mass., 1988—89; law clk. to Hon. Bailey Aldrich U.S. Ct. Appeals, First Cir., 1989—90; law clk. to Hon. A. David Mazzone U.S. Sentencing Commn. & U.S. Dist. Ct., Mass., 1990—91; instr. Harvard U. Extension Sch., 1993—95, Suffolk U., 1995—96. Author: Inevitability of Gay Marriage, 2004. Named one of best employment lawyers Boston, Boston Mag., 2002, top Boston lawyers, 2004; recipient Atty. Yr., Syracuse U. Law Sch., 2001. Fellow: Am. Assn. U. Women; mem.: Mass. Law Reform Inst., Women's Bar Assn., ABA, Boston Bar Assn.

VAN NESS, PATRICIA CATHELINE, composer, violinist; b. Seattle, June 25, 1951; d. C. Charles and Marjorie Mae (Dexter) Van N.; m. Peter Charles Marks. Student, Wheaton (Ill.) Coll., 1969-70, Gordon Coll., 1972. Composer: ballet score for Beth Soll, 1985, 87, 94, for Monica Levy, 1988, for Boston Ballet, 1988, 90, for Charleston Ballet Theatre, 1994; text and music for voices and early instruments with text translated into Latin for Evensong, 1991, Five Meditations, 1993, Cor Mei Cordis, 1994, Arcanae, 1995, Ego sum Custos Angels, 1995, Tu Risa, 1996, The Nine Orders of the Angels, 1996; various scores, 1985—; rec. violinist A&M Records, Private Lightning, 1980, Telarc Internat. Arcanae and Ego sum Custos Angela, 1996, Telarc Internat. Michael and Thronorum, 1999, Warner Classics Cor meum est templum sacrum, 2005, MDG Classics, The Nine Orders of the Angels, 2003; composer-in-residence First Church in Cambridge (Mass.), Congregational, 1996-, Coro Allegro, 1998, The Boston Athenaeum, 2002-03, Boston Landmarks Orch., 2003. Grantee Mass. Cultural Coun., 1993, 96, New Eng. Biolabs. Founds., 1989, Mass. Arts Lottery Coun., 1988, Meet the Composer, 1997, 98; recipient Spl. Recognition award Barlow Internat. Composition for Evensong, 1993, 1st prize His Majestie's Clerkes Choral Competition, 1997. Mem.: ASCAP (Std. award 1996—2004), Alliance Women in Music, Am. Music Ctr., Am. Composers Forum. Avocation: major league baseball.

VAN NESS, PATRICIA WOOD, religious studies educator; b. Peterborough, NH, Sept. 12, 1925; d. Leslie Townsend and Bernice E. (Coburn) Wood; m. John Hasbrouck Van Ness, June 13, 1953; children: Peter Wood, Stephen Hasbrouck, Timothy Coburn. BA, U. Wash., 1947; MA, Inst. Transpersonal Psychology, Palo Alto, Calif., 1993. Leader various workshops and retreats, 1979—; records mgr. dept. pub. rels. Std. Oil Co., NJ, (now Exxon Corp., NYC), 1948-50, sec. pub. rels. dept., 1951—53; sec. law dept. Johnson & Johnson, New Brunswick, NJ, 1953-54; reporter Hudson Valley Newspapers, Highland, NY, 1972-74; acting assoc. dir. office of pub. rels. SUNY, New Paltz, 1974; ednl. cons. Ulster County Assn. for Mental Health, Kingston, NY, 1973-76; Christian educator Meth. Ch., New Paltz, NY, 1976—78, White Plains Presbyn. Ch., NY, 1978—81; coord. pub. rels., adminstrv. asst. Inst. Transpersonal Psychology, Menlo Park, Calif., 1981-83; adminstrv. asst. Ctr. for Cont. Edn. Calif. Econ., Palo Alto, Calif., 1983-84; profl. rep. pvt. practice Palo Alto, 1984; adminstrv. asst. Inventory Transfer Systems Inc., Palo Alto, 1984-85; Christian studies educator Bedford Presbyn. Ch., NH, 1986—88. Workshop leader and cons. Author: Transforming Bible Study with Children, 1991; assoc. editor and writer Bible Workbench, 1993—; contbr. numerous articles to profl. jours. Trustee Peterborough (NH) Players, 1998—2001. Mem. Assn. Presbyn. Ch. Educators. Avocations: swimming, reading, contra dancing, theater. Home: 11 Jaquith Rd Jaffrey NH 03452-6406 Office Phone: 603-532-6834. Personal E-mail: pwvn@monad.net.

VAN NEST, ANN MARIE, science educator; d. Hal Everett Van Nest and Carol Ann Miller. BS, Mt. Mercy Coll., Cedar Rapids, Iowa, 1987; MEd, U. Mo., Columbia, 1997. 1st grade tchr. Holy Trinity, Davenport, 1987—88; 2d grade tchr. Hayes Elem., Muscatine, 1988; 3rd-8th grade sci. tchr. St. Joseph's Sch., Marion, 1990—92; 4th-6th grade sci. specialist Columbia Pub. Schs., Mo., 1992—93, upper elem. tchr., 1993—95, 6th & 7th grade sci. tchr., 1995—98; 8th grade sci. tchr. Lina-Mar Cmty. Sch. Dist., Mo., 1998—. Presenter in field. Mem.: NSTA. Office: Excellsior Mid Sch 3555 N 10th St Marion IA 52302

VAN NESTE, KAREN LANE, librarian, editor; b. Washington, Oct. 18, 1951; d. Wilbur Lane and Phyllis Worthington Van Neste; m. Howard Wayne Owen, Aug. 18, 1973. BA, U. Va., 1973; MS in Libr. Sci., U. N.C., 1976. Libr. divsn. disorders devel. and learning U. N.C., Chapel Hill, 1976—77; libr. Fla. State U., Tallahassee, 1977—78; libr., rschr. Media Gen., Inc., Richmond, Va., 1979—88; libr. Richmond (Va.) Times-Dispatch, 1988—98; restaurant critic Richmond Times-Dispatch, Richmond, Va., 2003—04, libr., 2004—; pub. Van Neste Books, Midlothian, Va., 1996—2001. Copy editor Richmond Times-Dispatch, 1999—2002; freelance editor, Richmond, 2001—. Author: The Question Finder, 1986; editor: Littlejohn, 1992, Fat Lightning, 1994, Answers to Lucky, 1996, The Measured Man, 1997, Styll in Love, 1998, One August Day, 1998, The Edge of Things, 1999, Floating in a Most Peculiar Way, 1999, Lumen, 1999, Survivors, 2000, A Better Man, 2000, Steal My Heart, 2000 (Peace Corps Fiction award, 2001), Harry and Ruth, 2000, Divisible by One, 2001, Liar Moon, 2001, The Rail, 2002, Turn Signal, 2004, Rock of Ages, 2006. Mem. Edgehill Condominium Assn., Richmond, Va., 1981—83; contbr. James River Writers Festival, Richmond, 2002—06; editor, writer newsletter The Prestwould Condominium Assn., Richmond, 2001—06. Mem.: Am. Biographical Inst., Va. Mus. Fine Arts, Spl. Libraries Assn., Profl. Women's Adv. Bd., U. Va. Alumni Assn. (life), 2300 Club (house rules com. 2006, mem. house rules com.). D-Liberal. Avocations: travel, interior decorating, cooking. Home: 612 West Franklin St Apt 6-B Richmond VA 23220 Office: Richmond Times-Dispatch 300 E Franklin St Richmond VA 23219 Office Phone: 804-649-6074. Business E-Mail: kowen@timesdispatch.com.

VANN-HAMILTON, JOY, academic administrator; d. Lloyd and Rosella Vann; m. Willis Hamilton, Jan. 1, 1993; children: Abner Hamilton, Elijah Hamilton, Willis Hamilton, Varonica Hamilton. BA, Wichita State U., 1987; MBA, U. Notre Dame, Ind.; student, Andrews U., Berrien Springs, MI, 2000—. Admissions counselor Wichita State U., Kans., 1987—89; asst. dir. of admissions St. Mary's Coll., Notre Dame, Ind., 1989—90; employment specialists Workforce Devel. Services, South Bend, Ind., 1990—91; dir., minority engring. program U. Notre Dame, 1991—2001, asst. provost, 2000—06; v.p. program ops. Kauffman Scholars, Inc., 2006—. Cons. BP/Amoco, Chgo.; dir., faculty learning communities U. Notre Dame, 2002—, dir., ameritech pre-college minority engring. program, 1993—2000. Leadership com. Young Life, South Bend, Ind., 2004—06; pastoral team River of Life Ch., South Bend, Ind., 2006, dir., new members class; liaison Early Childhood Devel. Ctr., Notre Dame, Ind., 2000—06; parent bd. New Creation Acad., Granger, Ind., 2005—06; vol. Expanding Your Horizons, Notre Dame, Ind., 2003—06. Recipient Notre Dame Presdl. award, U. Notre Dame, 1999, Outstanding Young Alumni award, Ft. Scott C.C., 1995; Veda Lesher Endowed scholarship, Andrews U., 2003, Exec. MBA scholarship, U. Notre Dame, 1996. Mem.: ASCD, Syllabus, Am. Assn. of Colleges and U. Associates, Coun. for Opportunity in Edn., Soc. for Applied Learning Tech., Am. Assn. for Higher Edn., Assn. fior Ednl. Comm. and Tech., Phi Lambda Theta, Phi Kappa Phi. Office: Kauffman Scholars Inc 4801 Rockville Rd Kansas City MO 64110 Personal E-mail: willisandjoy@yahoo.com. E-mail: jhamilton@kauffman.org.

VAN NOORD, DIANE C., artist, educator; b. Muskegon, Mich., Dec. 12, 1950; d. Ernest Raymond and Judith Ann Olsen; m. Calvin G. Van Noord, Sept. 26, 1981; children: Tawn Star, Brian Calvin, Timothy John. BA, Hope Coll., 1991; MA, We. Mich. U., 1994. Artist, Holland, Mich.; tchr. pvt. and group art, 2000—. Guest lectr. Counterpart Assn., Grand Haven, Mich., 1997, Lakeland Painters, Grand Haven, 1997, Traverse City (Mich.) Art Assn., 1997, Holland Christian Schs., 1998, 99, 2000. Exhbns. include Neville Pub. Mus., Green Bay, Wis., 1994, Carillon Gallery, Ft. Worth, 1995, 97, Sedona (Ariz.) Arts Ctr., 1995, 96, 99, Holland Area Arts Coun., 1995, Pitts. Ctr. for the Arts, 1995, Miss. Mus. Art, Jackson, 1995, Unitarian Universalist Ch., Phoenix, 1996, Lakeland Painters, Grand Haven, Mich., 1996, Sun Cities Mus. Art, Sun City, Ariz., 1997, Art Inst. Phoenix, 1998, Hill Country Arts Found., Ingram, Tex., 1998, Mus. Tex. Tech. U., Lubbock, 1998, Dunton Gallery, Arlington Heights, Ill., 2000, Internat. Mus. Art, El Paso, 2000; one-woman shows include Gallery Upstairs, Grand Haven, 1996, Moynihan Gallery, Holland, 1997, Trinity Presbyn. Ch., Denton, 1997, Show Sabbatical, 1998, 99, Freedom Village, Holland, 2000, Acad. Artists Assn., Springfield, Mass., 2001, Hilton Head Art League, 2001, Oil Painters Am., Chgo., 2002, Audubon Artists N.Y., 2002, Magnum Opus XIV, Sacramento, 2002, Am. Artists Profl. League, N.Y.C., 2002, Celebration of Western Art, San Francisco, 2002, Hilton Head Art League, 2003, 2004, Oil Painters Am., Taos, N.Mex., 2003, Scottsdale Artists Sch, 2004, Nat. Watercolor Soc., 2004, Rocky Mountain Plein Air Painters, 2004, Allied Artists, Inc., N.Y.C., Biennale Internazionale Dell'Arte Contemporanea, Florence, Italy, 2005—, Catharine Lorillard Wolfe Art Club, NY, 2006; group Shows include: Gallery Uptown, 2006, El Presido Gallery, Ariz., 2006; permanent collections in Fla., Ariz., Mich., Nebr., Ind.; contbng. author: How Did You Paint That? 100 Ways to Paint the Landscape, 2004, How Did You Paint That? 100 Ways to Paint Flowers and Gardens, 2004, Art Still on the Easel, Am. Art Collector Mag., 2006; contbr. articles to profl. jours. Recipient Mcht.'s award Lakeland Painters, 1996, No. Ariz. Watercolor Soc., Sedona Arts Ctr., 1999, Diane Parssinen Meml. award No. Ariz. Watercolor Soc., 2001, 2d prize Internat. Artist Mag., 2002, Honorable Mention, Artists Mag., 2002, 2004. Mem. Ariz. Watercolor Assn., No. Ariz. Watercolor Assn., Oil Painters Am. (assoc.), Nat. Watercolor Soc. (assoc.), Allied Artists (assoc.), Tucson Plein Air Painters Soc., Great LAkes Pleun Air Painters. Republican. Home: 6418 Oakridge Dr Holland MI 49423-8999 Personal E-mail: dvn@dianevannoord.com.

VAN NOY, CHRISTINE ANN, restaurateur; b. Oakland, CA, Mar. 25, 1948; d. Julio Ceaser and Bernice Thelma (Rose) Lucchesi; m. David Craik Van Noy, July 10, 1971; children: James Allan, Joseph Julio. Student, U. Calif., Berkeley, 1971-73, U. Phoenix, 1994—. Exec. sec. Kaiser Permanente Med. Care Program, Oakland, 1966-76; owner Secret Closet Boutique, Moraga, Calif., 1972-82; owner, operator The Wordshop, Moraga, 1976-86; owner, cons. Van Noy & Assocs., Moraga, 1979—; exec. sec. to sr. v.p., regional mgr. Kaiser Permanente Med. Care Program, 1986-88, chmn., CEO, 1988-92, dir. adminstrv. svcs., 1992-98, v.p. adminstrv. svcs., 1999-2000; owner Giulio's Catering, 1999-2000; pres. Kaiser Permanente Internat.; owner Cafe Dolce, 2000—02; prin. Guillio's Catering, 2002—. Instr. U. Calif., Santa Cruz, 1983-84, Diablo Valley Coll., Concord, Calif., 1984; cons. Nat. Alliance Homebased Businesswomen, San Francisco, 1981-84. Author: Homebased Business Guide, 1982, (with others) Women Working Home, 1982. Mem. bd. Joaquis Moraga Sch. Dist., 1983-84, Calif. Federated Jr. Women's Clubs, 1972-77; bd. dirs. Orinda/Moraga Recreational Swimming Assn., 1984-85, St. Mark's United Methodist Ch., Moraga, 1983-84; pres. bd. Protect Our Nation's Youth Baseball Assn., 1987-90; dir. Ctr. for Living Skills, 1990—. Mem. Women Health Care Execs. Democrat. Roman Catholic. Avocations: graphic design, painting, writing. Home: 181 Paseo Del Rio Moraga CA 94556-1641 Office: Cafe Dolce 100 Pringle Ave #120 Walnut Creek CA 94596 E-mail: cafedolce@hotmail.com.

VANNOY, VICKI LYNNE, mathematics educator, department chairman; d. Harry Lawrence VanNoy, Jr. and Betty June VanNoy. BS in Edn., Ind. U., Pa., 1973; MS in Edn., Mansfield U., Pa., 1980, MEd in Math/Sci., 1984. Substitute tchr. Troy Area Sch. Dist., Pa., 1974; math tchr./interactive media specialist Canton Area Sch. Dist., Pa., 1974—. Substitute tchr. math. Liberty H.S., Pa., 1973. Author: (articles) Gifted/Talented Jour. Choir mem. Canton Ecumenical Parish, 1989—. Finalist Tchr. of Yr., Pa., 1997; grantee for gifted edn., Reston, Va., 1984. Avocations: reading, piano, gardening, home improvement. Office: Canton Area Sch Dist 139 E Main St Canton PA 17724 Office Phone: 570-673-5134.

VAN ORDEN, PHYLLIS JEANNE, librarian, educator; b. Adrian, Mich., July 7, 1932; d. Warren Philip and Mabel A. Nancy (Russell) Van O. BS, Ea. Mich. U., 0954; AMLS, U. Mich., 1958; EdD, Wayne State U., 1970. Sch. librarian East Detroit (Mich.) Pub. Schs., 1954-57; librarian San Diego Pub. Library, 1958-60; media specialist Royal Oak (Mich.) Pub. Schs., 1960-64; librarian Oakland U., Rochester, Mich., 1964-66; instr. Wayne State U., Detroit, 1966-70; asst. prof. Rutgers U., New Brunswick, NJ, 1970-76; prof. library science Fla. State U., Tallahassee, 1977-91, assoc. dean for instrn., 1988-91; prof. libr. sci. program Wayne State U., Detroit, 1991-93; dir. Grad. Sch. of Libr. and Info. Sci. U. Wash., Seattle, 1993-96; cons. in field, 1996—. Author: Collection Program in Schools, 2001, Library Service to Children, 2005, Selecting Books for the Elementary School Library Media Center, 2000; editor: Elementary School Library Collection, 1974—77. Fla. State Libr. grantee, 1984, 86, 88; Lillian Bradshaw scholar Tex. Woman's U., 1993. Mem.: ALA (libr. resources and tech. svcs. divsn., Blackwell/N.Am. scholarship award 1983), Assn. for Libr. and Info. Sci. Edn. (pres. 1990, Svc. award 1997), Assn. Libr. Svc. to Children (past pres., Dist. Svc. award 2002), Pi Lambda Theta. Avocations: music, knitting, physical fitness, cooking, travel. E-mail: vanordp@u.washington.edu.

VAN OST, LYNN, physical therapist, Olympic team official; b. Englewood, N.J., Sept. 7, 1960; d. William Carlisle and Marijane Dorward Van Ost. BSN, West Chester State Coll., Pa., 1982; MEd, Temple U., Phila., 1987; BS Phys. Therapy, Temple U., 1988. RN Pa, 1982; cert. athletic trainer Nat. Athletic Trainer's Assn., 1984. Staff nurse Abington Meml. Hosp., Pa., 1982—84; nurse/ athletic trainer U.S. Sports Acad., Mobile, Ala., 1984—85; coord. sports medicine Providence Hosp., Mobile, 1985—86, Del. County Meml.

Hosp., Drexel Hill, Pa., 1988—90; staff phys. therapist Hunterdon Phys. and Sports Therapy, Flemington, NJ, 1990—91, Sports Phys. Therapy, Somerset, NJ, 1991—92; clin. specialist sports medicine Thomas Jefferson U. Hosp., Phila., 1992—98; asst. dir. Sports Phys. Therapy Inst., Princeton, NJ, 1998—2000, dir. Flemington, 2000—02; clin. specialist, sports phys. therapy Hunterdon Med. Ctr., Flemington, 2002—. Vol. athletic trainer U.S. Olympic Com., Colorado Springs, 1989—96, U.S. Field Hockey, Colorado Springs, 1993—96, U.S. Short Track Speed Skating, Lake Placid, NY, 1994—99. Author: (study guide) Athletic Training Student Guide to Success, 2003, 3d edit., 2006, (cd rom) Goniometry, 1999. Scholar Athletic Tng., Temple U., 1982—84. Mem.: Nat. Athletic Trainer's Assn., Abbes' Soc., Panhellenic (pres. 1981—82), Alpha Phi (panhellenic rep. 1980—81). Achievements include patents for Athletic Tng. Jacket. Avocations: golf, travel. Home: 2 Riverview Drive West Trenton NJ 08628 Office: Hunterdon Med Ctr 2100 Wescott Drive Flemington NJ 08822-4604 Office Phone: 908-782-1095. Personal E-mail: kmanfre@comcast.net.

VAN OUWERKERK, ANITA HARRISON, reading educator; b. Oakdale, La., Feb. 16, 1942; d. Otto Joseph and Nora Land Harrison; m. Clyde Carter, Dec. 31, 1962; m. William Van Ouwerkerk, June 28, 1969 (dec.); children: Kathryn, Jeffrey, Joseph. BA, Northwestern State U., Natchitoches, La., 1963; student McNeese State U., 1965; MEd, U. New Orleans, 1968; student, Lamar State U., Beaumont, Tex., 1978—83. Cert. tchr. K-8 and mentally retarded La., 1963, Tex., 1979. Various tchg. and cons. positions, La., 1963—70; edn. cons. Allen Paris, Elizabeth, La., 1974—75; tchr. spl. edn. West Orange Cove Inst. Sch. Dist., Orange, Tex., 1978—95; instr. Lamar State Coll., Orange, Tex., 1988—2001; instr. reading Blinn Coll., Bryan, Tex., 2001—. Dir. Greater Orange Area Lit. Svc., Orange, 1999—2001, bd. dirs., 1998—2001. Fellow spl. edn., U. New Orleans, 1967—68. Mem.: Coll. Reading and Learning Assn. (mem. nominating com.), Nat. Assn. Devel. Educators, Tex. Coll. Reading and Learning Assn. (pres. 2002—), League of Women Voters, Toastmasters, Delta Kappa Gamma (pres., sec. 1996—2000). Unitarian Universalist. Avocations: writing, singing, sewing. Office: Blinn Coll PO Box 6030 Bryan TX 77802 Personal E-mail: anita.vanouwerkerk@verizon.net. Business E-Mail: avanouwerkerk@acmail.blinncol.edu.

VAN PELT, DARA, mathematics educator; b. Charleston, S.C., Jan. 11, 1974; d. Larry and Carol Hahn; m. Dennis Robert Van Pelt, Jr., Oct. 25, 1998; children: Dayna Jennie, Darren Thomas. BS, Monmouth U., Long Branch, Wis., 1996; student in Ednl. Adminstrn. Cert. tchr. N.J., 1996. Tchr. math. Manasquan H.S., NJ, 1996—2003, Hazlet Bd. Edn., NJ, 2003—. Coach Manasquan H.S., 1996—2003, Hazlet Bd. Edn., 2003—05. Mem.: N.J. Edn. Assn. Home: 918 16th Ave Belmar NJ 07719 Office: Hazlet Board of Education Middle Road Hazlet NJ Office Phone: (732) 264-8411. Personal E-mail: davp25@yahoo.com.

VAN PELT, FRANCES EVELYN, management consultant; b. Oregon, Ill., Aug. 25, 1937; d. Henry Benjamin and Bessie May (Himes) Ulferts; m. R. Richard Van Pelt, Oct. 28, 1953; children: R. Richard Jr., Robin F. Van Pelt Dobbs, Raymond Scott, Ronda Jean. Student, Waubonsee Coll., Sugar Grove, Ill., 1971-75. Adminstrv. asst. Sears, Roebuck & Co., Aurora, Ill., 1960-73; owner, mgr., pres. Outdoor World, Inc., Aurora, 1973-87; 20 group facilitator Spader Mgmt. Groups, Inc., Sioux Falls, SD, 1988—. Bd. dirs. RV Consumer Care Commn., Fairfax, Va., 1985-88. Contbr. articles to profl. jours. Bd. dirs. Breaking Free, Aurora, 1988-90; cellist Fox Valley Symphony, Aurora, 1961-81. Recipient J.B. Summers award for disting. svc. to RV industry, 2002. Mem. Aurora C. of C. Recrational Vehicle Dealers Assn. (bd. dirs. 1978-79, exec. bd. 1980-82, pres. 1983, chmn. bd. dirs. 1984), Ill. RV Dealers Assn. (pres., bd. dirs. 1978-79, exec. bd. 1980-82, pres. 1983, chmn. bd. dirs. 1984). Avocations: music, tennis. Office: 46900 Bermont Rd 63 Punta Gorda FL 33982 Personal E-mail: franevanpelt@cs.com.

VAN RAALTE, BARBARA G., retired realtor; b. Rochester, N.Y., Apr. 11, 1932; d. Maurice Harry and Estelle Belle (Breman) Goldman; m. John Alan Van Raalte, Sept. 5, 1954 (div. July 1974); children: John Alan Jr., Peter Baird, Thomas Douglas, Skye Van Raalte Herzog. BA in Econs. and Polit. Sci., Wellesley Coll., 1954; postgrad., Harvard Grad. Sch. Design, 1993, 95. Cert. buyer rep., N.C. Dir. devel. Stowe (Vt.) Sch., 1975-77; assoc. dir. devel. NYU Med. Ctr., The Rusk Inst. Rehab. Medicine, N.Y.C., 1977-80; dir. devel. Planned Parenthood of Vt., Burlington, 1980-83; realtor, sr. assoc. Foulsham Farms Real Estate, South Burlington, 1983-95, Trombley Real Estate, Burlington, 1995-97; sr. assoc. CBR Re/Max Preferred Real Estate, South Burlington, 1997-99; sr. assoc. Pall Spera Co. Real Estate, Stowe, Vt., 1999—2002; ret., 2002. Bd. dirs., treas. Hist. Soc., Stowe, 1974-75; bd. dirs. emeritus Katonah (N.Y.) Mus. Art, 1980—; mem. Nat. Spkrs. Bur., United Jewish Appeal, 1982-84; guide Shelburne (Vt.) Farms, 1994-, vol. Lake Champlain Maritime Mus., 2000—. Mem. Hadassah (bd. dirs. Mid. East affairs 1996-98). Jewish. Avocations: architecture, landscape design, photography, travel, gardening. Home: 5 Southwind Dr Burlington VT 05401-5463

VAN RAALTE, POLLY ANN, reading and writing specialist, photojournalist; b. N.Y.C., Sept. 22, 1951; d. Byron Emmanuel and Enid (Godnick) Van R. Student, U. London, 1972; BA, Beaver Coll., 1973; MS in Edn., U. Pa., 1974, EdD, 1994, West Chester State Coll., 1977. Title I reading tchr. Oakview Sch., West Deptford Twp. Sch. Dist., Woodbury, N.J., 1974-75, title I reading supr., 1975 summer; lang. arts coord. Main Line Day Sch., Mitchell Sch., Haverford, Pa., 1975-76; reading supr. Salvation Army, Phila., summer 1976; reading Huntingdon Jr. H.S., Abington (Pa.) Sch. Dist., 1976-78; reading specialist No. 2 Sch., Lawrence Pub. Sch., Inwood, N.Y., 1978-87; high sch. reading specialist Cedarhurst, N.Y., 1988-93, Lawrence (N.Y.) H.S., 1988-93; elem. reading specialist No. 5 Sch., 1992—; reading specialist Hewlett (N.Y.) Elem. Sch., Hewlett-Woodmere Pub. Sch., 1987-88, Lawrence Mid. Sch., 1993-95; instr. reading and spl. edn. dept. Adelphi U., 1979—. Columnist South Shore Record, featured columnist, 1992—; columnist Boulevard Mag., 1995-97; photojournalist Manhattan Reports, 1997-2002; feature columnist www.15minutesmagazine.com. Bd. dirs., mem. exec. bd. Five Towns Cmty. Ctr., 1991-93, co-chmn. ednl. youth svcs. edn. com., 1991-93; cons. to sch. dists.; advisor Am. Biog. Inst., Inc.; coord. Five Towns Young Voter Registration, Hewlett, N.Y., summer 1971; chmn. class fund Beaver Coll., also mem. internat. rels. com. U. Pa. scholar, 1977-78; mem. assoc. divsn. Jewish Guild for Blind; mem. N.Y. City Sports Commn.; co-chair youth svcs. com. Mem. Internat. Reading Assn., Wis. Reading Assn., Nat. Coun. Tchrs. English, Nassau Reading Coun., N.Y. Reading Assn., Coun. Exceptional Children, Coun. for a Beautiful Israel, Nat. Assn. Gifted Children, Am. Assn. of the Gifted, Nat./State Leadership Tng. Inst. on the Gifted and Talented, Children's Lit. Assembly, N.Y. State English Coun., Assn. Curriculum Devel., Am. Israel Pub. Affairs Com., New Leadership Com. of Jewish Nat. Fund, State of Israel Bonds New Leadership, Simon Wiesenthal New Leadership Soc., Nat. Polit. Action Com., Am. Friends of Hebrew U. (torch com.), Technion Soc., Am. Friends David Yellin Tchr.'s Coll., Am. Friends Israel Philharm., Am. Friends of Tel Aviv U., Am. Israel Cultural Found., Hadassah, Film Soc. Lincoln Ctr., U.S. Olympic Soc., Friends of N.Y.C. Sports Commn., Cooper-Hewitt Mus., Mus. Modern Art, Met. Mus. Art, Whitney Mus., Phila. Mus. Art, Smithsonian Inst., Friends of Carnegie-Hall, Friends of Am. Ballet Theatre, Friends of Am. Theatre Wing, Women's Am. Orgn. for Rehab. Through Tng. (citi women divsn. N.Y.C.), U. Pa. Alumni Assn. N.Y.C., Dorot Soc., Human Rels. Club (sec.), Actors'Fund, Pi Lambda Theta, Kappa Delta Pi (sec., Internat. Tennis Hall of Fame). Home: 26 Meadow Ln Lawrence NY 11559-1828 Office: #5 Sch Cedarhurst Ave Cedarhurst NY 11516

VANREKEN, MARY K., psychologist; b. E. Grand Rapids, Mich., Dec. 13, 1947; d. Donald L. and Elsa M. (De Wind) vanR. Cert., Trinity Christian Coll., Palos Heights, Ill., 1967; BA magna cum laude, Hope Coll., Holland, Mich., 1969; MA in Psychology, Appalachian State U., Boone, N.C., 1970; PhD in Clin. Psychology, Purdue U., 1977. Vis. asst. prof. psychology Ind. U., Bloomington, 1977-78; asst. prof. psychology Ind. State U., Terre Haute, 1978-80; psychologist Valley Psychiatric Hosp., Chattanooga, 1980-82, adolescent program dir., 1983, chief psychologist, 1982-84; pvt. practice Chattanooga, 1982-94; rehab. psychologist HCMC, Mpls., 1994—95, Bethesda Luth. Hosp., St. Paul, 1995—99; pvt. practice Bloomington, Minn., 2000—. Cons. in field. Contbr. chpt. to book. Mem. adv. coun. Family & Children's Svcs., Chattanooga, 1981-85. Mem. LWV, Am. Psychol. Assn., Assn. Women in Psychology, Southeastern Psychol. Assn., Tenn. Psychol. Assn. (profl. affairs com. 1986-1994, com. chair 1989-1993), Ga. Psychol. Assn., Chattanooga Area Psychol. Assn. (treas. 1983, ethics com. 1984-86), NOW (sec. Tenn. chpt. 1985-86), Minn. Psychol. Assn., Am. Assn. Clin. Hypnosis. Avocations: photography, camping, skiing, bicycling. Office: 7800 Metro Pky #300 Bloomington MN 55425 Office Phone: 952-854-4116.

VAN RY, GINGER LEE, school psychologist; b. Alexandria, Va., June 26, 1953; d. Ray Ellsworth Hensley and Bernice Anne (Weidel) Wolter; m. Willem Hendrik Van Ry, Aug 23, 1986; 1 child, Anika Claire. AA, U. Nev., Las Vegas, 1973; BA, U. Wash., 1983, MEd, 1985. Cert. sch. psychologist (nationally). Psychometrist The Mason Clinic, Seattle, 1980-84, supr., psychology lab., 1984-86; sch. psychologist Everett (Wash.) Sch. Dist., 1986—. Mem. profl. ednl. adv. bd. U. Wash. Sch. Psychology, Seattle, 1995—; mem. early childhood devel. del. to China, 2000. Author: (with others) Wash. State Assn. of Sch. Psychologists Best Practice Handbook, 1993. Co-pres. Lake Cavanaugh Hghts. Assn., Seattle, 1994-95, chmn. long-range planning com., 1995—. Mem. AAUW, NEA, NASP (nationally cert. sch. psychologist), Wash. State Assn. Sch. Psychologists (chair profl. devel. com. 1995-2001), Wash. State Edn. Assn., U. Wash. Alumni Assn. Democrat. Avocations: reading, travel, fgn. cultures, woodworking, horticulture. Office: The Everett Sch Dist PO Box 2098 Everett WA 98203-0098 Office Phone: 425-385-5312.

VAN RY, KIMBERLY ANNE, secondary school educator; b. Chgo., Apr. 5, 1970; d. Daniel Joseph Gruber and Noreen Elgene Dalton; m. Jeff Ronald Van Ry, Mar. 13, 1993; children: Tessa Mary, Lilith Olivia. BS in Sci., U. Tampa, Fla., 1988—92, BA in English Lit. and Writing, 1988—92; Masters, Stanford U., Palo Alto, Calif., 1993. Cert. tchr. OSPI Wash., 2000. Honors biology and English tchr. Wilson H.S., Tacoma, 2000—. Author poetry. Vol. Habitat for Humanity, Tacoma, 2001—06. Mem.: NASA (assoc.). Avocations: research in medicine, travel, reading, writing. Office: Wilson High School 1202 N Orchard St Tacoma WA 98406 Office Phone: 253-571-6000. Business E-Mail: kvanry@tacoma.k12.wa.us.

VAN SANT, JOANNE FRANCES, academic administrator; b. Morehead, Ky., Dec. 29, 1924; d. Lewis L. and Dorothy (Green) Van S. BA, Denison U., Granville, Ohio; MA, The Ohio State U.; postgrad., U. Colo. and The Ohio State U.; LLD (hon.), Albright Coll., 1975. Tchr., health and phys. edn. Mayfield (Ky). H.S., 1946—47; instr. Denison U., Granville, Ohio, 1948; instr. women's phys. edn. Otterbein Coll., Westerville, Ohio, 1948-52, assoc. prof., 1955-62, dept. chmn., 1950-62, chmn. div. profl. studies, 1961-65, dean of women, 1952-60, 62-64, dean of students, 1964-93, v.p. student affairs, 1968-93; v.p., dean student affairs emeritus, 1993—; cons. Instnl. Advancement, 1993—. Co-pres. Directions for Youth, 1983-84, pres., 1984-85; bd. dirs. North Area Mental Health; trustee Friendship Village of Columbus, 1996—, pres. bd., 1998—2004; trustee Westerville Civic Symphony at Otterbein Coll., 1983-88; active numerous other community orgns.; ordained elder Presbyn. Ch., 1967. Named to hon. Order of Ky. Cols., 1957; recipient Focus on Youth award Columbus Dispatch, 1983, Vol. of the Yr. award North Area Mental Health Svcs., 1982, citation Denison U., 1996. Mem. Am. Assn. Counseling and Devel., Ohio Personnel and Guidance Assn., Ohio Assn. Women Deans, Adminstrs., Counselors (treas., exec. bd. 1972-73), Nat. Assn. Student Personnel Adminstrs., Ohio Coll. Personnel Assn., Mortar Bd. (hon.), Zonta Internat. (pres. Columbus, Ohio club 1978-80, dist. gov. 1988-90, internat. svc. chmn. 1996-98, internat. found. bd. 1997-2001), Vocal Arts Resource Network (chair bd. dirs. 1994-96), Cap and Dagger Club, Torch and Key Hon., Order Omega, Alpha Lambda Delta, Theta Alpha Phi, others. Avocations: musical and children's theater production, choreography. Home: 9100 Oakwood Pt Westerville OH 43082-9643 Office: Otterbein Coll Instnl Advancement Westerville OH 43081 Business E-Mail: jvansant@otterbein.edu.

VAN SCHENKHOF, CAROL DOUGHERTY (CAROL DOVAN), soprano, educator; b. Reading, Pa., Apr. 20, 1942; d. Harry Hammond Dougherty and Magdalen Mary Doviak; m. Mark Anton van Schenkhof, Feb. 18, 1995; m. John William Heierman, Sept. 4, 1965 (div. July 6, 1986). BA, Chatham Coll., 1964; student, Julliard Sch., N.Y.C., 1964—65, Julliard Sch., 1970; MA Ethno-musicology, Hunter Coll., 1970, student, 1971, Mannes Coll., 1980, Westminster Choir Coll., Princeton, N.J., 1992, Westminster Choir Coll., 1996, Oberlin Conservatory, 2000, student, 2002, Westminster Choir Coll. Conservatory, 2004. Tchr. voice Sch. Music Lab. Chatham Coll., Pitts., 1964; resource profl. Lincoln Ctr., N.Y.C., 1972; vis. artist, lectr. Ewha U., Seoul, 1975, Emissora Nacional de Radioifusao, Lisbon, Portugal, 1976, Conservatorio Nacional, Lisbon, 1976; lectr. opera C.W. Post Coll., L.I. U., Greenvale, NY, 1982—83; profl. coord. Port Washington Libr.-Music Adv. Coun., NY, 1985—87; tchr. voice Stony Brook U., NY, 1998—99, Carol Dovan-van Schenkhof Studios, Port Washington, 1980—. Singer: Rhodesia TV Ltd., 1974, Rhodesia Orgn., 1974, South African Broadcasting, 1974, Emissora Nacional de Radiodifuŝao, 1976, (soloist) Met. Opera Studio, 1971—72, Alice Tully Hall, 1983, recitals with composer Jeanne Singer, 1983—87, Nat. Grand Opera, 1983, (Operas) Best of Opera, Carnegie Hall, 1982, La Boheme, 1981, Ninth Symphony of Beethoven- Reading Sympony Orch., 1983, others. Recipient 1st Pl. award, Competition Pitts. Musicians Club, 1962, Pitts. Concert Soc. Youth Auditions, 1962, Pitts. Concert Soc. Major Auditions, 1963; scholar, Chautauqua (NY) Inst. Music, 1962—63, Aspen (Colo.) Music Festival, 1964. Mem.: N.Y. Singing Tchrs., Am. Guild Musical Artists, Nat. Assn. for Music Edn., Nat. Assn. Tchrs. Singing (adjudicator, Ea. Region auditions), Associated Music Tchrs. League (exec. bd. 1994—). Epsicopalian. Avocations: gardening, sailing. Home and Studio: 6 Hillview Ave Port Washington NY 11050 Office Phone: 516-944-5140. Personal E-mail: caroldov@optonline.net.

VAN SICKLE, BARBARA ANN, special education educator; b. Dubuque, Iowa, Apr. 29, 1932; d. Ralph and Grace Elizabeth (Dennis) Browne; m. Marvin Allen Van Sickle, June 7, 1953; children: Mark, Lee Ann Van Sickle Back, David, Karen Van Sickle. BA, U. No. Iowa, 1954; MA, Clarke Coll., 1971. Cert. tchr., Iowa. Tchr. remedial reading Dubuque schs., 1967-76; spl. edn. tchr. Indianola (Iowa) schs., 1976-92. Pub. info. chair Nat. Balloon Classic, Indianola, 1990-91, 93-94, 95—; pres. Warren County Assn. for Children with Learning Disabilities, Indianola, 1978-80. Mem. NEA, AAUW, Iowa State Edn. Assn., Indianola Edn. Assn. (pres. 1988-89, chair govtl. affairs 1990-92), Learning Disabilities Assn. Iowa (chair book room 1978-91, 2d v.p. 1994, 95, 2001, 02, 03, 04, 1st v.p. 1996, 97, 98, 99, bd. dirs. 2005, 06, Appreciation award 1980, Pres. award 1989, 99, Helping Hands award 1993). Democrat.

VAN SLYKE, ROSEMARY, tax specialist; b. Albany, NY, June 23, 1939; d. William and Edna Elizabeth (Lawler) Van Slyke; children: Rosemary Van Vorse, Christopher Van Vorse, Elizabeth Hudson. Assoc. Bus. Adminstrn., Albany Bus. Coll., NY, 1969; cert. med. asst., Mildred Elley Coll., Colonie, NY, 1993. With NY Staet Dept. Labor, Albany, 1969—96, Albany County Mental Health, Albany, 1997—2001, NY State Tax Dept., Albany, 2002—04, GE Corp. Tax, Albany, 2005—. Mem.: ACLU, NOW, CSEA (sec. 1981—88). Democrat. Roman Catholic. Avocations: exercise, reading, internet. Home: 2 Oceanspray Blvd Clifton Park NY 12065

VAN SLYKE, SHERRIE MARIE, psychotherapist; b. Oceanside, Calif., Sept. 15, 1945; m. George Dudley Van Slyke, June 11, 1966; children: Sandra Marie, Kathryn Suzanne. AA, Palomar Jr. Coll., 1965; AA summa cum laude, Met. State Coll., 1977, BS summa cum laude, 1979; MSW, U. Denver, 1982. Lic. clin. social worker. Probation officer Denver Juvenile Ct., 1978; psychotherapist Jefferson County Mental Health, Lakewood, Colo., 1978, 1979, 1981-82; social worker Kunsmiller Jr. High Sch., Denver, 1980-81; pvt. practice psychotherapy Littleton, Colo., 1982—2002; ret., 2002. Cons. Columbine United Ch., Littleton, 1982-88, also lectr., 1982-88, Christian Edn. dir., 1983-85, 89, divorce group leader, 1985-87; leader Incest Support Group, 1993, Women's Support Group, 1994. Bd. dirs. VOICES in Action. Democrat. Avocations: painting, gardening, reading.

VANSTROM, MARILYN JUNE CHRISTENSEN, retired elementary school educator; b. Mpls., June 10, 1924; d. Harry Clifford and Myrtle Agnes (Hagland) Christensen; m. Reginald Earl Vanstrom, Mar. 20, 1948; children: Gary Alan, Kathryn June Vanstrom Marinello. AA, U. Minn., 1943, BS, 1946. Cert. elem. tchr NY, Ill., Minn. Tchr. Pub. Sch., St. Louis Park, Minn., 1946-47, Deephaven, Minn., 1947-50, Chicago Heights, Ill., 1950-52, Steger, Ill., 1964, substitute tchr. Dobbs Ferry, N.Y., 1965-72, Yonkers, N.Y., 1965-92. Mem. Ch. Women, Christ Meml. Luth. Ch. Mem. AAUW (life, pres. So. Westchester br. 1988-90, Ednl. Found. award 1990), Evening Book Club (Met. West br. Minn., So. Westchester br. N.Y.), Yonkers Fedn. Tchrs., U. Minn. Alumni Assn. Democrat. Avocations: painting, sketching, piano, travel. Home: 12300 Marion Ln W Apt 2105 Minnetonka MN 55305-1317

VAN SUSTEREN, GRETA CONWAY, newscaster, lawyer; b. Appleton, Wis., June 11, 1954; d. Urban Peter and Margery (Conway) Van Susteren; m. John Purcell Coale, Oct. 12, 1987. BA in Econs (with distinction), U. Wis., 1976; JD, Georgetown U., 1979, LLM, 1982; LLD (hon.), Stetson Law Sch. Bar: D.C. 1979, U.S. Supreme Ct. 1982, Md. 1985, Wis. 1987, U.S. Ct. Appeals (D.C., 2d and 4th cirs.). Ptnr. Milliken, VanSusteren & Canan, Washington, 1982—; with CNN, 1991—2002, host The Point with Greta Van Susteren, co-host Burden of Proof, legal cons. The World Today; host On the Record With Greta Van Susteren Fox News Channel, 2002—. Adj. prof. Georgetown Law Ctr., Washington, 1984—99; lectr., panelist Jud. Conf., Washington, 1986. Co-author: My Turn at the Bullypulpit: Straight Talk About the Things That Drive Me Nuts. Bd. dirs. Stuart Stiller Found., Washington, 1982—. Named one of 100 Most Powerful Women, Forbes; recipient Sandra Day O'Conner Medal of Honor, Seton Hall Univ., 2000—01, 1st Place, "Attack on America", Nat. Headliners award, 2002; Stiller fellow, Georgetown Law Ctr., 1980. Mem.: ATLA (lectr. conf. 1986—), ABA (Presdl. award for Excellence in Journalism 2001), D.C. Bar Assn. Office: FOX News Channel 1211 Avenue of the Americas New York NY 10036

VAN TILBURG, JOANNE, archaeologist, educator, foundation administrator; b. Mpls., Apr. 20, 1942; d. Everton George and Ruth (Butler) Becker; m. Johannes Franciscus Pieter Van Tilburg, Aug. 10, 1968; 1 child, Marieka Joanna. BS, U. Minn., 1965; MEd, UCLA, 1976, PhD, 1986. Rsch. assoc. Inst. Archaeology UCLA, 1986—, dir. Rock Art Archive, Cotsen Inst. Archaeology, 1996—; assoc. rschr. Inst. de Estudios U. de Chile, Isla de Pascua, 1986—. Lectr. Archaeol. Inst. Am., 1995—, Brit. Mus., 1990—; instr. UCLA Extension, 1990—. Author: Easter Island Archaeology, Ecology and Culture, 1994, H.M.S. Topaze on Easter Island, 1992; editor: Ancient Images on Stone, 1983; contbr. articles to profl. jours. Pres. Mana Found. Grantee Nat. Geog. Soc., 1989, Calif. Coun. for the Humanities, 1980, 95. Fellow Royal Geog. Soc.; mem. Archaeol. Inst. Am. (Golden Trowel campaign medallion 1999), Soc. for Am. Archaeology, Pacific Arts Assn. Office: UCLA Inst Archaeology Fowler Mus Cultural History 405 Hilgard Ave Los Angeles CA 90095-9000

VAN TREASE, SANDRA ANN, insurance company executive; b. St. Louis, Dec. 11, 1960; m. Virgil Van Trease; children: Shawna, Erin. BSBA, U. Mo., St. Louis, 1982; MBA, Washington U., St. Louis, 1992. CPA, Mo.; cert. mgmt. acct., Mo. Sr. mgr. audit divsn. Price Waterhouse, St. Louis, 1982-94; v.p. fin. rep. and investor rels. Alliance Blue Cross/Blue Shield, St. Louis, 1994-95, sr. v.p., CFO, 1995-97, exec. v.p., COO, CFO, 1997—. Author practice cases, 1988, 90. Treas. Art-St. Louis, 1992-94, St. Louis County Fair and Air Show, 1993-94; chmn. adminstrn. Fair St. Louis, 1994-96; bd. dirs. Nat. Multiple Sclerosis Soc., 1997-98, Caring Program for Children, 1998—. Mem. AICPA, Fin. Execs. Inst., Inst. Mgmt. Accts., Mo. Soc. CPA's. Office: Alliance Blue Cross/Blue Shield 1831 Chestnut St Saint Louis MO 63103-2231

VANTREESE, LINDA FAY RAINWATER, retired medical/surgical nurse; b. Jackson, Tenn., Nov. 17, 1949; d. Robert Alson and Frances Marie (Stepp) Rainwater. ADN, Union U., 1973. Staff nurse, orthopedics Jackson Madison County Gen. Hosp.; ret., 1997. Home: 146 Bolivar Hwy Jackson TN 38301-7813 Personal E-mail: linlinpearl@jaxnet.net.

VAN ULFT, STEPHANIE ANN, health facility administrator; b. Lockwood, Mo., Oct. 8, 1959; d. Harlan Henry and Natalie Ann Wehrman; m. Carlo Josef Van Ulft, July 31, 1999. BS in Biology, Washington U., St. Louis, 1981; MD, U. Mo., Columbia, 1986. Bd. cert. adult psychiatry, bd. cert. geriatric psychiatry. Physician, corp. co-owner Psychiat. Assoc., St. Louis, 1990—96; physician St. Alexius Hosp., St. Louis, 1997—99, St. Anthony's Hosp., St. Louis, 1999—2003; med. dir. Heartland Human Svcs., Effingham, Ill., 2003—. Guest expert On Main St. Syndicated TV, St. Louis, 2001—03; mem. task force Mo. Divsn. Aging, Jefferson City, 1998—2002; mem. adv. com. Mo. Medicare, St. Louis, 1997—2002; mem. spkr.'s bur. Alzheimer's Assn., St. Louis, 1991—2003; monthly guest expert Radio Sta. KFUO, St. Louis, 1997—2006. Bd. dir. so. Ill. dist. Luth. Ch. Mo. Synod, Belleville, 2000—03, bd. dir., 2006—. Mem.: Am. Psychiat. Assn., Christian Med. and Dental Soc., Am. Assn. Geriatric Psychiatrists. Office: Heartland Human Svcs 1200 N Fourth Effingham IL 62401 Office Phone: 217-347-7179.

VAN UMMERSEN, CLAIRE A(NN), academic administrator, biologist, educator; b. Chelsea, Mass., July 28, 1935; d. George and Catherine (Courtovich); m. Frank Van Ummersen, June 7, 1958; children: Lynn, Scott. BS, Tufts U., 1957, MS, 1960, PhD, 1963; DSc (hon.), U. Mass., 1988, U. Maine, 1991; LHD (hon.), U. New Eng., 2005. Rsch. asst. Tufts U., 1957-60, 60-67, grad. asst. in embryology, 1962, postdoctoral tchg. asst., 1963-66, lectr. in biology, 1967-68; asst. prof. biology U. Mass., Boston, 1968-74, assoc. prof., 1974—86, assoc. dean acad. affairs, 1975-76, assoc. vice chancellor acad. affairs, 1976-78, chancellor, 1978-79, dir. Environ. Sci. Ctr., 1980-82; assoc. vice chancellor acad. affairs Mass. Bd. Regents for Higher Edn., 1982-85, vice chancellor for mgmt. systems and telecom., 1985-86; chancellor Univ. System NH, Durham, 1986-92; sr. fellow New Eng. Bd. Higher Edn., 1992-93; sr. fellow New Eng. Resource Ctr. Higher Edn. U. Mass., 1992-93; pres. Cleve. State U., 1993—2001, pres. emerita, 2001—; v.p., dir. Office of Women Am. Coun. Edn., Wash., DC, 2001—05, v.p. Ctr. for Effective Leadership, 2005—. Cons. Mass. Bd. Regents, 1981-82, AGB, 1992—, Kuwait U., 1992-93; asst. Lancaster Course in Ophthalmology, Mass. Eye. and Ear Infirmary, 1962-69, lectr., 1970-93, also coord.; reviewer HEW; mem. rsch. team which established safety stds. for exposure to microwave radiation, 1958-65; participant Leadership Am. program, 1992-93; bd. dirs. Nat. Coun. Sci. Environment, 1998—, mem. subcom. for future and fin. Active NH Ct. Systems Rev. Task Force, 1989-90, Leadership Cleve. Class '95, Ohio Gov.'s Coun. on Sci. and Tech., 1996-98, Strategy Coun. Cleve. Pub. Schs., 1996-98, Cleve. Sports Commn., 1999-2001, Cleve. Mcpl. Sch. Dist. Bd., 1999-2001; New Eng. Bd. Higher Edn., 1986-92, exec. com., 1989-92, NH adv. coun., 1990-92; chair Rhodes Scholarship Selection Com., 1986-91; bd. dirs. NH Bus. and Industry Assn., 1987-93; governing bd. NH Math. Coalition, 1991-92; exec. com. 21st Century Learning Cmty., 1992-93; state panelist NH Women in Higher Edn., 1986-93; bd. dirs. Urban League Greater Cleve., 1993-2001, strategic planning com., chair edn. com., 1996-99, sec., exec. com., 1997-99; bd. dirs. Great Lakes Sci. and Tech. Ctr., 1993-2001, edn. com., 1995-2001; bd. dirs. Greater Cleve. Growth Assn., 1994-2001, Civic Vision 2000 and Beyond, Cleve., 1997-98; bd. dirs., exec. com. Sci. and Tech. Coun. Cleve. Tomorrow, 1998-99; rep. NE Ohio Tech. Coalition, 1999-2001; trustee Ohio Aerospace Inst., 1993-2001, exec. com., 1996-2001; strategic planning com. United Way, 1996-2000, chair environ. scan subcom. 1996-2001; leadership devel. com. ACE, 1995-98, women's commn., 1999-2001; bd. dirs. United Way, 1995-2001; co-chair Pub. Sector Campaign, 1997-98; bd. dirs. NCAA, divsn. 1, exec. com., 1999-2001; mem. AGB Ctr. for Pub. Higher Edn. Trusteeship and Goverance, 2001-03, Assn. Liaison Officers Adv. Com., 1998-2001. Recipient Disting. Svc. medal U. Mass., 1979, Woman of the Yr. Achievement award YWCA, 1998; Am. Cancer Soc. grantee Tufts U., 1960. Mem. Am. Coun. on Edn. (com. on self-regulation 1987-91), Nat. Conf. Cmty. and Justice (program com. 1996-2001), Nat. Coun. for Sci. and the Environment (bd. dirs. 1999-, fin. and futures coms.), State Higher Edn. Exec. Officers (fed. rels. com., 1986-92, cost accountability task force, exec. com. 1990-92), ACE (com. leadership devel.), Nat. Assn. Sys. Heads (exec. com. 1990-92), Nat. Ctr. for Edn. Stats. (network adv. com. 1989-92), New Eng. Assn. Schs. and Colls. (commn. on higher edn. 1990-93), North Ctrl. Assn. Schs. and Colls. (evaluator 1993-2001, chair accreditation teams 1986-90), Greater Cleve. Round Table (bd. dirs. 1993-2001, exec. com. 1995-2001), Cleve. Playhouse (trustee 1994-2001), Nat. Assn. State Univs. and Land Grant Colls. (exec. com. on urban agenda, mem. commn. tech. transfer), Am. Assn. State Colls. and Univs. (state rep. 1994-96, commn. on urban agenda 1996-2001, bd. dirs. 1996-99, mem. emerging issues task force 1996-98), Phi Beta Kappa, Sigma Xi. Office: American Coun on Edn One DuPont Cir NW Washington DC 20036-1193 Office Phone: 202-939-9376. Business E-Mail: claire_van_ummersen@ace.nche.edu.

VAN VLECK, PAMELA KAY, real estate company officer; b. St. Cloud, Minn., Aug. 26, 1951; d. Kipp James Gillespie and Lorraine Marie (Johnson) Storck; m. Clinton Eugene Van Vleck, Jan. 29, 1985. Student, St. Cloud State U., 1969-70, Washburn U., 1971-72. Lic. pilot; lic. cmty. assn. mgr. Mgr. and broker Coldwell Banker-Pioneer Realty, Jackson, Wyo., 1980—85; owner and broker Tri-Corp Realty, Ltd., Scottsdale, Ariz., 1985—87, Affiliated Properties Group, Inc., Phoenix and Las Vegas, 1987—91; mgr. and broker Machan Hampshire Properties, Las Vegas, Nev., 1990—91; v.p. Affiliated Property Mgmt. Corp., 1990-92; retail properties specialist Grubb & Ellis, Tucson, 1991-92; dir., comml. broker Cameron Real Estate Svcs., Naples, Fla., 1992-98; dir. Lee County Cameron Real Estate Svcs., Inc., Ft. Myers, 1994—98, v.p., 1997—98; ptnr. and dir. property mgmt. Grubb & Ellis, 1998—; broker and mgr. VIP Comml. and Comml. Property Mgmt. Svcs., 1998—. Bd. dir., owner Affiliated Properties Group Inc./Affiliated Property Mgmt. Corp., Phoenix, 1985-92; bd. dir., cons. Realty Software Svcs. Ariz., Inc., Phoenix, 1986-91, MHP Realty & Mgmt., Inc., Las Vegas, 1989-91. Developer, copywriter computer software program REMMI (Real Estate Matching, Mktg. and Inventory). Grad. Leadership Lee County, 1996, chair steering com., 1997-98. Mem.: NAFE, Real Estate Investment Soc., Internat. Coun. Shopping Ctrs., Women's Comml. Sales Assn., Nev. Devel. Authority, Women in Comml. Real Estate, Exec. Women's Golf League (grad. advanced leadership 2005). Republican. Avocations: reading, skiing, biking, golf, hiking. Office: 13131 University Dr Fort Myers FL 33907-5716 Office Phone: 239-489-3303 x 284. E-mail: pvanvleck@viprealty.com.

VAN VLIET, CAROLYN MARINA, physicist, researcher; b. Dordrecht, Netherlands, Dec. 27, 1929; arrived in U.S., 1960, naturalized, 1967; d. Marinus and Jacoba (de Lange) Van V.; m. A.J. Cappon, Dec. 29, 1953 (div. 1983); children: Elsa Marianne, Mark Edward, Cynthia Joyce, Renata Annette Carolina. BS, Free U. Amsterdam, Netherlands, 1949, MA, 1953, PhD in Physics, 1956. Rsch. fellow Free U. Amsterdam, 1950-54, rsch. assoc., 1954-56, asst. dir., 1958-60; postdoctoral fellow U. Minn., Mpls., 1956-57, faculty, 1957-58, 60-70, prof. elec. engring. and physics, 1965-70; prof. theoretical physics U. Montreal, Que., Can., 1969-95, sr. rschr. math. rsch. ctr. Que., 1969-2000, prof. emerita, 1998—. Vis. prof. U. Fla., 1974, 78-88; prof. elec. and computer engring. Fla. Internat. U., 1992-2000; adj. prof. physics U. Miami, 2001—. Contbg. author: Fluctuation Phenomena in Solids, 1965; contbr. articles to profl. jours. Rsch. grantee, NSF, Air Force OSR, Nat. Sci. and Engring. Rsch. Coun., Ottawa. Fellow IEEE (life); mem. Am. Phys. Soc., NY Acad. Scis. Office: U Miami James L Knight Physics Bldg 1320 Campo Sano Dr Coral Gables FL 33146 Office Phone: 305-284-2325. Business E-Mail: vanvliet@physics.miami.edu.

VAN VLIET, CLAIRE, artist; b. Ottawa, Ont., Can., Aug. 9, 1933; d. Wilbur Dennison and Audrey Ilene (Wallace) Van Vliet. AB, San Diego State Coll., 1952; MFA, Claremont Grad. Sch., 1954; DFA (hon.), U. of the Arts, Phila., 1993, San Diego State U., 2002. Instr. printmaking Phila. Coll. Art, 1959-65; owner The Janus Press, 1954—; vis. lectr. printmaking U. Wis.-Madison, 1965-66. Mem. bd. advisors Hand Papermaking. One-man exhbns. include Print Club Phila., 1963, 66, 73, 77, Wiggin Gallery, Boston Pub. Libr., 1977, Rutgers U. Art Gallery, 1978, AAA Gallery, Phila., 1980, Dolan/Maxwell Gallery, Phila., 1984, 91, Mary Ryan Gallery, NYC, 1986, Mills Coll., 1986, U. of the Arts, Phila., 1989, Victoria and Albert Mus., London, 1994, Ottawa Sch. of Art Gallery, Can., 1994, Bates Coll. Mus. of Art, Lewiston, Maine, 1994, 99, ND Mus. Art, 1999, Rosenwald Wolf Gallery U. Arts. Phila, 2001, Grolier Club, NY, 2006, Nat. Gallery Art Libr., 2006, Humanities Gallery, Scripps Coll., 2006; group exhbns. include Bklyn. Nat., Phila. Arts Festival, Kunst zu Kafka, Germany, Paper as Medium, Smithsonian Instn., Washington, Paper Now, Cleve. Mus. Art, 1986, Boyle Arts Festival, Ireland, 1993, Libr. Congress, 1997—, ND Mus. Art, 1999; represented in permanent collections Nat. Gallery Art, Phila. Mus. Art, Boston Pub. Libr., Libr. of Congress, Cleve. Mus. Art, Montreal Mus. Fine Arts, Victoria and Albert Mus. London, Tate Gallery, London, US Dept. of State, Nat. Libr. Canada, British Libr. Grantee, Ingram-Merrill Found., 1989; NEA grantee, 1976—80, MacArthur fellow, 1989—94. Mem.: Nat. Acad., Soc. Printers Boston, Vt. Arts and Scis. Home and Office: 101 Schoolhouse Rd West Burke VT 05871-9773 Office Phone: 802-467-3335.

VAN VLIET, HEATHER AGNES JOAN DEVLIN, elementary school educator; b. Luton, Eng., Dec. 26, 1953; came to U.S., 1958; d. Peter and Mary Jopp Melville (Menzies) Devlin; m. Herb A. Van Vliet, Dec. 6, 1975; children: Peter Devlin, David Stuart, Evelyn Mary. AA, Ocean County Coll., Toms River, N.J., 1976; BA, Georgian Ct. Coll., Lakewood, N.J., 1990; MA, Kean Coll., Union, N.J., 1997. Lic. tchr. K-8, N.J. Reporter, writer Ocean County Observer, Toms River, 1974-75; writer Ocean County Reporter, Toms River, 1975-77; tchr., substitute Howell Bd. Edn., Farmingdale, N.J., 1983-90, tchr., 1991—. Freelance writer. Mem. Howell Twp. Edn. Assn. (v.p.), Phi Kappa Phi, Delta Kappa Pi. Avocations: rock and roll collectibles, travel. Home: 35 Roberta Dr Howell NJ 07731-2720 E-mail: hvanvliet@yahoo.com.

VAN VOORST, CAROL, ambassador; BA, Hope Coll.; MA, Nat. War Coll., 1998; MA, PhD, Princeton U. Tchr. City U. NY; spl. asst. to dep. sec. US Dept. State, 1984—85, Norway/Denmark desk officer, 1989—91, spl. asst. to under sec. polit. affairs, 1991—92, assigned to Panama, 1992—95, dir. Office Nordic & Baltic Affairs, 1995—97, chief polit. dept. to dep. high rep. office of high rep. Sarajevo, 1998—99; dep. chief of mission Am. Embassy, Helsinki, 1999—2002; dir. Austrian, German, Swiss affairs, Bur. European and Eurasian Affairs US Dept. State, 2002—04, US. amb. to Iceland Reykjavik, 2005—. Office: Am Embassy 5640 Reykjavik Pl Washington DC 20521*

VAN WERT, LINDA, elementary school educator; b. Morris County, N.J., May 28, 1945; d. Grant and Doris (Smith) Van Wert; m. Stanley J. Tokarz, Jr., July 18, 1993. BA, Kean Coll., Union, N.J., 1967; MA, Seton Hall U., 1982. Cert. ESL educator, N.J. Tchr. pub. schs., N.J., 1967—; ESL tchr. Dover (N.J.) Pub. Schs., 1969—. Founder Collection Connections, Morris County, N.J., 1994. Mem. Nat. Mus. of Women in the Arts, N.J. Conservation Found., Nat. Trust Hist. Preservation, Am. Littoral Soc., Kappa Delta Pi. Avocations: world travel, environmental activism. Home: PO Box 329 Cedar Knolls NJ 07927-0329

VAN WETTERING, CAROLYN, elementary school educator; d. Elton R. Stroud; m. David A. Van Wettering, Aug. 8, 1980; children: Michael, Kristen. BS in Edn., Ea. N.Mex. U., Portales, 1993. Tchr. Portales HS, 1994—2004, Portales Jr. HS, 1994—.

VANZANT, IYANLA, writer; b. Bklyn., 1953; married; 3 children. BS summa cum laude, Medgar Evers Coll., 1983; JD, Queens Coll. Law Sch., 1988. Host Iyanla (TV talk show), 2001; founder, exec. dir. Inner Visions Worldwide Network, Inc., Silver Spring, Md.; lawyer; ordained minister; inspirational spkr. Author: Tapping the Power Within: A Path to Self-Empowerment for Black Women, 1992, Acts of Faith: Daily Meditations for People of Color, 1993 (BlackBoard Book Yr., 1994), The Value in the Valley: A Black Woman's Guide Through Life's Dilemmas, 1995 (BlackBoard Book Yr., 1995), Interiors: A Black Woman's Healing in Progress, 1995, Faith in the Valley: Lessons for Women on the Journey to Peace, 1996 (BlackBoard Book Yr., 1996), The Spirit of a Man: A Vision of Transformation of Black Men and the Women Who Love Them, 1997, The Big Book of Faith, 1997, Success Gems: Your Personal Motivation Success guide, 1997, In the Meantime: Finding Yourself and the Love You Want, 1998, One Day My Soul Just Opened Up: Forty Days and Forty Nights Toward Spiritual Strength and Personal Growth, 1998, Yesterday I Cried: Celebrating the Lessons of Living and Loving, 1999, Don't Give It Away: A Work Book of Self Awareness and Self Affirmation, 1999, The Good Company: A Woman's Journal for Spiritual Reflection, 1999, Daily Ghetto Mediations: Affirmations for the Ghetto in You, 1999, Until Today!: Daily Devotions for Spiritual Balance and Peace of Mind, 2001, Up from Here: Reclaiming the Male Spirit, 2002, Every Day I Pray, 2001, Living Through the Meantime, 2001. Nat. spokesperson Literacy Vol. Am. Recipient Alumni Yr., Nat. Assn. Equal Opportunity Edn., 1994, Oni award, Internat. Congress Black Women. Mailing: Inner Visions Worldwide Network Inc 926 Phila Ave Silver Spring MD 20910 Office Phone: 301-608-8750. Office Fax: 301-608-3813.

VAN ZANTE, SHIRLEY M(AE), magazine editor; b. Elma, Iowa; d. Vernon E. and Georgene (Woodmansee) Borland; m. Dirk C. Van Zante. AA, Grandview Coll., 1950; BA, Drake U., 1952. Assoc. editor Mchts. Trade Jour., Des Moines, 1952-55; copywriter Meredith Pub. Co., Des Moines, 1955-60, book editor, 1960-67; home furnishings editor Better Homes and Gardens Spl. Interest Publs., Meredith Corp., 1967-74; home furnishing and design editor Better Homes and Gardens mag., 1974-89; writer, editl. cons., 1989-98. Named Advt. Woman of Yr. in Des Moines, 1961; recipient Dorothy Dawe award, 1971, 73, 75, 76, 77, Dallas Market Ctr. award, 1983, So. Furniture Market Writer's award, 1984. Mem. Alpha Xi Delta. Address: 1905 74th St Des Moines IA 50322-5701

VANZURA, LIZ (ELIZABETH K. VANZURA), automotive executive; b. May 1964; m. Rick Vanzura; children: Danielle, Jacqueline. BS, GMI Engring. and Mgmt. Inst.; MBA, Harvard U. With GM Corp., 1984—96, global dir. mktg. Hummer, 2001—06, mktg. dir. Cadillac, 2006—; dir. mktg. Volkswagen of Am., 1995—2000. Exec. bd. mem. Internat. Automotive Advt. Awards. Named Marketer of Yr., Advertising Age, 1998; named one of Top 100 Mktg. Profls., 1999; recipient Top Women to Watch Award, 2001, All Star award, Automotive News, 1999, 2000. Office Phone: 313-556-5000. Office Fax: 313-556-5108.*

VARDALOS, NIA, actress, screenwriter; b. Winnipeg, Can., Sept. 24, 1962; d. Constantine and Doreen Vardalos; m. Ian Gomez, 1993. Attended, Ryerson U. Actor: (films) No Experience Necessary, 1996, Men Seeking Women, 1997, Short Cinema, 1998, Meet Prince Charming, 1999, (also writer) My Big Fat Greek Wedding, 2002, (also writer, exec. prodr.) Connie and Carla, 2004, (voice): (TV series) Team Knight Rider, 1997, (guest appearance): High Incident, 1996, Common Law, 1996, The Drew Carey Show, 1997, Boy Meets World, 1998, It's Like, You Know, 1999, Two Guys, a Girl, and a Pizza Place, 1999, Curb Your Enthusiasm, 2000. Office: c/o Brillstein Grey Mgmt 9150 Wilshire Blvd Ste 350 Beverly Hills CA 90212

VARDAVAS, STEPHANIE J., lawyer; b. Balt., Aug. 3, 1956; d. John and Elaine V. BA, Yale U., 1979; JD, Fordham U., 1985. Bar: NY 1986. Exec. trainee Maj. League Baseball Office of Commr., N.Y.C., 1979-80, asst. counsel, 1986—89; mgr. waivers and player records Am. League of Profl. Baseball Clubs, N.Y.C., 1980-85; v.p. legal and bus. affairs ProServ, Inc. (SFX Sports), 1989—97; atty. endorsement and league affairs Nike, Inc., N.Y.C., 1997—. Vol. D'Amours for U.S. Senate, N.H., 1984, Kanjorski for U.S. Ho. of Reps., Pa., 1986, Mark Green for U.S. Senate, N.Y., 1986, Dukakis for Pres., N.Y., 1988, Clinton-Gore, 1992-96, Gore-Lieberman, 2000, Howard Dean for Pres., 2004; pres. Friends of the Multnomah County Libr. Mem.: ABA (forum com. on the entertainment and sports law industries), Sports Lawyers Assn. (bd. dirs. and co-chair tech. com.). Democrat. Greek Orthodox. Avocations: reading, writing, photography, travel. Office: Nike World Headquarters One Bowerman Dr Beaverton OR 97005-6453

VARELLAS, SANDRA MOTTE, judge; b. Anderson, S.C., Oct. 17, 1946; d. James E. and Helen Lucille (Gilliam) Motte; m. James John Varellas, July 3, 1971; children: James John III, David Todd. BA, Winthrop U., 1968; MA, U. Ky., 1970, JD, 1975. Bar: Ky. 1975, Fla. 1976, U.S. Dist. Ct. (ea. dist.) Ky. 1975, U.S. Ct. Appeals (6th cir.) 1976, U.S. Supreme Ct. 1978. Instr. Midway Coll., Ky., 1970-72; adj. prof. U. Ky. Coll. Law, Lexington, 1976-78; instr. dept. bus. adminstrn. U. Ky., Lexington, 1976-78; ptnr. Varellas, Pratt & Cooley, Lexington, 1975-93, Varellas & Pratt, Lexington, 1993-97, Varellas & Varellas, Lexington, 1998—. Fayette County judge exec., Ky., 1980—; hearing officer Ky. Natural Resources and Environ. Protection Cabinet, Frankfort, 1984-88; bd. trustees Lexington Network 1994-98, 2002-2004, sec., 1994-98. Committeewoman Ky. Young Dems., Frankfort, 1977-80; pres. Fayette County Young Dems., Lexington, 1977; bd. dirs. Ky. Dem. Women's Club, Frankfort, 1980-84, bd. dirs., Bluegrass Estate Planning Coun., 1995-98; grad. Leadership Lexington, 1981; chairwoman Profl. Women's Forum, Lexington, Ky., 1985-86, bd. dirs., 1984-87, Aequum award com., 1989-92; mem. devel. coun. Midway Coll., 1990-92; co-chair Gift Club Com., 1992; mem. pub. svc. sector com. United Way of Bluegrass, 2004. Named Outstanding Young Dem. Woman, Ky. Young Dems., Frankfort, 1977, Outstanding Former Young Dem., Ky. Young Dems., 1983. Mem. Ky. Bar Assn. (treas. young lawyers divsn. 1978-79, long range planning com. 1988-89), Fla. Bar, Fayette County Bar Assn. (treas. 1977-78, bd. govs. 1978-80), LWV (nominating com. 1984-85), Greater Lexington C. of C. (legis. affairs com. 1994-95, bd.ed irs. coun. smaller enterprises 1992-95), The Lexington Forum (bd. dirs. 1996-99), Lexington Philharm. Guild (bd. dirs. 1979-81, 86—), Nat. Assn. Women Bus. Owners (chmn. cmty. liaison/govtl. affairs com. 1992-93). Office: Varellas & Varellas 167 W Main St Ste 1310 Lexington KY 40507-1398

VARGA, DEBORAH TRIGG, music educator, entertainment company owner; b. Dayton, Ohio, Dec. 15, 1955; d. Ernest Cushman and Phyllis Ann (Martz) Trigg; m. Ali M. Abadi, Dec. 30, 1980 (div. July 1987); 1 child, Darren Vincent; m. Richard Charles Varga, June 25, 1994; 1 child, Kathryn Lenore. B of Music Edn. in Violin Performance, Converse Coll., Spartanburg, S.C., 1977. Music educator Seminole County Sch. Bd., Sanford, Fla., 1978-92, Howard County Pub. Schs., Ellicott City, Md., 1993—. Co-founder, co-owner Gold Star Entertainement, Inc., Orlando, Fla., 1984-86, Ctr. Stage Entertainment, Inc., Maitland, Fla., 1986-92; owner Varga Music Entertainement, Highland, Md., 1993—, Composer: children's songs, 1990—, Martin Luther King Tribute, Human Rights Commn., Howard County, 1997—2000. Mem. Am. Fedn. Musicians, Music Educators Nat. Conf., Am. String. Tchrs. Assn., Nat. Orch. Assn. Avocations: waterskiing, whitewater rafting, tennis, golf, reading. Home: 13464 Allnutt Ln Highland MD 20777-9743 Office Phone: 443-812-9437. E-mail: vargaent@comcast.net.

VARGAS, ELIZABETH, newscaster; b. Paterson, NJ, Sept. 6, 1962; m. Marc Cohn, July 20, 2002; children: Zachary Raphael, Samuel Wyatt; 2 stepchildren. BA in Journalism, U. Mo., Columbia. Reporter/anchor KOMU-TV, Columbia, Mo.; reporter KTVN-TV, Reno; lead reporter KTVK-TV, Phoenix, 1986—89; reporter/anchor WBBM-TV, Chgo., 1989—93; corr./anchor NBC News, NYC, 1993—97; corr. Dateline, NBC, NYC, 1993—96; news anchor, substitute co-host Good Morning Am., NBC, NYC, 1996—97; corr. ABC News, NYC, 1997—2005, co-anchor, 20/20 newsmagazine, 2004—; interim anchor ABC World News Tonight, NYC, 2005, co-anchor, 2006. Recipient Emmy award for Outstanding Instant Coverage of News Story (Elian Gonzales case), 2000. Office: ABC News Press Rels Fl 2 47 W 66th St New York NY 10023-6201*

VARGAS, LENA BESSETTE, nursing administrator; b. Hardwick, Vt., Dec. 26, 1922; d. Leon Alphonse and Dorilla Leah (Boudreau) Bessette; m. Jose Emilio Vargas, Sept. 3, 1949; children: Jose Emilio, Maria del Carmen, J. Ramon, Vicente Andres, Yolanda Teresa. BS in Nursing Edn., U. Vt., 1949. Instr. basic nursing Mary Fletcher Hosp., Burlington, Vt., 1947-49; clin. instr. St. Francis Hosp., Evanston, Ill., 1949-50; nurse participant streptomycin therapy research H.M. Biggs Meml. Hosp., Ithaca, N.Y., 1950-51; supr. ancillary personnel Providence Hosp., Washington, 1953-55, asst. dir. nursing, 1965—87, adminstrv. supr., 1987—2005. Mem. coun., del. coop. congress Greenbelt Coop., Savage, Md., 1983-86; bd. dirs. Providence Hosp. Fed. Credit Union, Washington, 1977-80, v.p. bd. dirs., 1983-85. Mem. AAUW (chmn. various coms., chair Kensington del. to nat. conv. 1991, gift to Ednl. Found. named in her honor by Kensington br. 1992, del. US/China Conf. on Women's Issues, Beijing 1995), Am. Nurses Assn. (cert. nursing adminstr.), Christ Child Soc Roman Catholic. Avocations: bridge, travel, real estate, horseback riding. Home: 10706 Keswick St Garrett Park MD 20896-0130 Personal E-mail: lenavargas@earthlink.net.

VARGAS, SYLVIA ELIA, dentist, small business owner; d. Jose Elio and Sylvia Yolanda Vargas; 1 child, Luis Gerardo. M Spanish, Tex. A&M Internat. U., Laredo, 2003. Cert. tchr. Tex. Sec. ed. Spanish tchr. United Ind. Sch. Dist., Laredo, 1995—; adj. faculty mem. Laredo C.C., 1998—2006. Author: (poetry) Letter To My Mother (SECOND Pl. -ADULT CATEGORY, 2000). Office: 3600 E Del Mar Boulevard Laredo TX 78045 Office Phone: 956-473-2216.

VARGAS STIDVENT, VERONICA, federal agency administrator; m. Chris Stidvent. BA, Tex. U.; JD, Yale U. Law clk. to Hon. Sidney Fitzwater U.S. Dist. Ct. Tex. (no. dist.), Dallas; assoc. Vinson & Elkins, LLP, Austin, Tex.; spl. asst. to adminstr. of info. and regulatory affairs Office Mgmt. and Budget, Washington; spl. asst. to Pres. for policy The White House, Washington; asst. sec. for policy U.S. Dept. Labor, Washington, 2004—. Office: US Dept Labor 200 Constitution Ave NW Rm S2006 Washington DC 20210 Office Phone: 202-693-5959. Office Fax: 202-693-5960.

VARGAS-TONSING, TIFFANYE, medical educator; b. El Paso, Tex. BA in Psychology, U. Tex., Austin, 2000; MA in Counseling Psychology, Mich. State U., E. Lansing, 2002, PhD in Sport and Exercise Psychology, 2004. Asst. prof. U. Tex., San Antonio, 2004—. Presenter in field. Contbr. articles to profl. jours., chapters to books. Grantee, U. Tex., Coll. Edn. and Human Devel., 2005, 2006. Mem.: APA, N.Am. Soc. Psychology Sport and Phys. Activity, Am. Alliance Health, Phys. Edn., Recreation and Dance, Nat. Assn. Sport and Phys. Edn., Nat. Coun. Accreditation Coaching Edn., Assn. Advanced Applied Sport Psychology (cert. cons.). Office: Univ Tex San Antonio Dept Health and Kinesiology 6900 North Loop 1604 W San Antonio TX 78249 Office Phone: 210-458-6228.

VARGAS-WILLIAMS, TRACI JUNELLE, special education educator; b. Wichita, Kans., Mar. 30, 1964; d. Judith Ann and James Dwayne Hilliard (Stepfather); m. Vance Allen Williams; children: Steven Dwayne, Christopher Jordan. BS, Northeastern State U., 1997, BEd, 2005. Emotional disturbance Okla. State Dept. Edn., learning disability Okla. State Dept. Edn., other health impairment Okla. State Dept. Edn., autism Okla. State Dept. Edn. Spl. educator Claremore Pub. Schs., Okla., 1997—2006; spl. educator Cherry Tree Elem. Sch. Carmel-Clay Sch. Dist., 2006—. Trainer Crisis Prevention and Intervention, Claremore, 2000—; presenter Diffusing Volatile Situations in Classrooms Okla. Edn. Assn. Conv.; candidate Nat. Bd. Profl. Tchg. Standards, 2005. Named Tchr. of Yr., 1998, 2004. Mem.: NEA (corr.), CEC (corr.), Okla. Edn. Assn. (corr.), Union H.S. Key Club (assoc.; pres. 1981—82), Future Tchrs. of Am. (assoc.; treas. 1993—94). Democrat. Avocations: gardening, reading. Home: 203 E 36th St Anderson IN 46013 Office: Cherry Tree Elem Sch 13989 Hazel Dell Pl Carmel IN 46033 Office Phone: 317-846-3086. E-mail: vanceandtraci@sbcglobal.net.

VARGHESE, MARY, secondary school educator; b. Mavelikara, Kerala, India, May 30, 1952; d. Joshua Puthenmadhom Zachariah and Kunjamma Joshua; m. Manalel Varghese, May 24, 1976; children: Renju Annu, Roger. BS, U. Kerala, 1973, BEd, 1975. Cert. secondary tchr. Tchr. St. John's High Sch., Kerala, 1977-81, Leulu Moega Fou Coll., Apia, AS, 1981-84, Leone (AS) High Sch., 1984—. Sponsor, advisor Sci. Club, 1984—; chair com. judging Sci. Fair, 1989-90. Recipient Commendation award Internat. Sci. and Engring. Fair, Washington, 1990, recipient Excellence in Teaching Sci. award (U.S. Ter.), 1993. Mem. ASCD, Nat. Assn. Biology Tchrs. (Outstanding Tchr. 1990), Sci. Tchrs. Assn. AS., (recipient Presdl. award), 1992 Avocation: gardening. Home: PO Box 4740 Pago Pago AS 96799-4740 Office: Leone HS Pago Pago AS 96799

VARGO, JERI, librarian; b. Easton, Pa., Mar. 30, 1948; d. Louis Harry and Ethelyn Theitis (Adam) V. BA in English, Wells Coll., 1970; MLS, Simmons Coll., 1976; MA in English Lit., U. Mass., 1984. Acquisitions librarian U. Mass., Boston, 1973-76, head acquisitions librarian, 1976-78, chief acquisitions librarian, 1978-85; acquisitions librarian Syracuse (N.Y.) U., 1985-86; head librarian Wells Coll., Aurora, N.Y., 1986—. Mem.: Aurora Wells. Democrat. Home: PO Box 143 Aurora NY 13026-0143 Office: Wells Coll Libr Main St Aurora NY 13026

VARGO, LOUISE ANN, landscape artist, music educator; b. LaGrange, Ill., Oct. 30, 1974; d. Charles Patrick and Loretta Ann Vargo. BA, Benedictine U., Lisle, Ill., 1997. Irrigation designer Century Rain Aid, Downers Grove, Ill., 1996—99; piano tchr. Louise Vargo Studio, Plainfield, Ill., 1997—; irrigation designer John Deere Landscapes, Downers Grove, 2002—05, irrigation design mgr., 2006—. Sales cons. Mary Kay Cosmetics, Plainfield, 2003—. Mem.: Music Educators Nat. Conf. Avocations: gardening, cooking. Home: 13605 Golden Meadow Dr Plainfield IL 60544 Personal E-mail: louisevargo@hotmail.com.

VARILEK, JULIE, music educator; b. Fort Dodge, Iowa, Mar. 14, 1956; d. Earl and Mavis Freeman; m. Charles Varilek, Aug. 5, 1978; children: Jennifer Marie, Audra Ann. BFA, U. SD, Vermillion, 1974—78. Music tchr. Bon Homme Sch. Dist., Tyndall, SD, 1980—85, Centerville Pub. Sch. Dist., SD, 1985—89, Thompson Sch. Dist., Loveland, Colo., 1990—95, Pk. Sch. Dist., Estes Park, Colo., 1995—. Ch. choir dir. Our Lady Mountains Cath. Ch., Estes Park, 1995—2006; mem. Fine Arts Guild Rockies, Estes Park, 2003—06. Recipient Outstanding Women Educator of Yr., AAUW, 2000. Mem.: Delta Kappa Gamma (mem. tchrs. orgn. 1993—2003, v.p. 1995—97), Rotary (hon.). Home: 1010 Acacia Dr Estes Park CO 80517 Office: Estes Park Intermediate Sch 1505 Brodie Ave Estes Park CO 80517

VARIS, AGNES, pharmaceutical executive; b. Lowell, Mass., 1930; d. Dionysis and Demetroula Koulovaris; m. Karl Leichtman. B in English and Chemistry, Brooklyn Coll.; D of Public Service (hon.), Tufts U., 2003. From entry-level chemist to exec. v.p. Fine Organics Inc., 1950—70; founder Agvar Chemicals, 1970—; co-founder Marsam Pharmaceuticals, 1985—; founder, pres. Aegis Pharmaceuticals, 1992—. Mem. consolidated corp. fund Lincoln Ctr.; pres., trustee MAKK Found.; bd. overseers Tufts Sch. Veterinary Medicine; bd. dirs. Nat. Org. Rare Disorders (NORD), Eleanor Roosevelt Legacy Com.; mng. dir. Met. Opera; bd. trustees Tufts U., 2004. Recipient Industry Leadership award, Nat. Org. Rare Disorders (NORD), 1999. Mem.: Sales Assn. Chemical Industry, Drug Chemical Allied Trade Assn., Chemist Club. Office: Agvar Chemicals 58 Rte 15 Little Falls NJ 07424*

VARKEY, PRATHIBHA, preventive medicine physician, medical educator; b. N.Y., Apr. 12, 1974; MD, Christian Med. Coll., Dr. M.G.R. Med. U., Vellore, Tamil Nadu, India, 1995; MPH in Health Care Mgmt., Harvard Sch. Pub. Health, 2001. Resident internal medicine Hosp. St. Raphael, New Haven, 1997—2000; fellow gen. preventive medicine and pub. health Mayo Clinic, Rochester, 2001—03, asst. prof. preventive medicine and internal medicine, dir. assoc. program preventive medicine fellowship. Mem.: AMA Found. (Excellence in Medicine Leadership award 2004). Office: Mayo Clinic 200 First St SW Rochester MN 55905*

VARLEY, ELIZABETH GAIL, social worker; b. Chapel Hill, N.C., Nov. 5, 1954; d. Robert Sr. and Anne Dysart V.; m. Roger Douglas Perk; 1 child, Justin. BA, U. N.C., Wilmington, 1976; MSW, U. N.C., 1980. Social worker II Dept. Social Svcs., Wilmington; sr. social worker Children's Home Soc. Fla., Ft. Myers, 1983-93; sr. children and families counselor Dept. Health and Rehab. Svcs., Ft. Myers, 1993-94; field instr. profl. devel. ctr. U. S.Fla., Tampa, 1994-99; med. social worker Lee Meml. Health Sys., Ft. Myers, 1999—. Founder, adminstrv. cons. Family Connection Ctr., Ft. Myers, 1994—; adj. faculty Coll. Profl. Studies, Fla. Gulf Coast U., 1998-2005. Mem. NASW (Fla. chpt., S.W. unit, legis. chair, newsletter editor). Democrat. Episcopalian. Avocation: fencing. Home: 15341 Thornton Rd Fort Myers FL 33908-6802 Office: Lee Meml Health Sys Health Pk Campus 9981 Health Park Cir Fort Myers FL 33908 Fax: 941-489-3543. Personal E-mail: gailvarley@comcast.net.

VARNER, CHARLEEN LAVERNE MCCLANAHAN, nutritionist, educator, administrator, dietitian; b. Alba, Mo., Aug. 28, 1931; d. Roy Calvin and Lela Ruhama (Smith) McClanahan; student Joplin (Mo.) Jr. Coll., 1949-51; BS in Edn., Kans. State Coll. Pittsburg, 1953; MS, U. Ark., 1958; PhD, Tex. Woman's U. 1966; postgrad. Mich. State U., 1955, U. Mo., 1962; m. Robert Bernard Varner, July 4, 1953. Apprentice county home agt. U. Mo., 1952; tchr. Ferry Pass Sch., Escambia County, Fla., 1953-54; tchr. biology, home econs. Joplin Sr. H.S., 1954-59; instr. home econs. Kans. State Coll., Pittsburg, 1959-63; lectr. foods, nutrition Coll. Household Arts and Scis., Tex. Woman's U., 1963-64, rsch. asst. NASA grant, 1964-66; assoc. prof. home econs. Central Mo. State U., Warrensburg, 1966-70, adviser to Colhecon, 1966-70, adviser to Alpha Sigma Alpha, 1967-70, 72, bd. adv. Honors Group, 1967-70; prof., head dept. home econs. Kans. State Tchrs. Coll., Emporia, 1970-73; prof., chmn. dept. home econs. Benedictine Coll., Atchison, Kans., 1973-74; prof., chmn. dept. home econs. Baker U., Baldwin City, Kans., 1974-75; owner, operator Diet-Con Dietary Cons. Enterprises, cons. dietitian, 1973—, Home-Con Cons. Enterprises; adj. prof. Highland (Kans.) CC, 2004—. Active Joplin Little Theater, 1956-60. Mem. NEA, AAUW, AAUP, Mo. State Tchr. Assn., Kans. State Tchr. Assn., Am. Dietetic Assn., Mo. Dietetic Assn., Kans. Dietetic Assn., Am. Home Econs. Assn., Mo. Home Econs. Assn., Kans. Home Econs. Assn., Mo. Acad. Scis., U. Ark. Alumni Assn., Alumni Assn. Kans. State Coll. of Pittsburg, Am. Vocat. Assn., Assn. Edn. Young Children, Sigma Xi, Beta Sigma Phi, Beta Beta Beta, Alpha Sigma Alpha, Delta Kappa Gamma, Kappa Kappa Iota, Phi Upsilon Omicron, Theta Alpha Pi, Kappa Phi. Methodist (organist). Home: PO Box 1009 Topeka KS 66601-1009

VARNER, CHILTON DAVIS, lawyer; b. Opelika, Ala., Mar. 12, 1943; d. William Cole and Frances (Thornton) Davis; m. K. Morgan Varner, III, June 19, 1965; 1 child, Ashley Elizabeth Davis. AB with distinction, Smith Coll., 1965; JD with distinction, Emory U., 1976. Assoc. King & Spalding, Atlanta, 1976-83, ptnr., 1983—. Bd. dirs. Wesley Woods Healthcare, 11th Cir. Ct. Appeals Hist. Soc.; trustee Emory U., Atlanta, 1995—, Product Liability Adv. Coun. Found., 1996—2004; mem. Adv. Com. Fed. Civil Rules, 2004—. Author: Appellate Handbook for Georgia Lawyers, 1995. Mem. Leadership Atlanta, 1984—85; mem. exec. com. Atlanta Arts Alliance, 1981—85; mem. Atlanta Symphony Chorus, 1970—74; asst. clk., elder, bd. elders Trinity Presbyn. Ch., Atlanta, 1975—88. Recipient Disting. Alumna award, Emory U. Law Sch., 1998. Fellow: Am. Coll. Trial Lawyers; mem.: ABA (mem. adv. com. fed. civil rules 2004—), Atlanta Bar Assn., Ga. Bar Assn., Phi Beta Kappa, Order of Coif. Office: King & Spalding 191 Peachtree St NE Ste 4900 Atlanta GA 30303-1740 Office Phone: 404-572-4789.

VARNER, HELEN, communications educator; b. Biddeford, Maine, Jan. 21, 1946; d. E. Harold Kemper and Darlene Ruth (Marcus) Meeks; m. Foy E. Varner, Jr., May 26, 1977; children: Dawn Hedgpeth, Jennifer Thompson, Foy E. III. B in Applied Arts and Scis., Stephen F. Austin State U., 1981, MA, 1983; EdD, Tex. A&M U., 1990. Reporter Galveston (Tex.) Daily News, 1964-65; acct. exec. John Gilbert Advt. Agy., Miami, Fla., 1965-67; chief Correspondence Sch., U.S. Army Edn. Ctr., Mannhiem, Germany, 1967-70; coord. pub. info. Galveston Coll., 1970-74; pub. rels., advt. dir. Sea-Arama Marineworld, Inc., Galveston, 1974-77; owner, chief exec. officer The Varner Pub. Rels. & Advt. Agy., Galveston, 1977-81; instr. Stephen F. Austin State U., Nacogdoches, Tex., 1981-88; assoc. prof. journalism N.E. La. U., Monroe, La., 1988-90, Chaminade U. of Honolulu, 1990-91; assoc. prof. comm. Hawaii Pacific U., Honolulu, 1991—, v.p. univ. rels. and dean of comm., 1998. Pres. Galveston Conv. & Vis. Bur., Galveston, 1978-79. Pres. Galveston Press Club, 1977, ARC, Galveston Chpt., 1976, Nacogdoches Chpt., 1980; dir. Girl Scouts Am, Gulf Coast, Galveston, 1976. Named Outstanding Adviser Pub. Rels. Student Soc. Am., 1989, Outstanding Prof. Omicron Delta Kappa, 1989, Favorite Prof. Alpha Lambda Delta, 1988; recipient Mentor award Mortarboard Sr. Leadership Soc., 1990, Outstanding Adviser award Women In Communication, Inc., 1986-87, 85-86, Lifetime Achievement award Internat. Assn. Bus. Com., 2004. Mem. Assn. for Edn. in Journalism and Mass Communication, Tex. Pub. Rels. Assn. (pres. 1987-88), Pub. Rels. Soc. Am. (Gregg W. Perry award 2004), Pub. Rels. Assn. La. (sec. 1989), So. Pub. Rels. Fedn., Women In Communications (pres. Honolulu Profl. chpt. 1995-96), Orgn. of Women Leaders (Woman Leader of Yr. 1995-96), Pub. Rels. Found. Tex. Avocation: dragon collection. Home: PMB 22008 PO Box 190 Jefferson OR 97352-0190 Office Phone: 808-544-0825. E-mail: hvarner@hpu.edu, communication@hpu.edu.

VARNER, JOYCE EHRHARDT, retired librarian; b. Quincy, Ill., Sept. 13, 1938; d. Wilbur John and Florence Elizabeth (Mast) Ehrhardt; m. Donald Giles Varner, Sept. 12, 1959; children: Amy, Janice, Christian, Matthew, Nadine. BA, Northeastern Okla. State U., 1980; MLS, U. Okla., 1984. Lab. analyst Gardner Denver Co., Quincy, 1956-60; sales rep. Morrisonville, Ill., 1963-69; libr. clk. U. Ill., Urbana, 1973-75; libr. tech. asst. Northeastern Okla. State U., Tahlequah, 1976-86; asst. reference libr. Muskogee (Okla.) Pub. Libr., 1986-90; libr. Jess Dunn Correctional Ctr., Taft, Okla., 1990-98; ret., 1998; field office supr. Census 2000 Dept. of Commerce, Welling, Okla., 1998. Editor Indian Nations Audubon Nature Notes, 1977-81, 96—; contbr. articles to newspaper. Vol. Lake-Wood coun. Girl Scouts U.S.A., 1975-98, bd. dirs. 1992-98, pres., 1995-96; sec.-treas. Cherokee County Rural Water Dist. 7, 1987—; edn. chmn. Indian Nations chpt. Nat. Audubon Soc., 1989-2000, pres., 2000-04; project dir. Tahlequah Friends of the Libr., 2002-04, pres. 2004—. Recipient Thanks Badge, Lake-Wood coun. Girl Scouts U.S.A., 1990. Mem. AAUW (chair diversity com. 2000), Okla. Libr. Assn. (nominating com. 1989), Okla. Acad. Sci., Okla. Ornithol. Soc. (chmn. libr. com. 1978-88, Award of Merit 1990, pres.-elect 1994, pres. 1995-96), Alpha Chi, Beta Beta Beta, Phi Delta Kappa (Found. rep. 1984-86, historian 1992-2006). Avocations: nature study, needlecrafts, square dancing, genealogy.

VARNER, MARLEEN ALLEN, retired academic administrator; b. West Chester, Pa., May 6, 1932; d. Lester Rueben and Florance Winegar Bengel; m. William Theodore Allen (dec. June 1965); children: David Avery Allen, Paul Charlton Allen; m. James Edward Ingle (div. Oct. 1980); 1 child, Jay Edward Ingle; m. Carroll H. Varner, Apr. 8, 1998 (dec. Apr. 2006); stepchildren: Carolyn R. Stone, Katherine M., Corinne, Caroll H. III. Student, U. Buffalo, 1949—51; AB, Coll. Wooster, Ohio, 1953; MA, Syracuse U., NY, 1956. Sec. World U. Svc., NYC, 1953—54; asst. instr. edn. Syracuse U., 1956—57; dir. reading and study skills lab. Franklin & Marshall Coll., Lancaster, Pa., 1958—59; dir. fin. aid and placement U. South, Sewanee, Tenn., 1967—69; dir. state grant programs Ky. Higher Edn., Frankfort, 1974—80; dir. fin. aid U. NC, Greensboro, 1980—93; ret. Counselor, tchr. history Elizabethtown Area High Sch., Pa., 1957—58. Contbr. articles to profl. jours. Tax aide instr., vol. Am. Assn. Ret. Persons, 2002—; sec. Carpenter's Home Estates Resident Assn., 2002—06; life mem. Fla. Life Care Residents Assn., 2005—, sec., 2002—05; life mem. Nat. Continuing Care Residents Assn., 2005, v.p., 2006—; comty. vol.; mem. Friends of the Libr., U. South Lakeland, Fla., 2001—, Sewanee Civic Assn., Tenn., 1993—, pres., 1996—97. Recipient Leadership award, U.S. Dept. Edn. Qualityh Control Project, 1991; fellow, Soc. Advancement Fin. Aid Mgmt. in Higher Edn., 1991. Mem.: Assn. Retarded Citizens (Tenn. pres. trust 1995—), Junaluska Assocs. (assoc.; life mem., v.p. 2000—02), EQB Club Sewanee (pres. 1997—99), Sewanee Woman's Club (EH Hosp. aux., life mem., pres. 1964—65), Pi Sigma Alpha, Phi Delta Kappa, Pi Lambda Theta, Delta Kappa Gamma. Democrat. Methodist. Avocations: travel, music, reading, bridge. Home: 1001 Carpenters Way G106 Lakeland FL 33809

VARNER, VICKY JO, actor, counselor; d. Robert Greer and Vera Fern Varner; m. Robin Wiley, May 1, 2002. BFA, Stephens Coll., Columbia, Mo., 1979. Cert. profl. co-active coach Coaches Tng. Inst., Calif., qualified MBTI practitioner TRI, Calif., cert. MBTI practitioner Myers-Briggs Found., job and career devel. coach Career Trainer Inc. Computer cons., Hollywood, Calif., 1980—96; self-discovery specialist Type Insights, Hollywood, 1996—. Editl. advisor Interstrength Assocs., Santa Ana, Calif., 1996—. Editor: 8 Keys to Self-Leadership (Dario Nardi), An Introduction to the Personality Type Code (Linda V. Berens and Dario Nardi), Dynamics of Personality Type (Linda V. Berens); actor: (movie) Cannibal Women in the Avocado Jungle of Death. Vol. advisor Foshay HS, LA, 2004—. Mem.: SAG, AFTRA, Assn. for Psychol. Type, Internat. Coach Fedn., Mensa, Acad. Magical Arts (assoc.). Avocations: travel, Celtic mythology, quilting. Office: Type Insights 7095 Hollywood Blvd # 333 Hollywood CA 90028 Office Phone: 323-469-1844. E-mail: vj@vickyjo.com.

VARNEY, CHRISTINE A., federal official; Degree in Politics, Philosophy and Econs. (hon.), Trinity Coll., Dublin, Ireland, 1975; BA in Polit. Sci. and History magna cum laude, SUNY, Albany, 1977; MPA in Policy Analysis, Legislation and Rsch. magna cum laude, Syracuse U., 1978; JD cum laude, Georgetown U., 1986. Legis. asst. N.Y. Senate, Albany, 1977; econ. analyst GAO, Washington, 1978; econ. devel. dir. El Centro, Calif., 1979; dir. Neighborhood Outreach Program, San Diego, 1980-82; assoc. Surry & Morse, Washington, 1984-86, Pierson, Semmes & Finley, Washington, 1986-88; counsel Hogan & Hartson, Washington, 1990-92; chief counsel Clinton for Pres. Primary Campaign, 1992, Clinton-Gore Campaign, 1992; gen. counsel Dem. Nat. Com., 1992, Presdl. Inauguration Com., 1993; dep. asst. to President U.S., sec. to Cabinet The White House, Washington, 1993-94; commissioner FTC, Washington, 1994—97; ptnr. Hogan & Hartson LLP, Washington, 1997—, mem. exec. com. Active Women's Legal Def. Fund. Mem. D.C. Bar Assn., N.Y. State Bar Assn., Nat. Lawyer's Coun. Office: Hogan & Hartson Columbia Sq 555 Thirteenth St NW Washington DC 20004-1109 Office Phone: 202-637-6823. Office Fax: 202-637-5910. Business E-Mail: cavarney@hhlaw.com.

VARNUM, CHARIS, writer, educator; MPA, Columbia U., NYC, 1991. Writer, cons., NYC, 1994—. Adj. prof. Columbia U., NYC, 2002—. Contbr. book. Mem. Nat. Orgn. Men Against Sexism, Woman's Nat. Dem. Club, Com. Status of U. Women. Pub. Affairs fellow, Columbia U., 1991. Mem.: NOW. Personal E-mail: clv15@columbia.edu.

VAROGLU, MARY, wholesale distribution executive; b. Mt. Vernon, N.Y., Apr. 11, 1960; d. Jack Walter and Jean (Kish) Milder; m. Salih Varoglu, Oct. 9, 1982. Student, Pace U., 1979-81. Adminstrv. dir. Jingles Internat., N.Y.C., 1982-85; pres. Elite Salon Svcs., Colorado Springs, Colo., 1985—. Mem. Beauty and Barber Supply Inst. Roman Catholic. Home: 2955 Electra Dr Colorado Springs CO 80906-1075

VARRA, DAWN RENEE, elementary school educator; b. Warsaw, Ind., Feb. 24, 1970; d. Gloria Wigent and Samuel Grubb; m. Sudheer Varra, Feb. 24, 1970; children: Ashutosh, Elias; children: Samuel Albertson, Emily Albertson. BS in Math., Purdue U., Ft. Wayne, Ind., 1996—2001. Cert. Secondary Math. Tchr. SBEC, 2002. Math tchr. Pflugerville Ind. Sch. Dist., Tex., 2002—. Student coun. sponsor Dessau Mid. Sch., Austin, 2003—06. Sponsor Student Coun., Pflugerville, 2003—06. Office: Dessau Mid Sch 12900 Dessau Rd Austin TX 78617

VARRO, BARBARA JOAN, retired editor; b. East Chicago, Ind., Jan. 25, 1938; d. Alexander R. and Lottie R. (Bess) V. BA, Duquesne U., 1959. Feature reporter, asst. fashion editor Chgo. Sun-Times, 1959-64, fashion editor, 1964-76, feature writer, 1976-84; v.p. pub. rels. Daniel J. Edelman Inc., Chgo., 1984-85; v.p. PRB/Needham Porter Novelli, Chgo., 1985-86; editor Am. Hosp. Assn. News, Chgo., 1987-94; editor spl. sects. Chgo. Tribune, 1995-2000; ret. Recipient awards for feature writing Ill. AP, 1978, 79, 80 Mem.: PEO. Home: 219 Autumn Trail N Michigan City IN 46360

VARTANIAN, ISABEL SYLVIA, retired dietician; b. Duquesne, Pa. d. Apel and Mary (Kasparian) V. BS, U. Ala., 1957; MS, Columbia U., 1962. Registered dietitian. Dietetic intern N.Y. Hosp./Cornell Med. Ctr., N.Y.C., 1957-58; therapeutic dietitian Vets. Affairs Med. Ctr., Bronx, N.Y., 1958-60, adminstrv. dietitian, 1960-62, nutrition clinic dietitian, 1962-63, rsch. and nutrition clinic dietitian Coral Gables, Fla., 1963, nutrition clinic dietitian Richmond, Va., 1963-66, chief nutritional therapy edn. and rsch. sect., 1966-83, nutrition support dietitian, 1983-2000; ret. Bd. dirs. Richmond Cmty. Action Program, 1978—83, Hopewell Preservation, Inc.; mem. adv. com. Social Svcs., Hopewell, Va., 1991—2001; mem. Sr. Citizens Adv. Commn., 2000—05; bd. trustee Appomattox Regional Libr. Sys., 2000—; mem. Hopewell, Prince Geoge C. of C., 2006—. Recipient Outstanding awards Vets. Affairs Med. Ctr., Superior Performance awards, Outstanding award. Mem. Richmond Dietetic Assn. (chair diet therapy sect. 1966-67, pres.-elect 1967-68, pres. 1968-70, chair Dial-A-Dietitian 1972-74, chair pub. rels. 1973-74, 78-81, chair Divsn. Cmty. Dietetics 1983-85, chair program planning com. 1985), Va. Dietetic Assn. (chair career guidance com. 1963-65, ednl. exhibits 1967, Dial-A-Dietitian 1972-74, pub. rels. 1982-84, visibility campaign 1984, exhibit com. 1984, program planning com. 1988, divsn. cmty. dietetic 1989-91), Va. Soc. Parenteral and Enteral Nutrition (chair program planning com. 1988-89, membership com. 1990), Am. Dietetic Assn. (life), Profl. Va. Dietetic Assn., Woodman World Lodge, Rotary, Am. Legion Aux., Fort Lee Cmty. Action Coun. Home: 2005 Jackson St Hopewell VA 23860-3633

VARY, EVA MAROS, retired chemicals executive; b. Kecskemet, Hungary, Apr. 13, 1933; arrived in U.S., 1958; d. Anthony and Kathleen (Czencz) Maros; m. Eugen Szent-Vary, June 13, 1956 (div. 1958); 1 child, Susan Marie. Chem. engrng. diploma, Tech. U. Budapest (Hungary), 1956; PhD in Phys. Chemistry, UCLA, 1966. Chem. engrng. area supr. Ujpesti Textile Plant, Budapest, 1956-57; chemist geology dept. UCLA, 1958-65; rsch. chemist, staff chemist Fabrics and Finishes Dept. Dupont, Phila., 1966-71, rsch. supr., 1971-79, tech. area supt. Parlin, NJ, 1979-80, asst. plant mgr. Parlin, Toledo, 1980-85; product supt. mng. Tedlar plant Dupont Fabricated Products, Buffalo, 1985-87, environ. cons. Wilmington, Del., 1987-90; dir. product safety, regulatory affairs pigments divsn. Ciba-Geigy Corp., Newport, Del., 1990-98; ret., 1998. Inventor, patentee release coatings. Com. chair Zonta Internat., Toledo, 1984, Buffalo, 1987. Mem. Am. Chem. Soc. Roman Catholic. Avocations: tennis, skiing, travel, photography. Home: 1100 Lovering Ave Apt 1508 Wilmington DE 19806-3288 Personal E-mail: varyeva@aol.com.

VARZEGAR, MINOO, literature educator, reading specialist; b. Kerman, Iran; d. Abdolrahim and Amjad (Vali) Varzegar; m. Saeid Fatemi, May 8; children: Delaram, Arezou. BA in English summa cum laude, U. Tehran, 1966, MA in Psychology, 1969; MA in Tchg. English, U. Tchr. Edn., 1967; MA in Tchg. ESL, U. Ill., 1971, PhD in Tchg. ESL, 1975, postgrad., 1994. Cert. tchr. English, cert. high acad. adminstrn. Asst. prof. U. Tehran, 1979—84, assoc. prof., 1984—94, prof. dept. English, 1984—97, head dept. English of Evening Classes, 1975—83, dir. Lang. Lab., 1975—80, dir. lang. ctr., 1981—83, head dept. English, 1983—97. Vis. prof. U. Ill., Champaign-Urbana, 1997-99, rsch. scholar, 1997-99; assoc. faculty Columbia U., N.Y.C., 1999-2001, exec dir PCF, 2004—; faculty English dept. Rutgers U., Newark, 1999—, William Paterson U., Wayne, NJ, 1999-2001; dir. Ctr. Testing and Psychometrics, Min. of Culture and Higher Edn., Tehran, 1975-77; mem. mng. editl. bd. and adv. bd. PCF Who's Who in The Iranian-Am. Cmty. Author: Children's English series, 1990-95, Reading Through Reading (Best Acad. Book), 1992, Testing and Measurement (Best Acad. Book), 1993, A Comprehensive Grammar of English, 1996, Testing TEFL, 1997; author/editor: Issues in Teaching English as a Second Language, 1990, English for the Students of Medicine, 1989; co-author: English for Medical Students, 1974; editor: English for the Students of Medicine (II), 1993, Novin English-Persian Dictionary, vols. I and II, 1993; co-editor: Yadvareh Persian-English Dictionary, vols. I, II, III, 1991, Yadvareh English-Persian Dictionary, vols. I and II, 1991, Yadvareh Unabridged English-Persian Dictionary, 1993, others; contbr. numerous articles to profl. jours. Mem. com. Ctr. Studying and Compiling Univ Books in Humanities Min. Culture and Higher Edn., 1984—97, mem. com. curriculum devel., 1984—97, com. for testing, 1977—79; mem. com. lang. testing Lang. Ctr., 1979—81. Recipient award for creating an Innovative Model of Reading Comprehension, U. Ill., 1975, Cert. of Appreciation for best adminstrn. U. Mich., 1998, award for extraordinary ability INS, 1998, Disting. Prof. award, 2000, Disting. Rschr. award, 2000, Woman of Achievement award BBC, 2002; U. Ill. grantee, 1975; Fulbright scholar, 1970-75, Profl. Devel. scholar TESOL, 1999; fellow in rsch. U. Ill., 1973-75. Mem. TESOL, U. Ill. Alumni Assn., Am. Assn. for Applied Linguistics, Nat. Coun. Tchrs. English, Internat. Reading Assn. Avocations: reading, painting, tennis, swimming. Home: 290 Anderson St # 6K Hackensack NJ 07601 Office: Rutgers Univ Dept English 156 Conklin Hall 175 Univ Ave Newark NJ 07102 Personal E-mail: varzegar@gmail.com.

VASANA, SUSAN (CHUN-YE), engineering educator; d. De-Jun and Yi-Hua Ye; m. William Vasana, Feb. 14, 2001; children: Danica Hill Chang, Anna Ye Vasana. BS, Shanghai Jiaotong U., 1983; MS, Tongji U., 1986; PhD, Queen's U., Can., 1994. Lectr. Tongji U., Shanghai, 1986—89; scientist Nat. Inst. Sci. Rsch., Montreal, Que., Canada, 1994; sr. staff engr. Motorola Inc., Boynton Beach, Fla., 1994—2002; adj. prof. Fla. Atlantic U., Boca Raton, Fla., 2000—01; prof. U. North Fla., Jacksonville, 2002—. Recipient Silver Quills award, Motorola Inc., 2000. Mem.: IEEE, Internat. Assn. Sci. and Tech. for Devel. Achievements include patents for communication device having antenna switch diversity and method therefor; method and apparatus for demodulating a frequency shift keyed signal; method and apparatus for decoding a 2-level radio signal; method in a selective call receiver for synchronizing to a multi-level radio signal; method and apparatus for baud detection in a communication device; method and apparatus for accurate synchronization using symbol decision feedback; method and apparatus for correlation detection of multi-level signals with non-standard deviations; method and apparatus for automatic simulcast correlation for a correlation detector; method and apparatus for gain normalization of a correlation demodulator. Office: U North Fla 4567 St Johns Bluff Rd S Jacksonville FL 32224

VASEY, ANN L., pre-school administrator, counselor; b. Cleve., May 3, 1949; d. Albert and Norma (Miller) Ringler; m. Graham C. Vasey, Feb. 20, 1972; children: Rachel Nora Vasey, Corinne Elisabeth Vasey. BS in Elem. Edn. and Early Childhood, Boston U., 1972; MEd in Counseling Psychology, Northeastern U., Boston, 1974. Lic. mental health counselor State of Mass., marriage and family therapist State of Mass., cert. clin. mental health counselor Nat. Bd. Cert. Counselors; supr. and dir. K-12 Mass. Dept. Edn., prin. pre-K-6 Mass. Dept. Edn., registered tchr. Yoga Yoga Alliance, cert. Parent Child Home Program, Parent Leadership Tng., EMDR. Adolescent and family therapist SHARE, Lowell, Mass., 1974-76; instr. Framingham (Mass.) State Coll., 1976; instr. psychol. Quinsigamond C.C., Worcester, 1978—92; founding head The Learning Experience Elem. Sch., Marlborough, 1981—88; early childhood coord. Southbridge (Mass.) Pub. Schs., 1993—; psychotherapist YOU, Inc. Family Svcs., 1995—; founding supr. Family Ctr., 2000—. Psychol. cons. Childcare Lab. Sch., Worcester, Mass., 1989—91; founding chair Family Literacy Coalition, Southbridge, 1998—; presenter Assn. Early Childhood Dirs., Oxford, 2002; ednl. and psychol. cons. HMEA Children's Svc., Hudson, 2003; team mem. comprehensive rev. and site visits Mass. Dept. Edn., 2004, 05. Co-author: (tchrs. guide) Some Psychological Issues Concerning Adolescent Debvelopment, 1987. Mem. Mass. Cmty. Partnerships Children, Northboro; bd. mem. Ashland Cultural Coun., Ashland, Mass., 1992—98; pres. bd. dir. Early Childhood Coun., 1993—; steering com. Cmty. Connections, Southbridge, Mass., 1998—. Grantee, Mass. Dept. Edn., 1993—. Mem.: Nat. Assn. Edn. Young Children (validator), Mass. Mental Health Counselors Assn., Delta Kappa Gamma. Avocations: yoga, travel. Home: 83 Woodland Rd Ashland MA 01721-1411 Office: Southbridge Pub Sch 156 West St Southbridge MA 01550 Personal E-mail: arvasey@aol.com.

VASILEFF, LILI ALEXANDRA, financial planner; b. Flushing, NY, Feb. 26, 1955; d. Henry David and Martha Schober Vasileff; m. Stephen Penfield Kressen, Aug. 23, 1980 (div. Jan. 1, 1991); children: Nathaniel David Penfield Kressen, Alexandra Marta Kressen. BA cum laude, Mt. Holyoke Coll., 1977; M Internat. and Pub. Affairs, Columbia U., 1979; cert. in European rels., Inst. d'Etudes Politiques, Paris, 1976. CFP, cert. divorce specialist, investment advisor Conn. Internat. officer Am. Express Internat. Bank, N.Y.C., 1979—80; assoc. Arthur Andersen, Denver, 1980—81; officer Bank of Denver, 1981—84; v.p., internat. treas. Security Pacific Corp., L.A., 1984—89; owner Money Matters!, Woodbridge/Greenwich, Conn., 1991—. Adj. prof. Quinnipiac U., Hamden, Conn., 1993—96. Mem. adv. com. Children With Spl. Health Care Needs., New Haven, 1995—; mem. Conn. Coun. Divorce Mediation, 1997—; bd. dirs. Friends of Yale-New Haven Children's Hosp., New Haven, 1991—. Recipient Dr. Barbar award, Yale-New Haven Children's Hosp., 1996. Mem.: Inst. Divorce Fin. Planners and Fin. Divorce Assn. (cert.), Sarah (ARC), Conn. Coalition for Inclusive Edn., Fin. Planning Assn. (bd. dirs. New Haven chpt.), Assn. Divorce Fin. Planners (pres.). Avocations: ballet, theater, travel, advocate for children with special health care needs. Office: Money Matters! 26 Maple Vale Dr Woodbridge CT 06525 E-mail: lvasileff@aol.com.

VASILYEVA, ANNA, artist, writer; b. Kiev, Ukraine, Nov. 24, 1977; d. Tamara Balenko and Vladimir Vasylyev. Fine Art Degree, T.G. Shevchenko State Art Sch., 1997; BA in Art, Calif. State U., Northridge, 2005. Tchr. asst. KidsArt, Tarzana, Calif., 1999; designer, illustrator Pub. Ho. KM Academia, Kiev, 1996, All Electronics Corp., Van Nuys, Calif., 2002—; tchr. art Marina's Sch. Music and Art, Northridge, Calif., 2001; tchg. assoc. Calif. State U., Northridge, 2004—; graphic designer Big Screen Network Prodns., Westlake Village, Calif., 2005—. Exhibitions include State Fall Exhbn. Art, 1993, First Internat. Exhbn. -Presentation of Periodical Publs. about Pets, 1995, Art Gallery of U. Kiev-Mogila Acad., 1996, Art Acad. L.A., 1999, Svitozor Gallery, 1999—2001, L.A. Valley Coll., 2000, L.A. Mission Coll., 2002, Limner Gallery, 2003, Pacific Design Ctr., L.A., 2004, Art Assn. Harrisburg's 76th Ann. Juried Exhbn., 2004; film editor, designer: Streetlight Cinema, 2004—; contbr. articles to mags. Recipient Biography Pub., The Nat. Dean's List, 2002—03; State U. Fee grant, Calif. State U., Northridge, 2003—, Campus Fee grant, 2003—. Avocations: reading, travel, horseback riding. Office: All Electronics Corp 14928 Oxnard St Van Nuys CA 91411 Office Phone: 818-904-0529. Personal E-mail: anya@artistanya.com.

VASOLI, GLENNA ISAAC, elementary school educator, school system administrator; d. Richard Henry and Pansy (Williams) Isaac; children: Angela Vasoli DeMara, Christopher John. BS, East Tenn. State U., 1971; MEd, Temple U., 1978; MS, Gwynedd Mercy Coll., 2005. Cert. K-12 prin. Pa., K-12 reading specialist Pa., elem. tchr. Pa. Elem. tchr. Greenville County Sch. Dist., SC, 1971—74, Polk County Sch. Dist., Bartow, Fla., 1974—75; reading specialist Remedial Edn. and Diagnostic Services, Inc., Langhorne, Pa., 1976—78; mid. sch. tchr. St. Stanislaus Parish Sch., Lansdale, Pa., 1985—87, reading specialist, libr., 1993—99; reading specialist, mid. sch. tchr. Sch. Dist. Allentown, Pa., 1999—2000; reading specialist Pennridge Sch. Dist., Perkasie, Pa., 2000—; profl. devel. grad. course instr. Reg. Tng. Ctr., 2006—. Mem. profl. devel. com. Pennridge H.S., 2005—06; ednl. adminstrv. practicum Gwynedd Mercy Coll., Gwynedd Valley, Pa., 2004—05. Art works in pvt. collections. Eucharistic min. St. Stanislaus Ch., Lansdale, Pa. Home: 1119 Forrest Ave Lansdale PA 19446 Office: Pennridge Sch Dist 1506 N Fifth Str Perkasie PA 18944 Personal E-mail: gvasoli@msn.com.

VASQUEZ, JO ANNE, retired science educator; BS in biology, No. Ariz. U., 1965, MA in early childhood edn., 1968; PhD in curriculum and instrn., Kennedy-Western U., 1999. Assoc. prof. sci. and edn. Ariz. State U.; lead curriculum developer, sci. specialist Mesa Pub. Schs.; profl. devel. cons. Macmillan/McGraw Hill, 2000—. Writer MacMillan/McGraw-Hill K-6 Sci., 1998—; bd. dirs. Nat. Sci. bd., 2002—; chair elem. sci. tchg. and assessment standards Nat. Bd. Profl. Tchg. Standards; mem. exec. bd. Nat. Acad. Sci. Ctr. for Sci., Math., and Engring. Edn.; former com. chair, reviewer Nat. Sci. Found.; cons. in field. Past pres. adv. bd. Sally Ride's TOYChallenge. Named Tchr. Yr., Nat. Environ. Assn.; recipient honoree, Nat. Assn. Latino Elected and Apptd. Officials, 2004, Gustave Oahus Elem. Sci. Tchg. award, Robert H. Carleton award, Nat. Sci. Teachers Assn., 2006. Mem.: Nat. Coun. Elem. Sci. Educators (past pres.), Internat. Coun. Sci. Edn. Orgn. (past pres.), Ariz. Sci. Tchrs. Assn. (past pres.), Nat. Sci. Edn. Leadership Assn. (pres.-elect), Nat. Sci. Tchrs. Assn. (past mem. nat. bd. dirs., elected first Hispanic pres., Disting. Svc. to Sci. Edn. award Search for Excellence in Elem. Sci. Edn. and Supervision). Achievements include first K-12 tchr. apptd. to bd. dirs. NSF Nat. Sci. Bd. Office: Nat Sci Found 4201 Wilson Blvd Arlington VA 22230*

VASS, JOAN, apparel designer; b. N.Y.C., May 19, 1925; d. Max S. and Rose L.; children: Richard, Sara, Jason. Student, Vassar Coll., 1941; BA, U. Wis., 1946. Pres. Joan Vass, Inc., N.Y.C., 1977—, Vass-Ludacer, N.Y.C., 1993—. Recipient Prize de Cashet, Prince Machiabelli, 1980, Coty award, 1979, Disting. Woman in Fashion award Smithsonian Instn., 1980. Address: 214 W 39th St New York NY 10018-6850 E-mail: joanvass@worldnet.att.net.

VASSILOPOULOU-SELLIN, RENA, researcher; b. Dec. 29, 1949; MD, Albert Einstein Coll. Medicine, 1974. Resident Montefiore Hosp., Bronx, 1974-77; fellow Northwestern U., Chgo., 1977-80; prof. Univ. Tex., Houston, 1980—. Fellow ACP, Am. Assn. Clin. Endocrinol.; mem. AAAS, AMA, Am. Soc. Bone and Mineral Rsch., Am. Diabetes Assn., Am. Soc. Clin. Oncology, Endo Soc. Office: Anderson Cancer Ctr 1515 Holcombe Blvd # 15 Houston TX 77030-4009

VASULKA, STEINA (STEINUNN BRIEM BJARNADOTTIR), artist, educator; b. Reykjavik, Iceland, 1940; m. Woody Vasulka. Student, Music Conservatory, Prague, Czech Republic. Mem. Icelandic Symphony Orch., 1964; freelance musician N.Y.C., 1965; co-founder The Kitchen media arts theater, 1971; mem. faculty Ctr. for Media Study State U. N.Y., Buffalo, 1974; artist-in-residence Nat. Ctr. for Experiments, KQED-TV, San Francisco, WNET-TV, N.Y.C., U.S./Japan Friendship Com., 1993; artist Art and Sci. Lab., Santa Fe, 1980—. Instr. Acad. for Applied Arts, Vienna; instr. Inst. for New Media Staedelschule, Frankfurt, Germany; instr. Coll. Arts and Crafts, Reykjavik. Organizer A Special Video Tape Show, Whitney Mus. Modern Art, N.Y.C., (exhibitions) Eigenwelt der Apparate-Welt: Pioneers of Electronic Art, Linz, Austria, 1992. Recipient Maya Deren award, Am. Film Inst., 1992, Siemens Media Art prize, 1995; grantee, NY State Coun. on Arts, Corp. for Pub. Svc., Nat. Endowment Arts, Corp. Pub. Broadcasting, Guggenheim Found., N.Mex. Arts Divsn.; scholar, Czechoslovak Ministry of Culture, 1959.

VAUCLAIR, MARGUERITE RENÉE, communications and sales promotion executive; b. Englewood, NJ, Jan. 26, 1945; d. Maurice Joseph and Yvonne Jeanne (Reynaud) V.; m. William Augustus Peeples II, (div. 1986). BS in Journalism, Bowling Green State U., 1967. Asst. promotion mgr. Internat. Herald Tribune, Paris, 1967-70; Europe promotion mgr. Vision-The European Bus. Mag., London, 1971; dir. programs and promotion Am. C. of C. in France, Paris, 1973-76; promotion and rsch. mgr. Johnston Internat. Pubs., N.Y.C., 1977-80; prin. Marguerite Vauclair Promotion-Pub. Rels.-Advt., 1981—; promotion mgr. L.A. Times Syndicate, 1985-88; advt. promotions and spl. sects. mgr. Soundings Publs. Inc., Essex, Conn., 1990. Collaborator on books, author: (guide) Guest Houses, Bed-and-Breakfasts, Inns and Hotels in Newport, R.I., 1982; contbr. articles to mags. and newspapers. Mem. Pub. Rels. Soc. Am. (Prisms awards com. LA 1988), Women in Comm. (bd. dirs. LA 1987-89), French-Am. C. of C. in U.S., Inc. (publs. com. 1993-98), Alliance Francaise de Westchester (bd. dirs. 2002—), Alliance Francaise de Greenwich, Advt. Club of Westchester (bd. dirs. 1994-97), Fairfield County Pub. Rels. Assn., Conn. Press Club (bd. dirs. 2000—), Kappa Delta (bd. dirs. UCLA chpt. 1986-88, U. Conn. 1990-91).

VAUGHAN, DORIS CELESTINE WALKER, retired librarian, educator; b. Lawrenceville, Va., Aug. 21, 1930; d. Warner L. and Otelia R. (Collier) Walker; m. Clyde Wilson Vaughan Sr., Nov. 6, 1954 (dec.); children: Sharon Maria, Clyde Wilson Jr., Gregory Andre. BS, St. Paul's Coll., Lawrenceville, 1952; MLS, U. Mich., 1979. Tchr. Loudoun County Sch. System, Leesburg, Va., 1953-54, Nottoway (Va.) County Sch. System, 1954-55, Brunswick County Sch. System, Lawrenceville, 1956-70; libr. asst. Cen. State U., Wilberforce, Ohio, 1971-80, libr. reference and gifts, adj. instr., 1980-92; ret. Libr., archivist Letterkenny Army Depot, Chambersburg, Pa., 1986—87; adj. instr. Ctrl. State U., Wilderforce, Ohio, 1993—96; sub. tchr. Xenia Cmty. Sch., Xenia, Ohio, 1999—2005. U. Mich. fellow, 1978. Mem. AAUP, Southwestern Ohio Coun. for Higher Edn., Alpha Kappa Alpha. Democrat. Avocations: reading, cooking, writing. Home: 1062 Frederick Dr Xenia OH 45385-1649

VAUGHAN, ELIZABETH JEAN, education educator; d. Richard Curtis and Ida Martell Vaughan. BSEd, Stephen F. Austin State U., 1974, MEd, 1977; PhD, U. South Fla., 1984. Assoc. prof. Stephen F. Austin State U., Nacogdoches, Tex., 1983—92; prof. Shippensburg (Pa.) U., 1992—. Author: (book) Learning Centers for Child-Centered Classrooms, 1992, Teaching Numeracy, Language and Literacy with Blocks, 2006. Mem. Success by 6 Leadership Coun., Carlisle, Pa., 2001—06; bd. dirs. Montessori Acad. of Chambersburg, Pa., 2006—. Mem.: Pa. Assn. for Edn. of Young Children (pres. 2005—), Mid-Atlantic Assn. for Edn. of Young Children (pres. 2001—03), Assn. Childhood Edn. Internat., Nat. Assn. for Edn. of Young Children. Home: 8 Lynn Ave Newburg PA 17240 Office: Shippensburg U 1871 Old Main Dr Shippensburg PA 17257 Office Phone: 717-477-1379.

VAUGHAN, ELIZABETH L., school nurse practitioner; b. Boston, Oct. 3, 1956; d. Robert J. Williams and Ella L. Gilstrap; m. Roscoe D. Vaughan, Nov. 22, 1980; children: Nathan C., Rebecca L. Student, Okla. Christian Coll., 1975—77; BSN, U. Okla., 1979. RN, cert. sch. nurse. Staff nurse Vis. Nurse's Assn., Okla. City, Okla., 1979—80, Nursing Svc. Inc., Tulsa, Okla., 1980—82, field supr., 1982—84; staff nurse St. Francis Hosp., Tulsa, 1985—91, field supr., 1991—94; with quality assurance St. Francis Home Health, Tulsa, 1994—98; nurse Tulsa (Okla.) Pub. Schs., 1998—. Vol. tchr. ARC, Tulsa, 1998—; vol. Day Shelter Homeless, Tulsa, 1991—; leader Magic Empire Chpt. Girl Scouts Am., Tulsa, 1992—. Mem.: NEA (del. 1998—), Nat. Assn. Sch. Nurses, Sigma Theta Tau. Republican. Avocations: reading, camping, national parks. Home: 6720 E 24th St Tulsa OK 74129 Office: Hamilton Middle Sch 2316 N Norwood Pl Tulsa OK 74115

VAUGHAN, FRANCES ELIZABETH, psychologist; b. N.Y.C., Jan. 1, 1935; d. Frederick V. and Caroline (Willis) V.; m. Reece R. Clark, July 12, 1957 (div. 1975); children: Reece Robert, Leslie Elizabeth; m. Roger N. Walsh, June 30, 1985. BA with great distinction, Stanford U., 1956; MA, Calif. State U., Sonoma, 1969; PhD, Calif. Sch. Profl. Psychology, Berkeley, 1973. Lic. psychologist, Calif. Pvt. practice, Mill Valley, Calif., 1975—. Prof. psychology, Inst. Transpersonal Psychology, Menlo Park, Calif., 1975-85; presenter workshops, 1975-2005; asst. clin. prof. U. Calif. Med. Sch., Irvine, 1987-96. Author: Awakening Intuition, 1979, The Inward Arc, 1986, 2d edit., 2000, Shadows of the Sacred, 1995, 2d edit., 2005; co-editor: Beyond Ego, 1980, Accept This Gift, 1983, A Gift of Peace, 1986, A Gift of Healing, 1988, Paths Beyond Ego, 1993. Fellow Am. Psychol. Assn.; mem. Calif. Psychol. Assn., Assn. Transpersonal Psychology (pres. 1975-77), Assn. Humanistic Psychology (pres. 1987-88), Internat. Transpersonal Assn. (bd. dirs. 1982-84, 89-91, trustee Fetzer Inst., 1996-), Phi Beta Kappa. Democrat. Episcopalian. Avocations: gardening, hiking, writing. Office: 10 Millwood St Ste 3 Mill Valley CA 94941-2064 Business E-Mail: email@francesvaughan.com.

VAUGHAN, MARTHA, biochemist, educator; b. Dodgeville, Wis., Aug. 4, 1926; d. John Anthony and Luciel (Ellingen) V.; m. Jack Orloff, Aug. 4, 1951 (dec. Dec. 1988); children: Jonathan Michael, David Geoffrey, Gregory Joshua. Ph.B., U. Chgo., Ill., 1944; MD, Yale U., New Haven, Conn., 1949. Intern New Haven Hosp., Conn., 1950-51; research fellow U. Pa., Phila., 1951-52, Nat. Heart Inst., Bethesda, Md., 1952-54, mem. research staff, 1954-68; head metabolism sect. Nat. Heart and Lung Inst., Bethesda, 1968-74; acting chief molecular disease br. Nat. Heart, Lung and Blood Inst., Bethesda, 1974-76, chief cell metabolism lab., 1974-94; dep. chief pulmonary and critical care medicine br. Nat. Heart, Lung, and Blood Inst., Bethesda, 1994—. Mem. metabolism study sect. NIH, 1965-68; mem. bd. sci. counselors Nat. Inst. Alcohol Abuse and Alcoholism, 1988-91. Mem. editl. bd. Jour. Biol. Chemistry, 1971-76, 80-83, 88-90, assoc. editor, 1992—; editl. adv. bd. Molecular Pharmacology, 1972-80, Biochemistry, 1989-94; editor: Biochemistry and Biophysics Rsch. Comms., 1990-91; contbr. articles to profl. jours., chpts. to books. Bd. dirs. Found. Advanced Edn. in Scis., Inc., Bethesda, 1979-92, exec. com., 1980-92, treas., 1984-86, v.p., 1986-88, pres., 1988-90; mem. Yale U. Coun. com. med. affairs, New Haven, 1974-80. Recipient Meritorious Svc. medal HEW, 1974, Disting. Svc. medal HEW, 1979, Commd. Officer award USPHS, 1982, Superior Svc. award USPHS, 1993. Mem. NAS, Am. Acad. Arts and Scis., Am. Soc. Biol. Chemists (chmn. pub. com. 1984-86), Assn. Am. Physicians, Am. Soc. Clin. Investigation. Home: 11608 W Hill Dr Rockville MD 20852-3751 Office: Nat Heart Lung & Blood Inst Nih Bldg 10 Rm 5N 307 Bethesda MD 20892-0001 Business E-Mail: vaughanm@nih.gov.

VAUGHAN, MITTIE KATHLEEN, journalist; b. Waycross, Ga., Mar. 18, 1950; d. Charles N. and Kathleen (Howell) V.; m. Bill Crews, Apr. 21, 1975 (div. Oct. 1978); 1 child, R. Hannah. Student, Abraham Baldwin Coll., 1968-70. Women's editor Waycross (Ga.) Jour.-Herald, 1970-73; staff writer Daily Tifton (Ga.) Gazette, 1973-74; news editor Wiregrass Shopper, Alma, Ga., 1976-78; assoc. editor The Alma Times, 1978-79; pub. Pierce County Press, Blackshear, Ga., 1980—; founder, pub. The Express, 1983—; pub. Brantley County Express, 2004—. 2d vice chmn. Pierce County Dem. Exec. Com., Blackshear, 1988-96; chmn. parent anonymous program Child Abuse Coun., 1988-89; sec. Pierce County Adv. Coun., United Way, 1996-98, chmn., 1998; Pierce County C. of C., 1987-98, bd. dirs., 1999-2002; charter mem., bd. dirs. Pierce County Hist. and Geneal. Soc., 1999-2005, sec., 2000-05. Recipient 4-H Vol. Leader award, 1991. Mem. Ga. Collegiate Press Assn. (dir. 1969-70, sec. 1970-71), Ga. Dist. Exch. Clubs (bd. dirs. 2002—, Exchangite of Yr. award 2000, Pres. of Yr. award 2005), Blackshear Exch. Club (sec.-treas. 1988-89, sec. 1989-91, 94-95, 99-00, bull. editor 1988-97, 99-00, club history book chmn. 1999-2002, publicity chmn. 1999-2000, Exchangite of Yr. 2000), Blackshear Woman's Club (publicity chmn. 1986-88, sec. 1994-96, chmn. pub. affairs dept. 1992-94, 96-98, chmn. 1998, Outstanding Cmty. Svc. award 1995, 97, 98, outstanding new mem. 1987, legis. chmn. 1994-96, 2000-2001, sec. 2003—), Christian Coalition, Eagle Forum, Brantley County Exch. Club (charter pres. 2004-2005, bull. editor 2004—, club history book chmn. 2004—, pres. 2005—), Pierce County Exch. Club (sec. 2003-05, pres.-elect 2005—). Democrat. Methodist. Avocations: gardening, singing solos, reading, ch. choir, playing piano. Office: Pierce County Press 138 Central Ave Blackshear GA 31516

VAUGHAN, NADINE, psychologist; b. Tampa, Fla., Aug. 30, 1947; d. Joseph Marcus and Velna Pearl (Jones) Williams; m. E.L. Vaughan III, 1966 (div. Aug. 1976); children: Edward L. Vaughan, Heather Vaughan Oyarzun, Melanie Sage; m. Richard S. Traum, Sept. 2002. BA in Criminal Justice, U. South Fla., 1974, MA with honors in Rehab. Counseling, 1975; PhD in Psychology, Saybrook Inst., 1990. Lic. clin. psychologist, Calif., Wash., Fla. Co-founder Women's Resource Ctr., Tampa and Nevada City, 1973—; cons., trainer N. Vaughan, PhD, 1982—; regional trainer APA Hope Program, 1994—98; clin. dir. dist. 13, Fla., 2002—06. Adj. prof. Rollins Coll., Valencia Coll., U. Ctrl. Fla. Assoc. prodr.: (movie) The Touch. Mem. APA, Am. Coll. Forensic Examiners (diplomate psychol. spltys., med. psychology). Democrat. Avocations: theatrical directing and producing, scriptwriting.

VAUGHAN, NANCY KING, school system administrator; b. Pampa, Tex., Feb. 23, 1957; d. Betty Morman and Ellis Leon King. BS, U. Tex., 1979; MEd, Tex. A&M U., 1991, MS, 1993, EdD, 2002. Cert. spl. edn. tchr. Tex., elem. math. tchr. Tex., elem. reading tchr. Tex., mid. mgmt. adminstr. Tex., supt. Tex. Prin. Lancaster (Tex.) Ind. Sch. Dist., 1993—96; ednl. cons. Edn. Svc. Ctr. Region XI, Ft. Worth, 1996—2004; asst. supt. instructional svcs. Decatur (Tex.) Ind. Sch. Dist., 2004—; v.p. Les Evans Tex. ASCD, Decatur, 2005—. V.p. Pink Pink Rose, 2002—. Bd. advs. Tarrant County Courage to Teach, Ft. Worth, 1999—. Mem.: Tex. Coun. Women Sch. Execs. (v.p. 2003—, pres.-elect 2004—05, pres. 2005—), Assn. Compensatory Educators Tex. (pres. 2004—, past pres. 2005). Home: 5884 Echo Bluff Fort Worth TX 76137 Office: Decatur Independent Sch Dist 501 E Collins Decatur TX 76234 Office Phone: 940-393-7107. Personal E-mail: nkvaughan@aol.com. Business E-Mail: nancy.vaughan@decatur.esc11.net.

VAUGHAN, STEPHANIE RUTH, water aerobics business owner, consultant; b. Winchester, Va., Feb. 27, 1956; d. Robert Hall Sr. and Peggy (Owen) Hahn; m. Ward Pierman Vaughan, Nov. 29, 1980; children: Carol Owen, Eva Virginia, Robert Alexander. BS in Biology, Shenandoah U., 1983, MBA, 1985; postgrad., George Mason U., 2003—. Sales rep., cashier Best Products, Roanoke, Va., 1977-78; dir. Peg-Ell Sch. Modeling, Winchester, 1978-79; mgr. purchasing and metal fabrication materials Fabritek Co., Inc., Winchester, 1979-84, sec. bd. dirs., 1980—; CEO, owner Splash Internat., Winchester, 1991—, internat. mktg. dir. original cabinet; internat. mktg. dir., v.p. Aquatic Alliance Internat., 1998—2004; safety dir. Fabritech Co., 2004—. Tennis instr. Camp Camelot, Wilmington, N.C., summer 1978; cons. Fabritek Co., Inc., 1993-95; membership dir. Stonebrook Swim and Racquet Club, Winchester, 1992-93, corp. fitness dir., 1993; instr. Workout in Water class Crooked Run Fitness and racquet Club, Front Royal, Va., 1992—, Winchester Parks and Recreation Dept., 1991-92; instr., designer Children's Water Fitness Classes Winchester County Club, Va., 1993, Stonebrook Country Club, 1994; instr. arthritis aquatic class and designer class Ida Lee Recreation Ctr., 1999-04; faculty Shenandoah U., 1998, Lord Fairfax C.C., 1998—; staff phys. therapy dept. Winchester Med. Ctr., 1998-99; aquatic dir. Signal Knob Recreation Ctr., Strasburg, Va., 1999-04; prof. aquatic exercise and swimming Lord Fairfax CC, 1999-05; keynote spkr., presenter in field. Author: Water Exercises for Physicians, Physical Therapists and Water Fitness Instructors, 1994 (award); contbr. articles to profl. jours.; internat. aquatic exercise and therapy presenter. Steering com. mem. Habitat for Humanity, 1995; bd. dirs. Winchester Fred County. Patentee for water fitness product. Mem. AAHPERD, NAFE, AAUW, AMA, Am. Coll. Sports Medicine, Va. Assn. Health, Phys. Recreation and Dance (conf. presenter, chair aquatic coun. 1994-95, v.p. recreation coun. 1996—), Va. Recreation and Parks Soc. (conf. presenter), U.S. Water Fitness Assn. (adv. bd., chair tech. com. 1993—, mem. nat. tech. com. 1992—, C. Carson Conrad Top Water Fitness Leader for Va. award 1993, Deep Water Running Champion 1993, BEMA Nat. Water Fitness Champion 1993, cert. pool coord., cert. instr., nat. conf. aquatic fashion show dir. 1992, 93, 94, conf. presenter, leader 1st Nat. Aquatic Summit, Washington, Team Water Aerobics aquatic champion 1994, June Andrus Entrepreneur of Yr. award 1995, Champion Deep Water Instr. 1995), United Daus. of Confederacy, Aquatic Exercise Assn. (conf. presenter, regional rep. 1994-96), U.S. Synchronized Swimming, Shenandoah U. Alumni Assn. (bd. dirs.), Aquatic Alliance Internat. (internat. mktg. dir. 1996—, v.p. 1997-98), Aquatic Edn. Assn. Achievements include patents in field. Avocations: water and snow skiing, flying, scuba diving, sewing, smocking. Home: 202 Brookneil Drive Winchester VA 22602-6627 Business E-Mail: stephanie@splashinternational.com.

VAUGHAN, THERESE MICHELE, insurance educator; b. Blair, Nebr., June 12, 1956; d. Emmett John and Lonne Kay (Smith) V.; m. Robert Allen Carber, Aug. 15, 1993; children: Kevin Leo Vaughan-Carber, Thomas S. Vaughan-Carber. BBA, U. Iowa, 1979; PhD, U. Pa., 1985. CPCU. Asst. prof. Baruch Coll., CUNY, 1986-87; cons. Tillinghast, N.Y.C., 1987-88; dir. ins. ctr. Drake U., Des Moines, 1988-94; ins. commr. State of Iowa, Des Moines, 1994—2004; Robb B. Kelley Disting. prof. ins. and actuarial sci. Drake U., 2005—. Bd. dirs. Endurance Splty. Holdings, Prin. Fin. Group, Nat. Coun on Corp. Ins. Chair Jour. of Ins. Regulation Bd., Kansas City, Mo., 1995-99; co-author: Fundamentals of Risk and Insurance, 1996, 99, 2003, Essentials of Insurance: A Risk Management Approach, 1995, 2001; contbr. articles to profl. jours. S.S. Huebner fellow U. Pa., 1979-82; recipient Outstanding Young Alumnus award U. Iowa, 1996; named to Iowa Ins. Hall of Fame, 2003. Mem. Nat. Assn. Ins. Commrs. (pres. 2002), Ins. Marketplace Stds. Assn. (bd. dirs. 2004—), Beta Gamma Sigma, Omicron Delta Epsilon. Avocations: hiking, biking, reading. Home: 4632 Elm St West Des Moines IA 50265-2993 Office: Drake Univ 2507 University Ave Des Moines IA 50311 Business E-Mail: terri.vaughan@drake.edu.

VAUGHN, BEVERLY JEAN, music educator, mezzo soprano; b. Warren, Ohio; d. Otis and Marion Jane Vaughn. BA Spanish, Loma Linda U., 1971; MusM, Ohio State U., 1973, DMA, 1982. Asst. prof. music Richard Stockton Coll. N.J., Pomona, 1982—90, assoc. prof. music, 1990—2000, prof. music, 2001—. Project dir., coord. 2002 Project Malawi, Atlantic County, NJ, 2002—03; condr. workshops on African-Am. music in Israel, Austria, Zimbabwe, Malawi, others. Singer: opera houses and concerts throughout Europe and U.S. Mem. coms., adv. bds. various activities. Recipient over 30 civic/cmty. awards. Mem.: NAACP, Internat. Fedn. Choral Music, Am. Choral Dirs. Assn. (state chair com.), Assn. for Study of African-Am. Life and History, Coll. Music Soc., Nat. Music Educators Assn., N.J. Am. Choral Dirs. Assn., Alpha Kappa Alpha. Avocations: travel, bicycling, reading, making new friends. Office: Richard Stockton Coll NJ 195 Jimmie Leeds Rd Pomona NJ 08240 Office Phone: 609-652-4264.

VAUGHN, CHRISTINE L., lawyer; b. Camden, NJ, Dec. 20, 1949; BA, Rutgers U., 1972; JD, Georgetown U., 1975, LLM, 1981. Bar: DC 1975. Dir. tax policy US C of C, 1979—81; spl. asst. to asst. sec. for tax policy US Treasury Dept., 1981—84; ptnr. Vinson & Elkins LLP, Washington, DC. Office: Vinson & Elkins LLP Willard Office Bldg 1455 Pennsylvania Ave NW, Ste 600 Washington DC 20004 Office Phone: 202-639-6517. E-mail: cvaughn@velaw.com.

VAUGHN, CONNIE MARIE, marketing professional, writer, consultant; b. Cin., Mar. 10, 1965; d. Richard and Susan Harless Halley, adopted d. William Edward and Carol Welling Vaughn. BA in Math. & Stats., Miami U., Oxford, Ohio, 1987; MA in Devel. Psychology, Loyola U., Chgo., 1993; MBA in Mktg. & Orgnl. Behavior, U. Chgo., 2001. Account dir. Epsilon Data Mgmt., Burlington, Mass., 1995—2000; brand planner Rapp Collins, Chgo., 2000—01; dir. strategic/database mktg. GSP Mktg., Chgo., 2001—02; modeling & database mktg. mgr. JC Whitney, Chgo., 2002—03; sr. mgr. mkt. devel. Quill Corp., Lincolnshire, Ill., 2004—06; instr. Loyola U., Chgo., 2006—; mktg. cons. Grayslake, Ill., 2006—. Contbr. articles and poems to jours. Scholar, Nat. Merit Scholarship Corp., 1983—84; Alumni scholar, Miami U. Ohio, 1983—87, Regents scholar, Ohio Bd. Regents, 1983—87, Dean's fellow, Loyola U. Chgo., 1989—92. Mem.: Guild Complex, Chgo. Songwriters Collective, Poetry Ctr. Chgo., Psi Chi, Pi Mu Epsilon. Home and Office: 1293 Karyn Ln Grayslake IL 60030 Office Phone: 847-876-3714, 847-223-5619. Personal E-mail: cmvaughn1@aol.com.

VAUGHN, CYNTHIA STARK, elementary school educator; b. Memphis; d. Wade Ashley and Mary Jean (Jones) Stark; m. Maurry Lynn Vaughn, July 11, 1981; children: Cody Lynn, Ethan Skinner. BS in Elem. Edn., U. Memphis, 1983. 5th grade lang. arts tchrs. Horn Lake Elem., Miss., 1983—85; 6th grade math tchr. Olive Branch Middle Sch., Olive Branch, Miss., 1985—86; 6th grade math and sci. tchr. Hernando Middle Sch., Miss., 2001—05, 7th grade pre-algebra tchr., 2005—. Boys soccer coach Hernando Middle Sch., 2006. Baptist. Avocations: sewing, water-skiing, history.

VAUGHN, GLADYS GARY, federal agency administrator, researcher, not-for-profit executive; m. Joseph B. Vaughn (dec. 2000). BS, Fla. A&M U., 1964; MS in Clothing and Textiles, Iowa State U., 1968; PhD in Home Econs. Edn. and Adminstrn., U. MD.-College Park, 1974; LHD (hon.), Fontbonne U., 2006. Nat. program leader for human scis. rsch. Families, 4-H and Nutrition Unit Cooperative State Rsch., Edn. and Extension Svcs., US Dept. of Agr., Washington. Named one of Most Influential Black Americans, Ebony mag., 2006. Mem.: The Links, Inc. (pres. 2002—), Black Women's Agenda, Nat. Coalition of Black Devel. in Home Econs., Delta Sigma Theta Sorority. Office: The Links, Inc 1200 Massachusetts Ave, NW Washington DC 20005*

VAUGHN, GLORIA C., state representative; b. Corpus Christi, Tex., June 25, 1936; m. James M. Vaughn; children: James, Melodie. Student, Del Mar Jr. Coll., Salvation Army Coll., N.Mex. State U. State rep. dist. 51 N.Mex. State Legis., Santa Fe, 1996—. Mem. Bus. and Industry com. N.Mex. State Legis., Santa Fe, mem. legis. judiciary labor and human resources com. Mem.: FEMA (bd. dirs.), LVA (bd. dirs.), ARC (sec.), Salvation Army, Salvation Army (pres.), Am. Cancer Bd., Boy Scouts Am., Habitat for Humanity (bd. dirs.), Alamogordo Women's Connection. Republican. Home: 503 E 16th St Alamogordo NM 88310 Office: New Mexico State Capitol Rm 203 ICN Santa Fe NM 87503

VAUGHN, LINDA F., musician, educator; b. Morrison, Ill., Feb. 3, 1952; d. Edwin J. and Nora E. Bush; m. Charles W. Vaughn, Apr. 23, 1999; children: Timothy M. Deal, Andrew E. Deal, Peter G. Deal. MusB, BA, Hope Coll., 1974; MusM, U. Ill., 1975, MA, 1979. Cert. tchr. Ill. Vocal music tchr. Urbana (Ill.) Sch. Dist., 1990—; tchr. Danville (Ill.) Area C.C., 1996—99. Organist, choir dir. First Bapt. Ch., Urbana, 1984—93; organist Cmty. United Ch. of Christ, Champaign, Ill., 1993—; accompanist The Chorale, Champaign, 1994—2001; mem., performer Evening Etude Mozart Music Club, Champaign-Urbana. Mem.: Music Educator's Assn., Am. Choral Dir.'s Assn. (life), Delta Phi Alpha (life), Delta Omicron (life). Avocations: sewing, crocheting, cooking, baking, needlecrafts. Home: 2606 Wadsworth Ln Urbana IL 61802 Office Phone: 217-384-3685. Business E-Mail: lvaughn@usd116.org.

VAUGHN, LINDA MARIE, municipal official; b. Moline, Ill., Aug. 6, 1947; d. Merwin Perry and Margaret Anne Baker; m. Jeffery M. Vaughn, Aug. 16, 1969; children: Jason P., Eric M. Student, Moline Inst. Commerce, 1965. Clk. data entry Eagle Warehouse, Milan, Ill., 1966—69, Lennox Heating/AC, Marshalltown, Iowa, 1970—73, Farmall (Internat. Harvester), Rock Island, Ill., 1973—75, Ingersoll, Rockford, 1975—87; trustee Village of Machesney Park, Ill., 1987—89, clk., 1989—2001, mayor, village pres., 2001—. Guest columnist Parks Jour., 1997—; charter mem. Parks Chamber Women's Network, Loves Park, Ill., 1995; 8 gal. mem. Rock River Valley Blood Ctr. Mem. Northwestern Ill. Mcpl. Clks. Assn. (sec. 1990-92, treas. 1997-99), C. of C. (ambassador 1987—). Democrat. Roman Catholic. Avocations: writing, fishing, reading, walking. Home: 9519 Shore Dr Machesney Park IL 61115-2058 Office: Village Machesney Park 300 Machesney Rd Machesney Park IL 61115-2495

VAUGHN, NOEL WYANDT, lawyer; b. Chgo., Dec. 15, 1937; d. Owen Heaton and Harriet Christy (Smith) Wyandt; m. David Victor Koch, July 18, 1959 (div.); 1 child, John David; m. Charles George Vaughn, July 9, 1971. BA, DePauw U., 1959; MA, So. Ill. U., 1963; JD, U. Dayton, 1979. Bar: Ohio 1979, U.S. Dist. Ct. (so. dist.) Ohio 1979, U.S. Cir. Ct. (6th cir.) 1987. Lectr. Wright State U., Dayton, 1965-67; communications specialist Charles F. Kettering Found., Dayton, 1968-71; tchr. English Miami Valley Sch., Dayton, 1971-76; law clk. to judge Dayton Mcpl. Ct., 1978-79; coordinator Montgomery County Fair Housing Ctr., Dayton, 1979-81, 85-89; atty. Henley Vaughn Becker & Wald, Dayton, 1981-90; pvt. practice Noel W. Vaughn Law

Offices, Dayton, 1990—. Chmn. Dayton Playhouse, Inc., 1981—92; pres. Freedom of Choice Miami Valley, 1980—83, 1986—87; com. mem. Battered Woman Project-YWCA, 1983—84; pres. Legal Aid Soc., 1983—84; chmn. Artemis House, Inc., 1985—88, bd. dirs., 1988—97, ACLU, 1982—86, Miami Valley Arts Coun., 1985—86, AIDS Found., 1988—90, Miami Valley Fair Housing Ctr., Inc., 1992—94, Human Race Theatre Co., Inc., 1995—2000, Housing Justice Fund, 1979—, Dayton Sister City Com., 2001—02. Recipient Order of Barristers award U. Dayton, 1979. Mem.: ABA, Ohio State Bar Assn., Ohio Fair Plan Underwriting Assn. (bd. govs. 1986—92), Dayton Bar Assn. (chmn. delivery legal svcs. com. 1983—84, family law com. 1991—, chmn. juvenile law com. 2001—03). Office: 1205 Talbott Tower 131 N Ludlow St Dayton OH 45402-1110 Office Phone: 937-222-6635.

VAUGHN, PAMELA W., music educator; MusB, U. Wyo., 1973. Cert. music tchr. Vocal music tchr. Ralston (Nebr.) Pub. Sch., 1973-75, Millard Pub. Sch., Omaha, 1980-84; vocal accompanist Papillion (Nebr.) Pub. Sch., 1987—2001; pvt. piano tchr. Omaha, 1976—. Min. of music Presbyn. Ch., Omaha, 1977—87; choral dir. Trinity United Meth. Ch., Ralston, Nebr., 1987—97, dir. music ministries, 1997—; All-State vocal accompanist Nebr. Music Educators Assn., 1994—2001. Bd. mem. Nebr. Summer Music Olympics, 2000—. Mem. Nat. Music Tchrs. Assn., Nebr. Music Tchrs. Assn., Omaha Music Tchrs. Assn., Pi Kappa Lambda, Pi Kappa Pi. Methodist. Avocation: family history.

VAUGHNDORF, BETTY RACHEL, executive secretary, artist; b. Savannah, Ga., Aug. 18, 1924; d. Morris Vaughndorf and Lena Stanley. Degree, Ryans Bus. Coll., 1944; student, Corcoran Art Sch., 1948, Abbott Art Sch., 1950. Stenographer U.S. Maritime Commn., Savannah, Ga., 1942—47, Smithsonian Instn., Washington, 1948—50, U.S. Info. Agy., Washington, 1951—56; sec. Dept. Interior, Washington, 1957—63; ret. Cons. Nat. Rep. Congl. Com., Savannah, 1997—2005. Recipient Outstanding Achievement in Amateur Photography award, Internat. Soc. Photographers, 2004, 2005. Mem.: Savannah Art Assn., Am. Assn. Ret. Persons.

VAZ, KATHERINE ANNE, language educator, writer; b. Castro Valley, Calif., Aug. 26, 1955; d. August Mark and Elizabeth (Sullivan) Vaz; m. Michael Trudeau, May 1, 1994. BA, U. Calif., Santa Barbara, 1977; MFA, U. Calif., Irvine, 1991. Assoc. prof. English U. Calif., Davis, 1995-99; lectr. Harvard U. Briggs-Copeland, 2003—. Keynote spkr. Libr. of Congress, 1997; keynote spkr. lit. confs. U. Ariz., Ariz., U. Calif., Berkeley, U. Mass., Dartmouth U., Rutgers U.; mem. U.S. Presdl. del. to Expo 98/World's Fair, Lisbon, Portugal; Briggs-Copeland lectr. Harvard U., Cambridge, Mass., 2003. Author: (novels) Saudade, 1994, Mariana, 1997, (short stories) Fado & Other Stories, 1997 (Drue Heinz Lit. prize, 1997). Grantee, Nat. Endowment Arts, 1993, Davis Humanities Inst., U. Calif., Davis, 1998—99. Mem.: PEN, Portuguese-Am. Leadership Coun. U.S., Authors Guild. Democrat. Roman Catholic. Personal E-mail: katherineavaz@hotmail.com. Business E-Mail: kvaz@fas.harvard.edu.

VAZIRANI-FALES, HEEA, legislative staff member, lawyer; b. Calcutta, India, Apr. 1, 1938; d. Sunder J. Vazirani; m. John Fales Jr., 1978; children: Deepika, Reetika, Ashish, Monika, Jyotika, Denise. AB, Guilford Coll., 1959; JD, Howard U., 1979. Staff/legis. dir. Montgomery County Del, Gen. Assembly of Md., 1981-87; legis. counsel to Congresswoman Constance A. Morella, US Ho. of Reps., Washington, 1987-94, counsel subcom. on postal svc. com. govt. reform, 1995—2000, dep. staff dir. and counsel subcom. on DC govt. reform, 2000—02, counsel subcom. on civil svc., 2003—. Mem. staff Vols. for Visually Handicapped, 1973-79, bd. dirs., 1979-81; bd. dirs. Manipal Edn. and Med. Found., 1970-92. Mem. Phi Delta Phi. Office: Subcom on Civil Svc B-373A Rayburn Bldg Washington DC 20515

VÁZQUEZ, MARTHA ALICIA, federal judge; b. Santa Barbara, Calif., Feb. 21, 1953; d. Remigio and Consuelo Medina Vazquez. BA in Govt., U. Notre Dame, 1975, JD, 1978. Bar: N.Mex. 1979, admitted to practice: US Dist. Ct. (Dist. N.Mex.) 1979. Atty. Pub. Defender's Office, Santa Fe, 1979-81; ptnr. Jones, Snead, Wertheim, Rodriguez & Wentworth, Santa Fe, 1981-93; chief judge U.S. Dist. Ct. N.Mex., Santa Fe, 1993—. Democrat. Roman Catholic. Office: US Courthouse PO Box 2710 Santa Fe NM 87504-2710 Office Phone: 505-988-6330. Business E-Mail: mvazquez@nmcourt.fed.us.

VAZQUEZ RIVERA, ORNELA AMLIV, psychologist; b. Malaga, Spain, Feb. 23, 1978; d. Sigfredo Vazquez Calderon and Vilma Celenia Rivera Merced. BA in Soc. Work magna cum laude, U. PR, 2001; MA, CAS in Sch. Psychology, Alfred U., NY, 2004. Lic. Sch. Psychologist NC, 2004. Intern, bilingual sch. psychologist Buffalo Pub. Schs., Buffalo, 2003—04; student svc. specialist Albemarle Rd. Elem., Charlotte, NC, 2004—. Leader Girl Scouts, Caguas, PR, 1999—2001, Charlotte, NC, 2004—. Recipient Gold Medal award, Girl Scouts, 1996. Mem.: NC Assn. of Educators, Nat. Assn. of Sch. Psychologist. Office: Charlotte Mecklenburg Schs Charlotte NC

VEACH, JENNIFER JEANNE, elementary school educator; b. Fort Morgan, Colo., Sept. 15, 1958; d. Edward Lee Nelson and Joan Horton Wright; m. Walter Anthony Veach, June 30, 1979; children: Mariah Rose, Walter Levi, Caleb Nelson. BA cum laude, Bethany Coll., Lindsborg, Kans., 1980; MA, U. Colo., Boulder, 2005. Lic. profl. educator Colo. Dept. Edn., 1990. Custom combining crew cook Tupper & Unruh Custom Cutting, Great Bend, Kans., 1976—78; substitute tchr. Unified Sch. Dist. #428, Great Bend, 1981, elem. tchr., 1981—90, Thompson R2-J, Loveland, Colo., 1990—; artist's asst. DeMott Fine Art, Loveland, 2000—; bookkeeper Gateway Garden Ctr., Loveland, 2000—. Co-dir. Thompson Summer Reading, Loveland, 2001—02. Author poetry and essays. Scholar, U. Colo., 2003. Mem.: Thompson Edn. Assn., Nat. Assn. for Bilingual Edn. (assoc.), Colo. Coun. Internat. Reading Assn. (assoc.), Thompson Coun. Internat. Reading Assn. (assoc.), Colo. Edn. Assn. (assoc.). Republican. Avocations: reading, crafts, sewing, travel. Office: Namaqua Elementary 209 N County Rd 19 E Loveland CO 80537 Office Phone: 970-613-6642. Business E-Mail: veachj@thompson.k12.co.us.

VEACO, KRISTINA, lawyer; b. Sacramento, Mar. 4, 1948; d. Robert Glenn and Lelia (McCain) V.; 1 child, Nina Katherine. BA, U. Calif., Davis, 1978; JD, Hastings Coll. Law, 1981. Legal adv. to commr. William T. Bagley Calif. Pub. Utilities Commn., San Francisco, 1981-86; sr. counsel Pacific Telesis Group, San Francisco, 1986-94; sr. counsel corp. and securities and pol. law AirTouch Comms., San Francisco, 1994-98; asst. gen. counsel, asst. sec. McKesson Corp., San Francisco, 1999—2006, corp. governance advisor, 2006—. Mem.: ABA, Soc. Corp. Secs. and Governance Profls. (pres. San Francisco chpt. 2001—02, mem. adv. com. San Francisco chpt., nat. bd. dirs.), San Francisco Bar Assn., Phi Beta Kappa. Office: 2470 16th Ave San Francisco CA 94116

VEATCH, SHEILA WILLIAMSON, retired counselor; b. Fitchburg, Mass., Jan. 10, 1950; d. William Robert Barse and Joan Jessie (Tothill) Williamson; stepfather George P. Williamson; m. Michael Alan Veatch, July 3, 1993; children: Michael and Katie Pitts. BSEd, U. Ga., 1971; MEd in Counseling, West Ga. Coll., 1991, EdS in Counseling, 1992. Nat. bd. cert. counselor; lic. profl. counselor. Tchr. Cobb County Schs., Marietta, Ga., 1971-73, 86-91, counselor, 1991—2006. Instr. Cobb Staff Devel., Marietta, 1992-93; workshop leader Kennesaw (Ga.) State U. Assn. Student Educators, 1993; presenter Cobb Mega Conf., 1992. Co-author: Manners Mania, 1993 (rsch. grantee 1992); contbr. articles to profl. jours. Active Cobb Co. Child Advocacy Ctr., Habitat for Humanity; validated innovative program "Project Improve" Ga. Dept. Edn., 1999. Named Elem. Counselor of Yr., Cobb County, 1997; rsch. grantee social skills program Cobb County, 1991-92, 92-93, anger/aggression reduction, 1993-94, parenting edn., 1994-95; Innovation grantee State Ga. Dept. Edn., 1998—; Cobb County Radiance Lifetime Achievement award, 2002. Mem. Ga. Sch. Counselors Assn. (fall conf. presenter 1992, 97, 99), Am. Sch. Counselor Assn., Lic. Profl. Counselor Assn. Ga., Cobb Sch. Counselor Assn. (v.p. 1995-96, pres. 1996-97), PTA (hon., life State of Ga. 1992), Homeowners Assn. of Due West Estates (pres. 2002-05). Avocations: travel, horseback riding. Home: 724 Moore Rd Columbus NC 28722 Office: Cobb County Sch Sys Glover St Marietta GA 30060

VEAZEY, DORIS ANNE, retired state agency administrator; b. Dawson Spring, Ky., Feb. 16, 1935; d. Bradley Basil and Lucy Mable (Hamby) Sisk; m. Herman Veazey Jr., Aug. 15, 1964 (dec. Sept. 1987); 1 child, Vickie Dianne Veazey Kicinski.. Murray State U., 1952-54. Unemployment ins. examiner Dept. for Employment Svcs., Madisonville, Ky., 1954-73, unemployment ins. supr., 1973-85, field office mgr., 1985-96; ret., 1996. Bd. dirs., adv. bd. region II Vocat. Tech. Schs., Madisonville, 1988-92. Mem. Mayor's Work Force Devel. Com., 1993-96, Ky. Indsl. Devel. Com., 1992-96; dept. dir. Adult III Sunday Sch., 1994-96, tchr., 2005-, ch. choir, 1990—; mem. staff devel. com. Madisonville First Bapt. Ch., 1997-99 Mem. Internat. Assn. of Pers. in Employment Svcs., Tenure, Order of Ky. Cols., Greater Madisonville C. of C. (dir. leadership 1988-93). Baptist. Avocations: reading, travel, photography. Home: 697 Brown Rd Madisonville KY 42431-2258

VEDOURAS, ANNA, federal lawyer; b. Cleve., Feb. 21, 1960; d. John and Emily (Peters) Vedouras; m. Jack Ramsey, 2004. BA, U. Mich., 1981; JD, Cleve. State U., 1985. Bar: Ohio 1989. Atty. LIGHTNET, New Haven, Conn., 1985-86; contract adminstr. Constrn. Control Svcs., Inc., Boston, 1986-87; project mgr. Legal Support Svcs., Boston, 1987-89; sr. assoc. counsel Dept. of Defense, Cleveland, Ohio, 1989—. Adj. faculty Malone Coll., 2004—. Pres. Young Friends Cleve. Mus. Art, 1993—95; trustee, v.p. Ctr. for Prevention of Domestic Violence, 1993—98; trustee Cleve. Play House, 1991—96; v.p. Cleve. Ctr. Contemporary Arts, 1996—2000, Spaces, 1999—2004; pres. Cleve. Mediation Ctr., 2001—; bd. dirs. Near West Theatre, 1996—2000. Recipient No. Ohio Live award of achievement, 1996, Disting. Fed. Svc. award, 1999; named one of 50 most interesting people Cleve. Mag., 1995; named Titan of Style, Sun Newspapers, 1995. Mem. Cleve. Bar Assn., Cleve. Film Soc. (v.p. 1993—, pres. 2006—).

VEECH, LYNDA ANNE, musician, educator; b. Montclair, NJ, July 19, 1969; d. Robert Gerald, Sr. and Josephine Veech. B in Music Edn., Rutgers U., New Brunswick, 1991, MA in Music History, 1995; MusM in Piano Performance and Pedagogy, Westminster Choir Coll., Princeton, N.J., 1998. Cert. tchr. N.J. Faculty mem. Westminster Conservatory, Princeton, 1995—2000; pvt. studio dir. Studio of Lynda A. Veech, Verona, NJ, 1995—; faculty mem. Essex County Coll., Woodbridge, NJ, 1996—98, Caldwell (N.J.) Coll., 2000—01; choral dir. Caldwell and West Caldwell Pub. Schs., 2000—02; music tchr. Bartle Elem. Sch., Highland Park, NJ, 2002—03, Morris Cath. HS, Denville, NJ, 2003—, chmn. Dept. Performing Arts, 2005—. Cons. freelance work, Verona, NJ, 1995—; participant Hands Across the Water Internat. Tchr. Exch. Program, Australia, 2002. Performer Ameropa Internat. Music Festival, Prague, Czech Republic, 2001, Montclair Music Festival, 2005. Bd. dirs. Music and More Booster Club, Caldwell, NJ, 2001—02; ch. musician 1st Bapt. Ch., Montclair, 2000—01; organist, choir dir. Calvary Luth. Ch., Verona, NJ, 2003—04; organist St. Luke's and All Saints Ch., Union, NJ, 2001—, 1st Reformed Ch., Pompton Plains, NJ, 2006; organist, vocalist Canticle AIDS Benefit Ensemble, NJ, 1999—2000; organist St. Anne's Ch., Hoboken, NJ, 2005—. Grantee, Rutgers U., 1991—95, Westminster Choir Coll., 1995—97. Mem.: Music Edn. Assn. (co-founder 2000—), Nat. Conf. Piano Pedagogy, Piano Tchrs. Guild, N.J. Edn. Assn., Am. Choral Dir.'s Assn., Music Educator's Nat. Conf. (treas. 1987, v.p. 1991). Roman Catholic. Avocations: reading, swimming, ballet, poetry, music. Home: 124 Sunset Ave Verona NJ 07044 Office: Morris Cath High Sch 200 Morris Ave Denville NJ 07834-1360 Personal E-mail: notenut@comcast.net.

VEEDER, NANCY WALKER, social work educator; b. Albany, N.Y., Mar. 17, 1937; d. Harold Gerit and Alice (Walker) V. AB, Smith Coll., Northampton, Mass., 1959; MS, Simmons Sch. Social Work, Boston, 1963; PhD, Brandeis U., 1974; MBA, Boston Coll., 1990. Prof., grad. sch. social work Boston Coll., Chestnut Hill, 1968—. Home: 53 Lake Ave Newton Center MA 02459-2110 E-mail: veeder@bc.edu.

VEGA, CAROLYN JANE, elementary educator, consultant, writer; b. Loma Linda, Calif., June 29, 1949; d. Ora Harrison Miller and Magil Muriel Rhodes; children: Matthew Harrison, Sarah Christine. AA, Orange Coast Coll., Costa Mesa, Calif., 1970; BA in Fine Arts and Humanities, San Diego State U., 1972; MA in Ednl. Tech., US Internat. U., San Diego, 1987. Std. elem. tchg. credential Calif., specially designed academic instrn. in English and lang. devel. Calif., cert. gifted and talented edn. Calif. Classroom tchr. San Diego Unified Sch. Dist., 1973—, edn. tech. resource tchr., 1988—95. Lectr. U. Calif. San Diego, La Jolla, 1989—95; cons. AAAS, Washington, 1994—2000; project 2061 team contb. Benchmarks for Sci. Literacy, 1993. Author: (textbooks) SRA Real Science, SRA Science Math and You. Del. NEA, Washington, 2000—; bd. dirs. San Diego Educators Assn., San Diego, 2004—06. Mem.: NEA (del. 2000—), San Diego Educators Assn. (elem. seat 2004—), San Diego Edn. Assn. (bd. dirs. 2004—), Calif. Tchrs. Assn. (svc. ctr. coun. 2001—06, We Honor Ours award 2005), Delta Kappa Gamma. Democrat. Achievements include research in implementing technology in the curriculum. Home: 6218 Winona Ave San Diego CA 92120 Office: San Diego Unified Sch Dist 4100 Normal St San Diego CA 92103 Office Phone: 619-582-0136. Personal E-mail: cjvega@cox.com.

VEGA, SUZANNE, singer, songwriter; b. Santa Monica, Calif., July 11, 1959; m. Paul Mills, Feb. 11, 2006. Grad., Barnard Coll., 1982. Singer, songwriter, concert performer, 1975—. Began performing in Greenwich Village coffeehouses, N.Y.C., 1975; albums include Suzanne Vega, 1985, Solitude Standing, 1987, Days of Open Hand, 1990, 99.9 F, 1992, Nine Objects of Desire, 1996, Songs in Red and Gray, 2001; songs include Cracking, Marlene on the Wall, Tom's Diner, Luka, Solitude Standing, (song for Pretty in Pink soundtrack) Left of Center; concert tours of U.S., Can., Europe and Far East, 1987. Buddhist.*

VEIT, CLAIRICE GENE TIPTON, measurement psychologist; b. Monterey Park, Calif., Feb. 20, 1939; d. Albert Vern and Gene (Bunning) Tipton; children: Steven, Barbara, Laurette, Catherine. BA, UCLA, 1969, MA, 1970, PhD, 1974. Asst. prof. psychology Calif. State U., L.A., 1975—77, assoc. prof. psychology, 1977—80; rsch. psychologist Rand Corp., Santa Monica, Calif., 1977—2004; ret., 2004. Rsch. cons. NATO Tech. Ctr., The Hague, The Netherlands, 1980-81; faculty Rand Grad Sch., Santa Monica, 1993—97. Mem. NOW, L.A. Opera League, Sierra Club. Achievements include development of subjective transfer function method to complex sys. analysis and the mental health inventory. Avocations: mountain climbing, playing piano, travel, music, theater. Personal E-mail: cveit@sbcglobal.net.

VELASCO, ESDA NURY, speech and language professional; b. Cali, Colombia, Oct. 1, 1953; d. Florentino and Dominga (Castro) Rivera; m. William Lubin Velasco, July 29, 1972; children: Martin Hernando, Monica Marie, Jaime Mauricio, Christopher Michael. BA in Psychology and Spanish cum laude, Cleve. State U., 1989, MEd. Spanish tchr. Berlitz Sch. of Langs., Cleve., 1979-85; interpreter Fed. Ct., Cleve., 1980-87; founder, pres. ENV Global Comm. Inc., Cleve., 1987—, Spanish instr., interpreter, translater, 1987—. Interpreter various orgns., 1980-87. Mem. MLA, N.E. Ohio Translators Assn., Am. Translators Assn. (cert.). Roman Catholic. Avocations: music, reading, dance, horseback riding, camping. Office: ENV Global Comm 5005 Rockside Rd Ste 600 Cleveland OH 44131-6827 Office Phone: 216-573-3744. E-mail: nury@env.global.com.

VELASCO, JODI MARIE, military lawyer; b. Elk Grove Village, Ill., July 19, 1969; d. John Edward and Margaret Ann Velasco; m. Anthony Michael Elavsky, Mar. 2, 1993. AA, U. Md., 1993; BA in Women's Studies, U. Okla., 1997, BA in Polit. Sci., 1997, JD, 2001. Enlisted U.S. Air Force, 1989, advanced through grades to sr. airman, 1993; asst. judge advocate, capt. USAF Res. 507th Air Refueling Wing, Tinker AFB, Okla., 2003—. Mem. NOW (state treas. 1996-98), ACLU (chpt. v.p. 1999-2000), Res. Officer Assn., Phi Alpha Delta (chpt. clk. 1999-2000, chpt. justice 2000-01), Pi Sigma Alpha. Democrat. Roman Catholic. Avocations: triathlon, feminism, vegetarianism, animal rights. Office: 507 ARW/JA 7435 Reserve Rd Tinker Afb OK 73145 E-mail: jodi.velasco@tinker.af.mil.

VELASQUEZ, ROSE, realtor; b. N.Y.C., Feb. 27, 1947; d. Pascual Negrón and Maria Luisa Vazqueź; (div. 1985); 1 child, Lisa Marie Velasquez. Student, Bronx C.C., 1994. Lic. notary N.Y.; lic. in real estate sales. Sec. Commonwealth P.R., N.Y.C., 1966-72; exec. sec. Combustion Equipment Assn., N.Y.C., 1972-81; group adminstr. for internat. Ruder Finn & Rotman, N.Y.C., 1981-86; v.p. adminstrn. GCI Group Internat., N.Y.C., 1986-91; sales agt./broker assoc., sales mgr. Metro-Star, Bronx, N.Y., 1992-97; broker, owner Rose Velasquez, Inc., Realtor, Bronx, 1998—. Sales assoc. rep. Century 21 Met. N.Y./L.I. Brokers Coun., 1993-95, team leader sales assocs. round table discussions, 1994. Fellow Nat. Notary Assn., N.Y. State Assn. Realtors, Bronx-Manhattan Assn. Realtors (grievance com. 1996—, MLS subcom. 1999). Democrat. Avocations: reading, gardening, family activities, theater. Office: Rose Velasquez Inc Realtor 1301 Allerton Ave Bronx NY 10469-5610

VELAZQUEZ, LYZETTE EILEEN, neurologist; b. San Juan, P.R., Sept. 15, 1958; d. Marcos Antonio and Lydia Velazquez; divorced; children: David, Alexander. BS, U. P.R., 1979; MD, Ross U., 1983. Diplomate Am. Bd. Neurology. Intern N.Y. Health, Bklyn., 1984-85; resident in neurology Sci. Ctr. at Bklyn., 1985-88; attending physician Interfaith Med. Ctr., Bklyn., 1988-89; neuromuscular fellow Samaritan Hosp., L.A., 1992-93; rschr. Good Samaritan Hosp., L.A., 1993-94; attending neurologist Geisinger Med. Ctr., Danville, Pa., 1995-97; pvt. practice Bronx, N.Y., 1997—. Mem. Acad. Neurology. Office: Neuro Care Assocs 1811 Hone Ave Bronx NY 10461-1406 also: 4 Lorraine Pl Scarsdale NY 10583-2808

VELÁZQUEZ, NYDIA MARGARITA, congresswoman; b. Yabucoa, PR, Mar. 28, 1953; BA magna cum laude in Polit. Sci., U. PR, Rio Piedras, 1974; MA in Polit. Sci., NYU, 1976. Mem. faculty U. PR, Humacao, 1976—81; adj. prof. Puerto Rican studies CUNY Hunter Coll., 1981—83; spl. asst. Staff of US Rep. Edolphus Towns from NY, 1983; mem. City Coun., NYC, 1984—86; dir. Migration Divsn. Office Puerto Rico Dept. Labor and Human Resources, 1986—89; dir. Dept. Puerto Rican Cmty. Affairs in the US for the Commonwealth of PR, 1989—92; mem. US Congress from 12th NY dist., 1993—. Ranking minority mem. small bus. com. US Congress, 1998—, mem. fin. svcs. com. Named Woman of Yr., Hispanic Bus. Mag., 2003; recipient Small Bus. Beacon award, Nat. Small Bus. United, 2000, HerMANA award, MANA, 2002, Champion of Small Bus. Devel. award, Assn. Small Bus. Devel. Ctr., 2005. Democrat. Achievements include being the first Puerto Rican woman elected to the US Congress. Office: US Ho Reps 2241 Rayburn Ho Office Bldg Washington DC 20515-2104 Office Phone: 202-225-2361.*

VELAZQUEZ, OMAIDA CARIDAD, vascular surgeon, researcher; b. Pinar del Rio, Cuba, Oct. 25, 1966; d. Telesforo and Andrea Velazquez; m. Romulo Cuy, 1991; 1 child, Peter James Cuy. MD, U. Medicine and Dentistry N.J., 1991. Lic. physician N.J. Instr. gen. surgery U. Pa. Med. Sch., Phila., asst. instr. gen. surgery, 1992—96; attending surgeon Hosp. U. Pa., Phila., 1999—. Clin. faculty gen. and vascular surgery U. Pa. Med. Sch., Phila., 1999—; adj. asst. prof. Wistar Inst., Phila., 2001—, vis. scientist, 1999—2001; attending surgeon Presbyn. Med. Ctr., Phila., 1999—, Phila. VA Med. Ctr., 2001—03, Children's Hosp. Phila., 2001—; asst. prof. surgery U. Pa. Med. Sch., 1999—, ednl. coord. vascular divsn., 2002—. Contbr. articles to sci. rsch. jours. (Joel J. Roslyn award Assn.for Acad. Surgery, 2003); external reviewer: med. jours. Recipient Scholarship for the Advancement of Med. Edn., William F. Grupe Found., Inc., 1988, 1990, Krans-Henle Meml. Fund Scholarship, Krans-Henle Meml. Fund, 1989, von Liebig Found. Award for Excellence in Vascular Surg. Rsch., von Liebig Found., 2001, Residents Rsch. award, Phila. Acad. of Surgery, 1996, Young Careerist award, N.J. Bus. and Profl. Women, 1995, Surg. Student Rsch. award, Assn. for Academic Surgery, 1991, Dr. Gertrude Ash Meml. award, N.J. Med. Women's Assn., 1991, Merck Manual award for highest grade in internal medicine, 1990; grantee, NIH, 2003—. Fellow: ACS; mem.: AMA, AAAS, John Morgan Soc., Internat. Acad. Clin. and Applied Thrombosis/Hemostasis, Pa. Med. Soc., Am. Soc. Angiology, Soc. U. Surgeons, Phila. Acad. Surgery, Internat. Soc. Vascular Surgery, Bus. and Profl. Women, Assn. Women Surgeons, Assn. for Acad. Surgery, Am. Surg. Assn. Found., Am. Assn. Vascular Surgery, Soc. Clin. Vascular Surgery, N.Y. Acad. Sci., N.J. Med. Sch. Alumni Assn., Sigma Xi, Alpha Omega Alpha. Office: Hosp of Univ of Pa 3400 Spruce St 4 Silverstein Philadelphia PA 19104 Office Phone: 215-662-6451.

VELDEY, BONNIE, special education educator; b. Mpls., Jan. 24, 1960; d. George Joseph III and Ethel Annette Acko;m. Steve Douglas Veldey, June 13, 1991; 1 child, Tyler George. AA, Inver Grove C.C., Inver Grove Heights, Minn., 1989; BA, Coll. St. Catherine, 1991; MA in Spl. Edn., U. St. Thomas, 1998. Sci. tchr. Roma (Tex.) Ind. Sch. Dist., 1991-92; spl. edn. tchr. Clark County Sch. Dist., Las Vegas, Nev., 1996-99; pvt. practice spl. edn. tchr. Mpls., 1999—2001; tchr. spl. edn. Mpls. (Minn.) Pub. Schs., 2001—. Democrat. Roman Catholic. Home: 4331 Minnehaha Ave Minneapolis MN 55406-3908

VELEZ, INES, oral pathologist, educator; b. Bogota, Colombia, Apr. 15, 1946; arrived in US, 1999; d. Jose and Emilia (Marulanda) Velez; m. Eduardo Tamara (div.); children: Luis Tamara, Clara Lucia Tamara; m. Guillermo Torres, Mar. 30, 1992. DDS, Colombian Coll. Odontology, 1979; postgrad., U. Fla., 1982—84; MEd, U. Los Andes, 1989; M in Laser Dentistry, Acad. Laser Dentistry, 1997. Cert. tchr. Fla. Chair., prof. pathology Colombian Coll. Odontology, 1984—92, pres. asst., 1989—92, dir. biopsy svc., 1984—95; chair, prof., dir. biopsy svc. Columbian Sch. Medicine, 1991—98, dir. bioclinical area, 1997—98; asst. prof. to assoc. prof., dir. oral and maxillofacial pathology, dir. biopsy svc. Nova Southeastern U., Ft. Lauderdale, Fla., 2000—. Lectr. in field. Contbr. articles to profl. jours. Recipient Best Student award, Coll. Sans Facon, 1963, Colombian Coll. Odontology, 1979, Educator award, Fla. Dental Assn., 2003, Golden Apple award, Nova Southeastern U., 2003, Ctr. of Excellence award, 2004. Mem.: ADA, Broward County Dental Assn., Fla. Dental Assn., Pierre Fouchard Acad., Acad. Laser Dentistry, Columbian Acad. Oral Pathology (founder), Am. Acad. Oral and Maxillofacial Pathology, Omicron Kappa Upsilon. Home: 3524 Parkside Dr Davie FL 33328 Office: Nova Southeastern U 3200 S University Dr Fort Lauderdale FL 33328 Office Phone: 954-472-7810. Business E-Mail: ivelez@nova.edu.

VELISEK, CARYL ANNE, journalist; b. Cleve., Apr. 8, 1932; d. Frank Emil Masl and Emma Julia Stone; m. Aldrich Francis Velisek, Jr., Feb. 11, 1950; children: Aldrich Francis Velisek, III, Jamie Lynn Razga, Michael Henry, Douglas Allen, Peter Alexander. Editl. corr. The Delmarva Farmer, Easton, Md., 1980—. Author: (autobiographical) I Studied To Be An Opera Singer But I Married A Cowboy; editor: (yearbook) American Angus Auxiliary Yearbook. Choir mem. United Meth. Ch., Balt., 1952—, regional conf. lay leader, 2005—06, DC, 2005—06. Recipient Dorothy Emerson Citizenship award, Md. 4-H Program, 1991, Roy Porter Meml. award, Md. Pork Prodrs., 1992, Svc. to 4-H Adv. Coun. award, Howard County Md., 4-H Gold & Silver clover awards, Howard County 4-H Ext. Program. Mem.: Pa. Angus Assn. (exec. sec. 1968—72), Md. Angus Woman's Club (pres. 1990—2006), Md. Beef Coun. (chmn. bd. 1991—92), Md. Angus Assn. (exec. sec. 1972—90, Svc. award). Home: 5593 Cottonwood Ct Frederick MD 21703 Office: Am Farm Publs Inc PO Box 2026 Easton MD 21601 Office Fax: 410-822-5068. Personal E-mail: caryldefarm@yahoo.com. Business E-Mail: editorial@americanfarm.com.

VELLA, APRIL, mathematics educator; b. Bklyn., Apr. 28, 1972; d. Roy Thomas and Diana Mary Vella. BA in Secondary Edn., Boston Coll., Chestnut Hill, Mass., 1994; MS in Natural Scis., Rensselaer Poly. Inst., Troy, NY, 1998. Tchr. math. No. Valley Regional H.S., Old Tappan, NJ, 1994—. Scholar, Govs of NJ, 1990—94, Japan Fulbright Meml. Fund, 2006. Mem.: No. Valley Edn. Assn. (bldg. rep. 2006—06), Assn. Math. Tchrs. NJ, Nat. Coun. Tchrs. Math. Roman Catholic. Avocations: travel, skiing, hiking. Office: Northern Valley Regional High School 150 Central Ave Old Tappan NJ 07675 Office Phone: 201-784-1600. E-mail: vella@nvnet.org.

VELLA, RUTH ANN, real estate executive; b. West Chester, Pa., Aug. 18, 1942; d. Eric and Carmella Tanberg; children: Michele Francette Vella, Nicole Renae Vella. Grad., Realtor's Inst. Real estate sales assoc. Reeve Realty, Wilmington, Del., 1966-72; owner Realtor Heritage Realty, Wilmington, 1972—92; instr. sales Wilmington Coll., 1978-85; mem. faculty Del. State Coll., 1979—; prin., owner Omega Real Estate Sch., Newark, Del., 1989—; mgr. Weichert Realtors, 1996—2002; profl. devel. coord. Prudential Fox & Roach Realtors, 2002—. Instr. Realtor's Inst., dean, 1983, asst. dean, 1983—; owner, pres. Corporate Fitness of Del., 1991—; mem. ednl. com. Del. Real Estate Commn., 2003—; spkr. in field. Edn. com. Real Estate Commn., 2002—06, Del. Real Estate Commn.; dir. Del. Assn. Realtors, 2004—06. Named Educator of Yr., New Castle County, 1996. Mem. New Castle County Bd. Realtors (dir. 1983-86, edn. com.), Womens Coun. Realtors (past state pres., gov.), Nat. Assn. Realtors (nat. speaker, energy conservation instr., Cert. Real Estate Broker instr.), Leading Edge Soc. Roman Catholic. Avocation: aerobics instr. and personal trainer. Office Phone: 302-999-9999. Business E-Mail: omega@realestateschool.com.

VELLENGA, KATHLEEN OSBORNE, retired state legislator; b. Alliance, Nebr., Aug. 5, 1938; d. Howard Benson and Marjorie (Menke) Osborne; m. James Alan Vellenga, Aug. 9, 1959; children: Thomas, Charlotte Vellenga Landreau, Carolyn Vellenga Berman. BA, Macalester Coll., 1959. Tchr. St. Paul Pub. Schs., 1959-60, Children's Ctr. Montessori, St. Paul, 1973-74, Children's Ho. Montessori, St. Paul, 1974-79; mem. Minn. Ho. of Reps., St. Paul, 1980-94, mem. tax. com. and rules com., 1991—94, chmn. St. Paul del., 1987—90, chmn. criminal justice div., 1987—90, mem. Dem. steering com., 1981—94, chmn. judiciary, 1991, 92, chmn. edn. fin., 1993—94. Mem. St. Paul Family Svcs. Bd., 1994-95; exec. dir. St. Paul/Ramsey County Children's Initiative, 1994-2000. Chmn. Healthstart, St. Paul, 1987-91; mem. Children, Youth and Families Consortium, 1995-99, Macalester Coll. Bd. Alumni, 1995-2001; chair Minn. Higher Edn. Svcs. Coun., 2000—05, mem. 1995—; mem. Citizens League Bd., Minn., 1999-2002, State Commn. Cmty. Svc., 2000-04; bd. dirs. Sexual Violence Ctr., 2004-06; mem. U. Minn. Out of School Time Commn., 2004; mem. H.B. Fuller Found. Bd., 2005—. Mem. LWV (v.p. St. Paul chpt. 1979), Minn. Women Elected Ofcls. (vice chair 1994). Democrat. Presbyterian.

VENABLE, DIANE DAILEY, retired elementary school educator; b. Sedro Woolley, Wash., June 11, 1939; d. Howard A. and LaVerne L. Dailey; m. Thomas C. Venable, June 28, 1974; 1 child, Erin Dailey. B, Simpson Coll., 1962; B of Elem. Edn., Seattle Pacific U., 1966. Tchr. elem. sch. Kent Schs., Calif., 1966—69, Seattle Schs., 1969—76, Calif. Schs., Simi Valley, 1996—98; ret., 1998. Chair 37th Dem. Assembly Dist., 1993—94; missions elder Emmanuel Presbyn. Ch., Thousand Oaks, Calif., 2000—03. Mem.: Red Hat Soc. Avocations: scrapbooks, reading, travel, golf. Home: 1024 Via Palermo Thousand Oaks CA 91320 E-mail: ddvenable@adelphia.net.

VENABLE, SARAH, art educator; d. James Venable and Martha Buxton. BS, U. Mich. K-12 Art Tchr. Mich., 2001. Art tchr. North Mid. Sch., Saginaw, Mich., 2002—. Author of poems. Recipient Advanced Studio Art Achievement award, Mott C.C., 2000. Master: Viking Art Club (leader 2004—05); fellow: Saginaw Bay Nat. Writing Project; mem.: Mich. Art Edn. Assn., Nat. Art Edn. Assn. Avocations: singing, piano, painting, drawing, cross country skiing, travel. Office: North Mid Sch 1101 North Bond St Saginaw MI 48602 Office Phone: 989-399-5400.

VENABLES, NORINNE, administrative assistant, dancer, educator; d. Norman and Lily Venables. AA, Crafton Hills Coll., Yucaipa, Calif., 1994; AS, Loma Linda U., Calif., 1996; BS, Calif. State U. San Bernardino, 2004. Phys. therapy aide Redlands Cmty. Hosp., Calif., 1998—99; monitoring and adminstrv. position Office of Hearings and Appeals Social Security Adminstrn., San Bernardino, 1999—2001; receptionist/adminstrv. asst. Conservatory of Dance, Yucaipa, 1991—, dance instr., 1993—, retail sales Studio II Dancewear, 1994—. Named to Student Governing Bd., Loma Linda U., 1995—96, Dean's List, Calif. State U. San Bernardino, 2003. Office Phone: 909-794-6485.

VENDELA, model; b. Sweden; With Ford Models, Inc., N.Y., 1986, Elizabeth Arden, 1988. Appeared on cover of Sports Illustrated Swimsuit Edition, 1993.

VENDITTI, CLELIA ROSE See PALMER, CHRISTINE

VENDLER, HELEN HENNESSY, literature educator, poetry critic; b. Boston, Apr. 30, 1933; d. George and Helen (Conway) Hennessy; 1 son, David. AB, Emmanuel Coll., 1954; PhD, Harvard U., 1960; PhD (hon.), U. Oslo, 1981; DLitt (hon.), Smith Coll., 1980, Kenyon Coll., 1982, U. Hartford, 1985, Union Coll., 1986, Columbia U., 1987, Washington U., 1991, Marlboro Coll., 1989, Yale U., 2000; DHL (hon.), Fitchburg State U., 1990, Dartmouth Coll., 1992, U. Mass., 1992, Bates Coll., 1992, U. Toronto, Ont., Can., 1992, Trinity Coll., Dublin, Ireland, 1993, U. Cambridge, 1997, Nat. U., Ireland, 1998, Wabash Coll., 1998, U. Mass, Dartmouth, 2000, Yale U., 2000, U. Aberdeen, 2000, Tufts U., 2001, Amherst Coll., 2002, Colby Coll., 2003; DHL, Bard Coll., 2005. Instr. Cornell U., Ithaca, NY, 1960-63; lectr. Swarthmore (Pa.) Coll. and Haverford (Pa.) Coll., 1963-64; asst. prof. Smith Coll., Northampton, Mass., 1964-66; assoc. prof. Boston U., 1966-68, prof., 1968-85. Fulbright lectr. U. Bordeaux, France, 1968-69; vis. prof. Harvard U., 1981-85, Kenan prof., 1985—, Porter U. prof., 1990—, assoc. acad. dean, 1987-92, sr. fellow Harvard Soc. Fellows, 1981-93; poetry critic New Yorker, 1978-99; mem. ednl. adv. bd. Guggenheim Found., 1991-01, Pulitzer Prize Bd., 1991-99; Jefferson lectr. NEH, 2004. Author: Yeats's Vision and the Later Plays, 1963, On Extended Wings: Wallace Stevens' Longer Poems, 1969, The Poetry of George Herbert, 1975, Part of Nature, Part of Us, 1980, The Odes of John Keats, 1983, Wallace Stevens: Words Chosen Out of Desire, 1984; editor: Harvard Book of Contemporary American Poetry, 1985, Voices and Visions: The Poet in America, 1987, The Music of What Happens, 1988, Soul Says, 1995, The Given and the Made, 1995, The Breaking of Style, 1995, Poems, Poets, Poetry, 1995, The Art of Shakespeare's Sonnets, 1997, Seamus Heaney, 1998, Coming of Age as a Poet, 2003, Poets Thinking, 2004, Invisible Listeners, 2005. Bd. dirs. Nat. Humanities Ctr., 1989—93. Recipient Lowell prize, 1969, Explicator prize, 1969, award Nat. Inst. Arts and Letters, 1975, Radcliffe Grad. Soc. medal, 1978, Nat. Book Critics award, 1980, Keats-Shelley Assn. award, 1994, Truman Capote award, 1996; Fulbright fellow, 1954, Guggenheim fellow, 1971-72, Am. Coun. Learned Socs. fellow, 1971-72, NEH fellow, 1980, 85, 94, 04, 05, fellow Churchill Coll., Cambridge, 1980, Charles Stewart Parnell fellow Magdalene Coll., Cambridge, 1996, hon. fellow, 1996—; NEH Jefferson Lectr. scholar US Fed. Govt., 2004-05. Mem. MLA (exec. coun. 1972-75, pres. 1980), AAAL, English Inst. (trustee 1977-85), Am. Acad. Arts and Scis. (v.p. 1992-95), Norwegian Acad. Letters and Sci., Am. Philos. Soc. (Jefferson medal 2000), Phi Beta Kappa. Home: 54 Trowbridge St 2 Cambridge MA 02138-4113 Office: Harvard U Dept English Barker Center Cambridge MA 02138-3929 Office Phone: 617-496-6028.

VENERABLE, SHIRLEY MARIE, retired gifted and talented educator; b. Washington, Nov. 12, 1931; d. John Henry and Jessie Josephine (Young) Washington; m. Wendell Grant Venerable, Feb. 15, 1959; children: Angela Elizabeth Maria Venerable-Joyner, Wendell Mark. PhB, Northwestern U., 1963; MA, Roosevelt U., 1976, postgrad., 1985; student in Life Long Studies, Triton C.C., River Grove, Ill., 2002. Cert. in diagnostic and prescriptive reading, gifted edn., finger math., fine arts, Ill. Tchr. Lewis Champlin Sch., 1963-74, John Hay Acad., Chgo., 1975-87, Leslie Lewis Elem. Sch., Chgo., 1988-99, Robert Emmet Sch., Chgo., 1999—; self employed tutorial programs, 1999—2003; ret., 2003. Sponsor Reading Marathon Club, Chgo., 1991—; co-creator Project SMART-Stimulating Math. and Reading Techniques John Hay Acad., Chgo., 1987-90, curriculum coord., 1985-87; creative dance student, tchr. Kathryn Duham Sch., N.Y.C., 1955-56; creative dance tchr. Doris Patterson Dance Sch., Washington, 1953-55; recorder evening divsn. Northwestern U., Chgo., 1956-62; exch. student tchr. Conservatory Dance Movements, Chgo., 1958-59; art cons. Chgo. Pub. Sch., 1967. Author primary activities Let's Act and Chat, 1991-94, Teaching Black History Through Classroom Tours, 1989-90. Solicitor, vol. United Negro Coll. Fund, Chgo., 1994; sponsor 37th Ward Reading Assn. Marathon, Chgo., 1991-94, 99; active St. Giles Coun. Cath. Women, 1985-96; vol. REAC Ctr. Programs Books, Info., Literacy and Learning, 1997-98. Recipient Meritorious award United Negro Coll. Fund, 1990, 94, Recognition award Alderman Percy Giles, Chgo., 1993, Hall of Fame award Nat. Women in Achievement, Inc., 2005. Mem.: ASCD (assoc. Recognition of Svcs. award 1989), Internat. Reading Assn., Nat. Women of Achievement Assn. (Chgo. chpt.), Phi Delta Kappa, Sigma Gamma Rho (Delta Sigma grad. chpt. 1963—93, Sigma chpt. 1992, Eta Xi Sigma chpt.), Eta Xi Sigma (Pearl award for excellence in edn. 1997). Roman Catholic. Home: 1108 N Euclid Ave Oak Park IL 60302-1219

VENNEMAN, SANDY S., biology professor; b. St. Louis, Sept. 12, 1958; d. Francis Joseph and Grace Venneman. BA in Biology, U. Mo., St. Louis, 1981; MS in Exptl. Psychology, St. Louis U., 1992, PhD in Exptl. Psychology, 1996. Chemistry faculty Notre Dame H.S., St. Louis, 1982—86; chemistry alb. supr. St. Louis U., 1986—97; postdoctoral rschr. UCLA Neuropsychiat. Inst., 1997—99; assoc. prof. dept. biology and physiology U. Houston, Victoria, Tex., 1999—. Owner Sunshine Stables LLC, Yoakum, Tex., 1999—. Sunshine Rsch. Assocs., Yoakum, 2005—. Contbr. articles to profl. jours. Steering com. Victoria Ethics Com., 2001—; mem. DeTar Hosp. Ethics Com., 1999—; mem. human rights com. Gulf Bend Mental Health/Mental Retardation, Victoria, 1999—2005. Recipient Enron Tchg. Excellence award, U. Houston, 2002—03, Faculty Svc. award, 2005—06, Outstanding Rsch. award, Sigma Xi, 1992. Mem.: AAAS, Am. Psychol. Soc., Phi Kappa Phi (chpt. pres. 2004—05). Avocation: equestrian. Home: 4209 Edgar-Leesville Rd Yoakum TX 77995 Office: University of Houston 3007 N Ben Wilson Victoria TX 77901 Office Phone: 361-570-4213. Business E-Mail: VennemanS@uhv.edu.

VENRICK, KRISTIE LUND, mathematics educator; b. Longmont, Colo., Oct. 7, 1955; d. Myron Joseph and Christine Lorraine Thompson; m. James Thomas Venrick, Feb. 14, 1986; 1 child, Emily Lund. BS, Bethany Coll., 1977; MA, U. No. Colo., 2002. Tchr. St. Vrain Valley Schs., Longmont, Colo., 1978—2000, math. coord., 2000—. Named Educator of Yr., Longmont C. of C., 1996; recipient Presdl. award for Excellence in Math. and Sci. Tchg., White House and NSF, 2000. Mem.: AAUW, Nat. Coun. Suprs. Math., Nat. Coun. Tchrs. Math., Phi Delta Kappa. Republican. Lutheran. Home: 3567 Columbia Dr Longmont CO 80503 Office: St Vrain Valley Sch Dist 395 S Pratt Pky Longmont CO 80501

VENTERS, TERESA ANNE, elementary school educator; d. William Edward and Rosalie Scott Venters; 1 child, Kelly Nicole McMullen. BS, Ea. Ky. U., 1974; edn. cert., Pikeville Coll., 1988; MA, Morehead State U., 1991. Interior designer Continental Interiors, Pikeville, 1974—76; ins. clk. Pikeville Nat. Bank, 1979—85; dep. clk. County Clk. Ky., Pikeville, 1985—87; tchr. Pikeville Ind. Schs., 1988—. Mem. piloted-Ky. edn. learning profile State of Ky., Frankfort, 1991—92, mem. primary adv. com. for continued assessment, 1992—93. Contbr. poetry to anthologies. Mem. Pike County Humane Soc., Pikeville, 1987—; sponsor 4-H, Pikeville, 2000. Mem.: NEA, Pikeville Edn. Assn., Ky. Edn. Assn. Baptist. Avocations: painting, reading. Office: Pikeville Elem 105 Bailey Blvd Pikeville KY 41501

VENTO, M. THÉRÈSE, lawyer; b. N.Y.C., June 30, 1951; d. Anthony Joseph and Margaret (Stechert) V.; m. Peter Michael MacNamara, Dec. 23, 1977; children: David Miles, Elyse Anne. BS, U. Fla., 1974, JD, 1976. Bar: Fla. 1977, U.S. Dist. Ct. (so. and mid. dists.) Fla. 1982, U.S. Ct. Appeals (5th and 11th cirs.) 1981, U.S. Supreme Ct. 1985. Clk. to presiding justice U.S. Dist. Ct. (so. dist.) Fla., Miami, 1976-78; assoc. Mahoney, Hadlow & Adams, 1978-79, Shutts & Bowen LLP, 1979-84, ptnr., 1985-95; founding ptnr. Gallwey Gillman Curtis & Vento, P.A., 1995—2004; ptnr. Shutts & Bowen, LLP, 2004—. Trustee Miami Art Mus., 1988—, v.p., 1999—; trustee The Beacon Coun., 1995-97, Law Sch. Alumni Coun., U. Fla., 1994-2004. Fellow Am. Bar Found.; mem. Dade County Bar Assn. (dir. young lawyers sect. 1978-83, editor newsletter 1981-83), Fla. Assn. for Women Lawyers, Fla. Bar Assn. (bd. govs., young lawyers div. 1983-85, civil procedure rules com. 1983-90, exec. coun. trial lawyers sect. 1996-2004), The Miami Forum (v.p. 1987-88, bd. dirs. 1989-91, co-pres. 2001-2002). Home: 3908 Main Hwy Miami FL 33133-6513 Office: Shutts & Bowen LLP 201 S Biscayne Blvd Ste1500 Miami FL 33131 Office Phone: 305-347-7318. E-mail: TVento@shutts-law.com.

VENTOLA, FRANCES ANN, mathematics professor; d. Joseph Robert Kenny and Katherine Julia Franek; m. Ralph Frank Ventola, July 6, 1975; 1 child, Lauren Katherine. BA, Montclair State Coll., Upper Montclair, NJ, 1971; MEd, Rutgers U., New Brunswick, NJ, 1974. Cert. math. tchr. NJ, 1971. Math. tchr. Hazlet Bd. Edn., NJ, 1971—82; prof. math. Brookdale CC, Lincroft, NJ, 1982—. Coord. summer inst. for new precalculus tchrs. & leadership inst. Rutgers U., 1991—91; site coord. for sci. edn. grant NSF. Recipient Outstanding Colleague award, Brookdale C.C., 2000; Rsch. grant, Steven's Inst. Tech., 1994—95. Mem.: NEA, NJ Edn. Assn. Office: Brookdale CC Newman Springs Rd Lincroft NJ 07738

VENTURA, JACQUELINE N., retired nurse; b. Chgo., Sept. 17, 1942; d. Frank Joseph and Ellen Sarah (Healey) Ventura. Diploma, St. Francis Sch. Nursing, Evanston, Ill., 1963; BS, DePaul U., Chgo., 1967; MS, U. Wis., 1972, PhD, 1975-80. RN, Ill. Staff nurse Hines VA Hosp., Maywood, Ill., 1963-67; team leader US AID, Vinh Long, Vietnam, 1967-69; staff nurse Childrens Meml. Hosp., Chgo., 1969-70; clin. nurse specialist U. Wis. Hosps. and Clinics, Madison, 1972-75; nurse cons., instr. U. Wis. Sch. Nursing, Madison, 1975-78; asst. prof. nursing U. Calif., San Francisco, 1981-89, nurse rschr. dept. radiology, 1989-95; clin. rsch. assoc. Dendreon Corp., Seattle and Mountain View, Calif., 1996—2002, ret., 2003. Recipient Civilian Svc. award Govt. of South Vietnam, 1969. Mem.: AAUW, Drug Info Assn., Women's Overseas League, Sigma Theta Tau. Home: 1530 5th Ave San Francisco CA 94122-3835 Personal E-mail: jacquelineventura@hotmail.com.

VENTURACCI, TONI MARIE, artist; b. Battle Mountain, N.V., Nov. 19, 1958; d. Tony Simone Ancho and Deanna Paul; m. Steven Louie Venturacci, July 28, 1979; children: Daniel Steven, Kassi Marie. A in Bus., W.N.C.C., Fallon, N.V., 1999. Substitute educator Churchill County Sch. Dist., Fallon, Nev., 1998—2001; pvt. art tchr. Nev., 2000—01. Organizer fundraisers Nev. State H.S. Rodeo, 1998—2001. Mem.: Am. Paint Horse Assn. (accomplished painter), Am. Qtr. Horse Assn. (accomplished breeder). Republican. Roman Catholic. Avocations: horses, art work, sewing, cooking, rodeoing. Home: 445 Venturacci Ln Fallon NV 89406

VENTURINI, JUDITH ANNE, education educator; b. Oakland, Calif. d. Arthur Francis Venturini and Germaine Junet. BS, Calif. State U., Hayward, 1969, MS in Phys. Edn., 1985, MS in Edn. Leadership, 1991; MS in Edn., Nat. U., San Jose, Calif., 1999. Practitioner of science of mind RScP. Tchr., adminstrv. intern Redwood City (Calif.) Elem. Sch. Dist., 1970—91; ednl. cons., exec. dir. Kids-at-Heart, Fremint, Calif., 1991—94; D.A.T.E. coord. Hayward Unified Sch. Dist., 1994; regional dir. Sonoma County Office of Edn., Santa Rosa, Calif., 1994—95; prin. tchr. San Jose Unified Sch. Dist., 1995—2000; spl. edn. tchr. for autistic students Santa Clara County Office of Edn., San Jose, 2001—02; adj. prof. Calif. State U., Hayward, 2000—, Nat. U., San Jose, 2000—, Nat. Hispanic U., San Jose, 2000—. Facilities chair Bay Area Career Women, San Francisco, 1987—90; chair Sonoma County Phys. Edn. Com., Santa Rosa, Calif., 1994—95; dir. Sonoma County Office of Edn. Gang Prevention Network Task Force, Santa Rosa, 1994—95. Contbr. poetry to anthologies. Bd. dirs. Ardenwood Homeowners, Fremont, Calif., 1987—88; practitioner, divinity student Ctr. of Positive Living, 2000—. Recipient multiple honors in athletics, Playmates award, Calif. Dept. Edn., 1994, Healthy Start award, 1994, 1996, award for inspirational programs for children, Housing Authority of Santa Clara County, 2000. Mem.: NEA, Calif. Tchrs. Assn. Avocations: dancesport, poetry, art, golf, writing songs. Home: 5206 Tacoma Ln Fremont CA 94555 Office: Kids-at-Heart 5206 Tacoma Ln Fremont CA 94555 Personal E-mail: junu@earthlink.net.

VENTURINI, TISHA LEA, professional soccer player; b. Modesto, Calif., Mar. 3, 1973; Degree in phys. edn., U. N.C. Mem. U.S. Women's Nat. Soccer Team. Mem. championship team CONCACAF, Montreal, 1994. Named Player of Yr., Mo. Athletic Club, 1994; recipient Gold medal, Centennial Olympic Games, 1996, Silver medal, World Univ. Games, 1993, Hermann trophy, 1994. Achievements include 1999 World Cup Champion. Office: c/o US Soccer Fedn 1801 S Prairie Ave # 1811 Chicago IL 60616-1319

VENZER, DOLORES, artist; b. Atlanta, Ga., May 21, 1933; d. Simon Seymour I and Pearl Levy Moltack; m. Stanley Jerry Sater, June 1955; children: Robyn Degnan, Simon Sater, Denise Landwerlen; m. Alan Marvin Venzer, June 29, 1974; children: Sherrie Nowacki, Diane Ransen, Ellen Venzer. BFA, U. Ga., 1954. Artist 21st Century Gallery, Denver, Philinda Gallery, Edwards, Colo., Forms Gallery, Del Ray, Fla., Naked Horse Gallery, Scottsdale, Az., Artists Atelier of Atlanta, S.W. Accents Gallery, Woodstock, Vt., Hansen Gallery, Knoxville, Tenn. Co-owner past pres. Artist's Atelier of Atlanta, 1992-99; judge Callaway Garden's Art Exhibit, 1998. Recipient Merit award, Seasoned Eye 3, Modern Maturity Mag., 1990, Honorable Mention award, Grumbacher Hall of Fame, 1995, Artist's Choice award, Callaway Garden's, 1999, Grumbacher Choice Creative Artists Guild, Dalton, Ga., 1994. Mem. Ga. Coun. Arts, Artists Atelier Atlanta, Atlanta Arts Ctr., A.R.T. Station, S. Cobb Arts Alliance, Dekalb Coun. Arts. Republican. Jewish. Office: Artists Atelier Atlanta 800 Miami Cir NE Ste 200 Atlanta GA 30324-3048

VERAY, BRUNILDA, psychologist, educator; b. Mayaguez, Puerto Rico, June 11, 1948; m. Alberto J. Rivas, Sept. 12, 1970; children: Lisa Joanna, Ana Cristina, Alberto Juan. BA Social Work, Catholic U. PR, 1969; MA Psychology, U. PR, San Juan, 1976; MS in Clin. Psychology, Caribbean Ctr. Advanced Studies, 1983; PhD Clin. Psychol., Carribean Ctr. Advanced Studies, San Juan, P.R., 1985; Cert. in Geriatrics, Med. Scis. U. PR, 1990. Cert. Clin. Psychologist Bd. Psychologist Examiners, P.R. Instr. Cath. U. P.R., Ponce, 1973—76; psychologist Anti Addiction Svcs. Dept., Ponce, PR, 1975—79; prof. U. P.R., Ponce, 1979—; dir social sci. dept. U. P.R. Ponce, 1987—90, 2004—. Clin. psychol. cons. Mental Health Cmty. Clinic, Ponce, 1985—87; clin. psychologist Pvt. Practice, Ponce, 1997—2001; mem. ethics com. Psychologists Exam. Bd., San Juan, PR, 1989—91. Mem. adv. bd. protection of minors Social Svcs. Dept., Ponce, PR, 1983—92. Recipient Golden Lion award, Am. Union of Women Ponce chpt., 1988, Productivity award, U.P.R. Ponce, 1997. Mem.: APA, Interam. Psychology Assn., P.R. Psychol. Assn. Achievements include development of forensic psychology program leading to BA degree at U. PR Ponce. Avocations: drawing, painting, reading. Office: Univ PR at Ponce PO Box 7186 Ponce PR 00732 Office Phone: 787-944-8181. E-mail: bveray@hotmail.com.

VERDILL, ELAINE DENISE, artisan; b. Bellefontaine, Ohio, Nov. 5, 1955; d. Margaret (Miller) V. BS, Bowling Green State U., 1978. Coord. info. svcs. JILA, U. Colo., Boulder, 1990-96, budget analyst, 1996—. Mem. Hand-Weavers' Guild of Boulder. Avocation: photography. Office: JILA U Colo Cb 440 Boulder CO 80309-0001

VEREB, TERESA B., psychiatrist; b. Poland; d. Joseph and Henryka Biskup; m. Bartholomew Vereb, Aug. 3, 1968; children: Bartholomew Jr., Teresa Tilden. MD, Acad. Medicine, Warsaw, 1966. Cert. stress mgmt. Am. Acad. Experts in Traumatic Stress, 2005. Resident psychiatry Hosp. Wolsky, Warsaw, 1966—68, Med. Sch. Safarik U., Kosice, Czech Republic, 1968—70, staff psychiatry, 1971—72; resident psychiatry SUNY, Buffalo, 1977—78; clin. instr. psychiatry Meyer Meml. Hosp., Buffalo, 1977—78; resident psychiatry U. Fla., Gainesville, 1978—80; pvt. practice gen. psychiatry Bradenton, Fla., 1980—; staff psychiatrist Blake Hosp., Bradenton, 1980—, Manatee Meml. Hosp., Bradenton, 1980—, chief psychiatry, sectional chief psychiatry, 1981—85, 1987—91, chairperson psychiat. sect., 2000. Active Sacred Heart Cath. Ch., Bradenton, 1980—. Named Am. Top Psychiatrist, Consumer's Rsch. Coun. Am., 2006; recipient Disting. Physician award, Fla. Med. Assn., 2005. Mem.: AMA (Physician Recognition award 1995—2002, 2005—06), Am. Acad. Experts in Traumatic Stress, Manatee County Med. Soc., Fla. Psychiat. Assn., Fla. Med. Assn. (Physician Recognition award 1995—2005, Rogeriem Pfizer Re-Commn. 1999, Am. Top Rate Physician 1999, Top Psychiatrist 2004—05, Boar Cert. for stress mgmt. 2005), Am. Psychiat. Assn. Achievements include successfully climbed Mount Kilimanjaro, 1997. Avocations: water-skiing, skiing, swimming, hiking, mountain climbing. Office: Vereb and Vereb MDs PA 5015 Manatee Ave West Bradenton FL 34209

VERED, RUTH, art gallery director, owner; b. Tel Aviv, Sept. 26, 1940; d. Abraham and Helen Rosenblum; children: Sharon, Oren. BA in Art History with honors, Bezalel U., Jerusalem, 1964. Freelance art cons., Israel and N.Y.C., 1965-75; dir. Vered Gallery, East Hampton, N.Y., 1977—. Exhibited at Vered Gallery. Sgt. paratroops Israeli Army, 1958-60. Home: 891 Park Ave New York NY 10021-0326 Office: Vered Gallery 68 Park Pl East Hampton NY 11937-2407 E-mail: vered@mindspring.com.

VERGARA, LORENDA, retired physician; AA, U. Santo Tomas, Manila, Philippines, 1947, MD, 1952. Intern Marymount Hosp., Garfield Heights, Ohio, 1953—54, resident in internal medicine, 1954—56; fellow in pediat. Mt. Sinai Hosp. and Babies Children's Hosp., Cleve., 1956—58; physician in internal medicine and pediat. Manila, Philippines, 1960—67; physician Bedford, Ohio, 1967—69, Sagamore Children's Psychiat. Hosp., Northfield, Ohio, 1968—70, 1970, ckub, dur, 1971, staff physician, 1971—76; med. dir. Broadview Nursing Home, Parma, Ohio, 1975—77, Pleasantview Nursing Home, Parma, Ohio, 1976—77; staff psychiatrist Sagamore Children's Psychiat. Hosp., Northfield, Ohio, 1976—77; staff physician, surgeon Lanternman State Hosp., Pomona, Calif., 1977—78; physician Hygeia Health Ctrs., L.A., 1978—91; ret., 1991. Contbr. articles to profl. jours. Mem.: L.A. County Med. Assn., Calif. Med. Assn. Home: 21401 Miramar Mission Viejo CA 92692

VERGEREAU DEWEY, SYLVIE PASCALE, French and Spanish language educator; b. Limoges, France, Mar. 26, 1947; came to U.S., 1969; d. Albert Emile and Simone Jeanne (Massonneau) Vergereau; m. Michael Thompson Dewey, Mar. 30, 1974; children: Daniel Albert, Caroline Nicole. MA, Rice U., 1974, PhD, 1976. Cert. in secondary edn., double cert. in French and Spanish. Instr. French U. Southwestern La., Lafayette, 1969-71, 74; tchg. asst. Rice U., Houston, 1972-74; tchr. Latin Rolla (Mo.) H.S., 1977-78; tchr. French and Spanish R.80 Salem (Mo.) Sch. Dist., 1978-84; instr. English U. Lyon, France, 1985-88; assoc. prof. French and Spanish Kutztown (Pa.) U., 1990—2004, prof. French and Spanish, 2004—. Vis. lectr. French and Spanish Pa. State U., State College, 1988-90; methodology specialist, student tchr. supr. Coll. Edn., Kutztown U., 1990-93. Contbr. articles to profl. jours. and books. Mem. MLA, Am. Assn. of Tchrs. of French (pres. Lehigh Valley chpt. 1991—), Alliance Française (v.p. 1993—), N.E. Am. Soc. for 18th-Century Studies, Women in French, French for Bus. and Internat. Trade, Mid. Atlantic and New Eng. Conf. for Can. Studies, Pa. State MLA, Pi Delta Phi, Phi Sigma Iota. Avocations: gardening, hiking. Home: 247 E Main St Kutztown PA 19530-1516 Office: Kutztown U DF 104 Dept Fgn Langs Kutztown PA 19530 Office Phone: 610-683-4430. Business E-Mail: dewey@kutztown.edu.

VERGES, MARIANNE MURPHREE, writer; b. Oklahoma City, Apr. 19, 1939; d. Buren Thomas and Ellen Marie (Kanaly) Murphree; m. James Thomas Verges, Aug. 6, 1960; children: Keith, Philip, John, Stasi. BA, U.

Okla., 1962; postgrad., U. Tex., 1980-84. Interior designer A.J. Bullard, Oklahoma City, 1962-64; owner, ptnr. Stuff Novelty Co., Westport, Conn., 1972-79; freelance writer Dallas, 1983—. Author: On Silver Wings, 1990; columnist Children's Pages, 1982—; contbr. articles to various regional publs. Bd. dirs. Westport Young Women's League, 1972-79, Youth Adult Council, 1975-76, Alcohol Guidance Ctr., 1975-77; mem. Republican Women, Dallas, 1980—; bd. dirs. Frontiers of Flight Mus., 1989—. Mem. Greater Dallas Writers. Roman Catholic. Avocations: community volunteer work, travel, dog breeding and training, distance walking, sewing. Address: 6801 High Field Trl Plano TX 75023-1326

VERGEZ, SANDRA S., retired secondary school educator; d. Elmer R. and Lura B. (Harrison) Smith; m. Vergez Paul L., Mar. 17, 1979; children: Christopher, Brian, Laura. BA, Miami U., 1977; MA in Counseling Psychology, U. No. Colo., 2005. Cert. tchr. Wright State U., 1978, lic. profl. educator. Social studies tchr. Dist. 20, Colo. Springs, 1995—96; substitute tchr. Dist. 38, Monument, Colo., 1997—99; cath. edn. coord. U.S. Airforce Comty. Ctr., Colo. Springs, 2002—03; ret., 2003. Mem.: Pi Lambda Theta.

VERGONA, KATHLEEN DOBROSIELSKI, biology educator, researcher; b. Pitts., Dec. 6, 1948; d. Raymond Henry and Sophie Bernice (Rabazinski) Dobbs; m. Ronald Joseph Vergona, Sept. 1, 1973; 1 child, Raymond. BS, U. Pitts., 1970, PhD, 1976. Rsch. fellow Cancer Rsch. Ctr. Allegheny Gen. Hosp., Pitts., 1976; rsch. fellow dept. anatomy and cell biology Sch. Medicine U. Pitts., 1977-79, asst. prof. dept. anatomy and histology Sch. Dental Medicine, 1976-81, assoc. prof. dept. anatomy and histology, 1982—, rsch. asst. prof. dept. neurobiology, anatomy and cell sci. Sch. Dental Medicine, 1982—, chairperson dept. anatomy/histology, 1990-92, assoc. chairperson dept. anatomy/histology, 1997—. Lectr. Carnegie Mus. of Natural History, Pitts., 1984-85; faculty fellow Geriat. Edn. Ctr., Pitts., 1986—, dental curriculum coord. Editor: The Biology of Salivary Glands; contbr. articles to profl. jours. Judge Pa. Jr. Acad. of Sci., Pitts., 1976—, Am. Student Dental Assn., Pitts., 1978—. Recipient Achievement of Excellence award Geriat. Edn. Ctr. Pa., 1987, Outstanding Instr. award Am. Student Dental Assn., 1981, 83; Nat. Inst. on Aging rsch. fellow, 1976. Mem. Am. Soc. Cell Biology, Am. Assn. Oral Biologists (founding mem., pres.), Am. Assn. Dental Rsch. (councilor Pitts. chpt. 1989-92), Am. Assn. Dental Schs. (chair anatomic scis. sect. 1995-96), Tissue Culture Assn., Salivary Rsch. Group, Sigma Xi, Beta Beta Beta. Democrat. Roman Catholic. Avocations: piano, tennis, reading, puzzles. Home: 4943 Oakhurst Ave Gibsonia PA 15044-8393 Office: U Pitts Sch Dental Medicine 615-1 Salk Hl Pittsburgh PA 15261-0001

VERHAALEN, MARION, music educator; b. Milw., Dec. 9, 1930; d. Carl John Verhaalen and Agnes Rose Sieberlich. MusB, Alverno Coll., 1954; MusM, Cath. U., 1962; EdD, Columbia U., 1970. Tchr. music, organist, Milw. and Elgin, 1954—58; asst. prof. music Alverno Coll., Milw., 1958—78; instr. Wis. Conservatory Music, Milw., 1978—2005, Cardinal Stritch U., 2005—. Instr. various univs., conservatories, Brazil, 1973-90; cons., clinician Nat. and Internat. Piano Tchg. Founds. Editor: Musica Para Piano & Criando e Aprendendo, vols. 1-5, 1974-76; author: Keyboard Dimensions, 1984, Explorando Musica, 2 vols., 1988-90, Adult Piano Express, vols. 1-2, 1992, A Journey in Faith, 1997 (Gambinus award Milw. County Hist. Soc. 1998), Camargo Guarnieri Expressões de uma Vida, 2001, John Downey: A Creative Profile, 2005, Camargo Guarnieri: Brazilian Composer, 2005; contbr. articles to profl. jours.; staff editor Musart mag., 1963-69; editor Notes of Interest newsletter, 1983-90; solo and two piano recitals with Milw. Cath. Symphony; composer vocal and choral works including Let Us Now Praise Water, 1979, Hymn of Glory, 1979, The Prairie Woman, 1979-81, Judith, 1981, Lord God, Let Your Spirit Come, 1981, Nunc Transitus, 1982, Marian Litany, 1987, Songs of the Way, 1990, Paean of Praise, 1992, On Children, 1994, Psalms, 1996, also compositions and arrangements for piano including Duets on Four Brazilian Songs, 1973, Modes in Miniature (collection), 1975, Concertino for Piano Solo, 1978, Songs from Brazil, 1981, Fantasy Suite, 1983, Johnny Has Gone for a Soldier, 1983, Folksongs of America, Set I and II, 1984, Canon in D for 8 hands, 1984, Canon in D for solo piano, 1984, Contemporary Christian Classics (collection), 1988, Suite for Friends, 1988, More Folk Songs from Here and There, 1993, 12 Bars of Blues, 1994, Solo Adventures I, II, III and IV, 1997. Tchrs. Coll. scholar, 1969; grantee OAS, 1969-70, Wis. Arts Bd., 1981; Fulbright tchg. grantee, 1988; recipient Career Achievement award Milw. Panhellenic Assn., 1976, Outstanding Milw. Musician award Wis. Fedn. Music Clubs, 1980, Citation for Outstanding Svc. to Music Edn. in Wis., Wis. Fedn. Music Clubs, 1985. Mem. Wis. Music Tchrs. Assn. (editor newsletter 1997-99), MacDowell Club Milw., Delta Omicron (local and state chpt. pres. 1972-80, Outstanding Mem. award 1974). Avocations: travel, photography. Home: 2259 S 31st St Milwaukee WI 53215-2435 Personal E-mail: mverhaalen@aol.com.

VERHESEN, ANNA MARIA HUBERTINA, social worker; b. Heerenveen, Friesland, Netherland, Dec. 6, 1932; came to U.S., 1968; d. Hendrikus H. and Henrika C. (Kluessjen) V. BS, Mercy Coll., Detroit, 1981; MA, Sienna Height, Adrian, Mich., 1992. Childcare worker Schiedam, Netherland, 1952-54; social worker Rotterdam Halfweg, Netherland, 1954-59; childcare worker Mt. St. Ann's Home, Worcester and Lawrence, Mass., 1968-70; chem. dependency social worker St. Vincent Med. Ctr., Toledo, 1970-75; social worker St. Joseph Hosp., Nashua, N.H., 1975-78; vocation dir. Grey Nuns, Lexington, Mass., 1978-79; coord. community svcs. St. Vincents Med. Ctr., Toledo, 1981-91; pvt. practice Sylvania, Ohio, 1992—. Alcohol/drug addiction/mental health counselor for ex-prisoners; founder St. Vincent Med. Ctr. Alcoholism Detox and Rehab. Unit, Toledo, 1970-75. Co-founder Transitional Residences for the Homeless, Toledo, 1981-90, Ohio Coalition for the Homeless, Columbus, 1982-89; co-founder of a home for persons with AIDS; co-chair City of Toledo Housing Policy, 1985-90; coord. Housing Now, Toledo, 1988-90. Recipient Woman of Achievement award Women in Communication, Toledo, 1986, Spirit of '87 award N.W. Ordinance and U.S. Constn. Bicentennial Commn., Toledo, 1987, Gov.'s Spl. Recognition award, 1988, Man for Others award St. John's High Sch., 1991; named Woman of Toledo, St. Vincent Med. Ctr. Aux., 1988, Ohio Ho. of Reps., 1987; featured in various mags. Roman Catholic. Home: Apt 127 2015 N Mccord Rd Toledo OH 43615-3071 Office: Elliott and Assocs Inc Sophia Counseling Ctr 6832 Convent Blvd Sylvania OH 43560 Office Phone: 419-885-1910.

VERHOEK, SUSAN ELIZABETH, botany educator; b. Columbus, Ohio, 1942; m. S.E. Williams; 1 child. Student, Carleton Coll., 1960-62; BA, Ohio Wesleyan U., 1964; MA, Ind. U., 1966; PhD, Cornell U., 1975. Herbarium supr. Mo. Bot. Garden, St. Louis, 1966-70; asst. prof. Lebanon Valley Coll., Annville, Pa., 1974-82, assoc. prof., 1982-85, prof., 1985—. Vis. researcher Cornell U., Ithaca, N.Y., 1982-83; content cons. Merrill Pub. Co., 1987-89; vis. profl. Chgo. Bot. Garden, 1991. Author: How to Know the Spring Flowers, 1982; contbr. articles to profl. jours., newspapers, and bulls. Trustee Lebanon Valley Coll., Annville, 1979-82, 84-90, 92-98; dir. Lebanon Valley Coll. Arboretum, 1996—. Mem. Soc. for Econ. Botany (pres. 1985-86), Bot. Soc. Am., Am. Pub. Gardens Assn. Office: Lebanon Valley Coll Dept Biology Annville PA 17003-0501 Office Phone: 717-867-6178. Business E-Mail: verhoek@lvc.edu.

VERI, FRANCES GAIL, musician, educator; b. Lancaster, Pa., Dec. 6, 1942; d. Frank Americus Veri and Ada Margaret Kirk; m. Michael George Jamanis, Aug. 29, 1964; 1 child, Michael Thomas Jamanis. BS, Juilliard Sch., 1964, MS, 1965. Faculty Hartt Coll. Music, Hartford, Conn., 1964—66, Lebanon Valley Coll., Annville, Pa., 1966—71; artist-in -residence Franklin Marshall Coll., Lancaster, 1971—74; duo-pianist Veri & Jamanis, Columbia Artists, NYC, 1974—88; co-founder Pa. Acad. Music, Lancaster, 1989, dean, 1991—; pres. Prince Prodns., Inc., Lancaster, 1999—. Advisor Nat. Fedn. Music Clubs, 1991—96. Walter Damrosch scholar, Fontainebleau Sch. Fine Arts, 1969. Mem.: ASCAP. Episcopalian. Avocations: poetry, writing. Home: 1109 Marietta Ave Lancaster PA 17603 Office: Pa Acad Music 42 N Prince St Lancaster PA 17603 Office Phone: 717-399-9733. Personal E-mail: verijamanis@princeproductions.com. Business E-Mail: fveri@pamusacad.org.

VER KUILEN, MARION JANE, retired instructional aide; b. Junction City, Wis., July 22, 1928; d. Fred A. and Mary Swanson; m. Theodore William Ver Kuilen, Feb. 8, 1947 (dec. Oct. 24, 1990); children: Victor Vernon, Van Vardon, Valerie Victoria, Venetta Venise Parrish, Vincent Vaughn. Student, Mt. San Antonio Coll., Walnut, Calif., 1977—78. Asst. mgr. Plz. Stationers and Book Store, West Covina, Calif., 1971—77; instrnl. aid Hacienda La Puente Unified Sch. Dist., La Puente, Calif., 1985—2005; ret., 2005. Photographer Reflections from the Past: Desert Twilight, America at the Millennium- The Best Photos of the 20th Century. Sec. Sunset Wesleyan Ch., La Puente, 1985—86; pres. Am Vets Auxillary, La Puente, 1958—61; den mother Boy Scouts Am., Rockford, Ill., 1954—57, San Pedro, Calif., 1958—59, La Puente, 1969—71. Named Outstanding Salesperson of Yr., West Covina C. of C., 1977, Outstanding Classified Employee of the Yr., Hacienda-La Puente Unified Sch. Dist., 1997; recipient In Svc. of Our Youth award, Mayor of Rockford, 1956, Best Photos of 2003 award, Editors Choice award, Internat. Libr. Photography, 1998—99. Mem.: DAV (assoc.), Nat. Geog. Soc. (corr.), Mt. Vernon Assn. (corr.), Colonial Williamsburg Assoc. (assoc.), WWII Veterans Meml. (life Charter Mem.), History (assoc.), WWII Mus. (assoc.), Sierra Club (corr.). Avocations: photography, reading, gardening. Home: 16105 Harvest Moon St La Puente CA 91744-1337

VERLEY, BARBARA ANN, music educator; b. Nashville, Aug. 4, 1953; d. James Edward and Mary Leila Goodwin; m. Robert Alan Verley, Dec. 21, 1990. Elem./Jr. High Adminstrv. Lic., Ind. State U., 1994—96; BA, U. of Evansville, MS in sch. guidance and counseling, 1992—94, MA, 1976—79. Music tchr. Castle Jr. HS, Newburgh, Ind., 1976—, Wash. Elem. Sch., Evansville, Ind., 1975—76. Choral condr. Castle Jr. HS, Newburgh, 1976—92, tchr.'s credit union faculty rep., 1979—, departmental lead tchr., 1980—, academic bowl coach for dramatic interpretation, prose, and poetry, 1985—2001, talent show coord., 1987—, student/tchr. sponsorship program leader for at-risk students, 1988—90, performance-based accreditation correlate chair, 1988—90, faculty adv. chair, 1992—93, adminstrv. intern, 1993—94, reality store project co-chair, 1993—94, profl. devel. com. mem., 1999—2002, student discipline-free com. chair, 1999—2002, sch. improvement com. team mem., 2001, student facilitator for strengthening families program, 2002—03, sect. 504 com. mem.; castle h.s. summer band camp coach Castle HS, Newburgh, 1984—86; Ind. state sch. music assn. judge ISSMA, 1988; north ctrl. assn. team mem. Ind. State U., Terre Haute, 1993—94. Musician Bethel Temple Cmty. Ch., Evansville, Ind., 1989—2002, First Christian Ch., Newburgh, Ind., 2001—. Nominee Disney's Outstanding Tchr. of the Yr. award, Disney, 1998, 2001; recipient musician, All-American Youth Honor Band in Europe, 1971. Mem.: NEA (assoc.), Ind. State Tchrs. Assn. (assoc.; faculty rep. 1983—85), Music Educators Nat. Conf. (assoc.), Phi Kappa Phi (assoc.), Chi Sigma Iota (assoc.), Sigma Alpha Iota (assoc.). Avocations: computer, cars, flute, keyboards, bass. Home: 5999 Hunter Rd Boonville IN 47601-8410 Office: Castle Junior HS 2800 HWY 261 PO Box 677 Newburgh IN 47629-0677 Office Phone: 812-853-7347. Personal E-mail: zyaa35@netzero.net.

VERLICH, JEAN ELAINE, writer, public relations executive, consultant; b. McKeesport, Pa., July 5, 1950; d. Matthew Louis and Irene (Tomko) V.; m. S(tanley) Wayne Wright, Sept. 29, 1979 (div. June 1988). Student, Bucknell U., 1968-69; BA, U. Pitts., 1971. Pres. sec. Com. to Re-elect Pres., S.W. Pa., 1972; adminstrv. asst. Pa. Rep. James B. Kelly III, 1972-73; reporter Beaver (Pa.) County Times, 1973-74; proofreader Ketchum, MacLeod & Grove, Pitts., 1975-76; cmty. rels. specialist PPG Industries, Pitts., 1976-77; editor PPG News, 1977-79, sr. staff writer, 1979-84, comm. coord., 1984-85; pub. rels. assoc. Glass Group, 1986-87; mgr. pub. rels. Glass Group PPG Industries, 1987-92; account mgr. Maddigan Comm., Pitts., 1992-93; owner JV Comm., Pitts., 1993—; news editor Clovis News Jour., 2006—. Mem. Internat. Assn. Bus. Communicators (bd. dirs. Pitts. chpt. 1981, v.p. pub. rels. Pitts. chpt. 1982, v.p. programs Pitts. chpt. 1985, pres. Pitts. chpt. 1986), Travelers Aid Soc. Pitts. (bd. dirs. 1992-95, v.p. 1994-95), Phi Beta Kappa, Delta Zeta, Automotive Pub. Rels. Coun. Office Phone: 505-693-6991. Business E-Mail: jverlich@jvcommunications.com.

VERMEER, MAUREEN DOROTHY, sales executive; b. Bronxville, N.Y., Mar. 21, 1945; d. Albert Casey and Helen (Valentine Casey) Vermeer; m. John R. Fassnacht, Feb. 11, 1966 (div. 1975); m. George M. Dallas Peltz IV, Oct. 26, 1985. Grad., NYU Real Estate Inst., 1976. Lic. real estate broker, NY. With Douglas Elliman, N.Y.C., 1965-74, mgmt. supr., 1974-78, v.p., 1978-83; real estate broker Rachmani Corp., N.Y.C., 1983-84; v.p. sales and mktg. Carol Mgmt. Corp., N.Y.C., 1984-90; v.p. mktg. The Sunshine Group, N.Y.C., 1990; v.p., sec., bd. dirs. H.J. Kalikow & Co., N.Y.C., 1991—. Mem. Real Estate Bd. N.Y. (bd. dirs., residential mgmt. com.), Assn. Real Estate Women (bd. dirs.officer, chmn. charitable fund) Republican. Presbyterian. Avocations: skiing, scuba diving. Home: 111 Broadway Norwood NJ 07648-1412 Office: H J Kalikow & Co 101 Park Ave Fl 25 New York NY 10178-0002

VERMILION, MARSHA RENEE, secondary school educator; b. Columbia City, Ind., Oct. 23, 1964; d. James Melvin and Vonne Ann McKinley; m. Ronald Lee Vermilion, July 24, 1993; children: Lane McKinley, Chloe Elysse, Shaylee Adele. BS, Ind. State U., Terre Haute, 1987. Tchr, Oak Hill H.S., Mier, Ind.; tchr. Chatard H.S., Indpls., Marion H.S., Ind., 1998—. Tchr. Grant County Sheriff's Dept., Marion. Actor: (Marion civic theatre) Various Plays (Clarence Slusser Award); dir.:, (various h.s. prodns.); singer: (oldies band) The Posse. Home: 130 North Washington Street Marion IN 46952 Office: Marion High School 750 West Twenty-Sixth Street Marion IN 46953

VERMILLION, JULIA KATHLEEN, music educator; b. Beardstown, Ill., June 28, 1958; d. Beulah Mahalah and Charles Francis Warden; m. Danny Lee Vermillion, July 15, 1978; 1 child, Erica. BA, We. Ill. U., 1980. Tchr. Beardstown (Ill.) Cmty. Sch. Dist., 1993—; choir dir. Beardstown United Meth. Ch., 1992—. Cmty. choir dir. Beardstown Cmty. Choir, 1991—. Named Most Inspirational HS Tchr., Western Ill. U., 2004; recipient Tchr. of Yr. award, Wal Mart, 1998, Tchr. of Month award, Beardstown Rotary Club, 1995. Mem.: Ill. Music Educators Assn. (dist. IV jr. high choral chair 1997—2005, dist. IV H.S. choral chair 2005—). Methodist. Avocation: travel. Home: 6256 Crooked Ln Beardstown IL 62618 Office: Beardstown Community Unit Sch Dist 200 East 15th St Beardstown IL 62618

VERNAZZA, TRISH BROWN (TRISH EILEEN BROWN), visual artist, art therapist, sculptor; b. Tampa, Fla., Mar. 22, 1958; d. Burrell Joseph and Katharine Stowell (Weekly) B. BFA in Art History, U. South Fla., 1993; MA in Clin. Feminist Psychology, New Coll. Calif., 1997; postgrad., U. Calif., Berkeley, 1997. Lic. marriage and family therapist, art therapist; older adult tchr. Flight attendant Pan Am. World Airways, N.Y.C., 1989—91; art therapist jail psychiat. svcs. Haight Ashbury Free Clinics, San Francisco, 1997—99; art instr. to older and disabled adults, 1999—; pvt. practice psychotherapy Carlsbad, Calif., 2003—. Judge John's Seafood Festival, Madeira Beach, Fla., program mgr., Mental Health Sys., 2002—04; expert Starting Over, NBC Warner Bros., 2006; presenter in field. Artist: worked with HIV Women/AIDS Artreach phase 3, sculpture, 1994; group shows include Centre Gallery, U. So. Fla., 1994, U. Mobile Ala., 1994, Ctr. for Contemporary Art, Tampa, 1994, Fla. State U. Gallery and Mus., Tallahassee, 1994, Valencia C.C., Orlando, Fla., 1993, Tandemn Art Ctr., Venice, Fla., 1993, Richmond Art Ctr., Calif., 1996, calendar Richmond Art Ctr., 1997, Sonoma Art Festival, 1997, Napa Valley Mustard Festival, 1998, Sebastopol Art Ctr., 1999, Vista Utility Box, Calif., 2003, 2004; author: Women Art & Mental Illness; works included in pvt. collections; co-chair VAgina Monologues, Carlsbad, Calif., 2006; quest expert, art therapist TV reality NBC Show Starting Over, 2006—; contbr. articles to profl. jours. Vol. art/crafts instr. Substance Abused Mothers Against Drugs, Tampa, 1993; vol. docent Salvador Dali Mus., St. Petersburg, Fla., 1986-88; mem. Women's Caucus for Art; active multicultural workshops arts & crafts for children, Clearwater, Fla., 1995; intersession instrs. arts & crafts for children, Alameda, Calif., 1995-98; vol. art therapist chronic mentally ill adults Berkeley Creative Living Ctr., 1996-97. Recipient Hillsborough County Emerging Artist award; named to Wall of Tolerance So. Poverty Law, Ala.; named Woman of Merit, North County San Diego; grantee Serpent Source Found. women, San Francisco. Mem. Women in Psychology, Calif. Assn. Marriage and Family Therapists, San Diego North County Assn. Marriage Family Therapists, North County African-Am. Women's Assn., Oceanside Mus. Art. Democrat. Avocations: art therapist and visual artist with a feminist, female and feminine voice addressing social, political and gender issues. Office Phone: 760-439-8874. Personal E-mail: info@trishv.com.

VERNERDER, GLORIA JEAN, retired librarian; b. Ft. Wayne, Ind., June 2, 1930; d. John Otto and Vergie W. Krieg; m. Carl Penrod Vernerder, Dec. 25, 1952 (dec. Sept. 1984); children: Carla Jeanne Vernerder Kelly, Nina Marie Vernerder Anderson. Grad., Midway (Ky.) Coll.; student, Ind. U., Ft. Wayne, U. Ky. Br. libr. Pub. Libr. of Ft. Wayne and Allen County, 1950-52; children's libr. La Grange (Ill.) Pub. Libr., 1952-59, Hinsdale (Ill.) Pub. Libr., 1961-68, head of youth svcs., 1969-95. Editor: Sunlight and Shadows, 1983, 87, 90, 92; contbr. articles to profl. jours. Mem. adminstrv. bd. First United Meth. Ch., La Grange, 1986-88, Stephen Ministry, 1986—, v.p. United Meth. Women, 1995-98, pres., 1998-00, mem. adminstrv. bd., 1996-00; mem. Interfaith Cmty. Ptnrs., 2005-, Aging Well, 2004-, Newcomers' Alumnae Club, 2005-. Mem. ALA, Ill. Libr. Assn., Libr. Adminstrs. Conf. of No. Ill. (treas. 1969), La Grange Woman's Club (v.p. 1998-00, pres. 2000-02), Gen. Fedn. Women's Clubs, Ill. Fedn. Women's Clubs (6th dist. pres. 2002-04). Republican. Methodist. Avocations: storytelling, theater, reading.

VERNON, ANN, educator, therapist; d. Maurice Eugene and Ethyl Mae Suhumskie; m. Nile D. Vernon, Aug. 15, 1970; 1 child, Eric John; m. Ronald D. Nazette (dec.). BA, U. Iowa, Iowa City, 1968, MA in Edn., 1971, PhD, 1980, DSc (hon.). Cert. NCC, LMHC. Tchr. English, Suhn Cmty. Schs., Iowa, 1968—70; elem. counselor Iowa City Schs., 1971—72; tchr. English, Holona Jr. H.S., Cedar Falls, Iowa, 1972—73; elem. counselor Price Lab. Sch., Cedar Falls, Iowa, 1973—83; therapist Covenant Psychiatry, Cedar Falls, Iowa, 1989—; prof. U. No. Iowa, Cedar Falls, 1983—. Author: What Works When with Children and Adolescents, 2002, Counseling Children and Adolescents, 2004, Thinking,k Feeling, Behaving, 2006. Recipient Outstanding Svc. award, Iowa Assn. Counseling, Regents Faculty award, Iowa Bd. Regents. Mem.: Am. Counseling Assn., Assn. for Counselor Educators and Suprs. (Outstanding Svc. award). Avocations: travel, reading, writing. Home: 37721 S Desert Sun Dr Tucson AZ 85739 Office Phone: 319-273-2221. Fax: 319-273-5195.

VERNON, DORIS SCHALLER, retired newswriter, publishing executive; b. Petoskey, Mich., Mar. 7, 1915; d. Harve and Edna (Covey) Fredrickson; m. William Albert Schaller, Oct. 18, 1938; children: Kirk, Karen, Brent. Student, Cleary Coll., 1936-37, North Cen. Mich. Coll., 1960-61, 66-69. Sec. Mr. Beebe, Dean Freshman Coll., Petoskey, Mich., 1934-35, Dr. Dean C. Burns, Burns Clinic, Petoskey, 1937-38; with Probate and Juvenile Ct. Register, Petoskey, 1956-60; sec. bd. No. Mich. Rev., Inc., Mich., 1960-93; ret., 1996. Bd. dirs., Petoskey Friendship Ctr., gardening com., 2001—. Contbr. travel stories to profl. publs. Cub scout leader, Petoskey; treas. Camp Daggett Bd.; pres. Bus. and Profl. Women's Club, Petoskey, 1974-75; state bd. Don't Waste Mich., Riga and Lansing, 1989—, bd. dirs. No. bd., 1988—; civic gardening chair Petoskey Area Garden Club, sec., 1986; program chair Keenagers, First Christian Ch.; choir mem. First Christian Ch.; dir. Friendship Chorus for Care Ctrs. Singing Monthly Programs, Emmet County; bd. dirs. Friendship Ctr. Petosky, Mich., 1997-2001. Recipient cert. of commendation Guardian of the Earth, No. Mich., 1997. Avocations: square dancing, quilting.

VERNON, JANE HARPER, music educator; b. Kinston, N.C., Aug. 10, 1955; d. James Thurman and Anita Smith Harper; m. Richard Thomas Vernon, June 11, 1977; children: Ryan Harper, Will Thomas. BMus in Edn., East Carolina U., Greenville, 1977; MMus in Edn., East Carolina U., 1990. Cert. music tchr. 2005. Gen. music k-12 Southwood Elem. Sch., Kinston, NC, 1979—. Dir. of music Southwood Meml. Christian Ch., Kinston, 1980—2006. Named Tchr. of the Yr., Southwood Elem. Sch., 1984—85. Mem.: NEA, Music Educators Assn. Office: Southwood Elementary School 1245 Hwy 58 S Kinston NC 28504 Office Phone: 252-527-9081. E-mail: jvernon@lenoir.k12.nc.us.

VERNON, LILLIAN, mail order company executive; b. 1927; d. Herman and Erna Menasche; m. Paolo Martino; children: Fred, David. DCS (hon.), Mercy Coll., Dobbs Ferry, N.Y., 1984, Coll. New Rochelle; DSc in Bus. Adminstrn. (hon.), Bryant Coll.; LLD (hon.), Baruch Coll.; LHD (hon.), Old Dominion U.; DCS (hon.), Mercy Coll.; DCS Coll. New Rochelle (hon.); D. in Bus. Adminstrn. (hon.), Bryant Coll.; LLD (hon.), Baruch Coll. Founding chmn. Lillian Vernon, Rye, NY, 1951—. Lectr. in field. Contbr. articles to profl. jours. Trustee Coll. Human Svcs., Bryant Coll.; mem. adv. bd. Giraffe Project Girl Scout Coun. Tidewater; mem. adv. bd. Women's News; mem. bd. overseers Columbia U. Bus. Sch., NYU; mem. adv. com. Citizens Amb. Program; mem. bus. com. Met. Mus. Art; bd. govs. The Forum; mem. nat. com. The Kennedy Ctr. for Performing Arts, Washington; active The Ellis Island Reopening Com.; Bd. dirs. Westchester County, Ctr. Preventive Psychiatry, Va. Opera, Children's Mus. Arts, Retinitis Pigmentosa Found. Named Va. Press Women Newsmaker of Yr., woman of Yr., Women's Direct Response Group and Westchester County Fedn. Women's Clubs, Hampton Rds. Woman of Yr., So. New Eng. Entrepreneur of Yr.; named to Acad. Women Achievers, YWCA, Direct Mktg. Assn. Hall of Fame, Conn. Women's Hall of Fame; recipient Disting. Achievement award, Lab. Inst. Merchandising, Entrepreneurial award, Women's Bus. Owners of N.Y., 1983, Bravo award, YWCA, Woman of Achievement award, Woman's NEws, Nat. Hero award, Big. Bros./Big Sisters, Legend in Leadership award, Emory U., A Woman Who Has Made a Differene award, Inter. Womens Forum, medal of honor, Ellis Island, Bus. Leadership award, Gannett Newspapers, Outstanding Bus. Leader award, Northwood Inst., Congl. Record Commendation award, Crystal award, Coll. Human Svcs., City of Peace award, Bonds of Israel, Svc. award, Sr. Placement Bur., Excellence award, Westchester Assn. Women Bus. Owners, Commendation in Cong. Record, Magnificent Seven award, Bus. and Profl. Women, Woman of Distinction award, Birmingham So. Coll. Mem.: Nat. Retail Fedn. (bd. dirs.), Women's Forum, Com. of 200, Am. Stock Exch. (listed co. adv. com.), Am. Bus. Conf. (dir.), Lotos Club. Office: Lillian Vernon Corp 445 Hamilton Ave White Plains NY 10601-1836

VERNON, OLYMPIA FLECHET, writer; b. Bogalusa, La., May 22, 1973; d. Fletcher Williams, Jr. and Faye Ann Williams. BA in Criminal Justice, S.E. La. U., 1999; MFA, La. State U., Baton Rouge, 2002. Writer-in-residence S.E. La. U., Hammond, La., 2004—; Hallie Brown Ford chair Willamette U., Salem, Oreg., 2006—. Author: (novel) Eden (AAAL Richard and Hinda Rosenthal Found. award, 2004), (short story) Guts, The Humble I, Diary, (poem) Untitled, (novel) Logic, A Killing in This Town, (short story) Redemption, In His Favor, Schekovski; painting, Pre and Post, oil pastel, Eden. Spkr. Bluffton (S.C) H.S., 2006, Nat. Mus. Women in Arts, Washington, 2006; mentor Ronald McNair Program, Baton Rouge, 2005; spkr. Tangipahoa Parish Sch., Hammond, Kentwood, and Baton Rouge, La., 2005. Recipient Dir.'s award for Profl. Outstanding Achievement, La. State U., 2001, Alumnus of Yr., Southeastern La. U., 2004, Profl. Artist of Yr., Gov. State of La., 2005; Matt Clark Meml. scholar, La. State U., 1999, 2000, Words and Music scholar, Tenn. Williams Festival, 2000. Mem.: PEN. Office: Willamette Univ Dept English 900 State St Salem OR 97301 Office Phone: 5033706210 (HR Dept). Personal E-mail: vernonof@yahoo.com.

VERONICA, DEBRA CLARISSE, principal; b. Buffalo, Sept. 17, 1966; d. John Thomas Owczarek and Dolores Pauline Evans; m. Mark David Veronica, Apr. 7, 1989; 4 children. BSc, State U. of NY at Buffalo, 1988, MSc, 1995. Cert. Teaching NY, 1996. Tchr. St. Barnabas Sch., Depew, NY, 1988—89, St. Amelia Sch., Tonawanda, NY, 1989—91, Buffalo Pub. Sch., 1991—2003; adj. prof. Canisius Coll., Buffalo, 2001—03; asst. prin. Lancaster Pub. Sch. Sys., NY, 2003—04; elem. prin. Maryvale Sch. Sys., Cheektowaga, NY, 2004—. Summer sch. prin. Sweet Home Sch., Amherst, NY, 2003; ednl. cons. Discovery Toys. Vol. tchr. St. Amelia Religious Edn. Dept., 1988—90, 1992; pres. Mother of Twins Club of Buffalo, 2002—04, corresponding sec., 2000, 2001, club adv., 2004—06. Mem.: Internat.

Reading Assn., Sch. Admin. Assn. of NY State, Assn. for Supervision and Curriculum Devleop., Nat. Assn. of Elem. Sch. Prin., Phi Alpha Theta, Kappa Delta Pi. Avocation: reading. Office: Maryvale Sch Sys 1 Nagel Dr Buffalo NY 14225

VERONNEAU-TROUTMAN, SUZANNE, retired ophthalmologist; b. Coaticook, Que., Can., Oct. 30, 1928; d. Sarto Veronneau and Victorine Marcoux; m. Richard C. Troutman, July 12, 1967; stepchildren: David Troutman, Anne Troutman, Richard Troutman. BA, Coll. St. Maurice, St. Hyacinthe, Que., 1951; BSc II, U. Montreal, Que., 1952, MD, 1957; postgrad. in ophthalmology/pathology, Inst. Ophthalmology, London, 1960—61. Diplomate ophthalmology Royal Coll. Physicians of London, Royal Coll. Surgeons of Eng., lic. Med. Coun. Can., physician N.Y. State, diplomate ophthalmology Coll. of Physicians and Surgeons Province of Que., Royal Coll. of Physicians and Surgeons of Can., Am. Bd. of Ophthalmology. Sr. plastic surgery, neurosurgery resident Notre Dame Hosp., Montreal, 1957—58; resident in ophthalmology Hosp. Maisonneuve, Montreal, 1958—59; asst. in ophthalmology Hosp. Edouard Herriot, Lyon, France, 1959—60; clin. asst., OPD officer Royal Eye and Moorfields Eye Hosps., London, 1961; ophthalmic surgeon Ghandi Eye Hosp., Aligarh, India, 1962; instr. basic scis. Maisoneuve Hosp., Montreal, 1963—67; clin. assoc. prof. ophthalmology SUNY Downstate Med. Ctr., Bklyn., 1971—82; clin. instr. dept. ophthalmology Cornell U. Med. Coll., N.Y.C., 1971—74, clin. asst. prof. ophthalmology, 1974—77, clin. assoc. prof. ophthalmology, 1977—98, clin. prof. ophthalmology, 1998—2000; clin. prof. emeritus Weill Med. Coll. of Cornell U., N.Y.C., 2000—. Dir. strabismus clinic and orthoptics Maisoneuve Hosp., Que., 1963—67; chief ocular motility clinic Manhattan Eye Ear and Throat Hosp., N.Y.C., 1970—2000; asst. attending physician dept. surgery, divsn. ophthalmology Hosp. of the Holy Family, 1973—77, assoc. attending physician, 1977—80; asst. dir. dept. motor anomalies N.Y. Eye and Ear Infirmary, 1974—78, assoc. dir., 1978—82, assoc. attending surgeon, 1974—82; adj. attending ophthalmologist Bronx Lebanon Hosp. Ctr., 1975—77, assoc. attending ophthalmologist, 1977—79; cons. dept. ophthalmology Beth Israel Med. Ctr., 1979—87; lectr. in field. Editor, transl.: Hugonniers' textbook Strabismus, Heterophoria, Oculomotor Paralysis; author: (textbook translated in French, Japanese and Portuguese) Prisms in the Medical and Surgical Treatment of Strabismus; contbr. 32 chpts. to books, articles more than 35 articles to scientific jours. Established endowment of bienniel internat. prize Pan Am. Asssn. Ophthalmology, 1991; established ann. prize Women in Ophthalmology, San Francisco, 1997; established perpetual endowment for ann. scholarships and prize dept. edn. U. Que., Montreal, 1997; established perpetual endowment for annual scholarships Dept. of Ophthalmology, U. Montréal, 2006. Recipient Residents award for outstanding tchg., N.Y. Eye and Ear Infirmary, 1970, Spl. Achievement medal, U. Montreal, 1993. Fellow: ACS (life), Royal Coll. Surgeons Can.; mem.: AMA (life), Am. Ophthalmol. Soc., Am. Acad. Ophthalmology (life Honor award 1981), Pan Am. Assn. Ophthalmology (life; bd. dirs. 1993—2003), Med. Soc. of the State of N.Y. (life), Am. Assn. Pediat. Ophthalmology and Strabismus (life; charter mem.).

VER PAULT, CAROLYN, science educator; b. Rockville Centre, NY, Oct. 20, 1960; d. Alfred Charles and Gladys Veronica Ver Pault; m. Colin Nigel Ver Pault, Jan. 13, 1996; children: Mikayla Lynn, Mia Ann. BS, Adelphi U., 1981, MS, 1984. Cert. sci. tchr. NY. Doctoral tchg. fellow St. John's U., Jamaica, NY, 1987—89, Clare Boothe Luce doctoral fellow, 1989—91; sci. tchr. Holy Cross HS, Flushing, NY, 1991—96, East Meadow (NY) HS, 1996—2001, Waldorf Sch. of Garden City, NY, 2001—. Bd. dirs., coach West Hempstead Chiefs Soccer Club, 2001—06; co-founder, ec. NY Assn. Blind Athletes, East Meadow, 1984—88. Mem.: NSTA, Sci. Tchrs. Assn. NY, Lions Club (sec. West Hempstead-Garden City club 1986—94). Avocations: reading, crafts. Office: Waldorf Sch of Garden City 225 Cambridge Ave Garden City NY 11530 Office Phone: 516-742-3434. Office Fax: 516-742-3457.

VERSACE, DONATELLA, fashion designer; b. Reggio di Calabria, Italy, May 2, 1955; d. Antonio and Francesca V.; m. Paul Beck (div.); children: Allegra, Daniel. Degree in lit., U. Florence, Italy. Head designer Versus label Gianni Versace Group, 1978—97, vice chmn., style and image dir. N.Y.C., 1997—. Released fragrance Versace Woman, 2001. Achievements include created children's line, 1993; launched fragrance Versace Woman, 2001. Office: Gianni Versace SpA Via Ges 12 20121 Milan Italy Address: Instante Vesa srl Via Spiga 25 20121 Milan Italy Office Phone: 02 7610931. Office Fax: 02 798572.*

VERSCH, ESTHER MARIE, artist; b. Santa Monica, Calif., May 27, 1927; d. Claro Contreras Santellanes and Juana Hernandez; m. Chester Ray Fraelich, Nov. 14, 1943 (div. Nov. 1964); children: Joe Fraelich, Diane Fraelich Foster Viramontes; m. Terry Lee Versch, June 21, 1969; stepchildren: Fred, Roman, Joseph, Terry Jr., Michael. Student, East L.A. Coll., Pasadena City Coll. Lic. vocat. nurse. Nurse pvt. dr.'s office, L.A., 1968-69, U. So. Calif. Med. Ctr., L.A., 1963-68; artist Altadena, Calif., 1972—. Artist: (front cover) Library Services L.A., 1983, Christmas card for Western Greeting Inc., (back cover) Moccasin Tracks, 1984-85; one woman shows include Republic Fed. Savings, Altadena, Calif., Pasadena Pub. Libr., Whites Art Store and Gallery, La Canada, Calif., 1979, Windmill Gallery, 1985; group exhbns.: Women Artists of the West Internat. Exhbn. and Sale, Cody Western and Wildlife Classyc, 1979, Nat. Cowgirl Hall of Fame, Hereford, Tex., 1978, Beauty for the Beast Benefit, 1980, Ducks Unltd. Invitational Art Show, Taylor, Mich., 1986-87, Lawrence (Kans.) Indian Art Show, Mus. Anthropology, 1989-90, Snake River Showcase, Lewiston, Idaho, 1992, Women Artists of the West, 1992, 98, 99, Death Valley 49's Invitational Art Show, 1994-2000, 2001, George Ohr Cultural Arts and Cultural Ctr., Biloxi, Miss., 1998, Western and Wildlife Invitational Art Show, Estes Park, Colo., 2000, WAOW Art Show Pinedale, Wyo, 2002, Art and Music Festival, Dublin, Ohio, 2002, West Wind Gallery, Casper, Wyo., 2003-04, Pomerene Ctr. for the Arts, 2004, Zanesville Ctr. for the Arts, 2004, 05, Red River Valley Mus., Vernon, Tex., 2004, Ronald Reagan Mus., Simi Valley, Calif., 2004, Johnson Humrickhouse Mus., 2004-05, Dogwood Festival Artists Tour Studio, 2006, others; collections: Johnson Humrickhouse Mus., Coshocton, Ohio, other pvt. collections; illustrator back cover Moccasin Tracks, 1984-85. Vol. nurses aide City View Hosp., L.A., 1960-63; vol. Arroyo Rep., Pasadena, Calif., St. Luke Hosp., Pasadena, 1990-94, flu immunization ARC, 1977-78. Recipient Gold medal for watercolor San Gabriel Fine Arts, 1979, Best of Show award for watercolor Am. Indian and Western, 1990, Hon. mention San Gabriel Fine Arts, 1990, 3rd Place Watercolor Women Artists of the West Saddle Back Art Gallery, 1982. Mem. Women Artists of the West (emeritus mem., treas., asst. sec., editor West Wind, membership chmn.), Ohio Art League, Coshocton Art Guild (v.p. Juried Art Show 2004-05). Republican. Roman Catholic. Avocations: walking, gardening, sewing. E-mail: everschart@newsguy.com.

VERSIC, LINDA JOAN, nursing educator, research company executive; b. Aug. 27, 1944; d. Robert and Kathryn I. (Fagird) Davies; m. Ronald James Versic, June 11, 1966; children: Kathryn Clara, Paul Joseph. RN, Johns Hopkins Sch. of Nursing, 1965; BS in Health Edn., Ctrl. State U., 1980; MS in Edn., Nova Southeastern U., 2000. Asst. head nurse Johns Hopkins Hosp., Balt., 1965—67; staff Nurse Registry Miami Valley Hosp., Dayton, Ohio, 1973—90; instr. Miami Jacobs Jr. Coll. Bus., Dayton, 1977—79; pres. Ronald T. Dodge Co., Dayton, 1979—86, chmn. bd., 1987—. Instr. Warren County Career Ctr., Ohio, 1980—84, coord. diversified health occupations, 1984—2003, career pathways coord., 2003—04, Greentree Acad., 2004—. Coord. youth activities, mem. steering com. Queen of Apostles Cmty.; active Miami Valley Mil. Affairs Assn., Glen Helen, Friends of Dayton Ballet, Dayton Art Inst. Recipient Excellence in Tchg. award, 1992, award for Project Excellence, 1992. Mem.: Am. Vocat. Assn., Ohio Vocat. Assn., Welsh Soc. Cin., South Slavic Club of Greater Dayton, Johns Hopkins Club, Vocat. Indsl. Clubs Am. (chpt. advisor 1982—). Roman Catholic. Home: 1601 Shafor Blvd Dayton OH 45419-3103 Office: Ronald T Dodge Co PO Box 41630 Dayton OH 45441-0630 Office Phone: 937-439-4497. Personal E-mail: lversic@rtdodge.com.

VER STEEG, DONNA LORRAINE FRANK, nurse, sociologist, educator; b. Minot, ND, Sept. 23, 1929; d. John Jonas and Pearl H. (Denlinger) Frank; m. Richard W. Ver Steeg, Nov. 22, 1950; children: Juliana, Anne, Richard B. BSN, Stanford, 1951; MSN, U. Calif., San Francisco, 1967; MA in Sociology, UCLA, 1969, PhD in Sociology, 1973. Clin. instr. U. ND Sch. Nursing, 1962-63; USPHS nurse rsch. fellow UCLA, 1969-72; spl. cons., mem. adv. com. on physicians' assts. and nurse practitioner progs. Calif. State Bd. Med. Examiners, 1972-73; asst. prof. UCLA Sch. Nursing, 1973-79, assoc. prof., 1979-94, asst. dean, 1979-81, chmn. primary ambulatory care, 1976-87, assoc. dean, 1983-86, prof. emeritus, chair primary care, 1994-96, prof. emeritus, 1996—. Co-prin. investigator PRIMEX Project Family Nurse Practitioners, UCLA Ext., 1974—76; assoc. cons. Calif. Postsecondary Edn. Commn., 1975—76; spl. cons. Calif. Dept. Consumer Affairs, 1978; accredited visitor Western Assn. Sch. and Coll., 1985; mem. Calif. State Legis. Health Policy Forum, 1980—81; mem. nurse practitioner adv. com. Calif. Bd. RN, 1995—97; mem. Edn. Industry Interface, Info. Devel. Mktg. Sub Com., 1995—99, recruitment, 1999—2001; archivist Calif. Strategic Planning Com. Nursing/Colleagues in Caring Project, 1995—. Contbr. chpts. to profl. books, articles to profl. jours. Recipient Leadership award Calif. Area Health Edn. Ctr. Sys., 1989, Commendation award Calif. State Assembly, 1994; named Outstanding Faculty Mem., UCLA Sch. Nursing, 1982. Fellow Am. Acad. Nursing; mem. AAAS, AAUW, ANA (pres. elect Calif. chpt. 1977-79, pres. 1979-81, interim chair Calif. 1995-96), Nat. League Nursing, Calif. League Nursing, N.Am. Nursing Diagnosis Assn., Am. Assn. History Nursing, Stanford Nurses Club, Sigma Theta Tau (Alpha Eta chpt. Leadership award Gamma Tau chpt. 1994), Sigma Xi. Home: 708 Swarthmore Ave Pacific Palisades CA 90272-4353 Office: UCLA Sch Nursing Box 956917 Los Angeles CA 90095-6917 Business E-Mail: dverste@ucla.edu.

VERSTEGEN, DEBORAH A., finance educator; b. Neenah, Wis., Oct. 27, 1946; d. Gerald C. and Margaret A. (Lamers) V. BA, Loretto Heights Coll., 1969; EdM, U. Rochester, N.Y., 1972; MS, U. Wis., 1981, PhD, 1983. Adminstr. Iditarod Area Sch. Dist., McGrath, Alaska, 1976-79; rsch. asst. Wis. Ctr. for Edn. Rsch., 1981-84; dir. asst. prof. mid-mgmt. program U. Tex., Austin, 1984-86; asst. prof. edn. fin. and policy U. Va., Charlottesville, 1986-91, assoc. prof. edn. in fin. and policy, 1992-99, prof., 2000—04, U. Nev., Reno, 2004—, chair, 2004—06. Assoc. rsch. fellow Oxford U., Eng., 1991; adv. bd. U.S. Dept. Edn., 1989-92. Author over 250 books, reports, chpts., articles and revs., latest being The Impacts of Litigation and Legislation on Public School Finance, 1990, Spheres of Justice in Education, 1991; editor Jour. Edn. Fin., 1990-93, editor edn. policy, 1993—. Treas. LVW, 1986, mem. Va. state bd., 1995—97, Va. edn. chair, 1993—2001. Recipient Alumni Achievement award, U. Wis., Madison, 1997. Mem.: AAUP (exec. bd. Va. 1999—, pres.-elect 2003, pres. 2003—04), U. Coun. on Ednl. Adminstrn. (adv. bd. fin. ctr. 1991—, disting. svc. award 1991), Women Edn. Leaders Va. (chair 1998, pres. 1999—2000, founder), Am. Ednl. Rsch. Assn. (SIG chair fiscal issues and policy 2002—04), Am. Ednl. Fin. Assn. (bd. dirs. 1986—89,, disting. svc. award 1989), Phi Kappa Phi, Phi Delta Kappa. Home: 6525 Monticello Ln Reno NV 89515 Office: U Nev Dept Edn Leadership MS 283 Coll Edn Rm 4054 Reno NV 89557-0201 Office Phone: 775-784-6518 x2300.

VERTEFEUILLE, CHRISTINE SIEGRIST, state supreme court justice; b. New Britain, Conn., Dec. 10, 1950; BA in Polit. Sci., Trinity Coll., 1972; JD, U. Conn., 1975. Pvt. practice, 1975-89; judge Conn. Superior Ct., 1989—99; adminstrv. judge Waterbury Jud. Dist., 1994-99, complex litig. judge, 1999; judge Appellate Ct., 1999-2000; assoc. justice Conn. Supreme Ct., 2000—. Alternate mem. Waterbury and New Haven (Conn.) Grievance Panels, 1985-89; faculty Conn. Judges Inst., 1989-94. Recipient Jud. award Conn. Trial Lawyers Assn., 1995. Mem. Conn. Bar Assn. (mem. exec. com. real property 1988-89). Office: Conn Supreme Ct 231 Capitol Ave Hartford CT 06106 Office Phone: 860-757-2117.

VERVILLE, ELIZABETH GIAVANI, federal official; b. N.Y.C., July 13, 1940; d. Joseph and Gertrude (Levy) Giavani. BA, Duke U., 1961; LLB, Columbia U., 1964. Bar: Mass. 1965, U.S. Supreme Ct. 1970, D.C. 1980. Assoc. Snow Motley & Holt, successor Gaston Snow & Ely Bartlett, Boston, 1965-67; asst. atty. gen. Commonwealth of Mass., Boston, 1967-69; atty. advisor for African affairs U.S. Dept. State, Washington, 1979-72, asst. legal adviser for East Asian and Pacific affairs, 1972-80, dep. legal adviser, 1980-89; dep. asst. sec. state Bur. Politico-Mil. Affairs Bur. Politico-Mil. Affairs, Washington, 1989-92, sr. coord., 1992-95; dir. for global and multilateral affairs Nat. Security Coun., Washington, 1995-98; dep. dir. Critical Infrastructure Assurance Office, Washington, 2000—01; spl. rep. Bur. Narcotics and Law Enforcement, Washington, 2000—02, 2005—; acting dep. asst. sec. Bur. Internat. Narcotics and Law Enforcement, Dept. State, Washington, 2001—02, sr. advisor, 2002—05, acting dep., asst. sec., 2005—. Recipient presdl. rank of meritorious exec., 1985, 90, 2003, presdl. rank disting. exec., 1988. Mem. Am. Soc. Internat. Law, Coun. on Fgn. Rels. Home: 3012 Dumbarton Ave NW Washington DC 20007-3305 Office: Bur Internat Narcotics & Law Enforcement State Dept Washington DC 20520-0001 Office Phone: 202-647-9822.

VESELY-RICE, ALISON C., theater director, actress, educator; b. Long Beach, Calif., July 23, 1957; adopted d. Ervin Joseph and Rosalie Constance (Brozowski) Vesely, d. Jean Stewart-Chandler; m. David Rice, Aug. 15, 1981; 1 child, Hayley Laura Rice. BFA, Ill. Wesleyan U., 1979. Classics project/ednl. program dir. Footsteps Theatre Co., Chgo., 1991—95; artistic dir. First Folio Shakespeare Festival, Oak Brook, Ill., 1996—. Bd. pres. First Folio Shakespeare Festival, Oak Brook, 1997—. Recipient After Dark award, Gay Chgo. Mag., 1996. Mem.: Soc. Stage Dirs. and Choreographers. Home: 146 Juliet Ct Clarendon Hills IL 60514 Office: First Folio Shakespeare Festival 1717 31st St Oak Brook IL 60523 Office Phone: 630-986-8067. Personal E-mail: firstfolio@firstfolio.org.

VESPER, VIRGINIA ANN, librarian; b. Washington, Dec. 3, 1944; d. Frank Frederick and Ellen Clare Vesper; m. Ronald Albert Messier, Dec. 27, 1967 (div.); children: Samantha Hope Messier, Benjamin Frank Messier. MA in Libr. Sci., U. Mich., 1972. Asst. acquisitions libr. Mid. Tenn. State U., Murfreesboro, Tenn., 1982—87; head, monograph acquisitions Winthrop U., Rock Hill, SC, 1988—94, coord. of libr. instrn., reference, 1994—95; collection mgmt. libr. Mid. Tenn. State U., 1995—2000, coord. of collection mgmt., 2000—. Author: (monograph) Criteria for Promotion and Tenure for Academic Librarians, (book reviews) Tennessee Librarian. Tutor York County Literacy Assn., Rock Hill, SC, 1988—93; conf. presenter Am./Popular Culture Assn., Instrnl. Tech. Conf., Charleston Conf., Tenn. Libr. Assn. Mem.: AAUW (v.p. and program chair 1985—87), ALA, TennShare (chair collection devel. com. 2001—02), Mid State Libr. Assn. (chair 1992—2000, vice chair 1998—99, newletter editor 2004—05), Tenn. Libr. Assn. (round table pres. 1997—98). Office: James E Walker Libr 1301 East Main St Murfreesboro TN 37132 Office Phone: 615-898-2806. Office Fax: 615-904-8224.

VEST, GAYLE SOUTHWORTH, obstetrician, gynecologist; b. Duluth, Minn., Apr. 7, 1948; d. Russell Eugene and Brandon (Young) Southworth; m. Steven Lee Vest, Nov. 27, 1971; 1 child, Matthew Steven. BS, U. Mich., 1970. Diplomate Am. Bd. Ob-Gyn. Intern in ob-gyn. Milw. County Gen. Hosp., 1974-75, So. Ill. U. Sch. Medicine, 1975-78; pvt. practice Chapel Hill (N.C.) Ob-Gyn., 1978-80; asst. attending physician dept. ob-gyn. U. N.C. Sch. Medicine, Chapel Hill, 1978-80; clin. assoc. dept. ob-gyn. Duke U. Med. Ctr., Durham, NC, 1978-80; pvt. practice Big Stone Gap (Va.) Clinic, 1980-88, Norwise Ob-Gyn. Assocs., Norton, Va., 1988—. Fellow: ACOG; mem.: Wise County Med. Soc., Med. Soc. Va., Va. Ob-Gyn. Soc., Christian Med. and Dental Assn. Avocations: skiing, kayaking, travel.

VEST, ROSEMARIE LYNN TORRES, secondary school educator; b. Pueblo, Colo., Jan. 16, 1958; d. Onesimo Bernabe and Maria Bersabe (Lucero) Torres; m. Donald R. Vest, May 1, 1982. BA, U. So. Colo., 1979, BS, 1991; cert. travel agt., Travel Trade Sch., Pueblo, 1986. Cert. secondary tchr., Colo.; lic. local pastor United Meth. Ch. Tutor U. So. Colo., Pueblo, 1977-79; sales rep. Intermountain Prodns., Colorado Springs, Colo., 1979-80; tutor, Pueblo, 1980-82, 84-85; travel agt. So. Colo. Travel, Pueblo, 1986-88; children's program facilitator El Mesias Family Support Program, Pueblo, 1987-88; substitute tchr. social studies Sch. Dist. 60, Pueblo, 1990—, Freed Mid. Sch., Pueblo, 1991, 92. Chpt. 1 Summer Reading Program, 1992, 93, 94, 95; instr. Travel and Tourism Dept. Pueblo C.C., 1994-95, Dept Social Studies, 1996-97. Tchr. Sunday sch., chairperson adminstrv. bd. cert. lay spkr., lay rep. to ann. conf. Ch. Evangelism, co-chmn. Trinity United Meth. Ch., Pueblo, 1989-94, parish coun. rep. to Trinity/Bethel Coop. Parish; sponsor United Meth. Youth United Meth. Ch.; tchr. Sunday Sch., co-coord. vacation Bible sch., edn. chairperson, 1994-1998, cert. lay spkr., ministerial program asst., lay leader Bethel United Meth. Ch., 1994-1998; craft facilitator Integrated Health Svcs., Pueblo, 1991-2004; spiritual devotions/worship leader Pueblo Manor Nursing Home, 1993-2004; vol. resident svcs. Pueblo County Bd. for Developmental Disabilities, 1989—; mem. conf. leadership team, parliamentarian Rocky Mountain Conf. United Meth. Ch., 1995, dist. rep., 1997-2000; ministerial candidate United Meth. Ch.; conf. rep. Rocky Mountain Conf. Coun. on Fin. and Adminstrn., 1996—. Recipient Excellence in Tchg. award Freed Mid. Sch., 1992, Vol. of Yr. award IHS of Pueblo, 1995. Mem. Assn. Am. Geographers, Nat. Oceanog. Soc., Nat. Geog. Soc. Democrat. Avocations: crafts, photography, reading, cross-stitch, listening to music. Home: 516 Lincoln St Pueblo CO 81004-1422

VESTAL, JOSEPHINE BURNET, lawyer; b. Iowa City, June 13, 1949; d. Allan Delker and Dorothy (Walker) V. Student, Williams Coll., 1970; BA, Mt. Holyoke Coll., 1971; JD, U. Wash., 1974. Bar: Wash. 1974, U.S. Dist. Ct. (we. dist.) Wash. 1974, U.S. Ct. Appeals (9th cir.) 1984, U.S. Ct. Appeals (D.C. cir.) 1984, U.S. Dist. Ct. (ea. dist.) Wash. 1993. Ptnr. Selinker, Vestal, Klockars & Andersen, Seattle, 1974-80; assoc. Williams, Kastner & Gibbs, Seattle, 1981-87; mem. Williams, Kastner & Gibbs, PLLC, Seattle, 1988—. Mem. ABA (labor and employment sect.), Def. Rsch. Inst. (labor and employment sect.), Wash. State Bar Assn., King County Bar Assn. Office: Williams Kastner & Gibbs PLLC 4100 Two Union Sq PO Box 21926 Seattle WA 98111-3926 Office Phone: 206-233-2894. E-mail: jvestal@wkg.com.

VETERE, KATHLEEN MARIE, athletic trainer; b. Anderson, Ind., Sept. 3, 1979; d. Michael Joseph Vetere, Jr. and Mary Theresa Vetere. BS, W.Va. U., Morgantown, 2004. Athletic trainer West Penn Allegheny Health Systems, Pitts., 2004—. Mem.: Nat. Athletic Trainers Assn. (cert. athletic trainer 2004). Home: 850 Baldwin St Apt 504 Pittsburgh PA 15234 Personal E-mail: kvetere@hotmail.com.

VETTEL, CHERYL ELYNORE, mathematics educator; b. Chgo., Aug. 31, 1946; d. Stanley Hamilton and Eleanor A. (Borgeson) Larson; m. Milton C. Stewart, June 16, 1973 (div. May 1991); children: Kristen J., Craig W.; m. James A. Vettel, July 18, 1992. BA in Math., San Jose State Coll., 1968; MEd, Nat. U., 1995. Cert. tchr., Calif.; cert. adminstr., Calif. Math. tchr. Fremont Union High Sch. Dist., Sunnyvale, Calif., 1969—. Mem. NEA, ASCD, Nat. Coun. Tchrs. Math, Calif. Tchrs. Assn., Calif. Math. Coun., Santa Clara Valley Math. Assn., Fremont Edn. Assn. Avocations: golf, tennis, stitchery. Office: Fremont High Sch 1279 Sunnyvale Saratoga Rd Sunnyvale CA 94087-2593 Business E-Mail: Cheryl_Vettel@fuhsd.org.

VETTER, VICTORIA L., pediatric cardiologist, educator; b. Louisville, Aug. 15, 1946; d. Albert Elmo and Mildred Irene Vetter; m. Anthony S. Jennings, June 8, 1974; children: Jennifer, Jonathan, Jason. BA in Chemistry, U. Ky., 1968, MD, 1972. Bd. cert. Am. Bd. Pediat. in Pediat. and Pediat. Cardiology. Intern pediat. Johns Hopkins Hosp., Balt., 1972—73, resident pediat., 1973—74; sr. resident pediat. Vanderbilt U. Hosp., Nashville, 1974—75; fellow pediat. cardiology The Children's Hosp. Phila., 1975—78, asst. cardiologist, 1978—82, assoc. cardiologist, 1982—89, sr. cardiologist, 1989—, dir. pediat. electrophysiology lab., 1978—95, dir. pediat. electrocardiography lab., 1978—, chief divsn. cardiology, 1993—; sr. physician dept. pediat. U. Pa. Sch. Medicine, 1989—. Instr. pediat. U. Pa. Sch. Medicine, 1978, asst. prof. pediat., 1978—81, prof. pediat., 1999—; asst. prof. pediat. The Children's Hosp. Phila., U. Pa. Sch. Medicine, 1981—87, assoc. prof. pediat., 1987—99, Evelyn R. Tabas chair in pediatric cardiology, 2005—; lectr. in field. Sci. reviewer: jours. Circulation, Am. Jour. Cardiology, Jour. Am. Coll. Cardiology, Pediat. Cardiology, Pacing and Clin. Electrophysiology, Pediat. Rsch., Clin. Pediat., Annals of Internal Medicine, New Eng. Jour. Medicine, Jour. Cardiovasc. Electrophysiology, Jour. Pediat., Am. Jour. Diseases of Children, Pediat. Emergency Care; contbr. chapters to books, articles and abtracts to jours. Grantee in field. Fellow: Am. Coll. Cardiology (mem. emergency cardiac care com. 1992—98, mem. pediat. cardiology com. 1994—96, mem. 1996 annual sci. session program com. 1995—96, mem. credentials com. 1997—2000), Am. Acad. Pediat. (mem. exec. com. pediat. cardiology subsect. 1989—92, Young Investigator award sect. on cardiology 1978); mem.: AMA, NHLBI Pediatric Network (prin. investigator 2001—), John Morgan Soc., Phila. Arrhythmia Group, Pediat. Arrhythmia Group (mem. steering com.), Phila. County Med. Soc., Internat. Registry for Drug-Induced Arrhythmias (mem. sci. adv. com.), Sudden Arrhythmia Death Syndromes Found. (mem. sci. adv. bd.), Cardiac Arrhythmias Rsch. and Edn. Found., Inc. (mem. sci. adv. bd., Heart of the Child award 1996), N.Am. Soc. Pacing and Electrophysiology (mem. annual sci. sessions program com. 1998—2001, mem. pediat. com. 1998—2001), Pediat. Electrophysiology Soc., Am. Heart Assn. Coun. on Cardiovasc. Disease in the Young (mem. exec. com. 1993—98, mem. com. on tng. in pediat. cardiology 1994—96, mem. com. on electrocardiography and arrhythmias 1995—97, mem. membership com. 1996—97, chair Rashkind lecture selection com.), Am. Heart Assn. (med. spokesperson), Am. Heart Assn. Southeastern Pa. Affiliate (mem. rsch. peer rev. com. 1987—92, program chairperson 1988—90, mem. exec. com. 1988—93, v.p. 1989—90, pres.-elect 1990—91, pres. 1991—92, past-pres. 1992—93, mem. bd. dirs. 1993—96, mem. bd. govs. 1994—96, mem. pediat. sub-com. cardiac support coalition 1997—, post-doctoral fellow 1976—77, 1978—79), Alpha Omega Alpha, Phi Beta Kappa. Home: 110 Willow Way Cherry Hill NJ 08034-3049 Office: The Childrens Hosp Phila 34th St & Civic Center Blvd Philadelphia PA 19104 Office Phone: 215-590-3529.

VEVERKA, RUTH TONRY, retired secondary school educator; b. Martinsburg, W.Va., June 24, 1918; d. James Charles and May Elizabeth (Matthews) Tonry; m. Rudolph Edward Veverka, Sept. 18, 1948; 1 child, Karen Elizabeth. BS in Home Econs., W.Va. U., 1940; MA, U. Nebr., 1950; postgrad., U. Nebr., Omaha, 1970. Cert. tchr., W.Va., Nebr. Tchr. Ft. Ashby (W.Va.) High Sch., 1940-41, Bunker Hill (W.Va.) High Sch., 1941-42; cryptanalyst USN, Washington, 1946-48; libr. sci. worker Westside Community Schs., Omaha, 1970-88. Mem. ARC, Arlington, Va., 1953-56, Navy Relief Soc., San Diego, 1959-61. Lt. USN, 1942-46. Mem. AAUW, Home Economists in Homemaking, Women Accepted for Vol. Emergency Svc., Feminine Vets. World War II, Order Ea. Star, 1918 Club, Phi Upsilon Omicron, Kappa Delta Pi, Pi Lambda Theta, Pi Mu Epsilon, Alpha Xi Delta. Republican. Lutheran. Avocations: reading, swimming, needlepoint.

VICE, SUSAN F., medicinal chemist; b. Oshawa, Ont., Can., Apr. 19, 1956; m. Andrew S. Thompson, Nov. 27, 1987. BS in Chemistry, U. We. Ont., London, Can., 1980; PhD, U. Waterloo, Ont., 1984. Postdoc. fellow U. Calif., Irvine, 1984—86; rsch. scientist Polysar Ltd., Sarnia, Canada, 1986—88; sr. prin. scientist Schering Plough Rsch. Inst., Kenilworth, NJ, 1988—2000; freelance tech. writer, 2001—05; mng. editor John Wiley & Sons, Inc., Hoboken, 2005—. Recipient Thomas Alva Edison Patent award, Rsch. and Devel. Coun. N.W., 2004; fellow Charles S. Humphrey grad. fellow, Guelph-Waterloo Ctr. Grad. Work in Chemistry, 1983, postdoc. fellow, Natural Scis. and Engring. Rsch. Coun., 1984—86, inds. postdoc. fellow, 1986; scholar, 1981—84. Mem.: Am. Soc. Microbiology, Editl. Freelancers Assn., Chem. Inst. Can. and Soc. Chemistry, Am. Chem. Soc. Home: 1144 Sawmill Rd Mountainside NJ 07092-2213 Personal E-mail: vicesf@yahoo.com.

VICENTE, RACHEL, real estate agent; b. Hoboken, NJ, Apr. 15, 1973; d. Robert and Nancy Vicente. BA, Barry U., 1995, BS, 1997. Lic. real estate agt. Fla. IT specialist Foote Cone Belding, Miami, Fla., 1997—2000; v.p. mktg. Camelot, Coral Gables, Fla., 2000; real estate agt. Miami. Vol. SART

Program, Miami, 2001—02, Miami Children's Telethon, 2000, AIDS Walk, Miami, 2000—05. Mem.: Realtors Assn. Miami-Dade, Rotary Club. Home: 817 Venetia Ave Coral Gables FL 33134 Office: Camelot 2600 Galiano St Miami FL 33134

VICK, MARSHA COOK, writer, humanities educator; b. Charlotte, N.C. d. Conley and Elizabeth (Voltz) Cook; m. Paul Allen Vick, Apr. 6, 1968 (div. 2005); children: Paul Allen Jr., Brian Conley. BA, U. N.C., 1963, MEd, 1965, PhD, 1996; MA, Duke U., 1985. Spanish translator Transl. Svc. Duke U., Durham, NC, 1974—76, speech writer for v.p., 1976—77, speech writer for pres., 1977—85; rsch. and editl. asst. U.S. Senate, Durham, 1986—92; lectr. Afro-Am. studies U. N.C., Chapel Hill, 1990—97; writer Durham, 1996—. Contbr. essays to various publs Mem. MLA, Coll. Lang. Assn., Sigma Delta Pi, Alpha Chi Omega. Home: 3405 Olney Dr Durham NC 27705-5497

VICKERS, NANCY J., academic administrator; BA, Mt. Holyoke Coll., 1967, LHD (hon.), 1999; MA, Yale U., 1971, PhD, 1976. Prof. French and Italian Dartmouth Coll., 1973—87; prof. French, Italian, and comparative literature U. Southern Calif., 1987—97, dean curriculum and instrn. Coll. Letters, Arts and Scis., 1994—97; pres. Bryn Mawr Coll., 1997—. Vis. prof. Harvard U., U. Pa., UCLA; bd. dirs. Bryn Mawr Bank Corp.; bd. govs. Coun. Dante Soc. Am. Recipient Presdl. medal Outstanding Leadership and Achievement, Dartmouth Coll., 1991; fellow vis. fellow, Princeton U. Office: Bryn Mawr Coll 101 N Merion Ave Bryn Mawr PA 19010-2899

VICKERY, ANN MORGAN, lawyer; b. Anderson, S.C., June 25, 1944; d. Joseph Harold and Doris (Rogers) Morgan; m. Raymond Ezekiel Vickery, Jr., June 23, 1979; children: Raymond Morgan, Philip Dickens. AB History, Mary Baldwin Coll., 1965; JD, Georgetown U., 1978. Bar: D.C. 1978. Elem. sch. tchr., Chesterfield County, Va., 1965-66; legal publs. specialist Nat. Archives and Record Svc., Washington, 1966-69; speech writing staff to Pres., rsch. asst., chief rschr., staff asst. The White House, Washington, 1969-74; summer clerk Graham & James, Washington, 1975; various positions Dept. Treasury, Washington, 1975-78; atty. Hogan & Hartson, LLP, Washington, 1978—, mng. ptnr.-D.C. office, dir. health practice group. Health group dir. Hogan and Hartson, LLP, Washington, 1991—, exec. com., 1992-95, 96-99, Washington office mng. ptnr., 1999—; outside legal counsel Nat. Hospice and Palliative Care Orgn., 1982— (named Woman of the Yr. 1986); spkr. in field. Contbr. articles to profl. jours. Dir. Hospice No. Va., Arlington, 1987-93; trustee Nat. Hospice Found., 1996—. Mem. ABA, Am. Health Lawyers Assn., D.C. Bar, Health on Wednesday, Phi Alpha Theta. Office: Hogan & Hartson LLP Columbia Square 555 13th St NW Ste 12E-300 Washington DC 20004-1161 Office Phone: 202-637-8605. Office Fax: 202-637-5901. Business E-Mail: amvickery@hhlaw.com.

VICKIE, CASH C., elementary school educator; b. Bremen, Ga., Aug. 13, 1960; d. Max and Carolyn Carroll; m. Garry H Cash, July 19, 1980; children: Brandon Harold Cash, Andrew Carroll Cash. BS in Early Childhood Edn., West Ga. Coll., Carrollton, 1980, M in Early Childhood, 1993; EdD in Early Childhood, State U. West Ga., Carrollton, 1997. Tchr. elem. sch. Haralson County Sch. Sys., Buchanan, Ga., 1982—. Recipient Tchr. Yr., Haralson County Sch. Sys., 2006. Mem.: PA of Ga. Educators PAGE (assoc.), Delta Kappa Gamma. Home: 130 Biggers Road Buchanan GA 30113 Office: Buchanan Elementary School 215 College Circle Buchanan GA 30113 Office Phone: 770-000-0000. Personal E-mail: vrcc13@aol.com.

VICKREY, HERTA M., microbiologist; b. San Gregorio, Calif. m. William David Vickrey; children: Ellean H., Carlene L. Smith, Corrine A. Pochop, Arlene A.; m. Robert James Fitzgibbon, Dec. 28, 1979. BA, San Jose State U., 1957; MA, U. Calif., Berkeley, 1963, PhD in Bacteriology and Immunology, 1970. Cert. immunologist, pub. health microbiologist, clin. lab. scientist. Pub. health microbiologist Viral & Rickettsial Diseases Lab., Calif. State Dept. Pub. Health, Berkeley, 1958-60, 61-62, 1964; postgrad. rsch. bacteriologist dept. bacteriology U. Calif., Berkeley, 1963-64; bacteriologist Children's Hosp. Med. Ctr. No. Calif., Oakland, 1958-70; asst. prof. U. Victoria, B.C., Can., 1970-72; rsch. assoc. rsch. dept. Wayne County Gen. Hosp., Wayne, Mich., 1972-83; lab. supr. med. rsch. and edn. U. Mich., Ann Arbor, 1977-83; pub. health lab. dir. Shasta County Pub. Health Svcs., Redding, Calif., 1983-84; sr. pub. health microbiologist Tulare County Pub. Health Lab., Tulare, Calif., 1984—, tech. supr. Visalia, Calif., 1992-93; med. technologist Hillman Health Clin. Lab., Tulare, Calif., 1994-96, clin. lab. scientist, 1996—. Vis. scientist MIT, Cambridge, 1982; organizer, lectr. mycology workshop Tulare County Health Dept. Lab., Visalia, 1988; USPHS trainee U. Calif., Berkeley, 1965, 66. Author: Isolation and Identification of Mycotic Agents, 1987-88; contbr. articles to profl. jours. Fundraiser Battered Women's Shelter, Redding, 1983, Real Opportunities for Youth, Visalia, 1985, 86, Open Gate Ministries, Dinuba, Visalia, 1987-94, 97-99, 2003, Leukemia and Lymphoma Soc., 2003, 04, 05, 06. Fellow NIH, 1966-69, Dr. E.E. Dowdle rsch. fellow, U. Calif., 1969-70; grantee U. Victoria, 1970-72, Med. Rsch. and Edn. and Med. Adminstrn., U. Mich., 1973-83. Mem. No. Calif. Assn. Pub. Health Microbiologists, Calif. Scholarship Soc., Am. Soc. Clin. Pathologists (assoc.), Phi Beta Kappa, Delta Omega, Phi Kappa Phi, Beta Beta Beta. Avocations: biking, hiking, swimming. Home: 3505 W Campus Dr Apt 5 Visalia CA 93277-1869 Office: Tulare County Pub Health Lab 1062 S K St Tulare CA 93274-6421 Office Phone: 559-687-6984.

VICTOR, LORRAINE CAROL, critical care nurse; b. Duluth, Minn., June 14, 1953; d. George E. and Phyllis M. (Pierce) Drimel; m. Robert G. Victor BA in Nursing, Coll. St. Scholastica, 1975; MS in Nursing, U. Minn., 1984; postgrad., Coll. St. Catherine. Cert. regional trainer for neonatal resuscitation program; cert. neonatal nurse practitioner. Staff nurse St. Mary's Hosp., Rochester, Minn., 1975-79, 80-81, U. Wis. Hosp., Madison, 1979-80, U. Minn. Hosps., Mpls., 1981-84, 85-86; clin. instr. neonatal ICU, Children's Hosp., St. Paul, 1984-86; clin. nurse specialist neonatal ICU, Orlando (Fla.) Regional Med. Ctr., 1986-88, Children's Hosp., St. Paul, 1988—2001; neonatal nurse practitioner Children's Hosp., St. Paul, 2001—. Mem. AACN (Critical Care Nurse of Yr.award Greater Twin Cities chpt. 1992), Nat. Assn. Neonatal Nurses, Acad. Neonatal Nursing, Sigma Theta Tau. Office: Children's Hosps & Clinics St Paul Birth Ctr 345 Smith Ave N Saint Paul MN 55102-2369 Office Phone: 651-220-6210. Business E-Mail: lorraine.victor@childrensmn.org.

VIDAL, MAUREEN ERIS, theater educator, actress; b. Bklyn., Mar. 18, 1956; d. Louis and Lillian (Kaplan) Hendelman; m. Juan Vidal, June 25, 1974 (div. Sept. 1981); m. Guillermo Eduardo Uriarte, Dec. 22, 1986. BA, Bklyn. Coll., 1976, MS, 1981. From English tchr. to drama tchr. N.Y.C. Bd. Edn., 1976—, chair women's history dept., 1984—, dean, 1997—, drama tchr., 2002—. Mem PETA Humane Soc. Mem.: AFTRA, Gorilla Soc., Nat. Anti-Vivisection Soc. (mem. physicians' com. responsible medicine), Heights Players Theater Co. (arranger theatrical performance for residents of homeless shelters 1986—2003, exec. bd., sec. 1993—, actress), Doris Day Animal League, Delta Psi Omega. Avocations: travel, white-water rafting, scuba diving, skydiving, theater. Office: I S 318 101 Walton St Brooklyn NY 11206-4311 also: Heights Players 26 Willow Pl Brooklyn NY 11201-4513 Office Phone: 718-782-0589. E-mail: MVidal4942@aol.com.

VIDAVER, ANNE MARIE, plant pathology educator; b. Vienna, Mar. 29, 1938; came to U.S., 1941; d. Franz and Klara (Winter) Kopecky; children: Gordon W.F., Regina M. BA, Russell Sage Coll., 1960; MA, Ind. U., 1962, PhD, 1965. Lectr. U. Nebr., Lincoln, 1965-66, rsch. assoc., 1966-72, asst. prof., 1972-74, assoc. prof., 1974-79, prof. plant pathology, 1979—, interim dir. Ctr. Biotech., 1988-89, 97-00, head dept. plant pathology, 1984-2000, 2003—; chief scientist USDA's NRICGP, 2000—02. Contbr. articles to profl. jours. and books; patentee in field. Recipient Pub. Svc. award Nebr. Agri-Bus., 1977, Sci. award for excellence NAMA, New Orleans, 1991. Fellow AAAS, Am. Phytopath. Soc., Am. Soc. Microbiology; mem. Intersoc. Consortium for Plant Protection, Internat. Soc. Plant Pathology, Alliance for Prudent Use of Antibiotics. Avocations: indoor gardening, reading. Office: U Nebr Dept Plant Pathology Lincoln NE 68583-0722 Office Phone: 402-472-2858. E-mail: avidaver1@unl.edu.

VIDERGAR, TERESA, musician, educator; b. San Barnardino, Calif., Oct. 9, 1963; d. John August and Frances Vidergar. MusB in Piano Performance, Calif. State U., Fullerton, 1986; MusM in Piano Performance, Eastman Sch. Music, 1990. Cert. multiple subject tchr. 2003. Piano instr. Teresa Vidergar Piano Studio, Fontana, Calif., 1981—; staff accompanist Temple Beth Israel Synagogue, Pomona, Calif., 1984—87, St. Anne Cath. Ch., San Bernardino, 1986—87, accompanist San Barnardino, Calif., 1991—96; accompanist for diocese Holy Rosary Cathedral, San Bernardino, 1986—87; piano accompanist CCD Congress, Cath. Convention, Anaheim, Calif., 1987; piano soloist, recitalist city colls. and recital series, Calif. and NY, 1986—94; piano instr. Music Maker Music Sch., Anaheim, 1996—. Piano adjudicator South Western Youth Music Festival, Southern Calif., 2000—. Bd. dirs., chmn. regional festival So. Calif. Jr. Bach Festival, 2001—. Recipient 3d prize, Joanna Hodges Internat. Piano Competition, 1985, Cert. of Merit, So. Calif. Jr. Bach Festival. Mem.: Music Tchrs. Assn. Calif. (state adjudicator chmn. for Composers Today program 2001—, 2d v.p. San Bernardino br. 1997—, award for Young Artist Debut Concert 1985, award for performance at state conv. 1985, Cert. of Merit Piano Exams), Music Tchrs. Nat. Assn. Office: Music Maker Music Sch 5701 E Santa Ana Canyon Rd Anaheim CA 92807

VIDERMAN, LINDA JEAN, legal assistant, corporate financial executive; b. Follansbee, W.Va., Dec. 4, 1957; d. Charles Richard and Louise Edith (LeBoeuf) Roberts; m. David Gerald Viderman Jr., Mar. 15, 1974; children: Jessica Renae, April Mae, Melinda Dawn. AS, W.Va. No. C.C., 1983; cert. income tax prep., H&R Block, Steubenville, Ohio, 1986. Cert. surg. tech., fin. counselor; lic. ins. agt. Food prep. pers. Bonanza Steak House, Weirton, W.Va., 1981—83; ward clk., food svcs. Weirton Med. Ctr., 1982—84; sec., treas. Mountaineer Security Systems, Inc., Wheeling, W.Va., 1983—86; owner, operator The Button Booth, Colliers, W.Va., 1985—; paralegal, adminstr. Atty. Dominic J. Potts, Steubenville, Ohio, 1987—92; gen. ptnr., executrix Panhandle Homes, Wellsburg, W.Va., 1988—96; sec.-treas., executrix Panhandle Homes, Inc., 1996—; ins. agt. Milico, Mass. Indemnity, 1991—92, L&L Ins. Svcs., 1992—94; paralegal Atty. Fred Risovich II, Weirton, 1991—93; sec. The Hon. Fred Risovich II, Wheeling, 1993; paralegal Cipriani & Paull, L.C., Wellsburg, W.Va., 1993—2004; owner Wellsburg Office Supply, 1993—94; owner, operator Viderman Child Care Svcs. Co., Wellsburg, 1997—; owner, dir. Viderman & Assocs., Wellsburg, 1997—; legal asst. Cassidy, Myers, Cogan, Voegelin, & Tennant, L.C., 2004—05, Cassidy, Myers, Cogan & Voegelin, L.C., 2005—. Notary pub., 1991—. Contbr. articles to profl. jours.; author numerous poems. Chmn. safety com. Colliers (W.Va.) Primary PTA, 1985-87; founding mem. Brooke County Homeschoolers/Panhandle Homeschoolers Assn., 1999; editor Panhandle Homeschoolers Newsletter, 2000; mem., sec. LaLeche League, Steubenville, Ohio, 1978-80; vol. counselor W.Va. U. Fin. Counseling Svc., 1990—; IRS vol. Vol. Income Tax Assistance Program, 1991—. Mem. W.Va. Manufactured Housing Assn. (bd. dirs. 2001-02), W.Va. Writers Assn., Legal Assts. of W.Va., Inc., Am. Affiliate of Nat. Assn. Legal Assts., W.Va. Trial Lawyers Assn., Wellsburg Art Assn., Brooke County Genealogical Soc., Phi Theta Kappa Jehovah'S Witness. Avocations: christian ministry, home computing, camping, genealogy, home schooling. Home: RR2 Box 28 Wellsburg WV 26070-9500 Office: Panhandle Homes Inc RR 2 Box 27A Wellsburg WV 26070-9500 Personal E-mail: lviderman@aol.com.

VIDWANS, SMRUTI JAYANT, microbiologist; b. India; BS in biology, MIT; PhD in microbiology, U. Calif., San Francisco, 2001. Amgen rsch. fellow Irvington Inst. Immunological Rsch., 2003; postdoctoral fellow in microbiology and immunology U. Calif., San Francisco, 2004; co-founder Phenotypica. Contbr. articles to profl. jour. Named one of Top 100 Young Innovators, MIT Tech. Review, 2004. Office: U Calif Ctr Bioentrepeneurship 185 Berry St Ste 4603 San Francisco CA 94143-1016

VIEIRA, MEREDITH, television personality; b. Providence, Dec. 30, 1953; d. Edwin and Mary Elsie Vieira; m. Richard Cohen June 14, 1986; children: Benjamin, Gabriel, Lily Max. BA in English (magna cum laude), Tufts U., 1975. News announcer WORC-Radio, Worcester, Mass., 1975; reporter, anchor WJAR-TV, Providence; reporter WCBS-TV, NYC, 1979-82; from reporter, Chgo. bur. to news correspondent CBS News, NYC, 1982—84; Chgo. bur. chief, contbg. nat. corr. CBS Evening News with Dan Rather, NYC, 1982—84; substitute co-anchor Morning, 1984—85; prin. corr. West 57th, 1985—89; corr., co-editor 60 Minutes, 1989—91; contbg. corr., CBS Primetime series Verdict, 1991; co-anchor CBS Morning News, 1992—93; host, chief corr. Turning Point, 1993—97; chief correspondent ABC News, NYC, 1993; co-host, moderator The View, NYC, 1997—2006; co-host Today Show, NYC, 2006—. Narrator ABC TV special Open Sesame: The Making of Arabian Nights, 2000; host 78th Ann. Miss America Pageant, 1998, Lifetime's Intimate Portrait, 1999—, ABC special The Beatles Revolution, 2000, ABC TV Network's Countdown to Oscar, 2000, Who Wants to Be a Millionaire, 2002—, co-exec. prodr., 2005—; host ABC News Spl. Fat Like Me: How to Win the Weight War, 2003. Broadway debut Thoroughly Modern Millie, 2003, cameo appearance The Stepford Wives, 2004, guest host Larry King Live, 2005, host (spl. featurette) Desperate Housewives Season 1 DVD Set, 2005, guest appearances Sports Night, 1998, Walt Disney World Christmas Day Parade, 2002, Party Planner with David Tutera, 2005, Hi-Jinks, 2005, Celebrity Jeopardy, Between the Lions (PBS), (TV series) Healthy Kids, 1998, Spin City, 2000, All My Children, 2001, General Hospital, 2003, The Practice, 2003, (talk shows) The Tonight Show with Jay Leno, Late Show with David Letterman, Late Night with Conan O' Brien, Charlie Rose and Live with Regis and Kelly, appeared in (nat. TV commercials) Bayer Aspirin, Got Milk?, featured on the cover of numerous magazines including TV Guide, Ladies Home Journal and others. Frequent contbr. several charitable foundations; co-founder, mem. sr. adv. bd. Club Mom's, 2004—. Recipient Front Page award Newswoman's Club of N.Y., 1991, Robert F. Kennedy journalism award, 1995, Woman of Yr. award, City of Hope, 2001, six Emmy awards for reporting; honored by Anti-Defamation League; Found. Am. Women Radio and T.V., 1997. Achievements include hosting more episodes as a game show host than any women in TV history. Office: ABC 320 W 66th St New York NY 10023-6304*

VIEREGGER, SUSAN WAYNETTE, marketing professional, educator; d. James Wayne and Hazel May Skaggs; m. Terry Michael Vieregger, Oct. 29, 2005. B in Mktg. Mgmt., Bellevue U., Omaha, 1995, MA in Mgmt., 1997. Lic. massage therapist Nebr., 1991. Purchasing mgr. Union Pacific RR, Omaha, 1999—2000, ops. planning mgr., 2000—02, transload chem. mgr., 2002—04, regional dir. shortline mktg., 2004—. Prof. Metro C.C., Omaha, 1998—; v.p. S&V Transp. Corp, Omaha, 2005—. Supporter Nebr. Humane Soc., Omaha, 2000—06; fund raiser YWCA, Omaha. Mem.: Am. Mgmt. Assn. (assoc.), Animal Advocacy (assoc.). Office: Union Pacific Railroad 1400 Douglas St Omaha NE 68179 Office Phone: 402-544-1295. Home Fax: 402-501-2310; Office Fax: 402-501-2310. Business E-Mail: swvieregger@up.com.

VIETRI, LINDA SMITH, gifted and talented educator; b. Norristown, Pa., Aug. 28, 1951; d. George John (Stepfather) and Laura MacMullen Herdegen; m. Robert Vietri, Aug. 25, 1973; children: Patrick Robert, Jeffrey Thomas, Andrew Joseph. BA in English, Ursinus Coll., 1973; MSLS, Villanova U., 1974; M of Elem. Edn., Arcadia U., 1990. Cert. elem. edn. Pa., 1990. Tchr. 4th and 5th grades Centennial Sch. Dist., Warminster, Pa., 1990—98, tchr. gifted, 1998—. Curriculum resource representative-technology Centennial Sch. Dist., 1991—93; vol. tchr. students spl. needs Gen. Nash Elem. Sch., Kulpsville, 1987—90; cmty. mentor h.s. students North Penn H.S., Lansdale, 1986—87. Coord. distribs.clothing and household items Campbell Am. M.E.Ch., Phila., 2001—05. Mem.: AAUW (assoc.), ALA (assoc.), Pa. Assn. Gifted Edn. (assoc.). Lutheran. Achievements include development of distribution of needed items to less fortunate individuals and families. Avocations: volunteer and charity work, tutoring, reading, art, travel. Home: 102 Chester Cir North Wales PA 19454 Office: Centennial Sch Dist Centennial Rd Warminster PA 18974 Office Phone: 215-441-6087. Personal E-mail: vietli@centennialsd.org.

VIEUX, CARLEE ANNANETTE NOLAND, special education educator; b. Boulder, Colo., Nov. 26, 1949; d. James W. Noland and Donna L. (Cromwell) Noland Kirby; m. Philip C. Vieux, June 3, 1972; children: Alexander N., Andrew P. AA, Dodge City Community Coll., Kans., 1969; BSE, Emporia (Kans.) State U., 1971. Tchr. English Shawnee Hts. Jr. High Sch., Tecumseh, Kans., 1973-76, Copeland (Kans.) High Sch., 1976-77, Garden City (Kans.) High Sch., 1977-78, Abe Hubert Middle Sch., Garden City, 1978-90; tchr. spl. edn. Kenneth Henderson Middle Sch., Garden City, 1990—93; tchr. English Garden City C.C., 1989; tchr. Garden City H.S. Alternative Learning Ctr., 1993—97, Bernadine Sitts Intermediate Ctr., 1997—2004; family resource coord. Unified Support Agy., Hugoton, Kans., 2004—05; tchr. Lakin H.S., Kans., 2006—. Tchr. cons. Kans. Writing Project, Wichita, 1984—; state leader Nat. Coun. Tchrs. English Excellence in Lit. Mag. Prog., 1988—. Editor: Writers' Slate, 1987. Exec. bd. Finney County Hist. Soc., Garden City, 1985-90. Mem. Nat. Coun. Tchrs. English, Kans. Assn. Tchrs. English (sec. 1985-87), Coun. for Exceptional Children, Coun. of Children with Behavior Disorders, Am. Fedn. Tchrs., Assn. for Supervision and Curriculum Devel., Kans. Assn. for Supervision and Curriculum Devel. Republican. Methodist. Avocations: community theatre, gardening, walking, reading. Home: 706 E Hamline St Garden City KS 67846-3425 Office: Lakin HS 407 N Campbell Lakin KS 67860 Office Phone: 620-355-6411. E-mail: vieuxc@usd215.pld.com.

VIGEANT, MICHELE A., mental health counselor; b. Bklyn., Mar. 13, 1975; d. Joanne M. and Felix C. Vigeant. MEd, Columbia U., 2001. Lic. mental health counselor N.Y. State, cert. counselor Nat. Bd. Cert. Counselors. Dir. sexual assault and clin. svcs. Safe Horizon, NYC, 2003—05, dir. program integration project, 2005—06, dir. programs, 2006—. Rsch. cons. Safe Horizon, 2002—05. Mem.: ACA. Office: Safe Horizon 2 Lafayette St New York NY 10007 Office Phone: 212-577-7700. Business E-Mail: mvigeant@safehorizon.org.

VIGEE, KIMBERLY DENISE, anatomy and physiology educator; b. Eunice, La., Aug. 3, 1970; d. Harvey Patrick and Shelva Dean Vigee; m. Patrick Shannon MacDanel II, May 22, 2004. BS, La. State U., Baton Rouge, 1993; MS, La. State U., 1995; Dr. Naturopathy, Honolulu U., 1999. Exercise physiologist Sports/Spa and Clinic, Sandestin, Fla., 1991; exercise/pulmonary rehab. specialist Heart and Fitness Ctr., Baton Rouge, 1993—96; adj. instr. Southeastern La. U., Hammond, 1996, La. State U., Baton Rouge, 1996—2002; faculty instr. Our Lady of the Lake Coll., Baton Rouge, 2001—. Named Most Outstanding Tchr. in Arts and Sci., Our Lady of the Lake Coll., 2005—06; recipient Endowed Professorship, 2006. Mem.: Human Anatomy and Physiology Soc., Am. Naturopathic Med. Assn. Avocation: Ironman triathlons and marathons. Office: Our Lady of the Lake College 5345 Brittany Dr Baton Rouge LA 70808

VIGEN, KATHRYN L. VOSS, nursing administrator, educator, dean; b. Lakefield, Minn., Sept. 24, 1934; d. Edward Stanley and Bertha C. (Richter) Voss; m. David C. Vigen, June 23, 1956 (div. 1977); children: Eric E., Amy Vigen Hemstad, Aana Marie. BS in Nursing magna cum laude, St. Olaf Coll., 1956; MEd, S.D. State U., 1975; MS, Rush U., 1980; PhD, U. Minn., 1987. RN. Staff nurse various hosps., Mpls, Boston, Chgo., 1956-68; nursing instr. S.E.A. Sch. Practical Nursing, Sioux Falls, SD, 1969-74; statewide coord. upward mobility in nursing Augustana Coll., Sioux Falls, SD, 1974-78; cons./researcher S.D. Commn. Higher Edn., 1974-79; gov. appointed bd. mem. S.D. Bd. Nursing, 1975-79; RN upward mobility project dir., chair/dir. div. of nursing Huron Coll. S.D. State U., 1978-79, mobility project dir., 1980-84; head dept. nursing, assoc. prof. Luther Coll., Decorah, Iowa, 1984-94; prof. nursing Graceland Coll., Independence, Mo., 1994-2001; dir., dean Sch. Nursing North Park U., Chgo., 2001—06. Cons. in field; developer outreach MSN programs Graceland Coll.; governing bd. mem. Midwest Alliance in Nursing, S.D. and Iowa, 1984-92, Mo., 1998—; founder Soc. for Advancement of Nursing, Malta, 1992; developer Health Care in the Mediterranean Study Abroad Program, Greece and Malta, 1994, 96, 98; developer summer internship for Maltese nursing students Mayo Med. Ctr. and Luther Coll.; presenter on internat. collaboration with Malta for nursing leadership 2d Internat. Acad. Congress on Nursing, Kansas City, 1996; presenter in field. Author: Role of a Dean in a Private Liberal Arts College, 1992; devel. and initiated 3 nursing programs in S.D., 1974-84 (named Women of Yr., 1982). Lobbyist Nursing Schs. in S.D., 1974-79; task force mem. Sen. Tom Harkin's Nurse's Adv. Com., 1986-94. Fellow to rep. U.S.A. ANA cand. in internat. coun. nursing 3M, St. Paul, 1978; recipient Leadership award Bush Found., St. Paul, 1979; Faculty fellow Minn. Area Geriatric Edn. Ctr. U. Minn., 1990-91; Fulbright scholar to Malta, 1992; recipient Fulbright award Malta Coun. Internat. Exch. of Scholars, Washington, 1992—; named Disting. Alumna, St. Olaf Coll., 2003. Mem. AAUW, ANA, AACN (hon. mem.), Am. Assn. Colls. Nursing (hon., exec. devel. subcom. 1990—, Hon. Mem. award), Internat. Assn. Human Caring, Iowa Nurse's Assn. (bd. dirs. 1989-92, mem. nursing edn. com. 1989—, co-pres. 1989—), Inst. Medicine Chgo., Midwest Alliance in Nursing (gov. bd. rep. Iowa 1989-92, chair membership com. 1989-92, Mo., 1998—, S.D. gov. bd. rep. 1984-86, Rozella Schlotfeldt Leadership award 1993), Iowa Acad. Sci., Iowa Assn. Colls. Nursing Soc., Gerontol. Soc. Am., Am. Assn. Colls. Mich., Rotary, Sigma Theta Tau. Democrat. Lutheran. Avocations: singing, travel and other cultures, meeting people, sailing, reading. Home: 5360 N Lowell Ave # 412 Chicago IL 60630 Office: North Park U 3225 W Foster Ave Chicago IL 60625 Office Phone: 773-244-5235.

VIGIL, ELIZABETH LEE, music educator; d. James Austin and Verla Lee Garrison; children: Benjamin, Timothy, Esther. BME, U. Colo., Boulder, 1983; MS in Counseling, Denver Sem., Englewood, Colo., 1990. Cert. tchr. K-12 Colo. Elem. music tchr. Dist. II, Colorado Springs, Colo., 1983—84; jr. high/h.s. music tchr. Sheridan Sch. Dist., Colo., 1985—87; asst. pastor Ref. Ch. Am., Denver, 1990—95; practice mgr. Body Mechanix Phys. Therapy, Brighton, Colo., 1995—2005; music./drama tchr. K-12 Jefferson County Schs., Bromfield, Colo., 2005—. Aurora Pub. Schs., Brighton, 2005—. Contbr. articles to profl. jours., newspapers. Vol. leader Homestead Home Sch. Corp., Prospect Valley, Colo., 2004—06; cellist Rocky Mountain Chamber, Denver, 2004—06; mem. Keenesburg Chamber, 2001—06. Mem.: NRA, Am. Choral Dirs. Assn., Music Educators Nat. Conf., Sigma Alpha Iota. Republican. Baptist. Avocations: reading, hiking, writing, dramatic works (directing and performing), performing vocal, cello, guitar. Home: PO Box 16 Keenesburg CO 80643

VIGIL-GIRON, REBECCA, state official; b. Taos, N.Mex., Sept. 4, 1954; d. Felix W. and Cecilia (Santistevan) Vigil; 1 child, Andrew R. AA in Elem. Edn., N.Mex. Highlands U., 1978, BA in French, 1991. Sec., project monitor, customer svc. rep. Pub. Svc. Co. N.Mex., 1978-86; sec. of state State of N. Mex, 1987—90, 1999—2006; exec. dir. N.Mex. Commn. Status of Women, 1991; electoral observer UN, Angola, Africa, 1992, Internat. Found. Electoral Sys., Dominican Republic, 1994, Equatorial Guinea, Africa, 1996, Washington, 1996. Participant AMPART, Mex., 1991. Dem. nominee U.S. Ho. Reps., 1990. Named among 100 Most Influential Hispanics in Nation, Hispanic Bus. Mag., 1990; recipient Trio Achievers award S.W. Assn. Student Assistance Programs, 1993, Gov.'s award Outstanding N.Mex. Women, 1994. Mem. Albuquerque Hispano C. of C. (membership rep., sr. sales mktg. rep., corp. rels. coord.) Democrat. Office: Office Sec of State State Capitol North Annex Ste 300 Santa Fe NM 87503

VIGLIOTTI, PATRICIA NOREEN, metal products executive, sculptor; b. Poughkeepsie, N.Y., May 13, 1955; d. James George and Florence Violet (Terwilligar) Dingee; Grad. h.s., Stratsbough. Welder Argos Inc., Brester, NY, 1989—; owner Vigliotti Sculpture Gallery & Studio, Balwinville, NY. One woman shows include Ward Lawrence, N.Y.C., Gallery 84; exhibited in group shows at Tannery Brook Collections Gallery, Woodstock, N.Y., Samagundi

Club Galleries, New Rochell Art Assn. (hon. mention), Gregg Chim Gallery, 1992, Conn. Acad. of Fine Arts, 1992, Orgn. of Ind. Artists, N.Y.C., represented in Providence Town of Mass. by Ester Lastique; featured as a sculptor in New Art International, 1997-98. Avocation: raising cockatiels and iguanas. Home: 8 Parker Dr E Mahopac NY 10541-2059

VIKANDER, LAURA A., lawyer; b. Florissant, Mo., Dec. 21, 1956; BA magna cum laude, Duke U., 1978; JD, U. Va., 1983. Bar: DC 1983, US Dist. Ct. DC 1984, Va. 1985, US Ct. Appeals (4th cir.). Assoc. Dickstein Shapiro Morin & Oshinsky LLP, Washington, 1983—95, counsel, vice chmn. hiring com. Mem.: Women's Work & Family Action Coun., Va. State Bar, Women's Legal Defense Fund, Va. Bar Assn., DC Bar Assn. (litig. sect.), ABA. Avocations: volleyball, coaching youth soccer, basketball & softball. Office: Dickstein Shapiro Morin & Oshinsky LLP 2101 L St NW Washington DC 20037-1526 Office Phone: 202-828-2246. Office Fax: 202-887-0689. Business E-Mail: vikanderl@dsmo.com.

VILA, ADIS MARIA, lawyer, business government executive; b. Guines Habana, Cuba, Aug. 1, 1953; d. Calixto Vila and Adis C. Fernandez. BA with distinction, Rollins Coll., 1974; JD with honors, U. Fla., 1978; LLM with high honors, Institut Universitaire de Hautes Estudes Internationales, Geneva, 1981; MBA, U Chgo., 1997. Bar: Fla. 1979, DC 1984. Assoc. Paul & Thomson, 1979-82; White House fellow Office Pub. Liaison, Washington, 1982-83; spl. asst. to sec. state for inter-Am. affairs Dept. State, Washington, 1983-86; dir. Office of Mex. and Caribbean Basin, Dept. Commerce, Washington, 1986-87; sec. Dept. Adminstrn., State of Fla., 1987-89; asst. sec. for adminstrn. USDA, Washington, 1989-91; vis. fellow Nat. Def. U., Washington, 1992-93; v.p. internat. devel. Vigoro Corp., Chgo., 1994-95; v.p. govt. affairs regulatory policy, Carribean & Latin Am. Nortel Networks, 1997-2000; pres., CEO Vila & Assocs., 2001—. Vis. asst. prof. Fla. Internat. U., 1993—94; mem. adv. bd. Ams. Global Asset Mgmt. Fund, 1999—; v.p. external affairs Miami Dade C.C., 2002—03; adj. faculty bus. law various not-for-profit, for profit instns., 2002—. Trustee So. Ctr. Internat. Studies, 1987—. Named one of 100 Most Influential Hispanics, 1988; Paul Harris fellow, Rotary Internat., 1983, U.S.-Japan Leadership fellow, 1991—92, Eisenhower Exch. fellow, Beca Fiore, Argentina, 1992. Mem.: Women Execs. in State Govt. (bd. dirs. 1987—89), Am. Coun. Young Polit. Leaders (bd. dirs. 1984—), Internat. Women's Forum, Coun. Fgn. Rels. (term mem. 1987—92), Dade County Bar Assn. (bd. dirs. young and lawyers sect. 1979—87). Republican. Roman Catholic. Avocations: tennis, skiing, golf, theater, art. Office Phone: 954-458-4080. E-mail: adisvila@bellsouth.net.

VILADAS, PILAR, editor; BA, Harvard Coll., 1977. With Interiors mag., 1979—81; with Progressive Architecture, 1981—88; home design editor NY Times mag., 1997—, House & Garden, 1989—93; contbg. writer Archtl. Digest, 1993—96. Author: Los Angeles: A Certain Style, 1995, Domesticities: At Home with the NY Times Magazine, 2005; co-author: California Beach Houses: Style, Interiors, & Architecture, 1996. Office: NY Times 229 W 43rd St New York NY 10036 Office Phone: 212-556-5183. Office Fax: 212-556-7382.

VILAR, SUSAN ANN, elementary school educator; b. Chilton, Wis., May 20, 1965; d. Kenneth Edwin and June Ann Smasal; m. Manuel Benigno Vilar, June 14, 2002. BA, Concordia U., Mequon, Wis., 1988. Cert. tchr. 1-8 Tex. Elem. sch. tchr. Laredo Ind. Sch. Dist., Tex., 1988—96, 4th grade gifted and talented tchr., 1996—2004; 4th grade tchr. Houston Ind. Sch. Dist., 2004—06; math interventionist Tulsa Pub. Sch., 2006—. Tech. facilitator Laredo ISD, 1997—2000; curriculum writer. Baseball scorekeeper Laredo Apaches, 1995; baseball/softball scorekeeper Laredo Parks and Recreation Dept., 1988—2004. Recipient Sch. Bell award, Laredo C. of C. Ednl. Com., 2002. Mem.: Tex. Classroom Tchrs. Assn. (exec. v.p. ea. dist. 2004—06). Home: 6801 S Birch Ave Broken Arrow OK 74011 Office: Tulsa Public Schools John Burroughs Elementary School 1924 N Cincinnati Tulsa OK 74106 Office Phone: 918-833-8780. Personal E-mail: sue3407@yahoo.com.

VILARDI, VIRGINIA ANN, secondary school educator, department chairman; d. Robert and Jacqueline Theresa Penson; m. Carmine Francis Vilardi, June 18, 1977; children: Nicholas Fredrick, Robert Peter Francis, Jacquelyn Concetta Vilardi LeFevre. BS in Biology, U. Mass., Loweel, 1989; M in Secondary Sci. Edn., Wright State U., Dayton, Ohio, 1994. Cert. tchr. Ala. State Bd. Edn., 1994. Tchr./sci. dept. chair Calhoun H.S., Letohatchee, Ala., 1994—96, Wetumpka H.S., Ala., 1996—. Club advisor Jr. Civitan, Wetumpka, 1996—; internat. sci. fair coord. Ala. Acad. Sci., Wetumpka, 1999—; Elmore County sci. fair coord. Elmore County Bd. Edn., Wetumpka, 1999—. Named Jr. Civitan Advisor of Yr., Jr. Civitan Internat., 2000, 2001; recipient Golden Apple award, WAKA TV, 1999; fellow, Woodrow Wilson Found., 2001; grantee, Ctrl. Electric Coop., 2002, 2003, 2004; Environ. Edn. fellow, Home Owners Boat Owners Lake Jordon and Ala. Power, 2003, 2004. Mem.: Ala. Sci. Tchrs. Assn. (assoc.; presenter 2000—06). Methodist. Achievements include research in Leaf Cutter Ants in Costa Rica. Avocations: travel, farming, research. Office: Wetumpka High School 1251 Coosa River Pkwy Wetumpka AL 36092 Office Phone: 334-567-5158. Business E-Mail: virginia.vilardi@elmore.k12.al.us.

VILARDO, CAROLE, retired small business owner, research association administrator; b. Bronx, N.Y., Mar. 11, 1941; d. Thomas and Victoria Vilardo. Cert., Tobe-Coburn Sch., 1960. Group mgr. Gimbel Bros., N.Y.C., 1960-63; gen. mgr. Showcase Shops, N.Y.C., 1963-71; owner Fashion Gallery, Las Vegas, Nev., 1971-79, Whatever, Ltd., Las Vegas, 1979-85; pres. Nev. Taxpayers Assn., Las Vegas and Carson City, 1986—. Pub. mem. Legis. Interim Tax Commn., Nev., 1979-81, 93-95; adv. mem. Gov.'s Health Care Study, Nev., 1996-98, Water Infrastructure Funding, Clark County,Nev., 1996-97. Contbr. articles to profl. publs.; editor rsch. papers in field. Bd. dirs. Winchester Town Bd., 1989-92; founding mem. Secret Witness, Clark County, 1979-92; bd. dirs. Nat. Kidney Found. of Nev., 1996—, v.p., 1992-93; bd. dirs. YMCA of So. Nev., 1992—. Recipient Free Enterprise award Las Vegas C. of C., 1981, Women of Achievement award Las Vegas C. of C., 1991, Homer Rodriquez award Nev. Assessors' Assn., 1997. Mem. Nat. Taxpayers Conf. (bd. dirs. 1995—). Avocations: gardening, cooking, reading. Office: Nev Taxpayers Assn 2303 E Sahara Ave Ste 203 Las Vegas NV 89104-4138

VILAS, FAITH, aerospace scientist; b. Evanston, Ill., Apr. 14, 1952; d. Jack Jr. and Faith McCrea (Lehman) V.; m. Larry Wayne Smith, July 5, 1986. BA, Wellesley (Mass.) Coll., 1973; MS, MIT, 1975; PhD, U. Ariz., 1984. Sr. rsch. asst. Cerro Tololo Inter-Am. Obs., La Serena, Chile, 1975-77; sr. assoc. scientist Lockheed Electronics Co., Houston, 1977-78; vis. rsch. scientist NRC, Johnson Space Ctr., Houston, 1984-85; space scientist NASA, Johnson Space Ctr., Houston, 1985—2005; discovery program scientist NASA Hdqs., Washington, 2001—02; chief planetary astronomy group Johnson Space Ctr., 2002—05; dir. MMT Obs., Tucson, 2005—. Editor: (with C.R. Chapman and M.S. Matthews) Mercury, 1988; mem. editl. bd. Icarus, 2001—03. Bd. dirs. Vatican Observatory Found., 1996—. Mem. Am. Astron. Soc. (div. planetary scis. nominating com. 1988-91, sec. 1992-95, vice chmn. 1995-96, chmn. 1996-97, prize com. chmn. 1997-98), Johnson Space Ctr. Nat. Mgmt. Assn. (chair Am. enterprise com. 1987-88, Shield Excellence award 1988). Episcopalian. Avocations: travel, flying, emergency medicine. Office: MMT Obs PO Box 210065 U Ariz Tucson AZ 85721 Office Phone: 520-621-1269. E-mail: fvilas@mmto.org.

VILCHEZ, VICTORIA ANNE, lawyer; b. Tampa, Fla., Aug. 10, 1955; d. Angel and Mary Ida (Guarisco) V.; m. Louis J. Deutsch; children: Matthew Stephen Williams, Michael Paul Williams, Heather Margaret Williams. BA, Fla. State U., 1977; JD, Mercer U., 1980. Bar: Fla. 1980. Trial atty. Office Pub. Defender, Miami, Fla., 1980-83; pvt. practice, 1983—. Rep. Nat. Conf. on Women and Law, Atlanta, 1978; traffic magistrate Palm Beach County Ct., 1991-95. Vol. Cath. Home for Children, Miami, 1983-84; mem. Coun. Cath. Women; class 1994 Leadership Palm Beach County; bd. dirs. Girl Scouts coun., Palm Glades, Fla., 1995-04, first v.p., 2003-04. Recipient cert. of achievement 8th Nat. Conf. Juvenile Justice, 1981, Livingstone Hall award Juvenile Justice ABA, 1998; grantee Mercer U., 1977. Mem. Fla. Bar, Fla. Assn. Women Lawyers (sec., newsletter editor Palm Beach County chpt. 1985-86, mentor chair 2003, pres.-elect 2004-05, pres. 2005-06), Palm Beach County Bar Assn., Fla. State U. Alumni Assn., Palm Beach County Hispanic Bar Assn. (pres.-elect 1990-91, pres. 1991-92, bd. dirs. 1990—, treas. 1993-94, 94-97), Legal Aid Soc. Palm Beach (bd. dirs. 1992—, v.p. 1999-2001, pres. 2001-03), West Palm Beach Kiwanis Club, Leadership Palm Beach County (grad. 1994, bd. govts. 1999-2001). Roman Catholic. Office: Ste 401 2161 Palm Beach Lakes Blvd West Palm Beach FL 33409 Office Phone: 561-471-0001. Business E-Mail: Vilchezlaw@palmbeachbar.org.

VILE, SANDRA JANE, leadership training educator; b. Oceanside, N.Y., Oct. 4, 1939; d. John Oliver and Roberta May (Wood) Ryan; m. Joseph Charles Vile, June 27, 1964; children: Jonathan Charles, Susan Jane. BS in Christian Edn. cum laude, Nyack Coll., 1961; MS in Edn., SUNY, Oneonta, 1963; diploma, Childrens Ministries Inst., Warrenton, Mo., 1974; Cert. in Visual Comm., Faith Venture Visuals, Inc., Lititz, Pa., 1979. Cert. elem. tchr., N.Y. Tchr. Hudson (N.Y.) City Sch. Dist., 1961-64, South Orangetown Ctrl. Sch. Dist., Orangeburg, N.Y., 1964-67; local dir. Child Evangelism Fellowship of Empire State, Afton, N.Y., 1972-88, state tng. instr., 1988-92; leadership tng. instr. Child Evangelism Fellowship, Inc., Warrenton, 1992—2002, vol. leadership tng. instr., 2002—. Vis. lectr. Nyack (N.Y.) Coll., 1967; tng. cons. Faith Venture Visuals, Inc., 1980-96. Contbr.: Children's Ministry Resource Bible, 1993. Lay leader Teen Missions, Inc., Merritt Island, Fla., 1982. Recipient Alumna of Yr. award Faith Venture Visuals, Inc., 1993. Mem. Pro Merito Soc., Logicians Soc. Avocations: computers, travel, counted cross-stitch. Home and Office: PO Box 679 Claverack NY 12513-0679

VILIM, NANCY CATHERINE, advertising executive; b. Quincy, Mass., Jan. 15, 1952; d. John Robert and Rosemary (Malpede) V.; m. Geoffrey S. Horner, Feb. 16, 1992; children: Matthew Edward Cajda, Megan Catherine Cajda, Margaret Horner. Student, Miami U., Oxford, Ohio, 1970-72. Media asst. Draper Daniels, Inc., Chgo., 1972—74; asst. buyer Campbell Mithun, Chgo., 1974—75; buyer Tatham, Laird & Kudner, Chgo., 1975—77; media buyer Adcom, Inc. div. Quaker Oats Corp., Chgo., 1977—79; media supr. G.M. Feldman, Chgo., 1979—81; v.p. media dir. Media Mgmt., 1981—83; v.p. broadcast dir. Bozell, Jacobs, Kenyon & Eckhardt, Chgo., 1983—88; v.p., media mgr. McCann-Erickson, Inc., 1989—2002; broadcast supr. OMD USA, Chgo., 2002—04; sr. media buyer GSD&M, Chgo., 2004—05; media dir. Jordan, Ross & Rose, Northfield, Ill., 2005—. Judge 27th Internat. Broadcast Awards, Chgo., 1987. Co-pres. Immaculate Conception Religious Edn. Parents Club, 1995-96. Recipient Media All Star awards Sound Mgmt. Mag., N.Y.C., 1987. Mem. Broadcast Advt. Club Chgo., Mus. Broadcast Communications, NAFE. Office: JRR Advt 790 Frontage Rd Northfield IL 60093

VILKER-KUCHMENT, VALERIA, violinist; Student Gnesiny Sch. Music, Gnesiny Acad. Music, Moscow Tchaikovsky Conservatory Music, violin studies with Yuri Yankelevich. Mem. Boston Symphony Orch. Former faculty Tchaikovsky Conservatory; faculty New Eng. Conservatory Music, Longy New Eng. Conservatory Sch. of Music, The Tanglewood Music Ctr. Appeared as recitialist, soloist, chamber musician throughout the U.S., USSR, Poland, Germany, and Czechoslovakia; concert mistress Boston Philharm., the Harvard Chamber Orch., and SinfoNova. Recipient prizes The Internat. Violin Competition, Prague, Internat. Chamber Music Competition, Munich. Office: New Eng Conservatory 290 Huntington Ave Boston MA 02115-5018

VILLACIAN, VANESSA LUISA, psychologist; b. Miami, Fla., Sept. 14, 1973; d. Fernando and Tania Luisa (Alvarez) Villacian; m. Robert Pagés, Dec. 23, 2004. Psy.D. utmost distinction, Carlos Albizu U., Miami, 2000. Cert. hypnotherapist. Pres. The Answers Centre, Miami, 2002—. Clin. dir. Oasis, Miami, 2005. Mem.: APA, Psi Chi. Avocation: exercise. Home: 199 Edgewater Dr Coral Gables FL 33133 Office: The Answers Centre 7171 SW 62nd Ave 301 South Miami FL 33143 Office Phone: 305-308-2178. Personal E-mail: drvpages@yahoo.com.

VILLAGOMEZ, DEBORAH LYNN, medical/surgical nurse, horse breeder; b. Calumet, Mich., Sept. 29, 1962; d. Rudolph J. Kela and Lyla Lillian Seppala. Grad. in nursing, Coll. of Lake County, Grayslake, Ill., 1991. RN Wis., N.Mex. Arabian and Quarter Horse rancher, Edgewood, N.Mex. Home: 1138 Mountain Valley Rd Edgewood NM 87015

VILLAIRE, HOLLY HENNEN HOOD, theater producer, director, actress, educator; b. Yonkers, NY, Apr. 11, 1944; d. John Wilson and Adele Jelonek (Deer) Hood. BA (summa cum laude), U. Detroit, 1964; MA, U. Mich., 1967. Cert. of studies Centre Dramatique Nat. du Sud Est, France, 1965. Assoc. artistic dir. Hamm & Clov Stage Co., Yonkers, NY, 1973—2001, producing artistic dir., 2001—; prodr. Olympic Arts Festival (Ensemble Studio Theatre), 1984; asst. prof. Allentown Coll. (now De Sales U.), 1991—92, Vassar Coll., 1992. Dir. grad. showcases Am. Musical and Dramatic Acad., 1992—95; screening, finals judge U. Resident Theatre Assn. Auditions, 1993—95; finals judge Region 2 Am. Coll. Theatre Festival, 1993—94; guest spkr. Disting. Artist Forum with James Earl Jones, U. Mich., 1993; guest artist, S.W. Gas Disting. Artist lectr. UNLV, Las Vegas, 1994; forum prodr. Actor's Ctr., 1996; casting cons. Stratford Festival Theatre, Conn., 1998; adj. prof. Mercy Coll., 2000—. Actor: Antony and Cleopatra (Pitts. Press award as Best Actress, 1989), (Off-Broadway) God Bless You, Mr. Rosewater, Bklyn. Acad. Music Theatre Company (BAM); dir.: Car, Berlin Festival, 1973; actor: Coming Around Again: A Concert in Tribute to Christopher Reeve, 1997; (Broadway plays) Habeas Corpus, Scapino, (theatre) On Borrowed Time, 1965, Our Town, 1966, Return the Rain, 1971, This Property is Condemned, 1972, Eyes of Chalk, 1972, Talk to Me Like the Rain and Let Me Listen, 1972; dir.: Anam, 2001, An Aisling Christmas, 2002, Anam Cara, 2003, Of Pubs and Parishes, 2004, Ardnaglass on the Air, 2005, A Touch of the Playright, 2006; prodr.: The Ring, 2006, Hispanic Heritage Cultural Weekend, 2006. Arts Alive grantee, Westchester Arts Coun. (NYSCA), 2003, 2004, 2005, 2006, NEA, 2006. Mem.: Actor's Equity Assn., AFTRA, SAG. Office Phone: 914-963-6222. Business E-Mail: hvillaire@hammandclov.org.

VILLA-KOMAROFF, LYDIA, molecular biologist, educator, academic administrator; b. Las Vegas, N.Mex., Aug. 7, 1947; d. John Dias and Drucilla (Jaramillo) V.; m. Anthony Leader Komaroff, June 18, 1970. BA, Goucher Coll., 1970; PhD, MIT, 1975; DSc (hon.), St. Thomas U., 1996, Pine Manor Coll., 1997; PhD (hon.), Goucher Coll., 1997. Rsch. fellow Harvard U., Cambridge, 1975-78; asst. prof. dept. microbiology U. Mass. Med. Ctr., Worcester, 1978-81, assoc. prof. dept. molecular genetics micro, 1982-85; assoc. prof. dept. neurology Harvard Med. Sch., Boston, 1986-95; sr. rsch. assoc. neurology Children's Hosp., Boston, 1985-95, assoc. dir. mental retardation rsch. ctr., 1987-94; prof. dept. neurology Northwestern U., Evanston, Ill., 1995—2002, assoc. v.p. rsch., 1995-97, v.p. rsch., 1998—2002; v.p. for rsch., COO, Whitehead Inst. for Biomed. Rsch., Cambridge, Mass., 2003—05; chief sci. officer Cytonome, Inc., 2005—. Mem. mammalian genetics study sect. NIH, 1982-84, mem. reviewers rsch., 1989, mem. neurol. disorders program project rev. com., 1989-94; mem. adv. bd. Biol. Sci. Directorate, NSF, 1994-99; bd. dirs. Nat. Ctr. Genome Rsch., 1995-00. TransKaryotic Therapies, 2003-05, chair 2005; mem. adv. coun. Nat. Inst. Neurol. Disorders and Stroke, NIH, 2000-04; bd. trustees Pine Manor Coll., 2004—; sr. lectr. Sloan Sch. Mgmt. MIT, 2003--05 Contbr. articles and abstracts to profl. jour.; patentee in field. Recipient Hispanic Engr. Nat. Achievement award, 1992, Nat. Achievement award Hispanic Mag., 1996; inducted Hispanic Engr. Nat. Achievement Hall of Fame, 1999; selected 50 most important Hispanics by "business & Tech., Hispanic Engr. & Info. Tech." mag. 2003; Helen Hay Whitney Found. fellow, 1975-78; NIH grantee, 1978-85, 89-96. Mem. AAAS (bd. dirs. 2000-05), Am. Soc. Microbiology, Assn. for Women in Sci., Soc. for Neurosci., Am. Soc. Cell Biology, Soc. for Advancement Chicanos and Native Ams. in Sci. (founding, bd. dir. 1987-93, v.p. 1990-93). Office Phone: 617-330-5030 ext. 354. Business E-Mail: lvk@alum.mit.edu.

VILLALON, DALISAY MANUEL, nurse, real estate broker; b. Angat, Bulacan, Philippines, Apr. 27, 1941; came to U.S., 1967; d. Federico Manuel and Librada (Garcia) Manuel; divorced; children: Ricky, May, Liberty, Derrick, Dolly Rose. BSN, Manila Ctrl. U., 1961; postgrad. in nursing, U. Ill., Chgo., 1972—74. RN Ill. Instr. nursing Ctrl. Luzon Sch. Nursing, Philippines, 1966-67; staff nurse St. Alexis Hosp., Cleve., 1968-70, Augustana Hosp., Chgo., 1972-74; nurse mgr. Holy Child Med. Clinic, Chgo., 1976-80; nurse auditor 1st Health Care, Rosemont, Ill., 1982-83; dir. nurses North Shore Terr., Waukegan, Ill., 1983-90, Carlton House, 1991-94. Columnist Philippine News. Bd. dirs. Filipino Am. Coun., Chgo., 1978-80, v.p., 1980-82; bd. dirs. Asian Human Svcs., Chgo.; pres. Am.-Filipino Profl. Civic Alliance, Chgo., 1984-90, Philipino-Am. United for Svc.-Oriental Objective, 1991—; chmn. Philippine Week Com., 1979; past v.p. Filipino Ams. Concerned for Elderly; trustee Rizal-MacArthur Found.; past v.p. Filipino Svc. League, 1989-91; past exec. v.p. Asian Festival, Inc.; past chmn. various civic coms.; mem. Asian-Am. Adv. Coun. Mayor Daley, 1989-97. Recipient Cert. Appreciation Rizal-MacArthur Found., 1977, Most Outstanding Filipino in Midwest award Cavite Assn. Am., 1980, Outstanding Cmty. Svc. Appreciation award Filipino Am. Coun., 1981, 89, NGHIA Sinh Internat., Inc., 1989, Outstanding Svc. award Asian-Am. Coaliton, 1989, Outstanding Contrn. award Dirs. Nursing and Adminstrs. Conf., 1988, Nat. Prism award for Women of Style & Achievement Phil Time USA and People Mag. 2003, Cert. of Recognition, Cir. Empowered Women of Midwest, 2004; named to Filipino Hall of Fame for cmty. svc. Phil Reports TV, 1996; named Outstanding Alumnus, Manila Ctrl. U. Coll. Nursing Alumni Assn., 2004. Mem. Ill. Nurses Assn. (bd. dirs., dist. senator 1989-91, human rights and ethics commn. 1990-91), Philippine Med. Assn. Aux. (pres. 1980, Outstanding Leadership award 1989), Chgo. Med. Soc. Aux. (v.p. 1980), Chgo. Philippine Lioness Club (pres. 1983-84, Outstanding Svc. award 1985, Mrs. Chgo. Philippine Independence, 2003, Melvin Jones fellow 2004), Filipino Woman's Club Chgo. (Outstanding Woman in Leadership 1992, Chgo. Filipino Hall of Fame award 1998), Filipino Am. Polit. Assn. Democrat. Roman Catholic. Home: 1070 Sanders Rd Northbrook IL 60062-2904 Office: Vitas Health Care Corp Vitas Innovative Care 700 N Sacramento Chicago IL 60612 Personal E-mail: delyvillalon@netzero.com.

VILLANO, CHRISTINE PEARSALL, elementary school educator; b. East Orange, N.J., Jan. 23, 1952; d. Raymond Wesley and Anne Dorothy (Simmons) Pearsall; m. James George Villano, May 19, 1977; children: Lisa, Katie, Theresa, Gabriel. Student, Seton Hall U., 1970-72; BEd, U. Alaska, 1978, postgrad. Cert. elem. tchr. Tchr., curriculum coord. St. Charles Kids Sch., Newark, 1971-74; vol. tchr., student advisor St. Mary Million Sch./Jesuit Vol. Corps, St. Mary's, Alaska, 1974-77; substitute tchr./aide tchr. Fairbanks (Alaska) No. Star Borough Sch. Dist., 1985—. Tchr. trainer Denali Discovery Sch., Fairbanks, 1990—. Named Vol. of Yr. Girl Scouts USA, 1987, 88, 93, Tchr. of Yr. Delta Kappa Gamma, 1992; recipient Presdl. award NSF, 1994. Fellow Alaska State Writing Consortium (steering com.); mem. NSTA (Presdl. award 1994), NEA, Internat. Reading Assn., Nat. Coun. Tchrs. Math., Fairbanks Edn. Assn. (bldg. rep.). Democrat. Roman Catholic. Avocations: community volunteering, swimming official. Home: 2142 Bridgewater Dr Fairbanks AK 99709-4103

VILLAR, MARIA, information technology executive; BS in Computer Sci., Fla. Internat. Univ.; MS in Info. Systems, Univ. Miami; MBA in Info. Systems, Miami Univ. With IBM, 1982—, v.p., e-business transformation planning and strategic alliances, v.p., info. and bus. intelligence transformation, 2003—. Named to Elite Women, Hispanic Bus. Mag., 2004; recipient New Media Leadership award, US Black and Hispanic Engrs. and Info. Tech. Mag., 2000. Office: IBM New Orchard Rd Armonk NY 10504 Office Phone: 914-499-1900. Office Fax: 914-765-7382.

VILLAREAL, PATRICIA J., lawyer; b. Sonora, Calif., Aug. 27, 1951; BA in Polit. sci., Mount Vernon Coll., 1975; JD, Harvard U., 1980. Bar: Tex. 1980. Law clk. to Judge H. Barefoot Sanders U.S. Dist. Ct. (no. dist.) Tex., 1980-82; mem. Jones Day (formerly Jones, Day, Reavis & Pogue), Dallas; ptnr. and chair, new assoc. recruiting Jones Day, Dallas. Spl. asst. Ho. Reps. Judiciary Com., 1975-77 Office: Jones Day 2727 N Harwood St Dallas TX 75201-1515 Office Phone: 214-969-2973. Business E-Mail: pjvillareal@jonesday.com.

VILLAROSA, SHARI, ambassador; BA in Internat. Studies, U. NC, Chapel Hill; JD, Coll. William and Mary. Diplomat in residence East-West Ctr., Honolulu; desk officer Office Investment Affairs US Dept. State, Washington, Singapore and Indonesia desk officer, dep. dir. Office Burma, Cambodia, Laos, Thailand and Vietnam Affairs, spl. asst. to undersecretary econ. affairs, dir. Philippines, Malaysia, Brunei, Singapore Affairs, East Asia and Pacific Bur., US chargé d'Affairs in Burma Rangoon, 2005—. Office: DOS Amb 4250 Rangoon Pl Washington DC 20521-4250*

VILLARREAL, CHRISTIE M., lawyer; b. Laredo, Tex., Dec. 9, 1976; BA cum laude, St. Mary's U. San Antonio, 1998, JD cum laude, 2001. Bar: Tex. 2001, US Dist. Ct. (no. dist. Tex.). Briefing atty. to Chief Justice Alma L. Lopez 4th Ct. Appeals, San Antonio, 2001—02; assoc. Godwin, Pappas, Langley & Ronquillo, L.L.P., Dallas, 2002—. Named a Rising Star, Tex. Super Lawyers mag., 2006. Mem.: Dallas Hispanic Bar Assn., Dallas Assn. Young Lawyers, Hispanic Nat. Bar Assn., ABA, Dallas Bar Assn. Office: Godwin Pappas Langley Ronquillo LLP Renaissance Tower Ste 1700 1201 Elm St Dallas TX 75270 Office Phone: 214-939-8675. E-mail: cvillarreal@godwinpappas.com.*

VILLARREAL, JUNE PATRICIA, retired sales executive; b. Atlantic City, Sept. 26, 1929; d. Edmund N. and Dorothy R. (McDowell) Ricchezza; m. Ottavio Gelmi, Dec. 16, 1954 (div. 1964); 1 child, Alessandra; m. Robert Joseph McElroy, Oct. 16, 1970 (dec. May 1974); m. Carlos Castañeda Villarreal, Oct. 3, 2002. Student, Temple U., 1947-48, Georgetown U., 1951-53. Staff mem. Am. Consulate Gen., Milan, 1954; legis. asst. U.S. Senate, Washington, 1956; social sec. Amb. of Finland, Washington, 1958; adminstrv. asst., translator Roosevelt and Clark Lobbyists, 1958—59; legis. asst. to congressman Washington, 1960-65; sr. assoc. Gillmore M. Perry Co., Washington, 1965-76; sales exec., cons., 1980-87; ptnr. Mfrs. Representatives Internat., Washington, 1987-97; ret. Pres. Spanish-Portugese Study Group, 1994—95. Mem.: Alliance Française, D.C. League Rep. Women, Pan Am. Round Table, John Carroll Soc., Georgetown U. Alumni Assn., Equestrian Order Holy Sepulchre of Jerusalem (Lady Comdr. 2003—), Army Navy Club (Washington). Republican. Roman Catholic. Home: 4000 Cathedral Ave NW Apt 208B Washington DC 20016-5254 Personal E-mail: jprvilla@verizon.net.

VILLARRUBIA, GLENDA BOONE, reading specialist, reading coordinator, educational consultant, educator; d. Albert Jewel and Tommie Lee Boone; m. David Daniel Villarrubia, Apr. 2, 1977; children: David Daniel Jr., Steven Joseph, John Albert. BA, Southeastern La. U., 1976, MBA, 1978. La. Teaching Certificate 1976, Reading Specialist Certification 1978, Behavior Specialist Certification 2000. Tchr. Wash. Parish Schools, Franklinton, La., 1976—79; tchr./coord. Jefferson Parish Schools, New Orleans, 1979; tchr. Ouachita Parish, Monroe, La., 1980; tchr. edn. Bogalusa City Schools, La., 1981—82, tchr., 1982—96, individualized edn. program cons., 1999—2005, individualized edn. program facilitator, resource teachers spl. edn., 1998—2000, dir./supr. spl. edn., 2000—01, individualized edn. program facilitator, 2001—04, compliance monitoring facilitator, 2005—. Spl. edn. cons., 2000; owner The Tchrs. Desk, 1989—99. Mem. Crisis Prevention Inst.; troop supporter Bogalusa, La, 2002—05; tiger cub leader Boy Scouts Am., Bogalusa, 1985; 4-H leader sponsor Bogalusa City Schools, 1985; beta club leader Wash. Parish Schools, 1977. Recipient Tchr. of Yr., Bogalusa City Schools, 1983, 1993, La. Dept. Edn., 1992. Mem.: Associated Profl. Educators of La., La. Pub. Sch. Rels. Assn., La. Ednl. Rsch. Assn., La. Assn. Supervision and Curriculum Devel., La. Assn. Educators, Learning Disability Assn., La. Assn. Sch. Execs., Nat. Edn. Assn., Coun. Exceptional Children,

Southeastern La. Alumni Assn., Alpha Signa Tau. Avocations: travel, gardening, church, reading. Home: 21486 Hwy 436 Bogalusa LA 70427 Office Phone: 985-281-2148. Personal E-mail: glenda90@hotmail.com.

VILLASENOR, BARBARA, book publisher; b. L.A., Sept. 17, 1946; d. Charles Belmont and Zita (Lewis) Bloch; m. Victor Edmundo Villasenor, Dec. 29, 1974 (div. Dec. 1999); children: David Cuauhtemoc, Joseph Edmundo. BA in Sociology, U. Calif., Berkeley, 1967; postgrad., Radcliffe Coll., 1967. Media buyer Diener Hauser Greenthal, L.A., 1971-76; editor Charles Pub., Oceanside, Calif., 1976-87, pub., 1987—. Ptnr. Strategies, San Diego, 1998—99; breath worker Heart to Heart, San Diego, 1988—94; event coord. Snow Goose Global Thanksgiving, Oceanside, 1992—; mem. Interfaith Alliance, San Diego, 1996—; CEO First Reads, 2000—; bd. dirs. A Future Without War, 2003—. Recipient award, Small Press Mag., 1996. Mem.: San Diego Publishers and Writers. Democrat. Avocations: creative expression, peace in the Mid. East. Office: Charles Publishing 1308 Stewart St Oceanside CA 92054-5448

VILLEMAIRE, DIANE DAVIS, science educator; b. Burlington, Vt., Nov. 21, 1946; d. Ellsworth Quinlan and Elizabeth Charlotte (Galvin) Davis; m. Bernard Philip Villemaire, Aug. 16, 1969; 1 child, Emily Jane. BS, U. Vt., 1968, MA, 1994; PhD, McGill U., Montreal, Que., Can., 1999. Cert. secondary sch. tchr., Vt., nat. bd. profl. tchr. aya sci. Rsch. asst. U. Vt., Burlington, 1965-68; tchr. biology Burlington H.S., 1968-71, Harwood Union H.S., Moretown, Vt., 1971—. Adj. faculty U. Vt., 1998—; equity specialist Harwood Union HS, Duxbury, Vt., 2002—. Author: E.A. Burtt, Historian and Philosopher, A Biography of the author of the Metaphysical Foundations of Modern Physical Science, 2002. Mem. NEA, AAUW (discussion leader), Am. Assn. Biology Tchrs. (Outstanding Biology Tchr. award 1978), Soc. for Advancement of Am. Philosophy, Phi Alpha Theta. Democrat. Avocations: antique flowers, art, travel, science and scientific advancements. Office: Harwood Union HS Vt Rt 100 South Duxbury VT 05660-9404 Office Phone: 802-882-1174. Personal E-mail: vilmaire@madriver.com. Business E-Mail: villemad@harwood.org.

VILLICA—A, TAUNYA, corporate financial executive; b. 1972; Co-founder, mng. ptnr. Affinity Fin. Grp. Mem. Ariz. Town Hall; former pres. Kiwanis de Amigos; Cmty. Needs and Preparedness com. chair Am. Red Cross; bd. treasurer Tucson Hispanic Chamber of Commerce; mem. Agua Prieta Shelters. Named one of 40 Under 40, Tucson Bus. Edge, 2006. Office: Affinity Financial Group 5363 E Pima St Tucson AZ 85712 Office Phone: 520-795-3360.*

VILLINES, BENITA CURTIS, language educator; b. Lewisburg, Tenn., June 8, 1953; d. George Edward and Edith Holbert Curtis; m. Harry Eugene Villines, May 24, 1975. BS, Mid. Tenn. State U., Murfreesboro, 1975, Med, 1981, Edn. Specialist, 1989. 5th and 6th grade tchr. Jones Sch., Lewisburg, Tenn., 1976—83; 6th-8th grade lang. arts tchr. Connelly Mid. Sch., Lewisburg, Tenn., 1983—97; 8th grade lang. arts tchr. Lewisburg Mid. Sch., 1997—. Lang. arts textbook com. Tenn. Dept. Edn., Nashville, 1997, Nashville, 2004; tech. coord. Lewisburg Mid. Sch., 1995—. Mem. vis. com. So. Assn. Schs. and Colls., Tenn., 1990. Named 21st Century Classroom Tchr., Marshall County Sch. Dist., 1998, Mid. Sch. Tchr. of Yr., 2002; Tech. grant, Tenn. Dept. Edn., 1997, Writing grant, Fed. Govt., 1998, Tech. grant, 2000. Mem.: Nat. Coun. Tchrs. English, Profl. Educators Tenn. Home: 3453 Clegg Dr Spring Hill TN 37174 Office: Lewisburg Middle Sch 500 Tiger Blvd Lewisburg TN 37091 Office Phone: 931-359-1265.

VILLOCH, KELLY CARNEY, art director; b. Kyoto, July 22, 1950; d. William Riley and stepdaughter Hazel Fowler Carney; m. Joe D. Villoch, Aug. 9, 1969; children: Jonathan, Christopher, Jennifer. A in Fine Arts, Dade C.C., Miami, Fla., 1971; student, Metro Fine Arts, 1973-74, Fla. Internat. U., 1985-88. Design asst. Lanvin, Miami, 1971—74, Fieldcrest, Miami, 1974-77; art dir. Advercolor, Miami, 1977-78; art dir. copywriter ABC, Miami, 1978-89; writer Armed Forces Radio & TV Network; multimedia dir. ADVITEC, 1989-91; art dir. writer Miami Write, 1979—89; owner Beach Point Prodns., 1992—; editor-in-chief L'Avenue Mag., 1998—. Lectr. Miami Dade C.C., cons. Studio Masters, North Miami, 1979-89; writer Lucent Techs., Telephonetics, Algorhythm, Inter-tel, 1997—; creative mktg. dir. Raintree Media, 2000. Prin. works include mixed media, 1974 (Best of Show 1974), pen and ink drawing, 1988 (Best Poster 1988); writer, dir., editor, prodr. (video film) Bif, 1988, Drink + Drive = Die, 1994; scriptwriter (film) The Raft, 1994, (charity video) Rosie O'Donnell, 2002; writer, dir., prodr. (pub. svc. announcement) Reading is the Real Adventure, 1990; film editor Talent Times Mag.; author: Winds of Freedom, 1994; art dir., exec. com. Miami Hispanic Media Conf., 1992, 93, 94; editor-in-chief, film editor: In Grove Miami Mag., 1994-96; webmaster, web content provider, website design cons., writer, graphic artist Guru Comms., 1996; editor-in-chief L'Avenue Mag., Miami Mag., Fla. Journey and Miami Guide, 1998-99, Paladar mag., 2002, Decasa mag., 2002, Flash Animation: Passionate Nomad-A Journey Through Cairo, 2002, Collins Ave. Mag., Markee Mag., 2006; web content provider WEBCOM; webmaster Miami Metro Mag., 2000; sr. editor Channels Intl. Mag., 2001; web site designer, multimedia dir.; creative mktg. dir. Light Sculptor Jim Morrison, 2005. State of Fla. grantee LimeLite Studios, Inc., 1990, William Douglas Pawley Found. grantee, Frances Wolfson scholar, Cultural Consortium grantee, 1993. Mem. Am. Film Inst., Phi Beta Kappa. Avocations: animation, printmaking, skin diving, boating, painting. Personal E-mail: villochk@bellsouth.net.

VINCENSI, AVIS A., sales executive, medical educator; b. Hazardville, Conn., July 10, 1949; d. George P. Vincensi and Hilda G. (Boucher) Vincensi(dec.). AS in Bus., Holyoke (Mass.) CC, 1987. Registered diagnostic med. sonographer, radiologic tech., radiography, mammography. X-ray technologist Baystate Med. Ctr., Springfield, Mass., 1969—73, Cooley Dickinson Hosp., Northampton, Mass., 1971—73, Holyoke Hosp., 1974—87, sonographer, 1973—82; sonographer, supr. Providence Hosp., Holyoke, 1982—87; sonographer Diagnostic Imaging, Springfield, Mass., 1987—90; product specialist/product mktg. sales Corometrics Med. Sys., Wallingford, Conn., 1991—96; diagnostic reagent rep. Sigma Diagnostics, St. Louis, 1996—2002; clin. adj. prof. Springfield Tech. CC, 1999—2002, assoc. prof., 2002—06, bd. dirs., 1999—2006, chair dept. sonography, 2002—06; staff sonographer Hartford (Conn.) Hosp., 2006—. Recipient 2 Gold medals and 1 Silver medal Tai Chi competition, 2002. Mem.: Am. Inst. Ultrasonic Medicine, Am. Registry Diagnostic Med. Sonographers. Home: 101 Acushnet Ave Springfield MA 01105-2218 E-mail: avincensi@harthosp.org.

VINCENT, CHRISTINE, academic administrator; m. David Chambers; 2 children. BA in visual arts, Ill. State U. Founder Cmty. & Cultural Resource Devel. Inc., N.Y.C.; dep. dir. Ford Found., N.Y.C., 1991—2001; pres. Maine Coll. Art, Portland, 2001—. Office: Office of President Maine College of Art 97 Spring St Portland ME 04101

VINCENT, SUZANNE SAWYER, physiologist, educator; d. Clarence Réal Sawyer and Mabel Viena Lawrence; m. Floyd Vincent, Dec. 7, 1996; 1 child, Patrick Palmer. PhD, U. Wash., 1982; postgrad., Boston U., 2000. Cert. sr. fitness instr. Am. Sr. Fitness Assn. Postdoctoral fellow VA Med. Ctr., Mpls., 1982—84; asst. prof. St. Lawrence U., Canton, NY, 1984—85, U. Iowa, Iowa City, 1985—86, U. Ill., Urbana, 1986—89; assoc. prof. Tex. Tech U. Sch. Allied Health, Lubbock, 1990—94, St. George's (Grenada) U. Sch. Medicine, 1994—98, Oral Roberts U., Tulsa, Okla., 2001—. Author: (journal articles and book chapters) Parkinson's disease, Neuromuscular control, brain and neurology, exercise for older adults; contbr. articles to profl. jours., chapters to books. State sci. fair judge Okla. Jr. Acad. of Sci., other sci. clubs, Ada, Okla., 2002—06. Intramural grantee, U. Ill., Urbana-Champaign, 1985. Mem.: Creation Rsch. Soc., Internat. Soc. Aging and Phys. Activity, Am. Physiol. Soc. Achievements include research in exercises to counteract movement disorders and aging. Avocation: camping. Office: Oral Roberts U Dept Biology 7777 S Lewis Ave Tulsa OK 74171 Office Phone: 918-495-6950. E-mail: svincent@oru.edu.

VINENT-CANTORAL, AIDA R., mediator; b. Havana, Cuba, Nov. 8, 1948; arrived in U.S., 1959; d. Roberto M. Vinent and Carmen; m. Ennio Cantoral, Dec. 26, 1979 (div. 1981); 1 child, Alfredo Cantoral. BA, Alverno Coll., 1969; MA, Marquette U., 1971, cert. dispute resolution, 1998; cert. negotiating labor agreements, Harvard U., 2000, U. Mich., 2002, Northwestern U.; cert. mediation sys. design, U. Tex.; postgrad., U. So. Tex. Coll. Law, 2004, Fed. Mediation and Conciliation Inst., 2004. Family health asst. Milwaukee County Dept. Human Svcs. & Hosp., 1975—; human svcs. case coord. Milwaukee County Dept. Human Svcs. and Hosp., 1998—; mediator pvt. practice Milw., 1979—; mediator Milwaukee County Family Ct., 1998—, USPS, 1998—, Bus. to Bus., 1998—, CHIPS, 1997, Wis. Spl. Edn. Mediation Sys., 2001—; case mgr. Milw. Co. Disability Svs., 1996—. Cons. in field. Active ACR, 1998—, Wis. Assn. Homicide Investigators, 2000—; parent educator Centro Legal, Milw., 1998—. Named Human Svcs. Worker of Yr., Wis. Foster Parents, 1980. Mem.: Wis. Coun. Problem Gambling, Wis. Assn. Mediators. Republican. Address: PO Box 462 Greendale WI 53129-0462 Office Phone: 414-550-8772. E-mail: avinent@aol.com.

VINOGRADOVA, NATALYA, mathematician, educator; b. Russia, Aug. 10, 1969; MS in Math., St. Petersburg State U., Russia, 1991; PhD in Math. Edn., SUNY, Buffalo, 2005. Cert. tchr. N.Y. Instr. math. Pedagogical U., Russia, 1991—99, Phillips Exeter Acad., NH, 2000—01; prof. dept. math. Plymouth State U., NH, 2005—. Spkr. in field. Author: (book) The First Steps in the Theory of Probability, 1996. Mem.: Math. Assn. of Am., Nat. Coun. Tchrs. of Math. Home: PO Box 433 Plymouth NH 03264 Office Phone: 603-535-3235. Personal E-mail: nvinogradova@hotmail.com.

VINSON, AUDREY LAWSON, retired literature and language professor; b. Temple, Tex., July 4, 1928; d. John McGregor and Jemima Belle (Hamilton) Lawson; m. James Vinson, Dec. 23, 1948 (dec.); 1 child, Paul Everett. BA, St. Augustine Coll., Raleigh, NC, 1948; MA, Fisk U., Nashville, 1962; CAS, Wesleyan U., Middletown, Conn., 1970. Tchr. Nashville City Schs., 1958—62; prof. Ala. A&M U., Huntsville, 1962—93, prof. emeritus, 1993—. Dept. chair Ala. A&M U., 1980—84. Co-author: The World of Toni Morrison, 1985. Bd. chair Huntsville Sickle Cell Ctr., 1968—72. Fellow, Rockefeller Found., 1968. Mem.: Modern Lang. Assn. Episcopalian. Avocations: poetry, writing. Home: 19950 Hueber Rd #1501 San Antonio TX 78258

VINSON, DEBORAH, secondary school educator, speaker; b. Bklyn., June 16, 1950; d. William and Odell Vinson; m. William Vinson, Sept. 1, 1946; children: William (dec.), Molly Lou (dec.), George (dec.), LaVern (dec.), Esther, Diane. BA, York Coll., Queens, N.Y., 1974; MA in Early Childhood Edn., Bklyn. Coll., 1978. Cert. tchr., N.Y.; lic. in real estate, N.Y.; fashion designer. Tutor math and English, evening classes Bd. Edn., Bklyn., 1968-90; tchr., cons. Salvation Army, Bklyn., 1982-83; tchr. Children's Day Care, Bklyn., 1974-76, Maxwell H.S., Bklyn., 1977-82, tutor evening GED program, 1983-85; tchr. GED Programs, Bklyn., 1985-90, Pitt C.C., Greenville, N.C., 1992-93; personal care attendant for the handicap, 2002—05; prin., owner Deborah Vinson Sch. Higher Learning, St. Thomas, 2005—. Tchr. disabled women, Bethany, Israel, 1993-95; vol. with heart disabled patients, Raleigh, N.C., 1995—. Author poetry. Avocations: travel, song writing, swimming, tennis, reading. E-mail: zzyaklb99@yahoo.com.

VINSON, LEILA TERRY WALKER, retired gerontological social worker; b. Lynchburg, Va., July 28, 1928; d. William Terry and Ada Allen (Moore) Walker; m. Hughes Nelson Vinson, Aug. 11, 1951; children: Hughes Nelson, William Terry. Student, Agnes Scott Coll., 1946-48; BA, U. Ala., Tuscaloosa, 1950; postgrad., U. Ala., Birmingham, 1980-81, U. Va., 1950-51. Cert. gerontol. social worker, Ala. Tchr. English and Latin Marion County Bd. Edn., Hamilton, Ala., 1952-59; social worker I Marion County Dept. Pensions and Security, 1963-72, gerontol. social worker II, 1972-85; ret., 1985. Bd. dirs. Marion County Dept. Human Resources, 1985—; bd. mem. Clye Nix Libr., Bevill Coll. Cmty. Theatre, 1992—; spkr. gen. subjects. Recipient Ala. Woman Committed to Excellence award Tuscaloosa coun. Girl Scouts U.S., 1987; named Mrs. Marion County, PTA, Gwin, Ala., 1969, Woman of Yr. Town of Hamilton, 1980, New Retiree of Yr. Ala. Ret. State Employees Assn., 1988, Woman of Yr. BPW, 1985; Gessener Harrison fellow U. Va., 1950-51. Mem. AAUW, DAR (flag chmn. Bedford chpt. 1988-90), UDC, Bus. and Profl. Women's Club (dist. dir. 1984-86, Outstanding Dir. award 1986), Ala. Fedn. Women's Club. Home: PO Box 1112 Hamilton AL 35570-1112 also: Military Rd Hamilton AL 35570

VIOLA, MARY JO, art history educator; b. Yonkers, N.Y., July 25, 1941; d. William F. and May (Cleary) O'Connor; m. Jerome Joseph Viola, June 21, 1967 (dec. Feb. 1990). BA in Fine Arts, Coll. of Mt. St. Vincent, Riverdale, N.Y., 1963; MA in Art History, NYU, 1966; MPhil in Art History, CUNY, 1983, PhD in Art History, 1992. Art history tchr. Georgian Ct. Coll., NJ, 1965-66, Hollins Coll., Roanoke, Va., 1966-67, Marymount Coll., Tarrytown, NY, 1967-71, Baruch Coll., CUNY, N.Y.C., 1974-97, Bklyn. Coll., 1990-97, Parsons Sch. of Design, N.Y.C., 1991-93, Rutgers U., 1993-95, Bronx C.C. CUNY, 1997—. Curator exhbns. Baruch Coll. Gallery, N.Y.C., 1987-88. Editor: A World View of Art History, 1985; art exhibited at Tribes Gallery, N.Y.C., 1996; creater ednl. videos. Rschr. for ethnic festivals, N.Y.C., 1993—. Fellow Nat. Trust for Hist. Preservation, 1964, Marymount Coll., 1970, Boston Mus. Fine Arts/CUNY, 1978, Luce Found., 1988. Mem. Coll. Art Assn., Historians of Am. Art, City Lore. Avocations: tai chi, dance. Home and Office: 37 Roosevelt St Yonkers NY 10701-5823

VIORST, JUDITH STAHL, writer; b. Newark, Feb. 2, 1931; d. Martin Leonard and Ruth June (Ehrenkranz) Stahl; m. Milton Viorst, Jan. 30, 1960; children: Anthony Jacob, Nicholas Nathan, Alexander Noah. BA, Rutgers U., 1952; grad., Washington Psychoanalytic Inst., 1981. Author: (children's books) Sunday Morning, 1968, I'll Fix Anthony, 1969, Try It Again Sam, 1970, The Tenth Good Thing About Barney, 1971 (Silver Pencil award 1973), Alexander and the Terrible, Horrible, No Good, Very Bad Day, 1972, My Mama Says There Aren't Any Zombies, Ghosts, Vampires, Creatures, Demons, Monsters, Fiends, Goblins or Things, 1973, Rosie and Michael, 1974, Alexander, Who Used to Be Rich Last Sunday, 1978, The Good-Bye Book, 1988, Earrings!, 1990, The Alphabet from Z to A (with Much Confusion on the Way), 1994, Alexander, Who's Not (Do You Hear Me? I Mean It!) Going to Move, 1995, Super-Completely and Totally the Messiest, 2001, Just in Case, 2006; (poetry) The Village Square, 1965-66, It's Hard to Be Hip Over Thirty and Other Tragedies of Married Life, 1968, People and Other Aggravations, 1971, How Did I Get to Be Forty and Other Atrocities, 1976, If I Were in Charge of the World and Other Worries, 1981, When Did I Stop Being Twenty and Other Injustices, 1987, Forever Fifty and Other Negotiations, 1989, Sad Underwear and Other Complications, 1995, Suddenly Sixty and Other Shocks of Later Life, 2000, I'm Too Young to be Seventy and Other Delusions, 2005; (with Milton Viorst) The Washington Underground Gourmet, 1970, Yes Married, 1972, A Visit From St. Nicholas (To a Liberated Household), 1977, Love and Guilt and the Meaning of Life, Etc., 1979, Necessary Losses, 1986, Murdering Mr. Monti, 1994, Imperfect Control, 1998, You're Officially a Grown-Up, 1999, Grown-up Marriage, 2003; (musical) Love and Shrimp (book and lyrics), 1990; (HBO children's movie) Alexander and the Terrible, Horrible, No Good, Very Bad Day (book and lyrics), 1990, (children's stage musical) Alexander and the Terrible, Horrible, No Good, Very Bad Day, 1998, Alexander, Who's Not Not Not Not Not Not Gong to Move (book and lyrics), 2003. Recipient Emmy award for poems used in Anne Bancroft Spl., 1970. Jewish.

VIRDEN, KAREN FRANCES, elementary school educator; b. Akron, Ohio, May 7, 1941; d. Wilburn and Alice D. Crites; m. William Wayne Virden, June 11, 1965; children: Scott William, Dean Michael. BS in Edn., Ohio State U., Columbus, 1963, MA in Elem. Edn., 1968. Tchr. 2-3rd grade Huy Elem., Columbus, 1963—70; tchr. 3rd grade Lexington Ave., Columbus, 1971—72, Violet Elem., Pickerington, Ohio, 1974—2001, Heritage Elem., Pickerington, 2001—. Presenter in field. Named Dist. Tchr. of Yr., Pickerington Local Schs., 1993; Jennings scholar, Martha Holden Jennings Found., 1983, 2000. Mem.: NEA, Pickerington Edn. Assn. (chair calendar com.), Ohio Edn. Assn. Avocation: sports. Home: 13804 Carlstead Dr Pickerington OH 43147 Office: Heritage Elem Sch 100 N East St Pickerington OH 43147

VIRK, SUBHDEEP, psychiatrist; b. Jalandhar, Punjab, India, Nov. 03; d. Devinder Singh and Manjeet Virk; m. Arvinder S. Bhinder, Nov. 30, 2000; 1 child, Panya Gurbax Bhinder. MBBS, Amritsar Med. Coll., India, 1993; MD, SUNY, Syracuse, 2005. Intern Gen. Hospita, Chandigarh, India; med. officer Lamba Nursing Hosp., Chandigarh, 1995—95; ho. officer Gen. Hosp., Chandigarh, 1995; jr. resident psychiatry Govt. Med. Coll., Chandigarh, 1996; clin. observer oncology Alameda County Med. Ctr., Oakland, Calif., 1998—99; clin. extern VA Med. Ctr., Syracuse, NY, 1999—2000; clin. rsch. assoc. SUNY, Upstate Med. U., Syracuse, 2000—01, resident psychiatry and behavioral sci., 2001—. Vol. Helpage India, Chandigarh, 1994, Govt. Rural Health Ctr., Dadumajra, Punjab, India, 1994, Highland Gen. Hosp., Oakland, 1998; student advisor Kaplan Ednl. Ctr., Berkeley, Calif., 1998—99, med. advisor, med. coll. admissions test instr., Syracuse, 1999—2000, med. advisor, Hackensack, NJ. Contbr. articles to profl. jours. Scholar, Am. Psychosomatic Soc., 2005; All India Army scholar, ESSA, India. Mem.: AMA, Am. Psychosomatic Soc., Assn. Psychiat. Medicine, Am. Assn. Physicians, Am. Psychiatry Assn., Med. Coun. India (licentiate). Achievements include research in psychiatry and behavioral health. Office: Erie County Med Ctr 462 Grider St Buffalo NY 14215 Home: Apt A 90 Arielle Ct Williamsville NY 14221 Home Fax: 315-464-3178. Personal E-mail: virks@upstate.edu, panyabhinder@gmail.com. Business E-Mail: svirk@buffalo.edu.

VIROSTKO, JOAN, elementary school educator; b. Jackson Heights, N.Y., Feb. 6; d. John and Dorothy Veronica (Eckert) Virostko. Cert. of Studies, Oxford U., 1972, 73; B.S., St. John's U., 1968, M.S., 1970, P.D., 1972, 85, M.B.A., 1980, Ph.D., 1983, SAS, SDA, 1985. Cert. elem. tchr., N.Y.; cert. sch. bldg. adminstr., sch. dist. adminstr., N.Y. Educator Half Hollow Hills Paumanok Sch., Dix Hills, N.Y.; instr. Oxford U., England, summer 1985, 86; instr., 1987—. Contbr. Ellis Island Found, 1984-86; lector Sacred Heart Cath. Ch., Glendale, N.Y., 1986-87; sustaining mem. Rep. Nat. Com., 1980—, sponsor 1980—. Recipient Disting. Dissertation award, 1983; named Educator of Yr., N.Y. State Assn. Tchrs., 1985, 92, 95, 99, 2001. Mem. N.Y. State United Tchrs. Assn., Kappa Delta Pi, Phi Delta Kappa, Alpha Sigma Alpha, Delta Sigma Chi. Republican. Avocations: traveling, music, water and snow skiing, water sports. Office: Half Hollow Hills Paumanok Sch 1 Seamans Neck Rd Dix Hills NY 11746-7114 Home: PO Box 107 Maspeth NY 11378-0107

VISCELLI, THERESE RAUTH, materials management consultant; b. Bitburg, Germany, Nov. 18, 1955; d. David William and Joyce (Kelly) Rauth; m. Eugene R. Viscelli, Feb. 4, 1978; children: Christopher, Kathryn, Matthew. BS, Ga. Inst. Tech., 1977; postgrad., So. Tech. Inst., 1977—78; MBA, Ga. State U., 1997. Mktg. engr. Hughes Aircraft Corp., Carlsbad, Calif., 1978—79; indsl. engr. Kearfott-Singer, San Marcos, Calif., 1979—80; product analyst Control Data Corp., Atlanta, 1981—84; dir. R&D Am. Software, Inc., Atlanta, 1984—92; acct. mgr. The Coca-Cola Co., 1992—93; dir. info. sys. Mizuno, USA, Norcross, Ga., 1993—98; mgr. tech. implementation and support E3 Corp., 1998—99; adj. prof. DeVry Inst. Am., 1999—2000; instr. Ga. State U., 2000—05; pres., CEO V-Shell, Inc., 2000—. Support faculty Kennesaw State U., 2006—. Mem. Am. Prodn. and Inventory Control Soc. (program chmn. 1982-83, v.p. 1983-84). Republican. Roman Catholic.

VISCUGLIA, JENNY LOU, music educator; b. Englewood, Colo., Sept. 12, 1967; d. Dwight B and Lynda Lee Eames; m. Felix Alfred Viscuglia, Apr. 5, 1997; m. Andrew Norvelle, Nov. 19, 1989 (div. Sept. 27, 1996). BS in Music Edn., U. Nev., Las Vegas, 2003. Cert. nursing asst., Colo., 1986; music tchr. K-12 Nev., 2003. Cert. nursing asst. Cherry Creek Nursing Ctr., Aurora, Colo., 1986—87; class a alarm operator Regent Security, Englewood, Colo., 1987—88; waitress, asst. mgr. McCoy's Family Restaurant, Littleton, Colo., 1988—89; clerical Kelly Services, Las Vegas, Nev., 1989—90; adminstrv. asst. Nathan Adelson Hospice Found., Las Vegas, Nev., 1990—95; sec. Rio Suites Hotel and Casino, Wine Cellar, Las Vegas, Nev., 1996—97; libr. Nev. Symphony, Las Vegas, Nev., 1994—98; pers. mgr., libr., clarinet sub The Las Vegas Philharm., Las Vegas, Nev., 1998—2004; k-8 music tchr. Clark County Sch. Dist., Las Vegas, Nev., 2003—. Mem. Goodsprings Citizens Adv. Coun., Goodsprings, Nev., 1998—2004; treas., mem. Goodsprings Hist. Soc., Goodsprings, 2001—04. Mem.: NEA, Music Educators Nat. Conf., Am. Orff-Schulwerk Assn., Nat. Assn. Music Educators. Avocations: travel, music, sewing. Home: Post Office Box 664 Goodsprings NV 89019 Office: Sandy Valley Elem Mid Sch Sandy Valley NV 89019 Office Phone: 702-799-0935. Personal E-mail: viscuglia@aol.com.

VISOCKI, NANCY GAYLE, information services consultant; b. Dumont, N.J., May 13, 1952; d. Thomas and Gloria Visocki. BA in Math., Manhattanville Coll., 1974; MS in Ops. Rsch. and Stats., Rensselaer Poly. Inst., 1977. Rsch. asst. Coll. Physicians and Surgeons Columbia U., N.Y.C., 1974-75; programmer analyst R. Shriver Assocs., Parsippany, NJ, 1977-79; sr. tech. rep. GE Info. Svcs. Co., East Orange, NJ, 1979-81, mgr. project office Morristown, NJ, 1981-83, tech. dir., 1983-87, tech. mgr., 1988-89, area mgr. sys. devel. and consulting Parsippany, 1989-92, area tech. mgr. sys. devel. and cons., Fin. Info. Sys., 1992-93, sr. cons. info. svcs., 1993-98, project mgr. e-commerce sys. integration, 1998-2000; mgr. Major e-commerce Applications Practice, 2000—03. Active Western Hills Christian Ch., Tranquility, N.J., 1986—; vol. Women's Ctr., Hackettstown, N.J., 1989-93; class fund-raising and gift chmn. Rensselaer Poly. Inst., Troy, N.Y., 1991-95; vol. Elfun Soc., 1981—; vol. bd. dirs., treas. NJCFS Assn., 2004— Manhattanville Coll. grantee, Purchase, N.Y., 1970-71; tuition fellow Rensselaer Poly. Inst., 1975-77. Mem. NAFE, Elfun, Women of Accomplishment. Avocations: tai chi, hiking, bicycling, reading, yoga.

VISSAT, MAUREEN, art educator; b. Pitts., Feb. 12, 1958; d. James William and Margaret McDonnell; m. David John Vissat, Sept. 26, 1987; children: Livia, Evan. BA in History, Georgetown U., 1979; MA in Art History, U. Pitts., 1983. Asst. prof. art history Seton Hill U., 1982—; art history instr. Lucca, Italy, 1984—86. Contbr. Newborns in Need, Pitts., 2005—06. Mem.: Am. Assn. U. Prof., Dante Soc. Cath. Avocations: travel, reading, yoga. Home: 1122 Lincoln Way Mc Keesport PA 15131 Office: Seton Hill Univ Art Dept Greensburg PA 15601

VISSER, LESLEY, sports correspondent; b. Quincy, Mass., Sept. 11, 1953; m. Dick Stockton. BA cum laude in English, Boston Coll., 1975; PhD (hon.), Coll. Our Lady of Elms, Mass., 1995. Sports staff Boston Globe, 1974-88; feature reporter, sports staff CBS Sports, 1988—94, 2000—; corr. GameDay (now NFL Countdown), SportsCenter ESPN, Bristol, Conn., 1994-98; sideline reporter ABC, N.Y.C., 1994-00, reporter Monday Night Football, 1998-00. Sideline reporter coll. football, NFL and Super Bowl ABC, 1994—; reporter Monday Night Football, 1998—. Trustee Women's Sports Found., 1993—. Named outstanding woman sportswriter in Am., 1983, New England Newswoman of Yr., WISE Woman of the Yr., 2002; named to the New England Sports Hall of Fame; recipient Journalism award Women's Sports Found., 1992, Pioneer award AWSM, 1999, Compass award, 2003, Pete Rozelle Radio Television award, Pro Football Hall of Fame 2006, Pop Warner Female Achievement award, 2006, Gracie Allen award Am. Women in Radio & Television, 2006 Office: CBS Sports 524 W 57th St New York NY 10019-2924*

VITALE, PATTY A., pediatrician, consultant, medical educator; MD, Jefferson Med. Coll., 1998; MPH in Epidemiology, U. Calif., San Diego. Diplomate American Board of Pediatrics. Intern pediat. U. Calif., San Diego, 1998—99, resident pediat., 1999—2001, fellow cmty. pediat.; fellow pub. health San Diego State U., 2001—03; asst. prof. pediat. U. Medicine and

Dentistry, NJ; full-time cons. child abuse. Mem.: AMA (Excellence in Medicine Leadership award 2004), Am. Acad. Pediat. Office: U Docs Pavilion #1100 42 E Laurel Rd Stratford NJ 08084*

VITANZA, JOANNE MARIA, allergist, pediatrician; b. Balt., May 8, 1959; MD, Tulane U., 1985. Cert. in allergy and immunology; cert. in pediats. Intern St. Christophers Children Hosp., Phila., 1985-86, resident in pediats., 1986-88, fellow in allergy and immunology, 1988-90; staff Presbyn. Hosp., Colo., St. Lukes Hosp., Colo.; with Childrens Hosp., Littleton (Colo.) Hosp., Porter Hosp. Mem. AMA, Am. Acad. Allergy and Immunology, Assn. Am. Physicians, Am. Coll. Allergy and Immunology. Office: 1450 S Havana St Ste 500 Aurora CO 80012-4030

VITEK, CAROLYN ROHRER, geneticist, educator; d. Curtis R. and Jane Simmons Rohrer; m. John M. Vitek; children: Sairey M., Keiran E., Jonathan R. MS, U. Minn., Mpls., 1993. Sr. lectr. St. Mary's U. Minn., Winona, 1987—2005; edn. specialist Mayo Clinic, Rochester, Minn., 2005—. Critical thinking coord. St. Mary's U. Minn., Winona, 2003—05. Pres. Early Childhood and Family Edn., Winona, Minn., 1989—94. Office: Mayo Clinic 200 First St SW Rochester MN 55905

VITETTA, ELLEN S., microbiologist, educator, immunologist; BA, Conn. Coll.; MS, NYU, 1966, PhD, MD, 1968. Prof. microbiology Southwestern Med. Sch., U. Tex., Dallas, 1976—; dir. Cancer Immunobiology Ctr., U. Tex., Dallas, 1988—; Sheryle Simmons Patigian Disting. chair in cancer immunobiology Southwestern Med. Sch., U. Tex., Dallas, 1989—. Bd. sci. coun. NCI Cancer Treatment Bd., 1993; sci. adv. bd. Howard Hughes Med. Inst., 1992—; Kettering selection com. GM Cancer Rsch. Foun., 1987-88; task force NIAID in Immunology, 1989-90; mem. sci. bd. Ludwig Inst., 1983—. Mem. editl. bd.: Advances in Host Defense Mechanisms, 1983—, Annual Review of Immunology, 1991—, Bioconjugate Chemistry, 1989-93, Cellular Immunology, 1984-93, Current Opinions in Immunology, 1992—, FASEB Journal, 1987—, Internat. Jour. of Oncology, 1992—, Internat. Soc. Immunopharmacology, 1989—, Jour. of Immunology, 1975-78, Molecular Immunology, 1978-93; assoc. editor Cancer Research, 1986—; Immunochemistry sect. editor: Jour. of Immunology, 1978-82; co-editor in chief: Therapeutic Immunology, 1992—. Recipient Women's Excellence in Sci. award Fedn. Am. Soc. Exptl. Biology, 1991, Taittinger Breast Cancer Rsch. award Komen Found., 1983, Pierce Immunotoxin award, 1988, NIH Merit award, 1987—, U. Tex. Southwestern Med. Sch. Faculty Teaching awards 1989, 91, 92, 93, 94, FASED Excellence in Sci. award, 1991, Abbot Clinical Immunology award Am. Soc. Microbiologists, 1992, Past State Pres. award Tex. Fed. Bus. Profl. Women's Club, 1993, Richard and Hinda Rosenthal Found. award Am. Assn. Cancer Rsch 1995, Charlotte Friend award Am. Assn. Cancer Rsch., 1995, AAAS Mentreny award, 2002. Mem. Am. Assn. Immunologists (pres. 1994), Nat. Acad. Scis., Am. Acad. Microbiology (hon.). Achievements include co-discovery of IL-4, development of immunotoxins and identification of IgD on murine B cells. Office: Univ Texas Cancer Immunobiol Ctr 6000 Harry Hines Blvd Dallas TX 75235-5303 Address: 6914 Pemberton Dr Dallas TX 75230-4260 E-mail: ellen.vitetta@utsoutheastern.edu.

VITO, MARILYN ELAINE, business educator; b. Louisville, Oct. 24, 1947; d. Gerald E. and Eleanor M. (Spencer) Bowles; m. Louis J. Vito, May 22, 1971; children: Louis Vito Jr., Linda, Sandra, Steven. BS in Bus., Stockton State Coll., 1980; MBA, Monmouth Coll., 1985; postgrad., Stonier Grad. Sch. Banking, 1989. CPA N.J., Pa., cert. mgmt. acct. Supr. Golden Nugget Casino/Hotel, Atlantic City, N.J., 1980-81; v.p., contr. Security Savs. & Loan, Vineland, N.J., 1981-85; sr. v.p., CFO Horizon/Marine Nat. Bank, Pleasantville, N.J., 1985-89; exec. v.p., CFO Meridian Mortgage Corp., Wayne, Pa., 1989-93; assoc. prof. bus. studies Richard Stockton Coll., Pomona, N.J., 1993—. Delegation leader Citizen Amb. Program Women Accts. to Ea. Europe, 1998. Mem. host com. Hillary Clinton/Tipper Gore reception Dem. Nat. Com.Women's Coalition, Phila., 1996. Grantee Disting. Faculty grant, Richard Stockton coll., 1996. NSF, 1999. Mem.: AICPA (campus liaison 1997—), N.J. Soc. CPA (bd. dirs. 1987—89), Am. Soc. Women Accts (Phila. chpt. pres. 1987—89, nat. pres. 1992—93, bd. dirs. South Jersey chpt. 1996—97, nat. nominating com. 1999). Office: Richard Stockton Coll PO Box 195 Pomona NJ 08240-0195 Office Phone: 609-652-4273. Personal E-mail: mevito2002@hotmail.com. Business E-Mail: mev@stockton.edu.

VITSON, ROBYN STANKO HOYE, singer, pianist, educator; b. Erie, Pa., June 1, 1963; d. Edward Richard and Lucille Ann (Smith) Stanko; m. Thomas Joseph Hoye, Oct. 1, 1988 (div. June 1993); m. James Michael Vitson, May 5, 2003. MusB in Piano Performance and Pedagogy, Wheaton (Ill.) Coll., 1985; MusM in Vocal Performance and Pedagogy, No. Ill. U., 1992. Clk.-typist, receptionist Tellabs, Naperville, Ill., 1985-86; clk.-typist United Parcel Svc., Addison, Ill., 1987-89; adminstrv. asst. Ednl. Assistance, Ltd., Wheaton, 1994-95; music and sound cons. Sound of Music, Mundelein, Ill., 1996-97; pvt. tchr. piano, Chgo., 1985-99; pvt. tchr. piano Nashville, 1999—2001. Pianist, singer Nat. Anthem at fundraisers Chgo. Rep. Com., 1997—. Avocations: reading, walking, attending church. Home: 4030 N Adams St Westmont IL 60559-1309 Office Phone: 630-768-5010.

VITTETOE, MARIE CLARE, retired clinical laboratory science educator; b. Keota, Iowa, May 19, 1927; d. Edward Daniel and Marcella Matilda Vittetoe. BS, Marycrest Coll., 1950; MS, W.Va. U., 1971, EdD, 1973. Staff technologist St. Joseph Hosp., Ottumwa, Iowa, 1950-70; instr. Ottumwa Hosp. Sch. Med. Tech., 1957-70, St. Joseph Hosp. Sch. Nursing, Ottumwa, 1950-70; asst. prof. U. Ill., Champaign-Urbana, 1973-78; prof. clin. lab. scis. U. Ky., Lexington, 1978-94. Mem. Sisters of Humility of Mary, 1946—; chair Congregation of Humility of Mary; clin. lab. asst., lab. cons. 6 clinics in Haiti, 2000—. Author: Vittetoe Family Tree and Scrapbook, 2000, Peiffer-Berg Family Tree and Scrapbook, 2000, Lutz/Peiffer Family Tree Update, 2002, Vittetoe Family Tree Update, 2002; contbr. articles to profl. jours. Vol. hosp. labs., Haiti, 1999—; apptd. to advisory bd. CRUDEM Found., 2005—. Named Ky. Col., Marie Vittetoe award for excellence in svc. named for her, U. Ky., 1999; recipient Kingston award for Creative Tchg., Recognition award for svc. to edn., Commonwealth of Ky. Coun. on Higher Edn., disting. grad. award, Nat. Cath. Ednl. Assn., 1995, devel. of youth award, Iowa 4-H Found., 1996, award for devel. Best Little Lab. in Haiti, 2002. Mem. Am. Soc. for Med. Tech. (chmn. 1986-89, Profl. Achievement award 1991, Ky. Mem. of Yr. award 1994), Am. Soc. Clin. Lab. Scis., Am. Soc. Clin. Pathologists (assoc.), Alpha Mu Tau, Phi Delta Kappa, Alpha Eta. Avocations: walking, genealogy.

VITTITOW, SUSAN, librarian, writer; b. Dayton, Ohio, Oct. 29, 1967; d. Orville L. and Willa M. Vittitow; life ptnr. Brian Mark. B in History, U. Dayton, Ohio, 1989; MLS, Clarion U., Pa., 2005. Edn. and bus. reporter Pk. Record, Park City, Utah, 1993—94; pub. Tongue River News, Ranchester, Wyo., 1994—95; asst. mng. editor Sheridan (Wyo) Press, 1995—98; pub. info. specialist Wyo. State Libr., Cheyenne, 1998—2001, pub. specialist, 2004—; found. dir. Laramie County Libr. Found., Cheyenne, 2002—04. Staff writer Wyo. Library Roundup. Recipient Pacemaker award for Column writing, Wyo. Press. Assn., 1996, High Plains Register Poetry prize, Laramie County C.C., 2003; Presdl. scholar, U. Dayton, 1985—89. Mem.: Mountain Plains Libr. Assn., Wyo. Libr. Assn., Western Writers Am., Wyo. Writers Inc. (webmaster 2004—06, pres. 2000—01, Emmie Mygatt award 2003, Western Horizon award 2005), Mensa. Democrat-Npl. Mem. Unitarian Ch. Avocations: skiing, music. Office Phone: 307-777-5915.

VITT-MAUCHER, GISELA MARIA, German educator; b. Berlin, Nov. 15, 1934; came to U.S., 1962; d. Maximilian H. and Valeria (Seitz) M.; m. Lawrence D. Vitt, 1966; 1 child, Mark Alan. Statsexam, J.W. Goethe U., Frankfurt/Main, Fed. Republic Germany, 1961; PhD in Comparative Lit., Washington U., St. Louis, 1964. Asst. prof. German Ohio State U., Columbus, 1964-70, assoc. prof., 1971-86, prof. German, chair dept., 1987-91, prof. German, 1987—, chair dept. comparative studies, 1978-80, prof. emeritus, 1992. Vis. prof. Middlebury Coll., 1966, 68. Author: E.T.A. Hoffmann's Fairy Tales, 1989; contbr. articles to profl. jours. Mem. MLA, Am. Assn. Tchrs. German, AAUP

VIVELO, JACQUELINE JEAN, writer, language educator; b. Lumberton, Miss., Jan. 23, 1943; d. Jack and Virginia Olivia (Bond) Jones; m. Frank Robert Vivelo, June 19, 1965; 1 child, Alexandra J. BA, U. Tenn., Knoxville, 1965, MA, 1970. Caseworker N.Y.C. Dept. Welfare, 1965-66; instr. reading Knoxville Coll., 1968-70; instr. English Middlesex County Coll., Edison, N.J., 1970-72, U. Mo., Rolla, 1975-77, Middlesex County Coll., Edison, 1978-80, Lebanon Valley Coll., Annville, Pa., 1981-87, asst. prof. English, 1987-91. Author: Super Sleuth, 1985 (Best Book award), Beagle in Trouble, 1986, A Trick of the Light, 1987, Super Sleuth and the Bare Bones, 1988, Writing Fiction: A Handbook for Creative Writing, 1993, Reading to Matthew, 1993 (Best Book award), Mr. Scatter's Magic Spell, 1993, Chills Run Down My Spine, 1994, Have You Lost Your Kangaroo?, 1995, Chills in the Night, 1997, Miss Topple Walks on Air, 1998; editor: College Education Achievement Project's Handbook for College Reading Teachers, 1969; co-editor: American Indian Prose and Poetry, 1974: contbr. articles/short stories to various publs. Recipient Best Book award Am. Child Study Assn., 1985, Young Book Trust, U.K., 1994, Pa. Coun. of the Arts Fellowship award for Lit., 1992; NIMH grantee, 1969-70. Mem. Children's Lit. Coun. Pa. (v.p. 1991), Soc. Children's Book Writers, Mystery Writers Am., Sigma Tau Delta (sponsor Omicron Omicron chpt. 1988-90), Pi Lambda Theta. Home: 5117 Brittany Dr Old Hickory TN 37138-1262

VIVIAN, SHIRLEY FULL, secondary educator; b. Mendota, Ill., Oct. 1, 1949; d. Lester J. and Eileen (McConville) Full; m. Richard T. Vivian, Dec. 26, 1970; children: Christopher, Jeremy. BS in Edn., Ill. State U., 1970; MS in Edn., No. Ill. U., 1974. Cert. tchr., Ill. Elem. and kindergarten tchr. Amboy (Ill.) Sch. Dist., 1970-78, libr., 1982-83; tchr. Chpt. I reading and kindergarten Dixon (Ill.) Pub. Schs., 1978-82, tchr. Chpt. 1 reading, gifted and lang. arts edn., 1983—. Workshop presenter, 1980—. Recipient Those Who Excel award Ill. Bd. Edn., 1988, Employee of Yr. award Dixon Pub. Schs., 1989, Tchr. of Yr. award Madison Jr. High Sch., 1989. Mem. Internat. Reading Assn., Ill. Assn. Tchrs. English, Ill. Edn. Assn., Ill. Reading Coun. (asst. editor jour. 1988-90), No. Ill. Reading Coun., Sauk Valley Reading Coun. (officer 1983-90). Avocations: reading, gardening, walking. Home: 1776 Clearview Rd Dixon IL 61021-8740

VIZENOR, ERMA J., Native American tribal leader; b. Cass Lake, Minn. d. Albin and Norma Nordstrom; m. Dallas Vizenor (dec.). MEd, Minn. State U., Moorhead; EdD, Harvard U. Tchr.; sec.-treas. White Earth Band of Ojibwe, 1996—2002, chairwoman, 2004—. Office: White Earth Reservation PO Box 418 White Earth MN 56591 Office Phone: 218-983-3285. Office Fax: 218-983-3641.

VIZYAK, LINDY L., retired elementary school educator; b. Pueblo, Colo., May 19, 1949; d. Charles Eugene and Edna Leatha (Pennington) Berry; m. Joe A. Vizyak, Dec. 20, 1969; 1 child, Sean Joseph. BS, U. So. Colo., 1971. Tchr. first grade Adam County Five Star Schs., Northglenn, Colo., 1978—2004, ret., 2004. Freelance cons. Westminster, Colo., 1994. Author: Student Portfolios: A Practical Guide to Evaluation K-6, 1993, Student Portfolios: A Practical Guide to Evaluation, 1995; contbr. articles to profl. jours. Mem. NEA, Colo. Edn. Assn., Colo. Coun. Tchrs. Math. (Math Tchr. of Yr. 1991, state finalist for presdl. award for execllence in tchg. elem. math.), Colo. Coun. Internat. Reading Assn., Internat. Reading Assn., Univ. So. Colo. Alumni Assn., Dist. Twelve Educators Assn., Phi Delta Kappa. Democrat. Avocations: reading, writing, travel. Home: 10001 Julian Ct Westminster CO 80031-6769 Office: Arapahoe Ridge Elem Sch 13095 Pecos St Westminster CO 80234

VIZZINI, CAROL REDFIELD, symphony musician, educator; b. San Diego, Jan. 3, 1946; d. Ernest Sylvester and Eleanor Diana (Soneson) Redfield; m. Edward Tracy Browning (div. 1981); children: Victor, Charlotte; m. Joseph Russell Vizzini, Apr. 12, 1997. MusB, Phila. Musical Acad., 1968, Prin. cellist Somerset Hills Symphony, Basking Ridge, NJ, 1971-81, New Philharm. of N.W. NJ, Morristown, 1978-87; asst. prin. cellist Princeton (NJ) Chamber Symphony, 1985-95; prin. cellist Orch. St. Peter-by-the-Sea, Point Pleasant, NJ, 1987-92; instr. in cello Westminster Conservatory, Rider U., Princeton, 1987—, head string dept., 1992—. Chamber music coach Vt. Music and Arts Ctr., Lyndonville, 1980-81; coach Greater Princeton Youth Orch., 1989-92; chamber music coach NJ Youth Symphonies, Summit, 1989—; chamber music coord. Westminster Conservatory, 1991-98. Author: Cello Scales, Volume One (One and Two Octave Scales), 1997, Cello Scales, Volume Two (Three and Four Octave Scales), 2004. Mem. Am. String Tchrs. Assn., Am. Fedn. Musicians, Music Tchrs. Nat. Assn. (string coord. 1989-93). Avocations: gardening, fly fishing, travel. Office: Westminster Conservatory of Music Rider Univ 101 Walnut Ln Princeton NJ 08540-3819 Office Phone: 609-921-7104. E-mail: cjvizzini@earthlink.net.

VLADECK, JUDITH POMARLEN, lawyer; b. Norfolk, Va., Aug. 1, 1923; BA, Hunter Coll., 1945; JD, Columbia U., 1947. Bar: NY 1947, US Supreme Ct. 1962. Assoc. Conrad & Smith, N.Y.C., 1947-51; sole practice N.Y.C., 1951-57; mem. Vladeck, Elias, Vladeck & Engelhard P.C., N.Y.C., 1957—; sr. ptnr. Vladeck, Waldman, Elias & Englehard, P.C., N.Y.C. Adj. prof. Fordham Law Sch. Mem. adv. bd. Inst. for Edn. and Rsch. on Women and Work, Cornell U.; bd. dirs. N.Y. Civil Liberties Union, 1963-68; bd. dir., counsel Tamiment Inst., Inc.; mem. advisory bd. R. Wagner Labor Archives, Tamiment Inst. Libr.; bd. dirs. lawyers' coordinating com. AFL-CIO; bd. mem. Non-Traditional Employment for Women. Recipient Hunter Coll. Profl. Achievement award, 1992, Edith Spivack award, 1998, Women of Power and Influence award NY NOW, 1998, ORT Jurisprudence award, 1996; elected to Hunter Coll. Hall of Fame, 1988; Non-Taditional Employment for Women named building Judith P. Vladeck Ctr. for Women, 1989; Margaret Brent Award, ABA 2002; Columbia Law Sch. Assoc. Medal for Excellence, 2003; NEW 25th Anniv. Equity Leadership Award, 2003, 60th Ann. NYS Human Rights Law award for Excellence, NYS Divsn. Human Rights, 2005, Peggy Browning Fund Lifetime Achievement award, 2006. Fellow Am. Bar Found., Coll. of Labor and Employment Lawyers; mem. ABA (co-chmn. labor law and equal employment coms., N.Y. State Bar Assn. (labor law com.), Assn. of Bar of City of N.Y., N.Y. County Lawyers Assn., Fed. Bar Assn., Women's Bar Assn., Am. Arbitration Assn. (panel of arbitrators), Columbia Law Sch. Alumni Assn. (bd. dir.), Harlem Inst. Fashion (counsel, bd. dir.). Home: 115 Central Park W New York NY 10023-4153 Office: Vladeck Waldman Elias & Engelhard 1501 Broadway Ste 800 New York NY 10036-5560 Office Phone: 212-403-7300. Business E-Mail: jvladeck@vladeck.com.

VLAHAC, MARY ANN RITA, marketing executive; b. Bridgeport, Conn., June 11, 1954; d. John S. and Catherine R. (Landor) V.; 1 child, Christopher James Westerman. AS, Housatonic C.C., 1974; BS, U. Conn., 1976; MBA, U. Bridgeport, 1980; postgrad., U. New Haven. Market rschr. Remington Arms/duPont, Bridgeport, Conn., 1976-79; mem. sr. market rsch. staff Pitney Bowes, Stamford, Conn., 1979-86; asst. v.p., dir. mktg. rsch. People's Bank, Bridgeport, Conn., 1986—2004; mktg. dir. Sikorsky Fin. Credit Union, Bridgeport, Conn., 2004—. V.p. mktg. Mar-Kris Trading Co., Stratford, Conn., 1985-89; owner Gewgaw, Stratford, 1980—; ptnr. Glass & Crafts, Bridgeport, 1980—; adj. prof. MBA programs. Adv., Housatonic C.C., 1985-86. Mem. bus. adv. bd. So. Conn. Stat U., 1995-96. Mem. Rotary. Avocations: art, music, travel, community work. Home: 545 Windsor Ave Stratford CT 06614-4211

VLAMING, CARRIE, theater educator; d. Mike and Gloria Fenger; m. Patrick Vlaming, June 21, 2001; 1 child, Katherine. Master, Lesley Coll., Boston, 2000. Theatre tchr. Las Vegas Acad., 1993—95, Palo Verde HS, Las Vegas, 1997—. Nev. thespian chpt. dir. Ednl. Theatre Assn., 2001—06. Office: Palo Verde HS 333 Pavilion Ctr Dr Las Vegas NV 89144 Office Phone: 702-799-1450. E-mail: fengeca@paloverde.org.

VLIET, DONNA LOVE, education educator; b. Hammond, Ind. d. Edwin Faye Love and Laura Viola (Seitz) Love-Calnon; m. Garry Clark Vliet, Dec. 15, 1962; children: Kirsten Lynn, Joanne Maria, David Paul. BA, Fresno State Coll., Calif., 1961; MEd, U. Tex., 1987, PhD, 1994. Cert. tchr., Calif., Tex. Tchr. Palo Alto Sch. Dist., Calif., 1961—63; educator collaborative programs sch. and mus. U. Tex. and Austin Ind. Sch. Dist., 1979—98; lectr. Tex. State U., 1997—98, U. Tex., Austin, 1998—2002. Author: (catalogue) Museums, Muses & Me!, 1985, 3d edit., 1992, Curriculum Connections, 1995, Museum/School Collaborations: Resources for School Research and Curricula, 1996 Pres. Gullett Elem. Sch. PTA, Austin, 1977-78, Lamar Jr. H.S. PTA (life mem.), Austin, 1981-82, McCallum H.S. Band Parents Assn., Austin, 1984-85; elder Covenant Presbyn. Ch., Austin, 1989-91; founder, dir. Access to Learning, Inc., 2003 Recipient Outstanding Achievement Art Edn. resolution Austin Ind. Sch. Dist., 1989 Mem. Tex. Art Edn. Assn. (chmn. mus. divsn. 1990-93, Outstanding Art Educator of Yr. award mus. divsn. 1988), Tex. Assn. Mus Avocation: tennis. Business E-Mail: donnavliet@mall.utexas.edu.

VOCE, JOAN A. CIFONELLI, retired elementary school educator; b. Utica, N.Y., Mar. 22, 1936; d. Albert and Theresa (Buono) Cifonelli; m. Eugene R. Voce Sr., Aug. 16, 1958; children: Eugene R. Jr., Lisa V. Stewart, Mark L., Daniel A. BS in Elem. Edn., Coll. St. Rose, Albany, N.Y., 1958; MS in Elem. Edn., SUNY, Cortland, 1981. Elem. tchr. Utica (N.Y.) Pub. Schs., 1958-59, 61-62, 64-67; tchr. Deerfield Elem. Sch., Whitesboro (N.Y.) Ctrl. Sch. Dist., 1968-91. Vol. Presbyn. Home for Ctrl. N.Y.; mem. Our Lady of the Rosary Ch., New Hartford, NY, Our Lady of Hope Ch., Port Orange, Fla. Mem. AAUW (Mohawk Valley br.), N.Y. State United Tchrs., Whitesboro Ret. Tchrs. Assn., Am. Assn. Ret. Persons, Oneida County Ret. Tchrs. Assn. (sec.), N.Y. State Ret. Tchrs. Assn., Coll. of St. Rose Alumni Assn., Utica Symphony League, Mohawk Valley Performing Arts, Pelican Bay Country Club (Daytona Beach, Fla.), Skenandoa Golf and Country Club (Clinton, NY), Alpha Delta Kappa (v.p. 1974-76, pres. 1976-78, corr. sec. 1972-74, rec. sec. 1986-88, 90-91). Avocations: reading, travel, golf, gourmet cooking, theater. Home (Winter): 201 Surf Scooter Dr Daytona Beach FL 32119 Home (Summer): 109 Birchwood Ln Whitesboro NY 13492 Personal E-mail: jcvoce@webtv.net.

VOCE, PATRICIA MARIA, medical/surgical nurse; b. N.Y.C., May 20, 1965; d. James Joseph Massi and Patricia Elvira Bozza; m. Frank William Voce, Jr., Sept. 17, 1988; children: Frank IV, Christopher. BSN, Dominican Coll., 1987. RN N.Y. Staff nurse White Plains (N.Y.) Hosp., 1987—89; RN Nyack Hosp. Cmty. Health, Orangeberg, NY, 1989—; per-diem skills lab. instr. Rockland Boces and LPN Program, 2001—04. Vice chair Clarkstown Rep. Com., NY, 1999—. Home: 4 Foltim Way Congers NY 10920

VOEGELE, KAREN E., social worker; b. Summit, N.J., Dec. 30, 1973; d. James Paul Adorna (Stepmother) and Shirley Ann ((Ruppert)) Schmidt; m. John Richard Voegele, Oct. 13, 2001. BA, U. Mass., 1996; MSW, U. Pa., 2000. Social worker Big Brothers Big Sisters, Eatontown, NJ, 1996—98; counselor Thomas Jefferson U., Phila., 2000—01; therapist Life Counseling Svcs., Paoli, Pa., 2001—02, Northwestern Human Svcs., 2000—. Home: 629 Kenilworth Rd Ardmore PA 19003 Office Phone: 215-248-6720. Business E-Mail: kvoegele@nhsonline.org.

VOEGTLIN-ANDERSON, MARY MARGARET, music educator, small business owner; b. Seattle; d. Joseph Walter and Veronica Margaret (Conroy) Voegtlin; m. Terry Lee Anderson, Mar. 19, 1977 (div. July 20, 1982). BA cum laude, Marylhurst U., 1963; postgrad., U. Wash., 1963—65, Oakland U., 1968, Seattle Pacific U., 1982—84. Cert. std. tchg. grades K-12 Wash. Profl. cellist Oreg. Symphony, Portland, 1962—63; tchr. music and humanities Chinook Mid. Sch., Seattle, 1963—89, gifted edn. specialist, 1983—89; tchr. music, music dept. chair Highline H.S., Seattle, 1989—2004, tchr. honors English, 1989—2004; owner, tchr. Anderson Music Studio, Seattle, 2004—. Contralto soloist Mt. Baker Pk. Presbyn. Ch., 1966—68, U. Congl. Ch., Seattle, 1968—73; profl. singer Seattle Opera Co., 1968—70; vocal coach, advisor Highline Jazz Ensemble, Seattle, 1990—2004; pvt. piano, cello and voice tchr., Seattle, 1991—; astronomy club advisor Highline H.S., Seattle, 1998—2004; dir. Highline Dist. Youth Orch., 2003—04, Burien Sr. Choir, 2003; trustee Sunlight Waters Corp., 2002—; pres., owner Anderson Music Studio. Contbr. articles to profl. jours. Officer, sec. 46th Legis. Dist. Dem. Party, Seattle, 1974—78, chairperson Initiative 314 Campaign, 1975; Wash. state conv. del. Dem. Party, Olympia, 1976, Dem. precinct chairperson Seattle, 1976—77. Fulbright Scholarship grantee, Nat. Tchrs. Performance Inst., Oberlin Coll., Ohio, 1970. Mem.: NEA, Planetary Soc., Nat. Coun. Tchrs. English, Seattle Astron. Soc., Music Educators' Nat. Conf. Roman Catholic. Avocations: astronomy, reading, bicycling, writing, hiking. Personal E-mail: mvanderson03@aol.com.

VOEHRINGER, HEIDI L., history educator; b. Durango, Colo., June 20, 1979; d. Marvin Walter and Jimmie Joan Voehringer. BA in History, U. No. Colo., Greenley, 2001; MA in Edn. Adminstrn., Grand Canyon U., Phoenix, 2006. Tchr. Montrose (Colo) H.S., 2001—, asst. coach volleyball, 2001—, asst. coach basketball, 2002—. Mem.: Am. Assn. Geographers, Nat. Coun. for Social Studies. Office Phone: 970-249-6636. Business E-Mail: voehringer@mcsd.k12.co.us.

VOELKEL, JANE CLAUDETTE, retired elementary school educator, home economist; b. Lexington, Ky., Jan. 30, 1937; d. George Edward Ross and Esther (Brigman) Hayes; m. Eugene Voelkel, Dec. 31, 1957; children: Claudette Ann, Robert Scott, Janet Elizabeth. BS, Tex. Woman's U., 1958, postgrad., 1966-67; MEd, Tarleton State U., Stephenville, Tex., 1981. Profl. home economist; cert. elem. tchr., kindergarten, learning lang. disabilities, Tex. Tchr. Mineral Wells (Tex.) Ind. Sch. Dist., 1965-66, Holly Hill (Fla.) Sch., Volusia County, 1967, Lawton (Okla.) Ind. Sch. Dist., 1978-79, Three Way Common Sch. Dist., Hico, Tex., 1979-81, Bryan (Tex.) Ind. Sch. Dist., 1981-98, ret., 1998. Mem. curr. coun. Bryan Ind. Sch. Dist., 1986-87, mem. supts. forum, 1988-90, chmn. forum, 1990-91, bldg. rep. book selection in lang. arts, 1988-89, in sci., 1990-91, grade level chmn., 1994-95, book selection in social studies, 1996-97. Deacon 1st Presbyn. Ch., Bryan, 1988-91; vol. Hospice, Bryan and College Station, 1990-93, v.p., 1989-92; vol. LOVES (Loving Outreach and Visitation to Elderly and Shut=Ins), 1985-95. Mem. Tex. Woman's U. Nat. Alumnae Assn. (life, v.p. 1989-92), Tex. Woman's U. Brazos Valley Alumnae Assn. (pres. 1986—), Assn. Tex. Profl. Educators, Internat. Reading Assn., Tex. State Reading Assn., Sam Houston Area Reading Coun. Republican. Home: 4 Ravens Perch St Bryan TX 77808-9719

VOGEL, CHRISTY RAE, secondary school educator; b. Butler, Pa., Aug. 12, 1974; d. Leonard Henry and Susanne Vogel. BS in Edn., Slippery Rock State U., Pa., 1996; MA in Tchg., Marygrove Coll., Detroit, 2001. Teller Nextier Bank, Butler, Pa., 1992—97; substitute tchr. Butler Sch. Dist., 1997—98; tchr. sci. Sch. Dist. Penn Hills, 1998—99, West Mifflin Area Mid. Sch. Dist., 1999—. Sci. club advisor West Mifflin Sch. Dist., 1999—, volleyball coach, 2001—05, newspaper co-editor, 2004—. Vol. Butler County Blind Assn., 2005—. Republican. Roman Catholic. Avocations: scrapbooks, travel. Office: West Mifflin Area Mid Sch Dist 371 Camp Hollow Rd West Mifflin PA 15122 Office Phone: 412-466-3200. Personal E-mail: vogelc@wmasd.org.

VOGEL, GLORIA JEAN HILTS, secondary school educator; b. Detroit, Mar. 24, 1947; d. Roy Ellis and Helen Amanda (Ludwig) Hilts; m. Charles Orville Vogel, Oct. 6, 1973; children: Mark Robert, Amanda Jean. BA in English and History, Mich. State U., 1969; MA Tchg. in English, Fitchburg State U., 1978. English tchr. Woodbury Sch., Salem, NH, 1969-73, No. Mid. Sch., Westford, Mass., 1973-76, Westford Acad., 1976—98, Leominster HS, 1998—. Dealer 19th century Am. art, Townsend, Mass., 1973—. Webelos leader Boy Scouts Am., Townsend, 1989-91; mem. choir Townsend Congl. Ch.; founding mem. Wall of Tolerance, Nat. Campaign for Tolerance, 2002, Nat. Women's History Mus., 2002. Recipient Excellence in Tchr. award,

Acad. Devel. Ctr., 2000, Woman of the Yr., Am. Biog. Inst. Bd. Internat. Rsch., 2006. Mem. AAUW, NEA, Nat. Coun. Tchrs. English, Mass. Tchrs. Assn., Westford Edn. Assn., Nat. Women's History Mus., Leominster Edn. Assn. Democrat. Home: 3 Sycamore Dr Townsend MA 01469-1312 Office: Leominster High Sch 122 Granite St Leominster MA 01453 Office Phone: 978-534-7715 x442. Personal E-mail: cvogel2503@comcast.net.

VOGEL, H. VICTORIA, psychotherapist, educator, writer, stress disorder and addiction recovery counselor; BA, U. Md., 1968; MA, NYU, 1970, MA, 1975; MEd, postgrad., Columbia U., 1982—; cert., Am. Projective Drawing Inst., 1983; CASAC, New Sch. U. for Social Rsch., 2000. Diplomate Am. Acad. Experts in Traumatic Stress; cert. addiction recovery counselor, expert in traumatic stress, alcohol and substance abuse counselor, addictions treatment, addiction counseling alcohol and substance abuse. Art therapist Childville, Bklyn., 1962-64; tchr. Montgomery County (Md.) Jr. H.S., 1968-69; with H.S. divsn. N.Y.C. Bd. Edn., 1970—; guidance counselor, instr., psychotherapist in pvt. practice. Guidance counselor, instr., psychotherapist in pvt. practice; clin. counseling cons. psychodiagnosis and devel. studies, art/play therapy The Modern Sch., 1984—; art/play therapist Hosp. Ctr. for Neuromuscular Disease and Devel. Disorders, 1986—; employment counselor-adminstr. N.Y. State Dept. Labor Concentrated Employment Program, 1971-72; intern psychotherapy and psychoanalysis psychiat. divsn. Ctrl. Islip Hosp., 1973-75, Calif. Grad. Inst., L.A.; intern psychol. counseling and rehab. N.J. Coll. Medicine, Newark, 1979. Author: The Never Ending Story of Alcohol, Drugs and Other Substance Abuse, 1992, Variant Sexual Behavior and the Aesthetic Modern Nudes, 1992, Psychological Science of School Behavior Intervention, 1993, Joycean Conceptual Modernism: Relationships and Deviant Sexuality, 1995, Electronic Evil Eyes, 1995 (U.S. Cert. of Recognition, 1996), Psychological Paradigms of Alcohol Violence Suicide Trauma Addiction Variant Pathologies PTSD and Schizophrenia, 1999. Mem. com. for spl. events NYU, 1989; participant clin. and artistic perspectives Am. Acad. Psychoanalysis Conf., 1990, participant clin. postmodernism and psychoanalysis, 1996; aux. police officer N.Y. Police Dept., 1994—; chair bylaws com. Columbia U., 1995—. Mem.: ACA, AAAS, APA, NY Acad. Sci., Tchrs. Coll. Adminstrv. Women in Edn., Assn. Humanistic Psychology (exec. sec. 1981), Art/Play Therapy, N.Y. Art Tchrs. Assn., Am. Acad. Experts Traumatic Stress (diplomate in expert traumatic stress), Am. Soc. Group Psychotherapy and Psychodrama (publs. com. 1984—), Am. Orthopsychiat. Assn., Am. Psychol. Soc., Phi Delta Kappa (editor chpt. newsletter 1981—84, exec. sec. Columbia U. chpt. 1984—, chmn. nominating com. for chpt. officers 1986—, rsch. rep. 1986—, pub. rels. exec. bd. dirs. 1991, NYU chpt. v.p. programs 1994—).

VOGEL, JENNIFER, lawyer; BBA, U. Iowa; JD, U. TX Sch. Law, Austin, TX, 1987. Atty. Vinson & Elkins LLP; v.p., gen. counsel Enron Global Power & Pipelines; v.p. legal & asst. sec. Continental Airlines, Inc., Houston, 1995—2001, gen. counsel, 2001—, sr. v.p., corp. compliance officer, corp. sec., 2003—. Mailing: Continental Airlines Inc PO Box 4607 Houston TX 77210-4607 Office Phone: 713-324-2950.

VOGEL, JENNIFER LYN, lawyer; b. Queens, N.Y., June 20, 1969; d. Bernard Henry and Alyce Susan Vogel. BA, Washington U., St. Louis, 1991; JD, Bklyn. Law Sch., 1994. Assoc. Seavey Vogel & Oziel, Mineola, N.Y., 1994—. Office: Seavey Vogel & Oziel LLP 33 Willis Ave Ste 200 Mineola NY 11501-4411

VOGEL, PAULA ANNE, playwright; b. Washington, Nov. 16, 1951; d. Donald Stephen and Phyllis (Bremerman) Vogel. BA, Cath. U., 1974; doctoral studies, Cornell U., 1974-77. Instr. theatre and women's studies Cornell U., Ithaca, N.Y., 1978-81; prodn. supr. Theatre on Film & Tape, N.Y.C., 1983-85; Adele Kellenberg Seaver prof. Creative Writing Program, Brown U., Providence, 1985—. Author: (plays) Meg, 1977 (Nat. Playwright award Am. Coll. Theatre Festival), And Baby Makes Seven, 1984, Desdemona, 1985, The Oldest Profession, 1988, The Baltimore Waltz, 1992 (Obie award for best play, 1992), Hot 'N' Throbbing, 1994, The Mineola Twins, 1996, How I Learned to Drive, 1996 (Pulitzer prize, 1998, Obie award, 1997, N.Y. Drama Critics Drama Desk award for best play, 1997, Lucille Lortel award, 1997, Outer Critics' Circle award, 1997). Recipient Bunting award, Radcliffe-Harvard Colls., 1990, Pew Charitable Trust Sr. Residency award, 1995, Laura Pels award, 1999; grantee Fund for New Am. Plays, 1994; playwright fellow NEA, 1981, 1990, Guggenheim fellow, 1995. Fellow: Am. Acad. Arts & Sciences, McDowell Colony; mem.: New Dramatists. Office: Brown U PO Box 1852 Providence RI 02912-1852*

VOGEL, SALLY THOMAS, psychologist, social worker, educator; b. Joplin, Mo., July 3, 1925; d. Clyde Albert Thomas and Kathryn (Waite) Thompson; m. F. Lincoln Vogel, Sept. 4, 1946; children: Kathryn Duchin, Linda, Robert L. BA, Beaver Coll., 1947; MEd, North Adams State Coll., 1969; EdS, Seton Hall U., 1995. Case worker Pa. Dept. Welfare, Phila., 1947-48; high sch. tchr. Downington High Sch., Coatesville, Pa., 1969—70; sch. social worker Delaware Valley High Sch., Frenchtown, N.J., 1970-84; study team coord. Holland Twp. Sch., Milford, N.J., 1975-85, sch. social worker, 1975-90, guidance counselor, 1990-94, intern, cons., 1994—98; sch. psychologist Lake Shore Sch. Dist., St. Clair Shores, Mich., 1998—2005. Instr. in Parent Effectiveness and Tchr. Effectiveness, Hunt County Adult Edn., N.J., 1975-84; advanced trainee Edn. Tng. Inst., Calif., 1984-89; presenter in field. Acting exec. dir. Big Bros./Big Sisters (founder), Hunterdon County, N.J., 1976. Recipient Ed Kiley Svc. award Big Bros./Big Sisters, 1978; named to Hunt County Women of Distinction. Mem.: AAUW, NASP, MASP. Office: Lake Shore Sch Dist Admin Bldg Harper St Clair Shores Saint Clair Shores MI 48081

VOGEL, SARAH ELIZABETH, music educator; b. Fort Morgan, Colo., Mar. 4, 1980; d. Edward James and Patricia Ann Kembel; m. Edwin charles Vogel, Mar. 20, 2004. MusB, Colo. State U., 2003. Music tchr. Akron Sch. Dist., Colo., 2004; band dir. Ft. Morgan Schs. RE-3, Colo., 2004—05; music dir. Stratton Schs., Colo., 2005—. Mem. Sugar Beats Swing Band, Ft. Morgan, 2003—04, Luth. Ch. of Our Redeemer Choir, Ft. Morgan, 2004—. Republican. Lutheran. Avocations: hunting, fishing, running, cooking. Home: 522 Lake St Fort Morgan CO 80701-3122

VOGEL, SUSAN CAROL, nursing administrator; b. Hartford, Conn., Oct. 9, 1948; d. Morton B. and Esther (Riback) Worshoufsky. Diploma in nursing, Grace Hosp., New Haven, 1969; B in Healthcare Mgmt., U. La Verne, 1991, M in Health Adminstrn., 1994. RN, Calif.; cert. nephrology nurse, Nephrology Nurse Cert. Bd. Oper. rm. nurse New Britain (Conn.) Gen. Hosp., 1970-72; staff nurse oper. rm. Parkview Cmty. Hosp., Riverside, Calif., 1972-74; staff nurse dialysis, IV team Cedars-Sinai Med. Ctr., L.A., 1974-82; clin. nurse III dialysis UCLA, 1982-88; nurse mgr. inpatient dialysis UCLA Med. Ctr., 1988-93; adminstr. South Valley Regional Dialysis Ctr., Encino, Calif., 1993—; pres. Renal Replacement Therapies, Inc. Bd. dirs. End Stage Renal Disease Network 18, med. rev. bd., 1996—2000, treas.; chmn. bd. Renal Support Network, 2006—. Author: (with others) Review of Hemodialysis for Nurses and Dialysis Personnel, 7th edit., 2002, Vascular Access, Principles & Practices, 4th edit., 2002; editor Nephrology Nursing Jour., 2000-02. Med. rev. bd. End Stage Renal Disease Network 18, 1996-2000, treas., 2004—06; pres. Calif. Dialysis Coun., 2002-05, past pres. 2005-; trustee Am. Kidney Fund, 2005—; bd. chmn. Renal Support Network, 2006. Mem. NAFE, Am. Nephrology Nurses Assn. (pres. LA chpt. 1990-92, 96-98, nat. chair hemodialysis spl. interest group 1993-95), Nat. Kidney Found. Avocations: travel, skiing. Office: South Valley Regional Dialysis Ctr 17815 Ventura Blvd Ste 100 Encino CA 91316-3600 Office Phone: 818-757-4520. Business E-Mail: svogel@svrde.com.

VOGEL, SUSAN MULLIN, museum director, art and archaeology professor; BS in French and English Literature, Georgetown U., 1964; MA, NYU, 1971, cert. mus. tng., 1977, PhD in Art History, 1977. Libr. asst. USIS Libr., Abidjan, 1964-65, Mus. Primitive Art, N.Y.C., 1966-67, asst. registrar, 1967-70, asst. curator, 1971-74; assoc. curator Met. Mus. Art, N.Y.C., 1975-82, sr. cons. African Art, 1982-84; exec. dir. The Ctr. for African Art, N.Y.C., 1982-1994; dir. Yale U Art Gallery, 1995—; prof. art history & archeology Columbia U., 2004—. Lectr. in field. Arranged exhbns. including The Art of Black Africa: Nigeria and Cameroon, Met. Mus. Art, 1971, The Sculpture of Black Africa: Upper Volta, Mus. Primitive Art, 1972, Faces (Africa only), Mus. Primitive Art, 1973, Gods of Fortune: The Cult of the Hand in Nigeria, Mus. Primitive Art, 1974, Rapacious Birds and Severed Heads: Early Bronze Rings from Nigeria, Art Inst. Chgo., 1979, The Buli Master: An African Artist of the 19th Century, Met. Mus. Art, 1980, For Spirits and Kings: African Art from the Paul and Ruth Tishman Collection, Met. Mus. Art, 1981, Michael C. Rockefeller Meml. Wing permanent installation of African art, Met. Mus. Art, 1982, African Masterpieces from the Musee de l'Homme Paris, Ctr. for African Art, 1984, African Aesthetics: The Carlo Monzino Collection, Ctr. for African Art, 1986, African Masterpieces from the Staatliches Mus. fur Volkerkunde Munich, Ctr. for African Art, 1987, Perspectives: Angles on African Art, Ctr. for African Art, 1987, Art/Artifact, Ctr. for African Art, 1988, The Art of Collecting African Art, Ctr. for African Art, 1988, Closeup: Lessons in the Art of Seeing African Art, Ctr. for African Art, 1990, Africa Explores: 20th Century African Art, Ctr. for African Art and New Mus. Contemporary Art, 1991, Home and the World: Archtl. Sculpture of two contemporary African Art, 1993, Fusion: West African Artist and the Venice Bienniale, Italy Mus. for African Art, 1993, Exhibition-ism: Mus. and African Art, Mus. for African Art, 1994; author exhbn. catalogues Ctr. for African Art: African Masterpieces from the Musee de l'Homme, 1985, African Aesthetics: The Carlo Monzino Collection, 1986, Africa Explores: 20th Century African Art, 1991, Closeup: Lessons in the Art of Seeing African Art, 1990; editor For Spirits and Kings, Met. Mus. Art, 1981; editor chpts. of books; contbr. articles to profl. jours. and many books in field. Office: Yale U Art Gallery PO Box 208271 New Haven CT 06520-8271

VOGELGESANG, SANDRA LOUISE, former ambassador, writer, consultant; b. Canton, Ohio, July 27, 1942; d. Glenn Wesley and Louise (Forry) Vogelgesang; m. Geoffrey Ernest Wolfe, July 4, 1982. BA, Cornell U., 1964; MA, Tufts U., 1965, MA in Law and Diplomacy, 1966, PhD, 1971. With Dept. State, Washington, 1975-97, policy planner for sec. state and European Bur., 1975-80, dir. Econ Policy Office, Orgn. Econ. Coop. and Devel., 1981-82, econ. minister U.S. Embassy, Ottawa, Can., 1982-86, dep. asst. sec. Internat. Orgn. Affairs Bur., 1986-89, dep. asst. adminstr. Office Internat. Activities Environ. Protection Agy., Washington, 1989-92; with Dept. State, Washington, 1992; sr. policy advisor Agy. for Internat. Devel., 1993; US amb. to Nepal Dept. State, Washington, 1994-97; pres. Everest Assocs. and Himalaya, 1997—2004. Bd. dirs. Ctr. for Econ. Devel. and Population Activities; mem. women and conservation com. World Wildlife Fund, 1997—2004, mem. Nat. Coun., 1999—2004; bd. advisors Am.'s Soc., N.Y.C., 1986—89; mem. Pres.'s Coun. of Cornell Women Cornell U., 1998—; adv. com. Dept. of Treasury com. on Internat. Child Labor Enforcement, 1999—; mem. global coun. Internat. Mus. Women, 2004—; writer, cons. internat. devel. issues. Author: Long Dark Night of the Soul, The American Intellectual Left and the Vietnam War, 1974, American Dream-Global Nightmare: The Dilemma of U.S. Human Rights Policy, 1980. Bd. dirs. Crafts Ctr., 1999-2000. Recipient Meritorious Service awards, 1973, 74, 82, 83, 86, Disting. Honor award, 1976 Dept. State, Pres.' Disting. Service award, 1985. Mem. Council on Fgn. Relations. Office: 9009 Charred Oak Dr West Bethesda MD 20817-1923 Business E-Mail: everest.associates@erols.com.

VOGELSONG, DIANA LOUISE, librarian; b. Morristown, N.J., Jan. 16, 1951; d. James Howard and Doris May (Kehr) V.; m. Wallace Cutting Duncan, Jr., Apr. 24, 1976; children: Matthew, Andrea. BA, Kalamazoo Coll., 1973; MLS in Libr. and Info. Sci., U. Md., 1975; MA in Art History, Am. U., 1981. Cataloger U.S. Book Exch., Washington, 1974; searcher McKeldin Libr., U. Md., College Park, 1975; reference libr. Am. U. Libr., Washington, 1975-80, head media svcs., 1980-96, asst. univ. libr. for info. svcs., 1993—2005, acting U. Libr., 2006—. Project coord. Mus. Ednl. Site Licensing Project, Getty Art History Info. Inst., 1995-1997. Author: Guide to the Microforms Collection of the National Gallery of Art, Washington, D.C., 1990, Landscape Architecture in America: A Guide to Resources on the History and Practice of Landscape Architecture in the United States, 1997; reviewer Video Rating Guide, 1990-91; contbr. chpts. to books and articles to profl. jours. Juror Am. Film and Video Festival, 1981, 87-93, jury chairperson, 1987, 93; mem. undergrad. studies com. Am. U. Senate, 1985-91, mem. computer resources com., 1994-96, chair faculty senate com. on info. resources, 2003-2005; chair audiovisual adv. com. Consortium of Univs., Washington, 1986-88; chair Am. Univ. Libr. Faculty Coun., 1991-93, 2003-2005. Recipient Alliance Francaise prize, sr. French fellow Kalamazoo Coll.; named Outstanding Young Women of Am., 1984; Rsch. Support grantee Am. U., 1985-86. Mem. ALA (video round table 1992-94), Assn. Coll. and Rsch. Librs. (copywright com.), Consortium of Coll. and Univ. Media Ctrs. (editl. bd. Coll. and Univs. Media Rev., mem. govt. regulations and pub. policy com., ad hoc task force on copyright), Art Librs. Soc. N.Am. Regional Assn., Alpha Lambda Delta, Phi Kappa Phi, Beta Phi Mu. Avocations: gardening, dance. Office: Am Univ Libr 4400 Massachusetts Ave NW Washington DC 20016-8046 Office Phone: 202-885-3236. Business E-Mail: dvogel@american.edu.

VOGELZANG, JEANNE MARIE, professional society administrator, lawyer; b. Hammond, Ind., Apr. 15, 1950; d. Richard and Laura Ann (Vanderaa) Jabaay. BA, Trinity Christian Coll., Palos Heights, Ill., 1972; MBA, U. Minn., 1981; JD, U. Chgo., 1987. Bar: Ill. 1987; CPA, Ill.; CAE. Tchr. Timothy Christian HS., Elmhurst, Ill., 1972-74; tchg. assoc. fin. U. Minn., Mpls., 1980-81; fin. analyst Quaker Oats Co., Chgo., 1982-84; assoc. Baker & McKenzie, Chgo., 1987-89, Jenner & Block, Chgo., 1989-91; pres., owner J.M. Vogelzang & Assocs., Western Springs, Ill., 1991-99; exec. dir. Structural Engrs. Assn. Ill., Chgo., 1992—2005, Nat. Coun. Structural Engrs. Assn., Chgo., 1996—, Structural Engrng. Cert. Bd., 2004—; pub., editor Structure mag., 1996—. Com. mem. Western Springs Planning Commn., 1991—95; village trustee Village of Western Springs, 1995—99, chmn. fin., chmn. gen. govt. com.; adv. bd. Coll. DuPage Internat. Trade Ctr., Glen Ellyn, Ill., 1992—94; bd. dirs., acad. affairs com., planning com., exec. com. sec. Trinity Christian Coll., 1992—98; trustees' evaluation com. Christian Ref. Ch. N.Am., 1998—; treas. The Tower Party of Western Springs, 1999—2001; jud. code com. Christian Reformed Ch. N.Am., Grand Rapids, Mich., 1991—97; bd. dirs. Austin Christian Law Ctr., Chgo., 1989—92, Barnabas Found., Palos Heights, Ill., 1989—95; treas. Ctrl. Park Chapel, Holland, Mich., 2002—. Fellow Ill. Lincoln Excellence in Pub. Svc., 1999. Mem. ABA, Am. Soc. Assn. Execs., Ill. Bar Assn., Chgo. Bar Assn., Elim Work Svcs. Bus. Roundtable. Presbyterian. Office: 645 N Michigan Ave Ste 540 Chicago IL 60611 Office Phone: 312-649-4600. Business E-Mail: execdir@ncsea.com.

VOGT, CHRISTY, music educator; M in Music Edn., Piano Pedagogy, U. Okla., 1992—95; DMA in Piano Pedagogy, U. Miami, 2000—03. Suzuki, Philosophy and Level 1A Suzuki Assn. of the Americas, 1997, MusikGarten MusikGarten, Inc., 1999. Group piano and pre-college piano instr. Wheaton Coll., 1995—98; lesson coord. Brook Mays Music Co., Dallas, 1998; early childhood music tchr. Tex. Christian U. Prep. Dept., 1999—2000; dir., keyboard for kids prep. piano program U. of Miami, 2000—03; asst. prof. piano, piano pedagogy McNeese State U., 2003—. Adjudicator Nat. Fedn. of Music Clubs, Miami, 2002—03. Mem.: Coll. Music Soc., Music Teachers Nat. Assn.

VOGT, KATHLEEN CUNNINGHAM, musician, educator; b. Ellwood City, Pa., July 3, 1951; d. Joseph Edward and Dorothea Cunningham Vogt. BS summa cum laude in Music Edn., Duquesne U., 1973, M in Music edn., 1975. Cert. Tchr Nat. Bd., 2003. Tchr., band and choral dir. Diocese of Pitts. Schs., 1973—79; tchr., band dir. Carrick HS, 1980—84; band dir., drama tchr. Hanahan (SC) HS, 1984—2004, Sangaree Mid. Sch. Instr. percussion Duquesne U., Pitts., 1975—79; adj. prof. Charleston So. U., SC, 2001—; guest clinician and conductor, 1975—. Musician: Pitts. Symphony Orch., Charleston Symphony Orch., Lowcountry Winds, Charleston (SC) Cmty. Band. Mem. Hanahan Area Arts Coun. Mem.: Nat. Bd. Cert. Tchrs., All Berkeley County Music Educators, Nat. Band Assoc., Nat. Baton Twirling Assn., Nat. Twirling Judges Bur. (Inducted into Baton Twirling Hall of Fame 2002), Am. Sch. Band Dirs. Assn., SC Band Dirs. Assn. (Outstanding Performance award 1985—2004, SC State Marching Band Champions 1986, 1987, 1988, 1991), SC Music Educators Assn., Music Educators Nat. Conf., Pi Lambda Theta, Phi Beta Mu. Home: 504 Greenmeadow Rd Goose Creek SC 29445 Personal E-mail: katyvogt@aol.com.

VOGT, LORNA CORRINE, retired librarian, small business owner; b. Rochelle, Ill., Feb. 18, 1936; d. Chester Floyd and Vera Mae (Worthington) Patton; m. Norman E. Vogt, Aug. 18, 1957; 1 child, Cindy Jean Vogt Welch. BE, No. Ill. U., 1957, MA, 1972; postgrad., Western Ill. U., 1989-90. Tchr. speech and English Harlem High Sch., Loves Park, Ill., 1957-58; tchr. English, libr. Alden-Hebron (Ill.) Jr.-Sr. High Sch., 1958-59; traffic mgr. Sta. WLBK Radio, DeKalb, Ill., 1964-65; libr. No. Il. U., DeKalb, 1967, Malta (Ill.) Schs., 1968-71, Sycamore (Ill.) High Sch., 1971-94; ret., 1994; owner Sesquicentennial Farm. Mem. Ogle County (Ill.) Farm Bur.; presenter in field. Author: The Heritage of the Lafayette Township Schools, 1990; compiler (book) James Reed Family, 1991, William Patton Family, 1987, Lafayette Township Officers, 1993. Chmn. Books South Africa Commn., DeKalb, 1991-92; co-chmn. Literary Festival Little 7 Conf., 1991-93; chmn. bd. deacons Conglist. Ch., 1993-94, vice moderator, 1994-95; mem. Ill. Conf. United Ch. of Christ Bd., 1996-98, exec. bd., 1996-98, vice moderator Prairie Assn., 1996-97, moderator, 1997-98, United Ch. of Christ Gen. Synod, Providence, del. conf., Ill., 1999, Kansas City, Mo., 2001, Stephenson County Hist. Soc., 2002-; former mem. Assn. Gravestone Studies. Mem. NEA, Popular Culture Assn. (presenter 1989), Ill. Assn. Tchrs. English (presenter 1988-90), Nat. Coun. Tchrs. English (presenter 1991, 93), Ill. Edn. Assn., Ill. Assn. Media Edn., Midwest Gilbert and Sullivan Soc., Somerset County Pa. Hist. and Geneal. Soc., Ill. Ret. Tchrs. Assn., Ret. Tchrs. Assn. Stephenson County (sec. 2004-), Ret. Educators Assn. Sarasota, Freeport Area Camera Club, Stephenson County Hist. Soc., Alpha Sigma Alpha (life), Nat. Coun. Tchrs. English Ctr. of Excellence (co-dir., 1989-1991). Congregationalist. Avocations: writing, genealogy. Home: 3167 Sandy Pointe Dr Freeport IL 61032-2824 Personal E-mail: lornapat218@aol.com.

VOIGT, CYNTHIA, writer; b. Boston, Feb. 25, 1942; d. Frederick C. and Elise (Keeney) Irving; married, 1964 (div. 1972); m. Walter Voigt, Aug. 30, 1974; children: Jessica, Peter. BA, Smith Coll., 1963. High sch. tchr. English, Glen Burnie, Md., 1965-67; tchr. English Key Sch., Annapolis, Md., 1968-69, dept. chmn., 1971-79, tchr., dept. chmn., 1981-88. Author: Homecoming, 1981, Tell Me If the Lovers Are Losers, 1982, Dicey's Song, 1982 (John Newbery medal 1983), The Callender Papers, 1983 (Edgar award 1984), A Solitary Blue, 1983, Building Blocks, 1984, Jackeroo, 1985, The Runner, 1985 (Silver Pencil award 1988, Deutscher Jugend Literator Preis 1989, ALAN award 1989), Come a Stranger, 1986, Izzy, Willy Nilly, 1986 (Calif. Young Reader's award 1990), Stories About Rosie, 1986, Sons From Afar, 1987, Tree by Leaf, 1988, Seventeen Against the Dealer, 1989, On Fortune's Wheel, 1990, The Vandemark Mummy, 1991, Orfe, 1992, Glass Mountain, 1991, David and Jonathan, 1992, The Wings of a Falcon, 1993, When She Hollers, 1994, Bad Girls, 1996, Bad, Badder, Baddest, 1997, Elske, 1999, It's Not Easy Being Bad, 2000, Bad Girls in Love, 2002, From Bad to Worse, 2003, Angus and Sadie, 2005.

VOIGT, ELLEN, literature educator; b. 1943; BA, Converse Coll.; MFA, U. Iowa. Prof. poetry MIT; prof. Goddard Coll., Vt.; prof. MFA program for writers Warren Wilson Coll., Asheville, NC, 1981—; Vt. State Poet, 1999—2003. Tchr. Bread Loaf Writers' Conf., Aspen Writer's Conf., Ind. Writers' Conf., Napa Writer's Conf., Catskills Writers' Conf., RopeWalk Writers' Conf. Author: (poems) Claiming Kin, 1976, The Forces of Plenty, 1983, The Lotus Flowers, 1987, Two Trees, 1992, Shadows of Heaven, 2002 (Nat. Book award finalist), (sonnet) Kyrie, 1995 (Nat. Book Critics' Circle award finalist, Teasdale Poetry prize); co-editor (with Gregory Orr): Poets Teaching Poets: Self and the World; author: The Flexible Lyric, 2001. Recipient Pushcart prize; fellow, Acad. Am. Poets, 2002; grantee, Vt. Coun. Arts, NEA, Guggenheim Found. Fellow: Am. Acad. Arts and Sciences; mem.: Acad. Am. Poets (chancellor 2003—). Achievements include developing and directing the nation's first low-residency writing program at Goddard College in 1976; the program has since been emulated by other colleges and universities. Office: Warren Wilson Coll PO Box 9000 Asheville NC 28815*

VOJTA-OSWALD, CLARICE GERTRUDE, educational diagnostician; b. Artesian, SD, Oct. 9, 1940; d. Raymond Fenton and Bertha Grace (Berg) Connor; m. Ralph Duane Vojta, June 20, 1964 (div. Dec. 1986); m. Larry Dale Oswald, Nov. 22, 1989; children: Patrick, Susan, Sandra. BA, U. S.D., 1962; MEd, No. State U., 1982, 86, 88. Instr. music Roscoe (S.D.) Schs., 1962-63, Glenham (S.D.) Sch., 1963-65; instr. Latin Belle Fourche (S.D.) Schs., 1965-67; instr. music Dupree (S.D.) Sch., 1967-68; libr. Herreid (S.D.) Sch., 1970-74; chpt. I tchr. Timber Lake (S.D.) Schs., 1976-77; elem. tchr. Smee Schs., Wakapala, SD, 1977-88; psychol. examiner Midland (S.D.) Schs., 1988-89, Milbank (S.D.) Schs., 1989-90; ednl. diagnostician El Paso Ind. Schs., 1990—. Recipient Blue Ribbon Mobridge Art Assn., 1985. Mem. AAUW (program chmn. 1981-84), Assn. Sch. Psychologist, S.D. Counselor's Assn., Eagles (sec. 1974-76), Moose (music chmn. 1983-85), Gamma Delta Theta (sec. 1986-88). Democrat. Roman Catholic. Avocations: painting, spectator sports, reading. Office: 5900 Enterprise Ct Apt 1E El Paso TX 79912-4751

VOKIC, HEATHER MAUREEN, artist, educator; b. Euclid, Ohio, Jan. 1, 1975; d. John L. and Patricia E. Pund; m. Miroslav A. Vokic, June 21, 1997; children: Lawrence R., Alexis M., Andrew J. BS summa cum laude, Case Western Res. U., 1993; Cert. of Completion in Art Edn., Cleve. Inst. Art, 1997; MA magna cum laude, Southeastern U., Fla., 2004. Visual arts educator Ohio Dept. of Edn. Art tchr. The Andrews Sch., Willoughby, Ohio, 1997—2001; art educator Meml. Jr. H.S., Mentor, Ohio, 2002—03, Wiley Mid. Sch., University Heights, Ohio, 2003—. Exhbn. and commn., Stained Glass & Textile Work. Educator, designer Christ Luth. Ch., Willoughby, 2001—05. Recipient Silk Heros grant, Reaching Heights Found., 2004—05; Martha Holden Jennings scholar, 2005—06. Mem.: Ohio Mid. Sch. Assn. (assoc.). Lutheran. Avocations: painting, stained glass, textiles. Home: 496 E 319th St Willoughby OH 44095 Office Phone: 216-371-7270. Personal E-mail: vglassdesigns@adelphia.net. E-mail: h_vokic@chuh.org.

VOLDEN, STEPHANIE KAY, science educator; b. Viroqua, Wis., Nov. 17, 1975; d. Richard Alan and Judy Ann Volden. BS in Zoology, U. Wis., Madison, Wis., 1998. Edn. specialist Discovery Ctr. Mus., Rockford, Ill., 1998—2001; mid. sch. sci. tchr. Wilmot Grade Sch., Wilmot, 2001—. Office: Wilmot Grade Sch PO Box 68 Wilmot WI 53192 Office Phone: 262-862-6461. Personal E-mail: svolden@hotmail.com.

VOLFSON-DOUBOVA, ELENA, psychiatrist, researcher; b. St. Petersburg, Russia, Oct. 27, 1971; d. Valeriy Dmitrievich Dubov and Larisa Alexandrovna Dubova; m. Ilya Alexander Volfson, Aug. 18, 2000; children: Veronique Anna Volfson, Erik Robert Volfson. BS, St. Petersburg State Pavlov Med. U., Russia, 1992, MD, 1996; MPH, SUNY, Albany, 2000. Lic. Med. NJ, St. Petersburg Acad. Postgraduate Edn., Russia. Internal medicine resident St. Petersburg State Med. Acad. Postgraduate Edn., 1996—98; psychiatry resident U. Med. Dental NJ, Robert Wood Johnson Med. Sch. Psychiatry Residency Program, Piscataway, 2001—06; fellowship addiction psychiatry U. Med. Dental NJ, 2006—. Rschr. addiction psychiatry U. Med. Dental NJ, 2004—05; rschr. mental illness, health policy Health Policy Rsch. Ctr., New Sch. U., N.Y.C., 2000; rschr. infectious diseases epidemiology Pub. Health Rsch. Inst., N.Y.C., 2000; med. interpreter St. Petersburg City Health Dept., 1995—98. Contbr. articles various profl. jours. Grantee, Fogarty Internat. Ctr., 1999-2000; Prof. Eichvald scolarship, St. Petersburg Med. Acad. Postgraduate Edn., 1997, Edmund S. Muskie, FREEDOM Support Act Grad. Fellowship Program, US Dept. State, Bur. Cultural, Ednl. Affairs, 1998-2000. Mem.: APHA (assoc.), NJ Psychiat. Assn. (assoc.), Am. Psychiat.

Assn. (assoc.). Office: U Med Dental NJ Robert Wood Johnson Med Sch 671 Hoes Ln C 205 Piscataway NJ 08854 Home: 26110 Cherry Blossom Ct Lawrenceville NJ 08648 Office Phone: 732-235-4341. Home Fax: 732-235-4649; Office Fax: 732-235-4277. Personal E-mail: volfsone@yahoo.com. Business E-Mail: volfsoel@umdnj.edu.

VOLGMAN, ANNABELLE SANTOS, cardiologist, educator; b. Quezon City, The Philippines, Oct. 30, 1957; arrived in U.S., 1970; d. Raymundo Jocson and Purificacion Villatuya Santos; m. Keith Allen Volgman, Apr. 23, 1988; children: Robert Keith, Caroline Annabelle. BA, Barnard Coll., 1980; MD, Columbia U., 1984. Internal medicine resident U. Chgo. Hosps. and Clinics, 1984—87; cardiology fellow Northwestern Meml. Hosp., Chgo., 1987—90; asst. prof. Rush U., Chgo., 1990—2000, assoc. prof., 2001—. Cons. and spkr. in field. Contbr. articles to profl. jours. Fellow: Am. Coll. Cardiology; mem.: Am. Heart Assn. (med. chair women's legacy luncheon 2000—02, bd. dirs. 2002—, Spl. Merit award 2001—02, Women with Heart award 2005), Menomonee Club (bd. dirs. 2002—04). Avocations: running, bicycling, triathlons, reading, swimming. Office: Rush Heart Inst Ste 1159 1725 W Harrison St Chicago IL 60612 Office Phone: 312-942-6569. Business E-Mail: annabelle_volgman@rush.edu.

VOLIN, SUZANNE, retired lab administrator; b. Detroit, Sept. 27, 1921; d. Kean Leo and Mignonne Bader Cronin; m. Verlynne Vincent Volin, Sept. 8, 1945; children: Suzanna, James, Virginia, Mignonne, André, Richard, Michelle, John. BA, U. Western Ont., London, Can. With Providence Hosp., Detroit, Childrens Hosp., Detroit, Evanston (Ill.) Clin. Lab., Detroit. Fellowship grantee Sioux Falls Branch STate. Mem. AAWU (ednl. rsch. and project grantee), Am. Soc. Clin. Pathologists (cert. med. technologist). Republican. Roman Catholic. Avocations: bridge, travel, golf, tennis. Home: 1325 S 2nd Ave Sioux Falls SD 57105-1907

VOLK, KRISTIN, advertising agency executive; b. Phila., Feb. 26, 1953; d. Richard H. and Doris (Colasanti) V. BS in Biology, Tufts U., 1976; MPH, Boston U. Sch. Med., 1981. Rsch. technician Beth Israel Hosp., Boston, 1976; rsch. asst. Dana-Farber Cancer Inst., Boston, 1976-78; sr. rsch. asst. Beth Israel Hosp., Boston, 1978-81; rsch. supr. Schneider Parker Jakuc Advt., Boston, 1981-86; v.p., assoc. rsch. dir. HBM/Creamer, Boston, 1986-88, Della Femina McNamee, Boston, 1988-90; v.p., dir. rsch. Lawner Reingold Britton & Ptnrs., Boston, 1990-93; sr. v.p., dir. consumer insight group Arnold Fortuna Lawner & Cabot, Boston, 1993-95; exec. v.p., dir. consumer insight group Arnold Comm., Inc., Boston, 1995-99; exec. v.p., dir. strategic planning Deutsch Boston, 1999—2001; exec. v.p., chief mktg. officer Arnold Worldwide, N.Y.C., 2001—. Guest lectr. colls. and univs., Boston. Contbr. articles to profl. jours. Mem. Am. Assn. Advt. Agencies (account planning group com., chmn. conf. 1998), Ad Club N.Y. Home: 252 7th Ave Apt 15k New York NY 10001-7349

VOLK, PATRICIA GAY, writer, essayist; b. NYC, July 16, 1943; d. Cecil Sussman and Audrey Elaine (Morgen) Volk; m. Andrew Blitzer, Dec. 21, 1969; children— Peter Morgen, Polly Volk BFA cum laude, Syracuse U., 1964; student, Sch. Visual Arts, N.Y.C., 1968, New Sch., 1975, Columbia U., 1977-88. Art dir. Appelbaum & Curtis, N.Y.C., 1964-65, Seventeen Mag., Triangle Publs., N.Y.C., 1966-68; copywriter Doyle, Dane, Bernbach, Inc., N.Y.C., 1969-88, also sr. v.p., creative mgr., 1969-87, sr. v.p.- assoc. creative dir., 1987-88; columnist N.Y. Newsday, 1995-96; fiction instr. Yeshiva Coll. Fiction instr. Playwrights Horizon Theater Sch., Marymount Coll. Author: The Yellow Banana, 1985 (Word Beat Press Fiction Book award 1984), White Light, 1987, All it Takes, 1990, Stuffed: Adventures of a Restaurant Family, 2001; contbr. articles to N.Y. Times mag., Redbook, Allure, Mirabella, Family Circle, The New Yorker, The Atlantic, Playboy, others; contbr. short stories to popular and small press publs. and anthologies. Recipient Stephen E. Kelly award, 1983, Various Andy, Clio, Effie and One Show awards, 1970—88, Yaddo fellow, 1983, 1999, 2001—05, MacDowell fellow, 1984, 2000. Mem.: PEN, Century Assn., Author's Guild, Juliana Berner's Anglers.

VOLKERING, MARY JOE, retired special education educator; b. Covington, Ky., Mar. 13, 1936; d. Everett Thomas and Edna Mae (Bohmer) Foley; m. Jack Lawrence Volkering, Aug. 19, 1961 (dec. Jan. 11, 1989); 1 child, Tara. BA, Thomas More Coll, 1961; MEd, U. Cin., 1977. Cert. educator of mentally handicapped, Ohio, Ky. Asst. engr. AT&T Co., Cin., 1956-63; tchr. severe & profound Comprehensive Care, Covington, Ky., 1970-76; tchr. mentally retarded Riverside Good Counsel Sch., Ft. Mitchell, Ky., 1976-79; tchr. trainable handicapped Covington (Ky.) Ind. Sch., 1979-99, spl. edn. cons., 1999—2006; ret. Bd. dir. No. Ky. Assn. Retarded, Covington, 1980—; adj. prof. No. Ky. U., Highland Heights, 1987-88. Leader Girl Scout Troop, Ft. Wright, Ky., 1973. Named John Bauer Spl. Edn. Tchr. of the Yr. North Ky. Assn. Retarded, 1979, Tchr. of the Yr. G.O. Swing Sch., Covington Ind. Schs., 1986, Golden Apple Nominee Tchr., Ky. Post and Jaycees, 1988. Mem. No. Ky. Assn. Retarded (treas. 1984-86, sec. 1980-82). Democrat. Roman Catholic.

VOLKMAN, BEATRICE KRAMER, special education educator; b. New Hampton, Iowa, May 7, 1940; d. Pinkey and Bernice Beatrice (Babcock) K.; m. Dale Volkman, Feb. 10, 1961; children: Valarie Volkman Bane, Todd Kramer, Jason Dale. BS, Drake U., 1962; MS, U. South Ala., 1976, cert., 1989. Tchr. 1st grade Kelly (Iowa) Elem. Sch., 1962-63; tchr. Holy Cross Kindergarten, Mobile, Ala., 1967-76; tchr. visually impaired S.W. Regional Sch. for Deaf/Blind, Mobile, 1976-77; reading specialist St. Paul's Episc. Sch., Mobile, 1977-80; dir. learning disabled IDEALS Sch., Mobile, 1980-82; spl. edn. resource tchr. Semmes Elem. Sch., Mobile, 1984-90; arts facilitator Magnet Schs. for Creative and Performing Arts, Mobile, 1990—. Cons. South Ala. Rsch. and Insvc. Ctr., Mobile, 1988—. Bd. dirs. Children's Theatre, Pixie Playhouse, Mobile, Children's Mus., Exploreum, Mobile. Named Tchr. of Yr., Mobile County, 1986-87, Ala. Tchr. of Yr. State Dept. Edn., 1990-91, Nat. Tchr. of Yr. Washington OCSSO, 1990-91; Mobile Arts Coun. grantee, 1985, 86, Mobile Jr. League grantee, 1987, 88, 90. Mem. ASCD (program presenter), Internat. Reading Assn., Mobile Reading Assn., Ala. Reading Assn. (program presenter), Mobile County Edn. Assn., Ala. Edn. Assn. (program presenter). Republican. Lutheran. Office: Old Shell Road Elem Sch 1706 Old Shell Rd Mobile AL 36604-1324

VOLKOVA, JULIA OLEGOVNA, singer; b. Moscow, Feb. 20, 1985; Attended, Moscow State Music Sch., Faculty of Vocals, 2000. Singer t.A.T.u., 1999—. Rep. for Russia Eurovision Song Contest, 2003. Singer: (albums) 200 km/h in the Wrong Lane, 2002, Dangerous and Moving, 2005. Recipient 3rd Place for song "Ne ver', ne bojsia", 2003. Mailing: tATu Interscope Records 2220 Colorado Ave Santa Monica CA 90404

VOLKOW, NORA DOLORES, medical researcher, director; b. Mexico City, Mar. 27, 1956; m. Steven Adler. BA, Modern Am. Sch., Mexico City, 1974; MD, Nat. U. Mex., 1980; postgrad. in Psychiatry, NYU, 1980-84. Diplomate Am. Bd. Psychiatry and Neurology. Rsch. asst. Registro Nacional de Anatomia Patologica, Mexico City, 1975-76, Miles Lab. Experimental Therapeutics, Mexico City, 1977-78; intern St. Anne Psychiat. Hosp., Paris, 1979-80; residency NYU Dept. Psychiatry, 1981—84; asst. prof. U. Tex. Med. Sch., Houston, 1984-87; attending physician psychiat. unit Herman Hosp., Houston, 1985-87; assoc. scientist dept. medicine Brookhaven Nat. Lab., Upton, NY, 1987-89, assoc. chief of staff, Clinical Rsch. Ctr., 1990, dir. Nuclear Medicine, 1994—2003, dir, NIDA/DOE Imaging Ctr., 1997—2003, assoc. dir. life sciences, 1999—2003; assoc. prof. dept. psychiatry SUNY, Stony Brook, 1991—2003, assoc. dean, Sch. Med., 1997—2003; lecturer, Psychiatry Dept. Columbia Univ.; dir. Nat. Inst. on Drug Abuse (NIDA), Washington, 2003—. Mem. Adv. Com. for Minority Tng. in Psychiatry, Washington, 1991—; mem. study sect. in clin. neuroscis. NIH, Washington, 1992—; elected mem., Inst. Medicine, 2000. Co-editor: Positron Emission Tomography in Schizophrenia Research, 1991. Named Innovator of the Yr., U.S. News and World Report, 2000; recipient Premio Robins award, U. Mex., 1978, Premio Gabino Barrera award, 1981, Laughlin fellowship, Am. Coll. Psychiatry, 1984, Scanditronix scholarship, 1985, Paul C. Aebersold award, Soc. of Nuclear Medicine, 2003. Office: Nat Inst on Drug Abuse NIH Rm 5274 6001 Executive Blvd Bethesda MD 20892-9581

VOLLACK, LIA, broadcast executive; Joined Sony Pictures Entertainment, 1997, sr. v.p., 1999—2000, exec. v.p., 2000, pres. worldwide music Columbia Pictures, 2002—. Named one of top women in music, Billboard, 2005. Achievements include becoming first female theatrical sound designer on Broadway. Office: Columbia Pictures 10202 West Washington Blvd Culver City CA 90232 Office Phone: 310-244-4000. Office Fax: 310-244-2626. E-mail: lia_vollack@spe.sony.com.*

VOLLINTINE, CAROL LOUISE, art educator; m. Lonnie Allen Vollintine, Aug. 17, 1974; children: Bryan Lee, Carissa Anne. BA in Elem. Edn., Greenville Coll., 1974; MA in Ednl. Leadership/Adminstrn., U. Ill., Springfield, 2003. Tchr. Title I program Witt (Ill.) Sch. Dist. 66, 1988—97, tchr. gifted program, 1985—97; instr. youth enrichment Lincoln Land C.C., Springfield, 1992—2001; tchr. kindergarten Hillsboro (Ill.) Comty. Unit 3, 1997—2002, coord. gifted program, 2002—03; Breakaway dir. 1st Presbyn. Ch., Witt, 2003—; tchr. K-5 art Hillsboro Comty. Unit 3, 2003—. Treas. Coffeen (Ill.) Free Meth. Ch., 2001—. Mem.: Cen. Ill. Photography/Imaging Club. Free Methodist. Avocation: photography. Home: 415 N Stuart St Witt IL 62094

VOLLMAR, ALICE MARY, writer; b. Sioux City, Iowa, May 14, 1940; d. Ralph Everet Speakman and Ella Margaret Kirkholm; m. Craig Lee Vollmar, Jan. 31, 1960; children: Jill, Frank, Amy Sunderman, Margaret Mumper, Bob, Alyssa Record. Student, State U. S.D., 1960, State U. Utah, 1962; BA, Met. State U., Mpls., 1984. Freelance writer, Mpls., 1984—. Author: (travel guidebook) Minnesota-Wisconsin Travel Smart, 1999; co-author: (nonfiction) Pay Dirt, 1998, 2000, Spirits of Canyon Creek, 2001; contbg. writer: Twins Mag., 1986—98. Named Travel Writer of Yr., St. Paul Conv. and Visitors Bur., 1993; recipient Travel Media award, Minn. Office Tourism, 1990. Mem.: Penn-Lake Libr. Writers, Midwest Travel Writers Assn. (Mark Twain award 2000, 2001, 2003). Avocations: reading, skiing, travel. Office: 3750 Inglewood Ave S Minneapolis MN 55416

VOLLWEILER, CHERYL P., lawyer; b. NYC, Dec. 4, 1963; BA, Brandeis U., 1985; JD, Hofstra U., 1988. Bar: NY 1989, NJ 1989, US Dist. Ct. Ea. Dist. NY, US Dist. Ct. So. Dist. NY, US Dist. Ct. Dist. NJ. Ptnr. Wilson, Elser, Moskowitz, Edelman & Dicker LLP, NYC. Mem.: ABA, Internat. Alliance Exec. & Profl. Women (bd. dirs.), Assn. Profl. Ins. Women (bd. dirs.), NY State Bar Assn. (co-chair toxic tort com.). Office: Wilson Elser Moskowitz Edelman & Dicker LLP 150 E 42nd St 23rd Fl New York NY 10017-5639 Office Phone: 212-490-3000 ext. 2674. Office Fax: 212-490-3038. Business E-Mail: vollweilerc@wemed.com.

VOLONTS, MARGUENTE LOUISE, music educator, singer; b. Jamaica, N.Y., July 21, 1954; d. Louis John Rub and Marquerite Signe Gustafson; children: Alex, Julia. BFA in Music, magna cum laude, Ithaca Coll., NY, 1976; MA, SUNY, Stony Brook, 1979. Permanent tchg. cert. NY. Tchr. Dalton Sch., N.Y.C., 1976, Rocky Point Schs., 1977—82, William Floyd Schs., 1982—87, Riverhead Schs., 1987—. Staff mem., camp dir. Frost Valley YMCA, 1969—95, trip leader, 1974—79; musical dir., condr., treas., pres. Riverhead Faculty Cmty. Theatre, 1982—; chairperson Long Island String Festival Assn., 1985—95, condr., 1997; chairperson Suffolk County Music Educator's Assn., 1985—95, condr., 1984, 2001, Three Village Festival, 1990, 1995; vocalist Gordon Hurley Big Band, 1994—2006, Sound Symphony, North Shore Chamber Orch.; youth choir dir. Wading River Congregational Ch., 1989—2002. Home: 51 Northside Rd Wading River NY 11792 Personal E-mail: mrub2@aol.com.

VOLPE, DEBORAH L, mathematics educator; b. Williamsport, Pa., Feb. 17, 1954; d. James William and Dorothy A. Love; m. Steven A. Volpe, June 18, 1977; children: Michelle Renee, Marie Elizabeth. MS, Ohio State U. Cert. tchr. math. Ohio, tchr. Nat. Bd. Tchr. math. Westerville City Schs., Ohio, 1976—; praxis III assessor Ohio Dept. Edn., Columbus, 2002—06; adj. prof. Columbus State C.C., Otterbein Coll. Home: 4311 Wilson Rd Sunbury OH 43074 Office: Westerville S HS 303 S Otterbein Ave Westerville OH 43081 Office Phone: 614-797-6000. Office Fax: 614-797-6001. Personal E-mail: deborahlvolpe@msn.com.

VOLPE, EILEEN RAE, retired special education educator; b. Fort Morgan, Colo., Aug. 23, 1942; d. Earl Lester and Ellen Ada (Hearting) Moore; m. David P. Volpe, July 28, 1965 (div. 1980); children: David P. Jr., Christina Marie. BA, U. No. Colo., Greeley, 1964, MA, 1978. Cert. fine art tchr., learning handicapped specialist, resource specialist. 5th grade tchr. Meml. Elem. Sch., Milford, Mass., 1967-68; fine arts jr./sr. high tchr. Nipmuc Regional Jr. Sr. H.S., Mendon, Mass., 1968-69; substitute tchr. K-12 Greeley (Colo.) Dist. 6 Schs., 1976—79; spl. edn. tchr. Saugus (Calif.) H.S., 1979—98, Valencia (Calif.) H.S., 1998—2003; ret., 2003; substitute tchr. grades K-12 Dist. 6, 2005—. Publicity dir. Sacred Heart Ch. Sch., Milford, Mass., 1974-75, float coord. bicentennial parade, 1975; substitute tchr. K-12 Dist. 6 Sch., Greeley, Colo., 2005-. Author: (poetry) Seasons to Come, 1994, Best Poems of 1997, 04, The Other Side of Midnight, 1997, Best of 2001 Poems, Best Poems and Poets of 2003, Best of 2005 Poems; contbr. to Best of Millennium Poetry, 1999-2000, Best of 2002 Poems, Best Poems of 2004, Labours of Love, 2006, Best of 2006 Poems. Mem. Calif. Tchr. Assn., Coun. for Exceptional Children, DAR, Phi Delta Kappa, Kappa Delta Pi. Republican. Avocations: arts and crafts, photography, travel, doll collecting and creation. Personal E-mail: purplewriter42@comcast.net.

VOLPE, KATHY A., elementary school educator, consultant; b. Chgo., June 5, 1951; d. John P. and Irene F. King; m. Martin F. Volpe, June 21, 1975; 1 child, John Patrick; 1 child, Mary Megan. BS in Edn., Loyola U., Chgo., 1973; MEd, Benedictine U., 1999. Cert. reading specialist Ill. Asst. buyer Marshall Field & Co., Chgo., 1971—74; tchr. Chgo. Pub. Schs., Chgo., 1974—77, Cmty. Unit Sch. Dist., Westmont, Ill., 1977—99, reading specialist, 1999—. Sec. troop governing com. Boy Scouts Am., Naperville, Ill., 1996—2002; religious edn. coord. St. Margaret Mary Parish, Naperville, 1986—98, chmn. religious edn. commn., 1988—91; reading cons. All Saints Cath. Acad., Naperville, 2005; v.p. bd. dirs. Ill. br. Internat. Dyslexia Assn., Glen Ellyn, Ill., 2005—. Mem.: Ill. Reading Assn., Internat. Reading Assn. Office: Cmty Unit Sch Dist 201 200 N Linden Westmont IL 60559 Office Phone: 630-468-8088. Business E-Mail: kvolpe@cusd201.org.

VOLZ, ANNABELLE WEKAR, learning disabilities educator, consultant; b. Niagara Falls, N.Y., May 24, 1926; d. Fred Wekar and Margaret Eleanor (McGillivray) Wekar Treadwell; m. William Mount Volz, May 9, 1958; children: Amy D., William M. Jr. BA, Seton Hill Coll., 1948; MS in Elem. Edn., N.Y. State Univ. Coll., 1956. Cert. learning disabilities cons. N.J. Georgian Ct. Coll., 1981. Lab. technician Moore Bus. Forms Inc., Niagara Falls, 1948-50, Niagara Falls Health Dept., 1950-53; tchr. Niagara Falls Bd. Edn., 1953-56, Am. Dependent Sch., Ashiya, Japan, 1956-58, Mehlville Bd. Edn., St. Louis County, Mo., 1968-70, U.S. Dependent Schs. European Theatre, Weisbaden, Fed. Republic of Germany, 1970-74; para-profl. Medford (N.J.) Bd. Edn., 1978-81; learning disabilities tchr., cons. Southampton Bd. Edn., Vincentown, N.J., 1981-91. Mem. Womens Fin. Info. Program, Burlington County, 1990-91; vol. N.C. Bapt. Hosp., 2000—. Mem. LWV (sec. 1994-96, mem. chair 199 6-99, voter's guide chair 1996, 98, LWV Piedmont chpt.), AAUW (N.J. chpt. Medford chpt. 1982-91, N.C. Winston Salem chpt. 1992—, treas. 1993-2000, scholarship com. 2006), Nat. Ret. Edn. Assn., N.J. Ret. Edn. Assn., Assn. Learning Cons., Mil. Officers Assn. Am. (bd. dirs. Winston Salem chpt. 2005—, membership chmn. 2005—), Seton Hill Alumnae Assn., Kappa Delta Pi.

VOM BAUR, DAPHNE DE BLOIS, artist; d. Francis Trowbridge vom Baur and Carolyn Bartlett Laskey; m. David Verner Hamilton, Sept. 3, 1973; children: Zoe Hamilton-vom Baur, Nerissa Alexandra Hamilton-vom Baur. BFA, Boston U., 1968. Fellow Atlantic Ctr. for Arts, New Smyrna Beach, Fla., 1986; mem. acquisitions com. S.C. Arts Commn., Columbia, SC, 1989—91. Vis. artist Susquehanna Studio, Union Dale, Pa., 1985—86. Exhbn., The Frye Mus., Seattle, 2002. Recipient Purchase award, S.C. State Art Collection, 1986. Mem.: Cosmos Club (mem. arts coun. 2001—05). Avocations: cross country skiing, swimming, opera, horses, especially the Connemara mural painting, painting. Office: Verner Gallery LLC 1 West Washington St PO Box2270 Middleburg VA 20118 Office Phone: 540-687-6875. Business E-Mail: vombaur@earthlink.net.

VON BAILLOU, ASTRID, executive search consultant; b. Neutitschein, Czech Republic, Mar. 2, 1944; d. Karl von Baillou and Angela Stillfried; m. Dennis Hallam Bigelow, Oct. 21, 1967 (div. Oct. 1994). BA in English, Sweet Briar Coll., 1965. Creative dir. Freeman Advt., Washington, 1969-72; on-air reporter, prodr. PBS, BBC, London Weekend TV, N.Y.C., 1972-80; v.p. Sci. Program Group TV, Washington, 1980-82; pres. Cullen & Casey, N.Y.C., 1982-86; sr. v.p. Ruder Finn, N.Y.C., 1986-87; pres. Baillou Internat., N.Y.C., 1988-94; prin., mgmt. dir. Kinser & Assocs., N.Y.C., 1994-2000; ptnr. Kinser & Baillou, N.Y.C., 2000—. Home: 1245 Park Ave Apt 19F New York NY 10128-1740 Office Phone: 212-534-2161. Business E-Mail: search@kinserbaillou.com.

VON BRANDENSTEIN, PATRIZIA, production designer; Prodn. designer The Mirisch Agy., L.A., 1978—. Prodn. designer: (films) Heartland, 1979, Breaking Away, 1979, Ragtime, 1981 (Academy award nomination best art direction 1981), Silkwood, 1983, Amadeus, 1984 (Academy award best art direction 1984), A Chorus Line, 1985, The Money Pit, 1986, No Mercy, 1987, The Untouchables, 1987 (Academy award nomination best art direction 1987), Working Girl, 1988, The Lemon Sisters, 1990, Postcards From the Edge, 1990, Billy Bathgate, 1992, Sneakers, 1992, Leap of Faith, 1993, Six Degrees of Separation, 1993, The Quick and the Dead, 1995, Just Cause, 1995, The People vs. Larry Flynt, 1996, A Simple Plan, 1998, Man on the Moon, 1999, Shaft, 2000, It Runs in the Family, 2002, The Emperor's Club, 2002, Ice Harvest, 2006, All the King's Men, 2006, Goya's Ghosts, 2006; costume designer: (films) Between the Lines, 1977, Saturday Night Fever, 1977, A Little Sex, 1982.

VON BRAUNSBERG, MARY JANE, clinical psychologist; b. N.Y.C. d. Thomas Charles and Margaret Mildred (Bradley) V.; m. Charles A. Gealish; children: Justin, Jeffrey, Luke, Sheridan, Jenny, Joshua, Maria, Amy, Bryon, Jordan. BS, Syracuse U., 1985, MS, 1990, PhD, 1993. Licensed Clin. Psychologist, N.Y. State. Clin. psychologist Hutchings Psychiatric Ctr., Syracuse, N.Y., 1991—; clin. dir. Dissociative Disorders Diagnostic & Treatment Ctr., Syracuse, 1998—. Chairperson Ctr. Human Policy, Syracuse, 1978-80. Co-Author: Amy Maura, 1979, Hackett McGee, 1980, The Sneely Mouthed Snerds, 1980. Mem. Am. Psychological Assn., Internat. Soc. Study of Dissociative Disorders.

VON DECK, MERCEDES DINA, orthopedist, surgeon; b. Iowa City, Iowa, Sept. 26, 1961; d. Marvin von Deck and Margaret Ann Fairbanks; m. Robert Michael Bojar, June 9, 1996; children: Alana Rachel, Rebecca Anna, Michelle Elana. BA, Wash. U., 1983; MD, Harvard Med. Sch., 1992. Diplomate Am. Bd. Orthopedic Surgeons, 1999. Orthopedic surgeon Cambridge Health Alliance, Mass., 1997—. Home: 47 Montclair Rd Waban MA 02468 Office: Cambridge Health Alliance 1493 Cambridge St Cambridge MA 02139

VONDERHAAR, BARBARA K., medical researcher; Grad., Clarke Coll., Dubuque, Iowa, 1965; PhD, U. Wis., Madison. Postdoctoral training in mammary gland biology NIH; now chief Mammary Biology and Tumorigenesis Lab. Ctr. Cancer Rsch., Nat. Cancer Inst., head Molecular and Cellular Endocrinology Sect., Mammary Biology and Tumorigenesis Lab.; chair Breast and Gynecologic Malignancies Faculty Nat. Cancer Inst.; co-chair Intramural Program for Rsch. on Women's Health NIH. Recipient Award for Excellence in Mentoring, Bethesda Assn. for Women in Sci., 2000, Helen F. Cserr Award for outstanding woman scientist, Mt. Desert Island Biol. Laboratories, 2004. Office: Mammary Biology and Tumorigenesis Lab Ctr Cancer Rsch 37 Convent Dr Bldg 37 Rm 1106A1 Bethesda MD 20892-4254 Office Phone: 301-435-7587. Office Fax: 301-402-0711. E-mail: bv10w@nih.gov.

VON DOHLEN, ELIZABETH K., secondary school educator; b. Houston, Tex., Sept. 26, 1943; d. Arthur Paul and France Elizabeth Kelley; m. Donald R. von Dohlen, Jr., Aug. 4, 1967; children: Sarah Alice von Dohlen Ojeda, Donald R. III. BA, U. St. Thomas, Houston, Tex., 1966. Lab. asst. Dental Sch. U. Tex., Houston, 1966—67; tchr. Dallas (Tex.) Ind. Sch. Dist., 1968—71; bookkeeper Titsch-Goettinger Dept. Store, Dallas, 1971—72; editor Accelerated Christian Edn., Lewisville, Tex., 1972—75; tchr., asst. prin. Pasadena (Tex.) Christian Sch., 1977—82; tchr. Bethel Christian Sch., Arlington, Tex., 1985—90; tchr. The Vestride Sch. Acad. Hall, Houston, 1990—93, N.E. Christian Acad., Kingwood, Tex., 1994—. Precinct judge Rep. Party, Arlington, Tex., 1983. Mem.: Daus. of King. Republican. Episc. Avocations: piano, organ, crossword puzzles, reading, aerobics. Office: Northeast Christian Acad 1711 Hamblen Rd Kingwood TX 77339

VONDRAK, ROBERTA G., counselor; b. Chgo., Sept. 7, 1951; d. Robert G. Gruntorad and Lorraine A. Hanopulus; m. Ross G. Vondrak, June 26, 1976; children: Sandra, Christine. AA, MacCormac Jr. Coll., Chgo., 1971; BS in Psychology, Elmhurst Coll., Ill., 1992; MA in Counseling Psychology, St. Xavier U., Chgo., 1997. Lic. counseling profl. Ill. Dept. Profl. Regulation, CADC. Project coord. Sch. Dist. 105, Ill., 1996—97; residential therapist City Girls, Chgo., 1998; substance abuse assessment counselor Chgo. Christian Indsl. League, 1999—2000; assessment counselor, supr. Meier Clinics, Wheaton, Ill., 1998—99, 2000—01, day program therapist, 2003—04, outpatient therapist, 2000—05, facilitator, 2004—05; outpatient therapist Heritage Counseling Ctr., Plainfield, Ill., 2005—. 12-step facilitator Meier Clinics, Wheaton, Ill., 2004—; parenting class facilitator Lyons Township Task Force, La Grange, Ill. Contbr. articles to profl. jours. Mem. Brookfield Jaycees, Ill., 1982—85; mem. caucus com. Sch. Dist. 204, La Grange, Ill., 1994—96. Mem.: Ill. Mental Health Counseling Assn., Ill. Counseling Assn., Am. Assn. Christian Counselors. Avocations: reading, walking, writing, travel. Home: 5707 S Ashland Ave Countryside IL 60525 Office Phone: 815-577-8970 x 204. Personal E-mail: rgvondrak@sbcglobal.net.

VONDRAN, JANET ELISE, physician; b. Wynne, Ark., July 4, 1951; d. Charles Aaron and Joyce Jean (Edwards) Proctor; children: Tony, Michael. MD, East Tenn. State U., JohnsonCity, 1987. Diplomate Am. Bd. Neurology and Psychiatry for Geriactrics, Am. Bd. Forensic Examiners, Am. Coll. Forensic Examiners. Resident U. Va., Charlottesville, 1987-91; pvt. practice Lewisburg, W.Va., 1991-95, Beckley, W.Va., 1991-95; med. dir. Jefferson Place Recovery, Lewisburg, 1993-94, Raleigh Gen. Hosp., Beckley, 1991-95, Harrison Meml. Hosp., Bremerton, Wash., 1995—. Mem. Am. Psychiat. Assn., Wash. State Psychiat. Assn., Kitsap County Med. Soc. Home: 9916 Dishman Rd NW Bremerton WA 98312-9105 Office: Harrison Meml Hosp 2520 Cherry Ave Bremerton WA 98310-4270

VONES, CYNTHIA LOUISE, art educator; b. Yukon, Fla., Feb. 13, 1947; d. Clinton Warren and Rose Marie Jones; 1 child, Patrick Scott Tyree. Student, U. Va., 1968; BS in Secondary Art Edn., Radford U., 1969, MS in Secondary Art Edn., 1974; cert. advanced studies Hollins U., 1991. Cert. profl. tchr. Va. Art tchr. Roanoke (Va.) City Schs., 1970—77, 1984—; prodn. and traffic mgr. Groseclose and Poindexter Advt., Roanoke, 1978; comml. and fine art instr. Va. Western C.C., Roanoke, 1978—79; freelance comml. artist, 1979—81; aid to dependent children case worker Dept. Social Svcs., Roanoke, 1981—84. Lectr., instr. art adult continuing edn. Va. Western C.C., Roanoke, 1979—82. Mem.: Arts Coun. of the Blue Ridge, Va. Art Edn. Assn., Nat. Art Edn. Assn. Avocations: art, gardening, horseback riding, hiking. Home: 8860 Willow Branch Rd Boones Mill VA 24065 Office: Roanoke City Schs Roanoke VA

VON ESCHEN, LISA A., lawyer; BA, Coll. of William and Mary, 1986; JD, NYU, 1991. Bar: Calif. 1991. Mem. bd. dirs. Western Law Ctr. for Disability Rights. Mem.: Women Lawyers Assn. L.A., Assn. Bus. Trial Lawyers, L.A. County Bar Assn. (vol. Pro Bono Domestic Violence Project, mem. labor and employment sect.). Office: Latham and Watkins LLP 633 W Fifth St Ste 4000 Los Angeles CA 90071

VON FETTWEIS, YVONNE CACHÉ, archivist, historian; b. L.A., Nov. 28, 1935; d. Boyd Eugene and Georgette Louisa (Tilmann) Adams; m. Maurice Lee Caché, Jan. 8, 1955 (div. 1962); children: Maurice C.B. II, Michele-Yvonne (Mrs. Vernon Young Sr.); m. Rolland Phillip von Fettweis, July 22, 1967. BA, Wagner Coll., 1954; postgrad, Am. U., 1973, Bentley Coll., 1981. Legal sec., asst. Judge, Davis, Stern, Orfinger & Tindall, Daytona Beach, Fla., 1961-66; head rec. sect., bd. dirs. 1st Ch. Christ Scientist, Boston, 1969-71, rsch. assoc., 1971-72, adminstrv. archivist, 1972-78, sr. assoc. archivist, 1979-84, records adminstr., 1984-91, div. mgr. records mgmt./orgnl. archives, 1991-92, divsn. mgr. ch. history, 1992—, divsn. mgr. ch. history and healing ministry, 1995; divsn. mgr. ch. history, 1995-96; ch. historian 1st Ch. Christ Scientist, Boston, 1996—. Cons. Christian Sci. Bd. Dirs., 1999—, pres. of Mother Ch., 2002-; mem. Religious Pub. Rels. Coun. Co-author: Mary Baker Eddy: A Lifetime of Healing, 1996, Mary Baker Eddy: Christian Healer, 1997, The New Woman and the New Church: The Lincoln Women, 2001. Trustee Ch. Hist. Trust, 1995—; exec. sec. Volusia County Goldwater campaign, Daytona Beach, 1964; mem. Christian Sci. Bd. Lectureship, 1998. Mem. Soc. Am. Archivists (editor The Archival Spirit), Automated Records and Techniques Task Force, Am. Mgmt. Assn., Orgn. Am. Historians, Ctr. for Study Presidency, Religious Pub. Rels. Coun., New Eng. Archivists, Assn. Records Mgrs. and Adminstrs. (bd. dirs. 1983—), Assn. Coll. and Rsch. Librs., Bay State Hist. League, Order Ea. Star, Order Rainbow (bd. dirs. 1972-77). Republican. Christian Scientist. Home: 147 Bosarvey Dr Ormond Beach FL 32176-6662

VON FRAUNHOFER-KOSINSKI, KATHERINA, bank executive, advertising executive; b. NYC; m. Jerzy Kosinski, Feb. 15, 1987 (dec. May 3, 1991). Student, St. Joseph's Convent, London, Clark's Coll. Various positions Robert W. Orr & Assocs., N.Y.C.; with traffic dept. Compton Advt., Inc., N.Y.C., 1956-63; acct. exec. J. Walter Thompson Co., N.Y.C., 1963-69; product mgr. Natural Wonder line Revlon Co., N.Y., 1969-71; pres. Scientia Factum, Inc., N.Y.C., 1971—, Polish Am. Resources Corp., N.Y.C., 1992—2000, pres., CEO, 1992—2002. Chmn. Am. Bank in Poland, 1990—2001. Co-founder Westchester Sports Club. Assoc. fellow Timothy Dwight Coll./Yale U., 1997—. Avocations: skiing, horse/polo, swimming, photography. Office: 60 W 57th St New York NY 10019-3909 Office Phone: 212-246-0128. Personal E-mail: sfi440@aol.com.

VON FRIEDERICHS-FITZWATER, MARLENE MARIE, researcher; b. Beatrice, Nebr., July 14, 1939; d. Paul M. and Velma B. (von Friederichs) Fitzwater; children: Richard Nielson, Kevin T. Young, James L. Nielson, Paul M. Nielson. BS, Westminster Coll., 1981; MA, U. Nebr., Omaha, 1981; PhD, U. Utah, 1987; cert. in death edn., Temple U., 1982. Various pub. rels., writing and editing positions, 1957-78; teaching fellow in comm. U. Nebr., Omaha, 1978-83, U. Utah, Salt Lake City, 1978-83; asst. prof. mass comm. U. So. Colo., Pueblo, 1983-85; prof. comm. studies Calif. State U., Sacramento, 1985—, chair comm. studies, 1996-2000; assoc. clin. prof. family practice Sch. Medicine U. Calif., Davis, 1987—, asst. adj. prof. internal medicine, 2003—, adj. asst. prof. hematology and oncology, 2005—; dir., outreach rsch. and edn. US Davis Cancer Ctr., 2005—. Condr. workshops on communication skills for health care profls. Bergan Mercy Hosp., Omaha, 1980-81, Mercy Care Ctr., Omaha, 1980-81, Am. Cancer Soc., 1981-82, Hospice of Salt Lake, Utah, 1981-82; condr. seminars, workshops and courses on health communication, death and dying, patient edn. and compliance, other related topics, 1983—; presenter in health communication various profl. orgn. meetings and confs., 1981—; dir., co-founder The Health Communication Rsch. Inst., Sacramento, 1988—. Contbr. articles to profl. jours. Trainer United Way, Sacramento, project mgr., 1986—; pres. bd. dirs. Hospice Care Sacramento, Inc., 1986-87; instr. vol. tng. program Hospice Consortium Sacramento; hospice vol. 1980—. Recipient Lifetime Achievement award Sacramento Pub. Rels. Assn., also numerous state, regional and nat. awards for writing, editing, publ. design and photography. Fellow Am. Acad. on Physician & Patient; mem. Internat. Communication Assn. (health communication div., newsletter editor 1987-89, sec. 1989-91), AAUP, Assn. Behavioral Scis. and Med. Edn., Assn. Women in Sci., Pub. Rels. Soc. Am. (bd. dirs. Calif. Capital chpt. 1987-91), Soc. Tchrs. Family Medicine, Soc. Health Care Pub. Rels. and Mktg. No. Calif. Home: 5020 Hackberry Ln Sacramento CA 95841-4765 Office: Calif State U Communication Studies Dept 6000 J St Sacramento CA 95819-2605 Address: 3550 Watt Ave Ste 140 Sacramento CA 95821 Office Phone: 916-734-8810. E-mail: fitzm@heri.com.

VON FURSTENBERG, BETSY, actress, writer; b. Neiheim Heusen, Germany, Aug. 16, 1931; d. Count Franz-Egon and Elizabeth (Johnson) von F.; m. Guy Vincent de la Maisoneuve (div.); 2 children.; m. John J. Reynolds, Mar. 26, 1984. Attended Miss Hewitt's Classes, N.Y. Tutoring Sch.; prepared for stage with Sanford Meisner at Neighborhood Playhouse. Made Broadway stage debut in Second Threshold, N.Y., 1951; appeared in Dear Barbarians, 1952, Oh Men Oh Women, 1954, The Chalk Garden, 1955, Child of Fortune, 1956, Nature's Way, 1957, Much Ado About Nothing, 1959, Mary Mary, 1965, Paisley Convertible, 1967, Avanti, 1968, The Gingerbread Lady, 1970 (toured 1971), Absurd Person Singular, 1976; off Broadway appearances include For Love or Money, 1951; toured in Petrified Forest, Jason and Second Man, 1952; appeared in Josephine, 1953; subsequently toured, 1955; What Every Woman Knows, 1955, The Making of Moo, 1958 (toured 1958), Say Darling, 1959, Wonderful Town, 1959, Season of Choice, 1959, Beyond Desire, 1967, Private Lives, 1968, Does Anyone Here Do the Peabody, 1976; appeared in Along Came a Spider, Theatre in the Park, N.Y.C., 1985; appeared in film Women Without Names, 1950; TV appearances include Robert Montgomery Show, Ed Sullivan Show, Alfred Hitchcock Presents, One Step Beyond, The Mike Wallace Show, Johnny Carson Show, Omnibus, Theatre of the Week, The Secret Storm, As the World Turns, Movie of the Week, Your Money or Your Wife, Another World; writer syndicated column More Than Beauty; contbr. articles to newspapers and mags. including N.Y. Times Sunday Arts and Leisure, Saturday Rev. of Literature, People, Good Housekeeping, Art News, Pan Am Travel; co-author: (novel) Mirror, Mirror, 1988; author, illustrator Grandmothers Surprise, 2004. Avocations: tennis, painting, photography.

VON FURSTENBERG, DIANE, fashion designer, writer, entrepreneur; b. Brussels, Dec. 31, 1946; arrived in US, 1969, naturalized, 2002; d. Leon L. and Liliane L. (Nahmias) Halfin; m. Eduard Egon von Furstenberg, July 16, 1969 (div. 1983); children: Alexandre, Tatiana; m. Barry Diller, Feb. 2, 2001; m. Barry Diller, Feb. 2, 2001. Student, U. Madrid, 1965-66, U. Geneva, 1966-68. Founder, pres. Diane von Furstenberg Studio, L.P., N.Y.C., 1970—; pres. Diane von Furstenberg Ltd., N.Y.C.; founder Salvy, Paris, 1985. Pioneer TV shopping with creative and live on-air selling Silk Assets collection, 1992; returns to retail as designer DIANE line of signature dresses, including the wrap, 1997. Author: Diane Von Furstenberg's Book of Beauty, 1977; Beds, 1991, The Bath, 1993, The Table, 1996, DIANE: A Signature Life, 1998; contbg. editor Vanity Fair mag., 1993; exec. prodr.: (films) Forty Shades of Blue, 2005, Andy Warhol: A Documentary Film, 2006. Recipient Ellis Island Medal of Honor, 1986. Mem.: Coun. of Fashion Designers of Am. (pres. 2006—).*

VON GENCSY, EVA, dancer, choreographer, educator; b. Csongrad, Hungary, Mar. 11, 1924; arrived in Can., 1948; d. Joseph and Valery Von G.; m. John S. Murray, May 13, 1957 (div. 1967). Student V.G. Troyanoff, Russian Ballet Acad., Budapest, Hungary, 1934-41, Szineszegyesuleti Iskola Theatre Sch., 1941-44; diploma, Royal Acad. Dance, London, 1953. Solo debut Salzburg (Austria) Landes Theatre, 1945-47; soloist Royal Winnipeg (Can.) Ballet, 1948-53; with Ballets Chiriaeff TV Co. (now Les Grands Ballet Canadiens), 1953-57, TV performer, 1957-70. Jazz instr. Banff Sch. Fine Arts, 1962-75; founder, dir. jazz workshop Saidye Bronfman Ctr., Montreal, Que., Can., 1965-72; with Les Grands Ballets Canadiens, 1962-72; co-founder, artistic dir., resident choreographer Les Ballets Jazz de Montreal Sch. and Co., 1972-79; guest tchr. Can., U.S.A., Europe, Malta, Marrocco, 1979-97; choreographer; adjudicator dance festivals. Past bd. dirs. Dance in Can. Recipient Best Dancer award French TV, 1967, Queen's medal, 1977, Lifetime Achievement award U. Que., Montreal, 1997, Rossetti Lifetime Achievement award, 1997. Mem.: Equity (hon.). Achievements include having a documentary film about her career, Eva, produced for television by Mireille Dansereau. Home: Apt 508 3650 Rue de la Montagne Montreal PQ Canada H3G 2A8 E-mail: louise.schratz@mcgill.ca.

VON GIZYCKI, ALKISTIS ROMANOFF, research scientist, writer; b. Famagusta, Cyprus; arrived in U.S., 1967; d. Costas and Evangelia Lillian Victoria Kyprianou; m. Nicholas Romanoff, 1977 (dec.); m. Walter Von Gizycki, Sept. 19, 1981 (div. Dec. 1992); children: Bernard, Elsa. BA with honors, RMWC, Lynchburg, Va., 1967-71; MA in Psychology, New Sch. U., 1976-78. Educator, counselor Bilingual Bd. Edn., Nicosia, Cyprus, 1971-86; bus. devel. Bucci Trading Co., Nicosia, Cyprus, 1981-86; rschr., writer freelance, 1986—. Officer ch. bd. Fifth Ave. Presbyn. Ch. 1979—; vol. ch. and civic leader. Fulbright grantee; recipient Gen. Excellence award, valedictorian Am. Acad., Nicosia, Cyprus, 1967, Vol. award J.P. Morgan Chase Found., 1995, Outstanding Performance award J.P. Morgan Chase, 1997. Mem. NOW, AAUW, NY Acad. Sci. (assoc.), Am. Psychol. Assn. Avocations: theater, films, reading, music, ballet.

VON HAKE, MARGARET JOAN, librarian; b. Santa Monica, Calif., Oct. 27, 1933; d. Carl August and Inez Garnet (Johnson) von Hake. BA, La Sierra Coll., 1955; MS in Library Sci., U. So. Calif., 1963. Tchr. Newbury Park (Calif.) Acad., 1955-60, librarian, 1957-60; circulation librarian Columbia Union Coll., Takoma Park, Md., 1962—67, library dir., 1967—, assoc. prof., 1990—2005, prof., 2005—. Mem. ALA, Md. Libr. Assn., Congress of Acad. Libr. Dirs. of Md. (pres. 1999-2000), Md. Ind. Coll.and Univ. Assn. Libr. Dirs. Round Table (chair 1996-98), Assn. Seventh Day Adventist Librs. (newsletter editor 1981-83, pres. 1989-90), Adventist Libr. Info. Cooperative Council (chair 2005—), Sligo Federated Music Club (pres. 1988-89, yearbook co-editor 2000—). Republican. Office: Columbia Union Coll 7600 Flower Ave Takoma Park MD 20912-7796 Office Phone: 301-891-4219.

VONHERRLICH, PHYLLIS HERRICK, academic administrator; d. Phillip Carl and Elisabeth Lingberg Herrick; children: Charles Phillip children: Kaarin Elien. Cert. in Maine Studies, U. Maine, Orono, 2001, B in Univ. Studies, 2002. Adminstrv. staff Am. Heart Assn., Greater Boston Divsn., Brookline, Mass., 1972—77, Mass. Med. Soc., Waltham, 1983—88, Brookline (Mass.) Sch. Com., 1983—88, U. Maine Sys., Bangor, 1988—. Author: (monograph, web site) Augusta (Maine) Women's History Trail. Mem. Augusta (Maine) Hist. Preservation Commn. Mem.: Norlands Living History Mus., Friends of the Maine State Mus., Old Ft. Western, Kennebec Hist. Soc. (mem. hist. preservation com. 2002—03), Alpha Sigma Lambda. Democrat. Avocations: historical research on 19th century Maine women, writing, reading, walking, needlecrafts. Office: Univ So Maine Muskie Sch 295 Water St Augusta ME 04330 E-mail: phyllis.vonherrlich@maine.gov.

VON HOLT, LAEL POWERS, retired psychotherapist, psychiatric social worker; b. Boston, Apr. 9, 1927; d. Merritt Adams and Rea Francisca (Hunt) Powers; m. Henry William Von Holt, Jr., Sept. 18, 1954; children: Gardner, Dudley, Edward. BA, U. Mass., 1950; MSW, U. Mo., 1972, postgrad., 1978; postgrad. Menninger Found., Topeka, 1977-85. Diplomate Bd. Clin. Social Work, Internat. Acad. of Behavioral Medicine Counseling and Psychotherapy; lic. clin. social worker, Mo. Psychiat. social worker N.Y. Dept. Mental Hygiene, Wingdale, 1950-51, Mass. Dept. Mental Health, Worcester, 1951-54; instr., social worker U. Oreg., Eugene, 1954-59; psychiat. social worker Mo. Dept. Mental Health, Fulton State Hosp., 1973-81, Columbia (Mo.) Regional Hosp. Psychiat. Svcs., Inc., 1977-82, Family Mental Health Ctr., Jefferson City, Mo., 1982-91, 99-2001; ret., 2001; mental health cons. Midland Counseling Ctrs./Focus, Inc., Hermann, Mo., 1991-99; field instr. U. Mo., Columbia, 1988. Bd. dirs. PTA, 1970-74, 77-78; mem. health com. Boone County Cmty. Svcs. Coun., 1975-76; vol. Meals on Wheels, 1972-73, 76-79; den mother Boy Scouts Am., 1968-69, 71-72; mem. by-laws com. Springdale Neighborhood Assn., 1977. Named Social Worker of Yr. Cen. Mo., 1986. Mem. Nat. Assn. Social Workers, Acad. Cert. Social Workers, LWV (state bd. dirs. 1995—, city coun. observer 1976-82, chmn. local action com. 1979-80, sec. 1974-77, chmn. Observer Corps 1981-83, chmn. com. mental health 1988-89, chair health com. 1991-94, co-pres. 1992-94, state v.p. 1997—), Stephens Coll. Faculty Wives (pres. 1979-80, 89-90, 1997—), Kappa Kappa Gamma. Republican. Methodist. Home: 378 Crown Pt Columbia MO 65203-2242

VON HUTTEN, GAIA THERESA, performing company executive, choreographer, educator; b. Pretoria, South Africa, Sept. 11, 1953; arrived in U.S., 1985; d. Hubert Cornelus Herzog Hutten and Theresa M.J. Vermeulen; 1 child, Theresa Van Niekerk. Associates, Royal Acad. Dancing, London, 1986; BA in Psychology, U. Pretoria, South Africa. Diplomate Corps S. Africa. Ballerina dancer PACT Ballet, Johnannesburg, Calif., 1970—74; dir. Pro Press Fundraising, Bramley, South Africa, 1979—80; sr. info. and accompanying offcl. Dept. Fgn. Affairs and Info., Pretoria, South Africa, 1980. Office: Ballet and Arts Acad 4 Son Morell Laguna Niguel CA 92677-8602

VON KAENEL, MICHELLE LISA, elementary school educator; b. Elyria, Ohio, Feb. 27, 1966; d. Burton and Ann Bursley; m. Joseph Arthur Von Kaenel, July 15, 1995; 1 child, Christian David. MusB, U. Akron, Ohio, 1989; M in Counseling, Ohio U., Athens, 1998. Cert. tchr. Ohio. Vocal music tchr. Oberlin (Ohio) Schs., 1989—93, Amherst Schs., Amherst, Ohio, 1993—. Group leader Weight Watchers, Sheffield Village, Ohio, 1991—. Singer: Wind Jammers Big Band. Opera scholar, U. Akron, 1988. Office: Amherst Exempted City Schs Forest St Amherst OH 44001 Office Phone: 440-988-4441.

VON KLAN, LAURENE, museum administrator; b. NY; BS in Econ., Williams Coll.; MS in Internat. Rels., Univ. Chgo. Dir. devel. Nature Conservancy, Ill. chpt., 1986—92; exec. dir. Friends of Chgo. River, 1992—2005; pres., CEO Peggy Notebaert Nature Mus., 2005—. Founding mem. Coalition to Restore Urban Waters (nat. steering com.); bd. dir. River Network; steering com. Chgo. Wilderness. Founding mem., nat. steering com Coalition to Restore Urban Waters (CRUW); citizen mem. Ill. River Coordinating Coun., 1998—; bd. dir. Nat. River Network, 2002—. Named one of 100 Most Influential Women, Crain's Chgo. Bus., 2004; recipient Protector of Environment award, Chgo. Audubon, 2003. Office: Notebaert Nature Mus 2430 N Cannon Dr Chicago IL 60614 Office Phone: 773-755-5100.

VON MOSCH, WANDA GAIL, middle school educator; b. Richmond, Va., Jan. 21, 1952; d. Jesse James, Sr. and Thelma Arleen (Bruce) Perdue; m. Carl Allan Von Mosch, June 24, 1978; children: Carl Allan Jr., Sarah Ashley, Katie Danielle. BS, Longwood Coll., 1974; MS in Ednl. Leadership, Old Dominion U., 2005. Tchr. pub. schs. City of Hampton, Va., 1974-77, City of Virginia Beach, Va., 1977—. Mem., planning coun., mem. faculty coun. Gt. Neck Mid. Sch., coord. ptnrs. edn., comm. liaison; coord., forensics coach Odyssey of Mind, Gt. Neck, 1997—98; adj. instr. career switcher program Old Dominion U. Sunday sch. tchr. Va. Marine Sci. Mus., Virginia Beach, 1983—, Bethel Bible grad., tchr., 1990—; participant Malcolm Baldridge TQM procedure U.S. Congress for Ind. Learning; mem. PTA; mem. adminstrv. bd. Francis Asbury United Meth. Ch., Virginia Beach, 1986—, supt., 1991. Named Tchr. of the Yr., Walmart, 2002, Gt. Neck, 2002; recipient PTA award for Disting. Svc., 1990. Mem.: NEA, Virginia Beach Tchr. Forum, Virginia Beach Reading Coun., Va. Math. League, Va. Reading Coun., Virginia Beach Edn. Assn., Va. Edn. Assn. Republican. Avocations: reading, cooking, music, board games, golf. Office: Great Neck Middle Sch North Great Neck Rd Virginia Beach VA 23454-1112

VON PRINCE, KILULU MAGDALENE, retired occupational therapist, sculptor; b. Bumbuli, Lushoto, Tanzania, Jan. 9, 1929; arrived in U.S., 1949; d. Tom Adalbert and Juliane (Martini). BA in Occupl. Therapy, San Jose State U., 1958, MS in Occupl. Therapy, 1972; EdD, U. So. Calif., 1980; doctorate in Higher Edn., 1978. Registered occupl. therapist; cert. work evaluator, work adjustment specialist. Commd. 2d lt. U.S. Army, 1959, advanced through grades to lt. col., staff asst. Denver, 1959-62; hand rehab. asst., hand therapy Walter Reed Army Med. Ctr., 1962-65; hand rehab. asst. occupl. therapist 97th Gen. Hosp., U.S. Army, Frankfurt, Germany, 1965-68; sr. occupl. therapist Inst. Surg. Rsch. U.S. Army, Ft. Sam Houston, Tex., 1967-70; dir. occupl. therapy clinic, sr. dir. clinics Tripler Army Med. Ctr., Honolulu, 1972-75; adminstr. occupl. therapy clinic, cons. LAMC U.S. Army, Presido, Calif., 1975; asst. evening coll. program San Jose CC, Calif., 1976-77; fellow allied health adminstrn. SUNY, Buffalo, 1978, Commonwealth U., Richmond, Va., 1978-79; staff project devel. pre-retirement program older adults De Anza Coll., Cupertino, Calif., 1980—81; project dir. Ctr. of Design, Palo Alto, 1980; part-time instr. Stroke Activity Ctr. Cabrillo Coll., Santa Cruz, Calif., 1981; dir. occupl. therapy clinics Presbyn. Med. Ctr., 1981-86; ptnr., mgr. retail store, 1986-89; dir. rehab. therapy Merrithew Meml. Hosp. Contra Costa Med. Ctr., Martinez, Calif., 1990-93; sculptor, 1993—; activity program coord. Calif. Womens Detention Facility, Chowchilla, 1994-97; ret., 1997. Co-author: Splinting of Burned Patients, 1974; producer videos: Elbow Splinting of the Burned Patient, 1970, Self-Instruction Unit: Principles of Elbow Splinting, 1971; contbr. articles to profl. jours. With U.S. Army, 1952—55. Decorated Legion of Merit; recipient Disting. Alumni Honors award San Jose State U., 1982, Best of Show award Nat. Veteran's Creative Arts Competition, Fresno Local Vet Art Show, 2004; honored by having Ballon painting to be first mosaic mural on Hwy. 168, Rotary Club, Fresno., 2006; scholar U.S. Surgeon Gen., 1972; fellow Kellogg Found., 1979. Mem.: Occupl. Therapy Assn. Calif. (v.p. 1981—84, state chair pers. 1981—84, state chair continuing edn. 1984—86, award of excellence 1986, Lifetime Achievement award 1994), Am. Occupl. Therapy Assn., Am. Soc. Hand Therapists (life), Alliance Calif. Artist. Avocations: stone sculpture, painting, kayaking, travel, fossil hunting. Home: 172 N Karen Ave Clovis CA 93612-0112 E-mail: kiluluv@aol.com.

VON RAFFLER-ENGEL, WALBURGA (WALBURGA ENGEL), retired language educator; b. Munich, Sept. 25, 1920; came to U.S., 1949, naturalized, 1955; d. Friedrich J. and Gertrud E. (Kiefer) von R.; m. A. Ferdinand Engel, June 2, 1957; children: Lea Maxine, Eric Robert von Raffler. DLitt, U. Turin, Italy, 1947; MS, Columbia U., 1951; PhD, Ind. U., 1953. Free-lance journalist, 1949-58; mem. faculty Bennett Coll., Greensboro, NC, 1953-55, U. Charleston (formerly Morris Harvey Coll.), W.Va., 1955-57, Adelphi U., CUNY, 1957-58, NYU, 1958-59, U. Florence, Italy, 1959-60, Istituto Postuniversitario Orgn. Aziendale, Turin, Italy, 1960-61, Bologna Center of Johns Hopkins U., 1964; assoc. prof. linguistics Vanderbilt U., Nashville, 1965-77, prof. linguistics, 1977-85, prof. emerita, sr. rsch. assoc. Inst. Pub. Policy Studies, 1985—2002, dir. linguistics program, 1978—85; chmn. com. on linguistics Nashville U. Ctr., 1978—85; Italian NSF prof. Psychol. Inst. U. Florence, Italy, 1986-87; prof. NATO Advanced Study Inst., Cortona, Italy, 1988; pres. Kinesics Internat., 1988—, ret. Vis. prof. linguistics Shanxi U., Peoples Republic China, 1988-2002; vis. prof. U. Ottawa, Ont., Can., 1971-72, Lang. Scis. Inst., Internat. Christian U., Tokyo, 1976, U. Paris, Sorbonne, 1965-67, 1978-79; grant evaluator NEH, NSF, Can. Coun.; manuscript reader Ind. U. Press, U. Ill. Press, Prentice-Hall; advisor Trinity U., Simon Frazer U.; dir. internat. seminar Cross-Cultural Comm., 1986-87; mem. Ctr. for Global Media Studies, 1999; State Dept. Italy del. to Congress of the Hague; lectr. in field; specialist in non-verbal comm. Author: Il prelinguaggio infantile, 1964, The Perception of Nonverbal Behavior in the Career Interview, 1983, The Perception of the Unborn Across the Cultures of the World, Japanese edit., 1993, English edit., 1994 (transl. into Chinese), A Traveler's Guide to Cross-Cultural Business Communications, 2000; co-author: Language Intervention Programs, 1960-75; editor, co-editor 12 books; author films and videotape; contbr. of 500 articles to profl. jours. in Engish, Italian, French, German, Chinese, Japanese. Grantee Am. Coun. Learned Socs., NSF, Can. Coun., Ford Found., Kenan Venture Fund, Japanese Ministry Edn., NATO, UNESCO, Finnish Acad., Meharry Med. Coll., Internat. Sociol. Assn., Internat. Coun. Linguists, Tex. A&M U., Vanderbilt U., others. Mem. AAUP, Internat. Linguistic Assn., Linguistic Soc. Am. (chmn. Golden Anniversary film com. 1974, emerita 1985—), Linguistic Assn. Can. and the U.S., Internat. Assn. for Applied Linguistics (com. on discourse analyses, sessions chmn. 1978), Lang. Origins Soc. (exec. com. 1985-97, chmn. internat. congress, 1987), Internat. Sociol. Assn. (rsch. com. for sociolinguistics, session co-chmn. internat. conf. 1983, session chmn. profl. conf. 1983), Internat. Coun. Psychologists, Internat. Assn. for Intercultural Comms. Studies, Internat. Assn. for Study of Child Lang. (v.p. 1975-78, chmn. internat. conf. Tuscan Acad. Scis., Florence, Italy 1972), Inst. for Nonverbal Comm. Rsch. (workshop leader 1981), Southeastern Conf. on Linguistics, 1980— (hon. mem. 1985—), Semiotic Soc. Am. (organizing com. Internat. Semiotics Inst. 1981), Nat. Assn. Scholars, Tenn. Assn. Scholars (bd. dirs. 1998-99), Internat. Assn. for Intercultural Comms. Studies (panel organizer 1999), United Europe Movement (sect. chmn. 1944-45), Internat. Comm. Assn., Internat. Pragmatics Assn. Achievements include being instrumental in forcing Vanderbilt U. to enroll women on an equal basis with men. Home and Office: 2455 Brighton Oaks San Antonio TX 78231

VON RYDINGSVARD, URSULA KAROLISZYN, sculptor; b. Deensen, Germany, July 26, 1942; came to U.S., 1950; d. Ignacy and Konegunda (Sternal) Karoliszyn; m. Paul Greengard. BA, MA, U. Miami, Coral Gables, Fla., 1965; postgrad., U. Calif., Berkeley, 1969-70; MFA, Columbia U., 1975; PhD (hon.), Md. Inst. Art, 1991. Instr. Sch. Visual Arts, N.Y.C., 1981-82; asst. prof. Pratt Inst., Bklyn., 1978-82, Fordham U., Bronx, NY, 1980-82; assoc. prof. Yale U., New Haven, 1982-86; prof. grad. divsn. Sch. Visual Arts, N.Y.C., 1986—. One-woman shows include Laumeier Sculpture Gallery, St. Louis, 1988, Capp St. Project San Francisco, 1990, Lorence-Monk Gallery, N.Y.C., 1990-91, Zamek Ujazdowski Contemporary Art Ctr., Warsaw, Poland, 1992, Storm King Art Ctr., Mountainville, N.Y., 1992-94, Galerie Lelong, N.Y.C., 1994, Weatherspoon Art Gallery, Grensboro, N.C., 1994, Univ. Gallery, Amherst, 1995, Mus. Art, Providence, 1996, Mus. Art R.I. Sch. Design, Providence, 1996, Yorkshire Sculpture Pk., Wakefield, England, 1997, Nelson-Atkins Mus., Kansas City, Mo., 1998, Madison (Wis.) Art Ctr., 1998, Chgo. Cultural Ctr., 1998, Indpls. Mus. Art, 1999, The Contemporary Mus., Honolulu, 1999, Barbara Krakow Gallery, Boston, 1999, Galerie Lelong, Zurich, 2000, N.Y.C., 2000, Doris C. Freedman Plz., Ctrl. Pk., N.Y.C., 2000, Neuberger Mus. Art, SUNY, Purchase, 2002; exhibited in group shows at Contemporary Arts Ctr., Cin., 1987, Damon Brandt Gallery, N.Y.C., 1989, Met. Mus. Art, N.Y.C., 1989-93, Whitney Mus. Contemporary Art, 1990, Cultural Ctr., Chgo., 1991, Ctrl. Bur. Art Exhbns., Warsaw and Krakow, Poland, 1991, The Cultural Space/Exit Art, N.Y.C., 1992, Galerie Lelong, N.Y.C., 1993, Denver Art Mus. and Columbus Art Mus., 1994—, others; outdoor exhbns include Pelham Bay Park, Bronx, N.Y., 1978, Neuberger Mus., Purchase, N.Y., 1979, Artpark, Lewiston, N.Y., 1979, Laumeier Sculpture Park, St. Louis, 1989-94, Walker Art Ctr., Mpls., 1990-93, Oliver Ranch, Geyserville, Calif., Storm King Art Ctr., Mountainville, N.Y., 1992-93; contbr. articles to profl. jours. Fulbright Hays travel grantee, 1975; grantee N.Y. State Coun. Arts, Am. the Beautiful Fund, Nat. Endowment for Arts, Creative Artists Program Svc.; Griswald traveling grantee Yale U., 1985; Guggenheim fellow, 1983-84; Nat. Endowment for Arts individual artists grantee, 1986-87; recipient Acad. award in Art, Am. Acad. Arts and Letters, 1994, Alfred Jurzykowski Found. Fine Arts award, 1996, Joan Mitchell award, N.Y., 1997. Office: Sch Visual Arts 209 East 23rd St New York NY 10010 Home: 78 Ingraham St Brooklyn NY 11237-1406 E-mail: art@galerielong.com.

VONSCHLEGEL, PATRICIA, artist; b. Fayetteville, N.C., Aug. 3, 1941; d. Robert Blackburn and Margaret (Scull) Slagle; m. John Lee Jordan, July 16, 1960 (div. Feb. 1975); children: John Christopher Jordan, Lisa Nicole Jordan. B of Creative Arts, U. N.C., Charlotte, 1978. Tchr. aide Children's Adventure, Nederland, Colo., 1978; kindergarten tchr. Charlotte Acad., 1980-81; tchr., supr. San Francisco Head Start, 1981-82; art tchr. Our Lady of Consolation,

Charlotte, 1982-83. Exhbns. include McKnight Gallery/U. N.C., 1978, Charlotte Printmakers, 1978, Princeton U., 1979, Davis (Calif.) Art Fair, 1982, Queens Gallery Group Show, Charlotte, 1983, Springs Mills Show, Lancaster, S.C., 1987, Art on the River, Savannah, Ga., 1989, Ann Gleason Interiors, Savannah, 1989, Spotlight on So. Artists, Atlanta, 1991, 92, 93, 94, 95, Coastal Nat., St. Simon Island, Ga., 1992, The Checkered Moon Gallery, 1993, Evening of the Arts/Hilton Head Island, S.C., 1992, 93, 94, 95, 96, Tin Can Alley Exhibit/Self Ctr.,Hilton Head, 1996; solo show at Patton and Howell, Savannah, 1990; contbr. to publd. Sanskrit, So. Accent. Roman Catholic. Avocations: theater, symphony, reading. Home: 322 E Taylor St Apt 1207 Savannah GA 31401-5059

VONSCHULZE-DELITZSCH, MARILYN WANDLING (LADY VONSCHULZE-DELITZSCH), artist, writer; b. Alton, Ill., May 16, 1932; d. Ralph Marion and Mary Mildred (Branson) W.; m. Sir Georg W.W. Herzog VonSchulze-Delitzsch; children: Jeffrey, Douglas, Pamela. Student, Monticello Coll., Godfrey, Ill, 1950-51, U. Ill., 1951-53; BA in Art, Webster U., St. Louis, 1968; MA Edn. in Art Edn., Washington U., St. Louis, 1975. Cert. tchr. art Kindergarten-Grade 12, Mo. 4th grade tchr. Alton (Ill.) Pub. Schs., 1961-62; art. buying dept. Gardner Advt. Co. Inc., St. Louis, 1962-63; art tchr. mid. sch. Lindbergh Sch. Dist., St. Louis, 1968-75; cons., designer V.P. Fair, Inc., St. Louis, 1982; adminstrv. asst. to headmaster, coll. counseling dept. John Burroughs Sch., St. Louis, 1979-82; dir. pub. rels. and advt. Dance St. Louis, 1983-85; freelance art and design St. Louis, 1970—; tchr. art mid. sch. St. Louis Pub. Schs., 1987-90, tchr. art Elem. Magnet Sch. for Visual and Performing Arts, 1990-98. Tchr. drawing and painting Summer Arts Inst., St. Louis Pub. Schs., 1992, graphic arts designer, cons. comty. affairs divsn., 1985-96, sch. vol. divsn., 1990-92, Webster Groves (Mo.) Sch. Dist., 1989-90, Pub. Sch. Retirement Sys., St. Louis, 1991; implementer classroom multi-cultural art edn. projects, 1987-98; summer participant Improving Visual Arts Edn., Getty Ctr. for Edn. in Arts, 1990; book illustrator-McGraw Hill Inter-Americana de Mexico, Mexico City, 1994-95, Simon & Schuster, Mexico City. Designer (cover and icons) English Language Teaching Text, 1996; designer Centennial Logo for St. Louis Pub. Schs. Sesquicentennial, 1988; painter, designer murals for Ctrl. Presbyn. Ch. Nursery, 1978-79, St. Nicholas Greek Orthodox Ch., 1980; designer two outdoor villages VP Fair, Arch Grounds, St. Louis, 1982; published writer. Patron St. Louis Symphony Orch. Recipient merit and honor awards Nat. Sch. Pub. Rels. Assn., 1990, 91, 92, 93, 95, Mo. Sch. Pub. Rels. Assn., 1989-90, 91, 92, 93. Mem. St. Louis Art Mus., PEO Sisterhood, Nat. Soc. DAR, Colonial Dames of 17th Cent., United Daus. of Confederacy, Chi Omega Alumnae. Avocations: Native American arts and culture, paintings, drawings, portraits.

VON SELDENECK, JUDITH METCALFE, career planning administrator; b. High Point, N.C., June 6, 1940; d. Frederick Maurice and Harriet (Curtis) Metcalfe; m. George Clay von Seldeneck, Apr. 8, 1972; children: Rodman Clay, Kevin Clay. BA, U. N.C., 1962; postgrad., Am. U., 1963—64. Senatorial asst., 1963—72; pres., CEO Diversified Search Cos., Phila., 1972—. Diversified Health Search. Bd. dirs. Corestates Fin. Corp., Keystone Life Ins. Co., Tasty Baking Co. Bd. dirs. Greater Phila. C. of C., Com. of 200; mem., co-founder, bd. dirs. Forum Exec. Women. Mem.: Assn. Search Cons., Wharton Club Phila. (bd. mem.), Sunneybrook Golf Club, Phila. Cricket Club. Democrat. Episcopalian. Avocations: golf, reading, fishing. Home: 8124 St Martins Ln Philadelphia PA 19118-4103

VON THURN, JELENA, health science specialist; b. Skopje, Macedonia, Yugoslavia, Jan. 1, 1939; came to U.S., 1972; d. Miladin and Hedy (Hem) M.; m. Ernst Anzbock, Dec. 14, 1959 (div. 1971); children: Harald, Evelyn; m. Ranko Caric, Nov. 3, 1973 (div. 1980); 1 child, Peter. Student, Molloy Coll., 1979-81, L.I. U., 1981-82, Rockland C.C., 1985, Vt. Coll., 1985-86. Orange County C.C., 1988, Empire State Coll., 1990—. Ordained to ministry Universal Spiritualist Assn. U.S.A., 1985; lic., real estate agt., N.Y.; registered and cert. reflexologist, N.Y. Owner Walter's Bake Shop, 1973-79; nurse's aide Hillside Manor, 1980; clerical worker Molloy Coll., 1980-81, L.I. U., 1981-82; chiropractor asst. Steven R. Siegel D.C., 1982; owner Linden Motel, 1983; lectr. on Shiatsu and reflexology New Age Ctr., 1985-86; v.p., min. Universal Ctr. New Age Consciousness, Inc., Milford, Pa., 1985—; with Abatelli Realty, 1988; owner Athena Spa, 1993-94, Jelena's Skin Care and Anti-Aging Clinic, Carmel, Calif., 1998—; esthetician The Spa, Pebble Beach, Calif., 1999. Gen. agt. Intern Cons. Exchange, San Diego, Calif., 1986; spa and skincare therapist, Pebble Beach, Calif., 1995, Carmel Valley Ranch, 1995, Hyatt Regency, 1996. Mem. Alliance of Massage Therapists, Inc., Universal Spiritualist Assn., Assoc. Bodywork and Massage Profls., Carmel Art Assn. Avocations: painting, piano, guitar, dance, estate auctions.

VON TROTTA, TAMARA JANE, art educator; b. Weymouth, Mass., Oct. 16, 1947; d. Salvatore F. Trotta and Jane F. Howe; m. Richard F. Cubi, Sept. 19, 1969; 1 child, Heather Noel Cubi Walker. BA, Bridgewater State Coll., Mass., 1976; MEd, Cambridge Coll., Mass., 1979. Sec. med. rsch. Boston U., 1968—78; art educator Silver Lake Regional H.S., Kingston, Mass., 1979—. Instr. skiing Igon Mountain, Lincoln, NH, 1997—; U.S. Forest Ranger USDA, White Mountain Nat. Forest, 2001—; v.p. Halifax Hist. Soc., Mass., 1978—79; apptd. hist. commn. Town Halifax, 1978—79. Vol. host German student Face the World, Halifax, 2002—03. Recipient Wilderness First Responder, White Mountain Nat. Forest, Bronze medal, Roller Skating Rink Operators Am., 1962. Mem.: NEA, Profl. Ski Instrs. Am., Mass. Edn. Assn., Am. Sailing Assn. Avocations: hiking, skiing, sailing, bicycling, Learning German.

VOORHESS, MARY LOUISE, pediatric endocrinologist; b. Livingston Manor, NY, June 2, 1926; d. Harry William and Helen Grace (Schwartz) V. RN, City Hosp. Sch. Nursing, Binghamton, N.Y., 1946; BA in Zoology, U. Tex., 1952; MD, Baylor Coll., Houston, 1956. Diplomate Am. Bd. Pediatrics and Pediatric Endocrinology. Rotating intern Albany (N.Y.) Med. Ctr., 1956-57, asst. resident pediatrics, 1957-58, chief resident pediatrics, 1958-59; rsch. fellow pediatric endocrinology and genetics SUNY Health Sci. Ctr., Syracuse, 1959-61, asst. prof. pediatrics, 1961-65, assoc. prof. pediatrics, 1965-70, prof. pediatrics, 1970-76, SUNY Sch. Medicine and Biomed. Scis., Buffalo, 1976-91, prof. pediatrics emeritus, 1991—; co-chief div. endocrinology Children's Hosp. Buffalo, 1976-91; retired, 1997. Mem. nat. adv. environ. health scis. coun. NIH, 1980-83. Ad hoc reviewer Jour. Pediat., Pediat., Am. Jour. Diseases Children, others, 1960-97; contbr. sci. articles to profl. jours., chpts. to books. Mem. adv. bd. Interim Healthcare inc., 1991-97; mem. devel. coun. Children's Hosp. Buffalo Found., 1991-97; med. dir. Children's Growth Found., Buffalo, 1976-97; cmty. advisor Assn. for Rsch. Childhood Cancer, Buffalo, 1990-97. Recipient rsch. career devel. award Nat. Cancer Inst., 1961-71, Dean's award SUNY Sch. Medicine and Biomed. Scis., 1991. Fellow Am. Acad. Pediatrics, AAAS; mem. Soc. Pediatric Rsch. (emeritus), Am. Pediatric Soc. (emeritus), Endocrine Soc. (emeritus), Lawson Wilkins Pediatric Endocrine Soc. (emeritus), Phi Beta Kappa, Alpha Omega Alpha. Presbyterian. Home: 6311 Chiswick Park Williamsburg VA 23188-6369 Personal E-mail: mlv6311@msn.com.

VORCE-TISH, HELENE R., writer; d. Palmer Lemuel Vorce and Adelaide Catherine Miller; m. Charles Ronald VanBuren, Dec. 23, 1950 (div. Aug. 1967); children: Gail Rae, Karen Helene; m. William David Tish, Oct. 20, 1978 (dec.). BA in Psychology, Mich. State U., 1950, tchrs. cert. in English, 1961; M in English, U. N.Mex., 1968. Secondary tchr. English and creative writing Grant Unified Tchrs. Dist., Sacramento. Spkr. in field; instr. workshops in field. Author: (novels) The Wounds of Hate, 2001, Challenging the Forces of Hate, 2002, Fencing With Danger, 2006; regular contbr.: Foothill Times; contbr. articles to profl. jours. and popular mags. Fellow: Am. Soc. Journalists and Authors, Calif. Writers Club (bd. mem. 1999—2000). Avocations: tennis, swimming, jogging. Home: 3473 Santos Cir Cameron Park CA 95682 Office Phone: 530-677-3327. Personal E-mail: tish@directcon.net.

VOSBECK, ELIZABETH JUST, retired geneticist; b. Mankato, Minn., May 24, 1925; d. Frederick William and Frances Beneta (Johnson) Just; m. William Frederick Vosbeck, Aug. 2, 1947; children: Lee, William Frederick III, Lynn, Jon Scot, James Stephen. BBA, U. Minn., 1947; MS in Anatomy, George Washington U., Washington, 1965; PhD in Human Genetics, George Washington U., 1975. Mktg. rsch. dir. Mpls. C. of C., 1947—48; embryology lab. instr., lectr., human genetics rschr. George Washington U., Washington, 1965—75; lab. dir. cell chromosome analysis Reprodn. Genetics Ctr., McLean, Va., 1976—87; ret., 1987. Grantee, NIH grantee, 1968—70. Mem.: DAR, Sigma Xi, Beta Gamma Sigma. Republican. Avocations: golf, bridge, genealogy, astrology, ice skating. Home: 7512 Fort Hunt Rd Alexandria VA 22307 E-mail: vosbeck01@aol.com.

VOSE, KATHRYN KAHLER, marketing executive, communications executive; b. Denton, Tex., Aug. 18, 1953; d. James and Martha Kahler; m. William O. Vose, June 1, 1996. BA in Sociology, Sophie Newcomb Coll. Tulane U., 1975; MA in Mass Communications, U. Minn., 1977. Health/scis. reporter The Jour.-News, Nyack, NY, 1977—83; nat. corr. Newhouse Newspapers, Washington, 1983—93; comm. dir. U.S. Dept. Edn., Washington, 1993—96; dir. comm. and mktg. Campaign for Tobacco-Free Kids, Washington, 1996—99, v.p. comm. and mktg., 1999—2000; sr. v.p., worldwide dir. anti-tobacco group Porter Novelli, Washington, 2001—02, exec. v.p., 2002—, dir. health and social mktg. practice, 2002—. Panelist Washington Week In Review; vis. fellow Woodrow Wilson Nat. Fellowship Found; adviser World Health Orgn.; bd. mem., chair mktg. com. Nat. Partnership for Women and Families; mem. steering com. for the women, tobacco and cancer initiative Nat. Cancer Inst.; mem. program and comm. coms., chmn. subcom. on comm. 11th World Conf. on Tobacco and Health; contbr. Nat. Acad. Scis. Recipient Crystal Medallion award AMA, Clarion award Assn. Women Comm., Silver Inkwell award Internat. Assn. Bus. Communicators, Mercury Grand award MerComm Internat., Thoth (2) awards Pub. Rels. Soc. Am., Assoc. Press Mng. Editors Pub. Svc. award. Mem. Nat. Press Club (pres. 1991, bd. govs.), Pub. Rels. Soc. Am. Home: 3351 Tennyson St NW Washington DC 20015-2442 Office Phone: 202-973-5800. Personal E-mail: kkahlervose@porternovelli.com.

VOSEVICH, KATHI ANN, writer, editor; b. St. Louis, Oct. 12, 1957; d. William and Catherine Mildred (Kalinowski) V.; m. James Hughes Meredith, Sept. 6, 1986. AB with honors, St. Louis U., 1980, MA, 1983; PhD, U. Denver, 1988. Tchg. fellow St. Louis U., 1980-83, acad. advising fellow, 1983-84; tchg. fellow U. Denver, 1985-87; prof. ESL, BNM Talensch., Uden, The Netherlands, 1988-91; instr. English, mentor U. Ga., Athens, 1992-94; vis. asst. prof. Colo. Coll., Colorado Springs, 1994; sr. tech. writer and editor Titan Client/Server Techs., Colorado Springs, 1994-96, head documentation, libr., 1996-97; documentation mgr. Beechwood, Colorado Springs, 1997-98, tech. mgr., 1998-99; tech. writer Microsoft, Redmond, Wash., 1999-2000; documentation and process mgr. Sprint, Denver, 2000; practice and group mgr. e-bus. Sprint Corp., Denver, 2000—02, svc. launch mgr. Mobile Computing Svcs., 2002—03, strategic market mgr., 2003—05, strategic alliances mgr., 2005, lead bus. strategist, 2005—. Forensic judge USAF Acad., Colo., 1987-88; edn. officer Volkel (The Netherlands) Air Base, 1988-91; instr. English European divsn. U. Md., The Netherlands and Belgium, 1989-91. Author: Customer Care User's Guide, 1996, Interview with Joseph Heller, 1999, Conversations with Joseph Heller in Understanding the Literature of World War II, 1999, Office Update, 1999-2000, Tutoring the Tudors, 2000, Sprint Takes Messaging into the Future, 2003; editor: Subscription Services System Documentation, 1996, Titan Process Documentation, 1994-96; copy editor: Language, Ideas, and American Culture; War, Literature and the Arts; contbr. over 100 electronic texts and articles to profl. jours. Colo. scholar U. Denver, 1985-86, grad. dean scholar, 1988; NEH fellow U. Md., 1994 Mem. MLA, Phi Beta Kappa, Alpha Sigma Nu. Roman Catholic. Avocations: writing, drawing, raising Bernese mountain dogs. Office: Sprint Ste 1400 1099 18th St Denver CO 80202

VOSKA, KATHRYN CAPLES, consultant, facilitator; b. Berkeley, Calif., Dec. 26, 1942; d. Donald Buxton and Ellen Marion (Smith) Caples; m. David Karl Nehrling, Aug. 15, 1964 (div. Nov. 1980); children: Sandra E. Nehrling, Barbara M. Nehrling, Melissa A. Nehrling-Holmgren; m. James Edward Voska, Aug. 31, 1985. BS, Northwestern U., 1964; MS, Nat.-Louis U., 1989. Cert. teacher, Ill.; cert. career mgmt. fellow practitioner Inst. Career Cert. Internat. Tchr. pub. schs., Northbrook and Evanston, Ill., 1964-65; acting phys. dir. YWCA, Evanston, Ill., 1975; quality control technician Baxter Travenol, Morton Grove, Ill., 1978-80; sr. quality assurance analyst Hollister Inc., Libertyville, Ill., 1980-85; info. ctr. trainer, tech. training mgr. Rand McNally, Skokie, Ill., 1985-92; cons., facilitator Capka & Assocs., Skokie and Kansas City, 1992—; dir. edn. Nat. Office Machine Dealers, 1992-94; career and mgmt. cons. Right Mgmt. Cons., Overland Park, Kans., 1994—. Pvt. practice estate conservator. Telephone worker Contact Chgo. Crisis Hotline, 1989-90; CPR instr. trainer Amer. Heart Assn., Chgo., 1977-89; aquatic dir. YMCA, Evanston, Ill., 1969-80; rep. Alumnae Panhellenic Coun., Evanston, 1969-75; grad. Leadership Overland Park, 1996, mem. 15th anniv. special task force. Mem. ASTD (bd. dirs. Kansas City chpt. 1997-99), ASCD, Soc. Human Resource Mgmt., Midwest Soc. Profl. Cons., Assn. for Mgmt. Orgn. Design, Chgo. Orgn. Data Processing Educators, Chgo. Computer Soc., Info. Ctr. Exch. of Chgo., Assn. Quality and Participation, Am. Soc. for Quality (teller N.E. Ill. sect. 1982-84), Internat. Soc. for Performance Improvement, Assn. Career Profls. Internat. (founding pres. Kansas City chpt. 2000-02, nat. bd. dirs. 2000—, nat. bd. v.p., pres.-elect 2002-04, nat. bd. pres. 2004-06, past pres.,k 2006—, chmn. internat. membership drive 2004), Learning Resource Network. Presbyterian. Avocations: scuba diving, swimming, hiking, camping, travel. Home: 1001 E 118th Ter Kansas City MO 64131-3828 Office: Right Mgmt Cons 7300 W 110th St Ste 800 Overland Park KS 66210-2387 Office Phone: 913-323-2309. Personal E-mail: kvoska@kc.rr.com. Business E-Mail: kathy.voska@right.com.

VOSS, MARGARET A., biology professor; b. Houston, Apr. 18, 1962; d. Margaret A. and adopted d. Richard B. Voss, Gary T. Garrison; m. Richard J. Ruby, Dec. 21, 2005; m. Charles A. Pike, May 14, 1982 (div. June 1995). BSc, SUNY, Syracuse, 1992, MSc, 1995; PhD, Syracuse U., 2001. Asst. prof. biology Pa. State U., Behrend Coll., Erie, 2002—, SUNY Coll. at Potsdam, 2000—02. Mem. Ctr. for Math. Biology Pa. State U., Behrend Coll., Erie, 2004—. Contbr. chapters to books, articles to profl. jours. Recipient Ralph T. King award in Wildlife/Fisheries Biology, SUNY, Coll. Environ. Sci. and Forestry, 1993, Outstanding Grad. Tchg. award, 1994, Helen I. Battle award, Can. Soc. Zoologists, 1997, Edn. Found. Citation of Merit, Assn. Women in Sci., 1998, Grad. Sch. Outstanding Tchg. Asst. award, Syracuse U., 1998, Coun. Fellows Excellence in Tchg. award, Pa. State U. Erie, Behrend Coll., 2005; Leroy C. Stegeman scholar, SUNY, Coll. Environ. Sci. and Forestry, 1994, Am. Fellowship Publ. grantee, AAUW, 2004—50. Mem.: Soc. for Coll. Sci. Tchrs. (newsletter editor 2001—03), Assn. for Women in Sci., Internat. Soc. for Behavioral Ecology, Assn. For Field Ornithology, Am. Ornithol. Union, Sigma Xi. Roman Catholic. Avocations: painting, travel. Office: Penn State Erie Behrend College 5091 Station Rd Erie PA 16563 Office Phone: 814-898-6292. Business E-Mail: mav11@psu.edu.

VOSS, MELINDA, health care association administrator; MPH, U. Minn, 1999. Staff writer The Des Moines Register; exec. dir. Assn. Health Care Journalists. Coord., health journalism masters program U. Minn., adj. instructor; chair Council Nat. Journalism Organizations. Casey Journalism Fellow, American Press Institute Fellow on Aging, Mini-Fellow, Henry J. Kaiser Family Found., 1997. Mem.: Investigative Reporters and Editors, Journalism and Women Symposium. Office: U Minn Sch Journalism 206 Church St SE Minneapolis MN 55455 Office Phone: 612-624-8877. Office Fax: 612-626-8251. Business E-Mail: melinda@umn.edu.

VOSSLER, DEBORAH J., mathematics and science educator; b. Portland, Oreg., May 15, 1954; d. Louis Paul and Ruth Ella Varga; m. V. Vic Vossler, June 30, 1972; children: Christopher Isaac, Erin Renee, Sierra Amira. BA in Bus. Adminstrn., U. Wash., 1977; M in Tchg., Wash. State U., 1995. CPA Wash., 1980; profl. educator Wash., 1998. Acct. Rainier Nat. Bank, Seattle, 1977—79; bus. adminstr. Luth. Family Svcs., Portland, Oreg., 1979—81; tchr., administr. Maasae Girls Luth. Secondary Sch., Monduli, Tanzania, 1995—98; math, sci. tchr. Frontier Mid. Sch., Vancouver, Wash., 1998—. Math dept. chair Frontier Mid. Sch., Vancouver, Wash., 2003—; leadership tchr. Ptnr. for Reform in Secondary Sci. and Math., Vancouver, 2004—. Vol. libr. Moringe Secondary Sch., Monduli, Tanzania, 1994; chair youth and family ministry Family of Christ Luth. Ch., Vancouver, 2000—06; bd. mem. Interracial Family Assn., Portland; bd. dirs. Orgn. Developmentally Accelerated Youth, Vancouver, 1981—85; leader Camp Fire, Vancouver, 1987—90; asst.leader Boys Scouts of Am., Vancouver, 1990—95; referee Evergreen Soccer League, Vancouver, 1992—94. Mem.: Nat. Sci. Tchrs. Am., Nat. Coun. Tchrs. Math. Lutheran. Avocation: travel. Home: 3106 NE 146 Pl Vancouver WA 98682 Office: Frontier Mid Sch 7600 NE 166 Ave Vancouver WA 98682 Office Phone: 360-604-3200. Personal E-mail: uwdog@comcast.net. Business E-Mail: dvossler@egreen.wednet.edu.

VOTROBECK, BARBARA JAN, music educator; b. Ida Grove, Iowa, May 11, 1950; d. John Stuart and Lucy Lenora Huldeen; m. Rick Lon Votrobeck, June 19, 1971; children: Nicholas Huldeen, Collin Steven. MusB in Edn., Morningside Coll., 1972. Cert. K-14 Music Instr. Iowa Dept. Edn. Choral, instrumental music instr. Jefferson (SD) Cert. Sch. Dist., 1971—75; 7-12 choral instr. Akron (Iowa) Cert. Sch. Dist., 1975—78; 5-8 vocal, instrumental music instr. Odebolt-Arthur (Iowa) Mid. Sch., 1978—2002; 5-12 instrumental music instr. Odebolt-Arthur (Iowa) Cert. Sch. Dist., 2002—. Pvt. music instr., Arthur, Iowa, 1971—; choir dir. First Presbyn. Ch., Odebolt, Iowa, 1986—. Dir.: (various musicals, variety shows). Chairperson Prospect Hill Presbyn. Christian Edn. Com., Storm Lake, Iowa; pres. Siouxland Master Chorale, Sioux City, 2002—04; boutique mgr. Iowa Choral Dirs. Assn., 2002—06; North ctrl. rep. Iowa Music Educators' Assn. Mem.: Iowa Music Educators' Assn, Iowa Bandmasters' Assn., Music Educators' Nat. Conf. (North ctrl. rep.), Iowa Choral Directors' Assn. (boutique mgr. 2002—06). Independent-Republican. Presbyn. Avocations: gardening, baking, singing, travel, home remodeling. Home: 2924 Buchanan Ave Arthur IA 51431-7505 Office Fax: 712-668-2631. Business E-Mail: barbara@revision8.com.

VOWELL, EVELENE C., retired real estate broker; b. May 11, 1940; d. Haughty Chester and Lottie Bell (Williams) Craddock; m. Darrell Odine, Dec. 27, 1959 (dec. Oct. 30, 2005); children: Amy Darlene, Kerry Don, Dal Keith. Student, Memphis State U., 1976—85; cert. residential specialist, Realtors Inst., 1988, grad., 1988. Lic. real estate affiliate broker. County agrl. extension sec., Hickman, Ky., 1957—59; payroll sec. Roper Pecan Co., Hickman, 1961—63; PR3 inspector Gen. Electric Co., Memphis, 1969—71; sec. Swift and Co., Memphis, 1971—73; affiliate broker John R. Thompson Realtors, Memphis, 1976—83, Crye Leike Realtors, Memphis, 1983—90, Pyramid Realtors, Cordova, Tenn., 1990—95; with New Concepts in Mktg., Charlotte, NC, 1995—. Mem.: Ind. Order Foresters, Memphis Bd. Realtors. Home: 10147 Walker Springs Cove Lakeland TN 38002 Office: New Concepts in Mktg PO Box 68370 Charlotte NC 28216-0007 Office Phone: 800-799-6246. Office Fax: 901-383-2891.

VOWELL, SARAH, writer, radio personality; b. Muskogee, Okla., Dec. 27, 1969; BA, Mont. State U., Bozeman, 1993; MA, Sch. of Art. Inst. Chgo., 1996. Former columnist Time, Salon.com, San Francisco Weekly; has contbd. to magazines and newspapers including Esquire, GQ, LA Times, The Village Voice, Spin, The NY Times Book Rev., and McSweeney's; contbg. editor This Am. Life Nat. Pub. Radio, 1996—. Guest op-ed columnist NY Times, 2005. Author: Radio On: A Listener's Diary, 1997, Take the Cannoli: Stories from the New World, 2000, The Partly Cloudy Patriot, 2003, Assassination Vacation, 2005; actor(voice): (films) The Incredibles, 2004. Office: This Am Life WBEZ Radio Navy Pier 848 E Grand Ave Chicago IL 60611

VOYTEK, MARY SULLIVAN, sculptor; b. Memphis, July 26, 1957; d. Herbert Dean and Mary Josphine Sullivan; m. Lawrence Voytek, June 30, 1986; children: Alexa, Zachary. BFA, Calif. Coll. of the Arts, Oakland, Calif., 1980; MFA, R.I. Sch. of Design, Providence, R.I., 1982. Vis. prof. R.I. Sch. of Design, Providence, 1980—81, Brown Univ., Providence, 1981—82; adj. prof. Fla. Gulf Coast Univ., Ft. Myers, Fla., 2000—04, asst. prof., 2004—. Pvt. cons. Fla. Gulf Coast Univ., Ft. Myers, Fla., 2000—01. Pub. commns., Dream to Connect, 2004 (Fla. Arts in Pub. Pl. award), exhibitions include Matsumoto Gallery, Sanibel, Fla., 2003, TVS Internat., Atlanta, Ga., 2000, Atla. Internat. Mus. Art and Design, 2000, Gallery Camino Real, Gallery Ctr., Boca Raton, Fla., 2004, Zenith Gallery, Washington, 2005, H.W. Gallery, Naples, Fla., 2005, numerous others, Represented in permanent collections Hsinchu Mus. Art, Taiwan, Sherman Gallery, Chgo., R.I. Sch. Design Mus., numerous others. Art in pub. places bd. City of Ft. Myers, Fla., 2004—; bd. mem. Fla. Arts, Ft. Myers, Fla., 2002—05. Mem.: DAR, Internat. Sculptors Ctr. Avocations: hiking, travel. Office Phone: 239-590-7241.

VOZHEIKO WHEATON, LENA, musician, educator; b. Alma-Ata, Kazakhstan, Dec. 30, 1951; d. Vladimir Isidorovich and Enessa Vasilyevna Vozheiko; m. Charles S. Wheaton, Dec. 20, 1995; 1 child, Anton A. MS, Conservatory of Music, Frunze Kyrgyzstan, 1975; PhD in Piano Performance, Tchaikovsky Music Conservatory, Moscow, 1989. Instr. Conservatory of Music, Frunze, 1975-93. Accompanist at various nat. and internat. competitins; pianist for Carmina Burana, Vancouver Symphony, Washington, 1997. Author: Principles of Duo Piano Playing, 1992. Mem. Music Tchrs. Nat. Assn. Avocation: painting rock animal figures.

VRATIL, KATHRYN HOEFER, federal judge; b. Manhattan, Kans., 1949; BA, U. Kans., 1971, JD, 1975; postgrad., Exeter U., 1971-72. Bar: Kans. 1975, Mo. 1978, U.S. Dist. Ct. Kans. 1975, U.S. Dist. Ct. (we. dist.) Mo. 1978, U.S. Dist. Ct. (ea. dist.) Mo. 1985, U.S. Ct. Appeals (8th cir.) 1978, U.S. Ct. Appeals (10th cir.) 1980, U.S. Ct. Appeals (11th dist.) 1983, U.S. Supreme Ct., 1995. Law clk. U.S. Dist. Ct., Kansas City, Kans., 1975-78; assoc. Lathrop Koontz & Norquist, Kansas City, Mo., 1978-83; ptnr. Lathrop & Norquist, Kansas City, 1984-92; judge City of Prairie Village, Kans., 1990-92. Bd. dirs. Kans. Legal Bd. Svcs., 1991-92; mem. adminstrv. com. Jud. Conf. of the U.S., 2000—. Bd. editors Kans. Law Rev., 1974-75, Jour. Kans. Bar Assn., 1992—. Mem. nat. adv. bd. U. Kans. Ctr. for Environ. Edn. and Tng., 1993-95. Fellow Kans. Bar Found., Am. Bar Found.; mem. ABA (editl. bd. Judges Jour. 1996—), Am. Judicature Soc., Nat. Assn. Judges, Fed. Judges Assn., Kans. Bar Assn. (mem. bench bar com., 2000—), Mo. Bar Assn., Kansas City Met. Area Bar Assn., Johnson County Bar Assn., Assn. Women Judges, Lawyers Assn. Kansas City, Kans. State Hist. Soc., U. Kans. Law Soc. (bd. govs. 1978-81, 2005—), Kans. U. Alumni Assn. (mem. Kansas City chpt. alumni bd. 1990-92, nat. bd. dirs. 1991-96, bd. govs. Adams Alumni Ctr. 1992-95), Native Sons and Daus of Kans. (life), Jr. League Wyandotte and Johnson Counties, Order of Coif, Kans. Inn of Ct. (master 1993—, pres. 1999-2000), Phi Kappa Phi. Republican. Presbyterian. Office: 511 Robert J Dole US Courthouse 500 State Ave Kansas City KS 66101-2403

VREDENBURGH, JUDY, youth organization executive; m. Donald Vredenburgh; 1 child. BA, U. Pa., 1970; MBA, U. Buffalo, 1975. Various positions in retail; exec. v.p., gen. mdse. mgr. Sizes Unlimited/Lerner Women; CEO Chess King; sr. v.p. March of Dimes, 1993—99; CEO and pres. Big Brothers Big Sisters of Am., 1999—. Bd. dirs. Generations United. Big Sister; bd. overseers Sch. Arts and Sciences. U. Penn. Office: Big Brothers Big Sisters of Am Nat Office 230 N 13th St Philadelphia PA 19107

VREDEVOE, DONNA LOU, academic administrator, microbiologist, educator, biomedical researcher; BA in Bacteriology, UCLA, 1959, PhD in Microbiology, 1963. USPHS postdoctoral fellow Stanford (Calif.) U., 1963—64; instr. bacteriology UCLA, 1963, postgrad. rsch. immunologist dept. surgery Ctr. Health Scis., 1964-65, asst. rsch. immunologist dept. surgery Ctr. Health Scis., 1964-67, asst. prof. Sch. Nursing, Ctr. Health Scis., 1967-70, assoc. prof., 1970-76; prof. Sch. Nursing, Ctr. Health Scis., 1976—, assoc. dean Sch. Nursing, 1976-78, acting assoc. dean Sch. Nursing, 1985-86, asst. dir. space planning Cancer Ctr., 1976-78, dir. space planning, 1978-90, cons. to lab. nuc. medicine and radiation biology, 1967-80, acting dean Sch. Nursing, 1995-96. Chair acad. senate UCLA, 1999—2000, vice chancellor acad. pers., 2001—. Contbr. articles to profl. publs. Postdoctoral fellow USPHS, 1963-64; Mabel Wilson Richards scholar UCLA, 1960-61; rsch. grantee Am. Cancer Soc., Calif. Inst. Cancer Rsch., Calif. divsn. Am. Cancer

Soc., NIH, USPHS, Am. Nurses Found., Cancer Rsch. Coordinating Com. U. Calif., Dept. Energy, UCLA. Mem Am. Soc. Microbiology, Am. Assn. Immunologists, Am. Assn. Cancer Rsch., Nat. League Nursing (2d v.p. 1979-81), Sigma Xi, Alpha Gamma Sigma, Sigma Theta Tau (nat. hon. mem.). Office: UCLA Chancellors Office 2147 Murphy Hall PO Box 951405 Los Angeles CA 90095-1405

VREELAND-FLYNN, TRACY LYNN, elementary school educator; b. San Antonio, Oct. 18, 1966; d. James Chester and Mary Lou (Meighan) V.; m. Russell Brian Flynn; 1 child, Brian Russell Flynn. BS in Edn., Shippensburg (Pa.) U., 1989; MEd, St. Francis Coll., Loretto, Pa., 1994. women's and men's varsity asst., swim team coach Altoona Area H.S., 1991-92. Tchr. Altoona (Pa.) Area Sch. Dist., 1990—, tchr. 3d grade, 1990—96, tchr. 4th grade, 1996-98, tchr. 6th grade, 1998-99, tchr. 5th-6th grade, 1999—, webmaster, 1998—. Computer trainer; dist.-wide tech. coord. com. Altoona Area Sch. Dist.; parent-cmty. study team ACT 178 dist. com. Outcomes Bd. Edn.; tchr. computer camps Altoona Area Sch. Dist., 1993-96; instr. in field. Mem. NEA, ASCD, Nat. Reading Assn., Pa. State Edn. Assn., Altoona Area Edn. Assn. Republican. Roman Catholic. Home: 4 Woodland Terrace Duncansville PA 16635 Office: Logan Elem Sch 301 Sycamore St Altoona PA 16602 Office Phone: 814-946-8370 x 206. Business E-Mail: trflynn@pennwoods.net.

VRINCEANU, ALINA DANIELA, psychiatrist; b. Bucharest, Romania, Dec. 15, 1968; arrived in U.S., 1995; d. Alexandra Mihaela and Marin Sandu (Stepfather); 1 child, Michael. MD, Carol Davila U. of Medicine, Bucharest, 1994. Diplomate Am. Bd. Psychiatry and Neurology, in addiction psychiatry Am. Bd. Psychiatry and Neurology. Internal medicine intern MCP Hahnemann U., Phila., 1997—98; psychiatry resident U. Medicine and Dentistry NJ, Piscataway, 1998—2001, addiction fellow, 2001—02; staff psychiatrist, med. dir. So. Highlands Cmty. Mental Health Ctr., Princeton, W.Va., 2002—. Presenter in field. Mem.: Am. Psychiat. Assn. (licentiate). Achievements include research in buprenorphine/naloxone versus clonidine for outpatient opiate detoxification. Office: Southern Highlands CMHC 200 12th St Extension Princeton WV 24740 Office Phone: 304-425-9541. Office Fax: 304-425-9219. Business E-Mail: alinavrinceanu@shcmhc.com.

VROMAN, BARBARA FITZ, writer, educator; b. Chgo., Mar. 31, 1933; d. William Edwin and Pearl Asenith (Coombs) Fitz; m. Dale Duane Vroman, June 30, 1951; children: Guy, Kim, Marc, Ryan. News editor Waushara Argus Newspaper, Wautoma, Wis., 1966-72; pub. Pearl-Win Pub. Co., Hancock, Wis., 1981-91; tchr. summer sessions The Clearing, Ellison Bay, Wis., 1989—; presenter pvt. seminars Rhinelander Sch. of Arts, U. Wis., 1975—. Author: Sons of Thunder, 1981, Linger Not at Chebar, 1992; co-author: Tomorrow is a River, 1977, Small Celebration Summer, 2003, Small Celebrations: Autumn., 2004, The Experiment, 2005. Home: N4721 9th Dr Hancock WI 54943-7617 Business E-Mail: pearlwin@uniontel.net.

VUCINICH, JANET, language educator; b. Cheyenne, Wyo., Aug. 4, 1947; d. Marlowe and Betty Woods Brecht. PhD, U. N.Mex, 1998. Mem. English faculty Santa Fe C.C., 1986—2001, head dept. devel. studies, 2001—06. Fulbright scholar Manipal Inst. Mass Comms., India, 2000—01. Editor: (textbooks) Journeys Through Our World, Self and Beyond. Mem.: Nat. Coun. Tchrs. Englisy. Home: 141 Sombrio Santa Fe NM 87501 Office: Santa Fe CC Richards Ave Santa Fe NM 87508-4887 Office Phone: 505-955-1831. Personal E-mail: jvucinich@yahoo.com. Business E-Mail: jvucinich@sfccnm.edu.

VUKODER, VELDA JANE, social worker; b. East St. Louis, Ill., Jan. 26, 1956; d. Kenneth Ray and Edith Lucille (Hansford) C.; m. Kenneth Thornton, Jan. 26, 1974 (div. 1982); m. Peter Vukoder, 1994. BS, Lindenwood Coll., 1982, postgrad. in Bus. Adminstrn., 1984-85; MSW, Washington U., 1992. Therapist Youth In Need, St. Charles, Mo., 1989-92, Father Flanagan's Boystown, Omaha, 1992-95, Seguin Health Resources, New Braunfels, Tex., 1995-97, Vericare, 1997—. Mem. NASW, ACSW, Tex. Cert. Social Workers. Personal E-mail: canyoncliff@hotmail.com.

VULGAMORE, ALLISON, performing arts association administrator; BMus, Oberlin Coll. Former gen. mgr., artistic adminstr., mgr. ops. Nat. Symphony Orch., Washington; former gen. mgr. N.Y. Philharm. Orch., N.Y.C.; pres., mng. dir. Atlanta Symphony Orch., 1993—. Hon. dir. Oberlin Coll.; mem. arts challenge panel in music NEA. Bd. dirs. Midtown Alliance; mem. Vision 2000 Econ. Devel. Collaborative; Cultural Olympiad and opening ceremonies coord. Centennial Olympic Games, Atlanta, 1996. Am. Symphony Orch. League fellow, 1980. Mem. Atlanta Rotary. Office: Atlanta Symphony Orchestra Robert W Woodruff Arts Ctr 1293 Peachtree St NE Ste 300 Atlanta GA 30309-3552

VUMBACO, BRENDA J., elementary school educator; b. Meriden, Conn., July 11, 1941; d. Frank and Mary (Zipoli) V. BA with honors, Seton Hill Coll., Greensburg, Pa., 1963; MA, Trinity Coll., Hartford, Conn., 1966. Cert. adminstrv. psychology. Assoc. editor Holt, Rinehart and Winston, Inc., N.Y.C.; mng. editor population reports George Washington U., Washington; mgr. publs. NAS, Washington; feature editor, news reporter The Cath. Transcript, Hartford, Conn.; tchr. Archdiocese of Hartford. Exec. dir. Am. Silver Mus., Meriden, Conn.; dir. devel. St. Thomas Aquinas H.S., New Britain, Conn. Recipient Community Svc. awards, numerous writing awards. Avocations: reading, travel, embroidery.

VYDARENY, KAY HERZOG, radiologist, medical educator; b. Chgo., Nov. 26, 1942; MD, U. Mich., 1968. Diplomate Am. Bd. Radiology. Intern Blodgett Meml. Med. Ctr., Grand Rapids, Mich., 1968—69; resident in diagnostic radiology Mich. State U., Grand Rapids, 1975—80; prof. radiology Emory U., Atlanta; radiologist Emory U. Hosp., Atlanta. Mem.: Am. Roentgen Ray Soc., Am. Assn. Women in Radiology, Assn. Univ. Radiologists, Am. Coll. Radiology (pres. 2001—02), Radiol. Soc. N.Am.

VYN, ELEANOR MEARS, physical therapist; d. David A. and Mary A. Mears; divorced; children: Michael, Katherine, Mary. AA, Colby Jr. Coll., 1968; BS, Columbia U., 1970. Phys. therapist Kindred Hosp., Peabody, Mass., 1997—. Avocations: dance, music, art, swimming, gardening. Office Phone: 978-397-9402. Personal E-mail: elievyn@comcast.net.

VYSKOCIL, MARY KAY, lawyer; b. NYC, May 22, 1958; d. Gerard John and Kay Theresa (Murphy) V. BA summa cum laude, Dominican Coll., Blauvelt, N.Y., 1980; JD, St. John's U., Jamaica, N.Y., 1983. Bar: N.Y. 1984, U.S. Dist. Ct. (so., ea. and no. dists.) N.Y. 1984, U.S. Dist. Ct. Conn. 1988, U.S. Dist. Ct. (no. dist.) Calif. 1988, U.S. Ct. Appeals (2d cir.) 1984, U.S. Ct. Appeals (3d cir. 1985), U.S. Ct. Appeals (4th and 6th cirs.) 1993, U.S. Ct. Appeals (9th cir.) 1992, U.S. Ct. Appeals (11th cir.) 1996, U.S. Supreme Ct. 1989; cert. in secondary edn., N.Y. Assoc. Simpson Thacher & Bartlett, NYC, 1983-90, ptnr., litigation dept., 1991—. Co-chair consumer subcom., gender working group 2d cir. Task Force on Racial, Ethnic and Gender Fairness, N.Y.c., 1995-97. Co-author: Modern Reinsurance Law and Practice, 1996, 2d. edit., 2000. Trustee St. Joseph's Sem., Yonkers, N.Y., 1986—, Dominican Coll., 1987—; 2nd v.p. alumni bd. dirs. St. John's U. Sch. Law, 1996—, dean search comm., 1998—. Recipient 40 Under Forty award Nat. Law Jour., 1995. Mem. Assn. Bar City N.Y. (fed. cts. com. 1996-99, chair ins. com. 1993-96), ABA (co-chair subcom. ins. coverage com. of litigation sect. 1997—). Roman Catholic. Avocations: swimming, reading, travel, horseback riding. Office: Simpson Thacher & Bartlett 425 Lexington Ave New York NY 10017-3954 Office Phone: 212-455-3093. Office Fax: 212-455-2502.

WAAGNER, SHARON FLANNERY, library media specialist; b. Teaneck, N.J., Nov. 4, 1941; d. Frederick Worth Sr. and Virginia Mae (Rhode) Flannery; m. Louis Leonard Jr., Sept. 7, 1963; children: Gregory Louis, Susan Lynne Waagner Diaferio. BS in Edn., Empire State Coll., 1990; MLS, SUNY, Albany, 1992. Customer svc. rep. N.J. Bell, Ridgewood, N.J., 1961-64; bookkeeper The Times Press, Rutherford, N.J., 1967-79; libr. media specialist Long Lake (N.Y.) Ctrl. Sch., 1990—. New corrs. The Post Star, Glen Falls, N.Y., 1980-88, Hamilton County News, 1980-88, Tupper Lake Free Press, 1980-88. Mem. EMT Long Lake Resque Squad, 1980-93; past pres. Wood-Ridge PTA, 1977-79; dir. Hamilton County Red Cross, Speculator, N.Y., 1985; treas. Long Lake Fire Dept., 1980-82; mem. Long Lake Cmty. Choir, 1980—. Trustee Wood-Ridge Pub. Libr., 1975-79, So. Adk. Libr. System, Saratoga Springs, N.Y., 1985-90, Friends of Long Lake Libr., 1992—; adv. bd. F-E-H Sch. Libr. Systems, Malone, N.Y., 1992—; class advisor Long Lake Ctrl. Class of 1999; children's program coord. Long Lake Libr. Mem. N.Y. State Libr. Assn., Long Lake Ctrl. Sch. Tech. Com., Adirondack Mus. Republican. Roman Catholic. Avocations: choir, community theatre, children. Home: PO Box 155 Newcomb Rd Long Lake NY 12847 Office: Long Lake Central Sch School St PO Box 217 Long Lake NY 12847-0217

WAAK, PATRICIA ANN, political organization administrator, environmental association executive; b. Muskogee, Okla., Feb. 1, 1943; d. Boxly William and Anne Nell (Smith) W.; children: Cinira Anne Baldi, Rachel Nell Carter. Student Tulane U., 1961-62, U. Houston, 1964-65, George Mason U., 1976-77; diploma Mather Sch. Nursing, 1964. R.N., Va. notary public, N.Y. Peace Corps nurse, Maceio, Alagoas, 1966-68; staff nurse U. Wis. Children's Hosp., Madison, 1968-70; dir. counseling Planned Parenthood, Washington, 1973-75; spl. asst. Devel. Support Bur., U.S. AID, Washington, 1977-78; assoc. dir. Office of Population, AID, Washington, 1978-82; asst. dir. Ctr. for Population and Family Health, Columbia U., N.Y.C., 1982-85; dir. population Nat. Audubon Soc., 1985—, state chair, Colo. Dem. Party, 2005-; U.S. del. UN Population Commn., 1981-82; cons. Family Planning Internat., 1973, Global Com. of Parliamentarians on Population and Devel., 1984-85; project design team U.S. AID, Zimbabwe, 1985, evaluation team, Kenya, Uganda, Nigeria, 1987; NGO participant UN Mid-Decade Conf. of Women, Copenhagen, 1981; moderator global population anniversary Peace Corps Conf., 1981; mem. U.S. del. 2nd and 3d preparatory com. meetings UN Internat. Confs. on Population Devel.; mem. environ. strategy and planning commn. World Conservation Union; lectr. in field. Exec. producer (population videotape) What is the Limit, Sharing the Earth, Finding the Balance, Population and Wildlife. Mem. McGovern-Shriver Presdl. Campaign Staff, 1972; vice chmn. Arlington Democratic Com., 1974; chmn. Arlington Com. on Status of Women, 1975; dep. campaign mgr. Shriver for Pres. Com., 1976; del. Va. Dem. Conv., 1976, 82; mem. Population Task Force, 1986—, Internat. Union Conservation Nature and Natural Resources, NGO steering com. on Devel., Environment and Population; del. World Conservation Strategy Conf. Recipient Population Fellows award Population Ref. Bur., 1993. Mem. Am. Pub. Health Assn. (population sect. council, com. on women's rights), Nat. Council for Internat. Health (pub. policy com.), Assn. for Women in Devel., Nat. Women's Polit. Caucus, Soc. Internat. Devel., Women in Def. of Environment. Home: 4225 Weld Co Rd 1/2 Erie CO 80516 Office: 777 Santa Fe Ave Denver CO 80204 Business E-Mail: pwaak@coloradodems.org.

WAAS, HARRIET ISSNER, elementary school educator; b. Miami, Fla., July 6, 1949; d. Martin and Hildegard (Wimpfheimer) Issner; m. George L. Waas, July 18, 1971; children: Elaine Beth, Amy Michelle. BS, Fla. State U., 1971, MS, 1978. Cert. elem., reading, lang. arts, gifted-talented tchr., ESL, Fla. Elem. tchr. Leon County Schs., Tallahassee; mem. Fla. Title I Statewide Team Dist. Educators, 1997—2002, ETS/Region XIV Comprehensive Ctr. Leadership Team, Pineview. Mem. Fla. Elem. Reading Adv. Bd., 2006—. Contbr. articles to profl. jours. Recipient Extra Mile award, 1986, 1987, 1988. Mem.: SACS, Internat. Reading Assn. Home: 3797 Sally Ln Tallahassee FL 32312-1018

WACHENHEIM, CHERYL J., agricultural studies educator; b. Rogers, Minn., Oct. 11, 1966; d. Arnold and Jacqueline Lee; children: Ellie, Hunter. BS, U. Minn., St. Paul, 1988; MS in Agrl. Econs., Mich. State U., Lansing, 1991, MBA in Materials Logistics and Mgmt., 1993, PhD in Agrl. Econs., 1994. Asst. prof. Ill. State U., Normal, 1993—98; assoc. prof. ND State U., Fargo, 1998—. Cons. in field. Chmn. bd. dirs. Northland Educators Fed. CU, Fargo, 1999—. 1st lt. Minn. Nat. Guard, 1998—. Recipient Excellence in Tchg. award, ND State U. Coll. Agr., 2001. Office: ND State U Dept Agribus and Applied Econs Box 5636 Fargo ND 58105

WACHHOLTZ, ANDREA MARIE, professional ballet dancer, choreographer; b. Bklyn., Aug. 15, 1969; d. Donald E. and Carol Ann Wachholtz. BFA, Adelphi U., Garden City, N.Y., 1991. Cert. CPR ARC, first aid ARC, kinder accreditation tchrs. USA Gymnastics. Soloist Empire State Ballet Co., Buffalo, Xing Ballet Co., Toronto, Ont., Buffalo City Ballet; performer Mime Internationale; soloist Royal Ballet Theatre, Hamburg, NY; ballet dancer Staten Island Ballet Co. Outreach resource coord. and children's ednl. rep. Empire State Ballet Co. Sch., Buffalo; tchg. artist Arts in Edn. Inst. Western N.Y.; gymnastic coach and routine choreographer Summit Gymnastics & Fitness Ctr.; gymnastics team coach Paragon Gymnastics, NJ; ballet instr./choreographer Staten Island Ballet Co. Sch., NY; substitue tchr. H.S. Performing Arts, Buffalo, 1994—95. Scholar, New Ballet Sch. Assoc. Sch. The Feld Ballet. Office: Staten Island Ballet Company 460 Brielle Ave Staten Island NY Office Phone: 718-980-0500. Personal E-mail: neondancer@aol.com.

WACHNER, LINDA JOY, former apparel marketing and manufacturing executive; b. NYC, Feb. 3, 1946; d. Herman and Shirley W.; m. Seymour Applebaum, Dec. 21, 1973 (dec., 1983) BS in Econs. and Bus., U. Buffalo, 1966. Buyer Foley's Federated Dept. Store, Houston, 1968-69; sr. buyer R.H. Macy's, N.Y.C., 1969-74; v.p. Warner divsn. Warnaco, Bridgeport, Conn., 1974-77; v.p. corp. mktg. Caron Internat., N.Y.C., 1977-79; chief exec. officer U.S. divsn. Max Factor & Co., Hollywood, Calif., 1979-82, pres., CEO, 1982-83, Max Factor & Co. Worldwide, 1983-84; mng. dir. Adler & Shaykin, N.Y.C., 1985-86; pres., CEO, chmn. Warnaco Inc., N.Y.C., 1986—2001. Bd. dirs. Applied Graphics Tech., N.Y. Stock Exch. Presdl. appointee Adv. Com. for Trade, Policy, Negotiations; trustee U. Buffalo Found., Carnegie Hall, Aspen Inst.; bd. overseers Meml. Sloan-Kettering Cancer Ctr. Recipient Silver Achievement award L.A. YWCA; named Outstanding Woman in Bus. Women's Equity Action League, 1980, Woman of Yr., MS. Mag., 1986, one of the Yr.'s Most Fascinating Bus. People, Fortune Mag., 1986, one of 10 Most Powerful Women in Corp. Am., Savvy Woman Mag., 1989, 90, Am.'s Most Successful Bus. Woman, Fortune Mag., 1992, Queen of Cash Flow, Chief Exec. Mag., 1994. Mem. Am. Mgmt. Assn., Am. Apparel Mktg. Assn. (bd. dirs.), Bus. Roundtable, Coun. on Fgn. Rels. Republican. Jewish.

WACHOWSKI, SUSAN MARIE, elementary school educator; b. Chgo., Oct. 23, 1956; d. Giles A. and Mary Catherine Wachowski. BA in Polit. Sci., Loyola U., Chgo., 1979; M of Math Edn., DePaul U., Chgo., 1995. Tchr. 8th grade St. John Cross Sch., Western Springs, Ill., 1981—88; tchr. math. Argo Cmty. H.S., Summit, 1989—90; tchr. h.s. Ombudsman Edn. Svcs., Palos Heights, 1990—91; tchr. 6, 7, 8 grades Hinsdale Mid. Sch., 1991—. Presenter in field. Recipient Pomegranate award, Spertus Mus., 1995, Golden Apple award, Golden Apple Found., 2002. Mem.: NEA (assoc.), Nat. Coun. Tchrs. Math., Ill. Edn. Assn. (assoc.). Office: Hinsdale Middle School 100 S Garfield Hinsdale IL 60521 Office Phone: 630-887-1370. Business E-Mail: swachowski@d181.org.

WACHS, CARYN LEE, psychologist, researcher; b. New Haven, July 27, 1972; d. Marvin Dennis and Irena (Twiddy) Wachs. BA, Emory U., 1994; MS, U. La., Lafayette, 1998; PsychD, Argosy U., 2005. Therapist Atlanta Ctr. Eating Disorders, 2001—05; postdoctoral fellow Cambridge Eating Disorder Ctr., Mass., 2005—06. Mem.: APA, Mass. Psychol. Assn. Democrat. Presbyterian. Avocations: travel, pets, billiards. Home: 67 Perry St 7 Newport RI 02840 Office Phone: 508-678-7542, clwox@hotmail.com.

WACHTELL, CYNTHIA JUNE, academic administrator, director, literature educator; BA, MA, Yale U., New Haven, Conn., 1989; AM, Harvard U., Cambridge, Mass., 1992, PhD, 1998. Dir. S. Daniel Abraham Hons. Program, Yeshiva U., N.Y.C., 1999—, asst. prof. English, 2000—. Office: Stern College for Women Yeshiva Univ 245 Lexington Avenue New York NY 10016 Office Phone: 212-340-7702. Business E-Mail: wachtell@yu.edu.

WACHTELL, ESTHER, non-profit management executive, consultant; b. June 30; m. Thomas Wachtell, Jan. 27; children: Roger Bruce, Wendy Anne, Peter James. BA in Phil., Conn. Coll.; MA in Literature, Cornell U. Pres. Music Ctr. of Los Angeles County; founder, pres. The Wachtell Group, TWG, Inc. Lectr. UCLA Grad. Sch. of Mgmt. Bd. visitors George L. Graziadio Sch. of Bus. Pepperdine U.; bd. dirs. The Ventura County Mus. of History and Art; chair U. So. Calif Ctr. Philanthropy and Pub. Policy; bd. dirs. Children's Hosp. L.A. Mem.: Regency Club (bd. dirs.). Fax: 805-649-3303.

WACHTER, SUSAN MELINDA, finance educator; b. June 22, 1943; d. Nathaniel and Edith (Dubow) Jaffe; m. Michael Lawrence Wachter, June 23, 1968; children: Jessica, Jonathan. BA, Radcliffe Coll., 1965; PhD, Boston Coll., 1974; MA (hon.), U. Pa., 1978. Lectr. Bryn Mawr Coll., Pa., 1969-72; lectr. Wharton Sch. U. Pa., Phila., 1972-74, asst. prof. fin., 1974-78, assoc. prof., 1978-95, prof. real estate and fin., 1995—, chmn. real estate dept., 1997—99; asst. sec., policy devel. and rsch. HUD, 1999—2001; Richard B. Warley prof. fin. mgmt., 2003—. Bd. dirs. Beneficial Corp., Beneficial Mortgage Corp. Author: Latin American Inflation: The Structuralist-Monetarist Debat, 1976, Inflation and Pensions, 1987; co-author: Redlining and Public Policy, 1980; co-editor: Towards a New U.S. Industrial Policy?, 1981, Removing Obstacles to Economic Growth, 1984, Real Estate Economics, 1997, Savings and Capital Formation: The Policy Options; editor: Social Security and Private Pensions: Planning for the 21st Century, 1988; bd. editors Jour. Real Estate Rsch., Jour. Am. Real Estate and Urban Econs., Jour. Housing Econs., Jour. Real Estate Fin. and Econs. Recipient Lindbach award Lindbach Soc., 1974-75; Rsch. fellow Harvard U., 1966. Mem. Am. Econ. Assn., Am. Fin. Assn., Econometric Soc., Am. Real Estate and Urban Econs. Assn. (bd. dirs. 1984-91, pres. 1988), Lambda Alpha. Home: 355 Margo Ln Berwyn PA 19312-1453 Office: U Pa Finance Dept Philadelphia PA 19104 Office Phone: 215-898-6355. Business E-Mail: wachter@wharton.upenn.edu.

WACHTMAN, JEANETTE MARIE, art educator, artist, writer; d. John and Margaret Wachtman. BS in Art Edn., State U. Coll., Buffalo, 1971, MS in Art Edn., 1972. Cert. permanent tchg. State U. Coll. -Buffalo, 1972, tchr. 1-5 Ga., 1991. Tchr. art Phoenix Sch. Dist., 1973—83, Suzuki Internat. Learning Ctr., Atlanta, 1984—85, Clayton State Coll., Ga., 1984—85, Chastain Art Ctr., Atlanta, 1984—86, Atlanta Coll. Art, 1988—92, Steeple Art Ctr., Marietta, Ga., 1990—92, Kennesaw State U., Ga., 1988—, Cobb County Schs., Marietta, 1991—. Mem. bd. Ga. Art Edn. Assn., 1995—2001, chair state capitol art exhibit, 1995—2000, co-chair office of govt. art exhibit, Ga., 1996—2000, chair elem. divsn., 1999—2001, art advocacy rep., 2000; mem. elem. divsn. devel. com. Nat. Art Edn. Assn., 1999—2000; presenter, lectr. in field. Author: (book) The How of It - A Cultural Program Resource Guide, 1995, Artists, Elements, and Principles of Art, 2001; co-author: Rhythm-ongs - The History of Art, 2000; one-woman shows include The Octagon House, Camillus, NY, 1977, Seneca Wall Gallery, Liverpool, NY, 1979, Woman in the Arts Festival, Syracuse, NY, 1980, Penfield Libr., SUNY, Oswego, 1981, Liverpool Art Gallery, NY, 1982, Trail of Tears Art Gallery, Atlanta, 1984, Inner Space Gallery, 1993, Istanbul Ctr. for Culture and Dialogue, Norcross, Ga., 2006. Organizer and presenter cmty. based arts edn. program Blackwell Elem. Sch., Cobb County, Marietta. Named Tchr. of Yr., Bryant Elem. Sch., 1996—97, Ga.'s Elem. Art Educator of Yr., Ga. Art Edn. Assn., 1997—98, Elem. Art Educator of Yr., Nat. Art Edn. Assn., 1999; recipient Youth Art Month award of Excellence, Ga. Art Edn. Assn., 1999, Outstanding Continuing Educator award, Kennesaw State U., 1993, Target, 2002; grantee, CVS, 2001, So. Bell, 1992—93, N.Y. State Edn. Dept., 1979. Mem.: Ga. Art Edn. Assn., Nat. Art Edn. Assn. Avocations: travel, art, writing. Home Fax: 770-894-3934. Personal E-mail: rajean@tds.net.

WACKER, SUSAN REGINA, graphics designer, consultant; b. Red Bank, NJ, Apr. 29, 1954; d. Durward Richard and Margaret Rose (Williams) Wacker; m. Edward W. Donle. BFA, Pratt Inst., 1978, cert. computer graphics/electronic pub., 2001. Asst. art dir. Lesley-Hille Inc., N.Y.C., 1975-79; art dir. Kasica, Lefton, Brown, Inc., N.Y.C., 1979-80, Marinelli & Hnath Assoc., Inc., N.Y.C., 1980-82, L'Oreal Retail Divsn., N.Y.C., 2000—02; sr. design dir. Elizabeth Arden Co., N.Y.C., 1982-99; creativie cons., pres. SRW Design, Inc., Pittsfield, Vt., 2002—. Author: Fragrances of the World/Parfums du Monde-21st Anniversary edit., 2005; exhibitions include Mus. Natural History, N.Y.C., 1997—98; photographer Fragrances of the World/Parfums du Monde, 21st Anniversary Edit., 2005. Named CPA Package of the Month Elizabeth Arden's 5th Avenue fragrance line, 1996; recipient 4 DESI awards, 1980, ANDY award, 1980, Fragrance Found. award, 1988, 1991, 1992, Silver award, N.J. Packaging Execs. Club, 1990, ADDY Excellence citation, 1991, Edison Best New Products Gold Medal award, 1991, 2 Gold awards, Nat. Paperbox & Packaging Assn., 1992, 1994, Silver Excellence award, 1993, 10 Silver Excellence awards, 1994, Silver award, Paperboard Packaging Coun., 1993, Excellence award, 1993, Mobius 1st Pl. Statuette award, 1995, Gold award, Nat. Paperboard Coun., 1995, Prix Francois 1st de L'Emballage de Luxe, 1995, OMA Gold award, 1995, Oscar de L'Emballage Prestige á Lyon, 1995, Mobius award 1st Pl. Statuette for Elizabeth Taylor's Black Pearls perfume product line/package design, 1996, OMA Gold award for Elizabeth Arden's 5th Avenue tester display, 1996, OMA Bronze award for Elizabeth Taylor's Black Pearls tester display, 1996, Lagerfeld, Jako Mdsg., 1998, Nat. Paperboard Packaging Conc. award, 1996, OMA Bronze award Lagerfeld JAKO Mdsg. Program, 1998. Mem.: Am. Inst. Graphic Arts, Fashion Group Internat. (mem. publ. com.), Cosmetic Exec. Women Found., Internat. Perfume Bottle Assn. Achievements include patents in field. Avocations: skiing, tennis, horseback riding, photography. Office: SRW Design Inc 19 Schoolhouse Dr PO Box 567 Pittsfield VT 05762 Office Phone: 888-666-7380. E-mail: srwacker@aol.com, srwdesign@comcast.net.

WACKER-B. DEBORAH, secondary Spanish and special education educator; b. San Diego, Dec. 22, 1945; d. Robert Eugene and Marion Llewella (Bancroft) Wacker; m. William E. Calvert, Dec. 22, 1966 (div. Aug. 1984); 1 child, William E. Calvert II; m. John Steven Bertram, Mar. 8, 1985 (div. Feb. 2001). BA, Belhaven Coll., Jackson, Miss., 1967. Cert. tchr., Miss., Tex. Mid. sch. spl. edn. tchr. Killeen Ind. Sch. Dist., Tex., 1982-85; elem. sch. spl. edn. tchr., tchr. ESL, Mansfield Ind. Sch. Dist., Tex., 1985-86; jr. high sch. spl. edn. tchr., head dept. Arlington Ind. Sch. Dist., Tex., 1986-90; jr. high sch. spl. edn. tchr. Conroe Ind. Sch. Dist., Tex., 1990-92, high sch. spl. edn. tchr., 1992-93, tchr. Spanish, 1993—99; v.p. Bertram Cons., Inc., 1995—96; tchr. spl. edn. Cy-Fair Ind. Sch. Dist., Tex., 1996—97; substitute tchr. Northland Christian Sch., 1997—2003; Spanish tchr. Klein Intermediate Sch., 2000—, Alief (Tex.) Taylor H.S., 2003—. Co-sponsor Tex. Future Tchrs. Assn., Pan Am. Student Assn./Club Leon; mem. various coms. Conroe (Tex.) Ind. Sch. Dist., 1991-96 Soprano Montgomery County Choral Soc., Conroe, 1991—94, sect. leader, 1995—96; mem. Campus Site-Based Decision Making Team, 1996—97, Arlington Choral Soc., 1986—89; sponsor Tex. Future Tchrs. Am., 1995—97; mem. Houston Symphony League, 1997—2003, Houston Mus. Fine Arts, 1996—97, 1998—, Houston Mus. Natural Sci.; soprano Houston Choral Soc., 2001—. Mem.: NEA, AAUW, Alief Educators Assn. (v.p. 2004—), Klein Edn. Assn. (v.p. 2002—03), Am. Coun. Tchrs. Fgn. Lang., Conroe Edn. Assn. (pres.-elect 1990—92, exec. com. 1994—97, pres.-elect 1995—97), Tex. State Tchrs. Assn. (1st pres. 1991, spl. edn. caucus), Tex. Fgn. Lang. Assn., Internat. Club (sponsor 1995—2002). Methodist. Avocations: music, reading, travel, internet. Home: 1333 Eldridge Pkwy Apt 212 Houston TX 77077-1611 Personal E-mail: soyyarnalady@aol.com. Business E-Mail: deborah.wacker@aliefisd.net.

WACTAWSKI-WENDE, JEAN, epidemiologist, educator, researcher; d. John Stanley Wactawski and Elizabeth Louise Ramsay; m. Karl Edward Wende, 1989; children: Alexandra Grace, Marilyn Elizabeth. BA in Biology, Canisius Coll., 1981; MS in Natural Scis., U. Buffalo, 1983, PhD in Epidemiology, 1989. Rsch. scientist Roswell Park Cancer Inst., Buffalo, 1982-89; clin. asst. prof. U. Buffalo, 1989-98, asst. prof., 1998—. Mem. faculty coun. U. Buffalo Sch. Medicine, 1994—. Contbr. articles to sci. and profl. jours. Bd. dirs. Niagara Hospice, Niagara County Bd. Health, N.Y., 1996-2002. Grantee Women's Health Initiative, NIH, 1993—, U.S. Army, 1996-2001, Women's Health Inst., 1995—, NIDR, 2002-. Mem. Am. Coll. of Epidemiology, Soc. for Epidemiologic Rsch., Soc. for Bone and Mineral Rsch. Presbyterian. Avocations: golf, sailing. Office: U Buffalo Sch Medicine 270 Farber Hall 3435 Main St Buffalo NY 14214-3001 E-mail: JWW@Buffalo.edu.

WADDELL, SARAH KATHERINE, elementary school educator; b. Portland, Oreg., Feb. 25, 1975; d. Charles Tannert Pinney, Jr. and Pamela Marie Pinney; m. Kevin Franklin Waddell, July 7, 2002; 1 child, Atticus Charles. BS in Liberal Arts, Oreg. State U., Corvallis, 1998, MA in Tchg., 2000. Cert. tchr. Oreg., 2000. Instrnl. tech. specialist Tigard Tualatin Sch. Dist., Oreg., 2000—02, 7th grade lang. arts/social studies tchr., 2002—. Office Phone: 503-431-4000.

WADDILL, CYNTHIA KAY, nurse; d. Owen Lee and Epsie Adrias Sugg; m. Dale Alin Waddill, July 16, 1993; children: Stacy Kay Emfinger, Christopher Ryan Emfinger, Jamison Matthew Emfinger. ADN, U. Ark. at Little Rock, 1981—84; BSN, U. of Phoenix, 1998—2000, MSN, 2000—01; MSN FNP, Graceland U., 2001—03. Certified Nurse of the Operating Room, AORN Colo., 1994, Orthopaedic Nurse Certified, NAON, 2001. Ortho trauma charge nurse Univ. Ark. Med Sci. Campus, Little Rock, 1991—96, Shands Hosp., Jacksonville, Fla., 1996—2001; nurse Shands UF Hosp., Jacksonville, Fla., 2004—. Sr. nurse cons. Ortho Trauma Practice Cons., Jacksonville, Fla., 2001—. Recipient Nat. Nurse Honor Soc., Sigma Theta Tau, 2002. Mem.: Am. Nursing Assn., Fla. Nurses Assn., Am. Acad. of Nurse Practitioners, Nat. Assn. of Orthopaedic Nurses, Sigma Theta Tau. Avocations: scuba diving, golf, fishing. Office: McLeod Orthopaedic Assocs 901 E Cheves St Ste 500 Florence SC 29501 Personal E-mail: cbones100k@aol.com.

WADDINGTON, BETTE HOPE (ELIZABETH CROWDER), violinist, educator; b. San Francisco; d. John and Marguerite (Crowder) Waddington. BA in Music, U. Calif., Berkeley, 1945, postgrad., Julliard Sch. Music, 1950, San Jose State Coll., 1955; MA in Music and Art, San Francisco U., 1953; studied with, Joseph Fuchs, Melvin Ritter, Frank Gittelson, Felix Khuner, Daniel Bonsack, D.C. Dounis, Naoum Blinder, Eddy Brown. Cert. gen. elem. and secondary tchr., Calif.; life cert. music and art for jr. coll.; cert. in librarianship for elem. sch. to jr. coll., Calif. Violinist Erie (Pa.) Symphony, 1950-51, Dallas Symphony, 1957-58, St. Louis Symphony, 1958-95. Toured alone and with St. Louis Symphony U.S., Can., Middle East, Japan, China, England, Korea, Europe, Africa; concert master Peninsula Symphony, Redwood City and San Mateo, Calif., Grove Music Soc., N.Y.C.; violinist St. Louis Symphony, 1958-95, violinist emeritus; numerous recs. St. Louis Symphony, 1958—. Julliard Sch. Music scholar 1950, San Jose State Coll. scholar 1955. Mem. Am. String Tchrs. Assn., Am. Musicians Union (life, St. Louis and San Francisco chpts.), U. Calif. Alumnae Assn. (life, Berkeley), San Francisco State U. Alumni Assn. (life), San Jose State U. Alumni Assn. (life), Sierra Club (life), Alpha Beta Alpha. Avocations: travel, art, archeology, history, drawing, painting. Office: St Louis Symphony Orch care Powell Symphony Hall 718 N Grand Blvd Saint Louis MO 63103-1011

WADDINGTON, IRMA JOANN, music educator; b. Nokomis, Ill., June 7, 1929; d. Albert William and Rose Minnie (Hueschen) Miller; m. Ralph Roger Waddington, Nov. 3, 1946; children: Joann, Janet, Jennifer. Cert. piano, organ Ill. State Music Tchrs. Assn. Music tchr. pvt. studio, Pana, Ill., 1957—2003; ch. organist, choir dir. St. Paul Luth. Ch., Pana, 1957—; keyboard player Waddington Trio, Pana, 1987—98, 2000—02. Composer: Memories of Kerri, 1983, Rejoice! Rejoice!, 1993, Praise! Praise!, 1993. Organist Rotary Club, Pana, 1985—, sr. citizens, Pana, 1970—, local nursing homes, Pana, 1974—. Named Best Piano Teacher, Decatur (Ill.) Herald & Review, 1987, Member of Yr. Decatur Area Music Tchrs. Assn., 1997. Mem. Am. Fedn. Musicians (pres., 1965-68), Music Tchrs. Nat. Assn., Decatur Area Music Tchrs. Assn. (pres. 1983, 84, 90, 94, 95, clinician, 1979-2005), Ill. Music Tchrs. Assn. (clinician 1991 conv.). Republican. Lutheran. Avocations: travel, golf. Home: 709A Kitchell Ave Pana IL 62557-1875 Personal E-mail: irmamusic@consolidated.net.

WADDY, PATRICIA A., historian, architecture educator; b. Cannelton, Ind., July 29, 1941; d. Luther and Gertrude Viola (Brandyberry) W. BA, Rice U., 1963; MA, Tulane U., 1965; PhD, NYU, 1973. Vis. lectr. Carnegie-Mellon U., Pitts., 1970-71, asst. prof., 1971-77; assoc. prof. archtl. history Syracuse U., NY, 1977-91, prof., 1991—2002, disting. prof. architecture, 2002—. Vis. lectr. Cornell U., Ithaca, N.Y., 1977, vis. assoc. prof., 1980; Frederic Lindley Morgan prof. archtl. design U. Louisville, 2006. Author: Seventeenth-Century Roman Palaces: Use and The Art of the Plan, 1990 (Alice Davis Hitchcock award 1992); co-author: (with D. DiCastro and A.M. Pedrocchi) Il Palazzo Pallavicini Rospigliosi e la Galleria Pallavicini, 2000; editor Nicodemus Tessin the Younger, Traicté dela decoration interieure (1717), 2002. Fulbright grantee, Rome, 1968-69; fellow Am. Acad. in Rome, 1970, Nat. Humanities Ctr., 1984-85, Samuel H. Kress sr. fellow Nat. Gallery Art, 1994-95, NEH fellow, 1998-99, Guggenheim fellow, 1999-00, Am. Coun. Learned Soc. fellow, 1978. Mem. Soc. Archtl. Historians (book rev. editor Jour. 1985-88, editor 1990-93, 2d v.p. 1993-94, 1st v.p. 1994-96, pres. 1996-98), Coll. Art Assn., Renaissance Soc. Am. Office: Syracuse U Sch Architecture Syracuse NY 13244-1250 E-mail: pwaddy@syr.edu.

WADE, ALLISON MUIA, orthopedic surgeon; b. NYC, Feb. 11, 1974; d. Carolyn Muia; m. Richard Scott Wade, June 17, 2000. BA in Psychology and Italian, U. Tenn., Knoxville, 1996, MD, 2003. Rsch. asst. Univ. Historian's Office, Knoxville, 1992—96; state govt. intern State of Tenn., Nashville, 1995—96; orthop. asst. Campbell Clinic Orthops., Memphis, 1998—99. Co-founder St. Jude's Life and Laughter Program, Memphis, 1999—2003; co-organizer Al Gore: Friends and Family Re-Union, Nashville, 1996. Fred M Roddy Coll. scholar, 1992—96, Salutatorian scholar, U. Tenn., 1992, Italian Study Abroad scholar, 1996. Mem.: AMA, Mo. State Orthop. Assn., Am. Acad. Family Physicians, Student Surg. Soc. (v.p. 2002—03), Ruth Jackson Orthop. Soc., Golden Key (v.p. 1995—96), Phi Kappa Phi, Phi Beta Kappa.

WADE, AMY MICHELLE, elementary school educator; b. Hot Springs, Ark., Sept. 2, 1962; d. Roger Michael and Madelyn Ruth Shields; m. Douglas Lee Wade; children: Julianna Michelle LoPorto, Zachary Levi Chantry. BS, Ark. Tech U., Russellville, 1990. Cert. tchr. Ark. Tchr. Lamar (Ark.) Elem. Sch., 1990—91, Plainview (Ark.) Elem. Sch., 1992—2003, Dardanelle (Ark.) Elem. Sch., Ark., 2003—. Musician Apostolic Gospel Tabernacle, Russellville, Ark., 1976—2006. Home: 14759 N State Hwy 28 Dardanelle AR 72834 Office: Dardanelle Elem Sch 2306 N State Hwy 7 Dardanelle AR 72834 Office Phone: 479-229-3707.

WADE, DEANNA JO, retired elementary school educator; b. New Castle, Ind., July 29, 1939; d. Joseph Floyd and Agnes Marie (Jordan) McGuire; m. Denzel Wm. Barricklow, Aug. 1, 1959 (dec. apr. 1992); children: Susanna, Timothy; m. Allen Wade. BS, Ball State U., 1961, MA, 1987. Cert. tchr., Ind. Music tchr. Muncie (Ind.) Community Schs., 1961-63; substitute tchr. Fayette County/Western Wayne Sch. Corps., Connersville/Cambridge, Ind., 1963-86; 6th grade tchr. Fayette County Sch. Corp., Connersville, Ind., 1987—2004; ret. Dir. Outdoor Edn. Sumemr Sch., 1987-2003. Contbr. articles to Ind. Audubon Quar., 1975-90. Sec., Three Rivers Solid Waste Dist. Adv. Com., Fayette County, 1991-2000; 3d v.p. Treatyline coun. Girl Scouts U.S., 1980-81; choir dir. Cambridge City (Ind.) Christian Ch., 1992. Mem. Ind. Audubon Soc. (edn. chair 1990-2004, Brooks award 1981), Connersville Area Reading Coun., Hoosier Assn. Sci. Tchrs., Psi Iota Xi (pres. 1975-76). Avocations: birding, camping, environmental activities. Home: 14096 Milton Rd Milton IN 47357-9756

WADE, EARLINE, elementary school educator; d. Earl and Betty Jean Wade. BS in Elem. Edn., Bowie State Coll., Md., 1983, MEd in Guidance Counseling, 1990. Cert. adminstr. I and II Md. State Dept. Tchr. 3d grade Oak Hill Elem., Severna Park, Md., 1990—93, tchr. 1st grade, 1983—90, 1993—2005, tchr. 2d grade, adminstr. in charge Summer Acad., 2005—. Nominee PTO, 2003—04, Kiwanis Club, 2003—04. Mem.: Md. State Tchrs. Assn., Tchrs. Assn. Anne Arundel County, Delta Sigma Theta. Office: Oak Hill Elem 34 Truck House Rd Severna Park MD 21146

WADE, ERNESTINE, public health nurse; b. Franklin, La., Aug. 18, 1941; d. Phillip and Emma (Bettis) Miller; m. James Wade Jr., Dec. 25, 1965; 1 child, Kevin Troy. ASN, Lamar U., 1980. Nurse asst. U. Tex., Galveston, 1961; pharmacy technician St. Mary Hosp., Port Arthur, Tex., 1963-64, lic. vocat. nurse, 1967-80, RN, 1980-81, Bapt. Hosp., Beaumont, Tex., 1981-82, UpJohn Home Health Agy., Port Arthur, 1982-83, Pub. Health Dept., Port Arthur, 1983-96; dir. health Port Arthur City Health Dept., 1996—. Mem. Star Enterprise Corp., Port Arthur, 1996—, UpJohn Healthcare, 1981-83, Port Arthur Ind. Sch. Dist. Head-Start, 1994-96. Mem. Southeast Tex. Nursing Assn. Avocations: reading, walking. Home: 4918 Austin Ave Port Arthur TX 77640-2505 Office: Port Arthur City Health Dept 603 5th St Port Arthur TX 77640-6540

WADE, ESTELLE B., psychologist, psychoanalyst; b. Bklyn., July 20, 1938; d. David and Selma Jobyna Schwartz; m. Donald E. Wade (div.); m. Alan L. Cantor, Apr. 3, 1992. BA, Clark U., 1959; MA, Brandeis U., 1961; PhD, Columbia U., 1971. Lic. psychologist NY, 1972, cert. profl. qualification psychology Assn. State Provincial Bds., 2001; bd. cert. found. fellow Am. Coll. Advanced Practice Psychologists, 1999. Postdoctoral fellowship in psychoanalysis Post-grad. Ctr. Mental Health, N.Y.C., 1980—83; counselor Inst. Crippled & Disabled, N.Y.C., 1961—62, N.Y.C. Dept. Hosps., Bklyn., 1962—65, Queens, 1962—65; psychology intern VA, N.Y.C., 1966—68; tchg. asst. Columbia U., N.Y.C., 1968—69; lectr. psychology CUNY, 1969—70; staff psychologist Queens County Neuropsychiatric Inst., Jackson Heights, 1969—71, chief psychologist, 1971—81; supervising psychologist Fifth Ave. Ctr. Psychotherapy, N.Y.C., 1981—84; pvt. practice psychoanalysis & psychotherapy N.Y.C., 1977—. Host several radio programs, 1971—75. Mem. Pinewoods Folk Music Soc., 1966—75, program chair, 1971—75; mem. Queens Ind. Democrats, Jackson Heights, 1967—69, Sloop Clearwater-NYC Chapter, 1969—75, program chair, 1973—75. Mem.: APA (program chair divsn. independent practice 1980—81, psychologist psychoanalyst practitioner, divsn. psychoanalysis 1984—), NY State Psychological Assn., Nat. Register Health Svc. Providers Psychology (platinum registrant 1994), Phi Beta Kappa. Democrat. Jewish. Avocations: classical music, opera, reading, walking. Office: 730 Fifth Ave 9th Fl New York NY 10019 Office Phone: 212-659-7799.

WADE, GAYLE PANAGOS, literature and language professor; b. Alexandria, Va., Mar. 25, 1950; d. Gus and Amber Henry Panagos; m. Sonny Wade, Aug. 26, 1972; children: Jess, Danny, Greg. BA, Emory and Henry Coll., Emory, Va., 1972; MA, Concordia U., Montreal, 1976. Asst. prof. English Patrick Henry C.C., Martinsville, Va., 1990—. Home: 943 Jones Ridge Rd Axton VA 24054 Office: Patrick Henry Community College 645 Patriot Ave Martinsville VA 24115 Office Phone: 276-656-0207.

WADE, GAYLIA SUZANNE, secondary school educator; d. Paul Hamilton Garrett and Sylvia Maurice Smith; m. Lorrin Louis Dreier (div.); children: Lorri Anne Dreier(dec.), Christopher Eric Dreier; m. Richard Merrill Wade, Dec. 20, 1997; 1 stepchild, Staci Lanell Wade Watkins. BA cum laude, So. Nazarene U., Bethany, Okla., 1967; postgrad., U. N.Mex., Albuquerque, 1985—97. Secondary tchg. cert. N.Mex., Tex. Tchr. Burges HS, El Paso, Tex., 1967—68, Albuquerque Pub. Schs., 1968—70, 1985—, Socorro (Tex.) Ind. Sch. Dist., 1980—84. Coord. mid. sch. initiative at-risk students City of Albuquerque/Albuquerque Pub. Schs., 1995—97; mentor gateway to tchg. program Golden Apple Found., U. N.Mex., Albuquerque Pub. Schs., 2005—; tutor Advantage Tutoring, Albuquerque, 2005—06. Sponsor World Vision, 1992—94, Voice of Martyrs, Bartlesville, Okla., 2005—06; contbr., supporter Albuquerque Rescue Mission, Storehouse, Joy Junction, 2005—06. Named Best All-Around Tchr., Truman Mid. Sch., 1988; recipient Tchg. Excellence award, 2005, Golden Apple award, N.Mex. Golden Apple Found., 1997. Fellow: Golden Apple Found. (life); mem.: Phi Delta Lambda. Republican. Baptist. Avocations: quilting, gardening, literature, piano. Office: Grant Mid Sch 1111 Easterday Dr NE Albuquerque NM 87112 Office Phone: 505-299-2113.

WADE, JANICE ELIZABETH, musician, educator, conductor; b. Decorah, Iowa, May 20, 1937; d. Lloyd Edward and Vivian Lois (Caskey) Richards; children: Kendall Anne, Craig Patrick. B in Music Edn., Drake U., 1959, M in Music Edn., 1960; DMA in Violin Performance, U. Iowa, 1992. Pvt. tchr. music, freelance violinist, Des Moines, 1960-87; prof. music Wartburg Coll., Waverly, Iowa, 1987—, chair, music dept. Prin. 2d violin Des Moines Symphony, 1965—87, chmn. players com., 1978—85, mem. negotiating team, 1983—87; tchr. instrumental music Des Moines pub. schs., 1966—76; founder, music dir., condr. Des Moines Cmty. Orch., 1976—87; concertmaster Bijou Players, Des Moines, 1980—; dir., condr. Wartburg Cmty. Symphony, 1987—. Editor: Am. String Tchr. Jour., 1976—84; contbr. articles to profl. jours. Active Planned Parenthood, Mus. Panel Iowa Arts Coun., 1989—90. Mem.: AAUP, Am. Symphony Orch. League, Am. String Tchrs. Assn., Condrs'. Guild, Iowa String Tchrs. Assn. (past pres.). Avocations: sewing, jogging, home decorating, reading, woodworking. Office: Wartburg Coll Dept Music 100 Wartburg Blvd # 1003 Waverly IA 50677-2215

WADE, REBA, musician, educator; b. Dresden, Tenn., Apr. 30, 1938; d. John Buford and Willie Ruth (Todd) Tilley; m. Ronald Lee Wade, July 22, 1956; children: Tony Lee, Randy Neal. Student, U. Tenn., Martin, 1976-80. Tchr. pvt. studio, Martin, 1962-70, 76—, Sharon (Tenn.) Sch., 1968, Westview H.S., Martin, 1976--79, Greenfield (Tenn.) Sch., 1984-86; mgr., dir. Wade Bros., Martin, 1965-71, High Variety Show Mems., Martin, 1994—. Tchr., accompanist for students, shows, groups, auditions and on radio and TV; profl. pianist. Prodr. Wade Bros. Rec., 1969, student recs., 1988-90, 97-2005; author lyrics, music original compositions including Little Cowboy, 1963, I Love My Jesus, 1963, Christmas Time, 1964, Happy Happy Day, 1964, Love, 1964, Oh How I Love You, 1965, Dear Mis-Fortune, 1965, Red Lace, 1965, Crazy Little Feeling, 1967, All Because of Christmas Day, 1968, Mean Mean Mama, 1968, God is Like This, 1979, Little Dreams, 1992, also tnr., prodr., 1988-90, 97-2001; performer Christmas music The White House, 1997-98, Pentagon Party, 1998; performer World Wide Air Show RAF, Fairford, Eng., London, 1999; recorded 3CDs (total 32 songs and pieces on piano), Nasville, Tenn., 2000, 2001, Christmas CD (9 songs), 2003; recorded 18 songs and pieces on piano, Hilltop Rec. Studio, Nashville, 2000, 12 others, 2001, 10 more songs, 2003; prodr. five rec. sessions Hilltop Rec. Studio, Nashville, 2004; tnr. students Cerebral Palsy Telethon WBBJ TV, Jackson, Tenn., 1995-2002, 05. Active in civic affairs, 1947-; judge music festival U. Tenn., Martin, 2000-01, 2002, 2004-05, fall performance, 2000-01, 2002-03, 04, 05, Kiwanis Club Talent Show, 2000-01; active Martin Elem. Chorus, 2001; fundraiser Big Cypress Tree State Park, 2000-01, Dickson (Tenn.) Police Dept., 2000, Relay for Life, 1992-2005; invited charter mem. 1st Women's History Mus., Washington; planner, tnr. fund raiser program local fire dept. to buy new fire truck, 2000, entertainment fund raiser local town to install new lights in town, 2000; trained and provided entertainment for various charities. Recipient Vol. Svc. award State of Tenn. Recreation and Parks Assn., 2001, Companion Honor award, 2002, Salute to Greatness award, 2005; named Internat. Woman Yr., 2001, Internat. Musician, 2004, Internat. Musician Yr., 2004; nominated for Am. Medal Honor, 2002, 03-04, Lifetime Achievement award United Cultural Convention, 2005. Fellow Internat. Biog. Assn. (life, dir. deputy gen., 2006, advisor to dir. gen., 2006, Top 100 Musicians Pinnacle Achievement award, 2006, Internat. Order Merit, 2006); mem. SAI (life, social chmn. 1979), Songwriters Guild Am., Music Tchrs. Nat. Assn., Philharm. Music Club (v.p. 1983-84, pres. 1985), Am. Coll. Musicians, Den. Women, Am. Biog. Inst. (profl. women's adv. bd., 2006—, World Lifetime Achieve award, 2004, Woman of Yr., 2006, 500 Greatest Geniuses of 21st Century, 2006, Am. Medal Honor, 2006) Baptist. Achievements include being ivvited to become a charter member of the first women's history museum in Washington DC. Avocations: music writing, interior decorating and designing, travel, church and charity work. Home: 208 Melody Dr Martin TN 38237-5535

WADE, SUSAN PRINCE, retired music educator; b. Columbus, Ohio, Apr. 22, 1949; d. William James and Anita Jane Staiger Prince; m. Michael Alan Wade, Dec. 28, 1985; 1 child, Tiffany Marie Wade Appell. MusB in Edn., Ohio State U., Columbus, 1972. Music educator Worthington City Schs., Ohio, 1973—. Choir dir. Northminster Presbyn. Ch., Columbus, 1968—85; singer Indian Run United Meth. Ch., Dublin, 1992—, Orange Johnson Singers, Worthington, 1980—, Columbus Symphony Chorus, 1982—. Mem. worship com. Indian Run United Meth. Ch., Dublin, 1994—2000. Recipient Sr. Women Leaders award, Ohio State U., 1972, Innovation award, Ohio Ho. of Reps., 1992. Mem.: NEA, Ohio Edn. Assn., Worthington Edn. Assn., Music Educators Nat. Conf., Ohio Music Educators Assn., Delta Omicron. Methodist. Avocations: gardening, travel. Home: 6980 Concord Bend Powell OH 43065 Office: Worthington City Schs 200 E Wilson Bridge Rd Worthington OH 43085 Office Phone: 614-883-2700. Personal E-mail: singersusie49@sbcglobal.net. Business E-Mail: swade@worthington.k12.oh.us.

WADE, THELMA J., lawyer, mental health nurse; d. Curtis E. and Laura B. Wade; children: Caleb, Mackenzie. ADN, S.W. Va. CC, Richards, 1908; BS, Bluefield Coll., Va., 1993; JD, Appalachian Sch. Law, Grundy, Va., 2000. Bar: Va. 2000; RN Va., 1992, Critical Care RN, Va., 1998. Staff nurse Clinch Valley Med. Ctr., Richlands, 1988—2001; ptnr. Bates & Wade, PLC, Bristol; staff nurse S.W. Va. Mental Health Inst., Marion. Office: Bates & Wade PLC 111 Commonwealth Ave Bristol VA 24201

WADE, TONYA SUE, religious studies educator, small business owner; d. Tommy and Linda Staten, Audrey Staten (Stepmother); m. John L. Wade. BSE in Early Childhood Edn., Ouachita Bapt. U., Ark., 1997; MA in Edn., U. Miss., 2005—06. Cert. Profl. Tchr. Ark. Dept. Edn., 1997. Pre-k kindergarten tchr. So. Bapt. Ednl. Ctr., Southaven, Miss., 1998—2000, elem. bible tchr., 2000—; bus. mgr. John Wade's Karate and Gymnastics, Southaven, Miss., 2003—. Autism art camp dir. John Wade's Karate and Gymnastics, Southaven, Miss., 2005—. Actor: (ouachita traveling drama team performances); contbr. ouachita puppet ministry presentations; dir.(participant): (ouachita clown troupe ministry). Children's ministry dir. Calvary Bapt. Ch., Horn Lake, Miss., 2004—06. Grantee Tchrs. Grant, Desoto Excellence Found., 2005—06; scholar Amb., Rotary Internat., 1997—98; SBEC Tchrs. Scholarship, U. Miss., 2005—06, Internat. Study Scholarship, 2006. Baptist. Avocations: travel, ballroom dancing, scrapbooks. Office: So Baptist Ednl Ctr 7400 Getwell Rd Southaven MS 38672 Office Phone: 662-349-5013.

WADLEY, SUSAN SNOW, anthropologist; b. Balt., Nov. 18, 1943; d. Chester Page and Ellen Snow (Foster) W.; m. Bruce Woods Derr, Dec. 28, 1971 (div. July 1989); children: Shona Snow, Laura Woods; m. Richard Olanoff, July 4, 1992. BA, Carleton Coll., Northfield, 1965; MA, U. Chgo., 1967, PhD, 1973. Instr. Syracuse U., 1970-73, asst. prof., 1973-76, dir. fgn. and comparative studies program, 1978-83, prof., 1982, dir. So. Asia Ctr., 1985—, Ford-Maxwell prof. South Asian Studies, 1996—, chair anthropology dept., 1990-95, assoc. dean Coll. of Arts and Scis., 2003—. Trustee Am. Inst. Indian Studies, Chgo., 1984-93, exec. com., 1991-94; mem. joint com. South Asia Social Sci. Rsch. Coun., 1982-89. Author: Shakti: Power in the Conceptual Struture of Krimpur Women, 1975, Women in India: Two Perspectives, 1978, revised, 1989, 95, Struggling with Destiny in Karimpur, 1925-84, 1994; editor: Power of Tamil Women, 1980, Oral Epics in India, 1989, Media and the Transformation of Religion in South Asia, 1995, Raja Nal and the Goddess: The North Indian Oral Epic Ahola with Performance, 2004. Pres. Edward Smith Parent Tchr. Orgn., Syracuse, 1988-89; pres. bd. dirs. Open Hand Internat. Mask and Puppet Mus., 2000-2003. Grantee NSF, 1967-69, U.S. Dept. Edn., 1983-84, Smithsonian Instn., 1983-84, Am. Inst. Indian Studies, 1989, Social Scis. Rsch. Coun., 1989, NEH, 1995, 98. Mem. Am. Anthropological Soc., Am. Folklore Soc., Assn. for Asian Studies. Home: 302 Carlton Dr Syracuse NY 13214-1906 Office: Syracuse U Maxwell Sch Syracuse NY 13244-0001 Business E-Mail: sswadley@syr.edu.

WADLOW, JOAN KRUEGER, retired academic administrator, retired construction executive; b. LeMars, Iowa, Aug. 21, 1932; d. R. John and Norma I. (IhLe) Krueger; m. Richard R. Wadlow, July 27, 1958; children: Dawn, Kit. BA, U. Nebr., 1953, PhD, 1963; MA, Fletcher Sch. Law and Diplomacy, 1956; cert., Grad. Inst. Internat. Studies, Geneva, 1957. Mem. faculty U. Nebr., Lincoln, 1966-79, prof. polit. scis., 1964-79, assoc. dean Coll. Arts and Scis., 1972-79; prof. polit. sci., dean Coll. Arts and Scis., U. Wyo., Laramie, 1979-84, v.p. acad. affairs, 1984-86; prof. polit. sci., provost U. Okla., Norman, 1986-91; chancellor U. Alaska, Fairbanks, 1991-99. Cons. on fed. grants; bd. dirs. Alaska Sea Life Ctr., Key Bank Alaska; mem. Commn. Colls. N.W. Assn.; pres. Lan Constrn., Inc., 1999-2004. Contbr. articles to profl. jours. Bd. dirs. Nat. Merit Scholarship Corp., 1988-97, Lincoln United Way, 1976-77, Bryan Hosp., Lincoln, 1978-79, Washington Ctr., 1986-99, Key Bank of Alaska, Alaska SeaLife Ctr.; v.p., exec. commr. North Ctrl. Assn., pres., 1991; pres. adv. bd. Lincoln YWCA, 1970-71; mem. def. adv. com. Women in the Svcs., 1987-89; mem. cmty. adv. bd. Alaska Airlines; mem. Univ. Pres.'s Mission to Israel, 1998; mem. bd. dirs. Netarts Oceanside Sanitary Dist., 2002-04. Recipient Mortar Board Tchg. award, 1976, Alumni Scholar Achievement award Rotary Internat., 1998, Alumni Achievement award U. Nebr., 2003; Seacrest Journalism fellow 1953-54, Rotary fellow, 1956-57, fellow Conf. Coop. Man, Lund, Sweden, 1956. Mem. NCAA (divsn. II pres. coun. 1997-99), Internat. Studies Assn. (co-editor Internat. Studies Notes 1978-91), Nat. Assn. State Univs. and Land-Grant Colls. (exec. com. coun. acad. affairs 1989-91, chair internat. affairs counsel 1996-97), Western Assn. Africanists (pres. 1980-82), Assn. Western Univs. (pres. 1993), Coun. Colls. Arts and Scis. (pres. 1983-84), Greater Fairbanks C. of C., Gamma Phi Beta. Republican. Congregationalist. Address: Chancellor Emerita PO Box 246 Oceanside OR 97134-0246 Personal E-mail: wadlow@hughes.net.

WAGER, DEBORAH MILLER, researcher, consultant; b. Phila., Sept. 5, 1938; d. Albert S. and Pauline (Goldberg) Miller; m. Robert J. Wager, July 3, 1966; 1 child, James M. BA, Skidmore Coll., 1960; MAT, Columbia U., 1963. Editor Toy Quality and Safety Report, Washington, 1972-88; cons. Wager Rsch., Washington, 1989—. Devel. rschr. Sidwell Friends Sch., Washington, 1988-89, 92-98, 2003—, Georgetown Day Sch., 1995—; trustee Sheridan Sch., Washington, 1978-84. Author: Good Toys, 1986. Mem. Assn. Profl. Rschrs. Advancement. Office: Wager Rsch Consulting 4545 29th St NW Washington DC 20008-2144 E-mail: dwager@erols.com.

WAGER, PAULA JEAN, artist; b. Lansing, Mich., Dec. 19, 1929; d. Mervin Elihu and Cora Della (Raymer) Fowler; m. William Douglas Wager, May 4, 1952; children: Pamela Ann, Scott Alan. Student, Mich. State U., 1949-52. Music tchr., Toledo, Ohio, 1968-72, Union Lake, Mich., 1972-76; tchr. art, artist Paula Wager's Art Studio, Commerce Twp., Mich., 1984—. Hostess Artistic Touch with Paula, Media Network of Waterford, 1999—, (Cable Comcast channel 44), Waterford, Mich., 1991-94, 96—, AT&T (formerly called TCI West Oakland), Walled Lake, Mich., Channel 10, 1991-94, Channel 14, 1996—. Exhibited in group shows including Village Art Supplies, 1982-88, Pontiac Oakland Soc. Artists, 1983—, Pontiac Galleria, 1983, 99, Oakland C.C., Commerce Twp., 1985, Red Piano Gallery, Hilton Head, S.C., 1985-89, Mich. State U., East Lansing, 1986, Silver Pencil Gallery, Pontiac, 1987-89, Wooden Sleight, Vestaburg, Mich., 1988-93, Art Pad, Keego Harbor, Mich., 1990-93, Local Color Gallery, Union Pier, Mich., 1992-94, Mich. Assn. Artists, Southfield Civ. Ctr. Mich. 1995, 97, 98, Swann Gallery, Detroit, 1995—, Kiva Gallery, Waterford, 1999, Southfield Ctr. arts, 1999; solo exhbns. include Waterford Pub. Lib., 1996, Waterland Pub. Libr., 1996—, Millers Artist Supplies, Ferndale, Mich., 1996, Waterford Twp. Hall, 1996, 99, Masonic Lodge, Milford, 1997, 98, 99, Livonia Libr., 1999; represented in pvt. collections; juror Village of Fine Arts Assn., 1996. Recipient Outstanding Achievement award in instructional programming

Comcast Cable TV, Waterford, 1992, 1st place, Waterford Friends of the Arts Art Show, 1988, Pontiac Oakland Soc. Artists Cmty. Rm., 1990, Am. Biog. Inst. Woman of Yr. Commemorative medal, 1995; Waterford Cable Commn. grantee, 1991, 93, Charter Twp. of Waterford grantee, 1991-94, 98. Mem. Nat. Assn. Female Exec. Pontiac Oakland Soc. Artists, Waterford Friends of the Arts, Mich. Watercolor Soc., Birmingham Bloomfield Art Assn., Colored Pencil Soc. Am., Colored Pencil Soc. Detroit, Village Fine Arts Assn., Paint Creek Ctr. for the Arts. Avocations: music, art. Home: 1426 Birchwood Dr Okemos MI 48864-3033

WAGGONER, KATHLEEN ALICE, psychotherapist; b. St. Louis, Jan. 10, 1954; d. William Dale Jerry Siebe and Doris Ilene Hanson; m. Robert Douglas Clark, July 24, 1974 (div. 1980); children: Angel Mae, Andrew Miles, Jason Allen; m. Curtis Lee Waggoner, Jr., Sept. 6, 1981; children: Amanda Jane, Jennifer Lee, Elizabeth Anne, Kathleen Rose. AA, St. Louis CC, 1983; BS, Southeast Mo. State, 1989, MA, 2003. Cert. NCC, LPC. Tchr. Cinemon Bear Day Care, Cape Girardeau, Mo., 1985—87; supr. infant toddlers San Jose Hosp., Calif., 1989—91; pvt. cons. Molene, Ill., 1991—93; clin. staff Pathways Cmty. Supports, Cape Girardeau, 1995—97, Cmty. Counseling Ctr., Cape Girardeau, 1999—. Pres. WELA, 2002—; sec. Sedgewickville Luth. Ch., Mo., 2004—. E-2 USN, 1973—76, Key West, Fla. Mem.: ACA. Personal E-mail: katecila@hotmail.com.

WAGNER, ALYSON KAY (ALY WAGNER), professional soccer player; b. San Jose, Calif., Aug. 10, 1980; Majored in combined scis., Santa Clara U., Calif., 1999—2002. Soccer player, midfielder U.S. Women's Nat. Team, 1998—; team mem. San Diego Spirit, 2003—. No. 1 draft pick San Diego Spirit, WUSA, 2003. Finalist Hermann trophy, 2001, Mo. Athletic Club award, 2001; named second team All-Am, NSCAA, 2000, first team All-Am, 2001, first team All-Am., 2002, Offensive MVP, NCAA Final Four, 2001, Female Player of Yr., Soccer Am., 2001; recipient Top VII award, NCAA, 2002, Mo. Athletic Club Hermann trophy, 2002. Office: US Soccer Fedn 1801 S Prairie Ave Chicago IL 60616

WAGNER, ANGELA DAWN, social studies educator; b. Canton, Ohio, Apr. 7, 1979; d. Olivia Alice Lowry. BS in Edn., Kent State U., Ohio, 2002. Lic. tchr. Ohio. Tchr. Lifeskills Ctr. Canton, Ohio, 2003—. Mem.: Ohio Coun. Social Studies, Nat. Coun. Social Studies. Democrat. Roman Catholic. Avocations: reading, scrapbooks, exercise.

WAGNER, ANN LOUISE, ambassador, former political organization executive; m. Ray Wagner; children: Raymond III, Stephen, Mary Ruth. BSBA, U. Mo., 1984. Mem. com. Lafayette Twp.; chmn. com. St. Louis County Republican Ctrl. Com.; mem. Mo. Fedn. Republican Women; dir. ho. and senate redistricting commn. Mo. Rep. Party, 1991, chmn. Jefferson City, 1999—2001; Mo. state exec. dir. Bush/Quayle Campaign, 1992; advisor Ashcroft for Senate Campaign, 1994; 2nd congl. dist. chair Dole for Pres. Campaign, 1996; co-chmn. Rep. Nat. Com., Wash., 2001—05; US amb. to Luxembourg US Dept. State, 2005—. Mem.: Republican Nat. Conv. Midwestern State Chmn.'s Assn. (com. on arrangements 2000, del. 2000, del. chmn. 2000). Office: Am Embassy Luxembourg Unit 1410 APO APO AE 09126

WAGNER, ANNICE MCBRYDE, judge; b. D.C. BA, JD, Wayne State U. Administrative aide to pres. Barnstable County Mental Health Assn.; with Houston and Gardner; gen. counsel Nat. Capital Housing Authority; people's counsel D.C.; assoc. judge Superior Court D.C., 1977-90, D.C. Ct. Appeals, 1990—94, 2005—, chief judge, 1994—2005. Mem. bd. directors Conference of Chief Justices; mem. bd. trustees United Planning Organization, 1979—, v.p. bd. trustees, 1988—; chair Task Force On Gender Bias In The Courts, D.C. Judicial Conference Arrangements Com., Com. On Selection & Tenure of Hearing Commissioners; mem. teaching team, trial advocacy workshop Harvard U. Office: DC Ct of Appeals 500 Indiana Ave NW Ste 6000 Washington DC 20001-2131*

WAGNER, BARBARA LEE, musician; b. Lockport, N.Y., Feb. 5, 1937; d. Richard Lee and Flora May McCarthy; m. William George Wagner, June 15, 1957 (dec. Apr. 17, 2003); children: Molly Heller-Wagner, Carrie Martin. BFA, SUNY, Buffalo, 1958; studies with Raymond Harvey, Buffalo, 1988—95; studies with Karl Richter, Munich Conservatory, 1974. Condr. Orchard Pk. Chorale, NY, 1975—79; dir. vocal activities Nichols Mid. Sch., Buffalo, 1977—97, Nichols Upper Sch., Buffalo, 1997—2001, Buffalo Sem., 2001—03; artistic dir. Buffalo Gay Men's Chorus, 2001—. Music dir. Peace Odyssey Concert Choir, 1989; guest condr. City of Good Neighbors Chorale, 1992; condr. Freudig Singers, 1998. Condr.: premier of Requiem by Kurt Vonnegut and Edgar Grana, 1988; co-author: Singing the Living Tradition, 1993. Min. music Unitarian Universalist Ch., Buffalo, 1963—; music dir. Temple Beth Am. Choir, Williamsville, NY, 1964—78, Unitarian Universalist Gen. Assembly Choir, 1986, 1992. Recipient award for Choral Excellence, Buffalo Philharm. Orch., 2002, Erie County Music Educators, 2002, NY State Pride Agenda award for cmty. svc., 2005. Mem.: Wednesday Morning Musicale, Erie County Music Educators Assn., N.Y. State Sch. Music Assn., Music Educators Nat. Assn., Am. Choral Dirs. Assn., Am. Guild Organists (sub-dean Buffalo chpt.), Unitarian Universalist Musicians Network (chair new hymns supplemental task force 2003, former v.p., former exec. bd., program chair), Chromatic Club (former bd. dirs.). Democrat. Avocations: reading, gardening. Home: 9 John Brian Ln Buffalo NY 14227 Office: Unitarian Universalist Ch 695 Elmwood Ave Buffalo NY 14222 Office Phone: 716-885-2136. Personal E-mail: wagschoir@aol.com.

WAGNER, BROOKE, secondary school educator; b. Allentown, Pa., Mar. 28, 1976; d. Barry J. and Lorraine M. Wagner. AB in History, Muhlenberg Coll., Allentown, Pa., 1994—98. Cert. Secondary Social Studies Tchr. N.J. Dept. Edn., 1999. Tchr. Northampton County Juvenile Justice Ctr., Easton, Pa., 2003—05, Scotch Plains-Fanwood Bd. Edn., NJ, 1998—. Ap reader Coll. Bd., Princeton, NJ, 2006. Author (curriculum writer): U.S. & Comparative Govt. Curriculums. Mem. PTA, Scotch Plains, 1998—2006. Grantee Eagleton Express, Eagleton Inst. Politics, Rutgers U., 2004—05. Independent. Mem. Christian Ch. Avocations: sports, reading. Office: Scotch Plains-Fanwood High School 667 Westfield Rd Scotch Plains NJ 07076 Office Phone: 908-889-8600. Business E-Mail: bwagner@spfk12.org.

WAGNER, CHARLENE BROOK, secondary school educator; b. LA; d. Edward J. and Eva (Anderson) Brook; children: Gordon, Brook, John. BS, Tex. Christian U., 1952; MEd, Sam Houston U., 1973; postgrad., U. Tex., Austin, 1975, Tex. A&M U., 1977. Sci. educator Spring Branch Ind. Sch. Dist., Houston, 1970-98; ret., 2000; dir. CompuKidZ, Houston, 1998—2000; cons. Scott Foresman, Addison Wesley, Ginn, Houston. Cons. Scott Foresman Pub. Co., Houston, 2000-01; owner Sci. Instrnl. Sys. Co., 1988—; dir. Compukidz. Mem. Houston Symphony League, 1992, Mus. Fine Arts, Mus. of Art of Am. West, Houston, 1989, Mus. Natural Scis., Women's Christian Home, Houston, 1991; mem. Houston Grand Opera Guild, mem. exec. bd. 1999-2000, rec./corr. sec.; social chmn. Encore, 1988; mem. Magic Circle Rep. Women's Club. Mem.: AAUW, NAFE, NEA, Internat. Platform Assn., Spring Branch Edn. Assn., Tex. State Tchrs. Assn., Heather and Thistle Soc., Wellington Soc. for Arts (Houston chpt.), Clan Anderson Soc., Art League Houston, Shepherd Soc., Watercolor Arts Soc. (Houston), Houston Highland Games Assn., Space City Ski Club. Episcopalian. Avocations: painting, watercolor media. Home: 2670 Marilee Ln Apt B54 Houston TX 77057-4264 E-mail: wagner2670@aol.com.

WAGNER, CHERI J., business owner; b. Mar. 9, 1963; Owner, mgr. Wagner Constrn., Lake Arrowhead, Calif., 1980-94, Blind Ambitions, Skyforest, Calif., 1994—. Mem. C. of C., Soroptomists, Nat. Fedn. Ind. Bus., Humane Soc., Arrowhead Bldg. Contractors Assn., Mountain Women's Assn. E-mail: poker4me247@msn.com.

WAGNER, CHERYL JEAN, elementary school educator; AS, CC Allegheny County, Pitts., 1994; BA, U. Pitts., 1998, MAT, 1999. Cert. elem. tchg. Pa. Kindergarten tchr. Bethel Park Sch. Dist., Pa., 1999—2002, 1st grade tchr., 2002—. ESL tutor Bethel Park Sch. Dist., Pa., 1999—2000, pvt. tutor, 1999—2005, homebound tutor, 1999—2005, class size reduction initiative tchr., 2000—02, stepping up tutor, 2004—05, mem. wellness com., 2004—, mem. assessment com., 2006—; participant Western Pa. Wellness Coll., 2004, 05, 06. Nominee Extra Mile award, Bethel Park Sch. Dist., 2005, Tchr. Excellence award, 2005, 2006; named Keystone Tech. Integrator, Pa. Dept. Edn., 2006. Mem.: Bethel Park Fedn. Tchrs. Republican. Avocations: reading, exercise. Home: 1300C Rosewood Ct Pittsburgh PA 15236-4721

WAGNER, CHRISTINA IRENE, elementary school educator; b. Chgo., Mar. 17, 1980; d. Alfred G. and Irene C. Wagner. BS in Edn. and Biology, U. Wis., Eau Claire, 2002. Tchr. mid. sci. Trevor Grade Sch., Wis., 2004—. Recipient, State of Ill., 1998.

WAGNER, CYNTHIA GAIL, editor, writer; b. Bethesda, Md., Oct. 3, 1956; d. Robert Cheney and Marjory Jane (Kletzing) W. BA in English, Grinnell Coll., 1978; MA in Comms., Syracuse U., 1981. Editl. asst. The Futurist/World Future Soc., Bethesda, Md., 1981—82, staff editor, 1982-85, asst. editor, 1985-91, sr. editor, 1991-92, mng. editor, 1992—. Editor: (newsletter) Futurist Update, 2000—, (book) Foresight, Innovation, and Strategy: Toward a Wiser Future, 2005; columnist: 3-2-1 Contact, 1994; contbr. Encyclopedia of the Future, 1995, The 21st Century, 1999; contbg. writer/music reviewer BeaversonIdol.com., 2004—. Mem. Theatre Comm. Group, Washington Shakespeare Reading Group. Avocation: theater. Office: The Futurist World Future Soc 7910 Woodmont Ave Ste 450 Bethesda MD 20814-3066 Business E-Mail: cwagner@wfs.org.

WAGNER, DEBORAH RAE, musician, educator; b. Las Vegas, Nev., Mar. 28, 1963; d. Raymond Duane and Julia Lois Wagner. BA, U. Nev., Las Vegas, 1985; MusM, Northwestern U., 1987; D in Musical Arts, Ariz. State U., 1997. Adj. prof. U. Nev., Las Vegas, 1989—90, Scottsdale (Ariz.) Cmty. Coll., 1995—2000; vis. prof. N.Mex. Highlands U., Las Vegas, 2000—. Freelance accompanist Nev., N.Mex., Ariz., Ill., 1990—; pianist Willow Entertainment, Scottsdale, 1991—95; aux. pianist Phoenix Symphony Orch., 1996—97. Musician: numerous concerts and recitals. Piano instr. The Christmas House, Phoenix, 1998—2000. Mem.: Music Tchrs. Nat. Assn. Avocations: birding, reading, cooking, horseback riding. Office: NMex Highlands Univ 800 W National Ave Las Vegas NM 87701 Office Phone: 505-454-3569. Business E-Mail: dwagner@nmhu.edu.

WAGNER, DOROTHY MARIE, retired senior creative designer, artist; b. Chgo., Jan. 12, 1926; d. William Christopher and Margaret Frances (Rowell) W. Student, Kalamazoo Coll., 1943-45; BS, Western Mich. U., 1947; BFA, Art Ctr. Coll. Design, L.A., 1962. Dir. electroencephalography lab. Bronson Hosp., Kalamazoo, 1945-51; dir. EEG lab. Terr. Hosp., Kaneohe, Hawaii, 1951-55, UCLA Med. Ctr., 1955-60; sr. creative designer GM Tech. Ctr. Styling, Warren, Mich., 1962-82. Cons. in EEG, Army Hosp., Honolulu, 1950-55; dir. sales and rental gallery Pt. Huron (Mich.) Mus., 1989-93, art and painting instr., 1992-96. Recipient Best of Show award Ea. Mich. Internat. Art Show, 1992, 1st pl. award, 1988, 89, 94. Mem. Blue Water Art Assn. (pres. 1990-96), Orion Art Ctr. Episcopalian. Avocations: horseback riding, showing in dressage, breeding and raising racing greyhounds, water color and acrylic painting, stained glass design and fabrication. Home: 14841 Pine Knoll Rd Capac MI 48014-1913 E-mail: dot@glis.net.

WAGNER, GERALDINE MARIE, nursing educator, consultant; b. Renton, Wash., Apr. 12, 1948; d. Ernest F. and Vera P. (Temiraeff) W. AA, Pasadena City Coll., 1970; BA cum laude, Calif. State U., Northridge, 1977; BSN, Calif. State U., L.A., 1982; MEd summa cum laude, Azusa Pacific U., 1993. Cert. pub. health nurse, Calif. Dept. Health Svcs. In utilization mgmt. Blue Cross, Woodland Hills, Calif., 1987-88, Healthmarc, Pasadena, Calif., 1988-90; nursing educator, asst. dir. vocat. nursing program Casa Loma Coll., L.A., 1991-92, dir. program planning and devel., and coord. continuing edn. Lake View Terrace, 1992-93; dir. vocal. nursing program Glendale (Calif.) Career Coll., 1994-95; with patient care rev. svcs. U. So. Calif. U. Hosp., L.A., 1996—; med.-legal nurse cons., 2000—. Docent Mission La Purisima Concepcion. Capt. Nurse Corp, U.S. Army, 1979-84. Mem.: VFW, Civil War Preservation Trust, Calif. Mission Studies Assn., Assn. for Women in Math., Fellowship Cath. Scholars, Nat. Assn. Cath. Nurses, Computer Using Educators, Nat. Coun. Tchrs. Math., Am. Math. Soc., Blue Army Our Lady Fatima, Nat. Maritime Hist. Soc., Soc. Cath. Social Scientists, Civil War Soc., Order of Preachers, Mil. Officer Assn. Am., U.S. Naval Inst., Cath. War Vets, Res. Officers Assn. U.S., Army Nurse Corps. Assn., AMVETS, Assn. U.S. Army, Inst. Religious Life, Assn. Hebrew Catholics, Disabled Am. Vets., Am. Legion, Sigma Theta Tau, Pi Lambda Theta. Roman Catholic. Home: 924 Rock Rose Ln Lompoc CA 93436 Office Phone: 805-735-3575. E-mail: srgmwagnerop@earthlink.net, srgmwagnerop@verizon.net.

WAGNER, GRETCHEN S., dance educator; b. Lexington, Oct. 14, 1979; d. John Alfred and Suzanne Tuttle Wagner. BA, U. Richmond, Va., 2002; MA, NYU, NYC, 2005. Educator dance Barbara Annis Sch. Dance, Lexington, Ky., 1996—2006; instr. U. Ky., 2005—. Adj. faculty Ea. Ky. U., Richmond, 2005. Choreographer Sayre Sch., Lexington, 2005—06. V.p. Ky. Ptnrs. Dance, Lexington, 2005; trustee, parliamentarian Dance Masters of Bluegrass, 2002—. Recipient Cheography award, U. Richmond, 2002. Mem.: Nat. Dance Alliance, Nat. Dance Edn. Orgn. Home: 1345 E Cooper Dr Lexington KY 40502

WAGNER, JODY M., treasurer; b. Canton, Ohio; m. Alan L. Wagner; children: Rachael, Jason, Elizabeth, Maxwell. Degree in econs., Northwestern U., Evanston, Ill., 1977; grad. degree in law, Vanderbilt U., Nashville, 1980. Bar: Tenn. 1980, Va. 1984. With Kaufman and Canoles PC, Norfolk, Va., 1981—2002; state treas. Va., 2002—. Office: Commonwealth of Va Dept of Treasury 101 N 14th St Richmond VA 23218 Office Phone: 804-371-6013. Business E-Mail: jody.wagner@trs.virginia.gov.

WAGNER, JUDITH BUCK, investment firm executive; b. Altoona, Pa., Sept. 25, 1943; d. Harry Bud and Mary Elizabeth (Rhodes) B.; m. Joseph E. Wagner, Mar. 15, 1980; 1 child, Elizabeth. BA in History, U. Wash., 1965; grad., N.Y. Inst. Fin., 1968. Registered Am. Stock Exch., N.Y. Stock Exch., investment advisor. Security analyst Morgan, olmstead, Kennedy & Gardner, L.A., 1968-71, Boettcher & Co., Denver, 1972-75; pres. Wagner Investment Mgmt., Denver, 1975—. Chmn. The Women's Bank, N.A., Denver, 1977-94, organizational group pres., 1975-77; chmn. Equitable Bankshares Colo., Inc., Denver, 1980-94; pres. Equitable Bank of Littleton, Colo., 1985; lectr. Denver U., Metro State, 1975-80. Author: Woman and Money series Colo. Woman Mag., 1976, moderator "Catch 2' Sta. KWGN-TV, 1978-79. Pres. Bit Sisters Colo., Denver, 1977-82, bd. dirs., 1972-83; bd. fellows U. Denver, 1985-90; bd. dirs. Red Cross, 1980, Assn. Children's Hosp., 1985, Colo. Health Facilities Authority, 1978-84, Jr. League Cmty. ADv. Com., 1979-82, Bros. Redevel., Inc., 1979-80; mem. agy. rels. com. Mile High United Way, 1978-81, chmn. United Way Venture Way, 1978-81, chmn. United Way Venture Grant com., 1980-81; bd. dirs. Downtown Dener, Inc., 1988-95; bd. dirs., v.p., treas. The Women's Found. Colo., 1987-91; treas., trustee, v.p., Graland Country Day Sch., 1990-97, pres., 1994-97; trustee Denver Rotary Found., 1990-95, Hunt Alternatives Fund, 1992-97; trustee The Colo. Trust, 1998—, chmn., 2003-05. Recipient Making It award Cosmopolitan Mag., 1977, Women on the Go award, Savvy Mag., 1983, Minouri Yasoui award, 1986, Salute Spl. Honoree award, Big Sisters, 1987; named one of the Outstanding Young Women Am., 1979, Woman Who Makes A Difference award Internat. Women's Forum, 1987, Maverick Thinker award Urban Park, 2003; named Disting. Citizen award U. Colo., 2005. Fellow Assn. Investment Mgmt. & Rsch.; mem. Women's Forum Colo. (pres. 1979), Women's Found. Colo., Inc. (bd. dirs. 1986-91), Denver Soc. Security Analysts (bd. dirs. 1976-83, v.p. 1980-81, pres. 1981-82), Colo. Investment Advisors assn., Rotary (treas. Denver chpt. found., pres. 1993-94), Leadership Denver (Outstanding Alumna award 1987), Pi Beta Phi (pres. U. Wash. chpt. 1964-65). Office: Wagner Investment Mgmt Inc Ste 240 3200 Cherry Creek South Dr Denver CO 80209-3245 Office Phone: 303-777-1800.

WAGNER, LESLIE, lawyer; b. Houston, July 18, 1953; d. Jacob and Geraldine (Harris) W. BA cum laude, U. Tex., 1975; JD, U. Houston, 1980. Bar: Tex. 1980, U.S. Dist. Ct. (so. dist.) Tex. 1981. Trial atty. civil rights EEOC, Houston, 1981—84; pvt. practice Houston, 1984—85, 1987—88, 2004—; dir. law placement U. Houston Law Ctr., 1985—87; employee rels. atty, sr. employee rels. analyst The Meth. Hosp. System, Houston, 1988—97; employee rels. cons. Prudential Fin., Houston, 1997—2003; equal employment affirmative action cons., 2004—. Cons. EEOC, Houston, 1984—; v.p., treas. Houston Soc. Healthcare Human Resources Adminstrns., 1995-97; dir., gen. counsel Hematology/Oncology Assistance Resource Coalition, 1995-2002. Editor: U. Houston Law Rev., 1979, assoc. editor, 1980. Mem. health and edn. com. Jewish Cmty. Ctr., Houston, 1983-85; polit. cons. Houston, 1984-85. Named Honors Day Honoree U. Tex., 1971; Arts and Scis. scholar U. Tex., 1971-74. Mem. ABA (com. employee and labor rels. 1983-85, employment rights com. gen. practice sect. 1986), ATLA, Houston Bar Assn., Tex. Young Lawyers Assn. (job fair com.), Tex. Hosp. Assn., Soc. of Human Resources Mgmt., Nat. Assn. Law Placement (careers com. 1986-87, minority placement com. 1987), Am. Studies Assn., Houston Festival Dancers (treas. 1976-77), Eta Phi Sigma. Democrat. Avocations: creative writing, dance, reading. Home: 5407 Wigton Dr Houston TX 77096-4005 Personal E-mail: leslie.wagner@earthlink.net.

WAGNER, MARILYN FAITH, retired elementary school educator; b. Salinas, Calif. d. Clay Chester and Gladys Edna (Wiley) W. AA, Hartnell Coll., Salinas, 1956; BA, San Jose (Calif.) State U., 1958; MA in Computer Edn., U.S. Internat. U., San Diego, 1987; diploma, Inst. Children's Lit., Redding Ridge, Conn., 1981. Cert. elem. tchr., cross-cultural lang. acad. devel., tech. in edn., Calif. Tchr. Hollister (Calif.) Elem. Sch., 1958—60, Greenfield (Calif.) Schs., 1958—2000, Alum Roc, Union Sch. Dist., San Jose, 1960—2000; ret., 2000; substitute and contract tchr. Alum Roc Union Sch. Dist., San Jose, Calif., 2001—. Tester Alum Rock Union Sch. Dist., 2006. Mem. Calif. Ret. Tchrs. Assn., Spartan Found., Monterey Bay Aquarium.

WAGNER, MARTHA JO, lawyer; b. Chgo., Apr. 6, 1951; d. Joseph Richard and Mary Marjorie W. BA summa cum laude, U. Md., 1979; JD cum laude, Georgetown U., 1982. Bar: DC 1982, Pa. 1985, Ga. 1997, U.S. Dist. Ct. D.C. 1983, U.S. Dist. Ct. (we. dist.) Pa. 1985, U.S. Ct. Appeals (3d cir.) 1985. Motions clk. DC Ct. Appeals, Washington, 1982-83; atty. Pension Benefit Guaranty Corp., Washington, 1983-85; assoc. Reed, Smith, Shaw & McClay, Pitts., 1985-88, Kilpatrick & Cody, Washington, 1988—91, ptnr., 1991, Kilpatrick & Stockton, Atlanta and Washington, 1999; ptnr., employee benefits practice Venable LLP, Washington. Editor (lead articles): The Tax Lawyer; contbr. articles to profl. jours. Fellow Am. Coll. Employee Benefits Counsel; mem. ABA (co-chmn. Employee Benefits Com., Labor & Employment Law sect.), State Bar Ga., DC Bar Assn., Phi Beta Kappa, Phi Kappa Phi, Phi Alpha Theta. Democrat. Office: Venable LLP 575 7th St NW Washington DC 20004 Office Phone: 202-344-4002. Office Fax: 202-344-8300. Business E-Mail: mjwagner@venable.com.

WAGNER, MARY MARGARET, library and information scientist, educator; b. Mpls., Feb. 4, 1946; d. Harvey F.J. and Yvonne M. (Brettner) W.; m. William Moore, June 16, 1978; children: Lebohang Y.C., Nora M. BA, Coll. St. Catherine, St. Paul, 1969; MLS, U. Wash., 1973; PhD, U. Minn., 2003. Asst. libr. St. Margarets Acad., Mpls., 1969-70; libr. Derham Hall High Sch., St. Paul, 1970-71; youth worker The Bridge for Runaways, Mpls., 1971-72; libr. Guthrie Theater Reference and Rsch. Libr., Mpls., 1973-75; asst. br. libr. St. Paul Pub. Libr., 1975; prof. dept. info. mgmt. Coll. St. Catherine, St. Paul, 1975—. Del. Minn. Gov.'s Pre-White House Conf. on Librs. and Info. Svcs., 1990; mem. Minn. Pre-White House Program Com., 1989-90, Continuing Libr. Info. and Media Edn. Com. Minn. Dept. Edn., Libr. Devel. and Svcs., 1980-83, 87-2002; mem. cmty. faculty Met. State U., St. Paul, 1980—; mem. core revision com. Coll. St. Catherine, 1992-93, faculty budget adv. com., 1992-95, faculty pers. com., 1989-92, 2001-04, acad. computing com. 1991-96, ednl. policies com., 1998-01; chair curriculum subcom. Minn. Vol. Cert. Com., 1993—. Contbr. articles to profl. jours. Bd. dirs. Christian Sharing Fund, 1976-80, chair, 1977-78. Grantee U.S. Embassy, Maseru, Lesotho, Africa, Brit. Consulate, Maseru, Fed. Inst. for Mus. and Libr. Scis., various founds.; Upper Midwest Assn. for Intercultural Edn. travel grantee Assoc. Colls. Twin Cities. Fellow: Higher Edn Consortia for Urban Affairs (bd. dirs. 1998—); mem.: ALISE (chair internat. rels. com. 2001—03), ALA (libr. book fellows program 1990—91), Minn. Ednl. Media Orgn., Minn. Libr. Assn. (pres. 1981—82, chair continuing edn. com. 1987—90, steering com. Readers Adv. Roundtable 1989—91), Spl. Libr. Assn., Am. Soc. Indexers, Am. Soc. Info. Sci. Office: Coll St Catherine Dept Info Mgmt 2004 Randolph Ave Saint Paul MN 55105-1750 Office Phone: 651-690-6843. Business E-Mail: mmwagner@stkate.edu.

WAGNER, MARY S., education center administrator; b. Jamestown, N.D., May 13, 1948; d. Thomas Charles Heydweiller and Lila Mae Clemens; m. David Wagner (div.); children: Kristen, James. BS, Cameron U., 1982; MBA, Okla. City U., 1984; graduate, Army Mgmt. Staff Coll., 1995; EdD, Nova Southeastern U., 1998. Cert. tchr. Okla., 1982. Adminstrv. asst. Electronics Command, Ft. Monmouth, NJ, 1972—74, Army Audit Agy., Frankfurt, Germany, 1974—80, Civilian Pers. Office, Ft. Sill, Okla., 1980—83; guidance counselor Army Edn. Ctr., Germany, 1983—86; test specialist Military Entrance Processing Sta., Springfield, Mass., 1986—88; vocat. aptitude battery, 1988—90; edn. svcs. officer 415 Base Support, Bn. Kaiserstlantern, Germany, 1990—96, Western Corridor, Republic of Korea, 1996—97, Area Support Group, Kuwait, 1997—. Named Vol. of Yr., Boy Scouts Am., 1986; recipient Outstanding Svc. award, Area Support Group, Kuwait, 2005, Commdrs. medal, U.S. Army, 1991. Avocations: reading, travel, cooking. Office: Area Support Group Kuwait Edn ASG Kuwait APO AE 09366 Business E-Mail: mary.wagner@arifian.arcent.army.mil.

WAGNER, MARY SUSAN, academic administrator; b. Troy, N.Y., Oct. 28, 1952; BS in Music Edn., Coll. St. Rose, 1974; MS, SUNY, 1977. Cert. sch. dist. adminstr. Music educator South Colonie Sch. Dist., Albany, NY, 1974—95; elem. sch. prin. East Greenbush CSD, NY, 1995—. Mem.: NAFE, Nat. Assn. Elem. Sch. Prins., Assn. for Curr. Devel., N.Y.State Assn. Women Adminstrs. Office: Green Meadow Sch 234 Schuurman Rd Castleton On Hudson NY 12033 Office Phone: 518-477-6422. Business E-Mail: wagnermary@egcsd.org.

WAGNER, MELINDA, musician, composer; b. Phila., 1957; m. James Saporito; children: Benjamin, Olivia. Grad., U. Chgo., U. Pa. Studied with Richard Wernick, George Crumb, Shulamit Ran, Jay Reise. Instr. U. Pa., Swarthmore Coll., Syracuse U., Hunter Coll. Works performed by: Chgo. Symphony, Am. Composers Orchestra, Chamber Music Soc. of Lincoln Ctr., Ill. Chamber Orchestra, Oakland East Bay Symphony; commissioned works: Barlow Found., Fromm Found. Harvard U., Mary Flagler Carey Charitable Trust, Chgo. Symphony Orchestra, N.Y. New Music Ensemble, Am. Brass Quintet; composer Falling Angels, commissioned by Chgo. Symphony Orchestra, premiered in 1993, performed by Am. Composers Orchestra, 1995, Chgo. Symphony, 1996, Concerto for Flute, Strings, and Percussion (Pulitzer prize in Music 1999), commissioned and premiered by Paul Lustig Dunkel and Westchester Philharmonic, 1998, Extremity of Sky, premiered by Emanuel Ax, Chicago Symphony Orch., 2003. Fellow Guggenheim Meml. Found., Howard Found., 1996; resident fellow MacDowell Colony, Yaddo; grantee Ill. Arts Coun., N.Y. State Coun. on Arts; recipient three ASCAP Found. Young Composer awards. Mem. ASCAP (panelist ASCAP Deems Taylor Competition, ASCAP Found. Morton Gould Grants to Young Composers Program; recipient numerous ASCAP Standard Special awards).

WAGNER, MURIEL GINSBERG, nutrition therapist; d. Irving A. and Anna Ginsberg; 1 child, Emily Lucinda Faith. BA, MS, Wayne State U.; PhD, U. Mich., 1982. Registered dietitian. Nutritionist Merrill-Palmer Inst., Detroit; pvt. practice, nutritional therapist Southfield, Mich., 1976—. Cons. select com. on nutrition U.S. Senate, Ford Motor Co., Dearborn, Mich., Detroit Dept. Consumer Affairs, 1979—; adj. faculty mem. Wayne State U., Detroit, U. Mich., Dearborn, 1974-79. Author: (cookbook) Tun.ahhh, 1993; contbr. articles to profl. publs.; writer, publisher (newsletter) Eating Younger. Vol. Am. Heart Assn. of Mich.; also various local and nat. govtl. groups Recipient Outstanding Cmty. Svc. award Am. Heart Assn., 1990; named Outstanding Profl., Mich. Dietetic Assn., 1974. Fellow Am. Dietetic Assn. (organizer Dial-A-Dietitian); mem. Am. Diabetes Assn. Avocations: cooking, recipe development, gardening. Office: 4000 Town Ctr Ste 8 Southfield MI 48075-1401 Office Phone: 248-350-1190.

WAGNER, PAULA, film company executive, film producer; b. Youngstown, Ohio, 1948; m. Robin Wagner (div.); m. Rick Nicita, 1984. BFA in Drama, Carnegie-Mellon U. Agent Creative Artist Agy.; cofounder (with Tom Cruise) Cruise/Wagner Productions, 1993—; CEO United Artists Corp., 2006—. Actress on & off Broadway, (TV miniseries) Loose Change, 1978; co-author: Out of Our Father's House; prodr.: (films) Mission: Impossible, 1996, Without Limits, 1998, Mission: Impossible II, 2000, Vanilla Sky, 2001, The Last Samurai, 2003, Suspect Zero, 2004, Elizabethtown, 2005, Ask the Dust, 2006, Mission: Impossible III, 2006; exec. prodr.: The Others, 2001, Narc, 2002, Shattered Glass, 2003, War of the Worlds, 2005; prodr.: (TV miniseries) Nightmares and Dreamscapes: From the Stories of Stephen King, 2006. Bd. trustees Carnegie-Mellon U.; bd. dir. Nat. Film Preservation Found., UCLA Sch. Theater, Film and TV. Co-recipient Nova award for outstanding achievement by new or emerging prodr. in theatrical motion pictures, Producer's Guild, 1997. Office: United Artists Corp 0250 Constellation Blvd Los Angeles CA 90067

WAGNER, RUTH JOOS, elementary school educator; b. L.A., June 1, 1933; d. Walter Joos and Ruth McKenzie (Edwards) J.; m. Gerald Dayton Wagner, Dec. 17, 1960; 1 child, Gregory Dayton. BA, UCLA, 1955, MA, 1976. Cert. primary Tchr., Calif. Kindergarten tchr. Inglewood (Calif.) Unified Sch. Dist., 1955—59, 1963—93, Coronado (Calif.) Unified Sch. Dist., 1959-62; pres. Rainbow West Assocs., L.A., 1986—. Ball chmn. League for Crippled Children, L.A., 1984, pres., 1988; bd. trustees L.A. Orthopaedic Hosp. Found., 1996-98; bd. dirs. L.A. Orthopaedic Hosp., 1998—; pres. League for Crippled Children, 2003-04; docent Getty Mus., 1997-2006. Named Tchr. of Yr., Inglewood Sch. Dist., 1984. Mem. NEA, Calif. Tchrs. Assn, Inglewood Tchrs. Assn., Greater L.A. Zoo Assn., World Affairs Coun., Lake Arrowhead Country Club. Republican. Episcopalian. Avocations: tennis, watercolor painting. Home: 2117 Eric Dr Los Angeles CA 90049-1816

WAGNER, SALLY STERRETT, music educator; b. Pitts., Sept. 24, 1951; d. Walter Renwick and Dorothy Grimpe Sterrett; m. Michael David Wagner, June 16, 1991; children: Caroline Elaine, Michael David Wagner Jr. MusB, U. Del., 1973; M Music Edn., Mich. State U., 1980. Cert. tchr. Md. Tchr. gen. music Dover Air Force Base Schs., Del., 1973—74; dir. bands Smyrna High Sch., 1974—77; choir dir. Portland Mid. & High Schs., Mich., 1979—80; dir. bands Beltsville Jr. High Sch., Md., 1980—81, Eleanor Roosevelt High Sch., Greenbelt, 1981—. Adjudicator Heritage Festivals, Salt Lake City, 1987—. Contbr. articles to profl. jours. Dir. youth choir Laurel Presbyn. Ch., 1995—2002. Recipient Outstanding Educator award, Prince Georges County C. of C., 1985, Outstanding Music Educator award, Md. Music Educators Assn., 2001. Mem.: Music Educators Nat. Conf., Md. Band Dirs. Assn., Women Band Dirs. Internat. Avocations: reading, counted cross stitch, travel. Office: Eleanor Roosevelt High Sch 7601 Hanover Pky Greenbelt MD 20770 E-mail: sally_wagner@comcast.net, swagner@pgcps.org.

WAGNER, SUSAN ALISON, physical education educator; d. Jean Katherine Wagner; m. Charles Madison Rhea, Nov. 21, 2004; children: Zach Guidry Lowy, Gabe Wagner Lowy, Marshall Emil Lowy. BS, SUNY, Cortland, 1972; MS, U. Colo., Boulder, 1975. Cert. tchr. NY, Colo., Ariz. Tchr. Dorothy Nolan Sch., Saratoga Springs, NY, 1972—74, Madison Meadows Sch., Phoenix, 1976—77; sr. lectr. Tex. A&M U., College Station, 1977—. Camp dir. Camp Adventure, College Station, Tex., 1987—96; program coord. Camp Aggieland, College Station, Tex., 1993—. Author: (textbook) Physical Education for Children: Building the Foundation, 1987, 2d edit., 1994. Sch. bd. trustees College Station Ind. Sch. Dist., Tex., 1995—2004. Named Fish Camp Namesake, Tex. A&M Fish Camp, 2002, Tchr. of Yr. Kinesiology, Dept. Health and Kinesiology,Tex. A&M U., 1999, 2002; recipient Fish Camp Namesake, Tex. A&M Fish Camp, 1995, Disting. Achievement in Tchg. award, Assn of Former Students, Tex. A&M, 2001. Mem.: AAHPERD, Tex. AHPERD (chair profl. devel. 2006). Office: Tex A&M Univ Tamu 4243 College Station TX 77843-4243 Office Phone: 979-845-2063. Office Fax: 979-847-8987. Business E-Mail: swagner@tamu.edu.

WAGNER, SUSAN JANE, sales and marketing consulting company executive; b. Englewood, N.J., Aug. 11; d. Jules A. and Florence I. (Froeba) W.; m. Mark E. McKenna, May 4, 1984. MusB with honors, Syracuse U., 1974; MPA with honors, Fairleigh Dickinson U., 1983. Dir. music, theater dependant sch. U.S. Dept. Def., Fed. Republic Germany, 1976-82; grad. asst. Fairleigh Dickinson U., Rutherford, N.J., 1982-83; account exec. Katz Radio/Katz Communications, Inc., N.Y.C., 1983-85; account mgr. network Katz Radio Group, N.Y.C., 1985-87, v.p., dir. mktg., 1987-90, sr. v.p. dir.mktg., 1990-91; v.p. corp. mktg. Katz Comm., Inc., N.Y.C., 1992-93; owner Exec. Dynamics Inc., Mahwah, N.J., 1993—. Mem. Am. Women in Radio and TV, Electronic Media Mktg. Assn., Am. Mktg. Assn., Promotion Mktg. Assn. Am., Broadcast Promotion Mktg. Execs., Sigma Alpha Iota, Gamma Phi Beta. Avocations: sailing, skiing, singing. Office: Exec Dynamics 2 James Brite Cir Mahwah NJ 07430-2527 Office Phone: 201-327-9070. Personal E-mail: edi1@iglide.net.

WAGNER CHAPPELEAR, MARIA, director; d. Cathy Wagner; m. Fred Chappelear, Aug. 19, 2005. Degree in Counseling Psychology, Chapman U., Orange, Calif. Lic. marriage and family therapist Calif. Clin. dir. Rossier Pk. Sch., Buena Park, Calif., 1995—2002, dir. sch., 2000—. Mem.: CAMFT (assoc.). Office Phone: 714-562-0441.

WAGNER-WESTBROOK, BONNIE JOAN, educational consultant, director; b. Watertown, N.Y., July 18, 1953; d. Elmer Ethan and Joan Eleanor (Niedermeier) Wagner; m. John Drewry Westbrook Jr., Aug. 21, 1982. BS, SUNY, Geneseo, 1975, MS, 1981; EdD, Rutgers U., 1989. Tchr. elem. Rochester (N.Y.) Sch. for the Deaf, 1975-80; instr. adult basic edn. Rochester City Sch. Dist., 1981-82; profl. interpreter Nat. Tech. Inst. for the Deaf, Rochester, 1981-83; instr., interpreter Henrietta (N.Y.) Ctrl. Sch. Dist., 1983-84; intern Middlesex County Vocat. Tech. Schs., New Brunswick, N.J., 1985; adminstr. Pub. Svc. Electric and Gas Co., Newark, 1990-91; cons. on urban initiative for N.J. Dept. Edn. Rutgers U., New Brunswick, 1985-86, program specialist, 1987-88, rsch. assoc. for N.J. Commn. on Employment and Tng., 1988-89, also senator Grad. Sch. Edn., 1985-87, program dir. New Brunswick, 1991—2005, dir. and faculty leadership devel. and fin. programs, 1991—2005; pres., prin. People Devel. Ptnrs., LLC, Lebanon, NJ, 2005—. Cons. Blueprint Project, Hudson County C.C., 1992-93, Pub. Svc. Electric and Gas Co., Newark, 1986-89. Vol. Rochester Sch. for the Deaf, 1977; mem. Rochester Oratorio Soc., 1978-81, SUNY Geneseo Chamber Singers, 1971-75. Rutgers U. scholar, 1986; Rutgers U. fellow, 1987. Mem. Am. Coun. on Edn. of Deaf, Nat. Registry Interpreters for Deaf, Rochester Amateur Radio Assn., Rutgers U. Alumni Assn., Omicron Tau Theta. Republican. Avocations: photography, gardening, computers, music, hiking. Home and Office: 7 Burlinghoff Ln Lebanon NJ 08833 Office Phone: 732-437-6162. E-mail: bonnie.westbrook@gmail.com.

WAGNON, JOAN, retired banker, retired mayor; b. Texarkana, Ark., Oct. 17, 1940; d. Jack and Louise (lucas) D.; m. William O. Wagnon Jr., June 4, 1964; children: Jack, William O. III. BA in Biology, Hendrix Coll., Conway, Ark., 1962; MEd in Guidance and Counseling, U. Mo., 1968. Sr. rsch. technician U. Ark. Med. Sch., Little Rock, 1962-64, sr. rsch. asst. Columbia, Mo., 1964-68; tchr. No. Hills Jr. HS, Topeka, 1968-69, J.S. Kendall Sch., Boston, 1970-71; counselor Neighborhood Youth Corps, Topeka, 1973-74; exec. dir. Topeka YWCA, 1977-93; mem. Kans. Legislature, 1983-94; exec. dir. Kans. Families for Kids, 1994-97; mayor City of Topeka, 1997-2001; pres. Ctrl. Nat. Bank, Topeka, 2001—03; sec. of revenue State of Kansas, 2003—. Chair Multistate Tax Commn.; v.p. Streamlined Sales Tax Governing Bd. Mem. Health Planning Rev. Commn., Topeka, 1984-85; nat. bd. Girl Scouts USA. Recipient Service to Edn. award Topeka NEA, 1979, Outstanding Achievement award, Kans. Home Econs. Assn., 1985, Equity in Action award Kans. B & PW Clubs, 1991, Disting. Svc. award Kans. Ct. Svcs. Officers, 1992, Womens Rights Star award NOW, 1994; named Woman of Yr. Mayors Council Status of Women, 1983, named one of Top Ten Legislators Kans. Mag., Wichita, 1986, Legislator of Yr., Kans. NASW, 1989. Mem. Topeka Assn. Human Svc. Execs. (pres. 1981-83), Topekans for Ednl. Involvement (pres. 1979-82), Women's Polit. Caucus (state chair). Lodges: Rotary. Democrat. Methodist. Avocations: music, swimming, boating. Office: 915 Harrison St Topeka KS 66612 Home: 4036 NE Kimball Road Topeka KS 66617 Business E-Mail: wagnon@kdor.state.ks.us.

WAGO, MILDRED HOGAN, retired municipal official; b. N.Y.C., Aug. 16, 1918; d. Andrew James and Gunhild (Olsen) Hogan; m. Charles Leonard Wago, Nov. 24, 1949 (dec.); children: Linda G., Richard Herbst, Charlene C., and William Decker. Grad. bus. sch., White Plains, N.Y. Clk. Met. Life Ins. Co., N.Y.C., 1938-50; publican Town of North Castle, Armonk, NY, 1960—2001. Mem. N.Y. State Assn. Receivers and Collectors (v.p. 1983-2001), Westchester County Assn. Receivers and Collectors (v.p., pres. 1987—), Nat. Assn. Exec. Females. Republican. Home: 3 Wago Ave Armonk NY 10504-1447

WAGONER, ANNA MILLS S., prosecutor; b. 1949; BA, Agnes Scott Coll.; JD, Wake Forest U. Assoc. Woodson, Linn, Sayers, Lawther, Short and Wagoner, 1985—87, ptnr., 1987—90; chief judge Dist. 19-C, NC, 1990—2001; US atty. (mid. dist.) NC US Dept. Justice, 2001—. Office: US Attys Office PO Box 1858 Greensboro NC 27402*

WAGONER, DEBORAH ANNE, social studies educator; d. Connie Nelsen; m. Terry Leroy Wagoner; children: Tucker, Tanner. BS in Elem. Edn., Ctrl. Mo. State U., Warrensburg, 1990, MS (hon.) in Curriculum and Instrn., 2002. Tchr. 1st grade Crest Ridge North Elem., Centerview, Mo., 1990—94; tchr., dir. preschool Puddle Jumpers Preschool, 1994—95, First Bapt. Ch., 1995—98; tchr. Holden Mid. Sch., 1998—. Tchr. Sunday sch. Heritage Bapt. Ch., Lee's Summit, Mo., 2001—06. Project Read grantee, State of Mo., 1998, Write Stuff grantee, 1999. Mem.: Mo. Mid. Sch. Assn. (assoc.), Mo. State Tchrs. Assn. (assoc.). Office: Holden Middle School 301 Eagle Drive Holden MO 64040 Office Phone: 816-732-4125.

WAGONER, JOHNNA, elementary school educator; d. Homer LaMarr and Ruth Ann Moore; m. Rick Wagoner, Oct. 29, 1974; 1 child, Leah Brooke Tooke. BSc in Elem. Edn., U. Ark., Pine Bluff, 1990. Tchrs. aide England (Ark.) Elem. Sch., 1979—86, sec. spl. edn., 1986—89; tchr. England (Ark.) Mid. Sch., 1990—. Republican. Bapt. Avocations: reading, crafts, gardening. Office: England Mid Sch 1500 NE 1st St England AR 72046

WAGONER, M. DEANNA, advocate; b. Miami, Fla., Aug. 29, 1940; d. Hasty Dean Wagoner. BA with honors, Columbia U., NYC, 1975, MA, 1976. Adminstrv. asst. Columbia U., 1963—64, 1966—70; ednl. asst. Congrès pour la liberé tde la couture, Paris, 1965; adminstrv. asst. Ch. World Svc., NYC, 1977—78; fraternal worker United Presbyn. Ch. N.S.A., Kathmandu, Nepal, 1979—85; founder, dir. Clown's Bazaar and Tax Exempt Fine Art, Charleston, SC, 1986—. Tchr. A-level English Godanary Alumni Assn., Kathmandu, 1981—85. One-woman shows include Broadway Nat. Bank, 1978, exhibitions include. Vol. Elder Craftsman, NYC, 1975—79; lay chaplain NY Chaplaincy, NYC, 1976—79; econ. devel. adviser Nepal Jesuits, Kathmandu, 1979—85. Recipient 3 Sisters award, Com. to Save the City, 2002, 3d Pl. award for oil painting, Women's Nat. Rep. Club Exhibit, 1998, English-speaking Union traveling fellowship, Jesuit Coll. Oxford Internat. Summer Sch., 1978. Mem.: DAR, NAACP, Columbia U. 1754 Soc. Avocation: painting. Office: Clown's Bazaar 56 Broad St Charleston SC 29401

WAGSCHAL, KATHLEEN, education educator; b. Woburn, Mass., May 30, 1947; d. John Kenneth and Elizabeth (Ginivan) Lanpher; m. Peter Henry Wagschal, July 17, 1971; 1 child, Adam Colin. MEd, U. Mass., 1972, MEd, 1975. Cert. secondary tchr., Calif. Adminstrv. dir. lab. sch. Greenfield (Mass.) Community Coll., 1978-83; adj. faculty mem. Sch. Edn. Nat. U., San Diego, 1985-87, dir. student tchr. program, 1987-88, chair tchr. edn. program, 1987—, dean Sch. Edn., 1988—. Cons., co-dir. Futures Unltd., N.Y. and Mass., 1972-85. Grantee Mass. Dept. Social Svcs., Mass. Dept. Edn., Bur. Nutrition and Edn., 1981-84. Mem. Calif. Assn. Colls Tchr. Edn., Calif. Coun. Edn. of Tchrs. Avocations: reading, pool. Office: Nat U 4141 Camino Del Rio S San Diego CA 92108-4103

WAHL, CHRISTINA M., biology professor, researcher; d. Wilburt Charles Wahl and Sonja Christine Oehme; m. Ellis Roger Loew, Aug. 6, 1983; children: Marina Loew, Fredrika Loew. BS, Cornell U., Ithaca, NY, 1980; MS, Cornell U., 1985, PhD, 1990. Instr. dept. physiology Cornell U., 1985—88, postdoctoral rsch. assoc. dept. anatomy, 1991—92, NIH postdoctoral fellow dept. anatomy, 1992—97, lectr. dept. physiology, 1994—2000; instr. Cornell Coll. Vet. Medicine, Ithaca, 1997—2000; assoc. prof. biology Wells Coll., Aurora, NY, 2000—. Courtesy assoc. prof. dept. biomed. sci. Cornell U., 2000—; chair instl. animal care and use com. Wells Coll., 2005—. Bd. dirs. Magic Garden Puppets, Cortland, NY, 1998—. Mem.: Assn. Rsch. in Vision and Ophthalmology, Am. Soc. Cell Biology, NY Acad. Scis. Avocations: sailing, gardening, sculpting, handwork, swimming. Office: Well Coll Dept BCS Main St Aurora NY 13026 Office Phone: 315-364-3473. E-mail: cwahl@wells.edu.

WAHLERS, JENNIFER ANN, art educator; b. Elgin, Ill., Sept. 10, 1977; d. Barbara Jean and Michael David Wahlers. BFA, U. Ill., 2000; MS, No. Ill. U., 2003. Art specialist Huntley Sch. Dist. 158, Lake in the Hills, Ill., 2000—. Mem. Ch. Of Christ. Office Phone: 847-659-5300. Personal E-mail: jwahlers@sbcglobal.net.

WAHLIN, SHELLY R., voice educator; d. Robert Marcel and Grace Harriet Christenson; m. J. Reid Wahlin, Aug. 16, 1980; children: Joshua, Jesse. BA in Elem. Edn., Concordia U., 1980, BA in Music, 1980; MEdn, St. Scholastica U., 2001. Music tchr. Mentor (Minn.) Pub. Sch., 1980—85; elem. tchr. Erskine (Minn.) Pub. Sch., 1985—86; music tchr. Win-E-Mac Sch., Erskine, 1986—94; choir dir. Fertile (Minn.)-Beltrami Sch., 1994—. Mem.: Minn. All State Choir (choral asst. 2004—06), Minn. Edn. Assn., Am. Choral Dirs. Assn., Minn. Music Educators Assn. (bd. dirs. 2004—06, All-State Choir Sect. Leader 2002—03). Democrat. Lutheran. Avocations: skiing, swimming, piano. Home: 39980 160th Ave SE Erskine MN 56535

WAHRMUND, PEGGY STIELER, artist, rancher; b. Kerr County, Tex., Sept. 22, 1927; d. Edgar and Anna W. Stieler; m. Emil T. Wahrmund, Oct. 14, 1950 (dec. Aug. 1998); 1 child, Warren. BS, Tex. Women's U., 1949; MA, N.Mex. Highlands U., 1960. One-woman shows include Southwest Tex. State U., Sam Marcos, 1961, Tex. Women's U., Denton, 1963, Springfield City Libr., Mass., 1964, Kerrville Art Club, Tex., 1965, Hill County Arts Found., Ingram, Tex., 1968, Am. Embassy, San Salvador, El Salvador, 1978, Am. Internat. Quilt Assn., Frankfort, Germany, 1996, exhibited in group shows at Am. Crafts Coun., San Antonio, 1957, Austin, 1965, Lubbock, 1968, N.Mex. Highlands U., Las Vegas, 1960, Southwest Crafts Ctr., San Antonio, 1978, Hill Country Arts Found., Ingram, Tex., 1978, 1986, Kaffe Gallery, Corpus Christi, Tex., 1979, Bright Shawl Gallery, San Antonio, 1985, Am. Internat. Quilt Assn., 1986, Houston, 1995, 1995, Quilter's Guild East Tex., Tyler, 1987, Am. Quilt Assn., Houston, 1990, West Coast Quilters' Conf., Sacramento, 1991, City Mus., Marshall, Tex., 1993, Southwest Parks and Monuments Assn., Stonewall, Tex., 1994, Am. Internat. Quilt Invitational, Portland, 1995, Represented in permanent collections Jeep Collins Jewelry, San Antonio, Bank One, Fredericksburg, Tex., Security State Bank, Bass Anglers Sportsman Assn., Montgomery, Ala., James Avary Craftsman, San Antonio, Austin, Houston, Kerrville, Tulsa, Southwest Tex. U. Art Dept., San Marcos, Am. Embassy, San Salvador, Nat. Mus. Art, Smithsonian Instn., Washington. Mem.: Am. Quilters Soc., Internat. Quilt Assn. (award 1996). Home: 474 Cir Ranch Rd Fredericksburg TX 78624-6462

WAHWEAH, LINDA MCNEIL, insurance agent, writer; b. Albuquerque, Apr. 2, 1955; d. Ernest Neil and Elizabeth Ann (Murane) Lemke; m. Eugene Gerald Wahweah, Feb. 14, 1979 (div. June 2001). Bus., Cannon's Internat. Bus. Coll., 1976. Legal sec. Manpower Gen. Dynamic, San Bernardino, Calif., 1980—82; ins. c.s.r. p.l. and comml. Ctrl. City Ins. Agy., San Bernardino, 1982—84; ins. office mgr. Bankers Life Ins., Riverside, Calif., 1984—85; ind. ins. agt. Am. Family Life Ins., Redlands, Calif., 1985—88; civil rights adv. Walker River Palute Tribe, Schurz, Nev., 1989—95; freelance writer Native Am. Civil Rights, San Clemente, Calif., 1996—2003; chronical specialist Native Am. Civil Union, San Bernardino, West Cajon, Calif., 2000—03. Promotor specialist Karaoke of Inland Empire, San Bernardino, 2000—03; council mem. Native Am. Civil Rights Union, 1992—95, fellow founder, 1993. Author: Poetry's "Guardian" Best Poems and Poets of 2003. Lobbyist Walker River Piaute Tribe, Schurz, Nev., 1993—95, civil rights adv. San Clemente, 1995—96. Named World Champion Amateur Poet, Internat. Soc. Poets, 2002, No. Am. Poet of Merit, Internat. Libr. Poetry, 2002, New Country Female Vocalist, CCMA of Inland Empire, 1999; recipient Editor's Choice award, Internat. Libr. Poetry, 2003, Outstanding Achievement in Poetry award, Internat. Soc. Poets, 2004, Poet of Merit award, Internat. Soc. Poetry, 2005. Mem.: ACLU, San Bernardino County Bar Assn., European Soc. Lit., Humane Soc., Am. Poetry Assn., Am. Lit. Guild, N.Am. Fishing Club. Democrat. Ch. Of Christ. Avocations: writing, karoke, cooking, sewing. Office Phone: 909-648-4112. Personal E-mail: wllply9@aol.com.

WAIHMAN, LISA GIRARD, mathematics educator; b. Suisun, Calif., Apr. 5, 1955; d. H. D. and June S. Girard; m. Vernon Ross Waihman, May 19, 1974 (dec. Aug. 13, 1996); children: Nicole Leigh, Nanci Lynete Waihman-Szafarz. BA in Liberal Arts and Scis., U. Ill., Champaign, 1976; EdM in Curriculum and Instrn., U. Houston, 1987; Tech. Instrn. Endorsement, Houston Bapt. U., 2001. English tchr. Hambrick Jr. H.S., Aldine, Tex., 1981—85; English and math. tchr. Crosby Mid. Sch., Tex., 1985—89; math. tchr. Crosby H.S., Crosby, 1989—99, John Foster Dulles H.S., Sugar Land, Tex., 1999—. Faculty sponsor Mu Alpha Theta, Sugar Land, 2002—05; faculty advisor Key Club, Sugar Land, 2002—. Treas. Lion's Club, Crosby, 1996—99. Gift fellow, GTE, 1992—93. Mem.: Fort Bend Coun. Tchrs. Math. (treas. 2005—), Nat. Coun. Math. Tchrs. Avocations: travel, reading. Office: John Foster Dulles High School 550 Dulles Ave Sugar Land TX 77478 Office Phone: 281-634-5600. Business E-Mail: lisa.waihman@fortbend.k12.tx.us.

WAINIO, MELODY F., registrar; b. Coshocton, Ohio, Feb. 25, 1948; d. Francis W. and Dorothy M. Burkhart; m. Edwin A. Wainio, July 20, 1985; m. Robert H. Vaughn, Sept. 7, 1968 (div. 1983); children: Eric R. Vaughn, Bryan S. Vaughn. AA, Lakeland C.C., Mentor, OH, 1982; BS in Tech. Edn., U. Akron, 1987; MSEd, Capella U., 2003. Adj. instr. Bryant and Stratton Coll., Richmond Heights, Ohio, 1990—90, full-time instr., 1990—91, faculty advisor, 1991—98, assoc. dean instrn. Willoughby Hills, Ohio, 1998—2003, dean student svcs., 2003—05, registrar, 2005—. Mem.: ASCD, Nat. Acad. Advising Assn. Home: 181 Meriden Rd Painesville OH 44077 Office: Bryant and Stratton Coll 27557 Chardon Rd Wickliffe OH 44092 Personal E-mail: mwainio@ameritech.net. E-mail: mfwainio@bryantstratton.edu.

WAINSCOTT, CYNTHIA, medical association administrator; BA, Metropolitan Coll. Edn. dir. Mental Health Assn. Minn., 1987—90; exec. dir. Nat. Mental Health Assn Ga., 1990—2003; now bd. chair, CEO Nat. Mental Health Assn., Alexandria. Nat. Mental Health Adv. Coun. Ctr. for Mental Health Svcs., 2000—04; adv. coun. Ga. Gov. Mental Health, Mental Retardation and Substance Abuse Adv. Coun.; drug utilization rev. bd. Ga. Medicaid Agy.; bd. dir. Ga. Parent Support Network; adv. com. Fuqua Ctr. for Late Life Depression, Emory Univ., Ga. Cmty. Trust. Mem.: Ga. Prevention Credentialing Consortium (founding mem.). Office: Nat Mental Health Assn 12 fl 2001 N Beauregard St Alexandria VA 22311 Office Phone: 703-684-7722. Business E-Mail: cwainscott@nmha.org.*

WAINWRIGHT, CYNTHIA CRAWFORD, banker; b. N.Y.C., July 5, 1945; d. Townsend Wainwright and Rosalie deForest (Crosby) Gevers; m. Stephen Berger, Sept. 24, 1977; children: Robin Wainwright Berger, Diana Wainwright Berger. MBA, Columbia Bus. Sch., 1984. Sec., adminstrv. asst. Time-Life Broadcast, N.Y.C., 1965-68; adminstrv. asst. Downe Comms., N.Y.C., 1968-69, Office of the Mayor, N.Y.C., 1969-71; program mgr. Dept. of Correction, N.Y.C., 1972-73, dir. adminstrn., 1973-75, dep. commr., 1978-79; dir. of spl. projects N.Y. State Dept. Correctional Svcs., Albany, 1975-76; asst. dir. Offender-Based Transaction Svcs./Divsn. Criminal Justice, Albany, 1976-77. Various positions Chem. Bank, N.Y.C., 1979-96; dir. corp. soc. resp. Chase Bank, N.Y.C., 1996—. Mem. adv. coms. N.Y. State Office of Parks, N.Y.C., 1986-95; bd. dirs., chmn. Hist. House Trust of N.Y.C., 1989—; bd. dirs., past pres. The Bridge, Inc., N.Y.C., 1984—; trustee, past pres. Preservation League of N.Y. State, Albany, 1984—; trustee The Chapin Sch., Ltd., N.Y.C., 1989—. Named Woman of the Yr. East Manhattan C. of C., 1984; recipient Mental Health award The Bridge, Inc., N.Y.C., 1992, award for acad. excellence Columbia Bus. Sch., N.Y.C., 1983. Avocations: horseback riding, tennis, cooking. Office: Chase Bank 600 5th Ave Fl 3 New York NY 10020-2302

WAISS, ELAINE HELEN, retired physician; b. Gary, Mar. 1, 1941; d. Frank and Helen Waiss; 1 child, Elizabeth Elaine Blok. AB in Russian, BS in Chemistry, Ind. U., Bloomington, 1963; MD in Medicine, Ind. U., Indpls., 1968. Lic. Am. Bd. Family Practice. Mem. hon. staff St. Catherine Hosp., E. Chgo., 1974—2002, Comty. Hosp., Munster, Ind., 1975—2002; ret., 2002. Mem.: Ind. State Med. Assn., Am. Acad. Family Practice (life). Byzantine. Avocations: gardening, reading, interior decorating.

WAIT, LEA, writer, small business owner; b. Boston, Mass., May 26, 1946; d. George W Wait and Sally Eleanor Smart; m. Robert Joseph Thomas, Oct. 28, 2003; children: Caroline Yoon Kyung Childs, Alicia Yupin Gutschenritter, Rebecca Siu Kuen Wynne, Elizabeth Purnima. BA, Chatham Coll., Pitts., 1968; MA, NYU, 1974, DWD, 1978. Author: (mystery novel) Shadows At The Fair: An Antique Print Mystery, 2002 (nominated for Agatha for best first mystery, 2003), Shadows On The Coast Of Maine: An Antique Print Mystery, 2003, Shadows On The Ivy: An Antique Print Mystery, 2004, Shadows at the Spring Show: An Antique Print Mystery, 2005, (historical novels) Seaward Born, 2003, Wintering Well, 2004, (historical novel) Stopping To Home, 2001, Finest Kind, 2006. Mem.: Maine Antique Dealers Assn., Mystery Writers Am., Sisters in Crime, Maine Alliance Writers and Pubs. (sec. 2002—), Nat. Coun. for Single Adoptive Parents. Home: PO Box 225 Edgecomb ME 04556 Personal E-mail: leawait@clinic.net.

WAITE, BARBARA L. (PIXIE), lawyer; b. Columbus, Miss., July 7, 1952; BA summa cum laude, Memphis State Univ., 1980; JD, Georgetown Univ., 1984. Bar: DC 1984, DC Ct. Appeals 1985, US Dist. Ct. (DC, Ariz.), US Ct. Internat. Trade 1985, US Ct. Appeals (DC, Fed. cir.) 1985, US Supreme Ct. 1989. Ptnr., Copyright & Unfair Trade practice Venable LLP, Washington, 2000—. Editor (mng.): Am. Criminal Law Rev. Mem.: Copyright Soc. USA. Office: Venable LLP 575 7th St NW Washington DC 20004 Office Phone: 202-344-4811. Office Fax: 202-344-8300. Business E-Mail: blwaite@venable.com.

WAITE, CHERYL SIEBERT, history professor, researcher; d. Elton Theodore and Marguerite Elizabeth Siebert; m. Steven James Waite, July 13, 2002; children: Rochelle Marie Siebert, Scarlett Elisabeth Siebert. BA, U. Colo., Denver, 2001, MA, 2006. Asst. mus. curator Aurora History Mus., Colo., 2002—; adj. prof. history C.C. of Aurora, Colo., 2004—. Docent Byers-Evans Ho. Mus., Denver, 2001—02; rschr. Colo. Hist. Soc., Denver, 2002—03. Mem.-at-large Sandy Creek Homeowners Assn., Aurora, 2005—. Recipient scholarship, Coulter Family, 2004—05, David Owen Tryba Preservation award, David Owen Tryba Archs., 2002. Mem.: Nat. Trust for Hist. Preservation (assoc.). Independent. Methodist. Avocations: travel, reading. Office: CC of Aurora 16000 E CenterTech Pkwy Aurora CO 80011 Office Phone: 303-360-4740. Personal E-mail: cheryles2@comcast.net.

WAITE, FRANCES W., librarian, genealogist; b. Newberrytown, Pa., Jan. 7, 1944; d. Jacob Kister and Mary Fisher (Conley) Wise; m. Arthur Owen Waite, May 22, 1937; children: Catherine Ann, Douglas Arthur, Mary Virginia. BS in Edn., Shippensburg U., 1964; MS, Kutztown U. Elem. sch. tchr. Cen. Bucks Sch. Dist., Doylestown, Pa., 1964-65, 67-68; receptionist Bucks County Hist. Soc., Doylestown, 1981-86, libr., 1987—2005. Lectr., tchr. family history rsch.; verifying genealogist for Nat. Soc. Colonial Dames of Am. Com. of Pa., 1998-2002. Co-author: (books) Bucks County Tax Records 1693-1778, 1982, Bucks County Declarations and Naturalizations 1802-1906, 1985; author: (books) Descendants of Thomas Connelly, 1980, Descendants of Hans Detweiler, 1976, expanded and updated edit., 1995, Desendants of Johannes Weiss of Dover, Pa., 1997, White Families of Lower Bucks, 1999, Anderson Families of Upper York County, Pa., 1999, Connelly-Conley Descendants of Thomas Connelly of Rapho Township Lancaster County PA, 2002, 2d edit., 2003; editor numerous geneal. reference books, 1980-2005. Charter mem. Bucks County Choral Soc., Doylestown, 1972-99. Mem. Nat. Geneal Soc. (award of merit 1997), Geneal. Soc. of Pa (past co-chair program com. 1991-97, publs. com. 1990-99), Bucks County Geneal. Soc. (founder, v.p., pres., newsletter editor 1981-90). Avocations: choral singing, travel, crocheting, gardening. Home: 649 S Chubb Dr Doylestown PA 18901-4547

WAITE-FRANZEN, ELLEN JANE, academic administrator; b. Oshkosh, Wis., Feb. 17, 1951; d. Earl Vincent and Margaret (Luft) W.; m. Thomas H. Dollar, Aug. 19, 1977 (div. July 1984); m. Kent Hendrickson, Mar. 26, 1994 (div. Dec. 1995); m. Scott Franzen, Apr. 4, 1998. BA in English Lit., U. Wis., Oshkosh, 1973; MLS, U. Wis., Milw., 1977. Head of cataloging Marquette U., Milw., 1977-82; head catalog libr. U. Ariz., Tucson, 1983-85; assoc. dir. libr. Loyola U., Chgo., 1985-86, acting dir. libr., 1986-87, dir. libr., 1987-94, v.p. acad. svcs., 1994-97; assoc. provost for info. svcs. U. Richmond, 1997-99, v.p. for info. svcs., 1999—2002; v.p. for computing and info. svcs. Brown U., Providence, 2002—. Cons. Loyola U., Chgo., 1984, Boston Coll., 1986, U. San Francisco, 1989; bd. trustees Online Computer Lib. Ctr., Dublin, Ohio, 1994-2000. Contbg. author: Research Libraries and Their Implementation of AACR2, 1985; author: (with others) Women in LC's Terms: A Thesaurus of Subject Headings Related to Women, 1988. Bd. trustees Online Computer Libr. Ctr., Dublin, Ohio, 1994—2000. Mem.: ALA. Avocation: photography. Office: Brown U Computing and Info Svcs Box 1885 Providence RI 02912-1885 E-mail: ewaite@brown.edu.

WAITES, CANDY YAGHJIAN, former state official; b. N.Y.C., Feb. 21, 1943; d. Edmund Kirken and Dorothy Joanne (Candy) Yaghjian; children: Jennider Lisa, Robin Shelley. BA, Wheaton Coll., Mass., 1965; MPA, U. S.C., 1997. County councilwoman, Richland County, SC, 1976—88; mem. S.C. Ho. of Reps., 1988—94; lectr. polit. sci., assoc. dean Leadership Inst. Columbia Coll., 1993—99, dir. Leadership Inst., 2004—; dir. divsn. children's svcs. Gov.'s Office, 1999—2003. Vice chmn. Adv. Commn. on Intergovtl. Rels., S.C., 1977-87; bd. dirs. Interagy. Council on Pub. Transp., S.C., 1977-85, Central Midlands Regional Planning Council, Columbia, S.C., 1977-84; dir. Wachovia Bank. V.p. bd. dirs. United Way of Midlands, 1977-89; trustee Columbia Mus. Art, 1982-88; bd. dirs. Rape Crisis Network, 1984-87, Nat. ATHENA Found., 1999-2001; chmn. County Coun. Coalition; mem. C. of C. Leadership Forum, S.C. Fedn. of Blind; mem. adv. bd. U. S.C. Humanities and Social Scis. Coll., Family Shelter, Nuturing Ctr.; pres. Trinity Housing Corp.; found. bd. Palmetto Richland Meml. Hosp., 1995-2000, bd. mem., 2005—; mem. Columbia Housing Authority Bd., 1997-2000 Named Outstanding Young Career Woman, Columbia YWCA, 1980, YWCA Hall of Fame, 1993, Columbia Housing Authority Bd., Outstanding Young Woman of Yr., Columbia Jaycees, 1975, Pub. Citizen of Yr. NASW; recipient Ann. Legis. award Common Cause S.C., 1990, 91. Mem. S.C. Women in Govt. (vice chmn. 1984-86), S.C. Assn. Counties (bd. dirs. 1982-88, Pres.'s award 1983, Legislator of Yr. award 1992), Columbia C. of C. (Athena award 1998), Network Female Execs., LWV (pres. 1973-76), Unic. Assocs. Club, Mortar Bd. (hon.), Omicron Delta Kappa. Democrat. Episcopalian. Avocations: exercising, drawing, gardening, walking. Home: 3419 Duncan St Columbia SC 29205-2705

WAITES, TRINA SULARIN, history educator; b. Huntsville, Ala., Oct. 9, 1976; d. Phillip Wayne Sularin and Janice Cook Mann; m. George Berkeley Waites, June 19, 2004. BA, U. Montevallo, Ala., 1999, M, 2000. History tchr. Oak Mountain H.S., Birmingham, Ala., 2001—05, Bob Jones H.S., Madison, 2005—. Blood drive sponsor Oak Mountain H.S., Birmingham, Ala., 2002—05; sponsor Interact Club Bob Jones H.S., Madison, 2005—06; Sunday sch. tchr. First Bapt. Ch., Gardendale, 1999—2001. Grantee, Madison City Bd. Edn., 2006. Mem.: Ala. Edn. Assn. (assoc.), Phi Kappa Phi (assoc.), Chi Omega Alumnae Assn. (assoc.). Avocations: travel, reading, research, gardening, baking. Office Phone: 256-895-2547.

WAJSFELD, ANNIE R., volunteer; b. Antwerp, Belgium, Jan. 19, 1936; arrived in U.S., 1949; d. Szloma Chaskel and Hinda (Labin) Wajsfeld. BA, Bklyn. Coll., 1972. Cert.: Bklyn. Coll. (paralegal). With CUNY Grad. Ctr., N.Y.C., 1965—70, Kingsborough C.C., Bklyn., 1970—90, Bklyn. Coll., 1991—96. Del. Dem. Party, Bklyn., 1990, Nat. Coun. Young Israel, Manhattan, 1975—99; office mgr., treas. Young Israel of Vanderveer Park Synogogue, Bklyn., maintained meml. book. Named Woman of the Yr., Young Israel Synagogue, 1988, 1996. Mem.: Dem. Club (inspector 41 assembly dist. 2000—). Jewish. Avocations: reading, outdoor activities, attending cultural events, racquetball. Office: Am Mizrahi Women's Orgn HQ 7th Ave New York NY

WAKE, JUDITH ANN VAN BUREN, secondary school educator; b. Grand Rapids, Mich. d. John and Joan Van Buren; children: Rhonda L., Brenda A., Travis E., Nathan C. BS in English Edn., Mo. Western State Coll., 1987; MS in Edn. Guidance, N.W. Mo. State U., 1988; PhD in Interdisciplinary Edn., U. Mo., Kans. City, 1995. Guidance counselor North Kansas City, 1990—. Mem. NEA, MNEA, MSCA, GKCSCA, Phi Kappa Phi, Kappa Delta Pi, Sigma Tau Delta.

WAKE, MADELINE MUSANTE, academic administrator, nursing educator; Diploma, St. Francis Hosp. Sch. Nursing, 1963; BS in Nursing, Marquette U., 1968, MS in Nursing, 1971; PhD, U. Wis., Milw., 1986. Clin. nurse specialist St. Mary's Hosp., Milw., 1971-74, asst. dir. nursing, 1974-77; from dir. continuing nursing edn. to provost Marquette U., Milw., 1977—2002, provost, 2002—. Mem. devel. team Internat. Classification for Nursing Practice, Geneva, 1991-99. Chmn. bd. dirs. Trinity Meml. Hosp., Cudahy, Wis., 1991-96; bd. dirs. Blood Ctr. Wis., 2003-. Recipient Profl. Svc. award Am. Diabetes Assn.-Wis. affiliate, 1978, Excellence in Nursing Edn. award Wis. Nurses Assn., 1989; named Disting. Lectr. Sigma Theta Tau Internat., 1991. Fellow: Am. Acad. Nursing; mem.: ANA, Am. Assn. Colls. and Univs., Vis. Nurs Assn. Wis. (bd. dirs.), Am. Assn. Coll. Nursing (bd. dirs. 1999—2002). Office: Marquette Univ O'Hara Hall Milwaukee WI 53201-1881 Office Phone: 414-288-7511.

WAKE, MARVALEE HENDRICKS, biology professor; b. Orange, Calif., July 31, 1939; d. Marvin Carlton and Velvalee (Borter) H.; m. David B. Wake, June 23, 1962; 1 child, Thomas A. BA, U. So. Calif., 1961, MS, 1964, PhD, 1968. Tchg. asst., instr. U. Ill., Chgo., 1964, asst. prof., 1968—69; lectr. U. Calif., Berkeley, 1969—73, asst. prof., 1973—76, assoc. prof., 1976—80, prof. zoology, 1980—89, chmn. dept. zoology, 1985—89, chmn. dept. integrative biology, 1989—91, 1999—2002, assoc. dean Coll. Letters and Sci., 1975—78, prof. integrative biology, 1989—2003, Chancellor's prof., 1997—2000, prof. of the Grad. Sch., 2004—. Mem. NAS/NRC Bd. on Sustainable Devel., 1995-99, NSF Bio Adv. Commn., 1997-2002; Smithsonian Sci. Commn., 2001-02. Editor, co-editor: Hyman's Comparative Vertebrate Anatomy, 1979, The Origin and Evolution of Larval Forms, 1999, Ecology and Evolution in the Tropics, 2005; co-author: Biology, 1978; contbr. articles to profl. jours. NSF grantee, 1978—; Guggenheim fellow, 1988-89. Fellow: AAAS (chair Biology Sect. G 1998), Calif. Acad. Sci. (trustee 1992—98, hon. trustee 1998—), Am. Acad. Arts and Scis.; mem.: Internat. Soc. Vertebrate Morphology (pres.-elect 2004—07), Am. Inst. Biol. Sci. (pres. 2005), World Congress of Herpetology (sec. gen. 1994—97), Internat. Union Biol. Scis. (U.S. nat. com. 1986—, chair 1992—95, sec. gen. 1994—2000, pres. 2000—04), Soc. Integrative Comparative Biology (pres. 2001—03), Am. Soc. Ichthyologists and Herpetologists (bd. govs. 1978—, pres. 1984). Office: U Calif Dept Integrative Biology 3060 VLSB Berkeley CA 94720-3140 E-mail: mhwake@socrates.berkeley.edu.

WAKEFIELD, MARIE CYNTHIA, performing arts educator, playwright, poet; b. Chgo., Feb. 11, 1945; d. Daniel Jesse Armstrong and Margaret M. Jenkins; m. Donald Wakefield; children: Adolphus Beal III, Donald Wakefield II, Walter McIntyre Jr., Michele McIntyre, Reyna, Candace. Student, Cortez W. Peters Bus. Coll., Chgo., 1962—63. Founder Creative Works, Etc., Inc., Inglewood, Calif. Poet/playwright: Quiet Storm, 1994. Named Poet of Yr., Famous Poets Soc., 1995, 1998, 2000. Avocations: writing, singing, producing plays. Office: Creative Works Etc 9717 S 8th Ave Inglewood CA 90305 Office Phone: 323-777-0251. Personal E-mail: mwake9717@aol.com.

WAKEMAN, MARTHA JANE, artist, educator; b. Bridgeport, Conn., Jan. 8, 1948; d. Norman Burr and Muriel (Evitts) Wakeman; m. Robert E. Proctor, Mar. 15, 1980; children: Rebecca Anne Proctor, Andrew Wakeman Proctor. BS, Skidmore Coll., 1970; MA, Villa Schifaroia-Rosary Coll., Florence, Italy, 1972, MFA, 1978. Cert. art tchr. K-12, Conn. Instr. art Gonzaga U. Jr. Yr. Abroad Program, Florence, 1974-79, Conn. Coll., 1980-81, instr. art Return to Coll. program, 1984—; instr. painting Umbra Inst., Pengra, Italy, 2002. Exhibited in one-woman shows in Milan, Florence, N.Y.C. and Conn., 1972-96; group shows include Alan Stone Gallery, N.Y.C., Skidmore Coll., Vangarde Gallery, New London, Conn., MS Gallery, Hartford, Conn., No-Ho Gallery, N.Y.C., Conn. Women Artists, New Haven; paintings included in more than 100 pvt. collections in Europe, U.S. and Can.; subject of articles. Class coord. St. Joseph Sch., New London, 1998-99, Pine Point Sch., Stonington, Conn., 1995-97; mem. parish coun. St. Joseph Ch., New London, 1993-96, lector, 1995—/ Democrat. Roman Catholic. Avocations: swimming, travel, studying foreign languages, reading. Home: 105 Oneco Ave New London CT 06320-4120 Office: Conn Coll Box 5573 New London CT 06320

WAKEMAN, OLIVIA VAN HORN, marketing professional; b. Starkville, Miss. d. Thomas Oliver and Mary Jeanne Wakeman. BA in Mgmt., Eckerd Coll., St. Petersburg, Fla., 1980; MIM in Mktg./Advt., Am. Grad. Sch. Internat. Mgmt., 1982. Bus. analyst Dun & Bradstreet, Tampa, Fla., 1980; mgmt. cons. Cardinal Mgmt. Assocs., L.A., 1982-83; asst. account exec. McCann-Erickson, N.Y.C., 1984-86; account exec. Hearst Mag., N.Y.C., 1986-87, Ribaudo & Schaefer, N.Y.C., 1987-88; dir. pub. affairs/bus. soc. and ethics program Carnegie Coun. on Ethics and Internat. Affairs, N.Y.C., 1989-93; mgr. client svcs. Burson-Marsteller, Inc., N.Y.C., 1994-97, Young & Rubicam, Inc., N.Y.C., 1994-99, Cohn & Wolfe, N.Y.C., 1997-99; sr. writer TManage, Inc., 2000—. Adult edn. mktg. prof. Touro Coll., N.Y.C., 1989; mktg. comm. cons. Hoffmann-La Roche, Inc., McGraw-Hill Inc., Daniel J. Edelman, Inc., Dilenschneider Group, Stingray Ptnrs., N.Y.C., 1993-94; sr. writer T Manage, Inc., 2000—. Reading vol. Vol. Svcs. for Children, N.Y.C., 1991-93. Episcopalian. Avocation: scuba diving.

WAKOSKI, DIANE, poet, educator; b. Whittier, Calif., Aug. 3, 1937; d. John Joseph and Marie Elvira (Mengel) W. BA in English, U. Calif., Berkeley, 1960. Writer-in-residence Mich. State U., East Lansing, 1976—, Univ. disting. prof., 1990—. Vis. writer Calif. Inst. Tech., 1972, U. Va., 1972-73, Wilamette U., 1973, Lake Forest Coll., 1974, Colo. Coll., 1974, U. Calif., Irvine, 1974, Macalester Coll., 1975, U. Wis., 1975, Hollins Coll., 1974, U. Wash., 1977, Whitman Coll., 1976, Emory U., 1980-81, U. Hawaii, 1978. Author: Coins and Coffins, 1962, Discrepancies and Apparitions, 1966, Inside The Blood Factory, 1968, The George Washington Poems, 1967, The Magellanic Clouds, 1969, The Motorcycle Betrayal Poems, 1971, Smudging, 1972, Dancing On The Grave of A Son Of A Bitch, 1973, Trilogy, 1974, Virtuoso Literature For Two and Four Hands, 1976, Waiting For the King of Spain, 1977, The Man Who Shook Hands, 1978, Cap of Darkness, 1980, The Magician's Feastletters, 1982, The Collected Greed: Parts I-XIII, 1984, The Rings of Saturn, 1986, Emerald Ice: Selected Poems 1962-87, 1988 (William Carlos Williams prize 1989), Medea The Sorceress, 1991, Jason the Sailor, 1993, The Emerald City of Las Vegas, 1995, Argonaut Rose, 1998, The Butcher's Apron: New & Selected Poems, 2000. Named Univ. Disting. Prof., Mich. State U., 1990, Author of Yr., Mich. Libr. Assn., 2003; recipient award, Mich. Arts Found., 1989, Disting. Faculty award, Mich. State U., 1989; grantee Cassandra Found., 1970, N.Y. State Cultural Coun., 1971—72, Guggenheim Found., 1972—73, Fullbright, 1984, Mich. Arts Coun., 1988. Office: Mich State U 207 Morrill Hall East Lansing MI 48824-1036 E-mail: dwakoski@aol.com.

WAKSBERG, NOMI, painter, photographer, artist; b. Dresden, Germany, July 16, 1947; d. Isaac and Mollie Waksberg; BFA, Ohio State, 1967; MFA, Rutgers U., 1972. Coord. Mable Douglass Liberty Women Artists, New Brunswick, NJ, 1971—75, MUSE Found., Phila., 1979—82; art instr. State U. NJ, Lawrence, NJ, 1982—84. Panelist WCA, Newark, 1972—79, NJ Arts Coun., Newton, NJ, 1979—80. One-woman shows include Morristown Mus., 1989, Trenton State Mus., 1984, Islip Mus., NY, 2006, Lemieux Gallery, New Orleans, La., 2006. Mem.: Pa. Humanities, NJ Arts Coun. Office Phone: 908-782-1753. Personal E-mail: click@patmedia.net. Business E-Mail: nwaksberg@patmedia.net.

WALBERT, KATE, writer, educator; b. Aug. 13, 1961; Lectr. writing Yale U. Author: Where She Went, 1998 (N.Y. Times Notable Book, 1998), The Gardens of Kyoto, 2001, Our Kind: A Novel in Stories, 2004 (Nat. Book Award finalist, 2004); contbr. articles to newspapers. Recipient NEA Fellowship, Conn. Commn. on Arts Fellowship. Office: Yale U 63 High St PO Box 208302 New Haven CT 06520-8302 E-mail: kate.walbert@yale.edu.

WALCHER, JENNIFER LYNNE, city official; b. Denver, Feb. 8, 1956; d. Donald Robert and Winifred Edmunde (O'Dell) W. AS in Adminstrn. of Justice, Arapahoe C.C., Littleton, Colo., 1984; BS in Criminal Justice, Columbia Coll., Aurora, Colo. and Columbia, Mo., 1986; AS in Occupl. Safety, Trinidad State Jr. Coll., 1994. Cert. water distbn. sys. technician, Colo. Security patrolman Mission Viejo, Highlands Ranch, Colo., 1983-84; security officer Denver Water Dept., 1985-87, water serviceman I, 1987-88, safety and loss control specialist, 1988—. Contbr. articles to profl. publs. Instr. CPR and first aid Colo. Safety Assn., Denver, 1988—; instr. defensive driving Nat. Safety Coun., 1988—. With USN, 1974-81. Mem. Am. Soc. Safety Engrs., Phi Theta Kappa. Lutheran. Avocations: golf, camping, fishing, ceramics, poetry. Home: 2720 S Newland St Denver CO 80227-3519 Office: Denver Water Dept 1600 W 12th Ave Denver CO 80204-3412

WALCK, CAMILA CROCKETT, biology educator; b. Newport News, Va., Mar. 6, 1963; children: Natalie, Danielle children: Blaine Allen. MS in Biology Edn., Old Dominion U., Norfolk, Va, 2005. Tchr. biology Princess Anne HS, Va., 1986—. Adj. instr. Va. Wesleyan Coll., Virginia Beach, 2002—. Author: Tapestry of Knowledge (Pub. in Book, 2000). Named Tchr. Yr., Princess Anne H.S., 2003; recipient Radioshack Nat. Tchr. award, Radioshack, 2003; grantee, Scott and Springfellow, 2003, NEA, 2005. Avocations: exercise, reading. Home: 8508A Altantic Avenue Virginia Beach VA 23451 Office: Princess Anne High School 4400 Virginia Beach Blvd Virginia Beach VA 23462 Office Phone: 757-473-6000. Personal E-mail: ccwalck@vbschools.com.

WALCOTT, DELORES DEBORAH, psychologist, educator; BA in Psychology, Chgo. State U., 1976, MS in Corrections, 1978; cert. group treatment with adolescents, Youth Guidance Tng. Inst., 1981; cert. law program for cmty. developers and social workers, John Marshall Law Sch., 1982; cert. MMPI-2 and MMPI-A clin. workshops, Western Mich. Psychol. Assn., 1992; PhD in Clin. Psychology, Ill. Sch. Profl. Psychology, Chgo., 1993. Cert. in sex edn.; cert. family life edn. tng.; licensed clin. psychologist, Ill., Mich. Psychologist, correction specialist, alcohol youth prevention specialist Bobby E. Wright Comprehension Inc., Chgo., 1978-84; child welfare worker Habilitative Sys., Inc., Chgo., 1984-85; program coord. Brass Found., Essence House, Chgo., 1985-86; social worker Kaleidoscope, Inc., Chgo., 1986-87; psychology extern, adult unit Ill. State Psychiat. Inst., Chgo., 1990-91; coord. family life edn. program Nia Comprehensive Ctr. for Developmental Disabilities, Inc., Chgo., 1987-92; clin. psychology intern Western Mich. U., Kalamazoo, 1992-93; clin. psychologist Onarga (Ill.) Acad.-Nexus Inc., 1993-95; asst. prof. Counseling Ctr. Western Mich. U., Kalamazoo, Mich., 1995—. Mem. APA, Am. Profl. Soc. Abuse of Children, Nat. Black Alcoholism Coun., Nat. Black Psychol. Assn., Western Mich. Psychol. Assn., Chem. People Task Force, Human Resource Devel. Inst. (Vol. award), Westside Youth Booster (bd. dirs. 1983-84), Alumni Assn. The Family Inst. Home: 8122 S Green St Chicago IL 60620-3143 Office: Western Mich U Counseling Ctr Kalamazoo MI 49008

WALD, DONNA GENE, advertising executive; b. Peekskill, NY, July 24, 1947; d. David and Blossom (Karlin) W. BA, Rider Coll., 1969; MA, Hunter Coll., 1974. Broadcast traffic rep. SSC&B, Inc., N.Y.C., 1969-74; broadcast buyer J. Walter Thompson, N.Y.C., 1974-78; regional broadcast supr., v.p. Dallas, 1978-81; prof. UCLA, 1984; sr. v.p., account dir. Western Internat. Media, Calif., 1985-95; exec. v.p., regional dir. account svcs., 1995; exec. v.p., dir. account svcs. Pacific region, 1998—2002; sr. v.p., group acct. dir. Inter/Media, Encino, Calif., 2002—. Mem. Advt. Industry Emergency Fund, Hollywood Radio and TV Soc., Assn. Broadcast Execs. of Tex. (bd. dirs. 1979-80, s ec. 1980-81), L.A. Advt. Club (bd. dirs. 1997-98). Home: 14844 Dickens St Apt 106 Sherman Oaks CA 91403-3655 Office: Inter Media 15760 Ventura Blvd 1st Fl Encino CA 91436

WALD, INGEBORG, librarian, translator; b. Oberrissdorf, Germany, Apr. 24, 1933; children: Alexander Lieb, Gregory Lieb. Student, Freie U., Berlin, 1953—57, Friedrich Schiller U., Jena, Germany, 1952—53; MA, Boston U., 1969; MLS, Calif. State U., San Jose, 1975. Libr. Goethe Inst., Boston, 1968—71; libr. asst. Lane Med. Libr., Stanford U., Palo Alto, Calif., 1971—75; various positions Cornell U., Ithaca, NY, 1976—91; libr. German Sch. NY, White Plains, 1991—2000; cons. La. State Dept. Edn., Baton Rouge, 2002; gen. libr. Hill Meml. Libr., La. State U., Baton Rouge, 2004. Coun. mem. Westchester BOCES Sch. Libr. Sys., 1991—2000; lectr. in field; cons. in field. Translator: An Ark of Stars, 1989, 12 Poems, 12 Paintings, 1991. Recipient Poetic Achievement award, Arcadia Poetry Press, Editor's Choice award, Nat. Libr. Poetry, 1997; grantee, NY Coun. on the Arts, 1979, Whitney Found., 1981, Kress Found., 1984—85, Coun. of the Creative and Performing Arts, 1985, 1988, Deutscher Akademischer Austauschdienst, 1986, 1986, 1987. Address: 316 Shady Lake Pkwy Baton Rouge LA 70810-4320

WALD, PATRICIA MCGOWAN, retired federal judge; b. Torrington, Conn., Sept. 16, 1928; d. Joseph F. and Margaret (O'Keefe) McGowan; m. Robert L. Wald, June 22, 1952; children: Sarah, Douglas, Johanna, Frederica, Thomas. BA, Conn. Coll., 1948; LLB, Yale U., 1951; HHD (hon.), Mt. Vernon Jr. Coll., 1980; LLD (hon.), George Washington Law Sch., 1983, CUNY, 1984, Notre Dame U., John Jay Sch. Criminal Justice, Mt. Holyoke Coll., 1985, Georgetown U., 1987, Villanova U., Amherst Coll., NY Law Sch., 1988, Colgate U., 1989, Hofstra U., 1991, New Eng. Coll., 1991, Vermont Law Sch., 1995; LLD, Yale U., 2001. Bar: DC 1952. Clk. to Hon. Jerome Frank US Ct. Appeals, 1951—52; assoc. Arnold, Fortas & Porter, Washington, 1952—53; mem. DC Crime Commn., 1964—65; atty. Office of Criminal Justice, 1967—68, Neighborhood Legal Svc., Washington, 1968—70; co-dir. Ford Found. Project on Drug Abuse, 1970, Ctr. for Law and Social Policy, 1971—72, Mental Health Law Project, 1972—77; asst. atty. gen. for legis. affairs US Dept. Justice, Washington, 1977—79; judge US Ct. Appeals (DC cir.), 1979—99, chief judge, 1986—91; judge Internat. Criminal Tribunal for Former Yugoslavia, The Hague, Netherlands, 1999—2001. Bd. dirs. Am. Constn. Soc., 2002—. Author: Law and Poverty, 1965; co-author: Bail in the United States, 1964, Dealing with Drug Abuse, 1973; bd. editors: ABA Jour., 1978—86; contbr. articles to profl. jours. Mem. Commn. on Intelligence Capabilities of the US Regarding Weapons of Mass Destruction, 2004—05; trustee Ford Found., 1972—77, Phillips Exeter Acad., 1975—77, Agnes Meyer Found., 1976—77, Conn. Coll., 1976—77; active Carnegie Coun. on Children, 1972—77; bd. dirs. Mental Disability Rights Internat., 2002—. Recipient Lifetime Achievement award, The Am. Lawyer, 2004. Mem.: ABA-Ctrl. and Ea. European Law Inst. (exec. bd. 1994—99), Am. Constitution Soc. (bd. dirs. 2004—), Am. Philos. Assn., Inst. Justice Initiative, Am. Acad. Arts and Scis., Am. Law Inst. (coun. mem. 1979—, exec. com. 1985—99, 2d v.p. 1988—93, 1st v.p. 1993—98), Open Soc. Inst. (chair justice initiative 2002—04), Phi Beta Kappa. Office: 2101 Connecticut Ave NW Washington DC 20008 Personal E-mail: patwald2@cs.com.

WALD, PRISCILLA B., language educator; b. Newark, July 31, 1958; d. Stanley Irwin and Audrey Katzman Wald; m. Joseph Paul Donahue III, Apr. 4, 1987; children: Evan Michael Donahue, Nathaniel Wald Donahue. BA in english, Yale U., 1980; MA in english, Columbia U., 1981, PhD in english, 1989. Asst. prof. english Columbia U., N.Y.C., 1988—95, assoc. prof. english, 1995, U. Wash., Seattle, 1996—99, Duke U., Durham, NC, 1999—, assoc. prof. women's studies, 2002—06, prof. English, prof. women's studies, 2006—. Assoc. editor Am. Lit. Jour., Duke U., 2000—; adv. bd. Duke U. Press, 2000—; assoc. editor Lit. and Med. Jour., N.Y.C., 2001—. Author: Constituting Americans: Cultural Anxiety and Narrative Form, 1995; editor: Am. Lit. Jour., 2006—, co-editor articles various profl. jours. Grantee Sci. and Religion fellow, Ctr. for Theology & Nat. Sci., 2002—03, Soc. for the Humanities fellow, Cornell U., 1999—2000, Mellon fellow, Stanford U., 1990—92. Mem.: MLA, Am. Studies Assn. (Exe. Com. of Divsn. 1997—2001). Avocations: camping, hiking, running, weightlifting. Office: Duke U Dept of English Box 90015 Durham NC 27708 E-mail: pwald@duke.edu.

WALD, SYLVIA, artist; b. Phila., Oct. 30, 1915; Student, Moore Inst. Art, Sci. and Industry. One-woman shows include U. Louisville, 1945, 49, Kent State Coll., 1945, Nat. Serigraph Soc., 1946, Grand Central Moderns, N.Y.C., 1957, Devorah Sherman Gallery, Chgo., 1960, New Sch., 1967, Book Gallery, White Plains, N.Y., 1968, Benson Gallery, Bridgehampton, L.I., 1977, Knoll Internat., Munich, 1979, Amerika Havs, Munich, 1979, Aaron Berman Gallery, N.Y.C., 1981, Hirschtladler Gallery, 1994, New Britain (Conn.) Mus., 1994, Dongah Art Gallery, Seoul, Korea, 1995, Hanlim Art Gallery, Daejun, 1995-96, Kwangju City Art Mus, Pusan, Korea, Dong Shin U., Kwangju, 1996, Chosun U. Mus., Kwangju City, 2001, Chosun Univ. Mus. Art, Kwangju, Korea, 2002, 05, Tenri Gallery, N.Y.C., 2004, 05; exhibited in group shows at Nat. Sculpture Soc., 1940, Sculpture Internat., Phila., 1940, Chgo. Art Inst., 1941, Bklyn. Mus., 1975, Libr. of Congress, 1943, 52, 58, Smithsonian Instn., 1954, Internat. Print Exhbn., Salzburg and Vienna, 1952, 2d Sao Paulo Biennial, 1953, N.Y. Cultural Ctr., 1973, Mus. Modern Art, N.Y.C., 1975, Benson Gallery, Bridgehampton, L.I., 1982, Dumon-Landis Gallery, New Brunswick, N.J., 1982-83, Suzuki Gallery, N.Y.C., 1982, Sid Deutch Gallery, N.Y.C., 1983, Aaron Berman Gallery, N.Y.C., 1983, Full House Gallery, Kingston, N.J., 1984, Nabi Gallery, Sag Harbor, N.Y., 1989, Worcester Mus., 1991, Boston Mus. Fine Arts, 1991, Hirschl & Adler Gallery, N.Y.C., 1993, Parrish Mus., Southampton, 2002, Tenri Galleru, NYC, 2005, 2x13 Gallery, 2006, Korea Gallery, 2006, others; represented in permanent collections Aetna Oil Co., AAUW, Ball State Tchrs. Coll., Bibliotheque Nat., Paris, Bklyn. Mus., Howard U., State U. Iowa, Libr. of Congress, U. Louisville, Nat. Gallery, Mus. Modern Art, Phila. Mus., N.C. Mus., Rose Mus. Art at Brandeis U., Whitney Mus., N.Y.C., Finch Coll. Mus., N.Y.C., U. Nebr., Ohio U., U. Okla., Princeton, Victoria and Albert Mus., Walker Gallery, Worcester (Mass.) Art Mus., Guggenheim Mus., N.Y.C., Grunewald Mus., UCLA, Rutgers Mus., N.J., Aschenbach Collection Mus., San Francisco, Grunewald Coll. Mus. UCLA, Wellesley Coll.; acquisitions Yale U. Art Gallery, 1998, Cleve. Mus., 1998; contbr. articles to profl. jours. Address: 417 Lafayette St New York NY 10003-7005

WALDBAUM, JANE COHN, art history educator; b. Jan. 28, 1940; d. Max Arthur and Sarah (Waldstein) Cohn. BA, Brandeis U., 1962; MA, Harvard U., 1964, PhD, 1968. Rsch. fellow in classical archaeology Harvard U., Cambridge, Mass., 1968-70, 72-73; from asst. prof. to assoc. prof. U. Wis., Milw., 1973-84, prof. art history, 1984—2002, chmn. dept., 1982-85, 86-89, 91-92, adj. prof. anthropology, 2002—. Dorot rsch. prof. W.F. Albright Inst. Archaeol. Rsch., Jerusalem, 1990-91; vis. scholar Hebrew U. Jerusalem, 1989-91. Author: From Bronze to Iron, 1978, Metalwork from Sardis, 1983; author (with others), co-editor: Sardis Report I, 1975; mem. editl. bd. Bull. Am. Schs. Oriental Rsch., 1994-98, Near Eastern Archaeology, 2000-2002; contbr. numerous articles to profl. jours. Woodrow Wilson Found. fellow, dissertation fellow, 1962-63, 65-66, NEH postdoctoral rsch., Jerusalem, 1989-90; grantee Am. Philos. Soc., 1972, NEH, summer 1975, U. Wis.-Milw. Found., 1983. Mem. Am. Schs. Oriental Rsch. (bd. trustees 2003—), Soc. for Archaeol. Sci., Israel Exploration Soc., Archaeol. Inst. Am. (exec. com. 1975-77, chmn. com. on membership programs 1977-81, nominating com. 1984, chmn. com. on lecture program 1985-87, acad. trustee 1993-98, 1st v.p. 1999—2002, pres. 2003-, com. profl. responsibilities 1993—, fellowships com. 1993-99, gold medal com. 1993-99, chair 1996-97, Near East Archaeology interest group 1993—, chair ann. meeting com. 1999—2002, chair regional meetings com. 1999—2002, pers. com., governance com., devel. com., fin. com.), W.F. Albright Inst. Archaeol. Rsch. (trustee 1996-2006, mem. governance com. 1996-2006), Wis. Soc. Jewish Learning (trustee 1993-99), Milw. Soc. Archaeol. Inst. (bd. dirs., pres. 1983-85, 91-95, 97-99), Phi Beta Kappa Office: U Wis Dept Anthropology PO Box 413 Milwaukee WI 53201-0413 Business E-Mail: JCW@uwm.edu.

WALDEN, DANA, broadcast executive; BA in Comm., U. So. Calif. Formerly with Bender, Goldman & Helper; former v.p. mktg. Arsenio Hall Comm., Paramount; former sr. v.p. media and corp. rels. 20th Century Fox TV, v.p. current programming, 1994—96, former v.p. drama, former sr. v.p. drama, former exec. v.p. drama devel., co-pres., 1999—. Named one of 100 Most Powerful Women in Entertainment, Hollywood Reporter, 1999—2005. Mem.: Hollywood Radio and TV Soc. (v.p. 2003—). Office: 20th Century Fox TV 10201 W Pico Blvd Bldg 88 Rm 29 Los Angeles CA 90035*

WALDINGER SEFF, MARGARET, special elementary education educator; b. N.Y.C., June 12; d. Herbert Francis Waldinger and Michelle (Rubin) Cohen; children: Dylan Paul Seff, Cortney Sara Seff, Blake Adam Seff. BA, Hofstra U., 1971; postgrad., NYU, 1971-73; MA, Fairleigh Dickinson U., 1986. Cert. elem. sch. tchr., tchr. of handicapped, learning disability tchr. cons., N.J. Tchr. pub. schs., N.J., N.Y., 1984-88; learning specialist Manchester (Vt.) Elem. Sch., 1988—. Adv., ednl. therapist, N.J., 1983-88. Reading grantee Tuxedo Park Sch., 1986, Bennington Rutland Supervisory Union, 1992. Avocations: tennis, golf, home restorations, drawing. Home: 5823 Main St Manchester Center VT 05255

WALDMAN, AMY, journalist; BA, Yale U., 1991. Freelance journalist, prof. U. Western Cape, South Africa, 1992—94; editor, writer Washington Monthly; editor Washington Post; metro desk reporter NY Times, 1997—2002, co-bur. chief New Delhi, 2002—05; nat. corr. Atlantic Monthly, Washington, 2005—. Recipient Disting. Feature Writing award, NY Newspaper Pub. Assn., Front Page award, Newswomen's Club NY, Overseas Press Club award for best bus. reporting in newspapers, 2006. Office: The Atlantic Monthly 600 New Hampshire Ave NW Washington DC 20037 Office Phone: 202-266-6000.*

WALDMAN, GLORIA, art gallery owner, artist; b. Bronx, NY, July 18, 1932; d. Isidore and Irene Galitzer; m. Harry S. Waldman, Sept. 23, 1951; 1 child, Helene. Art dealer, gallery owner, artist agt. Artcetera, Inc., Boynton Beach, Fla., 1982—, glass artist, 1999—, jewelry designer, 2003—. Vol. Kravis Ctr. Performing Arts, West Palm Beach, Fla., 1995—2000, Palm Beach Internat. Film Festival, West Palm Beach, 1997—2006. Mem.: Valencia Isles Visual Arts (pres. 2000—), Valencia Isles Players, Valencia Isles Culture Club. Avocations: singing, theater, swimming, tennis, art. Home: 6618 Bali Hai Dr Boynton Beach FL 33437-7048

WALDO, ANNA LEE, retired science educator, writer; b. Great Falls, Mont., Feb. 16, 1925; d. Lee William Van Artsdale and Cecelia Anna Prayzek; m. Willis Henry Waldo; children: Judith Ann, Sara Kendall, Dale Frederick, Patricia Gwyn, Richard Kirk. BS in Chemistry, Mont. State Coll., 1946; MS in Organic Chemistry, U. Md., 1949. Biochemistry instr. U. Dayton, Ohio, 1950—55, Mercy Coll., Frontenac, Mo., 1964—73; sci. instr. St. Louis C.C.-Meramec, Kirkwood, Mo., 1975—85, Calif. Poly. Tech. U., San Luis Obispo, 1995—97. Author: Sacajawea, 1979, rev. edit., 1984, Prairie, 1986, Circle of Stones, 1999, Circle of Stars, 2001; contbr. articles to profl. jours. Recipient L. White Quest award for writing, Women of the Globe Dem. newspaper, 1980, Woman of Distinction award, AAUW, 2001. Mem.: Authors Guild, Alpha Chi Sigma. Republican. Home: 49 Los Palos Dr San Luis Obispo CA 93401-7725 Personal E-mail: alwaldo@sbcglobal.net.

WALDRIP, KAREN MARIE, career planning administrator; b. Tacoma, Oct. 17, 1961; d. Mike and Ehtel Gray; m. Edwin Thomas Waldrip, Aug. 25, 1990; 1 child, Amy Lynn Ely. BS in Psychology, U. Puget Sound, 1984, M in Edn. and Counseling, 1987. Lic. profl. counselor Alaska. 2000. Counselor, social worker Ryther Child Ctr., Seattle, 1985—87; edn. specialist Petersburg (Alaska) Coun. on Alcoholism, 1987—88; adult treatment specialist Lakeside-Milam Recover Ctrs., Juneau, Alaska, 1988—90; employment career counselor State of Alaska Dept. Labor and Workforce Devel., Juneau, 1990—. Supporter Big Bros., Big Sisters, Boy Scouts of Am., Girl Scouts of Am., Juneau, 2002; doner ARC Assn., Juneau, 1999—2006; active Ptnr. in Hope donor registry St. Jude's Med. Ctr., Juneau, 2005; active Paralyzed Vets. Am., Juneau, 2000—06. Recipient 10 Yr. Svc. award, State of Alaska, 2000, E-Commerce 500+ Feedback award, 2005; grantee State Tng. and Employment Program, State of Alaska, 1993, 1994, 1995, 1995—2000. Mem.: Cmty. and Econ. Devel. (licentiate). Independent. Avocations: fishing, hunting. Home: 19935 Cohen Dr Tee Harbor AK 99801 Office: DOLWD Juneau Job Center 10002 Glacier Hwy Juneau AK 99801 Office Phone: 907-465-2963. Office Fax: 907-465-2984. Personal E-mail: etwaldrip75@msn.com. Business E-Mail: karen_waldrip@labor.state.ak.us.

WALDRON, ALLENE, insurance group executive; b. Jamestown, N.Y., Apr. 27, 1944; d. Sheridan Travers and Frances Marian Buck; m. Alton Guy Waldron, Sept. 8, 1962; children: Kimberly A. Kinnear, Tammy M., Robert A., Dan A. Grad., Edinboro (Pa.) U. Cert. in gen. ins. Assembler Elgin Electronics, Waterford, Pa., 1969-70, insp., 1972-75, Cherry Hill Ethan Allen, Union City, Pa., 1976-81; demonstrator Stanley HomePro, Waterford, 1981-82; mail clk. Erie (Pa.) Ins. Group, 1982-83, customer svc. rep., 1983-90, endorsement specialist, 1990—. Chair parish Asbury United Meth. Ch., 1991-93, chair adminstrv. coun., 1993-95. Mem. Nat. Assn. Ins. Women (CPIW), Order Eastern Star (worthy matron), Order of Amaranth (royal matron, royal patron, dist. dep.). Democrat. Avocations: piano, crocheting, knitting, reading, clown. Home: 136 E 1st St Waterford PA 16441-9711 Office: Erie Ins Group 100 Erie Insurance Pl Erie PA 16530-0001

WALDRON, JANET E., state commissioner; Sr. legis. analyst Legis. Office of Fiscal and Program Rev.; dir. legis. affairs Ctrl. Maine Power Co.; dir. adminstrn. Dept. Conservation; asst. sec. of state State of Maine, commr. dept. adminstrv. and fin. svcs., 1994—. Mem. Intergovernmental Task Force; co-chair Info. Tech. Task Force; chair Telecom. and Info. Tech. Planning Project. Office: Adminstrv & Fin Svcs Dept 78 State House Sta Augusta ME 04333-0078

WALDROP, ROSMARIE, writer; b. Kitzingen, Germany, Aug. 24, 1935; arrived in U.S., 1958; d. Josef and Friederike Sebald; m. Keith Waldrop, Jan. 20, 1959. Student, U. Wurzburg, 1954—56, U. Freiburg, 1957—58; MA, U. Mich., 1960, PhD, 1966. Asst. prof. Wesleyan U., 1964—70. Vis. writer Southeastern Mass. U., 1977; vis. lectr. Tufts U., 1979—81; vis. assoc. prof. Brown U., 1977—78, 1983, 97. Author: The Hanky of Pippin's Daughter, 1987, Reluctant Gravities, 1999, A Form of Taking It All, 2001, Lavish Absence: Recalling and Rereading Edmond Jabes, 2002, Blindsight, 2003, Dissonance (If you are interested): Collected Essays, 2005, Curves to the Apple, New Directions, 2006, translator books and poems. Recipient Writer's award, Lila Wallace Readers Digest, N.Y.C., 1999—2002; fellow, NEA, 1994; grantee, Found. for Contemporary Performance Arts, 2003; scholar, Brown U. Fellow: Am. Acad. Arts & Sciences; mem.: PEN. Home: 71 Elmgrove Ave Providence RI 02906

WALDT, RISA, psychotherapist, artist, writer; b. Tucson, Dec. 29, 1951; d. Carl J. and Jane D. Waldt. BA in Fine Arts, U. Ariz., 1973. Cert. Am. Soc. Experiential Therapists. Art therapist Miraflores ADL Facility, Tucson, 1993—94, Sierra Tucson Art Therapist, 1993—94; cons. and presenter in field. Author, artist: books A Story of Being, Grand Canyon, A River Trip; actor: (featured in) Artists of Arizona, Vol. I, Vol. II; one-woman shows include, exhibited in group shows, commd. work, to galleries. Facilitator Cir. Friends Job Corps, Tucson. Mem.: So. Ariz. Watercolor Guild (pres. 2003—04), Ariz. Watercolor Soc., Nat. League Am. Pen Women, Nat. Watercolor Soc., Nat. Mus. Women in Arts, Am. Watercolor Soc., Sweat Lodge. Episcopalian. Office: PO Box 41625 Tucson AZ 85717-1625 Office Phone: 520-825-9601.

WALENSKY, DOROTHY CHARLOTTE, language educator; b. N.Y.C., Mar. 23, 1941; d. Oliver L. and Henny T. (Schlesinger) Marton; m. Ernest Leonard Walensky, Aug. 17, 1968; 1 child. BA, Adelphi U., 1962; MA in Spanish, Middlebury Coll. and U. Madrid, 1963; MA in Teaching, Fairleigh Dickinson U., 1966. Bilingual sec. internat. div. Turner Jones Co., Inc., N.Y.C., 1963-64; prof. Spanish and German, Fairleigh Dickinson U., Teaneck, N.J., 1965—. Mem.: MLA, AAUP, Am. Assn. Tchrs. German, Am. Assn. Tchrs. Spanish and Portuguese, Delta Phi Alpha, Sigma Delta Pi. Avocations: travel, photography, stamp collector, tennis, ice skating. Office: Fairleigh Dickinson U 1000 River Rd Teaneck NJ 07666-1996

WALENTIK, CORINNE ANNE, pediatrician; b. Rockville Centre, N.Y., Nov. 24, 1949; d. Edward Robert and Evelyn Mary (Brinskele) Finno; m. David Stephen Walentik, June 24, 1972; children: Anne, Stephen, Kristine. AB honors, St. Louis U., 1970, MD, 1974, MPH, 1992. Diplomate Am. Bd. Pediat., Am. Bd. Neonatal and Perinatal Medicine, cert. physician exec. Certifying Commn. on Med. Mgmt., Am. Coll. Physician Execs. Resident pediat. St. Louis U. Group Hosps., 1974—76, fellow neonatalogy, 1976—78; neonatalogist St. Mary's Health Ctr., St. Louis, 1978—79; from co-dir. to dir. neonatal unit St. Louis City Hosps., 1979—85; dir. neonatalogy St. Louis Regional Med. Ctr., 1985—96; asst. prof. pediat. St. Louis U., 1990—94, assoc. clin. prof., 1994—98, assoc. prof. pediat., 1998—2001, prof. pediat., 2001—. Supr. nursery follow-up program Cardinal Glennon Children's Hosp., St. Louis, 1979—, neonatologist, physician exec. for managed care and pub. policy, 1997—; dir. nurseries St. Mary's Health Ctr., Richmond Heights, Mo., 2004—; chair provider svcs. adv. bd. St. Louis Regional Health Commn. Contbr. articles to profl. jours. Mem. adv. com. Mo. Perinatal Program., 1983-86; chair cmty. adv. bd. Mo. Found. for Health. Fellow: Am. Acad. Pediat. (pres. Mo. chpt., com. on child healthcare financing); mem.: APHA, St. Louis Met. Med. Soc., Mo. State Med. Assn., Nat. Perinatal Assn. (coun. 1984—87), Mo. Perinatal Assn. (pres. 1983), Mo. Pub. Health Assn. (pres. St. Louis chpt. 1995—96). Roman Catholic. Avocations: bridge, baseball, sports. Home: 7234 Princeton Ave Saint Louis MO 63130-3027 Office: Cardinal Glennon Children's Hosp 1465 S Grand Blvd Saint Louis MO 63104-1003 Office Phone: 314-577-5642. Business E-Mail: walentca@slu.edu.

WALHOUT, JUSTINE SIMON, chemistry professor; b. Aberdeen, SD, Dec. 11, 1930; d. Otto August and Mabel Ida (Tews) S.; m. Donald Walhout, Feb. 1, 1958; children: Mark, Timothy, Lynne, Peter. BS, Wheaton Coll., 1952; PhD, Northwestern U., 1956. Instr. Wright City Community Coll., Chgo., 1955-56; asst. prof. Rockford (Ill.) Coll., 1956-59, assoc. prof., 1959-66, 81-89, prof., 1989-96, prof. emeritus, 1996—, dept. chmn., 1987-95; cons. Pierce Chem. Co., Rockford, 1968-69; trustee Rockford (Ill.) Coll., 1987-91. Contbr. articles to profl. jours. Mem. Ill. Bd. Edn., 1974-81. Mem. AAUW (Ill. bd. dirs. 1985-87), Am. Chem. Soc. (councilor 1993-99), Rockford LWV (bd. dirs. 1983-85, 2002-04), Sigma Xi. Presbyterian. Home: 3204 Wesley Way Rockford IL 61101-8803 Office: Rockford Coll 5050 E State St Rockford IL 61108-2311

WALK, BARBRA DENISE, customer service administrator, tutor; b. Tacoma, Wash., Aug. 29, 1969; d. Robert Edward and Connie Lee Walk. A, Pierce Coll., Tacoma, 1993; BA, Wash. State U., Pullman, 1996. Office mgr. Comcast, Douglasville, Ga., 1999—2003; warranty adminstrn. coord. Rinnai, Peachtree City, Ga., 2004—; writer Gallopade Internat., Peachtree City, 2005—06; tutor Peachtree City, 2005—. Mem. edn. com. Japanese Am. Friendship Soc., Peachtree City, 2005—06. Named Miss Congeniality, Miss TEEN pageant, 1983; recipient Scholastic Achievement award, 1983, 5 achievement awards, Dale Carnegie. Mem.: Mensa, Phi Alpha Theta. Avocations: travel, tap dancing, music.

WALKER, ALICE, writer; b. Eatonton, Ga., Feb. 9, 1944; d. Willie Lee and Minnie (Grant) W.; m. Melvyn R. Leventhal, Mar. 17, 1967 (div. 1976); 1 dau., Rebecca Walker Leventhal, 1970. Attended, Spelman Coll.; BA, Sarah Lawrence Coll., 1966; PhD (hon.), Russell Sage U., 1972; DHL (hon.), U. Mass., 1983. Co-founder, pub. Wild Trees Pr., Navarro, Calif., 1984-88. Writer in residence, tchr. black studies Jackson State Coll., 1968-69, Tougaloo Coll., 1970-71; lectr. literature Wellesley Coll., 1972-73, U. Mass., Boston, 1972-73; disting. writer Afro-American studies dept. U. Calif., Berkeley, 1982; Fannie Hurst Prof. of Literature Brandeis U., Waltham, Mass., 1982; cons. Friends of the Children of Miss., 1967. Author: Once, 1968, The Third Life of Grange Copeland, 1970, Five Poems, 1972, Revolutionary Petunias and Other Poems, 1973 (Nat. Book award nomination 1973, Lillian Smith award So. Regional Coun. 1973), In Love and Trouble, 1973 (Richard and Hinda Rosenthal Found. award Am. Acad. and Inst. of Arts and Letters 1974) Langston Hughes: American Poet, 1973, Meridian, 1976, Goodnight, Willie Lee, I'll See You in the Morning, 1979, You Can't Keep a Good Woman Down, 1981, The Color Purple, 1982 (Nat. Book Critics Circle award nomination 1982, Pulitzer Prize for fiction 1983, Am. Book award 1983; movie Steven Spielberg, The Color Purple), In Search of Our Mothers' Gardens, 1983, Horses Make a Landscape Look More Beautiful, 1984, To Hell With Dying, 1988, Living By the Word: Selected Writings, 1973-1987, 1988, The Temple of My Familiar, 1989, Her Blue Body Everything We Know: Earthling Poems, 1965-1990, 1991, Finding the Green Stone, 1991, Possessing the Secret of Joy, 1992, (with Pratibha Parmar) Warrior Marks, 1993, (with others) Double Stitch: Black Women Write About Mothers & Daughters, 1993, Everyday Use, 1994, Alice Walker Banned: The Banned Works, 1996, Everything We Love Can Be Saved: A Writer's Activism: Essays, Speeches, Statements and Letters, 1997, The Same River Twice, 1997; editor: I Love Myself When I'm Laughing.And Then Again When I'm Looking Mean and Impressive, 1979, By The Light of My Father's Smile, 1998, The Way Forward is With a Broken Heart, 2000, Absolute Trust in the Goddness of the Earth: New Poems, 2003. Recipient first prize Am. Scholar essay contest, 1967, O. Henry award for Kindred Spirits, 1986, Nora Astorga Leadership award, 1989, Fred Cody award for lifetime achievement Bay Area Book Reviewers Assn., 1990, Freedom to Write award PEN Ctr. USA West, 1990; Bread Loaf Writer's Conf. scholar, 1966; Merrill writing fellowship, 1967; McDowell Colony fellowship, 1967, 77-78; National Endowment for the Arts grantee, 1969, 77; Radcliffe Inst. fellowship, 1971-73; Guggenheim fellow, 1977-78. Achievements include introducing the word "womanist". Address: Random House Inc 1745 Broadway #B1 New York NY 10019-4305

WALKER, ALICE R., mechanical engineer; b. Jackson, Wyo., May 19, 1965; d. Robert and Rosemary McIntosh; m. Kyle Walker; 2 children. BSME, U. Nev., 1991. Mech. engr. REECo., Las Vegas, 1991-92; sr. prodn. engr. Tyler Refrigeration MSD, Waxahachie, Tex., 1993-97; mech. engr. Sys. Engring. & Labs., Tyler, Tex., 1997-2000; sr. product engr. Carrier Corp., Tyler, Tex., 2000—. Registered engr. in tng. Mem. ASME (student v.p. 1990-91, 1st pl. speaking award 1991), Nat. Soc. Profl. Engrs. (assoc., pres.), Tex. Soc. Profl. Engrs. Avocations: horseback riding, camping, skiing, restoring classic pick-up, softball. Office: Carrier Corp 1700 E Duncan St Tyler TX 75702-2430

WALKER, AMAL KHAWAM, elementary school educator; d. Laurice Nouneh and Michel Khawam; m. Dale James Walker, May 13, 1984; 1 child, Carol Laurice. BS in Math., Physics, Chemistry, U. Damascus, Syria, 1978; BS in Elem. Edn. (hon.), Sam Houston State U., Huntsville, Tex., 1997. Cert. tchr. Tex., 1997. Sec. to purchasing dept. Shell Oil Co., Damascus, 1978—84; tchr. 7th grade, team leader York Jr. HS, Conroe, Tex., 2004—. Translator Pecten Oil Co., Damascus, Syria, 1978—84. Mem.: Kappa Delta Pi. Office Phone: 936-441-9297.

WALKER, ANN YVONNE, lawyer; b. San Francisco, Sept. 26, 1954; d. C. Richard and Athene (Henderson) Walker. BS with distinction in Math., Stanford U., 1976, JD, 1979. Bar: Calif. 1979. Assoc. Wilson, Sonsini, Goodrich & Rosati, Palo Alto, Calif., 1979-86, ptnr., 1986—. Violinist, bd. dirs. Redwood Symphony Orch., 1985—. Mem.: ABA (mem. fed. regulation securities com. 1992—, mem. com. lawyer bus. ethics 1993—, mem. standing com. professionalism 1996—99, chair 1997—2001, mem. bus. law sect. publs. bd. 2000—04, mem. bus. law sect. coun. 2001—05, mem. standing com. tech. and info. sys. 2005—), Palo Alto Area Bar Assn., Santa Clara County Bar Assn., Calif. State Bar Assn. (mem. corps. com. 1992—96, chair 1995—96, mem. exec. com. bus. law sect. 1996—, vice chair 1998—99, chair 1999—2000, advisor 2000—05, co-chair coun. state bar sects. 2001—02, advisor emeritus 2005—), Phi Beta Kappa. Office: Wilson Sonsini Goodrich and Rosati 650 Page Mill Rd Palo Alto CA 94304-1050 Office Phone: 650-320-4643. Business E-Mail: awalker@wsgr.com.

WALKER, ANNETTE, retired counseling administrator; b. Birmingham, Ala., Sept. 20, 1953; d. Jesse and Luegene (Wright) W. BS in Edn., Huntingdon Coll., 1974; MS in Adminstrn. and Supervision, Troy State U., 1977, 78, MS in Sch. Counseling, 1990, AA in Sch. Adminstrn., 1992; diploma, World Travel Sch., 1990; diploma in Cosmetology, John Patterson Coll., 1992; MEd in higher Edn. Adminstrn., Auburn (Ala.) U., 1995. Cert. tchr., adminstr., Ala.; lic. cosmetologist, Ala.; lic. funeral dir., Ala. Tchr. Montgomery (Ala.) Pub. Sch. System, 1976-89, sch. counselor, 1989—2000; lit. tchr. Fed. Bur. of Justice, 1997—2000; ret., 2000; acad. advisor Cmty. Coll. of Air Force; acad. counselor Maxwell Air Force Base, Ala., guidance counselor edn. office, 2001—. Tchr. Fed. Govt., 1997—, U.S. Bur. Justice, 1997—; gymnastics tchr. Cleveland Ave. YMCA, 1971-76; girls coach Montgomery Parks and Recreation, 1973-76; summer sch. sci. tchr. grades 7-9, 1977-88; chmn. dept. sci. Bellingrath Sch., 1987-90, courtesy com., 1987-88, sch. discipline com., 1977-84; recreation asst. Gunter AFB, Ala., 1981-83; calligraphy tchr. Gunter Youth Ctr., 1982; program dir. Maxwell AFB, Ala., 1983-89, vol. tchr. Internat. Officer Sch., 1985—, Adult Laubach Reading Prog., Ala. Goodwill Amb., 1985—, day camp dir., 1987, calligraphy tchr., 1988; trainer internat. law for sec. students, Ala., 1995—; leader of workshops in field; sales rep. Ala. World Travel, 1990—; behavior aid Brantwood Children's Home, 1996—; computer tchr. hs diploma program Montgomery County Sch., 1995—; behavior aide Brantwood Children's Home, 1995—; hotel auditor, 1995—; Am. del. to China, People to People Internat., 1998; acad. advisor C.C. of Air Force, Maxwell AFB, Ala., 2002—. Mem. CAP; vol. zoo activities Tech. Scholarship Program for Ala. Tchrs. Computer Courses, Montgomery; bd. dirs. Cleveland Ave. YMCA, 1976—80; sponsor Belle-Howe chpt. Young Astronauts, 1986—90, Pate Howe chpt., 1991—92; judge Montgomery County Children Festival Elem. Sci. Fair, 1988—90; bd. dirs. Troy State U. Drug Free Schs., 1992—; chmn. Maxwell AFB Red Cross-Youth, 1986—88; goodwill amb. sponsor to various families (award 1989, 95); State of Ala. rep. P.A.T.C.H.-Internat. Law Inst., 1995; founder Okinawa, Japan chpt., bd. dirs. People to People Internat., 2000; tchr. Sunday sch. Beulah Bapt. Ch., Montgomery. Named Tchr. of the Week, WCOV-TV, 1992, Ala. Tchr. in Space Program, summer, 1989, Local Coord. Young Astronaut Program, 1988, Citizen Amb. to China, People to People Internat., 1999; recipient Outstanding High Sch. Sci./Math. Tchr. award, Sigma Xi, 1989, Most Outstanding Youth Coun. Leader award, Maxwell AFB Youth Ctr., 1987, Outstanding Ala. Goodwill Amb. award, 1989, 1995, Tchr. of Yr. award, Paterson Sch., 1990, Career Infusion award (Most Appreciated Tchr. award), 1987, Montgomery Pub. Sch., 1982, 1984, Earthwatch Ednl. award, Israel, 1997, 20 Class award, Maxwell AFB Internat. Fgn. Officer Program, 25 Class award, 2003, 30 Class award, 2005, Ala. Goodwill Amb. award, Maxwell AFB Inernat. Officer Program 30 Class award, 2005; Fulbright scholar, Japan, 1999. Mem. NEA, Internat. Platform Assn., People to People Internat. (founder, bd. trustees, organizer, pres. Ala. chpt. 1998), Nat. Sci. Tchrs. Assn., Ala. Sch. Counselors, Montgomery Sch. Counselors Assn., Montgomery County Ednl. Assn., Space Camp Amb., Huntingdon Alumni Assn. (sec.-treas.), Ala. Goodwill Amb., Montgomery Capital City Club, Young Astronauts, Ea. Star, Japan Friends of Fulbright Meml. Fund Tchr. Prog., Water Watch, Montgomery, AL, Zeta Phi Beta, Chi Delta Phi, Kappa Pi. Avocations: international travel, calligraphy, international food, cruising. Personal E-mail: Awalker2001@yahoo.com.

WALKER, ATHENA MARIE, secondary school educator; b. Aurora, July 22, 1975; d. Carol Jean Yates; 1 child, Melia Norene. BS in Elem. Edn., U. Idaho, Moscow, 2003. Cert. tchr. K-8. Family cons. Early Head Start, Coeur d'Alene, Idaho, 2004—05; sci. tchr. Trinity Luth. Sch., Evansville, Ind., 2005—. With USN, 1993—96. Recipient full scholarship, Oreg. State Colls., 1993, Music award, USMC, 1993. Mem.: Nat. Soc. Collegiate Scholars. Republican. Avocations: music, snowboarding, travel, writing.

WALKER, AUDREY THAYER, social worker, psychotherapist; b. Quincy, Mass., June 29, 1935; d. Paul Clifton and Dorothy Ritchie Thayer; m. David A. Walker, Aug. 21, 1982; children: Elizabeth Penniman Billett Bilhartz, Matthew Thayer Billett. AB, Wheaton Coll., 1957; MSS/MSW, Smith Coll., 1959. Cert. social worker, LICSW D.C., cert. diplomate in clin. social work. Caseworker Ch. Home Soc., Boston, 1959—61; caseworker, family therapist Family Svc. Agy. of Sacramento, 1961—63; chief psychiat. social worker, supr. dept. psychiatry George Washington U., 1969—90, adj. assoc. prof., 1971—, dir. social work tng., 1975—90; adj. assoc. prof. Smith Coll. Sch. for Social Work, Northampton, Mass., 1971—2003; pvt. practice clin. social worker, psychotherapist, 1990—; adj. faculty Counseling and Psychiat. Svcs., Georgetown U., 1993—2005; field faculty advisor Smith Coll. Sch. for Social Work, Northampton, Mass., 1996—2003, adj. assoc. prof., 2006—. Adj. faculty, cons. Clin. Social Work Inst., 1999—2006; co-leader theoretical integrative seminar Smith Coll. Sch. for Social Work, 2003—. Co-sponsor Life Cycle Courses George Washington U. Dept. Psychiatry, Washington Psychoanalytic Inst., 1975—85; co-chair benefit ann. lectures Smith Coll. Sch. for Social Work Alumni Assn., Washington, 1978—88. Named Disting. Practitioner, Nat. Acads. of Practice, 2005; recipient Day-Garreit award for significant and maj. contbns. to social work, Smith Coll. Sch. Social Work, 2005; Grad. Study scholar, Episcopal Ch. of Am., Youth Svcs. Divsn., 1957-1959, Sr. Class Grad. Study awardee and scholar, Wheaton Coll. Sr. Class, 1957. Mem.: Nat. Academics of Practice (disting. practitioner, social work 2005—), Wash. Psychoanalytic Inst., Am. Group Psychotherapy Assn. (full clin. mem. 1982—2004), Smith Coll. Sch. for Social Work Alumni Assn. (Greater Washington chpt. steering com. 1974—93, co-chair Psychoanalytic Jour. Club 1975—76), Greater Washington Soc. for Clin. Social Work (v.p. profl. affairs 1990—94, bd. mem.-at-large, advisor 1994—2005, continuing edn. com. 1995—, founding chair consultation svcs. com. 1997—98, ad hoc ethics com. 2006—, Cert. of Appreciation 1991—97, 2002—04), Nat. Membership Com. on Psychoanalysis in Social Work (Washington area chair 1997—2003), Smith Coll. Club (Washington) (bd. dirs. 1983—87), Pi Gamma Mu. Democrat. Unitarian. Avocations: study group: the brain and psychoanalysis, travel, reading/book clubs, theatre, ballet/dance. Home: 4416 Q St NW Washington DC 20007 Office: 3 Washington Cir NW Ste 406 Washington DC 20037 Office Phone: 202-331-1547. Business E-Mail: audrey.walker@msb.edu.

WALKER, BARBARA ROSS, secondary school educator; b. Texarkana, Ark., Feb. 3, 1946; d. Ervie J. and Ella R. (Keel) Ross; m. Emory L. Walker, Oct. 10, 1969; children: Daphne, Brandon, Christel, Justin. BA, So. Ark. U., Magnolia, 1969; MS, Tex. A&M U., Texarkana, 1983, MEd, 1985. Cert. secondary tchr. social studies, history and govt., Ark., tex. Registrar Texarkana (Tex.) Hist. Mus., 1977-78; tchr. Am. history and African-Am. history Texarkana (Ark.) Sch. Dist. 7, 1980—2003. Mem. Texarkana Hist. Mus. Systems, 1993—. Asst. dir. music Lonoke Bapt. Ch. NEH grantee 1984, 85, 92, 93, 94, 95, 96, 97, 1999, 2001, 2002, Fulbright fellow Ghana and Guinea, West Africa, 2000. Mem. NAACP, NEA, ASCD, Nat. Coun. for Social Studies, Ark. Coun. for Social Studies, Ark. Edn. Assn. (mem. state human rels. commn. 1984-87, ACT 963 history com. 1994), Texarkana Classroom Tchrs. Assn. (chmn. gov.'s com., dist. social studies curriculum writing team 1994), Ark. Hist. Assn., Ark. Ret. Tchrs. Assn. (life). Democrat. Baptist. Avocations: piano, reading historical fiction/nonfiction, travel, tutoring. Home: 1207 Louisiana St Texarkana AR 71854-4665

WALKER, BERNICE BAKER, artist; b. Carbondale, Pa., Dec. 25, 1928; d. William Robert and Bernice Mary (Parry) Baker; m. Joseph Henry Walker, Sept. 13, 1952. Student, Richmond Profl. Inst., 1946-47; BFA, R.I. Sch. Design, 1952. Artist Highlights for Children, 1952-55, Studio K, Lancaster, Pa., 1959-64; tchr. Heintzelman Art Assn., Manheim, Pa., 1975-86; owner The Design Corner, Lancaster, 1989—2003. Tchr. Lancaster County Art Assn. Mem. Pa. Watercolor Soc., Venice Art Ctr., Englewood Art Ctr., Longboat Key Ctr. of the Arts, Am. Soc. Portrait Artists, Sarasota Portrait Soc., S.W. Pastel Soc., Am. Portrait Soc Avocations: spinning, natural dyeing, reading, photography, bridge. E-mail: bernspin1@aol.com.

WALKER, BETTE, automotive executive; BS in Bus. Mgmt., U. NH; student, Bosotn U.; completed Global Leadership Executive Development Program, Harvard U. Tech. dir. Latin Am. Digital Equip. Corp.; IT exec. auto. sector safety restraint sys. AlliedSignal, Inc.; v.p., CIO, energy & chassis divsn. Delphi Corp., Troy, Mich., 1997—. Office: World Hdqrs 5725 Delphi Dr Troy MI 48098-2815*

WALKER, BEVERLY ANN, minister, health facility administrator; b. Baltimore, Md., Mar. 17, 1950; d. Morris Allen and Mary Estelle Johnson; children: Tyrone Anthony Jeffries, Towanda Tonette Fortune, Bernard Alexander Jeffries, Charlotte Shrae Young, Harold Lawrence. BA, Va. Sem. and Coll., 1998; M. Religious Edn., Andersonville Bapt. Sem., 2000, DRE, 2002; MDiv, Va. U.-Lynchburg, 2005. Supr. ins. processing Va. Health Svcs. Found., Charlottesville, 1982—95; pastor North River Bapt. Ch., Bridgewater, Va., 1983—2001; founder Va. Women in Ministry, Charlottesville, 1990—95; moderator Berean Bapt. Assn., Bridgewater, 1994—98; founder God Called and Chosen Vessels, Stuarts Draft, 2002—; pastor Rising Sun Bapt. Ch., North Garden, 2004—. Counselor Harrisonburg Jail, Va., 1998—2001; bd. dirs. Helping Hand Ministry, Harrisonburg, 2002—. Contbr.: ch. adminstrn. book and handbook Decently and In Order. Mem. NAACP, Harrisonburg, Va., 1985. Recipient Female Ministerial award, Shenandoah Valley Hit Newspaper, 1994, Outstanding Svc. award, Va. Women in Ministry, 1995. Mem.: Hampton's Min. Conf., Bapt. Gen. Conf., Va. Bapt. Conf., Berean Valley Bapt. Assn. (life). Liberal. Baptist. Avocations: travel, reading, singing, dance, exercise. Home: 2410 Berkshire Pl Apt 42 Charlottesvle VA 22901-2444 Office Phone: 434-972-1800. Personal E-mail: beverlyrnrd3@aol.com.

WALKER, CARLENE MARTIN, state senator; BS, Brigham Young U., 1969. Supr. coding & data entry the Wirthlin Group, 1982-86; cons. D.K. Shifflet & Assocs., 1987-88; ptnr., mgr. Covecrest Properties, 1978-99; dir. adminstrn. Energy Lock, Inc., 1992-99; tech. recruiter Manpower Tech., 1999-2000; mem. Utah State Senate, Salt Lake City, 2001—. Cons. Wash. Times Newspaper, 1987-88. Bd., chair fundraising com. Granite Edn. Found., 1989-90; chmn., founder of the bd. Repub. Womens Political Action Com. Office: 4085 E Prospector Dr Salt Lake City UT 84121

WALKER, CAROL ELLEN BURTON, retired elementary school educator; b. Owensboro, Ky., July 23, 1934; d. Merle Wilson and Helen Mildred (Thomas) Burton; m. William Marvin Walker, June 28, 1958; children: Sara Helen, David William. BA, Ky. Wesleyan Coll., 1956; postgrad., Ind. U., 1957, U. Louisville, 1972. Cert. elem. music tchr. Tchr. Owensboro Pub. Schs., 1956-58; tchr. Jefferson County Pub. Schs., Louisville, 1958-63, 71-91; master dir. nat. leadership team Oxyfresh, USA, Inc., 1991—. Curriculum writer, music textbook selection com., music workshop leader Jefferson County Pub. Schs., Louisville; supr. for student tchrs. Bellarmine Coll., U. Ky., Murray State U., U. Louisville, 1971-91. Named Elem. Music Tchr. of Yr., Ky. Music Educators, 1988. Mem. NEA, Ky. Edn. Assn., Jefferson County Edn. Assn., Nat. Fedn. Music Clubs (nat. bd. dirs. 1991—), Ky. Fedn. Music Clubs (pres. 1987-91), Music Educators Nat. Conf., Ky. Music Educators Assn. (pres. Dist. 12 1986-88), MacDowell Music Club (pres. 1969-71), Thoroughbred Ladies Aux. (treas. 1980-93, Woman of Yr. 1987), Delta Kappa Gamma. Republican. Methodist. Avocations: bridge, cooking, reading, knitting. Home: 4029 Brookfield Ave Louisville KY 40207-2003

WALKER, CAROLYN MAE, retired secondary school educator; b. Neptune, N.J., Apr. 29, 1941; d. Frank and Estella (Matutis) W. BA in Sci., Montclair State Coll., 1963; MA in Edn., Newark State Coll., 1970. Cert. tchr., N.J. Elem. tchr. Howell (N.J.) Twp. Bd. Edn., 1963-65, Englishtown (N.J.)-Manalapan Regional Schs., 1965-67, Freehold (N.J.) Borough Schs., 1967-70, Freehold Regional H.S., 1970-73, North Brunswick (N.J.) Twp. Bd. Edn., 1975—; ret. Mem. NSTA, N.J. Sci. Tchrs. Assn., N.J. Schoolwomen's Club, Alpha Delta Kappa (chair pres. 1972-74, state sec. 1974-76, state v.p. 1976-78). Roman Catholic. Avocations: cruising, dressmaking, needlecrafts, gardening, classical/popular music. E-mail: caramwalker@juno.com.

WALKER, CHERYL A., literature educator; b. Litchfield, Ill., Sept. 1, 1954; d. Norman E. and Roleen A. Henke; m. James R. Walker; children: James R. Jr., Jeremy, Jason. BA in Elem. Edn., Blackburn Coll., 1975; MS in Edn., So. Ill. U., Edwardsville, 1989. Tchr., asst. Bunker Hill (Ill.) Pub. Schs., 1987—90; reading, math. tchr. Keystone (Okla.) Elem. Sch., 1990—93; reading recovery tchr. Sapulpa (Okla.) Pub. Schs., 1993—94, Belleville (Ill.) Dist. #118, 1994—. Fin. bd. St. John's Luth. Ch., Red Bud, 2006. Literacy grant, Ill. Reading Coun., 2000, 2002, 2005. Mem.: Lewis and Clark Reading Coun. (pres., treas. 1995—2006), Ill. Reading Coun. (treas. 2003—), Internat. Reading Assn. Home: 8908 S Prairie Rd Evansville IL 62242 Personal E-mail: ido4120@htc.net.

WALKER, DANIELLE, engineering executive; Engr. Progressive Engring. Group, LLC, Phila. Named one of 40 Under 40, Phila. Bus. Jour., 2006. Office: Progressive Engring Group, LLC 3001 Market St 2nd Fl Philadelphia PA 19104-2897 Office Phone: 215-222-0606. Office Fax: 212-222-0400.*

WALKER, DIANE, assistant principal; B, U. Montevallo, Ala., 1979; MEd, Valdosta State U., Ga., 2002. Cert. ednl. adminstrn. Ga. Music specialist Hahira Elem. Sch., Ga., 1986—2006; asst. prin. Dewar Elem. Sch., Valdosta, 2006—.

WALKER, DORI, biology educator; d. Diane Richter and Art Bassett; m. Seth Walker, July 6, 1996. B in Biology, Met. State Coll., Denver; M in Biology, Denver U. Honors biology tchr. Wheat Ridge H.S., Colo., 2000—. Mem.: Colo. Biology Tchrs. Assn. Office Phone: 303-982-7695.

WALKER, E. ANN, minister, writer, pastoral counselor, consultant; b. Avon Park, Fla., Aug. 3, 1951; d. Litton Meredith and Harriet Elizabeth (Williams) W. BA in Sociology, Lake Erie Coll., 1973; MS in Criminology, Fla. State U., 1975; MDiv, Drew U., 1997; PhD, Cornerstone U., 2005. Cert. neuro-emotional technique practitioner 2003, attractor field therapy practitioner 2004, lic. clin. pastoral counselor 2005. Correctional counselor I Fla. Dept. Corrections, Tampa, 1976-79; renovation cons. Libbey Apts., Sebring, Fla., 1978-81; program dir. Heart of Fla. Coun. Girl Scouts, Lakeland, 1980-87; dep. dir. West Pacific Girl Scouts, Okinawa, Japan, 1988-91; exec. dir. Becky Thatcher Area Coun. Girl Scouts, Hannibal, Mo., 1991—94; pastor United Meth. Ch., 1994—. Cons. USN Chaplains, CREDO, Okinawa, 1990-91, United Meth. Women Mo., 1993, Assn. Girl Scouts Exec. Staff, 1980-1993. Officer Hannibal Arts Coun., 1992-94; lay speaker Mo. East conf. United Meth. Ch., 1993-94; ordained elder, United Meth. Ch., 2001. Mem. Girl Scouts U.S.A. (life), AAUW (pres. 1993-95), Assn. Girl Scout Exec. Staff (sustaining mem.), Toastmasters Internat. (treas. 1992-94, Competent Toastmaster 1991, Able Toastmaster 1994).

WALKER, GWENDOLYN KAYE, real estate agent; b. Houston, Aug. 11, 1956; d. Willie Lee Sr. and Juanita W.; 1 child, Nika Ayanna Sewell. Student, U. Nev., 1973-74, Massey Bus. Coll., Houston, 1978-79; grad., So. Nev. Sch. Cosmetology, Las Vegas, 1988. Lic. manicurist. Mgr. snack shop St. Lukes Hosp., Houston, 1976-80; svc. rep. Centel Tel., Las Vegas, 1980-85; owner Nika's Gifts, Las Vegas, 1985-87; co-owner Genesis Nails and Gifts, 1987-89; loan officer Clark County Libr. Dist., Las Vegas, 1988—2000; co-owner Nika's Afrocentric Gifts, Las Vegas, 1992—. Author: (poetry) Feelings, 1996, Memories, Book II, 1997, Mommie and Me, 2003; co-author: From the Kitchen to the Boardroom, Nevada's Black Women, Courage, Strength and Faith, Nevada's Black Men; columnist Las Vegas Sentinel Newspaper, 1988-95, (cd) DaSpell Mem. bd. City North Las Vegas Crime Prevention Task Force, 1992-95; mem. North Las Vegas Police Area Command Children's Adv. Bd., 2005—; co-chmn. North Las Vegas Traffic and Parking Bd., 2005—; adv. bd. Kyle Ranch, 1982-84; capt. neighborhood watch Valley View Estates, 1984—; founder, pres. Walker African-Am. Mus. and Rsch. Ctr., Las Vegas, 1992—; sec., chmn. souvenir booklet and food basket com. Dr. Martin Luther King Jr. Com., 1985-88; mem. Mems. and Advs. for Minority Adoptions, 1982-84, Dem. Ctrl. Com., 1984-85, Nev. Black C. of C., various election coms.; leader 4-H, 1969-73; leader Swappett drill team, 1970-73. Recipient Cmty. Svc. award North Las Vegas City Coun., 1992, Clark County Commn., 1997, Outstanding Mem. and Sec. award Dr. Martin Luther King Jr. Com., 1987-88. Mem. NAACP, Nat. Assn. African-Am. History Preservation, Nev. Women in History, Tuskegee Airmen, Inc. (Nev. Chpt. sec. 1996—). Baptist. Avocations: sewing, poetry, singing, crafting, collecting. Office: Walker African-Am Mus 705 W Van Buren Ave Las Vegas NV 89106-3042 Office Phone: 702-649-2238.

WALKER, HELEN SMITH, retired real estate broker; b. Grovania, Ga., Jan. 29, 1917; d. George Washington and Mattie (Ellis) Smith; m. James Lee Walker, Apr. 21, 1946; 1 child, James Kenneth. Student, Ga. Wesleyan Coll., 1934-35, U. Ga., 1935-36, Wesleyan Conservatory, 1936-37. Sales rep. Thornton Realty Co., Macon, Ga., 1959-68; owner, operator Klondike Farms, Houston County, Ga., 1960—; co-owner, v.p. Warno Corp., Macon, 1964-69; v.p. O'Neal-Willingham Realty, Macon, 1968-71; assoc. broker Fickling & Walker Realty, Macon, 1971-77; pres., co-owner Hibble, Walker & Douglas, Macon, 1977-82; assoc. broker Fickling & Walker, Macon, 1982-91; ret. Tchr. primary tng. Union Bapt. Ch., 1950-65; mem. Make Am. Better Commn., 1971; group capt. Am. Cancer Crusale, 1978; active Ga. Trust for Hist. Preservation, Macon Hist. Soc., Macon Symphony. Mem. Am. Forestry Assn., Wesleyan Alumnae Club (awards com. 1988-89, 91—), Civic Woman's Club Macon. Democrat. Avocations: reading, poetry, gardening, music.

WALKER, JANIE SUZANNE, music educator; b. Pensacola, Fla., Mar. 26, 1974; d. Robert Lee Jr. and Anna Kathleen Newbold; m. Christopher James Walker, June 3, 2000; 1 child, Andrew James. BS in Edn., U. Ala., Tuscaloosa, 1997. Cert. tchr. Ala., Fla. Band dir. UMS Wright Prep. Sch., Mobile, Ala., 1997—99, Ransom Mid. Sch., Cantonment, Fla., 1999—. Pvt. music tchr., Pensacola, 1999—. Musician Mobile Pops Orch., 1997—99, 1st Bapt. Ch. Orch., Pensacola, 1991—2002. Mem.: Percussive Arts Soc., Fla. Bandmasters Assn., Million Dollar Band Alumni Assn. Republican. Baptist. Avocations: music, bicycling, shelling. Office: Ransom Mid Sch 1000 W Kingsfield Rd Cantonment FL 32533

WALKER, JERI A., psychiatrist; b. Burnsville, Miss., Dec. 26, 1944; d. Caire Agnew Walker and Ruthie Lillian Honeycutt-Walker; children: Jennifer Leigh McCarthy, Meghan Suzanne McCarthy. MD, U. Miss., Jackson, 1969. Diplomate Am. Bd. Psychiatry and Neurology. Resident in psychiatry Mendocino State Hosp., Talmage, Calif., 1970—71, Agnews State Hosp., San Jose, Calif., 1971—72, Langley Porter Neuropsychiat. Inst., San Francisco, 1972—73; physician Juvenile Hall, Dept. Youth Svcs., Ukiah, Calif., 1970—71; pvt. practice Palo Alto, Calif., 1973—80; sr. psychiatrist Dept. Mental Health, Palo Alto and San Jose, Calif., 1973—76; program physician, psychiatrist Agnews State Hosp., San Jose, Calif., 1973—74; officer of the day Palo Alto VA Hosp., Menlo Park, Calif., 1974—76; staff, psychiatrist VA Hosps., Menlo Park and Memphis, 1976—80; asst. prof. U. Tenn., Memphis, 1977—78; sr. staff psychiatrist, group ptnr. Permanente Med. Group, San Jose, Calif., 1980—85; psychiat. cons. Herbert Lipton MHC, Leominister, Mass., 1985—87, 1998; psychiatrist, asst. med. dir. Burbank Hosp., Fitchburg, Mass., 1986—87; psychiatrist, med. dir. North Ctrl. MHC, Gardner, Mass., 1989—93; psychiatrist Bolton and Fitchburg, Mass., 1987—93; psychiatrist, dept. chair Fallon Clinic, Worcester, Mass., 1993—97; psychiatrist Worcester, Mass., 1997—2004, Westwood Lodge, Mass., 1998—99, Cambridge Psychiat. Svc., Walham and Newton, Mass., 1998—2004; attending psychiatrist Newton-Wellesley Hosp., Mass., 1999—2002; prin. clin. investigator Boston Clin. Rsch., Wellesley, Mass., 2001—04; attending psychiatrist, pres. profl. staff orgn. Westboro State Hosp./U. Mass., Mass., 2004—; intern French Hosp., San Francisco, 1969—70. Vol. Bolton Emerson Sch., Mass., 1988—95, RSVP/Vista, Worcester, Mass., 2005—06. Mem.: Mass. Psychiat. Assn., Am. Psychiat. Assn. Avocations: gardening, art, needlecrafts, travel, reading. Office: Westboro State Hosp 288 Lyman St Westborough MA 01581 Office Phone: 508-616-2873. E-mail: drlady69@yahoo.com.

WALKER, JOAN H., marketing and communications executive; m. George Walker. BA, Rutgers U., New Brunswick, 1968, MA in Sociology, 1973. Sr. exec. mktg. and govt. N.J. State Govt., 1973-83; pres. Richmann & Ptnrs., 1983-88; exec. v.p. Saatchi & Saatchi, 1988-90; mng. dir. mktg. comm. NYNEX Corp., 1990-93; pres., CEO Bozell Pub. Rels., N.Y.C., 1993-96; ptnr. Bozell Sawyer Miller Group, 1996; sr. v.p. corp. comm. Ameritech, Chgo., 1996-99; sr. v.p. global pub. affairs Monsanto (merged with Pharmacia & UpJohn, now Pharmacia), Skolie, Ill., 1999—2002; exec. v.p. corp. mktg. and comm. Qwest Comm. Internat., 2002—. Dir. Qwest Found.; mem. bd. trustees Colo. Symphony Orch. Office: Qwest Comm Internat 1801 California St Denver CO 80202 E-mail: Joan.H.Walker@am.pnu.com.

WALKER, JOYCE L., music educator; b. Rochester, July 8, 1949; d. Albert Leroy and Doris Lucille Eshelman; m. David B. Walker, July 1, 1972; children: Julie L., Jacqueline L. BS, Ind. State U., Terre Haute, 1972; MA in Liberal Studies, Valparaiso U., Ind., 1976. Tchr. music Porter Twp. Sch. Corp., Valparaiso, Ind., 1972—; ch. organist, pianist Hebron United Meth. Ch., Hebron, Ind., 1972—. Home: 205 W Sigler St Hebron IN 46341 Office: Porter Lakes Elem Sch 208 S 725 W Hebron IN 46341 Office Phone: 219-988-2727. E-mail: djwalker@netnitco.net.

WALKER, KARA, artist; b. Stockton, Calif., Nov. 26, 1969; BA in Painting/Printmaking, Atlanta Coll. Art, 1991; MFA in Painting/Printmaking, R.I. Sch. Design, 1994. One-woman shows include Gallery 100, Atlanta, 1991, Ctr. Curaltorial Studies, Bard Coll., Annandale-on-Hudson, NY, 1995, Nexus Contemporary Arts Ctr., Atlanta, 1995, Wooster Gardens/Brent Sikkema, NYC, 1995, 1998, Bernard Toale Gallery, Boston, 1996, Huntington Beach Arts Ctr., Calif., 1997, U. Chgo., 1997, Contemporary Arts Ctr., Cin., 1997, Henry Art Gallery, U. Wash., Seattle, 1997, The Carpenter Ctr., Harvard U., Cambridge, Mass., 1997, San Francisco Mus. Modern Art, 1997, The Forum, St. Louis, 1998, Vienna State Opera House, Austria, 1998, The Print Ctr., Phila., 1998, Galleri Index, Stockholm, 1998, Contemporary Arts Mus., Houston, 1999, Calif. Coll. Arts and Crafts, Oliver Art Ctr., Oakland, 1998, Brent Sikkema, NY, 1998, McKinney Ave. Contemporary, Dallas, 1999, Des Moines Art Ctr., 2000, The Emancipation Approximation, Tel Aviv Mus. Art, 2001, Disturbing Allegories, Vanderbilt U. Fine Arts Gallery, Tenn., 2001, American Primitive, Brent Sikkema Gallery, NYC, 2001, Nat Turner's Revelation (an Important Lesson from our Negro Past You Will Likely Forget to Remember), Galerie Max Hetzler, Berlin, 2002, For the Benefit of All the Races of Mankind (Mos' Specially the Master One, Boss), Germany, 2002, Mannheimer Kunstverein, Germany, 2002, Internat. Bienal of Sao Paolo, Brazil, 2002, An Abbreviated Emancipation, U. Mich. Mus. Art, 2002, Narratives of a Negress, Tang Tchg. Mus. and Art Gallery, Skidmore Coll., 2003, Drawings, Brent Sikkema, 2003, Excavated from the Black Heart of a Negress, Studio Mus., Harlem, 2003, Centro Nazionale per le Arti Contemporanee, Rome, 2003, Fibbergibbet and Mumbo Jumbo, Fabric Workshop and Mus., Phila., 2004, Grub for Sharks: A Concession to the Negro Populace, Tate Liverpool, 2004, Museo de Arte Carrillo Gil, Mexico City, 2005, Event Horizon, New Sch. U., 2005, Song of the South, REDCAT, LA, 2005, exhibited in group shows at New Visions Gallery, Atlanta, 1991, MU Gallery, Boston, 1993, Sol Koffler Gallery, Providence, 1994, Paul Morris Gallery, NYC, 1995, Mills Gallery, Boston, Inst. Contemporary Art, 1996, Greg Kucera Gallery, Seattle, 1997, Stephen Friedman Gallery, London, 1998, Looking Forward Looking Backward, Elaine L. Jacob Gallery, Wayne State U., 1999, Istanbul Biennial: The Passion and the Wave, 1999, This Is Not the Place, Ramapo Coll. NJ, 2000, Blurry Lines, John Michael Kholer Arts Ctr., Wis., 2000, The Print World, Ljubljana Biennial, Slovenia, 2001, The Americans, Barbican Art Galleries, London, 2001, Form Follow Fiction, Castello di Rivoli Museo d'Arte Contemporanea, 2001, Moving Pictures, Solomon R. Guggenheim Mus., NYC, 2002, Telling Tales: Narrative Impulses in Recent Art, 2002, Tempo, MoMAQNS, NYC, 2002, Black President: The Art and Legacy of Fela Anikulapo-Kuti, New Mus., NYC, 2003, Comic Release: Negotiating Identity for a New Generation, Carnegie Mellon U., 2003, Provocations, Bronx Mus. Art, 2004, Monument to Now, DESTE Found. Contemporary Art, Athens, Greece, 2004, Fairy Tales Forever: Internat. Homage to H.C. Andersen, Copenhagen, 2005, Kiss the Frog! The Art of Transformation, Nat. Mus. Art, 2005, Getting Emotional, Inst. Contemporary Art, Boston, 2005, The Shadow, Vestsjaellands Kunstmuseum, Denmark, 2005, The World is a Stage, Mori Art Mus., Tokyo, 2005, Trials and Terrors, Mus. Contemporary Art, 2005, numerous others; author: Freedom, A Fable, A Curious Interpretation of the Wit of a Negress in Troubled Times; contbr. articles to profl. jours. Recipient MacArthur fellow, John D. and Catherine T. MacArthur Found., Lucelia Artist award, Smithsonian Am. Art Mus., 2004; fellow Individual Artist's fellow, Art Matters, Inc.; scholar Presdl. scholar, Atlanta Coll. Art, Ida Blank Ocko scholar. Office: c/o Sikkema Jenkins & Co 530 West 22d St New York NY 10011*

WALKER, KAREN D., lawyer; b. Tampa, Feb. 24, 1968; BS in Comm. studies, Fla. State U., 1990; JD with high honors, U. Fla. Coll. Law, 1993. Bar: Fla. 1993, US Dist. Ct. (No. and So. Districts Fla.) 2000. Ptnr. Holland & Knight LLP, Tallahassee, ptnr., pub. policy and regulation group, mem. state and local govt. contracts team; mem., telecommunications team; mem. dir. com. Holland & Knight LLP. Mng. editor U. Fla. Law Review, 1991—92, title standards editor, 1992—93. Past chair bd. dirs. United Way of the Big Bend, Inc. Mem.: Tallahassee Women Lawyers, Tallahassee Bar Assn., Order of the Coif, ABA (chair, young lawyers divsn., com. on women in the profession 2000—01, mem., standing com. on pub. edn. 2000—02, chair, young lawyers divsn., com. on women in the profession 2001—02, Fla. state chair pub. contract law sect. state/local procurement divsn 2002—, mem. sect. on pub. utilities, comm., and transportation law, chair IT procurement com.), Fla. Bar (mem. adminstrv. law sect.). Office: Holland & Knight LLP 315 S Calhoun St Ste 600 Tallahassee FL 32301 Office Phone: 850-425-5612. Business E-Mail: karen.walker@hklaw.com.

WALKER, KATHLEEN MAE, health facility administrator; b. Springfield, Ill., Sept. 23, 1947; d. Warren H. and Ruth E. (Berlin) Wille; m. Truman G. Walker, Jan. 29, 1972 (div. June 1988); 1 child, Janet Marie. BA in History, Valparaiso U., 1969; MBA, Regis U., 1997. Registered respiratory therapist. Staff respiratory therapist Michael Reese Med. Ctr., Chgo., 1976; supr. respiratory care Community Meml. Gen. Hosp., LaGrange, Ill., 1976-81; mgr. cardiopulmonary svcs. Longmont (Colo.) United Hosp., 1981-95; coord. field mgmt. devel. First Am. Home Care, Ft. Collins, Colo., 1995-96; pulmonary rehab. coord. Spalding Rehab. Outpatient Facility, Longmont, Colo., 1997—; respiratory therapist Community Hosp., 1997—; cons. Front Range Respiratory Cons. Svcs., Boulder, 1998—. Vice chmn. accountability & accreditation com. St Vrain Valley Schs., 1989—, chmn., 1990-97; vol. Bruce Fischer Div. Class, Longmont, 1989, 90. Mem. Am. Assn. Respiratory Care, Colo. Soc. Respiratory Care (no. chpt. pres. 1985, chmn. respiratory dirs. 1984). Lutheran. Avocation: softball. Home: 636 Wade Rd Longmont CO 80503-7010

WALKER, KATHRYN A., telecommunications industry executive; B in Civil Engring., SD State U.; MS, U. Mo., degree in Engring. Asst. v.p. human resources Sprint Tech. Svcs., 1995—97; v.p. product mgmt. Sprint Bus., 1997—2002; sr. v.p. network svcs. global Markets group Sprint Corp., 2002—03, exec. v.p. network svcs., 2003—. Office: 6200 Sprint Pkwy Overland Park KS 66251

WALKER, KATHY LE MONS, history professor; b. SC; PhD, UCLA, 1986. Assoc. prof. history Temple U., Phila., 1988—. Mem. editl. adv. bd. Jour. Peasant Studies, 2006—. Avocation: acting. Office: Temple U Dept History Philadelphia PA 19122 Office Phone: 215-204-5601. Business E-Mail: kwalker@temple.edu.

WALKER, KELLEY, painter; b. Columbus, Ga., 1969; BFA, Univ. Tenn., Knoxville, 1995. Exhibited in group shows at Paula Cooper Gallery, NYC, 2003, Curious Crystals of Unusual Purity, PS1 Contemporary Art Ctr., 2004, Tuesday Is Gone, Club 22, Tbilisi, Ga., 2004, La Lettre Volée, F.R.A.C. Franche-Comté Musée des Beaux-Arts de Dole, 2004, Galerie Peter Kilchmann, Zurich, Switzerland, 2004, Last One On is a Soft Jimmy, curated by Kelley Walker, Paula Cooper Gallery, NYC, 2004, La Salle de Bains, Lyon, France, 2005, Situational Prosthetics, New Langton Center for the Arts, San Francisco, Calif., 2005, Log Cabin, Artists Space, NYC, 2005, 7th Shorjah Biennial, United Arab Emirates, 2005, Invisible Hands and the Common Good, Champion Fine Art, LA, 2005, Bridge Freezes Before Road, Barbara Gladstone Gallery, 2005, Crash/Cars, Museo de Arte Contemporanea de Vigo (MARCO), Vigo, Spain, 2005, Whitney Biennial, Whitney Mus. Art, 2006.*

WALKER, KELLYE L., lawyer; b. Little Rock, Aug. 1966; BS, La. Tech. U., 1987; JD, Emory U., 1992. Atty. Boult, Cummings, Conners & Berry PLC, Nashville; assoc. Chaffe, McCall, Phillips, Toler & Sarpy LLP, New Orleans, 1995—98, ptnr., 1998—2000; mem., counsel Hill & Barlow LLP, Boston, 2000—03; sr. v.p., gen. counsel, sec. BJ's Wholesale Club Inc., Natick, Mass., 2003—. Achievements include Developed "Women in Bus. Series" at Chaffe, McCall, Phillips, Toler & Sarpy LLP. Office: BJ's Wholesale Inc One Mercer Rd Natick MA 01760-0023

WALKER, KIM A., lawyer; BA, U. Va., 1988; JD, Columbia U., 1991. Spl. counsel, Intellectual Property Dept. Willkie Farr & Gallagher LLP, NYC. Mem.: ABA, Black Entertainment and Sports Lawyers Assn., Internat.

Trademark Assn., Assn. Bar of City NY (mem. Com. Entertainment Law 2004—). Office: Willkie Farr & Gallagher LLP 787 Seventh Ave New York NY 10019 Office Phone: 212-728-8776. E-mail: kwalker@willkie.com.

WALKER, LINDA LEE, lawyer; b. Phila., Jan. 24, 1954; d. M. Lorenzo and Romaine Yvonne (Smith) W.; m. Steve Collins; children: Jessica Marie McIntyre, Nicole Yvonne McIntyre. BA, U. Penn., 1975; JD, Yale U., 1978. Bar: N.Y. 1979, U.S. Dist. Ct. (so. and ea. dists.) N.Y. 1982, U.S. Ct. Appeals (1st cir.) 1982; NASD. Asst. regional atty. HHS, N.Y.C., 1978-82; assoc. Shea and Gould, N.Y.C., 1982-85; v.p., sr. assoc. counsel Chase Manhattan Bank, N.A., N.Y.C., 1985-89; v.p., assoc. gen. counsel Citicorp Credit Svc., N.Y.C., 1989-97; asst. gen. counsel Prudential Ins. Co. Am., Iselin, 1997—2000, v.p., chief compliance officer for Prudential Retirement, 2000—04; dir. compliance UBS Fin. Svcs., Inc., Weehawken, NJ, 2004—. Mem., Phi Beta Kappa. Office Phone: 201-352-4959. Business E-Mail: linda.walker@ubs.com.

WALKER, LORENE, retired elementary school educator; b. Clovis, N.Mex., July 27, 1911; d. Jessie H. and Tille Eula (Harlan) Black; m. Carl Westley Walker, June 9, 1934; children: Wesley, Charles. BS, N.Mex. State U., 1933; M of Family Life, Ctrl. Wash. U., 1959, postgrad., 1956—74. Tchr. home econs. Floyd Sch., near Portales, N.Mex., 1933-34, Navajo Meth. Mission, Farmington, N.Mex., 1947-48; home agt. ext. svc. Wash. State Coop. Ext. Svc., Yakima, 1948-56; family life, counseling tchr. West Valley Sch., Yakima, 1956-71, spl. elem. reading tchr., 1971-75; tour organizer, leader Mission Tour, Yakima, 1966-98; trainer missioners United Meth. Ch., Yakima, 1998—. Coord. 4-H camps, fairs and programs Wash. Coop. Ext. Svc., Yakima, 1950-56. Chairperson Experiment for Internat. Living, Yakima Valley Rep. Women's Club, 1960-67; docent, tour leader Yakima Valley Mus., 1976—; trustee Found. Pacific Northwest United Meth. Ch., 1984—; pres. Columbia River dist. United Meth. Ch., 1987-88, chairperson global missions, 1993-94; chair Tour With a Mission, 1966-1993; del. World Meth. Conf., Brighton, Eng., 2001. Mem. AAUW (treas. 1962-66, bd. dirs., chair internat. rels. 1962-89; spl. honor award 1989), United Meth. Women (pres. 1987-89, active local, dist. confs. Pacific N.W. Conf., spl. recognition 1989), Wesleyan Svc. Guild Meth. Women. (officer 1964-68), Yakima Woman's Century Club (active local orgns.), Ret. Tchrs. Yakima County Assn. (active local orgns.), Alpha Delta Kappa (pres. 1967-69). Achievements include donating profit from tours to schools, hospitals and other charities. Avocations: gardening, travel, needlecrafts, international political and cultural news. Home: 101 N 48th Ave Apt 25A Yakima WA 98908-3179

WALKER, LOUISE CONVERSE, obstetrician, gynecologist; b. Urbana, Ill., Feb. 11, 1927; m. James L. Walker, May 17, 1952 (dec.); children: Teresa, Karen. MD, U. Ill., Chgo., 1951. Lic. ob-gyn. ACOG. Bd. dirs., vol. Planned Parenthood of Rocky Mountains, Denver, 1980—91, Evergreen Nature Audubon Soc., Colo., 1994—2000. Recipient Am. Indian Svc. award, 1991, Svc. award for Project Concern, CARE, 1960. Mem.: AMA, Colo. Gynecol. and Obstetrics Soc. (past pres.), Am. Med. Women's Assn. (past pres., Commitment to Women's Health Care award 2000). Home: # 104 6155 S Ammons Way Littleton CO 80123

WALKER, LUCY DORIS, secondary school educator, writer; b. Ridgeway, NC, May 6, 1951; d. Edgerton Verl and Mary Ellen (Williams) Plummer; m. William A. Walker Jr., June 21, 1969 (div. Aug. 1974); 1 child, Lucretia Marie. BA in English Edn., Fairleigh Dickinson U., 1975; MA in Theater Arts, Montclair State U., 1977. Cert. English and theater arts tchr., N.J. Tchr., dir., actor, writer Ctr. Modern Dance Edn., Hackensack, NJ, 1978; writer, dir. Am. Theater Actors, NYC, 1978-79; tchr. multicultural hub Ctr. Internat. Studies, Cultural Events, Teaneck HS, Teaneck, NJ, 1979—; coord. Teaneck Arts Acad. at Teaneck HS, Teaneck, NJ, 2002—. Artistic dir. Teaneck H.S. dance ensemble, 1989—; program coord. African and African-Am. Studies Resource Ctr., 1990—; instructional leader for fine and performing arts, coord. Teaneck Arts Acad. Writer and choreographer various plays, 1979-95. Recipient Acad. Achievement award Fairleigh Dickinson U. Opportunities Program, 1974, Black Heritage award Nat. Assn. Negro Bus. & Profl. Women's Clubs, 1991. Mem. NEA, NJ Edn. Assn. Democrat. Baptist. Avocations: sewing, gardening, hiking, painting, music. Home: 363 Washington Pl Englewood NJ 07631-3232 Office: Teaneck HS 100 Elizabeth Ave Teaneck NJ 07666-4713 E-mail: plumwalk@msn.com.

WALKER, MARTHA M., special education educator; b. Norristown, Pa., Jan. 11, 1965; d. J. Russell and Lois Miriam (Naylor) McC. BS in Edn., U. Del., 1986; MEd, Loyola Coll., Balt., 1992. Cert. tchr., Md., N.C. Spl. edn. tchr. Anne Arundel County Pub. Schs., Annapolis, Md., 1986-94, elem. Least Restrictive Environment resource tchr., 1992-94; tchr. Camp Lejeune Dependents Schs., NC, 1994—96, Onslow County Pub. Schs., NC, 1996—97, Anne Arundel County Pub. Schs., Annapolis, Md., 1997—, student assessment team, 2000—. Mem. Ascd, Coun. for Exceptional Children, Phi Delta Pi, Phi Kappa Phi. Home: 322 Rosslare Dr Arnold MD 21012-3006

WALKER, MARTHA YEAGER, state agency administrator, former state senator; b. May 15, 1940; m. H. Jarrett Walker; children: Meredyth, Brent, Melissa. BS, W.Va. U. Speech therapist Charleston Meml. Hosp., W.Va. Bureau Public Health, Kanawha Charleston Health Dept., Eye & Ear Clinic, Charleston, W.Va.; mem. W.Va. Ho. of Reps., Charleston, 1990-92, W.Va. Senate, Charleston, 1993—2001; sec. W.Va. Dept. Health & Human Resources, Charleston, 2005—. Mem. fin. com., govt. orgn. com., health and human resources com., pensions com., rules com., enrolled bills com.; with Byrd Inst. Studies, U. Charleston. Mem. W.Va. Dem. Exec. Com., Charleston Zoning Appeals Bd., Ctr. for Econ. Options, Byrd Inst. Govt. Studies, U. Charleston; former mem. Cabin Creek Health Ctr.; former treas. Kanawha County Pvt. Industry Coun.; active Literacy Vols. W.Va.; bd. dirs. Poison Control Ctr., Cabin Creek Health Ctr., Multiple Sclerosis Soc. W.Va., W.Va. Children's Health Policy Bd., Gov.'s Cabinet on Children and Families, Regional Contracting Assistance Ctr., Charleston Capitol Market, Literacy Vols. of Am.; sustaining mem. Jr. League Charleston; treas. PIC Kanawha County. Mem. Charleston C. of C., W.Va. U. Alumni Assn., Rotary. Democrat. Presbyterian. Office: Dept Health & Human Resources Bldg 3 Rm 206 State Capitol Complex Charleston WV 25305*

WALKER, MARY ALEXANDER, author; b. Beaumont, Tex., Sept. 24, 1927; d. James Cosper Alexander and Mary Helen (Johnson) Alexander Shelley; m. Tommy Ross Walker, Dec. 23, 1952; children— Timothy Ross, Mark Thomas, Miles Stephen. A.A., Lamar Inst. Tech., 1945; B.S., Tex. Women's U., 1950; M.A., San Francisco State U., 1981. Cert. community coll. tchr., Calif. Instr., Dominican Coll., San Rafael, Calif., 1972-80, coordinator writers conf., 1979-80, cons. writing program, 1984; lectr. U. San Francisco, 1983-84; cons. bus. writing Marriott Hotels, Santa Clara, 1983. Author: Year of the Cafeteria (Breadloaf Writers' Conf. fellow for disting. book for young people 1972), 1971; To Catch a Zombi, 1979; Maggot, 1980, Scathach and Maeve's Daughters, 1990; also short stories, articles, revs., reader of plays; Recipient 1st prize for short story Pacific N.W. Writers' Conf., 1976, 79, award for play adaptation Actor's Workshop, Santa Rosa, Calif., 1978; Lilly Endowment fellow, 1977. Mem. Soc. Children's Book Writers, Mystery Writers Am. Democrat. Unitarian. Home: 22 Corte Lodato San Rafael CA 94904-1225

WALKER, MARY L., lawyer; b. Dayton, Ohio, Dec. 1, 1948; d. William Willard and Lady D. Walker; 1 child, Winston Samuel. Student, U. Calif., Irvine, 1966-68; BA in Biol. Scis./Ecology, U. Calif., Berkeley, 1970; postgrad., UCLA, 1972-73; JD, Boston U. Law Sch., 1973. Bar: Calif. 1973, U.S. Supreme Ct. 1979, U.S. Dist. Ct. (no., ctrl., ea. and so. dists.) Calif. Atty. So. Pacific Transp. Co., San Francisco, 1973-76; assoc. Richards, Watson & Gershon, LA, 1976—77, ptnr., 1979-82, ptnr., chair environ. dept. San Francisco, 1989-91; prin. dep. asst. atty., environment and natural resources divsn. U.S. Dept. Justice, Washington, 1982-84; dep. solicitor U.S. Dept. Interior, Washington, 1984-85; asst. sec. for environment, safety and health U.S. Dept. Energy, Washington, 1985-88; spl. cons. to chmn. bd. Law Engring. Inc., Atlanta, 1988-89; v.p., West Coast and the Pacific Law Environ., Inc., San Francisco, 1989; ptnr. Luce, Forward, Hamilton & Scripps, San Diego, 1991-94; ptnr. and chair San Diego Environ. Law Group Brobeck, Phleger & Harrison, LLP, San Diego, 1994—2001; gen. counsel and chief of ethics U.S. Dept. Air Force, U.S. Dept. Defense, Washington, 2001—. U.S. commr. InterAm. Tropical Tuna Commn., 1988—95; mem. adv. bd. Floresta, Inc.; instr. natural resources law U. Calif., San Diego. Author of opinion pieces on environ. regulation, energy policy and nuclear power. Bd. dirs. Endowment for Cmty. Leadership, 1987—2000, Global Involvement Through Edn., 1998—2001; chair, environ. com. San Diego C. of C., 1993—94; adv. bd. Endowment for Cmty. Leadership, Washington. Named Outstanding Young Women of Am., 1984; recipient Women Who Mean Business award, Inaugural award for Law, San Diego Bus. jour., 1994. Mem. Calif. Bar Assn., San Diego Bar Assn., BIOCOM (bd. dirs. 1991-2001, pres. 1994, chair/co-chair environ. and safety com., 1991-2001), Profl. Women's Fellowship-San Diego (co-founder, bd. dirs. 1996-2001, pres. 1996-97), World Affairs Coun., Renaissance Women. Republican. Office: Air Force Gen Counsel Rm 4E856 1740 Air Force Pentagon Washington DC 20330-1740 Office Fax: 703-693-9355, 703-697-3796. E-mail: maryl.walker@pentagon.af.mil.

WALKER, MINERVA E. GILARA, poet, retail executive; b. Dauphin County, Pa., June 23, 1924; d. Daniel Snavely Ensminger and Nora Alice Hostetter; m. Stanley Michael Gilara, July 11, 1942 (div. Aug. 1972); children: Jerry, Stanley, Paul, Connie; m. John Henry Walker, Nov. 25, 1976 (dec. June 1993); 1 child, Tina. Student, Harrisburg Area C.C. Freelance writer, reporter Lebanon (Pa.) Daily News, 1954—60; hostess, retail advt. Welcome Wagon Internat., Hummelstown, Pa., 1958—60; tour guide, pub. rels. Indian Echo Caverns, Hummelstown, 1967—72; staff writer Middletown (Pa.) Press and Jour., 1960—66; retail rep. Svc. Advantage, Indpls., 1994—2000, Office Max, Shaker Heights, Ohio, 2000—04. Lutheran. Avocations: poetry, writing, art, travel, needlecrafts. Home: 28905 229th Pl SE Black Diamond WA 98010 Personal E-mail: minervawalker@comcast.net.

WALKER, NANCY ANNE, small business owner, history and art educator; b. Palo Alto, Calif., May 27, 1942; d. John Clarence and Dorothy May (Mole) Cheney; 1 child, Shelley Marie. BS, U. Oreg., 1964; MA, San Fernando State U., 1968; PhD, U. Colo., 1975. Lic. real estate broker, Calif. Instr. U. Md., Fed. Republic Germany, 1970-74; instr. history Modesto Jr. Coll., Calif., 1977-80, 88-93; owner, pres. Lockeford Clock Co., Inc., Stockton, Calif., 1978—; lectr. Calif. State U., Stanislaus, 1992; art and history docent Haggin Mus., 2002—. Owner Lockeford Antiques, 1974—, Nancy Walker Rentals. Contbr. articles to jours. including The Pioneer, Lockeford-Clements News, East European Quar., among others. Mem. Mayor's Task Force on Affirmative Action, Stockton, 1984—; pres. San Joaquin chpt. Nat. Orgn. for Women, 1988; mem. Del Tor Excavation, Israel, summer 1985; area rep. Youth for Understanding, 1987, 88; activities chmn. 6th Ward Ch. of Jesus Christ of Latter-day Saints, 1984; mem. Stockton Opera Guild; bd. dirs. Stockton Beautiful, 2002. Austrian Govt. grantee, 1970. Mem. DAR, Daus. Am. Colonists, Soc. Mayflower Descs., Am. Hist. Assn., Clements-Lockeford C. of C. (dir. 1977-79), Delta Assn. Investment Club (treas. 2004—), Kiwanis, Kappa Alpha Theta. Avocations: writing local history, travel. Office: 18880 N Highway 88 Lockeford CA 95237-9519

WALKER, OLENE S., former governor; b. Ogden, Utah, Nov. 15, 1930; d. Thomas Ole and Nina Hadley (Smith) W.; m. J. Myron Walker, 1957; children: Stephen Brett, David Walden, Bryan Jesse, Lori, Mylene, Nina, Thomas Myron. BA, Brigham Young U., 1954; MA, Stanford U., 1954; PhD, U. Utah, 1986; HHD (hon.), Weber State U., 1997. V.p. Country Crisp Foods, 1969-92; mem. Utah Ho. of Reps. Dist. 24; lt. gov. State of Utah, 1993—2003, gov., 2003—05. Mem. Salt Lake Edn. Found. bd. dirs. 1983-90; dir. community econ. devel.; mem. Ballet West, Sch. Vol., United Way, Commn. on Youth, Girls Village, Salt Lake Conv. and Tourism Bd.; mem. adv. coun. Weber State U. Mem. Nat. Assn. Secs. of State (Western chmn., nat. lt. gov.'s conf., pres. 1997-98). Republican. Mem. Lds Ch. Achievements include becoming first female elected to office of governor of Utah.*

WALKER, PAMELA, mathematics educator; BS, Utah State U., Logan, 1974. Cert. early childhood/elem. edn. and libr. media tchr. Utah. 4th grade tchr. A.W. Johnson Elem. Sch., Firth Sch. Dist., Idaho, 1974—83, Wash. Ter. Elem. Sch., Weber Sch. Dist., Ogden, Utah, 1984—89; 3rd grade tchr. Mcpl. Elem. Sch., Weber Sch. Dist., Roy, Utah, 1989—91; math tchr. Sand Ridge Jr. HS, Weber Sch. Dist., Roy, 1991—92, Roy Jr. HS, Weber Sch. Dist., Roy, 1992—. Named Tchr. of Yr., Firth Sch. Dist., 1983; recipient Apple for Tchr. award, Std. Examiner Newspaper, 1992—2006, Teacher's Recognition award, Remax Realtors, 1996. Mem.: Utah Edn. Assn. (assoc.). Avocations: sewing, needlecrafts. Business E-Mail: pwalker@weber.k12.ut.us.

WALKER, PATRICIA ANN DIXON, retired elementary school educator, real estate rehabilitator; b. Somerset, Pa., Nov. 26, 1937; d. Telford Miles and Bernice Irene Dixon; m. Paul J. Kuty, Nov. 2, 1957 (div. Nov. 1974); 1 child, Paul Dixon Kuty; m. James William Walker, Mar. 23, 1991. BS in Elem. Edn., Ind. State Coll., 1960; MA in Elem. Edn., Trenton State Coll., 1966. Tchr. grade 1 Neshaminy Sch. Dist., Langhorne, Pa., 1960—93; real estate investor Phila., 1985—. Vol. tutor NAACP, Bucks County, Pa., 1967—68; mem. Levittown Hist. Preservation Com., 2002—; committeewoman Dem. Party, Bucks County, 1974—78; chair Dem. Assn. Middletown Twp., Bucks County, 1974—75. Recipient Gift of Time tribute, Am. Family Inst. Valley Forge, 1992. Mem.: Homeowners Assn. Phila., Neshaminy Fedn. Ret. Tchrs., Pa. Assn. Sch. Retirees (mem. Bucks County chpt.). Avocation: travel. Home: 24 June Rd Levittown PA 19056 Office Phone: 215-945-4239.

WALKER, PATRICIA SINES, elementary school educator; b. Pitts., Jan. 29, 1959; d. Wayne Urmson and Patricia Cox Sines; m. Gilford Buchanan Walker, Sept. 21, 1985; children: Samuel, Maude, Henry. BA, Fla. Atlantic U., Boca Raton, Fla., 1984. Tchr. St. Edwards Sch., Vero Beach, Fla., 1999—. Commodore Sea Scouts Boy Scouts Am., Palm Beach, Fla., 1998—; bd. dirs. U.S. Sailing Ctr. Martin County, Jensen Beach, Fla., 2004—. Recipient Silver Beaver award, Boy Scouts Am., 2006. Mem.: NOW, Jr. League, Planned Parenthood. Democrat. B'Hai Brith. Avocation: designing jewelry.

WALKER, RHONDA GILLUM, announcer; b. Detroit; d. Ron and Harriet Gillum; m. Derrick Walker, 1996. B of Comm., Mich. State U., 1991. Weather and traffic reporter, style trend reporter WJBK-TV, Detroit; co-host WDIV-TV, Deroit, 2003—. Office: WDIV-TV 550 W Lafayette Blvd Detroit MI 48226

WALKER, RUTH CHARLOTTA, language educator, real estate broker; b. Kirksville, Mo., Oct. 3, 1931; d. Marion S. and Fern Thomas Schott; m. Dennis O. Walker, Nov. 21, 1954 (dec.). BS in Edn., Ctrl. Mo. State Coll., Warrensburg, 1952. Lic. real estate broker Wis., 1982. Tchr. English and speech, Warrensburg, Mo., 1951—53; pvt. tutor English and speech Mexico, 1956—57, Milw., 1968—95; profl. spkr., 1970—95; real estate broker, 1982—90; writer profl. book revs., 1990—. Author: (booklet) What Does P.E. Mean?, 1983. Pres. Woman's Club of Am. Fedn. Women, So. Milw., 1975—78, P.E.O. Sisterhood, So. Milw., 1979—81; sec. Woman's Courtroom Civic Conf., Milw., 1980. Mem.: Book Club So. Milw., Delta Zeta. Republican. Presbyterian. Achievements include raising funds for police department equipment, establishing camp Wil-o-Way in Grant Park, Milwaukee, creating drive for civic auditoriums. Avocations: travel, writing, reading.

WALKER, SALLY BARBARA, retired glass company executive; b. Bellerose, NY, Nov. 21, 1921; d. Lambert Roger and Edith Demerest (Parkhouse) W. Diploma, Cathedral Sch. St. Mary, 1939; AA, Finch Jr. Coll., 1941. Tchr. interior design Finch Coll., 1941-42; draftsman AT&T, 1942-43; with Steuben Glass Co., N.Y.C., 1943—, exec. v.p., 1959-62, exec. v.p. ops., 1962-78, exec. v.p. ops. and sales, 1978-83, exec. v.p., 1983-88, ret., 1988. Pres. 116 E. 66th St. Corp. Mem. Fifth Ave. Assn., Rockaway Hunting Club, Lawrence Beach Club, Colony Club, English-Speaking Union, Garden Club of Lawrence, City Garden Club of N.Y.C. Republican. Episcopalian. Home: 4031 Kenneth Pike #93 Greenville DE 19807

WALKER, SALLY M., writer; b. NJ; m. James Walker. Author: (children's books) Volcanoes, 1994, Rhinos, 1996, Earthquakes, 1996, Opossum at Sycamore Road, 1997, Hippos, 1997, The 18-Penny Goose, 1999, Dolphins, 1999, Seahorse Reef: A Story of the South Pacific, 2001, Wheels and Axles, 2001, Levers, 2001, Screws, 2001, Work, 2001, Inclined Planes and Wedges, 2001, Pulleys, 2001, Sea Horse's Surprise, 2001, Fireflies, 2001, Life in an Estuary: The Chesapeake Bay, 2002, Jackie Robinson, 2002, Fossil Fish Found Alive: Discovering the Coelacanth, 2002, Rays, 2002, Bessie Coleman: Daring to Fly, 2003, Secrets Of A Civil War Submarine: Solving The Mysteries Of The H. L. Hunley, 2005 (Am. Libr. Assn.'s Sibert Internat. Book award, 2006), Mystery Fish: Secrets Of The Coelacanth, 2005. Recipient Outstanding Trade Books for Children award (twice), Children's Choice award, 2001. Mailing: Author Mail CarolHoda Books Lerner Pub Group 1251 Washington Ave N Minneapolis MN 55401-1036*

WALKER, SUE ALBERTSON, retired school system administrator, consultant; b. Bloomsburg, Pa., May 1, 1943; d. Robert Wilson Albertson and Sara Porter; m. Robert Smith Walker, Apr. 13, 1968. BS in Edn., Millersville State Coll., Pa., 1964; MLS, Syracuse U., 1967. Cert. instrnl. II, curriculum and instrn. Pa. Sch. libr. Benton (Pa.) Area Sch. Dist., 1964—68; media coord. Fairfax (Va.) County Sch. Dist., 1968—73; libr., supr. Sch. Dist. of Lancaster, Pa., 1973—88, dir. curriculum, 1988—99. Adj. faculty Millersville U., 1983—85, Drexel U., Phila., 1984—91; ednl. cons., East Petersburg, Pa., 1980—; del., mem. steering com. Pa. Gov.'s Conf. on Librs., Harrisburg, 1976; del. White Ho. Conf. on Librs., Washington, 1978; advisor Gov.'s Adv. Coun. on Librs., Harrisburg, 1983—88. Author: Standards of Practice for Teachers, 2004. Chair Millersville U. Coun. Trustees, 1997—; sec. Lancaster Found. Ednl. Enrichment, 1999—; co-chair Millersville U. 150th Anniversary Celebration, 2002—. Named Outstanding Contbr., Pa. Sch. Librs. Assn., 1988. Mem.: ASCD, ALA, Am. Assn. Sch. Librs. (bd. dirs. 1986—89, conf. co-chair 1986), Phi Delta Kappa (Disting. Educator 1986). Republican. Presbyterian. Avocations: reading, travel, volunteer work. Home: 6065 Parkridge Dr East Petersburg PA 17520

WALKER, SUZANNAH WOLF, language educator; b. Akron, Ohio, May 3, 1954; d. Robert Patton and Katherine Jane (Guglielmi) Wolf Jr.; m. Timothy Gordon Walker, Dec. 23, 1988 (div. Dec. 21, 1992). BA in Secondary Edn., U. Akron, 1976; MA in Pub. Rels., Kent State U., 1987. Tchr. English, Spanish Cuyahoga Falls (Ohio) City Sch., 1977—96; tchr. English DOD Dependents Sch., Wurzburg, Germany, 1981—82; tchr. English, Spanish Canton (Ohio) City Schs., 1999—. Mem. supt. adv. com. Cuyahoga Falls City Sch., 1995, bldg. rep., 1992—95, Canton City Schs., 2000—03. Pub. rels. intern Ronald McDonald House, Cleve., 1985. Mem.: NEA, Canton Profl. Educators Assn. (mem. exec. com. 2003—), N.E. Ohio Fgn. Lang. Assn., Ohio Fgn. Lang. Assn., Cuyahoga Falls Edn. Assn., Ohio Edn. Assn. Home: 3430 E Prescott Cir Cuyahoga Falls OH 44223 Office Phone: 330-454-7717.

WALKER, SUZANNE ROSS, mathematics and education educator; b. Johnston, RI, Aug. 14, 1960; d. Raymond Henry Ross and Matilda Marion DeChristofaro; m. Paul Joseph Walker, Feb. 17, 1990; 1 stepchild, William Braeden Pierce. BA in Math./Math Edn. magna cum laude, Providence Coll., 1982, EdM in Guidance Counseling summa cum laude, 1992. HS math tchr. Bay View Acad., East Providence, RI, 1983—85, LaSalle Acad., Providence, 1985—87, Woonsocket Edn. Dept., RI, 1987—, math curriculum coord., 1998—. Math instr. Hall Inst. Tech. Sch., Pawtucket, RI, 1983—90; adj. faculty mem. calculus RI Coll., 1987—; advisor advanced placement calculus class Woonsocket HS, 1997—; prof. edn. Providence Coll., 2000—, math prof., 2006—. Chairperson Johnston H.S. Class of 1978, RI, 1988—. Mem.: Am. Math. Soc., Am. Tchrs. Math., R.I. Math. Tchrs. Assn. (advisor to student math team), Nat. Coun. Tchrs. Math., Math. Assn. Am., Phi Sigma Tau, Pi Mu Epsilon. Roman Catholic. Avocations: aerobics, yoga, walking, movies, music. Home: 39 Roger Williams Dr Greenville RI 02828 Office: Woonsocket HS 777 Cass Ave Woonsocket RI 02895 Office Phone: 401-767-4730. Personal E-mail: suzy814@msn.com.

WALKER, VICKI L., state senator; m. Steven Walker; children: Adam, Sara. Ct. reporting program, Lane C.C., 1980—83; BS in Polit. sci., U. Oreg., 1978. State sen. Oreg. State Senate, Salem, 1999—; ct. reporter Salem, 1983—. Mem.: Oreg. Ct. Reporters Assn. Democrat. Office: 900 Court St NE S-210 Salem OR 97301 Office Phone: 503-986-1707.

WALKER, WANDA MEDORA, retired elementary school educator, consultant; b. San Diego, Aug. 28, 1923; d. Bryant Hereford and Anna Genevieve (Barnes) Howard; m. Elmer Manfred Walker, Nov. 23, 1949 (dec. Aug. 1978); children: Kathleen May Stewart (dec.), Mary Ellen Quessenberry, Sydney Edward, Jessie Ann Meacham. BA, San Diego State U., 1947; MA, U. Wash., 1948; PhD, Calif. Western U., 1967. Cert. (life) spl. secondary music tchr., elem. tchr., sch. adminstr. Elem. tchr. Lakeside (Calif.) Elem. Dist., 1948-50, La Mesa (Calif.) Sch. Dist., 1951-53, San Diego City Schs. Dist., 1953-57, cons. gifted, 1957-59, vice prin., 1959-62; prin. San Diego Schs. Dist., 1962-88. Rep. San Diego City Schs. War Against Litter, 1971—76; pres. Assn. Calif. Sch. Adminstrs. Ret., 1992—94. Recipient Am. Educators medal Freedoms Found. Valley Forge, 1973, Woman of Yr. award Pres. Coun. Women's Svc., Bus. & Profl. Clubs San Diego, 1980, Woman of Action award Soroptimists Internat. El Cajon, 1992. Mem.: AAUW (parliamentarian 1989—98, Appreciation award 1992), Sr. Resource Ctr. (adv. bd., vol. 1989—), Assn. Calif. Sch. Adminstrs. (pres.), San Diego City Sch. Adminstrn. Assn. (pres. 1976—77), Calif. Retired Tchrs., Singing Hills Women's Golf Club. Avocations: photography, painting, gardening, golf, music. Home: 13208 Julian Ave Lakeside CA 92040-4312

WALKER, WINNETTA DORREAN, social studies educator; b. Prescott, Ariz., May 12, 1947; d. Samuel George Graves and Elizabeth Ava Henderson; m. Marcus Rockford Walker, July 16, 1977; children: James Marcus, Marla Ruth Payne, Elizabeth Margaret Martz. BA Edn., U. Ariz., Tucson, 1969. Cert. Std. Secondary Tchr. with Gifted Endorsement Ariz. Dept. Edn., 1969, Trainer Project READS, 1987, ATLES Instr. Ariz. Bar Found., 1990. Substitute tchr. Tucson Unified Sch. Dist., 1969—70; classroom tchr. Ganado Pub. Schs., Ganado, Ariz., 1970—73, Red Mesa H.S., Ariz., 1974—75, Chinle Pub. Schs., Ariz., 1975—89, Prescott Unified Sch. Dist., 1989—. Adj. faculty Prescott Coll., 1993—94; sponsor We the People Team Prescott H.S., 2002—, sponsor Mock Trial Team, 1989—; cooperating tchr. No. Ariz. U., Flagstaff, 1999—2002. Vol. fund raiser Chino Valley Swimming Pool com., Ariz.; dir. toys for tots program Chinle Jr. High Student Coun., dir. coats for kids program; advisor adopt a family for Christmas Prescott H.S. Cmty. Works Class, 2004—05; advisor Prescott Teen Ct., 1996—2006; site coun. mem. Prescott H.S. Site Coun., 1997—2003; mem. feeding displaced persons from the Indian fire com. Red Cross, Prescott; leader bill of rights issues book discussion group Humanities Coun., Prescott and Chino Valley, 1992; mem. com. to create a libr. Gen. Dynamocs, Chinle; served Christmas dinner to the elderly and homeless Chino Valley Ministerial Assn.; mem. Chino Valley Cmty. Ch., Yavapai Fed. Credit Union, Prescott, 2005—06; mem. interest based negotiations team Prescott Edn. Assn., 2002—06. Nominee Ariz. Tchr. of Yr., Ariz. Dept. Edn., 1985, Yavapai County Tchr. of Yr., Prescott H.S., 2002; named to Who's Who Among Am. Tchrs., Who's Who, 2006; recipient John J. Ross Meml. Award, Ariz. Bar Found., 1995, Cmty. Svc. award, Alpha Delta Kappa, 1983, Hon. Jack Ogg award, Yavapai County Bar Assn., 2004, Women Educators honoree, Delta Kappa Gamma, Eta chpt., 2004, 2006; Scholarship Tchr. for Nat. We The People Finals, Constl. Rights Found., 2006. Mem.: NEA (life), Ariz. Edn. Assn. (bd. dirs. 1985—89, legis. and govtl. task force 2002—05, small and rural sch. task force 2005—, Region 10 Bill Hodge award 1990), Prescott Edn. Assn. (pres. 2002—06), U. Ariz. Alumni Assn.

R-Conservative. Avocations: travel, yardwork, politics. Home: 1929 W Rd 4 North Chino Valley AZ 86323 Office: Prescott High School 1050 North Ruth Street Prescott AZ 86301 E-mail: dorrean.walker@prescottschools.com.

WALKER BONNER, LINDA CAROL, music educator; b. Nashville, Aug. 18, 1953; d. John Louis and Caronia Walker; m. Divorced; children: Jordan Bonner III, Angela Jonelle Bonner. BS, Tenn. State U., 1975; M, Vanderbilt U., 1977. Music specialist Williamson County Schools, Franklin, Tenn., 1976—. Contbr. articles to profl. jours. Vol. Habitat For Humanities, Nashville, 2000—05; v.p. Missionary Soc., Nashville, 2002—05. Mem.: WCEA (life; minority rep. 1986—92), TEA (life; minority affairs com. 1988—90). Home: 756 Garrison Dr Nashville TN 37207 Office: Grassland Elem Sch 6803 Manley Ln Brentwood TN 37027 Office Phone: 615-472-4480. Personal E-mail: lcwbonner@comcast.net. E-mail: lindab1@wcs.edu.

WALKER-LAROSE, LINDA WALESKA, elementary school educator; b. New Haven, June 19, 1952; d. Edward Lawrence and Waleska Katherine (Bussmann) W.; m. Mr. LaRose, Aug. 17, 1996. BS, So. Conn. State Coll., 1974, postgrad., 1979. Tchr. 4th grade Union Sch., West Haven, Conn., 1974-75, tchr. 2d grade, 1975-76; tchr. 3d grade Washington Sch., West Haven, 1976-81; tchr. 1st grade Washington Magnet Sch., West Haven, 1981—. Coop. tchr., mentor Conn. Dept. Edn., West Haven, 1987—. Mem. PTA. Mem. Conn. Fedn. Tchrs, Shorline Time Machine. Avocations: knitting, restoration of Victorian home, making Victorian lampshades, collecting and restoring old cars and trucks.

WALKER-TAYLOR, YVONNE, retired academic administrator; b. New Bedford, Mass., Apr. 17, 1916; d. Dougal Ormonde and Eva Emma (Revallion) Walker; m. Robert Harvey Taylor (dec.) BS, Wilberforce U., 1936; MA, Boston U., 1938; Edn. Specialist, U. Kans., 1964; L.H.D. (hon.), Morris Brown Coll., 1985; Dr. Pedagogy (hon.), Medaille Coll., 1985, Northeastern Coll., 1985. Asst. acad. dean Wilberforce U., Ohio, 1967-68, v.p., acad. dean Ohio, 1973-83, provost Ohio, 1983-84, pres. Ohio, 1984-88; Disting. Presdl. prof. Edn. Ctrl. State U., 1990-96. Bd. dirs. Nat. Commn. on Coop. Edn., 1977-82, 83-88, United Way, Xenia, Ohio, 1985-88; chmn. culture planning council Nat. Mus. Afro-Am. History; sec. Greene Oaks Health Ctr., 1983-87; bd. trustees, Dayton Art Inst; v.p. jud. coun. AME Ch.; mem. Ohio Humanities Coun., 1994—, Greene City Violence Bd. Named Woman of Yr., Met. Civic Women's Assn., Dayton, 1984, one of Top Ten Women, Dayton Newspapers-Women's Coalition, Dayton, 1984, Outstanding Woman of Yr., Iota Phi Lambda, Dayton, 1985; recipient Drum Major for Justice award So. Christian Leadership Conf., 1986; named to Greene County Hall of Fame, 1990. Mem. Com. on Ednl. Credit and Credentials of the Am. Council on Edn., Alpha Kappa Alpha, Phi Delta Kappa. African Methodist Episcopalian. Club: Links (past pres.) Avocations: reading, swimming, horseshoes, tennis, bicycling. Home: 1279 Wilberforce-Clifton Rd Wilberforce OH 45384-9999 Office: Wilberforce U Brush Row Rd PO Box 336 Wilberforce OH 45384-0336 E-mail: deonwt@aol.com.

WALKER TUCKER, DANA, lawyer; b. St. Louis, Oct. 23, 1963; d. Donald Edward and Mary Louis Walker; m. Mark Avery Tucker, May 29, 1998; 1 child, Jackson Miles Tucker. BS, U. Mo., 1986; JD (scholar 1991-94), St. Louis U., 1994. Bar: Mo. 1995, Ill. 2003. With Husch and Eppenberger, St. Louis, 1994—96, Banks and Assocs., 1996—2000; atty. Gary, Williams, Parenti, et. al., Stuart, Fla., 2000—02; atty., ptnr. Fox Galvin LLC, St. Louis, 2002—. Adj. prof. Washington U. Law Sch., 2004—. Mem.: Bar Assn. Met. St. Louis, Mound City Bar Assn., Def. Resource Inst., Nat. Bar Assn., Delta Sigma Theta. Democrat. Baptist. Office: Fox Galvin LLC #1 Memorial Dr Saint Louis MO 63102 Office Phone: 314-588-7000. Home Fax: 314-588-1965; Office Fax: 314-588-1965. Personal E-mail: dtucker@foxgalvin.com.

WALKER VICKERS, STEPHANIE CAROLE, special education educator; b. Huntsville, Ala., Feb. 26, 1974; d. John Ed and Carole Ann Vickers; m. Patrick Herbert Walker, Dec. 27, 1997. BS in Spl. Edn., Jacksonville State U., Ala., 1996, MS in Spl. Edn., 2002. Spl. edn. tchr. emotional/behavioral students McHenry Primary in Floyd County Schs., Rome, Ga., 1996—. Home: 120 Co Rd 691 Cedar Bluff AL 35959 Office: McHenry Primary 100 McHenry Dr Rome GA 30161 Office Phone: 706-236-1833. Personal E-mail: swalker@floydboe.net.

WALKINSHAW, NICOLE M., performing arts educator; B in Com. Processes & Disorders, U. Fla., 1988—92, B, 1988—92; M in Social Foundations in Multicultural Edn., Fla. Atlantic U., 2004—05. Cert. in Adolescent Young Adulthood/English Lang. Arts U.S. Nat. Bd. Edn., Fla., 2003, Speech, English & English for Speakers of Other Lang. Fla. Dept. Edn., 1992. Educator Nova HS, Davie, Fla., 1992—. S.t.a.r. mentoring program dir. Nova HS, 1996—, broadway series interactive achievers program dir., 2001—, e.a.g.l.e. tolerance tng. initiative program dir., 2002—. Facilitator (seminar) Integrating Literary Circles Across the Curricular Disciplines, Honae vs Tatamya: Exploring the Multifaceted & Mystical World of Japan; editor: (pub.) SNAPSHOT Entertainment Newsletter. Fundraiser project dir. Until There's A Cure, Davie, 1997—98; youth vol. coord. Read Across Am., Davie, 2002—05; fundraiser project coord. Broadway Cares Equity Fights A.I.D.S., Davie, 2003—05; vol. supr. Kids In Distress, Davie, 2003—05. Recipient Broward's Best, Broward County Sch. Bd., 2003, Alumni Assn. Appreciation award, U. Fla., 2004; Team Mentor grant, Citibank, 2002—03, Fulbright Meml. Fund. scholar, 2002. Mem.: NEA, Fla. Edn. Assn., Nat. Assn. Multicultural Edn., Fla. Humanities Coun., So. Poverty Law Ctr. Avocations: writing, travel, cinematic & arts appreciation. Office: Nova HS 3600 College Ave Davie FL 33314 Office Phone: 754-323-1650.

WALKLEY, MARY L., voice and music educator; b. Storm Lake, Iowa, Oct. 17, 1947; d. Leonard Leroy Gustafson and Betty Angelyne Barnes; m. Robert Wayne Gustafson, Feb. 10, 1965 (div. Feb. 11, 1983); children: Robert Scot, Andrea Lynn Jenkins. MusB in performance, U. of Tampa, Fla., 1983. Cert. level V speech level singing Instr. Seth Riggs Speech Level Singing Internat., 2000. Founder and dir., pre-coll. music program U. of Tampa, Fla., 1983—93; fine arts dir. Tampa Prep. Sch., 1983—96, 1983—97; founder and music dir. The Broadway Theatre Project, 1990—; founder and program dir. The Speech Level Singing Inst., L.A., 1998—2002; guest artist and workshop presenter Internat. Thespian Assn., Tampa, 1998—. Vocal cons. Busch Gardens Entertainment, Tampa, Fla., 1998—. Musician (arranger): (vocal arrangements, orchestrations) Broadway Theatre Project. Grantee study with Seth Riggs, Benedict Found., 1997. Mem.: NARAS, Nat. Assn. of Teachers of Singing, Inc. Avocations: travel, reading, singing, piano. Home: 775 NE 76th Street Miami FL 33138 Office: FloridaSings 775 NE 76th Street Miami FL 33138 E-mail: mary@floridasings.com.

WALKOWSKI, BARBARA A., lawyer; BA, JD, U. Mich., Ann Arbor. V.p. legal affairs, corp. counsel Siebel Sys., Inc., San Mateo, Calif. Bd. dirs. Meals On Wheels, San Francisco, V Found. Wine Celebration bd.

WALL, AUDREY G., secondary school educator; b. Concord, N.C., June 6, 1920; d. William Henry and Barbara (Golns) Gillis; m. Melvin Lloyd Wall, Sr., Nov. 7, 1973 (dec. Sept. 24, 1983); 1 child, Melvin Lloyd, Jr. BA, Barber-Scotia Coll., 1951; MS, A&T State U., 1958. Educator Stanly County Bd. Edn., Albemarle, N.C., 1962-65, Mecklenburg County Bd. Edn., Charlotte, N.C., 1965—. Reporter Stanly News & Press, 1951-53; feature writer Charlotte Post, 1982-85. Reader Am. Assn. for Blind, Charlotte, 1977-79; vol. Mercy Hosp., Charlotte, 1983-94; pres. Charlotte chpt. World Fedn. Meth. Women, 1986-88; vol. Carolinas Med. Ctr., 1994-97; planning com. Charlotte Women's Commn., 1995—; pres.-elect local chpt. Ch. Women United, Charlotte, 1994-96, pres., 1996-98, statewide comms. dir., 1998-99, state v.p., 1999—; moderator Presbyn. Women, 2000—. Mem. NEA (life), Order Eastern Star, Delta Sigma Theta. Home: 3115 Clearview Dr Charlotte NC 28216-3624

WALL, BARBARA WARTELLE, lawyer; b. New Orleans, Sept. 30, 1954; d. Richard Cole and Ruth Druhan (Power) Wartelle; m. Christopher Read Wall, June 21, 1980; 2 children. BA, U. Va., 1976, JD, 1979. Bar: N.Y. 1980, U.S. Dist. Ct. (so. and ea. dists.) N.Y. 1980. Assoc. Satterlee & Stephens, N.Y.C., 1979—85; asst. gen. counsel Gannett Co., Inc., Arlington, Va., 1985—90, sr. legal counsel, 1990—93, v.p., sr. legal counsel, 1993—2004, v.p. assoc. gen. counsel, 2004—. Mem.: ABA (past chair forum comm. law), Assn. Bar City of N.Y., N.Y. State Bar Assn. Republican. Episcopalian. Home: 5026 Tilden St NW Washington DC 20016-2334 Office: Gannett Co Inc 7950 Jones Branch Dr Mc Lean VA 22102-0320 Office Phone: 703-854-6951. Business E-Mail: bwall@gannett.com.

WALL, BETTY JANE, real estate consultant; b. Wichita Falls, Tex., Mar. 23, 1936; d. Albert Willis and Winnie Belle (Goodloe) Beard; m. Richard Lee Wall, Feb. 21, 1959; 1 child, Cynthia Lynn. BS in Vocat. Home Econs. Edn, U. Okla., Norman, 1958; MEd, Midwestern U., Wichita Falls, Tex., 1959. Lic. real estate salesperson, Tex. Tchr. San Diego County Schs., 1959-60, Long Beach (Calif.) City Schs., 1960-61, Norman (Okla.) Kindergarten Assn., 1961-65; real estate salesperson WestMark Realtors, Lubbock, Tex., 1983-85; now ind. real estate salesperson Lubbock, 1985—. Coll. adviser Nat. Panhellenic Conf., Tex., 1979-91; judge talent and beauty pageants, Tex. N.Mex., Okla., 1984—. Treas. Lubbock Symphony Guild, 1985-87, v.p. ways and means com., 1987-88, chmn. ball, 1990, pres. elect, 1993-94, pres., 1994-95; bd. dirs. Tex. Assn. of Symphony Orchs., 1994-95, Ballet Lubbock, 1996-98, 2000—; bd. dirs. Miss Lubbock Pageant, 1992—; co-chmn. Performance Lubbock' 96, 1996; mem. Lubbock Arts Festival Com., 1997-98. Recipient Tex. Tech. U. Outstanding Greek Alumni award, 1994, Tex. Tech. Chancellor's Coun. Mem. Tex. Real Estate Assn., Jr. League Lubbock (treas. 1976-78, sustaining advisor fin. com. 1979-83, hdqrs. commn. advisor 1989-94), Mus. Tex. Tech. Univ. (chmn. planetarium com. 1996, trustee 1997—, bd. dirs., mus. league 1992-2002, pres. 2002) Mus. of Tex. Tech. U. Assn. (v.p. 2002-2003), Lubbock C. of C., Lubbock Women's Club Hist. Found. (bd. dirs. 1996-2000, pres. 1999-2000, pres. hist. found. 1999-2000), Tex. Tech. U. Faculty Women's Club (v.p. and pres. 1967-69, Lubbock chpt. Achievement Rewards for Coll. Sci. bd. 1995-96), Alpha Chi Omega (nat. coun., nat. panhellenic del. 1978-83, 88-90, nat. v.p. membership 1985-88, nat. v.p. collegians 1990-92), Mus. Tex. Tech U. Assn. (v.p. mus. league 2002-2003), Lubbock Alumnae Panhellenic (pres. 2003-04). Avocations: needlepoint, travel, music. Home and Office: 3610 63rd Dr Lubbock TX 79413-5308

WALL, DELLA, human resources specialist, manufacturing executive; Various positions SupeRx Drug Stores, Kroger Mfg., 1971—2000; v.p. deferred benefits Kroger Co., Cinn., 2000—01, v.p. compensation and benefits, 2001—03, corp. v.p. human resources, 2003—04, group v.p. human resources, 2004—. Bd. dirs. Profit Sharing Coun. Am. Office: Kroger Co 1014 Vine St Cincinnati OH 45202-1100 Office Phone: 513-762-4000. Office Fax: 513-762-1160.

WALL, DIANE EVE, political science professor; b. Detroit, Nov. 17, 1944; d. Albert George and Jean Carol Bradley. BA in History and Edn., Mich. State U., 1966, MA in History, 1969, MA in Polit. Sci., 1979, PhD in Polit. Sci., 1983. Cert. permanent secondary tchr., Mich. Secondary tchr. Corunna (Mich.) Pub. Schs., 1966-67, N.W. Pub. Schs., Rives Junction, Mich., 1967-73; lectr. Tidewater C.C., Chesapeake, Va., 1974-77; instr. Wayne State U., Detroit, fall 1980, Lansing (Mich.) C.C., 1981-83, Ctrl. Mich. U., Mt. Pleasant, 1982; prof. dept. polit. sci. Miss. State U., 1983—, undergrad. coord., 1993—. Pre-law advisor Miss. State U., 1990—93, chair, 1993—. Co-editor spl. issue Southea. Polit. Rev.; contbr. articles, revs. to profl. jours., chpt. to book, entry to ency. Evaluator Citizen's Task Force, Chesapeake, Va., 1977; panelist flag burning program Ednl. TV, Mississippi State, 1990, prayer in pub. sch., Starkville Cmty. TV, 1995; scholar, judge Ctr. Civic Edn., Miss., 2001—; gubernatorial appointee Miss. Task Force on Local Govt. Info. Systems, 2003. Recipient Paideia award Miss. State U. Coll. Arts and Scis., 1988, Miss. State U. Outstanding Woman Tchg. Faculty award Pres.'s Commn. on Status of Women, 1994, Acad. Advising award Miss. State U., 1994, Outstanding Advisor award Nat. Acad. Advising Assn. and ACT, 1995, Miss. State U. Upper Level Undergrad. Tchg. award Miss. State U. Alumni Assn., 2000, Outstanding Prof. award Miss. State U., Polit. Sci. Dept., 2005; Grad. Office fellow Mich. State U., 1980; Miss. State U. rsch. grantee, 1984 Mem. ASPA (exec. bd. Sect. for Women 1987-90, Miss. chpt. pres. 1992-93), LWV (Chesapeake charter pres. 1976-77), Miss. Polit. Sci. Assn. (exec. dir. 1991-93), Miss. State U. Soc. Scholars (pres. 1992-93), Miss. State U. Faculty Women's Assn. (v.p. 1985-86, pres. 1986-88, scholar 1987-89), Phi Kappa Phi (v.p. 1985-86, pres. 1986-88), Pi Sigma Alpha (Ann. Chpt. Activities award 1991). Democrat. Methodist. Avocations: dog obedience training, corvette activities, gardening. Office: Miss State U PO Drawer PC Mississippi State MS 39762 E-mail: dew1@ps.msstate.edu.

WALL, GLENNIE MURRAY, historic preservation professional; b. Roseburg, Oreg., Oct. 8, 1931; d. James Matheny and Emily Lenore (Aten) Corbin; m. Louis Samuel Wall, Jan. 3, 1975; 2 daus. BS, Portland (Oreg.) State U., 1965, postgrad., 1966, U. Mo., Springfield, 1969, U. Mich., 1978, Practicing Law Inst., N.Y.C., 1980-82. Historian, Pipestone (Minn.) Nat. Monument Nat. Pk. Svc., 1966-68, historian, pk. supt. Herbert Hoover Hist. Site West Branch, Iowa, 1968-69; historian, landmark specialist western regional office Nat. Park Svc., San Francisco, 1969-72, div. chief Denver Svc. Ctr., 1974-83, mus. mgr. (maritime) San Francisco, 1983-89, cultural resources specialist, curator Presidio Project, 1989-90; prin. Hist. Preservation Planning, San Francisco, 1990—. Instr., lectr. on preservation law and policy Nat. Pk. Svc., 1974-83; lectr. Nat. Trust for Hist. Preservation, washington, 1971-89; dir. Coun. Am. Maritime Mus., Phila., 1987-88, Nat. Maritime Mus. Assn., San Francisco, 1983-88; chair Equal Opportunity Com., Nat. Pk. Svc., Denver, 1979-81. Author, editor: Maritime Preservation, 1987, Agency Guidelines for Cultural resources Management, 1979-83; photographer: Pipes on the Plains, 1967; co-author, photographer: Design Guidelines: Santa Rosa, Calif., Kodiak Historic District Management Plan, 1993; author: Cultural Resources Management Guide, 1994, Bessie's Sourdough, 1999. Treas. Colo. Corral of Westerners, Denver, 1974-76; mem. Com. for Green Foothills, San Mateo, Calif., 1984-88, Sta. KQED-TV, San Francisco, 1985—. Recipient spl. achievement awards Dept. Interior, 1969, 72, citation for excellence, 1976; Nat. Preservation award President's Adv. Coun., Washington, 1988., 72; Hoover scholar, 1993. Mem. Am. Assn. Mus., Internat. Coun. Mus., Internat. Congress Maritime Mus., Sierra Club. Avocations: photography, travel. Office: PO Box 370634 Montara CA 94037-0634

WALL, JENNIFER GREY, assistant principal; b. South Boston, Va., Aug. 12, 1973; d. Sarah Snow and Robert Thompson Wall. BS, Va. Tech., 1994, MA in Curriculum and Instrn., 2000. Lic. ednl. leadership. Tchr. math Blacksburg Mid. Sch., Va., 1994—2005, Dublin Elem. Sch., Va., 2005—. Math dept. chair Blacksburg Mid. Sch., 1997—2005, bldg. mentor coord., 2000—05, sch. improvement co-chair, 2001—04, team leader, 2003—05; math mentor coach Montgomery County Schools, Christiansburg, Va., 2004—05; profl. devel. presenter, Va., 1997—2005. Band mem. Blacksburg Cmty. Band, 1994—2001. Recipient Leila Stalker Math. Tchr. of the Yr., Blue Ridge Coun. of Teachers of Math., 2000; Hatcher Meml. scholarship, Va. Tech Math. Dept., 1991—93, Nat. Sci. Scholars, Nat. Dept. of Edn., 1991—93, Future Educator scholarship, Phi Delta Kappa, 1991. Mem.: VAESP, ASCD, Va. Coun. Tchrs. Math., Phi Delta Kappa, Pi Mu Epsilon, Phi Kappa Phi, Phi Beta Kappa. Avocations: music, walking. Home: 705 McBryde Dr Blacksburg VA 24060 Office: Dublin Elem Sch 600 Dunlap Rd Dublin VA 24084 Office Phone: 540-643-0337. Personal E-mail: jwall.vt@verizon.net.

WALL, KATHY ELLIOTT, secondary school educator; b. Kershaw, S.C., Nov. 13, 1955; d. Alton Leonard and Myrtle Mildred Elliott; m. Ronald Lee Wall, June 19, 1976; children: Noel E., Elliott Lee, Oliver Lawrence. BMus, Furman U., Greenville, S.C., 1978; MEd, U. S.C., 1983. Cert. tchr. S.C. Tchr. Heath Springs (S.C.) Elem. Sch., 1978—85, Andrew Jackson Mid. Sch., Kershaw, SC, 1985—99, Andrew Jackson H.S., Kershaw, SC, 1992—. Keyboard accompanist Covenant Bapt. Ch., Lancaster, SC, 2001—; children and youth music dir. First Bapt. Sch., Kershaw, 1990—2001; interim music dir. Heath Springs Bapt. Sch., 1980—84. Vol. Meals on Wheels, Kershaw, 1999—. Mem.: Palmetto State Tchrs. Assn., Music Educators Nat. Conf. Home: PO Box 91 Kershaw SC 29067

WALL, SHERRY HODGES, elementary school educator; b. Meriwether County, Ga., Nov. 21, 1951; d. William Henry and Leta (Reeves) Hodges; m. Charles R. Wall, Feb. 13, 1970; children: Christiane, Kera Leigh. BA in Mid. Grades Edn. cum laude, LaGrange (Ga.) Coll., 1986; student, Upson County Vocat.-Tech. Sch., Thomaston, Ga., 1971; MEd in Mid. Grade Edn., Columbus (Ga.) Coll. Cert. mid. grades Math and English tchr., Ga. Tchr.'s aide, tchr. Flint River Acad., Woodbury, Ga.; tchr. 5th grade math. and English, Pike County Bd. Edn., Zebulon, Ga. 4th grade inclusion tchr. Nat. Coun. Tchrs. Math., Ga. Tchrs. Math., Nat. Coun. Tchrs. Sci. Mem. NEA, Ga. Assn. Educators.

WALL, SONJA ELOISE, nursing administrator; b. Santa Cruz, Calif., Mar. 28, 1938; d. Ray Theothornton and Reva Mattie (Wingo) W.; m. Edward Gleason Holmes, Aug. 1959 (div. Jan. 1968); children: Deborah Lynn, Lance Edward; m. John Aspesi, Sept. 1969 (div. 1977); children: Sabrina Jean, Daniel John; m. Kenneth Talbot LaBoube, Nov. 1, 1978 (div. 1989); 1 child, Tiffany Amber; m. Charles Borsic, July 2002. BA, San Jose Jr. Coll., 1959; BS, Madonna Coll., 1967; postgrad., Wayne State U., 1967—68; student, U. Mich., 1968—70. RN, Calif., Mich., Colo. Staff nurse Santa Clara Valley Med. Ctr., San Jose, Calif., 1959-67, U. Mich. Hosp., Ann Arbor, 1967-73, Porter and Swedish Med. Hosp., Denver, 1973-77, Laurel Grove Hosp., Castro Valley, Calif., 1977-79, Advent Hosp., Ukiah, Calif., 1984-86; motel owner LaBoube Enterprises, Fairfield, Point Arena, Willits, Calif., 1979—; staff nurse Northridge Hosp., L.A., 1986-87, Folsom State Prison, Calif., 1987; co-owner, mgr. nursing registry Around the Clock Nursing Svc., Ukiah, 1985—; critical care staff nurse Kaiser Permanente Hosp., Sacramento, 1986-89; nurse Snowline Hospice, Placerville, Calif., 1989-92; carepoint home care and travel nurse Hosp. Staffing Svcs. Inc., Placerville, 1992-94, interim home health nurse, 1994-95; nurse Finders Home Health Care, 1996; owner Sunshine Manor Residential Care Home, Placerville, 1995—, Rainbow Manor Residential Care Home, 2000—02; psychol. and trauma RN Folsom State Prison, 2002—04, Calif. Dept. Mental Health, Placerville, Calif., 2004—. Owner Royal Plantation Petites Miniature Horse Farm. Contbr. articles to profl. jours. Leader Coloma 4-H, 1987-91; mem. mounted divsn. El Dorado County Search and Rescue, 1991-93; docent Calif. Marshall Gold Discovery State Hist. Park, Coloma, Calif. Mem. AACN, NAFE, Oncology Nurses Assn., Soc. Critical Care Medicine, Am. Heart Assn. (CPR trainer, recipient awards), Calif. Bd. RNs, Calif. Nursing Rev., Calif. Critical Care Nurses, Soc. Critical Care Nurses, Alzheimers Aid Soc. No. Calif., Am. Motel Assn. (beautification and remodeling award 1985), Nat. Hospice Nurses Assn., Cmty. Residential Care Assn. Calif., Soroptimist Internat. Calif., Am. Miniature Horse Assn. (winner nat. grand championship 1981-83, 85, 89), DAR (Jobs Daus. hon. mem.), C. of C. of El Dorado County, Kiwanis, Cameron Park Country Club. Republican. Episcopalian. Avocations: pinto, paint and miniature horses, real estate development, swimming. Home and Office: Sunshine Manor Residental Care Home Care and Around Clock Nursing Svc 2500 Cold Springs Rd Placerville CA 95667-5825 Fax: 530-622-2233. Office Phone: 530-622-3940. E-mail: sunshinemanor@directcon.net.

WALLA, CATHERINE ANNE, nursing administrator, educator; b. Chgo., Oct. 18, 1948; d. Louis Bernard and Mary Louise W.; m. Robert Joseph Murphy, July 2, 1972 (div. Oct. 1979); 1 child, Meghan Anne. BS, Loyola U., 1971, BSN, MA, 1978; M of Nursing, UCLA, 1988. RN Calif. Staff nurse Wadsworth VA Hosp., L.A., 1978-79; charge, staff nurse UCLA Med. Ctr., L.A., 1979-81; clin. rsch. nurse specialist L.A. County & U. So. Calif. Med. Ctr., L.A., 1981-84; asst. prof. Bethune-Cookman Coll., Daytona Beach, Fla., 1984-86; dir. perinatal rsch. L.A. County & U. Soc. Calif., 1986-90; coord. ob-gyn. rsch. Cedars-Sinai Med. Ctr., L.A., 1990—; asst. clin. prof. UCLA Sch. Nursing, 1990—. Cons. in field. Co-author: (chpts.) Maternity Nursing, 1991, 97, Diagnostic Medical Sonography, 1992, 97, Protocols for High Risk Pregnancy, 1996, Genetic Disorders and Pregnancy Outcome, 1997; Fetal Therapy, 1999; contbr. articles to profl. jours. Rsch. grantee Bethune Cookman Coll., 1985. Mem. APHA, Am. Inst. Ultrasound Medicine, Monterey Bay Aquarium, Long Beach Aquarium. Avocations: herptology, salt water aquariums, hiking, fictional writing, multi-cultural cooking. Home: 29044 Lake Dr Agoura Hills CA 91301-2947 Office: Cedars-Sinai Med Ctr Dept Ob-Gyn 8700 Beverly Blvd Los Angeles CA 90048-1865

WALLACE, ARDELIA LESLENE, elementary school educator; d. Robert J. and Billie Loyce Turner; m. Kenneth Carson Wallace, Oct. 26, 1946; 1 child, Carson Wayne. BS, SW Tex. State U., San Marcos, Tex. Cert. Tchr. State Bd. of Educators, Tex., 1997. Fifth grade tchr. Dripping Springs ISD, Dripping Springs, Tex., 1999—. Mem.: ATPE. D-Conservative. Achievements include Innovative Teaching Award for 2004. Avocations: reading, gardening. Office Phone: 512-858-4903 207.

WALLACE, BARBARA BROOKS, writer; b. Soochow, China, Dec. 3, 1922; arrived in U.S., 1938; d. Otis Frank and Nicia Brooks; m. James Wallace, Jr., Feb. 27, 1954; 1 child, James V. BA, UCLA, 1945. Script sec. Foote, Cone & Belding, Hollywood, Calif., 1946-49; tchr. Wright MacMahon Secretarial Sch., Beverly Hills, Calif., 1949-50; head fund drive Commerce and Industry Divsn. ARC, San Francisco, 1950-52. Author: Claudia, 1969 (Nat. League Am. Pen Women Juvenile Book award, 1970), Andrew the Big Deal, 1970, The Trouble with Miss Switch, 1971, Victoria, 1973, Can Do, Missy Charlie, 1974, The Secret Summer of L.E.B. (Nat. League Am. Pen Women Juvenile Book award, 1974), Julia and the Third Bad Thing, 1975, Palmer Patch, 1976, Hawkins, 1977, Peppermints in the Parlor, 1980 (William Allen White award, 1983), The Contest Kid Strikes Again, 1980, Hawkins and the Soccer Solution, 1981, Miss Switch to the Rescue, 1981, Hello, Claudia, 1982, Claudia and Duffy, 1982, The Barrel in the Basement, 1985, Argyle, 1987, 1992, Perfect Acres, Inc., 1988, The Twin in the Tavern, 1993 (Edgar award Mystery Writers Am., 1994), Cousins in the Castle, 1996, Sparrows in the Scullery, 1997 (Edgar award, 1998), Ghosts in the Gallery, 2000, Secret in St. Something, 2001, Miss Switch Online, 2002, The Perils of Peppermints, 2003. Mem.: Authors Guild, Children's Book Guild of Washington, Alpha Phi. Episcopalian. Home: 6251 Old Dominion Dr Apt 436 Mc Lean VA 22101-4810 E-mail: bbwallace@cox.net.

WALLACE, BEATRICE LESLIE, secondary school educator; b. Decker, Mich., Dec. 7, 1934; d. Albert Wheeler Leslie and Florence Eleanor (Jickling) Hacker; m. Robert Donald Wallace, Aug. 22, 1959; children: Julie Anne, Leslie Jayne BS Edn., Ctrl. Mich. U., 1985, MA, 1970. Tchr., libr. Hemlock Pub. Schs., Mich., 1965—95; libr., supr. Hemlock Pub. Schs., 1990—95; ret., 1995. Author: Haflinger Horses in North America and the People Who Belong to Them: 1958-1999, 2004; contbr. articles to various publs Sec. fin. com. Hemlock United Meth. Ch., 1974-85 Mem. AAUW (pres. Hemlock chpt. 1980), Haflinger Assn. Am. (v.p., registrar 1987-98), World Haflinger Assn., Gt. Lakes Haflinger Assn. (sec. 1985-86), Order Ea. Star Avocations: antiques, reading, haflinger horses, writing. Home: 14570 Gratiot Rd Hemlock MI 48626-8451

WALLACE, BECKY WHITLEY, protective services official; BA in Criminal Justice, Montgomery C.C. Police officer City of Troy (N.C.), 1974-75; deputy sheriff Montgomery County (N.C.), 1975-78, 82-94; alcohol law enforcement agt. N.C. Dept. Crime Control & Pub. Safety, Greensboro, 1978-82; U.S. marshal N.C., 1994—. Recipeint Leadership N.C. Stanley Frank award, Breaking the Glass Ceiling award Nat. Ctr. Women in Policing; named Disting. Woman of N.c., Coun. Women. Mem. Fed. Law Enforcement Officers' Assn., N.C. Women's Law Enforcement Assn., Nat. Sheriffs Assn., N.C. Sheriff's Assn., Montgomery County Law Enforcement Assn., Profl. Women's Assn. Office: US Post Office 324 W Market St Greensboro NC 27401-2544

WALLACE, BERTHA, retired elementary school educator; b. Pompano, Fla., Aug. 22, 1939; d. Eddie Williams and Francis Wilkins-Smith; m. James Wallace; children: James III, Dareo, Angela, Jamie. As, SUNY, Farmingdale, NY, 1975; BS, SUNY, Old Westbury, 1978. Therapy aide Devel. Ctr., Melville, NY, 1970, habitiational specialist Hicksville, NY, 1989.

WALLACE, BETTY JEAN, retired elementary school educator, lay minister; b. Denison, Tex., Dec. 5, 1927; d. Claude Herman and Pearl Victoria (Freels) Moore; m. Billy Dean McKneely, Sept. 2, 1950 (div. Nov. 1964); children: Rebecca Lynn, Paul King, David Freels, John Walker, Philip Andrew McKneely. Student, Tulane U., New Orleans, 1947; BA, Baylor U., Waco, Tex., 1949; postgrad., U. Houston, Tex., 1949-50, 74, 81, Rocky Mountain Bible Inst., 1959, U. Colo., 1969-70, U. No. Colo., 1965, 68, 72, U. St. Thomas, 1992, Autonomous U. Guadalajara, summer 1993; MEd, Houston Bapt. U., Tex., 1985. Cert. life profl. elem., high sch., life profl. reading specialist, secondary field ESL tchr., Tex. Tchr. Galena Park (Tex.) Ind. Sch. Dist., 1949-50, 52-53, 72-98, Corpus Christi (Tex.) Independent Sch. Dist., 1950-51, Denver Pub. Schs., 1953-54, 63-72, Wackenhut Cleveland (Tex.) Correctional Ctr., 1999—2003; ret. Author: The Holy Spirit Today, 1989, Our God of Infinite Variety, 1991, God Speaks in a Variety of Ways, 1991. Sunday sch. tchr. So. Bapt. Conv. chs., Tex., 1946-50, Denver, 1952-56; tchr. kindergarten Emmanuel Bapt. Ch., Denver, 1956-63; missionary, Queretaro, Mex., 1977-78; active Rep. Senatorial Inner Circle, Washington, 1989-91, 2002, Round Table for Ronald Reagan, Washington, 1989-90, Round Table for Pres. Bush, 2004; founding mem. RNC Presdl. Trust; helper Feed the Poor, Houston, 1983-85; active Suicide Prevention, Houston, 1973-76, Literacy, Houston, 1978-81; rep. NEA, Denver, 1966-72; mem. Retirement Com., Denver, 1970-72; bd. adv. Oliver North, 1994; mem. Rep. Presdl. Task Force, 2006. Recipient Rep. Senatorial medal of freedom, 1994, Rep. Senatorial medal of Victory, Justice, Freedom and Liberty, 2002, Congl. Order of Merit, 2003; grantee, NSF, 1969—70. Mem. Tex. Classroom Tchrs. Assn. (officer rep., pres. Galena Park chpt. 1988-91), Pres.'s Club, Delta Alpha Pi (pres. Waco chpt. 1948-49), Alpha Epsilon Delta. Republican. Avocations: writing, archaeology, gardening, reading. Home: 14831 Anoka Dr Channelview TX 77530-3201

WALLACE, BONNIE ANN, biochemist, biophysicist, educator; b. Greenwich, Conn., Aug. 10, 1951; d. Arthur Victor and Maryjane Wallace. BS in Chemistry, Rensselaer Poly. Inst., 1973; PhD in Molecular Biophysics and Biochemistry, Yale U., 1977; DSc (hon.), U. London, 1995. Postdoctoral rsch. fellow Harvard U., Boston, 1977-78; asst. prof. dept. biochemistry and molecular biophysics Columbia U., N.Y.C., 1979-86, assoc. prof., 1986; prof. dept. chemistry, dir. Ctr. for Biophysics Rensselaer Poly. Inst., 1987-92; reader in crystallography U. London, 1991—2001, prof. molecular biophysics, 2001—; dir. Ctr. for Protein and Membrane Structure and Dynamics, Daresbury Lab., 1999—. Vis. scientist MRC Lab. Molecular Biology, Cambridge, Eng., 1978; Fogarty sr. fellow Birkbeck Coll., U. London, 1990; Disting. vis. prof. Tzu-Chi U. and Academia Sinica, Taiwan, 2004. Assoc. editor Peptide and Protein Letters; mem. editl. adv. bd. Biochemistry; contbr. numerous articles to profl. jours. and books. Jane Coffin Childs fellow, 1977-79; recipient Irma T. Hirschl award, 1980-84, Sci Web award, 1998; Camille and Henry Dreyfus tchr.-scholar, 1986; named Hot Young Scientist Fortune Mag., 1990; Subject of Documentary Film: Hypertension Research for the Future, 1995. Fellow: AAAS, Inst. Biology, Royal Soc. Chemistry; mem.: Brit. Crystallographic Assn. (BSG award 1994), Biophysics Soc. (nat. coun., mem. internat. rels. com., Dayhoff award 1985), Phi Lambda Upsilon, Sigma Xi. Office: U London Birkbeck Coll Dept Crystallography London WC1E 7HX England

WALLACE, DEE, actress; b. Kansas City, Mo., Dec. 14, 1948; d. Robert Stanley and Maxine (Nichols) Bowers; m. Christopher Stone, June 28, 1980 (dec.); m. Skip Belyea; 1 child, Gabriella. BA, U. Kans., 1971. Actress feature films The Christmas Visitor, Secret Admirer, Cujo, E.T., Jimmy the Kid, The Howling, 10; actress ABC movies of the week Eminent Domain, Hostage Flight, A Whale for a Killing; actress CBS movies of the week An Enemy Among Us, Sin of Innocence, The Sky is No Limit, Happy, Surprise, Surprise, The Five of Me, Young Love, First Love; actress NBC movies of the week Wait Til Your Mother Gets Home, Child Bride of Short Creek, Skeezer; actress CBS After School Special Dad's Out of a Job; actress ABC After School Special Run Don't Walk; actress CBS series Police Story, Together We Stand/Nothing is Easy, Lou Grant; actress stage prodns. including Annie Get Your Gun, Oklahoma, My Fair Lady, Applause, Butterflies are Free, Middle of the Night. Spkr. in field; mgr. DWS Acting Studio, Burbank, Calif. Appeared in films including Nevada, 1997, Mutual Needs, 1997, Black Circle Boys, 1997, Bad As I Wanna Be: The Dennis Rodman Story, 1998, Flamingo Dreams, 1998, To Love, Honor and Betray, 1999, Invisible Mom II, 1999, Pirates of the Plain, 1999, Out of the Black, A Month of Sundays, Dead Canaries, Spice of Life, Total Rex, Abominable, Expiration Date, others; appeared on TV shows Cold Case, 2005, Crossing Jordan, 2005, Sons and Daughters, 2005. Fundraiser Actors and Others for Animals, L.A., 1980—, Amanda Found., L.A., 1986, 87; co-host, fundraiser Children's Hospital Telethon, Sta. KCET, L.A., 1985—; spokesperson Nat. Assn. of Children of Alcoholics, 1987—. Mem. Screen Actors Guild, Actors Equity, AFTRA. Methodist. Avocations: dance, singing. Office Phone: 818-876-0386. E-mail: totoent@aol.com.

WALLACE, DOROTHY MAE ADKINS, educator; b. Danville, Va., Nov. 14, 1941; d. George Burton and Ruby Mae (Law) A. BS, Radford Coll., 1964; MS in Bus. Edn., Va. Poly. Inst., 1966. Grad. teaching asst. Va. Poly. Inst., Blacksburg, 1964-65; prof. bus. Chowan Coll., Murfreesboro, N.C., 1965—, chairperson dept. bus., 1985—. Contbr. articles to profl. jours. Mem. Northampton County Hist. Soc., Jackson, N.C., 1979—; treas., sec. Woodland (N.C.) Community Club, 1979—, Woodland Civic Club, 1979—. Mem. Am. Acctg. Assn. Democrat. Baptist. Office: Chowan U One University Pl Murfreesboro NC 27855

WALLACE, ELIZABETH A., music educator; b. Crane, Tex., June 13, 1949; d. Charles Ray and Annie Lea Ellis; m. Alan Craig Wallace, Aug. 22, 1970; children: Elisa Annette West, Jesse Alan. B of Music Edn., Howard Payne U., 1971; MusM, Southwestern Bapt. Theol. Sem., 1977; PhD, Tex. Tech. U., 1990. Tchr., owner pvt. studio, Brownwood, Tex., 1972—73, Ft. Worth, 1973—77; tchr. owner pvt. studio Houston, 1977—79; tchr. owner of pvt. studio Lubbock, 1979—90; prof. music Howard Payne U., Brownwood, 1991—. Accompanist Howard Payne U., Tex. Tech. U., Lubbock Christian U., Bapt. chs., 1971—, Tex. Bapt. Women's Choir, 1995, Tex. Bapt. All State Youth Choir, 1997; tchg. asst., adj. tchr. Tex. Tech. U., Lubbock, 1983-89; adj. tchr. Lubbock Christian U., 1986-90. Soloist, accompanist numerous recitals and concerts. Mem. Music Tchrs. Nat. Assn., Nat. Guild Piano Tchrs., Tex. Music Tchrs. Nat. Assn. (student affiliate bd. 1997-99), Creative Motion Alliance (pres. 1998-2000). Southern Baptist. Home: 3412 3d St Brownwood TX 76801 Office: Howard Payne U Sch Music 1000 Main St Brownwood TX 76801 Business E-Mail: ewallace@hputx.edu.

WALLACE, ELIZABETH ANN (BECKY WALLACE), educator; b. Bartlesville, Okla., Jan. 28, 1939; d. Vernon Harold and Thelma Elizabeth (Ellis) W. BA in English Edn., U. Tulsa, 1962, postgrad., 1965. Cert. secondary English tchr., Okla. Substitute tchr. Bartlesville Pub. Schs., 1963—; clk. U.S. Post Office, Bartlesville, 1970. Publicist Bartlesville Civic Ballet Guild, 1975-94, pres., 1977, 92-94; publicist Bartlesville Civic Ballet Inc., 1974-85, bd. dirs. 1973-83, 94-97, named premier danseuse, 1994; chmn. scholarship com. Green County Rep. Women's Club, Bartlesville, 1990-95, sec., 1992—; mem. Bartlesville Mus., TAPROOTS Oral History Project; pres. Highland Park Ext. Homemakers, 1987, 92-93, publicist, 1986-90, 91-92; sec. adminstrv. coun. Oak Park United Meth. Ch., 1992, fin. chair, 2000, 01, sec., 2004, 05, 06; mem. publicity com. Allied Arts and Humanities Coun., 1980-81. Named Homemaker of Yr., Highland Park Ext. Homemakers, 1990; recipient award for outstanding contbns. and svc. to cmty. Allied Arts and Humanities Coun., 1993. Mem. AAUW (v.p. 1967-69, program v.p. 1993-95), LWV (co-chair local survey com.), Women's Network (program chmn. 1985-87, Meritorious Svc. award 1985-87), Bartlesville Symphony Soc. Avocations: quilting, books, gardening, culinary arts. Home: RR 3 Box 4050 Bartlesville OK 74003-9544

WALLACE, EVELINA VELVIA JOETHA, elementary school educator; arrived in U.S., 1979; d. Milton Rodon Cox Sr. and Leanna Sara Cox; m. Sydney Alexis Wallace IV, Dec. 9, 1989; children: Alexia Justina, Sydney Alexis V. AA, Miami Dade C.C., 1983; BS, Miami Fla. Meml. Coll., 1984. Tchr. S.C. Pherson High Sch., Nassau, The Bahamas, 1984—91, Bayharbor Elem. Sch., Miami, 1991—92, Oak Grove Elem. Sch., 1992—93, North Miami Mid. Sch., 1993—94, Lake Steven Elem. Sch., 1994—97, Meml. Mid. Sch., Orlando, 1997—98, Ctrl. Ave. Elem. Sch., Kissimmee, 1998—99, Kissimmee Elem. Sch, 1999—. Dir. women of region Caribbean Internat. Mins., Kissimmee, 1997, v.p., 1994, marriage counselor, 1994. Mem.: Arts Complete Edn., Fla. Music Educators Assn. Avocations: cooking, travel, singing. Home: 2080 Pine Needle Trail Kissimmee FL 34746 E-mail: evelinawallace@cim.com.

WALLACE, FANNIE MARGARET, minister, religious organization administrator; b. Corpus Christi, Tex., Apr. 20, 1942; d. Isaac Herron and Etha Lena Madison; m. William Taft Wallace, Nov. 1, 1973; children: Robert Terrance Hill, Prinston Damone Hill, Kevin Claudell Hill, Charisma Pitre. BTh, Cornerstone U. & Sem. of Jerusalem, Israel, 1994. Pastor, founder pvt. sch., adminstr., bus. developer Praise Assembly Ministries/Harbor Christian Acad., Del City, Okla., 1993—; CEO Praise Assembly Full Gospel Ministries, Del City, 1993—. Author: Prosperity Belongs to You, 1999, How To Go From Victory to Victory, 1999, Called to Separate, 2000, No More Issues, 2001, Next Level, 2002. Office: Praise Assembly Full Gospel Ministries 3540 SE 15th St Del City OK 73115 Office Phone: 405-677-3553. Business E-Mail: praiseassembly@sbcglobal.net.

WALLACE, FAY MARY, columnist; d. Bruno Francis and Amy Patricia Ferreira; m. Christopher Mullen Wallace, Sept. 8, 1974; children: Roxanne, Rowena, Flora, Victoria. BA, U. Bombay, 1962—66. Licenstrate piano Trinity Coll., London, 1967. Overseas rep. India AFS Internat. Scholarships, NYC, 1967—74; religious edn. tchr. Holy Family Cath. Ch., Dale City, Va., 1984—98; substitute tchr. Prince William Co. Schs., Va., 1994—; columnist Potomac News, Woodbridge, Va., 2003—. Mem. consumer bd. Giant Food, 1980—83; mem., sub-com. chair County Commn. Future, Prince William, 1989—92; co-chair parents' orgn. Cath. U. Am., 2004. Catholic. Avocations: photography, cooking, travel, reading, piano. Home: 13309 Old Delaney Rd Woodbridge VA 22193

WALLACE, GLADYS BALDWIN, librarian; b. Macon, Ga., June 5, 1923; d. Carter Shepherd and Dorothy (Richard) Baldwin; m. Hugh Loring Wallace Jr., Oct. 14, 1941 (div. Sept. 1968); children: Dorothy, Hugh Loring III. BS in Edn., Oglethorpe U., 1961; MLS, Emory U., 1966; EdS, Ga. State U., 1980. Libr. pub. elem. schs., Atlanta, 1956-66; libr. Northside HS, 1966-87, Episc. Cathedral St. Philip. Author: The Time of My Life, 1994, Just a Moment, a Book of Poetry, 2005, Glorious Grass, 1999. Mem. Madison-Morgan Cultural Ctr. Recipient Poet of Merit award, 1999; Ga. Dept. Edn. grantee, 1950, NDEA grantee, 1963, 65. Mem.: Am. Assn. Univ. Women, Am. Assn. Ret. Persons, Atlanta Bot. Garden. Home: NC 6 136 Peachtree Memorial Dr NW Atlanta GA 30309-1096

WALLACE, HELEN MARGARET, pediatrician, preventive medicine physician, educator; b. Hoosick Falls, NY, Feb. 18, 1913; d. Jonas and Ray (Schweizer) W. AB, Wellesley Coll., 1933; MD, Columbia U., 1937; MPH cum laude, Harvard U., 1943. Diplomate Am. Bd. Pediat., Am. Bd. Preventive Medicine. Intern Bellevue Hosp., NYC, 1938-40; child hygiene physician Conn. Health Dept., 1941-42; successively jr. health officer, health officer, chief maternity and newborn div., dir. bur. for handicapped children NYC Health Dept., 1943-55; prof., dir. dept. pub. health NY Med. Coll., 1955-56; prof. maternal and child health U. Minn. Sch. Pub. Health, 1956-59; chief prof. tng. US Children's Bur., 1959-60, chief child health studies, 1961-62; prof. maternal and child health U. Calif. Sch. Pub. Health, Berkeley, Calif., 1962-80, 99; prof., head divsn. maternal and child health Sch. Pub. Health San Diego State U., Calif., 1980—; Univ. Rsch. lectr. San Diego State U., Calif., 1985—. Cons. WHO numerous locations, including Uganda, The Philippines, Turkey, India, Geneva, Iran, Burma, Sri Lanka, East Africa, Australia, Indonesia, China, Taiwan, 1961—, traveling fellow, 1989—; cons. Hahnemann U., Phila., 1993, Ford Found., Colombia, 1971; UN cons. to Health Bur., Beijing, China, 1987; fellow Aiiku Inst. on Maternal and Child Health, Tokyo, and NIH Inst. Child Health and Human Devel., 1994; dir. Family Planning Project, Zimbabwe, 1984-87; vis. prof. U. Calif., Berkeley, 1999, 00, prof. emeritus, 2000—; mem. adv. com., faculty APHA Com. on Continuing Edn. Author, editor: 20 textbooks; editor (sr.): Health and Social Reform for Families for the 21st Century, 2d edit., 2003, Health and Welfare for Families in the 21st Century, 2003 (award Am. Coll. Nursing, Am. Jour. Nursing); contbr. 335 articles to profl. jours. Mem. coun. on Disabled Children to Media, 1991; dir. San Diego County Infant Mortality Study, 1989—, San Diego Study of Prenatal Care, 1991. Recipient Alumnae Achievement award Wellesley Coll., 1982, U. Minn. award, 1985; Ford Found. study grantee, 1986, 87, 88; fellow World Rehab. Fund, India, 1991-92, Fulbright Found., 1992—, NIH Inst. Child Health and Human Devel., 1994, Aiiku Inst. of Maternal-Child Health, Tokyo, 1994. Fellow: APHA (officer sect., chmn. com. on internat. maternal and child health, mem. faculty and adv. com. maternal and child health program 2000, Martha May Eliot award 1978, award in Internat. Maternal and Child Health 2001), Am. Acad. Pediatrics (Job Smith award 1980); mem.: AMA, Am. Sch. Preventive Medicine, Ambulatory Pediatric Assn., Am. Acad. Cerebral Palsy, Assn. Tchrs. Maternal and Child Health. Home: 850 State St San Diego CA 92101-6046 Office Phone: 619-235-4670.

WALLACE, JANE HOUSE, retired geologist; b. Ft. Worth, Aug. 12, 1926; d. Fred Leroy and Helen Gould (Kixmiller) Wallace. AB, Smith Coll., 1947, MA, 1949; postgrad., Bryn Mawr Coll., 1949—52. Geologist U.S. Geol. Survey, 1952—97; chief Pub. Inquiries Offices, Washington, 1964—72, spl. asst. to dir., 1974—97, dep. bur. ethics counselor, 1975—97, Washington liaison Office of Dir., 1978—97; ret., 1997. Recipient Meritorious Service award Dept. Interior, 1971, Disting. Svc. award, 1976, Sec.'s Commendation, 1988, Smith Coll. medal, 1992. Fellow Geol. Socs. Am., Washington (treas. 1963-67); mem. Sigma Xi (assoc.)

WALLACE, JOYCE IRENE MALAKOFF, internist; b. Phila., Nov. 25, 1940; d. Samuel Leonard and Henrietta (Hameroff) Malakoff; m. Lance Arthur Wallace, Aug. 30, 1964 (div. 1974); 1 dau. Julia Ruth; m. Arthur H. Kahn, Oct. 7, 1979 (div. 1986); 1 son, Aryeh N. Kahn. AB, Queens Coll., CUNY, 1961; postgrad., Columbia U., 1962-64; MD, SUNY, 1968. Diplomate Am. Bd. Internal Medicine. Intern St. Vincent's Hosp. Med. Ctr., N.Y.C., 1968-70; practice medicine N.Y.C., 1970-71; resident Manhattan VA Hosp., N.Y.C., 1972, Nassau County Med. Ctr., East Meadow, N.Y., 1972-73; practice medicine North Conway, NH, 1973—74; practice medicine specializing in internal medicine N.Y.C., 1976—; med. dir. FROST'D Primary Care, 1999—2003. Mem. attending staff Nassau County Med. Ctr., 1974, St. Vincent's Hosp. and Med. Ctr., N.Y.C., 1977—; asst. prof. medicine Mt. Sinai Med. Sch., N.Y.C.; pres. Found. for Rsch. on Sexually Transmitted Diseases, Inc., 1986-89, exec. and med. dir., 1989-2003. Fellow ACP, N.Y. Acad. Medicine; mem. Am. Med. Women's Assn., N.Y. County, N.Y. State Med. Socs.

WALLACE, JULIA DIANE, newspaper editor; b. Davenport, Iowa, Dec. 3, 1956; d. Franklin Sherwood and Eleanor Ruth (Pope) W.; m. Doniver Dean Campbell, Aug. 23, 1986; children: Emmaline Livingston Campbell, Eden Jennifer Campbell. BS in Journalism, Northwestern U., 1978. Reporter Norfolk Ledger-Star, Va., 1978-80, Dallas Times Herald, 1980-82; reporter, editor News sect. USA Today, Arlington, Va., 1982-89, mng. editor spl. projects, 1989-92; mng. editor Chgo. Sun-Times, 1992-1996; exec. editor Statesman Jour., Salem, Oreg., 1996—98; mng. editor Ariz. Republic, Phoenix, 1998—2000, Atlanta Jour.-Constitution, 2001—02, editor, 2002—. Mem. Am. Soc. Newspaper Editors. Mailing: Atlanta Journal-Constitution PO Box 4689 Atlanta GA 30302*

WALLACE, KATHY JOAN, secondary school educator; b. Wagoner, Okla., Jan. 4, 1958; d. Albert Buckmaster and Wanda Swadley; children: Amber Parnell, Kristi, Megan. M in Curriculum and Instrn., Okla. City U., 2001; EdB, Northeastern State U., Okla. Standard Teaching Certificate Okla. State Dept. of Edn., 1988. Part-time bus. instr. Northeastern State U., Tahlequah, Okla., 1989; h.s. bus., elem. classroom tchr. Okay Pub. Schools, Okla., 1988—97; bus. tchr. Bemidji H.S., Minn., 1998—99; assoc. dir. rsch. Okla. City U. Evaluation Team for FILM (Family Intergenerational Literacy Model Even Start Programs), 2000—01; classroom tchr. Mustang Mid. Sch., Okla., 2001—03; edn. instr. Mo. Western State U., St. Joseph, 2004—. 1st v.p. Women's C. of C., St. Joseph, Mo., 2006—06. Recipient Grad. with High Honors for Academic Achievement, Okla. City U., 2001—02, Outstanding Med Grad. award, Okla. City U. Edn. Dept., 2001—02. Mem.: ASCD, Nat. Sci. Tchrs. Assn., Nat. Assn. of Multicultural Edn, Kappa Delta Pi, Pi Lambda Theta. Avocations: travel, gardening, reading. Home: 2001 N 34th Terrace Saint Joseph MO 64506 Office: Mo Western State U 4525 Downs Dr Saint Joseph MO 64507 E-mail: jwallace@missouriwestern.edu.

WALLACE, LINDA KAY, mathematics professor; d. John Edward and Marion Sue Wallace. BS, Radford U., 1989, MS, 1991. Educator Prince William County Pub. Sch., Manassas, Va., 1991—98, math. instrnl. specialist, 1998—2001, algebra readiness coord., 2001—06; math. coord. Roanoke City Pub. Schs., Va., 2006—. Ednl. cons. Casio, Inc., Dover, NJ, 2004—. Mem.: Nat. Coun. Tchrs. Math. (assoc.), Nat. Coun. Suprs. Math. (assoc.), Phi Delta Kappa (assoc.; pres. chpt. 1448 2004—05, Outstanding Student of Yr. 1991). Office: 40 Douglass AveNW Roanoke VA 24012 Office Phone: 540-853-6052. Office Fax: 703-441-4497. E-mail: wallaclk@pwcs.edu.

WALLACE, MARY COLETTE, architectural researcher, designer; m. Clay Wallace. BArch, U. Okla., 1986, BA in Philosophy, 1989. Design rschr. various architecture and design firms, 1989—97; pres. Wallace Rsch. Group, Bellevue, Wash., 1998—. Task force mem. NW Regional Sustainable Bldg. Action Plan, Seattle, 1998—99. Contbr. articles to profl. jours.; editor (author): The WRG Newsletter. Cons. Overlake Pk. Presbyn. Ch. /Habitat for Humanity Townhome Project, Bellevue, Wash., 1991—94. Mem.: MENSA, AIA (assoc.), Assn. Ind. Info. Profls. (electronic comm. com. chair list coord. 2003—04). Democrat. Presbyterian. Avocations: swimming, drawing. Office: Wallace Research Group POB 50128 Bellevue WA 98015 Office Phone: 425-637-9049. Business E-Mail: info@wallaceresearch.net.

WALLACE, MARY MONAHAN, elementary, secondary schools and university educator; b. Teaneck, N.J., Nov. 22, 1943; d. Thomas Gabriel and Louise Grace (Monaco) Monahan; m. James Anthony Wallace, Nov. 22, 1978; (dec. May, 1992); 1 child, Meg. BS, Fordham U., 1967; MA, 1971; postgrad. in Supervision, Montclair U., 1978; postgrad. in Edn., various colls. Cert. tchr. language arts, supr., N.Y. 1st and 4th grades tchr. Holy Rosary Sch., Harlem, N.Y., 1963-65; 7th grade tchr. Immaculate Conception Sch., Bronx, N.Y., 1965-66; 8th grade tchr. St. Finbar Sch., Bklyn., 1966-68, St. Patrick Mil. Acad., Harriman, N.Y., 1968-69; English tchr. St. Stephen H.S., Bklyn., N.Y., 1969-70, Holy Rosary Acad., Union City, N.J., 1970-71, Harriman (N.Y.) Coll., 1971-72, Montclair (N.J.) U., 1981-82; English tchr. elem. and secondary schs. Fairlawn (N.J.) Schs., 1972—2003; clin. faculty Montclair U., 1999—2003, adj. faculty, 2004—. Advisor Fair Lawn H.S. Yearbook, 1977-80, Nat. Lang. Arts Olympiad, Fair Lawn, 1987-89; mem. Mid. Sch. Task Force Fair Lawn Schs., 1991-93, dist. wide steering com. Edn. Recognition Day, Fair Lawn, 1992-93, steering com. Fair Lawn Mid. Schs., 1994-97; exec. bd. Profl. Devel. Schs., Montclair U., 2000-03; mem. Fairlawn Bd. Edn., 2004—, bd. v.p., 2006; presenter in field Editor (newsletter) Concern, 1970-72; mem. editorial staff (newsletter) Flea Bytes, 1988-90. Participant Summer in the City U.S. Antipoverty Program, Staten Island, N.Y., 1965; pres. Bear Pond Improvement Assn., 1996—; chairperson spl. events com. marathon '99; mem. Fair Lawn Bd. Edn., 2004—, v.p., 2006 Named Meml. Sch. Tchr. of Yr., NJ Gov.'s Recognition Program, 1993; recipient Ansell Watson award for outstanding contbns. to edn., Montclair U., 2003. Mem.: NEA, Am. Fedn. Tchrs., Fair Lawn Edn. Assn. (treas. 1990—93, pres. 1993—2003), Bergen County Edn. Assn., N.J. Edn. Assn., Montclair U. Adj. Union (first v.p. 2006—). Roman Catholic. Avocations: reading, swimming, boating, travel. Home: 20-18 Saddle River Rd Fair Lawn NJ 07410-5933 E-mail: fairlawn@aol.com.

WALLACE, MARYJEAN ELIZABETH, science educator; b. Cedar Grove, NJ, July 19, 1963; d. Albert Joseph and Jean Wallace. BS summa cum laude, Adelphi U., Garden City, NY, 1985; MA summa cum laude, Ind. State U., Terre Haute, Ind., 1987. Cert. elem. tchr. NJ, secondary edn. earth sci. tchr. NJ, ednl. supr. NJ. Sci. tchr. Meml. Mid. Sch., Cedar Grove, NJ, 1987—91, Burnet Mid. Sch., Union Township, NJ, 1991—2000, Briarcliff Mid. Sch., Mountain Lakes, NJ, 2000—. Eucharistic min. Notre Dame of Mt. Carmel Ch., Cedar Knolls, NJ, 2002—. Named one of Outstanding Softball Players in NJ, Star Ledger, 2000; named to Athletic Hall of Fame, Adelphi U., 2000; Postgraduate scholar, NCAA, 1985. Mem.: NSTA, NJ Sci. Tchrs. Assn., Mountain Lakes Edn. Assn. (v.p. and membership chmn. 2005—), Phi Kappa Pi, Delta Tau Alpha, Kappa Delta Phi. Roman Catholic. Avocations: photography, travel, camping, hiking. Office: Briarcliff Mid Sch 93 Briarcliff Rd Mountain Lakes NJ 07046 Office Phone: 973-334-0342. Personal E-mail: mjwallace15@optonline.net. Business E-Mail: mwallace@mtlakes.org.

WALLACE, MICHELE, writer, educator; b. NYC, Jan. 4, 1952; d. Robert Earl Wallace and Faith Ringgold; m. Eugene Nesmith, Dec. 22, 1989 (div. Nov. 2002). BA, CCNY, 1974, MA in English, 1990; PhD in Cinema Studies, NYU, 1998. Asst. prof. English CUNY, 1989—91; assoc. prof. English, women's studies and film CUNY and CUNY Grad. Ctr., 1991—97, prof., 1998—2006. Pres. Art Without Walls, 1974. Author: Black Macho and the Myth of the Superwoman, 1979, Invisibility Blues: Pop to Theory, 1990, Black Popular Culture, 1992, Dark Designs and Visual Culture, 2004; columnist: The Village Voice, 1996; editor: Women in Art, 1971; mem. editl. bd.: Social Identities, Souls; contbr. to newspapers and popular mags. including Ms., The Village Voice, The Nation, The N.Y. Times, Art Forum, Art In America. Founding mem. Nat. Black Feminist Orgn., 1974; pres. Women Students and Artists for Black Art Liberation, 1970—76. Mem.: PEN, MLA, Oscar Micheaux Soc., Soc. Cinema Studies, Am. Studies Assn., Phi Beta Kappa. Office Phone: 212-650-6367. Personal E-mail: olympiax@aol.com. Business E-Mail: mfw28@cornell.edu.

WALLACE, NICOLLE (NICOLLE DEVENISH), former federal official; b. Orinda, Calif. m. Mark Wallace. BA, U. Calif., Berkley; MA, Medill Sch. of Journalism, Northwestern U. With Calif. Assembly Rep. Caucus, 1997—98, Calif. Rep. Party, 1998; former press aide to CEO Grassroots.com; former press secretary to Gov. Jeb Bush State of Fla.; former communications dir. Fla. State Tech. Office; spl. asst. to Pres. & dir. of media affairs The White House, Washington, 2000—05, asst. to Pres. for comm., 2005—06. Communications dir. Bush-Cheney '04 campaign.

WALLACE, NORA ANN, lawyer; b. Phila., May 24, 1951; AB, Vassar Coll., 1973; JD cum laude, Harvard U., 1976. Bar: N.Y. 1977. Mem. Willkie Farr & Gallagher, N.Y.C. Trustee Vassar Coll., Bklyn. Acad. Music, Bklyn. Acad. Music Endowment Trust; bd. dirs. Joseph Collins Found. Office: Willkie Farr & Gallagher 787 7th Ave New York NY 10019-6099

WALLACE, PATRICIA ELLEN, evangelist, minister; b. Rockville Centre, N.Y., July 29, 1950; d. Bertram Earl Wallace, Jr. and Lorraine Marie File; children: Russell, Ryan, Alicia, Richard, Peter, Jonathan. AA in Theology and Missions, Cathedral Bible Coll., 1999, BA summa cum laude in Theology and Missions, 2005. Lic. minister, pastor Pentecostal Holiness, ordained pastor Ch. of God; cert. victim's advocate N.C., 2005; victim svc. practioner N.C.

Victim Assistance Network Acad., 2005. Evangelist and recording artist Patricia Wallace Ministries, NY, 1975—; pastor Burlington, Vt., 1981—84; pastor and counselor Pentecostal Holiness Ch., Lake City, SC, 1995—99; pastor and chaplain Ch. of God, Cleve., Tenn., 2000—04; pastor and counselor New Harvest Ch. of God, Mint Hill, NC, 2004—. Performer: (albums) Hope in My Darkest Hours, 1992; author: Nine Steps to Being Whole, 2000, When the One You Love Hurts: A Guide to Aid in the Recovery of Domestic Abuse, 2003. Founder, chmn. bd. dirs. Six-Mile Crisis Intervention, Mt. Pleasant, SC, 1995—97; victims advocate, crisis counselor United Way-Turning Point Battered Woman's Shelter, Monroe, NC, 1999—; counselor West Main Crisis Counseling Ctr., Rock Hill, SC, 2002—04. Recipient Cert. of Recognition, Calvary Protestant Ch., 1964, Baldwin Sr. H.S., 1968, United Way, 2002. Avocations: art, singing, guitar. Office: PO Box 952 Monroe NC 28111 Home: 12411 Bain Sch Rd Charlotte NC 28227 Office Phone: 704-545-0550. E-mail: beautifulhawaii@hotmail.com.

WALLACE, PAULA S., academic administrator; 3 children. BA, Furman U.; MEd, EdS, Ga. State U. Co-founder Savannah Coll. Art and Design, 1979, pres., 2000—. Author of children's books. Mem. Skidaway Island United Meth. Ch., Savannah, Ga. Film and Videotape Commn., Ga. C. of C.; bd. dirs. B. B. & T. Bank, Nat. Mus. Women in the Arts. Recipient Oglethorpe Bus. and Profl. Women award, James T. Deason Human Rels. award; named Outstanding Young Woman of Am., Ky. Col.; named to Savannah Bus. Hall of Fame. Office: Savannah Coll Art and Design PO Box 3146 622 Drayton St Savannah GA 31402-3146 Office Phone: 912-525-5200.

WALLACE, PERMELIA FRANKLIN, artist; b. Lexington, Tenn., Oct. 21, 1935; d. Hulon Woodard and Etta Mae (Wood) Franklin; m. Clifford Franklin Wallace; children: Linda Dianne Wallace Lodes, Randy DeWaine Wallace. Grad., Am. Sch., Chgo., 1954. Sec. AT&T, Lucent, 2000—. One woman show includes Fall Art Show, Carnegie Ctr. for History and Arts, Jackson, Tenn., Jackson City Hall; respresented in permanent collections at Jackson Med. ctr., Starlights FCE Club, Smithsonion Art Mus., Washington; Exbhns. incude White House Blue Room, 2004. Mem. Family Community Edn. (reporter 1990, Woman of Yr. 1994), West Tenn. Decorative Painters (pres. 1992), Soc. Decorative Painters (charter mem. 1972), Jackson Art Assn. (reporter 1989), Jackson Bus. Women's Club, Artistic Stampers Anonymous Club (reporter 2002-05), Order Ea. Star. Roman Catholic. Home: 175 Summar Dr Jackson TN 38301-4274

WALLACE, SARAH REESE, banker; b. Newark, Ohio, Apr. 30, 1954; m. John H. Wallace; children: Sarah Hollman, John Gilbert, John Gerald. MBA, Ind. U., 1979; BA, DePauw U., 1976. Mgmt. trainee City Nat. Bank, Columbus, Ohio, 1976-78; with First Fed. Savs. and Loan Assn., Newark, 1980—, pres., 1982-99, chmn., 1999—, also bd. dirs. Trustee Ohio Savs. and Loan League, 1987—94, Thomas J. Evans Found., Newark Campus Devel. Fund, 1999—, DePauw U., 2000—; pres., sec. Thomas J. Evans Found., 1980—; trustee, treas. exec. com. Licking County Found., 1993—95; trustee A Call to Coll., Ctrl. Ohio Tech. Coll., Newark. Recipient Woman of Achievement award, 1993, Oustanding Young Alumni award DePauw U., 1990. Office: PO Box 4460 Newark OH 43058-4460

WALLACE, SHERRY LYNN, speech-language pathologist; b. Omaha, Feb. 27, 1947; d. Don Melvin and Reba Pauline (Cooper) Johnson; m. Rod Wayne Webb, June 16, 1989. BS, U. Kans., 1970, MA in Speech Pathology, 1972. Lic. speech pathologist, Kans., Mo. Speech pathologist Truman Neurol. Ctr., Independence, Mo., 1972-76; program dir. Johnson County (Kans.) Mental Retardation Ctr., 1976-77; dir. speech pathology Shawnee Mission (Kans.) Med. Ctr., 1977—. Cons. Johnson County Devel. Supports, Lenexa, Kans., 1995—. Bd. dirs. Kans. Bapt. Convention, 1968; sec. deacon bd. prairie Bapt. Ch., Prairie Village, Kans., 1997. Mem. Kans. Speech and Hearing Assn., Am. Speech and Hearing Assn., Sertoma Club Lenexa (pres. 1997). Avocations: reading, horseback riding, swimming. Home: 10223 Melrose St Overland Park KS 66214-2323 Office: Shawnee Mission Med Ctr 9100 W 74th St Shawnee Mission KS 66204-4019

WALLACE, STEPHANIE ANN, music educator, conductor; b. Denver, Mar. 28, 1956; d. Carmen Reilly Sutley and Gladys Jane Stults; m. Brett Lee Wallace, July 28, 1979; children: Lindsey Annette, Robin Christine. B of Music Edn., Colo. U., Boulder, 1979. Cert. music tchr. grades K-12 Colo. Tchr. orch. Dist. 12 Five Star Schs., Northglenn, Colo., 1979—82; tchr. cello Broomfield, Colo., 1982—90, Boulder, 1982—90; tchr. orch. Boulder Valley Sch. Dist., 1990—. Condr. and music dir.: Front Range Youth Symphony Orchestras, 1991—, Auspices of the Arvada Ctr. for Arts and Humanities, —, cellist: Cameo String Quartet, 1980—, music arranger: string quartets and orchs., guest conductor:. Mem.: Music Educators Nat. Assn., Am. String Tchrs. Assn. (condr. all-state string orch. 2003), Pi Kappa Lambda (mem. Alpha Tau chpt.). Avocations: scuba diving, snorkeling, bicycling, hiking, fishing. Home: 4343 Eldorado Springs Dr Boulder CO 80303 Office: Boulder Valley Schs Fairview HS Boulder CO 80305

WALLACE, STEPHANIE JEAN, language educator; b. San Diego, Jan. 31, 1978; d. Warren D. and Mary Jo Hoover; m. Jonathan Rexford Wallace, July 1, 2000; children: Bréanna F., Nathanael R. B English Edn., U. NC, Greensboro, 2000. Cert. Nat. Bd. Profl. Tchg. Stds. Tchr. East Forsyth HS, Kernersville, NC, 2000—. Contbr. to textbook, 2006. Ladies Bible study leader Grace Bapt. Temple, Winston-Salem, NC, 2006. Recipient Tchg. Excellence award, NEA, 2005; NC Tchg. Fellows scholar. Mem.: Forsyth Assn. Educators (pres. 2004—), Forsyth Assn. Tchrs. (exec. bd. 2000—), NC Tchr. Cadet Cadre, NC Assn. Educators (exec. bd. 2001—), Kappa Delta Pi. Avocations: reading, writing, cooking. Office: East Forsyth HS 2500 W Mountain St Kernersville NC 27284

WALLACE, TERESA LYNN, art educator; b. Springfield, Mo., Dec. 8, 1962; d. Joe Mack and Lanora Nadine Sanders; m. Richard Everett Wallace, June 6, 1986; children: Hannah Kate, Allison Rae. BA in Elem Edn., Coll. Ozarks, 1986; art cert., Southwest Mo. State U., 2002. Art tchr. Couch Sch., Myrtle, Mo., 1999—2001, Alton Elem. Sch., Alton, Mo., 2002—. V.p. Parent Tchr. Orgn., Alton, 1999; co-creator art scholarships, Alton, 2001. Prin. works include (paintings) The Wailing Wall, Harlin Mus., 1997—, French City Sidewalks, 2001, Mexico, 2003, Mexico Moment, 2004, Open Air Market, Art Show, 1998—, Visions of China, West Plains, Mo., 2000—. Leader PTO, Youth Cmty. Betterment, Alton, 1999. Outstanding Achievement honoree, Internat. Reading Assn., 2005. Baptist. Avocations: flute, reading.

WALLACE DOUGLAS, JEAN, conservationist; b. Des Moines, Iowa, June 30, 1920; d. Henry A. and Ilo Wallace; m. Wallace Leslie Douglas, Oct. 12, 1946; children: David, Joan, Ann. BA, Connecticut Coll., 1943. Pres. Wallace Genetic Found., Washington, D.C., 1965—. Past bd. dirs. America The Beautiful, Am. Bird Conservancy, Cornell Lab. of Ornithology, The Land Inst., Wallace House Birthplace, The Accokeek Found., Am. Farmland Trust, Concern, Henry A. Wallace Inst. for Alternative Agr. Office: Wallace Genetic Found Ste 221 4910 Massachusetts Ave NW Washington DC 20016-4358

WALLACE-HOUSE, MARY ELAINE, writer; m. Robert House. BFA cum laude, U. Nebr., Kearney, 1940; MusM, U. Ill., 1954; postgrad., Music Acad. West, Santa Barbara, Calif., 1955, Eastman Sch. Music, 1960, Fla. State U., 1962. Prof. voice, dir. opera La. Tech. U., Ruston, 1954-62, SUNY-Fredonia, 1962-69, So. Ill. U.-Carbondale, 1969-79; dir. Marjorie Lawrence Opera Theatre, Opera on Wheels; adminstrv. adviser Summer Playhouse, Carbondale; stage mgr. Chautauqua Opera Co., N.Y., 1963; asst. mus. dir., condr. Asolo Festival, Sarasota, Fla., 1961; music editor, critic The Chautauquan Daily; adjudicator Met. Opera auditions; exec. sec. Nat. Opera Assn., 1981-91. Co-author: Opera Scenes for Class and Stage, 1979, (with Robert Wallace) More Operas Scenes for Class and Stage, 1990, Upstage Downstage, 1992. Founding mem. bd. dirs. Rockwall Alliance for the Arts, 2001; founding bd. dirs. Rockwall Musicfest, Rockwall, 2002. Recipient Lifetime Achievement award Nat. Opera Assn., 1998, Alumni award U. Nebr., 1998, Disting. Alumna Kearney Pub. Schs., 2004. Mem. Nat. Opera Assn. (pres. 1974, 75), Music Tchrs. Nat. Assn., Nat. Assn. Tchrs. Singing, AAUP, AAUW, Met. Opera Guild, Mortar Bd., Sigma Tau Delta, Pi Kappa Lambda, Phi Beta, Alpha Psi Omega, Delta Kappa Gamma

WALLACH, ANNE JACKSON See JACKSON, ANNE

WALLACH, CAROL ODILE, elementary school educator; b. New London, Conn., Mar. 4, 1941; d. Russell Earl Newton and Odile Patricia (Bussell) Newton-LeBlanc; m. William Michael Wallach, Aug. 22, 1964; children: James, Andrew, Michael. BA in English, Regis Coll., Weston, Mass., 1963; MS in Edn., So. Conn. State U., 1983. Tchr. grade 5 Sacred Heart Acad., Newton Center, Mass., 1963-64; part-time tchr. chpt. I East Haven (Conn.) Sch. Sys., 1976-88, tchr. grade 5, 1988-91, tchr. grade 6, 1991—. Workshop presenter for tchrs., parents, bds. of edn., regional confs. on math. teaching ideas; adv. bd. for math. frameworkConn. Dept. Edn., 1993—; rep. from sch. dist. to Program Improvement Inst. for Sci. Edn., 1993-95. Prodr./presenter: (video) Discovery Math, 1995. Initiator series parent math and sci. nights R. Carone Sch., 1993—. Recipient Presdl. Award for Excellence in Math. Teaching, NSF, 1994, Celebration of Excellence award Conn. Dept. Edn., 1993; NSF scholar to NASA Tchr. Program, 1993, Wesleyan U. Pimms Program scholar, 1988-89; East Haven/Goals 2000 grantee, 1994—. Mem. Nat. Coun. Tchrs. Math., Nat. Sci. Tchrs. Assn. Avocations: reading, hiking, biking, travel, gardening. Office: Robert Carbone Elem Sch 67 Hudson St East Haven CT 06512-1524

WALLACH, KENYA, mathematics educator; b. Dothan, Ala., Mar. 13, 1977; m. Adam Wallach, Apr. 12, 2003; 1 child, Maya. BS in Math., U. Ala., Tuscaloosa; M in Adminstrn., Cambridge Coll., Mass. Math. tchr. Richmond (Va.) Pub. Schs., 2003—. Recipient R.E.B. award for Tchg. Excellence, Cmty. Found., 2004. Office: 5800 Patterson Ave Richmond VA 23226-2599 Office Phone: 804-285-1015. Business E-Mail: kwallach@richmond.k12.va.us.

WALLACH, MAGDALENA FALKENBERG (CARLA WALLACH), writer; b. Brussels; d. Carl Albert and Renee Antoinette (Meunier) Falkenberg; m. Philip Charles Wallach, Mar. 5, 1950. Student, Columbia U., Hunter Coll., New Sch. for Social Rsch. Ptnr. Williams-Falkenberg Advt. Assocs., Inc., N.Y.C., 1951-55. Author: Reluctant Weekend Gardener, 1971, Interior Decorating with Plants, 1976, Gardening in the City, 1976, Garden in a Teacup, 1978; contbr. articles to N.Y. Times, Glamour, Working Woman, Greenwich Time, Stamford Adv, others. Former bd. dirs. ARC, NYC; active Bruce Mus., 1987-2001, chmn. spl. events 75th anniversary gala, chmn. Renaissance Ball, bd. dirs., also other fundraising activities; founder Greenwich Adult Day Ctr., bd. dirs., v.p., chair annual fund raiser. Mem. Nat. League Am. PEN Women (pres. Greenwich br. 1987-92, Owl award 1996), Authors Guild, Garden Writers Assn., English-Speaking Union (past bd. dirs. Greenwich br.), Alliance Francaise, Nat. Inst. Social Scis. Roman Catholic. Avocations: gardening, reading, travel, music, theater. Home: 126 W Lyon Farm Dr Greenwich CT 06831-4352

WALLACH, PATRICIA, councilman, retired mayor; b. Chgo. m. Ed Wallach; 3 children. Grad., Pasadena City Coll. Mem. city coun. City of El Monte, Calif., 1990-92, mayor, 1992-99, elected mem. of city coun., 2003—. Ret. tchr.'s aide Mountain View Sch. Dist. Past trustee El Monte Union High Sch. Dist., L.A. County High Sch. for the Arts; amb. of goodwill Zamora, Michoacan, Mex., Marcq-en-Baroeul, France, Yung Kang, Hsiang, Republic of China, Minhang, Peoples Republic of China; bd. dirs. Cmty. Redevel. Agy., El Monte Cmty. Access TV Corp.; mem. PTA, Little League Assns.; del. Foothill Transit. Mem. League of Calif. Cities, San Gabriel Valley Coun. of Govts., Independent Cities Assn., U.S./Mex. Sister Cities Assn., Sister Cities Internat., Women of the Moose, El Monte Women's Club. Office Phone: 626-580-2001.

WALLACH-LEVY, WENDEE ESTHER, astronomer; b. N.Y.C., Dec. 29, 1948; d. Leonard Morris and Annette (Cohen) Wallach; m. David H. Levy, Mar. 23, 1997; 1 child, Nanette R. Vigil. BS in Edn., SUNY, Cortland, 1970; MA in Teaching, N.Mex. State U., 1975. Cert. tchr. N.Mex. Tchr. phys. edn. Las Cruces (N.Mex) Pub. Schs., 1970—96; mem. Shoemaker-Levy Observing Team, 1996—; dir. Jarnac Obs., Vail, Ariz., 1997—; mem. Jarnac Sky Survey Team, Vail, 2001—. Intramural and athletic coord. White Sands Sch., 1970—93; instr. swimming N.Mex. State U. Weekend Coll., Las Cruces, N.Mex., 1986—96; dir., coord. learn to swim program ARC, Las Cruces, N.Mex., 1970—96; instr. phys. edn., coach volleyball and track, athletic coord. Sierra Mid. Sch., 1993—96; bd. dirs. Nat. Sharing the Sky Found., 2005—. Co-author: Making Friends with the Stars, Cosmic Discoveries, 2001; co-host (internet radio show) LetsTalkStars.com, 2000, (internet radio show for Meade instruments) Ask David, 2005. Instr., trainer water safety ARC, 1973—98, instr., trainer CPR, 1974—98; instr., trainer life guard, health and safety specialist Doña Ana County, N.Mex., 1988—96, instr. trainer std. first aid N.Mex., 1991—98; chair com. health and safety svcs. Doña Ana County Red Cross, N.Mex.; vol. MDA chairperson Telescopes for Telethon Fundraising Com., 1998—. Named Water Safety Instr. of the Yr., ARC, 1986, 1989, Asteroid 6485 in her honor, 1997; recipient 25 yr. Svc. award, ARC, 1992, 30 Yr. Svc. award, 1997. Mem.: AAHPERD, Nat. Intramural-Recreational Sports Assn., N.Mex. Alliance Health, Phys. Edn. Recreation and Dance (spkr., aquatic chmn. 1990—92), Internat. Dark Sky Assn. (life). Democrat. Jewish. Avocations: skywatching, swimming, needlecrafts, astro photography.

WALLACK, RINA EVELYN, lawyer; b. Pitts.; d. Erwin Norman and Gloria A. (Schacher). AD in Nursing, Delta Coll., 1973; BS cum laude in Psychology, Eastern Mich. U., 1980; JD cum laude, Wayne State U., 1983. Registered nurse Mich.; bar: Calif. 1983. Psychiat. head nurse Ypsilanti (Mich.) State Hosp., 1973-77, instr., nursing educator, 1977-80; teaching asst. contracts Wayne State U., Detroit, 1981-83; legal asst. Wayne County Prosecutor's Office, 1982-83; atty. NLRB, L.A., 1983-86, dir. employee rels. legal svcs. Paramount Pictures Corp., L.A., 1986-89, v.p., 1989-98, v.p., sr. counsel, 1998-2002, sr. v.p., 2002-; Contbr. articles to profl. jours. Instr. ARC, Mich., 1978-80. Recipient Am. Jurisprudence Book award, 1983. Mem. ABA, L.A. County Bar Assn., Am. Trial Lawyers Assn., Mich. Bar Assn., Calif. Bar Assn., Order of Coif. Avocations: shooting, movies, dancing, reading, photography.

WALLEN, SHELIA RENEE, counseling administrator, educator; d. Joel and Shirley Ann Stumbo; m. Jeffrey Don Wallen, Feb. 4, 1989; children: Brandy Alise, Jonathan Richard. MEd, Lindsey Wilson Coll. Sch. Profl. Counseling, Prestonsburg Campus, 2005. Coord. Sch. Profl. Counseling, Prestonsburg, Ky., 2004—. Vol. Paintsville Lake Clean-up Project, Paintsville, 2001—02, Jenny Wiley Clean-up Project, Prestonsburg, 2001—02, Mountain Manor Nursing Home, Prestonsburg, Ky., 2002; cheerleading sponsor, vol. Betsy Layne Elem. Sch., Betsy Layne, 1999—2004; lifetime mem. DAV Ladies Aux., Betsy Layne, 2003; mem. Mayflower Unity Bapt. Ch., Pikeville, 1991—2006. Mem.: ACA, Ky. Counseling Assn., Ky. Mental Health and Counseling Assn., Chi Sigma Iota, Alpha Chi, Phi Theta Kappa. Office Phone: 606-886-3863 67237.

WALLENTINE, KATHIE JO, special education educator; b. Topeka, May 31, 1953; d. Oliver Otis and Dolly Lang; m. Jerry Lee Wallentine, Sept. 10, 1971; children: Jerry, Andrew, Jeremy. MEd, Washburn U., Topeka, 2005. Tchr. Cair Paravel-Latin, Topeka, 1986—92, Unifed Sch. Dist. 501, Topeka, 1991—94, Unified Sch. Dist. 330, Eskridge, Kans., 1993—96, Heritage Christian Sch., Topeka, 1996—99, Unified Sch. Dist. 437, Auburn, Kans., 2002—. Personal E-mail: kathiewallentine@yahoo.com.

WALLENTINE, MARY KATHRYN, secondary educator; b. Moscow, Idaho, Dec. 27, 1943; d. Elwood Vernon and Mary Berenice (Hillard) White; m. William Edward Wallentine, Dec. 29, 1977; 1 child, Vicki. BA, Whitman Coll., 1966. Tchr. math. and art Mt. Rainier H.S., Des Moines, Wash., 1966-85; pres. Highline Edn. Assn., Seattle, 1985-89; tchr. math., dept. head Tyee H.S., SeaTac, Wash., 1988-96, ret. Tchr. leadership cadre Highline Sch. Dist., 1988-92, co-chair dist. site-based decision making com., 1989-92; tchr. leadership cadre Tyee H.S., 1995—, sr. class advisor, graduation advisor, 1994-96. Dir., editor, photographer, prodr. sr. class video Fly Me to the Moon, Tyee H.S., 1995. Precinct committeeperson Dem. Ctrl. Com., King County, Wash., 1980—, state committeewoman, 1982-88, del. nat. conv., 1980—; campaign office mgr. Supt. of Pub. Instrn., 1996, 2000; mem. Bellevue Park Bd. Dirs., 1997-98; sch. grants reader Melinda and Bill Gates Found., 1999-2003. Recipient award Women's Polit. Caucus, 1997. Mem. NEA (resolutions com. 1987-92, ret. adv. coun. 2003-06, nat. del. 1980—, comp. task force 2000—), Nat. Coun. Tchrs. Math. (spkr.), Wash. Edn. Assn. (ret., pres. 2002-06, bd. dirs. 2002-06, mem. retired bd. dollars scholars 2003—, editor We-too, 2006-). Episcopalian. Avocations: gardening, politics, visual arts, community service. Home: 860 100th Ave NE Apt 34 Bellevue WA 98004-4132

WALLER, EUNICE MCLEAN, retired elementary school educator; b. Lillington, N.C., June 29, 1921; d. Absolom and Mary W. (Tucker) McLean; m. William DeHomer Waller, Aug. 9, 1958; m. Henry W. Ferguson, June 29, 1942 (div. June 1954). BS summa cum laude, Fayetteville (N.C.) State U., 1942; MS in Edn., U. Pa., 1952; 6th yr. Cert., U. Vt., 1965. Tchr. Harnett H.S., Dunn, NC, 1942—46, Shawtown H.S., Lillington, NC, 1946—56; demonstration tchr. Fayetteville State U., NC, 1956—58; tchr. 2d and U. Elem. Sch., Washington, 1958—60; tchr., asst. to prin. Fitch Elem. Sch., Washington, 1960—62; 7th grade tchr. Sarah Nance Elem. Sch., Columbia, SC, 1963—64; tchr. 8th grade Clark Lane Mid. Sch., Waterford, Conn., 1969—93; ret., 1993. Instr. dept. edn. Conn. Coll., New London, 1970—2001. Corporator Lawrence Meml. Hosp., New London; commr. ethics City Coun. of New London, Conn., 1990—2001; mayor, dep. mayor Dem. Town Com., New London, 1986—88; Civil Rights commr. City New London, 2006—; state convener State of Conn. Nat. Coun. Negro Women, Inc. sects., Washington, 2006—; v.p. NAACP, New London, 1990—2001; pres. Nat. Coun. Negro Women, New London, 1993—2000; trustee Mitchell Coll., New London, Waterford Country Sch., Conn. Named Woman of the Yr., Nat. Coun. Negro Women, 1993; recipient Lifetime Achievement award, W.E.B. DuBois, 1999, Cmty. Svc. award for outstanding achievement, Opportunities Industry Coun., 1983, Dr. E.E. Smith Highest Honors award, Fayetteville State U., 1942; grantee, NSF, 1965. Mem.: NEA (life; Conn. state dir. 1984—88), Conn. Edn. Assn. (Pub. Relations Achievement award 1988), New London Lions (v.p. 1989—99). Democrat. Baptist. Avocations: civic volunteer, civil rights activitst.

WALLER, NEOLA SHULTZ, retired secondary school educator; b. Canadian County, Okla., Feb. 14, 1929; d. Lewis Ray and Alma Marie (Liebscher) Shultz; m. William Waller, May 28, 1949; children: Mary Ann, Jeffrey Scott. BA, Okla. State U., 1949; M in Tchg. of Sci., Coll. William and Mary, 1972. Secondary math. tchr. Virginia Beach (Va.) City Pub. Schs., 1963—93. Mem. Virginia Beach Arts and Humanities Commn., 1978—79; del. joint conf. U.S./Russia on edn., 1994; mem. Va. Women's Leadership Project; chmn. bd. Baylake United Meth. Ch., Virginia Beach, 1982—83, 1984—86, lay leader; co-chair Va. Ann. Conf. United Meth. Ch. Commn. on Status and Role of Women, 2001—06. Named Secondary Math. Tchr. of Yr. for Va., Va. Coun. Tchrs. of Math., 1985. Mem.: AAUW (Va. treas. 1995—97, Va. membership v.p. 1997—98, Va. pres. 1998—2002, mem.-at-large ednl. found. 2003—), Delta Kappa Gamma. Avocations: travel, reading, hammered dulcimer. Home: 3100 Shore Dr PH 52 Virginia Beach VA 23451-1199

WALLER, STACEY, psychologist; b. Charleston, W. Va., Feb. 12, 1974; d. Clarence V and Glenna J Waller. BA, W. Va. U., 1996; MA, Western Mich. U., 2000, PhD, 2004. Lic. Psychologist. Post doctoral fellow W. Va. U., 2002—04; clin. psychologist W. Va. U. Med. Corp., 2004. Contbr. articles to profl. jours. Mem.: Am. Psychological Assn. Office: W Va U Dept Behavioral Medicine and Psychiatry 930 Chestnut Ridge Rd Morgantown WV 26506 Business E-Mail: swaller@hsc.wvu.edu.

WALLER, WILMA RUTH, retired secondary school educator, librarian; b. Jacksonville, Tex., Nov. 15, 1921; d. William Wesley and Myrtle (Nesbitt) W. BA with honors, Tex. Woman's U., 1954, MA with honors, 1963, MLS with honors, 1976. Tchr. English Dell (Ark.) High Sch., 1953-54, Jefferson (Tex.) Ind. Schs., 1954-56, Tyler (Tex.) Ind. Schs., 1956-68; librarian Wise County Schs., Decatur, Tex., 1969-71, Thomas K. Gorman High Sch., Tyler, 1971-74, Sweetwater (Tex.) Ind. Sch. Dist., 1974-86; ret. Lectr., book reviewer for various clubs. Active in past as vol. for ARC, U. Tex. Health Ctr. Ford Found. fellow, 1959; recipient Delta Kappa Gamma Achievement award, 1992. Mem. UDC, Smith County Ret. Sch. Pers., Bible Study Group, Delta Kappa Gamma. Republican. Baptist. Avocations: reading, gourmet cooking, piano, writing. Home: 1117 N Azalea Dr Tyler TX 75701-5206

WALLERSTEIN, BETTY COOPER, clinical social worker, family therapist; b. Ohio, Mar. 24, 1936; d. Joseph and Adele (Haberfeld) Cooper; m. David D. Wallerstein, May 29, 1966; children: Andrew Jonathan, Susan Eva AB, Goucher Coll., 1958; MSW, Howard U., 1960; postgrad. cert. in social agy. supervision/adminstrn., Hunter Coll., 1980. Cert. clin. social worker. Caseworker Mass. SPCC, Boston, 1960—62; psychotherapist Jewish Bd. Guardians, Manhattan, 1962—65; caseworker Georgetown Adolescent Clinic, Washington, 1965; family therapist Family Mental Health Clinic Jewish Family Svcs., Manhattan, 1966—71, supr. casework, 1968; pvt. practice N.Y.C., 1971—. Guest lectr. various colls.; presenter Am. Ortho psychiat. Assn., 1966; presenter in field. Co-chair, founder Coalition to Save City and Suburban Housing, Inc., N.Y.C., 1985—94; founder, pres. 40 Blocks E. 79th St. Neighborhood Assn., N.Y.C., 1984—2006; founder Neighbors R Us, 1996, Cmty. Coalition, 1998; co-founder CPR Zoning Coalition, 2001; apptd. Cmty. Planning Bd. 8. Recipient Disting. Pub. Svc. award, Goucher Coll., Our Town Leadership awards, Mayor's award for Vol. Leadership Excellence, Boro Pres. award for Vol. Pub. Svc., Ralph Menapace award in Historic Preservation, August Hecksher award in Zoning Planning, East Sider award, 2001, 2005, State Senate Woman of Distinction award, Jane Brown award for Housing Adv., 2005, Brooke Russell Astor award, Jane Brown award. Mem. NASW Avocations: philanthropic work for N.Y.C. arts groups, hospitals and Jewish/Israeli causes, travel, opera, classical music, theater.

WALLEY, VICKY CABANISS, medical/surgical consultant; b. Hattiesburg, Miss., Dec. 5, 1952; d. Tolly C. and Dorothy Ann (Dearman) Cabaniss; children: Sara Suzanne Walley, Laurel Elizabeth Walley. BS in Nursing, U. Miss. Med. Ctr., 1975, M of Nursing, 1978; postgrad., La. State U. Med. Ctr., 1986—. Asst. prof. U. So. Miss., Hattiesburg, 1979-86; staff nurse Tulane Med. Ctr., New Orleans, 1986; staff nurse telemetry Drs. Hosp. of Jefferson, Metairie, La., 1987-89; instr. La. State U. Med. Ctr. Sch. Nursing, New Orleans, 1990—94, U. So. Miss., Hattiesburg, 1994—2004; assoc. prof. William Carey U. Sch. Nursing, Hattiesburg, 2004—. Mem. Am. Nurses Assn., Sigma Theta Tau. Home: PO Box 1737 Purvis MS 39475-1737 Office Phone: 601-318-6112. Business E-Mail: vicky.walley@wmcarey.edu.

WALLINGFORD, ANNE, freelance/self-employed writer, marketing professional, consultant; b. Chgo., June 29, 1949; d. Lester Arlyn and Roseanne (Jones) W. BS in Edn., Chgo. State U., 1975. Cert. elem. and mid. sch. tchr., Ill. Profl. dressmaker Annie's Original's, Chgo., 1968-72; instr., asst. prin., St. Bonaventure Sch., Chgo., 1972-81; instr., chair sci. dept. Our Lady of Lourdes Sch., Chgo., 1981-87; product designer, catalog mgr. FSC Ednl., Inc., Mansfield, Ohio, 1988-91; interim dir. pub. rels. Shelby Meml. Hosp., 1991-92; founder, dir. Anne Wallingford WordSmith, Chgo., 1992—. Instr. English lit. and bus. writing North Ctrl. Tech. Coll., 1991-92; catalog/project developer ETA, 1992-95, Sargent-Welch, 1993-2002, Basic Sci., 2003—; permissions editor McGraw-Hill, 2000—; tech. writer United Sci., 2002—; cons. in field. Contbr. articles to profl. jours. and newspapers. Active The Vol. Ctr., Mansfield, 1992-93, steering com. Wright Community Ctr., 1991; treas. Wolfram St. Block Club, Chgo., 1975-78. Recipient Gold award Adler Planetarium, Chgo., 1985. Mem. Nat. Writers Union, Chgo., Women in Pub. (Individual Excellence in Prodn., 1994, 95), Soc. Tech. Communicators, Profl. Freelance Assn. (founder, pres., 1991-92), Editl. Freelancers Assn., Mensa. Avocations: telecommunications, reading, theater, museums.

WALLINGTON, PATRICIA MCDEVITT, computer company executive; b. Phila., July 29, 1940; d. James J. and Mary (Eschbach) McDevitt; m. William R. Wallington; 1 child, Colleen Xydis. BBA, U. Pa., 1975; MBA, Drexel U., 1978; postgrad. mgmt. devel., Harvard U., 1981. Project mgr. Fidelity Mut., Phila., 1965-72, Penn Mut. Ins. Co., Phila., 1972-77; mgr. info. systems Sun Info. Svcs., Phila., 1977-81; dir. info. systems Sun Exploration & Prodn. Co., Dallas, 1981-87; sr. v.p., chief info. officer Mass. Mut. Life Ins. Co., Springfield, 1987-89; corp. v.p., chief info. officer Xerox Corp., Rochester, NY, 1989—99; pres. CIO Assocs., Sarasota, Fla., 2000—. Mem. MBA adv. bd. Baylor U., Waco, Tex., 1986-88; bd. dirs. FINA, Inc., Middlesex Mut. P&C Co. Mem. adv. bd. Handicap Ctr.-HUP, Phila., 1978-80; v.p. fin. Girls Club Dallas, 1986-87. Named one of Top 100 Women in Tech., 1994, Hall of Fame, 1997, CIO mag., 1997. Mem. Soc. for Info. Mgmt.

WALLIS, DIANA LYNN, artistic director; b. Windsor, Eng., Dec. 11, 1946; d. Dennis Blackwell and Joan Williamson (Gatcombe) W. Grad., Royal Ballet Sch., Eng., 1962-65. Dancer Royal Ballet Touring Co., London, 1965-68; ballet mistress Royal Ballet Sch., London, 1969-81, dep. ballet prin., 1981-84; artistic coord. Nat. Ballet of Can., Toronto, 1984-86, assoc. artistic dir., 1986-87, co-artistic dir., 1987-89; free-lance prod., tchr. London; dep. artistic dir. English Nat. Ballet, London, 1990-94; artistic dir. Royal Acad. Dance, 1994—. Fellow Imperial Soc. Tchrs. Dancing. Office Phone: 020 7326 8012. Business E-Mail: lwallis@rad.org.uk.

WALLIS, HALEY HICKMAN, elementary school educator; d. James Ellis and Rita Hemphill Hickman; m. Haley Hickman Hickman, July 7, 2001. BA in Elem. and Spl. Edn., U. Miss., Oxford, 2001. Tchr. 6th grade Rankin County Schs., Brandon, Miss., 2001—. Recipient Tchr. Yr., NW Rankin Mid. Sch. 6th Grade, 2005. Mem.: Miss. Assn. Educators (assoc.). Home: 212 Faith Way Brandon MS 39042 Office: Northwest Rankin Middle School 1 Paw Print Place Brandon MS 39047 Office Phone: 601-992-1329.

WALLIS, MARY CAMILLA, civic leader; b. Albany, N.Y., Nov. 3, 1923; d. Huntington and Mary Camilla (McKim) Williams; m. Richard Fisher Wallis, Aug. 20, 1955; children: Maria Fisher, Sylvia Camilla. BA, Bryn Mawr Coll., 1946. Research asst. Cryogenic Lab Johns Hopkins U., Balt., 1946-52, research assoc. Applied Physics Lab. Silver Spring, Md., 1952-55; pres. Natural History Found. Orange County, Newport Beach, Calif., 1978. Docent Newport-Mesa Unified Sch. Dist., 1972-80, Smithsonian Inst., Washington, 1956-64. Contbr. articles profl. jours. Vol. curator Natural History Found. Orange County, 1980-91; bd. dirs. Orange County Natural History Mus., 1996—; pres. Carderock Springs (Md.) PTA, 1967; v.p. Newport Beach Parent Faculty Orgn., 1971; pres. U. Calif. Irvine Town and Gown, 1976-77. Mem. Geol. Soc. Am., Univ. Club (Irvine) Republican. Episcopalian. Avocations: fossil collecting, photography. Home: 2635 Alta Vista Dr Newport Beach CA 92660-4102

WALLISCH, CAROLYN E., principal; b. Denver, Aug. 23, 1939; d. Morgan Franklin and Margaret C. (Kopf) White; m. Darrell Dean Wallisch, June 9, 1963; children: Michael Dean, Kerri Elise. BA in Elem. Edn., U. No. Colo., 1961, MA in Elem. Edn., 1965; postgrad., Denver U., 1989. Cert. tchr. grades K-8, adminstrn. grades K-12. Tchr. grade 1 San Jose Unified Sch. Dist., 1961-62, Greeley (Colo.) Pub. Schs., 1962-69; tchr. grades 2-8, dean of students Jefferson County Schs., Lakewood, Colo., 1984-94; prin. grades K-5 Littleton (Colo.) Pub. Schs., 1994—2001; ret., 2001. Adj. prof. dept. edn. Colo. Christian U., Lakewood, Colo. Contbr. articles to profl. jours. Leader 4-H Clubs of Am., Littleton, 1982-84, Girl Scouts U.S.A., Littleton, 1979-82; den leader Boy Scouts Am., Littleton, 1976-78; precinct committeewoman Littleton, 1984-90. Named one of Outstanding Young Women of Am., 1965, Model Tchr., ABC News Peter Jennings Who's Happening in Edn., 1993, Instr. Mag., 1993. Mem. ASCD, Internat. Reading Assn. (Colo. coun. 1989—), Colo. Coun. Tchrs. Math. (conf. presenter), Colo. Assn. Sch. Execs. (conf. presenter), PTO (v.p. 1994—), Kiwanis, Kappa Delta Pi (bd. dirs.), Sigma Sigma Sigma (bd. dirs.), Alpha Delta Kappa (bd. dirs.), Phi Delta Kappa (bd. dirs., rsch. chmn. 1987—). Republican. Avocations: tennis, golf. Home: 5549 W Hinsdale Ave Littleton CO 80128-7021 Office: Colo Christian U Sch Edn 180 South Garrison St Lakewood CO 80226

WALLISON, FRIEDA K., lawyer; b. N.Y.C., Jan. 15, 1943; d. Ruvin H. and Edith (Landes) Koslow; m. Peter J. Wallison, Nov. 24, 1966; children: Ethan S., Jeremy L., Rebecca K. AB, Smith Coll., 1963; LLB, Harvard U., 1966. Bar: N.Y. 1967, D.C. 1982. Assoc. Carter, Ledyard & Milburn, N.Y.C., 1966-75; spl. counsel divsn. market regulation SEC, Washington, 1975; exec. dir., gen. counsel Mcpl. Securities Rulemaking Bd., Washington, 1975-78; ptnr. Rogers & Wells, N.Y.C. and Washington, 1978-83, Jones, Day, Reavis & Pogue, N.Y.C. and Washington, 1983-98; mem. Govtl. Acctg. Standards Coun., Washington, 1984-90, Nat. Coun. on Pub. Works Improvement, Washington, 1985-88; vice chair environ. fin. adv. bd. EPA, 1988-92. Contbr. articles to profl. jours. Fellow Am. Bar Found.; mem. N.Y.C. Bar Assn.

WALLNER, AMANDA OBER, retired music educator; d. William and Louise Ober; m. William Wallner, June 27, 1964. BS, Ithaca Coll., 1964; postgrad., Conn. Coll., 1988-89, U. Freiburg, Germany, 1972. Cert. tchr. Music educator Guilford (Conn.) Pub. Schs., 1978—99. Founder, dir. Checkerberry Theater Prodns., Guilford, Conn., 1981-82. Performer Conn. Artist Prodns., 1977-82, Young Audiences Inc., 1974-75; recitalist, Mich. State U. Lansing C.C. Prodn., 1975-76. Founder, pres. E. Lansing (Mich.) Com. for Children's TV, 1973-76, founder Citizen's United for Better Broadcasting, E. Lansing, 1973; mem. adv. com. WGRS, WMNR Fine Arts Radio, 1996—; mem. scholarship com. Shoreline Alliance for Arts. Recipient Resolution of Tribute, citation LVW, 1996, Diana award Senate Concurrent Resolution, East Lansing, 1975, Gen. Assembly Official Citation, the Conn. House, 1995, Celebration of Excellence, Conn. State Bd. of Edn., Hartford, 1995, Katherine Dunham award, Conn. Edn. Assn., Human and Civil Rights Com., Hartford, 1995, selected Internat. Festival Arts & Ideas Youth Summit, New Haven, 1996, Internat. Voice Contest, Vienna, 1972, Susan B. Anthony award Conn. Edn. Assn., 1997; Hilda Maehling grant Nat. Found. Improvement of Edn., 1995. Mem.: AAUW.

WALLNER, MELISSA KAY, music and theater educator, director; d. Stephen John and Barbara Kay Wallner. MusB, Pa. State U., 1995; MusM, U. Wyo., 1997; student, U. Nebr., 1997—99. Grad. tchg. asst. U. Wyo., Laramie, Wyo., 1995—97, U. Nebr., Lincoln, 1997—99; choral dir. Rio Rancho HS, N.Mex., 2000; substitute tchr. Poudre Sch. Dist., Fort Collins, Colo., 2000—02, Cherry Creek Schs., Greenwood Village, 2002, Lincoln Pub. Schs., 2002—03; choir, drama tchr. Poudre Sch. Dist., Fort Collins, Colo., 2003—. Adjudicator, clinician Lesher Jr. HS Solo and Ensemble Festival, Fort Collins, 2000; coll. instr., Fort Collins, 2000—04; diction instr. U. Nebr., Lincoln, 2003; voice instr. Concordia U., Seward, 2003; dir. music Blessed John XXIII Univ. Ctr., Fort Collins, 2004—. Actor: (musical) On the Town, 2002, Carnival, 1998, Oklahoma!, 1997, Carousel, 1997, Into the Woods, Nuncrackers, 2001, Titanic, Do Patent Leather Shoes Really Reflect Up?, 2001, The Sound of Music, 2000, The Taffetas, Sweeney Todd, 1999, Big River, 1998, (musical revue) Some Enchanted Evening, 1998; singer: (opera scenes) Manon, 1999, (opera) Amahl and the Night Visitors, 2000; dir.: (opera) Amahl and the Night Visitors, 1995; singer: (opera) The Medium, 1995, Riders to the Sea, 1994, (reunion concert) Play it Again Sam, 2000, three doctoral voice recitals, doctoral lecture recital; singer: (soloist) National Anthem; featured soloist (play) A Christmas Carol, 1998; singer (soprano soloist): Carmina Burana, (vespers) Mozart Vesperae solennes de Domenica, 1997, (requiem) Brahms Requiem, 1996. Com. mem. U. Nebr., Lincoln, 1998—99. Recipient Marjorie Jane Brewster award for Grad. Study Music, 1996; Grad. fellowship, Wheeler, McDonald, Reichenbach, 1998, Wheeler fellowship, 1999. Mem.: Nat. Pastoral Musicians, Colo. Music Educators Assn., Profl. Educators Assn., Nat. Assn. Tchrs. Singing (Vocal Excellence award 1994), Soc. Am. Fight Dirs., U. Wyo. Alumni Assn. Roman Catholic. Avocations: running, cross-training, stage combat, reading. Office: Lesher Jr High Sch 1400 Stover St Fort Collins CO 80528 Office Phone: 970-472-3846.

WALLOWICZ, MARCELLA LOUISE, mathematics professor; b. Phila., Nov. 7, 1955; d. John Michael Wallowicz Sr. and Marcella Ann (Sayre) Wallowicz. Masters in Math, Villanova U., 1988; postgrad., U. of Pitts., 2000—. Math. instr. Nazareth Acad., 1983—93, dept. chair, 1992—93; instr. of math. Holy Family U., Phila, 1993—96, asst. prof. of math. Phila., 1996—. Mem. Sisters of the Holy Family of Nazareth, Phila., 1978. Fellow Tchg. Assistantship, U. of Pitts., 2000-2002. Mem.: Math. Assn. Am. (corr.), Nat. Honor Soc. (corr.), Kappa Mu Epsilon (corr.). Roman Catholic. Avocations: reading, music. Home: 4800 Stevenson St Philadelphia PA 19114 Office: Holy Family U 9801 Frankford Ave Philadelphia PA 19114 Office Phone: 215-637-7700. Personal E-mail: smwallowicz@holyfamily.edu.

WALLS, MARTHA ANN WILLIAMS (MRS. B. CARMAGE WALLS), publishing executive; b. Gadsden, Ala., Apr. 21, 1927; d. Aubrey Joseph and Inez (Cooper) Williams; m. B. Carmage Walls, Jan. 2, 1954; children: Byrd Cooper, Lissa Walls Vahldiek. Student pub. schs., Gadsden. Pres., dir. Walls Newspapers, Inc., 1969-70; sec., treas., dir. Summer Camps, Inc., Guntersville, Ala., 1954-69; CEO, pres., dir. So. Newspapers, Inc., Houston, 1970—; pres., dir. So. Newspapers of Ala., Inc., Scottsboro. V.p., dir. Ft. Payne (Ala.) Newspapers, Inc., Galveston Newspapers, Inc.; dir. Monroe (Ga.) Newspapers, Inc.; bd. dirs. Jefferson Pilot Corp., Greensboro, N.C., 1990-98, Jefferson-Pilot Life Ins. Co., 1990-98, Jefferson Pilot Comm., 1990-98. Bd. dirs. Montgomery Acad., 1970-74. Mem.: Soc. Profl. Journalists. Episcopalian. Office: 5701 Woodway Ste 300 Houston TX 77057 Personal E-mail: mwalls@sninews.com.

WALLSKOG, JOYCE MARIE, nursing educator, retired psychologist; b. Melrose Park, Ill., Apr. 20, 1942; BSN, Alverno Coll., 1977; MSN, U. Wis., Milw., 1982; PhD, Marquette U., Milw., 1992. RN, Wis.; lic. psychologist; diplomate Am. Coll. Forensic Examiners. Staff nurse St. Mary's Hill Hosp., Milw., 1977—78, Waukesha (Wis.) Meml. Hosp., 1978—80, clin. nurse specialist, 1980—87; asst. prof. nursing Marquette U., Milw., 1986—2005; psychotherapist Psychiat. Assocs. Comprehensive Services, Ltd., Milw., 1982—85; nurse psychotherapist Counseling and Wellness Ctr., Waukesha, 1982—2005; adv. practice nurse prescriber, 1995—2005; guest lectr. Concordia U., Milw., 2005. Cons. Alverno Coll., Milw., 1983-84, Health Care Cons., Sussex, Wis., 1985—; coord. Waukesha Premenstrual Syndrome Program, 1980—; nurse psychotherapist Stress Mgmt. and Mental Health Svcs., Waukesha, 1991-94; co-founder Turning Point Mental Health and Cons. Svcs., Waukesha, 1994—; advanced practice nurse prescriber, 1995—. Contbr. articles to profl. jours. Bd. dirs. Waukesha County Mental Health Assn., 1982; mem. Waukesha County Unified Svcs., 1984; adv. bd. Northwest Rehab. Ctr., 1992-94; advisor Resolve Through Sharing, 1986-2001, Women's Health Svcs., 1987-2001; advisor Parish Nurse Program. Mem. APA, ANA (coun. psychiat. and mental health nursing), Wis. Nurses Assn. (rep. Wis. Coalition on Sexual Misconduct by Psychotherapists and Counselors 1988-93), Delta Upsilon Sigma, Phi Lambda Delta. Personal E-mail: wallskogj@aol.com.

WALRATH, MARY THERESE, elementary school educator; b. Ann Arbor, Mich., Nov. 4, 1946; d. Orville Joseph and Rita Agnes (Morrissey) Iott; m. Warren Kelly Walrath, Sept. 15, 1996; m. Patrick Michael Tuell (div.); children: Matthew J. Tuell, Daniel S. Tuell, Michael P. Tuell. BS in Edn., Siena Heights U., Adrian, Mich., 1968; M in Guidance & Counseling, Ea. Mich. U., Ypsilanti, 1991. Cert. Tchr. Mich. Dept. Edn., 1991. Religious edn. coord. St. Alphonsus Ch., Deerfield, Mich., 1980—81; musician liturgist St. Peter Ch., Eaton Rapids, 1981—83; pastoral min. Holy Spirit Ch., Hamburg, 1983—85; music educator Immaculate Heart/St. Casimir, Lansing, 1985—86; musician/liturgist, choir dir. St. Mary Ch., Charlotte, 1987—96; 5th-8th grade lang. arts tchr. Holy Cross Sch., Lansing, 1986—91; 5th grade lang. arts/social studies tchr. Charlotte Mid. Sch., 1991—. Co-dir. Gt. Lakes Camp & Trail Assn., Lansing, 1989—93; bd. mem. Youth Advocate Program, Eaton Rapids, 1982—83. Soloist St. Mary Cathedral, Lansing, 1985—2000; music worship leader Diocese of Lansing Jail Ministry, 1993—. Mem.: NEA, Mich. Edn. Assn. Avocations: piano, guitar, knitting, singing, reading. Home: 358 Stratford Ct Dimondale MI 48821 Office: Charlotte Mid Sch 1068 Carlisle Charlotte MI 48813

WALRATH, PATRICIA A., state legislator; b. Brainerd, Minn., Aug. 11, 1941; d. Joseph James and Pansy Patricia (Drake) McCarvill; m. Robert Eugene Walrath, Sept. 1, 1961; children: Karen, Susan, David, Julie. BS, Bemidji State U., 1962; MS, SUNY, Oswego, 1975. Cert. secondary math. tchr., N.Y., Mass. Programmer analyst Control Data Corp., Mpls., 1962-65; crewleader dept. commerce U.S. Census, Middlesex County, Mass., 1979-80; selectman Town of Stow, Mass., 1980-85; tchr. math. Hale Jr. High Sch., Stow, 1981-82; instr. math. Johnson & Wale Coll. Hanscom AFB, Bedford, Mass., 1983-84, test examiner, 1983-84; state rep. 3d Middlesex dist. State of Mass., Boston, 1985—. Many coms. including most recently; chmn. com. long term debt and capital expenditures Mass. Ho. of Reps., 1997—2001, asst. whip, floor chair, 2001—04, chmn. healthcare financing com., 2005—. Chmn. Mass. Indoor Air Pollution Commn., Boston, 1987-88; mem. Stow Dem. Com., 1988—. Recipient Disting. Svc. award Auburn N.Y. Jaycees, 1976. Mem. LWV (pres. 1973-76, dir. fin. 1977-78), Mass. Legislators' Assn., Mass. Dem. Leadership Coun. (v.p. 1991-92, co-chmn. 1993-94, treas. 1995-99), Mass. Women's Legis. Caucus (chair 1986). Roman Catholic. Avocations: gardening, stamp collecting/philately, travel. Home: 20 Middlemost Way Stow MA 01775-1363 Office: State Capital RM 236 Boston MA 02133 Office Phone: 617-722-2430. Business E-Mail: Rep.PatriciaWalrath@hou.state.ma.us.

WALSH, ALANA JOY, science educator; b. Mineola, N.Y., July 3, 1976; d. Patrick Joseph and Diane Anita Walsh. BS, U. of the Incarnate Word, San Antonio, 1999. Cert. phys. sci. 8-12 Tex. Sci. tchr. Del Rio H.S., Tex., 2003—. With USN. Mem.: STAT. Office Phone: 830-765-0004. E-mail: awalsh45@yahoo.com.

WALSH, ALEXANDRA M., lawyer; b. 1972; BA summa cum laude, Bowdoin Coll., 1995; JD, Stanford Univ., 2001. Bar: Md. 2004. Law clk. U.S. Ct. Appeals (D.C. cir.), Washington, 2001—02; assoc. Latham & Watkins, Washington, 2003; law clk. to Hon. Stephen G. Breyer U.S. Supreme Ct., Washington, 2003—04; assoc. Baker Botts, Washington, 2004—. Mem.: Order of the Coif. Office: Baker Botts LLP The Warner 1299 Pennsylvania Ave Washington DC 20004-2400

WALSH, ARLINE MARIE, retired alcohol/drug abuse services professional; b. NY, Nov. 09; d. Henry George and Agatha Rita Lubatty. BA in English and Anthropology, Hunter Coll., N.Y.; MEd in Guidance and Counseling, Coll. of Staten Island, N.Y., 1984; postgrad., Rutgers U., 1983. Nat. cert. counselor, credentialed substance abuse counselor. Clin. dir. Residential Care Ctr. for Adults Cath. Charities, Queens Village, N.Y., 1985-86; supr. Luth. Med. Ctr., Bklyn., 1986-89; guidance counselor Ditmas Intermediate Sch., Bklyn., 1989-90, Wm. McKinley Intermediate Sch., Bklyn., 1990—2003; ret. Mem. Am. Mental Health Counselor Assn. Avocations: bicycling, dance, swimming, walking, travel. Home: 5147 E Hermosa Dr Cornville AZ 86325

WALSH, DIANA CHAPMAN, academic administrator, sociologist, educator; b. Phila., July 30, 1944; d. Robert Francis and Gwen (Jenkins) Chapman; m. Christopher Thomas Walsh, June 18, 1966; 1 child, Allison Chapman. BA in English, Wellesley Coll., 1966; MS in Journalism, Boston U. Sch. of Pub. Comm., 1971; PhD in Health Policy, Boston U., 1983; LHD (hon.), Boston U, 1994, Amer. Coll. of Greece, Athens, 1995, U. Mass., Amherst, 1999; LHD, Northeastern U., 2003. Dir. info., edn. Planned Parenthood League, Newton, Mass., 1971—74; sr. program assoc. Dept Pub. Health, Boston, 1974—76; assoc. dir. Boston U. Health Policy Inst., 1985—90; prof. Sch. Pub. Health, Sch. Medicine, Boston U., 1987—90, adj. prof. pub. health, 1990—; Florence Sprague Norman and Laura Smart Norman prof., chair dept. health and social behavior Harvard Sch. Pub. Health, 1990—93, adj. prof., 1993—; pres. Wellesley Coll., 1993—. Author: (book) Corporate Physicians, 1987; editor: Women, Work and Health: Challenges to Corporate Policy, 1980, (book series) Industry and Health Care, 1977—80; co-author: Payer, Provider, Consumer, 1977; contbr. articles to profl. jours. Bd. dirs. Planned Parenthood League of Mass., 1974—79, 1981—85, bd. overseers, 1993—94; trustee Occupl. Physicians Scholarship Fund, 1987—94, WGBH Ednl. Found., 1993—2000. Recipient Book of the Yr. award, Am. Jour. Nursing, 1980; fellow, Kellogg Nat. fellow, 1987—90. Mem.: AHA, AAAS, Consortium on Financing Higher Edn., State Street Corp. (chair 2003—04), Mass. Pub. Health Assn., Soc. for the Study of Social Problems, Am. Sociol. Assn. Avocations: gender and health, social policy, writing, skiing. Office: Wellesley Coll Office of the Pres 106 Central St Wellesley MA 02481-8268 Office Phone: 781-283-2237. E-mail: president@wellesley.edu.*

WALSH, DIANE, pianist; b. Washington, Aug. 16, 1950; d. William Donald and Estelle Louise (Stokes) W.; m. Henry Forbes, 1969 (div. 1979); m. Richard Pollak, 1982. MusB, Juilliard Sch. Music, 1971; MusM, Mannes Coll., 1982. N.Y.C. debut Young Concert Artists Series, 1974; founding mem. Mannes Trio, 1983-94; solo appearances include: Kennedy Ctr. for Performing Arts, Washington, 1976, Met. Mus., N.Y.C., 1976, Wigmore Hall, London, 1980, Merkin Concert Hall, 1989, Miller Theatre, 1994, 96; with Mannes Trio: Lincoln Ctr.'s Alice Tully Hall, Libr. of Congress, 1987; appeared with maj. orchs. worldwide, including St. Louis Symphony, Indpls. Symphony, San Francisco Symphony, Am. Symphony, Austin (Tex.) Symphony, Bavarian Radio Symphony of Munich, Berlin Radio Symphony, Radio Symphony Frankfurt, Radio Symphony Stuttgart; has toured Europe, N.Am., S.Am., C.Am., Russia; Marlboro Festival, 1982, Bard Festival, 1990-99, Santa Fe (N.Mex.) Festival, 1995; recs. for Nonesuch Records, 1980, 82, Book-of-Month Records, 1985, Music and Arts, 1990, CRI, 1991, Koch, 1995, Biddulph Records, 1998, Stereophile, 1998, Newport Classic, 1998, Sony, 2000, Bridge, 2004; artistic dir. Skaneateles Festival, 1999-2004; mem. piano and chamber music faculty Mannes Coll. Music, 1982—. Recipient 3d prize Busoni Internat. Piano Competition, Italy, 1974, 2nd prize Mozart Internat. Piano Competition, Salzburg, Austria, 1975, 1st prize Munich Internat. Piano Competition, 1975, Naumburg Chamber Music award, 1986, Classical Recording Found. award, 2004, Classical Internet award, 2004; NEA grantee, 1981. Office Phone: 212-580-0210.

WALSH, ELIZABETH JAMESON, musician; b. Panhandle, Tex., Oct. 23, 1913; d. Edwin Reece and Lela (Blackshear) Jameson; m. Thomas Norris Walsh, Nov. 1, 1951 (dec. May 5, 1990); children: Thomas Edwin, Richard Malcolm, Lela Elizabeth. MusB, U. North Tex., Deuton, 1941, MusM, 1942. Cert. tchr. music. Piano tchr. U. North Tex., Denton, 1940-42; music tchr. Perryton HS, Tex., 1942-43, Plainview HS, Tex., 1943-45; choir dir. Presbyn. and Disciples Ch., Plainview, 1943-45; music tchr. Dallas Pub. Sch., 1945-53; organist, choir dir. Midway Hills Ch., Dallas, 1954-60; piano tchr. Hockaday Pvt. Sch., Dallas, 1960-70; music tchr. Dallas Pub. Sch., 1970-82; organist, choir dir. Greenville Ave. Christian Ch., Dallas, 1975-82, Grace Meth. Ch., Dallas, 1982-91, St. Andrews Episcopal Ch., Farmers Branch, Tex., 1991—, Christ United Meth. Ch., 2001—. Composer (operetta) Day in Mexico, 1971, various titles for choir, 1996—; author: The Echo Tower, 1987, The House on the Hill, 1989, Uncle Willie (biography); appeared as Cleopatra as Caesar and Cleopatra, Dallas Little Theatre, 1933, Jane in Jane Eyre, Amarillo Little Theatre, 1935, Anna in Anna and the King of Siam, Northway Ch. Players, 1971, Uncle Willie (biolgraphy), 2004. Mem. Dallas Civic Chorus, 1960-65, Dallas Symphony Chorus, 1970-75, Farmer's Br. Women's Club, 1995—; v.p. Mus. Arts, 2003—. Recipient 2nd prize in Nat. Recording Contest, Nat. Piano Guild, 1973. Mem. Dallas Music Tchr. Assn., Dallas chpt. Am. Guild Organists, Musical Arts Club (sec. 2001-03, 1st v.p. 2005-), Daus. Republic of Tex. (chaplain 1993-95, pres. James Butler Bonham chpt. 1997—, sec. 2005—, Mamie Wynne Cox award 1995, sec. 1995-97, 2003, chmn. yearbook), Pro Musica (pres. 1976-77, 85-86, 2001—, sec. 2003-05, asst. sec. 2003—, treas. 1980-81, 96-97), Pi Beta Phi, Mu Phi Epsilon. Avocations: reading, travel. Home: 14339 Tanglewood Dr Farmers Branch TX 75234-3855

WALSH, ERIN KATHLEEN, social studies educator; m. Ronald Walter Sauber, Jr. MA in Tchg., Lewis and Clark Coll., Portland, Oreg., 1999. Cert. 6-12 social studies tchr. Oreg., 1999. Tchr. social studies Canby H.S., Oreg., 1999—. Advisor OHSIRL, Salem, Oreg., 2000—. Office: Canby HS 721 SW 4th Canby OR 97013 Office Phone: 503-263-7200.

WALSH, JOAN, editor-in-chief; Freelance writer; with In These Times, Chgo., Santa Barbara News & Review; news editor Salon.com, San Francisco, 1998—99, v.p. news, 1999—2003, v.p., co-mng. editor, 2003—04, sr. v.p., editorial ops., 2003—04, editor-in-chief, 2005. Office: Salon Media Group 101 Spear St 203 San Francisco CA 94105-1517 Office Phone: 415-645-9200. Business E-Mail: jwalsh@salon.com.

WALSH, JOANNE ELIZABETH, retired elementary school educator, librarian; b. Chgo., Nov. 25, 1942; d. Joseph Frank and Elizabeth Margaret (Gretz) Fiali; m. John Kerwin Walsh, July 17, 1976; 1 child, Kevin Joseph. BA in English, Mundelein Coll., Chgo., 1965; MEd Ednl. Adminstrn. and Supervision, Loyola U., Chgo., 1969. Tchr. Chgo. Pub. Schs., 1965-83, prin., 1983-89; tchr. libr. Burbank, Ill., 1990—93; tchr. art Tate Sch. of Discovery, Knoxville, Tenn., 1994-95; ret., 1995. Vol. Palos Cmty. Hosp., Palos Park, Ill., 1990, Palos Heights Libr., 1993, Bapt. West Hosp., Knoxville, 2005—06; active St. John Neumann Cath. Ch.; decorating com. City of Farragut. Named Tchr. of Yr. award, McCord Sch., 1992—93. Mem.: Friends of Libr., Knoxville Symphony League, Omni Woman's Club, Knoxville Newcomers Club (pres. 2002—03), Knoxville Welcome Wagon Club (pres. 1999—2000). Avocations: reading, crafts, painting. Home: 607 Gwinhurst Rd Knoxville TN 37922 E-mail: ndisgr8@aol.com.

WALSH, JUANITA, theater educator, actress; b. Milw., May 03; d. Melvin John and Evelyn Dorothy (Heinrich) Walsh; m. Mark Jeffrey Rowen, Sept. 14, 1980. BFA, Stephens Coll., 1972; cert. speech, U. Wis., Milw., 1981. Mem. faculty NYU, N.Y.C., 1985-89, prof., 1997-2000; mem. faculty Marymount Manhattan Coll., 1989-92, Temple U., Phila., 1991, Rutgers U., New Brunswick, NJ, 1992-93, HB Studio, N.Y.C., 1985-2000. Founder, artistic dir. Actors Alliance Inc., N.Y.C., 1986—90. Actor: (plays) Grandma Sylvia's Funeral, 1997—98, Tribute to Uta Hagen, 1995, Glass Menagerie, 2001, Baker's Wife, 2002; (TV series) Ed, 2002; (TV miniseries) War of China's Fate, 1999; (films) The Two Henrys, Fresh Cut Grass, Crutch, 2003, The Color of Truth, 2004, Days Like This, 2004. Mem.: AFTRA, SAG, Actors Equity Assn. Avocation: gardening. E-mail: jwract@yahoo.com.

WALSH, KATHLEEN, lawyer; b. Madison, Wis., Apr. 16, 1951; d. William Patrick and Joan Iris Walsh; m. Stephen Michael Glynn, Mar. 17, 1981; stepchildren: Stephen Michael Jr., Theron Benson. BS, U. Wis., La Crosse, 1973; JD, U. Wis., Madison, 1984. Bar: Wis. 1984, U.S. Dist. Ct. (ea. and we. dists.) Wis. 1984. Investigator Office State Pub. Defender, Milw., 1977-80, adminstrv. asst., 1980-81; asst. city atty. City of Milw., 1984-85; staff atty. Legal Aid Soc. Milw., Inc., 1985-92, 95—. Adj. prof. Marquette U. Law Sch., Milw., 1986-92, 99; bd. dirs. Ctr. for Pub. Representation, Madison, 1986-90; mem. faculty Supreme Ct. Wis., 1987-93, Milw. Young Lawyers Assn., 1985-92. Contbr. chpt. to book, articles to profl. pubs. Coord., dir. Milw. Clinic Protection Coalition, 1992-95. Named Civil Libertarian of Yr., Wis. Civil Liberties Union, 1993. Mem. ACLU, NARAL, State Bar Wis. (bd. dirs. Individual rights and responsibilities sect. 1986-99), Milw. Young Lawyers Assn. (Pro Bono Tng. Seminars), Milw. Bar Assn. (faculty 1985-92, Def. Lawyer of Yr. award 1991), NOW, Planned Parenthood Wis. (Voice for Choice award 1993), Wis. Coalition Against Death Penalty, Nature Conservancy, World Wildlife Fund, Natural Def. Resources Coun. Democrat. Avocations: reading, snorkeling, biking, ceramics, sculpture. Home: 929 N Astor St Milwaukee WI 53202-3436 Office: Legal Aid Soc Milw Inc 521 N 8th St Milwaukee WI 53233

WALSH, KERRI LEE, Olympic athlete; b. Aug. 15, 1978; d. Tim and Margie. BA in Am. studies, Stanford U., 1999. Player BVA Tour, 2001, FIVG Internat. Tour, 2001—, AVP Tour, 2003—; beach volleyball player Team USA, Sydney Olympic Games, 2000, Team USA, Athens Olympic Games, 2004. Named First Team All-Am., 1995—99, Pro Beach Volleyball Rookie of the Yr., 2001, AVP Best Offensive Player, 2003, AVP Most Valuable Player, 2003, AVP Team of the Yr. (With Misty May), 2003. Achievements include being the second person in history named First Team All-American four years in a row, Stanford U., 1995-1999; winning FIVB World Champions with partner Misty May, 2002, 2003; winning gold medal (with Misty May) in Athens Olympic games, beach volleyball, 2004. Office: c/o USOC One Olympic Plz Colorado Springs CO 80909

WALSH, MARIE LECLERC, nurse; b. Providence, Sept. 11, 1928; d. Walter Normand and Anna Mary (Ryan) Leclerc; m. John Breffni Walsh, June 18, 1955; children: George Breffni, John Leclerc, Darina Louise. Grad., Waterbury Hosp. Sch. Nursing, Conn., 1951; BS, Columbia U., 1954, MA, 1955. Team leader Hartford (Conn.) Hosp., 1951-53; pvt. duty nurse St. Luke's Hosp., N.Y.C., 1953-57; sch. nurse tchr. Agnes Russel Ctr., Tchrs. Coll. Columbia U., N.Y.C., 1955-56; clin. nursing instr. St. Luke's Hosp., N.Y.C., 1957-58; chmn. disaster nursing ARC Fairfax County, Va., 1975; course coord. occupational health nursing U. Va. Sch. Continuing Edn., Falls Church, 1975-77; mem. disaster steering com. No. Va. C.C., Annandale, 1976; adj. faculty U. Va. Sch. Continuing Edn., Falls Church, 1981; disaster svcs. nurse ARC, Wichita, Kans., 1985-90, disaster svcs. nurse Seattle-King County chpt. Seattle, 1990-96; ret. Rsch. and statis. analyst U. Va. Sch. Continuing Edn. Nursing, Falls Church, 1975; rsch. libr. Olive Garvey Ctr. for Improvement Human Functioning, Inc., Wichita, 1985. Sec. Dem. party, Cresskill, N.J., 1964-66; county committeewoman, Bergen County, N.J., 1965-66; pres., v.p., Internat. Staff Wives, NATO, Brussels, Belgium, 1978-80; election officer, supr. Election Bd., Wichita, 1987, 88; v.p. McLean Newcomers, 1997-99, pres., 1999-2000. Mem. AAAS, AAUW, N.Y. Acad. Sci., Pi Lambda Theta, Sigma Theta Tau. Avocations: travel, gardening. Home: 8800 Prestwould Pl Mc Lean VA 22102-2231

WALSH, MARY CASWELL, psychotherapist; b. San Jose, Calif., Jan. 19, 1949; d. Dwight Alan and Doris Helen (Rayburn) Caswell; m. Matthew Brian Walsh, Aug. 5, 1972; children: Teresa Helen, Elizabeth Mary BA, U. San Francisco, 1976, MA Marriage, Family-Child Counseling, 1988, postgrad., 1989; MA English, U. Mich., 1976; cert., Detroit Inst. Addiction Rsch., 1979; postgrad., Loyola U., Chgo., 1997. Lic. marriage, family and child counselor, Calif.; cert. in addiction rsch. and tng.; cert. in child abuse and assessment, Calif.; lic. marriage and family threapist, Ill. Tchg. fellow U. Mich., Ann Arbor, 1974—76; focal counselor family svcs. Sacred Heart Rehab. Ctr., Detroit, 1977—80; clin. coord. aftercare svcs., family therapist Marin Gen. Hosp. Adolescent Recovery Ctr., Greenbrae, Calif., 1982—92; clin. coord., family therapist Sober Classroom (Now Sobriety H.S.), San Rafael, Calif., 1992—94; psychotherapist Cath. Charities, Chgo., 1998—; pvt. practice Oak Park, Ill., 1998—. Pvt. practice therapy, San Rafael and San Francisco, 1992-94; presenter Nat. Conf. Cath. Charities, N.Y.C., 1980, Marin Gen. Hosp., 1989-91; presenter on clin. pastoral edn. Loyola U., 1996-97; clin. cons. student attendance rev. bd. Marin County Pub. Schs., 1993-94 Author: The Art of Tradition: A Christian Guide to Building a Family, 1997, St. Francis Celebrates Christmas, 1998, Hidden Springs of Hope: Finding God in the Desert of Suffering, 2001; compiler: Prayers in Times of Crisis, 2003, Prayers Out of the Depths, 2003, Prayers for Expectant Parents, 2003 Event coord. auction fundraiser San Francisco Girls Chorus, 1992-94; mem. choir Holy Name Cathedral, Chgo.; mem. found. coun. Monastery of the Holy Cross, Chgo., 1999—, mem. oblate, 1999— U. San Francisco Swig scholar Hebrew U., Israel, 1988 Mem. Am. Assn. Marriage and Family Therapy (clin.), Ill. Assn. Marriage and Family Therapy (clin., presenter conf. 1998), Calif. Assn. Marriage and Family Therapy Democrat. Avocations: playing harp and viola, gardening. Office: One E Superior St Ste 500 Chicago IL 60611 also: 1103 Westgate St Oak Park IL 60301-1088

WALSH, MERIDETH A., secondary school educator, director; b. Port Jefferson, N.Y., Apr. 30, 1979; d. James E. and Alicia B. Walsh. M in Edn. Leadership and Supervision, St. Johns U., Oakdale, NY, 2006. Cert. tchr. and prin. endorsements Kans., Vt., N.Y., N.H., 2006. Tchr., adminstr. Springfield (Vt.) H.S., 2005—. Presenter in field. Office Phone: 802-885-7900. Personal E-mail: meriwalsh@hotmail.com.

WALSH, NAN, artist, painter, sculptor, consultant; b. NYC, Nov. 4, 1932; d. Joseph Edward and Mary Ellen (White) Heinl; m. Albert Anthony Walsh, July 10, 1954 (dec. Oct. 9, 2002); children: Maryellen, Nanette, Mark, Gregg (dec.). BS in Elem. Edn., Fordham U., 1954; postgrad., Nat. Acad. Sch. Fine Arts, Art Life Studio Inc., White Plains and Portchester, N.Y., 1984-94, V.K. Jonynas, L.I., N.Y., 1968-88, Art Ctr. No. N.J., 1996—2002. Fashion model Martha Clyde, N.Y.C., 1951-54; tchr. Yonkers (N.Y.) Pub. Schs., 1953-55; gallery dir. Mamaroneck Artists Guild, Larchmont, NY, 1988-95; fine artist, art juror, cons., 1995—. Membership juror Mamaroneck Artists Guild, Larchmont, 1982-84, membership juror chair, 1996-98, mem. adv. bd., 1996-98; mem. Ctr. for Contemporary Printmaking, 1998—. One-woman shows and juried exhbns. Westchester and N.Y.C., 1976—; works represented in corp. and pvt. collecitons. Hostess chairperson Citizens for John Lindsay, Gracie Mansion, N.Y., 1970; mem. Studio Twelve, pres., show chair, 1972-80; mem. Katonah Mus. Art. Recipient numerous 1st place awards for art. Mem. Nat. League Am. Penwomen (corr. sec. and membership chair 1992-96), Nat. Mus. Women in the Arts, N.Y. Soc. Women Artists, Guild Creative Art, N.J. Artists Equity, Mamaroneck Artists Guild (v.p. 1982, 83, membership chair 1992-95 Fordham U. Art Club (show chair 1965-80). Avocations: gardening, bridge, tennis, swimming, travel.

WALSHAK, MARY LYNN, academic librarian; b. Taft, Tex., Mar. 11, 1931; d. Wylie Ray and Vida Marie (Ingram) Grice; m. Donald James Walshak, Dec. 26, 1949 (div. 1966); 1 child, John Mark. BS, S.W. Tex. State Coll., 1968; MLS, North Tex. State U., 1970. Catalog libr. Ga. So. Coll., Statesboro, 1971-76; head govt. documents Henderson Libr., Ga. So. U., Statesboro, 1973—2000; ret. Presenter in field. Contbr. numerous articles to profl. jours. Acting chair, co-chmn. usher team Pittman Park Meth. Ch., 1991-2003, lay liturgist, 1993. Faculty devel. and welfare grant, 1987. Mem. ALA (editl. rev. bd. publs. com. 1993—, govt. documents roundtable, ACRL divsn. U. Librs. and Law and Polit. Sci. sect.), Ga. Libr. Assn. (acad. librs. divsn., documents interest group vice chair 1987-89, chair 1989-91, vice chair interest group coun. 1989-91, mem. exec. bd. 1989-91), Nat. Soc. DAR, Nat. Soc. Daus. of Am. Colonists, Univ. Optimist Club (youth activities com. 1992, Deen Day Smith award for Svc. 1992), League of Women Voters, Alpha Chi, Kappa Delta Pi. Avocations: genealogy, historical preservation. Home: 14207 Misty Meadow Ln Houston TX 77079-3103

WALSH-HUNT, LINDA ANN, social worker, consultant, poet; b. Syracuse, May 24, 1952; d. Edmond Charles and Jane Kathleen (Hudson) Walsh; m. Francis Edward Hunt, Sr., June 11, 1976; children: Francis Hunt III, Patrick Hunt, Elizabeth Hunt, James Hunt. BS, MSW, Syracuse U. Patient svcs. dir. Am. Cancer Soc., Syracuse, NY, 1973—; therapist Dept. Mental Health, Syracuse, 1993—; social worker Syracuse City Sch. Dist., 1995—. Cons. in field. Author: numerous poems. Bd. dirs. Mental Health Assn., 1991—92. Mem.: NASW, Am. Group Psychotherapy Assn., Clin. Soc. Social Work. Democrat. Avocations: piano, poetry, writing. Home: 115 Ruskin Ave Syracuse NY 13207

WALSH-PIPER, KATHLEEN A., museum director; b. Chgo., Aug. 17, 1947; d. James Clement and Jane (Burnham) W.; m. Michael G. Rubin, May 17, 1969 (div. 1978); m. Rubin H. Piper, Dec. 19, 1987. BA, Washington U., St. Louis, 1969, MA in Art History, 1973; postgrad., St. Louis U. Cert. tchr., Mo. Tchr. St. Louis Archdiocesan Schs., 1970-73; asst. prof. Mo. Bapt. Coll., St. Louis, 1973; tchr. Hazelwood Jr. High Sch., St. Louis, 1974-77; mus. tchr. St. Louis Art Mus., 1976, coord. rsch. ctr., 1977-80; asst. dir. mus. edn. Art Inst. Chgo., 1980—85; dir. edn. Terra Mus. Am. Art, Chgo., 1985-88; head dept. tchr. and sch. programs Nat. Gallery Art, Washington, 1988—95; cultural specialist U.S. Info. Agency, 1995; dir. edn. and pub. progs. Dallas Mus. Art, Tex., 1995—2002; dir. U. Ky. Art Mus., Lexington, 2002—. Mus. guest scholar J. Paul Getty Mus., Malibu, Calif., 1997. Author: Image to Word: Art and Creative Writing, 2002; contbr. articles to profl. jours. Robert E. Smith fellow Nat. Gallery of Art, 1994. Mem. Nat. Art Edn. Assn. (regional mus. educator 1984, nat. mus. educator 1985, dir. mus. divsn. 1992—), Am. Assn. Mus. (chair midwest edn. ccom. 1983-84). Avocation: writing. Office: U Ky Art Mus 116 Singletary Ctr Rose St and Euclid Ave Lexington KY 40506-0241 Office Phone: 859-257-1152. E-mail: kwpiper@email.uky.edu.

WALTEMATH, JOAN M., artist; b. Nebr., Oct. 6, 1953; Student, U. Nebr., 1971-73; BFA, RISD, 1976; MFA, Hunter Coll., 1993. Asst. prof. Sch. Arch. of Cooper Union, 2000—06. Vis. lectr. Princeton U., 1999-2003. One-woman shows include Barbara Braathen Gallery, N.Y., 1983, 87, 89, Willoughby Sharp Gallery, N.Y., 1990, Stark Gallery, N.Y., 1991, 92, 94-2000, P. Bungert Projects, 1996, S. Moody Gallery, 1998, Gallery Joe, Phila., 2001, Newspace, LA, 2002, White-Out Studio, Belgium, 2003, Victoria Munroe Gallery, Boston, 2005, Galerie Niklas von Bartha, London, 2006; group shows include Andrea Rosen Gallery, N.Y., 1990, Stark Gallery, 1992, Harvard U. Art Mus., Cambridge, 1992, Beth Urdang Gallery, Boston, 1994, Condeso-Lawler Gallery, 1995, Musee de Beaux Arts, La Chaux-de-Fords-Switzerland, 1996, Cunningham Gallery, N.Y., 2005, Univ. Nebr., 2006. Recipient H. R. Eagleton scholarship award Hunter Coll., 1990, Graf Travel award Hunter Coll., 1991, BRA Architecture award Edward Albee Found., 2003, Jent el Found., 2005.

WALTER, ANN L., special education educator; b. Maxton AFB, N.C., Aug. 22, 1945; d. Jack and Loraine (Lips) Stanek; m. Gary Walter, Dec. 18, 1966; children: Lynda S., Greg S BA Spl. Edn. and Elem. Edn., U. No. Colo., 1966; M Spl. Edn., Norfolk State U., 1981. Cert. elem., learning disabled, emotionally/mentally handicapped, gifted tchr., Ariz., elem. and spl. edn. tchr., Colo. Tchr. West Springfield Sch. Dist., Mass., 1968; tchr. 5th and 6th grade Briggsdale Sch. Dist., Colo., 1967—68; tchr. 1st grade Fife Sch. Dist., Wash., 1968—72; tchr. kindergarden and 1st grade Panama Canal Zone Sch., 1972—78; tchr. emotionally handicapped and learning disabled Hampton Sch. Dist., Va., 1976—81, Ellicott Sch. Dist., Colo., 1981—86; tchr. gifted kindergarten-8th grades Maricopa Accommodation Sch., Williams AFB, Ariz., 1986—88; tchr. spl. edn., chair dept. Carson Jr. H.S. Mesa Pub. Schs., Ariz., 1988—93, tchr. spl. edn. 1-2 Nathan Hale Elem. Sch., 1993—. Tchr. GED Ft. Kobbe Army Edn. Ctr., Panama Canal Zone, 1972-76; presenter in field Bd. dirs. Marcos De Niza H.S. Booster Club, Tempe, Ariz., 1990-91; charter mem. Marcos De Niza Grad Night, 1989-92; coach Spl. Olympics, Williams AFB, 1986-88; mem. Mesa Self Esteem Com., 1990-91 March of Dimes scholar, 1970; named Star Coach, Spl. Olympics, 1986, Tchr. of Yr. MARC, 1997 Mem. NEA, Ariz. Edn. Assn., Mesa Edn. Assn., Beta Sigma Phi (sec., v.p., pres. 1978-90, Woman of Yr. 1985) Lutheran. Avocations: bridge, counted cross stitch, baking, walking, soccer. Home: 1858 E Cornell Dr Tempe AZ 85283-2227 Office: Mesa Pub Schs 848 N Mesa Dr Mesa AZ 85201-4302

WALTER, BARBARA SYKES, reading educator; b. Amsterdam, NY; d. Julius Frank and Hermine (Kapsa) Sykes; m. George Robert Walter, June 28, 1952 (dec. Apr. 2000); children: George Robert, Allison Jane. BA, U. Rochester, 1950; MA, Syracuse U., 1951. Cert. Reading Specialist N.J., 1968. Tchr. Rochester (N.Y.) Schs., 1951—52, Syracuse (N.Y.) Jr. HS, 1952—54, Ridgewood (N.J.) HS, 1964—67; reading specialist Leonia (NJ) H.S., 1967—68, Racine Unified Sch. Dist., Racine, Wis., 1969—74; lectr. U. Wis., Kenosha, Wis., 1972—76; co-owner Tour-About, Inc., Racine, 1980—84. Co-author: Renewing Our Roots: Northside, 1979. Safety commnr. Borough of Ho-Ho-Kus, NJ, 1966; adv. bd. Racine Theatre Guild; mem. Mayoral commn. Bldg. Bd. Appeals; active Preservation-Racine, Inc.; tutor Laubach-Racine Literacy Coun.; mem. bd. Racine Pub. Libr.; bd. dir. Frank Lloyd Wright/Wis. Heritage Tourism Bd., Madison, Wis., Racine United Arts Fund Dr.; bd. dirs. Wustum Mus. Fine Arts, Racine Arts Coun. Recipient Woman of Distinction award, YWCA, 1990, Annual Arts award, Racine Arts Coun., 1993. Republican. Roman Catholic. Avocations: tennis, history, bridge, reading, archaeology. Home: 3726 North Bay Drive Racine WI 53402

WALTER, CARMEL MONICA, security firm executive, writer; b. Dublin, July 24, 1943; arrived in U.S., 1961; d. Albert and Anastatia Woods; m. Michael William Walter, June 15, 1963; children: Coleen, Daniel, Eileen. BS magna cum laude, Madonna U., Livonia, Mich., 1987. Co-founder, co-owner Am. Security Alarm Co., Madison Heights, Mich., 1969—72, Alarm Supply Co., Inc., Livonia, Mich., 1969—89, founder, owner Milford, NJ, 2001—. Intro.and product tng. for first wireless security sys. Resident Sentry, Madison Heights, 1967—72; co-owner CMD Co., Flemington, NJ, 1989—2002; established ongoing comprehensive tech. support sys. Alarm Supply Co., Milford, 2003—. Co-author (with Michael Walter): (security products and application manual) The Security Store. Mem. cert. nat. emergency response teams emergency support function #13 public safety and security Am. Bd. Cert. in Homeland Security, Springfield, Mo., 2005. Mem.: Am. Coll. Forensic Examiners Inst. (cert. homeland security-II), Kappa Gamma Pi. Roman Catholic. Avocations: travel, golf, theater, cooking, interior design. Office Phone: 908-995-2449. Business E-Mail: alarmsply@aol.com.

WALTER, JENNIE, elementary school educator; Tchr. Upper Arlington Schs., Ohio, 1986—. Home: 1249 Briarmeadow Dr Columbus OH 43235 Office: Upper Arlington City Schs 1850 Hastings Ln Upper Arlington OH 43220 Office Phone: 614-487-5100. Business E-Mail: jwalter@uaschools.org.

WALTER, JESSICA, actress; b. Bklyn., Jan. 31, 1941; m. Russ Bowman, 1966 (div. 1978); m. Ron Leibman, 1983; 1 child, Brooke Student, Bucks County Playhouse, Neighborhood Playhouse. Actor: (Broadway plays) Advise and Consent, 1961; other stage prodns. include: Rumors, 1988; (films) include Lilith, 1964, The Group, 1966, Grand Prix, 1966, Bye Bye, Braverman, 1968, Number One, 1969, Play Misty for Me, 1971, Going Ape, 1982, Spring Fever, 1983, Flamingo Kid, 1984, PCU, 1994, Dark Goddess, 1994, Slums of Beverly Hills, 1998, My Best Friend's Wife, 2001, Dummy, 2002; (TV series) Love of Life, 1962-65, For the People, 1965, Amy Prentiss, 1974-75, All That Glitters, 1977, Trapper John M.D., 1979-1986; ltd. series Amy Prentiss, 1974-75 (Emmy award for Outstanding Lead Actress in Ltd. Series) Bare Essence, 1983, (voice) Wildfire, 1986, Aaron's Way, 1988, (voice) Pirates of Darkwater, 1991-92, (voice) Dinosaurs, 1991-94, The Round Table, 1992, One Life to Live, 1996-97, Oh Baby, 1998-2000, Arrested Development, 2003-; (TV miniseries) Wheels, 1978; (TV films) Kiss Me Kate, 1968, The Immortal, 1969, Three's a Crowd, 1969, They Call It Murder, 1971, Women in Chains, 1972, Home for the Holidays, 1972, Columbo: Mind Over Mayhem, 1974, Hurricane, 1974, Having Babies, 1976, Victory at Entebbe, 1976, Black Market Baby, 1977, Wild and Wooly, 1978, Dr. Strange, 1978, Secrets of Three Hungry Wives, 1978, Vampire, 1979, She's Dressed to Kill, 1979, Miracle on Ice, 1981, Scruples, 1981, Thursday's Child, 1983, The Return of Marcus Welby, M.D., 1984, The Execution, 1985, Killer in the Mirror, 1986, Jenny's Song, 1988, Aaron's Way: The Harvest, 1988, Leave of Absence, 1994, Mother Knows Best, 1997, Doomsday Rock, 1997, I Do (But I Don't), 2004; TV guest appearances include Route 66, 1963, The Nurses, 1964, It Takes a Thief, 1969, Mission: Impossible, 1970, The Name of the Game, 1971, Night Gallery, 1972, Banacek, 1973, Barnaby Jones, 1974, Ironside, 1974, Hawaii Five-O, 1974, McCloud, 1975, McMillan and Wife, 1976, Quincy, 1978, Knots Landing, 1982, Joanie Loves Chachi, 1982, Matt Houston, 1982, Three's a Crowd, 1984, 85, Murder, She Wrote, 1985, 91, Magnum P.I., 1986, Coach, 1994, Babylon 5, 1994, Law & Order, 1995, Just Shoot Me!, 1998, Jack & Jill, 2000, 01, Touched by an Angel, 2003. Office: Judy Shane & Assocs 606 N Larchmont Ste 309 Los Angeles CA 90004

WALTER, PATRICIA L., psychotherapist, consultant; b. Logansport, Ind., Mar. 15, 1935; d. William Marion and Doris May (Duddleston) Sievers; m. Raymond C. Walter Jr., Mar. 28, 1968; m. Keith A. Erny (div.); children: Rodney Erny, Jeffrey Erny, Mark Erny, Troy Erny. BS in Edn., Ind. U., 1973, MS in Edn. & English, 1976, MS in Counseling, 1984. Cert. English tchr., lic. mental health counselor Ind., cert. nat. cert. addictions prevention specialist III, forensic counselors 1998. Tchr. English Logansport Sch. Corp., Ind., 1973—97; psychotherapist Four County Counseling, Peru, 1993—2000; high sch. counselor Logansport Cmty. Schs., 1997—2003; mental health cons. Texas Migrant Headstart, Kokomo, 2004—; psychotherapist RAJ Clinic, Logansport, 2004—. Coord. Adminstrv. Counsel, Logansport, 2001—03; coach Acad. Competitions, 1987—98, Girls 6th Grade Basketball, 1975—78. Vol. First Call Home Health and Hospice, 2004. Mem.: Call County Carousel, Am. Mental Health Counselors Assn., Kiwanis (sec. 1997—98, pres. 2005—), Zeta Tau Chapter of Sigma Phi Gamma Sorority. Republican. Avocations: golf, ballroom dancing, reading, exercise, gardening. Home: 5209 Canterbury Ln Logansport IN 46947

WALTER, SANDRA S., social worker; b. Quincy, Ill., Apr. 15, 1952; d. Merle G. and Margaret A. Walter. BA, Iowa Wesleyan Coll., 1974. Lic. Bachelor Social Worker Iowa Bd. Social Work Examiners, 1999. Program coord. Planned Parenthood S.E. Iowa, Fort Madison, 1974—82; social worker 2 Iowa Dept. Human Svcs., Burlington, 1982—82, 1983—87, social worker 3; family based counselor Iowa Children and Family Svcs., Burlington, 1982—82, family counselor, 1982—83; social worker 3 Iowa Dept. Human Svcs., Sigourney, Iowa, 2000—. Democrat. Methodist. Avocations: travel, genealogy, reading. Home: 307 West Stroup Richland IA 52585 Office Phone: 641-622-2090. Personal E-mail: sandyw@iowatelecom.net.

WALTER, SHERYL LYNN, lawyer; b. Morris, Ill., July 18, 1956; d. C. Frank and Margaret (Juhl) W. BA in History cum laude, Grinnell (Iowa) Coll., 1978; JD cum laude, U. Minn., 1984; MPA John F. Kennedy Sch. of Govt., Harvard U., 2003. Bar: Minn. 1984, U.S. Dist. Ct. Minn. 1987, U.S. Ct. Appeals (8th cir.) 1987, D.C. 1989, U.S. Dist. Ct. D.C. 1989, U.S. Ct. Appeals (D.C. cir.) 1989. Law clk. to presiding judge 3d Jud. Dist. of Minn., Rochester, 1984-85; law clk. to Chief Judge Donald P. Lay U.S. Ct. Appeals (8th cir.), St. Paul, 1985-87; assoc. Mayer, Brown & Platt, Washington, 1987-89; gen. counsel Nat. Security Archive, Washington, 1989-94, Assn. Records Review Bd., Washington, 1994-95, Commn. Protecting and Reducing Govt. Secrecy, Washington, 1995-97, dep. spl. counsel U.S. Senate Vets. Affairs com., 1997-98; minority staff dir., chief counsel U.S. Senate Jud. Com., Youth Violence Subcom., 1998-2000; with Office of Legis. Affairs U.S. Dept. of Justice, 2000—03, acting asst. atty. gen., 2001, chief of staff Office of Intelligence & Policy Rev., 2003—. Cons. Amnesty Internat., Washington, 1988-89. Vice chair bd. dirs. Rosemont Ctr. Head Start Sch., 2004—. Mem. ABA (vice chmn. adminstrv. law sect. govt. info. subcom. 1990-96), D.C. Bar Assn. (steering com., adminstrv. law sect. 1990-97), Am. Soc. Access Profls. (bd. dirs. 1990-98, pres. 1996-97), Brit.-Am. Security Info. Coun. (bd. dirs. 1994-2000), Lawyers Alliance for World Security (bd. dirs. 1994-2000). Office: US Dept Justice 9th and Pennsylvania Ave NW Washington DC 20530

WALTER, VIRGINIA LEE, psychologist, educator; b. Temple, Tex., Oct. 30, 1937; d. Luther Patterson and Virginia Lafayette (Wilkins) W.; m. Glen Ellis, 1958 (div.); children: Glen Edward, David Walter; m. Robert Reinehr, 1963 (div.); 1 son, Charles Allen; m. Robert Bruininks, 1975 (div.). BS, U. Tex.-Austin, 1959, M.Edn., 1967; postgrad. internship program in spl. Edn. Adminstrn., 1970; Ed.D., U. Houston, 1973. Prof. ednl. psychology dept. ednl. psychology U. Minn., Mpls., 1973-85; pres. Sch. Resource Ctr., Austin, Tex., 1985-90; tchr. Llano Pub. Schs., 1988-97; dir. Walter Resources, 1998—. Chmn. State Adv. Coun. for Inservice Tng. Regular Classroom Tchrs., 1977-79; cons. spl. ednl. various sch. dists., state depts. and agys. Editl. cons.: Jour. Ednl. Psychology, 1979, Reading Rsch. Quar., 1982; assoc. editor: Exceptional Children, 1979-84; assoc. editor Teaching Exceptional Children, 1985-89; contbr. articles to profl. jours., papers to profl. confs. Named Minn. Spl. Educator of Yr., 1978; recipient Svc. award Internat. Coun. Exceptional Children, 1978; HEW Office of Human Devel. Svcs. grantee, 1976-80; Dept. Edn. contractee, 1980-83 Mem. Coun. for Exceptional Children, Nat. Assn. Children with Learning Disabilities (dir. Minn. chpt. 1978-80), Nat. Assn. Retarded Citizens, AAUP, Assn. Supervision and Curriculum Devel. Home and Office: 7108 Running Rope Austin TX 78731-2128

WALTERS, ANNA LEE, writer, educational association administrator; b. Pawnee, Okla., Sept. 9, 1946; d. Luther and Juanita Mae (Taylor) McGlaslin; children: Anthony, Daniel. BA, Goddard Coll. Dir. Navajo C.C. Press, Tsaile (Navajo Nation), Ariz., 1982—. Contbg. author: The Man to Send Rainclouds, 1974, Warriors of the Rainbow, 1975, Shantih, 1976, The Third Woman, 1979, The Remembered Earth, 1979, American Indians Today, Thought, Literature, Art, 1981, Spider Woman's Granddaughters, Traditional Tales and Contemporary Writing by Native American Women, 1989, Tapestries of Life, Women's Work Women's Consciousness and the Meaning of Daily Experience, Talking Leaves, Contemporary Native American Short Stories, Growing Up Native American-An Anthology, Native Heritage-Personal Accounts by American Indians 1790- to Present, Walking the Twilight-Women Writers of the Southwest, Reinventing the Enemy's Languages, Contemporary Native Women Writings of Native America; co-author textbook: The Sacred Ways of Knowledge, Sources of Life, 1977; author: The Otoe-Missouria Tribe, Centennial Memoirs, 1881-1981, 1981, Earth Power Coming, 1983, The Sun is Not Merciful, 1985, Ghost Singer, 1988, The Spirit of Native America, 1989, Talking Indian, 1993, Neon Pow Wow, Reflections of Survival and Writing the Two-Legged Creature-An Otoe Story (retold by Anna Lee Walters); contbr. articles to jours.; guest editor Frauen Offensive, 1978; also poet, feature writer; editor: Neon Pow-Wow, 1994, The Two Legged Creature, 1994. Recipient Am. Book award The Before Columbus Found., 1986, Virginia Scully McCormick Lit. award, 1986. Office: Dine Coll Humanities Dept Tsaile AZ 86556

WALTERS, BARBARA JILL, broadcast journalist; b. Boston, Mass., Sept. 25, 1931; d. Lou and Dena (Selett) Walters; m. Robert Katz, June 21, 1955 (div. 1958); m. Lee Gruber, 1963 (div. 1976); 1 adopted child, Jacqueline; m. Merv Adelson, 1986 (div. 1992). BA in English, Sarah Lawrence Coll., 1953, LHD (hon.), Ohio State U., Marymount Coll., 1975, Wheaton Coll., 1983, Temple U., Hofstra U., Ben-Gurion U. Former producer WNBC-TV; former writer CBS News; then with Stas. WPIX and CBS-TV; writer, reporter-at-large Today Show, 1961—63, regular panel mem., 1964—74, co-host, 1974—76; moderator syndicated program Not For Women Only, 1972—76; founder, pres. Barwall Productions, NYC, 1976—; newscaster ABC Evening News (now ABC World News Tonight), 1976—78; host The Barbara Walters Spls., 1976—; co-host ABC TV news show 20/20, 1984—99, anchor, 1999—2004; host The 10 Most Fascinating People, 1993—; co-exec. prodr., co-owner, co-host The View, ABC, NYC, 1997—; exec. prodr. The Iyanla Show, 2001. Contbr. NBC Radio Network. Contbr. ABC programs Issues and Answers; author: (book) How to Talk With Practically Anybody About Practically Anything, 1970; contbr. to Reader's Digest, Good Housekeeping, Family Weekly. Honorary chair Nat. Assn. Help for Mentally Retarded Children, 1970. Named Woman Yr. Comm., 1974, Broadcaster Yr., Internat. Radio and TV Soc., 1975, Woman Yr., Theta Sigma Phi; named one of Am.'s 75 Most Important Women, Ladies' Home Jour., 1970, 200 Leaders Future, Time Mag., 1974, 10 Women Decade, Ladies' Home Jour., 1979, Most Important Women, Roper Report, 1979, Women Most Admired Am. People, Gallup Poll, 1982, 1984, Am.'s 100 Most Important Women, Ladies' Home Jour., 1983, America's 100 Most Important Women of the Century, Good Housekeeping, 2000, Ladies' Home Journal, 2000; named to 100 Women of Accomplishment, Harper's Bazaar, 1967, 1971, Museum of Television and Radio, Los Angeles, 2004; recipient Award Yr., Nat. Assn. TV Program Execs., 1975, Daytime Emmy award, Nat. Acad. TV Arts and Scis., 1975, Emmy award, 1980, 1982, 1983, Daytime Emmy award for outstanding talk show, 2003, Mass Media award, Am. Jewish Com. Inst. Human Relations, 1975, Barbara Walters' Coll. Scholarship in Broadcast Journalism established in her honor, Ill. Broadcasters Assn., 1975, Matrix award, N.Y. Women in Comm., 1977, Hubert H. Humphrey Freedom prize, Anti Defamation League B'nai B'rith, 1978, Pres.'s award, Overseas Press Club, 1988, inducted Hall of Fame, Acad. TV Arts and Scis., 1990, Lowell Thomas award, Marist Coll., 1990, Lifetime Achievement award, Internat. Women's Media Found., 1991, saluted, Am. Mus. Moving Image, 1992, Lifetime Achievement award, Women's Project and Prodn., 1993, honored for contbn. to broadcast journalism, Mus. TV and Radio, 1996, George Foster Peabody award for her interview with actor Christopher Reeve, 1996, Muse award, NY Women in Film and TV, 1997, Lifetime Achievement award, Daytime Emmy Awards, 2000, Nat. Acad. TV Arts and Scis., 2000, Silver Satellite award, Am. Women Radio and TV, Sherry Landing Leadership award, The Hollywood Reporter, 2005. Achievements include first woman to co-anchor the Network News, 1976; interviewed every U.S. president and first lady since Nixon; conducted several historic interviews including the Nov. 1977 joint interview with Egyptian President Anwar Sadat and Israel's Prime Minister Menachem Begin; hour-long primetime interview with Cuba's President Fidel Castro, June 9, 1977 and a second interview 25 years later in 2002; conducted the first interview with Monica Lewinsky, which became the highest-rated news program, 48.5 million viewers, ever broadcast by a single network, 1999. Office: The View 320 W 66th St New York NY 10023-6304

WALTERS, BETTE JEAN, lawyer, investor; b. Norristown, Pa., Sept. 5, 1946; BA, U. Pitts., 1967; JD, Temple U., 1970, LLM in Taxation, 1974. Bar: Pa. 1970, U.S. Dist. Ct. (ea. dist.) Pa. 1971. Law clk., assoc. William R. Cooper, Lansdale, Pa., 1969-72; spl. asst. to pub. defender Montgomery County (Pa.), 1973; pvt. practice North Wales, Pa., 1972-73; assoc. counsel Alco Standard Corp., Valley Forge, Pa., 1973-79, group counsel mfg., 1979-83; v.p., gen. counsel, sec. Alco Industries, Inc., Valley Forge, 1983—2003; pvt. practice, 2005—. Mem. corp. sponsors com. Zool. Soc. of Phila.; adv. environ. studies program U. Pitts.; bd. visitors Beasley Sch. Law Temple U. Mem. ABA, DAR, Pa. Bar Assn., Montgomery County Bar Assn. Republican. Office Phone: 215-540-0234. Personal E-mail: b.j.walters@verizon.net.

WALTERS, BRIDGET C., science educator; b. Ironton, Ohio, Oct. 5, 1975; d. Franklin Jim and Eleanor O. Dickess; m. Shane A. Walters, July 31, 1999; children: Burgundy A., Brandy A. BSc in Edn., Ohio U., Athens, 1998; MSc in Edn., U. Dayton, Ohio, 2001. Cert. tchr. Ohio Dept. Edn. Sci. tchr. Clinton Massie H.S., Clarksville, Ohio, 1998—2003, Princeton H.S., Cin., 2003—. Grantee NBC funding, Ohio Dept. Edn., 2006—. Mem.: NSTA. Office: Princeton HS 11080 Chester Rd Cincinnati OH 45246 Office Phone: 513-552-8200.

WALTERS, CAROLYN MARIA, secondary school educator; b. White Plains, NY, Aug. 15, 1947; d. Theodore William and Elizabeth Marie W. BA, Mercy Coll., Dobbs Ferry, N.Y., 1969; MS, Yeshiva U., 1974. Cert. permanent math. tchr., N.Y. Tchr. math. and computer sci. Mt. Vernon (N.Y.) High Sch., 1970—2004, coach varsity cheerleading, 1975-87; tchr. Sch. of the Holy Child, Westchester, NY, 2004—. Adj. prof. Mercy Coll., 1976-80; asst. tchr. Tchr. Tng. Inst., Hofstra U., Hempstead, N.Y., 1989; class advisor Mt. Vernon High Sch., 1982, 87, 93, 95, 98. Mem. choir Cath. Ch., Tarrytown, N.Y., 1975—; mem. exec. bd. Mt. Vernon Parents, Tchrs. and Students Assn., 1986—; coach Tex. Star Acad. Challenge Team; mem. Transfiguration Ch. Recipient Jenkins Meml. award Mt. Vernon Parents, Tchrs. and Students Assn., 1988, Mt. Vernon HS Parents, Tchrs., Students award, 1998; grantee NSF, 1985, 87-88, 89. Mem. Nat. Coun. Tchrs. Math., Mercy Coll. Alumni Assn. (chmn. awards com. 1975-88, 89-92, mem. fundraising com. 1989-92, Alumni Svc. award 1989), Mt. Vernon High Sch. Faculty Club (pres., chairperson sr. awards com., convocation com.). Democrat. Avocations: reading, trivia games, solving cryptoquotes, singing. Home: 222 Martling Ave AM Tarrytown NY 10591-4756 Office: Sch Holy Child 2225 Westchester Ave Rye NY 10580

WALTERS, DORIS LAVONNE, retired religious organization administrator, human services manager; b. Peachland, NC, Feb. 24, 1931; d. H. Lloyd and Mary Lou (Helms) W. AA, Gardner Webb U., Boiling Springs, NC, 1959; BA cum laude, Carson-Newman Coll., Jefferson City, Tenn., 1961; MRE, Southwestern Bapt. Theol. Sem., 1963; MA in Pastoral Counseling, Wake Forest U., Winston-Salem, N.C., 1982; DMIn in Pastoral Counseling, Southeastern Bapt. Theol. Sem., 1988. Min. of edn. and youth First Bapt. Ch., Orange, Tex., 1963-66; assoc. prof. Seinan Jo Gakuin Jr. Coll., Japan, 1968-72; dir. Fukuoka Friendship House, Japan, 1972-88, pastoral counselor, chaplain, 1983-86; Tokyo lifeline referral counselor (in English) Hiroshima-South, Fukuoka, 1983-86; supr. Japanese and Am. staff Fukuoka Friendship House, 1972-86; with chaplaincy Med. Coll. Va., Richmond, 1976; resident chaplain N.C. Bapt. Hosp., Winston-Salem, 1981-82, counselor-in-tng. pastoral care dept., 1986-88; dir. missionary counseling and support svcs. Pastoral Care Found. N.C. Bapt. Hosp., Winston-Salem, 1989-93; dir. Missionary Family Counseling Svcs., Inc., Winston-Salem, 1993—2003. Mem. Japan Bapt. Mission Exec. Com., Tokyo, 1973-76. Author: An Assessment of the Reentry Issues of the Children of Missionaries, 1991, 2d printing with title Missionary Children: Caught between Cultures, 1996; translator: The Story of the Craft Dogs, 1983. Trustee Gardner Webb U., 1999-2002. Named Alumnus of Yr., Gardner Webb U., 1993; J.M. Price scholar Southwestern Bapt. Theol. Sem., 1962; First Bapt. Ch. Blackwell grantee Southeastern Sem., 1986-88. Mem. Am. Assn. Pastoral Counselors, Am. Psychotherapy Assn. (diplomate). Democrat. Avocations: photography, travel, reading, classical music, concerts. Home: 5006 Carleton Dr Unit 113 Wilmington NC 28403 Personal E-mail: mfcs@juno.com.

WALTERS, ERICA SCHEFFLER, special education educator; b. Marietta, Ga., Sept. 5, 1975; d. Rick Scheffler and Kathi Lou Bagley, Kerry Bagley (Stepfather) and Jennifer Scheffler (Stepmother); m. Craig Walters; 1 child, Elizabeth Hope. BE, LaGrange Coll., Ga., 1994—98; MEd, Clemson U., SC, 1998—99. Spl. edn. tchr. East Lake Elem., McDonough, Ga., 2000—05, James M. Brown Elem., Walhalla, SC, 2005—. Recipient Teacher of Year award, 2002—03. Mem.: Coun. Exceptional Children, Kappa Delta Pi.

WALTERS, MARJORIE ANNE, interior designer, consultant; b. Flushing, N.Y., Dec. 5, 1925; d. Walter Bowne Williams, Florence Clara (Bach) Williams; m. Robert Leslie Walters, Sept. 17, 1949; children: Robert Bowne(dec.), Richard James. BS, Coll. William & Mary, 1947; AA, N.Y. Sch. Interior Design, 1958. Owner, pres. M.W. Walters, Interiors, Hohokus, NJ, 1958—86; pres. N.J. Ridgwood Art Inst., 1980—86; owner, pres. M.W. Walters, Interiors, Richfield Springs, NY, 1986—. Dir. Art & Program Commn., Richfield Springs, 1993—; chmn. Baker's Beach Art & Programs Commn., Richfield Springs; exec. dir. Cooperstown N.Y. Art Assn., 1986—90. Smithy-Pioneer Gallery, Cooperstown, N.Y., 2001—. Pres. Richfield Springs Hist. Assn., 1997—; v.p. Richfield Springs Libr. Bd., 1999—; sec. zoning bd. of appeals Town of Richfield Springs, 1999—; organizer of restoration and dedication of hist. town clock of 1918 Richfield Springs, NY, 2005. Recipient Cmty. Svc. award, Richfield C. of C., 1994, Good Citizenship award, DAR, 1994, Good Neighbor award, WBUG AM/FM, 1994, Ostego 2000 Historic Landmark award, Ostego County, 2006. Mem.: Nat. Mus. Women in Arts (charter mem.), Internat. Visual Artists (Eng.), Lake and Valley Garden Club (pres. 1998—2000). Avocations: landscape painting, flower arranging, swimming, skiing. Home and Office: 217 Walters Way Richfield Springs NY 13439 Office Phone: 315-858-0027. E-mail: mbwalt@aol.com.

WALTERS, REBECCA RUSSELL YARBOROUGH, medical technologist; b. Lancaster, S.C., Mar. 9, 1951; d. William Peurifoy and Anna Beth (Cheatham) Yarborough; m. Thomas Edward Walters, Oct. l5, 1983; l child, Katherine Rebecca. BA, Winthrop Coll., l972; postgrad. in med. tech., Palmetto Bapt. Med. Ctr., Columbia, S.C., l974; MA, Cen. Mich. U., 1978. Diplomate in Lab. Mgmt. ASCP. Teaching asst. in biology Winthrop Coll., Rock Hill, S.C., 1972-73; microbiology technologist Palmetto Bapt. Med. Ctr., 1974-76, evening shift supr., 1976-77, asst. adminstrv. dir., 1977-97, dir. lab., 1997—. Article reviewer Med. Lab. Observer; mem. Nat. Cert. Agy. for Med. Lab. Personnel. Hycel, Inc. scholar, l976, 77. Mem. Am. Soc. for Med. Tech. (scholar 1977), S.C. Soc. Med. Tech. (pres. 1979-80, scholar 1976), Am. Soc. Clin. Pathologists (assoc.), Clin. Lab. Mgmt. Assn., Beta Beta Beta, Alpha Mu Tau (scholar 1977). Republican. Presbyterian. Avocations: reading, aerobics, gardening. Home: 104 Turtle Pointe Ct Chapin SC 29036-7695 Office: Palmetto Health Bapt Taylor At Marion Columbia SC 29220-0001

WALTERS-TRAPASSO, SUSAN DIANE, secondary school educator; b. Palm Springs, Calif., July 21, 1967; adopted d. Charles Lee Walters and Janet Ilene Sterliing-Walters; m. Frank Anthony Trapasso II, Jan. 28, 2006; m. Gregory Scott Yeasley, July 20, 1985 (div. Apr. 23, 2003); children: Nathanael Jacob Yeasley, Tabitha Nachelle Yeasley, Hannah MaRee Yeasley. MA in Music, Hope Internat. U., 1986. Cert. tchr. Calif. Commn. Tchr. Credentialing, 2003. Head vocal music Thunderbolt Mid. Sch., Lake Havasu City, Ariz., 1996—2000; tchr. music Bakersfield (Calif.) City Schs., 2000—03, Taft (Calif.) Union H.S., 2003—. Pvt. music tchr., Calif., 1986—. Musician (composer) songs. Mem.: Calif. Music Educators Assn., ACDA, Music Educators Nat. Conf. Republican. Avocations: bicycling, camping, rollerblading, gardening, boogie boarding. Home: 3100 Chuckwagon St Bakersfield CA 93312 Office: Taft Union High School 701 7th St Taft CA 93268 Office Phone: 661-763-2300. Business E-Mail: syeasley@taft.k12.c.a.us.

WALTON, ALICE LOUISE, bank executive; b. Newport, Ark., Oct. 7, 1949; d. Sam and Helen (Robson) Walton BBA, Trinity U., 1971; D. of Bus. Adminstrn. (hon.), S.W. Bapt. U., 1988. Investment analyst First Commerce Corp., New Orleans, 1972-75; dir., v.p. investments Walton Enterprises, Bentonville, Ark., 1975—; retail & investment broker E.F. Hutton Co., New Orleans, 1975-79; vice chair, investment dir. Walton Bank Group, Bentonville, Ark., 1982-88; founder, former pres., chair, CEO Llama Co./Llama Asset Mgmt. Co., Fayetteville, Ark. Mem. dean's adv. coun. U. Ark. Coll. Bus. Adminstrn., Fayetteville, 1989-90. Bd. trustees Amon Carter Mus., Ft. Worth, Tex. Named Disting. Bus. Lectr. Ctrl. State U., Edmond, Okla., 1989, Arkansan of Yr., Ark. Easter Seals Soc., 1990; named one of Top 100 Women in Ark., Ark. Bus., 1995, Top 200 Collectors, ARTnews mag., 2006, Forbes Richest Americans, 2006. Mem.: Northwest Ark. Coun. (first chairperson 1990). Achievements include #13 on Forbes' World's Richest People List, 2005.*

WALTON, ANN THORSON, art historian, writer, curator, educator; d. George A. and Mern M. Thorson; m. Matt Savage Walton, June 21, 1970; children: Anne E.R. von Bergen, Owen H.R. BA in Humanities, U. Denver, 1958, MA in Art History, 1960; PhD in Art History, U. Minn., 1986. Asst. curator Denver Art Mus., 1959—60, curator, 1964—73; chief curator Minn. Mus. Art, St. Paul, 1974—76; corp. curator Burlington Northern, Inc., Seattle, 1981—86; pvt. practice St. Paul, 1986—. Adj. prof. art history U. Colo., Denver, 1970—73; adj. prof. Regis Coll., Denver, 1964—68; guest curator Royal Acad. Fine Arts, Stockholm, 1992; cons. Swedish Mus. Arch., Stockholm, 1990—92; guest lectr. Stockholm U., 1996—98; guest curator Nat. Mus. of Art, Stockholm, 1997. Author: The Burlington Northern Collection, 1982, Ferdinand Boberg, Architect, 1994, Ferdinand Boberg: arkitekten som allkonstnar, 1997; contbr. articles to profl. jours. Active St. Paul-Mpls. Com. on Fgn. Rels., 1983—. Fellow, Kress Found., 1980—81; grantee, Govt. Finland, 1981, Berit Wallenbergs Stiftelse, Stockholm, 1989—92, Swedish Coun. Bldg. Rsch., 1991—93; Thord-Gray Meml. Fund grant, Am.-Scandinavian Found., 1996, Egon Thun scholar, 1991. Mem.: Nat. Mus. Women in Art, Soc. Archtl. Historians, Am.-Scandinavian Found. Avocations: drawing, painting.

WALTON, CAROLE LORRAINE, clinical social worker; b. Harrison, Ark., Oct. 20, 1949; d. Leo Woodrow Walton and Arlette Alegra (Cohen) Armstrong. BA, Lambuth Coll., Jackson, Tenn., 1971; MA, U. Chgo., 1974. lic. clin. social worker. Social worker Community Mental Health, Flint, Mich., 1971-72, clin. social worker Westchester, Ill., 1974-76; dir. self-travel program Chgo. Assn. Retarded Citizens, 1973; coord. family svcs. Inner Harbors Psych. Hosp., Douglasville, Ga., 1976-83; sr. mental health clinician Northside Mental Health Ctr., Atlanta, 1983—; pvt. practice clin. social work Atlanta, 1997—2001. Mem.: NASW, Ga. Soc. for Clin. Work (pres. 1981—82, 1993—95, ethics co-chair 2003—05). Avocation: tennis. Office: Northside Mental Health Ctr 1140 Hammond Dr Ste J-1075 Atlanta GA 30328-7145 Office Phone: 770-842-3761.

WALTON, FLORENCE GOODSTEIN See GOODSTEIN-SHAPIRO, FLORENCE

WALTON, HELEN, philanthropist; m. Sam M. Walton (dec. 1992, founder of Wal-Mart) BA, U. Okla. Co-owner Arvest Bank; founder (with Sam M. Walton) Walton Family Found., 1987; contbr. Walton Family Arts Center. Mem. bd. trustees Univ. Osarks, 1975—. Known for philanthropic contributions, specifically to Arkansas and education. Named one of World's Richest People, Forbes, 2001—04, Forbes Richest Americans, 2006. Office: Walton Family Found PO Box 2030 Bentonville AR 72712

WALTON, JENNIFER REBECCA, middle school educator; b. Atlanta, Oct. 14, 1977; d. Donald Walton and Regina Crutchfield. B, Ga. State U., Atlanta, 2000. Cert. mid. grades educator Ga. Tchr. Thomson Mid. Sch., Centerville, Ga., 2003—, Clayton County, Ellenwood, Ga., 2000—03. Coach Thomson Mid. Sch., 2003—. Office Phone: 478-953-0489.

WALTON, KATHLEEN ENDRES, librarian; b. Columbus, Ohio, Mar. 24, 1961; d. Kenneth Raymond and Mary Margaret (Brown) Endres; m. Thomas Walton, Dec. 7, 1985; children: Tristan James, Arden Siobhan. BA, U. Md., 1982; MLS, Cath. U. Am., 1985. Head engring./architecture/math libr. Cath. U. Am. Libr., Washington, 1985-87; libr. Congl. Quarterly Inc., Washington, 1987-90, head libr., 1991-92, libr. dir., 1992—. Mem. ALA, Am. Assn. Law Librs., D.C. Libr. Assn., Spl. Librs. Assn. Roman Catholic.

WALTON, SHIRLEY DAWN, retired medical technician; b. Jamestown, N.Y., Dec. 12, 1935; d. Kenneth Everett and Wilma Alene Lewis; m. Okley Homa Walton, May 3, 1963 (dec.); 1 child, William W. Cert. respiratory care practioner Fla., 1993. Trainee Women's Christian Hosp., Jamestown, 1956—61; nurse's aid St. Joseph's Hosp., Tampa, Fla., 1963—64, cardiology technician, 1964—74; cardiology tech. U. Hosp., Tampa, 1975—82, respiratory therapist, 1982—88; cardiology tech. East Pasco Med. Ctr., Zephyrhills, Fla., 1988—98; ret., 1998. Methodist. Home: 6801 Woodsman Dr Zephyrhills FL 33544 Personal E-mail: wwaltonz@aol.com.

WALTON, SUZANNE W., elementary school educator; b. Clarksdale, Miss., Nov. 29, 1957; d. George Wayne and Rubie Winter; m. Gary Louis Walton, June 11, 1978; 1 child, Christy Louise. BS Edn., Delta State U., 1978, MA Elem. & Reading, 1980, MA Adminstrn., 1991. Tchr. Clarksdale Mcpl. Schs., Miss., 1978—89, title 1 supr., 1989—99, tchr., 2001—; coord. Pearl River C.C., Poplarville, 2000—01. Co-chair discipline com. Clarksdale Mcpl. Schs., 1993—94, mem. calendar com., 1995—99, mem. handbook com., 1995—99, tchr. evaluator, 1992—98. Sec., treas. Clarksdale Mcpl. Sch. Bd. Election Com., 1996. Mem.: Miss. Reading Assn., Delta Kappa Gamma (pres., treas. 1996—2000). Roman Catholic. Home: 1746 Bennett Rd Clarksdale MS 38614-9424

WALTON, TYLA JOHNSON, secondary school educator; b. Salt Lake City, Nov. 7, 1947; d. Bland Romell and Margaret Ada (Penney) Johnson; m. Kent Allen Walton, Dec. 24, 1974 (dec. May 10, 2005); 1 child, Danielle Caldwell. BS, Utah State U., Logan, 1970. Cert. tchr. Utah. Tchr. Jordan Sch. Dist., Sandy, Utah, 1970—76, Salt Lake Sch. Dist., 1996—. Advanced placement test reader Ednl. Testing Svc. Coll. Bd., NYC. Mem.: NEA, Salt Lake Tchrs. Assn., Utah Edn. Assn., Utah Coun. Social Studies, Utah State Hist. Soc., Orgn. Am. Historians. Mem. Lds Ch. Avocations: reading, travel, crafts. Home: 541 N Coleman Tooele UT 84074 Office: East High Sch 840 S 1300 E Salt Lake City UT 84102 Office Phone: 801-583-1661.

WALTZ, JUDITH A., lawyer; b. Apr. 20, 1956; BA, Ind. U., 1977, MPA, JD, Ind. U., 1981. Bar: Calif. 1982. Asst. regional counsel U.S. Dept. Health & Human Svc., 1986—98; ptnr. Foley & Lardner LLP, San Francisco, 1998—, chairperson health payments/compliance practice group. Co-author: Injunctive Relief Health Care Insolvencies, 1998, Payment Suspensions & Withholds, 2002. Office: Foley Lardner Llp PO Box 7274 San Francisco CA 94120-7274 Office Phone: 415-434-4507. Office Fax: 415-438-6412. Business E-Mail: jwaltz@foley.com.

WALTZ, KATHLEEN M., publishing executive; b. Mar. 6, 1954; m. Bill Raffel, 1990; stepchildren: Jamie, Jenny. BA, DePaul U.; postgrad., Northwestern U. Telemarketer Chgo. Tribune, 1973, mgr. recruitment advt., 1987, dir. customer satisfaction, 1989—90, dir. classified advt., 1990—95, v.p./dir. of developing bus., 1995—97; v.p., gen. mgr. Sun-Sentinel Co., Fla., 1997—98; CEO, pres., pub. Daily Press, Newport News, Va., 1998—2000, Orlando Sentinel Comm., 2000—. Bd. dirs. United Way. of Va. Peninsula, Peninsula Allice for Econ. Devel. WHRO Found. and Greater Peninsula Now; bd. dirs., exec. com. Hampton Roads Partnership; ABC/NAA liaison com., sr. exec. resource corps. Coll. of William and Mary. Mem. So. Newspapers Pub. Assn. (diversity com.). Avocations: travel, golf, gardening. Office: Orlando Sentinel 1000 N Garland Ave Orlando FL 32801

WALTZ, SUSAN, political scientist, educator; Former chmn. Amnesty Internat., London, England, 1993-98; prof. internat. pub. policy Gerald Ford Sch. Pub. Policy U. Mich., Ann Arbor, 2001—. Bd. dirs. Am. Friends Svc. Com., 2000—. Office: Ford Sch Public Policy Michigan U 611 Tappan St Ann Arbor MI 48109 Office Phone: 734-615-8683. Business E-Mail: swaltz@umich.edu.

WALZ, ANGELA, retired secondary school educator; b. Salt Lake City; d. Albert Richard and Emma (Boehnke) Riedel; m. Marvin Gideon Walz, Nov. 21, 1967; children: Gregory Marvin, Richard David. BS, U. Utah, Salt Lake City, 1959; student, Brigham Young U., Provo, Utah, 1963—81, Utah State U., Logan, 1985, Boston U., 1987—92, U. San Diego, 1994—97, U. Minn., 1994, U. Md., 1997—99. Sec. MIA music com. LDS Ch., 1955—64; elem. tchr. SLC, 1959—60; tchr. Eval. Utah Dep. Pub. Instr., 1960—61, Kelly Girl Agy., 1961—64; adminstrv. asst. music dept. Brigham Young. U., 1963, U. Utah Ednl. Rsch., 1966; sec. Am. Embassy, Germany, 1964—65; bus. tchr. Granite H.S., Salt Lake City, 1961—64, Dept. Def. Overseas Sch., Sasebo, Japan, 1966—67, Bitburg H.S., 1967—84, Baumholder H.S., Germany, 1985—94; bus. and work experience tchr. Hanau H.S., Germany, 1994—2001. Mem. curriculum develop. com. Dept. Def. Dependent Sch., Wiesbaden, Germany, 1995—2000, Washington, 1995—2000; prin. adv. bd. Baumholder H.S., 1990—91; admin. asst. music programs Ch. of Jesus Christ Latter Day Saints, Salt Lake City, 1956—64. Soloist: various musical prodns. Mem. cmty. choral groups Rheinlandpfalz Internat. Choir, Germany, 1961—90; ch. pianist and organist Latter Day Saints Ch., 1953—2006. Recipient Outstanding Tchr. award, Bitburg Sch. Dist., 1971, Baumholder Sch. Dist., 1991, Hanau Sch. Dist., 1995, Outstanding FBLA adv., Future Bus. Leaders of Am., 1990. Republican. Ch. Jesus Christ. Avocations: music, swimming, skiing, travel, community involvement. Home: 477 E Peak Ridge Way Draper UT 84020

WALZER, JUDITH BORODOVKO, academic administrator, educator; b. NYC, May 27, 1935; d. Isidore and Ida (Gins) Borodovko; m. Michael L. Walzer, June 17, 1956; children— Sarah, Rebecca BA, Brandeis U., 1958, MA, 1960, PhD, 1967. Dir. office women's edn. Radcliffe Coll., Cambridge, Mass., 1974-77, assoc. dean., 1976-77; Allston Burr sr. tutor, asst. dean for co-edn. Harvard Coll., Cambridge, Mass., 1977-80; asst. to the pres. Princeton U., N.J., 1980-85; provost New Sch. U., N.Y.C., 1985-98, prof. lit., 1998—. Mem. adv. com. Overseas Sch., Hebrew U. in Jerusalem, 1989—. Democrat. Jewish. Office: New Sch U 65 W 11th St New York NY 10011 E-mail: walzer@newschool.edu.

WAMBACH, ABBY (MARY ABIGAIL WAMBACH), Olympic athlete; b. June 2, 1980; Grad., Univ. of Florida. Mem. U.S. Nat. Soccer Team, 2001—; professional soccer player Washington Freedom, 2002—03; mem. U.S. Women's Olympic Soccer Team, Athens, 2004. Named WUSA All-Star game MVP, 2002, WUSA Rookie of the Year, 2002, WUSA First Team All-Star, 2003, MVP Founders Cup Champions match, 2003; named to WUSA All-Star Team, 2002—03. Achievements include member of US Women's Gold medal Soccer Team, Athens Olympic games, 2004; scored overtime game winning goal in Olympic gold medal game, Athens Olympic games, 2004; member of Founders Cup Championship Team, Washington Freedom, 2003. Office: c/o US Soccer Federation 1801 S Prairie Ave Chicago IL 60616

WAND, KIMBERLY JOANNE, assistant principal; b. Colo. Springs, Calif., Feb. 21, 1957; d. William James and Joanne Alice Craig; m. Michael Floyd Wand, May 12, 1979; children: Emily, Steven, Maribeth. MusB, Delta State U., 1979, MusM, 1985; AA in Gifted Edn., 1993; EdS, Miss. State U., 2002. English Certification Hinds Cmty. Coll., 1999. Gen. music tchr. Ruleville Ctrl. Elem., Miss., 1979—81; kindergarten tchr. St. Luke Meth. Ch., Cleveland, Miss., 1981—83; gen. music tchr. grades 1-6 Parks Bell Elem., Cleveland, 1984—86; k-2d grade tchr. Ruleville Ctrl. Elem., 1988—94; music tchr. Brandon Mid. Sch., Miss., 1994—98; fine arts coord. Richland Mid. Sch., 1998—99; asst. fine arts coord. Brandon H.S., 1999—2001; reading specialist, gifted program coord., asst. fine arts coord. Rankin County Sch. Dist., Brandon, 2000—02; dir. of academics Miss. Sch. of the Arts, Brookhaven, 2002—04; asst. prin. grades 7-8 Brookhaven Sch. Dist., 2004—. Presenter in field. Named Star Tchr., Brandon H.S., 2002; recipient Karen Semple Tchr. of Yr., Brandon Mid. Sch., 1997, Leadership award, Miss. State U., 2002. Mem.: Miss. Sci. Tchrs. Assn., Miss. Coun. of Tchrs. of Math., Miss. Assn. for Children Under Six, Music Educators Nat. Conf., Miss. Music Tchrs. Assn., Nat. Coun. of Tchrs. of English, Miss. Coun. of Tchrs. of English, Nat. Assn. for Gifted Children, Miss. Assn. for Gifted Children, Miss. Alliance for Art Edn. (pres. elect 2005—), Mu Phi Epilson. Home: 135 Ken Dr Brandon MS 39042

WAND, PATRICIA ANN, librarian; b. Portland, Oreg., Mar. 28, 1942; d. Ignatius Bernard and Alice Ruth (Suhr) W.; m. Francis Dean Silvernail, Dec. 20, 1966 (div. Jan. 19, 1986); children: Marjorie Lynn Silvernail, Kirk Dean Silvernail. BA, Seattle U., 1963; MAT, Antioch Grad. Sch., 1967; AMLS, U. Mich., 1972. Vol. Peace Corps, Colombia, S.Am., 1963-65; secondary tchr. Langley Jr. High Sch., Washington, 1965-66; asst. libr. Wittenberg U. Libr., Springfield, Ohio, 1967-69; secondary tchr. Caro (Mich.) High Sch., 1969-70; assoc. libr. Coll. of S.I. (N.Y.) Libr., 1972-77; head, access svcs. Columbia U. Librs., N.Y.C., 1977-82; asst. univ. libr. U. Oreg., Eugene, 1982-89; univ. libr. The Am. U., Washington, 1989—. Cons. Bloomsburg (Pa.) U. Libr., 1990, Banco Ctrl., Ecuador, 1998, Am. U. Sharjah, UAE, 1999-2003; bd. dirs. CAPCON, 1997-2003, chair, 2002-03; bd. dirs. ERIC Clearinghouse on Higher Edn. Adminstrn. Contbr. articles to profl. jours. Pres. West Cascade Returned Peace Corps Vols., Eugene, 1985-88; v.p. Friends of Colombia, Washington, 1990—; speaker on Peace Corps, 1965—, libr. and info. svcs., 1979—; bd. mem. Nat. Peace Corps Assn., 2005—. Honors Program scholarship Seattle U., 1960-62, Peace Corps scholarship Antioch U., 1965-66; recipient Beyond War award, 1987, Fulbright Sr. Lectr. award Fulbright, 1989, Disting. Alumnus award Sch. of Info. and Libr. Studies, U. Mich., 1992. Mem. ALA (chmn. com. on legislation 1997-98, coun. 2001-04, internat. rels. com. 2004—), Assn. Coll. and Rsch. Librs. (chair budget and fin. bd. dirs. 1987-89, 2001-04, chair WHCLIS task force 1989-92, chair govt. rels. com. 1993-94, chair internat. rels. com. 1996-98), On-line Computer Librs. Ctr. (adv. com. on coll. and univ. librs. 1991-96), D.C. Libr. Assn. (bd. dirs. 1993-98, pres. 1996-97, Disting. Svc. award 2003). Home: 4854 Bayard Blvd Bethesda MD 20816-1785 Office: Am Univ Libr 4400 Massachusetts Ave NW Washington DC 20016-8046 Office Phone: 202-885-3237.

WANDEL, SHARON LEE, sculptor; b. Bemidji, Minn., Mar. 19, 1940; d. Roy J. and Bonnie (Englund) Opsahl; m. Thaddeus Ludwik Wandel, Oct. 17, 1970; children: Holly, Erika. BA, Gustavus Adolphus Coll., 1962; MSW, Columbia U., 1965; Cert. in Arts Mgmt., SUNY, Purchase, 1993. Caseworker Manhattan State Hosp., N.Y.C., 1963-64; caseworker/rschr. Cmty. Svc. Soc., N.Y.C., 1965-67; teaching asst. dept. medicine NYU Med. Ctr., N.Y.C., 1967—71. Adv. bd. Lamia, Inc., NYC, 1999—2003. One-woman shows at

Silvermine Guild of Artists, New Canaan, Conn., 1993, 97, 2000, Pen and Brush, NYC, 1994, Clark Whitney Gallery, Lenox, Mass., 1994, James Cox Gallery, Woodstock, NY, 1994, 96, Cortland Jessup Gallery, Provincetown, Mass., 1998, NYC, 2000, 02, Gallery Marya, Osaka, Japan, 1999, Laura Barton Gallery, Westport, Conn., 2000, Firehouse Gallery, Damaviscotta, Maine, 2000, Gallery Irohane, Osaka, Japan, 2001; exhibited in group shows at Nat. Acad. Design, NYC, 1988, 90, 92, 94-95, 97-2000, 04-06, Cortland Jessup Gallery, Provincetown and NYC, 1998-2002, Canyon Ranch, Lenox, Mass. 1999-2003, Chesterwood, Lenox, Mass., 2000-01, Butler Inst. Am. Art., Youngstown, Ohio, 2000, Cavalier Gallery, Nantucket, Mass., 2001, Berkshires Bot. Garden, Mass., 2001, Paesaggio Gallery, West Hartford, Conn., 2001-04, Leighton Gallery, Blue Hill, Maine, 2001-06, Munson Gallery, Chatham, Mass., 2002-06, Sakai (Japan) City Mus., 2002, Craven Gallery, Martha's Vineyard, Mass., 2002-06, Berta Walker Gallery, Provincetown, Mass., 2002, Elan Fine Arts, Rockport, Maine, 2003-05, 2006, Clarke Galleries, Stowe, Vt., 2003-06, Palm Beach, Fla., 2003-04, NYC, 2003-04, Westchester Arts Coun., White Plains, NY, 2004, Gallery Yellow, Cross River, N.Y., 2006; permanent collections at Art Students League, Westinghouse Corp. Collection, Pitts., Nat. Acad. Design, Housatonic Mus., CT, C. of C., Toyamura, Japan, Pfizer Corp. Collection, Armonk, NY; commns. include two 8' bronze figures for Ihilani Resort, Kapolei, Hawaii, 1993, 2 5" figures Silvermine Galleries, 1993. Mem. rsch. com. Arthritis Found., N.Y.C., 1968-69. Recipient N.Am. Sculpture Exhbn. 2d place, 1991, Three River Arts Festival (Carnegie Inst.) Purchase award, 1990, Hakone Open Air Mus. (Japan) 3d and 4th Rodin Grand Prize Exhbn. Excellent Maquettes, 1990, 92, Matrix Gallery 1st prize for sculpture, 1990, Ariel Gallery Internat. Competition Group Show award, 1989, Salmagundi Club McReynolds award, 1989, Barret Coleco award, 1988, 1st place nat. competition Sundance Gallery, Bridgehampton, N.Y., 1997; Vt. Studio Ctr. fellow, 2000; elected Nat. Academician Nat. Acad. Design, 1994. Mem. Silvermine Guild of Artists (Solo Show award 1992), N.Y. Soc. Woman Artists (past pres.), Knickerbocker Artists USA, The Pen and Brush (Meisner award 1990, Solo Show award 1993), Nat. Acad. Design (elected nat. academician 1994, Cleo Hartwig award 1990), Nat. Sculpture Soc. (Meisner award 1994, Hexter award 1993, Spring award 1991, Meiselman award 1990), Audubon Artists (Chaim Gross Found. award 1993), Sculptors Guild (past bd. dirs.). Avocations: travel, cooking, reading. Studio: PO Box 314 Croton On Hudson NY 10520-0314 E-mail: wandel_s@hotmail.com.

WANDER-PERNA, LUCY, film company executive; Sr. v.p. Sony Pictures Entertainment, Inc., Culver City, Calif.

WANDERSMAN, LOIS PALL, psychologist; b. Bklyn., Feb. 4, 1950; d. Irving John and Gertrude (Weisner) Pall; m. Abraham Harold Wandersman, Sept. 12, 1970; children: Seth, Jeffrey. BA, SUNY, Stony Brook, 1970; PhD, Cornell U., 1977; postdoctoral, U. S.C., 1984. Rsch. assoc. Peabody Coll., Nashville, 1975-78; adj. asst. prof. psychology U. S.C., Columbia, 1978—; rsch. asst. prof. preventive medicine Sch. of Medicine U. S.C., Columbia, 1979—; pvt. practice Columbia, 1985—. Intern Yale Child Study Ctr., New Haven, 1985; clin. supr. U. S.C., Columbia, 1987-90; dir. therapeutic svcs. Nurturing Ctr., 1989-96. Contbr. chpts. to books in field and articles to profl. jours. Mem. APA, Soc. for Rsch. in Child Devel., S.C. Psychol. Assn. Home: 4128 Sandwood Dr Columbia SC 29206-2224 Office: 1512 Laurel St Columbia SC 29201-2623

WANDRO, KATHLEEN MARY, secondary school educator; b. Chgo., Oct. 19, 1953; d. James Joseph and Mildred Marie O'Rourke; m. William Donald Wandro, June 26, 1982; children: Jennifer Marie, Sean William. BFA, Drake U., Des Moines, Iowa, 1971—75; MEd, Roosevelt U., Chgo., 1982—85; Theatre & Edn. Studies, Northwestern U., Evanston, Ill., 1998—99. Cert. Tchrf. Ill. Dept. Edn., 1977. English tchr. Hoffman Estates HS, Ill., 1977—, musical dir., 1980—. Theatre play dir. Hoffman Estates HS, 1978—92, auditorium mgr., 1982—, mentoring program dir., 2003—; scholar instr. Golden Apple Found., Chgo., 1998—. Prodr.: Student produced films & ann. HEHS Film Festival. Recipient Those Who Excel award, Ill. Dept. Edn., 2005. Fellow: Golden Apple Acad. (life Excellence in Tchg. award 1998). Roman Catholic. Avocations: music, literature, travel, theater, films. Office: Hoffman Estates HS 1100 W Higgins Rd Hoffman Estates IL 60195 Office Phone: 847-755-5805. Office Fax: 847-755-5759. Business E-Mail: kwandro@d211.org.

WANG, AN-YI (ANNE) CHOU, real estate broker; b. Taipei, Taiwan, Aug. 9, 1946; arrived in U.S., 1984; d. Chin-Yung and Fei-Ying Chou; m. An Tai Wang, Apr. 14, 1971; 1 child, Stewart Sei-Yu. BA in Journalism, Nat. Cheng Chi U., 1970. Analyst Ctrl. Daily News, Taipei, 1970; reporter China Daily News, Taipei, 1970—71, Taiwan Times, Kaohsiung, Taiwan, 1971—72; chief editor Gen. Instrument of Taiwan Ltd., Taipei, 1972—77; reporter, chief editor Broadcasting Co. of China, Taipei, 1977—84; reporter Ctrl. Daily News, San Francisco, 1984—86, Internat. Daily News, San Francisco, 1986—87; sales rep. Century 21-City Properties, San Francisco, 1987—94; broker, owner Evergreen Realty, San Francisco, 1995—. Author (short story): Heart of Women, 1984; author: (essay) Stories of Artist, 1980, Group Image of Journalists and Pub., 1981. Mem.: San Francisco Assn. Realtors, San Mateo County Assn. Realtors, Calif. Assn. Realtors. Avocations: photography, travel, reading. Home: 2266 34th Ave San Francisco CA 94116 Office: Evergreen Realty 2124 Taraval St San Francisco CA 94116 Office Phone: 415-682-2888. Personal E-mail: evergree@pacbell.net.

WANG, CONG, electrical engineer; b. Hangzhou, Zhejiang, China, Nov. 1, 1965; came to the U.S., 1989; d. Ben Zuo Wang and Xia Ren Shieh. BSEE, U. Southwestern La., 1991; MSEE, U. Tex., Dallas, 1993. Elec. engr. Tex. Instruments, Dallas, 1993—, tech. ladder, 1998—. Recipient 1st place in math contest South Region, La., 1991. Mem. Chinese Orgn. Tex. Instrument (co-chair 1998—), Tau Beta Pi. Avocations: reading, hiking, volleyball, tennis, music. Office: Tex Instruments Inc MS947 13536 N Central Expy Dallas TX 75243-1108 also: PO Box 852638 Richardson TX 75085-2638

WANG, DIANE, music educator; b. San Francisco, Aug. 25, 1954; d. Hsih-Heng and Louise Siu-Tuan (Chen) W.; m. Stacy Dean Rodgers; children: Christopher Wang Rodgers, Heather Marie Rodgers. MusB, Ind. U., 1977; MusM, U. Tex., Austin, 1979. Tchr. piano and flute pvt. studio, 1969—. Instr. music U. Miss., University, 1998—. Performer Wang Rodgers Piano Duo, Oxford, Miss., 1986—, U. Miss., 1996—. Vol. Oxford Cmty. Park Assn., 1997-98, mem. flute/piccolo Tupelo Symphony Orch., 2004—. Mem. Oxford Piano Tchrs. Assn. (pres. 1991—), Miss. Music Tchrs. Assn. (pre-coll. auditions area chair 2000—). Avocation: tennis. Office: U Miss Music Dept University MS 38677 Office Phone: 662-915-7029.

WANG, JOSEPHINE JUNG-SHAN, language educator, translator; d. Hsiian Chang and Yen-Yi Lan; children: Charlotte C., Kenneth C. BA, Queens Coll., CUNY, Flushing, 1966; MA, George Washington U., 1969. Lang. instr. Montgomery Coll., Rockville, Md., 1975—2002; spl. asst. U.S. Dept. Edn., Washington, 1988—89; mem., Pres.'s Intergovtl. and Adv. Coun. of Edn., 1989—92; instr., Mandarin Montgomery City Pub. Schs., Md., 1990—. Mem., sr. coun. City of Gaithersburg, Md., 2003—; mem. St. Raphael's Cath. Ch. Taft sr. fellow, Catholic U. Mem.: NEA, Montgomery Retired Tchrs. Assn., West Deer Park Homeowners Assn., Queens Coll. Alumni Assn., George Washington U. Alumni Assn., Mid-Montgomery Rep. Club. Republican. Roman Catholic. Home: PO Box 3394 Gaithersburg MD 20885

WANG, JOSEPHINE L. FEN, physician; b. Taiwan, China, Jan 2, 1948; came to U.S., 1974; d. Pao-San and Ann-Nam (Chen) Chao; m. Chang-Yang Wang, Dec. 20, 1973; children: Edward, Eileen. MD, Nat. Taiwan U., Taipei, 1974. Diplomate Am. Bd. Pediatrics, Am. Bd. Allergy and Immunology. Intern Nat. Taiwan U. Hosp., 1973-74; resident U. Ill. Hosp., Chgo., 1974-76; fellow Northwestern U. Med. Ctr., Chgo., 1976-78, instr. pediatrics, 1978—; cons. Holy Cross Hosp., Chgo., 1978—, Meth. Hosp. Ind., 1979—, St. Anthony Hosp., 1985—, Christ Hosp., 1995—. Fellow Am. Coll. Allergy; mem. AMA, Am. Acad. Allergy. Office: 9012 Connecticut Dr Merrillville IN 46410-7170 also: 4901 W 79th St Burbank IL 60459-1554

WANG, KIM, commissioner, librarian; m. Harry Wang; children: Elaine, Steve, Leslie. BA in History, U. Colo.; MLS, U. Calif., Berkeley. Former libr. U. So. Calif., Hughes Aircraft; property mgr. and real estate broker. Mem. Nat. Mus. & Libr. Services. Bd., Inst. Mus. & Libr. Services, Washington, 2004—. V.p. La Terrazza Homeowners Assn.; former parks and recreation commr., planning commn. mem. City of Rancho Palos Verdes; bd. mem. Libr. Calif. Bd.; mem. Cultural Arts Commn., Torrance, Calif.; trustee Marymount Coll., Palos Verdes, Calif.; former bd. mem. Am. Heart Assn., Torrance. Mem.: AARP, AAUW (Torrance br.), LWV (Torrance br.), Am. Contract Bridge League, Torrance Sister City Assn., Torrance Hist. Soc., Torrance Hist. Assn., Torrance Chamber Toastmasters, Torrance Area C. of C. Office: Inst Mus and Libr Svcs 1100 Pennsylvania Ave NW Washington DC 20506

WANG, LIYAN, product design engineer; b. Guiyang, Guizhou, China, Oct. 30, 1962; came to U.S., 1990; d. Tongxing Wang and Zhirong Wu; m. Cheng Qian, Apr. 24, 1987; 1 child, Kathy Qian. BS, Northwestern Poly. U., Xian, China, 1984; MS, U. Ky., 1993, PhD, 1996. Engr. in tng. Tech. editor Nat. Def. Pub. House, Beijing, 1984-90; rsch. asst. mech. engring. dept. U. Ky., Lexington, 1991-96; rsch. assoc. Ctr. for Mfg. Sys., Lexington, 1996; project engr. Altair Engring. Inc., Allen Park, Mich., 1996-97, ICEMCFD Engring., Inc., Livonia, Mich., 1998; product design engr. Visteon Automotive Sys./An Enterprise of Ford Motor Co., Dearborn, Mich., 1998—. Project leader Computational Fluid Dynamics Simulation. Contbr. articles to jours. and papers to confs. Sect. chair Ford Yan Xin Qigong Club, Dearborn; pres. Northwestern Poly. U. Student Broadcasting Sta., Xian. Mem. ASME, Soc. Mfg. Engrs., Soc. Automotive Engrs. Avocations: ping pong/table tennis, swimming, jogging, yan xin qigong. Home: 6352 Marshall St Canton MI 48187-4700 Office: Visteon 17000 Rotunda Dr Dearborn MI 48120-1168 Fax: (313) 621-8004. E-mail: lwang@visteon.com.

WANG, NANCY, pathologist, educator; b. An-Wei, China, Sept. 2, 1944; m. Tingchung Wang; children: Jessie, Melissa. BS, Nat. Taiwan U., 1966; MS, U. Minn., 1968, PhD, 1978. Diplomate Am. Bd. Med. Genetics. Instr. Dept. Pathology & Lab. Med. U. Minn., Mpls., 1978-79, asst. prof., 1980-82, Dept. Pathology, Tulane Med. Sch., 1982-83, assoc. prof., 1984-86, U. Rochester, NY, 1986-93, prof. NY, 1993—. Mem.: Am. Assn. Human Genetics. Office Phone: 585-275-6597. Business E-Mail: nancy_wang@urmc.rochester.edu.

WANG, SONA, venture capitalist; b. South Korea; naturalized, US; BS in Indsl. Engring., Stanford Univ., 1980; MBA magna cum laude, Northwestern Univ., 1986. Mgr., engr. Intel Corp., Calif.; investment mgr. Allstate Venture Capital; co-founder, gen. ptnr. Batterson, Johnson & Wang, Ill., 1988—2001, Inroads Capital Ptnrs., Evanston, Ill., 1995—, Ceres Venture Fund, 2005—. Bd. dir. IKOS Sys., Answer Systems (now subs. of Platinum Technologies), Sigmedics, Inc., Array Technologies, Success Lab., Inc., Ultimo Enterprises, Ltd., High Tower Software, Grand Eagle Cos., Wine.com. Founding adv. coun. mem. Women's Bus. Devel. Ctr., Chgo.; mem. Coun. of 100, Northwestern Univ.; bd. trustees Northwestern Univ. Named one of 100 Most Influential Women, Crain's Chicago Business, 2004; recipient Leadership award for entrepreneurship, YWCA, 2001. Office: Inroads Capital Ptnrs Ste 2050 1603 Orrington Ave Evanston IL 60201 Office Phone: 847-864-2000. Office Fax: 847-864-9692.

WANG, VERA, fashion designer; b. NYC, June 27, 1949; d. Cheng Ching Wang; m. Arthur Becker, June 22, 1989; children: Cecilia, Josephine. BA in Art History, Sarah Lawrence Coll., New York, 1978. Various positions including accessories editor, European editor, sr. fashion editor Vogue mag., NYC, 1969—85; design dir. Ralph Lauren Women's Wear, NYC, 1987-89; prin. Vera Wang Bridal House Ltd., NYC, 1990—; expanded to ready-to-wear, fragrance, eyewear, footwear, fine jewelry, and a home collection. Designer for Olympic figure skaters including Nancy Kerrigan's silver medal performance at the 1994 Olympics. Costume designer (films) The Parent Trap, 1998, First Daughter, 2004; author: Vera Wang on Weddings, 2001. Recipient Womenswear Designer of the Yr., Coun. Fashion Designers Am., 2005. Achievements include first to successfully fuse high style and fashion with the tradition and symbolism of the bridal industry; designing wedding and red carpet gowns for Hollywood's elite. Office: Vera Wang Bridal House 225 W 39th St Fl 10 New York NY 10018-3103 Office Phone: 212-575-6400.*

WANG, YUFENG, science educator; arrived in U.S., 1995; d. Qiancai Wang and Jinzhu Chen. BS in Genetics, Fudan U., Shanghai, China, 1993; MS in Stats. and Genetics, Iowa State U., 1998, PhD in Bioinformatics and Computational Biology, 2001. Grad. asst. Iowa State U., Ames, 1995—2001; rsch. scientist Am. Type Culture Collection, Manassas, Va., 2001—03; asst. prof. U. of Tex., San Antonio, 2003—. Author to profl. jours. albums. Fellow James Cornette Rsch. fellowship, Iowa State U., 2001. Mem.: Am. Statis. Assn., Internat. Soc. Computational Biology, Genetics Soc. Am. Achievements include research in functional divergence and age distribution of human gene families, computational approach in drug discovery, evolutionary and population genetics of infectious diseases. Office: University of Texas San Antonio Dept of Biology 6900 N Loop 1604 West San Antonio TX 78249 Home: 12222 Vance Jackson Rd Apt 1538 San Antonio TX 78230-5947 Office Phone: 210-458-6492. Business E-Mail: ywang@utsa.edu.

WANGSNESS, GENNA STEAD, retired hotel executive, innkeeper; b. Detroit, Feb. 2, 1942; d. William Allen Stead and Genevieve Josephine Schreiber; m. Roger Carroll Wangsness, Dec. 1, 1967; children: Alison Lee Clement, Bijali Anne, Brian William. BA in Liberal Studies, Georgetown U., 1995. Vol. Peace Corps, Tehran, Iran, 1965—67; sec. Office of Pres. Georgetown U., Washington, 1984—86, coord. adminstrv. svcs. Office of Pres., 1986—89, adminstrv. officer dept. surgery, 1989—92, adminstrv. office Sch. Summer and Continuing Edn., 1992—95; exec. asst. to exec. v.p. Am. Soc. Clin. Oncology, Alexandria, Va., 1995—96; innkeeper The Inn at Folkston, Ga., 1997—2006; ret., 2006. Author: Folkston Then and Now 1881-2003, A Self-Guided Walking Tour of Historic Downtown, Folkston, Georgia, 2003. Mem.: Alpha Sigma Lambda. Achievements include establishment of womens studies section at Charlton Public Library.

WANGSNESS, HARRIET ANN, elementary school educator; b. Decorah, Iowa, Aug. 20, 1941; d. Emil Melvin and Hilda Marie Jevne; m. Clayton Elvin Wagnsness, May 25, 1974; children: Erik Clayton, Anne Marie, Jon Erik. BA, Luther Coll., Decorah, Iowa, 1962. 3rd grade tchr. Postville Cmty. Sch., Iowa, 1962—72; 2nd grade tchr. Decoran Cmty. Sch., 1972—73; title I/reading recovery tchr. N. Winneshier Cmty. Sch., 1983—. Sunday sch. tchr. Highland Luth. Ch., Rural Spring Grove, Minn., Bible sch. tchr. Mem.: Profl. Educators Iowa, Reading Recovery Coun. N. Am., Reading Recovery Coun. Iowa, Luren Ladies Aux. Republican. Lutheran. Avocations: reading, crocheting, walking. Home: 1549 N Bear Rd Spring Grove MN 55974 Office: N Winneshier Cmty Sch 3495 N Winn Rd Decorah IA 52101 Home Fax: 563-735-5981. Business E-Mail: hwangsness@n-winn.k12.ia.us.

WANLEY, PATRICIA ANN, medical/surgical nurse; b. Cin., Sept. 24, 1948; d. Charles Henry and Georgina Helen (Masterson) W. AS, U. Indpls., 1969. RN, Ark., Ind., Md. Staff nurse Ind. U. Hosp., Indpls.; staff nurse home health Bapt. Meml. Hosp., Hardy, Ark.; staff nurse to pvt. physician Chevy Chase, Md.; acting nurse mgr. Holy Cross Hosp., Silver Spring, Md.; rsch. nurse NIH, 2005—. Vol. Am. Diabetes Assn. Named Outstanding Vol. Am. Diabetes Assn.; Bus. and Profl. Women's Nursing scholar, Viva Campbell Nursing scholar. Mem. ANA, Md. Nurses Assn.

WANSBROUGH, ANN, legal assistant; b. Ft. Worth, Mar. 1, 1952; d. Frank and Hazel S. Hilton; 1 child, Trenton Scott Smith; m. Aaron Gregory Wansbrough, July 7, 1995. BS in Edn., Baylor U., Waco, Tex., 1974. Merchandiser J C Penney Co., Dallas, 1974—76, sr. merchandiser, 1976—78, pers. mgr., 1978—81; nat. sales mgr. T. Cappelli Handbags, Dallas, 1986—97; sales rep. Ann Smith and Assocs., Dallas, 1986—2002; legal asst. Ferrer Poirot & Wansbrough, Dallas, 2002—. Office: 2603 Oak Lawn Ave Dallas TX 75219-4021 Office Phone: 214-521-4412.

WANTZ, KATHY LYNN ZEPP, school nurse; d. Garland Edgar and Barbara Purdie Zepp; m. Stephen Albert Wantz, Apr. 8, 1979; children: Elizabeth Ann Chaney, Ashley May. RN, Catonsville C.C., 1979. RN Md., Md. From nurse's aid to in-svc. dir. WNCC, 1975—80; charge nurse Carroll County Gen. Hosp., 1980—86; residential client coord. Carroll County ARC, 1986—87; sch. nurse Carroll County Pub. Schs., 1987—91; staff nurse Critical Care Nursing Agy.-CCN, Inc., 1987—92; charge nurse PACU Carroll County Gen. Hosp./Dixon Outpatient Surg. Ctr., 1992—98; sch. nurse Carrolltowne Elem./Regional Spl. Edn. Ctr., 1998—. Lectr./presenter in field. Vol. Relay for Life, Md. Coop. Ext. Svc.; mem. Carrolltowne PTA, Carrolltowne Social Com.; former sec. and amb. attendant Pleasant Valley Cmty. Fire Dept.; former Sun. sch. tchr. and supt., choir mem. St. Mary's United Ch. of Christ. Named Md. Sch. Health Nurse of the Yr., Md. Assn. Sch. Health Nurses, 2004—05; recipient Spirit award, Carroll County Gen. Hosp. Mem.: Sch. Nurse Assn. Carol County, Carroll County Edn. Assn., Md. State Tchrs. Assn., Md. Assn. Sch. Health Nurses, Nat. Assn. Sch. Health Nurses. Republican. United Ch. Of Christ. Avocations: reading, gardening, scuba diving, snorkeling, travel.

WANWIG, ANNETTE CLARE, nursing administrator; b. Hudson, S.D., Oct. 2, 1948; d. Arnold Hartvig and Estella Ellen (Sorensen) Andersen; m. John Daniel Wanwig, June 3, 1973; children: Kirstin Anne, Bjorn Erik. BS, S.D. State U., 1970. RN. Nurse Harborview Med. Ctr., Seattle, 1970-72, U of Vt. Med. Ctr. Hosps., Burlington, 1972-75, St. Joseph's Hosp., Stockton, Calif., 1975-78; nurse, office mgr. Cascade Internal Medicine, Tacoma, 1978—. Mem. AAUW, Pierce County Med. Soc. Alliance, Sigma Theta Tau. Republican. Lutheran. Avocations: genealogy, nature, skiing. Home: PO Box 1609 Gig Harbor WA 98335-3609 Office: Cascade Internal Medicine 1901 S Union A-305 Tacoma WA 98405

WAPNER, DONNA, healthcare educator; d. Joseph and Sylvia Wapner; m. Peppino D'Agostino, Oct. 18, 1988. BS in Psychology, Pa. State U., 1976; MS, U. SC., 1979. Cert. addiction specialist Calif. Assn. Addiction Studies Educators. Asst. dir. U. SC, Office Health Promotion, Columbia, 1978—80; health edn. faculty Coll. Charleston, 1981—82; asst dir. Nat. Health Screening Coun., San Francisco, 1983—84; behavioral health educator Obesity, Risk Factor Program, San Francisco, 1984—90; part time faculty, health edn. San Francisco State U.; prof., health sci. Diablo Valley Coll., 1992—. Steering com. Health Access Coalition, Calif., 1990—93; chair, advocacy com. Soc. Pub. Health Educators, 1993—95; founding mem. Internat. Coalition Addiction Studies Educators, 1997—; adv. bd. mem. Nat. Addiction Tech. Transfer Ctr., 1997—. Radio columist Wellness Program, KQED, 1989; contbg. writer: website Power Web on Substance Abuse Issues, 2000—03. Chair bd. supr. Tobacco Master Settlement Adv. Bd., Solano County, Calif., 2003—06. Grantee FIPSE grant, 1997. Mem.: Calif. Assn. Alcohol, Drug Educators. Avocations: travel, kayaking, hiking. Office: Diablo Valley Coll 321 Golf Club Rd Pleasant Hill CA 94523 Office Phone: 925-685-1230 X 2467. Business E-Mail: dwapner@dvc.edu.

WARANIUS VASS, ROSALIE JEAN, artist; b. Fond du Lac, Wis., Dec. 10, 1938; d. John Stanley and Anna Francis (Jonaitis) Waranius; m. Kenneth James Vass, June 11, 1960; children: Kealie, Ross, Kenlyn, Jason. BA, Alverno Coll., 1960. Cert. art tchr., Ill. Art tchr. East Aurora (Ill.) H.S., 1979-83; dir. Doctor Scholl Art Gallery, Aurora, 1984-90; studio art tchr. Marmion Acad., Aurora, 1985-90. One-woman shows include Batavia (Ill.) Pub. Libr., 1987, The Holmstad, Ill., 1988, Bellarmine Coll., Ky., 1989, Aurora (Ill.) U., 1989, St. Charles (Ill.) Pub. Libr., 1989, Roberta Campbell Art Gallery, Ill., 1991, 95, Rolling Meadows (Ill.) Libr. Art Gallery, 1991, Alverno Coll. Art Gallery, Wis., 1991, Ill. Artisan Shop, 1992, Jesse Besser Mus., Mich., 1993, Beacon St. Gallery, Ill., 1995, Saginaw (Mich.) Art Mus., 1997, Alfons Gallery, Wis., 1998, Norris Cultural Arts Ctr., Ill., 1998, Balzekas Mus., Ill., 1999, Gallery 129, Ill., 2000, Lane Allen Gallery, Ill., 2005; exhibited in group shows including 17th Internat. Exhbn. Water Color Soc., Houston, 1994, NWS Signature Mem. Juried Exhbn., Norwalk, Calif., 1994, Aurora U., 1994, Invitational Batavia Artists, 1994, Women Artists: A Celebration, Youngstown, Ohio, 1994, No. Art Competition, Rhinelander, Wis., 1994, Watercolor Masters: Midwest Show, Lincolnwood, Ill., 1995, Norris Cultural Arts Ctr., St. Charles, 1989-98, Yello Gallery, Chgo., 1997, Alfons Gallery, Milw., 1998, Norris Cultural Arts Ctr., St. Charles, Ill., 1998, Balzekas Mus., Ill., 1999,, Gallery 129, Ill., 2000, Art & Whimsy, The Gallery, Batavia, 2001, Scribbles: Art & Text, The Gallery, Batavia, 2002, Northwest Area Arts Coun. Members Show, Woodstock, Ill., 2003, Womens Works, 2003, Vicinity Show, St. Charles, Ill., 2003, Midwest Winter Show, Wausau, Wis., 2004, The Modern Portrait Show, Lane Allen Gallery, Batavia, Ill., 2004, All the World's a Stage, 1st St. Playhouse Gallery, 2004, Artists on the Urban Edge VIII, Barrington, Ill., 2004, Contemporary Works, Taylor Kinzel Gallery, Roswell, Ga., 2004, An Eye for Color, Lane Allen Gallery, Ill., 2005, Vicinity Norris Gallery, Ill., 2005, Jane Meyer Gallery, Ill., 2005, Old Courthouse Gallery, Woodstock, Ill., Batavia City Hall Juried Exhibit, Ill., St. Charles Art and Music Festival Exhibit, Ill., 2005, Once Upon a Time, Orleans St. Gallery, St. Charles, Ill., 2005, Batavia Artist Showcase, First St. Playhouse Gallery, Ill., Batavia Art Guild Exhibit, Ill., Surroundings One Fine Art Gallery, Chgo., 2006, Wit and Whimsey CVA, Wausau, Wis., 2006, others; represented in permanent collections at Art and Music Festival, Ill., Whirlpool Corp., Ill., Security Bank, Iowa, First Chgo. Bank, Glenbrook North Western Healthcare, Jesse Besser Mus., Mich., Easter Seal, Ill., St. Francis Hosp., Ill. Delnor Cmty Hosp., Geneva, Ill., Kane County Courthouse, others. Mem. Nat. Watercolor Soc. (signature mem., life), Nat. Mus. Women in Arts, Chgo. Artists Coalition, Art Inst. Chgo. Avocations: travel, reading, cooking. Home: O S 888 Wenmoth Rd Batavia IL 60510-9711 Personal E-mail: rwaraniusvass@aol.com.

WARBERG, WILLETTA, concert pianist, music educator; b. Twin Falls, Idaho, June 2, 1932; d. George William Warberg and Ethel Margaret (Sargent) Warberg-Chandler; m. David Jacob Bar-Illan, Sept. 3, 1954 (div.); children: Daniela, Jeremy Oscar. Student, Colo. Women's Coll., 1950-51, Aspen Music Camp, 1951; studied with, Rudolph Firkusny, 1951-53; BS, Mannes Coll. Music, N.Y.C., 1954. Assoc. food editor Look mag., N.Y.C., 1956-61; food editor Status mag., N.Y.C., 1961-62, Ladie's Home Jour., N.Y.C., 1964-66; photog. stylist Gourmet mag., N.Y.C., 1961-64, freelance writer, photog. stylist, 1965-75; pres., owner Willetta Enterprises, advt. agy., Twin Falls, 1976-84; food columinst, music and arts critic Times News, 1978-87; duo-piano ptnr. with Robert Starer, N.Y.C., Woodstock, 1991—2000; piano coach Saugerties, NY, 1991—. Made feasibility study of restaurant situation in Israel, U.S. Dept. State ICA Point 4 Program, Washington and Israel, 1960; artist-in-residence Holy Cross Concert Series, Kingston, N.Y., 1994—. Concert pianist, Idaho, Oreg., Utah, Wash., Colo., N.Y.C., N.Y. State, 1940—; author: Cooking from Scratch, 1976, Space Age Cookery, 1977; syndicated food columnist Willetta Says, 1978-87; contbr. food and sci. articles to Cosmopolitan, Modern Maturity, Esquire, Sun Valley, Sci. Diegest, also other mags. Bd. dirs. N.W. Opera Assn., 1984-87; pres. bd. dirs. Woodstock Lyric Theatre, 1994-2000; v.p. bd. dirs. Woodstock Chamber Orch., 1993—; chmn. Friends of the Maverick Concerts Inc., Woodstock, N.Y., 1999—. Winner Rocky Mountain talent search contest Salt Lake Tribune and Salt Lake Telegram, 1949. Mem. Nat. Fedn. Music Clubs, Music Tchrs. Nat. Assn. (cert.), Kingston Music Soc. Avocations: designing and sewing clothes, painting still lifes, swimming, developing recipes, writing.

WARBURTON, SHELLY JO, music educator; d. Jerry and Mary Warburton. MusB in Edn., East Tex. State U., Commerce, Tex., 1992, MusM in Edn., 1994. Cert. tchr. music Tex., 1992, tchr. ESL Tex., 2004, tchr. Am. Orff-Schulwerk Assn., 2004. Asst. dir. band J.W. Nixon H.S. Laredo Ind. Sch. Dist.Z, Laredo, 1994—95; asst. dir. band Griffin Mid. Sch. Lewisville Ind. Sch. Dist., The Colony, Tex., 1995—98, music specialist Ctrl. Elem., 1998—. Pvt. instr. flute DeLay Mid. Sch. Lewisville (Tex.) Ind. Sch. Dist., 1999—.

Named Tchr. of Yr., Ctrl. Elem. Sch., 2006. Mem.: Am. Orff-Schulwerk Assn., Tex. Music Educators Assn., Tau Beta Sigma (life; v.p., treas.). Office: Central Elementary Lewisville ISD 400 High School Drive Lewisville TX 75057

WARCHOL, JUDITH MARIE, secretarial service company executive; b. Chgo., Apr. 20; d. Michael Henry and Rose Therese (Vito) Schmidt Fitpold; m. Daniel August Warchol, Aug. 17, 1963 (dec.); children— Kathleen Louise, Raymond Michael, Sherry Lynn. Exec. sec. N.W. Malt & Grain, Chgo., 1958-63; pres. Judy's Mailing & Secretarial Service, Northbrook, 1968—, Americano Motor Inn, Beaumont, Tex., 1976—; owner Jovies Family Restaurant, Beaumont, 1977-78, Chances R, Beaumont, 1978-80; v.p. Golden Triangle Limo Service, Beaumont, 1982—; mng. ptnr. Warchol Investments, Beaumont, Tex., 1982—. V.p. Band Booster Club, Stanley Field Jr. High Sch., Northbrook, 1975-77; leader Blue Bird Group, Camp Fire Girls, Northbrook, 1971-76; bd. dirs. Stanley Field Jr. High Parent Tchr. Club, Northbrook, 1970-78; foster parent, Sierra Leone, 1978-85. Mem. Women in Mgmt., Nat. Assn. Secretarial Services, Mail Advertisers Assn., Northbrook C. of C. (bd. dirs. 1984-86). Republican. Roman Catholic. Avocations: boating, golf, tennis, fitness programs, self-improvement studies. Home: 3493 Techny Rd Northbrook IL 60062-5066 Office: Judy's Mailing & Secretarial Service 33863392 Commercial Ave Northbrook IL 60062-1833

WARD, ANNE STARR MINTON, musician, educator; d. James Royster and Bobbie Lee (Clegg) Minton; m. Benjamin Kirby Ward, June 19, 1966; children: David Alexander, Karen Virginia. MusB cum laude, U. N.C., Greensboro, 1965, M Music Edn., 1966. Tchr. orch. Dade County Schs., Miami, Fla., 1967—68, Jacksonville County Schs., Fla., 1968—69; pvt. violin tchr. Florence, SC, 1974—; mem. faculty N.C. Suzuki Inst., Greenville, 1986—2005. Violinist Florence Symphony Orch., 1974—2005, concert master, 2000—; violinist Piedmont Trio, SC, 1996—2000; co-chmn. Florence Ctr. Arts, Inc., 2000—05. Lay leader Ctrl. United Meth. Ch., Florence, 1996—2003; chmn. Evangelistic awards S.C. conf. United Meth. Ch., 1997—2003; mem. Florence Downtown Devel. Bd., 2002—05; bd. dirs. Florence 2010 Com., 2001—02. Mem.: Music Educators Nat. Conf., Florence-Darlington String Assn. (co-founder 1998, pres. 1998—2006), Suzuki Assn. Am., AMA Alliance. Avocation: travel.

WARD, BESS B., oceanographer, educator; BS in Zoology, Michigan State U., East Lansing, 1976; MS in Biological Oceanography, U. Wash., Seattle, 1979, PhD in Biological Oceanography, 1982. Postgrad. rsch. biologist, Inst. Marine Resources, Scripps Instn. Oceanography U. Calif., San Diego, 1982—84, asst. rsch. oceanographer, Inst. Marine Resources, Scripps Instn. Oceanography, 1984—89, chair food chain rsch. group, Scripps Instn. Oceanography, 1987—88, assoc. mem. Ctr. Molecular Genetics, 1987—91, asst. prof. marine sci. Santa Cruz, 1989—91, assoc. prof. marine sci., 1991—95, prof., chair ocean sci. dept., 1995—98; prof. oceanography Princeton U., Princeton, NJ, 1998—. Visiting scientist Max Planck Inst. für Limnologie, Germany, 1993; disting. visiting biologist Woods Hole Oceanographic Instn., 1996. Fellow: Am. Acad. Arts & Sciences, Am. Geophysical Union, Am. Acad. Microbiology; mem.: AAAS, Am. Soc. Limnology & Oceanography (G. Evelyn Hutchinson medal 1997). Office: Princeton U Dept Geosciences M51 Guyot Hall Princeton NJ 08544

WARD, BRENDA ROBINSON, social worker; b. Gastonia, NC, Nov. 12, 1954; d. Elvin Franklin and Annie Sue (Clemmer) Robinson; m. Robert Crawford Ward, Aug. 29, 1981; children: Lauren Clemmer, Thomas Crawford. BSW, NC State U, 1977; MSW, U. N.C., 1980. LCSW NC. Social worker I Broughton Hosp., Morganton, NC, 1977—78; social worker II Smoky Mtn. Area Mental Health, Dillsboro, NC, 1980—81, Cherry Hosp., Goldsboro, NC, 1981—83; social worker III Piedmont Behavioral Healthcare, Concord, NC, 1983—91, local mental health unit coord., 1991—97, clin. social work specialist Kannapolis, NC, 1997—2002; clin. coord. Lifeworks Oupatient Program Rowan Reg. Med. Ctr., 2002—. Mem.: Cabarus County Mental Health Assn., NASW. Office: Lifeworks Outpatient Prgm Rowan Reg MC 612 Mocksville Ave Salisbury NC 28144

WARD, CHRISTINE L., elementary school educator; d. William C. and Rosemary Ward; m. Oscar Diaz, Aug. 4, 2006. BS in Elem. Edn., U. Scranton, Pa., 1996; MA in Environ. Studies, Montclair State U., NJ, 2001. Tchr. 5th and 6th grade Notre Dame Internat., Palisades Park, NJ, 1996—97; tchr. 6th and 8th grade Deerfield Sch., Mountainside, NJ, 1997—98; tchr. 5th grade East Brook Mid. Sch., Paramus, NJ, 1998—. Intern NASA-Stennis Space Ctr., Miss., 1999; fellow U.S. Dept. of Energy, Norfolk, Va., 2004—. Recipient Tchr. of Yr. award, Gov. of N.J., 2004. Mem.: NSTA, N.J. Sci. Leaders Assn. Office: East Brook Mid Sch 190 Spring Valley Rd Paramus NJ 07652 Office Phone: 201-261-7800 ext 8102. E-mail: chrissyleew@yahoo.com.

WARD, CONNIE MICHELE, psychologist, educator, environmentalist; b. Hampton, Va., June 11, 1954; d. Wallace W. and Elsie Saline (Polk) Ward. BA, U. Calif. Santa Cruz, 1976; MA, Ohio State U., 1978, PhD, 1980. Lic. psychologist. Asst. prof. Ga. State U., Atlanta, 1980—86, assoc. prof., 1986—95, adj. assoc. prof., 1995—. Counseling psychologist Counseling Ctr. Ga. State U., 1980—95; pvt. practice, Fayetteville, Ga., 1995—. Contbr. articles to profl. jours. Recipient Outstanding Adminstr. award, Intersorority Coun. Ga. State U., 1984. Mem.: APA. Methodist. Avocations: reading, cooking, music, volunteering. Home: 500 Concord Cir Jonesboro GA 30236-5519 Office: Ste E-F 115 Habersham Dr Fayetteville GA 30214-7341 Office Phone: 770-461-9944. Personal E-mail: cmwpsych@aol.com.

WARD, DOREE MAXINE, secondary school educator; b. Des Moines, Iowa, Oct. 17, 1955; d. Jeane and Wesley Ward. BSE in Edn., Drake U., 1977, MSEd, 1997. Tchr. Thomas Jefferson H.S., Council Bluffs, Iowa, 1978—82; tchr./coach Floyd Valley H.S., Alton, Iowa, 1982—84, Newton H.S., Newton, 1987—. Del. Russia and Hungary People to People Internat., 1993. Mem.: Iowa Assn. of Safety Edn. (pres. 1994—2002), Iowa State Edn. Assn. Avocations: swimming, horseback riding, softball, basketball. Home: 515 E 10th St S Newton IA 50208 Office: Newton High School 800 E 4th St S Newton IA 50208 Business E-Mail: wardd@newton.k12.ia.us.

WARD, DORIS M., county official; BA in Govt., Ind. U., MS in Edn.; MA in Counseling, San Francisco State U.; PhD in Edn., U. Calif., Berkeley. Tchr. Indpls. Pub. Schs., 1959-67, team leader, supr. tchg. interns, 1967-68; adviser, counselor San Francisco STEP program, 1969-70; coord. curriculum San Mateo County Office of Edn., Redwood City, Calif., 1968-89; mem. bd. govs. San Francisco C.C., 1973-79; mem. bd. suprs. City and County San Francisco, 1980-92, pres. bd. suprs., 1991-92, assessor, recorder, 1992—, elected assessor-recorder, 1996. Adj. assoc. prof. Sch. Edn. Calif. State U., 1969-70, 72-73; advisor to External Masters Degree Program, U. San Francisco, 1972-76; chief cons. Calif. Assembly on regional govt., 1989-92. Contbr. articles to ednl. and polit. jours. Bd. dirs. Nat. Dem. County Officials 1987—, pres. 1994—; mem. Dem. Nat. Com., 1992—, del. 1984, 88, 92, 96 convs. Named Woman of Yr., Zeta Phi Beta, 1984; recipient Disting. Alumni award San Francisco State U., 1993, Disting. Comty. award, U. San Francisco, 1994, Spl. Merit award Sun Reporter Newspaper and numerous other awards for comty. svc. by activist orgns; grantee: NDEA, 1967, 68, Ind. State U., Terre Haute, Ind., Lilly Found., 1967, Rockefeller Found., U. Calif., Berkeley, 1974. Mem. Bay Area Assessors Assn. (sec. 1994, v.p. 95, pres. 96), Calif. Assessors' Assn. (mem. legis. com. 1993, exec. com. 95), Nat. Assn. Counties (bd. dirs. 1989-91, chair human svcs. and edn., 1991-92), Nat. Assn. Black County Officials (bd. dirs. 1987—, regional dir. 1987—), Nat. League of Cities (bd. dirs. 1991-92, vice chair and steering com. Fed. Adminstrn. Intergovtl. Rels. 1990-91), Nat. Black Caucus of Local Elected Officials (bd. dirs. 1987-95), Pi Sigma Alpha, Pi Lambda Theta. Office: City County San Francisco Assessor Recorder Office Rm 190 1 Dr Carlton B Goodlett Pl San Francisco CA 94102-4603

WARD, ERICA ANNE, lawyer, educator; b. Okiyama, Japan, Oct. 20, 1950; d. Robert Edward and Constance Regina (Barnett) Ward; m. Ralph Joseph Gerson, May 20, 1979; children: Stephanie Claire Gerson, Madeleine Ward Gerson. BA, Stanford U., 1972; JD, U. Mich., 1975. Bar: Calif. 1975, DC 1976, US Ct. Appeals (5th and DC cir.) 1977, Temp. Emergency Ct. Appeals 1983, Mich. 1989. Assoc. Wilmer, Cutler & Pickering, Washington, 1975—77; staff counsel US Senate Ethics Com., Washington, 1977—78; exec. asst. gen. counsel Dept. Energy, Washington, 1978—79; counsellor to dep. sec., 1980; assoc. dir. energy and natural resources, domestic policy staff White House, Washington, 1980—81; counsel Skadden, Arps, Slate, Meagher & Flom., Washington, 1981—87; ptnr., 1987; adj. prof. law U. Mich., Ann Arbor, 1984—85; Editor Mich. Law Rev., 1975; commr. Mackinac Is. State Pk. Commn., Mich., 1989—95. Recipient Outstanding Svc. medal, Dept. Energy, 1981. Mem.: Women's Bar Assn. DC, ABA, U. Mich. Law Sch., Cranbrook Ednl. Cmty., Children's Hosp. Mich. Democrat. Jewish. Office: Skadden Arps Slate Meagher Flom 1440 New York Ave NW Ste 600 Washington DC 20005-6000 Office Phone: 202-371-7050. Business E-Mail: eward@skadden.com.

WARD, JACQUELINE ANN BEAS, nurse, healthcare administrator; b. Somerset, Pa., Oct. 23, 1945; d. Donald C. and Thelma R. (Wable) Beas; divorced; children: Charles L. Jr., Shawn M. BSN, U. Pitts., 1966; MA in Counseling and Guidance, W.Va. Coll. Grad. Studies, 1976; MBA, Columbus Coll., 1983; AS in Health Svcs. Mgmt./Nursing Home Adminstrn., St. Petersburg Jr. Coll., 1997. Cert. advanced nursing adminstrn.; adult living facility adminstr., nursing home adminstr. preceptor. Staff nurse W.Va. U. Hosp., Morgantown, 1966—67; staff nurse, head nurse Meml. Hosp, Charleston, W.Va., 1967—69; staff nurse Santa Rosa Hosp., San Antonio, 1969; staff nurse, supr. Bexar County Hosp., San Antonio, 1970; charge and staff nurse Rocky Mountain Osteo. Hosp., Denver, 1971; from staff nurse to asst. DON Charleston Area Med. Ctr., 1971—82; DON H.D. Cobb Meml. Hosp., Phenix City, Ala., 1982—84; v.p. nursing Venice Hosp., Fla., 1984—90, v.p. ops., 1990—94; exec. dir., v.p. Life Counseling Ctr., Osprey, Fla., 1994—95; dir. skilled unit and spl. projects Bon Secours/Venice Hosp., 1995—97; adj. clin. nursing faculty Manatee C.C., Venice, 1998—99; interim adminstr. DON contracting, Venice, 1999—2000; adminstr. Ctrs. for Long Term Care Venice Beach, 2000—01, Lake Towers/Sun Terrace Health Care Ctr., Sun City Center, Fla., 2002—05; exec. dir. Beneva Park Club, Sarasota, 2005; exec. dir. Tandem Health Care of Sarasota, 2005—. Clin. instr. Chattahoochie Valley C.C., Phenix City, 1982—84; support svcs. cons. Bon Secours Healthcare, Venice, 1996—97, Long Term Care, 1997—98. Office: Tandem Health Care of Sarasota 4783 Fruitville Rd Sarasota FL 34232 Office Phone: 941-378-8000.

WARD, JEANNETTE POOLE, retired psychologist, educator; b. Honolulu, June 19, 1932; d. Russell Masterton and Bessie Naomi (Hammett) Poole; children: John Russell Ward, Lisa Joy Ward. BA, Birmingham (Ala.) So. Coll., 1963; PhD in Psychology, Vanderbilt U., 1969. NSF summer rsch. asst. U. Iowa, Iowa City, 1962, Vanderbilt U., Nashville, 1963, NASA fellow, 1963-66, NIH postdoctoral fellow, 1966-67; spl. rsch. fellow Duke U., Durham, NC, 1970-71; asst. prof. psychology U. Memphis, 1967—72, assoc. prof., 1972—77, prof., 1977—2000; ret., 2001. Editor: Current Research in Primate Laterality, 1990, Primate Laterality, 1992; mem. editl. bd. Jour. Comparative Psychology, 1988-95, Internat. Jour. of Comparative Psychology, 1995—; contbr. chpts. to books and articles to profl. jours. Fellow APA; mem. Psychonomic Soc., Animal Behavior Soc., Am. Primatology Soc., Southeastern Psychol. Assn., Soc. for Neuroscis., Internat. Soc. for Comparative Psychology (treas. 1989-90, pres.-elect 1996-98, pres. 1998-2000), Sigma Xi (pres. Memphis State U. chpt. 1989-90, rsch. award 1985). Democrat. Avocations: reading, art, music. Personal E-mail: jeannetteward@cs.com.

WARD, JOYCE DIECKMANN, nurse midwife; b. Phila., July 8, 1955; d. Robert Holger and Joyce Olive Dieckmann; m. Daniel Allen Ward, Mar. 5, 1977; children: Janet Deanna, Dan Alan. BS in Nursing, Albright Coll., 1978; MS in Midwifery, Phila. U., 2001. Cert. midwifery, Phila. U., 1999. Medical/surgical nurse St. Joseph Hosp., Reading, Pa., 1978—79, labor & delivery nurse Lancaster, Pa., 1999—2003, Cmty. Gen. Hosp., Reading, 1980—96; substitute staff nurse Kutztown U., Pa., 1996—; owner, midwife Cmty. Women's Care of Baks Co., Reading, 2002—; cert. nurse midwife Ebersole, Zerby, Consoli, West Assoc PC, Reading, 2004—. CPR & first-aide instr. Am. Red Cross, Reading, 1989—; health care instr. Del. CC, Newtonsquare, Pa., 2001; nursing instr. Harrisburg CC, Lancaster, 2001—04. Leader Girl Scouts Am., Muhlenberg, Pa., 1984—; bd. mem. Muhlenberg Swimming Assoc., 2001—04; youth group leader Covenant Orthodox Presbyn. Ch., Reading, 2004—. Mem.: Penn. Assn. Legislative Midwives, Assn. Women Health, Obstetrics & Neonatal Nurses, Am. Coll. Nurse Midwives. Avocations: swimming, crafts, camping. Home: 1017 Duryea Ave Reading PA 19605 Office: Ebersole Zerby Consoli West Assoc PC 301 S 7th Ave Ste 365 Reading PA 19606

WARD, JUDITH A., elementary school educator; b. Brazil, Ind., Dec. 9, 1945; d. Stanley M. and J. Irene Cobley; m. William E. Norris, Aug. 18, 1967 (div.); 1 child, Edwin S. Norris; m. Don N. Ward, Nov. 1980 (dec.). BS cum laude, Ind. State U., 1967, MS, 1970. Elem. music tchr. Dekalb County Ctrl. United Sch. Dist., Auburn, Ind., 1967—71, Wabash (Ind.) City Schs., 1971—. Music dir. Wabash Christian Ch., 1978—; coord. Visual Performing Arts Cooperative, Wabash, 1996—; summer theatre dir., youth choir dir. Bd. dirs., music dir. Wabash Area Cmty. Theater, 1996—; music dir., mem. planning com. Cmty. Madrigal Dinner, Honeywell Ctr., Wabash, 1997—; dir., singer Market Street Beat, Wabash, 1999—. Recipient Disting. Citizen award, Wabash C. of C., 2001. Mem.: NEA, Assn. Disciple Musicians Ind. (sec., pres.), Assn. Disciple Musicians (nat. planning coun. 2001—03, sec. 2003), Ind. Gen. Music Educators Assn. (pres. 2000—02), Ind. Music Educators Assn. (area coord. Cir. the State with Song, state elem. chair Cir. the State with Song, Outstanding Elem. Music Educator 2003), Ind. State Tchrs. Assn., Delta Kappa Gamma, Sigma Alpha Iota (Ft. Wayne alum pres. 1970—72, Beta province v.p. 1978—87). Mem. Disciples Of Christ Church. Avocations: reading, latch hooking. Home: 3254 S 100 W Wabash IN 46992 Office: OJ Neighbours Elem 1545 N Wabash St Wabash IN 46992

WARD, LAKEYSHA MONIQUE, alcohol/drug abuse services professional, special education services professional; b. Milwuakee, Wis., June 8, 1980; d. Gary E. Harris and Belinda L. Ward. BA, U. Memphis, Tenn., 2001—04; MA, Capella U., Minn., 2004—. Therapist for autistic children, Arlington, Tenn., 2000—; clin. liasion Youth Villages, Memphis, 2004—05; alcohol and drug counselor Memphis Recovery Centers, Inc, 2005—06, Memphis Cts. for Rsch. and Addiction Treatment, 2006—. Recipient Nat. Dean's List, 2004—06. Personal E-mail: onlyelegant@hotmail.com.

WARD, MARILYN BEEMAN, commissioner; b. Oakland, Calif., June 6, 1929; d. Samuel William and Alice Lee (Turner) Beeman; m. Daniel Bridges Ward, Aug. 15, 1950; children: Anne Ward Ryan, Susan Ward Potts, Daniel E. Ward. Student, U. Calif., Berkeley, 1947-49; BA, Evergreen State Coll., 1978. Founding dir., loan officer Sound Savs. & Loan, Seattle, 1981-86; mng. ptnr. Bancroft Ctr., Berkeley, Calif., 2004—. Cons. Bellevue (Wash.) Pub. Schs., variety of social svc. agys., 1970s and 1980s. Chmn. Harborview Med. Ctr., Seattle, 1994, 1995, 1996; mem. Wash. State Med. Quality Assurance Commn., 1986—, chmn., 1993—94; mem. vis. com. U. Wash. Sch. Social Work, chmn., 1988; mem. vis. com. U. Wash. Sch. Pub. Health; bd. dirs. Facing the Future, vice chmn. Recipient Ralph Bunche Peace award Wash. State Bar Assn., 1985, Dorothy Bullitt Cmty. Leader award Jr. League, 1996, John H. Clark Leadership award Fedn. State Med. Bds. of U.S. Mem.: Sunset Club (pres.), City Club (co-founder 1985, pres. 1985—86). Episcopalian. Avocations: photography, gardening, golf, fishing, reading. Office: PO Box 465 Medina WA 98039-0465 E-mail: wardmarilynb@aol.com.

WARD, NINA GILLSON, jewelry store executive; b. Boston, Dec. 19, 1950; d. Rev. John Robert and Patricia (Gillson) Baker; m. Jorge Alberto Lievanos, June 6, 1981 (div.); children: Jeremy John Baker, Wendy Mara Baker, Raoul Salvador Baker-Lievanos; m. David Ward, July 24, 1998; stepchildren: Johnna Ward, Tavi Sterling. Student, Mills Coll., 1969-70; grad. course in diamond grading, Gemology Inst. Am., 1983; student in diamondtology designation, Diamond Coun. Am., 1986—. Cert. store mgr., Jewelers Cert. Coun., Jewelers Am. Artist, tchr., Claremont, Calif., 1973-78; escrow officer Bank of Am., Claremont, 1978-81; retail salesman William Pitt Jewelers, Puente Hills, Montclair, Calif., 1981-83, asst. mgr., 1983, mgr. Santa Maria, Calif., 1983-91, corp. sales trainer, 1988-89; sales and design specialist Merksamer Jewelers, Santa Maria, 1991, mgr. San Luis Obispo, Calif., 1991-92, Santa Maria, Calif., 1992-94, diamond specialist cons., 1994-96; pres., ops. mgr. Dancer House Designs, Santa Maria, Calif., 1996; pres. primary jewelry designer Dancer House Design Fine Jewelry, Inc., Kennebunk, Maine, 1997—. Artist tapestry hanging Laguna Beach Mus. Art, 1974; exhibited in Nat. Jeweler's Design Competition, 1999. Mem. Cen. Coast Pla. Adv. Bd., 1992; mem. Rep. Bus. Majority Coun. Recipient Cert. Merit Art Bank Am., 1968, 1st pl. Best of show award for jewelry design Maine Jeweler's Assn., 1998, design award, 2000, Rep. of Yr. Award Maine, 2000, 1st place award crystal divsn. nat. design competition Mfg. Jewelers and Suppliers of Am., 2001. Mem. NAFE, Internat. Platform Assn., Maine Jewelers Assn. (bd. dirs. 1999—), Speaker's Bur., Santa Maria C. of C., Compassion Internat. Republican. Avocations: tapestry weaving, creative writing.

WARD, PATRICIA S., theater educator; b. Houston, Aug. 28, 1945; m. Dale Ralph Ward, July 24, 1944; children: Steven Dale, Stefani Gail, Thomas Eldred. BS in Edn., Abilene Christian U., Tex., 1967. Tchr. Cooper H.S., Abilene, 1967—68, Spartanburg H.S., SC, 1970—71, Dallas Christian H.S., 1974—75, Mars Hill Bible Sch., Florence, Ala., 1984—90, David Lipscomb H.S., Nashville, 1990—2000, Centennial H.S., Franklin, Tenn., 2000—. Mem.: Ednl. Theatre Assn., Tenn. H.S. Speech and Drama League, Williamson County Edn. Assn., Tenn. Edn. Assn. R-Conservative. Mem. Church Of Christ. Avocations: travel, reading, theater. Office: Centennial High Sch 5050 Mallory Ln Franklin TN 07067 Office Phone: 615-472-4270 2373.

WARD, SARAH FRANCES, narcotic education consultant, counselor; b. Knightstown, Ind., Feb. 17, 1937; d. Ralph Smithson and Susannah Willard (Earnest). AB in Sacred Music summa cum laude, Lincoln Christian Coll., Lincoln, Ill., 1959; MME, Ind. U., Bloomington, 1961; MS in Counseling Psychology, George Williams Coll., Ill., 1981. Tchr. music Hanover Twp. Schs., Cedar Lake, Ind., 1961-64; nat. exec. dir. Youth Temperance Coun. Nat. WCTU, Evanston, Ill., 1964-69, narcotic edn. cons., 1984—; tchr. music Sch. Dist. 21, Wheeling, Ill., 1970-78; psychotherapist Pvt. Counseling Ctr., Knightstown, 1983-92; pres. Ind. Woman's Christian Temperance Union, 1992—2002, nat. pres., 1996—2006; pres. World Women's Christian Temperance Union, 2004—. Exec. dir. Ind. Youth Temperance Coun., 1980-91. Author ednl. materials on alcohol and drug use. Trustee Charles A. Beard Sch. Bd., Knightstown, 1982-90; community rep. Head Start Policy Coun., New Castle, Ind., 1985-88. Mem. AACD, Ind. Mental Health Counselor Assn., Henry County Mental Health Assn. (chmn. early childhood sect. 1986-89), Gamma Alpha Chi, Delta Epsilon Chi, Tau Beta Sigma, Pi Kappa Lambda. Avocations: needlecrafts, sports, travel. Home: 220 Hill Ave Knightstown IN 46148-1321

WARD, SARAH M., lawyer; b. Elizabeth, N.J., 1957; AB, Princeton U., 1981; JD, Fordham U., 1986. Bar: N.Y. 1987. Ptnr. Skadden, Arps, Slate, Meagher & Flom, N.Y.C. Office: Skadden Arps Slate Meagher & Flom 4 Times Sq Fl 24 New York NY 10036-6595

WARD, SELA, actress; b. Meridian, Miss., July 11, 1956; d. Granberry Holland and Annie Kate Ward; m. Howard Sherman May 23, 1992; children: Austin, Anabella. BA, U. Ala. Actor: (TV series) Emerald Point, N.A.S., 1983-84, Cameo By Night, 1987, Sisters, 1991—96 (Emmy award for Lead Actress in Drama Series 1994), Once and Again, 1999-2002 (winner lead actress in a drama series, Emmy award 2000, winner lead actress in a drama series, Golden Globe award 2001), House, 2005-; (TV films) The King of Love, 1987, Bridesmaids, 1989, The Haunting of Sarah Hardy, 1989, Rainbow Drive, 1990, Child of Darkness, Child of Light, 1991, Double Jeopardy, 1992, Killer Rules, 1993, Almost Golden: The Jessica Savitch Story, 1995 (winner lead actress in drama movie Cableace award 1996), The Rescuers: Stories of Courage: Two Women, 1997, Catch a Falling Star, 2000, Suburban Madness, 2004; (films) Rustler's Rhapsody, 1985, Nothing in Common, 1986, Steele Justice, 1987, Hello Again, 1987, The Fugitive, 1993, My Fellow Americans, 1996, 54, 1998, 54, 1998, Runaway Bride, 1999, The Reef, 1999, The Badge, 2002, Dirty Dancing: Havana Nights, 2003, The Day After Tomorrow, 2004, The Guardian, 2006; prodr. (Lifetime cable network) documentary Changing Face of Beauty, 2000, Lifetime "Intimate Portrait", 2001. Office: 289 S Robertson Blvd Ste 469 Beverly Hills CA 90211-2834*

WARD, SHARON DEE, secondary school educator; b. Tulsa, Okla., Sept. 15, 1958; d. Earl Edmond and Wilma Rose (Hurst) Walker; m. Ricky Lee Yates, Dec. 24, 1977 (div. Apr. 1986); children: Pamela, Lisa; m. William Eugene Ward, Apr. 8, 1988; children: Christian, William. AA, Rogers State Coll., 1987; BS cum laude, U. of the Ozarks, 1989; tchr. cert., Coll. of the Ozarks, 1992; M in Edn. leadership, Haring U. Cert. tchr. Ark. Bus. mgr. Dr. Phillips D.D.S., Owasso, Okla., 1982-85, Dr. Franklin D.D.S., Owasso, 1986; office asst. U. Ozarks, Clarksville, Ark., 1987-89; bus. mgr. M&R Container, Berryville, Ark., 1990; office bus. mgr. Carroll County News, Berryville, 1990; v.p. of fin. The Cookie Bouquet, Inc., Dallas, 1991; vocat. bus. educator Eureka Springs (Ark.) H.S., 1992—; asst. prin., curriculum coord. Gup-Perkins Schs. Mem. Eureka Springs Day Care, 1994-95; sponsor, leader First Eureka Springs Jr. Bank, Eureka Springs, 1993—; cons. Ark. Vocat. Bd., Little Rock, 1994—. Mem. cookie coun. Girl Scouts Am. Mem. Ark. Vocat. Assn., Bus. Edn. Assn., Ark. Edn. Assn. (sec. 1995—), Am. Vocat. Assn., Future Bus. Leaders of Am. Democrat. Methodist. Avocations: sewing, photography, computers. Home: PO Box 266 Guy AR 72061-0266

WARD, SOLVEIG MARIA, marketing professional; b. Stockholm, Aug. 22, 1954; d. Ingvar Erik and Inga Kronman; m. Edward L. Ward, Jan. 20, 1997; children: Johan Fredrick Mahrs, Lars Richard Mahrs. MSEE, Royal Inst. of Tech., Stockholm, 1977. Sales engr. Asea Ab, Vasteras, Sweden, 1977—80; supr. dept. sales ASEA SA de CV, Mexico City, 1980—82; product mktg. mgr. Abb (Asea) Ab, Vasteras, 1982—92; mgr. consulting engrng. ABB Inc., Coral Springs, Fla., 1992—99, product mgr. Allentown, Pa., 1999—2002; dir. product mktg. RFL Electronics Inc., Boonton Twp., NJ, 2002—. Mem.: IEEE. Achievements include patents for high speed single pole trip logic for use in protective relaying. Office: RFL Electronics Inc 353 Powerville Rd Boonton NJ 07005 Office Phone: 973-334-3100. Office Fax: 973-334-3863. Business E-Mail: solveig.ward@rflelect.com.

WARD, SUSAN ANNETTE, music educator; b. Frederick, Md., Aug. 18, 1962; d. Harold Edwin and Raetta Mildred Stotelmyer; m. James Arthur Ward, May 16, 1982; children: Cody, Lindsay. Student, Shenandoah Coll./Conservatory, Winchester, Va., 1980-81; cert., Inst. Children's Lit., West Redding, Conn., 1986. Cert. in web design Thomson Learning Direct, 2000, P.C. technician Thomson Learning Direct, 2001, in computer graphics Thomson Learning Direct, 2002, desktop pub. Thomson Learning Direct, 2003. Owner Simply Music, Jefferson, Md.; co-owner The Homeowner's Helper, Jefferson, Md., 1997—; owner Personally Yours, Jefferson, Md. Mem. wind ensemble Frederick C.C., 2003—. Vol., Valley Elem. Sch., Jefferson, 1992-2002, Brunswick (Md.) Mid. Sch., 1997-2000, Brunswick H.S. Band Boosters, 2000-04 Jordan Kitt grantee, 1998. Mem.: Frederick County Music Tchrs. Assn. (sec. 1998—99, pres. 2000—01, v.p. 2001—03), Md. State Music Tchrs. Assn., Music Tchrs. Nat. Assn. Lutheran. Avocations: reading, collectibles. Home: 5916 Broad Run Rd Jefferson MD 21755-9113 Office: Simply Music 5916 Broad Run Rd Jefferson MD 21755-9113 Business E-Mail: jsclward@musician.org.

WARD, VANESSA GAYLE, religious organization administrator, minister, consultant; b. Omaha, Mar. 24, 1953; d. Lillard William and Marcella Louise Loftin; m. Keith Dewayne Loftin, Sept. 29, 1973; children: Keith Dewayne Ward Jr., Torrey Glenn, Juana Chon-Ta', Va'Chona Reayle. Grad., Saul David Alinsky Leadership Tng. Inst., 2000; student, Gen. Dist. Ann. Sch. of Prophet, 1995. Overseer and CEO The Body of Christ Internat. (TBOC), Omaha, 2004—; founder and lead organizer Concerned Chs. and Citizens United (CCCU), Omaha, 2004—; founder, lead organizer 4Ward Leap. Founding pastor Afresh Anointing Ch., Omaha, 2002—, Spirit of God AME Zion Ch., Omaha, 1997—; cons. Luth. Metro Ministries ELCA, Omaha, 2002—, Evang. Covenant Ch., Omaha, 2003—; cmty. vol. Infinia Nursing Home, Omaha, 2004—, Maple Crest Nursing Home, Omaha, 1996—. Singer (dancer): (the musical) Working:. Cmty. activist; mem. Luth. Nebr. Senate Outreach (ELCA); steering com. Exec. Offices of Weed & Seed (North Omaha), Omaha, 2002; co-chair Omaha Together One Cmty. (OTOC), Omaha, 2002; pres. Ctrl. Pk. Neighborhood Assn., Omaha, 2000. Recipient, Exec. Offices of Weed and Seed award, 2003, Neighborhood Improvement grantee, 2000, Unsung Hero award, 2005. Mem.: Habitat for Humanity, Nat. Coun. of Negro Women. Office: The Body of Christ (TBOC) International 4757 N 24th St Omaha NE 68110 Office Phone: 402-451-6813.

WARDELL, LINDY CONSTANCE, non-profit organization administrator; b. Potsdam, NY, Apr. 28, 1928; d. Stewart A. and Mabel A. Henderson; m. David F. Constance, Sept. 6, 1947 (dec. Apr. 1984); children: John, Kathryn, Marie, Thomas, Richard; m. Frank M. Wardell, 1989. Student, Powellson Jr. Coll., Syracuse, N.Y., 1946-47, Ctrl. City Bus. Inst., Syracuse, 1946-47. Lic. realtor. V.p. Bicentennial Bus Co., Phila., 1974-77; assoc. cons. Constance & Wallace, Phila., 1976-84; v.p. Trade Devel. Corp., Phila., 1977-84; realtor assoc. Louis Gaev Realtors, Haverford, Pa., 1985-87; pres., chmn. bd. dirs. Darby (Pa.) Cmty. Forum, 1997—; pres., chmn. bd. Darby Borough Hist. Soc., Darby, 1998—. Chmn. Friends of Darby Meth. Meeting Cemetery, 1996—; mem. adv. bd. Delaware County Daily Times, Primos, Pa., 1998-99; bd. dirs. Darby Cmty. Project, 1991—. Author: Images of America, 2003; contbr. articles to newspapers. Pres., Coun. Rep. Women, Newtown Square, Pa., 1977-85; trustee Phila. Fairmount Pk. Hist. Sites com., 2002— Recipient Outstanding Individual Achievement award Delaware County Heritage Commn., 1999; Golden Rule Found. grantee, 1997. Mem Darby Hist. Soc. (founding mem. 1998), Delaware County Hist. Soc. (Coun. of Pres., Lee C. Brown award 2003). Republican. Avocations: genealogy, arts and crafts, historical research. Home: 16 Winthrop Rd Darby PA 19023-1116

WARDEN, KAREN BARBARA, special education educator; b. Camden, N.J., Jan. 19, 1949; d. Russell James Jr. and Harriet May (Tupper) W. BS, Vanderbilt U., 1971; student, NJ Tchr. Artist Inst., 1979, student, 1990—96, student, 2000—06, Peters Valley Ednl. Ctr., 1994, student, 1998—2005, Elkins/Davis Coll. Augusta Heritage Seminar 1994-96, 2001, W. Va., Cedar Lake Ctr., W.Va., 1998—2002. Cert. elem. edn., spl. edn., and art edn. tchr., N.J. Tchr. of handicapped Dept. Human Svcs. Region Sch., Cherry Hill, NJ, 1979-98; sch. art coord. Camden County Tng. Ctr., Cherry Hill, N.J., 1992—, spl. edn. art tchr., 1998—. Mem. N.J. Art Educators Assn., Third Star Fiber Arts Guild (sec.), Garden Patch Quilters (photographer), Am. Arts Action Group, U. Women, Crazy Patch Quilters. Avocations: weaving, spinning, quilting, painting, gardening. Home: 216 Atlantic Ave SW Magnolia NJ 08049-1716 E-mail: cathallowstudio@aol.com.

WARDEN, LENORE SPONSLER, physician; b. Muskogee, Okla., Nov. 25, 1929; d. Amick Charles and Marie Stanton Sponsler; m. Don Page Warden, Dec. 20, 1953; children: Shawn, Russell, David, Hank, Shay. Degree, Baylor U., Waco, Tex., 1951; MD, U. Tex., Dallas, 1955. Cert. Am. Bd. Quality Assurance. Intern Pierce County Gen. Hosp., Tacoma, 1956—57, gen. practice resident, 1957—58; assoc. instr. SWMS Woodlawn Hosp., 1958—59; health officer City of Weslaco, Tex.; cons. physician Weslaco Ind. Sch. Dist.; mem. exec. bd. Hidalgo County Health Care Corp.; med. dir. John Knox Med. Ctr., Valley Grande Nursing Home. Med. cons. Buckner's Children's Home. Mem. Knapp Med. Ctr. Found.; med. dir.local chpt. Am. Cancer Soc.; mem. consortium Regional Magnet HS; vol. lobbyist TMA and Christian Life Commn. Fellow, Am. Coll. Utilization Rev. Mem.: AMA, Tex. Acad. Family Practice (pres. Valley chpt. 1987, alt. del., mem. scholarship com.), Am. Acad. Family Practice, Tex. Med. Assn. (med. adv. com. 1982—90), Hidalgo County Med. Soc., Am. Assn. Family Physicians. Avocations: camping, travel, reading, crafts. Home: 5123 Osprey Rd Gilmer TX 75645-8348

WARDEN, WALDIA ANN, religious center administrator, director; b. New Orleans, Jan. 15, 1933; d. Walter Emmer and Lydia Eugenie (LeBlanc) W BS, St. Mary's Dominican Coll., 1961; MS Dietetics, St. Louis U., 1964; JCL, Cath. U. Am., 1988. Joined Dominican Sisters, Congregation of St. Mary, Roman Cath. Ch., 1953, coun. mem., 1976-84, 96-2004. Tchr. elem. schs., 1954—62; instr. foods and nutrition Dominican Coll., New Orleans, 1964—66, chmn. home econs. dept., 1966—69, asst. dean students, 1969—75, chmn. dept. home econs., 1975—78, chmn. Coll. Planning Coun., 1972—76; dir. Rosaryville Ctr., Ponchatoula, La., 1979—81; pres. St. Mary's Dominican Coll., New Orleans, 1983—86; defender Bond for Tribunal Archdiocese of New Orleans, 1989—2005; dir. Rosaryville Spirit Life Ctr., 2005—. Pres. St. Mary's Dominican H.S., 1990-94; coord. First Ct. Met. Tribunal, Archdiocese of New Orleans, 1994-2005 Trustee St. Mary's Dominican Coll., 1973-79, 83-86, 90-93; bd. regents Our Lady of Holy Cross Coll., New Orleans, 1992-98; bd. dirs. Henriette deLille Mid. Sch. for Girls, 2000-04, chair, 2004-05 Mem. La. Dietetic Assn. (editor jour. 1966-68), La. Leadership Conf. Women Religious, Am. Dietetic Assn., Am. Home Econs. Assn., Canon Law Soc. Am., Dominican Leadership Conf. (cluster coord. com. 2002-06, chair reconfiguration subcom. 2002-06) Home: 39003 Rosaryville Rd Ponchatoula LA 70454-7001 Office Phone: 225-294-5039. Personal E-mail: dawaldia@aol.com.

WARDLAW, KIM A. MCLANE, federal judge; b. San Francisco, July 2, 1954; m. William M. Wardlaw Sr., Sept. 8, 1984. Student, Santa Clara U., 1972—73, Foothill C.C., Los Altos Hills, Calif., 1973—74; AB in Comm. summa cum laude, UCLA, 1976, JD with honors, 1979. Bar: Calif., U.S. Dist. Ct. (ctrl. dist.) Calif. 1979, U.S. Dist. Ct. (so. dist.) Calif. 1982, U.S. Dist. Ct. Nev. 1985, U.S. Dist. Ct. (no. dist.) Calif. 1992, U.S. Dist. Ct. Mont. 1993, U.S. Dist. Ct. Minn. 1994, U.S. Dist. Ct. (no. dist.) Ala. 1994, U.S. Dist. Ct. (so. dist.) Miss. 1995, U.S. Supreme Ct. Law clk. U.S. Dist. Ct. Ctrl. Dist. Calif., 1979—80; assoc. O'Melveny and Myers, 1980—87, ptnr., 1987—95; judge U.S. Dist. Ct. Calif., LA, 1995—98, U.S. Ct. Appeals (9th cir.), 1998—. Presdl. transition team Dept. Justice, Washington, 1993; mayoral transition team City of LA, 1995—; bd. govs. UCLA Ctr. for Comm. Policy, 1994—, vice-chair, 1994—; cons. in field. Co-author: The Encyclopedia of the American Constitution, 1986; contbr. articles to profl. jours. Pres. Women Lawyers Pub. Action Grant Found., 1986—87; founding mem. LA Chamber Orch., 1992—; active Legal Def. and Edn. Fund Calif. Leadership Coun., 1993—; active Blue Ribbon of LA Music Ctr., 1993—; del. Dem. Nat. Conv., 1992. Named one of Most Prominent Bus. Attys. in LA County, LA Bus. Jour., 1995; recipient Buddy award, NOW, 1995. Mem.: NOW, ABA, Orgn. Women Execs., Assn. Bus. Trial Lawyers (gov. 1988—), LA County Bar Assn. (trustee 1993—94), Women Lawyers Assn. LA, Calif. Women Lawyers, Mex.-Am. Bar Assn. LA County, Hollywood Womens Polit. Com., Downtown Women Ptnrs., City Club Bunker Hill, Breakfast Club, Chancery Club, Phi Beta Kappa. Office: US Ct Appeals 9th Cir 125 South Grand Ave Pasadena CA 91105*

WARDRIP, ELIZABETH JANE, retired librarian; b. Lawrenceburg, Ind., Dec. 12, 1925; d. Estal Joseph Ackerman and Dorothy Leona Unthank; m. Schuyler Clark Wardrip, Dec. 20, 1953 (div. Dec. 24, 1981); children: Gregory Clark, Elizabeth Jane, Margaret Louise, Laura Anne, Mary Ann. BS in Gen. Studies, Columbia U., 1951; MLS, U. Md., 1972. Cert. libr. Md., 1972. Libr. adult svcs. Prince George's County Meml. Libr. Sys., Hyattsville, Md., 1972—92, ret., 1992. Fellow, U. Rochester, 1951. Mem.: DAR (regent 1999—2001). Democrat. Roman Catholic. Avocations: reading, theater, travel, museums, art galleries. Home: 6103 Sutters Place Bowie MD 20720

WARE, GWENDOLYN C., retired counseling administrator; m. Roy Ware, Mar. 28; 1 child, Sonja (Ware) Lucca. BA in English magna cum laude, U. Ark., Pine Buiff, 1970; MEd in Secondary Counseling with honors, U. Nev., Las Vegas, 1975. English instr. Clark County Sch. Dist., Las Vegas, 1971—77, guidance counselor, 1977—95, scholarship and coll. prep counselor, 1996—2003, ret., 2003. Fin. aid/scholarship workshop presenter Clark County Sch. Dist., Las Vegas, 1997—2003; coll. preparation workshop facilitator and presenter Kappa Alpha Psi Kappa League, Las Vegas, 2002—. Mem. Black Cmty. Orgn. Network, Las Vegas, 1988—2005. Mem.: AAUW, NAFE, Clark County Sch. Counselors' Assn., Western Assn. Coll. Admissions Counselors, Sickle Cell Anemia Found. (scholarship rev. and selection 1987—88), Phi Delta Kappa (2nd v.p. membership 1997—99, Mem. of Yr. 1997).

WARE, JANE ORTH, writer; b. Chgo., Feb. 23, 1936; d. Henry Walter and Mary Jane Orth; m. Brendan J. Ware, Oct. 7, 1961; children: Michael Orth, Henry William, Frieda Margaret. AB cum laude, Smith Coll., Northampton, Mass., 1958; MA, NYU, 1969. Rsch. editor This Week Mag., N.Y.C., 1959—65; staff writer Ridgewood (N.J.) News, 1978—80; freelance writer Columbus, Ohio, 1982—. Author: An Ohio State Profile, 1990, 2d edit., 1991, Other People's Business, 1993, Building Ohio: A Traveler's Guide to Ohio's Urban Architecture, 2001 (award Ohio Hist. Soc., 2001), Building Ohio: A Traveler's Guide to Ohio's Rural Architecture, 2002 (award Ohio Hist. Soc., 2002). Home: 2478 Bryden Rd Columbus OH 43209

WARE, MARILYN, ambassador, former utilities company executive; b. Lancaster, Pa., Nov. 4, 1943; d. John III and Marian Ware; children: Mark Strode, Amy Strode, Scott Strode. D of Pub. Services., Thaddeus Stevens Coll. Tech., 1998; LittD (hon.), Franklin & Marshall Coll., 2003. Vice-chmn. Am. Water Works Co., Inc., Voorhees, NJ, 1984-88, chmn., 1988—2003, chmn. emeritus Vorhees, NJ, 2003; US amb. to Finland US Dept. State, Helsinki, 2005—. CEO Ware Family Offices, Strasburg, Pa., 1991; dir. CIGNA Corp., Phila., 1993-2005, IKON Office Solutions, Malvern, Pa., 2000—2005, Am. Enterprise Inst., Washington, 1994, PENJERDEL Coun., Phila.; mem. Nat. Infrastructure Advisory Coun., 2002, Pew Oceans Commn., 2000-03 Editor: The Oxford Press, Lancaster, Pa., 1978-82. Trustee Nat. Osteoporosis Found., Washington, 1996-2000, U. Pa. Health Sys., Phila., 1991—, Gannon U., Erie, Pa., 1996-2000, Nat. Coun. of Conservation Fund, Washington, 1999—, Eisenhower Exch. Fellowships, Phila., 1995—, chmn. exec. com., 2000; founding mem., bd. dirs. Lancaster Farmland Trust, 1987—; founder, adv. bd. dirs. Janus Sch., Mt. Joy, Pa., 1991—; v.p., sec. Oxford Found., Strasburg, 1981—; chmn. Tom Ridge for Gov. Campaign, Harrisburg, Pa., 1993-94, Rep. Com. of Lancaster County, 1978-80, Woman for Bush, Pa., 1987-88; mem. Rep. State Com. of Pa., 1985-90. Recipient Samuel S. Baxter Meml. award Water Resources Assn., 2000, Paradigm award Greater Phila. C. of C., 1999, Dir.'s Choice award Nat. Women's Econ. Alliance Found., 1992; named Bus. Leader of Yr., Rep. Caucus, Pa. Ho. of Reps., 1993, Disting. Daus. of Pa., Gov. Tom Ridge, 2000. Office: Am Embassy 5310 Helsinki Pl Washington DC 20521*

WARE, SANDRA MARIE, minister, music educator, composer; d. Frank Ware, Sr. and Mary Lillie Ware. Degree in Ministry, Loman-Hannon Coll., 1971; BS cum laude, Ala. State U., 1980, MEd, 1998. Grad. asst., tchr. music dept. piano, music appreciation, and theory Ala. State U., Mont., 1978—80; music, choral tchr. St. Jude Cath. H.S., Mont., 1979—84; music tchr. Fews Elem. Sch., Mont., 1984—2001; pastor Varick-Star AME Zion Ch., Mont., 1996—2001; music tchr. E. D. Nixon Elem. Sch., Mont., 2001—. Composer: (songs) I'll Do My Best on the Stanford Achievement Test, 1996 (Recognition of Outstanding Music award, 1996), (various motivational songs and raps) Stanford Achievement Test, various inspirational gospel selections. Mem. Mt. Zion AME Zion Ch., Mont. Recipient Cert. of Appreciation award, Fed. Prison Camp, Maxwell AFB, 1975. Master: Montgomery Edn. Assn.; mem.: NEA, Ala. Edn. Assn., Delta Omicron Music Frat. Women (assoc.; dir. musical 1977—78). African Methodist Episcopal Zion. Avocations: singing, piano, typing, choral directing, hair braiding.

WARE, SUSAN JOY, elementary school educator; b. Mt. Pleasant, Pa., Feb. 20, 1956; d. John Louis and Nancy Martha Bauer; m. Keith Porter Ware, II, Dec. 17, 1976; children: Jason Michael, Zachary Todd. AA in Acctg., Westmoreland County C.C., Youngwood, Pa., 1976; BA in Family Studies, Seton Hill Coll., Greensburg, Pa., 1998; MA in Elem. Edn., Seton Hill U., 2002. Cert. elem. edn., early childhood edn. cert., mid. sch. social studies Pa. Bd. Edn. Various positions Stuart Med., Greensburg, 1988—96; tutor Seton Hill Coll., Greensburg, 1996—97, aide Child Devel. Ctr., 1997—98; tchr. St. John the Baptist Sch., Scottdale, Pa., 1999—. Vol. Boy Scouts Am., 1990—. Mem.: Pa. Assn. Edn. Young Children, Nat. Assn. Edn. Young Children. Roman Catholic. Avocations: camping, reading. Home: 182 Rolling Hills Rd Ruffs Dale PA 15679 Office: St John the Baptist Sch 504 S Broadway Scottdale PA 15683

WARFEL, SUSAN LEIGH, editor; b. LA, Aug. 5, 1959; Ba in Journalism, Sociology, U. So. Calif., L.A., 1981. Bus. reporter L.A. Herald Examiner, 1981-83, Investor's Bus. Daily, L.A., 1983-88, sr. editor, 1988-96, mng. editor, 1996—. Office: Investor's Bus Daily 12655 Beatrice St Los Angeles CA 90066-7303

WARFORD, PATRICIA, psychologist; d. Eldon J. Jameson and Rosa Kirschenman; m. Gary W. Warford, Sept. 5, 1955; children: Candice C. Zaniewski, Nathanael A. BS, S.D. State U., 1991; MS, George Fox Coll., 1993, D of Psychology, 1996. Lic. psychologist Oreg. Bd. Psychologist Examiners, 1998. Psychologist Western Psychol. & Counseling, Beaverton, Oreg., 1994—98, Yamhill County Adult Mental Health, McMinnville, 1998—2000, pvt. practice, Newberg, 2001—; co-owner Life Strategies Domestic Abuse Program, McMinnville, 2005—. Faculty State Victims Assistance Acad., Salem, Oreg., 2004—; presenter Boston Coll., Boston, 2002, George Fox U., Newberg, 2004. Co-author: (training manual chapter) Trauma Bonding. Oregon State Victims Assistance Academy Training ManualNumber 2002-VF-GX-KO23 awarded by the Office for Victims of Crime, Office of Justice Programs, U.S. Department of Justic, 2004. Appointee Oreg. Gov.'s Coun. Domestic Violence, Salem, 2004. Mem.: APA, Tri-County Batterers Intervention Providers, Yamhill County Domestic Violence Task Force. Office: 1013 N Springbrook PO Box 3279 Newberg OR 97132 Office Phone: 503-554-8172. Office Fax: 877-892-6114.

WARGO, ANDREA ANN, retired public health service officer; b. Pottsville, Pa., Dec. 27, 1941; d. John Andrew and Anna Mary (Blischok) W.; m. Roger Fredrick Sies, Mar. 31, 1981. BS in Biology, Chestnut Hill Coll., 1972; PhD in Biology, Georgetown U., 1978. Educator, adminstr. Cath. Archdiocese Phila., 1961-74; tchg. asst. Georgetown U., Washington, 1974-78, postdoctoral fellow, 1978-80; acting br. chief FDA, Silver Spring, Md., 1980-86, acting chief gen. hosp. and personal use devices, 1986-88; assoc. adminstr. Agy. for Toxic Substances and Disease Registry, Washington, 1988-2001; ret., 2001. Mem. Surgeon Gen.'s Policy Adv. Coun., 1996-2001. Contbr. articles to sci. publs. Grantee NSF, 1972, 73, Kidney Found., 19790-80. Mem. Assn. Women in Sci. (treas. Washington-Balt. chpt. 1979-80), Commd. Officers Assn., Georgetown U. Alumni Assn., Toastmistress Club (pres. Bethesda chpt. 1978-79), Pub. Health Svc. (scientist profl. adv. com., exec. sec. 1984-86, vice chmn. 1986-87), Sigma Xi. Avocations: languages, computers, financial planning, handwriting analysis, crossword puzzles. Home: 17604 N Stone Haven Dr Surprise AZ 85374

WARIAN, CHRISTINE BARBARA, elementary school educator; b. Somerville, Nj, May 7, 1967; d. Terence and Loretta Warian. MusB in Music Edn. and Therapy, Immaculata Coll., 1989; MA in Reading Specialization, Kean U., 2003. Cert. reading specialist, elem. tchr. NJ. Tchr. Christ the King Sch., Manville, NJ, 1997—2000, Our Lady of Peace Sch., Fords, NJ, 2000—01, Huntington Learning Ctr., Edison, NJ, 2005—; substitute tchr. Edison and Woodbridge Sch. Dists., 2001—04; reading specialist James Madison Intermediate Sch., Edison, 2004—05. Mem.: NJ Reading Assoc., Kappa Delta Pi. Avocations: singing, exercise, reading.

WARICHA, JOAN, publishing executive; BA, Boston U., 1967; MBA, Columbia U., 1980. V.p., editor-in-chief, assoc. pub. Scholastic, Inc., 1968-83; pres. Parachute Press, 1983-96; chmn., CEO Parachute Properties, 1996—; pres. Parachute Pub., 1996—, Parachute Entertainment, 1996—, Parachute Consumer Products, 1996—. Office: Parachute Properties 156 5th Ave New York NY 10010-7002 Office Phone: 212-691-1421. E-mail: jwaricha@parachuteproperties.com.

WARING, MARY LOUISE, retired social worker; b. Pitts., Feb. 15, 1928; d. Harold R. and Edith (McCallum) W. AB, Duke U., 1949; MSS, Smith Coll., 1951; PhD, Brandeis U., 1974. Sr. supervising social worker Judge Baker Guidance Ctr., Boston, 1955-65; dir. social svc. Cambridge (Mass.) Mental Health Ctr., 1965-70; assoc. prof. Sch. Social Work Fla. State U., Tallahassee, 1974-77; prof. Grad. Sch. Social Svc. Fordham U., N.Y.C., 1977-82; cons. Dept. Human Svc., N.J., 1983-84; cons., sr. staff mem. Family Counseling Svc. Bergen County, Hackensack, N.J., 1984-86; dir. Step One Employee Assistance Program Fortwood Ctr., Inc., Chattanooga, 1986-96; part-time psychotherapist Greenleaf Svcs., Chattanooga, 1996, pvt. practice, 1997-98; ret., 1999. Mem. ethics com. Chattanooga Rehab. Hosp., 1995. Contbr. articles to profl. jours. Mem. Citizen Amb. Program Human Resource Mgmt. Delegation to Russia, 1993; active Nat. Trust for Hist. Preservation, Hunter Mus. Am. Art, Chattanooga Symphony and Opera Assn., Friends of Hamilton County Bicentennial Libr.; mem. exec. coun. Friends of the Chattanooga-Hamilton County Bicentennial Libr., 2005—; docent Hunter Mus. Am. Art, Chattanooga, 2005. Recipient Career Tchr. award Nat. Inst. Alchohol and Alchohol Abuse, 1972-74; traineeship NIMH, 1949-51. Mem. NASW (charter), Acad. Cert. Social Workers, Nat. Mus. Women in Arts (charter), Nat. Trust for Hist. Preservation, Smithsonian Assocs., Cmty. Svcs. Club Greater Chattanooga (pres. 1995, 96, v.p. 1994, 97, membership chair 1998—).

WARMACK, WANDA LUCILE, education educator; b. Gadsden, Ala., Oct. 8, 1960; d. James Olin and Dorothy Lucile Warmack. BS in Elem. Edn., Ala. Christian Coll., Montgomery, 1983; MEd in Early Childhood Edn., Auburn U., Montgomery, 1990; PhD in Elem. Edn. Reading, Auburn U., Ala., 2006. Kindergarten tchr. BoPeep Childcare Ctr., Montgomery, 1983—85; office mgr., admissions Faulkner U., Montgomery, 1985—90; asst. dir., tchr. Green Oaks Preschool, Montgomery, 1990—93; asst. prof., edn. Faulkner U., 1993—. Mem., officer Friends for Faulkner, 1993—. Mem.: Ala. Reading Assn., Internat. Reading Assn.

WARMAN, LINDA K., retired language educator, retired art educator; b. Indiana, Pa., Mar. 25, 1942; d. James Edward and Elizabeth Josephine (Hawk) Warman. BA, Moravian Coll., Bethlehem, Pa., 1964. Tchr. Easton Area Sch. Dist., Pa., 1964—2001, chair dept. English, 1986—2001; ret., 2001. Contbr.: book Religious Literature of the West, 1970. Avocations: travel, reading, home decorating, gardening.

WARMAN, LYNNETTE R., lawyer; b. Willmar, Minn., Oct. 1, 1955; BA, U. Nebr., 1983; JD, Creighton U., 1986. Bar: Nebr. 1986, Tex. 1987, US Ct. Appeals 5th Cir., US Dist. Ct. No., Ea., We. & So. Districts Tex. Shareholder Jenkens & Gilchrist, P.C., Dallas, head bus. dept. Mem.: ABA, Tex. Bar Assn., Dallas Bar Assn. (bankruptcy sect.), John C. Ford. Am. Inn of Ct., Am. Bankruptcy Inst. (bd. dirs.). Office: Jenkens & Gilchrist PC 1445 Ross Ave Ste 3700 Dallas TX 75202-2799 Office Phone: 214-855-4792. Office Fax: 214-855-4300. Business E-Mail: lwarman@jenkens.com.

WARNATH, MAXINE AMMER, psychologist, arbitrator; b. NYC, Dec. 3, 1928; d. Philip and Jeanette Ammer; m. Charles Frederick Warnath, Aug. 20, 1952; children: Stephen Charles, Cindy Ruth. BA, Bklyn. Coll., 1949; MA, Columbia U., 1951, EdD, 1982. Lic. psychologist Oreg. Various profl. positions Hunter Coll., U. Minn., U. Nebr., U. Oreg., 1951-62; asst. prof. psychology Oreg. Coll. Edn., Monmouth, 1962-77; assoc. prof. psychology, chmn. dept. psychology & spl. edn. Western Oreg. U., Monmouth, 1978-83, prof., 1983—96, prof. emeritus, 1996—. Dir. organizational psychology program, 1983—96; pres. Profl. Perspective Internat., Salem, Oreg., 1987—; cons., dir. Orgn. R&D, Salem, Oreg., 1983—87; seminar leader Endeavors for Excellence program. Author: Power Dynamism, 1987. Mem.: APA (com. pre-coll. psychology 1970—74), Western Psychol. Assn., Oreg. Psychol. Assn. (pres. 1980—81, pres.-elect 1979—80, legis. liaison 1977—78), Oreg. Acad. Sci., N.Y. Acad. Scis., Am. Psychol. Soc. Office: Profl Perspectives Internat PO Box 2265 Salem OR 97308-2265 Office Phone: 503-371-6451. Personal E-mail: mwarnath@comcast.net. Business E-Mail: warnatm@wou.edu.

WARNELL, REBECCA E., social studies educator; b. Stamford, Conn., July 15, 1958; d. John Lewis and Mary H. Eavenson; m. Robin Scott Warnell, Aug. 1, 1992; 1 child, Rachel Rebecca. BS (hon.), Pa. State U., State College, 1980; MA (hon.), U. No. Colo., Greeley, 1981. Tchr. 8th grade social studies Aurora Pub. Schools, Colo., 1989—. Mem.: NEA. Office: Columbia Middle School 17600 East Columbia Avenue Aurora CO 80013 Office Phone: 303-690-6570.

WARNER, EMILY HANRAHAN HOWELL, retired pilot, writer; b. Oct. 30, 1939; m. Julius "Jay" Warner. BA in English, Souther U., Baton Rouge, La. Kindergarten and elem. sch. tchr.; flight instr. Clinton Aviation Co., 1961—67, rose to positions of chief pilot and flight sch. mgr., 1967—73; pilot Frontier Airlines, 1973—86, Continental Airlines, 1986—88, United Parcel Svc., 1988—90; aviation safety inspector FAA, 1990—2002, aircrew program mgr., 1992—2002. Bd. dirs. Internat. Air Mus., Dayton, Ohio. Author: (children's books) Lily of Watts- A Birthday Discovery, 1969, Lily Takes A Giant Step, (biography) Weaving the Winds, 2003. Co-founder Northeast Women's Ctr., Denver; active with Congress of Racial Equality, ACLU, NAACP. Named to Colo. Aviation Hall Fame, 1983, Nat. Women's Hall Fame, Seneca Falls, NY, 2001; recipient Amelia Earheart award as the Outstanding Woman in US Aviation, 1973. Mem.: Colo. Aviation Hist. Soc., Internat. Soc. Women Airline Pilots (founder), Ninety-Nines: Internat. Orgn. Women Pilots. Achievements include uniform installed in Smithsonian Inst. Air and Space Mus., 1976; first woman hired as pilot by major US airline, 1973.

WARNER, JAYNE LENA, academic administrator; b. Newport, Vt., Apr. 24, 1946; d. Newell D. and Eva L. (Leonard) W. BA in Classics and History, U. Vt., 1968, MA in Ancient History, 1970; PhD in Archaeology, Bryn Mawr Coll., 1976. Asst. editor Am. Sch. Classical Studies at Athens, Princeton, N.J., 1976-78; exec. dir. Poetry Soc. of Am., N.Y.C., 1978-79, Am. Turkish Soc., N.Y.C., 1979-82; dir. NY office Robert Coll. of Istanbul, Turkey, N.Y.C., 1982-95; dir. rsch. Inst. for Aegean Archaeology, Greenwich, Conn., 1996—. Author: Elmali-Karatas II--The Early Bronze Age Village of Karatas, 1994. Mem. Phi Beta Kappa. Home: 225 E 36th St Apt 12D New York NY 10016-3620 Personal E-mail: jaynewarner@earthlink.net.

WARNER, JO F., mathematics instructor; b. Kansas City, Kans., Nov. 22, 1949; d. William Halpin and Anna Lorene Fitzsimmons; m. Allen Robert Warner, July 22, 1978; children: Robin William, Gilbert Nathaniel, Lee Alexander. BS, Ea. Mich. U., 1971, MA, 1990; EdD, Grambling State U., 2001. Math. tchr. Ann Arbor (Mich.) Pub. Schs., 1983-86; vis. lectr. math. Washtenaw C.C., Ann Arbor, 1987—; instr. tchr., placement specialist Ea. Mich. U., Ypsilanti, 1989—. Author: Math Concepts for Algebra Prep, 1998, 3d edit., 2000; newsletter editor Mich. Devel. Edn. Cons. Mem.: AAUW, Mich. Devel. Edn. Consortium (pres.), Math. Assn. Am., Nat. Assn. for Devel. Edn. (chmn. rsch. com). Avocations: reading, walking, cross country skiing. Office: Ea Mich Univ 515 Pray-Harrold Ypsilanti MI 48197

WARNER, JOANNE RAINS, nursing educator, associate dean; b. Sioux Falls, S.D., June 27, 1950; d. Arnold D. and Arlene M. (Lawrence) W.; children: David Warner, Isaac Daniel. BA, Augustana Coll., 1972; MA, U. Iowa, 1976; D of Nursing Sci., Ind. U., 1990. Vis. nurse Delaware County Vis. Nurse Assn., Muncie, Ind., 1976-77; cons. Ind. State Bd. Health, Indpls., 1977-78; instr. Briar Cliff Coll., Sioux Falls, 1981-82; adj. faculty Okla. Bapt. U., Shawnee, 1985; assoc. prof. Ind. U., Indpls., 1990—, assoc. dean for grad. programs, 2002—. Mem. exec. com. Friends Com. on Nat. Legis., Washington, 1992—; fellow Primary Health Care Policy, Washington, 1996; bd. trustees Earlham Coll. Campaign mgr. Doug Kinser for State Rep. Ind. House Dist. 54, 1988-94; exec. com., mem. New Castle (Ind.) Healthy City Com., 1989-99; chair residential drive Am. Cancer Soc., New Castle, 1989. Mem. ANA, Assn. Cmty. Health Nurse Educators (bd. dirs.), Ind. Polit. Sci. Assn. (v.p. 1993-94,. pres. 1994-95). Mem. Soc. Of Friends. Office: Ind U 1111 Middle Dr Indianapolis IN 46202 Home: 3736 NE 36th Ave Portland OR 97212-1834 Office Phone: 317-274-3115.

WARNER, JUDITH (ANNE) HUSS, elementary school educator; b. Plainfield, N.J., June 15, 1936; d. Charles and Martha McMullen (Miller) Huss; m. Howard R. Warner, June 14, 1958; children: Barbara, Robert. BS in Elem. Edn., Russell Sage Coll., 1959. Elem. tchr. Pitts. Bd. Edn., 1959-60; home tchr. Napa (Calif.) Sch. Bd., 1974-77; substitute tchr. Allegheny Intermediate Unit, Pitts., 1977—94. Leader Girl Scouts U.S.A., Pitts., 1966-70; vol. Children's Hosp., Pitts., 1967-74, Jefferson Hosp., Pitts., 1977-88; pres., trustee Whitehall Libr., Pitts., 1984-92; pres., bd. dirs. Friends of Whitehall Libr., Pitts., 1969-94. Mem. AAUW, DAR. Republican. Methodist. Avocations: sailing, skiing, swimming, hiking, travel. Home: 4985 Wheaton Dr Pittsburgh PA 15236-2064

WARNER, KERSTIN JULIANNA, gifted and talented educator; d. Kerstin and John Warner; m. Louis Weinberg, June 23, 1995; 1 child, Sofia Weinberg. BS in Fine Art, Vassar Coll., Poughkeepsie, N.Y., 1986; MS in Spl. Edn., Bank St. Coll. Edn., 1994. Cert. tchr. K-8, spl. edn. 1-12, art 1-12 Conn., tchr. elem. K-6, art 1-12, spl. edn. 1 - 12 NY. Asst. tchr. St. Anne's Sch., Bklyn., 1987—90; tchr. spl. edn. preschool The League Sch., Bklyn., 1990—92; 2d grade tchr. Berkeley Carroll Sch., Bklyn., 1992—95; tchr. gifted St. Paul Pub. Schs., 1995—99, Bedford Mid. Sch., Westport, Conn., 1999—. Coach mock trial team Bedford Mid. Sch., Westport, 2002—; book discussion trainer Westport Pub. Libr., 2001—; Conn. chair Nicholas Green award, 2005—. Pres. Vassar Club of Fairfield County, Westport, Conn., 2002—. Recipient Golden Apple Achiever award, Ashland, 1998; Inter-district Archaeology Program, Conn. Assn. for the Gifted, 2004—05. Mem.: ASCD, Nat. Assn. for Gifted Children (state coord., chairperson Nicholas Green award 2006—), Conn. Assn. for the Gifted, Nat. Coun. Tchrs. Math., Vassar Club (pres. 2002—). Democrat. Avocations: creative writing, drawing, international travel. Office: Bedford Middle School 88 North Ave Westport CT 06880 Office Phone: 203-341-1582. E-mail: kerstin_warner@westport.k12.ct.us.

WARNER, MARY LOUISE, literature and language professor; d. Harvey Merritt and Agnes Mary Warner. MA in English, Creighton U., Omaha, 1985; ArtsD in English Lang. and Lit., U. Mich., Ann Arbor, 1992. Instr. English Mt. Mary Coll., Milw., 1985—89; tchg. asst. U. Mich., 1989—92, lectr., 1992—93; asst. prof. English edn. Black Hills State U., Spearfish, SD, 1994—96; prof. English, dir. English edn. Western Carolina U., Cullowhee, NC, 1996—2004; prof. English, dir. English credential program San Jose State U., Calif., 2004—. Presenter in field. Author: Adolescents in the Search for Meaning: Tapping the Powerful Resource of Story, 2006; editor: Winning Ways of Coaching Writing: A Practice Guide to Teaching Writing Grades 6-12, 2001. Mem. Sch. Sisters of Notre Dame, Mankato, Minn., 1971—. Mem.: ASCD, MLA, San Jose Area Writing Project (assoc. dir. 2005—), Nat. Writing Project, Calif. Assn. Tchrs. of English, Nat. Coun. Tchrs. of English (Assembly on Lit. for Adolescents). Avocations: walking, guitar, reading, cooking. Home: 1344 Fruitdale Ave # E2 San Jose CA 95126 Office: English Dept San Jose State U 1 Washington Sq San Jose CA 95192-0090 Office Phone: 408-924-4417. Office Fax: 408-924-4580. E-mail: mwarner@email.sjsu.edu.

WARNER, NEARI FRANCOIS, university president; b. New Orleans, July 20, 1945; d. Cornelius and Enell (Brimmer) Francois; m. Jimmie Duel Warner Sr., June 6, 1970 (div. Sept. 1983); 1 child, Jimmie Duel Jr. BS, Grambling (La.) State U., 1967; MA, Atlanta U., 1968; PhD, La. State U., 1992. Dir. Upward Bound So. U., New Orleans, 1976-89, dean jr. divsn., 1989-94; asst. v.p. acad. affairs Grambling State U., 1994-96, v.p. student affairs, 1996-97, v.p. devel., 1997-99, acting v.p. acad. affairs, 1999, provost, v.p. acad. affairs, 1999—. Sec. Conf. La. Colls./Univs., 1999—; mem. State Funding Task Force, State of La., 1998-99; bd. dirs. La. Endowment for Humanities, 1998—; pres. La. Assn. Student Asst. Program, 1986-88. Preface writer: Interdisciplinary Approach, 1998. Mem. adv. bd. Pupil Progression Commn., New Orleans, 1989-93; mem. task force Gov.'s Tech. Prep., Baton Rouge, 1991-93, Mayor's Task Force for Edn., New Orleans, 1992, Monroe (La.) City Sch., 1995. Named Role model YWCA, New Orleans, 1992, Disting. Alumnae Nat. Assn. Equal Opportunity, Washington, 1996. Mem. AAUW, NAACP, The Links, Inc. (treas. 1999—, Unsung Hero 1993), Alpha Kappa Alpha, Kappa Delta Pi, Pi Gamma Mu Democrat. Baptist. Avocations: reading, bowling. Office: Grambling State U PO Box 1170 Grambling LA 71245-1170 Home: 2518 Creekside Trce Jonesboro GA 30236-6189 E-mail: nfwarner@martin.gram.edu.

WARNER, ROBERTA ARLENE, retired accountant, financial services executive; b. Binghamton, N.Y., Dec. 31, 1938; d. Murrilan Earl and Ethel Margaret (Bell) W. BA, SUNY, Binghamton, 1960; MBA, Ind. U., 1962, MHA with highest distinction, 1973. CPA, N.Y.; lic. nursing home adminstr., N.Y. Sr. acct. Arthur Young & Co., CPA, Buffalo, 1962—66; acctg. supr. Children's Hosp., Buffalo, 1966—68; contr. King Manor Nursing Homes-Ave. Bldg. Corp., Buffalo, 1968—71; asst. dir. health fin. Hosp. Assn. N.Y. State, Albany, 1973—80, dir. health fin., 1980—93, Healthcare Assn. N.Y. State, Albany, 1994—97, dir. data analysis and stds., 1997—98; pres. Roberta A. Warner Co., 1999—2003, ret., 2003. Author articles in field. Trustee Ednl. Found. of Am. Women's Soc. CPA, Am. Soc. Women Accts., 1985-87. Fellow Healthcare Fin. Mgmt. Assn.; mem. AICPA, Am. Acctg. Assn., Am. Soc. Women Accts. (pres. Buffalo chpt. 1967-68), Am. Women's Soc. CPA, N.Y. State Soc. CPA, Ind. U. Alumni Assn. (life), SUNY Binghamton Alumni Assn. (life), Grange. Methodist. Home: 569 NY Rte 79 Windsor NY 13865-2714

WARNER, ROSEMARIE, elementary school educator; d. John and Mary Moraski; m. Paul J. Warner, Oct. 6, 1979; children: Joshua, Steven, Jonathan. BS, East Stroudsburg U., Pa., 1977; MS, U. Scranton, 1993. Cert. Instrnl. II Pa., 2003, Improving Math. and Sci. Elem. Schs. Pa., 2003. Tchr. St. Joseph's Sch., Scranton, 1979—82; adj. faculty Lackawanna Coll., Scranton, 1990—90, U. Scranton, 1990—95; tchr. North Pocono Sch. Dist., Moscow, Pa., 1995—. Mem. com. Nat. Night Out, Moscow, 2004—06; com. mem. Cub Pack 126, Moscow, 1994—97; mem. adult folk group St. Catherine of Siena Parish, Moscow, 1987—2006; race dir. Moscow Country Run North Pocono Booster Assn., 1999—2002. D-Conservative. Roman Catholic. Achievements include development of Hands on Math Course for Elementary teachers. Avocations: guitar, travel, reading. Personal E-mail: warner108@verizon.net.

WARNER, SUSAN, federal agency administrator; b. Rochester, N.Y., July 20, 1956; d. Harold J. and Jeannette (Nichols) Warner; divorced; children: Jennifer Lynn, Kathryn Alice. BA, Miami U., Oxford, Ohio, 1978; postgrad., Xavier U. Loan specialist HUD, Columbus, Ohio, 1978-79, Cin., 1979-83; fin. planner IDS Fin. Services, Inc., Cin., 1983-86, Manufacturer's Hanover Mortgage Corp., 1986, Shawmut Mortgage Corp., 1986-87, U.S. Dept. HUD, St. Louis, 1987—. Housing cons., Cin., 1985—. Author: Community Land Coop. Residents' Handbook, 1986. Adv. Cin. Tech. Coll., 1984—; mem. fin. com. Community Land Coop., Cin., 1985—; exhibits chair Conf. Cin. Women, 1985, corp. patrons chair, 1986, conf. coordinator, 1987—; vol. Am. Cancer soc., 1981-84, March of Dimes, 1996-2004; leader Girl Scouts. Recipient Mercury awards IDS, Cin., 1984, award for superior performance U.S. Inspector Gen. HUD, 1990, Profl. Team 2003 Excellence in Govt. award The Greater St. Louis Fed. Exec. Bd., 2003. Republican. Roman Catholic. Avocations: reading, costume designing, making teddy bears, softball, theater.

WARNKE, GEORGIA C., humanities educator; b. Washington, D.C. Aug. 22, 1951; d. Paul C. and Jean P. Warnke; children: Nathan W. Stern, Alexander W. Stern. BA, Reed Coll., Portland, Oreg., 1973; MA, Boston U., 1978, PhD, 1982. Asst. prof. Yale U., New Haven, Conn., 1982—89, assoc. prof., 1989—91; prof. U. Calif., Riverside, 1991—. Mem. Inst. Advanced Study, Princeton, NJ, 1991—92; assoc. dean, humanities, arts & scis. svcs. U. Calif., 2005—. Author: (book) Legitimate Differences, 1998. Grantee Sr. fellowship, Nat. Humanities Ctr., Rsch. Triangle Pk., N.C., 2004—05. Mem.: Am. Philos. Assn. (chair non-academic careers 2005—06). Democrat. Office: Univ Calif Dept Philosophy Riverside CA 92521

WARNKEN, PAULA NEUMAN, university library director, educator; b. La Crosse, Wis., Mar. 11, 1948; d. David M. and Gladys F. (Glickman) Neuman; m. Clifford H. Warnken, Sept. 12, 1970; children: Devin A., Jonathan D. BA, U. Wis., 1970; MLS, Kent State U., Ohio, 1980; M of Edn. and Personnel Tng. and Devel., Xavier U., 1985. Pub. service librarian Ohio U., Zanesville, 1976-80; head reader services Xavier U., Cin., 1980-84, dir. univ. libraries, 1984—, adj. instr. English, 1983—. Trustee OHIONET, 1987—. Mem. ALA, Acad. Library Assn. Ohio (pres. 1985-86).

WARONKER, CECILE C., secondary school educator; b. Clio, S.C., Sept. 25, 1935; d. Abe and Betty Mark Cohen; m. William L. Waronker, Dec. 28, 1958; children: Sherry Marah, Jay, Jody Para. BS in Edn., U. Ga., 1957. Tchr. DeKalb County Sch., Atlanta, 1957—60, City of Atlanta Sch., 1972—82, Lovett Sch., Atlanta, 1982—90. Writer (newspaper) Jewish Georgian. Recipient Woman of Achievement award, Jewish Fedn. of Atlanta, 2006. Democrat. Jewish. Home: 3649 Peachtree Rd #104 Atlanta GA 30319

WARREN, ALICE LOUISE, artist; b. Springfield, Mass., May 7, 1927; d. Roland D. and Ella May (McGrath) Eaton Von Der Lancken; m. John Homer Warren, June 5, 1948 (dec. Jan. 1988); children: John David (dec.), Daniel Wayne. Student, N.Y. Sch. Writing, 1952-55, Mansion House Art Sch., 1969, 70, 71; grad., Nat. Landscape Inst., 1960, Famous Writers Sch., 1965; Cert., United UMA Sch., 1967. Home nursing cert.; cert. home health aide paramedical. Nurses aide ARC, Springfield, 1942-45; vol. nurses aid, 1943—44; hot-line councilor Check Line, West Springfield, Mass., 1945-46; freelance columnist New England Homestead, Springfield, 1960-63; freelance columnist, editor Garden Page Woman's Circle, Horticulture mags. Author, photographer: (booklet) Evergreen Shrubs, 1964. solo art exhbns. Mercy Hosp., Arts Unltd. Gallery, 1997, Bay State Med., Springfield, Mass., 1999; featured artist Barnes and Noble Bookstore, Oct. 1999, Westfield Antheneum, 2000; on-line exhbns. MindsIsland.com, 2002, ArtRepsart.com, 2002--, Art-Exchange.com, 2003--. Recipient Bill Curtin award for watercolor, 1983. Mem. Amherst Writers & Artists Inst., Springfield Art League, Scriptures Writers, Mass. Writers Guild (treas. 1963), Tobacco Valley Artists Assn. Avocations: painting, travel, photography, reading. E-mail: artislalaw@comcast.net.

WARREN, BARBARA DENISE, special education educator; d. Willie D. and Earnestine Loretta Davis; m. Charles Eric Warren, Sept. 7, 1976; children: Tasha Shalace, TuJuana, Charles Jr. Cert. in practical nursing, Albany Vocat. Tech. Sch., 1983; BS, Albany State U., 1998; MEd, Clark-Atlanta U., 2002, EdS, 2003; postgrad., Walden U. LPN, Ga. Para profl. Dougherty County Sch., Albany, Ga., 1992—97; tchr. Dekalb County Sch., Atlanta, 1997—. Mentor tchr. Dekalb County Schs., Atlanta, 2000. Mem.: Coun. Exceptional Children, Ga. Assn. Educators (bldg. rep. 2000—). Avocations: reading, gardening, music, cooking. Home: 345 Lori Ln Riverdale GA 30296 E-mail: hsspid@aol.com.

WARREN, CINDY MICHELLE, author; b. Warren, Mich., Jan. 3, 1962; d William Henry and Margaret Helen (Cooper) W. Writer/journalist, Detroit, 1982—; bus. mgr. Detroit Writers Project, 1987—; founder, pres. Detroit Performance Army United, 1990—; asst. chair Women's Studies, Wayne State U., Detroit, 1991-92; poetry editor The Word Enamel, Detroit, 1995-96, fiction editor, 1992-93. Mgr. various poetry reading series, Detroit, 1987—; pub. Manque Mag., Detroit, 1980-83, Four Points of Love mag., Detroit, 1983-85. Author: Wayne Literary Review, 1990, 91, 92, Triage, 1991-94, Babyfish Lost Its Momma, 1989-94; contbr. articles to profl. jours. Fundraiser Detroit Writers Project, 1987—, Adrian (Mich.) Four, 1991, Poetry Resource Ctr., Detroit, 1989-94; mem. Detroit Zool. Soc., 1993—. Avocations: filmmaking, photography, dance, vocalist, performance artist.

WARREN, DIANE, lyricist; Staff writer Jack White, 1983; founder, owner RealSongs, LA. Author over 100 top ten pop songs including I'll Never Get Over You (Getting Over Me), How Do I Live, I Don't Want to Miss a Thing, If You Asked Me To, Don't Turn Around, Set The Night To Music, I'll Still Love You More, Because You Loved Me (Grammy award, song written specifically for a motion picture or TV, 1996), Rhythm of the Night, Nothing's Gonna Stop Us Now, Unbreak My Heart, Music of My Heart, My First Night With You (Nashville Songwriters Assn. Internat. award, superior creativity in the words and music of a song, 2000), I Will Get There (Nashville Songwriters Assn. Internat. award, superior creativity in the words and music of a song, 2000), There You'll Be, and many others. Hon. com. mem. PETA; founder, David S. Warren Weekly Entertainment Series, Jewish Home for the Aging; donor Wildlife Waystation, 10th Ann. Life Found., The Lange Found. Named Songwriter of Yr., Nat. Acad. Songwriters, 1996, No. 1 Pop Songwriter of Yr., Am. Songwriter Awards, 1997, Songwriter of Yr., Nashville Songwriters Assn. Internat., 2000; named to Songwriters Hall of Fame, 2001, Hollywood Walk of Fame, 2001; recipient Songwriter of Yr., Am. Soc. Composers, Authors & Publishers, 1990, 1991, 1993, 1998, 1999, Billboard, George and Ira Gershwin award, outstanding musical achievement, 1998, New Millennium Visionary award, Am. Cinema Awards Found., 1999, Legacy award, Orgn. For the Needs of the Elderly, 1999, Dream Maker's Cir. Award, Dream Found., 2000, Lifetime Achievement award, Bill Gavin Heritage Found., 2000, Angel award, Angels on Earth, 2000, Musician's Adv. award, Am. Soc. Young Musicians, 2001, Telly award, Found. for a Better Life, 2003. Achievements include songs features in over 80 motion pictures. Office: Realsongs 6363 W Sunset Blvd Fl 8 Hollywood CA 90028-7330 Mailing: c/o The Chasen Co 8899 Beverly Blvd Ste 405 West Hollywood CA 90048*

WARREN, ELIZABETH A., law educator; 1 child, Amelia Warren Tyagi. BS, U. Houston, 1970; JD, Rutgers U., 1976. Bar: NJ, Tex. Lectr. law Rutgers Sch. Law, Newark, 1977—78; asst. prof. law U. Houston Law Ctr., 1978—80, assoc. dean academic affairs, 1980—81, assoc. prof. law, 1981—83; rsch. assoc. Population Rsch. Ctr. U. Tex., Austin, 1983—87; prof. law U. Tex. Sch. Law, 1983—87, Conoco Faculty Fellow in Law, 1985—86, Jay H. Brown Centennial Fellow in Law, 1986—87; prof. law U. Pa. Law Sch., Phila., 1987—90, William A. Schnader Prof. Comml. Law, 1990—95; Leo Gottlieb prof. law Harvard Law Sch., Cambridge, Mass., 1995—. Vis. assoc. prof. law U. Tex. Sch. Law, 1981—82; vis. prof. law U. Mich., 1985; Robert Braucher Vis. Prof. Comml. Law Harvard U., 1992—93; proposal reviewer NSF, 1985—; bd. editors Am. Bankruptcy Law Jour., 1989—92; editl. adv. bd. Little Brown & Co. Law Sch. Divsn. (now Aspen Press), 1990—; com. on jud. edn. Fed. Jud. Ctr., 1990—99; bd. trustees Am. Bankruptcy Bd. Certification, 1992—96; exec. com. Nat. Bankruptcy Conf., 1993—95, 2002—05; advisor German Govt. Task Force on Bankruptcy Reform, 1993; reporter, cons., sr. advisor Nat. Bankruptcy Rev. Commn., 1995—97; regular commentator All Things Considered program Nat. Pub. Radio. Co-author: (books) As We Forgive Our Debtors: Consumer Credit and Bankruptcy in America, 1989 (Silver Gavel Award, ABA, 1990), The Law of Debtors and Creditors, 1991, 1996, 2001, Secured Transactions: A Systems Approach, 1995, 1998, 2000, 2003, Comml. Law: A Systems Approach, 1998, 2003, The Fragile Middle Class: Americans in Debt, 2000 (Scholarship Award, Am. Coll. Consumer Fin. Services Lawyers, 2000); co-author: (with Amelia Warren Tyagi) The Two-Income Trap: Why Middle-Class Mothers and Fathers Are Going Broke, 2003; author: numerous books chapters and jour. articles. Named one of 50 Most Influential Women Attorneys, Nat. Law Jour., 1998; recipient Frankel Publ. Award for Outstanding Writing, 1982, Commedation for Svc., Am. Bankruptcy Bd. Certification, 1998, Brown Award for Jud. Scholarship and Edn., Fed. Jud. Ctr., 1998, Champion of Consumer Rights Award, Nat. Assn. Consumer Bankruptcy Attorneys, 2000, Excellence in Edn. Award, Nat. Conf. Bankruptcy Judges, 2001, Lawrence P. King Award, Comml. Law League Am., 2002, Outstanding Tchr. Award, U. Houston Law Ctr., 1981, L. Hart Wright Teaching Excellence Award, U. Mich. Sch. Law, 1986, Harvey Levin Award for Excellence in Tchg., U. Pa. Sch. Law, 1989, 1992, Lindback Award for Disting. Tch., U. Pa., 1994, Albert A. Sacks-Paul A. Freund Award for Tchg. Excellence, Harvard Law Sch., 1997. Fellow: Am. Coll. Bankruptcy (Commendation for Outstanding Pub. Svc. 1998); mem.: Assn. Am. Law Schools (chair comml. and related consumer law sect. 1983—84, chair comml. law workshop 1984, planning com. conf. on tchg. contract law 1989, profl. devel. com. 1988—91, chair debtor-creditor sect. 1989—90, chair legislation com. debtor-creditor sect. 1990—93), Am. Law Inst. (exec. com. coun. 1994—95, US Adviser, Transnat. Insolvency Project 1995—, mem. nominating com. 1995—, exec. com. coun. 1998—, 2nd v.p. coun. 2000—04). Office: Harvard U Law Sch Hauser 200 Cambridge MA 02138

WARREN, ELIZABETH CURRAN, retired political science professor; b. St. Louis, Aug. 23, 1927; d. Maurice Donovan and Florence Schulte Curran; m. Geoffrey Spencer Warren, June 26, 1949; children: Kathryn Lloyd, Patricia, Michele, Deborah Perry. BA, Bryn Mawr Coll., Pa., 1949; MA, U. Kans., Lawrence, 1965; PhD, U. Nebr., 1970. Adj. prof. polit. sci. Loyola U. Chgo., 1977—80, asst. prof. polit. sci., 1980—87, ret., 1987. Cons. Dept. Housing, City of Chgo., 1981; cons. on subsidized housing City of Crystal Lake, Ill., 1982. Author: Legacy of Judicial Policy-Making, 1988, God, Caesar and the Freedom of Religion, 2003; co-author: Impact of Subsidized Housing on Property Values, 1983. Village pres. Village of Glencoe, Ill., 1985—93, trustee Ill., 1974—83; organizer, sec.-treas. Sr. Housing Aid, Glencoe, 1982—2001; mem. Glencoe Garden Club, 1989—, pres., 1997—99. Mem.: Skokie Country Club. Avocations: gardening, skiing, music, swimming, writing. Home: 24 Ct of Greenway Northbrook IL 60062

WARREN, IVORY JEAN, counselor, educator; b. Pocomoke City, Md., Jan. 25, 1954; children: Donnell Bland II, Shayla Denise, Vahson Alexander. BSW, Norfolk State U., Va., 1995, MSW, 1998. Customer svc. rep CCCI, Virginia Beach, Va., 1995—98; counselor TCC/The Women's Ctr., Norfolk, 1998—. Motivational spkr., Virginia Beach, 2000—06; outreach vol. The Women's Ctr., Norfolk, 2000—06. Bd. mem. Friends of Women's Studies, 2004—06. Recipient Outstanding Provost award, Tidewater C.C., 2004. Mem.: NOW, NASW, NAACP. Home: 701 Bolero Ct Virginia Beach VA 23462 Office: Tidewater CC/Women's Ctr 300 Granby St Norfolk VA 23510 Office Phone: 757-822-1116. Home Fax: 757-822-1174; Office Fax: 757-822-1174. Personal E-mail: iwarren@tcc.edu.

WARREN, JANE CAROL, psychologist; b. Dec. 25, 1938; d. George Stafford Harris and Helen Virginia (Swift) Swift-Harris; m. Philip Clinton Warren (div.); children: Charles, Susan Warren Sohn; m. Richard Karl Hertel, July 19, 2001. BA, U. Mich., Ann Arbor, 1961, MA, 1964, PhD, 1985. Lic. psychologist Mich. Tchg. asst. in botany U. Mich., Ann Arbor, 1960—61, asst. in counseling, 1967—68; sci. tchr. Belleville (Mich.) HS, 1961—63; clin. psychologist Huron Valley Cons. Ctr., Ann Arbor, 1980—85; pvt. practice Ann Arbor, 1985—. Past pres. Mich. Psychoanalytic Found., Farmington Hills; founding mem. Allen Creek Presch., Ann Arbor. Fellow, U. Mich., 1963—64. Mem.: APA, Mich. Psychol. Assn., Am. Psychoanalytic Assn. (assoc.; steering com. 2004—05, chair com. on psychotherapist assoc.). Office: 555 E William #16-I Ann Arbor MI 48104

WARREN, KATHERINE VIRGINIA, art gallery director; b. Balt., Aug. 10, 1948; d. Joseph Melvin and Hilda Virginia (Thiele) Heim; m. David Hardy Warren; 1 child, Gabriel Kristopher Coy; 1 stepchild, Michael Jonathan Warren. BA, U. Calif., Riverside, 1976, MA, 1980. Asst. curator Calif. Mus. Photography, Riverside, 1979-80, acting dir., 1980-81, asst. dir., curator of edn., 1981-84; dir. univ. art gallery U. Calif., Riverside, 1980—2003, ret., 2003—. Bd. dirs. Riverside Arts Found., 1980-89, chmn. bd., 1986-88. Marius De Brabant fellow U. Calif., 1977-79. Mem. Am. Assn. Mus., Western Mus. Conf. Office: Sweeney Art Gallery U Calif Riv Side Riverside CA 92521-0001

WARREN, MAREDIA DELOIS, music educator; d. Odis Franklin and Mary Velma Lewis; m. Charles Augustus Warren, July 9, 1966; children: John Charles, Maredia Dionne. B in Music Edn. magna cum laude, Howard U., 1965; MA, Columbia U., 1967, EdD, 1989. Tchr. elem. music Hartford Pub. Schs., 1965—66; adj. faculty Herbert H. Lehman Coll., CUNY, 1972—79, Fairleigh Dickinson U., 1975—79, Montclaire State U., 1984—93; tchr. music grades K-6 Teaneck Pub. Schs., NJ, 1979—87; dir. vocal music Teaneck H.S., 1987—99; asst. prof. music educator William Paterson U., Wayne, NJ, 1999—2000; assoc. prof., coord. music edn. N.J. City U., Jersey City, 2000—. Condr. N.J. All-State Chorus, N.J. State Music Tchrs. Assn., 1994, 2006, Mass. ACDA Women's Honor Choir, Amherst, Mass., 2003, Cape Cod H.S. Festival, 2005; dir. music, organist Presbyn. Ch. Teaneck, 1995—; presenter Choral Music Workshop, Ghana, 1995; presenter in field. Bd. mem., cons. Bergen County Divsn. Hist. and Cultural Affairs, 2002—; People to People amb. to China, 1998. Named Disting. Secondary tchr., Princeton U., 1993; recipient Trailblazer award in arts and culture, Nat. Coalition of 100 Black Women, 2005. Mem.: NEA (life), Coll. Music Soc., N.J. Music Educators Assn., Am. Choral Dirs. Assn., Am. Orff Schulwerk Assn., Orgn. Am. Kodaly Educators, Music Educators Nat. Conf. (collegiate advisor 2003—), N.J. Am. Choral Dirs. Assn. (Repertoire and Standards chair multicultural 1999—2003, bd. mem.), N.J. Edn. Assn. (life), Alpha Kappa Alpha, Inc. Office: NJ City Univ 2039 Kennedy Blvd Jersey City NJ 07305 Office Phone: 201-200-2158. E-mail: mdlwarren@aol.com.

WARREN, MELISSA ALLISON, lawyer; BA magna cum laude, Duke U., Durham, N.C., 1983; JD cum laude, U. Pa. Law Sch., 1988. Bar: Md. 1988. Ptnr. bus. transactions, securities, practices Venable LLP, Balt., 2001—. Office: Venable LLP 1800 Mercantile Bank & Trust Bldg 2 Hopkins Plz Baltimore MD 21201 Office Phone: 410-244-7695. Office Fax: 410-244-7742. Business E-Mail: mawarren@venable.com.

WARREN, PAMELA A., psychologist; d. James Herbert Trail, Jr. and Jacqueline Joann Trail; m. Bruce E. Warren, 1982; 1 child, Rachel M. B.A., MA, So. Ill. U., PhD, 1991. Lic. clin. psychologist Ill., 1993. Counselor So. Ill. U., Carbondale, 1986—89, instr., 1989—91; head psychology dept. Carle Clinic Assn., Urbana, 1991—; faculty U. Ill. Med. Sch., Dept. Psychiatry, 1994—; clin. supr. Resolutions Employee Assistance Program, Champaign, 1996—2001; faculty U. Ill., Psychology Dept., 2000—. Faculty SmithKline-Beecham Pharms., 1993—96; mem. work injury network steering com. Carle Clinic Assn., Urbana, 1999—; nat. psychol. cons. Work Injury Network, 1999—; cons. WebilityMD.com, Wayland, Md., 2001—04, Blue Cross Blue Shield Ins., Dallas, 2002—, CompPartners, Irvine, Calif., 2003—; psychol. cons. Ill. State Univs. Retirement Sys., Champaign, 2001—; mem. supported employment com. Disability Mgmt. Employer Coalitions, Eugene, Oreg., 2002—; mem. complimentary and alternative medicine steering com. Carle Clinic Assn., Urbana, 2003—; adv. bd. Reed Group Med. Disability, Colo., 2004—, Am. Coll. Occupational & Environ. Medicine Practice Guidelines Newsletter; mem. adv. bd. Job Demands Project, Disability Rsch. Inst.; presenter in field. Author: Managing Workplace Mental Health Issues and Appropriate Disability Management, 2004. Hospice vol. Meml. Hospice, Carbondale, Ill., 1984—91; ticket to work adv. bd. Social Security Adminstrn., 2004—. Scholar, So. Ill. U., 1983—91. Fellow: Prescribing Psychologists' Register; mem.: APA, Assn. Applied Psychophysiology and Biofeedback, Assn. Behavior Analysis, Psi Chi. Achievements include development of state-of-the-art model to assess and treat psychological concerns in order to prevent psychological disability. Avocations: travel, art, reading, sports. Office: Carle Clinic Assn 602 W Univ E-6 Urbana IL 61801 Office Phone: 217-383-3442. E-mail: pawarren@mchsi.com.

WARREN, RITA SIMPSON, manufacturing executive; b. Borger, Tex., Jan. 17, 1949; d. William D. and Bobbie J. (Hindman) S.; m. Harry E. Warren, jr., June 10, 1978. BA in Sociology, U. Tex., 1977; MBA, North Tex. State U., 1982. V.p. comms. Tetra Pak, Inc., Dallas, 1977-85; v.p. mktg. Devex, Inc., Dallas, 1986-87; v.p. Neotech Industries, Inc., Irving, Tex., 1987-88; sales mgr. worldwide Optek Tech., Inc., 1989-2001; key account mgr. Alcatel Optronics Inc., 2001—02, Sanmina-SCI, Allen, Tex., 2003—04; acct. mgr. Avnet, Columbia, Md., 2004—. Bd. dirs. Dallas Women's Found., 1999-2003; mem. women's resource ctr. adv. com. YWCA of Dallas, 1993-2001. Recipient various awards Dairy and Food Industries Supply Assn., 1979-84, Soc. Visual Comm., 1979, Dallas Ad League TOPS, 1984. Mem. Sportscar Vintage Racing Assn., Hist. Sportscat Racing Assn., Pub. Rels. Soc., Jaguar Owner's Assn. S.W. (co-pres. 1979-83), The Women's Ctr. of Dallas (bd. dirs. WISER 1991-92, Women in Leadership 1993, pres.-elect 1994, pres. 1995, past pres. 1996), Imagine Dallas (pres. 1997-98, bd. dirs. 1995-98). Avocations: classic European automobiles, driving vintage race cars, sailing. Office: Avnet 7134 Columbia Gateway Dr Columbia MD 21046

WARREN, ROSANNA, poet; b. Fairfield, Conn., July 27, 1953; d. Robert Penn Warren and Eleanor Clark; m. Stephen Scully, 1981; children: Katherine, Chiara; stepson, Benjamin. BA summa cum laude, Yale U., 1976; MA, Johns Hopkins U., 1980. Pvt. art tchr., 1977-78; clerical worker St. Martin's Parish, N.Y.C., 1977-78; asst. prof. English Vanderbilt U., Nashville, 1981-82; vis. asst. prof. Boston U., 1982-88, asst. prof. English and modern fgn. langs., 1989-95, assoc. prof. English, 1995—, Emma MacLachlan Metcalf prof. humanities, 2000—. Poetry cons., contbg. editor Partisan Rev., 1985-98; poet-in-residence Robert Frost Farm, 1990. Author: The Joey Story, 1963, Snow Day, 1981, Each Leaf Shines Separate, 1984, Stained Glass, 1993, Departure, 2003; editor, contbr.: The Art of Translation: Voices from the Field, 1989; editor: Eugenio Montale's Cuttlefish Bones, 1993, Satura, 1998; translator (with Stephen Scully) Euripides' Suppliant Women, 1995, poetry anthologies include In Time, 1995, From This Distance, 1996, Springshine, 1998; contbr. to periodicals including Agni Rev., Am. Poetry Rev., Antioch Rev., Atlantic Monthly, Chelsea, Chgo. Rev., Georgia Rev., Nation, New Republic, New Yorker, N.Y. Times, Paris Rev., Threepenny Rev., Partisan Rev., Ploughshares, Southern Rev., Washington Post. Recipient McLaughlin English prize Yale U., 1973, Charles E. Clark award Yale U., 1976, Nat. Discovery award in poetry 92nd St. YMHA-YWCA, 1980, Newton Arts Coun. award, 1983, Lavan Younger Poets prize Acad. Am. Poets, 1992, Lamont Poetry prize Acad. Am. Poets, 1993, Lila Wallace Writers' Fund award, 1994, Witter Bynner prize in poetry Acad. Arts and Letters, 1994, May Sarton award New Eng. Poetry Club, 1995, Pushcart prize, 2004, 06, award of merit in poetry Am. Acad. Arts and Letters, 2004, Ellen Maria Gorrissen Berlin prize Am. Acad. Berlin, 2006; named Scholar of House Yale U., 1975-76; Yaddo fellow, 1980, Lannan Found. fellow, 2005; Ingram Merrill grantee, 1983, 93; Guggenheim fellow, 1985-86; Am. Coun. Learned Socs. grantee, 1989-90. Fellow: Am. Acad. Arts and Sci.; mem.: PEN, ALTA, MLA, Acad. Am. Poets (chancellor 1999—2005), Assn. Literary Scholars and Critics (v.p. 2004, pres. 2005). Office Phone: 617-358-1782.

WARREN, SHIRLEY M., respiratory therapist; d. Martin Edgar Davis and Grace Marie Collins; m. Charles Earnest Holmes (div.); stepchildren: Charles Jr., Zann; m. Gary Don Warren, Jan. 2, 1984; children: Byron Keith, Dena Nicole, Theophilus Terrell. Attended, El Centro C.C., 1976, Calif. Coll. Health Sci., 1989. Cert. Respiratory Therapy Practioner Tex. Dept. State Health Svc., 1988. Respiratory therapist Baylor Med. Ctr., Dallas, 1974—81, 1990—91, Meth. Med. Ctr., Dallas, 1981—84, S.W. Med. Ctr., Dallas, 1984—90; respiratory therapist practioner Lancaster Med. Ctr., Tex., 1990—96, Vencor Hosp., Dallas, 1994—2003, Respiratory Assocs., Arlington, Tex., Ingenium Resources, Arlington, wellness care with the elderly; educator respiratory therapy Our Children's Ho., Dallas, 1999—2005. Pastor's aide, usher, mem. coms. Bayside Ch. Living God, Dallas. Home: 210 Indian Trail Cedar Hill TX 75104

WARREN, STACEY A., music educator; b. Ft. Dix, N.J., Oct. 6, 1956; d. R. Winston and Lyndall H. Warren; 1 child, E. Philip Heyde. BME, DePauw U., Ind., 1978; MusM, Northwestern U., Ill., 1980. Choir dir. Macona Quah Jr. High and HS, Bunker Hill, Ind., 1985—95, Caston Schs., Fulton, Ind., 1996—97; choral dir., sr. voice instr. Culver Acads., Ind., 1997—. Mem. Indpls. Symphony Choir, 2001. Mem.: Ind. Choral Dirs. Assn., Am. Choral Dirs. Assn. Roman Catholic. Avocations: skiing, cooking, travel, reading. Office: Culver Academies 1300 Academy Rd Culver IN 46511 Office Phone: 574-842-8283. Personal E-mail: warrens@culver.org.

WARREN, SUSAN HANKE MURPHY, international marketing business development executive; b. Detroit, Nov. 26, 1949; d. Homer Graf and Catherine H. (Fly) Hanke; m. William Joseph Murphy, Sept. 14, 1974 (div. 1984); m. Philip Hamilton Warren, Nov. 12, 1989; 1 child, Catherine Jane; 1 stepchild, Sarah Kate. MA in French and Spanish Langs./History, Denison U., 1971; MA in Internat. Studies, Am. U., 1979; MBA, Harvard U., 1981. Cert. tchr., Ohio. Br. chief, Africa, Office of Academic Exch. Programs, U.S. Dept. State, Washington, 1975-79; fin. and project mgr. corp. devel. Corning (N.Y.) Inc., 1981-83; mgr. strategic planning Ciba-Corning Diagnostics, Medfield, Mass., 1983-88, new venture mgr., 1988-91, dir. customer and mktg. svcs. U.S. comml. ops., 1991-93; dir. bus. planning U.S. comml. ops. Chiron Diagnostics, Emeryville, Calif., 1993-95, dir. worldwide mktg., immunoassays, 1995-98; dir. disease focus mktg. Bayer Diagnostics, Tarrytown, N.Y., 1999-2000; v.p. mktg. and sales Mosaic Technologies, Waltham, Mass., 2000-01; v.p. mktg. Parexel, Inc., 2001—. Alumni advisor Harvard Bus. Sch., Cambridge, Mass., 1995—. Editl. adv. bd.: Clinical Lab Products. Trustee First Parish, Westwood, Mass., 1985-88; mem. project funding com. The Junior League, Washington, Elmira, N.Y., Boston, 1972-85; mem. sch. site coun. Meml. Sch., Medfield, 1998-99. Recipient The Beacon Soc. award, 1989. Mem. Biomed. Mktg. Assn., Am Assn. Clin. Chemistry, Am. Mgmt. Assn. Republican. Avocations: sailing, alpine skiing, water-skiing, golf. Office: Mosaic Technologies 1 Financial Ctr Boston MA 02111-2621 E-mail: skh@aol.com.

WARREN-BILLINGS, JANET MARIE, language educator; b. Shawnee, Okla., Apr. 24, 1955; d. Billy Earl Billings and Sue Billings-Westmoreland; m. Michael Allen Warren, Dec. 8, 1973; children: Angie Marie Cloer, Ashley Michelle Thomas, Amber Jane Conner. BA in English Edn., U. Ctrl. Okla., Edmond, 1977; MEd, U. Okla., Norman, 1994. Chmn. English dept. Choctaw HS, Okla., 1980—. Home: PO Box 733 Choctaw OK 73020 Office: Choctaw HS 14300 NE 10th St Choctaw OK 73020 Office Phone: 405-390-8899. Business E-Mail: jwarren@cnpschools.org.

WARRES, MARGIE BLACK, retired social work administrator, human services manager; b. Phila., Feb. 17, 1918; d. Harry M. and Eva (Stulbaum) Black; m. H. Leonard Warres, June 11, 1939; children: Stephen Elliot, Neil Eric. Student, Goucher Coll., 1936-38; BA magna cum laude, Bklyn. Coll., 1941; MSW, U. Pa., 1944. Cert. ACSW, LCSW. Past caseworker Pub. Welfare Office, Kent County, Del.; exec. sec. pub. welfare com. Md. Conf. Social Concern, 1947—50; exec. dir. Cen. Scholarship Bur., 1952-88, ret., 1988. Condr. workshops for pub. sch. counselors Balt. Dept. Edn., 1967. Author: The Birth and Blossoming of a Bureau: CSB 1924-88, 1991; editor Med. Chi Alliance Md. Black Eyed Susan pub., 1996-98, co-editor, 2002-2003; contbr. articles to profl. jours. Vol. Care-Medico, Afghanistan, 1973; counc. State & Eastern regl. councilor of Southern Med. Assn. Aux.; mem. Jewish Bd. Edn., 1964—70; repeatedly past bd. electors Balt. Hebrew Congregation; past mem. Parents Coun. of Balt.; asst. to pres. Eastern regl. ARZA org., 1980—85; bd. dirs., chair search com. Md. Higher Edn. Loan Corp., 1986—96; past pres. Child Study Assn. of Balt. and Md., Balt. City Med. Aux., Alliance to the Med. and Chirurgical Faculty Md.; v.p. Balt. Hebrew Congregation Sisterhood, 1997—2002; spkr. Goucher Coll. scholarship luncheon, 1999; chair Uniongram Luncheon, 1998, 2002, Bernice Kramer Meml. Hebrew Congregation, Balt., 2002; Ea. regional chair Internat. Health Com. of AMA Aux., 1970—73, nat. chair, 1973—75; past bd. dirs. AMA Alliance; chair Ann. Interfaith Inst. Balt. Hebrew Congregation, 1996; Steering Com. Cir. of Giving Assoc: Jewish Cmty. Fedn., Balt., 2002—; bd. dirs. Ctl. Scholarship Bur. for Life, Med. Chi Alliance, STEP, Inc., 1991—2005. Recipient Harry Greenstein award, 1977; Disting. Mem. honoree Child Study's 75th Anniversary Gala, 1999. Mem. Child Study Assn. Md. (adv. bd., Natalie Hoffman Meml. award 2005). Jewish. Achievements include organizing first overseas travellers charter groups for Baltimore City and Maryland Med. Chi. orgs., 1965; Established scholarships at Goucher Coll. & Central Scholarship Bureau for special needs students, 1970. Avocations: travel, theater, art, music, writing.

WARRICK, KIMBERLEY KAYE, language and social studies educator; b. Lake Wales, Fla., Apr. 13, 1963; d. Bonnie Dawn and Edward Milo Dunagin (Stepfather); m. Robert Kelly Warrick, Nov. 30, 1986 (div. Apr. 0, 1995); 1 child, Kalegh Rebekah. BA, Capital U., 1989; MA, Ohio State U., 1999. Cert. elem. tchr. Mont., Ohio, learning disablities tchr. Mont., Ohio. Tchr. kindergarten/kindergarten afterschool program Columbus Torah Acad., Ohio, 1990—96, tchr. resource/ESL, 1990—96, tchr. 1st grade, 1990—96; tchr. 6th grade English/Social Studies Groveport Madison Local Schs., Ohio, 1996—2003; tchr. spl. edn. 8th grade Bozeman Pub. Schs., Mont., 2003—05, tchr. spl. edn. 9th grade, 2005—. English curriculum com. Bozeman Pub. Schs., Mont., 2004—05. Facilitator Ctr. for Civic Edn., Bozeman, Mont., 2004—05; del. Mont. Rep. Party State Conv., Big Sky, 2004. Mem.: Phi Delta Kappa (pres. MSU chpt. 2006), Coun. Tchr. Cert. Profl. Develop. (state bd. pub. edn. 2005—), Nat. Coun. for History Educators, Bozeman Edn. Assn. (bldg. rep. 2004—05), Gallatin County Rep. Women. Avocations: reading, volleyball, needlepoint. Office: Bozeman HS 205 N 11th Ave Bozeman MT 59715 Office Phone: 406-522-6354. Office Fax: 406-522-6222. Business E-Mail: kwarrick@bozeman.k12.mt.us.

WARRICK, LOLA JUNE, management consultant; b. San Francisco, June 19, 1923; d. Sigfrid Oscar and June Vesta (Merrifield) Bjorkqvist; m. Enos Barnie Warrick, June 12, 1948 (dec. June 1983); children: James Daryl, Nancy Jean, Gary Elton. AA, Merrit Bus. Sch. Col. McClellan AFB, Sacramento; spl. svcs. U.S. Govt.; owner, mgr. Burke-Warrick Theatre, Sacramento; mgr., asst. Naify Enterprises, Sacramento; asst. mgr. Fox West Coast Theatre; booking agt. Burke-Warrick Theatres, 1999—. Author: Merifield A to Z, 1995. Hon. vice-mayor City of North Highlands, Calif., 1999—. Named Citizen of Yr., North Highlands Cmty., 1999. Mem.: DAR (regent 1998—2000, State and Nat. awards 1998—2000), Nat. Assn. Ret. Fed. Employees (past v.p. chpt. 1680, pres. 1998—99), North Highlands Garden Club. Avocations: genealogy, computers.

WARRIOR, DELLA C., academic administrator, art educator; BA in Sociology, Northeastern State U.; MA in Edn., Harvard U. Pres. Inst. Am. Indian Arts, Santa Fe, devel. dir. CEO Otoe-Missouria Tribe, 1989—92; exec. bd. mem. World Indigenous Nations Higher Edn. Consortium; mem. U.S. Pres. Bd. Adv. on Tribal Coll. & U., 2002—.

WARRIOR, PADMASREE, communications executive; BSChemE, Indian Inst. Tech., New Delhi, India; MSChemE, CornellU. Joined Motorola, Inc., Schaumburg, Ill., 1984, v.p., gen. mgr., energy sys. group, corp. v.p., chief technology officer, semiconductor products sector, v.p., 1999, corp. officer, 2000, sr. v.p., 2003—05, chief tech. officer, 2003—, exec. v.p., 2005—. Gen. mgr. Thoughtbeam, Inc. (subsidiary of Motorola); mem. coun. digital economy Tex. Gov.; mem. rev. panel Tex. Higher Edn. Bd.; dir. Ferro Corp. Recipient Women Elevating Sci. and Tech. award, Working Woman Mag., 2001. Office: Motorola Inc 1303 E Algonquin Rd Schaumburg IL 60196 Office Phone: 847-576-5000.*

WARSHAUER, IRENE C., lawyer; b. NYC, May 4, 1942; m. Alan M. Warshauer, Nov. 27, 1966; 1 child, Susan. BA with distinction, U. Mich., 1963; LLB cum laude, Columbia U., 1966. Bar: N.Y. 1966, U.S. Dsit. Ct. (so. and ea. dist.) N.Y. 1969, U.S. Ct. Appeals (2d cir.) 1969, U.S. Dist. Ct. (no. dist.) N.Y. 1980, U.S. Supreme Ct. 1972. With 1st Jud. Dept., N.Y. State Mental Health Info. Svc., 1966-68; assoc. Chadbourne Parke Whiteside & Wolff, 1968-75; mem. Anderson Kill & Olick, P.C., N.Y.C., 1975-99, Fried & Epstein, N.Y.C., 2000—. Mediator U.S. Dist. Ct. (so. dist.) N.Y., N.Y. State Supreme Ct.; lectr. Columbia Law Sch., Def. Rsch. Inst., Aspen Inst. Humanistic Studies, ABA, Rocky Mountain Mineral Law Found., CPR Inst. Dispute Resolution; arbitrator NASD EEOC, NYSE, Am. Arbitration Assn. Contbr. chpts. to books, articles to profl. jours. Mem. County Dem. Com., 1968—. Named to Hon. Order Ky. Cols. Mem.: ABA, N.Y. State Bar Assn. (chmn. subcom. mentally disabled and cmty. 1978—82), Assn. Bar City N.Y. (judiciary com. 1982—84, mem. alternative dispute resolution com. 2000—). Avocations: gardening, cooking, birding, theater. Office: Fried & Epstein 1350 Broadway New York NY 10018-7702

WARSHAW, ROBERTA SUE, lawyer; b. Chgo., July 10, 1934; d. Charles and Frieda (Feldman) Weiner; m. Lawrence Warshaw, July 5, 1959 (div. June 1978); children: Nan R., Adam; m. Paul A. Heise, Apr. 2, 1994. Student, U. Ill., 1952-55; BFA, U. So. Calif., 1956; JD, Northwestern U., 1980. Bar: Ill. 1980. Atty., fin. specialist Housing Svcs. Ctr., Chgo., 1980-84, Chgo. Rehab. Network, 1985-91, 92-95; dir. housing State Treas., State of Ill., Chgo., 1991; sole practitioner, 1995—. Legal worker Sch. of Law, Northwestern U. Legal Clinic, Chgo., 1977-80; real estate developer, mgr., marketer, Chgo., 1961-77; bd. dirs. Single Room Housing Assistance Corp., Lebanon County Mediation Svcs., mediator, sec., 2001; asst. dir. Lebanon Valley Coll. Program, Hania, Crete, 1998. Co-author: (manual) The Cook County Scavenger Sale Program and The City of Chicago Reactivation Program, 1991, (booklet) Fix the Worst First, 1989; co-editor: The Caring Contract, Voices of American Leaders, 1996. Alderman 9th ward City of Evanston, Ill., 1985-93, mem. planning and devel., rules com., unified budget com., chair flood and pollution control com.; pres. Sister Cities Found.; mem. cmty. and econ. devel. policy Nat. League Cities, 1990-93; active Dem. Nat. Com.; bd. dirs. Dem. Ctrl. Com. Evanston, 1973—; elected committeeman Evanston Twp. Dem. Com., 1994-98, dem. committeeman Mt. Gretna Borough, 2000—; del. Dem. Nat. Conv., 1996; Dem. committeeman Mt. Gretna Borough, 2000—; vol. tax preparer; tax counseling for elderly, 2000—; bd. dirs., mediator Lebanon County Mediation Svcs., 2000—, sec., 2001-03, pres., 2003—. Mem. AAUW (Pa. bd. dirs., pub. policy chair), ABA (affordable housing com.), Ill. State Bar Assn., Chgo. Bar Assn. (real estate coms.), Decalogue Soc. Lawyers, Chgo. Coun. Lawyers (housing com.), IRS Tax Counseling for the Elderly (vol. tax preparer). Avocations: politics, travel, hiking, camping, athletic activities. Home: 104 Brown Ave PO Box 537 Mount Gretna PA 17064-0537 Personal E-mail: femdem1@narl.com.

WARTELLA, ELLEN ANN, communications educator, consultant; b. Kingston, Pa., Oct. 16, 1949; d. Nicholas and Margaret (Lipko) W.; m. D. Charles Whitney, Aug. 1, 1976; children: David Charles, Stephen Wright. BA, U. Pitts., 1971; MA, U. Minn., 1974, PhD, 1977. Asst. prof. Ohio State U., Columbus, 1976-79; rsch. asst. prof. communications U. Ill., Champaign, 1979-83, rsch. assoc. prof., 1983-89, rsch. prof., 1989-93; dean Coll. Comm., Walter Cronkite Regents Chair in Comm. U. Tex., Austin, 1993—. Vis. prof. U. Calif., Santa Barbara, 1992-93; cons. Children's TV Workshop, N.Y.C., 1988-89, FTC, Washington, 1978, 1991-92, FCC, Washington, 1979. Co-author National Television Violence Study, 1994-98, The Audience and Its Landscape, 1996, The American Communication Research: The Remembered History, 1996. Mem. bd. advisors Am. Children's TV Festival, Chgo., 1988; bd. trustees Children's TV Workshop, 1996—; bd. dirs. Headliners Found., Austin, Sta. KLRU-TV (ex officio), Austin. Recipient Krieghbaum award Assn. for Edn. in Journalism and Mass Communication, 1984; Univ. scholar U. Ill., 1989-93; Gannett Ctr. for Media Studies fellow, 1985-86. Fellow Internat. Comm. Assn. (pres. 1992-93), Broadcast Edn. Assn. (bd. dirs. 1990-94), Speech Comm. Assn., Soc. for Rsch. in Child Devel.

WARTMAN, MARY JANE, family practice nurse practitioner; b. Holton, Kans., Sept. 7, 1955; d. Henry Jr. and Marjorie Isabel (Taylor) Brockelman; children: Sarah Jane, Spencer Gregory. BSN, U. Kans., 1978; MSN, Wichita State U., 1994. RN, ARNP, Kans. Labor and delivery staff nurse St. Joseph Med. Ctr., Kansas City, Mo., 1978; staff nurse Bob Wilson Meml. Hosp., Ulysses, Kans., 1979-83, 91; sch. health nurse Stanton County Health Dept., Johnson, Kans., 1986-90, clin. nurse specialist, 1994-95; OB resource pool staff nurse S.W. Med. Ctr., Liberal, Kans., 1992-95; clin. nurse specialist St. Catherine Hosp., Garden City, Kans., 1995—. Nursing cons. Bob Wilson Meml. Grant County Hosp., Ulysses, 1996—. Cmty. leader, parents adv. com. Cimarron 4-H Club, Ulysses, 1992-94, cmty. leader, 1995—; swim team bd. dirs. Ulysses Sharks, 1991-94; chairwoman home products dinner C. of C., 1994. Parent-Child Nursing scholarship Wesley Women's Assn., 1994. Mem. AWHONN, U. Kans. Nurses Alumni, Gt. Plains Orgn. for Perinatal Health, Sigma Theta Tau. Republican. United Methodist. Avocations: walking, sewing, reading. Home: 5084 Firestone Ct Santa Rosa CA 95409-5531

WARWICK, DIONNE, singer; b. East Orange, N.J., Dec. 12, 1940; m. Bill Elliott (div. 1975); children: David, Damon. Student, Hartt Coll. Music, Hartford, Conn. As teen-ager formed Gospelaires and Drinkard Singers, then sang background for rec. studio, 1966; debut, Philharmonic Hall, N.Y. Lincoln Center, 1966; appearances include London Palladium, Olympia, Paris, Lincoln Ctr. Performing Arts, N.Y.C.; records include Don't Make Me Over, 1962, Walk On By, Do You Know The Way to San José, What The World Needs Now, Message To Michael, I'll Never Fall In Love Again, I'll Never Love This Way Again, Deja Vu, Heartbreaker, That's What Friends are For; albums include Valley of the Dolls and Others, 1968, Promises, Promises, 1975, Dionne, 1979, Then Came You, Friends, 1986, Reservations for Two, 1987, Greatest Hits, 1990, Dionne Warwick Sings Cole Porter, 1990, Hidden Gems; The Best of Dionne Warwick, Vol. 2, 1992, (with Whitney Houston) Friends Can Be Lovers, 1993, Dionne Warwick and Placido Domingo, 1994, Aquarela Do Brasil, 1994, From the Vaults, 1995, Sings the Bacharach and David Songbook, 1995, Dionne Sings Dionne, 1998, I Say a Little Prayer for You, 2000; TV appearance in Sisters in the Name of Love, HBO, 1986; screen debut Slaves, 1969, No Night, So Long, also, Hot! Live and Otherwise; co-host: TV show Solid Gold; host: TV show A Gift of Music, 1981; star: TV show Dionne Warwick Spl. Founder Dionne Warwick Scholarship Fund, 1968, charity group BRAVO (Blood Revolves Around Victorious Optimism), Warwick Found. to Help Fight AIDS; spokeswoman Am. Sudden Infant Death Syndrome; participant U.S.A for Africa; Am. Amb. of Health, 1987. Recipient Grammy awards, 1969, 70, 80; NAACP Key of Life award, 1990.

WARWICK, MARGARET ANN, health science facility administrator, consultant; b. Camden, N.J., June 7, 1931; d. Ralph Arthur and Margaret Wilson (Dilworth) W. BS, Fairleigh Dickinson U., 1955. Staff mem., med. tech. Jefferson Med. Coll. Hosp., Phila., 1955—61; clin. chemist West Jersey Health System, Camden, NJ, 1961—68, lab. supr. Voorhees, 1968—80, mgr. clin. lab. services, 1980—85, quality assurance mgr. clin. lab svcs., 1985—96; founder, pres. Clin. Lab. Cons. Services, Inc., Cherry Hill, 1985—96; ret., 1996. Mem. faculty chemist dept. Harcum Jr. Coll., Bryn Mawr, Pa., 1958-64; ednl. coordinator West Jersey Hosp. Sch. of Med. Tech., Voorhees, 1963-81. Vice pres. Wilderness Acres Civic Assn., Cherry Hill, 1980-81; chmn. com. Respond Inc. at Asbury United Meth. Ch., Camden, 1985-94, trustee, 1984-93. Mem. Am. Assn. for Clin. Chemists (secret treas. 1966-70, chmn. elect 1971-72, chmn. 1972-73 Phila chpt.), Clin. Lab Mgmt. Assn., Am. Soc. of Clin. Pathologist, Am. Soc. for Med. Tech., N.J. Soc. for Med. Tech. (bd. dirs. 1978-79). Republican. Methodist. Avocations: golf, boating.

WASCHER, DEBORAH LYNN, elementary school educator; BS in Edn., Ea. Ill. U., Charleston, 1999. Cert. tchr. Ill. Tchr. Heritage Sch. Dist. #8, Homer, Ill., 2000—. Vets. Day program dir. Homer Elem. Sch., Ill., 2000—. Organist/Sunday sch. tchr./bd. mem. Broadlands United Cmty. Ch., Ill., 1983; scoutmaster/denleader Boy Scouts of Am., Broadlands, Ill., 1988—96; dir./organizer After Sch. Break, Broadlands, Ill., 2001. Mem.: Heritage Edn. Assn. (assoc.). Home: 2516 County Rd 300 N Broadlands IL 61816 Office: 512 W First St Homer IL 61849 Office Phone: 217-896-2421. Personal E-mail: jdwascher@yahoo.com.

WASHBURN, GLADYS HAASE, retired church musician, educator, director; b. San Antonio, Feb. 19, 1919; d. Henry August and Rosa Sophie (Sundermeyer) Haase; m. Jost Brainard Washburn, Dec. 29, 1942 (dec.); children: Yvonne Rosalind, Henry Brainard, Diane Louise. Tchg. cert. in piano/organ, St. Louis Coll. Music, 1940. Cert. piano St. Louis Coll. Music, 1940. Ch. pianist Friedens Evang. Ch., 1932—38; organist, choir dir. St. Martin's Ch., High Ridge, Mo., 1939—40; choir dir. Bethany Evang. and Ref. Ch., San Antonio, 1940—42, organist, choir dir. New Orleans, 1952—55, St. Paul's Evang. and Ref. Ch., Corpus Christi, Tex., 1944—51, Bethlehem United Ch. of Christ, Buffalo, 1964—70, First Congl. United Ch. of Christ, Dwight, Ill., 1970—72, St. Michael's Episcopal Ch., Independence, Mo., 1985—92; dir. jr. choir Bethlehem Evang. and Ref. Ch., Buffalo, 1956—61; interim organist, choir dir. St. Paul's and St. Marks Ch., Buffalo, 1963, Village United Ch. of Christ, Blue Springs, Mo., 1992—93; interim organist chs. Greater Kansas City area, 1993—97; ret., 1997. Cons. chs. seeking organists, Buffalo, Blue Springs, Mo. Organ recitalist S.W. Conf. Nat. PTA Meeting, San Antonio, 1941, 1942; accompanist Harlandale Sch. Dist., San Antonio, 1941, 1942. Recipient Cert. in Ministry in Music, United Ch. Christ, 1992. Mem.: Am. Guild Organists. Republican. United Ch. Of Christ. Avocations: sewing, cooking, reading. Home: 300 SW 19th Terr Blue Springs MO 64015

WASHBURN, HARRIET CAROLINE, secondary school educator; b. Hallock, Minn., Mar. 15, 1920; d. John W. and Anna Melinda (Younggren) Swanson; m. Edward James Washburn, Jan. 22, 1971 (dec. 1993); m. Ohis Batt; 1 child, Jacqueline Ann Batt 1 stepchild, Margaret. BA cum laude, Macalester Coll., 1941; MA in Pupil Personnel Svcs., San Jose State U., 1969. Tchr. Latin, English, phys. edn. Renville (Minn.) Pub. Sch., 1941-43; tchr. phys. edn. St. Cloud (Minn.) Jr. H. S., 1943-44, Fremont (Calif.) Unified Sch. Dist., 1958-69; recreation specialist City Recreation Dept., Lincoln, Nebr., 1946-50; dir. youth activities Trinity Meth. Ch., Lincoln, 1950-53; counselor Milpitas (Calif.) Unified Sch. Dist., 1969-75, head counselor, 1975-80; cons., trainer, speaker Stockton, Calif., 1980—; coord. bank acct. Bank of Stockton, 1989—99. Presenter Internat. Tng., Anaheim, 1978—; cons. personal, profl. devel. Personal Dynamics, Inc., Mpls., 1980—87; spkr., presenter in field. Moderator Presbyn. Women of the Stockton Presbytery PC, 2002—. With USN, 1944—46. Recipient Sch. Counselor Svc. award, Calif. Sch. Counselor Assn., 1980, Hon. Membership award, Presbyn. Women, 2004. Mem.: AAUW, Alliance Mentally Ill San Jose County, Internat. Tng. Comm. (life), Lodi Investment Club. Avocations: bridge, bible study, reading, writing.

WASHBURN, JOAN THOMAS, small business owner; b. N.Y.C., Dec. 26, 1929; d. Frank B. and Josephine (Hartman) Thomas; m. Alan Lindsay Washburn, Sept. 26, 1953; children: Brian, Susan. BA, Middlebury Coll., Vt., 1951. Asst. Kraushaar Gallery, N.Y.C., 1951—53; dir. pub. rels. Wadsworth Atheneum, Hartford, Conn., 1953—55; dir. contemporary art Graham Gallery, N.Y.C., 1955—67; asst. Cordier-Ekstrom Gallery, N.Y.C., 1967—69; dir. Am. painting dept. Sotheby Parke-Bernet, N.Y.C., 1973—75; pres., dir. Washburn Gallery, N.Y.C., 1971—. Mem. Art Dealers Assn. (bd. dirs., v.p. 1991—) Home: 20 W 57th St New York NY 10019-3917 Office Phone: 212-397-6780. Personal E-mail: jwashburn@earthlink.net.

WASHBURN, NAN, conductor; BM in Performance with highest honors, U. Calif., Santa Barbara, 1976; MM in Performance, New England Conservatory of Music, 1979. Mem. faculty New England Conservatory, Boston, 1979-80; artistic dir. Women's Philharmonic, San Francisco, 1980-90, assoc. condr., 1988-90; mem. faculty, condr. classical ensembles Cazadero Music & Arts Ctr., 1982-87; resident condr. Am. Jazz Theater, Oakland, Calif., 1987-97; music dir., condr. Camellia Symphony Orchestra, Sacramento, 1990-96, Orchestra Sonoma (formerly the Rohnert Park Chamber Orch.), 1995—; condr. San Francisco State U. Symphony, 1996-97, Acalenes Chamber Orch.,

Lafayette, Calif., 1997-98, Channel Islands Symphony Orch., Thousand Oaks, Calif., 1997—. Mem. commissioning program panel Minn. Composer's Forum, 1988, music presenter's panel Calif. Arts Coun., 1992, 93, artist fellowship panel, 1995; guest condr. Antelope Valley Symphony Orch., Lancaster, Calif., 1987, Napa Valley (Calif.) Symphony Orch., 1990, Rudolf Steiner Coll., Sacramento, 1991, Sacramento Symphony Orch., 1989, 91, Women's Philharmonic, San Francisco, Oakland, 1991, Oreg. Mozart Players, Eugene, 1993, Eugene Symphony Orch., 1993, 94, Calif. All-State Honor Orch., Santa Clara, 1994, Columbus (Ohio) Women's Symphony, 1992, 94, Cumberland Valley Chamber Players, Chambersburg, Pa., 1994, Honor Festival Orch., Sacramento, 1993, 95, Berkeley (Calif.) Symphony Orch., 1995, 96, Richmond (Va.) Symphony Orch., 1996, Colo. Symphony Orch., Denver, 1997; lectr. Internat. Congress Women in Music, Atlanta, 1986, Festival New Am. Music, Sacramento, 1987, 90, Condrs. Inst., Columbia, S.C., 1988, conf. Calif. Music Educators Assn., Santa Clara, 1994. Recipient N.Y. Women Composers award, 1992, Role Model award Girl Scouts, 1996, Indy award Sonoma County Independent, 1998, 13 ASCAP awards Am. Symphony Orch. League, 1983, 85-90, 92-97. Mem. Am. Symphony Orch. League, Assn. Calif. Symphony Orchs., Condr.'s Guild, Musicians Union Local 6 (San Francisco), Pi Kappa Lambda.

WASHBURN, PATRICIA CHEYNE, retired psychologist, environmental scientist, conservationist; b. Plattsburgh, N.Y., Apr. 27, 1941; d. Gerald Kenneth and Doris Rothermel Cheyne; m. Christopher Hiram Washburn, July 24, 1965; children: Diane, James. BA Psychology, Hartwick Coll., 1963; MA Counseling Psychology, Immaculata Coll., 1991. Juvenile probation officer Oneida County, Utica, NY, 1963—64; elem. sch. tchr., 1964—86; play therapist, cons. Children Unltd., Pottstown, Pa., 1991—2001; co-founder Coventry Land Trust; planning commr. North Coventry Planning, 2001—. Mem.: Nat. Mus. Am. Indian (charter mem.), Natural Lands Trust, Phila. Zoo, Nat. Trust Historic Preservation, Nature Conservancy, Assn. for Play Therapy.

WASHBURN, SANDRA PAYNTER, art educator; b. Warrenton, N.C., Oct. 23, 1952; d. Claude Jackson and Evelyn Gupton Paynter; m. Frank Elton Washburn, Jr., May 11, 1973; 1 child, Reaves Avery 1 stepchild, Frank E. III. BFA in Art Edn., U. N.C., Greensboro, 1976. CETA art resource person Guilford County Schs., Greensboro, 1976—77; art tchr. J.F. Webb H.S., Oxford, NC, 1978—81; watermedia instr. Cultural Arts Divsn.-Pks. and Recreation, Chattanooga, 1994—97, Mountain Art Guild, Signal Mountain, Tenn., 1996—; art tchr. Brainerd Bapt. Sch., Chattanooga, 2001—03, David Brainerd Christian Sch., Chattanooga, 2002—. Panel of selection juror Assn. for Visual Artists, Chattanooga, 2000—; discussion facilitator Art in Pub. Places-Mayor's Office, Chattanooga, 2002—03. Two person exhbn., Stone, Steel and Acrylics, 2002, Surface and Substance, 2002, exhibited in group shows at Gallery 1401, Chattanooga, 2003. Vol. Hospice Chattanooga, 1995—2000; participant Art for Healing Ann. Exhbn. & Auction Meml. Hosp., Chattanooga, 2001—03; participant Cancer Awareness Through the Arts Meml. Hosp. Cancer Ctr., Chattanooga, 2002—03. Recipient Art for Healing Purchase award, Cam Busch Endowment, Chattanooga, 2001. Mem.: Nat. Mus. Women in the Arts, So. Watercolor Soc. (signature, Tenn. state rep. 1998—), Nat. Watercolor Soc. (signature), Tenn. Watercolor Soc. (signature, treas., v.p., exhbn. chair 1995—, workshop instr. 2002—03, award 2000, Mabel Larson award 2002). Independent. Avocations: painting, exercise, reading, gardening, music. Home: 77 Dogwood Ln Soddy Daisy TN 37379 Office: David Brainerd Christian School 7553 Igou Gap Rd Chattanooga TN 37421-7119

WASHER, BARBARA MOCHRIE, performing arts educator, director; b. Willimantic, Conn., Feb. 19, 1952; d. Richard D. and Helene Buchanar Mochrie; m. Steven Lloyd Washer, Feb. 15, 1982; 2 children. BA in Speech Edn., NC Stat U., Raleigh, 1974; MA in Theatre, U. New Orleans, 1976, MFA, 1978. Cert. tchr. NC, 1974. Waterfront dir., unit leader, program dir. Camp Mary Atkinson, Clayton, NC, 1972, 1973, 1974; speech instr., grad. asst. U. New Orleans, 1974—78; actor Regional Dinner, Outdoor Drama Children's Theatre, various, 1976—82; acting coach, speech and theatre instr. N.C. State U., Raleigh, 1984—90; theatre instr. U. Hartford, Hartford, Conn., 1993—94, U. Conn., 1992—95; musical theatre dir. Renbrook Summer Adventure, West Hartford, Conn., 1993—; drama coord. grades 1-9 Renbrook Sch., West Hartford, Conn., 1994—. Edn. cons. Hartford Stage Co., Hartford, 1993—96. Dir., author (plays, original children's musicals), 1985—. Leader Girl Scouts, 1992—94, 1998—2000; mem. quality and diversity com. Bd. of Edn., Windsor, Conn., 1995; mem. drama ministry Trinity United Meth. Ch., Windsor, Conn., 2000—. Avocations: swimming, reading. Office: Renbrook Sch 2865 Albany Ave West Hartford CT 06117

WASHINGTON, ANNIE RUTH, retired elementary school educator, minister; b. Five Points, Ala., Mar. 6, 1929; d. William German and Sallie Lee Hicks; m. Jacob Earl McQueen (dec.); 1 child, Irma Ruth McQueen Rhodes; m. Otis James Washington, Sr.; 1 child, Sharon Denise Washington Williams. BS in Elem. Edn., Ala. State Coll., Montgomery, 1954; advanced courses, St. John Coll., Cleve., 1972; Master's degree, Baldwin Wallace, Cleve., 1977. Tchr. elem. edn. Linden Acad. Jr. HS, Ala., 1955—60; asst. registrar, tchr. Selma U.-Jr. Coll., Ala., 1960—62; tchr. elem. edn. Hazeldell Sch., Cleve., 1962—82, Miles Standish Elem. Sch., Cleve., 1982—87; tchr. Selma U., Cleve., 1960; ret., 1987. Bd. dirs., asst. fin. adviser, adviser children/youth dept., mem. fin. com., tchr. Confirmed Word Faith Ctr., Cleve. Democrat. Baptist. Avocations: reading, writing, walking, singing, needlecrafts. Home: 1404 Timberland Ln Twinsburg OH 44087-1090 Personal E-mail: wash215@aol.com.

WASHINGTON, BARBARA J., language educator; b. Crystal Springs, Miss., Mar. 02; d. Julius Edward and Minnie Lee (Gilmore) Powell; children: Pamela B. Washington, Larry D. Washington. BS in English, Miss. Valley State U., 1972; MEd, U. Miss., 1977. Tchr. English, Leflore County H.S., Itta Bena, Miss., 1972-74; asst. prof. English and speech Miss. Valley State U., Itta Bena, 1974—, asst. prof., mem. honors faculty, 1991—, dir. honors program, 1993—, instr. Upward Bound, 1975—. Cons., com. chmn. So. Assn. Colls. and Schs., Blue Mountain, Miss., 1987—. Cons., parliamentarian local PTSA, Itta Bena, 1989—. Named Tchr. of Yr., Miss. Valley State U., 1995; recipient 30 Yrs. Svc. award. Mem. AAUW, Miss. Valley State U. Nat. Alumni Assn., Miss. Valley State U. Local Alumni Assn., Alpha Kappa Mu (Advisor award, 2003, Dirs. award 2005), Sigma Tau, Phi Delta Kappa, Alpha Kappa Alpha (corr. sec. 1995—, named Soror of Yr. 1997, 99). Home: PO Box 382 Itta Bena MS 38941-0382 Business E-Mail: bjpw@musu.edu.

WASHINGTON, EARLINE, health facility administrator; b. Balt., Dec. 6, 1947; d. Clifton Lee Cox and Dorothy Mae (Cooper) Ford; m. Curtis Washington, June 6, 1964; children: Curtis Jr., Kimberly. Student, Essex (Md.) C.C., 1978, Towson State U., Balt., 1985, Balt. City C.C., 1997. Nursing asst. Md. Gen. Hosp., Balt., 1965-66; optical asst. Greater Balt. Med. Ctr., optician; enrollment coord. Cmty. Family Health Ctr., Balt.; admissions dir. Elder Health Inc., Balt., 1996—. Sec. Empowerment Zone, East Harbor Village Ctr., Balt., 1994-96; mem. F.O.F. Family Support Adv., Balt., 1995-96, flaghouse Cts. Adv. Bd., Balt., 1994-96; cmty. activist Greater Balt. Med. Ctr., 1989-96; mem. Provider Network Group, Balt., 1996—; chmn. bldg. fund New Antioch Bapt. Ch., 1993-95, pres. Flower Cir., 1990-96; mentor Women Entrepreneur Bus., balt., 1993-95. Named Outstanding Cmty. Liaison, Flag House Cts., 1993; recipient Outstanding Vol. award City Springs Elem. Sch., 1993; T. Rowe Price Corp. Acad. scholar, 1994. Democrat. Baptist. Avocations: flora design, cooking, travel. Office: 1154 Sherwood Ave Baltimore MD 21239-2230

WASHINGTON, JOANN, elementary school educator; b. Nashville, Sept. 11, 1943; d. Jasper G. and Ruby William Green; m. James Washington; children: Rickey L., Angela. BS, U. Tenn., 1974; MS, Vanderbilt U., 1977. Cert. tchr. Tenn. Tchr. Williamson County Bd. Edn., Nashville, 1974-85; tchr. adult edn. Metro Bd. Edn., Nashville, 1986—. Leader Girl Scouts U.S. Named Tchr. of Yr., Jere Baxter Mid. Sch., 1989—90, 1996—97, 2003—04. Mem. Met. Bd. Edn., Urban League, Tenn. Edn. Assn. (adult edn. com.), Nashville Met. Alumnae Assn., Delta sigma Theta, Phi Delta Kappa Clubs: Ceramic. Avocations: ceramics, reading, tennis. Home: 2634 Delk Ave Nashville TN 37208-1919 Office Phone: 615-262-6710. E-mail: washingtonj2634@aol.com.

WASHINGTON, KERRY, actor; b. Bronx, NY, Jan. 31, 1977; BFA theatre, George Washington Univ., 1998. Actor: (TV films) Magical Make-Over, 1994; (films) Our Song, 2000, 3D, Save the Last Dance, 2001, Lift, 2001, Take the A Train, Bad Company, 2002, United States of Lelan, 2003, The Human Stain, 2003, Sin, 2003, Against the Ropes, 2004, Strip Search, 2004, She Hate Me, 2004, Ray, 2004, Sexual Life, 2005, Mr. & Mrs. Smith, 2005, Fantastic Four, 2005, Wait, 2005, Little Man, 2006. Nominee Best Female Actress, Ind. Spirit Awards, 2002.*

WASHINGTON, MICHELE, educational consultant; BA in Edn., Capitol U., 1978, MA in Edn. and Counseling, 1993. Instr., counselor, reading tutor Oakland Cmty. Jr. Coll., St. Louis, 1975—88; counselor student career planning, advisement, sexual harassment, tchr. Dallas Ind. Sch. Dist., 1988—90; instr. Dallas CC Dist., 1990—99; owner Elehcims Art Works, Lewisville, Tex., 2000—. Spkr., presenter in field. Bd. dirs. YWCA, Womens Halfway House; program devel. com. Pheonix House. Mem.: ASTD.

WASHINGTON, NANCY JANE HAYES, librarian; b. High Point, Dec. 31, 1936; d. Lester Eli and Annie Rose (Caldwell) Hayes; m. Charles D. Washington, Dec. 26, 1969 (div. June 1981). AA, Mars Hill Coll., 1957; BA, U. S.C., 1959; MA, U. West Fla., 1980; MLS, Fla. State U., 1982. Music tchr. private studio, Columbia, SC, 1959-67; asst. dir. film libr. State Dept. Edn., Columbia, 1967-68; elem. sch. tchr. Richland County Schs., Columbia, 1969-71; serials cataloging and acquisitions asst. U. West Fla., Pensacola, 1972-83, serials acquisitions libr., reference libr., 1983-84; bibliographer humanities, arts and social scis. U. SW La., Lafayette, 1984-86; asst. dir. sys. libr. svcs. U. SC, Columbia, 1986-94, dir. publs. univ. librs., 1994—. Author: Univ. SC Regional Campuses Faculty Senate: It's First 25 Years, 1993, (children's book) Miss Penny's Condo, 2005; editor Ex Libris, 1994-2000; editor: Renovation and Restoration of the USC Horseshoe: A Memoir, 2002; contbr. articles to profl. jours. Bd. dirs. Columbia Mus. Art, 1992-94. Mem. Am. Libr. Assn., SE Libr. Assn., SC Lib. Assn., Richland Kiwanis Club (sec.), Phi Kappa Phi, Beta Phi Mu. Episcopalian. Avocations: reading, gardening, photography, attending concerts and plays, singing. Office: Thomas Cooper Libr Univ SC 1322 Greene St Columbia SC 29208-0001 Office Phone: 803-777-2166. E-mail: nancyhw@gwm.sc.edu.

WASHINGTON, OLIVIA GRACE MARY, psychotherapist, educator, counselor, researcher; m. Lewis Washington, Sept. 21, 1970. BS, SUNY, Buffalo, 1966, MS, 1968; PhD, Wayne State U., 1997. Diplomate Am. Psychotherapy Assn.; ANCC bd. cert. advance psychiat. RN, cert. nurse practitioner, Mich. Treatment rm. nurse Roswell Pk. Meml. Cancer Inst., Buffalo, 1966—68; team leader, staff nurse E. J. Meyer Meml. Hosp., Buffalo, 1966—68; insvc. educator Lane Bryant Psychiat. Hosp., Buffalo, 1968—69; clin. specialist, adult psychiat. nursing/supt. 10 Lafayette Clinic, Detroit, 1968—69; asst. DON, chair dept. psychiat. nursing Grace Hosp. Sch. Nursing, Detroit, 1971—75; assoc. prof. Wayne State U., Detroit, 1979—; internat. nursing edn. external examiner, cons. U. Botswana, Gaborone, 1995—97; site liaison John A. Hartford Ctr. Geriatric Nursing excellence and the Gerontological Nursing Interview Rsch. Ctr Regional Tng. Consortium, 2003—. Contbr. articles to profl. jours. Active rsch. and svc. to homeless various orgns., 1998—; bd. dirs. Renaissance Home Health Care, Vis. Nurse Assn. of S.E. Mich., Inc., Detroit, 1997—2002. Recipient Pillar award, 2005, Devel. chair award, Wayne State U., 2005—06; grantee, Wayne State U. Ctr. for Health Rsch., 1999, Nat. Inst. Aging and Mich. Ctr. for Urban African Am. Aging Rsch., 1999—2000, NIH/Nat. Ctr. on Minority Health and Health Disparities, Nat. Inst. of Nursing Rsch., 2001—, Rsch. Grant award, Wayne State U. Alumni Assn., 2003, Nat. Inst. Aging, 2001—04; Brookdale fellow, 2002, Humanities Ctr. Faculty fellow, Wayne State U. Mem.: APHA, Internat. Soc. Psychiat.-Mental Health Nurses, Gerontol. Soc. Am., Am. Counseling Assn. (licentiate), Midwest Nursing Rsch. Soc. (licentiate Harriet H. Werley New Investigator award 2003). Avocations: travel, tennis, racquetball, playing alto saxophone, reading. Office: Wayne State U 5557 Cass Ave Detroit MI 48202 Office Phone: 313-873-2926.

WASHINGTON, TYONA, adult education educator; d. William and Juanita Washington; 1 child, Derick Reed. AAS, CUNY, Bklyn., 1983, BS, 1993, MS, 1997; MS in Supervision, Coll. of St. Rose, 2004. Advanced cert. in supervision. Tchr. Frederick Douglass Ctr.-N.Y.C. Dept. Edn., Bklyn., 1994—2002, ctr. adminstr., 2002—03; adult literacy tchr. Aux. Svcs. H.S., Bklyn., 1999—; dist. recruitment cert. specialist Dept. Human Resources/Dept. Profl. Devel., Bklyn., 2002—; prin. NYC Leadership Acad., 2004—. Chairperson sch. leadership team Frederick Douglass Ctr., Bklyn., 2002—03. Mem.: Nat. Alliance Black Sch. Educators, N.Y. Alliance Black Sch. Educators, Assn. Black Educators N.Y., United Fedn. Tchrs. (chpt. leader 1999—2003, Ely Trachtenberg award 2002), Am. Fedn. Tchrs. (del. NY State Unified Tchrs. 2000—). Avocations: reading, travel, music. Home: 177 Kingston Ave #3B Brooklyn NY 11213 Office: NYC Dept Edn 832 Marcy Ave Brooklyn NY 11216 Office Phone: 718-636-5770.

WASHINGTON, YVONNE, surgical nurse; b. Pascagoula, Miss., Jan. 23, 1955; d. Clarence C. and Gloria Mae (Bivins) Turner; m. Eugene Washington Jr., Mar. 11, 1987. AS, Jackson County Jr. Coll., 1987. RN, Miss. Med. asst. VA, Houston; unit clk. Singing River Hosp., Pascagoula, staff nurse neurol. surgery. Home: 4819 King James Dr Pascagoula MS 39581-5126

WASHKUHN, ERIN LYNNE, elementary school educator; b. San Bernardino, Calif., July 15, 1975; d. Dennis Dean and Susan Jean Swick; m. Reeve Wilson Washkuhn, July 8, 2000. BS in Phys. Edn., Ill. State U., Normal, 1999; MA in Edn., Roosevelt U., Schaumburg, Ill., 2006. Cert. tchr. grades K-12 phys. edn. Ill. State Bd. Edn. Phys. edn. tchr. Normal Unit Sch. Dist. 5, 1999—2000; preschool tchr. Kensington Sch., Geneva, Ill., 2001—02; phys. edn. tchr. Lily Lake Elem. Sch., Dist. 301, Ill., 2002—03, Anderson Elem. Sch., Dist. 303, St. Charles, Ill., 2003—. Wellness task force mem. St. Charles Sch. Dist. 303, Ill., 2005—. Mem.: Ill. Assn. for Health, Phys. Edn., Recreation and Dance. Avocations: running, travel, softball. Home: 421 Vaughn Circle Aurora IL 60502 Office: Anderson Elementary Sch 35W071 Villa Marie Rd Saint Charles IL 60174 Office Phone: 847-697-5040. Personal E-mail: erin.washkuhn@sbcglobal.net. Business E-Mail: ewashkuhn@d303.org.

WASIK, BARBARA ANN, psychologist, researcher; b. Newark, July 18, 1957; d. Thomas Joseph and Ruth Ann W.; m. James Patrick Byrnes, May 3, 1986; children: Julia, Thomas. BA in Psychology, Rutgers U., 1979, MA in Psychology, 1982; PhD in Devel. Psychology, Temple U., Phila., 1986. Postdoctoral fellow Johns Hopkins Med. Inst. dept. pediat., Balt., 1986-87, U. Mich., Ann Arbor, 1987-88; prin. scientist Johns Hopkins U., Balt., 1988—. Cons. Nat. Sr. Corp., Washington, 1995. Co-author: Preventing Early School Failure, Success for All: A Relentless Approach to Prevention & Early Intervention in Elementary Schools, 1995. Avocations: reading, running. Office: Johns Hopkins Univ 3003 N Charles St Ste 200 Baltimore MD 21218-3888 Home: 57 Lenfant Ct Glen Mills PA 19342-1668

WASIK, BARBARA HANNA, psychologist, educator; b. Douglas, Ga., May 29, 1942; d. Frank Joseph and Josephine (Nahoom) Hanna; m. John L. Wasik, June 24, 1966; children— John Gregory, Mark Timothy, Jeffrey Joseph AB, U. Ga., 1963; MA, Fla. State U., 1965, PhD, 1967. Lic. psychologist, N.C. Postdoctoral research fellow Duke U., Durham, NC, 1967-68; dir. research Ford Found. grant, Durham, NC, 1968-69; from asst. prof. to assoc. prof. U. N.C., Chapel Hill, 1969-77, prof., 1977—, William R. Kenan Jr. disting. prof., 2003—, assoc. dean Grad. Sch., 1972-75, chmn. div. human devel. and psychol. services, 1975-77, assoc. dean Sch. Edn., 1977-83, 1988—92, sr. investigator Child Devel. Ctr., 1972—. Mem. commn. NAS, 1998—2000; co-facilitator Nat. Forum Home Visiting, 1999—. Assoc. editor Jour. Applied Behavior Analysis, 1972; mem. editorial bd. Behavioral Assessment, 1984-85; contbr. chpts. to books and articles to profl. jours. Mem. N.C. Psychological Assn. (sec. 1982-85, pres. 1988-89), Am. Psychol. Assn. (divsn. 25 sec-treas. 1983-86, coun. rep. 1994-99, bd. edn. affairs 1999-2001, chair bd edn. affairs 2001), Soc. Research in Child Development, Southeastern Psychol. Assn., Assn. Advancement Behavior Therapy. Democrat. Roman Catholic. Home: 609 Brookview Dr Chapel Hill NC 27514-1402

WASKO, DEBORAH ANN, music educator; b. Beaufort, SC, July 1, 1967; d. Thomas Walter and Florence Ann Misiorowski; m. Steven Michael Wasko, June 22, 1991; children: Brittany Ann Kelly, Ashley Elizabeth. B Music Edn., U. Mo., Kansas City, 1991. Cert. music tchr. Mo. Orch. dir. North Kansas City Sch. Dist., Mo., 1991—99, Blue Springs Sch. Dist., Mo., 1999—. Orch. v.p. Kansas City Metro Dist., 2003. Mem. mariacho band, string quartet. Mem.: Music Educators Nat. Conf. Roman Catholic. Home: 5208 NW Downing St Blue Springs MO 64015 Business E-Mail: dwasko@bssd.net.

WASKO-FLOOD, SANDRA JEAN, artist, educator; b. NYC, Mar. 12, 1943; d. Peter Edmund and Margaret Dalores (Kubek) Wasko; m. Michael Timothy Flood, June 28, 1969. BA, UCLA, 1965, postgrad., 1968-69, Calif. State U., Northridge, summer 1968; student, Otis Art Inst., L.A., 1969, Marie Kaufman, Rio de Janeiro, 1970-72, Museo de Arte Moderno, 1970-73, Foothill Coll., Los Altos, Calif., 1973-74, Claremont (Calif.) Coll., 1975, U. Wis., Janesville, 1977, Beloit (Wis.) Coll., 1977-78, U. Wis., 1977-78; grad. etching student, Warrington Colescott. Instr. printmaking Washington Women's Arts Ctr., 1983; artist-in-residence U. Md., College Park, 1985; instr. printmaking Arlington (Va.) Arts Ctr., 1984-85; prof. St. Mary's (Md.) Coll., 1985; instr. printmaking Arlington County Lee Arts Ctr., 1989-97; workshop coord. cultural affairs div. Arlington County Cultural Affairs, 1989-97; printmaking instr. Home Studio, Alexandria, Va., 1987—2005; founder, pres. Living Labyrinths Peace, Inc., 2005—. Condr. workshops Washington Performing Arts Soc., 2002—; founder, pres., bd. dirs. Living Labyrinths for Peace, Inc., 2005—. One woman shows include Wisconsin Women in the Arts Gallery, Madison, 1977, Mbari Art, Washington, 1981, Miya Gallery, Washington, 1981, Slavin Gallery, Washington, 1982, Stuart Mott House, Washington, 1983, Washington Printmakers Gallery, 1986, 88, 91, St. Peter's Ch., N.Y.C., 1989, Montana Gallery, Alexandria, Va., 1991, Montpelier Cultural Arts Ctr., Laurel, Md., 1992, Gallery 10, Washington, 1994, 96, Sch. 33, Balt., 1996; mus. and internat. shows include Boston Printmakers: The 39th North Am. Print Exhbn., Framingham, Mass., Jan.-Mar., 1986, Internat. Graphic Arts Found. and Silvermine Guild Arts Ctr., New Canaan, Conn., Feb., 1988, Prints: Washington, The Phillips Collection, Washington, Sept.-Oct., 1988, Contemporary Am. Graphics, Book Chamber Internat., Moscow, 1990, Gallery 10 Artists of Washington D.C. Vartai Gallery, Lithuania, 1994, Peninsula Fine Arts Ctr., Newport News, Va., 1995-96, Riva Sinistra Arte, Florence, Italy, 1997, Contemporary Art Ctr. Va., Virginia Beach, 2000, Charles Sumner Sch. Mus., Washington, D.C., 2001, numerous others; juried shows include Washington Women's Arts Ctr.: Printmakers VII show, 1985, Washington Women's Arts Ctr., 1981, 82, Seventh Ann. Faber Birren Color Show Nat. Juried Open Exhibit, Stamford, Conn., 1987, Acad. of the Arts 25th Ann. Juried Exhbn., 1989, Fla. Printmakers Nat., 1994, S.W. Tex. State U., 1995, Peninsula Fivie Arts Ctr., Newport News, Va., 1998, Washington Women Artists, Women's Caucus for Art, 2001, Rockville Art Place, Md., 2002, Internat. Photography, 2003, and numerous others; invitational shows include Office of the Mayor, Mini Art Gallery, Washington, "Glimpses: Women Printmakers", 1981, Pyramid Paperworks, Balt., 1984, Gallery 10 "Nightmare Show": Washington, D.C., 1987, The Intaglio Process, The Benedicta Art Ctr. Gallery, St. Joseph, Minn., 1988, Women's Caucus for Art, Washington Artists in Perspective, Westbeth Gallery, N.Y.C., 1990, 91, Wesley Theol. Sem., 1992, Balt. City Hall, N.Am. Print Alliance, 1993, The Five Elements Women's Caucus For Art, 1994, WPA/Corcoran Auction, 1999, Washington Theological Union, Washington, 1999, Cannon Rotunda, U.S. House of Reps., Washington, 2000, Charles Sumner Sch. Mus., Washington, 2001, Washington Women Artists Marching into the Millennium, Women's Caucus for Art, 2001, Anne C. Fisher Gallery, Wash., 2005 and numerous others; galleries: Slavin Gallery, Washington, D.C., 1981-83, Washington Printmakers Gallery, Washington, 1985-96, White Light Collaborative, Inc., N.Y.C., 1988-89, Montana Gallery, Alexandria, Va., 1989-91, Gallery 10, Washington, 1992-97, Charleuoix Gallery, Albuquerque, NM, 1999, and numerous others; collections include Nat. Mus. of Women in the Arts, Washington, Corcoran Gallery of Art, Washington, Museo de Arte Moderno, Buenos Aires, Cultural Found., USSR, Coll. Notre Dame, Balt., Potomac Hosp., Woodbridge, Md.; dir. Labyrinths for Peace 2000, U.S. Capitol, 2002; featured artist Kali Guide: A Directory of Resources for Women, 2d reprint, 2002. Pres. Washington Area Printmakers, Washington, D.C., 1985-86; pub. rels. dir. Washington Women's Arts Ctr., 1980; bd. dirs. Washington Women's Arts Ctr., 1981-82; program chair D.C. chpt. Women's Caucus for Art, 1998—; founding mem. the Labyrinth Soc., 1998-; spl. projects dir. Labyrinth Soc., 2000; cons. Labyrinth Making and Products. Recipient Award of Honorable Mention Nat. Gallery of Art, 1989, Best of Show, Artists Equity Exhibit, Gallery 901, Washington, 1997; grantee Friends of the Torpedo Factory Art Ctr., Alexandria, Va., 1989, DC Commn. on Arts and Humanities Summer Edn. and Sports Program Artist in Schs., 2000, 01, 05, Wash. Performing Arts Soc., 2002-06; individual artists fellow Va. Commn. for Arts, 1994. Mem.: Arts/Sci. Collaborative, Inc. (N.Y.C.), Artists Using Sci. and Tech. (San Francisco), YLEM, The Labyrinth Soc., Washington Sculpture Group, Am. Print Alliance, Md. Printmakers, Women's Caucus for Art, So. Graphics Coun., Pyramic Atlantic, Nat. Print Orgn., Corcoran Gallery/Washington Project for the Arts. Avocations: classical music, hiking, reading. Studio: Living Labyrinths Peace Ctr 57 N St NW Washington DC 20001-1254 Home: 2229 Lake Ave Baltimore MD 21213-1015 Office Phone: 703-217-6706. Personal E-mail: waskoart@cox.net.

WASLIEN, CAROL IRENE, educator, academic administrator; b. Mayville, N.D., Sept. 24, 1940; d. Palmer Jennings and Ann Helen (Larson) W.; m. Amir N. Ghazaii, Aug. 30, 1981. BA, U. Calif., Santa Barbara, 1961; MS, Cornell U., 1963; PhD, U. Calif., Berkeley, 1968. Registered dietitian. Rsch. assoc. Vanderbilt U., Nashville, 1968-72; chmn., assoc. prof. Auburn (Ala.) U., 1972-76; cons. A T Kearney, Tunis, Tunisia, 1977-79; exec. dir. League Internat. Food Edn., Washington, 1979-81; chmn., prof. CUNY, Hunter Coll., NYC, 1981-90, U. Hawaii, Honolulu, 1990—2006; prof. Kuiwait U., 2006—. Bd. dirs. Universal Foods Corp., Milw., 1981-2000. Mem. APHA, Am. Inst. Nutrition, Am. Dietetic Assn. Office: U Hawaii 1960 E West Rd Honolulu HI 96822-2319

WASNAK, DIANE MARIE, comedian; b. Canton, Ohio, Sept. 22, 1961; d. Richard Dale and Lynn Iverne Wasnak. Grad. Antic Arts Acad., SUNY, Purchase, N.Y., 1983; apprenticeship with Tony Montanero, Celebration Barn, South Paris, Maine, 1985—88; studied with master trainer Lu Yi, Pickle Family Circus, San Francisco, 1989—2001. Cert. dog trainer San Francisco Dog Tng. Acad. Actress, comedian, stunt double: (films and TV prodns.) Matrix 2; Matrix 3; Ripley's Believe It Or Not; Ginger Snaps; Midnight Caller; Pro "7"; (theatrical prodns.) Tananai; A Midsummer Night's Dream (Backstage West Bouquet award, 1996); Woman Behind Bars; Peter Pan; Pino Stands Alone; Pickle Family Circus. Named Performer of Yr. runner-up, San Francisco Chronicle, 1994. Mem.: SAG, AFTRA, Assn. for Pet Dog Trainers, Actor's Equity Assn.

WASOW, MONA, social worker, educator; b. Rome, June 29, 1933; came to the U.S., 1933; d. Nathaniel F. and Thelma (Kottek) Cantor; children: Robin Murie, David Murie, Oliver Wasow. BS, U. Wis., 1966, MSW, 1968. Prof. sch. social work U. Wis., Madison, 1970—2003; prof. emeritus, 2003—. Author: Coping With Schizophrenia, 1982, The Skipping Stone: Ripple Effects of Mental Illness on the Family, 1995; contbr. numerous articles to profl. jours. Mem.: Nat. Alliance for Mentall Ill (Disting. Svc. award 1988, Cert. of Recognition 1988, Exemplary Program award 1988). Democrat. Jewish. Avocations: classical music, skiing, hiking, reading, travel. Business E-Mail: mwasow@wisc.edu.

WASS, HANNELORE LINA, educational psychology educator; b. Heidelberg, Germany, Sept. 12, 1926; came to U.S., 1957, naturalized, 1963; d. Hermann and Mina (Lasch) Kraft; m. Irvin R. Wass, Nov. 24, 1959 (dec.); 1 child, Brian C.; m. Harry H. Sisler, Apr. 13, 1978. BA, Tchrs. Coll., Heidelberg, 1951; MA, U. Mich., 1960, PhD, 1968. Tchr. W. Ger. Univ. Lab. Schs., 1958-60; mem. faculty U. Mich., Ann Arbor, 1958-60, U. Chgo. Lab. Sch., 1960-61, U. Mich., 1963-64, Eastern Mich. U., 1965-69; prof. ednl. psychology U. Fla., Gainesville, 1969-92, prof. emeritus, 1992—, faculty assoc. Ctr. for Gerontol. Studies Gainesville. Cons., lectr. in thanatology. Author: The Professional Education of Teachers, 1974, Dying-Facing the Facts, 1979, 2d edit., 1988, 3d edit., 1995, Death Education: An Annotated Resource Guide, 1980, vol. 2, 1985, Helping Children Cope With Death, 1982, 2d edit., 1984, Childhood and Death, 1984; founding editor (jour.) Death Studies, 1977-92; cons. editor: Ednl. Gerontology, 1977-92, (book series) Death Education, Aging and Health Care, 1980-96; contbr. approximately 200 articles to profl. jours. and chpts. in books. Mem. Am. Psychol. Assn., Gerontol. Soc., Internat. Work Group Dying, Death and Bereavement (bd. dirs.), Assn. Death Edn. and Counseling. Home: 6014 NW 54th Way Gainesville FL 32653-3265 E-mail: wass@nersp.nerdc.ufl.edu.

WASSENBERG, EVELYN M., retired medical/surgical nurse, educator; b. Oct. 8, 1933; d. Patrick A. and Mary A. (Kieffer) L'Ecuyer; m. Maurice P. Wassenberg, Oct. 29, 1955; children: Sherry Ann Gaines, Laura Marie O'Neil. Diploma in nursing, Marymount Sch. Nursing, Salina, Kans., 1955; BS in Nursing, Marymount Coll. of Salina, 1982; MN, Wichita State U., 1987. Cert. nurse specialist. Dir. nursing svc. Community Meml. Hosp. Inc., Marysville, Kans., 1962-79; house supr. Luth. Hosp., Beatrice, Nebr., 1980-82; primary nurse Beatrice Cmty. Hosp., 1983; instr. Ft. Scott C.C., Kans., 1983-2001, 2004—06; nurse Girard Hosp., 2001; ICU nurse Nevada Regional Health Ctr., Mo., 2001—03; retired, 2006. Mem. Mary Queen of Angels Cath. Ch. Named Nurse of Yr. Bourbon County Kans., 1992. Mem. Am. Nursing Assn., Kans. State Nursing Assn., Sigma Theta Tau. Address: 216 S Crawford St Fort Scott KS 66701-3231

WASSENICH, LINDA PILCHER, retired health policy analyst; b. Washington, Aug. 27, 1943; d. Mason Johnson and Vera Bell (Stephenson) Pilcher; m. Mark Wassenich, May 14, 1965; children: Paul Mason, David Mark. BA magna cum laude with honors, Tex. Christian U., Fort Worth, 1965; MSW, U. N.C., Chapel Hill, 1970. Licensed advanced practitioner, cert. social worker, Tex. Counselor family ct. Dallas County Juvenile Dept., 1970-73, 75-76; dir. govt. rels. Vis. Nurse Assn., Dallas, 1980-84, exec. officer of hospice, 1984-85; exec. dir. Incest Recovery Assn., Dallas, 1985-86; assoc. exec. dir. Lone Star Coun. Camp Fire, Dallas, 1986-89; exec. v.p. Vis. Nurse Assn. Found., Dallas, 1989-91; dir. policy and resource devel. Vis. Nurse Assn. Tex., 1992-99; ret. Field instr. U. Tex. Arlington Sch. Social Work, 1993-99. Contbr. articles to profl. publs. Mem. Leadership Dallas, 1988—89; bd. dirs. Women's Coun. Dallas County, 1986—95, 1999—2001, pres., 1992—93; mem. adv. bd. Maternal Health and Family Planning Dallas, 1990—94; chmn. Dallas County Welfare Adv. Bd., 1991—95; bd. dirs. United Way of Met. Dallas, 1992—94, Youth Impact Ctrs., Dallas, 1993—94; trustee Simmons Family Found., Dallas, 2000—; mem. cmty. coun. Greater Dallas, 2004—; chair governance com. Human Rights Initiative of North Tex., Dallas, 2004—; chair adv. coun. Dallas Area Agy. on Aging, 2005—. Recipient Heart award Lone Star Coun. Camp Fire USA, 1990, Laurel award AAUW, Dallas, 1995, Valuable Alumna award Tex. Christian U. Alumni Assn., 2003, Women of Spirit award Am. Jewish Congress, Dallas, 2005; named Field Inst. of Yr., U. Tex. Arlington Sch. Social Work, 1999, Golden Rule award finalist JC Penney, 2000. Mem.: LWV (bd. dirs. Dallas 1974—80, pres. 1995—99, bd. dirs. Tex. 1999—, Tex. v.p. pub. rels. 2001—, Myrtle Bales Bulkley award 2000, Pres. award 2005), NASW (co-chmn. Dallas unit 1981—82, chair Tex. nominating com. 1990—92, Tex. bd. dirs., Social Worker of Yr. award 1988, Lifetime Achievement in Social Work award 2002), Assn. Fundraising Profls. (bd. dirs. Dallas chpt. 1994—97, v.p. governance 1995—96, cert., Outstanding Fund Raising Exec. of Yr. 1999), Acad. Cert. Social Workers. Home: 5221 Pebblebrook Dallas TX 75229-5504

WASSER, LAURA ALLISON, lawyer; b. LA, May 23, 1968; d. Dennis Wasser. BA, U. Calif. Berkeley, 1991; JD, Loyola Law Sch., 1994. Bar: Calif. 1994. Ptnr. Wasser, Cooperman & Carter, LA. V.p. fin. devel., bd. dirs. Harriet Buhai Ctr. Family Law. Mem.: LA County Bar Assn., Beverly Hills Bar Assn. Office: Wasser Cooperman & Carter Ste 1200 One Century Plz 2029 Century Park E Los Angeles CA 90067 Office Phone: 310-277-7117. Office Fax: 310-553-1793.

WASSERMAN, ABBY LOIS, child, adolescent and family psychiatrist; b. Passaic, N.J., Aug. 8, 1945; d. Robert Sidney and Marjorie Dorothy (Hurevitz) W.; m. Daniel Paul Jaffe, May 19, 1974; children: Rachel, Robert. BA, Johns Hopkins U., 1967, MD, 1970. Diplomate Am. Bd. Pediatrics, Nat. Bd. Med. Examiners; diplomate, cert. sub-specialist in child psychiatry Am. Bd. Psychiatry and Neurology. Intern, then resident in pediatrics U. Wash. Hosp./Children's Orthopedic Hosp. and Med. Ctr., Seattle, 1970-72; fellow in pediatrics U. Wash. Sch. Medicine, Seattle, 1970-72; fellow, resident in psychiatry Henry Phipps Psychiatry Clinic Johns Hopkins U. Sch. Medicine, Balt., 1972-74; fellow in child psychiatry Judge Baker Guidance Ctr. Children's Hosp. and Med. Ctr., Harvard U. Med. Sch., Boston, 1974-76; resident in child psychiatry Children's Hosp. Med. Ctr., Boston, 1974-76; clin. asst. in psychiatry Mass. Gen. Hosp., Boston, 1976-81; chief divsn. psychiatry LeBonheur Children's Med. Ctr., Memphis, 1981-84; dir. divsn. psychiatry and psychology St. Jude Children's Rsch. Hosp., Memphis, 1984-87; dir. residency tng., dir. cons.-liaison child psychiatry Washington U. Sch. Medicine/Children's Hosp., St. Louis, 1987-90; dir. child, adolescent and family psychiatry St. Luke's Hosp., Chesterfield, Mo., 1990-93; med. dir. United Behavioral Systems, St. Louis, 1993-97; area med. dir. Merit Behavioral Care Corp., Maryland Heights, Mo., 1997—. Psychiat. cons. Greenery Nursing Home and Rehab. Ctr., Brighton, Mass., 1976-79, Charles River Hosp., Wellesley, Mass., 1979-80, Suffolk County Jail, Boston, 1980-81; instr. Harvard U. Med. Sch., Boston, 1976-81; asst. prof. pediatrics, 1981-87; cons. staff St. Jude Children's Rsch. Hosp., 1982-84, Bpat. Meml. Hosp. and Lakeside Hosp., Memphis, 1983-87; asst. prof. psychiatry and pediatrics Washington U., St. Louis, 1987—. Author tng. materials for parents in apnea home monitoring program; reviewer Jour. Devel. and Behavioral Pediatrics, 1981—, Jour. Clin. Oncology, 1985—, Pediatrics, 1985—, Jour. Am. Acad. Child and Adolescent Psychiatry, 1985—, Am. Jour. Mental Deficiency, 1986, JAMA, 1989; contbr. articles to profl. jours. Fellow Am. Acad. Pediatrics, Am. Acad. Child Psychiatry; mem. Ambulatory Pediatric Assn., Acad. Psychosomatic Medicine, Am. Psychiat. Assn., Ea. Mo. Psychiat. Soc. Avocations: house renovation, travel, bicycling, reading. Office: Merit Behavioral Care Corp 13736 Riverport Dr Ste 500 Maryland Heights MO 63043-4820

WASSERMAN, HARRIET M., academic administrator; BS in Chemistry, U. Wash. Assoc. dean., dir. info. tech. services Seattle Ctrl. Cmty. Coll. Named one of Premier 100 IT Leaders, Computerworld, 2005. Office: Seattle Ctrl Cmty Coll 1701 Broadway Seattle WA 98122 Office Phone: 206-344-4344. E-mail: hwasse@sccd.ctc.edu.

WASSERMAN, KRYSTYNA, librarian, art historian; b. Lodz, Poland, Aug. 10, 1937; came to U.S., 1971; d. Henryk and Polina (Volk) Ostrowski; m. Paul Wasserman, Apr. 14, 1973. M in Journalism, U. Warsaw, Poland, 1963; MLS, Pratt Inst., 1972; MA, U. Md., 1981. Reporter Ekran-The Screen Mag., Warsaw, 1960-62; sec. edn. com. Inst. Sci., Tech. and Econ. Info., Warsaw, Poland and Internat. Fedn. for Documentation, The Hague, Netherlands, 1962-71; ind. editor reference books College Park, Md., 1972-82; libr. Nat. Mus. Women Arts, Washington, 1982—2002, curator book arts, 2002—. Curator numerous art exhbns. Contbr. articles to profl. jours.; editor: A Guide to the World Training Facilities in Documentation and Information Work, 1965, 2nd edit., 1969. ASTEF fellow Govt. of France, 1967. Avocations: photography, walking, travel, collecting socks, collecting masks. Office: Nat Mus Women in Arts 1250 New York Ave NW Washington DC 20005-3970

WASSERMAN, SUSAN VALESKY, accountant, artist, yoga instructor; b. St. Petersburg, Fla., June 5, 1956; d. Charles B. Valesky and Jeanne I. (Schulz) Morgan; m. Fred Wasserman, III, May 19, 1990; 1 child, Sara Elisabeth. BS in Merchandising, Fla. State U., Tallahassee, 1978; BA in Acctg., U. South Fla., Tampa, 1983. CPA Fla.; ChFC, cert. yoga tchr. Fla. Inst. for Integrated Yoga Studies, 2002, yoga therapist Integrated Yoga Therapy, 2004. Store mgr. Levi Straus Inc., San Francisco, 1979; pvt. practice acct. St. Petersburg, 1980—; acct., tax and fin. planning specialist Barber, Stowe & Co., St. Petersburg, 1997—98; owner White Egret Yoga Studio, South Pasadena, Fla., 2002—. Exhibitions include Longboat Key (Fla.) Art Ctr., 1993, Fla. Suncoast Water Color Soc., Sarasota, 1994, South Pasadena Artspring, 1998—2000 (Judges award, 1998), 2005. Mem.: Internat. Assn. Yoga Therapists, Suncoast Yoga Tchrs. Assn. (pres.), Yoga Alliance. Home and Studio: 7015 Grevilla Ave S Saint Petersburg FL 33707-2050 Office: 5800 4th St N Saint Petersburg FL 33703-1402 Office Phone: 727-347-7354. E-mail: yogisue@tampabay.rr.com.

WASSERMAN-SCHULTZ, DEBBIE, congresswoman; b. Forest Hills, N.Y., Sept. 27, 1955; BA in Polit. Sci., U. Fla., 1988, MA, 1990. Mem. Fla. Ho. of Reps., 1992—2004, US Congress from 20th Fla. dist., 2005—; mem. Ho. Judiciary com. Mem. Gov.'s Commn. on Edn., 1996—; mem. legis. adv. coun. So. Regional Edn. Bd., 1995—; bd. dirs. Fla. Distance Learning Network, 1994; mem. Classrooms First Task Force, 1993. Recipient award for outstanding family advocacy Dade County Psychol. Assn., 1993, Giraffe award Women's Advocacy Majority Minority, 1993, Legis. Svc. award Fla. Assn. Women Lawyers, 1993, Quality Floridian award Fla. League of Cities, 1994, AMIT Woman of Yr. award, 1994, Outstanding Legislator of Yr. award Fla. Fedn. Bus. and Profl. Women, 1994, Rosemary Barkett award Acad. Fla. Trial Lawyers, 1995, Woman of Vision award Weizmann Inst. Sci., others; named one of Six Most Unstoppable Women, South Fla. Mag., 1994. Mem. Omicron Delta Kappa. Democrat. Jewish. Avocations: bowling, golf, politics, old houses. Office: US House of Representatives 118 Cannon House Office Bldg Washington DC 20515-0920 also: 10100 Pines Blvd Pembroke Pines FL 33026 Office Phone: 202-225-7931.

WASSILAK, JANET MARIAN, choral director; b. Framingham, Mass., Sept. 8, 1947; d. Asa Bedford Vear and Marian Leona McCabe; m. Frank Joseph Wassilak, July 10, 1971. MusB, Boston U., 1969, MusM, 1972. Choir dir. 1st Congl. Ch., Holliston, Mass., 1967—71; music tchr. East Mid. Sch., Braintree, Mass., 1969—70, Gibson Sch. for Gifted, Dearborn, Mich., 1972—74, Halston Mid. Sch., Dearborn Heights, Mich., 1975—76, Divine Child HS, Dearborn, 1985; choir dir., dir. music Cherry Hill Presbyn. Ch., Dearborn, 1972—94; dir. music ministries 1st United Meth. Ch., Farmington, Mich., 1995—. Dir. Novi Choralaires, Mich., 1977—. Basic reading tchr. Washtenaw Literacy, Ann Arbor, Mich., 1995. Mem.: Am. Choral Dirs. Assn., US Equestrian Assn. Avocations: horseback riding, reading, cooking, calligraphy. Home: 8640 Nollar Rd Whitmore Lake MI 48189

WASSON, BARBARA HICKAM, music educator; b. Spencer, Ind., Feb. 12, 1918; Student, DePauw U., 1937-38; BA, Vassar Coll., 1939; MusM, Chgo. Mus. Coll., 1944; postgrad., Ind. U., 1962-63. Founder, co-dir. Wasson Piano Studios, Dayton, 1946—; instr. Cedarville Coll., Dayton, Ohio, 1970-72; adj. prof. Wright State U., Dayton, Ohio, 1973-78; asst. prof. U. Cin., 1982-87; prof. Wright State U., 2005—. Instr. U. Dayton, Ohio, 2004—. Named Cert. Tchr. of Yr., Western Dist. of Ohio, 1998, 2001, Family of Yr., Ohio Fedn. Music Clubs, 2002; recipient Family of Yr. award Ohio Fedn. Music Clubs, 2002; MTNA Found. fellow, 2004. Fellow Music Tchrs. Nat. Assn.; mem. Ohio Music Tchrs. Assn. (pres. 1980-82, chmn. western dist. 1976-78), Calif. Assn. Bilingual Edn. (pres. chpt. 2005-06, Tchr. of Yr. 2006), Dayton Music Club (pres. 1989-91), Mu Phi Epsilon (pres. Dayton alumnae chpt. 1986-88), Dayton Piano Tchrs. Study Club (v.p. 2004-2006). Home: 9620 Belfry Ct Dayton OH 45458-4157 Office Phone: 937-885-3983. Personal E-mail: wassonpno@aol.com.

WASSON, CAROL R., music educator; b. Dayton, Ohio, Feb. 8, 1951; d. Audley Jackson and Barbara (Hickam) Wasson; children: Tiffany Elise Shaw, Tia Nicole Cundiff-Shaw. BMusic in Piano Performance, Wright State U., Fairborn, Ohio, 1978. Pvt. tchr. piano, 1965—; pvt. tchr. violin and viola, 1980—; owner, mentor to music tchrs. Wasson Music Ctr., Centerville, Ohio, 1993—. Lectr., tchr. piano to preschoolers. Chmn. jr. philharm. Dayton Philharm. Vol. Assn., 1979-80, asst. treas., 2005; hospitality chmn. Dayton Visual Arts Ctr., 2004—; chmn. fundraiser South Dayton Montessori, Kettering, Ohio, 1987-88. Mem. Nat. Guild Piano Tchrs. (chmn. Dayton-Wasson Audition Ctr. 1998—), Music Tchrs. Nat. Assn., Centerville Arts Commn., Dayton Music Club (chmn. judges Dist. IIIB Jr. Festival 1994—, co-chmn. 1999-2002, chmn. 2001—), Mu Phi Epsilon, Centerville Noon Optimists. Office: Wasson Music Ctr 35 Marco Ln Centerville OH 45458-3818

WASSON, CATHERINE CHURCH, education educator; b. Memphis, Jan. 11, 1948; d. Eugene Conner Sr. and Effie Mae (Harpole) Church; m. David George Wasson Sr., Nov. 4, 1966; children: David George Jr., Walter Eugene Harpole Wasson. BS, Miss. State U., Starkville, 1970; MEd, Delta State U., Cleveland, Miss., 1980; PhD, U. Miss., 1997. Cert. elem. and secondary edn. tchr., Miss. Tchr. Miss. Pub. Schs., Gulfport and Greenville, 1970-80; curriculum coord. Leland (Miss.) Pub. Schs., 1980-85; dir. migrant edn. project Cen. Delta Coop., Leland, 1983-85; instructional coord. Greenville Pub. Schs., 1985-89; program mgr. Sch. Exec. Mgmt. Inst. Miss. Dept. Edn., Jackson, 1989-93, dir. Office of Profl. Devel., 1993—2002; prof., grad. tchr. edn. Belhaven Coll., Jackson, Miss., 2002—. Cons. Anguilla (Miss.) Sch. Dist., 1983-84; local coord. Program for Rsch. and Evaluation in Pub. Schs., Leland, 1983-85; trainer Miss. Dept. Edn., Jackson, 1987-89, lead project dir., 1989-1991; dir. Office Leadership Devel. and Enhancement, 1991-1996; interim assoc. supt. edn. Academia Edn., 1996-1998; prof. U. Miss., 1998-1999; dir. grad. tchr. edn., 1999—. Mem. Presbyn. Women, Greenville, 1978-89, Washington Sch. PTA, Greenville, 1980-89, Washington Sch. Athletic Boosters, Greenville, 1980-89, Greenville Edn. Found., Greenville, 1988-89. Mem. Miss. Assn. Supervision and Curriculum Devel., AAUW (com. on women, auction chair 1987-89), Phi Delta Kappa, Millsaps Prin. Inst. (bd.), Little Light House (bd.). Republican. Avocations: restoring old homes, antiques, reading, water-skiing, travel. Home: 113 Belle Pointe Madison MS 39110-8287 Office: Belhaven Coll 1500 Peachtree Jackson MS 39202

WASSON, KRISTI BYAS, secondary school educator; b. Port Arthur, Tex., Nov. 28, 1964; d. Freddy Ray and Virginia Sue Byas; m. James W Wasson, Feb. 11, 1989; children: James Aubrey Zachary, Susie Lynn, James Walker. BS in Math. and Physics, Lamar U., Beaumont, Tex., 1987. Cert. tchr. Tex. Tchr. Spring Ind. Sch. Dist., Tex., 1990—; data entry/systems adminstr. Gordon Food Brokers, Houston, 1993—96. Active mem. Klein United Meth. Ch., Spring, Tex., 1996—2006. Office: Spring HS 19428 I-45 N Spring TX 77373-2999 Office Phone: 281-353-3465. Business E-Mail: kristiw@springisd.org.

WATANABE, NANA, photographer; b. Tokyo, Jan. 12, 1952; came to U.S., 1974; d. Kenji and Mie Watanabe; m. Julian Mark Fifer, Nov. 3, 1988; 1 child, Anais Fifer. BA in English Lit., Keio U., Tokyo, 1971. Freelance photographer, N.Y.C., Tokyo, Paris, 1980—. Author: Changemakers, 2005. Named Photographer of Yr., Am. Photographer mag., 1987. Avocations: languages, tennis. Home: 1010 5th Ave New York NY 10028-0130 Office: 1202 Lexington Ave 131 New York NY 10028 Office Phone: 212-288-6070.

WATER, LINDA GAIL, public relations executive; b. Cleve., Jan. 21, 1946; d. Kenneth and Suzanne Ellen (Bergman) Water; children: Bradley Katz, Douglas Katz. BA in Mktg., John Carroll U., 1967. Feature writer, reporter Fairchild Publs., Inc., Cleve., 1963—67; asst. account exec., copywriter Dix & Eaton, Inc., Cleve., 1967—71; mgr. consumer rels. Club Products Co. div. Standex Internat., Cleve., 1971—74; mgr. advt. pub. rels. and sales promotion mgr., mktg. Hauserman, Inc., Cleve., 1974—77; comm. program mgr., mktg. comm. group Herman Miller, Inc., Zeeland, Mich., 1977—79, program mgr. market programs group, 1979—80; corp. dir. comm. and mgmt. devel. Am. Seating Co., Grand Rapids, Mich., 1980—85; dir. mktg. comm., internat. ops. and leather divs. Wolverine World Wide, Inc., Rockford, Mich., 1985—87; dir. pub. rels. and Detroit ops. Sefton Assocs. Inc., Southfield, Mich., 1988—. Mem. YWCA. Mem.: Women in Comm. (inductee Acad. Women Achievers 1986), Pub. Rels. Soc. Am., Am. Mktg. Assn.

WATERBURY, DEBORAH KAY, minister; b. Lakeland, Fla., Dec. 27, 1962; d. William Ray and Jacqueline Rosalie Willis; m. Jeffrey Paul Waterbury, Mar. 2, 1985; children: Jeffrey Spence, Gregory Miles. BS in English and History, Mid. Tenn. State U., Murfreesboro, 1984; MA in Tchg., Grand Canyon U., Tempe, Ariz., 2003. English and reading tchr. Lily Hill Mid. Sch., Philippines, 1986—89; reading tchr. NE Mid. Sch., Clarksville, Tenn., 1991—93; English tchr. Mt. Juliet HS, Mt. Juliet, Tenn., 1995—96; history tchr. Amphi Mid. Sch., Tucson, 1996—97, Catalina Foothills HS, Tucson, 1997—2006; dir. women's ministries Faith Com. Ch., 2006—. Dir. womens ministries Faith Cmty. Ch., Tucson, 2006—. Avocations: running, writing, singing. Home: 1051 W Antelope Creek Way Oro Valley AZ 85737 Office: Faith Com Church 2551 W Orange Grove Rd Tucson AZ 85741

WATERER, BONNIE CLAUSING, retired secondary school educator; b. Toledo, Sept. 25, 1940; d. Kermit Henry and Helen Ethel (Waggoner) Clausing; m. Louis P. Waterer, June 17, 1961; children: Ryan, Reid. BS in Home Econs. Edn., Ohio State U., 1962; MA in Home Econs. Edn., San Jose State U., 1966. Tchr. James Lick H.S., San Jose, 1963-67, 1973-76; adult edn. instr. Met. Adult Edn. Program, San Jose, 1968-75; home econs. instr. Independence H.S., San Jose, 1976-99, home econs. dept. chair, 1976-80; home econs. coord. East Side Union H.S. Dist., San Jose, 1980-99, coord. coll. and career resource ctrs., 1995-99, ret., 1999—. Child care occupations instr. Ctrl. County Occupl. Ctr., San Jose, 1989-99; child devel. instr. Evergreen Valley Coll., San Jose, 1995. Bd. dirs. NAMI Yavapai County, Ariz., 2001—, West Yavapai Guidance Clinic, 2005—; mem. Family Resource Ctr. adv. coun. Yavapai Regional Med. Ctr., 2004—. Mem.: AAUW (v.p. Prescott br. 2004—06), Home Econs. Tchrs. Assn. Calif. (pres. 1989—91, Outstanding Tchr. award 1987), Calif. Assn. Family and Consumer Sci. (Tchr. of Yr. award 1994), Am. Assn. Family and Consumer Sci., Phi Upsilon Omicron, Delta Kappa Gamma (sec. Prescott br. 2002—06), Omicron Nu. Democrat. Methodist. Avocations: travel, computers, cooking, sewing. Home: 1052 Vantage Pt Cir Prescott AZ 86301 E-mail: bh2oer@aol.com.

WATERHOUSE, BETH ELAINE, writer, editor, environmental educator; b. Aurora, Ill., July 3, 1950; d. Robert C. and Elaine S. Waterhouse; m. Don D. Maronde; 1 child, Rachel Christine Hager. BS, U. Minn., Mpls., 1972. Tchr. pub. schs., Mpls., 1972—79; adminstr. Cooperating Fund Dr., St. Paul, 1980—83; cons. Corp. Philanthropy, Minn., 1984—89; exec. dir. Minn. Coun. Nonprofits, St. Paul, 1990—91, The Minn. Project, St. Paul, 1991—98; writer and editor various environ. orgns., Minn.; tchg. specialist U. Minn., St. Paul, 2001—. Editor: (stories) Renewing the Countryside: Minnesota; contbr. (nonfiction) The Farm as Natural Habitat, Time Soil and Children. Chair or bd. dirs. Land Stewardship Project, White Bear Lake, Minn., 1984—91; moderator Judson Meml. Bapt. Ch., Mpls., 1990—92, treas., 1993—99; bd. dirs. E. Oberholtzer Found., Marshall, Minn., 2004—. Fellow, Minn. Inst. Sustainable Agr., 2003—04. Baptist. Avocations: canoeing, travel. Home and Office: 818 3d Ave # 305 Excelsior MN 55331

WATERHOUSE, LYNETTE, mathematics educator; m. Robert Waterhouse; 1 child. BA in Sociology, Iona Coll., New Rochelle, NY, 1973; MS in Edn., Lehman Coll., Bronx, NY, 1987, Manhattan Coll., NY, 1991. Teacher NY State, 1984, Special Education Teacher NY State, 1991, Teacher 7-12 Social Studies NY State, 1995. Tchr. N.Y.C. Bd. Edn., 1984—93; math specialist Greenburgh Ctrl. Sch. Dist. 7, Hartsdale, NY, 1994—. Pres. Greenburgh Teachers Fedn., Hartsdale, NY, 2005—. Mem. Ethics Com., Yorktown, NY, 2005; pres., trustee John C. Hart Meml. Libr., Shrub Oak, NY, 2001—06; dir. NY State Theatre Inst., 2005—06. Scholarship, Manhattan Coll., 1989—91. Mem.: ASCD, Nat. Coun. for Social Studies, Nat. Coun. of Teachers of Math (assoc.), Kappa Delta Pi. Office: Greenburgh Ctrl Sch Dist#7 33 West HIllside Ave White Plains NY 10607 Office Phone: 914-948-8107. Business E-Mail: lwaterhouse@greenburgh7.com.

WATERMAN, DIANNE CORRINE, artist, educator, writer, religious organization administrator; b. Bklyn., Feb. 9, 1949; d. Beverly D. and Bernice Iona (Dowling) Waterman; children: Christopher, Tutankhamon, Joy, Derrick, Idiah, Kia, Sadid. BA, Hunter Coll., N.Y.C., 1984; postgrad., L.I. U., 1984-86; grad., N.Y.C. Cmty. Police Acad., 2000. Cert. leisure profl., NY; cert. correctional case mgr. Correctional Inst. Women, NC, 2005. Art instr./adminstr. Afro-Am. Experience, Hempstead, N.Y., 1968-73; art specialist/adminstr. MLK Youth Ctr., Westbury, N.Y., 1968-71; substance abuse counselor 5 Town Cmty. Ctr., Lawrence, N.Y., 1969-71; adminstr., counselor UJAMAA Acad., Hempstead, 1971-75; adminstr. asst. Inservice Learning Program Hunter Coll., 1981-84; unit mgr., youth divsn. counselor N.Y. State Divsn. for Youth, Bklyn., 1986-89; dean of women Claflin U., Orangeburg, SC, 1989-90; dir. recreation and art therapy Dept. Homeless Svcs., NYC, 1984-95; adj. prof. Touro Coll., Bklyn., 1995—; corrections officer Haynesville Correctional Ctr., Va., 1998-99; program dir. Hempstead Cmty. Action Program, 1999—; spiritual leader Loving Spirit Ministries Internat., 1999—, Women 2 Women, 2000—; clientele specialist GAP, Inc., 2000—. Founder Renaissance Woman Cons. Internat., NYC, 1984—, Artist in Focus, NYC, 1991-94; pres., founder Better Living Gen. Svc., NYC, 1990; designer Ethnic Wear, Empress Fashions, NYC, 1993—; project dir. Ednl. Alliance, 2001-03, Lillian Wald Cmty. Ctr; tech. assistance tng. coord., CJH Educational Svcs, Mission Tree Project, 2003-. Mem. PTA (pres. Bklyn. 1985), Citizens Com. N.Y.C., 1986, Dynamics of Leadership, Bklyn., 1995; dir. ednl. alliance Families First Project, 2000; founder/exec. dir. Women in Need Nationally for Econ. Resources and Spirituality (WINNERS), 2005; teen dir. Boys and Girls Club Metro of Atlanta, Douglasville, Ga., 2006. Recipient Outstanding Cooperation award Dept. Homeless Svcs., 1994, Outstanding Svc. award N.Y.C. Tech. Coll., 1987, Cert. of Appreciation Edwin Gould Svcs. for Children, 1984. Mem. Dress for Success Profl. Women's Group, Lioness Club, Zeta Iota Phi (sec. 1968—). Mem. Working Families Party. Avocations: art, writing, dance, jogging, public advocacy. Home and Office: 4065 Willow Ridge Rd Douglasville GA 30135 Personal E-mail: diannewaterman@yahoo.com.

WATERS, BETTY LOU, newspaper reporter, writer; b. Texarkana, Tex., June 13, 1943; d. Chester Hinton and Una Erby (Walls) W. AA, Texarkana Jr. Coll., 1963; BA, East Tex. State U., 1965. Gen. assignment reporter Galveston County Pub. Co., Galveston and Texas City, 1965-68; news and feature writer Ind. and Daily Mail, Anderson, S.C., 1968-69; reporter Citizen-Times newspaper, Asheville, N.C., 1969-74; edn. and med. reporter News Star World Pub. Co., Monroe, La., 1974-79; reporter, writer Delta Democrat Times, Greenville, Miss., 1980-89; staff writer Tyler (Tex.) Morning Telegraph, 1990—. Named Citizen of Yr., Sigma Sigma chpt. Omega Psi Phi, 2001; recipient hon. mentions, Tex. AP, 1966, news media award, N.C. Easter Seal Soc., 1973, 1st place award for articles, La. Press Women's Contest, 1978, 1st place for interview, 1979, for gen. news, Miss. Press Assn., 1983, 3d place award for feature writing, 1984, for investigative reporting, 1988, 1st place for best series of articles, 1990, Sch. Bell award for outstanding series, 1997, award for outstanding edn. series, Tex. State Tchrs. Assn., 1998, Tex. Coll. Women Changing the World award, 2000, Sch. Bell award for outstanding continuous coverage, Tex. State Tchrs. Assn., 2004. Mem. Sigma Delta Chi.

WATERS, CHARLOTTE ANN, investment management company executive; b. Millen, Ga., Oct. 2, 1947; d. Charles Redmond and Gracie Evelyn (Ellison) Waters. BA, Coll. Notre Dame, 1979; MBA, Loyola Coll., 1981. Office mgr. DESA Industries, Inc., Hunt Valley, Md., 1973—76; asst. corp. sec. Arundel Corp., Balt., 1976—78, corp. sec., 1978—81, corp. sec., legal adminstr., 1981—87; asst. corp. sec. T. Rowe Price, 1987—. Cons. project bus. div. Jr. Achievement; grad. Balt. County C. of C. Leadership Program; mem. Balt. County C. of C., small bus. coun., 1986—87; bd. dirs. Meals on Wheels Cen. Md., 1981—85, Jr. Achievement Met. Balt., 1983—87. Mem.: Nat. Soc. of DAR, Am. Soc. Corp. Secs.

WATERS, JENNIFER NASH, lawyer; b. Bridgeport, Conn., Dec. 21, 1951; d. Lewis William and Patricia (Cousins) W.; m. Todd David Peterson, Sept. 19, 1981; children: Elizabeth, Andrew. BA, Radcliffe, 1972; JD, Harvard, 1976. Bar: D.C. 1977, U.S. Supreme Ct. 1980. Clk. U.S. Ct. Appeals (D.C. cir.), Washington, 1976-77; assoc. Jones, Day, Reavis & Poque, Washington, 1977-79, Crowell & Moring, Washington, 1979-83, ptnr., 1983—. Mem. ABA (ho. of dels. 1997-99), Fed. Energy Bar Assn. (bd. dirs. 1988-99, v.p. 1994-95, pres. 1996-97). Office: Crowell & Moring LLP 1001 Pennsylvania Ave NW Fl 10 Washington DC 20004-2505

WATERS, JESSICA L., elementary school educator, psychologist; d. Sharyn K. Rigg. BS in Elem. Edn., U. St. Mary, Leavenworth, Kans., 1994; MA in Psychology, Regis U., 2001; postgrad., Inst. Transpersonal Psychology, 2003. Cert. elem. tchr. Colo. Elem. art tchr. Douglas County Schs., Castle Rock, Colo., 2002—; exec. dir. HeArtWork, Castle Rock. Exec. dir. WE Cancer-Care, Castle Rock. Pres. Am. Excellence USA Pageants, Tremont, Ill., 2005. Recipient Presidential Volunteer Service award, Presidential Call to Service award for Lifetime Achievement, Douglas County Outstanding Achievement award. Mem.: NOW, APA (assoc.), Am. Assn. Sch. Prins. (assoc.), Colo. Assn. Sch. Execs. (assoc.), Kappa Delta Phi (assoc.). Democrat. Office Phone: 720-979-6081.

WATERS, LISA LYLE, airport administrator, consultant; b. Hialeah, Fla., Dec. 11, 1962; d. Richard Donald and Marthal Annette Lyle; m. Edward Carl Waters, Mar. 8, 1986; children: Valerie Nicole, Rebecca Elizabeth. BS in Aviation Mgmt., Fla. Inst. Tech., Melbourne, 1984, AS in Flight Tech., 1984. Lic. comml. pilot. Airport planner Reynolds, Smith & Hills, Tampa, Fla., 1985-88; sr. airport planner LPA Group Inc., Tampa, 1988-89; noise abatement officer Palm Beach County Dept. Airports, West Palm Beach, Fla., 1990-93, mgr. noise abatement and cmty. affairs, 1994-96, dir. noise and tech. svcs., 1996—2000; owner, v.p. MEA Group Inc., West Palm Beach, 2000—. Mem. editl. bd.: Airport Noise Report, 1999—2001. Mem. bd. advisors Fla. Inst. Tech. Sch. of Aeronautics. Mem. Am. Assn. Airport Execs., Fla. Airport Mgrs. Assn., Fla. Aero Club. Avocations: children, cooking. Home: 2001 Palm Beach Lakes Blvd Ste 500 West Palm Beach FL 33409-6517

WATERS, MARY BRICE KIRTLEY, former federal agency administrator; B, U. Ill.; JD, George Mason U. Bar: D.C. Dir. agrl. task force Rep. Rsch. Com., 1981—82; legis. asst. Rep. Larry Hopkins, Ky., 1982—86; sr. dir., legis. counsel ConAgra Foods, 1986—2001; asst. sec. congl. rels. USDA, Washington, 2001—05. Past chair Washington Agrl. Roundtable; mem. Trade Policy Forum.

WATERS, MARY CATHERINE, sociology educator; b. Bronx, N.Y., Nov. 18, 1957; d. Michael Francis and Margaret Mary (O'Carroll) W.; m. Ric W. Bayly, Sept. 10, 1993. BA in Philosophy, Johns Hopkins U., 1978; MA in Sociology, U. Calif., Berkeley, 1981, MA in Demography, 1983, PhD in Sociology, 1986. Acting instr. dept. Sociol. U. Calif., Berkeley, 1983—85; asst. prof. dept. Sociol. Harvard U., Cambridge, Mass., 1986—90, John L. Loeb assoc. prof., 1991—93, prof., 1993—, chmn. dept. Sociol., 2001—05; prof. Harvard Coll., 1999—2004, M.E. Zukerman prof. sociology, 2006—. Mem. immigration com. Social Sci. Rsch. Coun., NYC, 1994; bd. dirs. Population Assn. Am., 2005—; cons. US Census Bur., Washington, 1993—95, adv. com. profl. associations, 1999—2005; cons. Bklyn. Children's Mus., 1994—98; cons. radio coverage of immigration WGBH Radio; cons. exhibits on African Am. history, immigration Strong Mus. of History, Rochester, NY, 1994; cons. project on social context of Puerto Rican child health and growth Wellesley Coll. Ctr. Rsch. on Women, 1995—97; internat. adv. bd. Ethnicities; consulting editor Am. Jour. Sociology, 1995—98; editl. bd. mem. Internat. Migration Rev. Author: (books) From Many Strands: Ethnic and Racial Groups in Contemporary America, 1990, Ethnic Options: Choosing Identities in America, 1990, Black Identities: West Indian Immigrant Dreams and American Realities, 1991 (Mira Komorovsky award Ea. Sociol. Soc., Otis Dudley Duncan award, Am. Sociol. Assn., Best Book in Ethnic Incorporation Am. Polit. Sci. Assn., Disting. Book award Cornell U. Ctr. Study Inequality, Thomas and Znaniecki award best book internat. migration Am. Sociol. Assn., 1999); co-editor (with Peggy Levitt): The Change Face of Home: The Transnational Lives of the Second Generation, 2002; co-editor: (with Joel Perlmann) The New Race Question: How the Census Counts Multiracial Individuals, 2002; co-editor: (with Fiona Devine) Social Inequalities in Comparative Perspective, 2003; co-editor: (with Philip Kasinitz and John H. Mollenkopf) Becoming New Yorkers: Ethnographies of the New Second Generation, 2004; contbr. articles to profl. jour., chapters to books. Bd. trustees Russell Sage Found., 2002—07; adv. bd. Ctr Rsch. on Immigration U. Houston; mem. Rsch. Network on Transition to Adulthood MacArthur Found., 2001—. Recipient Gertrude Jaeger prize, U. Calif. Berkeley, 1984, Hoopes award excellence in teaching, 1990, 1996, George R. Kharl award excellence in teaching, 1991, Shannon award, Nat. Inst. Child Health and Human Development, 1995—97; fellow Walter Channing Cabot Faculty, 2003—04; grantee Radcliffe Inst. Advanced Study, 2005—06; vis. scholar Russell Sage Found., 1991—92; Guggenheim fellow, 1993—94. Fellow: Am. Acad. Arts and Sciences; mem.: Regional Sci. Assn., Soc. for Study of Social Problems, Sociol. Rsch. Assn., Am. Philosophical Soc., Population Assn. Am., Ea. Sociol. Soc. (chair Candace Rogers award com. 1994, disting. contribution to scholarship com. 2002), Am. Sociol. Assn. (nom. com. mem. sect. race and ethnic minorities 1992, coun. mem. sect. race and ethnic minorities 1994—96, nom. com. mem. sect. race and ethnic minorities 1995, coun. mem. sect. population 1995—97, nominations com. 1995—97, chair sect. internat. migration, Thomas and Znaniecky Book Award Com. 2000). Democrat. Office: Dept Sociology Harvard Univ 540 William James Hall Cambridge MA 02138-2044 Office Phone: 617-495-3947. Office Fax: 617-496-5794. E-mail: mcw@wjh.harvard.edu.

WATERS, MAXINE, congresswoman; b. St. Louis, Aug. 15, 1938; d. Remus and Velma (Moore) Carr; m. Sidney Williams, July 23, 1977; children: Edward, Karen. Grad. in sociology, Calif. State U., L.A.; doctorate (hon.), Spelman Coll., NC Agrl.& Tech. State U., Morgan State U. Former tchr. Head Start. Mem. Calif. Assembly from dist. 48, 1976-91, Dem. caucus chair, 1984; mem. U.S. Congress from 35th Calif. dist., 1991—; mem. Banking, Fin., Judiciary, Urban Affairs com., Ho. subcom. on banking, capitol subcom. on banking, employment and tng. subcom. on vets., veterans affairs com., banking and fin. svcs. com., ranking house subcom. on gen. oversight and investigations; chair Congl. Black Caucus. Mem. Dem. Nat. Com., Dem. Congrl. Campaign com.; del. Dem. Nat. Conv., 1972, 76, 80, 84, 88, 92, mem. rules com. 1984; mem. Nat. Adv. Com. for Women, 1978—; bd. dirs. TransAfrica Found., Nat. Women's Polit. Caucus, Ctr. Nat. Policy, Clara Elizabeth Jackson Carter Found. Spellman Coll., Nat. Minority AIDS Project, Women for a Meaningful Summit, Nat. Coun. Negro Women, Black Women's Agenda; founder Black Women's Forum; dep. City Councilman David Cunningham, 1973-76, chief dep. Minority Whip; mem. Congl. Children's Working Group, Congl. Progressive Caucus, Dem. Nat. Com.; chair Dem. Caucus Spl. Com. election Reform; vice chair Steering Com. Mem. Calif. Peer Counseling Assn., Nat. Com. Econ. Conversion and Disarmament; mem. bd. Ctr. Study Sport in Soc., L.A. Women's Found. Named one of 100 Most Influential Black Americans, Ebony mag., 2006. Democrat. Office: US Ho Reps 2344 Rayburn Ho Office Bldg Washington DC 20515-0535 also: 10124 S Broadway Ste 1 Los Angeles CA 90003 Office Phone: 202-225-2201, 323-757-8900. Office Fax: 202-225-7854, 323-757-9506.*

WATERS, ROSEMARY R., biology professor; d. Leon H. and Margaret M. Rockwell; m. Jerry Waters, July 3, 1964; children: Craig R., David W. BA in Zoology magna cum laude, Calif. State U., Fresno, 1966, MA in Microbiology with distinction, 1972. Cert. ALS instr. Am. Heart Assn., 1975; dental asst. ADAA, 1962, registered Calif., 1972, cert. CC instr. Calif., 1972. Asst. quality control dir. Burton Parsons Pharmaceuticals, Seat Pleasant, Md., 1966—69; HS biology tchr. Queen of the Valley Acad., Fresno, 1969—72; dental assisting coord. Reedley Coll., Calif., 1972—94; biology prof. Fresno City Coll., 1994—. Infection control cons., Fresno, 1989—94. Author: (manual) Microbiology-A Manual of Laboratory Experiments. Mem. Chancellors Cir. State Ctr. C.C. Dist., Fresno, 2003—06; marriage ministry facilitator St. Paul Parish Newman Ctr., Fresno, 1984—96. Mem.: Calif. State U. Fresno Alumni (life), Cath. Bus. and Profl. Breakfast Club, Kappa Alpha Theta (Gamma Chi facility corp. sec. 1998—2006), Phi Kappa Phi (life). Avocations: marriage ministry, travel. Home: 1754 West Dovewood Ln Fresno CA 93711 Office: Fresno City Coll 1101 East University Ave Fresno CA 93741 Office Phone: 559-442-4600. Personal E-mail: rwatersfcc@comcast.net. Business E-Mail: rosemary.waters@fresnocitycollege.edu.

WATERS, SYLVIA, dance company artistic director; BS in Dance, Juilliard Sch.; studied with, Antony Tudor and Martha Graham; PhD (hon.), SUNY, Oswego, 1997. Prin. dance Alvin Ailey Am. Dance Theater, N.Y.C., 1968—74; artistic dir. Alvin Ailey Repertory Ensemble, N.Y.C., 1974—. Panelist Nat. Endowment for the Arts, N.Y. State Council on the Arts.

WATERS, ZENOBIA PETTUS, retired finance educator; b. Little Rock, Mar. 4, 1927; d. Henry Augustus and Lillie Liddell (Edwards) Pettus; m. Willie Waters, Jr., Jan. 29, 1949 (div. Feb. 1955); children: Pamela E. Reed, Zenobia W. Carter. BA cum laude, Philander Smith Coll., Little Rock, 1964; MEd, U. Wash., 1968. Cert. tchr. Ark., 1966. Office mgr. United Friends of Am., Little Rock, 1946—52; sec. State Dept. Edn., Little Rock, 1958—64; lectr. bus. Philander Smith Coll., Little Rock, 1965—67, asst. prof. bus., 1968—88, assoc. prof. bus. adminstrn., 1988—92, bd. dirs., faculty rep., 1976—80; asst. prof. bus. Ark. Bapt. Coll., Little Rock, 1970—84. Asst. bus. mgr. Philander Smith Coll., Little Rock, 1970—74, dir. summer sessions, 1970—81; spkr. in field. Mem. adv. bd.: Two Centuries of Methodism in Arkansas, 2000; contbr. articles to profl. jours. Dean West Gulf Regional Sch., 1975—77; founder Nat. Campaign Tolerance, Mont, Ala., 2005; vol. Dem. Party, Little Rock, 1986—92; contact person U.S. Presdl. Campaign, Little Rock, 1992; cert. lay spkr. United Meth. Ch., 1979—; pres. so. ctrl. juris United Meth. Women, 1984—88; bd. dirs. Gen. Bd. of Global Ministries, N.Y.C., 1984—88, Aldersgate Camp, Little Rock, 1976—79, St. Paul Sch. Theology, Kansas City, Mo., 1984—88, Mount Sequoyah, Fayetteville, Ark., 1984—88. Named Legend, Union Am. Meth. Ch., 2005; recipient Edn. Found. award, AAUW, 1983, Svc. award, Gen. Bd. Global Ministries/Women's Divsn., 1988; fellow, Nissan, 1989; grantee Ford Found. grantee, 1967. Mem.: AAUW, Nat. Campaign for Tolerance (founding mem.), Nat. Trust for Historic Preservation, United Meth. Women (pres. recognition pins 1963—2004, recognition pins 1963—2005), Phi Delta Pi, Iota Phi Lambda. Mem. Ame Ch. Avocations: reading, walking, writing. Home: 1701 Westpark Dr Apt 219 Little Rock AR 72204

WATERS BARHAM, TREVA RUTH, director; d. Daniel and LaNell Waters; m. Russell Barham, June 29, 2002. BA, East Tex. Bapt. U., Marshall, 2000; MA in Family Psychology, Hardin-Simmons U., Abilene, Tex., 2002. Dir. of first yr. experience LeTourneau U., Longview, Tex., 2003—. Mem. Ch. on the Rock, Longview, Tex., 2005—06. Mem.: Assn. for Christians in Student Devel. Office Phone: 903-233-4467.

WATFORD, DOLORES, elementary school educator; b. Feb. 26, 1951; BS in Edn., U. Hartford, 1973; MA in Psychol. Remedial Reading, Tchrs. Coll. Columbia U., 1974; MS in Spl. Edn., LI U., 1990, MS in Edn., 1993, profl. diploma in Sch. Adminstrn., 1997. Tchr. asst. Dalton Sch., Manhattan, NY, 1974—76; tchr. Pub. Sch., Conn., 1976—77; elem. tchr. Pub. Sch. 169, Bklyn., 1981—85; reading tchr. Pub. Sch. 167, Bklyn., 1985—2005; tchr. Pub. Sch. 191, Bklyn., 1985—99, Pub. Sch. 255, Bklyn., 1999—. Sec. Sch. Leadership Team, Bklyn., 2004—05. Pres. Bklyn. Reading Council, 2002. Recipient Svc. award, Bklyn. Reading Coun., 2004. Mem.: Internat. Reading Assn., NY State Reading Assn. (v.p. 2005—). Avocations: singing, aerobics, volleyball, reading. Home: One Rundle Ct Hempstead NY 11550 Personal E-mail: doloresbrc2002@msn.com.

WATKIN, VIRGINIA GUILD, retired lawyer; b. Clinton, Mass., July 28, 1925; d. George Cheever and Dorothy Louise (Springer) Guild; m. Donald M. Watkin, June 22, 1946; children: Henry M., Mary Ellen, Edward G., Ann Kymry. BA, Wellesley Coll., 1946; LLB, Columbia U., 1949; LLD (hon.), Norwich U., 1986. Bar: N.Y. 1949, D.C. 1952, Mass. 1963, U.S. Ct. Appeals (D.C. cir.) 1952, U.S. Supreme Ct. 1954, U.S. Dist. Ct. Mass. 1968, U.S. Ct. Appeals (1st cir.) 1968, U.S. Ct. Appeals (9th cir.) 1976, U.S. Ct. Appeals (4th cir.) 1980, U.S. Ct. Fed. Claims 1983, U.S. Ct. Appeals (5th cir.) 1993. Assoc. Covington & Burling, Washington, 1952-58; assoc. counsel Mass. Crime Commn., 1963-64; from assoc. to ptnr. Herrick, Smith, Donald, Farley & Ketchum, Boston, 1966-74; ptnr. Covington & Burling, Washington, 1974-2000; ret., 2000. Bd. vis. Columbia U. Sch. Law; bd. overseers Wellesley Coll. Stone Ctr. for Develop. Svcs. and Studies, 1989—, Wellesley Coll. Ctr. for Rsch. on Women, 1990—. Author: Taxes and Tax Harmonization in the Central American Common Market, 1967; contbr. articles to profl. jours. Trustee Northfield (Mass.) Mt. Hermon Sch. Bd., 1978-83, Norwich U., Northfield, Vt., 1977-90, Wellesley Coll., 1989—. Mem. ABA, Am. Law Inst., D.C. Bar Assn. (pres. 1993—), Soc. Woman Geographers, Columbia Law Sch. Alumni Assn. (regional v.p.), Wellesley Coll. Alumnae Assn. (bd. dirs. 1985-88), Cosmos Club. Home: 3001 Veazey Ter NW Washington DC 20008-5454 Office: Covington & Burling PO Box 7566 1201 Pennsylvania Ave NW Washington DC 20044-7566

WATKINS, ANN ESTHER, mathematics professor; b. L.A., Jan. 10, 1949; d. Rex Devere and Burnice Gordine (Duckworth) Hamilton; m. William Earl Watkins, Oct. 5, 1973; children: Mary Ann, Barbara Lee. BA, Calif. State U., Northridge, 1970, MS, 1972; PhD, UCLA, 1977. Instr. math. Los Angeles Pierce Coll., Woodland Hills, Calif., 1975-90; prof. math. Calif. State U., Northridge, 1990—. Editor: (with Albers, Rodi) New Directions in Two Year College Mathematics, 1985; co-author: (with Landwehr) Exploring Data, 1986, 2d edit., 1994, (with Landwehr, Swift) Exploring Surveys, 1987, (with Albers, Loftsgaarden, Rung) Statistical Abstract of Undergraduate Programs in the Mathematical Sciences and Computer Science, 1992 (with Scheaffer, Gnanadesikan, Witmer) Activity-Based Statistics, 1996, 2d edit., (with Scheaffer, Cobb) Statistics in Action, 2004; assoc. editor: American Mathematical Monthly, 1996-2000; editor Coll. Math. Jour., 1989-94; co-editor: (with Apostol, Mugler, Scott and Sterrett) A Century of Calculus, Part II, 1992; mem. editl. bd. Jour. Statis. Edn., 1992-95; mem. adv. bd. Math. Horizons mag., 1992-2001. Grantee NSF, 1987-90, 92—. Fellow Am. Statis. Assn.; mem. Math. Assn. Am. (2d v.p. 1987-88, pres. 2001-03, chair So. Calif. sect. 1988-89, gov. So. Calif. sect. 1995-98), Nat. Coun. Tchrs. Math. Business E-Mail: ann.watkins@csun.edu.

WATKINS, BRENDA L., music educator; b. Norfolk, Va., Apr. 18, 1946; d. Rosser Lee and Constance Norsworthy Jones; m. Claude William Watkins, Nov. 1, 1964; 1 child, Kimberly Lynn, Cynthia Anne, Katherine Lee. Student, William & Mary Coll., 1964, Old Dominion U., 1964-68. Adminstrv. asst. Va. Nat. Bank, Norfolk, 1964-71; pre-sch. tchr. asst. Westwood Hill Bapt. Ch., Virginia Beach, 1972-74; pre-sch. music tchr. Bellamy Manor and Broad Bay Manor, Virginia Beach, 1993-96; music tchr. Court House Pre-Sch., Virginia Beach, 1994-97, Great Neck Pre-Sch., Virginia Beach, 1994-97; ind. music tchr. Music and Arts Music, Chesapeake, Va., 1998—. Author, editor: Childhood Memories, 1994. Vol. info. desk Assn. for Rsch. and Enlightment, Virginia Beach, 1999. Mem. Music Tchrs. Nat. assn., Tidewater Music Tchrs. Assn., Order of Ea. Star (Kempsville chpt.), Ladies Oriental Shrine N.Am. (Zulekia Ct. #35), U.S. Amateur Ballroom Dancers Assn., Inc., Va. Dept. Game and Inland Fisheries (cert. boat safety). Lutheran. Avocations: writing, music, boating, walking. Home: 612 Cardamon Ct Virginia Beach VA 23464-1901

WATKINS, CAROLE S., human resources specialist, medical products executive; b. 1960; BA in Bus., Franklin U., Columbus, Ohio. With O.M. Scott & Sons, Lazarus, Huntington Banks; mem. staff Ltd. Brands, Columbus, Ohio, 1989—96; v.p. human resources Pharm. Distbn. Cardinal Health, Inc., Columbus, Ohio, 1996—2000, sr. v.p. pharm. distbn. and provider svcs., 2000, exec. v.p. human resources, 2000, chief human resources officer. Office: Cardinal Health 7000 Cardinal Pl Dublin OH 43017

WATKINS, CHERYL DENISE, special education educator; b. Chgo., Dec. 15, 1963; d. Henry Eugene and Jean (Ingram) W. BS Edn. in Spl. Edn., Chgo. State U., 1987; MEd, U. Ill., 1992. Tchr. children with spl. needs Chgo. Bd. Edn., 1987—. Cons. in field; adj. faculty Columbia Coll., Chgo., 1993, Nat. Louis U., Chgo. State U., Elmhurst Coll.; spkr. ednl. topics Chgo., St. Louis, Ill., Iowa, Fla., Md., Ala., Tex. Author: You Can Do Anything: A Story for Ryan, 1993, Living with Autism, 1995. Vol. workshops Cabrini Green Tutoring Program, Chgo. Recipient Golden Apple award Golden Apple Found., 1991, Disting. Alumni award Nat. Assn. for Equal Opportunity in Higher Edn./Chgo. State U., 1992, Kizzy award, 1992, Tchr. Achiever award Michael Jordan Found. Edn. Club, 1993, Swanegan Tchr. award Trinity United Ch. of Christ, 1996, Kathy Osterman award for superior pub. svc., Chgo., 1997; named Outstanding Young Woman in Am., 1986. Mem. Nat. Bd. Profl. Teaching Standards (spl. needs com.), Kappa Delta Pi, Phi Delta Kappa, Delta Sigma Theta. Avocations: roller skating, reading, cake decorating, writing, travel.

WATKINS, DAPHNE C., entrepreneur, consultant, advocate; b. Newport News, Va., July 5, 1981; d. Donald C. and Lucy B. Watkins. BA in Anthropology, U. N.C., Wilmington, 2002; PhD in Health Edn., Tex. A&M U., College Station, 2006. Rsch. asst. Ctr. Study of Health Disparities, College Station, Tex., 2003—06; rsch. fellow Inst. Social Rsch. NIMH, Ann Arbor, Mich., 2006—. Dir., CEO, Vernell Cons. Group, Ann Arbor; cons. in field, 2003—. Mem. bd. med. advisors: Black Health Mag.; contbr. scientific papers. Adv. bd. mem. Supernova Mentoring Program, Bryan, Tex.; vol. Ch. Media. Named Grad. Student of Yr., Dept. Health and Kinesiology, 2006; Mentorship and Edn. Program scholar, NIMH and U. N.Mex, 2005—07, Minority scholar, U. Tex. Permian Basin, 2006. Mem.: AAPHERD, APHA, Emerging Scholars Interdisciplinary Network, Delta Sigma Theta. Achievements include research in Black men and mental health; health education of minority populations; first African American news anchor, WSFX Fox 26 in Wilmington, N.C. Avocations: reading, writing, travel, dancing.

WATKINS, DEBORAH KAREN, epidemiology investigator, educator; b. Mt. Pleasant, Pa., Sept. 10, 1950; d. Thomas Earl and Berniece Helen (Kapelewski) W. AB, George Washington U., 1972; MS, Georgetown U., 1990. Production editor Am. Pub. Health Assn., Washington, 1972-79; exec. dir. Soc. for Occupational and Eviron. Health, Washington, 1979-81; dir. legis. affairs Pa. Environ. Coun., Phila., 1982-83; rsch. asst. prof. dept. family medicine Georgetown U., Washington, 1983—2002, dep. dir. divsn. occupl. health studies, 1990—2002; mng. scientist Exponent, Inc., Washington, 2004—. Adj. asst. prof. Georgetown U., Washington, 2002—. Mem. Soc. Occupl. and Eviron. Health (gov. coun. 1987-93), Soc. Epidemiologic Rsch., Soc. Profl. Journalists. Avocations: British history, needlepoint. Office: Exponent Inc 1730 Rhode Island Ave NW Washington DC 20036 Business E-Mail: dwatkins@exponent.com.

WATKINS, ELIZABETH SIEGEL, history professor; b. Providence, Feb. 24, 1962; d. Edward Phillip and Judith Semerik Siegel; children: Emily Rachel, Ellen Michelle. AB cum laude, Harvard U., Cambridge, Mass., 1984, PhD, 1996. Assoc. prof. history of health scis. program U. Calif., San Francisco, 2004—. Author: On the Pill: A Social History of Oral Contraceptives, 1950-1970, 1998, The Estrogen Elixir: A History of Hormone Replacement Therapy in America, 2007. Office: U Calif San Francisco 3333 California St Ste 485 San Francisco CA 94143-0850 Office Phone: 415-476-1245.

WATKINS, ESTHER SHERROD, secondary school educator, school librarian; b. Port Gipson, Miss., June 4, 1939; d. Raphael Sherrod and Carrie Powell Sherrod Peterson; m. John H. Watkins (dec.); children: Glenna Watkins Tolbert, MD, John Timothy. BA, Tougaloo Coll., Miss., 1960—64; Calif. tchng. credential, Calif. State U. Los Angeles, 1966—72; MA, U. of San Francisco, 1978—79. Sch. reading coord. Samuel Gompers Mid. Sch., Los Angeles, 1968—69, English/reading tchr., 1963—69; English tchr. Robert Frost Mid. Sch., Granada Hills, 1969—79, Sun Valley Mid. Sch., 1979—84; sch. writing coord. Verdugo HS, Tugunga, 1984—95; English tchr. Verdugo Hills HS, 1984—95, libr., 1995—2001. Del. NEA, 2000—01; active union mem. UTLA, 1995—2001. Author: Using Novels to Help High School Students to Cope, 1979. Elder Pasadena Christian Ch., 1969—; nat. bd. Delta Sigma Theta. Recipient 5 awards for fostering excellence in writing, L.A. Sch. Dist. Mem.: YWCA, Delta Sigma Theta. Achievements include serving as interim counselor co-dept. chair, reading compter coord. and training tchr. supr. Office Phone: 818-371-4096.

WATKINS, JOAN MARIE, osteopath, physician; b. Anderson, Ind., Mar. 9, 1943; d. Curtis David and Dorothy Ruth (Beckett) W.; m. Stanley G. Nodvik, Dec. 25, 1969 (div. Apr. 1974). BS, West Liberty State Coll., 1965; Cert. of Grad. Phys. Therapy, Ohio State U., 1966; DO, Phila. Coll. Osteo., 1972; M of Health Professions Edn., U. Ill., Chgo., 1986; MPH, U. Ill., 1989. Diplomate Osteo. Nat. Bds., Am. Bd. Preventive Medicine, Am. Bd. Occupl. and Environ. Medicine, Am. Bd. Emergency Medicine. Resident in phys. medicine and rehab. U. Pa., 1973—74; emergency osteo. physician Cooper Med. Ctr., Camden, 1974-79, Shore Meml. Hosp., Somers Point, NJ, 1979-81, St. Francis Hosp., Blue Island, Ill., 1981-82, Mercy Hosp. and Med. Ctr., Chgo., 1982-90, dir. emergency ctr., 1984-88; resident in occupl. and preventive medicine U. Ill., 1988-90; corp. med. dir. occupl. health svc. Univ. Cmty. Hosp., Tampa, 1992—. Fellow Am. Coll. Occupl. and Environ. Medicine, Am. Soc. Preventive Medicine, Fla. Assn. Occupl. and Environ. Medicine (pres. 1999-2001). Avocations: sailing, needlecrafts, swimming. Home: 4306 Harbor House Dr Tampa FL 33615-5408 Office: Univ Community Hosp Occupational Health Svcs 3100 E Fletcher Ave Tampa FL 33613-4613 Office Phone: 813-390-6558. Office Fax: 813-615-7711.

WATKINS, KAREN J., librarian; b. Albuquerque, July 5, 1947; d. Clifford Ray and Glenys Bell (Frevert) Jurgensen; m. William Gray Watkins, May 15, 1976. BA magna cum laude, St. John's Coll., Santa Fe, 1967; MA, U. Denver, 1972; postgrad., U. Calif., Berkeley, 1980-82. Libr. Santa Fe Pub. Schs., 1972-78; libr. cons. N.Mex. State Libr., Santa Fe, 1978-84, adminstr., 1984-89, dir., 1989—. Mem. AAUW (pres. Santa Fe chpt. 1991), N.Mex. Libr. Assn. (pres. 1988-89), N.Mex. Libr. Found. (bd. dirs. 1994), Rotary (bd. dirs. 1994).

WATKINS, LINDA THERESA, retired educational association administrator; b. York, Pa., Sept. 29, 1947; d. Nathan Franklin and Madelyn Marie (Mandi) Watkins; m. Hugh Jerald Silverman, June 22, 1968 (div. Apr. 1983); children: Claire Christine Goberman, Hugh Christopher Silverman; m. Patrick Grim. BA, Muhlenberg Coll., 1968; MA, San Jose (Calif.) State Coll., 1970; PhD, Stanford (Calif.) U., 1977; cert., Hofstra U., 1991. Rsch. asst. prof. LI Rsch. Inst., Stony Brook, NY, 1977-79; asst. prof. NYU, N.Y.C., 1979-85; rsch. assoc. dept. psychiatry SUNY, Stony Brook, 1985-87; dir. rsch., planning and grants mgmt. Bd. Coop. Ednl. Svcs. Eastern Suffolk, Patchogue, NY, 1987—2004; ret., 2004. Cons. Tele-Niger Evaluation Project, Paris, 1972, Dowling Coll., Oakdale, NY, 1991, Mid. States Assn. Colls. and Schs.; interviewer Am. Inst. Rsch., Kensington, Md., 1973; survey cons. Redbook mag., NY, 1987; adj. lectr. SUNY Sch. Soc. Welfare, 1994. Contbr. articles to profl. jours. NDEA fellow, 1972, Rsch. grantee, ABC, 1978, Ronald McDonald Children's Charities, 1988. Mem.: APA. Avocation: house restoration. Home: 99 Sweezey St Patchogue NY 11772-4160 Business E-Mail: ltwatkin@suffolk.lib.ny.us.

WATKINS, M(ARTHA) ANNE, family practice nurse practitioner; b. Vicksburg, Mich., Feb. 9, 1961; d. George H. and Coleene M. (Shearer) W. ADN, S.W. Mich. Coll., 1984; BSN, U. Mich., 1988, MSN, 2003. RN, Mich. Staff nurse Lee Meml. Hosp., Dowagiac, Mich.; clin. nurse II thoracic intensive care U. Mich. Hosps., Ann Arbor; emergency nurse Lee Meml. Hosp., Dowagiac, Mich.; critical care nurse Mercy Meml. Hosp., St. Joseph, Mich.; house supr. Lee Meml. Hosp., Dowagiac, Mich., dir. med. surg. pediat., 1995, v.p. patient care svcs., 1996—2001; family nurse practioner Planned Parenthood Mid Mich. Alliance, Benton Harbor, Mich., 2004—. Mem. Phi Theta Kappa. Home: 303 Mcphil Dr Dowagiac MI 49047-1012 Office: Planned Parenthood Mid Mich Alliance 1161 E Napier Benton Harbor MI 49022 Office Phone: 269-926-2042.

WATKINS, MELYNDA, chemist, researcher; b. Shaw AFB, S.C., Jan. 23, 1971; d. Leonard Virgil and Nancy Ruth Watkins. Student, Monash U., Melbourne, Victoria, Australia, 1992; BS in Chemistry, U. Ill., 1994. Asst. scientist Fujisawa USA, Melrose Park, Ill., 1995-96; assoc. scientist Solvay Pharms., Marietta, Ga., 1996-97; sr. rsch. scientist Triangle Pharms., Durham, N.C., 1997—. Adv. Rape Crisis Svcs., Urbana, Ill., 1993-95. Mem. Am. Chem. Soc., Pharm. Stability Discussion Group. Avocations: volleyball, exercise, travel. Home: 8004 Crichton Ln Durham NC 27713-6334

WATKINS, RENEE E., adult education educator; b. Berlin, Feb. 7, 1932; arrived in US, 1941; d. Kirt Max and Ruth Warburg Neu; 1 child, Cynthia Ruth. PhD, Harvard U., 1959. Tchr. Ithaca Coll., NY, 1961—63, Smith Coll., 1963—67, U. Mass., Boston, 1967—91. Assoc. prof. U. Mass., Boston, 1967—91. Grantee, Fulbright Found., Italy, 1959—60. Mem.: Phi Beta Kappa. Home: 855 Indian Rock Ave Berkeley CA 94707

WATKINS, SARA, musician; b. June 8, 1981; Mem. bank Nickel Creek; with Sugar Hill Records, 1998—. Musician: (recordings) Nickel Creek, 2000 (Cert. Gold, 2002, 2 Grammy nominations, 2001), This Side, 2002 (Cert. Gold, 2003, Grammy award for Contemporary Folk Album, 2003), (CD) Ten From Little Worlds, Not All Who Wander Are Lost, G.I.gantic, Faraway Land, Let it Fall, 26 Miles, More Than Words, Pickin' on ZZ Top, Philadelphia Folk Festival: 40th Anniversary, Telluride Bluegrass Festival: Reflection, Vol. 1, This is Americana, Vol 1: A View From Sugar Hill, Pickin' on the Rolling Stones, Prancer Returns, Further Down the Old Plank Road. Named Southwest Regional champions, Pizza Hut Internat. Bluegrass Music Showdown, 1994, Ariz. State Fiddle Champion, 1996, Emerging Artist of Yr., IBMA, 2000, Instrumental Group of YR., 2001; named one of Five Music Innovators for the Millennium, Time mag., 2000. Office: Q-Prime 131 S 11th St Nashville TN 37206

WATKINS, SHERRY LYNNE, elementary school educator; b. Bloomington, Ind., Oct. 13, 1944; d. Quentin Odell and Velma Ruth W. BSEd, Ind. U., 1966, MSEd, 1968. Tchr. 4th grade North Grove Elem. Sch., Ctr. Grove Sch. Dist., Greenwood, Ind., 1966-68; tchr. 4th and 6th grades John Strange Sch., Met. Dist. of Wash. Twp., Indpls., 1968-91; tchr. 4th grade Allisonville Sch. Met. Sch. Dist. of Wash. Twp., Indpls., 1991—. Bd. dirs. ISTA Ins. Trust and Fin. Svcs. Mem. People for Ethical Treatment of Animals. Mem.: AAUW, ACLU, NEA (nat. del. 1978—), World Confedn. Orgn. of Tchg. Profls. (del. Costa Rica 1990), Washington Twp. Edn. Assn. (pres. 1986—89), Ind. Tchrs. Assn. (state del. 1966—), Alpha Omicron Pi, Delta Kappa Gamma (chpt. pres. 1992—94, chmn. coordinating coun. Indpls. area 1994—96, state legislature chair 1997—99, state profl. affairs chair 2001—03). Avocations: travel, cultural activities. Office: Allisonville Sch 4920 E 79th St Indianapolis IN 46250-1615 Personal E-mail: sherryindy3@aol.com. Business E-Mail: swatkins@msdwt.k12.in.us.

WATLEY, NATASHA, Olympic athlete; b. Canoga Pk., Calif., Nov. 27, 1981; d. Edwin and Carolyn. Grad., UCLA, 2003. Mem. U.S. Nat. Team, 2002—, U.S. Women's Softball Team, Athens Olympic Games, 2004. Named NFCA First Team All-Am., 2000, 2001, 2002, 2003, MVP of ISF World Championships, 2002, Pac-10 Player of the Yr., 2003; recipient Honda award for Top College Female Athlete, 2003. Achievements include invention of mem. Gold medal U.S. Nat. Team, ISF World Championships, 2002, Pan Am. Games, 2003, Athens Olympic Games, 2004; mem. NCAA Champion UCLA Bruins, Women's Coll. World Series, 2003.

WATNE, DARLENE CLAIRE, county official; b. Minot, N.D., Feb. 11, 1935; d. Charles A. and Anna Marie Widdel (Fjeld) W.; m. Clair A. Watne, Mar. 27, 1954; children: Carmen, Steven, Nancy, Matthew. Court reporting diploma, Minot (N.D.) Bus. Coll., 1975; grad., Real Estate Inst., 1991. Cert. residential real estate specialist, N.D. Exec. sec. Grand Exalted Ruler Elks, Minot, ND, 1964-75; pres. Bus. Coll., Minot, 1974-76; ct. reporter N.W. Judicial Dist., Minot, 1976-90; real estate broker Watne Realtors Better Homes & Gardens, Minot, 1990-99; mem. N.D. Senate from 5th dist., Bismark, 1994—2001; commr. Ward County, ND, 1994—. Active Joint Civil Svcs. to the Poor, 1995-2001. Bd. dirs. ARC, Salvation Army, Red Cross; numerous state polit. interim senate coms. Named Minot Woman of Distinction in Bus. and Industry, 1993, Liberty award ND Bar Assn., 2000, named Citizen of Yr. ND Builders Assn., 2001. Republican. Avocations: reading, laking. Home: 520 28th Ave SW Minot ND 58701-7065

WATROUS, NAOMA DICKSION, retired clinical psychologist; b. Pauls Valley, Okla. d. William M. and Almeda (Cosby) Dickson. BS, Okla. Coll. for Women, 1940; EdD, Okla. U., 1960; MS, Okla. State U., 1950; cert. in gerontology, U. Calif., Long Beach, 1993. Lic. clin. psychologist, Washington; lic. marriage, family and child counselor, gerontologist. Clin. psychologist VA Hosp., Washington, 1961-72; supervisory clin. psychologist Washington D.C. Mental Health Svc., 1972-76, clin. psychologist, 1988-96, VA Hosp. and Med. Svcs., Long Beach, Calif., 1976-88; ret., 1996. Cons. KDH Mental Health Svc., Noble, Okla., 1996-97. Amb. Noble C. of C., Okla., 1997-98; vol. Ret. Srs. Vol. Program, 2000—. Recipient Cert. of Commendation Dept. Human Svcs., Govt. of D.C., 1990, 95. Mem. APA (group psychotherapy charter mem.). Avocations: painting, art therapy. Home: 1419 Prospect Dr Wynnewood OK 73098-1015 Personal E-mail: dick4139_ou@ionet.net.

WATSON, BETTY, artist; b. Passaic, N.J., Feb. 19, 1928; d. Joseph Francis and Doris Lillian (Wilcox) Rean; m. Robert Watson; children: Winthrop, Caroline Watson Keens. Student, Phoenix Sch. of Design, N.Y.C., 1946, Pa. Acad. Fine Arts, 1947, Art Students League, N.Y.C., 1947, 48, 49-51; BA, Wellesley Coll., Mass., 1949; postgrad., NYU, 1950-51; MFA, U. N.C., 1965. Asst. in art Barnard Coll., N.Y.C., 1949-51; asst. to Ferdinand Roten, Art Dealer Balt., 1952; instr. art Calif. State U., Northridge, 1968-69. One-woman shows include U. NC, Greensboro, 1962, East End Gallery, Provincetown, Mass., 1965, Place Gallery, Provincetown, Mass., 1966, Newsweek Gallery, NYC, 1966, Gallery Saint, Norfolk, Va., 1966, Elliott U. Ctr., 1972, High Point NC Theatre and Exhbn. Ctr., Morehead Gallery, 1982, GAL Gallery, Greensboro, 1993, Francis Marion U., SC, 1995, Jackson Libr. U. NC, Greensboro, 2000, retrospective exhbn. Green Hill Ctr. for NC Art, Greensboro, 2006; exhibited in group shows at Nat. Acad. Design, NYC, Am. Gallery, NYC, A.M. Sachs Gallery, NYC, Beilin Gallery, NYC, Waverly Gallery, NYC, Jack Tanzer Gallery, NYC, Grand Rapids Mich. Art Mus., Provincetown Mass. Art Assn., NC Mus. Art, Raleigh, Montclair (NJ) Arts Mus., South Eastern Ctr. Contemporary Art, Winston-Salem, NC, Calif. State U., Northridge, Collector's Gallery at NC Mus. Art, Raleigh, Weatherspoon Mus., U. NC, Greensboro, Ctr. for Creative Leadership, Greensboro, NC, 305 West Cameron Gallery, Chapel Hill, NC, Corp. Art Directions, NYC, 1991-95; author: Betty Watson Paintings: Five Decades, 1999. Mem. Phi Beta Kappa. Home: 4321 Galax Trail Greensboro NC 27410

WATSON, BETTY A., mathematics educator; b. Marion, Ohio, Aug. 3, 1965; d. Norma L. and Robert L. Horne; m. William B. Watson, July 25, 1992; children: Kasi Paige, Adrian Blair. BS Secondary Edn. Math., Ea. Ky. U., Richmond, 1987; MA Edn., Morehead State U., Ky, 1995. Tchr. math. Johnson Ctrl. H.S., Paintsville, Ky., 1987—. Named to Who's Who Among Am. Tchrs., Who's Who, 1998, 1999, 2000, 2002, 2003, 2004, 2005. Mem.: NEA, East Ky. Coun. Tchrs. Math. (sec. 1998—, Disting. Math Tchr. 2004), Ky. Coun. Tchrs. Math., Nat. Coun. Tchrs. Math., Ky. Edn. Assn. Home: PO Box 642 Paintsville KY 41240 Office: Johnson Central High School 257 North Mayo Trail Paintsville KY 41240 Personal E-mail: bwatson@foothills.net. E-mail: bwatson@johnson.k12.ky.us.

WATSON, BETTY ANN, early childhood education professor; b. Detroit, June 30, 1942; d. Lucien B. and Laura (Scholes) Work; m. Zearl David Watson, Nov. 21, 1970. AA, Rochester Coll. (formerly Mich. Christian), 1962; BA, Harding U. (formerly Harding Coll.), 1964; MA, Mich. State U., 1969; EdD, U. Memphis (formerly Memphis State U.), 1992. First grade tchr. Anderson Elem. Sch., Trenton, Mich., 1964-68; prof. early childhood and children's lit. elem. edn. Harding U., Searcy, Ark., 1969—98, dir. early childhood edn., 1998—. Mem. Diamond Reading Com. Recipient Disting. Tchrs. award, Harding U., 1997. Mem.: Am. Assn. Colls. for Tchr. Edn., Internat. Reading Assn., Southern Early Childhood Assn., Nat. Assn. for Edn. Young Children, Kappa Delta Phi (counselor). Church Of Christ. Office: Harding U Searcy AR 72149-0001 Office Phone: 501-279-4532.

WATSON, BRENDA BENNETT, insurance company executive; b. Decatur, Ga., Aug. 26, 1940; d. Robert Joseph and Clarissa Mae (Weekes) Bennett; m. James H. Pair Jr., Apr. 4, 1969 (div. Aug. 1993); children: Richard S. Pair, Randall J. Pair, Ronald G. Pair; m. James Leigh Watson, Sept. 9, 1995. Student, DeKalb Coll., 1971. Lic. property and casualty agt., Fla., Ga., Okla., Tenn., Tex. Underwriter W. K. Stringer Co., Atlanta, 1961-65, Tharpe & Assocs., Atlanta, 1965-68; sr. v.p. Alexander - Howden, Atlanta, 1968-82; exec. v.p., ptnr. Pair Underwriting Mgrs. Inc., Atlanta, 1982-86; pres. Walkingstick-LaGere-Pair Underwriting Mgrs., Inc., Chandler, Okla., 1986-88; exec. v.p., dir. LaGere-Walkingstick Ins. Agy., Chandler, Okla., 1988—. Exec. v.p. Nat. Am. Ins. Co., Chandler, Okla., 1987—, Austin, Tex., 1999—; exec. v.p., bd. dirs. Chandler Ins. Ltd., Cayman Islands, 1985—. Dir., past pres. Gateway to Prevention and Recovery, 1994-98. Mem. Nat. Assn. Ins. Women (pres. Atlanta chpt. 1978-79, Woman of Yr. 1979-80). Republican. Episcopalian. Office: Wells Fargo Bank Bldg 2028 E Ben White Blvd Ste 200 Austin TX 78741 E-mail: bwatson@naico.com.

WATSON, CAROLINE, secondary school educator; b. Huntington, NY, July 14, 1941; d. Edwin Shepard Watson and Helen Obiedzeuski. BS, NYU, 1964; MA, CW Post, 1976. Tchr. Middle Island Sch., NY, 1965—67; dance specialist Ward Melville HS, Setauket, NY, 1967—69; dance specialist, coord. Smithtown Sch. Dist., NY, 1969—96; choreographer, dir. Waldo Theater, 1998—2003. Choreographer, dir. Waldo Theatre, Waldo Boro, Maine, 1998. Choreographer (various theatre groups), 1967—80; performer choreographer NY Area, 1964—75, performer Summer Stock Cmty. Theatre. Mem.: Smithtown Lions. Achievements include development of dance program that fulfilled a physical edn. requirement for HS. Home: 30 Ledgewood Dr Boothbay ME 04537

WATSON, CATHERINE ELAINE, journalist; b. Mpls., Feb. 9, 1944; d. Richard Edward and LaVonne (Slater) W.; m. Al Sicherman (div.); children: Joseph Sicherman, David Sicherman. BA in Journalism, U. Minn., 1966; MA in Teaching, Coll. of St. Thomas, 1971. Reporter Mpls. Star Tribune, 1966-72; editor Picture mag., 1972-78, Travel sect., 1978—2004; editor in chief Galena (Ill.) Gazette, 1990-91. Instr., online mentor Split Rock Arts Program, U. Minn., 1996-2006; sr. travel editor Star Tribune, 2001-04. Author: Travel Basics, 1984, Roads Less Traveled: Dispatches from the Ends of the Earth, 2005 (named Best Book Soc. Am. Travel Writers - Ctrl. States, 2001); contbr. articles to newspapers and travel mags. and books. Recipient Newspaper Mag. Picture Editor's award Pictures of Yr. Competition, 1974, awards for writing and photography Soc. Am. Travel Writers, 1983-2004, Photographer of Yr. award, 1990, Alumna of Notable Achievement award U. Minn. Coll. Liberal Arts, 1994; rsch. grant Jerome Found./Gen. Mills Found., 2004; named Lowell Thomas Travel Journalist of Yr., 1990, Lowell Thomas Bronze awards 1994, 96, 2003. Mem. Am. Newspaper Guild, Soc. Am. Travel Writers, Phi Beta Kappa, Alpha Omicron Pi.

WATSON, DIANE EDITH, congresswoman; b. LA, Nov. 12, 1933; d. William Allen Louis and Dorothy Elizabeth (O'Neal) Watson. AA, L.A. City Coll., 1954; BA, UCLA, 1956; MS, Calif. State U., L.A.; PhD, Claremont Grad. Sch., 1987. Tchr., sch. psychologist L.A. Unified Sch. Dist., 1960-69, 73-74; assoc. prof. Calif. State U., L.A., 1969-71; health occupations specialist Bur. Indsl. Edn., Calif. Dept. Edn., 1971-73; mem. L.A. Unified Sch. Bd., 1975-78, Calif. Senate from dist. 26, 1978-98, chairperson health and human svcs. com.; US amb. to Micronesia US Dept. of State, 1999-2001; mem. U.S. Congress from 33d Calif. dist., 2001—, mem. govt. reform com. and internat. rels. com. Mem. Legis. Black Caucus, edn. com., budget and fiscal rev. com., criminal procedure com., housing and land use com. Calif State Sen.; del. Dem. Nat. Conv., 1972—; mem. Dem. Nat. Com.; mem. exec. com. Nat. Conf. State Legislators Author: Health Occupations Instructional Units-Secondary Schools, 1975, Planning Guide for Health Occupations, 1975; co-author: Introduction to Health Care, 1976. Recipient Mary Church Terrell award, 1976, Brotherhood Crusade award, 1981, Black Woman of Achievement award NAACP Legal Def. Fund, 1988; named Alumnus of Yr., UCLA, 1980, 82. Mem. Calif. Assn. Sch. Psychologists, L.A. Urban League, Calif. Tchrs. Assn., Calif. Commn. on Status Women. Democrat. Roman Catholic. Office: US Ho Reps 125 Cannon HOB Washington DC 20515-0533 also: 4322 Wilshire Blvd Ste 302 Los Angeles CA 90010 Office Phone: 202-225-7084. Fax: 202-225-2422. Office Phone: 323-965-1422. Office Fax: 323-965-1113.*

WATSON, DOROTHY COLETTE, real estate broker; b. Boston, Oct. 26, 1938; d. Edward Vincent and Ethel May (Sanford) Walsh; m. Gerald C. McDonald, May 23, 1959 (dec.); children: Gerald C., Deborah L., McDonald Hermanson, Gregory Christopher (dec.); m. William G. Watson, May 29, 1993. Student, Regis Coll., 1957-59; BS, Harvard U., 1960. Various secretarial positions, 1958-59; model, 1958-75; guidance counselor Newton H.S., 1959-60; model, personal shopper Filene's, Chestnut Hill, Mass., 1974-78; designer program covers Boston Red Sox, 1974-76; real estate broker Channing Assocs., Inc., Wellesley, Mass., 1976-81, Boca Blossom Realty Co., Boca Raton, Fla., 1979-81, N.B. Taylor & Co., Inc., Sudbury, Mass., 1986—; fashion coord Ava Botélle Fashions, Natick, Mass., 1988-90; mgr. Newton Store, 1990-93. TV facts girl for TV comml. T.V. Facts mag., 1974-75. Roman Catholic. Home (Winter): 10352 Quail Crown Dr Naples FL 34119-8832 Home (Summer): 11 Highbank Tr Plymouth MA 02360 Personal E-mail: dcw2001@aol.com.

WATSON, EASTER JEAN, psychotherapist, financial program consultant; b. Leland, Miss., U.S.A., Mar. 15, 1948; d. Tom and Louise B. Watson; m. Boisie Lee Watson, Oct. 24, 1965 (div. Apr. 1983); children: LaTonia Deonnette, Lorenzo Tomas, Derek Ondrea(dec.). BA in Sociology & Minority Studies, U. Notre Dame, 1974; MSW, Atlanta U., 1987. Psycho-therapist Oak Park & River Forest Mental Health Ctr., Ill., 1991—92; program cons. child welfare program Assn. House of Chicago, Chicago, Ill., 1993—94; exec. dir. Easter Watson, MSW & Assoc., Chicago, Ill., 1994—95; child welfare admin. Kinara Com. Svcs., Chicago, Ill., 2000—01; psycho-therapist cons. Self employed, Chicago, Ill., 2001—03; asst. dir. of child welfare YMCA of Metro, Chicago, Ill., 1996—2000. Cons. alternative sch. Chgo. Pub. Sch., Mgmt. Planning Inst., Chgo., 2001—; field instr. Chgo. State U., Chgo., 2001—, Nat. Louis U., Chgo., 2001—, Roosevelt U., 2001. Coord. (parent conference) The Power of Parents, 2003. Mem. Operation PUSH, Chgo., 1996—. Grantee, U. Notre Dame, 1972. Protestant. Home: 8049 South Sacramento Ave Chicago IL 60652 Office: Holistic Comprehensive Profl Svs Inc 10630 South Western Ave Chicago IL 60642 Personal E-mail: eastwats@aol.com.

WATSON, ELIZABETH MARION, protective services official; b. Phila., Aug. 25, 1949; d John Julian and Elizabeth Gertrude (Judge) Herrmann; m. Robert LLoyd Watson, June 18, 1976; children: Susan, Mark, David. BA in Psychology with honors, Tex. Tech. U., 1971. With Houston Police Dept., 1972-92, detective homicide, burglary and theft, 1976-81, lt. records div. northeast patrol div., 1981-84, capt. inspections div., auto theft div., 1984-87, dep. chief west patrol bur., 1987-90, police chief, 1990-92; with Austin, Tex. Police Dept., 1992—, police chief, 1992—. Mem. adv. bd. S.W. Law Enforcement Inst., Richardson,Tex., 1990—. Mem. editorial bd. Am. Jour. Police, 1991—. Mem. Internat. Assn. Chiefs of Police (mem. major cities chiefs, mem. civil rights com.), Police Exec. Rsch. Form, Tex. Police Chiefs Assn. Roman Catholic. Home: 725 County Road 136b Kingsland TX 78639-3943

WATSON, ELLEN I., academic administrator; b. Sioux City, Iowa, Jan. 14, 1948; d. Homer V. and Elsie (Bertelsen) W. AB, Wellesley Coll., 1970; MLS, U. Md., 1973. Cataloger Eisenhower Libr. Johns Hopkins U., Balt., 1970-74; appointments sec. to mayor City of Balt., 1974-75; libr. C.C. Balt., 1975-82, acting dir. librs., 1982-83; dir. learning resources ctr. Ark. Coll., Batesville, 1983-88; dir. Cullom-Davis Libr. Bradley U., Peoria, Ill., 1988-95, assoc. provost info. resources and tech., 1995-97; assoc. v.p. for info. svcs., dean of libr. Ind. State U., 1997—. Adv. bd. Ill. Valley Libr. System, Pekin, 1989-95. Contbr. articles to profl. jours. and chpts. to books. Mem. ALA, Assn. Coll. and Rsch. Librs., Libr. Adminstrn. and Mgmt. Assn., Libr. and Info. Tech. Assn., Ill. Libr. Assn., Ill. Assn. Coll. and Rsch. Librs., Phi Kappa Phi. Avocations: morgan horses, reading. Office: Bradley Univ 106 Bradley Hall 1501 W Bradley Ave Peoria IL 61625-0003

WATSON, EMILY, actress; b. London, Jan. 14, 1967; m. Jack Waters, 1995. Grad., Bristol U. Motion picture and stage actress. Films include Breaking the Waves, 1996 (nominee Best Actress Oscar 1997, nominee Golden Globe award 1997, Robert award 1997, N.Y. Film Critics Circle award 1996, Nat. Soc. Film Critics award 1996, L.A. Film Critics Assn. New Generation award 1996, European Film award 1996, others), The Mill on the Floss, 1997, Metroland, 1997, The Boxer, 1997, Hilary and Jackie (nominee Best Actress Oscar 1999, nominee Golden Globe award 1999), The Cradle Will Rock, 1999, Angela's Ashes, 1999, Trixie, 2000, Gosford Park, 2001 (SAG award outstanding performance by the cast, 2002), In Search of the Assasin, 2001, Equilibrium, 2002, Punch-Drunk Love, 2002, Red Dragon, 2002, Equilibrium, 2002, Blossoms and Blood, 2003, (voice) Back to Gaya, 2004, The Life and Death of Peter Sellers, 2004, Separate Lies, 2005, (voice) Corpse Bride, 2005, Wah-Wah, 2006. Office: c/o SAG 5757 Wilshire Blvd Los Angeles CA 90036-3635*

WATSON, GAIL H., retired librarian; b. Hattiesburg, Miss., May 12, 1941; d. Robert Elkin and Virginia Lucille (Swann) Hill; m. Tommy Gene Watson, June 4, 1963; children: James Todd, Thomas Gregory. BA, U. So. Miss., 1963; M in Librarianship, U. S.C., 1975; MEd, Tenn. State U., Nashville, 1983. Tchr. Hawkins Jr. H.S., Hattiesburg, 1963-64, Seminary (Miss.) H.S., 1965-66; libr. Bush River Elem. Sch., Newberry, S.C., 1973-74, Prosperity (S.C.) Elem. Sch., 1974-76; tchr. Franklin County H.S., Winchester, Tenn., 1977-83; libr. South/J.D. Jackson Jr. H.S., Cowan, Tenn., 1983—2003; ret., 2003. Mem. SACS rev. teams, Tenn., 1985—. Tenn. Dept. Edn. grantee, 1995. Mem. ALA, Soc. for Promotion of Christian Knowledge, Franklin County Librs. (chair 1998-2003), Franklin County Ret. Tchrs. Assn. (pres. 2006-09), Delta Kappa Gamma (pres. 2006—), Kappa Delta. Democrat. Episcopalian. Avocations: reading, travel. Home: 143 S Carolina Ave Sewanee TN 37375-2405 Personal E-mail: gailwatson@bellsouth.net.

WATSON, JOYCE LESLIE, elementary school educator; b. Riverside, N.J., May 31, 1950; d. Robert Eugene and Doris Virginia (Robinson) Stockton; 1 child, Michelle Leslie. BS, Trenton State Coll., 1972, MEd, 1978. Cert. elem. tchr., N.J., Pa. Tchr. elem. Willingboro (N.J.) Sch. Dist., 1972-81, Pennsbury Sch. Dist., Fallsington, Pa., 1987—, tchr. gifted/talented, advanced math. tchr., 1987-88, 92—, elem. demonstration tchr., 1995—97, 1998—2000, 2001—03. Coach Odyssey of the Mind, Pennwood Mid. Sch., Yardley, Pa., 1993—94; participant 8th Ann. Capital Area Space Orientation Program, Washington, 1996, NASA Educators Workshop, Kennedy Space Center, Fla., 2000, Pa. Gov.'s Inst. on Math, College Park, 2000, Share-a-thon at Nat. Congress on Aviation and Space Edn., 2002, Pa. Gov's Inst. on Personal Fin. and Entrepreneurship Edn., 2005. Mem.: NEA, Exptl. Aircraft Assn., Women in Aviation Internat., Nat. Aero. Assn., Airplane Owners and Pilots Assn., Pa. State Edn. Assn., Pa. Assn. for Gifted Edn., Kiwanis (Pa. dist. kids adminstr. 2005—06, lt. gov. divsn. 21 2005—06), Phi Delta Kappa. Home: 2293 Seabird Dr Bristol PA 19007 Office: Makefield Elem Sch Makefield Rd Yardley PA 19067

WATSON, JOYCE MORRISSA, forensic and clinical psychologist; d. Joseph Morris and B. Joyce Watson; 1 child, Matthew Joseph. BA, Maryville Coll., 1985; MSc summa cum laude, Troy State U., 1989; D magna cum laude in Psychology, Forest Inst. Profl. Psychology, 1994. Cert.: Fed. Bur. Prisons (fed. law enforcement officer) 1996; lic. psychologist Dept. Health, Fla., 1996. Sr. psychologist Fla. Dept. Corrections, Zephyrhills, 1995—96, regional mental health cons. Ft. Lauderdale, 1997—2000, dir. mental health Tallahassee, 1999—2002; staff psychologist, fed. law enforcement officer Fed. Bur. Prisons, Sumterville, Fla., 1996—97; dir. Sarasota Psychol. Svcs., Fla., 2002—. Faculty U. Sarasota, Tampa, 1997—2000; adv. coun. Governor's Commn. Mental Health and Substance Abuse, Tallahassee, 1999—2000; coun. mem. Fla. State Mental Health Planning Coun., Tallahassee, 1999—2001; bd. mem. hosp. North Fla. Reception Ctr. Hosp., Lake Butler, 1999—2001; presenter in field. Author jour. articles, book articles, essays in book. Vol. tchr. Fruitville Elem. Sch., Sarasota, 1989; vol. Bright Beginnings, Sarasota, 2003—05, Little League, Sarasota, 2005. Recipient Exceptional Performance award, Dept. Justice, Time-Off award, Bureau of Prisons; grantee, Pfizer, Glaxo Wellcome. Mem.: APA, Fla. Psychol. Assn., Soc. Personality Assessment. Avocations: show dogs, music, water sports. Office: J Morrissa Watson PsyD 4411 Bee Ridge Rd #353 Sarasota FL 34233 Business E-Mail: morrissawatson@aol.com.

WATSON, LORETTA, medical/surgical nurse; d. Thomas Louis and Mary Louise Watson. LPN, Young Meml. Vocat., Morgan City, 1978; AS, RN, Prince George's C.C., Largo, Md., 2000. LPN Lakewood Hosp., Morgan City, 1978, South La. Med. Ctr., Houma, 1979—87, D.C. Gen. Hosp., Washington, 1991—2000, RN, 2001, Hunter Med., Vienna, Va., 2002, Park Plaza Hosp., Houston, 2002—, charge nurse, 2003—; RN D.C. Gen. Hosp. Deaconess Mount Olive Bapt. Ch., 1997—. Mem.: Black Nurses Assn. Democrat. Avocations: reading, collecting angels, travel, decorating. Home: 1802 Spring Green Ct Missouri City TX 77489 Office Phone: 713-527-5800.

WATSON, MARILYN FERN, writer; b. Oklahoma City, July 30, 1934; d. Charles Haddon and Mary Perle (Knotts) Rounds; m. Donald Wayne Watson, Aug. 14, 1954; 1 child, Lyndon Lee. BS in Psychology magna cum laude, Ea. N.Mex. U., 1973, postgrad., 1980-81. Apprentice technician, Sante Fe Opera, 1982. Geol. draftsman Lion Oil Co., Roswell, N.Mex., 1956-57; freelance writer, artist Roswell, N.Mex., 1960—; pvt. tutor learning disabled, gifted children, 1976-77; founder, owner Creativity Unltd., Roswell, N.Mex., 1994—. Contbr. articles to mags. and profl. jours. Ofcl. centennial historian, artist United N.Mex. Bank, Roswell, 1990; chairperson/sponsor Heritage awards Hist. Ctr. S.E. N.Mex., Roswell, 1995, found. bd., 1996-97. Recipient Writer's Digest Mag. award, 1959, Guideposts Fedn. award, 1978. Mem. Psi Chi, Phi Kappa Phi. Methodist. Avocations: gardening, hiking, reading/collecting classic literature, designing stained glass, sculpture. Home: 100 S Pennsylvania Ave Roswell NM 88203-4533 Office: Creativity Unltd 100 1/2 S Penn Ave Roswell NM 88203-4533 Home: # 8 Hall St Napier Hawkes Bay New Zealand

WATSON, MARY ANN, marriage and family therapist; b. Quitman, Ga., Dec. 14, 1933; d. Paul Hansel and Mary Rebecca (Bowman) Bennet; m. Edgar Lee Watson, Oct. 23, 1954; children: Edgar Lee, Rebecca Watson Stansell, Elizabeth Watson Alford. BA magna cum laude, Shorter Coll., Rome, Ga., 1954; MA, West Ga. Coll., Carrollton, 1972. Cert. employee assistance profl., substance abuse profl. Alcohol and drug counselor Floyd

County Health Dept., Rome, 1971-73; psychologist Ga. Dept. Human Resources, Rome, 1972-79; counselor Harbi Clinic, Rome, 1971-80; employee assistance counselor Peachtree-Parkwood Hosp., Atlanta, 1978-81; program cons. Windwood/Floyd Hosp., Rome, 1981—; pres. Southeastern Employee Assistance Svcs., Rome, 1981—; family therapist in pvt. practice Rome, 1981—. Chmn. wellness com. Bekaert Corp., Rome, 1987—; chmn. disaster response Floyd Med. Ctr., Rome, 1992-93. Author articles; presenter, author seminars; presenter on radio talk shows. Mem. APA, Am. Assn. Marriagy and Family Therapists (clin. mem.), Employee Assistance Profls. Assn., Christian Counselors, Nat. Assn. Addiction Counselors, Rome Rotary Club, Greater Rome C. of C. (chmn. Women in Mgmt. 1989-90), Bartow County C. of C. (mem. Drugs Don't Work 1994—), Gordon C. of C. Presbyterian. Avocations: music, swimming, gardening, cooking, decorating. Home: 105 Pine Valley Rd Rome GA 30165-4339 Office: Southeastern Employee Assistance and Counseling 1012 N 5th Ave NE Rome GA 30165-2602

WATSON, PATRICIA PULLUMS, school system administrator; b. Chgo., June 3, 1949; d. James and Aletha (Pearline) Pullums; m. Charles Michael Watson, Aug. 10, 1985; 1 child, Kevyn Charles. BA, Chgo.State U., 1973; MS in Edn. and Reading, Chgo. State U., 1981; MA in Adminstrn. and Supervision, Gov.'s State U., University Park, Ill., 1997; postgrad., Ill. State U., 2004—. Cert. tchr. Ill. Tchr. Theodore Herzl Sch., Chgo., 1973—74; program dir. Accounters Cmty. Ctr., Chgo., 1974—83, asst. exec. dir., 1989—98, exec. dir., 1998—2002, pres., CEO, 2002—03; head tchr., asst. prin. Accounters Prep. Acad., Chgo., 1980—89; tchr., dept. chair., program coord. Cullen Elem. Sch., Chgo., 1991—98; asst. prin. Shoesmith Elem. Sch., Chgo., 1998—. Mem. People To People Citizen Amb. Program, Spokane, Wash., 1997—. Grantee grant, Chgo. Found. for Edn., 1996. Mem.: NAACP, Chgo. Area Alliance Black Sch. Educators, Assn. Supervision and Curriculum Devel., Nat. Assn. Secondary Sch. Prins., Nat. Coun. Negro Women, Internat. Reading Assn., Nat. Alliance Elem. Sch. Prins., Chgo. Prins. and Adminstrs. Assn., Chgo. Asst. Prin. Assn., Phi Delta Kappa, Delta Sigma Theta. Avocation: golf. Office Phone: 773-535-1764. Office Fax: 773-535-1877. Personal E-mail: wats1612@sbcglobal.net. E-mail: ppwatson@cps.k12.il.us.

WATSON, PATTI RAE, counselor, psychologist; b. Phoenix, Oct. 3, 1958; d. Kenneth Wayne Watson and Janice Lee Schramke Motley; m. Donald Leo Miller, Jan. 4, 1994. BS in Psychology, Emporia State U., 1988; MA in Counseling and Guidance, U. Ariz., 1991; EdD in Counseling Pschology, No. Ariz. U., 1996. Dir., vol. coord. Ariz. AIDS Info. Line, Phoenix, 1986; co-chair So. Ariz. Task Force on Domestic Violence, Tucson, 1990; counseling-practicum Tucson Ctr. for Women and Children, 1990; counseling intern Cath. Social Svcs., Tucson, 1990-91; counselor in pvt. practice Tucson, 1991-92, Mayer, Ariz., 1993-95; counselor Wahkiakum County, Cathlamet, Wash., 1992-93; instr. No. Ariz. U., Flagstaff, 1993; psychologist in pvt. practice Tucson, 1996—. U. Ariz. Regent's scholar, 1986-87, Nesbit Agrl. scholar, 1989, U. Ariz. grad. tuition scholar, 1989-91, Ruth R. Cowden scholar, 1990. Mem. Emporia State U. Alumni Assn., Psi Chi, Chi Sigma Iota. Avocations: quilting, gardening, drawing.

WATSON, PATTY JO, anthropology educator; b. Superior, Nebr., Apr. 26, 1932; d. Ralph Clifton and Elaine Elizabeth (Lance) Andersen; m. Richard Allan Watson, July 30, 1955; 1 child, Anna Melissa MA, U. Chgo., 1956, PhD in Anthropology, 1959. Archaeologist-ethnographer Oriental Inst.-U. Chgo., 1959—60, rsch. assoc., archaeologist, 1964—70; instr. anthropology U. So. Calif., Los Angeles, 1961, UCLA, 1961, L.A. State U., 1961; asst. prof. anthropology Washington U., St. Louis, 1969—70, assoc. prof., 1970—73, prof., 1973—2004, Edward Mallinckrodt disting. univ. prof., 1993—2004, prof. emerita, 2004—; faculty affiliate anthropology U. Mont., 2003—. Mem. rev. panel NSF, Washington, 1974-76; fellow Ctr. Advanced Study in Behavioral Scis., Stanford, Calif., 1981-82, 91-92. Author: The Prehistory of Salts Cave, Kentucky, 1969, Archaeological Ethnography in Western Iran, 1979; author: (with others) Man and Nature, 1969, Explanation in Archeology, 1971, Archeological Explanation, 1984, Girikihaciyan, A Halafian Site in Southeastern Turkey; author: (editor) Archeology of the Mammoth Cave Area, 1974, Prehistoric Archeology Along the Zagros Flanks, 1983; co-editor: The Origins of Agriculture, 1992, Of Caves and Shell Mounds, 1996, Archaeology of the Middle Green River Region, Kentucky, 2005. Recipient Arthur Holly Compton Faculty Achievement award Washington U., St. Louis, 2000, Peter H. Raven award for lifetime achievement Acad. Sci. St. Louis, 2002; grantee NSF, 1959-60, 68, 70, 72-74, 78-79, NEH, 1977-78, Nat. Geog. Soc., 1969-75, Southeastern Arch. Conf. Lifetime Achievement award, 2004. Fellow Am. Anthropol. Assn. (editor for archaeology 1973-77, Disting. Lectr. award 1994, Disting. Svc. award 1996), AAAS (chair sect. H 1991-92); mem. Cave Rsch. Found., Am. Acad. Arts and Scis., Am. Philos. Soc., Soc. Am. Archaeology (exec. com. 1974-76, 82-84, editor Am. Antiquity 1984-87, Fryxell medal 1990), Assn. Paleorient (sci. bd.), Nat. Speleological Soc. (hon. life, editorial bd. bull. 1979—, sci. award), Archaeol. Inst. Am. (Gold Medal for Disting. Archaeol. Achievement 1999), Nat. Acad. Scis. Business E-Mail: pjwatson@artsci.wustl.edu.

WATSON, PAULA D., retired librarian; b. N.Y.C., Mar. 6, 1945; d. Joseph Francis and Anna Julia (Miksza) De Simone; m. William Douglas Watson, Aug. 23, 1969; children— Lucia, Elizabeth AB, Barnard Coll., 1965; MA, Columbia U., 1966; MSLS, Syracuse U., 1972. Libr. reference U. Ill., Urbana, 1972—77, libr. city planning and landscape architecture, 1977—79, head documents libr., 1979—81; asst. dir. gen. svcs. U. Ill. Libr., Urbana, 1981—88, acting dir. gen. svcs., 1988—93, dir. ctrl. pub. svcs., 1989—93, asst. libr., 1993—95, dir. electronic info. svcs., 1995—2004, dir. scholarly comm., 2003—04; ret., 2004. Author: Electronic Journals: Acquisition and Management, 2003, E-Publishing Impact on Acquisition and Interlibrary Loan, 2004; contbr. articles to profl. jours. N.Y. State Regents fellow Columbia U., N.Y.C., 1965-66; Council on Library Resources profl. edn. and tng. for librarianship grantee, 1983 Mem. ALA (sec. univ. librs. sect. ALA-Assn. Coll. and Rsch. Librs. 1989-91, com. on instnl. coop., chair pub. svcs. dirs. group, 1997-99, mem. com. inst. coop./OCLC virtual electronic libr. steering com.), Ill. Library Assn. Avocation: gardening. Home: 715 W Delaware Ave Urbana IL 61801-4806

WATSON, PAULA SUE, pre-school educator; b. Akron, ohio, July 10, 1957; d. Anthony Charles and Fay Patricia Caracciolo; m. Lawernce A. Watson, Mar. 20, 1976; children: Allan R., Annalee, Andrew P. EdB, U. Akron, Akron, Ohio, 1980. Cert. early childhood edn., elem. edn., speical edn., mild mental disablities and emotional distrubance. 4th grade tchr. Morton Elem., Sinpsonville, SC, 1987—97; tchr. special edn. W. Oxford Elem., Oxford, NC, 1997—98, Ellen Woodside Elem., Pelzer, SC, 1998—99; dir. Christ Ch. Episc. Pre Sch., Greenville, SC, 1999—2000; child develop. tchr. Southern Child Develop. Ctr., Pelzer, SC, 2000—01; pre sch. develop. delay tchr. Harleyville-Ridgeville Elem., Dorchester, SC, 2001—06; tchr. presch. disabilities North Augusta Elem., SC, 2006—. Com. mem. Sch. Leadership Program, Dorchester, SC, 2003—06; com. mem. sch. rep. Supt. Coun., St. Geroge, SC, 2004—06. Mem.: SC Autism Soc., SC Early Childhood Assn., Coun. for Exceptional Children. Methodist. Avocations: embroidery, scrapbooks, interior decorating, gardening. Office: North Augusta Elem Sch 400 E Spring Grove Ave North Augusta SC 29841 Office Phone: 803-442-6280.

WATSON, REBECCA ELAINE, human resources specialist, consultant; b. Dallas, Nov. 11, 1960; d. John Cephas and Mary Magdeline (Rhea) Bishop; m. Billy Don Wilkinson, July 31, 1982 (div.); children: Eric Tyler Wilkinson, Kristen Rhea Wilkinson; m. David John Watson, June 12, 1999; children: Laura Nicole, David John II. BEd, U. Dallas, 1982, MBA, 1995. Adminstrv. asst. IBM, Irving, Tex., 1982-85, equal opportunity coord., 1985-90, human resources data analyst Roanoke, Tex., 1990-94; sr. human resources/payroll application specialist Westinghouse Security Sys., Irving, 1994-97, team leader fin. and adminstrv. sys., 1996-97; sr. cons. Cambridge Tech. Ptnrs., 1997-98; sr. assoc. dir. Comp-U-Temp, USA, Tex., 1998-2000; v.p. WW Cons., 2000—. Mem.: NOW, NAFE, Greenpeace, Sigma Iota Epsilon. Democrat. Episcopalian. Avocations: needlepoint, rollerblading, reading, golf, bowling.

WATSON, REBECCA WUNDER, federal agency administrator, lawyer; b. Chgo., Feb. 17, 1952; d. David Hart and Shirley May (Dahlin) Wunder; m. Keith C. Thomson, Oct. 6, 1979 (div. Dec. 1989); m. Gregory B. Watson, Jan. 20, 1996. BA, U. Denver, 1974, MA in LS, 1975, JD, 1978. Bar: Bar: Wyo. 1978, Colo. 1989, D.C. 1995, Mont. 1995. Law clk. U.S. Dist. Ct. for Dist. Wyo., Cheyenne, 1978-80; assoc., then ptnr. Burgess & Davis, Sheridan, Wyo., 1980-88; pvt. practice, Denver, 1988-90; asst. gen. counsel for energy policy US Dept. Energy, Washington, 1990-93; of counsel Crowell & Moring, Washington, 1993-95; ptnr. Gough Shanahan Johnson & Waterman, Helena, Mont., 1995—2002; asst. sec. land & minerals mgmt. US Dept Interior, Washington, 2002—. Contbr. author: ABA Natural Resource Law Handbook, 1993; contbr. articles to law jours. Mem. ABA (chmn. natural resource com. sect. adminstrv. law 1994-97, chmn. pub. lands com. sect. natural resources, energy and environ. law 1997-99), Wyo. Bar Assn., Mont. Bar Assn., Phi Beta Kappa. Republican. Avocations: cooking, reading, travel, hunting. Office: US Dept Interior Land and Materials Mgt 1849 C St NW Washington DC 20240 Home: 72 W Ranch Trl Morrison CO 80465-9503 Office Phone: 202-208-6734. E-mail: Rebecca_Watson@ios.doi.gov.

WATSON, RENÉE, marketing professional, consultant; b. San Antonio, Apr. 1, 1962; d. Clarence and Lettye Watson. BBA, U. Tex., San Antonio, 1987; MPA, CUNY, 1989. Chief staff to Councilman George Stevens, San Diego, 1991-95; dep. chief staff for Senator Rodney Ellis, Tex. Senate, Houston, 1995-97; dir. field mktg. UniverSoul Circus, Atlanta, 1997-99; cons. Watson Consulting, 1999—; program coord. planning and resource mgmt. Bexar County Courthouse, San Antonio, 2000—; mgr. Small Minority Women Owned Bus. Enterprise. Mem. Leadership San Antonio, 1991, Leadership Calif., Pasadena, 1993, Leadership Am., N.Y.C., 1995, Leadership Tex., 2002; mem. China del. People to People Amb. Program, 1997. Fellow Nat. Urban Fellows, 1989; named 40 under 40 Rising Stars in San Antonio San Antonio Bus. Jour, Alamo Area Coun. of Govts. Project of Yr. award, 2004. Democrat. Baptist. Avocations: reading, travel, walking, gardening, dance. E-mail: powernae@hotmail.com.

WATSON, RUBIE S., museum director; BS in Archaeology and Anthropology, U. Calif., Berkeley; MS in Anthropology, Rice U.; PhD in Social Anthropology, London Sch. Econs. Assoc. prof. anthropology, acting dir. Asian Studies program U. Pitts.; assoc. curator Peabody Mus. Archeology & Ethnology, sr. lectr. dept. anthropology Harvard U., Cambridge, Mass., 1992-95, assoc. dir., then Howells dir. Peabody Mus., 1995—. Author several books including Inequality Among Brothers: Class and Kinship in South China, 1985; editor: Memory, History, and Opposition under State Socialism, 1994; co-editor: Marriage and Inequality in Chinese Society, 1990, Harmony and Counterpoint: Ritual Music in Chinese Context, 1996. Fellow: Am. Acad. Arts. & Sci. Office: Peabody Mus Archeology Harvard U 11 Divinity Ave Cambridge MA 02138-2019

WATSON, SHARON DIANE, principal; b. Gulfport, Miss., Aug. 25, 1953; d. Wendell Howard and Thais (Cox) Watson. BS Edn., MA Edn., Memphis State U., 1976; EdS Supervision and Adminstrn., U. Memphis, 1996. Instr. Briarcrest Christian Sch., Memphis, 1976—2002, prin. mid. sch., 2002—. Dean women Briarcrest Christian Sch., 1998—2002, coach varsity volleyball, 1976—95. Named Coach of Yr., Tenn. State Volleyball Assn., 1981; named to Who's Who Among Am. Tchrs., 1992, Who's Who in Tenn., 1990. Mem.: Nat. Assn. Secondary Sch. Prins. Achievements include coach Tenn. State Champion Volleyball teams 1981, 1987, 1989, 1990. Avocations: videography, percussionist. Office: Briarcrest Christian Sch 6000 Briarcrest Ave Memphis TN 38120

WATSON, SHARON GITIN, psychologist; b. N.Y.C., Oct. 21, 1943; d. Louis Leonard and Miriam (Myers) Gitin; m. Eric Watson, Oct. 31, 1969; 1 child, Carrie Dunbar. BA cum laude, Cornell U., 1965; MA, U. Ill., 1968, PhD, 1971. Psychologist City N.Y. Prison Mental Health, Riker's Island, 1973-74, Youth Services Ctr., Los Angeles County Dept. Pub. Social Services, L.A., 1975-77, dir. clin. services, 1978, dir. Youth Services Ctr., 1978-80; exec. dir. Crittenton Ctr. for Young Women and Infants, L.A., 1980-89, Assn. Children's Svcs. Agys. of So. Calif., L.A., 1989-92, L.A. County Children's Planning Coun., 1992-99; cons. L.A. County Chief Adminstrv. Office, 2001—04, Edn. Coordinating Coun., 2004—; mem. L.A. City Commn. for Children, Youth and Their Families, 2000—. L.A. County Children's Planning Coun., 2001—. Mem. L.A. delegation Pres.'s Summit for Am.'s Future, 1997. Mem. Commn. for Children's Svcs. Family Preservation and Family Support Policy Com., 1989—99, Interagy. Coun. Child Abuse and Neglect Policy Com., 1993—99, Mayor's Com. on Children, Youth and Families, 1993—95; bd. dirs. Adolescent Pregnancy Childwatch, 1985—89, L.A. Ednl. Partnership, 1999—2003, LISC Health Sector, 1996—99, L.A. Roundtable for Children, 1988—94; trustee L.A. Ednl. Alliance for Restructuring Now, 1992—99. Mem.: APA, Assn. Children's Svcs. Agys. So. Calif. (sec. 1981—83, pres. elect 1983—84, pres. 1984—85), Calif. Assn. Svcs. for Children (sec.-treas. 1983—84, pres. elect 1985—86, pres. 1986—87), U.S. Figure Skating Assn. (chmn. sanctions and eligibility 1993—96, membership com. 1996—99, strategic planning com. 2000—02, regional vice chmn. competitions com. 2000—02, sec. 2002—, bd. dirs. 1992—, mem. exec. com. 2002—, nat. competition judge), U.S. Olympics Com. (Jr. Olympics com. 1998—2000), Pasadena Figure Skating Club (pres. 1985—87, 1989—90), So. Calif. Inter-Club Assn. of Figure Skating Clubs (vice chair 1989—91, chair 1991—93). Home and Office: 4056 Camino Real Los Angeles CA 90065-3928 E-mail: sharonla12@aol.com.

WATSON, VERA K., music educator, pianist; b. Voronezh, Russia, Oct. 13, 1972; d. Stepan Efremovich and Valentina Vasilevna Kulinchenko; m. Lee Watson, Sept. 20, 1997; 1 child, Leeann. BM, South-Ukrainian State Pedagogical U., Odessa, Ukraine, 1990—95; MM, Russian Acad. of Music, Moscow, Russia, 1995—97; postgrad., Moscow State Open Pedagogical U. Cert. tchr. of music in piano MTNA. Music tchr. Odesskya Secondary Sch., Odessa, Ukraine, 1994—95; condr. children's chorus Moscow Mcpl. Choir, Moscow, Russia, 1995—96; tchr. of chorus classes The Acad. of Chorus Art, Moscow, Russia, 1996—97; music tchr. St. John's Gramma Sch., Jacksonville, Fla., 1997—98; condr. Palms Presbyn. Ch., Jacksonville, Fla., 1998—; chair piano dept., artist-in-residence Douglas Anderson Sch., Jacksonville, Fla., 1999—, recitalist, 2001—. Dir. of d.a. piano concerto competition Douglas Anderson Sch., Jacksonville, Fla., 1999—; judge Smta, Fsmta, Fla., 1998—; piano instr. U. of North Fla. Summer Camp, Jacksonville, Fla., 2000—. Harmony grantee for the best piano program in NE Fla., Jacksonville Symphony, 2000, Surdna Outstanding Tchr. fellow, 2003. Mem.: Nat. Guild of Piano Teachers, Jacksonville Music Teachers Assn. (scholarship chairperson 1997—2002), Federated Clubs of Am. (v.p. Jacksonville dist. 1997—).

WATSON-BOONE, REBECCA A., dean, researcher, library and information scientist, educator; b. Springfield, Ohio, Mar. 7, 1946; d. Roger S. and Elizabeth Boone; m. Dennis David Ash, 1967 (div. 1975); m. Frederick Kellogg, 1979 (div. 1988); m. Peter G. Watson-Boone, May 26, 1989. Student, Earlham Coll., 1964-67; BA, Case Western Res. U., 1968; MLS, U. N.C., 1971; PhD, U. Wis., 1995. Asst. reference libr. Princeton (N.J) U., 1970-76; head cen. reference dept. U. Ariz., Tucson, 1976-83, assoc. dean Coll. Arts and Scis., 1984-89. Loaned exec. Ariz. Bd. Regents, 1988-89; pres. Ctr. for Study of Info. Profls., 1995—2002. Author: Constancy and Change in the Worklife of Research University Librarians, 1998; contbr. articles to profl. jours. Mem. ALA (div. pres. 1985-86, councilor 1988-92), NAFE, Assn. for Libr. and Info. Sci. Edn. Mem. Religious Soc. Of Friends. Office: 30 Camino de la Vina Vieja Placitas NM 87043 Business E-Mail: rebeccawb@earthlink.net.

WATT, ABBY NAITOVE, elementary school educator; b. N.Y.C., Oct. 26, 1952; d. Arthur and Constance Stever (Epstein) Naitove; m. Peter Watt, Aug. 18, 1973; children: Ezzy, Aaron, Iain. Student, London Contemporary Dance Sch.; MEd, Cambridge Coll., Mass. Performer KATS, Sesame Inst., London, 1971—75; dance tchr. YMCA, Needham, Mass., 1980—82; phys. edn. tchr. Needham Pub. Schs., 1988—96, mid. sch. tchr., 1996—; field hockey coach Pollard Mid. Sch., 1997—98; varsity gymnastics coach Needham H.S., 1996—. Guest dancer various Shubert Theater, Boston, 2001; dancer, presenter Royal Gala Performance for Her Majesty Queen Elizabeth, 1974. Actor: (films, documentary) Leavesdon Hosp. Movement Therapy, 1972—73, Smith Hospital School Autistic Project, 1973—75. Vol. tchr. Walker Home and Sch., Needham, 1983—85; head of com. Creative Arts for Pub. Schs., Needham, 1982—85; fundraising project dir. Needham Athletics, 2002. Named Coach of the Yr. in Gymnastics, Bay State League Ea. Mass., 2001—02, 2005—06. Mem.: AAHPERD, USA Gymnastics, Sesame Inst. Gt. Britain (life), Needham Soccer Club (pres. 1996—97, v.p. 1995—96). Avocations: dance, music. Office: Needham Public Schools 200 Harris Ave Needham MA 02492

WATT, MAUREEN R., retired secondary school educator; b. Helena, Mont., Dec. 1, 1947; d. B.A. and Lorraine (LaHood) Thompson; m. Philip R. Watt, Aug. 14, 1976. BA in Math., Ft. Wright Coll. Holy Names, Spokane, Wash., 1970; MATM, U. Mont., 1974. Cert. tchr., secondary math. and chemistry tchr., Mont. Tchr. math. Anaconda (Mont.) Cen. High Sch., Sch. Dist. 10, Anaconda, ret. Presenter insvc. workshops. Mem. Nat. Coun. Tchrs. Math., Mont. Coun. Computer Edn. (bd. dirs.), Anaconda Tchrs. Union (sec.-treas., v.p., chmn. curriculum com., past pres.), Delta Kappa Gamma (1st v.p. chpt., pres. chpt. 1992-94, state parliamentarian). Home: 1112 Heather Dr Anaconda MT 59711-2634 Personal E-mail: mrwatt2000@yahoo.com.

WATT, STEPHANIE DENISE, musician, educator, department chairman; d. Edmund Hudson and Joan Elizabeth (Patterson) Watt. BFA in Music Performance, LI U., 1984, MA in Composition and Performance, 1988, MS in Computer Sci. and Engring., 1999. Adj. asst. prof. music LI U., C.W. Post Campus, Brookville, NY, 1988—97, assoc. prof. music, 1997—; adj. asst. prof. music Suffolk County CC, Ammerman Campus, Selden, NY, 1988—97; adj. asst. prof. music Dowling Coll., Oakdale, NY, 1989—91; guest lectr. in music history Alvin Ailey Am. Sch. Dance, NYC, 1996—98. Founder EastWest Sch. Performing Arts, NY, 1979—2006; coord. seminar divsn. LI U. Chamber Music Program, Brookville, 1994—97; dir. piano studies LI U., C.W. Post Campus, 1988—, co-dir. student concert series, 1990—96, dir. theory studies, 1999—; adjudicator LI Philharm. Young Artist Piano Competition, 1994—2004, Music Lovers Club Young Artist Competition, 1994—2006, 8th and 9th NY Young Artist Piano and Violin Competition, 2005, 06; piano master classes Müvészeti Szakközepiskola és Gimnázium, Szombathely. Author: Information Theory Analyses of Bach Chorales and a Learning Classifier System, 1999; musician: (CD recording on Capstone Records) Duo for Cello and Piano by Allen Brings, 2006; dancer (dance exhbn.) Argentine Tango & Salsa Exhbn.; performer: Camerata Pro Musica, 2000, Carnegie Hall, 2005, The Hecksher Mus. Art, 2005, Park Ave. United Meth. Ch., 2005, Brick Gallery, 2005, LI U., C.W. Post Campus, 2005, 2006, Clarinet & Piano Concert, 2006, Concert Tour of Hungary, Communidad de Palermo Symphony Orch., 2006; guest artist, clinician LI Choral Festival and Inst., 2004, 2005, (DuoLeo performace) Weill Hall Carnegie Hall, NYC, 2005, Park Ave. United Meth. Ch., 2005, LI U., C.W. Post Campus, Brookville, 2005, 2006, (DuoLeo performace and solo performance) Brik Gallery, Catskills, NY, 2005, (Martino and Watt duo performace) Steinway Hall, NYC, 2006, Blueport Libr., 2006, LI Philharm. Choir, 2006, (DuoLeo performace one-woman shows) The Heckscher Mus. Art, Huntington, NY, 2005; dancer (dance exhbns.) Babylon Village Fair, NY, 2005, New Life Cmty. Ch., Sachem, NY, 2006, LI U., C.W. Post, 2006; featured Strings mag., 2002; contbr. articles to profl. confs. Recipient First Pl. award Foxtrot Exhbn., Kings Ball Dancesport Championships, SI, NY, 2001, First Pl. award Am. Tango Exhbn., 2001, First Pl. award Viennese Waltz Exhbn., Stardust Ball Competition, Melville, NY, 2002, First Pl. award Open Tango Exhbn., Stardust Ball, Melville, NY, 2002, Cert. of Recognition music performance, Mayor of Inc. Village of Hempstead, 1995, Second Pl. award slow waltz exhbn., NJ Open Championships, Rutherford, 2003, Third Pl. award Dance Team Exhbn., Northeastern Open Championships, Weston, Conn., 2003. Mem.: AAUW (assoc.), NY State Music Assn. (assoc.), Coll. Music Soc. (assoc.), Phi Eta Sigma. Achievements include research in the history of the tango and its political influence in Argentina. Office: LI U CW Post Campus 720 Northern Blvd Greenvale NY 11548 Office Phone: 516-299-2474. Office Fax: 516-299-2884. Personal E-mail: stefani1435@aol.com.

WATTLETON, FAYE (ALYCE FAYE WATTLETON), educational association administrator, advocate; b. St. Louis, July 8, 1943; d. George and Ozie (Garrett) Wattleton; m. Franklin Gordon (div.); 1 child, Felicia. BS in Nursing, Ohio State U., 1964; MS in Maternal and Infant Health Care, Columbia U., 1967; LHD (hon.), St. Paul's Coll., 1985, Spelman Coll., 1986; LLD (hon.), Northeastern Univ. Law Sch., 1990; LHD (hon.), Long Island Univ., 1990, U. Pa., 1990, Bard Coll., 1991; HHD (hon.), Oberlin Coll., 1991; LLD (hon.), Wesleyan Univ., 1991; LHD (hon.), Hofstra U., 1992, Haverford Coll., 1992, Meadville-Lombar Sem./U. Chicago, 1992; D in Pub. Svc. (hon.), Simmons Coll., 1993. Tchr. Miami Valley Hosp. Sch. Nursing, Dayton, Ohio, 1964-66; asst. dir. Montgomery County Combined Pub. Health Dist., Dayton, 1967-70; exec. dir. Planned Parenthood, Dayton, 1970-78; pres. Planned Parenthood Fedn. Am., Inc., NYC, 1978-92, Ctr. for Advancement of Women, NYC, 1995—. Author: How to Talk to Your Child About Sexuality, 1986, Life on the Line, 1996. Bd. dirs. Pardee Rand Grad. Sch., Quidel Corp., Savient Pharm., Jazz at Lincoln Ctr., Well Choice Inc., Eisenhower Fellowship, UNA/USA; trustee Columbia U. Recipient Am. Humanist award, 1986, John Gardner award, 1987, APHA award of excellence, 1989, Humanitarian award Congrl. Black Caucus Found., 1989, Claude Pepper Humanitarian award Internat. Platform Assn., 1990, Pioneer of Civil Rights and Human Rights award Nat. Conf. Black Lawyers, 1990, Florina Lasker award NY Civil Liberties Union Found., 1990, Whitney M. Young Jr. Svc. award Boy Scouts Am., 1990, Ministry of Women award Unitarian Universalist Women's Fed., 1990, Spirit of Achievement award Albert Einstein Coll. Medicine Yeshiva U., 1991, 20th Anniversary Advocacy award Nat. Family Planning and Reproductive Health Assn., 1991, Women of Achievement award Women's Projects and Prodn., 1991, Margaret Sanger award, 1992, Jefferson Pub. Svc. award, 1992, Dean's Disting. Svc. award Columbia Sch. Pub. Health, 1992, Fries prize, 2004; named one of Best Mgrs. of Non-Profit Orgns. in Am., Bus. Week, Outstanding Mother Nat. Mother's Day Com., 1997; named to Nat. Women's Hall of Fame, 1993. Office: Ctr for Advancement of Women 25 W 43rd St Ste # 1120 New York NY 10036 Office Phone: 212-391-7718. Business E-Mail: fwattleton@advancewomen.org.

WATTLEWORTH, ROBERTA ANN, physician; b. Sioux City, Iowa, Dec. 26, 1955; d. Roland Joseph and Elizabeth Ann (Ahart) Eickholt; m. John Wade Wattleworth, Nov. 7, 1984; children: Adam, Ashley. BS, Morningside Coll., Sioux City, 1978; D of Osteopathy, Coll. Osteo. Medicine/Surgery, Des Moines, 1981; M.Healthcare Adminstrn., U. Osteo. Med. and Health Scis., Des Moines, 1999; MPH, Des Moines U., 2004. Intern Richmond Heights (Ohio) Gen. Hosp., 1981-82, resident in anesthesiology, 1982-84; anesthesiologist Doctor's Gen. Hosp., Plantation, Fla., 1984-85; resident in family practice J.F. Kennedy Hosp., Stratford, NJ, 1985-87; educator family practice U. Osteo. Medicine and Health Scis., Des Moines, 1987-89; family practitioner McFarland Clinic, P.C., Jewell, Iowa, 1989-94; lectr. family practice Osteopath. Med. Ctr., Des Moines U., 1999—, prof., chair dept. family medicine, 2003—. Med. dir. nursing home Bethany Manor, Story City, Iowa, 1990-99, Jewell Vol. Fire and Rescue Squad, 1990-99. Bd. dirs. Heartland Sr. Svcs., 1995—99, Iowa Rural Health Assn. Named Nat. Outstanding Osteo. Educator of Yr., Nat. Student Osteo. Med. Assn., 2001—02. Fellow Am. Coll. Osteo. Family Physicians; mem. Am. Osteo. Assn., Am. Med. Dirs. Assn. (sec.-treas. Iowa chpt. 1997-99), Am. Coll. Osteo. Family Physicians (pres. Iowa chpt. 1995-96), Iowa Osteo. Med. Assn. (trustee 1995-99, v.p. 1999—, pres.-elect 2000-01, pres. 2001-02, Physician of Yr. 2004-05), Soc. Tchrs. Family Medicine. Lutheran. Avocations: gardening, cooking, painting. Office: 3200 Grand Ave Des Moines IA 50312-4104 Office Phone: 515-271-7816. E-mail: Roberta.Wattleworth@dmu.edu.

WATTOFF, ELIZABETH, special education educator; b. Houston, May 28, 1981; d. Geoff and Joanie Wattoff. B, Oral Roberts U., Tulsa, Okla., 2003. Cert. spl. education tchr. Okla., 2003. Tchr. spl. edn. Tulsa Pub. Schs., 2003—. Named Outstanding Tchr., Tulsa Pub. Schs., 2004—06, Oustanding Tchr. Yr., 2004—05.

WATTON, RHONDA KAY, social studies educator; d. Paul and Jan Plachetka. BA in Elem. Edn., Carthage Coll., Kenosha, Wis., 1992, Master's in Edn., 2000. Cert. elem. tchr. Wis. Tchr. 7th grade Milw. Pub. Schs., 1992—98; tchr. 8th grade Templeton Mid. Sch., Sussex, Wis., 1998—. Primary del. leader People to People, Spokane, Wash., 2003—. Recipient Class Act Tribute award, Hamilton Edn. Found., 2004. Mem.: Wis. Coun. Social Studies, Wis. Geographic Alliance (bd. dirs.), Nat. Coun. History Edn. Avocations: reading, travel, scrapbooks. Office Phone: 262-246-6477 4525. Fax: 262-246-0465. Business E-Mail: wattrh@hamiltondist.k12.wi.us.

WATTS, ALICE L., nurse; b. Kremlin, Mt., Dec. 15, 1920; d. Joseph Martin and Lucia Marie (Meyr) Mangels; m. Everett Bowen Watts, Jan. 25, 1946; children: James Everett, Donald Elton, Sheila Ann, Sandra Elaine. LPN. Nurse/lpn Phillips Co Hosp., Malta, Mont., PCH-Home Health, Malta. Leader Brownie Scouts, Malta, Mont., 1963-64, 4-H club, 1966-68; deaconess Congregational Ch., 1989-99. Named Sr. Citizen of Yr., Phillips County, Mont., 2003. Mem.: Order Eastern Star. Avocations: knitting, crocheting. Home: PO Box 924 Malta MT 59538-0924 Office: Phillips Co Hosp Health Malta MT 59538

WATTS, CLAIRE A., retail executive; b. Feb. 26, 1960; BA in Marketing, U. Cin. With Limited Stores, Lands End, May Dept. Stores; divisional merchandising mgr. product devel. Wal-Mart Stores Inc., Bentonville, Ark., 1997—2001, sr. v.p. product devel., 2001—03, exec. v.p., product devel., apparel, & home merchandising, 2003—. Named one of 50 Most Powerful Women in Bus., Fortune mag., 2006. Office: Wal-Mart Stores Inc 702 SW 8th St Bentonville AR 72716*

WATTS, DORIS EARLENE, retired librarian; b. Palatka, Fla., Jan. 7, 1923; d. Charles Franklin and Elouise A.C. (Hagler) Foster; m. Fernand Cortez Watts, Aug. 30, 1950 (dec. 1955); children: Varick Steven, Franklin Cortez. AB, Howard U., 1950; postgrad., Cath. U. Am., 1960-61, postgrad., 1965. Clk. War Dept., Washington, 1942-46, VA, Washington, 1949; editorial clk. Dept. Army, Washington, 1950-52, clk., 1953-59, Dept. Commerce, Washington, 1959; with ICC, Washington, 1959—, librarian, to 1983. Recipient Spl. Achievement award ICC, 1983; recipient Spl. Achievement award, 1984 Mem. ALA, Delta Sigma Theta. Democrat. Methodist. Home: 2502 Perry St NE Washington DC 20018-3133

WATTS, EMILY STIPES, retired English language educator; b. Urbana, Ill., Mar. 16, 1936; d. Royal Arthur and Virginia Louise (Schenck) Stipes; m. Robert Allan Watts, Aug. 30, 1958; children: Benjamin, Edward, Thomas. Student, Smith Coll., 1954-56; AB, U. Ill., 1958, MA (Woodrow Wilson Nat. fellow), 1959, PhD, 1963. Instr. English U. Ill., Urbana, 1963-67, asst. prof., 1967-73, assoc. prof., 1973-77, prof., dir. grad. studies dept. English, 1977—2005, prof. emerita, 2005—; bd. dirs. U. Ill. Athletic Assn., chmn., 1981-83; mem. faculty adv. com. Ill. Bd. Higher Edn., 1984—, vice chmn., 1986-87, chmn., 1987-88. Author: Ernest Hemingway and The Arts, 1971, The Poetry of American Women from 1632 to 1945, 1977, The Businessman in American Literature, 1982; contbg. editor: English Women Writers from the Middle Ages to the Present, 1990; contbr. articles on Jonathan Edwards, Anne Bradstreet to lit. jours. John Simon Guggenheim Meml. Found. fellow, 1973-74 Mem. AAUP, Am. Inst. Archaeology, Assn. Lit. Scholars Critics, Authors Guild, Ill. Hist. Soc., The Phila. Soc., Phi Beta Kappa, Phi Kappa Phi. Presbyterian. Home: 1009 W University Ave Champaign IL 61821-3317

WATTS, GINNY (VIRGINIA C. WATTS), artist; b. Chester, Pa., Jan. 24, 1931; d. Edwin Swoope Craig and Ruth Irene Tonge; m. Lynch S. Watts, Jr., July 21, 1951 (wid.); children: L. Kenneth, Karen Elizabeth Watts Dick, Monica Faye Watts Malandruccolo, Dawn Ellen Watts Eller; m. Alfred E. Meeds, May 5, 1948 (div. Nov. 1950); children: Brenda Joyce Meeds Parker, Edwin Lewis, Michael Alfred. Student, Del. Tech. and C.C., Georgetown, 1998—99. County coord. Easter Seals, Wilmington, Del., 1985-86; resident advisor Dept. Mental Retardation Kencrest Svcs., Dover, 1986-87, program mgr., 1987-90; fine arts instr. Del. Tech. and C.C., Georgetown, 1998—, 2002—. Instr. workshops Millsboro Art League, Del., 1998—. One person shows include Millsboro Art Gallery, 2000; exhibited in group shows at Del. Art Ctr., 1942—, Del. Tech. and C.C., 1997—, Millsboro Art League and Gallery, Del., 1997—, Fine Arts Event, Rehoboth Beach, Del., 2000, Geyers Art Gallery, Milford, Del., 2000, 01, 2002, others; artist oil, graphite and watercolor paintings, 1942—; group mural: wall of Art Gallery/Del. Tech. C.C., 1998; mural for lobby of Presentations, 2000; fine art work exhibited in offices of U.S. Sen. from Del.; contbr. articles to area newspapers. Vice-pres. Adult Art League, Del. Tech. C.C., 1997—; bd. dirs. Millsboro Art League, 1998—, pres., 2001—; mem. Sussex County Arts Coun., 1997—, Nat. Mus. Women in the Arts; bd. advisors Del. Tech. adult plus program Del. Tech. and C.C.; pres. Adult PLUS Art League, 1998—; pres. Millsboro Art League, 2001-. Recipient Excellence of Artistic Achievement award DAPA and Del. Tech. C.C., award for excellence Del. Tech. C.C., 2006. Avocations: swimming, hiking, bicycling, camping, gardening. Personal E-mail: vrcmw@aol.com.

WATTS, HELENA ROSELLE, military analyst; b. East Lynne, Mo., May 29, 1921; d. Elmer Wayne and Nellie Irene (Barrington) Long; m. Henry Millard Watts, June 14, 1940; children: Helena Roselle Watts Scott, Patricia Marie Watts Foble. BA, Johns Hopkins U., 1952, postgrad., 1952—53. Assoc. engr. Westinghouse Corp., Balt., 1965—67; sr. analyst Merck, Sharp & Dohme, Westpoint, Pa., 1967—69; sr. engr. Bendix Radio divsn. Bendix Corp., Balt., 1970—72; sr. scientist Sci. Applications Internat. Corp., McLean, Va., 1975—84; mem. tech. staff The MITRE Corp., McLean, 1985—94; ret., 1994. Adj. prof. Def. Intelligence Coll., Washington, 1984-85. Contbr. articles to profl. jours. Mem. IEEE, AAAS, AIAA, Nat. Mil. Intelligence Assn., U.S. Naval Inst., Navy League U.S., Air Force Assn., Assn. Former Intelligence Officers, Assn. Old Crows, Mensa, N.Y. Acad. Sci. Republican. Roman Catholic. Avocations: photography, reading.

WATTS, JILL MARIE, history educator; b. Pomona, Calif., May 28, 1958; d. Thomas H. and Doris Ruth (Hohlfeld) W. BA in History, U. Calif., San Diego, 1981; MA in History, UCLA, 1983, DPhil in History, 1989. Asst. prof. Weber State U., Ogden, Utah, 1989-91, Calif. State U., San Marcos, 1991-94, assoc. prof., 1994—96, dir. history program, 1994, 1995—96, prof. history, 2002—, and assoc. dept. chair, 2005—. Author: God, Harlem USA: The Father Divine Story, 1992, Mae West: An Icon in Black and White, 2001, Hattie McDaniel: Black Ambition, White Hollywood, 2005; editl. adv. bd. Jour. Popular Culture, 2005-, contbr. articles to profl. publs. (Theodore Salautos award). Carey McWilliams fellow, 1986-87, Rosecrans fellow, 1986-87, Inst. for Am. Cultures fellow, 1986-87, Cornell U. Soc. for Humanities fellow, 1994-95. Mem. Am. Hist. Assn., Orgn. Am. Historians, Am. Studies Assn., Western Assn. Women Historians, Oral History Assn., Popular Culture Assn., Am. Culture Assn. Office: Calif State U History Program San Marcos CA 92096-0001 Business E-Mail: jwatts@csusm.edu.*

WATTS, KAREN YOUNG, mathematics educator; m. David Jonathan Watts, June 8, 1974. MS, Jacksonville State U., Ala., 1978. Cert. tchr. Nat. Bd. for Profl. Tchg. Standards, 2001. Tchr. Talladega City Bd. of Edn., Ala., 1974—90, Jefferson County Bd. of Edn., Birmingham, Ala., 1990—2002, Marshall County Bd. of Edn., Guntersville, Ala., 2002—. Contact person and originator So. Wesleyan U., Central, SC, 2004. Named Secondary Tchr. of the Yr., Marshall County Bd. of Edn., 2005—06; scholar, So. Wesleyan U., 2005. Mem.: Nat. Coun. of Tchrs. Math. Office Phone: 256-593-2810.

WATTS, KISHA MANN, school system administrator, secondary school educator; b. Pensacola, Fla., June 3, 1980; d. Robert Darryl and Karen Theresa Watts. BA, Williams Coll., Williamstown, Mass., 2002. Membership intern Assn. Women in Sci., Washington, 2000; rsch. asst. Marine Biol. Lab., Woods Hole, Mass., 2001; sci. tchr., admissions coord., mid. sch. diversity dir. Thayer Acad., Braintree, Mass., 2002—. Del. for diversity Nat. Assn. Ind. Schs., India. Author: (short abstract) Physiological Characterization of Supramedullary 1 Dorsal Neurons of the Cunner Tautogolabrus Adspersus. Co-chair Nat. Assn. Independant Schs. People of Color Conf., 2007. Named to Wall of Tolerance, So. Poverty Law Ctr., 2003. Mem.: NAACP, Tchg. Tolerance, Nat. Mus. Am. Indian Art, Nat. Scholars Honor Soc. Avocations: yoga, travel, reading, fitness. Office: Thayer Academy 745 Washington St Braintree MA 02184 Office Phone: 781-664-2271. Office Fax: 781-843-2916. Personal E-mail: kishamw2002@yahoo.com. Business E-Mail: kwatts@thayer.org.

WATTS, MARY ANN, retired elementary school educator; b. Harrisburg, Pa., Sept. 13, 1927; d. Major Allan and Ellana Susan (Robinson) Brown; m. Spencer R. Watts, June 23, 1951; children: Shelley Lynn, Allison Dee, Howard Allan. BS, Cheyney U., 1949; postgrad., Temple U., 1965—67, Pa. State U., 1969—72, student, 2003—. Tchr. Harrisburg Sch. Dist., 1949-51, 59-69, Balt. Sch. Dist., 1951-57, Reading (Pa.) Sch. Dist., 1969-89. Mem. sch. dist. dress and discipline code com., 1977-79. Corr. Hamburg Item. Bd. dirs. Pa. State Assn. Boroughs, mem. resolutions and policy com.; mem. Bernville Borough Coun., 1976-2003, v.p., 1988-93, 96-98; sec., treas. Berks County Borough Assn., 1977-2003; Reach to Recovery vol. Am. Cancer Soc. Recipient Disting. Alumna award for achievement in govt. and politics Cheyney U., 1999. Mem. Pa. State Edn. Assn. (life), Pa. Assn. Sch. Retirees, Reading Assn. Sch. Retirees, Bernville Woman's Club (pres. 1978-80, 86-88, Woman of Yr. 1985, Grange Cmty. Svc. award 1988), Pa. State U. Alumni Assn., Cheyney Alumni Assn. Democrat. Mem. United Ch. of Christ.

WATTS, NAOMI, actress; b. Shoreham, Kent, Eng., Sept. 28, 1968; d. Peter Watts. Spl. envoy on HIV/AIDS UN, 2006—. Actor: (films) For Love Alone, 1986, Flirting, 1991, Matinee, 1993, Wide Sargasso Sea, 1993, Gross Misconduct, 1993, The Custodian, 1993, Tank Girl, 1995, Children of the Corn IV: The Gathering, 1996, Persons Unknown, 1996, Under the Lighthouse Dreaming, 1997, Dangerous Beauty, 1998, A House Divided, 1998, Strange Planet, 2001, Ellie Parker, 2001, Down, 2001, Mulholland Drive, 2001, The Ring, 2002, Plots with a View, 2002, Rabbits, 2002, Ned Kelly, 2003, Le Divorce, 2003, 21 Grams, 2003 (Acad. Award nomination for best actress, 2004, Screen Actors Guild Award nomination for best actress, 2004), We Don't Live Here Anymore, 2004, The Assassination of Richard Nixon, 2004, I Heart Huckabees, 2004, Ellie Parker, 2005, The Ring Two, 2005, Stay, 2005, King Kong, 2005; (TV films) Bermuda Triangle, 1996, Timepiece, 1996, The Christmas Wish, 1998, The Hunt for the Unicorn Killer, 1999, The Wyvern Mystery, 2000, The Outsider, 2002; (TV miniseries) Brides of Christ, 1991; (TV series) Home and Away, 1991, Sleepwalkers, 1997. Mailing: Creative Artists Agy 9830 Wilshire Blvd Beverly Hills CA 90212-1825*

WATTS, PAMELA RAE, elementary school educator; b. Parkersburg, W.Va., Oct. 9, 1952; d. William Ray and Luella Veda (Snider) Maze; m. Jack Lee Watts, Dec. 16, 1972; children: Bret Lee, Lachelle Rae, Raquel Dawn. BS cum laude, W.Va. U., 1975; grad., Wood County Tchrs. Acad., 1989; MEd, Marshall U., 1999. Cert. elem. tchr. math. and home econs., W.Va. Clk., sec. Walker/Parkersburg (W.Va.), 1971, 1972; lab. sec. Dupont, Washington, W.Va., 1973, sec. Zytel, 1974; tchr. 4th grade Cedar Grove Elem. Sch., Parkersburg, 1975-78, 79-84, tchr. 3d grade, 1983-89; tchr. 4th grade Kanawha Elem. Sch., Davisville, W.Va., 1989—. Sec. Cedar Grove PTA, Parkersburg, W.Va., 1987-89; fundraising chmn. Kanawha Elem. PTA, Davisville, 1989-93, improvement team, 1989—, coach track team, 1989—; mem. 4th Grade Steering Com. Wood County, Parkersburg, 1991-94; cons. Mary Kay, 1994—. Walking for books coord.; coord. Wood County Social Studies Fair, 2000—. Named Tchr. of Yr., Arch Coal, 2005, 2006. Mem. AAUW (Kanawha faculty senate rep. 1991-94, faculty senate treas. 1996), PTA (v.p., treas. Kanawha chpt. 1999-2001) Wood County Edn. Assn. (sch. rep. 1987-2005), W.Va. Edn. Assn., Phi Theta Kappa, Phi Upsilon Omicron, Alpha Delta Kappa Democrat. Mem. Ch. of Christ. Avocations: cross-stitching, tennis, ceramics, running, walking. Home: 2919 Fairview Ave North Parkersburg WV 26104-2238 Office: Kanawha Elem Sch RR 2 Box 38A Davisville WV 26142-9801 Office Phone: 304-420-9557.

WATTS, SUSAN HELENE, theater educator; d. Howard Harold and Madelyn Rebecca (Moore) Watts. BA, Mich. State U., 1963; MS, U. Kans., 1984. Tchr. Douglas County Schs., Castle Rock, Colo., 1964—74; owner/mgr. Old Bank Cafe, Oskaloosa, Kans., 1976—80; tchr. Valley Falls H.S., 1984—86; instr. Highland C.C., 1986—89; tchr. Oskaloosa H.S., 1986—89; communication coord./actor Omaha Magic Theatre, 1989—90; instr./divsn. chair McCook C.C., 1990—. Charter mem. Leadership McCook, 1990—; bd. mem. S.W. Nebr. Cmty. Theater Assn., 1990—2001; del. Nebr. Transfer Initiative, 1995—; chair local integrity subcom. North Ctrl. Accreditation Com., 1998—2001; adv. bd. Bright Beginnings, 1997—2001; mem. Campus Pres.'s Adv. Coun., 1993—97. Actor: (plays) Marvin's Room, Pools Paradise, Morning's At Seven, (stand up comedy) An Evening with Cassandra; author: (humor column) Dear Cassandra; dir.: (over sixty plays and musicals) (Outstanding Kans. Theatre Tchr., 1983). Banquet com. writer/performer McCook C. of C., 1998—2002; mem. goal setting task force McCook City Coun., 1998—98; mem. McCook Humane Soc., McCook, 1995—2003; bd. dirs. SpringFest, 1998—2000. Named Outstanding Kans. Theatre Tchr., Assn. Kans. Theatre, 1983. Mem.: NEA, Soc. Stage Dir. Choregraphers, Mid-Plains Edn. Assn., Nebr. State Edn. Assn., Kiwanis, Alpha Delta Kappa, Delta Kappa Gamma. Avocations: golf, gardening. Office: McCook Cmty Coll 1205 E Third Mc Cook NE 69001 Office Phone: 308-345-8173.

WATTS, VIRGINIA AGNES, retired special education educator; b. Hampstead, Md., Mar. 14, 1925; d. Thomas Leister and Anna (Freyer) Beam; m. Ervin Olman Watts., Sr., Feb. 9, 1946 (dec. 1972); 1 child, Ervin. RN, St. Agnes Hosp. Sch. Nursing, Balt., 1945; BS, U. Md., 1969, MS, 1974. Nurse St. Agnes Hosp., 1945-46; spl. edn. tchr. Anne Arundel Bd. Edn., Annapolis, Md., 1958-85. Mem. AARP (state housing coord. 1992-93, local health coord. 1993-96, bd. dirs. Capitol City task force 1997—, state legis. coun. 1997—, pres. Md. chpt. 2006), Anne Arundel County Retired Tchrs. Assn. (pres. elect 1997), Md. Sr. Citizen Hall of Fame (bd. dirs. 1999-). Republican. Home: 714 Cotter Rd Glen Burnie MD 21060-7330

WATTS, VIVIAN EDNA, state legislator; b. Detroit, June 7, 1940; d. Edward William and Dorothy Beatrice (Price) Walker; m. David Allan Watts, Jan. 30, 1960; children— Cynthia, Jeffery. B.A., U. Mich., 1962. Pres., Fairfax Area LWV, 1975-77; dir. research Fairfax C. of C., 1977-79; legis. aide U.S. Congress, 1980, Va. Gen. Assembly, 1980-81; legislator Va. Ho. of Dels., 1982-86; sec. Transp. and Pub. Safety, State of Va., 1986—; chmn. joint com. on in-state tuition, 1983. Editor, chmn. report Sch. Closing Task Force, 1978. Bd. dirs. Pre-Paid Legal Services, 1983—. Gov.'s Regulatory Reform Adv. Bd., 1982—, No. Va. Community Coll. Child Care Bd., 1980—; exec. bd. Nat. Capital United Way, 1976—; chmn. Tax and Revenue of Fairfax Fiscal Commn., 1978; founding mem. Fairfax Com. 100, 1975; chmn. 1978 Sch. Bond Referendum, 1978; mem. Gov.'s Cabinet; cons. Arthur Young & Co., 1985-86; child care bd. No. Va. Community Coll., 1980-85. Named Co-Fairfax County Citizen of Year, Washington Star, 1978, Citizen of Yr. Annandale (Va.) C. of C., 1986. Mem. No. Va. Consortium for Continuing Higher Edn. (dir.), Friends of Victim Assistance Network (dir.), No. Va. Coalition for Children (dir.), Bus. and Profl. Women (Woman of Yr. 1983), Woman Execs. in State Govt.

WATTS, WENDY HAZEL, wine consultant; b. York, Pa., Oct. 9, 1952; d. Alphonso Irving and Daphne Jean (Gainsford) Watts; m. Frederic Joseph Bonnie, (div. 1986); m. Kenneth Scott Herron, Feb. 14, 1987 (div. Jan. 1992). BS, U. Cin., 1975. Store mgr. The Grapevine, Inc., Birmingham, Ala., 1978-81; sales rep. Supreme Beverage Co., Birmingham, 1981-84, Internat. Wines Co., Birmingham, 1984-90; nat. sales exec. Kermit Lynch Wine Mcht., Berkeley, Calif., 1990-91; on-premise mgr., fine wine mgr. Premier Beverage Co., Birmingham, 1991-94; key accounts mgr. Ala. Crown Distbg. Co., Birmingham, 1994-95; dir. of wine Mountain Brook location Western Supermarkets, 1995—2001; dist. mgr. Winebow Italian Imports, 2001—05, state mgr., 2005—. Instr. ednl. wine tasting classes, 1996—; spkr., instr. various groups, Birmingham; co-chmn. Sonoma Wine Tour of Birmingham, 1987—88, chmn., 1989—90, Wine Tour of France, Birmingham, 1988—89; mem. exec. com. Taste of the Nation, 1992—98. Wine radio show host, 1992. Co-chmn. Multiple Sclerosis Wine Auction, 1992—93, mem. exec. com., 1997—; co-chair Share Our Strength Taste of the Nation, Birmingham, 1996-98; bd. dirs. Magic City Harvest, 1999—, vice chair, 2005—; mem. com. So. Environ. Ctr. Democrat. Avocations: wine and food tasting, designing, films, hiking, Italian language and culture.

WAVLE, ELIZABETH MARGARET, academic administrator; b. Homer, NY, Jan. 18, 1957; d. John Andrew Jr. and Louise Hayford (Estey) W. BMus, SUNY, Potsdam, 1979; AM in Libr. Sci., U. Mich., 1980; MS in Edn., Elmira Coll., 1990. Sr. libr. asst. U. Mich., Ann Arbor, 1979-80; pub. svcs. libr. Elmira (N.Y.) Coll., 1980-84, instr. music, 1981-97, head tech. svcs., 1984-97, coord. women's studies, 1992, 96-97, 2005—, dir., 2004—; assoc. dir. Ithaca (N.Y.) Coll., 1998—2004. Mem. South Ctrl. Rsch. Libr. Coun. Interlibr. Loan Adv. Com., Ithaca, N.Y., 1991-93; regional automation com. South Ctrl. Rsch. Libr. Coun., Ithaca, 1994-95, resource sharing com., 1996-97, pers. com., 2000-05, bd. trustees, 2003-05, fin. com., 2004-05, exec. com., 2005—, pres., 2006—; bd. trustees Steele Meml. Libr., Elmira, 2004-05, Chemung County Libr. Dist., 2006—, pres., 2006—. Contbr. revs., essays to profl. publs. Trustee Chemung County Libr. Dist., 2005—, pres., 2005—; trustee Steele Meml. Libr. Found., 2006—. Mem.: First Unitarian Soc. Ithaca. Democrat. Avocations: music, reading, antiques. Office: Elmira Coll Gannett-Tripp Libr One Park Pl Elmira NY 14901 Office Phone: 607-735-1865. Business E-Mail: ewavle@elmira.edu.

WAWRZASZEK, SUSAN V., university librarian; MSLS, SUNY Buffalo. With Brandeis U., Mass., 1995—, assoc. univ. libr. Mass., 2002—03, acting univ. libr. Mass., 2003—05, univ. libr. Mass., 2005—. Office: Brandeis U Mailstop 045 PO Box 549110 Waltham MA 02454-9110 Office Phone: 781-736-4700. Office Fax: 781-736-4719. E-mail: wawrzaszek@brandeis.edu.*

WAX, AMY LAURA, law educator; BS summa cum laude, Yale U., 1975; MD cum laude, Harvard U., 1981; JD, Columbia U., 1987. Bar: NY 1988. Resident in neurology NY Hosp.-Cornell Med. Ctr., 1982—85; cons. neurologist Bronx Cross County Clinic, NY, 1985—87, Brooklyn North Med. Group, 1985—87; law clk. to Hon. Abner J. Mikva US Ct. Appeals, DC Cir., 1987—88; asst. to solicitor gen. Office of Solicitor Gen., US Dept. Justice, Washington, DC, 1988—94; assoc. prof. U. Va. Law Sch., 1994—99, prof., 1999—2000, Class of 1948 prof. scholarly rsch. in law, 2000—01; vis. prof. U. Pa. Law Sch., Phila., 2000, prof. law, 2001—. Contbr. articles to profl. jours. Office: U Pa Law Sch 3400 Chestnut St Philadelphia PA 19104 Office Phone: 215-898-5638. Office Fax: 215-994-0496. E-mail: awax@law.upenn.edu.

WAX, NADINE VIRGINIA, retired bank executive; b. Van Horne, Iowa, Dec. 7, 1927; d. Laurel Lloyd and Viola Henrietta (Schrader) Bobzien; divorced; 1 child, Sharlyn K. Wax Munns. Student, U. Iowa, 1970-71; grad. Nat. Sch. Real Estate and Fin., Ohio State U., 1980-8l. Jr. acct. McGladrey, Hansen, Dunn (now McGladrey-Pullen Co., CPAs), Cedar Rapids, Iowa, 1944-47; office mgr. Iowa Securities Co. (now Wells Fargo Mortgage Co.), Cedar Rapids, 1954-55; asst. cashier Mchts. Nat. Bank (now U.S. Bancorp.), Cedar Rapids, 1956-75; asst. v.p. Mchts. Nat. Bank (now U.S. Bancorp), Cedar Rapids, 1976-78, v.p., 1979-90; ret., 1990. Vol. St. Luke's Hosp. Aux., Cedar Rapids, 1981—85, SCORE, 1999—2006; bd. dirs., v.p. Kirkwood C.C. Facilities Found., 1970—2006; bd. dirs., treas. Kirkwood C.C., 1984—91; trustee Indian Creek Nature Ctr., Cedar Rapids, 1974—2006, pres., 1980—81; mem. Linn County Regional Planning Commn., 1982—92, Cedar Rapids-Marion Fine Arts Coun., 1994—97; bd. suprs. Compensation Commn. for Condemnation, 1987—92; bd. dirs. Am. Heart Assn., Cedar Rapids, 1983—94; mem. Iowa Employment and Tng. Coun., Des Moines, 1982—83. Recipient Outstanding Woman award, Cedar Rapids Tribute to Women and Industry, 1984. Mem. Fin. Women Internat. (state edn. chmn. 1982-83), Am. Inst. Banking (bd. dirs. 1968-70), Soc. Real Estate Appraisers (treas. 1978-80), Linn County Bankers Assn. (pres. 1979-80), Cedar Rapids Bd. Realtors, Cedar Rapids C. of C. (bus.-edn. com. 1986-91), Cedar Rapids Country Club. Lutheran. Avocations: travel, reading, walking. Home: 147 Ashcombe SE Cedar Rapids IA 52403-1700

WAXBERG, EMILY STEINHARDT, special education educator, administrator; b. NYC, Nov. 19, 1918; d. Samuel M. and Leonora Steinhardt; m. Ira L. Waxberg; children: Ronald, Drew, Kelton. BA in Art, Empire State U., 1974; MS, C.W. Post, 1975; MA, PhD, Nova U., 1976—79. Lic. spl. edn. tchr. N.Y. Tchr. Bd. Edn., N.Y., 1980. Tchr. Bd. Edn., N.Y.; cons. Wartburg Day Health Care Ctr., Bklyn.; recreation therapist, supr. Pilgrim State Hosp., Brentwood, N.Y.; subs. tchr. BOCES, L.I.; ret., 1985. Past pres. Town of Oyster Bay (N.Y.) Arts Coun., Suburban Art League, L.I. Docent Nassau County Art Mus., Roslyn, N.Y., 1990—, Coe Mansion, Oyster Bay, 1990—; ombondsman United Presbyn. Home, Syosset, N.Y., 1996—. Grantee, N.Y. State, 1995; named Woman of Yr. in Arts in 2001, Town of Oyster Bay, L.I., Woman of Distinction in Arts, 2002. Mem.: Ind. Art Soc., BACCA Ind. Art League, L.I. Arts Coun., Art League Nassau County, Nat. League Am. Pen Women. Avocations: music, reading, travel, art. Home: 37 Fox Pl Hicksville NY 11801-5752

WAXLER, BEVERLY JEAN, anesthesiologist, physician; d. Isadore and Ada Belle (Gross) Marcus; m. Richard Norman Waxler, Dec. 24, 1972; 1 child, Adam R. BS in Biology, No. Ill. U., 1971; MD, U. Ill., Chgo., 1975. Diplomate Am. Bd. Anesthesiology, Am. Bd. Pathology. Intern dept. pathology Northwestern U., Chgo., 1975—76, resident, 1976—79; instr. Rush Presbyn. St. Luke's Med. Ctr., Chgo., 1979—81; asst. prof. pathology Loyola U., Maywood, Ill., 1981—84; resident dept. anesthesiology Stroger Hosp. Cook County (formerly Cook County Hosp.), Chgo., 1984—87; attending anesthesiologist Stroger Hosp. Cook County, Chgo., 1987—; chmn. divsn. postanesthetic care Stroger Hosp. of Cook County, Chgo., 2004—; clin. asst. prof. U. Ill., Chgo., 1988—95; asst. prof. Rush Med. Coll., Chgo., 1996—. Contbr. articles to profl. jours. Grantee, Varlen Corp., 1982; Nat. Rsch. Svc. fellow, Nat. Cancer Inst., 1980. Mem.: AAAS, Ill. Soc. Anesthesiologists, Chgo. Soc. Anesthesiologists, Am. Soc. Anesthesiologists, Internat. Anesthesia Rsch. Soc. (B. B. Sankey Anesthesia Advancement award 1989), Sigma Xi. Office: Stroger Hosp Cook County Dept Anesthesiology 1901 W Harrison St Chicago IL 60612 Office Phone: 312-864-2140. Business E-Mail: bwaxler@rush.edu.

WAXMAN, ANITA, theater producer; Prodr. (plays) Mrs. Klein, Below the Belt, Wild Honey (Drama Desk award nomination), The Foreigner, Music Man, 2000-01, One Flew Over the Cuckoo's Nest, 2001 (Tony award for Best Revival of a Play), Noises Off, 2001-02, Top Dog/Underdog, 2002 (Tony award for Best Play and Pulitzer Prize), The Elephant Man, 2002, Flower Drum Song, 2002-03, Gypsy, 2004 (Tony award for Best Revival of a Musical), Bombay Dreams, 2004—; co-prodr. (plays) Present Laughter (Tony award nomination), Breaking the Code, Circle & Bravo, Long Day's Journey Into Night, Annie get Your Gun, Mr. & Mrs. Nobody. Founder Noah's Ark Found.; creator Passin-Waxman Ctr., Moscow. Office: Waxman Williams Entertainment 260 W 44th St Ste 500 New York NY 10036-3900

WAY, BARBARA HAIGHT, retired dermatologist; b. Franklin, NJ, Dec. 27, 1941; d. Charles Padley and Alice Barbara (Haight) Shoemaker; m. Anthony Biden Way; children: Matthew Shoemaker Way, Sarah Shoemaker Way. AB in Music cum laude, Bryn Mawr Coll., 1962, postgrad., 1963-64; MD, U. Pa., 1968. Diplomate Am. Bd. Dermatology. Systems engr. IBM, Balt., 1962—63;

mem. dean's staff Bryn Mawr (Pa.) Coll., 1963—64; med. intern U. Wis. Hosps., Madison, 1968—69, resident in dermatology, 1969—72; physician emergency rm. St. Francis Hosp., La Crosse, Wis., 1969—72, founder dept. dermatology, 1972; asst. prof. dept. dermatology Tex. Tech U. Sch. Medicine, Lubbock, 1972—73, from asst. clin. to assoc. clin. prof., 1973—74, asst. prof., assoc. chair, 1974—76, assoc. prof., chair, 1976—81, assoc. clin. prof., 1981—92; clin. prof. Tex. Tech. U. Health Scis. Ctr., Lubbock, 1995—2005, founder, dir. dermatology residency tng. program, 1978—81, pvt. practice, 1973—74, 1981—2006; acting dir. Lubbock City Health Dept., 1982—83; ret., 2006. Courtesy staff Covenant Hosp., Lubbock, subsect. chief, 1992, 94; courtesy staff Covenant Lakeside Hosp., Lubbock, mem. credentials com., 1990, 92, 94, 95, founding dir. phototherapy unit, 1990-91, 93, mem. exec. com., 1991, 93, 98, chief dermatology sect., 1991, 93, 98. Alumna admissions rep. Bryn Mawr Coll., 1972-75, 87-96; mem. selection com. outstanding physician Lubbock chpt. Am. Cancer Soc., 1991-94, chmn., 1991; bd. dirs. Tex. Tech. U. Med. Found., 1987-89, Double T. Connection, 1988-90. Fellow Am. Acad. Dermatology (reviewer jour.); mem. Tex. Dermatol. Soc. (chmn. roster com. 1980), Tex. Med. Assn. (mem. sexually transmitted diseases com. 1986-90, mem. coun. pub. health 1990-92, vice councillor dist. III 1992-98, councillor dist. III 1998-2000, chmn. reference com. fin. and orgnl. affairs ann. session 1992), Lubbock County-Garza County Med. Soc. (mem. various coms. 1980-2000, chmn. sch. and pub. health com. 1983, mem. bd. censors 1983-85, chair 1985, sec. 1986, v.p. 1987, liaison with Tex. Tech. U. Health Scis. Ctr. com. 1988-91, co-chmn. pub. rels. com. 1988-89, alt. Tex. Med. Assn. del. 1988-89, del. 1990-95, 98-2000, pres.-elect 1989, pres. 1990, chmn. ad hoc bylaws com. 1991-94, chmn. Hippocratic award 1991), Women's Dermatologic Soc. (founding sec.). Office Phone: 214-353-0195. Personal E-mail: anthony.way@ttuhsc.edu.

WAYBOURN, KATHLEEN ANN, lawyer, consultant; BA magna cum laude, Queens Coll., Flushing, N.Y., 1978; JD, St. John's U. Law Sch., Jamaica, N.Y., 1984. Bar: N.Y. 1985, U.S. Supreme Ct. 2000, U.S. Dist. Ct. (so. dist.), N.Y. 2002; cert. chemist Am. Chem. Soc. Ind. legal cons. Office of Corp. Counsel City N.Y., 1985—86; atty. Aaron J. Broder, PC, NYC, 1988—92; pvt. practice, 1991—; assoc. atty. Mangiatordi, Maher and Lemmo, LLC, 1998—99; contract atty. Steven R. Harris and Assocs., 1999—. Pres. Toxic Tort Cons., Inc., N.Y.C., 2001—. Author: Informed Consent, 1994—97. Pro bono homeless shelter advocacy project NY County Lawyers Assn., 1991—92, with sex discrimination clinic and no sweatshop coalition, 1994—. Recipient cmty. svc. awards, N.Y. County Lawyers Assn.; tchg. fellow scholarship, NYU Grad. Sch. Arts and Scis., 1978—79. Mem.: NY County Lawyers Assn., Assn. Trial Lawyers Am., NY State Trial Lawyers' Assn., Beta Delta Chi. Avocations: photography, skindiving, swimming, scuba diving. Office: 110 E 59th St Ste 3200 New York NY 10022

WAYLONIS, JEAN LYNNETTE, elementary school educator; b. Brookville, Pa., Mar. 9, 1953; d. Leslie Edwin Gray and Lillian Wanita Bryant; m. Anthony John Waylonis, June 16, 1973; children: Anthony James, Ellen Claire. BS in child devel. and early childhood edn., Pa. State U., 1971—75; MA in early childhood spl. edn., George Wash. U., 1997—99. Postgraduate Professional License Va. Dept. of Edn., 2000. Pre-kindergarten tchr. Norfolk Pub. Schools, Norfolk, Va., 1976—78; dir. Subic Bay Naval Base Nursery Sch. Assn., Philippines, 1979—81; family adv. Family Advocacy Ctr., Subic Bay Naval Base, Philippines, 1981—82; multi-age inclusion tchr. FCPS - Belvedere Elem., Falls Church, Va., 1989—. Mentor Fairfax County Pub. Schools, Falls Ch., Va., 1992—99; trainer Project Realign, Washington, 1995—98; cons./trainer/presenter Collaborative Inclusion Project Team, Washington, 1992—99; presenter Fairfax County Pub. Schools, Fairfax, Va., 1992—. Composer: (song) Five Little Bunnies; contbr. article George Mason U. TAC Newsletter. Presenter Child Day Care Coun., Richmond, Va., 1997. Recipient Outstanding Leader award, Girl Scout Coun. Nation's Capital, 1996, Exceptional Inclusion Tchr., Va. Divsn. of Early Childhood, 1995; grant, Coun. for Exceptional Children, 1995. Mem.: AAUW (assoc.), NEA (assoc.), Nat. Assn. for Educators of Young Children (assoc.). Catholic. Avocations: sewing, travel. Home: 7201 Galgate Dr Springfield VA 22153 Office: FCPS - Belvedere Elementary School 6540 Columbia Pike Falls Church VA 22041 Personal E-mail: waylonis@erols.com. E-mail: jean.waylonis@fcps.edu.

WAYNE, JANE ELLEN, author; b. Phila., Apr. 6, 1936; d. Jesse Allen and Eleanor Mae (Brundle) Stump; student Grove City Coll., 1956, NYU, 1956, Am. Acad. Dramatic Arts, 1957; m. Ronald R. Wayne, May 26, 1958 (div. 1967); 1 dau., Elizabeth Jo. Mem. promotion staff NBC, NYC, 1957-65; mgr. V.I.P. div. NY World's Fair, 1966; v.p. Abbot & Abbot Corp., NYC, 1974-87; creator Beauty and Poise pvt. classes for bus. women, 1963-66. Mem. The Author's Guild, Sigma Delta Phi. Republican. Author: The Life of Robert Taylor, 1977; Kings of Tragedy, 1977; Tiffany, 1979; Lividia, 1979; The Love Gap, 1979; Kings of Tragedy II, 1982; Kings and Queens of Tragedy, 1983; The Barbara Stanwyck Story, 1985, Gable's Women, 1987, Joan Crawford's Men, 1988, Gary Cooper's Women, 1988, Robert Taylor, 1989, Ava's Men: The Private Life of Ava Gardner, 1990, Grace Kelly's Men, 1991, Lana: The Life and Loves of Lana Turner, 1995, The Golden Girls of MGM, 2002, The Leading Men of MGM, 2005; contbr. to Nat. Enquirer, Star mag.

WAYNE, JUNE CLAIRE, artist; b. Chgo., Mar. 7, 1918; d. Albert and Dorothy Alice (Kline) LaVine. DFA (hon.), Rutgers U., 2005. Indsl. designer, N.Y.C., 1939-41; radio writer, mem. staff sta. WGN, Chgo., 1942-43; founder, 1959; since dir. Tamarind Lithography Workshop, Inc. (funded by Ford Found.), Los Angeles; Tamarind Inst., U. N.Mex., 1970—. Mem. vis. com. Sch. Visual and Environ. Studies, Harvard, 1972-74, chancellors adv. com., arts mgmt. program Grad. Sch. Adminstrn., U. Calif. at Los Angeles, 1969-80, Calif. Confederation of Arts adv. bd., 1988, Calif. State U. dept. of art adv. coun., Long Beach, 1988, Rutgers U. Mason Gross Sch. Arts prof. of rsch. printmaking and paper, New Brunswick, NJ, 2002-. Contbr. articles to profl. publs.; subject TV programs.; Numerous one-woman exhbns., 1935—, latest being, Art Mus., U. N.Mex., 1968, Cin. Art Mus., 1969, Iowa Art Mus., U. Iowa, 1970, Grunwald Graphics Arts Found., U. Calif. at Los Angeles, 1971, Municipal Art Gallery, Barnsdall Park, LA, 1973, Van Doren Gallery, San Francisco, 1974, La Demeure, Paris, 1974, Musée de Brest, France, 1976, Montgomery Gallery, Pomona Colls., Calif., 1978, Ariz. State U. Galleries, 1978, ICA travelling exhbn., Rennes, 1976, Nancy, 1977, Brussels, 1978, Reims, 1978, Lyons, 1979, Neuberger Mus., Purchase, NY, 1997, Skirball Mus., Cin., 1998, LA County Mus. Art, 1998, Palm Springs Desert Mus., Calif., 1999, A.R.T. Gallery, NY, 2003, Rutgers U., Newark, 2005, The Armory Ctr. for Arts, Pasadena, Calif., 2005, Stedman Gallery, Newark, 2005, Mason Gross Galleries, New Brunswick, NJ, 2006, Birmingham Mus. and Art Gallery, UK, 2006, Tama Art U. Mus., Tokyo, 2006; rep. permanent collections, Library of Congress, The British Mus., London, Mus. Modern Art, NYC, Art Inst. Chgo., Houghton Library at Harvard, Smithsonian Instn., Rosenwald Collection, The Victoria and Albert Mus., London, Nat. Gallery Art, NY Pub. Library, Cin. Art Mus., Pasadena (Calif.) Mus. Art, Phila. Mus. Art, Phila. Print Club, Birmingham Mus. and Art Gallery, Walker Art Center, Mpls., Zimmerli Art Mus., New Brunswick. Bd. dirs. Grunwald Center Graphic Arts, 1965-80. Recipient numerous prizes, 1950—, latest being Prix de la Biennal Internat. de L'Estampe d'Epinal, France, 1971; Purchase prize Biennal d'Epinal, 1973; Golden Eagle Cine award and Acad. award nomination for film Four Stones for Kanemitsu, 1974; Silver Life Achievement award YWCA, 1983; Communicator award Women in Media, 1983; Woman of the Year, Palm Springs Desert Mus., 1999; Zimmerli award Women in Arts Com., Coll. Arts Assn., 2003; Mason Gross Sch. Disting. Svc. Arts award, 2004. Mem. Writers Guild Am., Women in Film, AFTRA, Women's Caucus for Art, Soc. Am. Graphic Artists, Soc. Washington Printmakers, LA Printmakers Soc., The Trusteeship, Internat. Women's Forum. Address: 1108 Tamarind Ave Los Angeles CA 90038-1906

WAYNE, KYRA PETROVSKAYA, writer; b. Crimea, USSR, Dec. 31, 1918; arrived in U.S., 1948, naturalized, 1951; d. Prince Vasily Sergeyevich and Baroness Zinaida Fedorovna (Fon-Haffenberg) Obolensky; m. George J. Wayne, Apr. 21, 1961; 1 child, Ronald George. BA, Leningrad Inst. Theatre Arts, 1939, MA, 1940. Actress, concert singer, Russia, 1939-46; actress, 1948-59; enrichment lectr. Royal Viking Line cruises, Alaska-Can., Greek Islands-Black Sea, Russia/Europe, 1978-79, 81-82, 83-84, 86-8, 88. Author: Kyra, 1959, Kyra's Secrets of Russian Cooking, 1960, 1993, The Quest for the Golden Fleece, 1962, Shurik, 1971, 1992, The Awakening, 1972, The Witches of Barguzin, 1975, Max, The Dog that Refused to Die, 1979 (Best Fiction award Dog Writers Assn. Am., 1980), Rekindle the Dreams, 1979, Quest for Empire, 1986, Li'l Ol' Charlie, 1989, Quest for Bigfoot, 1996, Pepper's Ordeal, 2000, The Chaperone, 2006. Founder, pres. Clean Air Program, Los Angeles County, 1971—72; mem. Seattle Art Mus.; mem. women's coun. Sta. KCET-Ednl. TV; mem. Monterey County Symphony Guild, 1989—91, Monterey Bay Aquarium, Monterey Peninsula Mus. Art, Friends of La Mirada, Fresno Art Mus., Fresno Met. Mus., Valley Children's Hosp. Served to lt. Russian Army, 1941—43. Decorated Red Star, numerous decorations USSR; recipient award, Crusade for Freedom, 1955—56, Los Angeles County, 1972, Merit award, Am. Lung Assn. Los Angeles County, 1988, award of Merit, Congress Russian Ams., 1999. Mem.: Seattle Art Mus., Idyllwild Sch. Music, Carmel Music Soc. (bd. dirs. 1992—94), Authors Guild, Soc. Children's Book Writers, PEN, Fresno Philharm., UCLA Affiliates (life), L.A. Lung Assn. (life; pres. and founder clean air program 1972—74), Art and Theatre Assn. (trustee 1987), Friends Lung Assn. (pres. 1988), UCLA Med. Faculty Wives (pres. 1970—71, dir. 1971—75), Club 25, Los Angelenos Club (life). Home: 25875 Canyon Rd NW Poulsbo WA 98370 Office Phone: 360-779-4480. Personal E-mail: kyrapwayne@aol.com.

WAYNE, SHARON H., mathematics professor; BS in Edn., U. Ga., Athens, 1970; MEd, Ga. State U., Atlanta, 1976. Math tchr. Chapel Hill City Schs., NC, 1970—72, DeKalb County Schs., Tucker, Ga., 1972—76; math tchr., dept. head Henry County Schs., Martinsville, Va., 1976—94; assoc. prof. Patrick Henry CC, Martinsville, 1997—. Vol. Va. Shares Food Program, Martinsville, 2002—06; asst. treas. Starling Ave. Bapt. Ch., Martinsville, 1997—. Recipient Disting. Faculty Achievement award, Patrick Henry CC, 1998. Mem.: ASCD, Va. Math. Assn. Two-Yr. Colls., Nat. Coun. Tchrs. Math., Va. CC Assn. (Showcase award 1999), Nat. Assn. Devel. Educators. Office Phone: 276-656-0284.

WAYNICK, CATHERINE ELIZABETH MAPLES, bishop; b. Nov. 13, 1948; d. Sevedus A. and Janet E. (Wilcox) Maples; m. Larry Wade Waynick, Nov. 28, 1968; 2 children. Student, Ctrl. Mich. U., 1966—68; BA in Religious Studies, Madonna Coll., 1981; MDiv, St. John's Provincial Sem., Plymouth, MI, 1985; DD (hon.), The Gen. Sem., NYC, 1998. Ordained deacon, 1985, priest, 1986; rector All Saints' Parish, Pontiac, Mich., 1994—97; consecrated bishop, 1997; bishop Episcopal Diocese of Indpls., 1997—. Mem. bd. Bexley Hall Sem., Rochester, NY. Office: Episcopal Diocese Indpls 1100 W 42nd St Indianapolis IN 46208 Office Phone: 317-926-5454. Office Fax: 317-926-5456.

WEAN, KARLA DENISE, secondary school educator; BS in Biology and Gen. Sci., Wheeling Jesuit Coll., W.Va., 1978, BA in Art, 1981; MS in Art Edn., Fla. State U., Tallahassee, 1990; grad. Arts Mgm. Sch., N.C. State U., Raleigh, 1980. Cert. tchr. Nat. Bd. Tchrs., 2000. Tchr. art, chmn. dept. Mt. de Chantal Acad., Wheeling, 1978-81; tchr. fine arts Montverde (Fla.) Acad., 1981-83; instr. art Lake Sumter C.C., Leesburg, Fla., 1981-82; art and sci. tchr. Sante Fe Cath. High Sch., Lakeland, Fla., 1983-85; art tchr. Kathleen (Fla.) Jr. High/Mid. Sch., 1985-95; instr. Polk Mus. Art, Lakeland, Fla., 1989—91; musician, composer Nav Videos, Lakeland, 1990-91; tchr. art Bartow (Fla.) H.S., 1995-97, Auburndale (Fla.) H.S., 1997—99, Mulberry H.S., 1999—. Bd. dirs. Arts on the Park, Lakeland, 1989-95, performer original music in concert entitled Seasons of Time, 1993; children's choir dir. St. John Neuman's Ch., Mulberry, Fla., 1991-95, St. Matthews, Winter Haven, Fla., 1995-96; singer, violinist, guitarist, flutist Ch. of the Resurrection, Lakeland, 1989-90, St. John Neuman's Ch. Folk Choir, 1991—; mem. Up With People, internat. song and dance group, 1978; musician, cantor, violinist, flutist, guitarist St. Anthony's Ch., Lakeland, Fla., 2003-04; singer, instrumentalist St. David's Ch., Lakeland, 2005-. Composer, performer videos Look and Draw, Faces and Figures; one woman show includes Wheeling Jesuit Coll.; exhibited in group shows at Lakeland Electric, 1990, Bartow Bloomin' Arts, 1990, Lakeland Art Guild Show, 1991 (Best in Show award 2001), Strawberry Festival, 1999, 2002 (1st pl. award 1999, 3d pl. award 1999). Goodwill amb. State of W.Va., 1978; vol. sheltered workshop of handicapped, 1984-85; sec.-treas. Coastal State Rabbit Club, 1996-97, bd. dirs., 1997-98. Recipient Disting. Leadership award in teaching, 1985, Jim Harbin Fame video award State of Fla., Tallahassee, 1991, Excellence in Edn. Bahai award Bahai Assn., Lakeland, 1991, Merit award Arts on the Park Mixed Media Show, 1995, awards in various art shows including 1st Pl. Sculpture Lakeland Art Guild, 2003, 2d Pl., 2004, 3d Pl. Mixed Media Ridge Art, Winter Haven, 2004, Lakeland Art Guild, 2005; selected to attend Disting. Fellows Symposium, Art Edn. Assn., 2004; commd. local radio sta., Lakeland, 2006. Mem. Nat. Art Edn. Assn., Fla. Art Edn. Assn.

WEARE, SALLY SPIEGEL, artist, educator; b. Chgo., Dec. 11, 1942; d. Manuel and Janice (Gottlieb) Spiegel; m. Shane Weare, June 7, 1964; children: Tobias, Kate. BA, U. Iowa, 1964; postgrad., St. Martin's Sch. of Art, 1966-67; MFA in Painting, Mills Coll., 1977. Lectr. Calif. Coll. of Arts and Crafts, Oakland, 1979; vis. artist Art Inst. of Chgo.; instr. Vista Coll., Berkeley, 1980, 87-90, Ctr. for Exptl./Interdisciplinary Art San Francisco State U., 1979-84. Leader round table discussion U.S. Embassy, Belgrade, Serbia, 1996. Exhibited works in solo show at Chaos Gallery, Belgrade, Yugoslavia, 1996; group shows at Berkeley (Calif.) Art Ctr., Sonoma County Mus. Visual Art, Santa Rosa, Calif., 1997, 98. Mem. Women's Caucus for Art Coll. Art Assn., 1979-83; bd. dir. Women Environ. Artists Directory. Va. Ctr. for the Arts fellow, 1991, Millay Colony fellow, N.Y., 1992. Studio: 2663 Bennett Ridge Rd Santa Rosa CA 95404 E-mail: sallyweare@hotmail.com.

WEATHERBEE, ELLEN GENE ELLIOTT, botanist, educator; b. Lansing, Mich., Sept. 16, 1939; d. Eugene Bradley and Wilma Alcott (Gardner) Elliott; m. Lee Weatherbee, Aug. 18, 1958 (dec. 1996); children: Anne Susan, Brent Robert, Julie Patricia. BA in Edn., U. Mich., 1960, postgrad., 1972-77; MA in English Lit., Eastern Mich. U., 1962. Cert. tchr. Tchr. adult edn. Schoolcraft Coll., Livonia, Mich., 1983-85; tchr. adult edn. lifelong learning program U. Mich./Wayne State U., Ann Arbor and Detroit, 1973-84; tchr. adult edn. Leelanau Schs./Sleeping Bear Nat. Lakeshore, 1982-86; tchr., nature trip leader adult edn. program Matthaei Bot. Gardens, U. Mich., Ann Arbor, 1984—, dir., founder adult edn. program, 1984—2004; cons. botanist U. Mich., Ann Arbor, 1977—. Cons. on plant and mushroom identification Mich. Hosps. Poison Control Ctr., 1978—; mem. editl. bd. Mich. Botanist, 1978-2003; founder, dir. Weatherbee's Bot. Trips, 1990—; field worker for wetlands and threatened and endangered species Mich. Dept. Natural Resources and Army Corp of Engrs.; bot. cons. for wetlands permits, 1991—; botany instr. for in-svc. tng. Mich. Dept. Environ. Quality Wetland Regulators; botany trainer Mich. Dept. Environ. Quality Corps Engrs., USDA Soil Scientists in Wetland Tng., 1999. Author: Coastal Plants of the Great Lakes Region, 2006; co-author: Edible Wild Plants, A Guide to Collecting and Cooking, 1982. Former constable Dem. party, Ann Arbor Twp., Mich. Mem. Fedn. Ont. Naturalists, Mich. Bot. Club, Nature Conservancy, N.Am. Mycological Assn., Pipsissewa Chamber Music Soc. Avocations: plants and habitats, backpacking, sea kayaking, playing cello, swimming. Home: 11405 Patterson Lake Dr Pinckney MI 48169-9748 Business E-Mail: eew@umich.edu.

WEATHERFORD, HAZEL ALICE, minister; d. Charles Augustus and Irma Hazel (Sample) Stief; m. Joe L. Weatherford (dec. Dec. 1965); children: Rebecc Anne Weatherford Irwin, John Charles. Student, Newspaper Inst. Am. Corr. Sch., Chgo., 1947—49, Lower Columbia Coll., 1966—69, Famous Writer's Corr. Sch., LA, 1966—68, Portland CC, Oreg., 1986—87, Zion Christian Fellowship, Melbourne Beach, Fla., 1991—93; grad., Inst. Children's Lit., West Redding, Conn., 2005. X-ray technician then office mgr. Dr. E.A. Grauer D.C., Longview, Wash., 1957—58; owner, mgr. Crown Photo Svc., Inc., Longview, 1958—72; cost-effective adminstr. Hope Christian Fellowship, Forrest Grove, Aloha, Oreg., 1986—87; editor New Creation Ministries, Inc., Medford, Oreg., 1988—90, Grover City, Calif., 1988—90; pastor Bible studies and counseling Ch. of the Nazarene, Frostburg, Md., 2003—. Bridal cons. Crown Photo Svc., Inc., Cowlitz County, Wash., 1962—72; pres. Bus. Women's Assn., Longview, 1964—66. Pres. Columbia Valley Garden PTA, Longview, 1948—51; bd. chmn. Alcohol and Drug Prevention/Treatment, Cowlitz County, 1968—71; Wash. and Oreg. pres., nat. spkr. Women's Aglow Internat., 1973—2001; mgr. State Senatorial Campaign Senator Tom Hall, Longview, 1963—64, State Senatorial Campaign Tom Gregg, Forrest Grove, Oreg., 1987; chairwoman bd. deaconesses Valley Bapt. Ch., Longview, 1955—59. Named Poet of Merit, Am. Poetry Assn., 1989; recipient First Place award, Eastman Acad. Awards Internat., 1963—64, Poetic Excellence award, Poetic Voice Am. Anthology, 1998. Mem.: Soc. Children's Book Writers and Illustrators. Avocations: sewing, reading, interior decorating, exercise. Office: Frostburg Ch of the Nazarene 150 Center St Frostburg MD 21532 Home: 84 Lesser Ave Apt 235 Nashville TN 37210-4263 E-mail: gramzell@bellsouth.net.

WEATHERINGTON, LAVETA HINSON, visual arts specialist; d. Charles Brantley and Helen Marie Hinson; children: Virginia Marie, Clifton Brantley. BS, East Carolina U., 1973, MA in Edn., 1977. National Board Certification EMC Art Nat. Bd. of Profl. Tchg. Std., 2005, Mentor and Art K-12 Certification NC Dept. of Pub. Instrn., 1973. Grad. asst. East Carolina U., Greenville, NC, 1973—74; visual arts specialist Greenville City Schools, 1974—81, Wahl Coates, Ea., Elmhurst Schools, Greenville, 1981—86, Wahl Coates Sch., Greenville, 1986—. Chmn. Cmty. Appearance Commn., Greenville, NC, 2005—06; conv. del. Dem. Party, Washington, 1992—2004; chmn. Dem. Precinct, Greenville, 1993—2000; conv. del. Pitt County Dem. Party, Greenville, 1992—2004, Third Congl. Dist. Dem. Party, Greenville, 1992—2004; state conv. del. NC Dem. Party, Raleigh, 1992—2004, state exec. com., 2005—06. Recipient Outstanding Young Educator award, Wahl Coates Sch., 1984, Tchr. Exec. Inst., Pitt County Schools, 1989—90, Tchr. Exch. Participant to Japan, Global Partnership Schools Consortium, 1999, Esther Page Hill award, NCAEA Com. for Multi-Ethnic Concerns, 2000—01, Tchr. Exch. Participant to Japan, Global Partnership Schools Consortium, 2001, Summer Study Program to China and Japan, NCTAN, 2001—02, Above and Beyond the Call of Duty (ABCD) award, Pitt County Schools, 2001, Wahl Coates Tchr. of Yr., Faculty of Wahl Coates Sch., 2001—02, Fulbright Meml. Fund Tchr. Program, Govt. of Japan, 2001, Kay Trull Outstanding Educator award, NC Assn. of Educators, 2004, Global Study Tour to Ghana, West Africa, NC Ctr. for Internat. Understanding, 2005, GlaxoSmithKline Art Educator award, NC Mus. of Art, 2005; grant, NC Found. for Pub. Sch. Children, 2000, Wellington Benefits Staff Devel. scholarship, Wellington Benefits, 2002, 2005. Mem.: NEA (rep. assembly del. 1988—2006), Pitt County Assn. of Educators (treas. 1983—2006), NC Art Edn. Assn. (elem. divsn. chair 2001—03), NC Assn. of Educators (bd. dirs. 1993—96), Nat. Art Edn. Assn., Delta Kappa Gamma Soc. (pres. elect 2006—), Phi Delta Kappa (v.p. programs 1996—98). Avocations: travel, cooking. Home: 203 Dupont Circle Greenville NC 27858 Office: Wahl Coates Sch 2200 East Fifth St Greenville NC 27858-3000 Office Phone: 252-752-2514. Office Fax: 252-758-6205. Personal E-mail: laveta51@earthlink.com. E-mail: weathel.wahl@pitt.k12.nc.us.

WEATHERS, VIVIAN JOY, physician administrator; b. Louisville; MD, Howard U., 1986; postgrad., Loyola U. Med. Ctr., 1993-95; cert., East Carolina U., 1997. Lic. physician, N.C.; cert. drinkwise provider. Tchr.'s asst. dept. math. Vassar Coll., 1976-78, lab. asst. dept. anatomy, 1980-83; co-chief resident dept. psychiat. medicine East Carolina U. Sch. Medicine, Greenville, 1996-97, dir. residency tng. dept. psychiat. medicine, 1997—. Cons. Hines Vets. Hosp., Chgo., 1993-95, Chgo. Sch. Bd., 1993-95, McNeal Hosp., Chgo., 1993-95, Pitt County Mental Health Ctr., Greenville, 1995-96, Pitt County Mental Health Ctr. for Adult Svcs., Greenville, 1997—, Rural U. Psychiat. Svc., East Carolina U., Chowan, N.C., 1997—, Albemarle Mental Health Ctr., Elizabeth City, 1997—, U. Psychiat. Svc., East Carolina U., Greenville, 1997—, P.O.R.T. Program, Pitt County Mental Health Ctr., Greenville, 1997—; bd. dirs. sickle cell disease chartered chpt. Howard U. Sch. Medicine, 1980-97; bd. dirs. bd. for substance abuse treatment for minorities Hines VA, 1993-95; bd. dirs. Mental Health Assn. Pitt County; mem. psychiat. peer rev. com. Pitt County Mental Health Ctr., 1997—; lectr. in field. Regular cons., author The Reflector newspaper, 1997—; author The Loyola Psych. Forum, 1994. Bd. dirs. Minority Excellence, 1989-90, Cmty. Action Com., 1997—; mem. Nat. Coun. for Negro Women, 1990—, Westend Cmty. Coun., 1995—. Named Resident of Yr., Pfizer Pharms., 1997, Spl. Cons., 1999. Mem. Nat. Med. Assn. (bd. dirs., minority affairs divsn. 1992—), Am. Assn. Dirs. of Psychiat. Residencies, Am. Assn. Dirs. Psychiat. Residency Tng., Am. Psychiat. Assn., Obsessive Compulsive Found., Putnam Math. Soc., Pitt County Mental Health Assn., N.C. Psychiat. Assn., N.C. Med. Soc., Vassar Alumni Assn. Office: East Carolina U Sch Medicine Dept Psychiat Medicine 6 Doctors Park Greenville NC 27834-2801 E-mail: vweathers@brody.med.ecu.edu.

WEATHERSPOON, MARY DARLINGTON, middle school educator; b. Richmond, Va., July 2, 1940; d. Jared and Reba M. (Michener) Darlington; m. Raymond Morton, Apr. 6, 1966 (div. Oct. 1971); 1 child, Matthew Darlington; m. Forrest Robert Weatherspoon, Dec. 20, 1990. AA, Hershey Jr. Coll., 1960; BEd, Ohio State U., 1965; MEd, Miami U., Oxford, Ohio, 1975. Cert. health, phys. edn., driver edn. tchr., Ohio. Tchr. Bethel Tate Jr. and Sr. H.S., Ohio, 1965-68; sr. H.S., Jr. H.S. and elem. phys./health/driver edn. tchr. Felicity-Franklin Sch. Sys., Ohio, 1969—97. Bd. dirs. Classic Fedr. Credit Union; life mem. Girl Scouts U.S.A., Columbus, 1961-65, Cin., 1966—; vol. for local polit. campaigns; instr. water safety, swimming, canoeing ARC, Harrisburg, Columbus and Cin., 1981—. Mem. AAHPERD (life), Ohio Edn. Assn. (treas. Alpha/Unisen coun. 1985—, rep. SWOA 1989), Felicity Edn. Assn. (pres. 1970—). Republican. Avocations: cooking, sewing, knitting, needlecrafts, gardening. Home: 2512 State Route 133 Bethel OH 45106-8513

WEATHERSPOON, TERESA GAYE, professional basketball player; b. Jasper, Tex., Dec. 8, 1965; Grad., La. Tech. Inst., 1988. Guard Blusto, Italy, 1988—89, 1990—93, Magenta, Italy, 1989—90, Como, Italy, 1996—97, CSKA, Russia, 1993—95, WNBA - N.Y. Liberty, N.Y.C., 1997—2003, L.A. Sparks, 2004—. Named, NCAA Women's Basketball Team Decade, 1980, La. State Player of Yr., 1988, Kodak All-Am., 1987, 1988, WNBA defensive player of yr., 1997, 1998, WNBA All-Star, 1999—2002; named to All-WNBA 2nd team, 1997—2000; recipient Gold medals, World Championship, 1986, Goodwill Games, 1986, World Univ. Games, 1987, Broderick Cup, Wade Trophy. Achievements include first player in WNBA history to record 1,000 career assists. Office: c/o Los Angeles Sparks 555 N Nash St El Segundo CA 90245

WEATHERUP, WENDY GAINES, graphic designer, writer; b. Oct. 20, 1952; d. William Hughes and Janet Ruth (Neptune) Gaines; m. Roy Garfield Weatherup, Sept. 10, 1977; children: Jennifer, Christine. BA, U. So. Calif., 1974. Lic. ins. agt. Freelance graphic designer, desktop pub., Northridge, Calif. Mem. NAFE, U. So. Calif. Alumni Assn., Alpha Gamma Delta. Republican. Methodist. Avocations: photography, travel, writing novels, computers. Home: 17260 Rayen St Northridge CA 91325-2919 E-mail: weatherw@aol.com.

WEAVER, ANN ROGERSON, art educator; b. Wilson, N.C., Oct. 22, 1948; d. James Emblic and Crecia (O'Neal) Rogerson; m. Johnny Douglas Weaver, July 7, 1983; children: Crecia, Jamie; stepchildren: John, Scott. BS in Art Edn., East Carolina U., 1971, MEd, 2002. Cert. Nat. Bd. EMC/Art 2003, Environ. Educator. Art tchr. Johnston County Schs., Smithfield, NC, 1972—75, art, 1985—; bookkeeper, receptionist, sec. John Hackney Ins./Hackney & Harris Realty, Wilson, 1976-80; owner, mgr. Ann's Sewing Rm., Wilson, 1980-85. Organizer, facilitator student art auctions, Glendale-Kenly Elem. Sch., Micro-Pine Level Elem. Sch., N.C., 1992-95; mem. Johnston County Tchr. Advisory Coun., Smithfield, 1994-2004. Designer Tobacco Farm Life Mus. logo, 1990, Kenly So. Heritage Festival logo, 1991. Bd. dirs. Johnston Meml. Hosp. Found., Smithfield, 1992-2002, Johnston Soil & Water Conservation Dist. Bd., Smithfield, 1989-94. Named Tchr. of Yr. Glendale-Kenly Elem., 1991-92, 94, 2000; Johnston County Edn. Found.

grantee, 1991-2005; recipient Environ. Educator of the Yr., NC Gov., 1999, Conservation award NC Bluebird Assn., 2002. Mem. Nat. Art Edn. Assn.(N.C. Elem. Art Educator of Yr. 1994 (N.C. Entomol. Tchr. award 1995, East Carolina U. Disting. Educator award 1996), N.C. Real Estate Assn. (broker's lic.), Kenly Area C. of C. Democrat. Baptist. Avocations: painting, gardening, designing. Home: 235 Beulahtown Rd Kenly NC 27542-8686

WEAVER, BARBARA FRANCES, librarian, consultant; b. Boston, Aug. 29, 1927; d. Leo Francis and Nina Margaret (Durham) Weisse; m. George B. Weaver, June 6, 1951; 1 dau., Valerie S. Clark. BA, Radcliffe Coll., 1949; MLS, U. R.I., 1968; EdM, Boston U., 1978. Head libr. Thompson (Conn.) Pub. Libr., 1961-69; dir. Conn. State Libr. Svc. Ctr., Willimantic, 1969-72; regional adminstr. Ctrl. Mass. Regional Libr. Sys., Worcester, 1972-78; asst. commr. of edn., state libr. State of N.J., Trenton, 1978-91; dir. R.I. Dept. State Libr. Svcs., Providence, 1991-96; chief info. officer State of RI, 1996—2001; govt. cons. in tech. mgmt., orgnl. devel. and libr. adminstrn., 2001—. Lectr. Simmons Coll., Boston, 1976-78. Mem. Conn. Libr. Assn.

WEAVER, DIANE CELESTE, music educator; b. Peoria, Ill., May 31, 1947; d. Harlan Richard and Frances Lucille Berger; m. Roger William Weaver, June 19, 1977; children: Noah Star, Benjamin Brooks, David Morgan. BA, Lawrence U., Appleton, Wis., 1969. Cert. tchr. Wash., 1989. French tchr. Crystal Falls Sch. Dist., Mich., 1969—70; builder-owner-mgr. Mountain Song Restaurant, Marblemount, Wash., 1974—86; substitute tchr. Darrington Sch. Dist., Wash., 1979—98; music specialist Sedro-Woolley Sch. Dist., Wash., 1989—; creator and dir. Sedro-Woolley Youth Orch., Wash., 1999—. Musician (concertmistress) Skagit Valley Symphony Orch. Many positions, including dist. tng. chmn. Boy Scouts of Am., Skagit Valley, Wash., 1987—97; elder Mt. Baker Presbyn. Ch., Concrete, Wash., 1995—98; mem. and bd. mem. Marblemount Presch., Wash., 1980—90. Named Scouting Family of the Yr., Boy Scouts of Am., 1995; recipient Dist. Award of Merit, 1994, nominee for profl. exch. to South Africa, People to People Ambs., 2003. Mem.: Music Educators Nat. Conf., Am. String Tchrs. Assn., Nat. Kodaly Educators Assn., Wash. Edn. Assn. Protestant. Avocations: being a loving mom to 3 sons who are valedictorians and eagle scouts, French, travel, reading, hosting exchange students. Home: 1216 Independence Blvd Sedro Woolley WA 98284 Office: Sedro-Woolley Schl Dist 801 Trail Rd Sedro Woolley WA 98284 Office Phone: 360-855-3500. Personal E-mail: weaver@sos.net.

WEAVER, DIANNE JAY, lawyer; b. Kansas City, Mo., June 28, 1944; d. Thomas G. and Anna Jeanette Jay; m. Benjamin J. Weaver, Sept. 16, 1970; children: Jay, Jenny, Scott, Elizabeth. BS, U. Kans., 1965; JD, Ind. U., 1970. Bar: Ind., Fla., Colo.; bd. cert. trial lawyer. Ptnr. Weaver & Weaver, P.A., Ft. Lauderdale, Fla.; of counsel Krupnick Campbell Malone Roselli Buser Slama & Hancock P.A., Ft. Lauderdale; ptnr. Harrell & Johnson, P.A., Jacksonville, 2002—. Speaker in field. Contbr. articles to profl. jours. Trustee Civil Justice Found.; bd. dirs. Trial Lawyers for Pub. Justice; chmn. publicity com. Civil Justice Found. Fellow Roscoe Pound Found. (life); mem. ATLA (bd. govs., sec.), Acad. Fla. Trial Lawyers (bd. dirs.), So. Trial Lawyers Assn. (bd. govs.), Fla. Bar Assn. (chair trial advocacy com.),. Fed. Bar Assn., Broward County Women Lawyers Assn. (founding pres.). Office: Harrell & Harrell PA 4735 Sunbeam Rd Jacksonville FL 32257 Office Phone: 904-251-1111. Business E-Mail: dweaver@forjustice.com.

WEAVER, DONNA KAY, writer, genealogist, former actress, stuntwomam; b. Waco, Tex., Jan. 15, 1955; d. Walter Harold Eaton and Bertha Beatrice Jackson; adopted d. Doyle H. and Vera Helen (Howze) Elliott; m. Carl Odell Weaver, Oct. 15, 1977. Grad., Univ. H.S., 1974. Former mem. Cen-Tex. Dance Co. Stuntwoman Tex. Gunfighters. Author: Sierra and Company, Castle on the Cliff; contbr. to periodicals; appeared in motion pictures A Matter of Time, 1974, Action USA, 1988; TV programs Better Living, Light of the World, CrimeStoppers, also theatrical prodns. at Waco Civic Theater. Active in assisting adoptee's and birth parents locate each other. Recipient awards Tex. State Geneal. Soc., also from local, state and national horse shows. Mem. Am. Miniature Horse Assn., Am. Miniature Horse Registry. Avocations: horseback riding, camping, fishing, travel, spelunking. Home and Office: PO Box 102 China Spring TX 76633-0102 E-mail: minihorseowner@yahoo.com.

WEAVER, DONNA L., engraver; Grad. in Fine Arts, Art Acad. Cin., 1966. Sculptor Kenner Toys, 1966—80; sculptor, engraver US Mint, 2000—. Avocation: bas-relief.

WEAVER, DONNA RAE, winery executive; b. Chgo., Oct. 15, 1945; d. Albert Louis and Gloria Elaine (Graffis) Florence; m. Clifford L. Weaver, Aug. 20, 1966; 1 child, Megan Rae. BS in Edn., No. Ill. U., 1966, EdD, 1977; MEd, De Paul U., 1974. Tchr. H.L. Richards High Sch., Oak Lawn, Ill., 1966-71, Sawyer Coll. Bus., Evanston, Ill., 1971-72; asst. prof. Oakton Community Coll., Morton Grove, Ill., 1972-75; vis. prof. U. Ill., Chgo., 1977-78; dir. devel. Mallinckrodt Coll., Wilmette, Ill., 1978-80, dean, 1980-83; campus dir. Nat.-Louis U., Chgo., 1983-90, dean div. applied behavioral scis., 1985-89; dean Coll. Mgmt. and Bus., 1989-90; pres. The Oliver Group, Inc., Kenilworth, Ill., 1993-97; mng. ptnr. Le Miccine, Gaiole-in-Chianti, Tuscany, Italy, 1996—. Cons. Nancy Lovely and Assocs., Wilmette, 1981-84, North Ctrl. Assn., Chgo., 1982-90. Contbr. articles to Am. Vocat. Jour., Ill. Bus. Edn. Assn. Monograph, Nat. Coll. Edn.'s ABS Rev., Nat. View. Mem. Ill. Quality of Work Life Coun., 1987-90, New Trier Twp. Health and Human Svcs. Adv. Bd., Winnetka, Ill., 1985-88; bd. dirs. Open Lands Project, 1985-87, Kenilworth (Ill.) Village House, 1986-87. Recipient Achievement award Women in Mgmt., 1981; Am. Bd. Master Educators charter disting. fellow, 1986. Mem. Nat. Bus. Edn. Assn., Delta Pi Epsilon (past pres.). Avocations: reading, travel, decorating. Home and Office: 144 Woodstock Ave Kenilworth IL 60043-1262 Address: Azienda Agricola Le Miccine S Traversa Chiantigiana 53013 Gaiole in Chianti Italy E-mail: drw@lemiccine.com.

WEAVER, ELIZABETH A., state supreme court justice; b. New Orleans; d. Louis and Mary Weaver. BA, Newcomb Coll.; JD, Tulane U. Elem. tchr. Glen Lake Cmty. Sch., Maple City, Mich.; French tchr. Leelanau Sch., Glen Arbor, Mich.; pvt. practice Glen Arbor, Mich.; law clk. Civil Dist. Ct., New Orleans; atty. Coleman, Dutrey & Thomson, New Orleans; atty., title specialist Chevron Oil Co., New Orleans; probate and juvenile judge Leelanau County, Mich., 1975—86; judge Mich. Ct. Appeals, 1987—94; justice Mich. Supreme Ct., Lansing, 1995—. Chief justice Mich. Supreme Ct., 1999—2000, re-elected, 2002—; chief justice Peter Rellected Superior Ct. Justice, 2002—; instr. edn. dept. Ctr. Mich. U.; mem. Mich. Com. on Juvenile Justice, Nat. Conv. State Adv. Groups on Juvenile Justice for U.S.; chair Gov.'s Task Force on Children's Justice, Trial Ct. Assessment Commn., Office Juvenile Justice and Delinquency Prevention; jud. adv. bd. mem. Law and Orgnl. Econs. Ctr. U. Kans.; treas. Children's Charter of Cts. of Mich. Chairperson Western Mich. U. CLE Adv. Bd.; mem. steering com. Grand Traverse/Leelanau Commn. on Youth; mem. Glen Arbor Twp. Zoning Bd.; mem. charter arts north Leelanau County; mem. citizen's adv. coun. Arnell Engstrom Children's Ctr.; mem. cmty. adv. com. Pathfinder Sch. Treaty Law Demonstration Project; active Grand Traverse/Leelanau Mental Health Found. Named Jurist of Yr., Police Officers Assn. of Mich.; named one of five Outstanding Young Women in Mich., Mich. Jaycees; recipient Eastern award, Warren Easton Hall of Fame, Lifetime Dedication to Children award, Mich. Champions in Childhood Injury Prevention, 2000, Recognition award for outstanding svc. to Mich. children and families, Gov. Engler and Family Independence Agy., 2000, Profls. award, Mich. Assn. Drug Cts., 2002, Mary S. Coleman award, Ctr. for Civic Edn. Through Law, 2002. Fellow: Mich. State Bar Found.; mem.: ABA, Antrim County Bar Assn., Leelanau County Bar Assn., Grand Traverse County Bar Assn., La. Bar Assn., Nat. Coun. Juvenile and Family Judges, Mich. Bar Assn. (chair CLE adv. bd., chair crime prevention ctr., chair juvenile law com.), Delta Kappa Gamma (hon.). Office: Mich Supreme Ct 3300 Grandview Plz 10850 E Traverse Hwy Traverse City MI 49684-1364*

WEAVER, F. LOUISE BEAZLEY, curator, director; b. Jacksonville, Fla., Apr. 26, 1953; d. Donald William Beazley and Frances Ann Weaver; 1 child, Elizabeth. BA in Humanities, Am. Coll. Switzerland, 1975; BA in Art History, U. Ariz., 1979; MA in Art History, U. Va., 1982. Co-curator Nat. Mus. Am. Art, Washington, 1983—84; assoc. dir. Konglomerati Book Art, St. Petersburg, Fla., 1985—86; dir., curator Derby Lane, St. Petersburg, 1991—. Commr. Pub. Arts for the City, St. Petersburg, 1994—2001; adv. bd. Fla. Gulf Coast Art Mus., Largo, Fla., 1997—2001. Contbr. articles Greyhound Review, 2001—02. Mem. bd. Fla. Orch. Symphony, Tampa, Fla., 2000—. Mem.: Soc. Am. Archivists, Am. Assn. Mus. Office: Derby Lane 10490 Gandy Blvd Saint Petersburg FL 33702 E-mail: history@derbylane.com.

WEAVER, JANET S., editor; m. Mark Weaver; children: Sam, Rachel. B in journalism, U. Mo., 1984. Reporter, asst. city editor Stuart (Fla.) News, 1986—89; from reporter to dep. mng. editor/features and sports Virginian-Pilot, Norfolk, Va., 1989—94; mng. editor The Wichita (Kans.) Eagle, 1994—97, Sarasota (Fla.) Herald-Tribune, 1997—99, exec. editor, 1999—2003; dean faculty Poynter Inst., St. Petersburg, Fla., 2003—04; mng. editor The Tampa Tribune, Fla., 2004—05, exec. editor, v.p. Fla., 2005—. Mem.: Am. Soc. Newspaper Editors (bd. dirs.). Office: Tampa Tribune 202 S Parker St Tampa FL 33606

WEAVER, JENNEFER JEAN, musician, educator; b. Greenville, Sc, Feb. 27, 1959; d. James Neville Jean and Ensign Joy Wilson; m. Keith Lamar Weaver, Sept. 17, 1983; children: Joshua, Jeremiah, Josiah, James, Jerusha, Joy. BS, James Madison U., Harrisonburg, VA, 1982. Dental asst. Dr. Owen Graves, Harrisonburg, Va., 1982—86; piano accompanist JMU, Harrisonburg, Va., 1999—; piano instr. Harrisonburg, Va., 1987—. Pres. Piano Teachers Forum, Harrisonburg, Va., 1999—2000, vice-president, 1997—99, reception coord., 2000—. Membership chmn. Alpha Gamma Delta, Harrisonburg, Va., 1978—79, ho. mgr., 1979—80, rush chmn., 1980—81. Fellow Gamma Gamma Greek Honor Soc., JMU Panhellenic Coun., 1982. Mem.: NGPT, VMTA, MTNA. R-Conservative. Presbyterian. Avocations: soccer mom, band booster, choral booster, choir accompanist, pta member. Home: 276 Franklin Street Harrisonburg VA 22801 Office: Piano Studio of Jennefer Weaver 276 Franklin Street Harrisonburg VA 22801 Personal E-mail: jenneweaver@msn.com.

WEAVER, JOE LE ANN, biology educator; d. Jerry Wayne and Cheryl Greer Weaver. BS in Biology, Angelo State U., San Angelo, Tex., 1997. Math/sci. tchr. grade 6 Dillard Mid. Sch., Goldsboro, NC, 1997—99; sci. tchr. grade 8 East McDowell Jr. High, Marion, NC, 1999—. Toyota Tapestry and Bright Ideas grantee, Toyota and Rutherford Electric, 2000, 2003. Home: 107 New St Marion NC 28752 Office: East McDowell Junior High 676 State St Marion NC 28752 Office Phone: 828-652-7711. Personal E-mail: jannweaver@aol.com.

WEAVER, KAREN JOHNSON, elementary school educator; d. Robert Lee and Phyllis Waugh Johnson; m. James David Weaver, July 9, 1983; children: Brad, Hunter. BA in Elem. Edn., Va. Tech., Blacksburg, 1983; EdM in Reading Edn., James Madison U., Harrisonburg, Va., 2003. Collegiate profl. cert. reading specialist and tchr. Va. Tchr. Louisa County Pub. Schs., Mineral, Va., 1983—91; tchr., tutor Grymes Meml. Sch., Orange, Va., 1994—2000; reading specialist Orange County Pub. Schs., Va., 2000—. Vol. Am. Cancer Soc., Va. Recipient Shirley Merlin Reading award for excellence in grad. sch. program, James Madison U., Harrisonburg, Va., 2001. Mem.: Va. Edn. Assn., Internat. Reading Assn. Avocations: antiques, history, reading. Home: 322 Harper Dr Orange VA 22960 Office: Orange County Pub Schs Waugh Blvd Orange VA 22960

WEAVER, KAREN LYNN, writer, performing arts educator, actress, poet; b. Boston, Mar. 9, 1970; d. Alfred George and Eileen Francis Weaver. Post Baccalaureate-Secondary English & Edn., Framingham State Coll., Mass., 1998; BS, Emerson Coll., Boston, 1991. Cert. tchr., Secondary English Fla. and Mass. Personal asst. to exec. prodr. Vin Di Bona Prod., Los Angeles, 1992; exec. asst. to v.p. Smith Barney, Beverly Hills, 1993—94; drama tchr., head of drama dept. Sarasota HS, 1998—2000, English tchr., 9th grade, 1998—2000; sr. casting agent Parker Agy., Sarasota, 2000—02; creator/head writer animated TV series, Heidi's World, Los Angeles, 2003—; tchr. honors English, honors writing, drama Marlborough H.S. Post-prod. TV movie, The Movie Break, Los Angeles, 2003; theater dir. Sarasota HS, 1998—2000, tutor, SAT prep and English, 1998—2000, student adv. bd., 1998—2000; liason Sarasota Film Festival, 2000—01. Author: (poem) Inner Darkness, 2004 (Editor's Choice Award, 2004), Shattered, 2004. Vol. AIDS Hospice for Men, Los Angeles, 1992—93; dir. of dramatic presentation United Nations Dev. Fund, Sarasota, 1998. Recipient Internat. Poet of Merit, Internat. Soc. of Poets, 2004, Outstanding Achievement in Poetry Silver Award/Cup, 2004. Mem.: Internat. Soc. of Poets (hon.), Alpha Upsilon Alpha, Kappa Delta Pi. Avocations: yoga, walking, hiking.

WEAVER, KITRA K., sales and marketing executive; b. Tawas City, Mich., Apr. 12, 1957; d. James Elmer Jr. and Glenda Kay (Ray) Weaver; m. Mark William Goldstein, Apr. 20, 1985 (div. Mar. 1989). Grad. h.s., Houston, 1975. Contract sales rep. Gen. Office Outfitters, Dallas, 1982-85; v.p. Money Saver Advertising, Dallas, 1985-88; dir. mktg. One Hour Moto Photo, Dallas, 1985-88; br. mgr. Metagram Am., Dallas, 1988-90; sales rep. Rollins Protective Svc., Atlanta, 1990-92; regional sales mgr. The Marlin Co., North Haven, Conn., 1992—2006. Mentor The Marlin Co., Orlando, Fla., 1993-98. Chair ticket com. SOS/Taste of the Nation, Orlando, 1991-2000; chair ticket sales UCP.Ctrl. Fla. Chili Cookoff, Orlando, 1990-93; co-founder Bus. Womens Network, 2000—. Republican. Methodist. Avocations: cooking, reading, sports, fundraising, the arts.

WEAVER, L. KAREN, retired reading specialist; b. Nyack, N.Y., Aug. 16, 1945; d. Roland Oswald and Louise (Castaldo) Lyle; m. Kenneth Allen Weaver, Apr. 27, 1968; children: Allison Nicole, Danielle Beth. BS Elem. Edn., SUNY, Brockport, 1967; MS Elem. Edn., SUNY, New Paltz, 1971; postgrad., Coll. New Rochell/L.I. Univ., 1981-92. Cert. tchr. reading, adminstr., N.Y. Tchr. grades 3 and 4 Ramapo Cen. Sch. Dist., Hillburn, N.Y., 1967-71; substitute tchr. North Rockland Cen. Sch. Dist., Garnerville, N.Y., 1971-81; reading tchr. Westwood Regional Sch. Dist., NJ, 1981-83; remedial reading specialist North Rockland Cen. Sch. Dist., Garnerville, NY, 1984—2001; ret., 2001. Sch. improvement planning team, West Haverstraw Elem. Sch., 1992—; adj. prof. CCNY, 1995. Sec. bd. trustees King's Daus. Pub. Libr., Haverstraw, N.Y., 1985—, trained reading recovery tchr. 1997; vestry person Trinity Episcopal Ch., Garnerville, N.Y., 1978-80, ch. sch. supt., 1975-81. Recipient Tchr. of Excellence award N.Y. State Coun. English Tchrs., 2000. Mem. Internat. Reading Assn., N.Y. State Reading Coun., Rockland Reading Coun., N.Y. State United Tchrs., NEA, Assn. Sch. Dist. Adminstrs. Republican. Avocations: reading, exercise. Home: 3 Lyle Ter Garnerville NY 10923-1734

WEAVER, LINDA MARIE, pharmacist, education educator; d. John William and Lorraine Marie Miller; m. Daniel Jacob Weaver. BA in Edn. and Spanish, Western Mich. U., 1974; BS in Pharmacy, Ferris State U., 1984; PharmD, Midwestern U., Chgo. Coll. of Pharmacy, 2000. Registered Pharmacist Mich., 1984. Ambulatory pharmacist Perry Drugs, Midland, Mich., 1984—87, Revco Drugs, Tucson, 1987—89, Walgreens Drug, Tucson, 1989—93; compliance officer Ariz. State Bd. of Pharmacy, Phoenix, 1993—99; clin. hosp. pharmacist John C. Lincoln Hosp., Phoenix, 1999—2001; med. sci. liaison Wyeth Pharmaceuticals, Scottsdale, 2001—03; med. liaison Abbott Labs., Scottsdale, 2003—04, clin. sci. mgr., 2004—. Adj. faculty mem. Midwestern U. Coll. of Pharmacy, Glendale, Ariz.; instr. Rio Salado C.C., Phoenix, 1997—98, Ariz. Pharmacy Assn., 1987—; adv. bd. mem. SCP Comm., Inc., Phoenix, 2001—01. Vol. Am. Diabetes Assn., Scottsdale, 1994—2004, Am. Heart Assn., Scottsdale, 1994—2004, Am. Cancer Assn., Scottsdale, 1994—2004. Recipient Golden Key Nat. Honor Soc., Mich. State U., 1981, Rho Chi Honor Soc., Midwestern U., 2000. Mem.: Am. Soc. of Health Sys. Pharmacists (licentiate), Am. Colleges of Clin. Pharmacists (licentiate), Am. Pharmacists Assn. (licentiate; del. 2001—03), Ariz. Pharmacy Assn. (licentiate; co-chair profl. affairs com. 1999—2000, maricopa rep. 2001—02, 2nd v.p. 2002—03, cert. of appreciation for outstanding svc. to Ariz. pharmacy assn. 2000, exec. bd. mem. award 2003). Avocations: scuba diving, cooking, jazz, travel, wine tasting. Home: 6120 E Gold Dust Ave Scottsdale AZ 85253 Office: Abbott Laboratories 6120 E Gold Dust Ave Scottsdale AZ 85253 Office Phone: 480-951-0366. Personal E-mail: lwpharmd@juno.com.

WEAVER, LOIS JEAN, physician, educator; b. Wheeling, W.Va., May 23, 1944; d. Lewis Everett and Ann Weaver. BA, Oberlin Coll., 1966; MD, U. Chgo., 1970. Pulmonary fellow Northwestern U., Evanston, Ill., 1975-77; trauma fellow U. Wash. Harborview Hosp., Seattle, 1977-79, research assoc., instr. medicine, 1979-81, clin. asst. prof. medicine, 1983—; clin. research fellow Virginia Mason Med. Research Ctr., Seattle, 1981-82; mem. med. staff Swedish Hosp., Seattle, 1984-92. Pulmonary cons. Fred Hutchinson Cancer Research Inst., Seattle, 1984-86, regional med. advisor and med. cons., disability quality br. Social Security, Seattle, 1985—. Contbr. sci. articles to profl. jours. La Verne Noyes scholar U. Chgo., 1966; Parker B. Francis fellow Northwestern U., 1975. Mem. AMA, Wash. Lung Assn., Sigma Xi. Avocations: gardening, music. Home: PO Box 2098 Kirkland WA 98083-2098 Office: 701 5th Ave Ste 2900 MIS 105 Seattle WA 98104-7075

WEAVER, LYN ANN SIMMONS, psychologist; b. Harrisonburg, Va., Oct. 27, 1944; d. Sidney Linwood and Annye Mae Simmons; m. Norris Elwood Weaver, May 27, 1967; 1 child, Tonya Lyn Bowers. BS, James Madison U., 1967, MS, 1973; EdD, U. Va., 1986. Lic. psychologist, sch. psychologist. Psychologist Woodrow Wilson Rehab. Ctr., Fisherville, Va., 1973-74; asst. to supt. Highland County Schs., Monterey, Va., 1974-81; owner NorLyn Enterprises, Dayton, Va., 1983-89; psychologist Mecklenburg County Schs., Boydton, Va., 1989-90, asst. prin. high sch., 1990-92; instr. psychology Southeastern C.C., Whiteville, N.C., 1992; psychologist Columbus County Schs., Whiteville, N.C., 1992-99, Brunswick County Schs., Bolivia, N.C., 1999—, pvt. practice, Chadbourn, N.C., 1993-99, Ocean Isle, N.C., 1999—. Psychologist, mgmt. First Mental Health EPA's, HMO, N.C., 1996—; psychologist Dept. Human Resources, Raleigh, N.C., 1999. Author: The Virginia Principal, 1990. Mem. ERA Summit, N.C. Equity, Women's Activist. Mem. AAUW, APA, N.C. Sch. Psychologist Assn., Bus. and Profl. Women (com. mem. 1999—, pres. 2000-01). Avocations: reading, travel, music. Office: Mgmt Solutions PO Box 6275 Shallotte NC 28470-6275 E-mail: lynw@2khiway.net.

WEAVER, MARTHA, newscaster; Degree, St. Olaf Coll., 1990. Aide to Gov. Arne Carlson State Dept. Adminstrn., Minn., 1990—94; reporter, anchor Sta. WEYI-TV, Flint, Mich., 1994—95; anchor Sta. WRTV-TV, Indpls., 1995—. Office: WRTV TV 1330 N Meridian St Indianapolis IN 46202

WEAVER, MELINDA YVONNE, secondary school educator; b. Harlingen, Tex., Feb. 1, 1978; d. Miguel Weaver, Jr. and Viola Weaver. Bachelors Degree, SW Tex. State U., San Marcos, 2001. Cert. dance edn. Tex., 2001, health and wellness promotion edn. Tex., 2001. Dance tchr. Medina Valley H.S., Castroville, Tex., 2002—03; 6th grade social studies tchr. Medina Valley Mid. Sch., Castroville, Tex., 2002—03; dance tchr. Samuel Clemens H.S., Schertz, Tex., 2003—05, Steele H.S., Cibolo, Tex., 2005—. Mem.: Dance Team Dirs. Am. (assoc.). Office: Steele High School 1300 Fm 1103 Cibolo TX 78108 Office Phone: 210-945-6568. Office Fax: 210-945-6510.

WEAVER, MOLLIE LITTLE, lawyer; b. Alma, Ga., Mar. 11; d. Alfred Ross and Annis Mae (Bowles) Little; m. Jack Delano Nelson, Sept. 12, 1953 (div. May 1970); 1 dau., Cynthia Ann; m. 2d, Hobart Ayres Weaver, June 10, 1970; stepchildren: Hobart Jr., Mary Essa, Robert. BA in History, U. Richmond, 1978; JD, Wake Forest U., 1981. Bar; N.C. 1982, Fla. 1983; Cert. profl. sec.; cert. adminstrv. mgr. Supr., Western Electric Co., Richmond, Va., 1952-75; cons., owner Cert. Mgmt. Assocs., Richmond, 1975-76; sole practice, Ft. Lauderdale, Fla., 1982-86, Emerald Isle, N.C., 1986-89, Richmond, 1989—. Author: Secretary's Reference Manual, 1973. Mem. adv. coun. to Bus. and Office Edn., Greensboro, N.C., 1970-73, adv. com. to bus. edn. Va. Commonwealth U., Richmond, 1977. Recipient Key to City of Winston-Salem, N.C., 1963; Epps award for scholarship, 1978. Mem. ABA, N.C. Bar Assn., Fla. Bar Assn., Word Processing Assn. (v.p., founder Richmond 1973-75), Adminstrv. Mgmt. Soc. (com. chmn. Richmond, 1973-75), Phi Beta Kappa, Eta Sigma Phi, Phi Alpha Theta. Republican. Home: 12301 Renwick Pl Glen Allen VA 23059-6959 E-mail: Legal311@aol.com.

WEAVER, NAOMI M., retired medical/surgical nurse, educator; b. Ephrata, Pa., June 13, 1933; d. Daniel H. and Lizzie (Martin) W. BSN, Eastern Mennonite Coll., Harrisonburg, Va., 1962; MSN, U. Pa., 1968; cert. adult nurse practitioner, U. Rochester, 1984. RN, Pa. Staff nurse St. Luke's Hosp., Denver, 1959-60; nurse educator, adminstr. Shirati Hosp. and Sch. Nursing, Musoma, Tanzania, 1962-74, 79-81; asst. prof. nursing Marion (Ind.) Coll., 1974-75, Eastern Mennonite Coll., 1975-79, Elmira (N.Y.) Coll., 1981-84; nurse educator Karanda Sch. Nursing, Harare, Zimbabwe, 1984-85; dep. prin. tutor Macha Enrolled Nurse Tng. Sch., Choma, Zambia, 1986-88; supr. Landis Homes Retirement Ctr., Lititz, Pa., 1988; staff nurse Hershey (Pa.) U. Med. Ctr., 1989; coord. practical nurse program Nazareth (Israel) Hosp., 1989-92; instr. U. Guam Coll. Nursing, 1993—95; nutritionist, leprosy nurse World Concern, Somalia, 1998; curriculum cons. in nursing Sch. Medicine and Allied Scis., U. Vietnam, Ho Chi Minh City, 1998-99; ret., 1999. Tchr. continuing edn. workshop Overseas Continuing Edn. Am. Nurses, Inc., Haiti, 1975, Kenya and Zambia, 1982; asst. prof. nursing, dir. transcultural nursing course Eastern Mennonite Coll., 1979-81; maternity relief nurse, Ombo Hosp., Migori, Kenya, 1980; mem. statewide planning com. nursing edn. N.Y. State Nurses Assn., 1982-84; mem. exam. com. Zambia Nursing Coun., 1987-88; bd. dirs. Shirati Hosp., Tanzania, 1971-74. Ch. worship leader, hospitality com., immigrant resettlement com., 2006—. Mem. Mennonite Nurses Assn. (exec. com. 1982-84). Avocations: travel, reading, walking, tennis, writing. Home: 1001 E Oregon Rd Lititz PA 17543 E-mail: nweaver@epix.net.

WEAVER, NORMA J., medical/surgical nurse; b. Tuskegee, Ala., Mar. 5, 1962; d. Estella (Keys) Weaver; div. BSN, Troy (Ala.) State U., 1984; MA, NOBTS, 1995. Cert. med.-surg. nurse. Charge nurse DePaul Hosp., New Orleans; charge nurse acute care unit detox United Med. Ctr., New Orleans; charge nurse Community Hosp., Tallassee, Ala., VA Med. Ctr., New Orleans; first dir. nursing Home Health Agys. Mid-Am. Home Care, NIA Home Health Care Agys.; flex pool agy. nurse Advantage Nursing Care. Mem. ANA. Home: 7720 Swift St New Orleans LA 70126-1336 Personal E-mail: secondcominjesus@aol.com.

WEAVER, PAMELA ANN, education educator; b. Little Falls, N.Y., July 7, 1947; d. Floyd Aron Weaver and Norma May (Putnam) Hoyer; m. Ken Ward McCleary, Mar. 2, 1947; children: Brian Wilson, Blake McCleary, Ryan McCleary. AA, Fulton Montgomery C.C., Amsterdam, NY, 1968; BA, SUNY, 1970; MA, U. South Fla., 1973; PhD, Mich. State U., East Lansing, 1978. Mem. math. dept. Riviera Jr. H.S., Miami, Fla., 1970-72; grad. asst. Office Med., Edn. R & D Mich. State U., East Lansing, 1973-74, grad. asst. dept. mktg., 1974-75, instr. mktg.; asst. prof. mktg., hospitality svcs. adminstrn. Ctrl. Mich. State U., Mt. Pleasant, 1978-79, 1982-86, chair acad. senate, 1985-86, prof. mktg., hospitality svcs. adminstrn., 1986-89; prof., undergrad. program coord. dept. hospitality and tourism mgmt. Va. Poly. Inst. and State U., Blacksburg, 1989—, undergrad. program coord., 2005—. Contbr. over 100 articles to profl. jours. Mem. Coun. on Hotel, Restaurant and Instl. Edn. (John Wiley & Sons, Inc. award for Lifetime Achievement to Hospitality Industry 1994). Office: Va Poly Inst and State U Wallace Hall Blacksburg VA 24061-0429 Business E-Mail: weaver@vt.edu.

WEAVER, PATRICIA ELLA, mathematics educator; b. Reading, Pa., Aug. 29, 1945; d. Lewis Jacob and Margie (Sherman) Kintzer; m. Theodore Orris Weaver, Nov. 22, 1969; children: Benjamin B., Jennifer K., Erika L. BS,

Kutztown State Coll., 1967; postgrad., Wilkes U., 1989-94, Pa. State U., 1992; Masters Equivalency, Kutztown State Coll., 1992. Cert. tchr., Pa. Tchr. math. Tulpehocken Sch. Dist., Bernville. Pa., 1967-73; homebound instr., daily subs. tchr. Ea. Lebanon County Sch. Dist., Myerstown, Pa., 1979-87, tutor math., daily subs. tchr., 1987-88, tchr. math. sr. high sch., 1988—, class advisor, 1991—96, student support team advisor, 1997—. Sec. Tulpehocken Edn. Assn., Bernville, 1971-72; insvc. planning com. Tulpehocken Sch. Dist., Bernville, 1971-73. Leader Eastern Neighborhood coun. Girl Scouts Am., Myerstown, 1984-90, Lebanon County coun. Boy Scouts Am., Myerstown, 1983-84; coord. Myerstown Girls Summer Softball Team, 1986-92; sec., mem. Girls Basketball Boosters, 1990-93; active Girls Hockey Boosters, sec., 1990-92, Band Boosters, United Ch. of Christ Coun., v.p., 1992; women's fellow Grace United Ch. Christ, 1996—, coun. sec., 2006. Mem. NEA, Pa. Edn. Assn., Ea. Lebanon County Edn. Assn., R-N Women's Club (pres. 1970-72), Lebanon County Women's Club (treas., 2000-2002). Republican. Avocations: church choir, recreational ladies softball team. Office: Ea Leanon County Sch Dist 180 Elco Dr Myerstown PA 17067

WEAVER, PAULINE ANNE, lawyer; b. Hornchurch, Eng., Mar. 31, 1949; came to U.S., 1960; d. George Henry and Eunice Mary (Obee) W.; m. Charles Franklin Scribner, Mar. 2, 1974. BA, Memphis State U., 1971, JD, 1979. Bar: Tenn. 1979, Calif. 1980, U.S. Dist. Ct. (no. dist.) Calif. 1980. Law clk. Shelby County Office Pub. Defender, Memphis, 1977-79, Alameda County (Calif.) Office Pub. Defender, Oakland, 1980-82, atty., 1982—. Adj. prof. law John F. Kennedy U., Orinda, Calif. Legal advisor LWV, Fremont, Calif., 1980-83, Parent Info. Network, Fremont, 1979-84, bd. dirs., 1981-84; bd. dirs. Shelter Against Violent Environs., Fremont, 1981—; consumer rep. Alameda County Emergency Med. Care com., 1980-83; mem. Fremont/Newark Philharm. Guild, 1981—; vol. Parole Project, 1984—; vol. tutor Alameda County Adult Literacy Project; past pres. Washington Hosp. Healthcare Found.; bd. dir. Eden Housing. Donnelly J. Hill Meml. scholar Memphis State U. Law Alumni Assn., 1978. Mem. ABA (chmn. domestic violence com. 1984-85, screening subcom., Outstanding State Membership chmn. 1981, Gavel awards, ho. del., bd. gov. 2003-), State Bar Calif. (past v.p.), Found. of State Bar Calif. (pres. 2004-), So. Alameda County Bar Assn., Women Lawyers of Alameda County (treas. 1983—), Nat. Women's Polit. Caucus (chmn. 1982-83), Calif. Women Lawyers (past pres.), Nat. Conf. Women's Bar Assn. (past pres.), Alameda County Pub. Defenders Assn., Alameda County Dem. Lawyers Club, Order of Barristers, Alpha Gamma Delta (pres. 1981-83), Delta Theta Phi, Omicron Delta Kappa. Office: Alameda County Public Defender 1401 Lakeside Dr 4th Fl Oakland CA 94612

WEAVER, PEGGY (MARGUERITE MCKINNIE WEAVER), plantation owner; b. Jackson, Tenn., June 7, 1925; d. Franklin Allen and Mary Alice (Caradine) McKinnie; children: Elizabeth Lynn, Thomas Jackson III, Franklin A. McKinnie. Student, U. Colo., 1943-45, Am. Acad. Dramatic Arts, 1945-46, S. Meisner's Profl. Classes, 1949, Oxford U., 1990, 91. Actress, 1946-52; mem. staff Mus. Modern Art, N.Y.C., 1949-50; woman's editor radio sta. WTJS-AM-FM, Jackson, Tenn., 1952-55; editor, radio/TV Jackson Sun Newspaper, 1952-55; columnist Bolivar (Tenn.) Bulletin-Times, 1986—2000; chmn. Ho. of Reps. of Old Line Dist., Hardeman County, Tenn., 1986—91, 1994—97. Pres. Hardeman County chpt. Assn. Preservation of Tenn. Antiquities, 1991—95; charter mem. adv. bd. Tenn. Arts Commn., Nashville, 1967—74, Tenn. Performing Arts Ctr., Nashville, 1972—; chmn. trustees br. Tenn. Libr. Assn., Nashville, 1973—74; Henry County regional chmn. Opera Memphis, 1979—91; mem. nat. coun. Met. Opera, N.Y.C., 1980—92, Tenn. Bicentennial Com., Hardeman County, 1993—96; bd. sec. Memphis Brooks Mus. League, 1997—98; docent Dixon Gallery and Gardens, Memphis; founder Paris-Henry County (Tenn.) Arts Coun., 1965. Mem. DAR, Nat. Soc. Colonial Dames Am. (chmn. Memphis Town com. 2002-04), Oxford Alumni Assn. N.Y., English Speaking Union (London chpt.), Jamestown Soc., Crescent Club, Dilettantes. Methodist. Avocations: horseback riding, travel, theater. Office: 402 Heritage Plantation Hickory Valley TN 38042 Office Phone: 731-764-6009. Business E-Mail: pweaver@heritagecompanies.net.

WEAVER, SANDRA KAE, nurse anesthetist; b. L.A., Oct. 5, 1957; d. Clarence P. and Lorene K. W. ASN, Union U., 1979, BS in Nursing, 1981; MS in Nursing, U. Tenn., Memphis, 1985; B in Nurse Anesthesia, U. Ala., Birmingham, 1993. Staff nurse Regional Hosp., Jackson, Tenn., 1979-91; nursing instr. Dyersburg (Tenn.) State Community Coll., 1986-89, Union U., Jackson, Tenn., 1989-90; staff nurse Jackson Gen. Hosp., 1990-91, critical care nurse, 1990-91; nurse anesthetist Jackson (Tenn.) Clinic Profl. Assn., 1993—2003, Cardiac Anesthesia Group, 2003—05, Jackson Gen. Hosp., 2005—. Mem. Am. Assn. Nurse Anesthetists.

WEAVER, SIGOURNEY (SUSAN ALEXANDRA WEAVER), actress; b. NYC, Oct. 8, 1949; d. Sylvester (Pat) Weaver and Elizabeth Inglish; m. Jim Simpson, Oct. 1, 1984; 1 child, Charlotte. BA in English, Stanford U., 1971; MA in Drama, Yale U., 1974. Actress: (theatre) including Watergate Classics, 1973, The Frogs, 1974 The Nature and Purpose of the Universe, 1974, Daryl and Carol and Kenny and Jenny, The Constant Wife, 1975, Titanic, 1976, Das Lusitania Songspiel (also co-writer), 1976, Marco Polo Sings a Song, 1977, A Flea in Her Ear, 1978, Conjuring an Event, 1978, Beyond Therapy, 1981, As You Like It, 1981, Hurlyburly, 1984-85, Sex and Longing, 1996, The Merchant of Venice, 1986, The Guys, 2002, The Mercy Seat, 2002, Mrs. Farnsworth, 2004, (films) Annie Hall, 1977, Madman, 1978, Alien, 1979, Eyewitness, 1981, The Year of Living Dangerously, 1982, Deal of the Century, 1983, Ghostbusters, 1984, Une femme ou deux, 1985, Aliens, 1986 (Acad. Award nomination for best actress, 1987), Half Moon Street, 1986, Gorillas in the Mist, 1988 (Acad. Award nomination for best actress, 1989, Golden Globe for best actress - drama, 1989), Working Girl, 1988 (Acad. Award nomination for best supporting actress, 1989, Golden Globe for best supporting actress in a motion picture, 1989), Ghostbusters II, 1989, 1492: Conquest of Paradise, 1992, Dave, 1993, Death and the Maiden, 1994, Jeffrey, 1995, Copycat, 1995, Snow White: A Tale of Terror, 1997, The Ice Storm, 1997 (BAFTA Film Award for best supporting actress, 1998), A Map of the World, 1999, Galaxy Quest, 1999, Airframe, 1999, Company Man, 2000, Speak Truth to Power, 2000, Heartbreakers, 2001, Big Bad Love (voice), 2001, Tadpole, 2002, The Guys, 2002, Holes, 2003, The Village, 2004, Imaginary Heroes, 2004, (TV series) Somerset, 1976, (TV miniseries) The Best of Families, 1977, (TV movies) 3 by Cheever: The Sorrows of Gin, 1979, 3 by Cheever: O Youth and Beauty!, 1979; co-prodr., actress: (films) Alien 3, 1992, Alien: Resurrection, 1997. Recipient Star on the Walk of Fame, 1999, Lifetime Achievement award, Chicago Internat. Film Festival, 2001. Office: William Morris Agy One William Morris Pl Beverly Hills CA 90212

WEAVER, SUSAN JEANNE, sociology educator; b. Huntington, W.Va., Dec. 11, 1950; d. John Francis and Sherley Rae (Wells) Marnell; m. Douglas W. Weaver, Jan. 28, 1970; children: Sarah Marnell, Nathaniel Heath. BA in Sociology, Marshall U., 1975, MA in Sociology, 1980; EdD in Leadership Studies, W.Va. U., 2000. Instr. in sociology Marshall U., Huntington, 1980—99, Ashland (Ky.) C.C., 1985—99, Ky. Christian Coll., Grayson, 1988—89; asst. prof. sociology Miami U. Oxford, Ohio, 1999—2005; dir. tchg. and learning Univ. of the Cumberlands, Williamsburg, Ky., 2005—. Bd. dirs. Sojourner's Recovery Svcs. Inc. Vol. Contact of Huntington, 1992—99; leader Girl Scouts U.S., Proctorville, Ohio, 1985—92; cub scout den mother Boy Scouts Am., Proctorville, 1990—92; bd. dirs. Touching and Learning, U. Cumberlands, Williamsburg, Ky. Mem. Am. Sociol. Assn., So. Sociol. Assn., Profl. Orgn. Devel. Network. Avocation: writing. Home: 100 Sycamore St Apt 9 Williamsburg KY 40769 Office: 6000 College Station Dr Williamsburg KY 40969 Office Phone: 606-539-4325.

WEAVER, SYLVIA, information technology executive; BA in English, Lafayette Coll.; MS in Telecommunications and Computing Mgmt., Polytechnic U. With Bell Atlantic, 1978—95; joined Johnson & Johnson, 1995; assoc. dir., global project planning in the clin. R&D orgn. R.W. Johnson Pharm. Rsch. Inst.; dir. customer svc., Independence Technology Johnson & Johnson; v.p., quality assurance & process excellence Johnson & Johnson Services, Inc., Networking & Computing Svcs., 2000—. Office: Johnson & Johnson NCS 1003 US Hwy 202 Raritan NJ 08869

WEAVER, TANYA LEA, elementary school educator; b. Monroe, La., Aug. 3, 1976; d. Edward Bradley and Joanne Louise Carpenter; m. Bradley Thomas Weaver, Aug. 15, 1998; children: Ryan, Cameron. AA, San Jacinto Coll., 1996; BA, U. Houston, 1998. Cert. Teaching Certificate State of Tex. Tchr. Pearland Jr. High West, 1999—2000, Morales Elem., Pasadena, Tex., 2000—01, 2001—02, Jennie Reid Elem., La Porte, Tex., 2002—04, 2004—. Curriculum mapper La Porte ISD, 2003—04, differential instructional coach, 2003—; mem. Social Studies Core Leadership Team, LaPorte ISD, 2003—04. Grantee La Porte Edn. Found., 2002—03, 2003—04. Mem.: Tex. Classroom Tchrs. Assn. Republican. Meth. Business E-Mail: weavert@lpisd.org.

WEAVER-STROH, JOANNE MATEER, education educator, consultant; b. May 21, 1930; d. Kenneth Hall and Jean (Weakley) Mateer; children: Karen, Mark, Laurie. BS in Edn., U. Pa., 1952, elem. and secondary prin. cert., 1979; MS in Psychology Reading, Temple U., 1968. Tchr. Paoli (Pa.) Sch., 1952-53, Somerville Sch., Ridgewood, NJ, 1953-55, Bryn Mawr (Pa.) Sch., 1955-57, Erdenheim Sch., Springfield, Pa., 1957-58; reading specialist Abington (Pa.) Sch. Dist., 1966-67, curriculum specialist, 1967-73, coord. human rels. programs, 1973-80; prin. Rydal Elem. Sch., Abington, 1980-88, Willow Hill Elem. Sch., 1988-96; ret., 1996. Cons., tchr. Marywood Coll., Scranton, Pa., 1972—; coord. drug and alcohol abuse program Abington Sch. Dist., 1989-96; cons. Conflict Resolution, 1996—. Chmn. Abington Human Rels. Adv. Coun., 1973-88; chmn. Cmty. Rels. Com. Abington Twp., 1978—; mem. Ea. Montgomery County Human Rels. Adv. Coun., 1981-83, 2006—; chmn. No Place for Hate project Abington Twp., 2003—; mediator Abington Twp.; leader Stephen Ministry program Abington Presbyn. Ch.; mem. ctr. internat. leadership and comm. bd. advisors Pa. State U., Abington, 2006—. Named Citizen of the Week Times Chronicle Newspaper, 1976; recipient award Four Chaplains Temple U., 1979, Disting. Citizens award Roslyn Jr. C. of C., 1981, Citizens for Progress Humanitarian award, 1982, Cmty. award Abington YMCA, 1987, Dr. Martin Luther King Jr. award Abington Twp., 1989, East Montgomery County/Pa. State Human Rels. Intergroup award, 2000, Citizens That Care award Abington Cmty. Taskforce, 2003, Disting. Cmty. Svc. award Intersvc. Clubs of Glenside, 2003. Mem. ASCD, NASEP, Internat. Coop. Learning Assn., Pa. Assn. Elem. Prins., Phi Delta Kappa, Delta Kappa Gamma. Republican. Home: 109 Durham Ct Maple Glen PA 19002-2854 Personal E-mail: rwstroh@att.net.

WEAVIL, VICKI LEMP, library director; b. Peoria, Ill., Sept. 16, 1956; d. John Frederick and Barbara King Lemp; m. Kevin Gilbert Weavil, Mar. 20, 2002; m. Robert Ellwyn Montle (div.); 1 child, Thomas. BA in Theatre, U. Va., 1978; MLS, Ind. U., 1988; MA in Liberal Studies, U. N.C., 2005. Reference libr. Lincoln Ctr. N.Y. (N.Y.) Pub. Libr., 1988—90; dir. reference and rsch. Mus. TV and Radio, N.Y., 1990—92; dir. libr. svcs. Semans Libr. N.C. Sch. Arts, Winston-Salem, NC, 1992—. Mem.: ALA, Theatre Libr. Assn., Beta Phi Mu, Phi Beta Kappa. Avocations: writing, gardening, travel, singing. Office: Semans Libr NC Sch Arts 1533 S Main St Winston Salem NC 27127 Office Phone: 336-770-3266.

WEAVING, CHRISTINE A., personal trainer; b. Winsted, Conn., Dec. 1, 1972; d. Edward Nelson and Katherine Elizabeth Weaving. AS in Phys. Edn./Athletic Tng., Mitchell Coll., New London, Conn., 1992; BS in Phys. Edn./Athletic Tng., Ctrl. Conn. State U., New Britain, 1996; EdM in Adminstrn./Supervision in Health Svcs., U. Hartford, West Hartford, Conn., 1999. Cert. athletic trainer Rehab Dynamics, Bristol, Conn., 1999—. CPR, first aid and automated external defibbrilator instr. ARC, Farmington, Conn., 2003—. Sport safety instr. coaches Berkshire League Conn. Interscholastic Athletic Conf., New Hartford and Terryville, Conn., 2005—06. Recipient Hero award, ARC, 1997, Outstanding Employee award, Bristol Hosp., 1999—2005. Mem.: Conn. Athletic Trainers Assn. (assoc.), Nat. Athletic Trainers Assn. (assoc.; cert. athletic trainer). Avocations: bowling, softball, darts. Home: 60 Birdsall St Winsted CT 06098 Office: Rehab Dynamics 975 Farmington Ave Bristol CT 06010 Office Phone: 860-589-3587. Office Fax: 860-589-1872. Business E-Mail: cweaving@brishosp.chime.org.

WEBB, ANN MARIE, literature and language educator, department chairman; b. Butler, Pa., Feb. 26, 1970; d. Richard and Carole Mack; m. Anthony Webb, Apr. 13, 1996; children: Megan Ann, Jacob Charles. BA in Mid. Grades Edn., U. N.C., Charlotte, 1993; MA in Mid. Sch. Reading and Supervision, U. of NC at Greensboro, Greensboro, NC, 2001. Cert. tchr. academically gifted N.C. Tchr. English Kernersville Mid. Sch., NC, 1998—. Dept. chairperson Kernersville Mid. Sch., NC, 1998—, academic team leader, 1999—. Mid. sch. youth group leader First Bapt. Ch. Greensboro, NC, 2002—. Baptist. Avocations: reading, exercise, scrapbooks. Home: 3395 Fallswood Court Colfax NC 27235 Office: Kernersville Mid Sch 110 Brown Rd Kernersville NC

WEBB, DEBBIE, elementary school educator; d. Donna Marie and Robert Leroy Johnson; children: Jason Scott, Jeremy Dean, Justin John. BS, Bethany Coll., Lindsborg KS, 1989—90; M in Curriculum & Devel., Kans. State U., Manhattan, 1999—2002, English as a Second Lang., 2002—03. Cert. Elem. Edn. K-9 Kans. State Dept. Edn., 1990. 6th grade Garden City Sch. Dist., Kans., 1990—92; mid. sch. grade 6 Wichita Sch. Dist., 1992—93; 6th grade tchr. Salina Sch. Dist., 1993—. Grantee Fulbright Hays Group grant, U. Kans., 1997, scholarship, Target Store, 1998. Democrat. Lutheran. Avocations: reading, walking, travel. Office: Lakewood Mid Sch 1135 Lakewood Cir Salina KS 67401 Office Phone: 785-309-4033.

WEBB, DIANA KAY, music director; b. Greenville, Ohio, Dec. 30, 1945; d. Carl and Mary Irene Dietrich; m. Myron Douglas Webb, June 15, 1968; children: Marc Douglas, Darron Ray. B Music Edn., Western Ky. U., Bowling Green, 1968; MA, No. Ky. U., Highland Heights, 1976. Cert. Orff level I and II. Music tchr. Meade County Bd. Edn., Brandenbury, Ky., 1968—69, Kenton County Bd. Edn., Erlanger, Ky., 1973—99; pvt. sch. kindergarten tchr. National City, Calif., 1970—71; music dir. Blessed Sacrament Ch., Diocese of Covington, Ft. Mitchell, Ky., 1988—. Clinician Music Tchr. Insvc., 1980—90. Recorded: music CDs for ednl. use. Mem.: Nat. Pastoral Musicians, Am. Orff Schulwerk, Ky. Music Educators Assn. Republican. Roman Catholic. Avocations: cooking, reading. Home: 105 Farmdale Ct Covington KY 41019 Office: Blessed Sacrament Ch 2409 Dixie Hwy Fort Mitchell KY 41017

WEBB, DONNA LOUISE, academic director, educator; b. Yakima, Wash., Aug. 12, 1929; d. Manuel Lawrence and Rena May (Sewell) Matson; (div.); children: Marlene Park, Ed Webb III. AA in Vocat. Edn., Portland (Oreg.) Community Coll., 1976; BA in Psychology, Warner Pacific Coll., 1980; MEd in Career and Vocat. Edn., Oreg. State U., Corvallis, 1980, EdD in Career and Vocat. Edn., 1983. Dir. placement Andrews U., Mich., 1969-74; dir. career edn. and coop. work experience Portland, 1976-78; coord. youth program Fed. Experiment/Chronically Unemployed Youth, Vancouver, Wash., 1979; dir. career counseling Clark Coll., Vancouver, 1979; tchr. coop. edn. project Multnomah County ESD, Portland, 1981; pvt. practice counselor Portland, 1982-84; dir. career devel. & coop. edn. Walla Walla (Wash.) Coll., 1984-87; assoc. dir. Ctr. for Lifelong Learning Loma Linda (Calif.) U., 1987-91; corp. trainer Pacific Inst., Seattle, 1991-94, account mgr. consulting and rsch., 1994—. Home decorator Frederick & Nelson; payroll and computerized bookkeeper Hilo Care Ctr.; with pers. office Flour-Utah Mining; employment counselor Snelling & Snelling Employment Agy.; tchr. bus. edn. Portland Adventist Acad. Contbr. articles to profl. jours. Mem. ASTD, Assn. Per. Adminstr. (columnist San Bernardino Sun newspaper), Coun. for Adult and Exptl. Learning, Calif. Assn. for Counseling and Devel., Coop. Edn. Assn., Nat. Commn. for Coop. Edn., Phi Delta Kappa. Office: 4501 W Powell Blvd Apt 72 Gresham OR 97030-5070

WEBB, DORIS MCINTOSH, human resources specialist; b. Aliquippa, Pa., May 26, 1930; d. Hayward Victor and Elaine Eloise (Kiernan) McIntosh; m. Alan D. Webb Sr. JD, Aug. 15, 1953 (dec. Sept. 1979); children: Alan D. Jr., Amy E. Webb-Burke. Student, Western Coll. for Women, 1949-51; BS in Bus. Adminstrn., Geneva Coll., 1953, tchr. cert., 1968; MEd, U. Pitts., 1972. Mgr. Crestmont Home Supply Co., Aliquippa, 1953-57; real estate mgr. McIntosh Constrn. Co., Aliquippa, 1957-62; tchr. bus. Rochester (Pa.) H.S., 1968-78; bus. tchr. adult edn. Allegheny C.C., Pitts., 1972-75, Draughon's Jr. Bus. Coll., Knoxville, Tenn., 1979—81, Hartford C.C., Bel Air, Md., 1981—85; corp. sec. McIntosh & Webb Inc., Cockeysville, Md., 1981-88; exec. dir., CEO housing authority City of Havre de Grace, Md., 1989-98; v.p. human resources, tng., devel. McIntosh and Webb Assocs., Charlottesville, Va., 1999—. Chmn. North Boroughs, WQED, Pitts., 1964-68; mem. fin. com. Housing Authority Risk Retention Corp. of Housing Authority Ins. Co., Cheshire, Conn., 1995-97, mem. fin. com. Housing Authority Ins. Co., 1995-97; housing cons. for pub. housing and modernization programs, 1989-97; Sect. 8 Fed. Housing insp., 1996—; owner Ebenezer House bed and breakfast, Rochelle, Va., 2003—. Co-author: Self-Esteem and Empowerment Recovering from Transitions, 2006. Recipient Geneva Coll. Alumni Disting. Svc. award, 1993. Mem.: The Profl. Woman Network, Profl. Woman Spkrs. Bur., Colonial Williamsburg Found. Republican. Lutheran. Avocations: fox hunting, beagling, travel, remodeling homes, decorating. Office Phone: 540-948-3695. Personal E-mail: dmwebb@ntelos.net.

WEBB, ELAINE MARIE, reading specialist; d. Nicholas and Mary Josephine Karhut; m. Donald Dean Webb, Aug. 13, 1977. BS in Edn., Kans. State U., Manhattan, 1971; MA in Spl. Edn., U. Mo., Kansas City, 1983. Cert. reading specialist Kans. and Mo., tchr. visually impaired Kans., learning disabilities Kans., home economics Kans. Tchr. home econs. Unified Sch. Dist., Osawatomie, Kans., 1972—74, Holy Name H.S., Omaha, 1974—75, Unified Sch. Dist., Scandia, Kans., 1975—76, St. Joseph's H.S., Shawnee, Kans., 1976—78; reading specialist St. Joseph's Grade Sch., Shawnee, 1980—85; tchr. learning disabilities Wyandotte H.S., Kansas City, 1985—86; reading specialist Cure' of Ars Cath. Sch., Leawood, Kans., 1986—91, Bluejacket-Flint Elem., Shawnee, 1991—. Com. chair various bldg. coms. Bluejacket-Flint Elem. Recipient Tchr. Recognition award, Bluejacket-Flint Elem. staff, 1995, 2001. Mem.: Internat. Dyslexia Assn., Internat. Reading Assn., Delta Kappa Gamma. Avocations: reading, needlecrafts, hiking, antiques. Office: Bluejacket-Flint Elem 11615 W 49th Ter Shawnee KS 66203

WEBB, EMILY, retired plant morphologist; b. Charleston, S.C., Apr. 10, 1924; d. Malcolm Syfan and Emily Kirk (Moore) W.; m. John James Rosemond, Apr. 23, 1942 (div. 1953); 1 child, John Kirk; m. Julius Goldberg, Sept. 9, 1954; children: Michael, Judith. Student, Coll. Charleston, 1951—54; AB in Liberal Arts and Sci. with honors, U. Ill., Chgo., 1968, MS in Biol. Scis., 1972, PhD in Biol. Scis., 1985. Undergrad. fellow in bacteriology Med. Coll. S.C., Charleston, 1952-54; teaching asst. U. Ill., Chgo., 1969-72, 77-84, rsch. asst., 1977; teaching fellow W.Va. U., Morgantown, 1974, instr., 1974-75. Rsch. in N.Am. bot. needlework art, 1986—. Author: Studies in Several North American Species of Ophioglossum, 1986; translator Nat. Transl. Ctr., Chgo., 1976; contbr. articles to profl. jours. James scholar U. Ill., 1968-69. Mem. DAR, ACLU. Democrat. Episcopalian. Avocations: gardening, writing, money management. Home and Office: 1356 Mandel Ave Westchester IL 60154-3433

WEBB, JULIA JONES, elementary school educator, minister; b. Portsmouth, Va., Apr. 3, 1962; d. William Edward Jones Jr. and Fannie Ford Jones; m. Alexander Maurice Webb Sr., Nov. 17, 1990; children: Brittany Alexandria, Alexander Maurice II. BA in Early Childhood Edn., Norfolk State U., 1988; postgrad., Va. Union U., 2004—. Lic. early edn. Va. Educator Chesapeake (Va.) Pub. Schs., 1988—, chmn. grade level II Southwestern Elem., 2005—. Assoc. minister First Bapt. Ch. Gilmerton, Chesapeake, 1999—2002, New Hope Bapt. Ch., Chesapeake, 2002—05, Grove Bapt. Ch., Portsmouth, Va., 2005—. USAA All-Am. scholar, Norfolk State U., 1989. Mem.: Va. Edn. Assn. (del. 1990—91), Chesapeake Tchr. Forum. Democrat. Baptist. Avocations: coaching cheerleading, gardening, cooking, interior decorating, reading. Home: 2701 Dockside Ct Chesapeake VA 23323 Office: Southwestern Elem Sch 4410 Airline Blvd Chesapeake VA 23321 Office Phone: 757-465-6310.

WEBB, KARRIE, professional golfer; b. Ayr, Queensland, Australia, Dec. 21, 1974; Profl. golfer, 1994—; mem. LPGA Tour, 1996—; mem. Australian Team Women's World Cup of Golf, 2005. Named Rookie of Yr., Women Profl. Golfers' European Tour, 1995, Rolex Rookie of Yr., LPGA, 1996, Rolex Player of Yr., 1999, 2000, Outstanding Women's Golf Performer of Yr., ESPN Espy awards, 1997, 2001, Female Player of Yr., Golf Writers Assn. Am., 2000, Queesland Sportswomen of Yr., 2000—02, 2001, 2002; recipient Vare Trophy, LPGA, 1997, 1999, 2000, Crowne Plaza Achievement award, 2000. Achievements include winning LPGA Tour events including the Weetabix Women's Brit. Open, 1995, 97, 2002, Healthsouth Inaugural, 1996, Sprint Titleholders Championship, 1996, SAFECO Classic, 1996, 1997, ITT LPGA Tour Championship, 1996, Susan G. Koman Internat., 1997, Australian Ladies Masters, 1998, 99, 2000; winner, LPGA Tour events including the City of Hope Myrtle Beach Classic, 1998, Wegmans Rochester Internat., 1999, Mercury Titleholders Championship, 1999, Standard Register PING, 1999, The Office Depot, 1999, 2000; winner, LPGA Tour events including the du Maurier Classic, 1999, Nabisco Championship, 2000, Oldsmobile Classic, 2000, LPGA Takefuji Classic, 2000, AFLAC Champions presented by Southern Living, 2000, US Women's Open, 2000, 01; winner, LPGA Tour events including the McDonald's LPGA Championship presented by AIG, 2001, Tyco/ADT Championship, 2001, Wegmans Rochester LPGA, 2002, John Q. Hammons Hotel Classic, 2003, Kellogg-Keebler Classic, 2004, Kraft Nabisco Championship, 2006, Michelob Ultra Open, 2006, Evian Masters, 2006; winner, international events including the AAMI Women's Australian Open, 2002, ANZ Ladies Masters on the Robe di Kappa Ladies European Tour, 2005; inducted into World Golf Hall of Fame, 2005; first LPGA player to achieve the Super Career Grand Slam by winning all 5 majors available in her career, 2002. Avocations: reading, basketball, fishing. Office: c/o LPGA 100 Internat Golf Dr Daytona Beach FL 32124-1092*

WEBB, LINDA KAY, elementary school educator; m. Darrin Webb. BA, Oral Roberts U, 1981. 5th grade tchr. Westwood Elem. Sch., Broken Arrow, OK. Mem. Okla. Tchr's Advisory Coun. Volunteer, Okla. Dept. of Wildlife Conservation. 1994-95 Okla. Tchr. of the Yr.

WEBB, LUCY JANE, actress, film producer, consultant; d. Phillip Carlen and Marcia Jane Webb; m. Kevin Pollak, Dec. 19, 1995. BA, U. Tenn.; student, New Sch. Social Rsch. Lyndon Baines Johnson intern Congressman Joe Evans, Tenn.; Congl. intern Congressman Albert Gore, Jr., Tenn.; pres. Calm Down Prodns., Inc., LA; prodr. Warner Bros. TV, CBS. V.p. spl. events, chair for Sundance Film Festival, Women in Film, LA; cons. Hollywood Symphony Orch. Actor: (TV series) Private Benjamin, Laughtrax, Not Necessarily the News; exec. prodr.: FX TV, 2005; prodr.: (plays) All Grown Up and No Place to Go; exec. prodr.: (Crystal/Lucy Awards) Women in Film, 2004—05. Chair AIDS charity Angel Women at Risk. Recipient ACE award, Cable ACE Assn., 1985, 1986, 1987, 1988, 1990. Mem.: Beverly Hills Country Club. Democrat. Roman Catholic. Avocations: piano, antiques, travel, films. Office Phone: 323-650-4027.

WEBB, MARTY FOX, principal; b. Des Moines, July 15, 1942; d. Joseph John and Jean (Way) Fox; m. Andrew H. Rudolph, Aug. 17, 1963 (div. Jan. 1988); children: Kristen Ann, Kevin Andrew; m. Eugene J. Webb, Nov. 23, 1991. BS, U. Mich., 1964; MEd, Houston Bapt. U., 1982; EdD, U. San Francisco, 1993. Cert. adminstr., Tex., elem. and spl. edn. educator, Mich., Tex. Tchr. spl. edn. Hawthorn Ctr., Northville, Mich., 1964-70; tchr. Bellaire (Tex.) Sch. for Children, 1977-80; prin. Corpus Christi Sch., Houston, 1980-97; founder, head of sch. The Monarch Sch., Houston, 1997—. Spkr. in field. Bd. dirs. DeBusk Found. Recipient Elem. Sch. Recognition award U.S. Dept. Edn., 1989-90, Blue Ribbon Sch. award, 1990, Outstanding Doctoral Student award, 1994. Mem. ASCD, U. Mich. Alumni Assn. Avocations: reading, fly fishing, camping, hiking, bodybuilding. Home: 3531 Sun Valley Dr Houston TX 77025-4148 Office: The Monarch Sch 1231 Wirt Rd Houston TX 77055-6852 Office Phone: 713-479-0800. Business E-Mail: mwebb@monarchschool.org.

WEBB, MARY GREENWALD, cardiovascular clinical specialist, educator; b. Tecumseh, Mich., Jan. 15, 1945; m. William R. Webb, Sept. 9, 1967; children: Adam, Stephanie. Diploma, Toledo Hosp. Sch. Nursing, 1966; BS, U. South Fla., 1986, MS, 1988; PhD, U. Fla., 1993. Instr. Pasco Hernando C.C., New Port Richey, Fla., 1993-95; assoc. prof. nursing U. South Fla., Tampa, 1995—. Recipient Mentors Sci. Rsch. award, NIH; fellow, Kellogg Found. Mem. Sigma Theta Tau (Excellence in Nursing Edn. award, 1999), Phi Kappa Phi. Home: 6422 Wisteria Loop Land O Lakes FL 34639-3116

WEBB, NANCY HUTCHINSON, elementary school educator; b. Washington, D.C., Apr. 14, 1948; d. Albert Cecil and Elizabeth Namminga Hutchinson; m. Lewis Norman Webb, Jr., Nov. 13, 1998; children: Eric Marshall Brittle, Ryan Coleman Brittle, Nancy Renee Brittle. BS, Va. Poly. Inst. and State U., Blacksburg; PhD, Va. Poly. Inst. and State U., 2004; MS, Va. State U., Petersburg, Va., 1988. Lic. tcdhr. Va. Tchr. Tidewater Acad., Wakefield, Va., 1971—75, Smithfield Elem. Sch., Va., 1981—84; adj. prof. Radford U., Va., 1988—93; tchr. English 6th grade Radford City Schs., 1993—. Adj. prof. Va. Poly. Inst. and State U., 2002—; field supr. Literacy Corp., Radford, 1990—93; grad. asst. S.W. Va. Writing Project, Blacksburg, 2002—04; tchr.-cons. Nat. Writing Project, 2000; panel reviewer Excellence in Edn. Conf.; presenter Phila. Ethnography in Edn. Rsch. Forum. Contbr. articles to profl. jours., chapters to books. Scholar, Fulbright Hayes Found., Africa, 2004, Va. Poly. Inst. and State U., 2000—04. Mem.: Va. Assn. for Tchrs. of English, Nat. Coun. Tchrs. English, Phi Delta Kappa. Avocations: photography, gardening, quilting, reading, writing. Home: 7040 Young Rd Dublin VA 24084 Office: Radford City Schools 810 Second Ave Radford VA 24141 Business E-Mail: nwebb@vt.edu.

WEBB, TARA YVETTE, music educator; d. Harey and Rachel Webb. BA in Music Edn., Baldwin Wallace Conservatory, Berea, Ohio, 1985. Cert. Orff Schulwerk level 1, 2, 3, Kodaly level 1. Music specialist Taft and Franklin Schs., Lakewood, Ohio, 1986—87; substitute tchr. Lakewood Pub. Schs., 1987—89; dir. children's choir and youth orch. Lakewood Presbyn. Ch., 1987—; music specialist K-8 Sts. Joseph and John Sch., Strongsville, Ohio, 1988—. Mem. guidance com. St. Joseph and John Sch., Strongsville, 2001—. Singer, actress, orch. mem. Singing Angels Comty. Theater; goodwill amb. Ohio Light Opera, 1977—81; mem. West Surbon Philharm. Orch. Recipient Latin Am. Art and Music grant, Eva and Joseph M. Bruening Found., 1998, Native Am. Music grant, McGinty Found., 2001. Mem.: Smithsonian Nat. Mus. of the Am. Indian, Rock and Roll Hall of Fame and Mus., Am. Orff Schulwerk Assn., Orgn. Am. Kodaly Educators. Home: 1508 Bunts Rd Lakewood OH 44107 Office: Sts Joseph and John Sch 12580 Pearl Rd Strongsville OH 44136

WEBB, YVONNE M., secondary school educator; b. Watertown, S.D., May 27, 1954; d. Lloyd T. and Rose V. Hanks; m. Melvin R. Webb; children: Justin, Grant, Forrest, Grace. BSc, No. State U., 1974. Tchr. German S.D. Sch. Visually Handicapped, Aberdeen, SD, 1974—77; tchr. Roscoe (S.D.) H.S., 1977—79, Cheyenne Eagle Butte (S.D.) H.S., 1994—, chmn. Dept. English, 1994—. Adv. student coun. Cheyenne Eagle Butte (S.D.) H.S., 1990—92, adv. H.S. class, 1983—2006. Vol. YMCA, Eagle Butte, 1996—2004, All Saints Cath. Ch., Eagle Butte, 1996—2000. Named Tchr. of Yr., Indian Office Edn., 2000. Mem.: Eagle Butte (S.D.) Edn. Assn. (sec. 1995, treas. 1995). Democrat. Roman Cath. Avocations: reading, gardening. Home: Box 27 Eagle Butte SD 57625

WEBBER, CAROLYN ANN (MRS. GERALD E. THOMSON), pathologist, educator; b. Aiken, SC, Mar. 28, 1936; d. Paul Rainey and Clemmie Vivian (Embly) Webber; BS, SC State Coll., 1956; MD, Howard U., 1960; m. Gerald Edmund Thomson, July 26, 1958; children— Gregory Alan, Karen Blair. Rotating intern Kings County Hosp., Bklyn., 1960-61, resident in pathology, 1961-63, 64-66, Am. Cancer Soc. clin. fellow in pathology, 1962-63, 64-65, attending physician, 1969-; instr. pathology SUNY Downstate Med. Ctr. Bklyn., 1966-69, asst. prof., 1969-73, clin. asst. prof., 1973-, attending physician, 1970- . Diplomate Am. Bd. Pathology. Mem. Am. Soc. Cytology, Assn. Women in Sci., Am. Med. Women's Assn. (pres. 2005-2006), NY Pathol. Soc., fellow, Am. Coll. Physicians; Contbr. articles to profl. jours. Office: SUNY Downstate Med Ctr Pathology Box 25 450 Clarkson Ave Brooklyn NY 11203-2056 Office Phone: 718-245-5401. Business E-Mail: cwebber@netmail.hscbklyn.edu.*

WEBBER, DIANA L., management consultant executive, engineering educator; b. Sacramento, May 12, 1960; d. Ralph and Mary P. (Chace) Van Tuyl. BS, Tex. A&M U., Coll. Station, 1983; M in Computer Systems Mgmt., Creighton U., Omaha, 1987; PhD, George Mason U., Fairfax, Va., 2001. Aerospace engr. USAF, Crystal City, Va., 1978—2001, Scitor Corp., Chantilly, Va., 1995—2001; adj. prof. George Mason U., Fairfax, Va., 2001—; prin. Booz Allen Hamilton, McLean, Va., 2001—. Mem. adv. bd., assoc. editor: Booz Allen Tech. Jour.; contbr. articles to profl. jours. Capt. USAF, 1978—94, Pentagon. Mem.: ACM, IEEE Computer Soc. Democrat. Achievements include research in The Variation Point Model. Avocations: walking, reading, swimming. Office: Booz Allen Hamilton 8283 Greensboro Dr Mc Lean VA 20191 Office Phone: 703-902-4062. Personal E-mail: drwebber@comcast.net. Business E-Mail: webber_diana@bah.com.

WEBBER, HELEN, artist; b. NYC; d. David and Frieda (Berlin) Ross; children: Joel Benjamin (dec.), Daniel Saul, Rachel Frieda. BA, Queens Coll., 1951; postgrad., Columbia U., 1953; MA, RI Sch. Design, 1963. Site specific artist in tapestry, clay, metal, wood and glass; tchr. in design dept. Calif. Coll. Arts, Oakland, 1982, 1984, 1987; lectr. U. Calif. Keynote spkr. ASID, San Diego and Kansas City, 1983, Nat. Home Furnishings League, San Francisco, 1980, Chgo., 1982; lectr., exhibitor Internat. Congress Women Archs., Paris, 1983, U. Calif., Santa Cruz, 1988, Commnwealth Club, San Francisco, 1989, guest lectr. RI Sch. Design Alumni Conf., 1996; instr. Hussian Coll. Art, Phila., 2003-04. Author, illustrator: Good-Night, Night, The Sea Is My Blanket, 1963, My Kite it the Magic Me, Summer Sun; prin. commissions for 6 Carnival Cruise Line ships; Festival, Tropical Fantasy, Holiday, Celebration, Destiny, Pittsburg Calif. Civic Ctr., Metro Commerce Bank, San Francisco, Statendam/Holland Am. Cruise Lines, VA Med. Ctr., Cleve., Vets. Cemetery, Riverside, Calif., VA Hosp., Lyons, NJ, East Tex. Med. Ctr., Tyler, St. Patrick's Hosp., Lake Charles, La., Gatwick Penta Hotel, London, Jewish Home for the Aged, Houston, Jewish Home for Aging, Riverdale, NY, Betty Ford Pavilion, Palm Springs, Fla., Sphohn Hosp., Corpus Christi, Tex., St. Agnes Hosp., Fresno, Calif., Chevron Corp., San Ramon, Calif., Merck & Co., Rahway, NJ, Kodak, Kingsport, Tenn., Kaiser Permanente, Bristol Hosp., Conn., Sacramento and San Jose, Calif., Quail Lodge Resort, Carmel Valley, Calif., Episcopal Homes Found., San Francisco, Menorah Manor, Dunedin, Fla., Hyatt Regency, Phoenix, 1st United Meth. Ch., Wichita Falls, Tex., Ctrl. Maine Hosp., Lewiston; designer, artist textile, wallpaper, sheets, towels, children's games for Collins & Aikman, Burlington, Covington, Peerage of Eng., Edward Fields, Pastime Industries. Mem. Design Internat. (pres., co-founder San Francisco 1984-85), Women -in-Design Internat. (founder, pres. 1977-83, Outstanding Contbn. to Design award 1980), Urban Art Internat. (bd. dirs.). Office: Helen Webber Art Design 103 S Village Ave Exton PA 19341-1216 Office Phone: 610-363-9241. Personal E-mail: helenwebber@comcast.net.

WEBBER, LINDA JUDITH RITZ, interior designer; b. Bronx; d. Murray and Marilyn Ritz; children: Ronald Alan, Amy Beth. BFA, Boston U., 1964; MEd, U. Hartford, 1967. Lic. interior designer, Conn. Elem. art supr., Winthrop, Mass., 1964-65; jr. high sch. art tchr. Wethersfield, Conn., 1965-66; freelance artist various bus. and industries; interior designer A. J. Skenderian, West Hartford, Conn., 1975-77, John LaFalce Inc., Canton, Conn., 1978-97; art tchr. Avon Mid. Sch., 1995-96; art curator U. Conn. Health Ctr., 2001. Art career counsellor Bloomfield (Conn.) Mid. Sch., 1979-81; lectr. in found. studies and interior design Paier Coll. of Art, 1988-89. One-woman shows include Reno Gallery, Hartford, Conn., 1971, Represented in permanent collections U. Conn. Health Ctr., Farmington, created mural, Forces of Life, Ctr. for Women's Health at U. Conn. Health Ctr. Mem. adv. com. for fine arts Bloomfield Bd. Edn., 1975-78; mem. title VII com., 1978-81; mem. bd. for student publs. Boston U., 1962-64; curator Weyerhauser and Musser Mansions, Historic Homes on Miss., 1997; cons. art. adv. com. U. Conn. Health Ctr., 1998—. Recipient Graphic Artist award West Hartford Art League, 1975, Carriage House prize Art League of New Britain, 1996, 99, Color Explorations painting prize West Hartford Art League, 1996, Wintonbury Art League award, 2004, Quru award Conn. Acad. Fine Arts, 2006. Mem. Conn. Women Artists, Clinton Art Soc. (merit award 1971), Wintonbury Art League (pres. 1991-93, Leonard Waller Meml. award 1981, Pritchett prize, Freidman Floor Covering award for a watercolor 1988, Honorable Mention award Essex 1989), Conn. Watercolor Soc. Avocation: ballroom dancing. E-mail: webberbydesign@comcast.net.

WEBBER, PAMELA D., information technology executive; Sr. mgr. applications devel. eCommerce Arrow Electronics, Inc., Melville, NY. Mem.: The Computer Tech. Industry Assn. (bd. mem. electronics industry data exch. leadership 2003—). Office: Arrow Electronics 50 Marcus Dr Melville NY 11747

WEBBER, SABRA JEAN, humanities educator, department chairman; d. Cecil Littlefield and Jean McKenzie Webber; 1 child, Michael Alexander McDougal-Webber. MA, U. Calif., Berkeley, 1975; PhD, U. Tex., Austin, 1981; BA, Occidental Coll., Eagle Rock, Calif. Asst. prof. Ohio State U., Columbus, Ohio, 1983—91, chair comparative studies in the humanities, 1989—95, assoc. prof., 1991—. Author: (ethnography) Romancing the Real: Folklore and Ethnographic Representation in North Africa; editor, field rschr.: childrens' book Lisagharina (For Our Children), author, co-editor (with Margaret Lynd): edited volume Fantasy or Ethnography: Irony and Collusion in Subaltern Representation. Recipient rsch. fellowship, Am. Rsch. Ctr. Egypt, 1983—84; Ind. Rsch. Fellow, NEH, 1982—83, Rockefeller Residency fellow, Wash. U., 1988—89, Sr. Regional Rsch. fellow, Fulbright, 1997—98, Sr. fellow, Social Sci. Rsch. Coun., 1998. Mem.: Mid. Ea. Studies Assn., Am. Anthrop. Assn., Am. Folklore Soc. Home: 103 East Third Ave Columbus OH 43201 Office: Ohio State University Hagerty 300 1775 College Rd Columbus OH 43210 Office Phone: 614-292-2559. Business E-Mail: webber.1@osu.edu.

WEBER, ADELHEID LISA, retired nurse, chemist; b. Cottbus, Germany, June 1, 1934; came to the U.S., 1958; d. Johannes Gustav Paul and Johanna Katinka (Askevold) Haertwig; m. Joseph Cottrell Weber (dec. 1986), Oct. 25, 1957; children: Robert Andreas, Miriam Lisa. RN, Stadtisches Hosp., Dortmund, Germany, 1956; BS in Distributive Sci., Am. U., 1983; MBA, U. Md., 1991; postgrad., New Eng. Acupuncture Sch., 2000. RN. Nurse Krankenhaus, Wuppertal, Germany, 1956—57; pvt. nurse Wellesley, Mass., 1969—74; lab. tech. Microbiol. Assoc., Bethesda, Md., 1979—84; switchboard operator Best Products Co., Bethesda, 1983—87; lab. tech. Uniformed Svcs. U. Health Scis., Bethesda, 1984—90; info. rsch. tech. Info. Rsch. Internat. Inc., Bethesda, 1987; chemist USDA, Beltsville, Md., 1990—93, ret., 1993; distbr. Morinda Health Product-Noni Juice, 1999—; nurse Comfort Keepers In Home, Cape Cod, Mass., 2005—. Vol. Sibley Meml. Hosp., Washington, 1991. Recipient Cert. award County of Montgomery, Md., 1988, Whitman Walker Clinic, 1987. Mem. NAFE, Soc. for Rsch. Adminstrs., Am. Chem. Soc., Nat. Assn. for Amputees, Soc. for Applied Spectroscopy, Nat. Trust for Historic Preservation, Hemlock Soc. Nat. Capital Area, Nat. Mus. for Women in Arts, Wash. Performing Arts Soc. Avocations: stained glass, pottery, gardening, needlecrafts, reading. Home: 23 Sunset Ln Osterville MA 02655-2036 E-mail: heidiweb_2003@yahoo.com.

WEBER, ALOIS HUGHES, principal; b. Clay County, Mo., Dec. 19, 1910; d. William Swan and Nora Mildred (Elam) Hughes; m. Frank Thomas Ewing Weber, May 28, 1934 (dec. 1980); children: Patricia Katherine Weber Brusuelas, Susan Weber Mills. BA, William Jewell Coll., Liberty, Mo., 1932; MA, U. Mo., Kansas City, 1971. Elem. prin. Linden (Mo.) Sch. Dist. #72, 1931-34; elem. tchr. Eugene (Mo.) Sch. Dist., 1935-38, Sycamore Sch., Boone County, Mo., 1938-41; reserve tchr. Kansas City (Mo.) Schs., 1941-55, contract tchr., 1955-63; head tchr. Allen Sch., Kansas City, 1963-67; remedial reading tchr. Benjamin Franklin Sch., Kansas City, 1967-69; reading cons. Div. Urban Edn., Kansas City, 1969-73; coord. Title I Elem. Reading and Compensatory Edn., Kansas City, 1974-79; ret. Instr., trainer ARC, Am. Assn. Ret. Persons, Staying Healthy After Fifty, State of N.Mex., 1987-89, Growing Old with Health and Wisdom, 1989-95; tutor Literacy Vols. of Am., Inc., Rio Rancho, N.Mex., 1990-93; spkr. AARP Health Care Reform, Health Care Am., 1992—, Lovelace Sr. Adv. Group, 1993-98. Vol. Corrales Libr., 1980-88; bd. dirs. Read West, Literacy Vols. Am., Rio Rancho, 1989-92; bd. dirs. Adobe Comty. Theatre, Corrales, 1989-90; lectr. in field; mem. State of N.Mex. steering com. Growing Old with Health and Wisdom, 1989-95; asst. state coord. Am. Assn. Ret. Persons, Health Advocacy Svcs., N.Mex., 1995-98; pres. adv. bd. Meadowlark Sr. Ctr., Rio Rancho, 1997-2003. Recipient Area Cmty. Svc. award AARP, Nat. award for HAS Outstanding Project Achievement, 1993; Area Cmty. Svc. award State of N.Mex., 1988, Cert. of Appreciation, ARC, 1988, Cert. of Appreciation for outstanding cmty. svc. N.Mex. Legislature, State Senate, 1997, Cert. of Appreciation Rio Rancho, N.Mex. Dept. Pub. Safety Srs. and Law Enforcement Together, 1997; NSF grantee, 1973. Mem. AAUW, N.Mex. Assn. Edn. Retirees (exec. com. 1987-89), Albuquerque Assn. Edn. Retirees (exec. sec., bd. dirs. 1990-95), PEO (chpt. BD chaplain, 1990-94), West Mesa Assn. Ednl. Retirees (membership chmn. 1991, v.p. 1993, pres. 1994), Grad. Club Albuquerque. Democrat. Baptist. Avocations: bridge, reading, travel. Home: 3321 Esplanade Cir SE Rio Rancho NM 87124-2198

WEBER, AMELIA LUCI, music educator; b. Wausau, Wis., July 20, 1982; d. James Dodd and Rosanne Christine Weber; m. Zachary Ryan Armstrong, July 1, 2006. BME summa cum laude, Wartburg Coll., Waverly, Iowa, 2004. Cert. K-12 profl. music educator Iowa, Wis. Vocal music tchr. Platteville H.S., Platteville, Wis., 2004—. Choir dir. St. Peter Ch. ELCA, Denver, 2003—04, First English ELCA, Platteville, 2005—; pvt. voice tchr., Wausau, Wis., 2002—04. Actor: Great Midwestern Ednl. Theatre Alliance, 2005; singer: Platteville Chorale, 2004. Mem. exec. bd. Music Boosters, Platteville, 2004. Mem.: Music Educators Nat. Conf., Am. Choral Dirs. Assn. Lutheran. Avocations: cooking, reading, running. Office: Platteville HS 710 E Madison Platteville WI 53818

WEBER, CHRISTINE RUTH, artist; b. London, Dec. 18, 1949; came to U.S., 1959; d. Thomas and Margorie Grace (Smith) Rock; m. Alan Dion Weber, Nov. 23, 1973; 1 child, Michele Elizabeth. BA in Psychology, Calif. State U., Northridge, 1974; cert. comml. design, U. Calif., Santa Barbara, 1980. Self employed artist, Oxnard, Calif., 1974—. Exhibiting artist Oxnard Art Assn., Buenaventura Art Assn., Ojai Ctr. for the Arts, Plein Aire Peintres. Avocations: travel, pvt. pilot, walking, music.

WEBER, DENISE E., retired history educator; b. Johnstown, Pa., Oct. 12, 1946; d. Stephen F. and Agnes L. Dusza; m. Thomas W. Weber, Oct. 4, 1969; children: Heidi A., Gretchen L., Michael T. BS in History Edn., Ind. U. Pa., 1964—68, MA in History, 1968—69. Cert. tchr. Pa. Dept. Edn., 1972. Old world history tchr. Ind. Area Jr. HS, Pa., 1969—83; advanced placement European history tchr. Ind. Area Sr. HS, 1983—99; part-time temp. instr. Lock Haven U. Pa., Clearfield, Pa., 2000—05. Advanced placement European history reader Ednl. Testing Svc., Trenton, NJ, 1991—2005. Author: Delano's Domain: A History of Warren Delano's Mining Towns of Vintondale, Wehrum and Claghorn, Vol. I, 1789-1930, 1991. Regional coord. U. Md. Nat. History Day Contest, 1992—96, Lock Haven U. judge, 2002—03; judge Pa. State History Day Contest, 1985—91. Rsch. grantee, U. Pa., 1984, Carnegie Mellon U., 1990, Ohio Wesleyan U., 1992, Fulbright scholar, 1989, 1993. Mem.: Pa. Hist. Assn. (exec. bd. mem. 1990—94), St. Andrew's Soc. Ind. County (exec. bd. 1999—2006), Cambria & Ind. Trail Coun. (life; sec. 2001—06). R-Conservative. Roman Catholic. Avocations: gardening, travel. Home: 291 Olive St Indiana PA 15701

WEBER, ELIZABETH ANN, academic administrator, music educator; b. Murphysboro, Ill., Jan. 8, 1941; d. Everett George and Lena Mae (Storey) W.; m. Gary Wayne Hornik, Dec. 19, 1970 (div. Jan. 1980). EdB in Music, MusB, Roosevelt U., 1964, M in Music, 1965; D in Musical Arts, U. Ill., 1980. Mem. Mid-America Chorale, Iowa, 1967-69; instr. music Coe Coll., Cedar Rapids, Iowa, 1969-72; prof. music Chgo. State U., 1972—98, chmn. music dept., 1985-91; ret., 1998. Instr. part-time Roosevelt U., Chgo., 1972-74. Mem. alumni bd. Roosevelt U., Chgo.; choral singer Chgo. area. Iowa Arts Coun. grantee, 1970-71. Mem. Coll. Music Soc., Nat. Assn. Tchrs. Singing, Music Edn. Nat. Conf., Phi Kappa Phi, Mu Phi Epsilon (4th v.p. 1983-89). Republican. Episcopalian. Avocations: golf, swimming.

WEBER, GAIL MARY, lawyer; b. Austin, Minn., Dec. 7, 1954; d. Clemence Peter and Aryls Marion (Mulick) W.; m. Thomas Jeffrey Miller, Sept. 24, 1983; 1 child, Paula Suzanne. AA, Austin C.C., 1975; BA in Psychology and English with high scholastic honors, St. Cloud State U., 1978; JD, Hamline U., 1983. Bar: Minn. 1983, U.S. Supreme Ct. Minn. 1983, U.S. Dist. Ct. Minn. 1984. Child care specialist Gerard Schs., Austin, 1978-80; legal intern St. Paul Dept. Edn., 1981-82; law clk. Alton, Severson, Sovis & Groves, Apple Valley, Minn., 1982, Heuer Madden & Gruesner, Mpls., 1983, assoc., 1983-85, Heuer, Weber & Assocs., Mpls., 1986-88, Robbins & Rashke, Mpls., 1986-93; ptnr. Robbins Rashke & Weber, Edina, 1993—; pvt. practice Edina, Minn., 1985-93. Coach high sch. mock trial program, Mpls., 1986-94, vol. Chrysalis, Mpls., 1986—; co-chmn. Legis. Action Com., Minn. Women Lawyers, 1987-89. Mem. ACLU, 1990, Minn. Civil Liberties Union, 1990, Big Sisters, St. Paul, 1980-82, Greenpeace; Sunday sch. tchr., 1995-98; co-leader Daisy Scouts, 1996-97. Recipient Appreciation award Chrysalis Ctr. for Women, 1989-97. Mem. Minn. Trial Lawyers Assn., Nat. Employment Lawyers Assn. (Minn. chpt.), Fed. Bar Assn., Minn. Soc. Criminal Justice (sec. 1988, v.p. 1989, bd. dirs.), Minn. Women Lawyers (bd. dirs. 1989-91), Minn. Trial Lawyers Assn., LWV (asst. editor newsletter 1987-89, bd. dirs., chair edn. study 1994-95), Delta Theta Phi. Democrat. Roman Catholic. Avocations: reading, theater, Karate, opera, golf. Home: 7205 Heatherton Cir Minneapolis MN 55435-4117

WEBER, GLORIA RICHIE, retired minister, retired state legislator; married; 4 children. BA, Washington U., St. Louis; MA, MDiv, Eden Theol. Sem., Webster Groves, Mo. Ordained to ministry Evang. Luth. Ch. Am., 1974. Family life educator Luth. Family and Children's Svcs. Mo.; mem. Mo. Ho. of Reps., 1993-94. Mo. state organizer, dir. comm. Mainstream Voters C.A.R.E., 1995. Editor: Interfaith Voices for Peace and Justice, 1996—2000. Exec. dir. Older Women's League, 1990—95. Named Woman of the Yr., Variety Club, 1978, Woman of Worth, Older Women's League, 1993; recipient Woman of Achievement award, St. Louis Globe-Dem., 1977, Unselfish Cmty. Svc. award, St. Louis Sentinel Newspaper, 1985, Faith in Action award, Luth. Svcs. St. Louis, 1994. Mem.: Older Wiser Luths. in Svc. (devotion leader), Assn. Lutheran Older Adults (mem. nat. bd. 2004—), N.Am. Interfaith Network (bd. dirs. 1993—2003), Phi Beta Kappa. Democrat. Personal E-mail: gloriaweber9@aol.com.

WEBER, GRACE T., school system administrator; b. Buffalo, Apr. 25, 1940; d. Leslie F. and Wanda A. Weber. BA, Valparaiso U., 1962; MA in Tchg., St. Louis U., 1966. Cert. tchr., Mo. Tchr. L.I. Luth. High Sch., Brookville, N.Y., 1962-65, Pattonville Sch. Dist., St. Louis, 1966-96, curriculum coord., 1996—. Mem. steering com. Mo. Geog. Alliance, St. Louis, 1998—; participant Fulbright Summer Seminar, U.S. Dept. Edn., India, 1990, Egypt and Zimbabwe, 1995. Mem. Cmty. Leadership for Tchrs., Focus St. Louis, 1991-92. Recipient Springboard to Learning Travel award, 1986. Mem. NEA, Mo. Edn. Assn., Nat. Assn. Gifted Educators, Nat. Assn. Geog. Educators, Nat. Coun. Social Studies, Delta Kappa Gamma (rec. sec. Delta state orgn. 2001—, 1st and 2d v.p. Pi chpt. 1990-94, pres. Pi chpt. 1994-98). Avocations: travel, reading, walking.

WEBER, IDELLE, artist, educator; b. Chgo., Mar. 12, 1932; d. J. Earl and Min (Wallach) Feinberg; m. Julian L. Weber, Apr. 17, 1957; children: Jonathan Todd, Suzanne. BA, UCLA, 1954, MA, 1955. Adj. assoc. prof. art, grad. div. NYU, 1974-88; assoc. prof. Carpenter Ctr. Harvard U., 1988-91; prof. Nat. Acad., 2004-2006. Exhibited one-woman shows: Bertha Schaefer Gallery, N.Y.C., 1963, 64, Hundred Acres Gallery, N.Y.C., 1973, 75, 77, Chatham Coll., Pitts., 1979, O.K. Harris Gallery, N.Y.C., 1979, 82, Ruth Siegel Gallery, N.Y.C., 1984, 85, 87, Antony Ralph Gallery, N.Y.C., 1989, Arts Club of Chgo., 1986, Homart, Houston, 1987, Barbara Fendrick Gallery, Washington, 1987, Jean Albano Gallery, Chgo., 1994, Victorian Coll. of Arts, Melbourne, U., Australia, 1995, Contemporary Arts Forum, San Francisco, 1995, Nassau Mus. Art, 2004, Ferregut Tower Gallery, N.Y., 2005; group shows: Pa. Acad. Fine Arts, San Antonio Mus., Larry Aldrich Ctr. for Contemporary Arts, Ridgefield, Conn., 1981, Mus. Modern Art, N.Y.C., 1956, Guggeheim Mus., N.Y.C., 1964, Wadsworth Atheneum, Hartford, Conn., 1964, 66, Darnstadt (W.Ger.) Mus., Yale U. Mus., New Haven, 1975, Va. Mus., Richmond, Nat. Collection Fine Art, Washington, Butler Inst., Youngstown, Ohio, Fendrick Gallery, Washington, 1978, 85, Nat. Acad. 2002, 05, 06, Danforth Mus., Framington, Mass, 1980, San Francisco Mus. Art, 1985-86, Contemporary Art Ctr., New Orleans, 1986, Indpls. Mus. Art, 1986, Graham Modern Mus., N.Y.C., 1986, Ft. Wayne Mus. Art, 1988, Carpenter Ctr. Harvard U., 1988, Met. Mus. Art, N.Y.C., 2001, U. Va. Art Mus., 2002, Gracie Mansion, Chelsea, N.Y.C., 2002, Nat. Acad. Design Mus., 2003, Neuberger Mus. Art, 2004, Nat. Acad., 2004, Ferregut Tower Gallery, Southampton, N.Y., 2005; represented permanent collections: Nat. Collection Fine Art, Va. Mus., Sydney and Francis Lewis Found., Richmond, Yale U. Art Gallery, Albright Knox Gallery, Buffalo, Worcester (Mass.) Art Mus., Rochester (N.Y.) U. Mus., McNay Art Inst., N.Y. Pub. Library, Met. Mus. Art, N.Y.C., Pacific Bell, Calif., Bklyn Mus., Albright-Knox Gallery, Buffalo, Nelson -Atkins Mus. Art, Kansas City, Mo., Met. Mus. Art, Art Inst. Chgo., Kranert, U. Ill., Urbana, Whitney Mus. Art, Nat. Acad. and Sch. Fine Arts. Recognized in various publs. including: Arts Mag., 1979, 82, 84, 86, Photo Realism (L. Meisel), 1980, San Antonio Mus. Catalogue (L. Nochlin), 1981, Art in Am. (E. Lubell), Am. Women Artists (C.S. Rubenstein), 1982, Wall St. Jour., 1985, Christian Sci. Monitor, 1985, 86, Art in America, 1986, Washington Post, 1986, Chgo. Tribune, 1986, Washington Post, 1986, 87, Art Examiner, 1986; subject of work: American Realist Painting, 1945-1980 (John L. Ward), 1989; Scholastic Arts mag. scholar, 1950. Mem. Coll. Art Assn., Women's Caucus for Art, Artists Equity, Nat. Acad.

WEBER, JANICE ANN, library director, grant writer; b. Baytown, Tex., Aug. 28, 1952; d. James Thelmer Jr. and Doris Geraldine (Bush) Foster; m. Louis Haldane Weber, Feb. 1, 1983. BS, Tex. Women's U., Denton, 1982, MLS, 1985. Libr. dir. Dimmit County Libr., Carrilo Springs, Tex., 1985-86, Val Verde County Libr., Del Rio, Tex., 1986-89, Laredo (Tex.) Pub. Libr., 1989—. Sec., bd. dirs. Literary Vol. of Am., Laredo, 1989-95, bd. dirs. Webb County Heritage Found., Laredo, 1990-94; chmn. Webb County Hist. Commn., 1989-94; mem. Tuesday Music & Lit., Laredo, 1997—. Grantee numerous orgns., 1990—. Mem. Nonprofit Mgmt. Assn., Tex. Libr. Assn., Tex. Mcpl. Libr. Dirs. Assn. Avocations: gourmet cooking, weaving. Office: Laredo Pub Libr 1120 E Calton Rd Laredo TX 78041-7328

WEBER, JOAN GEIGER, music educator; d. Lawrence Earl and Adeline Alberta Geiger; m. Anton Paul Weber, Jr., Aug. 12, 1962; children: Lisa Adeline Nelson, Anton Paul III. BA in Music Edn., St. Olaf Coll., Northfield, Minn., 1962; BS in Elem. Edn., U. Minn., St. Paul, 1964; MS in Spl. Edn., No. Ill. U., DeKalb, 1989. Cert. K-12 music tchr. Ill., 1962, K-8 elem. tchr. Minn., 1964, K-12 spl. edn. in learning disabilities tchr. Ill., 1989, K-12 spl. edn. in behavior disorders tchr. Ill., 1989. Tchr. elem. sch. Bloomington Sch. Dist., Minn., 1962—64, Rockford Sch. Dist., Ill., 1964—65, Bloomington Sch. Dist., Minn., 1965—66; ch. organist Our Savior Luth. Ch., Pekin, Ill., 1967—70, Good Shepherd Luth. Ch., Prospect Heights, Ill., 1971—80; pvt. piano tchr. Pekin, Ill., 1967—70, Wheeling, Ill., 1971—78; tchr. elem. sch. music Sch. Dist. 21, Wheeling, Ill., 1978—; dir. of music Gloria Dei Luth. Ch., Northbrook, Ill., 1980—; vocal music coord. Sch. Dist. 21, Wheeling, Ill., 2004—. Ins. rep. for sch. Sch. Dist. 21, Wheeling, Ill., 1994—; bd. dirs. AAEC - Sch. Credit Union, Arlington Heights, Ill., 2001—. Mem.: Dist. Edn.

Assn. (assoc.; sch. rep. 1995), Ill. Edn. Assn. (assoc.). Lutheran. Avocations: reading, sewing, baking, pianist, organist. Office Phone: 847-520-2780. Home Fax: 847-419-3077; Office Fax: 847-419-3077. E-mail: jweber@d21.k12.il.us.

WEBER, KATIE, retired special education educator; b. Delhi, La., Dec. 6, 1933; d. Sullivan and Teresa McClain Aytch; m. Hilliard Weber Jr., June 16, 1956; children: Barrett Renwick, Sandra Anita, Dawna Lynn, Thaddeus Marc. BA, So. U., 1957; MEd, Tex. So. U., 1982. Cert. elem. and spl. edn. tchr., La., Tex. Elem. tchr. Port Arthur Ind. Sch. Dist., Tex., 1957-73, elem. spl. edn. tchr. Tex., 1974-85, secondary spl. edn. tchr. Tex., 1985—93; ret., 1993. Part-time prin. Port Arthur Ind. Sch. Dist., 1976-83, interim prin., 1983-85; mem. Tex. assessment acad. skills test Tex. Edn. Agy., Austin, 1988-90, scorer master tchr. test, 1990; also curriculum writer. Candidate for city coun. City of Port Arthur, Tex., 1974; active Brentwood Bapt. Ch., Houston, Tex., 1998-, Bapt. Women Mission III, Sr. Adult Ministry, Class 10 Sunday Sch, Buchanan Cir., 1980—, Port Child Svc. League, Port Arthur, 1989—, Life PTA-Tex. PTA, 1985, Clean Cmty. Commn., Port Arthur, 1990—. Named One of Top 20 Tchrs. in Tex., Leadership Edn., 1984-85, Bus. Assoc. of Yr. plaque Energy City chpt. Am. Women Bus. Assn., 1984. Mem. Assn. Tex. Profl. Educators (Leadership cert. 1989), Zeta Phi Beta. Democrat. Avocations: walking, gardening, cooking, reading, classical music. Address: 1819 Thornbrook Dr Missouri City TX 77489-2207

WEBER, LINDA HORTON, secondary school educator; d. Clyde and Edna Horton; m. John Mauch, July 14, 2001; children: Michelle Elizabeth Tochtrop, Jennifer Marie, Alison Christine. MS, Kent State U., Ohio, 1975; MEd, Lesley U., Cambridge, Mass., 1991. Chemistry tchr. Belmont (Mass.) Pub. Schs., 1993—2001, Natick (Mass.) Pub. Schs., 2001—. Finalist Presdl. Award for Excellence in Math and Sci. Tchg., NSF, 2005; recipient Outstanding Secondary Sch. Chemistry Tchr. award, New Engl. Inst. Chemists, 2002. Mem.: Am. Chem. Soc. (sec. h.s. test com. 2005—, Theodore Williams Richards award 1999, Aula Laudis 2000). Office: Natick HS 15 West St Natick MA 01760 Office Phone: 508-647-6613. E-mail: linda_weber@natick.k12.ma.us.

WEBER, LISA M., insurance company executive; BA in Psych., SUNY, Stony Brook. With Painewebber, 1988—98; sr. v.p. human resources MetLife, Inc., NYC, 1998—2003, sr. v.p., 1999, exec. v.p., 1999—2001, sr. exec. v.p., chief adminstrv. officer, 2001—04, pres. individual bus., 2004—. Bd. dirs. New Eng. Fin., Gt. Am. Fin., Reinsurance Grp. of Am.; bd. dirs. benefits com. MetLife, Inc.; mem. social responsibility com. MetLife Found. Bd. Named one of 50 Most Powerful Women in Bus., Fortune mag., 2006. Mem.: Phi Beta Kappa. Office: MetLife Inc 200 Park Ave New York NY 10166*

WEBER, LORI ANN, elementary school educator; b. Rhinelander, Wis., Feb. 23, 1959; d. Howard Francis and LoisAnn Evelyn Steiner; m. Patrick Phillip Weber, Nov. 10, 1953; children: Julia Suzanne, Evan John. BS, U. Wis., Stevens Point, 1985; MEd, Olivet Nazarene U., Bourbonnais, Ill., 2004. Tchr. title 1 remedial reading and math. Northland Pines Sch. Dist., Eagle River, Wis., 1981—84, tchr. first grade, 1984—85, tchr. second grade, tchr. fifth grade, 1987—. Curriculum cons. Camp Awesome, Saint Germain, Wis., 2004—05; chair outdoor classroom project Northland Pines Sch. Dist., 1996—98. Vol. Eagle River Recreation Assn. Silver Blades Ice Show, 1996—2006, master ceremonies, 1995—; treas. hockey booster club Northland Pines H.S., 2005—06; choir mem., cantor St. Peter's Cath. Ch., Eagle River, 1998—2005. Grantee, Land O'Lakes Fish and Game Club, 1998. Mem.: Northland Pines Edn. Assn. (bldg. rep. 1998—2001). Roman Catholic. Avocations: gardening, cooking, horseback riding, reading. Office: Eagle River Elementary School 1700 Pleasure Island Road Eagle River WI 54521 Office Phone: 715-479-6471.

WEBER, MARGARET LAURA JANE, retired accountant; b. Fairview, Mo., Jan. 4, 1933; d. Mert James and Margaret Orr (Mortensen) Joel; m. James E. Jennings, Mar. 1953 (div.); children: James Edward Jennings, Janie Lea Franks, David Alan Jennings; m. Albert H. Weber, June 1956; children: Luhwanna Stonecipher, Margaret Anne Shadwick. AA, Crowder Coll., Mo., 1972; postgrad. Mo. So. Coll., 1988. Teller, First State Bank, Joplin, Mo., 1951-53; clk. Mo. Lic. Dept., Joplin, 1954-57, U. Mo. Ext. Dept., Neosho, 1967-68; cashier Crowder Coll., Neosho, Mo., 1968-83, acct., 1983-98m, ret., 1998. Mem., Newton County Welfare Com., 1984—. Mem. Am. Bus. Women's Assn. (Woman of Yr. 1982, Bus. Assoc. of Yr. 1987), Nat. Assn. Female Execs., Mo. Assn. Community Jr. Colls. (bd. dirs. 1978-82). Republican. Baptist. Home: 1205 Ozark Dr Neosho MO 64850-1363 Office: Crowder Coll 601 Laclede Ave Neosho MO 64850-9165

WEBER, MARILYN ANN, history educator; d. Emileo and Mary Orsucci; m. Glenn Weber, Sept. 22, 1973; 1 child, Brian. BA, Rosary Coll., Ill., 1967; MS, North Ill. U., 1972. U.S. History tchr. Oliver Wendall Holmes, Wheeling, Ill., 1967—69, Ind. Trail Sch., Addison, Ill., 1969—93, De Soto HS, Tex., 1993—94; A.P. U.S. History tchr. Grapevine HS, Tex., 1994—. Mem. Ill. Edn. Leadership Coun., 1990, 1992; pres. Ladies Aux. Knights of Columbus, Tex., 2002—, HOA Social Com., Tex., 2000—06; S.S. tchr. St. Francis, Tex., 1998—2005. Named Ill. State Tchr. of Year, Ill. State Bd. Edn., 1973; recipient Golden Apple award, 1987, 1990, Disting. Educators award, U. Tex. at Austin. Mem.: Midwest Council for Social Studies, Nat. Coun. for Social Studies. Business E-Mail: marilyn.weber@gcisd.net.

WEBER, MARYANN, language educator; b. Cleve., Mar. 9, 1943; d. Richard James and Charlotte (Pfahl) W. BA in English, Notre Dame Coll., Cleve., 1965; MA in French, Middlebury Coll., 1976, MA in Spanish, 1985, D of Modern Langs., 1985. Tchr. Regina Sch., South Euclid, Ohio, 1965-71, Notre Dame Acad., Middleburg, Va., 1971-72; instr. to assoc. prof. Notre Dame Coll., Cleve., 1972-93; assoc. prof., then prof. Mo. So. State U., Joplin, 1993—. Bibliographer Modern Language Jour., 1998—; contbr. articles to profl. jours. Co-recipient Cmty. Svc. award Ohio Fgn. Lang. Assn., 1990; scholar AATF, 1988, NEH, 89, 91, French Govt., 1995; grantee NEH, 1995-96, Title VI U.S. Dept. Edn., 1997-98. Mem. MLA, Am. Assn. Tchrs. French., Am. Coun. Tchg. Fgn. Langs., Mo. Fgn. Lang. Assn., Rocky Mountain MLA, Phi Sigma Iota. Roman Catholic. Avocations: reading, hiking, volunteer work. Office: Mo So StateU Dept Fgn Langs 3950 Newman Rd Joplin MO 64801-1595

WEBER, PAULA M., lawyer; b. Washington, Pa., June 6, 1959; BA magna cum laude, Colgate Univ., 1981; JD with high honors, George Washington Univ., 1985. Bar: Calif. 1985. Ptnr., chmn. Employment & Labor practice Pillsbury Winthrop Shaw Pittman, San Francisco. Mem.: Phi Beta Kappa, Order of the Coif. Office: Pillsbury Winthrop Shaw Pittman 50 Fremont St San Francisco CA 94105 Office Phone: 415-983-7488. Office Fax: 415-983-1200. Business E-Mail: paula.weber@pillsburylaw.com.

WEBER, RITA FAYE, science educator; d. Everett O. and Alice V. Elsenrath; m. Ernest H. Weber, June 18, 1977. BS, William Woods Coll., Mo., 1978; MEd, William Woods U., Mo., 1996. Tchr. So. Callaway R II Schs., Mokane, Mo., 1978—. Presenter SucessLink Sci. Wish, Jefferson City, Mo., 2000—06. Mem.: STOM, NSTA. Methodist. Avocations: sewing, clogging, scuba diving. Office: So Callaway R II Mokane MO 65059

WEBER, SUSAN A., lawyer; b. 1958; BA, Drake U., 1984; JD, MBA, SUNY, Buffalo, 1989. Bar: Pa. 1990, D.C. 1992, Ill. 1993, U.S. Ct. Appeals (4th cir.) 1990, U.S. Ct. Appeals (3d cir.) 1991, U.S. Ct. Appeals (7th cir.) 1992. Clk. to Justice Byron White U.S. Supreme Ct.; clk. to Judge James Sprouse U.S. Ct. Appeals (4th cir.); with Sidley Austin Brown & Wood, Chgo., 1993—, ptnr., 1997—. Office: Sidley Austin Brown and Wood One Bank Plz 10 S Dearborn St Chicago IL 60603

WEBER, VICKIE FEY, secondary school educator; b. Cedar Rapids, Iowa, Feb. 25, 1954; d. Keith E. and Marilyn (Utter) W.; m. Donald E. O'Neill, July 3, 1982. BA, Coe Coll., Cedar Rapids, Iowa, 1976. Teaching Cert., Iowa. Tchr. Wellsburg (Iowa) High Sch., 1976-77, Springville (Iowa) High Sch., 1977—. Named Tchr. of Yr. Springville (Iowa) High Sch., 1979. 1999; recipient Tchr. Recognition award Northwestern Coll., Orange City, Iowa, 1992, Spl. Tchr., Greater Cedar Rapids Found., 2002. Office: Springville High Sch Academy St Springville IA 52336

WEBER, WENDY A., mathematics professor; d. Melvin and Darlene Weber; m. Tom J. Linton, May 25, 2005. BA, Coll. St. Benedict, St. Joseph, Minn., 1993; MA, U. Ky., Lexington, 1995, PhD, 1999. Assoc. prof. math. Ctrl. Coll., Pella, Iowa, 1999—. Mem.: Math. Assn. Am. (assoc.; sec./treas. Iowa sect. 2002—06). Office: Central Coll 812 University St Pella IA 50219 Office Phone: 641-628-5100.

WEBER, YVONNE ROEBUCK, research administrator; educator; b. McKeesport, Pa., Oct. 22; d. Raymond Henry and Clara Maria (Roberts) Roebuck; B.A., U. Pitts., 1947, M.Litt., 1952, Ph.D., 1973; postgrad. Kent State U., 1950; Ecole Normale, Paris, 1953, Goethe Institut, 1960; m. William Frederick Weber, June 16, 1961; children— Laurel, Wendy. Tchr. French, German, English, history Carrollton (Ohio) High Sch., 1947-51, Canton, Ohio, 1951-52, Munhall (Pa.) High Sch., 1952-58, Wilkinsburg (Pa.) High Sch., 1958-61, Upper St. Clair (Pa.) High Sch., 1963-65; asst. prof. French and German, California (Pa.) State Coll., 1965-66, Point Park (Pa.) Coll., 1968-72; asst. prof., supr. edn. Washington and Jefferson Coll., 1976-79; scholar/discussion leader Pa. Humanities Coun., 1993. Recipient Good Citizenship award DAR, 1943, Doctoral Assn. Outstanding Svc. award U. Pitts., 1989; U. Pitts. scholar, 1943-47, Panhellenic Assn. scholar, 1946-47, disting. alumni award Sch. Edn., U. Pitts., 1985, Alumnae award, 1993; Fulbright grantee to Germany, 1960; program scholar Nat. Endowment for the Humanities, Am. Library Assn., 1986; named Disting. Alumna, U. Pitts., 1971-82; initial inductee hall of fame McKeesport High Sch., 1987. Mem. Modern Lang. Assn., Doctoral Assn. Educators, Pa. State Modern Lang. Assn., Pa. Assn. Tchr. Educators, U.Pitts. Alumni Council, Delta Kappa Gamma Soc. Internat. (Scholarship 1972-73, Eunah Temple Holden Golden Anniversary award 1979, head internat. research project, 1979-82), Mensa Internat., Pi Lambda Theta, Phi Delta Gamma, Zeta Tau Alpha. Club: McKeesport Coll. Author: A Beacon to the Future: Charting a Course for Advancement; contbr. articles to profl. jours. Home: 639 S 77th St Mesa AZ 85208-6453

WEBER-ROOCHVARG, LYNN, English as a second language educator, communications consultant; b. Long Beach, Calif., Jan. 5, 1945; d. Bernard R. and Ruth M. (Oehler) Weber; m. Edward A. Birge (div.); 1 child, Colin E.; m. Alan C. Roochvarg. BA, U. Wis., 1966, MA in Libr. Sci., 1967; PhD, Ariz. State U., 1980. Teaching asst. U. Wis., Madison, 1966-67; libr. Madison Pub. Libr., 1967-70, New Haven Free Pub. Libr., 1970-72; ESL instr. Tempe (Ariz.) Adult Basic Education Program, 1972-77, supr., 1977-80; archival cons. Phoenix, 1980-82; libr. Phoenix Coll., 1982-84, Lansdale (Pa.) Sch. Bus., 1985-92; pres. LWR Assocs., Colmar, Pa., 1991—. Author: Serving Adult Learners, 1981. Ford Found fellow, 1966; Ariz. Dept. Edn. grantee, 1978-80. Mem. ALA, Phi Beta Kappa. Office: LWR Assocs PO Box 501 Colmar PA 18915-0501

WEBSTER, CAROLYN LUCY, elementary school educator; b. St. Genevieve, Mo., June 9, 1952; d. Richard Nicholas and Helen Elizabeth Flieg; m. Darrell Duane Webster, Oct. 31, 1944; children: Daniel, Reta, Patricia. AAS in Early Edn., John Wood CC, 1994; BS in Elem. Edn., Quincy U., 2003. Tchr. Early Childhood Ctr., Quincy, Ill., 1992—2005; tchr. pre-sch. project program Eugene Fields Sch., Hannibal, Mo., 2005—06; tchr. early childhood spl. edn. Vets. Sch., Hannibal, Mo., 2006—. Child devel. assoc. advisor West Ctrl. Child Care Connection, Quincy, Ill., 1994—. Girl scout leader Two Rivers Girl Scouts, Quincy, 1989—94; Sunday sch. tchr. St. Peter's Ch., Quincy, 1987—92, instr. parish sch. religion, 1990—97. Mem.: Phi Theta Kappa, Kappa Delta Pi. Democrat. Roman Catholic. Home: 1106 Ohio St Quincy IL 62301 Office: Vets Sch 790 Vets Rd Hannibal MO 63401 Office Phone: 573-221-0649. Business E-Mail: cwebster@hannibal.k12.mo.us.

WEBSTER, CATHERINE T., telecommunications industry executive; B in Econs., NJ City U. CPA. With Bell Atlantic NJ, 1978, dir. fin. planning and analysis for Telecom/Network, 1993; asst. v.p. fin. planning Corp. Fin. Grp. Bell Atlantic, 1996; v.p. fin. Network Svcs. and Wholesale Markets Verizon Comm., v.p. fin., sr. v.p. investor rels., 2005—. Office: Verizon Comm 140 West St New York NY 10007*

WEBSTER, COLLEEN MICHAEL, language educator; b. Sunnyvale, Calif., Sept. 21, 1965; d. E. Patrick and Patricia Colleen Webster. BA in English, Coll. of Notre Dame of Md., 1987; MA in English, U. Del., 1989, ABD, 1992. Adj. faculty Coll. of Notre Dame, Balt., 1990-94, Harford C.C., Bel Air, Md., 1991-94, assoc. prof., 1994—2004, prof., 2004—; adj. faculty Goucher Coll., Balt., 1992-93, Towson State U., Balt., 1992-93. Organizer/moderator book club Coll. of Notre Dame, Balt., 1994-95, moderator book club Pikesville C.C., 1994-95, moderator Bel Air book club, 2000—; poetry reading coord. Steppingstone Mus., Havre de Grace, Md., 1993-98; spkr. Md. Humanities Coun., 2000—. Contbr. more than 70 poems to lit. publs. Pres. Md. Jr. Coll. Women's LaCrosse League, 1999; lacrosse coach Hartford C.C., 1994-99; literacy dir. Harford Arts Project. Recipient Judson Jerome Poetry scholar Antioch Writer's Conf., 1995, O'Henry award for lit. excellence, 2004; named Coach of Yr. Am. Juco Assn., 1996, 97; nominated Pushcart prize for Poetry, 2002, 04. Mem.: Md. Orinthological Soc. (chair field trip com. Harford chpt.). Democrat. Avocations: running, mountain biking, kayaking, marathons. Office: Harford Cmty Coll 401 Thomas Run Rd Bel Air MD 21015-1627

WEBSTER, DEBBIE ANN, social worker; b. Jamestown, N.Y., Jan. 29, 1959; d. George Thomas and Nicolina Marie (Lupica) Shagla; m. Otis Lee Webster, Mar. 19, 1986; children: Jordan Lee, Justin Thomas, Jasmine Nicole. BA in Psychology, St. Bonaventure U., 1981. Cert. child protectives svcs., S.C.; cert. mental health profl., S.C., Ga.; cert. mental retardation profl., S.C., Ga.; cert. qualified developmental disabilities profl., N.C. Telephone operator Midstate Telephone Co., Jamestown, N.Y., 1981-82; supr. Hillside Children's Ctr., Rochester, N.Y., 1982-86; tchr. Family Resource Ctr., Seaside, Calif., 1986, Aliamanu Child Devel. Ctr., Honolulu, 1987-88; med. social worker Hale Nani Health Ctr., Honolulu, 1988-90; supr. case mgmt. svc. Bibb County Mental Health, Macon, Ga., 1991-94; supr. child protective svcs. Richland County Dept. Social Svcs., Columbia, 1994-98; quality assurance coord. Thomas S. Svcs. Cumberland County Mental Health, Fayetteville, NC, 1998—99; MH program mgr. divsn. MH/DD/SAS NC DHHS, Raleigh, 1999—. Mem. NAFE, County Dirs. and Suprs. Assn., Nat. Assn. Devel. Disabilities. Democrat. Avocations: exercise, reading, computers. Home: 2721 Red Ruby Ln Raleigh NC 27610 Office: Mail Svc Ctr 3005 Raleigh NC 27699-3005 Office Phone: 919-715-2774. Personal E-mail: debbie.webster@ncmail.net, webd9@aol.com.

WEBSTER, LESLEY DANIELS, bank executive; married; 2 children. PhD in Econs., Stanford U. Asst. prof. Wash. U., 1977-83; with Chase Securities, 1983—90; mng. dir., head arbitrage trading group Union Bank Switzerland, N.Y.C., 1990-94; exec. v.p. market risk mgmt. Chase Manhattan Corp. (now JPMorganChase), N.Y.C., 1994—. Bd. dirs. United Way of N.Y.C., chair Women United in Philanthropy for N.Y.C. Named one of 25 Women to Watch, US Banker Mag., 2003. Mem.: Securities Industry Assn. (risk mgmt. com.). Office: Chase Manhattan Corp 270 Park Ave Fl 12 New York NY 10017-2036

WEBSTER, LINDA JEAN, communications executive, media consultant; b. L.A., July 16, 1948; d. Stanley Stewart and Irene M. (Sabo) W. BS, So. Conn. State U., New Haven, 1981, MA, 1983; PhD, La. State U., Baton Rouge, 1987; BA, St. Gregory U., 2002. CEO CBE Enterprises, Inc., Baton Rouge, 1984-89; rsch. fellow La. State U., Baton Rouge, 1983-87; instr. speech Southeastern La. U., Hammond, 1984-89, Hancock Coll., Santa Maria, Calif., 1989; curator of edn. Lompoc (Calif.) Mus., 1989; asst. prof. speech U. Ark., Monticello, 1990-95, assoc. prof. speech, dir. honors program, 1995-2000, prof. speech and journalism, 2000—, chmn. faculty senate, 2003—. Faculty advisor The Weevil student newspaper, U. Ark.; dir. journalism program; exec. dir. Drew County Hist. Mus., Monticello, 1992—95; media dir. Oasis Resources-Homeless Shelter, Warren, Ark., 1991—99, chair bd. dirs., 1998—99; bur. chief Pine Bluff (Ark.) Comml., 1992—94; media cons. Sta. WZXS-FM, Holly Ridge, NC, 1995—97; apptd. State Ark. Mus. Svcs. Rev. Panel, 1997—98, re-apptd., 1999—2000, elected chmn. panel, 1999; chair Drew County Salvation Army, 1999—2000; mem. faculty Exec. MBA program U. Chgo., 2001, 02; cons. William Blair & Co., Chgo., 2004. Editor Jour. Comm. Studies, 1997-2000, on-line version, 2001-04; assoc. editor; asst. Popular Measurement, 1998-2003; S.E. regional corr. Ark. Cath., 1999-2000, columnist, 2003—; writer, dir., prodr. (CD) Voices, 2004; contbr. chpts. to books, articles to profl. jours. Vol. Boys/Girls Club, Monticello, 1992—93; campaign dir. Gloria Wright Election, Monticello, 1995, dir. re-election campaign, 2000; campaign media dir. Ken Harper Election-Dist. 82, 1996; sec. Drew County Rep. Conv., 1998—2000; vice chair St. Mark Parish Coun., 2001—02; chair Migrant Worker Ministry to S.E. Ark., 1998—2000; diocesan coms. on adult faith formation Catechist Tng. Faculty; faculty Diocesan Theology Program. Recipient Noel Ross Strader award Coll. Media Advisors, Inc., 1991, Coll. Tchr. of the Yr. award Ark. State Commn. Assn., 1993, Alpha Chi Tchr. of Yr. award, 1999, Faculty Excellence Gold award, 1999, Walter L. Brown award, Ark. Hist. Assn., 2006; Master fellow Ark. Distance Learning Acad., 2000-01, Guest fellow Haverford Coll., 2006. Mem. AAUW, AAUP, Assn. Edn. in Journalism and Mass Comm., Nat. Women's Studies Assn., Am. Soc. History of Rhetoric, Ark. Press Women (state pres. 1993-95, Communicator of Achievement award 1991), Ark. State Comm. Assn. (1st v.p.-elect 1997-98, 1st v.p. 1998-99, pres. 1999-2000, Stds. Bearer 1997—), So. State Comm. Assn. (chair honors session 1995, constitution com. 1997-2000), Internat. Comm. Assn., Oral History Assn. (nat. planning com. nat. meeting 2006), Speech Comm. Assn. (commn. chair 1993-96), Nat. Comm. Assn. (sec. sr. coll. and univ. sect. 1997-99, min. Cath. campus 1993—, com. on revision of comm. competencies, 2005-06), Edn. Comm. Assn., Assn. Edn. Journalism and Mass Comm. Roman Catholic. Avocations: historic preservation, gardening. Office: U Ark-Arts & Humanities Monticello AR 71656 Business E-Mail: webster@uamont.edu.

WEBSTER, MARY JO, music educator; b. Algoma, Wis., Sept. 18, 1961; d. Kenneth Louis and Mary Ann Feld; life ptnr. Charles Wayne West. MusB, SUNY, Potsdam, 1983; MusM, VanderCook Coll. of Music, Chgo., 1989. Band dir. Algoma (Wis.) Mid. Sch., 1983—91, St. Mary's Internat. Sch., Tokyo, 1991—94, Cerro Coso C.C., Ridgecrest, Calif., 1994—97; band dir., dept. leader George Mason HS, Falls Church, Va., 1997—. Examiner in music Internat. Baccalaureate Orgn., Cardiff, Wales, 2004—06; cadre trainer NEA, Richmond, Va., 2002—06; musical theatre condr. Am. Music Stage, Burke, Va., 2000—06. Author: Teaching Point Textbook. Named Agnes Meyer Tchr. of Yr., Washington Post, 2005; recipient Tchr. of Yr. award, Kewaunee County, Wis., 1989. Mem.: Women's Band Dir. Nat. Assn., Va. Music Educators Assn. Office: Falls Church City Schs 7124 Leesburg Pike Falls Church VA 22043 Office Phone: 703-248-5500. Personal E-mail: mjowebster@aol.com.

WEBSTER, SUSAN, lawyer; b. Hartford, Conn., Dec. 21, 1956; BA, Wesleyan U., 1977; JD, Fordham U., 1984. Bar: N.Y. 1985. Ptnr., corp. Cravath, Swaine & Moore, N.Y.C. Mem. ABA, N.Y. State Bar Assn., Assn. of Bar of City of N.Y. Office: Cravath Swaine & Moore Worldwide Plz 825 8th Ave Fl 38 New York NY 10019-7475 Office Phone: 212-474-1660. Office Fax: 212-474-3700. Business E-Mail: swebster@cravath.com.

WECHSLER, JESSICA See JOSELL, JESSICA

WECHSLER, MARY HEYRMAN, lawyer; b. Green Bay, Wis., Jan. 8, 1948; d. Donald Hubert and Helen (Polcyn) Heyrman; m. Roger Wechsler, Aug. 1971 (div. 1977); 1 child, Risa Heyrman; m. David Jay Sellinger, Aug. 15, 1981; 1 stepchild, Kirk Benjamin; 1 child, Michael Paul. Student, U. Chgo., 1966-67, 68-69; BA, U. Wash., 1971; JD cum laude, U. Puget Sound, 1979. Bar: Wash. 1979. Assoc. Law Offices Ann Johnson, Seattle, 1979-81; ptnr. Johnson, Wechsler, Thompson, Seattle, 1981-83; pvt. practice Seattle, 1984-87; ptnr. Mussehl, Rosenberg et al, Seattle, 1987-88, Wechsler, Becker LLP, Seattle, 1988—. Mem. Bd. Ct. Edn., 1998—2006, sec., 2003—05, vice chair, 2006; bd. dirs. U. Wash. Law Sch. Child Advocacy Clinic, 1996—99; mem. Wash. State Commn. on Jud. Selection, 1995—96, Wash. State Commn. on Domestic Rels., 1996—97, 1999—2004; chair edn. com. Access to Justice Bd., 1996—99, mem. pub. trust and confidence com., 2000—05; mem. Jud. Coll. Bd. Trustees, 2005—; moderator Wash. State Summit on Jud. Independence and Jud. Selection, 2005; presenter in field. Author: Family Law in Washington, 1987, rev. edit., 1988, Marriage and Separation, Divorce and Your Rights, 1994; contbr. articles to legal publs. Mem. Wash. State Ethics Adv. Com., 1992-95; bd. dirs. Seattle LWV, 1991-92. Named Super Lawyer, Wash. Law and Politics, 2000—06; named one of Seattle's Top Lawyer's, Seattle Mag., 2003, 2004, 2005, 2006. Fellow Am. Acad. Matrimonial Lawyers (Wash. state chpt., sec.-treas. 1996, v.p. 1997-98, pres. 1999-2000, nat. arbitration com. 1999-2000, nat. interdisciplinary com. 1999-2000, nat. admissions procedure com. 2000-02, nat. long range planning com. 2003-05, chair 2003—, nat. bylaws com. 2005, nat. budget com. 2004-06); mem. ABA (chmn. membership Wash. state 1987-88), Wash. State Bar Assn. (exec. com. family law sect. 1985-91, chair family law sect. 1988-89), profl. devel. com. 2002-03, media project com. 2001, ct. improvement com. 1998-2000, legs. com. 1991-96, Outstanding Atty. of Yr. family law sect. 1988, comms. com. 1997-98, disciplinary hearing officer 1998—), Wash. Women Lawyers, King County Bar Assn. (legis. com. 1985-2000, vice-chair 1990-91, chair family law sect. 1986-87, chair domestic violence com. 1986-87, trustee 1988-90, policy planning com. 1991-92, 2d v.p. 1992-93, 1st v.p. 1993-94, pres. 1994-95, long-range planning com. 1998-99, awards com. 1997-99, nominations com. 2003, co-chair Bench-Bar Conf. 2003, Outstanding Atty. award 1999), Nat. Conf. of Bar Pres., King County Bar Found. (trustee 1997-2000), Am. Judicature Soc. (v.p. Washington chpt. 2000-03, pres. 2003—). Office: Wechsler Becker LLP Ste 4550 701 5th Ave Seattle WA 98104-7097 Office Phone: 206-624-4900. Business E-Mail: mhwechsler@wechslerbecker.com.

WECHSLER, SUSAN LINDA, business operations director, research and development software manager; b. Burbank, Calif., Oct. 7, 1956; d. Robert Edward and Sharron Ilene Wechsler; m. Gary Daniel Grove, Aug. 24, 1975 (dec. Dec. 1980); m. Dane Bruce Rogers, Feb. 28, 1987; children: Shayna Marneen Rogers, Ayla Corinne Rogers. BA in Math., Calif. State U., Long Beach, 1979. R&D software design engr. Hewlett-Packard Co., Corvallis, Oreg., 1980-97, R&D project mgr. sys. integration team for laptops, 1997—2002, software project mgr. web svcs. devel., 2002—06, bus. ops. mgr., 2006—. Presenter in field. Contbr. articles to profl. publs.; co-developer nine calculators and handheld computers; patentee in field; co-designer HP 200LX Palmtop PC/Organizer, 1994; writer user interface DMI and BIOS software for laptop computers, 1994-97. Pres. Gifts for a Better World, Corvallis, Oreg., 1994, bd. dirs. 1990-1995. Democrat. Avocations: sewing, gardening, raising orchids, reading. Business E-Mail: susan@hp.com.

WECHTER, CLARI ANN, manufacturing executive; b. Chgo., June 1, 1953; d. Norman Robert and Harriet Beverly (Golub) W.; m. Gordon Jay Siegel, Feb. 10, 1980; 1 child, Alix Jessica. BA, U. Ariz., 1975; BE, Loyola U., Chgo., 1977. Cert. tchr., Ill. Saleswoman, v.p. sales Federated Paint Mfg. Co., Chgo., 1979—. Republican. Jewish. Avocation: travel. Home: 25 E Cedar St Chicago IL 60611-1109 Office: Federated Paint and Pioneer Powder Mfg Co 1521 N 31st Ave Melrose Park IL 60160 Office Phone: 708-345-4848 x622.

WECHTER, MARILYN R., psychotherapist; b. N.Y.C., Aug. 25, 1952; d. William H. and Dorothy (Tannenbaum) W. BA, Washington U., St. Louis, 1973, MSW, 1975. Cert. social worker. Psychotherapist Quad City Mental Health Ctr., Granite City, Ill., 1975-76, Growth Ctr., St. Louis, 1976-80; pvt. practice psychotherapy St. Louis, 1980—. Adj. faculty Washington U., 1984-85, Webster U., St. Louis, 1988-2000; mem. faculty child devel. project

St. Louis Psychoanalytic Inst., 1981-84; mem. St. Louis Study Group for Applied Psychoanalysis, 1983-88. Mem. Mo. Psychol. Assn., Nat. Assn. Social Workers, Soc. Advancement Self Psychology, St. Louis Women's Commerce Assn. Home: 225 Woodbourne Dr Saint Louis MO 63105-2318 Office: 130 S Bemiston Ave Ste 703 Saint Louis MO 63105-1929 Office Phone: 314-721-2181.

WECK FARRAG, KRISTIN W., bank executive; b. Elgin, Ill., Nov. 5, 1959; d. John Francis and Florence Elaine (Ebel) W.; married Nov. 6, 2004. BBA, Augustana Coll., Rock Island, Ill., 1981. Lic. real estate broker, Ill., life/health ins. producer; registered securities rep. (series 7 and series 24); registered uniform investment advisor series 65. Intern with investment banking group First Chgo. Bank, London, 1980; intern Prudential-Bache Co., Ft. Lauderdale, Fla., 1981; residential appraiser Fox Valley Appraisal Counselors, Ltd., West Dundee, Ill., 1982-84; asst. real estate loan officer First Nat. Bank, Barrington, Ill., 1982-84; savs. and loan field examiner III Office of Thrift Supervision, Chgo., 1984-90; mng. agt. Resolution Trust Corp., Elk Grove Village, Ill., 1990-91; pres., treas., bd. dirs. Cardunal Savs. Bank, West Dundee, Ill., 1991—; dir. Prairie State Bank, Marengo, Ill., 1998—2002. Project Bus. cons. Jr. Achievement, 1992-96; literacy tutor Vols. of Am., 1998-99; dist. chmn. Found. Ednl. Excellence, 2003-04. Recipient Outstanding Achievement award Fed. Home Loan Bank Bd., 1985, Leading Us In Commerce and Industry award for fin. svcs., 1998, Sam Walton Bus. Cmty. Leader award, 1999. Mem. Nat. Assn. Securities Dealers (registered rep., registered prin.), Rotary Club Dundee Twp. (pres. 2001-02, Rotarian of Yr. 1997-98, Disting. Pres. 2002). Republican. Lutheran. Avocations: scuba diving, golf, walking, reading. Home: PO Box 930 Dundee IL 60118-0930 Office: Cardunal Savings Bank PO Box 839 Dundee IL 60118-0839 Personal E-mail: kweck@cardunal.net.

WEDDINGTON, ELIZABETH GARDNER (LIZ GARDNER), actress; b. NYC, Oct. 13, 1932; d. A. Adolph and Anne Mary (Gardner) Blank; m. George Lee Weddington, Jr., Oct. 23, 1965; 1 child, Georgiana Marie. Student, Moravian Sem. for Girls. Freelance writer NYC Tribune, others. Columnist polit. commentary, 1984—; appeared in over 300 TV commls., also TV and radio voice-overs. Mem. County Com., Conservative Party, N.Y.C., 1988-90, 94-96, 17th Precinct Comty. Coun., N.Y.C., 1974-96; rep. Yorkville Area Cath. Coun., N.Y.C., 1986-93. Recipient Mayor's Vol. Action Ctr. award, N.Y.C., 1981-82, Cert. Recognition N.Y.C. Dept. Police Dep. Commr. Community Affairs, 1981. Mem.: Nat. League Am. Pen Women, Am. Fedn. Radio and TV Artists, Screen Actors Guild, Hereditary Order Descendants of Loyalists and Patriots Am. Revolution, Friends of Va. Archives, N.Y. State Soc. Children Am. Revolution (sr. historian 1988—90, sr. 2d v.p. 1990—92), Colonial Dames Am. (N.Y. claims com. 1993—96, chpt. XXIX N.C. 1999—, courtesy mem. parent chpt.), Daus. Colonial Wars, United Daus. of Confederacy (pres. N.Y. divsn. 1988—90, nat. chmn. revision of gen. bylaws com. 1989—91, McMath Scholar gen. com. 1991—92, nat. chmn. gen. bylaws com. 1992—96, gen. chmn. radio and TV com. 1998—2000, mem. Mrs. Simon Baruch Univ. award com. 2000—02, chmn. chpt. bylaws com. 2002—04, gen. bylaws com. 2004—), N.Y. State Soc. Dames of Ct. of Honor (pres. 1984—88), N.Y. State Soc. Daus. 1812, Nat. Soc. U.S. Daus. of 1812 (organizing pres. Pres. James Madison chpt. 360 1988—98), Nat. Soc. Children of the Am. Revolution - Fraunces Tavern Soc. (sr. pres. 1985—89), Nat. Soc. DAR (assoc.; corr. sec. 1992—94, Washington colonial chpt. 1996—, Mary Washington Colonial chpt. 1996—, mem. Warren chpt. 1996—, treas. 2001—, chmn. nat. def. com. 2001—, Warren chpt., chmn. com. Mary Washington Colonial chpt.). Republican. Roman Catholic. Avocations: genealogy, military, opera, antiques, porcelains, English, Am. constl. and religious hist. Home and Office: 316 N Main St Warrenton NC 27589-1826 Office Phone: 252-257-4663. Business E-Mail: betsy1013@vance.net.

WEDDINGTON, SARAH RAGLE, lawyer, educator; b. Abilene, Tex., Feb. 5, 1945; d. Herbert Doyle and Lena Catherine Ragle. BS magna cum laude, McMurry Coll., 1965, PhD (hon.), 1979; JD, U. Tex., 1967; PhD (hon.), Hamilton Coll., 1979, Southwestern U., 1989, Austin Coll., 1993, Nova Southeastern U., 1999; PhD in Human Letters (hon.), Fitchburg State Coll., 2004. Bar: Tex. 1967, D.C. 1979, U.S. Dist. Ct. (we., no. and ea. dists.) Tex., U.S. Ct. Appeals (5th cir.), U.S. Supreme Ct. Pvt. practice law, Austin, 1967-77; gen. counsel Dept. Agr., Washington, 1977-78; spl. asst. to U.S. pres. Washington, 1978—79; asst. to U.S. pres., 1979—81; chmn. Interdepartmental Task Force on Women, 1978-81; mem. Pres.'s Commn. on Exec. Exchange, 1981; Carl Hatch prof. law and pub. adminstrn. U. N.Mex., Albuquerque, 1982-83; pvt. practice law Austin, Tex., 1985—; dir. Tex. Office State-Fed. Rels., Austin, Washington, 1983-85. Vis. prof. govt. Wheaton Coll., Norton, Mass., 1981-83; sr. lectr. Tex. Woman's U., Denton, 1981-90, 93, U. Tex., Austin, 1986-1989, adj. assoc. prof. 1989-2001, adj. prof., 2001-. Author: A Question of Choice, 1992; contbr. articles to various mags.; contbg. editor Glamour mag., 1981-83. Mem. Tex. Ho. of Reps., 1973-77; named hon. chair San Francisco Bar Assn. Breast Cancer Hotline/Network, 2001, named hon. chair ann. benefit for Breast Cancer Rsch. Ctr., Austin, 2002, named lecture showcase presenter Nat. Assn. Campus Activities, 2003. Named Lectr. of Yr., Nat. Assn. Coll. Activities, 1990, Tex. Woman of Century, Tex. Women's C. of C., 1999, Face of Century, San Antonio Express News, 1999, 2000, Outstanding Alumnus, McMurry U., 2004, Nat. Pub. Health Hero, U. Calif., Berkeley, 2005; named one of Most Influential Lawyers of the 20th Century, Tex. Lawyer, 2000; recipient Woman of Yr. award, Tex. Women's Polit. Caucus, 1973, Outstanding Young Am. Leaders, Time Mag., 1979, Leadership award, Ladies Home Jour., 1980, Spl. Recognition award, Esquire mag., 1984, Elizabeth (Betty) Boyer award, Equity Action League, 1992, Woman Who Dares award, Nat. Coun. Jewish Women, 1993, Woman of Distinction award, Nat. Conf. for Coll. Women Student Leaders, 1993, Colby award for Pub. Svc., Sigma Kappa, 1996, Hummingbird award, Leadership Am., 1998, Tallest Texan award, Houston Chronicle, 2000, Speaking Out for Justice award, AAUW Legal Advocacy Fund, 2001, AAUW Ednl. Found., 2001, Ally award, Possible Woman Leadership Conf., 2001, Sarah Weddington Leadership Conf. named in her honor, Tex. Woman's U., 2001, Humanitarian of Yr. award, Planned Parenthood, Tex., 2003, Courage award, Women Lawyers LA, 2004, Reproductive Equity award, Lilith Orgn., 2005. Mem. Tex. Bar Assn. Office: The Weddington Ctr 709 W 14th St Austin TX 78701-1707 Business E-Mail: sw@weddingtoncenter.com.

WEDDLE, REBECCA RAE, education educator; b. Elkhart, Ind., Sept. 20, 1942; d. Virgil Westover and Ardis Carol (Thornton) Harvey; divorced; children: Jodi Lynn Holloway, Julia Anne Sinn, Mark Douglas BA in Spanish and English, Goshen Coll., 1964; MS in Edn., Pittsburg State U., 1995. Tchr. Wakarusa (Ind.) High Sch., 1964-65, Ben Davis Jr. High, Indpls., 1965-68; Spanish, adult basic edn. and ESL Fort Scott (Kans.) C.C., 1989—. VISTA vol. Ft. Scott C.C., 1988-89; mem. sch. bd. Unified Sch. Dist. 234, Ft. Scott, 1981-2000; chair Good Ol' Days Steering Com., Ft. Scott, 1986-2006 Mem.: PEO. Republican. Mem. Christian Ch. (Disciples Of Christ). Avocations: reading, cooking. Home: 1610 Clairmont St Fort Scott KS 66701-3428 Office: Ft Scott Cmty Coll 2108 S Horton Fort Scott KS 66701 Office Phone: 620-768-2907. Business E-Mail: beckyw@fortscott.edu.

WEDEL-COWGILL, MILLIE REDMOND, secondary school educator, performing arts educator, communications educator, education educator; b. Harrisburg, Pa., Aug. 18, 1939; d. Clair L. and Florence (Heiges) Aungst; m. T.S. Redmond, 1956 (div. 1967); children: T.S. Redmond II; m. Frederick L. Wedel, Jr., 1974 (div. 1986); m. Paul R. Cowgill, May 19, 2001. BA, Alaska Meth. U., 1966; MEd, U. Alaska, Anchorage, 1972; postgrad. in comm., Stanford U., Calif., 1975-76. Lic. third class broadcasting, FCC. Profl. actress Charming Models & Models Guild of Phila., 1954-61; asst. dir. devel. in charge pub. rels. Alaska Meth. U., Anchorage, 1966, part-time lectr., 1966, 73; comm. tchr. Anchorage Sch. Dist., 1967-96; owner Wedel Prodns., Anchorage, 1976-86; cons. comms., media and edn., owner Cowgill Cons., 2003—. Pub. rels. staff Alaska Purchase Centennial Exhibit, U.S. Dept. Commerce, 1967; writer gubernatorial campaign, 1971; instr. Chapman Coll., 1990-93; adj. instr. U. Alaska, Anchorage, 1972, 77-79, 89-2001; cons. Cook Inlet Native Assn., 1978, No. Inst., 1979; judge Ark. Press Women's Writing Contest, 1990-91; sec. exec. bd. Alaska Dept. Edn. Profl. Tchg. Practices Commn., 1993-94. Bd. dirs. Sta. KAKM, Alaska Pub. TV, membership chmn., 1978-80, nat. lay rep. to Pub. Broadcasting Svc. and Nat. Assn. Pub. TV Stas., 1979; bd. dirs. Ednl. Telecom. Consortium for Alaska, 1979, Mid-Hillside Cmty. Coun., Municipality of Anchorage, 1979-80, 83-88, Hillside East Cmty. Coun., 1984-88, pres., 1984-85; rsch. writer, legal asst. Vinson & Elkins, Houston, 1981; v.p., bd. dirs. Inlet View ASD Cmty. Sch., 1994-95, pres., 1995-97; Valley Forge Freedoms Found., Murdoch Scholarships; bd. dirs. Rev. Richard Gay Trust, Alaska and Pa., 1992-2000. Recipient awards for newspapers, lit. mags.; award Nat. Scholastic Press Assn., 1981, 82, 83, 84; Alaska Coun. Econs., 1982, Merits award Alaska Dept. Edn., 1982-93, Legis. commendation State of Alaska, Nat. Blue Ribbon Outstanding Sch. award, 1993. Mem. NEA (AEA bldg. rep., state del. 70s, 80s, 94-95), Assn. Pub. Broadcasting (charter mem., nat. lay del. 1980), Indsl. TV Assn. (San Francisco and Houston 1975-81), Alaska Press Club (chmn. high sch. journalism workshops, 1968-69, 73, awards for sch. newspapers 1972, 74, 77), Alaska Fedn. Press Women (dir. 1978-86, 94-95, pres. 1995-96, h.s. journalism competition youth projects dir., award for brochures 1978, chair youth writing contest 1994-95), World Affairs Coun., Chugach Electric (chair 1990, nomination com. for bd. dirs. 1988-90), Hood Coll. Alaska Alumni Assn., Stanford U. Alumni Club (Alaska pres. 1982-84, 90-92, 99-2000, v.p. 1998-99), Rotary Club of Naples (photographer and asst. program chair 2003), Imperial Golf Course Country Club, Club at Pelican Bay, Naples (Fla.) Philharm. League, Naples Players Theatre Guild, Pelican Bay Women's League, Naples Fla. U. Pa. Club, English Speaking Union. Presbyterian. Home: PO Box 111489 Anchorage AK 99511-1489 Office: Cowgill Cons PO Box 770662 Naples FL 34107-0662

WEDER, NATALIE DANITZA, psychiatrist; b. Princeton, NJ, Aug. 7, 1977; d. Ricardo Alberto Weder and Teresa Cisneros; m. Juan Phillip Highland, May 8, 2004. MD, Nat. Autonomous U. Mex., Mexico City, 2003. Rsch. fellow Inst. Nat. Sciences Medicine and Nutrition Salvador Zubiran, Mexico City, 2003; psychiatry resident Yale U., New Haven, 2004—. Author (research): (myastenia gravis, cephalea in lupus) Cephalalgia, Acta Neurologica Scandinavica, Eur J Neurology, Journal Of Clinical Neuromuscular Disease (Best Clin. Rsch. award, Latin-American Neurophysiology Soc., Boehringer-Ingelheim Clin. Rsch. award). Minority fellow, Substance Abuse and Mental Health Svcs. Adminstrn., Am. Psychiat. Assn., 2006. Mem.: Am. Psychiat. Assn. Office Phone: 203-785-2095. Personal E-mail: natalie.weder@yale.edu.

WEDGE, BARBARA JANE, women's health nurse; b. Springfield, Ill., June 24, 1940; d. Allan Thomas and Susannah Alice (Barnes) Goodwin; children: John Thomas, Michelle Louise. AS, Forest Pk. C.C., St. Louis, Mo., 1968; BSN, Webster U., 1990. RN Mo., 1968. Clin. nursing supr. Ob-Gyn Clinic Barnes-Jewish Hosp., St. Louis, 1972—90, clin. nurse mgr. Women's Wellness Ctr., 1990—2002; ret. Cons. BJC-Home Health Profl. Adv. Bd., St. Louis, 1995—2002. Contbr. articles clinical rsch. to profl. jour. Hostess & mentor World Affairs Coun. of St. Louis, St. Louis, 1994—98; mem. Internat. Sister Cities-Stuttgardt, St. Louis; mem. chairperson Friends of Thomas Dunn Meml. Adult Edn., St. Louis, 2002—03. D-Conservative. Roman Cath. Achievements include development of and implemented advanced practice nurse collaborative practice with Wash. Univ.faculty; teen pregnancy ctr. for an underserved population. Personal E-mail: rayita@aol.com.

WEDGE, CAROLE C., architectural firm executive; B in Environ. Design, U. Colo., 1981; student, Alliance Francaise, 1982; BArch, Boston Archtl. Ctr., 1990. With J. & W. Seligman & Co., 1983—86; joined Sheple Bulfinch Richardson & Abbott, Boston, 1986, assoc., 1996, sr. assoc., 1998, prin., 2000, pres., 2004—. Lectr. in field. Mem.: ALA, AIA, Soc. Coll. and Univ. Planners, Assn. Coll. and Rsch. Librs. Office: Shepley Bulfinch Richardson & Abbott 40 Broad St Boston MA 02109-4306

WEDGEWORTH, ANN, actress; b. Abilene, Tex., Jan. 21, 1935; m. Rip Torn (div.); 1 child, Danae; m. Ernest Martin; 1 child, Dianna. Attended, U. Tex.; BA in Drama, So. Methodist U. Actor: (Broadway debut) Make A Million, 1958, (Broadway appearances) Chapter Two (Tony award), Thieves, Blues for Mr. Charlie, The Last Analysis, (off-Broadway appearances) Line, Chapparal, The Crucible, Days and Nights of Beebee Fenstermaker, Ludlow Fair, The Honest to God Shnozzola, A Lie of the Mind, Elba, The Aunts, The Debutante's Ball, (premiers) In the Moonlight Eddie at Pasadena Playhouse, Natural Affection in Pheonix, The Dream in Phila., (toured with nat. cos.) The Sign in Sidney Brustein's Window and Kennedy's Children, (appeared in TV series) Three's Company, The Edge of Night, Another World, Somerset, Filthy Rich, Evening Shade, (TV appearances) All That Glitters, The Equalizer, Roseanne, Bronk, Twilight Zone, Trapper John, M.D.; (TV films) The War Between the Tates, Right to Kill, Cooperstown, Fight for Justice: The Nancy Conn Story, Bogie, A Stranger Waits; (films) Handle With Care (Nat. Soc. Film Critics award), Thieves, Bang the Drum Slowly, Scarecrow, Catamount Killing, Law and Disorder, One Summer Love, Dragon-Fly, Birch Intervals, Soggy Bottom, USA, No Small Affair, Sweet Dreams, The Mens Club, A Tiger's Tale, Made in Heaven, Far North, Miss Firecracker, Green Card, Steel Magnolias, Love and a 45, The Whole Wide World, The Hunter's Moon, Hard Promises, Andy, My Science Project, The Hawk is Dying; TV host Evening at the Improv, A&E; actor: (play) Mother and Child, The Glass Menagerie. Address: 70 Riverside Dr Apt 6E New York NY 10024-5716

WEDGWOOD, RUTH, law educator, international affairs expert; b. NYC; d. Morris P. and Anne (Williams) Glushien; m. Josiah Francis Wedgwood; May 29, 1982; 1 child, Josiah Ruskin Wedgwood. BA magna cum laude, Harvard U., 1972; fellow, London Sch. Econs., 1972—73; JD, Yale U., 1976. Bar: D.C., N.Y., U.S. Supreme Ct. Law clk. to judge Henry Friendly U.S. Ct. Appeals (2d cir.), N.Y.C., 1976—77; law clk. to justice Harry Blackmun U.S. Supreme Ct., Washington, 1977—78; spl. asst. to asst. atty. gen. U.S. Dept. Justice, Washington, 1978—80; asst. U.S. atty. U.S. Dist. Ct. (so. dist.) N.Y., N.Y.C., 1980—86; prof. law Yale U., New Haven, 1986—2002, fellow Inst. for Social and Policy Studies, 1989—2002; fellow Berkeley Coll., Yale U., 1989—. Mem. Sec. of State's Adv. Com. Internat. Law, 1993—; sr. fellow for internat orgns. and law Coun. Fgn. Rels., 1994—2004; Charles Stockton prof. internat. law U.S. Naval War Coll., Newport, RI, 1998—99; mem. Hart-Rudman Commn. on Nat. Security in the 21st Century, Nat. Sec. Study Group, Dept. Def. Adv. Comm., 1999—2001; mem. acad. adv. com. to spl. rep. UN Sec.-Gen. for Children and Armed Conflict, 1999—2002; dir. studies Am. Soc. Internat. Law, 2000—03; guest scholar U.S. Inst. Peace, 2001—02; dir. studies Hague Acad. Internat. Law, 2001—02; elected U.S. mem. UN Human Rights Com., Geneva, 2002—06, Geneva, 2006—; mem. Hist. Rev. Panel, adv. to dir. CIA, 2002—; mem. Def. Policy Bd., advisor to U.S. Sec. Def., 2002—; prof. du Droit Internat. U. Paris I (Sorbonne), 2004; Berlin Prize fellow Am. Acad., 2006. Exec. editor Yale Law Jour., 1975-76; author: The Revolutionary Martyrdom of Jonathan Robbins, 1990, The Use of Force in International Affairs, 1992, American National Interest and the United Nations, 1996, Toward an International Criminal Court?, 1999, After Dayton: Lessons of the Bosnian Peace Process, 1999; mem. bd. editors Yale Jour. Law and Humanities, 1988-98, Am. Jour. Internat. Law, 1998-, World Policy Jour. (New Sch. Social Rsch.), 2001—, Am. Interest, 2005—, The Nat. Interest, 2005—, adv. coun.; contbr. articles to profl jours. and popular publs. including N.Y. Times, Washington Post, Christian Sci. Monitor, Internat. Herald Tribune, Wall St. Jour., Washington Times, Fin. Times, L.A. Times, Die Zeit, Fgn. Affairs, Fgn. Policy, Nat. Interest, Time mag.; commentator for CNN, PBS, Fox, Nat. Pub. Radio, MSNBC, BBC, Lehrer News Hour, PBS. Prin. rapporteur U.S. Atty. Gen.'s Guidelines on FBI Undercover Ops., Informant Use and Racketeering and Gen. Crime Investigations, 1980; bd. dirs. Lawyers Com. for Human Rights, N.Y.C., 1988-94; mem. policy adv. com. UN Assn. U.S.A., 1998-2003; bd. dirs. Freedom House, 2003-, UN Watch, 2004—. Recipient Israel Peres prize, 1976, Disting. Contbn. to Internat. Law award N.Y. State Bar Assn., 2000; Ford Found. Rsch. grantee; Rockefeller Found. fellow; Am. Acad. Berlin prize fellow, 2006. Mem. ABA (standing com. on law and nat. security 2002—, coun. Internat. Law sect. 2003—), Am. Law Inst., Am. Soc. Internat. Law (exec. com. 1995-98, v.p. 2005—), Internat. Law Assn. (v.p. 1994—, program chmn. Am. br. 1992), Assn. Am. Law Sch. (chmn. sect. internat. law 1995-96), Assn. Bar City N.Y. (chmn. arms control and internat. security affairs com. 1989-92, chmn. internat. affairs coun. 1992-95, exec. com. 1995-99), Union Internationale des Avocats, U.S.A. (chpt. bd. govs. 1993-98), Women in Internat. Security (bd. dirs. 2006—), Ctr. for Global Prosperty (bd. dirs. 2006—), Coun. on Fgn. Rels., Internat. Inst. for Strategic Studies, Elizabethan Club, Mory's Assn., Yale Club (N.Y.C.). Office: Johns Hopkins Sch Advanced Internat Studies 1619 Massachusetts Ave NW Washington DC 20036 Office Phone: 202-663-5618. Business E-Mail: rwedgwood@jhu.edu.

WEDIG, CINDY MARTINEZ, director; d. Arthur John and Elizabeth Eleanor Wedig; m. Jose de Jesus Martinez, Apr. 11, 1965; children: Yanette Guadalupe Martinez, Yadira Elizabeth Martinez, Yesenia Alexis Martinez. BS, U. Wis., 1981; MS, U. Ill., 1985, PhD, 1988. Program coord. U. Tex. - Pan Am., Edinburg, 1993—. Lectr. Calif. Poly. Inst., San Luis Obispo, 1988—90, U. Wis., Platteville, 1990—91; instr. Tex. State Tech. Coll., Harlingen, 1993—97; adj. instr. Baylor Coll. Medicine, Houston, 1994—. Office: Univ Texas - Pan American 1201 W University Dr Edinburg TX 78541 Office Phone: 956-316-7025. Home Fax: 956-381-2430; Office Fax: 956-381-2430. Business E-Mail: cindy@utpa.edu.

WEDL, LOIS CATHERINE, counselor, educator; b. Cold Spring, Minn., Mar. 5, 1931; d. John Michael and Marie Eva (Lill) W. BA, Coll. of St. Benedict, St. Joseph, Minn., 1966; MEd, Ohio U., 1982, PhD, 1986. Jr. high sch. tchr. Holy Angels Sch., St. Cloud, Minn., 1956-60, St. Mary's Schs., Long Prairie, Minn., 1960-64; tchr., adminstr. Colegio San Benito, Humacao, P.R., 1964-70, Colegio San Antonio, Humacao, 1970-74; prof. Coll. of St. Benedict, 1986—, St. Cloud State U., 1986-88. Cons. gerontology Order of St. Benedict, 1949—, dir. Elderhostel program. Editor Dept. Edn. Newsletter, Sch. Applied Behavioral Scis. and Ednl. Leadership, Ohio U., 1981-84. Mem. athletic adv. com. Coll. of St. Benedict, 1989—; bd. dirs. Assumption Home Complex. Recipient 2 Nat. Literary awards Am. Rehabilitating Counseling Assn., 1983-84, Breaking Barriers award, 2005; Bremer Found. gerontology grantee, 1988. Mem. Am. Assn. Adult Devel. and Aging (chairperson aging/religion com., chairperson awards com., del.-at-large, membership chair, Nat. Disting. Svc. award 1998), Chi Sigma Iota (internat. sect., chair awards com., Faculty Advisor of Yr. 1995, Nat. Lit. awards, Outstanding Leadership award 1995). Home and Office: 37 College Ave S Saint Joseph MN 56374-2001 Office Phone: 320-363-5586. Business E-Mail: lwedl@csbsju.edu.

WEE, CHRISTINE DIJOS, elementary school educator; b. Honolulu, Jan. 8, 1968; d. Cosme Wayne and Victoria Amparo Dijos; m. Phillip Ying Kin Wee, July 15, 2000; children: Deanna Rae Patacsil, Logan Wayne. BEd, U. Hawaii, Manoa, 1991. Cert. tchr. Hawaii, prof. diploma in elem. edn. Univ. Hawaii, 1992. Kindergarten tchr. Island Paradise Sch., Honolulu, 1992—93, Pauoa Elem. Sch., Honolulu, 1993—94, choral dir., 1997—2005, 6th grade tchr., 1994—2002, 5th grade tchr., 2003—04, 3d grade tchr., 2004—; spl. edn. summer sch. aide Wailupe Valley Elem. Sch., Honolulu; Challenger Ctr.-trained educator, NASA program Barber's Point Elem. Sch., Kapolei, Hawaii, 1996—2002. Regional conf. del. Sch.-to-Work, Honolulu, 1998; cadre mem. Roosevelt Complex Writing Inst., Honolulu, 1999, student svcs. coord., 2002—03; mem. music action rsch. team Hawaii State Dept. Edn., 1999—2001. Mem. coun. Sch. Cmty.-Based Mgmt. Coun., Pauoa Elem. Sch., 2001—03; vol., chmn. Honolulu Dist. Choral Festival, 1994—2002, 2005; mem. ch. choir; asst. dir. Sweet Adelines Internat.; bd. dirs. Pauoa Elem. Sch. PTA, 1996—97, 2005—06. Mem.: Hawaii Orff-Schulwerk Assn., Am. Choral Dirs. Assn., Hawaii State Tchrs. Assn. (union rep. 1995—96, 2000—01), Hawaii Music Educators Assn. (3d v.p. 2000—02, chmn. 2001—02), Delta Kappa Gamma. Avocations: walking, collecting keychains and unicorns, singing. Home: 823 9th Ave Honolulu HI 96816 Office: Pauoa Elem Sch 2301 Pauoa Rd Honolulu HI 96813 E-mail: tiniwee86@hawaii.rr.com.

WEED, MARY THEOPHILOS, psychology educator; b. Miami, Fla., Nov. 11, 1928; d. John George and Elizabeth Theophilos; m. Perry L. Weed, Mar. 29, 1963 (div. 1969); 1 child, Heather. BA, U. Miami, 1953; MA, U. Chgo., 1960. Sch. psychologist Chgo. Bd. Edn., 1960-62; asst. prof. psychology Chgo. City Colls., 1962—88. Pvt. practice clin. psychology, Chgo., 1963—. Mem. Am. Coll. Forensic Examiners, Am. Psychol. Assn. (assoc.), Ill. Psychol. Assn. Home and Office: 5534 S Harper Ave Chicago IL 60637-1830

WEEDERMANN, MARION, mathematics professor; d. Werner and Ute Weedermann. BS, József Attila Tudómány Egyetem, Szeged, Hungary, 1990, MS, 1995; PhD, Ga. Inst. Tech., Atlanta, 2000. Asst. prof. math. U. Wis., Green Bay, Dominican U., River Forest, Ill., 2003—. Mem.: Math. Assn. Am., Am. Math. Soc. Avocations: travel, running, tennis. Office: Dominican U 7900 W Division St River Forest IL 60305 Business E-Mail: mweederm@dom.edu.

WEEDMAN, JEAN M., secondary school educator; b. Milw., May 18, 1948; d. Warren Leroy and Betty Jean Carolyn (Flach) Reddemann. BS, U. Wis., Milw., 1972; MEd, Nat. Louis U., 1990. Secondary tchr. Oak Creek (Wis.) Schs., 1972—, mentor Young Authors Conf., 1993—2001. Chmn. journalism Milw. Area Tech. Coll. Skills Olympics, 1985-86; writer, mentor Young Author's Conf., Milw. Art Mus., 1988-90. Editor, originator hist. archtl. and preservation issues Preserve Milw., quar. mag., 1988-92. Tour leader Hist. Milw., 1981-92, bd. dirs., 1987-92. Mem.: Lady Bird Johnson Wildflower Ctr., Dirt Divas (founding mem.). Avocations: prairie gardening, landscaping. Home: W343S9768 Red Brae Dr Mukwonago WI 53149-9264 Office: Oak Creek Schs 340 E Puetz Rd Oak Creek WI 53154-3230

WEEDN, SONNEE D., psychologist; b. Mpls., Apr. 19, 1947; d. John E. Stallman and Delight M. Jaax; m. Robert A. Weedn, Aug. 16, 1969; children: Isaiah, Simon. BS in Social Sci., U. So. Calif., 1968, MS in Edn., 1969, MS in Counseling Psychology, 1973; PhD in Clin. Psychology, Calif. Grad. Sch. Psychology, 1988. Lic. psychologist. Pvt. practice marriage & family therapist, Novato, Petaluma, Calif., 1980—; pvt. practice psychologist, 1992—. Mem.: APA, Soc. Personality Assessment, Calif. Psychol. Assn. Democrat. Prebyterian. Office: 3 Hamilton Landing #230 Novato CA 94949

WEEKS, EDYTHE E., writer, educator; b. St. Louis, July 14, 1962; d. John and Garnetta L. Weeks. JD, U. Mo., Columbia, 1987; PhD in Polit. Sci. and Internat. Rels., No. Ariz. U., 2006. Author: (book) Outsiders' Guide to Understanding Outer Space Development, Understanding Legal Forms to Jumpstart a Business; contbr. articles to profl. publs. Founder Profl. and Amateur Artists Recognized, Inc., St. Louis, 1994—97. Recipient Flag of Learning and Liberty, Flagstaff Pub. Schs., 2000. Mem.: Internat. Inst. Space Law. Achievements include first to analysis of current legal trends on future space industry trends. Office: No Ariz U Dept of Political Science Box 15036 Flagstaff AZ 86011 Office Phone: 928-523-0957. Business E-Mail: Edythe.Weeks@nau.edu.

WEEKS, HEIDI K., mathematics educator; d. Steve T. and Linda A. Lunt (Stepmother); m. Sean A. Weeks, Aug. 4, 2001; children: Ryan, Connor. MA in Tchg., Aurora U., Ill., 2002. Tchr. math grade 8 Westfield Cmty. Sch., Algonquin, Ill., 1999—. Office: Westfield Comty Sch 2100 Sleepy Hollow Rd Algonquin IL 60102 Office Phone: 847-458-1900.

WEEKS, JANET HEALY, retired supreme court justice; b. Quincy, Mass., Oct. 19, 1932; d. John Francis and Sheila Josephine (Jackson) Healy; m. George Weeks, Aug. 29, 1959; children: Susan, George. AB in chemistry, Emmanuel Coll., Boston, 1954; JD, Boston Coll., 1958; LLD (hon.), U. Guam, 1984. Bar: Mass. 1958, Guam 1972. Trial atty. U.S. Dept. Justice, Washington, 1958-60, Trapp & Gayle, Agana, Guam, 1971-73; ptnr. Trapp, Gayle, Teker, Weeks & Freidman, Agana, 1973-75; judge Superior Ct. Guam, Agana, 1975-96; assoc. justice Guam Supreme Ct., Guam, 1996-99, retired assoc. justice Guam, 1999. Chmn. task force cts., prosecution and def. Terr. Crime Commn., 1973-76; mem. Terr. Crime Commn. Bd., 1975-76, Guam Law Revision Commn., 1981—; rep. Nat. Conf. State Trial Judges, 1982.

Mem. Cath. Sch. Bd. Guam, 1973. Mem. ABA, Nat. Assn. Women Judges (charter), Am. Judges Assn., Fed. Bar Assn. (chpt. sec. 1974), Guam Bar Assn., Internat. Club (Guam). Office: 120 W Obrien Dr Hagatna GU 96910-5174

WEEKS, LORI D., elementary school educator; b. Clinton, NC, Aug. 21, 1980; d. Tony B. and Connie S. Weeks. BS, Mount Olive Coll., NC, 2002. Cert. tchr. East Carolina U., 2002. Tchr. Union Mid. Sch. Sampson County Sch. Sys., Clinton, 2002—. Cheerleading coach Union Mid. Sch., Clinton, NC, 2005—. Named Tchr. of Yr., Union Mid. Sch., 2005—06.

WEEKS, MARTA JOAN, retired priest; b. Buenos Aires, May 24, 1930; arrived in U.S., 1932; d. Frederick Albert and Anne (Newman) Sutton; m. Lewis Austin Weeks, Aug. 17, 1951; children: Kermit Austin, Leslie Anne. BA in Polit. Sci., Stanford U., 1951; MDiv, Episcopal Theol. Sem. S.W., 1991; LHD (hon.), U. Utah, 2005; DDiv (hon.), Episcop. Theol. Sem. of the S.W., 2006. Ordained priest Episcopal Ch., 1992. Legal libr., sec. Mene Grande Oil Co., Caracas, Venezuela, 1948; English tchr. Centro-Venezolano Americano, Caracas, 1948; sec. Household Fin. Corp., Salt Lake City, 1951; legal sec. McKelvey & McKelvey Attys., Durango, Colo., 1952; sec., dir. Weeks Air Mus., Miami, Fla., 1985—2001; chaplain Jackson Meml. Hosp., 1992-93; interim asst. St. James Episcopal Ch., Salt Lake City, 1994-95; assisting priest St. Andrew's Episcopal Ch., Miami, Fla., 1999—2002; priest-at-large Episcopal Diocese of S.E. Fla., 2002—04. Trustee Beloit Coll., Wis., 1980—82, U. Miami, 1983—88, 1995—, Bishop Gray Inns, Lake Worth and Davenport, Fla., 1992—2002; advisor Ctr. for Sexuality and Religion, 1997—; mem. adv. coun. U. Utah, 1998—; dir. S.E. Fla. Episcopal Found., 2002—05. Mem.: Am. Soc. Order St. John of Jerusalem. Address: 7350 SW 162nd St Miami FL 33157-3820 Personal E-mail: msweeks24@bellsouth.net.

WEEKS, PATSY ANN LANDRY, librarian, educator; b. Luling, Tex., Mar. 3, 1930; d. Lee and Mattie Wood (Callihan) Landry; m. Arnett S. Weeks, Dec. 2, 1950; children: Patsy Kate, Nancy Ann, Janie Marie. BS, Southwest Tex. State U., 1951; MLS, Tex. Woman's U., 1979. Tchr. art, reading, math. Grandview Ind. Sch. Dist., Tex., 1950—52; tchr. phys. edn. Beaumont Ind. Sch. Dist., Tex., 1953; tchr. art, coll. algebra Cisco Jr. Coll., Tex., 1957—58; tchr. remedial reading Taylor County Schs., Tuscola, Tex., 1965—66, Anson Ind. Sch. Dist., Tex., 1971—73; libr. Bangs Ind. Sch. Dist., Tex., 1973—79, learning resources coord., 1979—90; dir. Heart of Tex. Ctr. for the Rev. and Exam. of Children's and Young Adults' Lit., 1988—2001; cons. Heart of Tex. Lit. Ctr., 2001—03. Bd. dirs. Anson Pub. Libr., Tex., 1971—72, Brownwood Pub. Libr., 2003—; mem. adv. com. Edn. Svc. Ctr., 1978—83; coord. Reading is Fundamental Program, 1978—83; counsilor Children's Round Table, 1993—; cons. Heart of Tex. Lit. Ctr., 2000—03, dir. projects, 2003—. Exhibitions include oil paintings, pastels various Tex. Fairs (1st prize, 1952, 1960), Gary Air Force Base, San Marcos, 1952. Named Coming Home Queen, Howard Payne U., 2006. Mem.: ALA, Tex. Assn. Sch. Libr. Adminstrs., Teenage Libr. Assn. Tex. (chmn. audio-visual award com. 1984), Tex. Assn. Improvement Reading, Tex. Assn. Sch. Librs. (media prodns. award com. 1985—86), Tex. Libr. Assn. (mem. intellectual freedom and profl. responsibility com. 1979—81, mem. Tex. Bluebonnet award com. 1982—85, chair adv. com. 1987, chair children's round table 1987, sec. young adult round table 1991—92, publs. com. 1991—, round table coun. 1993—95), Intellectual Freedom Round Table, Am. Assn. Sch. Librs., Young Adult Libr. Svcs. Assn. (outstanding books for coll.bound-fine arts com., publ.'s liaison com.), Assn. Libr. Svc. to Children (Caldecott award com. 1986, Grosset and Dunlap Group award selection com. 1988, nominating com. 1989, chair 1989—91, Newbery award com. 1999, Disting. Svc. award com. 2002—, Disting. Svc. award com. chair 2003—, cons. priority gorup III profl. devel.), Tex. State Tchr. Assn. (life), Bangs Prog. Women's Club (treas. 1974—76), Delta Kappa Gamma, Beta Phi Mu, Alpha Chi, Kappa Pi, Phi Delta Kappa. Bapt. Office: Howard Payne Univ Sta Walker Memorial Library Heart of Tex Ctr Brownwood TX 76801 Office Phone: 325-649-8606. Business E-Mail: pweeks@hptux.edu.

WEEKS, RANDI LYN, performing arts and language educator; b. Jeffersonville, Ind., Apr. 17, 1973; d. Randall Kent and Janna Dee Hogan; m. Timothy Howard Weeks, July 18, 1998; children: Maci Lola Krishelle, Kaylee Colleen, Timothy Howard Jr. BA summa cum laude, DePauw U., Greencastle, Ind., 1995. Cert. speech comm., theatre, English tchr.grades 9-12 Ind. Dept. Edn., 1995. Actress Showboat Becky Thatcher, Marietta, Ohio, 1995; prodn. mgr. StageWorks, Terre Haute, Ind., 1995—96; tchr. English and math remediation, drama dir. South Vermillion Mid. Sch., Clinton, Ind., 1996; tchr. speech and drama Broad Ripple H.S., Indpls., 1996—2000, dir. student activities, 1999—2000; tchr. English, speech, drama Kokomo H.S., Ind., 2000—. Mktg. and prodn. intern Beef and Boards Dinner Theatre, Indpls., 1993; prodn. intern Live with Regis and Kathie Lee, N.Y.C., 1994; reporting and editing intern WTHI - Channel 10, Terre Haute, 1995; creative dramatics camp instr. South Vermillion Sch. Corp., Clinton, 1996; dramatics instr. StageWorkShops, Terre Haute, 1997—2000, Terre Haute, 1997—2000. Actor: Under the Gaslight and other melodramas; dir.: (sch. theatrical performances) Little Shop of Horrors; Bye Bye Birdie The Hobbit; The Lion, The Witch, and The Wardrobe etc.; author: (short historical play) A World of Difference - Kokomo Rescue Mission, Radio Years - Vigo County Hist. Soc. Creative arts team mem., actor, singer, dir. Crossroads Cmty. Ch., Kokomo. Named Outstanding Tchr., Broad Ripple H.S., 1997; recipient Nat. Honor Roll for Outstanding Am. Tchrs., 2005—06. Conservative. Protestant. Avocations: singing, acting, directing, reading. Office: Kokomo HS 2501 S Berkley Rd Kokomo IN 46902 Office Phone: 765-455-8040 506. Business E-Mail: rweeks@kokomo.k12.in.us.

WEEKS, RANDI MONTAG, science educator; b. Mankato, Minn., Jan. 24, 1954; d. William B. and Mary Ann Montag; m. Daniel W. Weeks, June 7, 2003; children: Rachel Thompson, Rebecca Peterson. BS in Psychology & Sociology, Mankato State U., 1976; MA, U. No. Iowa, Cedar Falls, 1994. Tchr. Bellevue Elem. Sch., Iowa, 1990—92; curriculum developer Environ. Issues Instrn., Cedar Falls, 1993—2002; instr. sci. Des Moines Pub. Schs., 1994—, Global Youth Orgn., Des Moines, 1995—2001; specialist gifted and talented test Des Moines Pub. Schs., 1998—2004; tchr. educator AEA II, Johnston, 2001—03; instr. scie. Iowa State U., Ames, 2000—. Presenter in field. Author of poems. Named Tcht. of Yr., Disney Corp., 2001—03. Mem.: NEA, Iowa Acad. Sci. (pres. 2002—03), Nat. Sci. Tchrs. Assn. Office: Des Moines Pub Schs 4827 Madison Ave Des Moines IA 50310

WEEKS, SKYLA GAY, music educator; b. Kansas City, Mo., Jan. 16, 1963; d. Milfred Dale and Willo Dean (Vest) Hammerbacher; m. Russell Dwaine Weeks, June 8, 1990; 1 child, Tyler Blair. B Music Edn., U. Mo., 1985. K-12 vocal music tchr. Malcolm Pub. Schs., Nebr., 1986—87, Sheldon Sch., Mo., 1993—94; K-8 vocal music tchr Westview Sch., Neosho, Mo., 1993—94; entertainer Bur. Lecturers & Concert Artists, Lawrence, Kans., 1995—96; K-12 music tchr. Hermitage R-IV, Mo., 1998—2002, Macks Creek R-V, 2003—. Author: (songs) All I Need, 2001. Recipient tchr. appreciation award, Mo. Scholars Acad., 2001. Mem.: Mo. Music Educators Conf. Office Phone: 573-363-5911.

WEEKS, TRESI LEA, lawyer; b. Brownwood, Tex., Dec. 3, 1961; d. Dean Moore and Patsy Ruth (Evans) Adams; m. Kevin Weeks, Oct. 26, 1998. BA in Fgn. Svc., BA in French, Baylor U., 1984, JD, 1987. Bar: Tex. 1987, U.S. Dist. Ct. (no. dist.) Tex. 1988, U.S. Ct. Appeals (5th cir.) 1989. Atty. Richard Jackson & Assocs., Dallas, 1987-91, Amis, Bell & Moore, Arlington, Tex., 1992-98; sole practitioner Plano, Tex., 1999—. Vol. Legal Svcs. of North Tex., Dallas, 1988-97, Dallas Com. for Fgn. Visitors, 1989-92. Recipient Pro Bono Svc. award Legal Svcs. of North Tex., 1989, 90, 91. Mem. AAUW (pub. policy dir. Plano, Tex. br. 1992, 93-94, v.p. 1994-95), State Bar Tex. (mem. mentor program for lawyers com. 1994-98, mem. local bar svcs. com. 1994-96), Dallas Bar Assn., Dallas Women Lawyers Assn. (bd. dirs. 1989-90, v.p. 1992, pres. 1993). Avocations: scuba diving, reading, hiking, gardening, writing. Office: 555 Republic Dr Ste 200 Plano TX 75074

WEEKS, WENDY L., chemistry professor, consultant; b. Pomona, Calif., July 12, 1963; d. Joseph B. and Shirely A. Weeks; children: Tristan, Cheyenne. AS in Sci., Chaffey Coll., Calif., 1992; BS in Chemistry, U. La Verne, Calif., 1995; MS in Chemistry, U. Ariz., 1998. Chemistry faculty Pima CC, Tucson, 1996—; chief adminstrv. officer Desert Mosaic Sch., Tucson, 2000—. Author: (book) Chemistry Case Studies for Allies Health Students, 2006. Office: Pima CC 2202 W Anklam Rd Tucson AZ 85709-0290 Business E-Mail: wendy.weeks@pima.edu.

WEEMS, LORI K., lawyer; b. Lubbock, Tex., Sept. 26, 1968; BA, Baylor Univ., 1990, JD summa cum laude, 1994. Bar: Fla. 1996. Law clerk U.S. Ct. Appeals, 5th Cir., Fla., 1994—96; ptnr. Holland & Knight, Miami, 1996—. Recipient Lynn Futch Most Productive Young Lawyer, Fla. Bar, 2003, Vol. Atty. of Yr., Lawyers for Children Am., 2004. Mem.: Dade County Bar Assn., ABA (bd. gov. 2002—). Office: Holland & Knight LLP Suite 3000 701 Brickell Ave Miami FL 33131

WEERTMAN, JULIA RANDALL, materials engineering educator; b. Muskegon, Mich., Feb. 10, 1926; BS in Physics, Carnegie-Mellon U., 1946, MS in Physics, 1947, DSc in Physics, 1951. Physicist U.S. Naval Rsch. Lab., Washington, 1952-58; vis. asst. prof. dept. materials sci. and engring. Northwestern U., Evanston, Ill., 1972-73, asst. prof., 1973-78, from asst. prof. to assoc. prof., 1973-82, prof., 1982-99, Walter P. Murphy prof., 1989, chmn. dept., 1987-92, asst. to dean grad. studies and rsch. Tech. Inst., 1973-76, Walter P. Murphy prof. emeritus, 1999—. Mem. various NRC coms. and panels. Co-author: Elementary Dislocation Theory, 1964, 1992, also pub. in French, Japanese and Polish; contbr. numerous articles to profl. jours. Mem. Evanston Environ. Control Bd., 1972-79. Recipient Creativity award NSF, 1981, 86; Guggenheim Found. fellow, 1986-87. Fellow Am. Soc. Metals Internat. (Gold medal 2005), Minerals, Metals and Materials Soc. (leadership award 1997, Robert Mehl lectr. 2006); mem. NAE, Am. Acad. Arts and Scis., Am. Phys. Soc., Materials Rsch. Soc. (Von Hippel award 2003), Soc. Women Engrs. (Disting. Engring. Educator award 1989, Achievement award 1991). Home: 834 Lincoln St Evanston IL 60201-2405 Office: Northwestern U Dept Material Sci & Engring 2220 Campus Dr Evanston IL 60208-0876 Office Phone: 847-491-5353. Business E-Mail: jrweertman@northwestern.edu.

WEGMAN, COLLEEN, food service executive; m. O'Donnell Chris Wegman; 2 children. Grad., U. Colo., 1994; MBA, Simon Sch., U. Rochester, 2000. With Wegmans Food Markets, Inc., Rochester, 1991—, various positions, including store mgr. to dir., e-commerce, 1991—2002, sr. v.p., merchandising, 2002—05, pres., 2005—. Developed Wegmans' Nature's Marketplace depts. Named one of Rochester's Influential Women, Rochester Bus. Jour., 2005. Avocation: skiing. Office: Wegmans Food Markets Inc 1500 Brooks Ave Rochester NY 14624*

WEGMAN, DORIS JEAN, retired nursing administrator; b. Boston, May 9, 1939; d. Arthur Brother and Leah Gorstein Brother; m. Allan Mark Wegman, Sept. 20, 1959; children: Shelley Ilene Wegman Langenauer, Neil Howard. Diploma in nursing, Beth Israel Hosp., Boston, 1959; BS, St. Joseph Coll., Patchogue, NY, 1981. RN Mass., 1959, NY, 1964, cert. cmty. health nurse, 1981. Per diem substance abuse nurse Suffolk County Health Dept., Hauppauge, NY, 1978—82, staff substance abuse nurse, 1982—85, nursing coord. substance abuse, 1985—2002; ret., 2002. Pres. Commack Jewish Ctr., NY, 1988—89, Ea. L.I. br. Women's League for Conservative Judaism, 2001—02; mem. youth commn. United Synagogue for Conservative Judaism, 2004—. Named Nurse of Distinction, NY State Legislature, 1990; recipient Woman of Achievement award, Commack Jewish Ctr., Woman of Valor award, Woman of Achievement award, Ea. L.I. br. Women's League, Cmty. Svc. award, Suffolk County Jewish Orgn., Commack, 2005. Mem.: Profl. Women in Govt., NY State Nurses Assn., Suffolk County Nurses Assn. Avocations: crafts, reading.

WEGMANN, MARY KATHERINE, art director; b. New Orleans, Sept. 18, 1948; d. Joseph A. and Catherine (Lyons) W. BA in English lit., Spring Hill Coll., Mobile, Ala., 1970; MA in English Lit., U. New Orleans, 1972. Asst. mgr., actor, dir. La Mise En Scene Theatre, New Orleans, 1970-72; loan processor First Homestead Savs. and Loan, New Orleans, 1972-74; home improvement contractor Superior Distbrs., New Orleans, 1974-75; adminstr. Freeman-Anacker, Inc., New Orleans, 1975-77; assoc. dir. Contemporary Arts Ctr., New Orleans, 1978-91, acting dir., 1986-88, 88-89; owner MK Arts Co., New Orleans, 1991—; mng. dir. Junebug Prodns., 1993-99; pres., CEO Nat. Performance Network, 2001—. Cons. Junebug Prodn., New Orleans, 1985-93, Alternate Roots, Atlanta, 1986, 92, Cultural Arts Coun. Houston, 1988-89, Seven Stages Performing Arts Ctr., Atlanta, 1989, 91, Nat. Endowment Arts, Washington, 1983-93, Assn. Performing Arts Presenters, 1994, Arts Coun. New Orleans, 1991, 92, La. Philharm. Orch., New Orleans, 1992, Melanie Beene and Assocs., 1991-93, La. Divsn. Arts, 1992—, Arts Coun. New Orleans, 1991—; mem. various panels, juries and adv. coms., 1980—. Bd. dirs. Dog & Pony Theatre Co., New Orleans, 1993—; bd. dirs., treas. Junebug Prodns., 1985—, Nat. Performance Network, 1998—, Contemporary Arts Ctr., 1999—. Office: M K Arts Co 2019 Chartres St New Orleans LA 70116-2052 E-mail: mkw@npnweb.org, mkarts@earthlink.net.

WEGNER, DARLENE JOY, civic worker, event coordinator; b. Pasadena, Calif., May 2, 1953; d. Glenn Raymond and Evelyn Pryor (Ingram) Thornton; m. Robert Culbertson, July 25, 1975 (div. May 1977); m. Karl James, June 21, 1986; 1 child, Heather Joy. Student, East L.A. Jr. Coll., 1971-72; grad., Chaffey Coll., Rancho Cucamonga, Calif., 2002; student, King's Coll. and Seminary, 2002—. Exec. sec. Wells Fargo Bank, Rosemead, Calif., 1972-76; adminstrv. sec. Ford Aerospace, Pasadena, 1977-78; sales sec. A&F Sales Engring., Pasadena, 1979-84; sr. sec. Xerox Med., Pasadena, 1984-89; cmty. activist Ontario (Calif.) City Hall, 1991-92; vice chmn. Concerned Citizens Commn. on Pornography and Obscenity, Ontario, 1992-93; project dir. Inland Empire Prayer Gathering Nat. Day of Prayer, Ontario, 1993-94; office adminstr. Prayer Command Post, Ontario, 1995-96; adminstrv. svcs. dir. Inland Empire Secretarial Svcs., Ontario, 1996-98; adminstrv. asst. Somebody Cares-Inland Empire, 1998-99, Inland Empire, 2000—. Author: Beauty Instead of Ashes, 1994; freelance writer, 1997-98. Republican. Mem. Community Ch. Avocations: doll making, gardening, crafts, writing, reading.

WEGNER, JUDITH WELCH, lawyer, educator, dean; b. Hartford, Conn., Feb. 14, 1950; d. John Raymond and Ruth (Thulen) Welch; m. Warren W. Wegner, Oct. 13, 1972. BA with honors, U. Wis., 1972; JD, UCLA, 1976. Bar: Calif. 1976, D.C. 1977, N.C. 1988, U.S. Supreme Ct. 1980, U.S. Ct. Appeals. Law clk. to Judge Warren Ferguson, U.S. Dist. Ct. for So. Dist. Calif., L.A., 1976-77; atty. Office Legal Counsel and Land & Natural Resources Divsn. U.S. Dept. Justice, Washington, 1977-79; spl. asst. to sec. U.S. Dept. Edn., Washington, 1979-80; vis. assoc. prof. U. Iowa Coll. Law, Iowa City, 1981; asst. prof. U. N.C. Sch. Law, Chapel Hill, 1981-84, assoc. prof., 1984-88, prof., 1988—, assoc. dean, 1986-88, dean, 1989-99; sr. scholar Carnegie Found. for Advancement of Tchg., 1999—2001; chmn. faculty U. N.C., 2003—. Spkr. in field. Chief comment editor UCLA Law Rev., 1975-76; contbr. articles to legal publs. Mem. ABA (chmn. planning com. African Law Sch. Initiative 1994, co-chmn. planning com. 1994 mid-yr. deans meeting sect. on legal edn. and admission to bar), N.C. Assn. Women Attys. (Gweneth Davis award 1989), N.C. State Bar Assn., Assn. Am. Law Schs. (mem. exec. com. sect. on law & edn. 1985-88, mem. exec. com. sect. on local govt. law 1989-92, mem. accreditation com. 1986-88, chmn. 1989-91, program chmn. 1992 ann. meeting, program chmn. 1994 ann. meeting, mem. exec. com. 1992-96, pres. 1995), Soc. Am. Law Tchrs., Nat. League Cities (coun.-mentor program 1989-91), Women's Internat. Forum, Order of Coif (nat. exec. com. 1989-91), Phi Beta Kappa. Democrat. Office: U NC Sch Law Van Hecke Wettach Hall Campus Box 3380 Chapel Hill NC 27599-3380 Office Phone: 919-962-4113. Business E-Mail: judith_wegner@unc.edu.

WEHN, KAREN SWANEY, education educator, consultant; b. Chillicotne, Ohio, Mar. 1, 1950; d. Glenn Warren and Joyce Wood Swaney; m. David Carl Wehn, Apr. 8, 1989; 1 child, Glenn Ian Taylor. BA, Ohio State Univ., Columbus, Ohio, 1980; MS, Kent State Univ., Kent, Ohio, 1986. Cert. Profl. Geologist 1996. Rsch. asst. Ohio State Univ., Columbus, Ohio, 1976—92; project geologist Conestaga Rover 3 Assoc., Niagara Falls, NY, 1992—97, Golder Assoc., Niagara Falls, NY, 1997—; lectr. Buffalo State Coll., Buffalo, 1997—; asst. prof. Erie CC, Buffalo, 2000—. Rschr., Antarctica, 1980—85; pres. Buffalo Assn. of profl. Geologists, Buffalo, 1997—98. Contbr. articles pub. to profl. jour. Lay leader Warrens Corners United Meth. Ch., 2004—05. Grantee travel to Australia, Nat. Sci. Found., 1982, travel and work in Nigeria, Earth Watch, 1990—91. Mem.: Air and Waste Mgmt. Assn. (bd. mem.). Meth. Business E-Mail: wehnks@bscmail.buffalostate.edu.

WEHRMAN, NATALIE ANN, retired music educator; b. Springfield, Mo., Apr. 11, 1928; d. William Herman Seboldt and Isabel Johanna Browser; m. Harlan Henry Wehrman, June 22, 1952; children: Marcel Alyce, Nathan Scott, Stephanie Ann, Brian Lee, Denise Kay. BS, Mo. State U., 1950; postgrad., U. Mo., 1951, Concordia Coll., Seward, Nebr., 1951—52. Bus. and music tchr. Concordia HS, Seward, Nebr., 1951—52; bus. tchr. Lockwood (Mo.) Sch., 1952—54; pvt. music instr., piano, organ and voice Lockwood, 1953—88; ret., 1988. Music coord., adult choir Immanuel Luth. Ch., Lockwood, 1967—2001, head organist, adult choir accompanist, 1967—. Mem.: Assn. Luth. Ch. Musicians, Assn. Guild Organists, Bus. and Profl. Women (officer 1952—80, Woman of Yr. 1955), Nat. Music Tchrs. Assn., Luth. Women's Missing League, Mo. Music Tchrs. Assn., Am. Legion Aux. Lutheran. Avocations: quilting, travel. Home: 105 North State Hwy 97 Lockwood MO 65682

WEIANT, ELIZABETH ABBOTT, retired biology professor; b. New Britain, Conn., July 4, 1913; d. William Armstrong and Flora (Abbott) W. BS, MS, Tufts U., 1943; MA, Radcliffe Coll., 1952; EdD, Boston U., 1970. Instr. biology Tufts Coll., Medford, Mass., 1943-56, asst. prof., 1957-61; asst. prof. biology Simmons Coll., Boston, 1961-71, assoc. prof., 1972-79, chmn. dept., 1977-79, ret., 1979; corr. Evening Citizen, Laconia, N.H., 1987-98, Franklin-Tilton Telegram, Franklin, N.H., 1990-2000. Rschr. OSRD, USPHS, NSF, 1943-61; sr. rsch. fellow Max-Planck Inst., Seewiesen, Fed. Republic Germany, 1958; physiologist for product validation Cordis Corp., Miami, Fla., 1970 Contbr. articles to profl. jours. Active Hist. Dist. Commn., Sanbornton, NH, 1979-83; sec., Sanbornton Conservation Commn., 1979-83, Trustees of Trust Fund, Sanbornton, 1985-96; bd. dirs., sec. NH affiliate Am. Heart Assn., Manchester, 1981-85; bd. dirs., com. mem. Franklin, NH, Regional Hosp., 1984-91; pres. Sanbornton Hist. Soc., 1980-82; publicity chmn. Friends NH Music Festival; alumna trustee Tufts U., 1974-81, trustee emeritus, 1981. Recipient Disting. Svc. award Tufts U., 1970, Tower award Westbrook Coll., Portland, Maine, 1974, Woman of Yr. award Tilton-Northfield Bus. and Profl. Women, 1980, Heart of Gold award Am. Heart Assn., 1986, award for Pub. Svc. Belknap County Pomona Grange, 1990, Gov.'s Outstanding Vol. award, 1992. Mem.: Am. Inst. Biol. Scis., Grange, Sigma Xi (sec. Tufts U. chpt. 1947—59). Republican. Home: PO Box 11 Sanbornton NH 03269-0011

WEICKERT, WANDA OPAL, child welfare and attendance counselor, psychotherapist, educator; b. LaCygne, Kans., Apr. 10, 1941; d. Frank W and Opal M Weickert. BS in Phys. Edn., Kans. State Coll., 1959—63, MS in Phys. Edn., 1963—66; MA in Marriage and Family Therapy, Phillips Grad. Inst., 1983—85; Pupil Personnel Services Credential, Calif. Luth. Coll., 1987—89. Marriage Family Child Therapist Bd. of Behavioral Sciences-California, 1991; Teaching Credential Kans., 1963, Calif., 1969. Health phys. edn. tchr. Circle HS, Towanda, Kans., 1963—69; phys. edn. tchr. Nightingale Mid. Sch., LA, 1969—73; coach & phys. edn. tchr. Reseda Sr. HS, LA, 1973—81; career edn., coach, tchr. Kennedy Sr. HS, LA, 1981—89; child welfare & attendance counselor LA Unified Sch. Dist., 1989—; marriage family child therapist Self Employed, LA, 1991—; dist. counselor LA Unified Schs., 1994—2001. Coord. cheerleaders, kayettes and pep club Circle HS, Towanda, Kans., 1963—69; dir. camp waterfront Young Women's Christian Assn., Wichita, Kans.; counselor San Fernando Valley Mental Health Clinic, Van Nuys, Calif., 1985—88; drug prevention program dir. Kennedy HS, LA, 1987—89; counselor Valley Cmty. Clinic, North Hollywood, Calif., 1989—92; adv. bd. Sch. Attendance Rev. Bd. LAUSD, LA, 1991—2001; coach 1st pl. gymnast fl. exercise, city championships LA Unified Schs., 1976, coach 3d pl. volleyball team city championships, 79, coach 3d pl. gymnast all-around events, city championships, 80, crisis team leader, 1996—2001. Choreographer (drill team performance) LA Coliseum, 1977, Hollywood Christmas Parades, 1984—86, (1st pl. band and drill team championships) LA Unified Schs., 1978. Vol. Girl Scouts, LA, 1994—95; contbr. Civitan, Burbank, Calif.; presidents club contbr. Pitts. State U., Kans. Recipient Commendation for 32 years Pub. Sch. Svc., Mayor Jim Hahn, LA, 2001. Mem.: Calif. Assn. of Marriage and Family Therapists, Calif. Teachers Assn., Delta Psi Kappa (life), Alpha Sigma Alpha (life). Avocations: quilting, gardening, camping, swimming, walking. Office Phone: 818-893-2756. Personal E-mail: res1fosk@verizon.net.

WEIDE, JANICE LEE, librarian; b. Baker, Oreg., Aug. 12, 1948; d. Albert L. and Woodie Rue (Jeffords) Crowson; m. Roy Karl Weide, June 13, 1971; children: Megan, Alison. BA, Oreg. State U., 1971; MLA, U. Oreg., 1974. Online coord. Salem (Oreg.) Pub. Libr., 1974—. Contbr. articles to profl. publs. Recipient On the Frontline award OCLC, 1991. Avocations: reading, bicycling, swimming. Office: Salem Pub Libr 585 Liberty St SE Salem OR 97301-3591

WEIDEMANN, CELIA JEAN, social sciences educator, management consultant, financial consultant; b. Denver, Dec. 6, 1942; d. John Clement and Hazel (Van Tuyl) Kirlin; m. Wesley Clark Weidemann, July 1, 1972; 1 child, Stephanie Jean. BS, Iowa State U., 1964; MS, U. Wis., Madison, 1970, PhD, 1973; post grad., U. So. Calif., 1983. Advisor UN FAO, Ibadan, Nigeria, 1973—77; ind. rschr. Asia and Near East, 1977—78; program coord., asst. prof., rsch. assoc. U. Wis., Madison, Wis., 1979—81; chief inst. and human resources US AID, Washington, 1982—85; team leader, cons. Sumatra, Indonesia, 1984; dir. fed. econ. program Midwest Rsch. Inst., Washington, 1985—86; founder, pres. emeritus Weidemann Assoc., Arlington, Va., 1986—2000; pres. Weidemann Found., Arlington, Va., 2000—. Cons. U.S. Congress, Aspen Inst., Ford Found., World Bank, Egypt, Nigeria, Gambia, Pakistan, Indonesia, AID, Thailand, Jamaica, Panama, Philippines, Sierra Leone, Kenya, Jordon, Poland, India, Egypt, Russia, Finnish Internat. Devel. Agy., Namibia, pvt. client Estonia, Latvia, Russia, Japan, Internat. Ctr. Rsch. on Women, Zaire, UN FAO, Ghana, Internat. Statis. Inst., The Netherlands, Global Exch., 1986-87, Asian Devel. Bank, Mongolia, Nepal, Vietnam, Bangladesh, Indonesia, Philippines; bd. visitors Sch. Human Ecology, U. Wis., 2002—; bd. dirs. Cmty. Counseling and Edn. Ctr, Santa Barbara, Calif.; peer reviewer NRC, NAS Author: (book) Planning Home Economics Curriculum for Social and Econ. Develop., Agrl. Ext. for Women Farmers in Africa, 1990, Fin. Services for Women, 1992, Egyptian Women and Micro.: The Invisible Entrepreneurs, 1992, Small Enterprise Development in Poland: Does Gender Matter?, 1994, Micro. and Gender in India, 1995, Supporting Women's Livelihoods: Micro Fin. That Works for the Majority, 2002; contbr. chapters to books and articles to profl. journals. Bd. dirs. Cmty. Counseling Ctr., Santa Barbara, Calif., 2004—. Am. Home Econ. Assn. Fellow, 1969-73; grantee Ford Found., 1987-89. Mem. Soc. Internat. Devel., Am. Sociol. Assn., Assn. for Women in Devel. (pres. 1989, founder, bd. dirs.), Women in Devel. (steering com.), Coalition for Women's Econ. Devel. and Global Equality, Internat. Devel. Conf. (bd. dirs., exec. com.), Internat. Platform Assn., Pi Lambda Theta, Omicron Nu. Avocations: mountain trekking, piano and pipe organ, canoeing, photography, poetry. Office: Weidemann Found 749 Westwood Drive Santa Barbara CA 93109 Office Phone: 805-965-2902. Personal E-mail: jweidemann@aol.com.

WEIDENFELD, SHEILA RABB, television producer, writer; b. Cambridge, Mass., Sept. 7, 1943; d. Maxwell M. and Ruth (Cryden) Rabb; m. Edward L. Weidenfeld, Aug. 11, 1968; children: Nicholas Rabb, Daniel Rabb. BA, Brandeis U., 1965. Assoc. prodr. Metromedia, Inc., Sta. WNEW-TV, N.Y.C., 1965-68; talent coord. That Show with Joan Rivers, NBC, N.Y.C., 1968-71; coord. NBC network game programs, N.Y.C., 1968-71; prodr. Metromedia, Inc., Sta. WTTG-TV, Washington, 1971-73; creator/prodr. Take

It From Here, NBC (WBC-TV), Washington, 1973-74; press sec. to first lady Betty Ford, spl. asst. to Pres. Gerald R. Ford, 1974-77; mem. Pres.'s Adv. Commn. on Hist. Preservation, 1977-81; TV prodr., moderator On the Record, NBC-TV, Sta. WRC-TV, Washington, 1978-79; pres. D.C. Prodns., Ltd., 1978; prodr., host Your Personal Decorator, 1987; mem. Sec. State's Adv. Commn. on Fgn. Svc. Inst., 1972-74; founding mem. Project Censured Panel of Judges, 1976—. Bd. dirs. First Star. Author: First Lady's Lady, 1979. Mem. U.S. Holocaust Meml. Coun., 1987-97; corporator Dana Hall Sch., Wellesley, Mass.; bd. dirs. Wolf Trap Found., Women's Campaign Fund, 1978-79; bd. dirs. D.C. Contemporary Dance Theatre, 1986-88, D.C. Rep. Ctrl. Com., 1984—, D.C. Preservation League, 1987-90; chmn. C&O Canal Nat. Hist. Park Commn., 1988—; bd. dirs. Am. Univ. Rome, 1988—96, Friends of the Scuola San Rocco, 2002—. Recipient awards for outstanding achievement in the media AAUW, 1973, 74, Silver Screen award A Campaign to Remember for the U.S. Holocaust Meml. Coun., 1989, Bronze medal Internat. Film and Video Festival N.Y., 1990; named hon. consul gen. of Republic of San Marino to Washington; knighted by Order of St. Agatha, Republic of San Marino, 1986. Mem. NATAS (Emmy award 1972), Washington Press Club, Am. Newspaper Women's Club, Am. Women in Radio and TV, Cosmos Club, Consular Corps, Sigma Delta Chi. Home: 3059 Q St NW Washington DC 20007-3081 E-mail: Sheila.Weidenfeld@verizon.net.

WEIDMAN, SHEILA, marketing professional; b. Bradenton, Fla., July 11, 1961; BS in sci., Journalism and Comm., U. Fla., 1983. Mgr. comm. ASHRAE, 1983—88; mgr. corp. comm. Georgia-Pacific Corp., 1988—90, dir. external comm. and corp. advt., 1990—98, dir., spl. asst. to chmn. and CEO, 1998—2000, sr. dir. corp. mktg. and sales excellence, 2000—01, v.p. corp. mktg., 2001—02, v.p. corp. comm. and mktg. Atlanta, 2002—. Com. mem. Am. Heart Assn., Atlanta Hist. Soc.; mem. Leadership Atlanta, Class of 2004. Recipient Women of Achievement awards, YWCA, 1995. Mem.: Atlanta Sports Coun. (bd. dirs., chmn. mktg. com.), Atlanta CMO Roundtable, CMO Group of N.Am., Ga. Press Assn., Ga. State CMO Roundtable, Met. Atlanta C. of C. (vice chair chmn.'s campaign 2003), Mktg. Leadership Coun. (vice chair chmn.'s campaign 2004), Pub. Rels. Soc. Am., Sales and Mktg. Execs., Atlanta Press Club. Office: Georgia-Pacific Corp 133 Peachtree St NE Atlanta GA 30303

WEIGHTMAN, ESTHER LYNN, emergency trauma nurse; b. Tawas City, Mich., June 13, 1966; d. Garrie Lee and Naomi Ruth (Atwood) Schneller; m. Robert Thomas Weightman, Dec. 31, 1996; children: Erin Elizabeth, Kaili Marie. BS in Christian Secondary Edn., Ozark Bible Inst. & Coll., Neosho, Mo., 1988; BSN, Ind. Wesleyan U., Marion, 1991; MS in Cmty. Health Nursing, U. Colo. Health Scis. Ctr., Denver, 1995. RN, Colo.; cert. ACLS, pediatric advanced life support, trauma nurse core course; Profl. Spl. Svcs. licensee Colo. Dept. Edn. Staff nurse emergency dept. Marion Gen. Hosp., 1991-92, Penrose-St. Francis Healthcare Sys., Colorado Springs, Colo., 1992-95; staff nurse registry QS Nurses Corp., Colorado Springs, 1992-2001; staff devel. nurse 302d ASTS-USAFR, Peterson AFB, Colo., 1994-2001; staff nurse emergency dept. Med. Ctr. of Aurora, Colo., 1997-2001; staff nurse ICU St. Peter's Hosp., Helena, Mont., 2001—02, VA Mont. Healthcare Sys., Ft. Harrison, Mont., 2002—04; staff devel. nurse Mont. Air N.G., Great Falls, 2003—05; nurse surg. intensive care unit VA, Omaha, 2004—05, charge nurse urgent care, 2005—; clin. nurse 710th Med. Squadron, USAFR, Offutt AFB, Nebr., 2005—. Mentor various healthcare instrnl. facilities, 1991—; vol. tchr. health classes Knowledge is Power, Red Cross Shelter, Colorado Springs, 1995-96; health fair vol. Mem.: Emergency Nurses Assn., Res. Officers Assn., Sigma Theta Tau. Avocations: cooking, orchestra (trumpet).

WEIGLE, PEGGY, information technology executive; BA in philosophy cum laude, U. Mass. V.p. N. Am. sales Arbor Software, 1996; v.p. worldwide field operations Hyperion (merged with Arbor Software), v.p., gen. mgr. performance mgmt. divsn.; CEO Perfecto Tech. (now Sanctum, Inc.), 1999—. Chmn. application sub-com. BENS Silicon Valley Cyber Security Working Group; mem. tech. sub-com. Silicon Valley Blue Ribbon Task Force on Aviation Security and Tech. Named one of 50 Most Powerful Women in Networking, Network World mag., 2003.

WEIHMULLER, PATRICIA ANN, minister, artist, retired executive secretary; m. Fred H. Weihmuller, Aug. 31, 1957; children: Fredric, Susan Smith, Steven, Amy Kovanda. Secretarial Diploma, Blair Bus.Coll., Colorado Springs, 1955; cert., William Rainey Harper Coll., Palatine, Ill., 1983, Mgmt. Cert., 1992; leadership diploma, Stephen Ministries, St. Louis, 1993. Cert. profl. sec. Profl. Secs. Internat., 1983. Exec. sec. State Farm Ins. Co., Dearborn, Mich., 1959—60; exec. sec. Unocal, Schaumburg, Ill., 1971—92, Motorola (temp.), Schaumburg, Ill., 1993—94; Stephen ministry leader Prince of Peace Luth. Ch., Schaumburg, Ill., 1993—98, Stephen min., 1991—2006; oil painter Hoffman Estates, Ill., 1996—2006. Active Star, Schaumburg, 1967—2006; election judge Cook County Bd. of Elections, Schaumburg Twp., 1995—2005; exec. sec. parish planning coun. Prince of Peace Luth. Ch., Ill., 1989—92, bible study leader, mem. Naomi Cir., 1967—2006. Avocations: bridge, painting, reading, sewing, travel. Personal E-mail: fpweih@aol.com.

WEIKEL, SANDRA G., music educator; b. Hamilton, Ohio, Apr. 1, 1955; d. Heather P. Gilbert; 1 child, Derek Vaughn. B in Music Edn., U. Louisville, 1978. Cert. Tchr. N.Mex, 1984, Ky., 1979, S.D., 1980. Band dir. Roswell Ind. Sch. Dist., N.Mex., 1986—, Hagerman H.S., N.Mex., 1984—86, Viborg H.S., 1982—83, South Shore H.S., SD, 1980—82. French horn player SW Symphony, Hobbs, N.Mex., 1986—, Roswell Symphony, 1986—94; trumpet player Nacho Average Jazz Band, 1990—97; horn player ENMUR Cmty. Band, 2002—, Pecos Valley Brass, 1988—. Dir.(orch.): The Music Man. Rec. sec. Delta Kappa Gamma Soc., Roswell, 1992—2003. Mem.: SE N.Mex. Music Assn. (licentiate). Democrat-Npl. Methodist. Avocations: softball, travel, piano, music box collector, tennis. Home: 3411 Highland Rd Roswell NM 88201 Office: Berrendo Middle School 800 Marion Richards Rd Roswell NM 88203 Personal E-mail: sgweikel@wmconnect.com. E-mail: sweikel@risd.k12.nm.us.

WEIKERT, BARBARA RUTH, librarian; b. Kalispell, Mont., June 26, 1931; d. Austin D. and Ruth (Dinwiddie) W. Assoc. degree, John Muir Jr. Coll., Pasadena, Calif., 1951; BS, San Jose State U., 1954; MS, U. So. Calif., 1957. Tchr. elem. edn. Ashley Creek Elem. Sch., Kila, Mont., 1951-52; libr. Fall River Mills High Sch., McArthur, Calif., 1954-56; asst. libr. Spokane (Wash.) County Libr., 1961-62; br. libr. Pierce County Libr., Tacoma, 1962-66, coord. ext. svcs., 1966-76, coord. circulation and interloan, 1976-82, reference and supervising reference libr., 1982—96. Mem. policy adv. com., LWV rep. Citizen's Land Use Policy Com., Tacoma, 1974; mem., citizen-at-large N.E. Tacoma Citizen's Adv. Com., 1977; com. mem. Land Use Mgmt. Plan, 1975, Land Use Planning N.E. Tacoma Plan, 1979; mem. dist. and conf. com. of ch. and women's orgn. United Meth. Ch., 1970—. Mem. LWV (bd., 2002-2005, policy adv. com., newsletter editor 1972-74), AAUW (pres. 1966-68, state chair internat. rels. 1968-70), UN Assn. of U.S.A. (pres. 1977-79, state sec. 1984-88), Wash. Libr. Assn. (rep. to steering com. status 1980, mem. tech./energy cmty. forums 1980, interlibr. loan chpt. 1982-84), Pacific N.W. Libr. Assn. (circulation chair 1979-81, ref. chair 1993-1995). Avocations: walking, reading, church activities, travel.

WEIKERT, BARBARA SLIKER, music educator; b. Norristown, Pa., Aug. 20, 1978; d. Frank Joseph and Barbara J. Sliker; m. Joshua John Weikert, Aug. 1, 2003. BS in Music Edn., Chestnut Hill Coll., 2000; MA in Ednl. Leadership, Villanova U., 2003. Music tchr. Norristown Area Sch. Dist., 2000—. Music tchg. and learning facilitator Norristown Area Sch. Dist., 2003—. Office: Eisenhower Mid Sch 1601 Markley St Norristown PA 19401 Office Phone: 610-277-8720. E-mail: bweikert@nasd.k12.pa.us.

WEIKSNER, SANDRA S., lawyer; b. Washington, Nov. 9, 1945; d. Donald B. and Dick (Cutter) Smiley; m. George B. Weiksner, Aug. 19, 1969; children: Michael, Nicholas. BA in Psychology, Stanford (Calif.) U., 1966, JD, 1969. Tchg. fellow Stanford U., 1969-70; assoc. Cleary, Gottlieb, Steen & Hamilton, N.Y.C., 1970-77, ptnr., 1978—2003, sr. counsel, 2004—. Vis. lectr. Yale Law Sch., 1991-92. Bd. dirs. N.Y. Law Sch.; mem. Union Theol. Sem. Fellow Am. Bar Found., Am. Coll. Trusts and Estates Counsel, Internat. Acad. Estate and Trust Law; mem. Assn. Bar City of N.Y. Democrat. Unitarian Universalist. Home: 164 E 81st St New York NY 10028-1804 Office: Cleary Gottlieb Steen & Hamilton 1 Liberty Plz Fl 43 New York NY 10006-1404

WEIL, LEAH, lawyer; b. LA, 1960; m. Fred Schulcz; children: Stephen, Elizabeth. BA, U. Calif., 1982, JD, 1985. Bar: 1985. Assoc. Hill, Wynne, Troop & Meisinger, LA; pvt. practice, 1992—96; various positions including sr. counsel, sr. v.p. legal affairs, dep. gen. counsel Sony Pictures Entertainment, Culver City, Calif., 1996—2001, gen. counsel, 2001—. Office: Sony Pictures Entertainment Inc 10202 W Washington Blvd Culver City CA 90232 Office Phone: 310-244-4000. Office Fax: 310-244-2626.

WEIL, LYNNE AMY, communications executive, writer; b. Santa Monica, Calif., Apr. 29, 1963; d. Robert Harry and Miriam Ruth Weil; m. Nils Johan Axel Bruzelius, Aug. 10, 2002; 1 child, Emilie Anna Bruzelius. BA in Comm., U. Calif., L.A., 1985; M in Pub. Policy, Princeton U., 2001. Freelance fgn. corr. Nat. Pub. Radio, Monitor Radio, Marketplace pub. radio, BBC, various others, Bonn, Germany, 1993—96; prodr., reporter Radio Deutsche Welle, Cologne, 1991—92; European corr. Cath. News Svc., Rome, 1996—99; reporter UPI, L.A., 1986—88; prodr., reporter Calif. Pub. Radio Network, Long Beach, 1988—91; press sec. Senate Fgn. Rels. Com., Washington, 2001—03; comm. dir. Ho. Internat. Rels. Com. Dem. staff, 2003—. Cons. Woodrow Wilson Sch., Princeton U., NJ, 2003. Contbr. articles to profl. jours. Recipient Coll. journalism award with stipend, Pub. Interest Radio and TV Soc., 1985; scholar, Woodrow Wilson Sch., Princeton U., 2000—01; Congl. fellow, Am. Polit. Sci. Assn., 1999—2000. Mem.: Fgn. Corr. Assn. Germany (pres. 1995—96, v.p. 1994—95), Women in Internat. Security. Avocations: skiing, tennis, various musical instruments. Office Phone: 202-225-6735.

WEILER, BERENICE, theater producer, consultant; d. Sidney and Lillian Hammer Weiler. BA, Hunter Coll.; student, New Sch. Social Rsch. Sec. treas. Assn. of Theatrical Press Agents and Mgrs., 1991—97; prodr. Smithville Theatre for ABC; adminstr. BAM Theatre Co., 1977—78; mng. prodr. Am. Shakespeare Theatre, Stratford, Conn., 1960—73; prin., owner Weiler/Miller Assocs., N.Y. Adj. prof. U. Miami; lectr. and cons. in adminstrn. and mgmt.; stage mgr. USO, The Late Christopher Bean. Co-prodr.: American premiers of Graham Greene's Carving a Statue, Gorki's Country People; casting dir. Hallmark Hall of Fame, assoc. prodr. Caesar's Hour, Colgate Comedy Hour, exec. dir. Univ. Resident/Theatre Assn., 1975—93. Mem.: League Profl. Theatre Women (founder, past co-pres.), Nat. Theatre Conf., Assn. Theatrical Press Agents and Mgrs. Home and Office: Weiler/Miller Assoc 340 East 52 St New York NY 10022

WEILER, KATHLEEN, education educator, researcher; b. Fresno, Calif., July 9, 1941; d. Conrad and Nadine Becktold; m. Peter Weiler, June 27, 1963; children: Sarah, Emma. BA, Stanford U., 1963; M, Harvard U., 1966; EdD, Boston U., 1985. Assoc. prof. Tufts U., Medford, Mass., 1994—98, prof. edn., 1998—. Dir. peace and justice studies Tufts U., Meford, 1995—97, 2003—04, chair dept. edn., 2002—05. Author: (scholarly book) Women Teaching for Change, Country Schoolwomen; editor: Feminism and Social Justice in Education, What Schools Can Do, Rewriting Literacy, Feminist Engagements, Telling Women's Lives; series editor feminist ednl. thinking: Open U. Press, 1995—. Fellow, NEH, 1992—93; grantee, Spencer Found., 1999; scholar, Fulbright, 1995; Spencer Postdoctoral fellow, Nat. Acad. of Edn., 1987—89, Bunting fellow, Radcliffe Inst., 1992—93. Mem.: John Dewey Soc. (editl. bd. mem. 2004—), Am. Ednl. Rsch. Assn. Avocations: travel, gardening, swimming. Office: Tufts Univ Dept of Edn Medford MA 02155 Office Phone: 617-627-2394. Office Fax: 617-627-3901. E-mail: kathleen.weiler@tufts.edu.

WEILERT, MARY E., communications educator; b. Youngstown, Ohio, May 7, 1964; d. Chester E. Young and Sue E. Ayers; m. Tim D. Weilert, Nov. 17, 1984; children: Adam D., Amy M., Alex K. BA in Comm., Avila Coll., Kansas City, Mo., 1985; MA in English, Pitsburg State U., Kans., 1989. Tchr. Allen County CC, Iola, Kans., 1989—93; instr. Neosho County CC, Chantue, 1993—. Home: 802 S Highland Chanute KS 66720 Office: Neosho County CC 800 W 14 Chanute KS 66720 Office Phone: 620-431-2820.

WEIL-GARRIS BRANDT, KATHLEEN (KATHLEEN BRANDT), art historian; b. Surrey, Eng. d. Kurt Hermann and Charlotte (Garris) Weil; m. Werner Brandt (dec. 1983). BA with honors, Vassar Coll., Poughkeepsie, N.Y., 1956; postgrad., U. Bonn, Germany, 1956-57; MA, Radcliffe U., 1958; PhD, Harvard, 1966; MA, Oxford U., 1998. Asst. prof. NYU, N.Y.C., 1963-67, assoc. prof., 1967-72, prof., 1973—; asst. prof. NYU Inst. Fine Arts, N.Y.C., 1966-67, assoc. prof., 1967-72, prof., 1973—; vis. prof. Harvard U., Cambridge, Mass., 1980; editor in chief The Art Bulletin, N.Y.C., 1977-81; Slade prof. Oxford U., 1998. Cons. on Renaissance art Vatican Mus., 1987—; vis. fellow Bibliotheca Hertziana (Max-Planck Inst.) Rome. Author: Leonardo and Central Italian Art, 1974, Problems In Cinquecento Sculpture, 1977; author: (with J. d'Amico) The Renaissance Cardinal's Ideal Palace, 1981, (with C. d'Acidini, J. Draper, N. Penny) Giovinezza di Michelangelo, 1999-2000; editor: Michelangelo: la Cappella Sistina: documentazione e interpretazione, vol. III, 1996; contbr. articles to profl. jours. Mem. Am. com. Medici Archive Project, 1996—; bd. dirs. Raccolta Vinciana, 1997—. Decorated officer Order of Merit (Italy); recipient Rsch. award Humboldt Found., 1985, Disting. Tchg. award Lindback Found., 1967, Golden Dozen Tchr. award NYU, 1993, Alumni Great Tchr. award, 1996; Guggenheim fellow, 1976; grantee Henkel Found., 1987, Samuel H. Kress Found., 1999. Mem. Coll. Art Assn. (bd. dirs. 1973-74, 77-81), Renaissance Soc. Am. (editl. bd. 1992—), Soc. Archtl. Historians, Friends of the Frances Lehman Loeb Art Ctr. (bd. mem. 2005—), N.Y. Acad. Scis., Phi Beta Kappa (v.p. NYU chpt. 1979-81). Avocations: art films, conservation, music, dance. Office: NYU Inst Fine Arts 1 E 78th St New York NY 10021-0119 Business E-Mail: kathleen.brandt@nyu.edu.

WEINBAUM, BATYA, artist, writer; b. Ann Arbor, Mich., Feb. 2, 1952; d. Jack and Barbara Weinbaum; 1 child, Ola. BA, Hampshire Coll., 1976; MA, SUNY, Buffalo, 1986; PhD, U. Mass., Amherst, 1996. Asst. prof. English Cleve. State U., 1998—2003; founder, developer Red Serpent Threads, 2004—; self-employed artist, writer, editor. Working with a family learning cmty. Cleve. Heights, Ohio, 2003; lectr. Pacifica Grad Inst., 2006. Author: Curious Courtship of Women's Liberation & Socialism, 1978, Pictures of Patriarchy, 1984, Island of Floating Women, 1993, Islands of Women & Amazons, 2000; editor: Femspec, 1999—; mem. editl. bd.: Women and Judiasm; contbr. over 250 articles and reviews to profl. jour. Founder, co-chair Feminist Mothers and Their Allies Task Force/Nat. Women's Studies, 1998—2005. Grantee, Robert Fleming Fund, 1976, Rabinowitz Found., 1978, Equity Fund, Women's Classical Caucus, 2004. Mem.: Assn. Am. U. Women Legal Advocacy Fund (scholars support 2006), Sci. Fiction Rsch. Assn., Am./Popular Culture Assn., Nat. Assn. Women's Studies (acad. discrimination adv. bd. 2005). Jewish. Avocations: swimming, music, dance, painting, meditation. Home: 1610 Rydal Mount Cleveland Heights OH 44118

WEINBERG, ALEXANDREA, music educator; b. Litchfield, Ill., Feb. 22, 1971; d. Pamela Elaine and Steve Vernon Rademacher; m. Steven Carl Weinberg, July 11, 1998; children: Isaac Benjamin, Aaron James. BA in Music Mgmt. and Performance, Blackburn Coll., Carlinville, Ill., 1993. Lic. K-12 music edn. Ill. State Bd. Edn., 2000. K-12 vocal music tchr., drama instr. Panhandle Sch., Raymond, Ill., 1999—2003, Staunton CUSD, Ill., 2003—05; K-6 music tchr. Southwestern CUSD, Piasa, Ill., 2005—. Leader, tng. officer Cub Scouts of Am., Gillespie, 2005—06; sec., musical dir. Lyric Theatre Guild, Gillespie, Ill., 2005—06. Mem.: Ill. Edn. Assn. Home: 18437 Washer Rd Gillespie IL 62033 Office: Southwestern Sch Dist #2 201 E City Limits Rd Brighton IL 62012 Office Phone: 618-372-3162. Office Fax: 618-372-4915. Personal E-mail: teach_musick12@hotmail.com. E-mail: aweinberg@piasabirds.net.

WEINBERG, DALE GLASER, writer, consultant; b. N.Y.C., Oct. 21, 1948; d. Milton and Joyce I. (Litsky) Glaser; m. Howard Weinberg, June 20, 1971 (separated); 1 child, Tracy J. BS in English Edn., NYU, 1971; MS in English Edn., Iona Coll., New Rochelle, N.Y., 1975. Lic. secondary tchr. English, N.Y. Programmer, documentation adminstr. ITT Continental Baking, Rye, N.Y., 1971-78; owner, pres. Techically Write, Eastchester, N.Y., 1978—. Cons., course leader, tchr. writing seminars throughout U.S., Am. Mgmt. Assn., N.Y.C., 1980; designer, tchr. bus. writing Am. Mgmt. Assn.-Operation Enterprise, Hamilton, N.Y., 1998; ind. tech. writing and tng. cons., 1978—. Editor: Money Smarts, 1982, A Funny Thing Happened on the Way to the Interview, 1995; designer, editor, prodr. 3 major publs. Eastchester (N.Y.) Mid. Sch., 1993—; assoc. editor Calif. Ride Reporter, 1993—. Recipient Spl. Svc. award/citation for publs. Eastchester Mid. Sch., 1994. Mem. IEEE Profl. Comm. Soc. (assoc.), Soc. Tech. Comm. (sr.), Assn. Computing Machinery. Avocations: scuba diving, yoga, skiing, theater, reading, travel. Office: Technically Write 19 Soundview Dr Eastchester NY 10709-1526

WEINBERG, ELISABETH H., physical therapist, health facility administrator; b. Chgo., Jan. 18, 1934; d. Hermann Heckel and Alice Matilda Lodoen; m. Elliott Weinberg, Nov. 1956; children: Pamela, Arthur, Rachel. Student, Coll. of Wooster, 1952-54; BS, Med. Coll. Va., 1954-56. Staff therapist Med. Coll. Va., Richmond, 1956-57; dir. phys. therapy Soc. Crippled Children and Adults, Balt., 1957-67; cons. Health Care Agy., Cin., 1975-84; v.p. Weinberg Rehab., Inc., Cin., 1984-96, adminstr., advisor, 1996-97, ret., 1997. Cons. Health Dept. Ohio, Columbus, 1984-96. Sec.-treas. Nat. Coun. Jewish Women, Frederick, Md., 1957-67; active Nat. Rep. Party, Cin., 1990-99, State Rep. Women, Columbus, 1998-99; mem. sisterhood Beth de Filloh Temple, Brunswick, Ga., 1998-99. Mem. AAUP. Home: 101 Enclave Ln Saint Simons Island GA 31522-5293

WEINBERG, ELIZABETH, education educator, researcher, retired small business owner; b. Greensburg, Ky., Apr. 6, 1923; d. Edward Shaikun and Eugenia Sophia Lerner; m. Jerry K. Weinberg (dec.); children: Ilean Rowe, Daniel Louis, James Harris. BS, MS, U. Ky., Lexington, 1943. With Linden H.S., Mich., 1944—45, Henderson State Tchrs. Coll., Arkadelphia, Ark., 1945—49; owner Plaza Shop, Madison, Ind., 1964—80. Officer Ark. Bus. Tchrs., 1946. Pres. LWV, Madison, Ind., 1964; benefactor Jewish Fedn., Louisville, 1998—2005, Cmty. Found., Madison, Ind., 2000—05. Fellow, U. Ky. Bus. Sch., 1944, U. Ky., 2005; scholar, 2004. Mem.: AAUW (pres. 1965), Ind. Jewish Hist. Soc. (bd. mem. 1974—94, Irma Rosenthal Frankenstein award 2005, Disting. Svc. award). Democrat. Jewish. Home: Apt 1022 5100 US Hwy 42 Louisville KY 40241-6046

WEINBERG, H. BARBARA, art historian, educator, curator; b. NYC, Jan. 23, 1942; d. Max and Evelyn Kallman; m. Michael B. Weinberg, Aug. 30, 1964. AB, Barnard Coll., 1962; MA, Columbia U., NYC, 1964, PhD, 1972. Prof. art history Queens Coll. Grad. Sch., CUNY, 1972—94; curator Am. paintings sculpture Met. Mus. Art., NYC, 1990—98; Alice Pratt Brown curator Am. paintings sculpture Met. Mus. Art, NYC, 1998—. Author: The Decorative Work of John La Farge, 1977, The American Pupils of Jean-Léon Gérome, 1984, The Lure of Paris: Nineteenth-Century American Painters and Their French Teachers, 1991, Thomas Eakins and the Metropolitan Museum of Art, 1994, co-author: American Impressionism and Realism: The Painting of Modern Life, 1885-1915, 1994, American Drawings and Watercolors in The Metropolitan Museum of Art: John Singer Sargent, 2000, John Singer Sargent in The Metropolitan Museum Art, 2000, Childe Hassam, American Impressionist, 2004, Americans in Paris, 1860-1900, 2006; mem. editl. bd. Am. Art Jour., 1984—. Mem.: Phi Beta Kappa. Office: Met Mus Art 1000 5th Ave New York NY 10028-0198 Office Phone: 212-879-5500.

WEINBERG, LILA SHAFFER, editor, writer; d. Sam and Blanche (Hyman) Shaffer; m. Arthur Weinberg, Jan. 25, 1953; children: Hedy, Anita, Wendy Clare. Editor Ziff-Davis Pub. Co., 1944—53; assoc. chief manuscript editor jours. U. Chgo. Press, 1966—80, sr. manuscript editor books, 1980—98; mem. faculty Sch. for New Learning DePaul U., Chgo., 1973—89. Vis. faculty continuing edn. programs U. Chgo., 1984-92. Author: (with A. Weinberg) The Muckrakers, 1961 (selected for White House Library 1963), Verdicts Out of Court, 1963, Instead of Violence, 1963, Passport to Utopia, 1968, Some Dissenting Voices, 1970, Clarence Darrow: A Sentimental Rebel, 1980; contbr. articles and revs. to various publs. Bd. dirs. Hillel Found. U. Chgo., 1988-96. Recipient Friends of Lit. award Chgo. Found. Lit., 1980, Social Justice award Darrow Community Ctr., 1980, Disting. Body of Work award Friends of Midwest Authors, 1987, John Peter Altgeld Freedom of Speech award, 2001. Mem. Soc. Midland Authors (dir. 1977-83, pres. 1983-85, Best Midwest Biography award 1980), ACLU, Clarence Darrow Commemorative Com., YIVO, Authors' League, Work in Progress. Home: 5421 S Cornell Ave Chicago IL 60615-5646

WEINBERG, LORETTA, state legislator; b. NYC, Feb. 6, 1935; d. Murray Isaacs and Raya Hamilton; m. Irwin S. Weinberg, July 25, 1960 (dec. Feb. 1999); children: Daniel J., Francine S. BA, UCLA, 1956. Former aide NJ Assemblyman D. Bennett Mazur, Trenton; mem. NJ Assembly, Trenton, 1992—, NJ State Senate, 2005—. Mem. Teaneck Coun., 1990-94. Recipient Legis. Leadership award No. NJ Chiropractic Assn., 1992, Woman of Achievement award Bus. and Profl. Women's Club of East Bergen, 1993, Carrie Chapman Catt award No. NJ NOW, 1997, Ethical Recognition award Ethical Culture Soc. of Bergen County, 1998, Barbara Boggs Sigmund award, Women's Polit. Caucus, 2004, Legis. Recognition, Consumers for Civil Justice; named Citizen of Yr. NJ Jewish War Vets., Legislator of Yr., NJ State Nurse's Assn., 2000; named Women in Govt., Good Housekeeping, 2005. Mem. Nat. Coun. Jewish Women (life mem., Hannah G. Solomon award 1995, Disting. Achievement award Women's Commn.). Democrat. Jewish. Office: State of NJ 545 Cedar Ln Teaneck NJ 07666-1740 Office Phone: 201-928-0100. Business E-Mail: senweinberg@njleg.org.

WEINBERG, LOUISE, law educator, writer; b. NYC; m. Steven Weinberg; 1 child, Elizabeth. AB summa cum laude, Cornell U.; JD, Harvard U., 1969, LLM, 1974. Bar: Mass. Sr. law clk. Hon. Chas. E. Wyzanski, Jr., Boston, 1971-72; assoc. in law Bingham, Dana & Gould, Boston, 1969-72; teaching fellow Harvard Law Sch., Boston, 1972-74; lectr. law Brandeis U., Waltham, Mass., 1974; assoc. prof. law Suffolk U., Boston, 1974-76, prof., 1977-80; vis. assoc. prof. law Stanford U., Palo Alto, Calif., 1976-77; vis. prof. law Sch. Law, U. Tex., Austin, 1979, prof. law, 1980-84, Thompson prof. law, 1984-90, Andrews and Kurth prof. law, 1990-92, Fulbright and Jaworski regents rsch. prof., 1991-92, Angus G. Wynne, Sr. prof., 1992-97, Fondren chair faculty excellence, 1995—, Eugene R. Smith Centennial rsch. prof. law, 1993-97, holder William B. Bates chair, 1997—. Vis. scholar Hebrew U., Jerusalem, 1989; Forum fellow World Econ. Forum, Davos, Switzerland, 1995—; pub. spkr., lectr. in field. Author: Federal Courts: Judicial Federalism and Judicial Power, 1994; co-author: Conflict of Laws, 1990, 2d edit., 2002; contbr. chpts. to books, articles to profl. jours. Bd. dirs. Ballet Austin, 1986-88, Austin Coun. on Fgn. Affairs, 1985—, Austin Civil War Round Table, 1998—. Recipient Disting. Educator award Tex. Exes Assn., 1996. Mem.: Supreme Ct. Hist. Soc., Am. Constn. Soc., Maritime Law Assn., Tex. Asian C. of C., Assn. Am. Law Schs. (chair sect. on conflict laws 1991—93, chair sect. on fed. cts. 2003—04, acting chair 2004—05, chair sect. admiralty 2005—06), The Philos. Soc. Tex., Am. Law Inst. (consultative com. complex litigation 1989—93, consultative com. enterprise liability 1990—95, adv. group fed. judicial code revision project 1996—2001, mems.' consultative group, intellectual property 2004—, internat. jurisdiction and judgments 2004—, aggregate litigation 2006—), Phi Kappa Phi, Phi Beta Kappa. Office: U Tex Sch Law 727 Dean Keeton St Austin TX 78705-3224 Business E-Mail: lweinberg@law.utexas.edu.

WEINBERG, MYRL, medical association administrator; Exec. Assn. for Retarded Citizens, Joseph P. Kennedy, Jr. Found., Am. Diabetes Assn.; pres. Nat. Health Coun. Office: Nat Health Coun 1730 M St NW Ste 500 Washington DC 20036

WEINBERG, RUTHMARIE LOUISE, special education educator, researcher; b. Woodbury, N.J., Feb. 9, 1953; d. Louis Albert Schopfer, Sr. and Ruth Marie (Bilse) Schopfer; m. Robert Weinberg, June 26, 1982. AS Human Svcs., Camden County Coll., 1973; BA Tchr. of the Handicapped, Glassboro State Coll., 1975; MA Sch. Adminstrn., Rowan U., 1998. Cert. tchr. of the handicapped 1975, supr. 1998, prin./supr. 1998. Supr. of cottage life, tchr. and supr. of mentally retarded Am. Inst. Mental Studies, Vineland, NJ, 1975—79; spl. edn. tchr. Haddon Heights (N.J.) H.S., 1979—. Girl Scout leader for clients Am. Inst. Mental Studies, Vineland, NJ, 1975—79, supr. summer recreation program, 1975—79. Recipient Gov.'s award for excellence in tchg., Gov. Florio and Commr. John Ellis, N.J., 1991. Mem.: Haddon Heights Ednl. Assn., N.J. Ednl. Assn., Nat. Ednl. Assn. Avocations: music, dance, sports, nature walks, exploring new horizons. Home: 422 Austin Ave Barrington NJ 08007 Office: Haddon Heights Jr & Sr HS 301 2nd Ave Haddon Heights NJ 08035-1407

WEINBERGER, ADRIENNE, artist, art appraiser; b. Washington, Apr. 28, 1948; d. Samuel Aaron and Marta (Barta) W.; m. Edward Herschel Egelman, Mar. 21, 1980; children: Serge Maurice, Liana Dora. BA, Goucher Coll., 1970; MEd, Johns Hopkins U., 1973; MA, Northwestern U., 1974; postgrad., Sch. of Mus. of Fine Arts, 1979-82. Lectr. Art Inst. Chgo., 1973-75; lectr., docent trainer Mus. of Fine Arts, Boston, 1978-82; mus. educator Yale Ctr. Brit. Art, Yale Art Gallery, New Haven, 1984-86; instr., coord. alumni coll. Albertus Magnus Coll., New Haven, 1987-89; instr. Mpls. C.C., 1989-94; propr. Studio 95, Edina, Minn., 1995-99, Charlottesville, Va., 1999—. Panelist New England Regional Confs., Am. Assn. Muss., Mass., Conn., 1976-77; workshop leader New Haven Green Found., New Haven 350 Com., 1987-88; pres. Cmty. Art Fund., 2000—. Author, illustrator: New Haven Coloring Book, 1987, CulchaMan Visits New York City, 1988, CulchaMan Visits Washinton, D.C., 1988. Participant Edina Futures Forum, 1990; dir. Edina-Woodhill Assn., 1997—98; active State Affirmative Action Commn., 1996—98; del. chair, mem. nominating com. Dem. State Conv., St. Paul, 1994, del., chair Rochester, 1996, St. Cloud, 1998, del. Norfolk, 2000, Roanoke, 2004; active Dem. State Exec. Com., 1997—99; sec. Dem.-Farmer Labor Party, Edina, Eden Prairie, 1990—94, chair, 1994—96, treas. 3d Congl. Dist., 1996—99; active Dem. State Cen. Com., 1994—99, Albemarle County Dem. Com., 2005; adv. bd. gifted edn. svcs. Edina Pub. Schs., 1993—96; bd. dirs. Consortium for Advancement of Arts, 2001—03, Leadership Charlottesville, 2002—, Northwestern U. Alumni Club, 2003—, Northwestern U. Club Va. Recipient Juror's award Berkshire Mus., Pittsfield, Mass., 1981, New Haven Brush & Palette Club, 1985, Edina Art Ctr., 1991. Mem. Am. Soc. Appraisers (accredited sr. appraiser; sec. Twin Cities chpt. 1997-99, pres. Richmond chpt. 2000-01, 3d v.p. Richmond chpt. 2001-03), Charlottesville C. of C. (Amb. Corps. 2000, legis. action com. 2000—2006, legal action com. 2000-2006), U. Va. Art Mus.(vol. bd. 2003-), Leadership Charlottesville Alumni Assn. (bd. dirs. 2006—), Northwestern U. Alumni Club Va. (bd. dirs. 2003—), Alumni Assn. Avocations: travel, reading, politics. Office: Studio 95 3100 Waverly Dr Charlottesville VA 22901-9576 Office Phone: 434-297-0694. Business E-Mail: studio95@guanotronic.com.

WEINBERGER, JANE DALTON, retired nurse, volunteer; b. Maine, Mar. 29, 1919; m. Caspar Willard Weinberger, Aug. 16, 1942; children: Caspar Willard and Arlin Weinberger. Student, U. Maine, 1936-38, student, 1938-41; BSN, Somerville Hosp. Sch. Nursing, 1940; postgrad., Boston U., 1941. Reg. nurse Calif. Vol. St. Luke's Hosp., San Francisco, 1947-77; owner, editor, author Windswept House Pubs., Mt. Desert, Maine, 1984—; ret., 1999—. Author: (Children's Books) The Little Ones, Lemon Drop, Tabitha Jones, Wee Peter Puffin, Fanny and Sarah, Cory the Cormorant, That's What Counts, VIM: A Very Important Mouse, Mrs. Witherspoon's Eagles; (adult biography): As Ever, Canned Plums and Other Vissitudes of Life. Bd. Trustees Nat. Symphony Assn., 1970—, Capitol Children's Mus., 1970-85; bd. dirs. Folger Shakespeare Libr., 1970—, chmn. 1981-86; founding mem. New Globe Theatre, London, 1999; bd. vols. D.C. Gen. Hosp., 1970-75, hon. bd. mem. 1975—; bd. dirs. Jackson Lab. (Cancer Rsch. Inst.), 1984—, mem. Internat. Coun. Jackson Lab., 1990—; mem. women's com. Washington Performing Arts Soc., 1970—; sponsor The Internat. Hospitality Soc., Washington, 1970-85, other vol. orgns.; Rep. coms. campaign mgr., San Francisco, 1964-68. 2nd lt. U.S. Army Nurse Corps, 1942-43, PTO. Recipient Svc. to Humanity award, Alpha chpt. Chi Eta Phi, 1974, Deborah Morton award, Westbrook (Maine) Coll., 1992. Mem. Maine Media Women, Nat. News Women, Maine Writers and Pubs. Alliance, Jr. Army Navy Guild (hon.), Soc of Sponsors USN, The Century Club of Calif., Congressional Club (Washington), Pal's Club, (Sacramento,Calif.). Episcopalian. Avocations: cooking, gardening, swimming, boating, collecting glass paperweights, minature porcelain boxes. Office: Windswept House PO Box 159 Mount Desert ME 04660-0159

WEINBERGER, LILLA GILBRECH, bookseller; b. Pasadena, Calif., Oct. 8, 1941; d. George Herbert and Lilla Dorothy Gilbrech; m. Christopher Pearce (div. 1969); m. Andrew Harvey Weinberger, Nov. 10, 1974; children: Gideon, Tobias. Student, Occidental Coll., 1959-61; BA in Comparative Lit., U. Calif., Berkeley, 1963. Child care officer London County Coun., 1964-65; libr. asst. Huntington Libr., San Marino, Calif., 1965-66; rschr., edn. pub. welfare rsch. svc. Libr. Congress, Washington, 1966-72; freelance photographer, writer LA, 1973-84; dir., cmty. coord. Women's Svc. Ctr., Pittsfield, Mass., 1984-91; co-owner Reader's Books, Sonoma, Calif., 1991—. Pres., bd. dir. Women's Statewide Legis. Network, Mass., 1988-90; mem. Gov.'s Commn. on the Status of Women, Mass., 1987-91. Recipient poetry award Bantam Doubleday Dell Pub., 1994; named Woman of Yr. Berkshire County Women's Groups, 1990, Indy award Sonoma County Ind., 1998. Mem. No. Calif. Ind. Booksellers Assn. (former sec., exec. bd. dir.), Am. Booksellers Assn. (former bd. dir.), Sonoma Valley Cmty. Health Ctr. (vice-chair bd. dirs.). Democrat. Office: Readers Books 130 E Napa St Sonoma CA 95476-6709

WEINEL, PAMELA JEAN, nurse administrator; b. Olney, Md., Dec. 14, 1956; d. Clarence Dawson and Jean Elizabeth (Woodward) Weinel; m. Nathan Richards, May 6, 1995. AA in Edn., Montgomery Coll., Rockville, Md., 1976; BSN, U. Md., Balt., 1986, M in sci. Adminstrn., 1998; MBA, U. Balt., 2001. Oncology staff nurse George Washington U. Med. Ctr., Washington, 1986—88, Bone Marrow Transplant coord., 1988—90; adminstrv. coord. Walter Reed Army Med Ctr., Washington, 1990—98; advice nurse Kaiser Permanente, Kensington, Md., 1991—98; rsch. program mgr. Clin. Rsch. and Protocol Mgmt. Office U. Md. Greenebaum Cancer Ctr., Balt., 1999—2002; IVF nurse Shady Grove Fertility Ctr., Rockville, Md., 2003—04; project mgr. Social and Sci. Sys., Inc. CODA Divsn. FDA MedSun Project, Silver Spring, Md., 2004—06; nurse cons. FDA Ctr. for Med. Devices and Radiol. Health, 2006—; faculty assoc., grad. nursing program U. Md., Rockville, 2006. Cons., mem. People to People Internat., Russia, 1992, Vietnam, 93; roundtable facilitator Internat. BMT Symposium, Omaha, 1992; lectr. Contemporary Forums, San Francisco, 1994. Contbr., 1993—94. Sponsor for adults Resurrection Roman Cath. Ch., Burtonsville, Md., 1997—2000, CCD instr. 7th grade, 2001—02. Named One of Outstanding Young Women in Am., 1997. Mem.: Oncology Nursing Soc. (Bone Marrow Transplant spl. interest group), Am. Soc. for Reproductive Medicine, Sigma Iota Epsilon, Phi Kappa Phi, Phi Theta Kappa, Sigma Theta Tau (scholar 1996). Avocations: travel, photography, writing, Tae Kwon Do. Office: FDA CDRH ODE Divsn DRARD 9200 Corporate Blvd 320D Rockville MD 20850 Business E-Mail: pam.weinel@fda.hhs.gov.

WEINER, ANNE LEE, social worker; b. Chelsea-Malden, Mass., Nov. 2, 1932; d. Nathan and Edith E. (Sigel) Varnick; m. Paul J. Weiner, Jan. 25, 1959; children: Berdine R., Ronald M. Diploma in med. sec., Chandler Sch. for Women, 1952; AA in Social Work, Middlesex C.C., 1974; BSW, Salem Coll., 1987. Med. sec. New Eng. Med. - Boston U. Hosp., Boston, 1952-1960; social worker Lynn-Union Hosp., Lynn, Mass., 1968-1982; home care social worker Mass. Elder Care, Peabody, 1982-1987; dir. Dept. Social Work Logan Homes, Wingate Homes, Hill Haven Homes, Mass., 1987-99. Mem. region bd. Hadassah steering com. social work, Hadassah Boston and Fla. Atlantic region; pres. Chessed, 2003—06; active Hist. Soc. Peabody; organizer social work support groups North Shore, Mass., 2003—04. Personal E-mail: lighthouse@bellsouth.net.

WEINER, CLAIRE MURIEL, freelance writer; b. Bronx, N.Y., Dec. 18, 1951; d. David and Norma (Berry) W. BA, U. Miami, Coral Gables, Fla., 1973; MA, U. Md., 1980. Pub. rels. specialist Hialeah Recreation Div., Hialeah, Fla., 1974-77; freelance writer North Miami Beach, 1977-78, Germantown, Md., 1989—, Montgomery County, Md., 1981—. Govt. affairs liaison for new ednl. data base co. being formed, Montgomery County, 1982—; acting comm. dir. Ednl. Info. Svcs., 1996—. Contbr. articles to local newspapers; contbr. travel articles to profl. jours, mags. Active membership com. newsletter Greater Miami Jewish Fedn., 1974-77; charter mem. Women for Today chpt. B'nai B'rith Women, Washington, 1985-89. Named Hon. Citizen of Historic Williamsburg. Life fellow Am. Biog. Inst. Rsch. Assn., World Lit. Acad.; mem. NAFE, Internat. Platform Assn., Nat. Trust for Hist. Preservation. Jewish. Home: 18828 Sky Blue Cir Germantown MD 20874-5398

WEINER, FERNE, psychologist; b. N.Y.C., June 14, 1928; d. Irving Kapp and Peggy (Finkelstein) Hessberg; m. Howard Weiner, July 20, 1948; children: Irving Kenneth, Laurie. BA, Skidmore Coll., 1965; MA, Sarah Lawrence Coll., 1971; PhD, U. Hawaii, 1975. Lic. psychologist, Calif., Hawaii. Asst. prof. West Oahu Coll. U. Hawaii, Honolulu, 1975—77; staff psychologist Cmty. Guidance Clinic, Manchester, Conn., 1978—83; chief cons. psychologist Consultation and Evaluation Ctr., Meriden, Conn., 1984—85; psychologist cons. Disability Determination Svcs., Hartford, Conn., 1986—87, Honolulu, 1988—; police psychologist Honolulu Police Dept., 1988. Pvt. practice, Greenwich, Conn., 1983-87, Honolulu, 1988—; cons. Adopt-A-Sch. Project, Honolulu, 1991-94; interviewer, therapist Sexual Abuse Treatment Team, Manchester, 1979-83; cons., trainer Conn. schs., day care, ch. groups, 1979-87. Contbr. articles to profl. jours. Active Disaster Assistance Mgmt. Team, Hawaii, 1994-95; v.p., sec. Queens Court at Kapiolani Bd., Honolulu, 1992-95; admissions rep. Hawaii Sarah Lawrence Coll., Honolulu, 1970-80; cons. to adoptees search Orphan Voyage, Conn., 1980-87; mentor Girl Scout Coun. Am., Oahu, 1993-94. Mem. Am. Psychol. Assn. (clin. psychotherapy and neuropsychology divsn.), Hawaii Psychol. Assn., Nat. Registry Health Svcs. Providers, Outrigger Canoe Club, Shiley Sports Club. Democrat. Jewish. Avocations: aerobics, interior design, property renovation, gourmet cooking, travel. Personal E-mail: wferne1@san.rr.com.

WEINER, JENNIFER AGNES, writer; b. De Ridder, La., Mar. 28, 1970; m. Adam Bonin, Oct. 27, 2001; 1 child, Lucy Jane. BA summa cum laude, Princeton Univ., 1991. Intern Poynter Inst. for Media Studies, St. Petersburg, Fla., 1991; reporter Centre Daily Times, State College, Pa., 1991—94; features writer Lexington Herald-Leader, Ky., 1994—95; gen. assignment, features reporter Phila. Inquirer, 1995—2001. Contbg. editor: Mademoiselle Mag., 1998—; author: (novels) Good in Bed, 2001 (NY Times Bestseller list), In Her Shoes, 2002 (made into feature movie starring Cameron Diaz), Little Earthquakes, 2004 (Best Women's Fiction Novel nominee, Romantic Times Mag., Publishers Weekly Bestseller paperback list, 2005), Goodnight Nobody, 2005 (Publishers Weekly Bestseller hardcover list, 2005). Office: c/o Joanna Pulcini PO Box 1829 Bridgehampton NY 11932 Business E-Mail: jen@jenniferweiner.com.*

WEINER, KAREN COLBY (KAREN LYNN COLBY), psychologist, lawyer; b. Oak Park, Ill., Oct. 28, 1943; d. Leonard L. and Mildred Irene (Berman) Colby; m. J. Laevin Weiner, July 26, 1964; children: Joel Laevin, Doren Robin, Anthony Justin. BA, Mich. State U., East Lansing, 1964; JD, U. Detroit, 1977, MA, 1986, PhD, 1988. Bar: Mich. 1977, D.C. 1978. Speech therapist Oak Park Sch. Dist., 1965-68; law clk. justice G. Mennen Williams Mich. Supreme Ct., Lansing, 1977-79; assoc. Dickinson, Wright, Moon, Van Dusen & Freeman, Detroit, 1979-83; intern in psychology Detroit Psychiat. Inst., 1986-88; psychologist Northland Clinic, Southfield, Mich., 1987-88; postdoctoral intern Wyandotte (Mich.) Hosp. and Health Ctr., 1988-90; psychologist Counseling Assocs., Southfield, 1988—2004, dir. psychol. svcs., quality assurance coord., 1991-99; bd. dirs. Mich. Psychoanalytic Inst. Found., 2004—. Hearing panelist Atty. Discipline Bd., Detroit, 1982-95; hearing referee Mich. Civil Rights Commn., Detroit, 1983-91; mem. Mich. Bd. Psychology, 1999—, vice chair, 2004—; adj. prof. U. Detroit Mercy, 2001-03; ethics com. Internat. Coaching Fedn., 2003—; adj. prof. Inst. Life Coach Tng., 2004—. Author: The Little Book of Ethics for Coaches, 2004; contbr. articles to profl. jours. Adv. bd. Mich. chpt. Anti-Defamation League, 1981-90. Fellow Mich. Psychol. Assn. (mem. ethics com. 1992—2000, chmn. legis. com. 1993, chmn. ethics com. 1997-99); mem. APA, Internat. Coaching Fedn. (ethics and stds. com.), Mich. Soc. for Psychoanalytic Psychology (pres. 1995-97, sec. 1991-92, treas. 1992-94), Women Lawyers Assn. Mich. (pres. 1981-82, pres. Found. 1982-83), Mich. Bar Assn. (chmn. spl. com. for expansion under represented groups in law 1980-83). Jewish. Home: 2501 Long Lake Rd West Bloomfield MI 48323 Office: 29260 Franklin Rd Ste 115 Southfield MI 48034-1144 Office Phone: 248-353-1020. Personal E-mail: drkcw@comcast.net.

WEINER, MINA RIEUR, museum consultant, civic worker; b. NYC, Oct. 20, 1936; d. Charles Isaac and Gertrude (Levinson) Rieur; m. Stephen A. Weiner, Sept. 1, 1958; children: Karen Lessall Goss, Paul Rieur (dec.), James Rieur. BA, Cornell U., 1957; MA, NYU, 1987. Life mem. Cornell Univ. Coun., Ithaca, NY, 1958—; guest curator N.Y. Hist. Soc., 1995—96, 1999—2004; dir. N.Y. City Fire Mus., 1995-98; exhbn. cons. Norman Rockwell Mus., 1995-97; guest curator Mus. City of N.Y., 1988-94, spl. projects coord., 1990-95; guest curator South St. Seaport Mus., 1989; exhbn. cons. NYC Bar Assn., 2005—; cons. Inst. Classical Architecture and Classical Am., 2006. Mem. exec. bd. dirs. LWV, Port Washington, N.Y., 1970-73; trustee Sands Point Civic Assn., N.Y., 1975-79; creator, coord. Vols. in Port Schs., Port Washington, 1976-78; mem. Sands Point Planning Bd., 1977-81; bd. dirs. Port Washington Pub. Schs., 1979-85, v.p., 1979-81, pres., 1981-85; mem. State Legis. Network, N.Y. State Sch. Bds. Assn., 1980-85; founder Port Washington Youth Coun.; mem. adv. bd. dirs. Mediation Alternative Project, Edn. Assistance Ctr., Port Washington, 1981-86; cons. Cow Neck Peninsula Hist. Soc., 1987-92, N.Y.C. Bar Assn., 2005—. Editor: Survey on Port Washington Pub. Schs., 1972-73; contbr. articles to profl. jours. Avocations: reading, tennis. Home: 190 Harbor Rd Port Washington NY 11050-2636

WEINER, SANDRA SAMUEL, critical care nurse, consultant; b. NYC, Jan. 12, 1947; d. Herbert A. and Ruth (Wallerstein) Samuel; m. Neil D. Weiner, June 15, 1969 (div. June 1980); 1 child, Jaime Michelle. BS in Nursing, SUNY, Buffalo, 1968; cert. in critical care, Golden West Coll., 1982; postgrad., UCLA, U. West L.A. Sch. Law, 1992—95. RN, Pa., Calif. Staff nurse N.Y. Hosp.-Cornell Med. Ctr., 1968-69; head nurse med.-surg. nursing Abington (Pa.) Hosp., 1969; assoc. prof. Sch. Nursing, U. Pa., Phila., 1970; instr. nursing Coll. Med. Assts., Long Beach, Calif., 1971-72; surg. staff nurse Med. Ctr. of Tarzana, Calif., 1978-79, Cedars-Sinai Med. Ctr., L.A., 1979-81; supr. recovery rm. Beverly Hills Med. Ctr., L.A., 1981-92; post anesthesia care unit nurse Westside Hosp., 1992-96, Midway Hosp., Beverly Hills, Calif., 1996-99, Encino (Calif.) - Tarzana Med. Ctr., 1996—, Four Seasons Surgery Ctr., 2001—. Med. cons. RJA & Assocs., Beverly Hills, Calif., 1984-92; instr. CPR, L.A., 1986-95. Mem. women's aux. Ctr. Theater Group Vols., L.A., 1986-94, Maple Ctr., Beverly HIlls, 1987-96. Mem. ANA, Am. Soc. Post-Anesthesia Nursing, Am. Assn. Critical Care Nurses, Heart and Lung Assn., Post Anesthesia Nurses Assn., U.S. Ski Assn. Democrat. Jewish. Avocations: skiing, aerobics, travel, theater, ballet. Home: 12633 Moorpark St Studio City CA 91604-4537 Office Phone: 818-793-2050.

WEINER, WENDY L(OU), elementary school educator, writer; b. Milw., Jan. 2, 1961; d. Kenneth J. and Jessie M. Weiner. AA, U. Wis. Washington County, West Bend; BS, MS, U. Wis., U. Wis., Milw., 1993; prin. lic., Marian Coll. Cert. nat. cert. early childhood edn. Nat. Bd. Profl. Tchg. Standards, tchr. Wis. Tchr. Milw. Pub. Schs. Contbr. articles to profl. jours. Mem. Milw. Pub. Mus. Tchr. Adv. Coun., TV and Tech. Com., Vision and Tech. Com., Learning Mag.'s Student Best Adv. Coun. Recipient Presdl. Award in Sci. Tchg. Excellence, AT&T Recognition in Sci. Tchg. Excellence, Wis. Aerospace Educator of Yr., Milw. Tchr. of Yr., Grad. Last Decade award U. Wis. Milw. Alumni Assn., Warner Cable-Tchg. Creativity with Cable award, Excellence in Sci. Tchg. award. Wis. Elem. Sci. Tchrs. Assn., Nat. Urban Tech. in Edn. award Coun. Great City Schs., Sen. Herb Kohl Tchr. Achievement award, Ameritech-Wis. Bell Gold Tchr. Recognition award, Presdl. award for elem. sci. tchg. excellence; grantee Greater Mil. Edn. Trust, Wis. Space Grant Consortium/NASA, NSF. Mem. PTA, Wis. Aerospace Edn. Assn. (instr. mag. adviser, Sam's Club Tchr. of Yr.), YMCA-Young Astronauts, Nat. Arbor Day Assn., NSTA, Wis. Elem. Tchrs. Assn., Milw. Kindergarten Assn., Wis. Secondary Sci. Assn., Wis. Assn. Sch. Adminstrs., Milw. Reading Assn., Midwest Devel. Corp., Assn. Presdl. Awardees in Sci., Soc. for Elem. Presdl. Awardees, Coun. Elem. Sci. Internat., Civil Air Patrol (sr. officer). Avocations: crafts, walking. Office: Parkview Sch 10825 W Villard Milwaukee WI 53225 Personal E-mail: wlw23@prodigy.net.

WEINER-HEUSCHKEL, SYDELL, theater educator; b. N.Y.C., Feb. 18, 1947; d. Milton A. and Janet (Kay) Horowitz; children: Jason, Emily; m. Rex Heuschkel, Sept. 3, 1992. BA, SUNY, Binghamton, 1968; MA, Calif. State U., L.A., 1974; postgrad., Yale U., 1968—70; PhD, NYU, 1986; MS, Calif. State U., Dominguez Hills, 1996. Lic. marriage and family therapist. Prof. theater arts, chmn. dept., dir. honors program Calif. State U. Dominguez Hills, Carson, 1984—. Guest lectr. Calif. Inst. Arts, 1988. Appeared in play Vikings, Grove Shakespeare Festival, 1988; dir. Plaza Suite, Brea (Calif.) Civic Theatre, 1982, Gypsy, Carson Civic Light Opera, 1990, Same Time Next Year, Muckehthaler, 1987, Slow Dance on the Killing Ground, Alternative Repertory Theatre, 1989; co-author: School and Community Theater Problems: A Handbook for Survival, 1978, (software) Public Speaking, 1991; contbr. Am. Jour. Psychotherapy, 1997, Jour. Clin. Psychology, 1998. Yale U. fellow, 1969; recipient Lyle Gibson Disting. Tchr. award, 1989. Mem. Screen Actors Guild, Am. Fedn. TV and Radio Artists, Calif. State U. Women's Coun. (treas. 1989-91), Phi Kappa Phi. Office Phone: 310-243-3534. Business E-Mail: sweiner@csudh.edu.

WEINGAND, DARLENE ERNA, librarian, educator; b. Oak Park, Ill., Aug. 13, 1937; d. Edward Emil and Erna (Heidenway) W.; m. Wayne Anthony Weston, Sept. 7, 1957 (div. June 1976); children: Kathleen Mary, Lynda Anne, Judith Diane, Barbara Jeanne; m. James Elberling, May 1977 (div. 1980); m. Roger Paul Couture, Apr. 7, 1984. BA in History and English, Elmhurst Coll., 1972; MALS, Rosary Coll., 1973; PhD in Adult Edn./Libr. Sci., U. Minn., 1980. Asst. prof. U. Wis., Madison, 1981-86, assoc. prof., 1986-92, prof., 1992-99, prof. emerita, 1999—, SLIS acting dir., 1991, summer 86, SLIS asst. dir., 1990-94, adminstr. SLIS Continuing Edn. Svcs., 1981-99; adj. prof. and mem. affiliate grad. faculty. U. Hawaii Manoa, Manoa, 1999—2006. Cons. in mktg., continuing edn., libr. futures, info. issues, and mgmt., 1980—; invited mentor Snowbird Leadership Inst., 1990, 92; vis. fellow Curtin U. Tech. Perth, Australia, 1990; Fulbright lectr. U. Iceland, 1988; lectr. 2d World Conf. on Continuing Edn. for Libr. and Info. Sci., Barcelona, 1993, Internat. Fedn. Libr. Assn. Author: Customer Svc. Excellence: A Concise Guide for Librarians, 1997, Future Driven Library Marketing, 1998, Marketing/Planning Library and Information Services, 1999, 4th edit., 2001, Administration of the Small Public Library, 4th edit., 2001, Budgeting and the political Process in Libraries, Simulation Games, 1992 (with others), Connections: Literacy and Cultural Heritage: Lessons from Iceland, 1992, Managing Today's Public Library: Blueprint for Change, 1994, author (with others) Continuing Professional Education and Internat. Fed. of Libr. Assoc.: Past, Present, and a Vision for the Future, 1992; contbr. articles to profl. jours. Recipient excellence award Nat. Univ. Continuing Edn. Assn., 1989, Econ. and Cmty. Devel. award, 1989, outanding achievement in audio applications award Internat. Teleconferencing Assn., 1991, LITA/Libr. Hi-Tech award, 1996, disting. alumna award Dominican U., 1998; Russia project fellow Assn. Libr. and Info. Sci., 1994. Mem. ALA, AAUW, Wis. Assn. for Adult and Continuing Edn., Beta Phi Mu. E-mail: weingand@lava.net.

WEINGARTEN, KAETHE, clinical psychologist; b. Bklyn., Jan. 13, 1947; d. Victor and Violet (Brown) W.; m. Hilary Goddard Worthen, June 15, 1969; children: Benjamin, Miranda Eve. BA, Smith Coll., 1969; PhD in Arts and Sci., Harvard U., 1974. Pvt. practice, Newton, Mass., 1974—; asst. prof. dept. psychology Wellesley (Mass.) Coll., 1975-78; rsch. assoc. Wellesley (Mass.) Coll. Ctr. for Rsch. on Women, 1975-79; founder, dir. family tng. program, Dept. Psychiatry Judge Baker Children's Ctr. Harvard Med. Sch., Boston, 1979-87, teaching assoc., cons. Dept. Psychiatry, 1979-94; asst. prof. psychology dept. psychiatry Harvard Med. Sch., Boston, 1994—2000, assoc. prof. psychology, 2000—. Co-dir. program systemic therapies Family Inst. Cambridge, Watertown, Mass., 1982—90, co-dir. program narrative therapies, 1991—; presenter for psychol., med. and family therapy orgns. Author: The Mother's Voice: Strengthening Intimacy in Families, 1994, Common Shock: Witnessing Violence Every Day, 2003, How We Are Harmed, How We Heal, 2003; co-author: Sooner or Later: The Timing of Parenthood in Adult Lives, 1982; editor: Cultural Resistance: Challenging Beliefs About Men, Women and Therapy, 1995; editl. bd. Family Process, Jour. of Feminist Family Therapy; contbr. articles to profl. jours. Fellow Mass. Psychol. Assn.; mem. APA, Am. Family Therapy Acad. (bd. dirs.). Office: Family Inst of Cambridge 51 Kondazian St Watertown MA 02472-2830

WEINGARTEN, RHONDA (RANDI WEINGARTEN), labor union administrator, lawyer; b. NYC, Dec. 18, 1957; d. Gabriel and Edith (Appelbaum) W. BS, Cornell U., 1980; JD cum laude, Benjamin N. Cardozo Sch. Law, 1983. Bar: N.Y. 1984, U.S. Dist. Ct. (so. and ea. dists.) N.Y. 1984. Legis. asst. Labor Com. N.Y. State Senate, Albany, 1979-80; assoc. Stroock, Stroock and Lavan, NYC, 1983-86; counsel to pres. United Fedn. Tchrs., NYC, 1986—98; tchr. Clara Barton HS, Brooklyn, 1991—97; asst. sec. United Fedn. Teachers, NYC, 1995, treas., 1997, pres., 1998—; v.p. Am. Fedn. Teachers. Bd. dirs. N.Y. State United Teachers; adj. instr. Cardozo Sch. Law, N.Y.C., 1986; mem. Mayor Bloomberg's transition com., N.Y.C., 2001. Mediator Bklyn. Mediation Ctr. Victim Services Agy., 1981-82 (outstanding achievement award, 1981); mem. N.Y. Com. Safety and Health, 1986, Park Slope Safe Homes Project, 1984—. Dem. Nat. Com.; bd. dirs. Justice Resource Ctr., Coun. for Unity, N.Y. Com. on Occupational Safety and Health, N.Y. Region Anti-Defamation League, United Way Greater N.Y., Internat. Rescue Com. Mem. ABA (labor and employment sect.), N.Y. State Bar Assn., Women's Bar Assn., Council N.Y. Law Assocs., Cardozo Sch. Law Alumni Assn. (treas., bd. dirs. 1983—). Democrat. Jewish. Avocations: gardening, running, music, theater. Office: United Fedn Tchrs 52 Broadway New York NY 10004

WEINGOLD, MARJORIE NASSAU, retired special education educator; b. Hartford, Conn., Oct. 27, 1929; d. Joseph Nassau and Ruth Klein; m. Allan Byrne Weingold, Dec. 21, 1952; children: Beth Plavner, Roberta Greenberg, Matthew, Daniel. BA, Oberlin Coll., 1951; MA, Columbia U., 1952; cert. diagnostic therapeutic reading disability, George Washington U., 1974. Elem. edn. tchr. Hartsdale (NY) Bd. Edn., 1952—55, USN Sch. Sys., San Juan, PR, 1958—59; presch. tchr. White Plains (NY) Sch. Sys., 1959—60; diagnostician, remediator George Washington U. Reading Ctr., Washington, 1978—83. Pvt. tutor, Potomac, Md., 1981—90. Founder, chmn. Com. for George Washington Med. Ctr., Washington, 1992—2003; trustee George Washington U. Club, Washington, 1998—2003; chmn. host com. ACOG, Washington, 1984—88; mem. women's bd. George Washington Hosp., Washington, 1997—2006; trustee Contemporary Am. Theater, 1999—, Luther Brady Art Gallery, George Washington U., 2002—; bd. dirs. Literacy Vols. Am.,

Washington, 1988—97, Watergate East Inc., Washington, 1996—2001. Mem.: Heritage Soc. George Washington U. Avocations: reading, travel, tennis, swimming. Home: 2510 Virginia Ave NW Washington DC 20037-1904

WEINHOLD, LINDA LILLIAN, psychologist, researcher; b. Reading, Pa., Nov. 9, 1948; d. Aaron Zerbe Weinhold and Nancy Louise (Spotts) Weikel; m. Jack Wayne Prisk, Jan. 21, 1967 (div. 1969). Lic. practical nurse, AVTS, 1970; BS, Penn State U., 1975; MS, C.W. Post Ctr., 1982; PhD, Fordham U., 1986. LPN; cert. profl. counselor. Instr., asst. prof. Gettysburg (Pa.) Coll., 1985-86; post doc. fellow John Hopkins U., Balt., 1986-88; staff fellow NIH NIDA Addiction Rsch. Ctr., Balt., 1988-93; cons. NIH NIDA Medications Devel., Rockville, Md., 1993-94; soc. sci. program coord. Med. Ctr. NIDA Rsch., Washington, 1994-95; cons. The Clin. Cons. Group Antech, Inc., Balt., 1995; substance abuse counselor Hope Village, Inc., Washington, 1996—. Various presentations. Mem. Am. Psychological Assn., Phi Kappa Phi, Sigma Xi. Democrat. Avocations: singing, dance, painting, photography, reading. Home: 2611 Bowen Rd SE Apt 203 Washington DC 20020-6623 Office: Hope Village Inc 2840 Langston Pl SE Washington DC 20020-3241

WEINKAUF, MARY LOUISE STANLEY, retired clergywoman, educator; b. Eau Claire, Wis., Sept. 22, 1938; d. Joseph Michael and Marie Barbara (Holzinger) Stanley; m. Alan D. Weinkauf, Oct. 12, 1962 (dec. Nov. 2000); children: Stephen, Xanti. BA, Wis. State U., 1961; MA, U. Tenn., 1962, PhD, 1966; MDiv, Luth. Sch. Theology, Chgo., 1993. Grad. asst., instr. U. Tenn., 1961-66; asst. prof. English Adrian Coll., 1966-69; prof., head dept. English Dakota Wesleyan U., Mitchell, SD, 1969-89; instr. Columbia Coll., 1989-91. Pastor Calvary Evang. Luth. Ch., Siloa Luth. Ch., Ontonagon Faith, White Pine, Mich., Gowrie, Iowa. Author: Hard-Boiled Heretic, 1994, Sermons in Science Fiction, 1994, Murder Most Poetic, 1996. Trustee The Ednl. Found., 1986-90; bd. dirs. Ontonagon County Habitat for Humanity, 1995-97, Lakeland Area Food Pantry, 2000—; mem. bd. Luth. Campus Ministry for Wis. and Upper Mich., 1996—2002, Fortune Lake Bible Camp, 2003-04. Mem. AAUW (divsn. pres. 1978-80), Nat. Coun. Tchrs. English, S.D. Coun. Tchrs. English, Sci. Fiction Rsch. Assn., Popular Culture Assn., Milton Soc., S.D. Poetry Soc. (pres. 1982-83), Delta Kappa Gamma (pres. local chpt., mem. state bd. 1972-89, state v.p. 1979-83, state pres. 1983-85), Sigma Tau Delta, Pi Kappa Delta, Phi Kappa Phi. E-mail: woodwork@nnex.net.

WEINNER, BRENDA LYNNE, director, education educator, special education educator; d. William and Alna Purves; m. Paul Karl Weinner, Oct. 21, 1983; children: Karl William James, Rebekah Ann Camille, Victoria Elizabeth Grace. BS, Ea. Mich. U., Ypsilanti, 1982; postgrad., Mich. State U., East Lansing, 1987, Atlantic Bapt. Bible Coll., Richmond, Va., 2005. Cert. spl. edn. tchr. Mich., 1982, music edn. Mich., 1982, elem. edn. tchr. Mich., 1982. Tchr. severely multiply impaired Mich. Sch. Blind, Lansing, 1984—87; tchr. 1st grade and music HOPE Acad., 1987—88; tchr. spl. edn., cons. New Covenant Christian Sch., 1990—91; dir. spl. edn. and fine arts dept. Capitol City Bapt. Sch., Holt, 1996—; tchr., mgr., designer Paper Trends, 2004—; prof. edn. Capitol City Bapt. Bible Inst., 2005—. Master tchr., reading cons., tchr. trainer Riggs Inst., Beaverton, Oreg., 1990—2006; choir dir. Home Sch. Singers, Lansing, 1988—93; curriculum cons. Area Home Schoolers, 1988—96; choir dir., organist Berean Bapt. Ch., 1991—2001; instrumentalist, soloist Capitol City Bapt. Ch., 2002—; reading curriculum cons., tchr. trainer Whitmore Lake Elem. Sch., 1997—2001, Elmhurst Elem. Sch., Lansing, 1998—2001; curriculum devel. North Liberty Christian Sch., Ind., 1999—2001. Music dir. Nursing Home Programs, Lansing, 1996—2006; home bldg. Cross Treks Missions, Tijuana, Mexico, 1995—2005. Mem.: Mich. Assn. Christian Schs., Am. Guild English Handbell Ringers. Avocations: scrapbooks, piano, reading, golf, camping. Office: Capitol City Baptist School 5100 W Willoughby Rd Holt MI 48842 Office Phone: 517-694-6122. E-mail: ccbsmrsweinner@yahoo.com.

WEINROTH, LOIS L., lawyer; b. NYC, 1941; AB cum laude, Barnard Coll., 1963; LLB cum laude, Columbia U., 1968. Bar: N.Y. 1968. Ptnr., co-adminstrv. ptnr., structured fin. practice area Stroock & Stroock & Lavan LLP, N.Y.C. Office: Stroock & Stroock & Lavan LLP 180 Maiden Ln New York NY 10038-4982 Office Phone: 212-806-5868. Office Fax: 212-806-6006. Business E-Mail: lweinroth@stroock.com.

WEINSTEIN, ANNA, music educator; d. Naum and Revekka Goykhman; m. David Weinstein, Dec. 30, 1972; children: Yana, Anthony. BS (hon.), Melitopol Pedagogical Inst., Melitopol, Ukraine, 1992. Lic. tchr. Ohio. Piano instr., pvt. piano tchr. Sch. Creative and Performing Arts, Cin., 1999—. Music dir. Russian Amateur Theatre JCC, Cin., 2004—06; judge World Piano Competition. Musician: (teaching piano) Regional Judge For World Piano Competition. Music dir. Jewish Cmty. Ctr., Cin., 2004—06. Recipient Talent award for tchg., World Piano Competition, 2000, Bronze medal, 2001. Mem.: Am. Music Scholarship Assn. Office: Sch Creative and Performing Arts 1310 Sycamore St Cincinnati OH 45202 Office Phone: 513-363-8000.

WEINSTEIN, DEENA, sociology professor; b. NY; BS, Queens Coll., N.Y., 1964; MA, Case Western Res. U., Cleve., 1967; PhD, Purdue U., West Lafayette, Ind. Prof. sociology DePaul U., 0971—. Author: Bureaucratic Opposition: Challenging Abuses in the Workplace, 1979, Postmodern(ized) Simmel, 1993, Heavy Metal: The Music and Its Culture, 2006. Office Phone: 773-325-7824. Office Fax: 773-325-7821.

WEINSTEIN, JOYCE, artist; b. June 7, 1931; d. Sidney and Rose (Bier) W.; m. Stanley Boxer, Nov. 28, 1952. Student, CCNY, 1948-50, Art Students League, 1948-52. Exec. coord. Women in Arts Found., Inc., 1975-79, 81-82, coord. bd., 1983-87. One-person shows include Perdalma Gallery, N.Y.C., 1953-56, L.I. U., Bklyn., 1969, U. Calif.-Santa Cruz, 1969, T. Bortolazzo Gallery, Santa Barbara, Calif., 1972, Dorsky Gallery, N.Y.C., 1972, 74, Galerie Ariadne, N.Y.C., 1975, Gloria Cortella Gallery, N.Y.C., 1976, Meredith Long Contemporary Gallery, N.Y.C., 1978, 79, 88-90, Martin Gerard Gallery, Edmonton, Alta., Can., 1981, 82, 84, Galerie Wentzel, Cologne, Fed. Republic of Germany, 1982, 87, Haber Theodore Gallery, N.Y.C., 1983, 95, Gallery One, Toronto, Ont., Can., 1983, 2002, Paul Kuhn Gallery, Calgary, 1985, Eva Cohn Gallery, Highland Park, Ill., 1985, Meredith Long & Co., Houston, 1988, 90, Alena Adlung Gallery, N.Y.C., 1989, Flanders Contemporary Art, Mpls., 1999, 2005, Harmon-Meek Gallery, Naples, Fla., 2000, Gallery One, Toronto, 2002, Flanders Contemporary Art, Mpls., 2005; exhibited in group shows at Marlborough Gallery, N.Y.C., 1968, Bula Mus. Art, Calcutta, India, 1970, Phoenix Gallery, N.Y.C., 1988, Provident Nat. Bank, 1988, Alena Adlung Gallery, 1989, 90, Edmonton Art Mus., 1975, 77, 83, 85, 89, Rose Fried Gallery, N.Y.C., 1970, Hudson River Mus., 1971, Dorsky Gallery, 1972, 94, Suffolk Mus., Stony Brook, N.Y., 1972, N.Y. Cultural Ctr., 1973, Stamford (Conn.) Mus., 1973, Landmark Gallery, N.Y.C., 1974, Women's Interart Ctr., N.Y.C., 1974, 75, 78, New Sch. Social Rsch., N.Y.C., 1975, Bklyn. Mus., 1975, Galerie Ariadne, 1975, Mus. of Modern Art, N.Y.C., 1981, The Queens Mus. N.Y., 1984, The Centre de Creacio Contemporania, Barcelona, Spain, 1987, Fairleigh Dickinson U., Hackensack, N.J., 1976, Gloria Cortella, Inc., 1976, Northeastern U., Boston, 1977, Lehigh (Pa.) U., 1977, Meredith Long Contemporary Gallery, 1977, 78, 79, 80, Galerie Wentzel, 1981-85, Martin Gerard Gallery, 1981-84, Gallery One, 1983, 84, Haber Theodore Gallery, 1982-85, Jerald Melberg Gallery, Charlotte, N.C., 1984, Richard Green Gallery, N.Y.C., 1986, Rosel Art Fair, Basel Switzerland, 1986, Meredith Long & Co., 1988-90, Broome St. Gallery, N.Y.C., 1991, 97, Andre Zarre Gallery, N.Y.C., 1990, Cork Gallery, N.Y.C., 1990, Chgo. Internat. Art Exbn., 1990, Queens Coll., N.Y.C., 1991, Miami Art Fair, 1993, Bklyn. Botanic Gardens, 1994, Dorothy Blau Gallery, Bay Harbor Islands, Fla., 1997-98, Harmon-Meek Gallery, Naples, Fla., 1998-99, Flanders Contemporary Art, Mpls., 1999, 2005, Hubert Gallery, N.Y.C., 2003; represented in permanent collections: Pa. Acad. Fine Arts, N.J. State Mus., Ciba-Geigy Corp., New Sch. Social Rsch., Bula Mus. Art, U. Calif., Mus. Modern Art, N.Y.C., McMullen Gallery, Edmonton, Ga., De Spisset Mus., U. Santa Clara, Edmonton Art Gallery Mus., The Hines Collection, Boston, others; represented by Flanders Contemporary Art, Mpls., Gallery One, Toronto, Yellow Bird Gallery, Newburg, NY, Amy Simon Fine Art, Westport, Conn. Recipient Lambert Fund award Pa. Acad. Fine Arts, 1955, Susan B. Anthony award NOW, 1983. Home: 46 Fox Hill Rd Ancramdale NY 12503-5311 Office Phone: 518-329-0614. Personal E-mail: weinsteinjoyce@aol.com.

WEINSTEIN, MARGO, lawyer; b. Chgo., July 25, 1960; BA, Yale Univ., 1982; JD, Northwestern Univ., 1987. Bar: Ill. 1988. Law clerk U.S. Ct. Appeals 7th circuit, Ill., 1987—88; ptnr. Sonnenschein Nath & Rosenthal, Chicago. Named to Order of the Coif, Northwestern Univ. Mem.: Women's Bar Assn. Ill. Office: Sonnenschein Nath & Rosenthal Sears Tower Suite 8000 233 S Wacker Dr Chicago IL 60606

WEINSTEIN, MARIE PASTORE, psychologist; b. N.Y.C., Oct. 3, 1940; d. Edward and Sarah (Mancuso) Pastore; children: Arielle Rebecca Dorros, Damon Alexander. BA in Polit. Sci. and Lit., Ind. U.; MS in Psychology, L.I. U.; PhD in Ednl. Psychology, CCNY, 1986. Cert. sch. psychologist; lic. psychologist, N.Y. Pvt. practice, 1978—; dir., adminstr. learning ctr. Guidance Ctr. Flatbush, Bklyn., 1978—82; clin. team coord./psychologist Lorge Upper and Lower Sch., N.Y.C., 1982—85; psychologist devel. disabilities ctr. Roosevelt Hosp., N.Y.C., 1985—87; chief psychologist Blueberry Treatment Ctrs., Bklyn., 1987—89; cons. psychologist Safe Space, N.Y.C., 1989—2003; law guardian Panel of Forensic Psychologists, 1994—. Cons. psychologist United Cerebral Palsy Hearst Presch., Bklyn., 1988-89, Charles Drew Day Ctr., Queens Village, N.Y., 1982-85, Warbasse Nursery Sch., Bklyn., 1981-85, YWCA Montessori Sch., 1993-94; adj. asst. prof. Baruch Coll. CUNY, 1989; pvt. practice, Bklyn.; rsch. cons. Children's TV Workshop, N.Y.C., 1979; clin. cons. Bedford Stuyvesant Mental Health Ctr., Bklyn., 1990, Youth Counseling League, N.Y.C., 1993; cons. dist. 2 N.Y.C. Bd. Edn., 1988; guest lectr. Met. Hosp. Dept. Psychiatry, N.Y.C., 1988, Dist. 3 Bd. Edn., 1993; edn. cons. Lit. Vols. N.Y., 1974-76. Contbg. author to children's ency., 1970. Fellow Am. Orthopsychiat. Assn. (program com. 1990—); mem. APA, Internat. Congress on Child Abuse and Neglect, Manhattan Fedn. Child and Adolescent Svcs. Office: 26 Court St Ste 2112 Brooklyn NY 11242-1121

WEINSTEIN, RUTH JOSEPH, lawyer; b. N.Y.C., Mar. 26, 1933; d. David Arthur and Toby (Landau) J.; m. Marvin Walter Weinstein, June 3, 1962; children: Rosalyn S., Steven M., Barbara E. AB magna cum laude, Radcliffe Coll., 1954; LLB, Harvard U., 1957. Bar: N.Y. 1957, D.C. 1966. Assoc. Hale Russell & Gray and predecessor firms, N.Y.C., 1957-66, ptnr., 1966-85, Winthrop Stimson Putnam & Roberts, N.Y.C., 1985-98, sr. counsel, 1999-2000, Pillsbury Winthrop, N.Y.C., 2000—05, Pillsbury Winthrop Shaw Pittman LLP, N.Y.C., 2005—. Chairperson Practising Law Inst. Forum, N.Y.C., 1978. Mem. sch. bd. Union Free Sch. Dist. 5, Rye Town, N.Y., 1976-79, pres., 1978-79. Mem. ABA, Assn. of Bar of City of N.Y. (com. on Aeronautics Assn. 1987-90). Avocations: boating, skiing. Home: 156 Ridgecrest Rd Stamford CT 06903 Personal E-mail: rjwein@sbcglobal.net.

WEINSTEIN, SHARON SCHLEIN, corporate communications executive, educator; b. Newark, Apr. 15, 1942; d. Louis Charles and Ruth Margaret (Franzblau) Schlein; m. Elliott Henry Weinstein, May 7, 1978. BA, U. Pa., 1964; MA, New Sch. for Social Rsch., N.Y.C., 1985. Sr. editor Merrill Lynch, N.Y.C., 1972-74; pub. rels. officer Chase Manhattan Bank, N.Y.C., 1974-79; mgr. corp. communication Sanford C. Berstein & Co., N.Y.C., 1980-83; v.p. corp. affairs Nat. Westminster Bancorp, N.Y.C., 1983-95; dir. corp. comms. Nat. Securities Cleaning Corp., N.Y.C., 1995-98; asst. v.p. corp. comm. Guardian Life Ins. Co., N.Y.C., 1998—2002; comms. mgr. Zurich N.Am., N.Y.C., 2002—. Adj. asst. prof. NYU, 1988—. Home: 161 W 15th St New York NY 10011-6720

WEINSTOCK, DEBORAH, psychologist; b. Montevideo, Uruguay, Mar. 20, 1958; came to U.S., 1977; d. David and Olga (Betech) Slomiuc; children: Ezra, Freide, Shlomo. BA in Psychology, Touro Coll., 1997, postgrad. in sch. psychology and sch. adminstrn. Proficiency in Am. Sign Language, Spanish, and Yiddish. Interpreter N.Y.C. Bd. Edn., 1996—; bilingual sch. psychologist Com. on Spl. Edn. N.Y.C. Dept of Edn., 2003—. Mem. APA, NASP, APT, NYASP. Avocations: Karate, guitar. Home: Apt 5B 1270 E 18th St Brooklyn NY 11230-5340 Personal E-mail: debrawein@yahoo.com.

WEINSTOCK RAD, KATHERYN LOUISE, music educator; d. Henry Robert and Jeanallan Joyce Weinstock; m. Jalal Rad, Aug. 23, 1993; 1 child, Jason Shyaan Rad. Aux. music study, U. Birmingham, England, 1983—84, U. Keele, Staffordshire/Newcastle, 1983—84; MusB, U. Tulsa, 1985, MusM, 1988. Cert. Okla. Tchr. Cert. State of Okla., 1988. Cellist Signature Symphony Okla. Sinfonia, Tulsa, 1982—, Tulsa (Okla.) Philharm., 1982—; adj. cello instr. Northeastern State U, Tahlequah, Okla., 1988—90; music tchr. Tulsa Pub. Sch., 1989—96; dir. of strings, tchr. Broken Arrow (Okla.) Pub. Sch., 1996—99; music curriclum coord. Tulsa Pub. Sch., 1999—2002; music coord. Tulsa Cmty. Music Sch., 2003; adj. cello instr. Performing Arts Ctr. Edn. Tulsa C.C., 2000—; fine arts coord. Cent. High Sch. Acad. Arts, 2003—. Mem. bd. fine arts task force Tulsa Pub. Sch., 1996—; adv. Barthelmes Conservatory, 2000—02; bd. mem. Chamber Music Tulsa(Okla.), 2001—; performer cellist Tulsa Philharmonic, Tulsa Signature Symphony, Okla. City Philharmonic; prin. cellist Light Opera Orchestra of Okla.; performer has performed with many classical, pop/rock, jazz and blues artists, including a live performance on NPR. Grandstand, judge Vet. Day Parade, Tulsa, 1999—2002; mem. Tulsa Now Task Force - Mayor Bill Fortune, 2002—; fundraiser raised over one half million dollars music programs Tulsa Pub. Schs. Recipient Tchr. Touching Tomorrow Award, Tulsa Pub. Sch., 1996, Superior Civilian Svc. Award, Dept. of the U.S. Army, 1999—2000; grantee VH-1 save the Music Grant, VH-1, 2001, U.S. Dept. Edn., 2002, music study at Internat. Music Workshops in Graz, Austria, Found. for Tchrs., 2004. Mem.: Hyetchka, Am. Federation of Musicians. Avocations: playing cello in variety of genres, cooking, exercise. Home: 630 Pioneer Rd Sapulpa OK 74066 Office: Tulsa Central HS Acad Fine Arts 3101 W Edison Tulsa OK 74127 Office Phone: 918-833-8492. Business E-Mail: radka@tulsaschools.org.

WEINTRAUB, ELLEN L., commissioner; b. 1957; m. Bill Dauster; 3 children. BA cum laude, Yale Coll.; JD, Harvard Law Sch. Bar: NY, DC and Supreme Court. Chair Fed. Election Commn., Washington, 2002—03, vice chair, 2004—; of counsel Perkins Coie, Political Law Group; litigator Cahill Gordon & Reindel; counsel Com. on Stds. of Ofcl. Conduct for U.S. Ho. Reps. Office: 999 E St NW Washington DC 20463

WEIR, CATHERINE GRANT, psychology educator; b. Balt., Oct. 5, 1943; d. Gilvary Preston and Royce (Barnett) Grant; m. Robert Struthers Weir, Sept. 23, 1967 (div. 1987), m. Edward H. Parker, 2001; 1 child, Peter. BA, Colo. Coll., 1965; PhD, U. London, 1970. Prof. psychology Univ. Coll., U. London, 1970-90, Rockford (Ill.) Coll., 1990-91, Colo. Coll., Colorado Springs, 1991—. Contbr. articles to profl. jours. Marshall Commn. scholar, 1965-68; Woodrow Wilson fellow, 1965. Mem. APA, Brit. Psychol. Soc., Assn. Psychological Sci., Internat. Soc. Infant Studies. Office: Colo Coll 14 E Cache La Poudre St Colorado Springs CO 80903-3298 Business E-Mail: cweir@coloradocollege.edu.

WEIR, DAME GILLIAN CONSTANCE, musician; b. Martinborough, New Zealand, Jan. 17, 1941; d. Cecil Alexander and Clarice M. Foy (Bignell) W. Grad., Royal Coll. Music, London, 1965; Mus D (hon.), U. Victoria of Wellington, New Zealand, 1983; DLitt (hon.), Huddersfield U., 1997; Mus D (hon.), Hull U., 1999, Exeter U., 2001; Doctorate (hon.), U. Ctrl. Eng., 2001; Mus D (hon.), Leicester Univ., 2003; MusD (hon.), U. Aberdeen, Scotland, 2004. Artist-in-residence numerous univs. including Yale U, Washington U., St. Louis, U. Western Australia, Johns Hopkins U., 2005, others; vis. lectr. Royal No. Coll. Music, Manchester, Eng., 1974-89; vis. prof. organ Royal Acad. Music, London, 1997-98; Prince Consort prof. Royal Coll. of Music, London, 1999—; spkr. BBC programs on music and performance; subject of Melvyn Bragg's TV documentary South Bank Show, 2000; apptd. Disting Artist-in-residence Peabody Inst., John Hopkins U., Balt., 2005. Concert appearances with leading Brit. Orchs. and Boston Orch., Seattle Orch., Australian ABC Orch., Wurttemberg Chamber and other fgn. orch.; appeared in major internat. festivals including Edinburgh, Flanders, Aldeburgh, Bath, Proms, Europalia; appeared at concert halls including Royal Festival Hall, Royal Albert Hall, Lincoln Ctr., NY, Sydney Opera House; numerous radio and TV appearances in Brit. and world-wide including Royal Festival Hall Jubilee; organ cons.; adjudicator internat. competitions; contbr. The Messiaen Companion, 1995; contbr. articles to profl. jour.; recs. include complete organ works of Olivier Messiaen, others; TV documentary film on career, 1982, BBC TV programs The King of Instruments, 1989. Decorated comdr., dame comdr. Order Brit. Empire; recipient Turnovsky award 1985, Evening Std. award for outstanding solo performance, 1998-99, Lifetime Achievement award The Link Found., London, 2005; winner 1st prize St. Albans Internat. Organ Competition, 1964. Fellow Royal Coll. Organists (hon., mem. coun. 1977—, mem. exec. 1981-85, pres. 1994-96, 1st Woman pres.), Royal Can. Coll. Organists (hon.), Royal Coll. Music (London); mem. Royal Acad. Music (hon.), Inc. Soc. Musicians (1st woman pres. 1992-93), Albert Schweitzer Assn. (Silver medal 1998). Office: care Karen McFarlane Artists 2385 Fenwood Rd Cleveland OH 44118-3803 Office Phone: 216-397-3345. Personal E-mail: gillianweir@gillianweir.com.

WEIR, RITA MARY, retail executive; b. Ft. Dix, N.J., Aug. 28, 1955; d. Rynart Barnabas and Teruko (Yokota) Haling; m. Mark Adrian Weir, Oct. 25, 1986. AA, Austin C.C., 1988; BA summa cum laude, Granite State Coll., 1990; MBA cum laude, N.H. Coll., 1997. Store mgr. KFC, El Paso and Austin, Tex., 1973-86; asst. mgr. Stuart Shaines, Portsmouth, NH, 1989-90; mkt. fasion mechandiser Wal-Mart, 1991—. Bd. govs. Seacoast Learning Ctr., 2005—06. Mem. NAFE, Am. Bus. Women's Assn. (pres. 1992-93, bull. chair 1993-94, hospitality com. 1993-94, 94-95, membership com. 1993-94, 94-95, Woman of Yr. 1993, 95, v.p. 1994-95, chpt. del. 1994-95, program chair 1995), Top Ten 2000 (nominating chair 2006), Phi Theta Kappa (leadership seacoast). Avocations: reading, walking, travel. Home: 44 Lamprey Ln Lee NH 03824-6552 Office: Wal-Mart 702 SW 8th St Bentonville AR 72716 Office Phone: 479-273-8800 51320.

WEIR, SONJA ANN, artist; b. Hazleton, Pa., Oct. 12, 1934; d. Stephen and Anna (Prehatny) Tatusko; m. Richard Clayton Weir, Jan. 14, 1956; children: Robert, Carl, Donna, Lisa, and Nancy. Studied with Mary Ellen Silkotch, 1963—83; student, Art Students League, N.Y.C., 1985—87. Artist Knickerbocker Toy Co., Middlesex, NJ, 1980; represented by Agora Gallery, Soho, NY, 1999. Tchr. adult art edn. in Jointure, NJ., 2001-03; guest spkr. career day Bridgewater H.S., 1993-94. One-woman shows include Johnson & Johnson, Piscataway, N.J., 1992, Stillman, N.J., 2003 (Meml. award), Somerset County Libr., Bridgewater, N.J., 1992—94, Manville (N.J.) Pub. Libr., 1994—99, exhibited in group shows at Raritan Valley Art Assn., 1982—83, 1995, 1998 (Best in Show award, 1983, 2d prize, 1995, 1st pl. for oil, 1998), Ariel Gallery, N.Y.C., 1991, Am. Artists Profl. League, 1991, 1994, Barren Art Ctr., Woodbridge, N.J., 1993, Agora Gallery, N.Y.C., 1995—99, 2001, Somerset County Libr., 1998—99, Am. Artists Profl. League, 1999, Atrium Gallery, Morristown, N.J., 2001, Somerset County Cultural and Heritage Gallery, 2003, Johnson & Johnson, Stillman, N.J., 2003, Children's Specialized Hosp., N.J., 2003, Barrons Art Ctr., Woodbridge, N.J., 2003, Art Extraordinaire, Bernardsville, N.J., 2004, N.J. Soc. Watercolor Show, 2004 (award of excellence, 2004), Amsterdam Whitney Gallery, N.Y.C., 2005, Taiwan Ctr., Flushing, NY, 2006, Lamington Ch., Bedminster, NJ, 2006, Represented in permanent collections N.W.B. Bank of South Bound Brook, N.J., Summit Bank; featured in Artis Apectrum mag., vol. 11/6, 1999, Star Ledger, 2000; Star Ledger, 2003, Chronicle, Bound Brook, N.J., 2003. Judge Essex Watercolor Soc. Recipient Peter Matulavage award Salmagundi Club, Meml. award Am. Artists Profl. League, NYC, Samual Lightment Meml. award Salmagundi Club, 2003; Sr. Artist Exhbn. Citation award, Bd. of Chosen Freeholders in Somerset County, NJ, 2005. Fellow: Nat. Am. Artists Profl. League (v.p. N.J. chpt. 1988—91, publicity com. 1988—91, show chmn. 1989—91, pres. N.J. chpt. 1992—95, editor newsletter 1992—99, nat. exec. bd. 1998—2000, show chmn. 2001—04, nat. pres. 2001—05); mem.: Am. Artists Profl. League (nat. pres. 2001—05), Miniature Art Soc. Fla., Nat. Miniature Assn. (assoc.), Raritan Valley Arts Assn. (pres. 1982—84), Nat. Mus. Women in the Arts. Home: 25 Madison St South Bound Brook NJ 08880-1244

WEIRES, SALLY L., paralegal; b. L.A., Calif., June 14, 1941; d. Henry L. and Sarah L. (Minor) Walleck; m. Thomas C. Cockle (div. 1979); children: Susan, John; m. Norman E. Weires, June 11, 1988; children: Todd, Scott, Kathleen, Dean. Student, UCLA, 1960—62; BA, Dominican U., San Rafael, Calif., 1980. Cert.: Calif. (paralegal). Legal asst. Prieston Law Firm, San Rafael, 1994—99, Green & Green Law, San Rafael, 1999—2002, Tishgart Law Firm, Greenbrae, Calif., 2002—04, Glenn, Sites & Reeder, Madras, Oreg., 2005—. Intern Prison Law Office, San Quentin, Calif., 1980—81. Sec., clk. Marin County Grand Jury, San Rafael, 1975—76; receptionist, dispatcher Sr. Coun. on Aging, Richmond, Oreg., 2005—06; monitor ct.-ordered visitation Apple Family Ctr. Mem.: Oreg. Paralegal Assn. Democrat. Roman Catholic. Avocations: traveling in RV, reading, walking. Office: Glenn Sites & Reeder LLP 205 SE 5th St Madras OR 97741

WEIR-SOLEY, DONNA AZA, language educator, writer; b. Bois Content, St. Catherine, Jamaica, Oct. 17, 1965; arrived in U.S., 1983; d. Kenneth Weir and Daisy Mae McCalla; m. Norman Washington Soley, Dec. 24, 1995; children: Chenjerai C., Iyah, Kai. BA in English summa cum laude, Hunter Coll., NYC, 1990; MA in English, U. Calif., Berkeley, 1993, PhD in English, 2000. Grad. instr. dept. English U. Calif., Berkeley, 1994—99; asst. prof. English Fla. Internat. U., North Miami, 1999—. Mem. adv. bd. African New World studies Fla. Internat. U., 2000—, affiliate instr. Honors Coll., 2004—. Author: (poetry book) First Rain, 2006. Mem.: African Lits. Assn., Assn. Caribbean Women Writers & Scholars, Caribbean Studies Assn. Democrat. Christian. Avocations: performance poetry, weightlifting, singing gospel music. Office: Fla State Univ Coll Arts/Scis 3000 NE 151st St Miami FL 33181 Business E-Mail: weirsole@flu.edu.

WEIS, JUDITH SHULMAN, biology professor; b. N.Y.C., May 29, 1941; d. Saul B. and Pearl (Cooper) Shulman; m. Peddrick Weis; children: Jennifer, Eric. BA, Cornell U., 1962; MS, NYU, 1964, PhD, 1967. Lectr. CUNY, 1964-67; asst. prof. Rutgers U., Newark, 1967-71, assoc. prof., 1971-76, prof., 1976—. Congl. sci. fellow U.S. Senate, Washington, 1983—84; mem. grant rev. panel NSF, Washington, 1976—82, program dir., 1988—90; mem. rev. panel EPA, 1984—92; mem. NOAA Nat. Sea Grant Rev. Panel, 1997—; vis. scientist EPA Lab., Gulf Breeze, Fla., 1992. Mem. marine bd. NAS, 1991—94. Grantee NOAA, 1977—, N.J. EPA Rsch., 1978-79, 81-83, N.J. Marine Scis. Consortium Rsch., 1987—; NSF fellow, 1962-64, U.S. Geol. Survey, 1996—, NSF, 1998—. Mem.: NOW (pres. Essex County 1972), AAAS (chair biology sect. 1999), Assn. Women in Sci. (councilor 2002—05), Ecol. Soc. Am., Estuarine Rsch. Fedn., Soc. Environ. Toxicology and Chemistry (bd. dirs. 1990—93), Am. Inst. Biol. Scis. (bd. dirs. 1986—88, 1989—91, 1997—99, pres.-elect 2000—01, pres. 2001), Sierra Club (bd. dirs. N.J. chpt. 1986—88). Avocations: choral singing, swimming, light opera. Office: Rutgers U Dept Biol Scis Newark NJ 07102 Business E-Mail: jweis@andromeda.rutgers.edu.

WEIS, KRISTINE ERICA, secondary school educator; b. Aurora, Ill., Feb. 23, 1975; d. Jack Weis and Terri Moe. BA, North Ctrl. Coll., Naperville, Ill.; MA in Ednl. Leadership, U. St. Francis, Joliet, Ill. Tchr. Plainfield (Ill.) Ctrl. H.S., 1998—. Office: Plainfield Central High School 611 West Fort Beggs Drive Plainfield IL 60544 Office Phone: 815-436-3200.

WEIS, MARGARET EDITH, writer, editor; b. Independence, Mo., Mar. 16, 1948; d. George Edward and Francis Irene (Reed) W.; m. Robert William Baldwin, Aug. 22, 1970 (div. 1981); children: David William (dec.), Elizabeth Lynn; m. Donald Bayne Stewart Perrin, 1996 (div. 2003). BA in Creative Writing, U. Mo., 1966-70. Proofreader Herald Pub. House, Independence, Mo., 1970-73, advt. dir., 1973-82; dir. div. Independence Press, 1977-82; editor TSR Inc, Lake Geneva, Wis., 1982-86. Freelance writer; owner Sovereign Press, Williams Bay, Wis., margaretweis.com, Margaret Weis

Prodns., Ltd. Author: (short story) The Test of the Twins, 1984, (books) The Endless Catacombs, 1984, Tower of Midnight Dreams, 1984, (with Tracy Hickman) The Dragonlance Chronicles, Vols. 1-3, 1984, 85, Dragonlance Legends, Vols. 1-3, 1985, 86, The Darksword Trilogy, Vols. 1-3, 1987, (with Roger Moore) Riddle of The Griffon, 1985, (under Margaret Baldwin) The Boys Who Saved The Children, 1982, Kisses of Death, 1983, (with Pat O'Brien) Wanted: Frank and Jesse James, The Real Story, 1981, (with Janet Pack) Children of The Holocaust, 1986, My First Thanksgiving, 1983, (with Gary Pack) Computer Graphics, 1984, Robots and Robotics, 1984, (short story) The Thirty Nine Buttons, 1987, (novella) (with Tracy Hickman) The Legacy, 1987, Wanna Bet?, 1987; editor: The Art of Dungeons and Dragons, 1985, Leaves of the Inn of the Last Home, 1987, The Art of Dragonlance, 1987, Dragonlance Tales, vol. 1, 2, 3, 1987, (with Tracy Hickman) The Rose of the Prophet, 1989, (with Tracy Hickman) Death's Gate, vol. 1, 1990, vols. 2, 3, 4, 5, 6, 7, Star of the Guardian, vol. 1, The Lost King, 1990, King's Test vol. 2, 1991, King's Sacrifice Vol. 3, 1991, Ghost Legion Vol. 4, 1991, Dragons of Summer Flame, 1996, (with Don Perrin), Doom Brigade, 1997, Mag Force 7 novels, 3 vols., The Soulforge, 1998, Brothers in Arms, 1999, (with Tracy Hickman) Starshield, Vols. 1-3, 1997, Legacy of the Darksword, 1997, War of Souls, 3 vols., 2000; editor: Kender, Gully Dwarves and Gnomes, 1989, Love and War, 1991, Reign of Istar, 1993, Dragons of War, 1996, Dragons of Chaos, 1997, Relics and Omens, 1998, Sovereign Stone Role-Playing Games, 1999, Sovereign Stone novels, (with Tracy Hickman) vol. 1, Well of Darkness, 2000, vol. 2, Guardians of the Lost, 2001, Journey Into the Void, vol. 3, 2003, Mistress of Dragons, 2003, Draconian Measures, 2000, Dragon's Son, 2004, Ashes and Amber, 2004, Master of Dragons, 2005, Ashes and Iron, 2005, (with Tracy Hickman) The Lost Chronicles, vol. 1 Dragons of the Dwarven Depths. Named to Writer's Hall of Fame, 2002, Adventure Gaming Hall of Fame, 2002; recipient Origins award, 2001. Avocations: role-playing games, flyball, agility. Office Phone: 262-248-2419.

WEISBART, JENNIFER RACHEL, mathematician, educator; b. Canoga Park, Calif., July 16, 1970; d. Monica Berit Stellert-Weisbart and Marvin Weisbart, Carolyn Weisbart (Stepmother). BA, U. Wash., 1994; tchr. credential, Ctrl. Wash. U., 1997; MEd (hon.), U. Wash., 2003; postgrad., Claremont U., Calif., 2006—. Cert. tchr. math, spl. edn., & elem. Wash., 1997, math. tchr. Calif., 2001, edn.specialist mild/moderate disabilities instruction Calif., 2001. 9-12 math, 3rd grade tchr. Chabad Cheder K-12 Sch., Seattle, 1998—99; 7-8 math and sci., 10-12 spl. edn. tchr. Northshore Sch. Dist., Bothell, Wash., 1999—2001; 9-12 math and sci., spl. edn. tchr. Oxnard (Calif.) Union H.S. Dist., 2001—02; 9-12 math. spl. edn. tchr. Walnut (Calif.) Valley Unified Sch. Dist., 2003; devel. math prof. Mt. San Antonio Coll., 2004—; 8-10 math. tchr. for ELL students Fontana (Calif.) United Sch. Dist., 2004—. Instr. math. Fullerton Coll., 2005; presenter in field. Mem.: Coun. for Exceptional Children, ASCD, Am. Math. Assn. 2 Yr. Colls., Nat. Coun. Tchrs. Math., Kappa Delta Pi, Pi Lambda Theta. Avocation: dance. Office Phone: 909-357-5000 ext 7370. E-mail: weisjr@fusd.net.

WEISBERG, BARBARA, writer, editor; b. Phila., Apr. 3, 1946; d. Samuel Weisberg and Miriam (Rosenbach) Weisberg-Kind; m. David Black, June 20, 1996; stepchildren: Susannah Black, Tobiah Black. BA, U. Pa., 1968; MPhil, Yale U., 1972; MFA, Bklyn. Coll., 1992. Prodr., writer Harcourt Brace Jovanovich, N.Y.C., 1973-77; writer WNET/Thirteen, N.Y.C., 1977-80; assoc. dir. TV devel. Scholastic, N.Y.C., 1980-83; dir. TV devel. Consumer Reports, Mt. Vernon, N.Y., 1983-87; writer, prodr., editor N.Y.C., 1987—. Poetry editor Bklyn. Review (lit. jour.), 1992. Co-creator (TV series) Charles in Charge, 1984; author: (children's books) Susan B. Anthony, 1989, Coronado's Golden Quest, 1993, Knights and Castles, 1994, (adult nonfiction) Talking to the Dead, Kate and Maggie Fox and the Rise of Spiritualism, 2004, paperback, 2005. Mem. Hadassah, 1970—, NOW, 1970—, Planned Parenthood, 1985—. Recipient fellowship Yale U., 1971, MacArthur scholarship in poetry Bklyn. Coll., 1991, Wallace fellow for creative artists and writers Am. Antiquarian Soc., 1998, D. Scott Rogo award for Parapsychol. Lit., Parapsychology Found., 1998. Mem. Writers Guild of Am. East, Am. Antiquarian Soc., Authors Guild, Phi Beta Kappa. Democrat. Jewish.

WEISBERG, RUTH, artist; Laurea in Painting and Printmaking, Acad. di Belle Arti, Perugia, Italy, 1962; BA, U. Mich., 1963, MA, 1965. Lectr., demonstrator, juror, curator U. Mich., 1987, 88, U. Hawaii, Honolulu, 1988, Pa. Acad., Phila., 1987, Queens Coll., N.Y.C., 1987, CCNY, 1987, U. Iowa, 1978, 87, U. N.D., Grand Forks, 1987, Fresno (Calif.) Arts Ctr. and Mus., Carnegie Mellon U., Pitts., 1986, 87, U. Tenn., Knoxville, 1986, U. Calif., Santa Cruz, 1985, U. Washington, Seattle, U. Kans., Lawrence, Skirball Mus. Hebrew Union Coll., Los Angeles, Calif. Inst. Arts, Valencia, Otis Art Inst., Los Angeles, Mass. Coll. Art, Boston, Norwegian Graphic Artists' Assn., Oslo, Coll. Art Assn. Conf., Detroit, many others; current chairperson art dept., U. So. Calif. Solo and two-person exhibitions include: Pollack Gallery, Toronto, 1969, 71, Richard Nash Gallery, Seattle, 1971, 72, 74, Seaberg-Isthmus Gallery, Chgo., 1972, Mcpl. Art Gallery, Oslo, 1972, Triad Gallery, Los Angeles, 1974, Norwegian Graphic Arts Assn., Oslo, 1976, Palos Verdes (Calif.) Art Gallery, 1976, El Camino Coll., Los Angeles, 1977, Oglethorpe U., Atlanta, 1978, Peppers Art Gallery, U. Redlands (Calif.), 1980, Kellas Gallery, Lawrence, Kans., 1979-81, M. Shore and Sons, Santa Barbara, Calif., 1981, U. Richmond, Va., 1985, U. Tenn., Knoxville, 1986, Sierra Nev. Mus. Arts Reno, 1987, The Alice Simsar Gallery, Ann Arbor, Mich., 1968, 69, 72, 74, 77, 88, Associated Am. Artists, N.Y.C., 1987, Jack Rutberg Fine Arts, Los Angeles, 1983, 85, 88; group exhibitions include: Chgo. Art Inst., 1978, E.B. Crocker Art Mus., 1978-80, Contemporary Arts Ctr., New Orleans, 1980, Pratt Graphic Ctr., N.Y.C., 1978-80, U. Art Mus., U. N.M., 1981, Loyola Marymount U., Los Angeles, 1982, Kenkeleba House, N.Y.C, 1984, The Design Ctr., Los Angeles, 1984, Palos Verdes Art Ctr., 1984, Gallery in the Plaza, Security Pacific Bank, Las Angeles, 1985, Thomas Ctr. Gallery, Gainesville, Fla., Associated Am. Artists, N.Y.C, 1987, many others; works published in The Survey Exhibition Catalogues, 1968-88; permanent collections include: The Achenback Found. for Graphic Arts, Fine Arts Mus., San Francisco, Ariz. State U. Mus., Tempe, The Art Inst. Chgo., The Dance Collection, Lincoln Ctr., N.Y.C., Detroit Inst. Arts, Grunwald Found. for Graphic Arts, U. Calif., Los Angeles, The Bibliotheque Nat. France, Paris, Los Angeles County Mus. Art, The Jewish Mus. N.Y.C, The Nat. Gallery, Washington, The Nat. Musl Women in the Arts, many others; contbr. articles to profl. jours. Mem.: L.A. Printmaking Soc., L.A. Artists Equity (adv. bd.), Tamarind Inst., Coll. Art Assn. (past pres., co-chair studio sessions, nat. adv. bd.). Office: Sch Fine Arts U S Calif Watt Hall 104 Los Angeles CA 90089-0001

WEISBERGER, BARBARA, artistic director, advisor, educator; b. Bklyn., Feb. 28, 1926; d. Herman and Sally (Goldstein) Linshes; m. Sol Spiller, Sept. 3, 1945 (div. 1948); m. Ernest Weisberger, Nov. 15, 1949; children: Wendy, Steven. BS in Edn., Psychology, Pa. State U., 1945; L.H.D. (hon.), Swarthmore Coll., 1970; D.F.A. (hon.), Temple U., 1973, Kings Coll., 1978, Villanova U., 1978, U. New England, 1996. Founder, dir., tchr. Wilkes-Barre (Pa.) Ballet Theater, 1953-63; founder, dir. Pa. Ballet, Phila., 1962-82, Carlisle (Pa.) Project, 1984—96; artistic advisor Peabody Dance, Balt., 2001—. Vice chmn. dance panel Nat. Endowment for the Arts, Washington, 1975-79. Performed with Met. Opera Ballet, N.Y.C., 1937, 38, Mary Binney Montgomery Co., Phila., 1940-42, ballet mistress, choreographer, Ballet Co. of Phila. Lyric Opera, 1961-62; choreographic works include Italian Concerto, Bach, Symphonic Variations, Franck; also operas for, Phila. Lyric Opera Co. Named Disting. Dau. of Pa., 1972, Disting. Alumna, Pa. State U., 1972; recipient 46th ann. Gimbel Phila. award, 1978. Mem. Psi Chi. Home and Office: 571 Charles Ave Kingston PA 18704-4711 Office Phone: 570-287-8349.

WEISBERG-SAMUELS, JANET S., psychologist; b. N.Y.C., Mar. 21, 1940; d. Morris and Vivian (Wank) Weisberg; m. Richard Samuels, Jan. 16, 1983; children: Debra Samuels, David Samuels. BBA, CCNY, 1960; MS, CUNY, 1967; PhD, Yeshiva U., 1984. Lic. psychologist, cert. sch. psychologist N.Y. Psychologist, administr. Bklyn. Jewish Hosp., 1969—75, Beth Israel Hosp., N.Y.C., 1975—87; dir. edn. Interfaith Med. Ctr., Bklyn., 1987—; pvt. practice psychology, N.Y.C., 1985—. Cons. Westchester Jewish Comm. Svcs., 2000—; team leader N.Y. State Dept. Mental Hygiene, N.Y.C., 1977; cons. N.Y.C. Bd. Edn., 1977, Parent-Child Consultation Ctr., 1980—; program dir. Brotherhood Synagogue, N.Y.C., 1968—75, dir. edn. and tng., 1987—, dept. psychiatry Interfaith Med. Ctr. Pres. singles divsn. Park Ave. Synagogue, N.Y.C., 1980—83; bd. dirs. Couples Club, 1986—, pres., 1988—90. Mem.: APA, Manhattan Psychol. Assn. (exec. bd. 1993—, pres.-elect 1997—98), Ea. Psychol. Assn., N.Y. State Psychol. Assn. (chair internship dirs. 2003—06). Avocations: opera, museums, ballet. Office: 160 E 89th St Apt 1B New York NY 10128-2306 Office Phone: 212-410-4391.

WEISBLATT, BARBARA ANN, secondary school educator; b. New Brunswick, N.J., Mar. 21, 1958; d. Stanley Herman and Clara Armel Friedelbaum; m. Alan Joel Weisblatt, Dec. 27, 1992. BA in French/Spanish, Rutgers U., 1979, MAT in French, 1986, supr. cert., 1991. Cert. French, Spanish tchr. K-12 N.J. Tchr. Somerville (N.J.) H.S., 1980—; supr. Somerville Pub. Schs., 1993—94. Mem. Holocaust H.S. and Dist. Coms., Somerville, 1995—. Mid. States Steering Com., Somerville, 2000—02, H.S. Renaissance Com., Somerville, 2000—, H.S. Quality Coun., Somerville, 2002—. Author: (test) French Placement Test for Middle School Students, 1995. Mem. Hebrew HS bd. edn. Temple Sholom, Bridgewater, NJ, 1995—. Recipient Tchr. Recognition award, Gov. State of N.J., 2001; NEH grantee, Figaro Inst., 1991. Mem.: NEA, Assn. for Supervision and Cirriculum Devel., Fgn. Lang. Educators N.J., Am. Assn. Tchrs. French, Somerville Edn. Assn., N.J. Edn. Assn. Avocations: reading, photography, travel, exercise. Home: 85 Perrine Pike Hillsborough NJ 08844 Office: Somerville HS 222 Davenport St Somerville NJ 08876 Office Phone: 908-218-4157.

WEISBROD, TARA LYNN, secondary school educator; d. Wayne and Linda Frana; 1 child, Maxwell Freeman. BA in Secondary Edn./Polit. Sci., Gustavus Adolphus Coll., St. Peter, Minn., 1995. Tchr. Deerfield (Wis.) Sch. Dist., 2000—. Office Phone: 608-764-5431.

WEISBURGER, ELIZABETH KREISER, retired chemist; b. Greenlane, Pa., Apr. 9, 1924; d. Raymond Samuel and Amy Elizabeth (Snavely) Kreiser; m. John H. Weisburger, Apr. 7, 1947 (div. May 1974); children: William Raymond, Diane Susan, Andrew John. BS, Lebanon Valley Coll., 1944, DSc (hon.), 1989; PhD, U. Cin., 1947, DSc (hon.), 1981. Rsch. assoc. U. Cin., 1947-49; col. USPHS, 1951-89; postdoctoral fellow Nat. Cancer Inst., Bethesda, Md., 1949-51, chemist, 1951-73, chief carcinogen metabolism and toxicology br., 1972-75, chief Lab. Carcinogen Metabolism, 1975-81, asst. dir. chem. carcinogenesis, 1981-89, ret. Cons. in field; lectr. Found. for Advanced Edn. in Scis., Bethesda, 1980-95; adj. prof. Am. U., Washington, 1982-83. Asst. editor-in-chief Jour. Nat. Cancer Inst., 1971-87; mem. editl. adv. bd. Chem. Health and Safety, 1994-99, Jour. Applied Toxicology, 1996—; contbr. articles to profl. jours. Trustee Lebanon Valley Coll., 1970—, pres. bd. trustees, 1985—89. Recipient Meritorious Svc. medal USPHS, 1973, Disting. Svc. medal, 1985; Hillebrand prize Chem. Soc. Washington, 1981, Charles Gordon award, 1999. Fellow AAAS (nominating com. 1978-81); mem. Am. Chem. Soc. (Garvan medal 1981, Tillmanns-Skolnick award divsn. chem. health and safety 2001), Am. Assn. Cancer Rsch., Soc. Toxicology, Am. Soc. Biochem. and Molecular Biology, Royal Soc. Chemistry, Am. Conf. Govtl. Indsl. Hygienists (Herbert Stokinger award 1996, William Wagner award 2003), Grad. Women in Sci. (hon.), Iota Sigma Pi. Lutheran. Office Phone: 301-309-0078.

WEISENFELD, CAROL ANN TRIMBLE, marketing executive, consultant; b. Port Arthur, Tex., Jan. 6, 1939; d. Vance Henry and Elzene Miller Trimble; m. Ronald John Nordheimer, Sept. 3, 1977; children: Diane Carol Nordheimer, David Douglas Nordheimer, Rex Robert Nordheimer. BA in Journalism, U. Pa., Phila., 1960; MA in Comm., Annenberg Sch. Comm. U. Pa., Phila., 1962. Wire editor Westchester County Pubs., Inc., Tarrytown, NY, 1960—61; interview asst. Samuel Lubell, N.Y.C., 1961; editor U. City News Bartash Pubs., Phila., 1961—62; coord. cmty. rels. West Phila. Corp., 1962—71; comm. cons. Schnader Harrison Segal & Lewis, 1962—63; dir. comm. U. City Sci. Ctr., 1971—73; campaign cons. Heinz for U.S. Senate, 1976—77; dir. devel. Fox Chase Cancer Ctr., 1977—80; campaign cons. Holtzman for US Senate, N.Y.C., 1980—81; asst. mng. dir. City of Phila., Philadelphia, Pa., 1981—83; dir. transition team Holtzman to N.Y.C. Comptr., N.Y.C., 1990—91; chmn. and CEO Gauge Corp., Wilmington, Del., 1991—94; pres. and CEO Market Tech Assoc., Inc., 1994—. Adj. lectr. comm. Widener U. Brandywine Divsn., Wilmington, Del., 1988—89; mem. bd. dir. Forum Exec. Women, Phila., 1983—85, pres., Wilmington, Del., 1993—94. Prodr.(host): (weekly radio program) Pathways to Service. Pres. Caesar Rodney Rotary Club, Wilmington, Del., 1996—97; gov. dist. 7630 Rotary Internat., 2001—02; regional vice chair Rotary Leadership Inst., 2004—, faculty mem., 2004—; commr. Commn. Women, Del., 1994—; mem. Governor's Pub. Works and Procurement Coun., 2002—; pres. Organized Classes of U. Pa., 1982—83; mem. bd. Pub. Allies (Del. chpt.), 1994—2004. Mem.: Del. Assn. Nonprofit Agencies (mem. bd. 2004—06), U. & Whist Club, Kappa Kappa Gamma. Office: Market Tech Assoc Inc 1304 Hilltop Ave Wilmington DE 19809-1628 Office Phone: 302-792-0100. Home Fax: 302-792-0111; Office Fax: 302-792-0111.

WEISENTHAL, REBECCA G., clinical psychologist; b. Detroit, Dec. 23, 1965; d. Lee Avery and Fredrika Phyllis Weisenthal; m. Michael Anthony Cataldo, Sept. 5, 1995. BA, Oberlin Coll., 1988; EdM, Harvard U., 1989; PsyD, Ill. Sch. Profl. Psychology, Chgo., 1994. Lic. clin. psychologist, Ill., Calif. Youth counselor MaComb County Youht Interim Care Facility, Warren, Mich., 1989-90; psychology intern U. Chgo., 1991-92, Women's Health Resources, Chgo., 1992-93, U. Calif., Berkeley, 1993-94; postdoctoral fellow Kaiser Permanent, Martinez, Calif., 1994-95; psychologist No. Ill. U., Dekalb, 1995—. Author: Group Therapy for Learning Disabilities, 1997. Chair, bd. dirs. social programs Congregation Beth Shalom, Dekalb, 1999—; vol. Friends We Care Network, Dekalb, 1999. Mem. APA, Calif. Psychol. Assn. Democrat. Jewish. Avocations: running, swimming, travel, reading, film. Office: No Ill U Counseling & Student Ctr 200 Campus Life Bldg Dekalb IL 60115

WEISER, KATHY M., highway designer; b. Harrisburg, Pa., Oct. 8, 1961; d. William Frederick Sr. and Jessie Marie (Conrath) Finkbone; m. John Peter Kruleski, Oct. 22, 1983 (div. 1990). Student, Dauphin County Technical, Harrisburg, 1979, Harrisburg Area C.C., 1985, 91. Draftsperson Gannett Fleming Inc., Camp Hill, Pa., 1979-83; geotechnical draftsperson F.T. Kitlinski & Assocs., Harrisburg, 1984-85; highway technician Baker Engrs., Inc., Harrisburg, 1985-90; highway designer Sheladia Assocs., Inc., Camp Hill, 1992-95, McCormick, Taylor & Assocs., Inc., 1995—. Active Rep. State Com., Harrisburg, 1980—, Ctrl. Pa. Ashtray Assn., Harrisburg, 1985—, Penbrook Fire Co., Harrisburg, 1990—. Mem. VFW, Venture Clubs of Am. (sec. 1992—), Am. Soc. of Hwy. Engrs., Harrisburg. Lutheran. Avocations: community service, antiques, camping. Home: 5618 Stradford Dr Harrisburg PA 17112

WEISER, LAURA ANN, judge; b. Denver, Feb. 6, 1959; d. Alva Myron and Rosalie Ellen Caster; m. Juan Velasquez III, Dec. 30, 1995; 1 child, Juan Velasquez IV; children: Jessica Katherine, Scott Thomas. BA, Houston Bapt. U., Houston, Texas, 1977—80; JD, U. Houston, 1995; cert., Tex. Coll. New Judges, 1990, Tex. Coll. Jud. Studies, 2005. Bar: Tex. 1986. Briefing atty. Cole, Cole and Easley, Victoria, Tex., 1985—86; staff atty. Coastal Bend Legal Svcs., Victoria, 1986—88; asst. criminal dist. atty. Victoria County Criminal Dist. Atty., Victoria, 1988—90; judge County Ct. at Law No. 1, Victoria, 1990—. Chmn. Tex. Ctr. for Judiciary, Austin, 2005—, mem. bench book com., mem. curriculum com. Mem. adv. bd. Victoria Coll. Police Acad., 2000—06, Crossroads Prog. Women, Victoria, 2005—06; trustee First United Meth. Ch., Victoria, 2000—06. Named Friend of Edn., Victoria Classroom Tchrs. Assn., 1991—93. Mem.: State Bar of Tex. (jud. liaison 2005—, chmn. jud. sect. 2005—), Victoria County Bar Assn. (hon.), Jr. League Victoria. Methodist. Avocations: reading, music, travel. Office: Victoria County Ct at Law No 1 115 N Bridge St Rm 203 Victoria TX 77901 Office Phone: 361-575-4550. Home Fax: 361-575-7181; Office Fax: 361-575-7181. Personal E-mail: lweiser@cox-internet.com. Business E-Mail: lweiser@vctx.org.

WEISERT, MARY CAROL, language educator; b. Quincy, Ill., Oct. 9, 1947; d. John Alphonsus and Ruth Margaret (Sullivan) Mayerle; m. John Steven Weisert, Nov. 27, 1971; children: Michael John, Lisa Ann. BS, U. Minn., 1969, MA, 1973. Spanish instr. North Harris County Coll., Houston, 1979—86, St. Luke Catholic Sch., Indpls., 1987—88, St. Monica Cath. Sch., Indpls., 1988—90; subs. tchr. Eagle-Union Schs., Zionsville, Ind., 1990—95; instr. tchg. Eng. second lang. Ivy Tech. State Coll., Indpls., 2001—. French and Spanish instr. OASIS, 2004—; pvt. tutor. Vol. Conner Prairie Mus., Fishers, Ind., 1999—, Julian Ctr., Indpls., 1996—, Ind. Transportation Mus., Noblesville, 1996—. Personal E-mail: ninji19@yahoo.com.

WEISKOPF, WANDA, mezzo soprano, writer, poet; b. Jefferson City, Mo., Aug. 2, 1921; d. Elmer and Stella Jane (Buster) Connell; m. Herbert Weiskopf (dec.); children: Douglas McK., Marta Jane. Student, L.A. Conservatory, 1950—55. Pvt. practice, Portland, Oreg., 1970—80. Activities dir., editor Skylines Portland Ctr., 1970—85; adjudicator Met. Opera Auditions, Seattle, 1990. Singer: (Operas) Portland Cathedral and St. Michael's, 1970—85, appeared in maj. opera houses, leading roles in Mo., Calif., Oreg., Italy, San Remo; author: All Is Not Winter, 1976, On the Wings of Song: My Life with the Maestro, 1995, Listen To The River, 2001. Organizer meml. concert Am. Heart Assn., Portland, 1971; active Dem. Party, Burbank, Calif., 1990. With U.S. Army, 1942. Mem.: Nat. Assn. Tchrs. Singing, Nat. Writers Assn. (sec. LA chpt. 1989—2005). Democrat. Avocation: walking. Home: 1207 N Cordova St #105 Burbank CA 91505-2218

WEISMAN, DIANE BOYD, elementary school educator; b. Pine Bluff, Ark., Aug. 21, 1949; d. Dale Duaine and Mary Charles (Smith) Boyd; m. Gary Reed, Apr. 15, 1947 (div. Sept. 1976); 1 child, Alan David; m. Robert Alan Weisman, June 9, 1990. BS, Miami U., Oxford, Ohio, 1971; MS, Corpus Christi State U., 1977. Cert. elem. educator, counselor. Tchr. Rolling Hills Ind. Sch. Dist., Byesville, Ohio, 1972-74; tchr. reading Calallen Ind. Sch. Dist., Corpus Christi, Tex., 1975-82; counselor Corpus Christi Ind. Sch. Dist., 1981—, gifted/talented tchr., 1982-90; tchr. middle sch. Stafford (Tex.) Ind. Sch. Dist., 1990-91, Ft. Bend Ind. Sch. Dist., 1991-93; v.p. Weisman & Assocs., Inc., Tampa, 1993—. Mem. Fla. Orchestra Guild, Sword of Hope Cancer Soc. Corpus Christi State U. grantee, 1983; named Notable Woman of Tex., 1986. Mem. ASCD, Nat. Coun. Tchrs. Math., Internat. Reading Assn., Tex. State Tchrs. Assn., Tex. Assn. Gifted and Talented, Alpha Delta Kappa, Tampa Women's Club. Avocations: reading, needlwork, cooking, music, travel. Home: 4306 Hudson Ln Tampa FL 33618-5343

WEISMILLER, ELEANOR KOVACS, library director; b. Perth Amboy, NJ, July 28, 1942; d. Louis T and Ethel D Kovacs; m. David L Weismiller (dec.); children: Chris, David. BA, Duquesne U., 1964; tchg. cert., Wash. Montessori Inst., 1967. Cert. Notary Public State of Calif. Tchr. Montessori Child Develop., West Covina, Calif., 1978—80; sch. libr. Rowland Unified Sch. Dist., Rowland Hts., Calif., 1981—87; libr. asst. County of Los Angeles Pub. Libr., 1987—96, cmty. libr. mgr. Whittier, Calif., 1996—. Founding mem. Friends of the Sorensen Libr., Whittier, Calif., 1989—. Mem. West Whittier Cmty. Coun., Population Stabilization, Washington. Avocation: art. Office: Sorensen Libr 11405 E Rose Hedge Dr Whittier CA 90606 Office Phone: 562-695-3979.

WEISS, BARBARA G., artist; b. Phila., Mar. 14, 1917; d. Carl Jacob Greenspan, Nellie Ellen Moyed; m. Victor Hugo Jr., May 6, 1942 (div. Dec. 1945); m. John Weiss, Nov. 10, 1946; children: Warren P., Willard Eric. Student, Calif. Art Ctr., Los Angeles, 1962—64. Owner, creator Balema Hugo Studio, Phila., 1942—49; interior designer L.A., 1953—63. Organizer workshops Charles Reid and other Artists of note, Thousand Oaks, 1994—96; creator gallery City of Thousand Oaks Civic Arts Plaza, 1996; creator mo. art show Umbrella Artists, Westlake Village, 1997—. Represented in permanent collections, L.A., Tucson, San Francisco, Paris, Rome; dir.(show): (art) The Gallery/Barnsdal Mcpl. Art Gallery, 1993—95, Heritage Gallery/Ventura County Adminstrn. Bldg., 1994—96; Exhibited in group shows at Viva Gallery, Los Angeles, 1996—97, collections, Still life, Corina/M. & Mme René BoeuF (Chagal collectors), Á Cap Martin Morning on Santarini, Anne Murphy (Collects Calif. Arts), geometrics, Dr. Francoise Farneti, Rome, Le Lac, Pamela Peterson Gallery Dir., Rythmns, Á LeMarché, Le Petit Pont, Mme Monique Salvie, Tuscon, Ar. Social chmn. San Fernando Valley for John F. Kennedy campaign, Pierre Salinger Senatorial Campaign; pres. Westlake Village Art Guild, Calif., 1994—96, program dir., 1993—2001; art show dir. Caruso Holdings Ltd., Westlake Village, Calabasas, Calif., 1997—. Recipient 1st prize, Westlake Village Art Guild, 1996, Best of Show, Dr. Winefrid Higgins, Judge, U. Calif./San Diego, 1998, 1st prize, Westlake Village Art Guild, 2000. Mem.: Valley Watercolor Soc. Home: 31756 Bedfordhurst Ct Westlake Village CA 91361

WEISS, CAROL ANN, writer; b. St. Louis, Sept. 6, 1947; d. Isidore and Annette (Cohen) Kalishman; m. Jay H. Weiss, Dec. 25, 1969; children: Benjamin Robert, Ivan Jay. BA in English, U. Mo., St. Louis, 1969; MS in Social and Philos. Edn., U. Ky., Lexington, 1975. Tchr. English Horton-Watkins H.S., Ladue-St. Louis, Mo., 1969—73; visual arts editor, columnist, feature writer Arts Ind., Indpls., 1984—94; spl. projects writer Hudston Inst. Consortium of Arts Adminstrs., Indpls. Author: The Encyclopedia of Indianapolis, 1994; co-author (with Judith Vale Newton): Take Care, 1988, A Grand Tradition: The Art and Artists of the Hoosier Salon 1925-1990, 1993, Beyond Realism: The Life and Art of Frederik Grue, 1995, Skirting the Issue: Stories of Indiana's Historical Women Artists, 2004; contbr. columns in newspapers, articles to periodicals. Recipient Penrod award,; Clio grant, Ind. Hist. Soc., 1999. Jewish. E-mail: cakweiss@yahoo.com.

WEISS, CAROL JULIET, psychiatrist; b. N.Y.C., Mar. 5, 1957; d. Eugene and Rose (Schwartz) Weiss. BA, Wesleyan U., 1977; MD, Johns Hopkins U., 1983. Diplomate Am. Bd. Psychiatry and Neurology. Intern N.Y. Hosp., N.Y.C., 1983—84; resident Payne Whitney Clinic, N.Y. Hosp., N.Y.C., 1984—87; asst. psychiatrist Payne Whitney Clinic - N.Y. Hosp., N.Y.C., 1983—87; clin. fellow Cornell U., N.Y.C., 1987—89, instr. and clin. affiliate in psychiatry and pub. health, 1989—91, clin. asst. prof. in psychiatry and pub. health N.Y.C., 1992—; pvt. practice N.Y.C., 1987—. Cons. in field. Contbr. articles to profl. jours., chpts. to books. Mem. Am. Psychiat. Assn., Am. Soc. Addiction Medicine, Phi Beta Kappa. Office: 1044 Madison Ave New York NY 10021-0138 Office Phone: 212-988-1209.

WEISS, ELIZABETH, anthropologist, educator; b. San Francisco, Feb. 26, 1974; d. David Alexander and Gisela Elisabeth Weiss. BA, U. Calif., Santa Cruz, 1996; MA, Calif. State U., Sacramento, 1998; PhD, U. Ark., Fayetteville, 2001. Rsch. assoc. Can. Mus. Civilization, Hull, Quebec, Canada, 2002—04; asst. prof. anthropology San Jose (Calif.) State U., 2004—. Contbr. articles to profl. jours. Recipient Mildred Trotter Student Prize for Rsch. on Bones and Teeth, 2002; Coll. Social Sciences Rsch. grantee, San Jose State U., 2004—06, Jr. Faculty Career Devel. grantee, San Jose State U. Found., 2005—06, Coll. Social Sciences Profl. Devel. grantee, San Jose State U., 2005—06. Mem.: Am. Anthrop. Assn., Paleopathology Assn., Southwestern Anthrop. Assn., Am. Assn. Phys. Anthropologists. Achievements include research in ancient bone biology. Office: San Jose State University Anthropology One Washington Sq San Jose CA 95192-0113 Office Phone: 408-924-5546. Business E-Mail: eweiss@email.sjsu.edu.

WEISS, JOAN OPPENHEIMER, social worker, educator; b. Balt., Apr. 10, 1930; d. Reuben and Selma (Levy) Oppenheimer; m. Milton Gottesman, Oct. 19, 1952 (div. 1958); m. Stanley Weiss, Nov. 6, 1960; children: Betsy, Michael, Jonathan (dec.). BA, Barnard Coll., 1952; MSW, Cath. U., Washington, 1956. Caseworker Jewish Social Svc. Agy., Washington, 1956-62, Family and Child Svcs., Washington, 1962-64; social worker divsn. med.

genetics Johns Hopkins U., Balt., 1968-88; founding exec. dir. Alliance of Genetic Support Groups, Chevy Chase, Md., 1988-96; co-dir. Human Genome Edn. Model Project, 1993—2001; cons. in genetics support. Instr. Child Devel. Ctr., Georgetown U., Washington, 1981—95; cons. Genetics Ctr., Johns Hopkins U., 1988—90; chmn. GenEthics Consortium, 1997—98; chmn. genetic standards for clin. practice com. NASW. Co-author Starting and Sustaining Genetic Support Groups, 1996; co-editor: Genetic Disorders and Birth Defects in Families and Society, 1983, Genetic Support Groups: A Partnership of Volunteers and Professionals, 1986; contbr. articles to profl. jours. Mem. profl. adv. bds. several vol. genetic orgns., 1973—. Maternal and Child Health grantee, 1989-96, March of Dimes Birth Defects Found. grantee, 1991. Mem. NASW (vice-chmn.found. bd. dirs.), Am. Soc. Human Genetics (social issues com.), Am. Coll. Med. Genetics, Nat. Soc. Human Genetics, Nat. Soc. Genetic Counselors, Genetic Alliance, Nat. Coalition Health Profl. Genetics in Edn. (bd. dirs.). Avocations: painting, travel, theater, reading, music. Personal E-mail: weissjns@erols.com.

WEISS, JUDITH ANN, music educator; d. Robert and Florence Weiss; m. Richard Rubin, Aug. 31, 1983 (dissolved 1993); children: Robert, Jonathan. BA in Edn., U. Hartford, 1977; MS in Edn., CUNY81. Cert. music tchr. N.Y., N.J. Vocal music tchr. Meml. Jr. HS, Huntington Sta., NY, 1977—80, Rocky Point (N.Y.) Jr.-Sr. HS, 1980—83, South Side HS, Rockville Ctr., NY, 1983—84; music tchr. Meml. Elem. Sch., East Brunswick, NJ, 1984—86, Farmingdale (N.J.) Sch., 1987—90, Ctrl. Elem. Sch., East Brunswick, 1994—. Condr. elem. divsn. Dist. Wide Vocal Music Festival, East Brunswick, 2003—04, co-founder, 2003, co-dir., 04. Prodr.(dir.): (musicals), 1977—99; dir.: (plays), 1977—99; author: Elementary Music Curriculum, 1985; dir.: (musical prodns.) Meml. Jr. H.S., 1977—80, Rocky Point (N.Y.) Jr.-Sr. H.S., 1980-83, South Side H.S., Rockville Ctr., 1984, Meml. Elem. Sch., 1994, Ctrl. Elem. Sch., 1994—98. Recipient Tchg. Recognition award, State of N.J., 2001; grantee Blue Ribbon grant tchg. mentor, East Brunswick (N.J.) Edn. Found., 1999—2000, 2003—04. Mem.: N.J. Music Educators Assn., Music Educator's Nat. Conf., East Brunswick Edn. Assn. Avocations: gardening, reading, crafts, home improvement, music. Office: Central Elementary School 371 Cranbury Rd East Brunswick NJ 08816 Office Phone: 732-613-6820.

WEISS, LISA ANN, lawyer; b. Chgo., Dec. 6, 1958; d. Benjamin B. and Suzanne (Harris) W. BA, Yale U., 1980; JD, Columbia U., 1983. Bar: N.Y. 1984. Assoc. Stroock Stroock & Lavan, NYC, 1983-86, Rosenman & Colin, NYC, 1986-92, ptnr., 1992—2000; dep. gen. counsel Sony Music, 2000—01, gen. counsel, 2001—05, Sony BMG, 2005—06; ptnr. Morrison & Foerster LLP, NYC, 2006—. Bd. dirs. Lightspeed Audio Labs., 2006—. Mem. NYC Bar Assn. (corp. law com. 1992-95). Office: Morrison & Foerster LLP 1290 Ave of the Americas New York NY 10104-0050 Office Phone: 212-468-8003. E-mail: lweiss@mofo.com.

WEISS, LOUISE ANNETTE, music educator; b. Litchfield, Ill. m. Dennis R. Weiss. BME, So. Ill. U., 1979, MME, 1996. Cert. tchr. K-12, Ill. Tchr. music Greenfield (Ill.) Cmty. Unit, 1979-81, Mulberry Grove (Ill.) Schs., 1981-87; asst. prof. music Greenville (Ill.) Coll., 1988—. Adjudicator various mus. contests, 1979—; conducted band clinic Ramsey (Ill.) High Sch., 1992; guest condr. Bond County Band Festival, 2002; accompanist Greenville Coll. H.S. Choir Festival, Tri-County Choir Festival, 1989—; chmn. tchr. edn. com. Greenville Coll., 2001—. Ch. musician Mulberry Grove Meth. Ch., 1981—, tchr. Sunday sch., 1996—2006. Mem. Nat. Assn. Coll. Wind and Percussion Instrs., Music Tchrs. Nat. Assn., Music Educators Nat. Conf., Kappa Delta Pi. Office: Greenville Coll Dept Music 315 E College Ave Greenville IL 62246-1145

WEISS, LYN DENISE, physician; b. Bethpage, N.Y., Apr. 13, 1959; d. Eugene and Lois Zanger; m. Jay M. Weiss, Apr. 7, 1984; children: Ari, Helene, Stefan, Richard. BA, U. Va., 1981; MD, SUNY, Bklyn., 1985. Diplomate Am. Bd. Electrodiagnostic Medicine, Nat. Bd. Med. Examiners, Am. Bd. Phys. Medicine and Rehab. Resident Dept. Phys. Medicine & Rehab. Nassau U. Med. Ctr., East Meadow, NY, 1985—89; attending physician Dept. Phys. Medicine & Rehab. Nassau U. Med. Ctr., 1989—94, dir. Electrodiagnostic Medicine Dept. Phys. Medicine Rehab., 1991—; dir. residency tng. Dept. Phys. Medicine & Rehab. Nassau U. Med. Ctr., 1993—; acting chmn. Dept. Phys. Medicine & Rehab. Nassau U. Med. Ctr., 1994—96; chmn. Dept. Phys. Medicine & Rehab. Nassau U. Med. Ctr., 1996—. Bd. dirs. Ctr. for Rehab. Rsch. Tech., Massapequa, N.Y., 1996— Author: Cumulative Trauma Disorders, 1997, Skin Care Triad, 2000, Easy EMG, 2004.

WEISS, LYNNE S., pediatrician, educator; MD, Hahnemann Med. Coll., Phila., 1974. Diplomate Pediatrics Am. Bd. Pediatrics, 1979, Pediatric Nephrology Am. Bd. Pediatrics, 1982. Intern in Pediatrics Michael Reese Hosp., Chgo., 1974—75, resident in Pediatrics, 1975—77, fellow in Nephrology (pediatric), 1977—79; physician, chief divsn. pediat. nephrology & hypertension UMDNJ-Robert Wood Johnson Med. Sch., New Brunswick, NJ, 1985—. Prof. Pediatrics Robert Wood Johnson Univ. Hosp., New Brunswick, NJ, 1987—, dir. Pediatric Nephrology Ctr., 1987—. Office: UMDNJ-Robert Wood Johnson Med Sch Pediatric Nephrology and Hupertension 98 French St 2221 New Brunswick NJ 08901 Office Phone: 732-235-7880.

WEISS, MARIANNA SHRENGER, psychotherapist; b. Pakrac, Croatia, Dec. 10, 1941; arrived in U.S., 1951; d. Edoardo and Vanda Schrenger Weiss; 1 child, Jacob Solomon. BA, MA, U. Calif., Berkeley, 1966; MS, Calif. State U., Hayward, 1985. Lic. marriage, family, and child counselor Bd. of Behavioral Scis., Calif. Workshop leader, hotline response worker Rape Crisis Ctr., Richmond, Calif., 1987—89; coord., group facilitator, newsletter editor and contbr. Tikvah, Holocaust survivors self-help group, San Francisco and Berkeley, 1989—94; therapist Family and Children's Svcs. of Contra Costa County, Walnut Creek and Richmond, Calif., 1989—93; therapist, dir. svcs. to Holocaust survivors Family Svc. of Silicon Valley, Los Gatos, Calif., 1999—2001; therapist Ctr. for Cmty. Counseling, Eugene, Oreg., 2002—; leader chronic illness workshop PeaceHealth Med. Ctr., Eugene, 2003—. Actor: (residential theater). Office: CCC 1465 Coburg Rd Eugene OR 97401

WEISS, MARILYN ACKERMAN, artist; b. Bklyn., Sept. 4, 1932; d. Max and Anna (Haber) Ackerman; m. Howard Jerry Weiss, Nov. 24, 1972; children: Jodi Kim Magaliff Gittelman and Barry Todd Magaliff (twins). BS magna cum laude, NYU, 1953. Exhibited solo shows: Alper-Goldberg Gallery, Cedarhurst, N.Y., 1977, Fred Leighton Madison Ltd., 1975, Port Washington (N.Y.) Libr., 1974, Adelphi U., 1974, Hewlett Woodmere Libr., 1972, Bodley Gallery, N.Y.C., 1983, Discovery Gallery, Glencove, N.Y., 1990, Z Gallery, N.Y.C., 1995, Allen Sheppard Gallery, Piermont, N.Y., 1995, 97, Sundance Gallery, Bridgehampton, N.Y., 1998, Westhampton Libr., Westhampton Beach, N.Y., 1999, 2001, Shelter Rock Art Gallery, Manhasset, 2000, Omni Gallery, Uniondale, W.Va., 2003, Gayle Willson Gallery, Southampton, NY, 2003, Studio 389 A Ea., Quogue, N.Y., Harvest Gallery, East Dennis, Md., 2005, 06, Gayle Wilson Gallery, Southampton, N.Y, 2004, 05, 06, Treasure Rm. Gallery, The Interchurch Ctr., N.Y., 2005, Madeline Hegeler Semerjian Gallery Rogers Nat. Libr., Southampton, N.Y., 2005, others; exhibited in group shows Firehouse Gallery Nassau Community Coll., Garden City, 1971, Pallazzio Vechio, Florence, Italy, 1972, Palazzio Nat., Naples, Italy, 1972, Brockton (Mass.) Library, 1972, Roanoke (Va.) Fine Arts Ctr., 1972, Milliken U., 1972, U. Okla., 1973, Southeastern Ark. Art and Sci. Ctr., 1973, Tuskegee Inst., 1974, Albrecht Gallery, 1974, Bergen Community Mus., 1974, 84, 85, Jesse Besser Mus., 1976, Cen. Wyo. Mus. Art, 1977, U. Wis., 1978, City Gallery, N.Y.C., 1981, Community Mus., 1974, Equitable Gallery, N.Y.C., 1979, Fed. Bldg., N.Y.C., 1979, 81-91, 92, U.S. Painting Exhbn., 1983-85, 85-88, 91-93, Traveling Painting Exhbn. U.S.A., 1972-74, 88-90, Traveling Watermedia Exhbn. U.S.A., 1976-78, Oil and Watermedia Exhbn., 1978-80, Cayuga Mus. History and Art, Auburn, N.D., 1983, Stephanie Roper Gallery, 1985, Sarah Lawrence Coll., 1985-92, Lighthouse Gallery, Fla., 1986, McPherson Coll., 1986, Schenectady Mus., N.Y., 1987, Adelphi U., N.Y., 1987, Nabisco Art Gallery, N.J., 1987, Pace U. Art Gallery, N.Y., 1988, Maier Mus. Art, Va., 1988, Lever House, N.Y.C., 1988, 91, Fine Arts Mus. Nassau County, 1988, Fine Arts Mus. L.I., 1988 (Bronze award 1988), Midge Karr Gallery L.I., 1989, Discovery Gallery, 1989-91, Cork Gallery, Lincoln Ctr., N.Y.C., 1989, 91, 92, 94, 98, Marbella Gallery, N.Y.C., 1989, Firehouse Gallery, Garden City, 1990, Printmaking Exhbt. U.S.A., 1990-91, 92-93, Adams State Coll. Co., 1991, Smithtown Twp. Arts Coun., N.Y., 1991, Jain Marunouchi Gallery, N.Y.C., 1991-94, Broome St. Gallery, N.Y.C., 1992-99, Richmond Art Mus., Ind., Concordia Gallery, N.Y., Thomas KJ Walsh Art Gallery, Conn., 1993, Mus. Southwest Tex., 1990, Cultural Ctr., Carmel, Calif., 1990, Lever House, N.Y.C., Sarah Lawrence Coll., N.Y., 1992, Gallery 420 Broadway, N.Y.C., 1995, 96, Seagate, Princeton, N.J., 1995, Blue Hill Gallery, Hudson, N.Y. 1995, Global Focus, Beijing, 1995, Millennium Gallery, East Hampton, N.Y., 1996, Morani Gallery, Phila., 1997, Shelter Rock (N.Y.) Art Gallery, 1997, Gallery 54, N.Y.C., 1997, Heckscher Mus. Art, Roslyn, N.Y., 1998, New World Art Ctr., N.Y., 1998, World Fine Art Ctr., N.Y., 1998-99, Salmagundi Club Gallery, N.Y., 1998, Sundance Gallery, Bridge Hampton, N.Y., 1998, New World Art Ctr., NYC, 1999, Cork Gallery, Lincoln Ctr., NYC, 1999, 2003, ISE Art Found., NYC, 2000, Sarah Lawrence Coll., Bronxville, NY, 2001, Gallery Fairlawn Libr., 2001, Elizabeth Found. for Arts, NYC, 2001, New Century Artists, NY, 2002, Freyberger Gallery, Pa. State U., Reading, 2002, Banana Factory, Bethlehem, Pa., 2002, Hiddenite (NC) Ctr., 2002, Paint Creek Ctr. Arts, Rochester, 2002, Long Beach Art Assn., 2002, BJ Spoke Gallery, Huntington Sta., NY, 2002, Broome St. Gallery, N.Y.C., 2002, 03, 04, 05, 06, The Gallery at 80 5th Ave, N.Y.C., 2003, Art Trium, Melville NY, 2004, Goggle Works Ctr. Arts, Reading, Pa., 2006, numerous others; represented in permanent collections including Mus. Southwest, Midland, Tex., Nat. Mus. Women in Arts, Washington, Sarah Lawrence Coll., Bronxville, N.Y., Sloan Kettering Art Collection. Recipient maj. prize Suburban Art League Ann. Show, 1968, 71, Elizabeth Morse Genius Found. prize for water media, 1983, Cecil Shapiro Meml. award, 1988, Spl. award Innovation Drawing Show, 1989, Miriam E. Halpern Meml. award, 1991, Dr. Irving H. Silver award Nat. Assn. Women Artists, 2000, Donald Pierce Meml. award Am. Soc. Contemporary Artists, 2002, Excellence award Long Beach Art League, 2002, 03, 04, Cleo Hartwig award, NAWA Ann., 2004, others. Mem. Contemporary Artists Guild, Nat. Assn. Women Artists (bd. dirs., Canady-Karasik Meml. award "Work on Paper" 1997, Cleo Hartwig award for sculpture 2004), Am. Soc. Contemporary Artists Guild (Harriet Febland Art Workshop award "Work on Paper" 1993), Artists Equity. Address: 1100 Park Ave New York NY 10128-1202 also: 35 Library Ave 7 I Westhampton Beach NY 11978 Personal E-mail: mawart1@yahoo.com.

WEISS, MILI DUNN, artist, educator; b. Phila., July 15, 1920; d. Max Dunn and Rebecca Rubin; m. Emanuel Gordon Weiss, June 21, 1942; children: Randall Dunn, Linda Weiss Levitsky. BFA, Tyler Sch. of Art, Temple Univ., Phila., 1942; BS in Practical Arts, Boston Univ., 1943; post graduate study, Mus. Sch., Boston, Mass., 1945. Tchr., painting and related media Cheltenham Ctr. for the Arts, Cheltenham, Pa., 1957—95; lectr., Looking at Art Mus. Galleries, Phila., 1980—90; dir. edn. Cheltenham Ctr. for the Arts, Cheltenham, Pa., 1985—95. Exhibitions include Eng., France, Holland, China U.S. Mus., Pa. Acad. of Fine Arts, Butler Inst. of Am. Art, Nat. Acad. of Design, N.Y., Represented in permanent collections Phila. Mus. Art, Harvard U., The Sichuan Inst. Fine Art in China, Nat. Mus. Am. Jewish History in Phila., The Berman Mus. at Ursinus Coll., Widener U., Bibliotheque Nat., Paris; contbr. articles to profl. jour.; prints reproduced, Making Art Safely, drawings reproduced, Voices of Marshall St. Recipient Outstanding Artist Educator, Cheltenham Twp., 1985, Outstanding Aquisitions Exhibit, Biliotheque Nat., 1992, Phila. Treasures, Mayor Edward Rendell, 1998. Mem.: Cheltenham Ctr. for the Arts (bd. mem., pres.), Phila. Water Color Soc. (bd. mem.), Artists Equity (sec.). Avocations: shell collecting, raising orchids, gardening, poetry. Home: 411 Randall Rd Wyncote PA 19095

WEISS, MYRNA GRACE, management consultant; b. NYC, June 22, 1939; d. Herman and Blanche Ziegler; m. Arthur H. Weiss; children: Debra Anne Huddleston, Louise Esther Pennington. BA, Barnard Coll., 1958; MA, Hunter Coll., 1968; MPA, NYU, 1978; cert. in Mktg., U. Pa. Tchr., N.Y.C. and Vallejo, Calif., 1959-68; dir. admissions Columbia Prep. Sch., N.Y.C., 1969-72; dir. PREP counselling NYU, N.Y.C., 1973-74; dept. head Hewitt Sch., N.Y.C., 1974-79; mgr. Met. Ins. Co., N.Y.C., 1979-84; mktg. exec. Rothschild, Inc., N.Y.C., 1984-85; pres. First Mktg. Capital Group Ltd., N.Y.C., 1985—; mng. dir. Wrap Co. Internat. N.V., 1992-97; advisor Lared Group, N.Y.C., 1987-97; CEO, pres., bd. dirs. Ibnet, 1998—2002. Adv. Gov.'s Hwy. Safety Com., NYC, 1985-88; pres. Fin. Women's Assn. NY, 1984-85; faculty SUNY, 2005—. Bd. dirs. 92nd Y, NYC, 1972—90, ARC, NYC, 1989—2006, asst. treas., 1993—. Mem. Internat. Women's Forum (bd. dirs. 1990-92), Econ. Club N.Y., Women's Econ. Roundtable (bd. dirs. 1988-90). Office: 1st Mktg Capital Group Ltd 1056 5th Ave New York NY 10028-0112 E-mail: mzweiss@nyc.rr.com.

WEISS, NANCY P., artist; b. Chgo., June 12, 1938; d. Manny and Helen (Spero) Passman; m. Lenard Garsen Weiss, Aug. 30, 1958; children: Pamela Lee, Elizabeth Susan. Student, U. Colo., 1956-57, U. Calif., Berkeley, from 1958, CCAC, Oakland, Calif., 1980-81, San Francisco Art Inst., 1984-85. Artist, 1950—. Exhibited in shows at Bolinas (Calif.) Mus., 1992-2002, Galleria Le Logge, Assisi, Italy, 1997, 98, 99; contbr. to The Calif. Art Rev., 1990. Chair Berkeley Civic Arts Commn. City of Berkeley, 1980-85; mem. adv. bd. No. Calif. chpt. Nat. Mus. Women in the Arts; bd. dirs. Eureka Theatre Co., San Francisco. Democrat. Jewish. Avocations: walking, yoga, tennis. Fax: (415) 362-3110.

WEISS, RENÉE KAROL, editor, musician; b. Allentown, Pa., Sept. 11, 1923; d. Abraham S. and Elizabeth (Levitt) Karol; m. Theodore Weiss. BA, Bard Coll., 1951; student, Conn. Sch. Dance; studied violin with, Sascha Jacobinoff, Boris Koutzen, Emile Hauser, Ivan Galamian. Mem. Miami U. Symphony Orch., 1941, N.C. State Symphony, 1942-45, Oxford U. Symphony, Opera Orchs., Eng., 1953-54, Woodstock String Quartet, 1956-60, Bard Coll. Chamber Ensemble, 1950-66, Hudson Valley Philharmonic, 1960-66, Hudson Valley String Quartet, 1965, Princeton Chamber Orch., 1980-93; orchestral, chamber work, 1966—. Participant Theodore and Renée Weiss poetry writing workshops Princeton U., 1985, Hofstra Coll., 1985, modern poetry workshop Cooper Union, 1988, Princeton Adult Edn.; tchr. modern dance to children Bard Coll., Kindergarten Tivoli, NY Pub. Sch., 1955-58 Author: (children's books) To Win A Race, 1966, A Paper Zoo, 1968 (best books for children N.Y. Times, Book World 1968, N.J. Author's award 1968, 70, 88), The Bird From the Sea, 1970, Biography: David Schubert: Works and Days, 1984; co-editor, mgr. Quar. Rev. Lit., 1945-2005; author: (with Theodore Weiss) The Always Present Present, 2005; author of poems. Mem.: PEN (Nora Magid Lifetime Achievement award with Theodore Weiss 1997). Office: Q R L Poetry Series Princeton U 185 Nassau St Princeton NJ 08544-4914 Office Phone: 609-759-3366. Business E-Mail: qrl@princeton.edu.

WEISS, SHIRLEY F., retired urban and regional planner, economist, educator; b. NYC, Feb. 26, 1921; d. Max and Vera (Hendel) Friedlander; m. Charles M. Weiss, June 7, 1942. BA, Rutgers U., 1942; postgrad., Johns Hopkins U., 1949-50; M in Regional Planning, U. NC, 1958; PhD, Duke U., 1973. Assoc. research dir. Ctr. for Urban and Regional Studies U. N.C., Chapel Hill, 1957-91, lectr. in planning, 1958-62, assoc. prof., 1962-73, prof., 1973-91, prof. emerita, 1991—; joint creator-sponsor Charles and Shirley Weiss Urban Livability Program, U. N.C., Chapel Hill, 1992—; research assoc. Inst. for Research in Social Sci., U. N.C., 1957-73; research prof. U. N.C., Chapel Hill, 1973-91, acting dir. women's studies program Coll. Arts and Scis., 1985, faculty marshal, 1988-91. Grad. edn. advancement bd. U. NC, Chapel Hill, 2001—, tech. com. Water Resources Rsch. Inst., 1976-79; adv. com. on housing for 1980 census Dept. Commerce, 1976-81; cons. Urban Inst., Washington, 1977-80; rev. panel Exptl. Housing Allowance Program, HUD, 1977-80; adv. bd. on built environ. Nat. Acad. Scis.-NRC, 1981-83, program coordinating com. fed. constrn. coun. of adv. bd. on built environ., 1982-83; mem. Planning Accreditation Bd., Site Visitation Pool, Am. Inst. Cert. Planners and Assn. Collegiate Schs. Planning, 1985—; discipline screening com. Fulbright Scholar awards in Architecture and City Planning, Coun. for Internat. Exchange of Scholars, 1985-88; N.Mex. adv. bd. Enterprise Found., Santa Fe, 1997-2002; governing bd. Acad. Freedom Fund, AAUP, 1997-2000. Author: The Central Business District in Transition: Methodological Approaches to CBD Analysis and Forecasting Future Space Requirements, 1957, New Town Development in the United States: Experiment in Private Entrepreneurship, 1973; co-author: A Probabilistic Model for Residential Growth, 1964, Residential Developer Decisions: A Focused View of the Urban Growth Process, 1966, New Communities U.S.A., 1976; co-author, co-editor: New Community Development: Planning Process, Implementation and Emerging Social Concerns, vols. 1, 2, 1971, City Centers in Transition, 1976, New Communities Research Series, 1976-77; mem. editl. bd.: Jour. Am. Inst. Planners, 1963-68, Rev. of Regional Studies, 1969-74, 82-92, Internat. Regional Sci. Rev., 1975-81. Trustee Friends of Libr., U. N.C., Chapel Hill, 1988-94, Santa Fe Chamber Music Festival, adv. coun., 1990-91, 97-98, trustee, 1991-97, 98-2004, trustee emerita, 2004-; bd. dirs. Triangle Opera, 1986-89, 91-2002, Chamber Orch. of the Triangle, 1997-2005, hon. life mem., 2005-. Recipient Cornelia Phillips Spencer Bell award U. NC, Chapel Hill, 1996, Disting. Alumni award Alumni Assn. Dept. City and Regional Planning, U. NC, Chapel Hill, 1996, Mary Turner Lane award Assn. Women Faculty, 1994, (with Charles M. Weiss) Gifford Phillips award Santa Fe Chamber Music Festival, 2000, Disting. Alumni and Alumnus award U. NC, Chapel Hill, 2003; Adelaide M. Zagoren fellow Douglass Coll., Rutgers U., 1994. Emeritus fellow Urban Land Inst. (sr. fellow, exec. group, cmty. devel. coun. 1978—); mem. Am. Inst. Planners (sec., treas. southeast chpt. 1957-59, v.p. 1960-61), Am. Inst. Cert. Planners, Am. Planning Assn., Am. Econ. Assn., So. Regional Sci. Assn. (pres. 1977-78), Regional Sci. Assn. (councillor 1971-74, v.p. 1976-77), Nat. Assn. Housing and Redevelopment Ofcls., Interamerican Planning Soc., Internat. Fedn. Housing and Planning, Town and Country Planning Assn., Internat. Urban Devel. Assn., Econ. History Assn., Am. Real Estate and Urban Econs. Assn. (regional membership chmn. 1976-82, 84-85, dir. 1977-80), AAUP (chpt. pres. 1976-77, pres. N.C. Conf. 1978-79, mem. nat. coun. 1983-86, William S. Tacey award Assembly of State Confs.), Douglass Soc., Order of Valkyries, Phi Beta Kappa. Home: 750 Weaver Dairy Rd # 2114 Chapel Hill NC 27514-1483

WEISS, SIMONA, retired paralegal; d. Leon and Rose Weiss; m. Morton B. Elliot, Apr. 14, 1951 (div. May 10, 1972); children: Russell Wayne Elliot, Linda Beth Elliot-Morris. BA cum laude, Fairligh Dickinson U., 1974; postgrad., Columbia U., 1968—70, NYU, 1974—76, William Patterson U., 2001—03. Cert. paralegal Upsala Coll. N.J., 1980. Paralegal adminstr. Witco Chem. Corp., N.Y.C., 1980—81; paralegal supr. Pitney, Hardin, Kipp & Szuch, Morristown, NJ, 1982—82; real estate paralegal Willkie Farr & Gallagher, N.Y.C., 1983—84; real estate and corp. paralegal Robinson Silverman Pearce Aronsohn & Berman, N.Y.C., 1984—90; real estate paralegal Freddie Mac, New York, NY, 1991—91; legal asst. Gen. Investment Sect. Legal Dept. The Prudential Ins. Co. of Am., Newark, 1992—94; comml. real estate paralegal Cleary, Gottlieb, Steen & Hamilton, N.Y.C., 1994—96; real estate and corp. paralegal Hannoch Weisman, Roseland, NJ, 1996—98; comml. real estate paralegal Unilever Bestfoods, Englewood Cliffs, NJ, 1998—2002. Chmn. Haworth (N.J.) Parks & Playgrounds Com., 1972—78; county com. mcpl. chmn. Haworth (N.J.) Rep. Orgn., 1973—79; candidate Non-Partisan Bergen County (N.J.) Charter Study Commn., 1973—74; primary candidate Bergen County (N.J.) Bd. of Chosen Freeholders, 1977—77; fin. and corr. sec. Temple Beth El, Closter, NJ, 1968—72; program and publicity chmn. 1st Bergen County Women's Ctr., Teaneck, NJ, 1972—74; v.p. fund raising Haworth (N.J.) Home and Sch. Assn., 1967—69. Recipient Mayor's Cert., Borough of Haworth, 1979; scholar, Fairleigh Dickinson U., 1971—74. Mem.: Legal Asst. Mgmt. Assn., Nat. Paralegal Assn., Phi Omega Epsilon. Independent. Avocations: theater, movies, opera, ballet, reading. Home: 2000 Linwood Ave 19U Fort Lee NJ 07024 Personal E-mail: simona_wei@msn.com.

WEISS, SUSAN, newspaper editor; Mng. editor Life Section, USA Today, Arlington, Va. Office: USA Today 7950 Jones Branch Dr Mc Lean VA 22108-0001

WEISS, SUSAN F., accountant; b. Providence, Mar. 9, 1965; d. Frank and Maria (Felsner) Weiss. BS in Accig., R.I. Coll., 1988; postgrad., Bryant Coll., 2000—. Cert. mgmt. acct. Acctg. intern Ann & Hope Svc. Corp., Cumberland, R.I., 1986-88; sr. cost acct. Quebecor Printing, Inc., Providence, 1988-98; cost acct., material requirements project mgr. Union Industries, Inc., Providence, 1998; cost acctg. mgr. AAI.Fostergrant, Smithfield, R.I., 1999—. Mem. Am. Soc. Women Accts. (pres. R.I. chpt. 2001-02), Inst. Mgmt. Accts. Avocation: ballet. Home: 86 Meadowcrest Dr Cumberland RI 02864-6434 Office: 500 George Washington Hwy Smithfield RI 02917-1926 E-mail: sweiss@aaifgg.com.

WEISS, SUSAN FORSCHER, musicologist, educator; b. NYC, July 22, 1944; d. Joseph L. and Mollie G. Forscher; m. James L. Weiss, June 23, 1967; children: Ethan, Lisa. BA, Goucher Coll., 1965; MA, Smith Coll., 1967; PhD, U. Md., 1985. Teaching fellow, music dept. Smith Coll., 1965-67; elem. music instr. Conn. Pub. Sch. System, West Haven, 1967-68; teaching fellow, music dept. U. Mich., 1968-70; elem. music instr. The Georgetown Hill Sch., Bethesda, Md., 1971-72, The Valley Sch., Owings Mills, Md., 1972-74; lectr. of music Goucher Coll., Towson, Md., 1985-87; chair music dept. The Garrison Forest Sch., Owings Mills, Md., 1973-94; faculty music history The Peabody Inst. of the Johns Hopkins U., Balt., Md., 1987—. Mem. local arrangements com. Am. Musicological Soc. Nat. Meeting, Balt., 1988, chair, 1996; mem. vis. com. music dept. Swarthmore Coll., 1989; peer reviewer Nat. Endowment for the Humanities, 1990; mem. exec. bd. The Baltimore Consort, 1991—; mem. exec. com. Chamber Music Soc. of Baltimore, 1991—, music dir., 1996; chair adv. bd. Arthur Friedheim Libr., Peabody Inst., 1991-98; joint appt. in Romaine langs. and lit. The Krieger Sch. of Arts & Scis., John Hopkins U., 2000—. Contbr. chpts. to books and articles to profl. jours. Chair acad. issues subcom. Provost's Com. on the Status of Women, 1995—. John M. Ward fellow in Dance and Music for the Theatre, The Houghton Libr., Harvard U., 1991, Folger Shakespeare Libr. Short Term fellow, 1992; Travel grantee Am. Coun. of Learned Socs., 1987, NEH Summer Inst. for Coll. and Univ. Profs. Northwestern Univ.: Culture in Crisis: Italy 1494-1527, 1993; Provost's grantee for Distance Edn., Johns Hopkins U., 1996, 2002-03, Collaborative Rsch. Grant NEH, 2004-05. Home: 8302 Tally Ho Rd Lutherville MD 21093-4719

WEISS, SUSETTE MARÉ, technical and photographic consultant, mass communications and media relations specialist, investor; b. New Orleans, La., June 14, 1959; d. Stanley and Dorothy Lee (Cambre) Weiss. AA in Photojournalism, La. State U., Monroe, 1977; PhD in Comparative Religion, Universal Life Coll., Modesto, Calif., 1990. Cert. retinal angiographer; cert. ophthalmic asst. Prodn. supr., lab. mgr. Colorpix Custom Photogs., Inc., New Orleans, 1978-84; ophthalmic photographer Ochsner Clinic, New Orleans, 1984-85; dir. ophthalmic photography Omni/Medivision, Metairie, La., 1986-87; audiovisual meeting planner, technician and cons. New Orleans, 1988-89; tech. and photographic supr. Retina and Vitreous Assocs. of Ala., Mobile, 1989; dir. photography Dauphin West Eye, Ear, Nose and Throat Specialists, Mobile, 1989-91; tech. sales rep., tech. specialist Nikon, Inc., Melville, N.Y., 1992-95; contractual cons. Simply Susette, Inc., New Orleans, 1995—, pvt. investor, 2001—. Mass comm. specialist with emphasis in photographic imaging and media rels. Inventor stereo-imaging calibrator and quantitative stereopsis technique; author: Redefining the Wheel: Stereo-Photomicroscopy and Ophthalmology, 150 Years of Advancement; contbr. photography to Inc. Mag., Mademoiselle, Good Housekeeping, Income Opportunities, Mari Times, 1998-99; videographer Chrysler Corp. comml.; Rep. Conv. speech coverage aired by ABC, CBS, NBC, C-SPAN, 1998; exclusive media coverage and photos for New Orleans Mus. of Art's Famous Native-Am. Painting Acquistion, Times Picayune Newspaper, 1998; nat. test trial photos selected to demonstrate the tech. advancements in Neopan 400 film, Fuji Film, Photokina 1990 World News Conf. Recipient Best of Show photography award Biol. Photographers' Assn., 1991, 1st pl. gen. photography award Biol. Photographers' Assn., 1991. Mem. Ophthalmic Photographers' Soc. (audio-visual chair 1991, audio-vusial co-chair 1992 nat. edn. meeting), Am. Soc. Mag. Photographers, Profl. Photographers Am., Biol. Photographers

Assn., Jr. League of Ft. Meyers, Fla. Achievements include ongoing rsch. and devel. in new techniques and applications of teletronic comms. and imaging for the med. and comml. field. Home and Office: 14031 W Hyde Park Dr # 101 Fort Myers FL 33912 E-mail: etparley@earthlink.net.

WEISS, TAMMY LEE, information technology manager; b. Scranton, Pa., Sept. 25, 1969; d. Terrance and Evelyn Weiss. BS in Computer Info. Systems, Franciscan U. Steubenville, Ohio, 1991; MBA, Marywood U., 1996. Cert. webmaster 2000. Computer programmer Metlife, Clarks Summit, Pa., 1991—99, info. tech. project mgr., 1999—. Mem.: ASPCA, Humane Soc. U.S., Alpha Epsilon Lambda, Sigma Phi. Roman Catholic. Avocations: travel, animals. Home: 312 S Abington Rd Clarks Green PA 18411 Office: Metlife 1028 Morgan Hwy Clarks Summit PA Personal E-mail: tweiss@metlife.com.

WEISS-CORNWELL, AMY, interior designer; b. Mpls., Dec. 8, 1950; d. August Carl and Margaret Amelia (Wittman) Weiss; m. Dan Cornwell, July 31, 1995; 1 child, Emma Cornwell. AA in Home Econs., Cerritos Coll.; student, Long Beach State U., Santa Ana Jr. Coll. Asst. to interior designer Bobbi Hart at Pati Pfahler Designs, Canoga Pk., Calif., 1974-75; interior designer B.A. Interiors, Fullerton, Calif., 1976-78, Birns Co., Rancho Mirage, Calif., 1978-79; staff interior designer Assoc. Design Studios, Costa Mesa, Calif., 1979-81; interior designer Carole Eichen Interiors, Fullerton, 1981, Sears, Roebuck and Co., Alhambra, Calif., 1982-84; sr. corp. designer, mgr. design studio Barratt Am., Irvine, Calif., 1984-88; owner, retail designer Amy Weiss Designs, Coronado, Calif., 1988—; office, yacht designer, 1997—. Designer in residence San Diego Design Ctr., 1990—92; participant Pacific Design Ctr.; Designer on Call program, 1994—95. Prin. works include interior designs for residences, yachts; comml. interiors including lobbies and offices. Mem. Am. Soc. Interior Designers (Globe-Guilders steering com. 1989-92, chmn. Christmas party, co-chmn. Christmas on Prado 1989, 89, designer for ASID showcase house 1992, 93), Bldg. Industry Assn. (sales and mktg. coun. awards com. 1993, mem. sales and mktg. coun. 1986-88, mem. home builders coun. 1994, 2d place M.A.M.E. award 1987, 1st place M.A.M.E. award 1986, 2d place S.A.M. award 1987), Building Industry Assn. Remodeler's Coun., Nat. Kitchen and Bath Assn., Coronado C. of C., Coronado Cays Yacht Club. Office: Amy Weiss Designs 1123 Marysville Ave Chula Vista CA 91913 Office Phone: 619-216-6002. Personal E-mail: amyweissdesigns@cox.net.

WEISSLER, FRAN, theatrical producer; m. Barry Weissler. Co-prodr. plays Othello, Medea, Zorba, My One and Only, Cabaret, Cat on a Hot Tin Roof, Gypsy, Fiddler on the Roof, Bye Bye Birdie, My Fair Lady, Falsettos, Chicago, Full Gallop, Wonderful Town, Sweet Charity; prodr. (play) Chicago. Co-recipient 5 Tony awards. Office: Shubert Theatre 225 W 44th St New York NY 10036-3991

WEISSMAN, ANN PALEY, artist, educator, consultant; b. NYC, Aug. 20, 1931; d. Bernard and Sylvia Paley; m. Arthur Weissman, Jan. 27, 1951; children: Nili, Kenneth, Margot. BA in Psychology and Sociology, Hunter Coll., 1952; student, fine and applied art, Broome C.C., 1983—. Social worker Learning Ctr., Binghamton, NY, 1968—70; dir. Hope Lodge (Am. Cancer Soc.), 1970—73; consumer advisor, cons. Cuisinarts, Greenwich, Conn., 1970—85; designer, owner Arbor Art, Binghamton, 1998—; tchr., cons. Discovery Ctr., Binghamton, 2000—. Archtl. guide Preservation Assn. S Tier, Binghamton, NY, 1981—; fin. advisor, tchr. Broome C.C. and Office for Aging, Binghamton, 1989—; fin. advisor Discovery Ctr., Binghamton, 1985—. 1850 Christmas, 2001; inventor flower collars and tree masks. V.p. bd. Preservation Assn. of Binghamton, 1991—; docent So. Tier Roberson Meml. Mus., Binghamton, 1962—69; cons. Binghamton Planning Commn., 2000—; bd. dirs. Commn. of Arch. and Urban Design, Binghamton, NY, 1998—, SOS Shelter for Abused Women and Children. Mem.: Abused Women and Children Shelter (bd. mem.), Madrigal Choir of Binghamton (mem. bd. pub. rels. 1985—). Avocations: gardening, ceramics, music, cooking, decorating. Home: 5 Vincent St Binghamton NY 13905

WEISSMAN, MYRNA M., epidemiologist, researcher, medical educator; PhD in Chronic Disease Epidemiology, Yale U., 1974. Prof. psychiatry and epidemiology Yale U.; prof. epidemiology and psychiatry Coll. Physicians and Surgeons, Columbia U., N.Y.C. Chief divsn. clin. and genetic epidemiology N.Y. Psychiat. Inst., N.Y.C. Office: NY Psychiatric Inst Columbia U 1051 Riverside Dr Unit 24 New York NY 10032 Office Phone: 212-534-5880. Business E-Mail: mmw3@columbia.edu.

WEISZ, RACHEL, actress; b. London, Mar. 7, 1971; 1 child. BA, U. Cambridge, England. Motion picture and T.V. actress. Actor (films) Death Machine, 1995, Stealing Beauty, 1996, Chain Reaction, 1996, Going All the Way, 1997, Amy Foster, 1997, Land Girls, 1998, I Want You, 1998, Swept From the Sea, 1998, The Mummy, 1999, Sunshine, 1999, Beautiful Creatures, 2001, Enemy at the Gates, 2001, The Mummy Returns, 2001, About a Boy, 2002, The Shape of Things, 2003 (also prodr.), Confidence, 2003, Runaway Jury, 2003, She Died on Canvas, 2003, Envy, 2004, Constantine, 2005, The Constant Gardener, 2005 (Best Performance by an Actress in a Supporting Role in a Motion Picture, Hollywood Fgn. Press Assn. (Golden Globe award), 2006, Outstanding Performance by a Female Actor in a Supporting Role, Screen Actors Guild award, 2006, Performance by an Actress in a Supporting Role, Acad. Motion Picture Arts & Sciences, 2006); (TV films) Scarlet and Black, 1993, My Summer with Des, 1998; (plays) Design For Living, 1994, Last Summer, 1999, The Shape of Things, 2001. Office: c/o Creative Artists Agency 9830 Wilshire Blvd Beverly Hills CA 90212

WEITZ, JEANNE STEWART, artist, educator; b. Warren, Ohio, Apr. 30, 1920; d. William McKinley and Ruth (Stewart) Kohlmorgan; m. Loyal Wilbur Weitz, Aug. 1, 1940 (dec. 1986); children: Gail, Judith, John, Marc. BS in Art and English, Youngstown U., 1944; MEd in Art, U. Tex., El Paso, 1964; postgrad., Tex. Tech U., 1976. Indsl. engr. Republic Iron & Steel, Youngstown, Ohio, 1942-43; art tchr. pub. schs., Bessemer, Pa., 1943-44, El Paso Ind. Sch. Dist., 1944-50, 54-78, art. cons., 1978-87; art tchr. Hermosa Beach (Calif.) Ind. Sch. Dist., 1950-53, El Paso Mus. Art, 1960-65; lectr. in art U. Tex., El Paso, 1963-66; instr. El Paso C.C., 1970-78; free-lance artist, lectr. El Paso, 1987-91; supr. student tchr. U. Tex., El Paso, 1989-91; mgr. Sunland Art Gallery, 1994-95. Author: high sch. curriculum guide; Exhibited in group shows at Sun Carnival Exhbn., 1961, El Paso Mus. Art, 1962, LVAA Shows, 1990, 1992, Westside Art Guild, 1992, N.Mex. State Art Fair, 2001—05, Fuller Lodge Art Gallery, Los Alamos, N.Mex., 2004—06, Rio Grand Art Assn., 2000—06, Signature Mem. Show, Albuquerque Mus. Art, 2005, Palcitas Art Series, 2005—, N.Mex. Watercolor Soc., 2002—06, PSNM Nat., 2004. Coordinator art edn. El Paso Civic Planning Coun., 1985-86; chmn. art edn., art resources dept. City of El Paso, 1982-83. Recipient Purchase award El Paso Art Assn. Spring Show, 1995, 1st pl. award KCOS (PBS), 1996, 1st pl. award Westside Art Guild, 1996, 2d pl. El Paso Art Assoc., 1998, 1st pl. award West Side Art Guild, 1998, 99, H.M. El Paso Pastel Soc. Show, 1998. Mem.: Pastel Soc. N.Mex. (v.p. 2001, pres. 2003), Rio Grande Art Assn., N.Mex. Watercolor Soc. (signature mem. 2004), Pastel Soc. El Paso (v.p. 1999—2000), Rio Bravo Watercolorists (sec. 1998), Nat. Soc. Am. Pen Women, Westside Art Guild (pres. 1993—95), Nat. Art Edn. Assn. (sec. 1988—93, two 1st place award LVAA shows 1989), Lower Valley Art Assn. (Hon. Mention award 1988), El Paso Mus. Art Guild, Nat. Soc. Arts and Letters (sec. El Paso chpt. 1988—), Tex. Art Edn. Assn. (local orgn. 1981, conf. planner, Hon. Mention award 1972). Republican. Presbyterian. Avocations: printmaking, travel. Home: 22 Canon Escondito Sandia Park NM 87047 Office Phone: 505-281-0881. E-mail: jeanne@moo-vee.com.

WEITZE, TEENA, science educator; b. Charlotte, N.C. m. Charles Weitze; children: Scott, Brian. BS, U. Wis., Milw., 1969; MEd, Fitchburg State Coll., Mass., 1973. Cert. tchr. biology Mass., 2005. Tchr. sci. Gardner H.S., Mass., 1973—. Cons. Biolink Biotechnology. Home: 115 Crestwood Dr Gardner MA 01440 Office: Gardner HS 200 Catherine St Gardner MA 01440 Office Phone: 978-632-1600 1101. Business E-Mail: weitzet@gardnerk12.org.

WEITZEL, GINGER M., entrepreneur, critical care nurse; b. Richland, Wash., Dec. 28, 1952; d. Carl Benton and Margaret Allee White; m. Gregory L. Weitzel, Aug. 28, 1978; children: Skylar Benjamin, Spencer Cameron. AA, Pima CC, Tucson, 1976; student, U. Ariz., 1971—73, U. Denver, 1995—98. RN, cert. ACLS. Nat. sales support mgr. Valleyrab, Boulder, Colo., 1984—90; exec. sales mgr. 3M, St. Paul, 1990—96; sales mgr. Am. Telecare, St. Paul, 1998—99; nurse emergency dept. Exempla Health Care, Wheat Ridge, Colo., 2000—02; pvt. practice Arvada, Colo., 2002—. Nat. acct. mgr. Sims-Deltec, St. Paul, 1994—96. Mem.: Legal Nurse Cons., Emergency Nurses Assn. Democrat. Methodist. Avocations: gardening, walking, reading, politics. Home: 5975 Braun Way Arvada CO 80004 Office: Weitzel and Assoc 5975 Braun Way Arvada CO 80004

WEJCMAN, LINDA, retired state legislator; b. Dec. 1939; m. Jim. Student, Iowa State U. Minn. State rep. Dist. 61B, 1991—2000, ret., 2000. Home: 3203 5th Ave S Minneapolis MN 55408-3248

WEJMAN, JANET P., information technology executive, air transportation executive; BS, Northwestern U., Evanston, Ill. Programmer United Airlines; dir. sys. devel. Covia Technologies, 1988—92; with Chgo. & Northwestern R.R., 1992—96; sr. v.p. and chief info. officer Continental Airlines, Inc., Houston, 1996—. Office: Continental Airlines PO Box 4607 Houston TX 77210-4607

WELBES, DIANE M., literature and language educator; b. Miles City, Mont., June 12, 1948; d. Richard Allen and Velda Nadine Welbes. AA, Miles City Coll., 1968; BS, Ea. Mont.Coll., 1970. Tchr., prin. Sacred Heart Sch., Miles City, Mont., 1970—91; tchr., asst. prin. Rosebud Sch., Mont., 1991—2006. Mem. Curriculum Consortium, 1992—2006. Author: (books of poetry) Anthology of Poetry, 1994; adv. (newspaper) The Wrangler, 1991—2006. Mem. Suicide Prevention, Miles City, Mont., 1974. Recipient Young Adult of Yr., Dioceses, 1995. Mem.: Am. Assn. Health, Physical Edn. and Recreation. Avocations: crafts, tennis. Home: 1506 Palmer Miles City MT 59301

WELBORN, CARYL BARTELMAN, lawyer; b. Phila., Jan. 29, 1951; d. Raymond C. and Helen Ann Bartelman; m. Lucien Ruby, Apr. 11, 1987. AB, Stanford U., 1972; JD, UCLA, 1976. Bar: Ill. 1976, Calif. 1978. Assoc. Isham Lincoln & Beale, Chgo., 1976—78; from assoc. to ptnr. Morrison & Foerster, San Francisco and L.A., 1978—95; prin. Law Office of Caryl Welborn, 1995—2004; ptnr. DLA Piper US LLP, San Francisco, 2004—. Lectr. real property law. Named Best Lawyers in America. Mem. ABA (chmn. com. on partnerships, real property sect. 1989-93), Am. Coll. Real Estate Lawyers (bd. govs. 1994-2002, pres. 2001), Anglo-Am. Real Property Inst. Office: DLA Piper US LLP 153 Townsend St Ste 800 San Francisco CA 94105-2150 Business E-Mail: caryl.welborn@dlapiper.com.

WELBORN, VICTORIA LEE, science librarian, educator; b. Thomasville, N.C., Feb. 17, 1953; d. Ivan Edward and Mary Christine (Murphy) W.; m. Craig K. Weatherington, Apr. 20, 1993. BA, Wake Forest U., 1975; MLS, Kent State U., 1979. Ref. libr. Health Scis. Libr. Ohio State U., Columbus, 1980-83, head Biol. Scis. Libr., 1983-88; head sci. libr. U. Calif., Santa Cruz, 1988—. Adj. instr. Libr. Sch., Kent (Ohio) State U., 1987-88. Mem. Internat. Assn. Marme Scis. Librs. and Info. Ctrs. Office: U Calif Sci Libr Santa Cruz CA 95063

WELCH, CHERIE LYNN, healthcare educator; b. Detroit, Feb. 5, 1966; d. Charles and Judith Welch. BS, Western Mich. U., 1990, MS, 1998. Secondary phys. edn. instr. Dept. Edn., Agana, Guam, 1992—93; secondary health, phys. edn. tchr. Hackett Cath. Ctrl. H.S., Kalamazoo, 1994—96; secondary phys. edn. tchr. Our Lady of Mercy H.S., Farmington Hills, Mich., 1996—97; phys. edn. instr. Western Mich. U., Kalamazoo, 1997—98; elem. and mid. sch. phys. edn. tchr. Grand Rapids Pub. Schs., Mich., 1998—2000; aquatic instr. Oakland CC, Farmington Hills, Mich., 2004—06; wellness instr. Rochester Cmty. Schs., Mich., 2000—06. Home: 3721 Barberry Cir Wixom MI 48393 Office Phone: 248-726-5400.

WELCH, FRANCES SUZANNE, director; d. James and Martha Welch. BS in Elem. Edn., U. Tex., Austin, 1987; Masters Degree, U. Houston, Clear Lake, Tex., 2004. Cert. tchr. Tex., 1987. Pre-kindergarten tchr. Lamar CISD, Rosenberg, Tex., 1989—90, kindergarten tchr., 1990—95, 5th grade tchr., 1995—98, 7th-8th grade sci. tchr., dept. head, 1998—2003, curriculum and instrnl. specialist, 2003—. Active Clavery Bapt. Ch., Rosenberg, 1991—2006. Recipient Outstanding Leader award, Lone Star Girl Scout Coun., 1988. Mem.: NSTA. Home: 1410 Caslyn Rosenberg TX 77471 Office: Lamar CISD 3911 Avenue I Rosenberg TX 77471 Office Phone: 832-223-0140. Personal E-mail: fswelch@aol.com. Business E-Mail: fwelch@lcisd.org.

WELCH, JEANIE MAXINE, librarian; b. LA, Jan. 22, 1946; d. Howard Carlton and Roberta Jean (Dunsmuir) W. BA, U. Denver, 1967, MA, 1968; M in Internat. Mgmt., Thunderbird, The Garvin Grad. Sch. Internat. Mgmt., 1981. Asst. libr. Am. Grad. Sch. Internat. Mgmt., Glendale, Ariz., 1968-83; reference libr. Lamar U., Beaumont, Tex., 1983-85, head reference, 1985-87; reference unit head U. N.C., Charlotte, 1988-98, asst. coord. reference svcs., 1998-2000, bus. ref. libr., 2000—. Author: The Spice Trade, 1994, The Tokyo Trial, 2002; contbr. articles to profl. jours. Rsch. grantee Tex. Libr. Assn., 1986; recipient Best Bibliographies in History, 2003; named Dun & Bradstreet Info. Svcs. Online Champion of Yr., 1996; recipient Highly Commended award Literati Club, 2000 Mem.: ALA, Western Assn. of Women Historians, Assn. Coll. Rsch. Libr., N.C. Libr. Assn. (ref. and adult svcs. sect. exec. bd. 2004—), Phi Beta Delta. Democrat. Methodist. Office: U NC Atkins Libr Charlotte NC 28223 Business E-Mail: jmwelch@email.uncc.edu.

WELCH, JOAN MINDE, elementary school educator; b. Auburn, N.Y., May 25, 1940; d. Arland E. and Alice (Stoker) Minde; m. Richard J. Welch (div. Oct. 1989); children: Mindy Aileen, James Edward. Student, Merrill Palmer Inst., Detroit, 1960-61; BS magna cum laude, SUNY, Buffalo, 1962; postgrad., Syracuse (N.Y.) U., 1970-71, SUNY, Cortland, 1973-74. Cert. tchr. home econs. N-6, N.Y. 4-H agt. N.Y. State Coop. Ext., Cortland, 1961-62; tchr. spl. edn. Cayuga County BOCES, Auburn, N.Y., 1969-72; instr. YMCA-Women's Ednl. and Indsl. Union, Auburn, 1997—; elem. tchr. Moravia (N.Y.) Ctrl. Schs., 1980—. 4-H evaluator N.Y. State Coop. Ext., Ithaca, 1990—; mgr., tchr. Responsive Classroom, Moravia, 1995—. Coleader Auburn Divorced, Separated, Widowed Group, 1985-92. Mem. Am. Fedn. Tchrs., N.Y. State United Tchrs., Nat. Soc. DAR (Children of Am. Revolution chair Owasco chpt. 1974—), N.Y. State DAR, Delta Kappa Gamma (v.p. 1996—), Phi Upsilon Omicron (chaplain 1961—). Roman Catholic. Avocations: genealogical research, historical collections. Office: M Fillmore Elem Sch 24 S Main St Moravia NY 13118-2307

WELCH, KATHY JANE, information technology executive; b. San Antonio, Aug. 5, 1952; d. John Dee and Pauline Ann (Overstreet) W.; m. John Thomas Unger, Jan. 8, 1977. BAS in Computer Sci., So. Meth. U., 1974; MBA in Fin., U. Houston, 1978. Programmer, analyst Tex. Instruments, Houston, 1974-76, project leader, 1976-78, br. mgr., 1978-81; mgr. systems and programming Global Marine, Houston, 1981-84, mgr. office automation, 1984-85, mgr. user systems, 1985-88; dir. MIS Advanced Tech. divsn. Browning-Ferris Industries, Houston, 1988-89; dir. Telecom. and Computer Svcs., 1989-93; v.p. info. tech. Talent Tree Svcs., Inc., Houston, 1993-96; info. tech. cons. Tech. Ptnrs., Inc., Houston, 1996—2000, project dir., 2000—03, v.p. info. tech., 2003—. Mem. Mensa, Beta Gamma Sigma. Office: Tech Ptnrs Inc Ste 200 10055 Grogans Mill Rd The Woodlands TX 77380 E-mail: kathy.welch@tpi.net.

WELCH, LISA RENEA, biology professor; b. Midland, Tex., Mar. 14, 1967; d. Jeff Eugene Williams and U. Sue Boardman; m. Clay Eugene Welch; children: Meggan, Jacob, Jennifer. BS, U. Wyo., Laramie, 1989; MS, Tex. Tech. U., Midland, 2003. Biology instr. Midland Coll., 1997—. Faculty advisor Pre-Physician Asst. Soc., Midland, 1999—2006; v.p. faculty senate Midland Coll., 2004—06. Mem.: Phi Kappa Phi. Home: 1320 NCR 1090 Midland TX 79706

WELCH, LYNNE BRODIE, nursing school dean; b. Norwalk, Conn., Oct. 19, 1941; d. John and Jeannette Brodie; m. C. William Welch, Aug. 1965 (div. Dec. 1980); children: John, Andrew. BS, U. Conn., 1963; MSN, Cath. U. Am., 1968; EdD, Columbia U., 1979. From staff nurse to instr. Sch. of Nursing Stamford (Conn.) Hosp., 1963-65; staff nurse, instr. Children's Hosp. Ctr., Washington, 1965-66; staff nurse CCU Washington Hosp. Ctr., 1966-67; staff nurse ICU/CCU Danbury (Conn.) Hosp., 1968-69; asst. prof. Western Conn. State U., Danbury, 1970-79; assoc. prof., chairperson Pace U., Pleasantville, N.Y., 1979-82; prof., dean Sch. Nursing So. Conn. State U., New Haven, 1982-86; prof., dean Coll. of Nursing and Allied Health U. Tex., El Paso, 1986-89; statewide dir. S.C. Area Health Edn. Consortium Med. U. of S.C., Charleston, 1989-91; prof., dean Sch. of Nursing Marshall U., Huntington, W.Va., 1991—98, dean Coll. of Health Professions, 1998—. Mem. joint bd. Kellogg Community Partnership, Morgantown, W.Va., 1991—; mem. bd. W.Va. Ptnrs. of the Americas, Charleston, 1992—; chairperson W.Va. Health Care Planning Commn. Task Force, Charleston, 1992—. Editor: Women in Higher Education: Changes and Challenges, 1990, Minority Women in Higher Education, 1992, Roles of Nursing Faculty in Higher Education, 1992, Strategies for Promoting Pluralism in Education and the Work Place, 1997. Mem. Leadership Tri State, Ashland, Ky., 1992, Leadership W.Va., 1993, Leadership El Paso, Class 10, 1988. Mem. ANA, Nat. League for Nursing, Am. Assn. Acad. Adminstrs. (state commr. 1979-92), Sigma Theta Tau, Phi Kappa Phi. Republican. Presbyterian. Avocations: gardening, cooking, travel. Home: 3200 Orchard Dr Huntington WV 25701-9534 Office: Marshall U Pritchard Hall 426 1 John Marshall Dr Huntington WV 25755-0003

WELCH, MARTHA GRACE, physician, researcher; b. Buffalo, June 21, 1944; d. Thomas Harris and Jane Elizabeth (Todd) W.; m. Anthony H. Horan, July 11, 1970 (div. May 1985); 1 child, Thomas Bramwell Welch Horan. BA, N.Y.U., 1966; MD, Columbia U., 1971. Diplomate Am. Bd. Psychiatry and Neurology. Intern Greenwich (Conn.) Hosp. Assn., 1971-72; resident Albert Einstein Coll. Med., Bronx, N.Y., 1972-74, fellow, 1974-77, instr., 1977-79; dir., founder The Mothering Ctr., Greenwich, 1978—; asst. clin. prof. psychiatry Columbia U., N.Y.C., 1997—. Author: Holding Time, 1989, (with others) Autistic Children, 1983; contbr. articles to profl. jours. Pres. alumni coun. Columbia U. Coll. Physicians and Surgeons, 2001-2002 Recipient Alumni Achievement award Middlebury (Vt.) Coll., 1995. Mem. Am. Psychiat. Assn., Internat. Soc. for Devel. Psychobiology, Soc. for Neuroscience. Avocations: reading, skiing, tennis, sewing, biking, music. Office: 15 E 91st St New York NY 10128-0648 Office Phone: 212-369-8566.

WELCH, MARTHA LYNN, environmentalist, educator; d. Margaret Melvina Sandifer and Richard Charles O'Connell; m. John Tyler Welch II, Aug. 28, 1987. BA in Environ. Studies, U. N.C., Wilmington, N.C., 1983; MS in Edn., Old Dominion U., 1996; EdD, Fla. Internat. U., 2004. Asst. edn., exhibits coord. N.C. Aquarium, Ft. Fisher, 1984—86; owner, operator Manatee Tours, Inc., Islamorada, Fla., 1990—93; marine edn. specialist Coll. William and Mary, Va. Inst. Marine Sci., Gloucester Point, 1996—97; field leader, instr. Audubon Fla., Miami, 1999—2003; dir. edn. Fla. Flora and Fauna, Inc., Hutchinson island, 1999—. Cons. Sch. Dist. Palm Beach County, Fla., 2002—. Author: Mandy the Manatee Saves the Day; contbr. articles to profl. jours. Mem.: ASCD, NSTA (assoc.), Fla. Assn. Sci. Tchrs., Nat. Marine Edn. Assn. (assoc.), Nat. Audubon Soc., Fla. Marine Sci. Edn. Assn., Phi Kappa Phi. Avocations: travel, snorkeling, boating. Home and Office: 137 Queens Rd Hutchinson Island FL 34949 Office Phone: 561-951-9313. Personal E-mail: jwelch261@sprintpcs.com.

WELCH, MARY ROSE DWYER, secondary school educator; b. Sparta, Wis., Feb. 5, 1946; d. Robert Edward and Margaret Ann (Gregor) Dwyer; m. Theodore William Welch, June 29, 1968. Student, U. Wis., 1967; BS, U. Wis., La Crosse, 1968, MEd in Profl. Devel., 1986. Cert. English tchr., Wis. Secondary tchr. English Sparta Area Schs., 1968—2001. Sr. class play dir. Sparta Sr. High Sch., 1968-71, forensic coach, 1968-90; ednl. cons. McDougal, Littell & Co., Evanston, Ill., 1985; forensic judge La Crosse dist. Wis. High Sch. Forensic Assn., Arcadia, 1986—; goal, devel. English tchr., WWTC, La Crosse, 2002—. Active Friends of Terry Musser for Assembly and Senate, Melrose, Wis., 1983-84, Friends of Tommy Thompson for Gov., Mauston Wis., 1985-86, Friends of Terry Madden for Assembly, Elroy, Wis., 1986; bd. dirs. Wilton (Wis.) Fun Fest Com., 1985-90; mem. Wilton Swimming Pool Fund Com., 1985-88; mem. Tax Incremental Dist. Com., Wilton, 1987; bd. dirs. Winding Rivers Libr. System, 1991-97, Wilton Pub. Libr., 1990-2002, sec. 1992-2002; parish coun. St. John the Bapt. Cath. Ch., 2005— Mem. NEA, Wis. Edn. Assn., Western Wis. Edn. Assn., Sparta Edn. Assn., Wis. Regional Writers Assn., Parish Council Cath. Women, Wilton Pub. Libr. Book Discussion Group Avocations: walking, card playing, bicycling, sewing, reading. Home: 701 Walker St PO Box 271 Wilton WI 54670-0271 Office: WWTC 103 S Water St Sparta WI 54656 Office Phone: 608-269-3791.

WELCH, MURIEL RUTH, religious organization administrator; d. Dewey J. and Ruth Elizabeth (Wright) Frye; m. Richard Dale Welch, July 8, 1951; children: Linda, Dale Michael, James Martin, Richard Lee, Elaine Ruth, Brian Daniel, Karen Lynn, Alecha Reace. Student, Mich. State U., East Lansing, Mich., 1950—57; degree, Full Gospel Bible Inst., Phila., 1972; degree in Real Estate, San Antonio Realtors U., 1982. Administrator The Master's Ho., Lansing, Mich., 1972—80; chaplain Lorton (Va.) Correction Facility, 1981—83; founder, dir. Project James 1:27, San Antonio, 1992—. Chaplain Ingham County Jail, Mason, Mich., 1975—80, Wainwright Ret. Home, Lansing, Mich., 1975—80; missionary, Romania, 1992, Mex. orphanages, 1985—94. Publisher: The Light Ho., 1972—80. Home: 6331 Forest Village San Antonio TX 78250

WELCH, RAQUEL, actress; b. Chgo., Sept. 5, 1940; d. Arm and Josepha (Hall) Tejada; m. James Westley Welch, May 8, 1959 (div.); children: Damon, Tahnee; m. Patrick Curtis (div.); m. Andre Weinfeld, July 1980 (div.). Actress: (films) including Fantastic Voyage, 1966, One Million B.C, 1967, The Biggest Bundle of Them All, 1968, Fathom, 1967, The Queens, 1967, 100 Rifles, 1969, Magic Christian, 1970, Bedazzled, 1971, Fuzz, 1972, Bluebeard, 1972, Hannie Caulder, 1972, Kansas City Bomber, 1972, Myra Breckinridge, 1970, The Last of Sheila, 1973, The Three Musketeers, 1974 (Golden Globe award for best actress), The Wild Party, 1975, The Four Musketeers, 1975, Mother, Jugs and Speed, 1976, Crossed Swords, 1978, L'Animal, 1979, Chairman of the Board, 1998, (TV movies) The Legend of Walks Far Woman, 1982, Right to Die, 1987, Scandal in a Small Town, 1988, Trouble in Paradise, 1989, Torch Song, 1993, Naked Gun 33 1/3, 1994, Folle d'elle, 1998; (Broadway debut) Woman of the Year, 1982; star Victor/Victoria (on Broadway), 1997; (TV series) Central Park West, 1995; author: The Raquel Welch Total Beauty and Fitness Program, 1984.

WELCH, RHEA JO, special education educator; b. Jacksonville, Ill., Jan. 26, 1957; d. James Daniel and Bobbye Jo (Weatherford) W.; 1 child, James Alexander. BA, William Woods U., Fulton, Mo., 1980; cert., U. Ill., Springfield, 1981; postgrad., MacMurray Coll., 1985, 86, 88, So. Ill. U., 1990, 91. Cert. 6-12 tchr., spl. edn., Ill. Tchr. recreational skills Ill. Sch. for Visually Impaired, Jacksonville, 1984; cross categorical tchr. Sangamon Area Spl. Edn. Dist., Springfield, 1988-89; tchr.'s aid Four Rivers Spl. Edn. Dist., Jacksonville, 1981, substitute tchr. spl. edn., 1982-86, tchr. learning disabilities, 1987, tchr. students with severe behavioral disorders, 1989—. Mem. human rights com. Jacksonville Devel. Ctr., 1992—; pub. speaker; project dir. for community svc. programs Garrison Sch., Ill. Adv. Coun. on Voluntary Action-Serve Ill.; originator Class Time Community Svc. Volunteerism Four Rivers Spl. Edn. Dist.; coord. Spl. Olympics Ivan K. Garrison Sch., 1992-93; speaker Ill. Coun. Children With Behavior Disorders, 1997. Vol. ARC, instr. HIV-AIDS, CPR, First Aid. Named Staff Mem. of Month, Ivan K. Garrison Alternative Sch., 1992, 2001; recipient 2 Disting. Svc. citations, 1992;

grantee, Kraft Food Co., 1991—92. Mem. Coun. for Exceptional Children, Nat. Soc. for Experiential Edn. Episcopalian. Office: Four Rivers Spl Edn Dist 936 W Michigan Ave Jacksonville IL 62650-3113

WELD, ALISON GORDON, artist; b. Ft. Knox, Ky., June 10, 1953; d. Paul Woodbury and Mary Jean (Cameron) W.; m. Charles Robert Russell, July 1, 1990. Student, Wolverhampton (Eng.) Poly., 1974-75; BFA, Alfred U., 1975; MFA, Art Inst. Chgo., 1979. Curatorial asst. Am. Mus. Natural History, N.Y.C., 1980-83; curator Robeson Gallery, Rutgers U., Newark, N.J., 1983-88; asst. curator fine art N.J. State Mus., Trenton, 1988-99. One-woman shows include E.L. Stark Gallery, NYC, Morris Mus., Morristown, NJ, Susan Schreiber Gallery, NYC, U. Bridgeport, Conn., 1996, Ednl. Alliance, NYC, 1997, Ajira, Newark, 1997, Hunterdon Mus. Art, 1998, Pacifico Fine Art, NYC, 2001, Molloy Coll. Art Gallery, 2002, Robert Steele Gallery, NYC, 2003, 2005, Ben Shahn Gallery, William Patterson U., Wayne, NJ, 2003, Springfield (Ohio) Mus. Art, 2006, Rider U. Art Gallery, 2006; curator: Dream Singers, Story Tellers: An African American Presence, Pukul Fine Arts Mus., Japan, NJ State Mus., 1992—94, (show of self-taught and mainstream artists) A Density of Passions, NJ State Mus., 1989, Art by African Americans in the Collection of the NJ State Mus., 1998. Artist grantee N.J. State Coun. Arts, 1983-84, artist Rutgers Ctr. for Innovative Printmaking, 1994. Personal E-mail: agweld@comcast.net.

WELDON, LINDA JEAN, psychology educator; b. Cape Girardeau, Mo., Oct. 2, 1949; d. Cecil Elza and Ida (Zimmerman) W. AA, Coll. San Mateo, Calif., 1969; BA, Calif. State U., Chico, 1971, MA, 1974; PhD, U. Md., 1980. Rsch. psychologist Johns Hopkins U., Balt., 1978-80, ARRO, Washington, 1980-84; rsch. scientist U. Md., College Park, 1984-90; asst. prof. psychology CC Balt. Essex Campus, Balt., 1986-90, assoc. prof. psychology, 1990-94, Essex C.C., 1994—. Contbr. articles to profl. jours. Democrat. Home: 2515 K St NW Apt 202 Washington DC 20037-2052 Office: CC Balt Essex Campus 7201 Rossville Blvd Baltimore MD 21237-3855

WELDON, VIRGINIA V., retired food products executive, retired pediatrician; b. Toronto, Sept. 8, 1935; arrived in US, 1937; d. John Edward and Carolyn Edith (Swift) Vernal; children: Ann Weldon Doyle, Susan Weldon Erlinger. AB cum laude, Smith Coll., 1957; MD, SUNY-Buffalo, 1962; LHD (hon.), Rush U., 1985. Diplomate Am. Bd. Pediatrics, Am. Bd. Pediatric Endocrinology and Metabolism, Nat. Bd. Med. Examiners (bd. dirs. 1987-89). Intern Johns Hopkins Hosp., Balt., 1962-63, resident in pediatrics, 1963-64; fellow pediatric endocrinology Johns Hopkins U., Balt., 1964-67, instr. pediatrics, 1967-68; from instr. to assoc. prof. Washington U., St. Louis, 1968—79, prof., 1979-89, v.p. Med. Ctr., 1980-89, dep. vice chancellor med. affairs, 1983-89, dir. Ctr. Study Am. Bus., 1998-99; v.p. sci. affairs Monsanto Co., St. Louis, 1989, v.p. pub. policy, 1989-93, sr. v.p. pub. policy, 1993-98. Mem. gen. clin. rsch. ctrs. adv. com. NIH, Bethesda, Md., 1976—80, mem. rsch. resources adv. coun., 1980—84; advisor, dir. Monsanto Co., 1989—98. Contbr. articles to sci. jours. Mem. risk assessment mgmt. commn. EPA, 1992—97; commr. St. Louis Zool. Pk., 1983—92; mem. Pres.'s Com. Advisors Sci. and Tech., 1994—2000; trustee Calif. Inst. Tech., 1996—, Whitaker Found., 1997—99, St. Louis Sci. Ctr.; bd. dirs., vice chmn., chmn. St. Louis Symphony Orch., 1993—2005, hon. trustee, 2005—; bd. dirs. United Way Greater St. Louis, 1978—90, St. Louis Regional Health Care Corp., 1985—91; mem. adv. com. on agrl. biotech. USDA, 2000—01. Fellow: AAAS, Am. Acad. Pediat.; mem.: St. Louis Med. Soc., Soc. Pediat. Rsch., Endocrine Soc., Am. Pediat. Soc., Assn. Am. Med. Colls. (disting. svc. mem., del., chmn. coun. acad. socs. 1984—85, chmn. assembly 1985—86), Nat. Acads. (nat. assoc.), Inst. Medicine, Equestrian Order of Holy Sepulchre, Alpha Omega Alpha, Sigma Xi. Roman Catholic. Home: 242 Carlyle Lake Dr Saint Louis MO 63141-7544

WELDY, LANA GAIL, secondary school educator; b. Colorado Springs, Colo., Dec. 16, 1973; d. Bill Little and Lee Luetje; m. Steve Matthew Weldy; children: Joshua Matthew, Jonathan Micheal. M in Curriculum and Instrn., Coll. of the S.W., Hobbs, N.Mex., 2003; AA, 1996, BSc, 1999. Tchr. English Hobbs (N.Mex.) Mcpl. Schs., 1999—. Sponsor Nat. Jr. Honor Soc. Hobbs H.S., 2002—. Office: Hobbs Mcpl Schs Jefferson Hobbs NM 88240 Personal E-mail: weldyl@hobbsschools.net.

WELHAN, BEVERLY JEAN LUTZ, nursing educator, administrator; b. Phila., Dec. 7, 1950; d. Winfield E. and Mary Helen (James) Lutz; m. Robert John LeBar, Aug. 28, 1971 (div. July 1978); m. Joseph Welhan, Jan. 7, 1984; children: James Benjamin, Jillian Grace. Diploma, Montgomery Hosp. Sch. Nursing, 1971; BSN, Gwynedd Mercy Coll., 1974; MEd, Lehigh U., 1977; MSN, Villanova U., 1983; DNSc, Widener U., 2000. Staff nurse recovery room Montgomery Hosp., Norristown, Pa., 1971-72; charge nurse North Penn Convalescent Residence, Lansdale, Pa., 1972-74; instr. med./surg. nursing Episcopal Hosp., Phila., 1974-78; staff nurse Montgomery Hosp., Norristown, 1978-79; asst. dir. nursing edn. Episcopal Hosp., Phila., 1979-85, assoc. dir. nursing edn., 1985-89, dir. nursing edn., 1989-98; dir. nursing program, prof. Montgomery County C.C., 1998—. Adj. instr. Pa State U., 1983-84. Author: Testing Program for Scherer's Introductory Medical/Surgical Nursing, 1986. Mem. Nat. League for Nursing Accrediting Commn. (program evaluator 1990—, bd. rev. 1993-96, edn. rev. panel 1997-98), Southeastern Pa. League for Nursing (mem. nominating com. 1982-83, bd. dirs. 1983-85, 1998-2000, chair-elect 2000-02, chair 2002-04), Pa. League Nursing (bd. dirs. 2004—), N.E. Coalition of Hosp. & Diploma Schs. of Nursing (bd. dirs. 1993-94, chair nominating com. 1993-94, nominating com. 1991-92, 98, mem. mktg. com. 1995-97), Montgomery Hosp. Alumni Assn., Nurses' Alumni Assn. of Episcopal Hosp. (hon.), Sigma Theta Tau, Phi Kappa Phi. Republican. Office: Montgomery County Cmty Coll 340 Dekalb Pike PO Box 400 Blue Bell PA 19422-1412 Office Phone: 215-641-6471. Office Fax: 215-619-7180. E-mail: bwelhan@mc3.edu.

WELKEN, JAN DENISE, elementary school educator; b. Valley City, ND, Apr. 2, 1949; d. Roland Edward and Charlotte Berneice Gessner; m. Kenneth Everett Welken Jr., May 31, 1969; children: Nathan Jeffrey, Nicholas Scott. BS in Phys. Edn. and Health and Bus. Edn., Valley City State U., 1970; M Curriculum and Instrn., St. Thomas U., St. Paul, 1996. Tchr. phys. edn., health and bus. Casselton HS, ND, 1970—77; tchr., kindergarten phys. edn. program, founder Moorhead Sch. Dist., Minn., 1989—94; phys. edn. tchr. Riverside Elem. Sch., Moorhead, 1994—2004, Hopkins Elem. Sch., Moorhead, 2005—. Named Phys. Edn. Teacher of Yr., Minn. Elem. Sch., 2002. Home: 16 11th Ave S Moorhead MN 56560-3362

WELKER, JENNIFER CAROL MARIE, artist; b. Conroe, Tex., May 9, 1977; d. Pamela Diane and Ronald Vaughn Welker. AA in Fashion Design, Fashion Inst. Tech., NYC, 1999. Co-founder, designer IC3D, N.Y.C., 1999—2002; mens designer Garren Inc., N.Y.C., 2002; artist Briefly Stated Inc., N.Y.C., 2003—. Co-founder D-Jeans, N.Y.C., 2003—; founder War Angels, N.Y.C., 2003—. Dir.: (documentary) Beyond The Ribbon. Mem. UNA-USA, N.Y.C., 2005—06; rev. World Christianship Ministries, Fresno, Calif., 2006—06; sponsor, mentor Save the Children, N.Y.C., 2005—06. Recipient Wall of Tolerance award, So. Poverty Law Ctr., 2005. Mem.: UN High Commn. for Refugees (life), Human Rights Watch (assoc.), Witness Orgn. (assoc.), Nat. Art Honor Soc. Achievements include design of digital custom clothing. Avocations: philanthropy, screen writing, human rights activist, sign language, actor. Home: 409 W 39th St Apt2A New York NY 10018 Personal E-mail: welker@beyondtheribbon.com.

WELKOWITZ, JOAN, psychology educator; b. N.Y.C; d. Abraham Jules and Ray (Jungfrau) Horowitz; m. Walter Welkowitz, June 17, 1951; children: David, Lawrence, Julie. BA, Queens Coll., 1949; MA, U. Ill., 1951; PhD, Columbia U., 1960. Lic. psychologist, N.J. Asst. prof. psychology NYU, 1964-68, assoc. prof., 1968-74, prof. psychology, 1975—, coord. clin. psychology program, 1988—. Statis. cons. NYU Med. Coll., 1980—. Author: Introduction to Statistics for the Behavioral Sciences, 1983; cons. editor Jour. Clin. and Cons. Psychology, 1977-82; contbr. articles to profl. jours. Mem. APA, Am. Assn. Applied and Preventive Psychology, Ea. Psychol. Assn., Am. Psychol. Soc. Home: 1 Washington Square Vlg Apt 6S New York NY 10012-1605 Office: NYU Dept Psychology 6 Washington Pl Dept New York NY 10003-6634

WELLEIN, MARSHA DIANE AKAU, military educator, director; d. George Herbert and Trude (Michelson) Akau; m. Daniel Navarro Atoigue; 1 child, Daniet Hokule'a; m. Lawrence Theodore Wellein (dec.); children: Geoffrey Michael, Nicholas Patrick. BA, U. Hawaii, 1966, tchg. cert., 1971; MEd, U. Guam, 1974; postgrad. in ednl. leadership, Argosy U., 2005. Instr. Hawaii Job Corps Ctr., 1969—71; tchr. spl. edn., reading, lang. arts, adults, pre-kindergarten to HS, U. Guam, 1972—80; reading specialist Waipahu Intermediate; instr. (full and part time) Leeward CC, U. Hawaii, 1981—85, instr. reading, 1983—85; full time guidance counselor US Army, Ft. Shafter Edn. Ctr., 1983—85, Larson Barracks, Germany, 1985—86, Dept. Army, Schofield Barracks, 1990; edn. svcs. officer, dir. Multinat. Force and Observers, North Camp, El Gorah, Sinai, Egypt, 1987—90; edn. svcs. officer Dept. Army, Soto Cano Air Base, Honduras, 1991—93, Ft. Kobbe, Panama, 1991—93; edn. svcs. specialist Dept. Army, Kuwait and Saudi Arabia (Desert Storm), 1993, Schofield Barracks Edn. Ctr. 25th Infantry, Hawaii, 1994—96, Camp Zama Edn. Ctr., Japan, 1996—98, 8th Army, Republic of Korea, 1998—99, Dept. Army, Ft. Shafter, 2000—01; dir. edn. and libr. svcs. US Army South, 1999—2000; svcs. and test control oficer USAR, Honolulu, 2006—. Author: (juvenile hardback novel) The Endless Summer, An Adventure Story of Guam, 1976; editor: Kalihi Kids Can Communicate, 1976. Bd. mem. Internat. Reading Assn., 1972—80, pres., 1980; mem. Oahu Com. Children and Youth, Honolulu, 1969. Named Outstanding Edn. Svcs. Officer, Dir. Edn., USAR, 2003; recipient Multinat. Force and Observers medal, US State Dept, 1987—89, Achievement medal civilian svc., Kuwait, 1993, Japan, 1997, Comdr.'s award civilian svc., 1986, 1987, 1988, 1998, Cold War cert., Camp Zama, Japan, 1998, Equal Opportunity award, 1998, Unsung Heroes award, Dir. Army Edn., Hdqrs., Washington, 2005, Lamp Lighters award, USAR, 2005. Mem.: Coun. Coll. and Mil. Educators, Am. Assn. Adult and Continuing Edn. Avocations: travel, reading, theater. Home: 95-086 Waihonu Pl Mililani HI 96789 Office: HQ G1 US Army Res APIX-PE 1557 Pass St Honolulu HI 96819-2135 Office Phone: 988-984-8727. Office Fax: 808-438-1379. Personal E-mail: welleinmd@hotmail.com.

WELLER, DEBRA ANNE, elementary school educator; b. New Orleans, Feb. 4, 1954; d. James Garretson and Elizabeth Gene (Blakely) Hyatt; m. Bruce Weller, June 15, 1974; children: Jenny, Todd. AA in Art, St. Petersburg Jr. Coll., 1974; BA in Art Edn., Glassboro State Coll., 1983; MS in Curriculum and Instrn., Nat. U., 1991. Cert. tchr. Profl. storyteller, Mission Viejo, Calif., 1980—; tchr. Capistrano Unified Sch. Dist., San Juan Capistrano, Calif., 1989—; elem. tchg. asst. prin. Bathgate Elem., 1998—. stds. curriculum specialist. Edn. dir. South Coast Storytellers Guild, Costa Mesa, Calif., 1990—; workshop presenter Orange County Dept. Edn., Costa Mesa, 1991—, Imagination Celebration, Irvine, Calif., 1993—; bd. mem. Calif. Kindergarten Assn; parenting instr. Author: (pamphlets) Image-U-Telling Clubs, 1995, Storytelling, the Cornerstone of Literacy, also articles. Adv. Eagles, Boy Scouts Am. Cultural Arts grantee Dana Point (Calif.) Cultural Commn., 1993; City of Mission Viejo grantee, 2003; Arts Orange County Storytelling Inst. grantee, 2005. Mem. NEA, Nat. Storytelling Network (liaison Pacific region), Calif. Tchrs. Assn., Calif. Kindergarten Assn. (bd. dirs., pres.-elect), South Coast Storytellers Guild (pres.), Storytellers Guild (pres. 1995-97, 2003—). Mem. Lds Ch. Avocations: calligraphy, composing, playing banjo, dulcimer and guitar.

WELLER, ELIZABETH BOGHOSSIAN, child and adolescent psychiatrist; b. Aug. 7, 1949; m. Ronald A. Weller, Feb. 18, 1978; children: Andrew, Christine. BS, Am. U., Beirut, Lebanon, 1971, MD, 1975. Lic. psychiatrist, Lebanon, Mo., Ohio, Pa. Intern Am. U. of Beirut, 1974-75; resident Renard Hosp./Washington U., St. Louis, 1975-78; fellow U. Kans. Med. Ctr., Kansas City, 1978-79; asst. prof. psychiatry U. Kans. Med. Sch., Kansas City, 1979-85; chief child/adolescent psychiatry Ohio State U., Columbus, 1985-94, assoc. chair dept. psychiatry, 1994-96; prof. psychiatry and pediat. U. Pa., 1996—, chmn. dept. psychiatry child and adolescent psychiatry, 1996-99, vice chmn. dept. psychiatry, prof. psychiatry/pediatrics, 1996—. Fred Allen chair dept. psychiatry Children's Hosp. of Phila., med. dir. Child Guidance Ctr., 1996-99; pres. Am. Bd. Psychiatry and Neurology, 2004. Co-author: Psychiatric Disorders in Child/Adolescent, 1990, Current Perspectives on Major Depressive Disorders in Children, 1984, Children's Interview for Psychiatric Syndromes, 1999. Fellow APA, Am. Acad. Child/Adolescent Psychiatry; mem. AMA, ACP, World Fedn. for Mental Health, Soc. Biol. Psychiatry, Am. Bd. Psychiatry and Neurology (pres. 2004). Office: 3440 Market St Philadelphia PA 19104-4399 Office Phone: 215-590-7573. Business E-mail: weller@email.chop.edu.

WELLER, LAURIE JUNE, artist, educator; b. Warsaw, N.Y., May 18, 1953; d. Charles M. and Mary (Loysen) W.; m. Gary B. Washmon, Sept. 5, 1980; children: Katelin, Jesse. BFA, U. Ill., 1976; MFA, Tyler Sch. of Art, Phila., 1980. Instr. Laguna Gloria Art Mus. Sch., Austin, Tex., 1980-83; lectr. S.W. Tex. State U., San Marcos, 1981-83; v.p. Austin Contemporary Visual Arts Assn., 1984-85; lectr. Tex. Woman's U., Denton, 1988-90, adj. asst. prof., 1990—. Vis. asst. prof. Tex. A&M U., Corpus Christi, 1997, Austin Coll., Sherman, Tex., 1999, 2006. One woman shows include Hadler/Rodriguez Gallery, Houston, 1981, 85, U. Gallery Southwest Tex. State U., San Marcos, Tex., 1983, Air Gallery, Austin, 1984, Amarillo Art Ctr., Tex., 1984, Objects Gallery, San Antonio, Tex., 1984, East & West Galleries Tex. Women's U., Denton, Tex., 1987, Gardiner Art Gallery Okla. State U., Stillwater, 1987, Patrick Gallery, Austin, 1989, Mountain View Coll., Tex., 1993, William Campbell Contemporary Art, Ft. Worth, 1993, Tex. Woman's U., Denton, 1994, Lakeside Gallery Richland Coll., Dallas, 1995, Harry Nohr Gallery U. Wis., Platteville, 1996; exhibited in two person shows at Illini Union Gallery U. Ill., Urbana, 1984, Patrick Gallery, Austin, Tex., 1986, Tarrant County Jr. Coll., Ft. Worth, Tex., 1990, Parkland Coll. Art Gallery, Champaign, Ill., 1990, Brookhaven Coll., Dallas, 1993, Irving Art Ctr., Irving, Tex., 1993, N. Lake Coll., Dallas, 1994, Okla. U., Norman, Okla., 2003, Visual Art Ctr., Denton, Tex., 2004, Hardin Simmons U. Abilene, Tex., 2006; exhibited in group shows at Butler Inst. Am. Arts, Youngstown, Ohio, 1976, Springfield (Mo.) Art Mus., 1979, Laguna Gloria Art Mus., Austin, 1982, San Antonio Mus. Art, Tex., 1985, Abilene Art Mus, Texas, 1988, William Campbell Contemporary Art, Ft. Worth, Tex., 1989, Matrix Gallery, Austin Tex., 1990, Charles P. Goddard Ctr. Visual Arts, Ardmore, Ohio, 1991, Laguna Gloria Art Mus., Austin, 1991, Longview Mus. Arts Ctr. Longview, Tex., 1992, Brookhaven Coll., Dallas, 1994, Meadows Gallery, Denton, 1994, Coll. of the Mainland, Texas City, Tex., 1995, Maurice Sternberg Gallery, Chgo., 1996; represented in permanent collections Pepsi-Cola South, Texas Instruments, Radisson Hotels, 3M Corp., Amoco Oil Co., Prudential Ins. Co., Steak & Ale Corp., Tambrands. Fellow Va. Ctr. for Creative Arts, Sweet Briar, 1982, 84. Office: Tex Woman's U PO Box 425469 Denton TX 76204-5469 Office Phone: 940-898-2538.

WELLER, MARTHA RIHERD, physics and astronomy professor, consultant; b. Charleston, SC, Oct. 20, 1952; d. Paul Markey and Martha Carroll Riherd; m. Robert Allen Weller, June 21, 1975; children: Rachel Weller Deaton, Robert Samuel, Rebecca Shelley. BA in Physics, Rice U., 1973; PhD in Physics, Calif. Inst. Tech., 1979. Rsch. physicist Naval Rsch. Lab., Washington, 1979—80; rsch. staff physicist, rsch. assoc. Yale U., New Haven, 1980—87; asst. prof. physics Mid. Tenn. State U., Murfreesboro, Tenn., 1988—93, assoc. prof. physics, astronomy, 1993—98, prof. of physics, astronomy, 1998—. Com. mem. Brentwood 2020, Tenn., 1998—98; pres. Edmondson Elem. PTO, Brentwood, Tenn., 1995—96, Centennial H.S. Parent Tchr. Student Orgn., Franklin, Tenn., 1998—99; sch. bd. rep. Williamson County Bd. of Edn., Franklin, Tenn., 2002—06. Mem.: Tenn. Acad. of Sci. (physics and astronomy editl. bd. 1991—, exec. bd. mem. 1995—97), Sigma Xi, Am. Assn. of Physics Tchrs., Am. Phys. Soc. Office: Mid Tenn State Univ PO Box 403 Murfreesboro TN 37132 Office Phone: 615-898-2792. Office Fax: 615-898-5303. E-mail: mweller@mtsu.edu.

WELLER, ROBIN LEA, elementary school educator; b. Jacksonville, Ill., Aug. 9, 1955; d. James Robert and Lois Lea Ford; m. Michael Lewis Weller, June 22, 1975; children: Christopher Lewis, Robert Michael, Morgan Lea. B in Elem. Edn., U. Ill., Springfield, 1985. Owner Robin's Nest Flower Shop, Greenfield, Ill., 1976—81; lang. arts instr., counselor Greenfield Elem. Sch., 1985—; GED instr. Greene County Ill. Impact Incarceration Program, Roodhouse, Ill., 1993—. Methodist. Avocations: painting, gardening, music. Home: 302 Walnut St Greenfield IL 62044 Office: Greenfield Elem Sch 115 Prairie St Greenfield IL 62044 Personal E-mail: rweller1955@yahoo.com.

WELLER, TRUDY A., psychotherapist; b. Lancaster, Pa., Feb. 14, 1948; d. Stearns H. Kline and Ruth N. (Kantner) Boyer; 1 child, Iris E. BS, Kutztown U., 1996, MA, 2000. Lic. profl. counselor Pa. Trainer Threshold, Reading, Pa., 1978—83; tchr. Headstart, Reading, 1983—89; counselor, foster care dir. Luth. Home, Topton, Pa., 1997—2001; clin. counseling supr. Cath. Social Agy., Reading, 2001—. Mem.: Am. Kite Flyers Assn., Am. Counseling Assn. Democrat. Achievements include development of therapeutic approach called the Nature Nurture Network. Avocations: hiking, collecting irises, ice skating, gardening, kite flying. Home: 604 Main St Oley PA 19547

WELLING, KATHRYN MARIE, editor; b. Ft. Wayne, Ind., Feb. 4, 1952; d. Arthur Russell Sr. and Genevieve (Disser) W.; m. Donald Robert Boyle, Oct. 21, 1978; children: Brian Joseph, Thomas Arthur. BS in Journalism, Northwestern U., 1974. Copy reader Dow Jones News Retrieval, N.Y.C., 1974-75; copy reader, reporter AP-Dow Jones, N.Y.C., 1975-76; copy editor Wall Street Jour., N.Y.C., 1976; reporter Barron's, N.Y.C., 1976-81, asst. to editor, 1981, mng. editor, 1982-92, assoc. editor, 1992—99; ltd. ptnr. Weeden & Co. L.P., Greenwich, Conn., 1999—; prin. Welling@Weeden, Greenwich, 1999—. Columnist Welling's Acute Observations, Traders Mag. Online. Charter mem. Northwestern U. Coun. of One Hundred. Avocations: sailing, skiing. Office: Weeden & Co LP 145 Mason St Greenwich CT 06830 Office Phone: 203-861-7643. Business E-Mail: welling@weedenco.com.

WELLING, MARY ANN, secondary school educator; b. Moline, Ill., Oct. 24, 1925; d. Camiel Joseph DeWitte and Margaret Carton De Witte; m. Vern Anthony Welling (dec.); children: John Joseph, James Anthony, Mary Lisa Faust. BA, Western Ill. U., 1977, MSc, 1980. Cert. ednl. specialist in edn. adminstrn. Western Ill. U., 1983, tchr. physical edn. State of Ill., 1977, tchr. elem. and sec. edn. State of Ill., 1980, ednl. adminstrn. State of Ill., 1983. Sec. Moline Pub. Hosp., Moline, Ill., 1943—60; tchr., athletic dir. St. Anne Sch., 1961—83; tchr., dept. head Rock Island H.S., Ill., 1983—95. Pres. Rock Is./Milan Fedn. of Teachers (Divsn. of Am. Fedn. of Teachers), 1985—95; sec. Peoria Diocese Commn. on Edn., 1985—. Past pres., bd. dirs. Assn. for Retarded Citizens, Rock Is., Ill., 1986—90; trustee Wilber L. Burress Endowment Found. Assn. for Retarded Citizens, Rock Is., Ill., 1991—; past v.p. Am. Cancer Soc. (NW region), 1986—2002; fund distbn. panel mem. United Way of the Quad Cities, 2000—02; v.p. Diocesan coun. of Cath. Women, Peoria, Ill., 2002—; pres. Sacred Heart Ch., Altar and Rosary Soc., Moline, Ill., 2001—; lay min. Sacred Heart Ch., 1975—. Recipient Evelyn Colbert ARC award for service (first recipient), 1988, Master Tchr. award, Rock Is./Milan Sch. Dist., 1995. Mem.: Ill. Ret. Tchrs. Assn., Quad City Bot. Ctr., Phi Delta Kappa. Roman Cath. Avocations: sewing, sports, church, politics. Home: 1143 45th St Rock Island IL 61201 E-mail: madewitte1@aol.com.

WELLINGTON, JEAN SUSORNEY, librarian; b. East Chicago, Ind., Oct. 23, 1945; d. Carl Matthew and Theresa Ann Susorney; m. Donald Clifford Wellington, June 12, 1976; 1 child, Evelin Patricia. BA, Purdue U., 1967; MA in LS, Dominican U., River Forest, Ill., 1969; MA, U. Cin., 1976. Head Burnam Classical Libr. U. Cin., 1970—. Compiler Dictionary of Bibliographic Abbreviations Found in the Scholarship of Classical Studies and Related Disciplines, 1983, 2d edit., 2002, revised and expanded edit., 2003. Mem. Art. Librs. Soc. N.Am. (chair Ohio br. 1984-85). Office: U Cin Classics Libr PO Box 210191 Cincinnati OH 45221-0191

WELLMAN, MARIAN C., social worker; b. Washington, July 23, 1934; d. Vivian Barnes Cole; m. William Wellman (div.). BA in Psychology, Calif. State U., L.A., 1965; MSW, UCLA, 1971. LCSW. Social worker L.A. County, L.A., 1965—71, adoptions worker and supr., 1971—90; therapeutic counselor and practitioner in pvt. practice L.A., 1990—2003. Oral examiner Bd. Behavioral Sci. State of Calif., 1992—98. Author: New Shades of Poetry, 1984, Living With the "I" Word, 2002. Mem. Black Women's Forum, L.A., 1995—; big sister Big Sister League, L.A., 1996—97; pres. Sat. Morning Lit. Workshop, L.A., 1982—; mem. St. Paul's Luth. Ch., L.A. Recipient Fannie Lou Hamer award, Internat. Black Writers of Am., 1997. Avocations: travel, music, theater, walking, bicycling. Office: PO Box 43722 Los Angeles CA 90043

WELLS, BETTE EVANS, psychotherapist; b. Hot Springs, Ark., Oct. 31, 1944; d. Basil Brent and Betty (Gandy) Evans; m. John W. Wells, July 25, 1969; 1 child, Karis Evan. BA, Bob Jones U., 1967; cert. edn. Fla. Atlantic U., 1976; MS, Nova U., 1979. Tchr. pvt. and pub. schs., Fla., 1967-76; pvt. group practice psychotherapy, Ft. Lauderdale, 1981-87; dir. Wells & Assocs., 1987—. Contbr. articles to profl. jours. Mem. Task Force Commn. on Status of Women, 1981-82. Mem. Nat. Council on Family Relations, Am. Mental Health Counselor Assn., Am. Assn. Counseling and Devel. Republican. Presbyterian. Office: Wells & Assocs Inc Bank Atlantic Bldg 10 Fairway Dr Ste 217 Hillsboro Blvd Deerfield Beach FL 33441

WELLS, CAROL MCCONNELL, genealogist, retired archivist; b. Phila., Feb. 21, 1918; d. William Hugh McConnell and Edith Mary Lower; m. Tom Henderson Wells, Dec. 31, 1943; children: Lucy, Sarah, Tom, Christopher, Julia, Peter. BA, Pa. State Coll., State College, 1939; MA, Northwestern State U., Natchitoches, La., 1973. Archivist Northwestern State U., Natchitoches, La., 1974-88; editor So. Studies, Natchitoches, 1982-88. Spkr. in field. Author: Williamson County, Tennessee: A Genealogical Abstract of the County Court Minutes, 1800-1804, 1987, 88, Davidson County, Tennessee, County Court Minutes 1783-1792, 1990, Davidson County, Tennessee, County Court Minutes, 1792-1799, 1991, Davidson County, Tennessee, County Court Minutes 1799-1803, 1991, Genealogical Abstracts of Edgefield, SC, Equity Court Records, 2002, Edgefield County, South Carolina, Probate Records, Boxes 1-3, 2004, many others Mem. Natchitoches Hist. Found., 1994—. Lt. (j.g.) USNR, 1944. Named Woman of Yr. C. of C., 1975; recipient Clio award Phi Alpha Theta, 1988. Mem. DAR, PEO Sisterhood, Phi Mu, Phi Beta Kappa, Phi Kappa Phi. Republican. Anglican Catholic. Avocation: gardening. Home: 607 Williams Ave Natchitoches LA 71457 Personal E-mail: carolwells@cp-tel.net.

WELLS, CAROLYN CRESSY, social work educator; b. Boston, July 26, 1943; d. Harris Shipman Wells and Marianne Elizabeth (Monroe) Glazier; m. Dale Reed Konle, Oct. 11, 1970 (div. Sept. 3, 1982); m. Dennis Alan Loeffler, Sept. 29, 1990. BA, U. Calif., Berkeley, 1965; MSW, U. Wis., 1968, PhD, 1973. Lic. clin. social worker, marriage and family therapist. Vol. VISTA, Espanola, N.Mex., 1965—66; social worker Project Six Ctrl. Wis. Colony, Madison, 1968, Milw. Dept. Pub. Welfare, 1969, Shorewood Manor Nursing Home, Wis., 1972; sch. social worker Jefferson County Spl. Edn., Wis., 1977—78; from lectr. sociology and social work to prof. Marquette U., Milw., 1972—94, prof. social work, 1994—99, U. Wis., Oshkosh, 1999—; social work therapist Lighthouse Counseling Assocs., Racine, Wis., 1989—91, The Cambridge Group, 1991—92, Achievement Assocs., 1992—95. Vis. lectr. social work U. Canterbury, Christchurch, N.Z., 1983; Edward R. Rudow endowed prof. U. Wis., Oshkosh, 2005. Author: Social Work Day to Day, 1982, 3d edit., 1999, Social Work Ethics Day to Day, 1986, Stepping to the Dance, the Training of a Family Therapist, 1998; co-author: The Social Work Experience, 1991, 4th edit., 2003. Mem. Wis. Coun. on Social Work Edn., pres., 1980-82, sec., 1985-87, mem. exec. com., 1993-96. Mem. NASW, Coun. on Social Work Edn. (mem. publs. and media com. 1989-91, site visitor for accreditation 1987—), Acad. Cert. Social Workers, Assn. Baccalaureate Program Dirs. (assoc.) Democrat. Avocations: writing, silent sports, celtic harp. Home: 4173 Sleeping Dragon Rd West Bend WI 53095-9296 Office: U Wis Oshkosh Dept Social Work 800 Algoma Blvd Oshkosh WI 54901 Office Phone: 920-424-7179. Business E-Mail: wellsc@uwosh.edu.

WELLS, CATHY ECKARD, elementary school educator; d. Merrill and Virginia Eckard; m. Lehman Dale Wells, Sr. (dec.). BS, Appalachian State U., Boone, N.C., 1971; Masters, Converse Coll., Spartanburg, S.C., 1981; postgrad., U. S.C., Spartanburg, 1981—85. Cert. notary pub. S.C., 1985, tchr. N.C., S.C. Tchr. 2d grade Glendale Elem. Sch., SC, 1971—79; homebound instr. Spartanburg Sch. Dist. 3, Glendale, SC, 1975—77; tchr. adult edn. R.D. Anderson Vocat. Ctr., Moore, SC, 1977—91; tchr. 4th grade Clifdale Elem. Sch., Spartanburg, SC, 1979—2000, tchr. 5th grade, 2001—. Mem. Clifdale Elem. Sch. PTO, 1979—. Named Tchr. of Yr., Vets. Fgn. Wars, Spartanburg, 2005; recipient Disting. Reading Tchr., Internat. Reading Assn., 1985, Reading Tchr. of Yr. award, Clifdale Elem. Sch., 1986, Tchr. of Yr. award, 1988, award, Walker E. Solomon Sch., 1998, numerous grants. Mem.: Alpha Delta Kappa. Avocation: travel. Office Phone: 864-579-8010. E-mail: cwells@spa3.k12.sc.us.

WELLS, CHRISTINE, foundation executive; b. Houghton Lake, Mich., Aug. 6, 1948; d. Chester John and Mary W.; m. David Mazzarella. BA in French and Eng., Mich. State U., 1970, MLIR, 1982; MLS, U. Mich., 1976. Head libr. Lansing State Jour., E. Lansing, Mich., 1973-82; mng. editor libr. svcs. USA TODAY, Washington, 1982-87; libr. dir. Gannett Co., Inc., Washington, 1985-87, chief staff, chmn. and CEO office, 1988-89; v.p. adminstrn. Gannett Found., Washington, 1989-90; v.p. internat. The Freedom Forum, Washington, 1991—; exec. dir. The Newseum, 1993-94; sr. v.p. internat. The Freedom Forum, 1994—. Dir., Al Neuharth Free Spirit Award Com. Mem. bd. overseers Internat. Press Ctr. and Club, Moscow; mem. bd. visitors Coll. Sci., Mich. State U. Recipient Dising. Alumni award U. Mich., 1991. Mem. ALA, Spl. Librs. Assn. (Profl. award 1994). Office: The Freedom Forum 1101 Wilson Blvd Ste 2300 Arlington VA 22209-2265

WELLS, CHRISTINE VALERIE, music educator; b. Flushing, N.Y., Sept. 25, 1948; d. Roland Clifford and Frances Marie (Da Ros) Stoehr; m. Jonathan Freda Wells, June 20, 1970 (dec. Nov. 1989); children: Jennifer Lee Magee, Kevin Michael, Frederick Joseph. BMus cum laude, Bucknell U., 1970; MA, U. Md., 1974. Elem. vocal music tchr. Prince George's County Pub. Schs., Upper Marlboro, Md., 1970—2003; cantor, substitute organist Holy Trinity Cath. Ch., Glen Burnie, Md., 1980-81, St. Stanislaus Kostka Ch., Balt., 1983-2000; organist Holy Rosary Ch., Balt., 2000—; vocal music tchr. Woodmont Acad., Cooksville, Md., 2003—. Choir dir. Gregorian Singers, Glen Burnie, 1981—90; music dir. numerous plays Pasadena Theatre Co., Millersville, Md., 1981—; music dir. for plays Act II Dinner Theatre, Rosedale, Md., 1994—95, Timonium (Md.) Dinner Theatre, 1994—95, Music and Drama and Goddard Space Flight Ctr., 1997—; soprano Friday Morning Music Club Chorale, Washington, 2001—. Active fundraising Leukemia Soc., Am. Heart Assn., Glen Burnie; cantor, organist, lector Good Shepherd Cath. Ch., Glen Burnie, 1982—; organist St. Alphonsus Rodriguez Ch., Woodstock, Md., 2001—; tchr. piano Langley Pk. Sr. Ctr., Prince George County, Md., 2005. Mem. Nat. Mus. Women in the Arts (charter). Republican. Roman Catholic. Avocations: travel, music and theater, baseball, swimming, reading. Home: 303 Glenwood Ave Glen Burnie MD 21061-2233 Office: Woodmont Academy 2000 Woodmont Ln Cooksville MD 21723-9502 E-mail: christine.wells@verizon.net.

WELLS, CYNTHIA, elementary school educator; b. Redwood City, Calif., Nov. 05; d. Ken and Alice Herndon; m. Joe Wells. BS in Elem. Edn., U. Nev., Reno, 1982. Tchr. 6th grade Kingsbury Mid. Sch., Lake Tahoe, Nev., 1983—2000, tchr. 7th and 8th grade, 2000—. Recipient Tchr. Yr., Kingsbury Mid. Sch., 1988, 2003. Avocations: bicycling, gardening, reading, travel. Office: Kingsbury Middle School PO Box 648 Zephyr Cove NV 89448 Office Phone: 775-588-6281. E-mail: cwells@dcsd.k12.nv.us.

WELLS, DEBRA ELAINE, parochial school educator; b. Circleville, Ohio, Feb. 12, 1958; d. Loring James and Teresa Mae Allen; m. Randall K. Wells, Aug. 26, 1977; children: Dawn Marie Gonzalez, Kellie Kathleen Berlean. B in Profl. Studies summa cum laude, Barry U., Miami, Fla., 1996; MA in Edn., Mt. Vernon (Ohio) Nazarene U., 2004. Substitute tchr. Knox County Schs., Mount Vernon, 2003—05; adj. instr. Mt. Vernon Nazarene U., 2004—, edn. field supr., 2005; tchr. Gilead Christian Sch., Mt. Gilead, Ohio, 2005—. Nat. honor soc. faculty advisor Gilead Christian Sch., 2005—06, academic counselor, Class of 2009 advisor, 2006—. Mem.: Assn. Christian Schs. Internat., Nat. Coun. Social Studies (corr.). Home: 18320 Paige Rd Mount Vernon OH 43050 Office: Gilead Christian Sch 3613 TR 115 Mount Gilead OH 43338 Office Phone: 419-946-5990. Personal E-mail: dewells1977@yahoo.com.

WELLS, EDIE CAROL, artist, educator; BS in Art Edn., Auburn U., Ala., 1985. Graphic artist Bapt. Pub. Ho., Monrovia, Liberia, 1988, Start Mag., Birmingham, Ala., 1990—92; artist/jewelry designer - co-owner The Elephant Crossing, Ft. Worth, 1995—2005; visual arts tchr. Ft. Worth Acad. Fine Arts, 2003—. Mem.: Tex. Art Edn. Assn., Nat. Art Edn. Assn. Avocation: travel. Home: 129 Berkshire Ln Fort Worth TX 76134-2926 Office: Fort Worth Academy of Fine Arts 3901 S Hulen Fort Worth TX 76109 Office Phone: 817-924-1482. Office Fax: 817-926-9932. Business E-Mail: edie.wells@fwafa.org.

WELLS, GERTRUDE BEVERLY, psychologist; b. Haverhill, Mass., July 14, 1940; d. True Franklyn Wells and Priscilla Eleanor (Browne) Duerstling. BS, SUNY, Fredonia, 1962; MA, Coll. St. Rose, Albany, N.Y., 1969; PhD, U. Mo., Columbia, 1976; PhD in Clin. Psychology, Fielding Grad. U., Santa Barbara, Calif., 1999. Tchr. speech pathology N.Y. Pub. Schs., Albany and Clifton Park, 1962-70; lectr. SUNY, Albany, 1970-73; asst. prof. Coll. St. Rose, Albany, 1975-77; assoc. prof. U. No. Iowa, Cedar Falls, 1977-78; prof. U. of La., Lafayette, 1978-85; prof., program dir. Calif. State U. Stanislaus, Turlock, 1985-87; prof. comm. Calif. State U., San Francisco, 1987—92; chief exec. officer West Coast Inst., 1992—2000; clin. psychologist, pvt. practice, 2001—. Author: Stuttering Treatment, 1987; contbr. articles to profl. jours. Health svc. provider Nat. Register of Health Svc. in Psychology. Mem.: APA, Calif. Psychol. Assn., Am. Acad. Health Care Providers in Addictive Disorders. Avocations: writing, bicycling, gardening. Office: 16 Joost Ave San Francisco CA 94131 Office Phone: 415-585-5212. Personal E-mail: doctorwells@earthlink.net.

WELLS, GLADYSANN, library director; BA in English, Greensboro Coll., NC, 1970; MLS, SUNY, Albany, 1972. Libr. Empire State Coll., 1972—73; legis. reference libr. N.Y. State Libr., Albany, 1973—78; with Senate Rsch. Svc., 1975—80; libr. Senate Libr., 1978—80; adminstr. N.Y. State Libr., 1980—95; interim dir. N.Y. State Libr. Rsch. Libr., 1995—97; state libr. Ariz. State Libr., 1997—. Editor several books on the economy of the northeast; contbr. articles to profl. jours. Avocations: horseback riding, cross country skiing, hiking, snow shoeing. Office: Ariz State Libr 1700 W Washington Ste 200 Phoenix AZ 85007-2896

WELLS, JULIA ELIZABETH See DAME ANDREWS, JULIE

WELLS, KAREN KAY, medical librarian; b. Petaluma, Calif., Jan. 9, 1956; d. Albert Lee and Miyoko (Kay) W.; m. John Edward Guth, Aug. 4, 1979 (div. 1986). BS with honors, U. Colo., 1977; MEd with honors, U. Ill., 1980, MS with honors, 1982. Cert. tchr., Colo., Ill. Grad. asst. grad. libr. U. Ill., Urbana, 1981—82; asst. prof. med. libr. svcs. sch. medicine Mercer U., Macon, Ga., 1982—88; libr., head dept. Presbyn. Denver and St. Luke's Med. Ctr., 1983; instr., cons. dialog pharm. database AMI-St. Luke's Hosp. Health Scis. Libr., Denver, 1985—87; head libr. Manville Health, Safety and Environ. Libr., Denver, 1988—91; info. cons. Wells Info. Svc., Denver, 1989—91, sr. adminstrv. assessor, 1996—98; libr. mgr. Exemple Luth. Med. Ctr., Wheat Ridge, Colo., 2000—. Mem. ALA, Med. Libr. Assn., Colo. Coun. Med. Librs. (cons. med.-sci. databases 1984—), U. Colo. Alumni Assn., U. Ill. Alumni Assn., Beta Phi Mu, Kappa Delta Pi. Democrat. Presbyterian. Avocations: racquetball, diving. Office: Exempla Luth Med Ctr 8300 W 38th Ave Wheat Ridge CO 80033

WELLS, KIMBERLY K., not-for-profit organization executive; BA in Psychology, MA in Counseling Psychology. Dir. youth svcs., dir. program svcs., assoc. exec. dir. Home Sweet Home Mission, 1987—97; exec. dir. Corp. Alliance to End Prtnr. Violence, 1997—. Mem. Workplace Com. Nat. Task Force to End Sexual and Domestic Violence Against Women; chair Promotion Com., State of Ill.; mem. Gov.'s Commn. on Status of Women in Ill. Violence Reduction Group, Ill. Corp. Citizenship Initiative; mem. steering com. Ill. Family Violence Coordinating Coun.; mem. 11th Jud. Cir. Family Violence Coordinating Coun. Planning Com.; co-chair McLean County Domestic Violence Task Force Youth and Children Work Group; treas., bd. dirs. Ill. Ctr. for Violence Prevention; grad. Leadership Am. Am. Issues Forum, 1999; guest lectr. Ill. State U., Heartland C.C. Office: 2416 E Washington St Ste E Bloomington IN 61704-4472

WELLS, KITTY (ELLEN MURIEL DEASON), musician; b. Nashville, Aug. 30, 1919; d. Charles Cary and Myrtle Bell (Street) Deason; m. Johnnie Robert Wright, Oct. 30, 1937; children: Ruby Jean Wright Taylor, Bobby Wright, Carol Sue Wright-Sturdivant. Grad. high sch. Country music singer; sang gospel in chs. as a child; formed group Deacon Sisters, performed on radio, early 30's; with Johnny and Jack and the Tenn. Mountain Boys, late 1930's-early 1940's, regular on Grand Ole Opry, from 1952, had own family TV show, late 1960's-early 1970's, now with Johnny Wright, Bobby Wright and the Tennessee Mountain Boys; songs include: Gathering Flowers for the Master's Bouquet, How Far is Heaven, Release Me, It Wasn't God Who Made Honky Tonk Angels, Making Believe, Thank You For the Roses; albums include Kitty Wells & Roy Drusky, Vol. 1 & 2, Back to Back Patsy Kline, 1995, (with Red Foley, Webb Pierce, others) Duets, 1995; author: Kitty Wells Cookbook. Bd. dirs. Nashville Meml. Hosp. Recipient award as number 1 female singer Cashbox Mag., 1953-62, Billboard 1954-65, award of yr. for top female country vocalist Record World mag. 1965, award for highest artistic achievement in rec. arts 1964, various awards Downbeat Mag., award as all-time queen of country music Music Bus. Mag. 1964, Woman of Yr. award 1974, Pioneer award Acad. Country Music 1985, Living Legend award Music City news 1991, voted nation's number one Country Female Artist for 14 consecutive years; named Top Female Artist of Decade, Record World Mag. 1974; named to Country Music Hall of Fame 1976. Mem. Country Music Assn., Nat. Assn. Rec. Arts and Scis. (Govs. award for Outstanding Achievement in Recording Industry, 1981, Grammy Lifetime Achievement award, 1991). Mem. Ch. of Christ. Achievements include being the first woman to hit No. 1 on the country charts with "It Wasn't God Who Made Honky Tonk Angels.".

WELLS, LESLEY, federal judge; b. Muskegon, Mich., Oct. 6, 1937; d. James Franklin and Inez Simpson Wells; m. Charles F. Clarke, Nov. 13, 1998; children: Lauren Elizabeth, Caryn Alison, Anne Kristin, Thomas Eliot. BA, Chatham Coll., 1959; JD cum laude, Cleve. State U., 1974. Bar: Ohio 1975, US Dist. Ct. (no. dist.) Ohio 1975, US Supreme Ct. 1989. Pvt. practice, Cleve., 1975; ptnr. Brooks & Moffet, Cleve., 1975—78; dir., atty. ABAR Litigation Ctr., Cleve., 1979—80; assoc. Schneider, Smeltz, Huston & Ranney, Cleve., 1980—83; judge Ct. Common Pleas, Cleve., 1983—94, U.S. Dist. Ct. (no. dist.) Ohio 6th Cir., Cleve., 1994—. Adj. prof. law and urban policy Cleve. State U., 1980-83, 90-93. Editor, author: Litigation Manual, 1980. Past pres. Cleve. Legal Aid Soc.; legal chmn. Nat. Women's Polit. Caucus, 1981-82; chmn. Gov.'s Task Force on Family Violence, Ohio, 1983-87; mem. biomed. ethics com. Case Western Res. U. Med. Sch., 1985-94; mem. NW Ordinance US Constn. Commn., Ohio, 1986-88; master William K. Thomas Inn of Ct., 1989—, counselor, 1993, pres., 1998-99; trustee Rosemary Ctr., 1986-92, Miami U., 1988-92, Urban League Cleve., 1989-90, Chatham Coll., 1989-94. Recipient Superior Jud. award Supreme Ct. Ohio, 1983, J. Irwin award Womenspace, Ohio, 1984, award Womens City Club, 1985, Disting. Alumna award Chatham Coll., 1988, Alumni Civic Achievement award Cleve. State U., 1992, Golden Gavel award Ohio Judges Assn., 1994, Outstanding Alumni award Cleve. Marshall Law Alumni Assn., 1994, Greater Cleve. Achievement award YWCA, 1995. Mem. ABA (coun. litigation sect. 1996-99), Am. Law Inst., Ohio Bar Assn., Ohio Womens Bar Assn., Cleve. Bar Assn. (Merit Svc. award 1983), Cuyahoga County Bar Assn., Nat. Assn. Women Judges, Philos. Club Cleve. Office: 328 US Court House 201 Superior Ave Cleveland OH 44114-1234 Office Phone: 216-615-4480. Business E-Mail: lesley_wells@ohnd.uscourts.gov.

WELLS, LINDA ANN, editor-in-chief; b. NYC, Aug. 9, 1958; d. H. Wayne and Jean (Burchell) W.; m. Charles King Thompson, Nov., 1993. BA in English, Trinity Coll., 1980. Edit. asst. Vogue Mag., N.Y.C., 1980-83, assoc. editor beauty, 1983-85; style reporter New York Times, N.Y.C., 1985, beauty editor, food editor, 1985-90; founding editor, editor-in-chief Allure Mag., N.Y.C., 1990—. Spkr. Am. Womens' Econ. Devel., N.Y., 1988-89, Brand Futures Group, N.Y., 1999. Contbr. numerous articles to N.Y. Times Mag., Allure Mag., 1985—; appearances on Today Show, The View, Entertainment Tonight, E!, CNN. Chmn. N.Y. Shakespeare Festival, 1993, 94; bd. fellows Trinity Coll., 1998—; bd. visitors Mary Inst. Country Day Sch., St. Louis. Recipient Fragrance Found. award 1991, 99, 2000, 2001, Nat. Mag. Design award, 1994, Legal Def. and Edn. Fund Equal Opportunity award NOW, 1994, Trinith Coll. Alumni Achievement award, 2000, Cosmetic Exec. Women Achiever award, 2001, Skin Sense Award, Skin Cancer Found., 2003. Mem. Am. Soc. Mag. Editors (bd. dirs. 1993-97). Office: Allure Mag Conde Nast Publs 4 Times Sq Fl 10 New York NY 10036-6522

WELLS, LINDA LEE, retired elementary school educator; b. Pine Bluff, Ark., Feb. 13, 1944; d. Charles Ray and Betty Lee Bryan; m. Danny Joe Wells, Sept. 29, 1961; children: Terri Harper, Gene Wells. BS in Elem. Edn., U. Ark., 1984. Elem. tchr. White Hall (Ark.) Sch. Dist., 1985—2004; ret. Charter mem. Redfield (Ark.) Hist. Soc., 1982. Mem. NEA, Ark. Edn. Assn. (Nat. Dean's List 1983, Chancellor's List 1983), Redfield C. of C. Avocations: painting, drawing, arts and crafts. Home: 1119 Wells Dr PO Box 69 Redfield AR 72132 Office: Hardin Elem Schoolwood Dr Redfield AR 72132

WELLS, MARY ELIZABETH THOMPSON, deacon, chaplain, director; b. Dallas, Oct. 9, 1936; d. Owen Perry and Ruth Marie Thompson; children: Tadd Whitney, Britony Ruth. BA in Sociology, Syracuse U., 1958; MA in Child Devel., Tufts U., 1964, MEd in Counseling Psychology, 1974; MA in Theology, St. Vincent de Paul Regional Sem., 2005. Ordained min. Diocese of Southeast Fla., 2002. Asst. dir. pub. rels. Inst. Crippled and Disabled, N.Y.C., 1958-59; head tchr. Eliot-Pearson Children's Sch., Tufts U., Medford, Mass., 1964-66; psychotherapist Mental Health Ctr. Greater Cape Ann, Gloucester, Mass., 1974-89; deacon, chaplain, spiritual dir. St. Paul's Episcopal Ch., Delray Beach, Fla., 1999—, dir. Diocesan Sch. S.E. Fla., 2003—. Mem.: APA, Spiritual Dirs. Internat., Assn. Profl. Chaplains, Assn. Clin. Pastoral Educators, Am. Orthopsychiatric Assn. Home: 1183 Canoe Point Delray Beach FL 33444 Office: Saint Pauls Episcopal Ch 188 S Swinton Ave Delray Beach FL 33444-3698

WELLS, MARY JULIA, psychologist; b. Arlington, Va., Nov. 23, 1958; d. John Murrell and Rollene Sumner Wells; 2 stepchildren. BS, Va. Commonwealth U., 1980; MPhil, George Wash. U., 1988, PhD, 1990. Lic. clin. psychologist Va., 1991. Psychology assoc. Wash. Pain and Rehab Ctr., Wash., DC, 1988—90; asst. prof. Med. Coll. Va., Richmond, Va., 1990—93; clin. psychologist Inst. Chronic Pain Mgmt., Richmond, 1993—96, pvt. practice, Richmond, 1996—2000, Sheltering Arm Hosp., Richmond, 2000—. Contbr. chapters to books. Pres. Richmond Acad. Clin. Psychologists, Richmond, Va., 1995—96, mem. chair, 2002—04, pres., 2005; anti racism trainer Unitarian Universalist Assn., Richmond, Va., 1999. Mem.: Am. Psychological Assn., Va. Psychological Assn., Richmond Acad. Clin. Psychologists. Democrat. Unitarian. Avocations: music, dogs. Office: Sheltering Arms Physical Rehab Hosp 8254 Atlee Rd Mechanicsville VA 23116 Office Phone: 804-723-3275. Business E-Mail: mwells@shelteringarms.com.

WELLS, MELISSA FOELSCH, retired ambassador; b. Tallinn, Estonia, Nov. 18, 1932; emigrated to U.S., 1936, naturalized, 1941; d. Kuno Georg and Miliza (Korjus) Foelsch; m. Alfred Washburn Wells, 1960; children: Christopher, Gregory. BS in Fgn. Service, Georgetown U., 1956. Fgn. svc. officer Dept. State, Washington, 1958-61, consular officer Trinidad, 1961-64; econ. officer mission OECD, Paris, 1964-66; econ. officer London, 1966-71; internat. economist, 1971-73; dep. dir. maj. export projects Dept. Commerce, 1973-75; comml. counselor Brazil, 1975-76; amb. to Guinea-Bissau and Cape Verde Dept. of State, 1976-77; U.S. rep. ECOSOC, UN, N.Y.C., 1977-79; resident rep. UNDP, Kampala, Uganda, 1979-81, dir. IMPACT program Geneva, 1982-86; amb. to Mozambique, 1987-90; amb. to Zaire, Kinshasa, 1991-93; under-sec. gen. for adminstrn. and mgmt. UN, N.Y., 1993-94; consul gen. Sao Paulo, Brazil, 1995-97; amb. to Republic of Estonia Dept. of State, 1998—2001; ret., 2001. Bd. dirs. U.S.-Baltic Found. Mem. Am. Fgn. Service Assn., Am. Acad. Diplomacy. Office: Casa Wells Plz Leoncio Bento 7 38830 Agulo Gomera Canary Islands Spain

WELLS, NINA MITCHELL, state official; b. 1950; m. Theodore V. Wells; 2 children. BA, Newton Coll. of Sacred Heart, 1973; JD, Suffolk U. Atty. Bell Comms. Rsch., 1985; dir. div. rate counsel NJ Pub. Advocate; dir. minority student program and fin. aid Rutgers U. Sch. Law, asst. dean, 1996—97; v.p. pub. affairs Schering-Plough Corp., Kenilworth, NJ, 1998—2004; sec. of state State of NJ, Trenton, 2006—. Pres. Schering-Plough Found. Recipient Garden State Bar Assn. award, 2005. Democrat. Office: Office Sec of State PO Box 300 Trenton NJ 08625 Office Phone: 609-984-1900. Office Fax: 609-292-9897. E-mail: feedback@sos.state.nj.us.*

WELLS, PENNY WHORTON, gifted and talented educator, history educator; d. Leonidas Preston and Danna Binder Whorton; m. William Howard Wells, June 16, 1973; children: Preston Wendell, Christopher John. BA in Am. Civilization, Brown U., 1966. Cert. tchr. Ohio Dept. Edn. Tchr. history H.S. Dallas (Tex.) Ind. Sch. Dist., 1968—69; tchr. history hons. and gifted jr. H.S. Youngstown (Ohio) Bd. Edn., 1969—. Tutor Prefreshman Program Brown U., Tougaloo, Miss., 1966; social studies curriculum improvement com. Youngstown (Ohio) City Schs., 2003—; co-chmn. making mid. grades work Volney Rogers Jr. H.S., Youngstown, 2002—; mem. curriculum improvement team Rogers Jr. H.S., 1995—. Author: Pacing Guide for 7/8 Social Studies series, 1995—2004. With Vol. In Svc. To Am., W.Va., 1966—68; mid. sch. delegation to China People to People Program, 2001; adv. Youth for Justice Team; sec. Southside Ministries, Youngstown, 1994—; treas. Richard Brown Meml. United Meth. Ch., 2001—, trustee Richard Brown Meml., 2001—, chmn. fin. Richard Brown Meml., 2001—. Named Tchr. of Yr., Youngstown (Ohio) Bd. Edn., 2002, Woman of Yr., YWCA, 2003; Martha Jennings Holden scholar, Jennings Found., 1996—97. Mem.: NEA, Ohio Edn. Assn., Civil War Roundtable, Delta Kappa Gamma (chmn. by-laws com. 2004—05). Avocations: reading, walking. Home: 4117 Oak Knoll Dr Youngstown OH 44512 Office: Volney Rogers Jr High School 2400 S Schenley Youngstown OH 44511 Business E-Mail: youn_pww@access-k12.org.

WELLS, REBECCA, writer; b. Alexandria, La. married. Student, Naropa Inst., Boulder, Colo. Founder Performing Artists for Nuclear Disarmament, Seattle. Author: (plays) Splittin' Hairs (nominee, Showtime's Excellence in Am. Theater), Gloria Duplex, (novels) Divine Secrets of the Ya-Ya Sisterhood, 1996 (Adult trade Abby award, 1999, #1 NY Times bestseller), Little Altars Everywhere, 1998 (Western States Book award, NY Times bestseller), Ya-Yas in Bloom, 2005 (NY Times bestseller). Roman Catholic. Mailing: c/o HarperCollins 10 E 53rd St New York NY 10022

WELLS, ROSEMARY, writer; b. NYC, 1943; Student, Boston Mus. Sch. Freelance illustrator, writer, 1968—. Author: (children's fiction) John and the Rarey, 1969, Michael and the Mitten Test, 1969, The First Child, 1970, Martha's Birthday, 1970, Miranda's Pilgrims, 1970, The Fog Comes on Little Pig Feet, 1972, Unfortunately Harriet, 1972, Noisy Nora, 1973, Benjamin and Tulip, 1973, None of the Above, 1974, Abdul, 1975, Morris's Disappearing Bag: A Christmas Story, 1975, Leave Well Enough Alone, 1977, Don't Spill It Again, James, 1977, Stanley and Rhoda, 1978, Max's series, 10 vols., 1979-86, When No One Was Looking, 1980, Timothy Goes to School, 1981, Good Night, Fred, 1981, A Lion for Lewis, 1982, Peabody, 1983, The Man in the Woods, 1984, Hazel's Amazing Mother, 1985, Through the Hidden Door, 1987, Forest of Dreams, 1988, Shy Charles, 1988 (Horn Book award for picture book, 1989), Max's Chocolate Chicken, 1989, Edward Unready for School, 1995, Edward in Deep Water, 1995, Edward's Overwhelming Overnight, 1995, My Very First Mother Goose, 1996 (Parents Choice award, ALA Notable Children's Book award), Max's Dragon Shirt, 1996, Max's Christmas, 1996, McDuff Comes Home, 1997, McDuff and the Baby, 1997, McDuff's New Friend, 1998, Bunny Cakes, 1997, Bunny Money, 1997, Max's First Word, 1998, Max's Bath, 1998, Max's Birthday, 1998, Max's Bedtime, 1998, Max's New Suit, 1998, Max's Ride, 1998, Max's Toys, 1998, Max's Breakfast, 1998, Mary on Horseback Three Mountain Stories, 1999, Morris's Disappearing Bag, 1999, Timothy Goes to School, 2000, Emily's First 100 Days of School, 2000 (NY Times bestseller list), Max Cleans Up, 2000, When No One Was Looking, 2001 (Edgar Allen Poe award), Yoko's Paper Cranes, 2001, Yoko & Friends School Days: Mama, Don't Go!, 2001, Yoko & Friends School Days: The School Play, 2001, Yoko & Friends School Days: The Halloween Parade, 2001, Yoko & Friends School Days: Doris's Dinosaur, 2001, Bunny Party, 2001, Ruby's Beauty Shop, 2003, Max Drives Away, 2003, Ruby's Tea for Two, 2003, Carry Me!, 2006, numerous others. Mailing: c/o Hyperion Books for Children 114 Fifth Ave New York NY 10011*

WELLS, TONI LYNN, accountant; b. Lexington, Ky., June 24, 1959; d. George Andrew and Noreta Florence (Collins) W. AA, Hinds Jr. Coll., 1979; BSBA in Fin., U. So. Miss., 1982, M in Profl. Acctancy, 1984. Internal auditor First Nat. Bank Co., New Orleans, 1984; staff auditor Touche Ross & Co., Jackson, Miss., 1984-85, semi-sr., 1985-87; staff auditor Occidental Petroleum Corp., L.A., 1987-88, sr. auditor, 1988, audit supr., 1988-92, gen. acctg. supr. Corpus Christi, Tex., 1992-95, regional accounts payable supr. Houston, 1995-96, sr. ops. analyst, 1996-97; contr. Laurel Industries (subs. of Occidental Petroleum Corp.), Cleve., 1997-98; fin. planning and analysis, fin. mgr. Dallas, 1998—. Vol. jr. achievement Calallen H.S., Spl. Olympics; alt. del. West Tex. Diocese, Episcopal. Ch. Coun., 1995. Mem. Am. Soc. Women Accts., U. So. Miss. Alumni Assn., U. So. Miss. Golden Eagles, Corpus Christi Plant Recreation Club (sec. bd. dirs.), Internat. Order of St. Luke, Scottish Heritage Soc. (advisor to treas. 1994-95). Episcopalian. Avocations: hiking, bicycling, antiques, travel.

WELNA, CECILIA, retired mathematics professor, dean; b. New Britain, Conn., July 15, 1927; d. Joseph and Sophie (Roman) Welna. BS, St. Joseph Coll., 1949; MA, U. Conn., 1952, PhD, 1960. Instr. Mt. St. Joseph Acad., 1949-50; asst. instr. U. Conn., 1950-55; instr. U. Mass., Amherst, 1955-56; prof., chmn. dept. math. and physics U. Hartford, 1956—82, dean Coll. Edn., Nursing and Health Professions, 1982—93, prof. math., 1993—. Mem.: Math. Assn. Am., Nat. Council Tchrs. Math., Assn. Tchrs. Math. Conn., Sigma Xi. Personal E-mail: seawell31@aol.com.

WELSH, CHRISTINE MARIE, small business owner, dance educator; b. Phoenix, Ariz., Jan. 30, 1979; d. Arthur Joseph and Dianne Marie Goldmann; m. Timothy Patrick Welsh, July 19, 2005. BFA, U. Iowa, Iowa City, 2001. Dancer, dance capt. Silver Tree Prodns., St. Louis, 1998—2001; dancer, choreographer Six Flags St. Louis, 2001; dancer, singer Busch Gardens, Tampa, Fla., 2002; dancer Milw. Bucks, 2004; dance instr. U. Wis., Milw., 2004, Danceworks, Inc., Milw., 2003—05; owner, dir., pres. Elation Dance Ctr., Delafield, Wis., 2006. Mem.: Delafield C. of C., Chi Omega Alumni Assn. Republican. Roman Catholic. Avocations: pilates, boating, swimming, golf. Office: Elation Dance Ctr 405 B Genesee St Delafield WI 53018 Office Phone: 262-646-3680. Business E-Mail: elationdance@msn.com.

WELSH, DORIS MCNEIL, early childhood education specialist; b. Kansas City, Mo. d. Zelbert Melbourne and Anna May (Main) McNeil; children: J. Randall, Valerie M. BA, U. Calif., Berkeley, 1950, MA, 1952; postgrad., U. San Francisco, 1980-82. Cert. tchr., counselor, supr., Calif. Asst. dir. Bing Sch., Stanford, Calif., 1966-76; family devel. specialist Children's Hosp., Stanford, 1976-78; rsch. cons. Stanford U. Med. Ctr., 1970-87; dir. One Fifty Parker Sch., San Francisco, 1978-99; assoc. Lawrence Hall of Sci., U. Calif., Berkeley, 1996—. Citizen amb. del. edn. and childcare People to People Internat., St. Petersburg, Russia, Vilnius, Lithuania, Budapest, Hungary, 1993; pres. bd. dirs. Support for Parents of Spl. Children, San Francisco, 1986-87; bd. dirs. Family Svc. Assn. Mid-Peninsula, Palo Alto, Calif., 1970-80; leader Summer Camp for Pre-Schoolers, East Palo Alto, 1970-73; leader parenthood discussion groups U. Chgo., 1963-64; lectr. in field; cons., 1999—. Vol. Irving Mental Hosp., Chgo., 1963. Mem. Nat. Assn. Edn. Young Children, Assn. Childhood Edn. Internat., World Affairs Coun., Audubon Soc., Sierra Club. Avocations: natural sciences, hiking, horseback riding, gardening. Office: 26630 Ascension Dr Los Altos CA 94022-2001 E-mail: Kharis6@cs.com.

WELSH, DOROTHY DELL, columnist, writer; d. Roland Fields and Martha Gladys (Sheppard) Butler; m. James Robert Welsh, June 26, 1965; children: Pamela Jeanne(dec.), James Michael, Julie Marie. BA, U. Okla., 1957, MA, 1964; postgrad., U. Tex., Austin, 1983-84, U. Tex., San Antonio, 1984. Newspaper reporter summer intern Pryor Jeffersonian, Okla., 1952—55; tchr. English and journalism Classen HS, Oklahoma City, 1957-61, Henderson Jr. HS, Nev., 1961-62, Desert HS, Edwards, Calif., 1965-66; dir. publs. Amarillo (Tex.) HS, 1962-64; tchr. English Palmdale HS, Calif., 1964-65; lectr. English San Antonio Coll., 1979-88; tchg. assoc. U. Tex., San Antonio, 1986-91; reporter Swimming World mag., Sedona, Ariz., 1980—2000; freelance writer, 1992—. Lectr. journalism John Brown U., 1992. Author: The Butlers of Oklahoma, 1957, A Good Man is Hard to Find, 1961, To Seattle for a Bone Marrow Transplant, 1982, Fact, Fiction and Poetic License, 1995, The Butlers: A Newspaper Family, 2003; editor: Crescent News, 1974—80, 1983—86, The Swimmer's Ear, 1983—84, Off the Blocks, 1985—86; contbr. articles to profl. jours. Bd. dirs., publicity chmn. S. Tex. Swimming Assn., Austin, 1982—84; mem. info. com. Tex. Swimming Assn., Dallas, 1983—84; v.p. Mayes County Geneal. Soc., Okla., 2002; mem. Mayes County Hist. Soc., Okla., Rogers County Hist. Soc., Okla., Okla. Hist. Soc. Recipient citation superior work journalism, U. Interscholastic League, Austin, 1964, Svc. award, San Antonio Aquatic Club, 1983, Outstanding Svc. award, U.S. Swimming/Phillips 66, 1989, Pres.'s award, Okla. Press Assn., 2003. Mem.: DAR, MLA, Clan Grant Soc. U.S., Okla. Anthrop. Soc., Journalism Edn. Assn., Soc. Profl. Journalists, Indian Women's Pochohontas Club, U. Okla. Assn., Tulsa Archeol. Soc., Okla. Geneal. Soc., Elks, Pryor (Okla.) Red Hat Soc., First Families Okla., Gamma Phi Beta (internat. officer 1992—94, pres. San Antonio 1972—73, 1987—88, v.p. 1973—74, Svc. award 1977, Internat. Merit Roll 1986). Baptist. Office Phone: 405-872-7172. Business E-Mail: jrwddw39@okplus.net.

WELSH, JUDITH SCHENCK, communications educator; b. Patchogue, NY, Feb. 5, 1939; d. Frank W. and Muriel (Whitman) Schenck; m. Robert C. Welsh, Sept. 16, 1961; children: Derek Francis, Christopher Lord (dec.). BEd, U. Miami, 1961, MA in English, 1968. Co-organizer Cataract Surg. Congress med. meetings, 1963-76; grad. asst. instr. Dale Carnegie Courses Internat., 1967; adminstr. Office Admissions, Bauder Fashio Coll., Miami, 1976-77, instr. comms., 1977—, also pub. coll. monthly paper. Freelance writer regional and nat. publs.; guest spkr. Optifair Internat., N.Y.C., 1980, Fla. Freelance Writers Assn. ann. conf., Ft. Lauderdale, 1991, Suncoast Writers' Conf., Tampa, Fla., 2000, Book Island Festival, Fernandina, Fla., 2000; guest spkr., mem. seminar faculty Optifair West, Anaheim, Calif., 1980, Optifair Midwest, St. Louis, 1980, Face to Face, Kansas City, Mo., 1981; conf. dir. So. Fla. Writers Conf., Nat. Writers Assn./U. Miami, 1997—98, 1999—2000; guest spkr. So. Fla. Writers Conf., Fla., 2002—03, Bapt. Health Systems seminar, So. Miami Hosp., 1999—2003. Co-editor: The New Report on Cataract Surgery, 1969, Second Report on Cataract Surgery, 1974; editor: Surgidev's Cataract Surgery N.O.W., 1982—; author: How to Write Powerful Press Releases, 2003, Miami's Coral Reef Yacht Club: 50 Years on Biscayne Bay, 2005; contbr. articles to newspapers and mags.; writer: internet cos. Mem. NAFE, Fla. Freelance Writers Assn., Nat. Writers Club (award), Nat. Writers Assn. (conf. dir. 1997-2000), Coral Reef Yacht Club, Riviera Country Club, Rotary Internat. (Paul Harris award), Delta Gamma. Congregationalist. Home and Office: 1135 Campo Sano Ave Coral Gables FL 33146 Personal E-mail: mipress@bellsouth.net.

WELSH, KATHERN DARLENE, artist, writer; b. Mansfield, Ohio, Apr. 8, 1942; d. Harold James and Alice Naomi Gillogly; m. Elihu Welsh, Apr. 3, 1993; children: Eric Anthony Grimes, Lorinda Rene Canales. Degree in interior design, Internat. Corr. Sch., Scranton, Pa., 1969; editing and proofing specialist, written English profl., Brainbench, Chantilly, Va., 2000; natural health counseling (hon.), Natural Health Sch. Com., Bridgeton, Mo., 2001. Artist Sebastian (Fla.) Art Club; editor Virtual Books Pub., College Station, Tex.; graphic designer Breakthrough Ministries, Columbus, Ohio; writer and artist K+ Designs, Columbus. Author: Raise Responsible Teens by 5, 2002, The Dark Side of Surgery, 2004, (column of articles) Natural Health and Herbs for Women, 1998; one-woman shows include Art Designs by K, Florida, 1999, Cmty. Ctr., Vero Beach, Fla., 2006, exhibitions include Images of Indian River County, 2005, Uncommon Gallery, Pompano Beach, Fla., 2006, exhibitions include in govt. offices, Vierra, 2005, exhibitions include in pub. libr., Barefoot Bay, Fla., 2004. Artist Brevard Cultural Alliance, Vierra, Fla., 2004—. Recipient award for poetry, Internat. Libr. Poetry, 2001, 2004, 2005. Mem.: Vero Beach Art Club, Sebastian Art Club (sec. 2005—). Avocations: designing poll historical and contemporary costumes, poetry, sewing. Personal E-mail: wordsindesign@yahoo.com.

WELSH, MELANIE MILLEN, secondary school educator; b. Atlanta, Ga., Oct. 24, 1980; d. Timothy Carl and Susan Ann (Millen) Welsh. B in Edn., U. Ga., Athens, 2003. Cert. tchr. Ga. Receptionist LA Fitness, Atlanta, 2003—; swim team coach Dekalb County Druid Hills HS, Atlanta, 2004—. Hope scholar, Ga. Dept. Edn., 1999—2003. Mem.: Kappa Delta (life). Democrat. Roman Catholic. Avocations: swimming, running, weight training, travel, acting. Home: 3044 Saint Helena Dr Tucker GA 30084 Office: Dekalb County- Druid Hills High Sch 1945 Haygood Dr NE Atlanta GA 30307 Office Phone: 678-874-6303. Personal E-mail: melabby143@yahoo.com. Business E-Mail: melanie_m_welsh@fc.dekalb.k12.ga.us.

WELSOME, EILEEN, journalist, writer; b. NYC, Mar. 12, 1951; d. Richard H. and Jane M. (Garity) Welsome; m. James R. Martin, Aug. 3, 1983. BJ with honors, U. Tex., 1980. Reporter Beaumont (Tex.) Enterprise, 1980—82, San Antonio Light, 1982—83, San Antonio Express-News, 1983—86, Albuquerque Tribune, 1987—94, Westword Newspaper, Denver, 2000—01. Author: The Plutonium Files, 1999 (PEN/Martha Albrand award for first nonfiction, 2000). Recipient Clarion award, 1989, News Reporting award, Nat. Headliners, 1989, John Hancock award, 1991, Mng. Editors Pub. Svc. award, AP, 1991, 1994, Roy Howard award, 1994, James Aronson award, 1994, Gold Medal award, Investigative Reporters and Editors, 1994, Sigma Delta Chi award, 1994, Investigative Reporting award, Nat. Headliners, 1994, Selden Ring award, 1994, Heywood Broun award, 1994, George Polk award, 1994, Sidney Hillman Found. award, 1994, Pulitzer Prize for nat. reporting, 1994, PEN/West Lit. award for rsch. nonfiction, PEN, 2000; John S. Knight fellow, Stanford U., 1991—92.

WELSTEAD, JEAN MAUDIE, artist, educator; b. Fremont, Nebr., Nov. 22, 1922; d. Edward C. and Irene Elizabeth (Hooper) Olson; m. Marvin Glenn Welstead, Feb. 21, 1942; children: Robert L., Jon A. Student, Joslyn Art Mus., Omaha, 1962—64, St. Mary's Coll., 1964—68, Midland Luth. Coll., Fremont, 1970—74, BA (hon.), 1988. Legal sec. law firm, Fremont, 1940—42; staff hdqrs. office Northrup Aircraft Co., Hawthorne, Calif., 1943; civil service wartime rationing officer 3d Air Force USAF, Stuttgart, Ark., 1943—46; adminstrv. clk. merit sys. Dodge County Assistance Office, Fremont, 1946—48. Art supr. Fremont Parks and Recreation, 1967—71; publicity dir. Fremont Area Art Assn. Gallery, 1963—85; pvt. instr. art, 1967—71. One-woman shows include Midland Luth. Coll. Gallery, 1970, 1976, 1981, Norfolk Art Ctr., 1982, Dana Coll., Blair, Nebr., 1982, Dahl Fine Arts Ctr., Rapid City, SD, 1987, Wesleyan U., Lincoln, 1986, Hayden Gallery, 1987, Columbus Area Art Gallery, 1988, exhibited in group shows at Sioux City Art Ctr., 1976—78, Elder Gallery Wesleyan U., 1976—87, U. Nebr., Omaha, 1982, Stuhr Mus., 1984, Dahl Fine Arts Ctr., Rapid City, 1985, Sheldon Art Gallery, Lincoln, Nebr., 1985, Joslyn Art Mus., Omaha, 1986, Represented in permanent collections Nebr. Artists, Appalachian State U., Boone, NC, Wesleyan U., Lincoln, Nebr., Wayne State Coll., Nebr., Kearney State Coll., Chmn. Art from the Heart Viet Nam Amputees, Oakland Naval Hosp., Calif. Active Boy Scouts Am.; pres. Linden Sch. PTA, 1955; active Rep. Party. Mem.: Fremont Art Assn. (charter, organizer, pres. 1965—71, Cmty. Art Svc. award 1985), Nat. League Am. Pen Women, Assn. Artists Omaha, Assn. Nebr. Art Clubs (bd. dirs. 1974—75, Excellence award 1974—79, Best of Show 1983), Order of Eastern Star. Meth. Home: 1943 Parkview Dr Fremont NE 68025-4479

WELTE, LINDA ANNE, music educator; d. Arthur Alexander and Anne Elizabeth Augugliaro; m. John Francis Welte, Oct. 19, 1985; children: Christopher John, Matthew John. BA, Western Md. Coll., Westminster, 1978. Cert. music tchr. N.J., 1978. Music tchr. Westampton Twp Pub. Schs., NJ, 1983—; dir. music ministry St Andrew the Apostle Ch., Gibbsboro, NJ, 1981—91. Registered music together tchr. Conservatory of Musical Arts, Haddonfield, NJ, 1994—. PTA pres. and vol. Berlin Cmty. Sch. and Home Assn., Berlin, NJ, 1997—2006; contbg mem. and vol. Berlin Borough Adv. Com., 1999—2004; sch. bd. mem. Berlin Borough Sch. Bd., 2006—; eucharist min. and music min. St Andrew the Apostle Ch., Gibbsboro, NJ, 1991—2006; trustee Berlin Borough Edn. Found., Berlin, NJ, 2003—06. Mem.: N.J. Edn. Assn. (assoc.). Avocations: reading, promoting youth activities. Office: Westampton Twp Public Schools Rancocas Rd Westampton NJ 08060 Office Phone: 609-265-8565.

WEMHOENER, DOLORES LUCILLE, cultural organization administrator, entertainer; b. Quincy, Ill., Aug. 20, 1929; d. George Joseph and Lillian Ella-Mae Mating; m. Gerald Junior Wemhoener, June 3, 1951 (dec. Dec. 1990); children: Theodore Jay, Pamela Diane, Jeffrey Stuart. Degree in music, Quincy Conservatory Music, 1950. Accompanist dancing sch., Quincy, 1945—50; sec. loan dept. Broadway Bank, Quincy, 1949—51; alumni sec. Franklin Coll, Ind., 1951—52; legal sec. Judge Robert Hunter, Quincy, 1952; tchr. piano Quincy Conservatory, 1955—, sec., 1965—70, v.p., 1975—80, pres., 1980—85. Accompanist ch. svc. Salem United Ch. of Christ, Quincy, Ill., 1991—. Home: 2130 State St Quincy IL 62301

WEN, GWEN GUOYAO, music educator; b. Nanjing, China, Nov. 3, 1947; arrived in U.S., 1986, naturalized, 1999; 1 child, Wen Shen. Diploma in Piano Performance, Cen. Conservatory of Music, Beijing, 1967; M in Piano Performance, St. Louis Conservatory of Music, 1990. Orchestra pianist Cen. Ballet, Beijing, 1973—86; accompanist Cen. Conservatory of Music, Beijing, 1976—86; soloist/accompanist Internat. Recording Co., Beijing, 1973—86; accompanist St. Louis Conservatory of Music, 1987—90, State Ballet Mo./Ballet Conservatory in St. Louis, 1990—95; piano instr. Beverly Milder's Musical Arts, St. Louis, 1990—99; ind. piano instr. Gwen Wen's Piano Studio, St. Louis, 1990—. Mem.: Piano Tchrs. Roundtable (v.p. programs 2003—), Nat. Fedn. Music Clubs (festival judge 1998, co-chmn. keyboard merit 2003), Music Tchrs. Nat. Assn.

WEN, SHEREE, computer company executive; BS in Physics, Natural Tsiug Hua U, Taiwan; PhD, U. Calif., Berkeley, 1979. Rsch. divsn. staff IBM, 1979-81, dept. mgr. Materials, Characterization and Analysis, 1981-84, program mgr. Tech., 1984-86, sr. mgr of Optics 1986, prog. mgr., tech. asst. to sr. v.p.; pres. WenLab USA Inc., N.Y.C. Patentee in field; Contbr. articles to profl. jours. Recipient John E. Dom Achievement award Am. Soc. for Metal, 1978, Outstanding tech. Achievement award, IBM, 1986, invention Achievement award, IBM, 1987; The Robert Lansing Hardy gold Metal The Metals, Materials & Minerals Soc. (TMS-AIME); the AIME as the most promising young Materials Scientist in Am., 1979 Mem. TMS-AIME's Process Monitor & Control Com. (chmn.), Materials Design & Mfg. Divsn. Award Com.; Indsl. Liaison for U. Calif. at Berkeley's ctr. for Materials. Office: Wen Technology Corp 22 Saw Mill River Rd Ste 5 Hawthorne NY 10532-1549 Fax: 914-376-7092.

WENDEL, JOAN AUDREY, music educator; b. N.Y.C., Dec. 1, 1931; d. Adam and Edna Sophia Wohlfart; m. Ralph Aurel Wendel, July 21, 1962 (dec. May 1998); 1 child, Tracy Lynn. BA summa cum laude, Dowling Coll., 1969; MA, Adelphi U., 1971. Cert. elem. tchr., N.Y. Sec. A.C. Edwards Inc., Sayville, NY, 1950-53; office mgr. John V. Potter Ins., East Islip, NY, 1953-59, Pilger Agy., Patchogue, NY, 1959-66; tchr. Connetquot CSD of Islip, Bohemia, NY, 1969-91; pvt. music tchr. Bohemia, 1979—; music dir. Christ Luth. Ch., Cape Coral, Fla., 1996—, Sounds of Fla., Cape Coral, 1999—2003. Mem. Music Tchrs. Nat. Assn., Music Educators Nat. Conf., Assn. Luth. Ch. Musicians, Ft. Myers Music Tchrs. Assn. (v.p. 1999), Order Eastern Star (worthy matron 1964, assoc. grand marshal 1973, grand musician 1987). Republican. Lutheran. Avocations: walking, golf, music, reading. Home: 2218 SE 10th Ter Cape Coral FL 33990-6217 Office: Christ Luth Ch 2911 Del Prado Blvd S Cape Coral FL 33904-7297

WENDELBURG, NORMA RUTH, composer, educator, pianist; b. Stafford, Kans. d. Henry and Anna Louise (Moeckel) W. MusB, Bethany Coll., 1943; MusM, U. Mich., 1947, Eastman Sch. Music, 1951, postgrad., 1964-65, 66-67, PhD in Composition, 1969; postgrd., Mozarteum, 1953-54, Vienna Acad. Music, 1955. Tchr. music edn., piano Wayne (Nebr.) State Coll., 1947-50; asst. prof. Bethany Coll., Lindsborg, Kans., 1952-53, U. Iowa, 1956-58; asst. prof. composition, theory, piano Hardin-Simmons U., Abilene, Tex., 1958-66, chmn. grad. com. Sch. Music, 1960-66, founder, chmn. ann. univ. festival contemporary music, 1959—; assoc. prof. music Dallas Bapt. Coll., 1973-75; rsch. asst. to dir. grad. studies Eastman Sch. Music, 1966-67; assoc. prof., chmn. dept. theory and composition S.W. Tex. State U., 1969-72; mem. faculty Friends Bible Coll., Haviland, Kans., 1977-83. Guest composer colls. including U. Ottawa, 1984; performed in Eng. and Prague; performed Am. Conservatory Mus., Charles Ives Ctr. for Am. Music, 1990—; various solo recitals and festivals. Composer: Symphony, 1967, Suite for Violin and Piano, 1965, Song Cycle for Soprano, flutes, Piano, 1974, Music for Two Pianos, 1985, Affirmation, 1982, Interlacings (organ), 1983, (recorded) Suite No. 2 for Violin and Piano, 1989, Fantasy for Trumpet and Piano, 1990, Sonata for Clarinet and Piano, Sinfonietta, 1994, Concerto for Clarinet and Orch., (albums) Sinfonietta, 1997, Mosaic, 2001, Concerto for Clarinet and Oroh, 2002, (CD) Warsaw Rhapsody, Warsaw Nat. Philharm. Orch., 2006; performances Mosaic, 2001, Symphony Orch. of Prague, Smetana Hall, 1999, Symphony Hall, Boston, 1998, Concertino for Oboe and String Orch., Alice Tully Hall Lincoln Ctr., N.Y.C., 1999, Warsaw Rhapsody, Warsaw Philharm. Orch., Lutoslawski Hall, 1999, Warsaw Rhapsody, Warsaw, 1999, Bratislava, Slovakia, 2006. Recipient Meet the Composer award N.Y. State Coun. Arts, 1979; named Kans. Composer of Yr., Kans. Fed. Music Clubs, 2000; Composition scholar Composers' Conf. Middlebury (Vt.), 1950, Berkshire Ctr., 1953; Fulbright awardee, 1953-55; Resident fellow Huntington Hartford Found., 1955-56, 58, 61; MacDowell Colony fellow, 1958, 60, 70; Nat. Festival Performing Arts fellow, 1989. Mem. ASCAP (Composition awards 1988-2006), Am. Soc. Univ. Composers, Minn. Composers Forum, Am. Women Composers, Music Club (Hutchinson), Sigma Alpha Iota. Republican. Avocations: travel, photography, gardening. Address: 2206 N Van Buren St Hutchinson KS 67502-3738

WENDELIN, DENISE KAY, performing arts educator, artist; d. James Brian and Linda Lee Shoults; m. Lynn Frederick Wendelin, June 24, 2005; 1 child, Presley Paige;children from previous marriage: Tarnie JoLee Prickett, Kristyna Keeta Pickett. AA in Biology Edn., Ea. Wyo. Coll., Torrington, 1991; BS in Art Edn., Chadron State Coll., Nebr., 1998. Substitute tchr. Goshen County Schs. & Platte County Schs., Torrington, Wyo., 1991—98; instr. dance Torrington H.S., 1992—94, D&M Dance Studio, 1993; choreographer Torrington H.S., 1998—2002, educator art, 1998—2002, Maxwell Pub. Schs., Nebr., 2002—. Prin. works include pastel on velour Fall Fantasy, 2004, prin. works include pastel on leather suede Prairie Winds, 2005, Unwavered Resolve, 2006. Mem.: Maxwell Edn. Assn., Nebr. Edn. Assn. Avocations: dance, art, fishing, running.

WENDELL, BARBARA TAYLOR, retired real estate agent; b. Ames, Iowa, Jan. 30, 1920; d. Harvey Nelson and Ruby (Britten) Taylor; m. Donald Thomas Davidson Sr., May 22, 1942 (dec. Oct. 1962); children: Donald Thomas Jr., John Taylor, Ann Elizabeth Davidson Costanzo; m. Connell S. Wendell, Oct. 10, 1992 (dec. Sept. 1995). BS in Home Econs. Sci., Iowa State U., 1943. Assoc. tchr. Ames (Iowa) Pub. Schs., 1970-73; retail mgr. Gen. Nutrition Ctr., Ames, 1974-77; sales assoc. Century 21 Real Estate, Ames, 1978-82, Friedrich Realty, Ames, 1982-89. Pres. Ames City PTA Coun., 1950; leader, advisor Boy Scouts Am., Ames, 1952-58; chmn. Campfire Leaders' Assn., Ames, 1959-61; sec. bd. dirs. Campfire Girls, Ames, 1964-66; property com. United Meth. Ch., Ames, 1964-67; vol. Para-Legal Svcs. for Elderly; active Octagon for the Arts, Brunier Gallery, Med. Ctr. Aux., Art Gallery Com.; vol. at Med. Ctr., 1962—. Mem. Nat. Home Econs. in Homemaking (chmn. fgn. student rels. com.), Internat. Orch. Assn., Iowa State U. Meml. Union (life), Iowa State U. Alumni Assn. (life), Ames Community Arts Coun. Republican. Avocations: floriculture, wildlife and forest conservation, indian culture, fitness and nutrition, gerontology. Home: 1110 Johnson St Ames IA 50010-4206

WENDER, PHYLLIS BELLOWS, literary agent; m. Ira Tensard Wender; children: Justin Bellows, Sarah Tensard. BA, Wells Coll., 1956. Publicity dir. Grove Press, NYC, Dell Pub. Co., NYC; theatrical agt. Artists Agy. Inc., NYC; agt. Wender & Assocs., NYC; prin., agt., ptnr. Rosenstone/Wender, NYC. Bd. dir. Just Women Inc., Bklyn., 1982, mem. adv. com., 1983-87; bd. dir. Fortune Soc., N.Y.C., 1977-80; trustee Wells Coll., Aurora, N.Y., 1981-90. Mem. Women's Media Group (dir. 1988-90), Cosmopolitan Club. Office: Rosenstone Wender 38 East 29th St 10th Flr New York NY 10016 Personal E-mail: pbwender@aol.com.

WENDLANDT, DOROTHEA SCHNEPF, artist, writer; b. Trenton, NJ, Aug. 17, 1927; d. Emil Ludwig Schnepf and Helen Dorothea Bruker, Cleveland A. Mulligan (Stepfather); m. Robert Jack Wendlandt, Aug. 14, 1974; children: Lynn Mioduszewski, Robert Jack Wendlandt, Jr., Leigh, Steven Daniel. Pictorial Illustration diploma, Newark Sch. of Fine and Indsl. Art, 1949. Artist Harold Pearson Advt., Edison, NJ, 1955—56; illustrator Joseph P. Schneider, N.Y.C., 1957—58; asst. art dir. Batista Advt., N.Y.C., 1959—60; ednl. exhibit designer/illustrator Binney and Smith, N.Y.C., 1960—68; corp. dir. of advt. art Fedders Corp., Edison, NJ, 1968—74; artist, co-owner Bob's Art Ctr., Old Bridge, NJ/Sarasota, Fla., 1974—. Mem. N.J. Art Dirs. Club, 1971—74; art tchr. Middlesex Jr. Coll., Edison, NJ, 1972—73; owner DS and W Creative Art Svc., Old Bridge, NJ, 1974—78. One-woman shows include Beaux Art Gallery, St. Petersburg, Fla., 1982, exhibitions include Phila. Mus. of Art Craft, 1966, Represented in permanent collections Fedders Exec. Offices, Edison, N.J., acrylic painting, Out of Gas (Meml. Award Nat. Soc. of Painters in Acrylics and Casein, 1983), Tools (Meml. Award Nat. Soc. of Painters in Acrylics and Casien, 1987), Birds in a Window (first prize Manatee Art League, 1983), acrylic and watercolor paintings, Four Artists, Bodies Of Work (Parade of Prize Winners, 1984), watercolor, Cactus Collection 1989 (Best of State Nat. League of Am. Penwomen State Show, 1989), Cactus Collection Two (Venice Art League Best of Show, 1990); author: An Artist's Life: A Tale of Love & Woe, 2006. Treas. Metuchen Arts Coun., NJ, 1970—74; pres. Art Uptown, Sarasota, Fla., 1982—83; bd. dirs. Sarasota Art Assn., Fla., 1981—88; dir. St. Boniface Conservatory of Visual Arts, Sarasota, Fla., 1984—86. N/a N/A. Recipient Grumbacher award, Grumbacher Inc./ Sarasota Art Assn., 1983. Mem.: Nat. Soc. of Painters in Acrylics and Casein (life), Nat. League of Am. Penwomen (life; v.p. 1984—86). Democrat-Npl. Christian. Avocations: opera management, singing, writing, reading. Home: 5577 Burnt Branch Cir Sarasota FL 34232 Office Phone: 941-378-3724. Personal E-mail: lowerball243@aol.com.

WENDLING, LOUISE, wholesale company executive; Sr. v.p., country mgr. Costco Wholesale, Ottawa, Ont., Canada. Office: 415 W Hunt Club Rd Ottawa ON Canada K2E IC5

WENDT, KRISTINE ADAMS, librarian; b. Beaver Dam, Wis., May 29, 1951; d. Howard Thomas and Dorothy H.M. (Bernhardt) Adams; m. Gene Richard Wendt, Oct. 29, 1977. BA in History/Broad Field Social Studies, Carroll Coll., 1973; MA in Libr. Sci., U. Wis., 1974. Cert. grade 1 pub. libr. Assoc. dir., children's libr. Rhinelander (Wis.) Dist. Libr., 1974—2001, assoc. dir., adult cmty. svc. coord., 2001—03, exec. dir., 1974—. Columnist North Star Jour., 1976—. Vol. Sta. WXPR Pub. Radio, Rhinelander, 1989—; co-chair Children's Book Fest, Rhinelander, 1988—; adv. bd. Wis. State Hist. Soc. Office Sch. Svcs., 1995—, Coop. Children's Book Ctr., 1986-89, 92-95, chair adv. bd., 1994-95; mem. State Supt. Adv. Coun. on Rural Sch., Libr., and Cmty., 2004—, Wis. Humanities Coun., 2004— Recipient Woman of Achievement award Rhinelander Bus. and Profl. Women, 1992, Exemplary Svc. in Promotion of Literacy award Internat. Reading Assn. and Headwaters Reading Coun., 1995, Friend of Edn. award State Supt. Wis., 2004 Mem. Antique Automobile Club Am., Wis. Libr. Assn. (libr. devel. and legis. com. 1997—, task force on statewide coop. libr. initiatives 1997-98, nominations com. 1995-96, long range planning com. 1992-95, chair long range planning com. 1993, ad-hoc com. affiliations 1993, sec. 1989, intellectual freedom com. 1985-88, youth svcs. sect. 1975—, chair youth svcs. sect. 1982, libr. legis. day com. 2000-02, named Libr. of Yr. 1993), Coun. Libr. and Network Devel., Wis. Lincoln Fellowship, Horseless Carriage Club. United Methodist. Avocations: antique automobiles, genealogy, history. Office: Rhinelander Dist Libr 106 N Stevens St Rhinelander WI 54501-3158 Office Phone: 715-365-1082. Business E-Mail: kwendt@wbls.lib.wi.us.

WENETSCHLAEGER, PATTY STRADER, lawyer; married; 2 children. MS in Clin. Psych., Abilene Christian U.; M of Dispute Resolution, Pepperdine U. Strauss Inst.; JD, Pepperdine U. Sch. Law, Malibu, Calif. Bar: Tex. Assoc. Brewer, Anthony & Middlebrook, P.C., Irving, Tex. Adj. grad. prof. family mediation Abilene Christian U. Named a Rising Star, Tex. Super Lawyers mag., 2006. Mem.: Am. Inn of Ct., ABA, Denton County Bar Assn., Tarrant County Family Law Bar Assn., Dallas Bar Assn. (mem. family law sect.). Office: Brewer Anthony & Middlebrook PC 5201 N O'Connor Blvd Ste 500 Irving TX 75039 Office Phone: 972-870-9898. E-mail: pwenetschlaeger@bamlawyers.net.*

WENGER, ELEANOR LERNER, retired science educator; b. N.Y.C., July 18, 1921; d. Herman and Sara Beatrice (Goodman) Lerner; m. Byron S. Wenger, Apr. 8, 1947; children: Sharon, Rhona, Jarrell, Ileana. BA, Bklyn. Coll., 1940; MA, Oberlin Coll., 1943; PhD, Washington U., 1948. Rsch. assoc. dept. anatomy U. Kans., Lawrence, 1951-69, U. Saskatchewan Sch. Medicine, Saskatoon, Can., 1971-85; assoc. prof. U. Saskatchewan, Saskatoon, Can., 1969-71, asst. prof., 1988-89, asst. prof. biology dept., 1972-88; lab. coord. U. Saskatchewan Sch. Vet. Medicine, Saskatoon, Can., 1985-89; assoc. prof. Ross U. Med. Sch., Dominica, 1989-91, St. Georges (Grenada) U., Med. Sch., 1991-92; ret., 1992. Reviewer of books and films AAAS, Washington, 1988—. Vol. tel. reader Audio Reader, Lawrence, 1993—; vol. Natural History Mus., U. Kans., Lawrence, 1996-99, Spencer Art Gallery, 1997— Mem. LWV, Can. Fedn. Univ. Women (pres. 1972-73), U. Kans. U. Women's Club, Ladies Literary League (pres. 1995-96, 2005—06). Democrat. Home: 1237 N 900 Rd Lawrence KS 66047-9601

WENGER, NANETTE KASS, cardiologist, researcher, educator; b. N.Y.C., Sept. 3, 1930; d. Aaron Zelig and Edith (Malkin) Kass; m. Julius Wenger; children: Deborah, Judith, Beth. BA summa cum laude, Hunter Coll., 1951; MD, Harvard U., 1954. Intern Mt. Sinai Hosp., N.Y.C., 1954—55, chief resident in cardiology, 1956—57; sr. resident in medicine Grady Meml. Hosp., Atlanta, 1958; fellow in cardiology Sch. Medicine, Emory U., 1958—59; instr. medicine Schs. Medicine and Dentistry, Emory U., Atlanta, 1959—62, assoc. in medicine, 1962—64, asst. prof. cardiology, 1964—68, assoc. prof., 1968—71, prof., 1971—; mem. med. staff Crawford W. Long Hosp., Atlanta, 1977—. Dir. cardiac clinics Grady Meml. Hosp., 1960—, chief cardiology, 1998—; cons. cardiology VA Med. Ctr., Atlanta, 1988—; participant numerous profl. symposiums and confs.; mem. cardiovas. and renal drugs adv. com. U.S. FDA, 1978-82; co-chair nat. plan for cardiac rehab. com. Div. Vocat. Rehab., Social and Rehab. Svcs., HEW, 1973-90; mem. Internat. Task Force for Prevention of Coronary Heart Disease, 1989—; founding fellow Soc. Geriatric Cardiology, 1986, bd. dirs., 1987—, pres., 1994-95. Mem. editl. bd. various profl. publs. including Cardiac Rehab. Quar., 1974-79, Primary Care, 1975-79, Internat. Jour. Sports Cardiology, 1983—, Med. Month, 1983-84, Jour. Cardiovasc. and Pulmonary Medicine, 1983—, Geriatric Cardiology, 1986—, Nutrition, Metabolism and Cardiovasc. Disease, 1989—; reviewer publs. including Am. Jour. Medicine, 1972—, Am. Jour. Cardiology, 1979—, Am. Heart Jour., 1975—, European Heart Jour., 1983—; editor Am. Jour. Geriatric Cardiology, 1992—. Active Ga. affiliate Am. Heart Assn., 1960—, chair Heart Sunday program, 1968-69, program chair Fulton County Heart Unit, 1969-71, bd. dirs., 1969-79, 80-82, pres., 1977-78; fellow coun. clin. cardiology, Am. Heart Assn., 1970, chair rehab. com., 1972-75, chair artheroscleroisis task force, 1973-74, program v.p., 1975-76, pres., 1977-78, bd. dirs., 1975-79, mem./past mem. numerous other coms.; mem. med. adv. and cardiovasc. health coms. Butler St. YMCA, 1980-82. Recipient Myrtle Wreath award Atlanta Hadassah, 1967, award of Achievement, Nat. Ctr. for Vol. Action, 1978, Bronze Disting. Svc. medallion Ga. affiliate Am. Heart Assn., 1970-71, Silver Disting. Svc. medallion, 1978, Gold Disting. Svc. medallion, 1979, Disting. Achievement award, Sci. Coun. Am. Heart Assn. and Women in Cardiol. Mentoring award, 1999, Juha P. Kokko award for Excellence in Cardiovascular Lecturing and Edu., Dept. Med. Housestaff, Emory Univ. Sch. Med., 1999-2000, Emory Williams Disting. Tchg. award, 2004, Evangeline Papageorge Alumni Tchg. award, 2004, Shining Star award Atlanta Women in Law and Medicine, 2000, R. Bruce Logue award for Excellence in Medicine, Am. Heart Assn., 2001, Gold Heart award, 2004; Disting. Fellow Soc. Geriatric Cardiology, 2002; honoree Women of Yr. issue Time Mag., 1976; named Joseph B. Wolff Meml. Lectr., Am. Coll. Sports Medicine, 2001. Fellow ACP (James D. Bruce Meml. award 2000), Am. Coll. Cardiology (gov. for Ga. 1983-86, trustee 1987-89, various coms.); mem. AMA, WHO (expert adv. panel on cardiovasc. disease 1989—), Am. Assn. Cardiovasc. and Pulmonary Rehab. (trustee 1985-88, chairperson ethics com. 1985—, 2d Ann. Lecture award 1987), Nat. Heart, Lung and Blood Inst., Internat. Soc. and Fedn. Cardiology (pres. sci. coun. on rehab. of cardiac patients 1984-88), Soc. Geriatric Cardiologists (officer, pres. 1994-95), Med. Assn. Ga., Med. Assn. Atlanta, Atlanta Clin. Soc.(emeritus), Soc. for Prevention of Heart Disease and Rehab. (hon.), Soc. Women's Health (bd. dirs. 2000—, vice chair 2002—), Philippine Heart Assn. (hon.), Philippine Coll. Cardiology (hon.), Omicron Delta Kappa. Office: Emory Univ Sch Medicine 49 Jesse Hill Jr Dr SE Atlanta GA 30303-3033 Office Phone: 404-616-4420.

WENGER, SHARON LOUISE, cytogeneticist, researcher, educator; b. Washington, Sept. 25, 1949; d. William Fred and Lois Helen (Compton) W.; m. George E. Fromlak Jr., Jan. 10, 1976; children: Nicholas Edward, Holly Louise, Andrea Lee. BA in Biology, Thiel Coll., 1971; MS in Human Genetics, U. Pitts., 1973, PhD in Human Genetics, 1976. Cert. in clin. cytogenetics Am. Bd. Med. Genetics. Asst. prof. U. Pitts. Sch. Med., 1980-89, assoc. prof., 1989—97; prof. pathology W. Va. U., 1997—. Contbr. articles to profl. jours. Mem. Am. Soc. Human Genetics, Am. Coll. Med. Genetics, Assn. Genetic Technologists, Assn. Molecular Pathology, Am. Soc. Hematology. Achievements include research of sister chromatid exchange and fragile sites, chromosome syndromes and mechanism of tissue limited mosaicism. Home: 50 Crescent Heights Morgantown WV 26505 Office: W Va U Dept Pathology PO Box 9203 Morgantown WV 26506-9203 Office Phone: 304-293-3212.

WENGERD, CAROL JOYCE, mathematics educator; b. Hazleton, Pa., Apr. 10, 1950; d. Albert Charles and Catherine Lucille Hinger; m. Eugene Robert Wengerd, July 5, 1975; children: Erin Rachel Young, Seth Allen. BS, Pa. State U., University Park, 1971, EdM, 1974. Permanent edl. cert. Pa., 1974. Adj. prof. Allegany Coll. Md., Cumberland, 1967—; tchr. Boyertown (Pa.) Area Sch. Dist., 1971—75, Salisbury (Pa.)-Elk Lick Sch. Dist., 1976—. Mem.: Phi Delta Kappa. Office Phone: 814-662-2741 104. Business E-Mail: wengerdc@selsd.com.

WENGLOWSKI, JOYCE, painter; b. Rochester, N.Y., Sept. 2, 1943; d. Harwin E. and Martha A. (Weit) Richards; m. Gary M. Wenglowski, Sept. 2, 1942; children: Gary M., Jr., Catherine J. Student, Rochester Inst. of Technology, 1961-63; BFA cum laude, Manhattanville Coll., 1980. Owner Joyce Wenglowski Gallery, Blue Hill, Maine, 1996-99; tchr. Artists Roster-Westchester Arts Coun., White Plains, 1995-2004; tchr., designer art program Waterview Hills Nursing Ctr., Purdy's, N.Y., 1989-99; tchr. painting, YMHA-YWHA, Pleasantville, N.Y., 1990-92; guest spkr. New Castle Pks. and Recreation, Chappaqua, N.Y.; tchr. artist-in.-residence New Rochelle Day Nursery, 2000-01, vis. artist, Empire State Partnership, Westchester Magnet Acad., 2005.; spkr. in field. One-woman shows include The Joyce Wenglowski Gallery, Blue Hill, Maine, 1996-99, Deer Isle (Maine) Artists Assn., Maine, 1993, 98, Landmark Gallery, Stamford, Conn., 1996, Island Fishermen's Wives Hardship Fund, Deer Isle, 1995, CARE, Pound Ridge, N.Y., 1993, The Annex., N.Y.C., 2002, Northern Westchester Hosp., 2000—, Katonah Mus. of Art, 2002; exhibited in group shows at The Katonah Mus. of Art studio tour, 2000, Paramount Ctr. for the Arts, Peekskill, N.Y., 1999, Westchester Arts Coun., White Plains, N.Y., 1999, 2000, 03, 04, 05, Mus. Gallery, White Plains, 1999, The Gallery at Macy Pavilion, Valhalla, N.Y., 1998, The Walter Meade Gallery, Roxbury, N.Y., 1997, Manhattanville Coll., Purchase, N.Y., 1997, Neiman Marcus, Westchester Art Coun., White Plains, N.Y., 1996, Silvermine Galleries, New Canaan, Conn., 1989, Mamaroneck Artists Guild, N.Y.C., 1994, Faber Birren Nat. Color Award Exhibit, Stamford, Conn., 1997, The Studio, Armonk, N.Y., 1999, 2000, 01, 02, 03, 05, 06, The Katonah Mus. Art, 2002, G. Watson Gallery, Stonington, Maine, 2001-06, The Hammond Mus. North Salem, N.Y., 2004, others; featured interview WFAS Radio, White Plains, 1999; represented in pvt. and corp. collectors, U.S. and Eng.; contbr. articles to profl. jours. Recipient Making a Difference award Westchester Arts Coun., 1993, Alumni Disting. in the Arts award Manhattanville Coll., 1991, Mixed Media award Stamford Conn., 1996, Katonah Mus. Artists' Assn., 2001; named NYNEX Patent Trader Vol. of Month, Westchester, 1992. Mem. Katonah Mus. Artsts Assn. (adv. bd. 1995—, pres. 2002-03, The Studio adv. bd., 2002—), Deer Isle Artists Assn. (adv. bd. 1993-97), Exhibiting Artists Ltd. (pres. 1982-83).

WENIG, CINDY L., lawyer; b. Queens, NY, Mar. 26, 1966; AB summa cum laude, Princeton U., 1988; JD, Columbia U., 1991. Bar: NY 1992. Ptnr., Real Estate Practice Group Chadbourne & Parke LLP, NYC. Adv. bd. Stewart Title Guaranty Co., Profl. Women's Alliance of NYC. Harlan Fiske Stone Scholar. Mem.: Real Estate Bd. NY, Women Exec. in Real Estate (WX) (sec.), Nat. Assn. Women Bus. Owners. Office: Chadbourne & Parke LLP 30 Rockefeller Plz New York NY 10112 Office Phone: 202-408-1188. Office Fax: 212-541-5369. Business E-Mail: cwenig@chadbourne.com.

WENTS, DORIS ROBERTA, psychologist; b. L.A., Aug. 26, 1944; d. John Henry and Julia (Cole) W. BA, UCLA, 1966; MA, San Francisco State U., 1968; postgrad., Calif. State U., L.A., 1989—90, Claremont (Calif.) Grad. U, 1990—. Lic. ednl. psychologist, credentialed sch. psychologist, Calif. Sch. psychologist Diagnostic Sch. for Neurologically Handicapped Children, L.A., 1969—86; pvt. practice Monterey Park, Calif., 1986—89; cons. rsch. psychologist orgnl. behavior, 1993—. Instr. Calif. State U., L.A., 1977. Co-author: Southern California Ordinal Scales of Development, 1977. Mem.: Western Psychol. Assn., Acad. Mgmt., L.A. Conservancy, Sigma Xi, Zeta Tau Alpha (officer Santa Monica alumnae chpt. 1970—, Cert. of Merit 1979). Avocations: travel, watersports, theater, bridge, photography. Personal E-mail: wentsd@uclalumni.net.

WENTWORTH, DIANA VON WELANETZ, author; b. L.A., Mar. 4, 1941; d. Eugene and Marguerite (Rufi) Webb; m. Frederic Paul von Welanetz, Nov. 2, 1963 (dec. Mar. 19, 1989); 1 child, Lexi Welanetz Bursin; m. Theodore S. Wentworth, Dec. 9, 1989; stepchildren: ChristinaWentworth Coyne, Kathryn Allison Wentworth Purdy. Student, UCLA, 1958-60. Ptnr. von Welanetz Cooking Workshop, L.A., 1968-85; host TV series New Way Gourmet, 1983-86; founder Inside Edge Found. Edn., Calif., 1985-93. Spkr. in field. Author: The Pleasure of Your Company, 1976 (Cookbook of Yr.), With Love from Your Kitchen, 1976, The Art of Buffet Entertaining, 1978, The Von Welanetz Guide to Ethnic Ingredients, 1983, L.A. Cuisine, 1985, Celebrations, 1985, Chicken Soup for the Soul Cookbook, 1995, Send Me Someone, 2001, Chicken Soup to Inspire The Body and Soul, 2003. Treas. Louise L. Hay Found., Carson, Calif., 1988—; advisor Women of Vision, Calif., 1995—. Mem. Internat. Food, Wine & Travel Writers Assn., Angels of Arts/Orange County Performing Arts Ctr., Ctr. Club, Confrérie de La Chaîne des Rôtisseurs, N. Am. Travel Journalists Assn. Avocations: painting, art, travel, design. Office: 4631 Teller Ave Ste 100 Newport Beach CA 92660-8105 E-mail: diana@dianawentworth.com.

WENTWORTH, LAVERNE WELLBORN, university program coordinator; b. Bryan, Tex., July 26, 1929; d. Charles Floyd and Ethel Berneice (Swanzy) Wellborn; m. Thomas Richard Wentworth (wid. 1986); children: Jason Charles, Rance Richard, Paige Lynn Wentworth Honkerkamp. BA, Baylor U., 1949, MA in Am. Civilization, 1954; postgrad., State Tchrs. U. N.J., Southwestern State Tchrs. U., San Marcus, Tex., U. Ky. Sch. tchr. Tex. and N.J., 1949—58; tchr. JFK White House Paper on Youth, 1963; comm. edn. instr. Georgetown (Ky.) Coll., 1988—90; elderhostel program coord. U. Ky., Lexington, 1992—2001; Boyce Sch. instr. So. Bapt. Theol. Seminary, Lexington, 1990; pers. dept. Cardinel Hill Rehab. Hosp., Lexington, 1987-93. Tchg. cons. U.S. Steel Co., Trenton, N.J., 1957; cons., instr. Interdenominational Young People Confs., Pocono Plateau, Pa., 1958-87; field supr. U.S. Dept. Commerce, Bur. of Census, Washington, 1970-88; guest lectr. Georgetown (Ky.) Coll. Author: (books) Manifest Destiny in Walt Whitman's Prose, 1954, Tryst, 1959 Pres. Princeton Theol. Sem. Wives, 1956-57, Rotary Anne, W.Va., 1982-83; mem. Scott County Women's Club, Georgetown, 1987-93; mem. by-laws com. Ky. Bapt. Fellowship, 2004—. Recipient Ship of State award W.Va. State of Sec., 1983. Mem. AAUW (pres. 1987-90), Scott County Hist. Soc. (program chmn. 2001-03), Georgetown Coll. Woman's Assn. (life), Faith Bapt. Ch. of Georgetown (tchr., chmn. by-laws 1998—2006), Ky. Bapt. Fellowship (by-laws com. 2004—).

WENTWORTH, LYNN A., telecommunications industry executive; BSBA, Babson Coll.; MS in Taxation, Bentley Coll.; MBA Ga. State U. Various positions with numerous depts. including handling tax, strategic planning, investor rels. and finl. planning Bellsouth Corp., 1985—2003, v.p., treas. Atlanta, 2003—. Tutor C.W. Hill Elem. Sch., Atlanta. Mem.: AICPA, Ga. Soc. CPA's.

WENTZEL, KAREN LYNN, secondary school educator; b. Granite City, Ill., May 22, 1949; d. Mike J. and Virginia L. (Prewett) Firtos; m. Joseph A. Wentzel Jr., June 2, 1967 (div. 1989); 1 child, David J. AA, St. Louis Community Coll., 1988; BA summa cum laude, Fontbonne Coll., 1990; MEd, U. Mo., St. Louis, 1994. Cert. secondary tchr., Mo. Instr. writing Meramec Coll., St. Louis, 1990-91; tchr. Div. of Youth Svcs., St. Louis, 1991; tchr. lang. arts North Kirkwood Mid. Sch., St. Louis, 1991—98; tchr. Kirkwood H.S., 1998—. Features editor newspaper Fontbanner, 1990; mng. editor newsletter Hogan Highlights, 1991. Recipient Meramec's Exemplary Svc. award, 1991. Mem. Mo. Mid. Sch. Assn., Nat. Coun. Tchrs. English, Phi Theta Kappa, Sigma Tau Delta, Phi Delta Kappa, Chi Sigma Iota, Phi Kappa Phi. Avocations: classical ballet, tap and jazz dancing. Home: 4908 Fite Dr Imperial MO 63052-1412 Office: Kirkwood HS 801 W Essex Kirkwood MO 63122 Office Phone: 314-213-6100 1271. E-mail: wentzel@gw.kirkwood.k12.mo.us.

WENZEL, ANN MARIE, music educator; b. Winona, Minn., Aug. 4, 1960; d. Walter John and Elaine Susan Wenzel. BS in Music Edn., Winona State U., 1982. Instrumental music tchr. Aquinas HS, LaCrosse, Wis., 1998—. Clarinetist Winona Mcpl. Band. Mem.: Music Educators Nat. Conf. (corr.). Home: 167 Mankato Ave Winona MN 55987 Personal E-mail: headtoad@hbci.com.

WENZEL, KAREN MARIE, writer; b. Grand Rapids, Mich., Sept. 8, 1937; d. Kennythe Thorma Thomsen; m. Richard E. Wenzel, June 28, 1958; children: Susan Smith, Lori Krueger, Jennifer Choe. Student, Ctrl. Mich. U. Substitute tchr. Rockford (Mich.) Pub. Schs., 1958—66, Pennfield Pub. Schs., Battle Creek, Mich., 1966—80; owner Kids' Stuff, Farwell, Mich., 1980—82; substitute tchr. Mecosta-Osceola Intermediate Sch. Dist., Mecosta County, Mich., 1984—88; leader children's writing workshops WNZ Publs., Mich., Ind., 1997—. Presenter Mich. Reading Assn., Grand Rapids, 1997—98. Author: (children's books) The Fantom Spider, 1997, A Flower Forest Wedding, 1999, The Legend of the First Sparkly Web, 2004. Mem. Humanities Coun. Mecosta County, 2003—05; participant Art Works, Mecosta County, 2003—05. Avocations: travel, golf, tennis, RVing. Home: 8277 Peninsula Dr Stanwood MI 49346 Office: WNZ Publs PO Box 393 Mecosta MI 49332 Office Phone: 231-972-8135. Business E-Mail: wnzpub@centurytel.net.

WENZEL, MARY JOAN, music educator; b. Massillon, Ohio, Aug. 26, 1960; d. Richard Thomas and Esther Elizabeth Wenzel. BMus in Music Edn. and Performance, U. Akron, Ohio, 1983. Music tchr. New Philadelphia City Schs., Ohio, 1983—90, Dover City Schs., Ohio, 1990—. Musician (clinician): Music From the Back of the Room: Creativity and the School Percussionist. Vol. Hospice of Tuscarawas County, Dover, 2006. Mem.: Ohio Music Edn. Assn. (sec./treas., dist. 8 1994—2000). Conservative-R. Christian. Avocation: fitness. Home: 206 N McKinley Ave Dover OH 44622-2019 Office: Dover (OH) City Schools 2131 N Wooster Ave Dover OH 44622-2019 Office Phone: 330-364-7121. Office Fax: 330-364-7127. Personal E-mail: wenzelj@adelphia.net. E-mail: wenzelj@dover.k12.oh.us.

WERA, SUZY E., science educator, golf and tennis coach; b. Pontiac, Mich., Oct. 13, 1953; d. Raymond Albert and Margaretha Louise Eick; m. Jeffrey Clark Wera, Aug. 20, 1977; children: Timothy L., Christopher T., Jeffrey C. BA in Biology and Physical Edn., Olivet Coll., 1975; MA in Edn., Northern Ky. U., 1982. Sci. tchr. Beechwood Sch., Ft. Mitchell, Ky., 1974—; sci. tchr., physical edn. tchr. Potterville Pub. Sch., Mich., 1975—79. Golf and tennis coach Beechwood Sch., 1992—, tutor, 2004—, site base decision making, 2005—06. Mem. habitat for humanity St. Joseph Ch., Crescent Springs, Ky., 2004—; chmn. Boy Scouts Am., Cin., 1992—94; recreation dir. City of Ft. Mitchell, 1996—99; tchr. leadership C. of C., Ft. Mitchell, 2000. Named to Northern Ky. U. Pinnacle Honor Soc., 2003; recipient Outstanding Mid. Sch. Sci. Tchr., Ky. Sci. Tchrs. Assn., 1997, Ky. Post Boys Tennis Coach of Yr., 2001, Ky. Post Boys Golf Coach of Yr., 1999, Presdl. award for Excellence in Sci., Coun. of Sci. and Math., 1993, Outstanding Earth Sci. Tchr., Geological Soc. Am., 1993, Golden Apple Tchr. award, Ky. Post, 1993. Mem.: Nat. Sci. Tchr. Assn., Ky. Sci. Tchrs. Assn., Phi Delta Kappa. Republican. Cath. Avocations: swimming, walking, golf, travel. Home: 1069 Carpenters Trace Villa Hills KY 41017

WERDEGAR, KATHRYN MICKLE, state supreme court justice; b. San Francisco; d. Benjamin Christie and Kathryn Marie (Clark) Mickle; m. David Werdegar; children: Maurice Clark, Matthew Mickle. Student, Wellesley Coll., 1954—55; AB with honors, U. Calif., Berkeley, 1957; JD with highest distinction, George Washington U., 1962; JD, U. Calif., Berkeley, 1990. Bar: Calif. 1964, U.S. Dist. Ct. (no. dist.) Calif. 1964, U.S. Ct. Appeals (9th cir.) 1964, Calif. Supreme Ct. 1964. Legal asst. civil rights divsn. U.S. Dept. Justice, Washington, 1962—63; rsch. atty., author Calif. State Study Commn. on Mental Retardation, 1963—64; assoc. U. Calif. Ctr. for Study of Law and Soc., Berkeley, 1965—67; spl. cons. State Dept. Mental Health, 1967—68; cons., author Calif. Ctr. Trial Judges, 1968—71; dir. criminal law divsn. Calif. Continuing Edn. of Bar, 1971—78; assoc. dean acad. and student affairs, assoc. prof. Sch. Law, U. San Francisco, 1978—81; sr. staff atty. Calif. 1st Dist. Ct. Appeal, 1981—85, Calif. Supreme Ct., 1985—91; assoc. justice Calif. 1st Dist. Ct. Appeal, 1991—94, Calif. Supreme Ct., San Francisco, 1994—. Regents' lectr. U. Calif., Berkeley, 2000. Author: Benchbook: Misdemeanor Procedure, 1971, Misdemeanor Procedure Benchbook rev., 1975, Misdemeanor Procedure Benchbook, 1983; contbr. California Continuing Education of the Bar books; editor: California Criminal Law Practice series, Discovery, 1975, California Uninsured Motorist Practice, 1973, I California Civil Procedure Before Trial, 1977. Recipient 5 Am. Jurisprudence awards, 1960—62, Charles Glover award, George Washington U., 1962, J. William Fulbright award for disting. pub. svc., George Washington U. Law Sch. Alumni Assn., 1996, Excellence in Achievement award, Calif. Alumni Assn., 1996, Roger J. Traynor Appellate Justice of Yr. award, 1996, Justice of Yr. award, Consumer Attys. of Calif., 1998, Citation award, Boalt Hall Sch. Law U. Calif., Berkeley, 2002. Mem.: Am. Law Inst., Nev./Calif. Women Judges Assn., Calif. Judges Assn., Nat. Assn. Women Judges, Calif. Supreme Ct. Hist. Soc. (bd. dir.), Order of the Coif. Office: Calif Supreme Court 350 McAllister St San Francisco CA 94102-4797 Office Phone: 415-865-7032.

WERDENSCHLAG, LORI B., psychologist, educator; b. Livingston, N.J., Apr. 20, 1965; d. Stephen Robert and Sandra Joyce Werdenschlag; m. William Alden Barbour, Aug. 5, 2000; 1 child, Jordan Sara Barbour. BA in Psychology and Anthropology, Emory U., Atlanta, 1987; MS in Developmental Psychology, Tulane U., New Orleans, 1990; PhD in Developmental Psychology, Tulane U., 1992. Prof. dept. psychology Lyndon State Coll., Lyndonville, Vt., 1992—; devel. home provider Washington County Mental Health, Vt., 1999—. Creator organizer Lyndon State Coll. Ann. Cultural Festival, 1996—; resource provider Coalition: Success by Six, Headstart, Vt. Dept. Health, 2003—, St. Johnsbury Daycare Provider Network, 2003—; condr. tng. workshops in field. Contbr. articles to profl. jours. Big sister Big Bro./Big Sisters, New Orleans, 1990—; exec. bd. dirs. AIDS Cmty. Awareness Project/Vt. Cares Orgn., 1996—2000. Fellow, PEW Found., 1991—92; Advanced Study grantee, Lyndon State Coll., 1995, 1999, 2000, Learning Communities Fund grantee, Vt. State Colls., 1996—97, Faculty fellow, 2002—04. Avocations: reading, travel, skiing. Office: Lyndon State College 1001 College Rd Lyndonville VT 05851 Office Phone: 802-626-6435. E-mail: lori.werdenschlag@lyndonstate.edu.

WERKMAN, ROSEMARIE ANNE, former public relations professional, volunteer; b. Washingtonville, N.Y., Apr. 21, 1926; d. Alexander and Michelina (Russo) Di Benedetto; m. Henry J. Werkman, June 29, 1947; children: Elizabeth, Kristine, Hendrik Student, U. Miami, Fla. Billing clk. Stern's Dept. Store, N.Y.C., 1945; clk., typist Doubleday-Doran Book Pub., N.Y.C., 1945—46; receptionist Moser & Cotins Advt. Agy., Utica, NY, 1947—48, Washingtonville Sch., NY, 1960—75. Instr. Personal Life History Class Orange County C.C. Author: (biography/autobiography) Love, War and Remembrance, 1992; author short stories; poetry pub. in several anthologies Mem. Dem. Com., Blooming Grove; bd. dirs. Blooming Grove Hist. Assn.; mem. com. Update: Blooming Grove Master Plan; mem. Orange County Coun. Disabled; bd. dirs. Rehab. Support Svcs; charter mem. Orange County Citizens Found.; mem. steering com. Blooming Grove BiCentennial Celebration, 1999; participant restorations Habitat for Humanity, 2001—; mem. steering com. Hist. Brotherhood Winery, Inc., 2003— Named Poet of Merit, Am. Poetry Assn., 1989, Poet Laureate Orange County, N.Y., 2002; recipient Notable Civic Contbns. award Blooming Grove/Washingtonville C. of C., 1996, Rose award, 1996 Mem. Blooming Grove C. of C. (v.p.), Orange County Classic Choral Soc., Clearwater (Fla.) Chorus Democrat. Roman Catholic. Avocations: reading, gardening, furniture refinishing, singing.

WERLEY, ANNMARIE, secondary school educator; d. James and Julia Moralis; m. Steven A. Werley, June 20, 1987; children: Danielle C., Steven E. BS in Human Ecology, Marywood U., Dunmore, Pa., 1983. Profl. tchg. cert. Pa. Tchr. Allentown (Pa.) Sch. Dist., 1983—87, Bethlehem (Pa.) Area Sch. Dist., 1987—. Treas. Women's 5K Classic, Orefield, Pa., 1999—2006.

WERLEY, KELLY, secondary school educator; BS in Secondary Edn., Pa. State U., University Park, 1996; MEd summa cum laude, Kutztown U., Pa., 2003. Cert. instrl. II Pa. Secondary social studies tchr. Brandywine Heights Area Sch. Dist., Mertztown, Pa., 1998—. Key Club advisor Brandywine Heights Area Sch. Dist., Mertztown, 1998—, sr. project advisor, 1998—; advanced placement US govt. and politics exam reader Coll. Bd., ETS, Denver, 2006—. Presdl. election vol. PA Victory '04, Reading, 2004. Mem.: Nat. Coun. for Social Studies (assoc.), Kutztown U. Alumni Assn. (assoc.), Pa. State Alumni Assn. (assoc.).

WERLLA, VANESSA LYNN, psychiatrist; b. Houston, Tex., Sept. 23, 1953; d. Charles Julius Werlla, Jr. and Virginia Bushnell Werlla; m. Richard Billings Noulles, July 7, 1979; children: Rebekah Lynn Noulles, Sarah Elizabeth Noulles, Mary Katherine Noulles. BA with Honors in Biology, U. of Tex. at Austin, 1971—74; MD, U. Okla. Coll. of Medicine, 1976—80. Diplomate Am. Bd. Psychiatry & Neurology, 1989. Chmn. dept. psychiatry St. John Med. Ctr., Tulsa, 1992—2002; med. dir. behavioral health Cmty. Care HMO, Tulsa, 1993—2002; clin. asst. prof., dept. psychiatry U. Okla. Coll. Medicine, 1994—; psychiatric med. reviewer Blue Cross/Blue Shield of Okla., Oklahoma City, 1996—; med. cons. Family Children's Svcs., Tulsa, 2002—05; pvt. practice Tulsa, 2004—. Mem. nat. cmty. mental health adv. bd. Eli Lilly Pharm., 2003—; nat. spkr. Forest Pharm., 2003—, Astra Zeneca Pharm., 2003—. Mem. Nat. Rep. Congl. Com., 2004; bd. mem. Tulsa Mental Health Assn. Bd., Tulsa, 2005—. Recipient Ronald Regan Gold Medal award, 2004; Michael DeBakey fellowship, Baylor Coll. Medicine, Houston, 1971—72. Mem.: AMA, Tex. Med. Assn., Okla. Med. Assn., APA, Tex. Execs. (life), Alpha Lambda Delta. Republican. Protestant. Avocations: painting, piano. Office: 2626 E 21st St Ste 6 Tulsa OK 74114 Office Phone: 918-712-7488.

WERMUTH, MARY LOUELLA, secondary school educator; b. Oakland County, Mich., May 2, 1943; d. Burt and Ila A. (Cole) W.; m. David J. Kohne, Dec. 28, 1975; 1 child, John B. BA, Oakland U., 1965, MA, 1969, 81. Tchr. Rochester Cmty. Schs., Rochester Hills, Mich., 1965—96; instr., counselor Internat. Acad., Bloomfield Hills, Mich., 1996—2001. Farmer, 1964—; presenter in field; bd. dirs. Mich. Future Problem Solving; exchange tchr. New South Wales, Australia, 1996; ptnr. Old Indian Enterprises, 1982—; faculty Internat. Acad., dean humanities, 1996-2000; mem. adv. coun. Honors Coll., Oakland U., 2002—; ednl. travel cons.; ESL tutor/cons., 2003-05 Author: Images of Michigan, 1981. Michigan Centennial Farm History, 1986. Pres. Horizons Residential Ctrs., Inc., New Baltimore, Mich., 1984—2006; artistic dir. Phoenix Theater Co., 1997—2001, prodr.; ptnr. Rediscovery Ctr., Holly, Mich., 2000—; bd. dirs. Honors Coll. Oakland U., 2002—; bd. dirs. Amerris Ind. Schs., 2000—06. Recipient Disting. Alumni award Oakland U., 1976. Mem. NEA, AAUW (scholarship chmn. Flator chpt. 2000—), Rochester Edn. Assn., Mich. Edn. Assn., Mich. Coun. Tchrs. English (coms. 1985, 87), Oakland U. Alumni Assn. (pres. 1971-73), Mich. Centennial Farm Assn. (bd. dirs. 1979-2004), Mich. Assn. Gifted Edn. (v.p. 1991-93), Oakland County Tchrs. English (coms. 1985-93, editor profl. writing ad copy). Office: Internat Acad 1020 E Square Lake Rd Bloomfield Hills MI 48304-1957

WERNER, CECELIA MARIE, counselor; b. Norfolk, Nebr., May 29, 1955; d. Lambert and Marion Rita (Koch) Podany; m. Lavern Eugene Werner, Dec. 28, 1974 (div. May 1983); children: Jesse, Sara. BFA in Art Edn. cum laude, Wayne (Nebr.) State Coll., 1984, MA in Counselor Edn., 1988. Waitress Hank's Place, Petersburg, Nebr., 1977-78; secondary tchr. art Pope John XXIII Cen. Cath. High Sch., Elgin, Nebr., 1978-80; grad. asst Adult Resource Ctr., Wayne State Coll., 1985, grad. asst. psychology dept., 1987-88; secondary tchr. art and Spanish, Pierce (Nebr.) Pub. Schs., 1985-87; secondary sch. counselor Red Oak (Iowa) Community Schs., 1988—. Officer Student/Tchr. Assistance Team, Red Oak, 1990—. Vol. tchr. art St. John's Sch., Petersburg, 1977-79. Scholar Wayne State Coll., 1983, 84. Mem. IACD, Iowa Assn. Counseling and Devel. Roman Catholic. Home: 905 E Prospect St Red Oak IA 51566-1631 Office: Red Oak High Sch 2011 N 8th St Red Oak IA 51566-1114 Office Phone: 712-623-6612.

WERNER, ELIZABETH HELEN, librarian, language educator; d. Fielding and Lucy Elizabeth McDearmon; m. Michael Andrew Werner, Aug. 21, 1976. BA, Mills Coll., 1966; MA, Ind. U., 1968; MLS, U. Md., 1973. Instr. Spanish McDaniel Coll., Westminster, Md., 1968—72; libr., assoc. prof. Clearwater (Fla.) Christian Coll., 1975—. Sec. Sunline Libr. users group Tampa Bay Libr. Consortium, Tampa, Fla., 1993—94, 1998—2000, 2002—03, 2006—, chmn., 2003—05. Contbr. book revs. to profl. jours. Com. mem. Upper Pinellas County Post Office Customers' Adv. Coun., Clearwater, 1992—2000. Recipient Vol. of Yr., Assn. Christian Libraries, 2003. Mem.: Fla. Assn. Christian Librs. (sec. 1987—90, pres. 1991—94, sec. 1995—98, 2000—), Assn. Christian Librs. (Christian libr. consortium team coord. 1998—2006), Fla. Libr. Assn., Friends of Clearwater Libr., DAR (chpt. libr. 2006—, chmn. constitution com. 2005—). Avocations: reading, choir, travel, languages, genealogy. Office: Clearwater Christian Coll 3400 Gulf-to-Bay Blvd Clearwater FL 33759 Business E-Mail: elizabethwerner@clearwater.edu.

WERNER, KAREN ELAINE, music educator; b. Mexico, Mo., July 14, 1953; d. Leroy Herbert and Myrtle Marie Sperry; children: Kristina, Angela. BS Music Edn., SW Mo. State U., 1975; MA Music History, U. Mo., 1980. Cert. music tchr. Mo. Tchr. music Niangua Pub. Schs., Mo., 1975—76; dir. choirs Ava Jr. and Sr. H.S., Mo., 1977—81; dir. choir Rolla Pub. Schs., Mo., 1981—84; head choral dept. McEvoy Music, San Diego, 1984—89; tchr. music La Jolla Elem., Calif., 1989—94; assoc. prof., dir. singers Moberly Area C.C., Mo., 1994—. Dir. music La Jolla Children's Theater Workshop, 1990—94; leader music workshop Choral Condrs. Guild, San Diego, 1991—94; clinician, adjudicator area h.s. music contests and festivals, 1994—; vis. instr. Christ Ch. U. Coll., Canterbury, Kent, England, 1999; presenter Global Edn. Conf., Kansas City, 2001. Bd. dirs. Moberly Area Coun. of Arts, 1997—2002; music dir. Palisades Presbyn. Ch., San Diego, 1991—94. Recipient Tchg. Excellence award, Gov. Mo., 2003, Alfred and Hazel Parrish award, 2005. Mem.: Mo. C.C. Assn. (chair salary com.), Am. Choral Dirs. Assn. (chair state repertoire and stds. 1999—2003), Mo. Assn. Depts. and Schs. Music (bd. dirs. 2001—04), Music Educator's Nat. Conf. (dist. choral v.p. 1981—84). Methodist. Avocations: running, gardening, travel. Office: Moberly Area Cmty Coll 101 College Ave Moberly MO 65270 Office Phone: 660-263-4110 ext. 357. Business E-Mail: karenw@macc.edu.

WERNER, PATRICE (PATRICIA ANN WERNER), academic administrator; b. Jersey City, May 31, 1937; d. Louis and Ella Blanche (Smith) W. BA in French, Caldwell Coll., 1966; MA in French, McGill U., 1970; PhD in French, NYU, 1976; postgrad. Inst. Ednl. Mgmt., Harvard U., 1991. Joined Dominican Sisters of Caldwell, 1954. Sch. tchr. Archdiocesan Sch. Systems, N.J., Ala., 1954-62; tchr. French, Latin Jersey City, Caldwell, NJ, 1962-72; instr. French Caldwell (NJ) Coll., 1973-76, dir. continuing edn., 1976-79, chair dept. fgn. langs., assoc. prof. French, 1979-85, acad. dean, prof. French, 1985-94, pres., 1994—. Trustee Caldwell Coll.; mem. corp., trustee Providence Coll.; mem. Dominican Higher Edn. Coun.; mem. NJ Pres.' Coun. accountability com., liaison com. to NJ Higher Edn. Partnership for Sustainability. Named Salute to Policy Makers award, Exec. Women NJ, 2006, Outstanding Woman in Am. History, DAR Maj. Joseph Bloomfield Chpt.; recipient Woman of Achievement award, N. N.J. Coun. of Boy Scouts of Am., 1999, The Archbishop T.E. McCarrick award for Disting. Svc. to the Ch., 2000, Cmty. Woman of Achievement, West Caldwell Hist. Soc. and West Essex Women's Club, 2000, Caldwell Cup, Excellence in Edn. award, N. Essex C. of C. Found., 2003; scholar AATF Summer Grant. Mem.: Assn. Gov. Bds. of Univs. and Colls., N.J. C. of C., Assn. Cath. Colls. and Univs., Nat. Assn. Ind. Colls. and Univs. (bd. dirs., sec. bd. dirs., com. policy analysis and pub. rels.), Coun. Ind. Colls. (bd. dirs., pub. info. com.), Ind. Coll. Fund. N.J. (trustee, vice chmn. exec. com.), Assn. Ind. Colls. and Univs. in N.J. (chmn. bd. dirs.). Avocations: tennis, reading, avid sports fan, travel. Office: Caldwell Coll 9 Ryerson Ave Caldwell NJ 07006-6195 Office Phone: 973-618-3217. Business E-Mail: spwerner@caldwell.edu.

WERNER-JACOBSEN, EMMY ELISABETH, developmental psychologist; b. Eltville, Germany, May 26, 1929; came to U.S., 1952, naturalized, 1962; d. Peter Josef and Liesel (Kunz) W. BS, Johannes Gutenberg U., Germany, 1950; MA, U. Nebr., 1952, PhD, 1955; postgrad., U. Calif., Berkeley, 1953-54. Research asso. Inst. Child Welfare, U. Minn., 1956-59; vis. scientist NIH, 1959-62; asst. prof. to prof. human devel., rsch. child psychologist U. Calif., Davis, 1962-94, rsch. prof., 1995—. Sr. author: The Children of Kauai, 1971, Kauai's Children Come of Age, 1977; author: Cross-Cultural Child Development: A View from the Planet Earth, 1979, Vulnerable, but Invincible, 1982, 3d edit., 1998, Child Care: Kith, Kin and Hired Hands, 1984, Overcoming the Odds, 1992, Pioneer Children on the Journey West, 1995, Reluctant Witnesses: Children's Voices From the Civil War, 1998, Through the Eyes of Innocents: Children Witness World War II, 2000, Unschuldige Zeugen, 2001, Journeys From Childhood to Mid Life: Risk, Resilience and Recovery, 2001, A Conspiracy of Decency: The Rescue of the Danish Jews in World War II, 2002, In Pursuit of Liberty, 2006; contbr. articles to profl. jours. Recipient Disting. Sci. Contbn. to Child Devel. award, Soc. Rsch. Child Devel., 1999, Dolly Madison Presdl. award for outstanding lifelong contbns. to devel. and wellbeing of children and families, Zero to Three, 1999, Arnold Gesell award, German Soc. Pediat., 2001, award for disting. career contbns. to sci. study of lifespan devel., Soc. for Study of Human Devel., 2005. Fellow: Assn. Psychol. Scis., Soc. Rsch. Child Devel., German Acad. Social Pediats. (hon.). Business E-Mail: eewerner@ucdavis.edu.

WERNICK, SANDRA MARGOT, advertising and public relations executive; b. Tampa, Fla., Sept. 13, 1944; d. Nathan and Sylvia (Bienstock) Rothstein. BA in English, U. Fla., 1966. Tchr. English Miami Beach (Fla.) Sr. H.S., 1967; adminstrv. asst. pub. rels. Bozell & Jacobs, Inc., N.Y.C., 1968-69; asst. to dir. pub. rels. Waldorf-Astoria, N.Y.C., 1969-70; dir. advt. and pub. rels. Hyatt on Union Sq., San Francisco, 1974-82; pres. Wernick Mktg. Group, San Francisco, 1982—; exec. dir. Sales and Mktg. Execs. of the Bay Area, 1995-2000; mng. ptnr. The Stanford Group, 1998-99; pres. Auction Magic, San Francisco, 2003—. Bd. dirs. Nat. Kidney Assn., San Francisco, 1985-87; advisor Swords to Plowshares, San Francisco, 1988-89; mem. mktg. com. to bd. Boy Scouts of Greater East Bay, 1995-2000. Recipient Award of Merit, San Francisco Advt. and Cable Car Awards, 1979, Award of Excellence, San Francisco Art Dirs. 1978, Disting. Mktg. award Sales and Mktg. Internat., 1997, awards Am. Hotel and Motel Assn., 1981, 82. Mem. NAFE, Women in Comms. (bd. dirs. 1987-89), Am. Women in Radio and TV (bd. dirs. 1989-90), Pub. Rels. Soc. Am., San Francisco Publicity Club (pres. 1989, awards of excellence 1990, 94, 95-98), Variety Club, Profl. Bus. Women's Assn., Calif. Pacific Med. Ctr. (aux. 1988-95). Democrat. Jewish. Office: 1690 Broadway Ste 705 San Francisco CA 94109-2107 E-mail: sandie@wernickmarketinggroup.com.

WERNICKE, MARIAN O'SHEA, language educator; b. St. Louis, Mo., May 21, 1943; d. Thomas James and Margaret Ward O'Shea; m. Robert Michael Wernicke, Sept. 25, 1976; children: Kristin, Timothy Joseph, John Michael. BA in English, Fontbonne Coll., St. Louis, 1965; MA in English, U. West Fla., Pensacola, 1985. Prof. English Pensacola Jr. Coll., 1988—, dept. head English/comm., 1997—2003. Editor: (literary mag.) The Hurricane Rev. Mem. bd. Kaleidoscope Ballet, Pensacola, 2005—06. Recipient Tchg. Excellence award, Pensacola Jr. Coll., 1993, Supr. of Yr., 2001. Democrat. Catholic. Avocations: poetry, writing. Home: 823 N 17th Ave Pensacola FL 32501 Office: Pensacola Jr Coll 1000 College Blvd Pensacola FL 32504 Office Phone: 850-484-1424.

WERRA, DONNA, elementary school educator; b. East Chicago, Ind., Nov. 7, 1965; d. Anthony and Barbara Werra; m. Danny Steven Torres; 1 child, Danielle Christine Torres Werra. BA, Ind. U., Bloomington, 1987. Cert. single subject English Calif., 1994, CLAD Calif., multiple subjects Calif., 1994. English/history tchr. Luther Burbank Middle Sch., San Francisco, 1994—96; lang. arts/social studies tchr. James Lick Mid. Sch., San Francisco, 1996—2002; lang. arts tchr. Creekside Mid. Sch., Patterson, Calif., 2002—06. Josephine Miles fellow. Office Phone: 209-862-0621.

WERSHING, JULIA M., pediatrician; d. Nicholas L. and Julia M. Wershing. BA, U. Mo., Columbia, 1954; MD, Georgetown U., Washington, 1958, ScD, 1984. Instr. pediat. U. Colo. Med. Sch., Denver, 1962—63; from instr. to assoc. prof. Georgetown U. Sch. Med., Washington, 1963—. Contbr. articles to profl. jours. Fellow: Am. Assn. Pediat.; mem.: Order British Empire (hon.). Roman Catholic. Avocations: gardening, golf, writing.

WERT, BARBARA J. YINGLING, special education consultant; b. Hanover, Pa., May 18, 1953; d. Richard Bruce and Jacqueline Louise (Myers) Yingling; m. Barry Thomas Wert, Aug. 23, 1975; children: Jennifer Allison, Jason Frederick. BS in Elem. Edn., Kutztown (Pa.) U., 1975; MS in Spl. Edn., Bloomsburg (Pa.) U., 1990; PhD, Pa. State U., 2002, cert. in autism, 2004. Cert. in elem. edn., spl. edn., Pa.; cert. early childhood, Pa. Dir. children's program Coun. for United Ch. Ministries of Reading, Reading, Pa., 1975-76; instr. Berks County Vo-Tech., Oley Valley, Pa., 1976-77; asst. tchr. Ostrander Elem. Sch., Wallkill, N.Y., 1982-85; spl. needs surp., instrnl. support tchr., cons. Danville (Pa.) Child Devel. Ctr., 1986—; dir. Little Learners Pre-Sch., Northumberland, Pa., 1991-94, ednl. cons., 1991—; asst. prof. Bloomsburg U., 2002—. Pvt. cons. Families with Spl. Needs, Northumberland, 1991—; adj. prof. spl. edn., Bloomsburg U., 1995, 97, 98, 99, 00. Recipient Parent Profl. Partnership award 1993. Mem. ASCD, Coun. for Exceptional Children (exec. bd. dirs. divsn. early childhood 1991—, sec. 1991-93, newsletter editor, v.p. 1993-94, pres. 1995-96, mem. tchr. edn. divsn.), Nat. Assn. for Edn. Young Children (v.p. Pa. divsn. for early childhood 1993—, tchr. edn. divsn., coun. for behavior disorders divsn., learning disabilities divsn.), Local Autism Support and Advocacy Group. Avocations: photography, needlecrafts, hiking, reading.: 230 Evergreen Dr Winfield PA 17889-9170 Office Phone: 570-389-4110. Business E-Mail: bwert@bloomu.edu.

WERTHEIM, MARY DANIELLE, educational coordinator; b. N.Y.C. d. Daniel Leo and Helen Loretta (Sudimick) Conroy; m. Stanley Claude Wertheim, Mar. 9, 1963. BA in English with honors, CCNY, 1960, MA, 1979. Coord. English and lang. arts Horace Mann Lower Sch., Riverdale, NY, 1969—. Pvt. investor Wertheim Trust, N.Y.C., 1985—; pres. winner's cir. Horace Mann Investment Club, Riverdale, 1989—. Founder, advisor Horace Mann Lower Sch. Cmty. Svc. Group, Riverdale, 1980—; active Rep. nat. Com., 1980—. Mem.: ASCD, Nat. Assn. Investors Corp., The Internat. Netsuke Soc. (sec. N.Y. chapter), Priory Scholars, Am. Firm, Mensa, The Grolier Club. Avocations: desk top publishing, manuscript collecting. Home: 180 Cabrini Blvd # 57 New York NY 10033-1138 Office: Horace Mann Lower Sch 4440 Tibbett Ave Bronx NY 10471-3416 E-mail: herbieboo@aol.com.

WERTHEIM, MITZI MALLINA, information technology executive; b. N.Y.C. d. Rudolf and Myrtle B. (McGraw) Mallina; m. Ronald P. Wertheim, Feb. 25, 1965 (div. July 1988); children: Carter, Tiana. BA, U. Mich., 1960. Asst. dir. div. research Peace Corps, Washington, 1961-66; sr. program officer Cafritz Found., Washington, 1970-76; dep. undersec. navy, 1977-81; with Fed. Sector Div. IBM, 1981-94; v.p. enterprise solutions SRA Corp., 1994-98, CNA Corp., 1998—. Woodrow Wilson vis. fellow, 1979, 80; founder, dir. The Energy Consensus, 2005—. Bd. dirs. Nat. Coalition Sci. and Tech., 1983—86; mem. vis. com. MIT, 1983—89; bd. dirs. Youth Policy Inst., 1986—91, VITA, 2001—, Cebrowski Inst., Naval Post Grad. Sch.; founder MIT Seminar XXI, 1985—. Recipient Federally Employed Women award Def. Dept., 1980; Disting. Pub. Svc. medal Navy Dept., 1981; fellow Maxwell Sch. Syracuse U., 1996-97. Mem.: Naval Studies Bd., Coun. on Fgn. Rels. Episcopalian. Home: 3113 38th St NW Washington DC 20016-3726

WERTHEIM, SALLY HARRIS, director, academic administrator, dean, education educator, consultant; b. Cleve., Nov. 1, 1931; d. Arthur I. and Anne (Manheim) Harris; m. Stanley E. Wertheim, Aug. 6, 1950; children: Kathryn, Susan B., Carole J. BS, Flora Stone Mather Coll., 1953; MA, Case Western Res. U., 1967, PhD, 1970. Cert. elem. and secondary edn. tchr. Ohio. Social worker U. Hosps., Cleve., 1953-54; tchr. Fairmount Temple Religious Sch., Cleve., 1957-72; mem. faculty John Carroll U., Cleve., 1969—, chair dept. edn., 1979—86, dean Grad. Sch., 1986—99, dir. planning and assessment, 1999—2004, interim dean Coll. Arts and Scis., 2004—05, cons. Office of Acad. V.P., 2005—, interim dir. Career Ctr., 2005—06. Cons. in field; cons. Jennings Found., Cleve.; chmn. sch. com. Cleve. Commn. on Higher Edn., 1987-99. Contbr. articles to profl. jours. Sec. Cuyahoga County Mental Health Bd., Cleve., 1978—82; pres. Montefiore Home, Cleve., 1987—90; bd. dirs. Mt. Sinai Med. Ctr., Cleve., 1984—93, Cleve. Edn. Fund, 1992—94; chair edn. com. Cleve. Found. Commn. on Poverty, 1988—93, Cleve. Cmty. Bldg. Initiative, 1993—95, United Way Svcs., 1994—2001; trustee Mt. Sinai Health Care Found., 1998, Gerson Found., 1998, Miller Found., 1998, Begun Found., 2001, Mandel Found., 2001; pres. Jewish Family Svc. Assn., Cleve., 1974—77; v.p. Jewish Cmty. Fedn., 1988—91, pres., 1994—97, trustee, 1975, life trustee, 1997—. Named One of 100 Most Influential Women, Cleve. mag., 1983, One of 29 Most Influential Women, Cleve. Mag., 1997; recipient award John Carroll U., Curtis Miles award for cmty. svc., 1997; grantee Jennings Found., 1984-87, Cleve. and Gund Found., 1987-90, Lilly Found., 1988; S.H. Wertheim scholarship and edn. excellence award established John Carroll U., 1997. Mem. Am. Assn. Colls. for Tchrs. Edn. (bd. dirs. 1982-85), Ohio Assn. Colls. for Tchrs. Edn. (pres. 1981-83), Coun. of Grad. Schs. Avocations: flower arranging, travel, antiques. Office: John Carroll Univ Office of Acad VP Cleveland OH 44118 Business E-Mail: wertheim@jcu.edu.

WERTHEIMER, MARILYN LOU, librarian, educator; b. Pueblo, Colo., Dec. 1, 1928; d. Louis Robert and Alice Erdine Schuman; m. Y. Ernest Satow, Jan. 4, 1953 (div. Oct. 1958); m. Michael M. Wertheimer, Sept. 12, 1970; stepchildren: Karen Anne, Mark David, John Benjamin. BA, Stanford U., 1950; MA, Columbia U., 1953; postgrad., U. Calif., Berkeley, 1961—62; MLS, U. Calif., L.A., 1967. Sec., proofreader various publ. firms, N.Y.C., 1953—56; sec. Rockefeller Bros. Fund, 1956—57; personal staff, sec. Nelson A. Rockefeller, 1957—58; sec. Gen. Dynamics Corp., San Diego, 1959—64; cataloguer U. Calif., 1965—68; reference libr. U. Colo., Boulder, 1968—93, prof. honors sem., 1972—91, prof. emeritus, 1993—. Mem. libr. del. U.S. Exch. China, 1985, U.S. Exch. U.S.S.R., 1988; cons. Archives of History Am. Psychology, Akron, Ohio, 1980. Co-author: Sources of Information in the Social Sciences, 1986; co-editor: History of Psychology: A Guide, 1979; one-woman shows include Boulder (Colo.) Pub. Libr., 2004, Sun Microsystems, Broomfield, Colo., 2004, Norlin Libr. U. Colo., Boulder, 2005, Classical Acad., Colorado Springs, Colo., 2005. Mem. del. vis. Tibet, Boulder-Lhasa Sister Cities Program, 1988; vol. Christian Sci. Ch., 1986—; bd. dirs. U. Club, U. Colo., Boulder, 1976—79. Recipient First prize, Internat. Libr. Photography, Owings Mills, Md., 1999—2000. Mem.: ALA. Democrat. Home: 546 Geneva Ave Boulder CO 80302 Office: Norlin Libr U Colo Campus Box 184 Boulder CO 80309-0184 Business E-Mail: wertheim@colorado.edu.

WERTHEIMER-SEXTON, WILLA RENEE, clinical psychologist; b. Chgo., May 10, 1964; d. William Ralph and Faye Ruth Wertheimer; m. Peter Patrick Sexton, Aug. 15, 1990; children: Maitiú Dáibhid, Liam Dainéal. BA Psychology, DePaul U., Chgo., 1987; PsychoID, Ill. Sch. Profl. Psychology, 1996. Cert. Clin. Pschologist Ill. Dept. Profl. Regulation. Intern Forest Hosp., Des Plaines, Ill., 1992—93; postdoctoral intern North Shore Counseling and Consulting, 1993—94, ind. contractor, therapist Bannockburn, Ill., 1994—98; pres. Advocacy Counseling Ctr., Woodstock, Ill., 1998—. Affiliated staff psychologist Centegra Meml. Hosp., 1998—. Mem. adv. bd. McHenry County Head Start, Woodstock, Ill., 2001—; vol. presenter Head Start, Woodstock, 2001—; vol. teen group leader (family relationships) Woodstock H.S., 2003; numerous free workshops to various groups McHenry County, Ill. Mem.: APA. Jewish. Avocations: art, reading, spiritual development. Office: Advocacy Counseling Ctr 115 E South St Woodstock IL 60098 Office Phone: 815-243-6789. Office Fax: 815-334-0312. E-mail: dr.willa@sbc.global.net.

WERTS, RUBY WOODWARD, elementary school educator; b. Cordele, Ga., Jan. 24, 1944; d. John Dewey and Marie Singletary Woodward; m. William Allen Werts, June 25, 1967; children: Jerbundy, Anna. BS in Elem. Edn., Ga. So. Coll., Statesboro, 1966; MEd, Ga. Coll., Milledgeville, 1976. Tchr. Radium Springs Elem., Albany, 1966—67, San Diego Sch. Dist., Calif., 1967—68, Ctrl. State Hosp. Sch., Milledgeville, Ga., 1970—73, Northside Elem., Milledgeville, 1974—89, Davis Elem., Milledgeville, 1989—2000; tchr., children's theatre Allied Arts, Milledgeville, 2000—. Student writing editor Ga. Coun. English Tchrs., 1989—93; Editor, Camp Good Grief Writing Hospice, Milledgeville. Playwright: children's plays Cats, Cats, Cats, Everybody Rocks, We Are America, Medieval Magic, Mother Goose Revue, Fable Follies. Sec. Milledgeville Music Club, 1994—, pres.; children's choir dir. First Bapt. Ch.; mem. adv. bd. Friends of Allied Arts, 1988—. Recipient Tchr. of Yr., Northside Elem., 1987, Davis Elem., 1997. Mem.: Milledgeville Players (bd. mem. 2000—). Avocations: theater, music, antiques, history. Home: 103 Partridge Rd NE Milledgeville GA 31061

WESELAK, ANNA MARIE SCHMIDT, educational association administrator, media consultant; b. Aurora, Ill., Oct. 28, 1949; d. John Joseph and Anna Florence (Sandor) Schmidt; m. Kevin John Weselak, May 20, 1972; children: Timothy Charles, Thomas John, Kristin Marie. BS, No. Ill. U., 1971, MS, 1974. Cert. early childhood edn. tchr., elem. edn. tchr. First grade tchr. Sch. Dist. 131, Aurora, 1971-75; kindergarten tchr. Pioneer Child Care Ctr., Lombard, Ill., 1987-92; sales and mktg. mgr. Minuteman Press, Addison, Ill.; owner, cons. Weselak & Assocs., 1994—; cons. Pearson Skylight, 1996—; sch. collaborative design team cons. The Ball Found., 1999—2000. Graphic media cons. Minuteman Press, Addison, Ill., 1991—; bd. dirs. DuPage regional unit Chgo. Assn. for Edn. Young Children; chmn. parent-child fair for Wk. of Young Child, 1988-89; program chmn., 1989-91, fall conf. chmn., 1991-92. Pres. Lombard PTA Coun., 1987-89, 5th dist. Gen. Fedn. Women's Clubs Ill., 1988-90, Lombard Newcomers, 1976-77, Lombard Svc. League, 1981-83; grand marshall Lombard Lilac Parade, 1993. Recipient 10 Yr. Svc. award No. Ill. U. Alumni Assn., 1980, Ill. State Bd. Edn. Those Who Excel award of merit, 1992-93; named gift AAUW, 1985, one of Outstanding Young Women Am., 1983, Lombard Woman Yr., 1989. Mem. Ill. PTA (bd. mgrs., dist. 32 dir. 1988-91, chair leadership tng. 1991-93, v.p. dist. dirs. 1993—, state conv. chmn. 1992, 93, Book of Recognition award 1990, hon. life mem.), Nat. PTA (hon. life mem., pres. elect 2003-05, pres. 2005-7), Ill. Fedn. Women's Clubs (chair budget and fin. 1990-92, editor Ill. Clubwoman mag. 1991—), Sigma Lambda Sigma (pres. 1970). Roman Catholic. Avocations: crafts, needlecrafts, sewing. Office: Nat PTA Ste 1300 541 N Fairbanks Ct Chicago IL 60611-3396

WESELY, MARISSA CELESTE, lawyer; b. NYC, Apr. 25, 1955; d. Edwin Joseph and Yolanda Teresa (Pyles) W.; m. Frederick Hamerman; 1 child, Emma Elizabeth Wesely Allen. BA magna cum laude, Williams Coll., 1976; JD cum laude, Harvard U., 1980. Bar: N.Y. 1981. Assoc. Simpson Thacher & Bartlett, NYC, 1980-82, 84-88, London, 1982-84, ptnr., 1989—. Lectr., cons. Harvard Inst. Internat. Devel., Beijing, 1981, Jakarta, Indonesia, 1982; guest lectr. Yale Law Sch., New Haven, 1991; spkr. Am. Conf. Inst., Practicing Law Inst., Bankers Assn. for Fgn. Trade, N.Y. State Bar Assn. confs., 1993—. Bd. dirs. City Lore, NYC; capital campaign com. Lawyers Alliance NY; bd. legal adv. Legal Momentum. Mem.: ABA, Internat. Bar Assn., N.Y. State Bar Assn., N.Y.C. Bar Assn., Phi Beta Kappa. Office: Simpson Thacher & Bartlett LLP 425 Lexington Ave Fl 20 New York NY 10017-3954 Office Phone: 212-455-7173. Office Fax: 212-455-2502. Business E-Mail: mwesely@stblaw.com.

WESEMAN, VICKI LYNNE, elementary school educator; b. Hastings, Nebr., Oct. 29, 1954; d. Virgil John and Vera Lillie (Berg) Kennedy; m. Creighton Lee Weseman, May 28, 1988 (div. Oct. 1999); 1 child, Jason K. BS, U. Nebr., 1977, MA, 1988. Cert. elem. tchr. Nebr., profl. tchr. Nebr. Elem. tchr. Hanover Elem. Sch., Glenvil, Nebr., 1977—2003, Lincoln Elem. Sch., Grand Isle., Nebr., 2003—. Pres. Adams County Edn. Assn., Hastings, Nebr., 1996—97; team leader stds. Adams County Schs., Hastings, 2000—01. Oregon Trail rodeo pageant coord. Adams County Agrl. Soc., Hastings, 1992—. Named Miss Rodeo, Nebr., 1977, Com. Person of Yr., Oregon Trail Rodeo, Hastings, 1999. Mem.: Nebr. Edn. Assn. (mem. selection com. 2000), Women's Profl. Rodeo Assn., Alpha Delta Kappa. Democrat. Lutheran. Avocation: barrel racing in rodeo. Office: Lincoln Elem 805 Beal St Grand Island NE 68801

WESLEY, RUBY LAVERNE, nursing educator, administrator, researcher; b. Detroit, Nov. 25, 1949; d. David Williams and Leatrice (Gragg) Williams; 1 child, Nathaniel Rogers Wesley III. Diploma, Providence Hosp. Sch. Nursing, Southfield, Mich., 1971; BS in Nursing, Wayne State U., Detroit, 1974, MEd, 1977; PhD, U. Md., Balt., 1987. Clin. instr. U. Tenn. Sch. Nursing, 1978-79; community health nursing instr. U. Md., Balt., 1984-85; assoc. prof. Bowie State U., 1985-89; asst. dean Coppin State Coll., Balt., 1989-90; asst. prof. Wayne State U., 1991—; nurse researcher Rehab. Inst. Mich., 1992, dir. nursing practice Detroit, 1992-93, dir. nursing, 1993-96; asst. v.p. med./surg. rehab. nursing Sinai Hosp. Detroit, 1996—98; chief oper. officer Detroit Inst. for Children, 1998—99; pres., CEO Big Bros./Big Sisters of Metro Detroit, 2000—02; v.p. programs Detroit Urban League, 2002—03; exec. dir. Wayne County Patient Care Mgmt. Sys., 2003—06; assoc. chief nurse educator VA Med. Ctr., Washington, 2006—. Henry C. Welcome fellow, 1986-87; Nat. Inst. Disability and Rehab. rsch. fellow, 1991-92. Office: Washington VA Med Ctr 50 Irving St NW Washington DC 20422-0002 Office Phone: 202-745-8486. Personal E-mail: drrlwesley@hotmail.com.

WESLEY, SUSAN BRAY, psychotherapist, music educator; b. Chgo., Nov. 21, 1948; d. Walter George Bray Jr. and Julia Balizs Bray; 1 child, Andrew Eric Bilyeu. B in Music Edn., Hope Coll., Holland, Mich., 1970; MALS, Valparaiso U., Ind., 1976; PhD, U. Akron, Ohio, 1984. Instl. rsch. intern Lorain (Ohio) County C.C., 1981—84; fine arts dir. Bangor (Maine) Sch., 1988—96; CEO Wesley Cons. & MESA, Bangor, 1996—2005, Wesley Cons., Soap Lake, Wash., 2005—. Music therapy cons. MSAD, Maine, 1984—2005; faculty U. Maine, Orono, 1986—2001; adult, human devel. tng. specialist St. Joseph's Hosp., Bangor, 1993—95; ministerial assessment specialist New Eng. region United Meth. Ch. - New Eng. Regio, Lawrence, Mass., 1994—2005; adv. bd. Internat. Acad. Design and Health, Stockholm, 2003—05; am. transl. cons. Klrara Kokas, Budapest, 2004—; faculty Husson Coll., Bangor, 2004—. Author: Guided Imagery and Music, Design & Health, Design & Heatlh, MasterClass. Edn. dir. Music For People, Keene, NH, 1986—93. Scholar Provost award for Grad. Study in Music, U. Akron, 1983—84. Fellow: Assn. Music and Imagery (corr.), Unkefer Acad. Neurologic Music Therapy (assoc.). Avocations: house plants, reading, fitness, travel. Office: Wesley Cons PO Box 1462 Soap Lake WA 98851 Office Phone: 509-771-2407. Office Fax: 509-246-1803. E-mail: wesleydsl1@yahoo.com.

WESLIN, ANNA THERESE, acute care nurse practitioner, dance consultant; d. Norman Uno and Mary Lou Weslin. AA, El Paso CC, Colorado Springs, 1977; BA, Dance Minor, St. Mary's Coll., Kans., 1981; BS in Nursing, Beth-El Coll. of Nursing, Colorado Springs, 1995; MSN, U. Colo., Colorado Springs, 2004. RN Colo. State Bd. of Nursing, Colo., 1995, cert. Clinical Nurse Specialist, Colo. State Bd. of Nursing, Colo., 2006. Assoc. dir., sec. treas. Colo. Springs Ballet Acad., 1981—2005; RN, charge nurse Health South Rehab. Hosp., Colorado Springs, 1996—2000; pres., CEO, tchr. La Sante et la Danse, Inc., Colorado Springs, 2003—; RN Pikes Peak Hospice & Palliative Care, Colorado Springs, 2006—; rn cardiology staff nurse Parkview Episcopal Hosp., Pueblo, Colo.; R&D plant mgr. Brown Disc Mfg., Colorado Springs. Recipient Best of Springs award (Best Pl. for Dancer's with a Broken Pointe), Gazette Newspaper, 2005. Mem.: Colo. Springs BBB, Colo. Springs C. of C., Assn. of Rehab. Nurses, Performing Arts Medicine Assn., Internat. Assn. Dance Medicine and Scis., Sigma Theta Tau Internat. Achievements include development of 1st nursing based dance medicine clinic in the State of Colo; research in common injuries of adolescent dance students. Office: La Sante et la Danse Inc 2935 N Prospect St Ste 200 Colorado Springs CO 80907 Office Phone: 719-329-0144. Business E-Mail: lasante@adelphia.net.

WESNER, PATRICIA, bank executive; m. Jim Hoffman. BA, Pa. State U.; MA Bus. Adminstrn., Marquette U. With First Wis. Nat. Bank, 1977; div. head Milw. branches Firstar Bank (now US Bank), v.p. Retail Payment

Solutions. Mem. Visa USA's Deposit Products Exec. Coun., Visa's Small Bus. Exec. Coun., Visa's Internat. Adv. Coun. Bd. dirs. LSS Found., 2005—, Florentine Opera Co. Mem.: Tempo Internat. Office: US Bank 777 E Wisconsin Ave Milwaukee WI 53202

WESOLOSKI, DEBORAH J., music educator; b. Garfield Heights, Ohio, Nov. 29, 1958; d. Leo S. and Virginia D. Kukwa; m. Steven Wesoloski, Aug. 1, 1992; children: Monty, Craig, Austin. MusB, U. Cin. Conservatory, 1980; MA in Tchg., Marygrove Coll., Detroit, 2000. Tchr. music Cin. Pub. Schs., 1980—84, Berea City Schs., Ohio, 1987—. Mem.: Nat. Sch. Orch. Assn., Am. String Tchrs. Assn., Ohio Music Edn. Assn., Nat. Conf. Music Educators.

WESSELKAMPER, SUE, academic administrator; m. Tom Wesselkamper; 2 children. BA History, Govt., Edgecliff Coll.; M Social Work, U. Mich.; PhD Social Welfare, CUNY. Head cmty., social svs. program New River Cmty. Coll.; dir. social work field instrn. program Radford U., Va.; dean sch. arts and scis., assoc. prof. social work Coll. New Rochelle, NY; pres. Chaminade U. Honolulu, 1995—. Author: Enhancing Ethnic Identity Through Cross-Cultural Interaction, An Intercultural Approach to Contemporary Ethnicity, Issues in Implementing Cultural Diversity Content, Role of the Social Worker in Health Planning. Chmn. bd. dirs. Family Svcs. Westchester County, NY; mem. adv. com. Pew Charitable Trust 3d Black Colls. Project on Student Retention; mem. Hawaii Cath. Conf., Hawaii State Network of Am. Coun. on Edn.'s Women Leaders in Higher Edn. Avocations: reading, movies, hiking, travel. Office: Chaminade U of Honolulu 3140 Waialae Ave Honolulu HI 96816

WESSELMANN, JANINE CAROL, artist; b. Utica, N.Y., June 13, 1947; d. Robert A. and Anita G. (Ziegler) W. BS in Design, Cornell U., 1969; BS in Art Edn., Ladycliff Coll., 1980. Vol. Peace Corps, 1969; mem. faculty, head art dept. All Saints, St. Thomas, V.I., 1970-73; mem. faculty Ladycliff Coll., Highland Falls, N.Y., 1979-80; art dir. Tepfer Pub. Co., Danbury, Conn., 1980-85. Designed murals for Pan Am. Hotel, Miami Beach, Fla.; instr. graphic arts, Switzerland and Caribbean; art cons. Cunard Lines; cultural emissary to France, 1997. Exhibited one-woman shows Columbia U., N.Y.C., 1994, U.S., Europe, Caribbean. Pres. Art Circle; art del. to France; art amb. to Rome, 1996. Recipient awards for painting Am. Bicentennial, Venice Art League, Nat. Design award for best mag. covers, 1985, Disting. Leadership award, 1985, award for Leadership in the Arts, Cambridge, Eng., Tribute des Arts, France, 1994; 1st Am. woman to show at Exposition d'Orange, France, 1994, Centro Culturale, Rome, 1995, Collection d'Art, Paris, 1997, 1st Am. woman included in permanent collection of Art Modern de la Ville de Paris; internat. recognition for painting Ground Zero, 2001. Studio: PO Box 627 West Redding CT 06896-0627 Office Phone: 203-794-1407. E-mail: jwesselmann@comcast.net.

WESSELS-MCCOY, DENISE WENDY, pre-school administrator, consultant; b. Windsor, NY, Aug. 18, 1955; d. Bess Marie Urbani and David Wilfred Wessels; children: Joseph J. McCoy, Ryan D. McCoy. BA in Child Devel., San Jose State U., 1977; MS, Nova Southeastern U., 1990, postgrad., 2002—. Owner Learning Tree Pre Sch., Santa Cruz, Calif., 1980—89; instr. U. Calif., Santa Cruz, 1989—91; child devel. program supr. Child Devel. Inc., Campbell, Calif., 1992—99; instr. Monterey Peninsula Coll., Monterey, Calif., 1996—2002, Cabrillo Coll., Aptos, Calif., 1999—2002, Ctrl. Sierra ROP, Placerville, Calif., 2002—05, Calif. State U., Sacramento, 2005—. Cons. Pathways Cons., Placerville, Calif., 2002—; county coord. ACT Against Violence, Santa Cruz, Calif., 2000—02; presenter in field. Active Human Rights Roundtable, Placerville, Calif., 2004—05; bd. dirs. Calif. Assn. for the Edn. of Young Children, Sacramento, 2000—04. Recipient Cert. of Appreciation, Santa Cruz County Children and Families Commn., 2002, Cabrillo Coll. ECE and Ctrl. Coast Assn. Edn. Young Children, 2002. Mem.: Nat. Assn. for the Edn. Young Children (sect. pres. 2002—04, acad. validator 1994—2005). Avocation: travel. Home: 1640 Pheasant Run Placerville CA 95667 Personal E-mail: travelerdenise@comcast.net.

WESSLER, MARY HRAHA, real estate company executive; b. Des Moines, Nov. 4, 1961; d. Francis M. and Shirley A. (Malone) Hraha; 1 child, Nick. BA in Mass Comm., Iowa State U., Ames, 1984; postgrad., U. Denver, 1990. Dir. mktg. Real Estate Mgmt. Corp., Scottsdale, Ariz., 1984—87; v.p. Great West Mgmt. and Realty, Ltd., Denver, 1987—97; reg. v.p. AIMCO, Denver, 1997—98; v.p. JPI, Denver, 1999—2001; sr. v.p. Omni Apt. Communities, Inc., Denver, 2001—. Instr. Multi-Housing World, NNat. Apt. Assn., Inst. of Real Estate Mgmt.; spkr. in field. Mem.: Apt. Assn. Metro Denver (bd. dirs. 1991—2003, pres. 1997—98), Colo. Apt. Assn. (bd. dirs. 1990—2003), Nat. Apt. Assn. (v.p. Region 8 2000—03, bd. dirs. 2000—03). Home: 4185 S Granby Cir Aurora CO 80014 Office Phone: 303-386-8404. Personal E-mail: marywessler@comcast.net.

WESSNER, DEBORAH MARIE, telecommunications industry executive, consultant; b. St. Louis, Aug. 15, 1950; m. Brian Paul Wessner, Sept. 15, 1972; children: Krystin, David. BA in Math. and Chemistry, St. Louis U., l972; M Computer Info. Sci., U. New Haven, l980. Statistitian Armstrong Rubber Co., New Haven, 1972-74; programmer analyst Sikorsky div. United Techs., Stratford, Conn., 1974-77; project engr. GE, Bridgeport, Conn., 1977-79, software mgr. Arlington, Va., 1979-81; mgr. software ops. Satellite Bus. Systems, McLean, Va., 1981-83; v.p. ops. DAMA Telecommunications, Rockville, Md., 1983-87; dir. network ops. and adminstrn. Data Gen. Network Svcs., Rockville, 1987-91; dir. bus. ops. Sprint Internat., Reston, Va., 1991-92; v.p. network adminstrn. Citicorp, Washington, 1992-93, v.p. telecomm. product mgmt. Reston, Va., 1994-95, v.p. product mgmt., 1996-97, v.p., dir. Yr. 2000 program, 1997-99; v.p. global procurement C&W, 2000—01; v.p. contracts SAIC, 2003—. Assoc., cons. KDB Assocs., Columbia, Md., 1986—. Mem. exec. bd. Howard County PTA. Mem.: NAFE, Am. Bus. Women's Assn. Avocations: sailing, windsurfing, tennis.

WEST, BETSY, broadcast executive; m. Oren Jacoby. Grad., Brown U.; MS, Syracuse U. Reporter WHEN Radio, Syracuse, N.Y., 1974; writer, editor ABC Radio, 1975; writer ABC News World News Tonight, Chgo., 1978-82; sr. prodr. ABC News Nightline, 1983-89; sr. broadcast prodr. ABC News Turning Point, 1989-98; exec. prodr. ABC News; v.p. primetime news CBS, N.Y.C., 1998—2004. Recepient 19 Emmy awards, Christopher award, duPont-Columbia award. Mem. Phi Beta Kappa (trustee).

WEST, CATHERINE G., retail executive; b. Sept. 6, 1959; BA, Lynchburg Coll. With People's Express Airline, 1981—85; v.p. credit card ops. Chevy Chase Bank FSB, 1985—91; sr. v.p. card mem. svcs. to exec. v.p. mktg. svcs. First USA Bank, 1991—2000; sr. v.p. U.S. consumer risk ops. Capital One, 2000—04, pres. U.S. card bus., 2004—06; exec. v.p., COO JC Penney Co., Inc., 2006—. Named one of 50 Most Powerful Women in Business, Fortune mag., 2006. Office: JC Penney Co Inc 6501 Legacy Dr Plano TX 75024-3698 Office Phone: 972-431-1000. Office Fax: 972-431-9140.*

WEST, DOE, psychotherapist, educator; b. Tucson, July 14, 1951; AA, Dutchess C.C., 1975; BS, SUNY, New Paltz, 1977; BA, Logos Bible Coll., 1986, MDiv, 1993; MS, Boston U., 1980; PhD, Northeastern U., 2001. Dir. 504/compliance officer dept. health and hosp. City of Boston, 1979-81, commr. handicap affairs, 1981-84; fellow Ctr. for Psychol. Rehab. Boston U., 1999—2002; pvt. practice psychotherapy, 2004—. Project coord. task force on human subject rsch. Fernald State Sch., 1994; sr. rsch. assoc. N.E. Family Study, Harvard Sch. Pub. Health, 2001-04, Columbia U. Internat. Rolandic Epilepsy Study, 2005—. Author: Internat. Perspectives on Family Violence and Abuse: A Cognitive Ecological Approach, 2004, Coping + Plus: Dimensions of a Disability, 1995, Appreciating Differences: A Textbook for Educators on How to Run Handicap Awareness Training in the Classroom, 1983, Stalking the Elusive Buck: Fundraising for Non-Profit, Profit and Individual Needs. Home: PO Box 985 Framingham MA 01701 Personal E-mail: doewest@aol.com.

WEST, DONNA J., language arts educator; b. Munich, June 9, 1962; d. Robert Charles and Joanne Mary Bevan; m. David Anthony West, Mar. 16, 1991; children: Victoria Rose, Katelyn Julia. BA, Ariz. State U., Tempe, 1985. Cert. tchr. secondary edn. Ariz., 1992. Lang. arts tchr. Independence H.S., Glendale, Ariz., 1992—. Sr. class advisor Independence H.S., 2000—. Office Phone: 623-435-6100.

WEST, EILEEN M., caseworker; b. Somerset, Pa. d. Casimir M. and Beatrice T. Stanis; m. Richard E. West (div. 1981); children: Theodore, Cynthia, Michael. BA, Pa. State U., 1970. Cert. FACTS program leader, Pa. Caseworker Susquehanna County Bd. Assistance, Montrose, Pa., 1970-73, Cumberland County Children & Youth Agy., Carlisle, Pa., 1988-89, Child-Line, Harrisburg, Pa., 1989—. Pa. Dept. Pub. Welfare liaison to Pa. Coalition Against Rape, Harrisburg, 1993-95. Chief shop stewart Svc. Employees Internat. Union 668, 1991—, alt. mem. statewide grievance appeal com., 1992-93, chair, 1993—, mem. statewide mobilization com. 1992-93, chpt. mobilizer, 1992-93, mem. statewide budget and fin. com., 1993, chpt. treas., 1993, chpt. v.p., 1994, area contract mobilizer, 1995—, del. Ea. Regional Women's Conf., Boston, 1995; mem. Molly Pitcher Stitchers Embroiderers' Guild Am., 1993—, publicity chairperson Susquehanna chpt., 1992-94, mem. Wyoming Valley chpt. 1995—, program chairperson Susquehanna chpt. 1996—, pres., 1996—; mem. 146 Knights of Lithuania Coun., 1991, v.p., 1992, pres., 1993, ritual chair, 1994—; tchr. Polyclinic Needlework Show, Harrisburg, 1993, 95. Republican. Roman Catholic. Avocations: needlecrafts, reading, herb gardening. Home: 410 Norman Rd Camp Hill PA 17011-6130 Office: Commonwealth of Pa DPW ChildLine PO Box 2675 Harrisburg PA 17105-2675

WEST, FRANCES LEE, retired doll artist, freelance writer; b. Groves, Tex., Jan. 31, 1934; d. Henry Brewer Crittenden and Nora Josephine Billiot Showalter; m. Ronald Bruce West, May 14, 1955; children: Berry Jo Carter, Melissa Alyce Nelson. Student, Credit Burs. Am., Houston, 1957. Owner Dälzenstuff, Flower Mound, Tex., 1992-98. Mem. The Crafter's Network, Artists' Breakfast Club. Democrat. Avocations: listening to opera, reading, sewing, houseboating, writing. Home: 3708 Spring Meadow Ln Flower Mound TX 75028-1221

WEST, GAIL BERRY, lawyer; b. Cin. d. Theodore Moody and Johnnie Mae (Newton) B.; m. Togo D. West, Jr., June 18, 1966; children: Tiffany Berry, Hilary Carter. BA magna cum laude, Fisk U., 1964; MA, U. Cin., 1965; JD, Howard U., 1968. Bar: D.C. 1969, U.S. Supreme Ct. 1978. Staff atty. IBM, 1969-76; spl. asst. to sec. HUD, 1977-78; staff asst. to spl. asst. to Pres., Washington, 1978-80; dep. asst. sec. for manpower res. affairs installations Dept. Air Force, 1980-81; atty. AT&T, Washington, 1983-84; exec. dir. govt. affairs Bell Comm. Rsch. Inc., Washington, 1984-95; dir. govt. rels. Armstrong World Industries, Inc., Washington, 1995—2003, cons., 2003—. Mem. exec. com. ARC, Washington, 1974-85; bd. dirs. Family and Child Svcs., Washington, 1974-87; trustee Corcoran Gallery Art, 1983-2000, Arena Stage, 1992-99, Decatur House, 1994—, WETA, 1995-2001, Fisher House Found., Inc.; bd. dirs. Meridian House, 1994-2000; mem. D.C. Commn. Fine Arts, 2003-; mem. cathedral chpt. Nat. Cathedral; bd. dirs. Nat. Mus. of Am. History, Smithsonian, 2005-. Ford Found. fellow, 1965-68. Mem. ABA, D.C. Bar Assn., Unified Bar D.C. Democrat. Episcopalian. Home: 4934 Rockwood Pkwy NW Washington DC 20016-3211

WEST, KAREN MARIE, musician, educator; d. Mario J. and Albertine C. Arduino; m. Billy Ray West, June 21, 1997; children: Billy Jr., Edward, Deborah Manna, Julia Harmelin, Nora Harmelin. B in Music Edn., Temple U., 1967. String tchr. Phila. Pub. Schs., 1968—72; violinist Colo. Philharm., Evergreen, Colo., 1968; orch. dir. Winslow Pub. Schs., Winslow Twp., NJ, 1985—; violinist Melodia Trio, Cedarbrook, NJ, 1990—. Adjudicator, mgr. All-South Jersey Orch., NJ, 1985—; adjudicator All-State Orch., NJ, 1985—; mem. Gifted and Talented Adv. Com., Winslow Twp., 2001—02. Mem.: South Jersey Band and Orch. Dirs. Assn., N.J. Edn. Assn., Music Educators Nat. Conf., Internat. Soc. Violin Bottle Collectors.

WEST, KARRIE L., school psychologist; d. Craig A. West and Mary A. d'Avignon. BA with honors, Calif. State U., 1998; MA, Gallaudet U., 1999, PsyS, 2001. Sch. psychologist Kings County Office Edn., Harford, Calif., 2001—02, Padaro Valley Unified Sch. Dist., Watsonville, Calif., 2002—. Mem.: Nat. Assn. Sch. Psychologists, Golden Key. Avocation: Am. sign language. Office: 294 Green Valley Rd Watsonville CA 95076 Office Phone: 831-786-2130.

WEST, MARJORIE EDITH, former elementary education educator; b. Lawrence, Kans., Aug. 18, 1940; d. Merwin Hales and Helen Aletha (Fellows) Wilson Polzin; m. Hammond Dean Watkins, Feb. 17, 1968 (div. 1971); 1 child, Michele Dawn; m. Merlin Avery West, Apr. 2, 1975 (div. 1984). BA in Elem. Edn., U. No. Colo., 1962, MA in Reading, 1970; postgrad., La. State U., 1981-82, U. New Orleans, 1981-82. Cert. tchr., Colo. Tchr. Sch. Dist. 11, Colorado Springs, Colo., 1962-64, Nat. Def. Overseas Teaching Program, Wiesbaden, Fed. Republic Germany, 1964-65, Alaska On-Base Schs., Fairbanks, 1965-66, Great Bend (Kans.) Sch. Dist., 1966-67, Killeen (Tex.) Sch. Dist., 1967-68, Jefferson County Schs., Lakewood, Colo., 1969-99; ret., 1999. Trustee Nat. Tchr. Hall of Fame, 2002—. Recipient Alumni Trail Blazer award U. No. Colo., 1988; named Colo. Tchr. of Yr., 1994, finalist Nat. Tchr. of Yr., 1994; named to Nat. Tchrs.' Hall of Fame, 1995. Mem. NAFE, AAUW, NEA, PTA (by-laws com. 1989-90, hon. life mem.), Colo. Edn. Assn. (del. to assembly 1985-90), Jefferson County Edn. Assn. (spl. svcs. com. 1989-90), Internat. Reading Assn., Phi Delta Kappa, Pi Lambda Theta, Epsilon Sigma Alpha (edn. chair 1989-90, chair ways and means com. 1990-91, publicity chair 1991-93). Democrat. Avocations: football, travel, golf, reading.

WEST, MARSHA, elementary school educator; b. DeQueen, Ark., Sept. 1, 1950; d. Marshall T. and Mildred L. (Davis) Gore; m. Larry T. West, May 19, 1972; 1 child, Zachary west. BS in Edn., So. State Coll., Magnolia, Ark., 1971; MEd, U. Ark., 1975; postgrad., Henderson State Coll., Arkadelphia, Ark., Purdue U.; specialist's degree, U. Ga., 1991. Cert. elem. and spl. edn. tchr., media specialist Ga. Spl. edn. resource tchr. Gatesville (Tex.) Ind. Sch. Dist.; tchr. early childhood spl. edn. Bryan (Tex.) Ind. Sch. Dist.; elem. tchr. Tippecanoe Sch. Corp., Lafayette, Ind., Clarke County Sch. Dist., Athens, Ga., media specialist. Mem.: NEA, ALA, Clarke County Assn. Educators, Ga. Libr. Media Assn. (dit. V chair, pres.), Ga. Assn. Instrnl. Tech., Ga. Assn. Educators, Am. Assn. Sch. Librs., Kappa Delta Pi. Office: David C Barrow Elem Sch 100 Pinecrest Dr Athens GA 30605-1459

WEST, MELANIE KIM, elementary school educator; b. Cedartown, Ga., Nov. 19, 1961; d. Kenneth Neal and Glenda Jane (Davis) Hackney; m. Martin D. West, Nov. 27, 2004; 1 child from previous marriage, Joshua Neal Kirkpatrick. BA in Polit. Sci., Jacksonville State U., 1983; paralegal cert., Nat. Ctr. Paralegal Tng., 1983; MEd in Early Childhood Edn., Berry Coll., 1986, EdS in Leadership in Tchg. & Curriculum, 1997, EdS in Adminstrn. and Supervision, 2000. Tchg. cert., Ga. Paralegal Smith Shaw Attys., Rome, Ga., 1984-85; kindergarten tchr. Polk Sch. Dist., Cedartown, 1985—. Mem., dir. children's choir, mem. sanctuary choir, mem. Chapel Bells, mem. adult ensemble First Bapt. Ch., Cedartown. Mem. Profl. Assn. Ga. Educators, Cedartown Jr. Svc. League, Cedartown Music Club (sec. 1996-97, patrons chmn. 1997), Kappa Delta Pi. Avocations: reading, volunteer work, travel. Office: Polk Sch Dist 120 Gordon St Rockmart GA 30153-1748 Office Phone: 770-684-6134. E-mail: khwest@charter.net.

WEST, MICHELLE, principal; b. Bronx, May 11, 1960; d. Thomas and Katherine Crowder; m. Kevin Farrior, Dec. 31, 2005; children from previous marriage: Angela, Khashif, Marquita. BA in Spl. Edn., Jersey City State Coll., 1998; MA in Adminstr. and Supr., NJ City U., 2000; postgrad., United BibleColl. Theol. Sem., 2005—. Tchr. pre-sch. The Learning Emporium, 1993—95; tchr. pre-sch. handicapped Urban League Hudson County, 1995—97; tchr. spl. edn. Jersey City Pub. Schs., 1997—2001; adminstrv. intern Dr. Charles P. Defuccle Sch., 2000—02; asst. prin. Whitney M. Young Jr. Primary Sch., Jersey City, 2002—. Recipient Govs. Tchr. Recognition award, NJ Dept. Edn., 2001. Mem.: NAACP, ASCD, Coun. Exceptional Children. Home: 78 Neptune Ave Jersey City NJ 07305 Office: Jersey City Pub Schs 135 Stegman St Jersey City NJ 07305

WEST, NETTIE J.R., music educator; b. Schoharie, N.Y., Oct. 12, 1925; d. Everett C. and Christina M. Maria (Youngs) Ruland; m. J. Russell Langwig, Sept. 11, 1948 (div. 1976); children: J. Russell, John Everett, Christina; m. Robert L. West, Oct. 8, 1983; stepchildren: Elizabeth Ann, Kathleen Suzanne, Laurel Marie. BS, BM cum laude, Skidmore Coll., 1947; MA, U. Buffalo, 1968; cert. Suzuki tchg., Sch. for Strings, N.Y.C., 1983, Ithaca Coll., 1978-79. Music instr. Suzuki Sounds Violin Sch., Lagrangeville, NY, 1984—; orch. tchr. Hyde Park (N.Y.) H.S., 1983-84; Suzuki violin tchr. The Music Box, Poughkeepsie, 1997-99, Hudson Valley Philharm. Music Sch., Poughkeepsie, 1979-80; sub. tchr. Arlington Sch., Wappingers Dist., 1976-80; violinist Woodstock (N.Y.) Chamber Orch., 1983—. Attendee internat. confs. Suzuki Method, Matsumoto, Japan, 1983, 89, 99, Alberta Canada, 1985, Berlin, Germany, 1987, Adelaide, Australia, 1991, Dublin, Ireland, 1995, Turin, Italy, 2006; tchr. Suzuki method Dutchess C.C., Poughkeepsie, N.Y., 2003—. Mem. Religious Soc. Friends, Bulls-Head Oswego Meeting, 1980—, mem. worship group Green Haven Corr. Fac., 1980—; facilitator Alternatives to Violence Project, 1980—, coord. at Green Haven Prison 1986-89; mem. Martha's Vineyard Hist. Assn. Mem. Suzuki Assn. Am., Inc., Music Educators Nat. Conf., N.Y. State Sch. Music Assn., Lagoon Pond Assn. Inc. of Martha's Vineyard. Avocations: swimming, skiing, bird watching, reading, attending concerts.

WEST, ROBIN LEA, psychology educator; b. Mpls., Jan. 28, 1951; BA with distinction, U. Nebr., 1973; MA in Psychology, Vanderbilt U., 1978, PhD in Psychology, 1980. Vis. asst. prof. psychology Memphis State U., 1980-83; postdoctoral rsch. fellow Aging and Devel. Lab. Washington U., St. Louis, 1983-84; vis. asst. depts. psychology and clin. health psychology U. Fla., 1984-87, asst. prof. psychology, 1987-90, dir. curriculum, assoc. dir., dir. Ctr. Gerontol. Studies, 1986—, assoc. prof., 1990—2004, prof., 2004—; ret. Rsch. cons. Memory Assessment Clinics, Inc., 1988-92; lectr., participant, presenter in field to confs. and workshops. Mem. editorial bd. Aging and Cognition, Experimental Aging Research, Psychology and Aging; reviewer numerous publs. including Jour. Gerontology, Psychology and Aging, Exptl. Aging Rsch., Applied Cognitive Psychology, Memory, Aging, Neuropsychology, and Cognition, Internat. Jour. Behavioral Development, Devel. Psychology; contbr., editor articles to profl. jours. Grantee U. Fla. Divsn. Sponsored Rsch., 1987, 88, 90, NIH, 1987, 96, Nat. Inst. Aging, 1986, 97; Brookdale Found. fellow, 1989, Retirement Rsch. Found. fellow, 2000, 2002, 2004; Fulbright scholar, 1995. Fellow Gerontol. Soc. Am., APA, Nat. Coun. on Aging, Soc. Applied Rsch. in Memory and Cognition. Office: U Fla Dept Psychology PO Box 112250 Gainesville FL 32611-2250

WEST, STACY KATHLENA, athletic trainer; b. Flint, Mich., Sept. 22, 1979; d. Jay Robert and Sonia Kathleen Kelso; m. Aaron Michael West, May 3, 2003. BS, Cen. Mich. U., Mt. Pleasant, Mich., 2002. Cert. atletic trainer Nat. Athletic Trainers Assn. Cert. athletic trainer Mclaren Sports Medicine, Davison H.S., Mich., 2003—. Mem.: Nat. Athletic Trainers Assn. (assoc.). Home: 3106 Reid Rd Swartz Creek MI 48473 Office: Mclaren Sports Medicine 1240 Fairway Dr Davison MI 48423 Office Phone: 810-653-3962. Personal E-mail: kelso1sk@yahoo.com.

WEST, SUSAN D., lawyer; b. Jackson, Miss., July 17, 1952; d. William Lloyd Smith, Jr. and Betty Jo Connolly; m. Thomas Mellen West, II, Feb. 26, 1994. BS in Anthropology, U. Tulsa, 1978, JD, 1981. Pvt. practice, Tulsa, 1981—84; title examiner, asst. counsel Hexter Fair Title Co., Dallas, 1984—89; asst. counsel Chgo. Title Ins. Co., Dallas, 1989—99; comml. underwriting counsel Ticor Title Co., Dallas, 1999—2000, Commerce Title Co., Dallas, 2000—. Mem.: Dallas Bar Assn., Okla. Bar Assn., Tex. Bar Assn. Home: 6831 E Grand Ave Dallas TX 75223 Office: Commerce Title Co 4th Fl 2728 N Harwood Dallas TX 75201

WEST, SYLVIA WANDELL, small business owner, director, educator, researcher; b. Harrisburg, Pa., Dec. 26, 1937; d. John George Wient and Kathleen Hill Wandell; m. Henry Earl Seidmeyer, Sept. 18, 1994; m. Jack Dennis West, Aug. 30, 1958 (div. June 15, 1971); children: Todd Conner, Jill Conner, Gary Conner, Susan Conner, Blake Conner. BFA, Tex. Christian U., 1961, MLA, 1988, MS, 1991, PhD, 1993. Tutor The Tutoring Rm., Ft. Worth, 1962—2005; founding dir. Lollypop Sch., 1964—67, Hill Sch., 1974—84; owner, dir. West Acad., 1984—. Rschr., presenter in field. Mem. Hill Sch., Ft. Worth, 1982—83. Achievements include research in Academic Achievement with Failure Avoidant Students. Avocations: swimming, reading, writing curriculum, cooking, interior remodeling. Home: 3821Arundel Ave Fort Worth TX 76109 Office: West Acad 3825 McCart Fort Worth TX 76110 Office Phone: 817-924-3535. Home Fax: 817-926-3399; Office Fax: 817-926-3399. E-mail: drsylviawest@yahoo.com.

WEST, TERESA L. (TERRI WEST), semiconductor company executive; BA in Journalism, U. North Tex., 1982. Student intern Tex. Instruments Inc., 1978, former mgr. media rels., former v.p. and mgr. strategic comm., currently sr. v.p. comm. and investor rels. Dallas. Dir. Dallas Pub. Broadcasting System affiliate, KERA-TV; mem. Nat. Investor Rels. Inst. and Conf. Bd.; founding mem. Women of TI Fund; v.p. Tex. Instruments Found.; chair comm. com. (during renewal of US-Japan Semiconductor Trade Arrangement) Semiconductor Industry Assn., 1992, 96. Chancellor's leadership coun. U. North Tex. Office: Tex Instruments Inc 12500 TI Blvd Dallas TX 75243 Office Phone: 972-995-2011, 972-995-4360.

WEST, VANETTE JANE, secondary school educator; b. San Diego, Nov. 24, 1943; d. Vance Edwin and Betty Jane Wainscott; m. Warren Leslie West, Apr. 25, 1962; children: Jane Alison, Jennifer Agnes, Jefferson Edwin. BA in Biology and minor in Chemistry, So. Oreg. U., Ashland, 1995, MS in Secondary Sci. Edn., 1995. Cert. tchr. in Biology and Integrated Scis. Oreg., 1994. Sci. tchr. Knappa H.S., Astoria, Oreg., 1996—. Recipient Inspirational Tchr. award, Ea. Oreg. U. Mem.: Oreg. Edn. Assn. (licentiate). Avocations: exercise, photography, reading, travel, horseback riding. Office: Knappa High School 41535 Old Hwy 30 Astoria OR 97103 Office Phone: 503-458-6166. Office Fax: 503-458-5466.

WEST, VIRGINIA, artist, educator; b. Boston, May 24, 1924; d. Alexander and Beatrice (Lowe) McWilliam; m. John Barth West, Sept. 4, 1941 (div. 1973); children: John Thomas, Lynnea Christine, Elise Anne, David Lowe, Michael; m. Frank Martin, Oct. 11, 1974. MFA, Coll. Art Md. Inst., 1974. Instr. Coll. Art Md. Inst., Balt., 1969-82. Author: Finishing Touches for the Handweaver, 1968, Weavers Wearables, 1976, The Virginia West Swatch Book (ltd. edit.), 1986, Designer Diagonals: A Portfolio of Bias-Designed Clothing, 1988, A Cut Above: Couture Clothing for Fibre Artists, 1992; contbr. articles to profl. jours; commd. fiber murals U.S. and abroad. Recipient purchase award Balt. Mus. Art, 1970, Del. Art Mus., 1972. Mem. Am. Craft Council (sec. 1968-70, pres. Md. chpt.), Balt. Weavers Guild (hon.), Weavers Guild Pitts. (hon.), Mo. Fiber Artists (life). Episcopalian. Avocations: archaeology, travel. Home and Office: 2901 Boston St # 216 Baltimore MD 21224

WESTBERRY, ANITA PARRISH, education educator; b. Clewiston, Fla., Oct. 5, 1946; d. Virgil Ennis and Onetta Armour Parrish; m. Lawrence Ray Westberry, Sr., Nov. 5, 1966; children: Danita Westberry Thomas, Lawrence Ray Jr. AA, Edison Cmty., Fort Myers, Fla., 1978; BS, Nova S.E. U., Fort Lauderdale, Fla., 1988; MEd, Tenn. State U., Nashville, 1999. Elem. tchr. Glades County Schs., Moore Haven, Fla., 1988—89, Hendry County Schs., LaBelle, Fla., 1989—97; ESL tchr. Franklin County Schs., Winchester, Tenn., 1997—98, Rutherford County Schs., Murfreesboro, Tenn., 1998—2004; instr. U. Phoenix, Nashville, 2002—, online instr.; instr. Western Internat. U., Phoenix, 2004—; online instr. Axia Coll., Western Internat. U. Rep. S.W. Fla.

Tchr. Edn. Ctr., Fort Myers, 1995—97. Named Leader of Yr., 4-H, 1980. Church Of Christ. Avocations: reading, travel. Home: 256 White Oak Dr Manchester TN 37355 Office Phone: 931-570-4140. Personal E-mail: 2awestberry@charter.net. Business E-Mail: purplenannie@netzero.net.

WESTBERRY, JENNY REBECCA, elementary school educator; b. Waycross, Ga., Dec. 27, 1976; d. James Riley, Jr. and Nancy J. Westberry. BFA, Brenau U., Gainesville, Ga., 2000. Preschool tchr. Primrose Sch. Buford, Buford, 1995—2000; dance tchr. grades 9-12 Person HS, Roxboro, NC, 2000—02; dance instr. North Ga. Acad. Dance, Suwanee, 2002—05; lead tchr. pvt. pre-K Legacy Acad., Sugar Hill, Ga., 2002—03; tchr. grade 2 Hopewell Christian Acad., Gainesville, Ga., 2003—04; lead tchr. pre-K Primrose Sch. Suwanee West, Ga., 2004—06; 1st grade tchr. Lawrenceville Elem. Sch., 2006—. Program instr. Primrose Scholars, Suwanee, 2005—; drill team coach Person HS, 2000—02, dance team coach, 2000—02, dance co. founder & artistic dir., 2000—02. Leader Girl Scouts Am., 2003—05. Mem.: Nat. Dance Assn., AAHPERD. Office Phone: 770-932-3900. Personal E-mail: sunnyballerina@hotmail.com.

WESTBERRY, PAULA I., nursing administrator; b. Worcester, Mass., Aug. 7, 1954; d. Richard R. and Patricia I. (Gilbert) Wood; m. Chuck Westberry, 2005; children: Laura, Andrew, Brian. Diploma summa cum laude, David Hale Fanning Sch., 1974; BS in Computer Sci. summa cum laude, Clark U., 1986; AAS summa cum laude, SUNY, Albany, 1988; BSN, Barry U., Miami Shores, Fla., 1996, MSN summa cum laude, 1998; PhD summa cum laude, Columbus U., 1999. Cert. nursing adminstrn. advanced. ANA, dir. nurses Nat. Assn. Dirs. Nursing Adminstrn./Long Term Care, nursing adminstrn. cert. legal nurse cons. Head nurse Seven Hills Adolescent Program, Worcester, 1985-88; coord. utilization rev. Worcester County Hosp., 1988-90, 45th St. Mental Health Ctr., West Palm Beach, Fla.; nurse mgr. N.Medico Neurol. Rehab. Ctr. of Palm Beach (Fla.), 1990-91; dir. nurses Edgewater Pointe Estates, Boca Raton, Fla., 1991-93; DON Empathy Care, Boca Raton, 1993-96; owner Traditional Home Health Svcs., Inc., Lake Worth, Fla., 1996-99; nurse mgr. Genesis Eldercare Network, Laconia, N.H., 1998-99; DON Hollywood Hills Nursing Home, 1999-2001; adminstr. Physician's Choice Home Health Svcs., 2001—03; v.p. clin. ops. Home Care Solutions Group, Ft. Lauderdale, 2003—06; adminstr. Total Home Health Inc., Sebring, Fla., 2006—. Mem. content expert panel ANCC Nurse Adminstrn., 2002—. Trustee Fla. Nurse Found., 2003—06, v.p., 2003—06. Mem.: ANA, Nat. Assn. Dir. Nursing Adminstrn. (chairperson home health coun., cert.), Fla. Nurses Assn. (Quality and Unity in Nursing coun. mem., dist. XI bd. mem.), Fla. Orgn. Nursing Execs., Sigma Theta Tau. Republican. Office Phone: 863-381-1958. Personal E-mail: docpaula54@yahoo.com.

WESTBIE, BARBARA JANE, retired graphics designer; b. Little Rock, Nov. 3, 1946; d. Freeman Bryant Davis and Virginia Lee Thompson; children: Suzanne Michelle, Derrek Christopher. Grad. in graphic design, U. Calif., Davis, 1992; student, Miramar Coll., San Diego, 1976, Chabot Coll., Hayward, Calif., 1974. Exec. dir. Ambiance, Danville, Calif., 1980—84; dir. Lake Gallery, Tahoe City, Calif., 1985—87; art cons. Reed Gallery, Tahoe City, 1988—90; ret., 1990. Art dir., creative cons. Associated Students Re-Entry Ctr. Chico State U., Calif., 2001—03. Inventor Fat Fuzzy/Iknonotrisc Family, 1981, artist (poster/logo) Project Mana Fundraising Event, 1988, (brochure/media kit) Chocolate Festival, 1989. Vol. crisis intervention counselor CIS/Tahoe Women's Svcs., Kings Beach, 1989—91; lead counselor Emotions Anonymous 12-Step Program, North Lake Tahoe Area, 1990—93; vol. pk. svc. Washoe Lake State Pk., Carson City, Nev., 1993—94; coord. new vols. ARC, Chico, 2000—01, vol. Butte County, 2000—, Emergency Animal Rescue Svcs., 2002—. Named Vol. of Yr., Tahoe Women's Svcs., 1989; recipient Disting. Svc. award, CIS/Tahoe Women's Svcs., 1989—90. Mem.: Smithsonian Instn. (assoc.). Protestant. Avocations: skiing, reading, gardening, writing, painting.

WESTBROOK, ARLEN RUNZLER, retired social worker; b. Milw., Nov. 17, 1928; d. Arthur Charles and Helen Olivia (Gilman) Runzler; m. Perry Westbrook, Dec. 29, 1961 (dec. Feb. 1998); adopted children: Tempa, Joyce stepchildren: Anne, Emily, Paul; m. Marshall B. Clinard; stepchildren: Marsha Clinard-Boast, Stephen Clinard. BS, U. Wis., Madison; MSW, SUNY, Albany, 1967. LCSW N.Y. Caseworker Dept. Social Svc. County of Albany, NY, 1952—62; social worker Northeastern N.Y. Speech Ctr., 1968—76; clin. social worker and founding ptnr. Capital Area Speech Ctr., Inc., 1976—2005; ret., 2005. Author (with Perry D. Westbrook): Writing Women of New England: 1630-1900, 1982. Bd. dir. Helderberg House, Inc., Altamont, NY, pres., 1979. Mem.: Acad. Cert. Social Workers, Nat. Assn. Social Workers, Gourmet Travel Club. Mem. Lds Ch. Home: 912 Hillcrest Dr Santa Fe NM 87501

WESTBROOK, LYNDA A., financial consultant; b. Jersey City, July 27, 1960; d. Nicholas and Mildred Lucarelli; m. Kevin J. Westbrook, Apr. 28, 2001; m. Erik Vikjaer, Apr. 7, 1984 (div. Mar. 30, 1991); children: Amanda Vikjaer, Andrew Vikjaer. Grad., Cliffside Park H.S., N.J., 1978. Asst. v.p., mgr. comml. RM team Fifth Third Bank, Cin., 2000—. Diversity bd. mem. Fifth Third Bank, Cin., 2006—. Office: Fifth Third Bank 38 Fountain Square Plaza MD10909A Cincinnati OH 45263 Office Phone: 513-534-3104. Office Fax: 513-534-0217. E-mail: lynda.westbrook@53.com.

WESTBROOK, REBECCA VOLLMER, secondary school educator; b. Hagerstown, Md., Jan. 12, 1943; d. Harry Frederick and Margaret Caldwell (Jack) Vollmer; m. John William Westbrook Jr., Apr. 4, 1972; children: Margaret Rebecca, John Williiam III. BA in French and Spanish cum laude, Thiel Coll., 1964; MAT in French and Spanish, Emory U., 1965; cert. in French studies, Inst. Am. U., Aiv-en-Provence, France, 1963. Cert. tchr. Ga., 1966, Fla., 1985. Tchr. French and Spanish Henry Grady H.S., Atlanta, 1966—70, Northside H.S., Atlanta, 1970—76, Forest H.S., Ocala, Fla., 1985—; instr. French and Spanish Jefferson C.C., Louisville, 1980—82. Cons. Itinerant Tutors, Louisville, 1983—84. Active Girl Scouts Am.; mem. Ocala Women's Club, 1989—92. Mem.: NEA, Alpha Delta Kappa, Phi Sigma Iota. Avocations: travel, antiques, reading. Home: 2630 SE 14th St Ocala FL 34471 Office: Forest High School 5000 Maricamp Rd Ocala FL 34478

WESTBY, MARCIA, language educator; d. Henry J. and Romola Waida, adopted d. Janice Thon; m. John Westby, Sept. 23, 1973. BA, Cornell U., Ithaca, NY, 1969. Cert. secondary English NY. English tchr. Belmont (Mass.) HS, 1978, Churchville (NY)-Chili Ctrl. Sch. Dist., 1985—. English dept. liaison Churchville-Chili Ctrl. Sch. Dist., 2003—. Bd. dirs. Genesee Valley Breeders Assn., Livonia, NY, 1988—2005. Mem.: NCTE (assoc.), Defenders of Wildlife (assoc.). Office Phone: 585-293-4540.

WESTEBBE, BARBARA LIEBST, writer, sculptor; b. Newton, Kans., Dec. 8, 1925; d. Harold Charles and Marie Josiphine (Whitcomb) Liebst; m. Richard Manning Westebbe, Dec. 18, 1947; children: Mark, Shelly, Bruce, Susy. Student, Kans. State Tchrs. Coll., 1945; grad., Utrecht (Holland) U., 1954; postgrad., George Washington U., 1955, 56, 57. Tchr. 8th grade Deerhead Sch., Medicine Lodge, Kans., 1945; illustrator, engr. Culver Aircraft Corp., Wichita, Kans., 1946; mem. Sen. Arthur Capper staff U.S. Senate, Washington, 1946-47; asst. to chmn. Nat. Assn. Motor Bus Operators, Washington, 1947-48; office mgr. to Dr. R. McFarland Human Engring. Dept. Sch. Pub. Health, Harvard U., Cambridge, Mass., 1949-51; prin. Am. H.S., Den Haag, Holland, 1953-54; editor of Den Haag transls. of Den Ramp series Am. Acad. Scis., Den Haag, Holland, 1954-56; writer weekly column Athens (Greece) Post Newspaper, 1961-65; founder, dir. Life Conservation, Inc., Fredricksburg, Va., 1973—. Exhibited in group exhbns. at Pierce Coll., Athens, 1966; editor (poems under pseudonym Colleen Cody) Fed. Poet, 1967-70; author poems; writer quar. column Downs Syndrome Mag., 1990-94. Bd. dirs. Nat. Womens Party, 1946-66; mem. archtl. review bd. Stafford County Svcs., Falmouth, Va., 1989—; mem. Fredricksburg Ctr. Creative Arts, 1990—. Recipient Citizen of Yr. award Am. Legion. Mem. Nat. Edn. Soc., Alpha Zigma Tau. Avocations: gardening, teaching special artists, pets, sculpting. Home and Office: 807 Holly Corner Rd Fredericksburg VA 22406-5360

WESTENFELDER, HARRIET ELLEN, retired elementary school educator; b. Buffalo, N.Y., Oct. 5, 1927; d. Berten Bradley and Ethel Karr Bean; m. Roy L. Westenfelder, Aug. 29, 1953 (dec.); children: Louis L., Frederick E., Karl R. BS, Syracuse U., N.Y., 1949; MEd, SUNY, Buffalo, 1953. Lab. technician Buffalo Children's Hosp., 1949—52; tchr. Buffalo Bd. Edn., 1953—56, Perry Township Schs., Indpls., 1970—90, ret., 1990. Contbr. poems to newspapers. Vol. tchr. Ind. State Mus., Indpls., 1995—; vol. house staff Clowes Hall Butler U., Indpls., 1997—; vol. United Way Ind., Indpls., 1990—; v.p. bd. Perry Sr. Citizen Svcs., Indpls., 1990—. Mem.: AARP, Alumni U. Buffalo, Southport OES, Phi Delta Kappa, Phi Lambda Theta. Avocations: travel, music, sports, skiing, bicycling. Home: 633 Griffin Rd Indianapolis IN 46227

WESTERBERG, MARY L., retired secondary school educator; b. Ironwood, Mich., Nov. 17, 1942; d. Rudolph Henry and Gertrude Ethel (Saari) W. BA, Mich. State U., 1964, MA in Teaching, 1969; postgrad., U. Minn., Duluth, U. N.H. Cert. life English, history and French tchr., Minn. Tchr. Alpena (Mich.) High Sch.; tchr. English and French, Anoka (Minn.) Sr. High Sch., also chmn. Bldg. Leadership Team; ret. Organizer, co-developer workshops for parents; mem. com. on religion in pub. schs. Bd. dirs., rec. sec., program com. Finn Fest '02 Minn. Alumni disting. scholar. Mem. NEA (del. rep. assembly), Nat. Coun. Tchrs. English, Mich. Coun. Tchrs. English (legis. liaison com., censorship com., resolutions chmn., rep. to Minn. Coalition against Censorship), Minn. Edn. Assn. (IPD state coun., exec. bd., chmn. profl. growth, conf. presenter, Univ. IPD award), AHEA (v.p., chmn. settlement task force, chmn. IPD), Midwestern River Project (cons., tchr., curriculum developer), Delta Kappa Gamma (local pres., v.p.).

WESTERMAN, LIANE MARIE, research scientist executive; b. Long Branch, NJ, June 20, 1949; d. Charles Wilson and Edith Doris (Johnson) Case; m. S. Thomas Westerman; children: David Aaron, Charles Paul. BA in Psychology, Monmouth U., West Long Branch, N.J., 1972; MA in Teaching, Coll. of N.J., 1979. Cert. tchr. of handicapped, N.J. Tchr. spl. edn., dir. afternoon program S.E.A.R.C.H., Ocean, NJ, 1972-74; tchr. spl. edn. Jackson (N.J.) Twp. Sch. System, 1974-79; exec. dir. Otologic Edn., Inc., Shrewsbury, NJ, 1980-88; dir. clin. rsch. Nat. Patent Analytical Systems, Inc., Roslyn Heights, NY, 1983-86, v.p. rsch., 1986-88; pres. Westerman Rsch. Assocs., Inc., Shrewsbury, NJ, 1988—. Participant numerous convs., profl. organs. and spl. interest groups, U.S.A., Israel and The Netherlands, 1974—; software devel. expert to knowledge engr. for Visual Perceptual System, 1984—; v.p. Otologic Edn., Inc., Shrewsbury, 1988—. Co-contbr. articles and chpts. to profl. publs.; U.S. and Can. patentee computer-aided drug-abuse detection. Fundraiser Am. Heart Assn., 1991; bd. dirs. Women's Coun. for Leon Hess Cancer Ctr. at Monmouth Med. Ctr., 2003—; active MADD; activist Nat. Audubon Soc. Mem. Am. Acad. Otolaryngology, Head and Neck Surgery (assoc.), Internat. Regulatory Affairs Profls. Soc., Nat. Graphic Soc., Assn. Clin. Pharmacologists, Regulatory Affairs Profls. Soc., Monmouth County Assn. Children with Learning Disabilities, Psi Chi, Sigma Xi. Avocations: travel, classical music, creative writing. Office: Westerman Rsch Assocs Inc 170 Ave at the Common Ste 6 Shrewsbury NJ 07702-4003

WESTERVELT, GAYLE GAETANO, physical education educator; b. Utica, N.Y., Mar. 26, 1950; d. Felix Louis and Jeanne LaQuay Gaetano; m. Terry E. Westervelt, Aug. 3, 1975; 1 child, Marisa G. BS in Edn., SUNY, Cortland, 1973; postgrad., SUNY, Oneonta, 1976, St. Rose, Albany, N.Y., 1977—78. Cert. phys. edn. N.Y. Lifeguard and instr. swimming Town of Boonville, NY, 1967—73, Adirondack Ctrl. Sch., 1971—72; recreation instr. Cortland Dept. Pks. and Recreation, 1972—73; encore team facilitator Cobleskill-Richmondville Ctrl. Sch., Cobleskill, NY, 1993, phys. educator, 1973—, asst. athletic dir., 2001—, dist. health coord., 2004—. Chmn. health adv. com. Cobleskill-Richmondville Ctrl. Sch. Sch. and Cmty., Cobleskill, 2004—, coord. sch. health index, 2004—; mem. fit before 5 com. Bassett Hosp., Cobleskill, 2004—05; advisor Gymnastics Club, 1973—2002; coach girls basketball, girls tennis. Recipient N.Y. State Sportsmanship awards, 2002—05; Fitness grantee, BOCES, 1996, 1997, Health and Fitness grantee, BOCO and NYSPHERD, 2006. Mem.: Am. Assn. Health, Phys. Edn., Recreation and Dance, N.Y. Assn. Health, Phys. Edn., Recreation and Dance. Avocations: painting, swimming, gardening, interior decorating. Home: 244 Philip Schuyler Rd Cobleskill NY 12043 Office Phone: 518-234-8368 2030. Fax: 518-234-3950. E-mail: catboy@telenet.net.

WESTFALL, CAROL ANN, artist, educator; b. Everett, Pa., Sept. 7, 1938; d. Carroll Francis and Doris Lucille (Hawkins) Dooley; m. Jon David Westfall, Jan. 27, 1962 (div. Aug. 1976); children: Camille, Maigann; m. Andrew J. Del Preore, Aug. 14, 1992. BFA, RISD, 1960; MFA, Md. Inst., 1972. Instr. Md. Inst., Balt., 1968-72; asst. prof. fine arts Montclair State Coll., NJ, 1972-79, assoc. prof., 1979-87, prof., 1987—2002, v.p. senate Sch. Fine, Performing Arts, 1987-89; ret., 2002; contbg. feature writer Shuttle, Spindle & Dyepot, 2002—. Vis. prof. Columbia U. Tchrs. Coll., NYC, 1976-86; artist-in-residence Memphis Coll. Art, 1985, Am. Craft Mus., NYC, 1987; artists in sch. panel NJ Coun. on Arts, Trenton, 1978-88; study leader India tour Textile Mus., Washington, 1987; resident Artpark, Lewiston, NY, 1989; guest prof. Seian Coll., Kyoto, Japan, 1992; adj. prof. We. Wash. U., 2004—. Co-author: Plaiting: Step by Step, 1976; exhibited at Lausanne Biennale, 1975, Am. Craft Mus., 1987, Kyoto (Japan) Internat. Textile Exhbn., 1989, 97, 99; contbr. articles to profl. jours Recipient purchase award NJ State Mus., 1975; Indo-Am. fellow, 1980-81, fellow NJ Coun. on Arts, 1987; Rsch. grantee Montclair State Coll., 1987, 89-91, 94, 98-2001. Mem.: Haji Baba Club. E-mail: carol@carolwestfall.com.

WESTFALL, LOIS LORENE, retired minister, nurse; b. Monroe, Nebr., Apr. 29, 1933; d. Roy William and Lorena Dorothea (Hoare) Johnson; m. Robert Harris Westfall (div.); children: Thomas, Laurie, Brenton, Ruth, Bridget, Michael, Tracy. Student, Cottey Women's Coll., 1950—51; RN, Clarkson Hosp. Sch. Nursing, 1954; BA, Dana Coll., 1976; MDiv, Austin Presbyn. Theol. Sem., Tex., 1980. RN State Bd. Nursing, Nebr., 1954, Tex.; ordained minister Presbytery No. Waters, Presbyn. Ch., 1986. Staff nurse U. Hosp., Omaha, 1954—55, Oak Pk. Annex Hosp., Lansing, Mich., 1955—56; nurse Gen. Practice Physician, Holt, Mich., 1956—58; emergency rm., fl. nurse Children's Meml. Hosp., Omaha, 1961—64; staff nurse ob. Clarkson Hosp., Omaha, 1964—65; staff nurse St. David's Hosp., Austin, 1979; office specialist Office Specialists, Austin, 1983—86; minister First Presbyn. Ch., Superior, Wis., 1986—98, ret., 1998. Chaplain YMCA, Superior; commr. Synod Gen. Assembly, Wis., 1993—94; mem. com. Presbytery No. Waters, Wis., vice moderator, 1996, moderator, 97, chmn. coun., 98. Chmn. Red Cross Bloodmobile, Albion, Nebr. Mem.: Austin (Tex.) Sem. Alumni Assn., Clarkson Coll. Alumni Assn., Dana Coll. Alumni Assn., Cottey Coll. Alumni Assn. Presbyterian. Avocations: genealogy, scrapbooks, antiques, fishing. Home: PO Box 503 702 So Ingram Madison NE 68748 Personal E-mail: loiswestfall@yahoo.com.

WESTHEIMER, RUTH SIEGEL (KAROLA WESTHEIMER), psychologist, television personality; b. Frankfurt, Fed. Republic Germany; came to U.S., 1956; m. Manfred Westheimer; children: Miriam, Joel. Grad. psychology, U. Paris Sorbonne; Master's degree, New Sch. for Social Research, N.Y.C., 1959; EdD, Columbia U., 1970. Research asst. Columbia U. Sch. Pub. Health, N.Y.C., 1967-70; assoc. prof. Lehman Coll., Bronx, N.Y., 1970-77; with Bklyn. Coll., West Point Milit. Acad.; counsellor, radio talk show hostess Sexually Speaking Sta. WYNY-FM, N.Y.C., 1980-90; hostess TV series Good Sex, Dr. Ruth Show, Ask Dr. Ruth, 1987-92; pvt. practice N.Y.C., 1976—. Adj. assoc. prof. NYU; leader seminars for residents and interns in pediats. on adolescent sexuality Brookdale Hosp. Author: Dr. Ruth's Guide to Good Sex, 1983, First Love: A Young People's Guide to Sexual Information, 1985, Dr. Ruth's Guide for Married Lovers, 1986, (autobiography) All In a Lifetime, 1987, Sex and Morality: Who is Teaching Out Sex Standards?, 1988, Dr. Ruth's Guide to Erotic and Sensuous Pleasures, 1991, Dr. Ruth's Guide to Safer Sex, 1992, Dr. Ruth Talks to Kids, 1993, The Art of Arousal, 1993, Dr. Ruth's Encyclopedia of Sex, 1994, Heavenly Sex, 1995, Sex for Dummies, 1995, The Value of Family, 1996; co-author: (with Steven Kaplan) Surviving Salvation; contbr. articles to mags.; appeared in film A Woman or Two, 1986; appeared on TV show Quantum Leap, 1993, Play Boy Making Love Series (video), 1996, All New Dr. Ruth Show (nominated 5 times by Ace awards, Ace award for excellence in cable TV, 1988), What's Up, Dr. Ruth (gold medal Internat. Film and TV Festival for excellence in ednl. TV), You're on the Air with Dr. Ruth, Never Too Late, 1992—, Dr. Ruth's House, (calendar) Dr. Ruth's Good Sex Night-to-Night Calendar, 1993, 94, (boardgame) Dr. Ruth's Game of Good Sex; exec. prodr. documentary on Ethiopian Jews Surviving Salvation, 1991; columnist Ask Dr. Ruth. Pres. YMHA, Washington Heights. Recipient Mother of Yr. award Nat. Mother's Day Com., Liberty medal City of N.Y. Fellow N.Y. Acad. Medicine. Office: Pierre Lehu Communication Connection 928 Broadway Ste 1206 New York NY 10010-8109

WESTHEIMER, RUTH WELLING, retired management consultant; b. Detroit, May 17, 1922; d. Benjamin Dennis and Elsa (Friedenberg) Welling; m. Robert Irvin BA, U. Wis., 1944. V.p., bd. dirs. Stepping Stones Ctr., Cin., 1976-85; chmn., developer Vol. Action Ctr., Cin., 1979-82; trustee United Way Community Chest, Cin., 1980-88; organizer Cooporate Voluntarism Council, Cin., 1982-85; v.p., exec. com. United Way Community Chest, Cin., 1983-85; chmn. Evaluation Com. United Way, Cin., 1985-88; advisor YWCA Career Women Achievement, Cin., 1981—; bd. dirs. Cancer Family Care, Cin., 1986—; chmn. United Way Agy. Partnership Devel., Cin., 1988—. Treas. Workum Scholarship Found., Cin., 1969-86; chmn. Fine Arts Fund, Trustee Cin. Psychoanalytic Found., 1974-78, Ohio Citizens Coun., Columbus, 1967-70; bd. dirs. Planned Parenthood Assn., Cin., 1991—. Mem. Woman's City Club, League of Women Voters (treas. 1959-68); bd. of trustees, American Classical Music Hall of Fame, Cincinnati. Avocations: tennis, golf, horticulture, travel.

WESTHOFF, LAURA M., history professor; d. Herbert H. and Mary Beth Westhoff; m. Darel Shelton, May 25; children: Henry, Jacob. BA, Northwest U., Ill., 1988; MA, Washington U., St. Louis, 1993, PhD, 1999. Asst. prof. U. Mo., St. Louis, 1999—. Office: Univ Mo St Louis 3832 Russel Blvd Saint Louis MO 63110-3708

WESTHOFF, PAMELA LYNNE, lawyer; b. Redondo Beach, Calif., Dec. 24, 1960; d. Frank Wade and Barbara Adrienne Fowler; m. Douglas James Westhoff, June 19, 1982; children: Steven Michael, Dylan James. BBA, Loyola Marymount U., 1982; MBA, JD, U. So. Calif., 1986. Bar: Calif. 1986, U.S. Dist. Ct. Calif. 1986. Assoc. O'Melveny & Myers, LLP, LA, 1986—95, ptnr., 1995—2002, Gilchrist & Rutter PC, Santa Monica, Calif., 2002, DLA Piper Rudnick Gray Cary LLP, LA, 2003—. Office: DLA Piper Rudnick Gray Cary LLP 550 S Hope Ste 2300 Los Angeles CA 90071 Office Phone: 213-330-7747. Office Fax: 213-330-7547. Business E-Mail: pam.westhoff@dlapiper.com.

WESTLUND, MARIBETH, secondary school educator; b. Chgo., Apr. 29, 1961; d. Francis Joseph and Catherine Marie Balda. BS, Ill. State U., 1983; MEd, DePaul U., 1993. Cert. ednl. adminstr., tchr. Ill. Tchr. Our Lady of Knock Cath. Sch., Calumet City, Ill., 1985—86; dept. chair of social studies, tchr. Schaumburg H.S., Schaumburg High School, Ill., 1986—. Bd. dirs. N.W. Ctr. Against Sexual Assault. Nominee Golden Apple Educator Nominee, Golden Apple Found., 2002. Mem.: AAUW, NOW, Nat. Coun. Social Studies. Avocations: travel, hiking, bicycling, tennis. Office: Schaumburg HS 1100 W Schaumburg Rd Schaumburg IL 60194 Personal E-mail: mbwestlund@yahoo.com. E-mail: mwestlund@d211.org.

WESTMORELAND, BARBARA FENN, neurologist, educator; b. 1940; BS in Chemistry, Mary Washington Coll., 1961; MD, U. Va., 1965. Diplomate in neurology and clin. neurophysiology Am. Bd. Psychiatry and Neurology. Intern Vanderbilt Hosp., Nashville, 1965-66; resident in neurology U. Va. Hosp., Charlottesville, 1966-70; fellow in electroencephalography Mayo Clinic, Rochester, Minn., 1970-71, assoc. cons. neurology, 1971-73; asst. prof. neurology Mayo Med. Sch., Rochester, 1973-78, assoc. prof., 1978-85, prof., 1985—. Vice chair exam. com. cert. clin. neurophysiology Am. Bd. Psychiatry and Neurology, 1998—2003, chair exam. com. cert. clin. neurophysiology, 2003—. Co-author: Medical Neurosciences, 1978, rev. edit., 1986, first author 3d edit., 1994. Recipient Herbert Jasper award, Am. Clin. Neurophysiology Soc., 2005. Mem.: Mayo History Medicine Soc. (pres. 1990—91), Am. Acad. Neurology (chair sect. clin. neurophysiology 2000—02, A.B. Baker award for lifetime achievement in edn. 2002), Ctrl. Assn. Electroencephalographers (sec.-treas. 1976—78, pres. 1979—80, chair neurology resident in-svc. tng. exam 1994—99), Am. EEG Soc. (sec. 1985—87, pres. 1991—92), Am. Epilepsy Soc. (treas. 1978—80, pres. 1987—88), Sigma Xi (pres. chpt. 1987—88).

WESTON, FRANCINE EVANS, secondary school educator; b. Mt. Vernon, NY, Oct. 8, 1946; d. John Joseph and Frances (Fantino) Pisaniello. BA, Hunter Coll., 1968; MA, Lehman Coll., 1973; cert., Am. Acad. Dramatic Arts, NYC, 1976; PhD, NYU, 1991. Cert. elem., secondary tchr., NY. Tchr. Yonkers Bd. Edn., NY, 1968—; aquatic dir. Woodlane Day Camp, Irvington-on-Hudson, NY, 1967-70, Yonkers Jewish Community Ctr., NY, 1971-75. Creative drama tchr. John Burroughs Jr. HS, Yonkers, 1971-77; stage lighting designer Iona Summer Theatre Festival, New Rochelle, NY, 1980-81, Yonkers Male Glee Club, 1981-89, Roosevelt HS, 1980-97; freelance, 1998—; rsch. specialist Scholarship Locating Svc., 1992-94, Yonkers Civil Def. Police Aux., 1994—; master electrician NYU Summer Mus. Theatre, 1979-80; appointed program developer for Cadet Acad. of Police & Fire Scis., Pub. Safety Magnet, Roosevelt HS, 2001, program dir., 2004-. Actress in numerous comty. theater plays including A Touch of the Poet, 1979; dir. stage prodns. including I Remember Mama, 1973, The Man Who Came to Dinner, 1975; author: A Descriptive Comparison of Computerized Stage Lighting Memory Systems With Non-Computerized Systems, 1991, (short stories) A Hat for Louise, 1984, Old Memories: Beautiful and Otherwise, 1984; lit. editor: (story and poetry collection) Beautifully Old, 1984; editor: Command Post Dispatch quar., 1997—. Mem. Yonkers Civil Def. Police Aux., 1994—, adminstrv. asst. to commanding officer, 1996—, capt. adminstrn., 2002—, capt., 2004—; steering com. chairperson Roosevelt H.S.-Middle States Assn. of Schs. and Colls. Self-Evaluation, 1985—88. Named Tchr. of Excellence, NY State English Coun., 1990, 95, 2000; recipient Monetary award for Teaching Excellence, Carter-Wallace Products, 1992; President's Call to Svc. award, Lifetime award, USA Freedom Corps, 2005; named to Arrid Tchrs. Honor Roll, 1992. Republican. Roman Catholic. Avocations: swimming, theater. Office: Roosevelt High Sch Tuckahoe Rd Yonkers NY 10710

WESTON, JANICE LEAH COLMER, librarian; b. Phila., Jan. 3, 1944; d. Robert Henry and Mildred Viola (Hale) Colmer; m. Stephen Paul Oksala, Aug. 21, 1965 (div. 1970); m. Leonard Charles Weston, Oct. 28, 1972. BA in History, U. Mich., 1966; MS in LS, Wayne State U., 1969; postgrad., Cath. U. Am., 1975, Brigham Young U., 1975. Cert. profl. libr., Va. Library clk. Edn. Libr., U. Mich., Ann Arbor, 1966-67; reference libr. John Tyler Community Coll., Chester, Va., 1969-70, Tech. Libr., Aberdeen Proving Ground, Md., 1971-72; br. libr. Chester Pub. Libr., 1969-70; libr. Gen. Equipment Test Activity, Ft. Lee, Va., 1970-71; chief libr. Army Ordnance Ctr. and Sch., Aberdeen Proving Ground, 1972-94. Mem. job analysis task force Dept. Army, Washington, 1976; chmn. Aberdeen Proving Ground Media Svcs. Com., 1978, 83, 88. Author: Operating Procedures, 1988. Mem. James Buchanan Found., Lancaster, Pa., 1977-2004, Fulton Opera House Found., Lancaster, 1985-2004, Friends Libr. So. Lancaster County, Quarryville, Pa., 1985-2004; Humane League Friends, Lancaster, 1988-2004, Friends of Atglen Susquehanna Trail, 1994—, Friends of the Libr., Cocoa Beach, Fla., 1996—; mem. St. David's by the Sea Episcopal Ch., Cocoa Beach, 1996—. Mem. Spl. Libr. Assn., Ret. Officers Assn., Red Hats Club Avocations: needlecrafts, reading, dance, travel, theater. Home: 520 S Brevard Ave 234 Cocoa Beach FL 32931

WESTON, JOAN SPENCER, communications executive; b. Barton, Vt., Aug. 11, 1943; d. Rolfe Weston and Dorothy Lena (Spencer) Schoppe. BA magna cum laude, U. Mass., 1965. Tchr. high sch. Gorham (Maine) Schs., 1965-66; tchr. Sherwood Hall Sch., Mansfield, Eng., 1966-67; tchr. middle sch. Meden Sch., Warsop, Eng., 1967-68; dept. head high sch. Goffstown (N.H.) Schs., 1968-82; dir. circulation T.H.E. Jour., Acton, Mass., 1982-83; prodn. mgr. The Robb Report, Acton, 1983-87, prodn. dir., 1988; prodn. cons. Spencer Weston Assocs., Portland, Maine, 1988-93; prodn. dir. New Age Jour. (now Body & Soul), Watertown, Mass., 1993-96; dir. editl. and prodn. Alloy Edn., Westford, Mass., 1996—2006. Mem. Boston Prodn. Mgrs. Group (charter), Phi Beta Kappa. Avocations: travel, music, psychology, antiques.

WESTON, PRISCILLA ATWOOD, library director; b. May 6, 1925; BA, U. N.H., 1947, cert. in libr. techniques, 1974. Libr. dir. Mansfield Libr., Temple, N.H., 1964—. Author: Deep Roots in Rocky Soil, 2005; co-author: A History of Temple, N.H. 1768-1976; co-author: (with Wilton, Temple, and Lyndeborough) Images of America. Curator Temple Hist. Soc., 1964—; mem., sec. Temple Conservation Commn., 1978-88; mem. Temple Sch. Bd., 1952-55, ch. historian; dir. Hillsboro County Farm Bur., 1964-65. Mem. Greenville Woman's Club, Miller Grange (master 1964-65). Avocations: reading, gardening, genealogy, choir. Office: Mansfield Libr PO Box 210 Temple NH 03084-0210

WESTON, REBECCA LYNN, forensic specialist, educator; b. Waren, Pa., Aug. 22, 1949; BS in Criminology, 1995. Sgt. Union Co. prosecutor office, Elizabeth, NJ, 1981—2000; instr. Warren Co. Cmty. Coll., Washington, NJ, 1996—.

WESTOVER, DIANA KAY, interior designer, executive recruiter; b. Clovis, N.Mex., Aug. 24, 1953; d. Martin B. and Mary Catherine (Eberwein) Goodwin; m. Dn Oliver Westover, June 14, 1975; children: Jacqueline Diona, Daniele Leigh. Student, Ea. N.Mex. U., 1971-73; Interior Design diploma, LaSalle U., 1973; BFA in Interior Design, N.Y. Sch. Interior Design, 1977. Cert. pers. cons. Mem. sales staff The Popular, El Paso, Tex., 1979-81; various sales and design positions Hollon's, Lubbock, Tex., 1981-82, Spears, Lubbock, 1982-84; instr. interior design N.Mex. Jr. Coll., Hobbs, 1986—; owner, mgr. EnerTech Research, mgmt. and tech. recruiting firm, Houston, 1991—. Interior designer, buyer Callaway's Hobbs, 1985-86; interior designer Designers II, Hobbs, 1986—; set designer Miss N.Mex. Pageant, Hobbs, 1984-85. Program chmn. Les County Rep. Women; bd. dirs. S.W. Symphony; active Christian Women, Hobbs, Altar Soc., Hobbs, St. Joseph's Circle, Hobbs, Rep. Women, Hobbs; v.p. Spring (Tex.) Rep. Women, 1992, bd. dirs., 1997; mem. fin. com. St. Ignatius Loyola Cath. Ch., 1993. Named Clovis Young Rep. of Yr., 1974; recipient Top Recuiter award CUF, 1997. Mem. Tex. Assn. Pers. Cons. Avocations: tennis, reading, bicycling, golf. Home: 9211 Godstone Ln Spring TX 77379-6508 also: Diana's 2400 N Grimes St Ste 6 Hobbs NM 88240-2131

WESTRICH, KATE ANN, web site editor, writer; b. Cin., Ohio, July 26, 1978; d. Paul Joseph and Catherine Marie Westrich. BS, Ohio U., Athens, 2000; MA, U. of Cin., 2003. Web editor, sr. mktg. assoc. Cin. Children's Hosp. Med. Ctr., 2000—; webmaster Ohio Coordinating Ctr. for Dual Diagnosis, Columbus, 2005—. Book and music critic Score! Rocks Mag., Akron, Ohio, 2003; webmaster MedCare Rehab, Chgo., 2004—; book critic X-Ray Mag., Cin., 2004—05; adj. prof. U. of Cin., Clermont Coll., Cin., 2005; writer Time Warner Cable, Cin., 2005—06. Vol. O'Bronville Animal Rescue, Cin., 2005—06; reading tutor Cin. Pub. Schs., Cin., 2004—05; vol. Susan G. Komen Race for the Cure, Cin., 2001—04. Recipient Outstanding Achievement in Web Site Devel. award, Web Mktg. Assn., 2005. Personal E-mail: katewestrich@hotmail.com.

WESTRICH, KATHLEEN MAUREEN, science educator; b. Milw. m. Craig A. Berg. BSc, Marquette U., Milw., 1991; MSc, U. Wis., Milw., 1997. Cert. tchr. sci. Wis., 1997, candidate in adolescent and young adulthood sci. Nat. Bd. Profl. Tchg. Stds., nat. trainer Coop. Discipline Behavior Mgmt. Model Linda Albert, founder, 2005. Sci. tchr. Milw. Pub. Schs., 1997—; instr. U. Wis., Milw., 2001—. Adj. faculty Nat. Louis U., Milw., 2005—; advisor Health Occupations Students Am. Avocations: reading, painting, knitting, motorcycling, travel. Office Phone: 414-393-6202.

WESTRICK, HEIDI LYNN, medical/surgical nurse; b. Johnstown, Pa., Dec. 15, 1966; d. Thomas and Karol Anne (Kirchner) Zwiener; m. Daniel D. Westrick, Sept. 4, 1999. Diploma, Conemaugh Valley Meml. Hosp., Johnstown, 1987; BSN, U. Pitts., Johnstown, 1993. RN Pa., cert. trauma nurse, in peritoneal dialysis, in cardiac monitoring, med. surg. nursing, acute head injuries/trauma care of acute rehab. patients, Am. nursing credential; in CPR. Nurse Conemaugh Valley Meml. Hosp., Johnstown, Pa., 1987—; admissions coord. Conemaugh Rehab. Unit, Crichton Ctr. Advanced Rehab., Johnstown, Pa., 1996—. Mem. Conemaugh Valley Meml. Alumni (sec. peer rev. com.), Alumni of U. Pitts. at Johnstown. Office Phone: 814-948-4261. Office Fax: 814-948-4393. Personal E-mail: daniel@forspeed.com.

WESTROPE, MARTHA RANDOLPH, psychologist, consultant; b. Gaffney, S.C., May 19, 1922; d. Gordon Robert and Hannah (Brown) W.; 1 adopted child, Ashley Randolph. BS, Winthrop Coll., 1942; MA, U. N.C., 1944; PhD, State U. of Iowa, Iowa City, 1952. Lic. psychologist, S.C. Pvt. practice, Greenville, S.C., 1960—; part-time pvt. practice, 1987-96; part-time staff mem. Spartanburg (S.C.) Mental Health Clinic, 1971-73, Greenville Mental Health Ctr., 1974-85, Patrick B. Harris Psychiat. Hosp., Anderson, S.C., 1985-87; med. cons. S.C. Vocat. Rehab. Dept., Greenville, 1987-91, part-time med. cons., 1993-99. Cons. S.C. Parole Bd. for Psychol. Evaluation, S.C. Dept. Corrections, 1983-87. Mem. Am. Psychol. Assn., Southeastern Psychol. Assn., S.C. Psychol. Assn., Am. Assn. for Advancement of Psychology, Greenville County Mental Health Assn., Am. Group Psychotherapy Assn., Coun. for the Nat. Register of Health Svc. Providers in Psychology. Democrat. Presbyterian. Avocations: wildlife preservation, fine arts, doll collecting, stamp collecting/philately. Home: 11 Darien Way Greenville SC 29615-3236

WESTWATER, MARTHA ELIZABETH, language educator; b. Boston, Jan. 3, 1929; d. Joseph James Westwater and Martha Elizabeth Early. BS in Secondary Edn., St. John's U., 1957, MA in English Lit., 1962; PhD in English Lit., Dalhousie U., 1974; LHD (hon.), Mt. St. Vincent U., 1996. Prof. English Mt. St. Vincent, Halifax, Can., 1972-98; prof. emeritus Massasoit C.C., Brochton, Mass., 2000—. Rsch. in field. Author: Nothing on Earth, 1967, The Wilson Sisters, 1984, Spasmodic Career of Sydney Dobell, 1992, Giant Despair Meets Hopeful, 2000; contbr. articles to scholarly jours. Mem. Sisters of Charity, 1949—; founder Mothers Advanvced Edn. Team, Dartmouth, Can., 1994—. Mem. MLA. Roman Catholic. Avocation: reading. Office Phone: 508-588-9100 x1812. Personal E-mail: westwtrl@aol.com.

WETHERBY, IVOR LOIS, retired librarian; b. Louisville, May 22, 1924; d. Luther Silas and Clara Morris (Hite) W.; m. Herbert Charles Howard, July 4, 1947; children: Ivor Jane, Elizabeth Wetherby, John Allen, Luther Hite, Ann Dell. AB, Ky. Wesleyan Coll., 1944; MS in Library Sci., Fla. State U. 1965; SEd, Fla. Atlantic U., 1984; EdD Fla. Internat. U., 1992. Various clerical and secretarial positions, 1944-50; tchr. Our Lady of Mercy Acad., Louisville, 1963-64; librarian Palm Beach Jr. Coll., Lake Worth, Fla., 1966-78; head librarian Sebring (Fla.) Pub. Library, 1978; health scis. reference librarian Miami (Fla.)-Dade CC, Med. Ctr. Campus, 1978-87; librarian med. library Moncrief Army Cmty. Hosp., Ft. Jackson, S.C., 1987-89; ref. libr. Fla. Internat. U., 1992, ret., 1992. Active New Life Alliance Ch., West Palm Beach, Fla., Pleasant Grove Bapt. Ch., Louisville. Mem. DAR, Palm Beach County Geneal. Soc., Daus. of Founders and Patriots of Am., Nat. Soc. Colonial Dames XVII Century, Holland Soc. NY, Huguenot Soc., Nat. Soc. Daus. Union 1861-65. Home: 615 Laurel Lake Dr Apt A224 Columbus NC 28722

WETHERILL-SMITH, LINDA MARIE, musician, educator, performing arts association administrator; b. Milw., Mar. 2, 1950; d. Albert Edward Christensen and Elsa Dorothea Etterman; m. Joseph David Smith, July 7, 2000. MusB, U. Rochester, 1972, performers cert., 1971; MusM, SUNY, Stony Brook, 1991. 1st flutist solo and ensemble Chamber Artists Garbarino of La Scala, Milan, 1973—76; solo and 1st flutist Frankfurt Radio Symphony Orch., 1975—76, IRCAM, Ensemble Intercontemporain, Paris, 1976—80; internat. soloist freelance, U.S.I.S. and McCann Artists, Ltd., London, 1973—; prof. music major Turkish univs., Istanbul, 1987—90; cultural amb. U.S. Info. Svc., Washington, 1985—; prof. music Adelphi U., Garden City, NY, 1994—; solo flutist Aspelete, 2006—, Salzburg Mozarteam, 2006—, Orch. of Our Time, N.Y.C., 2006—. Judge Internat. Competition, Salzburg, Austria, 2004—; solo performer, lectr. Internat. Soc. Cont. Music, Miami, 2004; performances and master classes in Argentina and Brazil; cons. various internat. programs, 1973—. Editor: L.I. Flute Notes, 1994—; editor, performer (solo CD) Sound and Repercussion, Far Amazon, 2000 (Amazon award, 2003), (book and CD) International Anthology of Solos for Alto and Bass Flutes, 2005; contbr. articles and interviews to profl. jours. Pres., founder Muzarte, Phila., N.Y.C., 1980—. Grantee, NY State Coun. for the Arts, 1997—2005. Mem.: L.I. Flute Club (bd. dirs., adv. bd. 1994—2005), Sigma Alpha Iota. Achievements include first woman to perform publicly for mixed audiences in Saudi Arabia in 1986; first American flute soloist to perform and teach in Hunan province of China in 2002. Avocations: travel, political diplomacy, world cultures. Home: 38 W 74th Ave Apt 3C New York NY 10023 Office: Adelphi U South Ave Garden City NY 11530 Office Phone: 917-861-4528. E-mail: muzarte@msn.com, muzarte@lindawetherill.com.

WETHINGTON, WILMA Z., artist, educator; b. Clinton, Iowa, Apr. 15, 1918; d. Marion Leslie and Marjorie Irene Russell; children: Roberla Ann, Paul Jr., Richard. Student, Marshall U., Huntington, W.Va., 1936—37, Wichita State U., Kans., 1955—64. Owner Wethington Studio and Gallery, Wichita, 1964—, Accent Frames and Gallery, Wichita, 1974—79. Judge art shows. 28 one-woman exhbns., 150 group shows, portraits, J.F. Kennedy, Space Ctr. Mus., retiring presidents, Wichita State U., Miss Am. Debbie Bryant. Mem.: Mo. Watercolor Soc., Wichita Artist Guild (bd. dirs.), Kans. Watercolor Soc. (bd. dirs.), Am. Watercolor Soc. (assoc.), Kappa Pi. Avocations: gardening, decorating, travel. Home: 2 Linden Wichita KS 67206

WETLE, TERRIE FOX, gerontologist, educator, dean; b. Bremerton, Wash., Nov. 7, 1946; d. Gerald Lee and Elinor Myrle (Martindale) Todd; m. Richard W. Besdine, July 2, 1981; children: Sarah, Molly. BS in Psychology, Portland State U., 1968, MS in Psychology, 1971, PhD of Urban Studies, 1976. Asst. prof. Portland (Oreg.) State U., 1976-78; social policy analyst Dept. Health, Edn. and Welfare, Washington, 1978-79; asst. prof. Yale U., New Haven, 1979-81, Harvard U., Boston, 1981-88; dir. Braceland Ctr., Hartford, Conn., 1988-95; assoc. prof. U. Conn. Health Ctr., Farmington, 1989—95; dep. dir. Nat. Inst. Aging, NIH, Bethesda, Md., 1995-2000; assoc. dean medicine, prof. cmty. health Brown U. Med. Sch., Providence, 2000—. Bd. dirs. Armed Forces Retirement Home, Washington. Editor: Older Veterans, 1984, Handbook of Geriatric Care, 1982; contbr. articles to profl. jours. Pres. Alzheimer's Assn. Greater Hartford, 1993-95; apptd. Alzheimer's Coalition Conn., 1991-95. Fellow: Gerontol. Soc. Am. (chair com.); mem.: APHA (del., governing coun.), Am. Soc. Aging. Office: Brown U Sch Medicine 97 Waterman St G-A2 Providence RI 02912

WETTER, VIRGINIA FORWOOD PATE, broadcast executive; b. Havre De Grace, Md., Aug. 10, 1919; BA, Coll. William and Mary, 1940, D (hon.) of Pub.Svc., 2006, PhD (hon.) in Pub. Svc., 2006. Pub. rels. Std. Oil Co. of Pa., 1940, Irwin and Leighton Contractor, 1941; pres., gen. mgr. WASA and WHDG radio Havre de Grace, MD, 1960—85; pres. Multiview Cable Co. (later Comcast), 1966—82; chmn. bd. Chesapeake Broadcasting Corp., 1985—. Trustee Harford CC Bd. of Trustees, 1959—69, chmn., 1966—69; pres. Md. Assn. Bds. of Edn., 1963—64, Md. Dist. of Columbia Del. Broadcaster's Assn., 1965—66; mem. Harford County Bd. Edn., 1959—69, pres., 1966—69; mem. radio code bd. Nat. Assn. of Broadcasters, 1966—71; libr. bd. Broadcast Pioneers, 1980—2004. Dir. Harford County Heart Assn. and Cancer Soc., Susquehanna Coun. of Girl Scouts; county chmn. Pres.'s Com. to Promote Employment of Physically Handicapped; plans bd. United Way; dir. Blood Bank of Md.; vol. Harford Meml. Hosp. Aux.; chmn. ann. fund drive Coll. William and Mary, 1985, endowment assn. trustee, pres.'s coun.; vestry St. John's Episcopal Ch., chair 150th anniversary celebration, co-chair bldg. com. Recipient Alumni Medallion award, Coll. William and Mary, 1969, Am. Broadcast Pioneer award, Broadcasters' Found., 2001, Disting. Svc. to Broadcasting award, Broadcast Pioneers of Washington Area, 2001. Mem.: Am. Women in Radio and Television (life; nat. pres. 1970—71, Bd. Dirs. award 1991, Radio Leadership award 2000), Md. Congress of Parents and Tchrs. (life), Delta Kappa Gamma (hon.). Home: 1000 Chesapeake Dr Havre De Grace MD 21078 Personal E-mail: vwetter@aol.com.

WETZEL, ANGELA DENISE, music educator; b. Dayton, Jan. 20, 1980; d. Glenn E. and Evelyn L. Wetzel. MusB in Edn., Wright State U., Dayton, 2002. Music educator London City Schs., Ohio, 2004—. Instr. winter guard Brookville Local Schs., Ohio, 2005—. Mem.: London Edn. Assn. (bldg. rep. 2006—), Ohio Music Edn. Assn. Avocations: travel, reading.

WETZEL, BETTY PREAT, writer; b. Roundup, Mont., Nov. 7, 1915; d. Alfred William and Rachel Preat (Johnston) Eiselein; m. Winston Warren Wetzel, June 5, 1940; children: Susan Hinman, Kurt, Gretchen Grafin von Rittberg, Rebecca. BA in Journalism, U. Mont., 1937. Columnist, reporter Roundup (Mont.) Rec.-Tribune, 1938-46; sec. SEATO Cholera Rsch. Lab. and Hosp., Dacca, Bangladesh, 1965-67; adminstrv. asst. to v.p. Wellesley (Mass.) U., 1969-73; dir. pub. rels. Oxfam-Am., Boston, 1973-77; book rev. editor Mont. Mag., Helena, 1989-91. Author: The Making of a Montanan, 1986, Missoula, The Town and The People, 1988, After You, Mark Twain, 1990; co-author: Older Women in the Outdoors, 1996. Bd. dirs. Flathead Lake Biol. Sta., Bigfork, Mont., 1980-86. Democrat. Avocations: mountain hiking, tennis, reading, politics. Home: 189 Pierce Ln PO Box 693 Bigfork MT 59911-0693 Personal E-mail: bwetzel@digisys.net.

WETZEL, KAREN J., nurse; b. Milw., Dec. 1, 1953; d. Carl William and Shirley Ann (McFarlane) Hoffman; m. David A. Wetzel, July 24, 1971; children: Michael David, Brian Lee, Terry Alan, Robyn Janel, Cassi Jo. Student, Good Samaritan Med Ctr. Sch., Milw., 1983, Carroll/Columbia Sch. Nursing. RN; cert. inpatient obstetric nursing. Clin. coord., oral surgery Marquette U., Milw.; nurse coronary ICU Sheboygan (Wis.) Meml. Med. Ctr.; head nurse Milw. Med. Clinic, Port Washington, Wis.; charge nurse obstetrics/gynecology L&D/nursery St. Mary's Hosp., Ozaukee, Port Washington; staff nurse pediatrics Cedar Mills Med. Group St. Mary's Health Ctr., Cedarburg, Wis. Lectr. nursing diagnosis, care plans, maternal and newborn assessment; researcher in self hypnosis, pain control and behavioral modification. Instr., trainer Neonatal Resuscitation, basic life support; active ARC, community health awareness programs, civil and animal rights causes, politics; active ch. leadership, women's and children's ministry, Bible studies, evangelism, motivational spkr. Friedens Ch. Port Wash., Wis. 2nd lt. U.S. Army, 1985-87. Mem. AWHONN (cert. inpatient obstetric nursing), NAFE. Avocations: health awareness programs, community programs, church. Home: 1390 Jay Rd Belgium WI 53004-9795 Office: 13111 N Port Washington Rd Mequon WI 53097-2416

WETZEL, MARLENE REED, freelance/self-employed writer; b. Jordan, Mont., Apr. 5, 1937; d. Frederick Edward and Alma Jane (Flippin) Reed; m. John Hall Wetzel, May 14, 1960; 1 child, Kurt. BA magna cum laude, U. Tulsa, 1987. Govt. affairs rschr. Arabian Am. Oil Co., Dhahran, Saudi Arabia, 1979, 1980—82; asst. to dir. The Philbrook Mus., Tulsa, Okla., 1987; freelance writer, editor, 1988—98; author, 1998—. Recipient award, PEN/Amazon.com, 2000. Avocations: tennis, skiing. Home: 11950 S Mingo Rd Bixby OK 74008

WEXLER, ANNE, government relations and public affairs consultant; b. NYC, Feb. 10, 1930; d. Leon R. and Edith R. (Rau) Levy; m. Joseph Duffey, Sept. 17, 1974; children by previous marriage: David Wexler, Daniel Wexler. BA, Skidmore Coll., 1951, LLD (hon.), 1978; DSc in Bus. (hon.), Bryant Coll., 1978. Assoc. pub. Rolling Stone mag., 1974-76; personnel adviser Carter-Mondale transition planning group, 1976-77; dep. undersec. regional affairs Dept. Commerce, 1977-78; asst. to Pres. of U.S., Washington, 1978-81; pres. Wexler and Assocs., Washington, 1981-82; govt. relations and pub. affairs cons., chmn. Wexler, Reynolds, Harrison & Schule, Inc., Washington, 1981-90; vice chmn. Hill and Knowlton PA Worldwide, Washington, 1990-92; chmn. The Wexler Group, 1992—. Bd. dirs. Methanex, Dreyfus Index Funds, Wilshire Mut. Funds, Dreyfus Family of Funds. Bd. dirs. Washington Econ. Club, WETA. Decorated officer Order of Australia; named Outstanding Alumna Skidmore Coll., 1972, recipient most disting. alumni award, 1984, Bryce Harlow award, 1989. Mem. Coun. on Fgn. Rels., Nat. Women's Forum. Jewish. Office: Wexler Group 1317 F St NW Ste 600 Washington DC 20004-1157

WEXLER, JOAN G., dean, law educator; b. NYC, Nov. 25, 1946; m. Marvin Wexler, June 16, 1968 (div.); children: Matthew Eric, Laura Page. BS (hons. and distinction), Cornell U., 1968; MA in tchg., Harvard U., 1970; JD, Yale, 1974. Bar: N.Y. 1976. Jud. law clk. for Judge Jack B. Weinstein U.S. Dist. Ct. (ea. dist.), NY, 1974-75; assoc. Debevoise & Plimpton, N.Y.C., 1975-77; asst. prof. law NYU Sch. Law, 1978-81, assoc. prof. law, 1981-85; prof. law Bklyn. Law Sch., 1985—87, assoc. dean acad. affairs, prof. law, 1987-94, acting dean, prof. law, 1994, dean, pres. and prof. law, 1994—. Spkr. in field; evaluator trust adminstrn. and estate adminstrn. courses N.Y. State Banking Assn., 1993; mem. planning com. Bench and Bar Conf. Fed. Bar Coun., 1995, 2003, chair Winter Bench and Bar Conf., Feb. 2002, bd. dirs. Fed. Bar Coun. Found.; mem. planning com. Workshop on Family and Juvenile Law Am. Assn. Law Schs., Washington, 1993; atty. mem. Jud. Conf. of State of N.Y., 2000—; with Bklyn. Legal Svcs. Corp. (mem. adv. com. 1994-). Contbr. articles to profl. jours. Bd. dirs. Downtown Bklyn. Devel. Assn., 1992-96, Fund for Modern Cts., 1994—, Assn. of the Bar of the City of N.Y. Fund, 1994-96; active Commn. on Alcohol and Substance abuse in the Profession, 1999—; mem. Commn. on Univ. Relations, Cornell U., 2001—. Recipient Spl. Recognition award, N.Y. Women's Bar Assn., 1996, Pres. Spl. award, 2002, award, Greater Boy Scout Soc. N.Y., 1999, William Schoenfeld award, Soc. Adolescent Psychiatry, 1999. Fellow Am. Bar Found.; mem. ABA (mem. continuing legal edn. com. 1997-98, 99-2001, ind. law schs. com. 1996-97, 2000-, sect. legal edn. and admissions to bar, new deans seminar planning com. 2001—), Am. Law Inst. (mem. mem's. consultative group-law family dissolution, spl. com. inst. size 1998-2000), Fed. Bar Coun. (pres.-elect 2002-, v.p. 2001-2002, chair Winter Bench and Bar Conf. 2001-2002, planning com. 2002-2003, pres. Fed. Bar Found. 1998-99, chair, Fed. Bar Coun. and Found. nominating com. 1998), N.Y. State Bar Assn. (mem. com. on children and law 1993-97, com. legal edn. and admission 1994—), N.Y. Women's Bar Assn. (v.p. 1987-88, 92-93, bd. dirs. 1998-91, Pres.'s Spl. award 2002, Spl. Recognition award 1996), Greater Boy Scouts Coun. N.Y. (William Schoenfeld award 1999), Soc. Adolescent Psychiatry (William Schoenfeld award 1999), Jud. Conf. State N.Y. (atty. 2000-2002), Downtown Bklyn. Coun. (mem. exec. com. 2000-), State N.Y. Office of Ct. Adminstrn. (commn. on alcohol and substance abuse in profession 1999-), Practicing Law Inst. (mem. com. on programs and pubs. 1998, alt. mem., exec. com. 2001-), Fund Moderate Cts. (mem. bd. dirs., task force ct. facilities 2001), Downtown Bklyn. Devel. Assn., Assn. Bar City N.Y. Fund Inc. (v.p. 1996-97, mem. nominating com. 92-93, 1999, chair com. on honors 1997-2000, mem. com. on honors 1994-97, com. matrimonial law 1985-89, 92-95, long range planning com. 1992-95, com. on family ct. and family law, 1989-92, ad hoc com. on AIDS 1987-88, ad hoc com. surrogate parenting 1986-88), Pres.'s Coun. of Cornell Women (com. on univ. rels. 2001-), Com. to Restore Thurgood Marshall Landmark Courthouse, Bklyn. Legal Svs. Corp. A (mem adv. com. 1994-), Cornell U. (mem. Cornell Coun. 2002-, pres.'s coun. Cornell Women 1995-, mem. com. on u. rels. 2001), Second Cir. Task Force on Gender, Racial and Ethnic Fairness in Cts., N.Y. State Supreme Ct.(adv. com. 18-B family ct. panel, appellate divsn. first dept.), Jud. Conf. Second Cir. (planning and programming com. 1999-2002), Am. Assn. Law Schs. Workshop on Family and Juvenile Law, Downtown Bklyn. Coun. Exec. Com.; trustee Practising Law Inst. (mem. com. on programs and pubs., 1998-, alt. mem. exec. com., 2001-). Home: 1045 Nine Acres Ln Mamaroneck NY 10543-4706 Office: Bklyn Law Sch 250 Joralemon St Brooklyn NY 11201-3700 Business E-Mail: joan.wexler@brooklaw.edu.

WEXLER, PATRICIA SUSAN, dermatologist, surgeon; b. 1951; MD, U. Libre de Bruxelles, Belgium, 1979. Cert. Am. Bd. Internal Medicine 1983, Am. Bd. Dermatology 1986. Intern Beth Israel Med. Ctr., NY, 1979—80, resident internal medicine NY, 1980—82, fellowship infectious disease NY, 1982—83, attending physician NY, Mt. Sinai Hosp., NY; private practice Wexler Dermatology, Manhattan, NY. Tchr. Beth Israel Med. Ctr. Dermatology Surgery Clinic; asst. clin. prof. Albert Einstein Sch. Medicine, Bronx, NY; cons. in the develop. of several skin care and make-up lines. Author medical rsch. publs. Recipient Am. Acad. Cosmetic Surgery award for Excellence in Cosmetic Surgery. Fellow: Am. Soc. Dermatologic Surgery. Office: 145 E 32nd St 7th Fl New York NY 10016-6055 Office Phone: 212-684-2626.

WEXLER, ROBERTA VAIL, volunteer; b. Windsor, Vt., Mar. 8, 1957; d. Edward Cowles and Emma Watson Vail; m. Robert Gregor Wexler, Apr. 28, 1979; children: Lisa, Gregory, Kevin. BA, Pa. State U., Univ. Pk., 1979. Coord. Down Syndrome Soc. R.I., Cranston, 1987—96; asst. dir. Ronald McDonald Ho., Providence, 1996—2002; dir. equipping ministry St. John's Episc. Ch., Barrington, RI, 2002—05; vol. program mgr. Home & Hospice Care R.I., Pawtucket, RI, 2005—. Administrator Myers Briggs Type Indicator. Avocations: crafts, needlecrafts. Home: 65 Seal Island Rd Bristol RI 02809

WEXLER, SANDRA M., artist, medical illustrator; b. NYC, Dec. 17, 1945; d. Irving and Sophie Engel; children: Jason, David. AA, Fashion Inst. Tech., 1965. Cert. medical asst. Balt., 1996. CMA Johns Hopkins Hosp., Lutherville, Md., 1996—97; CMA, clin. coord. Drs. Stanley Klatsky & Adam Basner, Balt., 1997—2000; CMA Dr. Eve Bruce, Lutherville, 2001—03, Dr. Seth Goldberg, Rockville, Md., 2004—. Exhibitions include Am. Inst. Architects Gallery, Sch. 33, Katzenstein Gallery, Slayton House Gallery, Women's Resource Ctr, Greater Balt. Med. Ctr., Gormley Gallery, Coll. Notre Dame, one-woman shows include Shainberg Gallery, Gallerie Elan, 2005, Represented in permanent collections The Art Resource, Balt., Susan Perrin Fine Art Balt., limited edit. greeting cards, Balt. Mus. Art Shop, Corporate Collections, Bloomingdales, NYC, Hyatt Regency, Balt., The Hammers Co., Greenbelt, Md., Wharton, Levin, Ehrmantraut, Klein & Nash, Bethesda, Md., Edward Friedman, CPA, Balt., Signature Mgmt., Balt., Levindale Hebrew Geriatric Ctr. & Hosp., Balt., Ampersand Inc., Reiserstown, Md., Penan & Scott, P.A., Rockville, Md., Martin, Junghans, Snyder & Bernstein, Balt., TCAG, Rockville, Potts & Potts, P.A., Balt., Royal Ins. Co., Balt., Cooper Wingard, Balt., Wiley, Rein & Fielding LLC, DC, Art Forms Gallery, Red Bank, NJ, A. Lee Dellon, MD, Balt., Arles Mgmt., Inc., NY, Gallerie Elan, Bethesda, Ellicott City, Md. Vol. surg. holding area Sinai Hosp., Balt., 1993—2000. Fellow, Vt. Studio Colony, 1990. Jewish. Avocations: art, reading, travel, cooking, photography.

WEXNER, ABIGAIL, apparel executive; m. Leslie H. Wexner. Dir. Ltd. Brands, Inc., Columbus, Ohio, 1997—. Past chair governing com. Columbus Found.; chair Ctr. for Child and Family Advocacy; mem. bd. trustees Children's Hosp., Inc, The Columbus Acad., The Wexner Ctr. Found.; founder, chair Columbus Coalition Against Family Violence. Named one of Top 200 Collectors, ARTnews Mag., 2004. Avocation: Collector of Modern and Contemporary Art; British Sporting Pictures. Office: Ltd Brands Inc Three Limited Pky PO Box 16000 Columbus OH 43216

WEYANT, ERIN KATHLEEN BEEGLE, athletic trainer, small business owner; b. Everett, Pa., June 2, 1981; d. Cliff and Jackie Beegle; m. Joe Weyant, June 30, 2004. BA, Gettysburg Coll., Pa., 2003. Cert. athletic trainer Nat. Athletic Trainers Assn. Bd. Cert., 2003, CPR ARC, Pa., 2005, First Aid instr. ARC, Pa., 2003, automated external defribillator ARC, Pa., 2003. Athletic trainer ProCare Health Sys., Inc., Everett, Pa., 2004—; co-owner Weyant Landscaping, New Paris, 2004—. Mem. Bedford United Meth. Ch., Pa., 1991—2006. Mem.: Nat. Athletic Trainers Assn. Methodist. Avocation: travel. Home: 508 East Penn St Bedford PA 15522 E-mail: erinweyant@yahoo.com.

WEYER, DIANNE SUE, health facility administrator; b. Anchorage, Aug. 15, 1954; d. Vernon H. and Myrtle M. Larson; m. Merlin D. Weyer; 1 child, Alison. BSW magna cum laude, Augustana Coll., Sioux Falls, S.D., 1976; MPA, U. S.D., Vermillion, 1989. LCSW 1996. Program dir. Threshold, Sioux Falls, SD, 1976—78; policy analyst S.D. Divsn. Law Enforcement Assistance, Pierre, SD; coord. youth projects Mountain Plains Youth Svcs. Coalition, Pierre, 1980—82; social worker S.D. Dept. Social Svcs., Pierre, 1983—85; child and adolescent program specialist S.D. Divsn. Mental Health, Pierre, 1985—96; mgr. Social Svcs. St. Mary's Healthcare Ctr., Pierre, 1996—2000, dir. outreach, 2002—. Social work adv. bd., adj. faculty Augustana Coll., Sioux Falls, 1977—79; interagy. coord. coun., state bd. mem. S.D. Dept. Edn., Pierre, 1989—96; state rep. for children and youth Nat. Assn. State Mental Health Program Dirs., Washington, 1985—96; chair S.D. Interagy. Coordination Network Coun., Pierre, 1991—96; social work adv. bd. Presentation Coll., Aberdeen, SD; adj. faculty Capital U., Pierre, 2000—06; exec. bd., past pres. S.D. Social Work Leaders in Health Care, Sioux Falls, 1999—2001. Healthcare com. Pierre C. of C., 1999—2003; tchr., confirmation guide Luth. Meml. Ch., Pierre, 1985—2001; bd. dirs. Missouri Shores Resource Ctr., Pierre, 1980—82; exec. bd. Healthy Cmtys./Healthy Youth, Pierre, 1999—. Recipient Spl. Recognition award, Capitol Area Counseling Svc., 2001, S.D. Family-Based Svcs. Assn., 1994, Outstanding Svc. award, S.D. Corrections Assn., 1990; grantee S.D. CASSP-Local Infrastructure Demonstration, Ctr. Mental Health Svcs., 1993—96, Rural Mental Health Demonstration, NIH, 1987—89, HHS Adminstrn., Children, Youth and Family Svcs., 1987—90. Mem.: NASW, S.D. Alliance for the Mentally Ill, S.D. Social Work Leadership in Healthcare (sec., v.p., pres. 1998—2001, Spl. Recognition award 1996), Nat. Social Work Leadership in Healthcare, Optimist Club (sec. bd. dirs. 2006). Home: 1217 Hilgers Dr Pierre SD 57501 Office: St Mary's Healthcare Ctr 801 E Sioux Pierre SD 57501 Personal E-mail: mdweyer@pic.midco.net. Business E-Mail: dianneweyer@catholichealth.net.

WEYGANDT, STACI, mathematics educator; d. William and Christel Quimby; m. Michael Weygandt, Aug. 9, 2003; 1 child, Cooper. BS in Math., Ea. Oreg. U., La Grande, Oreg., 1994, MEd, 1995. Tchr. math., specialist child devel. Five Oaks Mid. Sch., Beaverton, Oreg., 1995—96; tchr. math. Aloha (Oreg.) H.S., 1996—99, Southridge H.S., Beaverton, Oreg., 1999—, tchr. math., coach, 1999—. Mem.: Nat. Coun. Tchrs. Math. Office: Southridge High School 9625 SW 125th Beaverton OR 97008 Office Phone: 503-259-5400. Office Fax: 503-259-5425.

WEYMAN, SANDRA LEE, secondary school educator; b. Woodward, Pa., May 19, 1946; d. Harold George Ard and Beatrice Emma Stover; m. Michael Dane Weyman, Aug. 11, 1968; children: Michael Dane Jr., Brett Anthony, Kinsy Renee Weyman Lukasavage. BS, Mansfield U., Pa., 1976; MS, Wilkes U., Wilkes-Barre, Pa., 1991. English tchr. Lake-Lehman Jr. High, Lehman, Pa., 1988—93, Lake-Lehman Sr. High, 1993—. Advisor Knightlife sch. newspaper, Lehman, 1989—2003; mem. sr. project com. Lake-Lehman Jr.-Sr. HS, 2000—. Editor (lit. mags.) Sounds in the Knight, 1993—2003, Jr. High Lit. Mag., 2004—06. Mem. adv. bd. Back Mountain Meml. Libr., Dallas, Pa., 2003—; vol. Humanities Hwy. Clean-up, Lehman. Mem.: NEA, Nat. Coun. Tchrs. English, Pa. State Edn. Assn., Lake-Lehman Edn. Assn. Democrat. Avocations: reading, antiques, travel. Home: 30 Haddonfield Hills Dallas PA 18612 Office: Lake-Lehman Jr-Sr HS Box 38 Lehman PA 18627 Office Phone: 570-255-2882. Business E-Mail: weymans@lake-lehman.k12.pa.us.

WEYMOUTH, ELIZABETH (LALLY) GRAHAM, editor, columnist; children: Katharine, Pamela Bass. BA in Am. History and Lit. with honors, Harvard U. Reporter The Boston Globe, 1965—66, freelance writer, reporter, 1966—76; with Bedford Stuyvesant Restoration Corp. Senator Robert Kennedy, 1968—69; freelance journalist, contbg. editor numerous publs. including NY Times Mag., Esquire, Atlantic Monthly, Parade, LA Times, New York, 1977—83; contbg. editor LA Times, 1983—86, Washington Post, 1987—92; sr. editor, spl. diplomatic corr. Newsweek Mag., 1992—. Interviewer Washington Post, 1986—; mem. Coun. Fgn. Rels. Author: America in 1876: The Way We Were, 1976; editor, compiler Thomas Jefferson: The Man, His World, His Influence, 1973. Mem. Coun. Foreign Relations; mem. adv. com. Ctr. Strategic and Internat. Studies.

WEYMOUTH, TONI, social worker, writer, educator; b. L.A., May 17, 1945; d. William Morgan and Grace Lucille Allen; m. Ira Mark Smith, Jan. 15, 1972 (div. Jan. 1975); children: Jeffery Paul Smith, Jennifer Suzanne Smith; m. Donald Leroy Weymouth, Oct. 25, 1990. BA in Psychology, Calif. State U., Fresno, 1993, MSW, 1989; EdD in Sexology, Inst. Advanced Study of Human Sexuality, 1994. Social worker Big Bros./Big Sisters, Fresno, Calif., 1980-86, Fresno Mental Health Dept., 1989-91. Therapist, activist Parents of Prisoners Support Group, Fresno, 1995—; instr. Fresno Unified Sch. Dist., 1999—. Author: Outsiders Looking In: How to Keep from Going Crazy When Someone You Love Goes to Jail, 1998, Maiden Voyage: The Art of Romance, 1999. Activist, writer Amnesty Internat., Fresno, 1995—, Death Penalty Focus, Fresno, 1995—. Mem. NOW (v.p. 1981-83). Home: 4732 E Michigan Ave Fresno CA 93703-1653 Office: OLinc Pub PO Box 6012 Fresno CA 93703-6012

WHALEN, LORETTA THERESA, educational association administrator; b. Bklyn., May 21, 1940; d. William Michael and Loretta Margaret (Malone) Whalen; children: Ann Lindsay, Margaret Force. RN, St. Vincent's Hosp., N.Y.C., 1960; BSN, U. Pa., 1965; MA in Edn., Fordham U., 1971; cert. in sociology religion, Louvain U., Belgium, 1974; PhD in Global Edn., The Union Grad. Sch., 1994. Staff nurse Holy Family Hosp., Atlanta, 1967-69; Latin Am. communication dir. Med. Mission Sisters, Maracaibo, Venezuela, 1969-71; intensive care nurse St. Vincent's Hosp., N.Y.C., 1971-72; mem. ministry team Med. Mission Sisters, various locations, 1972-74, dir. communications Phila., 1974-77; asst. to exec. Interreligious Peace Colloquium, Washington, 1977; freelance writing, photography Ch. World Svc., N.Y.C., 1978-79; dir. Office Global Edn. Nat. Council Chs., N.Y.C., 1980-99. Co-author: Make a World of Difference: Creative Activities for Global Learning, 1990, Tales of the Heart: Affective Approaches to Global Education, 1991; mem. editorial bd., rev. editor Connections Mag., 1984-87; contbr. articles to profl. jours. Mem. Peace and Justice Commn., Archdiocese of Balt., 1985-89. Mem. Amnesty Internat., Bread for the World, NOW, World Wildlife Fund, Greenpeace, Sigma Theta Tau. Democrat. Roman Catholic. Avocations: photography, writing, racquetball, interior design, travel.

WHALEN, LUCILLE, retired academic administrator; b. L.A., July 26, 1925; d. Edward Cleveland and Mary Lucille (Perrault) W. BA in English, Immaculate Heart Coll., Los Angeles, 1949; MSLS, Catholic U. Am., 1955; DLS, Columbia U., 1965. Tchr. elem. and secondary parochial schs., L.A., Calif., 1945—52; tchr., libr. Conaty Meml. H.S., L.A., 1950—52; reference/serials librarian, instr. in library sci. Immaculate Heart Coll., 1955-58; dean Immaculate Heart Coll. (Sch. Library Sci.), 1958-60, 65-70; assoc. dean, prof. SUNY, Albany, 1971-78, 84-87, prof. Sch. Info. Sci. and Policy, 1979-87; dean grad. programs, libr. Immaculate Heart Coll. Ctr., Los Angeles, 1987-90; ref. libr. (part-time) Glendale Community Coll., 1990—. Dir. U.S. Office Edn. Instn. Author, editor (with others): Reference Services in Archives, 1986; author: Human Rights: A Reference Handbook, 1989; author: (with Nina Redman) Human Rights: A Reference Handbook, 2d edit., 1998. Mem. ACLU, Common Cause, Amnesty Internat. Democrat. Roman Catholic. Home: 320 S Gramercy Pl Apt 101 Los Angeles CA 90020-4542 Office: Glendale CC 1500 N Verdugo Rd Glendale CA 91208-2809 Personal E-mail: lucillew213@sbcglobal.net.

WHALEN, NORMA JEAN, special education educator; b. Albuquerque, N. Mex., Nov. 26, 1936; d. Ervin O'dell and Louise (Harcrow) Betts; m. Thomas Leo Whalen; children: Timothy, Patrick, Anna, Emily Wells, Kevin. BEd, Carson-Newman Coll., Jefferson City, Tenn., 1959. Cert. Tchr Secondary Edn. Fla., 1959, Tchr. - History Fla., 1959. Sec. sch. tchr. La Puente Jr. HS, La Puente, Calif., 1959—62; tchr. Umatilla (Fla.) Elem. Sch., 1969—70; substitute tchr. Lake County Schs., Leesburg, 1969—70, 1975—79; tchr., evening class Lee Adult H.S., Leesburg, Fla., 1979—80; elem. sch. tchr. St. Paul's Cath. Ch., Leesburg, Fla., 1980—81; spl. edn. tchr. Lee Opportunity Ctr. Lifestream Behavioral Ctr., Leeburg, Fla., 1990—2003. Cons. curriculum devel. St. Paul's Cath. Ch., Leesburg, 1986—89, tchr. 1st communion and confession classes, 1986—2003. Dir. learning resource ctr. St. Paul Cath. Ch., Leesbug, 1986—89; Bd. dirs. Melon Patch Theater, Leesburg, Fla., 1976—81. Recipient Best Supporting actress award, Melon Patch Theater, 1979, Disting. Svc. award, 1980, Svc. award, Lake County Bd. Edn., 1999, Nat. Assn. Mentally Ill Parents Org., 2000. Mem.: NEA, Leesburg Edn. Assn. Roman Catholic. Avocations: crocheting, reading, swimming, cooking, travel. Home: 1246 Estill Ave Lady Lake FL 32162-3732

WHALEY, BETH DOWLING, retired elementary school educator; b. Providence, R.I., Apr. 24, 1926; d. Henry Joseph and Agnes Josephine Dowling; m. Richard Charles Whaley, Apr. 28, 1951; children: Mark Michael, Richard Sean, Brian Timothy, Karen Marie. BEd, R.I. Coll. Edn., Providence, 1948; M of Adminstrn. and Reading, Loyola Coll., Balt., 1967. Classroom tchr. Anne Arundel County Pub. Schs., Annapolis, Md., reading resource tchr., vice prin.; cons. Anne Arundel County Bd. Edn., Annapolis, Md., 1987—88; ret., 1987. Founder Annapolis Fine Arts Festival, 1963, Md. Hall Story Theatre, 1981; founding bd. mem. Annapolis Arts Alliance, 2003; co-founder Md. Hall Creative Arts, 1979, Remember Inc., 1990. Author: (book) The Best I Can Be, 1988; editor-in-chief: book Annapolis Faces, 1965, For the Love of It, 1999. Vol. book recorder, narrator Md. Libr. Blind Handicapped; vol. St. Vincent dePaul Soc., St. Mary's Ch., Annapolis, Md. Named to Md. Hall Fame, 1985; recipient, County Exec. Citation, Carolyn Brady award, 1980, Arts Achievement award, Anne Arundel County Comm. Culture Arts, 1990, D.A.R. Cmty. Svc. award, 1994, Lifetime Achievement in Arts award, Arts Coun. Anne Arundel County, 2004. Mem.: Friends Md. Fed. Art, Annapolis Arts Alliance, Colonial Players (pres. 1962—64, 1991—92). Roman Catholic. Avocations: theater, reading, travel, walking, painting. Home: 31 Wilelinor Dr Edgewater MD 21037

WHAPLES, MIRIAM KARPILOW, music educator; b. Bridgeport, Conn., Dec. 16, 1929; d. Samuel and Mollie (Micklin) Karpilow; m. George Whaples, Aug. 24, 1949 (dec. May 1981); children: Tamar, Barbara, Jonathan (dec.) BA, Ind. U., 1950, MM, 1954, PhD, 1958. Instr. to asst. prof. We. Md. Coll., Westminster, 1960—66; asst. prof. U. Mass., Amherst, 1966—72, assoc. prof., 1972—79, prof., 1979—. Solo and ensemble performer on harpsichord Author: Bach Aria Index, 1971; editor: Carmina Burana: 20 Songs, 1975; contbr. articles to profl. jours Office: Dept Music and Dance Univ Mass Amherst MA 01003

WHARE, WANDA SNYDER, lawyer; b. Columbia, Pa., Nov. 5, 1959; m. James Robert Snyder, Nov. 14, 1987; 1 child, Eric James. BA, Franklin & Marshall Coll., 1981; JD, Dickinson Sch. Law, 1984. Bar: Pa. 1984. Asst. counsel Pa. Dept. Labor and Industry, Harrisburg, 1984-87; assoc. Gibbel, Kraybill & Hess, Lancaster, Pa., 1987-89; corp. counsel Irex Corp., Lancaster, 1990-98, chmn. awareness subcom., 1995-97, mem. continuous improvement con., 1995-97; corp. counsel Specialty Products & Insulation Co., Lancaster, 1998—2001; v.p., sec. Specialty Products Investments, Inc., Wilmington, Del., 1998—2001; asst. sec. Specialty Products & Insulation Co., Wilmington, Del., 2000—01; assoc. Nikolaus & Hohenadel LLP, 2001—. Class agt. Franklin and Marshall Coll., 1981—2005; parish-staff rels. com. First Meth. Ch., Lancaster, 1987—92, com. on status and role of women, 1989—95, chmn., 1992—95, adminstrv. team, 2001—04, chair lit. prodn. com., 2003; chmn. com. on status and role of women Ea. Pa. Conf. of United Meth. Ch., 1996—98. Mem.: Lancaster Bar Assn. (chair employment law sect. 2006). Office: Nikolaus & Hohenadel LLP 212 N Queen St Lancaster PA 17603 Office Phone: 717-299-3726. Business E-Mail: wwhare@n-hlaw.com.

WHARFF, JULIE DAWN, principal; d. Jearl and Ardythe Looper; children: Melissa Franca, Aaron. BA, Calif. State U. Stanislaus, Turlock, 1987; MEd, U. LaVerne, Calif., 2004. Cert. preliminary adminstrv. svcs. Calif. Commn. on Tchr. Credentialing, 2004, clear crosscultural lang. and academic devel. Calif. Commn. on Tchr. Credentialing, 1997, profl. clear multiple subjects tchg. Calif. Commn. on Tchr. Credentialing, 1990. Elem. tchr. Oakdale Joint Unified Sch. Dist., Calif., 1988—2004; vice prin. Shackelford Elem. Sch., Modesto, Calif., 2004—05; prin. Magnolia Elem. Sch., Oakdale, 2005—. Support provider Oakdale Joint Unified Sch. Dist., 1999—2004; tchr. in charge Magnolia Elem. Sch., 2002—04. Mem.: Assn. Calif. Sch. Adminstrs., ASCD, Stanislaus Reading Coun., AAUW. Avocations: reading, travel. Office: Magnolia Elem Sch 739 Magnolia St Oakdale CA 95361 Office Phone: 209-847-3056.

WHARTON, MARGARET AGNES, artist; b. Portsmouth, Va., 1943; BS, U. Md., 1965; MFA, Sch. of Art Inst. Chgo., 1975. Vis. artist Sch. of Art Inst. of Chgo., 1978, 89, 90, Columbia Coll., Chgo., 1994. One women shows include Phyllis Kind Gallery, Chgo., 1976, 80, 85, 88, 91, N.Y.C., 1977, 78, 79, 81, 83, 87, 90, Mus. Contemporary Art, Chgo. 1981-82, Laguna Gloria Art Mus., Austin, Tex., 1981-82, Zolla/Lieberman Gallery, Inc., Chgo., 1992, 94, Evanston Art Ctr., 1995, Rockford (Ill.) Coll., 2000, Jean Albano Gallery, Chgo., 1996, 97, 2000; exhibited in group shows at The Cinn. Art Mus., 1988-90, U. Wis. Art Mus., Milw., 1991, The Chgo. Cultural Ctr., 1992, Rockford (Ill.) Art Mus., 1994, and numerous others; represented in permanent collections Am. Med. Assn., Art Inst. of Chgo., Dallas Mus., Seattle Art Mus., State Ill. Collection, Whitney Mus. Am. Art, and others; comms. include Mus. of Contemporary Art, Chgo., 1985, Chgo. Pub. Libr., West Lawn Branch, Chgo., 1986. Founding mem. Artemesia Cooperative Gallery, Chgo., Ill. Recipient NEA grant 1979, 88, 93, Ill. Art Coun. grantee, 1999; recipient Visual Arts award, 1984. Home: 2147 S Halsted St Chicago IL 60608-4532

WHARTON, MARGARET MARY, nun, educator; b. San Diego, Calif., Sept. 2, 1948; d. John Philip Wharton and Mary Elizabeth Roundtree. BA in Math., Salve Regina Univ., Newport, R.I., 1976; MA in Math., Appalachian Univ., 1997. Cert. tchg. math/secondary N.C, 1994, R.I., 1982. Tchr. St. Anthony Sch., Guam, 1969—72, Cathedral Grade Sch., Guam, 1972—74, 1978—82, vice prin., 1973—74, Santa Barbara Sch., Guam, 1983—84, tchr., 1982—85; sub. tchr. Gaston/Charlotte-Mecklenburg Sch., 1990; tchr. St. Michael's Sch., Gastonia, NC, 1990—94, Acad. of Our Lady, Guam, 1976—78, 1985—88; tchg. asst. Appalachian State Univ., 1996; prof. Southern W.Va. Cmty. & Tech. Coll., 1998—2000, Marshall Univ., 2000—01, Shenandoah Univ., 2001—. Author: Tutor-Training Manual for Shenandoah University, 2003, Learning Styles, 2003, Study Skills, 2003, Math Anxiety, 2003; contbr. scientific papers; co-author: Collabrorative Learning Activties Manual, 2006, Introductory and Intermediate Algebra, 2006. Mem.: Kellogg Inst. Developmental Educators, Coll. Reading & Learning Assn., N.C. Coun. of Tchrs. of Math., Math. Assn. of Am., Nat. Assn. of Devel. Educators, Va. Assn. of Devel. Educators, Nat. Coun. of Tchrs. of Math. Democrat. Roman Cath. Avocations: astronomy, research, medicine. Office Phone: 540-542-6215. Business E-Mail: mwharton@su.edu.

WHARTON, MARY MERCHANT, secondary school educator; b. Martinsburg, W.Va., Nov. 13, 1942; d. Oliver Phillipps and Mary Belle (Maddox) Merchant; m. Stewart Boyd Wharton Jr., Sept. 28, 1963; children: Stewart B. III, Mary Ella Wharton Cogle. BA in Secondary Edn., Shepherd Coll., 1965, BA in Elem. Edn., 1975. Cert. tchr., W.Va. Tchr. 1st and 2d grade Middleway (W.Va.) Elem. Sch., 1967-72; tchr. 1st grade South Jefferson Elem. Sch., Charles Town, W.Va., 1972-77, tchr. 2d grade, 1977-83; tchr. 3d grade Shepherdstown (W. Va.) Elem., 1983-85, South Jefferson Elem. Sch., Charles Town, W.Va., 1985-90; tchr. lang. Arts 6th grade Blackville (S.C.) Mid. Sch., 1990-93, tchr. lang. arts 7th grade, 1991-93. Den mother troop 42, Cub Scouts Am., Charles Town, 1973-75; leader troop 595, Girl Scouts U.S.A., Charles Town, 1974-79, 2000—; leader 4-H Club, Charles Town, 1985-91, 2000; active PTA; tchr. spl. edn. Sunday sch. Meth. Ch., 1985-91, leader Asbury Children's Coun., 1983-85; Sunday sch. Meth. Ch., Blackville, S.C., 1995-00; membership com. Bolivar United Meth. Ch., 2004—. Mem. NEA, S.C. Edn. Assn., Blackville Edn. Assn., Blackville County Edn. Assn., Jefferson County Edn. Assn., Charlestown Jaycee-ettes (pres. 1968-70, Jaycee-ette of Yr. award 1969), UDC (W.Va. divsn. pres. 1983-1998, page 1987—, recorder of crosses 1977-90, historian 1990-92, 1st v.p. 1996-1998, 2001-03, pres. 2003—), Real Great Granddaus. Club (v.p. W.Va. divsn. 1989-90), Tops Club (Shenandoah Junction, W.Va., corr. com. 1987), DAR (chmn. edn., chair Indian and history 2001—), Am. Legion Aux. Post #91, Sigma Sigma Sigma. Democrat. Avocations: sewing, stitchery, travel, reading. Home: 144 Rural Retreat Dr Charles Town WV 25414-4103

WHATLEY, YVONNE MARIE TRAMONTANA, secondary school educator; b. Tampa, Fla., Sept. 9, 1952; d. Robert Scaffidi and Violet Rodriguez Tramontana; m. Donald Carey Whatley; children: Darin Seth, Erin Marie Griffith. BA in Biology, U. S. Fla., Tampa, 1976. Sci. tchr. Hudson (Fla.) HS, 1976—, sci. dept. head, 1996—. Tchr. Gateway Christian Ctr. Assembly of God, Tampa, 1999—2006. Republican. Pentecostal. Office: Hudson HS 14410 Cobra Way Hudson FL 34669 Office Phone: 727-774-4200.

WHEALEY, LOIS DEIMEL, humanities scholar; b. N.Y.C., June 20, 1932; d. Edgar Bertram Deimel and Lois Elizabeth (Hatch) Washburn; m. Robert Howard Whealey, July 2, 1954; children: Richard William, David John, Alice Ann. BA in History, Stanford U., 1951; MA in Edn., U. Mich., 1955; MA in Polit. Sci., Ohio U., 1975. Tchr. 5th grade Swayne Sch., Owyhee, Nev., 1952-53; tchr. 7th grade Ft. Knox (Ky.) Dependent's Sch., 1955-56; tchr. adult basic edn. USAF, Oxford, 1956-57; tchr. 6th grade Amerman Sch., Northville, Mich., 1957-58; tchr. 8th grade English, social studies Slauson Jr. High Sch., Ann Arbor, Mich., 1958-59; adminstrv. asst. humanities conf. Ohio U., Athens, 1974-76, 83. Part-time instr. Ohio U., Athens, 1966-68, 75, VISTA with Rural Action, 1996-98. Contbr. articles to profl. jours. Mem. Athens County Regional Planning Commn., 1974—78, treas., 1976—78; mem. Ohio coord. com. Internat. Women's Yr., 1977; v.p. Black Diamond Girl Scout Coun., 1980—86; chair New Day for Equal Rights Amendment, 1982; mem. Athens City Bd. Edn., 1984—90, v.p., 1984, pres., 1985; mem. Tri-County Vocat. Sch. Bd., Nelsonville, Ohio, 1984—90, v.p., 1988—89; mem. adv. com. Ohio River Valley Water Sanitation Commn., 1986—95; Ohio outreach liaison Nat. Town Meeting for Sustainable Am., 1999; bd. dirs. Ohio Environ. Coun., 1984—90, sec., 1986—90; bd. dirs. Ohio Alliance for Environ., 1994—98, v.p., 1998; bd. dirs. Organize Ohio, 1999—, bd. pres., 2001—; bd. dirs. Ohio Women, Inc., 1995—, sec., 1997—; bd. dirs. Unitarian Universalist Svc. Com., 2001—03, Ohio Meadville Dist. Unitarian-Universalist Assn., 1975—81; co-chair nat. vol. network Unitarian Universalist Svc. Com., 2003—05. Recipient Unsung Unitarian Universalist award Ohio-Meadville Dist. Unitarian Universalist Assn., 1984, Thanks badge Black Diamond Girl Scout Coun., 1986, How-to award Ednl. Press Assn. Am., 1990, Donna Chen Women's Equity award Ohio U., 1994, Cmty. Svc. award Athens County Cmty. Svcs. Coun., 1998, award for an individual contbn. over a lifetime Ohio Alliance for Environment, 2002; named Woman of Achievement, Black Diamond Girl Scout Coun., 1987, Peacemaker Appalachian Peace and Justice Network, 1998, Outstanding Feminist, Athens Herstory Celebration, 2002. Mem. AAUW (pres. Athens br. 1969-70, 89-90, 93-2001, AAUW/Ohio bd. 1995-2004), LWV (pres. 1975-77), Phi Lambda Theta, Phi Kappa Phi. Democrat. Avocations: classical music, genealogy. Home: 14 Oak St Athens OH 45701-2605

WHEAT, MARGARET ANN, marriage and family therapist; d. Thomas H. and Matilda K. Wheat; life ptnr. Thomas Scott McIntyre; children: Thomas Jigme, Caryn Yeshe, Rigzin Dorje, Alexander Miles, Marcus John, Tara Alice. BS in Orgnl. Behavior, U. San Francisco, 1992, MS in Counseling Psychology, 1994. Lic. marriage family therapist Bd. Behavioral Scs., Calif., 1998. Child protective svcs. -emergency response team Mendocino County, Ukiah, Calif., 1997—2000; clin. care mgr. Managed Health Network, Health Net, San Rafael, Calif., 2000—05; therapist Sonoma County, Santa Rosa, Calif., 2006—. Singer (wine country opera) from opera to rock and roll. Corp. sec. Wine Country Opera, Santa Rosa, Calif., 1994—2005. Mem.: Am. Assn. of Marriage Family Therapists, Calif. Assn. of Marriage Family Therapists. Office Phone: 707-321-2640.

WHEAT, SHEREE RENEE, elementary school educator; d. Jesse Robert and Irene Louise Pinkerton; children: Harold Christopher, Stephen Patrick, Brittany Alyce. BSc in Social Scis., Secondary Edn., U. Tenn., 1980; M in Ednl. Leadership, Tenn. Tech. U., 2002. Cert. Elem. Edn. Tchr. U. Tenn., Knoxville, 1982, in English Edn. U. Tenn., Knoxville, 1983, U. Tenn., Knoxville, 2001, Ednl. Specialist Tenn. Tech. U., 2003. Tchr. Chattanooga Pub. Schs., 1990—94, elem. adv. com. mem.; sci. tchr., math., lang. arts tchr. Hamilton County Schs., Chattanooga, 1996—, sci. coord.; flight dir. rep. Chattanooga pub. schs. U. Tenn., 1994—96. Workshop attendee in field, 1992—2003. Vol. homeless tutoring program. NEH fellowship, Trinity Coll., 1996, U. Va., Charlottesville, 2000, Tenn. Space grant, Tenn. Tchrs. Assn., Vanderbilt U., 2005. Mem.: Internat. Reading Assn., Assn. Supervision and Curriculum Devel., Tenn. Sci. Tchrs. Assn. (3d dist. exec. com. sci. rep., exec. bd. mem.), Nat. Sci. Tchrs. Assn., Chattanooga Edn. Assn., Tenn. Edn. Assn., Phi Lambda Theta, Alpha Kappa Alpha. Avocations: reading, writing, acting, singing, computers.

WHEATLEY, DEBORAH A., music educator; b. Mt. Clemens, Mich., Oct. 28, 1954; d. Ernest William Wheatley and Joanne Smith. AA with honors, Miami-Dade CC, 1975; BA magna cum laude, U. Ctrl. Fla., 1978; grad., US Army Element Sch. Music, 1984. Music tchr. Lecanto (Fla.) Primary, 1978—81; band dir. Lecanto Mid. Sch., 1981—83, fine arts tchr., 1986—96, band dir., 1996—; with signal corps band U.S. Army Elem. Sch. Music, Ft. Gordon, Ga., 1984; summer duty U.S. Army, 1986—92. With Signal Corps Band U.S. Army, 1984—86. Recipient U.S. Army Commendation medal, 1986. Republican. Avocations: running, promoting healthy lifestyle to middle school students. Home: 1801 Silverwood St Inverness FL 34453 Office: Lecanto Mid Sch 3800 W Educational Path Lecanto FL 34461 Office Phone: 352-746-2050. E-mail: debwheat@mailstation.com.

WHEATLEY, KATHERINE HOLBROOK, federal official, lawyer; AB, Harvard, 1976, JD, 1979. Asst. to assoc. gen. counsel Fed Res. Bd., Washington. Office: Fed Res Bd 20th And C Sts NW Washington DC 20551-0001

WHEATON, MARILYN, musician; b. Warren, Ohio, Feb. 1, 1933; d. Russell and Donabelle Irene Donehue; m. Warren Randall Wheaton, June 20, 1953; 1 child, Janean Renee Vaupel-Wilson. BS in Music Edn. cum laude, Kent State U., 1955. Cert. Yamaha music instr. Pvt. piano and organ tchr., Ohio and Ariz., 1950—; profl. pianist, organist, accompanist, 1946—; elem. music supr. Austintown Pub. Schs., Youngstown, Ohio, 1955-61. Founder, dir. Potter's Clay Christian singing group, Phoenix, 1981-85; choir dir., organist, pianist at various chs., Ohio and Ariz., 1942—; rep. for elem. music texts and programs Mahoning County Schs., Youngstown, 1959-60; tchr., organizer student trips to numerous concerts; tchr., dir. choirs and soloists for dist. and state competitions, 1955—. Composer (poems to music) Seven Last Words of Christ, also anthems, introits, reponses; arranges music for beginning and handicapped students. Dir., accompanist Terry's Variety Show, Austintown, 1951, Potter's Clay, 1980-85; pianist at various sr. citizens' groups Kent State

U. and Youngstown U. scholar, 1951-55. Mem. Music Tchrs. Nat. Assn., Delta Omicron (life, charter mem., pres. Delta Upsilon chpt.). Avocations: travel, camping, reading, walking, piano recitals. Home and Office: 3245 W Yucca St Phoenix AZ 85029-4133

WHEELAN, BELLE S., educational association administrator; 1 child, Reginald. BA in Psychology and Sociology, Trinity U.; MA in Devel./Ednl. Psychology, La. State U.; D in Ednl. Adminstrn., U. Tex., 1984. Asst. prof. psychology, dir. devel. edn., dir. acad. support svcs. San Antonio Coll., 1974—87; dean student svcs. Thomas Nelson C.C., Hampton, Va., 1987—89; provost Tidewater C.C., Portsmouth, Va., 1989—92; pres. Ctrl. Va. C.C., 1992, No. Va. C.C., 1998—2001; sec. of edn. Commonwealth of Va., Richmond, 2002—05; pres. Commn. on Colls. So. Assn. for Colls. and Schs., Decatur, Ga., 2005—. Mem. Am. Coll. Testing Bd., Nat. Commn. on NAEP 12th Grade Assessment and Reporting, 2003—. Recipient Outstanding Alumnus award, Trinity U., 2002, Strong Men and Women award, 2003. Mem.: Nat. Coun. on Black Am. Affairs (pres. roundtable). Office: Commn on Colls So Assn Colls and Schs 1866 Southern Lane Decatur GA 30033 Office Phone: 404-679-4512. Business E-Mail: belle.wheelan@sacscoc.org.

WHEELAND, JOYCE A., information technology executive; m. John Wheeland; 1 child, Nicole. Chmn., CEO Computer Cons. Am., Inc., Southfield, Mich. Supporter Nat. Football League's Detroit Lions' Charities, Juvenile Diabetes Found., Detroit, 2000. Mem.: Nat. Assn. Computer Consulting Businesses (founding mem. Open Door Found.). Office: Computer Cons Am Inc Ste 601 24901 Northwestern Hwy Southfield MI 48075

WHEELER, BARBARA J., management consultant; b. Coral Gables, Fla., June 1, 1960; d. Robert Henry and Mary Jean (Seiler) W. BA, Miami U., 1982. Commd. 2nd lt. USAF, 1984, advanced through grades to capt., 1988, chief command control comm., def. sect., XIDB project mgr., intelligence agency; resigned, 1992; prin. cons. Litton-PRC, McLean, Va., 1994-97; dir. TRW Mgmt. Cons., Reston, Va., 1998-2000; strategic and program mgmt. counsulting, writer Montgomery Village, Md., 2000—. Mem. Project Mgmt. Inst. (cert.). Avocations: reading, lecturing, travel, ice skating.

WHEELER, ELIZABETH DARRACOTT, volunteer; b. Richmond, Va., July 14, 1917; d. Clements Cawwin and Dorothy Hartung Darracott; m. Charles Horatio Wheeler, III, July 9, 1940 (dec. Sept. 16, 2000); children: Charles Horatio IV, Anne Wheeler Stratton, William Darracott. BA, U. Richmond, 1938. Cert. tchr. 1938. Instr., Varina, Va., 1938—40. Author: (book) Sir John Dodderidge, Celebrated Barrister of Britain, 1555-1628, 1992, Ten Remarkable Women of the Tudor Courts and Their Influence in Founding the New World, 1530-1630, 2000. Pres., sr. bd. mem. Va. Home, Richmond, 1961—62, pres., jr. bd. dirs., 1946—56; residential col. Richmond Area Cmty. Campaign, Richmond, 1957—57; tchr., mem. Grace Covenant Presbyn. Ch., Richmond, 1918—2002; mem., patriotic svc. com. Colonial Dames of Am., Richmond, 1944—64. Mem.: The Tuckahoe Woman's Club, The Woman's Club.

WHEELER, GENEVIEVE STUTES, library administrator, educator; b. Duson, La., Dec. 13, 1937; d. Noah and Natalie (Falcon) Stutes; m. Richard Anthony Musemeche, Feb. 3, 1956 (div. 1975); children— Sabrina Marie Musemeche Beckham, Susan Ann Lowrie; m. 2d, Berle Steele Wheeler, July 1, 1978. B.A., U. Southwest La., Lafayette, 1959; M.S. in Library Sci., La. State U., Baton Rouge, 1970. Cert. tchr. Tchr. Iberia Schs., New Iberia, La., 1959-60; sch. librarian Lafayette Parish Sch., 1960-69; tchr., librarian La. State Sch. Deaf, Baton Rouge, 1970-71; librarian East Baton Rouge System, 1971-78; library adminstr. St. Bernard Community Coll., Chalmette, La., 1978—, cons., 1978-92; dir. libr. sci. Nunez Community Coll., Chalmette, 1992—; cons. library La. State Dept. Edn., Baton Rouge, 1975-76. Author tchr. guides, 1975, 77. Co-organizer, co-sponsor Project LesEnfants, 1975. Mem. Am. Library Assn., Am. Assn. Jr. and Community Colls., La. Assn. Sch. Librarians (pres. 1982-83), ALA, La. Assn. Sch. Execs., La. Library Assn., Gov.'s Conf. Libraries, Delta Kappa Gamma (v.p. Baton Rouge 1975-76), Phi Kappa Phi. Home: 913 Cross Gates Blvd Slidell LA 70461-3919 Office: Nunez CC 3700 La Fontaine St Chalmette LA 70043-1249

WHEELER, GERALDINE HARTSHORN, historian, writer; b. Pomona, Calif., Feb. 5, 1919; d. Albion True and Beatrice Osa (Barnes) Hartshorn; m. Lloyd Franklyn Wheeler, Dec. 2, 1938 (dec. Mar. 1996); children: Russell Lloyd, Robert Gerald. AA, Santa Barbara (Calif.) C.C., 1950's. Co-owner Atheling's, Santa Barbara, Calif., 1971-76, Pomona, 1976-90; chmn. bd. trustees Atheling Heritage Trust, Claremont, Calif., 1994—. Pub., editor: mag. Atheling's, 1974—75, newsletter Grand Priory of America Order of St. Lazarus, 1974—86; editor: St. Margaret's Jour., 1975—; author: (essays) A World Full in 1891, 1975—, President John Adams - A Profile, 1975—, Ralph Waldo Emerson--A Profile, 1975, The Many Masks of Communism, 1975, A Tale of St. Nicholas, 1995, Post Cards and Postal Cards, 1996, Pocahontas Kinships, 1996. Vol. PTA, Fontana and Santa Barbara, 1945-60; mem. various coms. and choir First Congl. Ch., Santa Barbara, 1952-72; leader Cub Scouts Am., Santa Barbara, 1953-56; grey lady unit chmn. Santa Barbara chpt.-ARC, 1958-62; women's project bd. v.p., activities chmn., active various coms. Santa Barbara Hist. Soc., 1960-74; exec. sec. 1960 Nixon for Pres. Campaign, Santa Barbara, 1960; mem. spkrs. bur. Nixon for Gov. Campaign, Santa Barbara, 1962; mem. Rep. state ctrl. com. State of Calif., 1962-64; blitz chmn. Rockefeller for Pres. Campaign, Santa Barbara, 1964; coord. vol. svcs. Office of Civil Def., City of Santa Barbara, 1965-76; coord. tv series on earthquakes Sta. KEYT, Office of Civil Def., Santa Barbara, 1968; bd. dirs. Calif. Ctrl. Coast Area, U.S.O., 1968-76, treas. bd., 1970-76; supporter Vis. Nurses and Hospice Assn., 1994—; others. Decorated Dame of Grace, Mil. and Hospitaller Order of St. Lazarus of Jerusalem, Cert. of Merit, 1973, The Alan Weaver Hazelton award; recipient Cert. of Merit, Santa Barbara Jr. Coll., 1954-55, Medal of Appreciation SAR, 1972, Cert. of Award Nat. Soc. Daus. of Founders and Patriots of Am., 1977. Mem. Acad. Polit. Sci., Calif. Hist. Soc., New Eng. Hist. and Geneal. Soc., The Pomona Ebell (pres. 1998-2000), Wilson Ctr. Assocs., Smithsonian Assocs., Nat. Trust for Hist. Preservation, Am. Farmland Trust, Nat. Woman's History Mus., Nat. Arbor Day Found., Pomona Valley Hist. Soc., La Verne Hist. Soc., La Salle County Hist. Soc., Nat. Wildlife Fedn., Colonial Williamsburg Found., The Postcard Soc. (founder), Musicians Club Pomona Valley, Shakespeare Club Pomona Valley, Nat. Soc. DAR (past regent chpts.), Calif. Huguenot Soc., Nat. Soc. Daus. Founders and Patriots (past nat. officer, orgn. pres. So. Calif. chpt.), Colonial Dames Am. (orgn. pres. chpt. XX), Nat. Soc. Daus. Colonial Wars (state officer), Nat. Soc. Women Desc. Ancient and Honorable Artillery Co. (past nat. chaplain and state officer), Soc. Mayflower Desc. (past colony gov.), Nat. Soc. Dames of the Ct. of Honor, Nat. Soc. New Eng. Women, Hereditary Order Desc. Colonial Govs. (past nat. officer), Soc. Desc. Most Noble Order of the Garter, Ams. Armorial Ancestry, Ams. Royal Descent, Colonial Order of the Crown, The Plantagenet Soc., Nat. Soc. Magna Charta Dames, Order of the Crown of Charlemagne in USA, Nat. Soc. Ams. Royal Descent, Nat. Soc. Desc. Early Quakers (founding nat. clk.), Nat. Guild St. Margaret of Scotland (founder), Nat. Gavel Club, Mt. Vernon Ladies' Assn., Order of the Merovingian Dynasty. Republican. Avocations: book collecting, reading, genealogy, classical music, needlecrafts. Home: 1047 E Baseline Rd Claremont CA 91711-1577

WHEELER, GWEN, medical, surgical, and critical care nurse; b. Bogalusa, La., Oct. 5, 1949; d. John David and Marie (Taylor) Easterling; m. Thomas D. Wheeler, July 20, 1968; children: Thomas D. Jr., Daniel Blair. AD, S.W. Miss. Jr. Coll., Summit, 1986; student, St. Josephs Coll., 1990—95, U. So. Miss., 1995—98; M in Nursing Sci., Southeastern La. U., 2000. Cert. critical care nurse, ACLS, advance trauma life support system, RN, cert. adult nurse practitioner. Emergency rm. staff nurse Riverside Med. Ctr., Franklinton, La., 1992, nursing supr., 1992-94, staff nurse emergency room, 1998—2001; ICU staff nurse Bogalusa (La.) Cmty. Med. Ctr., Franklinton, La., 1994—98; adult nurse practitioner Franklinton Rural Health Clinic, 2001—. Mem. AACN, La. Nursing Assn., Emergency Nurses Assn. Office: FRHC 2004 S Marvin Magee Dr Franklinton LA 70438 Office Phone: 985-839-3555.

WHEELER, JANE FRANCES, protective services official; b. McAlester, Okla. Dir. Consumer Protection, Oklahoma City, 1984—. Office: Consumer Protection Atty Gen 313 NE 21st St Oklahoma City OK 73105

WHEELER, JANET MARILYN, retired special education educator; d. Ezra Lansing Wheeler and Muriel Celeste Fox. Diploma in nursing, Genesee Hosp. Sch. Nursing, Rochester, NY, 1955; MS in Counseling, No. Ariz. U., Flagstaff, 1958; BS in Edn., U. Tenn., Knoxville, 1966. RN NY. Pediat. nurse Lenox Hill Hosp., NYC, 1956—58; staff nurse Albany Med. Ctr., NY, 1958—60; med. and contagion nurse U. Rochester Med. Ctr., 1961—70; spl. edn. tchr. Avondale Elem. Sch., Ariz., 1972—94; ret. Home: 10905 W Santa Fe Dr Sun City AZ 85351-2519

WHEELER, KATHERINE WELLS, retired state legislator; b. St. Louis, Feb. 8, 1940; d. Benjamin Harris and Katherine (Gladney) Wells; m. Douglas Lanphier Wheeler, June 13, 1964; children: Katherine Gladney, Lucille Lanphier BA, Smith Coll., 1961; MA, Washington U., St. Louis, 1966. Founder auction N.H. Pub. TV, Durham, 1973-76; pub. mem. N.H. Pub. Broadcasting Coun., Durham, 1975-80; founding mem. bd. govs. N.H. Pub. TV, 1980-88; elected N.H. Ho. of Reps., Concord, 1988, 90, 92,94; mem. N.H. Senate, 1966—98, 1998—2000, 2000—02, chmn. health & human svcs. com. Coord. internat. visitors program N.J. Coun. World Affairs, 1981-95. Bd. dirs. Planned Parenthood No. New England, 1989-95, Gt. Bay Svcs., Newington, N.H., 1989-97, Behavioral Health and Devel. Svcs. Strafford County, Inc., 1991—; vice chairperson Strafford County Legis. Del., 1993-94; active Commn. on Health, Human Svcs. and Elderly Affairs N.H. Ho. of Reps., Concord, 1988-96; bd. dirs. N.H. Pub. Health Assn., 1996—, pres., 2003--; bd. dirs. NAMI N.H., 2002--, NARAL N.H. Found., 1998-- Named Woman of Yr., Union Leader Newspaper, 1984, Citizen of Yr., Homemakers of Strafford County, 1990, N.H. sect. NASW, 1993, Legislator of Yr., N.H. Nurses Assn., 1996, N.H. Acad. Pediat., 1996; recipient Elizabeth Campbell Outstanding Pub. TV Vol. award Nat. Friends Pub. Broadcasting, 1984, Meritorious Svc. award N.H. Women's Lobby, 1992, Dist. Contbn. award N.H. Psychol. Orgn., Inc., 1994, Cert. of Achievement for Outstanding Legis. Leadership N.H. Citizen Action, 1994; Fleming fellow Leadership Inst., Ctr. for Policy Alternatives, Washington, 1997-98. Mem. AAUW, LWV, Am. Assn. Ret. Persons, Order of Women Legislators, N.H. Smith Coll. Club (v.p. 1974-76, pres. 1976-78, v.p. class of 1961, 1991-96), N.H. Assn. Social Workers (Legislator of Yr. 1993), N.H. Psychol. Orgn. Inc. (Disting. Contbn. award 1994). Democrat. Mem. United Ch. of Christ. Home and Office: 27 Mill Rd Durham NH 03824-3006

WHEELER, KATHRYN S., editor; b. Grosse Ile, Mich. d. Emich Duane and Anna K. Solms; m. William Donald Wheeler, Sept. 23, 1989. BA, Hope Coll., 1976; student, U. Mont., 1981. Editor Herman Miller Inc., Zeeland, Mich., 1977-80; copywriter Exclamation Point Advertising, Billings, Mont., 1981-84; sr. copywriter Aves Advertising, Grand Rapids, Mich., 1985-89; staff writer David Perkins & Assocs., Grand Rapids, 1990-94; editor School Zone Publishing, Grand Rapids, 1994-95; sr. editor Instructional Fair Group (now McGraw-Hill Children's Pub.), Grand Rapids, 1998—. Cons. in ednl. writing, 1994—, adj. prof. Grand Valley State U., 1986-90. Editor: ednl. CD and book series; author: Tunnel 2000, 1999, The Suspicious Stranger, 1999, No Room for Neighbors, 1999, Finders Keepers, 2000, Patty Saves the Day, 2001, Patriotic Traditions, 2002. Advertising cons. Sara Smolenski Campaign, 1996, bd. mem. Carol Irons Com., 1989. Grantee Mich. Coun. for the Arts, 1988. Mem. Soc. Children's Book Writers and Illustrators. Democrat. Episcopalian.

WHEELER, SUSAN, poet, educator; b. Pitts., July 16, 1955; d. Ray Barton and Grace Louise (Skeen) W.; m. Philip Furmanski, Aug. 23, 1991; stepchildren: Lisa, Jonathan. BA in Lit., Bennington Coll., 1977; postgrad., U. Chgo., 1979-81. Dir. pub. programs and info. Art Inst. Chgo., 1981-85; freelance cons., editor and writer, 1983-91; dir. pub. affairs arts and sci. NYU, 1989-95. CETA writer and instr. Vt. Coun. on the Arts, 1977-78; instr. liberal arts Sch. of Art Inst. Chgo., 1984-85; instr. Poets in Pub. Svc., NYC, 1989-91; instr. New Sch. for Social Rsch., NYC, 1994—; Thornton writer-in-residence Lynchburg Coll., 1995; lectr. Rutgers U., 1995-96, NYU, 1997-98, U. Iowa Writers Workshop, 2000, Princeton U., 1999—, Columbia U., 2004. Author: (poetry collections) Bag o' Diamonds, 1993 (Poetry Soc. Am. Norma Farber 1st Book award 1994), (novels) Smokes, 1998 (Four Way Books award 1998), Source Codes, 2001, Ledger, 2005, The Record Palace, 2005; author numerous poems; contbr. articles to profl. jours. Recipient Grolier award for poetry, 1987, Pushcart prize 1994, 2001; Vt. Coun. Arts grantee, 1978-79, Fund for Poetry grantee, 1990; N.Y. Found. for Arts fellow, 1993-95, 97-99, John Simon Guggenheim Found. fellow, 1999-2000, Bynner prize Am. Acad. of Arts and Letters, 2002. Mem. PEN, Poetry Soc. Am., Poetry Project at St. Mark's Ch., Poets and Writers, Authors Guild. Office: Burnes And Clegg Inc 136 E 57th St Fl 18 New York NY 10022-2923 Office Phone: 212-331-9880.

WHEELER, SUSIE WEEMS, retired school system administrator; b. Cassville, Ga., Feb. 24, 1917; d. Percy Weems and Cora (Smith) Weems-Canty; m. Dan W. Wheeler Sr., June 7, 1941; 1 child, Dan Jr. BS, Fort Valley (Ga.) State U., 1945; MEd, Atlanta U., 1947, EdD, 1978; postgrad., U. Ky., 1959-60; EdS, U. Ga., 1977. Tchr. Bartow County Schs., Cartersville (Ga.) City Schs., 1938-44, Jeanes supr., 1946-58; supr., curriculum dir. Paulding Sch. Sys.-Stephens Sch., Calhoun City, 1958-64; summer sch. tchr. Atlanta U., 1961-63; curriculum dir. Bartow County Schs., 1963-79; ret., 1979. Pres., co-owner Wheeler-Morris Svc. Ctr., 1990—; mem. Ga. Commn. on Student Fin., 1985-95. Coord. Noble Hill-Wheeler Meml. Ctr. Project, 1983—. Recipient Oscar W. Canty Cmty. Svc. award, 1991, Woman in History award Fedn. Bus. and Profl. Women, 1995, New Frontiers Cmty. Svc. award, 1997, Outstanding Achievement for Preserving Georgia Hist., 2000, Life Achievement award Etowah Valley Hist. Soc., 2005; recognized for dedicated svc. on behalf of Bartow County Citizens Comm. Clarence Brown, 2003; named one of Women of Excellence, Star of the Past Bartow Women at Work, 2003. Mem. AAUW (v.p. membership 1989-91, Ga. Achievement award 1993, Edn. Found. award Cartersville-Bartow br.), Ga. Assn. Curriculum and Supervision (pres.-elect 1973-74, pres. 1974-75, Johnnye V. Cox award 1975), Delta Sigma Theta (pres. Rome alumnae chpt. 1978-80, mem. nat. bd. 1984, planning com. 1988—, Dynamic Delta award 1967, 78, Grand Chpt. cert. recognition 2002, recognition 50 plus years, Cartersville Rotary Club (Jean Harris award, 2004), Delta Sigma Theta Sorority, Inc., 2002), Ga. Jeanes Assn. (pres. 1968-70), Delta Kappa Gamma. Home: 105 Fite St Cartersville GA 30120-3410

WHEELER-HAPP, DARRA ANNE, secondary school educator; b. Bklyn., Apr. 5, 1961; d. Dennis Francis and Florence Elizabeth Wheeler; m. Gary Happ, Feb. 5, 1994; children: Jackson, Garrett. BS in Edn., SUNY, Cortland, 1983; M in Edn., SUNY, New Paltz, 1991. Tchr. lang. arts grades 7-8 Circleville (N.Y.) Mid. Sch., 1986—87; tchr. English grade 7 Shaker Jr. H.S., Latham, NY, 1986—87; tchr. grade 5 Roe-Jan Elem., Hillsdale, NY, 1991—98; compensatory edn. educator Taconic Hills Sch. Dist., Hillsdale, 1998—. Author: (newspaper column) Answers from the Teacher, 1999—. Mem.: NEA. Avocations: singing and playing guitar, bicycling, kayaking, walking.

WHEELER RUSSELL, GWENDOLYN KAY, education educator; b. Mt. Vernon, Ohio, Aug. 31, 1961; d. Windell and Cynthia Kay (Guthmann) Wheeler; m. Justin Gorman Russell, July 4, 1991; children: Cameron, Tsinnijinnie, Justin Jr. BS, Ea. Mich. U., Ypsilanti, 1983; MS, No. Ariz. U., Flagstaff, 1988; EdD, U. Cin., Cinn., 1996. Cert. sch. psychologist, spl. edn. tchr. and prin. Tchr. Harold Lewis Sch., Marysville, Ohio, 1984-85; tchr. Chinle Valley Sch., Chinle, Ariz., 1985-86, Chinle Pub. Sch., Chinle, 1986-89; program coord. No. Ariz. U. Inst. for Human Devel., Flagstaff, 1989-91; rsch. assoc. U. Cin., 1992-97; asst. prof. U. Tenn., Martin, 1997-98; dir., asst. prof. Mesa State Coll., Grand Junciton, Colo., 1998—2003; sch. psychologist Delta County Schs., Colo., 2003—. Chair Multicultural Cmty. Concerns, DEC/Coun. for Exceptional Children, 1997—. Co-author: (jour.) Multiple Voices, 1995; co-author: (2 book chpts.) 1997; asst. editor: (newsletter) 1995-96. V.p. Ohio Coun. for Exceptional Children/Divsn. for Culturally & Linguistically Diverse Exceptional Learners, pres.-elect, 1996-97; program chair Parents Coop. Pre Sch., 1996-97; publs. chair TED/Coun. for Exceptional Children Diversity Com., 1995-98. Mem. Coun. for Exceptional Children, Nat. Assn. Sch. Psychologists. Democrat. Lutheran. Home: # 14 38540 Bridgeport Rd Whitewater CO 81527-9434 E-mail: russell_gwen@hotmail.com.

WHEELES, EMILY S., biology educator; b. Alexander City, Ala., May 28, 1974; d. Jerry Thomas and Sherry Bradford Sasser; m. Michael Shane Wheeles, Dec. 21, 2002; 1 child, Michael. AA, Ctrl. Ala. C.C., Alexander City, 1994; BS, Faulkner U., Montgomery, Ala., 1998; MEd, Auburn U., Montgomery, 2002. Sci. tchr. Benjamin Russell H.S., Alexander City, 1997—. Bldg. leadership team Benjamin Russell H.S., Alexander City, 2002—04, mem. tech. com., 2004—05; adj. biology instr. Ctrl. Ala. C.C., Alexander City, 2002—; mem. textbook selection com. Auburn U., 2005—06. Named Tchr. of Quarter, Benjamin Russell H.S., 1999, Tchr. of Yr., Alexander City Bd. Edn., 2000. Home: 392 Crestline Cir Alexander City AL 35010 Office: Benjamin Russell HS 225 Heard Blvd Alexander City AL 35010

WHEELESS, CHARLOTTE ANN, science educator; d. Fred Simmons and Kathleen B Hattenhauer; m. Gene Wheeless, May 12, 1990; children: Patrick, Nicholas, Jessica. BS in Edn. summa cum laude, Williams Bapt. Coll., Walnut Ridge, Ark., 1994; postgrad., Grand Canyon U., Phoenix, 2005—06. Sci. tchr. Walnut Ridge Mid. Sch., Ark., 1996—. Tchr. tng. workshop facilitator Interactive Tng. Media, Orlando, Fla., 2003—05; tchr. adv. bd. mem. Williams Bapt. Coll., Walnut Ridge, 2000—01. Adult leader 4-H Western Wranglers Horse & Pony Club, Black Rock, Ark., 2001—06, Ark. 4-H State Tech. Team, Little Rock, 2005—06; bd. mem. Lawrence County Hist. Soc., Powhatan, 2000—06. Recipient Tchr. Yr., Walnut Ridge Pub. Sch., 1999, Wal-Mart Tchr. Yr., Wal-Mart Corp., 1999, Young Achievement award, Williams Bapt. Coll., 1999—2000; grantee, Ark. Sci. and Tech. Authority, 2002—06, 2003; scholar, Walnut Ridge Bus. & Profl. Women Assn., 2005; Japan Fulbright tchr. participant, 2006. Mem.: Ark. Sci. Tchrs. Assn., Nat. Sci. Tchrs. Assn., Bus. & Profl. Women Assn. Avocations: travel, reading. Office: Walnut Ridge Public School 508 East Free Street Walnut Ridge AR 72476 Office Phone: 870-886-6697.

WHEELOCK, PAM, financial executive; BA in History, Coll. St. Catherine; MA in Applied Econs., Marquette U. Exec. budget officer Minn. Dept. Fin., 1988—92; budget dir. City of St. Paul, 1992—94, dep. mayor, 1994—96, dir. dept. planning and econ. devel., 1996—99; commr. Minn. Dept. Fin., 1999—2002; sr. v.p., CFO Minn. Sports and Entertainment, 2002—. Office: Minn Wild 317 Washington St Saint Paul MN 55102

WHEELUS, ELIZABETH, mental health services professional; d. Elizabeth Wheelus; life ptnr. David Wheelus; children: Michael, Alec. Degree in Psychology Transitions (hon.), Jefferson State C.C., 1994; BA in Sociology, Human Svc. Social (hon.), U. Montevallo, 1977; MS in Cmty. Agy. Counseling, Jacksonville State U., 2001. Cert. sexual offender treatment specialist U.S., Ohio U. George E. Hill Ctr. Counseling, Rsch., criminal justice addictions specialist Am. Acad. Cert. Forensic Counselors, sentence mitigation specialist Am. Acad. Cert. Forensic Counselors, forensic addictions examiner Am. Acad. Cert. Forensic Counselors, domestic violence counselor - III Acad. Domestic Violence Counselors. Owner, forensic mental health counselor, contract vendor L.I.V.E.S., Lincoln, Pell City, Ala., 1999—, crisis rape ctr. Anniston, Ala., 2000—01; mhm Maximum State Correctional Facility, Springville, Ala., 2001—03; supr., counselor II Bridge Crisis Residential, Outpatient, Gadsden, Ashville, Ala., 2001; supr., mental health counselor Seraaj Family Homes, Oxford, Ala., 2002. Vol., social work asst., foster care adoption panelist com., quality assurance com. Ala. St. Clair Dept. Human Resources, Pell City, 1986—2001; cert. vol., prison life group facilitator, leader, angel tree area coord. Prison Fellowship Ministries Internat., Ala., 1991—99; vol., coord., mental health counselor cons. Surviving the Sys. and Recovery Guide, Miss. & Nevada, 2003—; substitute tchg. St. Clair County Bd. Edn., 2000; continuing edn. provider Ala. Bd. Social Worker Examiners, 2004. Designer www.harvestinthewilderness.org; spiritualist Our Father's Arms, Jacksonville, Ala., 2003—06. Named to President's List, Dean's List, Jefferson State C.C., 1988-1993, U. Montevallo, 1994-1997, Nat. Dean's List, Nat. Dean's List U.S., 2 years via University of Montevallo; recipient Coord., Treas., Chair, Phi Alpha Nat. Social Work Honor's Soc., U. Montevallo, 1994-1996, Spl. Honors Recognition Phi Alpha, U. Montevallo, 1995 (Life-Long), Phi Alpha Nat. Social Work Honor's Soc. Charter Mem. award, 1995 (Life-Long), Recognition Outstanding Scholastic Achievement and Excellence, Golden Key Nat. Honor Soc., U. of Montevallo, 1995 (Life-Long), Recognition of Conspicuous Attainments, Svc. Coll. Activities, Omicron Delta Kappa Honor's Soc. U. Montevallo, 1996 (Life-Long); Presidents Leadership scholarship, U. Montevallo, 1994-1997, Scholarship Achieve. Honors Cert., Faculty, Staff U. Montevallo, 1995. Mem.: ACA, Nat. Assn. Forensic Counselors, Assn. Treatment Sexual Abusers, Assn. Addiction Profls., Am. Mental Health Counselor's Assn., Am. Correctional Assn. Office: LIVES LLC PO Box 770 Lincoln AL 35096-0770 Office Phone: 205-763-7724. Business E-Mail: lives777@aol.com.

WHELAN, MARY JANE, accountant, writer, photographer; b. Canton, Ohio; d. William D. Rank and Marie E. Strahl; m. Thomas Whelan, Jan. 16, 1963; children: Thomas J., Michaela M. Rogers. Cert. tax cons. Acctg. and tax cons., Lawrenceville, Ga., 1984—2003; writer Royal Reign Publs., White City, Oreg., 1995—. Author: Accounting and Tax Consulting; author: (photographer) (poetry) Tides of Love, 2003. Nominee Bus. Woman of Yr., Atlanta, 1986; recipient 5 Editors Choice awards, Poet of Merit trophy. Avocations: travel, writing, singing, racquetball, hiking.

WHELAN, SUSAN, former Canadian government official; b. Windsor, Ont., Can., May 5, 1963; d. Elizabeth and Eugene Whelan. Degree in commerce, U. Windsor, B in Laws, 1988; JD, U. Detroit. Bar: Ont. 1990. Assoc. Yuffy, Roberts, Goldstein, Manzocco, Windsor, 1988-93; M.P. for Essex-Windsor House of Commons, 1993—2004, parliamentary sec. to Min. Nat. Revenue, 1993-96, mem. standing com. pub. accouts, 1994-96, assoc. mem. standing com. on fin., 1994-96, vice chair fin. com., 1996-97, mem. justice subcom. on draft regulations on firearms, 1996-97, mem. subcom. on rev. of spl. import measures act, 1996, chair industry com., 1997—2002, min. internal cooperation, 2002—03. Former dir. Essex Region Conservation Found., Alzheimer Soc. Windsor and Essex County. Named "Hon. Susan E. Whelan", Minister for Internat. Coop., 2002. Mem. Law Soc. Upper Can., Can. Bar Assn., Essex County Law Assn.

WHELCHEL, BETTY ANNE, lawyer; b. Augusta, Ga., Dec. 22, 1956; d. John Davis and Charnell (Ramsey) W.; m. Douglas Charles Kruse, June 20, 1987. AB, U. Ga., 1978; JD, Harvard U., 1981. Bar: D.C. 1981, N.Y. 1984, gaikokuho-jimu-bengoshi (fgn. lawyer) Japan, 1988-89. Atty.-advisor U.S. Dept. Treasury, Washington, 1981-84; assoc. Shearman & Sterling, N.Y.C., 1984-87, 89-90, Tokyo, 1987-89; dep. gen. counsel Deutsche Bank N.Am., N.Y., 1990—99; global gen. counsel Deutsche Bank Asset Mgmt., 1999—2004; gen. counsel-N.Am. BNP Paribas, 2005—. Lectr., NAS, 2003; staff atty. Depository Instns. Deregulation Com., Washington, 1983-84. Mem. Assn. of the Bar of the City of N.Y. (com. on fgn. and comparative law 1992-97, chmn. 1996-99, coun. on internat. affairs 1996-99, spl. task force on lawyer's role in corp. governance, 2005-). Home: 25 Broad St Apt 20C New York NY 10004 E-mail: bawhel@hotmail.com.

WHELCHEL, SANDRA JANE, writer; b. Denver, May 31, 1944; d. Ralph Earl and Janette Isabelle (March) Everitt; m. Andrew Jackson Whelchel, June 27, 1965; children: Andrew Jackson, Anita Earlyn. BA in Elem. Edn., U. No. Colo., 1966; postgrad., Pepperdine Coll., 1971, UCLA, 1971. Elem. tchr. Douglas County Schs., Castle Rock, Colo., 1966-68, El Monte (Calif.) schs., 1968-72; br. libr. Douglas County Librs., Parker, Colo., 1973-78; zone writer Denver Post, 1979-81; reporter The Express newspapers, Castle Rock, 1979-81; history columnist Parker Trail newspapers, 1985-93; columnist

Authorship Mag., 1991—, Gothic Jour., 1994; writing tchr. Aurora Parks and Recreation, 1985-91; writing instr. Arapahoe C.C., 1991-2000; exec. dir. Nat. Writers Assn., 1991—. Lectr. on writing and history Durango Writer's Workshop, 1996-97, Estes Park Writer's Retreat, 1996-97, Pikes Peak Writer's Workshop, 1997, Sinipee Writer's Workshop, 1998, Oasis for Seniors, 2000, Denver Women's Press Club, 1999, Rocky Mountain Gold Conf., 1999, Colo. Writers Fellowship, 2000, Colo. Ind. Publishers, 2000; spkr. Internat. Olympiad of Mind, Paris, 2000, Art Cafe, 2003; motivational spkr. various Optomist groups in Denver area; hist. tours, Parker, Colo. Editor Authorship mag., 1992-98; lit. agent NWLA, 1996-99; contbr. short stories and articles to various publs. including: The Writer, Writer's Open Forum, Writer's Jour., Reunions, Fresno Bee, Ancestry Newsletter, Calif. Horse Rev., Jack and Jill, Child Life, Children's Digest, Peak to Peak mag.; author (non-fiction books): Your Air Force Academy, 1982, A Guide to the U.S. Air Force Acad., 1990, Parker, Colorado: A Folk History, 1990, The Beginning Writer's Writing Book, 1996, A Folk History of Parker and Hilltop, 1996; co-author: The Writer's Office, 1998, Writing for Beginners, 2006, The Register, 1989, (coloring books) A Day at the Cave, 1985, A Day in Blue, 1984, Pro Rodeo Hall of Champions and Museum of the American Cowboy, 1985, Pikes Peak Country, 1986, Mile High Denver, 1987, (novel) Hide & Seek, 2006; contbr. chpts. to books Mem.: Nat. Writers Assn. (pres. 1990, 1991, 2003—04), Colo. Author's League (awards com. 1999—2000, who's who com. 2001), Parker Area Hist. Soc. (pres. 1987—89), Nat. Writer's Club (treas. Denver Metro chpt. 1985—86, v.p. membership 1987, sec. 1990, bd. dirs., pres. 1990—91, v.p. programs 1992, v.p. membership 2002, bd. dirs., pres. 2003). Office Phone: 303-841-0246.

WHETSTONE, JONI LEE, music educator; b. Cumberland, Md., July 25, 1955; d. John Moyer and Eleanor Mae Shambach; 1 child, Leanna Lynn. MusB in Edn., Lee U., 1977; MusM, Ind. U. Pa., 1982. Instr. vocal music Everett (Pa.) Area Jr. Sr. H.S., 1983—. Lectr. music Pa. State U., Altoona, Pa., 1986—; instr. vocal music Everett (Pa.) Christian Academy, 1977—78, 1980—83; dir. music First Evang. Luth. Ch., Altoona, 1987—89. Named Claes Nobel Educator Distinction, Nat. Soc. H.S. Scholars, 2004. Mem.: NEA, Pa. State Educators Assn., Am. Choral Dirs. Assn., Pa. Music Educators Assn., Music Educators Nat. Conf. Republican. Home: PO Box 1495 Altoona PA 16603 Office: Everett Area Jr Sr High Sch 1 Renaissance Cir Everett PA 15537-1406 Office Phone: 814-652-9114 1302. Business E-Mail: jwhetstone@everett.k12.pa.us.

WHICHELLO, CAROL, political scientist, educator, writer; b. Newton, N.J., Mar. 29, 1945; d. Arthur Frederick Whichello and M. W. Niper. BA, Salem Internat. U., 1967; MEd, Coll. N.J., 1978. Cert. tchr. N.J., Fla. Tchr. Freehold Twp. (N.J.) Bd. Edn., 1967—97; adj. prof. polit. sci. Indian River C.C., 1998—; sub. tchr. Martin County Sch. Bd., Fla., 2001—. Past exed. bd. dirs., legis. chairperson Freehold Twp. Edn. Assn. Mem. Stuart (Fla.) Heritage Mus., 1998—, bd. mem., 2002—. Recipient N.J. Mid. Sch.Tchr. of Yr. in Social Studies, N.J. Social Studies Tchrs., 1989. Democrat. Baptist. Avocations: writing, editing historical works. Home: 210 SE Kitching Cir Stuart FL 34994-5929 Personal E-mail: cwhichello@aol.com.

WHILDIN, LEONORA PORRECA, retired nursing educator; b. Boston, Mass., Dec. 7, 1926; d. John and Anna (Annunziata) Porreca; m. William Miller Whildin; children: Susan Lee, Robert Miller, Walter Thomas. BS, Boston U., 1954; MS, Columbia U., 1971. RN, Mass., N.Y., N.J.; cert. nurse midwife, N.Y. Cadet nurse corps. Boston City Hosp., 1943-46, staff, asst. head nurse neurology, neurosurgery, 1946-48, scrub nurse neurosurgery, 1948-50; civilian nurse Dept. of Army, Bremerhaven, Germany, 1948; pub. health nurse Bklyn. Vis. Nurse Assn., 1954-56; instr. Helene Fulde Sch. of Practical Nursing, N.Y.C., 1956-57; pub. health nurse V.N.A. Morris Co., Morristown, NJ, 1967; instr. All Souls Hosp. Sch. of Nursing, Morristown, NJ, 1968-69; guest lectr. Seton Hall U., South Orange, NJ, 1978. Del. Am. Nurses Assn, Mass., 1954; By-Laws Com. Am. Coll. Nurse Midwives, N.Y., 1972, By-Laws Com. Am. Coll. Nurse Midwives (N.J. chpt.), 1980; bd. mem. V.N.A. Morris Co., Morristown, N.J., 1977-78; v.p. bd. health, Randolph Twp., Randolph, N.J., 1972-74. Coun. woman Randolph Twp., 1972-78; mayor (1st woman mayor) Randolph Twp., 1977; Dem. party county com., Morris Co., Morristown, N.J., 1972-96; Dem. party state com., N.J., 1992-98; vol. United Way of Morris County. Mem. APHA, ANA, LWV, Mass., N.Y., N.J. (bd. mem. 1964-66), Sigma Theta Tau. Democrat. Avocations: ice skating, knitting, crafts, baking. Home: 82 Radtke Rd Randolph NJ 07869-3815

WHILEY, JULIA HELEN, writer, actress; b. Miami, Feb. 20, 1951; d. Maceo and Sherah Jones; m. Leroy Eugene Whiley, Oct. 26, 1990; m. Morgan Eugene Thomas, Aug. 8, 1982 (div. Oct. 20, 1990); children: Ayana Sheba Sanders, Aliscia Leala, Latasha Lanae. BA in Comm., Old Dominian U., 2002. Lic. message therapist Fla. Dept Profl. Regulations, 1995. Sec. Fla. Dept. Rehab. Svcs.- Vocat. Rehab., Miami, 1973—76; cert. worker II Fla. Dept. Health and Rehab. Svcs.- Food Stamps Office, 1976—80; veneral disease investigator Dade County Healt Dept., 1980—86; commd. USN, 1983, ret. petty officer, 1996. Actress, playwright, screenwriter, poet Norfolk Playwright Forum, Va., 2002—. Author of poems, (short stories) Love On The Fang Side Of The Moon, (screenplays) Detective Story, (plays) A lovely Day, One More Try; actor: (plays) Ti-jean, The Great Dismale Swamp, Everyman, Antigone, Abolishian Museum, African Kings and Queens; dir.: True West. Decorated Sailor Of The Month. Mem.: Dramatist Guild Am., Am. Screen Writers Assn. Liberal. Avocations: acting, writing. Personal E-mail: juliawhi51@aol.com.

WHIPPLE, JUDITH ROY, retired editor; b. N.Y.C., May 14, 1935; d. Edwin Paul and Elizabeth (Levis) Roy; m. William Whipple, Oct. 26, 1963. AB, Mount Holyoke Coll., 1957. Head libr. Am. Sch. Lima (Peru), S.A., 1957-59; asst. editor children's books G.P. Putnam's Sons, N.Y.C., 1959-62; assoc. editor W.W. Norton & Co., Inc., N.Y.C., 1962-68; editor Four Winds Press, 1968-75; editor-in-chief Scholastic Gen. Book Divsn., 1975-77; pub. Four Winds Press subs. Scholastic Inc., N.Y.C., 1977-82; pub., v.p. Macmillan Pub. Co., N.Y.C., 1982-89, exec. editor, 1989-94; editl. dir. Cavendish Children's Books, Tarrytown, NY, 1994—2002, ret., 2002. Mem.: PEN, Children's Book Coun. (pres. 1977, bd. dirs. 1970—79), Women's Nat. Book Assn., Soc. Children's Book Writers and Illustrators. Avocations: gardening, swimming, piano, travel. Personal E-mail: jrwhipple@stny.rr.com.

WHITAKER, DIANA MARIE, medical/surgical nurse; b. Utica, N.Y. d. Wendell Wolfred Witaker and Gail Ita Glenson. EMS tech. AS degree, Indian River C.C., 1995, ADN, 1999. RN, Fla.; nat. registered paramedic. Fire-fighter, rescue EMT Griffiss AFB, Rome, N.Y., 1993; paramedic Marint Meml. Hosp., Stuart, Fla., 1995-99, Indian River Meml. Hosp., Vero Beach, Fla.; RN Holmes Regional Med., Melbourne, Fla., 1999—. EMT course coord., instr. City Coll. of Chgo., 1990-91. Team capt. Relay for Life-ACS, Stuart, Fla., 1998; coord. Crop Walk, Stuart, 1998-99; mem. Women in Mil. Svcs. Meml. Found., 1998-99. Staff sgt. USAF, 1982-90. Mem. Nursing Student Assn. (project in touch recruiter, pub. rels. officer, runner ho. of dels. 1998, Cmty. Svc. award 1999), Am. Cancer Soc. (coord., leader 1998-99). Avocations: helping the homeless, bicycling, weightlifting, college.

WHITAKER, ELIZABETH D., lawyer; b. Washington, Feb. 20, 1953; BA in Anthropology magna cum laude, Wheaton Coll., 1979; JD cum laude, So. Meth. U., Dallas, 1980. Bar: Tex. 1980. Co-mng. ptnr. Bracewell & Giuliani, LLP, Dallas. With Carrington, Coleman, Sloman & Blumenthal LLP, 1980—81, 1982—99, Dallas County Dist. Atty. Office, 1981—82; exec. com., bd. dirs. Com. for Qualified Judiciary, 2000, 01; exec. com. So. Meth. U. Sch. Law, 1998—, Inst. Tech. Law; barrister Patrick Higginbotham Inns of Ct., 2004—; trustee Ctr. Am Internat. Law; spkr. in field. Contbr. articles to profl. law jours. Commr. State of Tex. Lottery Commn., 2000—03; mem. United Way, Women's Initiative, 2002; bd. dirs. Cmtys. in Schs., 2004—, Grammen Chiapas Initiative, 2004—. Recipient The Innovator award, Profiles in Leadership, 2004. Fellow: Am. Bar Found. (founder), Dallas Bar Found., Tex. Bar Found.; mem.: Am. Law Inst., Order of Coif, Coll. of State Bar Tex., State Bar Tex. (chair continuing legal edn. com. 1996—97, bd. dirs. 1996—99, chair bd. dirs. 1998—99, pres.-elect 2002—03, pres. 2003—04). Republican. Office: Bracewell & Patterson LLP 500 N Akard St Ste 4000 Dallas TX 75201-3387 Office Phone: 214-758-1000. Business E-Mail: betsywhitaker@hotmail.com. E-mail: betsy.whitaker@bracewellgiuliani.com.

WHITAKER, RUTH M., newswriter, photographer, horse breeder; b. Jacksonville, Fla., Feb. 18, 1935; d. Clifford Orville Bailey and Margaret Agnes Carlton Bailey Walden; m. Ray Gene Whitaker, Sept. 1, 1951; children: Raymond Eugene, Charles David, Frank Robert, Cynthia Ann, Wayne Douglas, Linda Ruth, Margaret Lee. Student, Palmer Inst. San Antonio Coll. Real Estate. Sales Lee Schwartz Shop, Uvalde, Tex., 1949—50; sales, window decorator Julian's, 1950—51, Levine's Dept. Store, San Angelo, 1951—52; asst. photographer Joske's Portrait Studio, 1952—54; photographer Studer's Aztec Theatre Bldg, 1954—55; reporter, photographer Hondo Anvil Herald, Hondo, 1960—62; reporter, photographer, columnist Medina Valley Times, Devine, 1970—84, Devine News, Devine, 1984—97, 2000—. Horse breeder Am. Quar. Horses, 1960—2002; owner dog kennel, 1985—99. Mem.: Biry Hermann Sons (sec.-treas. 1995—). Republican. Methodist. Avocations: hand tooled leatherwork, painting, genealogy. Office: The Devine News 216 S Bright Devine TX 78016 Office Phone: 830-665-2211. E-mail: rmw@devtex.net.

WHITAKER, RUTH REED, state legislator, retired newspaper editor; b. Blytheville, Ark., Dec. 13, 1936; d. Lawrence Neill and Ruth Shipton (Weidemeyer) Reed; m. Thomas Jefferson Whitaker, dec. 29, 1961; children: Steven Bryan, Alicia Morrow. BA, Hendrix Coll., 1958. Copywriter, weather person KTVE TV, El Dorado, Ark., 1958-59; nat. bridal cons. Treasure House, El Dorado, 1959; bridal cons. Pfeifers of Ark., Little Rock, 1959-60; dir. of continuity S. M. Brooks Advt. Agy., Little Rock, 1960-61; layout artist C. V. Mosby Co., St. Louis, 1961-62; editor, owner Razorback Am. Newspaper, Ft. Smith, Ark., 1979-81; ret., 1981; mem. from dist. 3 Ark. State Senate, 2000—. Host Crawford Conversations TV show; contbr. author indsl. catalog, 1979 (Addy award). State sec. Rep. Party of Ark., 1992-94, mem. Ark. Electoral Coll., 1996, del. Rep. Nat. Conv., 1996;; mem. Ben Geren Regional Park Commn., Sebastian County, Ark., 1984-89, pres., 1990; past pres. Jr. Civic League; mem. Ft. Smith Orchid Com.; mem. com. of 21 United Way; publicity chmn. Sebastian County Rep. Com., 1983-84; state press officer Reagan-Bush Campaign, 1984; exec. dir. Ark. Dole for Pres., 1995-96; pres. Women's Aux. Sebastian County Med. Soc., 1974; mem. Razorback Scholarship Fund; class agt. alumni fund Hendrix Coll., 1990, 91, 92; mem. Sparks Woman's Bd.; 1st vice chmn. 3d Dist. Rep. Party; state committee-woman Rep. Party Ark.; chmn. Crawford County Rep. Com.; apptd. by Gov. of Ark. to Commr. Ark. Ednl. TV Network Commn., sec. 1998-99; mem. city coun. City of Cedarville, Ark., 1998; dist. panelist NOW in Bux., 2003. Recipient Disting. Vol. Leadership award Nat. Found. March of Dimes, 1973, Appreciation award Ft. Smith Advt. Fedn., 1977, 78, Recognition award United Cerebral Palsy, 1980, Hon. Parents of Yr. award U. Ark., 1984, Firekeeper award Sparks Hosp. Women's Ctr., 2003. Mem. AAUW, Alden Soc. Am. (life), Ft. Smith C. of C., Ark. Nature Conservancy, Am. Legion Aux., Frontier Rschrs. Soc. (pres. 1995-96), Daus. Union Vets. Presbyterian. Avocations: philanthropy, genealogy, writing, photography, ornithology. Home: PO Box 349 Cedarville AR 72932-0349

WHITAKER, SHIRLEY ANN, retired communications executive; b. Asmara, Ethiopia, Oct. 13, 1955; (parents Am. citizens); d. Calvin Randall and Ruth (Ganeles) Peck; m. John Marshall Whitaker, June 16, 1973; 1 child, Kathryn Ann. AA, Tacoma C.C., 1974; BA, Wash. State U., 1977, MBA, 1978. Planning adminstr. for econ. rsch. GTE NW, Everett, Wash., 1978-80; specialist in demand analysis western region GTE Svc. Corp., Los Gatos, Calif., 1980-81, fin. analyst Stamford, Conn., 1981-83, staff specialist demand analysis and forecasting, 1983—84; group mgr. for rate devel. Nat. Exch. Carrier Assn., Whippany, NJ, 1984-87; mgr. pricing strategy and migration GTE Calif., Thousand Oaks, Calif., 1987—88; mgr. market forecasting GTE Tel. Ops. Hdqrs., Irving, Tex., 1989-90, dir. revenue analysis, 1990—92, dir. market rsch., 1992—93, dir. process re-engring., 1993—94, dir. network and resource mgmt., 1994—97; gen. sales mgr. customer contact GTE Network Svcs., Victorville, 1997—2000; dir. employee devel. Verizon Comm., NYC, 2000—01, dir. support and response ctrs. Trenton, NJ, 2001—03; ret., 2003. Mem. Beta Gamma Sigma, Phi Kappa Phi. Avocation: sailing. Personal E-mail: whitakerfamily@qwest.net.

WHITAKER, SUSAN LAVERNE, retired secondary home economics educator; b. Waynesburg, Ky., Oct. 5, 1945; d. Walter Carroll and Emma Rae (Smith) Caldwell; m. Otis Dean Whitaker, Nov. 26, 1964; children: Deana, Justin, Brent, LaTasha. BS, Ea. Ky. U., Richmond, 1965; MA, Del. State Coll, Dover, 1989, postgrad., 1992. Cert. tchr., Del. Tchr. Buckeye Elem. Sch., Lancaster, Ky., 1965-66, Garrard County High Sch., Lancaster, 1966-67, Bourne (Mass.) High Sch., 1968-70; sec. Reeder Ins. Co., Lexington, Ky., 1971-72; tchr. home econs. Milford (Del.) Christian Sch., 1978-79, Caesar Rodney HS, Camden, Del., 1982-84, 86-87, Dover Air Base Jr. HS, Camden, 1984—85, Caesar Rodney Jr. HS, Camden, 1987—95, asst. prin., 1995—2001; prin. Postlethwait Mid. Sch., 2001—05; ret., 2005. Mem. Del. Assn. of Secondary Prins., Nat. Assn. of Secondary Prins. Baptist. Avocation: sewing. Home: 756 Mud Mill Rd Marydel DE 19964-1903

WHITAKER, SUSANNE KANIS, veterinary medical librarian; b. Clinton, Mass., Sept. 10, 1947; AB in Biology, Clark U., 1969; MS in Library Sci., Case Western Res. U., 1970. Regional reference librarian Yale Med. Library, New Haven, 1970-72; med. librarian Hartford Hosp., Conn., 1972-77; asst. librarian Cornell U., Ithaca, NY, 1977-78; vet. med. librarian Coll. Vet. Medicine, Cornell U., 1978-98, vet. pub. svcs. libr., 1998—. Mem. Med. Libr. Assn. (vet. med. librs. sect. 1983-84, chmn. 1984-85, chmn. pub. rels. com. 2000—), Med. Libr. Assn. (Upstate NY and Ont. chpt.), Acad. Health Info. Profls. (disting. mem.), Am. Vet. Med. History Soc. (sec.-treas. 2004—). Home: 23 Wedgewood Dr Ithaca NY 14850-1064 Office: Cornell U Coll Vet Medicine Flower-Sprecher Libr Ithaca NY 14853-6401 Office Phone: 607-253-3499. Business E-Mail: skw2@cornell.edu.

WHITCOMB, LOIS ANN, retired academic administrator; b. Belfast, Maine, Dec. 31, 1934; d. Harold E. and Eleanor M. (Miller) W.; m. Robert A. Jones, June 28, 1958 (div. 1970); children: Robin, Laurie. BA in English with highest distinction, U. Maine, Orono, 1957; MEd, U. Mass., 1972, EdD, 1974. Cert. tchr. grades 7-12, Maine. Public sch. tchr. various locations, 1957-71; curriculum developer Ford Found. psychol. curriculum project U. Mass., Amherst, 1972-74; grad. asst. curriculum of affect for responsive edn. Montague Sch. Sys., Turners Falls, Mass., 1972-74; edn. specialist div. human devel. and guidance resources Maine Dept. Edn., Augusta, 1974-77, coord., 1977-82, asst. to commr., 1983-87, cons. office of compensatory edn., 1987-93, state title I dir., 1993—97; ret., 1997. Assessor NASSP Assessment Ctr., U. So. Maine, 1983-87; state pres. N.E. Coalition Ednl. Leaders, 1983-84; state coord. State Edn. Policy Seminars, 1986-92. Cons. Nat. Action Com. on Drug Edn., U.S. Office Edn., Washington, 1973-75; pres., bd. trustees All Souls Ch., Augusta, 1978-80, 85-87; mem., bd. dirs. Maine Facilitator Ctr., 1983-85, Maine Conservation Sch., 1984-87. N.E. Regional fellow Ford Found., 1971-72, State Exec. Policy fellow U.S. Dept. Edn., 1984. Mem. U. Maine Alumni Assn. (v.p. Class of 1957, 1982-97, pres. 1997—), Delta Kappa Gamma (pres. Gamma chpt. 1978-80, state communications chmn. 1981-83). Home: 26 Longwood Ave Augusta ME 04330-4131

WHITE, ANGELA PEARL, literature and language educator; b. Borger, Tex., Sept. 22, 1956; d. Ernest C. Johnson and Billie Moran, Cleo Moran (Stepfather); m. Larry White, July 9, 1956; children: Jason Duane, Courtney Rae Menefee. BA in English Edn. (hon.), Southwestern Okla. State U., Weatherford, 1988. Tchr. h.s. English Sharon-Mutual H.S., Mutual, Okla., 1988—97, Vici H.S., Okla., 1997—. Coord. advanced placement Vici H.S., 2006. Contbr. poetry to anthologies. Chair worship com. Vici United Meth. Ch., 1994—2000. Recipient Advance Placement English Lang. grant, Coll. Bd., 2000. Republican. Methodist. Avocations: travel, reading, singing, playing piano, scrapbooks. Home: 1100 N Houser Vici OK 73859 Office: Vici H S Miller Vici OK 73859 Office Fax: 580-995-3101. Business E-Mail: awhite@vicischools.k12.ok.us.

WHITE, ANNE J., lawyer; BA magna cum laude, St. Lawrence U., 1975; MA, U. Minn., 1977; JD, Boston U., 1980. Bar: Mass. 1980, U.S. Dist. Ct. Mass. 1981. Ptnr. Klieman, Lyons, Schindler & Gross, Boston. Author: Tax Policy & Health Maintenance Orgn.: Case For Sect. 501 (C)(3) Tax Exemption, 1980. Named an top Boston lawyers, Boston Mag., 2002; recipient Outstanding Leadership Award, E.P. Hepburn. Mem.: Internat. Women's Insolvency & Restructuring. Confederation, Am. Bankruptcy Inst., Mass. Bar Assn., Boston Bar Assn. (co-chmn. bankruptcy sect. 2003—05), Phi Beta Kappa. Office: Klieman Lyons Schindler & Gross 21 Custom House St Ste 920 Boston MA 02110 Office Phone: 617-443-1000. Office Fax: 617-443-1010.

WHITE, ANNETTE IRENE, marketing professional; b. L.A., Oct. 28, 1970; d. Fleming Leonard White and Jessica Frances Chavez-White. BBA, ASU, Tempe, Ariz., 1999; student Leadership Mgmt., ASU Leadership Inst., Tempe, Ariz., 2000—. V.p. mktg. mgr. Chicanos Por La Causa, Phoenix, 1994—. Pres. ASU Downtown Alumni Bd., Phoenix, 2003—, pres. elect., 2001—03; mem. at large DeColores Domestic Viol Shelter, Phoenix, 2001—; rep. Environ.-Comm. Action Coun., Phoenix, 2003—. Mem.: Amnestiy Internat., Nat. Coun. of La Raza, Am. Legion Post 41. Democrat. Cath. Avocations: music, interior decorating, research. Office: Chicanos Por La Causa 1112 E Buckeye Rd Phoenix AZ 85034

WHITE, BARBARA ANN, technologist; b. Beckley, W.Va., June 28, 1963; d. Robert Diehl and Jo Ann (Watson) Rhodes; m. Randy Dale White, Aug. 31, 1985 (div. Oct. 1999); 1 child, Julia Ann-Marie. BS in Zoology, Marshall U., 1985. Asst. mgr. Rt. 16 Gift Shop, Beckley, 1981-85; biol. scis. technician VA Med. Ctr., Huntington, W.V., 1986, 89-92; data entry clk. Navy Fed. Credit Union, Vienna, Va., 1987; med. technologist Nat. Health Labs., Vienna, 1987-89; phys. sci. technician Appalachian Farming Sys. Rsch. Ctr., USDA, Beaver, W.Va., 1992—, mem. chem. response team, 1993-95, chmn. ednl. outreach, 1996-97. Troop leader, recruiter Black Diamond coun. Girl Scouts U.S.A., 1992—, spl. event coord., 1993—; Career Day spkr. Raleigh County Bd. Edn., Beckley, 1993—; coord. children's ministry Mabscott (W.Va.) United Meth. Ch., 1995-98. Recipient honor award Beckley Area Fedn. Assn. Mem. AAUW (br. pres. 1995-97, W.Va. program v.p. 1999-01, organizer sister to sister summit 1999-00), Am. Chem. Soc. (technician affiliate group). Democrat. Office: USDA ARS Appalachian Farming Sys Rsch Ctr 1224 Airport Rd Beaver WV 25813-9423 Home: 1008 Girder Ct Fuquay Varina NC 27526-1667 E-mail: bawhite@citynet.net.

WHITE, BETTY, actress, comedienne; b. Oak Park, Ill., Jan. 17, 1922; m. Dick Barker 1945 (div. 1945), m. Lane Allen 1947 (div. 1949), m. Allen Ludden, 1963 (dec. 1981). Student pub. schs., Beverly Hills, Calif. Appearances on radio shows This Is Your FBI, Blondie, The Great Gildersleeve; actress: (TV series) including Hollywood on Television, The Betty White Show, 1954-58, Life With Elizabeth, 1953-55, A Date With The Angels, 1957-58, The Pet Set, 1971, Mary Tyler Moore Show, 1974-77, The Betty White Show, 1977, Mama's Family, 1983-86, The Golden Girls, 1985-92 (Emmy award for best actress 1986), Another World, 1988, The Golden Palace, 1992-93, Maybe This Time, 1995, (TV films) With This Ring, 1978, The Best Place to Be, 1979, Before and After, 1979, Eunice, 1982, Chance of a Lifetime, 1991, The Story of Santa Claus, 1996, A Weekend in the Country, 1996, The Retrievers, 2001, Annie's Point, 2005, (films) Advise and Consent, 1962, Dennis the Menace 2, 1998, Hard Rain, 1998, The Story of Us, 1999, Bringing Down the House, 2003, The Third Wish, 2004; guest appearances include Petticoat Junction, 1969, The Odd Couple, 1972, Fame, 1983, St. Elsewhere, 1985, Who's the Boss, 1985, Matlock, 1987, Empty Nest, 1989, 92, Carol & Company, 1990, Nurses, 1991, Diagnosis Murder, 1994, The Naked Truth, 1995, Suddenly Susan, 1996, (voice) King of the Hill, 1999, 2002, Ally McBeal, 1999, (voice) The Simpsons, 2000, Yes, Dear, 2002, Providence, 2002, That 70s Show, 2002, 03, Everwood, 2003, 04, The Practice, 2004, My Wife and Kids, 2004, Malcolm in the Middle, 2004, (voice) Father of the Pride, 2004, Boston Legal, 2005; frequent celebrity guest on numerous game shows including Hollywood Squares, Match Game; summer stock appearances Guys and Dolls, Take Me Along, The King and I, Who Was That Lady?, Critic's Choice, Bells are Ringing; author (book) Betty White's Pet-Lovers: How Pets Take Care of Us, 1987, Here We Go Again: My Life in Television, 1995; contbr. to forward(book) The Irrepressible Toy Dog, Dr. Fisher's Life on the Ark: Green Alligators, Bushman and Other "Hare Raising" Tales from America's Most Popular Zoo and Around the World, 2004, (preface) The Pets are Wonderful Family Album. Mem. Morris Animal Found., 1976—; zoo commr. Greater LA Zoo, 1998—. Recipient Emmy award NATAS, 1975, 76, 86; LA Area Emmy award, 1952, Living Legacy award, Women's Internat. Ctr., 1988, star on the Hollywood Walk of Fame; inducted into TV Hall of Fame, 1995; named Amb. to the Animals, Greater LA Zoo, 2006. Mem. AFTRA, Am. Humane Assn., Greater LA Zoo Assn. (dir.). Office: c/o William Morris Agy Betty Fanning 151 S El Camino Dr Beverly Hills CA 90212-2704*

WHITE, BEVERLY JANE, cytogeneticist; b. Seattle, Oct. 9, 1938; Grad., U. Wash., 1959, MD, 1963. Diplomate Nat. Bd. Med. Examiners, Am. Bd. Pediatrics, Am. Bd. Med. Genetics; lic physician and surgeon, Wash., Calif. Rsch. trainee dept. anatomy Sch. Medicine U. Wash., Seattle, 1960-62, pediatric resident dept. pediatrics, 1967-69; rotating intern Phila. Gen. Hosp., 1963-64; rsch. fellow med. ob-gyn. unit Cardiovascular Rsch. Inst. U. Calif. Med. Ctr., San Francisco, 1964-65; staff fellow lab. biomed. scis. Nat. Inst. Child Health and Human Devel. NIH, Bethesda, Md., 1965-67, sr. staff fellow, attending physician lab. exptl. pathology Nat. Inst. Arthritis, Metabolism and Digestive Diseases, 1969-74, acting chief sect. cytogenetics, 1975-76, rsch. med. officer, attending physician sect. cytogenetics lab. cellular biology and genetics, 1974-86, dir. cytogenetics unit, interinstitute med. genetics program clin. ctr., 1987-95; dir. cytogenetics Corning Clin. Labs., Teterboro, NJ, 1995-96; assoc. med. dir. cytogenetics Nichols Inst.-Quest Diagnostics, San Juan Capistrano, Calif., 1996-97, med. dir. cytogenetics, 1998—2000, med. dir. genetics divsn., 2000—02, med. dir. cytogenetics and genetic counseling, 2002—. Vis. scientist dept. pediat. divsn. genetics U. Wash. Sch. Medicine, 1983-84; intramural cons. NIH, 1975-95; cons. to assoc. editor Jour. Nat. Cancer Inst., 1976; cons. dept. ob-gyn. Naval Hosp., Bethesda, 1988-89; lectr., presenter in field. Recipient Mosby Book award, 1963, Women of Excellence award U. Wash. and Seattle Profl. chpt. Women in Comm., 1959, Reuben award Am. Soc. for Study Sterility, 1963. Fellow Am. Coll. Med. Genetics (founding), Am. Acad. Pediatrics; mem. AMA, Am. Soc. Human Genetics, Assn. Genetic Technologists (program com. 1989). Home: 14 Toulon Laguna Niguel CA 92677 Office: Nichols Inst Quest Diagnostics Inc Dept Cytogenetics San Juan Capistrano CA 92690-6130 Office Phone: 949-728-4301. E-mail: bjwsur@aol.com.

WHITE, BONNIE YVONNE, management consultant, retired educator; b. Long Beach, Calif., Sept. 4, 1940; d. William Albert and Helen Iris (Harbaugh) W. BS, Brigham Young U., 1962, MS, 1965, EdD in Ednl. Adminstrn., 1976; postgrad., Harvard U., 1987. Tchr. Wilson High Sch., Long Beach, Calif., 1962-63; grad. asst. Brigham Young U., Provo, Utah, 1963-65; instr., dir. West Valley Coll., Saratoga, Calif., 1965-76; instr., evening adminstr. Mission Coll., Santa Clara, Calif., 1976-80; dean gen. edn. Mendocino Coll., Ukiah, Calif., 1980-85; dean instrn. Porterville (Calif.) Coll., 1985-89, dean adminstrv. svc., 1989-93. Rsch. assoc. SAGE Rsch. Internat., Orem, Utah, 1975-99. Mem. AAUW, Faculty Assn. Calif., Cmty. Colls., Calif., Coun. Fine Arts Deans, Assn. Calif. C.C. Adminstrs., Assn. Calif. C.C. Adminstrs. Liberal Arts, Zonta (intern), Soroptimists (intern). Republican. Mem. Lds Ch.

WHITE, CAROLYN LOUISE, music educator; b. LaCrosse, Wis., Sept. 5, 1939; d. Julius Elmer and Nora Marie Forde; m. Ronald Glenn White, Aug. 18, 1962; children: Elizabeth, Sara, Andrea. BA, Luther Coll., 1961. Tchr.

Madison (Wis.) Pub. Schs., 1961—67; piano tchr. pvt. lessons, Madison, 1965—; substitute tchr. Verona Area Schs., Wis., 1970—85. Dir. music camp Bethel Horizons, Madison; sec., pres. Fitchrona EMS, Verona, 1978—83; accompanist children's choir Bethel Luth. Ch., Madison, Wis. Mem.: Verona Area Performing Arts Series (pres. 1998—2003), Madison Symphony Orch., Madison Symphony Orch. League (pres. 2000), Madison Area Piano Tchrs. Assn. (pres. 1992), Attic Angel Assn., Madison Civics Club (pres. 1998). Achievements include development of Verona Area Performing Arts Series. Avocations: gardening, travel, reading. Home: 6871 Sunset Dr Verona WI 53593

WHITE, CHERYL LOUISE, administrative assistant; b. Alexandria, La., Oct. 20, 1961; d. Richmond and Ellen White; 1 child, Dylan Kyle Bradford. BS in Bus. Adminstrn., Northwestern State U., Natchitoches, La., 1983. Dept. head, buyer Gus Kaplan, Alexandria, La., 1986—89; sec., asst. comptroller Sta. KALB-TV, Alexandria, 1989—92; staff asst. McPherson (Kans.) Coll., 1994—97; adminstr. coord. Centeon Pharm., Bradley, Ill., 1998. Founding mem. Nat. Campaign of Tolerance, Civil Rights Meml. Ctr., Montgomery, 2005; vol. ACT testing McPherson Coll.; vol. tutor W.O. Hall Magnet Elem., Alexandria, 2003; vol. LAJET Job Tng. Program, Alexandria. Mem.: AAUW, Am. Assn. Individual Investors, Nat. Assn. Female Exec., Home Gardening Club, Am. Shoppers Panel, Postal Commerative Soc., Nat. Assn. Cars Users, Cooking Club Am. (life). Democrat. Baptist. Avocations: photography, travel, movies, scrapbooks, music. Home: 415 Jacobs Alley Alexandria LA 71302 Office: Centeon Pharm 1201 N Kinzie Ave, Rt 50 Bradley IL 60915 Office Phone: 815-932-6771.

WHITE, CHRISTINE A., internist, oncologist, pharmaceutical executive; BA in Biology, U. Chgo., MD. Cert. Internal Medicine, Med. Oncology. With Scripps Meml. Hospitals, San Diego, 1984—94, med. dir. oncology rsch., 1990—94, chair, dept. medicine, 1994; dir., clin. oncology rsch. Sidney Kimmel Cancer Ctr., San Diego, 1994—96; several sr. positions, most recently served as sr. v.p., global med. affairs Biogen Idec, Cambridge, Mass., 1996—2005. Bd. dir. Pharmacyclics, Inc., Sunnyvale, Calif., 2006—, Arena Pharm., Inc., San Diego, 2006—. Mem. editl. bd. Cancer Biotherapy and Radiopharmaceutical, Expert Review of Anti-Cancer Therapy, Journal of Immunotherapy, and several others; contbr. articles to profl. jours. Office: Pharmacyclics Inc 995 E Argues Ave Sunnyvale CA 94085*

WHITE, CLARA JO, small business owner, consultant; b. County Cherokee, Tex., June 26; children: Anita, Jackie, Mona Lisa, Jeris, Gina. Diploma, Ft. Worth Bus. Coll., Tex., 1947; MS in Graphoanalysis, IGAS Congress Inst. Tng., Chgo., 1979; AA in Social Sci., Riverside City Coll., 1986; MA with honors in Social Sci., World Acad. Letters, Am. Biog. Inst., N.C., 2004. Cert. graphoanalyst 1977, mus. docent 1977, cert. graphoanalyst Internat. Graphoanalysis Soc., Inc., Chgo., 1977, diploma IGAS Congress Inst. Training, 1979, cert. mgmt. supr. devel. U. Calif., Riverside, 1986, counseling skills U. Riverside, 1990. Owner, pres. White Handwriting Analysis Svc., Riverside, Calif., 1982—. Instr. Internat. Congress and Resident Inst., Internat. Graphoanalysis Soc., 1989, discussion group leader, 88; analyzed handwriting Lady Margaret Beaufort, 1992, Mary Queen of Scots, 1994, Hillary Rodham Clinton, 1994, Pres. Bill Clinton, 1997, Georgia O'Keeffe, 1999, presidents George Washington, Abraham Lincoln, John F. Kennedy, 2000; participant 24th Internat. Congress on Arts and Comm. Oxford U., England, 1997; dir. gen. Internat. Biog. Ctr., Cambridge, 2002; cons. graphoanalysis, Riverside, Calif., 1977—; presenter and spkr. in field. Editor (asst. editor): Reflections, 1986; author: numerous poems; presenter (edn. symposium) ABI/IBC World Forum, Oxford U., Eng., 2006. Mem. children's conf. planning com. Riverside Mental Health Assn., 1981—; v.p. Heritage Ho. Mus., Riverside, Calif., 1981—, co-pres., 1985—86, pres; historian Riverside Juvenile Hall Aux., 1984—, pres., 1987—; mem. U.S. Olympic Com., 1984; bd. dir. Riverside Mus. Assoc., 1985—87, vol., 1985—88, aux. historian, 1984—, pres., 1987—88. Recipient Cert. of Appreciation Riverside County Probation Dept., 1986, County Riverside Suprs., 1988, Riverside Mental Health, 1990; award F.H. Butterfield Sch., 1980, Golden Poet award The Homer Honor Soc., 1987, 90, cert. appreciation Nat. Law Enforcement Officers Meml. Fund, 1998, cert. Libr. of Congress, 1998; named Vol. of Yr., recipient cmty. svc. cert. Riverside City Coll., 1982; named to Hall of Fame, Riverside Juvenile Hall Aux., 1984; recipient First pl. writing-poetry Am. Biog. Rsch. Assn., 1991, trophy Outstanding Svc. to Cmty. Sta. KQLH-FM, Trophy pl. Vol. Ctr. of Riverside, 1991, trophy and Individual Svc. award Riverside County Juvenile Hall of Fame, 1990-91, cert. Recognition Riverside County Probation Dept., 1991, Calif. Legis.-State Assembly, 1991, So. Calif. Chpt. IGAS, 1990-91, Riverside County Bd. Suprs. and Riverside County Probation Dept., 1993, 26th Children's Conf. Com., 1999; Participation award 21st Internat. Congress Arts and Comm., Scotland, 1994, Lisbon, Portugal, 1999, Internat. Gold Medal of Honor for disting. participation ABI/IBC 26th Congress On Arts and Comm., Lisbon, Portugal, 1999, Graphoanalyst of Yr. award So. Calif. chpt. Graphoanalysts, 2000, Disting. Svc. award City of Riverside, 2004, Order of Ambassadors Sovereign award ABI/IBC Inaugural World Forum, 2006. Master: Internat. Graphoanalysis Soc. (life; 2d then 1st v.p. so. Calif. chpt. 1984, Merit cert. 1981, Pres. Excellence award 1982, 1983, 1984, Pres. Merit citation 1988, Achievement cert. 1995); mem.: NAFE, YWCA, AAUW, DAV Aux. (life), Nat. Mus. Women in Arts, World War II Meml. Soc. (charter mem.), Smithsonian Assocs., Nat. Geographic Soc., Met. Mus. Assocs., Calif. Probation, Parole, and Corrections Assn. (cert. of tng. 1995), Top Cops Nat. Assn. Police Orgns., The Rsch. Coun. of Scripps Clinic and Rsch. Found., Riverside C. of C., U.S. Olympic Soc. (U.S. Olympic Team, U.S. Olympic Com. Sixth Ring charter mem. 2004, Replica Bronze medal 2004), Women's Networking Club (Riverside chpt.), Confederation of Chivalry (life; grand coun., dame officer). Avocations: sewing, music, collecting antiques, dance, exercise. Home and Office: 7965 Helena Ave Riverside CA 92504-3513

WHITE, COLLEEN TOY, judge; d. Ira Bass and Bula Olive Moore; m. E. Dale White (div.); children: Misty Dawn, Kevin B.; m. Art Bliss Jr., Aug. 7, 2002. JD, Ventura Coll. Law, Calif., 1977. Chief asst. Ventura County Dist. Atty.'s Office, Ventura, Calif., 1976—94; judge Ventura County Superior Ct., Ventura, 1994—2006, presiding judge, 2006—. Instr. So. Calif. colls.; presenter, spkr. in field; mem. task force Victim Svcs. Com., Atty. Gen.'s Serious Habitual Offender Adv. Com. Co-author: (manual) Raped - What Happens Now?. Founder Sr. Citizens Hotline, Ventura County; chmn. Ventura County Domestic Violence Task Force; vol. Ventura County Peri-natal Substance Abuse Com.; mem. City of Ventura Crime Prevention Com., Ventura County Teen Pregnancy Task Force; co-developer Rape and Awareness Prevention project; bd. dirs. Interface Children and Family Svcs. Named Calif. Legis. Woman of Yr., 1994; recipient honors, Coalition to End Domestic and Sexual Violence, 2002, JC Penney Golden Rule award, Cmty. Svc. award, KC, 1998, Vol. of Yr., Ventura County Med. Resource Found., 2002, Woody Deem award, 2002. Mem.: Ventura County Bar Assn. (Ben Nordman award 1992). Home: 800 S Victoria Ave Ventura CA 93009-0001

WHITE, DAPHNE MILBANK, writer; b. Vancouver, Can., Apr. 12, 1927; d. Robbins Milbank and Mary Lightfoot; m. Barrie M. White Jr., Sept. 13, 1947 (div. 1966); children: Deborah, Pamela, Ellen, Barrie. BA in Polit. Sci., Smith Coll., 1948; MS in Pub. Affairs, Am. U., 1979; postgrad., George Washington U., 1979—82. Co-mgr. four small bus., 1947—51; br. chief Am. U., Cultural Info. Analysis Ctr., Washington, 1967—68; voters svc. sr. staff specialist League of Women Voters Edn. Fund, Washington, 1969—72; comm. dir. Pub. Affairs Coun., Washington, 1973—74; writer, editor, paralegal, Office Gen. Coun. Nat. Oceanic and Atmospheric Adminstrn., Washington, 1975—78, writer, editor regulations. devel. analyst, Nat. Marine Fisheries Svc., 1979—90, program analyst, Ctr. Ocean Analysis and Prediction Monterey, Calif., 1990—92, program analyst, Monterey Bay Nat. Marine Sanctuary, 1992—93; ret., 1993. Contbr. articles to profl. jours. Enumerator and reviewer Census, 1960; bd. dirs. Youth Citizenship Fund, 1970—72; bd dirs. Memton Fund, Inc., 1981—95, pres., 1989—94; vol. guide Monterey Bay Aquarium, 1993—97; mem. adv. coun. subcom. Monterey Bay Nat. Marine Sanctuary, 1994—; bd. dirs. LWV Monterey Peninsula, 1994—97, Girl Scouts Am. Mem.: LWV, Elkhorn Slough Found., Nonprofit Devel. Ctr., U.N. Assn., Fgn. Policy Assn., Marine Mammal Ctr., Save Our Shores, Cmty. Found., Friends Long Marine Lab, Coyote Point Mus., Monterey History and Art Assn., Environ. Defense, Ocean Conservancy.

WHITE, DAUN ELOIS, professional society official; b. Winsted, Conn., Feb. 11, 1955; d. Robert Hamilton and Bessie Emma (Land) Daly; m. Stephen Scott White, Feb. 9, 1974; children: Stephen Scott Jr., Derik James. Student, Tri-Community Coll., Covina, Calif., 1974-76; BS in Bus. Adminstrn., U. of Redlands, Calif., 1982. Sec., bookkeeper Century 21 Comml., West Covina, Calif., 1978-80; sec. Century 21 Regional, West Covina, 1980-82; adminstrv. asst. Century 21 Real Estate, Covina, 1982-84, Covina Bd. Realtors, 1984-86; asst. to v.p. acquisitions Occidental Land Rsch., Diamond Bar, Calif., 1986-87; exhibits mgr. Soc. for Advancement Material and Process Engrs., Covina, 1987—91, exec. dir., 1991—2002, Soc. of Hispanic Profl. Engrs., LA, 2003—. Men. Nat. Assn. Expn. Mgrs., NAFE. Episcopalian. Office: SHPE Inc 5400 E Olympic Blvd Ste 210 Los Angeles CA 90022

WHITE, DAWN MARIE, elementary school educator; b. Providence, Oct. 1, 1961; d. Edgar George and Linda Joan Hamel; m. Steven Ralph White, June 19, 1982; children: Brandon John Michael, Karlyca Lee-Anne, Steven Ralph Edgar George. BS in Edn magna cum laude, R.I. Coll., Providence, 2000. Profl. tchr. elem. edn. R.I. Dept. Elem. and Secondary Edn., 2000, advanced religious cert. Diocese of Providence, 2001. Dietary aide Zambarano Meml. Hosp., Wallum Lake, RI, 1981—84; waitress Levesques Restaurant, Pascoag, 1990—91; bus monitor Burrillville Sch. Dept., Harrisville, 1991—94; prop. Pennies Consignment Store, Pascoag, 1993—94; tchr. aide and substitute tchr. Father Holland Elem. Sch., 1994—2000; tchr. grade 3 Greater Woonsocket Cath. Regional Sch. Sys., 2000—. Mem. prin. search com. Wiliam Callahan Sch., Harrisville, 1992; sch. coord. CAT testing Diocese of Providence, 2001—; revisor sci. and social studies curriculum com. Greater Woonsocket Cath. Regional Sch. Sys., 2003—. Sr. vol. resource instr. U.S. Army Reserve Family Readiness Program, Washington, 2001—; vol. Operation Stand Down for Homeless Veterans, Woonsocket, 1993—94; asst. den leader Boy Scouts Am., Pascoag, 1990—92; master trainer family team bldg. U.S. Army Cmty. and Family Support Command, Alexandria, Va., 1995—; family support coord. U.S. Army Reserves 94th Regional Support Command, Devens, Mass., 1996—2000; catechist St. Joseph Roman Cath. Ch., Pascoag, RI, 1993—2000. Carr scholar, Feinstein Sch. of Edn. and Human Devel., 1999—2000, Gilda R. Martone 38 Endowment scholar, 1999—2000, Phyllis Moorman Salk scholar, 1999—2000. Mem.: Nat. Cath. Ednl. Assn., Pi Epsilon Rho, Kappa Delta (life). Roman Catholic. Avocations: camping, travel, boating, foreign currency collecting.

WHITE, DEBORAH LEE, psychologist; b. Lawrence, Mass., Oct. 15, 1960; d. Albert Charles White and Elinor Beatrice Innes; m. Loren Eugene Mallory, Mar. 15, 1986; 1 child, Ian Andrew Mallory-White. MA in Theology, Fuller Theol. Sem., 1990, PhD in Clin. Psychology, 1990. Lic. psychologist Oreg., 1991. Asst. dir. The Ctr. for Aging Resources, Pasadena, Calif., 1990—91; psychologist, ptnr. in group pvt. practice Willamette Valley Family Ctr., Oregon City, 1991—. Mem. adult edn. com. St. John's Episcopal Ch., Milw., 2003—. Recipient Valerie Mossman Sharpe Excellence in Psychology, Gordon Coll., 1980. Mem.: APA (assoc.). Episcopal. Office: Willamette Valley Family Ctr 610 Jefferson St Oregon City OR 97045 Office Phone: 503-657-7235. Office Fax: 503-657-7676.

WHITE, DEBRA ANN, social worker, counseling administrator; b. Jersey City, Jan. 26, 1958; d. John Angelo Migliorisi and Mildred Fabrazzo; m. Jack Russell White, Feb. 16, 1991; 1 child, Russell John. BS in Human Ecology/ Svcs. and Edn., Marywood U., 1980; MA in Counseling, Rider U., 1990. Cert. social worker NJ; tchr. K-12 Pa., Pa. Tchr. human ecology Pinelands Regional H.S., Tuckerton, NJ, 1980—81; mem. Sisters of Mercy of Scranton, Dallas, Pa., 1981—85; group facilitator, educator Luth. Synod Drug and Alcohol Program, 1985—86; program supr. Fitzmaurice Resdl. Svcs., Inc., Stroudsburg, Pa., 1985—86; habilitation plan coord. Cmty. Svcs., Divsn. Devel. Disabilities State NJ, Howell, 1986—88; counselor sch. based youth svcs. program Long Branch (NJ) H.S. and Mid. Sch., 1988—89; guidance counselor G. Harold Antrim Elem. Sch., Pt. Pleasant Beach, NJ, 1989—92; social worker, counselor Brick Twp. Bd. Edn., 1993—. Religion tchr. Roman Cath. Ch., Brick, 2004—; sec. bd. dirs. Ocean County Adult Retarded Citizens, 2002—. Avocations: travel, going to the beach. Office: Brick Twp Bd Edn 103 Hendrickson Ave Brick NJ 08724 Office Phone: 732-785-3050 5504. Personal E-mail: migs613@aol.com.

WHITE, DENISE, mathematics professor, department chairman; d. Donald and Mary Jean (Thomas) Teegarden; m. Richard E. White, July 31, 2003; children: Jennifer Beach, Alyson Beach, Jeremy Beach. BA in Math., Mid-America Nazarene U., Olathe, Kans., 1976; MEd in Curriculum and Instrn. in Math., Wichita State U., Kans., 2000. Cert. tchr. Mo., Kans. Math. tchr., chmn. dept. Winfield HS, Kans., 1987—2000; math. instr. Cowley County CC, Arkansas City, Kans., 2000—03; chmn. math. dept. liberal arts divsn. Santa Fe CC, 2003—. Presenter workshops in field. Deacon First Presbyn. Ch., Winfield. Recipient Tchg. Excellence award, Nat. Inst. for Staff and Orgnl. Devel., 2003. Mem.: NEA, Nat. Coun. Tchrs. Math., N.Mex. Assn. Two-Year Colls. Democrat. Presbyterian. Avocations: travel, music, computers, reading. Office: Santa Fe CC 6401 Richards Avenue Santa Fe NM 87508 Office Phone: 505-428-1374. Office Fax: 505-428-1282. Business E-Mail: dwhite@sfccnm.edu.

WHITE, DONNA ANNETTE, retired secondary school educator; b. Kittanning, Pa, Jan. 27, 1940; d. Willard D. and Geraldine A. (Anthony) Hayes; children: Chad, Shane. BS, Syracuse U., 1961. Cert. tchr. Tchr. various HS and Jr. HS, Pa., 1961-72, Hillsborough County, Fla., 1972-74, Gibbs HS, Pinellas County, Fla., 1974—2005, ret., 2005. Sponsor Internat. Thespian Soc., 1974—; pres. Pinellas Assn. for Theatre Edn., 1977-79, 81-83, 85-90, 95-96, 97—; mem. Validation Com. for Theatre Certification Exam, 1988-89, Fla. Assn. for Theatre Edn., 1990-2005; co-chair The Rose Years Extravaganza, 1990; co-dir. Pinellahassee Day at the Capitol, 1990; bd. dir. Fla. Alliance for Arts Edn., 1990-91, Fla. Theatre Conf., 1990-97, v.p., 1992-98, chair secondary sch. divsn., 1998—, sec. 1999-2005; chair Tchr. Incentive Grant Panel for Fla. Alliance for Arts Edn., 1996-2003, Secondary Sch. Auditions for the Southeastern Theatre Conf., Fla. Alliance for Arts Edn., 1992-94. Recipient Disting. Career award for secondary sch. Fla. Theatre Conf., 1989, Theatre Leadership award Fla. Assn. for Theatre Edn., 1992; recipient Pin. Co. Ed. Found. Outstanding Ed. Award, 2002. Avocations: reading, beach walking. Home: 8401 W Gulf Blvd Treasure Island FL 33706-3421 Office Phone: 727-893-5452. Personal E-mail: whitelady@verizon.net. Business E-Mail: msblue@peoplepc.com.

WHITE, FLORENCE MAY, retired special education educator; b. Ottawa, Kans., Sept. 1, 1936; d. O.C. Robert and Effie Lynne (Walker) Arnold; m. Donald L. White, June 1, 1958 (dec. Jan. 1996); children: Tab Vincent, Jacque Sue, Michelle May. BA, Ottawa U., 1958; MS, Kans. U., 1974; postgrad., Kans. U. Med. Ctr., 1975—76. Cert. reading specialist, learning disabilities specialist; cert. elem. and mid. sch. edn.; lang. arts, social studies, elem. curriculum. Classroom tchr. 2d grade Wellsville (Kans.) Elem., 1958-59; learning disabilities tchr. Olatha (Kans.) Spl. Edn. Coop., 1971-74; learning disabilities specialist, tchr. 7-9 Ottawa Mid. Sch., 1974-77; learning disabilities specialist, tchr. Paola Spl. Edn. Coop., Richmond, Kans., 1980-95; tchr. learning disabilities classes elem. level Ctrl. Heights Elem. Sch., Richmond, Kans., 2001—02. Pub. rep., speaker on learning disabilities to civic groups and local orgns., 1972-75. Den mother Boy Scouts Am. and Brownies, Ottawa, 1968-70; chair state GOP women's polit. activities Rep. State Party, Topeka, 1964-67; chair scholarship contest DAR, Ottawa dist., 1984-96; Sunday sch. tchr. Meth. Ch., Ottawa; crafts tchr. local 4-H, Ottawa; mem. Central Heights PTA (projects com. 1980-95); mem. Ottawa Arts Coun. State of Kans. scholar State Spl. Edn. Dept., 1976. Mem.: PEO, Kans. Assn. Ret. Sch. Employees, Franklin County Reading Coun. (pres.-elect 1989—91, pres. 1991—92, mem. exec. bd. 1993—94, v.p.), Kans. Reading Assn., Internat. Reading Assn., Garden Club, Soroptimist, Ottawa Area C. of C., Franklin County Ottawa C. of C., Alpha Delta Kappa (projects com. 1988—, environment com., hospitality com., historian). Roman Catholic. Avocations: painting, reading, travel, music, flower arranging. E-mail: gramaflo@sbcglobal.net.

WHITE, FRANCES LAVONNE, academic administrator; b. Houston, Oct. 15, 1947; d. John Wesley Jr. and Irma Johnetta (Porter) Williams; m. Harley Sr. White, Dec. 22, 1971; 1 child, Ivan Whitney. AA in Edn., Merritt Coll., 1968; BS in Psychology, Calif. State U., Hayward, 1970, MS in Counseling and Psychology, 1972; PhD in Edn., U. Calif., Berkeley, 1990. Instr. psychology Peralta Colls., Oakland, Calif., 1980—90, dir. staff devel., 1990—91; dean social scis., arts, phys. edn. Laney Coll., Oakland, 1991—94, Evergreen Valley Coll., San Jose, Calif., 1994—96; interim chancellor San Jose/Evergreen Colls., 1996; exec. vice chancellor City Coll., San Francisco, 1996—99; pres. Skyline Coll., San Bruno, Calif., 1999—. Mem. Oakland Citizen's Adv. Bd., 1986—88; pres., bd. dirs. Adminstrs. Calif. C.C. Assn., Sacramento, 1994—2000; chmn. bd. dirs. Families on Track, South San Francisco, Calif., 1999—; mem. leadership com. United Way, San Mateo County, Calif., 2000—01; mem. cmty. adv. bd. Seton Med. Ctr., Daly City, Calif., 1999—; bd. dirs. C.C. League Calif., Sacramento, 1999—2000. Named Educator of Yr., Iota Phi Lambda, 2001; recipient Tom Lakin Leadership award, Calif. C.C. Africa American Trustees, 1997. Mem.: AAUW, San Bruno Rotary (bd. dirs. 1999—, Mem. of Yr. 2001). Avocations: reading, bicycling, singing, walking, meditation. Office: Skyline Coll 3300 College Ave San Bruno CA 94066 Home: Po Box 3029 San Rafael CA 94912-3029

WHITE, GAYLE COLQUITT, writer, journalist; b. Lamar County, Ga., Nov. 4, 1950; d. Albert Candler and Ethel Eugenia (Moore) Colquitt; m. Robert Eugene White, Jr., Apr. 9, 1972; children: Margaret Candler, Robert Eugene III. AB in Journalism, U. Ga., 1972. Reporter Atlanta Jour. & Constn., 1972—; pres. Religion News Writers' Assn., 1972—. Author: Believers and Beliefs, 1997. Named Templeton Reporter of Yr., Religion Newswriters Assn., 1992. Presbyterian. Office: Atlanta Journal & Constitution 72 Marietta St NW Atlanta GA 30303-2899

WHITE, GRETCHEN NANCE, education educator, writer; d. Virginia Lee Nance; m. Ronald Craig White (dec.); children: Loronzo De'Warren, David Lee, Mark Du'Pree, Paul Keith, Anthony O'Lunte, Michelle Ja'Nesse Jefferson. Diploma in child daycare, ICS, Pa., 1995; diploma in mgmt. in health care, Calif. Coll. of Health Scis., 1998, diploma in bus. comm., 2001. Cert. ordination Tex., 2001, Tex. Notary Pub. Commn. Pvt. duty nurses asst. Meth. Hosp., Houston, 1984—87; vocat. coord. Richmond (Tex.) State Sch., 1988—. Founder, pres. White's Internat. Scholarship, Inc., Wharton, Tex., 2001—. Author: (book) It's Vision Time, 2000, The Four F''s/Faith, Fear, Failure, Forgiveness, 2000, A Nation on the Rise to Be Educated or Not to Be Educated, 2003. Host bible study chat group, vol. Read-A-Thon; sponsor free hot meal program for low-income housing project area, 2004—; pastor A Nation on the Rise Youth/Teen Ministry Explosion. Grantee, Wal-mart Super Ctr., 2004. Avocations: cooking, reading, health glider, sports. Office: Whites Internat Scholarship Inc PO Box 1283 Rosenberg TX 77471 Office Phone: 281-846-8558. Business E-Mail: gretchen.white@dads.state.tx.us.

WHITE, H. KATHERINE, lawyer; b. Salina, Kans., May 21, 1945; BS, MIT, 1967; JD, Rutgers U., 1975. Bar: Calif. 1975, NJ 1982. Joined Sealed Air Corp., Saddle Brook, NJ, 1982, v.p., gen. counsel, sec., 1998—. Mem.: NJ Corp. Counsel Assn. (dir. 1994—96), Am. Corp. Counsel Assn., Am. Soc. Corp. Secretaries, State Bar Calif., NJ State Bar Assn., ABA. Office: Sealed Air Corp Pk 80 E Saddle Brook NJ 07663-5291

WHITE, HELEN LOU, school nurse practitioner; b. Caldwell, Kans., Aug. 24, 1936; d. Orville George and Mildred Estelle (Garrison) Fauchier; m. Wayne Lee White, Sept. 1, 1957; children: Michelle Lee, Dana Lynn, Jacki Lou. Diploma, St. Francis Sch. Nursing, Wichita, Kans., 1957; cert. sch. nurse, Pittsburg State U., Kans., 1983. RN Kans., nat. cert. sch. nurse. Staff nurse St. Francis Hosp., Wichita, Kans., 1957—60, St. Lukes Hosp., Wellington, Kans., 1961—63, Wellington Hosp. and Clinic, 1971—74; sch. nurse and dir. health svcs. Unified Sch. Dist. # 353, Wellington, 1974—94; ret., 1994. Mem. planning com. for implementing sch. nurse cert. programs Wichita State U., 1984—90; advisory coun. on health and physical edn., Kans., 1984—90; human sexuality tchr. trainer Kans. Dept. Edn., 1988; human sexuality, AIDS edn. trainer for elem. tchrs., 89. Mem.: Am. Nurses Assn., Nat. Assn. Sch. Nurses (Kans. dir. bd. dirs. 1985—89), Kans. Sch. Nurse Orgn. (pres.-elect 1981—83, pres. 1983—85, Kans. Sch. Nurse of Yr. 1991, legis. co-chair 2000—05), Kappa Kappa Iota. Democrat. Methodist. Avocations: acting, theater directing, piano, singing, travel. Home: 438 E 20th St N Wellington KS 67152

WHITE, IRENE, insurance professional; b. Tamuning, Guam, Jan. 3, 1961; d. Antonio Gill and Irma Magdalena (Idrogo) Gill; m. William Paul Franck, Aug. 4, 1979 (div. July 1984); m. Richard Nelson White, May 12, 1989 (div. Dec. 1993); 1 child, Karen Elizabeth. Cert. ins. adjuster, Tex., assoc. in claims; chartered property casualty underwriter, 1997. Ins. adjuster Gen. Accident Group, San Antonio, 1983-85, Crum & Forster Ins., San Antonio, 1985-89, Aetna Life & Casualty, San Antonio, 1979-83, adjuster, analyst, cons., complex case mgr. Dallas, 1989-96; sr. account exec., regional mgr. St. Paul Travelers, Dallas, 1996—. Big sister Big Bros. and Sisters, San Antonio, 1987—89; vol. counselor March of Dimes, San Antonio, 1988—89; team mgr. Destination Imagination, Plano, 2004—06, volleyball coach, 2005; catechist St. Mark the Evangelist Cath. Ch., Plano, Tex., 1999—. Republican. Avocation: gardening. Office: Ste 200 1301 E Collins Blvd Richardson TX 75081 Business E-Mail: irene.white@stpaultravelers.com.

WHITE, JENNIFER SULLIVAN, secondary school educator; adopted d. Bill R. and d. Jean A. Sullivan, d. Thomas C. Bullock; m. Mark A. White, Jan. 1, 1997; children: Kase A., Gage A., Taylor B. BA, U. Tex., Austin, 1992. Cert. tchr. Tex. Tchr. Longview (Tex.) Ind. Sch. Dist., 2002—04, Pine Tree HS, Longview, 2004—. Coach, sponsor Nat. Forensic League, Longview, 2004—, rep., Ripon, Wis., 2004—. Mem.: Tex. Ednl. Theatre Assn. (assoc.). Avocations: travel, politics. Home: 261 PR 3538 Gladewater TX 75647 Office: Pine Tree HS 1001 W Fairmont Longview TX 75604 Office Phone: 903-295-5031. Home Fax: 903-297-2899; Office Fax: 903-295-5029. Personal E-mail: jwhite2813@aol.com. E-mail: jwhite1@ptisd.org.

WHITE, JILL CAROLYN, lawyer; b. Santa Barbara, Calif., Mar. 20, 1934; d. Douglas Cameron and Gladys Louise (Ashley) W.; m. Walter Otto Weyrauch, Mar. 17, 1973. BA, Occidental Coll., L.A., 1955; JD, U. Calif., Berkeley, 1972. Bar: Fla. 1974, Calif. 1975, U.S. Supreme Ct. Staff mem. U.S. Dept. State, Am. Embassy, Rio de Janeiro, 1956-58; with psychol. rsch. units Inst. Human Devel., Inst. Personality Assessment and Rsch., U. Calif., Berkeley, 1961-68; adj. prof. criminal justice program U. Fla., Gainesville, Fla., 1976-78; pvt. practice immigration and nationality law, Gainesville, 1976—2002. Contbr. articles to profl. jours. Mem.: Fla. Bar (immigration and nationality law cert. com. 1994—99, chmn. cert. com. 1997—98, cert. in immigration and nationality law 1995—), Bar Assn. 8th Jud. Cir. Fla., Am. Immigration Lawyers Assn. (bd. dirs. Ctrl. Fla. chpt. 1985—94, 1995—96, 1997—2000, chmn. Ctrl. Fla. chpt. 1988—89, co-chmn. so. regional liaison com. 1990—92, nat. bd. dirs. 1988—89), Altrusa. Democrat. Office Phone: 352-380-9122. Personal E-mail: jwhite49@earthlink.net.

WHITE, JOY KATHRYN, retired claims consultant, artist; b. Pawnee, Okla., Jan. 12, 1941; d. Stephen G. Gover, Vera Fay Gover; m. Bob Al White, Aug. 10, 1962; children: Stephen, Robert. H.S. diploma, Weatherford H.S., 1959. Ins. filing clk. Jane Phillips Med. Ctr., Bartlesville, Okla., 1986—; Am. Indian Beadworker The Silver Quail, Dewey, Okla., 1972—, ret., 2003—. Artist Am. Indian Beadwork Indian Colors, 1989 (2d Pl., 1989), Eagle Woman, 1996 (1st Pl., 1996), Justice?, 1992 (1st Pl., 1992), Blue Cut Glass Beaded Staff, 1994 (1st Pl., 1994), Buckskin Dress, 1993 (1st Pl., 1993), Magistic, 2000 (1st Pl., 2000), Unnamed- Green Cut Glass Medallion, 1998

(1st Pl., 1998), Unnamed- White Cut Glass Bolo, 2001 (1st Pl., 2001, 2002, 2nd Pl., 2002, 3d Pl., 2002, Honorable Mention, 2003), Cut Glass Beaded Cane, 2002 (1st Pl., 2002), Beaded Turtle Medallion, 2002 (1st Pl., 2003), Beaded Bolo, 2002 (2d Pl., 2002), Beaded Fan, 2000 (2d Pl., 2003). Tribal mem. Pawnee Nation; pres. Pilot Club of Dewey, 1986—87; mem., adv. Indian Summer Art Festival Com., Bartlesville, 1990—. Mem.: Am. Women in Arts, Pani Art Assn., Osage Gem and Mineral Soc., Bartlesville Indian Women's Club (pres. 1998—2000). Democrat. Baptist. Avocations: canning, cooking, sewing, gardening, art. Home: 505 E Third Dewey OK 74029

WHITE, JOY MIEKO, retired communications executive; b. Yokohama, Japan, May 1, 1951; came to U.S., 1951; d. Frank Deforest and Wanda Mieko Mellen; m. George William White, June 5, 1948; 1 child, Karen. BA Comm., Calif. State U., Fullerton, 1974, student, 1977, Orange Coast C.C., 1981, Golden West C.C., 1990. Cert. secondary tchr., Calif.; cert. tchr. Coast C.C.s Dist. Secondary tchr. Anaheim Union H.S. Dist., Calif., 1977—80; tech. writer Pertec Computer Corp., Irvine, Calif., 1980—81; supr. large sys. disvn. Burroughs, Mission Viejo, Calif., 1981—83; mgr. Lockheed divsn. CalComp, Anaheim, 1983—86; owner, pres. Communicator's Connection, Irvine, 1986—90; pres. Info Team, Inc., 1989—2004; ret., 2004. Adj. faculty, coord. tech. comm. program Golden West Coll., Huntington Beach, Calif., 1987-90; instr. U. Calif., Irvine, 1987-89, Calif. State U., Fullerton, 1988-91; sec. Santa Ana Dist. chpt. U.S. SBA Assn. for Minority-Owned Bus., 1991-96; presenter in field Active Performing Arts, Costa Mesa, 1986— Fellow Soc. Tech. Comm. (assoc., internat. assoc., sr., Orange County chpt. 1987, Mem. of Yr.); mem. NAFE, Soc. Profl. Journalists, Women in Comm. (pres. Orange County Profl. chpt. 1989-90), Nat. Assn. Women Bus. Owners, Rembrandts Wine Club (Yorba Linda), Girl Scouts U.S. (life, active 1994—, troop leader 1995-2003) Republican. Avocations: writing short stories, needlecrafts, camping, fishing. Home: 3531 Brentridge Dr Corona CA 92881-8445 Personal E-mail: joywhitemk@comcast.com. Business E-Mail: infoteam@comcast.com.

WHITE, JOYCE LOUISE, librarian; b. Phila., June 7, 1927; d. George William and Louisa (Adams) W. BA, U. Pa., 1949; MLS, Drexel U., 1963; MA in Religion, Episc. Sem. S.W., 1978. Head libr. Penniman Libr. Edn. U. Pa., Phila., 1960-76; archivist St. Francis Boys' Home, Salina, Kans., 1982-84; libr. Brown Mackie Coll., Salina, 1983-86; libr., dir. St. Thomas Theol. Sem., Denver, 1986-95; libr., dir. Archbishop Vehr Theol. Libr. Archdiocese of Denver, 1995-96. Author: Biographical and Historial Yarnall Library, 1979, Colorado Episcopal Clergy in the 19th Century: A Biographical Register, 2003; asst. editor: Women Religious History Sources, 1983; contbr. articles to profl. jours. and chpts. to books. Vol. libr. St. John's Cath., Denver, 1993—. Mem. Ch. and Synagogue Libr. Assn. (life, founding, pres. 1969-70, exec. sec. 1970-72, exec. bd. 1967-76, ann. conf. chair 1996). Avocations: gardening, cats, church libraries. Office: 1350 Washington St Denver CO 80203-2008

WHITE, JULIE, actress; b. San Diego, June 4, 1962; d. Edwin and Sue Jane W.; m. Carl Pandel, 1984 (div.); 1 child, Alexandra. Student, Fordham U., Tex. State U. Actress Carsey-Werner Co., CBS-MTM Studios, Studio City, Calif. TV appearances: Grace Under Fire, 1993-97, Six Feet Under, 2001-03; stage appearances: Dark of the Moon, 1984-85, The Geography of Yearning, 1985-86, Lucky Stiff, 1988, Early One Evening at the Rainbow Bar, Grille, 1989, Largo Desolato, 1990-91, Marathon '91, 1991, The Stick Wife, 1991, Spike Heels, 1992, Money and Friends, 1992-93, Absurd Person Singular, 1992-93, The Heidi Chronicles, 1995, Over Texas, The Family of Mann, Just Say No, Dinner With Friends, 1999, Barbra's Wedding, Bad Dates, Fiction, Marvin's Room, The Little Dog Laughed, 2005 (OBIE award Village Voice 2006); film appearances: Take Down, 1978, Flypaper, 1997, Say It Isn't So, 2001, Slap Her.She's French, 2002, War of the Worlds, 2005. Office: Carsey-Werner Co CBS-MTM Studios 4024 Radford Ave Studio City CA 91604-2101*

WHITE, KAREN JEAN, artist; d. Patrick and Bonnie Jean W.; m. W. Michael Shuster, Aug. 12, 1988 (div.). BFA, Ohio State U., 1969; postgrad., Met. State Coll., 1976-77, U. Colo., 1985. Tchr. Arapahoe C.C., Denver, 1988, U. No. Colo., Denver, 1990, Colo. Inst. Art, Denver, 1991, Colo. Art Tchrs. Conf., Denver, 1991; front range cmty. tchg. educator State Coll., Colo., 1996. Co-founder Women's Art Gallery, Denver, 1995. Exhibited in numerous solo and group shows, including Denver Art Mus., 1974, Sandy Carson Gallery, Denver, 1987, Arvada (Colo.) Ctr. for Arts, 1987, Foothills Art Ctr., Golden, Colo., 1987, Emmanual Gallery, Denver, 1987, New Dawn Gallery, Edina, Minn., 1988, Contemporary Crafts Ctr., Denver, 1988, Core New Art Space, Denver, 1988, Boulder Ctr. for Visual Arts, 1989, Am. Craft Mus., Denver, 1989, Foothills Arts Ctr., 1990, Del Mano Gallery, L.A., 1989, Western Colo. Ctr. for Arts, Grand Junction, 1989, Grant St. Arts Ctr., Denver, 1989, Mariani Gallery, U. No. Colo., Greeley, 1989, Steamboat Springs (Colo.) Art Ctr., 1989, Technic Gallery, St. Paul, 1990, Banaker Gallery, Walnut Creek, Calif., 1990, Katie Gingress Gallery, Santa Fe, N.Mex., 1990, Gallery bel eTage, Basel, Switzerland, 1991, Internat. Gallery, San Diego, 1991, UMC Fine Arts Ctr., Boulder, Colo., 1992, Colo. Gallery of Arts, Littleton, 1992, J. Jevitts Ctr., N.Y.C., 1992, Emmanual Gallery, Denver, 1992, Nora Eccles Harrison Mus. Art, Utah, 1990, Loveland Art Mus., 1990, Bergen Mus. of Art, 1991, Nat. Libr., Royal Palace, Hungary, 1992, Mini Biennial Invitational, Olfstrom, Sweden, 1993, Concordia U., Que., Can., 1993, Musee du pays et Val de Charmeney, Switzerland, 1993, Nat. Assn. Women Artists, N.Y.C., 1994, Anna Blake Gallery, 1994, Mus. Papierfabrik Scheufen, Lenningen, Germany, 1995, others. Pres. Neighborhood Partnership Team, Denver, 1995-96; founder Clean Air Coalition, Denver, 1988, Broadway Corridor Arts Alliance, Denver, 1996, Women's Arts Ctr. and Gallery, Denver, 1997. Pub. art grantee Neighborhood Cultures of Denver, 1995, Neighborhood Arts Program grantee Weed & Seed Dept. of Justice, Denver, 1995; recipient Juror's Choice award FIBER/texture, 1993, 1st prize Mannings Nat. Fibre Show, 1977, Colo. Lawyers for Arts Ann. Show, 1988. Mem. Nat. Assn. Women Artists, Women's Caucus on the Arts. Democrat. Avocation: reading. Home: 282 Delaware St Denver CO 80223-1306

WHITE, KAREN RUTH JONES, information systems executive; b. Ft. Meade, Md., Oct. 8, 1953; d. Frank L. Jones and Inge H. Lesser; m. M. Timothy Heath, Apr. 23, 1973 (div. Aug. 1976); m. Carl W. White, May 30, 1993 AS Electronic Data Processing, N.H. Tech. Inst., Concord, 1977; BS MIS high honors, Northeastern U., Boston, 1984, MS Info. Sys., 1997. Prof. Project Mgmt. Inst., 2001. Programmer Chubb Life Ins. Co., Concord, NH, 1977—79, Retailers Electronics Account Processing, Woburn, Mass., 1979—82; sr. programmer, analyst N.H. Ins. Group, Manchester, 1982—84; prin. sys. analyst Wang Labs., Inc., Lowell, Mass., 1984—89; project mgr. TASC, Inc., Reading, Mass., 1989—2000; sr. dir. consulting svcs. PM Solutions, Havertown, Pa., 2000—. Bd. dirs. Brandywyne Common Assn., Derry, N.H., 1991-94; mem. St. Paul's Sch. Advanced Studies Program Alumni Assn., Concord With U.S. Army Res., 1974-84 Decorated Army Commendation medal, 1980 Mem.: NAFE, IEEE (program chair 5th reengring. forum 1996, exec. adv. bd. 1996—99, ep. conf. chair 6th reengring. forum 1998, computer soc., tech. com. in software engring.), Project Mgmt. Inst. (Mass. Bay chpt. program dir. 1992—93, project chair 1994—96, dir. seminars/symposium 1996—98, adv. group 1999—2000, ethics rev. com. 2000—02, awards rev. com. 2001—03, chair ethics rev. com. 2003—06, ethics stds. rev. com. 2004—, chairperson ethics stds. implementation planning com. 2006, bd. dirs. Edn. Found.), Sigma Epsilon Rho. Home: 50 Merrill Rd Weare NH 03281-4708 Office: PM Solutions 50 Merrill Rd Weare NH 03281-4708 Business E-Mail: kwhite@pmsolutions.com.

WHITE, KATE, editor-in-chief; m. Brad Holbrooke; 2 children. BA, Union Coll. Editor Child mag., 1988—89; editor-in-chief Working Woman mag., NYC, 1989—91, McCall's mag., NYC, 1991—94, Redbook, NYC, 1994—98, Cosmopolitan mag., NYC, 1998—. Author: Why Good Girls Don't Get Ahead and Gutsy Girls Do, 1995, (novels) If Looks Could Kill, 2002, A Body to Die For, 2003, 'Til Death Do Us Part, 2004, Over Her Dead Body, 2005. Recipient Matrix award, Women in Comms., 2003. Office: Cosmopolitan Hearst Magazines 224 W 57th St New York NY 10019-3299 also: Sandra Dijkstra Lit Agy 1237 Camino Del Mar Del Mar CA 92014 Office Phone: 212-649-3561. Office Fax: 212-397-7581.*

WHITE, KATHARINE STONE, museum administrator; b. Lexington, Mass., Nov. 5, 1914; d. Edward Carleton and Katharine (Brooke) Stone; m. John Warren White, Dec. 20, 1941; children: Susan White West, Patience H., John F. (dec.). BA, Vassar Coll., 1936. Rschr. film libr. Mus. Modern Art, N.Y.C., 1938-41; film programmer DeCordova Mus., Lincoln, Mass., 1962-63; film programmer dept. edn. Boston Mus. Fine Arts, 1970-74; trustee Mus. Fine Arts, Boston, 1974-90, hon. trustee, 1990—. Editor, chair trustee handbook com. Assn. Am. Mus., 1982. Chmn. Planning Bd., Lincoln, 1955-60; pres. Lincoln Hist. Soc., 1963-65.

WHITE, KATHERINE E., law educator; BSE elec. engring. and computer sci., Princeton U., 1988; JD, U. Wash., 1991; LLM in Intellectual Property, George Washington U., 1996. Bar: Mich. 1996, U.S. Supreme Ct, U.S. Ct. Appeals (fed. cir.), U.S. Ct. Appeals Armed Forces, U.S. Army Ct. Mil. Rev., U.S. Patent and Trademark Office, Wash. 1992. Intellectual property counsel U.S. Army Corps Engrs., Washington, 1992—95; jud. law clk. for Hon. Randall Rader U.S. Ct. Appeals (fed. cir.), 1995—96; assoc. prof. Wayne State U. Law Sch., Detroit, 1996—. Adj. prof. George Washington U. Law Ctr., Washington, 1994—96; regent U. Mich., Ann Arbor, 1999—; mem. patent pub. adv. com. U.S. Patent and Trademark Office, 2000—02. Actor: Intellectual Property Litigation, Pretrial Practice Guide, 1999; co-author (with Eric Dobrusin): Intellectual Property Litigation, Pretrial Practice Guide, 1999; contbr. articles to profl. publs. CPT JAG U.S. Army, 1992—95, maj. JAG USAR, 1995—. Recipient Fulbright Sr. Scholar award, Max-Planck Inst. for Fgn. Internat. Patent, Copyright and Competition Law, 1999—2000; grantee, Max-Planck-Inst. for Fgn. Internat. Patent, Copyright and Competition Law, 2000; scholar, ROTC, Washington Law Found., 1988—91; Shaw fellow, 1994—96, White House Fellow, special coun. to the sec. of agr., 2001—02. Mem.: AAUP, ABA, Wolverine Bar Assn., Wash. State Bar Assn., Nat. Bar Assn., Mich. Patent Lawyer's Assn., Am. Intellectual Property Law Assn., Am. Assn. Law Schs., State Bar Mich. (mem. coun. intellectual property law sec., co-chmn. student liaison com., co-chmn. com. pattent issues in legislation), Princeton Club Mich. Office: Wayne U Law Sch 471 W Palmer Detroit MI 48202

WHITE, KATHERINE ELIZABETH, retired pediatrician; b. Syracuse, N.Y., Mar. 23, 1920; d. Rufus Macandie and Marguerite Mary (Eselin) W.; m. Nicholas V. Oddo, Feb. 12, 1947 (dec. 1966); 1 child, Sandra S. Qualls. BA, Syracuse U., 1941, MD, 1943. Intern Syracuse U. Med. Ctr., 1944-45; asst. resident Buffalo Children's Hosp., 1945-46, chief resident, 1946-47; instr. pediatrics L.A. Children's Hosp., 1947; pvt. practice, Long Beach, Calif., 1947-90; mem. med. staff Miller Children's Hosp., Long Beach, 1966—, trustee, 1968—. Adv. bd. Children's Clinic, Long Beach, Calif., bd. dirs. 1968-87, 2004—, mem. founders cir. care; bd. trustees Long Beach Meml. Med. Ctr. Mem. Friends of Miller's Children's Hosp. Leadership Cir., 2002. Recipient award Meml. Med. Ctr. Found., 1990, Found. for Children's Health Care, 1984, 87, Humanitarian award Kiwanis, 1990, Katherine White, M.D. Philanthropy award, Long Beach Kiwanis Club, 1990, Recognition award Children's Clinic, 1991, Achievement award Long Beach, Calif., Meml. Med. Ctr., 1997, Tribute award Children's Clinic, Long Beach, 2005. Fellow Am. Acad. Pediatrics; mem. AMA, Am. Med. Women's Assn., Calif. Med. Assn., L.A. County Med. Assn., Long Beach Med. Assn., Soroptimist (Woman of Distinction 1989, Hall of Fame award 1990), Women and Philanthropy Calif. State, Laurel Soc. Soroptimist Internat. (life, archivist), Phi Beta Kappa. Republican. Roman Catholic. Home: 4538 Clubhouse Drive Lakewood CA 90712 Personal E-mail: bknlb@aol.com.

WHITE, KATHLEEN, director; b. St. Louis, July 10, 1959; d. Thomas Ray Halterman and Nancy Corine (Dexheimer) Rutsaert. BS in Edn., Ill. State U., 1984; MA in Edn., Chapman U., 1996; MA in Edn. Adminstrn., Calif. State U., Bakersfield, 2002. Elem. tchr. St. Mary's Sch., Cheyenne, Wyo., 1984-89, Earlimart (Calif.) Sch. Dist., 1989—. Peer coach for pre-interns, new tchr. mentor, leadership team, BTSA support provider. Recipient Anna Keaton scholarship Assn. Residence Halls, Ill. State U., 1984. Mem.: Assn. Calif. Sch. Adminstrs. Democrat. Roman Catholic. Avocations: reading, music, crafts, travel, silhouette rifle competitions. Office: Earlimart Sch Dist PO Box 11970 Earlimart CA 93219-1970

WHITE, KATHLEEN MAE, social worker, marriage and family therapist; b. Lamar, Colo., Feb. 12, 1941; d. Cornelius William and Lillian Mae (Oswald) Hogan; m. Larry F. White, Mar. 30, 1959; children: Thomas William, Richard Edward, July Lynn, Ramona Marie. AA, U. Md., 1969; BS cum laude, Tex. A&M U., 1972; MSW, Our Lady of the Lake U., 1976. Lic. profl. counselor, Tex. Dept. Health, chem. dependency counselor, LCSW, lic. marriage and family therapist. With Vol. Svcs., ARC, Wright Patterson AFB, Ohio, 1964-65, Randolph AFB, Tex., 1965-66, Sembach AFB, Germany, 1966-69; tchr. St. Augustines Cath. Sch., Laredo, Tex., 1970-71; social worker Tex. Dept. Pub. Welfare, San Antonio, 1972-74; tchr. Edgewood Ind. Sch. Dist., San Antonio, 1976-78; coord. teenage mothers sch. Harlandale Ind. Sch. Dist., San Antonio, 1978-83; pvt. practice mental health social work, 1976—. With dept. of psychiatry Tex. Health Sci. Ctr., 1996-99, with dept. of adult psychiatry Meth. Healthcare Sys., San Antonio, 1999—. Recipient VA stipend, 1975-76. Mem. Acad. Cert. Social Workers, Am. Assn. Social Workers, Tex. Soc. Clin. Social Workers, Our Lady of the Lake U. Alumni Assn. Republican. Roman Catholic. Office: 1201 Pat Booker Rd Universal City TX 78148-3936 Home: 261 Westway Dr Universal City TX 78148-4347 Office Phone: 210-658-7337.

WHITE, LANI NYLA, real estate developer, real estate broker; d. Fleet Russell and Nyla Marie White. BA in Art, Mills Coll.; MFA in Art, U. Calif., Irvine; MA in Drama, U. Calif., Santa Barbara. Cert. real estate broker, Colo. Owner/broker Lani White & Assoc., Aspen, Colo.; pres., owner Aspen Polo Club. Horse trainer, polo sch. Mem. Colo. Assn. Realtors, Nat. Assn. Realtors, Aspen Soc. for Animal Rights (co-dir), U.S. Polo Assn. (del.), Maroon Creek Country Club, El Dorado Polo Club. Avocations: polo, skiing, tennis. Office Phone: 970-948-9464. Business E-Mail: apsenrealestate@aol.com.

WHITE, LEANDRES, history educator; d. Edward and Leatha McDonald; children: Lois, Freda, Karen. BA in History, U. Ill., Chgo., 1970; MA in History, Chgo. State U., 1975, MA in Curriculum Instrn., 1983, MA in Adminstrn. Supervision, 1986. History tchr. Chgo. Bd. Edn., 1970. Mem. adv. bd. trustees Chgo. State U., 1983—86, mem. exec. bd., 2001—04; chmn. Cohaere, 1999—2004; softball coach, basketball referee, baseball umpire. Mem.: LWV, NAACP (mem. exec. com. 2006—), Chgo. Tchrs. Union (trustee 2001—04). Avocations: bowling, swimming, softball, volleyball.

WHITE, LIBBY KRAMER, librarian; b. Boston, Sept. 30, 1934; d. Samuel and Ida (Drucker) Kramer; m. Gerald Milton White, June 6, 1956; children: Charles, Andrew, Judith White Cuttler, Abigail White D'Costa. BS in Social Sci., Simmons Coll., Boston, 1956; MLS, SUNY, Albany, 1972; MALS, SUNY, 1998. Librarian Temple Israel, Albany, N.Y., 1966-73; bookmobile librarian Schenectady County Pub. Library, 1973, br. librarian, 1973-76, ref./YA librarian, 1976-85, ref./ethnic culture librarian, 1985—; libr. Jewish Vocat. Svc. Balt., 1998—, Beth Israel Congregation, Owings Mills, Md., 1998—. Chmn. Nat. Library Wk., Schenectady, 1985, 96; resident advisor Summer Seminars in Judaic Studies, Skidmore Coll., Saratoga Springs, N.Y., 1987-95. Book reviewer Sch. Libr. Jour., 1980—, Libr. Jour., 1989, Assn. Jewish Librs. Newsletter, 1994—; cons. various encys., mags.; contbr. articles profl. jours. Trustee Beth Israel Synagogue, Schenectady, 1986-94, 95-98. Mem. Md. Libr. Assn., Assn. Jewish Librs. (mem. Sydney Taylor awards com. 1999—). Jewish. Avocations: reading, writing short stories, travel. Office: Jewish Vocat Svc 1515 Reisterstown Rd Baltimore MD 21208-4353 also: Beth Israel Congregation 3706 Crondall Ln Owings Mills MD 21117-2205 E-mail: white_libby@juno.com, lwhite@jvsbaltimore.org, llibbylib@aol.com.

WHITE, LILLIAS, actress; Appeared in Broadway plays Titanic, Cats, Once on This Island, Dreamgirls, Rock 'n' Roll: The First 5000 Years, Barnum, How to Succeed in Business., The Life (Tony award 1997), Chicago, 2006; (off-Broadway) Waiting for Godot, The Princess and The Black-eyed Pea, Antigone Africanus, Romance in Hard Times (Obie award); (nat. and internat. tour) Ain't Misbehavin', The Wiz, Tintypes, Dreamgirls (Drama-Logue award), Purlie, 2005, South Pacific, 2005; (TV series) Sesame Street (Emmy award), Law & Order, NYPD Blue; (film) (voice) Hercules; concert appearance include Carnegie Hall, Lincoln Ctr., The White House. Office: Don Buchwald & Assocs 10 E 44th St Fl 2 New York NY 10017-3654*

WHITE, LINDA DIANE, lawyer; b. NYC, Apr. 1, 1952; d. Bernard and Elaine (Simons) Schwartz; m. Thomas M. White, Aug. 16, 1975; 1 child, Alexandra Nicole. AB, U. Pa., 1973; JD, Northwestern U., 1976. Bar: Ill. 1976. Assoc. Walsh, Case, Coale & Brown, Chgo., 1976-77, Greenberger & Kaufmann (merged into Katten, Muchin), Chgo., 1977-82, ptnr., 1982-85, Sonnenschein Nath & Rosenthal LLP, Chgo., 1985—. Mem. trustees coun. Penn Women; mem. Samuel Zell and Robert Lurie Real Estate Ctr., Wharton Sch., U. Pa. Mem.: ABA (mem. real property fin. com., mem. comml. leasing com., mem. real property, probate and trust law sect. 1987—), Practicing Law Inst. (chmn. program negotiating comml. leases 1995—99, mem. real estate law adv. com.), Chgo. Bar Assn., Ill. Bar Assn. Office: Sonnenschein Nath & Rosenthal LLP 7800 Sears Tower 233 S Wacker Dr Ste 7800 Chicago IL 60606-6491 Office Phone: 312-876-8950. Business E-Mail: lwhite@sonnenschein.com.

WHITE, LINDA MARIE, former fraternal organization administrator; b. Cleve., Apr. 21, 1942; BA, Clark Coll., 1963; MA, U. Chgo., 1969. Mgmt analyst HHS, Washington; social security adminstr. Chgo.; area dir. Chgo. East Dist. Office. Bd. dirs. United Negro Coll. Fund. Named one of Most Influential Black Americans, Ebony mag., 2006. Mem.: NAACP (life), Alpha Kappa Alpha Sorority (supreme basileus, internat. pres. 2002—06). Office: Alpha Kappa Alpha Sorority, Inc 5656 S Stony Island Ave Chicago IL 60637*

WHITE, LUCETTE DARBY, painter, sculptor; b. Springfield, Ill., Nov. 22, 1931; d. William Edson and Maurine McVicar Darby; married, July 19, 1962; children: Elizabeth, Darby, Matthew, Esther. At, Newcomb Coll., New Orleans, La., 1950—51, U. Ark., Fayetteville, 1951—53, Sarasota Sch. Art, Fla., Inst. Contemporary Art, Boston, Ark. Arts Ctr., Little Rock; studied with, Helen Terry Marshall, Russellville, Ark., Edwin Brewer, Little Rock, James Valone, Ark. Arts Ctr., Hilton Leech, Sarasota, Fla., George Demetrios, Boston. Bd. trustees Ark. Arts Ctr., Little Rock, 1972—76; mem. acquisition com. Cape Ann Mus., Gloucester, Mass., 1988—90; bd. trustees Montserrat Sch. Art, Beverly, Mass., 2000. Prin. works include Black Light, Storm Fantasy, one-woman shows include U. Ark. Med. Sch., Little Rock, 1959, Lakewood Ho. Gallery, North Little Rock, 1966, ML Gallery Fine Arts, N.Y.C., 1976, La. Tech. U., Ruston, 1976, Judi Rotenberg Gallery, Boston, 1990, Endicott Coll., Beverly, Mass.1990, Turnbridge (Vt.) Pub. Libr., 1995, Mercury Gallery, Boston, 1996, 1998, Rockport, Mass, 2002, Hill Country Arts Found., Ingram, Tex., 1997, Granite Shore Gallery, Rockport, 2000, 2001, exhibitions include 62d Ann. Exhibit Allied Artists in Am., N.Y.C., 1975, 63d Ann. Exhibit Allied Artists in Am., 1976, Nat. Acad. Design 153d Ann. Exhbn., 1978, Judi Rotenberg Gallery, Boston, 1987, 1991, 1992, DeCordova & Dana Mus., Lincoln, Mass., 1988—90, Boston - "90, 1990, West End Gallery, Gloucester, Mass., 1997, Acacia Gallerey, 1998, 2000, Cape Ann Hist. Mus., 1999, Mercury Gallery, Boston, 2000, 2002, 2003, 2004, U.S. Artist Am. Fine Art Exhibit, Phila., 2002, Represented in permanent collections Bank Am., Little Rock, First Nat. Bank, Harrison, Ark., Nat. Old Line Ins. Co., Little Rock, St. Vincent Infirmary, William J. Clinton Presdl. Libr. Mem.: Nat. Acad. Design (assoc.), Allied Artists Am. (assoc.). Democrat. Avocations: swimming, hiking, outdoor painting. Home: 24 Bass Rocks Rd Gloucester MA 01930

WHITE, LUCIE E., law educator; b. NC, June 13, 1949; BA, Radcliffe Coll., 1972; grad. studies in comparative lit., Yale U., 1972—74; JD, Harvard U., 1981. Bar: DC 1981, NC 1982, Calif. 1987. Law clk. to Judge James McMillen US Dist. Ct. We. Dist. NC, Charlotte, 1981—82; staff atty. Legal Services of So. Piedmont, Charlotte, 1982—84; supervising atty. U. NC, 1984—86; asst. prof. UCLA, 1986—89, acting prof., 1989—90, prof., 1990—95; prof. law Harvard Law Sch., Cambridge, Mass., 1995—, Louis A. Horvitz Prof. Law, 1998—. Office: Harvard Law Sch 1563 Massachusetts Ave Cambridge MA 02138 Office Phone: 617-496-3358. Office Fax: 617-495-4299. Business E-Mail: lwhite@law.harvard.edu.

WHITE, MARILYN DOMAS, information science educator; b. Franklin, La., Aug. 16, 1940; d. George Julian and Norma Domas; m. Roger Stuart White, Aug. 31, 1968; 1 child, Joshua Stuart. BA, Our Lady of the Lake Coll., San Antonio, 1962; MS, U. Wis., 1963; PhD, U. Ill., 1971. Dir. Commerce Libr. U. Wis., Madison, 1963-65; head Social Sci./Bus. Libr. So. Ill. U., Edwardsville, 1965-67; cons. So. Ill. U./U.S. AID Adv. Team, South Vietnam, 1967; asst. prof. SUNY, Buffalo, 1972-74; lectr., vis. asst. prof. U. Md., College Park, 1976-77, asst. prof. info sci., 1977-82, assoc. prof. info. sci., 1982—2006, prof. emerita, 2006—. Cons. USIA, Washington and abroad, 1977—83, Inst. for Def. Analyses, Bowie, Md., Supercomputing Rsch. Ctr., 1990—91, Am. Health Care Assn., Washington, 1990—92, Am. Coun. on Edn., 1995, U.S. Bur. of Census, 2003—04. Contbr. articles to profl. jours. including Libr. Quar., Libr. & Info. Sci. Rsch., Jour. Documentation, Jour. Am. Soc. for Info. Sci. James Lyman Whitney grantee ALA, 1983, Spl. Libr. Assn. rsch. grantee, 1993-94, Coun. Libr. Resources grantee, 1995-96, Info. Sci. Abstracts grantee, 1997-98. Mem. Am. Soc. for Info. Sci., Spl. Libr. Assn. Office: U Md Coll Info Studies Hornbake 4117E South Wing College Park MD 20742-0001 Office Phone: 301-405-2058. Business E-Mail: whitemd@umd.edu.

WHITE, MARJORIE MARY, retired elementary school educator; b. LaCrosse, Wis., May 10, 1944; d. Knute Emil and Florence Catherine (Frederich) Johnson; m. David James White, July 6, 1985; stepchildren: Christopher Howard, Wendy Marie White Ehnert. BSE, Winona State U., 1966, MSEd, 1971. Cert. elem. tchr., Minn. Tchr. Lacrosse Cath. Schs., Wis., 1966-68, Winona County Schs., Dakota, Minn., 1968-72, Ind. Sch. Dist., Winona, Minn., 1972—2001. Mem. NEA, AAUW (treas. 1990-92, membership co-chair 2001-03, mem.-at-large 2003—), Minn. Edn. Assn., Winona Edn. Assn. (faculty rep. 1970-96, membership chmn. 1986-96), Phi Delta Kappa (newsletter editor 1988-89, 94-98, del. 1985-91, 94-96, v.p. membership 1989-91, Svc. Key award 1991), Delta Kappa Gamma (sec. 2002-04). Democrat. Roman Catholic. Avocations: needlecrafts, hiking, gardening, reading, travel. Home: 705 W Wabasha St Winona MN 55987-2764

WHITE, MARNELLE ROSALIE, real estate broker; b. San Andreas, Calif., July 28, 1937; d. Adolph Benjamin and Bertha Evalena (Cresswell) Reusser; m. David Howard White, Apr. 8, 1956; children: Lou Ellen Garner, David Edward, Beth Evelyn Salie. AA, Modesto Jr. Coll., Calif., 1971; BA, Calif. State U., Turlock, 1973, M in Lang. Arts and Lit., 1975. Lic. real estate broker Calif. Instr. Modesto Jr. Coll., 1975—85; real estate broker Marnelle White Real Estate, Copperopolis, Calif., 1981—. Polit. action com. Modesto Bd. Realtors, 1985—87; adv. com. Assembly Subcom. on Edn. Reform, Sacramento, 1986. Author: 30 Pages, 1977, Sometimes the Wind Blows, 1982, Iris, 2002. Chair adv. coun. Stanislaus County Area Agy. on Aging, Modesto, 2000, Area 12 Agy. on Aging, Sonora, Calif., 2006; del. Dem. Nat. Conv., San Francisco, 1984; chair Dem. Ctrl. Com., Modesto, 1986. Named Outstanding Woman, Stanislaus County Commn. for Women, 2003; recipient Gertrude Parker award, Stanislaus County Dem. Ctrl. Com., 1988, Svc. award, Stanislaus County Area Agy. on Aging, 2005. Mem.: AAUW, Nat. League Am. Pen Women (pres. 2002—03), Calif. Fedn. Chaparrel Poets (pres. 1984—86). Democrat. Avocations: poetry, crossword puzzles, gardening. Office: Marnelle White Real Estate PO Box 383 Copperopolis CA 95228

WHITE, MARTHA VETTER, allergist, immunologist; b. Richmond, Va., Oct. 23, 1951; d. Robert Joseph and Miriam Ernestine (Thomas) Vetter; m. Frederick Joseph Kozub, Oct. 11, 1975 (div. June 1982); m. John Irving White, Feb. 18, 1984; children: Josh, Christie. Student, Vanderbilt U., Nashville, 1969-71; BA, U. Richmond, 1973; MD, Va. Commonwealth U., Richmond, 1978. Cert. m. Bd. Pediatrics, Am. Bd. Allergy and Immunology. Pediatric intern and resident Va. Commonwealth U., Richmond, 1978-81; locum tenans Pub. Health, Richmond, Va., 1981-82; fellow Allergy and Immunology U. Southern Calif., L.A., 1983-84, Georgetown U., 1983-84; sr. staff fellow Food and Drug Adminstrn., Bethesda, Md., 1984-85; NSRA fellow Nat. Inst. Allergy and Infectious Diseases, Bethesda, Md., 1985-88; sr. staff fellow, 1988-93; rsch. dir. Inst. for Asthma and Allergy, Wheaton, Md., 1993—. Cons. Sandoz Pharms., Marion Merrell Dow, Glaxo, Boehringer Ingleheim, Ciba-Geigy, Miles Genentech; rschr. Glaxo, Abbott, Pfizer, Marion Merrell Dow, Miles, Rhône Poulenc Rhoen, Sanofi, Adams, Astra, Merck, Neurbiol. Techs., 3M, Zeneca, Wyeth, Smith-Kline Beecham; bd. dirs. Allery & Asthma Network/Mothers of Asthmatics, 1987—; med. editor MA Report, 1986—; assoc. editor Allergy, Asthma and Immunology Guide, 1989-90. Contbr. numerous scientific papers, abstracts, chpts. and reviews in field. Recipient Norwich Eaton Rsch. award, 1987; Merrell Dow scholar in allergy, 1989; Geigy fellow, 1984. Mem.: Soc. Prin. Investigators (pres. 2002—03), Am. Thoracic Soc., Am. Coll. Allergy and Immunology, Adm. Acad. Allergy and Immunology, Am. Acad. Pediat., Am. Assn. Immunologists, Gamma Sigma Epsilon, Psi Chi, Beta Beta Beta. Office: Inst Asthma and Allergy 11002 Veirs Mill Rd # 414 Wheaton MD 20902 Office Phone: 301-962-5800.

WHITE, MARY ANN, bank executive; b. Blackey, Ky., June 21, 1932; d. William Bradley and Audrey Ison; divorced; 1 child, William R. Student, Cannon Trust Sch., Charlotte, NC, 1974; grad., Nat. Grad Trust Sch., Evanston, Ill., 1978. With 1st Nat. Bank and Trust Co., Georgetown, Ky., 1953—, asst. trust officer, 1962-64, asst. cashier, 1964-74, asst. trust officer, asst. v.p., 1974-76; v.p., trust officer Whitaker Bank-Georgetown (formerly 1st Nat. Bank and Trust Co.), Georgetown, 1976—. Treas. Sr. Citizens Exec. Bd., Georgetown; bd. dirs. Urban Renewal and Cmty. Devel. Agy. Bd., Georgetown, C. of C., Georgetown; pres. Scott County Bus. Women's Club, Georgetown. Mem. Fin. Women Internat. (sec., treas., v.p.). Avocations: flower gardening, cooking, travel. Office: Whitaker Bank-Georgetown 101 W Main St Georgetown KY 40324-1320

WHITE, MARY BETH, counseling administrator, adult education educator; b. Nashville, Aug. 10, 1951; d. Roy William and Myra Kathryn (De Cleene) Huffman; m. Frank White, Feb. 21, 1976 (div. Aug. 1997); children: Andrew Huffman, Leigh Ann. BA in Psychology, Quincy U., 1973; MS in Edn., Vanderbilt U., 1977; cert. guidance and counseling, Tenn. State U., 1997. Tchr. Wilson County Devel. Ctr., Lebanon, Tenn., 1977-79, Mt. Juliet (Tenn.) Jr. High, 1979-80; guidance counselor Holy Rosary Acad., Nashville, 1992-97; instr. Vol. State C.C., Gallatin, Tenn., 1999—; owner Hermitage Learning Ctr., 2000—. Roman Catholic. Avocations: tennis, travel. Office: Hermitage Learning Ctr 3441 Lebanon Pike Hermitage TN 37076-2097 Home: 423 Jaywood Ln Mount Juliet TN 37122-3756

WHITE, MARY JO, lawyer, former prosecutor; b. Kansas City, Mo., Dec. 27, 1947; d. Carl and Ruth King Monk; m. John W. White, Jan. 24, 1970. BA, Coll. William and Mary, 1970; MA in Psychology, New Sch. for Social Rsch., 1971; JD, Columbia U., 1974. Bar: NY 1975. Law clk. to Hon. Marvin E. Frankel US Dist. Ct. (So. dist.) NY, 1975—76; assoc. Debevoise & Plimpton LLP, 1976—78, litig. ptnr., 1983—90, ptnr., chair of litig., 2002—; asst. U.S. atty., chief appellate atty. criminal divsn. (So. dist.) NY US Dept. Justice, 1978—81; instr. in profl. responsibility and ethics Columbia Law Sch., 1981—; chief asst., acting U.S. Atty. (ea. dist.) NY US Dept. Justice, Bklyn., 1990—93, U.S. atty. (So. dist.) NY Manhattan, 1993—2002. Chair Atty. Gen. Janet Reno's Adv. Com. of U.S. Attys., 1993—94. Recipient "Magnificent 7" award, Bus. & Profl. Women USA, Law Enforcement Person of the Year award, Soc. of Profl. Investigators, Human Relations Award, Anti-Defamation League Lawyer's Div., 1996, Edward Weinfeld award for distinguished contbn. to Admin. of Justice, N.Y. County Lawyers' Assn., 1998, Nat. Law Jour. 2002 list of Top Women Litigators, John P. O'Neill Pillar of Justice award, Respect for Law Alliance, 2002, Sandra Day O'Connor award for Distinction in Public Svc., 2002, dir. of FBI's Jefferson Cup award for contbn. to Rule of Law in the fight against terrorism and crime, 2002, George H. W. Bush award for excellence in counter-terrorism and the Agency Seal Medallion, CIA, 2002, Women of Power and Influence award, NOW. Fellow: Am. Coll. Trial Lawyers; mem.: ABA, N.Y. State Bar Assn., Assn. Bar City of N.Y. Achievements include First women to serve as U.S Atty. for So. Dist. of N.Y; first chairperson of Atty. Gen. Janet Reno's Advisory Com.of U.S. Attys. Office: Debevoise & Plimpton LLP 919 Third Ave 46t Fl New York NY 10022 Business E-Mail: mjwhite@debevoise.com.

WHITE, MARY RUTH WATHEN, social services administrator; b. Athens, Tex., Dec. 27, 1927; d. Benedict Hudson and Sara Elizabeth (Evans) W.; m. Robert M. White, Nov. 10, 1946; children: Martha Elizabeth, Robert Miles, Jr., William Benedict, Mary Ruth, Jesse Wathen, Margaret Fay, Maureen Adele, Thomas Evan. BA, Stephen F. Austin State U., Nacogdoches, Tex., 1948. Chmn. Regional Drug Abuse Com., San Antonio, 1975-81, Met. Youth Coun., San Antonio, 1976-78; state chmn. Citizens United for Rehab. Errants, San Antonio, 1978-91; sec. Bexar County Detention Ministries, San Antonio, 1979-88; chmn. Bexar County (Tex.) Jail Commn., 1980-82; chmn. com. on role of family in reducing recidivism Tex. Dept. Criminal Justice, Austin, 1985—; chmn. Met. Cmty. Corrections Com., San Antonio, 1986-90. Bd. dirs. Tex. Coalition for Juvenile Justice, 1975-93, Target 90 Youth Coordinating Coun., San Antonio, 1986-89; local chmn. vol. adv. bd. Tex. Youth Commn., 1986-87. Pres. San Antonio City Coun. PTA, 1976-78, Rep. Bus. Women Bexar County, San Antonio, 1984-86, North Urban Deanery, San Antonio Alliance Mental Illness, 1995-96, also legis. chmn.; bd. dirs. CURE, 1978-92; legis. chmn. Archdiocese of San Antonio Coun. Cath. Women; mem. allocation com. United Way, San Antonio, 1986-91; founder chmn. South Tex. Consumer and Family Support Consortium, 1996-97. Named Today's Woman, San Antonio Light newspaper, 1985, Outstanding Rep. Woman, Rep. Bus. Women Bexar County, 1987; honoree Rep. Women Stars over Tex., 1992. Mem. Am. Corrections Assn., Assn. Criminal Justice Planners, LWV (pres. San Antonio chpt. 1984-86), Conservation Soc., Fedn. Women (bd. dirs. 1984-90), DAR (regent), Colonial Dames (pres.), Cath. Daus. Am. (profl. registered parliamentarian, past regent Ct. of St. Anthony), Tex. Cath. Daus. Am. (state legis. chair), San Antonio Alliance for Mentally Ill (pres. 1996-97). Office: 5372 Fredericksburg Rd Ste 114 San Antonio TX 78229-3559

WHITE, MEG (MEGAN MARTHA WHITE), musician, vocalist; b. Grosse Pointe, Mich., Dec. 10, 1974; m. John Gillis, 1996 (div. 2000). Drummer, vocalist The White Stripes, 1997—; toured with Pavement and Sleater-Kinney, 1999, 2000. Performer: (albums) The White Stripes, 1999, De Stijl, 2000, White Blood Cells, 2001, Maximum, 2002, Elephant, 2003, Get Behind Me Satan, 2005; actor: (films) Coffee and Cigarettes, 2003, Cold Mountain, 2003. Office: Monotone Inc 150 S Rodeo Dr # 200 Beverly Hills CA 90212-2408

WHITE, MELINDA ELOIS, retired elementary school educator; d. Richard Ellis and Clara Mae Powell; m. Charles White (dec.); 1 child, Angela White-Smith. BS, Ind. U., 1953, MA, 1956; postgrad., Purdue U., 1976, Ind. U., 1976; Assoc. in Bible Studies, Moody Bible Inst., Chgo., 2001. Ordained deacon-min. 2004. Tchr. Gary Pub. Schs., Ind., 1953—76, asst. prin., 1976—84, prin., 1984—92; edn. workshop presenter Nat. Sch. Svcs., Chgo., 1992—99; ret., 1999. Past pres. Jack and Jill Am., Gary. Author: Doves in the Verbena Pot, 2004, numerous poems, prose and short stories. Chair youth membership NAACP, Gary; supt. Sunday schs. More Like Christ Christian Fellowship Ministries Ch., Chgo. Recipient Outstanding Svc. to Youth award, ABJ Cmty. Svc. Org., 2004. Mem.: Saturday Bridge Club, Phi Delta Kappa. Democrat. Baptist. Avocations: bridge, ceramics, golf, walking, writing.

WHITE, MICHELLE JO, economics professor; b. Washington, 1945; d. Harry L. and Irene Rich; m. Roger Hall Gordon, July 25, 1982. AB, Harvard U., 1967; MSc in Econs., London Sch. Econs., 1968; PhD, Princeton U., 1973. Asst. prof. U. Pa., Phila., 1973-78; from assoc. prof. to prof. NYU, N.Y.C., 1978-83; prof. econs. U. Mich., Ann Arbor, 1984—2001, dir. PhD program in econs., 1992—94, Ann Arbor, 1998—99; prof. econs. U. Calif., San Diego, 2000—. Vis. asst. prof. Yale U., New Haven, 1978; vis. prof. People's U., Beijing, 1986, U. Warsaw, 1990, U. Wis., Madison, 1991, U. Munich, Germany, 1992, 2002, Tilburg U., The Netherlands, 1993, 95, U. Chgo., 1993, Copenhagen Bus. Sch., 1995, Uppsala U., Sweden, 1997, Hebrew U., Israel, 1997, U. Calif. Law Sch. Berkeley, 1999, Harvard Law Sch., 2004; rsch. assoc. Nat. Bur. Econ. Rsch., 2002—; cons. Pension Benefit Guaranty Corp., Washington, 1987, World Bank, 1999; chmn. adv. com. dept. econs. Princeton U., 1988-90. Editor: The Non-profit Sector in a Three Sector Economy, 1981, Financial Distress and Bankruptcy: Economic Issues, 1997; assoc. editor Jour. Econ. Perspectives, 2004—; contbr. numerous articles to profl. jours. Bd. dirs. Com. on Status of Women in Econs. Profession, 1984-86. Resources for Future fellow, 1972-73; grantee NSF, 1979, 82, 88, 91, 93, 96, 2002, Sloan Found., 1984, Fund for Rsch. in Dispute Resolution, 1989; Fulbright scholar, Poland, 1990. Mem. Am. Econ. Assn., Am. Law and Econ. Assn. (bd. dirs. 1991-92, 2001-04, chair nominating com. 2002, sec.-treas. 2006—), Am. Real Estate and Urban Econs. Assn. (bd. dirs. 1992-95), Social Scis. Rsch. Coun. (bd. dirs. 1994-2000, treas. 1996-2000), Midwest Econs. Assn. (1st v.p. 1996-97). Office: U California-San Diego Dept Economics 9500 Gilman Dr La Jolla CA 92093-0508

WHITE, MILDRED VIRGINIA, secondary school educator, retired counseling administrator; d. Stanis Augustus and Elsie Emma Watkins; m. Richard Clarence White, Jan. 1, 1949; children: Michael Kenneth, Valerie Clarissa. BSc, Tuskegee Inst., 1948; MA, Atlanta U., 1965. Cert. counseling Ala., 1965. H.S. health and phys. edn. tchr. Macon County Tng. Sch./Macon County Bd. Edn., Tuskegee, Ala., 1950—65; career counselor for adult students Manpower Tng. Act/Labor Dept. Fed. Govt., Tuskegee, Ala., 1965—66; guidance dir. /job developer H.S. equivalency program OEO, Tuskegee, 1966—67, 1968—69; program dir. for rsch. and demonstrational program Adult Edn. Rsch. Program HEW, Tuskegee, 1967—68; career devel. specialist for head start teachers Head Start Supplementary Program for Tchrs., Tuskegee, 1970—71; world history instr. for headstart tchrs. Tuskegee Inst. Fed. Govt., 1971—72; h.s. guidance counselor Deborah Cannon Wolfe H.S./Macon County Bd. Edn., Shorter, Ala., 1972—81; coord. health program Tuskagee Inst. Health, Edn. and Welfare, 1984; career coord. Explorer Pk., Tuskagee, 1994—95. Cons. Adult Edn. State Workshop for Tchrs., Tuskegee, 1970—70; coun. mem. for tng. program Tng. and Preparation for Employment, Montgomery, Ala., 1970—72; dir. Consortium Minorities in Engring., 1984—86; mem. state retirement com. representing Macon County State Retirement and Membership Com./Ala. Tchrs. Assn., Tuskegee, 1995—97. Co-author: Handbook for Counselors for Disadvantaged Adults, 1956. Den mother Macon County Cub Scout Pack, Tuskegee Inst., 1962—64; rsch. coord. Tuskegee Inst./HEW, 1974; explorer career coord. Explorer Post of Tuskegee, 1995—95; neighborhood chmn. United Way, Tuskegee, 1998—2003. Fellow, Tuskegee Inst., 1944, Kellogg Found./Tuskegee Inst. Resource Devel. Ctr., Ohio State U., Columbus, 1969. Mem.: NEA, Ret. Tchrs. Assn., Ala. Ednl. Assn., Macon County Ret. Tchrs. Assn. (v.p. 1992—94, pres. 1994—96), Tuskegee Optimist Mrs. Club (pres. 1997—98), Delta Sigma Theta (life; founder, dir. Delteen youth club 1984—91, pres. 1990—91). Home: 903 N Marable Dr Tuskegee AL 36083 Personal E-mail: mildredgreta@aol.com.

WHITE, NORA LIZABETH, language educator; d. Ralph Senter and Carol L. Hay; m. Donald S. McSheehy; children: Daniel Stuart McSheehy, Luke Adam. BA, Urbana U., Ohio, 1982; MA, Ohio State U., 1989, PhD, 1992. Cert. tchr. State Of Ohio Dept. of Edn., 1989. Postdoctoral rsch. fellow U. of Western Sydney, Penrith, New South Wales, Australia, 1997—99; assoc. prof. U. of Alaska, Fairbanks, 1992—2000, Tex. Woman's U., Denton, Tex., 2000—. Coord. grad. lang. and literacy edn. program U. of Alaska, Fairbanks, 1999—2000, coord. elem. edn. program, 1992—95, coord. Russian far east student exch. program, 1992—94. Contbr. articles to profl. jours. Field coun. rep. Nat. Reading Conf., Alaska, 1992—99, internat. com. mem. Washington, 2001—03. Recipient Vol. award, Newton Rayzor Elem. Sch., 2002, Outstanding Vol. award, Denton Ind. Sch. Dist., Adopt a Sch. Program, 2002, Top Vol. award, 2004; grantee, Alaska Schools Rsch. Project, 1995, 1992, Lang. Australia, 1999; Ulir Endowed fellow in higher edn., 2004—05. Mem.: Denton Reading Coun., Australian Literacy Educator's Assn., Am. Anthrop. Assn., Nat. Coun. of Teachers of English, Am. Ednl. Rsch. Assn., Internat. Reading Assn., Nat. Reading Conf., Family, Sch., Cmty. Partnership Spl. Interest Group (newsletter editor 2002—), Phi Delta Kappa. Avocations: travel, reading, writing, swimming. Office: Texas Woman's U PO Box 425769 Denton TX 76204-5769 Home: 5201 W Oak Shores Dr Crossroads TX 76227 E-mail: nwhite@mail.twu.edu.

WHITE, OTHELL, interior designer; b. Valley Head, Ala., Dec. 30, 1942; d. Charles Ray and Lily Cleo (Couch) White; children: Thomas Gregory Owens, Steven Craig Adams, Pamela Gayle Adams. Student, McKenzie Coll., Chattanooga, 1961, Delgado Coll., New Orleans, 1977-79. Interior designer Smartt Cabinets, Chattanooga, 1981-83; decorator cons. J.C. Penney, Chattanooga, 1983-85; owner, interior designer Pizzazz, Chattanooga, 1985-88; freelance interior designer Chattanooga, Boca Raton, Fla., 1988-89; interior designer Concepts in Kitchens, DelRay Beach, Fla., 1990-91, Othell Interior Design, Chattanooga, 1993—. Mem. Am. Soc. Interior Design, Interior Design Soc. Republican. Roman Catholic. Avocations: walking on beach, writing, reading, painting.

WHITE, PAMELA JANICE, lawyer; b. Elizabeth, NJ, July 13, 1952; d. Emmet Talmadge and June (Howlett) W. BA, Mary Washington Coll., 1974; JD, Washington and Lee U., 1977. Bar: Md. 1977, U.S. Dist. Ct. Md. 1978, D.C. 1979, U.S. Dist. Ct. D.C. 1979, U.S. Ct. Appeals (4th cir.) 1979, U.S. Ct. Appeals (D.C. cir.) 1981, U.S. Ct. Claims 1981, U.S. Ct. Appeals (2d cir.) 1983, N.Y. 1983, U.S. Dist. Ct. (so. dist.) N.Y. 1983, U.S. Ct. Appeals (9th cir.) 1988, U.S. Supreme Ct. 1981. Assoc. Ober, Grimes & Shriver, Balt., 1977-84; prin. Ober, Kaler, Grimes & Shriver PC, Balt., 1985—. Chair Employment Group, 1994—; mem. bd. law examiners, 1986-94, select com. on Gender Equality, 1989-2000, chair, 1997-99, judiciary pub. trust and confidence com., 2001-05, spl. com. on ethics 2002-04, jud. campaign conduct com., 2005—; mem. fed. dist. ct. adv. group Civil Justice Reform Act, 1990; exec. com. Md. Inst. Continuing Profl. Edn. Lawyers, 2000-02, vol. faculty; adv. bd. Md. Mediation and Conflict Resolution Ctr., 2001-02; equal justice coun. Legal Aid Bur., 2000-06. Note and comment editor Washington and Lee Law Rev. 1976-77, Washington and Lee Law Council 1983-87, pres. 1991-92. Mem. Fed. Ct. Bicentennial Com., 1988-90; vol. Profl. Gov.'s Drug-Free Workplace Initiative, 1990-93; bd. trustees Washington and Lee U., 1995-2004; trustee Balt. Hist. Soc., 2002—. Recipient Leadership in Law award Md. Daily Record, 2001, Exemplary Svc. award Legal Aid Bur. 2002, Outstanding Pro Bono Cert., 2004; named Disting. Alumna, Washington and Lee U., 1994, Mary Washington Coll., 2001; named among Md. Top 100 Women, 2000, 04. Fellow Am. Bar Found., Md. Bar Found. (award for excellence 1996, bd. dirs. 2000-); mem. ABA (chair tort and ins. practice employer/employee rels. com. 1999-2000, del. 2000-02), Am. Arbitration Assn. (arbitrator, mediator employment and comml., large complex case panels), Balt. Bar Found. (bd. dirs. 2003—), Fed. Bar Assn., Md. State Bar Assn. (coun. legal edn. sect. 1987-96, chmn. 1992-93, labor sect. coun. 1992-96, professionalism com. 1991—, chmn. 1994-97, bd. govs. 1993-95, 1998-2003, exec. com. 1994-95, 99-01, pres. 2001-02, immediate past pres. 2002-03, task force on professionalism chair 1996-97), D.C. Bar Assn., Balt. City Bar Assn. (exec. coun. 1995-96, 1997-98), Md. Legal Svcs. Corp. (bd. mem. 2006-), U. Md. Washington Alumni Assn. (bd. mem. 2006-), Women's Bar Assn. Md. (treas. 1986-87, v.p. 1987-88, pres.-elect 1988-89, pres. 1989-90, bd. dirs. 1984-86, Rita C. Davidson award 2000), Md. Assn. Def. Counsel, Pro Bono Resource Ctr. (exec. com. 2000-02, bd. trustees 2002-03, Leaders of Equal Justice award 2002), Order of Coif, Phi Beta Kappa (hon. alumni), Omicron Delta Kappa (hon. alumni). Presbyterian. Avocation: baseball. Office: Ober Kaler Grimes & Shriver PC 120 E Baltimore St Ste 800 Baltimore MD 21202-1643 Office Phone: 410-347-7323. Business E-Mail: pjwhite@ober.com.

WHITE, PAMELA JO, elementary school educator; b. Lynchburg, Va., June 20, 1943; d. Robert E. and Josephine T. (Patterson) W. BA in Art and Elem. Edn., Lynchburg Coll., 1968, MA in Teaching, 1969; postgrad., U. Va., Kent State U. Elem. tchr. Baltimmore County Pub. Schs., Towson, Md., Bedford County Pub. Schs., Bedford, Va., Appomattox County Pub. Schs., Appomattox, Va.; ret., 1990. Recipient Outstanding Vol. award 4-H Club, Cystic Fibrosis Found. Mem. Am. Fedn. Tchrs., Nat. Trust for Hist. Preservation, Smithsonian Assocs., Kappa Delta Pi, Delta Kappa Gamma, Beta Sigma Phi.

WHITE, PATRICIA ANN, chemistry educator, medical technician; b. Bryan, Tex., Oct. 29, 1946; d. Philip Wayne and June Lavaughn Cadenhead; m. Lew David White, Sept. 29, 1976; children: Cade Warren, Ross Philip. BS, U. Houston, 1969. Registered med. technologist; cert. secondary and sci. tchr. Tex. Supervising med. technologist of chemistry Meth. Hosp., Houston, 1969—80; sci. dept. head, chemistry tchr. Lockhart HS, Tex., 1989—. Sunday sch. tchr. and vestry Episcopal Ch., Lockhart; sec. Beta Sigma Phi, Lockhart, 1983—93. Mem.: TSTC (corr.). Democrat. Episcopalian. Avocations: travel, reading, walking, piano, socializing. Home: 1215 Plum St Lockhart TX 78644 Office: Lockhart HS 1 Lion Country Dr Lockhart TX 78644

WHITE, PATRICIA DENISE, dean, law educator; b. Syracuse, NY, July 8, 1949; d. Theodore C. and Kathleen (Cowles) Denise; m. Nicholas P. White, Feb. 20, 1971 (div. 1997); children: Olivia Lawrence, Alexander Cowles; m. James W. Nickel, Sept. 15, 2005. BA, U. Mich., 1971, MA, JD, 1974. Bar: D.C. 1975, Mich. 1988, Utah 1995. Assoc. Steptoe & Johnson, Washington, 1975-76; vis. asst. prof. Coll. of Law U. Toledo, 1976-77; assoc. Caplin & Drysdale, Washington, 1977-79; asst. prof. Law Ctr. Georgetown U., 1979-84, assoc. prof. Law Ctr., 1985-88; vis. prof. Law Sch. U. Mich., Ann Arbor, 1988-94; prof. U. Utah, Salt Lake City, 1994-98; counsel Parsons, Behle and Latimer, Salt Lake City, 1995—98; dean, prof. Ariz. State U. Coll. Law, 1999—. Counsel Bodman, Longley and Dahling, Detroit, Ann Arbor, 1990-95. Contbr. articles to profl. jours. Fellow: Am. Coll. Tax Coun. Office: Ariz State Sandra Day O'Connor U Coll Law McAllister & Orange Sts PO Box 877906 Tempe AZ 85287-7906 Office Phone: 480-965-6188. Office Fax: 480-965-6125. Business E-Mail: patricia.white@asu.edu.

WHITE, PAULINE M., interior decorator; b. Kansas City, Mo., Oct. 2, 1933; d. George Francis and Anna Elizabeth (Schnase) Adams; m. Norman Edgar White, Aug. 7, 1952; children: Donna Jean, Norman Alan. BA, Kansas City U., 1951; cert., Elizabeth Bolden Sch. Design, 1952. With Southwestern Bell Telephone Co., Kansas City, 1950-52; supr. AT&T Telephone Co., Kansas City, 1957-61; with med. records divsn. Shawnee Mission Hosp., Overland Park, Kans., 1961-70; tchr. ceramics and crafts Donahues Plastics, Gladstone, Mo., 1970-72; recreation leader, tchr. City of Columbia, Mo., 1980-88; decorator, interior planner for home J.C. Penney, 1988—. Tchr. Broadway Christian Ch., 1973-96; vol. tchr., counselor Ctrl. Mo. Regional Ctr. for Developmentally Disabled, Columbia, 1980—. Mem. Ryan Club (pres. 1980). Republican. Avocation: work for learning impaired.

WHITE, REBECCA E., advocate; b. Washington, Nov. 17, 1945; d. Edward and Anna Pendleton White. BS, D.C. Tchrs. Coll., 1971; postgrad., Pepperdine U., Malibu, Calif., 1993, Calif. State U., L.A., 2003—04. Cert. tchr., D.C., Calif. Tchr. English D.C. Pub. Schs., Washington, 1971-73; paralegal specialist U.S. Dept. Justice, Washington, 1973-81; adminstr. U.S. Dept. Vet. Affairs VA Med. Ctr., L.A., 1982-89, 94-96, Sepulveda, Calif., 1992-94; patient/employee advocate U.S. Dept. Vet. Affairs, L.A., 1982-89, 92-96; tchr. English L.A. Unified Sch. Dist., 1989-91, children's advocate, 1989—2005; tchr. English Inglewood (Calif.) Unified Sch. Dist., 1996-97, children's advocate, 1996—98; tchr. spl. edn. Gladstone St. Elem. Sch., Azusa, Calif., 2003—04; freelance writer, 2005—; tchr. English Mpls. Pub. Schs., 2005—. Cmty. advocate Baldwin Hills Cmty., L.A., 1983—2004; children's advocate L.A. County Schs., 2005—; mem. L.A. World Affairs Coun., 1999-2004; mem. Nat. Campaign For Tolerance, 2006-. Mem. NEA, Calif. Tchrs. Assn. Avocations: writing, hiking, entertaining, reading. E-mail: rebecca.white@mpls.k12.minn.us.

WHITE, REBECCA HANNER, dean, law educator; BA, Ea. Ky. U.; JD, U. Ky. Judicial law clerk to Chief Judge George C. Edwards Sixth Cir. U.S. Ct. Appeals; atty. Dinsmore & Shohl, Cincinnati; prof. U. Ga. Sch. Law, 1989—, assoc. provost and assoc. v.p. academic affairs, interim dean, 2003—04, dean, 2004—, J. Alton Hosch Prof. Law. Co-author: Employment Discrimination, 2002, Cases and Materials on Employment Discrimination, 2003; editl. bd. The Labor Law Jour. Recipient Josiah Meigs Award, 2000, John C. O'Byrne Award, Woman of Distinction award, State Bar Ga. Younger Lawyers Div., 2004. Office: U Ga Sch Law Athens GA 30602 Office Phone: 706-542-7140. Office Fax: 706-542-5556. E-mail: rhwhite@uga.edu.

WHITE, RHEA AMELIA, library and information scientist; b. Utica, NY, May 6, 1931; d. John Raymond and Rhea Jane (Parry) White. BA, Pa. State U., 1953; MLS, Pratt Inst., Bklyn., 1965; postgrad., SUNY, Stony Brook, 1990-92. Rsch. fellow Parapsychology Lab. Duke U., Durham, NC, 1954-58; editor Jour. Am. Soc. Psychical Rsch., N.Y.C., 1959-62, 84-00, editor-in-chief, 2001—; libr. dept. psychiatry Maimonides Med. Ctr., Bklyn., 1965-67; dir. info. Am. Soc. Psychical Rsch., N.Y.C., 1965-80; reference libr. East Meadow (N.Y.) Pub. Libr., 1965-95; founder, dir. Parapsychology Sources of Info. Ctr., Dix Hills, NY, 1981-90; editor Rsch. in Parapsychology, Metuchen, NJ, 1981-85, Theta, Durham, NC, 1981-86; founder, editor Parapsychology Abstracts Internat., Dix Hills, 1983-89, Exceptional Human Experience, Dix Hills, 1990—; founder, producer PsiLine Database, Dix Hills, 1983—; mng. editor Advances in Parapsychol. Rsch., N.Y.C., 1977; founder, dir. Exceptional Human Experience Network, New Bern, 1990-94, 95—; with Exceptional Human Experience News, 1994—2002. Rsch. fellow Menninger Found., Topeka, 1963-65; abstractor Psychol. Abstracts, Washington, 1967-91; cons. Scarecrow Press, Metuchen, NJ, 1980-85; referee Jour. Parapsychology, Durham, 1981-85; chmn., keynote spkr. conf. on women and parapsychology Parapsychology Found., Dublin, Ireland, 1991; keynote speaker Acad. Religion and Psychical Rsch. Conf., 1992; founder, editor EHE News, Dix Hills, 1994, New Bern, 1995—; instr. exceptional human experience course Portland (Oreg.) State U., 1999. Author: Parapsychology: Sources of Information, 1973, Surveys in Parapsychology, 1975, Parapsychology: New Sources of Information, 1990; (with M. Murphy) The Psychic Side of Sports, 1978; parapsychology book reviewer Libr. Jour., NYC, 1974-86, Reprint Bull., 1974-79, (with Michael Murphy) In the Zone, 1995; regional editor European Jour. Parapsychology, 1975-90; mem. editl. bd. Advances in Parapsychol. Rsch., 1980-85, Archaeus, 1985-93, 3 books on key aspects of the transformative potential of non-ordinary exceptional hum. experiences; contbr. over 100 articles to profl. jours. Recipient Hans Peter Luhn award Am. Soc. Info. Sci., N.Y.C. chpt., 1965. Mem.: Assn. Near-Death Studies, Acad. Religion and Psychical Rsch. (mem. bd. 1982—84, publs. com. 1982—97), Parapsychological Assn. (mem. coun. 1958, 1962—63, 1982—85, pres. 1984, dir. 1986, Lifetime Outstanding Rsch. award 1992, conf. spkr. 1993), Ctr. for Psychology and Social Change, Soc. for Anthropology of Consciousness, Internat. Assn. Religion and Parapsychology, Internat. Soc. for Study Subtle Energies and Energy Medicine, Found for Shamanic Studies, Penn State Alumni Assn. Coll. Liberal Arts. Avocations: hiking, gardening, animals, reading, listening to music. Home and Office: 414 Rockledge Rd New Bern NC 28562-9553 Office Phone: 252-636-8734. Personal E-mail: ehenwhite@cox.net.

WHITE, ROBERTA LEE, financial analyst; b. Denver, Sept. 18, 1946; d. Harold Tindall and Araminta (Campbell) Bangs; m. Lewis Paul White, Jr., Jan. 23, 1973 (div. Sept. 1974). BA cum laude, Linfield Coll., 1976; postgrad., Lewis and Clark Coll. Lic. tax preparer, Oreg. Office mgr. Multnomah County Auditor, Portland, Oreg., 1977-81; rsch. asst. Dan Goldy and Assocs., Portland, 1981-83; regional asst. Vocat. Rehab., Eugene, Oreg., 1983-85;

internal auditor Multnomah County, Portland, 1985-89; cons. Portland, 1989-91; fin. analyst City of Portland, 1991-93; comptr. Wordsmith Svc., Portland, 1993-97; fin. analyst City of Portland, 1997—. Mem. Com. for Implementation of the ADA, Portland, 1991—93. Treas. Mary Wendy Roberts for Sec. of State, Portland, 1992, Re-Elect Mary Wendy Roberts, Portland, 1990, Elect Hank Miggins Com., 1994; mem. Oreg. Women's Polit. Caucus, Portland, 1982-85, City Club, Portland, 1978-81. Democrat. Mem. Disciples Of Christ. Avocations: reading, hiking, opera, symphony, ballet. Home: 6685 W Burnside # 336 Portland OR 97210 Office: City of Portland Office of Mgmt/Fin Facil Svc Divsn Rm 1204 1120 SW 5th Ave Portland OR 97204-1912

WHITE, SARAH ELIZABETH SLOAN, elementary school educator; b. Warren, Ark., Nov. 14, 1936; d. Clyde Van and Ruthie Moree Akens; m. Billy Gene White, July 1, 1960; children: Timothy Gene, James Edwin. BS Edn., Ark. State Tchrs. Coll., 1957; MEd, Memphis State, 1967. Cert. tchr., Mo. Home econs. tchr. Standford (Ark.) High Sch., 1957-60, Oak Grove High Sch., Paragould, Ark., 1960-63, Wardell (Mo.) High Sch., 1963—, Portageville (Mo.) High Sch., 1963-66, Hayti (Mo.) High Sch., 1966-67, Brookland (Ark.) High Sch., 1967-68, Southland High Sch., Arbyrd, Mo., 1968-69; elem. sch. tchr. Zalma (Mo.) Elem. Sch., 1970, Bourbon (Mo.) Elem. Sch., 1970-95. Pres. Bourbon Cmty. Tchrs. Assn., chmn. welfare com., grievance com.; mem. profl. devel. com., Bourbon, 1989-94, mem. career ladder dist. com., Bourbon, 1994. Contbr. to sch. curriculums. Sunday sch. supt., choir mem., adminstrv. coun. United Methodist Ch., Cuba, Mo., 1978-94; mem. Cuba Arts Coun., 1990-94; choir mem. Crawford County Community Choir, Cuba, 1980-92; sponsor Ben Franklin Stamp Club, Bourbon, 1985-93. Mem. NEA, MNEA (del./bldg. rep.), Bourbon Mo. Edn. Assn. (sec.), Mo. State Tchrs. Assn. (del., bldg. rep.), South Cen. Coun. IRA (sec./pub. chmn. 1975-95), Delta Kappa Gamma (pres. 1984-85), others. Democrat. Avocations: sewing, reading, swimming, working outdoors. Home: 639 Green Rd Paragould AR 72450

WHITE, SARAH JOWILLIARD, retired counselor; b. Oxford, N.C., Sept. 1, 1921; d. John Hiriam and Emma (Redfern) Isham; m. Hamilton B. Carson, Sept. 20, 1945 (div. 1968); 1 child, Lynne Denise. Student, Bennett Coll., 1939-42, Cornell U., 1979-82; BA, CCNY, 1973. Clk. N.Y. Dept. Law, N.Y.C., 1948—53; auditor U.S. Fed. Govt. Svc., N.Y.C., 1955—62; postal clk. U.S. Govt., Mt. Vernon, NY, 1963—66; prin. N.Y. State Dept. Labor, N.Y.C., 1966—88, ret., 1988; youth organizer N.Y. State Careerists Soc., Inc., N.Y.C., 1989—. Youth and employment counselor Women in Cmty. Svc., Nat. Coun. Negro Women, Manhattan sect., NYC, 1983—. Vol. Advanced Vocation Edn. Day, Albany, N.Y., 1988; vol., coord. Decade of the Youth, N.Y.C., 1989-90; corres. sec. Lower East Side United Neighbors, N.Y.C., 1989. Recipient Youth award, 1987, Recognition award, 1987, Internat. Assn. Pers. Employees Youth award, Plaque for Women in Cmty. Svcs., Outstanding Vol. Svc. award Gov. Mario Cuomo, 1994, Outstanding Vol. award, 1991-92, Outstanding Vol. award Women in Cmty. Svc., 1994, Cert. Appreciation, 1995, Appreciation award South Bronx Job Alumni chpt., 1995, Nat. Coun. Negro Women Recognition award, 1996; named one of N.Y.'s Finest Vols. Women in Cmty. Svcs. Mag., 1994, Woman on the Move, Cable TV, 1994, Outstanding Recognition award Women in Cmty. Svcs., 1996, Joint Action in Cmty. Svc. award, 1996, Nat. N.E. Regional award Women in Cmty. Svcs., 1997, Youth Recognition award Yale U., New Haven, 1997, award Joint Action in Cmty. Svc., 1997, N.E. Regional Pres. Vol. award, 1998, JAC Recognition award, 1998, Horthers Regional award, 1998, Nat. Coun. Negro Women Pres.'s award, 1998, 99, Cert., Women in Cmty. Svc. Northeast Regional Pres. award, 1998, Nat. Coun. Negro Women Pres. award, 1998, Joint Action Cmty. Svc. award, 1998, 99, Nat. Pres.'s award Women in Cmty. Svc., 1999, Samuel and May Rudin Cmty. Svc. award NYU, 1999. Mem.: NAFE, Internat. Assn. Pers. Employees, Nat. Coun. Negro Women (chairperson, Achievement award 1988—90, Cmty. Svc. award 2001, Legacy award 2002—05), Assn. U.S. Govt. Job Corps (Alumni Recognition award 1995), N.Y. Careerists Soc. (sec., Merit award 1988), Black Alumni CCNY (pub. rels. com., Outstanding award 1989). Democrat. 7th Day Sabbath Keeper House of God. Avocations: reading, writing, music.

WHITE, SHARMAN LYNELL, lawyer; b. Albany, Ga., Aug. 19, 1968; d. Frank Irvin and Annette Jones White; 1 child, Andrew Franklin White Cleary. BA in Govt. cum laude, Harvard Coll., Cambridge, Mass., 1990; JD, U. Tex., Austin, 1995. Bar: NY 1996. Assoc. Beveridge & Diamond, PC, Washington, 1995—97; atty., adviser U.S. Dept. Agr., 1997—. Mem. unexploded ordnance panel US Dept. Interior, Conf. Environment, Albuquerque, 2001; spkr. pub. lands and natural resources seminar US Dept. Justice, Nat. Advocacy Ctr., Columbia, SC, 2000; appointee Fed. Natural Resource Damage Assessment and Restoration Adv. Com.; mem. legal rsch. bd. U. Tex. Law Sch. Lead articles editor: Tex. Environ. Law Jour., 1994—95. Sponsor Christian Children's Fund. Recipient Performance awards, USDA Office Gen. Counsel, 1998—2004, On the Spot award, 1999, Extra Effort award, 2000, Departmental awards, USDA Hazardous Materials Mgmt. Group, 2001, 2005. Mem.: ACLU, Harvard Crimson, Harvard Club Washington, Potomac Pedalers Touring Club, MENSA. Avocations: travel, writing, bicycling, movies, boating. Office: US Department of Agriculture 1400 Independence Avenue SW Washington DC 20250 Office Phone: 202-720-6716. Personal E-mail: sharmian.white@post.harvard.edu. E-mail: sharmian.white@usda.gov.

WHITE, SHARON LARUE, social worker, therapist; b. Jefferson County, Tex., Oct. 3, 1950; d. Jack Dayton Sr. and Jessie Larue (Daniels) W. BSN cum laude, Tex. Christian U., 1976; BFA with honors, U. Tex., 1987, MS in Social Work with highest honors, 1988. RN Palo Pinto Gen. Hosp., Mineral Wells, Tex., 1976-77; RN, asst. head nurse All Saint's Hosp., Ft. Worth, 1977-78, charge nurse, 1979, supr. in-svc. edn., 1979-80, acting dir. nurses, 1980; team leader surg. fl. Harris Hosp., Ft. Worth, 1981-82, edn. coord., 1980-81; acting charge nurse cardiac fl. Med. Pla., Ft. Worth, 1982; psychiat. social worker intensive treatment unit Wyo. State Hosp., 1989-90; clin. therapist Pioneer Counseling Svcs., 1990—. Co-facilitatior Rape Crisis Ctr., Ft. Worth, 1985-87. Episcopalian. Avocations: music, painting, reading, needlecrafts.

WHITE, SHELBY, art association administrator; m. Leon Levy. BA, Mount Holyoke Coll; MA, Columbia U. Chmn. Shelby White-Leon Levy Prog. for Archaeol. Publs., 1997—. Mem. Cultural Property Adv. Com., 2000. Named one of Top 200 Collectors, ARTnews Mag., 2004, 2006. Avocation: Collector of Antiquities. Office: Semitic Mus Harvard U 6 Divinity Ave Cambridge MA 02138 Office Phone: 617-495-9317. E-mail: info@whitelevy.org.*

WHITE, SONYA RENEE, music educator; b. Islip, NY, Dec. 25, 1965; d. Ralph and Karloyne White. MusB in performance, Boston U., 1988, MusM in performance, 1990. Kodaly Method Cert. New England Conservatory, 2001, cert. Music Teacher K-12 State of Mass., 2001. Violin tchr., sectional coach Greater Boston Y1989outh Symphony Orch., 1989—98; viola faculty Cmty. Music Ctr. Boston, 1989—93; string tchr. Boston Latin Sch., 1992—; condr., worcester youth strings Performing Arts Sch. of Worcester, 2003—; instr., class strings Boston U., 2004—, tchg. asst., concert music, 2004—. Fellow Tanglewood Music Ctr., 1988. Musician (violist): Portland Symphony Orch., 1990—2003, Cambridge Cmty. Chorus Orch., 1996—, Boston Festival Orch., 1990—, Boston Classical Orch., 1990—92. Summer fellow, Northwestern U., 2003. Mem.: Boston Musicians Assn., Boston Teachers Union, Boston Area Kodaly Educators, Org. of Kodaly Educators, Am. String Tchr. Assn., Mass. Music Educators Assn., Nat. Assn. for Music Edn. Achievements include research in music education.

WHITE, SUSAN COLVIN, finance educator; b. Waco, Tex., Oct. 24, 1959; d. O. Herbert and Mary Ila Colvin; m. Gary D. White, June 4, 1988; children: Phoebe M., Toby C. BA, Baylor U., Waco, Tex., 1981; MBA, Baylor U., 1984; PhD, Tex. A&M U., College Station, 1994. Mgr. Phil van Duivendyk Studio, Waco, 1981—83; dir. health care markets analysis RRC, Inc., Bryan, Tex., 1985—88; instr. Northwestern State U., Natchitoches, La., 1988—91, Hibernia Bank prof. bus., 1994—2001; asst prof. decision scis. Sch. Bus. George Wash. U., Washington, 2001—. Lay leader Clarendon United Meth. Ch., Arlington, Va., 2002—04. Recipient Gubernatorial Commendation, Gov. Mike Foster, La., 1998. Office: George Washington University Sch Bus Decision Sci Dept Washington DC 20052 E-mail: scwhite@gwu.edu.

WHITE, SUSAN ROCHELLE, psychologist, investor; b. Highland Park, Mich., Jan. 23, 1957; d. John Tyree and Jayne Rochelle White. BA, U. Mich., 1979; MS, Ea. Mich. U., 1990. Lic. psychologist Mich. Disability examiner State of Mich. - Dept. Social Svcs., Southfield, 1980-88, group leader Whitmore Lake, 1988-92; case mgr. State of Mich. - Dept. Mental Health, Mt. Clements, 1992-93; group leader State of Mich. Family Ind. Agy., Whitmore Lake, 1993-94, psychologist, 1994—2002, youth residential dir., 2002—. Rschr. Aggression Replacement Tng., 1998. Mem.: APA (assoc.), Mich. Women Psychologists. Avocations: guitar, racquetball, bicycling, animal training, rental property renovation. Office: Family Ind Agy PO Box 349 Whitmore Lake MI 48189-0349 E-mail: whites@michigan.gov.

WHITE, SUSIE MAE, school psychologist; b. Madison, Fla., Mar. 5, 1914; d. John Anderson and Lucy (Crawford) Williams; m. Daniel Elijah White, Oct. 20, 1958 (dec. Sept. 29, 1968) BS, Fla. Meml. Coll., St. Augustine, 1948; MEd, U. Md., 1953; postgrad., Mich. State U., 1955, Santa Fe C.C., 1988; Cert. Child Care Supervision, W.T. Loften Edn. Ctr., Gainesville, Fla., 1994. Tchr. elem. Grove Park Elem. Sch., Fla., 1943; tchr. Douglas H.S., High Springs, Fla., 1944—55; sch. psychologist Alachua County Sch. Bd., Gainesville, Fla., 1956—69, coord. social svcs., 1970; owner, dir. Mother Dear's Child Care Ctr., Gainesville, 1988—. Author: Determined--in spite of.Autobiography of Susie Mae Williams White, 1998, Lord, Fix Me Inspirational Poems, 2000 Del. Bapt. World Alliance, Bapt. Conv. Fla., Tokyo, 1970; state dir. leadership Fla. Bapt. Gen. Conv., 1971-85 Recipient Cert. of Appreciation, Fla. State Dept. Edn., 1971, Appreciation for Disting. Svc. award, Fla. Gen. Bapt. Conv., 1979, Hall of Fame award, Martin Luther King Jr. Hall of Fame, 1994, Cert. Appreciation for Outstanding Svc. & Leadership, Mt. Sinai Woman's Conv., 1997, The Susie Mae White scholarship fund established, Mt. Sinai Congress Christian Edn., 1995, Cert. Appreciation, Friendship Bapt. Ch., 2000, Deloris Keith Meml. Good Neighbor award, East Gainesville Devel. Task Force, Inc., 1999, Trophy for Being Inspiration to Young Women, Alachua Practical Acad. Cultural Edn. Ctr. for Girls, Inc., 2001, Plaque for Appreciation of 60 Yrs. of Svc., Friendship Baptist Ch., 2001, Plaque for Appreciation of Leadership & Dedication to Cmty., Faith Tabernacle of Praise Mins., Inc., 2001. Mem. AAUW, Nat. Ret. Tchrs. Assn., Alachua County Tchrs. Assn., Fla. Meml. Coll. Nat. Alumni Assn., Heroines of Jericho, Masons Democrat. Avocations: gardening, speaking, working with police on crime prevention. Office: Child Care Ctr 811 NW 4th Pl Gainesville FL 32601-5049

WHITE, WILDA L., lawyer; BA, U. Vt., Burlington, 1980; JD, U. Calif., Berkeley, 1983; MBA, Harvard U., Boston, 1992. Bar: N.Y. 1984, Calif. 1986, Mass. 1990. Assoc. Sterns & Walker, San Francisco, 1986—88, mng. atty., 1988—90; asst. city editor Knight Ridder, Miami, Fla., 1992—93; mgmt. cons. McKinsey & Co., San Francisco, 1994—96; of counsel Law Offices of James Eggleston, Oakland, Calif., 1996—2003; ptnr. Walker, Hamilton & White, San Francisco, 2003—. Contbr. articles to profl. jours. Bd. dirs. Oakland Unified Sch. Dist., Oakland, 2000—02; founding bd. dirs. Growing Children Charter Sch., Oakland, 2001—02. Recipient President's award, Calif. Preservation Found., 2001, Ptnr. in Preservation award, Oakland Heritage Alliance, 2001. Mem.: San Francisco Trial Lawyers Assn. (bd. dirs. 2004). Office: Walker Hamilton & White 50 Francisco St Ste 460 San Francisco CA 94133-2100 Office Phone: 415-986-3339. Office Fax: 415-986-1618. E-mail: wwhite@walkerhamiltonwhite.com.

WHITE, YONSENIA S., artist, educator; BA, Va. Tech, Blacksburg, 1996, BFA, 1997; MFA, Rutgers U., New Brunswick, NJ, 1999. Instr. dept. art and art history Va. Tech., Blacksburg, 1999—2000, asst. prof. dept. art and art history, 2000—06, assoc. prof., 2006—. Manna from the Marquis: Spiritual Guidance from the Side of the Road, visual art exhibitions, Stereotypes & Catharsis, Hard to Ingest, Race (Enter Personal Politics), As I Am, 3rd Annual Women's Art Show. Prayer team leader St. Paul AME Ch., Blacksburg, Va., 2003—05. Recipient Minority Blueprint award, Rutgers U., Dept. Art, Mason Gross Sch. Arts, 1999; grantee, Peninsula Fine Arts Ctr., 1999, Va. Tech., U. Writing Program, 2003. Mem.: Women's Caucus Art, Nat. Mus.Women Arts, Southeastern Coll. Art Conf., Founds. Art Theory and Edn., Coll. Art Assn. Liberal. Avocations: fine and performing arts, poetry, sports, travel, jazz. Office Phone: 540-231-3807. Personal E-mail: yonsenia@yahoo.com.

WHITEBREAD, MELANIE JO, language educator; d. Raymond Earl and Shirley Jean Whitebread. BS, Bloomsburg U., Pa., 1986, MA, 1988; MS, Wilkes U., Pa., 1997. Cert. tchr. Pa. Substitute tchr. Berwick Area Sch. Dist., Berwick, Pa., 1988—89; adj. instr. Luzurne County CC, Nanticoke, Pa., 1990—93, asst. prof., 1994—96, assoc. prof., 1996—. Instr. Bloomsburg U., Pa., 1993. Mem.: NEA, Nat. Coun. Tchrs. English, Pa. State Edn. Assn. Office: Luzerne County Cmty Coll 1333 S Prospect St Nanticoke PA 18634

WHITE-HAMMOND, GLORIA E., pastor, pediatrician, human rights advocate; m. Ray A. Hammond, 1973; children: Mariama, Adiya. BA in Biology, Boston U.; MD, Tufts U., 1976; MDiv, Harvard Divinity Sch., 1997; LHD (hon.), Tufts U., 2006. Pediatrician South End Cmty. Health Ctr., 1981—; co-pastor (with husband Rev. Ray A. Hammond, M.D.) Bethel AME Ch., Boston, 1997—. Medical missionary in several African countries including Botswana, Cote D'Ivoire and South Africa. Co-founder My Sister's Keeper, Sudan, 2002—; chair Million Voices for Darfur campaign; founder, cons. Do the Write Thing, 1994—; co-convener The Red Tent Group; co-chair Mass. Coalition to Save Darfur; trustee Brigham and Women's Hosp.; bd. overseers Tufts U. Coll. Cmty. and Public Svc.; bd. dirs. Am. Anti Slavery Group, Boston, Christian Solidarity Internat., Zurich. Recipient Humanitarian award, Boston Theological Inst., 2004, Liberating Vision award, Greater Boston Sect. Nat. Coun. Negro Women, 2004, Impact award, Am. Assn. Retired Persons, 2004, Exceptional Women award, Magic 106.7, 2006. Achievements include being involved in obtaining the freedom of 10,000 women and children in Southern Sudan who were enslaved during the two decades long civil war. Office: Bethel AME Church 215 forest Hills St Jamaica Plain MA 02130-3302*

WHITEHAWK, ANN, secondary school educator; b. Sioux Falls, S.D., Aug. 9, 1951; d. A. Shirley Christensen and Eunice Elthea Ugland; m. Ronald Mario Whitehawk, Jan. 29, 1971; children: Jenine Nicole, Michael Christopher. BA in Comms., U. Tex., Arlington, Tex., 1973. Cert. speech, theater arts, ESL. Tchr. St. George Cath. Sch., Fort Worth, Tex., 1973—75; mus. dir. Republic Rio Grande, Laredo, Tex., 1984—85; tchr. United HS, Laredo, Tex., 1987—. Sponsor Laredo (Tex.) Youth Coun., 1985—87; mem. dist. edn. improvement coun. United Ind. Sch. Dist., Laredo, 1992—98; mem. site base decision making com. United High, Laredo, 1991—98; mem. liaison and ins. com. United Ind. Sch. Dist., Laredo, 1988—2002; tchr. speech, debate,and ESL speech. Founder El Paso (Tex.) Lupus Assn., 1979; co-founder Laredo (Tex.) Youth Coun., 1985—87. Named Woman of Yr., El Paso (Tex.) Lupus Assn., 1983. Mem.: So. Tex. Writing Project, Tex. Comm. Assn., Tex. Forensic Assn., Nat. Forensic League. Democrat. Roman Cath. Avocations: painting, furniture refinishing. Home: 323 Farrell Rd Laredo TX 78045-2322 Office: United High School 8800 McPherson Laredo TX 78045 Office Phone: 956-717-6100.

WHITEHEAD, JENNIFER SUE, choreographer; b. Houston, Mar. 7, 1973; d. Travis Wayne and Mary Sue Heisler; m. Kenneth Wayne Whitehead, Aug. 2, 1997; children: Patrick Wayne, Rebekah Kate. BFA in Secondary Edn., Stephen F. Austin State U., Nacogdoches, Tex., 1998. Instr., choreographer Showtime Internat., Lago Vista, 1991—97, Crowd Pleasers Dance Camps, Austin, Tex., 1997—2004; dance asst. dir., tchr. Katy (Tex.) H.S., 1999—2002; instr., choreographer United Spirit Assn. USA, Cypress, Calif., 2001—; dance dir., tchr. Cypress Ridge H.S., Houston, 2003—. Staff NCA Collegiate All-American Dancer, 1995. Dancer Houston Met. Dance Ctr., 2004—05, Planet Funk, Houston, 2004—05. Recipient NCA Collegiate Nat. Winner, 1993—95, Head Instr. and Choreographer award, United Sprit Assn. Jazz Staff, 2005—06. Mem.: TDEA (logo designer 2004—06). R-Liberal. Baptist. Avocations: dance, drawing, painting, travel. Office Phone: 281-807-8023.

WHITEHEAD, TANYA DIANNE GRUBBS, psychologist, educator, researcher; b. Scottsbuff, Nebr., June 23, 1953; d. William Elliott Grubbs and Esther Mary Cooper Grubbs; m. William Downing Whitehead, Aug. 12, 1971; children: Shana Alexandra, Thomas William, Bethany Rose. B in Psychology summa cum laude, Ottawa U., 1990; M in Clin. Psychology, Avila U., 1992; D in Psychology, U. Mo., 2001. Cert. specialist, developmental and handicapping conditions U. Kans. Sch. Medicine, 1993. Clin. instr. U. Kans. Sch. Medicine, Kansas City, 1987—96; rsch. prof. U. Mo., Kansas City, 1996—. Psychol. consulting burn unit, craniofacial team, spina bifida clinic, pediatric gastroenterology Sch. Medicine, U. Kans., Kansas City, 1987—96; state, regional and nat. advisor People First Self Advocacy Tng. Adults With Devel. Disabilities, 1997—2001; peer grant rev. facilitator and chair US Depts Health and Human Svcs., Corp. for Nat. Svc., Washington, 1999—; program evaluator, impact of asset bldg. on youth from disadvantaged circumstances Office of Cmty. Svc., US Dept. Health and Human Svs.; program evaluation: promoting higher edn. partnerships for global devel. US AID, Assn. Liaison Office for U. Cooperation in Devel., Cape Town, South Africa; dir. AmeriCorps VISTA Project in Self Advocacy, Statewide, Mo., 1998—2000; cons.: cmty. movement for urban progress cmty. devel. corp. Urban Core Cmty. Devel. Project, Kansas City, 2002—04; sr. program evaluator; assets for independence demonstration project, us hhs, office cmty. svcs. PeopleWorks, Inc., Washington, 2000—01. Author: (Self Determination Workshops) New Media Workshops for Adults with DD, (book) Exploring Self Advocacy from a Social Power Perspective, (film) Enslaved Minds: Final Barrier to Freedom and Justice; contbr. new media toolkit (Crystal Communicator Award, 2001); author: (disability accommodation guide) Exchange City Accommodation Guide. Fellow Ctr. for the City, U. Mo., 2004-2005; fellow, Studies in Cmty. Change, 2000. Mem.: ANA (mem. commn. accreditation), AAUP, AAUW, LWV, APA, Assn. for the Advancement Ednl. Rsch. (bd. mem.), Am. Nurses Credentialing Ctr. (bd. Commn. on Accreditation). Office Phone: 913-488-7722. Business E-Mail: whiteheadt@umkc.edu.

WHITEHILL, ANGELA ELIZABETH, artistic director; b. Leeds, Yorkshire, Eng., Oct. 21, 1938; came to U.S., 1952, naturalized, 1995; d. Donald Paul and Audrey May (Clayforth) Warner; m. Norman James Whitehill, Jr., Dec. 23, 1959; children: Norman James III, Pamela Elizabeth; m. William Parker Noble, Dec. 27, 1998. Student, Arts Ednl. Sch., London, 1955-59. With corps de ballet Ballet Paris, 1958-59; dir. London Sch. Ballet, St. Thomas, V.I., 1960-63; asst. dir. Ocean County Ballet Co., Toms River, NJ, 1965-68; founder, dir. Shore Ballet Sch., Toms River, 1968-76; artistic dir. Shore Ballet Co., Toms River, 1971-76; artist in residence Castleton State Coll., Rutland, Vt., 1977-79; founder, artistic dir. Burklyn Ballet Theatre, Johnson, Vt., 1977—2003, founding artistic dir., 2003—; dir. Ballet Umbrella, Dance Coun., Burklyn Designs, 2003—; artistic dir. Paradise Ballet Theatre, Key West, Fla., 2005—. Vis. prof. Colby Sawyer Coll., New London, N.H., 1978-79; resident designer Atlanta Ballet Co., 1982-83; designer, pub. relations N.J. Ballet Co., Orange, 1983-85; artistic dir. Vt. Ballet Theatre, Burlington, 1985-94; master tchr. 1st Congress Internat. de Ballet Classico Contemporaneo, Mex., 2000, Ft. Wayne Ballet, 2005, Regional Dance Am. SW Festival, 2006; interim artistic dir. Huntington Ballet Theatre, 2006. Choreographer Arensky Dances, 1983, A Deux, 1984, 4 Plus 2, 1986, Twins From A Time Gone By, 1987, Heart of the Island, 2002; co-author: Parent's Book of Ballet, 1988, 2d edit., 2003, The Young Professional's Book of Ballet, 1990, The Dancer's Book of Ballet, 2000, Ballet Magic, The Burklyn Story, 2001, Nutcracker Backstage, 2004; dir. artistic advisor Paradise Ballet Theatre, Nutcracker Key West, 2005; costumer designer Grand Rapids Ballet Swan Lake Act III, 1984, Scottish Am. Ballet, La Sylphide, 1984, Legend of Ench. Bird, 1994, Burklyn Youth Ballet, 1999-05, Hansel & Gretel, Alice in Wonderland, Cinderella & The Flower Fairies, Little Mermaid, Beauty and the Beast, Aladdin, Huntington Ballet Theatre, Cinderella, 2005, Nutcracker Key West ACT II, 2005, Burklyn Youth Ballet, 2006. Dir. Vt. Ballet Theatre Found., Calledonia County, 1986-96. Recipient Francis Hopkins award Ocean County, N.J., 1976, Woman of Achievement award Vt. Woman, 1989, Author's award N.J. Inst. Tech., 1989. Mem. Vt. Council on the Arts, Regional Dance Am. Mem. Soc. Of Friends. Home: 218 Ocean Ave Island Heights NJ 08732 Home (Winter): PO Box 907 Island Heights NJ 08732-0907 Office: Dance Counsel PO Box 493 Johnson VT 05656-0493 Office Phone: 732-288-2660. Personal E-mail: awhitehill@aol.com. E-mail: awhitehill@comcast.net.

WHITEHILL, MARY EVELYN, artist, retired librarian; b. Newburgh, N.Y., Mar. 9, 1920; d. David J. Perrott and Carrie Evelyn Pope; m. W. Hugh Whitehill, July 10, 1943 (dec. Oct. 1972); children: David H., Walter J., Joan W. Roth, Brian T. BA, Wells Coll., 1941; MS, SUNY, Albany, 1966. Libr. Newburgh Bd. Edn., 1966-86. Sec. Middletown (N.Y.) Art Group, 1994-2006. One-woman shows include Intercounty Savs. Bank, New Paltz, N.Y., 1982, Beck Gallery, Hurley, N.Y., 1984, Pine Bush Art Assn., 1987—89, Putnam Valley Hosp., Carmel, N.Y., 1989, Interlude Gallery, Rhinebeck, N.Y., 1990, Unitarian Fellowship, Poughkeepsie, N.Y., 1998, Rock Tavern, N.Y., 2000, Howland Cultural Ctr., Beacon, N.Y. Invitationals, 2002—04, Plein Air Register of N.Y., 2005, Korpeles Mus., 2005, Mus. Hudson Highlands, 2006, Orange Invitational, SUNY, 2006, Represented in permanent collections Glen Ridge (N.J.) Country Club, Putnam Valley Hosp., Mt. St. Mary Coll., Newburgh, N.Y., numerous pvt. collections. Fellow: Salmagundi Club (N.Y.C.); mem.: Ridgefield Art Assn., Ridgewood Art Assn., Catskill Art Soc., N.E. Watercolor Soc. (sec. 1987—91, signature mem.), Pa. Watercolor Soc. (signature mem.), Kent Art Assn. (signature mem.). Presbyterian. Avocations: golf, gardening, music.

WHITEHORTON, THELMA, educational administrator; b. Blyesville, Ark., Feb. 7, 1949; d. William Soloman and Corrine (Carrigans) White; m. Charles D. Horton, May 20, 1970 (div. 1991); children: Corrine Daniel Horton, Tiffany Louise, Charles William. Student, Fla. Internat. U.; BSW, Boise State U., 1975; D (hon.), World U.; student, St. Thomas U., 2006—. Team tchr. Dade County Pub. Schs., Parks and Recreation Coll., North Miami, 1979—80; lead tchr. gifted edn. Dade County Elem. Schs., Miami Dade C.C., Miami, 1980—; owner, dir. Hi School Day Care and Learning Ctr., Cutler Ridge, Fla., 1981—; reading tchr. Miami Dade CC, 1981—83. Lead tchr. gifted Naranja Elem. Sch.; owner Charisma, Fla.; tutor English, Perrine, Fla., 1982—; with Comet Lab, 1996-97; cons. WESTAT Rsch., Barr Industries, Perrine, 1981—, The Rand Co., Student Travel Svc. student placement; temp. Dade County Pub. Schs.; alternative edn. tchr. 5th grade Peskoe Elem. Sch.; advocate African-Am. voices; tchr. liberal arts Wardstone Coll.; adminstr. R.E.S.S. program for implementation of the Met. Test/Archdiocese of Miami; creator of The Horton Chart for Math; pvt. tchr. tap dance. Author: Have Your Cake and Eat it Too, The Black C, Reciprocal Reading, African Curriculum Integration for Intermediate Education in the Classroom, Reciprocal Reading 1996-97, Epinions.com., Ms. T. Tuttle's 2nd Grade Class T.E.A.M., The Reading Quagmire: ERIC, Lessonpro, The Dream Catcher, 2004; contbr. papers to profl. jours. Active Boy Scouts Am., PTSA, ARC; mem. usher bd. Martin Meml. Meth. Ch.; st. capt. Neighborhood Crime Watch; advocate for Nat. Tchr. Cert., 1995-96; vol. The Horton Chart Eisenhower Nat. Clearinghouse; advocate African Am. Voices; children's adv. Idaho Gov.'s ADvocacy Program, Boise, 1974-76. Named Comet Lab. Tchr. of Yr., 1996; recipient Equity and Excellence award, Magnet Innovative Programs, Cmty. Svc. award, JESCA orgn. Mem. ACLU, The Exec. Female, Children's Advocates (pres. 1975-83), United Tchrs. Dade County, Alumni Assn. Boise State U., Inst. Children's Lit., Miami C. of C., Fla. Assn. for the Gifted, Kappa Delta Pi. Home: 15905 SW 105th Ct Miami FL 33157-1571 Office: 13990 SW 264th St Homestead FL 33032-7402 Personal E-mail: pug@bellso.net. E-mail: chinatown48@yahoo.com.

WHITEHOUSE, ANNE CHERNER, writer; d. Marvin and Leona Roth Cherner; m. Stephen Compton Whitehouse, June 24, 1979; 1 child, Claire Landau. BA magna cum laude, Harvard U., 1972—76; MFA in Writing, Columbia U., 1976—79. Freelance journalist, 1988—; special projects mgr. Dorot, NYC, 1997—. Devel. cons. Am. Opera Projects, Bklyn., 1995—. Author: (poems) The Surveyor's Hand, 1981, Fall Love, 2001. Mem.: Phi Beta Kappa. Home: 340 Riverside Dr New York NY 10025 Office: Dorot 171 W 85th St New York NY 10024 E-mail: awhitehouse@dorotusa.org.

WHITEHURST, LUCINDA SNYDER, school librarian; d. Wilma Jones and William Franklin Snyder; m. Mark Alexander Whitehurst, May 20, 1989; children: Megan Macye, Alexander William. BA, Coll. William and Mary, 1986; MS, U. Ill., 1987. Children's libr. DC Pub. Libr., 1987—89; young adult libr. County of Henrico Pub. Libr., Richmond, Va., 1989—92; lower sch. libr. St. Christopher's Sch., Richmond, 1992—. Adj. instr. continuing edn. U. Va., Richmond, 2001—. Contbr. articles and reviews to profl. jours.; editor: (newsletter) The Open Book. Mem. Friends of the Richmond Pub. Libr., 2000—02, State Networking Users Adv. Bd., Richmond, 2000—02; pres. Garfield F. Childs Meml. Fund, Richmond, 2003—04. Lois Wells Irwin fellow, U. Ill. Grad. Sch. Libr. and Info. Sci., 1986. Mem.: Va. Ednl. Media Assn., ALA (com. chair 2004—05). Office: St Christopher's Sch 711 St Christopher's Rd Richmond VA 23226

WHITEHURST, MARY TARR, artist, poet, writer; b. Norfolk, Va., Nov. 20, 1923; d. Jenry Bennitt and Martha Ida Tarr; m. Jerry Rutter Whitehurst, Dec. 24, 1943; children: Henry Armistead, Jeffrey Tarr, Martha W. Bryant. Student, Coll. William & Mary, 1940-42, Wytheville C.C., 1968, Sullins Coll., 1976-80, Va. Western C.C., 1988. Docent Mus. Fine Arts, Roanoke, Va., 1973-75. Dir., endowing mem. Fine Arts Ctr. of New River Valley, Pulaski, Va., 1980-93; charter, endowing mem. Bristol Mus. Fine Arts, Va./Tenn., 1975-80; benefactor, mem. Arts Found. Radford U., Va., 1991—. One-woman shows include Mus. Fine Arts, Roanoke, Va., 1977, Emory & Henry Coll., Emory, Va., 1982, Radford U. Art Gallery, Va., 1991, Ashland Area Art Galery, Ky., 1993, Va. Polytech. Inst. & State U., Blacksburg, 1985—, New River C.C. Found., 1985—, Coll. William & Mary, Williamsburg, 1995; endowment Poly. Inst. & State U., Blacksburg, Va., 1998; author: (poetry) Silent As Birds, 1997. Endowing mem. Va. Polytech. Inst. & State U., Blacksburg, 1985—, New River C.C. Found., 1985—, Coll. William & Mary, Williamsburg, 1995; mem. Va. Polytech. Found., Blacksburg, Va. Recipient Clement Gueenberg award of distinction Mus. Fine Arts, Roanoke, 1976, Grumbacher Gold medal Soc. Water Color Artists, 1995; art dept. named in honor New River C.C., Dublin, Va., 1994. Mem. Catharine Lorillard Wolfe Art Club (Joyce Williams water color award 1985), Midwest Transparent Water Color Soc. (signature mem.), Va. Water Color Soc. (dir. 1994), Ala. Water Color Soc., Blacksburg Regional Artists Assn., Allied Artists (assoc.), So. Water Color Soc. (two awards 1997, Blue Ribbon winner 2000). Avocations: travel abroad, art collection, history, philanthropy. Home: Painters Wood 2492 Forest Hill Dr Draper VA 24324-3224

WHITELAW, DOLORES FAHEY, artist; b. Bklyn., June 12, 1941; d. John Michael and Irene Marie (Bulger) Fahey; m. Bruce David Whitelaw, June 23, 1962; children: Erin Carolyn, Casey Bruce. Student, Newark Sch Fine & Indsl. Arts, 1959, 60, Art Student League, 1962, 63. One woman shows include E3 Gallery, N.Y.C., 1996, 2004, Les Malamut Art Gallery, Union, N.J., 1998, 2005; exhibited in group shows at Carole Franklin Gallery, Emerson, N.J., 1997, JCB Internat., N.Y.C., 1997, La MaMa La Galleria, N.Y.C., 1998, Westbeth Gallery, N.Y.C., 1998. Mem. Orgn. Ind. Artists, City Without Walls. Home: 362 Forest Dr Union NJ 07083-7942 E-mail: dwstudio362@juno.com.

WHITELEY, EMILY C., biology professor; b. Charlevoix, Mich., Oct. 10, 1962; d. Daniel G. and Ruth O. Axt; m. Stephen J. Whiteley, May 25, 1986. AS, Western Piedmont C.C., Morganton, NC, 1995; BA in Biology, U. NC, Asheville, NC, 1997; MS, Western Carolina U., Cullowhee, NC, 2000. Biology instr. Catawba Valley C.C., Hickory, NC, 2001—. Mem.: Nat. Assn. of Biology Teachers (assoc.). Achievements include discovery of a new spider species in 1999, Spider was named Anthrobia whiteleyae in 2005. Avocations: hiking, horse rescue. Office: Catawba Valley Cmty Coll 2550 Hwy 70 SE Hickory NC 28602 Office Phone: 828-327-7000. Personal E-mail: dunhorse2003@yahoo.com. E-mail: ewhitele@cvcc.edu.

WHITELEY, KENDRA LEIGH, secondary school educator; d. Billie Whiteley. BA in Engish Lit. and African and African Am. Studies, U. Mich., Ann Arbor, 1990; MEd, Oklahoma City U., 1998. Cert. Mich. Tchr. English N.Y.C. Pub. Sch., 1990—91, Oklahoma City Pub. Sch., 1994—98; tchr. English and social studies Plymouth (Mich.) Canton Cmty. Sch. Advisor Mid. Ea. Student Assn., Plymouth/Canton, 2003—05, Indian Am. Student Assn., Plymouth/Canton, 2004—06; co-advisor Muslim Student Assn., Plymouth/Canton, 2004—06. Office: Plymouth Canton Cmty Sch 454 S Harvey St Plymouth MI 48170 Office Phone: 734-416-2700. Personal E-mail: kendrawhiteley@hotmail.com.

WHITELEY, SANDRA MARIE, librarian, editor; b. May 24, 1943; d. Samuel Smythe and Kathryn Marie (Voigt) Whiteley; m. R. Russell Maylone, Jan. 8, 1977; 1 child, Cybele Elizabeth. BA, Pa. State U., 1963; MLS, Columbia U., 1970; MA, U. Pa., 1975; postgrad., Northwestern U., 1985—. Tchr. Amerikan Kiz Koleji, Izmir, Turkey, 1967-69; reference libr. Yale U., New Haven, 1970-74; head reference dept. Northwestern U., Evanston, Ill., 1975-80; asst. editor Who's Who in Libr. and Info. ALA, Chgo., 1980-81, editor Reference Books Bull., 1985-96; lectr. Grad. Libr. Sch. U. Chgo., 1982-83; assoc. exec. dir. Assn. Coll. and Rsch. Librs., Chgo., 1981-85; editor Chase's Calendar of Events NTC/Contemporary Pub., 1997—2001; freelance editor, 2001—. Author: Purchasing an Encyclopaedia, 5th edit., 1996, The American Library Association Guide to Information Access, 1994. Mem. ALA (various coms. 1977-81), Beta Phi Mu. Democrat. Congregationalist. Avocations: reading, hiking, travel. Home: 1205 Noyes St Evanston IL 60201-2635

WHITELO, VELMA HOLLAND, special education educator; b. Memphis, Dec. 11; d. Willie Rogers and Lettie Sherrod Holland; 1 child, Valerie N. Jackson. BS, Lemoyne Owen Coll., 1973; MS in Edn., U. Memphis, 1986; student, Cumberland U., 1995. Spl. edn. tchr. Memphis City Sch., 1973—, homebound tchr., 1993—99. Coach Spl. Olympics, Memphis, 1978—; jr. deputy coord. Shelby County Sheriff Dept., 1983—; truant officer Memphis City Sch., 1993—99. Coord. Just Say No Club, 1985—99. Recipient United Way award, Nat. Children's Cancer Soc., Trust Officer of Year, Truancy Prevention Svc., Rotary award, Memphis Rotary Club, 1996; grantee Tchr. Initiative Grant, 1994. Mem.: Nat. Edn. Assn., Tenn. Edn. Assn., Memphis Edn. Assn., Delta Sigma Theta. Democrat. Baptist. Avocations: travel, dance.

WHITEMAN, LOUISE ANN, elementary school educator; d. Ronald George and Ruby Louise Hett; m. Gail Lynn Whiteman, Aug. 6, 1977; children: Justin, Jess, Jarvis. BA, Asbury Coll., Wilmore, Ky., 1975; MS in Curriculum & Instrn., Wichita State U., Kans., 2004. Tchr. 2d grade Florence Elem. Sch., Kans., 1975—78; tchr. 1st grade Bown-Corby Grade Sch., Marion, 1978—80; tchr. 3d & 4th grades Burns Elem. Sch., 1989—94; tchr. 2d grade Peabody-Burns Elem. Sch., 1994—. Mem.: ASCD. Methodist. Avocation: scrapbooks. Office: United Sch Dist 398 Peabody-Burns 506 Elm Peabody KS 66866

WHITEMAN RUNS HIM, HEATHER DAPHNE, prosecutor, artist; Diploma, Northfield Mt. Hermon Sch., Mt. Hermon, Mass., 1992; A.F.A., Inst. of Am. Indian Arts, Santa Fe, N. Mex., 1996; BFA, U. N.Mex, Albuquerque, 1999; JD, Harvard Law Sch., Cambridge, Mass., 2002. Bar: N.Mex 2002, Crow Tribe 2003. Assoc. atty. Nordhaus Law Firm, Albuquerque, 2002—04; adj. faculty U. of N. Mex, 2003—; assoc. atty. Sonosky Chambers Sachse Endreson & Perry, Albuquerque, 2004—05; atty. N. Mex Pub. Defender, 2005—. Alumni adv. coun. mem. Nat. Native Am. Law Students Assn., 2005—. Independent. Office Phone: 505-841-6980.

WHITE-MYERS, BARBARA JEANNE, artist, retired educator; d. Elmer Charles and Mary Jane (Shaw) Frye; m. Bob White, II (dec.); 1 child, Scott Christopher White; m. Charles Casper Myers, Mar. 20, 1999. B in Applied Arts, U. Cin., 1960, BS in Edn., 1960; MA in Profl. Studies, SUNY, 1990; postgrad., Union Coll., 1972—73, C.W. Post, 1973, Skidmore Coll., 1989, Coll. Santa Fe, 1990, Bard Coll., 1990, postgrad., 1997, Bennington Coll., 1992. Cert. Tchr. Kindergarten through Twelfth Grade 1973. Art tchr. Princeton Ctrl. Sch. Dist., Cin., 1960—61, Arlington Ctrl. Sch. Dist., Poughkeepsie, NY, 1961—96; ret., 1996. Core tchr. Total Edn. for the Total Environment, NY, 1971—72; mem. Art Curriculum Assessment Team Arlington Ctr. Sch. Dist., 1982—92, mem. Project Team, 1982—92; visiting artist Seven Springs Elem. Sch., New Port Richey, Fla., 2002; participant nat. conventions, nat. & internat. confs. Sculptor, Bad Sun Day, 1995 (1st Prize, Phylis Graff, NY Times Art Critic, 1995), juried exhibition, Remnants of Things Past, 1997 (1st Place award, Dutchess County Art Assn., 1997), exhibitions include Memorial Day, Remnants of Things Past, 1997 (1st Place award, curator Juror Francesca Consagra, Lehman Loeb Art Ctr., Vassar Coll., 1997), Three BoBo's in Paradise, Promising Picassos Exhibit, Fla., 2000 (People's Choice award, Pasco County Arts Coun., 2000), Millennium Madness, Seems Like Yesterday Exhibit, 2000 (award, David Prace, West Pasco Hist. Soc., 2000), Pasco's Pride & Joy, Fla. State Capitol Bldg., Tallahassee, 2001, West Pasco Govt. Ctr., Pasco/Hernando CC, Arts Desire Gallery. Chmn. Earth As Art Vasser Coll., Poughkeepsie, 1995, vol. Frances Lehman Loeb Museum, 1996—98; vol. Hudson River Clearwater Revival, Walkway Over the Hudson. Recipient Southeastern Art Educator of Yr., NY State Art Tchrs. Assn., 1995. Mem.: Nat. Art Edn. Assn., Nat. Trust Hist. Preservation, NY State Art Tchrs. Assn., Nat. Mus. Women Arts, Am. Assn. U. Women, Pasco Arts Coun., Fla. Humanities Coun., NY State United Tchrs. Retiree Coun., Progress Energy Art Gallery, Delta Phi Delta Nat. Art, Alpha Chi Omega. Home: 7710 Lakeside Woodlands Dr Hudson FL 34667

WHITENER, CAROLYN RAYE, artist; b. Corpus Christi, Texas, Feb. 2, 1941; d. Rayburn N. and Alice G. Hamilton; m. Howard Dwain Whitener; children: Mark Dwain, Rynn Rayna. Student, U. Sci. and Arts Okla., 1981-85. Co-owner Honk'n'Holler's, Stillwater, Okla., 1962-75; owner Clynn's Designs, Okla. City, 1969—; co-owner W&W Cattle Ranch, Okla., 1973—; comml. artist, co-owner Colorvision, Inc., Okla. and Tex., 1979—. Cons. Tele-Weight, Buena Vista, Colo., 1985-92, Craig Versus Boren, 1972-76; comml. design cons. for one and two dimensional rendering drawings Rynn's Lawncare & Landscaping, Oklahoma City, 1997—; freelance designer staging and backdrops, N.Y., 1973-74; mem. adv. coun., Status of Okla. Woman, 2001—. Active Grady County Environ. Coalition, 1991—92; adv. mem. Gov.'s Okla. Commn. on Status of Women, 2000—. Recipient Outstanding Cmty. Svc. award, 1992, One Person Who Made a Difference LWVOK, 1997, Pres. Prestigious award Okla. State U., 1996, First Adv. award Okla. Commn. on Status of Women, 2001, Gov. Commendation award Gov. Frank Keating, 2001, State of Okla. Citation award Rep. Richard Phillips and Sen. Mike Fair, 2001; named Woman of Yr. Okla. City Coun. of Beta Sigma Phi, 1997-98. Mem. Okla. Assn. Family Cmty. and Edn., Grady County Ext. Homemakers, Oklahoma City Newcomer's Club, Beta Sigma Phi (Woman of Yr. award 1997-98, Outstanding Svc. award 1992, Evening Lions Homecoming Window Design awards, 1966-68), Chickesha Okla. H.S. Alumni Class (decorations com. 1989—). Democrat. Methodist. Avocations: art, sewing, cooking, travel. Home: 12324 St Lukes Ln Oklahoma City OK 73142 E-mail: CrWhitener@aol.com.

WHITESELL, PATRICIA S., academic administrator; b. Ann Arbor, Mich., Mar. 22, 1950; d. Don McKinstry and Patricia Jane (Smith) W.; m. John R. Wolfe, Sept. 7, 1990 BA, Olivet Coll., 1972; MA, U. Mich., 1980, PhD, 1994. Fin. aid officer U. Mich., Ann Arbor, 1973—80; dir. fin. aid U. Mich. Law Sch., Ann Arbor, 1980—86; adminstrv. mgr. Rsch. Office U. Mich., Ann Arbor, 1986—94, asst. to v.p. Rsch. Office, 1994—. Author: A Creation of His Own: Tappan's Detroit Observatory, 1998-2004; contbr. articles to profl. jours Chair adv. com. Detroit Obs., U. Mich., 1994-98, dir., curator, 1998-2005, curator emerita 2005—; bd. dirs., curator Kempf House Ctr. for Local History, 1995-96. Mem. Washtenaw County Hist. Soc Avocations: university history, history of astronomy, hiking, travel, natural history. Office: U Mich Detroit Observatory 1398 East Ann St Ann Arbor MI 48109-2051

WHITESIDE, CAROL GORDON, foundation executive; b. Chgo., Dec. 15, 1942; d. Paul George and Helen Louise G.; m. John Gregory Whiteside, Aug. 15, 1964; children: Brian Paul, Derek James. BA, U. Calif., Davis, 1964. Pers. mgr. Emporium Capwell Co., Santa Rosa, 1964-67; pers. asst. Levi Strauss & Co., San Francisco, 1967-69; project leader Interdatum, San Francisco, 1983-88; with City Coun. Modesto, 1983-87; mayor City of Modesto, 1987-91; asst. sec. for intergovtl. rels. The Resources Agy., State of Calif., Sacramento, 1991-93; dir. intergovtl. affairs Gov.'s Office, Sacramento, 1993-97; pres. Great Valley Ctr., Modesto, Calif., 1997—. Trustee Modesto City Schs., 1979-83; nat. pres. Rep. Mayors and Local Ofcls., 1990; mem. Sierra Nev. Conservancy Bd., 2005-. Recipient Lifetime Achievement award League of Calif. Cities, 2002, Excellence in Pub. Svc. award, Fresno Bus. Coun., 2004; named Outstanding Woman of Yr. Women's Commn., Stanislaus County, Calif., 1988, Woman of Yr., 27th Assembly Dist., 1991; Toll fellow Coun. of State Govts., 1996, Champion of Am. Dream, Calif. State U., Stanislaus, 2002. Republican. Lutheran. Office: Great Valley Ctr 201 Needham St Modesto CA 95354-0903 E-mail: carol@greatvalley.org.

WHITESIDE, KAREN SOWARDS, mathematics educator; d. Irvin Thomas and Anne Questel Sowards; m. Donald Gene Whiteside, July 29, 1972; children: Christopher Michael, Shannon Marie Hull, Michelle Lenai Earley. BA, U. S.Fla., Tampa, 1968—72, MA, 2000—03. Cert. tchr. Fla. Dept. Edn., 1972. Math. tchr. Boca Ciega HS, Gulfport, Fla., 1972—80, Dunedin HS, Fla., 1981—2001, Pinellas Pk. HS, Largo, Fla., 2001—. Tchr. Forest Hills Ch. Christ, Tampa, 1970—72, Disston Ave Ch. Christ, St. Petersburg, Fla., 1972—75, Largo Ch. Christ, Fla., 1975—86, NE Ch. Christ, Clearwater, 1986—2001, Clearwater Ch. Christ, Clearwater, 2001—06. Edn. grants, Pinellas Edn. Found., 1996—97, 1999—2000, 2001—02, Edn. grant, City Clearwater & Dunedin Jr. League, 1996—97, 1999—2000. Mem.: Nat. Coun. Tchs. Math., Fla. Coun. Tchrs. Math., Pinellas Coun. Tchrs. Math., Phi Kappa Phi, Delta Kappa Gamma. R-Liberal. Church Christ.

WHITESIDE, PATRICIA LEE, fine art antique and personal property appraiser; b. Keokuk, Iowa, Dec. 29, 1957; d. Francis Lee and Ruby Elaine (Higbee) W. AA, Merced Coll., Calif., 1980; Cert. Appraisal Studies, NYU, 1997, Cert., 1999. Proprietor estate specialist Lexington Ave. Antiques, Magnolia, Mass., 1984-88; pub., editor, dir. The Art and Antique Tour Guide, 1988—; art advisor, pres. Fine Art and Antique Tour Assocs., 1988—; estate specialist East Coast region, 1981—, New Eng. Appraisers Assn., Palm Beach, Fla., 1988—. Contbr. articles to profl. jours., local newspapers. Active Palm Beach Civic Assn., 1995—, Palm Beach C. of C., 1990—, Children's Mus., Boca Raton, Fla., others. Recipient award Mass. Hist. Assn., Harvard U., 1987, others. Mem. New Eng. Appraisers Assn. (S. Fla. regional dir.), Soc. for the Preservation of New Eng. Antiquities, Compass Inc. Charities, Palm Beach Hist. Soc., Epilepsy Assn., Nat. Assn. Profl. Appraisers, others. Democrat. Avocations: painting, historical preservation, writing children's books, sailing, travel. Office: PO Box 2101 Palm Beach FL 33480-2101

WHITE-WALKER, ROXANA, elementary school educator; b. Beckley, W.Va., Sept. 13, 1947; d. George S. and Rosetta D. (Duey) White; m. Aug. 22, 1970; children: Joyce D., Walter W., Yalena A. BS in Edn., Lincoln U., Jefferson City, Mo., 1971; MEd, U. Louisville, 1989. Dir. presch. USAF, Eileson AFB, Alaska; elem. tchr. Wichita (Kans.) Pub. Schs.; tchr. kindergarten Westphalia (Mo.) Sch. Dist.; elem. tchr. Jefferson County Pub. Schs., Louisville. Former unit dir. Head Start, Phoenix. Treas. King Elem. Sch. PTA; rep. Jefferson County Pub. Sch. Mem. Ky. Edn. Assn. (rep. Jefferson County), Black Tchr. Caucus, Golden Key. Home: 316 Shawnee Dr Louisville KY 40212-2649

WHITFIELD, ANDREA BILLINGSLEY, elementary school educator; b. Birmingham, Ala., June 11, 1954; d. Arthur Brooke Billingsley, Ollie Lee (Bolden) Billingsley; children: Andrenetta, April, Amber. BS, Ala. A&M U., 1976; MA, U. Ala. Birmingham, 1978, cert. elem. edn., 1978, cert. principalship, 1993. Tchr. reading Blessed Sacrament Sch., Birmingham, 1977—79; tchr. reading Title I Birmingham Bd. Edn., 1979—85, tchr. elem., 1985—. Cons. in field. Author (poetry): The Essence of a Flower, 2001 (1st pl., 2001); choreographer praise dance I Believe I Can Fly, 1999 (cert., 2000); contbr. articles to profl. jours.; playwright Judgment Day, Wrongfully Accused; founder, dir. Melodies from Heaven Dance Acad. Named Outstanding Young Women Am., Poet of Yr., Inst. Poetry. Mem.: NEA (nat. black caucus 2001—), Birmingham Edn. Assn. (legis. contact team 2000—), Ala. Edn. Assn. (elections com. 2000—, SW minority leader 2000—), Birmingham West End Optimist Club (spkr. 2001—, Plaque 2001), Phi Delta Kappa, Delta Sigma Theta. Democrat. Baptist. Avocations: dance, reading, writing, backgammon, billiards, skiing. Home: 620 McCary St SW Birmingham AL 35211

WHITFIELD, ERICA SHARON, director, career planning administrator; b. Roanoke, Va., July 5, 1980; d. Edith Cookie (Peirce) and David James Whitfield. BS with honors, Lynchburg Coll., Va., 2001, MEd, 2004. Hall dir., grad. asst. residence life Lynchburg Coll., 2002—04, career counseling intern, 2003; counselor intern New Land Jobs, Lynchburg, 2003, Ctrl. Va. CC, Lynchburg, 2003—04; counselor Region 2000 Workforce Ctr., Lynchburg, 2003—04; dir. career devel. svcs. Mary Baldwin Coll., Staunton, Va., 2004—06; event planner, edn. coord. Alpha Sigma Alpha Sorority, Indpls., 2006—. Conf. chair Consortium of Va. Women's Coll. and Univ., Staunton, Va., 2005. Scholar, Mary Baldwin Coll., 2006. Mem.: ACA, Va. Found. for Ind. Coll., Va. Assn. Colleges and Employers, Nat. Assn. Colleges and Employers, Am. Coll. and Pers. Assn., Nat. Career Devel. Assn. (field editor for career convergence 2005—06), Alpha Psi Omega, Psi Chi, Kappa Delta Pi, Omicron Delta Kappa, Alpha Sigma Alpha (chpt. advisor 2004—06). Home: 3030 Bentwood Cir S Dr 1B Indianapolis IN 46268 Office: Alpha Sigma Alpha Sorority 9550 Zionsville Rd Ste 160 Indianapolis IN 46268 Office Phone: 317-871-2920. Personal E-mail: eryielle@yahoo.com. Business E-Mail: ewhitfield@alphasigmaalpha.org.

WHITFIELD, KAREN KAY, music educator; b. Wichita Falls, Tex., July 15, 1958; d. Harry L. and Glenda Thomas; m. Darrell Ray Whitfield, June 5, 1982; children: Kayla D'Ann Minchew, Lacey Dawn. B in Music Edn., Midwestern State U., Wichita Falls, 1980. Cert. tchr. Tex., 1980. Band dir. Throckmorton (Tex.) Ind. Sch. Dist., 1980—82; elem. music tchr. Seminole (Tex.) Ind. Sch. Dist., 1982—98; band dir. Seminole Jr. H.S., 1998—. Mem. South Seminole Bapt. Ch., 1982—2006. Named Wal-Mart Tchr. of Yr., Wal-Mart Industries, 2005. Mem.: Assn. Tex. Small Sch. Bands, Tex. Music Educators Assn., Seminole Music Club. Baptist. Avocations: music, camping, hunting, scrapbooks. Home: 503 Southwest 23rd Seminole TX 79360 Office: Seminole Jr High School 601 Southwest Ave B Seminole TX 79360 Office Phone: 432-758-9431. Personal E-mail: kwhitfield@seminole.k12.tx.us.

WHITFIELD, LYNN, actress; b. Baton Rouge, May 6, 1953; d. Valerian and Jean (Butler) Smith; m. Vantile Whitfield (div.); m. Brian Gibson, July 4, 1990 (div. 1992); 1 child, Grace; m. Van Whitfield (div.). Student, Howard U. Actor: (films) Doctor Detroit, 1983, A Thin Line Between Love and Hate, 1996, Gone Fishin', 1997, Eve's Bayou, 1997, The Planet of Junior Brown, 1997, Stepmom, 1998, A Time for Dancing, 2000, Head of State, 2003, Madea's Family Reunion, 2006, (TV films) The Women of Brewster Place, 1989, (lead role) The Josephine Baker Story, 1991, Sophie and the Moonhanger, 1995, (Emmy award), Deep in My Heart, 1999, Dangerous Evidence: The Lori Jackson Story, 1999, Love Songs, 1999 (TV miniseries) The Wedding, 1998, A Girl Thing, 2001, (TV series) Equal Justice, The Cosby Mysteries, 1994, Lost in Oz, 2002. Recipient Image award for outstanding performance in a youth or children's series/spl., 1997, Image award for outstanding supporting actress in a drama series, 1998.*

WHITFIELD, MARGARET DENNY, retired music educator; b. Richmond, Va., Apr. 18, 1936; d. Theodore Marshall and Elizabeth Denny (Dixon) Whitfield; children: David Yong Kim, Susanne Elisabeth Nelson. MusB cum laude, Western Md. Coll., 1958; MusM, Eastman Sch. Music, 1964; student, Cornell U., Western Md. U., U. Tenn. Tchr. Meth. Bd. Missions, Okadayama, Japan, 1958—61; instr. piano Hochstein Sch. Music, Rochester, NY, 1963—64; instr. piano Dept. Prep. Peabody Conservatory, Balt., 1964—65; orch. dir. Hanover (Pa.) Pub. Schs., 1968—70; dir. orch. Fairfax County (Va.) Pub. Schs., 1970—98. Ch. organist, 1957—58, 1963—; guest dir. orch. clinic James Madison U., Harrisonburg, Va., 1984; dir. H.S. orch. Carnegie Hall, N.Y.C., 1996. Piano concert soloist Western Md. Coll., 1957, Ithaca Coll. Orch., 1965; musician: Hanover (Pa.) Hall Nursing Home, 2003—04, various chs., 1960—61, Am. Cancer Soc., 2005. Vol. Eng. tchr., Japan, 1958—61; vol. driver Am. Cancer Soc., Falls Ch., 1999—; founder clothing shop Westminster (Md.) Meth. Ch., 1952; vol. Christian Witness Mission, Paducah, Ky., 1950, Christian Work Camp, Pharr, Tex., 1956, Seoul, Republic of Korea, 1959; missionary Meth. Bd. Missions and English Tchrs. Recipient Outstanding Intermediate Orch. award, Fairfax (Va.) Music Educators Assn., 1990, Citation award, Gov.'s Sch. of the Arts, 1993; scholar, Eastman Sch. Music, 1962—64. Mem.: Am. Guild Handbell Rings, Am. Guild Organists, Fairfax County (Va.) Ret. Educators Assn. Avocations: gardening, knitting, volunteering. Home: 7402 Monticello Blvd Springfield VA 22150 Office: Westover Baptist Ch 1125 N Patrick Henry Dr Arlington VA 22205

WHITFIELD, REBECCA WAVRIN, art educator; b. Little Rock, July 9, 1946; d. Clarence Peter and Johnnie Lou W.; m. Paul Douglas Whitfield, Aug. 17, 1968; children: Tracy Meredith, Michael Paul. BSE, U. Ctrl. Ark., 1969; MA, U. Ark., 1987, MAE, 1988. Tchr. math. Yale (Okla.) High Sch., 1973-75; chairperson art dept. Wilbur D. Mills U. Studies H.S., Little Rock, 1977—2002; visual arts instr. Ark. Gov.'s Sch., Conway, 1991—98; math. instr. Episc. Collegiate Sch., Little Rock, 2002—05. Instr. drawing Ark. Arts Ctr., Little Rock, 1987-90; visual arts program dir. AEGIS-Ark. Gifted Programs, Pine Bluff, 1988-90; art curriculum cons. State Dept. Edn., Little Rock, 1988—. Eight one-woman shows featuring abstracts. Recipient Outstanding Contbn. to Ark. Arts award Ark. Arts Coun., 1993. Mem. NEA, Nat. Art Educators Assn., Nat. Advocates for Gifted Children, Ark. Art Educators, Arkansans for Gifted and Talented Edn., Ark. Art Edn. (cons.). Democrat. Methodist.

WHITFIELD, TAMMY J., elementary school educator, director; b. June 2, 1963; BA, Grove City Coll., 1988; MS, Robert Morris Coll., 1996; EdD, Duquesne U., 2000. Cert. prin. K-12, Pa. Tchr. Chartiers Valley Sch. Dist., Bridgeville, Pa., 1988—2000, prin. spl. programs, 2000—04, asst. supt., 2004—. Address: 67 Cowan Rd Carnegie PA 15106-1409 Office Phone: 412-429-2217. E-mail: twhitfield@cvsd.net.

WHITING, MARTHA COUNTEE, retired secondary school educator; b. Marshall, Tex., Mar. 24, 1912; d. Thomas and Nannie Selena (Yates) Countee; m. Samuel Whiting, June 8, 1937; children: Jacqueline Bostic, Sammie Ellis, Nan Broussard, Tommye Casey, Martha Goddard. BA in Sci., Bishop Coll., 1934; M of Secondary Edn., Tex. So. U., 1959, postgraduate, 1962; postgrad., U. Colo., 1963. Tchr., sci., math. Houston Ind. Sch. Dist., 1942-73; researcher, local history Houston, 1973—. Lectr. in field. Mem. exec. com. (life mem.) Houston YWCA, 1977; advisor Preservation 4th Ward, Houston, 1991—; trustee Antioch Missionary Bapt. Ch., Houston, 1977; instrumental in getting the Antioch Missionary Bapt. Ch. in Christ Inc. on the Nat. Register of Hist. Places, 1976; presented Queen Elizabeth II with miniature history of Antioch Missionary Bapt. Ch. in Christ, 1991; author nomination form for Tex. hist. marker Antioch Missionary Bapt. Ch. in Christ, 1994; presenter to Harris County Heritage Soc. of Jack Yates House, the only house built by a former slave to be maintain ed by a U.S. city, and chmn. Pathfinder presentation of achievements of 64 Negro pioneers in Harris County, 1966-1986. Named Woman Courage, Houston Radcliffe Club, 1985, Black Womens Hall Fame Mus. Africal Am. Life, Dallas, 1986; recipient Friend of the Soc. award Harris County Heritage Soc., 1994. Mem. Tex. Ret. Tchrs. Assn., Houston Mus. Fine

Arts, Harris County Heritage Soc. (exec. com. 1984), Bluebonnet Garden Club (pres. 1968), Jack & Jill Am. (pres. Houston chpt. 1955-57), Smithsonian, Nationwide Trust for Historic Preservation. Avocations: writing, gardening, travel, sewing, singing. Home: 3446 Southmore Blvd Houston TX 77004-6349

WHITING DOBSON, LISA LORRAINE, video production educator, producer, director; b. Lansing, Mich., July 22, 1959; d. Lowell Stanton and Ruth Lorraine (Gregory) Whiting. BS in Psychology, Mich. State U., 1981, BA in Telecom. cum laude, 1984, MA in Telecom., 1988; AA in Dance magna cum laude, Lansing C.C., 1984. Prodr., dir. Cath. Diocese Lansing, 1984—; video instr., prodr., dir. dept. telecom., info. studies and media Mich. State U., East Lansing, 1987—; instr. media tech. Lansing C.C., 1999—. Dance instr. Synergy, 2002—. Mem. Jr. League of Lansing. Office: Mich State U Dept Telecom 409 Communication Arts Bldg East Lansing MI 48824-1212 E-mail: whiting3@msu.edu.

WHITIS, CYNTHIA M., secondary school educator; b. Augusta, Ga., Nov. 3, 1956; d. George W. and Lucy Alice Jenkins; m. James E. Whitis, Oct. 1, 1989; children: Alisa A. Mossbarger, David S. Mossbarger, Laura E. Mossbarger. EdB, Ind. U., Indpls., 1984; EdM, Ball State U., Indpls., 1994. Cert. tchr. Ind., 1984. Guidance counselor Ft. Gordon, Augusta, Ga., 1989—90; tchr. Atterbury Job Corp, Edinburgh, Ind., 1994—96, Indpls. Pub. Schs., 1996—. Author: (novels) Growing up in Fish Village. Sunday sch. tchr. New Bethel Bapt. Ch., Indpls., 1998—2006, children's ch. tchr., 2002—06. Recipient Fifteen Yr. Pin, U.S. Govt., 1974—94. Mem.: NEA (assoc.). Home: 9018 Imperial Dr Indianapolis IN 46239 Office: Indianapolis Public Schools 120 E Walnut St Indianapolis IN 46201 Office Phone: 317-226-4239.

WHITIS, GRACE RUTH, retired nursing educator; b. San Antonio, Sept. 14, 1942; d. Allan and Jewel (Conlee) Richardson; m. Robert E. Whitis, Mar. 6, 1965; children: Jay, Jennifer. PhD, U. Tex., 1981; BS, U. Mary Hardin - Baylor, 1968; MS, Baylor U., 1970; MSN, U. Tex., 1972. Staff nurse Providence Hosp., Waco, Tex., 1965-67; faculty U. Mary Hardin-Baylor, Belton, Tex., 1970-79, prof., dean, 1979-83; prof. nursing Ark. State U., Jonesboro, 1993-98, chmn. dept., 1985-93. Vis. prof. La. Tech. U., Ruston, 1982-84. Contbr. articles to profl. jours. Mem. ANA, Tex. Nurses Assn., Sigma Theta Tau. Home: 13070 W State Highway 36 Temple TX 76502-6933

WHITLATCH, CHRISTINE LYN, music educator; b. Pana, Ill., Nov. 5, 1955; d. Junior Henry Lawson and Alice Mae (Bender) Lilly; m. James E. Whitlatch, Apr. 24, 1976; children: Troy James, Jamie Lyn. MusB, Millikin U., Decatur, Ill., 1993. Music tchr. Pana Sch. Dist., 1994—2006, St. Anthony HS, Effingham, Ill., 2006—. Pvt. piano & voice tchr., Assumption, 1973—; choir dir. Pana Cmty. Coun. for Arts, 1999—. Choir dir. Meml. Presbyn. Ch., Assumption, Ill., 1980—2002. Mem.: Chorus Am., Am. Choral Dir.'s Assn., Music Educator's Nat. Presbyn. Avocations: victorian home decor, flower gardening. Home: 101 N St John Assumption IL 62510 Office: St Anthony HS 304 E Roadway Ave Effingham IL 62401

WHITLEY, L. TRACEE, lawyer; BA cum laude, Harvard U., 1988, MA Am. Govt., 1995; JD, Northeastern U., 1997. Bar: Mass. 1997, N.C. 1997. Dir., office chmn. Bingham McCutchen LLP, Boston, 2001—. Mem.: Ivy League Women's Silver Anniversary Soccer Team, 1998 (life), Harvard Varsity Club Hall Fame, 2003 (life). Office: Bingham McCutchen LLP 150 Federal St Boston MA 02110-1726 Office Phone: 617-951-8218. Office Fax: 617-951-8736. Business E-Mail: ltracee.whitley@bingham.com.

WHITLOCK, BETTY, retired secondary school educator; b. Somerset, Ky., Mar. 17, 1942; d. Rual Robert and Hazel Ellen (Biers) Wilson; m. L. Craig Whitlock, June 12, 1962 (dec. 2002); children: Michael Craig, Jeffrey Robert, Katherine Elizabeth. BA, Georgetown Coll., 1964; MA, Miss. Coll., 1980, EdS, 1982; postgrad., U. So. Miss., 1986. Nat. bd. cert. tchr. Adolescence and Young Adulthood/English Lang. Arts. Tchr. kindegarten First Bapt. Ch. Kindergarten, Clinton, Miss., 1970-72, Northside Bapt. Ch. Kindegarten, Clinton, Miss., 1972-73; tchr. high sch. Miss. Bapt. H.S., Jackson, 1973-75, Clinton H.S., 1975—2005; tchr. Pope H.S., Marietta, Ga. Bd. dirs. Miss. Youth Congress, 1985-2005; chmn. com. Lit. Map of Miss., 1985—; cons. Miss. H.S. Activities Assn., 1991-2005. Co-author: Mississippi Writers: An Anthology, 1987, Mississippi Writers: Reflections on Childhood and Youth, 1988, (textbook) Dramatic Interpretation, 1994. Tchr. Sunday sch. First Bapt. Ch., Clinton, 1969-2005. Named Tchr. of Excellence in ACTR-ACEL, 1997; named to Hall of Fame, Nat. Fedn. HS, 2005; recipient Miss. Tchr. of Yr., 1992. Mem. Nat. Coun. Tchrs. English, Nat. Forensic League, Miss. Coun. Tchrs. English (chmn. maps 1975—, Outstanding Tchr. award 1992), Miss. Speech Communication Assn. (dir. congress 1973-2004), Miss. Profl. Educators, Miss. Forensic League (chmn. 1988-99), Jackson Cath. Forensic League (moderator 1991-93), Miss. Coll. Faculty Wives, Phi Delta Kappa. Republican. Baptist. Avocation: writing. Office: Pope HS 3001 Hembree Rd Marietta GA 30062 Personal E-mail: nanawhit@aol.com.

WHITLOCK, VERONICA P., interior designer, educator; b. N.Y.C., Sept. 29, 1961; d. Emmet and Gloria Welch Whitlock; children: Alexander M. Laughlin, III, Julia W. Laughlin. BA in Studio Art and Art History cum laude, Duke U., 1983; BFA in Interior Design with distinction, N.Y. Sch. Interior Design, 1989. Cert. Nat. Coun. Interior Design Qualification, lic. interior designer Conn., cert. N.Y. Adminstrv. asst. William Doyle Galleries, N.Y.C., 1984—86; assoc. Timmins-Munn, Inc., N.Y.C., 1987—98; interior designer V.W. Interiors, Greenwich, Conn., 1994—; tchr. N.Y. Sch. Interior Design, N.Y.C., 2001—. Vol. Jr. League, Greenwich, 1999—. Mem.: Interior Designers for Licensing N.Y. (bd. mem.), Am. Soc. Interior Designers (profl.), Decorators Club (pres.). Home and Office: 25 Halsey Dr Old Greenwich CT 06870 Office Phone: 203-637-3348. E-mail: vwint@optonline.net.

WHITMAN, ANN ELIZABETH, retired elementary school educator, education educator; b. Burlington, Vt., May 17, 1941; d. Robert Royal and Elizabeth Ann (Page) Hinsdale; m. William Raymond Whitman, Nov. 22, 1962; children: Scott David, Andrew Wright. BS in Edn., U. Vt., Burlington, 1963; MS in Curriculum and Instrn., Del. State Coll., Dover, 1989. Cert. mid. childhood generalist tchr. Del. Tchr. grade 2 Helen Hunt Elem. Sch., Old Town, Maine, 1963—64, Quonset Point Elem. Sch., Quonset Point, RI, 1964—66; tchr. grades 7, 8, 9, 11 Sackville Jr-Sr. H.S., N.B., Canada, 1969, tchr. grades 7, 9, 1971—73; tchr. grades 1, 2 Sackville Ctrl. and Salem Sch., 1973—85; tchr. grade 3, writing specialist State of Del., Milford Sch. Dist., Milford, Del., 1986—2005; adj. instr. edn. Wilmington Coll., Dover, Del., 2005—. Profl. devel. chmn. Dist. 14 Tchrs., Sackville, 1983—85; writing specialist Milford Sch. Dist., 2000—02; workshop presenter in field; figure skating instr.; piano accompanist. Pianist, leader for song Genesis Eldercare, Milford, 1993—; singer baritone quartet Sweet Adelines, Milford, 2002—; treas. First St. Harmonettes, Milford, 2005—. Mem.: Sweet Adelines Internat. Avocations: reading, piano, singing, travel. Home: 1035 Rothermel Rd Milford DE 19963

WHITMAN, CHRISTINA BROOKS, law educator; b. 1947; BA, U. Mich., 1968, MA, 1970, JD, 1974. Law clk. to judge Harold Leventhal U.S. Ct. Appeals, Washington, 1974-75; law clk. to justice Powell U.S. Supreme Ct., Washington, 1975-76; asst. prof. U. Mich., Ann Arbor, 1976-79, assoc. prof., 1979-82, prof., 1982—, Francis A. Allen Collegiate Prof. Law. Contbr. articles to law jours. Office: U Mich Law Sch 338 Hutchins Hall 625 S State St Ann Arbor MI 48109-1215 Office Phone: 734-764-9535. Office Fax: 734-763-9375. E-mail: cwhitman@umich.edu.

WHITMAN, CHRISTINE TODD, former federal agency administrator, former governor; b. NYC, Sept. 26, 1946; d. Webster Bray and Eleanor Schley Todd; m. John Whitman, 1974; children: Kate, Taylor. BA in Govt., Wheaton Coll., 1968. Freeholder Somerset County, 1982—87; pres. NJ State Bd. Pub. Utilities, 1988—90; host radio talk show Sta. WKXW, Trenton, N.J.; gov. State of N.J., 1994-2001; adminstr. EPA, Washington, 2001—03. Chmn. Com. for an Affordable N.J.; bd. dirs. Texas Instruments Inc., 2003-, Millennium Challenge Corp., S.C. Johnson and Son, Inc., United Tech. Corp., 2003-, Chgo. Climate Exchange, Inc.; mem. steering com. Cancer Inst. NJ Leadership Coun.; co-chair Nat. Smart Growth Coun., Smart Growth Am.; mem. leadership coun. Rep. Pro-Choice Coalition, gov.'s bd. Oquirrh Inst., S&T presdl. and fed. adv. com. Appointments of Nat. Acads. Author: It's My Party Too: The Battle for the Heart of the GOP and the Future of America, 2005. Columnist newspapers. Bd. freeholders Somerset County, N.J., 1982-87; bd. pub. utilities, 1988-89; Rep. candidate for senator State of N.J., 1990.; mem. Ctr. Civic Engagement and Volunteerism adv. bd. Raritan Cmty. Coll., UN sec-gen. adv. bd. Water and Sanitation. Republican. Achievements include first female governor in N.J.; delivered Republican response to President Clinton's 1995 State of the Union address.

WHITMAN, KAREN, artist; b. N.Y., Feb. 22, 1953; d. Martin and Shirley W.; m. Richard Keith Pantell, Jul. 26, 1998 BFA Printmaking, SUNY, Buffalo, 1975; Cert. Graphic Design, Parsons Sch. Design, 1990; student, Art Students League, N.Y.C., Woodstock Sch. Art. Represented artist Old Print Shop, N.Y.C., 1995—. Lectr. Woodstock Sch. Art, 1999 One-woman shows at Bird-In-Hand Gallery, Washington, 2001, Old Print Shop, N.Y.C., 2002; New Rochelle Pub. Libr., N.Y., 2003; Azarian-McCullough Art Gallery, St. Thomas Aquinas Coll., Sparkill, N.Y., 2003, Perkins Gallery, Stoughton, Mass., 2004, Pen and Brush, Inc., N.Y.C., 2004, Woodstock Artists Assn., 2005; group exhbns. include: Woodstock Artists Assoc., N.Y., 1993—, Art Students League, N.Y.C., 1993, 94, Soc. Am. Graphic Artists Ann. Exhbn., 1994-, Market Theatre Gallery, Albany, N.Y., 1994, Northwest Print Coun., Portland, Oreg., 1994, McDermott, Will and Emery, N.Y.C., 1994, James Cox Gallery, Woodstock, N.Y., 1994, Walsh Art Gallery, Contemporary Am. Printmakers, Fairfield (Ct.) U., 1994, Firehouse Gallery, Nassau C.C., Garden City, N.Y., 1995, Lore Degenstein Gallery, Susquehanna U., Selinsgrove, Pa., 1995, Schenectady Mus., Print Club Albany, 1995, 97, 98, Gallery 479, N.Y.C., 1996, Fred Baker, Inc., Urban USA Portfolio Exhbn., Chgo., 1996, Old Print Shop, Urban USA Portfolio Exhbn., N.Y.C., 1996, Kala Inst. Gallery, Berkeley, Calif., 1996, Seton Hall U., South Orange, N.J., 1996, Olive Hyde Gallery, Fremont, Calif., 1996, Annex Gallery, East/West Print Exch. Exhbn., Santa Rosa, Calif., 1996, Coll. Art Gallery, Norwalk Cmty. Tech. Coll., Conn., 1996, Rensselaerville (N.Y.) Inst. Gallery, Kleinert Art Gallery, Woodstock, 1997, Cork Gallery, Lincoln Ctr., N.Y.C., 1997, SAGA Mems. Exhbn., Wagner Coll. Gallery, S.I., N.Y., 1998, Old Print Shop, N.Y.C. Centennial Portfolio Exhbn., 1998, Parkside Nat. Small Print Exhbn., U. Wis., Kenosha, 1998, 99, Catharine Lorillard Wolfe Art Club, 1999-2006, Nat. Arts Club, N.Y.C., (Medal of Honor for Graphics, 1999, Bronze medal 2001), Schoolhouse Galleries, Croton Falls, N.Y. "Street Life" Exhbn, 1999, Woodstock Sch. Art Instrs. and Lectrs. Exhbn, 1999, 2003, Prince St. Gallery, N.Y.C., 1999; Printwork Barrett Art Ctr., Poughkeepsie, N.Y., 2000, N.Y. Soc. Etchers, Nat. Arts Club, 2000, Silvermine Guild Nat. Print Biennial, New Canaan, Conn., 2000, 03, Audubon Artists Ann. Exhbn., Salmagundi Club, N.Y.C., 2000-06, Nat. Assn. Women Artists Ann. Exhbn., 2001-05, Contemporary Printmakers, Old Print Shop, 2001, 03, 05, Pen and Brush Regional Juried Exhbn., N.Y.C., 2001, Nat. Assn. Women Artists, N.Y.C., 2000—, Prints by Art Students League Artists, 1901-2001, UBS Paine Webber Gallery, N.Y.C., 2002, N.Y. by New Yorkers, Artist Views in Prints, Mus. City of N.Y., 2002, Artlink 23d Ann. Print Exhbn., Ft. Wayne, Ind., 2002, McNeese U. Nat. Works Paper Exhbn., Lake Charles, La., 2003, Wash. Printmakers Nat. Small Works Exhbn., 2003, Hofstra U. Mus., Hempstead, N.Y., 2003, N.Y. Transit Mus., 2003, Allied Artists Am. Ann. Exhbns., N.Y.C., 2003, 04, 05, Susan Teller Gallery, 2004, N.Y. Hist. Soc., 2004, Gallery Graphic Arts, N.Y.C., 2004, 05, Kleinert/James Gallery, Woodstock, 2004, Gallery 928-Nat. Assn. Women Artists, N.Y.C., 2004, Taiwan Internat. Mini Print Exhbn., Taipei, 2004, Object Image Gallery, N.Y., 2005, Noble Maritime Mus., S.I., 2006; represented in permanent collections N.Y. Pub. Libr., Mus. City of N.Y., Hofstra Mus., Brit. Mus., Portland Art Mus., Zimmerli Art Mus., Samuel Dorsky Mus. Art, N.Y. Transit Mus., N.Y. Hist. Soc., Nat. Mus. Printmaking of Print Club Albany, Norwalk Comm. Tech. Coll., Taiwan U. Inst. Fine Arts, Taipei; featured in Am. Artist Mag., 2002 Recipient medal of honor, Catharine Lorillard Wolfe Art Club, Nat. Arts Club, N.Y.C., 1999, Anna Hyatt Huntington bronze medal, 2001, Rembrandt Graphic Arts Printmaking award, Hunterdon Mus., Clinton, N.J., 2001, Yasuo Kuniyoshi Fund award, Woodstock, NY, 2001, Solo Exhbn. award, Pen and Brush, 2002. Mem.: Allied Artists Am. (Mary Lou Fitzgerald Meml. award 2004, Nat. Arts Club award 2005), Am. Soc. Contemporary Artists, Pen and Brush, Art Students League, Audubon Artists, Nat. Assn. Women Artists (Stelly Sterling Meml. Award for Printmaking 2003), Elizabeth Morse Genius Found. (award 2002, medal of honor 2002), Catharine Lorillard Wolfe Art Club (medal of honor 1999, Anna Hyatt Huntington Bronze medal 2001, 1st Pl. award for graphics members exhbn. 2005), Nat. Assn. Women Artists (medal of honor 2002), Woodstock Artists Assn. (hon. mention 1999, 2003, Alan Koff award for best in show 2004), Print Club Albany, Soc. Am. Graphic Artists (coun. mem. 1994, Roberta Waddell award 2004). Avocations: international folk dancing, playing violin, songwriting, singing. Home: PO Box 550 Bearsville NY 12409 Office Phone: 845-679-4435. Personal E-mail: karrick3@aol.com.

WHITMAN, MARGARET C. (MEG WHITMAN), Internet company executive; b. LI, N.Y., Aug. 4, 1956; m. Griffith R. Harsh IV; children: Griff, Will. BA in Econs., Princeton U., 1977; MBA, Harvard U., 1979. Brand asst. Procter & Gamble, 1979—81; v.p. Bain & Co., 1982—89; sr. v.p. mktg. & consumer products divsn. Walt Disney Co, Burbank, Calif., 1989—92; corp. v.p. strategic planning Stride Rite Corp., 1992—93, exec. v.p. Keds divsn., 1993—94, pres. Stride Rite Divsn., 1994—95; pres., CEO Florists' Transworld Delivery (FTD), 1995—97; gen. mgr. preschool divsn. Hasbro Inc., 1997—98; pres., CEO eBay, Inc., San Jose, Calif., 1998—. Bd. dirs. eBay, Inc., 1998—, Staples Inc., 1999, The Goldman Sachs Group Inc., 2001—02, Procter & Gamble Co., 2003—, The Gap Inc., 2003—06, DreamWorks Animation SKG, Inc. Bd. trustees Princeton U. Named Number One on List of Best CEO's, Worth, 2002; named one of 25 Most Powerful Business Mgrs. (annually since 2000), Business Week, 25 Most Powerful People in Business, Fortune, 2004, Most Powerful Women in American Business, World's 100 Most Influential People, Time Mag., 2004, 2005, 100 Most Powerful Women, Forbes mag., 2005—06, 2006, 50 Women to Watch, Wall St. Journal, 2005, 50 Most Powerful Women in Bus., Fortune mag., 2006. Avocation: fly fishing. Office: eBay Inc 2145 Hamilton Ave San Jose CA 95125*

WHITMAN, MARINA VON NEUMANN, economist, educator; b. NYC, Mar. 6, 1935; d. John and Mariette (Kovesi) von Neumann; m. Robert Freeman Whitman, June 23, 1956; children: Malcolm Russell, Laura Mariette. BA summa cum laude, Radcliffe Coll., 1956; MA, Columbia U., 1959, PhD, 1962; LHD (hon.), Russell Sage Coll., 1972; LLD (hon.), Cedar Crest Coll., 1973, Hobart and William Smith Coll., 1973; LHD (hon.), U. Mass., 1975, N.Y. Poly. Inst., 1975; LLD (hon.), Coe Coll., 1975, Marietta Coll., 1976. Mem. faculty U. Pitts., 1962-79, prof. econs., 1971-73, disting. pub. svc. prof. econs., 1973-79; v.p., chief economist Gen. Motors Corp., N.Y.C., 1979-85, group v.p. pub. affairs, 1985-92; disting. vis. prof. bus. adminstrn., pub. policy U. Mich., Ann Arbor, 1992-94, prof. bus. adminstrn., pub. policy, 1994—. Mem. Trilateral Commn., 1973-84, 88-95; mem. Pres. Adv. Com. on Trade Policy and Negotiations, 1987-93; mem. tech. assessment adv. coun. U.S. Congress Office of Tech. Assessment, 1990-95; mem. Consultative Group on Internat. Econs. and Monetary Affairs, 1979—; mem. U.S. Price Commn., 1971-72, Coun. Econ. Advisers, Exec. Office of Pres., 1972-73. Author: Government Risk-Sharing in Foreign Investment, 1965, International and Interregional Payments Adjustment, 1967, Economic Goals and Policy Instruments, 1970, Reflections of Interdependence: Issues for Economic Theory and U.S. Policy, 1979, New World, New Rules: The Changing Role of the American Corporation, 1999; bd. editors: Am. Econ. Rev., 1974-77; mem. editl. bd. Fgn. Policy; contbr. articles to profl. jours. Trustee Nat. Bur. Econ. Rsch., 1993—, Princeton U., 1980-90, Inst. Advanced Study, 1999—; bd. dirs. Inst. for Internat. Econs., 1986—, Salzburg Seminar, 1994—, Eurasia Found., 1992-95; bd. overseers Harvard U., 1972-78, mem. vis. com. Kennedy Sch., 1992-98. Fellow Earhart Found., 1959-60, AAUW, 1960-61, NSF, 1968-70, Social Security Rsch. Coun.; recipient Columbia medal for excellence, 1973, George Washington award Am. Hungarian Found., 1975. Mem. Am. Econ. Assn. (exec. com. 1977-80), Am. Acad. Arts and Scis., Coun. Fgn. Rels. (dir. 1977-87), Phi Beta Kappa. Office: U Mich Gerald Ford Sch Pub Policy Joan and Sanford Weill Hall Rm 3228 Ann Arbor MI 48109-3091 Office Phone: 734-763-4173. Business E-Mail: marinaw@umich.edu.

WHITMIRE, MARILYN THERESE, art educator; b. Chgo., Nov. 18, 1949; d. James Edward and Claire Therese (Guara) Bennett; m. Edward Lee Whitmire, June 20, 1990; children: Christopher Bernard Gray, Steven James Gray, Kyle Edward. BA, U. Ill., 1975; tchr.'s cert., Otterbein Coll., 1983; postgrad., U. S.C., 1989. Prof. educator cert. Ala. Dept. Edn. Bookkeeper, head teller State Savs. Bank, Canal Winchester, Ohio, 1974—75; substitute tchr. Watkins Mid. and HS, Licking County, Ohio, 1983—84, Reynoldsburg Schs., Ohio, 1984—86; art tchr. Kingstree Elem. Sch., SC, 1986—88, Fairforest Middle Sch., Spartanburg, S.C., 1988—90, Thomasville HS, Ala., 1990—. Sch. newspaper advisor Kingstree Elem. Sch., 1987—88; yearbook advisor Fairforest Middle Sch., 1989—90; sponsor Thomasville HS chpt. Nat. Art Honor Soc., 1995—. Sec. PTA, Spartanburg, 1989—90; 7th grade Peace Poster Contest sponsor Thomasville Lion's Club, 2000—; art theme exhibit Thomasville Women's Club Conv., 2003; sponsor Youth Day T-shirt design Thomasville HS Art Club, 2002—05. Mem.: NEA (mem. state chpts.), Ala. Alliance for Arts Edn., Nat. Art Edn. Assn. (mem. state chpts.). Avocations: painting, gardening, crafts. Office: Thomasville HS 777 Gates Dr Thomasville AL 36784 Business E-Mail: mwhitmire@thomasvilleschools.org.

WHITMORE, MENANDRA M., librarian; b. Ancash, Peru; d. Rafael and Jacinta (Moreno) Mosquera; m. Jacob L. Whitmore III, Jan. 7, 1965; children: Jacqueline Grace, Michelle Jacinta. Degree in social work, U. Catolica del Peru, 1967; MLS, U. P.R., 1974, Catholic U. Am., Washington, 1984. Social worker Cornell U., Vicos, Peru, 1960-62, Servicio de Extension Agricola del Peru, 1962-63, Am. Friends Svc. Com., Mex. and Peru, 1963-65; libr. Colegio Maria Auxiliadora, P.R., 1971, Country Day Sch., San Jose, Costa Rica, 1974-76, Colegio San Ignacio, P.R., 1976-77; dir. libs. Am. Coll. P.R., 1977-80; libr. Lib. Gov. Printing Office, 1981-84; chief acquisitions sect., mgr. Hispanic employment program Pentagon Libr., Washington, 1984-99, chief tech. and stds. divsn., 1999—2002, acting dir., 2002—03, dir., 2003—. Author: (all pub. under name Menandra Mosquera) Bibliography on Hypsipyla, 1976, Bibliography of Forestry of Puerto Rico, 1984, Useful Trees of Tropical North America, 1998. Recipient commendation Dept. Def., 1987-98. Mem. ALA, Soc. for Acquisition Latin Am. Libr. Materials, Reforma (treas. Washington chpt. 1988, pres. 1989-91, 95-99, nat. ways and means chair 1991-92). Office Phone: 703-695-2006. Business E-Mail: mena.whitmore@hqda.army.mil.

WHITNEY, CAROLYN, psychology professor; d. Robert Arthur and Frances Whitney Hockman. BA, Castleton State Coll., 1990; MA, U. Vt., 1995, PhD, 1997. Vis. prof. Trinity Coll., Burlington, Vt., 1999—2000, NH Coll., Manchester, 2000—01, St. Michael's Coll., Colchester, Vt., 2002—04, asst. prof., 2004—. Office: St Michael's Coll 1 Winooski Park Colchester VT 05439

WHITNEY, CONSTANCE CLEIN, psychologist, educator, consultant; b. Seattle; BA, Stanford U.; MA; PhD, Washington U., St. Louis; children: Mark Wittcoff, Caroline Wittcoff. instr. U. Mo., St. Louis, 1976-78; rsch. assoc., Wash. U. Med. Sch., 1977-78; dir. Motivation Rsch. Inst. U. Wash., 1979-83; post doctoral fellow Grad. Sch. Bus., Wash. U., 1983-86; dir., exec. edn. Town Hall Calif., 1989-92. Bd. dirs. UCLA Arts Coun., Club 100 Music Ctr., Leadership So. Calif., Stanford Alumni So. Calif., Nat. Commn. for UN Conv. to eliminate discrimination; cons. Orgn. Devel. & Leadership; pres. Strategic Leadership Consulting, 1986—; faculty mem. EMBA Nat. U., L.A. Mem. Am. Psychol. Assn., Calif. Psychol. Assn., AAUP, ASTD, Acad. Mgmt., Orgn. Behavior and Teaching Soc. Author, producer, dir.: (film) Women and Money: Myths and Realities. Home: # 1202 10601 Wilshire Blvd Apt 1202 Los Angeles CA 90024-4520

WHITNEY, LORI ANN, legislative staff member; b. Rhinelander, Wis, Feb. 20, 1968; d. Larry R. and Mary E. (Gaffney) Whitney. BA in Spanish/Polit. Sci. cum laude, U. Wis., Eau Claire, 1990. Messenger Wis. State Assembly, Madison, 1991—95, postal clk., 1995—2003, postmistress, 2003—. Fundraiser State Employees Combined Campaign, Madison, 1992—, mem. state coordinating com., 1996—; fundraiser Multiple Sclerosis Soc., 1993—; mem. Amnesty Internat., 1991—; monthly donor Planned Parenthood Nat. Leadership Coun.; fundraiser, vol. Am. Diabetes Assn.; vol., donor Planned Parenthood Advocates of Wis.; mem., donor YWCA; blood donor ARC; vol. Prevent Child Abuse Wis., 1994—; mem., donor So. Poverty Law Ctr., 1994—, People for the Am. Way, 1996—, Wis. Coalition Against the Death Penalty, 1993—; mem. Hoop Troop Booster Club U. Wis. Madison Women's Basketball, 1993—; campaign vol. David Clarenbach and Tammy Baldwin, Madison, 1992, State Rep. Tammy Baldwin, 1994, 1996, 1998, Fred Risser, 1996, 2000, 2004, Russ Feingold, 1998, 2004, Tammy Baldwin and Al Gore, 2000, Tammy Baldwin, Jim Doyle, Kathleen Falk, Barbara Lawton, 2002, 2004. Recipient Hopebuilder Habitat for Humanity award, 1995, 10 SECC Fundraising awards, Cmty. Vol. award, United Way, 2002, Hannah Needham Rogers award, Planned Parenthood Advocates of Wis., 2002, Backyard Hero award, Prevent Child Abuse Wis., 2004, Know Your Wis. State Jour. award, 2004, Top Fundraiser award, Madison Walk for Diabetes, 2004, Bob Alesch award, (Ptnrs. in Giving) State Employees Combined Campaign, 2005. Mem.: NOW. Democrat. Avocations: reading, sports, rock music, movies (comedy), travel. Home: 4322 Melody Ln # 211 Madison WI 53704

WHITNEY, MARILYN LOUISE, elementary school educator; b. Leominster, Mass., Mar. 6, 1943; d. Pasquale Vincent and Mildred Louise (Maxim) Marino; m. Thomas Despo Whitney, Aug. 16, 1968; 1 child, Jon Robert. BS in Edn., Fitchburg State U., 1965; MS in Edn., Duquesne U., 1970. Elem. tchr. Town of Leominster, 1966-68, Fox Chapel (Pa.) Country Day Sch., 1968-70, Town of Ware, Mass., 1970—2002; ret., 2002. Mem. Ware Tchrs. Assn. (v.p.), Mass. Tchrs. Assn. (rep. to NEA Assembly), NEA, Leominster Tchrs. Assn. (rep. 1967), AAUW, AARP. Democrat. Episcopalian. Avocations: skiing, swimming, travel.

WHITNEY, MARY ELLEN, not-for-profit developer, educator; b. Reading, Pa., Jan. 28, 1956; d. Charles Edward and Margaret Louise Snelson; m. Jonathan Thomas Whitney, Aug. 27, 1997. BS, East Stroudsburg U., Pa., 1978; MEd, Lehigh U., Bethlehem, Pa., 1981. Tchr. Questar III, Castleton, NY, 1983—; founder, CEO Stride, Inc., Reusselau, NY, 1986—. Named Woman of Yr., Woman's Day Mag., 2005, Woman of Distinction, N.Y. State Senate, 2005; recipient Jefferson award, Albany, N.Y., 2005. Mem.: AAPHERD, N.Y. State AAPHERD, PSIA (examiner 2005). Avocations: travel, skiing. Office: Stride Inc PO Box 778 Rensselaer NY 12144

WHITNEY, PHYLLIS AYAME, author; b. Yokohama, Japan, Sept. 9, 1903; d. Charles J. and Lillian (Mandeville) W.; m. George A. Garner, July 2, 1925 (div. 1945); m. Lovell F. Jahnke, 1950 (dec. 1973). Grad., McKinley High Sch., Chgo., 1924. Instr. dancing, San Antonio, 1 yr; tchr. juvenile fiction writing Northwestern U., 1945; children's book editor Chgo. Sun, 1942-46, Phila. Inquirer, 1947, 48; instr. juvenile fiction writing N.Y.U., 1947-58; leader juvenile fiction workshop Writers Conf., U. Colo., 1952, 54, 56. Pres. exec. bd. 5th Ann. Writers Conf., Northwestern U., 1944. Author: A Place for Ann, 1941, A Star for Ginny, 1942, (vocat. fiction for teenage girls) A Window for Julie, 1943, (mystery novel for adults) Red Is for Murder, 1943, The Silver Inkwell, 1945, Willow Hill, 1947, Writing Juvenile Fiction, 1947, Ever After, 1948, Mystery of the Gulls, 1949, Linda's Homecoming, 1950, The Island of Dark Woods, 1951, Love Me, Love Me Not, 1952, Step to the Music, 1953, A Long Time Coming, 1954, Mystery of the Black Diamonds, 1954, The Quicksilver Pool, 1955, Mystery on the Isle of Skye, 1955, The Fire and The Gold (Jr. Lit. Guild), 1956, The Highest Dream (Jr. Lit. Guild), 1956, The Trembling Hills (Peoples Book Club), 1956, Skye Cameron, 1957, Mystery of the Green Cat (Jr. Lit. Guild), 1957, Secret of the Samurai Sword (Jr. Lit. Guild), 1958, The Moonflower, 1958, Creole Holiday, 1959, Thunder Heights, 1960, Blue Fire, 1961, Mystery of the Haunted Pool, 1961 (Edgar award Mystery Writers

Am.), Secret of the Tiger's Eye, 1961, Window on the Square, 1962, Mystery of the Golden Horn, 1962, Seven Tears for Apollo, 1963, Mystery of the Hidden Hand, 1963 (Edgar award Mystery Writers Am. 1964), Black Amber, 1964, Secret of the Emerald Star, 1964, Sea Jade, 1965, Mystery of the Angry Idol, 1965, Columbella, 1966, Secret of the Spotted Shell, 1967, Mystery of the Strange Traveler, 1967, Silverhill, 1967, Hunter's Green, 1968, Secret of Goblin Glen, 1968, Mystery of the Crimson Ghost, 1969, Winter People, 1969, Secret of the Missing Footprint, 1970, Lost Island, 1970, The Vanishing Scarecrow, 1971, Listen for the Whisperer, 1971, Nobody Likes Trina, 1972, Snowfire, 1973, Mystery of the Scowling Boy, 1973, The Turquoise Mask, 1974, Spindrift, 1975, Secret of Haunted Mesa, 1975, The Golden Unicorn, 1976, Secret of the Stone Face, 1977, The Stone Bull, 1977, The Glass Flame, 1978, Domino, 1979, Poinciana, 1980, Vermilion, 1981, Guide to Fiction Writing, 1982, Emerald, 1983, Rainsong, 1984, Dream of Orchids, 1985, Flaming Tree, 1986, Silversword, 1987, Feather on the Moon, 1988, Rainbow in the Mist, 1989, The Singing Stones, 1990, Woman Without a Past, 1991, The Ebony Swan, 1992, Star Flight, 1993, Daughter of the Stars, 1994, Amethyst Dreams, 1997; sold first story to Chgo. Daily News; later wrote for pulp mags., became specialist in juvenile writing, now writing entirely in adult field. Spent first 15 years of life in Japan, China and P.I. (father in shipping and hotel bus.). Recipient Friends of Lit. award for contbns. to children's lit., 1974; Reynal and Hitchcock prize in Youth Today contest for book Willow Hill; Today's Woman award Coun. Cerebral Palsy Auxs., 1983, Agatha award Malice Domestic, 1990, Rita award Romance Writers Am., 1990, Lifetime award Romance Writers Am., 1990, Midland Authors award for a lifetime of literary achievement, 1995. Mem. Mystery Writers Am. (pres. 1975, Grandmaster award for lifetime achievement 1988), Am. Crime Writers League, Sisters in Crime, Authors League of Am., Authors Round Table (pres. 1943-44). Address: care McIntosh and Otis 353 Lexington Ave New York NY 10016-0941

WHITNEY, SHARRY JAN, science educator; b. Houston, Tex., Aug. 6, 1960; d. Lonie Gene and Elizabeth Janet Cook; m. Michael William Whitney, Nov. 15, 1997; children: Jennifer, Stephanie, Richard; children: David, Allie, Carson. BS, Baylor U., Waco, Tex., 1982. Cert. Tchr. grades 1-8 (sci. emphasis) Tex. Dept. Edn. 2d grade tchr. Hurst-Euless-Bedford Ind. Sch. Dist., Hurst, Tex., 1982—83, Gravette Pub. Schs., Ark., 1984—86; 5th grade tchr. Nashville Pub. Schs., Tenn., 1990—99; 7th grade sci. tchr. Lewisville Ind. Sch. Dist., Tex., 1999—2006, AIS instrnl. specialist, 2006—. Recipient Tchr. of Yr., Rosepark Mid. Sch., Nashville, 1998, Tchr. Who Makes a Difference award, Griffin Mid. Sch., The Colony, Tex., 2004, 2005. Mem.: ASCD. Avocations: mountain biking, reading, skiing, hiking. Office: Delay Middle Sch Lewisville TX 75057

WHITNEY, TAMORA ANN, literature educator; b. Omaha, Apr. 4, 1961; d. Robert William and Konnie Kay (Beeman) Whitney; m. Gordon Russell Mosher, Sept. 24, 2005. BA in English, Coll. St. Mary, Omaha, 1983; MA in English, U. Nebr., Lincoln, 1984, PhD in English, 1990. Instr. S.E. C.C., Lincoln, 1984—86; tchg. asst. U. Nebr., Lincoln, 1985—87; writing specialist Doane Coll., Crete, Nebr., 1986—90; instr. Iowa We. C.C., Coun. Bluff, Iowa, 1990—93, Met. C.C., Omaha, 1993—. Lectr. Creighton U., Omaha, 1991—; instr. Coll. Saint Mary, 1998—; freelance editor, Omaha, 2005. Mem. editl. bd.: Nebr. English Jour., 1991—93; author: History of Names, 1990, Wheel of The Year, 1995, Menopause Maze, 2005; contbr. poems to various pubs. Fellow, U. Nebr., 1983—85; scholar, 1985—87. Mem.: Omaha Altrusa (comms. officer 2000—), Mensa (comms. officer Nebr. chpt. 1995—, scholarship judge 1995—2006, named Poet Laureate Nebr.-We. Iowa chpt. 2003, Nat. Pub. award 2005), Ladies Ancient Order Hibernians, Sigma Tau Delta. Avocations: history, Irish folk music, culture. Office: Creighton Univ 2500 California Plz Omaha NE 68178

WHITSON, ELIZABETH TEMPLE, graphics designer; b. Washington, D.C., Oct. 1, 1959; d. Norman Burkey Musselman, Elizabeth Temple (Henry) Musselman; m. William Stuart Whitson, Dec. 21, 1985; 1 child, Ian Alexander. BA, Va. Tech. U., 1982. Artist, office asst. Artisan Graphics, Alexandria, Va., 1983—84; graphic artist, office asst. Gestalt Assocs., Alexandria, 1984—86; graphic artist, sales rep., prodn. mgr. Gestalt Prodns., Herndon, Va., 1986—89, ImageMatrix, Inc., Falls Church, Va., 1989—91; graphic designer, publ. dept. head CompuSlides, Vienna, Va., 1991—94, New Media Comms., Vienna, 1994—95; graphic designer, owner Port City Prodns., Inc., Alexandria, 1993—. Newsletter chmn.: Meeting House Coop. Pre-sch., 2000—03; editor (illustrator): Highlights of the Alexandria Com., 1988. Mem. Brookville/Seminary Valley Civic Assn., Alexandria, 1988—2002; vol. Torpedo Factory Art Ctr.; active mem. The Alexandria Libr. Co.; com. vol., tchr., mem. Old Presbyn. Meeting House. Mem.: DAR (corr. sec. 1995—98, chmn. two coms. Mt. Vernon chpt.), The Old Presbyterian Meeting House (worship com. 1995—97, childcare com. 2000—03, childhood edn. com. 2003—04, Godly Play tchr. 2003—), Friends of Gunston Hall, The Alexandria Assembly, Nat. Soc. Colonial Dames of Am. (rec. sec. 1999—2002, directory chmn. 2002—, vice chmn. 2004—, Alexandria com.). Presbyterian. Avocations: remodeling, gardening, painting, illustration, piano. Home and Office: 1701 Sherwood Hall Ln Alexandria VA 22306 Office Phone: 703-718-0105. E-mail: portcity23@verizon.net.

WHITSON, JANET SUSAN, biology professor; b. St. Louis, Nov. 29, 1949; d. Gilbert McLain and Florence Olga Ormerod; m. Craig E. Whitson, Sept. 5, 1970; children: Susan Marie Granfors, Clay E., Jonathan Scott. BS, Concordia Tchrs. Coll., River Forest, IL, 1971; PhD in Biology, U. Calif., Irvine, 1991. Asst. prof. U. Tex. Med. Sch., Houston, 1993—95; chair sci. dept. Concordia Luth. H.S., Tomball, 1997—2002, asst. prin., 2002—03; asst. prof. biology dept. Concordia U., Seward, Nebr., 2003—. Fellow, Baylor Coll. Medicine, Houston, 1991—93. Office: Concordia University 800 North Columbia Ave Seward NE 68434 Office Phone: 402-643-7319.

WHITSON, PEGGY ANNETTE, astronaut, biochemist; b. Mt. Ayr, Iowa, Feb. 9, 1960; d. Earl Keith and Beth Avalee (Walters) S.; m. Clarence Felton Sams, May 6, 1989. BS summa cum laude, Iowa Wesleyan Coll., 1981; PhD, Rice U., 1985. Welch predoctoral, then postdoctoral fellow Rice U., Houston, 1982-86; NRC RRA postdoctoral fellow Johnson Space Ctr., NASA, Houston, 1986-88, rsch. chemist, 1989-92, project scientist Shuttle-Mir, 1992-95; dep. divsn. chief med. scis. divsn., 1994—. Co-chair U.S./Russian Mission Sci. Working Group, 1995—. Contbr. articles to Biochemistry, Jour. Biol. Chemistry, Jour. Cellular Physiology. Mem. Am. Assn. Biochemistry and Molecular Biology, N.Y. Acad. Scis. Achievements include research in fluid and electrolyte physiology associated with spaceflight, renal stone risk assessments, receptor-ligand interactions, second messenger signaling, and gravitational effects on cytoskeletal structures. Office: Astronaut Office/CB NASA Johnson Space Ctr Houston TX 77058

WHITT, MARGARET JEAN, educator; b. Oklahoma City, Feb. 23, 1951; d. Arthur Francis and Margery Ann (Thilenius) W. BA in English magna cum laude, DePauw U., 1973; MS in Bus. magna cum laude, Abilene Christian U., 1983. Cert. tchr., Ind., Tex. Tchr. Jay County Schs., Portland, Ind., 1973-77; adminstr. Dallas County Community Colls., 1977-81, educator, cons., 1984—2000; adminstr. Children's Arts & Ideas Found., Dallas, 1981-83; pres. Peak Enterprises, Dallas, 1983-84, educator, cons., 1984—, Richardson Independent Schs., Dallas, 1984—. Instr. Young People's U., Dallas, 1979-81; tutor Meadow Creek Sch., Garland, Tex., 1983-85. Campaign worker Rep. Party, Dallas, 1983-86; fundraiser Tex. Cultural Alliance, Dallas, 1984-85. Named Tchr. of Yr., State of Tex. Regional, 1994—95, Elks Lodge, 1995. Mem. Richardson Edn. Assn., Assn. Tex. Profl. Educators, Greater Dallas Coun. of Tchrs. of English, Phi Beta Kappa. Avocations: travel, reading, cooking, dance. Home: 316 Heatherbrook Dr Murphy TX 75094-4018 Office: Richardson Independent Sch Dist 319 N Interurban St Richardson TX 75081-3312

WHITT, PAMELA P., mathematics educator; b. Spartanburg, S.C., Feb. 8, 1966; d. Bennie D. and Rachel T. Parker; m. Gregory D. Whitt, June 18, 1988; children: Gregory Clayton, Benjamin Alexander. BS in Secondary Edn., U. S.C., Spartanburg, 1989; EdM, So. Wesleyan U., 2006. Math. tchr. Cherokee County Sch. Dist. #1, Gaffney, SC, 1989—. Sunday sch. tchr. Macedonia Bapt. Ch., Gaffney, 2004—06. Home: 235 James Rd Gaffney SC 29341 Personal E-mail: pam.whitt@gw.cherokee1.k12.sc.us.

WHITTAKER, JEANNE EVANS, retired journalist; b. Detroit, Jan. 1, 1934; d. Alfred Heacock and Margaret (Evans) W.; m. Charles Martin Hines Jr., Sept. 29, 1962 (div. Feb. 1970); children: Charles M. Hines III, Margaret Helen Whittaker Zimmerman. Student, Northwestern U., 1952-53; BS in History, U. Mich., 1956. Clubmobile worker UN forces ARC, Republic of Korea, 1956—58; staff programmer ARC France, Chaumont, Evreux, 1958—61; dir. Bexar County chpt. youth ARC, San Antonio, 1961—62; staff writer/columnist Detroit Free Press, 1970—75; editor Mich. Social Register, 1975—77; Lifestyle editor Observer and Eccentric newspapers, Birmingham, Mich., 1977—87; staff writer, columnist Detroit News, 1987—91; cons. in field, 1992—. Mem. adv. com. Wayne State U. Press, 2000—. Contbr. articles to mags. Bd. dirs. Detroit chpt. ARC, 1989-92; Mem. Univ.-Liggett Sch. Aumni Bd., 2003—; mem. adv. bd. Greenfield Village Antiques Show, 2000-05. Recipient Penney-Mo. award U. Mo., 1984; 1st place lifestyles/Family award Mich. Press Assn., 1982, 84, Gen. Excellence award 1982, 86; Gen. Excellence award Suburban Newspaper Assn., 1979. Mem. Detroit Hist. Soc. (bd. dirs. 1986-91), Detroit Inst. Arts Women's Assn. Episcopalian. Avocations: writing, reading, travel. Home: 552 Cadieux Rd Grosse Pointe MI 48230-1508 Personal E-mail: jeannewhittaker@aol.com.

WHITTAKER, JUDITH ANN CAMERON, lawyer; b. N.Y.C., June 12, 1938; d. Thomas Macdonald and Mindel Cameron; m. Kent E. Whittaker, Jan. 30, 1960; children: Charles Evans II, Catherine Cameron. BA, Brown U., 1959; JD, U. Mo., 1963. Bar: Mo. 1963, U.S. Dist. Ct. (we. dist.) Mo. 1963, U.S. Ct. Appeals (8th cir.) 1965, U.S. Supreme Ct. 1980, D.C. 1987. Assoc. and ptnr. Sheffrey, Ryder & Skeer, Kansas City, Mo., 1963-72; asst. and assoc. gen. coun., exec. v.p. gen. coun. Hallmark Cards, Inc., Kansas City, 1972—2004; dir., v.p., gen. coun. Univision Holdings, Inc., Kansas City, 1988-92; sec., bd. dirs. Crown Media Holdings, Inc., 2000—04; of counsel Shook, Hardy & Bacon, Kansas City, Mo., 2004—. Bd. dirs. Am. Arbitration Assn., 1997-2003. Trustee Brown U. Providence, 1977-83, U. Mo. Law Found., Kansas City, 1977-90; dir. Kansas City (Mo.) Indsl. Devel. Authority, 1981-84, Legal Aid Kansas City, 1971-77, De La Salle Sch. Episcopalian. Avocations: reading, skiing, hiking, piano, golf. Office: Shook Hardy & Bacon 2555 Grand Blvd Kansas City MO 64198-2613

WHITTAKER, LYNN MARIE, elementary school educator; b. Corydon, Ind., Feb. 27, 1979; d. Fred and Ann Kellum; m. Trevor Lee Whittaker, June 27, 2003; children: Hunter Lathan, Hope Ann. BA in Sci. Edn., Ind. U. SE, New Albany, 2003; MA in Elem. Sch. Tchg., Oakland City U., Ind., 2006. 6th grade sci. tchr. Corydon Intermediate Sch., Ind., 2003—. Team capt. Harrison County Relay for Life, Corydon, 2002—06. Mem.: NEA. Catholic. Personal E-mail: lk2558@aol.com.

WHITTELL, POLLY (MARY KAYE WHITTELL), editor, journalist; b. Washington, Oct. 20; d. Alfred Whittell Jr. and Mary Halsey (Patchin) Hopper. BA in English, U. Calif., Berkeley; postgrad., Radcliffe Coll.; postgrad. in journalism, Columbia U. Rschr. Nat. Rev. Mag., N.Y.C., 1970-71; asst. to presdl. speech writer The White House, Washington, 1971-72; asst. editor TravelAge East Mag., Dun & Bradstreet Publs., N.Y.C., 1973-75; copy editor Ski Mag. Skier's Guides, Times Mirror Mags. and Am. Express, N.Y.C., 1975-76; asst. editor to sr. editor Hearst Mags., Motor Boating & Sailing Mag., N.Y.C., 1977-2000; contbg. editor Powerboat Mag., 2000—01, Hearst Mags., 2002—. Contbg. author: (anthology) Against the Sea, 1998; contbr. articles to other nat. and internat. consumer mags. Mem. charity benefit com. Youth Counseling League, N.Y.C., 1975-85, Am. Cancer Soc., 1998-99, and others; v.p. Knickerbocker Rep. Club, N.Y.C., 1979-80; elected mem. N.Y. Rep. County Com., N.Y.C., 1980-84. Mem. Boating Writers Internat. (award for environ. article 1995), Soc. Profl. Journalists, Princeton Club (N.Y.), SandBar Beach Club (v.p. membership 1980-82). Episcopalian. Avocations: photography, travel, boating, skiing. Personal E-mail: pollywhitt@aol.com.

WHITTEMORE, ALICE, biostatistician; b. NYC, July 5, 1936; BS, Marymount Manhattan Coll., 1958; MA, Hunter Coll., 1964; PhD in Mathematics, CUNY, 1967. From asst. prof. to assoc. prof. math. Hunter Coll., N.Y.C., 1967-74; adj. assoc. prof. environ. med. N.Y.U., 1974-76, mem. faculty dept. statistics, 1976-87; prof. epidemiology dept. health rsch. and policy Stanford U., Palo Alto, Calif., 1987—. Recipient Sloan Found. rsch. grant, Soc. Ind. and Applied Math. Inst. Math and Soc., 1974-76, Rockefeller Found rsch. grant 1976-77. Mem. NAS Inst. Medicine, AAAS, Soc. Indsl. and Applied Math, Am. Math Soc., Math Assn. Am., Sigma Xi Office: Stanford U Sch Medicine Dept Health Rsch and Policy HBP Redwood Bldg Stanford CA 94305-5092

WHITTEN, JEANIE G., physics educator; b. Anderson, S.C., Dec. 22, 1956; m. Tim M Whitten; children: Kathryn, John. MS, Clemson U., S.C., 1979. Cert. tchr. 2003. Physics tchr. Ft. Mill H.S., SC, 1984—. Mem.: Am. Assn. Physics Tchrs. (assoc.). Presbyterian. Home: 10014 Bora Bora Dr Tega Cay SC 29708 Office: Fort Mill High School 225 Munn Rd Fort Mill SC 29715 Office Phone: 803-548-1900.

WHITTEN, MARY LOU, nursing educator; b. Vandalia, Ill., Apr. 8, 1946; d. Otto M. and Lucille (Mattes) Elam; m. Dennis L. Whitten, Aug. 27, 1966; children: Michael, Christopher, Andrew. BSN, Baylor U., 1968; MS in Nursing, So. Ill. U., 1990. RN, Ill. Instr. health occupations Okaw Vocat. Sch., Vandalia, Ill.; head nurse med.-surg. Fayette County Hosp., Vandalia; DON Kaskaskia Coll., Centralia, Ill. CPR instr. Am. Heart Assn. Vol. ARC. Mem. Am. Assn. of Women in C.C. Ill., Ill. Coun. Dirs. of Nursing, Phi Kappa Phi. Home: RR 3 Box 848 Vandalia IL 62471-9204 Office: Kaskaskia Coll 27210 College Rd Centralia IL 62801-7800 Office Phone: 618-545-3331. Business E-Mail: mwhitten@kaskaskia.edu.

WHITTEN, NANCY BIMMERMAN, clinical social worker, marriage therapist; b. Wilmington, Del., Oct. 17, 1934; d. Harry Gordon and Marian Bimmerman; m. Robert Hunt Whitten, Jan. 2, 1960 (div. 1982); 1 child, Barbara Louise Whitten Debnam. BS in Biology, Bucknell U., 1956; postgrad., Stanford U., 1956-57, U. Del., 1957-59; M Social Svcs., Bryn Mawr Coll., 1995. Lic. clin. social worker, Del., Md. V.p. Robert Hunt Whitten Inc, Wilmington, 1960-81; br. mgr. Chase Manhattan Bank, Wilmington, 1985-88; realtor Patterson Schwartz Real Estate, Wilmington, 1988-95; clin. intern Penn Coun. for Relationships, Phila., 1995-96; med. social worker Chester River Home Care and Hospice, Chestertown, Md., 1997; clin. social worker S.O.A.R., Inc. (Survivors of Abuse in Recovery), Milford, Del., 1998—2003, bd. dirs., 1994-98; psychotherapist Nancy B. Whitten, LCSW, Easton, Md., 1997—. Crisis counselor Crime Victims Ctr., West Chester, Pa., 1992-95; condr. marriage seminars Mental Health Assn. Talbot County, Easton, Md., 1997-98, bd. dirs. 1996-99, pres.-elect 1998-99, pres., 2000—. Elks scholar Stanford U., 1956. Mem. NASW, Am. Assn. for Marriage and Family Therapy (clin. mem., cert.), Mortar Bd., Psi Chi, Phi Sigma. Unitarian Universalist. Avocations: sailing, fishing, tennis. Home and Office: 9660 Leeds Landing Cir Easton MD 21601-5562 Office Phone: 410-820-9191. Business E-Mail: nbwhitten@dmv.com. E-mail: nbwhitten@atbnticbb.net.

WHITTEN-FRICKEY, WENDY ELISE, entertainer; b. Silver Spring, Md., Mar. 15, 1963; d. Ray Sloan and Elsie Helen (Calderone) Whitten; m. Keith James Frickey, Nov. 24, 1990. BS in Agr. and Life Sci., U. Md., 1985. Mktg. and promotion asst. Pimlico and Laurel Racetracks, Balt., 1987-89; co-owner mktg. and advt. San Carlos Park Animal Hosp., Fort Myers, Fla., 1990-94; owner, pres. Ion Imagination Entertainment, Inc., Nashville, 1994—. Food technologist quality control Unilever USA-Shedds, Balt., 1987-88, dairy flavors applications-Quest, 1989-90. Author, songwriter, singer, narrator: (book and tape) The Adventures of Flumpa and Friends, Someday.Someday, Book 1, 1994 (Parents Choice award 1996, Nat. Parenting Ctr. award 1997); songwriter, prodr., singer: (CD/tape) Flumpa's World-.Frogs, Rain Forests and Other Fun Facts, 1998 (Parents' Choice award 1998, others), Flumpa's World-Out of This World, 2000 (Film Adv. Bd. award 2000, Parent's Guide to Children's Media award 2000, Dr. Toy 100 Best award 2000, others), Flumpa's World--Water, Water Everywhere, 2003, 2004 (Film Adv. Bd. award 2004, Parenting Hot award 2004, Dr. Toy Best Ednl. CD 2005); entertainer with Flumpa and Friends Live!; performer White House, various festivals, schs. and zoos. Recipient Certificate of Merit Printing Industries Am., 1996. Mem. AFTRA, BMI, Pub. Mktg. Assn., Coun. for Agrl. Sci. and Tech., Inst. of Food Technologists, Small Pub. Assn. of N.Am., Nat. Sci. Tchrs. Assn., Nat. Acad. Rec. Arts and Scis. Avocations: photography, travel. Office: Ion Imagination Entertainment Inc PO Box 210943 Nashville TN 37221-0943 Office Phone: 615-202-5282. Personal E-mail: ionimagin@aol.com.

WHITTINGTON, CATHY DEE, chemist; b. Upland, Pa., Oct. 29, 1955; d. Frank Adam and Virginia Helen (Keil) W. AA in biology, Widenen Univ., 1984, BA, 1996; BSN, Neuman Coll. Nursing. Asst. mgr. McDonald's, Brookhaven, Pa., 1973-75; blood lab. tech. CCMC, Chester, Pa., 1976-77; environmental tech. Scott Paper Internat., Chester, Pa., 1979-83; paramedic V AmbulCare Ambulance, Phila., 1984-96; sr. rsch. assoc. Scott Paper Corp. R&D, Phila., 1996-97; rsch. cons. Kimberly Clark Corp., Chester, Pa., 1997; process specialist HIA Cons., Chester, 1997-99; chemist Novell Inc., Provo, Utah, 1999—2006; nurse Riddle Meml. Hosp., Media, Pa., 2006—. Network engr. Novell, Inc., Provo, Utah, Scott Paper House of Quality, team orgn. Scott Paper R&D. Amb. lt. Parkside Vol. Fire Co., Parkside, Pa., 1977—. Recipient Military History Excellence award Daughter's of Founders & Patriots of Am., 1977, tech. excellence award, 1987-91. Mem. Tech. Orgn. of Pulp & Paper Ins., Nat. Archieves (assoc.). Republican. Baptist. Avocations: walking, hiking, reading. Home: 139 W Roland Rd Brookhaven PA 19015-3217 Office: Riddle Meml Hosp Rt 1 Media PA 19065

WHITTINGTON, VIRGINIA CAROLINA, language educator, writer; b. Vandergrift, Pa., Sept. 4, 1931; d. Joseph Adam and Mary Bernice (Dlugos) Opoczenski; m. Len Kolasinski, Feb. 7, 1953; (div. Sept. 1982); children: Sheryl, Sharon, Diane, Kurt Kolasinski; m. William Tyre Whittington, Nov. 12, 1983 (div. 1994). BA, Pa. State U., 1953; MA, U. Pitts., 1972; MEd, Westminister Coll., 1978. Tchr. Spanish Villa Maria (Pa.) High Sch., 1972-75; instr. Spanish Westminster Coll., New Wilmington, Pa., 1972-75; tchr. Latin, English, Spanish Mohawk Area Sch., Bessemer, Pa., 1975—96. Freelance writer, vacation reporter Vindicator newspaper, Youngstown, Ohio, 1979-84. V.p. Citizens League Greater Youngstown, 1988-98; Clinton del. Dem. Nat. Conv., 1992, 96; bd. dirs. First Unitarian Ch. Youngstown; mem. Main Line Unitarian Ch., Devon, Pa., Chester County Exec. Com.; committeeperson Tredyffrin Twp. Democratic. Mem. LWV, NEA, NOW (pres. greater Youngstown chpt. 1988-91, mem. nat. child care task force), Pa. State Edn. Assn. (pres.), Nat. Women's Polit. Caucus of Pa. (bd. mem.), Phi Beta Kappa. Democrat. Home: 367 Paoli Woods Paoli PA 19301-1547 E-mail: gingerwhit@comcast.net.

WHITTINGTON-BROWN, VANESSA ELIZABETH, secondary school educator; b. Boston, Apr. 15, 1960; d. Samuel Wall and Ernestine (Brazand Hundley) Whittington; m. Alphonso Brown, July 25, 1992. BS, Bridgewater State U., 1978; postgrad., Cambridge Coll., 1992—. Elem. tchr. Boston (Mass.) Pub. Schs., 1983—, Pauline A. Shaw, Dorchester, Mass., 1987-92; tchr. The Josiah Quincy Sch., Boston, 1992—. Adult edn. sec. Boston Pub. Schs., 1982, 83, mem. graphic learning com., 1983, impact II tchr. adaptor; musician cable TV program Gospel Expressions Prodns.; tutor Metco (after sch. program); mem. Primary Summer Source Inst., 1991; local pres. Sunshine Band, 1986, state pres., 1989-92. Composer: Lord I'm Coming Home, 1986. Mem. Children's Mus. and the Mus. Sci., Women's Heritage Trail, 3 Regent St. Young Adult Choir, Women's Choir, Boston Writing Project, Professional Dev. Program; co-dir. Specially Trained Youth Leadership in Excellence (STYLE), 1997; church musician Church of God in Christ Church, 1976-92. With USAR, 1979-91. Mem. Assn. Supervision and Curriculum Devel., Greater Boston Reading Coun., Boston Tchrs. Union, Black Educators Alliance of Mass., Nat. Coun. Tchrs. English, Women's Heritage Trail, African Meeting House. Democrat. Avocations: music, bowling, racquetball, basketball, poetry. Office Phone: 617-635-8497. E-mail: vewb@myway.com.

WHITTLESEY, JUDITH HOLLOWAY, public relations executive; b. Bartlesville, Okla., Dec. 28, 1942; d. Harry Haynes and Suzanne (Arnote) Holloway; m. Dennis Jeffrey Whittlesey, Aug. 3, 1968; children: Kristin Arnote, Kevin Jeffrey. BA, U. Okla., 1964; postgrad., Tulsa U., 1965, U. Va., 1971-72. Staff aide Office of the V.P. of U.S., Washington, 1979-81, Com. for Future of Am., Washington, 1981-82; dep. dir. scheduling and advance Mondale-Ferraro Campaign, Washington, 1982-84; dir. media rels. Susan Davis Internat., Washington, 1986-87, v.p., 1987-88, exec. v.p., 1988—. Bd. dirs. Cultural Alliance of Greater Washington, 1983-93, Washington Project for the Arts, 1987-93, Levine Sch. Music, 1993-98, Food Rsch. and Action Ctr., 1993—; bd. dirs. Decatur House, Suited For Change, Leadership Washington, 2004. Avocation: contemporary art. Office: Susan Davis Internat 1350 I St NW Washington DC 20005 Office Phone: 202-408-0808. Business E-Mail: judy@susandavis.com.

WHITTY, MARY JANE, counselor; b. Baraboo, Wis., June 26, 1947; d. Robert Peter and Virginia (Marron) W. B.S. in Edn., U. Wis.-LaCrosse, 1970; M.Counseling, U. Wis.-Whitewater, 1979, M.Sch. Adminstrn., 1980. Cert. tchr., counselor, Wis. Tchr., New Berlin Schs. (Wis.), 1970-78, counselor elem., 1978-80, counselor secondary, 1980—, curriculum chmn. guidance dept., 1982—, chairperson dist. wide curriculum research, 1983; advisor student govt., student yearbook; adminstrv. asst. Eisenhower Middle Sch. Pvt. counselor parents of terminally ill children, Greendale, Wis., 1980—. Recipient Outstanding Tchr. award Zerox Corp., 1974. Mem. Wis. Guidance Profl. Assn., Nat. Guidance Profl. Assn. Democrat. Roman Catholic. Clubs: Ski (advisor), Track (New Berlin) (dir. 1980—), Health.

WHITWAM, EILEEN V., adult nurse practitioner, educator; b. Passaic, NJ, Jan. 18, 1949; d. Anselm A. and Louise J. Bagatti; m. Russell Whitwam, Aug. 1, 1970; children: Eric R., Hilary P. Akman. AS in Nursing, Broward C.C., Davie, Fla., 1968; AA, Daytona Beach C.C., Fla., 1982; BSN, U. Ctrl. Fla., Orlando, 1989; MSN, U. Fla., Gainesville, 1997. Asst. charge nurse pediat. Broward Gen. Med. Ctr., Ft. Lauderdale, Fla., 1968—70; staff nurse adult medical-surgical unit Doctor's Hosp., Hollywood, Fla., 1970—71; asst. charge nurse, adult and pediatric med.-surg. units Daytona Beach Gen. Hosp., Holly Hill, Fla., 1972—74; emergency rm. charge nurse Humana Corp., Daytona Beach, Fla., 1980—85, radiology spl. procedures scrub nurse, 1986—87; adj. nursing instr. Daytona Beach C.C., 1988—96, assoc. prof. nursing, 1996—2003, prof. nursing, 2003—; geriatric nurse practitoner Good Samaritan Nursing Ctr., Daytona Beach, 1998—2003. Textbook reviewer Mosby Corp., 2003—. Mem. adv. bd. Good Samaritan Soc., Daytona Beach, 2003—06. Mem.: Am. Acad. Nurse Practitioners (licentiate). Office: Daytona Beach CC 1200 International Speedway Boulevard Daytona Beach FL 32114 Office Phone: 386-506-3000.

WHITWORTH, KATHRYNNE ANN, professional golfer; b. Monahans, Tex., Sept. 27, 1939; d. Morris Clark and Dama Ann (Robinson) W. Student, Odessa Jr. Coll., tex., 1958. Joined tour Ladies Profl. Golf Assn., 1959—. Named to Hall of Fame Ladies Profl. Golf Assn., Tex. Sports Hall of Fame, Tex. Golf Hall of Fame, World Golf Hall of Fame; Capt. of Solheim Cup, 1990-92. Mem. Ladies Profl. Golf Assn. (sec. 1962-63, v.p. 1965, 73, 88, pres. 1967, 68, 71, 89, 1st mem. to win over $1,000,000). Office: care Ladies Profl Golf Assn 2570 Volusia Ave Daytona Beach FL 32114-8144

WHITWORTH, PEGGY AGNES, special education educator, consultant; b. Abilene, Kans., Jan. 2, 1949; d. Bruce Arthur and Mildred Violet (Woodring) Merrill; m. Robert Jeffrey Whitworth, Dec. 27, 1968; children: Amy, Kaysie. BA, Kans. Wesleyan U., 1971; MS, Kans. State U., 1976. Cert. tchr., Kans.; cert assistive technology apps., 1999; cert. spl. edn. supr., coord.,

1992. Tchr. Vernon Elem. Sch., Leesville, La., 1973; tchr. educator mentally handicapped Cen. Kans. Coop. in Edn., Salina, 1972, tchr. rehavior disabilities, 1984-86, tchr. learning disabilities, 1986-87, vision cons., 1989—. Cons. Junction City (Kans.) Sch. Dist. Grantee Tex. Tech. U., 1983; traineeship State Kans., 1974; recipient Elks Leadership award 1967. Mem. Coun. Exceptional Children, Assn. for Edn. and Rehab. of the Visually Handicapped and Blind. Methodist. Avocations: horseback riding, reading, tennis.

WHOBREY, VIRGINIA JEAN, retired director; b. Dorset, Ohio, May 21, 1931; d. Rufus Lowery and Ruth Emma Spencer; m. Anthony Herbert Whobrey, Mar. 13, 1960 (dec. 1989); children: Everett Brett, Raymond Henry, Gene Lowery, Antoinette Michele Pfenning. BA, Hiram Coll., Ohio, 1953; postgrad. in Counseling, Miami U. Oxford, Ohio, 1958—59, East Tenn. U., Johnson City, 1964—65; student, Lake Erie Coll., 1969. Lic. profl. counselor Ohio, 1988, Qualified Mental Retardation Profl. Ohio, 1980, cert. lifetime tchr. Ohio, 1979. Tchr. home econs./dramatics Maple Heights (Ohio) City Schs., 1953—58; tchr., slow learners Middletown (Ohio) City Schs., 1958—59; counselor BVR/State Hosp., Burlington, Vt., 1959—60; tchr. Marion (Ohio) City Schs., 1958—59; guidance dir. Haines City (Fla.) Jr. HS, 1965—66; dir. guidance, coord. spl. svcs. Union County Schs., Lake Butler, Fla., 1966—69; tchr. EDMR Jefferson (Ohio) City Schs., 1969—79; tchr. MI/Mental Retardation Dayton Mental Health Ctr., Dayton, Ohio, 1979—84, vocation evaluator-civil and forensic hosp. team leader, 1984—88; dir. - set up pilot program Mentally Ill/Mental Retardation Montgomery Co MRDD-County Mental Health Bd., Dayton, Ohio, 1998—99; dir. of ICF/Mental Retardation unit Dayton (Ohio) Mental Health Ctr., 1988—91; dir. new dimensions state operated svcs. Dayton Mental Health Ctr./Mental Health Bd., 1991—98. Bd. dirs. Miami Valley Housing Opportunities, Dayton, Ohio; bd. dirs. Pathways mental health, substance abuse, devel. disabilities svs. Gaston, Lincoln, Cleve. Counties, NC. Avocations: painting, crafts, reading, travel. Home: 125 Mark Twain Ct Mount Holly NC 28120 Personal E-mail: btwho647@aol.com.

WHORISKEY, KATHERINE JANE, theater director, educator; d. Peter Joseph and Phyllis Mary Whoriskey. BFA, NYU, 1988—92; grad. cert., ART Inst.-Harvard, Cambridge, Mass., 1996—98. Artistic assoc. Intiman Theater, Seattle, 2002—04, S. Coast Rep., Costa Mesa, Calif., 2004—; visiting lectr. Princeton U., NJ, 2006—. Freelance dir. Goodman Theater, Playwrights Hanigans, Labyrinth Theater, Shakespeare Theater, DC, A.R.T., Balt. Ctr. Stage. Dir.: (plays) Fabulation, 2004, Intimate Apparel, 2004, Rose Tattoo, 2004. Mem.: NEA (Mentorship grant 2002, fellowship 2000). Home: 301 E 10th St New York NY 10009-5009

WHYTE, BETTINA MARSHALL, financial crisis manager; b. LA, Apr. 4, 1949; d. William Robert and Inez E. Marshall. BS in Indsl. Econs., Purdue U., 1971; MBA in Fin. and Acctg., Northwestern U., 1974. Cert. Insolvency and Restructuring Acct. Lending officer Harris Trust & Savings Bank, Chgo., 1971-74; v.p. Continental Bank Chgo., 1974-82; pres. KRW & Assocs., Inc., Houston, 1982-88; ptnr. Peterson & Co. Cons., Houston, 1988-90, Price Waterhouse, Houston, 1990-97, nat. dir. of bus. turnaround svcs.; prin. Jay Alix & Associates, New York, NY, 1997—. Bd. dirs. Washington Group Internat. Inc., 2002—, Amerisure Mut. Ins. Co. Contbg. editor: Turnaround Topics column, Am. Bankruptcy Inst. Jour. Mem. Am. Assn. Bankruptcy Trustees, Am. Bankruptcy Inst. (exec. bd., 1998-, pres.-elect, 2002-03, pres., 2003-), Assn. Insolvency Accountants, Phi Beta Kappa, Beta Gamma Sigma, Phi Kappa Phi. Avocation: showing and breeding Irish Setters. Fax: 212-4901344.

WHYTE, NANCY GOOCH, microbiologist; b. Oak Hill, W Va., July 15, 1936; d. Benjamin Adair and Martha (Baker) Gooch; children: James, Nancy, David. BA, W. Va. Univ., Morgantown, W.Va., 1954—58; M Gen. Admin., U. Md., 1982. Registered Microbiologist, 1976. Supr., microbiology Alexandria Hosp. (Inova), Alexandria, Va., 1971—95; microbiologist US Environ. Protection Agy., Arlington, Va., 1998—. Assoc. prof. (adj.) Prince Georges Cmty. Coll., Largo, Md., 1996—2001. Elder, Presbytery Commr. Presbyn. Ch., NY Ave. Office: US EPA 1801 S Bell St 308G Arlington VA 22202 Home: 2802 Lumar Dr Fort Washington MD 20744-2037 Business E-Mail: whyte.nancy@epa.gov.

WHYTE, NANCY MARIE, performing arts educator; b. Myrtlepoint, Oreg., Mar. 12, 1948; d. Lawrence Edward and Carol Elizabeth (Johnson) Guderian; m. Anthony John Whyte, Aug. 7, 1967 (div. Sept. 1968); 1 child, Charles Lawrence; m. Douglas Brian Graff, June 27, 1971 (div. Oct. 1974); m. Lawrence Hanson, Mar. 12, 1976 (div. Aug. 1984); m. Joseph Paul Deacon, Aug. 10, 1985; 1 child, Nina Alexandra. Student, U. Wash., 1969-72, Am. Sch. Dance, 1972; BA, Evergreen State Coll., 1987. Owner, dir. Nancy Whyte Sch. Ballet, Bellingham, Wash., 1969—; artistic dir. Garden Street Dance Players, Bellingham, 1969-72, MT Baker Ballet, Bellingham, 1975—, Alpha and Omega Worship Dancers, 2003—; co-dir. Exptl. Performance Workshop, Bellingham, 1975-77; instr. creative dance St. Paul's Primary Sch., Bellingham, 1993-97; facilitator dance workshop Allied Arts/Whatcom Co., Bellingham, 1995—. Guest lectr. Western Wash. U., Bellingham, 1976—83, 1996—2003; guest faculty Dance Theatre N.W., Tacoma, 1995—; liturgical dance cons. Assumption Cath. Sch., 2001—05; artistic dir. Alpha and Omega Worship Dancers, 2003—. Author: Memoirs of a Child of Theatre Street, 1993; soloist Raduga Folk Ballet/N.Y. Character Ballet, N.Y.C., 1978-79; choreographer numerous ballets, 1972—. Mem. Nat. Dance Assn., Dancers Over 40, Sacred Dance Guild, Vancouver Ballet Soc. Democrat. Avocations: voice, writing. Office: MT Baker Ballet 1412 Cornwall Ave PO Box 2393 Bellingham WA 98227-2393 Office Phone: 360-734-9141. Personal E-mail: isadorables@msn.com.

WICHMAN, YVONNE BEARD, lighting designer, literature educator; b. Atlanta, July 21, 1949; d. Herbert Glyndon Beard and Maria DeMarco Messer; m. Bryant Michael Baker, Sept. 21, 2002; 1 child, Ty Christopher. MA in Profl. Writing, Kennesaw State U., Ga., 1999. English instr. Kennesaw State U., 1999—; lighting designer Juno Lighting, Chgo., 1997—2005. Office Phone: 404-680-4224.

WICK, ERIKA ELISABETH, psychologist, educator, researcher; b. Basel, Switzerland, July 31, 1937; came to U.S., 1964; d. Josef and Martha (Gabriel) W. Tchr.'s diploma, Tchr.'s Coll., Basel, 1958; MA, PhD, U. Basel, 1964. Diplomate Am. Bd. Psychol. Hypnosis; lic. psychologist, N.J.; cert. sch. psychologist, N.Y. From asst. to assoc. prof. St. John's U., Queens, N.Y., 1966-75, prof. psychology, 1975—. Author: Zur Psychologie der Reue, 1971. Fellow Soc. Clin. and Exptl. Hypnosis; mem. APA, N.J. Psychol. Assn. Office: St Johns Univ 8000 Utopia Pkwy Jamaica NY 11432-1343

WICKERHAM, DEBORAH LOUISE, elementary school educator; d. Louis G. and Georgia Ruth (Spinelli) DeMarco; m. Vaun-Lee Wickerham, Apr. 27, 1979; children: Adam, Amanda. BS in Elem. Edn., Bowling Green State U., Ohio, 1976; MA in Ednl. Leadership, U. Findlay, Ohio, 2001. Tchr. Findlay City Schs., 1976. Adj. prof. U. Findlay, 1999—; mem. sci. adv. bd. MacMillan McGraw Hill, N.Y., 2004—; coord. region Nat. Bd., Findlay, 2002—; cons. in field. Chmn. Mobile Sci. Bus, 2004. Recipient Edn. Tchr. award, Vermir, Oreg., 2006, award, Coun. Elem. Schs., 2006. Mem.: NEA, Nat. Sci. Tchrs. Assn. (Presdl. award 1989), Alumni Pres. Award Sci. Tchrs., Findlay Edn. Assn., Ohio Edn. Assn., Sarmu Elem. Pres. Alumni. Roman Cath. Avocations: reading, history, baseball. Office: Chamberlin Hill 600 W Yates Ave Findlay OH 45840

WICKHAM, CINDY SUE, principal; b. Saginaw, Mich., June 17, 1954; d. Donald Maxwell and Charlys Ione (Pierre) Ward; m. Robert Thomas Wickham, June 18, 1976; children: Kelly C., Jeffrey R. BS in elem. and spl. edn. with high honors, We. Mich. U., Kalamazoo, 1976; MA in early childhood edn. with high honors, Ctrl. Mich. U., Mt. Pleasant, 1981; degree in elem. adminstrn., Grand Valley State U., Grand Rapids, Mich., 2000. Tchr. spl. edn. Saginaw Township Cmty. Schs., Mich., 1976—87; tchr., early childhood coord. Greenville Pub. Schs., Mich., 1987—2002; prin. Niles Cmty. Schs., Mich., 2002—. Developer/dir. Mentor-A-Mom, Greenville, 1999—2002, Niles, 2002—. Finalist Mich. Tchr. of Yr., Mich. State Dept. Edn., Lansing, 1987; named Tchr. of Yr., Saginaw Township Cmty. Schs., 1986. Mem.: NAESP, ACISD, Nat. Assn. for the Edn. of Young Children. Avocations: skiing, swimming, reading. Office: Northside Sch Niles Cmty Schs 2020 N Fifth Niles MI 49120

WICKHAM, DIANNE, nursing administrator; b. Dillon, Mont., Feb. 26, 1952; d. William Byron Wickham and Margaret Dewalt (Lovell) Starkweather. ADN, No. Mont. Coll., 1974; BSN, Mont. State U., 1978, MSN, 1980. RN, Mont. Clin. dir. St. Patrick Hosp., Missoula, Mont., 1980-81; asst. prof. Lewis Clark State Coll., Lewiston, Idaho, 1981-83, Mont. State U., Bozeman, Mont., 1983-86; home health nurse West Mont. Home Health, Helena, 1986-87, dir. clin. svcs., 1987-90; critical care nurse St. James Hosp., Butte, Mont., 1986-87; exec. dir. Mont. State Bd. of Nursing, Helena, 1990—. Mem. long term care com. Gov. Task Force on Aging, Helene, Mont., 1993-95, mem. task force to devel. investigator tng. Nat. Com. of State Bds. Nursing, Chgo., 1993—, mem. adj. faculty Mont. State U., Bozeman, 1993—, cons. in field, 1994—. Judge Soroptomists scholarship award, 1993, JC Penneys Golden Rule award, Helena, 1995. Recipient State award for excellence Am. Acad. Nurses Practitioners, 1994.

WICKIEWICZ, JESSICA-LAUREN CHARLOTTE, academic administrator; b. Greensboro, N.C., Sept. 11, 1976; d. Janice E. Keegan. MA in Psychology, Adelphi U., 2002. Rsch. asst. Derner Inst., Garden City, 2002—03; program dir. Adelphi U., Garden City, NY, 2002—, sr. resident dir., 2003—, coord. Greek life, 2004—. Presenter White Ribbon Campaign, Garden City, 2004—05. Recipient Women's Recognition for Svc. award, Adelphi U., 2003, 2004, 2005. Master: Sigma Delta Tau (assoc.; advisor 2001—05); mem.: Psi Chi (life). Achievements include research in affect of an open adoption on the adoptee.

WICKIZER, CINDY LOUISE, retired elementary school educator; b. Pitts., Dec. 12, 1946; d. Charles and Gloria Geraldine (Cassidy) Zimmerman Sr.; m. Leon Leonard Wickizer, Mar. 20, 1971 (div. Oct. 2003); 1 child, Charlyn Michelle. BS, Oreg. State U., Corvallis, 1968. Tchr. Enumclaw (Wash.) Sch. Dist., 1968-99, ret., 1999. Mem. Wash. State Ret. Tchrs. Assn., Am. Rabbit Breeders Assn. (judge, chmn. scholarship found. 1986-87, pres. 1988-94, 96-98, 2003-04, dist. dir. 1994-96, 2003-04, pres., 2005—, Disting. Svc. award 1987, Hall of Fame 1998), Wash. State Rabbit Breeders Assn. (life, Pres.'s award 1983, 94, sec., dir., v.p. 1995-97), Vancouver Island Rabbit Breeders Assn., Wash. State Rabbit and Cavy Shows Inc. (sec. 1994-2005), Evergreen Rabbit Assn. (sec., v.p., pres.), Alpha Gamma Delta, Women of Vision (bd. dir. 2004-06, v.p. 2006-), Sons/Daughters Pearl Harbor Survivors Home: 20825 Star Rte 410 E PMB 196 Bonney Lake WA 98391 E-mail: CindyWick@aol.com.

WICKLUND, GERRI M., finance educator; b. Manitowoc, Wis., Mar. 6, 1946; m. Dennis G. Wicklund; children: Julia M., Elizabeth A. BS, U. Wis., Whitewater; MS, Viterbo U., LaCrosse, Wis., EdM, 1998. Bus. tech. instr. Madison Area Tech. Coll., Wis., 1978—. Creator and coord. online edn. program Madison Area Tech. Coll., 2001—. Named Outstanding Employee, Madison Area Tech. Coll., 2003. Mem.: Internat. Assn. Adminstrv. Profls. (assoc.; mem. at large 2001—06). Achievements include design of first Associate Degree Administrative Assistant program in the US. Avocation: gardening. Home: 5311 Scenic Ridge Trail Middleton WI 53562 Office: Madison Area Technical College 3550 Anderson St Madison WI 53704 Office Phone: 608-246-6336. Office Fax: 608-246-6880. Business E-Mail: gwicklund@matcmadison.edu.

WICKLUND, JUDITH K., language educator, writer; Bachelors, U. Wis., Superior, 1983. Tchr. Grantsburg Pub. Schs., Wis., 1985—90, Luth. Jr. Sem., Morogoro, Tanzania, 1991—94; English tchr. Luck Pub. Schs., Wis., 1994—. Theatre dept. dir. Luck Pub. Schs., Wis., 1985—2006; sports photographer Burnett County Sentinel, Grantsburg, Wis., 2001—06. Author plays, reader's theatre scripts. Advisor, dir. 4-H, Grantsburg, Wis., 1983—90; chmn. bd. Trinity Luth. Ch., Siren, Wis. Recipient George Olmstead award, Williams Coll., 1996. Conservative. Lutheran. Avocations: writing, photography, gardening. Office: Luck Schs 810 W 7th St Luck WI 54853 Business E-Mail: judyw@lucksd.k12.wi.us.

WICKLUND, KAREN JEAN, voice and health professional, educator; b. Mpls., Dec. 22, 1956; BA, St. Olaf Coll., 1978; MM, U. Mich., 1980; DM, Northwestern U., 1996. Cmty. outreach coord. Y-Me Nat. Program, Homewood, Ill., 1986-87; health edn. coord. MacNeal Hosp., Berwyn, Ill., 1987-89; lectr. Northwestern U., Evanston, Ill., 1993-94; prof. Wash. State U., Pullman, 1994-95, U. Nebr., Omaha, 1995-97, Western Mich. U., Kalamazoo, 1997—. Pres. Of Spl. Note, Inc., Kalamazoo, 1989—. Contbr. articles to profl. jours. including Jour. Singing. Grantee U. Nebr., 1995, PEO Sisterhood, 1993; Ragland fellow Northwestern U., 1991-93. Mem. Nat. Assn. Tchrs. Singing, Chgo. Singing Tchrs. Guild (sec.). Office: Western Mich U 1201 Oliver St Kalamazoo MI 49008-3804 E-mail: Karen.wicklund@wmich.edu.

WICKMAN, PATRICIA ANN, retired social worker; b. San Diego, Calif., Nov. 18, 1928; d. Charles King Warrington and Sylvia Elisabeth Howard; m. Glenn A. Wickman, June 30, 1951; 1 child, Stacy Ann. BSc with distinction, U. Minn., 1951; MA, Coll. Idaho, 1971; student in History, Boise State U., 1988—91. Social worker Settlement House Mpls. Dept. Welfare, Mpls., 1948—49; social worker State Dept. Pub. Assistance, Idaho, 1950—55; tchr. Eng., drama, speech Meridan Sch. Dist., Meridan, Idaho, 1955—57, libr., 1958; substitute tchr. Boise Sch. Dist., Boise, 1958—60, pilot counseling program elem. sch., 1969—70. Lectr. in field; workshop leader in field. Author: History of Environmental Movements in the United States, 1972, Militarizing America, Reagan years, 1982, (plays) Fashion, Folly and Feminism, 1982, History of the Boise Branch, AAUW, 2001; editor: Des Arab Newsletter, 1973—74; contbr. articles to newspapers; guest (TV series). Vol. counselor State of Idaho Corrections Program Dist. IV, 1970—73; pres. Ada County Citizens Crisis Coalition, Ada County, Idaho, 1984—86; leader 4-H, 1967—77; pres., chmn. Collister Sewer Bond Drive, 1968—72; mem. Ada County Adv. Com. Planning, 1978—82; bd. dirs. League of Women Voters, 1960—67; vol. AdaCo Spl. Olympics, 1972—82; precinct leader Ada County, Idaho; Sunday sch. tchr. Luth. & Unitarian Ch.; bd. dir. Ada County Citizens Crisis Coalition, 1983—88. Unitarian Universalist. Home: 1178 E Beacon Lt Rd Eagle ID 83616

WICKNER, SUE HENGREN, biochemist; BS, American U., 1967; MS, Georgetown U., 1970; PhD, Albert Einstein Coll. Med., 1973. Rsch. chemist lab molecular biology Nat. Cancer Inst., NIH, 1977—94, chief molecular biology, lab. molecular biology, 1994—. Recipient Merit award, NIH, 1995; Postdoctoral Rsch. fellow, 1974—76, Staff fellow, 1976—77. Mem.: Nat. Acad. Scis. Office: Nat Cancer Inst NIH Lab Molecular Biology Bldg 37 Rm 2D19 37 Convent Dr MSC 4255 Bethesda MD 20892-4255*

WICKS, DEBRA S., nursing educator; b. Long Beach, Calif., May 15, 1949; d. Harry Hap W. and Eleanor J. (Magri) McMillen; m. Edward C. Wicks, June 14, 1972; 1 child, Lara S. Byers. Assoc. Nursing, Coll. of Sequoias, Visalia, Calif., 1975; BSN, Calif. State U., Long Beach, 1986; BA in English, Calif. State U., San Luis Obispo, 1972; MSN, Calif. State U., Sacramento, 1993. Cert. AACN, 1991. ICU nurse Kaweah Delta Dist. Hosp., Visalia, Calif., 1975—79; ICU nurse, nurse mgr. ICU/telemetry, supr. Sierra Nev. Meml. Hosp., Grass Valley, Calif., 1979—95; oncology nurse U. Calif., Davis Med. Ctr., Sacramento, 1996—98, Mercy Gen. Hosp., Sacramento, 2002—04; tchr. nursing Sacramento City Coll., 1995—. Sr. warden Emmanuel Episcopal Ch., Grass Valley, 2003—06. Mem.: Nat. Intravenous Nurse Soc. (CRNI 1986), AACN. Episcopalian. Office: Sacramento City Coll 3835 Freeport Blvd Sacramento CA 95822-1386 Office Phone: 916-558-2276.

WICKWIRE, PATRICIA JOANNE NELLOR, psychologist, educator; d. William McKinley and Clara Rose (Pautsch) Nellor; m. Robert James Wickwire, Sept. 7, 1957; 1 child, William James. BA cum laude, U. No. Iowa, 1951; MA, U. Iowa, 1959; PhD, U. Tex., Austin, 1971; postgrad., U. So. Calif., UCLA, Calif. State U., Long Beach. Lic. ednl. psychologist, marriage and family therapist, Calif. Tchr. Ricketts Ind. Schs., Iowa, 1946-48; tchr., counselor Waverly-Shell Rock Ind. Schs., Iowa, 1951-55; reading cons., head dormitory counselor U. Iowa, Iowa City, 1955-57; tchr., sch. psychologist, adminstr. S. Bay Union H.S. Dist., Redondo Beach, Calif., 1962-82, dir. student svcs. and spl. edn. Cons. mgmt. and edn.; pres. Nellor Wickwire Group, 1981—; mem. exec. bd. Calif. Interagy. Mental Health Coun., 1968-72, Beach Cities Symphony Assn., 1970-82; chmn. Friends of Dominguez Hills, Calif., 1981-85. Contbr. articles in field to profl. jours. Pres. Calif. Women's Caucus, 1993-95, 2003—. Mem. APA, AAUW (exec. bd., chpt. pres. 1962-72), Nat. Career Devel. Assn. (media chair 1992-98), Am. Assn. Career Edn. (pres. 1991—), L.A. County Dirs. Pupil Svcs. (chmn. 1974-79), L.A. County Pers. and Guidance Assn. (pres. 1977-78), Assn. Calif. Sch. Adminstrs. (dir. 1977-81), L.A. County SW Bd. Dist. Adminstrs. for Spl. Edn. (chmn. 1976-81), Calif. Assn. Sch. Psychologists (bd. dirs. 1981-83), Am. Assn. Sch. Adminstrs., Calif. Assn. for Measurement and Evaluation in Guidance (dir. 1981, pres. 1984-85, 98-2000, 04-05), ACA (chmn. Coun. Newsletter Editors 1989-91, mem. com. on women 1989-92, mem. com. on rsch. and knowledge 1994—, chmn. 1995—, mem. and chmn. bylaws com. 1998-2001, rep. to joint com. on testing practices 2001—), Assn. Measurement and Eval. in Guidance (Western regional editor 1985-87, conv. chair 1986, editor 1987-90, exec. bd. dirs. 1987-91), Calif. Assn. Counseling and Devel. (exec. bd. 1984—, pres. 1988-89, jour. editor 1990—), Nat. Assn. for Ind.-Edn. Coop. (bd. dirs. 2002-05), Internat. Career Assn. Network (chair 1985—), Pi Lambda Theta, Alpha Phi Gamma, Psi Chi, Kappa Delta Pi, Sigma Alpha Iota. Office: The Nellor Wickwire Group 2900 Amby Pl Hermosa Beach CA 90254-2216 Office Phone: 310-376-7378.

WIDDER, EDITH ANNE, biologist; b. Boston, June 11, 1951; d. David Vernon and Vera Adela (Ames) Widder; m. David Charles Smith, Feb. 9, 1972. BS magna cum laude in Biology, Tufts U., Medford, Mass., 1973; MS in Biochemistry, U. Calif., Santa Barbara, 1977, PhD in Neurobiology, 1982. Cert. sci. rsch. pilot for atmospheric diving sys. submersibles 1984. Lab. asst. phycology U. Mass. Field Sta. Environ. Scis., 1968—69; rsch. assoc. NIH Resource Lab. Electron Probe Microanalysis Harvard U. Med. Sch., Boston, 1973-75; assoc. rschr. ONR bioluminescence prog. U. Calif., Santa Barbara, 1977-83, postdoctoral rsch. biologist, 1983-85, asst. rsch. biologist, co-prin. investigator Marine Sci. Inst. and Neuroscience Rsch. Inst., 1985-89; asst. scientist, prin. investigator Harbor Br. Oceanog. Instn., Ft. Pierce, Fla., 1989-91, assoc. scientist, prin. investigator, 1991—93, acting divsn. dir., 1993—94, sr. scientist, prin. investigator, 1993—2005; prof. biol. scis. Fla. Inst. Tech., 1991—; pres., sr. scientist Ocean Rsch. & Conservation Assn., 2005—. Sci. cons. Dynamics Tech., Inc., LA, 1987—89; disting. scientist adj. Monterey Bay Aquarium Rsch. Inst., 1998—; adj. rsch. prof. earth and planetary scis. dept. Johns Hopkins U., 2000—; affiliate prof. dept. biol. sci. Fla. Atlantic U., 2000—; adj. sr. rsch. scientist Bigelow Lab. Ocean Scis., 2005—. Contbr. articles to profl. jours.; mem. editl. bd.: Marine Tech. Soc. Named Earle C. Anthony fellow, 1978; recipient Women of Discovery award, Sea, Wings WorldQuest, 2006; grantee, NSF, 1986—88, 1990—91, 1991—; MacArthur Fellow, John D. and Catherine T. MacArthur Found., 2006. Mem. AAAS, Am. Soc. Limnology and Oceanography, Am. Soc. Zoologists, Soc. Neuroscience, Soc. Photo-Optical and Instrumentation Engrs., Internat. Soc. Bioluminescence and Chemiluminescence (councilor), Am. Acad. Underwater Scis., Explorers Club. Achievements include patents in field; first to make video recordings of bioluminescence in the ocean, 1985. Office: Ocean Rsch & Conservation Assn 1420 Seaway Dr Fort Pierce FL 34949 E-mail: ewidder@oceanrecon.org.*

WIDDOWS, MARIANNE SHUTA, orchestra director; b. Wilkes-Barre, Pa., June 18, 1960; d. Joseph and Matilda Marie Shuta; m. Donald Richard Widdows. B of Music Edn., Coll. Misericordia, Dallas, Pa., 1982; M of Music Edn. in String Pedagogy, U. NC, Greensboro, 1990. Orch. dir. Southview Jr. H.S., Fayetteville, NC, 1984—86, Terry Sanford H.S., Fayetteville, 1989—97, Ashley Elem., Fayetteville, 1985—, Van Story Elem., Fayetteville, 1986—, Max Abbott Mid. Sch., Fayetteville, 1986—. Violin coach Cumberland County Youth Orch., Fayetteville, 1984—; assoc. dir. Snyder Bapt. Ch. Youth Orch., Fayetteville, 2004—; violinist Cumberland Quartet, Fayetteville, 1984—. Mem.: Am. Fedn. Musicians, Am. String Tchrs. Assn., Nat. Sch. Orch. Assn., Music Educators Nat. Conf. Avocations: collecting nesting dolls, reading, animals. Office: Max Abbott Mid Sch 590 Winding Creek Rd Fayetteville NC 28305 E-mail: dwiddows@aol.com.

WIDEMAN, CAROL M., accountant, consultant; b. York, AL, July 7, 1949; d. Coleman and Martha J. W.; 1 child, Tangiera L. Loftis. BA in Acctg., Suffolk U., 1978; MA in Mgmt., Cambridge Coll., 1985. Auditor Dept. of Revenue, Boston, 1978-79; acct./analyst Mass. Port Authority, Boston, 1979-86; town acct. Town of Canton, Mass., 1986-96, Town of Littleton, Mass., 1996-99. Legis. com. Mass. Mcpl. Auditors/Accts. Assn., Boston, 1994—; fin. cons. Blue Hill Ave. Coalition, 1995-98. Mem. Meeting House Hill Assn., Dorchester, Mass., 1998—; chairperson, liaison Metco Parent Group, Roxbury, Mass., 1982-84. Recipient Foster Parent award Roxbury (Mass.) Svcs. for Children, 1998. Mem. Mass. Mcpl. Assn., Mass., Mcpl. Auditors & Accts. Assn., Eastern Mass. Mcpl. Auditors and Accts. Assn., Assn. Gov. Accts. Home: 39 Mount Everett St # 3 Dorchester MA 02125-2437

WIDEMAN, IDA DEVLIN, science educator; d. John Cole and Lillie Alma Devlin; m. Leroy Wideman, May 12, 1945; children: Michael Andre, Leroy Maurice. BS, SC State U., 1964—68; MAT, U. of SC, 1976—77. Sci. tchr. West Side H.S., Newark, 1971—73, Hopkins Jr. H.S., Hopkins, SC, 1976—83, St. Andrews Mid. Sch., Columbia, SC, 1983—. Co-dir. NSF grant Ctr. for Sci. Edn., U. S.C.; master tchr. sci. U. S.C., Columbia, Aiken; presenter in field. Mem. Nat. Assn. of U. Women, Columbia, SC, 1990. Named Tchr. of Yr., St. Andrews Middle Sch., state winner, Presdl. Awards for Excellence in Math. and Sci. Tchg. Mem.: Richland County Edn. Assn., SC Edn. Assn., NEA, SC Earth Sci. Teachers Assn. (past pres., v.p. 1988—90), SC Sci. Coun., NSTA, Delta Sigma Theta Sorority (life). United Methodist. Avocations: walking, reading. Home: 446 Koon Store Rd Columbia SC 29203 Office: St Andrews Middle Sch 1231 Bluefield Rd Columbia SC 29210 Office Phone: 803-731-8910. Home Fax: 803-333-0542; Office Fax: 803-731-8913. Personal E-mail: lwideman@sc.rr.com. E-mail: iwideman@richlandone.org.

WIDENER, MARY LEE, non-profit financial executive; b. Schaal, Alaska, July 6, 1938; d. Mert and Johnnie (Newton) Thomas; children: Warren Jr., Michael, Stephen. Diploma, Heald Bus. Coll., 1956; Pub. Adminstrn. Program, U. San Francisco Sch. Profl. Studies, 1978; LLD (hon.), John F. Kennedy U., 1979. Adminstrv. asst. to exec. v.p. U. Calif., Berkeley, 1959-69, office mgr. gifts and endowments, 1959-69; urban program coord. Fed. Home Loan Bank Bd., Washington, 1972-73; housing cons. Ford Found., N.Y.C., 1973-74; exec. dir. Oakland Neighborhood Housing Svcs., Oakland, 1973-76; program cons. Urban Reinvestment Task Force, Washington, 1974-76; pres., CEO Neighborhood Housing Svcs. of Am., Inc., Oakland, 1974—. Chmn., Fed. Home Loan Bank, San Francisco, 1994-2003, Social Compact, 2004-06; bd. dirs. The PMI Group, S.H. Cowell Found., The First Am. Corp.; bd. trustees Nat. Housing Conf., 2000—. Author: (with others) Housing America, 1993. Trustee, San Francisco Found., 1988-98, chair, 1996-98; trustee Ptnrs. for Livable Cmtys.; adv. bd. PEW Charitable Trusts Partnership for Civic Change, Phila.; former dir. KQED, San Francisco, United Way Bay Area, Univ. YWCA, BRIDGE Housing Corp., John F. Kennedy U., program adv. coun. Inst. Nonprofit Orgn. Mgmt., U. San Francisco; former state chair Calif. Dem. Ctrl. Com., San Francisco; former mem. U.S. Senate Housing Task Force, Washington, Commn. on Homelessness, Oakland; former chair affordable housing adv. coun. Fed. Home Loan Bank, San Francisco; former mem. Fannie Mae's Adv. Coun.; former participant Internat. Exch. Housing Profls. Recipient award Nat. Coalition of 100 Black Women, N.Y., 1989, San

Francisco LWV Women who could be Pres. award, 1996; named Housing Person of Yr., Nat. Housing Conf., Washington, 2000. Democratic. Methodist. Avocations: tennis, travel, golf. Office: Neighborhood Housing Svc Am 1970 Broadway Fl 4 Oakland CA 94612-2212 Office Phone: 510-287-4201.

WIDES, LOUISE D., small business owner, consultant; b. Chgo. married, Oct. 1965; 2 children. BA, Mount Holyoke Coll., 1962; MA in Internat. Rels., Tufts U., 1963. Editor Internat. Orgn., 1963-65; tchr. Fair Lawn H.S., N.J., 1965-66, Walden Sch., N.Y.C., 1966-68; rschr. Gen. Learning Corp., N.Y.C., 1968-69, Tchrs. Coll. Columbia U., N.Y.C., 1969-70; writer Fed. Election Commn., Washington, 1970-75, chief publs., 1975-85, asst. staff dir. info. divsn., 1985—2001; prin., owner Wides Consulting, LLC, 2001—. Bd. dirs. Micah House, 1989-95, pres., 1989. Recipient Blue Pencil award 2nd place Govt. Brochure for Tech. Audience Nat. Assn. Govt. Communicators, 1994, Gold award for the Record Newsletter on Newsletters, 1994. Jewish. Avocations: reading, walking, movies, theater, opera. Office: Fed Election Commn 999 E St NW Washington DC 20463-0002

WIDGER, TANYA MARIE, counselor; b. Astoria, Oreg., Feb. 11, 1977; d. William Earl and Michelle Elaine Fleming; m. Ernest Edward Widger, Nov. 1, 2002. AA, Lane C.C., 2003; BSc, U. Oreg., 2004. Crisis counselor Sexual Assault Support Svcs., Eugene, Oreg., 2003—05; libr. Women's Resource Ctr., Bend, Oreg., 2005—. Mem. steering com. Sexual Assault Support Svcs., 2004; facilitator Breaking Free, Eugene, 2000. Author: Signifying Nothing, 2006 (Editor's Choice award Internat. Libr. Poetry, 2006); contbr. articles to mags. Fundraiser Spl. Olympics, Bend, 1993; coord. Take Back The Night, Eugene, 2004; mem. team Project Saferide, Eugene, 2000—01. Recipient Hon. Mention award, Lane County Photography, 2003. Mem.: PETA, ACLU, Susan Komen Breast Cancer Found., Wall Tolerance, Native Am. Rights Fund, Campaign for Tibet, Greenpeace, So. Poverty Law Ctr., Amnesty Internat. Democrat. Avocations: writing, reading, yoga, photography, fishing.

WIDNALL, SHEILA EVANS, aeronautical educator, former secretary of the airforce, former university official; b. Tacoma, July 13, 1938; d. Rolland John and Genievieve Alice (Krause) Evans; m. William Soule Widnall, June 11, 1960; children: William, Ann. BS in Aero. and Astronautics, MIT, 1960, MS in Aero. and Astronautics, 1961, DSc, 1964; PhD (hon.), New Eng. Coll., 1975, Lawrence U., 1987, Cedar Crest Coll., 1988, Smith Coll., 1990, Mt. Holyoke Coll., 1991, Ill. Inst. Tech., 1991, Columbia U., 1994, Simmons Coll., 1994, Suffolk U., 1994, Princeton U., 1994. Asst. prof. aeros. and astronautics MIT, Cambridge, 1964-70, assoc. prof., 1970-74, prof., 1974-93, head divsn. fluid mechanics, 1975-79; dir. Fluid Dynamics Rsch. Lab., MIT, Cambridge, 1979-90; chmn. faculty MIT, Cambridge, 1979-80, chair com. on acad. responsibility, 1991-92, assoc. provost, 1992-93; sec. USAF, 1993-97; Inst. prof. MIT, Cambridge, 1997—. Bd. dirs. Gen. Corp., Chemfab Inc., Bennington, Vt., Aerospace Corp., L.A., Draper Labs., Cambridge, Gencorp; past trustee Carnegie Corp., 1984-92, Charles Stark Draper Lab. Inc.; mem. Carnegie Commn. Sci., Tech. and Govt, mem. Columbia Accident Investigation Bd, 2003-. Co-author: Lean Enterprise Value: Insights from MIT's Lean Aerospace Initiative, 2002 (Engring. Sci. Book award Internat. Acad. Astronautics 2003); contbr. articles to profl. jours.; patentee in field; assoc. editor AIAA Jour. Aircraft, 1972-75, Physics of Fluids, 1981-88, Jour. Applied Mechanics, 1983-87; mem. editorial bd. Sci., 1984-86. Bd. visitors USAF Acad., Colorado Springs, Colo., 1978-84, bd. chair, 1980-82; trustee Boston Mus. Sci., 1989-93, Sloan Found., 1998-. Named to Nat. Women's Hall of Fame, 2003; recipient Washburn award, Boston Mus. Sci., 1987. Fellow AAAS (bd. dirs. 1982-89, pres. 1987-88, chmn. 1988-89), AIAA (bd. dirs. 1975-77, Lawrence Sperry award 1972, Durand Lectureship for Pub. Svc. award 1996, pres. 2000-01), Am. Phys. Soc. (exec. com. 1979-82); mem. ASME (Applied Mechs. award 1995, Pres. award 1999), NAE (coun. 1992-93, v.p. 1998—), NAS (panel on sci. responsibility), Am. Acad. Arts and Scis., Soc. Women Engrs. (Outstanding Achievement award 1975), Internat. Acad. Astronautics, Seattle Mountaineers. Office: MIT Bldg 33-411 77 Massachussetts Ave Cambridge MA 02139 Office Phone: 617-253-3595. E-mail: sheila@mit.edu.*

WIDNER, ROBERTA ANN, accountant, artist; b. El Paso, Tex., Sept. 27, 1940; d. Wilburn Alton and Frances (Martin) Leavelle; m. Jerry Wesley Widner, Jan. 21, 1959; children: Kim, Mark. Attended, Fechin Inst., 1986. Civil svc. Fed. Govt., 1958, cert. state merit system State of N.Mex, 1958. Stenographer Employment Security Commn. Legal Dept., Albuquerque, 1958, Cannon AFB Comdr.'s Office, Clovis, 1958; sec. to pres. Walker Wholesale Hardware, Jacksonville, 1959; stenographer Household Fin. Corp., San Diego, 1960—61; temp. clk. U.S. Post Office, Clovis, 1974; sec./acctg. Coop. Ext. Svc./Dir. - 4-H - NMSU Rodeo Dept., Las Cruces, 1977—. Sec. N.Mex Employment Security Commn., Albuquerque, 1958; state triticale sec. N.Mex Triticale Assn., Clovis; profl. improvement com. Coop. Ext. Svc., Las Cruces, 1983—84. Oils, pastels, watercolors. Planning com. fashion fund raisers Am. Cancer Soc., Las Cruces, 1991—92; planning com. ann. renaissance fair Dona Ana Arts Coun., Las Cruces, 1985—85; planning com. nat. maid of cotton fashion show Cotton Inc., Las Cruces. Recipient Pres.'s Star Performer award, NMSU, 2002. Mem.: Border Book Festival, Dona Arts Coun., Mesilla Valley Arts Guild (treas. 1985). Achievements include juried Exhibit - El Paso Museum of Art, 1987; juried - Internat. Penwomens' Mex./U.S. Exhibit; juried Art - Cinco Pintores - Linda Lundeen Gallery/Las Cruces; juried - Southern New Mexico Arts Profls., 1999; juried - Rio Grande Arts Invitational, 1998. Avocations: painting, Mexican/European travel, ballooning, sewing, water-skiing. Business E-Mail: rwidner@nmsu.edu.

WIDSETH, JANE CHRISTINA, psychologist, psychotherapist; b. Mpls., Oct. 14, 1942; d. Edwin Clarance and Janet Christine (Hart) W.; m. Robert Bruce Partridge II, Aug. 28, 1976; children: John Ditton Widseth Partridge, Carl Erik Widseth Partridge. BA, U. Minn., 1964; AM, Boston U., 1966, PhD, 1972. Lic. psychologist, Pa. Psychol. counselor Haverford (Pa.) Coll., 1970-72, dir. counseling, 1972-84, psychol. counselor, 1984—. Vol. counselor Univ. Counseling Svcs., Cambridge, Eng., 1986; pvt. practice psychotherapy, Haverford, 1972—; bd. dirs. Phila. Ctr. for Psychoanalytic Edn., 1993—, pres., 1996-99. Contbr. articles to profl. jours. Mem. APA, Phila. Soc. for Psychoanalytic Psychology (past pres.), Haverford Faculty Swimming Club (bd. dirs. 1988-92, treas. 1988-90), Phi Beta Kappa. Avocations: sports, travel, music. Office: Haverford Coll CAPS Haverford PA 19041 Office Phone: 610-896-6385. E-mail: jwidseth@haverford.edu.

WIDYOLAR, SHEILA GAYLE, dermatologist; b. Vancouver, B.C., Can., June 11, 1939; d. Walter Herbert and Olive Louise (O'Neal) Roberts; Kithi K. Widyolar, 1960 (div. 1979); 1 child, Keith. BS, Loma Linda U., 1962; MD, Howard U., 1972. Resident U. Calif., Irvine, 1973-76; dermatologist pvt. practice, Laguna Hills, Calif., 1976—. Clin. instr. U. Calif. Sch. Medicine, 1978—86. Chmn. bd. dirs. Opera Pacific, Costa Mesa, Calif., 1996-97. Fellow Am. Acad. Dermatology, Am. Soc. Dermatopathology; mem. AMA, Calif. Med. Assn., Dermatol. Soc. Orange County (pres. 1983), Alpha Omega Alpha. Avocations: music, travel. Office: Ste 403 23911 Calle de Mag Dalena Laguna Hills CA 92653 Office Phone: 949-452-3814.

WIE, MICHELLE SUNG, professional golfer; b. Honolulu, Oct. 11, 1989; d. Byung-Wook and Hyun-Kyong Sung Wie. Played in major LPGA Tournaments US Women's Open, 2003, Kraft Nabisco Championship, 2003, 2004; winner Jennie K. Wilson Invitational, 2001, Hawaii State Women's Stroke Play Championship, 2001, USGA Women's Amateur Pub. Links Championship, 2003; profl. golfer, 2005—. Named one of 100 Most Influential People, Time Mag., 2006. Mem.: Hawaii State Jr. Golf Assn. Achievements include youngest player to win Hawaii State Women's Stroke Play Championship, Jennie K. Wilson Internat., and US Amateur Pub. Links Championship; youngest player to make an LPGA cut, playing in the Kraft Nabisco Championship; youngest player to ever compete and win the Curtis Cup, 2004. Avocations: reading, art, drawing, computers. Office: c/o LPGA 100 Internat Golf Dr Daytona Beach FL 32124-1092*

WIEBENSON, DORA LOUISE, architectural historian, editor, writer; b. Cleve., July 29, 1926; d. Edward Ralph and Jeannette (Rodier) W. BA, Vassar Coll., 1946; MArch, Harvard U., 1951; MA, NYU, 1958, PhD, 1964. Architect, N.Y., 1951-66; lectr. Columbia U., 1966-68; assoc. prof. U. Md., 1968-72, prof., 1972-77; vis. prof. Cornell U., 1974; prof. U. Va., Charlottesville, 1977-92, prof. emeritus, 1992—, chmn. div. archtl. history, 1977-79, assoc. fellow U. Va. Ctr. Advanced Studies, 1982-83; pres. Archtl. Publs., N.Y.C., 1982—; editor-in-chief Centropa, 2000—. Editor: Marsyas XI: 1962-64, 1965, Essays in Honor of Walter Friedlaender, 1965; Architectural Theory and Practice from Alberti to Ledoux, 1982, rev., 1983, Spanish transl., 1988; Guide to Graduate Degree Programs in Architectural History, 1982, rev., 1984, 86, 88, 90; co-editor: The Architecture of Historic Hungary, 1998, Hungarian transl., 1998; author: Sources of Greek Revival Architecture, 1969, Tony Garnier: The Cité Industrielle, 1969, Japanese transl., 1983, The Picturesque Garden in France, 1978, Mark J. Millard Architectural Collection, Vol. I: French Books: Sixteenth through Nineteenth Centuries, 1993; contbr. articles to profl. jours. Student fellow Inst. Fine Arts, 1961-62, 62-63; grantee Am. Philos. Soc., 1964-65, 70, Samuel H. Kress Found., 1966, 72-73, 98, Gen. Rsch. Fund, U. Md., 1969, 74, 76, NEH, 1972-73, Am. Coun. Learned Socs., 1976, 81, 85, Ctr. Advanced Studies, U. Va., 1980, 81, 97, Graham Found. Advanced Studies Fine Arts, 1982, 93, Archtl. History Found., 1996; fellow Yale Ctr. Brit. Art, 1983; sr. rsch. fellow NEH, 1986-87. Mem. Soc. Archtl. Historians (bd. dirs. 1974-77, 80-83, chair edn. com. 1976-90), Coll. Art Assn., Am. Assn. Advancement Slavic Studies, Am. Soc. Eighteenth Century (mem. exec. bd. 1991-94). Business E-Mail: centropa@rcn.com.

WIECHERT, BARBARA THERESA, school nurse practitioner; d. Dominick Michael and Lillian Kolar Marino; m. Paul Joseph Wiechert, July 1, 1972; children: Paul Joseph Jr., Sarah Anne. BSN, Loyola U., 1972; MEd, Govs. State U., 2003. Cert. vision technician, Ill., 1987, audiometric technician, Ill., 1987, type 73, Ill., 1990. Staff nurse Palos Cmty. Hosp., Palos Heights, Ill., 1976—80; staff nurse Med. Ctr. Loyola U., Maywood, Ill., 1980—85; staff nurse outpatient Mulchay Outpatient Ctr., Maywood, 1985—87; sch. nurse Aero Spl. Edn. Coop., Burbank, Ill., 1987—94, Ridgeland dist. 122, Oaklawn, Ill., 1994—. Supr. sch. nurse interns Nat. Coll. Edn., Evanston, Ill., 1989, 1997—98; involved with nat. incentive Every Child Needs a Sch. Nurse Am. Fedn. Tchrs., DC, 2003—. Exhibitions include Loyola U. Art Show, 1972 (Hon. Mention award, 72). Asst. leader Girl Scouts Am., Chgo., 1992—96. Grantee, Ill., 1988—90. Mem.: PTA (various coms. 1994—), Am. Fedn. Tchrs., Ill. Assn. Sch. Nurses, Nat. Assn. Sch. Nurses. Avocations: travel, ceramics, reading, music, walking. Office: Ridgelan Pub Schs 6500 W 95th St Oak Lawn IL 60453

WIECK, MARIE L., information technology executive; b. Oct. 22, 1960; BS in Engring., Cooper Union; MS in Computer Sci., Columbia U., MBA. With IBM Corp., 1986—, gen. mgr., industry solutions and bus. integration, application and integration middleware divsn., software group, v.p., WebSphere Platform, software group, 2005—. Co-chairperson, US Women's Coun. IBM Corp.; leader Work/Life Balance Initiative; created IBM Corp., Tri-State Networking Event; spkr. in field. Sponsored IBM Corp., Family 360 Pilot, IBM Corp., Talking to Children about Work initiative; mentor Mentor-Net. Recipient President's award, Cooper Union, 2004. Mem.: Women in Tech. Internat., Nat. Assn. Female Executives, Soc. Women Engineers (Work/Life Balance award 2005), IEEE. Achievements include having implemented several programs to help IBM's employees address the challenges of balancing work and personal family commitments. Office: IBM Corp 1133 Westchester Ave West Harrison NY 10604*

WIEDL, PRISCILLA, music educator; b. New Haven, Conn., Aug. 18, 1942; d. Clifford Guthrie and Susan Anna Anderson; m. Edward John Wiedl, Dec. 3, 1971; children: Noel Elaine Widel Gaussens, Seth Clifford. BS in Music, Houghton Coll., N.Y., 1964. Cert. tchr. N.Y. Tchr. music Filmore Ctrl. Sch., NY, 1964, Wyoming County BOCES, NY, 1964—65, No. Collins Ctrl. Sch., NY, 1965—68, Williamsville Ctrl. Sch., NY, 1968—69, Lake Shore Ctrl. Schs., Angola, NY, 1969—99, St. Aloisius Sch., Cheektowaga, NY, 2000—01, Our Lady of the Sacred Heart Sch., Orchard Park, NY, 2001—. Office: Our Lady of Scred Heart Sch 3144 Abbott Rd Orchard Park NY 14127-1039

WIEGAND, ELIZABETH, musician, educator; b. Michigan City, Ind., Sept. 25, 1931; d. Leo Theodore and Ella Martha Grieger; m. Lee Paul Wiegand, June 17, 1950; children: David Lee, Elaine Martha Johnson, Susan Elizabeth, Christine Mary. Cert. music tchr., Valparaiso U. Cert. Nat. Cert. Music Tchrs., permanent cert. Music Tchrs. Nat. Assn. Organist Queen All Sts. Ch., Michigan City, 1954—92; organist, choir dir. St. Stanislaus Kostka Consolation Choir, Michigan City, 1992—, spl. Eucharistic min., 1998—; chapel organist St. Anthony Meml. Hosp., Michigan City, 1998—; organist, pianist LaPorte Presbyn. Ch., Ind., 2001—. Competition judge Nat. Tchrs. Music Conf., Nat. Assn. Organ Tchrs. Musician: Tex. Women's U. Repository, 1999, Cath. of Antwerp, 1998, St. Williams Ch. Named Music Educator of the Yr., Am. Music Conf., 1995—2005. Fellow: Nat. Fedn. Music Clubs; mem.: ASCAP (Popularity award 1980—2006), Am. Coll. Musicians (1st Pl. gold medal Internat. Rec. Competition). Roman Catholic. Avocations: embroidery, art, photography. Home: 7421 W Johnson Rd Michigan City IN 46360 Office Phone: 219-878-9511.

WIEGAND, JULIE WILDS, elementary school educator; b. Galesburg, Ill., Apr. 14, 1954; d. John Wilson and Helen Arletta (Mitchell) Wilds; m. Michael Anthony Wiegand, Nov. 10, 1984; children: Joseph Michael, Margaret Eshe. BS, Ill. State U., 1975. Substitute tchr. Normal/Bloomington Schs., Ill., 1975—77; tchr. Immaculate Conception, Monmouth, Ill., 1977—79, Galesburg Unified Sch. Dist. #205, Ill., 1979—. Pres., sec., treas., parliamentarian Galesburg Jr. Woman's Club, 1980—; treas., sec. Ill. Fedn. of Women's Clubs, 1989-92. Mem. Galesburg Edn. Assn. (treas. 1981-85), Phi Delta Kappa (annual fund, rsch. rep. 1989-91). Democrat. Lutheran. Avocations: church outreach work, christian education, reading, travel. Home: 1173 N Academy St Galesburg IL 61401-2646 Office: Gale Sch 1131 W Dayton St Galesburg IL 61401-1507

WIEGAND, PENELOPE TARLETON, elementary school educator; arrived in US, 1946; d. John and Jean Mills; m. John Wiegand, July 30, 1988; m. Donald P. Eilmes, Dec. 26, 1968 (div. June 1975); children: John Eilmes, Judy Eilmes, Velma Eilmes. BA in Edn., Calif. State U., LA, 1964, M in Urban Edn., 1980; PhD in Spl. Edn., U. Calif., Riverside, 2003. Cert. tchr. Calif. Bank reconciler Security Pacific, LA, 1960—64; tchr. La Seda Sch., Rowland Heights, Calif., 1964—68, Rowland Unified Sch. Dist., 1975—87; resource specialist Shelyn Sch., Rowland Heights, 1987—2004. Recipient Ada Mae Warner award, Shelyn PTA, 1996, Hon. Svc. award, 2004; grantee, Dist. Grant Pools, 1993, San Gabriel Valley Pub. Schs. Credit Union, 1996—97. Mem.: Calif. Assn. Spl. Edn. Adminstrn., Nat. Assn. Sch. Psych., Calif. Reading Assn., Internat. Reading Assn. Democrat. Baptist. Home: 6345 Yale St Chino CA 91710

WIEGAND, SYLVIA MARGARET, mathematician, educator; b. Cape Town, South Africa, Mar. 8, 1945; came to U.S., 1949; d. Laurence Chisholm and Joan Elizabeth (Dunnett) Young; m. Roger Allan Wiegand, Aug. 27, 1966; children: David Chisholm, Andrea Elizabeth. AB, Bryn Mawr Coll., 1966; MA, U. Wash., 1967; PhD, U. Wis., Madison, 1972. Mem. faculty U. Nebr., Lincoln, 1967—, now prof. math.; program dir. Nat. Sci. Found., 2002—03. Vis. assoc. prof. U. Conn., Storrs, 1978-79, U. Wis., Madison, 1985-86; vis. prof. Purdue U., 1992-93, Spring 1998, Mich. State U., Fall 1997. Editor Communications in Math., 1990-2004, Rocky Mountain Jour. Math., 1991-2004; contbr. rsch. articles to profl. jours. Troop leader Lincoln area Girl Scouts U.S., 1988-92. Grantee NSF, 1985-88, 90-93, 94-96, 97-2002, NSA, 1995-97, 2002, 03-05; Vis. Professorship for Women, 1992, Nat. Security Agy., 1995-97. Mem. AAUP, Assn. Women in Math (pres.-elect 1995-96, pres. 1997-99), London Math. Soc., Math. Assn. Am., Am. Math. Soc. (mem. coun. 1994-96, chmn. policy com. on meetings and confs. 1994-96, mem. nominating com. 1997—), Can. Math. Soc. (bd. mem. at large 1997—). Avocation: running. Office: U Nebr Dept Math Lincoln NE 68588-0130 Office Phone: 402-472-7248. E-mail: swiegand@math.unl.edu.

WIEHL, LIS W., law educator, legal analyst; b. Seattle, Aug. 9, 1961; d. Richard Lloyd and Inga (Wolfsberg) W.; children: Jacob, Danielle. JD, Harvard U., 1987; MA, U. Queensland, Brisbane, Australia, 1985; BA, Columbia U., 1983, U. Helsinki, Helsinki, Finland, 1978-79. Bar: Wash., US Dist. Ct. Wash., US Ct. Appeals (9th cir.). Assoc. Perkins Coie Law Firm, Seattle, 1987-90; fed. prosecutor U.S. Attys. Office, Seattle, 1990-95; assoc. prof. Law Sch., dir. of trial advocacy program U. Wash., Seattle, 1995—. Counsel Perkins Coie Law Firm, Seattle; exec. asst. U.S. atty., Seattle, summer 1998; prin. dep. chief investigative counsel to U.S. Ho. of Reps. Com. on Judiciary, 1998-99; legal commentator Nat. Pub. Radio, NBC News, 2000-01, Sta. KIRO (CBS) News, 2001-02, legal analyst Fox-TV News Channel, 2001-; vis. prof., law and journalism dir. NY Law Sch. Contbr. to law rev. U. Wash., 1987, U. Mich., 1998; contbr. articles to New York Times, ABA Jour., Jour. Trial Advocacy, Harvard Blackletter Law Jour. Treas. Lawyers Students Engaged in Resolution, Seattle, 1995-99. Recipient Distinction in Teaching award Harvard U., 1987, Emil Gumpert award A. Coll. Trial Lawyers, Richardson S. Jacobson award for Excellence in Tchg. Trial Advocacy Roscoe Pound Inst., 2001. Mem. Fed. Bar Assn., Order of the Coif, Phi Beta Kappa. Business E-Mail: lis.wiehl@foxnews.com.

WIELE, PATRICIA GIORDANO, interior decorator; b. Houston, Aug. 29, 1947; d. Conrad Joseph and Ellen Patricia (Condon) Schoppe; m. Natale Joseph Giordano, Apr. 17, 1971 (dec. Sept. 1989); children: Keith Joseph Giordano, Michael David Giordano, Ryan Peter Giordano, Todd Christopher Giordano; m. Fred J. Wiele, Jan. 16, 1994; 1 child, Suzanne stepchildren: Robin, Scott, Brian, Craig. Student, U. Houston, 1965-67, NYU, 1969. Prin. Patricia S. Giordano Interiors, Ridgefield, Conn., 1975-94, Patricia G. Wiele Interiors, Los Gatos, Calif., 1994—2000, Beauchene Interiors, 2000—. Pub. spkr. various floral design and horticulture workshops. Bd. dirs. Family and Children's Aid, Inc., Danbury, Conn., 1976—78, program and rev. and nominating coms., 1978, pres. aux., 1976—79; v.p. Twin Homeowners Assn., Ridgefield, Conn., 1978—79, chmn. founder area beautification, 1978; pres. East Ridge Mid. Sch. PTO, 1988—89, PTA, 1991—92; co-coord. Katrina and Rita Hurricane Relief, Catholic Charities, Houston, 2005. Recipient Excellence award, Fed. Garden Clubs. Conn., 1984, Tricolor award, Nat. Coun. State Garden Clubs, 1984, Aboreal award, 1984, Hort. Excellence award, 1984. Mem.: Caudatowa Garden Club (v.p. 1987—89, 1990—91, pres. 1991—93), Allied Bd. Trade. Republican. Roman Catholic. Avocation: flower arranging.

WIELENGA, DIXIE KAY, music educator; b. Sioux Center, Iowa, Mar. 17, 1960; m. Kevin Jay Wielenga, Aug. 17, 1978; children: Erin Marie Wielenga-Edkin, Abby Jo Wielenga-Van Kley, Autumn Rose, Olivia Kay, Zachary Jay, Nicolas Cade, Emily Celeste, Klayton Andrew. BA, Northwestern Coll., Orange City, Iowa, 1982, Dordt Coll., Sioux Center, 1979. Music tchr. Ireton Christian Sch., 1982—83, Orange City Christian Sch., Orange City, Iowa, 1983—2006; pvt. music studio Orange City, Iowa, 1978—2006. Music dir. 1st Christian Ref. Ch., Orange City, Iowa, 1989—2004. Republican. Home: 715 Delaware Ave SW Orange City IA 51041 Office: Orange City Christian Sch 604 3rd St SW Orange City IA 51041 Office Phone: 712-737-2274.

WIENER, VALERIE, state senator, writer, communications executive; BJ, U. Mo., 1971, MA, 1972, U. Ill., Springfield, 1974; postgrad., McGeorge Sch. Law, 1976—79. Prodr. Checkpoint Sta. KOMU-TV, Columbia, Mo., 1972-73; v.p., owner Broadcast Assocs., Inc., Las Vegas, 1972-86; pub. affairs dir. First Ill. Cable TV, Springfield, 1973-74; editor Ill. State Register, Springfield, 1973-74; prodr. and talent Nev. Realities Sta. KLVX-TV, Las Vegas, 1974-75; account exec. Sta. KBMI (now KFMS), Las Vegas, 1975-79; nat. traffic dir. six radio stas., Las Vegas, Albuquerque and El Paso, 1979-80; exec. v.p., gen. mgr. Stas. KXKS and KKJY, Albuquerque, 1980-81; exec. adminstr. Stas. KSET AM/FM, KVEG, KFMS and KKJY, 1981-83; press sec. U.S. Congressman Harry Reid, Washington, 1983-87; adminstrv. asst Friends for Harry Reid, Nev., 1986; press sec. U.S. Senator Harry Reid, Washington, 1987-88; owner Wiener Comm. Group, Las Vegas, 1988—; mem. Nev. Senate, Dist. 3 Clark County, 1996—, minority whip, 2001—; owner PowerMark Pub., 1998—. Author: Power Communications: Positioning Yourself for High Visibility (Fortune Book Club main selection 1994, Money Book Club selection 1995), Gang Free: Friendship Choices for Today's Youth, 1995, 2d edit., 1996, The Nesting Syndrome: Grown Children Living at Home, 1997, Winning the War Against Youth Gangs, 1999, Power Positioning: Advancing Yourself as The Expert, 2000 (Nat. awards), Power-Master HandBook Series, 2000— (seven nat. awards); contbg. writer The Pacesetter, ASAE's Comm. News. Sponsor Futures for Children, Las Vegas, Albuquerque, El Paso, 1979—83; mem. El Paso Exec. Women's Coun., 1981—83; media chmn. Gov.'s Coun. Small Bus., 1989—93; mem. Clark Coun. Sch. Dist. and Bus. Cmty. PAYBAC Spkrs. and Partnership Programs, 1989—, chair legis. com. on juvenile justice, 1999—2000; chair Commn. on Sch. Safety and Juvenile Violence, 1999—2000; various state and nat. legis. commn.s and coms.; vice chmn. Congl. Awards Coun., 1989—93, Gov.'s Commn. on Postsecondary Edn., 1992—96; mem. Nev. Technol. Crimes Task Force, 2001—03, Nev. Drug Commn., 1997—2000, Nev. Commn. on Aging, 1997—, Nev. Anti-Bullying Task Force, 2001—03, Gov.'s Task Force on Corrections, 2002, chair legis. com. on obesity, 2003—04; mem. VIP bd. Easter Seals, El Paso, 1982; med. dir. 1990 Gov.'s Conf. on Women; steering com. Youth Recovery Network, 2001—02; founding mem. Nev. team Action Healthy Kids; bd. dirs. BBB So. Nev., 1994—, Pub. Edn. Found., 1997—. Named Nev.'s Disting. Sr. Athlete, 2000, Outstanding Vol., United Way, El Paso, 1983, SBA Nev. Small Bus. Media Adv. of Yr., 1992, Disting. Sr. Athlete in Nev., 2000, So. Nev. Health Care Policy Hero, 2003, Nev. Legislator of Yr., Soc. Pub. Health Educators, 2004; named one of 27 Healthy Sch. Heroes in U.S., 2002; named to Hall Fame, Leadership Las Vegas, 2006; recipient 165 Comm. awards, 1989—, Outstanding Achievement award, Nat. Fedn. Press Women, 1991, Disting. Leader award, Nat. Assn. Cmty. Leadership, 1993, Gold medals in fitness and weightlifting, Nev. Sr. Olympics, 1998—2003, 2005, Gold medals in swimming, 2002—03, 2005, Walking Silver medal, 2005, Outstanding Women Adv. for Edn. award, Va. Commonwealth U., 2000, Internat. Cmty. Svc. award, Internat. New Thought Alliance, 2001, Winner Nev. 100 Fitness Challenge, Nev. State Legis. Session, 2005. Mem. Nat. Assn. Women Bus. Owners (media chmn., nat. rep. So. Nev. 1990-91, Nev. Adv. of Yr. award 1992), Nev. Press Women, Nat. Spkrs. Assn., Small Pubs. Assn. N.Am., Dem. Press Secs. Assn., El Paso Assn. Radio Stas., U.S. Senate Staff Club, Las Vegas C. of C. (Circle of Excellence award 1993), Soc. Profl. Journalists. Democrat. Avocations: reading, writing, fitness and weighlifting training and competition, public speaking, community involvement. Office: 1500 Foremaster Ln Ste 2 Las Vegas NV 89101-1150

WIENS, ANN, artist, writer, editor, art critic; East Coast editor, then sr. editor, and editor New Art Examiner, 1991—98, art critic New City, 1998—2000; contbr. articles to Art and Antiques, Chicago Magazine, CS, dialogue, New City, Chicago Reader, Chicago Collection; exhibits paintings in numerous group and solo shows throughout the Midwest and East Coast, represented by Byron Roche Gallery, Chgo. Mem.: Chgo. Art Critics Assn. Address: 2010 W Eastwood Ave Chicago IL 60625 Office Phone: 312-344-8631. E-mail: a.wiens@comcast.net.

WIER, LEANNE M., life sciences educator; b. San Antonio, Tex., Aug. 29, 1977; adopted d. Glen W. and Shirley Diane Latimer Wier. BS in Agrl. Devel., Tex. A&M U., College Station, 2000; MS Animal Sci., Okla. State U., Stillwater, 2004. Lab. technician Okla. State U., Stillwater, 2001—05; lab. tech. Ultimate Genetics, Franklin, Tex., 2000—01; prof. Rose State Coll., Midwest City, Okla., 2005—. Lab. tech. OvaGenix, Bryan, Tex., 2001—05. Co-chair food ct. RSC Global Okla., Midwest City, Okla., 2006. Grantee, Rose State Coll., 2006—. Mem.: Nat. Sci. Tchrs. Assn., Classic Motorcycle and Scooter Riders Okla., Phi Kappa Phi. Achievements include research in evaluation of gene expression during development of the neonatal porcine uterus using suppression subtractive hybridization. Home: 9712 S Bryant Terrace Oklahoma City OK 73160 Office: Rose State College 6420 SE 15th Street Midwest City OK 73110 Office Phone: 405-733-7553. E-mail: lwier@rose.edu.

WIER, PATRICIA ANN, publishing executive, consultant; b. Coal Hill, Ark., Nov. 10, 1937; d. Horace L. and Bridget B. (McMahon) Norton; m. Richard A. Wier, Feb. 24, 1962; 1 child, Rebecca Ann. BA, U. Mo., Kansas City, 1964; MBA, U. Chgo., 1978. Computer programmer AT&T, 1960-62; lead programmer City of Kansas City, Mo., 1963-65; with Playboy Enterprises, Chgo., 1965-71, mgr. systems and programming, 1971; with Ency. Britannica, Inc., Chgo., 1971—; v.p. mgmt. svcs. Ency. Britannica USA, 1975-83, exec. v.p. adminstrn., 1983-84; v.p. planning and devel. Ency. Britannica, Inc., 1985, pres. Compton's Learning Co. divsn., 1985; pres. Ency. Britannica (USA), 1986-91, Ency. Britannica N.A., 1986—94; exec. v.p. Ency. Britannica, Inc., 1986-94; pres. Ency. Britannica N.Am., 1986—94; mgmt. cons. pvt. practice, Chgo., 1994—. Cons. pvt. practice, Chgo., 1994—; bd. dirs. Alcas Corp., Mannatech Inc. Life mem. coun. Grad. Sch. Bus., U. Chgo.; mem. bd. regents Lewis U. Mem. Direct Selling Assn. (bd. dirs. 1984-93, chmn. 1987-88, named to Hall of Fame 1991), Women's Coun. U. Mo. Kansas City (hon. life) Com. 200, The Chgo. Network. Roman Catholic. Office: Patricia A Wier Inc 175 E Delaware Pl Ste 8305 Chicago IL 60611-7748 Personal E-mail: wier@prodigy.net.

WIERSEMA, DONNA SANDERS, science educator; b. Houston, May 26, 1944; d. Leslie Eugene and Muriel Theresa Sanders; m. Vernon Lee Wiersema, Aug. 27, 1968; children: Kimberly, Geoffrey, Nicholas, Aimee. BS in Biology, U. Houston, Tex., 1967, MS in Biology, 1969; MBA, U. Houston, Tex.; MT (ASCP), Vet.'s Hosp./Baylor Coll. Medicine, Houston, 1974. Rsch. technician Vet.'s Adminstrn. Hosp., Houston, 1963—67; rsch. asst. U. Houston Grad. Sch., 1967—69, Tex. Rsch. Inst. Mental Sci., Houston, 1969—70; sr. med. technologist St. Luke's Episcopal Hosp., Houston, 1974—82; instr. microbiology/biology Houston C.C., 1987—. Chairperson gen. biology textbook subcom. Houston C.C., 1992—97, chairperson microbiology textbook subcom., 1997—. Co-editor: book Microbiology Lab Manual, 1997—. Libr. Houston Orchid Soc.; vol. Leukemia Soc., Houston. Mem.: Tex. Jr. Coll. Tchrs. Assn., Human Anatomy & Physiology Soc., Am. Soc. Microbiology. Republican. Avocations: gardening, painting, birds, antiques, astronomy. Office: Houston CC Southwest Coll 10141 Cash Rd Ste S-113 Stafford TX 77477

WIERWILLE, MARSHA LOUISE, elementary school educator; b. Springfield, Ohio, Mar. 19, 1951; d. Eugene Junior and Donna Catherine (Bodine) Randall; m. Bob Edward Wierwille, June 14, 1975; children: Benjamin Joseph Reuben, Jeremiah James Eugene, Samuel John Philip, Adam Joel David. BS, Ohio State U., 1973; MEd, Wright State U., 1976; postgrad., U. Dayton, Ohio, 1982, U. Dayton, 1984, postgrad., 1987, Coll. of Mt. St. Joseph, summer, 1985, postgrad., 1986. Cert. elem. edn. tchr., curriculum supr., Ohio. Tchr. 1st grade New Bremen (Ohio) Sch., 1973-76, tchr. 2d grade, 1976—. Mem. NEA, Ohio Edn. Assn., Western Ohio Edn. Assn., New Bremen Tchrs. Assn. (pres. 1976-77), Delta Kappa Gamma. Avocations: reading, walking, bicycling, travel. Office: New Bremen Sch 202 S Walnut St New Bremen OH 45869-1297

WIES, BARBARA, publishing executive, editor; b. Dec. 5, 1939; BA, U. Conn., 1961; student, New Sch. for Social Rsch., 1961-62. Product devel. Fearn Soya, Melrose Park, Ill., 1973-75; product devel. Modern Products, Milw., 1973-75; editor, pub. Bestways Mag., Carson City, Nev., 1977-89; pub. The Healthy Gourmet Newsletter, 1989-91, Fine Wine-Good Food Newsletter, 1991—; publicity dir. Nev. Artists Assn., 1994—; owner Gualala (Calif.) Galleries, 1989-90; assoc. pub., mgr. Edn. Range Mag., 1998—. Owner, operator cooking sch. Greensboro N.C. 1969-73; instr. Very Spl. Arts Nev., 1997. Author: Natural Cooking, 1968, Wok and Tempura, 1969, Japanese Home Cooking, 1970, The Wok, 1971, Super Soy, 1973, The Health Gourmet, 1981, International Healthy Gourmet, 1982; editor: Desert News, 2004—; one-woman show paintings Dolphin Gallery, Gualala, Calif., 1990, River Gallery, Reno, 1994; 2 women show 1992, 94, 96, Dolphin Gallery, Calif., 1994, solo exhbn. Nev. Artists Assn. Gallery, 1993, 95, 96, 97; featured artist Nev. State Libr., 1996, Silver State Gallery, Reno, 1998, West Nev. C.C., 1996, art show judge, 1997; restaurant critic Reno Gazette Jour., 1995-2001; editor, designer Nev. Episcopal Diocesan newsletter Desert Spirit, 2004—, Bishop's Staff, Episcopal Diocese of Nevada, 2005-06. Performer Nev. Arts sponsored Tumblewords, 2000—; staff assoc. Wilmington Children's Mus., NC; del. Nev. Episcopal Diocese Convention, 2002, Vestry St. Peter's Episcopal Ch., 2003—, sr. warden, 2005. Grantee Nev. Arts Coun., 2002; recipient First Place adult fiction Nev. State Lit. Co., 1995, First Place fiction State Lit. Comp., 1998, 2d Place fiction Writers Block; Nev. Arts Coun. fellow, 1999-2000. Mem. Nat. League Am. Pen Women (chair 1st and 2d ann. lit. competition Reno br., chairperson 1st Nat. Lit. award), Inst. Food Technologists, Pastel Soc. of the West Coast, Inst. Am. Culinary Profls.

WIESE, DENISE KAY, music educator; d. Bruce James and Janice Anita Smith; m. Paul Raymond Wiese, Dec. 14, 1991; 1 child, James Paul. BS in Music Edn., N.D. State U., 1984; MusM, U. St. Thomas, St. Paul, Minn., 1996. Tchr. music Chokio Alta. Pub. schools, Alberta, Minn., 1984—89, Fergus Falls Pub. Schs., Minn., 1989—. Recipient Heritage award, N.D. Gov., 1982. Mem.: NEA, Minn. Band Directors Assn, Minn. Music Edn. Assn.

WIESE, NEVA, critical care nurse; b. Hunter, Kans., July 23, 1940; d. Amil H. and Minnie (Zemke) W. Diploma, Grace Hosp. Sch. Nursing, Hutchinson, Kans., 1962; BA in Social Sci., U. Denver, 1971; BSN, Met. State Coll., 1975; MS in Nursing, U. Colo., Denvr, 1978; postgrad., U. N.Mex., 1986; PhD, Kennedy Western U., 1999. RN, N.Mex. Cardiac ICU nurse U. N.Mex. Hosp., Albuquerque; coord. critical care edn. St. Vincent Hosp., Santa Fe, charge nurse CCU, clin. nurse III intensive and cardiac care. Recipient Mary Atherton Meml. award for clin. excellence St. Vincent Hosp., 1986. Mem.: ANA. Home: 849 Rio Vista St Santa Fe NM 87501-1549

WIESENBERG, JACQUELINE LEONARDI, social sciences educator; b. West Haven, Conn., May 04; d. Curzio and Filomena Olga (Turrinziani) Leonardi; m. Russel John Wiesenberg, Nov. 23; children: James Wynne, Deborann Donna. BA, SUNY, Buffalo, 1970; postgrad., 1970-73, 80—. Interviewer, examiner U.S. Dept. Labor, New Haven, 1948-52; sec. W.I. Clark Co., Hamden, Conn., 1952-55; acct. VA Hosp., West Haven, 1956-60; acct.-commissary USAF Missle Site, Niagara Falls, N.Y., 1961-62; tchr. Buffalo City Schs., 1970-73, 79; acct. Erie County Social Svcs., Buffalo, 1971-73; lectr., 1973—. Contbr. articles to CAP, USAF mag. Capt., Nat. Found. March of Dimes, 1969—, com. mem. telethon, 1983-86; vol. VA, 1973—; den mother Boy Scouts Am., 1961-68; chmn. Meals on Wheels, Town of Amherst, 1975-76; leader, travel chmn. Girl Scouts U.S., 1968-77; mem. Nat. Congress Parents and Tchrs., 1957—; heart fund vol. Heart Assn., 1960-86; rep. Am. Diabetes Assn., 1994—, vol. diabetes collection, 1994-95; mem. Humane Soc. U.S., ASPCA, N.Y. Srs. Coalition. Mem. AAUW, NAFE, Internat. Platform Assn., Nat. Pks. and Conservation Assn., Am. Astrol. Assn., Nat. Arbor Day Found., Western N.Y. Conf. Aging, Nat. Geog. Soc., Wilderness Soc., Nat. Wildlife Fedn., Nat. Trust for Hist. Preservation, Nature Conservancy, Ctr. for Marine Conservation, Internat. Funds Animal Welfare, North Shore Animal League, The Nature Conservancy, The Libr. Congress, U. Buffalo Found., Pvt. Land Conservancy-Nat. Park Trust, Blue Planet Soc., U. Buffalo Alumni Assn., Epsilon Delta Chi, Alpha Iota.

WIESENBORN, CHARLENE M., science educator; b. Faulkton, S.D., Nov. 25, 1955; d. Leslie and Geraldine Hansen; m. William D. Wiesenborn, Sept. 27, 1980; children: Christina, Brent, Carly. BS, S.D. State U., Brookings, 1979. Tchr. sci. Beaver City Schs., Nebr., 1979—80, Mohave Valley Elem. Sch., Ariz., 1982—83, San Bernardino City Schs., Calif., 1984—91, Clark County Sch. Dist., Las Vegas, Nev., 1992—. Vol. coach Boulder City Recreation Dept., Colo., 1992—2000, Boulder City Little League, 2000—05. Named Jerrano Mid. Sch. Outstanding Tchr. of Yr., San Bernardino City Schs., 1989; grantee, State of Calif., 1990—91, Wells Fargo, 1998—99. Mem.: NEA, Clark County Sci. Tchrs. Assn., Nev. Sci. Tchrs. Assn., Nat. Sci. Tchrs. Assn. Avocation: softball. Home: 1410 Stacey Ln Boulder City NV 89005

WIESENFELD, BESS G., interior designer; b. Elizabeth, N.J., May 6, 1915; d. Morris and Rebecca (Sokolov) Gazevitz; m. Benjamin Wiesenfeld, Oct. 23, 1938 (dec.); children: Myra Judith Wiesenfeld Lewis, Elaine Phyllis Wiesenfeld Livingston, Ira Bertram (dec.), Sarah Ann Wiesenfeld Wasserman BFA, N.Y. Sch. Interior Design, 1982. Pres. Anasarca Corp., 1958—; real estate devel. Colonia, NJ, 1961—; pres. Carolier Lns., Inc., 1986—, BGW LLC, Bess & Co. Patron Met. Opera; sustaining mem. N.J. Symphony Orch. Mem.: AAUW, Am. Soc. Interior Designers (allied), Friends of Music at Princeton, Friends of Art Mus. Princeton, N.J., Mus. Modern Art, Met. Mus. Art. Jewish. Home: 374 New Dover Rd Colonia NJ 07067-2713 also: 2600 S Ocean Blvd Palm Beach FL 33480-5484

WIEST, DIANNE, actress; b. Kansas City, Mo., Mar. 28, 1948; Student, U. Md. Appeared in numerous plays including Ashes (off-Broadway), 1976, Leave It to Beaver is Dead, The Art of Dining (Obie award, 1979, Theatre World award 1983), Bonjour La Bonjour, Three Sisters, Serenading Louie (Obie award, 1983), Othello, After the Fall, Heartbreak House, Our Town, and Hunting Cockroaches, 1987, In the Summer House, 1993, Blue Light, 1994, Memory House, 2005, Third, 2005; appeared in films including It's My Turn, 1980, I'm Dancing as Fast as I Can, 1982, Independence Day, 1982, Footloose, 1984, Falling in Love, 1984, The Purple Rose of Cairo, 1985, Hannah and Her Sisters, 1986 (Acad. award for Best Supporting Actress 1987), Radio Days, 1987, Lost Boys, 1987, September, 1987, Bright Lights, Big City, 1988, Parenthood, 1989 (Acad. award nominee), Cookie, 1989, Edward Scissorhands, 1990, Little Man Tate, 1991, Cops and Robbersons, 1994, The Scout, 1994, Bullets Over Broadway, 1994 (Golden Globe award Best Supporting Actress-Drama 1995, Acad. award for Best Supporting Actress 1995), Drunks, 1995, The Birdcage, 1996, The Associate, 1996, Practical Magic, 1998, The Horse Whisperer, 1998, Portofino, 1999, I Am Sam, 2001, Dr. Rey!, 2002, (voice) Robots, 2005; TV appearances include The Wall, 1982, The Face of Rage, 1983, Simple Life of Noah Dearborn, 1999, The 10th Kingdom, 2000.

WIGFIED-PHILLIP, RUTH GENIVEA, genealogist, writer; b. Couer d' Alene, Idaho, Dec. 1, 1918; d. Arthur and Jenivea Caroline (Crisp) Wigfield; m. Milton Fred Phillip, May 14, 1942 (dec. Nov., 1984); children: Rochelle Ruth, Gloria Genivea, Nancy Lenore, Douglas Fred, Andrea Arleen. BA, U. Montana, Missoula, 1939; registered genealogist, Augustine Genealogy Sch., Torrance, Calif., 1985, Desc. of William the Conquerer, 1997, Desc. of Companion of William Conquerer, 1997. Med. technician Deaconess Hosp., Great Falls, Mont., 1939-42; social worker Mont. State Welfare Dept., Helena, 1944-46; musical instr. Mont. Music Tchrs. Assn., Great Falls, 1947-62, Missoula, 1962-72; genealogy rschr. Phillip Heritage House, Missoula, 1962-66, writer, author, 1972—. Author, editor: (5 newsletters on genealogy) Wigfield Genealogy, 1972—, Crisp Genealogy, 1981—, Lipscomb Genealogy, 1981, Martin Genealogy, 1981, New Race, 1985—. Mem. Immanuel Luth. Ch., Sunday sch. supt., 1965-72; sec. Mont. State Music Tchrs. Union, 1969-71. Recipient music scholarship Harlowtown Music Dept., Harlowtown, Mont., 1932-35. Mem. DAR (regent Bitterroot chpt. 1973-75, state Indian chmn. 1976-90, 25 yr. h on. award Bitterroot chpt. 1997), Guild of St. Margaret of Scotland (grand dame Mont., 1986—), Eastern Star (organist), Rebecca Lodge (organist). Avocations: bridge, garden club, travel, fishing, golf. Home and Office: Phillip Genealogy Heritage House 605 Benton Ave Missoula MT 59801-8633

WIGGERS, NANCY RHEA, education educator; b. Miss., Jan. 3, 1963; d. Rhea E. David and Frances E. Rhea; m. Frank T. Wiggers, Sept. 7, 1985 (div. Feb. 15, 2006); children: Maxey Rhea, Mary Keith, John David. BA, Delta State U., Cleveland, iss., 1984; MA, U. Miss., University, Miss., 1985, PhD, 1995. Lic. Teacher Miss. Dept. of Edn., 1986. Coord. intensive english program U. Miss., 1987—98, instr., 1988—89, Oxford City Sch., Miss., 1998—99; asst. prof. U. Miss., 2000—. Author: (book review) Am. Language Jour.; contbr. articles to profl. jours. Mem. U. Miss. Mus., 2003—06. Mem.: ASCD, TESOL, Phi Delta Kappa (pres. um chpt. 2005—06). Avocations: reading, music, cycling, golf, travel. Office: Univ Miss Guyton Hall University MS 38677 Office Phone: 662-915-7350. Office Fax: 662-915-6718. E-mail: nwiggers@olemiss.edu.

WIGGINS, DOROTHY L., retired primary school educator; b. Auburn, N.Y., Sept. 6, 1935; d. Kenneth Howard and Frances Emma Lefavor; m. Richard James Wiggins; children: Richard Jr., Robin, Marc. BA, SUNY, Brockport, 1956; M in Elem. Edn., SUNY, Oswego, 1976. Kindergarten tchr. Red Creek (N.Y.) Ctrl. Sch., 1956—94; ret., 1994. Bd. dirs., Literacy Vols., NY, 1999. Named Tchr. of the Yr., Wayne County Tchrs. Assn. Mem.: Butler Historical Preservation Soc. (town historian 2005—, sec. 2002—), Lioness Club (past pres.), Delta Kappa Gamma (past pres.). Avocations: reading, playing piano and organ, crossword puzzles, jigsaw puzzles. Home: 4885 Butler Center Rd Wolcott NY 14590

WIGGINS, GLORIA, not-for-profit developer, television producer; b. NYC, Jan. 17, 1933; d. John and Gladys (Jones) Pruden; m. Albert Wiggins, Jan. 15, 1954 (dec. Aug. 1982); children: Michael, Teresa. BA, Richmond Coll., S.I., N.Y.; MA, SUNY, Albany. Lic. practical nurse. Project dir. Suffolk County Black History Assn., Smithtown, NY, 1982; pres., chair, founder Zamanii Internat. Devel. Corp., Central Islip, NY, 1983—; chair, founder Ikeda Mandela Uhuru Cultural Ctr., Inc., Central Islip, NY, 1991—; LPN, 1952—. Chair Univ. Sons and Daus. of Ethiopia, Deer Park, N.Y., 1990-91. Prodr., artist: pub. access TV Celebration of Kwanzaa, 1993 (grant, 1993); prodr.: Living Arts, 1994 (grant, 1994); prodr.: (exhibit) Adventure to the Homeland, 1995 (grant, 1995), African Women/African Art, 1992 (grant, 1992), 2d Roots Internat. Homecoming Festival, 1998, Women Achievers of 1998, Black History Celebration Senegal, 1999, We Sing America, 2000, International Poets, 2000, Positive Images, 2000, African American Couples in the Arts, 2000, Public Library Exhibits, 2000, TV Public Access, 2001, African Americans in West Africa, Celebration of Black History Month, 2001, (TV pub. access program of Senegalese in N.Y.) A Naming Ceremony, (pub. access TV) 10th Birthday Celebration Pow Wow, 2002, TV Pub. Access programs 100th Birthday Celebration, 2002, African Immigrants in Harlem, 2003, Smithtown Art Exhibit, Sr. Citizen Art Exhibit, Nigerian Art Exhibit, 2003, West African Photography Exhibit, Ikeda Mandela Uhoru Cultural Ctr., 2003, The Art of Romare Bearden, TV Pub. Access, 2004, Exceptional Black Scientist Exhibit, Ikeda Mandela Uhoru Cultural Ctr., Inc., 2005, Nigerian Art Exhibit, photography exhibit, 2005; author (poem) Man of Two Worlds (prize, 2001). Pres. Mariners Harbor Tenant Assn., S.I., N.Y., 1968-70; vol. Peace Corps, 1980, Peace Corps, 1979. Named Donor of Yr., Help Hospitalized Vets., 2002; recipient Editors Choice award, Internat. Libr. Photography, 1998, Poet of Yr. medallion and Diamond Homer trophy, Famous Poets Soc., 1999, Internat. Poet Merit award, Internat. Soc. Poets African Woman, 2002, cert. of recognition, L.I. Hall of Fame, 2002, Famous Poets Soc. award Proud to Belong, 2004; grantee Chase Manhattan Bank, 1996, N.Y. Decentralization Coun. on the Arts, 1987—93, Suffolk County Office of Cultural Affairs, 1987—2002, 2002. Mem.: NAEIR, Smithsonian, Ikeda Mandela Uhucu Cultural Ctr. Inc., Nat. Tree Arbor Found., Zamani Internat. Devel. Corp. (life). Avocations: art, television production, swimming, writing, community service. Home: 248 Tree Ave Central Islip NY 11722-2745 Office Phone: 631-234-2533. Personal E-mail: mybang2003@yahoo.com. Business E-Mail: gwiggins@suffolklib.ny.us.

WIGGINS, IDA SILVER, elementary school educator; b. Bklyn., Apr. 23; d. Joseph C. and Alice V. (Carter) Silver; m. G. Franklin Wiggins, Dec. 27, 1955; children: Bryan Franklin, Sharon-Amy. BS, NYU, 1955, MA, 1966; D Christian Letters (hon.), Shaw Divinity Sch., Raleigh, N.C., 1988. Cert. tchr., N.Y. Tchr. Durham (N.C.) County Pub. Sch., 1955-56, Johnston County Pub. Sch., Clayton, N.C., 1956-60; ednl. cons. Child Care Ctr., N.Y., 1960-61; tchr. Lakeland Cen. Schs., Shrub Oak, N.Y., 1961-91, Hudson Valley Christian Acad., Mahopac Falls, N.Y., 1991—. Tchr. adv. panel Silver Burdett Pub. Co., Morristown, N.J., 1987-88; mem. lang. arts task force, elem. math com., social studies curriculum com. Lakeland Cen Schs., 1989—; bd. dirs. Tutorial Program, Peekskill, 1986—. Writer: (choral reading) Martin Luther King, Jr., 1970. Life mem. Peekskill Hosp. Aux., 1980; former bd. mem. Peekskill YWCA, 1982, Peekskill Mus., 1988; life mem. NAACP, Peekskill, 1989; trustee Shaw U., Raleigh, N.C.; former bd. dirs. Hudson Valley Hosp. Found. Mem. AAUW, Am. Fedn. Tchrs., N.Y. State United Tchrs., Lakeland Fedn. Tchrs., Nat. Black Child Devel. Inst., Nat. Coun. Negro Women, Blacks in Govt. (life W. Point chpt.), The Links, Inc., Delta Kappa Gamma, Alpha Kappa Alpha. Baptist. Home: 1282 Maple Ave Peekskill NY 10566-4853

WIGGINS, KAREN SUE, education educator, counselor; b. Houston, Tex., June 30, 1953; d. Jack Myrl Townsend and Elsie Jane Townsend (Head); m. Kenneth Lyle Wiggins, Dec. 30, 1994; children: Townsend Cade Norris, Adam Ryan. BSc in elem. edn., SW Tex. State U., 1971—77; MSc in edn., U. of Houston Clear Lake, 1982—84; PhD in human services, Capella U., 1997—2001. Cert. Tex. Sch. Counselor State Bd. for Educator, 2001, Reading Specialist State Bd. for Educator Cert., Tex., 1984, Generic Spl. Edn. Classroom Tchr. State Bd. for Educator Cert., Tex., 2000, Elem. Tchr. State Bd. for Educator Cert., Tex., 1977, Basic CRT Cert. Nat. Orgn. of Victims Assistance, Wash. DC, 2003, cert. Irlen Screener Irlen Scotopic Sensitivity Screening, Calif., 2003. Tchr. Aldine Ind. Sch. Dist., Houston, 1977—80, Dallas Ind. Sch. Dist., 1980—81, Pasadena Ind. Sch. Dist., Tex., 1982—86, Big Bend C.C., Grafenwhoer, Germany, 1986—88, Pasadena Ind. Sch. Dist., Tex., 1988—91, Clear Creek Ind. Sch. Dist., League City, Tex., 1991—99; sch. counselor Galveston Ind. Sch. Dist., Tex., 1999—; adj. prof. dept. of edn. U. of St. Thomas, Houston, 2002—; adj. prof. LeTourneau U., Houston, 2003—. Mem.: ACA, Nat. Orgn. of Victims Assistance, Tex. Sch. Counselor Assn., Am. Sch. Counselor Assn., Tex. Counseling Assn.

WIGGINS, MARIANNE, writer; b. Lancaster, Pa., 1947; m. Salman Rushdie, 1988 (div. 1993); 1 child. Prof. English U. Southern Calif., 2005—. Author: (novels) Babe, 1975, Went South, 1980, Separate Checks, 1984, Herself in Love and Other Stories, 1987, John Dollar, 1989, Bet They'll Miss Us when We're Gone: Stories, 1991, Eveless Eden, 1995 (nominee Orange prize, 1991), Almost Heaven, 1998, Evidence of Things Unseen (nominee for Nat. Book award, 2003). Recipient Whiting award, Nat. Endowment for the Arts Grant, Janet Heidinger Kafka prize. Office: USC Bldg THH 404 3551 Trousdale Pkwy Los Angeles CA 90089-0354

WIGGINS-ROTHWELL, JEANINE ELLEN, artist; b. Jacksonville, Fla., Apr. 15, 1967; d. Otis K. Wiggins and Minnie Lois (Odem) Martin; m. John Joseph Rothwell, Jan. 2, 1993. Student, Fla. CC, 1984, 85, U. Ga., 1985; BFA in Painting, U. Fla., 1995. Freelance illustrator Earth Art, Inc., Gainesville, Fla., 1990—; airbrush artist Shade Tree Creations, Inc., Gainesville, 1995, Cain Studios, Inc., Gainesville, 1994; artist, art dir. Themeworks, Inc., High Springs, Fla., 1997-98; art tchr. Flagler County Sch. Bd., 2000—. Horizons, 1995, Salamander, 1994 (Best in the West 1st pl. award, 1984); painter set design: (films) Spunk, 1994. Donater art works and graphic illustrations Artitorium Coop. Gallery, Gainesville, 1988, 1989, Dance Alive, Gainesville, 1994, 1995, Greens Alachua's Celebration Diversity, Gainesville, 1994; artist, rep. women's issues NOW, 1996. Recipient 1st pl. Sunday Afternoon with Artist, Flagler County Art League, 2001, Spring Art Show, Millenium Art Guild, 2002; scholar, Lions Club, 1984. Democrat. Avocations: swimming, canoeing, dance, camping, writing. Home: 615 NW 9th Ave Gainesville FL 32601 Personal E-mail: jrothwell36@yahoo.com.

WIGGLEWORTH, MARGARET, property manager; b. Potomac, Md. Student, U. Md. Staff mem. judiciary com. and govtl. affairs com. Senator Charles McC. Mathias, Jr., Md., 1980—85; asst. dir. nat. affairs NPR, 1985—87; exec. dir. U.S. Coalition Svc. Industries, Inc., 1987—98; pres., CEO Colliers Internat. Property Consultants USA Inc., Boston, 1998—. Office: Colliers Internat Property Consultants USA Inc 20th Fl 50 Milk St Boston MA 02109

WIGGS, SHIRLEY JOANN, retired secondary school educator; b. Johnston County, N.C., Nov. 6, 1940; d. William H. and Sallie P. (Barden) Wiggs. BA, Atlantic Christian Coll., 1963; postgrad., Duke U., 1966, East Carolina U., 1979-80; grad., Newspaper Inst. Am. Tchr. pub. schs., South Hill, Va., 1963-64; tchr. lang. arts and social studies Glendale Chapel H.S., Kenly, N.C., 1964-65, Benson (N.C.) H.S., 1965-69; tchr. advanced placement English, lang. arts, journalism South Johnston H.S., Four Oaks, N.C., 1969-96, chairperson dept. lang. arts, 1971-83; ret., 1996; historian, 2003—04. Evaluator profl. books Allyn and Bacon, Inc., 1974, 79; yearbook judge Columbia Scholastic Press Assn., 1986-92, yearbook advisor, 1980-94. Sunday Sch. tchr. 1st Bapt. Ch., Smithfield, N.C., 1964-66, assoc. supt. young people's dept., 1964-67, scholarship chair, 1987-91, ch. libr., 1992-2004, tutor, 2000, Clothes' Closet dir., 2004; dir. WMU, 2004; chmn. Keep Johnston County Beautiful, 1979-81. Named Woman of Yr., Atlantic Christian Coll., 1962; recipient Internat. Cheerleading Found. award 1972, Acad. Booster Club award, 1986. Mem. NEA, Nat. Coun. Tchrs. English, Assn. Supervision and Curriculum Devel., N.C. Assn. Educators), N.C. English Tchrs. Assn. (dir. dist. 12, 1980-85), Johnston County Assn. Educators (pres. 1979), Johnston Co. Retired Tchrs Assn. (historian 2003—). Home: 102 E Sanders St Smithfield NC 27577-4211

WIGHT, JULIA HELEN, secondary school educator; b. Rochford, England, May 19, 1945; arrived in US, 1965; d. Sigmund and Marion St. Bride Kohn; m. Richard Gordon Wight, June 8, 1968. BA in Art History, U. Wash., 1974, EdM, 1976. Cert. tchr. Montessori, 1965. Tchr. N.W. Montessori Sch., Seattle, 1966—74, asst. prin., 1976—79, prin., 1979—85, tchr., 1985—87; tutor Seattle, 1987—90; tchr. Eton Sch., Bellevue, Wash., 1991—93; pres. Who's New Internat. Women's Club, Panama City, Panama, 1995—98. Cons., lectr. in field. Author: (children's story) Beyond Time & Place. Mem.: Pacific N.W. Montessori Tchrs. Assn. (pres.). Democrat. Episcopalian. Avocations: walking, watercolors, languages, gardening, sewing. Home: 4163 Beach Dr SW # 301 Seattle WA 98116

WIGHT, PATRICIA ANNE, neuroscience educator; b. Providence, June 10, 1955; d. Howard Morrison Jr. and Nancy Lee (Phillips) W.; m. Mark David Crew, Jan. 15, 1988; children: Joseph David, Kyle Douglas, Michael Patrick. BS, U. Calif., Irvine, 1978; PhD, U. Calif., Riverside, 1988. Rsch. asst., tchg. asst. U. Calif., Riverside, 1981—88; postdoctoral fellow UCLA, 1988—92; asst. prof. U. Ark. Med. Scis., Little Rock, 1992—99, assoc. prof., 1999—2006, prof., 2006—. Contbr. articles to profl. jours. Mem. AAAS, Am. Soc. Neurochemistry, Am. Physiol. Soc., Soc. for Neurosci., Sigma Xi. Roman Catholic. Avocations: hiking, skiing, swimming. Office: U Ark Med Scis 4301 W Markham St # 750 Little Rock AR 72205-7101 Office Phone: 501-686-5366. E-mail: pwight@uams.edu.

WIGHTMAN, ANN, lawyer; b. Dayton, Ohio, July 29, 1958; d. William L. and Mary Ann (Lamb) W. AB, Ohio U., 1980; JD, Case Western Res. U., 1984. Bar: Ohio 1984, U.S. Dist. Ct. (so. dist.) Ohio 1984, U.S. Ct. Appeals (6th cir.) 1991, U.S. Ct. Appeals (7th cir.) 1992, U.S. Supreme Ct. 1993. Assoc. Smith & Schnacke, Dayton, 1984-89; sr. assoc. Faruki Gilliam & Ireland, Dayton, 1989-91, ptnr., 1991—. Adj. prof. U. Dayton Sch. Law, 1988-93; chmn. Artemis House, Inc., Dayton, 1988-90, bd. dirs., 1985-95; arbitrator Am. Arbitration Assn.; mem., bd. dirs. Legal Aid Soc. Dayton, Inc., 1996—; bd. dirs. Impact Weekly. Mem. Vol. Lawyer's Project, Dayton, 1988-96; mem. Challenge 95 Task Force, Dayton, 1989-90, Up and Comer, Dayton, 1990; vol. arbitrator Montgomery County Common Pleas Ct., 1989—; bd. dirs. ACLU of Ohio Found., 1991-94; mem. Leadership, Dayton, 1992. Mem. ABA (trial and environ. sects.), Ohio Bar Assn., Phi Beta Kappa. Office: Faruki Gilliam & Ireland 10 N Ludlow Sbl Ste 500 Dayton OH 45402-1854 Home: 1632 Ladera Trl Dayton OH 45459-1402

WIGHTMAN, SHARON LEILANI, librarian; d. Frank Bacon and Hazel Elizabeth Drake; m. James Ernest Wightman, Oct. 9, 1965; children: Wendy Joy, Kim Diane, Dawn Lyn, Robin Gail. BS in Liberal Arts, Cazenovia Coll., 1995; MLS, Syracuse U., 1999. Cert. pub. libr. N.Y. State. Tailor, owner Wightman Tailoring, Cazenovia, NY, 1982—88; admissions rep. Cazenovia Coll., 1988—95; sales lead coord. Inchcape Testing, Cortland, NY, 1995—97; children's libr. Fayetteville (N.Y.) Free Libr., 1999—2001; libr. ITT Tech. Inst., Liverpool, 2001—. Notary pub. N.Y. Dept. of State, N.Y.C., 2000—; bd. trustees Ctrl. N.Y. Libr. Resources Coun., 2006—. Author: (online publ.) Digital Libraries Initiative, 1998. Bd. dirs. 4-H Found., Madison County, 2001—04. Named Employee of the Quar., ITT Tech. Inst., 2002, Employee of the Yr., 2002; recipient Achievement in Profl. Devel., Reference Adult Svc. Sect., N.Y. Libr. Assn., 2004. Mem.: ALA, AAUW, Am. Soc. Notaries, NY Libr. Assn., Librn. Unltd. (v.p. 2004—05, pres. 2005—). Republican. Avocations: travel, reading, gardening, surf fishing. Office: ITT Tech Inst 235 Greenfield Pkwy Liverpool NY 13088 Office Phone: 315-461-8000. Business E-Mail: swightman@itt.tech.edu.

WIGSMOEN, SUSAN CATANIA, elementary school educator; b. Chgo., Sept. 13, 1964; d. Anthony Edward and Susan Catherine (Kmetty) Catania; m. David Andrew Wigsmoen, July 10, 1993. BA, St. Xavier Coll., 1986; MA, St. Xavier U., 1995. Tchr. kindergarten Bridgeport Cath. Acad., Chgo., 1986—99; tchr. Luther Burbank Elem. Dist. 111, Ill., 2004—, reading specialist dist. III, 1999—2004. Mem. pub. rels. com. Epilepsy Found. of Greater Chgo. 1994. Mem. Ill. Assn. for Supervision and Curriculum Devel. Republican. Roman Catholic. Avocation: piano. Home: 8745 S Utica Ave Evergreen Park IL 60805-1034 Office Phone: 312-376-6223, 708-499-0838. Personal E-mail: schwigs@msn.com.

WIJNBERG, SANDRA S., professional services company executive; b. Aug. 1, 1956; BA English, UCLA; MBA, U. So. Calif., L.A. With Morgan Stanley & Co. Inc.; joined PepsiCo as v.p., treas., 1994; sr. v.p., CFO KFC Corp. Divsn.; sr. v.p., treas. Tricon Global Restaurants Inc, 1997—2000; sr. v.p., CFO Marsh & McLennan Cos., N.Y.C., 2000—. Bd. dirs. Pvt. Sector Coun., 2001—, Tyco Internat. Ltd., 2003—. Corp. adv. bd. N.Y.C. Ballet. Office: Marsh & McLennan Co 1166 6th Ave New York NY 10036*

WIK, JEAN MARIE (JEAN MARIE BECK), librarian, media specialist; b. Aitkin, Minn., Feb. 10, 1938; d. Herman Otto Beck and Ferdina Mathilda (Petersen) Kalt; m. Richard Lyle Wik, Aug. 17, 1958; children: Steven L., Lori Jo. BS, No. State U., Aberdeen S.D., 1963; MA, U. Minn., 1972; cert. in media arts, Mankato State U., 1974. Elem. tchr. Howard Hedger Sch., Aberdeen, S.D., 1958-62; tchr. spl. edn. Westwood Sch., Bloomington, Minn., 1963-64; elem. tchr. Washburn Sch., 1964-71; media generalist elem. elem. and secondary schs., 1972-85; media generalist Kennedy High Sch., Bloomington, 1985-96; fashion coord. Weekender Casual Wear, 1993—2001. Dir. Annehurst Curriculum Classifications System project Bloomington Schs., 1976-85, dist. media leadership position, 1990-92. Chmn. Christian Women's Club, 1972-74, area rep., 1981-85. Mem. NEA, Minn. Edn. Assn., Minn. Ednl. Media Assn. Avocations: songwriting, singing, public speaking for christian groups.

WIKARSKI, NANCY SUSAN, writer; b. Chgo., Jan. 26, 1954; d. Walter Alexander and Emily Regina (Wejnerowski) W.; m. Michael F. Maciekowich, Dec. 5, 1976 (div. Feb. 1985). BA, Loyola U., Chgo., 1976, MA, 1978; PhD, U. Chgo., 1990. Paralegal Winston & Strawn, Chgo., 1978-79; real estate analyst Continental Bank, Chgo., 1979-84, systems analyst, 1984-88, ops. officer, 1988-89, automation cons., 1989-92; systems mgr. PNC Mortgage Co. of Am., Vernon Hills, Ill., 1992-94; ind. cons., 1994—. Author: German Expressionist Film, 1990, The Fall of White City, 2002, Dime Anthology, 2004, Shrouded in Thought, 2005; book reviewer Murder Past Tense, 2000-02, Deadly Pleasures, 2003—. Fellow U. Chgo., 1987-90. Mem. Mystery Writers Am., Sisters in Crime, Mensa. Avocation: gardening.

WIKE, D. ELAINE, small business owner; b. Ridgecrest, Calif., Sept. 26, 1954; d. Robert G. and Jimmie Mae (Sallee) Field; m. Mike Wike, Oct. 14, 1978; children: Mike II, Angelina Elaine, William V., Danielle Elizabeth, Edward Lawrence, Windy Gale. Student, U. Houston, 1975—77. Legal sec. Morgan, Lewis & Bockius, Washington, 1977—78; legal asst. Alfred C. Schlosser & Co., Houston, 1972—77, 1978—81, Jerry Sadler, atty., Houston, 1982—83; founder, owner DEW Profl. & Bus. Svcs., Houston, 1979—; office mgr. Law Offices Mike Wike, Houston, 1983—. Contbr. poetry to publs. including Internat. Libr. of Poetry, 2001. Treas. Wilhelm Schole Parents Orgn, 1981—82; mem. Free, Inc.; vol. campaign worker Ron Paul for Congress and Reagan for Pres., 1975, 1976. Recipient 3d place, Nassau Bay Tex. Christmas Boat Lane Parade First Ann. Photography Contest, 1990. Mem.: Nat. Paralegal Assn., Am. Soc. Notaries, Nat. Assn. Female Execs., Nat. Notary Assn., Young Ams. for Freedom. Republican. Libertarian. Mem. Christian Ch. Office: 2421 S Wayside Dr Houston TX 77023-5318

WIKSTROM, LORETTA WERMERSKIRCHEN, artist; b. Willow River, Minn., Mar. 2, 1938; d. Jacob Joseph and Anna Bertha (Doege) Wermerskirchen; m. Donovan Carl Wikstrom, Aug. 16, 1958; children: Bradley Donovan, Kendra Kay, Brock Karl. Student, St. Paul Sch. of Art, 1956-57, U. Minn., 1957-58, Honolulu Acad. of Art, 1963-66, Dayton Art Inst., 1985-87. Exhibited in group shows at Sinclair Coll., 1985, Arts Venture, 1985, one-woman shows include Bevercreek Libr., 1986, City of Englewood, 1986. Vol. artist Boy Scouts Am., Charleston, SC, Minn., 1967—74; vol. artist, tchr. Girl Scouts U.S., O'Fallon, Ill., 1975—76; vol. art judge pub. elem., jr. and sr. HS, Charleston, Mascoutah, Ill., 1969—78, Ill. State Hist. Libr., Belleville, 1979, Belbrook (Ohio) HS, 1988, 1989. Recipient 2d pl., hon. mention, Nat. Nature and Wildfowl Show, 1987, hon. mention, Wyoming (Ohio) Pub. Arts Comm. show, 1987. Mem.: Dayton Soc. Painters and Sculptors, Beavercreek Creative Artists Assn. (sec. 1987—, v.p. 1988—90), St. Louis Artists Guild, Gateway East Artists Guild, Minn. Artists Assn., Charleston Artists Guild, Guild S.C. Artists. Home: 395 12 Oaks Trl Dayton OH 45434-5873 Personal E-mail: lwikstrom@aol.com.

WILBANKS, DONNA MAE, editor; b. Grubbs, Ark., Jan. 4, 1945; d. Aubrey Lee Wilbanks and Zelda Ford; children: Josephine D. Travinski, Peter L. Schemberger, Paul A. Schemberger. Co-owner Real Graphics, Vancouver, Wash., 1998—2005; editor and co-owner Ctrl. Oreg. Sr. Times, Bend, 2005—. Achievements include funded, designed and created Central Oregon Senior Times. Office: Central Oregon Senior Times 61535 S Hwy 97 #9-299 Bend OR 97702 Office Phone: (541) 788-9476. Business E-Mail: seniortimes@comcast.net.

WILBANKS, JANICE PEGGY, special education educator; b. Boaz, Ala., Oct. 20, 1962; d. Olen Toliver and Evelyne Ziddie Brown; m. Charles Ray Ledon Wilbanks Sr., Nov. 4, 1978; 1 child, Charles Ray Ledon Jr. AS cum laude, N.E. State Coll., 1992; BSc in Edn., Athens State Coll., 1994; MA, U. Ala., 1997. Spl. edn. tchr. State of Ga., Atlanta, 1994—, State of Ala., Montgomery, Ala., 1994—. EBD tchr. Pennville Elem., Summerville, Ga., 2002—05. Mem.: Ga. Assn. Edn. Baptist. Avocations: reading, gardening, swimming, painting. Home: 1801 Adamsburg Rd E Fort Payne AL 35967

WILBANKS, MARY, artist; b. Lexington, Ky., Aug. 31, 1940; d. Marino Francis and Louise Traynor Peyrefitte; m. Robery Leroy Wilbanks, May 7, 1959; children: Ann Wilbanks Scarandville, Ken. Student, Glassel Sch. of Art, Houston, 1975-80. Painting tchr. Phoenix Art Mus., 1980—84, Fine Arts Ctr.-Bemis Sch., Colorado Springs, 1984-87, Juvenile Detention Ctr., Houston, 1989-94; collage painting tchr. various locations, 1994—, Art League of Houston, 1994—. Presenter in field. One-woman shows include Goldesberry Gallery, Houston, 2004, Envision Gallery, Taos, N.Mex., 2005, LKG Contemporary, Scottsdale, Ariz., 2005, exhibitions include Art League, Houston, 1994, The Jung Ctr., 2001, Art-Art-Bo-Bart Gallery, Taos, 2002, Goldesberry Gallery, Houston, 2002—03, Cynthia Woody Gallery, 1998, Deloney-Newkirk Gallery, Santa Fe, N.Mex., 2003, Mo. Art Mus., 2003, Shorelines Gallery, Austin, Tex., 2006, represented in books including, Best of Watercolor-Painting Texture, 1998, Best of Watercolor III, 1999, Art and Healing, 1999, cover art, Collage Techniques, 1997. Active Big Bros.-Big Sisters, 1996—2002, Art League of Houston, 1994—. Recipient 1st award Rocky Mountain Nat., 1997, 30 awards nat. shows, 1990-99. Mem. (signature) Nat. Watercolor Soc., Watercolor USA Honor Soc., Watercolor Art Soc. Houston (faculty), Art League of Houston, Soc. Layerists. Democrat. Roman Catholic. Avocations: studying spanish, travel, sailing, yoga, hiking. Home and Office: 18307 Champion Forest Dr Spring TX 77379-3973

WILBER, CLARE MARIE, musician, educator; b. Denver, Mar. 21, 1928; d. Thomas A. and Kathleen M. (Brennan) O'Keefe; m. Charles Grady Wilber, June 14, 1952 (dec. 1998); children: Maureen, Charles, Michael, Thomas (dec.), Kathleen, Aileen, John Joseph. AB, Loretto Heights Coll., 1948; MS, Fordham U., 1950; MM, Colo. State U., 1972. Instr. biology and music various colls. and univs., 1951-83; mgr. Ft. Collins (Colo.) Symphony, 1969-81, exec. dir., 1981-85, exec. dir. emerita, 1985—; pvt. music instr. Ft. Collins, 1973—. Trustee Ft. Collins Symphony, 1986-95, mem. young artist competition com., 1985—. Composer Fantasie Romantique, 1972, Mass in D, 1980, Seascapes for Suzanne, 1988, Panoramas for Polly, 1990, Journeys for Jennifer, 1994, Augustine's Lament, 1996, Collage for Cynthia, 1997, Daydreams for Drew, 2001, An Air For Audrey, 2004 Ballads for Bailee, 2004-05. Mem. adv. coun. Ft. Collins H.S., 1972—74; mem. adv. bd. Children's Sch. of Sci., Woods Hole, Mass., 1965—95. Recipient AT&T Crystal Clef award, 1982; Clare Wilber award named in her honor, Ft. Collins Symphony, 1992. Mem. Ft. Collins Music Tchrs. Assn. (treas. 1984-90), Colo. State Music Tchrs. Assn., Music Tchrs. Nat. Assn. (cert. music tchr. 1978—), Marine Biol. Lab. Assocs., Cosmos Club (assoc.), Sigma Xi (assoc.), Delta Omicron (local chpt. pres. 1970-72, sec. 1988—, Spl. Svc. award 1974, Star of Delta Omicron award 1995). Republican. Roman Catholic. Home and Office: 900 Edwards St Fort Collins CO 80524-3824

WILBUR, CAROL ANNE, literature and language educator, researcher; b. Jacksonville, Fla., Jan. 1, 1948; d. Kenneth Wilbur and Stella Francis Yull; children: Leigha Elizabeth, Andrew Ryan. BA in English, Ft. Lewis Coll., 1970; MA in English, U. Mont., 1993. Tchr. John Evans Jr. H.S., Greeley, Colo., 1972—74, Lone Rock Sch., Stevensville, Mont., 1977—78, Missoula County Pub. Sch., Mont., 1978—. Asst. dir. U.S./China Initiative, 2003—05. Mem.: Mont. Assn. Tchrs. (pres. 1991—93, v.p. 1990—91, Western Dist. pres. 1986—90), Mont. Weavers Guild. Avocations: poetry, kayaking, fiber arts. Office: Hellgate HS 900 Southwest Higgins Missoula MT 59801 Office Phone: 406-728-2400.

WILBUR, COLLEEN PATRICIA, elementary school educator, principal; b. Detroit, July 20, 1949; d. John Martin and Rita Marie (Hurley) Cooney; m. Otis Gray Wilbur, Dec. 16, 1972; 1 child, John. BS, Kent State U., 1971; BA in Edn., Fla. Atlantic U., Boca Raton, Fla., 1983; student MS tng., ednl. leadership program, Nova Southeastern Univ., Ft. Lauderdale, Fla., 2001—. Cert. Early Childhood, Elem. Edn., Fla. Tchr. Merrell Day Sch., Lauderdale Lakes, Fla., 1978-83, St. Coleman Sch., Pompano Beach, 1983-94, St. Mark's Sch., Ft. Lauderdale, 1994—99, lower sch. prin., prek3 - grade 4, 1999—2005, head lower sch., 2005—. Peer tchr. St. Coleman Sch., 1987-88, 92-93, coord. grades kindergarten through 4, 1992-94. Named Tchr. of Yr., St. Coleman Sch., 1987—88. Mem.: Fla. Kindergarten Coun. (bd. dirs. 2003—). Avocations: gardening, sailing, gourmet cooking. Home: 6731 NW 23rd Ter Fort Lauderdale FL 33309-1405 Office: St Marks Sch 1750 E Oakland Park Blvd Fort Lauderdale FL 33334-5299 Business E-Mail: cwilbur@saintmarks.com.

WILBUR, DORA LYNN, elementary school educator; b. Bellevue, Ohio, May 10, 1963; d. Doris Mae and Ron Milburn (Stepfather). BS, Olivet Nazarene U., Kankakee, Ill., 1985; M, Ashland U., Ohio, 1999. Tchr. Herscher Sch. Dist., Ill., 1985—90, Margaretta Local Sch., Castalia, Ohio, 1990—91, Berlin-Milan Local Schools, Ohio, 1991—. Coach Berlin-Milan Local Sch., 1991—98. Vol. Habitat for Humanity, Norwalk, Ohio, 2006. Named Wal Mart Tchr. of Yr., 2006; recipient Presdl. award for Sci., Eisenhauer, 1998; fellow, Christa McAuliffe Found., 1998. Mem.: Ohio Edn. Assn., NEA. Office: Berlin-Milan Local Sch 140 S Main St Milan OH 44846 Office Phone: 419-499-2471. Personal E-mail: dwilbur@berlin-milan.org.

WILBUR, JANIS A., financial consultant, sales professional; b. Canadian, Tex., June 18, 1940; d. Harry Samuel Jr. and Margaret Hervey Wilbur; m. Martin Alfred Wasserman, Oct. 18, 1969 (div. Dec. 1981); 1 child, Paul Scott Wasserman. Student, U. Hawaii, 1958; BS in Commerce, Tex. Christian U., 1962. Cert. sr. advisor. Exec. asst. First Nat. Bank, Dallas, 1962-65, So. Union Gas, Dallas, 1965-69; adminstrv. sec. IBM, Armonk, N.Y., 1969-72; owner Leisure Sports Sys., Dallas, 1972-79; sec. to econometrics prof. So. Meth. U., Dallas, 1989-95; part time sales assoc. Neiman Marcus, Dallas, 1989—; registered rep., cert. sr. advisor First Dallas Securities, Dallas, 2003—, 2003—. Pub. (quarterly newsletter) The Fin. News RE-View, 1999. Vol. Am. Diabetes Assn., Dallas Crippled Children Soc., Am. Heart Assn.; mem. Women's Guild Bd. Am. Cancer Soc.; organizer ann. golf tournament benefiting Parkinson Disease; vol. Dallas Ct. Apptd. Spl. Advs., bd. planned giving program, 2002—; membership com. Buckner Orphans Home, 2000—01; mem. women's coun. Dallas Arboretum and Bot. Garden, 2000. Mem.: DAR (nat. com. chmn. on Americanism and manual for citizenship 1999, Literacy Challenge chmn. 2001—02, chaplain 2002—03, vice regent 2003—04, regent 2004—06, 2005—06, Michael Stoner chpt.), NAFE, Internat. Exec. Guild, First Dallas Alumni Club (charter), Park Cities Bapt. Ch. Women's Bible Study, Water Skiing Club, Dallas Skiing Club, Kappa Alpha Theta Alumni (v.p. 1989—99, pres. 2000—01, advisor 2002—, treas. 2005—06). Republican. Baptist. Avocations: tennis, bridge, skiing, cooking, water rafting, hiking. Home: 9563 Windy Knoll Dr Dallas TX 75243-7561 Office: First Dallas Securities 2905 Maple Ave Dallas TX 75201 Office Phone: 214-349-2561. Personal E-mail: janiswilbur@sbcglobal.net.

WILBUR, MARCIA KAORU, writer; d. Willard Leroy and Masayo Wilbur; children: Tina, Zack, Cordell, Alex Emmett Marian. AAS, Three Rivers, Norwich, CT, 1999—2000; BS, Ariz. State U., 1998—2002. Intern Free Software Found., Cambridge, Mass., 2002; ind. contractor/writer Aries Tech., Tempe, 2003—04; contract tech. writer NCS Pearson, Mesa, Ariz., 2004. Author: (book) Digital Millennium Copyright Act; author: (subject matter expert) (computer based curriculum) Linux Essentials; editor: (online directory) DMCA editor, (online journal) Computing Life; author: Binary Freedom/ System Toolbox. Com. mem. Digital Speech Project - FSF, Cambridge, Mass., 2002—03. Personal E-mail: aicra@well.com.

WILCOX, BONITA DIANE, middle school educator; b. Chgo., June 10, 1943; d. Joseph Peter Jenkins and Angeline (Bonnie) Alice Sullivan; m. Joseph Paul Wilcox, Feb. 20, 1965; children: Kelly Kimberly Quiring, Joseph Paul, Michael Eaves, Brian Boehm, Regan Marie Wilcox-Price. B of Language Arts in Secondary Edn., U. Kans., Lawrence, 1965. Lic. secondary tchr. Colo. Tchr. lang. arts South Mid. Sch., Aurora, 1967—75; dir. religious edn. St. Francis Assisi, Castle Rock, Colo., 1976—85; tchr. theatre arts Castle Rock Mid. Sch., 1989—. Sponsor Green Keepers Environment Club; creator, former sponsor Pen Pal Brigade. Dir.: (plays) Flowers for Algernon, Go Ask Alice, David and Lisa, Angel in the Night, And Then They Came for Me, The Outsiders, The Village Fable, Secret Garden, many others; contbr. articles to mags. Facilitator social justice issues Pax Christi, Highlands Ranch, Colo., 2005—06. Named Tchr. of Yr., Colo. Middle Level Theatre Arts, 2003. Green Party. Roman Catholic. Avocations: activism, mountain climbing, hiking, writing. Home: 4663 North Lariat Dr Castle Rock CO 80108 Office Phone: 303-387-1327. Personal E-mail: bd.wilcox@comcast.net.

WILCOX, CHARLENE DELORIS, retired elementary school educator; b. Muncie, Ind., Jan. 8, 1932; d. Otto Orlando and Leona Irene (Forrest) Long;m. Arnold Henry Wilcox, Apr.17, 1955; children: George H., Roberta Lynn Cooley, Arnold Long. Student, Mexico City Coll., 1952; BS in Edn., Ohio State U., 1954. Tchr. 3d grade Jackson (Mich.) Pub. Schs., 1954-56; tchr. grades 2 and 3 Wyandotte (Mich.) Pub. Schs., 1956-60; tchr. grade 4 Consolidated Schs. of Salem, N.H., 1961-62; tchr. grades 1, 2 and 4 Jackson (Mich.) Pub. Schs., 1963-86; ret. Mem. United Meth. Ch., mem. edn. com., 2001—. Mem.: NEA, AAUW (membership chmn. 1990—92, social chmn. 1992—93, program v.p. 2001—05), Ch. Women United, Assn. of Childhood Edn. (corr. sec. 1954—56), Jackson Edn. Assn., Mich. Edn. Assn., Am. Assn. Ret. Persons, Red Hat Soc., Job's Daus., Peace Coun. (sec. 1991—92), United Meth. Women (pres. 1992—94, rec. sec. 2001, 2004—05), Woman's Club of Jackson (corr. sec. 2001—, v.p. 2003—04, pres. 2004—05), Delta Kappa Gamma Soc. (internat. Beta Beta chpt. membership v.p. 2002—03, 2005—06), Alpha Gamma Delta (pres. 1953—54). Methodist. Avocations: travel, reading, sewing, swimming, quilting, crafts. Address: 3144 Cypress Ct Jackson MI 49201-8690

WILCOX, DIANE MARIE, educational psychologist, software designer; b. Cin., June 26, 1957; d. Herbert Arthur and Doris Ann Beard; m. Thomas Minshull Wilcox, Sept. 18, 1982; children: Alexandra Frances, Annika Marie. BBA in Bus. Mgmt., Coll. William and Mary, 1979; MA in Ednl. Psychology, U. N.C., 1994, PhD in Ednl. Psychology, 1997. Sales and tech. support corr. Tax Mgmt., Inc., Washington, 1980-82; dist. rep. Bur. Nat. Affairs, Inc., Washington, 1982-86; freelance computer graphic designer, editor Diane Wilcox & Assocs., San Rafael, Calif., 1986-91; instr. psychology King's Coll., Charlotte, N.C., 1995; pres. Mindforge, Inc., Burlington, N.C., 1996-98, Wilcox Instrnl. Media, LLC, Hillsborough, N.C., 1998—; instnl. design mgr. Autodesk, Inc., San Rafael, 2000—04; asst. prof. James Madison U., Harrisonburg, Va., 2004—. Designer ednl. CD-ROM Mindforge Fractions, 1998. Cons. for gifted and talented programs River Mill Charter Sch., Saxapahaw, N.C., 1999-2000; vol. art instr. Grady Brown ELem. Sch., Hillsborough, N.C., 1997-98. Mem. APA, Shenandoah Valley Soc. for Human Resource Mgmt., Assn. for Advancement of Computing in Edn. Avocations: art, music, dance. Office Phone: 540-568-6707. E-mail: wilcoxdm@jmu.edu.

WILCOX, HELENA MARGUERITA (RITA), music educator; b. Manhattan, Kans., Feb. 16, 1930; d. Virgil Otis Jones and Helena Mary Viers-Jones; children: Charles E., Marguerita E., Patricia A. MusB, State U. Iowa, 1952, MA, 1959. Cert. music tchr. Ariz., 1959, Calif., 1967, Jr. Coll. Calif., 1972. Pvt. kindergarten, Springerville, Ariz., 1959—60; art supr. Yuma (Ariz.) Elem. Sch. Dist., 1960—67; violin tchr. Ariz. Western Cmty. Coll., Yuma, 1965—67; string instrument tchr. Stockton (Calif.) Unified Sch. Dist., 1967—2002; Suzuki violin tchr. San Joaquin Delta Coll., Stockton, 1972—; musician Stockton (Calif.) Symphony, 1967—; tchr. summer arts Stockton (Calif.) Arts Commn.; organ. Symphony Orch., Yuma, 1962—67. Production grant, Stockton Unified Sch. Dist., 1980. Mem.: Nat. Music Educators, Calif. Tchrs. Assn., Suzuki Assn. of the Am., Music Tchrs. Assn. of Calif., Stockton Br. (pres. 2003—), Am. String Tchrs. Assn. (pres. 1975). Democrat. Unitarian. Home: 2348 W Alpine Ave Stockton CA 95204 Personal E-mail: ritaviola@sbcglobal.net.

WILCOX, JUSTINE ELIZABETH, lawyer; b. NYC, Oct. 20, 1949; d. Harry W. and Colleen (Cerra) W.; m. Elizabeth H. Axelson. BA, Goucher Coll., Towson, Md., 1971; JD cum laude, Suffolk U., Boston, 1978. Bar: Mass. 1978, D.C. 1979. Atty. adviser HUD, Washington, 1978-80, program analyst, 1980-81; assoc. Lane and Edson, PC, Washington, 1981-86, ptnr., 1986-89, Kelley, Drye & Warren, Washington, 1989-93, Peabody & Brown, Washington, 1993—99; mng. ptnr. Nixon Peabody LLP, Washington, 1999—. Mem. dean's adv. bd. Suffolk U. LawSch., Fed. City Coun., Econs. Club. Mem. D.C. Bar Assn. Avocations: sailing, tennis, bridge. Office: Nixon Peabody LLP Ste 900 401 Ninth St, NW Washington DC 20004-2128 Office Phone: 202-585-8745. Office Fax: 202-585-8080. E-mail: jwilcox@nixonpeabody.com.

WILCOX, KRYSTA, social studies educator; b. Gainesville, Fla., Feb. 2, 1980; d. James and Frances Littleton; m. George Stephen Wilcox, July 17, 2005. BA in Pub. History, U. West Fla., Pensacola, 1998—2001. Cert. Tchr. Fla. Dept. Edn., 2003. Social studies tchr. Bailey Mid. Sch., Pensacola, Fla., 2003—. Relay for life team capt. Bailey Mid. Sch., 2004—. Mem.: Phi Alpha Theta (life; v.p. 2001—02). Office: Bailey Mid Sch 4110 Bauer Rd Pensacola FL 32506 Office Phone: 850-492-6136. Business E-Mail: kwilcox@escambia.k12.fl.us.

WILCOX, LYNN E., psychology educator; b. Huntsville, Ala., Sept. 4, 1935; d. William Francis and Anna Mae (Linthicum) Esslinger; 1 child, Gregory C. Haun BS cum laude, Southwest Mo. State U., 1959; MEd, U. Mo., 1961, PhD, 1968; postgrad., U. Catolica, Quito, Ecuador, 1976—78. Cert. sch. counselor and sch. psychologist, Calif.; lic. marriage, family and child counselor, Calif. Tchr. h.s., Springfield, Mo., 1958—60; grad. rsch. asst. U. Mo., Columbia, 1960—64; counselor Pub. Schs., Smyrna, Ga., 1965—67; asst. prof. Ga. State U., Atlanta, 1968—69; prof. edn. Calif. State U., Sacramento, 1969—; pvt. practice marriage, family and child counselor Sacramento, 1970—. Dept. chair Calif. State U., Sacramento, 1973-75, counselor, coord. edn., 1986-88, mem. women's studies bd., 1972; instr. in Sufi Meditation, M.T.O. Shahmaghsoudi, Sacramento and San Francisco, 1984— Author: Wayfinding, 1995, Sufism & Psychology, 1995, Women and the Quran, 2003; editor: Sayings of the Sufi Sages, 1996 Pres. Wayfinders Inc., Sacramento, 1986—; chmn. Am. Pers. & Guidance Assn. Com. for Women, 1972-74; bd. dirs. Cmty. Interaction Program, Sacramento, 1972; prof. adv. com. Suicide Prevention Svc., Sacramento, 1970-72; rep. Sacramento Cmty. Commn. for Women, 1971-73 Fellow Gregory 1962, Danforth 1975; recipient Profl. Promise award Calif. State U., Sacramento, 1986, Meritorious Performance award, 1988 Mem. APA, ACA, NOW, Calif. Assn. Marriage and Family Therapists, Suri Psychology Assn. (pres. 1998—), Nature Conservancy, League Women Voters, Sierra Club. Moslem. Office: Calif State U Dept Counselor Edn 6000 J St Sacramento CA 95819-6079

WILCOX, MARY MARKS, retired Christian education consultant, educator; b. Madison, Wis., Apr. 23, 1921; d. Roy and Mary Celia (Leary) Marks; m. Ray Everett Wilcox, Nov. 28, 1942; children: Peter, Anne, Susan, Steven. BA, U. Wis., 1942; MRE, Iliff Sch. Theology, Denver, 1968. Cert. Christian educator. Cons. local chs., Lakewood, Littleton, Wheat Ridge, Colo., 1963-74; instr., leader numerous seminars throughout U.S. and Can., 1963—; interim parish cons. 1st Presbyn. Ch., Lakewood, 1988-90, profl. assoc. for faith devel., 1993-97; adj. prof. Iliff Sch. Theology, 1970—; ret., 2002. Author: Developmental Journey, 1979; co-author: Viewpoints, 1998; contbr. articles to various publs., chpts. to books. Trustee, mem. exec. bd. Nat. Ghost Ranch Found., Abiquiu, N. Mex., 1983-93. Recipient award Iliff Alumni Assn., 1989. Mem.: Assn. Presbyn. Christian Educators (past mem. exec. bd.). Democrat. Presbyterian. Home: 3590 Estes St Wheat Ridge CO 80033-5933 E-mail: marywilcox@aol.com.

WILCOX, MAUD, editor; b. N.Y.C., Feb. 14, 1923; d. Thor Fredrik and Gerda (Ysberg) Eckert; m. Edward T. Wilcox, Feb. 9, 1944 (dec. 1998); children: Thor(dec.), Bruce, Eric, Karen. AB summa cum laude, Smith Coll., 1944; A.M., Harvard U., 1945. Teaching fellow Harvard U., 1945-46, 48-51; instr. English Smith Coll., Northampton, Mass., 1947-48, Wellesley Coll., Mass., 1951-52; exec. editor Harvard U. Press, 1958-66, humanities editor, 1966-73, editor-in-chief, 1973—89; freelance editorial cons. Cambridge, 1989—; ret. Cons., panelist NEH, Washington, 1974-76, 82-84; cons. Radcliffe Pub. Course, 1991. Mem. MLA (com. scholarly edits. 1982-86), Assn. Am. Univ. Presses (chair com. admissions and standards 1976-77, v.p. 1978-79, chair program com. 1981-82), Phi Beta Kappa. Democrat. Episcopalian. Home and Office: 63 Francis Ave Cambridge MA 02138-1911 Personal E-mail: maudwilcox@post.harvard.edu.

WILCOX, NANCY DIANE, nursing home administrator; b. Griffin, Ga., Oct. 28, 1951; d. Robert Wayne Birdwell and Eula F. (Maddox) Tatum; m. David Reed Wilcox, May 29, 1970; children: David Jr., Melanie, Bradley, Amy. AS, Panola Coll., 1971; lic. vocat. nurse, Kilgore Coll., 1990, ASN, 1993; BSN magna cum laude, U. Tex., Tyler, 1994; postgrad., St. Joseph's Coll., 1996—. RN, Tex.; cert. in home health nursing ANCC. Hemodialysis nurse Good Shepherd Hosp., Longview, Tex., 1990-91, critical care and telemetry nurse, 1993-94; staff nurse Roy H. Laird Hosp., Kilgore, 1991-93; case mgr. TLC Home Health Agy., Longview, 1994-95; owner, operator LifeCare Home Nursing, Inc., Longview, 1995—. Mem. ANA, Tex. Nurses Assn., Home Care Nurses Assn., Phi Theta Kappa, Alpha Chi, Sigma Theta Tau. Avocation: collecting dolls. Home: 3355 Sam Page Rd Longview TX 75605-7554

WILCOX, SHEILA MAUREEN, music educator; b. St. Paul, Jan. 12, 1965; d. Leonard Reuben and Bethel Elaine (Cottrell) Anderson; m. Mark Stephen Wilcox, July 11, 1992. BM, U. Wis., Superior, 1987; MM, U. Wis., Madison, 1992. Lic. tchr., Minn. Orch. tchr. Sch. Dist. of Superior (Wis.), 1987-88, Ind. Sch. Dist. #706, Virginia, Minn., 1988—. Section violinist Duluth Superior Symphony Orch., 1984-97. Mem. Mesabi Cmty. Orch., 1990—. Mem. Minn. Music Educators Assn., Music Educators Nat. Conf., Minn. Edn. Assn., Nat. Sch. Orch. Assn. (Minn. chpt.), Am. String Tchrs. Assn. Democrat. Swedish Baptist. Avocations: cross country skiing, aerobics, bicycling, sewing, cooking. Office: Ind Sch Dist 706 411 S 5th Ave Virginia MN 55792-2768 Office Phone: 218-749-5437 1248. Business E-Mail: swilcox@virginia.k12.mn.us.

WILCOX, SHIRLEY JEAN LANGDON, genealogist; b. Arcata, Calif., Dec. 10, 1942; d. Elmore Harold and Alberta May (Starkey) Langdon; m. Wayne Kent Wilcox, June 22, 1963; 1 child, Harold Bonner. BS, U. Md., 1964. Cert. Bd. for Certification of Genealogists. Tchr. Prince George's County (Md.) Sch. System, 1964-67, substitute tchr., 1968-73; profl. genealogist Lanham, Md., Arlington, Va., 1973—; genealogy tchr. Fairfax County Pub. Schs., 1995-99. Level II coord. Mid-Atlantic Genealogy and History Inst., George Mason U., Fairfax, Va., 1986; trustee Bd. for Certification of Genealogists, 2000—. Editor: A Bibliography of Published Genealogical Source Records, Prince George's County, Maryland, 1975, Prince George's County Land Records, Vol. A, 1696-1702, 1976, 1850 Census Prince George's County, Maryland, 1978, 1828 Tax List Prince George's County, Maryland, 1985; author: The National Genealogical Society: A Look at Its First One Hundred Years, 2003. Elder Presbyn. Ch., 1970-73, 95-98. Fellow Nat. Geneal. Soc. (chmn. conf. program subcom. 1990, 2d v.p. 1990-94, councilor 1994-96, pres. 1996-2000); mem. DAR (libr. Belle Air chpt. 1985—, Outstanding Jr. Mem. award 1979), Assn. Profl. Genealogists (pres. 1991-93, pres. Nat. Capital area chpt. 1994-96, dir. region 3 2004—06, Grahame Thomas Smallwood Jr. award of merit 1995), Va. Geneal. Soc. (gov. 2001—), Prince George's County Geneal. Soc. (pres. 1973, 75-76, book rev. editor 1976-96, Jane Roush McCafferty award of excellence 1985), Fairfax Geneal. Soc. (pres. 1986-89), Soc. Mayflower Descs. in D.C., Paperweight Collectors Assn. (pres. Md.-D.C.-Va. chpt. 1988-90), Clay Family Soc. (dir. 2002-06), numerous others. Avocation: collecting paperweights. Home: 1500 23rd St S Arlington VA 22202-1523

WILCOXSON, CAROL ANN, music educator; b. Greenville, S.C., Feb. 15, 1943; d. Carroll Raleigh and Dorothy Ann (Brunson) Greene; children: Danielle Elise, Paul Edwin. BS, East Tex. State U., 1965; MLA, So. Meth. U., 1996. Cert. Music Tchr.'s Nat. Assn., Am. Nat. Coll. Musicians' judge (piano). Caseworker Buckner Children's Home, Dallas, 1965-66; caseworker, supr. Dept. Human Resources, Dallas, El Paso, Tex., 1967-74; pvt. practice piano tchr. Dallas, 1981—; pianist Old San Francisco Steak House, Dallas, 1995—2004. Vol., interviewer White Rock Ctr. of Hope-Food Pantry & Short-Term Help, Dallas, 1989-93. Mem. Am. Coll. Musicians (piano guild judge 1989—), ADHD Parent Support (bd. dirs 1990-95), Dallas Music Tchr. Assn. (bd. dirs. 1996-2000), Mesquite (Tex.) Area Music Tchrs. (pres., v.p. 1998). Methodist. Avocations: hiking, reading, research study, creative writing, travel. Home and Office: Apt 226-C 333 N McDowell Blvd Petaluma CA 94954

WILCOXSON-UECKERT, CATHERINE ANN, science educator, consultant; b. Lemmon, SD, Nov. 13, 1948; d. Alvin Herman and Myra V. (Eggers) Thies; m. Dale Arthur Wilcoxson, Dec. 13, 1969 (div.); children: Blaine, Erik; m. Warren Ueckert, May 19, 2001 BS, Midland Luth. Coll., 1971; Masters, U. Nebr., Omaha, 1989; PhD, U. Nebr., 1994; D (hon.), Midland Coll., 2003. Tchr. North Bend (Nebr.) Ctrl. Sch., 1971-78, Fremont (Nebr.) H.S., 1978-81, 84-92; project coord. N.E. Dept. Edn., Lincoln, 1993-95; assoc. prof. No. Ariz. U., Flagstaff, 1995—. Cons. La. Dept. Edn., 1994, 95, Coun. Chief State Sch. Officers, Washington, 1994, 96, Ark. Dept. of Edn., 1996. Editor: N.E. Math/Science Frameworks, 1994, Guidelines for Teacher Preparation: Mathematics and Science, 1995, Middle School Idea Book, 1996. Recipient Master Tchr. award Midland Luth. Coll., 1993. Mem. Nat. Sci. Tchrs. (manuscript reveiw com. Jour. Coll. Sci. Tchrs. 1995-98), Am. Ednl. Rsch. Assn., Nat. Assn. Biology Tchrs. (sec./treas. 1996-2000, pres. 2003 Outstanding Biology Tchr. 1991, Excellence in Encouraging Equity award 1994), Nat. Assn. for Rsch. in Sci. Tchg., Ariz. Sci. Tchrs. Assn., Phi Delta Kappa Office: No Ariz Univ PO Box 5640 Flagstaff AZ 86011-0001 Office Phone: 928-523-7026. Business E-Mail: catherine.ueckert@nau.edu.

WILCZEWSKI, LYNN CHERYL, social studies educator, department chairman; d. David Joseph and Cheryl Ann Wilczewski. BA in History, SUNY, Geneseo, 1993; MEd, East Carolina u., Greenville, N.C., 1999. Lic. profl. tchr. social studies grades 7-12 N.C. Tchr. social studies and dept. chair Halifax County Schs., NC, 1996—99, Chesterfield County Schs., Va., 1999—. Mem.: NEA, Va. Edn. Assn., Va. Hist. Soc. Office: Chesterfield County Schs 990 Krause Rd Chesterfield VA 23832-6335

WILDE, CHRISTINE BUCEY, secondary school educator; b. Chula Vista, Calif., Nov. 9, 1949; d. Charles Clair Bucey and Clare Patricia Palardy; m. Daniel L. Wilde, June 12, 1983. Student, Russell Coll., 1967-71; BS, Stanford U., Calif., 1973, MA in Tchg., 1989. Cert. tchr., Calif. Chemistry and earth sci. tchr. Mercy High Sch., San Francisco, 1973-75; tchr. Yosemite Inst., Yosemite Nat. Park, Calif., 1975-76; physics, chemistry tchr., dept. head, gifted edn. coordinator Cen. Cath. High Sch., Modesto, Calif., 1986—. Cons., Modesto, 1983—; lectr. Calif. Assn. for Gifted state conv., Oakland, Calif., 1986, seminars on improving sci. teaching, Calif.; tchr. trainer Ethiopian Tchr. Trainer Inst., 2000—; owner, operator Yasmen's Navel Acad. Belly Dance Studio. Author: (with others) Chemistry Demonstrations, 1984; book reviewer Charles Merrill Publ. Co., 1985, 88. Host family Youth for Understanding, Turlock, Calif., 1985-86. Recipient Tandy Tech. Scholar award, 1992; named Tchr. of Yr. Modesto Rotary, 1997. Mem. Nat. Sci. Tchrs. Assn. (speaker conv. 1986), Calif. Sci. Tchrs. Assn. (contbr. articles to jour.), Am. Assn. Physics Tchrs., Calif. Assn. Chemistry Tchrs., Calif. Sect. Am. Chem. Soc., AAUW, Sierra Club, Sigma Xi (Sci. Tchr. of Yr. 1983). Roman Catholic. Avocations: sports, needlecrafts, gardening, reading, writing. Office: Cen Cath High Sch 200 S Carpenter Rd Modesto CA 95351-1938 E-mail: wildec@clearwire.net.

WILDE, KERRI DAWN, dance educator; b. Springfield, Mo., Aug. 18, 1967; d. Valerian K. and Edith Marie Lamy; m. Ryan John Wilde, Aug. 13, 1994; children: Hunter Michael, Chasten Valerian. B in Edn., U. Toledo, Ohio, 1991. Dance instr. Owens C.C., Toledo, 2002—05, Perrysburg Area Art Coun., Ohio, 2003—, Toledo Ballet, 2004—06; dancer tchr. Toledo Sch. for the Arts, 2005—. Choreographer Perrysburg Area Art Coun., 2004—. Office: Toledo Sch for the Arts 333 14th St Toledo OH 43624 Office Phone: 419-246-8732. Office Fax: 419-244-3979. E-mail: www.ts4arts.org.

WILDE, STEPHANIE, artist; b. Coalville, Utah, Jan. 7, 1952; d. Fred Robinson and Ruth Smith Wilde; m. Lane Stewart Bune, Feb. 21, 1982; 1 child, Seffan Palmer Bune. Self employed artist, Ogden, Utah, 1974, Boise, Idaho, 1988; artist, co-owner Stewart Gallery, Boise, 1989—. Pub. Smith & Wilde Press, Boise, 1986—. Pub.: books Wilde Birds, 1986, Slim (AIDS in Africa), 1993, Possessed by the Twins, 1998. Recipient Mayor's award, Artistic Excellence, 1999, Gov's award, Excellence in Arts, 2002, fellowship, Idaho Commn. on Arts, Boise, 2006; grantee, 1988, 1994. Office: Stewart Gallery 2212 Main Boise ID 83702

WILDEMAN, ROSE A., musician, educator; b. Evansville, Ind., July 2, 1949; d. Anthony John and Theresa Louise Wildeman. BS, Oakland City Coll., Ind., 1971; MA in Music, Ball State U., Muncie, Ind., 1981. Cert. tchr. Ind. Music tchr. Sacred Heart and St. John's Sch., Vincennes, Ind., 1971—73; music tchr., liturgist Christ The King Sch., Evansville, 1973—86, St. Joseph Ch., Evansville, 1986—2005; dir. initial formation Sisters of St. Benedict, Ferdinand, Ind., 2005—. Ex-officio mem. parish coun. St. Joseph Ch., 1991—2005. Composer: (tape/CD recording) Sounds of Peace, 1988, Open My Life, 1998, Time Made Holy, 1999. Chmn. Music Tchrs. of Diocese, Evansville, 1995—2005. Named Music Tchr. of Yr., Shuttler's Music Store, Evansville, 1986. Mem.: Nat. Pastoral Musicians, Music Educators' Nat. Conf. Roman Catholic. Avocations: swimming, counted cross stitch, entertaining. Home: 802 E 10th St Ferdinand IN 47532 Office: Sisters of St Benedict 802 E 10th St Ferdinand IN 47532

WILDER, JANELL LYNN, music educator; b. Sylvania, Ohio, June 17, 1975; d. Donald Kenneth and Cynthia Jean Koskie; m. Daniel Alan Wilder; 1 child, Ava Lorraine. MusB, Cleve. State U., 1997; MusM, Bowling Green State U., Ohio, 1999. Tchr. Brookfield Acad., Rochester Hills, Mich., Troy, Mich., 1999—2000, Waterford Sch. Dist., Mich., 2000—. Clinician Waterford Sch. Dist. Sponsored Diversity Conf., 2001, 58th Ann. Mich. Music Tchrs. In-Svc. Conf., 2002. Grantee, Waterford Found., 2003—04; Ednl. grantee, Metro N. Fed. Credit Union, 2004—05, Found. Future Edn. grantee, MEEMIC Ins. Co., 2005—06. Mem.: NEA (Innovation grantee 2004—05), Waterford Edn. Assn. Avocations: reading, writing, exercise. Home: 18320 Shadyside St Livonia MI 48152

WILDER, JANET MARY, performing company executive; d. Robert and Jean; m. Ward Wilder; children: Suzanne, Robert. BS, U. Colo., 1966. Cecchetti tchr. cert. Cecchetti Coun. Am., tchr. cert. Chgo. Nat. Dance Masters Assn., tchg. cert. Calif. Tchr. Santa Venetia Mid. Sch., San Rafael, Calif., 1967—68; fitness/dance instr. Am. Wives' Club, Ghedi, Brescia, Italy, 1969—71; instr. Julie Ward Sch. Dance, Rapid City, SD, 1972—77, Spokane Ballet, Wash., 1981—83, Capitol City Ballet, Sacramento, 1985—87, Marguerite Phares Sch. Dance, Sacramento, 1985—87; artistic dir. Dakota Repertory Dance Co., Rapid City, 1975—77, San Antonio Dance Theatre, 1983—85, Dance Theatre NW, Spokane, 1994—2004, Ballet Spokane, 2003—; instr., co-dir. Entenman Sch. Dance, Bellvue, Nebr., 1978—81; dancer Omaha Ballet, 1979—81; dir. Ballet Arts, San Antonio, 1983—85; co-dir. Ballet Arts Acad., Spokane, 1987—94; co-founder, dir. Theatre Ballet Spokane, 1987—94; choreographer/prodr./dir. Coeur d'Alene (Idaho) Summer Theatre, 1991—96; resident choreographer Spokane/Coeur d'Alene Opera, 1987—; owner, dir. Acad. Dance, Spokane Valley, Wash., 1994—. Founder/mem. Inland NW Dance Assn., Spokane, 1989—; ballet adv. bd. mem. Greater Spokane Music & Allied Arts Festival, 1988—2000, MusicFest NW, Spokane, 2000—; dance edn. del. to China People to People, Bejing, 1996. Author: (book) Terms Every Dancer Should Know; writer, prodr., dir.: (ballets) The Toy Shelf; choreographer (over 150 ballets, operas & musicals). Mem. Rapid City Svc. League, 1975—77; mem./officer PTA, Rapid City, 1975—77; com. mem. First Night Spokane, 2003; mem. entertainment com. Diamonds & Divas, Spokane, 2000—05. Recipient Outstanding Mem., Ghedi Air Force Wives' Club, 1971, Ellsworth Officer's Wives' Club, 1977, Outstanding Young Women of Am., Outstanding Young Women of Am. program, 1973, Wash. State Dance Sch. Dir., Dance Excellence Internat. Festival for Young Dancers, 1992—95, Bowl Games of Am./CocaCola Olympic City, 1996, Jim Chase Asset builder, Chase Youth Commn., 1997, Dir. in charge - Teen Group Creativity Award, 2000, Dir. in charge - Teen Group Cmty. Svc. Hon. Mention, 2001. Mem.: Nat. Dance Edn. Orgn., Nat. Dance Assn., MusicFest NW, Inland NW Dance Assn. (v.p. 2002—04). Avocations: writing, scuba diving, skiing, boating. Office Phone: 509-922-3023. Personal E-mail: janetwilder123@aol.com.

WILDER, LISA YVETTE, dancer, educator; d. John Edward Wilder and Eva Adelle Kingsberry. BS, U. N.C., Greensboro, 1990. Cert. dance edn. grades K-12 N.C. Dept. Pub. Instrn., 1990. Tchr. dance edn. grades K-12 Caldwell County Schs., Lenior, NC, 1990, Mooresville Graded Sch. Dist., NC, 1991; tchr. dance edn. grades 6-12 Clinton City Schs., NC, 1991—93, Durham Pub. Schs., 1993—2004; tchr. dance edn. grades 9-12 Wake County Pub. Schs., Raleigh, NC, 2004—. Instr. studio dance YWCA, Raleigh, 1979—83; summer recreation dance instr. Durham Pks. and Recreation, 1984—90; dir. dance co., colorguard, and cheerleaders Clinton H.S., 1991—93; dir. dance co. Neal Mid. Sch., Durham, 1993—95, Hillside H.S., Durham, 1995—2004, S.E. Raleigh Magnet H.S., 2004—. Mem.: N.C. Assn. Educators. Office: Southeast Raleigh Magnet HS 2600 Rock Quarry Rd Raleigh NC 27610 Office Phone: 919-856-2835. Home Fax: 919-856-2827; Office Fax: 919-856-2827. Personal E-mail: liwilder@earthlink.net. Business E-Mail: lwilder@wcpss.net.

WILDEROTTER, MAGGIE (MARY AGNES WILDEROTTER), software company executive, former cable television executive; b. Neptune, N.J., Feb. 9, 1955; d. Denis James and Constance Rosemary (Shields) Sullivan; m. Philip Jay Wilderotter; children: Christopher, Daniel. BA in Econs., Holy Cross Coll., 1977. Accts. receivable supr. CableData, Sacramento, 1979-80, mgr. acctg. svcs., 1980-82, mgr. reg. support, 1982, mktg. mgr., 1982-83, dir. mktg., 1983, dir. nat. accts., 1983-85, v.p., 1985—87, sr. v.p., sales & mktg., 1987—91; sr. v.p. McCaw Cellular Communications, 1991—95; exec. v.p., nat. ops. & CEO, Aviation Communications div. AT&T Wireless Svcs., 1995—97; pres., CEO Wink Communications, 1997—2002; sr. v.p., bus. strategy Microsoft Corp., 2002—04; pres., CEO Citizens Communications, 2004—05, chmn., CEO, 2005—. Bd. dirs. Phoenix Cable Ptnrs., San Rafael, Calif., 1988—, Satellite Video Ctr., Rancho Cordova, Calif., 1988—, CAble-Data Europe Ltd., Leeds, Eng., 1989—, Citizens Communications, 2004-, Xerox Corp., 2006-. Outstanding Mentor award, Women in Cable and Telecommunications Found., 1999. Mem. Nat. Cable TV Assn. (bd. dirs. 1987—), Women in Cable (exec. mem.), Cable TV Adminstrn. & Mktg. Soc., Calif. Cable TV Assn., Nat. Acad. Cable Programming. Republican. Roman Catholic. Office: Citizens Communications 3 High Ridge Park Stamford CT 06905

WILDING, DIANE, computer scientist, consultant; b. Chicago Heights, Ill., Nov. 7, 1942; d. Michael Edward and Katherine Surian; m. Manfred Georg Wilding, May 7, 1975 (div. 1980). BSBA in Acctg. magna cum laude, No. Ill. U., DeKalb, 1963; postgrad., U. Chgo., 1972—74; cert. in German lang., Goethe Inst., Rothenburg, Germany, 1984; cert. in internat. bus. German, Goethe Inst., Atlanta, 1994; cert. in Web page design, Kennesaw State U., Ga., 2000. Lic. cosmetologist. Sys. engr. IBM, Chgo., 1963-68, SAP cons. Atlanta, 1993—; data processing mgr. Am. Res. Corp., Chgo., 1969-72; system R & D project mgr. Continental Bank, Chgo., 1972-75; fin. industry mktg. rep. IBM Can., Ltd., Toronto, Ont., 1976-79; regional telecom. mktg. exec. Control Data Corp., Atlanta, 1980-84; gen. mgr. The Plant Plant, Atlanta, 1985-92. Pioneer installer on-line automatic teller machines Pos Equipment. Author: The Canadian Payment System: An International Perspective, 1977. Mem. Chgo. Coun. Fgn. Rels.; bd. dirs. Easter House Adoption Agy., Chgo., 1974—76. Mem.: Internat. Brass Soc., Mensa, Goethe Inst., Libertyville Racquet Club, Royal Ont. Yacht Club, Ponte Verde Club (Fla.). Avocations: travel, gourmet cooking, languages, antiques. Home: PO Box 723055 Atlanta GA 31139-0055 Office: IBM 1600 Riveredge Pkwy NW Atlanta GA 30328-4697 E-mail: diane.wilding@gmail.com.

WILDMAN, IRIS J., retired law librarian; b. Chgo., May 10, 1930; d. Isadore and Stella (Stark) W. BS, Northwestern U., Evanston, Ill., 1952; MLS, Case Western Res. U., 1954; JD, Santa Clara U., 1978. Asst. cataloger U. Chgo. Law Libr., 1952-53; cataloger Copyright Office/Libr. of Congress, 1954; law cataloger U.S. Army Libr./Pentagon, 1954-56; cataloger U.S. Dept. of Justice Libr., Washington, 1956-57; head tech. svcs. Ohio State U. Law Libr., Columbus, 1957-59, Skokie (Ill.) Pub. Libr., 1959-60; head cataloging and classification Northwestern U. Law Libr., Chgo., 1961-64; chief acquisitions and binding Yale Law Libr., New Haven, 1965-74; pub. svcs. libr. Stanford U. Law Libr., 1976-85; sr. reference and spl. projects libr. Robert Crown Law Libr. Stanford (Calif.) U., 1985-95; ret. Cons. Corp. Counsel, Govt., Washington D.C. Libr., 1957, U. P.R. Law Libr., 1968; faculty/dir. AALL Institutes on Cataloging, Classification and Acquisitions, 1966, 70, 73; libr./lectr. Stanford Law Sch., 1978-82, 85-93. Compiler: Federal Judges and Justices, 1987-2001; editor: Law Libraries in the U.S. and Can., 1958, Directory of Law Librs., 1964, 66; indexer: Index to Foreign Legal Periodicals, 1983-2000; contbr. articles to profl. jours. Mem. No. Calif. Assn. Law Librs. (v.p., pres. elect 1980-82), Am. Assn. Law Librs. Avocations: writing, reading, photography, gardening. Home: 1757 Pilgrim Ave Mountain View CA 94040-2363 Business E-Mail: iwildman@stanford.edu.

WILDONER, NANCY SCHAMU, music educator, fine arts department chairman; b. Syracuse, NY, June 8, 1957; d. Frederick William and Marlyn Meyer Schamu; m. Robert Sterling Wildoner, Aug. 15, 1987; children: Melody June, Robert Sterling III. BA in Music Edn., Fredonia State U., 1979; MusM, Binghamton U., 1983; studied organ with M. Searle Wright and Paul Jordan. Tchng. Cert. NY. Music tchr. Norwich Sch. Dist., NY, 1979—81; grad. asst. Binghamton U., NY, 1981—83; substitute tchr. Broome County, Binghamton, NY, 1983—85; K-12 music tchr. Chenango Forks Sch., Binghamton, NY, 1984—; choir dir., organist First Congregational Ch., Binghamton, NY, 2002—. Church organist various chs., 1977—2005; exec. coun. mem. Broome County Music Educators Assn., Binghamton, NY, 2000—05; pvt. piano and organ tchr., Binghamton, NY, 2001—05. Womens aux. mem. Sanitaria Springs Fire Dept., NY, 1989—2005. Mem.: Broome County Music Educators Assn., NY Sch. Music Assn., Music Educators Nat. Conf., Am. Guild of Organists. Protestant. Avocations: theater, travel. Home: 778 Brotzman Rd Binghamton NY 13901 Office: Chenango Forks elem Sch 6 Patch Rd Binghamton NY 13901 Business E-Mail: wildonern@cforks.org.

WILDT, JANETH KAE, small business owner; b. Bath, Mich., July 15, 1950; d. Gareth Macey and Mary Elizabeth (Shipley) Harte; children: Kimberly Kae, Larry Micheal. Owner Ceramics By George, Bath, Mich., 1979—; truck driver RJ Trucking, Inc., Auburndale, Fla., ETV Trucking, Inc., Grand Rapids, Mich. Avocations: cooking, yardwork, ceramics. Home and Office: Ceramics by George 13367 Center Rd Bath MI 48808 Office Phone: 517-641-6081. Personal E-mail: cbygeorge@earthlink.net.

WILE, JOAN, composer, lyricist, singer; b. Rochester, N.Y., July 17, 1931; d. Louis and Janet Louise (Wile) Meltzer; children: Ron Wasserman, Diana Wasserman McCloskey. BA, U. Chgo., 1952. Freelance composer, lyricist, singer, mus. book writer. Rec. artist Vanguard Records, 1954; singer Storyville, 1954, The Crystal Palace, 1957; mem. vocal-revue act The Neighbors performances include The Village Vanguard, Le Ruban Bleu, The Bon Soir and The Living Room; singer, lyricist feature film The Happy Hooker, 1974; singer radio and TV jingles, movie sound tracks, supper clubs, hotels, TV music spls. and variety shows; lyricist, composer mus. Tobacco Road, 1974, Seven Ages of Woman, 1987 (named most promising new musical); writer, producer When They Turned on the Tap at the Watergate, The Truth Come Pourin' Out; lyricist songs for Romper Room, 1983; lyricist, composer, writer People is People, 1983; lyricist, composer script for children's albums for Golden and Peter Pan Records, others; lyricist, composer material in Julius Monk's Upstairs at the Downstairs, 1958; lyricist, composer, performer Nancy's Economic Plan, 1980; lyricist, composer Mothers and Daughters, 1984; lyricist, composer, author The Symposium, 1987; lyricist, composer From There to Here, 1987; writer Rhyme, Women and Song; lyricist, librettist, composer Museum of Natural Sex History, 1992; composer Women Walking, 1997, composer-lyricist What A Woman (Homage to Peggy Lee), 2003; founder, singer The NY Granny Chicks, 2005. Organizer Women in Def. Eleanor Roosevelt, N.Y.C., 1989—; founder, dir. Grandmothers Against the War, 2003; founder, organizer Revolt Against the Tax Refund, 2001; founder Granny Peace Brigade, 2005; treas. bd. dirs. Soc. Singers, 2002. Runner-up Am. Song Festival, 1976 Mem.: ASCAP (Popular award 1970—2005), AFTRA, SAG, Theatre Artists Workshop, Dramatists Guild, Soc. of Singers (bd. dirs.). Avocation: political and musical activities. Home and Office: 263 West End Ave Apt 4B New York NY 10023-2613 E-mail: jwile@prodigy.net.

WILENSKY, GAIL ROGGIN, economist, researcher; b. Detroit, June 14, 1943; d. Albert Alan and Sophia (Blitz) Roggin; m. Robert Joel Wilensky, Aug. 4, 1963; children: Peter Benjamin, Sara Elizabeth. AB (hon.), U. Mich., 1964, MA in Econs., 1965, PhD in Econs., 1968; degree (hon.), Hahnemann U., 1993, Rush U., 1997, U. Scis., Phila., 2002. Economist President's Commn. on Income Maintenance Programs; exec. dir. Md. Coun. of Econ. Advs., 1969-71; sr. rschr. Urban Inst., Washington, 1971-73; assoc. rsch. scientist, pub. policy and pub. health U. Mich., Ann Arbor, 1973-75, vis. asst. prof. econs., 1973-75; sr. rsch. mgr. Nat Ctr. for Health Svcs. Rsch., Hyattsville, Md., 1975-83; assoc. profl. lectr. George Washington U., 1976-78; v.p. div. health affairs Project HOPE, Millwood, Va., 1983-90; adminstr. Health Care Fin. Adminstrn., Washington, 1990-92; dep. asst. to the pres. for policy devel. White House, 1992-93; sr. fellow Project HOPE, Bethesda, Md., 1993—, chair phys. payment rev. com., 1995-97; chmn. Medicare Payment Adv. Commn., 1997—2001; co-chair Pres.'s Task Force to Improve Health-care Delivery for Vets., 2001—03. Contbr. 100 articles in field to profl. jours. Dir. Am. Heart Assn., 1980-85, bd. dirs., 2002—; mem. health adv. com. Compt. Gen. U.S., 1987-90; bd. dirs. United Healthcare Corp., Cephalon, ManorCare, Gentiva Health Svcs., Inc., Quest Diagnostics; mem. vis. com. med. sch. U. Mich., 1993-97; trustee United Mine Workers Am. Retirement Fund, 1993—; commr. WHO Commn. on the Social Determinants of Health, 2005-. Flinn Found. distring. scholar, 1985; recipient Dean Conley award Am. Coll. Healthcare Execs., 1989. Mem. NAS (mem. inst. medicine 1989—), Am. Econ. Assn. (women's com. 1982-84), Fedn. Orgn. of Profl. Women (chmn. econ. task force 1981-83), Am. Statis. Assn., Nat. Tax Assn., Washington Women Economists, Assn. Health Svc. Rsch. (dir. 1984-87), Found. Health Svc. Rsch. (bd. dir. 1987-90), Acad. Health (chair bd. dir. 2000—, Cosmos Club (Washington). Home: 2807 Battery Pl NW Washington DC 20016-3439 Office Phone: 301-656-7401. Business E-Mail: gwilensky@projecthope.org.

WILES, LESSLEY DECKER, foundation administrator, preservationist; b. Pitts., Apr. 19, 1939; d. John Ellsworth and Irma Evelyn Decker; m. William Wharton Wiles, Aug. 20, 1961; 1 child, Kenneth William. BA, U. Ky., 1960. Statistician Wis. State Employment Svc., Madison, 1962—65, U.S. Dept. Labor, Wash., 1965—67; project mgr. HUD, Wash., 1967—72, new cmty. program officer, 1972—83, sr. program specialist, 1983—91, dir., coinsurance mgmt. divsn., 1991—92, sr. program officer, 1992—95; self-employed housing cons. York, Pa., 1996—. Mem., FHA commr.'s asset mgmt. strategy working team HUD, Wash., 1993—94. Mem. and com. chair Arlington/Tyson's Civitan Clubs, Fairfax County, Va., 1985—2005; ch. counsel sec. Walker Chapel United Meth. Ch., Arlington, 1988—97, flower com. chair, 1995—2002; mem. Arlington Cmty. Residences, Inc., 1982—88. Recipient Civitan of Yr., Arlington Civitan Club, 1991, 1992. Mem.: Pa.-Del. AHMA. Liberal. United Methodist. Avocations: crafts, gardening, volunteering. Home: 2635 Twin Lane York PA 17402-8248

WILEY, ELIZABETH ANN, theater educator, department chairman; b. Mpls., Apr. 21, 1962; d. Thomas Wiley and Elva Ann Rutter; m. David Andrew Doersch, Sept. 12, 1987; children: Miranda Eve, Kaliska Virginia. Student, Smith Coll., Northampton, Massachusetts, 1980—82; BA, U. Wis., Madison, 1984; MFA, U. Minn., Mpls., 1988. Asst. prof. U. Miss., Oxford, 1994—97; assoc. prof. Coll. William and Mary, Williamsburg, Va., 1997—. Actor, dir., voice coach. Actor: (theater production) Copenhagen by Michael Frayn (Port Folio Theatre Award for Best Actress in a Drama, 2004); prodr.(director): (theatre company) Wiley Coyote Productions; dir.: (theatre production) Shirley Valentine by Willy Russell; actor(vocal coach): Virginia Shakespeare Festival, Virginia Stage Company.; Playwrights Premiere Theatre, (jungle theatre, minneapolis) Betrayal by Harold Pinter, (television, film and video). Bd. dirs. First Night Williamsburg, Inc., Va., 2002—03; theatrics and ritual creator Cir. Sanctuary, Mt. Horeb, Wis., 1995—2006; ritual creator Earthspirit, Williamsburg, Mass., 1996—98; worship assoc., lay min. Williamsburg Unitarian Universalists, 1998—2006. Recipient Thirteen Club Tchg. award, William & Mary Students, 1999—2000, Tchg. award, Alumnae

Assn. William and Mary, 2003—04. Mem.: Voice and Speech Trainers Assn., Am. Fedn. TV and Radio Artists, Actors Equity Assn. Pagan. Office: College of William and Mary Department of Theatre Speech and Dance Williamsburg VA 23187 Office Phone: 757-221-2651. Office Fax: 757-221-2636. E-mail: eawile@wm.edu.

WILFERT, CATHERINE M., medical association administrator, pediatrician, epidemiologist, educator; b. LA, July 26, 1936; m. Samuel L. Katz; children: Rachel, Catherine stepchildren: John, David, William, Deborah, Susan, Penelope. BA with distinction, Stanford Coll., 1958; MD cum laude, Harvard U., 1962. Med. intern Boston City Hosp., 1962—63; resident in pediat. Children's Hosp., Boston, 1964—66, fellow in infectious diseases, 1966—68; asst. prof. pediat. and virology Duke U., 1969—73, assoc. prof. pediat., 1974—79, prof. pediat. and microbiology, chief pediatric infectious diseases, 1980—96, prof. emeritus; sci. dir. Elizabeth Glaser Pediat. AIDS Found., Santa Monica, Calif., 1997—. Chair Adv. Com. on Immunization Practices, 1980, Perinatal Working Group of Prevention Trials Network, NIH; mem. adv. com. Office of AIDS Rsch., 1999—2005. Mem.: NIH AIDS Coms., Inst. Medicine, Infectious Diseases Soc. Am. (pres. 2000). Office: Elizabeth Glaser Pediatric AIDS Found 1917 Wildcat Creek Rd Chapel Hill NC 27516-9786 Office Phone: 919-968-0008. Home Fax: 919-968-0447. Personal E-mail: wilfert@mindspring.com.

WILHARM, SHARON LYNETTE, religious studies educator, comedienne; b. Carrabelle, Fla., July 15, 1966; d. Sylvin Ray and Grace Earline Campbell; m. Fred Stephens Wilharm, Dec. 8, 1990; 1 child, Brittany Julianne. AA in Elem. Edn., Okaloosa Walton Jr. Coll., 1986; BA in Elem. Edn., U. West Fla., 1988. Cert. C.L.A.S.S. spkr. Educator East Hill Christian Sch., Pensacola, Fla., 1989—92; freelance writer mags. and newspapers, 1993—. Christian entertainer, spkr., 1996—2000. Author: (homesch. unit studies and curriculum) Patchwork Primers Unit Studies; lead actor (films) Homecoming. Chmn. Walton County Jr. Miss Scholarship Program, DeFuniak Springs, Fla., 2000—03; dir. Acteens, Pensacola, Fla., 1997—98; mem. Brentwood Baptist Ch.; v.p. Chautauqua Hall of Brotherhood Found., DeFuniak Springs, 2003—04; chmn. Walton County Heritage Mus., DeFuniak Springs, 2005. Named a Fred and Sharon Wilharm Walton County Heritage Rsch. Libr., Walton County Heritage Mus., 2006; grantee, N.W. Fla. Improvement Found., 2005; scholar, Destin Rotary Club, 1984—88, U. West Fla., 1986; Acad. scholar, Fla. Dept. Edn., 1984. Mem.: Christian Comedy Assn., Mid. Tenn. Home Educator Assn. R-Consevative. Baptist. Home: 278 Keswick Grove Ln Franklin TN 37067 Personal E-mail: mainstreetprod@bellsouth.net.

WILHELM, CATHY S., elementary school educator; m. Larry Joseph Wilhelm, July 30, 1988; 1 child, Melanie Elaine; 1 child, Michael Eric Kyle. M, U. Akron, Ohio, 1979. Permanent Tchg. Cert. State of Ohio, 1979. Instr. English and Reading Highland Local Schs., Medina, Ohio, 1976—. Treas. Highland Edn. Assn., Medina, 1989—; mem. Strategic Planning Com. Highland Local Schs., Medina, 2005—06; mem. scholarship com. Highland Edn. Assn., Medina, past pres., 1979—88; mem. text com. Medina County Bd. Edn., 1979—98. Dir.(drama performance): Thespis Awards (Life Time Achievement Award, 2001). Mem. exec. com. Highland Cmty. Support Network, Medina, 2004—06. Named Who's Who Among Am. Tchrs.; recipient Tchrs. Golden Apple award, Ashland Oil; fellow, Martha Holden Jennings Assn., 1983—84. Mem.: NOW, ACLU, LWV, AAUW, NEA (life), Ohio Edn. Assn., Nat. Campaign for Tolerance, Highland Found. for Ednl. Excellence, Phi Delta Kappa. Democrat-Npl. Office: Highland Local Schools 3880 Ridge Rd Wadsworth OH 44281 Home Fax: 330-239-7388.

WILHELM, GRETCHEN, retired secondary school educator, volunteer; b. Ames, Iowa, Sept. 30, 1938; d. Harley Almey Wilhelm and Orpha Elizabeth Lutton. BS in Math., Iowa State U., 1960; MS in Math., Oreg. State U., 1969. Permanent profl. endorsement for math. grades 7-12 and gen. sci. Iowa, life endorsement math. grades 7-12 and all scis. grades 7-12 Minn. Math. tchr. Shenandoah (Iowa) H.S., 1960—63, Robbinsdale (Minn.) Sr. H.S., 1963—68; jr. mathematician on faculty Inst. Atomic Rsch. Iowa State U., Ames (Iowa) Lab. U.S. Atomic Energy Commn., 1969; math. tchr. Robbinsdale Cooper Sr. High, New Hope, Minn., 1969—94, math. dept. chmn., 1974—76; ret., 1994. Dist. math. curriculum devel. com. Robbinsdale Sch. Dist., New Hope, 1984—89. Election judge, New Hope, 1994, 1996, 1998, 2000; charter mem. Plymouth (Minn.) Creek Christian Ch., 1978, bd. mem., 1978—79, 1982—84, 1989—91, 1997—2001. Recipient NSF Math. Inst. stipend, Oreg. State U., Corvallis, 1962, 1963, 1964, 1965. Mem.: AAUW (life; Mpls. br. bd. dirs., edn. rep. 1997—98), NEA (life), Minn. Geneal. Soc., Iowa Geneal. Soc., Women Descs. Ancient and Hon. Arty. Co., US Daus. War of 1812 (state registrar 2000—), Thomas Stanton Soc., Thomas Minor Soc., New Eng. Women Descs. (state registrar 2005—), Dau. Am. Colonists, Colonial Dames the XVII Century (state rec. sec. 1997—99), Colonial Dames Am., Nat. Soc. DAR (life; chpt. 2nd vice regent 1987—88, chpt. registrar 1988—94, State constn. week chmn. 1992—95, chpt. 1st vice regent 1994—96, state registrar 1995—97, state officers club v.p., chaplain 1995—97, chpt. chaplain 1996—98, state DAR good citizen chmn. 1997—99, chpt. regent 1998—2000, bd. mgmt., state regent 2001—03, charter mem. State Regents Club, Officers Club 2001—, hon. state regent 2003—, state membership chmn. 2003—05, chair Holt Cogswell Nursing scholar 2004—, speaker staff 2005—). Republican. Mem. Christian Ch. (Disciples Of Christ). Avocation: genealogy. Home: 3925 Winnetka Ave N Minneapolis MN 55427

WILHELM, KATE (KATY GERTRUDE), author; b. Toledo, June 8, 1928; d. Jesse Thomas and Ann (McDowell) Meredith; m. Joseph B. Wilhelm, May 24, 1947 (div. 1962); children: Douglas, Richard; m. Damon Knight, Feb. 23, 1963; 1 child, Jonathan. PhD in Humanities (hon.), Mich. State U., 1996. Writer, 1956—. Co-dir. Milford Sci. Fiction Writers Conf., 1963-76; lectr. Clarion Fantasy Workshop Mich. State U., 1968-94. Author: More Bitter Than Death, 1962; (with Theodore L. Thomas) The Clone, 1965, The Nevermore Affair, 1966, The Killer Thing, 1967, Let the Fire Fall, 1969, The Year of the Cloud, 1970, Abyss: Two Novellas, 1971, Margaret and I, 1971, City of Cain, 1971, The Clewiston Test, 1976, Where Late the Sweet Birds Sang, 1976, Fault Lines, 1976, Somerset Dreams and Other Fictions, 1978, Juniper Time, 1979; (with Damon Knight) Better Than One, 1980, A Sense of Shadow, 1981, Listen, Listen, 1981, Oh! Susannah, 1982, Welcome Chaos, 1983, Huysman's Pets, 1986; (with R. Wilhelm) The Hills Are Dancing, 1986, The Hamlet Trap, 1987, Crazy Time, 1988, Dark Door, 1988, Smart House, 1989, Children of the Wind: Five Novellas, 1989, Cambio Bay, 1990, Sweet, Sweet Poison, 1990, Death Qualified, 1991, And the Angels Sing, 1992, Seven Kinds of Death, 1992, Naming the Flowers, 1992, Justice for Some, 1993, The Best Defense, 1994, A Flush of Shadows, 1995, Malice Prepense, 1996, The Good Children, 1998, Defense for the Devil, 1999, No Defense, 2000, The Deepest Water, 2000, Desperate Measures, 2001, Skeletons, 2002, Clear and Convincing Proof, 2003, The Unhidden Truth, 2004, Storyteller, 2005, The Price of Silence, 2005; (multimedia space fantasy) Axoltl, U. Oreg. Art Mus., 1979, (radio play) The Hindenburg Effect, 1985; editor: Nebula Award Stories #9, 1974, Clarion SF, 1976; contbr. articles to popular mags., profl. jours. Mem. Nat. Writers Union, Mystery Writers Am., Authors Guild. Address: 1645 Horn Ln Eugene OR 97404-2957 E-mail: kate@katewilhelm.com.

WILHELM, MONICA L., music educator; d. Eric J. and Deberah R. Smith; m. Brad J. Wilhelm, Aug. 0, 2002. MusB in Music Edn., Millikin U., Decatur, Ill., 2001; postgrad., Ill. State U., Bloomington/Normal, 2001, VanderCook Coll. of Music, Chgo., Ill., 2004—06. Mid. sch. band/primary gen. music tchr. Manteno CUSD 5, Manteno, Ill., 2001—04, 2006—, tchr. spl. edn. dept., 2005—06; jr. high & h.s. band/music appreciation tchr. Beecher CUSD 200U, Ill., 2004—05. Tutor/mentor Manteno CUSD 5, Manteno, Ill., 2004; pvt. music lessons tchr., Morrisonville, Decatur, Manteno, Ill., 1999—; orch. pit musician Kankakee Valley Theatre Assn., Kankakee, Ill., 2003—; clarinetist & charter mem. River Valley Wind Ensemble, Kankakee County area, Ill., 2004—. Mem. sch. referendum com. Citizens for Good Schs. and Good Kids, Manteno, 2005—06; sch. referendum com. mem. Manteno F.I.V.E. Com., Manteno, Ill., 2003—04; pianist & praise band musician United Meth. Ch., Manteno, Ill., 2001; mentor (team swag vol.) Bands of Am., Bloomington/Normal, Ill., 1999—2001. Recipient Sigma Alpha Iota Coll. Honor Award, Sigma Alpha Iota (a nat. music frat.), 2001, Disney Hand in Tchg. Award Nomination, Disney, 2004. Mem.: Nat. Edn. Assn., Ill. Edn. Assn., Nat. Assn. for Music Edn. (MENC), Pi Kappa Lambda. Avocations: reading, travel, piano, clarinet, volleyball.

WILHELM, VIDA MEADOWS, counselor; b. Worth, W. Va., Dec. 27, 1944; d. Clyde Merlin and Nannie Belle (Crotty) Meadows; m. Wilbert Edward, Dec. 21, 1963; children: Sheryl Leigh, Byron scott. Diploma, Princeton High Sch., 1962, Ohio State U., 1978, Masters, 1981. cert. teaching, Ohio. Substitute tchr. Columbus (Ohio) City Schs., 1982-85, Worthington (Ohio) Schs., 1982-85; ESL tutor Columbus City Schs, 1982-84; English tutor Worthington, Ohio, 1982-88; undergraduate counselor ednl. curriculum and instrn. dept. Tex. A&M U., College Station, 1988-90, sr. acad. advisor, 1990—97; dir. academic svcs., dean's office Coll. Edn. and Human Devel., 1997—. Mem. Worthington Schs. Direction for Edn., Ohio, 1983; facilatator, Worthington Schs. High Sch. Study, Ohio, 1984; sec., PTA Council, Worthington, 1984-85, co-chair, global, Local Outreach Ministeries, Linworth, 1986-89, Bryan FUM Ch., 1994-97. Mem. AAUW (Edn. rep. 1982-87). Republican. Avocations: bridge, reading, sports. Home: 2912 Colton Pl College Station TX 77845-7720

WILHELMI, CYNTHIA JOY, information technology manager, information scientist, consultant; Student, Iowa State U., Ames, 1964—66, BA in Art and Edn., 1966; MA in Comm., U. Nebr., Omaha, 1996. Master Artist-in-Residence Nebr. Arts Coun., Omaha, 1985—91; grad. tchg. asst., tchg. fellow U. Nebr., Omaha, 1993—95; Family Friends of Eastern Nebr. program coord. Vis. Nurse Assn., Omaha, 1996—97; instr. Midland Luth. Coll., Fremont, Nebr., 1997—99; info. tech. cons., project mgr., test engr., bus. analyst Bass & Assocs., Omaha, 1999—2000; info. tech. cons. Robert Half Internat. Cons., 2000, Maxim Group/TEKSystems, 2000—02, Client Resources Inc., 2003; data mgr. TEKsystems, 2003; govt. bid proposal coord. NuGenSof cons. co., 2003—04; bus. sys. analyst Wells Fargo; data mgr. Raytheon, 2003, proposal coord., 2003—04; bus. sys. analyst Praxis Tech. Group, 2005; sr. quality assurance, testing engr. Acacia Tech. Svcs. Inc., 2006; sr. project mgr. and coord. Profl. Project Ptnrs., Inc., 2006—. Sr. project mgr., bus. analyst Alegent Health, Ameritrade, Omnium Worldwide, Lincoln Benefit Life, Raytheon, Wells Fargo, Praxis Tech. Group; IT data mgr., govt. info. tech. proposal coord.; sr. test engr. Ameritrade, Lincoln Benefit Life, Ameritas, Alegent Health, Nationwide Ins., 2006; project mgr. Alegent Health, Ameritrade, Lincoln Benefit Life; engr. Omnium Worldwide, Raytheon, Northrop Grumman Mission Sys., Ameritrade; 3d-party vendor mgr. Alegent Health, Lincoln Benefit Life; CD installation tester Lincoln Benefit Life; tech. documentor Alegent Health, Omnium Worldwide, Ameritrade, PerClick-dot-com, Ameritas, Raytheon Sys., Inacom; data mgr. Northrop Grumman Mission Sys.; bus. sys. cons. Wells Fargo, Nationwide Agribusiness Ins., Nationwide Insurance Agile Tech.; project mgr., enterprise field ops. release coord. Wells Fargo Corp. Offices; farmer, 2001—. Editor, pub., contbg. author Salaam mag., 1985-86. Mem. adv. coun. Foster Grandparents, Omaha, 1999-2005; bd. dirs., pub. rels./publicity chair U. Nebr. Friends of Art, Omaha, 1997-99; bd. dirs. Nebr. SIDS Found., 2002—03 Named Outstanding Grad. Tchg. Asst., U. Nebr., Omaha, 1995, Adm. in the Gt. Navy of Nebr., 1990. Mem. AAUW, Am. Meteor. Soc., Soc. for Tech. Comm. (bd. dirs., chair pub. rels. 1999), Nebr. Adms. Assn., Soc. for Collegiate Journalists (hon.), Phi Delta Gamma, Mensa (Nebr., Western Iowa exec. com. 2003-05, SIGHT coord. 2003-05, mem. nat. nominating com. 2004-05, ctrl. nominating com. 2006—). Republican. Personal E-mail: cwi813@earthlink.net.

WILHELMI, MARY CHARLOTTE, education educator, academic administrator; b. Williamsburg, Iowa, Oct. 2, 1928; d. Charles E. and Loretto (Judge) Harris; m. Sylvester Lee Wilhelmi, May 26, 1951; children: Theresa Ann, Sylvia Marie, Thomas Lee, Kathryn Lyn, Nancy Louise. BS, Iowa State U., 1950; MA Edn., Va. Poly. Inst. and State U., 1973, cert. advanced grad. studies, 1978. Edn. coord. Nova Ctr. U. Va., Falls Church, 1969—73; asst. adminstr. Consortium for Continuing Higher Edn. George Mason U., Fairfax, Va., 1973—78, adminstr., asst. prof., 1978—83; dir. coll. mktg., pub. affairs, assoc. prof. No. Va. C.C., Annandale, 1983—2004, dir. gov. affairs cmty. rels., 2005—. Bd. dirs. No. Va. C.C. Ednl. Found., Inc., No. Va. C.C. Real Estate Found.; v.p. audience devel. Fairfax Symphony, 1995-2003; chmn. Health Sys. Agy. No. Va., Fairfax; mem. George Mason U. Inst. for Ednl. Transformation Mem. Editl. bd. Va. Forum, 1990-93; contbr. articles to profl. jours Bd. dirs. Fairfax County chpt. ARC, 1981-86, Va. Inst. Polit. Leadership, 1995—, Fairfax Com. of 100, 1986-88, 90—, Arts Coun. Fairfax County, 1989—, Fairfax Spotlight on Arts, Inc., 2002—, bd. dirs. Va. Opera, Hospice No. Va., 1983-88, devel. bd., 1997-2000; mem. steering com. Hurrah for Hospice Gala, 1999, Nat. Capital Region Hospices Gala, 2002, 2003, No. Va. Mental Health Inst., Fairfax County, 1978-81, Fairfax Profl. Women's Network, 1981; vice chair Va. Commonwealth U. Ctr. on Aging, Richmond, 1978—; supt.'s adv. coun. Fairfax County Pub. Schs., 1974-86, No. Va. Press Club, 1978—; mktg. chair, exec. com. Internat. Childrens Festival, 1997—; pres. Fairfax Ext. Leadership Coun., 1995; mem. Leadership Fairfax Class of 1992, Commonwealth Va. Combined campaign, State Adv. Coun., 1999-2005 Named Woman of Distinction, Soroptomists, Fairfax, 1988, Bus. Woman of Yr., Falls Church Bus. and Profl. Women's Group, 1993; fellow Va. Inst. Polit. Leadership, 1995 Mem. State Coun. Higher Edn. Va. (pub. affairs adv. com. 1985—), Greater Washington Bd. Trade, Fairfax County C. of C. (legis. affairs com. 1984—, millenium steering com. 1999) Va. Women Lobbyists, No. Va. Bus. Roundtable, Internat. Platform Assn., Phi Delta Kappa (20-Yr. Continuous Svc. award 2001), Kappa Delta Alumni No. Va., Psi Chi, Phi Kappa Phi Roman Catholic. Avocations: piano, organ, reading, hiking. Home: 4902 Ravensworth Rd Annandale VA 22003-5552 Office: NVCC 4001 Wakefield Chapel Rd Annandale VA 22003-3796 Office Phone: 703-323-3750. Business E-Mail: mcwilhelmi@nvcc.edu.

WILHITE, NANCY JANE, evangelist; b. Knoxville, Tenn., Oct. 7, 1944; d. Melvin Bertrand Wilhite and Laura Brownlee Rogers. BS in Elem. Edn., U. Tenn., 1965; MDiv, Emory U., 1992. Cert. elders order (ordination) 1994, evangelist. Tchr. Knoxville City Schs., 1966, 1969—71; recreation dir. and social worker ARC mil. base hosp., 1966—68; tchr. Birmingham City Schs., Ala., 1968—69; field dir. Tanasi Girl Scout Coun., Knoxville, 1971—76; owner and dir. Kaleidoscope Pre-Sch., Gatlinburg, Tenn., 1981—86; exec. housekeeper Holiday Inn, Gatlinburg, 1986—87; pastor Holston Conf. United Meth. Ch., Harriman, Tenn., 1991—94; evangelist Kaleidoscope Ministries, Inc., Knoxville, 1994—, preacher, dramatist, tchr.; min. Greystone Circuit United Meth. Ch., Greensville, Tenn., 2004—. Author: (book) The Rev. William Hurd Rogers and His Descendants, 2004. Mem.: Nat. Assn. United Meth. Evangelists (v.p. 2000—03). Avocation: genealogy. Home: 6538 New River Rd Fairlawn VA 24141 Office: Kaleidoscope Ministries 2100 Greystone Rd Greeneville TN 37743-8601 E-mail: ladymin@earthlink.ne.

WILKE, SABINE, language educator; b. Wiesbaden, Germany, July 21, 1957; d. Hans and Klara Wilke; m. Richard T. Gray, Dec. 6, 1984; 1 child, Cora L. Wilke-Gray. MA, U. Mainz, Germany, 1982, PhD, 1986. Asst. prof. German, Stanford U., Calif., 1986—89, U. Wash., Seattle, 1989—92, assoc. prof., 1992—97, prof., 1997—. Vis. prof. Harvard U., Cambridge, Mass., 2000—. Author books. Fellow Fulbright-DAAD fellow, 1983—84, NEH, 1990—91, Humboldt Found., 1996—97; Fulbright fellow, 2003—04, Guggenheim fellow, 2003—04. Office: U Wash Dept Germanics Box 353130 Seattle WA 98195 Office Phone: 206-543-4580. Business E-Mail: wilke@u.washington.edu.

WILKE MONTEMAYOR, JOANNE MARIE, nursing administrator; b. Jerome, Ariz., Sept. 10, 1941; d. Karl Nickolas and Anna Linda (Worgt) Wilke; m. Casimiro L. Montemayor, Oct. 8, 1978. BS in Nursing, U. Colo., 1965; M in Nursing, U. Washington, 1974. Patient care coord. Vesper Hospice, San Leandro, Calif., 1989-93, RN case mgr., 1993-95, Summit Med. Ctr., 1995—. With USNR, 1959-79. Mem. Nat. Hospice Orgn. Democrat. Methodist. Avocations: music, gardening, cooking, silk flower arranging.

WILKEN, CLAUDIA, judge; b. Mpls., Aug. 17, 1949; BA with honors, Stanford U., 1971; JD, U. Calif., Berkeley, 1975. Bar: Calif. 1975, U.S. Dist. Ct. (no. dist.) Calif. 1975, U.S. Ct. Appeals (9th cir.) 1976, U.S. Supreme Ct. 1981. Asst. fed. pub. defender U.S. Dist. Ct. (no. dist.) Calif., San Francisco, 1975-78, U.S. magistrate judge, 1983-93, dist. judge, 1993—; ptnr. Wilken & Leverett, Berkeley, Calif., 1978-84. Adj. prof. U. Calif., Berkeley, 1978-84; prof. New Coll. Sch. Law, 1980-85; mem. jud. br. com. Jud. Conf. U.S.; past mem. edn. com. Fed. Jud. Ctr.; chair 9th cir. Magistrates Conf., 1987-88; mem. bd. Berkeley H.S. Sch. Site Com., 2004-. Mem. ABA (mem. jud. adminstrn. divsn.), Alameda County Bar Assn. (judge's membership), Nat. Assn. Women Judges, Order of Coif, Phi Beta Kappa. Office: US Dist Ct No Dist 1301 Clay St # 2 Oakland CA 94612-5217

WILKENFELD, JOHANNAH, labor union administrator; b. Chgo., Apr. 4, 1927; d. Julius and Lillyan Nathan; m. Robert Hoffman (dec.); children: Mallory Hoffman, Randi Rosenkrantz, Marshall Hoffman; m. Herschell Wilkenfeld, Feb. 14, 1999. Pres. Union Iron and Metal Co., Houston, 1992—2000. Bd. mem., head major gifts Houston Grand Opera, 1974—90; bd. mem., chmn. fundraiser com. Alzheimer Assn. Houston, 1987—90. Named Outstanding Vol., Mayor Houston, 1990; recipient Blue Chip Enterprise award, Houston Bus. Jour., 1998. Avocations: music, opera, theater, creative writing. Home: 10170 Memorial Dr Houston TX 77024

WILKENFELD, POLLY, librarian; m. Bruce M. Wilkenfeld, Sept. 7, 1969; children: Ari J., Joshua I., Daniel A. BA in Psychology, Barnard Coll., NYC, 1970; MS in Libr. Sci., Columbia U., NYC. Sch. libr. Mizrachi Sch., University Hts., Ohio, 1995—2002; head reference & instrn. svcs. Ursuline Coll., Pepper Pike, 2002—06; head patron svcs. & instrn. Ursuline Coll. Libr., 2006—. Contbr. book. Mem. coms. Congregation Shaarey Tikvah, Beachwood, Ohio. Mem.: Academic Libr. Assn. OH. Office: Ursuline College 2550 Lander Rd Pepper Pike OH 44124 Office Phone: 440-449-4080. Business E-Mail: pwilkenfeld@ursuline.edu.

WILKENING, LAUREL LYNN, academic administrator, aerospace scientist; b. Richland, Wash., Nov. 23, 1944; d. Marvin Hubert and Ruby Alma Wilkening; m. Godfrey Theodore Sill, May 18, 1974 BA, Reed Coll., Portland, Oreg., 1966; PhD, U. Calif., San Diego, 1970; DSc (hon.), U. Ariz., 1996. From asst. prof. to assoc. prof. U. Ariz., Tucson, 1973—80, dir. Lunar and Planetary Lab., head planetary scis., 1981—83, vice provost, prof. planetary scis., 1983—85, v.p. rsch., dean Grad. Coll., 1985—88; divsn. scientist NASA Hdqrs., Washington, 1980; prof. geol scis., adj. prof. astronomy, provost U. Washington, Seattle, 1988—93; prof. earth system sci., chancellor U. Calif., Irvine, 1993—98. Dir. Rsch. Corp., 1991-2003, Seagate Tech., Inc., 1993-2000, Empire Ranch Found., 1998-2003, 2005—; vice chmn. Nat. Commn. on Space, Washington, 1984-86, Adv. Com. on the Future of U.S. Space Program, 1990-91; chair Space Policy Adv. Bd., Nat. Space Coun., 1991-92; co-chmn. primitive bodies mission study team NASA/European Space Agy., 1984-85; chmn. com. rendezvous sci. working group NASA, 1983-85; mem. panel on internat. cooperation and competition in space Congl. Office Tech. Assessment, 1982-83; trustee NASULGC, 1994-97, UCAR, 1988-89, 97-98, Reed Coll., 1992-2002. Editor: Comets, 1982. Recipient trainee, NASA, 1967—70; grantee fellow, U Calif Regents, 1966—67. Fellow Meteoritical Soc. (councilor 1976-80), Am. Assn. Advanced Sci.; mem. Am. Astron. Soc. (chmn. div. planetary scis. 1984-85), Am. Geophys. Union, AAAS, Planetary Soc. (dir. 1994-2000, v.p. 1997-2000), Phi Beta Kappa. Democrat. Avocations: gardening, camping, swimming.

WILKERSON, LUANN, dean, medical educator; BA magna cum laude, Baylor U., 1969; MA in English, U. Tex., 1972; EdD, U. Mass., 1977. Tchg. asst. dept. English U. Tex., Austin, 1970-72; tchr. grade 8 lang. arts Quabbin Regional H.S., Barre, Mass., 1974-75; rsch. asst. Clinic to Improve Univ. Tchg. U. Mass., Amherst, 1974-76, staff assoc., 1976-77; dir. tchg. and media resource ctr., asst. prof. speech and theatre Murray (Ky.) State U., 1977-80; acting dir., coord. faculty devel. office ednl. devel. and resources Coll. Osteopathic Medicine Ohio U., Athens, 1980-81; assoc. dir. office curricular affairs, asst. prof. family medicine Med. Coll. Wis., Milw., 1981-83; ednl. specialist ednl. devel. unit Michael Reese Hosp. and Med. Ctr., Chgo., 1983-84; dir. faculty devel. office ednl. devel. Harvard Med. Sch., Boston, 1984-91, lectr. in med. edn., 1988-91; dir. Ctr. for Ednl. Devel. and Rsch. UCLA Sch. Medicine, 1992-99, asst. dean med. edn., 1992-94, assoc. prof. medicine, 1992-95, prof. medicine, 1996—, assoc. dean med. edn., 1995-97, sr. assoc. dean med. edn., 1998—. Mem. editl. bd. Advances in Health Scis. Edn., 1995—, Med. Edn., 1995—, Acad. Medicine, 2001—; reviewer: Acad. Medicine, 1989—, Tchg. and Learning in Medicine, 1990—, Jour. Gen. Internal Medicine, 1988—, Am. Ednl. Rsch. Assn., 1987—, Rsch. Med.Edn. Ann. Conf., 1988—; contbr. articles to profl. jours. and chpts. to books; lectr. in field. Recipient Clinician Tchr. award Calif. Regional Soc. Gen. Internal Medicine, 1995, Excellence in Edn. award UCLA Sch. Medicine, 1998. Mem. Am. Assn. Med. Colls. (mem. rsch. med. edn. com. 1990-93, western chair group on ednl. affairs 1995-97, co-dir. fellowship in med. edn. rsch. 1995-97, convenor spl. interest group on faculty devel. 1997-98, chair group on ednl. affairs 1997—), Am. Ednl. Rsch. Assn., Profl. and Orgnl. Devel. Network (mem. nat. core com. 1977-80, 84-86, exec. dir. 1984-85), Phi Beta Kappa. Office: UCLA Sch Medicine Ctr Ednl Devel & Rsch PO Box 951722 Los Angeles CA 90095-1722 E-mail: lwilkerson@mednet.ucla.edu.

WILKERSON, PATRICIA HELEN, director; b. Victoria, Tex., Aug. 2, 1936; d. Milo Andrew and Gertrude H. (Nichols) Beeman; children: Cheryl Lynn, Susan Leigh, Debra Ann, Jon Craig. Student, U. Corpus Christi, Tex., 1954—56, Del Mar Coll., 1970—71, student, 1986—88. Tax clk. Nueces County Tax Assessor, Corpus Christi, Tex., 1956—57; corr. sec. Boy Scouts of Am. Gulf Coast Coun., Corpus Christi, 1957—58; elem. dir, nursery sch. coord. First Bapt. Ch., Corpus Christi, 1972—73, pre-K tchr., sec., 1975—85; dir. child devel. ctr. 2d Bapt. Ch., Corpus Christi, 1985—99, Northway Bapt. Ch., Dallas, 1999—. ASSIST pre-sch. leader Corpus Christi Bapt. Assn., 1967-99; conf. leader, cons. Bapt. Gen. Conv., Dallas, 1967—; mem. early childhood adv. bd., Del Mar Coll., Corpus Christi, 1981-86; mem. adv. com. Tex. Bapt. Weekday Assn., Dallas, 1995-98, Gulf Coast Tng. coalition. Writer Presch. Sunday Sch. Curriculum, 1992-99, Southern Bapt. Conv. Sunday sch. tchr. various Tex. Bapt. chs., 1959—2006; conf. leader Dallas Bapt. Assn., 2000—02. Mem. Bay Area Assn. Edn. Young Children (sec. 1981-82, co-chair conf. 1991, Week of the Young Child chair 1995-96). Avocations: reading, sewing, cats, nature study. Office: Northway Bapt ChCtr 3877 Walnut Hill Ln Dallas TX 75229 Home: 2323 Anderson Irving TX 75062 E-mail: cdc@northwaybaptist.org.

WILKERSON, RITA LYNN, retired special education educator; b. Crescent, Okla., Apr. 22; BA, Cen. State U., Edmond, Okla., 1963; MEd, Cen. State U., 1969; postgrad., U. Okla., 1975, Kans. State U. Elem. tchr. music Hillsdale Pub. Sch., Okla., 1963-64; jr. high sch. music and spl. edn. Okarche Pub. Sch., Okla., 1965-71; cons. Title III Project, Woodward, Okla., 1971-72; dir. Regional Edn. Svc. Ctr., Guymon, Okla., 1972-81; dir., psychologist Project W.O.R.K., Guymon, 1981-90; tchr. behavioral disorders Unified Sch. Dist. 480, Liberal, Kans., 1990—2004; sch. psychologist Hardesty Schs., Okla., 1994; spl. ednl. cons., sch. psychologist, cons. Optima, Hardesty, Goodwell and Hooker, 2004—. Diagnostician Tyrone, Okla. Pub. Schs., 1992-95; home svcs. provider Dept. Human Svcs., Guymon, 1990; active Kans. Dept. Social and Rehab. Svcs., 1993—; adj. tchr. Seward County C.C., 1994—; cons. in field. Grantee Cen. State U., 1968-69, Oklahoma City Dept. Edn., 1988-89. Mem. ASCD, NAFE, NEA (liberal Kans. chpt.), AAUW, Coun. Exceptional Children, Okla. Assn. Retarded Citizens, Okla. Assn. for Children with Learning Disabilities, Phi Delta Kappa. Republican. Avocation: crafts. Home: 616 N Crumley St Guymon OK 73942-4341 Office: Unified Sch Dist 480 7th And Western Liberal KS 67901 Business E-Mail: rwnguy@ptsi.net.

WILKERSON WALLEY, HAZEL SARAH, music educator, lay worker; d. Gary Ward and Barbara Ann Wilkerson; m. Derrick Wayne Walley, June 17, 2006. BS in Music Edn., U. Mobile, Ala., 2004. Cert. tchr. music primary-12 Ala., 2005. Youth min. First Bapt. Ch., Mobile, Ala., 2002—; elem. music tchr. Mobile County Pub. Sch., 2005, Baldwin County Pub. Schools, Spanish Fort, 2005—. Youth missions leader First Bapt. Ch., Mobile, Ala., 2002—06. Named Miss U. Mobile, 2003; scholar, Bd. Trustees U. Mobile, 2000—04. Mem.: NEA, Music Tchr. Nat. Assn., Am. Orff Schulwerk Assn., Music Educators Nat. Conf. Baptist. Office: Rockwell Elem Sch 10183 Highway 31 Spanish Fort AL 36527 Office Phone: 251-626-5528. Office Fax: 251-621-7206. Business E-Mail: swilkerson@bcbe.org.

WILKEY, ELMIRA SMITH, illustrator, artist, writer, educator; b. Kankakee, Ill., Dec. 13, 1936; d. Edmond Anthony and Dorothy Agnes (Schilling) Smith; m. Lowell Gene Wilkey; children: Anthony, Eric, Martin, Barry, Tad, Jeremy. BA cum laude, Loretto Heights Coll. (now Regis U.), Denver, 1958. Mgr. Duncan Assocs., Champaign, Ill., 1960-61; English/drama speech tchr. Kankakee Sch. Dist., 1958-60; substitute tchr. Kankakee County, 1965-80; art instr. Kankakee C.C., 1988, 2000; behavior couns. Nutri-Sys., Bourbonnais, Ill., 1987-91; English tchr. Bishop McNamara H.S., Kankakee, 1994-2000; founder, co-owner, printer Studio Sans Serif Divsn., Bronte Press Ltd. Edits., Manteno, Kankakee, Bourbonnais, 1977—. Textbook art cons. DSP, Boston, 1965-74; art adj. Olivet Coll., Bourbonnais, 1993-94; writer, art presenter W.C. Workshops Olivet Coll., Kankakee Art League, 1980-90, design cons. for histories Sisters, Servants of the Holy Heart of Mary, 2002-04; lectr. in field. Illustrator: Come Spring, History of Rockville, Hoofbeats, 2001; with Children's Book Program, cable TV, Manteno, Ill., 1996-99, ten books including classic, historical prose, poetry, folklore, herbal subjects, and 2 children's books; columnist Pat's Meanders, 1992—; one woman shows include Galesburg Civic Art Ctr., 1984, Tall Grass Art Assn., ONU Brandenberg Gallery, 1994; exhibited in solo shows at Prairie State Coll., 1980, Western Mich. U.; group shows include Ill. Women in the Arts Invitation, Prairie State Coll., 1980, Copley Soc., Boston, 1986, Tall Grass Art Assn., 2001, 05, 06, Xavier U., 2004, 05, Vanderpoel, Chgo., 2004-05, Tall Grass Gallery, Park Forest, Ill., 2005, 06, Sanctuary Gallery, Ill., 2005, 06. Cmty. arts. coun. Kankakee; cmty. art adv. bd. Kankakee C.C.; donates artwork annually to Hospice, Catholic Charities, United Way. Recipient numerous awards in art; Straw Series Signature art technique, V.I.P. Mem. Nat. League Am. Penwomen (Ill. state pres, Chgo. br. v.p. 1979—, treas. 2002—04), Ill. State Poetry Soc. (charter), Transparent Watercolor Soc. Am., Nat. Mus. Women in Arts, Great Books (charter, pres. 1980-85), Miniature Book Soc., Christians in Visual Arts. Republican. Roman Catholic. Avocations: walking, herb/plant identification, singing, piano, camping. Home and Office: Studio Sans Serif Divsn The Bronte Press 4136 W 6940N Rd Bourbonnais IL 60914-4208 Office Fax: 815-936-9913. Personal E-mail: miraswilkey@yahoo.com.

WILKEY, MARY HUFF, investor, writer, publisher; b. Dayton, Ohio, Sept. 30, 1940; d. Charles Joseph and Frances Rose (Wintersteen) Huff; divorced; children: Christopher Tyson, Charles Cory, Jennifer Jo. Student, Sinclair C.C., Dayton, 1979—85. Pvt. sec. Dare, Inc., Troy, Ohio, 1962-63; legal sec. Smith & Schnacke, Dayton, 1963-68; adminstrv. asst. U.S. Magistrate, Dayton, 1971-74; legal technician Coolidge, Wall, Womsley & Lombard Co., L.P.A., Dayton, 1968-75, 81-85, Lair & Owen, Dayton, 1979-81; owner, operator Village Mill Country Store, Tipp City, Ohio, 1987-88; mgr. Happy Days Residence, Franklin, Ohio, 1989—2005. Author, pub. (directory) Your Personal Guide, 1988, 89, 'elf Expressions Ezine, 2001—. Phone support vol. Operation Golden Ring, Dayton, 1984-85; vol. Sta. WPTD Pub. TV, Dayton, 1983-85. Mem. NAFE, Mensa, Internat. Platform Assn., Greater Dayton Real Estate Investor Assn. Avocations: Bible study, creative writing, natural health, real estate, internet marketing. Office Phone: 937-746-4086.

WILKIN, ALANA ZIMMER, elementary school educator; b. Danville, Pa., June 3, 1961; d. Albert Arthur and Alma Clara Zimmer; m. Timothy Vail Wilkin; children: Brandon Zimmer Madura, Albert Peyton Madura. BA, Thiel Coll., Greenville, Pa., 1983; MS, U. South Ala., Mobile, 1998. Cert. med. technologist Am. Soc. Clin. Pathologists, 1984, specialist in blood banking Am. Soc. Clin. Pathologists, 1984. Med. technologist Montefiore Hosp., Pitts., 1984—85, St. Elizabeth Hosp., West Lafayette, Ind., 1985—86; blood bank specialist St. Lukes Episcopal Hosp., Houston, 1986—87; quality control technologist Gamma Biologicals, Houston, 1987—90; med. technologist - tng. specialist ARC, Mobile, 1990—97; quality control mgr./trainer Gamma Biologicals, Houston, 1997—2001; tchr. lang. arts Cypress-Fairbanks Ind. Sch. Dist., Houston, 2001—. Recipient Spotlight Tchr., Cypress-Fairbanks Ind. Sch. Dist., 2006. Mem.: Assn. Tex. Profl. Educators, Pi Lambda Theta, Kappa Delta Pi. Home: 13311 Blackbird Dr Cypress TX 77429 Office: Lowery Elem 15950 Ridge Park Houston TX 77095 Office Phone: 281-463-5900. Business E-Mail: alana.wilkin@cfisd.net.

WILKINS, ADDI L., retired lay worker; b. Gleason, Tenn., June 9, 1933; d. Roy Thomas and Sendy Estelle Wilkins; children from previous marriage: Raybarn, Regina, Theresa, Roscoe, Anthony. At, Stowe Coll., St. Louis, 1953—55, St. Louis U., 1987, Valparaiso U., Ind., 1988. Consecrated Luth. Deaconess Assn., 1989. Adminstrv. asst. All Nation and Transfiguration Luth. Ch., St. Louis, coord. social ministry. Sec. no. zone women's group Luth. Women's Missionary League, St. Louis; sec. dist. bd. social ministry Luth. Family Svc. Luth. Ch. Mo. Synod; spkr. to ch. and youth groups. Chmn. bd. Pruitt Igo Devel. Housing Corp., St. Louis; bd. dir. United Ch. Christ Neighbor Houses, Friends of Moms; bd. mem. Luth. Family and Children Svcs. Named Mother of Yr., Sigma Gamma Rho (St. Louis chpt.), 1989; recipient Cmty. Svc. award, Nat. Coun. Negro Women, 2004, Star Bethel Bapt. Ch., 2004. Mem.: Luth. Deaconess Assn. Democrat. Lutheran. Avocations: gardening, reading, crafts, quilting. Home: 1905 E Warne Ave Saint Louis MO 63107-1017 Office Phone: 314-385-2653.

WILKINS, AMY P., publishing executive; BA, Holy Cross Coll. Assoc. pub., advt. dir. Health Mag., 1994—95, pub., 1995—97; pres. Petersen Youth Group1, 1997—98; pub. Biography Mag., 1998—2000, Smithsonian, Smithsonian Air & Space Mag., 2000, Better Homes and Gardens Mag., Country Home, 2006—. Office: Country Home Mag Meredith Publ 375 Lexington Ave New York NY 10017-5514*

WILKINS, ARLENE, social worker; b. Balt., Oct. 20, 1936; d. Joseph Martin and Alice Gertrude (Mickey) Martin Patterson; m. E.J. Wilkins, Jan. 15, 1963; children: Del, Deirdre, Justin, Patrick. BA, Wilkes Coll., 1959; MA, U. Pa., 1962. Lic. social worker. Social worker Children's Svc. Inc., Phila., 1960-62, Western Psychiat. Inst. and Clinic, Pitts., 1966-67, Bethesda United Presbyn. Ch., Pitts., 1967-70; clin. social worker Allegheny Gen. Hosp., Northview Heights Health Ctr., Pitts., 1986-99, ret., 1999; pvt. practice Pitts., 1999—. Program chmn. St. Andrew United Presbyn. Ch., Sewickley, Pa., 1981-83, elder, 1999-00; bd. dirs., sec., Cmtys. Outreach Ministry, 1995-00; past bd. dirs. Open Door Crafton Cmty. Agy. Mem. NASW, MSW (bd. cert. diplomate). Republican. Home: 802 7th St Rochester PA 15074-1433

WILKINS, CAROLINE HANKE, advocate, political organization worker; b. Corpus Christi, Tex., May 12, 1937; d. Louis Allen and Jean Guckian Hanke; m. B. Hughel Wilkins, 1957; 1 child, Brian Hughel. Student, Tex. Coll. Arts and Industries, 1956—57, Tex. Tech. U., 1957—58; BA, U. Tex., 1961; MA magna cum laude, U. Ams., 1964. Instr. history Oreg. State U., 1967-68; adminstr. Consumer Svcs. divsn. State of Oreg., 1977-80, Wilkins Assoc., 1980—. Mem. PFMC Salmon Adv. subpanel, 1982-86. Author: (with B. H. Wilkins) Implications of the U.S.-Mexican Water Treaty for Interregional Water Transfer, 1968. Dem. precinct committeewoman, Benton County, Oreg., 1964-90; publicity chmn. Benton County Gen. Election, 1964; chmn. Get-Out-the-Vote Com., Benton County, 1966; vice chmn. Benton County Dem. Ctrl. Com., 1966-70; vice chmn. 1st Congl. Dist., Oreg., 1966-67, chmn., 1967-68; vice chmn. Dem. Party of Oreg., 1968-69, chmn., 1969-74; mem. exec. com. Western States Dem. Conf., 1970-72; vice chmn. Dem. Nat. Com., 1972-77, mem. arrangements com., 1972, 76, mem. Dem. Charter Commn., 1973-74; mem. Dem. Nat. Com., 1972-77, 85-89, mem. size and composition com., 1987-89, rules com., 1988; mem. ethics commn., Oreg. Govt., 1974-76; del., mem. rules com. Dem. Nat. Conv., 1988; 1st v.p. Nat. Fedn. Dem. Women, 1983-85, pres., 1985-87, parliamentarian, 1993-95, 99-2001, chair Pres.'s coun., 2001-2003, chair by-laws com., 2003-05, parlimentarian, 2005-, we. regional dir., 2005—, western region dir., 2005-; mem. Kerr Libr. bd. Oreg. State U., 1989-95, pres., 1994-95; mem. Corvallis-Benton County Libr. Found., 1991-2001, sec., 1993, v.p., 1994, pres., 1995, mission and goals com. chair 2000-01; bd. dirs. Oreg. chpt. U.S. Lighthouse Soc., pres., 1997-98; bd. dirs. Oreg. State U.-Corvallis Symphony, 1998-2001, v.p. 1999-2000, resources com.; pres. Oreg. Fedn. Dem. Women, 1997-2001, Oreg. State-Corvallis chpt., UNIFEM, 1998-2002; bd. dirs. Oreg. State U. Acad. Lifelong Learning, 2003—; mem. Women and Philanthropy, Oreg. State U. Giving Cir., 2003; mem. Oreg. Jud. Fitness and Disability Commn., 2004-, vice chair, 2006-. Named Outstanding Mem. Nat. Fedn. Dem. Women, 1992, Woman of Achievement, Oreg. State U. Women's Ctr., 1998. Mem.: Soc. Consumer Affairs Profls., Nat. Assn. Consumer Agy. Adminstrs., Oreg. State U. Folk Club (pres. faculty wives 1989—90, scholarship chair 2000—01, grants com. 2002—03), Zonta Internat. (vice area bd. dirs. dist. 8 1992—94, bd. dist. 8 1994—96, by laws and resolutions chair 1997—98, internat. rels. coord. dist. 8 2000—02, chair dist. 8 nominating com. 2003—06, chair 2005—06, parliamentarian 2006—). Office: 3311 NW Roosevelt Dr Corvallis OR 97330-1169

WILKINS, MARTHA ANN, secondary school educator; b. St Louis, Jan. 8, 1936; d. Donald Porter Rogers, Sr. and Anna Margaret (Ohle) Rogers; foster children: Richard Yu, Eileen Yu children: Margaret Elizabeth, Maria Paige, Gregory Todd, Melanie Rebecca, Garlan Hay. AB, Washington U., St. Louis, Mo., 1958, postgrad., 1958—60, McCormick Sem., Chgo., Ill., 1972—73, Fla. Christian Coll., Kissimee, 1984—86. Cert. secondary tchr. Mo. Rsch. asst. Washington U., St. Louis, 1958—60; lectr., rsch. assoc. So. Ill. U., Edwardsville, 1960—62; co-dir. pilot program Presbyn. Bd. Nat. Missions, St. Louis, 1962—63; co-dir. Kiddie Kollege, Ravenswood YMCA, Chgo., 1974—76; tchr. children's nursery Eustis 1st Presbyn. Ch., Fla., 1978—88; bus. mgr. Golden Triangle YMCA, Fla., 1988; ch. nursery caretaker 1st Ch. Christ, Fla., 1988—98; substitute tchr. Bd. Edn., Lake County, Fla., 1980—85; pub. assistance specialist Fla. Dept. Children and Families, Lake County, 1989—97. Pres. County Title I Parent Adv. Coun., Lake County, Fla., 1977—79. Editor: (yearbook) Washington U. Hatchet, 1957—58. Participant World Coun. Chs., Noisey-Le-Grand, France, 1960; v.p. City of Tavares Libr. Bd., Fla., 2001—; founding mem. Nat. Campaign for Tolerance, Montgomery, Ala., 2003—; leader Girl Scouts Am., 1974—80; pres. N.E. Presbyterial United Presbyn. Ch., 1984—85. Recipient Sr. Svc. award, Girl Scouts Am., 1953; scholar, Sophomore Commn. Mem.: DAR, United Presbyn. Women, Wildlife Fedn., Nature Conservancy, Sierra Club, Mortar Bd., Delta Gamma. Presbyn. Avocations: genealogy, sewing, camping, reading. Home: 415 W Caroline St Tavares FL 32778

WILKINS, RITA DENISE, product development, research and technology director; b. Detroit, June 21, 1951; d. William H. and Alice L. (Hayes) Smith. Student, George Peabody Coll., 1969-70, Cleveland (Tenn.) State C.C., 1973-75. Mgmt. coord., legal coord. Arlen Realty and Devel. Corp., Chattanooga, 1973-76; asst. v.p., office mgr. Newburger Andes & Co., Atlanta, 1976-78, asst. v.p., project mgr., 1978-79; acquisition devel. mgmt. rep. Cardinal Industries, Inc., Atlanta, 1983-86; pres., sr. cons. CPC/Foresite, Charleston, SC, 1986—96; dir. info. Sys., rsch. Charleston, 1996—2000; dir. product. devel. tech. Advantage West, Asheville, NC, 2000—01; info. architect, tech. cons. DataTech Resources, Hendersonville, NC, 2001—. Guest lectr. Ga. State U. Contbr. articles to profl. jours. E-mail: rita.robinette@datatechresources.com.

WILKINS, SALLY, writer; b. Melrose, Mass., Dec. 9, 1956; d. Malcolm C. and Nancy Grant Dunbar; m. Thomas A. Wilkins, Nov. 28, 1981; children: Rebekah, Aaron, Rachel, Kathryn, Isaac. BA summa cum laude, Boston Coll., 1981. Co-author: The Insiders Guide to N.H., 1997; author: Forests, 1999, When Jesus was Little, 1999, Sports and Games of Medieval Cultures, 2002; co-author (with others): Lousia May Alcott Ency., 1999. Mem. Amherst Planning Bd., NH, 1986—; vice chair Amherst Sch. Bd., 1993—2000; dir. Amherst Land Trust, 1997—. Recipient Hon. Mention Journalism award, Cath. Press Assn., 1996. Mem.: Soc. Children's Book Writers & Illustrators. Roman Catholic. Avocations: gardening, hiking. Home: PO Box 273 Amherst NH 03031

WILKINS, VIRGINIA KATHLEEN, government liason; b. Balt., Oct. 11, 1985; d. Donald Arthur and Geraldine Davis Wilkins. B, Moravian Coll., Bethlehem, Pa., 2004—06. Founder, dir. Camp Hollywood: Where Every Girl's a Star, Severna Park, Md., 2000—02; docent coord. William Paca Ho., Annapolis, Md., 2002—03; resident advisor Moravian Coll., Bethlehem, 2004—06; mentor, coord. The Learning Connection: Moravian Coll., Bethlehem, 2004—; scholars in svc. Americorps, Bethlehem, 2005—06; program asst. John's Hopkins Ctr. Talented Youth, Sandy Springs, Md., 2006; project amb., govt. liason One World Youth Project, Marston Mills, Mass., 2006—. Concert coord. Moravian Coll., Bethlehem, 2006—. Concert liason Amnesty Internat., Md., 2002—04; on-site coord. LeaderShape, Bethlehem, 2005—06; coord. Holiday Hope Chests, Bethlehem, 2005—06; vol. Spl. Olympics, Bethlehem, 2006, 2004 Stop AIDS Campaign, 2003—04; with Americorps, Bethlehem, 2005—06; lobbying Student Global AIDS Conf., 2004; mem. fundraising bd. God's Littlest Angels Orphanage, Haiti, 2005—06. Recipient Honoree, Nat. Campaign Tolerance, 2005. Mem.: Model NATO (assoc.; pres. 2004—06), Habitat for Humanity (assoc.; sec. 2006), Sierra Club (assoc.), Amnesty Internat. (assoc.; coll. pres. 2004—06, Freedom Writer's award 2003), History Honor Soc., Fgn. Lang. Honor Soc., Nat. Honor Soc., Polit. Sci. Honor Soc., Zeta Tau Alpha (life; v.p., svc. chair, panhellenic del. 2004—06, Outstanding New Mem. award 2004). Democrat-Npl. Presbyterian. Avocations: sailing, rugby, piano, figureskating, belly dancing. Home: 203 Springdale Ave Severna Park MD 21146 Home Fax: 410-647-1236. Personal E-mail: vkwilkins@yahoo.com.

WILKINS, WANDA FAYE, retired publishing executive; b. Denton, Tex., Sept. 28, 1939; d. William S. Sherman and Mineola Luttrell; m. Galyn S. Wilkins, Dec. 6, 1975; 1 child, Dana Ann Williams. Student, Tex. Christian U. Exec. sec. to pub. Star-Telegram, Ft. Worth, 1969—88, dir. human resources, 1988—99; ret., 1999. Recipient SWA Painting of the Yr., 2005. Mem.: Internat. Soc. Exptl. Artists, So. Watercolor Soc. (Hal P. Moore award for Exptl. Painting), Soc. Watercolor Artists (various). Home and Studio: 7709 Woodside Hill Fort Worth TX 76179 Personal E-mail: wilkinswanda@sbcglobal.net.

WILKINSON, ANNE, musician, educator; d. Alfred Erwin and Helen Marie Barrett; m. Charles Edward Wilkinson, Dec. 29, 1979; children: Kate Barrett, Elyse Barrett, Erin Barrett. MusB, Western Mich. U., Kalamazoo, 1979. Orch. dir. Thornton Acad. and Saco Schs., Maine, 1990—; dir. So. Maine String Acad. U. So. Maine, Gorham, 2000—. Pvt. music tchr., Dayton, Maine, 1984—; free-lance cellist, Maine, 1984—; part-time tchg. faculty U. So. Maine, Gorham. Dir. So. Maine String Acad., Gorham, 2000—06. Honors String Quartet scholar, Western Mich. U., 1977—79. Mem.: Am. String Tchrs. Assn. with the Sch. Orch. Assn. (mem. scholarship com. Maine unit 2000—06), Saco Edn. Assn. (assoc.), Music Educators Nat. Conf. (assoc.). Democrat. Unitarian Universalist. Avocations: home renovation, gardening, reading, walking, travel. Home: 65 Waterhouse Rd Dayton ME 04005 Office: Thornton Academy 438 Main St Saco ME 04072 Office Phone: 207-282-3361. Personal E-mail: barrett2@adelphia.net. Business E-Mail: anne.wilkinson@thornton.saco.org.

WILKINSON, BARBARA J., pediatrician, educator; b. Mitcham, Surrey, Eng., June 5, 1946; came to U.S., 1954, naturalized, 1963. d. Arthur Frederick and Elizabeth (Law) Wilkinson. BA in Zoology with highest distinction, U. Maine, 1969; MD, Boston U., 1973. Diplomate Am. Bd. Pediatrics, 1981. Pediatric intern Boston City Hosp., 1973-74; fellow in neonatology U. Rochester/Strong Meml. Hosp., Rochester Gen. Hosp., Rochester, N.Y., 1976-78; resident in pediatrics Maine Med. Ctr., Portland, 1974-76, assoc. neonatologist, outreach educator, 1979-83, attending staff, courtesy staff, 1979—, lectr. for pediatric med. students Portland, 1983—2003; clin. instr. pediatrics part time faculty U. Vt. Coll. Medicine/Maine Med. Ctr., Portland, 1980-83, clin. asst. prof. pediatrics part time faculty, 1983—2004. Participant at emergency and family practice grand rounds on bereavement Maine Med. Ctr., early 1990s, co-facilitator Sudden Infant Death Support Group, 1980-2004; adj. faculty in allied health scis. So. Maine Vocat. Tech. Inst., South Portland, 1984-86; adj. faculty pathophysiology courses So. Maine Tech. Coll., South Portland, 1998-2000. Mem. Maine SIDS Found.; mem., contact person Maine Children's Meml. Libr. for Bereaved Parents, 1990s-; precinct ward clk. Elections, Portland, 1990's-2001. Fellow Am. Acad. Pediatrics; mem. AAUW (life), Am. Acad. Pediat., Altrusa Internat., Nat. Honor Soc., Phi Beta Kappa, Phi Kappa Phi (life). Avocations: watercolor painting, silk screening, photography, reading. Home: 56 Garrison St Portland ME 04102-1933

WILKINSON, BETH A., lawyer; BA cum laude, Princeton U., 1984; JD, U. Va., 1987. Bar: DC 1999, NY 1988. Capt., asst. to Army Gen. Counsel for intelligence, spl. ops., and nat. security matters, 1987—91; asst. US atty. Eastern Dist. NY, 1991; ptnr., litig. dept. Latham and Watkins, Litigation Dept., 1998—. Co-chair Latham and Watkins' White Collar Crime Practice Group. Author: "When Talk is Not Cheap: Communications With The Media, The Government, And Other Parties in High Profile White Collar Criminal Cases", Am. Criminal Law Review, 2002; featured on news programs such as NBC "Today" show, Nightline, NewsHour with Jim Lehrer, Face the Nation & Good Morning America, featured in National Law Journal, American Lawyer & Legal Times. Trustee Nat. Youth Leadership Forum; co-chmn. Constn. Project's Death Penalty Initiative. Named one of 75 Best Lawyers in Washington, Washingtonian Mag., 2002. Achievements include received the Exceptional Svc. award twice, Atty. Gen. highest commendation; prosecutor in Okla. City Bombings case; lead trial counsel for Gen. Electric; represented Ford Motor Co. during Firestone investigation. Office: 555 Eleventh St NW Ste 1000 Washington DC 20004-1304 Office Phone: 202-637-2200. Office Fax: 202-637-2201.

WILKINSON, DENISE V., psychologist; b. Coral Gable, Fla., Apr. 17, 1953; d. John Edward Van Diver and Doris Helen Sandner; m. Michael Bert Wilkinson; children: Melissa Brittany, Justin Bert. BA, Univ. S. Fla., Tampa, Fla., 1979, MA, 1981, Edn. Specialist, 1988. Cert. sch. psychologist 1987; lic. 1988. Mental health tech. Upper Pinellas Assn. for Retarded Citizens, Clearwater, Fla., 1974—76; psychometrist pvt. practice, Tampa, Fla., 1976—79, Devel. Ctr., Tampa, Fla., 1979; sch. psychologist Pasco County Sch. Bd., Land O'Lakes, Fla., 1982—. Sch. psychologist pvt. practice, Land O'Lakes, Fla., 1989—. Contbr. articles pub. to profl. jour. Recipient Student Svcs. Tchr. of the Yr., Pasco County Sch. Bd., 1996. Mem.: Nat. Assn. of Sch. Psychologist, Fla. Assn. of Sch. Psychologist. Independent. Unitarian Universalist. Avocations: photography, travel, beach, seashell collecting, collecting postcards. Office: Pasco County Sch Bd 7227 US Hwy 41 N Land O Lakes FL 34639 Home: 22846 Chesterview Loop Apt 101 Land O Lakes FL 34639-5343

WILKINSON, DORIS, medical sociology educator; b. Lexington, Ky., June 13, 1936; d. Howard Thomas and Regina Wilkinson. BA, U. Ky., 1958; MA, Case Western Res. U., 1960, PhD, 1968; MPH, Johns Hopkins U., 1985; postgrad., Harvard U., summer 1991. Asst. prof. U. Ky., Lexington, 1968-70; assoc. prof., then prof. Macalester Coll., St. Paul, 1970-77; exec. assoc. Am. Sociol. Assn., Washington, 1977-80; prof. med. sociology Howard U., Washington, 1980-84; vis. prof. U. Va., 1984-85; prof. sociology U. Ky., Lexington, 1985—. Chmn. panel women in sci. program NSF, Washington, 1976; rev. panelist Nat. Inst. Drug Abuse, Washington, 1978—79; mem. bd. sci. counselors Nat. Cancer Inst., Bethesda, Md., 1980—84; vis. scholar Harvard U., Cambridge, Mass., 1989—90, vis. prof. (summers), 1992, 93, 94, 97; Rapoport vis. prof. social theory (summers) Smith Coll., 1995, 96; bd. dirs. Nat. Conf. for Cmty. Justice, 1992—96; dir. Heritage Project, 2000—. Author: Workbook for Introductory Sociology, 1968; editor: Black Revolt: Strategies of Protest, 1969; co-editor: The Black Male in America, 1977, Alternative Health Maintenance and Healing Systems, 1987, Race, Gender and the Life Cycle, 1991, Race, Class and Gender, 1996; social history photographic exhbn. "The African American Presence in Medicine" Harvard Med. Libr., 1991, Pearson Mus.- So. Ill. U. Med. Sch., 1992, N.J. Coll. Medicine and Dentistry, 1993, Louisville Mus. History and Sci., 1994, U. Cin. Med. Sch. Libr., 1994, Albert Einstein Coll. of Medicine, 1995, Midway Coll., 1996; contbr. articles to profl. jours. Bd. overseers Case Western Res. U., Cleve., 1982-87; apptd. Ky. Commn. on Women, 1993-96. Recipient Pub. Humanities award U. Ky., 1990, Midway Coll. Women's History Month award, 1991, Gt. Tchr. award Nat. Alumni Assn. U. Ky., 1992, Disting. Scholar award Assn. Black Sociologists, 1993, Cmty. Svc. award Frankfort-Lexington Links, Inc., 2005-, Cmty. Svc. award Girl Scout Wilderness Road Coun., Lexington, Ky., 2005; inducted into Hall of Disting. Alumni, U. Ky., 1989, Ida Lee Willis Mem. award, 2006, award Ky. Heritage Found., 2006; fellow Woodrow Wilson Found., 1959-61, Ford Found., 1989-90; grantee Social Sci. Rsch. Coun., 1975, Nat. Inst. Edn., 1978-80, Nat. Cancer Inst., 1986-88, Ky. Humanities Coun., 1988, 01, Am. Coun. Learned Soc., 1989-90, NEH, 1991; Disting. Prof. in Coll. Arts and Scis., U. Ky., 1992-93, Coll. of Social Work Hall of Fame, U. Ky., 1999; Disting. Lectureship named in hon. AASR Program, 2000. Mem.: Ea. Sociol. Soc. (v.p. 1983—84, pres. 1992—93, I. Peter Gellman award 1987), Soc. Study Social Problems (v.p. 1984—85, pres. 1987—88), DC Sociol. Soc. (pres. 1982—83), So. Sociol. Soc. (honors com. 1993—94), Am. Sociol. Assn. (exec. assoc. 1977—80, budget com. 1985—88, v.p. 1991—92, mem. coun. 1994—97, elected History of Sociology sect. 2003, Dubois-Johnson-Frazier award 1988), Phi Beta Kappa.

WILKINSON, FRANCES CATHERINE, librarian, educator; b. Lake Charles, La., July 20, 1955; d. Derrell Fred and Catherine Frances (O'Toole) W.; div.; 1 child, Katrina Frances. BA in Comm. with distinction, U. N.Mex., 1982, MPA, 1987; MLS, U. Ariz., 1990. Mktg. rsch. auditor Mktg. Rsch. N.Mex., Albuquerque, 1973—78; freelance photographer, 1974—75; from libr. supr. gen. libr. to assoc. dean libr. svcs. U. N.Mex., Albuquerque, 1978—2001, interim dean libr. svcs., 2001—02, assoc. dean librs., 2002—06, interim dean, 2006—. Cons., trainer ergonomics univs. and govt. agys. across U.S., 1986—; bd. dirs. Friends of U. N.Mex. Librs., Albuquerque, 1991-94; mediator Mediation Alliance, 1991-94, U. N.Mex. Faculty Dispute Resolution, 1999—; mediation coach U. N.Mex., 1999-2000. Author, editor books; editor jour. columns; contbr. articles to profl. jours. Counselor, advocate Albuquerque Rape Crisis Ctr., 1981-84. Recipient James Fulton Zimmerman award for adminstrv. excellence, Friends of U. N.Mex. Librs., Inc. Mem.: ALA (com. 1990—2000, 2003—, Leadership in Libr. Acquisitions award 2000), N.Mex. Assn. Rsch. Librs., N.Mex. Preservation Alliance (vice chair 1995—96), N.Mex. Libr. Assn., N.Am. Serials Interest Group (com. 1994—97, exec. bd. 1997—2001, com. 2001—03), Pi Alpha Alpha, Phi Kappa Phi (chpt. treas. 1991—92, chpt. pres. 1992—94). Home: PO Box 8102 Albuquerque NM 87198-8102 Office: U N Mex Univ Librs MSC 05 3020 1 University of New Mex Albuquerque NM 87131-0001 Office Phone: 505-277-4241. Business E-Mail: fwilkins@unm.edu.

WILKINSON, LOUISE CHERRY, psychology professor, dean; b. Phila., May 15, 1948; BA magna cum laude, Oberlin Coll., 1970; EdM, EdD, Harvard U., 1974. Prof., chmn. dept. ednl. psychology U. Wis., Madison, 1976-85; prof., exec. officer Grad. Sch. PhD Program CUNY, N.Y.C., 1984-86; disting. prof., dean Grad. Sch. Edn. Rutgers U., 1986—2003; dean Sch. Edn. Syracuse (NY) U., 2003—05, disting. prof. edn., psychology and comm. scis., 2003—. Chair ednl. strategic planning Rutgers U.; mem. nat. rev. bd. Nat. Inst. Edn., 1977, 85, 87; cons. Nat. Ctr. for Bilingual Rsch., 1982, 84, US Dept. Edn., 1995—96; adv. bd. Nat. Reading Rsch. Ctr., 1992—98; vis. prof. U. London, 2006—; honored guest prof. Beijing Normal U., 2001—05. Co-author: Communicating for Learning, 1991; editor: Communicating in Classroom, 1982, Social Context of Instruction, 1984, Gender Influences in the Classroom, 2002; co-editor: Literacy and Language Learning, 2004; contbr. articles to profl. jours.; mem. editl. bds. various publs.:. Fellow: APA, Am. Assn. for Applied and Preventive Psychology, Am. Psychol. Soc.; mem.: NJ Coun. Acad. Policy Advisors, Am. Ednl. Rsch. Assn. (v.p. 1990—92, program chair 1997). Home: 525 Plum St # 208 Syracuse NY 13204

WILKINSON, MARYE, mathematics educator; b. Orange, Tex., Oct. 25, 1945; d Richard E. and Eve (Michon) Wilkinson; m. Grady L. Dorrough, Apr. 28, 1968; children: Kathleen, Alan, Donald. Student, U. Ala., Huntsville, 1984-85; AS, Brevard Community Coll., Cocoa, Fla., 1987; BS summa cum laude, U. Cen. Fla., 1989, MEd, 1992, postgrad., 1993—. Br. mgr. Am. Express IBC, Schwaebisch, Gmuend, Fed. Republic Germany, 1970-73; sr. teller Minnequa Bank, Pueblo, Colo., 1978-80; tchr. math., math. dept. chairperson Astronaut High Sch., Titusville, Fla., 1989—. Fellow Martin Marietta U. Tenn., 1991, NASA, U. Ctrl. Fla., 1994; presenter state and local math. confs. Guardian, Fla. Guardian Ad Litem, Titusville, 1988, 89. Mem. Nat. Coun. Tchrs. Math., Fla. Coun. Tchrs. Math., Brevard Coun. Tchrs. Math. (pres. 1995-96), Kappa Delta Pi, Pi Mu Epsilon. Avocations: dog training, reading science fiction. Office: Astronaut High School 800 War Eagle Blvd Titusville FL 32796-2398

WILKINSON, ROSEMARY REGINA CHALLONER, poet, writer; b. New Orleans, Feb. 21, 1924; d. William Lindsay Challoner Jr. and Julia Regina (Sellen) Challoner/Schillo; m. Henry Bertram Wilkinson, Oct. 15, 1949; children: Denis James, Marian Regina, Paul Francis, Richard Challoner. Lifetime credential to teach poetry, San Francisco State U., 1978; LHD (hon.), Livre U., Pakistan, 1975; DLitt (hon.), World Acad. Arts & Culture, Rep. of China, 1981. Lectr./reader of poetry. Author: (poetry) A Girl's Will, 1973, California Poet, 1976, Earth's Compromise, 1977, It Happened to Me, 1978, I Am Earth Woman, 1979, The Poet and the Painter, 1981, Poetry and Arte, 1982, Gems Within, 1984, Nature's Guest, 1984, In the Pines, 1985, Longing for You, 1986, Purify the Earth, 1988, Sacred in Nature, 1988, Earth's Children, 1990, New Seed, 1991, Angels and Poetry, 1992, Cambrian Zephyr, 1993, Collected Poems, 1994, Poetry: Nature, 1996, Poetry: Spiritual, 1997, Poetry Calendar 2000, 1999, A Song in the Wind with Love, 2001, My Plea, 2001, Selected Verses, 2001, Blessing of Poetry, 2002, Living Spring Water, 2005, 2006, others, (epic) An Historical Epic, 1974, Epic of the Ships Captain, 1986. Founder Poetry-Fine Arts Divsn. of San Mateo (Calif.) County Fair, 1977, Dr. Williams Poetry Workshop, Burlingame H.S., 1985; sec.-gen. World Acad. Arts and Culture-USA, San Francisco, 1985—95, pres., 1994—2003. Mem.: Authors League Am., The Authors Guild, Acad. Am. Poets, Poetry Soc. of Am., Nat. League Am. Pen Women Inc. (Washington 4th and 5th v.p. 1986—90, Berkeley, Calif. pres. 1988—90, Lake Tahoe br. 1988—), World Acad. of Arts and Culture/World Congress of Poets, World Congress of Poets (Taipei, Taiwan bd. dirs. 1973—2003, San Francisco pres. 1981, sec.-gen. 1985—95, pres. 1994—2003), Soroptimist Internat. (hon.). Democrat. Roman Catholic. Avocations: reading, research, brush painting, lecturing. Home: 3146 Buckeye Ct Placerville CA 95667-8334

WILKINSON, SHARON ELIZABETH ROBERSON, elementary school educator; b. New London, Jan. 9, 1945; d. Raymond Benard and Georgia Elizabeth (Adair) Roberson; m. Stephen Thomas Wilkinson, June 4, 1966; 1 child, Shara Deeann. BA, Tex. A&M, 1966; MS, East Tex. State U., 1969; postgrad., Tex. Tech U. Cert. libr. sci., elem. and secondary edn. tchr., Tex. Tchr. English Edgewood (Tex.) High Sch., 1966-67; tchr. 5th grade Terrell (Tex.) Elem. Sch., 1967-69; tchr. English and reading Terrell High Sch., 1969-79; tchr. 4th grade, libr. Pringle-Morse Consolidate Ind. Sch. Dist., Morse, Tex., 1979-88; tchr. 6th grade English Dawson Elem. Sch., Wharton, Tex., 1989—. Part-time tchr. Henderson County Jr. Coll., 1973-79, Southwestern Christian Coll., 1973-79, Upward Bound, Southwestern Christian Coll., 1973-79; cons. Terrell Ind. Sch. Dist.; spl. friends adv. bd., at-risk students coord.; learning styles cons.; adminstrv. bd. Wharton UMC; dir. summer sch. program K-6 Camp Dawson, 1992—. Officer, bd. dirs. First United Meth. Ch., Stinnett, Tex., 1979-89, Wharton, 1989-91, Community Concerts, Wharton, 1990-91, 2nd v.p., organist, chancel choir, handbell choir, tap-dancing ladies group. Mem. ASCD, Tex. Gifted and Talented Assn., Tex. Tchrs. Assn. (pres. 1st v.p., 2d v.p., sec. 1970-76), Delta Kappa Gamma. Avocations: reading, travel, music, handbell choir, tap dance group. Home: PO Box 871 Wharton TX 77488-0871

WILKINSON, SIGNE, cartoonist; b. Wichita Falls, Tex. married. BA in English, 1972; student, Pa. Acad. Fine Arts. Reporter West Chester (Pa.) Daily Local News, Academy of Natural Scis., Phila.; freelance cartoonist Phila. and N.Y. publs.; cartoonist San Jose (Calif.) Mercury News, 1982-85, Phila. Daily News, 1985—. Illustrator: Abortion Cartoons in Demand, 1992, You Bet Your Tomatoes, 2002, How to Grow the $735 Tomato, 1999; contbr. to Univ. Barge Club News, various mags. Bd. dirs. Fair Hill Burial Ground. Recipient Pulitzer Prize for editl. cartooning, 1992, Overseas Press Club award, 1997, 2001, Robert F. Kennedy award, 2002. Mem. Assn. Am. Editl. Cartoonists (pres. 1994-95). Avocations: gardening, rowing. Office: Phila Daily News PO Box 7788 400 N Broad St Philadelphia PA 19130-4015 Business E-Mail: wilkins@phillynews.com.

WILKOF, MARCIA VALERIE, finance educator; b. Canton, Ohio, Oct. 2, 1950; d. Raymond G. and Rossetta G. (Alpiner) W. BA cum laude, U. Cin., 1972; MS, U. Pa., Phila., 1977, PhD, 1982. Asst. prof. bus. mgmt. Rutgers U., NJ, 1982-90; cons. Tom Peters Group; prin. mvwGroup. Adj. asst. prof. Wharton Sch. Bus. U. Pa.; guest lectr. Sch. Engring. and Applied Sciences U. Pa. Mem. Acad. Mgmt. Achievements include research in women-friendly companies.

WILKS, DANA LYN, protective services official, writer; b. Long Beach, Calif., Dec. 27, 1964; d. Donald Lee and Helen Arlene Wilks; m. Kim Kreimeyer, Apr. 3, 2004. BA, Colo. State U., Fort Collins, 1988, MA, 1993. Ordained to ministry Universal Life Ch., Calif., 2004; cert. corrections mgr. Am. Correctional Assn., 2004. Cert. addicitons counselor New Beginnings, Fort Collins, Colo., 1988—91; grad. tchg. asst. Colo. State U., 1992—93; case mgr. supr. The Restitution Ctr., Greeley, 1993—96; free-lance rschr. Denver, 1995—2006; probation officer 19th Jud. Dist., Greeley, 1996—2001; probation supr. 18th Jud. Dist., Centennial, 2001—; instr. U. No. Colo., Greeley, 2004—05. Trainer Colo. Jud. Br., Denver, 1995—; presenter in field. Author short stories, of poems. Mem. So. Poverty Law Ctr., Montgomery, Ala., 2005—06; mem., vol. Human Rights Campaign, Washington, 2003—06; vol. Shambhala Meditation Centers, Colo., 2003—06; project dir. Trek for Hospice, 2006—. Recipient Outstanding Svc. award, Colo. Alcohol and Drug Driving Safety Program, 2004. Mem.: Colo. Probation Supr. Assn. (chairperson 2004—06), Am. Correctional Assn., Am. Probation and Parole Assn. Achievements include first to pass testing and be granted the American Correctional Association's Certified Corrections Manager certification in Colorado. Avocations: travel, writing. Office: 18th Judicial Probation Dept 7305 S Potomac St 201 Centennial CO 80112-4041 Office Phone: 303-662-5946. Office Fax: 303-662-5900. E-mail: dana.wilks@judicial.state.co.us.

WILKSMAN, KAREN SONJIA, secondary school educator; d. Harvey Isaac and Elma Helen Wilksman; children: Dean Harvey Albert, Ted Eric Albert. M in Secondary Edn., Ala. A&M, Normal, 1979. Cert. tchr. Ala. English tchr. Huntsville (Ala.) City Schs., 1970—, Calhoun CC, Redstone, Ala., 1989—2006. Home: 3401 Pulaski Pike Huntsville AL 35810-3254 Office: Huntsville City Schs 2304 Billie Watkins Huntsville AL 35801 Office Phone: 256-428-8050. Personal E-mail: wilksman@bellsouth.net.

WILL, BETTY, elementary school educator; d. Rudy and Lillie Kaderka; m. Richard Will, Feb. 8, 1975; children: Melissa Ann, Amy Renee. BA, Dominican Coll., Tex, 1970. Cert. elem. edn. Tex., 1974. 4th grade tchr. All Saints Cath. Sch., Houston, 1974—75, 5th grade tchr., 1975—77. Mid. sch. math tchr. Wells Mid. Sch. - SISD, Spring, Tex., 1977—79; ec3 tchr. & asst. dir. St. Mary's Cath. Ch., Humble, Tex., 1984—87; media specialist St. Anthony Cath. Sch., San Antonio, 1991—. Dir.(asst.): (religious program) Agapaopolis. Vol. Over 1200 Hours Vol. Work Per Sch. Yr., Pasco County Pub. Schs., 1988—91. Mem.: Cath. Family Fraternal Tex. (life). Roman Catholic. Avocations: technology, gardening, cooking. Office: Saint Anthony Cath Sch 32902 Massachusetts Avenue San Antonio FL 33576 E-mail: bwill@tampabay.rr.com.

WILL, KATHERINE HALEY, academic administrator; m. Oscar Henry Will, III; 4 children. Student, Carleton Coll., 1970-73; BA in English, Tufts U., 1974; MA in English, U. Ill., Urbana, 1975, PhD in English, 1986. Instr. English Augustana Coll., Sioux Falls, S.D., 1977-86, asst. prof. English, 1986-90, faculty dir. new student seminar program, 1987-91, assoc. prof. English, 1990-96, dean grad. study, dir. gen. edn., 1991—96; provost, prof. English Kenyon Coll., Gambier, Ohio, 1996-99; pres. Whittier Coll., Calif., 1999—2004, Gettysburg Coll., Pa., 2004—. Participant Mgmt. Devel. Seminar for Higher Edn. Adminstrs., Harvard U., summer 1992; cons. and presenter in field. Contbr. articles to profl. jours. Bd. dirs. United Way Great L.A. NEH fellow Summer Seminar in Romanticism and Gender, UCLA, 1989. Mem.: Annapolis Group (exec. com.), Coun. Ind. Colls. (bd. dirs.), Nat. Assn. Ind. Colls. and Univs. (bd. dirs.). Office: Gettysburg Coll Pennsylvania Hall, 3 Fl W 300 N Washington St Gettysburg PA 17325 Office Phone: 717-337-6011. Office Fax: 717-337-6008. E-mail: will@gettysburg.edu.*

WILLANS, JEAN STONE, bishop, religious organization administrator; b. Hillsboro, Ohio, Oct. 3, 1924; d. Homer and Ella (Keys) Hammond; m. Richard James Willans, Mar. 28, 1966; 1 dau., Suzanne Jeanne. Student, San Diego Jr. Coll.; DD (hon.), Am. Coll. Sems., 1996. Ordained archdeacon, 1996, ordained priest 1997, consecrated bishop 1998, Ch. of the East. Asst. to v.p. Family Loan Co., Miami, Fla., 1946-49; civilian supr. USAF, Washington, 1953-55; founder, dir. Blessed Trinity Soc.; editor Trinity mag., L.A., 1960-66; co-founder, exec. v.p., dir. Soc. of Stephen, Altadena, Calif., 1967—; exec. dir. Hong Kong, 1975-81. Lectr. in field. Author: The Acts of the Green Apples, 1974, rev. edit. 1995, Chinese edit., 2003; co-editor: Charisma in Hong Kong, 1970, Spiritual Songs, 1970, The People Who Walked in Darkness, 1977, The People Who Walked in Darkness II, 1992, 2d edit., 2000; works archived at Fuller Theol. Sem., 2004. Recipient Achievement award Nat. Assn. Pentecostal Women, 1964; monument erected in her honor Kowloon Walled City Park, Hong Kong Govt., 1996. Republican. Office: Soc of Stephen PO Box 6225 Altadena CA 91003-6225

WILLARD, GARCIA LOU, artist; b. Huntington, W.Va., Apr. 15, 1943; d. Harry Lee and Laura Lillian (Riley) Hall; m. Victor Percy Young, Sept. 2, 1972 (dec. Mar. 1980); m. Roger Lee Willard, Aug. 22, 1988. Student, Marshall U., 1978—83, W.Va. U., 1993, U. N.D., 1994—95. Owner, pres. Young's Fine Art, Huntington, 1975-85, Dyna Line, Wheeling, W.Va., 1980-85; instr. pastel and drawing Oglebay Mus.'s Stifel Fine Art Ctr., Wheeling, 1984-87; instr. pastel and portraiture Ohio U., Athens, 1987; owner, operator Outlines, Phoenix, Ariz., 1988-91; contbg. artist Sonoran Gallery, Phoenix, 1993—. Mem. adv. bd. Profl. Art League, St. Clairsville, Ohio, 1984-85; lectr. and exhbn. juror various art orgns., Ohio, W.Va., Pa., 1987-88; art cons. Journey's End Designs, Wheeling, 1987. One woman shows include: Delf-Norona Mus., Moundsville, W. Va., Ariel Gallery, N.Y.C., Sonoran Gallery, Phoenix; Group shows include: Pen & Brush Club, N.Y.C., 1988, Hermitage Found. Mus., Va., 1988; contbr., illustrator: (book) Dr. Horton on African Art, 1985. Advisor Ariz. Fine Arts Commn., Phoenix, 1989-92. Recipient Best of Show award Delf-Norona Mus., 1985, Molly Guion award for graphics Catharine Lorillard Wolfe Art Club, 1988, Douglas Pickering Carnegie Mellon award, 1986. Fellow Am. Artists Profl. League (Pastel award 1988); mem. Pastel Soc. Am. (signature mem. artist mem., A & M design award, 1988), Acad. Artists Assn. (artist mem., award for pastel portrait 1989), Degas Pastel Soc. (artist mem., M. Grumbacher award for pastel excellence 1988), Nat. Drawing Assn., Art Assn. Harrisburg (artist mem.), Signature Mem. Pastel Soc. Am., N.Y.C. Republican. Avocations: archaeology, astronomy, paper-making, symphonies, travel. Office: Sonoran Gallery 8819 W Corrine Dr Peoria AZ 85381-8166 Office Phone: 623-773-1958. Personal E-mail: rrollo88@cox.net.

WILLARD, KAREN WALTERS, music educator; b. Concord, NC, Oct. 9, 1956; d. Earl Hoover and Maud Alice (Anderson) Walters; m. Michael Downing Willard, Dec. 29, 1979; children: William Karlton, Kristina Michelle. MusB, U. NC, Greensboro, 1978. Lic. collegiate. prof. Va. Music tchr. Isle Of Wight County Pub. Schs., Va., 1978—. Music dir. Smithfield Bapt. Ch., Va., 1978—. Actor Smithfield Cmty. Theatre; music dir. Cmty. Chorus, Smithfield. Recipient Elem. Tchr. of Yr., Isle Of Wight County Pub. Schs., 1991. Mem.: Music Educators Nat. Conf. (assoc.). Conservative. Baptist. Avocations: colonial dancing, reading, sewing, music, drama. Home: 311 Jefferson Dr Smithfield VA 23430 Office: Carrollton Elem Sch 14440 New Towne Haven Ln Carrollton VA 23314 Office Phone: 757-238-2452.

WILLARD, NANCY MARGARET, writer, educator; b. Ann Arbor, Mich. d. Hobart Hurd and Margaret (Sheppard) W.; m. Eric Lindbloom, Aug. 15, 1964; 1 child, James Anatole. BA, U. Mich., 1958, PhD, 1963; MA, Stanford U., 1960. Lectr. English Vassar Coll., Poughkeepsie, NY, 1965—. Author: (poems) In His Country: Poems, 1966; Skin of Grace, 1967; A New Herball: Poems, 1968, Testimony of the Invisible Man: William Carlos Williams, Francis Ponge, Rainer Maria Rilke, Pablo Neruda, 1970, Nineteen Masks for the Naked Poet: Poems, 1971, The Carpenter of the Sun: Poems, 1974, A Visit to William Blake's Inn: Poems for Innocent and Experienced Travelers, 1981 (Newbery Medal 1982), Household Tales of Moon and Water, 1983, Water Walker, 1989, The Ballad of Biddy Early, 1989; (short stories) The Lively Anatomy of God, 1968, Childhood of the Magician, 1973; (juveniles) Sailing to Cythera and Other Anatole Stories, 1974, All on a May Morning, 1975, The Snow Rabbit, 1975, Shoes Without Leather, 1976, T0e Well-Mannered Balloon, 1976, Night Story, 1986, Simple Pictures are Best, 1977, Stranger's Bread, 1977, The Highest Hit, 1978, Papa's Panda, 1979, The Island of the Grass King, 1979, The Marzipan Moon 1981, Uncle Terrible, 1982, (adult) Angel in the Parlor: Five Stories and Eight Essays, 1983, The Nightgown of the Sullen Moon, 1983, Night Story, 1986, The Voyage of the Ludgate Hill, 1987, The Mountains of Quilt, 1987, Firebrat, 1988; (novel) Things Invisible To See, 1984, Sister Water, 1993; (play) East of the Sun, West of the Moon, 1989, The High Rise Glorious Skittle Skat Roarious Sky Pie Angel Food Cake, 1991, A Nancy Willard Reader, 1991, Pish Posh said Hieronymus Bosch, 1991, Beauty and the Beast, 1992; illustrator: The Letter of John to James, Another Letter of John to James, 1982, The Octopus Who Wanted to Juggle (Robert Pack), 1990, (novel) Sister Water, 1993, (essays) Telling Time, 1993, (juvenile) A Starlit Somersault Downhill, 1993, (juvenile) The Sorcerer's Apprentice, 1993; author, illustrator: An Alphabet of Angels, 1994; (juvenile) Gutenberg's Gift, 1995, The Good Night Blessing Book, 1996, Cracked Corn and Snow Ice Cream, 1997, The Tortilla Cat, 1998; (poems, with Jane Yolen) Among Angels, 1995, Swimming Lessons, 1996, The Magic Cornfield, 1997; editor: (anthology of poems) Step Lightly: Poems for the Journey, 1998, The Tale I Told Sasha, 1999, (juvenile) Shadow Story, 1999, (juvenile) The Moon and Riddles Diner and the Sunny Side Cafe, 2001, (juvenile) The Mouse, the Cat and Grandmother's Hat, 2003, (scholastic) Cinderella's Dress, 2003, (young adult) Paradise Lost, 2004, Sweep Dreams, Little Brown, 2005 Recipient Hopwood award, 1958, Devins Meml. award, 1967, John Newbery award, 1981, Empire State award, 1996; Woodrow Wilson fellow, 1960; NEA grantee, 1987. Mem. The Lewis Carroll Soc. Office: Vassar Coll Dept English Raymond Ave Poughkeepsie NY 12604-0001

WILLE, KARIN L., lawyer; b. Northfield, Minn., Dec. 14, 1949; d. James Virginia Wille. BA summa cum laude, Macalester Coll., 1971; JD cum laude, U. Minn., 1974. Bar: Minn. 1974, U.S. Dist. Ct. Minn. 1974. Atty. Dresselhuis & Assoc., Mpls., 1974-75; assoc. Dorsey & Whitney, Mpls., 1975-76; atty. Dayton-Hudson Corp., Mpls., 1976-84; gen. counsel B. Dalton Booksellers, Edina, Minn., 1985-87; assoc. Briggs & Morgan, Mpls., 1987-88; shareholder Briggs and Briggs, Mpls., 1988—2005, of counsel, 2005—. Co-chair Upper Midwest Employment Law Inst., 1983—. Named Leading Minn. Atty., Super Lawyer, Mpls.-St. Paul Mag., Twin Cities Bus. Monthly and Minn. Law and Politics; named one of Best Lawyers in Am. Mem. ABA, Minn. State Bar Assn. (labor and employment sect., corp. counsel sect., dir. 1989-91), Hennepin County Bar Assn. (labor and employment sect.), Minn. Women Lawyers, Phi Beta Kappa. Office: Briggs & Morgan 80 S 8th St Ste 2200 Minneapolis MN 55402-2157 E-mail: kwille@briggs.com.

WILLE, LOIS JEAN, retired editor; b. Chgo., Sept. 19, 1931; d. Walter and Adele S. (Taege) Kroeber; m. Wayne M. Wille, June 6, 1954. BS, Northwestern U., 1953, MS, 1954; Litt.D. (hon.), Columbia Coll., Chgo., 1980, Northwestern U., 1990, Rosary Coll., 1990. Reporter Chgo. Daily News, 1958-74, nat. corr., 1975-76, assoc. editor charge editorial page, 1977; assoc. editor charge editorial and opinion pages Chgo. Sun-Times, 1978-83; assoc. editor editorial page Chgo. Tribune, 1984-87, editor editorial page, 1987-91, ret., 1991. Author: Forever Open, Clear and Free: the Historic Struggle for Chicago's Lakefront, 1972, At Home in the Loop: How Clout and Community Built Chicago's Dearborn Park, 1997. Recipient Pulitzer prize for public svc., 1963, Pulitzer prize for editorial writing, 1989, William Allen White Found. award for excellence in editorial writing, 1978, numerous awards Chgo. Newspaper Guild, numerous awards Chgo. Headline Club, numerous awards Nat. Assn. Edn. Writers, numerous awards Ill. AP, numerous awards Ill. UPI. Home: 1530 S State St Apt 1011 Chicago IL 60605 Personal E-mail: lowille@aol.com.

WILLE, ROSANNE LOUISE, educational consultant; b. Hackensack, N.J., Aug. 4, 1941; d. Albert Wille and Rose Marie (Rock) Eberhardt; m. George B. Jacobs, Mar. 12, 1980; children: Leigh, Steven, Alexander, Jeffrey. M Pub. Adminstrn., Rutgers U., 1986; PhD, N.Y.U., 1980. Dept. chair Rutgers U., Newark, 1978-84, Lehman Coll., Bronx, NY, 1984-87, dean, 1987-92, provost, sr. v.p., 1992—2002; cons. for higher edn., 2002—. Contbr. articles to profl. jours. Bd. dirs. Family Support Svcs., Bronx, N.Y., 1994-2002, bd. dirs. South Bronx Overall Economic Devel., Inc., Bronx, 1991-2002. Recipient Vision award Family Support Svcs., Bronx, 1996, Thousand Points of Light award Pres. George Bush, Washington, 1991. Mem. N.Y. Acad. Scis., N.Y. Acad. Medicine, Am. Assn. Higher Edn. Avocations: aviation, golf. Address: PO Box 4148 South Hackensack NJ 07606-4148 Personal E-mail: rlwille@earthlink.net.

WILLEFORD, PAMELA PITZER, former ambassador; m. George Willeford III; children: Emily Ann, Nancy Kathryn. BA in English and Spanish, U. Tex. Former tchr., Dallas; former dir. devel., coord. Tex. Capitol Rededication Tex. State Preservation Bd.; mem. Tex. Higher Edn. Coordinating Bd., Austin, 1995—, chair, 1998—2003; ptnr., pres. Pico Drilling Ltd., Breckenridge, Tex.; U.S. amb. to Switzerland and Liechtenstein US Dept. State, Bern, 2003—06.

WILLEMAN, FLORENCE KAY, secondary school educator, small business owner; b. Napoleon, Ohio, Mar. 8, 1948; d. Albert and Laurena (Plassman) Arps; m. David Martin Willeman, Aug. 6, 1978; children: Denise, Michael, Mark, Lynette, Angela. BS, Ohio State U., 1976. Cert. florist Ohio. Floral designer La Villa Florist, Napoleon, 1966-76; instr. horticulture Four County Jr. HS, Archbold, Ohio, 1976—. Owner Willeman's Flowers, Okolona, Ohio, 1986—, mail order, 1996—. Mem. NEA, NAFE, Am. Vocat. Assn., Ohio Vocat. Assn., Ohio Florists Assn., Shriners. Lutheran. Home: 815 Coon Hollow Dr Napoleon OH 43545-9701 Office: Willeman's Flowers PO Box 203 Okolona OH 43550-3203 E-mail: willeman@bright.net.

WILLEN, LIZ, reporter; Staff writer, edn. reporter Newsday, NYC, 1989—2000; reporter, sr. writer Bloomberg News, NYC, 2000—. Co-recipient Spl. citation, Edn. Writers Assn., 1994, George Polk award for health reporting, 2006, IRE award, Investigative Reporters & Editors Jour., 2006; recipient Breaking News Story award, Edn. Writers Assn., 1994. Office: Bloomberg News 731 Lexington Ave New York NY 10022 Office Phone: 212-617-2300. Office Fax: 917-369-5000. E-mail: ewillen@bloomberg.net.*

WILLENBRINK, ROSE ANN, retired lawyer; b. Louisville, Ky., Apr. 20, 1950; d. J.L. Jr. and Mary Margaret (Williams) W.; m. William I. Cornett Jr. Student, U. Chgo., 1968-70; BA in Anthropology with highest honors, U. Louisville, 1973, JD, 1975. Bar: Ky. 1976, Ind. 1976, U.S. Dist. Ct. (we. dist.) Ky. 1976, Ohio 1999. Atty. Mapother & Mapother, Louisville, 1976-79; v.p., counsel Nat. City Bank, Louisville, 1980-99, v.p., sr. atty. Cleve., 1999—2004, Louisville, 2004—05, ret., 2005. Mem. Ky. Bar Assn., Phi Kappa Phi. Home: 6803 Chadworth Pl Prospect KY 40059 Personal E-mail: willenbrink@yahoo.com.

WILLENZ, JUNE ADELE, writer, editor, playwright, scriptwriter, public relations executive; BS, U. Mich., 1945, MA, 1947; ABD, New Sch. for Social Rsch., 1951. Instr. English Montgomery Coll., Md. Exec. dir. Am. Vets. Com., 1965—2002; chair standing com. on women World Vet. Fedn., 1983—; conf. organizer Women In and After War, Bellagio, Italy, Rape in Armed Conflicts, Istanbul; lectr. USIA; radio and TV guest appearances; del. White House Conf. on Youth, White House Conf. Aging; planning com. 5th and 6th legis. confs. World Vets. Fedn.; scholar in residence Am. U., 1997—; rep. for U.S. Internat. Seminar on Peace Keeping, Baeria, Norway, 2001; lectr., spkr., presenter in field. Author: Women Veterans: America's Forgotten Heroines, 1983; co-author: Gender Differences, 1991; editor, author: Dialogue on the Draft, 1967, Human Rights of the Man in Uniform, 1969; editor: AVC Bull.; columnist Stars and Stripes; advisor, commentator (film) The GI Bill: The Law That Changed America, 1997; contbr. articles to profl. jours., local newspapers, popular mags., chapters to books. Exec. com. 1st VA Adv. Com. Womens Vets., 1983—86, First Lady's Women's Conf. Cir., 1995; head of working group on refugee women and women in armed conflict UN Decade for Women; accredited non-govtl. orgn. rep. World Vets. Fedn. UN, 1985—; organizer Workshops on Refugee Women, Armed Conflict, Gender Justice, and other issues at UN, N.Y.C. and Geneva; pub. mem. 19th Fgn. Officer Selection Bd. USIA; testified before congl. coms., exec. agys., chair Task Force on Vets. and Mil. Affairs for Leadership Com. on Civil Rights; advisor; co-chair Coordinating Com. on Voluntary Nat. Svc.; organizer nat. conf. Dialogue on Nat. Svc., 1989, The Draft, 1966, Human Rights of Man in Uniform, 1968, 1970; chair subcom. on disabled vets. Pres. Com. Employment of People with Disabilities, 1995—96; active Inter-Univ. Seminar Armed Forces & Soc.; adviser Vets. Brain Trust Conf., 1997. Recipient La Médaille de la Ville de Paris, Mayor of Paris, 2000, Human Rights award, UNA Nat. Capital, 2001, honored by Congl. Black Caucus, 1997, honored for outstanding leadership on behalf of disabled vets., U.S. Dept. Labor, 2002, Cross of Merit, Fedn. Women Vets., Helsinki, Finland, 2005. Mem. Non-Govtl. Orgn. Com. on Status of Women (convener task force on women in armed conflict, convener working group on refugee women), Authors Guild. Personal E-mail: june@junewillenz.com.

WILLERTON, BEVERLY KAY, mathematics educator; b. Borger, Tex., Apr. 23, 1951; d. Frank Quentin and Ozline M Ward; m. Donald L Willerton (div.); children: Justin, Joshua, Scott. BS, Midwestern State U., 1973. Math. tchr. Hirschi H.S., Wichita Falls, Tex., 1974—75; math. instr. U. N.Mex. at Los Alamos, 1987—, math. dept. chair, 1994—, divsn. chair, 2004—. Mem.: Nat. Assn. Devel. Edn., N.Mex. Assn. Two-Yr. Colls., Math. Assn. Am. Office: U NMex at Los Alamos 4000 University Dr Los Alamos NM 87544

WILLETT, ANNA HART, composer, painter; b. Bartlesville, Okla., June 18, 1931; d. Thomas Kellogg Willett and Mary Kathryn (Feist) Willett Dalferes; m. Roger Garland Horn, Aug. 1956 (div. June 1962). B in Music Edn., Southwestern La. Inst., 1954; studies with H. Gunderson, 1955—64; MA, La. State U., 1964, postgrad. in piano, voice majors, 1976-87; studies with K. B. Klaus, Jr., 1976—87, studies with D. Constanides, 1976—87. Lifetime tchr. cert. La. Pub. sch. vocal music tchr. Iberville Parish, Plaquemine, La., 1954-55, Orleans Parish, New Orleans, 1966-71; elem. music pedagogy tchr. St. Mary's Dominican Coll., New Orleans, 1972. Post-grad. rsch. history life scholar in late Medieval English Crown changes LSU. Composer: Dances for Solo Violin, 1981, Weaving Song, 1982, Entertainer's Song (from the opera Omar), 1983, Hercules Piano Variations, 1986, En Ivrez Solo Song, 1989, Solo Songson Poems of Alfieri, 1996, 2000, Variations on a Southern Folk Hymn for piano, Memories of New Orleans, variations for piano, voice Recital at Fest for All, (Operas) How to Murder Mother, 1982, Who Murdered Mother, 1982, Omar, 1984, Caught, 1986, Cellini the Opera, 1997, Lines on Wine, 1987, Druid Installation, 1992, Seven Gables, 1998, The Icey Road, 1999; exhibitions include La. State Archives, Baton Rouge,

Zeigler Gallery, Jennings, La., Old Bogan Fire Sta., Baton Rouge, Represented in permanent collections David S. Adler, MD; author: The Math. of History, 2000. Mem. ch. choir St. Albans Episc. chapel, 1976—. Scholar, Loyola U. South, New Orleans, 1972—73. Mem.: AAUW, Sigma Alpha Iota, Alpha Sigma Alpha. Avocations: gardening, bridge, local archeology. Home: 324 Roselawn Blvd Lafayette LA 70503-3910

WILLETT, HOLLY GENEVA, librarian, educator; b. Brunswick, Maine, Apr. 15, 1948; d. Hollis Eugene and Gene Edith (Stratton) W. BA magna cum laude, San Francisco State Coll., 1971; MLS, U. Calif., Berkeley, 1972; MA, Simmons Coll., Boston, 1980; PhD, U. N.C., 1986; postgrad., U. North Tex., Denton, 1993-94. Cert. tchr. Spanish, Tex., learning resources endosement, Tex. Libr. I, II Alameda County Free Libr., Fremont, Calif., 1972-78; coord. children's svcs. New Bedford Free Pub. Libr., Mass., 1980-81; asst. prof. U. Wis., Madison, 1985-92; asst. vis. prof. Tex. Woman's U., Denton, 1992-93, adj. asst. prof., 1993, 96; libr. media specialist Dallas Pub. Schs., 1993-97; asst. prof., libr. edn. coord. Rowan U., Glassboro, NJ, 1997—2003, assoc. prof., 2003—, chair dept. secondary edn., 2003—05. Planner, spkr. Children's Svcs. Inst., U. Wis.-Madison, 1989, 91. Editl. cons. Highsmith Press, Ft. Atkinson, Wis., 1992-93; author: Public Library Youth Services, 1995; author environ. rating scale for children's svcs., 1989— (Hannigan award 1991); contbr. articles to profl. jours. Bd. mem. Denton Unitarian Universalist Fellowship, 1994-96; life span religious edn. team leader Unitarian Univerlist Ch. of Christ, Cherry Hill, N.J., 2005-. Fellow Bush Inst. for Child & Family Policy, Chapel Hill, 1983-85, Margaret Kalp fellow U. N.C., Chapel Hill, 1981-83. Mem. ALA, Am. Folklore Soc., Assn. Libr. and Info. Sci. Edn. (Hannigan award 1991), Calif. Libr. Assn., Children's Lit. Assn., Nat. Storytelling Assn., six other nat. orgns. Democrat. Avocations: reading, gardening, choral singing. Office: Rowan Univ 201 Mullica Hill Rd Glassboro NJ 08028-1702 Office Phone: 856-256-4561.

WILLETT, JANE S., biology educator; b. Boston, Jan. 6, 1948; d. Allan J. and Ruth H. Stinchfield; m. Daniel G. Willett, July 3, 1971; children: Beth, Laura. BA, Colby Coll., Waterville, Maine, 1970; MEd, Univ. Maine, Orono, Maine, 1971. Biology tchr. Massabesic HS, Waterboro, Maine, 1971—78; paralegal Alfred, Maine, 1978—81; sci. tchr. Bonney Eagle Jr. High, Buxton, Maine, 1982—84; biology tchr., dept. chair Massabesic HS, Waterboro, Maine, 1984—2005. Bd. mem. Maine Sci. Tchrs., Augusta, Maine, 1990—94. Sch. com., Gorham, Maine, 1990—99; town coun., 1999—. Mem.: NEA, Am. Biology Tchrs., Alpha Delta Kappa. Avocations: tennis, skiing, reading, knitting, sewing.

WILLETT, MELISSA CAROL, art educator; m. James Robert Willett, Oct. 2, 2004. BA, Western Ky. U., 2003. Art tchr. Franklin (Ky.) Simpson Mid. Sch., 2004—. Baptist.

WILLETT, ROSLYN LEONORE, public relations executive, food service consultant, writer, editor; d. Edward and Celia (Stickler) Sternberg; m. Edward Willett (div.); 1 child, Jonathan Stanley. BA, Hunter Coll., NYC; postgrad., Columbia U., CUNY, NYU, New Sch. Dietitian YWCA, NYC; tech. and patents libr., food technologist in charge tech. svcs. and devel. Stein Hall & Co., NYC; editor McGraw-Hill, Inc., NYC, Harcourt Brace Jovanovich, Inc., NYC; pub. rels. writer Farley Manning Assocs., NYC; cons. pub. rels. and food svc. Roslyn Willett Assocs., Inc., NYC, 1959—. Adj. prof. Hunter Coll., Poly U., Columbia U. Sch. Pub. Health; dir. West End Writers Workshop, 1998—2002; seminar presenter in field. Author: The Woman Executive in Woman in Sexist Society, 1971, also short stories and essays; assoc. editor Timber Creek Rev., Words of Wisdom, 2001—, Bulls Head Creek Rev., 2004—. V.p. North Shore Ams. for Dem. Action; ofcl. rapporteur Post-Assembly Tech. Sessions, WHO; juror Am. Film Festival, Arts and Scis., 1962—88; chmn. Women's Polit. Caucus, Inc. NY, NJ, Conn, 1971—73; v.p. Mid Hudson Arts and Sci. Ctr., Poughkeepsie, NY; apptd. to regional adv. coun. Fed. SBA, 1976—78; chmn. image of woman com. NOW; bd. dirs. Small Bus. Task Force, Assn. for Small Bus. and Professions, 1981—85, Rhinebeck Chamber Music Soc., 1985—86, Will Inst., New Paltz, 1980—2001, Women Studies Abstracts, 1971—81; pres. Hunns Lake Assn., 1999—2001. Mem. Pub. Rels. Soc. Am. (accredited), Food Svc. Cons. Soc. Internat. (bd. dirs. 1978-80), NY Acad. Scis., Inst. Food Technologists, Juilliard Assn., Assn. for Japanese Art in Am., Inc., Alliance Française, Paris Club, NY Print Club. Avocations: writing, dance, art collecting, hiking, swimming. Home: 97 W Hunns Lake Rd Stanfordville NY 12581-5606 Office: 441 West End Ave New York NY 10024-5328

WILLETT, TERI KAY, art educator; b. Jefferson City, Mo., May 15, 1953; d. Robert Jewell and Esther Marie Cunningham; m. Roger Gregory Willett, Aug. 7, 1976; children: Sarah Ellen Willett-Otto, Jesse Timothy, Anthony Carter. BA, St. Mary Coll., 1975; M in religious Edn., Loyola U. New Orleans, 1987; MA, Ctrl. Mo. State U., 1997. Cert. tchr. Mo. Educator Holy Family Sch., Independence, Mo., 1985—87, Nativity of Mary Sch., Independence, 1986—87, St. Mary's H.S., Independence, 1987—. Workshop presenter Mo. Art Edn. Assn., 1996—. Exhibitions include St. Mary Coll., Leavenworth, Kans., 1975, 1993, 1994, Visitors Ctr., Arrow Rock, Mo., 1995, Rozier Gallery, Jefferson City, Mo., 1996, 1999, Ea. Mo. State U., Warrensburg, 1997, St. Joseph, Mo., 1998, Mo. Art Edn. Assn., Lake of the Ozark, 1999, Winston Churchill Meml., Fulton, Mo., 2001, 2002, 2005, Lake of the Ozarks, Mo., 2001, 2005, Period Gallery, Omaha, 2001, Parklane Gallery, Kirkland, Wash., 2001, Joyfeli Gallery, Kansas City, Mo., 2001—02, Images Gallery, Kansas City, 2003, 2005, 2006, St. Louis, 2004, Old Blake Mus., Independence, Mo., 2004, Goppert Gallery, Leavenworth, Kans., 2005, Unity Temple, Kansas City, 2005, North Ctrl. Mo. Coll., Trenton, 2005, Cornerstone Gallery, Independence, 2006, Blue Wolf Gallery, Kansas City, 2006. Merit badge counselor Boy Scouts Am., Kansas City, Mo., 1993—2003. Named Secondary Tchr. of Yr., Nat. Cath. Educators Assn., 1994; recipient Tchrs. Honor award, Nelson/Atkins Mus. Art, 1996, Grand prize, 1999. Mem.: Kans. Watercolor Soc. (assoc.), Mo. Watercolor Soc. (assoc. Signature Status 2002), Mo. Art Edn. Assn. (assoc.; dist. #3 rep. 1993—2006). Home: 3602 N Osage Independence MO 64050 Office: St Mary's High School 622 N Main Independence MO 64050 Personal E-mail: terikay@comcast.net. E-mail: twillett@stmhs.org.

WILLETTS, ELIZABETH M., humanities lecturer, actress; b. Toms River, N.J., Nov. 19, 1969; d. Ronald John Edwin and Virginia Ethel Willetts. BA, Rutgers U., 1992; MA, Montclair State U., 1994; postgrad., Drew U. Lectr. in humanities Ocean County Coll., Toms River, 1995—, coord. of recruitment, 1999—; actress N.J. and N.Y.; choreographer, 1992—. Spkr. Ocean County Spkrs. Bur., 1998—; vocalist First United Meth. Ch., Toms River, 1990—. Author poetry. Named Most Promising Actress, Newark Star Ledger, 1994. Mem. NOW, AAUW, Ocean County Pers. and Guidance Assn., Circle K. (advisor 1998—). Methodist. Avocations: writing, singing, dance, travel. Office: Ocean County Coll College Dr Toms River NJ 08754-2001 Home: 14 Brookside Ct Toms River NJ 08753-4327

WILLEY, FRIEDA ANDERS, adult education educator; b. Independence, VA, Aug. 17, 1936; d. David Alex Anders and Dixie Alice Snow; m. Edward Lake Willey, June 16, 1962; 1 child, Betsy Eden Hawthorne. AA, Bluefield Coll., 1958; BS in Elem. Edn., Salisburg U., 1977, MA, 1978. Elem. tchr. Cecil City Bd. of Edn., Elkton, Md., 1958—62, Dorchester City Bd. of Edn., Cambridge, Md., 1962—84; jr. high sch. tchr. Wythe City Bd. of Edn., Wytheville, Va., 1984—85, Harrington (Del.) Sch. Dist., 1985—86; secondary spl. edn. tchr. Orange County Bd. of Edn., Orange, Va., 1986—2003, adult educator, 1995—; interpreter Montpelier Found., Montpelier Station, Va., 1999—. Methodist. Avocation: reading, hist. places, writing fiction.

WILLIAMS, ADELLA JUDITH, elementary school educator, state representative; b. Barton, N.D., July 21, 1918; d. Bird J. and Clara (Adina Fluerog) Saude; m. Clifford James Williams, Aug. 31, 1941; children— Clark, Jerome, Konnie, Janet, Jane, Brian. B.A., Jamestown Coll., 1940. First class profl. teaching cert. Tchr., Lidgerwood, N.D., 1956-73; mem. N.D. Ho. of Reps., 1983-84, 85-86. Mem. Ret. Tchrs. Assn. (pres. 1978-83). Democrat. Methodist.

WILLIAMS, ALICE NOEL TUCKERMAN, retired foundation administrator; b. Bethesda, Md., Dec. 21, 1918; d. Walter Rupert and Edith (Abercrombie-Miller) Tuckerman; m. Robert Hugh Williams, June 21, 1939 (dec. 1983); children: Sarah Fenno Williams Lord, Edith Tuckerman Williams Ward. Mem. ladies bd. St. John's Child Devel. Ctr., Washington, 1960—69; pres. ladies bd. St. John's Devel. Ctr., Washington, 1969-72, v.p., trustee, 1970-72. Bd. dirs. Recording For The Blind and Dyslectic, Washington, 1990—94. Mem. Colonial Dames Am. (pres. Washington chpt. 1970-74), Sulgrave Club, The Investment Group (co-founder, pres. 2004—). Episcopalian. Avocations: volunteer work, reading.

WILLIAMS, AMY MCDANIEL, lawyer; b. Birmingham, Ala., Sept. 7, 1962; BA cum laude, Duke Univ., 1985; JD magna cum laude, Cornell Univ., 1990. Bar: Va. 1990. Assoc. Hunton & Williams LLP, Richmond, Va., 1992—99, ptnr., bus. practice group, 1999—, chmn. ethics com., 2002—. Sr. note editor Cornell Law Rev., 1990. Mem.: ABA, Met. Richmond Women's Bar Assn., Nat. Assn. Women Lawyers. Office: Hunton & Williams LLP Riverfront Plz East Tower 951 E Byrd St Richmond VA 23219-4074 Office Phone: 804-788-7388. Office Fax: 804-788-8218. Business E-Mail: awilliams@hunton.com.

WILLIAMS, ANITA JEAN, elementary school educator; b. Little Rock, July 14; d. Hoover and Clara Mae (Lewis) W BS Edn., Ark. State U., 1983, MS Edn., 1989. Tchr. Carver Washington YMCA Day Care, Little Rock, 1978—79, Annie Nannies Day Care, Memphis, 1986—87; tchr. elem. Parkin Sch. Dist., Ark., 1983—84; tchr. kindergarten Hughes Pub. Schs., Ark., 1984—86; clk. receipt and ctrl. IRS, Memphis, 1987—90; tchr. elem. English, kindergarten Earle Sch. Dist., Ark., 1988—. Sec., bookkeeper Lewis and Son Rice Processing Mill, Earle, 1977—; wedding dir. and coord., Earle, 1992— Coach/sponsor Cheerleading Squad Recipient Ednl. award Nacerima Club, Forrest City, Ark., 1977, 83, 89, award Bulter Chapel Christian Meth. Episcopal Ch., Earle, 1991, 92, 93 Mem. NEA, Ark. Edn. Assn., Ark. Cheerleading Coaches Assn., Nat. Cheerleading Assn., (25 trophies for safety, most spirited, and most improved team), Order Ea. Star, Kappa Delta Pi Methodist. Avocations: playing piano, listening to music, directing weddings, singing gospel music. Home: 1197 State Highway 149 S Earle AR 72331-9677 Office: Earle Sch Dist PO Box 637 Earle AR 72331-0637 Office Phone: 870-735-5252. E-mail: anitawilliams@west.grsc.k12.ar.us.

WILLIAMS, ANN CLAIRE, federal judge; b. Detroit, Aug. 16, 1949; m. David J. Stewart. BS, Wayne State U., 1970; MA, U. Mich., 1972; JD, U. Notre Dame, 1975; degree (hon.), Lake Forest Coll., 1987, U. Portland, 1993, U. Notre Dame, 1997. Law clk. to Hon. Robert A. Sprecher, 1975-76; asst. U.S. atty. U.S. Dist. Ct. (no. dist.) Ill., Chgo., 1976-85; faculty Nat. Inst. for Trial Advocacy, 1979—, also bd. dirs.; adj. prof., lectr. Northwestern U. Law Sch., 1979—, John Marshall Law Sch., 1979—; judge U.S. Dist. Ct. (no. dist.) Ill., 1985-99, U.S. Ct. Appeals (7th cir.), Chgo., 1999—. Chief Organized Crime Drug Enforcement Task Force for North Ctrl. Region, 1983-85; mem. ct. adminstrn. and case mgmt. com. Jud. Conf. U.S., 1990-97, chair, 1993-97. Sec. bd. trustees U. Notre Dame; founder Minority Legal Resources, Inc. Recipient Earl Burns Dickerson award, Chgo. Bar Assn., 1997, Tradition of Excellence award, Minority Legal Resources, Inc., 1997, Thurgood Marshall Jurist of Year, Legal Ministry of Second Baptist Church, 1997, Alumni of Year, Black Law Students Assn, U. Notre Dame, 1997, Morton A. Brody Disting. Jud. Svc. award, Colby Coll., 2002. Mem. FBA, Fed. Judges Assn., Ill. State Bar Assn., Ill. Jud. Coun., Cook County Bar Assn., Women's Bar Assn. Ill., Black Women's Lawyers Assn. Greater Chgo. Office: US Ct Appeals 7th Circuit 219 S Dearborn St Ste 2612 Chicago IL 60604-1803*

WILLIAMS, ANN MEAGHER, retired hospital administrator; b. Hull, Mass., May 28, 1929; d. James Francis Meagher and Dorothy Frances (Meagher) Mullins; m. Joseph Arthur Williams, May 15, 1954; children: James G., Mara A., A. Scott (dec.), Gordon M., Mark J., Antoinette M., Andrea M. BS, Chestnut Hill Coll., 1950; MS, Boston Coll., 1952. Radioisotope biologist Air Force Cambridge Rsch. Ctr., Bedford, Mass., 1952-55; asst. mgr. Roxbury Businessmen's Exch., Boston, 1956-66; owner, operator Chatterlane, Osterville, Mass., 1961-66; realtor James E. Murphy Inc., Hyannis, Mass., 1968-77; dir. cmty. affairs Cape Cod Hosp., Hyannis, 1977-95; realtor James E. Murphy, Inc., Osterville, 1995—. Bd. dirs. YMCA Cape Cod, Inc., 2004-, Cmty. Coun., Mid Cape, Mass., 1977-88, Cape Cod Mental Health Assn., 1977-82, Ctr. for Individual and Family Svcs., Mid Cape, 1982-87, Am. Cancer Soc., Mid Cape, 1981-96, Cape Cod C.C. Ednl. Found., 1997—, exec. com., 1999—; mem. sch. com. Cape Cod Regional Tech. High Sch., 1978—, exec. com., 1983—; mem. United Way of Cape Cod, 1988-89; chmn. fin. com. City of Barnstable, Mass., 1969-77. Named Woman of Yr. Bus./Profl. Women's Club, 1982; recipient cert. of appreciation Am. Cancer Soc., 1983, 88, Pres. Recognition award United Way Cape Cod, 1989. Life Achievement award Mass. Assn. Sch. Cos., 2000. Mem.: Nat. Assn. Hosp. Devel., SE Mass. Hosp. Mktg. & Pub. Rels., New Eng. Hosp. Mktg. & Pub. Rels., Am. Soc. Hosp. Mktg. & Pub. Rels., Chestnut Hill Coll. Alumnae Assn., Rotary Leadership Inst. (regional vice chmn. 2003—), Rotary Internat. (gov. 2002—03, Zone 31 membership coord. 2004—06, Zone 31 literacy coord. 2005—06), Rotary (bd. dir. Osterville 1993—98, pres. 1996—97, asst. gov. dist. 7950 1998—99, area rep. 1999—2000, gov. 2002—03), Hyannis Area C. of C. (bd. dir. 1993—98, ga 2002—03). Roman Catholic. Avocation: community theater. Home: 25 Wedgewood Dr Centerville MA 02632-3162

WILLIAMS, BARBARA ANNE, retired academic administrator; b. Camden, N.J., Oct. 14, 1938; d. Frank and Laura Dorothy (Szweda) W. BA cum laude, Georgian Ct. U., 1963; MLS, Rutgers U., 1965; MA, Manhattan Coll., 1973; postgrad., NYU, 1976—81, postgrad., 1993—. Cert. English tchr., N.J.; joined Sisters of Mercy, 1957. Sec. Camden Cath. H.S., 1956-57; registrar Georgian Ct. U., Lakewood, NJ, 1960-66, dir. libr. svcs., 1966-74, dean acad. affairs, 1974-80, pres., 1980-2000, sci. and math. libr., 2000—04, pres. emerita, 2000—, archivist, 2003—. Bd. dirs. N.J. Natural Gas Co., 1986-91 Mem. editl. bd. N.J. Woman mag. Bd. dirs., mem. edinl. adv. coun. Diocese of Trenton, N.J., 1983-90; mem. adv. bd. Ocean County Ctr. for Arts, Lakewood, N.J., 1983-91; mem. Ocean County Pvt. Industry Coun., 1983-92; bd. dirs. Monmouth/Ocean Devel. Coun., 1981-84; mem. State of N.J. Student Assistance Bd., 1995-99; mem. Ocean County School-to-Career Com., 1996-2000; mem. art adv. coun. Nat. Mus. Cath. Art and History, 2000—; mem. Mid-Atlantic Regional Archives Conf., 2003—; trustee Camden Cath. H.S., 2005—. Named Outstanding Woman N.J. Assn. Women Bus. Owners, 1983; recipient Humanitarian award Monmouth/Ocean Devel. Coun., 1985, Salute to Policymakers award Exec. Women N.J., 1986, Woman in Leadership award Monmouth Coun. Girl Scouts, 1987, Citizen of Yr. Alcoholism & Drug Abuse Coun. Ocean County, 1993, Brotherhood/Sisterhood award Monmouth/Ocean County chpts. NCCJ, 1994, Friend of Scouting award Boy Scouts Am. Jersey Shore Coun., 1999, Leadership award Mercy Higher Edn. Colloquium, 2000. Mem. Assn. Mercy Colls. (pres. 1981-83, sec. 1996-98), Mercy Higher Edn. Colloquium (mem. exec. com. 1980-87), Ocean County Bus. Assn. (trustee 1982-84), Nat. Assn. Ind. Colls. and Univs. (secretariat 1981-83, 87-91), NAIA (coun. of pres. 1997-2000), Soc. Am. Archivists. Home and Office: Georgian Ct Univ 900 Lakewood Ave Lakewood NJ 08701-2600 Office Phone: 732-987-2441. E-mail: williamssb@georgian.edu.

WILLIAMS, BARBARA KITTY, nursing educator; b. Kingsport, Tenn., July 14, 1944; d. Charles H. Penley and Ada Ruth Baldwin; m. Emerson Williams, Dec. 23, 1961. RN, Johnston Meml. Hosp. Sch. Nursing, Abingdon, Va., 1970; BS in Profl. Arts, St. Joseph's Coll., North Windom, Maine, 1981; BSN, East Tenn. State U., 1986; MSN, U. Va., 1991. RN Tenn., Va., clin. nurse specialist, Am. Nurses Credentialing Ctr., 1993. Critical care nurse Holston Valley Cmty. Hosp., Kingsport, 1971—74; faculty Kingsport Sch. Practical Nursing, 1974—76; asst. nursing dir. Johnson County Hosp., Mountain City, Tenn., 1976—78; dir. med. surg. svcs. Bristol (Tenn.) Regional Med. Ctr., 1978—85; asst. prof. nursing Virginia Highlands C.C., Abingdon, Va., 1988—. Adv. bd. YWCA, Bristol, Tenn., 1996—98; mem. bd. Shots for Tots, Rotary Club, Bristol, Tenn., 1995. Finalist Tribute to Women award, YWCA. Mem.: AAUP (award), Bristol Art Guild (pres. 1995—97), Pastel Soc. Am., Assn. Depot Artist, Bristol C. of C. (amb. 1995), Bristol Toastmasters (pres. 1982), Sigma Theta Tau. Methodist. Avocations: painting, travel. Office: Va Highlands Cmty Coll Box 828 Abingdon VA 24212 Business E-Mail: kwilliams@vhcc.edu.

WILLIAMS, BARBARA STAMBAUGH, editor; b. Jenkins, Ky., Nov. 22, 1937; d. James Cosby and Jessie Kate (Bise) Stambaugh; m. Manning Williams, Sept. 11, 1963. BS in Journalism, U. Tenn., 1959. Polit. reporter News and Courier, Charleston, S.C., 1961-63, 67-76, asst. mng. editor, 1976-81; city hall reporter Camden (N.J.) Courier Post, 1963-67; editor The Evening Post, Charleston, S.C., 1981-90, The Evening Post and News Courier, Charleston, S.C., 1990-91, The Post and Courier, Charleston, S.C., 1991—. Pres. Nat. Conf. Editl. Writers, Rockville, Md., 1992. Bd. dirs. Charleston Sci. and Cultural Edn. Fund. Named Outstanding Newspaper Woman in S.C., S.C. Press Assn., 1962. Mem. Sigma Delta Chi (ByLiner award 1973). Achievements include first woman editor of a daily newspaper in South Carolina. Office: The Post & Courier 134 Columbus St Charleston SC 29403-4800 Office Phone: 843-937-5526. E-mail: barbara@postandcourier.com.

WILLIAMS, BETHTINA QUBRÉ, minister; d. Cleophus Noble Marshall and Marilyn Etta Marshall-Pierce; m. Stanley Davis Williams, Feb. 28, 1986; children: Stanley II, Jonathan, Joshua. BA, Friends Internat. Christian U., Merced, Calif., 1990, MA, 1996, DMin, 2001. Ordained min. Living Word Christian Ctr., Inc., 1996. Adminstrv. asst. Tex. Tech. U., Lubbock, Tex., 1983—84; health and safety coord., tchr. Kinder Care Pre-Sch., Lubbock, 1985—87; assoc. mgr. Paul Harris Store, Lubbock, 1987—89; libr. asst. Torreion (Spain) AFB, 1990—91; co-founder, co-pastor, exec. adminstr. Lighthouse of Faith Cmty. Ch., Ft. Walton Beach, Fla., 1997—; network pastor Life Cmty. Fellowship, 2001—05. Adv. bd. West Navarre Elem. Sch., 2004—05. Author: Women of Character and Destiny, 2005. Dir. outreach in humanitarian svc. Landstuhl (Germany) Base Chapel, 1993. Recipient Appreciation cert., Wayland Bapt. U., 1986, Commdr.'s Commendation medal, USAF, Ramstein, Germany, 1995, Appreciation cert., USAF, 2000, Commdr.'s medal, Hurlbut Field AFB, Fla., 2000, cert. of honor, King of Shai State, Ghana, 2004. Avocations: writing, exercise, singing, travel, public speaking. Office: Lighthouse of Faith Church Inc 755 Lovejoy Rd NW Fort Walton Beach FL 32548

WILLIAMS, BETTY, peace activist; b. Belfast, Northern Ireland, May 22, 1943; arrived in US, 1982; m. Ralph Williams, 1961 (div.); 2 children; m. James T. PErkins, 1983. LL.D. (hon.), Yale U.; L.H.D. (hon.), Coll. Siera Heights, 1977. Co-organizer (with Mairead Corrigan) of movement Women for Peace (now Community of Peace People), Belfast, 1976-80; apptd. Tex. Commn. for Children and Youth, 1992; vis. prof. Sam Houston State U.; disting. vis. prof. Nova Southeastern U. Co-founder (with Mairead Corrigan) Peace by Peace mag. Head Global Children's Found.; pres. World Ctr. Compassion for Children; chair Inst. for Asian Democracy, Washington. Recipient Nobel Prize for Peace, 1976, Norwegian People's Peace prize, 1976, Carl von Ossietzky prize, German Fed. Republic, 1976, Schweitzer Medallion for Courage, Martin Luther King, Jr. award, Eleanor Roosevelt award, 1984, Child Care International Oliver Award, Frank Found.; Paul Harris Fellowship; and the Together for Peace Bldg. award, Rotary Club Internat., 1995. Roman Catholic. Address: PO Box 725 Valparaiso FL 32580-0725

WILLIAMS, BETTYE JEAN, language educator; b. Pine Bluff, Ark., July 2, 1946; d. Eunice and Dorothy (Willingham) W. BA in English, Agrl. Meth. and Normal Coll., 1968; M of English, Pittsburg State U., 1970; PhD in Am. Lit., Ind. U. Pa., 1993. Prof. English U. Ark., Pine Bluff, 1968-96, Ind. U. Pa., 1990-93, Pines Tech. Coll., Pine Bluff, 1995. NEH fellow, 1992-93. Mem. NAUW (pres. Pine Bluff br. 1989-90, 2001-2003, South Ctrl. sect. dir. 2005), Nat. Assn. Advancement of Coll. People, Nat. Urban League, Nat. Lang. Assn., Coll. Lang. Assn., Nat. Assn. U. Women (sectional dir., South Ctrl. section, 2005), Sigma Tau Delta, Delta Sigma Theta. Democrat. Baptist. Avocation: needlepoint. Home: 3402 W 36th St Pine Bluff AR 71603 Office Phone: 870-536-3073. Personal E-mail: bettye-williams@sbcglobal.net. Business E-Mail: Williams_bj@uapb.edu.

WILLIAMS, BOBBRETTA M., educational company executive; b. Des Moines, Dec. 11, 1948; d. Robert and Margaret (Preston) Elliston; m. Cecil H. Brewton, Jr.; 1 child, Ayana Michelle. BSE, N.E. Mo. State, 1971; MSE, Drake U., 1975, EdS, 1978, EdD, 1981; BA, Upper Iowa U., 1991. Cert. adminstr., supr., tchr. Tchr. Des Moines (Iowa) Pub. Schs., 1971—90; pres. ABC Diversified, ednl. communications tng. and consultation, Des Moines, 1990—93; coord. Hiatt Jr. High Sch., Des Moines; cons. Voluntary Transfer, Des Moines; elem. prin. Longfellow Sch., Des Moines; dir. Children and Families of Iowa, 1993—2000; cons. Exec. Resources Assistance, 2000—01; dir. The Outreach Project, 2001—.

WILLIAMS, BRENDA JEANNE, literature and language educator; b. Madison, Wis., May 8, 1980; d. Steven George and Mary Paula Wittmann; m. Bryon John Williams, Aug. 28, 2004. BA in English, Judson Coll., 2001. Cert. tchr. Concordia U., Wis. Office mgr. ARC Badger Chpt., Madison, Wis., 2001—02; substitute tchr. Oreg. (Wis.) Sch. Dist., 2002—03; English tchr. Montello (Wis.) HS, Montello, Wis., 2003—. Girls' volleyball, basketball asst. coach Montello HS, 2003—, advisor class 2008, 2004—. Avocations: travel, sports, writing, reading. Office: Montello HS 222 Forest Ln Montello WI 53949 Office Phone: 608-297-2126.

WILLIAMS, CANDICE L., special education educator; d. Robert Heyward Williams II and Connie Proctor Williams. BA, U. N.C., Charlotte, 2004. Student tchr. Cabarrus County Schs., Concord, NC, 2002—04, spl. edn. tchr., 2004—05. Membership chair, student coun. for exceptional children U. N.C., 2002—04; mem. Coun. for Exceptional Children, 2004—. Mem. Order of Omega, U. N.C., 2003—04. Mem.: Zeta Tau Alpha (Diamond Honor award 2004). Mem. Christian Ch. Avocations: music, reading.

WILLIAMS, CAROL H., advertising executive; b. Chgo. d. Clarence Earl Williams and Betty Jane Norment-Williams; m. Tipkins Hood; children: Tipkins Hood Jr., Carol Hood. Student, Northwestern U. Creative dir., sr. v.p. Leo Burnett Agy., Chgo., 1969—80, Foote-Cone & Belding, San Francisco, 1980—82; prin. owner Carol H. Williams Advt., Inc., Oakland, Calif., 1986—. Active US Dream Acad. Recipient Outstanding Women in Mktg. and Comms. award, Ebony Mag., 2001, Women to Watch award, Ad Age, 2002, Bus. Achievement award, Nat. Coalition 100 Black Women, Inc., 2003, Ad Agency of Yr., Black Enterprise Mag., 2004. Mem.: NAACP, TEC Internat., Rainbow/PUSH Coalition. Office: Carol H Williams Advertising Inc 555 12th St Ste 1700 Oakland CA 94607-4058

WILLIAMS, CAROL JORGENSEN, social work educator; b. New Brunswick, NJ, Aug. 12, 1944; d. Einar Arthur and Mildred Estelle (Clayton) Jorgensen; m. Oneal Alexander Williams, July 4, 1980. BA, Douglass Coll., 1966; MS in Computer Sci., Stevens Inst. Tech., 1986; MSW, Rutgers U., 1971, PhD in Social Policy, 1981. Child welfare worker Bur. Children's Svcs., Jersey City, 1966-67, Outagamie County Dept. Social Svcs., Appleton, Wis., 1967-69; supr. WIN N.J. Divsn. Youth and Family Svcs., New Brunswick, 1969-70; coord. Outreach Plainfield (N.J.) Pub. Libr., 1972-76; rsch. project dir. County and Mcpl. Govt. Study Commn., N.J. State Legislature, 1976-79; prof. social work Kean U., Union, 1979—, assessment liaison social work program, 1987-2000, dir. MSW program, 1995-2000. Chmn. faculty senate gen. edn. com. Kean U., N.J., 1990-94, chmn. faculty senate academic tech. com., 2004-, chmn. faculty senate ad hoc com. for 5-yr.

review of gen. edn. program, 1991-93, retention and tenure com. Sch. of Liberal Arts, 1988-94, 2004-05, vice chmn., 1992-94; cons. N.J. div. Youth and Family Svcs., 1979-93, 2003—, Assn. for Children N.J., 1985-88; cons., evaluator Thomas A. Edison Coll., 1977—, N.J. Dept. Human Svcs., 2003; cons. advanced generalist practice La. State U. Grad. Sch. Social Work, 2002. Adv. coun. Outdoor World, 2000—03. Named Grad. Tchr. of Yr., Kean U., 2001. Mem.: NASW (co-chair chpt. com. on nominating and leadership identification 1991—92), NOW, Publ. Com., Nat. Network Social Work Mgrs., Kean U. Fedn. Tchrs., Assn. Baccalaureate Program Dirs. (com. on info tech. and distance edn. 1995—, editor BPD Update 2005—, mem. editl. bd. Jour. Baccalaureate Social Work, pubs. com. 2005—), Coun. Social Work Edn. (dir. APM Med. Tech. Ctr. 1999—2002, chair subcom. on abstract rev. 2000—02, commn. on confs. and faculty devel. 2000—02, pers. com. 2003—04, bd. dirs. 2003—06, investment com. 2003—06, mem. editl. bd. 2006—), Good Sam Club. Democrat. Home: 32 Halstead Rd New Brunswick NJ 08901-1619 Office: Kean U Social Work Program Morris Ave Union NJ 07083-7117 Personal E-mail: caroljwilliams@worldnet.att.net.

WILLIAMS, CAROLYN LILLIAN, psychology educator; b. Coral Gables, Fla., Jan. 21, 1951; d. Robert L. and Irene (Kasa) Williams; m. James Neal Butcher, Nov. 8, 1979; 1 child, Holly Krista. BA, U. Ga., Athens, 1973, MS, 1977, PhD, 1979. Lic. consulting psychologist, Minn. Asst. prof. U. Minn. Sch. Pub. Health, Mpls., 1981-90, assoc. prof., 1990—2000, prof., 2000—01; prof. emeritus, 2001—. Cons. WHO, UN Border Relief Operation, Aranya prathet, Thailand. Editor: Refugee Mental Health in Resettlement Countries, 1986; co-editor: Mental Health Services for Refugees, 1991; co-author: Development and Use of the MMPI-2 Content Scales, 1990, Essentials of MMPI-2 and MMPI-A Interpretation, 2000, Users Guide to the Minn. Report: Adolescent Clinical System, 1992; co-developer: Minn. Multiphasic Personality Inventory for Adolescents, 1992; first author: MMPI-A Content Scales: Assessing Psychopathology in Adolescents, 1992; contbr. articles to profl. jours. Grantee NIH. Fellow APA; mem. APHA, Univ. of Minn. Twin Cities chpt. AAUP (pres. 1997-98), Soc. Pub. Health Edn. Office: U Minn Div Epidemiology 1300 S 2nd St Ste 300 Minneapolis MN 55454-1087 Home: 21955 Minnetonka Blvd Apt 8 Excelsior MN 55331-5601

WILLIAMS, CECELIA PEAY, retired psychologist; b. Boston, Sept. 29, 1924; d. Moses and Rosa Ophelia Peay; 1 child, Rosa. Grad., Boston Clerical Sch., 1944; BA, Calif. State U., L.A., 1966, MS, 1970. Legal secretary private practice Attorney's Office, Boston, Ma, 1944—45; sec. Washington D.C. Vet's Adminstrn., John Hay Whitney Found., N.Y.C., Crippled Children's Soc., L.A.; adminstrv. sec. Galton Inst., L.A., 1965—68; bus. tchr. L.A. Unified Sch. Dist., 1969—72, sch. psychologist, 1973—98, adminstrv. cons., 2000—. Oral commr. Bd. Behavioral Sci. Mem. Baldwin Hills Neighborhood Assn., L.A., 1988—. Mem.: L.A. Assn. Sch. Psychologists (pres. 1980—81), Delta Kappa Gamma Beta Xi (pres. 1993—94), Chi State Delta Kappa Gamma.

WILLIAMS, CECILIA LEE PURSEL, optometrist; b. Lewisburg, Pa., Nov. 15, 1948; d. Lee LaVerne and Geraldine May (Steininger) Pursel; m. Richard Lee Williams, May 17, 1975; 1 son, Kent Lee. Student, Lycoming Coll., 1966-68; BS, Pa. Coll. Optometry, 1970, OD, 1972. Lic. and/or cert. optometrist, D.C., Pa., N.Y., N.J., Va. Rsch. optometrist in soft lens materials Gumpelmayer Optik, Vienna, Austria, 1973; optometrist Sterling Optical Co. Contact Lens Ctr., Washington, 1974-79; pvt. practice optometry Springfield, Va., 1980—. Recipient Clin. Efficiency award Pa. Coll. Optometry, 1972; Women's Aux. of Pa. Optometrists scholar, 1968-70, 70-72; Pa. State grantee, 1968-70, 70-72. Mem. Optometric Ctr. of Nation's Capital (dir. 1977-80), Am. Optometric Assn., Va. Optometric Assn., No. Va. Optometric Soc., Nat. Honor Soc. for Optometry, Omega Delta. Home: 3600 Wilton Hall Ct Alexandria VA 22310-2176 Office: 7241 Commerce St Springfield VA 22150-3411 Office Phone: 703-866-9364.

WILLIAMS, CHARLOTTE EDWINA, secondary school educator, real estate manager; b. Phila., Jan. 5, 1945; d. Charles Edward and Elaine Frances Lydia (Scott) Williams; m. Charles Ross Woodson, III, Jan. 19, 1971 (div. June 1985); 1 child, Amber Charlotte BS, Cheyney (Pa.) State U., 1968; MEd, U. So. Miss., 1989; postgrad., Temple U., 1996—. Tchr. Phila. Pub. Schs., 1968—69, adminstr., 1968—69, tchr., 1972—, adminstr., 1972—. Majority inspector Election Bd., Phila., 1982-90; treas. West Ctrl. Germantown Neighbors, Phila., 1995—; sec. Jack and Jill of Am., Inc., Phila., 1980-82. Mem. Phi Delta Kappa, Alpha Kappa Alpha. Avocations: photography, real estate remodeling.

WILLIAMS, CHERYL A., secondary school educator; b. Neosho, Mo., July 7, 1957; d. Travestine Williams. BS in Math., Tex A&M U., 1978, postgrad., 1978-79, Rose State Coll., 1980-81, Sheppard Tech. Tng. Ctr., 1980-81; MS in Math., U. Tex., 1997. Computer scientist Tinker AFB, Oklahoma City, 1980-81, Defense Comm. Agy., Washington, 1986; tchr. Parent Child Inc., San Antonio, 1989; asst. sec. Antioch Bapt. Ch., San Antonio, 1989-92; substitute tchr. San Antonio Ind. Sch. Dist., 1990-93; instrnl. asst. Northside Ind. Sch. Dist., San Antonio, 1995-96, asst. tchr., 1994-95, North East Ind. Sch. Dist., San Antonio, 1996—2001; rep. West Telemarketing, 1998-99; math. tutor Alamo C.C. Dist., 1998—99, instr. math., 1998—, St. Philips Coll., 1998—2001; math. tutor Trave and G.G.'s Tutorial Svc., 1999—; instr. math. Guardian Angel Performing Arts Acad., 2002—. Asst. mgr. Fashion Pl., San Antonio, 1994—95; tax preparer H&R Block, 1994—95; distbr. Avon, 1999—2001; indep. beauty cons. Mary Kay Cosmetics, 1999—; scorer Harcourt Brace Corp., 2001, Randstad, 2001; rep. Express Svcs., 2001; cons. Prepaid Legal Svcs., Inc., 2003; ind. bus. owner Cyberwize, 2004. Counselor YMCA, San Antonio, 1989-91; active Girl Scouts U.S., 1964-86; mem. choir, asst. sec. area ch., 1972, tutor, 1970—, tchr. Sunday Sch., 1973-86, asst. sec. Sunday Sch., 1973-86, 88—, asst. ch. sec., 1988-91; mem. Dorcas Circle, Lupus Found. Am., Biomed. Rsch. U. Tex., 1995—; mem. Epilepsy Found. Am., Tex. Head Injury Assn., Nat. Head Injury Assn., Smithsonian Instn.; vol. Cancer Therapy Rsch. Ctr., 2003—, Am. Cancer Soc., 2003—. Mem. NEA, Tex. Edn. Assn., Mu. Alpha Theta. Avocations: jigsaw puzzles, bowling.

WILLIAMS, CHRISTIN MICHELE, elementary school educator; b. Phila., June 2, 1972; d. James Joseph Messina and Gail Ann Bruchko; m. Barry Joseph Williams, Apr. 7, 2001; children: Delaney Michele, Joseph James. BS in Edn., Bucknell U., Lewisburg, Pa., 1994; MS in Curriculum and Instrn., Loyola Coll., Balt., 2001. Cert. elem. tchr. NY. Mental health technician Friendship House Children's Ctr., Scranton, Pa., 1994—97; 1st and 2d grade tchr. Marlton Elem., Upper Marlboro, Md., 1997—2000; 5th and 2d grade tchr. Tioga Hills Elem., Apalachin, NY, 2000—. Vol. Habitat for Humanity, Lewisburg, Pa., 1991. Mem.: NEA, Nat. Sci. Tchrs. Assn., Delta Gamma (sec. Epsilon Beta chpt. 1991—94). Avocations: skiing, piano, golf. Office: Tioga Hills Elem 40 Glann Rd Apalachin NY 13732

WILLIAMS, CHRISTINE ALICIA, lawyer; m. Jason N. Williams; 1 child. BA in Psychology, Va. Wesleyan Coll., Norfolk, 1996; JD, U. N.C., Chapel Hill, 2001. Bar: Va. 2001, U.S. Ct. Appeals (4th cir.) 2002, U.S. Dist. Ct. (ea. and we. dists.) Va. 2002, U.S. Ct. Appeals (fed. cir.) 2005. Atty. Durrette-Bradshaw PLC, Richmond, Va., 2001—. Co-chmn. bd. TrePadges, Richmond, 2002—. Mem.: ABA (assoc.), Richmond Bar Assn. (assoc.), Va. Trial Lawyers Assn. (assoc.). Office: DurretteBradshaw PLC 20th Fl 600 East Main St Richmond VA 23219 Office Phone: 804-775-6838. Office Fax: 804-775-6911. Business E-Mail: cwilliams@durrettebradshaw.com.

WILLIAMS, CLAUDIA BAXTER, retired media specialist, school librarian; b. Houston County, Ala., Mar. 12, 1930; d. L. J. and Ilene Chambers Baxter; m. Henry, Jr. Williams; children: Michael Duryea, Yul Karen. BS in Edn., Ala. State U., 1951; MEd in media, Auburn U., Ala., 1984. Librarian Shelby County Sch. Sys., Columbiana, Ala., 1951—52, Houston County Sch. Sys., Dothan, 1953—54; office clk. Hansberry Enterprises, Chgo., 1955—56; tchr., librarian Madison County Schs., Greenville, Fla., 1957—59; elem. sch. tchr. Houston County Schs., Dothan, Ala., 1962—64; media specialist Dothan (Ala.) City Schs., 1965—94. Textbook com. Dothan (Ala.) City Schs., 1978—89, English tchr. to Vietnamese students, 1989—92; yearbook advisor Carver Mid. Sch., Dothan, Ala., 1989—94. Contbr. articles Wiregras Roots-Genealogy Quarterly. Voter activation Ala. Dist. 85, Dothan, 1985; coord. Houston County Centennial Com., Dothan, 2003; bd. dirs. NBCAR Hist. Dist., Dothan, 2001—, Wiregrass Genealogy Soc., Dothan, 1999—. Recipient Disting. Svc. award, Ala. Hist. Commission, 2004, Centennial award, Houston County Bd. Comrs., 2003, Cmty. Svc. award, Zeta Phi Beta Sorority, 2006. Mem.: Southeast Ala. Genealogical Soc. (recording sec. 1998—99, Achievement of Excellence 1999), Ala. Assn. Women's Club (scholarship chair 1999—2003, Mabel S. Neely Individual Achievement award 1999, 2000, 2001), Ala. Edn. Assn., Nat. Ed. Assn. (life), Alpha Kappa Alpha. Democrat. Baptist. Avocations: reading, sewing, gardening, fabric artwork. Home: 2187 E Burdeshaw St Dothan AL 36303

WILLIAMS, CONSTANCE, state senator; b. June 27, 1944; m. Sankey V. Williams; 2 children. BA, Barnard Coll., 1966; MBA, U. Pa., 1980. Rep. Pa. House of Reps., Harrisburg, 1996—2001; mem. Pa. State Senate, Harrisburg, 2001—. Democrat. Jewish. Office: 352 Main Capital Senate Box 203017 Harrisburg PA 17120-3017 Business E-Mail: chwilliams@pasenate.com.

WILLIAMS, CYNTHIA ANN, small business owner, pediatrics nurse, writer; b. Portsmouth, Va., Dec. 8, 1959; d. Kenneth Leroy Miller and Connie Lee Miller (Joyner); m. John Leonard Bibbins; m. Sidney Small III; children: Sidney Lekenny Small, Joshua Tadarrell Small; m. Ashton Mcgregor Smith Jr.; children: Ebony Ashtone Shannon, Ashley Mahogany Smith. Diploma in med. specialist, Acad. Health Sci., Fort Sam Houston, Tex., 1982, diploma for lic. practical nurse, 1986; AAS, U. Md., 1994; diploma in practical theology, Beacon U., 2004—. Cert. Basic Cardiac Life Support, 1982, Neonatal Advanced Life Support, 1986, lic. Practical Nurse, 1986, cert. Emergency Medical Technician Basic, 2001; Ordained Minister Victory New Testament Fellowship, 2000; foster parent Va. Enlisted US Army, 1981, advanced through ranks to staff sgt., ret., 2001; wardmaster mother baby unit Dewitt Army Cmty. Hosp., US Army, Fort Belvoir, Va., 1995—96; North Atlantic regional command retention Dewitt Army Cmty. Hosp., North Atlantic Regional Med. Command/US Army, Fort Belvoir, Va., 1996—98, in charge of ob-gyn clinic and well woman clinic, 1998—2000, in charge of ob-gyn clinic Seoul, Republic of Korea, 2000—01; in charge first replacement med. detachment,anthrax coord. 121st Gen. Hosp., 18th Med. Command, Seoul, Republic of Korea, 2001; owner, founder clothing line One of Those Women; owner NSE Enterprises; pvt. duty in- home pediat. nurse Continuum Pediatric Nursing, Virginia Beach, Va., 1998—. Combat lifesaver instr. US Army, Taegu, 1987—2000, customer svc. sch. excellence instr., Seoul, 2000—01; EMT, 2001—02; CEO It's a New Day Prodns., Newport News, Va., 2004; ind. advertiser The Greatest Vitamin in the World. Author: One Of Those Women, 2001, Marriage: Not Just A Simple "I Do", 2001. Dir., founder FreeWill Fellowship Ministry, Richmond, 2000—; ptnr. in many ministries. Decorated Expert Field Med. Badge U.S. Army, Meritorious Svc. medal, 4 Commendation Medals. Fellow: Am. Biog. Inst. (life), Internat. Biog. Assn. (life); mem.: VFW, Potter's House Bishops Cir., NonCommissioned Officer Assn., Mighty Warrior Intercessor Prayer Team, U.S. Official Presdnl. Prayer Team. Avocations: writing, gardening, art, crafts. Office: Free-Will Fellowship Ministry 87 Deer Run Tr Newport News VA 23602 Office Phone: 703-623-9981, 757-369-9673. E-mail: oneofthosewomen@yahoo.com.

WILLIAMS, CYNTHIA DENISE, secondary school educator; b. East St. Louis, Ill., Aug. 11, 1980; d. Charles Edward and Debra Denise Williams. BS in Elem. Edn., So. Ill. U., Edwardsville, 2002. Waitress Mazzio's Pizza, Fairview Heights, Ill., 1996—2002; office clk. records office So. Ill. U., Edwardsville, 1999—2002; tchr. mid. sch. lang. arts Cahokia Sch. Dist., Ill., 2002—. Tchr. Sabbath sch. Bethlehem Temple House of God, East St. Louis, 1996—2006. Recipient Johnetta Haley scholarship, So. Ill. U., 1998—2002. Home: 5 Lakewood Pl Alorton IL 62207 Office: Cahokia Sch Dist 1900 Mousette Ln Cahokia IL 62206 Office Phone: 618-332-3722. Personal E-mail: williamscd@stclair.k12.il.us.

WILLIAMS, CYNTHIA M., literature and language professor; b. Denver, Feb. 9, 1960; d. Fred M. and Clair A. Williams; 1 child, Alison A. BA in English, SW Mo. State U., Springfield, 1982; MA, U. Tex., Austin, 1986; PhD, U. Mo., Kansas City, 2004. Dir. English 2d lang. program U. Mo., Kansas City, 1986—96; asst. prof. English Pk. U., Parkville, 1996—. Adj. instr. English U. Mo., 1986—96. Author: Darkness Invisible, Dreams of Trees and Fingers. Rescue pets foster home Nat. Brittany Rescue and Adoption Network, Reno, 2000—05; rescue pets foster home, fund raiser Pet Connection, Overland Park, Kans., 1998—2006. Grantee, NEH, 2000; Aruthur Mag fellow, 1995. Mem.: Woman's Polit. Caucas, Greater Kans. City Interfaith Coun. Avocations: writing, reading, travel. Office: Park University 8700 NW River Park Drive Parkville MO 64152 Office Phone: 816-741-2000. Personal E-mail: cynatpark@yahoo.com. E-mail: cmwilliams@park.edu.

WILLIAMS, DANNA BETH, reading specialist; b. Aurora, Ill., Apr. 13, 1956; d. Daniel Strango and Roberta Arlene Roberts; m. Norman Charles Williams, June 25, 1988; children: Scott, Samuel, Spencer. BSc, U. Nev., Reno, 1978; postgrad. in Curriculum and Instrn., Concordia U., Irvine, Calif., 2006—. Cert. TESOL Nev. Lic. of Edn., tchg.credential Calif. Reading specialist Job Corps, Stead, Nev., 1979; tchr. Churchill County Schools, Fallon, 1979—88; sub. tchr. Irvine Sch. Dist., Calif., 1988—90, Mission Viejo Sch. Dist., 1989—90; tchr. pvt. schools Orange County, 1990—96; tchr. Orange Unified Sch. Dist., 1996—2000, reading specialist, 2000—. Lang. arts mentor, tchr. Orange Unified Sch. Dist., 1999—2001, English lang. learner adv., 2005—, Consortium on Reading Excellence trainer fifth grade tchrs., 2003—04. Religious educator San Francisca Solano, 1988—91, 2002—04, Cath. Ch., 1983—88. Mem.: ASCD, Calif. Teachers Assn., Internat. Reading Assn. Roman Catholic. Home: 21022 Los Alisos Blvd Apt 614 Rancho Santa Margarita CA 92688 Office: Cambridge Elem Sch 425 N Cambridge Orange CA 92866 Office Phone: 714-997-6103. E-mail: dwilliam@orangeusd.k12.ca.us.

WILLIAMS, DARCEL PATRICE, writer, editor; b. Houston, Nov. 23, 1958; d. Leroy and Estelle Forch Williams; m. Jason LaRue Williams, Sr., May 26, 1979 (div. Sept. 0, 1985); 1 child, Jason LaRue II. Student, Tex. So. U., 1977—81, U. Houston, 1985—88. Lic. massage therapist City of Tulsa, 1993. Acctg. Taft Broadcasting, Houston, 1981—85; office mgr. DeColores Prodns., Houston, 1989—90; cmty. ctr. dir. Helping Hands - Riverview Pk., Tulsa, 1995; author Am. Book Pub. Group, Salt Lake City, 1999—, sr. editor, 1999—2003. Creative adviser/cons. Various Ind. Entrepreneurial Enterprises, Tulsa, 1989—2003. Author: (novel) Soaring On Clipped Wings (Book of Month, 2004), (screenplay) Fighting to Love; senior editor: novels Cryer's Valley, Have No Mercy, writer, dir.: Sadie's Soap Suds TV Show, 2004; web designer, writer (web site) www.DarcelWilliams.com;, author poetry; contbr. Named Humanitarian of Month, 2003; recipient Best New Writer of Yr. Disilgold Mag. award, Younity Reviewers Guild, 2004. Mem.: Younity Revs. Guild Worldwide, Disilgold Lit. Network Assn., Nat. Writers Union, Authors Den Forum (life). Achievements include design of safety product for use in vehicular transportation of children; product for walking in hazardous environmental conditions. Avocations: singing, music, sewing and design, swimming, reading. Office Phone: 918-499-8722. Personal E-mail: eagledfly@yahoo.com.

WILLIAMS, DARLENE F., federal agency administrator; BA, Howard U.; MBA, Chgo. U.; PhD, Stanford U. Mgr. mktg., planning and rsch. Ryder Systems, Inc.; corp. policy mgr. TXU; gen. dep. asst. sec. policy devel. and rsch. HUD, Washington, 2003—05, gen. dep. asst. sec., 2005, asst. sec., 2005—. Office: HUD 451 Seventh St SW Mail Code R Rm 8100 Washington DC 20410-6000 Office Phone: 202-708-1600. Office Fax: 202-619-8000.

WILLIAMS, DAWN MONIQUE, theater director, educator; b. Oakland, Calif., July 2, 1978; d. Lee Otis Williams and Beth Irene Jennings; 1 child, Jordyn RayeLyn Millet. BA in Theatre, Calif. State U., Hayward, 2003—03; MA in Dramatic Lit., History, Theory and Criticism, San Francisco State U., 2006. Founder ReVerb Theatre, East Bay, Calif., 2006—. Assitant dir. Cal Shakes, Berkeley, Calif., 2005; asst. dir. TheatreWorks, Palo Alto, Calif., 2005; guest artist Calif. State U. East Bay, Hayward, 2004—. Dir.: (stage play) La Ronde, Children of Eden, Creon, Trojan Women, Medea, (edinburgh fringe festival) Scapin, the Cheat. Mem.: Assn. for Theatre in Higher Edn., Ednl. Theatre Assn., Soc. of Stage Dir. and Choreographers (assoc.). Home Fax: 510-991-9930. Personal E-mail: dmw@reverbtheatre.com.

WILLIAMS, DENISE, academic administrator; b. Iowa, 1972; BBA, Detroit Coll. Bus.; M, Marygrove Coll. Assoc. dir. U. Detroit Mercy, 2001, dir., dean of admissions, 2003—. Named one of 40 Under 40, Crain's Detroit Bus., 2006. Office: University of Detroit Mercy FAC 100 4001 W McNichols Rd Detroit MI 48221 Office Phone: 313-993-1245. Office Fax: 313-993-3326.*

WILLIAMS, DIANE, writer, editor; b. Chgo., Jan. 16, 1946; d. William Maurice and Mary Rosen Swartz; m. Paul Casey Williams, June 28, 1970 (div. 1993); children: Jacob, Alexander. BA in English Lit., U. Pa., 1968. Asst. editor J. G. Ferguson divsn. Doubleday, N.Y.C., 1969—71, Scott, Foresman Co., Glenview, Ill., 1971—73; assoc. editor Sci. Rsch. Assocs., Chgo., 1973—76; co-editor StoryQuarterly, Glenview, 1985—97; founding editor NOON, N.Y.C., 2000—. Vis. asst. prof. Syracuse (N.Y.) U., 1999; vis. assoc. prof. Bard Coll., Annandale-on-Hudson, NY, 2001. Co-editor: (anthology) The American Story: The Best of StoryQuarterly, 1990; author: (stories) This Is About the Body, the Mind, the Soul, the World, Time, and Fate, 1990, Some Sexual Success Stories Plus Other Stories in Which God Might Choose to Appear, 1992, (stories and novella) The Stupefaction, 1996, Excitability: Selected Stories, 1998, Romancer Erector, 2001; contbr. stories to jours.; author short stories, novellas. Recipient Pushcart prize, 1991, 1992, 2000. Office: NOON PMB 298 1324 Lexington Ave New York NY 10128

WILLIAMS, DIANE ELIZABETH, architectural historian, photographer; b. Glendale, Calif. BA, Calif. State U., L.A., 1973; MA, UCLA, 1988. Cert. elem. tchr., Calif. Tchr. L.A. area schs., 1975-78; editorial asst. L.A. Times, 1978-80, copyeditor, feature writer, 1980-83; preservation planning cons. Sierra Madre, Calif., 1983-94; assoc. planner Environ. Planning Assocs., L.A., 1989; asst. planner City of Burbank, Calif., 1989-90; assoc. planner City of Claremont, Calif., 1990-91; planner City of Glendale, Calif., 1991-94; sr. archtl. historian Hardy Heck Moore & Assocs., Austin, Tex., 1994, ptnr., 1995; preservation planning cons. Austin, 1996—. Instr. Cerritos Community Coll., Norwalk, Calif., 1990-94. Bd. dirs. Pasadena Heritage, 1984-90, sec., 1985-86; mem. steering com. Pasadena Residents in Def. of the Environment, 1988-90; reader Henry E. Huntington Libr. and Art Gallery, 1985—; commr. Cultural Heritage Commn., City of Pasadena, 1990-93; mem. state bd. of rev. Tex. Hist. Commn., 1999-2005, vice chmn., 2003-04, chmn. 2004-05. Recipient Cecilia Steinfeldt fellowship for Rsch. in the Arts and Material Cutlure, 2002. Mem. Soc. Archtl. Historians (bd. dirs. So. Calif. chpt. 1989-94, v.p. 1991-92, Tex. chpt. 1997-2000, founding editor SPECS 1997). Avocations: hiking, travel, photography. Office: Diane E Williams & Assocs PO Box 49302 Austin TX 78765-0921 Office Phone: 512-458-2367. Business E-Mail: texashistory@sbcglobal.net.

WILLIAMS, DOCIA SCHULTZ, small business owner; b. St. Louis, Mo., Sept. 12, 1930; d. John Frederic and Statira Jim (Thornton) Schultz; m. Stanley Good Southworth Jr. (div. 1983); 1 child, Sarah Elizabeth Southworth; m. Roy Donald Williams, Dec. 1, 1984. BA, Tex. Womans U., 1951. Fashion coordinator Ike Clark of Dallas, Dallas, 1951—53, Harveys Dept. Store, Nashville, Tex., 1953—55; model, coordinator Freelance, San Antonio, 1968; owner, boutique shop San Antonio, 1973—79; tour mgr. numerous travel co., 1979—89; owner, operator Mission City Tours, San Antonio, 1989—. With S.A. Writers Guild, San Antonio; writer C.S. Journal, San Antonio Conservation Soc., San Antonio, 2003—. Author: Spirits of San Antonio, 1992, When Darkness Falls, 1994, Ghosts Along The Texas Coast, 1993, Phantoms of the Plains, 1995, Best Tales of Texas Ghosts, 1998, Exploring San Antonio with Children, 2000, History and Mystery of the Menger Hotel, 2000; speaker (various profl. conventions). Nat. pres. Tex. Woman's U. Assn. of Former Students, 1982—84. Named one of Ten Outstanding Women in San Antonio, Express News Pub. Co., 1973; recipient Spirit of San Antonio award, San Antonio Hotel and Lodgings Assn., 2003. Mem.: Nat. Assn. Women Bus. Owners (Entreprenurial Spirit award 2004), Tour Guides Assn. of S.A. (charter mem., Disting. Svcs. award 2004), S.A. Coun. Presidents, San Antonio Hist. Soc., Nat. Soc. Arts and Letters. Republican. Meth. Avocations: music, travel, creative writing, antiques. Home and Office: 1319 Vista Del Monte San Antonio TX 78216 Office Phone: 210-493-2454. Personal E-mail: dociasw@aol.com.

WILLIAMS, DORIS W., rancher; b. West Bend, Wis., July 5, 1929; d. Wayne R. and Helen A. (Strasberg) Webster; m. George E. Williams, June 1951 (dec. 1968); 1 child, Lane G. Rancher Lazy J. Quarter Circle Ranch, New Rayner, Colo., 1953—; clk., trainer Wilson Leather Co., Greeley, Colo., 1998—99; bookeeper Milliken Potato Co., 1988. Pres. Pawnee Pioneer Trails-Byway; mem. Weld County Agrl. Coun., 1988—91; gov. Colo. Air Quality Control Commn., 1979—82. Recipient Cattle Woman of Yr., Colo. Cattle Women, 1994; Ranchers for Peace grant, 1982. Mem.: Weld County Livestock Assn., Weld County Hist. Soc. (pres. 1991—2006), Weld County Cattle Women (pres. 1969—2006). Democrat. Meth. Avocations: doll collecting, archaeology, history, paleontology. Home: 57875 Weld County Rd New Raymer CO 80742

WILLIAMS, DOROTHY STANDRIDGE, retired food products manager, civic worker; b. Powder Springs, Ga. d. Robert Anderson and Bertie Mae Standridge; m. Harold Thomas Barfield (div.); 1 child, H. Gregory; m. J. Arden Williams (div.). Student, DeKalb Coll., Atlanta, 1982—83, U. Que., 1997, U. Laval, Que., 1998, U. Paris-Sorbonne, 2000. Assoc. promotion mgr., promotion coord. Coca-Cola USA, Atlanta, 1978-83, promotions mgr., 1983-86; mgr. internat. promotion svcs. The Coca-Cola Co., Atlanta, 1986-90, mgr. global promotion svcs., 1990-94. Cons., judge Point-of-Purchase Advt. Inst., 1995. Attaché Atlanta Conv. and Visitors Bur., 1992—; vol. Welcome South Ctr., Atlanta, 1995—; bd. advisors Life Coll. for Knowledge and Tng., 1995—; chmn. cmty. rels. com. Life Coll., 1995-96, vice chmn. bd. adv. Knowledge and Tng. program, 1997-98, chmn. bd. advisors Knowledge and Tng. program, 1998-99. Mem. Ga. Trust for Hist. Preservation, Atlanta High Mus. Art, Atlanta Bot. Garden, Alliance Francaise, Smyrna Hist. Soc. Avocations: travel, french language, interior design, hiking, bridge.

WILLIAMS, E. FAYE, lawyer, political organization executive, health products executive; BS, Grambling State U.; MPA, U. So. Calif.; JD, Howard U.; PhD in Pub. Adminstrn., City Univ. of LA; D of Ministry, Wesley Theol. Seminary. Former counsel US Congress; legis. counsel DC City Coun.; chief of staff to DC Coun. Mem. Marion Barry; pres., CEO Natural Health Options, Inc., Washington. Former prof. internat. law So. U. Law Ctr., Baton Rouge; pub. affairs dir. WWGB, Washington; commentator La. Radio Network. Bd. mem. Shundahia Network. Named one of Most Influential Black Americans, Ebony mag., 2006; recipient Star Performer Award, Asian Benevolent Soc., Humanitarian Award, African Hebrew Israelites, Winnie Mandela Endurance with Dignity award, Support A Child Found., Inc., 2001, Cmty. Svc. award, Nation of Islam, Woman Entrepreneur of Yr. award, Indiana Black Expo. Mem.: Nat. Congress of Black Women (nat. chair 2006—, past gen. counsel). Office: Nat Congress of Black Women Ste 200 1224 W St, SE Washington DC 20020 Office Phone: 301-562-8000.*

WILLIAMS, EDNA ALETA THEADORA JOHNSTON, journalist; b. Halifax, N.S., Can., Sept. 19, 1923; d. Clarence Harvey and Edna May (Lewis) Johnston; m. Albert Murray Williams, Apr. 16, 1949 (dec.); children: Murleta, Norma, Martin, Charla, Kerrick, Renwick, Julia. Student, Maritime Bus. Coll., 1943. Typist Dept. Treas. (Navy), Halifax, 1944-49; with Bedford (N.S.) Mag., Halifax br., 1954-55, Presbyn. Office, New Glasgow, N.S., 1965-67, Thompson and Sutherland, New Glasgow, 1967-69; family editor, columnist, reporter New Glasgow Evening News, 1969-88, ret., 1988; soc.

corr. Evening News, 1997—. Mem. coun. Halifax YMCA; founding mem. Pictou County YM-YWCA, 1966—; ref. person media and religion Black History Month; New Glasgow Bapt. rep. Pictou County Coun. of Chs., 1978—82, sec., 1980—82; pres. ch. aux. 2d United Bapt. Ch., 1979—83; chorus dir. Men's Choir, 1980—, hon. mem. ch. aux., v.p., 1993—; treas. Ch.'s Men's Brotherhood, 1995—; organist St. James Anglican Ch., 1983—85, provincial organist, 1994—; organist St. Bee's Anglican Ch., 1996—2003; provincial pres. Women's Inst. of African United Bapt. Assn., 1983—86; bd. dirs. Pictou County YM-YWCA, 1967—77, corr. sec., v.p., 1974—75, 1975—77; past pres., past provincial dir., Home and Sch. provincial sec. African United Bapt. Assn. of N.S., 1988—90; sec. area IV Atlantic United Bapt. Conv., 1989—93; past officer local interracial com.; bd. dirs. Big Bros./Big Sisters, 1984—86, Pictou County United Way, 1983—96, Palliative Care Aberdeen Hosp., 1985—, Black United Front; chair Pictou County Srs. Festival, 1999—2001. Recipient Hon. award, United Way, 1993, Grot award, Black Cultural Ctr. N.S., 1999, honored by, Pictou County Music Festival, 1994, award, 2d United Bapt. Ch., 1997, Cultural Heritage award, Town of New Glasgow, 2004, Palliative Care Vol. award, 2005, Honored over 50 yr. mem. and 20 yr. organist, African United Bapt. Assn. Women's Inst., 2005. Mem. N.S. Sr. Secretate, Can. Press Assn., Black Journalists Assn. N.S., Can. Bible Soc. (pres. 2004—, Certificate, 1998), African United Baptist Assn. Women's Inst. Home: 230 Reservoir St New Glasgow NS Canada B2H 4K4 Office: Evening News 352 East River Rd Glasgow NS Canada B2H 5E2 Personal E-mail: karryw@ns.sympatico.ca.

WILLIAMS, ELEANOR JOYCE, retired government air traffic control specialist; b. College Station, Tex., Dec. 21, 1936; d. Robert Ira and Viola (Ford) Toliver; m. Tollie Williams, Dec. 30, 1955 (div. July 1978); children: Rodrick, Viola Williams Smith, Darryl, Eric, Dana Williams Robinson, Sheila Williams Watkins, Kenneth. Student, Prairie View A&M Coll., 1955-56, Anchorage Community Coll., 1964-65, U. Alaska-Anchorage, 1976. Clk./stenographer FAA, Anchorage, 1965-66, adminstrv. clk., 1966-67, pers. staffing asst., 1967-68, air traffic control specialist, 1968-79, air traffic control supr. San Juan, P.R., 1979-80, Anchorage, 1983-85, airspace specialist Atlanta, 1980-83, with Washington, 1985-87; area mgr. Kansas City Air Rt. Traffic Control Ctr., Olathe, Kans., 1987-89, asst. mgr. Quality Assurance, 1989-91, supr. traffic mgmt., 1991, supr. system effectiveness section, 1991-93, asst. air traffic mgr., 1993-94; air traffic mgr. Cleve. Air Route Traffic Control Ctr., Oberlin, Ohio, 1994-97; acting mgr. sys. mgmt. br. Des Plains, Ill., 1995-96; mem. human resource reform team task force Washington, 1996—; acting regional exec. mgr. Great Lakes Region Des Plaines, Ill., 1996-97. Propr. Williams Apts., Anchorage. Sec. Fairview Neighborhood Coun., Anchorage, 1967-69; mem. Anchorage Bicentennial Commn., 1975-76; bd. dirs. Mt. Patmos Youth Dept., Decatur, Ga., 1981-82; mem. NAACP; del. to USSR Women in Mgmt., 1990; v.p. A&M Consol. Lincoln H.S. Alumni Assn., 2000—; mem. citizens amb. program People to People Internat.; mem. adv. bd. Lincoln Recreation Ctr. Recipient Mary K. Goddard award Anchorage Fed. Exec. Assn. and Fed. Women's Program, 1985, Sec.'s award Dept. Transp., 1985, Pres. VIP award, 1988, C. Alfred Anderson award, 1991, Disting. Svc. award Nat. Black Coalition of Fed. Aviation Employees, 1991, Paul K. Bohr award FAA, 1994, Nat. Performance Rev. Hammer award from V.P. Al Gore, 1996, Regional Adminstrs. award for meritorious svc. Gt. Lakes Regional Adminstrn., 1997, Top Flight award for outstanding svc. FAA, 1997; A salute to Her Name in the Congl. Record 104th Congress, 1995, Execs. in Profile award for exemplary career performance Region Ten Blacks in Govt., 1998, Pres.'s award for outstanding svc. Lincoln Former Students Assn.; named Disting. Alumnus Lincoln H.S., 2000; named Youth Advocate Cmty. Champion State of Tex., Tex. Commn. Alcohol and Drug Abuse, 2001; inducted into Black Aviation Hall fame, 2001, Woman of Yr. award North to the Future Bus. and Profl. Women's Club, Anchorage, 2006 Mem.: Women in Mgmt. (del. Soviet Union), Internat. Platform Assn., Fed. Mgrs. Assn., Air Traffic Contrs. Assn., Profl. Women Contrs. Orgn., Nat. Black Coalition of Fed. Aviation Employees (pres. cen. region chpt. 1987—92, Over Achievers award 1987, Disting. Svc. award 1988, Sojourner Truth award Great Lakes region 1997), Blacks in Govt., Nat. Assn. Negro Bus. and Profl. Women USA Inc. (North to the Future club, charter pres. 1975—76), Gamma Phi Delta. Democrat. Baptist. Avocations: singing, sewing. Home: 7931 Old Seward Hwy Apt 8 Anchorage AK 99518-3265 Personal E-mail: ejw4atc@aol.com, ejtwmsent@msn.com.

WILLIAMS, ELIZABETH, human services administrator; d. Sylvester and Lucinda Williams; m. Willie Alfred Oden (div.); 1 child, Robert Earl Oden (dec.). Student, Hammel Bus. Coll., Akron, Ohio, 1960—61, Washtenaw CC, Ann Arbor, Mich., 1962—63, Econ. Inst. Christian Edn., Stanford, Conn., 1968, Norwalk CC, Conn., 1969—70, Roosevelt U., Chgo., 1972, City Coll. NY, Manhattan, 1972—74. LCSW Mich., 1974. Founder, owner Al's Restaurant, Akron, 1964—68; head sports dept. Lord and Taylors, Stanford, 1968—70; supr., planner, bd. dirs. Washtenaw County Neighborhood Svcs., Ypsilanti, Mich., 1970—76; founder, exec. dir. New Bethel Cmty. Ctr., Ypsilanti, 1976—80, People's Choice Multi Purpose Ctr., Inc., Ypsilanti, 1976—80, founder, pres. LA, 1981—87; program dir. Watts Labor Com. Action, LA, 1980—81; founder, pres. EOW Enterprises, LA, 1987—94, SLW Fin. and Investment Corp., 1993—, EW Capital Sys. Enterprises, 2002—. Founder Sr. Citizens Edn. and Tutoring Program, 1970—76; program dir. campus svc. E. Mich. U., Ypsilanti, 1979—80; coord. youth tng. Mich. Tech. Inst., Ann Arbor, 1980; program coord. U. Mich. Dept. Continuing Edn. for Women. Founder Washtenaw County Lit. Coun., Ann Arbor, Mich., 1976—80; mem. Solid Front for Unity in Am., 1982—85, Nat. Orgn. Black Lawyers, Calif., Nat. Coun. Aging, Calif., Ypsilanti Orgn. Social Workers, Nat. and State Orgn. Social Workers, Calif., Ypsilanti area Coll. Life-Long Learning, Wayne State U., Detroit; rep. Bd. Licenses and Regulations, Mich.; spl. program dir. Mt. Zion Ch. of God in Christ, Ypsalanti, 1973—81; bd. mem. YWCA, Stanford, Conn.; state chair Conf. Black Women, Stanford; mem. Stanford Housing Project, MLK Birthday Commn., LA, 1982—85; program planner, program dir., recruiter, trustee Hong Kong Internat. Humanitarian Self Liquidating Loan Program, 1991—2005; mem., bd. dirs. Nat. Orgn. Social Workers; mem. exec. com. United Way, Calif.; mem. Mich. State Steering Com.; mem. bd. dirs. extended opportunity program Boy Scouts of Am., Ypsilanti. Named Exec. Adminstr. of Yr., Compton, Calif., 1983—84, Bus. Woman of Yr., CBS TV, 1984, Citizen of Week, KNX News, 1985, Bus. Woman of Yr., ACC News, 1986, Miss Christianity, ACC Churches and Cmty. News, 1987; recipient Pauline award, Ministers Alliance, LA, 1983—84, Entrepreneur award, Philanthropist Christian Club, LA, 1983—84, Agy. of Yr. award, Calif., 1983—84, Excellent Cmty. Svc. award, NAACP, 1984, Outstanding Svc. to LA Cmty. award, IRS, 1985, Humanitarian award, People's Choice bd. dirs., 1986, Keys to the City, Compton, 1987, Feeding the Hungry spl. award, 1987; Unique Partnership in Conservation award grant, So. Calif. Gas Co., 1986. Avocations: checkers, chess, cooking, dominoes, interior decorating.

WILLIAMS, ELIZABETH EVENSON, writer; b. Sioux Falls, S.D., Sept. 25, 1940; d. A. Duane and Eleanor (Kelton) Evenson; m. Louis P. Williams Jr., Aug. 31, 1968; 1 child, Katherine. BS, S.D. State U., 1962; MA, U. Wis., 1964; postgrad., U. Minn., 1969-70; MA, S.D. State U., 1983, PhD, 1997. Dir. pubs. No. State Coll., Aberdeen, S.D., 1965-68; instr. journalism S.D. State U., Brookings, 1968—69, 1985—89; asst. editor Journalism Quar., Mpls., 1969-70; pub. info. specialist S.D. Com. on Humanities, Brookings, 1975-78; asst. and instr. speech dept. S.D. State U., Brookings, 1981-92, adj. journalism faculty, 1989—; part-time dir. Women's Ctr., Brookings, 1988-90; reading series coord. S.D. Com. on Humanities, Brookings, 1986-91. Adj. sociology faculty S.W. State U., Marshall, Minn., 1998—99, Marshall, 2000—01, Augustana Coll., Sioux Falls, SD, 2001, S.D. State U., Brookings, 2001—. Author: Emil Loriks: Builder of a New Economic Order, 1987, More Reflections of a Prairie Daughter, 1993, Free to Speak His Mind: W.R. Ronald, Prairie Editor and an AAA Architect, 1999; weekly columnist Brookings Daily Register, 1985-92, RFD News, 1992-95; contbr. articles to profl. jours. Vestry mem. St. Paul's Ch., Brookings, 1975-76, 84-86, 92-97, sr. warden, 1995-97, 2003-04; pres. LWV of S.D., 1985-89, treas., 1990-92, 99—; trustee Brookings Pub. Libr., 1994-2006. S.D. Humanities Com. grantee, 1984, 87, 90. Mem. Nat. Fedn. Press Women (1st place nat. writing contest 1977), Phi Kappa Phi, Pi Kappa Delta, Alpha Kappa Delta. Episcopalian. Avocations: golf, photography, travel. Home: 1103 3rd St Brookings SD 57006-2230 E-mail: lizerly@brookings.net.

WILLIAMS, ELIZABETH NUTT, psychologist, educator; BA in Psychology, Stanford U., 1989; MA in Counseling Psychology, U. Md., 1994, PhD in Counseling Psychology, 1997. Lic. psychologist Md. Asst. prof. psychology St. Mary's Coll. Md., St. Mary's City, 1997—2003, assoc. prof. psychology, 2003—, coord. women, gender and sexuality program, 2004—. Recipient Milton Dean Havron Social Scis. award, U. Md., 1996, Homer L. Dodge award for excellence in tchg., St. Mary's Coll. Md., 2003. Mem.: NOW, APA, Soc. Psychotherapy Rsch., Phi Beta Kappa (historian Zeta chpt. 1998—2001, pres. Zeta chpt. 2001—03). Office: St Mary's Coll Md Dept Psychology 18952 E Fisher Rd Saint Marys City MD 20686 Business E-Mail: enwilliams@smcm.edu.

WILLIAMS, ELIZABETH YAHN, writer, educator, lawyer; b. Columbus, Ohio, July 20, 1942; d. Wilbert Henry and Elizabeth Dulson (Brophy) Yahn. BA cum laude, Loyola Marymount U., 1964; secondary tchg. credential, UCLA, 1965; JD, Loyola U., 1971. Cert. tchr. h.s. and jr. coll. English and history. Writer, West Covina, Calif., 1964—; designer, 1966-68; tchr. jr./sr. h.s. L.A. City Schs., Santa Monica, Calif., 1964-65, La Puente H.S. Dist., Calif., 1965-67; legal intern, lawyer Garvey, Ingram, Baker & Uhler, Covina, Calif., 1969-72; lawyer, corp. counsel Avco Fin. Svcs., Inc., Newport Beach, Calif., 1972-74; pvt. practice Santa Ana, Calif., 1974—87; poetry project dir. Frank Craig Poetry Cub of the Solana Beach Libr., 2005—06. Mem. faculty continuing edn. State Bar of Calif., 1979; adj. prof. Western State U. Sch. Law, Fullerton, Calif., 1980; mem. fed. cts. com. Calif. State Bar, San Francisco, 1977-80. Author: (1-act plays) Acting-Out Acts, 1990, Grading Graciela, 1992, Boundaries in the Dirt, 1993; author: (lyricist) Peter and the Worry Wrens, 1995; author: (lyricist, narrator) Love in Our Midst, 2000; author: (poetry chapbook) A Medley of Cherry, 2000, Verses for Violins, 2001, Joy: Moments for Reflection, 2002; co-author (with Hither and Yahn): Hither & Yahn II: Partners in Rhyme Take on the Holidays, 2006; editor: The Music of Poetry, 1997, 1998; contbr. articles to profl. jours.; panelist (TV show) Action Now, 1971, interviewee Women, 1987; scriptwriter, dir.: TV show Four/Four, 1994; author: (3-act adaptation) Saved in Sedona, 1995, (play, screenplay) Showings, 2004; scriptwriter, prodr., host: TV show Guildelights to Success, 1996; developer board game Go With Your Goals!. Mem. alumni bd. Loyola-Marymount Coll., L.A., 1980-84; mem. adv. bd. Rancho Santiago Coll., Santa Ana, 1983-84; spkr. Commn. on Status on Women, Santa Ana, 1979. Grantee, Ford Found., 1964—65, SLS, St. Petersburg, Russia, 2006; scholar, Nat. Audio Theatre Found., 2004; Writer's grantee, Vt. Ctr. Studio, 2003, French scholar, Ohio State U., 1959, acad. scholar, Loyola-Marymount U., 1960—64, Book Expo 2000 scholar, Pubs. Mktg. Assn.-San Diego Pubs. Alliance Pub Mktg. U., 2000, Writing scholar, Episcopal Diocese of L.A., 1999. Mem.: Sunset Beach Poets, Nat. League Am. Pen Women, Magee Park Poets, Calif. Women Lawyers (life; bd. dirs. 1975—76, co-founder), Phi Theta Kappa (life most disting. hon.). Avocation: art. Address: PO Box 233 San Luis Rey CA 92068-0233 E-mail: dreywilliams@hotmail.com.

WILLIAMS, ELLA OWENS, writer; b. Skippers, Va., June 21, 1931; d. Thomas Walden and Mary Corine Owens; m. Charlie Lee Williams, Apr. 19, 1957; children: Kalimah Matthews, Karl Lin. BS, St. Paul's Coll., Lawrenceville, Va., 1952; MA, NYU, N.Y.C., 1957; ArtsD, Clark Atlanta U., Atlanta, 1987; EdD, Walden U., Naples, Fla., 1976. Cert. tchr. Calif., 1971. Prof. Pierce Coll., Tacoma, 1972—95; ret., 1995. Author: (novels) Blackberry Women; essayist Strength to Carry On, 1998. Pres. Pensacola Chpt., The Links, Inc, Fla., 2003—04; protocol chair Societas Docta, Inc., Atlanta. Recipient Inst. on Africa award, Hamlin U., Minn., 1986; fellow NEH fellow, U. of Pa., 1985. Mem.: Dela Sigma Theta (corr.; first v.p. 2003—04, Cert. 2003, 2004). United Methodist. Home: P O Box 5486 Navarre FL 32566 Home Fax: 850-939-8067. Personal E-mail: ellaowilliams@yahoo.com.

WILLIAMS, ENID ROBERTA (ENID W. TROLL), psychologist, nurse; b. Long Beach, Calif., Mar. 1, 1923; d. Clarence Strong and Zita Marie (Stafford) Williams; m. John Hans Troll, Sept. 4, 1963. BSN, St. Louis U., 1945; MA in Voc. Guidance, Columbia U., Tchrs. Coll., 1958, profl. diploma in Rehab. counseling, 1958; postgrad., Rutgers U., 1961; MS in Psychiat. Nursing, Boston U., 1976, EdD in Human Svcs. and Counseling, 1982. Intern psychology Child Study Ctr., Phila., 1961-62; pre-doctoral fellow psychology NJ Dept. Insts. and Agys., 1962-63; school psychologist NYC and Conn. Pub. Schs., 1964-68; staff psychologist Harlem Valley State Hosp., Wingdale, N.Y., 1969-70; staff nurse, psychiat. The Arbour Hosp., Jamaica Plain, Mass., 1974—98; post-doctoral fellow geriatric mental health Harvard Med. Sch., Dept. Psychiatry, Boston, 1985-86, rsch. on effects of anesthesia on neuropsychological functioning; post-doctoral intern psychology Metrowest Youth Guidance Ctr., Framingham, Mass., 1988-89; cons. in psychology Boston, 1989—98. Recipient U.S. Pub. Health Nursing scholar, 1942-45,; grantee NIMH, Sch. Nursing, Boston U., 1973-74. Mem. APA, Mass. Psychol. Assn., Sociologists Women Soc. Home: 1025 Chelwood Park Blvd NE Apt 134 Albuquerque NM 87112-5941

WILLIAMS, FREDA BERRY, administrative assistant; b. Petersburg, Va., June 9, 1956; d. William Lewis and Estella Virginia (Bouldin) Berry; m. LaMar Williams, Sr., Sept. 9, 1980 (div. Nov. 1992); children: LaMar Jr., Keana Trahearn, Genique Renee. Student, John Tyler C.C., Chester, Va., 1973-80; Diploma, United Truck Master, Clearwater, Fla., 1988. Lic. tractor trailer driver, reupholsterer, drafting technologist. Reupholstery worker Berry's Sewing Shop, Colonial Heights, Va., 1969-75; office asst. John Tyler C.C., 1975-76; domestic worker Ramada Inn, Richmond, Va., 1977-78; engr., drafter C.C. Towns & Assocs., Colonial Heights, 1979; owner, operator Williams Ind. and Assocs., Colonial Heights, 1981-88; sewing machine operator Crawford Mfg., Richmond, 1982-88; tractor trailer driver Capital Dist., Ashland, Va., 1988-91; transp. clk. Golden Capital Dist., Ashland, 1991, transp. adminstrv. asst., 1991-95. Network mgr. Pegasus Female Execs., 1985—88; cons. Williams Enterprises and Assocs--Cyberspace and Catalog Svc., 2000—. County exec. Women's Congl. Congress 4th Dist., Richmond, 1988—89; spokesperson Safety Coun. Transp. Dept., 1991—94; mem. policy coun. Chesterfield Head Start, 1998—, treas., 1998—99, mem. sch. yr. health adv. com., 1990—2000, merchandiser, 1996—; head of women's fellowship ministry Pavilion of Joy, 2001—, primary Sunday sch. tchr., 2001—. Mem. Newbridge Book Club, NAFE. Baptist. Avocations: drawing, painting, arts and crafts.

WILLIAMS, FREDA VIDELL, speech pathology/audiology services professional; d. Norman Freeman Williams and Coreen Videlle Davis; children: Shannon O'Neal Otwell, Michael Scott Otwell. MS in Speech-Pathology and Audiology, Fla. State U., Tallahassee. Speech-lang. pathologist Sunland Tng. Ctr., Marianna, Fla., 1979, Jackson County Schs., 1979—79, Houston County Schs., Dothan, Ala., 1980—80, Sunland Tng. Ctr., Marianna, 1980—80, Wash. County Schs., Chipley, Fla., 1981—83, pvt. practice, 1983—87, Leon County Schs., Tallahassee, 1987—88, Programs Infants and Children, Anchorage, 1988—89, Lauderdale County Schs., Meridian, Miss., 1989—90, Dothan City Schs., Ala., 1990—97, Programs Infants and Children, Anchorage, 1997—99, Bay Dist. Schs., Panama City, Fla., 1999—2002, coord. speech-lang. pathology, 2002—. Coord. Emerald Coast Speech-Lang. Pathology Consortium, Panama City, 2004—. Builder Habitat Humanity, Panama City, 2005—06; councilwoman Dem. Exec. Com., Marianna, 1981—82; builder United Meth. Ch., Oaxaca, Mexico, 1983—83. Mem.: Am. Speech-Lang.-Hearing Assn. (assoc.). Conservative. Avocations: painting, swimming, walking, travel.

WILLIAMS, GLENDA CARLENE, writer; b. Jefferson County, Ala., Jan. 17, 1946; d. Wilmer and Lucy Iris (Crowley) W.; three children: Shawna Dawn White, Crystal Lee, Tomas Lee. Ballroom dance instr. Continental Dance Studio, Birmingham, Ala., 1968-70; receptionist, instr. Occupl. Rehab., Birmingham, 1970-74; exec. sec. Educators Investment, Birmingham, 1974-76; sec., county agt. County Extension Office, Rusk, Tex., 1976-78. Freelance tchr. spl. needs children, Ala., 1990—; counselor natural healing and nutrition, Ala., 1990—; founder, dir. Healing Hands Ministry, Birmingham, 1998—. Author: Nutrition and Attention Deficit Disorder, 1991, Beyond this Hill, 1995, And When You Wake, 1995; editor: Legends of the Owl, 1995. Vol. Am. Cancer Soc., 2002-03. Avocations: writing, nutritional research, humanitarian projects, hymnbook angels. Home: PO Box 236 Elmore AL 36025-0236

WILLIAMS, GRETCHEN MINYARD, food store executive; b. Dallas, Dec. 18, 1956; d. Marvin Tipton and Clarine (Cooper) Minyard; m. Joseph Larry Williams, June 10, 1978. BBA, Tex. Christian U., 1978. Dir. employee rels. Minyard Food Stores, Inc., Coppell, Tex., 1978-80, v.p. employee rels., 1980-83, v.p. corp. rel., 1983-85, vice chmn. of bd. dirs., 1985-88, co-chmn. bd. dirs., 1988-98, co-CEO, co-chmn. bd. dirs., 1998—. Bd. dirs. Cullen/Frost Bank, N.A., Dallas. Adv. bd. mktg. edn. Dallas Ind. Sch. Dist., Dallas, 1981—; campaign mem. Old City Park, Dallas, 1988, Tex. Christian U. Fund Drive, Ft. Worth, 1987-88; adv. bd. Dallas Bapt. U., 1985—. Mem. Dallas/Ft. Worth Retail Grocers Assn. (chmn. bd. 1988—, avt. com.), AGAPE Social Svcs. Inc. (bd. dirs. 1987—), Baylor Health Care System (bd. dirs. 1989—), Zeta Tau Alpha (pres 1986-87). Avocations: reading, travel. Office: Minyard Food Stores Inc PO Box 518 777 Freeport Pky Coppell TX 75019-4411

WILLIAMS, HARRIET CLARKE, retired academic administrator; b. Bklyn., Sept. 5, 1922; d. Herbert Edward and Emma Clarke (Gibbs) W. AA, Bklyn. Coll., 1958; student, Art Career Sch., NYC, 1960; degree, Hunter Coll., 1965, CPU Inst. Data Processing, 1967; student, Chinese Cultural Ctr., N.Y.C., 1973; degree (hon.), St. Joseph's Coll., Mont., 1990. Adminstr. Baruch Coll., N.Y.C., 1959-85. Substitute math. dept. Baruch Coll., 1983-85; mktg. rschr. 1st Presbyn. Arts and Crafts Shop, Jamaica, N.Y., 1986-96; tutor in art St. John's U., Jamaica, 1986-96; founder, curator Internat. Art Gallery, Queens, N.Y., 1991—. Exhibited in group shows at Union Carbide Art Exhibit, N.Y.C., 1975, Queens Day Exhbn., N.Y.C., 1980, 1st Presbyn. Arts and Crafts Shop, N.Y.C., 1986, others; contbr. articles to profl. publs. Vol. reading tchr. Mabel Dean Vocat. High Sch., N.Y.C., 1965-67; mem. polit. action com. dist. council 37, N.Y.C., 1973-77; mem. negotiating team adminstrv. contracts, N.Y.C., 1975-78; mem. Com. To Save CCNY, 1976-77, Simon Wiesenthal Ctr., Calif., 2003-06, Statue Liberty Ellis Island Found., Woodrow Wilson Internat. Ctr. Scholars, Wilson Ctr. Assocs., Washington, St. Labre Indian Sch., Ashland, Mont., Nat. Law Enforcement Fund. Appreciation award Dist. Coun. 37, 1979; recipient Plaque Appreciation Svcs., Baruch Coll., Key award St. Joseph's Indian Sch., 1990, Key award in Edn. and Art, 1990, others. Mem. NAFE, AAUW, Women in Mil. Svc., Assn. Am. Indian Affairs, Nat. Mus. of Am. Indian, Artist Equity Assn. N.Y., Am. Indian Edn. Found., Lakota Devel. Coun., Am. Film Inst., Bklyn. Coll. Alumni, Nat. Geographic Soc., Nat. Mus. Woman in the Arts, Statue of Liberty Ellis Island Found., Inc., Alliance of Queens Artists, U.S. Naval Inst., El Museo Del Barrio, Am. Mus. Natural History, Internat. Ctr. for Scholars-Wilson Ctr. Assocs., Alumni of Baruch Coll., Arrow Club-St. Labre Indian Sch., Mus. of Television and Radio, Women in Mil. Meml. Found., Nat. Mus. of Am. Indian, U.S. Holocaust Mus., Navy Meml. (adv. coun.), U.S. Golf Assn. Roman Catholic. Avocations: aerobics, volunteer work, world travel, music. Office: Baruch Coll 17 Lexington Ave New York NY 10010-5518

WILLIAMS, HAZELYN MATTHIS, dancer, educator; b. Wilmington, NC, Feb. 3, 1981; d. Roland Elliott and Joanna Crumpler Matthis; m. Kimbrell Clark Williams, May 24, 2003. B, Meredith Coll., Raleigh, NC, 2003. Lic. tchr. K-12 NC, cert. CPR NC. Dance tchr. Cumberland County Schs., Hope Mills, NC, 2003—. Dance team coach Gray's Creek HS, Hope Mills, 2003—. Mem., bible sch. tchr. Elizabeth Missionary Bapt. Ch., Roseboro, NC, 2006; judge for governor's sch. Cumberland County Schs., Fayetteville, 2005. Named Gt. Am. Tchr., 2005; Teacher's Reimbursment scholar, Cumberland County, 2005. Mem.: Aerobics and Ftness Assn. Am. (licentiate; cert. aerobics instr.). Office Phone: 910-424-8589.

WILLIAMS, HELEN MARGARET, retired accountant; b. Fresno, Calif., Mar. 16, 1947; d. James Ray Jr. and Barbara (LaRue) Franklin; m. Phillip Dean Bangs, Apr. 16, 1977; children: Aluvia, Adevia, Rodney. AA in Home Economics, Sacramento City Coll., 1969, AA in Acctg., 1971; BS in Acctg. and Fin. cum laude, Calif. State U., Sacramento, 1988. Acct. tech. Sacramento Regional Transit Dist., 1974-87, revenue rm. contr., 1987-88, acct. I, 1988, acct. II, 1988-97. Editor employee newsletter Sacramento Regional Transit Dist., 1986-90. Past mother and worthy adv. Rainbow for Girls; past host parent Am. Field Svc., past chair host family selection com. Mem. Am. Soc. Women Accts. (chair scholarship com. 1992-94, chair pub. com. 1993-94, bd. dirs. 1993-96, 2000—, sec. 1994-95, 99-2000, 2002-04, chair roster com. 1995-96, chair hospitality com. 1996-98, 2001-2002, chair publicity com. 1998-99, treas. 2000-02, 2004-06), Calif. State U.-Sacramento Alumni Assn., Capital Investors Investment Club (fin. ptnr., recording ptnr. 1998—), Order Ea. Star, Precious Moments Collectors Club (newsletter editor 1992—, treas. 1993—). Avocations: sewing, interior design, needlecrafts, collectibles, genealogy.

WILLIAMS, HETTIE V., history professor; b. New Brunswick, N.J., Feb. 8, 1971; d. Freddie G. Williams, Sr. and Gloria A. Hill. BA, Rowan U., Glassboro, NJ, 1994; MA, Monmouth U., West Long Branch, NJ, 2000. Coord. tutoring AmeriCorps/Urban Schs. Svc. Corps, Red Bank Pub. Schs., NJ, 1995—96; instrnl. asst. E.D. classroom Matawan-Aberdeen Pub. Schs., NJ, 1997—98; adj. history instr. Brookdale C.C., Lincroft, NJ, 2000—06, Essex County Coll., Newark, 2001—; full time history instr. Monmouth U., West Long Branch, NJ, 2002—. Presenter and lectr. in field. Contbr. articles to profl. jours. Mem.: NJ Coun. on History Edn., Nat. Coun. on History Edn., Assn. for the Study of African Am. Life and History, Orgn. Am. Historians, Phi Alpha Theta. Avocations: painting, reading, writing, poetry. Office: Monmouth Univ 400 Cedar Ave West Long Branch NJ 07764

WILLIAMS, HOLLY THOMAS, retired business executive; b. Pitts., Dec. 24, 1931; d. Andrew Matthew and Elizabeth (Kuklinca) Thomas; m. Donald Evan Williams, May 14, 1961. AA cum laude, Keystone Jr. Coll., LaPlume, Pa., 1978; BS magna cum laude, U. Scranton, Pa., 1981. Dancer Arthur Murray Studios, Pitts., 1953-60, franchise owner Scranton, 1960-80; mgr. Nutri/System Weight Loss Ctr., Scranton, 1984-85, franchise owner, 1985-2001. Fund raiser United Cerebral Palsy of Lackawanna County, Scranton, 1970-79, St. Joseph's Children's Hosp., Scranton, 1962-76; exec. sec. Foxhowe Assn., Buck Hill Falls, Pa., 1984-85. Mem. AAUW (bd. dirs. 1985-86, 94-2001, br. pres. 1999-2001), Scranton Club. Republican. Mem. Christian Ch. Avocations: reading, golf, bridge, dance, travel. Home: 213 Karen Dr Scranton PA 18505-2207 also: PO Box 151 Buck Hill Falls PA 18323-0151

WILLIAMS, IDA JONES, consumer and home economics educator, writer; b. Coatesville, Pa., Dec. 1, 1911; d. William Oscar and Ida Ella (Ruth) Jones; m. Charles Nathaniel Williams, Mar. 17, 1940 (dec. July 1971). BS, Hampton Inst., 1935; MA, U. Conn., 1965. Cert. high sch. tchr., English, sci., home econs., Va., Pa. Tchr. sci. and home econs. Richmond County H.S., Ivondale, Va., 1935—36; tchr. English and home econs. Northampton County H.S., Chesapeake, Va., 1936—40, tchr. consumer and home econs. Machipongo, Va., 1940—70, Northampton Jr. H.S., Machipongo, 1970—76. Author: Starting Anew After Seventy, 1980 (plaque 1980), News and Views of Northampton County High Principals and Alumni, 1981, Great Grandmother, Leah's Legacy-Remember You're Free, 2000; co-author: The History of Virginia State Federation of Colored Women's Clubs, Inc., 1996; editor: Fifty Year Book 1935-1985 - Hampton Institute Class, 1985, Favorite Recipes of Ruth Family & Friends, 1986. V.p. Ea. Lit. Coun., Melfa, Va., 1987-89; active Ea. Shore Coll. Found., Inc., Melfa, 1988-2000, Gov.'s Adv. Bd. on Aging, Richmond, Va., 1992-94; instr. Ladies Community Bible Class, 1976-80 (Plaque 1980); sec., treas., v.p. Hospice Support of Ea. Shore, 1980-94; mem. Northampton/Accomack Adv. Coun., 1992-94; marshall 28th anniv. commencement Ea. Shore C.C., 1996; bd. dirs. Ea. Shore C.C. Found., 1998-2000; com. mem. Va. State Legis., 1995-2002 Named Home Econs. Tchr. of Yr., Am. Home Econs. Assn. and Family Cir., 1975, Woman of Yr., Prog.

Women of E.S., 1997, Ida J. Williams scholarship in her honor, Keller Ch. Christ, 1999; recipient Jefferson award, Am. Inst. Pub. Svc., Wavy-TV-Bell Atlantic and Mattress Discounters, 1991, Nat. Sojourner Truth Meritorious Svc. award, Negro Bus. and Profl. Women's Clubs, Gavel Ea. Shore Ret. Tchrs. Assn., 1994, Gov.'s award for vol. excellence, 1994, Contribution to Edn. award, Ea. Shore Coll. Found., 1997, plaque, Southeastern Assn. Colored Women's Clubs, Inc., 2001, Leadership award, 2001, Dedicated Svc. award, Nat. Assn. Colored Women's Club, 1998, Exemplary Svc. award, 2001, Svc. award, E.S. C.C. Found., Inc., 2000, plaque 1st Black Northampton County, Ea. Shore Va. C. of C., 2002, Black Achievement award, Ebenezer A.M.E. Ch., 2003, Achievement award, Chester County Hist. Soc. of Pa., 2003, Ednl. Achievement award, Northampton County H.S. Alumni Assn., 2003, Dedicated Svc. award, S.E. Assn. Colored Women's Clubs Inc., 2003—05; honored at ceremony for mother Ida Ella Ruth Jones at hist. road marker on Route 82, Pa., 2004. Mem. AARP (Citation award 1996, Mem. of Yr. 1997, v.p. Northampton chpt. 1998-2000), Progressive Women of Ea. Shore (pres. 1985-93, Gold Necklace 1993, Woman of Yr. 1997), C. of C., Univ. Women (v.p. Portsmouth br. 1985-87), Ea. Shore Ret. Tchrs. (pres. 1977-84), Dist. L Ret. Tchrs. (pres. 1989-91, chmn. legis. com. 1998, 99, 2001, chmn. edn. and scholarship com. 2001-05, Dedicated and Outstanding Svc. award 2003), Va. State Fedn. Colored Women's Club (pres. 1990-94, editor history com. 1994-96) Mem. Ch. of Christ. Avocations: crafts, travel, writing, lecturing. Home and Office: PO Box 236 14213 Lankford Hwy Eastville VA 23347-0236

WILLIAMS, IVORY LEE, special education educator; b. White Castle, La., Nov. 8, 1953; d. Johnny and Gussie Mae (Morris) W. BA in Elem. Edn., So. U., Baton Rouge, 1975, M of Elem. Edn., 1978; postgrad. thirty plus, So. U. & Southeastern U., Baton Rouge, Hammond, La., 1990. Spl. edn. tchr. Dorseyville Elem. Sch., White Castle, La., 1975—. Leader Dorseyville 4H Club, White Castle, mem. 4H Adv. Bd., Plaquemine, La., 1981—; mem. Very Spl. Arts Com., Plaquemine, 1991; sec. Greater Progressive Bapt. Ch. Named Outstanding 4H Leader Iberville Parish 4H Club, 1991. Mem. La. Assn. Eductors (Emerging Leader 1992), Iberville Parish Assn. Educators. Democrat. Avocations: reading, sewing. Office: Dorseyville Elem Sch PO Box 518 White Castle LA 70788-0370

WILLIAMS, JANELLE AUST, literature and language educator; b. Storm Lake, Iowa, Mar. 12, 1946; d. Fred G. and Valaria V. Aust; m. David A. Williams, Aug. 15, 1970. BA Edn., Ctrl. Wash. State Coll., Ellensburg, 1968; MEd, U. Portland, Oreg., 1991. Std. Tchg. Cert. Wash., 1968. Tchr. English, coach forensics W. F. West H.S., Chehalis, Wash., 1968—. Sec. Chief Examiner Chehalis Civil Svc. Commn., 1985—. Lewis County bd. trustee Timberland Regional Libr., Tumwater, Wash., 1994—2004. Recipient Disting. Svc. award, Wash. State Forensics Assn., 2003. Home: 1738 S Market Blvd Chehalis WA 98532 Office: W F West High School 342 SW 16th St Chehalis WA 98532 E-mail: jwilliams@chehalis.k12.wa.us.

WILLIAMS, JANICE H., business executive; d. William Leroy and Mamie Louise Abernathy; m. Ruben J. Williams, Sr., 1966; children: Ruben J. Williams, Jr., Chauncey J., Anjalon D.K. Assoc. Degree, Davenport Bus. Sch., 1981; Degree, Grand Rapids Jr. Coll., 1981; Bachelor Degree, Davenport Bus. Sch., 1987; Divinity Cert., Oral Roberts U., 1998. Cert. personal ins. Inst. Cert., 1976, comml. ins. Inst. Cert., 1977. Exec. sec. Christman Constrn., Grand Rapids, Wirhams Co., Grand Rapids; underwriter St. Paul Ins., Grand Rapids; asst. underwriter Aetna Ins., Grand Rapids; exec. sec. Spartan Stores, Grand Rapids; investigator Ford Motor Credit, Grand Rapids; pres., CEO Lakeside Orgn., Inc., Grand Rapids. Reporter St. Paul Ins., Grand Rapids, 1982—84; employment cons. Lakeside Orgn., Inc., 1994—2004; Power Point videographer Chrisman Constrn., Grand Rapids, 1999—2000. Amb., task force mem., vol. 4-H Mich. State U., 1990—2002; adult literacy trainer Kent County Lit. Coun., Mich., 1992—96; charter mem., fin. supporter Trail Blazer Girl Scouts, Grand Rapids, 1996—. Recipient Booker T. Washington Vol. Svc. to Children award, Kent County Child Abuse and Neglect, 1993, Vol. Svc. award, Nat. Assn. Negro Bus. Assn., 1994. Mem.: Cambridge England Adv. Coun. (hon.), Historic Mount Vernon Legacy (leader 2002—05), Girl Scouts of Am. (life). Avocations: poetry reading, golf, sewing, photography. Home: 2240 Delange Dr SE Grand Rapids MI 49506

WILLIAMS, JEANNE ELIZABETH, music educator; b. Greensboro, N.C., Aug. 23, 1950; d. James Henry and Mary Jessye Long Williams. BS in Music Edn., Winston-Salem State U., 1974. Cert. K-12 music N.C., kinder musick N.J. Reading tutor grade 3 Winston-Salem/Forsyth County Schs., NC, 2000—01, tchr. music, 2001—. Organist St. Phillips Moravian Ch. Mem. Watchfulnetwork Bus. Orgn.; performed with Maya Angelou Mt. Zion Bapt. Ch., 1984—87, mem. chancel choir, 2003; mem. Carver Sch. Rd. Adv. Libr. Bd.; organist Mt. Zion Bapt. Ch.; performerd with Robert Shaw Chorale Westminster Choir Coll., 1982. Recipient Cert. of Achievement in music, Appalachian State U., 2003. Mem.: N.C. Assn. Educators, Music Educators Nat. Conf., Nat. Assn. Music Edn., N.C. Music Educators, Nat. Women Achievement, Order Ea. Star, Zeta Phi Beta (mem. Rho Zeta chpt.). Avocations: reading, organ, dance, volleyball, traveling to the Caribbean.

WILLIAMS, JENNIFER ANN, public relations executive; b. Chgo., Jan. 15, 1965; children: Allen Pierre, Jason Austell, Jarvis Dominique. Cert. Office Automation Clk. U.S. Dept. Housing & Urban Devel., 1992; Office Asst. Ill. Dept. Human Svcs., 2002. Contracted hr profl. SPHERION, Chgo.; contracted adminstrv. profl. MANPOWER, Joliet, Genie Temp. Svcs., Joliet; pub. rels. mktg. profl. AFLAC, Joliet. Alumni Link Unlimited Scholarship Program, Chicago, Ill., —. Election judge Will County Clk.'s Office, Joliet. Named to Nat. Dean of Students List, 2005; recipient Grand Lady, Knights of St. Peter Claver, Jr. Daughters Divsn., 1980—81, Nat. Vice-Supreme Lady, Knights Of St. Peter Claver, Jr. Dau. Divsn., 1981—82; grantee scholarship, Knights of St. Peter Claver Orgn., 1982. Home: 611 E Cass St Joliet IL 60432 Office: Will County Clerk's Office 302 N Chicago Joliet IL 60435 Office Phone: 815-740-4616. Personal E-mail: jenniferhasadream@yahoo.com.

WILLIAMS, JENNIFER CATHERINE, elementary school educator; d. Danny Wayne and Mary Elizabeth Williams. AA in Liberal Arts, Allan Hancock Coll., Santa Maria, Calif., 1994; BA in Sociology, Calif. State U., Fullerton, 1996; Tchg. Credential, Chapman U., Orange, Calif., 2003. Residential counselor Maryvale Orphanage, Rosemead, Calif., 1996; instrnl. aide Orange County Dept. of Edn., Mission Viego, Calif., 1997; substitute tchr. Whittier City Sch. Dist., Calif., 1998, tchr. 7th grade English, 1999—. Youth group leader The Cause Cmty. Ch., Brea, Calif., 2005—. Mem.: Calif. Tchrs. Assn. Republican. Office: Whittier CSD-Dexter Mid Sch 11532 E Floral Dr Whittier CA 90601 Office Phone: 562-789-3090. Office Fax: 562-789-3095. E-mail: hislibra@hotmail.com.

WILLIAMS, JESSICA APRIL, elementary school educator; b. La Crosse, Wis., Apr. 21, 1981; d. Jeffrey Alan and Judith Anne Williams. BS, Viterbo U., La Crosse, Wis., 2004. Cert. tchr. elementary sch. Wis., 2004. Art tchr. Franklin Elem. Sch., La Crosse, 2000—02; tchr./daycare provider Noah's Ark Devel. Ctr., Cashton, Wis., 2004—05; pre-kindergarten/kindergarten tchr. Sacred Heart Sch., Cashton, 2004—05; music tchr. Wallace Elem. Sch., Parker, Ariz., 2005—. Tutor Wallace Elem. Sch., Parker, Ariz., 2005—; vol. music tchr./children's ch. choir dir. Sacred Heart Sch. Parish, Cashton, 2004—05. Campaign vol. Brad Pfaff for State Senate Campaign, La Crosse, 2004. Catholic. Avocations: cooking, singing, walking, scrapbooks. Office Phone: 928-669-2161. Personal E-mail: jwilluvzfrogs@hotmail.com.

WILLIAMS, JO KAREN KOBECK, artist, writer; b. Lawrenceburg, Tenn., Apr. 10, 1944; d. William Ethan and Ethel Marie (Hendrix) Kobeck; m. J.R. Benson, 1963 (div. 1974); children: Pamela Jo Benson Robinson, Anita Marie Benson Bosaw; m. Luther Williams, 2006. Cert. in drafting, Miss. Gulf Coast Jr. Coll., 1974; cert. in engring. graphics, U. Tenn., 1975; cert. in drafting, Mountain Empire C.C., 1980. Advt. asst. Rogers, Inc., Florence, Ala., 1966-67; drafter Litton Industries, Pascagoula, Miss., 1972-74; drafter, illustrator Cities Svc. Co., Copperhill, Tenn., 1974-78; design drafter Westmoreland Coal Co., Big Stone Gap, Va., 1978-88; design drafter, neon designer and illustrator Designs by Jo, East Stone Gap, Va., 1983—97; ind. cons. Mary Kay Cosmetics, 2001—. Mem. Copper Basin Redevel. Design Coun., 1975-77; lectr. Take off Pounds Sensibly, Appalachia, Va., 1985-87, 93-94, Coeburn, Va., 1999-2006; active Friends of Libr., Big Stone Gap, 1988; bd. dirs. H.E.L.P. Ctr., Big Stone Gap, 1988; pres. Va. Family and Cmty. Edn., 1991-98; election officer Dist. 3, Wise County, 1996, 97; mem. Christian Ch. Avocations: photography, wildlife rehabilitation, decorative artist, art. Home: 173 Beech Ave NE Coeburn VA 24230-3016

WILLIAMS, JOAN ELAINE, podiatric surgeon, educator; b. La Mesa, Calif. d. William E. and Dottie B. Williams; m. Edward Homewood Miller, 1987; children: Carol Martins, William Baerg, Michael Baerg. BS, Calif. Coll. Podiatric Med., 1978, D of Podiatric Medicine, 1981; MS, Pepperdine U., 1979. Diplomate Am. Bd. Podiatric Surgery, Am. Bd. Podiatric Orthopedics and Primary Podiatric Medicine. Chief podiatric medicine and surgery dept. vets. affairs Puget Sound Health Care System, Seattle, 1982—; clin. asst. prof. podiatric medicine Calif. Coll. Podiatric Medicine, San Francisco, 1982—, U. Osteo. Medicine and Health Sci., Des Moines, Iowa, 1982-90; clin. assoc. prof. U. Osteo. Medicine and Health Scis., Des Moines, Iowa, 1990—. Oral bd. examiner Am. Bd. Podiatric Orthopedics, Chgo., 1988; reviewer merit rev. grant Vets. Affairs Ctrl. Office, Washington, 1989; lic. exam reviewer Nat. Bd. Podiatric Med. Examiners, State College, Pa., 1993—. Editor: Preferred Practice Guidelines, 1992-94; contbr. articles to profl. jours. County del. Wash. State Rep. Party, Seattle, 1994. Recipient Acad. scholarship Pepperdine U., 1979. Fellow Am. Coll. Foot and Ankle Surgeons, Am. Coll. Foot and Ankle Orthopedics. Presbyterian. Avocations: classical music, playing cello. Office: Puget Sound Health Care Sys Dept Vets Affairs 1660 S Columbian Way Seattle WA 98108-1532

WILLIAMS, JOBETH, actress; b. Houston, Dec. 6, 1948; m. John Pasquin, 1982; children: Nick, Will. Grad., Brown U. Appeared in plays A Coupla White Chicks Sitting Around Talking, 1980, Gardenia, 1982, Idiot's Delight, 1986, Cat on a Hot Tin Roof, 1993; films include Kramer vs. Kramer, 1979, The Dogs of War, 1980, Stir Crazy, 1980, Poltergeist, 1982, Endangered Species, 1982, The Big Chill, 1983, American Dreamer, 1984, Teachers, 1984, Desert Bloom, 1986, Poltergeist II, 1986, Memories of Me, 1988, Welcome Home, 1989, Switch, 1991, Dutch, 1991, Stop! Or My Mom Will Shoot, 1992, Me, Myself and I, 1993, Wyatt Earp, 1994, Parallel Lives, 1994, Little City, 1997, Just Write, 1997, Jungle 2 Jungle, 1997, When Danger Follows You Home, 1997, Justice, 1998, Repossessed, 2002, The Rose Technique, 2002, Into the Fire, 2004, Fever Pitch, 2005; TV movies include Fun and Games, 1980, The Big Black Pill, 1981, Adam, 1983 (Emmy award nominee, Golden Globe award nominee), The Day After, 1983, Kids Don't Tell, 1985, Adam: His Song Continues, 1986, Murder Ordained, 1987, Baby M, 1988 (Emmy award nominee, Golden Globe award nominee), My Name is Bill W., 1989, Child in the Night, 1990, Victim of Love, 1991, Jonathan: The Boy Nobody Wanted, 1992, Sex, Love and Cold Hard Cash, 1993, Chantilly Lace, 1993, Voices from Within, 1994, Lemon Grove, 1994, Parallel Lives, 1994, Voices from Within, 1994, Season of Hope, 1994, Ruby Jean and Joe, 1996, Breaking Through, 1996, It Came From the Sky, 1998, A Chance of Snow, 1998, Justice, 1999, Jackie's Back!, 1999, Trapped in a Purple Haze, 2000, The Ponder Heart, 2001, Homeward Bound, 2002, 14 Hours, 2005; TV series include The Guiding Light, 1977-81, Somerset, 1975-76, (voice) Fish Police, 1992, John Grisham's The Client, 1995-96, (voice) Stories from My Childhood, 1998, Payne, 1999; co-exec. prodr.: (TV movie) Bump in the Night, 1991; dir. (films): On Hope, 1994 (Acad. award nominee for Best Live Action Short Film 1995), Winona's Web, 2001.

WILLIAMS, JODY, political organization administrator; b. Rutland, Vt., Oct. 9, 1950; BA, U. Vt.; MA, Sch. Internat. Tng.; MA in Internat. Studies, Johns Hopkins U.; PhD (hon.), Briar Cliff Coll., Marlboro Coll., U. Vt., Williams Coll., Pa. State U., Royal Mil. Coll. Canada, Wesleyan U., Franklin Pierce Coll., Regis U., Shensu U., Rockhurst U., Gustaus Adolphus Coll., Lehman Coll., Smith Coll. Former coord. Nicaragua-Honduras Edn. Project, Washington; assoc. dir. Children's Project Med. Aid El Salvador, L.A./El Salvador, 1986—92; founder Internat. Campaign to Ban Landmines Vietnam Vet. Found. Am., Washington, 1991—; amb. Internat. Campaign to Ban Landmines, Alexandria, Va., 1997—; founder Sponsor a Mine-Detection Dog program, 1998—. Patron Internat. Peace Found., Vienna, 1998—; adv. com., arms divsn. Human Rights Watch, 1998—; adv. com. Code of Conduct on the Arms Trade, Arias Found. for Peace and Human Progress, 1998—, Rep. Eddie Bernice Johnson's Women for World Peace Fund, 2003—; disting. vis. prof. social work and global justice Univ. Houston, Tex., 2004—. Contbr. articles to profl. jours, co-author: After the Guns Fall: The Enduring Legacy of Landmines, 1995. Founder Nobel Women's Initiative, 2006. Co-recipient Nobel Peace Prize, 1997; named one of 100 Most Powerful Women in World, Forbes Mag., 2004; recipient Distinguished Peace Leadership award, Nuclear Age Peace Found., 1998, Fiat Lux award, Clark U., Hollywood Humanitarian award, 2002. Address: ICBL 33 rue de Bruxelles 1470 Genappe Belgium E-mail: williams@icbl.org.

WILLIAMS, JOJO MACASAET, office administrator; b. Talisay, Batangas, The Philippines, Sept. 18, 1948; came to U.S., 1970, naturalized, 1990; d. Andrew Ricafort Macasaet and Petra (Casal) Arriola; m. Ernest Thomas Williams, Jr., June 2, 1973; children: Andrew (dec.), Enrico, Maria Elena, Frederick Mac. BS in Psychology, U. Santo Tomas, Manila, 1968; postgrad., Arellano U., Manila, 1970; spl. grad. specialized study in Cytology, U. Chgo., 1972. Tchr. Talisay High Sch., 1968-70, San Guillermo Acad., Talisay, 1968; instr. Mabini Jr. Coll., Talaga, The Philippines, 1968-70; sr. cytotechnologist U. Chgo. Hosp., 1970-73, St. Francis Hosp., La Crosse, Wis., 1973-74, VA Hosp. and Fargo (N.D.) Clinic, 1974-78; sr. histocytotechnologist St. Ansgar Hosp., Moorhead, Minn., 1974-78; bus. mgr., optometric asst. Office Dr. E. Williams, Optometrist, Hibbing, Minn., 1978—. Vice pres. Am. Cancer Soc., Hibbing, Minn., 1986-91, pres., 1993-94. Mem. AAUW (co-editor bull. Hibbing 1986-88, 3d v.p. 1988-90), Am. Assn. Clin. Pathologists, Am. Found. Vision Awareness (2d v.p. Minn affiliate 1992—, comm. trustee, pub. info. trustee 1993—), Internat. Acad. Cytology, Am. Soc. Cytology, Minn. Optometric Assn. (3d v.p. scholarship chmn. 1988-90, corr. sec. 1987—, coord. Save Your Vision Week 1992-97), Talisay Midwest Assn. (Chgo. chpt., bd. dirs.), Nashwauk C. of C. (v.p. 1980-82, sec.-treas. 1984-87), Mesaba Athletic Club, Hibbing Gourmet Club, Soroptimists, Quad Cities Internat. Toastmasters Club. Roman Catholic. Avocations: reading, craftwork, golf, bodywork, tennis. Home: 802 Aspen Knls Hibbing MN 55746-3848 also: 2932 1st Ave Hibbing MN 55746-2564

WILLIAMS, JOY, writer; b. Chelmsford, Mass., Feb. 11, 1944; d. William Lloyd and Elisabeth (Thomas) W.; m. Rust Hills; 1 child, Caitlin. MA magna cum laude, Marietta Coll., 1963; MFA, U. Iowa, 1965. Rschr., data analyst USN, Siesta Key, Fla., 1967-69; now writer. Vis. instr. U. Houston, 1982, U. Fla., 1983, U. Calif., Irvine, 1984, U. Iowa, 1984, U. Ariz., 1987. Author: State of Grace, 1973, The Changeling, 1978, Taking Care, 1982, The Florida Keys: A History and Guide, 1986, Breaking and Entering, 1988, Escapes, 1991, The Quick and the Dead (Pulitzer Prize finalist), 2000, Honored Guest, 2004; contbr. short stories to numerous anthologies and mags. Guggenheim fellow, 1974; NEA grantee, 1973; recipient Nat. Mag. award for fiction, 1980, Harold and Mildred Strauss Livings award Am. Acad. Arts and Letters, 1993, Rez Short Story award Ill Nature essays, 2002. Mem. Phi Beta Kappa. Democrat. Office: 1425 E magee Rd Tucson AZ 85718 also: Amanda Urban ICM 40 W 57th St New York NY 10019-4001

WILLIAMS, JOYCE HALL, secondary school educator; b. Viola, Tenn., Feb. 6, 1926; d. Albert White and Byrde Groom Hall; m. Lewis Blanton Williams, Dec. 14, 1948; children: Susan Joyce Boada, Nancy Hall West, Lewis B.(dec.). BA, U. Tenn., Knoxville, 1947; postgrad., U. Miami, 1967; MA, U. North Ala., 1982. Cert. tchr. Fla., Ala. Tchr. Gulliver Preparatory Sch., Coral Gables, Fla., 1967—70, 1975—79, Am. Internat. Sch., New Delhi, 1970—73, Internat. Inst. Tropical Agr., Ibadan, Nigeria, 1974—79; faculty Faulkner U., Florence, Ala., 1981—88, N.W. C.C., Muscle Shoals, Ala., 1981—88; adj. tchr. U. North Ala., 1994. Owner Off-Ctr. Pub. Co., Ala., 1985. Author: A Volunteer in Romania, 1999, Sunshine and Shadows, 2001, In the Cradle of Mankind, Let's Play Ball and the Taj Mahal!, Roamin Around Romania, 2004, (children's coloring book) Can Cousin Kunja Cut a Kanga?. Vol. tchr. Headstart, Handy Ctr., Florence, 2001—03; tchr., vol. Adult Basic Edn., Handy Ctr., 2001—03; vol. ch. libr. Edgemont Meth. Ch., 1987—. Named Tchr. of the Yr., Gulliver Acad.; recipient Diploma of Recognition, Israelite Heritage Instn. for excellence in Bible Study, 1967, winner, Ernest Hemingway Internat. Writing Competition, Key West, Fla. Mem.: AAUW, Assn. Ala. Writers, United Meth. Women. Avocation: golf. Home: 3412 Kolbe Ln Florence AL 35631-1842

WILLIAMS, JUANITA (TUDIE WILLIAMS), home health care nurse, administrator; b. Springfield, Mo., June 3, 1954; d. Clay Caldwell Deeds and Martaun LaVeda Smith; m. Phillip E. Williams, June 21, 1996; 1 child, Megan E. Deeds. BSN, U. of State N.Y., Albany, 1990. Cert. med.-surg. nurse. Staff nurse St. John's Regional Health Ctr., Springfield, 1975-78; head nurse cardiac Cox Med. Ctr., Springfield, 1978-92; dir. continuous quality improvement/edn. svcs., dir. clin. svcs. Cmty. Home Health Care, Springfield, 1992—. Mem. adv. bd. Columbia Health Ctr., Springfield, 1992—; coord. quality assurance bd. Cmty. Home Health, Springfield, 1992-96; mem. cardiac adv. bd. Cox Med. Ctr., Springfield, 1985. Contbr. articles to profl. jours. Mem. Mo. State Nurses Assn. Republican. Roman Catholic. Avocation: photography. Home: 7674 W Farm Road 128 Springfield MO 65802-9172 Office: Cmty Home Health 2828 N National Ave Springfield MO 65803-4306

WILLIAMS, JUANITA ROSALIE, artist; b. Zanesville, Ohio, Aug. 7, 1933; d. Joseph Russell and Gladys Lucille (Worden) Somers; m. Roy George Williams, Feb. 16, 1952 (div. 2002); children: Karin Sue Williams Brandi, Kenneth Roy. Grad. high sch., Zanesville. Juror Bexley (Ohio) Art Guild, Capital U., 1984. One-woman shows include Collector's Gallery Columbus Mus. Fine Art, Ohio, 1972, Pomerene Fine Arts Ctr., 1991, McDonough Gallery, Marietta Coll., 1991, Blue Sky Gallery, Columbus, 1992, exhibited in group shows at Zanesville Art Ctr., 1981, 1990, Franklin U., Columbus, Ohio, 1985, Marietta (Ohio) Coll., 1991, Pomerene Fine Arts Ctr., Coshocton, Ohio, 1991, No. Ariz. U., 1992, French Art Colony, Gallipolis, Ohio, 1992, Soc. Layerists in Multi-Media, San Miguel Allende, Mex., 1996, Marlborough, Eng., 1997, Sirius Gallery, Santa Fe, 2001, Represented in permanent collections Zanesville Art Ctr., Ohio, Soc. Bank Cleve., Edward Cherry Corp., Columbus, Nat. WaterColor Soc. Bd. dirs. Zanesville Art Ctr., 1986-90, 92-95. Recipient 1st award Rocky Mountain Nat., 1984, Elsie and David Wu-Ject Key award Am. Watercolor Soc., 1989, 4th award San Diego Watercolor Soc., 1993. Mem. Nat. Watercolor Soc., Soc. Layerists in Multi-Media, Ohio Watercolor Soc. (silver Buckeye award 1986), Southeastern Ohio Watercolor Soc. (co-founder, 1st pres. 1978-79). Avocations: gardening, interior decorating, reading, metaphyics, travel. Mailing: 9908 Wild Turkey NW Albuquerque NM 87114 Office Phone: 505-792-7782. E-mail: juan1aran@aol.com.

WILLIAMS, JUDITH ELLEN, educational association administrator; b. Oakland, Nebr., Jan. 9, 1953; d. Alva Charles and Helen Lanore (Bader) Tracy; m. Rudolph Edward Williams, Dec. 26, 1992; children: Stephanie, Ashley. BA, Antioch U., L.A., 1985. Tng. specialist St. Luke Med. Ctr., Pasadena, Calif., 1983-88; program dir. mental health unit Glendale (Calif.) Meml. Hosp., 1988-91; program dir. Psychiat. Mgmt. Resources, San Diego, 1991-93; dir. psychiatry program U. So. Calif., L.A., 1993-96; rsch. coord. Alzheimer Disease Ctr., Ind. U. Sch. Medicine, Indpls., 1996-99, dir. ops., 1999—. Avocations: reading, jet skiing, travel. Office: Ind U Sch Med 550 University Blvd # 3124 Indianapolis IN 46202-5149 E-mail: jwillia2@iupui.edu.

WILLIAMS, JULIE FORD, retired finance company executive, economist; b. Long Beach, Calif., Aug. 7, 1948; d. Julious Hunter and Bessie May (Wood) Ford; m. Walter Edward Williams, Oct. 20, 1984; 1 child, Andrew Ford. BA in Econs., Occidental Coll., 1970. Legal sec. Kadison, Pfaelzer, Woodard, Quinn & Rossi, L.A., 1970-71, 74-77; legal sec. Fried, Frank, Harris, Shriver & Jacobson, N.Y.C., 1971-72, Pallot, Poppell, Goodman & Shapo, Miami, Fla., 1973-74; adminstrv. asst. Capital Research-Mgmt., Los Angeles, 1978-82; corp. officer Cash Mgmt. Trust Am., 1982—, Bond Fund Am., 1982—, Tax-Exempt Bond Fund Am., 1982—, AMCAP Fund, 1984-98, 2000—, Am. Funds Income Series, 1985—, Am. Funds Tax-Exempt Series II, 1986—, Capital World Bond Fund, 1987—, Am. High-Income Trust, 1987—, Intermediate Bond Fund Am., 1987—, Tax-Exempt Money Fund Am., 1989—, U.S. Treasury Money Fund Am., 1991—, Fundamental Investors, 1992-2000, Ltd. Term Tax-Exempt Bond Fund Am., 1993—, Am. High-Income Mcpl. Bond Fund, 1994—; v.p. fund bus. mgmt. group Capital Rsch. Mgmt., 1986—; sec. Growth Fund of Am., 1998-2000, Am. Mutual Fund, 2000—05; ret., 2005. Pres. alumni bd. govs. Occidental Coll., 1997—98, bd. trustees, 1999—2003. Democrat. Episcopalian. Office: Capital Rsch & Mgmt Co 333 S Hope St 55th Floor Los Angeles CA 90071-1452

WILLIAMS, JULIE LLOYD, federal agency administrator, lawyer; b. Washington, May 24, 1950; d. Walter Herbert and Jean (Grabill) W.; m. Don Scroggin, May 9, 1981; 1 child, Patrick Conner. BA, Goddard Coll., 1971; JD, Antioch Sch. Law, 1975. Bar: Va. 1975, D.C. 1976. Assoc. Fried, Frank, Harris, Shriver, Washington, 1975-83; assoc. gen. counsel Fed. Home Loan Bank Bd., Washington, 1983-86, dep. gen. counsel, 1986-89; dep. chief counsel Office of Thrift Supervision, Washington, 1989-91, sr. dep. chief counsel, 1991-93; dep. chief counsel Comptr. of Currency, Washington, 1993-94, chief counsel, 1994-98, acting comptr., 1998, 2004—05, first sr. dep. comptr., chief counsel, 1999—; bd. dir. FDIC, 2004—. Co-author: (handbook) How to Incorporate: A Handbook for Entrepreneurs & Professionals, 1987; author: Savings Institutions: Mergers, Acquisitions & Conversions, 1988, National Banks and the Dual Banking System, 2003. Mem. ABA (banking law com.), Women in Housing and Fin. Home: 3064 Q St NW Washington DC 20007-3080 Office: Office of Comptroller Currency 250 E St SW Washington DC 20219

WILLIAMS, JULIE LYNNE, music educator; b. Arlington Heights, Ill., Nov. 14, 1972; d. William John and Patricia Marie Allen; m. Matthew Oliver Williams, July 12, 2003. B of Music Edn., U. No. Colo., Greeley, 1997, M of Music Edn., 2006. Choir tchr. Hill Mid. Sch., Denver, 1997—2001, Eaglecrest H.S., Centennial, Colo., 2001—. Bd. dirs. Colo. All-State Jazz Choir, Denver, 2002—. Democrat. Roman Catholic. Avocations: singing, travel, reading. Home: 9697 E Arbor Pl Englewood CO 80111 Office: Eaglecrest H S 51005 S Picadilly St Centennial CO 80015

WILLIAMS, JULIE MARIE, history educator; d. Arthur Gene and Marilyn Shirley Williams. BA in History, BS in Edn., U. Mo., 2001. Cert. social studies tchr. In-sch. suspension supr. McCluer HS, Florissant, Mo., 2001—02, social studies tchr., 2002—. Office: McCluer HS 1896 S New Florissant Rd Florissant MO 63031-8398

WILLIAMS, KAREN C., elementary school educator; BE, U. NC, Charlotte, 1986, M in Elem. Edn., 1997. Academically gifted tchr. Union County Pub. Sch., Monroe, NC, 1986—. Named AIG Tchr. of Yr., Elem. Math. Tchr. of Yr., Tchr. of Yr., Piedmont Mid. Sch. Office: Union County Pub Sch 4511 Unionville Rd Monroe NC 28110 Office Phone: 704-296-3055. Business E-Mail: karen.williams@ucps.k12.nc.us.

WILLIAMS, KAREN HASTIE, lawyer; b. Washington, Sept. 30, 1944; d. William Henry and Beryl (Lockhart) Hastie; m. Wesley S. Williams, Jr.; children: Amanda Pedersen, Wesley Hastie, Bailey Lockhart. Cert., U. Neuchatel, Switzerland, 1965; BA, Bates Coll., 1966; MA, Tufts U., 1967; JD, Cath. U. Am., 1973. Bar: DC 1973. Staff asst. internat. gov. relations dept. Mobil Oil Corp., N.Y.C., 1967-69; staff asst. com. Dist. Columbia U.S. Senate, 1970, chief counsel com. on the budget, 1977-80; law clk. to judge Spottswood Robinson III U.S. Ct. Appeals (D.C. Cir.), Washington, 1973-74; law clk. to assoc. justice Thurgood Marshall U.S. Supreme Ct., Washington, 1974-75; assoc. Fried, Frank, Harris, Shriver & Kampelman, Washington,

1975-77, 1975-77; adminstr. Office Mgmt. and Budget, Washington, 1980-81; of counsel Crowell & Moring, Washington, 1982, ptnr., 1982—2004; ret., 2005. Bd. dirs. Chubb Corp., Gannett Co., Inc., Sun Trust Bank, Inc., Washington Gas Light Co., Continental Airlines. Trustee, past chair Greater Washington Rsch. Ctr. Mem. ABA (pub. contract law sect., past chair), Nat. Bar Assn., Washington Bar Assn., NAACP (legal def. fund, bd. dirs.). Office: Crowell & Moring 1001 Pennsylvania Ave NW Ste 1100 Washington DC 20004-2595

WILLIAMS, KAREN JOHNSON, federal judge; b. Orangeburg, SC, Aug. 4, 1951; d. James G. Johnson and Marcia Johnson (Reynolds) Dantzler; m. Charles H. Williams, Dec. 27, 1968; children: Marian, Ashley, Charlie, David. BA, Columbia Coll., 1972; postgrad., U. S.C., 1973, JD cum laude, 1980. Bar: S.C. 1980, U.S. Dist. Ct. S.C. 1980, U.S. Ct. Appeals (4th cir.) 1981. Tchr. Irmo (S.C.) Mid. Sch., 1972—74, O-W H.S., Orangeburg, 1974—76; assoc. Charles H. Williams PA, Orangeburg, 1980—92; judge U.S. Ct. Appeals (4th cir.), 1992—. Exec. bd. grievance commn. S.C. Supreme Ct., Columbia, 1983—92. Child devel. bd. First Bapt. Ch., Orangeburg; bd. dirs. Orangeburg County Mental Retardation Bd., 1986—94, Orangeburg-Calhoun Hosp. Found., Columbia Coll., 1988—92, Reg. Med. Ctr. Hosp. Found., 1988—92; adv. bd. Orangeburg-Calhoun Tech. Coll., SC, 1987—92. Mem.: ABA, Nat. Assn. of Women Judges, Bus. and profl. Women Assn., S.C. Trial Lawyers Assn., Orangeburg County Bar Assn. (co-chair Law Day 1981), S.C. Bar Assn., Fed. Judges Assn., Am. Judicature Soc., Rotary, Order of Coif, Order of Wig and Robe. Home: 2503 Five Chop Rd Orangeburg SC 29115-8185 Office: Lewis F Powell Jr US Cthse Annex 1100 E Main St Ste 617 Richmond VA 23219-3517*

WILLIAMS, KATHRYN VANDERVOORT, science educator; d. Earl Crady and Betty Kathryn Vandervoort; m. Benjamin F. Williams, Aug. 2, 1980; children: Jared Thomas, Blake Anthony. BS, U. So. Miss., Hattiesburg, 1976. Cert. tchr. N.C., 1992. Environ. specialist Burns and McDonnell Engring., Co., Kansas City, Mo., 1976—79; chem. lab technician Ga. Pacific, Port Hudson, La., 1979—80; rsch. chem. technician Ethyl Corp., Baton Rouge, 1984—85; 8th grade sci. tchr. Shaw Mid. Sch., Wagram, NC, 1993—2000, Carver Mid. Sch., Laurel Hill, NC, 2000—01; sci. tchr. Scotland H.S., Laurinburg, NC, 2001—. Mem.: N.C. State Sci. Tchrs. Assn., NCAE. D-Liberal. Methodist. Avocations: reading, travel. Office: Scotland High Sch 1000 W Church St Laurinburg NC 28352 Office Phone: 910-276-7370.

WILLIAMS, LENA, sportswriter; b. Washington, Mar. 2, 1950; BA cum laude in English, Howard U., 1972; MS in Journalism, Columbia U., 1973. Assoc. editor Black Sports Mag.; clk. NY Times, 1974—76, reporter, 1976—88, sports writer, 1988—. Author: It's the Little Things: The Everyday Interactions That Get Under the Skin of Blacks and Whites, 2000. Named one of Outstanding Women in Mktg. and Comms., Ebony Mag., 2001; recipient Excellence award, Nat. Assn. Black Journalism, 1997, Black Achievers award, Young Men's Christian Assn. Mem.: Newspaper Guild (chair of Times-Guild unit). Office: NY Times Sports Desk 229 W 43d St New York NY 10036 Office Phone: 212-556-7371. Office Fax: 212-556-5848.*

WILLIAMS, LEONA RAE, small business owner, consultant; b. Fairfield, Nebr., July 1, 1928; d. Melton M. and Helga D. (Sorensen) Brown; m. Eugene F. Williams, June 6, 1946; 1 child, Dennis D. Grad. high sch., Fairfield. Owner Alice Rae Apparel Shop, Tucson, 1953—96, second location, 1967—96, Green Valley, Ariz., 1976—93, Sun City, Ariz., 1979—96; ret., 1996; owner Boutique on Wheels, 2001—, prin., 2001—. Cons. in field. Sponsor Distributive Edn. Program, 1978-82; coord. fashion shows Am. Cancer Soc., Tucson, 1987, 88, 89. Mem. DAR, Exec. Women's Internat. Assn. (chpt. pres. 1994), Mchts. Assn. (pres. 1987-89), Soroptomists, C. of C. Better Bus. Bur., Exec. Women's Internat. Christian Women. Republican. Baptist. Personal E-mail: leonagene@msn.com.

WILLIAMS, LINDA C., lawyer; b. Portsmouth, Va., Apr. 4, 1956; BA with high honors, Univ. Va., 1978, JD, 1982. Bar: Calif. 1984. Law clk. Judge Albert Tate, Jr., US Ct. Appeals (5th cir.), New Orleans; ptnr., head Corp. Securities & Fin. Inst. group Pillsbury Winthrop Shaw Pittman, San Francisco. Instr. Univ. San Francisco Sch. Law. Mem.: Order of the Coif. Office: Pillsbury Winthrop Shaw Pittman 50 Fremont St San Francisco CA 94105 Office Phone: 415-983-7334. Office Fax: 415-983-1200. Business E-Mail: linda.williams@pillsburylaw.com.

WILLIAMS, LINDA DIANNE, music educator; d. James Melvin and Essie Mae Bowman; m. Fred Lee Williams (dec.); 1 child, Ryan Christopher Harley. B in Music Edn., Ohio State U., Columbus, 1972. Tchr. vocal music Arts Impact, Columbus, Ohio, 1972—77, Marion-Franklin H.S., Columbus, Ohio, 1977—80, Beery Mid. Sch., Columbus, Ohio, 1980—. Min. of music 1st Ch. of God, Columbus, Ohio, 1982—2000. Democrat. Avocations: music, travel, reading, shopping. Home: 2578 Anderley Ct Grove City OH 43123 Office: Beery Mid Sch 2740 Lockbourne Rd Columbus OH 43207 Office Phone: 614-365-5414. Fax: 614-365-5412. E-mail: linda_williams124@hotmail.com.

WILLIAMS, LINDA STALLWORTH, literature and language professor; b. Atlanta, Dec. 13, 1951; d. James Owen Stallworth and Pearl Bell Willis; m. Max Virgil Williams, Sept. 29, 1972; children: Laura LeAnne, Max Brenton. BA, U. W.Ga., Carrollton, 1972; MA, U. Ctrl. Okla., Edmond, 1986; PhD, U. Okla., Norman, 1990. Vis. lectr. U. Okla., Norman, 1988—91; prof. English Rose State Coll., Midwest City, Okla., 1991—94; acad. coord. faculty devel. Bd. Regents, U. Sys. Ga., Atlanta, 1996—98; assoc. prof. English N.Ga. Coll. and State U., Dahlonega, 1997—. Recipient Dorothy Golden award for Excellence in Tchg. of Composition, Student Success in First-Year Composition Conf., 2001, Cert. of Appreciation for Patriotic Civilian Svc., Dept. of Army, 2005. Mem.: Conf. Coll. Composition and Comm., Assn. Bus. Comm., Nat. Coun. Tchrs. of English. Home: 11000 Big Canoe Big Canoe GA 30143 Office: North Georgia Coll and State Univ 100 College Cir Dahlonega GA 30597 Office Phone: 706-864-1681.

WILLIAMS, LISA A., special education educator; d. Ida M. Williams. B. Music Edn., Howard U., Washington, 2000, M. Music Edn., 2003; MEd in Spl. Edn., U. San Diego, Calif., 2002; EdS in Spl. Edn., Fla. State U., Tallassee, 2005. Cert. tchr. Music K-12 Calif., Va., Fla., 2000, tchr. spl. edn. Fla., 2004. Tchr. spl. edn. San Diego City Schs., San Diego, 2000—02; tchr. music Fairfax County Schs., Fairfax, Va., 2002—03; tchr. spl. edn. Leon County Schs., Tallahassee, 2004—06, San Diego Unified Sch. Dist., 2006—. Acad. counselor Fla. State U., Tallahassee, 2003—04; site coord. Leon County Schs., Title I Program, Tallahassee, 2004; dir. children's choir Bethel AME Ch., San Diego, 2000—02. Named Riley Minority Educator of Yr., 2006; Spl. Edn. and Minority scholar, Howard U., Grad. asst., 2002—03, Doctoral fellow, Phi Delta Kappa Internat., 2003—04, Childhood Edn., Reading and Disability Svcs. fellow, Fla. State U., 2005—06. Mem.: Nat. Assn. Music Educators, Phi Delta Kappa Internat., Internat. Clarinet Assn., Nat. Assn. for Black Sch. Educators, NEA, Coun. for Exceptional Children, Tau Beta Sigma, Alpha Kappa Alpha (Ednl. Advancement Found. scholar 2005), Sigma Alpha Iota (life). Personal E-mail: pindrop26@aol.com.

WILLIAMS, LUCINDA, country musician; b. Lake Charles, La., 1953; d. Miller W.; m. Greg Sowders (div.). Albums include: Ramblin' On My Mind, 1979, Happy Woman Blues, 1980, Lucinda Williams, 1988, Passionate Kisses, 1989 (Grammy award Best Country Song 1994), Sweet Old World, 1992, Car Wheels on a Gravel Road, 1998 (Grammy award for best contemp. folk album, 1999), Essence, 2002 (Grammy award for best female rock vocal); contbr. songs to: Sweet Relief, 1993, Born to Choose, 1993.

WILLIAMS, LUIDA K., retired elementary school educator; b. Valparaiso, Ind., May 15, 1942; d. Edgar Pricer and Velma (Cook) Williams. BS in Elem. Edn., Ind. U., Bloomington, 1965; MS in Elem. Edn., Butler U., Indpls., 1968. Cert. tchr. Tchr. Indpls. Pub. Schs., 1965—2004; ret., 2004. Basketball coach; tchr. Indpls. Pub. Libr. Summer camp organizer for at-risk children, Englishton, Ind.; agent Jameson Camp, Indpls., 1966—2004, Englishton Camp, Lexington, Ind., 1970—2004. Recipient Tchr. of Yr. award, IPS Sch., 1991, Mary McClelland Vol. award, Jameson Camp, 1995, Tchr. of Yr. award, Soc. Intensified Edn. Mem.: NEA, Indpls. Edn. Assn. (rep. 1965—2004), Indpls. Edn. Assn., Ind. State Tchr. Assn. (lobbyest Ind. Gen. Assembly 1970—2000, ethics com.). Avocation: tennis. Home: 7356 Mikesell Dr Indianapolis IN 46260

WILLIAMS, MARCIA PUTNAM, human resources specialist; b. Ossining, N.Y., July 3, 1948; d. Charles Samuel and Lois Barbara (Putnam) W. BA, U. Denver, 1970, MA, 1972. Warehouse person, truck driver Strear Foods/United Food Svc., Denver, 1977-79; truck driver Beverage Distributors Corp., Aurora, Colo., 1979-84; tour guide for morale, welfare, and recreation USN, Sigonella, Sicily, 1984-85; reservations sales agt. Western/Delta/United Airlines, Denver, 1986-88; unemployment ins. rep. Dept. Labor and Employment State of Colo., Denver, 1988-90; site mgr., sr. outplacement counselor Army Career and Alumni Program, Ft. Carson, Colo., 1990-91; labor and employment specialist Dept. Labor and Employment State of Colo., Denver, 1991—. Guidance counselor Mesa County Sch. Dist. 51, Grand Junction, Colo., 1976-77, Douglas County Sch. Dist., Castle Rock, Colo., 1975-76, Adams County Sch. Dist., North Glenn, Colo., 1974-75; world history tchr. Ithaca (N.Y.) City Sch. Dist., 1972-74. Author: National Job Hotline Directory, 1995-2000. Mem. Internat. Assn. Pers. in Employment Security (legis. chair 1997-98). Avocations: photography, travel, sports, cooking, motorcycles. Home: PO Box 211113 Denver CO 80221-0396

WILLIAMS, MARGARET M. (MEG WILLIAMS), insurance company executive; Joined Scottsdale Ins. Co., 2003, chief info. officer, v.p. info. tech. Named one of Premier 100 IT Leaders, Computerworld, 2005. Office: Scottsdale Ins Co 8877 N Gainey Ctr Dr Scottsdale AZ 85258 Office Phone: 480-365-4000. Office Fax: 480-483-6752.

WILLIAMS, MARSHA C., corporate financial executive; B in Econs., Wellesley Coll.; Masters, U. Chgo. Various positions Amoco Corp., 1989—93, treas., 1993—98, v.p., treas., 1997—98; chief adminstrv. officer Crate & Barrel, 1998—2002; exec. v.p., CFO Equity Office Properties, Chgo., 2002—. Office: Equity Office Properties 2 N Riverside Plz Chicago IL 60606

WILLIAMS, MARSHA E., broadcast executive; BA, Conn. Coll.; MA, Washington U. With The Psychological Corp., Cleve., San Antonio, Children's TV Workshop (now Sesame Workshop), 1991—95, MTV Networks Co., NYC, 1996—, v.p. rsch. and planning Nickelodeon Networks, sr. v.p. rsch. and planning Nickelodeon Networks, 2006—. Office: MTV Networks Co Nickelodeon Networks 1515 Broadway 42d Fl New York NY 10036*

WILLIAMS, MARTHA ETHELYN, information science educator; b. Chgo., Sept. 21, 1934; d. Harold Milton and Alice Rosemond (Fox) Williams. BA, Barat Coll., 1955; MA, Loyola U., 1957. With IIT Rsch. Inst., Chgo., 1957-72, mgr. info. scis., 1962-72, mgr. computer search ctr., 1968-72; adj. assoc. prof. sci. info. Ill. Inst. Tech., Chgo., 1965-73, lectr. chemistry dept., 1968-70; rsch. prof. info. sci., coordinated sci. lab. Coll. Engring. U. Ill., Urbana, also dir. info. retrieval rsch. lab., 1972—, prof. info. sci. grad. sch. of libr. info. sci., 1974—, affiliate, computer sci. dept., 1979—. Chair large data base conf. Nat. Acad. Sci./NRC, 1974, mem. ad hoc panel on info. storage and retrieval, 1977, numerical data adv. bd., 1979-82, computer sci. and tech. bd., nat. rsch. network rev. com., 1987-88, chair utility subcom., 1987-88, subcom. promoting access to sci. and tech. data for pub. interest; task force on sci. info. activities NSF, 1977; U.S. rep. review com. for project on broad system of ordering, UNESCO, Hague, Netherlands, 1974; vice-chair Gordon Rshc. Conf. on Sci. Info. Problems in Rsch., 1978, chair, 1980; mem. panel on intellectual property rights in age of electronics and info. U.S. Congress, Office of Tech. Assessment; program chmn. Nat. Online Meeting, 1980-2001; founder, pres. Info. Market Indicators, Inc., 1982-; cons. in field; invited lectr. Commn. European Communities, Industrial R&D adv. com., Brussels, 1992. Editor-in-chief: Computer-Readable Databases Directory and Data Sourcebook, 1976—89, founding editor:, 1989—; editor: Ann. Rev. Info. Sci. and Tech., 1976—2001, Online Rev., 1979—92, Online and CD-ROM Rev., 1993—2000; mem. editl. adv. bd.: Database, 1978—88, mem. editl. bd.: Info. Processing and Mgmt., 1982—89, The Reference Libr., founding editor: Online Info. Rev., 2000—; contbr. articles to profl. jours. Trustee Engirng. Info., Inc., 1974-87, bd. dirs., 1976-91, chmn. bd. dirs., 1982-91, v.p., 1978-79, pres., 1980-81; regent Nat. Libr. Medicine, 1978-82, chmn. bd. regents, 1981; mem. task force on sci. info. activities NSF, 1977-78; mem. nat. adv. com. ACCESS ERIC, 1989-91. Recipient best paper of year award H. W. Wilson Co., 1975; Travel grantee NSF, Luxembourg, 1972, Honolulu, 1973, Tokyo, 1973, Mexico City, 1975, Scotland, 1976 Fellow: AAAS (mem. nominating com. 1983, 1985), Nat. Fedn. Abstracting and Info. Svcs. (hon.), Inst. Info. Scis. (hon.); mem.: NAS (mem. joint com. with NRC on chem. info. 1971—73), Internat. Fedn. for Documentation (U.S. nat. com.), Assn. Sci. Info. Dissemination Ctrs. (v.p. 1971—73, pres. 1975—77), Assn. Computing Machinery (pub. bd. 1972—76), Am. Soc. Info. Sci. (councilor 1971—72, mem. publs. com. 1974—, pres. 1987—88, councilor 1987—89, contbg. editor bull. column 1974—78, Award of Merit 1984, Pioneer Info. Sci. award 1987, Watson Davis award 1995), Am. Chem. Soc. Home: 2134 Sandra Ln Monticello IL 61856-8036 Office: U Ill 1308 W Main St Urbana IL 61801-2307 E-mail: m-will13@uiuc.edu.

WILLIAMS, MARTHA GARRISON, lawyer; b. Greenville, S.C., July 3, 1942; d. William Theodore and Edith (Roberts) G.; m. Ray R. Williams Jr.; 1 child, Ray R. III. BA, Randolph-Macon Coll., 1964; JD, U. S.C., 1967. Bar: S.C. 1967, U.S. Dist. Ct. S.C. 1967, U.S. Ct. Appeals 1970. Atty. regulatory div. U.S. Dspt. Agr., Washington, 1967-68; atty. Liberty Corp., Greenville, S.C., 1971-72, asst. v.p., asst. sec., 1972-82, counsel, 1980-82, v.p., gen. counsel, sec., 1982—; atty. investment div. Liberty Life Ins. Co., Greenville, 1968-72, asst. sec., 1972-82, asst. v.p., 1976-79, v.p., 1979—, counsel, 1980-82, gen. counsel, sec., 1982—, also bd. dirs. Bd. dirs. ARC, Greenville, 1981-86, S.C. Dept. Health and Environ. Control, Greenville, 1985—. Mem. ABA, S.C. Bar Assn., Greenville County Bar Assn., Assn. Life Ins. Council, Am. Soc. Life Ins. Council, Am. Soc. Corp. Secs., Fedn. Ins. Counsel, Am. Corp. Counsel Assn., Am. Council Life Ins., Life Insurers Conf. Office: Liberty Corp PO Box 502 135 S Main St Greenville SC 29602 Office Phone: 864-241-5400. Office Fax: 864-241-5401.

WILLIAMS, MARTHA JANE SHIPE, psychologist, retired educator; b. Houston, June 28, 1935; d. Charles Edward and Florence Mae (Coons) Shipe; m. John Gregor Williams, June 4, 1958; children— John, David, Susan, Thomas. BA, U. Tex., Austin, 1957, MA, 1962, PhD, 1963. Sec. U. Tex., Austin, 1954-57; sec. pers. and sales div. Tenneco, 1957-58; teaching and rsch. asst. U. Tex., Austin, 1958-61, rsch. assoc., 1961-66, asst. prof., 1966-69, assoc. prof., 1969-75, prof., 1975-91, prof. emeritus, 1991—; asst. dir. Inst. Higher Edn. Mgmt., U. Tex. System Adminstrn., Austin, 1979-81; dean, centennial prof. Sch. Social Work, U. Tex., Austin, 1981-91; dean health scis. U. Wyo., Laramie, 1991—98, prof., 1998—2006, prof. emerita, 2006—. Author books, book chpts.; contbr. articles to profl. jours. Chairperson Tex. Gov.'s Commn. for Women, 1983-85. Univ. fellow, 1959; NSF fellow, 1960-61 Mem. APA, Coun. Social Work Edn., Am. Ednl. Rsch. Assn., Phi Delta Kappa, Sigma Xi. Home: 1312 E Park Ave Laramie WY 82070-4146 Office: U Wyo Wyo Hall 359 Laramie WY 82071-3432 Office Phone: 307-766-3457. Business E-Mail: mswllms@uwyo.edu.

WILLIAMS, MARTHA SPRING, psychologist; b. Dallas, Oct. 5, 1951; d. Thomas Ayers and Emma Martha (Felmet) Spring; m. James Walter Williams, June 30, 1979; children: Dane Ayers, Jake Austin BA, East Tex. State U., 1972, MEd, 1974, EdD, 1978. Cert. and lic. psychologist, Tex.; lic. profl. counselor, marriage and family therapist. Tchr. Dallas Ind. Sch.; grad. asst. to dean Coll. Edn. East Tex. State U., 1975—77; intern Terrell State Hosp. Outreach Clinic and Hunt County Clinic, Greenville, Tex., 1975—76; intern Counseling Ctr. East Tex. State U., 1976—77; learning dir. Man and His Environ. Program, 1978—85; pvt. practice psychology Dallas, 1981—. Adolescent group therapist in-patient psychiat. facility, 1986-91; mem. staff Baylor/Richardson (Tex.) Med. Ctr., clin. dir. allied mental health profls., 1992-94; v.p. for provider rels. Advanced Behavioral Health Care Sys., Inc., 1995—; mem. staff South We. Med. Sch., Lake Pointe Hosp., St. Paul Author: (with others) The Role Innovative Woman and Her Positive Impact on Family Functioning, 1981, Women and Intimacy, 1982, Premenstral Syndrome: A Family Affair, 1984, The Expanding Horizons of Traditional Private Practice: High Tech High/Touch, 1986, Adolescent Suicide: Consequences of an Anti-Child Society, 1986, Therapist as a Partner, 1987 Nat. del. Dem. Conv., San Francisco, 1984, 2000, 2004; Dem. county chair Kaufman County, 1993-98; mem. state Dem. Exec. Com. 1993— Mem. APA, Am. Assn. Marriage and Family Therapists, Am. Soc. Clin. Hypnosis Lutheran. Avocations: skiing, travel, politics, tap dancing. Home: PO Box 1119 Terrell TX 75160-7144 Office: 12860 Hillcrest Rd Ste 119 Dallas TX 75230 Office Phone: 214-384-1039.

WILLIAMS, MARY ELEANOR NICOLE, writer; b. Atlanta, May 14, 1938; d. Edward King Merrell and Bernice I. (Pitts) Smith; m. Charlie Lloyd Williams, July 25, 1993 (dec. June 1997); children: Mary Palmer, Susan Gober, Traci Bunch. Student, Fla. Jr. Coll., 1974. Lic. real estate broker, Fla. Editor, writer, former owner Southwestern Advt. and Pub., Carrollton, Ga., 1991-94; freelance writer children's stories, 1992—. Author, editor: West Georgia Area Guide, 1991-93. Avocations: writing, music, travel, walking, art. Home: 105 N Nixon St Carrollton GA 30117-4319

WILLIAMS, MARY ELLEN COSTER, federal judge; b. Flushing, NY, 1953; married; 2 children. BA in Latin and Greek summa cum laude, Cath. U., 1974, MA in Latin, 1974; JD, Duke U., 1977. Assoc. Fulbright and Jaworski, Washington, 1977—79, Schnader, Harrison, Segal and Lewis, Washington, 1979—83; asst. US atty. civil divsn. US Dept. Justice, Washington, 1983—87; ptnr. Janis, Schuelke and Weschler Law Firm, Washington, 1987—89; adminstrv. judge GSA Bd. of Contract Appeals, Washington, 1989—2003; judge US Ct. of Fed. Claims, Washington, 2003—. Editl. bd. Duke Law Jour. Fellow: Am. Bar Found. (life); mem.: DC Bar (sec.), DC Young Lawyers Sect. (chair), Bar Assn. of DC (found. pres., trustee, bd. dirs.), ABA (sect. rep. com. of ethics and professionalism 1998—2000, commn. on evaluation of rules of profl. conduct 1998—2000, presdl. task force on govt. lawyers 2000—01, chair sect. pub. contract law 2002—, chair elect, vice chair, sec., sect. rep. ho. delegates 2004—). Office: US Ct of Fed Claims 717 Madison Pl NW Washington DC 20005

WILLIAMS, MARY HICKMAN, social worker; b. Newton, Tex., July 09; d. Casey and Mattie Hickman; m. Herman Williams, Aug. 25, 1984; children: Michael, Mitchell, Marcus. BSW, Prairie View A&M U., Tex., 1980; MSSW, U. Tex., Arlington, 1982. Cert. social worker, Tex.; lic. profl. counselor, Tex. Clin. social worker Rusk (Tex.) State Hosp., 1982, Deep East Tex. Mental Health/Mental Retardation, Lufkin, 1982-87, Lufkin State Sch., 1987—. Mem. NASW. Home: 4424E State Hwy 103 Lufkin TX 75901-9170

WILLIAMS, MARY IRENE, business education educator; b. Hugo, Okla., June 30, 1944; d. Primer and Hylar B. (Tarkington) Jackson; m. Lee A. Williams (div. June 1981); 1 child, Monica Ariane. BS in Bus. Edn., Langston U., 1967; MS in Bus., Emporia State U., Kans., 1973; EdS, U. Nev., Las Vegas, 1977; DBA in Internat. Bus., Alliant U., 1992. Instr. Spokane (Wash.) C.C., 1967-70; tchr. bus. Topeka Pub. Schs., 1970-73; prof. C.C. So. Nev., Las Vegas, 1973—, assoc. dean of bus., 1978—93, dean acad. support svcs., 1993—95, prof. bus./mgmt., 1997—, chmn. bus. adminstrn. dept., 2006—; prof. bus./mgmt., asst. to assoc. v.p., asst. coord. bus. Langston U., Tulsa, 1995—97. Adj. prof. So. Nazarene U., 1996-97; adj. prof. Tulsa Jr. Coll., 1997. Author: A Journey Upward, 2004. Named Educator of Yr. Nucleus Plaza Assn., 1985, New Visions, Inc., 1986. Mem. AAUW, Nat. Bus. Edn. Assn., Alpha Kappa Alpha Avocations: exercising, studying languages, reading. Office: CCSN 6375 W Charleston Blvd W2C Las Vegas NV 89146-1164 Personal E-mail: marywmslvnv@aol.com.

WILLIAMS, MARY PEARL, judge; b. Brownsville, Tex., Jan. 12, 1928; d. Marvin Redman and Theo Mae (Kethley) Hall; m. Jerre Stockton Williams, May 28, 1950; children: Jerre Stockton, Shelley Williams Austin, Stephanie Williams Laden. BA, U. Tex., 1948, JD, 1949. Bar: Tex. 1949, U.S. Supreme Ct. 1955, U.S. Dist. Ct. (we. dist.) Tex. 1987. Asst. atty. gen. State of Tex., Austin, 1949-50; relief judge Mcpl. Ct., Austin, 1964; asst. instr. dept. govt. U. Tex., Austin, 1966-67; atty. Office of Emergency Preparedness, Exec. Office of Pres., Washington, 1968-70; labor arbitrator, mem. arbitration panel Am. Arbitration Assn., 1972-73; judge County Ct. Law 2, Travis County, Tex., 1973-80, 53d Jud. Dist. Ct., Austin, 1981-2000, sr. judge, 2000—. Cons. HEW, 1966—67. Mem. adv. com. Juvenile Bd. Travis County, 1964—67; trustee United Way, 1974—78. Named Outstanding Woman, Austin Am.-Statesman, 1974, Austin Citizen, 1978, Woman of the Yr., Austin Dist. Bus. and Profl. Women, 1977; named to Austin HS Hall of Fame, 1996. Fellow: ABA, Am. Bar Found.; mem.: Inst. Jud. Adminstrn., Am. Judicature Soc., Am. Law Inst., Travis County Bar Assn., Coll. State Bar Tex., State Bar Tex., Jr. League Austin, Kappa Alpha Theta, Delta Kappa Gamma (hon.). Democrat. Methodist. Home: Apt 137 4100 Jackson Ave Austin TX 78731-6034 Office: Travis County Courthouse PO Box 1748 Austin TX 78767-1748 E-mail: greatimpy@aol.com.

WILLIAMS, MAXINE ELEANOR, retired elementary school educator; b. Birmingham, Ala., Nov. 8, 1940; d. Ocie and Annie Bell (McCants) Easter; m. Ardre Dell Williams, Aug. 3, 1968 (div. 1988); children: Andrea Babett, Roxanne Denise, John Ashley. BS, Tuskegee Inst., 1963; MA, Mich. State U., 1970. Elem. tchr. Chester A. Moore Elem. Sch., Ft. Pierce, Fla., 1963-64, R.J. Wallis Elem. Sch., Kincheloe AFB, Mich., 1964-66, Alexander Elem. Sch., Grand Rapids, 1966-67, Brown St. Elem. Sch., Milw., 1967-68, Jefferson T.P.L.L., 1968-78; team leader Twenty First St. Sch., 1978-80; reading tchr. Bryant & Parkview Sch., 1980-81; reading resource tchr. Morse Mid. Sch., 1981-93, Parkman Mid. Sch., 1993—94, ret., 1994. Census ctr. vol. Morse Mid. Sch., 1990. Democrat. Avocation: bible study. Home: 3736 N Humboldt Blvd Apt 4 Milwaukee WI 53212-1766

WILLIAMS, MEG See WILLIAMS, MARGARET

WILLIAMS, MICHELLE, actress; b. Kalispell, Mont., Sept. 9, 1980; d. Larry and Carla; 1 child, Matilda Rose. Actor: (films) Lassie, 1994, Species, 1995, Timemaster, 1995, A Thousand Acres, 1997, Halloween H20: 20 Years Later, 1998, Dick, 1999, But I'm a Cheerleader, 1999, Perfume, 2001, Prozac Nation, 2001, Me Without You, 2001, The United States of Leland, 2003, The Station Agent, 2003, A Hole in One, 2004, Imaginary Heroes, 2004, Land of Plenty, 2004, The Baxter, 2005, Brokeback Mountain, 2005 (Critics Choice award, best supporting actress, Broadcast Film Critics Assn., 2006), The Hawk is Dying, 2006; (TV series) Raising Caines, 1995, Dawson's Creek, 1998—2003; (TV films) My Son Is Innocent, 1996, Killing Mr. Griffin, 1997, If These Walls Could Talk 2, 2000. Named one of 21 Hottest Stars Under 21, Teen People mag., 1999. Avocations: reading, boxing. Office: Creative Artists Agy 9830 Wilshire Blvd Beverly Hills CA 90212*

WILLIAMS, MICHELLE (TENETRIA MICHELLE WILLIAMS), singer; b. Rockford, Ill., July 23, 1980; Mem. Destiny's Child, 2000—05. Singer: (albums) Heart to Yours, 2002, Do You Know, 2004; singer: (with Destiny's Child) (songs) Say My Name, 2000 (MTV Video Music award, 2000, Grammy Award for best group R&B performance, best R&B song, 2001), (albums) Survivor, 2001 (MTV Video Music award, 2001, Am. Music award, Favorite Pop Album, 2002, Grammy award for best group R&B vocal performance, 2002), 8 Days of Christmas, 2001, Destiny Fulfilled, 2004 (Am. Music award, Favorite R&B Album, 2005); actor: (Broadway plays) Aida, 2002. Recipient Best Female Group, BET, 2001, Favorite R&B Group, Am. Music Awards, 2001, 2002, 2005, Image award for Outstanding Duo or Group, NAACP, 2001, 2005, 2006, Brit award, Best Internat. Group, 2002, World's Best-Selling Group, World Music Awards, 2002, World's Best-

Selling Pop Group, 2002, 2006, World's Best-Selling R&B Group, 2002, 2006, Best-Selling Female Group of All Time, 2006. Address: 1505 Hadley Houston TX 77002 Office Phone: 212-833-3000. Office Fax: 713-772-5175.*

WILLIAMS, MILDRED JANE, librarian; b. Charlotte, N.C., Nov. 9, 1944; d. Leonard Augustus William and Edith (Long) Frances; m. George E.J. Singleton. BA, Pfeiffer Coll., Misenheimer, N.C., 1966; MS in Libr. Sci., U. N.C., 1968. Reference libr. Pub. Libr. Charlotte and Mecklenburg County, NC, 1967—70, assoc. dir. NC, 1974—77; head dept. documents and serials Libr. Davidson Coll., NC, 1970—73; acting asst. dir. U. N.C.-Charlotte Libr., 1977—78; pub. libr. cons. N.C. State Libr., Raleigh, 1979—80, asst. state libr., 1980—85, state libr., 1986—89; rsch. assoc. U.S. Nat. Commn. on Librs. and Info. Sci., Washington, 1990—98; dir., planning and adminstrv. svcs. U. Md. Librs., College Park, 1998—. Office Phone: 301-405-9124.

WILLIAMS, MINNIE CALDWELL, retired educator; b. Chapel Hill, N.C., Feb. 25, 1917; d. Bruce and Minnie (Stroud) Caldwell; m. Peter Currington Williams Sr., July 25, 1938; children— Peter Jr., Bruce, James, Jacqueline, Charles. B.S. in English, N.C. Central U., 1938, M.A. in Elem. Edn., 1942; postgrad. U. Ill., 1962, U. South Fla., 1965, Fla. State U., 1967. Cert. elem. tchr., N.C.; cert. spl. edn., Fla. Tchr. Weldon pub. schs., N.C., 1940-60, Pinellas County Sch., St. Petersburg, Fla., 1961-80, reading specialist, 1961-80, spl. edn. tchr., 1961-80. Exec. Democratic committeeman, Pinellas County, Fla., 1983-85, local campaign and poll worker; co-chairperson United Way Com; bd. mem. St. Petersburg YWCA. Recipient Ret. Tchrs. award Dixie Hollins High Sch., 1984; Ret. Tchrs. award NAACP, 1980; Panhellenic Service award Greek Orgn., 1980. Mem. Nat. Assn. Ret. Tchrs., Am. Bus. Women Assn., Profl. Bus. Women, Garden Club of St. Petersburg, Delta Sigma Theta (NAACP rep.), Kappa Delta Pi. Baptist. Avocations: Travel; reading; gardening; arts; bowling. Home: 1726 28th Ave S Saint Petersburg FL 33712-3830

WILLIAMS, MONICA BERNARDETTE ELLEN, jewelry designer; b. Port Jefferson, N.Y., July 5, 1980; d. Bernard Gerard Williams and Monica Ellen Donnelly. BA summa cum laude, SUNY, Stony Brook, 2003; postgrad. in Art History and Criticism, SUNY Stony Brook, 2004—. Jewelry designer, costume jewelry dealer Grandma's Top Drawer Jewelry Boutique, Port Jefferson, 1998—. Mem.: Vintage Fashion and Costume Jewelry, Welcome Inn Soup Kitchen, Sigma Beta, Golden Key, Phi Beta Kappa. Roman Catholic. Personal E-mail: liquidsilver9@att.net.

WILLIAMS, NAN PARKER, secondary school educator; b. Dallas, Feb. 28, 1930; d. John Campbell and Leone (Gage) Parker; m. Clyde H. Williams, Jr., June 21, 1960 (div. 1980); 1 child, Wendy Williams Landry. BA, Principia Coll., Elsah, Ill., 1950; postgrad., Eastman Sch. Music, Rochester, N.Y., 1952-53; MFA, U. Iowa, 1956. Cert. theatre and art edn. tchr., Fla. Scenic designer, instr. art and theatre, chmn. art dept. Jacksonville (Fla.) U., 1958-66; tchr. art Bartram Sch., Jacksonville, 1966-67, Cushman Sch., Miami, Fla., 1968-72, Orange County Schs., Orlando, Fla., 1973—2002. Adj. faculty mem. in art edn. U. Cen. Fla., Orlando, 1975—, Rollins Coll., Winter Park, Fla., 1984-89; adj. instr. in art history and humanities Valencia C.C., Orlando, 1979-91; presenter, cons. in field; contbg. author Fla. art curriculum, 1974; Fla. master tchr., 1984-86. Contbr. articles and revs. to nat. art mags.; over 100 scenic designs, 1958-80; art exhbns., theater and piano performances, 1950—. Chmn. performing arts Jacksonville Arts Festival, 1958-66. Named Tchr. of Yr. Fern Creek Elem. Sch., Orlando, 1986, Nat. Elem. Art Educator of Yr., 1997; grantee Fla. Dept. Edn., 1984-87, Walt Disney World Co., 1992-95, 99, Arts for Complete Edn., 1992, 94. Mem. NEA, Nat. Art Edn. Assn. (dir. elem. divsn. 1999-2001, presenter nat. confs.), Fla. Art Edn. Assn. (pres. 2001-03, Fla. Art Tchr. of Yr. award 1990), Orange County Art Edn. Assn. (pres. 1990-92), Fla. League Tchrs. (charter mem.), Delta Kappa Gamma. Christian Scientist. Avocations: piano, travel. Home: 385 Grouse Ct Winter Park FL 32789-6128

WILLIAMS, NANCY, lawyer; b. Kansas City, Mo., Jan. 2, 1945; BS in Journalism, Northwestern U., 1967; JD magna cum laude, U. Mich., 1980. Bar: Wash. 1981, US Ct. Appeals (9th Cir.), US Dist. Ct. (We. Dist.) Wash., US Dist. Ct. (Ea. Dist.) Wash. Volunteer PeaceCorp, 1967—69; pub. info. officer US Dept. Labor, 1973—78; ptnr. Perkins Coie LLP, Seattle, mem. exec. com., chmn. Labor & Employment Practice Area Seattle Office. Co-editor: Washington Employment Law Letter, 1994—; rev. asst. Equal Employment Law Update, 1996, 1997, 1998; contbg. editor: (rev. asst.) Equal Employment Law Update, 2003—, Employment Discrimination Law, 1996. Mem.: ABA (Labor & Litig. Sect.). Office: Perkins Coie LLP 1201 Third Ave Ste 4800 Seattle WA 98101-3099 Office Phone: 206-359-8473. Office Fax: 206-359-9000. Business E-Mail: nwilliams@perkinscoie.com.

WILLIAMS, NANCY CAROLE, nursing researcher; b. Conover, N.C., Dec. 22, 1953; d. Howard G. and Edith (Hager) W. Diploma nursing, Gaston Coll., Dallas, N.C., 1981; student, U. N.C., 1990—. Charge nurse critical care unit Lincoln County Hosp., Lincolnton, N.C., 1981-83; primary charge nurse N.C. Meml. Hosp., Chapel Hill, N.C., 1983-85; charge nurse U. N.C. Clin. Rsch., Chapel Hill, 1985—. Mem. Nat. Assn. Rsch. Nurses and Dietitians, Am. Nurses Assn., N.C. Nurses Assn. Home: 202 6th St SW Conover NC 28613-2720

WILLIAMS, NATASHA BONDAREVA, information scientist, educator; b. Zaporozhye, Ukraine, Feb. 23, 1958; arrived in U.S., 1995; d. Alexander Michailovich Bondarev and Valentina Ivanovna Bondareva; m. Kendall Scott Williams, Apr. 22, 1995; children: Masha, Sasha. MS, Moscow State U., 1982; PhD in Biology, Ctrl. Siberian Bot. Garden, Russia, 1988. Sci. rschr. Ctrl. Siberian Bot. Garden, 1982—93; rsch. project mgr. Uvs-Noor Internat. Biosphere, Russia, 1993—95; info. tech. instr. Colo. Mountain Coll., 2000—. Computer cons. Highlight Internat., 1998—. Author: Population Morphology of Caragana Genus in Siberia, 2000; co-author: Flora of Siberia: Cyperaceae, 2001; contbr. articles to profl. jours. Mem. Environ. Bd., Carbondale, Colo., 2000—05. Named Mother of the Yr., The Valley Jour., Aspen/Carbondale, 2001. Avocations: gardening, travel, skiing, foreign languages. Home: 266 S 4th St Carbondale CO 81623

WILLIAMS, NELLIE JAMES BATT, secondary education educator; b. Nashville; d. Ivan C. and Lottie B. (Phillips) James; A.B., Stowe Coll., 1942; MS, U. Ill., 1945; postgrad. Ill. Inst. Tech., 1959, 64, Oberlin Coll., 1965, St. Louis U., 1962, 63, 67, 68, Rockhurst Coll., 1972, Webster Coll., 1984, 85, U. Mass, 1990; m. Napoleon Williams, July 21, 1973 (dec. 1989); 1 child by previous marriage, Charles W. Batt, Jr. Tchr. Sumner High Sch., St. Louis, 1949-54, Handly High Sch., 1954-63; tchr., head mathematics dept. Northwest High Sch., St. Louis, 1963-76; instr., dept. head, Acad. Math. and Sci., St. Louis, 1976-92; instr., head dept. Harris Teacher Coll., Forest Park C.C. Active NAACP, YWCA. NSF grantee, 1959, 62-65, 67, 72. Mem. Math. Club Greater St. Louis, Top Ladies of Distinction, Math. Assn. Am., Assn. Women in Math., Lane C. M. E. Church, Delta Sigma Theta Sorority (edn. com.). Methodist. Home: 7584 Amherst Ave Saint Louis MO 63130-2803

WILLIAMS, NETTIE, retired childcare facility administrator; d. Alexander Sr. and Elberta Young; children: Tamara Yolanda Bell, Ramon Monceal. Assoc., Ft. Lauderdale Tech. Coll., 1970, Waycross Tech. Coll., Ga., 1983. Cert. child devel. Ga., 1983. Substitute tchr. Ware County Sch. Dist., Waycross, Ga., 1993—96; child care dir., tchr. Episcopal Daycare, Waycross, 1996—2005; ret., 2005. V.p. Am. Legion Post 517 Auxilary, Waycross, Ga., 2005—06; mem. Am. Leagion Aux., Waycross, 2002—; Sunday sch. tchr. New Mt. Pleasant Bapt. Ch., Waycross, 1975—; sec. City Wide Usher's Ministry, Waycross, 1975—; youth dir. St. John Congress Christian Edn., Ga., 1980—; bd. mem. Ga. Legal Services, Waycross, Ga., 1997—2006. Named Vol. of Yr., Concerted Svcs., 2005—06, Parent of Year, Reedsville Head Start, 1983—84; named to, Wall of Tolerance; recipient Appreciation award, St. John Missionary Bapt. Assn., Cert. of Appreciation, Concerted Svcs., Outstanding/Dedicated Svc. award, Reedsville Head Start, 1984—85. Mem.: NAACP (pres. 2001—02, Woman of Yr. 1995).

WILLIAMS, PAT L., military officer; b. Sumner, Miss., May 19, 1961; d. Otha M. and Vera N. Williams; m. Not Married. BA in Comms., Miss. State U., 1982; MA in Nat. Security Affairs Western Hemisphere, Naval Postgrad. Sch., 1995; MA in Nat. Security and Strategic Studies, Naval War Coll., 2001. Joint profl. mil. edn. phase 1. Commd. 2d lt., 1984; advanced through grades to lt. comdr., 1984; yeoman Fleet Logistics Support Squadron 30, Naval Air Sta., N. Island, Calif., 1984—89; officer candidate Officer Candidate Sch., Newport, RI, 1989; adminstrv. budget and supply officer Pers. Support Activity New London, Groton, Conn., 1989—91; head message ctr. Naval Computer and Telecomms. Sta., Mauritius, 1991—92; officer in charge pers. support detachment Naval Hosp. Long Beach, 1992—94; br. head, program mgr. Bur. Naval Pers., Arlington, Va., 1996—97; flag aide Comdr. Navy Recruiting Command, Arlington, 1997—98; assignments officer Comdr. Naval Pers. Command, Millington, Tenn., 1998—2000; commdg. officer Mil. Entrance Processing Sta., San Antonio, 2002—. Mil. social aide The White House, Washington, 1997—98. Named Navy Marksman (Pistol), USN, 1991; recipient Achievement medal with two gold stars, 1991—92, Nat. Def. Svc. medal, 1991, Mil. Outstanding Vol. medal, 1996—98, Commendation medal with three gold stars, 1998—2000. Mem.: Nat. Naval Officers Assn. (life; Secretary 1993—94, None). Avocations: running, reading, travel. Office: Naval War Coll 1950 Stanley Rd Ste 103 Fort Sam Houston TX 78234 Home: 10501 Wyld Dr Upper Marlboro MD 20772-4600 Personal E-mail: plaquinn@msn.com. E-mail: sntcdr@mepcom.army.mil.

WILLIAMS, PATRICIA ANNE, philosopher, writer; b. Alexanderia, Va., May 26, 1944; d. Samuel Leonard and Kay Cloaninger Williams. BA, Coll.William and Mary, 1966; MA in English, U. Va., 1967, MA in Philosophy, 1985; PhD, U. Guelph, 1989. Lectr. La Trobe U., Melbourne, Victoria, Australia, 1968—71; asst. prof. Va. State U., Petersburg, 1990—95. Del. Citizen Amb. People to People Program, China, 1993. Author: (book) Doing without Adam and Eve: Sociobiology and Original Sin, 2001 (Outstanding Acad. Title award Choice Mag., 2002), Where Christianity Went Wrong, When, and What You Can Do About It, 2001, Hazardous Engagement: God Makes a Friend, 2006; editor: Evolution and Human Values, 1995, (Jour.) Universalist Friends, 2005—; contbr. articles to profl. jours. and encys. Mem. ACLU, 1973—; charter mem. U.S. Holocaust Meml. Mus., Washington, 1993—; mem. So. Poverty Law Ctr. Wall of Toleration, Montgomery. Fellow, Westar Inst., 2005—; NEH fellow, 1989. Fellow: Quaker Universalist; mem.: Inst. on Religion in an Age of Sci., Internat. Soc. for History, Philosophy, and Social Studies of Biology (program chmn. 1992—93), Philosophy of Sci. Assn., Am. Philos. Assn., Friends Assn. Higher Edn. Mem. Soc. Of Friends. Avocations: travel, hiking. Home: PO Box 69 Covesville VA 22931 Personal E-mail: theologyauthor@aol.com.

WILLIAMS, PATRICIA BADIA, retired counseling administrator; d. Robert Murray Johnson and Orienta Badia Bozynski; m. Robert F. Williams, July 6, 1989; children: Kristin Marie Tyson, Aaron William Harrison stepchildren: Celeste Anderson, Lisa Hubbard, Thomas, Kyle, Jody, Beth Thayden, Megan Clark. BA with Disting. in Psychology, U. Calif., San Jose, 1971; MA in Counseling Psychology, U. Santa Clara, Calif., 1976; postgrad., Kent State U., Ohio, U. Wash., Adams State Coll., U. N.Mex., U. Puget Sound, Youngstown State U., Ohio. Cert. clin. criminal justice specialist (CCCJS) Nat. Assn. Forensic Counselors, master addictions counselor AODA Cert. Bd., nat. sch. counselor, nat. bd. counselor, lic. tchr., counselor Ohio, 2006, cert. tchr. Colo., lic. counselor Ariz., cert. secondary sch. tchr., tchr. Wash., lic. counselor Wash., cert. tchr. Calif. Jr. h.s. math.tchr., 1971—77; instr. math Olympic Coll., Bremerton, Wash., 1978—79, instr. prevention of child sexual abuse, 1985; adj. prof. Seattle Pacific U., 1986; jr. high counselor, math. tchr. South Kitsap Sch. Dist. 402, Port Orchard, Wash., 1977—79; mid. sch. counselor Bainbridge Island Sch. Dist., Bainbridge Island, Wash., 1979—89; jr. high counselor Marana Unified Sch. Dist., Marana, Ariz., 1989—93; mid. sch. counselor Fremont RE-1 Sch. Dist., Canon City, Colo., 1993—98; tchr. math. Canfield Village Sch. Dist., Canfield, Ohio, 1999—2000; ret., 2000. Sch., cmty. trainer in prevention of child sexual abuse, 1985—87. Active numerous civic orgns./founds.; vol. tchr. Ceasar Chavez Farmer Worker Assn., 1970—71; charter bd. dirs. Storybook Mus.; bd. dirs. Mid. Sch. Alternative Program, Canon City, 1996—97; bd. mem. Salem Hist. Hope Cemetery, 2006; charter mem. Kitsap County Human Rights Commn., 1989. Named Outstanding Alumna of the Yr., U. Santa Clara, 1999, Lifetime Hon. Rotarian for Cmty. Svc., 1993, Mid. Sch. Counselor of Yr.; recipient Recognition for Svc. to Youth, Kiwanis, 1998. Mem.: Ohio Sch. Counselors Assn. (bd. dirs. 1999—2000, dist. 9 rep.), Nat. Assn. Forensic Counselors, Am. Sch. Counselors Assn., Am. Assn. Christian Counselors, Ohio Counselors Assn., Salem Preservation Soc. Achievements include initiated peer mediation programs in Colo. and Ariz. Personal E-mail: rwilliams4@neo.rr.com.

WILLIAMS, PATRICIA HILL, retired university administrator; b. Richmond, Va., May 3, 1939; d. Marshall Jerome and Virginia (O'Brien) H.; m. Arthur Esterbrook Williams, Sept. 6, 1958 (div. Aug. 1981); 1 child, Tory Therese. B.A., SUNY-Old Westbury, 1976; M.A., N.Y. Inst. Tech., 1981; MA in Liberal Studies, SUNY-Stony Brook, 1991, EdD Calif. Coast U., 1996; cert. Mgmt. Devel. Program, Harvard Grad. Sch. Edn., 1992. Assoc. editor Babylon Beacon, N.Y., 1972-79; columnist, editor N.Y. Amsterdam News, N.Y.C., 1971-83; tchr. English, North Babylon Sch. Dist., N.Y., 1976-77; pub. info. officer Am. Cancer Soc., Melville, N.Y., 1977-80; asst. to pres. SUNY/Farmingdale, 1980-99, v.p. external affairs, 1999-2004, ret. 2004; mem. coun. Farmingdale Coll., 2006—; Owner, pres. PHW Assoc. Inerntat. Devel. Cons.; mem. exec. bd. SUNY Confedn. Alumni Assns., 1983-86; bd. dirs. SUNY Coll. and Univ. Advancement and Devel. Council, 1984-86. Contbr. poetry to anthologies. Mem. allocations com. United Way L.I., 1976—; pres. bd. advisors Historically Black Colls.and U., 1991; adv. coun. African Devel. Found., 1992; exec. bd. Ptnrs. of Ams., Inc., 1992-94, treas. bd., 2004—; commr. Human Rights, Suffolk County, 1989—; apptd. by Pres. Clinton to Inter-Am. Found., 1995, vice chmn., 2000-04. Named Alumna of Yr. SUNY/Old Westbury, 1988, Hall Fame, SUNY, 2000; recipient Disting. Svcs. award, SUNY, 2000; W.K. Kellogg Internat. fellow, 1984-86. Mem. AAUW, Black Women in Higher Edn., 100 Black Women (charter mem. L.I. chpt. 1983—, pres. 1986-90, pres. 1994—), Nat. Adv. Council Women's Ednl. Programs (Pres. Reagan's), The Links, Inc., Alpha Kappa Alpha. Episcopalian. Avocations: writing, travel. Home: 15 Genoa St West Babylon NY 11704-1708

WILLIAMS, PATRICIA J., law educator; b. Boston, 1951; BA, Wellesley Coll, 1972; JD, Harvard Univ, 1975. Bar: Calif, US Ct Appeals, 9th cir. Dep. city atty. LA City Atty. Office, 1976—78; atty. Western Ctr. on Law & Poverty, LA, 1978—80; asst. prof. Golden Gate Coll., 1980—84, assoc. prof., 1984—85, CUNY, 1984—88; prof. Univ. Wis., Madison, 1988—93, Columbia U., NYC, 1991—, James L. Dohr prof. law. Trustee Wellesley Coll. Columnist The Nation; author: The Alchemy of Race & Rights, 1991, The Rooster's Egg: On the Persistence of Prejudice, 1995, Seeing a Color-Blind Future: The Paradox of Race, 1997. Grantee MacArthur Fellowship, 2000. Office: Columbia Law Sch 435 W 116th St New York NY 10027-7297 E-mail: williams@law.columbia.edu.

WILLIAMS, PATRICIA SUE, agricultural studies educator; b. Orange, Calif., Dec. 10, 1957; d. O. Dean and Cornelia Palmer Williams. B in Agrl. Sci., Calif. State Poly. U., San Luis Obispo, 1980; M in Agrl. Edn., Calif. Poly. State U., 1983. Clear single subject agr. sci. credential Calif., clear vocat. credential Calif. Agr. tchr. Hale Jr. High, Woodland Hills, Calif., 1981—82, Valenica HS, Placentia, Calif., 1982—85, Buena Pk. (Calif.) HS, 1985—94, Chino (Calif.) Unified Sch. Dist., 1994—98, Orange (Calif.) HS, 1998—. Dir. Mounted Assistance Unit, Silverado, Calif., 1999—2002; large animal rescue technician, Orange, 2001—; animal rescue US Humane Soc., 2005—; animal rescue technician LA Area B Emergency Animal Rescue Team, Redondo Beach, Calif., 2005—; pres., mem. Orange County Fair Auction Com., Costa Mesa, Calif.; mem., tchr. Calif. State Fairs and Shows Ethics Com., Sacramento; advisor FFA, Orange. Mem. choir First United Meth. Ch., Orange. Named Outstanding FFA Advisor, Calif. Agr. Tchrs. Assn., 1982—; recipient Crystal Apple award, KNBC News, 1981, Outstanding Young Mem. award, Calif. Agr. Tchrs. Assn., 1987. Master: ETI (v.p. 2000—04); mem.: MAU (pres.), Nat. Vocat. Agr. Tchrs. Assn., Calif. Teachers Assn., Calif. Agr. Tchrs. Assn. (Outstanding Young Mem. award 1987, Outstanding FFA Advisor 1982—), Am. Riding Club for the Handicapped. Avocations: horse camping, music, guitar, singing, travel. Home: 265 S Lime St Orange CA 92868 Office: Orange HS 525 N Shaffer St Orange CA 92867 Office Phone: 714-997-6299. Personal E-mail: appyonr@sbcglobal.net.

WILLIAMS, PAULA JO, nurse, educator; d. Roger H. and Marie T. Dumont; m. James F. Williams, Sept. 9, 1972; children: Holly A. McCarthy, Carol E., Shawn M., Shawn M. Diploma, Newton-Wellesley Hosp. Sch. of Nursing, Newton Lower Falls, Mass., 1972; BS, Fitchburg (Mass.) State Coll., 1979; MS in Nursing Adminstrn., U. Mass., Lowell, 1989; postgrad., U. Mass., 2000—. Med.-surg. and surg. nurse Lowell Gen. Hosp., Mass., 1972—76; surg. nurse Leominster Hosp., Mass., 1976—77; surg./PACU nurse St. Joseph Hosp., Nashua, NH, 1981; instr. nursing St. Joseph Hosp. Sch. of Practical Nursing, Nashua, 1984—92; asst. prof. nursing Rivier Coll., Nashua, 1992—, interim chair divsn. of nursing, 2002—04, chair divsn. of nursing, 2004—. Chair faculty staff capital campaign Rivier Coll., 1997—; mem. Pandemic Influenza Plan, Nashua, 2006; religious educator Resurrection Parish, Nashua, 1985—97; bd. dirs. Hollis (NH) Pre-Sch., 1981—84. Recipient St. Madeleine of Jesus award. Mem.: Sigma Theta Tau. Roman Catholic. Avocations: cooking, travel, walking. Office: Rivier Coll 420 S Main St Nashua NH 03060 Office Phone: 603-897-8628. Office Fax: 603-897-8628. E-mail: pwilliams@rivier.edu.

WILLIAMS, PEARL See GOOD, EDITH

WILLIAMS, PEGGY RYAN, academic administrator; b. Montreal, Que., Can., May 27, 1947; d. Fred Smith and Carol (Kennedy) Ryan; m. David A. Williams, May 30, 1970. BA psychology, U. Toronto, St. Michael's Coll., Can., 1968; MEd, U. Vt., 1976; EdD, Harvard U., 1983. Caseworker, children's svcs. Monroe County Dept. Social Svcs., Rochester, NY, 1968-72; med. social worker Med. Ctr. Hosp. of Vt., Burlington, 1972; coord. instrn, academic advisor CC of Vt., Lamoille County, 1973—75, project dir. Northwestern Vt., 1975—76, regional dir. Montpelier, 1976-82; part-time instr. C.C. Vt., 1978—85; asst. to the pres. Johnson (Vt.) State Coll., summer 1981; tchg. fellow Harvard U., 1981; dir. ednl. and pers. svcs., office of chancellor Vt. State Colleges, Waterbury, 1982-85; assoc. prof. Trinity Coll., Burlington, 1985—89, chair, dept. bus & economics, 1985-88, assoc. acad. dean, 1988-89; pres. Lyndon State Coll., Lyndonville, Vt., 1989-97, Ithaca (N.Y.) Coll., 1997—; dir. Coun. Ind. Colls. Adj. faculty Johnson State Coll., 1984—86. Active The Ithaca Downtown Partnership Cmty. Adv. Bd.; bd. mem. Sacred Heart Sch. Montreal, bd. chair, 1998—2001; bd. mem. Tompkins Trust Co., 1999—; com. mem. Cornell U. Johnson Mus. Art Cmty. Adv. Coun.; mem. adv. coun. Finger Lakes Land Trust, 2000—03. Recipient Jackie M. Gibbons Leadership award, Am. Coun. Edn./Nat. Identification Program, 1984, Margaret R. Williams Emerging Prof. award. Mem. Am. Assn. Higher Edn., 1973-, Am. Coun. on Edn., 1981- (bd. dirs., 2000-), Nat. Assn. Women in Edn., 1985-, Office: Ithaca Coll Job Hall Ithaca NY 14850

WILLIAMS, PETRA SCHATZ, antiquarian, director; b. Poughkeepsie, N.Y., Sept. 2, 1913; d. Grover Henry and Mayme Nickerson (Bullock) Schatz; m. J. Calvert Williams, Nov. 26, 1946; children: Miranda, Frederica, Valerie. AB, Skidmore Coll., 1936; JD, Fordham U., 1940. Founder Fountain House, Phoenix, 1953, Fountain House East, Jeffersontown, Ky., 1966. Author: Flow Blue China, An Aid to Identification, 1971, Flow Blue China II, 1973, Flow Blue China and Mulberry Ware, 1975, Staffordshire Romantic Transfer Patterns, 1979, Staffordshire III Romantic Transfer Patterns, 1986, L'Envoi, 1998. Past pres. Meml. Hosp. Aux., Phoenix, Heard Mus. Guild, Phoenix; bd. dirs. Ky. Humane Soc. Mem. Nat. Soc. Interior Designers (nat. dir. for Ariz. 1957-58, Ky. 1968, pres. Ky. 1967-68), DAR, Ky. Hist. Soc., Flow Blue Internat. Collectors Club (hon.). Clubs: Filson. Mem. Soc. Of Friends. Address: PO Box 99298 Jeffersontown KY 40269-0298

WILLIAMS, PHYLLIS CUTFORTH, retired realtor; b. Moreland, Idaho, June 6, 1917; d. William Claude and Kathleen Jessie (Jenkins) Cutforth; m. Joseph Marsden Williams, Jan. 21, 1938 (dec. 1986); children: Joseph Marlis, Bonnie Lou Williams Thompson, Nancy Kay Williams Stewart, Marjorie Williams Karren, Douglas Claude, Thomas Marsden, Wendy Kathleen Williams Clark, Shannon Irene Williams Ostler. Grad., Ricks Coll., 1935. Tchr. Grace (Idaho) Elem. Sch., 1935-38; realtor Williams Realty, Idaho Falls, Idaho, 1972-77; mem. Idaho Senate, Boise, 1977. Owner, mgr. river property. Compiler: Idaho Legisladies Cookbook, Cookin' Together, 1981. With MicroFilm Ctr., LDS Ch. Mission, Salt Lake City, 1989-90; former block chmn., vol. Cancer Drive; active Idaho State Legisladies Club, 1966-84, v.p., 1982-84; mem. Bonneville County (Idaho) Rep. Women. Avocations: genealogy, music, politics, cooking, attending grandchildren's special events.

WILLIAMS, REBA WHITE, corporate financial executive, writer, researcher; m. Dave H. Williams. BA in Enlgish, Duke U., Durham, N.C.; MBA, Harvard U., Cambridge, Mass.; MA in Art History, Hunter Coll., N.Y.C.; MA in Philosophy, CUNY, PhD in Art History. Former rschr. McKinsey & Co., Inc.; securities analyst Mitchell Hutchins, Inc. Dir. spl. projects, mem. bd. dir. Alliance Capital Mgmt.; vice chmn. White Williams Holdings, Ltd., 2001—. Mem. editl. bd. Print Quar.; contbr. articles to Am. Artist, Bus. and Soc., Instl. Investor Chgo. Daily News, Fin. Analysts Jour., others; author catalog essays. Mem. Manhattan Cmty. Bd. 8, 1999-2000; mem. Art Commn. City NY, 1995-98, pres., 1997-98; mem. NY State Coun. on the Arts, 1996-99, vice chmn., 1999; hon. keeper of Am. prints The Fitzwilliam Mus., Cambridge, Eng. Decorated Polish Order of Merit, cavalier of grand cross Order of Poland 1st class; recipient Pacesetter award NY City Coun., 1999, Disting. Cultural Leadership award NY Rep. County Com., 1999, Augustus Graham medal Bklyn. Mus., 1998; named one of Top 200 Collectors, ARTnews Mag., 2004, 2006, others. Mem. Cosmopolitan Club. Avocation: Collector of Am. Prints. Office: 258 Atlantic St Stamford CT 06901 Office Phone: 212-752-1705. Business E-Mail: reba@rebawhitewilliams.com.

WILLIAMS, RITA TUCKER, lawyer; b. Atlanta, Jan. 26, 1950; d. Claude Edward and Lillian Bernice (Barber) Tucker; m. Raymond Williams, Jr., Jan. 1, 1973; children: Monet Danielle, Brandon Raynard, Blake Hassan. BA, Spelman Coll., 1972; MA, U. Mich., 1976; JD, Emory U., 1987. Bar: Ga. 1987. Tchr. pub. schs., Suisun, Calif., 1977-82; assoc. Alston & Bird, Atlanta, 1987-89, Bernard & Assocs., Decatur, Ga., 1989-90; prin. Williams & Assocs., Decatur, Ga., 1990—. Instr. seminar Nat. Inst. Trial Advocacy, Emory U., Atlanta, spring 1992-95, tutor 1st yr. law students, 1996. Named Outstanding Alumna, Emory U. Law Sch., 1996. Mem. ABA, State Bar Ga. Assn., Ga. Trial Lawyers Assn., Omicron Delta Kappa. Democrat. Office: 220 Church St Decatur GA 30030-3328 Office Phone: 404-370-3783. Personal E-mail: ritw@atlonline.com.

WILLIAMS, RUBY JO, retired principal; b. Marshall, Tex., Sept. 26, 1936; d. Henry Clay and Luberta Smith; m. Q.D. Williams (dec. Apr. 1998). BA, Wiley Coll., Marshall, Tex., 1959; M in Edn., U. N. Tex., 1972; postgrad. in Mid-Mgmt., Tex. Woman's U., 1987. Cert. elem., secondary sch. educator, mid-mgr., Tex. Tchr. Gainesville (Tex.) Sch. Dist., 1962-69, Sherman (Tex.) Sch. Dist., 1969-86, appraiser, 1986-87, prin., 1987-96, Edison coord., 1996-98. Mem., past chmn. Grayson Coll. Trustees, Grayson County, 1992—, Comty. Block Grant, Sherman, Tex.; mem Hosp. Metraplex Bd., Sherman. Named Outstanding Citizen, City of Sherman, 1979. Mem. NAACP (life), AAUW (pres., v.p., Woman of Yr., Woman of Achievement, Outstanding Woman Educator 1978-79), Nat. Alliance of Black Sch. Educators, Tex. Elem. Prins. Assn., Goals for Sherman (multi-cultural chmn.) Mem. Ch. of Christ. Avocations: reading, travel, cooking, sewing. Home: 2015 E Alma Ave Sherman TX 75090-4006

WILLIAMS, RUTH LEE, clinical social worker; b. Dallas, June 24, 1944; d. Carl Woodley and Nancy Ruth (Gardner) W. BA, So. Meth. U., 1966; M Sci.in Social Work, U. Tex., Austin, 1969. Milieu coordinator Starr Commonwealth, Albion, Mich., 1969-73; clin. social worker Katherine Hamilton Mental Health Care, Terre Haute, Ind., 1973-74; clin. social worker, supr. Pikes Peak Mental Health Ctr., Colorado Springs, Colo., 1974—2000; pvt. practice social work Colorado Springs, 1978—2000; pres. Hearthstone Inn, Inc., Colorado Springs, 1978—; practitioner Jin Shin Jyutsu, Colorado Springs, 1978—2000; dir. cmty. rels. Walker Wear, 2001—. Pres., v.p. bd. dirs. Premier Care (formerly Colorado Springs Mental Health Care Providers Inc.), 1986-87, chmn. quality assurance com., 1987-89, v.p. bd. dirs., 1992-93; bd. dirs. Beth Haven, Inc., JAC Svcs. Author, editor From the Kitchen of The Hearthstone Inn, 1981, 2d rev. edit., 1986, 3d rev. edit., 1992. Mem. Am. Bd. Examiners in Clin. Social Work (charter mem., cert.), Colo. Soc. Clin. Social Work (editor 1976), Nat. Assn. Soc. Workers (diplomate), Nat. Bd. Social Work Examiners (cert.), Nat. Assn. Ind. Innkeepers, So. Meth. U. Alumni Assn. (life). Avocations: gardening, hiking, sailing. Office: 11555 Howells Rd Colorado Springs CO 80908-3735

WILLIAMS, SERENA, professional tennis player, apparel designer; b. Saginaw, Mich., Sept. 26, 1981; Prof. tennis player WTA Tour, 1995—; designer Aneres clothing line. TV appearances include: My Wife and Kids, 2002; Law and Order: Special Victims Unit, 2004; The Division, 2004; (voice) The Simpsons, 2001. Named WTA Most Improved Player, 1999, Player of the Year, TENNIS Mag., 1999, Female Athlete in the World, AP, 2002, WTA Tour Player of the Year, 2002, #1 most marketable female athlete, Sports Business Daily, 2003; recipient Espy award for Best Female Athlete, ESPN, 2003, Espy award for Best Female Tennis Player, 2003, 2004. Achievements include winner of 26 career singles titles, 10 career doubles titles, and 2 mixed doubles titles, WTA tour; Grand Slam Championships: US Open, 1999, 2002, Wimbledon, 2002, 2003, Roland Garros, 2002, Austalian Open, 2003, 2005; winner of doubles titles (with Venus Williams) at Australian Open 2001, 2003, Wimbledon, 2000, 2000, Roland Garros, 1999, US Open, 1999, Mixed Doubles (w/ Max Mirnyi), Wimbledon, 1998; winner of doubles gold medal (with Venus Williams), Sydney Olympic games, 2000; winning 4 Grand Slam tournaments in a row, 2002-2003; signing largest endorsement deal to date by a female athlete with Nike, 2003. Office: c/o USTA 70 W Red Oak Ln White Plains NY 10604-3602*

WILLIAMS, SHANNON RENEE, mental health services professional; d. Joyce Bromley Wright; m. Anthony Markell Williams, July 5, 1997; children: JaHarold, Justin, Jamilla. BS, Bowie State U., 1990, MA, 1993; PhD, Howard U., 2004. Lic. clin. profl. counselor Md. Mental health assoc. Regional Inst. for Children and Adolescents, Rockville, Md., 1990—94; correctional psychologist assoc. Dept. Pub. Safety and Correctional Svcs., Jessup, Md., 1994—2005; therapist Wash. Assessment and Therapy Svc., Lanham, Md., 2005—; psychotherapist Bowie Counseling Svcs., 2006—. Coord. Diamonds in the Rough womanhood tng. program Paramount Bapt. Ch., Washington, 2000—. Mem.: APA, Am. Counseling Assn. Avocations: reading, singing.

WILLIAMS, SHEILA A.T., elementary school educator, consultant; b. Columbus, Miss., Dec. 30, 1963; d. James Thurman and Lillian Augusta Thomas; divorced; children: Phillip James Thomas, Kristin Nicole Sims. BA in English, U. Miss., Oxford, 1986. Cert. in elem. edn. K-8, Miss. Tchr. Oxford City Schs., 1986-88; flight attendant Eastern Airlines, Miami, Fla., 1988-89; photographer Sears, Columbus, Miss., 1989-90; tchr. Cumberland County Schs., Fayetteville, N.C., 1994-95, Oktibbeha County Schs., Crawford, Miss., 1995-98, Lowndes County Schs., Columbus, 1990-94, 98—. Pres., founder S.H.A.K.E.R./Flight Buddies Aviation Program, Columbus, 1994—. Coord. Promote the Vote mock election, Crawford, 1996. Recipient Excellence in Tchg. award Nat. Coun. Negro Women, 1999; named Tchr. of Yr., Southview Mid. Sch., 1995. Fellow U.S. Space Found.; mem. AAUW, Air Force Assn. (Christa McAuliffe award 1998), Tuskegee Airmen (v.p. 1999—), Nat. Historic Preservation Soc. Democrat. Baptist. Avocations: flying, writing, swimming, hiking, reading.

WILLIAMS, STEPHANIE DIANE, music educator; b. Morristown, Tenn., Sept. 29, 1978; d. Samuel Keith and Linda Susan Moyers; m. Timothy Ellis Williams, July 24, 1999; 1 child, Carly Ann. AS, Walters State C.C., Morristown, 1998; MusB, East Tenn. State U., Johnson City, 2000. Elem. music tchr. Greene County Bd. Edn., Greeneville, Tenn., 2001, Cocke County Bd. Edn., Newport, Tenn., 2001—. Music dir. Southside Bapt. Ch., Newport, 2004—. Active Southside Bapt. Ch., Newport, 1979—. Mem.: East Tenn. Vocal Assn. Home: 282 Lower Bogard Rd Newport TN 37821 Office: Cocke County Bd Edn Hedrick Dr Newport TN 37821 Office Phone: 423-623-7821. Personal E-mail: stephaniedwilliams@hotmail.com.

WILLIAMS, SUE DARDEN, library director; b. Miami, Fla., Aug. 13, 1943; d. Archie Yelverton and Bobbie (Jones) Eagles; m. Richard Williams, Sept. 30, 1989. BA, Barton Coll., Wilson, N.C., 1965; M.L.S., U. Tex., Austin, 1970. Cert. librarian, N.C., Va. Instr. Chowan Coll., Murfreesboro, NC, 1966-68; libr.'s asst. Albemarle Regional Libr., Winston, NC, 1968-69; br. libr. Multnomah County Pub. Libr., Portland, Oreg., 1971-72; asst. dir. Stanly County Pub. Libr., Albemarle, NC, 1973-76, dir., 1976-80; asst. dir. Norfolk (Va.) Pub. Libr., 1980-83, dir., 1983-94, Rockingham County Pub. Libr., Eden, NC, 1996—2004, Albemarle Regional Libr., Winton, NC, 2004—. Mem. ALA (coun. 1987-91, orientation com. 1990-92, chair 1991), Libr. Adminstrv. and Mgmt. Assn. (pub. rels. sec. 1985-87bd. dirs. 2004—), Southeastern Libr. Assn. (staff devel. com. 1986-88, Rothrock award com. 1984-86, sec. pub. libr. sect. 1982-84), Va. Libr. Assn. (SELA rep. 1993-96, coun. 1984, 88-91, 93-96, ad hoc conf. guidelines com. 1985-86, chmn. conf. program 1984, awards and recognition com. 1983, mem. SELA outstanding libr. program award com. 2002), Pub. Libr. Assn. (bd. dirs.-at-large Met. area 1986-89), Va. State Libr. (coop edn. com. 88-89), N.C. Libr. Assn. (scholarship com. 1999-2005, chair 2001-2005), LAMS. Home: 109 Chowan Rd Murfreesboro NC 27855 Office: Albermarle Regional Libr PO Box 68 303 W Tryon St Winton NC 27986 Office Phone: 252-358-7832. E-mail: swilliams_arl@yahoo.com.

WILLIAMS, SUNITA L., astronaut; b. Euclid, Ohio, Sept. 19, 1965; d. Deepak N. and Ursaline B. Pandya; m. Michael J. Williams. BS in Physical Sci., U.S. Naval Acad., 1987; MS in Engring. Mgmt., Fla. Inst. Tech., 1995. Commn. ensign USN, 1987, advanced through grades to lt. comdr., various assignments, 1987—89, overseas combat, 1989—92; officer in charge Hurrican Andrew Relief Ops. USS Sylvania, 1992—93; various assignments USN, 1993—95; served on USS Saipan, Norfolk, Va., 1995—98; astronaut NASA, Houston, 1998—. Decorated Commendation medal USN, Achievement medal USN & USMC, Humanitarian Svc. medal USN. Mem.: Soc. Flight Test Engrs., Soc. Exptl. Test Pilots, Am. Helicopter Assn. Office: Astronaut Office CB NASA Johnson Space Center Houston TX 77058

WILLIAMS, SUSAN BULLARD, music educator; b. Clinton, N.C., July 28, 1957; d. William Alex and Catherine Lorraine Bullard; m. Michael Wilson Williams, Dec. 27, 1980; children: Terri Catherine, Alex Elizabeth. BS in Music, Pembroke State U., N. C., 1979. Tchr. music Pine Forest Jr. H.S., Fayetteville, NC, 1979—81, Armstrong Jr. H.S., 1981—86, Mac Williams Mid. Sch., 1996—. Mem. sch. improvement team; chair cultural arts. Named Tchr. of Yr., MacWilliams Mid. Sch., 2006. Mem.: N.C. Music Edn. Assn. (chair mid. sch. choral sect. 2001—03, Mid. Sch. Tchr. of Yr. 2003). Baptist. Home: 4132 Bentgrass Dr Fayetteville NC 28312-8712

WILLIAMS, SUSAN SHIDAL, language educator; b. Atlanta, Jan. 7, 1963; d. L. Neil and Sue (Sigmon) W. BA, Yale U., 1985, PhD, 1991. Asst. prof. English Ohio State U., Columbus, 1991-97, assoc. prof. English, 1997—2006, prof. English, 2006—. Author: Confounding Images: Photography and Portraiture in Antebellum American Fiction, 1997, Reclaiming Authorship: Literary Women in America 1850-1900, 2006; co-editor: Reciprocal Influences: Literary Production Distribution, and Consumption in America, 1999, American Periodicals; manuscript reviewer and contbr. articles to profl. jours. Mem. Columbus Symphony Orch. Chorus, 1992-98. Whiting fellow Yale Univ., New Haven, Conn., 1990-91, Steven Botein fellow Am. Antiquarian Soc., Worcester, Mass., 1997; Coca-Cola Crit. Difference for Women Rsch. grantee Ohio State U., 1996-97, Nat. Endowment for the Humanities, 2006. Mem. MLA, Am. Studies Assn., Soc. History of Authorship, Reading & Pub., Rsch. Soc. Am. Periodicals (mem. adv. bd. 1997-2005). Office: Ohio State Univ English Dpt 164 W 17th Ave Columbus OH 43210-1370 Office Phone: 614-688-3147. E-mail: williams.488@osu.edu.

WILLIAMS, SUZANNE, writer, community volunteer; b. Scottsbluff, Nebr., July 10, 1944; d. Norman William and Opal (Stafford) Adams; m. H. Douglas Williams, Sept. 14, 1968; children: Kate Lynn, Betsy Anne. BA in Speech, U. Calif., Berkeley, 1966; postgrad., U. Ill., 1966-68. Pers. analyst Santa Clara County, San Jose, Calif., 1969-70; pub. affairs rep., staff writer Santa Clara County Transp. Agy., San Jose, 1976-79; writer, rschr. self employed, San Jose, 1981—; pub. Birthday Matches Custom Cards, San Jose, 1989—. Mem., vice chair San Jose Pub. Libr. Commn., 1988-92; mem. San Jose Libr. Yes on E Com., 1994, San Jose Libr. Master Plan Task Force, 1995-97; mem. adv. joint libr. com. San Jose and San Jose State U., 1997-98; co-chair No on A Com. Campbell HS Dist., 1999; elder Stone Ch., San Jose, 1997-2000, 2003-06, libr., 1991—; bond oversight com. Campbell HS Dist., 2000—; mem. Project Diversity Screening Com., City of San Jose, 2004—. Recipient commendation City of San Jose, 1995; inducted into Prytanean Soc., U. Calif., Berkeley, 1966; named Mil. Wife of Yr., USAF Air Tng. Command, 1974. Mem. Presbyn. Women of Stone Ch. (life; mission sec. 1995—), Friends of San Jose West Valley Libr. Democrat. Avocations: reading, writing, book shopping. Office: Birthday Matches Custom Cards PO Box 10521 San Jose CA 95157-1521 Business E-Mail: dougwilliams@covad.net.

WILLIAMS, SUZANNE, state senator; b. Oklahoma City, Feb. 3, 1945; m. Ed Williams; 2 children. BA in Edn., Baylor U.; MA in Spl. Edn., U. Colo. Educator; state sen. dist. 41 Colo. Senate, Denver, 1996—, mem. edn. and transp. and energy coms. Recipient Gov.'s award for curriculum innovation, 1985, Gov.'s Action Plan award, 2000, Insider award, Aurora Sentinel, 1994, Leadership award, Colo. Edn. Assn., 1999, Outstanding Leadership Legis. award, AIA, Colo., 2001, cert. appreciation, Denver Indian Family Resource Ctr., 2002. Mem.: AAUW, Colo. Soc. Sch. Psychologists, Assn. Sch. Nurses, Colo. Assn. Edn. Young Children, Women in Govt., Aurora Sister Cities Internat., Delta Kappa Gamma. Democrat. Avocations: reading, music, exercising. Office: State Capitol # 271 200 E Colfax Ave Denver CO 80203 Office Phone: 303-866-3432.

WILLIAMS, TARA LYN, psychologist; b. Rome, Ga., May 10, 1973; d. Bill Rowney and Joan Marie Williams. BS, Vanderbilt U., Nashville, 1995; MS, Tex. A&M U., College Station, 1998, PhD, 2001. Staff psychologist Sheppard Pratt Hosp., Towson, Md., 2003—05, psychology contractor, 2005—; staff psychologist Psychiat. Inst. Washington, 2005—06. Cons. Retreat at Sheppard Pratt Hosp. Contbr. articles to profl. jours. Recipient Disting. Grad. Student award, Tex. A&M U., 2002; fellow, Sheppard Pratt Hosp., 2001—03. Mem.: APA, Internat. Soc. Study Dissociation, Md. Psychol. Assn. Avocations: reading, running, racquetball, snowboarding, dance. Office: Sheppard Pratt Hosp Trauma Disorders Program 6501 N Charles St PO 6815 Towson MD 21285-6815 Office Phone: 410-938-4363. Business E-Mail: twilliams@sheppardpratt.org.

WILLIAMS, TERRIE MICHELLE, public relations executive; b. Mt. Vernon, NY, May 12, 1954; MA, BA cum laude, Brandeis U., 1975; MS, Columbia U., 1977. Exec. dir. World Inst. of Black Community, NYC, 1982; dir. pub. rels. Essence Communications Inc., NYC, 1982-86, v.p., dir., 1986-88; pres. The Terrie Williams Agy., NYC, 1988—. Med. soc. worker N.Y. Hosp., NYC, 1977-80; program adminstr. Black Filmmaker Found., N.Y.C., 1980-81; exec. dir. Black Owned Communications Alliance, N.Y.C., 1981-82. Author: The Personal Touch, 1995. Recipient Entrepreneur of the Yr. award Nat. Assn. Market Developers, 1990, Flo Kennedy Media award, 1990, Matrix award N.Y. Women in Communications, 1991. Mem. Women in Communications, NOW, Brandeis U. Alumni Assn. (bd. dirs.), NY TV Acad. Arts and Scis., Pub. Rels. Soc. Am. (D. Parke Gibson award 1981). E-mail: tmwms@terriewilliams.com.

WILLIAMS, TESSA RENÉ, music educator; d. James Fay Carter, Jr. and Kay Helen Carter; m. Johnny Franklin Williams, Apr. 17, 2004; children: Marina Kay Gabrielle Huffman, Madison Faye Huffman, Jaden Ty. BA in Academic Studies, Sam Houston State U., Huntsville, Tex., 1993. Elem. tchr. Alvin Ind. Sch. Dist., Tex., 1993—96, Angleton Ind. Sch. Dist., Tex., 1996—2003, elem. music tchr., 2003—. Avocations: singing in church choir, softball, piano. Office: Southside Elementary 1200 Park Ln Angleton TX 77515 Office Phone: 979-849-5245.

WILLIAMS, THELMA B., retired principal; d. Joseph and Floria Bush; m. McDonald Williams, Oct. 9, 1955; children: Donald J., Patricia A. Johnson. BS in Edn., Paine Coll., 1963; EdM, U. Ga., 1974, EdS, 1981. Tchr. Levi White Elem., Augusta, Ga., 1963—72; reading specialist Richmond County Schs., Augusta, 1972—76; asst. prin. Glenn Hills High, Augusta, 1976—81; prin. W.S. Hornsby Elem., Augusta, 1981—99. Edn. vol. Richmond County Schs., 1999—2002; founder after-sch. tutorial program, 2005—. Mem. Augusta Richmond County Hist. Preservation Commn., 1995—2003, vice chair, 2006—; mem. several ministries Macedonia Bapt. Ch., organizer after school tutorial program, 2004; mem. Augusta Classic, 1998—, Alzheimer's Assn., Augusta, 1983—2003. Recipient Meritorious Svc. award, Richmond County Prin. Assn., 1999, Pres.'s award, Paine Coll., 2001, Disting. award of edn., Nat. Assn. Equal Opportunity in Higher Edn., 2002, United Negro Coll. Fund award, Tom Joyner Found., 2003, Yough Svc. award, Ga. Rep. Quincy Murphy, 2004, Outstanding Educators award, W.S. Hornsby and East Augusta Cmty. Neighborhood Assn. and PCS Nitrogen, 1998. Mem.: Richmond County Ret. Tchrs. Assn., Art Factory for Creative Arts (sec. 1990—92), Loyal Christian Women Civic Group (v.p. 2006—, vice chair 2006—), Paine Coll. Alumni Assn. (chmn. ballot com. 1997—99, pres. Augusta chpt. 2001—), Phi Delta Kappa (pres. Platinum Club 1983—, lectr. Founder's Day 1994, nat. chairballots 1997—99, chmn. ballots com. 1997—99, local pres. 2001—03, pres. Augusta chpt. 2001—), Zeta Phi Beta (Founder's Day Lectr. 1994). Avocations: travel, reading, baking, teaching. Personal E-mail: TBW51@comcast.net.

WILLIAMS, THOMASYNE HILL, speech pathology/audiology services professional; d. Thomas James and Ophelia Garrett Hill; children: Tressie Jamese, Thomas Carmichael Garrett Hill. BS Comm. Sci and Disorders, U. Montevallo, Ala., 1983, MS Comm. Sci and Disorders, 1987; EdD in Spl. Edn., U. Ala., Tuscaloosa, 1999. Lic. speech and lang. pathologist Ala., 1993, cert. Am. Speech Lang. Hearing Assn. Speech/lang. pathologist Escambia County Sch. Sys., Brewton, Ala., 1983—85, Coweta County Sch. Sys., Newnan, Ga., 1985—86, InSpeech Rehab., Daytona Beach, Fla., 1987—88, Volusia County Sch., Daytona Beach, 1988—90, Birmingham City Schs., Ala., 1990—93, Jefferson County Bd. Edn., Birmingham, 2002—; instr., asst. prof., clin. supr. U. Montevallo, 1993—2002. Pres., owner Hill Comm. Consultants, Inc, Birmingham, 2000—; event planner, owner Events for All Occasions, Birmingham, 2006. Bd. mem. Children's Literacy Guild Ala., Birmingham, 2002—, Black Assn. Speech-Lang. and Hearing. Recipient AAUW of Ala. Leadership Award, AAUW of Ala. Montevallo Br., 2006, Who's Who Among America's Teachers, Who's Who, 1999 and 2002; scholar Faculty Scholarship for Diversity, U. of Montevallo, 1995. Mem.: AAUW (Ala. state pres. 2004—06, assn. program devel. com. 2006—, programs v.p. 2002—04, div. team mem. 2001—03, div. chair 2002—04), Am. Speech, Language, Hearing Assn. (cert.), Alpha Kappa Alpha (graduate advisor 1994—96). Democrat. Baptist. Avocations: travel, football, basketball, music. Home: 904 Goldwire St SW Birmingham AL 35211 Office Phone: 205-401-7817. Home Fax: 205-322-6686. Personal E-mail: drtwaka@earthlink.net.

WILLIAMS, TIFFANY N., personal and athletic trainer; b. Englewood, NJ, May 20, 1982; d. Levi and Monique Williams. BS, Mo. State U., Springfield, 2004. Cert. NASM personal trainer, ACE personal trainer. Cert. atheltic trainer Pinnacle Therapy, Kansas City, Mo., 2004—; cert. personal trainer Front Door Fitness, Overland Park, Kans., 2006—. Mem.: Nat. Atheltic Trainers Assn. (cert.). E-mail: volleyblgl@aol.com.

WILLIAMS, TONDA, entrepreneur, consultant; b. NYC, Nov. 21, 1949; d. William and Juanita (Rainey) W.; 1 child, Tywana. Student, Collegiate Inst., N.Y.C., 1975-78, C.W. Post Coll., 1981-83; BA in Bus. Mgmt., Am. Nat. U., Phoenix, 1983; grad., L.I. Bus. Inst., 1996. Notary pub. N.Y. Asst. controller Acad. Ednl. Devel., N.Y.C., 1971-81; mgr. office Chapman-Apex Constrn. Co., Bayshore, NY, 1982-84; specialist computer RGM Liquid Waste Removal, Deerpark, NY, 1985-87; contr. LaMar Lighting Co., Freeport, NY, 1987—; owner, pres. Omni-Star, Bklyn., 1981—; pres. Omni-Data Tech., Bayshore, NY, 1996—. Author: Tonda's Songs in Poetry, 1978, The Magic of Life, 1991; co-author: Computer Management of Liquid Waste Industry, 1986. Recipient Golden Poet award World of Poetry, 1992. Mem. Am. Mus. Natural History, Am. Soc. Notary Pubs. Avocations: bowling, chess, singing. Home: 74 Cedar Dr Bay Shore NY 11706-2419 Office Phone: 631-968-0016. Office Fax: 631-968-1016. E-mail: tonda@omnidatatech.com.

WILLIAMS, UNA JOYCE, psychiatric social worker; b. Youngstown, Ohio, June 24, 1934; d. Samuel Wilfred and Frances Josephine (Woods) Ellis; children: Wendy Louise, Christopher Ellis, Sharon Elizabeth. BA, U. Ala., 1957; MSW, Adelphi U., 1963. Diplomate in profl. counseling Internat. Acad. Behavioral Medicine, Counseling and Psychotherapy. Dir. Huntington Program Sr. Citizens, 1963—67; psychiat. social worker-supr. N.Y. State Dept. Mental Hygiene, Suffolk Psychiat. Hosp., Central Islip, 1969—72; info.-referral counselor Mental Health Assn. Nassau County, Hempstead, NY, 1993—; therapist Madonna Heights Family Clinic, Dix Hills, NY, 1994—99; med. and psychiat. social worker Northport VA Med. Ctr., NY, 1994—2005, psychiat. social worker acute psychiat. treatment svcs., 2005—, med. social worker dialysis svcs., 2005—. Cons. on programs for aging Luth. Social Svcs. Met. N.Y., 1959, sr. citizens programs, Bd. Edn. Port Jefferson, N.Y., 1961-63. Chmn. Huntington Twp. Com. Human Rels., 1970; sec. bd. trustees Unitarian Universalist Fellowship Huntington, 1984. Mem. NASW (diplomate in social work), Am. Assn. Family Counselors and Mediators,Germany Philatelic Soc. (pres. chpt. 30, 1990, Mem. of Yr. 1987). Avocations: painting, stamp collecting/philately, music (voice & piano), genealogy. Home: 316 Lenox Rd Huntington Station NY 11746-2640 Office Phone: 631-261-4400 2349.

WILLIAMS, VANESSA (VANESSA LYNN WILLIAMS), recording artist, actress; b. Millwood, N.Y., Mar. 18, 1963; d. Milton and Helen; m. Ramon Hervey II, 1988 (div. 1997); children: Melanie, Jillian, Devin; m. Rick Fox, 1999 (div.); 1 child, Sasha Gabriella Fox. Recording artist, 1988—. Stage appearances include: (Broadway) Kiss of the Spider Woman, 1993-95 (Theatre World award, 1995), Into the Woods, 2002(nominee Drama Desk award for Outstanding Actress in a Musical, 2002, Tony award Best Actress in a Musical, 2002); film appearances include Pick-up Artist, 1987, Under the Gun, 1988, Another You, 1991, Harley Davidson and the Marlboro Man, 1991, Eraser, 1996, Hoodlum, 1997, Soul Food, 1997, Dance with Me, 1998, The Adventures of Elmo in Grouchland, 1999, Light It Up, 1999, Shaft, 2000, Johnson Family Vacation, 2004,(TV films) Full Exposure: The Sex Tapes Scandal, 1989, The Kid Who Loved Christmas, 1990, Perry Mason: The Case of the Silenced Singer, 1990, Stompin' at the Savoy, 1992, Jacksons: An American Dream, 1992, Nothing Lasts Forever, 1995, Bye Bye Birdie, 1995, The Odyssey, 1997, Futuresport, 1998, Courage to Love, 2000 (also exec. prodr.), Don Quixote, 2000, A Diva's Christmas Carol, 2000, WW3, 2001, Keep the Faith, Baby, 2002, (TV mini series) Nothing Lasts Forever, 1995, (TV series) Ugly Betty 2006-; guest appearances Partners in Crime, 1984, T.J. Hooker, 1986, The Love Boat, 1986, The Fresh Prince of Bel-Air, 1990, Between Brothers, 1997, Vanessa Williams and Friends: Christmas in N.Y., 1996, Star Trek: Deep Space Nine, 1996, L.A. Doctors, 1999, Ally McBeal, 2002, Boomtown, 2003, South Beach, 2006; albums: The Right Stuff, 1988, The Comfort Zone, 1991, The Sweetest Days, 1994, Star Bright, 1996, Next, 1997, Alfie, the Best of Vanessa, 1998; # 1 hit single Save the Best for Last; vocalist (soundtracks) Beverly Hills 90210, 1990, Harley Davidson and the Marlboro Man, 1991, Adventures of Priscilla, Queen of the Desert, 1994, The Mask, 1994, Pocahontas, 1995, Eraser, 1996, Dance with Me, 1998, The Adventures of Elmo in Grouchland, 1999, Isn't She Great, 2000; host Style World, 2000; spokesperson for Proactive Solution (Acne Medication); commercial appearances Radio Shack. Recipient 8 Grammy award nominations; named one of 50 Most Beautiful People, People Mag. Achievements include being the first Black to be named Miss America, 1983 (resigned title 1983). Office: Mercury Records care Dawn Bridges 825 8th Ave New York NY 10019-7416 also: Mercury Records 11150 Santa Monica Blvd Los Angeles CA 90025-3380 Address: William Morris Agy 151 El Camino Dr Beverly Hills CA 90212*

WILLIAMS, VENUS, professional tennis player; b. Lynwood, Calif., June 17, 1980; d. Richard and Oracene Williams. Profl. debut Bank of West Classic, Oakland, Calif., 1994; owner V Starr Interiors; designer Venus Williams Collection Wilson's Leather Co. Mem. U.S. Fed Cup Team, 1995, 99, 2003, U.S. Olympic Tennis Team, Sydney, 2000, Athens, 04. Recipient ESPY award for outstanding women's tennis player, 2001, Espy award for Best Female Tennis Player, 2001, 2006, Espy award for Best Female Athlete, 2002; named Most Impressive Network Newcomer award, 1997, TENNIS Mag. Most Improved Player, WTA Tour, 1998; winner mixed doubles (with Gimelstob) Australian Open, 1998, Roland Garros, 1998, doubles (with Serena Williams) French Open, 1999, U.S. Open, 1999, Australian Open, 2001, 03, Wimbledon, 2002, 2005, singles and doubles gold medal winner, Sydney Olympics, 2000, singles U.S. Open, 2000, 01, Wimbledon, 2000, 2001; winner 31 Career Singles Titles and 9 Career Doubles Titles, WTA Tour. Mem.: WTA Tour Players' Coun. Jehovah'S Witness. Avocations: interior decorating, fashion design. Office: US Tennis Assn 70 W Red Oak Ln White Plains NY 10604-3602*

WILLIAMS, VERONICA MYRES, psychotherapist, social worker; b. Shreveport, La., May 11, 1947; d. McEura and Margie Virgina (Reagan) Myres; divorced; children: Nicole Leann, Jennifer Lyn, Erica Maria. BA, La. Tech. U., Ruston, 1969; MSW, U. Mich., Ann Arbor, 1977; PhD, So. Calif. U., 2001. Diplomate Am. Bd. Clin. Social Workers, Am. Psychotherapy Assn.; cert. social worker, Mich. Probation counselor Citizens Probation Authority, Flint, Mich., 1970-72; unit dir., therapist Svcs. to Overcome Drug Abuse Among Teenagers, Flint, 1972-74; psychiat. therapist Psycho-Therapeutic Treatment Clin., P.C., Flint, 1974-77; psychiat. social worker Hurley Med. Ctr., Flint, 1977-79; field instr. Sch. Social Work U. Mich., Ann Arbor, 1978-79, 86—; psychiat. social worker Inst. Mental Health, Flint, 1979-81, Psychotherapeutic Treatment Clinic, 1981-83; clin. social worker Flint Bd. Edn., 1979-83; pupil apprasal spl. edn. Caddo Parish Sch. Bd., Shreveport, La., 1983—85; psychiat. therapist Mott Children's Health Ctr., 1986—92, Oakland Psychol. Clinic, P.C., 1991—92; owner and dir. V. Williams, PhD, MSW, ACSW, BCD, PC, Flint, Mich., 1992—. Developer dropout prevention program Flint Bd. Edn., 1986-98; Beecher Sch. Dist., 1998-2006. Bd. dirs. Boys & Girls Club. Mem. NASW, ACSW, NEA, Mich. Edn. Assn. Democrat. Office: Ste 110 225 E 5th St Flint MI 48502 Office Phone: 810-232-0018. E-mail: drvmw@yahoo.com.

WILLIAMS, WENDY, radio personality, writer; m. Kevin Hunter; 1 child. BA, Northeastern U., 1986. Intern Matt Siegel morning show, Kiss 108, Boston; radio personality WVIS, St. Croix, WOL-AM, Washington, DC, WQHT, NYC, WPLJ, WRKS, WQHT-FM, 1995—98, WUSL-FM, Phila., 1998—2001, WBLS-FM, NYC, 2001—, host The Wendy Williams Experience, 2003—; host Wendy Williams Is on Fire VH1, 2003—. Author: (memoir) Wendy's Got the Heat, 2003; co-author: The Wendy Williams Experience: Queen of Radio, 2004; author: (novels) Drama Was Her Middle Name, 2006. Office: WBLS-FM 3 Park Ave # 41 New York NY 10016*

WILLIAMS-BYRD, JULIE, electronics engineer; BS in Physics, Hampton Inst./U., 1984, MS in Physics, 1986. Contractor NASA Langley Rsch. Ctr., 1986—88, electro-optics engr., 1988, electronics engr., aerospace technologist. Mem. Langley Fed. Women's Program Com., 1993—96. Office: NASA Langley Rsch Ctr Bldg 1202 Rm 233 Hampton VA 23681-2199 Business E-Mail: j.a.williams-byrd@larc.nasa.gov.

WILLIAMS-DE SILVA, LISA ANNETTE, small business owner, adult nurse practitioner; d. Joice Renee and Charles Braden (Stepfather); m. Lionel De Silva, June 12, 2003. BS in Bus., Ariz. State U., 1988, BSN, 2000, MSN, Nurse Practitioner, 2003. Cert. Achievement Cynosure Laser, Cert. Proficiency, Aesthetic Laser Sys. Sciton Aesthetic. Pres. Medical-Legal Support Svcs., Inc., Scottsdale, Ariz., 1998—. Owner and nurse practitioner Ultra Smooth Skin, Inc., Scottsdale, 2003—. Faculty Wives Club scholar, Ariz. State U., 1998—2000, STAR Program scholar, 1998—2000. Mem.: Dermatology Nurses Assn., Internat. Acad. of Laser Medicine and Surgery (assoc.), Am. Assn. of Legal Nurse Consultants (assoc.), Am. Coll. of Phlebology (assoc.), Am. Acad. of Nurse Practitioners (assoc.), Am. Soc. of Laser Medicine and Surgery (assoc.). Avocations: hiking, travel, scuba diving. Office: Med-Legal Support Svcs Inc 14891 N Northside Scottsdale AZ 85260 Office Phone: 480-699-1244.

WILLIAMSEN, DANNYE SUE, publishing executive, writer; b. Memphis, Mar. 26, 1949; d. Roy Fauntly and Arliss Wyleen Goodroe; m. Jon Charles Beckum, Dec. 23, 1969 (div. Mar. 1972); m. John Dean Williamsen, Dec. 24, 1986. BA cum laude, U. Memphis, 1995. Adminstr. Security Investments, Inc., Memphis, 1972—75; nightclub owner, investor Memphis, 1976—78; internat. tech. analyst ContiCommodity, Inc., Memphis, 1977—80; owner, tech. analyst Commodity Cons., Inc., Memphis, 1981; project mgr. B&P Devel. Co., Austin, Tex., 1982—84; asst. to pres. Memphis C. of C., 1984—86; owner, dental technician Williamsen Dental Lab., Memphis and Prophetstown, Ill., 1986—; ptnr., editor Personal Edn. Network, Prophetstown, Ill., 2001—; owner Networx Pub., Prophetstown, 2002—05, Williamsen Pub., Smyrna, Ga., 2006—. Bd. dirs. Heartland Equine Assisted Therapeutic Ctr., Rock Falls, Ill., 2000—01; columnist Penmanship mag., 2005—; pub. Williamsen Pubs., 2006—. Author: Illusions, 1998, IT'S YOUR MOVE! Transform Your Dreams from Wishful Thinking to Reality, 2004; editor: Creative Living-an evolving approach to bus. life, 2001—, (e-newsletter) Metaphysical Minute, 2003—04; columnist: Penwomanship Mag, 2005; editor: (newsletter) MindSlap!; author: Metaphysical Minute-Philosophy on the Run, 2006. Mem. AAUW (pres. 1998-99), APA, NOW, NAFE, Am. Bus. Women's Assn., Assn. for Humanistic Psychology, Nat. Assn. Women Writers, Small Pubs. Assn. N.Am., Pubs. Mktg. Assn., Psi Chi, Chi Beta Phi. Avocations: reading, counseling. Office: Williamsen Publs PO Box 680924 Marietta GA 30068-0016 Office Phone: 770-438-0889. Business E-Mail: dannyew@williamsenpublications.com.

WILLIAMS EZELL, MARGARET (PEGGY), artist, educator; d. Ivor Williams and Hazel Brinker; children: Elizabeth Dancer, Amy Ezell, Victoria Lewis. Assoc. Degree, Moser Bus. Coll., Chgo., 1963; BA in Fine Art, Siena Heights U., Adrian, Mich., 2000; MA in Tchg./Fine Art, Olivet Coll., Mich., 2003. Asst. to the dean Northwestern U., Evanston, Ill., 1963—65; office mgr., designer Holland/Steed Archs., Deerfield, Ill., 1965—67; asst.to deisnger R. Buckminster Fuller So. Ill. U., Carbondale, 1965—69; cons. art edn. Title III-Art Edn., St. Louis, 1969—72; artist, writer, asst. editor Wendy's Food Corp., Chgo., 1976—79; historic preservationist St. Luke's Episcopal Ch., Kalamazoo, 1990—92; summer faculty Peninsula Art Sch., Fish Creek, Wis., 1992—; historic preservationist St. John's Anglican Ch., Southampton, Ont., 1993—98; instr. art and humanities Kalamazoo (Mich.) Valley C.C., 2000—. Exhbn., Mich. Women's Mus., 2000; contbr. articles to profl. jours. Sch. bd. mem. St. Augustine Elem. Sch., Kalamazoo, 1987—91; vol. coord. for academic testing for students with learning disabilities Hackett Cath. Ctrl. H.S., Kalamazoo; coord./spokesperson for stop pollution of open burning Colony Woods Assn., Kalamazoo, 2002—05; artist, muralist, renovator St. Augustine Elem. Sch., Kalamazoo, 1985—86. Mem.: Pendragons Calligraphy. Episcopalian/Anglican. Avocation: historic preservation. Office Phone: 269-488-4701 2240.

WILLIAMS GIFFORD, SUSAN, state legislator; m. Mark Williams Gifford. BA, Western Mich. U. Bd. of selectmen Wareham, 1999—2002; state rep. Mass. House, 2003—. Republican. Office: Rm 540 State House Boston MA 02133 Office Phone: 617-722-2090.

WILLIAMS MADDOX-BROWN, JANICE HELEN, nurse; b. Boston; d. Arthur Hamilton Wade and Edith Josephine (Weekes) Williams; m. Larry Maddox, May 21, 1977 (dec.); m. Richard Brown, Mar. 11, 2000. BS in Nursing, Boston U., 1957; MA, Atlanta U. Sch. Edn., 1971; MPH, Emory U., 1976; PhD, Union Inst., Cin., 1998. Staff nurse Beth Israel Hosp., Boston, 1958, N.Y. Hosp.-Cornell U. Med. Ctr., N.Y.C., 1958-59; ward supr. Jewish Meml. Hosp., Boston, 1959-61; staff and pvt. duty nurse Mass. Gen.Hosp., Boston, 1961-63; pub. health nurse Boston Health Dept., 1963-64; intravenous nurse Hughes Spalding Hosp., Atlanta, 1964-66; pub. health nurse Fulton County (Ga.) Health Dept., 1966-69; sr. tchr. Atlanta Southside Comprehensive Health Ctr., 1970-73, acting dir. edn., 1973-74, assoc. dir. clin. nursing, 1974-76; assoc. dir. mental health planning project So. Region Edn. Bd., Atlanta, 1976-78; nursing cons. Dept. Health and Human Svcs., Atlanta, 1978-81; head nurse VA Med. Ctr., Atlanta, 1982-85; br. mgr. Am. Home Health Care of Ga., Inc., Jonesboro, 1985-86; ind. contractor Med. Emergency Clinic-Grady Meml. Hosp., 1986—91; project dir. Morehouse Sch. Medicine Initiative, W.K. Kellogg Found., 1991-95; assoc. prof. Ctrl. Mich. U., 2000—01. Evening coord., instr. for innovative practical nursing program for health para-profl. Atlanta Area Tech Sch., 1971-83; admissions com. M. Pub. Health program Emory U. Sch. Medicine, 1979-91. Women's Day com. Ctrl. United Meth. Ch., Atlanta, Ben Hill United Meth. Ch Recipient spl. recognition Am. Cancer Soc., 1975.

WILLIAMSON, BRYNNE AMBER, paralegal; b. Glendale, Calif., July 25, 1972; d. John Park Williamson and Sharon Eileen Putterlik. Cert. in Paralegal Studies, San Joaquin Coll. Law, 2004. Cert.: (legal sec.); notary public Wash., notary signing agt. 2004. Asst. to editor recs. MacMillan/McGraw-Hill, N.Y.C., 1992—95; mgr. Sazarac Grove, Cambridge, Mass., 1995—96; bookkeeper Beckham Pl., Pasadena, Calif., 1996—97; data transcriber IRS, Fresno, Calif., 2002; paralegal Dietrich, Glasrud, Mallek & Aune, Fresno, Calif., 2004—05; tax preparer H&R Block, Calif. and Wash., 2004—05; legal sec. McNaul, Ebel, Nawrot & Helgren PLLC, Seattle, 2005—06, Graham & Dunn, PC, Seattle, 2006—. Mem.: Nat. Assn. Legal Secs. of Greater Seattle. Personal E-mail: brynnewilliamson@comcast.net.

WILLIAMSON, DIANA JEAN, nurse; b. Portland, Oreg., Dec. 21, 1956; d. Gerald George and Jean Elizabeth Musson; m. Bradley Alan Williamson, Dec. 12, 1981. Grad., Good Samaritan Hosp./Med. Ctr., 1977. RN, Oreg.; cert. psychiat. and mental health nurse. Staff nurse Western Lane Hosp., Florence, Oreg., 1977-79; asst. head nurse Providence Portland Med. Ctr., Portland, 1979-99, staff nurse, 1999—. Activist Oreg. Wildlife Fedn./Witness Against Lawless Logging, Portland and Rhododendron, Oreg., 1996. Mem. ANA, Am. Inst. Archaeology, Oreg. Nurses Assn. (unit rep.), Oreg. Wildlife Fedn., Defenders of Wildlife. Democrat. Avocations: reading, music, wine. Home: PO Box 239 Rhododendron OR 97049-0239 E-mail: Diana.Williamson@providence.org.

WILLIAMSON, DONNA MARIA, pastoral counselor; b. Oswego, N.Y., Feb. 26, 1944; d. Donald Carl and Helen Mary (Saber) Townsley; m. Patrick H. Williamson, July 7, 1962; children: Kevin Patrick, Michael Brian, Timothy Daniel. Grad. pub. schs., Fulton, N.Y. Cert. in clin. pastoral edn., pastoral care, Onondaga Pastoral Counseling Ctr.; weight loss counselor. Chaplain Loretto Geriatric Ctr., Syracuse, 1981-82; hosp. chaplain St. Rose of Lima Parish, Syracuse, 1982-84, pastoral counselor, 1984—. Weight loss counselor Nutri-System, Syracuse, 1988-91. Founding mem. Fulton Community Nursery Sch., 1967, Commn. on Women in Ch. and Society, Syracuse, 1984; mem. Alethea, Ctr. on Death and Dying, Inc., Syracuse, 1978, Syracuse Area Domestic Violence Coalition's Religious Task Force, 1994-2000; chair Syracuse Diocesan Commn. on Women in Ch. and Soc., 1997-98, 98-99. Mem. Charles F. Menninger Soc., Women Transcending Boundries. Roman Catholic. Avocations: flower arranging, vocalist. Office: St Rose of Lima Parish 409 S Main St North Syracuse NY 13212-2811 Fax: 315-458-1290. Personal E-mail: dmidilli1@verizon.net. E-mail: dmwilli1@verizon.net.

WILLIAMSON, DORIS, retired business education educator; b. Salt Lake City, July 1, 1937; d. Frank Farrow and Ruby Dean (Andersen) W. A.S., Coll. So. Utah, Cedar City, 1957; B.S. in Bus. Edn., Brigham Young U., 1959; M.S. in Bus. Edn., Utah State U., 1974. Cert. secondary tchr., Utah. Tchr., Salt Lake City Schs., 1959-64; tchr. typewriting Granite Sch. Dist., Salt Lake City, 1964-70; asst. prof. bus. edn. Idaho State U., 1973-76; assoc. prof. So. Utah State Coll., Cedar City, 1976—02, chmn. dept., 1985-2002, ret., 2002; pres. faculty senate, So. Utah State Coll., 1981-82; lectr. workshops in teaching methodology and secretarial sci. Trustee Utah Summer Games, 1985-1995; state advisor, 1985-91. EDPA fellow, 1971-73; recipient Leadership award Delta Pi Epsilon, 1976; Outstanding Tchr.-Bus. Edn. award Utah Bus. Edn. and Utah Vocat. Assns. 1979; Disting. Educator award So. Utah State Coll., 1983; named Advisor of Yr. So. Utah U., 1989, 90. Mem. Utah Bus. Edn. Assn., Utah Vocat. Edn. Assn., Nat. Bus. Edn. Assn., Am. Vocat. Assn., Bus. and Profl. Women Internat. (Woman of Achievement award Cedar City 1983), Utah Shakespeare Guild (pres. 1983-1991), Cedar City C. of C. (bd. dirs. 1981-83, pres. 1982-83, Outstanding Educator award 1985), Western Bus. Edn. Assn., Classroom Edn. of Bus. Assn., Delta Pi Epsilon, Delta Kappa Gamma, Phi Kappa Phi, Phi Beta Lambda (state advisor 1984-90). Mormon. Home: 17 Robbers Roost Ln Cedar City UT 84720-3524

WILLIAMSON, (EULAH) ELAINE, elementary school educator; b. N.Y.C., July 27, 1945; d. Eddie Lee and Eulah Genola (Hardie) Riley; m. George Leslie Williamson, Feb. 17, 1973 (div. 1999); children: George Todd, Michelle Elaine, Heather Dawn BA, Hampton U., 1967; MA in Urban Edn., Jersey City State Coll., 1998; postgrad., St. Peter's Coll., Jersey City. Cert. elem. tchr. K-8, supr., N.J. Tchr. elem. Englewood (N.J.) Pub. Schs., 1967-78, Irvington (N.J.) Pub. Schs., 1988-97; tchr. math. Hackensack (N.J.) Pub. Schs., 1997—. Mem. NEA, Nat. Mid. Sch. Assn., Nat. Coun. Tchrs. Math., Nat. Black Child Devel. Inst., N.J. Edn. Assn., Hackensack Edn. Assn., Profl. and Bus. Women NAACP, Phi Delta Kappa Democrat. Bapt. Avocations: photography, football, horseback riding. Office: Hackensack Mid Sch 360 Union St Hackensack NJ 07601-4394 also: 5/6 Sch 320 State St Hackensack NJ 07601 Office Phone: 201-646-8170. E-mail: blackie727@aol.com.

WILLIAMSON, MARILYN LAMMERT, literature educator, academic administrator; b. Chgo., Sept. 6, 1927; d. Raymond Ferdinand and Edith Louise (Eisenbies) Lammert; m. Robert M. Williamson, Oct. 28, 1950 (div. Apr. 1973); 1 child, Timothy L.; m. James H. McKay, Aug. 15, 1974. BA, Vassar Coll., 1949; MA, U. Wis., 1950; PhD, Duke U., 1956. Lectr. Duke U., Durham, NC, 1955-56, 58-59, N.C. State U., Raleigh, 1957-58, 61-62; asst. prof. Oakland U., Rochester, Mich., 1965-68, assoc. prof., 1968-72; prof. English Wayne State U., Detroit, 1972-90, Disting. prof. English, 1990-97, Disting. prof. emerita, 1997—, chmn. dept. English, 1972-74, 81-83, assoc. dean Coll. Liberal Arts, 1974-79, dir. women's studies, 1976-87, dep. provost Detroit, 1987-91, sr. v.p. for acad. affairs, provost, 1991-95, 98-200. Pres. Assn. Depts. English, 1976-77. Author: Infinite Variety, 1974, Patriarchy of Shakespeare's Comedies, 1986, British Women Writers 1650-1750, 1990, Tales of Two Dogs, 2005; editor: Renaissance Studies, 1972, Female Poets of Great Britain, 1981, Shakespeare Studies: Middle Comedies, 2003; contbr. articles to profl. jours. Pres. LWV, Rochester, 1963-65. Recipient Detroit Disting. Svc. award, 1986, Faculty Recognition award Bd. Govs., Wayne State U., 1991, 30 Yr. award Mich. Humanities Coun., 2004; Bunting Inst. fellow, 1969-70, AAUW fellow, 1982-83, J.N. Keal fellow, 1985-86. Mem.: MLA (exec. coun. 1977—80, mem. editl. bd. 1992—94), Fed. State Humanities Coun. (bd. dirs. 1994—2001, chair 1997—99), Mich. Coun. Humanities (bd. dirs. 1988—2001, chair 1991—93), Mich. Acad. (pres. 1978—79). Democrat. Home: 2275 Oakway Dr West Bloomfield MI 48324-1855

WILLIAMSON, MYRNA HENNRICH, retired career officer, lecturer, consultant; b. Gregory, S.D., Jan. 27, 1937; d. Walter Ferdinand and Alma Lillian Hennrich. BS with highest honors, S.D. State U., 1960; MA, U. Okla., 1973; grad., U.S. Army Command and Gen. Staff Coll., 1977, Nat. War Coll., 1980. Commd. 2d lt. U.S. Army, 1960, advanced through grades to brig. gen., 1985, bn. comdr. Mil. Police Sch. Fort McClellan, Ala., 1977-79, chief plans policy and service div. Jl 8th Army Korea, 1980-81, chief mgmt. support Office Dep. Chief Staff for Research, Devel. and Acquisition Washington, 1981-82, brigade comdr. Fort Benjamin Harrison, Ind., 1983-84, comdg. gen. 3d ROTC Region Fort Riley, Kans., 1984-87, dep. dir. mil. personnel mgmt. Washington, 1987-89, ret., 1989. U.S. del. com. on women in NATO Forces, 1986-89. Pres., bd. dirs. S.D. State U. Found., 1988—; bd. dirs. Women in Mil. Svc. to Am. Found.; mem. U.S. Olympic Com. on Sports for the Disabled; mem. bd. advisors The Army Distaff Found. Inc. Recipient Disting. Alumnus award S.D. State U., 1984. Mem. Assn. U.S. Army (trustee), United Svcs. Automobile Assn. (bd. dirs. 1988-98), The Internat. Alliance, Phi Kappa Phi.

WILLIAMSON, SANDRA KAYE, education educator; b. Greenville, Ohio, Aug. 28, 1951; d. James Sherman and Dortha Maria (Mikesell) Clapp; m. John Leslie Williamson, July 5, 1975; children: Bradley, Laura. BS, Ea. Ky. U., 1973, MEd, 1979; PhD, Kent State U., 1999. Cert. tchr., home economist. Educator West Clermont Schs., Amelia, Ohio, 1973—75, Fayette County Schs., Lexington, Ky., 1975—83, U. Akron, Ohio, 1990—93; tchg. fellow Kent State U., Ohio, 1993—95; instrl. technologist Neumann Coll., Aston, Pa., 1996—97; asst. prof. U. Del., Newark, 1997—99, Lincoln U., Pa., 2000—01, Wilmington Coll., Del., 2001—. Editor: Am. Assn. Family & Consumer Sci., Districts, 1990—93; author: Orientation to Professional Studies: Home Economics, 1992, Nutrition for Healthy Living, 1997, (on-line chat rooms) Treehouses, 2000. Chmn. PTA, Medina, Ohio, 1986—89; mem. AHEA reaccreditation U. Akron, Akron, 1992—93. Mem.: Am. Ednl. Rsch. Assn. (presenter Conf. 2005, 2006), Assn. Ednl. Comm. & Tech., Am. Assn. Family & Consumer Scis., Kappa Delta Pi. Avocations: computer technology, emerging technologies. Home: 126 Soltner Dr Kennett Square PA 19348-1445 Office: 320 DuPont Hwy New Castle DE 19720 E-mail: sandra.c.williamson@wilmcoll.edu.

WILLIAMS-PAISLEY, KIMBERLY, actress; b. Rye, NY, Sept. 14, 1972; d. Gurney and Linda W.; m. Brad Paisley, Mar. 15, 2003. Grad., Northwestern U. Actress Creative Artists Agy., Beverly Hills, Calif. Actor: (films) Father of the Bride, 1991, Secret Games, 1992, Indian Summer, 1993, Samuel Beckett Is Coming Soon, 1993, Coldblooded, 1995, Father of the Bride Part II, 1995, The War At Home, 1996, Safe House, 1998, Elephant Juice, 1999, Simpatico, 1999, Ten Tiny Love Stories, 2001, How to Go Out on a Date in Queens, 2006, How to Eat Fried Worms, 2006, (TV films) Stood Up!, 1990, Jake's Women, 1996, Follow the Stars Home, 2001, The Christmas Shoes, 2002, (TV series) Relativity, 1996-97, According to Jim, 2001-, (TV appearances) The MTV Movie Awards, 1992, Neil Simon;s Jake's Woman, 1996, The U.S. Olympic Open Golf Championship, 1986; stage appearances: The Last Night of Ballyhoo, 1997, The Vagina Monologues, Speed the Plow; actor, dir., prodr.: (films) Shade, 2006; actor, co-prodr.: (TV films) Lucky 7, 2003, Identity Theft: The Michelle Brown Story, 2004. Spokesperson Elizabeth Glazer Pediatric AIDS Found.; bd. dirs. Earth Comm. Office. Office: Creative Artists Agy 9830 Wilshire Blvd Beverly Hills CA 90212-1825*

WILLIAMS-PERRY, BRENDA LEE, pre-school educator; b. Colorado Springs, Colo., July 24, 1960; d. Arthur Lee and Rebecca Beard; m. Carl Eugene Perry, Jan. 11, 1991; 1 child, Kenneth Earl Williams Jr. AA in Child Devel., Almeda U., Boise, Idaho, 2006; BA in Early Childhood Edn., Almeda U., 2006; MA in Edn1. Adminstrn., Almeda U., Boise, 2006. Child Development Associate's Credential Coun. for Profl. Recognition, 2004, Directorship Certification Tex. Dept. of Protective & Regulatory Services, 2006, G-Tube Feeding Certification Gateway Child Devel. Ctr., 2004, Instructor CPR & First Aid Certified ARC, 2006, Infant Modules USAF, 2004. Dir. San Antonio Urban Ministries, 1999—2001; lead infant tchr. Jewish Cmty. Child Devel. Ctr., San Antonio, 2001—03; child devel. program technician Gateway Child Devel. Ctr., San Antonio, 2003—06; dir. St. Philip's Coll. Child Devel. Ctr., San Antonio, 2006—. Mem.: Nat. Black Child Devel. Inst. (assoc.). Home: 8021 W Military Dr Apt#807 San Antonio TX 78227-1861 Office: St Philip's College Child Dev Center 2207 Wyoming St San Antonio TX 78203 Office Phone: 210-271-7033. Personal E-mail: brendawilliamsperry@msn.com. E-mail: bwilliam@accd.edu.

WILLIAMS-THOMAS, ELIZABETH A., financial planner, consultant; b. San Francisco, Jan. 16, 1948; d. John and Myrtle Mary (Thierry) W.; children: Brian, Jonathan. Degree, U. Calif., 1979, MBA. Manpower coord., fed. programs U.S. Govt., San Francisco; patient svc. rep. Health Care Svc., Oakland, Calif.; ins. and real estate cons.; pres. Investments Unlimited, Oakland, EWJ & Assocs. Mktg. Firm; planning commr. City of Pitts.; CEO Ultimate Vacations Inc. Human rels. commr. Contra Costa County. Recipient Pub. Speaking award; European Investment fellow. Mem. AAUW, NAFE, NAACP, Nat. Real Estate Owners Assn., Nat. Notary Assn., Order Ea. Star, Heroines Jericho, Daus. Isis, Soroptimist Inc., Toastmistress Club, Beta Phi Sigma. Home: PO Box 523 Pittsburg CA 94565-0052

WILLIAMS-WENNELL, KATHI, human resources specialist; b. Danville, Pa., Sept. 22, 1955; d. Raymond Gerald and Julia Dolores (Higgins) Williams; m. Mark Kevin Wennell, Apr. 3, 1982; children: Ryan Christopher Wennell, Lauren Ashley Wennell. BA, Immaculata Coll., 1977; MEd, Pa. State U., 1978. Cert. rehab. counselor Pa., profl. human resources. From project dir. to coord. devel. activities Cmty. Interactions, Blue Bell, Pa., 1978-83; from mgmt. trainee to coord. coll. recruiting and rels. Meridian Bancorp, Inc., Reading, Pa., 1983-86, mgmt. recruiter, 1986-88, compensation analyst, 1989-93, recruiter, spl. projects, 1993-96; cons. Chet Mosteller & Assocs., Reading, Pa., 1996—. Cons. Norristown (Pa.) Life Ctr., 1981; instr. Immaculata (Pa.) Coll., 1981—83, Alvernia Coll., Reading, 1988—89. Meridian campaign coord. United Way Berks County, Reading, 1985. Named Recruiter of the Yr., LaSalle U., Phila., 1986; recipient Excellence in Programming award, Nat. Assn. Bank Women, Pa., 1986. Mem.: Soc. Human Resources Mgmt. Republican. Roman Catholic. Avocations: walking, golf, tennis, piano, reading. Home: 69 S Hampton Dr Wyomissing PA 19610-3108 Office Phone: 610-779-3870. Personal E-mail: kwennell@aol.com.

WILLIAMS-WETENHALL, TANYA DAWN, art appraiser, consultant; b. Spokane, Wash., June 17, 1967; d. Stanley T. and Tessa M.D. Williams; m. John Wetenhall. AAS, Fashion Inst. Tech., N.Y.C., 1987; BA, NYU, 1989. Cert. in appraisal studies, fine and decorative arts NYU, 2002, registered notary public Fla., 2003. Lang. specialist-consular asst. Immigration & Naturalization Svc. - U.S. Embassy, Moscow, 1992—93, overseas immigration specialist Rome, 1993—99; propr. Tanya Williams Fine Art Appraisals, Sarasota, Fla., 2002—; pres. Cultural Tours Internat. Inc., 2005—. Lectr. in field. Mem.: Appraisers Assn. Am., Inc. Avocations: tennis, travel, performing arts, internat. rels., vol. humane soc. Office: Tanya Williams Fine Art Appraisals PO Box 2275 Sarasota FL 34230 Office Phone: 941-355-8456. Business E-Mail: info@artappraisals.org.

WILLIFORD, SANDRA SIMMONS, music educator; b. Anderson, S.C., Nov. 6, 1972; d. Rocshell Simmons II; m. William Lamont Williford, June 22, 2006; children: Paris Monet, A'Lonzo Nygel. BA in Music, Ch., Charleston So. U., S.C., 1995; B in Music Edn., Anderson U., S.C., 1998; MEd, So. Wesleyan U., Central, S.C., 2003. Cert. tchr. music S.C. Tchr. gen. music, choir dir. Parker Acad., Greenville, SC, 1998—99; tchr. gen. music, chorus Hughes Acad., Greenville, 1999—2000; tchr. gen. music, instr. performing arts, choir dir., coach step team Varennes Elem. Sch., Anderson, 2000—. Chairperson Parents and the Cmty. Varennes Elem. Sch., 2005—06. Vol. Adopt-A-Hwy., Anderson, 2004—. Recipient Golden Apple, Anderson Sch. Dist. #5, 2005—06; grantee, Donors Choose Grants, 2005—06. Mem.: Zeta Phi Beta. Avocations: singing, reading, movies. Home: 2504 McGaha Dr Anderson SC 29626 Office: Varennes Elem Sch 1820 Hwy 29 S Anderson SC 29626 Office Phone: 864-260-5215. E-mail: sandrawilliford@andersons.net.

WILLIFORD, VELMA JEAN, minister; b. Anderson, S.C., May 15, 1947; d. Eugene and Zora Etrulia Hagood; m. Claude Riley Williford, Apr. 14, 1965; children: Claude Rodriques, Maximo Jermaine, William Lamont. DMin, Christian Life Sch. Theology, Columbus, Ga., 1994—2004. Pres. Tabernacle of Faith Min., Inc., Anderson, SC, 1991—2005. Mem.: Gold Reagents. Avocations: reading, cooking, camping. Office: Gospel Tabernacle Faith Ch 1613 S Main St Anderson SC 29624 Office Phone: 864-261-6107. Business E-Mail: gospeltfc@bellsouth.com.

WILLIG, BARBARA ADELE, music educator; b. Phila., Apr. 24, 1941; d. Paul and Jeanne Willig; 1 child, Julie Rose Braman. B Music Edn., Temple U., 1963, M Music Edn., 1976, supervision cert., 1982. Cert. music, vocal tchr., supr. Pa. Coord. music theater, accompanist Abington Mus. Theatre, Pa., 1984—87; co-dir. music theater workshop Bucks County CC, Richboro, Pa., 1990—98; mentor tchr. for student tchrs. Phila. Sch Dist.; supr. student tchrs. Drexel U., Phila.; cons., artist-in-residence Phila. Sch. Dist. Presenter, writer grants in field; leader arts groups, presenter Phila. Sch. Dist., 1988—96; devel. presch. music workshops Settlement Music Sch. Author curriculum materials; composer, condr.: sabbath svc. record and performance Chants for Peace, 1972; co-dir.: Pa. premier performance Alice in Wonderland. Vol. various election campaigns, 1990—; mem., sec., v.p. B'Nai B'Rith Educators Unit, Phila., 1992—. Recipient Svc. to Cmty. award, B'Nai B'Rith Educators Unit, 1993, Tchr. of Excellence award, Chapel of Four Chaplains. Mem.: LWV, Am. Choral Dirs. Assn., Nat. Orff Assn., Pa. Music Educators Assn., Music Educators Nat. Conf., Temple U. Boyer Coll. Music Alumni Assn. (pres.-elect 2005), Phi Delta Kappa. Avocations: fitness, tai chi, theater, travel, languages. Home: 813 Roslyn Ave Glenside PA 19038

WILLMAN, PAULINE, retired reporter, foundation administrator; b. Albany County, N.Y., Jan. 11, 1926; d. Harrison and Alta Allen (Hallenbeck) Salisbury; m. Raymond Willman, Jan. 11, 1947 (div. Oct. 1951). Grad., Albany Stenotype Secretarial, 1941-42. Cert. shorthand reporter. Staff reporter Empire Stenographers, Albany, 1942-46; exec. sec. Res. Officers Assn., Dept. of N.Y., Albany, 1947-49; ofcl. reporter N.Y. State Supreme Ct./Third Jud. Dist., Albany, 1958-64; ofcl. stenographer N.Y. State Senate, Albany, 1979-98; profl. shorthand reporter self employed, Albany, NY, 1949—2006; ret., 2006. Mem. Cert. Shorthand Reporter Licensure Bd., Albany, 1992-2004; specialized in reporting tech. engring. rev. procs. involving water supply and waste water treatment facilities throughout N.Y. state, 1952-94; mem. edn. and small bus. coms. Bus. Coun. N.Y. State, 1985-2000. Contbr. articles to profl. jours. Mem. RNSC Inner Circle, Washington, 1980-97; mem. Senatorial Bus. Adv. Bd., Washington, 1982-86. Recipient resolution and commendation for svc. N.Y. State Senate, 1998. Mem. Am. Water Works ASsn. (life), Nat. Ct. Reporters Assn., Kiwanis Internat. (club pres. 1997-99, award of excellence 1999). Republican. Mem. Dutch Reformed Ch. Avocations: golf, gardening, exercise, reading, music.

WILLINGER, RHONDA ZWERN, optometrist; b. Bklyn., Apr. 26, 1962; d. Jerome Max and Jeanette (Zwern) Willinger; m. Wayne Ken Chan, Aug. 26, 1990; children: Jamie S. Chan, Jared Max. BS, U. Miami, 1983; OD with honors, New Eng. Coll. Optometry, 1987. Resident in optometry VA Med. Ctr., Bedford, Mass., 1987-88; pvt. practice, Burlington, Mass., 1988-89; pvt. practice specializing in contact lenses Framingham, Mass., 1989—. Clin. investigator for contact lens companies. Scholar New Coll., U. South Fla., 1979-81; honors scholarship U. Miami, 1981-83. Mem. Am. Optometric Assn. (contact lens sect.), Mass. Soc. Optometrists. Avocation: violin. Home: 228 Lowell Ave Newton MA 02460-1830 Office: 659 Worcester Rd Framingham MA 01701-5204 Office Phone: 508-872-2722. E-mail: studio.optics@verizon.net.

WILLINGHAM, EMAGENE EMANUEL, social worker; BA in Psychology and Sociology, Jacksonville U., 1959; MSW, U. N.C., 1984; postgrad., UNC-Duke Psychoanalytic Edn. Program. Diplomate in clin. social work. Personnel asst. Jacksonville (Fla.) Paper Co., 1959-60; social worker Dept. Social Svc., Raleigh, N.C., 1984-86, Wake County Alcohol Treatment Ctr., Raleigh, N.C., 1986-88; psychotherapist pvt. practice, Chapel Hill, N.C., 1989—. Mem. NASW, Am. Psychoanalytic Assn., N.C. Psychoanalytic Soc., N.C. Psychoanalytic Found. Office: 727 Eastowne Dr Ste 300A Chapel Hill NC 27514-2209 Office Phone: 919-493-4815.

WILLINGHAM, JANICE ANN, secondary school educator; b. Frankfurt, Germany, Aug. 15, 1949; children: Leslie Ann Lawrence, Kristi Lynn Phipps. MA in Sci. Edn., U. Ctrl. Okla., Edmond, 1989. Tchr. Westmoore H.S., Oklahoma City, 1989—, AP chemistry tchr./dept. chair. Named Outstanding Sci. Tchr., Sigma Xi chpt. from U. of Ctrl. Okla., 1004, Sigma Xi chpt. of U. of Okla., 2000; recipient AP Tchr. of the Yr. for State of Okla., Siemens Award, 2006. Office Phone: 405-691-800.

WILLINGHAM, JEANNE MAGGART, performing arts educator, performing company executive; b. Fresno, Calif., May 8, 1923; d. Harold F. and Gladys (Ellis) Maggart. Student, Tex. Woman's U., 1942; student profl. dancing schs. worldwide. Tchr. dance Beaux Arts Dance Studio, Pampa, Tex., 1948—; artistic dir. Pampa Civic Ballet, 1972—. Mem. Tex. Arts and Humanities Coun. Mem. Tex. Arts Alliance, Pampa C. of C. (fine arts com.), Pampa Fine Arts Assn. Office: Pampa Civic Ballet Beaux Arts Dance Studio 315 N Nelson St Pampa TX 79065-6013 Office Phone: 806-669-6361.

WILLINGHAM, MARY MAXINE, fashion retailer; b. Childress, Tex., Sept. 12, 1928; d. Charles Bryan and Mary (Bohannon) McCollum; m. Welborn Kiefer Willingham, Aug. 14, 1950; children: Sharon, Douglas, Sheila. BA, Tex. Tech U., 1949. Interviewer Univ. Placement Svc., Tex. Tech U., Lubbock, 1964-69; owner, mgr. buyer Maxine's Accent, Lubbock, 1969—. Speaker in field. Leader Campfire Girls, Lubbock, 1964-65; sec. Cmty. Theatre, Lubbock, 1962-64. Recipient Golden Sun award Dallas Market, 1985, Woman of Excellence award in Bus., YWCA, 2001; named Outstanding Mcht., Fashion Retailer Mag., 1971, also Outstanding Retailer. Mem. Ranch and Heritage Ctr.

WILLIS, ANNA L., commissioner; b. Winchester, Ky., Jan. 11, 1941; d. Walter Jerome and Mary Frances Newell; m. Norman Lee Willis, Mar. 5, 1969; children: Mia Teresa Pugh, Angela Lee. BA in Sociology, Ky. State U., 1964; postgrad., U. Ill., 1975, cert. gerontology, 1996; MS in Mgmt., Nat. Louis U., 1981. Dir. social svcs. Columbus Hosp., Chgo., 1974-78; dir. Evanston (Ill.) Twp. Gen. Assistance, 1978-89; dep. commr. Chgo. Dept. on Aging, 1990-98, commr., 1998—. Adv. coun., bd. mem. Northwestern U. Ctr. for Gerontology, 1998—; created frozen meals program for seniors; created and implemented depts. response to city wide emergency. Mem. Ill. Alliance for Aging, Unity Fin. Network (pres. 1998), Chgo. Fund on Aging (bd. dirs. 1998), Zonta Internat. Democrat. Avocation: reading. Office: Chgo Dept on Aging 30 N Lasalle St Ste 2320 Chicago IL 60602-2504 Fax: 312-742-0699.

WILLIS, BEVERLY ANN, architect; d. Ralph William and Margaret Amanda (Porter) W. BFA, U. Hawaii, 1954; PhD in Fine Arts (hon.), Mt. Holyoke Coll., 1983. Registered architect, Calif. Prin. Willis Atelier, Honolulu, 1954-58, Willis & Assocs., Inc., San Francisco, 1958-88. Pres. Beverly Willis Architecture Found., 2002—; pres., dir. Architecture Rsch. Inst., Inc., NYC, 1993—2005; co-chair Rebuild Downtown Our Town Coalition, 2002; prof. Internat. Women's U., Kassel, Germany, 2000. Author: Invisible Images: The Silent Language of Architecture, 1997; contbg. author: City and Gender-International Discourse on Gender, Urbanism and Architecture, 2003, Creating Sustainable Urban Environments: Future Forms and Design for Sustainable Cities, 2005; prin. works include Union St. Stores (merit award San Francisco AIA, award of distinction State of Calif.), Nob Hill Cts. (merit award AIA), 1970, Margaret Hayward Park (grand and merit awards Pacific Coast Bldg. Con., Honor award Design Internat.), 1983, San Francisco Ballet Bldg., 1984, Manhattan Village Acad. H.S., N.Y.C., 1995; contbr. articles to profl. jours., chpts. to books. Founding trustee Nat. Bldg. Mus., Washington, 1976—, mem. bd. infrastructure and the constructed environ., 1971-79, chair fed. facility coun., 1976-79; pres. Beverly Willis Arch. Found., NYC, 2002-. Recipient Phoebe Hearst Gold Medal award, 1969. Fellow AIA (v.p. Calif. coun. 1979, pres. 1980); mem. Achievement Rewards for Coll. Scientists, Internat. Women's Forum, Lambda Alpha (pres. San Francisco chpt. 1981-82), Villa Taverna and Nat. Arts Club. Avocations: poetry, sketching, tennis. Office Phone: 212-577-1200. Business E-Mail: bevwillis@architect.org.

WILLIS, BURDENA, director; MA, Webster U., St. Louis; BA, U. Mo., St. Louis. Lifetime cert. tchr. Dept. Elem./Secondary Edn., Mo. Dist. pres. profl. devel. com. University City Sch., St. Louis; pres. profl. devel. com. University City H.S., chairperson English dept., chairperson career edn. com.; adj. prof. English St. Louis U.

WILLIS, CHERYL MARY, art educator; b. New Orleans, La., Jan. 8, 1947; d. Joseph Frank and Lena Marino Willis. BS, Our Lady of Holy Cross Coll., New Orleans, La., 1969; BFA, Univ. Wis., Milw., 1986; MA, Cardinal Stritch Univ., Milw., 1975; EdD, Temple Univ., Phila., 1991. Cert. Elem. Edn. Wis., La., elem. edn. Wash., Reading tchr., Dance. Tchr. Cath. Schs. Dioceses, Lafayette, La., 1969—70; owner, dir. The Dance Studio, Tripoli, Libya, 1971—72; tchr. Am. Oil Cos. Sch., Tripoli, 1971—72, Cath. Schs. Archdioceses, New Orleans, 1972—73; reading specialist Hartford Common Schs., Wis., 1974—76, West Bend Joint Sch. Dist., Wis., 1976—81; dance tchr. Allegro Sch. Dance and Gymnastics, West Allis, Wis., 1977—78; owner, dir. Melody in Motion Sch. Dance, West Bend, 1978—86; reading specialist Interboro Sch. Dist., Prospect Park, Pa., 1987—88; rhythm tap tchr. Bowman Sch. Dance, Cherry Hill, NJ, 1988—91; instr. Upper Darby Performing Arts Ctr., Pa., 1988—91; creative dance specialist Vancouver Sch. Dist., Wash., 1992—2006. Presenter and cons. in field; instr. dance dept. Bryn Mawr Coll., Pa., 1988; instr. acad. skills program Camden County Coll., Blackwood, NJ, 1991—92; instr. dance program Swarthmore Coll., Pa., 1991—92; instr. dance dept. Temple U., Phila., 1989—92; instr. edn. dept. Wash. State U., Vancouver, 1995—96. Author: Dance Education: Tips from the Trenches, 2002; contbr. chapters to books, articles to profl. jours. Named Dance Educator of Yr., Dance Educators' Assn. Wash., 1999, Nat. Dance Educator of Yr., Nat. Dance Assn., Am. Alliance Health, Phys. Edn., Recreation and Dance, 2000; Dance Historian fellow, Pa. Coun. on the Arts, 1992. Avocations: hiking, bicycling, kayaking, gardening, video production. Personal E-mail: cherylwillis@earthlink.net.

WILLIS, CONNIE (CONSTANCE E. WILLIS), writer; b. Denver, Dec. 31, 1945; m. Courtney Willis; 1 child. Tchr. elem. and jr. H.S., Branford, Conn., 1967-69. Author: (short stories) Letter from the Clearys, 1982 (Nebula award, 1982, Hugo award, 1983), Even the Queen, 1992 (Nebula award, 1992, Hugo award, 1993), Death on the Nile, 1993 (Hugo award, 1994), The Soul Selects Her Own Society, 1996 (Hugo award, 1997), (novels) Water Witch, 1982, Fire Watch, 1985 (Nebula award, 1982, Hugo award, 1983), Lincoln's Dreams, 1987 (John W. Campbell Meml. award), Doomsday Book, 1992 (Nebula award, 1992, Hugo award, 1993), Impossible Things, 1993, Unchartered Territory, 1994, Uncharted Territory, 1994, Remake, 1995, Bellwether, 1996, To Say Nothing of the Dog, 1997 (Hugo award, 1999), Miracle, 1999, Promised Land, 1997, Miracle and other Christmas Stories, 1999, Passage, 2001 (Locus award, Hugo award nominee, 2002, Nebula award nominee, 2002), Inside Job, 2005, (novellas) The Last of the Winnebagos, 1989 (Nebula award, 1988, Hugo award, 1989), The Winds of Marble Arch, 2000 (Hugo best novella nominee, 2000). Named Best Sci. Fiction/Fantasy Author of Nineties Locus Mag. Address: 1716 13th Ave Greeley CO 80631-5418 E-mail: conniewillis@juno.com.

WILLIS, DAWN LOUISE, legal assistant, small business owner; b. Johnstown, Pa., Sept. 11, 1959; d. Kenneth William and Dawn Louise (Joseph) Hagins; m. Marc Anthony Ross, Nov. 30, 1984 (div.); m. Jerry Wayne Willis, Dec. 16, 1989 (div.). Grad. high sch., Sacramento, Calif. Legal sec. Wilcoxen & Callahan, Sacramento, 1979-87, paralegal, 1987-88; legal adminstr. Law Office Jack Vetter, 1989-99; owner, mgr. Your Girl Friday Secretarial and Legal Support Svcs., 1991—; legal asst. Foley & Lardner, 1999-2001; case mgr. Larry Lockshin, Esq. Law Corp., 2001—02; legal asst. Hunter, Richey, Di Benedetto & Eisenbeis, 2002—03; legal sec. Downey Brand LLP, 2003—. Vol ARC, 1985, Spec Olympics, 1997—. Mem.: Sacramento Legal Secys Asn (pres. 2004—05, parliamentarian 2005—). Democrat. Avocations: water sports, camping, reading, cooking. Office: Downey Brand LLP 555 Capitol Mall Sacramento CA 95814 Personal E-mail: doe9121@cwnet.com.

WILLIS, ELEANOR LAWSON, not-for-profit development director; b. Nashville, Sept. 15, 1936; d. Harry Alfred Jr. and Helen Russell Lawson; m. Alvis Rux Rochelle, Aug. 25, 1956 (div. Mar. 1961); m. William Reese Willis Jr., Mar. 7, 1964 (div. June 1994); children: Alfred Russell Willis, William Reese III, Brent Lawson. BA cum laude, Vanderbilt U., 1957. Host children's syndicated TV show Sta. WSIX-TV, Nashville, 1961-64; tchr. head start program Metro Pub. Sch., Nashville, 1965-67; co-investigator cognitive edn. curriculum project Peabody Coll., Nashville, 1979-81; dir., founder Heads Up Child Devel. Ctr., Inc., Nashville, 1973-87; dir. devel. Vanderbilt Inst. Pub. Policy Studies Vanderbilt U., Nashville, 1988—. Bd. dirs. Vanderbilt Child Devel. Ctr. Author: (with others) I Really Like Myself, 1973, I Wonder Where I Came From, 1973. Pres. Nashville Bar Aux., 1967-68, Nashville Symphony Guild, 1984-85, W.O. Smith Nashville Cmty. Music Sch., 1987-03; founder, bd. dirs. Rochelle Ctr., Nashville, 1968-03; vice-chmn. Century III Com., Nashville, 1978-80; Homecoming 1986 Steering Com., Nashville, 1985-86; dir. Tenn. Vols. for Gore for Pres. Campaign, Nashville, 1987-88; mem. Cheekwood Fine Arts Ctr., Nashville City Ballet, Nashville Symphony Assn., Dem. Women of Davidson County; apptd. Metro Arts Commn., 1992, Metro Ednl. Access Corp.; exec. dir. Friends of Warner Park, 1994; leadership coun. John F. Kennedy Ctr., 1995—; founder Nashville Tree Found.; bd. dirs. Cumberland Region Tomorrow, 2001. Recipient Leadership Nashville award, 1982; Seven Leading Ladies award Nashville Mag., 1984; Eleanor Willis Day proclaimed by City of Nashville, 1987; named to Acad. for Women of Achievement, 2003. Mem. Exch. Club of Nashville (pres. 2005-2006), Vanderbilt Alumni Assn. Presbyterian. Avocations: reading, camping, running. Office: 50 Vaughn Rd Nashville TN 37221-3706 Office Phone: 615-370-8053. E-mail: eleanor.willis@nashville.gov.

WILLIS, EMMA K., mathematics educator; d. Ronald D. and Dealie M. Dodds; m. Charles D. Willis, Aug. 12, 1978; children: Amanda M., Molly C. MA in Edn., Ball State U., Muncie, Ind., 1982. Math. tchr. Owen County Sch. Corp., Owenton, Ky., 1978—80, New Castle Cmty. Sch. Corp., Ind., 1980—.

WILLIS, HEATHER NICOLE, science educator; b. Tenn., Dec. 1976; d. Danny and Teresa Puryear; m. Jason Willis. BS in Middle Grades Edn. first honor grad., Shorter Coll., Rome, Ga., 1999; M in Middle Grades Edn., Berry Coll., Rome, Ga., 2003. Tchr. 7th grade Coosa Mid. Sch., Ga., 1999—2003; tchr. sci. K-5 Cave Spring Elem. Sch., Ga., 2003—. Named Tchr. of Yr. for Cave Spring Elem., Floyd County Sch. System, 2006, Tchr. of Yr. for Floyd County Sch. System, 2006. Mem.: Nat. Sci. Tchrs. Assn., Assn. Supervsion and Curriculum Devel., Profl. Assn. Ga. Educators. Baptist. Home: 115 Melson Rd Cave Spring GA 30124 Office: Cave Spring Elem Sch 13 Rome St Cave Spring GA 30124 Business E-Mail: hwillis@floydbre.net.

WILLIS, JAKIE ARLETA, secondary school educator; b. Richland, Ga. d. Jacob C.W. and Ardella (Alford) Williams; m. Frank A. Willis (dec.); children: Beverly Donita, Reginald Tyronne. BS, Albany State Coll., 1951; MA, NYU, 1957. Cert. elem. edn. Tchr. Stewart County, Lumpkin, Ga., 1951-63; tchr. Stratford Bd. Edn., Stratford, Conn., 1963-92; interim prin. Honeyspot Ho., Stratford Acad.; ret., 1992—. Named Outstanding Tchr. Am., Fuller & Dees, Washington, 1975. Mem. Assn. for Supervision and Curriculum Devel., NEA (life), Stratford Edn. Assn. (sec. 1965-67, pres. 1980-81), Conn. Edn. Assn. (life), Alpha Kappa Alpha (pres. Bridgeport, Conn. chpt. 1985-89, Albany chptr. 1998-2000), Semper Fidelis Club, Inc. (sec. 1996—), Richland H&I Sch. Alumni Assn., Inc. (pres. 1995—), Alpha Kappa Alpha (life). Democrat. Methodist. Home: PO Box 71224 Albany GA 31708-1224

WILLIS, JUDY ANN, lawyer; b. Hartford, Conn., July 7, 1949; d. Durward Joseph and Angeline Raphael (Riccardo) Willis. BA, Ctrl. Conn. State U., 1971; postgrad., U. Conn. Law Sch., 1976—77; JD, Boston Coll., 1979. Bar: Mass. 1979, U.S. Dist. Ct. Mass. 1980, Calif. 1990. Sr. atty. H.P. Hood Inc., Charleston, Mass., 1979-83; v.p. law Parker Bros., Beverly, Mass., 1983-89; sr. v.p. bus. affairs Mattel, Inc., El Segundo, Calif., 1989—. Office: Mattel Inc M1-0848 333 Continental Blvd El Segundo CA 90245-5012 E-mail: judy.willis@Mattel.com.

WILLIS, LANI TYLER, elementary school educator; b. Clinton, Iowa, Oct. 5, 1940; d. Raymond Howes and Mary L. (Platt) Tyler; m. Robert J. Willis, Aug. 9, 1964; children: Eric, Barbara, James. BA, Cornell Coll., 1963; MA, U. Iowa, 1979. Tchr., Spanish/stringed instrument instr. Clinton Community Schs., 1963-64; tchr., Spanish Ames (Iowa) Schs., 1964-65; elem. tchr. Camanche (Iowa) Community Schs., 1966-69, 1976-93, Muscatine (Iowa) Cmty. Schs., 1995—2002. Methodist. Avocations: music, violin, gardening, choir director.

WILLIS, RUTH, freelance/self-employed theater director, actress; b. Toledo, Nov. 7, 1932; d. Thomas LeRoy and Ruth Caroline (Ehmann) Ramsey; m. Charles Perrin Willis, Nov. 14, 1956; children: David, Laura. BE cum laude, U. Toledo, 1954. Grade sch. tchr. Toledo Pub. Schs., 1954—61; acting tchr. Cin. Children's Home, 1958—59, Contemporary Arts Mus., Houston, 1972, Jewish Cmty. Ctr., 1969—72; dir. Exptl. Wing Country Playhouse, 1968—72; mem. Actor's Studio Ariz. State U., Phoenix, 1980—81; dir. Plays for Living Family and Children's Svcs., Pitts., 1984—87; adult acting tchr. Point Park Coll. Conservatory, 1987—2001; artistic dir. Open Stage Theatre, 1991—. Dir.: (over 100 major prodns.); actor: (plays) The Women (named Best Actress, Assn. Cmty. Theatres, Cin.), The Sleeping Prince (named Best Actress, Country Playhouse, Houston), Sweet Bird of Youth (named Best Actress, Stagebrush Theatre, Scottsdale, Ariz.); dir.: Candida (named Best Dir.), Lucia Mad (Best Top Ten Evenings of Theatre, Pitts. Gazette, 1997). Gen. bd. mem. Mariemont Players, Cin., 1958—60, Phoenix Children's Theatre, 1978—81; exec. bd. mem., sec. Phoenix Theatre, 1978—79, exec. bd. mem., v.p., 1980—81; founder Open Stage Theatre, Pitts., 1991. Recipient Svc. award, Phoenix Little Theatre Bd. Dirs., 1981. Mem.: Charlevoix Garden Club, Nat. Soc. Arts and Letters, Pi Epsilon Delta. Avocations: piano, painting, yoga, gardening, decorating.

WILLIS, SELENE LOWE, electrical engineer, application developer, consultant, information technology manager; b. Birmingham, Ala., Mar. 4, 1958; d. Lewis Russell and Bernice (Wilson) Lowe; m. André Maurice Willis, June 12, 1987. BSEE, Tuskegee U., Ala., 1980; postgrad., UCLA, 1993—94, U. So. Calif., 1996, UCLA, 1999. Component engr. Hughes Aircraft Corp., El Segundo, Calif., 1980—82; reliability and lead engr. Aero Jet Electro Sys. Corp., Azusa, Calif., 1982—84; sr. component engr. Rockwell Internat. Corp., Anaheim, Calif., 1984, Gen. Data Comm. Corp., Danbury, Conn., 1984—85; design engr. Lockheed Missile and Space Co., Sunnyvale, Calif., 1985—86; mgr. property Penmar Mgmt. Co., L.A., 1987—88; aircraft mechanic McDonnell Douglas Corp., Long Beach, Calif., 1989—93; unix sys. adminstrn. Santa Cruz Ops., Calif., 1994; bus. ops. mgr., cons. New Start, Santa Monica, Calif., 1995; software developer Nat. Advancement Corp., Calif., 1996; entrepreneur Datatronics, Calif., 1996—; exec. v.p., owner L.A. Network Engr. Jet Propulsion Lab., 1996—2000; software engr., network engr., application engr., lead engr. Jet Propulsion Lab, Pasadena, Calif., 1996—2000, project mgr., 1999—2000, lead UNIX engr. L.A., 1998—2000; mgmt. sys. engr. Tech. Jet Propulsion Lab., Pasadena, 1998—2000, mgr. project element, 1999—; cons., sr. project mgr. Amgen, Thousand Oaks, Calif., 1999—2000, sr. sys. engr., 2000—; mgr. project So. Calif. Edison, 2002—03, mgr., settlements, 2003—, mgr. energy supply and mgmt., 2003—05, mgr. structured contracts, 2005—. Cons., software designer Kern and Wooley, atty., Westwood, Calif., 1995; software developer Nat. Advancement Corp., Santa Ana, Calif., 1995—. Vol. Mercy Hosp. and Children's Hosp., Birmingham, Ala. 1972-74; mrm. L.A. Gospel Messengers, 1982-84, West Angeles Ch. of God and Christ, L.A., 1990; cons., mgr. bus. ops. New Start, Santa Monica (Calif.) Bay Area Drug Abuse Coun., 1995; vol. Pres. Clinton's Going-To-Coll. Program through Univ. Calif. at Los Angles, 1997—; chair Univ. Calif. at Los Angles Transfer Coll. Scholarship Program, 1998-99. Scholar Bell Lab., 1976-80, Univ. Calif. at Los Angles, 1994, Gem Award, UTA, 1999, Outstanding Group Award, JPL, 1999. Mem. IEEE, ASME, Aerospace and Aircraft Engr., So. Calif. Profl. Engring. Assn., Tuskegee U. Alumni Assn., UCLA Alumni Assn. (scholarship and adv. com.), Eta Kappa Nu, Christian Ch. Avocations: piano, computers, softball, real estate.

WILLISCROFT-BARCUS, BEVERLY RUTH, retired lawyer; b. Conrad, Mont., Feb. 24, 1945; d. Paul A. and Gladys L. (Buck) W.; m. Kent J. Barcus, Oct. 1984. BA in Music, So. Calif. Coll., 1967; JD, John F. Kennedy U., 1977. Bar: Calif. 1977. Elem. tchr., Sunnyvale, Calif., 1968-72; legal sec., legal asst. various law firms, 1972-77; assoc. Neil D. Reid, Inc., San Francisco, 1977-79; sole practice Concord, Calif., 1979—2004. Exam. grader Calif. Bar, 1979-2001; real estate broker, 1980-88; tchr. real estate King Coll., Concord, 1979-80; judge pro-tem Mcpl. Ct., 1981-93; mem. Stage Right Drama Group, Concord, Calif., 1999—; lectr. in adoption law. Co-author: Adoption Law in California, Adoption Practice, Procedure and Pitfalls in California; lectr. in field. Bd. dirs. Contra Costa Musical Theatre, Inc., 1978-82, v.p. adminstrn., 1980-81, v.p. prodn., 1981-82; mem. community devel. adv. com. City of Concord, 1981-83, vice chmn., 1982-83, mem. status of women com., 1980-81, mem. redevel. adv. com., 1984-86, planning commnr. 1986-92, chmn., 1990; mem. exec. bd. Mt. Diablo coun. Boy Scouts Am., 1981-85; bd. dirs. Pregnancy Ctrs. Contra Costa County, 1991-2001, chmn., 1993-2000 Mem. Concord C. of C. (bd. dirs., chmn. govt. affairs com. 1981-83, v.p. 1985-87, pres. 1988-89, Bus. Person of Yr. 1986), Calif. State Bar (chmn. adoptions subcom. north, 1994), Contra Costa County Bar Assn., Christian Legal Soc., Todos Santos Bus. and Profl. Women (co-founder, pres. 1983-84, pub. rels. chmn. 1982-83, Woman of Achievement 1980, 81), Soroptimists (fin. sec. 1980-81). Office: PO Box 981 Pittsburg CA 94565-0098

WILLITS, EILEEN MARIE, medical, surgical nurse, health facility administrator; b. Euclid, Ohio, 1953; d. John Francis and Geraldine Alice (Denoyer) Donohoe; m. Gary Eugene W., May 24, 1986; 1 child, William. Diploma, Providence Hosp. Sch. Nursing, 1974; BS in Human Svcs., U. Detroit, 1979; MS in Nursing Adminstrn., U. Mich., 1984. Diplomate Am. Coll. Healthcare Execs. From nurse to head nurse, then to adminstrv. asst. St. John Hosp., Detroit, 1974-84; v.p. patient svcs. E.L. Bixby Med. Ctr., Adrian, Mich., 1984-89; v.p. nursing Grandview Hosp. and Med. Ctr., Dayton, Ohio, 1989—. Mem. Am. Orgn. Nurse Execs., Ohio Orgn. Nurse Execs., Am. Coll. Healthcare Execs., Am. Hosp. Assn.

WILLMORE, LEANNA, music educator; b. Ogden, Utah, Sept. 11, 1943; d. Don Norman and Velma Beasley Read; children: Trent B. Florence, West Kenneth. BS in Music Edn., Weber State U., Ogden, Utah, 1971; M.Music Edn., U. Utah, 1983. Choir tchr. Valley Jr. H.S., Huntsville, Utah, 1971—73, Bonneville H.S., Ogden, Utah, 1973—90, Bingham H.S., South Jordan, Utah, 1990—99, Riverton High Sch., Utah, 1999—. Bd. dirs. WestEd, San Francisco, 2001—. Named Dist. Tchr. of the Yr., Jordan Sch. Dist., 1998, Music Educator of the Yr. award, Nat. Fedn. of H.S. sect. 7, 2000; recipient State Music Educator of the Yr. award, Utah H.S. Activities Assn., 1999, Music Educator of the Yr. award, Nat. Fedn. of H.S., 2002. Mem.: Music Educators Nat. Conf. (state pres. 1991—93, western divsn. pres. 1998—2000), Delta Kappa Gamma (state pres. 1989—91). Avocation: gardening. Home: 256 Sterling Dr Bountiful UT 84010 Office: Riverton High Sch 12476 S 2700 W Riverton UT 84065

WILLNER, ANN RUTH, political scientist, educator; b. N.Y.C., Sept. 2, 1924; d. Norbert and Bella (Richman) W. BA cum laude, Hunter Coll., 1945; MA, Yale U., 1946; PhD, U. Chgo., 1961. Lectr. U. Chgo., 1946-47, rsch. assoc. Ctr. for Econ. Devel. and Cultural Change, 1954-56, 61-62; advisor on orgn. and tng. Indonesian Ministry for Fgn. Affairs, Jakarta, 1952-53; expert for small scale indsl. planning Indonesian Nat. Planning Bur., Jakarta, 1953-54; fgn. affairs analyst Congl. Reference Svc., Libr. of Congress, 1960; asst. prof. polit. sci. Harpur Coll., Binghamton, NY, 1962-63; postdoctoral fellow polit. sci. and Southeast Asian studies Yale U., New Haven, 1963-64; rsch. assoc. Ctr. Internat. Studies, Princeton U., 1964-69; assoc. prof. polit. sci. U. Kans., Lawrence, 1969-70, prof., 1970-98. Vis. prof. polit. sci. CUNY, 1975; cons. govt. agys. and pvt. industry Polit. sci. editor: Ency. of the Social Scis., 1961; mem. editl. bd. Econ. Devel. and Cultural Change, 1954-57, Jour. Comparative Adminstrn., 1969-74, Comparative Politics, 1977—; author: The Neotraditional Accomodation to Political Independence, 1966, Charismatic Political Leadership: A Theory, 1968, The Spellbinders, 1984, 2004; also monographs, jour. articles, book chpts., newspaper columns. Grantee Rockefeller Found., 1965, Social Sci. Rsch. and Am. Coun. Learned Socs., 1966. Mem. Am. Polit. Sci. Assn. (gov. coun. 1979-81), Nat. Press Club. Home: 560 N St SW # N405 Washington DC 20024-4605 Office Phone: 202-484-2092. Personal E-mail: arwill@earthlink.net.

WILLNER, DOROTHY, anthropologist, educator; b. NYC, Aug. 26, 1927; d. Norbert and Bella (Richman) W. Ph.B., U. Chgo., 1947, MA, 1953, PhD, 1961; postgrad., Ecole Pratique des Hautes Etudes, U. Paris, France, 1950—51. Anthropologist Jewish Agy., Israel, 1955-58; tech. asst., adminstrn. expert in community devel. UN, Mexico, 1958; asst. prof. dept. sociology and anthropology U. Iowa, Iowa City, 1959-60; research assoc. U. Chgo., 1961-62; asst. prof. dept. sociology and anthropology U. N.C., Chapel Hill, 1962-63, Hunter Coll., N.Y.C., 1964-65; assoc. prof. dept. anthropology U. Kans., Lawrence, 1967-70, prof., 1970-90; professorial lectr. Johns Hopkins U. Sch. Advanced Internat. Studies, 1992. Cons. Washington Action for Youth, United Planning Orgn., 1964; rsch. in field. Author: Community Leadership, 1960, Nation-Building and Community in Israel, 1969. Contbr. numerous articles to profl. publs. Fellow Am. Anthrop. Assn., Soc. Applied Anthropology, Royal Anthrop. Inst.; mem. Cen. States Anthrop. Soc. (past pres.), Assn. Polit. and Legal Anthropology (past pres.). Home: N 407 560 N St SW Washington DC 20024-4605

WILLNER, JUDITH P., clinical geneticist, pediatrician, educator; b. Bay Shore, N.Y., July 27, 1945; d. Hyman and Edith (Sclank) Pleasure; m. Joseph Harrison Willner, June 22, 1969; children: Daniel, Rachel, Jonathan. AB, Harvard U., 1967; MD, NYU, 1971. Cert. Am. Bd. Pediatrics, Am. Bd. Med. Genetics. Asst. prof. ob-gyn. and pediatrics N.Y. Hosp./Cornell U. Med. Ctr., N.Y.C., 1982-89; asst. prof. pediatrics, clin. geneticist Mt. Sinai Sch. Medicine, N.Y.C., 1977-80, asst. prof. pediatrics, 1989-93, assoc. prof. human genetics and pediatrics, 1993—. Pres. N.Y. State Genetics Task Force, N.Y.C., 1996—. Mem. schs. com. Harvard U., Radcliffe Coll., 1974—; co-chair 30th reunion Radcliffe Coll., Cambridge, Mass., 1996—. Mem. Am. Soc. Human Genetics. Office: Dept Human Genetics Mt Sinai Hosp 1 Gustave L Levy Pl New York NY 10029-6500

WILLOCK, MARCELLE MONICA, retired medical educator; b. Georgetown, Guyana, Mar. 30, 1938; came to U.S. 1954; d. George and Renee W. BA, Coll. New Rochelle, 1958; MD, Howard U., 1962; MA, Columbia U., 1982; MBA, Boston U., 1989. Diplomate Am. Bd. Anesthesiology. Asst. clin. prof. med. ctr. NYU, 1968-72, assoc. clin. prof. med. ctr., 1972-74; asst. prof. clin. anesthesiology Columbia U., NYC, 1978-82; prof. Boston U., 1982, chmn. dept. anesthesiology, 1982—98, asst. provost cmty. affairs, 1998—2002; dean Coll. Medicine Charles R. Drew U., L.A., 2002—05; ret., 2005. Sec. The Med. Found., Boston, 1991-94. Contbr. articles to profl. jours. Pres. Louis and Marthe Deveaux Found., Panama, 1965—; trustee Coll. New Rochelle, NY, 1976-82, 2006—. Mem. Am. Soc. Anesthesiologists (del. 1986—, alt. dir. 1990-94, bd. dirs. 1994—, asst. sec. 1999-2001), Mass. Soc.

Anesthesiologists (pres. 1988-89), Soc. Acad. Anesthesia Chairs (sec.-treas. 1989-91, pres.-elect 1993-94, pres. 1994—), Alpha Omega Alpha. Roman Catholic. Home: 85 East India Rd Apt 31E Boston MA 02110

WILLOUGHBY, SARAH-MARGARET C., retired chemist, educator, chemical engineer, consultant; b. Bowling Green, KY, Oct. 15, 1917; d. Austin Burrell Claypool and Minerva Dallas Renfrow-Claypool; m. John Richard Evans, II, Aug. 30, 1938 (dec Dec. 1942); 1 child, Richard Claypool Evans; m. Olief Glenn Willoughby, June 18, 1948 (dec.); children: Sarah, Stephen(dec.). BS, Western Ky. U., 1938; PhD, Purdue U., 1950. Registered profl. engr., Ind., Tex. Chemist Devoe-Reynolds, Inc., Louisville, 1941—42; jr. engr. chem. lab. div. Curtiss-Wright Corp., Louisville, 1942—44; tech. asst. Purdue U., West Lafayette, Ind., 1944—46, fellow, 1946—50; rsch. chemist, coatings divsn. Monsanto Chem. Co., Boston, 1950—52; assoc. prof. of chemistry U. Tex., Arlington, 1954—84, co-dir. Ctr. for Microcrystalline Polymer Rsch. Studies, 1978—82, prof. emeritus chemistry, 1984. Cons. Albert H. Halff Assocs., Dallas, 1980—86. Co-edit., author Engineer-in-Training Manual, 1970. Nominee Dallas-Ft. Worth Trailblazer award, 1996; named to Hall of Disting. Alumni, Western Ky. U., 1994, Am. Men and Women of Sci., Personalities of the South, 1974, Cmty. Leaders and Noteworthy Americans, 1978, Notable Women of Tex., 1984—85, Daughters of Guilds of Colonial Artisans and Tradesmen, 2005; recipient Outstanding Chem. Engr. award, Purdue U., 1996, Cmty. Growth Contbn. award, Arlington Hist. Soc., Tex. Fellow: Am. Inst. Chemists; mem.: Am. Chem. Soc. (emeritus mem.), Peyton Soc. Va. (life), Gold Star Wives Am. (life), NY Acad. Sci. (life), Soc. Women Engrs. (sr.), Nat. Soc. Daughters of Founders and Patriots (v.p. N.E. Tex. chpt. 1997—, pres. N.E. Tex. chpt. 2006—08), Plantagenet Soc., Colonial Dames Am., Nat. Soc. DAR (chpt. regent 1967—69, nat. bicentennial com. mem. 1975—76, Nat. Women's Issues essay award 2006), Nat. Soc. Children of Am. Revolution (Tex. sr. state pres. 1968—70), Nat. Soc. Colonial Dames of XVII Century (chpt. regent 1980—82), Magna Charta Dames and Barons (formerly Nat. Soc. Magna Charta Dames) (Tex. state pres. 1986—88, nat. chmn. edn.), Colonial Order of the Crown, Soc. Descendants of Knights of the Most Noble Order of the Garter, Sovereign Colonial Soc. Ams. of Royal Descent, Friends of St. George, Order Ky. Cols., Sigma Xi (pres. 1966—68, emeritus mem.), Alpha Chi Omega (Lambda Epsilon chapt.). Home: 1630 Pecan Park Dr Arlington TX 76012

WILLOWS, MARY ROSE, special education educator; b. Chgo., Oct. 29, 1953; d. James Joseph and Mary Margaret McDonough; m. James Leroy Willows, Jr., Nov. 29, 1980; children: James Leroy III, Donald Jason. BA in Psychology, San Francisco State U., 1978, MA in Edn., 1979, Spl. Edn. Credential, 1992; Profl. Clear Multiple Subjects, Calif. State U., Hayward, 1991. Cert. educator Calif., 1991. Tchr. for the visually impaired Tri-Valley Spl. Edn. Local Plan Area, Livermore, Calif., 1991—96, Calif. Sch. for the Blind, Fremont, 1996—. Com. chairperson on parental concerns Nat. Fedn. of the Blind, Balt., 1985—95; curriculum com. mem. Calif. Sch. for the Blind, Fremont, 1997—98, judge braille bee, 1999—99, featured spkr. braille bee, 2000—00, mem. tchr. adminstr. adv. com., mem. mini grants com.; pres.-elect. No. Calif. chpt. Assn. for Edn. and Rehab., Pleasanton, 1994—96, pres. No. Calif. chpt., 1996—99, mem. conf. com., San Francisco, 1995. Author: The Story of the Earth Angels, 2003, Meeting the Challenge, 1998. Nominee Tchr. of the Yr., Disney, 1997; named Disting. Alumni of the Yr., Alvernia H.S., Chgo., 2003; recipient Youth Garden Grant award, Nat. Gardening Assn., 2004. Mem.: Nat. Fedn. of the Blind of Calif. (licentiate; sec. 1985—2005, Tri-Valley chpt., mem. Braille Readers are Leaders, coord. child care program 1993—97, corr. com. 1988—2005, chaiperson Calif. edn. com. 1982—86, chairperson com. on parental concerns 1994—97, Educator of Yr. 2002), Nat. Orgn. Blind Educators (assoc.; pres. 1998—2001). Home: 3934 Kern Ct Pleasanton CA 94588 Office: California School for the Blind 500 Walnut Ave Fremont CA 94536 Office Phone: 510-794-3800. Personal E-mail: marywillows@sbcglobal.net. Business E-Mail: mwillows@csb-cde.ca.gov.

WILLS, BETH LOUISE, elementary school educator, social worker; b. Modesto, Calif., Nov. 3, 1936; d. Laurence Walter Johnson and Christina Agnes Lasell; m. Morris L. Wills, Sept. 27, 1958; children: Susan Miller, Morris L. Jr., Karen McClelland. BS, Brigham Young U., 1958. Cert. tchg. cert. Calif., 1987, early childhood cert., nat. bd. cert. tchr. County social worker various locations, Calif., 1958—63; social worker Salvation Army, Modesto, Calif., 1965—68, Sierra Hosp., San Fernando, Calif., 1980, Santa Monica Hosp., 1980—82, Henry Mayo Hosp., 1982—83; ESL tchr. Los Angeles Sch. Dist., 1983—2003, elem tchr., 1983—2005; ret., 2005. Support provider Los Angeles Sch. Dist., 1998—, Calif. State Teach, 2002—03; mentor tchr. Calif. State Northridge, 2002—. Sec. block capt. Neighbor Watch, Sylmar, Calif., 1985—2002; co-chair Healthy Start Collaborative; crisis counselor Mission Coll., 2004; adv. Ch. Jesus Christ of Latter Day Saints, Sylmar, 2000—05. Mem.: Nat. Assn. Edn. Young Children. Republican. Avocations: hiking, crafts, knitting, crocheting. Home: 313 Remington Ct Sandpoint ID 83864 Personal E-mail: Willsfamily1@verizon.net, willsfamily@juno.com.

WILLS, LOIS ELAINE, art gallery owner, religious education educator; b. Dayton, Ohio, Feb. 26, 1939; d. Harold Otto and Marjorie Elizabeth (Schmidt) Wallen; m. David P. Wills, Sept. 26, 1960 (dec.); children: Marianne, Melody, Michele. Degree, Coll. Mount St. Joseph; BFA, Coll. Mt. St. Joseph, 2000, MA, 2004. Cert. catechist. Educator, substitute various schs., 1985-90; gallery dir. Studio San Giuseppe, Cin., 1987-90; curator Murdock Art and Antiques, Cin., 1990-92; mgr. Cin. Antique Mall, 1992-93; dir. religious edn. St. John the Bapt., Dover, Ind., 1993-96, Blessed Sacrament, Ft. Mitchell, Ky., 1996—2002; owner Fine Arts Gallery, Ga., 2002—. Group exhibits include Clermont County Libr., Batavia, Ohio, 1990, Murdock Gallery, Cin., 1990, Studio San Giusseppe, Mount St. Joseph Coll., Cin., 1990, Milford Libr., Cin., 1991, Cathedral Fresh Art Exhibit, Covington, Ky., 1998 (1st pl.); Coll. Mt. St. Joseph Studio San Guiseppi, Ga. State Fair, Ga., 2003; represented in pvt. collections. Mem. Youth Encouragement Svcs., Aurora, Ind., 1985—; active Dearborn Highland Arts Coun., Lawrenceburg, Ind., 1990-95; mem. Rev. Club, Lawrenceburg, 1985-2002; dir. religious edn. Blessed Sacrament Parish, Ft. Mitchell, Ky., 1996-2002; mem. Perry Players, Inc. Master Gardener. Avocations: art, reading, travel, gardening, swimming. Office: 203 River Valley Trl Kathleen GA 31047-2135

WILLSIE, SANDRA KAY, provost, dean, internist, educator; BS in Med. Tech., Pittsburg State U., Kans., 1975; DO, Kansas City U. Medicine and Bioscis., Mo., 1983. Diplomate in internal medicine, pulmonary diseases and critical care medicine Am. Bd. Internal Medicine, Am. Bd. Osteo. Internists, 2000. Rotating intern Univ. Hosp., Kansas City, Mo., 1983-84; resident in internal medicine U. Mo.-Kansas City Affiliated Hosps., 1984-87; fellow in pulmonary diseases and critical care medicine Truman Med. Ctr.-West, Kansas City, Mo., 1987-89; instr. medicine U. Mo.-Kansas City Sch. Medicine, 1984-89; med. dir. pulmonary clinic Truman Med. Ctr., 1991-2000; asst. prof. medicine U. Mo. Kansas City Sch. Medicine, 1989-94, assoc. prof. medicine, 1994-99, dep. asst. dean, 1994—97, asst. dean, 1997-2000, prof. medicine, 1999-2000, Kansas City U. Medicine and Bioscis., 2000—02, vice dean acad. affairs, adminstrn., med. affairs, 2002—, exec. v.p. acad. affairs, provost, dean, 2002—. Invited bd. question author Am. Bd. Internal Medicine, 1995—, relevance reviewer for pulmonary disease bd. exam, 1996—; internal medicine subspecialty program pre-reviewer Accreditation Coun. for Grad. Med. Edn., 1997—2000; credentials com. Truman Med. Ctr., Inc., 1990—96, med. intensive care unit com., 1992—2000, intermediate care unit com., 1992—2000, exec. com. Truman Health Sys., 1998—2000, profl. standards com., 1998—2000. Contbr. articles to profl. jours. Bd. dirs. Girls to Women, 1995—2000, v.p. bd. dirs., 1996—2000. Fellow: Am. Coll. Physicians (state activities com. 1991—95, chair, state activities com. 1994, scientific presentations judge 1995—96, coun. mem. 1998—2004), Am. Coll. Osteo. Internists (program com. 2002—, rsch. com. 2003—, Rschr. of Yr. 2004); mem.: Met. Med. Soc. (chair women in medicine com. 1995—2000, pres. com. 1995—2000, bd. dirs. 1997—2000, exec. com. 1999—2000, chair women in medicine com. 2002—), Am. Osteo. Assn., Kans. City Pulmonary Roundtable (pres.), Soc. Critical Care Medicine, Am. Lung Assn. Mo. (bd. mem.), Jackson County Osteo. Assn., Mo. Assn. Osteo. Physicians and Surgeons, Am. Thoracic Soc., Am. Coll. Chest Physicians (chair, basic sci. com. 1995—98, scientific program com. 1995—2003, membership com. 1997—2001, gov. for Mo. 1997—2001, chair, scientific presentations and awards com. 1998—2000, vice chair, scientific program com. 1999—2000, chair, scientific program com. 2000—01, regent 2004—, Young Investigator award 1992). Office: Kansas City Univ Medicine and Bioscis 1750 Independence Ave Kansas City MO 64106-1453 Office Phone: 816-283-2308. Business E-Mail: swillsie@kcumb.edu.

WILLSON, DORIS, librarian; b. Moro, Ark., 1928; d. James L. and Bertha Mae (Kirk) Willson. Degree, U. Ky., 1950, Louisville, 1962. Libr. Valley HS, Jefferson County Pub. Sch., Louisville, 1950—51, Ea. HS, Jefferson County Pub. Sch., Louisville, 1952—84; ret., 1984. Adv., libr. Middletown (Ky.) Hist. Mus., 1984—85; sec. libr. com. City of Middletown, 1984; vol. libr. Louisville (Ky.) Sci. Ctr., 1984—. Recipient Inst. on Asian Studies award, US State Dept., U. Hawaii, 1970, 20 Yr. Svc. award for Vol. Work, Louisville Sci. Ctr., 2005. Mem.: U. Louisville Alumni Assn., U. Ky. Alumni Assn., Ky. Retired Tchrs. Assn., Jefferson Co. Retired Teachers Assn. Democrat. Baptist. Avocations: reading, music, coin collecting/numismatics, golf. E-mail: dw40243@aol.com.

WILLSON, MARY FRANCES, ecology researcher, educator; b. Madison, Wis., July 28, 1938; d. Gordon L. and Sarah (Loomans) W.; m. R.A. von Neumann, May 29, 1972 (dec.). BA with honors, Grinnell Coll., 1960; PhD, U. Wash., 1964. Asst. prof. U. Ill., Urbana, 1965-71, assoc. prof., 1971-76, prof. ecology, 1976-90; rsch. ecologist Forestry Scis. Lab., Juneau, Alaska, 1989-99; sci. dir. Great Lakes program Nature Conservancy, 1999-2000. Prin. rsch. scientist, affiliate prof. biology, Inst. Arctic Biology and Sch. Fisheries and Ocean Scis., U. Alaska, Fairbanks-Juneau. Author: Plant Reproductive Ecology, 1983, Vertebrate Natural History, 1984; co-author: Mate Choice in Plants, 1983. Fellow Am. Ornithologists Union; mem. Brit. Ornithologists Union, Soc. for Study Evolution, Am. Soc. Naturalists (hon. mem.), Ecol. Soc. Am., Brit. Ecol. Soc. E-mail: mwillson@gci.net.

WILMOT, EVELYN MILLER, elementary school educator; d. Clifford Potter and Evelyn (Rodenbaugh) Miller; m. Peter Roberts Wilmot, Aug. 1, 1964; children: Kristie Wilmot Colwell, Peter Clifford Colwell. BS in Elem. Edn., U. Millersville, Pa.; postgrad., Temple U., Phila., Kutztown U., Harvard U. Cert. tchr. Pa., Ill., Colo., NJ. Kindergarten tchr. Plymouth Meeting Sch. Dist., Pa., 1963—64, Bethlehem Sch. Dist., Pa., 1964—66, Westmont Sch. Dist., Ill., 1966—67; substitute tchr. Cherry Creek and Denver Sch. Dists., 1969—78; chile study team tchr. Title I Rockaway Twp. Sch. Dist., NJ, 1979—83, 2d grade and kindergarten tchr., 1983—, mem. instnl. coun., 1986—88. Developer Mountain Lakes HS Ski Team, 1984; social chmn. Golden Shores Condo. Assn., Stone Harbor, NJ, 2005—; mem. pastoral com. Cmty. Ch., Mountain Lakes, NJ, 2006—. Grantee, Harvard U., 1996. Mem.: AAUW, NJ Assn. Kindergarten Educators. Avocations: reading, skiing, travel, bridge.

WILMS, ANNE M., information technology executive; Grad., Trinity Coll., Dublin, Ireland, 1979, U. Chgo., 1993. Dir. info. sys. Wis. Power and Light, Madison; with Oracle Corp., Redwood City, Calif.; mgr. info. tech. So. Nat. Gas Co. Sonat, Inc., 1995, v.p. info. tech. Sonat Svcs., 1996, v.p., CIO Sonat Svcs., 1998; v.p., CIO Rohm and Haas Co., Phila., 1999—. Bd. dirs. Elemica, CIDX. Mem. bd. councillors Hist. Soc. Pa.; bd. mem. Red Cross S.E. Pa.; mem. CIO adv. coun. Villanova U. Office: Rohm and Haas Co 100 Independence Hall West Philadelphia PA 19106-2399

WILMSHURST, LINDA ANNE, psychologist, writer; arrived in U.S., 1999; d. Wesley S. and Jean B. Werbowy; children: Luke P., Rachel L. BA, Univ. Windsor, Windsor, Can., 1972, MA, 1973, MA, 1974; PhD, Univ. Toronto, Tornto, Can., 1989. Registered pyschologist Can., 1992, lic. pyschologist, specialist in sch. pyscology Tex., 1999, sch. pyscology Fla., 2000, registered Can. Rsgister of Health Svc. Providers in Psychology Can., 1998, cert. profl. qualification 1999, diplomate psychology 2002. Sch. psychologist Metro Toronto Sch. Bd., Toronto, Canada, 1979—89, Lake County Sch., Howey in the Hills, Fla., 2002—05; univ. prof. Univ. Western Ontario, London, Canada, 1989—91; psychologist Ministry of Edn., London, Canada, 1991—93, Martin Bach & Assoc., London, Canada, 1994—95, Child & Parent Rsch., London, Canada, 1995—99, Madame Vanier Child Svc., London, Canada, 1995—99; prof. Univ. Houston, Victoria, Tex., 1999—2001, Tex. Woman's Univ., Denton, Tex., 2001—02; psychologist dept. psychology Elon U., NC, 2005—, asst. prof. psychology, 2005—. Chair humanities subjects Univ. Houston, Victoria, Tex., 2000—01; grad. adv. com. Tex. Woman's Univ., Denton, Tex., 2001—02. Author: (textbook) Child & Adolescent Psychopathology: A Casebook, 2004, Essentials of Child Psychopathology, 2005; co-author (with A. Brue): A Parent's Guide to Special Education, 2005; contbr. scientific papers. Mem.: Fla. Assn. Sch. Psychologists. Achievements include findings of a significant program summarized in Data Trends #61; data trends selected only the top 2% of rsch. pub. on childrens mental health for review. One of only randomized clin. trial studies to compare a residential treatment program for severly disturbed; youth with a cmty. based alternative. Cmty. based treatment was superior: some children actually became worse in residential treatment. Office: Elon U Dept Psychology Elon NC 27244 Office Phone: 336-278-6404. Business E-Mail: lwilmshurst@elon.edu.

WILNER, LOIS ANNETTE, retired speech and language pathologist; b. Newark, Jan. 15, 1935; d. Benjamin and Ida (Schwam) Friedman; m. Sherman Wilner, July 6, 1957 (dec. Apr. 1996); children: Bonnie Joy, Robert Steven. BS, Newark State Tchrs. Coll., 1953-57; MA, Newark State Coll., 1969-73. Tchr. 5th grade Maplewood-South Orange Bd. Edn., South Orange, N.J., 1957-58; permanent substitute Parsippany (N.J.)-Troy Hills Bd. Edn., 1967-68, speech and language pathologist, 1968-95, ret., 1995. Cons., speech and lang. pathologist Ctr. for Comm. Disorders, Livingston, NJ, 1987-89. Contbr. newsletter Condo Seabreeze Assn., 1995-97, asst. sec., 1996-97; program v.p. Palm Isles Singles Club, 1996-97. Mem. AAUW, NEA, NJ Edn. Assn., Morris County Edn. Assn., NJ Speech-Hearing Assn., Morris County Speech-Hearing Assn. (libr. 1987-90), Ret. NJ Educators of So. Fla. (co-pres. 2004-05, pres. 2005—06, pres. 2006-), Palm Isles Art Club (sec. 1995-96, sec./reservations chmn. 1996-97, pres. 1998-2000), B'nai B'rith Women (Roseland, Livingston and Suburban Essex chpt. pres. 1985-88), Alpha Delta Kappa (pres. Mu chpt. 1990-92, NJ state scholarship chmn. 1992-94). Home: 7609 Island Breeze Ter Boynton Beach FL 33437-5405

WILNER, MARION LEONARD, art educator; b. N.Y.C., Sept. 27, 1929; d. Jack Frank and Madeline (Leff) Leonard; m. Myron Wilner, May 28, 1950; children: Andrew, Matthew, David. BS, NYU, 1950, MA, 1952. Prof. of art, coord. art transfer program Bristol Community Coll., Fall River, Mass., 1966-89, prof. emerita, 1993. Advisor dean's adv. coun. coll. visual and performing arts U. Mass., Dartmouth, 1993; lectr. Sacred Hearts Convent, 1992, R.I. Jewish Hist. Soc., 1992, Brandeis U. Nat. Women's Com., 1991, 90, Universidade Nova, Lisbon, 1988, Universidade Dos Acores, 1987; vis. scholar U. Mass., Dartmouth, 1992; mem. Higher Edn. Nominating Coun., 1990; judge Ea. Edison Poster and Essay Contest, 1989, R.I. Regional Scholastic Art Awards, 1987, Ann. Regional Art Exhbn. Fall River Festival, 1985; writer art Fall River Herald News, 1994-. Prin. works exhibited in numerous one-woman and group shows including DeBlois Gallery, Newport, R.I., 1992, 94, Bert Gallery, Providence, 1991, Dodge House Gallery, Providence, 1990, Fall River Hist. Soc., 1988, Newport Art Mus., 1987, Escola Superior de Belas Artes, Lisbon, 1986, Eastbourne Gallery, Newport, 1977, Facets Gallery, Fall River, 1993, New England Ctr. Gallery, U. N.H., 1992, Fed. Res. Bank Boston, 1992, Deblois Gallery, Newport, RI, 2003, Perkins Gallery, Mass., 2004, Retrosptctive at Bristol C.C., Fall River, Mass., 2005, Bristol Art Mus., RI, 2006; prin. works represented in numerous collections including Duro Industries, Inc., Bristol C.C., Providence Art Club Mems. Show, Cianfarani award, 1998, R.I. Econ. Devel. Corp., 1999, Juried R.I. State Com., Nat. Mus. Women in Arts, 2000, Providence Art Club, Printmaking award, 2001, Deblois Gallery, Newport, R.I., 2001, Newport Art Mus., 2002, KRAUSE Gallery, 2003. Trustee Swain Sch. Design, New Bedford, Mass., 1977-91, Fall River Pub. Libr., 1978-91; active Fall River Cultural Commn., 1988—, Fall River Arts Lottery Coun., 1989—; mem. adv. bd. SMU Ctr. for Jewish Culture, 1983; visual arts dir. Festival '82; graphic designer for various community orgns. Gulbenkian grantee Lisbon, Portugal, 1986, 88; recipient Outstanding Cmty. Svc. award Fall River Area C. of C. and Industry, 1996, Ruth Findley award Providence Art Club, 2002. Mem.: Deblois Gallery, 19 on Paper. Home: 786 Madison St Fall River MA 02720-5718 E-mail: mandmwilner@yahoo.com.

WILPER, KIMBERLY DAWN, elementary school educator; b. St. Maries, Idaho, June 18, 1976; d. William and Jeanette Cuddy; m. John Kelly Wilper, June 1, 1996. BS in Elem. Edn., Lewis-Clark State Coll., Lewiston, Idaho, 1994—98. Cert. Elem. Edn. Tchr. Idaho Dept. Edn., 1998. 6th grade tchr. Meridian Sch. Dist., Idaho, 2000—. Office: Meridian Sch Dist Meridian ID

WILS, MADELYN, film company executive; b. Queens, NY, 1955; Owner, prodr. Bread and Butter TV; pres., CEO Tribeca Film Inst., NYC, 2004—. Trustee Alliance Downtown NY, Inc., Conservancy Hist. Battery Pk., Gateway Sch. NY; dir. Hudson River Park Trust; bd. mem. Lower Manhattan Devel. Corp., NYC, 2001—. Office: Tribeca Film Inst 375 Greenwich St New York NY 10013

WILSON, ANGELA K., chemistry professor; BSc in Chemistry with hons., Ea. Wash. U., 1990; PhD in Chem. Physics, U. Minn., 1995. Asst. prof. chemistry U. North Tex., Denton, 2000—05, assoc. prof. chemistry, 2005—, co-dir., Ctr. Advanced Sci. Computing and Modeling, 2005—. Vis. rsch. scholar U. Sydney, Australia, 2003; vis. rsch. scientist Oak Ridge Nat. Lab., 2003, 04; sci. adv. bd. program cons. EPA, 2003—04; US chair Chinese-Am. Frontiers Sci., NAS, 2006. Contbr. articles to profl. jours. Mem. adminstrv. bd. 1st United Meth. Ch., Denton, 2002—05. Recipient Career award, NSF, 2003, Young Investigator award, Wiley Internat. Jour. Quantum Chemistry, 2004, Alumnus Achievement award, Ea. Wash. U., 2006. Mem.: AAAS, Am. Phys. Soc., Am. Chem. Soc. (councilor to nat. coun. 2004—, mem. sci. com. 2005, 2006), Internat. Union Pure and Applied Chemistry (assoc.; mem. divsn. phys. and biophysical chemistry, mem. internat. leadership team, Young Observer award 2003, 2005), Sigma Xi. Achievements include research in method and basis set development in ab initio quantum mechanical computational chemistry. Office: Univ North Texas Dept Chemistry Box 305070 Denton TX 76203-5070 Office Phone: 940-565-4296.

WILSON, ANNE MARIE, chemistry professor; b. Rochester, NY; BA in Chemistry with honors, Oberlin Coll., Ohio, 1989; PhD, U. Utah, Salt Lake City, 1994. Postdoctoral assoc. Fla. State U., Tallahassee, 1995—96; assoc. prof. chemistry Butler U., Indpls., 1996—, dir. honors program, 2004—; vis. scientist Eli Lilly and Co., Indpls., 2004. Recipient Outstanding Faculty award, Butler U. Coll. Liberal Arts and Scis., 2003; grantee Discretionary award, Rsch. Corp., 2000; Type G Starter grantee, Am. Chem. Soc. Petroleum Rsch. Fund, 2000—02. Mem.: Am. Chem. Soc. (assoc.; outreach coord. nat. chemistry week, local chpt. 1997—2001, Spl. Svc. Award 2001), Phi Kappa Phi (assoc.), Sigma Xi (assoc.), Iota Sigma Pi (life; pres. Cobalt chpt. 1997). Office: Butler University 4600 Sunset Avenue Indianapolis IN 46208 Office Phone: 317-940-9405.

WILSON, ANNETTE SIGRID, elementary school educator; b. Harlan, Iowa, Jan. 30, 1953; d. Anker Christian and Ruth Edith Eastergard; m. John Roger Wilson, Dec. 21, 1974; children: Elicia Ruth, Elizabeth Annette. BS, Bob Jones U., 1975; diploma, Nancy Bounds Modeling and Finishing Sch., 1998; MAE, U. No. Iowa, 2001. Educator Arlington Bapt. Sch., Baltimore, Md., 1976—78, Calvary Bapt. Sch., Normal, Ill., 1978—80, Walnut (Iowa) Pub. Sch., 1986—2000, Council Bluffs (Iowa) Cmty. Schs., 2000—05; trainer Area Edn. Agy., Council Bluffs, 1991—97. Homebound spl. edn. instr., 1987. Contbg. author: Work on Creativity, 2004; co-author (with Benedicte Riis): Music Room, 2005. Recipient Optimist award for Youth Appreciation, 1992, 1996, Leadership award, Area XIII, 1998.

WILSON, AVON W., state representative; b. Wichita Falls, Tex., Sept. 24, 1929; m. Bill Wilson. BA, N. Tex. State U., 1949; MED, Ea. N.Mex. U., 1996. Tchr. Fort Stockton and Big Spring Schs., Tex., 1949—55, Roswell Ind. Sch. Dist., N.Mex., 1955—80; owner Gift Shop, Roswell, 1976—86; ednl. cons. Roswell, 1986—; state rep. dist. 59 N.Mex. State Legis., Santa Fe, 2001—. Mem. energy and natural resources N.Mex. State Legis., Santa Fe, mem. Human Resources/Labor com., mem. interim com. Indian affairs. Mem.: Altrusa Internat. Roswell (v.p./pres. 1992—). Republican. Methodist. Home: PO Box 381 Roswell NM 88202-0381 Office: New Mexico State Capitol Rm 202A Santa Fe NM 87501

WILSON, BERTINA IOLIA, retired music educator; b. Southampton, Va., Aug. 17, 1938; d. Purcell Lee and Clarine Branch; m. Aug. 25, 1963 (div. May 1977); children: Brian Keith, Linda Elizabeth. BA, Newark State Coll., 1960; MA, Kean Coll., 1981. Cert. elem. edn. tchr., N.J. Tchr. Newark Bd. Edn., 1960-77, project coord., 1977—95; ch. organist, choir dir. Zion Hill Bapt. Ch., Newark, 1974—; vice prin. Newark Pub. Schs., 1995—97. Mem. Newark Tchrs. Union, Project Coords. Assn. (exec. bd. Newark chpt. 1981—), Order of Eastern Star (Outstanding Ch. Musician 1986), Phi Delta Kappa (pub. rels. dir. 1987-89). Democrat. Avocations: singing, playing the organ. Home: 345 Mclean Pl Hillside NJ 07205-1748

WILSON, BETH A., college official; BA, Calif. State Coll., Sonoma; MBA, Nat. U. Asst. dir. Am. Bus. Coll., 1976-81; scholarship adminstr. Nat. U., 1982-84; v.p. br. ops. Nat. Coll., 1990-91; from exec. dir. bus. sch., group mgr. to v.p. adminstrn. United Edn. and Sofware, 1984-90; exec. dir. Capital Hill campus, then area ops. mgr. Nat. Edn. Ctrs., Inc., 1991-95; ops. dir., regional ops. dir. Corinthian Schs., Inc., Santa Ana, Calif., 1995-97, regional ops. dir. coll. region of Rhodes Colls. divsn., 1997-98, v.p. ops. parent co., 1998—. Office: Corinthian Colls Inc 6 Hutton Centre Dr Ste 400 Santa Ana CA 92707-5764

WILSON, BLENDA JACQUELINE, foundation administrator; b. Woodbridge, N.J., Jan. 28, 1941; d. Horace and Margaret (Brogsdale) Wilson; m. Louis Fair Jr. AB, Cedar Crest Coll., 1962; AM, Seton Hall U., 1965; PhD, Boston Coll., 1979; DHL (hon.), Cedar Crest Coll., 1987, Loretto Heights Coll., 1988, Colo. Tech. Coll., 1988, U. Detroit, 1989; LLD (hon.), Rutgers U., 1989, Ea. Mich. U., 1990, Cambridge Coll., 1991, Schoolcraft Coll., 1992; DHL (hon.), Marysville U., 1994, Mt. St. Mary's Coll., 1996, Antioch U., 1999, Cambridge Coll., 2001, Salve Regina U., 2002, Merrimack Coll., 2001; D Pub. Svc. (hon.), U. Mass., 2002, Mass. Coll. Liberal Arts, 2003. Tchr. Woodbridge Twp. Pub. Schs., 1962-66; exec. dir. Middlesex County Econ. Opportunity Corp., New Brunswick, N.J., 1966-69; exec. asst. to pres. Rutgers U., New Brunswick, N.J., 1969-72; sr. assoc. dean Grad. Sch. Edn. Harvard U., Cambridge, Mass., 1972-82; v.p. effective sector mgmt. Ind. Sector, Washington, 1982-84; exec. dir. Colo. Commn. Higher Edn., Denver, 1984-88; chancellor and prof. pub. adminstrn. & edn. U. Mich., Dearborn, 1988-92; pres. Calif. State U., Northridge, 1992-99, Nellie Mae Found., Quincy, Mass., 1999—. Am. del. U.S./U.K. Dialogue About Quality Judgments in Higher Edn.; adv. bd. Mich. Consol. Gas Co., Stanford Inst. Higher Edn. Rsch., U. So. Colo. Dist. 60 Nat. Alliance, Nat. Ctr. for Rsch. to Improve Postsecondary Tchg. and Learning, 1988-90; bd. dirs. Alpha Capital Mgmt.; mem. higher edn. colloquium Am. Coun. Edn., vis. com. Divsn. Continuing Edn. in Faculty of Arts and Scis., Harvard Coll., Pew Forum on K-12 Edn. Reform in U.S., The Coll. Bd., Federated Dorchester Neighborhood House, Fed. Res. Bank of Boston; bd. dirs. Ptnrs. Healthcare Sys., Medco Health Solutions, Inc. Dir. U. Detroit Jesuit High Sch., Northridge Hosp. Med. Ctr., 1993-99, Arab Cmty. Ctr. for Econ. and Social Svcs., Union Bank, J. Paul Getty Trust, James Irvine Found., 1996-99, Internat. Found. Edn. and Self-Help, Achievement Coun., L.A.; dir., vice chair Met. Affairs Corp.; exec. bd. Detroit area coun. Boy Scouts Am.; bd. dirs. Commonwealth Fund, Henry Ford Hosp.-Fairlane Ctr., Henry Ford Health System, Met. Ctr. for High

Tech., United Way Southeastern Mich.; mem. Nat. Coalition 100 Black Women, Detroit, Race Rels. Coun. Met. Detroit, Women & Founds., Greater Detroit Interfaith Round Table NCCJ, Adv. Bd. Valley Cultural Ctr., Woodland Hills; trustee assoc. Boston Coll.; trustee emeritus Cambridge Coll.; trustee emeritus, bd. dirs. Found. Ctr.; trustee Henry Ford Mus. & Greenfield Village, Sammy Davis Jr. Nat. Liver Inst. Mem. AAUW, Assn. Governing Bds. (adv. coun. of pres.'s), Edn. Commn. of the States (student minority task force), Am. Assn. Higher Edn. (chair-elect), Am. Assn. State Colls. & Univs. (com. on policies & purposes, acad. leadership fellows selection com.), Assn. Black Profls. and Adminstrs., Assn. Black Women in Higher Edn., Women Execs. State Govt., Internat. Women's Forum, Mich. Women's Forum, Women's Econ. Club Detroit, Econ. Club, Rotary. Office: Nellie Mae Edn Found 1250 Hancock St 205N Quincy MA 02169-4331 Business E-Mail: bwilson@nmefdn.org.

WILSON, BOBBI ELLEN, physical therapy assistant; b. Peoria, Ill., Nov. 4, 1980; d. Judy Stretch and Robert Wilson, Don Stretch (Stepfather); 1 child, Zachary Robert Baikie. AAS, Ill. Ctrl. Colege, Peoria, 2001; BS, Ill. State U., Bloomington, 2004. Athletic trainer, phys. therapy asst. ATI Phys. Therapy, Willowbrook, Ill., 2004—06, Joliet, Ill., 2006—. Mem.: Nat. Strength and Conditioning Assn., Gt. Lakes Athletic Trainer's Assn., Am. Coll. Sports Medicine, Nat. Athletic Trainer's Assn. (cert.), Am. Phys. Therapy Assn. (cert. phys. therapy asst.). Office: ATI Physical Therapy Joliet IL 60431

WILSON, BONNIE JEAN, lawyer, educator, investor; b. Alameda County, Calif. d. August and Violet Adeline (Lockard) Ritzenthaler; m. Allan Nicholas Wilson (dec.); children: Albert Clyde, Bruce Allan. BA, U. Calif., Berkeley, cert. in elem. tchg.; JD, Thomas Jefferson SOL, 1981. Bar: Calif.; cert. tchr., Calif. Elem. sch. tchr. Contra Costa and San Diego Counties; intern San Diego County Dist. Atty. Office, 1981; pvt. practice La Jolla, Calif., 1982—. Mem. La Jolla Presbyn. Ch., San Diego Symphony Assn., Friends of the La Jolla Libr.; adv. dir. San Diego Opera Assn.; edn. activist, 1972-76. Mem. Calif. State Bar Assn., San Diego County Bar Assn., La Jolla Newcomer's Club (bd. dirs. 1968-69), U. Calif. Berkeley Alumni Club (bd. dirs. San Diego chpt. 1961-62), Am. Assn. Ind. Investors (bd. dirs. 1991-97), Pi Lambda Theta, La Jolla Beach and Tennis Club. Presbyterian. Home: 2235 Bahia Dr La Jolla CA 92037-7007

WILSON, BRENDA MARIE, secondary school educator; b. New Orleans, Feb. 4, 1951; d. Chester Simmons, Jr. and Lillie Mae Simmons; m. Eli Wilson, Jr., June 19, 1971; children: Eli III, LaVar Antoine. AS, So. U., 1972; BSc, Rochester Inst. Tech., NY, 1984; MSc, LI U., 1990. Adj. prof. L.I. (N.Y.) U., 1987—89, asst. dean, 1989—93; tchr. Bd. Edn., Bklyn., 1997—98; with accts. payable Chempiah Ministries, Queens, NY, 1998—2000; tchr. Orange County Pub. Schs., Orlando, Fla., 2001—. Mem. sch. adv. com. Orange County Pub. Schs., 2002—. V.p. Eli Wilson Ministries, Orlando, 2002—03. Named Tchr. of Yr., Orange County Pub. Schs., 2004. Mem.: Phi Gamma Nu, Alpha Kappa Alpha. Baptist. Office: Cerokee School 550 S Eola Dr Orlando FL 32801-3999 Home: 6503 Hawdsmoor Dr Orlando FL 32818

WILSON, CAROL PERKINS, principal; d. Richard E. and Dorothy A. Perkins; m. Ronald K. Wilson; children: Ryan R., Megan A. BS in Elem. Edn., Slippery Rock U., Pa., 1970; MEd, Fla. Atlantic U., 1993. Elem. specialist Glendale Elem. Sch., Vero Beach, Fla., 1989—97; prin. Fellsmere (Fla.) Elem. Sch., 1997—2002, Beachland Elem. Sch., Vero Beach, 2002—. Office: Beachland Elem Sch 3350 Indian River Dr E Vero Beach FL 32963 Office Phone: 772-564-3300.

WILSON, CAROLYN ROSS, retired school system administrator; b. Lake Charles, La., June 25, 1941; d. Charles Wesley and Lucille Gertrude (Payne) Ross; m. James David Wilson, Apr. 10, 1971; 1 child, Charlise. BS in Music Edn. cum laude, Xavier U., 1962; MMus in Music Edn., Cath. U., Washington, 1968; postgrad., U. D.C., 1985-86, George Washington U., 1987-88, Harvard U., 1989. Tchr. Xavier U. Jr. Sch. Music, New Orleans, 1960-61, Orleans Parish Schs., New Orleans, 1962-63, D.C. Pub. Schs., Washington, 1964-87, curriculum writer, summer 1984, 85, adminstrv. intern Ea. High Sch., 1987-88, asst. prin. Cardozo High Sch., 1988-89, asst. prin. Duke Ellington Sch. of Arts, 1989-93; prin. Duke Ellington Sch. Arts, Washington, 1993-97—; proposal reader U.S. Dept. Edn., 1998, 98, 99. Curriculum writer music dept. D.C. Pub. Schs., Washington, 1984-85, dir. All City High Sch. Chorus, 1973. Composer: A Dedication to Federal City Alumnae Chapter of Delta, Sigma Theta Sorority, Inc., 1973. Lector Immaculate Conception Ch., Washington, 1986—; named D.C. Tchr. of Yr., 1987. Recipient Cert. of Merit-Outstanding Tchr. and Prin. award D.C. Govt., 1994; U.S. Dept. Edn. Effective Schs. grantee, Washington, 1992. Mem. ASCD, Instn. for Devel. Ednl. Activities (6th yr. fellow, session chair 1988, seminar leader 1991, 92, 93, 94), Delta Sigma Theta (Federal City Alumnae chpt.). Roman Catholic. Avocations: reading, travel, bowling, musical arranging, playing the piano.

WILSON, CAROLYN TAYLOR, librarian; b. Cookeville, Tenn., June 10, 1936; d. Herman Wilson and Flo (Donaldson) Taylor; m. Larry Kittrell Wilson, June 14, 1957 (dec.); children: Jennifer Wilson Rust, Elissa Anne Wilson. BA, David Lipscomb Coll., 1957; MLS, George Peabody Coll., 1976. Tchr. English Fulton County Sch. System, Atlanta, 1957-59; serials cataloger Vanderbilt U. Libr., Nashville, 1974-77; asst. libr. United Meth. Pub. House, Nashville, 1978-80; collection devel. libr. David Lipscomb U., Nashville, 1980—, acting dir. Beaman Libr., 1998, dir. Beaman Libr., 1999—. Cons. and rschr. in field; project dir. Tenn.'s Lit. Legacy for Tenn. Humanities Coun., 1994—, ALA grant. Frontier in Am. Culture, 1996-98; project dir. Tenn. Humanities Coun. grant, 1998—; rep. Tenn. Avd. Coun. Librs., Acad. Librs., 1999—. Rsch. asst. Handbook of Tennessee Labor History, 1987-89. Adv. bd. So. Festival of Books, Nashville, 1988-90, 90—, vol. coord., 1989, 90—; project dir. Women's Words (summer grant program) for Tenn. Humanities Coun., Tenn.'s Literary Legacy (summer grant program), 1994-96, Growing Up Southern (summer grant), 1996—, ALA grant The Frontier in Am. Culture, 1996—. Recipient Nat. Honor Soc. award Phi Alpha Theta, 1956, Internat. Honor Soc. award Beta Phi Mu, 1980, Frances Neel Cheney award Tenn. Libr. Assn., 1992; nominee Athena award, 1992; Growing Up Southern summer grantee, 1996—. Mem. ALA, Tenn. Hist. Soc., Tenn. Libr. Assn. (Frances Neel Cheney award 1992), Southeastern Libr. Assn. (chmn. outstanding S.E. author award com. 1991-92, chmn. So. Books competition 1992-94, sec. exec. bd. 1997—), Women's Nat. Book Assn. (pres., v.p., treas., awards chmn. 1980—), Disciples of Christ Hist. Soc. (bd. dirs. 2002—), Tenn. Writers Alliance (bd. dirs. 1995—). Democrat. Avocations: reading, cooking, jogging, sailing. Office: David Lipscomb U Beaman Libr # 310 Nashville TN 37204 Office Phone: 615-279-5837. Business E-Mail: carolyn.wilson@lipscomb.edu.

WILSON, CARRIE LEE STROUD, principal; b. Bellevue, La., Dec. 14, 1948; d. Jeffrie Edward Stroud and Mary Elizabeth Jones-Stroud; m. Victor George Wilson, Apr. 19, 1972; children: Geoffrey Victor, Kimberly Georgina Elizabeth, James Anderson Stuart. B.A, U. Redlands, 1971; MA in Edn., U. Calif.-Berkeley, 2003. Preliminary Adminstrv. Intern Servicing Credential Calif. Tchg. Credentialing Com., 2002, Preliminary Adminstrv. Servicing Credential Calif. Tchr. Credentialing, 2004, Emergency Tchg. Credential Calif. Tchg. Credentialing, 2001. Counselor Upward Bound/U. Redlands, Vallejo, Calif., 1967; asst. to teen post dir. Redlands City Recreation Dept., Redlands, Calif., 1968; recreation leader Redlands Recreation Dept., Calif., 1969—70, art instr., 1971; docent U. Calif., Berkeley, 1971—72; tchr./drawing and composition-photography Vallejo City Unified Sch. Dist., 1998—99, asst. prin., 2002—03, vice prin., 2004—; tchr. Berkeley Unified Sch. Dist., Berkeley, Calif., 1973—74; real estate agt. Calif. Sch. Real Estate, Oakland, 1979—80; substitute tchr. Vallejo City Unified Sch. Dist., 1980—84, tchr., 1884—2000; art instr./exploratory art for young people Calif. Coll. Arts and Crafts, Oakland, 1985—86; tchr./summer sch. Vallejo City Unified Sch. Dist., 1999—2000, tchr./secondary/jr. high-middle sch., 1983—98, tchr./art-photography, 1998—99; academic dir. Jesse Bethel HS, Vallejo, 1999—2001, asst. prin., 2002—03, vice prin., 2003—. Chairperson/facilitator Springstowne Jr. HS, Vallejo, 1985—98, dept. head, 1991—98; state conf. presenter Calif. League of Mid. Schs., San Francisco, 1991—92; mentor-master-coach tchr. Springstowne Jr. HS, Vallejo, 1992—98; tchr. leader Jesse Bethel HS, Vallejo, 1998—2001, chairperson digital grant application to the state, 1999—2001, state standardized test coord., 2000—, chairperson com. for accreditation, 2001—02, state sch. intervention program for student achievement, 2001—03. Author: (poetry) What Time Is Fishin Time (pub. Famous Poets Soc., 1995), (essay) The Importance of Nature (pub. Nat. Essay Press, 1967); exhibitions include oil & acrylic painting thesis Journey of Self Expression, ceramics, Vase (Nat. Mus. of Arts- Wash., D.C., 1968), portraits on canvas/oil paintings (Patton State Hospital-Rehabilitation Ctr. For Young Women, 1969), Personal Expressions of African American Suburb Experience (Participant in Exhibit, 1968); contbr. (Cert./Black History Month, 1969); Compilation of Perspectives of an African American Woman (Cert. of Participation/Watts Summer Festival of Arts, L.A., 1965). Mem. ednl. reform programs for student achievement Vallejo City Unified Sch. Dist., 1995—2005; min. Jehovah's Witnesses, Vallejo, 1973—2005; mem. Vallejo Artist Guild, 1990—96; contbr. Continental Omega Boys and Girls Club, Vallejo, 2001—05; advisor Willie B. Atkins Tanner Project, Vallejo, 1998—2005. Nominee Tchr. of Yr., Calif. League Mid. Sch.; recipient, Elks B.P.O.E.; grantee Ednl. Opportunity Grant, Fed. Govt., 1967—71; Behring Scholar, U. Calif. Berkeley, Prin. Leadership Inst., 2001—03. Mem.: Vallejo Schs. Mgrs. Assn., ASCD, Assn. Calif. Sch. Adminstrs. Jehovah'S Witness. Achievements include recipient Phillip Harris Memorial Scholarship; missionary Ministry for Jehovah's Witnesses. Avocations: writing, art. Home: 119 Toni Ct Vallejo CA 94591-4272 Office: Jesse Bethel HS 1800 Ascot Pkwy Vallejo CA 94591-4272 Office Phone: 707-556-5700.

WILSON, CHERYL YVONNE, elementary and secondary school educator; b. Dayton, Ohio, Sept. 25, 1958; d. Samuel Wesley Wilson Sr. and Hazel Oneida Wilson; m. Henry Heard Cofield Jr., July 27, 1985. Student, Ohio State U., 1976—81; AA, Miami U., 1987. Legal sec. Raymond W. O'Neal, Sr. Atty. at Law, Middletown, Ohio, 1982—83; reorder buyer Dason's Hardware Ctr., 1984—85; Writer's Digest Novel Writing Workshop Middletown City Sch. Dist., 1986—87; deputy clk. Butler County Clk. Cts., Hamilton, 1990—91; mail room clk. Butler County Printing Co., 1992—95; mail courier, security officer Johnson Controls Svcs., Inc., 1998—2000; mail room clk. Dayton Daily News Cox Ohio Publ., 2003—04. Pres., CEO Ohio Writer's Pub. Co., Middletown, 1987—, 1991—; dept. sec. House Reparations 40, 2005—. Columnist: Dept. Health Regulation Forty Indsl. Inst., 2004—; author: numerous poems, —. Mem. 2006-1966 U.S. Bicentennial Commn., 2003—, curator, exec. dir., 2003. Nominee 87th Spingarn medal award, NAACP, 1998, 2001, Coretta Scott King book award, 2002, Oprah Winfrey Angel Network Use Your Life award, 2003. Mem.: NAACP (life Bronze Plaque award 2002), Nat. African Am. Genealogy Rsch. Pub. Assn., Internat. African Am. Genealogy Rsch. Pub. Assn. (curator 2003—, exec. dir. 2003—), Middletown Hist. Soc. (life). Republican. Mem. Lds Ch. Avocations: writing, reading, photography. Office Phone: 513-424-7749. Personal E-mail: ohioafriamerhistmo@sbcglobal.net.

WILSON, CLEO FRANCINE, foundation administrator; b. Chgo., May 7, 1943; d. Cleo Antonio Chancey and Frances (Page) Watson; divorced; children: SuLyn Silbar. BA in English with distinction, U. Ill., 1976. Supr. Playboy Enterprises, Inc., Chgo., 1980-82; grants mgr. Playboy Found., Chgo., 1982-84, exec. dir., 1984—, v.p. pub. affairs, 2001—. Pres. Intuit: The Ctr. for Intuitive and Outsider Art, 1996—, 2000—. Pres. AIDS Found. Chgo., 1990-93; v.p. Donors Forum Chgo., 1986-88; sec. Chgo. Women in Philanthropy, 1986-87; advisor Chgo. Dept. Cultural Affairs, 1988-90. Recipient Kizzy Image award Black Woman Hall of Fame, 1984;, Friend for Life award Howard Brown Health Ctr, 1991, Handy L. Lindsey award for inclusiveness in philanthropy, 2004; honored by AIDS Found, Chgo, 1999; named one of Chgo's Up and Coming by Dollars & Sense mag., 1985, Phenomenal Woman award An Expo for Today's Black Woman, 1997. Home: 6571 N Glenwood Ave Chicago IL 60626-5121 Office: Playboy Enterprises Inc 680 N Lake Shore Dr Fl 15 Chicago IL 60611-4455

WILSON, DEBORA J., broadcast executive; m. Larry Wilson; 1 stepchild, Kevin; 1 child, Christine. BS in Fin. and Bus. Adminstrn., George Mason U. With Bell Atlantic Network Svcs.; joined The Weather Channel, 1994, sr. v.p. new bus. devel., exec. v.p., gen. mgr. online svcs.; pres., CEO The Weather Channel Interactive, 1999—2003; COO The Weather Channel Network and The Weather Channel Interactive, 2003—04; pres. The Weather Channel Cos., 2004—. Recipient Tami Award, 2000. Mem.: Interactive Adv. Bureau, Cable & Telecom. Assoc., National Cable Television Assoc., bd. of dir. Lightbridge, Inc. Office: 300 Interstate North Pkwy SE Atlanta GA 30339-2403

WILSON, DEBORAH GRIM, music educator; b. Reading, Pa., Jan. 24, 1955; d. Robert Frederick and Jean (LeMay) Grim; m. Michael Louis Wilson, Dec. 27, 1975; children: Michelle Josephine, Stephanie Nicole. BS in Music Edn., Indiana U. Pa., 1976; MA, Western State Coll., 1984. Cert. tchr. early adolescent and young adult music/band, board cert. tchr. 2003. Tchr. elem. music W. End Sch. Dist., Nucla, Colo., 1978—80, Clifton Elem. Sch., Grand Junction, Colo., 1980—81; elem. band dir. Sch. Dist. #51, Grand Junction, 1981—84; jr. high. band dir. Orchard Mesa Mid. Sch., Grand Junction, 1984—89; elem. music tchr. Wingate Sch., Grand Junction, 1989—98; mid. sch. band. dir. Grand Mesa Mid. Sch., Grand Junction, 1998—. Mem.: Colo. Band Masters Assn., Colo. Music Educators Assn., Am. Sch. Band Dirs. Assn. Home: 711 Jasmine Ln Grand Junction CO 81506 Office Phone: 970-254-6270. E-mail: dgwilson21@bresnan.net.

WILSON, DEBORRAH, physical education educator; b. Tachikowa, Japan, Aug. 18, 1950; BS in Phys. Edn. and Health, U. Del., 1972; MEd, Wilmington Coll., 2000. Elem. phys. edn. tchr. Downes Elem. Sch.; instr. of programs, teen dir. YWCA, 1972—78; phys. edn. specialist Christina Sch. Dist., 1978—. Recipient Outstanding Alumni award U. Del., 1993, Disting. Svc. award Maclary PTA, 1993, Del. Congress Parents and Tchrs. Inc.; named Ea. Region Elem. Sch. Phys. Edn. Tchr. of Yr., Nat. Assn. Sport and Phys. Edn., 1993, Elem. Phys. Edn. Tchr. of Yr., State of Del., 1993, Tchr. of Yr. Elem. Sch., 2000. Home: 731 Art Ln Newark DE 19713-1208 Office Phone: 302-454-2133. E-mail: dekeencat@aol.com.

WILSON, DEBRA JOANNE, vice principal; m. Frank Lamont Wilson, Apr. 2, 1977; children: Carrie Elizabeth, Jennifer Joy, Jeffrey Scott. BS, Olivet Nazarene U., Kankakee, Ill., 1972—76; MA, Trevecca Nazarene U., Nashville, Tenn., 1988—89; Ednl. Specialist, Mid. Tenn. State U., Murfreesboro, 2000—01. Lic. Tchr. Tenn. Dept. Edn., 1979. Interim tchr. Bradley East Elem., Ill., 1977—79; reservation sales agt. Piedmont, Nashville, 1980—83; tchr. Metro Davidson County Schs., Nashville, 1984—96, Warren County Schs., McMinnville, Tenn., 1996—2004, instrnl. coord., vice principal, 2004—. Dir., women's ministries First Ch. of the Nazarene, Nashville, 1985—90; sponsor Jr. Beta Club, McMinnville, 2004—06. Recipient Jr. of Yr., Ch. of the Nazarene, Fla. Dist., 1966, Miss Teenage Daytona Beach, Miss Am. Pageants, 1968, Tchr. of Yr., Metro Davidson County Schs., 1989. Mem.: Assn. Supervision & Curriculum Devel., Phi Kappa Phi. Protestant. Avocations: piano, reading, cross stitch. Office: West Elementary Sch 400 Clark Blvd Mc Minnville TN 37110 Office Phone: 931-473-3801 267. Office Fax: 931-473-0863. Business E-Mail: wilsond38@k12tn.net.

WILSON, DONNA MAE, academic administrator, language educator; b. Columbus, Ohio, Feb. 25, 1947; d. Everett John and Hazel Margaret (Bruck) Palmer; m. Steven L. Wilson, Nov. 16, 1968. BA, Ohio State U., 1973, MA, 1976; postgrad studies, U. Wash., Seattle Pacific U., U. Mass., 1980—93; cert., U. Salamanca, Spain, 1985; PhD in Higher Edn., U. Mass., 2003. Cert. oral proficiency Am. Coun. Tchrs. Fgn. Lang. Tchg. assoc. Ohio State U., Columbus, 1974—76; lectr. U. Wash., Seattle, 1977—78; grants officer Seattle U., 1978—82; adj. prof. Shoreline Coll., Seattle, 1982—84; coord. fgn. langs., prof. Spanish Bellevue Coll., Wash., 1984—87; prof. Spanish Highline Coll., Des Moines, 1987—98, chair fgn. lang. dept., 1990—94, chair arts and humanities, 1994—98; assoc. dean acad. affairs Greenfield Coll., Mass., 1998—2002; adminstr.'s policy rsch. assoc. U. Mass., 2003—04; fgn. lang. project editor Nat. Evaluation Sys., Amherst, 2004—. Editor: Fronteras: En Contacto, 1992-93; editor Modern Lang. Jour., 1991, 92, 94, 96, 97, 98, 2001, Hispania, 1993, 95, 98, 2001, 03; text editor D. C. Heath and Co., Harcourt, Brace and Jovanovich, Houghton Mifflin, Prentice Hall; contbr. articles to profl. jours., chpt. to English of Science and Technology Learning, 2000; manuscript cons. Modern Lang. Jour., 1999—. Mem. Mass. Bd. Higher Edn. Exit Assessment, 1999-2000; pres. Mass. Coun. Acad. Deans, 2000-2001; assoc. deans think tank New England Resource Ctr. Higher Edn., 2000-02. Recipient cert. of excellence Phi Theta Kappa, 1990, Pathfinder award Phi Beta Kappa, 1995; fellowship grant Coun. Internat. Edn. Exch., Santiago, Chile, 1992. Mem. Nat. Coun. Instr. Adminstrns., Am. Assn. Tchrs. Spanish (v.p. Wash.), Am. Coun. Tchrs. Fgn. Langs., Assn. Dept Fgn. Langs. (exec. bd. 1994-97), Pacific N.W. Coun. Fgn. Langs., 1986-98, Nat. Assn. Fgn. Lang. Suprs., Sigma Delta Mu. (nat. exec. sec. 1992-98), Nat. Assn. Women in Higher Edn. Achievements include assessment, organizational behavior theory, higher education leadership, research on second language. E-mail: dmslwilson@verizon.net.

WILSON, DORIS H., volunteer; b. Akron, Ohio, Jan. 26, 1921; d. Charles Peter and Emma Clara (Howald) Huff; m. Angus Francis Wilson, June 14, 1952; children: Ann Wilson Lambertus, Lea Wilson MacInnis. BS, U. Akron, 1945; postgrad., Framingham State Coll., 1965, Salem State Coll., 1968. Adminstrv. asst. divsn. comml. engr. Ohio Bell Tel. Co., Akron, 1941-52; adminstr. Framingham Ctr. Kindergarten and Nursery Sch., 1965-68. Author: (book) A History of Great Neck, Ipswich, 1984, 1996. Vol. nurse's aide ARC, Akron, 1940; active Gov.'s Coun. Civilian Def., Boston, 1960—66; cofounder, charter mem. Hospice at Home, Wayland, Weston, Natick, Sudbury, Mass., 1978; chmn. W. Suburban Area Boston Symphony Orch., 1978—81; docent Gt. Ho. at Castle Hill, Ipswich, Mass., 1984—2003, Whipple Ho., Ipswich, 1985—2002; treas. Nuc. Freeze Coun., Ipswich, 1986—87; charter mem., bd. dirs. Aplastic Anemia Found. Am. New Eng. region, Brookline, Mass., 1987—92; vol. office asst. Habitat for Humanity, St. Petersburg, Fla., 1988; mem. Ipswich Women's Club, 1981—2006. Recipient Election Poll Officer citation, Gov. of Mass., 1980, 1st pl. Ann. Short Story Contest, Gen. Fedn. Women's Club, 2002. Mem.: AAUW (Mass. state parliamentarian 1966—76, charter, pres. Framingham-Wellesley br., North Shore br., grantee 1974), Ipswich Citizens Advocating Renewable Energy, Friends Glen Magna (Danvers, Mass. dir. 1991—93), Ipswich Hist. Soc., Boston Symphony Assn. Vols., Peace Action, Ipswich Bay Yacht Club (dir. 1981—82), Wayland Women's Club (hon.; pres.). Democrat. Roman Catholic. Home: 8 Bowdoin Rd Ipswich MA 01938-2807

WILSON, ELEANOR MCELROY, county official; b. Lancaster, Pa., Sept. 10, 1938; d. Hartford Ford and Jane Ann McElroy; m. Frank Eugene Wilson, July 17, 1976 (dec. Jan. 1980). AA, Monterey Peninsula Jr. Coll., Monterey, Calif., 1959; BA in Edn., San Jose State U., 1963; MA in Bus. /Mgmt., Webster U., St. Louis, 1981; MA in Internat. Rels., Salve Regina Coll., Newport, R.I., 1990; MA in Nat. Security/Strategic Studies, Naval War Coll., Newport, 1991. Sec. Geo. Dovolis Real Estate, Monterey, 1957-59; legal sec. Thompson & Thompson Attys., Monterey, 1959-61; legal asst., supr. Thomson J. Hudson, Atty., Monterey, 1963-68, legal asst., 1972-74. Mem. Orange County Grand Jury Superior Ct., Santa Ana, Calif., 1982—83; citizen mem. Orange County Parole Bd., Santa Ana, 1993—96, 1999—2001; mem. Orange County Juvenile Justice Commn., Orange, 1992—2000, chair, 1995; nat. adv. coun., bd. advisors Flying Leatherneck Hist. Found., 2000—. Col. USMCR, 1968—98. Decorated Legion of Merit. Mem.: Sloan Found. (bd. dirs. 1996—98), Marine Corps Aviation Assn. (bd. dirs. 1980—94, bd. advisors 1994—), Marine Corps Heritage Found. (bd. dirs. 1992—98). Avocations: reading, golf, tennis, travel.

WILSON, EVELYN GLEEN, retired language educator; b. Kannapolis, N.C., July 1, 1941; d. Della Ree Thompson-Wilson, Robert Felton Wilson. BA, Livingstone Coll., 1963. Tchr. Rowan County Schs., Salisbury, NC, 1991—2000, Kannapolis City Schs., NC, 2000—; ret. Coord. Kannapolis out of sch. tutorial program FFLC Fishertown Learning Ctr., NC, 2000—. Human svc. coord. Nat. Multiple Sclerosis Soc.; vol. Laubach Literacy Action S.W. Edn. Alliance, Dem. Conv., Atlanta, 1988; bd. dirs. Sankofa Multi-cultural Coalition, 1988. Named Most Admired Tchr. of Rowan County Schs., Charlotte Hornets/Paramount, 1995—96; recipient Cmty. Svc. award, The Martin Luther King,Jr./Southern Christian Leadership Com., 1983. Mem.: NAACP, NEA (sch. chairperson 1997—99, Gold Key Chain award 1999). Baptist. Achievements include name placed on national campaign for tolerance honoring those who take a personal public stance against hate, injustice, and intolerance. Avocation: painting. Home: 231 Rosemont Ave Kannapolis NC 28081 Office: Kannapolis City Sch 525 E C St Kannapolis NC 28083 Office Phone: 704-467-3418. Personal E-mail: egwil@earthlink.net.

WILSON, F. JILL, real estate company executive, internet consultant; b. Dallas, Dec. 9, 1944; d. Earl Kenneth Wilson and Dorothy Ruth Bowers; m. David Holcomb, Sept. 1969 (div. Mar. 1971); m. Donald Lee McRee, Mar. 20, 1983. BBA, So. Meth. U., 1966; MBA, St. Mary's U., 1973. Cert. property mgr., comml. investment mem. Pres., owner Wilson Schanzer Inc., San Antonio, 1978-93; pres. Security Capital Group Realty Svcs., San Antonio, 1993-95; ptnr. Wilson-McRee Cons., San Antonio and Vail, Colo., 1992—; CEO ApartmentWorld.com, San Antonio, 1999—2000; mng. dir. RentPort, Inc., NY, 2000—01. Mem. exec. bd. dirs. St. Mary's U. Sch. Bus., San Antonio, 1990—; mem. adv. bd. Via Transit, San Antonio, 1998; sec. fin. bd. Health and Med. Facilities, San Antonio, 1986-92; mem. adv. bd. Housing Fin. Bd., San Antonio, 1984-89. Recipient Corp. award Tex. Coun. of Family Violence, 1992; named Bus. Woman of Yr., San Antonio Express News, 1992, Entrepreneur of Yr. Inc. Mag./Ernst & Young, 1991. Mem. Tex. Apt. Assn. (pres. 1991), Bus. and Profl. Women (pres. 1989), Internat. Women's Forum (Women and Corp. Who Make a Difference 1991), Tex. Women's Forum, Colo. Forum, North San Antonio C. of C. (vice chmn. 1990). Avocations: skiing, hiking, mountain climbing. Home: 3487 River Way San Antonio TX 78230

WILSON, FRANCELIA LATTING, retired elementary school educator; b. Pueblo, Colo., Sept. 28, 1943; d. Trimble Baggett and Patience Sewell Latting; m. Thomas Allen Wilson (dec.); children: Cynthia Anne, Robin Marie. AA, Christian Coll., Columbia, Miss., 1962—63; BA in Elem. Edn., Okla. City U., 1963—67; MEd, Our Lady Lake U., San Antonio, 1969—75. Tchr. Am. Assn. U. Women; ret. Mem.: Am. Assn. U. Women. Home: 4410 NW 122 Oklahoma City OK 73114

WILSON, FRANCES C., career military officer; BS, Mich. State U.; MEd, Pepperdine U.; MA in Psychology, U. No. Colo.; MS in Bus. Mgmt., Salve Regina Coll.; PhD in Edn., U. So. Calif. Commd. 2d lt. USMC, 1972, advanced through grades to maj. gen.; air traffic control officer Marine Corps Air Sta., Yuma, Ariz., Kaneohe, Hawaii, 1975; tchr. instrnl. mgmt. Marine Corps Devel. & Edn. Ctr., Quantico, Va.; staff sec. 3d Marine Divsn., Okinawa, Japan, 1980-81; asst. prof., co. officer brigade of midshipmen U.S. Naval Acad., Annapolis, Md.; mgmt. analyst HQ USMC, Washington; spl. asst. for gen. and flag officer matters Joint Staff, Pentagon, exec. asst. to vice dir., 1987; comdr. 4th Recruit Tng. Battalion, Parris Island, S.C., 1988-90, Camp H.M. Smith, Svc. Battalion Marine Corps Pacific; sec. Joint Staff, until 1997; commanding gen. Marine Corps Base, Quantico, 1997-99, Third Force Svc. Support Group, Okinawa, Japan, 1999—2001; dir. pers. mgmt. divsn. M&RA Hdqrs. USMC, 2001—03; comdt. Indsl. Coll. Armed Forces, Nat. Def. U., Ft. McNair, DC, 2003—. Decorated Def. Superior Svc. medal, Def. Meritorious Svc. medal, Meritorious Svc. medal, Navy Commendation medal, Navy Achievement medal.

WILSON, FRANCES EDNA, protective services official; b. Keokuk, Iowa, Aug. 4, 1955; d. David Eugene and Anna Bell (Hootman) W. BA, St. Ambrose Coll., 1982; MA, Western Ill., 1990; cert. massage therapist, Shocks Ctr. Edn., Moline, Ill., 1993. Lic. massage therapist, cert. instr. Rape Aggression Def. Sys., 2d degree blackbelt Tai Ho Jujitsu, instr. aerosol spray restraint Aresol Spray Restraint Coun., 1996. Trainer, defensive tactics

Davenport (Iowa) Police, 1990—2004, police corporal, 1985-94, police sgt., 1994—; apptd. recs. bur. comdr. Iowa Assn. Women Police, Davenport, 1996-98, pres., 1989-92, patrol supr., coord. comm. training operator, 1998—2001, CTO coord., 1999—2001, sr. sgt. day shift patrol, 2001—02, adminstrv. sgt. day shift, 2003—05; adj. instr. Kaplan Coll., 2003—. Cons., def. tactics Scott C.C., Bettendorf, Iowa, 1993-; owner Wilson Enterprises Ltd., Davenport, 1995—; spkr. workshops; guest spkr. Genesis Employee Assistance Program, 1996-2002; training com. Davenport Police Dept., 1996-2001, recruitment com., 2001-02; instr. Rape Aggression Def. Sys., 1997-, kids instr., 1999-, Women Key Chain Def. instr., 2004-05; with Davenport Cmty. Adult Edn., 2002; mem. Family Connection bd., 1996-2002; advisor to criminal justice bd. Kaplan U., Davenport. Bd. dirs. Scott County Family YMCA, Davenport, 1990-95, instr., 1989—, The Family Connection, Ltd., West Family YMCA, 2003-04; instr. Davenport Cmty. Adult Edn., 1991-94; mem. Iowa SAFE KIDS Coalition, 1992-2000; active First Presbyn. Ch., Davenport, 1986—, bd. deacons, 1995; vol. asst. sgts. planning com. on tng. Davenport Police Dept., 1991, K-9 Unit, 1990-94. Recipient Law Enforcement award Davenport Optimist Club, 1997. Mem. NOW, AAUW, Law Enforcement Alliance Am., Am. Women Self Def. Assn., Am. Soc. Law Enforcement Trainers, Nat. Ctr. for Women and Policing, Iowa Assn. Women Police (pres. 1989-92, Officer of Yr. 1995), Iowa State Police Assn., Iowa Assn. Chiefs of Police and Peace Officers, Internat. Assn. Women Police, So. Poverty Law Ctr. Avocations: photography, reading, education, massage therapy, enjoying life. Office: Davenport Police Dept 420 N Harrison St Davenport IA 52801-1304 Office Phone: 319-326-6125. E-mail: frankie_wilson@juno.com.

WILSON, FRANCES HELEN, retired occupational therapist; b. Pitts., Oct. 17, 1929; d. J. Vernon and Margaret Hassler (Prugh) Wilson. BA, Conn. Coll., 1951; advanced standing cert., Columbia Sch. Occupl. Therapy, 1953. Therapist Washington (Pa.) County Soc. Crippled Children and Adults, 1953-54; staff therapist Oakland VA Hosp., U. Pitts., 1955-66; supr. Occupl. Therapy Clinic, Aspinwall VA Hosp., Pitts., 1966-74, 81-85, Occupl. Therapy Clinic, Oakland VA Hosp., Pitts., 1974—85, ret., 1985. Active Jr. League Pitts., Inc.; vol. Pitts. (Pa.) Children's Mus. Mem. Western Pa. (treas. 1967-69), Am. Occupl. Therapy Assns., Presbyn. Univ. Hosp. Pitts. Vol. Assn., Pitts. (Pa.) Symphony Assn., Acad. Lifelong Learning, Conn. Coll. Club (treas. 1971-94), Twentieth Century Club (Pitts.). Republican. Presbyterian. Home: Washington Plz 1116 1420 Centre Ave Pittsburgh PA 15219

WILSON, GAYLE ANN, civic worker; b. Phoenix, Nov. 24, 1942; d. Clarence Arthur and Charlotte Evelyn (Davison) Edlund; m. Theodore William Graham, Sept. 14, 1963 (div. May 1983); children: Todd Chandler, Philip Edlund; m. Pete Wilson, May 29, 1983. BA, Stanford U., 1965; postgrad., U. San Diego, 1982. First lady State of Calif., Sacramento, 1991-99; bd. directors ARCO, Los Angeles, CA, 1999—. Adv. for early childhood health and improved math. and sci. edn.; bd. dirs. Ctr. for Excellence in Edn., McLean, Va., 1985—, also former chmn.; mem. Jr. League San Diego, 1968—, also past pres.; bd. dirs. Calif. Inst. Tech., Pasadena, 1995—, Children's Inst. Internat., Phoenix House; former spokesperson Access for Infants and Mothers (AIM), Calif. Breast Cancer Initiative, Never Shake a Baby Campaign, Partnership for Responsible Parenting; mem. Calif. Sesquicentennial Commn.; hon. chmn. Calif. Sci. Fair, Calif. 4-H Found., Calif. Perinatal Outreach-BabyCal, Calif. Commn. on Improving Life Through Svc., Keep Calif. Beautiful; hon. co-chmn. Calif. Mentor Initiative; mem. adv. coun. Ct. Apptd. Spl. Advs.; mem. adv. coun. computers in schs. program Detweiler Found.; hon. chmn. bd. dirs. Leland Stanford Mansion Restoration Found.; founding mem. Achievement Rewards for Coll. Scientists; mem. San Diego Park and Recreation Commn., 1980-83; regent Children's Hosp. L.A. Found., 1998—; bd. dirs. Center Theatre Group, L.A., 1998—, ARCO. Recipient Guardian Angel award L.A. ChildShare, 1995, lifetime achievemecnt award Jr. League L.A., 1996. Mem. Phi Beta Kappa. Republican. Avocations: lyric writing, singing, performing, watercolors. Office: 2132 Century Park Ln Apt 301 Los Angeles CA 90067-3320

WILSON, GRETCHEN, vocalist; b. Granite City, Ill., June 26, 1973; 1 child, Grace. Signed by Epic Records, 2003—. Singer: (singles) Redneck Woman, 2004 (Breakthrough Video of Yr., Country Music Television Music award, 2005), When I Think About Cheatin, 2004 (Female Video of Yr., Country Music Television Music award, 2005), (five singles) 5-Mo-Fo-Ya, 2005, (albums) Here for the Party, 2004, All Jacked Up, 2005; TV appearances include: In The Moment, 2004. Named Female Vocalist of Yr., Country Music Assn., 2005; recipient Horizon award, 2004, Favorite New Artist, Am. Music Awards, 2004, Favorite Female Country Artist, 2005, Female Country Artist of Yr., Billboard Music Awards, 2004, New Country Artist of Yr., 2004, Top New Artist, Acad. Country Music Awards, 2005, Top Female Vocalist, 2005. Achievements include first new artist to debut at #1 on Billboard's Country LP chart. Office: Sony Music 34 Music Sq E Nashville TN 37203-4323*

WILSON, HEATHER ANN, congresswoman; b. Keene, NH, Dec. 30, 1960; d. George Douglas Wilson and Martha Lou Wilson-Kernozicky; m. Jay Hone; 3 children. BS in Internat. Politics, USAF Acad., Colo., 1982; MPhil in Internat. Rels., U. Oxford, Eng., 1984, PhD in Internat. Rels., 1985. US mission NATO, Brussels, 1987—89; dir. def. policy and arms control NSC, Washington, 1989—91; pres. Keystone Internat., Inc., Albuquerque, 1991—95; cabinet sec. N.Mex. Dept. Children, Youth and Families, Santa Fe, 1992—98; mem. US Congress from 1st N.Mex. dist., 1998—, mem. energy and commerce com., mem. permanent select com. on intelligence, chair tech. and tactical intelligence subcommittee. Adj. prof. U. N.Mex.; mem. Def. Adv. Com. on Women in the Svcs. Contbr. articles to profl. jours. Capt. USAF, 1982—89. Named Rhodes scholar, 1982; recipient Hero of the Taxpayer award, Ams. for Tax Reform, 1999, 2002, Spirit of Free Enterprise award, US C. of C., 2000, Guardian of Small Bus. award, Nat. Fedn. Ind. Bus., 2000, Golden Bulldog award, Watchdog of Treasury, 2000, Disting. Cmty. Health Superhero award, Nat. Assn. Cmty. Health Ctrs., Inc., 2005, Javits-Wagner-O'Day Champion award, 2005. Mem.: Kiwanis. Republican. Methodist. Avocations: hiking, skiing. Office: US Ho Reps 318 Cannon Ho Office Bldg Washington DC 20515-3101 Office Phone: 202-225-6316.*

WILSON, JANE, artist; b. Seymour, Iowa, Apr. 29, 1924; d. Wayne and Cleone (Marquis) Wilson; m. John Gruen, Mar. 28, 1948; 1 child, Julia Gruen. BA, U. Iowa, 1945, MA, 1947. Mem. fine arts faculty Parsons Sch. Design, 1973-83, 89-90. Vis. artist U. Iowa, 1974; adj. assoc. prof. painting and drawing Columbia U., 1975—85, assoc. prof., 1985—86, prof., 1986—88, acting chair, 1986—88; Andrew Mellon vis. prof. painting Cooper Union, 1977—78. One-woman shows include Hansa Gallery, N.Y.C., 1953, 1955, 1957, Stuttman Gallery, 1958, 1959, Tibor de Nagy Gallery, 1960—66, Graham Gallery, 1968, 1969, 1971, 1973, 1975, Fischbach Gallery, 1978, 1981, 1984, 1988, 1990, 1991, 1993, 1995, 1997, Munson-Williams-Proctor Inst., Utica, N.Y., 1980, Cornell U., Ithaca, N.Y., 1982, Compass Rose Gallery, Chgo., 1988, Am. U., Washington, 1989, U. Richmond, Va., 1990, Earl McGratgh Gallery, LA, 1990—91, 1993, Dartmouth Coll., Hanover, N.H., 1991, Arnot Mus., Elmira, N.Y., 1993—94, Parrish Mus., Southampton, N.Y., 1996, Glenn Horowitz Gallery, East Hampton, N.Y., 1996, D. C. Moore Gallery, N.Y.C., 1999, 2001, 2003, 2004, Heckscher Mus., Huntington, N.Y., 2001, McKinney Ave. Contemporary, Dallas, 2003, Represented in permanent collections Met. Mus., Mus. Modern Art, Whitney Mus., Wadsworth Atheneum, Heron Art Mus., NYU Rockefeller Inst., Vassar Coll., Pa. Acad. Fine Arts, Hirsch Horn Mus., Washington, Nelson-Atkins Mus., Kansas City, Mo., San Francisco Mus. Modern Art, Heckscher Mus., L.I. Mus., Stony Brook, others. Recipient Eloise Spaeth award, Guild Hall, East Hampton, N.Y., 1968, Lifetime Achievement award, 2001, Purchase prize, Childe Hassam Fund, 1971, 1973, 1981, Ranger Fund Purchase prize, 1977; Ingram-Merrill grantee, 1963, Louis Comfort Tiffany grantee, 1967. Mem.: Nat. Acad. Design (academician 1974—, pres. 1992—94), Am. Acad. Arts and Letters (award in Art 1985), Phi Beta Kappa. E-mail: jwi1010@aol.com.

WILSON, JEAN LOUISE, retired state legislator; b. Phila., June 13, 1928; d. Horace and Catherine (Lennox) Terry; m. Benjamin H. Wilson (dec.); children: Sheryl J. Gordon, Denise T. Munn. BS in Edn., Pa. State U., 1949. Tchr. Columbia Inst., Phila., 1949-50, Wilkes Coll., Wilkes Barre, Pa., 1950-51; office mgr., exec. sec. Camden Fibre Mills, Warminster, Pa., 1969-82; mem. Pa. Ho. of Reps., 1988-92. Legis. chmn. Doylestown V.I.A.; active Benj. H. Wilson Sr. Ctr., Ctr. for Learning in Retirement, Del. Valley Coll.; former mem. bd. Bucks County Opportunity Coun.; former treas. Bucks County chpt. Fox Chase Cancer Ctr. Avocations: duplicate bridge, golf. Home: 12 Far View Rd Chalfont PA 18914-2511

WILSON, JILL MARIE, elementary school educator; b. St. Louis, Nov. 29, 1953; d. Arthur Walter and Mary Katherine (Heitzler) Buback; m. Gary Wayne Wilson, July 22, 1972 (div. Sept. 1997); children: Christopher, Patricia. AAS, East Ctrl. Coll., 1988; degree in spl. edn., U. Mo., 1990—. Advt. artist Christian Bd. Publ., St. Louis, 1972-77; paraprofl. Franklin County Spl. Edn. Coop., St. Clair, Mo., 1988-90; early childhood tchr., dir. Meramec Valley R-3 Early Childhood Ctr., Pacific, Mo., 1990—. Freelance artist, 1977—. Treas. Oak Hill Elem. PTO, St. Louis, 1984-85; mem., coach, mgr., treas. Union Girls Softball Assn., 1990-96; elem. sch. program facilitator Jr. Achievement, St. Louis, 1999. Mem. Assn. for Childhood Edn. Internat., Mo. Nat. Edn. Assn., Early Childhood Tchr.'s Club, Mo. Coun. for Exceptional Children, Phi Theta Kappa. Avocations: decorative painting, reading, computers, canoeing, walking. Office: Meramec Valley R-3 Early Childhood Ctr 2001 W Osage St Pacific MO 63069-1126 Home: 1416 S Vermont Ave Sedalia MO 65301-7218

WILSON, JUDITH ANN, secondary school educator; b. Cassville, Mo., Feb. 12, 1951; d. Joe Edward and Jean Bayless W.; m. David M. Wilson, June 2, 1973; 1 child, Melissa Jean. BS in Edn., Southwest Mo. State U., 1972, MA in English, 1976. Journalism adviser Butler H.S., Mo., 1972-73, Strafford H.S., Mo., 1974-75; instr. English Southwest Mo. State U., Springfield, Mo., 1977-81; journalism adviser Parkview H.S., 1981—2001, English tchr., 2002—. Coach Critical Friends Group Annenberg Inst. Sch. Reform, Providence, 1995-98. Mem. Journalism Edn. Assn., Ozarks Pub. Advisers. Home: 1904 E Lark St Springfield MO 65804-4346 Office: Parkview High Sch 516 W Meadowmere St Springfield MO 65807-1459

WILSON, JUDY, small business owner; b. Ohio; From order desk clk. to sales rep. Pacific Fasteners; sales rep. Wire & Cable; outside sales rep. Standard Wire & Cable Co., L.A.; owner Wilco Wire & Cable. Office: Wilco Wire & Cable Co 1035 Mission Ct Fremont CA 94539-8203

WILSON, JULIA ANN YOTHER, lawyer; b. Dallas, Sept. 6, 1958; d. Julian White and Mary Ann (Estes) Yother. BA, East Ctrl. U., Ada, Okla., 1980; JD, U. Okla., 1983. Bar: Okla. 1990, Calif. 1993, D.C. 1995; U.S. Ct. Appeals (9th cir.) Calif. 1993, U.S. Supreme Ct. 1993, U.S. Dist. Ct. (ctrl. dist.) Calif. 1993, U.S. Dist. Ct. (we. dist.) Okla., 1997. Assoc. Law Office of George Rodda Jr., Newport Beach, Calif., 1984-96; sole practice law Oklahoma City, 1996-97; assoc. Coldiron, Wilson & Assocs., Oklahoma City, 1997—2004; pvt. practice Oklahoma City, 2004—. Served to 1st lt. USAR, 1980-86. Mem. ABA, D.C. Bar Assn., Calif. Bar Assn., Oklahoma County Bar Assn., Okla. Bar Assn. (litigation sect.), Orange County Bar Assn. Office: 3233 E Memorial Rd Ste 107B Edmond OK 73013 Office Phone: 405-478-8889. Business E-Mail: julia.wilson@lawoklahoma.com.

WILSON, K. SHANNON, psychologist; b. Des Moines, Nov. 21, 1973; d. Robert Dennis and Nelda Bowers; m. William Franklin Wilson, Oct. 23, 1999; children: Susannah, Nicholas 1 stepchild, Sarah. BA in Psychology magna cum laude, Gettysburg Coll., 1995, BA in Religion, 1995; PhD, U. Tenn., 2001. Rsch asst. Gettysburg Coll. Dept. Psychology, Pa., 1993—95; intern Gettysburg Jr. High Sch., 1993—94; summer rsch. asst. Gettysburg Coll. Psychology Dept., 1994; sr. honors rschr., 1994—95; rsch asst. U. Tenn. Psychology Dept., 1995—96; therapist U. Tenn. Psychol. Clinic, Knoxville, 1996—99; diagnostic, evaluation cons. Resource Assocs., Inc., Knoxville, 1997—98; psychology assoc. Ridgeview Psychat. Hosp., Inc., Oak Ridge, 1997—98; doctoral intern Guidance Ctr., Murfeesboro, Tenn., 2000—01; pvt. practitioner Behavorial Health Ctr. Child and Adult Svcs., Knoxville, 2001—05, Bearden Psychological Ctr., 2005—. Psychologist health, support orgns. including law enforcement, 1996—; cons. parents; cons. stress training; presenter in field. Contbr. articles to profl. jours. Counselor, mentor Adams County Adolescent Pregnancy Intervention Program, Pa., 1991—93; tutor, study group discussion facilitator for psychology students Gettysburg Coll., 1993—95; sec. Gettysburg Coll. Cir. K Club, 1992—93, pres., 1993—94, advisory bd., fundraising chair, 1994—95. Recipient Girl Scout Gold award, 1991, Psi Chi Jr. Achievement award, 1994, Psi Chi Sr. Achievement award, 1995, Oscar W. Carlson award for Religion Students, 1995; MacCartney Scholarship award for Work Study Students, 1993, Milla Alihan Scholarship award, Soc. Clin. and Experimental Hypnosis, 1996, 1997. Mem.: APA, Nat. Assn. Female Exec., Equine Assisted Growth and Learning Assn., Knoxville Area Psychol. Assn., Phi Beta Kappa, Alpha Lambda Delta. Methodist. Avocations: camping, movies, reading, horses. Office: 5401 Kingston Pike Ste 170 Knoxville TN 37919 Office Phone: 865-584-4005. Personal E-mail: kswilsonphd@aol.com.

WILSON, KAREN LEE, museum staff member, researcher; b. Somerville, NJ, Apr. 2, 1949; d. Jon Milton and Laura Virginia (Van Dyke) W.; m. Paul Ernest Walker, 1980; 1 child, Jeremy Nathaniel. AB, Harvard U., 1971; MA, NYU, 1973, PhD, 1985. Rsch. assoc., dir. excavation at Mendes, Egypt Inst. Fine Arts, NYU, 1979-81; coord. exhbn. The Jewish Mus., N.Y.C., 1981-82, adminstrv. cataloguer, 1982-83, coord. curatorial affairs, 1984-86; curator Oriental Inst. Mus. U. Chgo., 1988-96, mus. dir., 1996—2003, rsch. assoc., 1988—; coord. Kish Project Field Mus. Natural History, Chgo., 2004—. Rsch. asso. Oriental Inst. U. Chgo. Author, editor: Mendes, 1982; contbr. articles to profl. jours. Mem.: Coll. Art Assn., Am. Oriental Soc. Office Phone: 312-665-7184. Business E-Mail: k-wilson@uchicago.edu.

WILSON, KAREN LYNN, esthetician; b. Hartford, Conn., Mar. 6, 1956; d. Derwood Alexander and Rita Harriet Briggs; m. Leo Franklin Wilson, Sept. 5, 2003; children: Jeffrey Thomas Haynes, Jason Brian Haynes. BS in Fin. (hon.), Williams Coll., Houston, 1999. Lic. Esthetician Conn. Cosmetology, 2004. Sales and mktg. dir. Bollitierri Tennis Acad., Bradenton, Fla., 1990—95; registrar Nortel Comm., Wethersfield, Conn., 1995—98; sr. fin. assoc. NextiraOne, Wethersfield, Conn., 1998—2002; mktg. staff Total Comm., East Hartford, Conn., 2001—04; esthetician Timeless Reflection @ Cutters' Edge, Rocky Hill, Conn., 2004—. Apptd. to employee counsel Williams Comm., Wethersfield, Conn., 1998—2000, AR task team, 2000—01. Team leader United Way, Wethersfield, Conn., 1998—2000; chairperson Diabetes Found., Wethersfield, 1998—2001; team leader disaster recovery Rebuilding After 911 Tragedy. Recipient Dedication to Customers during 911 Tragedy, NextiraOne, 2001, Tiffany award, Manpower Staffing Svcs., 1996, Cir. of Excellence award, Williams Comm., 2000, Superior Performance; Gold Level, 1996—97, Achieving Customer Excellence award, 2000. Mem.: Continuing Profl. Edn. (assoc.), ABMP (assoc.), Jr. Women's Club (assoc.). Home: 222 Chestnut Hill Rd East Hampton CT 06424 Office: Timeless Reflection @ Cutters' Edge 2162 Silas Deane Hwy Rocky Hill CT 06067 Office Phone: 860-563-0243. Personal E-mail: k_lunited@yahoo.com. E-mail: timeless@yahoo.com, skincarebykaren@sbcglobal.net.

WILSON, KRISTIN M., mathematics educator; d. Fred H. and Suzanne M. Wilson. BS in Secondary Math. Edn., Plymouth State Coll., NH, 1995; MEd in Curriculum & Instrn., New Eng. Coll., Henniker, NH, 2003; C.A.G.S. Ednl. Leadership, Plymouth State U., 2004. Cert. Math. Edn. Endorsement NH, 1995. Tchr. math. Mascoma Valley Regional HS, Canaan, NH, 1995—. Named to Who's Who in Am. Tchrs., 1999, 2003. Mem.: ASCD, NEA. D-Liberal. Roman Catholic. Avocations: travel, reading. Office: Mascoma Valley Regional HS 27 Royal Rd Canaan NH 03741

WILSON, L. MICHELLE, lawyer; b. Boise, Idaho, Jan. 20, 1963; d. Tom Martin and George Ann Wilson. BA, U. Wash., Seattle, 1985; JD, U. Chgo., 1988. Ptnr. Perkins Coie, Seattle, 1988—; assoc. gen. counsel Amazon.com Inc., Seattle, 1999—99, v.p., gen. counsel, sec., 1999—. Recipient Dow Jones award Wall St. Jour., 1985. Mem. ABA, Washington State Bar Assn., Order of Coif, Phi Beta Kappa, Beta Gamma Sigma. Office: Amazon.com Inc 1200 12th Ave S Ste 1200 Seattle WA 98144-2734 Office Phone: 206-266-1000. Office Fax: 206-266-1821.

WILSON, LAURA ANN, newspaper editor; b. Otis AFB, Mass., Oct. 3, 1967; d. Robert Carl Laidacker, Emmett Adkins, Jr. and Wanda June (Laidacker); m. Charles John Wilson, Dec. 12, 1992; children: Brendan, Emily. Cert., Lucas Travel Sch., 1988; AA, Pierce Coll., 1993; BS, U. So. Fla., 1997. Intern The Tampa Tribune, Fla., 1996, bus. clerk Fla., 1996; mgn. editor The Pinellas News, St. Petersburg, Fla., 96-98; cmty. editor The Star Democrat, Easton, Md., 1998-2000, spl. sects. editor, 2000—03; editl. specialist Shore Health System, 2003. Spkr. Career Day, Clearview Elem. Sch., St. Petersburg, Fla., 1997, Easton Middle Sch., Md., 1998; guest spkr. Md. Nonprofits, Balt., 1999; student mentor, Talbot Mentors, Easton, 1999—. Mem. The Writers Guild (v.p. USF chpt. 1994), Soc. Profl. Journalists (pres. USF chpt. 1996). Avocations: bowling, walking, reading, travel, movies. Office: Shore Health Sys 219 S Wash St Easton MD 21601 E-mail: lwilson@chespub.com.

WILSON, LAURA ELEANOR, landscape architect; b. Columbus, Ohio, July 9, 1930; d. Russell Brown and Geraldine Gertrude (Rang) W. BS in Landscape Architecture, Iowa State U., 1953. Landscape arch. Rose Greely Landscape Arch., Washington, 1953-55, Prentiss French Landscape Arch., San Francisco, 1955-57, Nat. Park Svc., San Francisco, 1957-72, Santa Fe, 1972-83; sculptor pvt. practice, Santa Fe, 1983—. Landscape architecture: designer and team capt. Visitor Ctr. Cabrillo Nat. Monument, 1969, (Garden Club award 1972), Lehman Caves New Mex., 1966, Redwoods NewMex., Visitor's Ctr., 1971; sculptor: solo exhibitions include Cadmium Gallery, San Francisco, 1962, Art Assocs. W. San Francisco, 1969, 71. St.John's Coll. Santa Fe, New Mex., 1972-1998, Concepts Gallery, Santa Fe, 1984, 86, 88, 90, 92, Santa Fe Contemporary Art, 1995; group show: New Mex. Sculptor's Guild Fuller Lodge Art Ctr., Los Alamos, 1992; invitational, juried incl. 1987's New Mexico Selections Coll. of Santa Fe, invitation to outdoor sculpture Coll. Santa Fe, 1991-2003, Friends of Contemporary Art, 2000, N.Mex. Sculptor's Guild, 2002, Gov.'s Gallery, N.Mex. State Capitol, 2002. Recipient Trailblazer award, State of New Mex. Commn., 1998, Muchas Gracias award, City of Santa Fe, 1998, Santa Fe Living Treasure award, 2003. Mem. emeritus Am. Soc. Landscape Architects, Don Diego Neighborhood Assn. (pres. 1995-2001, Santa Fe, New Mex.) Home: 1107 Don Cubero Ave Santa Fe NM 87505-1620

WILSON, LINDA, librarian; b. Rochester, Minn., Nov. 17, 1945; d. Eunice Gloria Irene Wilson. BA, U. Minn., Morris, 1967; MA, U. Minn., 1968. Libr. rsch. svcs. U. Calif., Riverside, 1968-69, head dept. phys. scis. catalog, 1969-71; city libr. Belle Glade (Fla). Mcpl. Libr., 1972-74; instr. part-time Palm Beach Jr. Coll., Belle Glade, 1973; head adult-young adult ext. Kern County Libr. Sys., Bakersfield, Calif., 1974-80; dir. dist. libr. Lake Agassiz Regional Libr. System, Crookston, Minn., 1980-85; supervising libr. San Diego County Libr., 1985-87; county libr. Merced (Calif.) County Libr., 1987-93; learning network mgr. Merced Coll., 1994-95; city libr. Monterey Park (Calif.) Bruggemeyer Libr., 1995—. Mem. Leadership Merced, 1987-88, East Site Based Coordinating Coun., Merced, 1990-92, Merced Gen. Plan Citizens Adv. Com., 1992-95, Sister City Com., Merced, 1992-95. Recipient Libr. award Eagles Aux., 1984, Woman of Achievement award Commn. on the Status of Women, 1990, Libr. award Calif. Libr. Trustees and Commrs., 1990, Woman of Yr. award Merced Bus. and Profl. Women, 1990, People Who Make a Difference award Monterey Pk. United Dems., 2003, Woman of Yr. award 29th Congl. Dist., 2004. Mem. ALA (sec. pub. libr. sys. sect. 1988-89), Met. Coop. Library Sys. (pres. 1999-2000), Calif. Libr. Assn. (sec. govt. rels. com. 1991-92, continuing edn. com. 1993-96, pub. rels. 1997-2000, nominations com. 2000-01), Minn. Libr. Assn. (pres. pub. libr. divsn. 1985), Merced County Mgmt. Coun. (pres. 1989), Merced Bus. and Profl. Women (Woman of Yr. 1987, pres. 1988-89), East L.A.-Montebello Bus. and Profl. Women (v.p. 1998-2002, pres. 2002-05), Rotary (pres. Monterey Park chpt. 1999-2000). Democrat. Lutheran. Avocations: travel, walking, reading, swimming, stamp collecting/philately. Home: 1000 E Newmark Ave Apt 22 Monterey Park CA 91755-3129 Office Phone: 626-307-1418. Business E-Mail: lwilson@montereypark.ca.gov. E-mail: lindalwilson@juno.com.

WILSON, LINDA EDMISTON, secondary school science educator; b. Youngtown, Ohio, Dec. 18, 1941; d. Ernest Lyle and Florence Jeannette (Hoover) Edmiston; m. Jon Rhodes Wilson, Aug. 16, 1942; children: Scott Lyle, Jon Todd, Michelle Lynn. AB in Secondary Edn., Asbury Coll., 1963; MA in Elem. Edn., Nova Southeastern U., 1979. Tchr. health and phys. edn., Millersport, Ohio, 1964-66; tchr. Newark, Ohio, 1966-67; tchr. 2d grade Univ. Sch., Davie, Fla., 1978-80; tchr. sci. Driftwood Middle Sch., Hollywood, Fla., 1980-85; tchr. sci. and KLAS Hollywood Hills H.S., Hollywood, 1985—. Coord. Silver Knights for Hollywood Hills, Miami Herald Newspaper, Ft. Lauderdale, Fla., 1991; coord at risk 10-12 grades Hollywood Hills H.S., 1985—. Illustrator: (Child's Book), The Loveable Lookalike, 1981; author, illustrator: Frankly Fortish, 1996. Named Christa McAuliffe Tchr. of Yr., Broward County Fla Engring. Soc., Ft. Lauderdale, Fla., 1989, Hills Silver Knight Tchr. of Yr., Hollywood, Fla., 1990; recipient Sunshine Medallion recognition, Sunshine State Sch. Pub. Rels. Assn., 1993. Methodist. Avocations: writing, crafts, reading, mountain climbing. Home: 4951 SW 29th Way Fort Lauderdale FL 33312-5823 Office: Hollywood Hills HS 5400 Stirling Rd Hollywood FL 33021-1602 Office Phone: 754-323-1050. Personal E-mail: micamtn93@aol.com.

WILSON, LINDA LEE, finance company executive; b. Lakewood, Ohio, Nov. 9, 1943; d. Jon E. and Virginia L. (Weaver) Brown; m. Curtis Wilson, July 30, 1983 (div. 1991); children: Catherine, Laura. BA in English, UCLA, 1970. Lic. ins. agt. Pres. Americorp Fin. Group, Inc., Bellevue, Wash., 1984—. Co-founder panel discussion Women in Transition. Mem. AAUW (bd. dirs.), Internat. Assn. Fin. Planners (bd. dirs. Wash. chpt.), Soroptimist Internat., Toastmasters Internat. Avocation: equestrian.

WILSON, LINDA SMITH, retired academic administrator; b. Washington, Nov. 10, 1936; d. Fred M. and Virginia D. Smith; m. Malcolm C. Whatley, June 29, 1957 (div. 1969); 1 child, Helen K. Whatley; m. Paul A. Wilson, Jan. 22, 1970; 1 stepchild, Beth A. BA, Tulane U., 1957, HLD (hon.), 1993; PhD, U. Wis., 1962; DLitt (hon.), U. Md., 1993. Rsch. assoc. U. Md., College Park, 1962—64, rsch. asst. prof., 1964—67; vis. asst. prof. U. Mo., St. Louis, 1967—68; asst. to vice chancellor for rsch., asst. vice chancellor for rsch., assoc. vice chancellor for rsch. Washington U., St. Louis, 1968—75; assoc. vice chancellor for rsch. U. Ill., Urbana, 1975—85; assoc. dean U. Ill. Grad. Coll., Urbana, 1978—85; v.p. for rsch. U. Mich., Ann Arbor, 1985—89; pres. Radcliffe Coll., Cambridge, Mass., 1989—99, pres. emeritus, 1999; sr. lectr. Harvard Grad. Sch. Edn., 1989—2003; bd. dirs. Myriad Genetics, Tulane U., Tulane Murphy Found., Friends of DaPonte String Quartet; ret., 2003. Rsch. resources adv. coun. NIH, Bethesda, Md., 1978—82; mem. Nat. Commn. on Rsch., Washington, 1978—80; dir.'s adv. coun. NSF, Washington, 1980—89; com. on govt.-univ. relationships NAS, 1981—83, govt.-univ.-industry rsch. roundtable, 1984—89, coord. coun. for edn., 1991—93; energy rsch. adv. bd. Dept. of Energy, 1987—90; chmn. adv. com. office sci. and engring. pers. NRC, 1990—96; adv. com. edn. and human resources NSF, Washington, 1990—95; sci., tech. and states task force Carnegie Commn. on Sci., Tech. and Govt., 1991—92; overser Mus. Sci., Boston, 1992—2001; trustee Mass. Gen. Hosp., 1992—99, hon. trustee, 1999—2002; trustee Com. on Econ. Devel., 1995—; bd. dirs. Inacom, Inc., 1997—2003, Citizens Fin. Group, Inc., 1997—2000, Value Line, Inc., 1998—2000; bd. vis. Coll. Letters and Sci. U. Wis., 1999—2005; dean's adv. coun. Newcomb Coll., 1999—2006. Contbr. articles to profl. jours. and book chpts. Adv. bd. Nat. Coalition for Sci. and Tech., Washington, 1983—87; bd. govs. YMCA, Champaign, Ill., 1980—83. Named One of 100 Emerging Leaders, Am. Coun. Edn. and

Change Mag., 1978; recipient Centennial award, Newcomb Coll., 1986, Disting. Alumni award, U. Wis., 1997, Radcliffe medal, 1999. Fellow: AAAS (bd. dirs. 1984—88); mem.: Am. Coun. Edn. (commn. on women in higher edn. 1991—93, chair 1993), Inst. Medicine (coun. mem. 1986—89, com. on setting NIH priorities, com. on govt.-industry collaboration in biomed. edn. and rsch.), Assn. for Biomed. Rsch. (bd. dirs. 1983—86), Nat. Coun. Univ. Rsch. Adminstrs., Soc. Rsch. Adminstrs. (Disting. Contbn. to Rsch. Adminstrn. award 1984), Am. Chem. Soc. (bd. coun. com. on chemistry and pub. affairs 1978—80), Phi Kappa Phi, Phi Delta Kappa, Alpha Lambda Delta, Sigma Xi, Phi Beta Kappa. Home: 47 Keene Neck Rd Bremen ME 04551

WILSON, LIZABETH ANNE, dean, library director; b. Waterloo, Iowa, May 21, 1954; d. Martin Lucien and Joanne Hausser Wilson; m. Dean August Pollack, Sept. 1, 1983. BA, Northwestern U., 1972—77; MLS, U. of Ill., 1977—78. Asst. architecture and art libr. U. Ill., 1979—80, asst. undergrad. libr., 1980—86, asst. dir. librs. undergrad. and instrnl. svcs., 1986—92; assoc. dir. librs. for rsch. and instrnl. svcs. U. Wash., Seattle, 1992—2000, dean univ. librs., 2001—. Chair of bd. of trustees OCLC, Inc., Dublin, 2003—; exec. dir. Leopoldo Cicognara Program+, Urbana-Champaign, Ill., 1987—2004; co-founder UWired collaboration at the University of Washington. Author (co-author): (journal article) The Bottom Line; contbr. chapters to books, articles. Recipient Margaret E. Monroe Libr. Adult Services award, RUSA/Am. Libr. Assn., 1995, Miriam Dudley Instrn. Libr. award, Assn. of Coll. and Rsch. Libraries, 1995, EDUCAUSE Award for Systemic Progress in Tchg. and Learning, EDUCAUSE, 2000. Mem.: Greater Western Libr. Alliance (pres. 2004), Digital Libr. Fedn. (mem. exec. com. 2004—), OCLC Membs. Coun. (pres. 1999—2000), Assn. Rsch. Librs. (bd. dirs. 2003—), Instrn. Sect. of ACRL (chair 1990—91), Assn. Coll. and Rsch. Librs. (pres. 2000—01, Excellence in Academic Libr. award 2004). Achievements include development of. Office: U Wash Box 352900 Seattle WA 98195-2900 Office Phone: 206-543-1763. Business E-Mail: betsyw@u.washington.edu.

WILSON, LOIS FAIR, retired school system administrator; b. Redlands, Calif., Mar. 17, 1924; d. James Albert and Emma (Lederer) Fair; m. Herbert Blair Wilson (dec. Nov. 1989). BA, U. Redlands, 1945; MEd, U. So. Calif., L.A., 1954; EdD, U. Ariz., 1972. Elem. tchr. Long Beach (Calif.) City Schs., San Bernardino County, 1945-51; curriculum cons. Office of San Bernardino (Calif.) County Schs., 1951-61; asst. prof., coord. elem. edn. U. Redlands, Calif., 1961-64, supr. student tchrs. Calif., 1988—; program asst. to coord. for kindergartens Tucson Unified Sch. Dist., 1965-72, curriculum coord. to elem. prin., 1972-84; supr. student tchrs. Calif. State U., San Bernardino, 1985-88, ret., 1988; travel escort Hillsen's Tours and Travels, Redlands, 1984-92, Laura's Travel Svc., Redlands, 1992—95; escort San Diego Opera Summer Music Festival, 1993, 94; supr. student tchrs. interim program Summer Demonstrations Sch. Tchr. hard of hearing Easter Seal Pre-Sch., 1964-65; summer faculty World Campus Afloat, Chapman Coll., 1974-75, No. Ariz. U., 1978, 80; mem. steering com. Ariz. Young Readers' Conf., U. Ariz., 1975-84; mem. kindergarten curriculum guide com. State of Ariz.; tchr. Stanford U., 1956-58, team staff curriculum workshop, 1959. Contbr. articles to profl. jours. Mem. pre-sch. com. Tucson, 1967-68; bd. dirs. Town and Gown U. Redlands, 1985-92, pres., 1991-92, membership, sec., historian (Hon. Svc. award 1993); chair San Bernardino County Agrl. Stabilization and Conservation Svc. Com., 1986-1990; mem. Assocs. of the Redlands Bowl, Assistance League of Redlands, 1988—, heritage aux. 4th grade program, 3d grade drug awareness program, Kimberly Jrs. Reunion Com., 1991; bd. dirs. Redlands Hist. Mus., 2d v.p Recipient Cert. of Appreciation Dept. Edn. State of Ariz., 1984. Mem. AAUW, PEO (chpt. treas. 1994-95), ASCD (pres. 1960, pres. Ariz. chpt. 1980), Calif. Women for Agr., Ret. Edn. Mgrs. of Calif. (region 12), Calif. Ret. Tchrs. Assn. (v.p. Redlands-Yucaipa div. 1990-92), U. Redlands Pan Hellenic Alumnae (bd. dirs. 1984-90, class rep. 1984-96, alumni bd. 1994-1998), Redlands Assn. and Symphony Guild (bd. dirs., 2d v.p. 1988-90, 2003-05, chmn. youth music com. 1988-91, mem. adv. com. 1994-99), Inland Orange Conservancy, Redlands Conservancy, Friends A.K. Smiley Libr., Lincoln Shrine Asns., Redlands Sister City Assn., Redlands Hist. Glass Mus., Redlands Contemporary Club, April Morning Club (membership com. 1988-89, publicity 1989-90, yearbook 1991-92, pres. 1994-95), Alpha Delta Kappa Fidelis Iota (sec., 2003-2004), Redlands Area Hist. Soc., U. Redlands Ret. Faculty Assn., Easter Seal Soc. (tchr. pre-sch. fostering learning deaf), Kimberly-Shirk Assn. Republican. Presbyterian. Avocations: travel, reading, classical music, research and writing, volunteerism. Home: 1131 Kimberly Pl Redlands CA 92373-6786

WILSON, LOIS M., minister; b. Winnipeg, Man., Can., Apr. 8, 1927; d. Edwin Gardiner Dunn and Ada Minnie (Davis) Freeman; m. Roy F. Wilson, June 9, 1950; children: Ruth, Jean, Neil, Bruce BA, United Coll., Winnipeg, 1947, BDiv, 1969; Diploma in TV prodn., Ryerson Tech. Inst., 1974; DDiv (hon.), Victoria U., Toronto, 1978, United Theol. Coll., Montreal, 1978, Wycliff Coll., 1983, Queens U., Kingston, 1984, U. Winnipeg, 1986, Mt. Allison U., 1988; LLD (hon.), LLD (hon.), Dalhousie U., 1989, Ripon Coll., Wis., 1992; LLD (hon.), U. Toronto, 2005, U. Manitoba, 2006; DCL, Acadia U., 1984; DHuml (hon.), Mt. St. Vincent, Halifax, 1984. Ordained to ministry United Church of Can., 1965. Minister, Thunder Bay, 1965-69, Hamilton, 1969-78, Kingston, 1978-80; moderator United Church of Can., Kingston, 1980-82, McGeachy sr. scholar, 1989-91; pres. Can. Council of Chs., Toronto, Ont., 1976-79; co-dir. Ecumenical Forum Can., Toronto, Ont., 1983-89; pres. World Council of Chs., Geneva, 1983-91; chancellor Lakehead U., Thurder Bay, Ont., 1990-2000; chmn. contemporary theology Lafayette-Orinda (Calif.) Presbyn. Ch., 1995; ind. senator Senate of Can., 1998—2002; apptd. ecumenist in residence Toronto Sch. Theology, 2006—. Mem. adv. coun. internt. devel. studies U. Toronto, 1987-93, Fair Oto Can., Across Boundries Multifaith Inst., Mining Watch Can.; spokesperson Project Ploughshares, 1st and 2d UN Conf. on Disarmament, N.Y.C., 1978-82; officer Human Rights Commn., Ont., 1973; mem. bd. regents Victoria U., 1990—; chief Can. Fact finding Mission to Sri Lanka, 1992; team mem. Ctrl. Am. Monitoring Group to El Salvador and Guatemala, 1993; spl. envoy of Can. to The Sudan, 1999-02; lectr. in field. Author: Like a Mighty River, 1980, Turning the World Upside Down, 1989, Miriam, Mary and Me, 1992, Telling Her Story, 1992, Stories Seldom Told, 1997, Nuclear Waste, 2000; mem. adv. bd.: Can. Woman Studies Jour., York U., 1993—2004; contbr. articles to profl. publs.; author: Transforming the Faith of Our Fathers. Apptd. Can. Senator, 1998; pres. Social Planning Coun., Thunder Bay, 1967—68, Can. Com. for Scientists and Scholars, Toronto, 1982; mem. Refugee Status Adv. Com., 1985—89; chmn. Urban Rural Mission, Can., 1990—96; mem. environ. assessment panel Can. Nuclear Fuel Waste Mgmt. and Disposal Concept, 1989—96; bd. dirs. Elizabeth Fry Soc., Hamilton, 1976—79, Amnesty Internat., 1978—90, Can. Inst. for Internat. Peace and Security, 1984—88, Energy Probe, 1981—86, Internat. Ctr. Human Rights and Dem. Devel., 1997—98, Can. Univ. Svc. Overseas, 1983—85; trustee Nelson Mandela Fund, 1990—92. Decorated Order of Can., Order of Ont., Companion of Order of Can.; sr. fellow Massey Coll. U. Toronto, 2005—; recipient Queens Jubilee medal, Commemorative medal for 125th Anniversary of Confederation of Can., 1992, World Federalist Peace award, 1985, Pearson Peace medal UN Assn. of Can., 1985; named hon. pres. Student Christian Movement of Can., Toronto, 1976. Mem. DPR Korea Assoc., Canada (chmn. 2002-), Women, Peace and Security (co-chair 2001-), CAW (pub. rev. bd. 1986—), Can. Assn. Adult Edn. (bd. dirs. 1986-90), Friends Can. Broadcasting (bd. dirs. 1986-94, v.p.), Civil Liberties Assn. (v.p. 1986—), UNIFEM (nat. v.p. 1993-95, mem. CCIC team to monitor El Salvador election 1994), World Federalists (pres. Can. chpt. 1996-2000, v.p. World Federalist Movement intern, 1998-, acting pres., 2004-), Parliament of World's Religions (del. 1993), Christian-Jewish Dialogue Jerusalem (keynote speaker 1994). Mem. United Ch. Of Can. E-mail: royandlois.wilson@sympatico.ca.

WILSON, LORI, newscaster; b. Columbus, Ind. Grad., U. Ind., Bloomington. Reporter, anchor Sta. WCIA-TV, Champaign, Ill.; anchor Sta. KSLA-TV, Shreveport, La., Sta. WGCL-TV, Atlanta, 2002—. Office: Sta WGCL-TV 425 14th St NW Atlanta GA 30377

WILSON, MAGGIE ISABELLE LOVELL, secondary school educator; b. Branchville, Ala., Jan. 26; d. Winston Porter and Ruth Kate (Buckner) Lovell. AB, Samford U., Birmingham, Ala., 1971; MA, EdS, U. Ala., 1978; MFA, Loyola U., 1979; PhD, Sussex (Eng.) U., 1981. Cert. elem./secondary tchr. Tchr. English Birmingham Pub. Schs., 1972-92; tchr. English secondary edn. Terrell County Schs., Dawson, Ga., 1992-93. Author, illustrator: Carousel of Creative Communication, 1976, Leeds, Her Story, 1979; author: Creative Expressions, 1980, Into Our Third Century, 1984, From Brush Arbor Days to the Twentieth Century, 1992. Historian Leeds (Ala.) First United Meth. Ch., 1990-99; docent Birmingham Mus. Art, 1970-80; pres. Sylacauga dist. United Meth. Women, 1981-84. Recipient numerous awards Ala. Watercolor Soc., Birmingham, 1970—. Pres. award Kappa Pi, Samford U., Birmingham, 1971, Art of Distinction Salon Des Nations, Paris, 1984. Mem. AAUW, Internat. Biog. Assn., Ala. Coun. Tchrs. English (bd. mem. 1976—), Leeds Art Coun., Leeds Hist. Soc., Birmingham Art Assn., Internat. Soc. Artists, Leeds Bus. and Profl. Women (pres. 1971-76, 86, 88—, Woman of Yr. 1996-97), Leeds United Meth. Women (pres. 1972-76, 84—, pres. Sylacauga dist. 1981-84), La. Watercolor Soc. (awards 1986-99), So. Watercolor Soc., Kappa Delta Epsilon, Phi Gamma Mu. Home: 1110 Montevallo Rd SW Leeds AL 35094-1926

WILSON, MARCIA LEE, secondary school educator; b. Morris, Ill., Apr. 2, 1952; d. Leland J. and Georgiabelle M. Wilson; children: Reagan L. Stevens, Jared W. Stevens, Jordan B. Stevens. BSEd, No. Ill. U., DeKalb, 1975. Cert. secondary tchr. Ill. Tchr. consumer econs. Aurora (Ill.) Sch. Dist. 131, Ill., 1975—79; bus. instr. Elgin (Ill.) C.C., 1979—91; tchr. keyboarding Marengo (Ill.) Cmty. H.S., 1990—91; tchr. lang. arts and social studies Morris (Ill.) Elem. Dist. #54, 1994—. Named Educator of Yr., Kiwanis Club, Morris, 2003. Mem.: NEA, Morris Elem. Edn. Assn., Ill. Edn. Assn., Nat. Honor Soc. Home: 1248 Brendan Dr Morris IL 60450 Office: Morris Elem Sch Dist 54 725 School St Morris IL 60450 Office Phone: 815-942-3605. Personal E-mail: mwilson@mornet.org.

WILSON, MARGARET BUSH, lawyer; b. St. Louis, Jan. 30, 1919; married; 1 child, Robert Edmund. BA cum laude, Talladega Coll., 1940; LL.B., Lincoln U., 1943. Ptnr. Wilson & Wilson, St. Louis, 1947-65; now with firm Wilson & Assocs. Asst. dir. St. Louis Lawyers for Housing, 1969-72; asst. atty. gen. Mo., 1961-62; atty. Rural Electrification Adminstrn., Dept. Agr., St. Louis, 1943-45; instr. civil procedure St. Louis U. Sch. Law, 1971; chmn. St. Louis Land Reutilization Authority, 1975-76; mem. Mo. Coun. Criminal Justice, 1972—; chmn. Intergroup Corp., 1985-87; bd. dirs. Mut. of N.Y. Mem. gen. adv. com. ACDA, 1978-81; trustee emeritus Washington U., St. Louis; chmn. bd. trustees Talladega Coll., Ala., 1988-92; nat. bd. dirs. ARC, 1975-81, United Way, 1978-84, Police Found., 1976-93; treas. NAACP Nat. Housing Corp., 1971-84, chmn. nat. bd., 1975-84; dep. dir./acting dir. St. Louis Model City Agy., 1968-69; adminstr. Mo. Commn. Svc. and Continuing Edn., 1967-68. Recipient Bishop's award Episcopal Diocese Mo., 1962; Juliette Derricotte fellow, 1939-40, Disting. Lawyer award Bar Assn. Metro St. Louis, 1997; Margaret Bush Wilson Endowed Professorship in Arts and Scis. established at Washington U., St. Louis, 2004. Mem. ABA (chmn. youth edn. for citizenship 1991-94, chmn. Nat. Law Day 1998-2000), Nat. Bar Assn., Mo. Bar Assn., Mound City Bar Assn., St. Louis Bar Assn., Alpha Kappa Alpha. Office: Wilson & Assocs 4054 Lindell Blvd Saint Louis MO 63108-3202 Office Phone: 314-534-4400. Office Fax: 314-534-4403.

WILSON, MARIE C., foundation administrator; b. Ga. 5 children. D in Cmty. Svc. (hon.), Drake U. Dir. women's programs Drake U.; mem. DesMoines City Coun.; pres. Ms. Found. for Women, N.Y.C., 1984—. Co-creator Take Our Daus. To Work Day, 1993—; U.S. govt. del. UN Fourth World Conf. on Women, Beijing, 1995; co-founder, pres. The White House Project, 1998—. Co-author: Mother Daughter Revolution, 1993; author: Closing the Leadership Gap: Why Women Can and Must Help Run the World, 2004. Recipient Robert W. Scrivner award for creative grantmaking, Leadership for Equity and Diversity award, Women & Philanthropy. Office: Ms Found for Women 120 Wall St 33rd Fl New York NY 10005

WILSON, MARY ALICE, musician, educator; b. Nov. 2, 1939; MusB, Northwestern U., Evanston, Ill., 1961. Orch. band dir., pvt. tchr. Luth. Schs., Deerfield Pub. Schs., 1961-64; pvt. tchr. violin and piano Cleve., 1964-77; dir. Suzuki Program, violin tchr. W.Va. U., 1977—, chmn. music divsn., 2005; founder, leader Seneca String Quartet, Morgantown, W.Va., 1986—. Accompanist. Ch. vol. tchg. and music, Cleve., Chgo., Morgantown, 1960—. Recipient Outstanding Tchr. award, W.Va. U. Music Dept., 2005. Mem.: Am. String Tchrs. Assn. (co-developer, chmn. 5th yr. state solo competition, state sect. 2003—05), W.Va. Music Tchrs. Assn. (dist. chmn. of strings 1977—, state officer pub. 1989—, State Outstanding Tchr. Yr. 1996), Music Tchrs. Nat. Assn. (state office of composition contest 1989—). Home: 237 Poplar Dr Morgantown WV 26505-2519 E-mail: cbwilson@mail.wvu.edu, bigmacwil@hotmail.com.

WILSON, MARY ELIZABETH, epidemiologist, physician, educator; b. Indpls., Nov. 19, 1942; d. Ralph Richard and Catheryn Rebecca (Kurtz) Lausch; m. Harvey Vernon Fineberg, May 16, 1975. AB, Ind. U., 1963; MD, U. Wis., 1971. Diplomate Am. Bd. Internal Medicine, Am. Bd. Infectious Diseases. Tchr. of French and English Marquette Sch., Madison, Wis., 1963-66; intern in medicine Beth Israel Hosp., Boston, 1971-72, resident in medicine, 1972-73, fellow in infectious diseases, 1973-75; physician Albert Schweitzer Hosp., Deschapelles, Haiti, 1974-75, Harvard Health Svcs., Cambridge, Mass., 1974-75; asst. physician Cambridge Hosp., 1975-78; hosp. epidemiologist Mt. Auburn Hosp., Cambridge, 1975-79, chief of infectious diseases, 1978—2002, dir. Travel Resource Ctr., 1996—2002, mem. consulting staff, 2003—05. Mem. adv. com. immunization practices CDC, Atlanta, 1988—92; mem. acad. adv. com. Nat. Inst. Pub. Health, Mexico, 1989—91; cons. Ford Found., 1988; site dir. GeoSentinel Network, 1999—2002, spl. cons., 2002—; instr. medicine Harvard Med. Sch., Boston, 1975—93, asst. clin. prof., 1994—99, assoc. prof. medicine, 1999—2004, assoc. clin. prof., 2004—; assoc. Ctr. Health and Global Environment, 1996—2000; asst. prof. depts. epidemiology and population and internat. health Harvard Sch. Pub. Health, 1994—99, assoc. prof. population and internat. health, 1999—; lectr. Sultan Qaboos U., Oman, 1991; chair Woods Hole Workshop, Emerging Infectious Diseases, 1993. Author: A World Guide to Infections: Diseases, Distribution, Diagnosis, 1991; editor (with Richard Levins and Andrew Spielman): Disease in Evolution: Global Changes and Emergence of Infectious Diseases, 1994; mem. editl. bd. Current Issues Pub. Health, 1999—2003, Emerging Infectious Diseases, Global Change and Human Health, 1999—2003; sect. editor travel medicine and tropical diseases: Infectious Diseases Clin. Practices; mem. editl. bd. Infectious Diseases Clin. Practices, 2006—; assoc. editor: Jour. Watch Infectious Diseases, 1997—; mem. editl. adv. bd. Clin. Infectious Diseases, 1999—2004, spl. sect. editor Emerging Infections, Clinical Infectious Diseases, 2006—. Mem. Cambridge Task Force AIDS, 1987—90; bd. dirs. Horizon Comm., West Cornwall, Conn., 1990—97. Recipient Lewis E. and Edith Phillips award, U. Wis. Med. Sch., 1969, Cora M. and Edward Van Liere award, 1971, Mosby Scholarship Book award, 1971, Leo Blacklow Tchg. award, 1999; fellow, Ctr. Advanced Study Behavioral Scis., Stanford, Calif., 2002; scholar-in-residence, Bellagio (Italy) Study Ctr., Rockefeller Found., 1996. Fellow: ACP, Royal Soc. Tropical Medicine and Hygiene, Infectious Diseases Soc. Am.; mem.: Soc. for Epidemiol. Rsch., Internat. Union Against Tuberculosis and Lung Disease, Soc. for Vector Ecology, Wilderness Med. Soc., Internat. Soc. Travel Medicine, Peabody Soc., Mass. Infectious Diseases Soc., Am. Soc. Tropical Medicine and Hygiene, N.Y. Acad. Scis., Am. Soc. Microbiology, Aesculapian Club, Alpha Omega Alpha, Phi Sigma Iota, Sigma Sigma. Avocations: flute, hiking, reading, travel. Business E-Mail: mary_wilson@harvard.edu.

WILSON, MARY ELLEN, retired project administrator; b. L.A., Aug. 7, 1927; d. Nels Efraim and Ellen (Matson) Lovemark; m. Richard Spencer Dyer, Mar. 6, 1952 (dec. July 1960); children: Robert Alan, Terry Ann; m. Edward LeRoy Wilson, Jan. 21, 1961 (dec. Jan. 1992); 1 child, Pamela Susan; stepchildren: Scott Stanton, Jefferey Kevin Wilson. Expediter C F Braun & Co., Alhambra, Calif., 1947-53; project expediter The Ralph M. Parsons Co., Pasadena, Calif., 1977-79, project coord., 1979-83, project adminstr., 1984-89. Docent Scott Gallery, Huntington Libr., Pasadena, 1992—, Huntington Gallery; publicity profl. Pasadena Rep. Women's Club, 1960s; pres. Pasadena Charity for Calif. Pediat. Ctr., L.A., 1955-60; First Lady, Pasadena Tournament of Roses, 1973-74; mem. L.A. World Affairs Coun., 1997—. Mem. Annandale Golf Club. Republican. Avocations: golf, tennis, bridge, travel. Home: 951 S Fair Oaks Ave #212 Pasadena CA 91105-2631

WILSON, MARY FLYNN, writer, educator; b. Bklyn., Nov. 15, 1938; d. Edwin Anthony and Ann Rita (Eckart) Flynn; children: Mary Kate, Colin, Daniel. BA in English Lit. magna cum laude, Merrimack Coll., 1960. Cert. initial educator, Conn.; cert. minister. Editl. asst. IEEE, N.Y.C., 1960-61; journalist Reporter-Dispatch, White Plains, N.Y., 1961-67; adminstrv. asst. Immaculate Conception Parish, New Hartford, Conn., 1981-86; exec. sec. to CEO Petroleum Meter & Pump, Avon, Conn., 1986-87; copy editor The Hartford (Conn.) Courant, 1987-96; adj. faculty N.W. Conn. C.C., Winsted, 1994—. Admissions rep. Merrimack Coll., North Andover, Mass., 1960-68, fund-raiser, 1990—. Author: Trinita at 75, 1999, (newspaper series) Reporter Dispatch, 1963; editor: Producing Patient-Centered Health Care, 1999, Hoist Your Sails.Attaining Life and Job Happiness, 1999. Campaign mgr. Dem. Party, New Hartford, 1970, 72; town co-chair United Way, Barkhamsted, Conn., 1974-75; group leader 4-H, Barkhamsted, 1978-82; lay min. Immaculate Conception Parish, New Hartford, Conn., 1978-88; vol. musician Valerie Manor Health Care, Torrington, Conn., 1995-2000; adv. bd. mem. Trinita Retreat Ctr., New Hartford, 1998—. Recipient Commendation, Sigma Delta Chi-N.Y. state chpt., 1963, Cmty. Svc. award N.Y. State Pubs. Assn., 1963, commendation Conn. Bd. Higher Edn., 1995. Mem. Congress Conn. C.C., Fedn. Christian Ministries, Merrimack Coll. Alumni Coun., Cancer Survivors Group. Roman Catholic. Avocations: water sports, art, handwork, opera, carpentry. Home: 26 Center Hill Rd Pleasant Valley CT 06063-4100 Office: NW Conn Cmty Tech Coll Park Pl East Winsted CT 06063 E-mail: MaryflynnWilson@yahoo.com.

WILSON, MELISSA ANN, athletic trainer; b. Brunswick, Maine, July 12, 1979; d. Ronald Eugene and Cynthia Ann Beyor; m. Terry Lynn Wilson II, May 15, 2004. BS, Catawba Coll., Salisbury, N.C., 2001; MS, Marshall U., Huntington, W.Va., 2003. Cert. athletic trainer Nat. Athletic Tng. Assn. Bd. of Certification, 2001. Cert. athletic trainer Excell Phys. Therapy, East Liverpool, Ohio, 2003—04, HealthSouth, Parkersburg, W.Va., 2004—05, Univ. Sports Medicine, Rochester, NY, 2005—. Named Frank Myers Athletic Trainer Of The Yr., Catawba Coll., 2001; recipient Stephen H. Wurster Sportsmanship award, 2001. Mem.: Nat. Athletic Trainers Assn. (assoc.). Office: University Sports Medicine 4901 LacDeVille Blvd Rochester NY 14618 Office Phone: 585-341-9150. Personal E-mail: missyatc@yahoo.com. E-mail: melissa_wilson@urmc.rochester.edu.

WILSON, MICHELINE, small business owner; b. Villotte-Sur-Aire, Meuse, France, Dec. 7, 1945; came to U.S., 1967; d. Jean Roger Clausse and Mauricette Marie Bohin; m. Steven Owen Wilson, June 1, 1976 (div. 1984). Bachelor's, Lycee de Jeunes Filles, Metz, Moselle, France, 1964. Lic. cosmetology. Hairstylist Mr. John's Beauty Salon, Augusta, Ga., 1968-70, Laurens, S.C., 1970-72; hairstylist, owner Micheline Hair Salon, Lakeland, Fla., 1973—. One-woman show Burdines, 1996. Recipient awards Lakeland Art Guild, 1990, 92, 95, Ridge Art Assn., Winterhaven, Fla., 1994, Fla. Strawberry Festival, Plant City, 1993, Chgo. Cosmetologists, 2000, Small Bus. award Lakeland Area C. of C., 2001, Sch.-to-Work Silver Zone award Polk County Sch. Bd., 2004, 2005; named one of Top 200 Fastest Growing Salons in the Nation 5 Yrs. in a Row, Best Philanthropic Program for Salons of Its Size in the Nation. Mem. The Salon Assn., Nat. Assn. Women Bus. Owners, Nat. Cosmetology Assn. Avocations: painting, world beat music, yoga, dance, nutrition. Office: Micheline Salonspa 5035 S Lakeland Dr Lakeland FL 33813-2558 Office Phone: 863-644-0102. E-mail: mail@michelinesalonspa.com.

WILSON, MICHELLE LERMOND, internist; b. Colorado Springs, Colo., Oct. 2, 1958; Student, Armstrong State Coll., 1988; DO, W.Va. Sh. Osteo. Medicine, 1992. Diplomate Am. Bd. Internal Medicine. EMT, Winston-Salem, N.C., 1979; med. lab. asst. N.C. Baptist Hosp., Winston-Salem, N.C., 1979-81, respiratory therapy tech. asst., 1981-82; vet. tech. Tibet Animal Hosp., Savannah, Ga., 1982-84; EMT Savannah, Ga., 1984; vet. tech. Island Vet. Clinic, Savannah, Ga., 1984-88; intern Roanoke (Va.) Meml. Hosp., 1992-93; resident Meml. Med. Ctr., Savannah, Ga., 1993-95, mem. staff, 1995—; temp. med. co-dir. Ga. Healthcare Partnership. Com. mem. Meml. Med. Ctr., Ga. Healthcare Ptnrship. Vol. EMT Winston-Salem Rescue Squad, 1979-81, Olympic Games, Savannah, 1996; organizer pet visits Moss Oaks Nursing Home, Savannah, 1986. Recipient Gates Pharm. cert. 1992. Mem. AMA, ACP, Am. Osteopathic Assn., Ga. Med. Soc., So. Med. Assn., Am. Med. Students Assn., Psi Sigma Alpha, Tri-Beta. Avocations: jet skiing, gardening, swimming, boating, pets.

WILSON, MIRIAM GEISENDORFER, retired physician, educator; b. Yakima, Wash., Dec. 3, 1922; d. Emil and Frances Geisendorfer; m. Howard G. Wilson, June 21, 1947; children— Claire, Paula, Geoffrey, Nicola, Marla. BS, U. Wash., Seattle, 1944, MS, 1945; MD, U. Calif., San Francisco, 1950. Mem. faculty U. So. Calif. Sch. Medicine, L.A., 1965—, prof. pediatrics, 1969—2004, emeritus prof. pediatrics, 2004—. Office: U So Calif Med Ctr 1129 N State St Rm 1g24 Los Angeles CA 90033-1044

WILSON, MIRIAM S., adult education educator; b. Massillon, Ohio, Nov. 8, 1949; d. Wilbert H. and K. Miriam Shaffer Jones; m. David S. Wilson, Aug. 4, 1997; children: Todd Donald Schenkenberger, Pamela Reed Suh. PhD, Ohio State U., Columbus, 1998. Asst. prof., MPA coord. Bowling Green State U., Ohio, 2001—06; instr. U. of Toledo, 2006—. Field rschr. Rockerfeller Inst., Albany, NY, 1998—2004. Contbr. rsch. reports and articles to profl. jours. Initiator Just Desserts, Bowling Green, 2006. Democrat. Lutheran. Home: 3130 Darlington Rd Toledo OH 43606 Office: Univ of Toledo 6600 Bancroft Ave Toledo OH 43606

WILSON, MOLLIE, retired music educator; d. William D. and Frances W. Wilson; BS, Pa. State U., 1974, MS, 1996. Orch. dir. Pennridge Jr. HS, Perkasee, Pa., 1974—75; band dir. Del. Valley Sch. Dist., Milford, Pa., 1975—; proprietor Pine Gables of Aberdeen Bed & Breakfast, NC, 2004—. Mem.: Elks (Port Jervis, Exalted Ruler). Office Phone: 910-944-9595, 845-551-6891. Personal E-mail: pinegablesofaberdeen@yahoo.com.

WILSON, MONICA DEANN, school guidance counselor; b. Ft. Worth, Feb. 6, 1968; BS, Tarleton State U., 1990; MS, Tex. Woman's U., 2002. Cert. tchr. Tex., counselor Tex. Sci. and math. tchr. Frisco (Tex.) HS, 1991—95, 1995—2001; membership devel. dir. Tex. Girl Scout Coun., Dallas, 1995; guidance counselor Wylie (Tex.) HS, 2001—02, Hebron HS, Lewisville, Tex., 2002—03, Hackberry Elem. Sch., Little Elm, Tex., 2003—05, Boswell HS, Saginaw, Tex., 2005—. Mem.: APA, Tex. Assn. Eoll. Edn. Counselors, Tex. Counseling Assn., ACA, Tex. Sch Counselors Assn. (elem. v.p. 2003—05, chmn. human rights com. 2002—03). Democrat. Home: 5304 Dillon Cir Haltom City TX 76137 Office: Boswell HS 5805 Bailey Boswell Rd Fort Worth TX 76179

WILSON, NANCY ESTHER, social worker; b. Ahoskie, N.C., June 15, 1915; d. Albert Raleigh and Hattie Bessie (Turner) L.; m. Robert E. Jackson (dec.); 1 child, Dwight E. Jackson-Wilson (dec.); m. James M. Wilson (dec.); children— Suzanne Wanda (dec.), James Albert (dec.). Student, Wycoff Heights Sch. Nursing, Bklyn., 1960. Supervising field monitor Dept. Social Services, N.Y.C., 1983—; mem. Social Services Employees Union Forum for Social Services. Mem. tng. program for social service employees Girl Scouts U.S.A. Recipient Appreciation award City N.Y. Human Resources Adminstrn.; Pub. Service award City N.Y. Dept. Welfare, 1983; Profl. Achievement award Bur. Spl. Services, 1963. Democrat. Roman Catholic. Clubs: Bowling Team (Bklyn., N.Y.); Bus. Women (Euclid, N.Y.), Holy Rosary Ch. Rosary Soc. Avocations: bowling; gardening; reading. Home: 3724 Polar St Brooklyn NY 11224-1245

WILSON, NANCY JEANNE, laboratory consultant, medical technologist; b. Neptune, N.J., Apr. 17, 1951; d. Harry E. Sr. and Kathryn E. (O'Shea) W. BS, Monmouth Coll., 1975; MPA, Fairleigh Dickinson U., 1988. Cert. assisted living adminstr. NJ Dept. Health. Clin. intern med. tech., staff med. technologist Riverview Med. Ctr., 1975; staff med. technologist Rush Clin. Labs., Red Bank, NJ, 1976, Kimball Med. Ctr., Lakewood, NJ, 1977—78, clin. lab. supr., 1978—86; infection control practice Jersey Shore Med. Ctr., Neptune, N.J., 1990; dir. lab. and diagnostic svcs. Carrier Clinic, Belle Mead, NJ, 1990—2002, lab. and infection control cons., 2002—04, clin. lab. adminstr., infectious control coord., 2004—. Mem. Am. Soc. Clin. Pathologists (diplomate lab. mgmt.), Am. Assn. Clin. Chemistry, Am. Soc. Microbiology, Clin. Lab. Mgmt. Assn., Am. Soc. Clinics Lab. Sci., Assn. for Profls. in Infection Control, Pi Alpha Alpha. Avocations: golf, walking, relaxing. Home: 42 Monument St Freehold NJ 07728-1721 Office Phone: 908-281-1340. Personal E-mail: nwwilson@carrierclinic.com.

WILSON, OLIVE FULLER, librarian; b. Martinsville, Tex., Feb. 18, 1922; d. Fulton and Lillian B. (Brewer) F.; m. William T. Lander, Jr., Mar. 31, 1943 (dec. 1968); children: Susan Lander, Margaret Lander Shaw, Mary Laura Lander Davis; m. Jack Crymes Wilson, Feb. 25, 1973 (dec. 2003). BMus., Mary Hardin Baylor Coll., 1943; LLM., U. S.C., 1979. Tchr. English, Williamston pub. schs. (S.C.), 1948-50; tchr. Spartanburg, S.C., 1952-53, Pelzer Elem. Sch. (S.C.), 1953-56; dean women, hostess S.C. Opportunity Sch., West Columbia, 1961-68, dir. music, 1965-68, tchr., 1967-68, trustee, 1976—96; tchr. Palmetto HS Williamston, 1968-70, libr., 1970—87; pvt. piano tchr., 1945-60. Sec. Williamston Democratic Com., 1969-70, 73-74; legis. appointee Anderson County Animal Shelter, 1976—78. Mem. S.C. Edn. Assn., Anderson County Mus. Bd., NEA, Alpha Delta Kappa (chpt. pres. 1974-76, chaplain 1982—84). Meth. Club: Williamston Garden (pres. 1958-60, 68-70, 74-76, 80-82, 86-88, 2004-06). Author: History of Williamston, S.C., 1970. Home: 950 Montague Rd Columbia SC 29209

WILSON, PAMELA K., corporate financial executive; BS, U. Ill.; MBA, NYU. With J.P. Morgan, 1980—2000; sr. v.p. WL Ross & Co. LLC, N.Y., 2000—. Office: WL Ross & Co LLC Manhattan Tower 19th Fl 101 East 52nd St New York NY 10022

WILSON, PATRICIA POTTER, library and information scientist, educator; b. Jennings, La., May 3, 1946; d. Ralph Harold and Wilda Ruth (Smith) Potter; m. Wendell Merlin Wilson, Aug. 24, 1968. BS, La. State U., 1967; MS, U. Houston-Clear Lake, 1979; EdD, U. Houston, 1985. Cert. tchr., learning resources specialist (libr.), Tex. Tchr. England AFB (La.) Elem. Sch., 1967-68, Edward White Elem. Sch./Clear Creek Ind. Schs., Seabrook, Tex., 1972-77; libr. C.D. Landolt Elem. Sch., Friendswood, Tex., 1979-81; instr./lectr. children's lit. U. Houston, 1983-86; with U. Houston/Clear Lake, 1984-87, asst. prof. libr. sci. and reading, 1988-94, assoc. prof. learning resources and reading edn., 1994—2001, assoc. prof. emerita, 2001—. Cons. Hermann Hosp., Baywood Hosp., 1986-87, Bedford Meadows Hosp., 1989-90, Wetcher Clinic, 1989; co-owner, v.p. Potter Farms, Inc., 1994—; devel. bd. NASA and CCISD, Longhorn, 2005-; pres. cabinet U. Houston, Central, Clear Lake, U. Tex. Med. Br. Author: Happenings: Developing Successful Programs for School Libraries, 1987, The Professional Collection for Elementary Educators, 1996, Premiere Events: Library Programs That Inspire Elementary Patrons, 2001, Leadership for Today's School Library, 2001, Igniting the Spark: Library Programs that Inspire High School Patrons, 2001, Center Stage: Library Programs That Inspire Middle School Patrons, 2002; editor: A Review Sampler, 1985—86, 1989—90; contbg. editor: Tex. Libr. Jour., 1988—94; contbr. articles to profl. jours. Trustee Freeman Meml. Libr., Houston, 1982—87, v.p., 1985—86, pres., 1986—87; trustee Evelyn Meador Libr., 1993—94, adv. bd., 1994—; mem. bd. dirs. Houston Symphony League-Bay Area, 2004—05, chair ann. fund campaign, 2005; founder Friends of Neumann Libr., 1998—2001; chmn. hospitality com. Lunar Rendevous Festival, 1998—2001; gen. chmn. Lunar Rendezvous Festival, 2002, mem. adv. bd., 2002—; mem. Assistance League of the Bay Area, 1997—; vol. Houston: A Visit from St. Nicholas Com., 2004—, co-chmn. kick-off event, 2005; mem. adv. bd. Bay Area Soc. Prevention Cruelty Animals, 1994—98, Bay Area Turning Point, 1998—; bd. dirs. Sta. KUHT-TV, 1984—87, Friends of Neumann Libr., 1998—99, Bay Area Houston Ballet and Theatre, 2001—04, vice chair bd. dirs., 2003—04, chmn. kickoff event, 2003; dir. Learning Resources Book Rev. Ctr., 1989—90; bd. dirs. Armand Bayou Nature Ctr., Houston, 1989—94; mem. Bay Area Houston Econ. Partnership, 2002—, mem. banquet com., 2002—. Named Outstanding Vol. of Yr., Houston's Nat. Philanthropy Day, 1999; named one of 10 Men and Women of Heart, Bay Area Turning Point, 2001; recipient Rsch. award, Tex. State Reading Assn., 1993, Pres. award, Tex. Coun. Tchrs. English, Disting. Tchg. award, Enron Corp., 1996, Disting. Alumni award, U. Houston-Clear Lake, 1998, Disting. Alumna award, U. Houston, Coll. Edn., 2002, Disting. Alumni award, Univ. Houston Ctrl., 2005, Bravo award, Bay Area Houston Ballet & Theater, 2006; grantee, Tex. Libr. Assn., 1993. Mem. ALA, NASA, Clear Creek Ind. Sch. Dist. (Longhorn devel. bd. 2005—), Am. Assn. Sch. Librs., Internat. Reading Assn., Nat. Coun. Tchrs. English (Books for You rev. com. 1985-88, 97-98, Your Reading rev. com. 1993-96), Tex. Coun. Tchrs. English, Antarctican Soc., Bay Area Houston Econ. Partnership (banquet com. 2002-), Clear Lake Panhellenic Assn., Lakewood Yacht Club, Travelers' Century Club, Bay Oaks Country Club, Phi Kappa Phi (sec. 1997-98, pres. 1998-99). Methodist.

WILSON, PEGGY MAYFIELD, retired chemist; d. Isaac Newton and Ella Lockwood Mayfield; m. Irving Ray Dunlap Jr. (dec.); m. William W. Wilson III, July 25, 1975 (dec.). BS in Chemistry, U. Tex., Austin, 1948, PhD in Chemistry, 1952. Spl. instr. U. Tex., Austin, 1952—53; from rsch. technologist to sr. rsch. technologist Mobil Rsch. Devel. Corp., Dallas, 1953—84, group mgr. dept. rsch., 1984—89; pres. Greater Duncanville Indsl. Corp., Tex., 1991—2000, Stone Gap Indsl. Corp., Duncanville, 1991—2000; ret., 2000. Regent East Tex. State U., Commerce, 1981—87. Founder, econ. devel. City of Cedar Hill, Tex., 1991—96; adv. bd. Cedar Valley C.C.; coun. mem. City of Cedar Hill, 1996—98; active State Rep. Exec. Com., Tex., 1971—80; bd. dirs., treas. Internat. Mus. Cultures. Named Outstanding Rep. Woman, Tex. Fedn. Rep. Women, 1973; recipient Jean Harris award, Rotary, 1998, Golden Cedar Lifetime award, Cedar Hill C. of C., 2001. Mem.: Am. Chem. Soc., Cedar Hill Assn. for Cultural Arts, Cedar Summit Book Club. Republican. Methodist. Achievements include patents in field. Avocation: gardening.

WILSON, PETA, actress; b. Sydney, Australia, Nov. 18, 1970; d. Darcy Wilson and Karlene White; 1 child, Marlowe. Studied with Arthur Mendoza, Tom Waits, Sylvana Gulado. Actor: (films) Sadness of Sex, 1995, Naked Jane, 1995, Loser, 1996, One of Our Own, 1997, Mercy, 2000, The League of Extraordinary Gentlemen, 2003, Superman Returns, 2006, (TV films) Woman Undone, 1996, Vanishing Point, 1997, Other People, 2001, Joe and Max, 2002, False Pretenses, 2004, (TV series) La Femme Nikita, 1997. Youngest member of the Australian Nat. Basketball Team. Home: 13001 Galewood St Studio City CA 91604-4048*

WILSON, REBECCA ANN, retired English and special education educator; b. Balt., Feb. 21, 1945; d. Bertram Bradford and Nancy Ann Wiley; m. David Lloyd Wilson, July 29, 1967; children: Laura Beth, Amy Lynn. BA in Secondary Edn., Shepherd Coll., 1967; postgrad., W.Va. U. Cert. Spl. Edn. Tchr. W.Va., 1968. Tchr. Jefferson County Schs., Charles Town, W.Va., 1967—72, substitute tchr., 1975—79. Vol. Jefferson County Spl. Olympics, Charles Town, W.Va., 1986—97; judge Jefferson County Fair, 1968—; chmn. W.Va. Adv. Coun. Edn. Exceptional Children, Charleston, 1986—92; adv. com. Jefferson County Bd. Edn., Charles Town, W.Va., 1990, mem., 1994—98, Gov. Sch. Adv. Coun., Charleston, 2001—; mem. bd. dir. Regional Edn. Svc. Agy.; mem. altar guild Trinity Episcopal Ch.; mem. bd. dir. Shepherdstown Day Care Ctr. Mem.: AAUW (life), Internat. Assn. Jazz Edn., Homemakers Club, Shepherdstown Women's Club (pres. 2000—06), Md. 4-H All Stars (life), Gen. Fedn. Women's Clubs (pres. Easter dist. W.Va. 2006—), Order of Ea. Star. Democrat. Episcopalian. Avocations: travel, attending national conventions, reading, cooking. Home: 27 Old Prospect Ave PO Box 624 Shepherdstown WV 25443 E-mail: rwilson6@hotmail.com.

WILSON, REBECCA JO, associate dean, education educator; b. Wabash, Ind., July 8, 1949; d. DeVon A. and Marcella Jean Wilson; adopted children: Abbi Kim, Amanda Faye. BS in Edn., Taylor U., 1972; MS in Edn., U. So. Calif., L.A., 1985; EdD, Ball State U., 1991. Life tchg. cert., Ind. Tchr. grade 4 Fayette County Schs., Connersville (Ind.) Sch., 1972; tchr. grade 1 Lancaster (Ohio) City Schs., 1972-81; tchr. grade 1 and 2 Seoul (Korea) Fgn. Sch., 1981-89; dir. student tchg., prof. edn. Bethel Coll., Mishawaka, Ind., 1991-96, assoc. dean instrn., 1996—. Adj. prof. Ind. Wesleyan U., Marion; spkr. in field. Author: Middle School English, 1988. Bd. dirs. Adoptions Alternative, South Bend, Ind., Harris Prairie Ch. of Christ Pre-sch.; orphan escort Holt Adoption Agy., Seoul, 1983, 84. Jennings scholar Martha Holden Jennings Found., Lancaster, 1976; doctoral fellow Ball State U., Muncie, Ind., 1989-90. Mem. ASCD, Internat. Reading Assn., Assn. Tchr. Educators, Ind. Assn. for Tchr. Educators, Ind. Assn. for Colls. Tchr. Edn., Ind. Reading Assn. (St. Joseph Valley Coun. v.p.-elect 1992-93, v.p. 1993-94, pres. 1994-95, past pres. 1995-96), Ind. Reading Profs., Phi Delta Kappa. Avocations: racquetball, reading, sewing, travel. Office: Bethel Coll 1001 W Mckinley Ave Mishawaka IN 46545-5509 E-mail: WilsonR@Bethel-IN.edu.

WILSON, RITA, actress; b. LA, Oct. 26, 1958; m. Tom Hanks; 2 children. Actor: (films) The Day It Came to Earth, 1979, Cheech & Chong's Next Movie, 1980, Volunteers, 1985, The Bonfire of the Vanities, 1990, Sleepless in Seattle, 1993, Mixed Nuts, 1994, Now and Then, 1995, That Thing You Do!, 1996, Jingle All the Way, 1996, No Dogs Allowed, 1996, Psycho, 1998, Runaway Bride, 1999, The Story of Us, 1999, Perfume, 2001, Auto Focus, 2002; (TV films) Barbarians at the Gate, 1993, If These Walls Could Talk, 1996, From the Earth to the Moon, 1998, Invisible Child, 1999; prodr.: (films) My Big Fat Greek Wedding, 2002, Connie and Carla, 2004; (TV series) My Big Fat Greek Life, 2003.

WILSON, ROBERTA BUSH, retired psychotherapist, accountant; b. Watertown, NY, Dec. 23, 1937; d. Robert King and Barbara P. (Wiggins) Banks; m. Marvin D. Bush, Feb. 28, 1959 (div. 1977); m. Asa A. Wilson, July 29, 2004. BA, Glenville State Coll., 1977; MS, W.Va. U., Morgantown, 1985. Lic. profl. therapist W.Va. Acct. GE Plastics, Parkersburg, W.Va., 1959—77; lit. vol. Parkensburg, 1977—89; outpatient site head Abraxas, Parkensburg, 1989—95; psychotherapist Westbrook Health Svc., Parkensburg, 1996—97; ret., 1997. Pres., bd. dirs. Lit. Vol. Program of Wood County, Parkersburg. Mem.: Profl. Women's Assn. (pres., bd. dirs., Hall of Fame 1995). Episcoplian. Home: 111 Canterbury Dr Parkersburg WV 26104-8057

WILSON, ROBERTA (BOBBI) GAIL, performing arts educator; d. Robert Wallace and Ruth Lorraine (Bayne) Wilson; m. Thomas D. Bachenberg, June 2, 1975 (div. Jan. 6, 1978). BA in Music Edn., U. No. Colo., 1975; student in voice, choral conducting, U. Nev., 1981—82; student in Shakespeare and Directing, U. So. Oreg., 1996; student in Theatre, Union Inst. and Univ., 1999—. Tchr. vocal music Lewis-Palmer Schs., Monument, Colo., 1975—79, Sheridan (Colo.) HS, Sheridan, Colo., 1975—79; singer, dancer, actor MGM Grand Hotel, Reno, 1980—82, Nev. Opera and Ballet, Reno, 1980—82; freelance singer, dancer, actor, dir. LA, 1982—93; performing arts dir., vocal music Inst. Music and Drama, Christian Bros. HS, Sacramento, 1993—97; dir. Arts Acad. Cotter HS and Jr. HS Acad. Performing Arts, Winona, Minn., 1997—2000; dir. music and drama Studio Acad. HS for Arts, Rochester, Minn., 2001—02; coord. Dist. Arts Fountain (Colo.) Ft. Carson Sch. Dist. 8, 2002—. Performer Colo. Opera Festival, Colo. Springs, 1976—78; dir., choreographer Ctrl. Minn. Children's Theatre, St. Cloud, Minn., 2001. Vol. Dem. Party, LA, 1992. Named Tchr. of Month, Kiwanis Club, 1993. Mem.: Ednl. Theatre Assn., Music Educators Nat. Conf. Democrat. Meth. Office: Fountain Fort Carson School Dist 425 W Alabama St Fountain CO 80817

WILSON, ROBERTA LOUISE, writer, editor, journalist, activist; b. Hollywood, Calif., June 2, 1954; d. Robert Louis and Noreen Irvine Wilson; life ptnr. Jeff Lynn Moore; stepchildren: Tyron, Dashal, Adrianne 1 child, Dova Lindsay Moore. BA in Psychology, Chapman U., 1976. Editor Career Publs., Orange, Calif., 1976—81; freelance journalist Agoura Valley News, Westlake Mag., Agoura Hills, Calif., 1977—79; tech. writer Ashton-Tate, Torrance, Calif., 1983—87; tech. writer/project lead Microsoft Corp., Redmond, Wash., 1988—2000; freelance tech. writer Aldus Corp., Seattle, 1989—91. Officer Washtech/CWA Local 37083, Seattle, 2002—. Performance art for antinuclear UNARM, Business as Usual; contbr. articles to mags., websites. Media/People Power coord. Gt. Peace Mar. for Global Nuc. Disarmament, L.A., 1986—86; state coordinating com. Green Party of Wash. State, Seattle, 2001—02; co-organizer/writer bill of rights resolution Bill of Rights Def. Com., Bainbridge Island, Wash., 2003. Mem.: Green Party of Kitsap County (v.p. 2000—05), Winslow Cohousing Group (bd. trustees 1991—93). Mem. Religious Soc. Of Friends. Achievements include walked across the country with the Great Peace March for Global Nuclear Disarmament; co-founding member of first owner-developed cohousing community in the United States.

WILSON, RUBY LEILA, nursing educator; b. Punxsutawney, Pa., May 29, 1931; d. Clark H. and Alda E. (Armstrong) Wilson. BS in Nursing Edn., U. Pitts., 1954; MSN, Case Western Res. U., 1959; EdD, Duke U., 1969. Staff nurse, asst. head nurse Allegheny Gen. Hosp., Pitts., 1951—52, night clin. instr., adminstrv. supr., 1951—55; staff nurse, asst. head nurse Fort Miley VA Hosp., San Francisco, 1957—58; instr. nursing Duke U. Sch. Nursing, Durham, NC, 1955—57, asst. prof. med. surg. nursing, 1959—66, assoc. in medicine, 1963—66, prof. nursing, 1971—, dean sch. nursing., 1971—84, asst. to chancellor for health affairs, 1984—; asst. prof. dept. community and family medicine Duke U. Sch. Medicine, 1971—; cons., vis. prof. Rockefeller Found., Thailand, 1968—71; vis. prof. Case Western Res. U., 1982—84. Mem. Gov.'s Commn. on Health Care Reform in N.C., 1994—96. Contbr. articles to profl. jours. Active N.C. Med. Care Commn., N.C. Ctr. for Nursing, 1990—; adv. bd. Duke U. Cancer Ctr., 1986—. Fellow: Inst. Medicine, Am. Acad. Nursing; mem.: N.C. Found. for Nursing (pres. 1990—94), Women's Forum N.C. (bd. dirs. 1984—88, 1995—), Assn. for Acad. Health Ctrs. (mem. inst. planning com.), Nat. League Nursing, Am. Assn. Higher Edn., Am. Assn. Colls. Nursing, ANA, Sigma Theta Tau. Office: Duke U Med Ctr PO Box 3243 Durham NC 27715-3243

WILSON, RUTH PESTER, elementary school educator, researcher; b. Elizabeth, N.J., Mar. 12, 1918; d. Julius and Harriet Choate Pester; m. Edward Wilson, June 1, 1940 (dec.); children: Robert Edward, Janet Louise Wilson Benson. BEd, Danbury Tchrs. Coll., Danbury, Conn., 1939; MS, Bridgeport U., Conn., 1965. Tchr. Cos Cob Sch./Greenwich System, Conn., 1951—79; ret. Pres. Diamond Hill Ch. Cmty. Svc., Cos Cob. Recipient Brava award, Greenwich YWCA, 1998. Mem.: NEA, Fairfield Ret. Tchrs. Assn., Conn. Ret. Tchrs. Avocations: painting, sewing, reading, historical biographies. Home: 98 Valley Rd #6 Cos Cob CT 06807

WILSON, RUTH YVETTE, artist, educator; b. St. John, Canada, July 5, 1933; d. James Ritson Wilson; m. James Blair Wilson, June 15, 1964; 1 child, James Blair. Staff promotion artist Zellers Ltd., Montreal, 1953—56; advertising artist All Fla. Mag., Ocala, Fla., 1956—57; asst. promo. dir. Charm Mag., N.Y.C., 1957—59; advertising mgr. Velcro Sales, N.Y.C., 1959—60; fashion co-coord. artist Haggertys, Beverly Hills, Calif., 1960—61; fashion co-coord. stylist Christenson Studios, N.Y.C., 1961—62; instr. Can. Bedminster Workshops, 1962—, Muncy Greeting Card Corp., 2003—. Instr. watercolor Somerset Art Assn., Peapack, NJ, 2003—; workshop instr. Corp. & Art Assn., Can., U.S.A.; pvt. classes Wilsons Watercolor Classes, Pluckermin, NJ, 1970—; gallery owner North Mountain Gallery, Muncy Valley, Pa., 1998—, Keystone Horseshoe Mountain Pk., 1995—. Prin. works include United States Equestrian, 1979—84, Tele. & Telegraph, 1981, greeting card co., 1996—98. Recipient Liquitex Art award, Bald Eagles art League, 2001, Best Non Equine award, Hunterdon County Edn. Found., 2002, Honorable Mention, Cultural Heritage Gallery, 2003, numerous others. Mem.: Am. Artist Profl. League, Sullivan Coun. of the Arts, Eagles Mere Friends of the Arts, Rartian Valley Arts Assn., Somerset Art Assn. (Award of Excellence 2003), Garden State Water Color Soc. (Silver Brush award 2000), N.J. Water Color Soc., Pa. Water Color Soc. (assoc.). Avocations: reading, painting, gardening, cooking, sewing. Office Phone: 908-526-9048.

WILSON, SAL, systems analyst; b. Cedar Rapids, Iowa, May 9, 1947; d. Joseph John and Alma (Klouda) Nemec; m. Robert Foster Wilson, Oct. 1982. BS in Computer Sci., Mt. Mercy Coll., 1985. Cert. netware engr., info. tech. specialist IV. Systems analyst State of Iowa Dept. Human Rights, Des Moines, 1987-97; exec. v.p. Lawyer Forms Inc., Cedar Rapids, Iowa, 1992—; client/server developer State of Iowa Dept. Human Svcs., Des Moines, 1997—. Home: 2179 Blake Blvd SE Cedar Rapids IA 52403- Office: State of Iowa Dept Human Svcs Hoover Bldg 1st St Fl N Des Moines IA 50319-0001 E-mail: rwilsonlaw@aol.com.

WILSON, SHAUNA B., psychologist, researcher; d. Janie and Charles Wilson (Stepfather), Charles Joye. BS, Ga. So. U., Statesboro, 2003. Math tutor Academic Success Ctr., Statesboro, 2002—04; grad. asst. Ga. So. U., Statesboro, 2004—05; rsch. asst. Fla. State U., Tallahassee, 2005—. Staff sgt. Air Force N.G., 2000—06. Decorated Achievement medal Air Force; Predoctoral Interdisciplinary Rsch. Tng. fellow, Fla. State U. and Fla. Ctr. for Reading Rsch., 2005—. Mem.: Assn. for Psychol. Sci. Achievements include research in differences among ethnicities with regard to dating.

WILSON, STEPHANIE D., astronaut; b. Boston, 1966; m. Julius B.J. McCurdy. BS in Engring., Harvard U., Divsn. Engring. and Applied Sciences, 1988; MS in Aerospace Engring., U. Tex., 1992. Loads and dynamic engr. astronautics group Martin Marietta, Denver, 1988—90; mem. attitude and articulation control subsystem for Galileo spacecraft Jet Propulsion Lab., Pasadena, Calif., 1992—96; astronaut NASA, Johnson Space Ctr., Houston, 1996—. Lead CAPCOM (capsule communicator) Columbia Mission, 2003; mission specialist, load master, operating robotic arm STS-121, Return-to-Flight test mission and assembly flight to Internat. Space Station, 2006. Mem.: AIAA. Achievements include research in control and modeling of large, flexible space structures; second African-American women in space. Avocations: skiing, music, astronomy, stamp collecting/philately, travel. Office: Astronaut Office/CB NASA Johnson Space Ctr Houston TX 77058*

WILSON, SUSAN BERNADETTE, psychologist; b. Pitts., May 3, 1954; d. Booker Talifero and Edna Jean (Marconi) W.; m. John C. Scott Jr., Feb. 1975 (div.); children: Sharmel D., Justin. BS cum laude, U. Pitts., 1974, MS, 1981, PhD, 1985; MBA, U. Mo., 2005. Lic. clin. psychologist, Mo. Tchg. asst., fellow U. Pitts., 1979-81; intern VA Med. Ctr., Pitts., 1983-84; staff psychologist, fellow Menninger Found., Topeka, 1984-89; clin. dir. Crittenton Kansas City (Mo.) Clinic, 1989-90; asst. prof. Med. Sch. U. Mo., Kansas City, 1990—; v.p. Swope Pky. Cmty. Mental Health Ctr., Kansas City, 1997—2005; CEO Rodgers Health, Kans. City, 2005—. Cons. clinician Kansas City Chiefs, Nat. Football League, 1999—; cons. The Kaufmann Found., Kansas City, 1990; mem. faculty Karl Menninger Sch. Psychiatry, Topeka, 1986-89; asst. prof. Sch. Medicine, U. Mo., Kansas City, 1990-2002. Creator workshop: Being the Best You Can Be: A Psychoeducational Program for an Urban Workforce, 1989. Commr. Mayor's Commn. on Human Rights, Kansas City, 1992—; regional adv. com. Dept. Mental Health, Alcohol and Drug Abuse, 1992. Provost Devel. Fund fellow U. Pitts., 1977-79; named one of 100 Most Influential African Americans in Kansas City, Kansas City Globe, 1995. Mem. Am. Psychol. Assn., Am. Group Psychotherapy, Prime Health Bd., Jack and Jill of Am., Delta Sigma Theta. Democrat. Roman Catholic. Avocations: gardening, singing, painting, drawing, travel. Home: 1257 SW Summit Crossing Dr Lees Summit MO 64081-3264 Office: United Meth Rodgers Health 825 Euclid Kansas City MO 64145 Office Phone: 816-889-4622.

WILSON, SUSAN RICE, vice principal; b. Brownsville, Tenn., Aug. 11, 1942; d. Moreau Estes and E. Estelle (Walker) Rice; m. Charles E. Scott, Feb. 28, 1969 (div. July 1985); children: Tamera W., David W.; m. Lloyd Curlin Wilson, Apr. 7, 1994. BS, U. Tenn., Martin, 1964; EdM, Memphis State U., 1979, EdD, 1989. Cert. master tchr., Tenn. Elem. tchr. Lauderdale County Bd. Edn., Ripley, Tenn., 1964-65; exchange tchr. USIA, Washington, Netherlands, 1986-87; chmn. English dept. Am. Sch. of The Hague, Netherlands, 1987-88; secondary tchr. Haywood County Bd. Edn., Brownsville, Tenn., 1974-86, tchr. vocat. English, 1989-90, dir. adult basic edn., 1990-95; vice prin. Haywood H.S., Brownsville, Tenn., 1995—. Mem. curriculum task force Tenn. Dept. Edn., Nashville, 1985-86, mem. collaborative task force, 1989-92; chair Tenn. Acad. Decathlon Bd., 1998—. Local elector Tenn. Pres.'s Trust, Knoxville, 1989—; mem. Sister Cities Commn., Brownsville, 1990; com. mem. Ptnrs. in Edn., Brownsville, 1992—93; mem. West Star Leadership, 1993, Tenn. Reorgnl. Improvement Mgmt. Sys., 1994—95; mem. steering com. Fayette County-Haywood County Cmty. Enterprise, Brownsville, 1994—2000; bd. dirs. YMCA, Brownsville, 1996—2001. Named Outstanding Tchr. by students U. Chgo., 1989. Mem. NEA, Nat. Coun. Tchrs. English (regional composition judge 1984-86), Tenn. Edn. Assn., Tenn. Tchrs. Study Coun. (state steering com. 1984-86), Tenn. Prins. Study Coun., Sigma Tau Delta, Phi Delta Kappa. Methodist. Avocations: reading, travel. Home: 321 N Washington St Brownsville TN 38012-2063 Office: Haywood HS 1175 E College St Brownsville TN 38012-2208

WILSON, SYLVIA ALYCE, musician, educator; b. Mpls., June 19, 1950; d. Robert Leighton and Doris Mae (Seim) Butts; m. Dennis Charles Wilson, Sept. 12, 1970; children: Ryan Bradley, Virginia Anne Herzog. BS in Music Edn. with high distinction, U. Minn., Mpls., 1972, MA in Music Edn., 1987. Orch. tchr. Anoka-Hennepin Sch. Dist. No. 11, Coon Rapids, Minn., 1972—77, music tchr., 1986—89, 1992—; substitute music tchr. St. Louis Park (Minn.) Sch. Dist. No. 283, 1978—85; orch. tchr. Wayzata (Minn.) Sch. Dist. #284, 1985—86; orch./choir tchr. Roseville (Minn.) Area Pub. Schs. #623, 1989—90. Musician Lake String Quartet, Mpls., 1982—85; piano tuner, pvt. music tchr., 1982—86; preschool music tchr. West Bank Sch. Music, Mpls., 1983—85; judge Minn. State HS League, St. Paul, 2003—; presenter in field; MMEA State mentor Minn. Music Edn. Assn., 2006—. Contbr. articles to profl. jours. Violinist, violist Cantati Evangelica, Mpls., 1995—2001, Mpls. Civic Orch., 1970—; VBS tchr. First Bapt. Ch. Mpls., 1990—94, choir dir., bell choir dir., 1992—2000. Named Outstanding Sr., Am. Legion, 1968; recipient Meritorious Orch. Program award, Minn. String Tchrs. Assn., 1987, 2002; grantee, Anoka-Hennepin Ednl. Found., 1999—2001; scholar, U. Minn., 1968. Mem.: NEA, Minn. Educators of the Gifted and Talented, Anoka-Hennepin Edn. Minn. (bldg. rep. 2000—05), Am. String Tchrs. Assn., Music Educators Nat. Conf., Pi Kappa Lambda, Sigma Alpha Iota (pres., v.p., treas., corr. sec. 1970—, co-chair benefit music scholarships, Music scholar 1970, Sword of Honor 1971, Svc. to Chpt. award 2005, Rose of Honor 2006). Home: 2700 Joppa Ave S Saint Louis Park MN 55416 Office: Northdale Mid Sch 11301 Dogwood St Coon Rapids MN 55448 Personal E-mail: swilsonusf@yahoo.com.

WILSON, TAMARA LEE, English educator; b. Terre Haute, Ind., Sept. 20, 1961; d. James Brown and Mary Ann Lindsey; m. James Michael Wilson, June 22, 1999. BA, Ind. U., Ft. Wayne, 1983; MA, San Jose State U., Calif., 1994; PhD, U. La., Lafayette, 1999. Tchg. fellow U. La., Lafayette, 1995—96; adj. U. North Fla., Jacksonville, 1997—98, Flagler Coll., St. Augustine, Fla., 1997—2000, asst. prof. English, 2000—. Lectr. in field. Contbr. articles to profl. jours. Foster coord. Siberian Husky Rescue of Fla., Seminole, 2004—06; mem. Oxford Roundtable Women and Leadership, Oxford, England, 2005. Fellow, U. La. fellow, 1994. Mem.: Popular Culture in the South. Democrat. Office: Flagler College 74 King St Saint Augustine FL 32084

WILSON, VALERIE PETIT, health science association director; b. New Orleans, Jan. 24, 1950; d. Alvin Joseph and Lorraine Catherine (Kelly) Petit; children: Daniel Lawrence, Craig Anthony. BS, Xavier U. La., 1970; PhD, Johns Hopkins U., 1976. Dir. policy USPHS, Washington, 1990—92, dept. dir., 1992, asst. dir. nat. AIDS policy office, 1992—93; dir. health scis. policy Inst. Medicine Nat. Acad. Scis., Washington, 1993—98; dep. dir. Tulane/Xavier Ctr. Bio-Environ. Rsch., New Orleans, 1998—2003; exec. dir. leadership alliance, clin. prof. cmty. health Brown U., Providence, 2004—. Cons. NIH, Fairfax County Schs. Contbr. articles to profl. jours. Mem. AAAS, Am. Soc. Biochemists and Molecular Biologists. Avocations: quilting, gardening. Office: Brown U Leadership Alliance Cranston RI 02920-2699 Office Phone: 401-863-1474. Business E-Mail: valerie_wilson@brown.edu.

WILSON, VICTORIA JANE SIMPSON, farmer, medical/surgical nurse; b. Floresville, Tex., Nov. 30, 1952; d. Joseph Eugene and Eva Gertrude (Ferguson) Simpson; m. Richard Royce Wilson, May 15, 1976; children: Sarah Beth, Nathan Lawrence. BSN, U. Cen. Ark., 1977; MS in Nursing, Northwestern State U., 1981. Charge nurse surg. St. Vincent Infirmary, Little Rock; staff nurse ICU La. State U. Med. Ctr., Shreveport, La.; patient edn. coord. White River Med. Ctr., Batesville, Ark.; co-owner, CEO Health Plus, Stuttgart, Ark.; co-owner Wilson Enterprises, Humphrey, Ark., 1992—99; staff nurse St. Vincent Health Sys., 2000—01; mem. faculty Southeast Ark. Coll., 2000; Level I coord. faculty Jefferson Sch. Nursing, Pine Bluff, Ark., 2001—06; instr. U. Ark., Pine Bluff, 2006—. Mem.: ANA, Ark. Nurses Assn., Sigma Theta Tau. Home: 51 Wilson Ln Humphrey AR 72073-9097 Personal E-mail: victoriarichardwilson@yahoo.com.

WILSON, WANDA O., nurse anesthetist, educator; Diploma, Holzer Med. Ctr. Sch. Nursing, Gallipolis, Ohio, 1969, Cin. Gen. Hosp. Sch. Nurse Anesthesia, 1972; BS magna cum laude, U. Cin., 1986, BSN summa cum laude, 1992, MSN, 1994, PhD in Nursing Sci. and Physiology, 1998; postgrad., J.L. Kellogg Grad. Sch. Mgmt., Chgo., 1993. RN Ohio, ACLS. Operating rm. nurse Holzer Med. Ctr., Gallipolis, 1969—70; anesthesia instr., mem. staff Cin. Gen. Hosp., 1972—79; anesthesia staff nurse Clermont Mercy Hosp., Batavia, Ohio, 1979—80; anesthesia instr., staff nurse Cin. Gen. Hosp., 1981—82; staff anesthetist Good Samaritan Hosp., Cin., 1982—84; anesthesia instr., staff nurse anesthesia program U. Cin., 1984—, chief nurse anesthetist, 1993—98; staff anesthetist Our Lady of Mercy Hosp., Cin., 1985—, Shriners Burns Inst., Cin., 1990—94; clin. coord. nurse anesthesia major U. Cin. Coll. Nursing, 1991—98, adj. asst. prof., 1994—2001, interim asst. dir. nurse anesthesia major, 1997—98, program dir., 1998—, assoc. prof. clin. nursing, 2001—03, assoc. prof. nursing tenure tract, 2003—; asst. dir. Anesthesia Svcs. U. Hosp., Cin., 1995—. Legal cons. case revs., 1998—; anesthesia cons. Baxter Pharm. Products Inc., 2001—02; spkr. in field. Mem.: Sigma Theta Tau, Ohio Coalition Nurses with Specialty Cert., Ohio Assn. Nurse Anesthetists (mem. edn. com. 1991—93, bd. dirs. 1995—98, chmn. edn. com. 1996—98, program chmn. 1998, co-chmn. fed. govt. rels. com. 1998—99, pres.-elect 1998—99, pres. 1999—2000), Am. Assn. Nurse Anesthetists (found. profl. devel. com. 1997—99, continuing edn. com. 1998—2000, nominating com. 2000—01, site-reviewer 2000—02, liaison edn. com. 2000—02, edn. com. 2000—02, rsch. proposal/posters judge 2000—04, regional bd. dirs. 2002—04, strategic planning com. 2002—06, nursing care performance measures steering com. 2003—04, fin. com. 2004—05, nat. treas. 2004—05, chmn. ad hoc com. for reviewing standing coms. 2004—05, found. trustee 2005—, profl. devel. com. 2005—, found. fundraising com. 2005—, cert., nat. v.p. 2005—06, nat. pres.-elect 2006—), Delta Tau Kappa, Alpha Sigma Kappa. Home: 900 Adams Crossing # 3600 Cincinnati OH 45202 Office: U Anestesia Assocs Inc U Cin Med Ctr Anesthesiology Dept 231 Albert Sabin Way Cincinnati OH 45267-0531 also: U Cin Coll Nursing William Procter Hall 3110 Vine St Cincinnati OH 45221-0038

WILSON, WENDY SCOTT, history educator; b. Litchfield, Ill., Jan. 21, 1946; d. John Denniston and Shirley Mansfield Wilson; m. Kenneth John Hilty, June 24, 2006; 1 child, Michaela Jane Thompson. BA, Wells Coll.; M of Letters, U. Aberdeen, Scotland, 1970. Tchr. Lexington H.S., Mass., 1971—. Sr. lectr. Northeastern U., Boston, 1972—2006; presenter in field. Author: (textbook) American History on the Screen, 2d edit., 2002, World History on the Screen, 2d edit., 2003, Differentiated Instruction for Social Studies, 2006. Sr. warden Grace Episcopal Ch., Newton, Mass., 1998—2000. Recipient Julia Taylor Martin prize in History, Wells Coll., 1968. Mem.: Phi Alpha Theta (life). Episcopalian. Avocations: travel, writing, gardening, auto restoration. Office: Lexington Pub Sch 251 Waltham St Lexington MA 02421 Office Phone: 617-921-1902. E-mail: wwhilty@yahoo.com.

WILSON-HUNT, SIMONE SONYA YEVETTE, elementary school educator; b. Augusta, Ga., Dec. 24, 1971; d. Solomon and Shirley Ann Wilson; m. Thomas Hunt, Sept. 1, 2001. BA, Clark Atlanta U., 1995; MEd (hon.), Mercer U., Atlanta, 1999. Tchr. Clayton County Bd. Edn., Riverdale, Ga., 1998—. Sec. St. Marion Bapt. Ch., Girad, Ga., 1996—2006. Recipient Tchr. of Month, Ch. St. Elem. Home: 110 New Oakridge Trail Fayetteville GA 30214 Office: Church Street Elementary 7013 Church Street Riverdale GA 30274 Office Phone: 770-994-4000.

WILSON-JONES, LINDA, guidance counselor; b. Hattiesburg, Miss., Apr. 11, 1955; d. Herman and Mary (Chapman) W.; m. James L. Jones, Jr., Aug 12, 1972 (div. Dec. 1986); children: Rhoda Grechelle Jones, James LeMontrell Jones III. BA, Miss. State U., 1995, MS, 1997, Ednl. Splst., 1998. Cert. guidance counselor Miss., La. Substitute tchr., adminstrv. asst. Meridian (Miss.) Pub. Schs., 1990-95; day treatment splst., mental health counselor Weems Mental Health, Meridian, 1995-96; counselor, facilitator, educator Choctaw Housing Authority, Phila., 1996-98; counselor, program supr., transition program coord. Youth Excitement Team, Inc., Meridian, 1998—; guidance counselor, sch. drug coord., test coord. Rankin County Schs., Brandon, Miss., 1999—. Cons. profl. devel., pres. JoLin Cons. Group, Meridian, 1998—, How to Plan a Workshop demonstration, 1998; counselor Classroom Guidance Lessons, 1999. Mem. task force, facilitator, cons. Miss. Coalition Against Domestic Violence, 1998; facilitator Sem. on Male Perspective about Domestic Violence, Green, Yellow and Red. Know the Signs, 1998; event coord. Meridian's Martin Luther King Parade and Celebration. Mem. Miss. Counseling Assn. (mem. exec. bd. 1997—), Miss. Assn. Multi-Cultural Counseling and Devel. (pres.) Doct. Student Assn. (sec.), Miss. Assn. Multi-Cultural Counseling and Devel. (conf. coord. 1997-99), Order of Ea. Star (grand sec. Bathsheba grand chpt. Miss. jurisdiciton 1997-99), Zeta Phi Beta, Inc. Democrat. Methodist. Avocations: reading motivational articles, travel, meeting new people, interacting with positive people.

WILSON-LAWSON, MELANIE, social worker, educator; d. Bobby L. and Mary Ann Wilson; m. Daniel Russell Lawson; children: Hannah LeAnn Lawson, Farryl Christina Lawson. BS, Tex. So. U., 1991; MPH, U. Tex., Houston, Tex., 1993; PhD in Social Work, U. Houston, Houston, Tex., 2002; cert. in Clin. Scientist Tng. Program, Baylor Coll. Medicine, 2005. Project mgr. U. Houston, 1996—98; supr. Ryan White Title 1 Program NAACP, Houston, 1999—2000; asst. prof. Coll. Pharmacy & Health Scis. Tex. So. U., Houston, 2002—. Mem. rsch. adv. com. Tex. So. U., 2003, mem. strategic plan 2001-2005 subcom., 2003—04, faculty liaison hiv/aids orientation and profl. edn., 2004, campus coord. elimination health disparities project, 03. Grad. rsch. Greater Houston (Tex.) Women's Found., 1998; adv. pub. health issues Lee P. Brown Mayoral Campaign, Houston, 1997; bd. dirs. The Sandra Organ Dance Co., Houston, 2003—05. Recipient Golden Vol. award, Congressional Office Sheila Jackson Lee, Exemplary Svc. award, Inst. Advancement Multicultural & Minority Medicine. Mem.: Cmty.-Campus Partnerships Health (corr.), The Houston Soc. (rep. univ. chpt. 2004—, mem. cmty. fund bd. 2004—), The LINKS, Inc., Delta Sigma Theta. Office: Texas Southern University COPHS 3100 Cleburne Ave Houston TX 77004 Business E-Mail: lawson_mw@tsu.edu.

WILSON-MCNAMARA, PAMELA, microbiologist, educator; b. Crockett, Tex., Nov. 25, 1948; d. Francis Corley Wilson and Gladys DeZelle; m. Robert Dale Alexander, Apr. 6, 1976 (div. Aug. 1987); children: Matthew Robert Alexander, Shane Gregory Alexander. BA in Microbiology, U. Tex., 1971. Cert. med. tech. Am. Assn. Clin. Pathologists. Adj. faculty Wenatchee (Wash.) Valley Coll., 1984—2003; microbiologist Ctrl. Wash. Hosp., 1987—2000; adj. faculty microbiology and chemistry N. Seattle C.C., 2004—. Pres. Wenatchee Jr. Hosp. Guild, 1994; vol. AIDS patients Multifaith Care Teams, Seattle, 2000—03; docent Burke Mus., Seattle, 2002—03. Mem.: DAR. Home and Office: 4549 18th Ave NE Seattle WA 98105 E-mail: wilsonmcnamara@aol.com.

WILSON-PLEINESS, CHRISTINE JOYCE, writer, columnist, poet; b. Chgo., July 27, 1951; d. Peter Joseph Thelen and Edna (Milewski) Dombrowski; m. Douglas A. Wilson, July 7, 1973 (div. Oct. 1986); children: Amy Kathleen, Lauri Ellyn; m. Glenn B. Pleiness, Dec. 5, 1998. BS in Edn., No. Ill. U., 1973; MFAW, Spalding U., 2003. Asst. store mgr. County Seat Co., Joliet, Ill., 1981-83; cash applicator Aurora (Ill.) Pump Co., 1984-85, accounts payable clk., 1986-89; accounts payable technician Horizon Sportswear, Inc., Madison Heights, Mich., 1989-90; accounts payable rep. Crain Comm., Inc., Detroit, 1990-95; accounts payable specialist Philip Svcs. Corp., Detroit, 1995-96, ORACLE project team, 1996, accounts payable team leader, 1996-97; accounts payable and expense supr. Superior Cons. Co., Inc., Southfield, Mich., 1997-98; accounts payable auditor The Profit Recovery Group Internat. Inc., Clawson, Mich., 1998-99; accounts payable supr. ACN Inc., Farmington Hills, Mich., 1999-2000, Roush Industries, Livonia, Mich., 2000—02; accounts payable coord. The Oakland Press, Pontiac, Mich., 2002—03; accounts payable specialist Omnicare, Inc., Covington, Ky., 2004—. Mem., bd. dirs. Somerset Square Condominium Assn., Sterling Heights, 1996, 97; rec. sec. Troy Cmty. Chorus, 1999-2003; mem. Citizen Participation Com., Covington, Ky., 2006—. Recipient Tchr. Edn. scholarship State of Ill., 1969. Mem. Parents Without Ptnrs. (treas. chpt. 761, 1996-98, Appreciation award 1997, 98, 99), Monday Night Writing Group (founding, facilitator 1997-2003), Friends of Peaselburg Neighborhood Assn., Beta Sigma Phi (Woman of Yr. award 1989, 98, Order of the Rose 2000). Avocations: writing, reading, dance, attending the theatre, singing. Personal E-mail: writerssoup@yahoo.com.

WILSON-STEWART, MARILYN LUCILLE, retired human resources leader; b. Lima, Ohio, Feb. 6, 1933; d. Russell A. and Ruth Alma Parcher; m. Billy A. Stewart, May 15, 1965 (div. Apr. 1991); m. Bobbie H. Wilson, Nov. 7, 1953 (div. Feb. 4, 1960); children: Bobbie Craig Wilson, Keith Russell Wilson. Exec. sec. specialized human resources program, Baker Bus. U., Flint, Mich., 1953. Stenographer, statistician Flint Child Guidance Clinic, 1953—64; human resources tng. Gen. Motors Corp., Marion, Ind., 1964—95; ret., 1995. Pres. bd. dirs. Marion (Ind.) Urban League, 1973, YWCA, Marion; pres. Women's Ministry; 1st v.p. Ch. Women United Grant County; Sunday Sch. dir., altar worker, trainer and coord. Recipient GM award for Excellance in Cmty. Svc., 1973, Pres. award, NAACP, local br., 1991. Mem.: Order Ea. Star (past worthy matron). Democrat. Baptist. Avocations: reading, Bible teacher, crafts, cooking.

WILSON-WEBB, NANCY LOU, educational association administrator; b. Maypearl, Tex., Jan. 20, 1932; d. Madison Grady Wise and Mary Nancy Pearson-Bedford (Haney) Wilson; m. John Crawford Webb, July 29, 1972. BS magna cum laude, Abilene Christian U., Tex., 1953; EdM (hon.), Tex. Christian U., 1985. Cert. tchr., mid-mgmt., sch. adminstr., Tex. Tchr. elem. grades Ft. Worth Ind. Sch. Dist., 1953-67, adult edn. tchr., 1967-73; dir. adult edn. consortium for 38 sch. dists. Tex. Edn. Agy., 1973-2000. Pres. Nat. Commn. on Adult Basic Edn., "Most Outstanding adult ed. Admin. in US" by AAAC; 1994-95; pres. Tex. Adult Edn. Adminstrn., 1994; apptd. mem. Tex. State Literacy Coun., 1987-94, Tex. State Sch. Bd. Commn., 1994-99; exec. bd. Tex. Coun. Co-op Dir., 1989-2001, Bd. Nat. Assn. of AAACE, 1988; pres., 1994—; apptd. to Gov. Ann Richard's Task Force for Edn.; ranch owner, mgr., 1998-2003. Cons. to textbooks, 1994-98; editor textbooks, 1999. Pres. Jr. Womans Club, Ft. Worth, 1969, Fine Arts Guild, Tex. Christian U., Ft. Worth, 1970-72, Ft. Worth Womens Civic Club Coun., 1970, pres. Aquarius Women's Club; active Exec. Libr. Bd., Ft. Worth, 1990-2003, Jewel Charity Ball, 1988-2003; bd. dirs. Literacy Plus in North Tex., 1988-99, pres., 2001—; bd. dirs. Greater Ft. Worth Literacy Coun., 1976-88, 2002—, pres., 2001-03; commr. Ed-16 Task Forces Tex. Edn. Agy., 1985-94; literacy bd. dir. Friends of Libr., 1967-2002, Opera Guild Bd. Ft. Worth, 1965-85, Ft. Worth Ballet Guild, Johnson County (Tex.) Corr. Bd., 1990-2000; bd. dirs. Salvation Army, Ft. Worth, 1996-2003, Ft. Worth Libr.; active Tarrant County Bd. on Aging, 1997-98, Commn. Status of Women, Ft. Worth, 1973-99, Southside Ch. of Christ. Recipient Bevy award Jr. Womans Club, 1968, Proclamation Commr. Ct. Outstanding 43 Yr. Literacy Svc. to Tarrant County Com. Ctr., 1994, Tarrant County Woman of Yr. award, Fort Worth Star Telegram, 1995, Outstanding Leadership award Ft. Worth ISD Sch. Bd., 1985, 95, Mayor's Proclamation of Nancy Webb Week, 1996; named one of Most Outstanding Educators in U.S. Nat. Assn. Adult Edn., 1983, Most Outstanding Woman Edn., City of Ft. Worth, 1991, others; nominated to Tex. Hall of Fame for Women, 1991; named to Ft. Worth Hall of Fame, 1992; scholar Germany, 1983. Mem. NEA, DAR (Mary Isham Keith chpt. 1985-2002, Nat. Literacy award 1992, Leadership Literacy award 1985-87, 89, 94, Nat. Educators award 2003), AAUW, Am. Assn. Adult and Continuing Edn. (v.p. 1987-89, chair 1993 internat. conv. 1992, Nat. Adminstr. of Yr. in Adult Edn. 1998, Most Outstanding Adminstr. Adult Edn. in US 1999), Tex. Assn. Adult and Cont. Edn. (pres. 1985-86, Most Outstanding Adult Adminstr. in Tex. 1984), Tex. Coun. Adult Edn. Dirs. (pres. nat. com. on edn., Nat. Dept. Labor award 1992), Coun. World Affairs (bd. dir. 1980-2002), Am. Bus. Women's Assn., Ft. Worth C. of C., Lecture Found., Internat. Reading Assn. (Literacy Challenge award 1991), Ft. Worth Adminstrv. Assn., Southwest Cattle Raisers Assn., Ligon Assn., Zonta, Tanglewood Garden Club, Ft. Worth Garden Club (exec. bd. dirs. 2000-03), Woman's Club, Ft. Worth Petroleum Club, Carousel Dance Club, Met. Dinner Dance Club, Ridglea Country Club, Girls Svc. League, Aquarius (pres. 2001-02), Crescent Club (Dallas), Alpha Delta Kappa (Nat. Literacy award 1992), Greater Ft. Worth Literacy Coun. (pres. 2000-03), Phi Delta Kappa, Mary Isham Keith DAR (Nat. award 1993, Nat. Found. award 2003). Democrat. Mem. Lds Ch. Home: 3716 Fox Hollow St Fort Worth TX 76109-2616

WIMBERLEY, CHERYL ANN, choreographer, educator; b. Needham, Mass., Sept. 8, 1954; d. Samuel Nelson and Josephine Murphy; m. David Merrill Wimberley, July 31, 1979; children: Todd Merrill, Sean David, Karrissa Marie. BFA in Dance, Jacksonville U., Fla., 1995, BS in Dance Edn., 1995. Cert. dir. dance studies Fla., 2006. Choreographer Godby High, Tallahassee, 1995—; tchr., choreographer US Choreographer. Cons. in field. Designer, choreographer Whispers of Women (Awards of Distinction for Choreography, 1995); dir.: Youth in The Arts. Dir., choreographer Dance, Baton, Tallahassee, 1995—2005. Named Outstanding Designer and Choreographer, 2000—. Home: 1599 Payne St Tallahassee FL 32303 Office: Godby High School 1717 West Tharpe St Tallahassee FL 32303 Office Phone: 850-488-1325. Business E-Mail: cheryl_wimberley@hotmail.com.

WIMBERLY, CYNTHIA DIANE, mathematics educator; d. Winnette Vinyard Wimberly; life ptnr. Patricia Rose Manning, Feb. 9, 1952; children: Marley Kim Boyd, Mary Shannon Boyd, Jonathan Matthew Boyd. MS, Sul Ross State U., Alpine, Tex., 1994. Cert. in secondary math. Tex. Math. tchr. Marfa (Tex.) Ind. Sch. Dist., 1999—. Home: 607 W Sul Ross Ave Alpine TX 79830 Office: Marfa Ind Sch Dist PO Box T Marfa TX 79843 Office Phone: 432-729-4252.

WIMBERLY, LINDA ROBERTS, music educator, artist; b. Lincoln, Nebr., Sept. 26, 1945; d. Arthur Thomas Roberts and Dorothy Mae Moore; m. Charles Augustus Wimberly, July 2, 1966 (div. Aug. 1985); children: Susan Lynn, Sheri Beth. Student, North Ga. Coll., 1963—64, Shorter Coll., 1964—67; BA, U. Ala., 1995. Pvt. music instr., Marietta, 1965—; entertainer, vocalist The Fireside Restaurant, Marietta, 1973—76; vocalist, contralto soloist N.W. Presbyn. Ch., Atlanta, 1988—96, dir. music, 1991—96; composer vocal, piano, choral works, 1995—; guitar instr. continuing edn. Kennesaw (Ga.) State U., 1996—2003; pres., owner Artist L'Inc Corp., Marietta, 2000—05. Edn. ptnr. Ga. Wildlife Fedn., Atlanta, 2000—05. One-woman shows include South Trust Bank, Mableton, 2001, Imagine Sta., Lehigh Valley, Pa., 2003, exhibitions include Period Gallery, Lincoln, Nebr., 2001—05, Upstream People Gallery, Omaha, 2002—05, exhibited in group shows at N.W. Presbyn. Ch., Atlanta, 1995, Mable House Artfest, Mableton, Ga., 2000, Mon-Dak Heritage Ctr., Sidney, Mont., 2000, 2001, Marietta/Cobb Mus. Art, 2002, 2004, myexpose.com, 2004—05, many others, Represented in permanent collections;, author articles, poetry and essays. Recipient Writing residency, Vt. Studio Ctr., 1997. Mem.: ASCAP, Acad. Am. Poets, Music Tchrs. Nat. Assn., Golden Key (life). Avocations: environment, nutrition, organic lifestyle, exercise.

WIMMER, KATHRYN, retired elementary school educator; b. St. Louis, May 8, 1929; d. Arthur Jordan and Louise Clara Sykes; m. Harry William Wimmer, Aug. 4, 1951; children: Robert William, Richard Jordan. BS in Edn., U. Mo., 1951; postgrad., U. South Fla., 1971—72. Cert. tchr. Mo., Fla. Tchr. Affton (Mo.) Sch., 1951—52, Heege Sch., Affton, 1965—67, Gulf Gate Sch., Sarasota, Fla., 1967—72; piano tchr. Crestwood, Mo., 1963—65. Artist, musician, tchr. music and art; tutor IQ, employment and aptitude testing. Oil paintings, watercolor paintings. V.p. Southgate Cmty., Sarasota, 1989—90; pres. bd. dirs. Assoc. Women's Club, Sarasota, 1990—91, bd. dirs., 1986—93; vol. Gulf Gate Libr., Sarasota, 1993—2006. Recipient tennis trophy, Bath and Racquet Tennis Club, Sarasota, 1979, swimming trophy, Southgate Cmty. Assn., 1987, 1988, Wall of Honor cert., Roosevelt H.S., St. Louis, 2003. Mem.: Roosevelt H.S. Alumni Assn., U. Mo. Alumni Assn., Mysterium High IQ Soc., Delta Gamma (scholarship chmn., treas., rush chmn., social chmn.). Democrat. Presbyterian. Achievements include thirteen of the tutored students who were tested successfully were sent to Pine View School for the gifted. Avocations: embroidery, literature, travel, history, genealogy, embroidery. Personal E-mail: HarryKay@peoplepc.com.

WIMSATT, ANNE MOSHER, retail bookstore owner; b. Joliet, Ill., May 18, 1943; d. Arthur Theodore and Alice Wynne (Hall) Mosher; m. Michael Hughes Winsatt, June 6, 25, 1966 (div. June 1988); children: Michael William, Theodore Hughes. BA, Swarthmore Coll., 1965; MA in Teaching, Cornell U., 1966. Lic. secondary English tchr., N.Y. English tchr. Boynton Jr. High Sch., Ithaca, N.Y., 1966-67, Brighton High Sch., Rochester, N.Y., 1967-71; activities dir. Mary Imogene Bassett Hosp., Cooperstown, N.Y., 1971-72, computer programmer, 1972; owner, mgr. The Book Shop, Lewistown, Pa., 1986—92. Bd. dir. United Way of Mifflin-Juniata, Lewistown, 1982-2005, pres., 1987; mem. Med. Soc. Aux., Lewistown, 1978-87, pres., 1982-83; sec. Parking Authority, Lewistown, 1987—; mem. Lewistown Planning Commn., 1990—, chmn. 2005—. Mem. AAUW (v.p. Lewistown br. 1980-81). Episcopalian. Avocations: gardening, reading, sewing. Office: The Book Shop 22 N Brown St Lewistown PA 17044-1733

WINANS, CECE, gospel vocalist; b. Detroit, Oct. 8, 1964; m. Alvin Love; children: Ashley, Alvin II. Albums with Bebe Winans include Lord Lift Us Up, 1985, Bebe and Cece Winans, 1987, Heaven, 1988, Different Lifestyles, 1991, Noel, 1993, Relationships, 1994, Bebe & Cece Winans Greatest Hits, 1996; solo albums include For Always (1987 Grammy award for Best Female Gospel Performance), Don't Cry (1989 Grammy award for Best Female Gospel Performance), Alone In His Presence, 1995 (Grammy award 1995), Everlasting Love, 1998, His Gift, 1998, Alabaster Box, 1999, CeCe Winans, 2001, Throne Room, 2001, Purified, 2005 (2 Grammy awards); appeared in films including White Men Can't Jump, 1992, Waiting to Exhale, 1995, The Prince of Egypt, 1998; appeared on TV shows including The Grammy Awards, Soul Train, Sesame Street, Martin, Living Single, Touched By an Angel, Christmas in Washington, Nat. Meml. Day Concert; host (TV program) Cece's Place, (radio program) On A Positive Note; author: Feel the Spirit, 1998. Recipient 10 Grammy awards, numerous Stellar and NAACP Image awards. Office: Capital Entertainment 1201 N St NW Apt A Washington DC 20005-5104*

WINBLAD, ANN, investment company executive; BA in Math. and Bus. Adminstrn., U. St. Thomas, St. Paul, Minn., MA in Internat. Econs. and Edn.; LLD (hon.), U. St. Thomas. Systems programmer Fed. Reserve Bank; co-founder Open Systems, Inc., 1976-83; strategic planning cons., IBM, Microsoft, Price Waterhouse, and many start-ups; co-founding ptnr. Hummer Winblad Venture Ptnrs., San Francisco, 1989—. Bd. dirs. Dean & Deluca, Intacct, Market Wire, The Knot, Voltage Security, Arbor Software, Berkeley Systems, Net Perceptions; advisor The Software Forum, San Jose Ctr. for Software Develop., Stanford/MIT Venture Forum. Co-author: Object-Oriented Software, 1990; contbr. articles to profl. publs. Trustee U. St. Thomas, St. Paul, Mich. Office: Hummer Winblad Venture Partners 1 Lombard St Ste 300 San Francisco CA 94111-1130*

WINBUSH, OLGA JOYCE, education educator, consultant; d. Harbart Theodore and Claudia Madeleine Tatum; m. Albert Steve Winbush, Oct. 19, 1976; children: LaKetta Denise, Albert Steve, Ari Solomon, Meko Meyatta. BA in Sociology, UCLA, 1976, PhD in Edn., 1999; MA in Human Devel., Pacific Oaks Coll., 1980. Multiple subject clear tchg. credential Commn. on Tchg. Credentialing, Calif., 1992. Tchg. asst. Westland Sch., L.A., 1982—83; tchr. Children's Cmty. Sch., Van Nuys, Calif., 1983—93; adj. faculty Antelope Valley Coll., Lancaster, Calif., 1993—98; core faculty, prof. Pacific Oaks Coll., Pasadena, Calif., 1998—. Adj. faculty Chapman U., Lancaster, 1994—98; curriculum cons. Children's Cmty. Sch., Van Nuys, 1996—2003; literacy curriculum cons. First 5/Pacific Oaks Coll., Pasadena, 2003—; literacy cons. Bridging Resources in Tech. and Edn. Afterschool Program, Pasadena, 2003—, CORAL, Pasadena, 2004—05; presenter in field. Editor: (jour.) Pathways, 1992—96; contbr. articles to profl. jours. Mem. Found. for Excellence, Van Nuys, 1985—. Recipient Unsung Hero award, Bridging Resources in Tech. and Edn. Afterschool Prgram, 2004; grantee, First 5 Early Literacy Tng., 2003. Mem.: ND Study Group on Evaluation, Rschrs. of Color, Nat. Black Child Devel. Inst., Jack and Jill Am. (assoc.). Democrat. Avocations: travel, reading, photography. Office: Pacific Oaks College 5 Westmoreland Pl Pasadena CA 91103-3592 Business E-Mail: owinbush@pacificoaks.edu. E-mail: asojwin@msn.com.

WINCH, DONNA GLADHILL, music educator; b. Frederick, Md., Oct. 9, 1950; d. Franklin Startzman and Bessie Mae Gladhill; m. Walter L. Winch, Aug. 3, 1982; children: Ashley, Tyler. BS, Lebanon Valley Coll., Annville, Pa., 1972. Cert. tchr. Pa., lic. vocal and instrumental music tchr. K-12 Pa. Pvt. piano tchr., Frederick, 1967—71, Lebanon, Pa., 1971—78; piano and voice tchr. Harrisburg, Pa., 1978—2006; gen. music and choral dir. Dover Sch. Dist., Pa., 1972—74, Susquehanna Twp. Sch. Dist., Harrisburg, 1974—; mus. dir. musicals Susquehanna Mid. Sch. and H.S., 1980—. Advisor YWCA/Dover Mid. Sch., 1972—74; youth choir dir. Christ Evang. Luth. Ch., Linglestown, Pa., 1990—97; dir. Macy's Day Parade, N.Y.C., 2003, Am. Sings, Washington, 1997—; mem. Stock Stalkers, Harrisburg, 1998—2005; pres. Lebanon Valley Alumni Chorale, Annville, 1978—83; com. woman Dem. Party, Dauphin County, Pa., 2002—03. Grantee, Hanna Found., 2002. Mem.: Susquehanna Twp. Edn. Assn. (treas., rep.), Pa. Edn. Assn., Pa. Music Educators Assn., Dauphin County Music Educators (1st v.p., pres. 1984—88), Delta Kappa Gamma (2d v.p. 2004—). Democrat. Lutheran. Avocations: gardening, needlecrafts. Home: 1060 Woodridge Dr Middletown PA 17057 E-mail: winch@comcast.net.

WINCHELL, MARGARET J., realtor; b. Clinton, Tenn., Jan. 26, 1923; d. Robert Love Webster and Mayme Jane Warwick; m. Charles M. Winchell, June 7, 1941; children: David Alan(dec.), Margaret Winchell Boyle; m. Robert George Sterrett, July 15, 1977 (dec. 1982). Student, Denison U., 1940, Miami U., Oxford, Ohio, 1947, 48. Saleswoman Fred K.A. Schmidt & Shirmer Real Estate, Cin., 1960-66, Cline Realtors, Cin., 1966-70; owner, broker Winchell's Showplace Realtors, Cin., 1972—; ins. agt. United Liberty Life Ins. Co., Cin., 1966—, dist. mgr., 1967-70, 77-82, regional mgr., 1982—; stockbroker Waddell & Reed, Columbis, Ohio, 1972—, Security Counselors. Annuity and ins. specialist Fin. Cons., 1982—, dir., 1984, 85, 86, 87, owner;

instr. evening coll. Treas., v.p. Parents Without Ptnrs., 1969, sec., 1968; pres. PTA, Hamilton Fairfield Singles; vol. leader, sr. dance leader Sycamore Sr. Str., 1990—2000; nat. spkr. Child Evangelism Fellowship and Nat. Sunday Sch. Convs., 1955—57; dir. Child Evangelism Cin.; pres. Christian Solos, 1974; chaplain Bethesda N. Hosp.; leader singles group Hyde Park Cmty. United Meth. Ch.; ordained Stephen min. Montgomery Comm. Bapt. Ch., 1990—2003. Mem.: Womens Coun. Real Estate Bd. (treas.), Nat. Assn. Real Estate Bds. West Schell Realtors (v.p.), Hamilton Singles Club (pres.), Guys and Gals Singles Club (founder, 1st pres.), Travel Go Go Club, Alfonta Club. Home and Office: 8221 Margaret Ln Cincinnati OH 45242-5309 E-mail: margaretwinchell@fuse.com.

WINDHAM, MELBA B., real estate broker; b. Royston, Ga., Jan. 15, 1947; d. Teasley Barton Burns and Willie Pauline Craft; m. Gene H. Windham, Dec. 31, 1969 (div.); 1 child, Charlee W. Alvarez. BA in Journalism, U. Ga., 1969. Lic. real estate broker S.C., 1986, Ga., 1986. With ins. sales Carswell of Carolina, Hilton Head Island, SC, 1991—98; broker in charge Del Webb Cmtys., Inc., Bluffton, SC, 1998—. Author: (weekly columns) Island Packet, 1993—98; contbr. articles to mags. Chmn. Relay for life American Cancer Soc.; bd. dirs. Low Country Players, Hilton Head Island, 1994, American Cancer Soc., Hilton Head Island, 1995—2003. Mem.: Hilton Head Island (S.C.) Assn. Realtors (bd. dir. 2002—), S.C. Assn. Realtors (state dir. 2003), Nat. Assn. Realtors. Democrat. Presbyn. Avocations: golf, writing. Home: P22 Acorn Ln Hilton Head Island SC 29928 Office: Del Webb Cmtys Sun City Hilton Head 127 Sun City Blvd Bluffton SC 29909

WINDHEIM, RANDI MACKLER, literature educator; b. Passaic, NJ, Aug. 27, 1955; d. Alfred and Helen Mackler; m. Robert G. Windheim, July 30, 1978; children: Justin L., Marc I. BA in Sociology, U. Pa., Phila., 1977; BS in Elem. Edn., U. Pa., 1977; MEd in Reading Specialist, Beaver Coll., Pa., 1980. Cert. instrnl. II reading specialist, elem. edn. Pa. Tchr. William Penn Sch. Dist., Darby, Pa., 1977—80; reading specialist Montgomery County IU, Pa., 1980—81; instr. Penn State U., Abington, Pa., 1985—89; reading specialist Upper Dublin Sch. Dist., Willow Grove, Pa., 1990—. Presenter Internat. Reading Assn., Keystone State Reading Assn., Upper Dublin Sch. Dist. Founder, advisor assistance program Upper Dublin Sch. Dist., 1996—; mentor Upper Dublin Edn. Found., Fort Wash., 2005—; bd. mem. Joseph Alexander Found., N.Y.C., 2001—. Named Upper Dublin Educator of Yr., Mongomery Cty. C. of C., 2004. Mem.: Internat. Reading Assn., Keystone State Reading Assn., Del. Valley Reading Assn. (former pres., bd. mem. 1998—). Avocations: reading, travel, spectator sports. Home: 1216 Duncan Dr Dresher PA 19025 Office: Thomas Fitzwater Elem Sch 30 Sch Ln Willow Grove PA 19090 Office Phone: 215-784-0381. Business E-Mail: rwindhei@udsd.org.

WINDHORST, JANE LOUISE, elementary school educator; b. Reading, Pa., July 11, 1957; d. MaryEllen and Jairus Edward Zerbe; m. David Paul Windhorst, June 13, 1987; children: David Paul, Bradley Davis. MEd, Millersville U., Pa., 1984. Pre first tchr. Hempfield Area Sch. Dist., Landisville, Pa., 1980—86; 4th grade tchr. Laurel Area Sch. Dist., New Castle, Pa., 1986—90; emotional support aide grades 4-6 Ellwood City Area Sch. Dist., Pa., 1997—. Com. mem. Boy Scouts Am., Ellport, Pa., 1999—; band booster mem. Lincoln High Blue Band Boosters for Ellwood City Area Sch. Dist., Pa., 2002—; com. chmn. Boy Scouts Am. Troop 870, Ellport, Pa., 2000—04; classroom plus tutoring and pvt. tutoring Tchg. Profession, Portersville and Ellwood, 1991—; vacation bible sch., music tchr. Mountville Presbyn. Ch., Portersville. Band booster mem. Ellwod City Area Sch. Dist.- Lincoln Blue Band, 2002—06; chmn. of auditors Perry Twp., Portersville, Pa.; vacation bible sch., music tchr. Mountville Presbyn. Ch., Portersville. Recipient Anne E. Beyers award for Outstanding Student Tchg., Millersville U., 1979, Who's Who of Executives and Professionals, Manchester Who's Who, 2005—06. Mem.: ASCD. Avocations: gardening, music, sewing, farming, nature studies. Home: 1766 Barkley Rd Portersville PA 16051 Office: Ellwood City Area Sch Dist 501 Crescent Ave Ellwood City PA 16117 Office Phone: 724-758-5609. Personal E-mail: wdjdb@aol.com.

WINDO, PAMELA ANN, administrative assistant, writer; b. Brighton, Sussex, UK, May 24, 1942; arrived in U.S., 1979; d. Aubrey Clifford Ayton and Muriel Tempest Stedman; m. Gary Windo, 1964 (dec.); children from previous marriage: Simon Russell, Jamie Russell. Asst. Axinn Veltrop & Harkrider, N.Y.C.; asst./editor-in-chief McCall's Mag., N.Y.C.; asst. and chief prodr. to Martin Scorsese for movie Kundun, Morocco; pub. rels./VIP attache Sheraton Hotel, Marrakesh, Morocco. Spkr., presenter, lectr. Brit. Coun., Am., Morocco Embassy, Alliance Francaise, Montclair U., Jersey City Mus. Author: (book) Escape to Morocco, 2000, Fodor's Guide to Morocco, 2000, (book) Zohra's Ladder, 2005. Recipient Letter, King Mohammah VI of Morocco, 2005. Avocations: travel, gardening, reading, cooking, music. Home: 154 Ogden Ave 2B Jersey City NJ 07302

WINDSOR, HARRIET SMITH, state official; children: James A. Smith Jr., Julia A. Smith-O'Hanlon. BA, Juniata Coll.; PhD, MA, U. Del. Cert. lay spkr. Peninsula Conf. Former English tchr. Seaford Sr. HS; dean instrn., dept. English Chmn. Del. Tech. and Cmty. Coll. Owens Campus; mem., dir. State Personnel Gov. Thomas R. Carper's Cabinet, 1993—2001; sec. of state State of Del., 2001—. Writer, spkr. numerous local, state and nat. bds. Serves Dist. Com. Ordained Ministry; mem., choir dir., organist, ch. sch. tchr., supt., adminstrv. bd. chmn., chmn. Pastor Parish Rels. Com. Millsboro Grace United Meth. Ch., lay leader, 2002—. Named Del. Mother of Yr., 1999, Woman of Yr., Sussex Ctrl. Jr. HS students; named to Del.'s Hall of Fame, 1997; recipient Millsboro's Woman of Year, 1989, Order of the First State, Governor Thomas R. Carper, Del., 2000. Democrat. Methodist. Office: Office Sec of State Townsend Bldg 401 Federal St Ste 3 Dover DE 19901 Office Phone: 302-739-4111. Office Fax: 302-739-3811. E-mail: hnsmith@state.de.us.

WINDSOR, KENDRA LINNETTE, elementary school educator; b. Norfolk, Va., Nov. 25, 1975; d. Randy and Deborah Vaughan; m. Shannon Mason Windsor, Sept. 5, 1998; children: Seth, Kennon. BS in Elem. Edn., Hannibal-LaGrange Coll., Mo., 1998; EdM, William Woods U., Fulton, Mo., 2002; student in Reading Recovery Program, 2004—05. Cert. tchr. Dept. Elem. and Secondary Edn., Mo., 1998. First grade tchr. Silex Elem., Mo., 1998—99, Williamsburg Elem., Mo., 1999—2001; kindergarten tchr. McIntire Elem., Fulton, 2001—04; reading recovery/title I tchr. Bush Elem., Fulton, 2004—. Kindergarten grade level chairperson McIntire Elem., Fulton, 2003—04; Fulton Edn. Assn. rep. Fulton Pub. Schs., 2005—. Sunday sch. dir., tchr. Mineola Bapt. Ch., Mo., 2004—. Recipient Disting. Educator award, Westminster Coll., 2004. Mem.: Mo. State Tchrs. Assn. (life). Avocations: singing, acting, reading, walking. Home: 1908 Lakeview Dr Fulton MO 65251 Office Phone: 573-642-2877. Personal E-mail: skwinds@ktis.net.

WINDSOR, MARGARET EDEN, writer; b. Flemington, Mo., Aug. 10, 1917; d. John Denny and Rhoda Belle (Morgan) Head; m. Eugene B. Windsor, Jan. 10, 1987. Instr. hematology; med. technologist, 1958; ret. med. technologist, 1982. Author: Murder in St. James, 1990, The Outhouse, 1996, Far Cry, 2004, Bell's Out House, 2004; editor: From Pandora's Box, 1993. Cpl. USAF, 1944-45. Mem. Columbia Chpt. Mo. Writers Guild (v.p. 1989-90). Democrat. Roman Catholic. Avocations: music, theater, reading, television.

WINDSOR, PATRICIA (KATONAH SUMMERTREE, PERRIN WINTERS, ANNA SEELING), author, educator, lecturer; b. NYC, Sept. 21, 1938; d. Bernhard Edward and Antoinette (Gaus) Seelinger; m. Laurence Charles Windsor, Jr., Apr. 3, 1959 (div. 1978); children: Patience Wells, Laurence Edward; m. Stephen E. Altman, Sept. 21, 1986 (div. 1989). Student, Bennington Coll., 1956—58, Westchester C.C.; AA, NYU. V.p. Windsor-Morehead Assoc., NYC, 1960—63; info. mgr. Family Planning Assn., London, 1974—76; faculty mem. Inst. Children's Lit., Redding Ridge, Conn., 1976—94, 1999—; editor-in-chief AT&T, Washington, 1978—80; instr. U. Md. Writers Inst., Open Univ., Washington, 1980—82; creative developer, faculty mem. Long Ridge Writer's Group, Danbury, Conn., 1988—2000, instr., 2006—; dir. Summertree Studios, Savannah, Ga., 1992—. Dir. Wordspring Lit. Cons., 1989—, Wordworks Writing Cons., 1999—, Born Author Lit. Cons., 2003-; dir. Devel. Writing Workshops, Katonah, NY, 1976-78; judge Internat. Assn. Bus. Communicators, Washington, 1979, 89; lectr. LI U., Jersey City State Coll., Skidmore Coll., others, 1987—; instr. Coastal Ga. Ctr. for Continuing Edn., 1996—, Armstrong Atlantic U. Continuing Edn., 1997-2000, Anne Arundel (Md.) C.C., 2000—, workshop coord., 2000—; dir., founder Born Author.com, 2002—; dir. Windsomethings Art & Crafts, 2004—; owner, designer Tiger Woman Crafts for Meditation, 2005-. Author: The Summer Before, 1973 (ALA Best Book award 1973, transl. 1980 Austrian State prize 1980, also Brit., Norwegian, German edits.), Something's Waiting for You, Baker D, 1974 (starred selection Libr. Jour., Brit., Japanese edits.), Home Is Where Your Feet Are Standing, 1975, Diving for Roses, 1976 (NY Times Outstanding Book for Young Adults award, starred selection Libr. Jour.), Mad Martin, 1976, Killing Time, 1980, Demon Tree, 1983 (pen name Colin Daniel), The Sandman's Eyes, 1985 (Edgar Allan Poe Best Juvenile Mystery award Mystery Writers Am.), How a Weirdo and a Ghost Can Change Your Life, 1986, The Hero, 1988 (highest rating Voice of Youth Advocate), Just Like the Movies, 1990, The Christmas Killer, 1991 (Edgar nominee, Brit., Danish, French edits.), Two Weirdos and a Ghost, 1991, A Weird and Moogly Christmas, 1991, The Blooding, 1996 (YALSA pick for reluctant readers), The House of Death, 1996, Nightwood (nominated Best Book 2006), 2006; columnist The Blood Rev., 1990-92, Savannah Parent, 1990-92; columnist Coastal Senior, 1997-99; also short stories in anthologies and mags.; actress: The Haunting of Hill House, City Lights Theatre Co., 1991; contr. articles Once Upon a Time Mag., 2003, 04, 05. Mem. City Lights Theatre Co., Savannah, Ga., 1991. Mem. Horror Writers Am., Internat. Women's Writing Guild, Children's Book Guild, Authors Guild, Poetry Soc. Ga., Savannah Storytellers. Avocations: skiing, painting, modern dance. Office: Born Author Dot Com PO Box 799 Severna Park MD 21146 E-mail: info@bornauthor.com.

WINDWARD, SHIRLEY, secondary school educator, poet; b. Washington, Jan. 10, 1919; d. Albert Carl Weimar and Della Jost; m. Erwin Windward, Aug. 8, 1942; children: Stephen, Rolfe. BA in Edn., U. Wis., 1940; MA in English, UCLA, 1964. Cert. tchr. Calif. Tchr. Ctrl. H.S., Sheboygan, Wis., 1940—42, L.A. Valley Schs., Northridge, Calif., 1955—60; tchr., adminstr. Paul Revere Sch., L.A., 1960—68; tchr., adminstr., founder Windward Sch., Santa Monica, 1971—76, L.A., 1977—2004. Author: Midwife Chronicles, 1998; author: (with Audrey Hargreaves) Slipping Honey In, Two Kisses; contbr. poetry to profl. jours.; author: (poetry) Web Songs, 2004. Buddhist. Avocations: choral music, travel, ceramics, public readings.

WINE-BANKS, JILL SUSAN, lawyer; b. Chgo., May 5, 1943; d. Bert S. and Sylvia Dawn (Simon) Wine; m. Ian David Volner, Aug. 21, 1965; m. Michael A. Banks, Jan. 12, 1980. BS, U. Ill., Champaign, Urbana, 1964; JD, Columbia U., 1968; LLD (hon.), Hood Coll., 1975. Bar: N.Y. 1969, U.S. Ct. Appeals (2d, 4th, 5th, 6th, 7th and 9th cirs.), U.S. Supreme Ct. 1974, D.C. 1976, Ill. 1980. Asst. press. and pub. rels. dir. Assembly of Captive European Nations, N.Y.C., 1965-66; trial atty. criminal divsn. organized crime & racketeering U.S. Dept. Justice, 1969-73; asst. spl. prosecutor Watergate Spl. Prosecutor's Office, 1973-75; lectr. law sem. in trial practice Columbia U. Sch. Law, N.Y.C., 1975-77; assoc. Fried, Frank, Harris, Shriver & Kampelman, Washington, 1975-77; gen. counsel Dept. Army, Pentagon, Washington, 1977-79; ptnr. Jenner & Block, Chgo., 1980-84; solicitor gen. State of Ill. Office of Atty. Gen., 1984-86, dep. atty. gen., 1986-87; exec. v.p., chief oper., officer ABA, Chgo., 1987-90; atty. pvt. practice, 1990-92; v.p., dir. transaction and govt. rels. Motorola Internat. Network Ventures, 1992-97; dir. strategic alliances Motorola Cellular Infrastructure Group, 1997—99; v.p. alliance mgmt. Maytag Corp., 1999-2001; CEO Winning Workplaces, Evanston, Ill., 2001—03; chief officer Chgo. Pub. Schs. Edn. to Careers, 2003—. Mem. EEC disting. vis. program European Parliament, 1987; chmn. bd. dirs. St. Petersburg Telecom., Russia, 1994-97, Omni Capital Ptnrs., Inc., 1994-97. Trustee Roosevelt U., 2004—; mem. adv. bd. Project Lead the Way, UIC Econ. Edn. Recipient Spl. Achievement award U.S. Dept. Justice, 1972, Meritorious award, 1973, Cert. Outstanding Svc., 1975; decorated Disting. Civilian Svc. Dept. Army, 1979; named Disting. Vis. to European Econ. Cmty. Mem.: The Chgo. Network, Internat. Women's Forum, Exec. Club (bd. dirs. 1999—2001), Econ. Club. Office: Chgo Pub Schs Edn to Careers 125 S Clark St 12th Fl Chicago IL 60603 Office Phone: 773-553-2460. Business E-Mail: jwine-banks@cps.k12.il.us.

WINEBERG, DANETTE, lawyer, apparel executive; m. Steve Wineberg; 1 child. Grad., Oberlin Coll., 1968; JD, U. Mich., 1980. Gen. counsel Little Caesar Enterprises, Inc., 1993—97; v.p., gen. counsel Timberland Co., 1997—, sec., 2001—. Bd. mem. Odyssey House, Inc. Avocations: jogging, reading, singing. Office: Timberland Co 200 Domain Dr Stratham NH 03885 Office Phone: 603-772-9500.

WINEBRENNER, SUSAN KAY, writer, consultant; b. Milw., Mar. 11, 1939; d. Samuel Bernard and Lillian (Ginsberg) Schuckit; m. Neil T. Winebrenner, Feb. 11, 1981 (dec.); children: Stacy Lynne Naimon, Kari Beth Naimon. BS, U. Wis., 1956; MS, U. Wis., Milw., 1979. Cert. tchr., Ill., Wis. Tchr. Shorewood (Wis.) Pub. Sch., 1961—81, River Forest (Ill.) Sch. Dist. 90, 1981—83; gifted coord. Forest Park (Ill.) Sch. Dist. 91, Ill., 1983—86; cons. Self-Edn. Cons. Svcs., San Marcos, Calif., 1986—. Author: Super Sentences Activity Book, 1987, Teaching Gifted Kids in the Regular Classroom, 2nd edit., 2000, Teaching Kids with Learning Difficulties in the Regular Classroom, 1996, Cluster Grouping Fact Sheet, 2001; contbr. numerous atricles on differentiating instruction for atypical learners. Recipient Outstanding Tchr. award Joint Coun. on Econ. Edn., Wis., 1979. Mem. ASCD (presenter), Nat. Assn. Gifted Children (presenter). Home and Office: 1450 La Loma Dr San Marcos CA 92069-4737 E-mail: susan.winebrenner@adelphia.net.

WINEINGER, BARBARA ANN, science educator; b. Washington, Ind., Feb. 22, 1941; d. Bernard and Audrey (Wagoner) Savage; m. Darrell Dean Wineinger, Aug. 27, 1961. Student, Asbury Coll., 1959-61; BS, Ky. Wesleyan Coll., 1964; MAT, Ind. U., 1968. Instr. Ky. Wesleyan Coll., Owensboro, 1964; asst. prof. life sci. Vincennes (Ind.) U., 1968-71, prof. Jasper, 1982—, chair dept. math. and scis., 1987—. Past pres. local, past dist. pres., gen. coun. Nazarene World Mission Soc. Recipient Disting. Svc. award Brownstown Ch. of Nazarene, 1980, S.W. Ind. Nazarene World Mission Soc., 1987, 90. Mem. Nat. Coun. Instrnl. Adminstrs., Ind. U. Alumni Assn., Hoosier Assn. Sci. Tchrs., Human Anatomy and Physiology Soc. Republican. Office: Vincennes U 850 College Ave Jasper IN 47546-9393 Home: 410 Reyling Dr Jasper IN 47546-1025

WINEMAN, JEAN D., architecture educator; BA in Psychology and Sociology, Wellesley Coll., 1971; M in Urban Planning, U. Mich., 1973, DArch, 1977. Asst. prof. arch. Ga. Inst. Tech., Coll. Arch., 1977—82, assoc. prof. arch., 1982—99, prof. arch., 1999—2000, acting dir. doctoral program, 1992—94, dir. doctoral program, 1994—2000; prof. arch. U. Mich., Taubman Coll. Arch. and Urban Planning, Ann Arbor, 2000—, assoc. dean, 2000—, chair doctoral program in arch., 2000—. Editor: Behavioral Issues in Office Design, 1986; contbr. chapters to books, articles to profl. jours. Office: U Mich Taubman Coll Arch and Urban Planning 2000 Bonisteel Blvd Ann Arbor MI 48109-2069

WINES, LYNNE, bank executive; Grad., Nova Southeastern U. Joined Union Bank, Sunrise, Fla., 1986, CEO; mem. exec. mgmt. team Colonial Bank, 2004—. Bd. mem. Fla. Bankers Assn. Named Bus. Women of Yr., South Fla. Bus. Jour., 2002. Office: Colonial Bank One Commerce St Montgomery AL 36104

WINFIELD, JOYCE HELEN, communications educator; b. Stromsburg, Nebr., May 22, 1952; d. Bert G. and Velma A. Gissler; m. Douglas Edward Winfield, June 23, 1990. BA, Midland Luth. Coll., 1974; MA, U. Nebr., Omaha, 1982; PhD, U. Minn., 1989. Asst. prof. journalism Midland Luth. Coll., Fremont, Nebr., 1988—89, assoc. prof. journalism, 1997—; instr. journalism and English Cambridge (Minn.) C.C., 1989—97. Coord. annual campus H.S. Journalism Day Midland Luth. Coll., Fremont, 1997—, coord. journalism intern, 1997—, adviser student mag., 2002—. Consulting editor: Diskus Brief, 1994—96. Mem. publicity com. Habitat for Humanity, Fremont, 1997—, coord. design workshops, 2005—; summer docent May Mus., Fremont, 2002. Named Outstanding Tchr., Cambridge C.C., 1997. Mem.: Nebr. Collegiate Media Assn., Nebr. Press Assn., Coll. Media Advisers, Dodge County Hist. Soc. Avocations: reading, writing, travel, volleyball. Office: Midland Luth Coll 900 N Clarkson Fremont NE 68025 Office Phone: 402-941-6375. Business E-Mail: winfield@mlc.edu.

WINFREY, MARCELLENE SEDETTA, music educator, church musician; b. Chgo., Dec. 4, 1949; d. Arthur Semon and Nellye Mae Winfrey; m. Darryl Jones, Nov. 27, 1988 (div. Sept. 0, 1994); 1 child, Troy Lamar. B in Music Edn., Roosevelt U., 1980; MS in Elem. Edn., Xavier U., 1994. Cert. Orff-Schulwerk tchr. U. Cin., Coll. Conservatory Music, OH, 2004. Distbn. clk. USPS, Chgo., 1969—74; instr. Chgo. City Wide Coll., 1980—82; educator Chgo. Pub. Schs., 1982—87; adminstr. So. Bapt. Day Care, Cin., 1988—88; min. music Union Bapt. Ch., 1988—93; music specialist Cin. Pub. Schs., 1988—; ch. organist Quinn Chapel AME, 1994—97; ch. musician Allen Temple AME, 1997—. Mem. Local Sch. Dist. Mgmt. Com., Cin., 2004—. Mem., mentor Excel Club, Cin., 2004—05. Mem.: ASCD (assoc.), Ohio Music Educators Assn. (assoc.), Phi Delta Kappa (life). Avocations: travel, genealogy, gardening, walking, dance. Office: Western Hills HS 2144 Ferguson Rd Cincinnati OH 45238-3799 Office Fax: 513-363-8751. E-mail: winfrem@cpsboe.k12.oh.us.

WINFREY, OPRAH, television talk show host, actress, television producer; b. Kosciusko, Miss., Jan. 29, 1954; d. Vernon Winfrey and Vernita Lee. BA in Speech Comm. and Performing Arts, Tenn. State U. News reporter Sta. WVOL Radio, Nashville, 1971-72; reporter, news anchorperson Sta. WTVF-TV, Nashville, 1973-76; news anchorperson Sta. WJZ-TV, Balt., 1976—78, host morning talk show People Are Talking, 1978—83; host talk show A.M. Chgo. Sta. WLS-TV, 1984; host The Oprah Winfrey Show, Chgo., 1985—, Oprah After the Show, Chgo., 2002—; nationally syndicated, 1986—; host series of celebrity interview spls. Oprah: Behind the Scenes; owner, prodr., chmn., CEO Harpo Prodns., 1986—. Ptnr., co-founder Oxygen Media, an Internet and cable TV co., 1998—; founder, editl. dir. O, The Oprah Magazine in conjunction with Hearst Mags., 2000; launched (mag.)first internat. edit., O, The Oprah Magazine in South Africa, 2002-, Oprah, After the Show, 2002-, O at Home, 2004-, Oprah & Friends, XM Satelite Radio Holdings, Inc., 2006-; online leader, Oprah.com, launched Live Your Best Life, 2003-; started Oprah Book Club. Appeared in films The Color Purple, 1985 (nominated Acad. award and Golden Globe award), Native Son, 1986, There Are No Children Here, 1993, Beloved, 1998 (prodr.), About Us: The Dignity of Children, 1997 (TV), Before Women Had Wings, 1997 (TV; also prodr. ABC series Oprah Winfrey presents); prodr. Dr. Phil (TV series), 2002—; Listen Up: The Lives of Quincy Jones (TV spl.), 1990; prodr., actress ABC-TV mini-series The Women of Brewster Place, 1989, also series Brewster Place, 1990; co-prodr. The Color Purple (Broadway), 2005; exec. prodr. (ABC Movie of the Week) Overexposed, 1992; host, supervising prodr. celebrity interview series Oprah: Behind the Scenes, 1992, ABC Aftersch. Spls., 1991-93; host, exec. prodr. Michael Jackson Talks.to Oprah-90 Prime-Time Minutes with the King of Pop, 1993; exec. prodr. (TV) Nine, 1992, Oprah Winfrey Presents: Their Eyes Were Watching God, 2005; host Oprah Winfrey's Legends Ball, 2006; exec. prodr. TV miniseries: Oprah Winfrey Presents: The Wedding, 1998, David and Lisa, 1998, Tuesdays with Morrie, 1999, Amy and Isabelle, 2001, Their Eyes Were Watching God, 2005; voice (video) Our Friend, Martin, 1999; guest appearances The Fresh Prince of Bel-Air, 1992, Ellen, 1997, Home Improvement, 1999, The Hughleys, 1999, Mad TV, 2002 and several others. Established Oprah Winfrey Found., 1987—, Oprah's Angel Network, 1997—, ChristmasKindness South Africa, 2002—, Oprah Winfrey Scholars Program. Recipient Woman of Achievement award NOW, 1986, Emmy award for Best Daytime Talk Show Host, 1987, 91, 92, 94, 95, 97, Hon. Nat. Book Award for influential contbn. to reading and books, 1999, Nat. Book Found's 50th Anniversary gold medal, 1999, America's Hope award, 1990, Industry Achievement award Broadcast Promotion Mktg. Execs./Broadcast Design Assn., 1991, Image awards NAACP, 1989, 91, 92, 94, Entertainer of Yr. award NAACP, 1989, CEBA awards, 1989, 90, 91, George Foster Peabody's 1995 Individual Achievement award, 1996, Gold Medal award IRTS, 1996, Lifetime Achievement award NATAS, 1998, People's Choice award, 1997, 98, Horatio Alger award, 1993, Bob Hope Humanitarian award, 54th Ann. Primetime Emmy Awards, 2002, Marian Anderson Award, Phila., 2003, AAP Honors award, Assn. Am. Publishers, 2003, Disting. Svc. award, Nat. Assn. Broadcasters, 2004, Global Humanitarian Action award, UN Assn. U.S.A., 2004, Nat. Freedom award, Nat. Civil Rights Mus., 2005; ranked #1 Most Powerful In Industry, Entertainment Weekly, 1998, 200 Greatest Pop Culture Icons, VH1, 2003; named Broadcaster of Yr. Internat. Radio and TV Soc., 1988, TV Performer of Yr., TV Guide, 1997, Most Important Person in Books and Media, Newsweek, 1997; named one of 50 Most Beautiful in the World, People, 1997, America's 25 Most Influential People of the 20th Century, Time, 1998, 100 Most Powerful Women in Entertainment, Hollywood Reporter, 2004, 100 Most Influential People, Time Mag., 2004, 2005, Most Powerful Women, Forbes mag., 2005-2006, 50 Women to Watch, Wall St. Journal, 2005, 100 Most Influential People, Time Mag., 2006, 100 Most Influential Black Americans, Ebony mag., 2006, 50 Most Powerful Women in Bus., Fortune mag., 2006; named to List American Billionaires, Fortune, 2003, 400 Richest Americans, 1999-, World's Richest People, 2003-; inducted to Television Hall of Fame, 1994, Broadcasting and Cable Hall of Fame, 2002, NAACP Hall of Fame, 2005; elected to Nat. Women's Hall of Fame, Seneca Falls, NY. Initiated a campaign to establish a national database of convicted child abusers, and testified before U.S. Senate Judiciary Committee on behalf of National Child Protection Act in 1991, as a result, President Clinton signed the "Oprah Bill" into Law on December 20, 1993, establishing the national database used by law enforcement agencies around the world; third woman in American entertainment industry to own her own studio; first African-American woman to reach billionaire status; after receiving Lifetime Acheivement Award in 1998, permanently withdrew name from Daytime Emmy Award consideration; Oprah and Oprah Winfrey Show received a total of 39 Daytime Emmy awards: seven for Outstanding Host; nine for Outstanding Talk Show; twenty-one in the Creative Arts categories; and one for supervising producer of the ABC School Special, Shades of Single Protein; celebrated the 20th year anniversary of the Oprah Winfrey Show in November, 2005. Office: Oprah Winfrey Show Harpo Studios 1058 W Washington Blvd Chicago IL 60607 Address: Harpo Prodn PO Box 909715 Chicago IL 60607 Office Phone: 312-633-0808.*

WING, ADRIEN KATHERINE, law educator; b. Aug. 7, 1956; d. John Ellison and Katherine (Pruitt) Wing; children: Che-Cabral, Nolan Felipe. AB magna cum laude, Princeton U., 1978; MA, UCLA, 1979; JD, Stanford, 1982. Bar: N.Y. 1983, U.S. Dist. Ct. (so. and ea. dists.) N.Y. 1983, U.S. Ct. Appeals (5th and 9th cirs.). Assoc. Curtis, Mallet-Prevost, Colt & Mosle, N.Y.C., 1982-86, Rabinowitz, Boudin, Standard, Krinsky & Lieberman, 1986-87; assoc. prof. law U. Iowa, Iowa City, 1987-93, prof., 1993—, disting. prof. law, 2001—, assoc. dean faculty R&D, 2006—. Mem. alumni council Princeton U., 1983-85, 96-2000, mem. exec. com., 2002—, trustee Class of '78 Alumni Found., 1984-87, 93—, v.p. Princeton Class of 1978 Alumni, 1993-98, trustee Princeton U. 1995; mem. bd. visitors Stanford Law Sch., 1993-96; vis. prof. U. Mich., 2002. Mem. bd. editors Am. J. Comp. Law, 1993—. Mem. Iowa Commn. on African Ams. in Prisons, 1999—. Recipient Disting. Alum award, Newark Acad., 2004, Gertrude Rush award, 2006. Mem.: ABA (exec. com. young lawyers sect. 1985—87, law sch. site inspector 2002—), U.S. Assn. Constl. Law (bd. dir.), Am. Assn. of Law Schs. (minority sect. bd. 1996—, chair 2002), Am. Friends Svc. Com. (bd. dirs. Mid. East 1998—2004), Am. Soc. Internat. Law (exec. coun. 1986—89, exec. com. 1988—99, nominating com. 1991, 1993, group chair S. Africa 1993—95, membership com. 1994—95, exec. coun. 1996—99, v.p. 2007—), Internat. Assn. Dem. Lawyers (UN rep. 1984—87), Nat. Conf. Black Lawyers (chmn. internat. affairs sect. 1982—95, UN rep.), Internat. Third World Legal Studies Assn. (bd. dirs. 1996—, nominating trustee Princeton com. 1997—2000), Coun. on Fgn. Rels., Iowa Peace Inst. (bd. dirs. 1993—95), Iowa City Fgn. Rels. Coun. (bd. dirs. 1989—94), Transafrica Scholars Forum Coun. (bd. dirs. 1993—95), Black Alumni of Princeton U. (bd. dirs. 1982—87). Democrat. Avocations: photography, writing, poetry. Office: U Iowa Sch Law Boyd Law Bldg Iowa City IA 52242 Office Phone: 319-335-9129. E-mail: adrien-wing@uiowa.edu.

WING, KERENSA SHOEMAKE, secondary school educator, assistant principal; b. Cumming, Ga., Sept. 4, 1968; d. Marvin Dean and Brenda Patricia Shoemake; m. States Williams Wing, July 11, 1992; children: Walker, Kyia. BA in History and Secondary Edn., Oglethorpe U., Atlanta, 1990; MEd, Ga. State U., Atlanta, 1995; EdS in Adminstrn. and Supervision, Lincoln Meml. U., Harrogate, Tenn., 2001. Cert. tchr. Ga. Tchr./coach Shiloh H.S., Lithonia, Ga., 1990—94; tchr./coach/adminstr. Collins Hill H.S., Suwanee, Ga., 1994—. Finalist Tchr. of Yr., Gwinnett County, Ga., 2001—02; named, Collins Hill H.S., 2001—02. Mem.: Local Sch. Adminstrs. Assn. (sec. 2006—), Nat. Assn. Secondary Sch. Prins., Assn. for Supervision and Curriculum Devel. Avocations: running, tennis, reading. Home: 3525 Chartwell Blvd Suwanee GA 30024 Office: Collins Hill HS 50 Taylor Rd Suwanee GA 30024 Business E-Mail: kerensa_wing@gwinnett.k12.ga.us.

WINGATE, BETTYE FAYE, librarian, educator; b. Hillsboro, Tex., Oct. 31, 1950; d. Warren Randolph and Faye (Gilmore) W. BA summa cum laude, Baylor U., 1971, MA, 1975; MLS, Tex. Womans U., 1985. Cert. prov. sec., learning resources endorsement. English tchr. Mexia HS, Tex.; reading tchr. Connally Ind. Sch. Dist., Waco, Tex.; reading tchr., libr. Grapevine-Colleyville Ind. Sch. Dist., Grapevine, Tex.; libr., ret., May 02 Crockett Mid. Sch., Irving, Tex. Mem. librs. coms., Campus Action Planning Com., 1989-93, Irving Ind. Sch. Dist. Site Based Decision-Making Com., 1992-94, mem. staff devel. coun., 1994-96, chair media fair com., 1996-2001; rev. Linworth Pub.; spkr., presenter in field. Founding sponsor Challenger Ctr., Air Force Meml. Found. Recipient Tex. Media awards, 1988, 89, 94. Mem. ALA, NEA, Am. Assn. Sch. Libr. (vol. libr. Kids Connect), Tex. State Tchr. Assn. (assn. rep.), Tex. Libr. Assn. (chmn. state media awards com. 1989-91), Tex. Assn. Edn. Tech., Tex. Computer Edn. and Tech., Assn. Ednl. Comm. and Tech., Planetary Soc., Nat. Space Soc., Nat. Parks & Conservation Assn., Baylor Alumni Assn. (life), Wilderness Soc., Sierra Club, Beta Phi Mu, Delta Kappa Gamma (scholar 1985). E-mail: bettye.winate@yahoo.com.

WINGATE, CONSTANCE BLANDY, retired librarian; b. Woodbury, N.J., Mar. 7, 1935; d. John Chase and Josephine Spond (Black) Blandy; m. Len B. Cooke Jr., 1978 (div. 1987); m. John B. Wingate, Mar. 12, 1999. BA, U. Pa., 1956; MA, U. Denver, 1957. Adult cons. Onondaga Library System, Syracuse, 1965-66; asst. dir. Mt. Vernon (N.Y.) Public Library, 1966-75; dep. dir. Queens Borough Public Library, Jamaica, NY, 1975-79, dir., 1980-94; ret., 1994. Founder pres. Literacy Vols. Mt. Vernon, 1972-74. Trustee METRO, 1980-91, v.p., 1985-88, pres., 1988-91; mem. N.Y. State Libr. Svcs. and Constrn. Act Adv. Coun., 1982-88, chmn., 1986-87; bd. dirs. Queens Coun. on the Arts, 1988-94, v.p., 1989-93; bd. dirs. Queens Mus. of Art, 1988-98, v.p., 1994-96, pres. 1996-98; bd. dirs. Queens Libr. Found., 1996-2003. Mem.: ALA, Circumnavigators Club (internat. sec. 2002—06, internat. bd. govs. 2006—). Republican. Episcopalian. Home: 166-25 Powells Cove Blvd Beechhurst NY 11357

WINGET, DALORES LORAINE, educator, freelance writer; b. Chicago Heights, Ill., Jan. 7, 1936; d. Earl Robert and Lila Elizabeth (Martin) Broome; m. Richard Owens Winget, Sept. 20, 1969; children: Richard, Susan. BS in Edn. and English, Andrews U., 1964, MA in Edn. and Psychology, 1964. Tchr. Berrien Springs (Mich.) Pub. Schs., 1964-65, Georgetown Elem. Sch., Montgomery, Md., 1968-69, Saukview Sch., Chicago Heights, Ill., 1969-70, Baton Rouge Jr. Acad., 1980-90, Twin Spring Farms Elem. Sch., Ambler, Pa., 1990-92, Greater Phila. Jr. Acad., Huntingdon Valley, Pa., 1992—. Contbr. articles to profl. jours. Republican. Adventist. Avocations: writing, tennis, reading. Home: 1008 Monroe Dr Warminster PA 18974-6162 E-mail: wingerdee@cs.com.

WINGFIELD, SUSAN, energy executive; b. Dallas, Feb. 24, 1952; d. Robert Lee and Eileen Fayetta (Murphy) W.; m. Jay Trent Copeland, Apr. 27, 1974 (div. July 1978). BS, Okla. State U., 1973. Credit analyst Worthington Pump, Shawnee, Okla., 1974-75; ad mgr. Herald Star Tribune, Casper, Wyo., 1975-76; mgr. Tipperary Oil & Gas, Grand Junction, Colo., 1976-77; v.p. transp. and sales Va. Energy Co., Bristol, 1977-81; spl. asst. U.S. Dept. of Commerce, Washington, 1981-84; v.p. MVCEC, New Orleans, 1984-87, pres., 1987-92, Energy and Environ. Svcs., Inc., New Orleans, 1992—. Mem. Miss. River Maintenance Forum, New Orleans, 1985—, Port Activity Com., New Orleans, 1985—, Lower Miss. River Safety Adv., New Orleans, 1990—, Chem. Transp. Adv. Com., Washington, 1987—; dir. World Trade Ctr., New Orleans, 1989—. Contbr. articles to profl. jours. Advisor Boy Scouts Am., New Orleans, 1990—, U. New Orleans, 1991—. Recipient Bertel award World Trade Ctr., 1990, Disting. Svc. award Women in Mining, 1990. Mem. Internat. Maritime Orgn. (del. 1990—), UN Coal Com. (del. 1985—), Coal Industry Adv. Bd. (assoc.). Avocations: reading, furniture restoration. Office: PO Box 659 Warner NH 03278

WINGSTON-JENKINS, MARY ALLYSON, secondary school educator; d. Alfonso and Rosa Wingston; children: Keenan Olajuwon Jenkins, Alfonso Jemas Jenkins. BS, Hampton U., Va., 1984; MS, Queens Coll., NY, 1986; EdS, Emory U., Atlanta, 1992; postgrad., Nova Southeastern U. Cert. tchr. Ga. Dept. Edn., 2003. Tchr. NYC Bd. Edn., Bklyn., 1984—88, Atlanta Pub. Schs., 1988—96; tchg. Clayton County Schs., Jonesboro, Ga., 1996—. Black history coord. Forest Pk. (Ga.) H.S., 2005—06, drama coach, 2005—. Vol. Hosea Feed the Hungry Program, Atlanta, 1990—2005. Grantee, Atlanta Pub. Schs., 1994. Democrat. Office Phone: 404-362-3885.

WINICK, BERNYCE ALPERT, artist, photographer; b. NYC; Student, Bklyn. Mus. Art Sch., 1938—41; BA in Fine Arts and Music, NYU; pvt. studies with, Mario Cooper, N.Y.C., 1969—86; student, Traphagen Sch. Fashion, 1958—61, Art Students League N.Y., 1961—64, Nat. Acad. Design Sch. Fine Arts, 1968—72. Artist, Woodmere, L.I., N.Y., 1969—. Designer, fashion artist, fashion con. in field. One-woman shows include Hewlett-Woodmere Pub. Libr., LI, 1969, Galerie Internat., NY, 1977, Thomas Moran (First prize Nat. Acad. Sch., 1972, Salmagundi Club 1981, 87, 90, Nat. Arts Club, 1985, Nat. Acad. Sch., 1972, First Prize Meml. award 2002), Gallery Internat. 57, NY, 1989, Discovery Art Gallery, Sea Cliff, LI, 1989, 96, 98, Glen Cove, NY, 1993-94, Chelsea Ctr., East Norwich, NY, 1993, 96, 98, 2000, 02, Z Gallery, SoHo, NY, 1994, County Exec. Bldg., 1997, Fine Arts Mus. LI, 1997, Town Hall, Hempstead, NY, 2000, Nat. Arts Club., NY 2002, NY Inst. Tech., 2004, Wisser Meml. Libr., 2003, N.Y. Inst. Tech., 2004; exhibited in group shows at Discovery Art Gallery, Glen Cove, NY, 1988, 91-93, 1996, 2000, 02, Nat. Acad. Sch. Fine Arts, NY, 1972, Long Beach Mus., LI, 1979, 81-85, 89 (2d prize 1989), Chen Chung Gallery of St. John's U., NY, 1980, Salmagundi Club, NY, 1980-81, 2002 (Thomas Moran Meml. award, 1st prize), Am. Watercolor Soc., NY, 1982, 85, 88, 92, Fine Arts Mus. LI, 1983, 88-89, 91-92, 96 (2d prize), 97, Nat. Arts Club, NY, 1985-86, 88-89, 2002, Nassau County Mus., LI, 1985-86, 88, Nat. Assn. Women Artists, NY, 1986, 88, 91-93, C.W. Post Coll., LI, LI Arts Coun. Freeport, 1995-96, 1999 (First prize in black and white photography), 2006 (Fabian Adler Meml. award), Chelsea Cultural Ctr., NY, 1995, 2001, (Suburban Art League award), Rockville Ctr. Guild for the Arts, NY, 1995, 97 (Best in Show for photography), Chelsea Ctr. (Peacock Showcase award, First prize 2000), (Merit award 2001), East Norwich, NY, Discovery Art Gallery, Sea Cliff, NY, 1998, Canton Art Inst. Ohio, Galerie Internat., Gallery Internat. 57, Z Gallery, Salle Augustin-Chenier, Quebec, Can., Town Hall, Town of Hempstead, NY, 2000, NY Inst. Tech., Wisser Meml. Libr., 2001, Nat. Arts Club (First photography prize 2002), Heckscher Mus., Huntington, NY, 2003, Mills Pond House, St. James, NY, 2002, 05 (1st prize watercolor), Nat. Arts Club, NY, 2001 (1st prize), NY Inst. Tech. Wissen Meml. Libr., Old Westbury, 2004, others; work included in U.S. Dept. State Art in Embassies program, pvt. and corp. collections; photographs in publs. including South Shore Record, 1995, Encyclopedia of Watercolour Landscape Techniques, 1996, Popular Photography, 1996-97, 99-00, 04, Photography on America Online, 1997, 99-2000, New York: Sterling Pub. Co., Inc., 1998, Watercolor Planning and Painting, 1998, Abstracts in Watercolor, 1996, NY Times, 1999, 2001, NY Inst. Tech., 2003, Wisser Meml. Libr., Old Westbury, NY, 2004, Mills Pond House (1st prize watercolor 2005), St. James, NY, 2005; photography in (books) Capturing the Seen and Unseen in Photographs, 2001, Thirty Nine Musical Photographs, 2003, Town and Country Mag.; photographs exhibited in Mill Pond House, Salmagundi Club, NYU, Nat. Assn. Women Artists, Artists Unlimited, Tampa, Fla. Recipient award, Salmagundi Club, 2004, 2005, other awards, Fabian Adler Meml. award, L.I. Arts Coun., 2006. Fellow Royal Soc. Encouragment Arts Manufactures and Commerce (London); mem. Am. Watercolor Soc., Nat. Assn. Women Artists, Tri County Artists, Long Beach Art League, Nat. Arts Club, Salmagundi Club, Harvard Club and Arts Group. Avocations: fashion design, piano, poetry. Home and Office: 923 Beth Ln Woodmere NY 11598-1507

WINIECKI, ALYSSA, elementary school educator; b. Maywood, Ill., Jan. 18, 1977; d. Gerald and Sylvia Winiecki. MA in Gifted Edn., Northeastern Ill. U., Chgo., 2003. Cert. tchr. elem. edn. grades K-8 State of Ill., 2006, candidate Nat. Bd. Profl. Tchg. Stds. Tchr. Cicero Dist. 99, Cicero, Ill., 2001—. Active Literacy Vols. Western Cook County, Oak Park, Ill., 2003—06. Mem.: Ill. Assn. Gifted Children, Nat. Assn. Gifted Children.

WINK, LAURA A., special education educator; b. Buffalo, Mar. 28, 1967; d. Charles P. and Audrey E. Hock; children: Brooke Love, Oliver Love, Graham Love. BS in Edn., SUNY, 1989; MS in Spl. Edn., Nazareth Coll., Rochester, NY, 2003. Activity therapist Greenwich Svcs., Phila., 1990—92; recreation and respite coord. Ontario ARC, Canandaigua, NY, 1992—93; tchr.'s aide Canandaigua Montessori Sch., NY, 2001—03; tchr. Canandaigua YMCA, NY, 1996—; tchr. spl. edn. Mary Casida Children's Ctr., Rochester, NY, 2003—. Mem.: Coun. for Exceptional Children. Home: 18 Lehigh Ave Manchester NY 14504

WINKIE, DUSTI KAI, director; b. Marengo, Iowa, Aug. 2, 1957; d. Wallace Benjamin and Beverly Mae Winkie. BA, U. of Iowa, Iowa City, Iowa, 1979—81, MA, 1983—86. Sec. Ctrl. States Theater Corp., Des Moines, 1975—76; spotwelder Amana Refrigeration, Amana, Iowa, 1976—77; nurse's aide Beverly Manor Convalescent Ctr., Belle Plaine, Iowa, 1978—80; rsch. asst. U. of Iowa, Iowa City, 1981—81; interviewer for 65+ rural health study U. Hospitals, Iowa City, 1981—82; substitute tchr. Dept. of Def. Dependents Schools, Idar-Oberstein, Germany, 1983—83, Darmstadt, Germany, 1986—88; reading, comm., and math. instr. US Army, Darmstadt, Germany, 1987—90; German instr. Kirkwood C.C. Continuing Edn., Belle Plaine, Iowa, 1991; scorer NCS, Iowa City, 1993—97; scoring dir. Pearson Ednl. Measurement, Iowa City, 1997—. German tutor pvt., Belle Plaine, Iowa, 1991—93. Mem. Am. Legion Aux., Belle Plaine, Iowa, 1993—2003; vol. in elem. sch. lang. arts instrn. Belle Plaine Cmty. Schools, Belle Plaine, Iowa, 1976—79, Dept. of Def. Dependents Schools, Idar-Oberstein, Germany, 1982—83, Darmstadt, Germany, 1986—89, Belle Plaine Cmty. Schools, Belle Plaine, Iowa, 1991—93. Recipient Graduation With Highest Distinction And Honors In Psychology, U. of Iowa, 1981, elected to Phi Beta Kappa, Phi Beta Kappa, 1981. Achievements include development of Children's Loneliness Scale; Online Scoring Training. Avocations: studying Germanic languages, translating letters and documents, restoring antique furniture, travel.

WINKLEBLECH, SHANNAN, music educator; b. Dayton, Ohio, Jan. 22, 1974; d. James Jones and Kathleen Kennedy; children: Arianne, Kendra. BS in Edn., Clarion (Pa.) U., 1996. Cert. instrnl. tchr. II Pa. Music tchr. Bishop Leonard Cath. Sch., Pitts., 2001—05; elem. music tchr. Ringgold Sch. Dist., Monongahela, Pa., 2005—. Music dir. Peace Luth. Ch., Greenock, Pa., 1999—. Mem.: Pa. Music Educators Assn. (assoc.). Lutheran. Home: 420 Worthington St Mc Keesport PA 15132 Office: Monongahela Elem Ctr 1200 Chess St Monongahela PA 15063 Office Phone: 724-258-2911.

WINKLER, AGNIESZKA M., marketing executive; b. Rome, Feb. 22, 1946; came to U.S., 1953; naturalized, 1959; d. Wojciech A. and Halina Z. (Owsiany) W.; children from previous marriage: children: Renata G. Ritcheson, Dana C Sworakowski; m. Arthur K. Lund. BA, Coll. Holy Name, 1967; MA, San Jose State U., 1971; MBA, U. Santa Clara, 1981. Tchg. asst. San Jose State U., 1968-70; cons. to Ea. European bus. Palo Alto, Calif., 1970-72; pres./founder Commart Communications, Palo Alto, 1973-84; pres./founder, chmn. bd. Winkler Advt., Santa Clara, Calif., 1984—; chmn. bd. SuperCuts, Inc.; chmn., founder TeamToolz, 2000—04, The Winkler Group, 2004—. Bd. dirs. Reno Air, Lifeguard, Lifeguard Life Ins., IP Locks, C200, Inter-tel, Western Folklife Ctr.; exec. com. C200. Author: Warp Speed Branding, 1999. Trustee Santa Clara U., 1991—; trustee O'Connor Found., 1987-93, mem. exec. com., 1988—, mem. Capital Campaign steering com., 1989; mem. nat. adv. bd. Comprehensive Health Enhancement Support System, 1991—; mem. mgmt. west com. A.A.A.A. Agy., 1991—, vice chair no. Calif. coun., 1996—; project dir. Poland Free Enterprise Plan, 1989-92; mem. adv. bd. Normandy France Bus. Devel., 1989-92; mem. bd. regents Holy Names Coll., 1987—; bd. dirs. San Jose Mus. Art, 1987; mem. San Jose Symphony, Gold Baton, 1986; mem. nat. adv. com. Chess, 1991—; dir. Bay Area Coun., 1994—. Recipient CLIO award in Advt., Addy award, others; named to 100 Best Women in Advt., Ad Age, 1988, Best Woman in Advt., AdWeek and McCall's Mag., 1993, one of 100 Best and Brightest Women in Mktg. & Advt., Nat. Assn. Women Bus. Owners, 1996. Mem. Family Svc. Assn. (trustee 1980-82), Am. Assn. Advt. Agys. (agy. mgmt. west com. 1991), Bus. Profl. Advt. Assn., Polish Am. Congress, San Jose Advt. Club, San Francisco Ad Club, Beta Gamma Sigma (hon.), Pi Gamma Mu, Pi Delta Phi (Lester-Tinneman award 1966, Bill Raskob Found. grantee 1965). Office: The Winkler Group 633 Post # 515 San Francisco CA 94109

WINKLER, DOLORES EUGENIA, retired health facility administrator; b. Milw., Aug. 10, 1929; d. Charles Peter and Eugenia Anne (Zamka) Kowalski; m. Donald James Winkler, Aug. 18, 1951; 1 child, David John. Grad., Milw. Bus. Inst., 1949. Acct. Curative Rehab. Ctr., Milw., 1949-60; staff acct. West Allis (Wis.) Meml. Hosp., 1968-70, chief acct., 1970-78, reimbursement analyst, 1978-85, dir. budgets and reimbursement, 1985-95; ret., 1995. Mem. adv. coun., fin. com. Tau Home Health Care Agy., Milw., 1981—83. Mem.: Inst. Mgmt. Accts. (pres. 1983—84, nat. dir. 1986—88, pres. Mid Am. Regional Coun. 1988—89, award of excellence 1989), Healthcare Fin. Mgmt. Assn. (pres. 1989—90, Follmer Bronze award 1980, Reeves Silver award 1986, Muncie Gold award 1989, medal of honor 1993), Beta Chi Rho (pres. 1948). Avocations: travel, photography, golf. Home: 12805 W Honey Ln New Berlin WI 53151-2652

WINKLER, REBECCA B., psychologist; b. Reno, Nev., Aug. 16, 1977; d. Anthony Clayton and Cathleen Ann Winkler; m. Jason Johnathan Bailey, May 17, 2003. BA, U. Ga., 1998; MA, DePaul U., Chgo., 2002, PhD, 2004. Orgnl. devel. assoc. Adv. Health Care, Oak Brook, Ill., 2001—04; corp. psychologist/mgmt. cons. Sperduto & Assocs., 2004—. Contbr. chapters to books. Vol. Ctr. for Sexual Assault Survivors, Athens, Ga., 1995—98. Scholar, Atlanta Jamaican Assn., 1995, DePaul U., 2000—04; Hope scholar, State of Ga., 1995—98, Robert C. Byrd scholar, 1995—98, Gov.'s scholar, 1995—98, Alumni scholar, U. Ga. Alumni Assn., 1995—98. Mem.: NOW (co-pres. U. Ga. chpt. 1997—98), APA, Soc. Indsl. and Orgnl. Psychology, Smithsonian Instn., Nat. Wildlife Fedn., Sierra Club, Phi Beta Kappa, Phi Kappa Phi. Democrat. Episcopalian. Avocations: travel, reading. Office: Sperduto & Assoc 235 Peachtree St NE Ste 300 Atlanta GA 30303 Office Phone: 404-577-1178.

WINKLER, SUE ELAINE, art psychotherapist, social worker; b. Ypsilanti, Mich., Nov. 5, 1932; d. Norman Julius and Thelma Evelyn (Rose) Fairbanks; m. William P. Marquardt, Nov. 1951 (dec. July 1959); 1 child, Scott Edward; m. Edward David Winkler, Dec. 17, 1960; children: Shenlei Elizabeth, Sheila Ellyn. BA in Psychology, U. Mich., Flint, 1979; MA in Edn., Wayne State U., 1987; postgrad., Vt. U.; A in Fine Arts, Lansing CC, 2005. Cert. social worker, Mich.; cert. human studies, Lansing CC, 2004. Substitute tchr. Brandon Community Schs., Ortonville, Mich., 1979-85; cons. Delta Psychol. Assn., Lansing, Mich., 1986—; pvt. practice art psychotherapy Psychiatry and Psychology Assoc., Lansing, 1988—. Author: Creative Cornhusks Crafts, 1976. Recipient art award Flushing (Mich.) Art Show, 1975, Mott Community Coll., Flint, 1976. Mem. Am. Art Therapy Assn. (registered), Mich. Art Therapy Assn., Phi Theta Kappa. Avocations: fine arts, piano, tennis, woodworking, dance. Home: 5908 Bradford Ln Lansing MI 48917-1205 Studio: Hemmingbird Studio 5908 Bradford Ln Lansing MI 48917 E-mail: hemmingbird-studio@sbcglobal.net.

WINKLEY-PIKES, SANDRA KAY, special education educator; b. Dallas, Tex., Jan. 17, 1959; d. Leon and Lillie Bell Steward; m. Clyde Pikes, Jr., July 20, 2002; children: Crysta LaDawn Pikes, Clyde Pikes III, Caleb Anthony Pikes; 1 child, Derek LaRussell Winkley II. EdB, Tex. A&M U., 1979; EdM, Tex. A&M Universtiy, 1987. Cert. tchr. Tex. Bd. of Certification, 1979. Spl. edn. tchr. W.W. Samuell HS, Dallas, 1980—, spl. edn. liaison, 2000—03. Named Outstanding Young Women of Am., Outstanding Young Women of Am., 1981; recipient Tchr. of the Yr. Finalist, Dallas Roatary Club, 2001, Unsung Hero award, WB33 TV, Dallas, Tex., 2002. Mem.: Alpha Kappa Alpha. Democrat. Baptist. Avocations: reading, movies, travel, gardening, volunteering at church. Home: 1313 Devonshire Lane Mesquite TX 75150 Office: WW Samuell High School 8928 Palisade Drive Dallas TX

WINN, JADE G., library science educator; b. Pitts., Oct. 3, 1966; d. Terry Lee Wien and Sandra Jane D'Amico; m. Christopher N. Hardaway, Dec. 13, 1993; 1 child, Jace Winn Hardaway. AA, Coll. Desert, Joshua Tree, Calif., 1997; BA, San Diego State U., 1999; MLIS, San Jose State U., 2001; PhD, U. San Diego, 2005. Rschr. San Diego State U., 1997—2001, U. San Diego, 2001—03, asst. prof., 2002—. Office: Univ San Diego 5998 Alcala Pk San Diego CA 92110 Office Phone: 619-260-6885.

WINN, JANICE GAIL, food products administrator; b. Springfield, Mass., Nov. 2, 1954; d. Rose Eleanor (Draskawich) W. BA, Western New Eng. Coll., 1976. Gen. mdse. mgr. Mott's Shop-Rite, East Hartford, Conn., 1979-84; sr. merchandiser Imperial Distbrs., Auburn, Mass., 1984-85; dir. of gen. mdse. Waldbaums Food Mart, Holyoke, Mass., 1985-91; dir. health, beauty care and gen. mdse. Big Y Foods, Inc., Springfield, 1991—. Republican. Avocations: travel, spending time with partner and family. Office: Big Y Foods Inc 2145 Roosevelt Ave Springfield MA 01104-1650 Office Phone: 413-504-4410. E-mail: winni@charter.net.

WINN, NELROY GRIFFIN, healthcare administrator; b. Spur, Tex., June 9, 1940; d. Sevy Elroy and Nelda Gay (Shields) W.; m. Herbert Thomas Winn, Nov. 8, 1958; children: Robin, Carol, Glen. BBA in Acctg., Tex. Wesleyan U., 1985. CPA, Tex. Bookkeeper All Sts. Health Care, Ft. Worth, 1971-73; dir. acctg. All Sts. Health Sys., Ft. Worth, 1973-89, dir. internal audit, 1989-95, dir. bus. office, 1995-96, dir. compliance, 1996—. Mem. acctg. adv. bd. Tarrant County Coll., Ft. Worth. Ch. treas. St. Paul United Meth. Ch., Ft. Worth, 1982—; mem. fin. com. Ft. Worth West Dist. United Meth. Ch., 1998—; conf. treas. Ctrl. Tex. conf. United Meth. Women, 1999—. Mem. Tex. Soc. CPAs, Health Care Compliance Assn. (regional bd. dirs. 1998—), Hosp. Fin. Mgmt. Assn., Vol. Hosps. Am. Compliance Affinity Group (mem. S.W. compliance com. 1998—). Avocations: travel, camping, grandchildren. E-mail: compliance@allsaintshealth.org.

WINN, STEPHENIE, senior program specialist; b. Albany, N.Y., Apr. 8, 1970; d. Stephen Allen and Sharon Lynn Jenkins Winn. BA in Art with honors, U. LaVerne, 1992; MS in Spl. Edn. magna cum laude, Nat. U., L.A., 1995, MS in Instnl. Leadership summa cum laude, 1996; postgrad., U. So. Calif., L.A., 1997—2005. Calif. multiple subject tchg. credential, Calif. specialist tchg. credentials learning handicapped and severely handicapped. Tchg. asst. art dept. U. LaVerne, Calif., 1991-92; tchr. L.A. County Office Edn., Downey, 1993-99, sr. program specialist, 1999—. Mem.: Phi Delta Kappa (USC chpt.). Avocations: the arts, dance, sailing, scuba diving. Home: 15529 S Normandie Ave Unit A1 Gardena CA 90247-4013

WINNER, KARIN E., editor; b. White Plains, NY, Dec. 27, 1945; BA in Journalism, U. So. Calif. Editor San Diego Union-Tribune, 1995—. Office: San Diego Union-Tribune Pub Co 350 Camino De La Reina San Diego CA 92112-0191 Office Phone: 619-293-1201. E-mail: Karin.winner@uniontrib.com.

WINNER, SONYA D., lawyer; b. Mountain Home AFB, Idaho, May 13, 1957; BA with honors, Mich. State U., 1979; JD magna cum laude, Harvard U., 1982. Bar: D.C. 1983. Law clk. to Judge Louis F. Oberdorfer U.S. Dist. Ct. for D.C., 1982-83; assoc. Covington & Burling, Washington, 1983—90, ptnr., 1990—, founding ptnr. San Francisco office, 1999—, co-chmn., Litig. Practice Group. Mem. Harvard Law Rev. 1980-82; co-author: Clean Air Deskbook, 1992. Office: Covington & Burling One Front St San Francisco CA 94111 Office Phone: 415-591-7072. Office Fax: 415-591-6091. Business E-Mail: swinner@cov.com.

WINNEY, GAYLE MARIE, music educator; b. Roseville, Calif., Aug. 11, 1968; d. Gary and Peg Winney. BA in Music Edn., Chico State U., Calif., 1995; MA in Edn., Nat. U., Sacramento, Calif., 2003. Tchr. music San Juan Unified Sch. Dist., Carmichael, Calif., 2001—; edn. dir. Sacramento Philharm. Orch., 2005—. Edn. cons. Collegio Flor Naciente, Santiago, Dominican Republic, 2002—06. Mem.: Am. River Orff-Schulwerk Soc. (treas. 2005), Am. Symphony Orch. League (assoc.), Orff-Schulwerk Soc. (assoc.). Avocations: travel, music, dance. Office: Sacramento Philharmonic Orchestra 3418 3rd Avenue Sacramento CA 95817 Office Phone: 916-732-9045. Office Fax: 916-732-9049. Business E-Mail: gayle@sacphil.org.

WINNIE, AMY E., music educator; b. Gloversville, NY, Dec. 9, 1971; d. Lorren G. and Mary E. Worden. MS in Music Edn., Coll. St. Rose, Albany, NY, 2001. Tchr. gen. music, dir. chorus, band Piseco Elem. Sch., NY, 1994—95; tchr. itinerant gen. music Ceww Boces, Plattsburgh, 1997—98; tchr. mid. sch. gen. music, choral dir. Corinth Ctrl. Sch., 1998—99; tchr. itinerant, spl. ed. music Hfm Boces, Johnstown, 1999—. Music dir. Bleecker Cmty. Ch., NY, 2004—; 1st clarinet A Pretty Good Band, Lake Pleasant, 2004—; 1st soprano Mountain Arts Consortium Chorus, 2004—. Conservative. Avocations: crafts, reading. Home: 107 Lake Rd Gloversville NY 12078 Office: Hamilton-Fulton-Montgomery BOCES 25 W Main Street Johnstown NY 12095 Office Phone: 518-725-7411.

WINOGRAD, AUDREY LESSER, retired advertising executive; b. NYC, Oct. 6, 1933; d. Jack J. and Theresa Lorraine (Elkind) Lesser; m. Melvin H. Winograd, Apr. 29, 1956; 1 child, Hope Elise. BA, U. Conn., 1953. Asst. advt. mgr. T. Baumritter Co., Inc., N.Y.C., 1953-54; asst. dir. pub. rels. and creative merchandising Kirby, Block & Co., Inc., N.Y.C., 1954-56; divsn. mdse. mgr., dir. advt. and sales promotion Winograd's Dept. Store, Inc., Point Pleasant, NJ, 1956-73, v.p., 1960-73, exec. v.p., 1973-86; pres., CEO AMW Assocs., Atlanta, 1976—2002, ret., 2002—. Editor bus. newsletters. Bd. dirs. Temple Beth Am, Lakewood, N.J., 1970-72, Temple Emanuel, Atlanta, 1999-2001; active Alley Cat Allies, Fund for Animals. Mem. NAFE, LWV, Jersey Pub. Rels. and Advt. Assn. (pres. 1982-83, bd. dirs.), Retail Advt. and Mktg. Assn. Internat., Monmouth Ocean Devel. Coun., Monmouth County Bus. Assn. (bd. dirs. 1985-97, pres. 1988-90, Woman of Yr. 1992-93, Person of Yr. 1995), N.J. Assn. Women Bus. Owners, Am. Soc. Advt. and Promotion, Ocean C. of C. (bd. dirs. 1994-97, award 1993, 94), Retail Advt. Conf. (Career Achievements and Contbns. to Soc. award 1993), Soc. Prevention Cruelty to Animals, Animal Protection Inst. Am., Human Soc., Internat. Fund Animal Welfare, World Wildlife Fund, Friends of Animals, Defenders of Wildlife, Nat. Humane Edn. Soc., In Defense of Animals, Atlanta Humane Soc., Sierra Club, Peta, Natural Resources Def. Coun., Delta Rescue, Last Chance for Animals, Best Friends, Humane Soc. of U.S., United Animal Nat., Wilderness

Soc., Lifesavers Wild Horse Rescue, Environ. Defense, Audobon, Greenpeace. Avocations: collecting animal collectibles, gourmet cooking, environmental protection, exercise. Office: AMW Assocs 5304 Vernon Lake Dr Atlanta GA 30338-3527 Personal E-mail: audwin@comcast.net.

WINOKUR, MARISSA JARET, actress; b. NYC, Feb. 2, 1973; Studied at, Am. Musical and Dramatic Acad. Actor: (plays, Broadway) Grease, 1995, Hairspray, 2002 (Tony award for best actress, 2003), 2005; (plays) Guys and Dolls, Peter Pan, Little Shop of Horrors, Romeo and Juliet, Nunsense II, Grandma Sylvia's Funeral, Hair, Happy Days; (films) Demo Real, 1998, Why Love Doesn't Work, 1999, Never Been Kissed, 1999, American Beauty, 1999, Sleep Easy, Hutch Rimes, 2000, Scary Movie, 2000, Amy's Orgasm, 2001, On Edge, 2001, Now You Know, 2002; (TV films) Beautiful Girl, 2003; co-exec. prodr. (TV films) Beautiful Girl, 2003; actor(guest appearances): (TV series) The Steve Harvey Show, 1998, Felicity, 1999, Dharma & Greg, 1999, 2000, Moesha, 2000, Curb Your Enthusiasm, 2000, Just Shoot Me, 2000, The Ellen Show, 2001, Boston Public, 2001. Office Phone: 310-288-5888. Office Fax: 310-288-5868.

WINSLETT, STONER, artistic director; b. Jacksonville, Fla., Aug. 17, 1958; m. Donald Paulding Irwin; children: Louise Gray Irwin, Elizabeth Irwin, Alexander Pankoff, Caroline Irwin. Student, Am. Ballet Theatre Sch., N.C. Sch. of the Arts; BFA summa cum laude, Smith Coll., 1980. Artistic dir. Richmond Ballet, 1980—. Pres. John Butler Found. Mem.: Phi Beta Kappa. Office: Richmond Ballet 407 E Canal St Richmond VA 23219-3811*

WINSLOW, ANNE BRANAN, artist; b. Waynesboro, Ga., July 28, 1920; d. Walter Augustus and Rubie (Griffin) Branan; m. James Addison Winslow Jr., May 8, 1943; children: Lu Anne, Jan Renee. BS in Fine Art, Queens Coll., 1941; postgrad., U. South Fla., 1974—75. One-woman shows include Dunedin (Fla.) Art Ctr., 1980, Tampa (Fla.) Originals Gallery, 1982, Pub. Libr., St. Petersburg, Fla., 1982, Lee Scarfone Gallery, 1983, 84, Studio 1212, Clearwater, Fla., 1983, 87, 90, Gallery 600, Largo, Fla., 1986, Gallery of State Capitol, Tallahassee, 1987, Berghoff Gallery, Clearwater, 1988, 92, Anderson-Marsh Gallery, St. Petersburg, 1989, 92, Loveland (Colo.) Mus., 1990, Gallery at City Hall of Tampa, 1990, Lawrence Charles Gallery, Tampa, 1993, Gallery Contemporanea, Jacksonville, Fla., 1994; painting, oil painting, Fla. Series II, Images II, 1980, Amagedon, 1974, Eastern Series III, 1984, original handpulled serigraphs, 1991, 92. Mem. Studio 1212, Fla. Artist Group, Mus. Women in Arts, Fla. Printmakers Soc., Generator Gallery (founding). Republican. Avocations: world travel, reading, gardening. Home: 3750 Peachtree Rd NE Apt 901 Atlanta GA 30919-1322 E-mail: annebwinslow@canterburycourt.org.

WINSLOW, BETTE KILLINGSWORTH, dance studio owner; b. Springfield, Mo., Dec. 10, 1919; d. Troy Kenwood andWinifred Elizabeth (Reed) Killingsworth; m. Kenelm Crawford Winslow, Sept. 5, 1947; children: Katherine, Jeanette, Kenelm, Elizabeth, Priscilla. Student, Christian Coll., 1937-39, Perry Mansfield Theater Arts Camp, summer 1938; studied with, George Balanchine, 1939-41, Pierre Vladimiroff, Anatole O'Boukhoff, Anatole Vilzak, Ludmila Shollar, Muriel Stuart, Jack Stanley, Jose Fernandez, Doris Humphrey, Jose Limon, Martha Graham, Nimura. Dancer Vogue Ballet, Rodeo, Vincent Youman Concert Revue, Met. Opera Ballet, N.Y.C., Boston and Can., 1939-44; program dir. overseas clubs ARC, New Guinea, Philippines and Korea, 1944-47; owner dance studios, pvt. tchr. dance Hermon, N.Y., Ishpeming, Mich., and Taos, N.Mex., 1947—. Dir. Dance Taos summer workshops, 1986-92. Choreographer numerous dance prodns., original ballets. Recipient Disting. Alumni award Columbia Coll., 1996, Taos Living Treasure award, 1998; special honor, Taos Dance, 2000. Avocation: sewing. Home: PO Box 927 El Prado NM 87529-0927 Office: PO Box 425 Taos NM 87571-0425

WINSLOW, HELEN LITTELL, lawyer; b. Wilmington, Del., May 11, 1952; d. Julian Dallas and Jean (Littell) W.; m. Jonathan David Jaffe, Nov. 8, 1980; children: Kenan Winslow Jaffe, Nathaniel Harrington Jaffe, Saul Handler Jaffe. AB, Bryn Mawr Coll., 1974; JD, U. N.C., 1977. Bar: Del. 1977, U.S. Dist. Ct. Del. 1977, U.S. Ct. Appeals (3d cir.) 1980, U.S. Supreme Ct.1980. Law clk. to presiding judge U.S. Dist. Ct. Del., Wilmington, 1977-79; assoc. Richards, Layton & Finger, Wilmington, 1979—2001; asst. gen. counsel H.D. Lee Co., Inc., 2001—. Mem. ABA, Fed. Bar Assn. (v.p. Del. chpt. 1985-86, pres. Del. chpt. 1987—89), Del. Bar Assn. (pres. 2005-06), Am. Judicature Soc. Democrat. Jewish. Avocation: singing. Office: HD Lee Co 3411 Silverside Rd Concord Pike Wilmington DE 19810

WINSLOW, JANET LUCAS, elementary school educator; b. Scotland Neck, N.C., May 2, 1939; d. Ernest and Cora Wilma (Dixon) Lucas; m. Roy L. Winslow, Dec. 27, 1969; 1 child, Sally L. BS in Edn., Old Dominion U., 1965; student, U. Va., Norfolk State U. Cert. collegiate profl. K-7. Tchr. Norfolk (Va.) City Schs., 1965-95, ret., 1995, mem. all city teaching team, tchr. mentor adv. coun., 1970, 85, 90, 91. Great books leader, tchr. corps. program. Program dir. Girl Scout Camp Matoaka. Recipient Sch. Bell award, 1989-90, 1990-91. Mem. NEA, Va. Edn. Assn., Edn. Assn. Norfolk, PTA (life). Home: 3378 Finch Ave Norfolk VA 23518-5713

WINSON, ELLEN-MARIE (MACONE), school system administrator, reading specialist; b. Woburn, Mass., Sept. 6, 1941; d. Fred Charles and Edna McKay Macone; m. Robert Arthur Winson, Aug. 7, 1971 (dec. Dec. 2005); children: Maura Jane Mann, Suzanne Marie DiPalma, Peter Robert. BS, U. of Mass., 1958—62; MEd, Northeastern U., 1963—66. Teacher Elementary K-8 Mass. Dept of Edn., 1962, Reading Specialist K-12 Mass. Dept of Edn., 1965, Supervisor of Reading K-12 Mass. Dept. of Edn., 1968. Elem. tchr. Woburn Pub. Schools, Woburn, Mass., 1962—66, reading specialist k-12, 1966—76, Title 1 tchr., 1987—2000, Title 1 dir., 2000—. Remedial reading coord. Woburn Pub. Schools, Mass., 1968—77. V.p. Friends of the Libr., Woburn, Mass., 2001; bd. dirs. Title 1 Dissemination Project, Melrose, Mass., 1990—2005. Recipient State Leadership award, Nat. Assn. of Fed. Edn. Program Administrators, 2005. Mem.: Coun. of Administrators of Compensatory Edn. (rec. sec. 2003—05), Internat. Reading Assn. Avocations: travel, reading. Home: 23 Clinton St Woburn MA 01801 Office: Woburn Public Schools 55 Locust St Woburn MA 01801 Office Phone: 781-937-8233 x 230. Office Fax: 781-937-0715. Personal E-mail: ewinson@aol.com. E-mail: emwinson@woburnpublicschools.com.

WINSTEAD, ANTOINETTE FAY, performing arts educator; b. Colorado Springs, Colo., Dec. 25, 1964; d. James R. and Jo A. Winstead. AA, San Antonio Coll., 1985; BFA, NYU, 1987; MA, Our Lady of the Lake U., San Antonio, 1995; MFA, Columbia U., N.Y.C., 1989. English lectr. Our Lady of the Lake U., San Antonio, 1994—95, asst. prof., 1995—2000, assoc. prof., 2000—05, prof., 2005—. Artistic chair The Renaissance Theater Guild, San Antonio, 2002—; book reviewer Choice Rev./ALA, Middletown, Conn., 2002—. Author (dramatic reading): (novel excerpt) God Done Blessed You; dramatic reading (novel excerpt) Their Eyes Were Watching God; actor: (play) Mother Knows Best, Black Lily/White Lily; dir: Innocent Thoughts, A Fool of Passion, Family Portrait, All the World's a Stage, Our Town, In the Blood, (choreographer) (musical) Forever Free; costume coord. (play) Bee-Luther- Hatchee; author: (poetry) A Garland of Poems: A Collection from Ten Female Poets, Poetic Voices of America, (short stories) The Thing Itself, (play) Too Long Coming, The Meeting; author: (director) One Drink Too Many; contbr. poetry ot profl. pubs.; author: (plays) The Interrogator, Somebody Else's Life. Co-chair Ad Hoc U.C. Libr. Fundraising Com., Universal City, Tex., 1999—2000; grant reviewer Tex. Commn. on the Arts Grant Rev. Panel, Austin, 1997—98; sec. Universal City Pub. Libr. Adv. Commn., 1996—2000, co-chair, 2002—03; sec. Universal City Pub. Libr. Found., Universal City, Tex., 1999—2002; pres. San Antonio Poets Assn., San Antonio, 2002—. Recipient Supt.'s Tchg. award, Judson Ind. Sch. Dist., 1993; scholar Honor sholar, NYU, 1987. Mem.: San Antonio Poets Assn. (pres. 2002—04), SAT Playwrights, The Internat. Women's Writing Guild, Sigma Tau Delta (life). Office: Our Lady of the Lake University 411 SW 24th St San Antonio TX 78207 Personal E-mail: winsa@lake.ollusa.edu.

WINSTEAD, MELODY, science educator; d. Teryl Washington. BA, Coll. New Rochelle, N.Y., 1980; MA, CCNY, N.Y.C., 1993. Cert. secondary sci. edn. tchr. NY State, 1987. Staff developer sci. NYC Dept. Edn. Dist. 5, NYC, 1979—2004, tchr., 1997—99, NYC Dept. Edn., NYC, 1987—. Sci. inquiry specialist, New Rochelle, NY. Home: 23 Lathers Park New Rochelle NY 10801-3910 Personal E-mail: melodywinstead@yahoo.com.

WINSTON, AMY DANIELLE PICARD, science educator, department chairman; b. Woonsocket, R.I., Nov. 16, 1975; d. Arthur Wilfred and Muriel F Picard; m. William Michael Winston, July 26, 2003. BA in Physics, Wellesley Coll., Mass., 1993—97; MA in Edn., Tufts U., Medford, Mass., 1999—2001. Lic. Tchr., Physics Mass. Dept. Edn. Physics tchr. Melrose HS, Mass., 1997—99, Newton North HS, 1999—2005, sci. dept. chair, 2005—. Mentor coord. Newton North HS, 2001—. Office: Newton North HS 360 Lowell Ave Newton MA 02460 Office Phone: 617-559-6380. Personal E-mail: apicard@alum.wellesley.edu.

WINSTON, JANET MARGARET, real estate agent, volunteer; b. Binghamton, N.Y., Sept. 30, 1937; d. Cornelius Adrian and Vera Helene (Strohman) Salie; m. Edmund Joseph Winston, Nov. 29, 1958 (dec. July 1981); children: Mark Edmund, Deborah Ann. Student, SUNY, 1955-57, Bliss Coll., 1978. Sales assoc. HER Real Living, Worthington, Ohio, 1979—. Dist. chair women's divsn. Cmty. Chest ARC, Kalamazoo, 1970; docent Indpls. Mus. Art, 1975, Columbus (Ohio) Mus. Art, 1976—, beaux art mem., 1976—87; docent Chinese Son of Heaven Exhibit, 1989, mus. fund drive, 1980—87, 1989—95; trustee Worthington Resource Ctr., 1979—84, v.p., 1984, chair youth employment svcs., 1980—83; trustee, sec. Worthington Hills Civil Assn., 1986—89. Recipient Nat. Sales award The Dozen, 1996, Top HER award, 1980-2002, Brass award HER Real Living, 2004. Mem.: Ohio Assn. Realtors, Nat. Assn. Realtors, Columbus Bd. Realtors (pub. rels. com. 1980, 1983, 1986, sales adv. com. 1987, pub. rels. com. 1988, svcs. task force 1989, 10 Million Dollar Club award), Sessions Soc. (bd. dir. 2001—03), Worthington C. of C., Worthington Women's Club, Worthington Hills Garden Club (bd. dir. 1989), Worthington Hills Women's Club. Republican. Episcopalian. Avocations: art, music, golf. Home: 8036 Golfview Ct Columbus OH 43235-1230 Office: HER Real Living 6902 N High St Worthington OH 43085-2555 Office Phone: 614-825-8852. Personal E-mail: janetwinston66@yahoo.com. Business E-Mail: janet.winston@realliving.com.

WINSTON, JUDITH ANN, lawyer; b. Atlantic City, Nov. 23, 1943; d. Edward Carlton and Margaret Ann (Goodman) Marianno; m. Michael Russell Winston, Aug. 10, 1963; children: Lisa Marie, Cynthia Eileen. BA magna cum laude, Howard U., Washington, 1966; JD, Georgetown U., 1977. Bar: DC 1977, US Supreme Ct. Dir. EEO project Coun. Great City Schs., Washington, 1971-74; legal asst. Lawyers Com. for Civil Rights Under Law, Washington, 1975-77; spl. asst. to dir. Office for Civil Rights, HEW, Washington, 1977-79; exec. asst., legal counsel to chair U.S. EEO Commn., Washington, 1979-80; asst. gen. counsel U.S. Dept. Edn., 1980-86; dep. dir. Lawyers Com. for Civil Rights Under Law, 1986-88; dep. dir. pub. policy Women's Legal Def. Fund, Washington, 1988-90, chair employment discrimination com., 1979-88, ednl. cons., 1974-77; asst. prof. law Washington Coll. Law of Am. U., 1990-93, assoc. prof. law, 1993-95; gen. counsel U.S. Dept. Edn., Washington, 1993-2001; exec. dir. Pres.'s Initiative on Race, 1997-98; undersec. U.S. Dept. Edn., 2000-01; rsch. prof law Washington Coll. Law Am. U., Washington, 2001—02; ptnr. Winston Withers & Assocs., LLC, Washington, 2002—. Author: (book) Desegregating Schools in the Great Cities: Philadelphia, 1970, Chronicle of a Decade 1961-70, 1970, Desegregating Urban Schools: Educational Equality/Quality, 1970; contbr. articles to profl jours. Pres. bd. dirs. Higher Achievement Program; bd. dirs. Ptnrs. for Dem. Change, Nat. Pub. Radio, So. Edn. Found., Nat. Law Ctr. on Poverty and Homelessness, Hist. Soc. DC Cir. Ct. Appeals, 2004—. Named Woman Lawyer of the Yr, Women's Bar Asn, 1997; recipient Margaret Brent, Am Bar Asn Comn Women in the Profession, 1998, Thurgood Marshall award, DC Bar, 1999. Fellow: ABA Found.; mem.: ACLU, Lawyers Com. Civil Rights Under Law, Nat. Bar Assn., Washington Bar Assn., Washington Coun. Lawyers, DC Bar Asn, Fed. Bar Assn., Links Inc., Phi Beta Kappa, Delta Theta Phi, Alpha Kappa Alpha. Democrat. Episcopalian. Home: 1371 Kalmia Rd NW Washington DC 20012-1444 Office: Winston Withers & Assocs 1730 M St NW # 413 Washington DC 20036 Office Phone: 202-887-8202. Business E-Mail: jwinston@winwithassocs.com.

WINSTON, KRISHNA, foreign language professional; b. Greenfield, Mass., June 7, 1944; d. Richard and Clara (Brussel) W.; 1 child, Danielle Billingsley. BA, Smith Coll., 1965; MPhil, Yale U., 1969, PhD, 1974. Instr. Wesleyan U., Middletown, Conn., 1970-74, asst. prof., 1974-77, assoc. prof., 1977-84, prof., 1984—, acting dean, 1993-94. Coord. Mellon Mays Undergrad. Fellowship, 1993—. Author: O v. Horváth: Close Readings of Six Plays, 1975; translator: O. Schlemmer, Letters and Diaries, 1972, S. Lenz, The Heritage, 1981, G. Grass, Two States, One Nation, 1990, C. Hein, The Distant Lover, 1989, G. Mann, Reminiscences and Reflections, 1990, J. W. V. Goethe, Wilhelm Meister's Journeyman Years, 1989, C. v. Krockow, The Hour of the Women, 1991, E. Heller, With the Next Man Everything Will be Different, 1992, R. W. Fassbinder, The Anarchy of the Imagination, 1992, G. Reuth, Goebbels, 1994, E. Lappin; editor: Jewish Voices, German Words, 1994, P. Handke, Essay on the Jukebox, 1994, P. Handke, My Year in the No-Man's-Bay, 1998, G. Grass, Too Far Afield, 2000, P. Handke, On a Dark Night I Left My Silent House, 2000, G. Grass, Crabwalk, 2003. Vol. Planned Parenthood, Middletown, 1972-77; mem. Recycling Task Force, Middletown, 1986-87; chmn. Resource Recycling Adv. Coun., Middletown, 1989—; trustee Ind. Day Sch., Middlefield, Conn., 1989—. Recipient Schlegel-Tieck prize for translation, 1994, 2001, Helen and Kurt Wolff prize for transl., 2001; German Acad. Exch. Svc. fellow, Kahn fellow Smith Coll., 2000-01. Mem. MLA, ALTA, Soc. for Exile Studies, Am. Assn. Tchrs. German, PEN, Phi Beta Kappa (pres. Wesleyan chpt. 1987-90). Home: 655 Bow Ln Middletown CT 06457-4808 Office: Wesleyan Univ German Studies Dept Middletown CT 06459-0040 Office Phone: 860-685-3378. E-mail: kwinston@wesleyan.edu.

WINSTON, MARY A., publishing executive; BS in Acctg. and Info. Sys., U. Wis.; MBA, Northwestern U. Sr. auditor Arthur Andersen & Co., 1983—87; various positions Ameritech, 1987—91; dir. bus. devel. and strategy Biotech Divsn. Baxter Internat., 1991—95; sr. mgmt. positions Warner-Lambert, 1995—2002; v.p. Visteon Corp., 2002—04, treas., 2002—03, controller, 2003—04; exec. v.p. Scholastic Corp., N.Y., 2004—, CFO, 2004—. Office: Scholastic Corp 557 Broadway New York NY 10012

WINSTON, ROBIN EUGENE, political party professional; b. Washington, Pa., Oct. 14, 1957; m. Charlitta Peterson Winston, Oct. 25, 1997; 1 child, Chloe. BA, U. Louisville. Chief of staff/legis. aide Bd. of Aldermen, Louisville, Ky., 1986-93; cmty. devel. specialist Ind. Dept. Commerce, Indpls., 1993-94; spl. asst. Office of the Lt. Gov., Indpls., 1994-96; polit. dir. Ind. Dem. Party, Indpls., 1996-99, chmn., 1999—. Pres. Polimark, Indpls., 1983—. Contbr. articles to profl. jours. Bd. trustees Indpls. Mus. of Art, 2000—; mem. Dem. Nat. Com., Washington, 1999—; del. 2000 Dem. Nat. Conv., Washington, 2000; bd. dirs. Indpls. Urban League Bd. Dirs. Named Rising star Campaigns and Elections mag., 2000; recipient Cmty. Svc. award Ministerial Alliance of Indpls., 2001, Outstanding Svc. award Ind. Dem. African-Am. Caucus, 1999, Ky. Col. Office of Gov., 1983. Mem. NAACP (Heritage award 2000), Am. Assn. of Polit. Cons., Fraternal Order of Police Supporter. Baptist. Avocations: golf, walking, historical sightseeing, family activities. Office: Ind Dem Party 1 North Capitol #200 Indianapolis IN 46204 Fax: 317-231-7109. E-mail: crwinston@aol.com.

WINSTON, SANDRA, health sciences administrator; b. Kansas City, Mo., Apr. 16, 1962; d. Roosevelt and Delilah Winston. BSBA, U. Ark., Fayetteville, 1984. Pharm. sales person Bristol-Myers Squibb, Little Rock, 1989-94; with legis. affairs divsn. Office of Lt. Gov. Huckabee, Little Rock, 1994-95; asst. for internat. office Family Life, Little Rock, 1995-96; health and human svcs. liaison Office of Gov. Huckabee, Little Rock, 1996-99; dir. Health Svcs. Agy., Little Rock, 1999—. Mem. Conway C. of C. (bd. dirs.).

WINTER, JANE, medical educator; b. N.Y.C., 1952; MD, U. Pa., 1977; intern, U. Chgo., 1977-78, resident int. medicine, 1978-80. Fellow in hematology and oncology Columbia P&S, N.Y.C., 1980-81, Northwestern U., 1981-83, prof., 1983—. Mem.: Ea. Coop. Oncology Group, Am. Soc. for Blood and Marrow Transplantation, Am. Assn. Cancer Rsch., Am. Fedn. for Clin. Rsch., Am. Soc. Clin. Oncology, Am. Soc. Hematology. Office: Divsn Hematology/Oncology 676 N St Clair St Ste 850 Chicago IL 60611-2978 Office Phone: 312-695-0990. E-mail: j-winter@northwestern.edu.

WINTER, JUDY ELAINE, freelance/self-employed journalist, speaker; d. Lester App and Marie Pitcowicz; m. Richard Kent Winter, Aug. 7, 1976; children: Jenna Marie, Eric Richard(dec.). BA in Comm., Mich. State U., 1980. From advt. mgr. to corp. devel. assoc. WKAR-TV, East Lansing, Mich., 1985—88, corp. devel. assoc., 1988—92; freelance columnist DeWitt, Mich., 1996—. Contbr.; co-author: Enabled in Words: The Real Lives. Real Victories of People with Disabilities, 2005; author: Breakthrough Parenting for Children with Special Needs: Raising the Bar of Expectations, 2006; contbr. articles to profl. jours. and periodicals. Co-chmn. Eric RicStar Winter Music Therapy Summer Camp, Mich. State U., 2003—. Named to Wall of Tolerance, Montgomery, Ala., 2003; recipient Cmty. Achievement award, Mich. Week, 2000, Disting. Achievement award, The Assn. Ednl. Pubs., 2000, 2002, Exceptional Parent award, Mich. Federated Chpts. Coun. Exceptional Children, 2002, Chief Everything Officer award, AOL and Dove, 2006. Avocations: travel, gardening, walking, photography, community outreach. E-mail: jappwinter@aol.com.

WINTER, KATHRYN, music educator, writer; b. Bratislava, Slovakia, May 16, 1934; arrived in U.S., 1946; d. Sigmund and Alice. MusB, Manhattan Sch. Music, 1956, MusM, 1957. Piano tchr. "Y" 92d St., N.Y.C., 1958—62, Rubin Conservatory of Music, Jerusalem, 1968—81; piano and music tchr. young musicians program U. Calif., Berkeley, 1982—; residency as writer Millay Colony for Arts, Steepletop, NY, 1997. Author: (short stories) Madison Review, Stories, Across the Generations, (novels) Katarina (translated to French, German, Chinese and Slovak), 1998. Avocations: dance, singing, walking.

WINTER, MIRIAM THERESE (GLORIA FRANCES WINTER), nun, religious studies educator; b. Passaic, N.J., June 14, 1938; d. Mathias William and Irene Theresa (Marton) W. BMus, Cath. U. Am., 1964; M in Religious Edn., McMaster Divinity Coll., Hamilton, Ont., Can., 1976; PhD in Liturgical Studies, Princeton Theol. Sem., 1983; LHD (hon.), Albertus Magnus Coll., 1991, St. Joseph Coll., 1993, Mount St. Vincent U., 2004. Joined Med. Mission Sisters, Roman Cath. Ch., 1955. Dir. liturgy and liturgical music Med. Mission Sisters, Phila., 1960-76, pub. rels. dir., coord., 1963-72; assoc. prof. liturgy, worship and spirituality Hartford (Conn.) Sem., 1980-85, prof., 1985—, prof. liturgy, worship, spirituality, and feminist studies, 1994—; founder, dir. Women's Leadership Inst., 1996—. Mem. faculty St. Therese's Inst., Phila., 1964-68, acad. dir., 1968-72, Immaculate Conception Sem. Summer Program, Mo., 1969, Cath. U. Summer Grad. Program, Washington, 1970, Hope Ecumenical Inst., Jerusalem, summer 1974, 75, 76, McMaster Divinity Coll. Grad. Program, 1976, Continuing Edn. Program, 1976, N.Y. Archdiocesan Sch. Liturgical Music, summer 1980, 82, Vancouver Sch. Theology, summer 1982, USN Chaplains through Auburn Theol. Sem., 1990; mem. adj. faculty Union Inst., Cin., 1992-94; with emergency relief work Internat. Rescue Com., Cambodia, 1979-80, Malteser-Hilfsdienst Auslandsdienst, Germany, 1984, Med. Mission Sisters, Ethiopia, 1985; lectr., instr., performer, worship leader, song leader for various groups by invitation, nat. and internat., 1967—. Author: Preparing the Way of the Lord, 1978, God-With-Us: Resources for Prayer and Praise, 1979, An Anthology of Scripture Songs, 1982, Why Sing? Toward a Theology of Catholic Church Music, 1984, WomanPrayer, Woman Song: Resources for Ritual, 1987, WomanWord: A Feminist Lectionary and Psalter, 1990, WomanWisdom: A Feminist Lectionary and Psalter, Women of the Hebrew Scriptures, Part I, 1992 (1st pl. award for books on liturgy Cath. Press Assn., 1992), Woman-Witness: A Feminist Lectionary and Psalter, Women of the Hebrew Scriptures, Part II, 1992 (1st pl. award for books on liturgy Cath. Press Assn., 1993), The Gospel According to Mary: A New Testament for Women, 1993; co-author: Defecting in Place: Women Claiming Responsibility for Their Own Spiritual Lives, 1994 (2d pl. award for books on gender studies Cath. Press Assn., 1995), The Chronicles of Noah and Her Sisters: Genesis and Exodus According to Women, 1995 (2d pl. award for books on gender studies Cath. Press Assn., 1996), Songlines: Hymns, Songs, Rounds and Refrains, 1996, The Singer and the Song: An Autobiography of the Spirit, 1999, Out of the Depths, The Story of Ludmila Javorova, Ordained Roman Catholic Priest, 2001 (1st pl. award for books on popular presentation of the Cath. faith Cath. Press Assn., 2002), Eucharist with a small "e", 2005 (3d pl. award for books on liturgy, 2006); author: numerous songs including albums Keepsake, Hymns Re-Imagined, SpiritSong, EarthSong, WomanSong, Remember Me, Sandstone, Songs of Promise, RSVP: Let Us Pray, Gold, Incense and Myrrh, In Love, Seasons (Christian Oscar award Nat. Evang. Film Found., 1971), Knock, Knock, Praise the Lord in Many Voices (live rec. of Mass of a Pilgrim People premiered at Carnegie Hall), 1967, I Know the Secret, Joy is Like the Rain (Gold album in USA and Australia); contbr. articles to profl. jours. Bd. dirs. Capitol Region Conf. Chs., 1984-91, v.p., 1986-88. pres. bd. dirs., 1988-90, past pres., 1990-91, Archdiocesan Office Urban Affairs, 1986-95; mem. Christian Conf. ann. event WINFEST, 1986, 87; mem. small christian communities design team Archdiocese of Hartford, 1987-91; mem. major events design team RENEW, 1986; subcommn. chair Archdiocesan Office of Synod, 1991; mem. New Eng. team Ministry of Money, 1984-90, 93; mem. The New Century Hymnal editl. com. United Ch. of Christ, 1993-95; active Pediats. AIDS Unit Yale-New Haven Hosp., Covenant to Care, Voices of Joy Gospel Choir women imprisioned at Niantic. Grantee Lilly Endowment, 1989-90, 91-93; recipient Ho. of Reps. citation Commonwealth of Pa., 1968, Women in Leadership Edn. award YWCA Conn., 1989, Convenant to Care award for ministry to children, 1993; named to McMaster U. Alumni Gallery, 1982, Celebration of 120 Women in Leadership, 1987, Bayley-Ellard H.S. Hall of Fame, 1993, Conn. Women's Hall of Fame, 2002. Mem. ASCAP (Popular Awards list 1968—), AAUW (Excellence in Equity award Conn. chpt. 1995), Nat. Assn. Pastoral Musicians, N.Am. Acad. of Liturgy, Societas Liturgica. Avocations: photography, calligraphy. Office: Hartford Sem 77 Sherman St Hartford CT 06105-2260 Office Phone: 860-509-9558.

WINTER, NANCY FITZ, retired media and public relations executive; b. Farmville, Va., Dec. 8, 1949; d. James Herbert Fitz Sr. and Hazel Virginia Adams; m. Louis Eugene Winter Jr., Feb. 3, 1973 (div. Nov. 1986); 1 child, Ross Monroe; m. Robert William Olney, June 8, 1991 (dec. Dec. 2001). BS, Va. Commonwealth U., 1972; MA, Am. U., 1976. Asst. editor of publs. Life Ins. Co. of Va., Richmond, 1972-75; reporter, photographer Hanover Herald Progress, Ashland, Va., 1975; reporter Sta. WTVR-TV, Richmond, 1976-77; CEO Media Dynamics, Richmond, 1977-80; morning anchor, reporter Sta. WWBT-TV, Richmond, 1978-80; field prodr. Newsweek Broadcasting, N.Y.C., 1977-80, Sta. WUSA-TV, Washington, 1977-80; polit. reporter Sta. WTVR-TV, Richmond, 1980-81; dir. devel. Richmond Meml. Hosp., 1982—84; v.p. mktg. and comm. Am. Heart Assn. Va., 1984-97; cons. in field Richmond, 1997-99; pub. rels. profl. Commonwealth of Va. Dept. Health, Richmond, 1999—2003; ret., 2004. Recipient awards, Va. Soc. Hosp. Mktg. and Pub. Rels. Mem.: Pub. Rels. Soc. Am., Nat. Pub. Health Info. Coalition, Richmond Pub. Rels. Assn. Episcopalian. Avocations: antiques, travel, reading, painting, genealogy.

WINTER, PATRICIA LEA, psychologist, researcher; b. Newport Beach, Calif., Dec. 17, 1958; d. William Sherman Stowell and Ruby Jean Thomas Koellisch; m. Christopher Scott Winter, Dec. 30, 1978 (div. 1998); children: William Ernest, Jacob Thomas. BA, U. Calif., Irvine, 1980; MA, Claremont Grad. Sch., 1984, PhD in Psychology, 1990. Rsch. coord. Casa Colina Rehab. Hosp., Pomona, Calif., 1984-88; asst. prof. Chaffey Coll., Rancho Cucamonga, Calif., 1988-89; lectr. Riverside (Calif.) C.C., 1990-92, Calif. State U., Fullerton, 1988-91, Calif. State Poly., Pomona, 1990-92, 94; rsch. social scientist USDA Forest Svc., Riverside, 1992—. External cons. Kaiser Permanente, Walnut Creek, Calif., 1990-92. Contbr. articles to profl. jours.

Mem. Am. Psychological Assn., Western Psychological Assn., Soc. Risk Analysis. Democrat. Christian. Achievements include evaluation of an innovative European head injury treatment program applied in the U.S.; research on cultural diversity, environmental attitudes and actions, social trust and agency/public interactions. Office: USDA Forest Svc 4955 Canyon Crest Dr Riverside CA 92507-6071 Business E-Mail: pwinter@fs.fed.us.

WINTER, RUTH, artist; b. N.Y.C., Jan. 17, 1913; d. Benjamin and Yetta (Rosenberg) Cohen; m. Alexander Winter, Apr. 4, 1941; 1 child, James. BS, NYU, 1931, MA, 1932. Artist Robert M. Coates Art Galleries, N.Y.C., 1957, Stuart Preston Art, N.Y.C., 1957, Painting Televised, Boston, 1958. Exhibited in shows at Silvermine, Conn., 1957-61, Nat. Assn. Women Artists, 1957-68, Gallery 15, 1959, Bklyn. Museum, 1960, Nat. Acad. Design, 1960, Lever House, 1963, 67, Pepsi Cola Exhibition, 1964; painting reproduced in N.Y. Times, 1957. Recipient Max Law award, 1959, Maylow award Mahopec Art League, 1959. Mem. Art Students League, Nat. Assn. Women Artists. Avocation: swimming. Home: 357 Malin Rd Newtown Square PA 19073-4318

WINTER, RUTH GROSMAN (MRS. ARTHUR WINTER), journalist; b. Newark, May 29, 1930; d. Robert Delmas and Rose (Rich) Grosman; m. Arthur Winter, June 16, 1955; children: Robin, Craig, Grant. BA, Upsala Coll., 1951; MS, Pace U., 1989. With Houston Press, 1955-56; gen. assignment Newark Star Ledger, 1951-55, sci. editor, 1956-69; columnist L.A. Times Syndicate, 1973-78, Register and Tribune, syndicate, 1981-85, isyndicate.com, 1999-2001. Columnist myskinMD.com, 2000-01; contbr. to consumer mags.; instr. St. Peters Coll., Jersey City.; vis. lectr. mag. writing Rutgers U. Author: Poisons in Your Food, rev. edits., 1971, 91, 99, 2004, How to Reduce Your Medical Bills, 1970, A Consumer's Dictionary of Food Additives, 1972, 3d rev. edit., 1994, 99, 2004, Vitamin E, The Miracle Worker, 1972, So You Have Sinus Trouble, 1973, Ageless Aging, 1973, So You Have a Pain in the Neck, 1974, rev. edit., 2000, A Consumer's Dictionary of Cosmetic Ingredients, 1974, 4th rev. edit., 1994, 6th rev. edit., 2005, Don't Panic, 1975, The Fragile Bond: Marriage in the 70's, 1976, Triumph Over Tension, 1976 (N.J. Press Women's Book award), Scent Talks Among Animals, 1977, Cancer Causing Agents: A Preventive Guide, 1979, The Great Self-Improvement Sourcebook, 1980, The Scientific Case Against Smoking, 1980, People's Guide to Allergies and Allergens, 1984, A Consumer's Guide to Medicines in Food, 1995, So What Can I Eat?, 2006; co-author: The Lean Line One Month Lighter Program, 1985, Thin Kids Program, 1985, Build Your Brain Power, 1986, Eat Right: Be Bright, 1988, A Consumer's Dictionary of Medicines: Prescription, Over-the-Counter and Herbal, 1994, 97, Super Soy,: The Miracle Bean, 1996, rev. edit., 2000, Pain in the Neck, 1997, rev. edit., 2000, Anti Aging Hormones, 1997, Brain Workout, 1997, 2003, Vitamin E: Your Protection Against Exercise Fatigue, Weakened Immunity, Heart Disease, Cancer, Aging, Diabetic Damage, Environmental Toxins, 1998, Smart Food, 1999, The Female Athlete's Body Book: Preventing and Treating Sports Injuries in Women and Girls, 2003, What Can I Eat? 2006. Recipient award of merit ADA, 1966, Cecil award Arthritis Found., 1967, Am. Soc. Anesthesiologists award, 1969, Arthritis Found. award, 1978; named Alumnus of Year Upsala Coll., 1971, Woman of Year N.J. Daily Newspaper Women, 1971, Woman of Achievement Millburn Short Hills Profl. and Bus. Women's Assn., 1991, Golden Triangle award Am. Dermatol. Assn., 1998. Mem. Soc. Mag. Writers, Authors League, Nat. Assn. Sci. Writers, Am. Med. Writers Assn. (Eric Martin Meml. award), N.J. Daily Newspaper Women (awards news series 1958, 70, named Woman of Achievement 1971, 83), Am. Soc. Journalists and Authors (pres. 1977-78, spl. service award 1983, Lifetime Achievement award 2004), N.J. Press Women (pres. 1982-84) Home and Office: 44 Holly Dr Short Hills NJ 07078-1318 E-mail: ruth@www.brainbody.com.

WINTER, SHAWNE NANISDILDA, small business owner; b. Nashville, Tenn., Sept. 19, 1974; d. Vincent Hillis Clifford and Susan Kay Lawrence; m. James William Winter, June 26, 1999; 1 child, Kalena Shaylee. Degree in Comm. and Dance with minor in Performing Arts, Beloit Coll., Wis., 1996. Posting supr. Adams Outdoor Advt., Madison, Wis., 1996—2000; asst. dir. Ptnrs. Dance Studio, Columbus, Wis., 1996—2002; receptionist Jerry's Sewing & Vacuum, Madison, 2000—02, Verona Press, Wis., 2001—02; owner, dir. Dance Dimensions Dance Studio, Stoughton, Wis., 2002—. Dir. Part II Dance Concert, Stoughton, 2002—05; founder Dance Dimensions Performance Group. Avocations: dance, music, movies. Office: Dance Dimensions 1401 E Main St Stoughton WI 53589 Business E-Mail: ddimensions@msn.com.

WINTERER-SCHULZ, BARBARA JEAN, graphics designer, writer; b. Manchester, N.H., Apr. 1, 1938; d. John Edward and Elizabeth Virginia Grace; m. Allen George Winterer, Mar. 30, 1959 (div. 1977); children: Audrey Lyn Winterer-Chavez, Amy Jo Winterer DeNoble. AA, Mesa (Ariz.) CC, 1980; BS summa cum laude, U. Md., Heidelberg, Germany, 1996; postgrad. Sheriff's Tng. Acad., Montezuma County, Colo.; grad., U. Colo., 2004. Art designer Morningstar Art Design Studio, Dolores, Colo., 1988—. Interpreter Colo. State Pk.; U.S. rail ranger Durango-Silverton R.R.; master gardener Colo. State U.; bd. dirs. S.W. Cmty. Resources; health care provider Archuleta County Sch. Dist., Pagosa Springs, Colo.; farm medic.; guest lectr. Northern Ariz. Univ., Mesa Verda Nat. Pk., UNESCO World Heritage Ctr. Contbr. articles to newspapers and jours. Asst. dir. Ariz. Myasthenia Gravis Found., 1977—80; ofcl. U.S. reporter World Eskimo Indian Olympics, Fairbanks, Alaska, 1994; mem. disaster response team ARC, Pagosa Springs, mem. Durango chpt.; bd. dirs., chmn. pub. rels. com. Habitat for Humanity, Pagosa Springs; interpreter Chimney Rock Hist. Archeol. Site; interpretive docent, vol. Bur. Land Mgmt., Anasazi Heritage Ctr. Mus., 2004—; mem. Friends of Libr., Dolores, Colo. Recipient Humanitarian award, Phila. Inst. Human Potential, 1972, Chancellor of Germany award for Acad. Achievement, 1986, citation of Meritorious Achievement award in the Arts and Humanitarianism, Internat. Biog. Ctr., 1997; scholar, Chancellor of Germany. Mem.: AAUW, Colo. Archeology Soc., Hihitsanom Archeol. Soc., Pub. Lands Interpretive Assn., Libr. of Congress (assoc.), Internat. Rotary Club, Nat. Fedn. Garden Clubs, Cortez Garden Club (pres.), Colo. Fedn. Garden Clubs, Phi Theta Kappa, Alpha Sigma Lambda. Avocations: gardening, gourmet cooking. Office: Morningstar Art Design Studio PO Box 388 Dolores CO 81323-0388

WINTERHALTER, DOLORES (DEE) AUGUST, art educator; b. Pitts., Mar. 22, 1928; d. Joseph Peter and Helen August; m. Paul Joseph Winterhalter, June 21, 1947 (dec.); children: Noreen, Audrey, Mark. Student, Yokohama, Japan, 1963-64, Paris, 1968-70, La Romita Sch. Art, Terni, Italy, 2001, Venice Art Ctr. Workshops Home Study Classes. Cert. tchr. Japanese Flower Arranging, Kamakuri Wood Carving. Tchr. YWCA, Greenwich, Conn., 1978-84, Friends of the Arts and Scis., Sarasota, Fla., 1992—; tchr./lectr. classes and workshops, 2004; tchr. workshops Venice Art Ctr. and Home Studios, 2004—. Staff Hilton Leech Art Studio and Gallery, Sarasota; events chmn. State of Fla. Watercolor Exhbn., Sarasota, 1995; cultural exch. tchr. univs., fine arts acads., China; tchr. Venice Art Ctr., Sarasota, 1996—2003, Art Ctr., Sarasota, 1999—2002; Hilton Leech Tchr., Sarasota, 1996—99; mem. Women's Caucus of Arts in Am., 1996—98; selected demonstrator Fine Arts of Sarasota, 1995—98; paper cons. D'Arches Watercolor Paper Co., Paris, 1983—2000; tchr., judge Sumie Inks; demonstrator Fla. Watercolor Conv., Ocala, 2000; workshop instr. Venice Watercolor/Monoprint and Sumi-e, Fla., 2006—; tchr. Our Lady of Mount Carmel, Osprey, Fla.; lectr., presenter in field. Exhbns. Xiam, China, 1994, Creators Tour of Fine Arts Soc. Sarasota, 1994-2001; exhibited in group shows at Womens Contemporary Art Soc., 2005 (2d prize); pvt. and corp. collections; judge Englewood Fla. Art Exhbn., 2005. Pres., Am. Women's Club, Genoa, Italy, 1962; fundariser for scholarships Collectors and Creators Tour of Fine Arts Soc. of Sarasota, 1994. Recipient numerous awards Old Greenwich (Conn.) Art Assn., 1971-84, Sarasota, 1985, Collectors and Creators Tour award Fine Arts Soc. Sarasota, 1994, Pat Buckman award, 2000; named Artist of Yr., Fine Arts Soc. Sarasota, 1994, Venice Art Ctr., 2000. Mem. Suncoast Fla. Watercolor Soc. (life), Fla. Watercolor Soc., Long Boat Key Art Assn., Sarasota Art Assn., Sumi-e Soc. Am., Nat. League Am. PEN Women (pres. 1994-96, scholarship bd. 1996-98), Internat. Soc. Marine Painters (signature mem.), Venice Art Ctr., Art Sarasota, Womens Contemporary Arts Soc. (tchr., lectr. 2004). Democrat. Roman Catholic. Avocations: wood carving, travel, bridge, creative design in crochet and fashion. Home and Office: 4027 Westbourne Cir Sarasota FL 34238-3249

WINTERHOF, SUZANNE, music educator; d. John Leonard and Vera R Johnson; m. Vernon Winterhof, Aug. 9, 1959; children: Jeanette Hinkeldey, Janece Valentine. BA, Buena Vista Coll., Storm Lake, Iowa, 1959. Cert. music tchr. Music Teachers Nat. Assn., 1985. Elem. music tchr. Aurelia Cmty. Sch., Aurelia, 1969—; dir. of ch. music St. John Luth. Ch., Storm Lake, 1958—. Pvt. piano tchr., Aurelia. 4-H leader and vol. Iowa 4-H, Aurelia, 1975—2006. Master: Iowa Music Tchrs. Assn. (local chair 1981—2006); mem.: Am. Guild of Organists (sec. 1995—2006), Hanover Hist. Soc. Avocations: genealogy, sewing. Home: 6194 Y Ave Aurelia IA 51005 Personal E-mail: swinterhof@aurelia.k12.ia.us.

WINTER-NEIGHBORS, GWEN CAROLE, special education educator, art educator, consultant; b. Greenville, S.C., July 14, 1938; d. James Edward (dec. 2002) and Evelyn (Lee) Walters (dec. 1998); m. David M. Winter Jr., Aug., 1963 (dec. Feb. 1980); children: Robin Carole Winter, Charles G. McCuen, Dustin Winter TeBrugge; m. Thomas Frederick Neighbors, Mar. 24, 1989. BA in Edn. and Art, Furman U., 1960, MA in Psychology, 1967; cert. in guidance/pers., Clemson U., 1981; EdD in Youth and Mid. Childhood Edn., Nova Southeastern U., 1988; postgrad., U. S.C., Spartanburg, 1981-89; cert. clear specialist instrn. with honors, Calif. State U., Northridge, 1991; art edn. cert., Calif. State U., L.A., 1991; JD, Glendale U., 1999. Cert. tchr. art, elem. edn., psychology, secondary guidance, S.C. Tchr. 7th grade Greenville Jr. H.S., 1960—63; art tchr. Wade Hampton H.S., Greenville, 1963—67; prin. adult edn. Woodmont H.S., Piedmont, SC, 1983—85, Mauldin H.S., Greenville and Mauldin, SC, 1981; tchr. ednl. psychology edn. dept. Allen U., Columbia, SC, 1969; activity therapist edn. dept. S.C. Dept. of Corrections, Columbia, 1973—76; art specialist gifted edn. Westcliffe Elem. Sch., Greenville, 1976—89; tchr. self-contained spl. day class Elysian Heights Elem. Sch., Echo Park and L.A., Calif., 1989—91; art tchr. med. drawing Sch. Dist. Greenville County Blue Ridge Mid. Sch., Greer, 1991—95; tchr./asst. head edn. dept. N. Creenville Coll., 2001—02. Participant nat. conf. U.S. Dept. Edn./So. Bell, Columbia, 1989; com. mem. nat. exec. com. Nova Southeastern U., 1988—89; asst. chmn., tchr. edn. dept. North Greenville Coll., 2001, adm., staff, 01, U. S.C., Spartanburg; adj., student tchr., supr. U. SC, 2002; adv. bd. S.C. Gov. Sch. for Arts and Humanities; parent/tchr. adv. bd. Spl. Edn.; adj. prof U. SC Univ. Ctr., Greenville, 2002—03; ind. rep. Primerica Fin. Svs., 2003—. Mozart Book, 1988; author: Let's Sing a Song About America, 1988 (1st pl. Nat. Music award, 1990), numerous poems; featured poet: Internat. Libr. Poetry, 2004. Life mem. Rep. Presdl. Task Force, 1970—; mem. voter registration com. Lexington County Rep. Party, 1970—80; grand jury participant 13th Jud. Ct. Sys., Greenville, 1986—88, guardian ad litem, 1988—2005; mem. arts educators adv. task force S.C. Gov. Sch. Arts and Humanities, 2002—04; mem. spl. edn. parent adv. bd. representing Sue Cleveland Elem. Sch. Greenville Co. Sch. Dist., Spl. Edn. Topics and Trends, 2001—06; poll mgr. Greenville Co.; bd. dirs., vice chmn. Webb-Atkins Inst. of Change, 2006—; vice chmn. bd. dirs. Webb-Akins Inst. Change. Tchr. Incentive grantee Sch. Dist. Greenville County, 1986-88, Project Earth grantee Bell South, 1988-89, 94-95, Edn. Improvement Act/Nat. Dissimination Network grantee S.C. State Dept. Edn., 1987-88, Targett 2,000 Arts in Curricular grantee S.C. Dept. Edn., 1994-95, Alliance grantee Bus. Cmty. Greenville, 1992-95, Greer Art Rsch. grantee, 1993-94, S.C. Govs. Sch. Study grantee, 1994, Edn. Improvement Act Competitive Tchr. grantee S.C. Dept. Edn., 1994-95, Alliance Grand grant, 1995-96; recipient Am. Jurisprudence Bancroft-Whitney award Glendale U. Sch. Law, 1997, 98, Excellence Recognition in Real Property award Glendale Law Faculty, 1997, Excellence in Art of Appellate Advocacy, Glendale U. Sch. Law, 1998, Am. Jurisprudence Bancroft-Whitney award Constl. Law I, 1998. Mem.: ABA, Palmetto State Tchr. Assn., S.C. Art Edn. Assn., S.C. Arts Alliance, Nat. Mus. Women in Arts, Nat. Art Edn. Assn., Furman U. Singer Alumni, Phi Delta Kappa. Baptist Avocations: computers, art, writing, music. Office Phone: 214-499-4619. Personal E-mail: gwen.neighbors@gmail.com.

WINTERS, BARBARA JO, musician; b. Salt Lake City; d. Louis McClain and Gwendolyn (Bradley) W. AB cum laude, UCLA, 1960, postgrad., 1961, Yale, 1960. Mem. oboe sect. L.A. Philharm., 1961-94, prin. oboist, 1972-94; ret. Clinician oboe, English horn, Oboe d'amore. Recs. movie, TV sound tracks. Avocation: painting. Home: 3529 Coldwater Canyon Ave Studio City CA 91604-4060 Office: 151 S Grand Ave Los Angeles CA 90012-3013

WINTERS, JACKIE F., small business owner, foundation administrator; b. Topeka, Apr. 19, 1937; m. Marc Winters; 4 children. Student, Oreg. State U. Cert. Policy Alternatives Flemming Fellow. Clk. Oreg. Med. Sch., 1959—69; asst. Oreg. Gov. Tom McCall, 1969—79, Oreg. Gov. Vic Atiyeh, 1979—81; owner Jackie's Ribs, 1985—; mem. Oreg. Ho. of Reps., 1998—2002, Oreg. Senate, 2003—. Campaign chair United Way Marion/Polk Counties; active Govs. Task Force on Mental Health, Cmty. Partnership Task Force Oreg. State Fair. Republican. Office: 900 Court St NE S-212 Salem OR 97301 Office Phone: 503-986-1710.

WINTERS, KAREN CRISPELL, educator; b. Wilkes-Barre, Pa., May 9, 1944; d. Loren Nathan and Mary (Jones) Crispell; m. Raymond Winters, May 12, 1973. BA, Coll. Misericordia, Dallas, Pa., 1965; MS in Edn., Mansfield (Pa.) U., 1985; PhD, Pa. State U., 1991. Lic. comprehensive English reading specialist, Pa. Tchr. Williamsport (Pa.) Area Sch. Dist., 1970-82, Am. Community Sch., Amman, Jordan, 1982-83; instr. English Williamsport Area C.C., 1984-85; asst. edn. theory and policy Pa. State U., University Park, 1986-87, instr. Hazleton, 1989; researcher, writer Nat. Commn. Employment Policy, Washington, 1987; instr. Piedmont C.C., Roxboro, N.C., 1988-89; asst. prof. Bloomsburg (Pa.) U., 1991, Lock Haven (Pa.) U., 1991—. Cons. EduSearch, State College, Pa., 1990—. Co-author, sr. project dir. An Investigation of Education Options for Youth-at-Risk Ages 9-15, 1988. Mem.: Phi Kappa Phi, Phi Delta Kappa. Home: 235 Spring St State College PA 16801-7161 Office: Lock Haven U Lock Haven PA 17745 Office Phone: 570-893-2487.

WINTERS, MARJORIE K., retired writer, editor, researcher; b. Chgo., Ill., Apr. 8, 1931; d. Daniel H. and Marian H. Knop; m. Harold A. Winters, Aug. 20, 1955. BS with honors, No. Ill. U., DeKalb, Ill., 1953, MS, 1954. Tchr. English DeKalb H.S., DeKalb, Ill., 1954—55, Glencoe Sch., Glencoe, Ill., 1956—59, Portland State U., Portland, Oreg., 1959—60, Justin Morrill Coll., Mich. State U., East Lansing, Mich., 1960—62; editor African Studies Ctr., Mich. State U., East Lansing, Mich., 1967—81; mktg. specialist Orval Kent Foods, Wheeling, Ill., 1983—83; restaurant critic & food columnist Lansing Mag., Lansing, Mich., 1981—82; cookware buyer & demonstrator Grande Gourmet, Lansing, Mich., 1984—86; restaurant critic Lansing State Jour., Lansing, Mich., 1988—90. Coord. of entries on African studies Ency. Brit., 1974—74; contest judge Mich. Pork Prodrs. Assn., Lansing, Mich., 1992; prodn. editor Rev. African Studies, African Urban Studies & Rural Africana, East Lansing, Mich. Author (with Duke Winters): Adventurous Eating in Michigan: 101 Special Restaurants & Recipes; editor (with Harold Winters): Applications in Geographic Research; author (with Duke Winters): Adventurous Eating in Michigan: A Restaurant Guide & Cookbook; author: (poem) Trial & Error; contbr. articles pub. to profl. jour., chapters to books. Mem.: Las Vegas Art Mus., Nat. Wild Horse Assn., Trout Unlimited. American Independent. Avocations: fly fishing, food & wine seminars & events, travel, reading. Home: 3024 High Range Dr Las Vegas NV 89134 Personal E-mail: marjduke@cox.net.

WINTERS, MARTHA PATRICE, history and language educator; d. Charles LeRoy and Jacqueline Cleve Winters. BA in Letters, U. Okla., Norman, 1975, MA in Latin, 1978. Tchr. Latin, world history Ardmore H.S., Okla., 1978—85, Ctrl. Mid-H.S., Norman, Okla., 1985—97; tchr. world history Norman North H.S., Okla., 1997—2005, tchr. Latin, world history, 2005—. Pres. Okla. Fgn. Lang. Tchrs. Assn., 1980—81; com. People to People-Social Studies, South Africa, 2004. Mem.: Nat. Coun. for Social Studies, Am. Classical League. Republican. Office: Norman North HS 1809 Stubbeman Ave Norman OK 73069 E-mail: mwinters@norman.k12.ok.us.

WINTER-SWITZ, CHERYL DONNA, travel company executive; b. Jacksonville, Fla., Dec. 6, 1947; d. Jacqueline Marie (Carroll) Winter; m. Frank C. Snedaker, June 24, 1974 (div. May 1976); m. Robert William Switz, July 1, 1981. AA, City Coll. of San Francisco, 1986; BS, Golden Gate U., 1990, MBA, 1992. Bookkeeper, agt. McQuade Tours, Ft. Lauderdale, Fla., 1967-69; mgr. Boca Raton (Fla.) Travel, 1969-76; owner, mgr. Ocean Travel, Boca Raton, 1976-79; ind. contractor Far Horizons Travel, Boca Raton, 1979-80; mgr. Tara/BPF Travel, San Francisco, 1981-84; mgr. travel. dept. Ernst & Whinney/Lifeco Travel, San Francisco, 1984-86; travel cons. Golden Gate U., San Francisco, 1986-99, Siemer & Hand Travel, San Francisco, 1989-99, Ravenel Travel, Charleston, SC, 1999-2000, Carlson Carolina Travel, Mt. Pleasant, SC, 2000—02, Sato/Navigant Travel, 2003—04; mgr. travel dept. WareOnEarth Comm., Inc., Charleston, 2004—. Instr. Golden Gate U., 1986-99, U. San Francisco. Mem. Amateur Trapshooting Assn., Hotel and Restaurant Mgmt. Club. Republican. Episcopalian. Avocations: trap shooting, gardening, cooking, travel, reading. Home: 1189 W Park View Pl Mount Pleasant SC 29466-7910 Office: WareOnEarth Comm Inc 2457 Aviation Ave Ste 200 N Charleston SC 29406

WINTHROP, EMILIE See CUTHBERT, EMILIE

WINTON, LINDA, international trainer, consultant; b. Phila. BA in Secondary Edn. and Spanish, La Salle Coll., Phila., 1971—75; MA in Spanish Lang. and Lit., NYU, Madrid, 1978—79; MS in Adult Edn. and Human Resource Tng. and Devel., U. So. Maine, Gorham, 1990—91. Cert. Tchr. Spanish Pa. Dept. Edn., 1975, NJ Dept. Edn., 1975, Tchr. French NJ Dept. Edn., 1977, Exhbn. Mgr. Internat. Assn. Exhbn. Mgmt., 2003. Spanish and French tchr. Willingboro HS, NJ, 1975—77; ESL instr. Camden Learning Ctr., NJ, 1975—77, Shell Oil Co., Madrid, 1977—79, Inst. Internat. Madrid, 1977—79, Aldeasa, Madrid, 1977—79; export sales Wheatland Tube Co., EMSI, Pa., 1979—81; Spanish and French tchr. Haddonfield HS, 1981—82; Spanish instr. U. Ky., 1982—84; dir. Gorham Adult and Cmty. Edn., Maine, 1989—93; prin. Tng. Assocs. Maine, 1990—91; sales rep., account exec. Diversified Expn., Maine, 1994—97; pres., CEO New Markets Internat. LLC, Falmouth, Maine, 1997—. Programmer Tampa Bay Coun. Internat. Visitors, Fla., 1986—87; sr. programmer Maine Coun. Internat. Visitors, 2000—. Recipient Ofines award for study linguistics, 1978; fellow, Nat. Endowment Humanities, 1984. Mem.: Meeting Profls. Internat. (internat. devel. com. 2000—01, global issues adv. group 2001—02, New Eng. chpt. fin. com. 2001—02, New Eng. chpt. internat. membership com. 2002—03, New Eng. chpt. membership com. 2002—04, New Eng. chpt. liaison to multicultural initiative 2003—05, New Eng. chpt. bd. dirs. 2004—05), Internat. Assn. Exhbn. Mgmt. (dept. commerce liaison com. 2001—03, CEM commn. 2003—). Office: New Markets Internat LLC 12 Arbor Rd Falmouth ME 04105 Office Phone: 207-781-2019. Business E-Mail: umi@maine.rr.com.

WINTOUR, ANNA, editor-in-chief; b. London, Nov. 3, 1949; arrived in U.S., 1976; d. Charles and Elinor Wintour; m. David Shaffer, Sept. 1984 (div. 2001); children: Charles, Kate; m. J. Shelby Bryan. Student, Queens Coll., 1963—67. Deputy fashion editor Harper's and Queen Mag., London, 1970—76; fashion editor Harper's Bazaar, NY, 1976—77; fashion and beauty editor Viva Mag., NY, 1977—78; contbg. editor fashion and style Savvy Mag., NY, 1980—81; sr. editor NY Mag., 1981—83; creative dir. US Vogue, NY, 1983—86; editor-in-chief British Vogue, London, 1986—87, House and Garden, NY, 1987—88, Vogue, NY, 1988—. Office: Vogue 4 Times Sq New York NY 10036*

WINTZ, MARILYN BELLE, retired elementary school educator; b. Aspen, Colo., Feb. 14, 1940; d. Fred Arthur and Mary Alta (Sturm) Cook; m. Rodney G. Wintz, June 16, 1963; children: Marilee, Shirrae. BA, U. No. Colo., 1962; MA, Adams State Coll., 1990; PhD, Denver U., 2005. Cert. administr., Colo. Tchr. El Paso Sch. Dist. 11, Colorado Springs, Colo., 1962-63, Creede Sch. Dist. 1, Colo., 1963—2003; ret., 2003. Ranch mgr. Wason Ranch Corp., Creede, 1963-2003. Named Tchr. of Yr., Creede Sch. Dist. 1, San Luis Valley Bd. of Coop. Ednl. Svcs. Mem. Nat. Coun. Tchrs. Math., Assn. for Curriculum and Devel., Internat. Reading Assn., Colo. Coun. Internat. Reading. Avocations: gardening, photography, guitar, canoeing, cross country skiing. Mailing: PO Box 750 Creede CO 81130

WINZER, P.J., lawyer; b. Shreveport, La., June 7, 1947; d. C.W. Winzer and Pearlene Hall Winzer Tobin. BA in Polit. Sci., So. U., Baton Rouge, 1968; JD, UCLA, 1971. Bar: Calif. 1972, U.S. Supreme Ct. 1986. Staff atty. Office of Gen. Counsel, U.S. HEW, Washington, 1971-80; asst. spl. counsel U.S. Office of Spl. Counsel Merit Systems Protection Bd., Dallas, 1980-82; regional dir. U.S. Merit Systems Protection Bd., Akexandria, Va., 1982—. Mem. Calif. Bar Assn., Fed. Cir. Bar Assn., Delta Sigma Theta. Office: US Merit System Protection 1800 Diagnol Rd Ste 205 Alexandria VA 22314-2840

WIRICK, LINDA JANE, medical/surgical nurse; b. Connellasille, Pa., Oct. 14, 1957; d. Eugene Smith and Rebecca Jane Miller; m. Brian Lee Wirick, July 25, 1985; children: Richard, Robert, Matthew, Christopher Theodore, Justin, Nicholas. Med. sec. degree, Westmoreland Cmty. Coll.; AA, Penn State. Oncology nurse Uniontown Hosp. Home: 106Spartan Ct Uniontown PA 15401

WIRKUS, CARRIE, elementary school educator; d. Edward and Carol Lary; m. Gary J. Wirkus, Apr. 25, 1992; children: Sawyer, Zara Jo, Croix. AS, U. Wis., Wausau, 1988; BS in Elem. Edn., U. Wis., River Falls, 1990; MEd in Profl. Devel., U. Wis., La Crosse, 2004. Tchr. St. Charles Sch., Lena, Wis., 1992—94, St. John's Sch., Edgar, Wis., 1994—97, Medford (Wis.) Area Mid. Sch., 1997—. Libr. bd., Dorchester, Wis., 2005—06; ch. tchr. Edgar, Wis., 1994—96. Mem.: Wis. Math. Coun. (assoc.), Nat. Coun. Tchrs. Math. (assoc.). Home: 5862 Reynolds Ave Dorchester WI 54425 Office: Medford Area Mid Sch 509 E Clark St Medford WI 54451 Office Phone: 715-748-2516.

WIRTH, KELLEY K., state representative; b. Panorama City, Calif., Aug. 2, 1965; children: Kennedy, Meghan. BS, Oreg. State U., 1989; MS, U. So. Calif., 1992. State rep., dist. 16 Oreg. House Rep., Salem, 2001—; sys. analyst, planning commr. City of Corvallis, Oreg., 1996—; sys. analyst Asst. to 3d Infantry Divsn. Chief of Staff, 1993—99. Adj. computer tech. faculty City Colls. Chgo.-Europe, 1992; bd. mem. Land Devel. Hearings Bd. City of Corvallis, 1998—, mem. Neighborhood Tech. Rev. Group, 1997—. Mem.: Corvallis LWV. Democrat. Episcopalian. Office: 900 Court St NE H-479 Salem OR 97301 Office Phone: 503-986-1416. Personal E-mail: wirthk@comcast.net.

WIRTH, TAMARA L., music educator; b. Steubenville, Ohio, July 18, 1968; d. William Harry and Elva Elizabeth Jones; m. Douglas Harry Wirth; children: Matthew Robert, Bradley Douglas. BS in Music Edn., Ind. U., Pa., 1990; MA in Edn., Marygrove Coll., 2005. Organist, choir dir. Paris (Pa.) Presbyn. Ch., 1985—92; organist Trinity United Meth. Ch., Spencerville, 1993—97; substitute tchr. various sch., Allen and Auglaize counties, Ohio, 1993—98; music tchr. St. Joseph Cath., Wapakoneta, Ohio, 1998—. Sec. St. Joseph PTO, Wapakoneta, 1999—2003, Spencerville PTO, 1998—2002. Democrat. Avocations: crafts, sewing, aerobics. Home: 8656 Deep Cut Rd Spencerville OH 45887 Office: St Joseph Cath Sch 1101 Lincoln Hwy Wapakoneta OH 45895

WIRTSCHAFTER, IRENE NEROVE, tax specialist, consultant, military officer; b. Elgin, Ill., Aug. 05; d. David A. and Ethel G. Nerove; m. Burton Wirtschafter, June 2, 1945 (dec. 1966). BCS, Columbus U., 1942. Cert. tax profl., enrolled agt., IRS. Commd. ensign Supply Corps, USN, 1944, advanced through grades to capt., 1975; comdg. officer Res. Supply Unit,

1974—75; ret., 1976; agt. Office Internat. Ops. IRS, 1967—75; internat. banking specialist; real estate profl., appraiser, 1976—80; pvt. practice tax cons. Cocoa Beach, Fla. Sr. intern program U.S. Senate, 1981; mem. Sec. Navy's Adv. Com. Ret. Pers., 1984—86, VA Adv. Com. Women Vets., 1987—90. Past troop leader Girl Scouts U.S.A.; lt. col. and mission pilot CAP, 21 air races; comml. instrument pilot land and sea; Navy liaison officer Commd.'s Retiree Coun., Patrick AFB, 1985—89; mem. Nat. Com. Internat. Forest of Friendship, Atchison, Kans., 1976—; elected silver rep. Nat. Silver Haired Congress, 1977—2001; elected rep. Silver Haired Legis., 1984, Silver Haired Senate, 1988—; trustee Internat. Women's Air and Space Mus., 1993—, bd. dirs., 1999—; state rep. Nat. Soc. to Preserve Social Security and Medicare, 1999; bd. dirs., treas. Honor Am., 2001—05; sec. Navy League, 2000; cons. Jr. Achievement, 1989—94; founder sr. action com. Brevard County, 1981; chmn. College Park Airport Johnny Horizon Day, 1975; elected dir. Fla. Space Coast Philharm., 1985—, treas., 1986—92; bd. dirs., adv. mgr. Cocoa Beach Citizen's League, 1990—92; co-chmn. Internat. Women's Yr. Take Off Dinner, Washington, 1976; 1st v.p. Friends of Cocoa Beach Libr., 1988—90, pres., 1990—92, bd. dirs., 1993—; apptd. to Cocoa Beach Libr. Br., 1996—; mem. Cocoa Beach Bus. Improvement Coun.; elected senator Silver Haired Legislature, Fla., 1985—; vol., founding mem. Brevard Zoo; chmn. Cocoa Beach Code Enforcement Bd., 1989—96; co-chmn. sr. adv. com. Cape Canaveral Hosp., 1994—; trustee Assn. Naval Aviation, 1988—. Named Hon. Citizen, Winnipeg, Man., Can., 1966, Atchison, 1989, New Orleans, 1988, Hon. Dep. State Fire Marshal, Fla., 1987, Ky. Col., La. Col.; recipient cert. of appreciation, Cocoa Beach Women's Club, 2000, Svc. Above Self award, Rotary, 1998. Mem.: RMGS, TROA, AAUW, Navy League (sec. 2001), WAVES Nat. (bd. dirs. chpt. 75 1989—, founder), Cocoa Beach Area C. of C., Assn. Enrolled Agts., Banana River Squadron (founder, comptr. 1984—), Assn. Naval Aviation (nat. trustee 1988—), Naval Order U.S. (treas. nat. capitol commandry), Naval Res. Assn. (nat. treas. 1975—77, nat. adv. com. 1985—, Nat. award of Merit 1992), Internat. Platform Assn. (life), Ninety Nines (past chpt. sect. and nat. officer, 99 achievement awards), Jazz Soc. Brevard, Patrick Women's Golf Assn. (treas. 1996—97), Silver Wings (nat. sec. 1986, bd. dirs. 1990—, nat. v.p. 2000—, Woman of Yr. award 1985), Tailhook Assn. (life), Rotary. Avocations: aviation, golf, music. Home: 1825 Minutemen Cswy Apt 301 Cocoa Beach FL 32931-2033 Personal E-mail: irenwirt@juno.com.

WIRUM, ANDREA A., lawyer; b. Okla. City, Feb. 24, 1956; BA, Mich. State Univ., 1977; JD, Univ. Calif., Hastings, 1980. CPA 1977; bar: Calif. 1980. Ptnr. Corp. & Securities practice, mem. mng. bd. Pillsbury Winthrop Shaw Pittman, San Francisco. Office: Pillsbury Winthrop Shaw Pittman 50 Fremont St San Francisco CA 94105 Office Phone: 415-983-1735. Office Fax: 415-983-1200. Business E-Mail: andrea.wirum@pillsburylaw.com.

WIRZ, MELODY, lawyer; d. William and Maureen Pimley; m. Trey Wirz, Dec. 18, 1998; 1 child, Jaxon. BS, Okla. State U., 1997; MBA, Okla. City U., 1999; JD, U. Okla., 2004. Bar: Okla. 2004, US Patent and Trademark Office 2003. Engr. Coon Engring., Oklahoma City, 1999—2002; assoc. Dunlap, Codding & Rogers, P.C., Oklahoma City, 2003—05, Baker Botts LLP, Houston, 2005—. Home: 8530 Westerbrook Ln Humble TX 77396 Office: Baker Botts LLP 910 Louisiana St Houston TX 77002 Office Phone: 713-229-1244. Office Fax: 713-229-2844. Personal E-mail: melody.wirz+who@gmail.com. E-mail: melody.wirz@bakerbotts.com.

WISBAR, REBECCA KITTOK, lawyer; b. New Orleans, May 31, 1960; d. Clarence D. Kittok and Joan M. Desemar; m. Frederick William Wisbar; children: Taylor, Ashley. BA, U. Va., Charlottesville, 1982; JD, La. State U., Baton Rouge, 1986. Bar: La. 1986, U.S. Dist. Ct. (ea, we. and mid. dists.) La., Tex. 6. Ptnr. AKers & Wisbar LLC, Baton Rouge. Mem.: Dsylexia Assn. Greater Baton Rouge (bd. dirs. 2006—). Office: Akers & Wisbar LLC 8280 YMCA Plz Dr Bldg 8-C Baton Rouge LA 70820

WISBEY, LOU ANN, radiologist, department chairman; d. Lewis and Shamieh Tanoos; m. Bradley A. Wisbey, Dec. 26, 1993; children: Alex, Aric, Aaron. BS, Ind. U., Indpls., 1990. Lic. radiol. technologist. Radiology evening supr. Union Hosp., Terre Haute, Ind., 1982—86; radiation therapist Hux Cancer Ctr., Terre Haute, 1990—2003; radiology instr. Ivy Tech. CC, Terre Haute, 2003—06, radiology program chair, 2006—. Mem.: Am. Soc. Radiol. Technologists (cert.). Office: Ivy Tech Cmty Coll 7999 US Hwy 41 S Terre Haute IN 47802

WISDOM, EMMA NELL JACKSON, writer, educator; b. Somerville, Tex., Dec. 19, 1942; d. Herbert R.B. and Linnell Ruth (Malone) Jackson; m. Edward Henry Wisdom Jr., May 27, 1962; children: Rolanda Michelle, Edward H. III. AS, U. Tenn., 1979; BAS cum laude, Tenn. State U., 1991, MA in Edn., 1995. Lic. cosmetologist, Tenn.; cert. profl. sec. Program coord. Meharry Med. Coll., Nashville, 1980, asst. to pres., 1980-84; exec. asst. Meharry Med. Group, P.C., Nashville, 1984-86, exec. dir., 1986-89; features editor Met. Times Newspaper, Nashville, 1990; instnl. aide Tenn. State U., Nashville, 1990-93; instr. Nashville Urban League, 1997-99; writer-cons. Nashville Pride Newspaper, 1996—. Mem. nat. adv. bd. Today's Sec., N.Y.C., 1981-82; mem. adv. bd. U.S. Postal Svc., Nashville, 1994-96. Author: A Practical Guide to Planning a Family Reunion, 1988, 2d edit., 1997, Family Reunion Organizer, 1992, So You Want to Write a Book?, 1997, Dreammaker, 2006; editor: Invisible Scars and Other Writing About Relationships, 1997. Bd. dirs. Nashville Symphony Guild, 1985-89, ARC, Nashville, 1989-95; ctr. dir. Sr. Ctr. Inc. at Hadley Pk. Sr. Ctr., 2004-06. Recipient Philanthropist award in edn. The Time is Now, 1991. Mem. Wordshop Writers Group (co-founder, pres., treas. 1990-93), Tenn. Writers Alliance (founding, chmn. 1995-98, bd. dirs.). Avocations: reading, crossword puzzles. Office: Post Oak Publs PO Box 70455 Nashville TN 37207-0455 Fax: 615-228-8073. E-mail: ewisdom@aol.com.

WISE, CHRISTINA RENÉE, school disciplinarian; b. Stillwater, Okla., June 29, 1970; d. Glenn Ray and Marlene Joy (Robinson) Wise. BA in Psychology, Our Lady of Lake U., 1992; BA in Counseling, U. Tex., San Antonio, 2001. Dir. birth family svcs. ABC Adoption Agy., Inc., San Antonio, 1993—; counselor San Antonio Coll., 2005—. Vol. Animal Defense League, San Antonio, 2000. Mem.: Am. Mensa, Am. Counseling Assn., Tex. Counseling Assn. Office: San Antonio Coll 1300 San Pedro Ave San Antonio TX 78212 Personal E-mail: chwise10625@yahoo.com.

WISE, HELENA SUNNY, lawyer; b. Ridgecrest, Calif., Dec. 3, 1954; d. Strother Eldon and Mary Helen (Harinek) W.; children: Marie Evelyn, Shawnie Helene. BA with honors, UCLA, 1976; JD with highest honors, Loyola Marymount U., 1979. Bar: Calif. 1979, Nev. 1992, U.S. Dist. Ct. (ctrl. dist.) Calif. 1980, U.S. Dist. Ct. (ea. dist.) Calif. 2001, U.S. Dist. Ct. Ariz. 1992, U.S. Ct. Appeals (9th cir.) 1980, U.S. Supreme Ct. 2000. Ptnr. Geffner & Satzman, Los Angeles, 1980-87; pvt. practice Burbank, Calif., 1987—. Arbitrator talent agy. disputes SAG. Columnist Los Angeles Lawyer mag., 1985-86. Chmn., founder Barristers Child Abuse Com., L.A., 1982-86; mem. exec. bd. Vols. in Parole, L.A., 1983-90; mem. Dem. Chair's Circle, L.A., 1985; mem. adv. bd. Over Easy Found., 1987—; vol. Love is Feeding Everyone; chair Celebrity Appreciation, OMNI Youth Music awards, 2005. Fellow ABA (exec. coun. labor and employment law 1986-89, liaison young lawyers sect., bd. dirs. young lawyers divsn. 1986-88, mem. MSN team Nat. Com. on Child Abuse, del., teller Ho. of Dels. 1978-79), L.A. County Bar Assn. (v.p. sr. bar 1984-86, pres. young lawyers sect.), State Bar Calif. (bd. dirs. Calif. Young Lawyers Assn., labor law ad hoc com. on wrongful discharge, mem. juv. law com., UCLA alumni rep., USAC 1992-94, student rels. com. 1992-94, mgr. 2001-), Am. Legion Women's Auz., Simply Marie and her Canyon Country Cowboys, Shawnie and her Sassy Sax. Avocations: photography, skiing, playing organ. Office: 3111 W Burbank Blvd Ste 101 Burbank CA 91505-2350 Fax: 818-843-7958. Office Phone: 818-843-8086.

WISE, JOAN S., lawyer; b. Trenton, NJ, Aug. 11, 1941; BS in Edn., George Wash. U., 1976; MA in Remedial Reading, U. Calif., 1979; JD, Georgetown U. Bar: Md. 1984, DC 1987, US Supreme Ct. 1988. Asst. atty. gen. State of Md.; atty. to assoc. gen. counsel Am. Assn. Retired People (AARP), 1987—99, gen. counsel, 1999—. Mem.: Md. State Bar Assn., Inc., DC Bar Assn. Office: AARP 601 E St NW Washington DC 20049*

WISE, JOANNE HERBERT, art director; b. Bryn Mawr, Pa., Aug. 11, 1943; d. Charles Nugent and Carolyn (Le Maistre) Herbert; m. Douglas Wise, Nov. 26, 1976. Student, Acad. Fine Arts, Phila. Sec. to corp. v.p. Fawcett Publs., N.Y.C., 1964-66; sec. to promotion dir. Weightman Advt., Phila., 1966-70; assoc. media mgr. Scott Paper Co., Phila., 1970-75; promotion dir. Jimmy Carters Nat. Campaign, Atlanta, 1976; dir. The Wise Collection, Tokyo, Houston and N.Y.C., 1980—. Curator Japan Hands, N.Y.C., 1987-89; coord. screen project Sculptor Jiro Okura, Roanoke, Va., 1990-91; moderator, presenter Shaker/Japanese North Country Studio Conf., 1993, exec. dir., 1995—. Pub.: newsletter Current Influences in Contemporary Art, 1986—95. Pres. Tokyo/Am. Club, 1980; founder Tex. Print Alliance, Houston, 1982; exec. dir. North Country Studio Conf., 1995—. Avocations: skiing, cooking, travel, art collecting, racquet sports. Office: The Wise Collection PO Box 286 Lyme NH 03768-0286

WISE, KATHRYN E, marketing professional; b. Alexandria, Va., June 7, 1980; d. Kathryn H. and Neal E. Wise. BFA, James Madison U., Harrisonburg, Va., 2002. Jr. graphic designer Senate Rep. Conf., Washington, 2002—04; graphic designer Infocus Mktg., Inc., Warrenton, Va., 2004—05; mktg. prodn. editor ESI Internat., Inc., Arlington, Va., 2005—. Office: ESI Internat 901 North Glebe Rd Ste 200 Arlington VA 22203 Office Phone: 703-558-3000. Personal E-mail: wiseke@gmail.com.

WISE, PATRICIA, opera singer, educator; b. Wichita, Kans. d. Melvin R. and Genevieve F. (Dotson) W.; 1 child, Jennifer. B. Music Edn., U. Kans., Lawrence, 1966. Prof. voice Ind. U. Sch. Music, Bloomington, 1995—; tchr. master classes San Francisco, Vienna Conservatory, Salzburg (Austria) Mozarteum; voice tchr. Domingo Young Artist program Washington Opera. Debut as Susanna in Marriage of Figaro, Kansas City, 1966; prin. roles include Lucia, Gilda, Micaela, Juliette, Zerbinetta, Pamina, Musetta, Lulu, Violetta, Nedda, others; appeared with leading Am. opera cos. including, Chgo., Santa Fe, N.Y.C., San Francisco, Houston, San Diego, Miami, Balt., Phila., Pitts.; European appearances, 1971-76, London Royal Opera, Glyndebourne Festival, Vienna Volksoper, Geneva Opera; guest artist with Vienna, Hamburg, Munich, Cologne, Frankfurt, and Berlin State Operas; guest appearances in Madrid, Barcelona, Rome, La Scala Milan, Nice, Paris Chatelet, Zurich, Dresden, Salzburg Festival, Theatro Colon, Buenos Aires; appeared with orchs. including, Chgo. Symphony Orch., Los Angeles Symphony Orch., N.Y. Handel Soc., Israel Philharm. Orch., Vienna Philharm. Orch., N.Y. Philharm., Cleve. Orch., Berlin Symphonic Orch., BBC Orch., Nat. Orch. France; Angel Recordings; internat. TV, film appearances. Recipient Morton Baum award N.Y.C. Ctr., 1971, Dealey Meml. award Dallas Symphony, 1966, Naftzger young Artist award Wichita Symphony, 1966, Midland Young Artist award Midland (Tex.) Symphony Orch., 1966; M.B. Rockefeller Fund grantee, 1967-70; Sullivan Found. grantee, 1967-68; named Kammersänger Vienna Staatsoper, 1989. E-mail: patwise@indiana.edu.

WISE, SANDRA CASBER, lawyer; BA, Macalester Coll., 1969; JD, U. Minn., 1972. Bar: Minn. 1972, D.C., 1986, W.Va., 1987. Legis asst. to Rep. Martha Keys, Washington, 1977-78; asst. to asst. to the pres. for women's issues Sara Weddington, The White Ho., Washington, 1979; staff sub-com. on pub. assistance Ho. Com. on Ways and Means, Washington, 1980, staff sub-com. on health, 1981-85; atty. White, Fine and Verville, 1986; staff dir. sub-com. on social security Ho. Com. on Ways and Means, Washington, 1987-94, minority counsel subcom. on social security, 1995-2000; first lady State of W.Va., 2001—.

WISE, VIRGINIA JO, law educator, librarian; b. Midland, Mich., Nov. 8, 1950; d. Lester Allen and Frances Irene (Schoch) W.; m. Frederick F. Schauer, May 25, 1985. B in Gen. Studies, U. Mich., 1973, MLS, 1975; JD, Wayne State U., 1977. Bar: Calif. 1977, Tex. 1979, U.S. Dist. Ct. (no. dist.) Calif. 1978. Acquisitions and serials clk. U. Mich. Law Libr., Ann Arbor, 1973-74; asst. libr. Miller, Canfield, Paddock & Stone, Detroit, 1975-77; reference libr. Tarlton Law Libr., U. Tex., Austin, 1978-79; assoc. law libr. Harvard U. Law Libr., Cambridge, Mass., 1979-82; assoc. prof. law, dir. law libr. Boston U. Sch. Law, 1982-85; lectr. ref. libr. U. Mich., 1986-87, sr. assoc. libr., 1987-88, asst. prof. libr. and info. studies, 1988-90; lectr. Harvard U. Law Sch., 1990—2004, sr. lectr. on law, 2004—. Cons. Houghton Mifflin Pub. Co., Boston, 1985-86, UN Devel. Program, 1997-2000, STAR Project, USAID Vietnam, 2002-2004. Book rev. editor, Tex. Bar Jour., 1978-79. Mem. ALA, Am. Assn. Law Librs. (rep. Spl. Librs. Assn. 1986-88), Calif. State Bar Assn., Tex. State Bar Assn. Office: Harvard Law Sch 126 Areeda Hall Cambridge MA 02138 E-mail: wise@law.harvard.edu.

WISEHART, MARY RUTH, retired religious organization administrator; b. Myrtle, Mo., Nov. 2, 1932; d. William Henry and Ora (Harbison) W. BA, Free Will Bapt. Bible Coll., 1955, George Peabody Coll. Tchrs., 1959, MA, 1960, PhD, 1976. Tchr. Free Will Bapt. Bible Coll., Nashville, 1956-60, chmn. English dept., 1961-85; exec. sec.-treas. Free Will Bapt. Women Nat. Active for Christ, 1985-98. Author: Sparks Into Flame, 1985, Beyond the Gate, 1998; contbr. poetry to jours. Mem. Scribbler's Club. Free Will Baptist. Avocations: photography, music, drama. Personal E-mail: wisemrw@aol.com.

WISELY, DONNA, secondary school educator, athletic trainer; d. Donald and Theresa Keller; m. John Wisely, Mar. 25, 1995; 1 child, Caroline. BS, So. Ill. U., Carbondale, 1990; MA, Northeastern Ill. U., Chgo., 2002. Cert. athletic trainer 1991, lic. Ill., 1991. Athletic trainer Twp. H.S. Dist., Hoffman Estates, Ill., 1991—2005, tchg. asst., 1992—2005; tchr. Larkin Ctr., Elgin, Ill., 2004—05, Cmty. Unit Sch. Dist., St. Charles, Ill., 2005—. Athletic trainer Mike Glenn Camp, Decatur, Ga., 1989—99, World U. Games, Buffalo, 1993—93, Am. Hearing Impaired Hockey Assoc., Chgo. area, 1995—99, Atlanta Com. for Olympic Games, 1996—96, Prairie State Games, Various, Ill. Vol. Women In Need Growing Stronger, Chgo. area, 2000. Dr. John Jevitz Continuing Edn. scholar, Ill. Athletic Trainers Assn., Inc., 2000—01, Grad. Merit scholar, Northeastern Ill. U., 2000—02. Mem.: NEA, Ill. Edn. Assn., Nat. Athletic Trainers Assn., Gt. Lakes Athletic Trainers Assn., Ill. Athletic Trainers Assn. (sec., v.p. 1995—2005, mem. Hall of Fame 2006). Avocation: travel. Office Phone: 630-513-2287.

WISEMAN, CYNTHIA SUE, language educator; b. New Albany, Miss., Sept. 8, 1952; d. Paul W. and Betty J. (Gore) W.; m. Ivan A. Tardio, Jan. 25, 1983 (div. Dec. 1997); children: E. Alexandra, Robert Paul. BA in English Lit., U. Miss., 1974; postgrad., La Sorbonne, Paris, 1978-79; MA in Tchg., Sch. for Internat. Tng., 1982; postgrad., Columbia U. With Peace Corps, Senegal, 1975-77; editor Guita Rev., N.Y.C., 1983-86; coord. evening program Hunter Coll., CUNY, N.Y.C., 1992-95; dir. Queensborough Adult Learning Ctr., CUNY, N.Y.C., 1991-92; adj. instr. ESL Am. lang. program Columbia U., N.Y.C., 1989-91; adj. instr. ESL, LaGuardia C.C., CUNY., 1987—; adj. prof. dept. culture and comm. NYU, N.Y.C., 1995—. Adj. prof. John Jay Coll. Criminal Justice, CUNY, 1995-98, instr. Internat. English Lang. Inst., 1989—; co-chmn. part-timers caucus TESOL, Alexandria, Va., 1996-99, mem.-at-large HEIS, TESOL, 1999—; chair signage TESOL, 1999; mem. exec. bd. CUNY ESL Coun., 1997-99. Active AIDS orgns., N.Y.C., 1990—. Mem. N.Y. State Tchs. English to Speakers of Other langs. (pres. 2001, v.p. 2000, exec. bd., chmn. sociopolit. com. 1995-97). Democrat. Avocations: bicycling, rollerblading. Home: 300 Cathedral Pky Apt 1E New York NY 10026-4051 Office: CUNY BMCC 199 Chambers St New York NY 10007

WISEMAN, GRETCHEN RENEE, special education educator; d. Richard Earl and Sandra Lee Wiseman. BA, Buena Vista U., Storm Lake, Iowa, 1996. Cert. tchr. Ohio, 2003. Camp counselor Easter Seals, Des Moines, 1994—98; k-8 multicategorical resource rm. tchr. Rockwell-Swaledale CSD, Rockwell, Iowa, 1996—98; residential specialist Sunshine Inc. of NW Ohio, Maumee, Ohio, 1998—2003; spl. educaiton tchr./tech. coord. The Aurora Acad., Toledo, 2000—03; intervention specialist George A. Phillips Acad., Toledo, 2003—. Home: 27695 Tracy Rd Lot 248 Walbridge OH 43465 Personal E-mail: unicorn_gw@yahoo.com.

WISH, LESLIEBETH BERGER, psychotherapist, writer, management consultant; d. Irving L. and Miriam Solomon Berger; m. Peter A. Wish, Nov. 16, 1984; 1 stepchild, Carly Sidra. AB in History & English, Carnegie Mellon U., 1970; MA in English, Ohio U., 1971; MA in Social Svc. Mgmt., Byrn Mawr Coll., 1976; EdD in Human Devel., U. Mass., 1996. Lic. clin. social worker Md., 1980, Mass., 1982, Fla., 2003, diplomate clin. social work Bd. Examiners, 1988; cert. aquatics fitness instr. 2005. Post doctoral tng. in marriage & family therapy sys. Georgetown U. Med. Sch., DC, 1979—82; dir. social work & families The Linwood Sch., Ellicott City, Md., 1980—81; dir. human resource devel. & clin. svcs. The New England Inst. Family Rels., Framingham, Mass., 1982—94; faculty coord., admissions acad. advisor Grad. Ctr. Bus. & Counseling Webster U., Sarasota, 2001—04; v.p. Gulfcoast Healthstyle, Sarasota, Fla., 1994—. Cons. in field. Author, contbg. editor: Trafalgar Publications, 2001—; author: (book) Incest, Women & Work, 1998; contbr. articles, fiction, and poems to numerous nat. magazines. Chair Sarasota Women's Advisory Commn., 1994—2001; pres. coun. Easter Seals, 2002—; co-coord. counseling network, spl. ops. Warrior Found., 2006—; co-coord. counselor network Spl. Ops. Warrior Found. Recipient Md.'s Best Small Press award, Md. Arts Commn., 1981. Mem.: Women's Leadership & Acad. Honor Society (mortar bd. 1970), Phi Kappa Phi. Achievements include pioneering the expansion of sex education and awareness of sexual issues at work and home for The New England Institute of Family Relations, the first sexual dysfunction clinic in New England; first to research, link and present in a book the connection between childhood sexual abuse and its impact on work and career in women; lecture in area of work and career; copyright on career-family history inventory; introduced seminars and counseling at places of work. Avocations: travel, opera, writing, painting.

WISHARD, DELLA MAE, former newspaper editor; b. Bison, S.D., Oct. 21, 1934; d. Ervin E. and Alma J. (Albertson) Preszler; m. Glenn L. Wishard, Oct. 18, 1953; children: Glenda Lee, Pamela A., Glen Ervin. Grad. high sch., Bison. Mem. S.D. Ho. of Reps., Pierre, 1984-96; pub., editor Bison (S.D.) Courier, 1996-2000; owner Wishards Rentals, Rapid City, SD, 2004—. Columnist County Farm Bur., 1970-96. Committeewoman state Rep. Cen. Com., Perkins County, SD, 1980-84, 98-01; Rep. precinct committeewoman Pennington County, 2006-. Mem. Am. Legis. Exch. Coun. (state coord. 1985-91, state chmn. 1991-96), Fed. Rep. Women (chmn. Perkins County chpt. 1978-84), S.D. Farm Bur. (state officer 1982), Perkins County Rep. (chmn. 2000-03). Lutheran. Avocations: writing, gardening. Home and Office: 3900 S Valley Dr Rapid City SD 57703 Personal E-mail: wishd@macomm.com.

WISHERT, JO ANN CHAPPELL, music educator, elementary and secondary school educator; b. Carroll County, Va., July 10, 1951; d. Joseph Lenox and Helen Alata (Wagoner) Chappell; m. Clarence Hinnant Wishert, Jr., June l0, l987; 1 child, Kelly Marie. BA, Oral Roberts U., 1974; MS, Radford U., 1977; degree in advanced postgrad. studies, Va. Poly. Inst. and State U., 1981; postgrad., U. SC, Spartanburg, 1990, U. SC, Columbia, 1995, The Citadel, 1996, Winthrop U., 1995—96, postgrad., 2003. Cert. elem. music supr., Va., elem. and secondary music tchr., SC, music tchr., ednl. specialist, NC. Head start tchr. Rooftop of Va., Galax, 1975; elem. music tchr. Carroll County Pub. Schs., Hillsville, 1975—78; grad. asst., supr., course advisor Coll. Edn., Va. Poly. Inst. and State U., Blacksburg, 1978—81, pregrad. interviewer placement svcs., 1981—83; music dir. Heritage Acad., Charlotte, NC, 1984—85, fine arts specialist, 1985—86; choral dir. Chester County Schs., Chester, 1986—2002; music tchr. Old Pointe Elem./Rock Hill Sch. Dist. #3, 2002—. Fine arts chair Chester H.S., 1995-2002, adept evaluator, 1996—; guest condr. workshop Patrick County Schs., Stuart, Va., 1980; liaison for Chester County Schs. to SC Gov.'s Sch. for Arts, 1990-91; faculty mem., sponsor Tri-M Music Honor Soc., Curriculum Leadership Arts, 2003. Soloist PTL TV Network, Charlotte, 1984-85. Guest spkr. on battered women and marital abuse to chs. and workshops; entertainer; co-dir. Chester City Schs. Choral Festival; active Arts Coun. Chester County, 1988—, SC Arts Alliance and Arts Advocacy, Winthrop Consortium for the Arts, Rock Hill Sch. Dist. Tchr. Forum, 2003—; sponsor Beta Club. Named Tchr. of Yr., Chester County Sch. Dist., 1988-1989, 1991-92, Educator of Yr., Chester County C. of C., 1992, Chester County Sch. Dist. Tchr. of Yr., 1992, Tchr. of the Week, The Herald, 1995, Old Pointe Elem. Tchr. of Yr., 2003-04; recipient Ednl. Improvement Act Tchr. award SC Dept. Edn., 2006. Mem. ASCD, AAUW (mem. bylaws com. Chester br. 1987-93, sec. 1988-89, fine arts chmn. 1995-2002), Music Educators Nat. Conf., SC Music Educators Assn. (del. pub. rels. network Chester County Schs. 1991), SC Edn. Assn., Palmetto State Tchrs. Assn., Am. Assn. Choral Dirs., Chester County Edn. Assn., Nat. Assn. Secondary Music Edn. (team evaluator divsn. tchr. edn. cert. 1989, 91-2002), SC State Coun. Internat. Reading Assn., SC Reading Assn., State So. Assn. Schs. and Colls. (mem. evaluation team, mem. steering com.), SC Arts Alliance for Art Edn., All U.S.A. Chorus Student Group (alumni), Tri-M Music Honor Soc. (sponsor), 4-H Club (life), Phi Delta Kappa., Old Pointe Elem. (spl. areas dept. chair, 2003-04). Republican. Baptist. Avocations: reading, cross stitch, needlepoint, music. Home: 1122 Virginia Dare Dr Rock Hill SC 29730-9669 Business E-Mail: jwishert@rock-hill.k12.sc.us.

WISHNICK, MARCIA MARGOLIS, pediatrician, educator, geneticist; b. N.Y.C., Oct. 10, 1938; d. Hyman and Tillie (Stoller) Margolis; m. Stanley Wishnick, June 12, 1960; 1 child, Elizabeth Anne. BA, Barnard Coll., 1960; PhD, NYU, 1970, MD, 1974. Diplomate Am. Bd. Pediatrics, Nat. Bd. Med. Examiners. Rsch. technician Lederle Labs./Am. Cyanamid, Pearl River, NY, 1960-66; postdoctoral fellow N.Y. Pub. Health Lab., N.Y.C., 1970-71; resident in pediatrics NYU-Bellevue Med. Ctr., N.Y.C., 1974-77, asst. prof. pediatrics, 1977-82; clin. assoc. prof. pediatrics Bellevue Med. Ctr. NYU Med. Ctr., N.Y.C., 1982-87; clin. prof. pediatrics NYU-Bellevue Med. Ctr., N.Y.C., 1987—2003; pvt. practice, N.Y.C., 1977—2003. Contbr. articles to profl. jours. Fellow Am. Acad. Pediatrics; mem. AMA, N.Y. Pediatric Soc., N.Y. Med. Soc. Office Phone: 808-937-0312. Business E-Mail: docwishnick@earthlink.net.

WISHY, SHAWNA NICOLE, special education educator; b. Kansas City, Mo., Dec. 16, 1981; d. Gregory Dee and Glenda Sue Hammond; m. Andrew Michael Wishy, Nov. 13, 2004. BA of Edn. Mild/Moderate Disabilities, Okla. Bapt. U., Shawnee, 2004. Cert. tchr. Okla. Bd. Edn., Mo. Bd. Edn. Dance instr. Layton's Dance Acad., Lee's Summit, Mo., 1995—2000; paraprofl. Rainbow Ctr., Blue Springs, Mo., 2000; pvt. tutor Shawnee, Okla., 2001; tutor Am. Reads, Okla., 2003; asst. tchr. YMCA Children's Ctr., Kansas City, Mo., 2001—03; spl. edn. tchr. Raytown Sch. Dist., Mo., 2004—. Pub. rels. cons. Coun. for Exceptional Children, Shawnee, 2001—04. Grantee Null Fulkerson award, Norman scholarship, Okla. Baptist U., 2004. Avocations: running, exercise, journaling. Home: 4020 S Jackson Dr Apt 209 Independence MO 64057

WISKOCIL, ANGIOLINA, telecommunications industry executive; b. Ecuador; B, Univ. Calif. Acctg. clerk Pacific Bell, 1973, v.p., network engring. West; now sr. v.p.-network svcs. AT&T Inc. (formerly SBC Comm., Inc.), San Antonio. Served on Calif. United Task Force to bridge digital divide; rep. to Leadership Am. Named one of 80 Elite Hispanic Women, Hispanic Bus. Mag., 2005, 50 Most Important Hispanics in Tech., Bus., Hispanic Engineer and Info. Tech. mag., 2005. Office: AT&T Inc 175 E Houston San Antonio TX 78205 Office Phone: 210-821-4105. Office Fax: 210-351-2071.*

WISLER, DARLA LEE, pastor; b. Balt., May 14, 1940; d. Hugh Charles Douglas and Angela Rita (Poffel) Mayer; m. Norman Marvin Wisler, Dec. 26, 1960; children: David Paul, Diane Lynn. A in Biblical Studies, Christian Internat. U., 1982, BTh, 1984, MDiv, 1990, D in Ministry, 1993. Asst. pastor Anderson Christian Assembly, SC, 1978-80; founder, apostle Living Water Ch., Anderson, 1981—; on call chaplain Anderson Area Medical Center,

2003—; apostle, dean Living Water Ministry Tng. Ctr., 2006. Mid-week devotion min. NHC Healthcare of Anderson, 1980—, pres. adv. bd., 1988—; dean Living Water Bible Coll., Anderson, 1982—; prin. Living Water Christian Sch., Anderson, 1983-88; regular host and co-host Dove Broadcasting TV-16, Greenville, S.C., 1984—; coord. Christian Internat. Network of Chs. Mid-East Region, 1994-96. Author: Basic Christian Teaching Made Plain and Clear, 1994, Advanced Christian Teaching Made Plain and Clear, 1995, Bible Lessons for Children, 2003, Tremendous Teens, 2004. Pres. clergy staff exec. com. Anderson Area Med. Ctr., 1993-94, on-call chaplain, 2003—; sec. Anderson County Sheriff's Dept. Chaplaincy, Anderson, 1996-98; chaplain Anderson County Sheriff's Dept., 1996-2004, bd. dirs., 1996-2004, vice chair bd. dirs., 2001-02, chair, 2002-04. Republican. Avocations: walking, reading, crocheting, cooking. Office: Living Water Ch PO Box 1823 Anderson SC 29622-1823 Office Phone: 864-224-9315. E-mail: dr_wisler@charter.net, dr_docki@peoplepc.com.

WISMER, PATRICIA ANN, retired secondary school educator; b. York, Pa., Mar. 23, 1936; d. John Bernhardt and Frances Elizabeth Loreen Marie (Fry) Feiser; m. Lawrence Howard Wismer, Aug. 4, 1961. BA in English, Mt. Holyoke Coll., 1958; MA in Speech/Drama, U. Wis., 1960; postgrad., U. Oreg., 1962, Calif. State U., Chico, 1963-64, U. So. Calif., 1973-74. Tchr., co-dir. drama program William Penn Sr. High Sch., York, 1960-61; instr. English, dir. drama York Jr. Coll., 1961-62; assoc. church editor San Francisco Examiner, 1962-63; reporter, publicist News Bur. Calif. State U., Chico, 1963-64; chmn. English Dept. Chico Sr. H.S., 1966-96; mentor tchr. Chico Sr. High Sch., Chico Unified Sch. Dist., 1983-93. Judge writing awards Nat. Coun. Tchr. English, 1970—; cons. No. Calif. Writing Project, 1977—; curriculum cons., freelance writer and photographer, 1996—. Author: My Life with Vanessa: A Journal of the Plagued Years, 1998, 40 Year Photo Retrospective, 2002; newsletter editor Chico Cat Coalition, 1999-2004; (poetry/ photo book project) Ambient Light and Shadow, 2005. Mem. Educators for Social Responsibility, Planetary Soc., Upper Calif. Coun. Tchrs. English (bd. dirs. 1966-85, pres. 1970-71), Calif. Assn. Tchrs. English, Nat. Coun. Tchrs. English, NEA, Calif. Tchrs. Assn., Chico Unified Tchrs. Assn. Democrat. Lutheran. Avocations: photography, play production, video production. Home: 623 Arcadian Ave Chico CA 95926-4504 Office: PO Box 1235 Cannon Beach OR 97110-1235 Personal E-mail: pwismer@aol.com.

WISNER, PAMELA L., social worker; b. Stevensville, Newfoundland, Can., Dec. 4, 1958; d. John R. Wisner, Leslie S. Wisner. BA in Psychology and Sociology, U. Mobile, 1980; M in Counseling, La. Bapt. U., 1998. LCSW Ala. Bd. Social Work Examiners, 1995, cert. Cognitive Behavioral Therapist 1999, Forensic Counselor 1999, Addictions specialist, Domestic Violence Counselor endorsement 1999. Dir. cmty. svc. RAPHA, Mobile, Ala., 1995—96; coord., counselor Charter of Mobile, 1996—2000; therapist, family cons. Gulf Coast Therapeutic Program, Inc., Mobile, 2000—. Mem.: Nat. Bd. Cognitive Behavioral Therapists, Am. Psychotherapy Assn. (diplomate 1999). Avocation: Avocations: travel, reading, cats, crafts, cooking. Office: Therapeutic Programs 601 Bel Air Blvd Ste 200 Mobile AL 36606-3524 Home: 6213 Burnt Wood Dr S Mobile AL 36695

WISNIEWSKI, P. MICHELLE, retired obstetrician, gynecologist; b. Oneida, NY, June 26, 1945; d. Henry Francis Wisniewski and Kathryn Starr Holloway; m. Anna Cebula Costello, Sept. 20, 1998; m. Louise Marie Benyovszky, Sept. 22, 1984 (div.); children: Ladislaus Michael, Alexander Paul. BS, Georgetown U., 1967; MD, Universidad Autonoma de Guadalajara, Mexico, 1975. Bd. Cert. Am. Bd. of Ob/Gyn, 1983, lic. Physican and Surgeon NJ, Pa., 1977, Residency in Ob/Gyn Hahnemann U., 1980. Chairperson, dept of ob/gyn Health Care Plan of NJ., Cherry Hill, NJ, 1980—82; attending physician ob/gyn NE Hosp., Phila., 1882—1987, Nazareth Hosp., Phila., 1984—90, Pa. Hosp., Phila., 1987—91; chairperson, dept. of ob/gyn Mercy Hosp., Wilkes-Barre, Pa., 1991—92. Author: (medical research) Journal of Reproductive Medicine (Fellowship, Internat. Soc. for the Study of Vulvovaginal Disease, 1987), (photographic exibit) The Natural and Scenic Beauty of the Florida Keys, 2003. Chairperson Fla. Keys Coun. for People with Disabilities, Key West, Fla., 2000—06; sr. dir. Disability and Disaster: Surviving the Fla. Keys; lobbyist Key West City Coun., Monroe County Commn., Key West, Fla., 2001—06; active plaintiff Assn. for Disabled Am., Miami, Fla., 2001—06, pres., 2006—. 1st lt. US Army, 1967—70, Rep. Vietnam. Decorated Air Medal for Valor USARV, Mil. Medal of Honor & Gallantry Cross Rep. Vietnam; recipient Hon. Conch Cert., Monroe Fla. County Mayor, 2002. Fellow: Am. Coll. Ob-Gyn. (life). Achievements include first to led the struggle to make the Florida Keys accessible for people with disabilities; aided passage of transgender civil rights legislation. Office: FKCFPWD Chairperson 1100 Simonton St Ste 2 257 Key West FL 33040 Personal E-mail: kwimages@bellsouth.net.

WISNIEWSKI, ROSEMARY, mathematics educator; b. Oceanside, N.Y., Oct. 18, 1976; d. Rolando and Estela Escobar; m. Lukasz Wisniewski, Aug. 29, 2004. MS, Hofstra U., Hempstead, N.Y., 2001. Cert. math. grades 7-12 N.Y., 2001. Tchr. East Hampton (N.Y.) UFSD, 2004—. Scholar, Assn. Math. Tchrs. N.Y. State, 2000. Mem.: Phi Beta Kappa.

WISS, MARCIA A., lawyer; b. Columbus, Ohio, May 15, 1947; d. John William and Margaret Ann (Cook) W.; m. Donald G. MacDonald (dec.); children: Christopher C. Wiss MacDonald, Joan Merle MacDonald. BS in Fgn. Svc., Georgetown U., 1969, JD, 1972. Bar: D.C. 1972. Econ. analyst World Bank, Washington, 1969; atty. U.S. Dept. Justice, 1972-73; atty. office gen. counsel Overseas Pvt. Investment Corp., 1973-78; gen counsel-designate Inst. for Sci. and Tech. Cooperation, 1979; ptnr. Kaplan Russin & Vecchi, 1987-92, Whitman & Ransom, 1992-93, Whitman, Breed, Abbott & Morgan, Washington, 1993-96; counsel Wilmer, Cutler & Pickering, 1996-2000; ptnr. Hogan & Hartson, 2000—. Gen. counsel Washington chpt., Soc. Internat. Devel., 1980-2001; gen. counsel, Assn. for Women in Devel., 1982—; bd. advisers, Procedural Aspects of Internat. Law Inst., 1985—; gen. counsel internat. policy coun. agr., adj. prof. of law Georgetown U. Law Ctr., 1984—, Johns Hopkins Sch. of Advanced Internat. Studies, 2001—. Editor Georgetown Law Ctr. Jour. Law and Policy in Internat. Bus., 1971-72. Chair Holy Trinity Parish Coun., Washington, 1976. Mem. Am. Fedn. Govt. Employees (chmn. 1975-76), D.C. Bar (steering com. divsn. 12, 1985-88, co-chmn. fin. and banking com. 1985), Am. Soc. Internat. Law (v.p. 1991-94, exec. coun. 1987-90), Washington Fgn. Law Soc. (pres. 1983-84). Roman Catholic. Office: Hogan & Hartson 555 13th St NW Washington DC 20004 Office Phone: 202-637-5429.

WISSLER-THOMAS, CARRIE, professional society administrator, artist; b. Ephrata, Pa., Nov. 2, 1946; d. Robert Uibel and Grace Urbane (Nicholas) Wissler; m. James Richard Gamber, June 12, 1968 (div. 1972); m. Scott Kerry Thomas, Mar. 3, 1972; 1 child, Dylan Crayton Llewellyn. BA, Hood Coll., 1968; MS, Temple U., 1986. Copywriter WGSA Radio, Ephrata, Pa., 1970-71, William Assocs., Harrisburg, Pa., 1977; correspondent Art Matters of Phila., Harrisburg, 1984-86; art columnist Pennsylvania Beacon, Harrisburg, 1983-85; writer Strictly Business, Harrisburg, 1985-86; painting instr. Art Assn. of Harrisburg, 1980-86; freelance artist Harrisburg, 1968—; exec. dir., pres. Art Assn. of Harrisburg, 1986—. Exhbn. panel Harrisburg City Govt. Ctr., 1983-89; art adv. panel Harrisburg Area C.C., 1985-95; gallery com. Univ. Ctr. at Harrisburg, 1988-95; chmn. Easter Seals Art Show by Disabled Artists, Harrisburg, 1983-86; trustee Pa. Coll. Art and Design, 1989—; mem. Harrisburg Multi-Cultural Coalition, 1992-94; chmn. Harrisburg Gallery Walk, 1989—; bd. dirs. Historic Harrisburg Assn., Better Bus. Bur.; pres. Allied Arts Affiliates Coun., 1993-95; mem. Dauphin Co. commn. on status of women, 2000-01. Prin. work includes Broadway Babies oil painting, 1982 (Grumbacher Gold Medallion 1982); over 30 solo exhibitions. Mem. Hist. Soc. Cocalico Valley, Ephrata, 1982—, Dauphin County Hist. Soc., Harrisburg, 1986—; minority inspector Paxtang Election Bd., Harrisburg, 1977-79; mem. ACLU, Pa., 1988-91; bd. dirs. Hist. Harrisburg Assn., 1992-98. Recipient Women Who Work award Communications and the Arts Pomeroy's, 1985, Disting. Svc. to Arts award Harrisburg Community Theatre, 1991, Arts Advocate award, Women Creat, 2005. Mem. Am. Coun. on Arts, Art Assn. Harrisburg (pres. 1980-84), Rotary. Democrat. Anglican. Avocations: reading, biographies, visiting museums/galleries, gardening. Home: 2721 N 2nd St Harrisburg PA 17110-1205 Office: Art Assn of Harrisburg 21 N Front St Harrisburg PA 17101-1606 Office Phone: 717-236-1432. Business E-Mail: carrie@artassocofhbg.com.

WISSMANN, CAROL RENEÉ, sales executive; b. Berkeley, Calif., July 9, 1946; d. Conrad Clayton and Carol Elizabeth Wissmann. BA, Whittier Coll., Calif., 1968; Montessori Diploma, Coll. Notre Dame, Belmont, 1970. Dist. mgr. U.S. C. of C., Washington; divsn. mgr. Classified Yellow Pages Inc., Cookeville, Tenn., 1986; pres. The BelleMann Corp., Gig Harbor, Wash., 1988—. Cons., writer, spkr. in field. Mem.: Seattle Free Lances (past pres.). Republican. Avocations: horseback riding, ballroom dancing. Home and Office: 3483 Edwards Dr Gig Harbor WA 98335-1151 Office Phone: 253-851-5101. E-mail: BelleMann@hotmail.com.

WISZ, KATHERINE, nurse; b. Chgo., Mar. 15, 1951; d. Sylvester and Patricia Wisz. A, Olive Harvey Coll., 1973. Trauma nurse specialist, Ill. Emergency Nurse Assn., 1990. Staff nurse emergency dept. Palos Cmty. Hosp., Palos Heights, Ill., 1980—91; staff nurse Apria Healthcare, Elmhurst, Ill., 1995—98, Omnicare Infusion Svc., Des Plaines, Ill., 1998—. Mem.: Infusion Nurse Soc. (bd. dirs. Chgo. area chpt. 2005—), MENSA. Avocations: travel, reading, needlepoint, archaeology. Home: 2013 Pepper Valley Dr Geneva IL 60134 Office: Omnicare Infusion Svc 2289 Mount Prospect Rd Des Plaines IL 60018 Office Phone: 800-633-4879. Office Fax: 847-375-0853.

WITCHER, PHYLLIS HERRMANN, secondary school educator; b. Wilmington, Del., Feb. 23, 1938; d. Carl Victor and Ruth Naomi (Ice) Herrmann; m. Murray H. Witcher, Apr. 8, 1961 (div. 1992); children: David, Stephanie Witcher Stewart. BS, U. Del., 1960; MEd, West Chester U., 1982. Cert. secondary tchr., Pa. Tchr. pub. schs., Pa., Tenn., Del., 1974—; textile analyst Sears Roebuck Labs., Chgo., 1977-79; ind. admissions counselor Coll. Selection Svcs., Chadds Ford, Pa., 1983—. Bd. dirs. Unionville-Chadds Ford Sch. Dist., 1986-91, Chester County Intermediate Unit, Exton, Pa., 1988-91; instr. family law policy U. Del. Acad. Lifelong Learning, 2003-06. Author, speaker, legis. witness No-Fault Div., 1996. Bd. dirs. Mental Health Assn. in Del., Wilmington, 1985-93; past pres. Del. Symphony League, Wilmington, 1985; founder, pres. Protecting Marriage, Inc., Chadds Ford, 1991. Recipient Giraffe Project Nat. Commendation, 1994. Republican. Roman Catholic. Avocations: sewing, travel. Home: 2304 Riddle Ave Apt 2C Wilmington DE 19806-2163 Office: Protecting Marriage Inc PO Box 7436 Wilmington DE 19803-0436 E-mail: phyllaw@comcast.net.

WITHEE, DIANA KEERAN, art historian, art dealer, educator; d. Royal Victor and Johanna Polterock Keeran; m. Gregory Wallace Withee, June 8, 1968 (div. 2006); children: Christopher Edward, Jefftrey Wallace, Brett Andrew. BA in Art History cum laude, Pomona Coll., Claremont, CA, 1969; MA in Art History, Tulane U., 1976; ABD in Art History, U. Md., College Park, 1994. Rsch. & prodn. asst., art documentaries Nat. Mus. of Am. Art, Washington, 1980—83; art history instr. Montgomery Coll., Rockville, Md., 1984—85; art history instr. & cons. Montgomery County Pub. Schs., Rockville, Md., 1986—87; curatorial asst., manuscripts and rare books Walters Art Gallery, Baltimore, Md., 1988—90; mus. educator Nat. Gallery of Art, Washington, 1990—93; guide supr., mus. educator Hillwood Mus., Washington, 1993—98; art dealer Sumner and Dene Gallery, San Diego, 1999—2002, Whitt-Krauss Objects of Fine Art, San Diego, 1999; art instr. Ctrl. Tex. Coll., San Diego, 2001—; art dealer Susan St. Fine Art Gallery, Solana Beach, Calif., 2002—; co-owner Keeran Properties, Helendale, Calif., 2004—. Cons. Time-Life Books, Alexandria, Va., 1992; bd. dirs. San Diego State U. Arts Coun.; panelist, art critic San Diego Inst. The Living Artist, 2002—05. Prodn. asst. (videotape) Anni Albers, William H. Johnson, Reuben Nakian, Jacob Kainen:Five Decades as an Artist, asst. prodr. Americans in Brittany and Normandy, curator (art exhibition) More than a Miniature: Works of Art in Medieval Manuscripts, (exhibition) The Power of the Press: Revolution & Communications 1450-1600; author: (mag. articles) The Walters Art Gallery Bulletin, (contributing author) Culture et Revolution: The French Revolution and Its Aftermath, (instructor's manual) The Inquiring Eye: The European Renaissance, (book) Teacher Programs in Art Museums: A Directory; contributing author (magazine) The Post, presenter (symposium paper) Intimate Portrayals of Napoleon's Family, (scholarly conference paper) Anatomical Observations of Women's Life Stages in the Frescoes of Thera, (scholarly conference presentation) An Altar in the Miniature Fresco at Thera and Its Implications, lecturer (scholarly lecture) Timeless Cycles: Youth, Beauty and Ag in the Bronze Age Frescoes of Thera, scholarly presenter (scholarly conference presentation) The Boxing Boys and Fishermen Frescoes at Thera: An Analysis of their Physical Ages and Its Implications, Physical Growth and Aging Characteristics Depicted in the Theran Frescoes at Thera, conference presenter (conference presentations) Developing Good Relationships Between Guides and Security, lecturer (museum lecture series) C.W.Post and the Breakfast Cereal Revolution, The Gilded Age: The Newport Mansions; editor: (newsletter) COVA Newsletter. Recipient Letter of Commendation, Nat. Gallery of Art, 1991, Cash Bonus award, 1992; scholar Grad. assistantship, U. Md., 1986-1988; Mus. fellowship, U. of Md., 1988-89, Travel fellowship, Wash. Chpt., Am. Inst. of Archaeology, 1991. Mem.: Phi Kappa Phi. Achievements include development of new methodology of deciphering Aegean Bronze Age art; ran numerous national programs in museum education for National Gallery of Art; re-organization of entire Hillwood guide program; volunteered to teach Navy & Marine personnel aboard the aircraft carrier John C. Stennis on its deployment to participate in war in Afghanistan two months after 9/11. Home: 850 State St #128 San Diego CA 92101 Personal E-mail: dkkeeran@cox.net.

WITHERELL, NANCY LOUISE, education educator; b. Bridgewater, Mass., Aug. 1, 1952; d. Anthony and Bertha Eunice (Smith) Kopcych; m. Peter Walker Witherell, Aug. 27, 1973; children: Paul William, Jonathan Lewis, Thomas Clayton. BA in Sociology, U. Mass., Dartmouth, 1974; EdM in Elem. Sch. Adminstrn., U. Md., 1979; EdD in Lang. Arts and Literacy, U. Mass., Lowell, 1993. Cert. tchr., Mass. Elem. tchr. Prince Georges County Pub. Sch., Hyattsville, Md., 1974-80, Norton (Mass.) Pub. Schs., 1980-81; tchrs. asst. U. Mass., Lowell, summer 1992; vis. lectr. Bridgewater (Mass.) State Coll., 1985-93, assoc. prof., 1993—, sec. media literacy task force, 1995—2000. Cons., 1993—. Co-author: Graphic Organizer and Activities to Differentiate Instruction in Reading, 2002, Focus on Fluency, 2004, Teaching Writing Through Differential Instruction With Leveled Graphic Organizers, 2005. Great Books coord., bd. dirs. Raynham (Mass.) Vol. Edn., 1986-2003; chairperson, bd. edn. Pilgrim Congl. Ch., Taunton, Mass., 1987-2005 Named Vol. of Yr. award, Raynham Area Vols. Edn., 2003. Mem.: ASCD, Nat. Coun. Tchrs. English, Internat. Reading Assn., Assn. Colls. U. Reading Educators (past pres.), Internat. Reading Assn. (publ. proposal reviewer), Southea. Regional Reading Coun. (past pres., Literary award 2005), Mass. Reading Assn. (com. parent-child comm. 1993—94, tech. com. 1996—, nominating chair 2002—03, bd. dirs. 2005—, Sylvia D. Brown scholar 1993), Pi Lambda Theta (Virginia B. Biggy scholar 1992). Avocations: reading, skiing, sailing. Home: 345 Elm St Raynham MA 02767 Office: Bridgewater State Coll Hart Hall Dept Elem Edn Bridgewater MA 02324 E-mail: nwitherell@bridgew.edu.

WITHERSPOON, CAROLYN BRACK, lawyer; b. Little Rock, Mar. 29, 1950; d. Gordon Paisley and Mildred Louise (Lemon) Brack; m. Joseph Roger Armbrust, July 25, 1970 (div. 1976); 1 child, Catherine Paisley Armbrust; m. John Leslie Witherspoon, June 15, 1979. Student, U. Ark., 1968—70, So. Meth. U., 1970; BA, U. Ark., 1974, JD with honors, 1978. Bar: Ark. 1978, U.S. Dist. Ct. (ea. and we. dists.) Ark. 1978, U.S. Ct. Appeals (8th cir.) 1979, U.S. Supreme Ct. 1981. Asst. atty. City of Little Rock, 1978, chief dep. atty., acting city atty., 1984—85; assoc. House, Wallace & Jewell, Little Rock, 1985—87, ptnr., 1987—90; dir. McGlinchey Stafford Lang, Little Rock, 1990—97, Cross, Gunter, Witherspoon & Galchus, Little Rock, 1997—. Mem. com. Fed. Ct. Practice, 1988—91; mem. civil practice com. Ark. Supreme Ct., 1989—97, mem. continuing legal edn. bd., 1998—2001; chair adv. com. Civil Justice Reform Act, 1993—95; chair State Bd. Bar Examiners, 2001—05. Contbr. articles to profl. jours. Commr. Ark. Real Estate Commn., 1978—81; past chmn. Little Rock Housing Authority Bd. Commn.; past pres., bd. dirs. Advs. for Battered Women; past pres. Women's Found. Ark., Ark. Women's History Inst. Recipient Labor Law award, Am. Jurisprudence, 1977. Fellow: Coll. Labor and Employment Lawyers, Am. Bar Found. (Ark. Fellows chair); mem.: ABA (ho. dels. 1997—, trial and ins. practice sect., equal employment opportunity com.), Am. Employment Law Coun., William R. Overton Inn of Ct. (pres. 1992—93), Nat. Inst. Mcpl. Law Officers (state chmn. 1985—87, v.p. 1987—89), Pulaski County Bar Assn. (pres. 1989—90), Ark. Assn. Women Lawyers (pres. 1982—83), Ark. Bar Assn. (pres. 1995—96, Golden Gavel award 1989, Ark. Inst. Cont. Legal Edn. award 1991, Golden Gavel award 1993, Charles L. Carpenter award 2005), Transp. Lawyers Assn. (mem. exec. com. 1997—99), Nat. Conf. Bar Pres. (mem. exec. coun. 1996—99), Am. Jur Soc., Am. Law Inst. Avocations: hunting, fishing, reading, travel. Office: Cross Gunter Witherspoon and Galchus 500 President Clinton Ave Ste 200 Little Rock AR 72201-1747 Office Phone: 501-371-9999. Business E-Mail: cspoon@cgwg.com.

WITHERSPOON, REESE (LAURA JEAN REESE WITHERSPOON), actress; b. New Orleans, Mar. 22, 1976; d. John and Betty Witherspoon; m. Ryan Phillippe, June 5, 1999 (separated); children: Ava Elizabeth, Deacon. Co-owner prodn. co. Type A Films. Actor: (films) The Man in the Moon, 1991, A Far Off Place, 1993, Jack the Bear, 1993, S.F.W., 1994, Freeway, 1996, Fear, 1996, Twilight, 1998, Overnight Delivery, 1998, Pleasantville, 1998, Cruel Intentions, 1999, Election, 1999, Best Laid Plans, 1999, American Psycho, 2000, Little Nicky, 2000, (voice only) The Trumpet of the Swan, 2001, Legally Blonde, 2001, The Importance of Being Earnest, 2002, Sweet Home Alabama, 2002, Vanity Fair, 2004, Just Like Heaven, 2005, Walk the Line, 2005 (Best Actress, NY Film Critics Circle, 2005, Boston Soc. Film Critic award, 2005, Broadcast Film Assn., 2006, Nat. Soc. Film Critics award, 2006, Best Performance by an Actress in a Motion Picture-Musical or Comedy, Hollywood Fgn. Press Assn. (Golden Globe award), 2006, Outstanding Performance by a Female Actor in a Leading Role, Screen Actors Guild award, 2006, Actress in a Leading Role, British Acad. Film and TV Arts, 2006, Performance by an Actress in a Leading Role, Acad. Motion Picture Arts & Sciences, 2006, Choice Movie Actress: Drama/Action Adventure, Teen Choice awards, 2006); actor, exec. prodr.: (films) Legally Blonde 2: Red, White & Blonde, 2003; actor, prodr.:(films) Penelope, 2006; actor: (TV films) Wildflower, 1991, Desperate Choices: To Save My Child, 1992; (mini-series) Return to Lonsome Dove, 1993 (TV appearances) Friends, 2000, (voice only) King of the Hill, 2000, The Simpsons, 2002 Named 25 Most Intriguing People, People, 2001, 50 Most Beautiful People, 2002, Favorite Female Film Star, 2004; named one of 100 Most Influential People, Time Mag., 2006, 50 Most Powerful People in Hollywood, Premiere mag., 2006; recipient Catalan Internat. Film Festival Award Best Actress, 1997, Movieline Young Hollywood Award for Breakthrough Performance (Female), 1999, Online Film Critics Soc. Award for Best Actress, 1999, National Soc. of Film Critics Award for Best Actress, 1999, Favorite Leading Lady, People's Choice Award, 2006. Office: c/o 360 Mgmt 9111 Wilshire Blvd Beverly Hills CA 90210 Address: Endeavor 9601 Wilshire Blvd Beverly Hills CA 90210 also: Baker Winokur Ryder c/o Nancy Ryder 9100 Wilshire Blvd 6th Fl W Tower Beverly Hills CA 90212*

WITHHART, CAROL JOYCE, mathematician, educator; d. Orville Franklin and Esther Opal Mozena; m. John Philip Withhart, June 7, 1970; children: Misty Jo Kudrna, Christopher John. BS, Buena Vista Coll., Storm Lake, Iowa, 1971; MA in Tchg., U. St. Mary, Leavenworth, Kans., 2004. Cert. secondary tchr. Iowa, 1971. Mid. sch. math/sci. tchr. Ida Grove Mid. Sch., Iowa, 1971—72; mid. sch./H.S. sci. tchr. Battle Creek H.S., Iowa, 1973—74; substitute tchr. local schs., Ida Grove, Iowa, 1973—79; mid. sch. Chpt. I tchr. Ida Grove Mid. Sch., Iowa, 1979—81; mid. sch./H.S. math tchr. Schleswig Cmty. Schs., Iowa, 1983—94; H.S. math. instr. Denison Cmty. Schs., Iowa, 1994—. Math bee coach Schleswig Cmty. Schs., Iowa, 1983—94; negotiator Schleswig Edn. Assn., Iowa, 1985—94; Odyssey of the Mind coach Denison H.S., Iowa, 1996—2000; advisor Nat. Honor Soc., Denison, Iowa, 2005—; faculty rep. Denison Edn. Assn., Iowa, 2005—. Vol. Our Savior Luth. Ch., Denison, Iowa, 1994—2006. Mem.: NEA, DEA (faculty rep. 2005—06), ISEA, ICTM. Home: 2106 7th Ave N Denison IA 51442 Office: Denison HS 819 N Sixteenth Denison IA 51442 Office Phone: 712-263-3101.

WITHINTON, NANCY KAY, elementary school educator; b. Breese, Ill., Aug. 2, 1958; d. Robert Frank and Wilma Ann (Junker) Beckemeyer; m. Jerry William Withinton, June 7, 1989 AA, Kaskaskia Jr. Coll., 1978; BS Elem. and Spl. Edn., Ea. Ill. U., 1980; cert. Early Childhood Edn., We. Ill. U., 1983. Cert. tchr., Ill., Mo. Substitute tchr. Decatur Pub. Sch. Dist. 61, Ill., 1980; tchr. behavior adjustment Roach Elem. Sch., Decatur, 1980—81; tchr. early childhood Westmer Elem. Sch., New Boston, Ill., 1981—82; cons., tchr. early childhood/behavior disorder Aledo Cmty. Schs., Ill., 1982—84; tchr. behavior disorders, then tchr. 2d grade Orchard Farms Elem. Sch., St. Charles, Mo., 1984—86; tchr. kindergarten, 1st, 2d and 3d grade Athena Elem. Sch., DeSoto, Mo., 1988—2004, libr., 2004—. Girls' volleyball coach St. Teresa H.S., Decatur, 1980, Aledo H.S., 1982; vol. leader Westmer Elem. Singing Warriors, 1981-82; counselor Touch of Nature Spl. Populations Camp, So. Ill. U., Carbondale, 1984 Gymnastics coach Spl. Olympics, YMCA, Decatur, 1980-81; youth leader 1st Congl. Jr. High Youth Fellowship, Decatur, 1980-81; youth counselor United Meth. Sr. Youth Fellowship, Aledo, 1983-84; girls' softball coach Aledo YMCA, 1983 Mem. NEA, Mo. State Tchrs. Assn., DeSoto Tchrs. Assn., Coun. Exceptional Children, Coun. Children with Behavior Disorders, Phi Delta Kappa Avocations: flying, fishing, travel, reading. Home: 2000 Linhart Dr Festus MO 63028-3644 Office: Athena Elem Sch 3775 Athena School Rd De Soto MO 63020-4588

WITHROW, LUCILLE MONNOT, nursing home administrator; b. Alliance, Ohio, July 28, 1923; d. Charles Edward Monnot and Freda Aldine (Guy) Monnot Cameron; m. Alvin Robert Withrow, June 6, 1945 (dec. 1984); children: Cindi Withrow Johnson, Nancy Withrow Townley, Sharon Withrow Hodgkins (dec.), Wendel Alvin. AA in Health Adminstrn., Eastfield Coll., Mesquite, Tex., 1976. Lic. nursing home adminstr., Tex.; cert. nursing home ombudsman. Held various clerical positions, Dallas, 1950-72; office mgr., asst. adminstr. Christian Care Ctr. Nursing Home, Mesquite, Tex., 1972-76; head adminstr. Christian Care Ctr. Nursing Home and Retirement Complex, Mesquite, 1976-91; nursing home ombudsman Tex. Dept. Aging and Tex. Dept. Health, Dallas, 1991-93; legal asst. Law Offices of Wendel A. Withrow, Carrollton, Tex., 1993—. Com. on geriatric curriculum devel. Eastfield Coll., Mesquite, 1979, 87; ombudsman adv. com. Sr. Citizens Greater Dallas; cons. in field. Vol. Dallas Arboretum and Bot. Soc.; mem. Ombudsman adv. com. Sr. Citizens of Greater Dallas; charter mem. Stage Show Prodns. Recipient Volunteerism award, Tex. Atty. Gen., 1987, Tex. Gov., 1992. Mem. Tex. Assn. Homes for Aging, Am. Assn. Homes for Aging, Health Svcs. Speakers Bur., White Rock Kiwanis. Mem. Ch. Of Christ. Avocations: reading, travel, theater. Home: 11344 Lippitt Ave Dallas TX 75218-1922 Office: Law Office of W A Withrow 1120 Metrocrest Dr Ste 200 Carrollton TX 75006-5872

WITHROW, MARY ELLEN, federal agency administrator; b. Marion, Ohio, Oct. 2, 1930; d. Clyde Welsh and Mildred (Stump) Hinamon; m. Norman David Withrow, Sept. 4, 1948; children: Linda Rizzo, Leslie Legge, Norma, Rebecca Gooding. Mem. Elgin Local Bd. Edn., Marion, Ohio, 1969-73, pres., 1972; safety programs dir. ARC, Marion, 1968-72; dep. registrar State of Ohio, Marion, 1972-75; dep. county auditor Marion County, Ohio, 1975-77, county treas. Ohio, 1977-83; treas. State of Ohio, Columbus, 1983-94; treas. of the U.S. Dept. Treasury, Washington, 1994—2001. Chmn. Ohio Bd. Deposits, 1983—. Mem. exec. com. Ohio Dem. Com., mem. exec. com. women's caucus; mem. Dem. Nat. Com.; mem. Met. Women's Ctr.; pres. Marion County Dem. Club, 1976; participant Harvard U. Strategic Leadership Conf., 1990; mem. Dem. Leadership Coun.; mem. Internat. Currency News Bd., 2002—, Robert Wood Johnson Fellowhisp Bd, 1997—. Recipient Donald L. Scantlebury Meml. award, 1991, Women of Achievement award YWCA of Met. Columbus, 1993, Outstanding Govt. Svc. award Am. Numis. Assn., 1995; inducted Ohio Women's Hall of Fame, 1986; named Outstanding Elected Dem. Woman Holding Pub. Office, Nat. Fedn. Dem.

Women, 1987, Advocate of Yr., SBA, 1988, Most Valuable State Pub. Ofcl., City and State newspaper, 1990; Women Execs. in State Govt. fellow Harvard U., 1987. Mem. LWV (dem. leadership coun.), State Assn. County Treas. (legis. com. 1979-83, treas. 1982), Nat. Assn. State Treas. (pres. 1992, Jesse Unruh award 1993, chair long range planning com., mem. exec. com.), Nat. Assn. State Auditors Comtps. and Treas. (pres. 1990, strategic planning com., intergov. rels. com., chair state and mcpl. bonds com.), Treasury Hist. Assn., I Safe Bd, Coun. State Govts. (exec. com., internat. affairs com., orgnl. planning and coord. com., strategic planning task force), Women Execs. in State Govt. (chair fund devel. com.), Altrusa Bus. and Profl. Women's Club (hon.), Delta Kappa Gamma (hon.), Delta Sigma Pi (hon.). Clubs: Bus. and Profl. Women's.

WITHROW, SHAWANNA NICOLE, paralegal, entrepreneur; b. Charlotte, NC, Apr. 22, 1979; d. Calvin Cunningham and Paulette Withrow; life ptnr. Jared Bruton, Apr. 20, 2003; 1 child, Javaryon Nikhi Bruton. Assoc., King's Coll., 2000. Paralegal McDowell St. Ctr. for Family Law, Inc., Charlotte, 2000—; cert. paralegals NC State Bar, 2006—. Owner Paralegals Pro Se, Inc. & Legal Self Help Solutions, Charlotte, 2002—, exec. dir., owner, 2004—. Active So. Poverty Law Ctr., Washington, 2002. Mem.: Nat. Notary Assn., Metrolina Paralegal Assn., Nat. Assn. Legal Assistance. Office: NC Legal Enterprise for Paralegals Inc 5340 Grafton Dr Charlotte NC 28215-3145 Office Phone: 704-537-9424. Business E-Mail: paralegalsforprose@hotmail.com.

WITHROW, SHERRIE ANNE (JIMIE JEAN PEARL), financial specialist; b. Sacramento, Mar. 10, 1960; d. Jim and Ilene (James) Withrow. Student, Diablo Valley C.C., Pleasant Hill, Calif., 1975—76, Tarrant County Jr. Coll., Ft. Worth, 1982—83, Coll. of Marin, Kentfield, Calif., 1988, Merritt Coll., Oakland, Calif., 1990; AA in Bus. Adminstrn. and Mgmt., St. Louis C.C., Florissant, Mo., 1981. Cert. regional occupations program-web design program course Calif., 2006. Internal cashier AAA Automobile Club Mo., St. Louis, 1977-79; receiving clk. Dayton-Hudson Target Stores, Florissant and Ft. Worth, 1979-81; supr. credit and collection World Svc. Life Ins. Co., Ft. Worth, 1982-83; bank br. balancer, data processing divsn. Tex. Am. Bank Svcs., Inc., Ft. Worth, 1984-85; asst. to contr. Positive Video-Post Prodn., Orinda, Calif., 1985-87; with contractor's desk adminstrn. dept. Shell Oil Co., Martinez, Calif., 1987-88; asst. to CFO J.T. Thorpe & Son, Inc., Richmond, Calif., 1988-89; founder, gen. ptnr. HomeVisions Constrn. Svcs., El Sobrante, Calif., 1989-99, AudioVisions Sound and Lighting Co., El Sobrante, 1990-2000; corp. acctg. and investments Liquidity Fund Mgmt., Inc., 1990-92; founder, gen. ptnr. AV Electric, El Sobrante, 1994-2000; tax and payroll benefits specialist, founder WorldMediaVisions, Martinez, 2001—. Audio engr., cons. and project fin. cons. Contbr. (poetry) The Brilliance of Night, Internat. Libr. of Poetry Compilation, 2000, The Best Poems and Poets of 2001, 2001, The Silence Within, 2001, Nature's Echoes, 2001, Internat. Libr. Poetry, 2003; contbr.: poetry Theatre of the Mind, 2004, Noble House Collection, 2004, audio recs.: The Sound of Poetry, 2001; audio recs. The Best Poems and Poets of 2002, Eternal Portraits, 2004, Expressions, 2004, Noble House Collection Labours of Love, 2005. Fundraiser Sr. Citizen Subsidized Housing Complex, Martinez, 1987-88. David L. Underwood scholar Florissant Valley (St. Louis) C.C., 1980-81. Mem.: Internat. Platform Assn., Phi Theta Kappa. Democrat. Office: WorldMediaVisions PO Box 2919 Martinez CA 94553-7919 Personal E-mail: pearl4u713@yahoo.com.

WITKIN, EVELYN MAISEL, retired geneticist; b. NYC, Mar. 9, 1921; d. Joseph and Mary (Levin) Maisel; m. Herman A. Witkin, July 9, 1943 (dec. July 1979); children— Joseph, Andrew. AB, NYU, 1941; MA, Columbia U., 1943, PhD, 1947; DSc honoris causa, N.Y. Med. Coll., 1978, Rutgers U., 1995. Mem. staff genetics dept. Carnegie Inst., Washington, 1950-55; mem. faculty State U. N.Y. Downstate Med. Center, Bklyn., 1955-71, prof. medicine, 1968-71; prof. biol. scis. Douglass Coll., Rutgers U., 1971-79, Barbara McClintock prof. genetics, 1979-83, Waksman Inst. Microbiology, 1983-91; Barbara McClintock prof. emerita Waksman Inst. Microbiology, Rutgers U., 1991—. Author articles; mem. editorial bds. profl. jours. Postdoctoral fellow Am. Cancer Soc., 1947-49; fellow Carnegie Instn., 1957; Selman A. Waksman lectr., 1960; Phi Beta Kappa vis. scholar, 1980-81; grantee NIH, 1956-89; recipient Prix Charles Leopold Mayer French Acad. Scis., 1977, Lindback award, 1979, Nat. Medal of Science award, 2002. Fellow AAAS, Am. Acad. Microbiology; mem. NAS, Am. Acad. Arts and Scis., Environ. Mutagen Soc., Am. Genetics Soc. (Thomas Hunt Morgan medal, 2000), Am. Soc. Microbiology. Home: 1 Firestone Ct Princeton NJ 08540-5220 E-mail: ewitkin@aol.com.

WITMAN, LAURA KATHLEEN, writer, security professional; b. Pottstown, Pa., Mar. 4, 1957; d. William Tedford and Kathleen (Nieman) W. Student, San Bernardino Valley Coll., 1976-79; Degree in Actg. magna cum laude, Adelphi Bus. Coll., San Bernardino, Calif., 1985. Cert. acctg. bookkeeper. Silent alarm monitor, payroll acct. Comml. Security Alliance, San Bernardino, Calif., 1985—87. Author: The Sun, 1994; (poetry) World of Poetry, 1990, National Library of Poetry, 1992, 94, 95, 96, 98, Sparrowgrass, 1993; (short story) Antivivesection Soc., 1993, Animal Voice, 1994, Paws Newsletter, 1993, 94, 96, A Dogs Day Newsletter, 1994, House Rabbit Soc., 1994, 95, songs. Mem. Gay and Lesbian Ctr. Inland Empire, Heartland Christian Fellowship Met. Cmty. Ch., Inland Empire Pride Coun. Mem. People for Ethical Treatment of Animals, House Rabbit Soc. Democrat. Home: 7877 Willow Ave Riverside CA 92504-2624

WITOSHYNSKY, RUTH ELLEN, mathematics educator; b. Hialeah, Fla., Nov. 16, 1962; d. Joseph J. and Martha Elizabeth Brailsford; m. Michael N. Witoshynsky, July 27, 1985; children: Leah Elizabeth, Kayla Noel. Degree in secondary social sci. & mid. math, Fla. Gulf Coast U., Fort Myers, 1998—2002. Tchr., coach Pinellas County Sch., St. Petersburg, Fla., 2004—. Literacy coun. Charlotte County Sch., Punta Gorda, Fla., 2002—04. Coach SunCoast All Star, Olsmar, Fla., 2005—06.

WITSCHGER, MARY ANN, medical/surgical nurse; b. Cin., Apr. 5, 1962; d. Donald E. and Loraine E. (Schack) W. BSN, Thomas More Coll., Crestview Hills, Ky., 1984. Cert. med.-surg. nurse, oncology nurse, RN. Staff nurse Bethesda Oak Hosp., Cin., 1984-97, Bethesda North Hosp., Cin., 1997—. Recipient Nurse Profl. award, 1992, Roberta Scofield Meml. Cert. award, 2005. Mem. Trihealth Orgn. Office: Bethesda North Hosp 10500 Montgomery Rd Cincinnati OH 45242-4415

WITSCHI, EMILY, art educator; b. Detroit, May 25, 1957; d. Ralph William and Elizabeth (Toler) Witschi; children: Jason Daniel, Jason Joseph. BFA, Lake Erie Coll., Painesville, Ohio, 1979. Cert. tchr. visual arts K-12, indsl. tech. K-12. Pottery instr. City of Pontiac, Mich., 1975-79; youth art instr. Willoughby (Ohio) Sch. Fine Art, 1979-80; human resources staff May Co., Mentor and Cleve., Ohio, 1980-93; art dir. Fairmont Fine Arts Ctr., Russel, Ohio, 1994-98; art tchr. Cuyahoga Heights (Ohio) Bd. Edn., 1993—. Gallery dir. Fairmont Fine Art Ctr., 1995-98; artist Griswold Creek Pottery, Chesterland, Ohio, 1995—; dept. coord. Cuyahoga Heights Sch., 2003, Artfest coord., 2006. Group shows (pottery) include Four Coll. Invitational Art Show, 1977, Willoughby Regional Art Show, 1978, Womansart Show, 1979, Elise Newman Gallery, 1995, The Treehouse, Avonlake, Ohio. Advisor student coun. Cuyahoga Heights H.S., 1993-95; vol. demonstrating pottery various schs. N.E. Ohio. Mem. Clay Arts Guild, Art Educators Assn., Psi Beta. Unitarian/Universalist. Avocations: hiking, bicycling, reading, museums, gardening. Home: 12836 Opalocka Dr Chesterland OH 44026-2614

WITT, ALICIA, actress; b. Worcester, Mass., Aug. 21, 1975; d. Robert and Diane W. Home edn. Actress Internat. Creative Mgmt., Beverly Hills, Calif. TV appearances: Cybill, 1995-98, The Disappearance of Vonnie, 1994, Blackout, 1993, Twin Peaks, 1991, Hotel Room, Ally McBeal, 2000, Ring of the Nibelungs, 2004; film appearances: Dune, 1984, Liebestraum, 1991, Bodies, Rest and Motion, 1993, Fun, 1994 (Spl. Jury Recognition award Sundance Film Festival 1994), Four Rooms, 1995, Mr. Holland's Opus, 1995, Citizen Ruth, 1996, The Reef, 1997, Bongwater, 1998, Urban Legend, 1998, (voice) Gen 13, 1998, Cecil B. DeMented, 2000, Playing with Mona Lisa, 2000 (Best Actress award U.S. Comedy Arts Festival 2000), Vanilla Sky, 2001, Ten Tiny Love Stories, 2001, American Girl, 2002, Two Weeks Notice, 2002, The Upside of Anger, 2005; prodr. On the Wise, 2005; actor, prodr. Girls' Lunch, 2004; TV guest appearances Twin Peaks, 1990, Hotel Room, 1993, The Sopranos, 2000, Ally McBeal, 2000, The Twilight Zone, 2003, (mus. theater) The Gift, 2000. Recipient Spl. Jury Recognition for acting, Sundance Film Festival, 1994, Ind. Spirit Award nomination, 1995. Avocations: listening to big-band recordings, chess, backgammon, bowling.

WITT, CATHERINE LEWIS, neonatal nurse practitioner, writer; b. Burlington, Iowa, Nov. 21, 1957; d. Rodney Darrell and Neola Ann (Wharton) Lewis; m. John Robert Witt, Mar. 31, 1984; children: Jeffrey Lewis, Jennifer Diane. BSN, U. No. Colo., 1980; MSN, U. Colo., 1987. Cert. neonatal nurse practitioner. Staff nurse St. Joseph's Hosp., Denver, 1980-85; neonatal nurse practitioner Denver Children's Hosp., 1986-88; coord. neonatal nurse practitioner and neonatal transport Presbyn.-St. Luke's Med. Ctr., Denver, 1988—2002; neotal nurse practitioner NNP Svcs. of Colo., 2003—. Mem clin faculty neonatal nurse practitioner program Regis U. Column editor: Advances in Neonatal Care; contbr. chapters to books, articles to profl. jours. Troop leader Girl Scouts US; children's Bible tchr., altar guild Episcopal Ch. Mem. Nat. Assn. Neonatal Nurses (co-chair program com. 1992-94, bd. dir., dir.-at-large 1997-99, sec. 1999-2000, pres. 2003-04, past pres. 2005—), Nat. Cert. Corp. (test. com. 1994-96, nominations com. 2004-05). Democrat. Episcopalian. Avocations: altar guild, reading, sewing, dance. Home: 17586 E Dickenson Pl Aurora CO 80013-4180 Office: Presbyn-St Luke's Med Ctr 1719 E 19th Ave Denver CO 80218-1235 Office Phone: 303-839-7735. Personal E-mail: 70044.2401@compuserve.com, catherine.witt@healthonecares.com.

WITT, DOREEN MARIE, sales executive; b. Dubuque, Iowa, Apr. 28, 1960; d. John Dale and Janet Louise (Chunat) Kenkel; m. Carey Michael Witt, Oct. 4, 1986; children: Zachariah Harding, Cody Michael, Greyson Jacob. Student, Loras Coll., 1979; BS in Mktg., Iowa State U., 1983. Asst. mgr. Sanger Harris, Dallas, 1983, sales mgr., 1983, area mgr., 1983-85; product devel. specialist County Seat Stores, Dallas, 1985; S.W. account exec. Perry Ellis Sportswear, Dallas, 1985-86; account exec. Radio Stas. KOKE, KKMJ, Austin, Tex., 1986-90, 93-98; sr. acct. exec. Radio Sta. KKMJ, Austin, 1990-93; dir. sales tng. Radio Stas. KKMJ, KFGI, KJCE, Austin, 1993-96, key acct. mgr., 1996-97, Radio Stas. KKMJ, KFGI, KJCE, nontraditional revenue devel., Austin, 1998—2001; sr. account exec. KKMJ, 2001—06; with Time Warner Cable TV Media Sales, 2006—. Vol. Volente (Tex.) Vol. Fire Dept., 1986—; voter registrar Williamson County, Leander, Tex., 1987; lay reader, sunday sch. tchr. St Lukes on the Lake Episcopal Ch. 1986—. Mem. Am. Mktg. Assn., Austin Bus. Forum (sec. 1987-88, v.p. membership 1988-90, 92—), Am. Women in Radio and TV (v.p. membership 1986-88, membership co-chair 1992—, v.p. scholarship 1988-91, del. 1988, 90, Appreciation award 1986, 87-88, 89-91). Republican. Avocations: waterskiing, skiing, jogging, travel, bible study. Home: 7328 Reed Dr Leander TX 78641-9147

WITT, FELICIA LESTAGE, biology educator; b. Lewisville, Ark., Jan. 26, 1958; d. Charles Weymon and Beatrice Lestage; m. Dennis D. Witt, Nov. 22, 1997; m. Gerald Wade Dodgen, Jan. 26, 1991 (div. June 19, 1994); 1 child, Patrick Wade Dodgen; children: Paul Wayne Perry, Michael Travis Perry. A, Tyler Jr. Coll., Tex., 1977; BS in Biology and Phys. Edn., East Tex. State U., Commerce, 1980; MS in Secondary Edn., Tex. A&M U., Commerce, 2000. Tchr. sci. Wylie ISD, Tex., 1981—82; tchr. anatony and biology Allen H.S., 1982—, tchr. sci., 2005—. Tchr. aide, future tchrs. Am. advisor Allen H.S., 1982—86, asst. student coun. advisor, 1987—2005, coach women's athletics, 1987—91, sr. class advisor, 2000—05, acad. assoc. for sci., 2005—. Recipient Outstanding Am. Tchr., Nat. Honor Roll's, 2006. Mem.: Sci. Tchrs. Assn. Tex., Tex. Assn. Biology Tchrs., Nat. Assn. Biology Tchrs., Alpha Delta Kappa (dist. II chaplain 2004—06). Avocations: reading, gardening, travel. Office: Allen High School 300 Rivercrest Blvd Allen TX 75002 Office Phone: 972-727-0400. Personal E-mail: flwitt@comcast.net. E-mail: felicia_witt@allenisd.org.

WITT, NANCY CAMDEN, artist; b. Richmond, Va., Oct. 24, 1930; d. Roland Parker and Lucy Catherine (Haydon) Riddick; m. Robert Roy Camden, 1951 (div. 1960); children: John Bradley, Matthew David; m. John Temple Witt, Apr. 2, 1966 (div. June 1990); 1 child, Jeremy Temple. BA, Old Dominion U., 1965; MFA, Va. Commonwealth U., 1967; DFA (hon.), Randolph-Macon Coll., 1997. Comml. artist, 1952-60; chmn. art dept. Richard Bland Coll., Petersburg, Va., 1960-63; studio artist Ashland, Va., 1965—; owner Cross Mill Gallery, Ashland. One woman shows include Sharon Bennett Gallery, Atlanta, 1973, Asheville (NC) Mus. Fine Arts, 1976, Longwood Coll., Farmville, Va., 1974, 77, Randolph-Macon Woman's Coll., Lynchburg, Va., 1974, 79, Phillip Morris, Inc., Richmond, 1978, VMI, Lexington, 1965, 79, Touchstone Gallery, NYC., 1974, Roanoke Coll., Salem, 1979, 20th Century Gallery, Williamsburg, Va. 1974, 82, 93, Randolph-Macon Coll., Ashland, Va., 1974, 79, 84, 98, 2005, SECCA, Winston-Salem, 1980, U. Ill., Chgo., 1989, Portsmouth (Va.) Mus., 1984, Cudahy's, Richmond, Va., 1990, 92, 94, 96, 98, 2000, 2002, Between the Muse Gallery, Camden, Maine, 1996, Nancy Moore Fine Art, NYC., 1996, 98, Élan Fine Arts, Rockport, Maine, 2003, Rentz Gallery, Richmond, 2004, others; exhibited in group shows at Valentine Mus. Biennial, Richmond, 1962, Mint Mus., Charlotte, 1971, Miss. Mus. Art, 1979, Chrysler Mus., Norfolk, 1983, Touchstone Gallery, NYC., 1986, Huntington (W.Va.) Mus. Art, 1992, Ridderhof Martin Gallery, Mary Washington Coll, Fredericksburg, Va., 2001, Sweet Briar Coll., Va., 2004; represented in permanent collections Markel Corp., Richmond, David Rockefeller Collection, Phillip Morris Co., Fed. Res. Bank, U. Va., Charlottesville, Va., Norfolk, Ethyl Corp., Richmond, CSX Corp., Richmond, Wheat First, Richmond, others; author: On Alternate Days: The Paintings of Nancy Witt, 1995, (film) Vanishing Point, 1973. Named Va. Artist of Yr., Woman's Caucus for Art, Va., 1993; recipient award for achievement in arts, Randolph-Macon Coll., 2005. Mem. Jungian Venture (co-founder, convener 1984-86). E-mail: wittn@rcn.com.

WITT, RUTH HUTT, management consultant; b. Columbus, Aug. 8, 1957; d. Thomas Micijah and Mary Barnes; children: Jeffrey Tyler Sheppar, William Fisher III. B of Elec. Engring. Tech., Ohio Inst. Tech., Columbus, 1979. Metallurgical tech. Reynolds Metal, Richmond, Va.; bus. analyst Va. Power, Lavisa; mng. prin. Oracle, Reston. Home: 15255 Brazil Cir Dale City VA 22193 Office: Oracle 1910 Oracle Way Reston VA 20190

WITT, SALLY ELEANOR, psychologist, educator; b. Indpls. d. Boyd and Eleanor (Huffman) Graves; m. Donald W. Witt (dec. 1987); children: Leslie, Alison, Donald. BA, Calif. State U., Fullerton, 1965; MEd, Nat. Coll. Edn., 1974; PhD, Northwestern U., 1985. Lic. clin. psychologist. Prof. psychology Oakton Coll., Des Plaines, Ill., 1980—94; pvt. practice Counseling and Hypnosis Ctr., Arlington Heights, Ill., 1985—. Bd. dirs. Chgo. Psychol. Assn., 1990. Prodr. audiotapes Counseling Psychology Self-Hypnosis Tapes, 1989. Mem. APA (approved cons. Clin. Hypnosis), Am. Soc. Clin. Hypnosis, Soc. Psychol. Hypnosis, Chgo. Soc. Clin. Hypnosis (v.p., cons.), Mensa. Office: Counseling and Hypnosis Ctr 1635 N Arlington Heights Rd Arlington Heights IL 60004-3944

WITTENBORG, KARIN, university librarian; m. Michael B. Sullivan. BA, Brown U., 1969; MLS, SUNY-Buffalo, 1976. Positions with SUNY-Buffalo, 1976—79; libr. mgmt. intern MIT, 1981—82; chief gen. reference dept. and curator social sci. collections Stanford U., 1979—85; assoc. univ. libr. collections UCLA, 1985—93; univ. libr. U. Va., 1993—. Adv. coun. Academic Computing and Libr. Stanford U.; mem. com. info. resources Brown U.; exec. com. Digital Libr. Fedn. Avocations: cooking, running, gardening. Office: U Va Libr PO Box 400113 Charlottesville VA 22904 Office Phone: 434-924-7849. Fax: 434-924-1431. E-mail: kw7g@virginia.edu.*

WITTENSTEIN, SHIRLEY ANN, retired branch assistant; b. Kansas City, Mo., Feb. 25, 1924; d. Harry and Jeanette Delphine (Markowitz) Herowitz; m. Harlan Wittenstein (dec. 1992); adopted children: Hal Gregory, Jodi Lynn. BA, Ind. U., Bloomington, 1946. Cert. braillist. Asst. libr. Westport Libr., Kansas City, 1946—48; sales rep., office clk. Macy Co. and Hartzfeld Store, Kansas City, 1948—51; ret. Tutor foreign lang., Des Moines, 1977—85; temporary office worker Meredith Pub. Co., Des Moines, 1977—. Vol. libr. worker Clive Sch. and Franklin Libr., Des Moines, 1973—85; sec. B'nai B'rith Women; vol. Temple B'nai Jeshurun. Avocations: singing, gardening, reading, cooking, walking.

WITTER, KAREN ACKERMAN, museum administrator; b. Peoria, Ill., June 13, 1954; d. Raymond J. and Margaret J. Ackerman; m. Randall F. Witter, Dec. 1, 1979; children: Dorothy, John. BS in Zoology, Iowa State U., Ames, 1976; MS in Ecology, U. Wales, Bangor, 1978. Resource planner Ill. Dept. Conservation, Springfield, 1978—82; dir. Ill. Nature Preserves Commn., Springfield, 1982—85; asst. to Gov. for natural resources Office of Gov., Springfield, Ill., 1985—88; dir. Ill. Dept. Energy & Natural Resources, Springfield, 1988—91; exec. dir. Gov.'s Sci. Adv. Com., Springfield, Ill., 1991—95; asst. to dir. Ill. Dept. Natural Resources, Springfield, 1995—99; assoc. mus. dir. Ill. State Mus., Springfield, 1999—. Cabinet dir. Gov. James R. Thompson, Ill., 1988—91. Mentor U. Chgo. Mentor Program, 1993—; bd. dir. Springfield Pub. Schs. Found., Ill., 2001—, pres., 2005—06. Recipient Cyrus Mark Conservation Award, The Nature Conservancy, 1985; fellow, Rotary Found., 1976—78. Mem.: Ill. Assn. Mus. (bd. mem. 2000—), Assn. Midwest Mus. (bd. mem. 2001—, v.p. 2004—05). Avocations: running, travel. Office: Ill State Mus 502 S Spring St Springfield IL 62706-5000 Office Phone: 217-782-7011.

WITTIG, REBECCA C., community health educator; b. Waukesha, Wis., Oct. 11, 1977; d. Phillip and Christine Wittig. BS in Cmty. Health Edn., U. Wis., La Crosse, 2001; MEd in Health Edn., Carroll Coll., Waukesha, Wis., 2006. Cert. health edn. specialist. Health educator - preceptorship Marquette U. - Ctr. for Health Edn. and Promotion, Milw., 2001; cmty. edn. specialist The Women's Ctr., Inc., Waukesha, Wis., 2002—. Contbr. manual. Mem.: AAHPERD. Roman Catholic. Avocations: yoga, reading.

WITTMAN, BRITTANY LYN, design educator; b. Williamsport, Pa., Apr. 23, 1974; d. Kenneth Lynn Wittman and Linda Diane Cardene. BS in Textile Design cum laude, Phila. Coll. Textiles and Sci., 1997; MFA in Sculpture, U. Arts, 2004. Designer, project mgr. Knoll Textiles/Suzanne Tick, Inc., NYC, 1997—98; assoc. M. Finkel & Dau. Antiques, Phila., 2000; tech. assoc. Phila. U., 2000—04, co-dir. nonwovens design & engring. lab., 2004—05, prof., 2004—05. Adj. prof. Phila. U., 2002—04, vis. asst. prof., 2004—05; studio asst. Peters Valley Craft Ctr., Layton, NJ, 1996, Haystack Sect. Crafts, Deer Isle, Maine, 1999; adj. prof. Art Inst. Pitts. Online, 2006—. Exhibitions include Convergence, 2000, Da Vinci Art Alliance, Phila., 2001, Convergence, 2002, Phila. U. Faculty Show, 2002, Daegu Internat. Textile Design Exch., Korea, 2002, Convergence, 2003, East Falls, Phila., 2005, Premiere Vision, Paris, 2005, Gallery in the Garden, 2005. Asst. curator Lycoming County Hist. Soc., Williamsport, 1995. History Textiles & Costumes fellow, 1994—97. Address: 817 Rural Ave Williamsport PA 17701-3035

WITTMAN, VANESSA AMES, communications executive; b. New London, Conn., Apr. 16, 1967; m. Drew M. Wittman; children: Parker, Mason. BS, U. N.C., 1989; MBA, U. Va., 1993. Assoc. Anderson Consulting, 1989—91; investment banker Morgan Stanley, 1993—96; ptnr. Sterling Payot, 1996—97; CFO Metricom, Inc., 1997—99; sr. dir. corp. devel. Microsoft Corp., 1999—2000; v.p., corp. devel. 360networks, 2000—02, CFO broadband network svcs., 2002—03; exec. v.p., CFO Adelphia Comm. Corp., 2003—. Bd. dirs. InfoSpace, Inc., Bellevue, Wash. Avocations: tennis, skiing. Office: Adelphia Comm Corp 5619 DTC Pkwy Greenwood Village CO 80111 Office Phone: 303-268-6300. Office Fax: 303-268-6495.*

WITTMANN, JANE GORDON, volunteer; b. Salinas, Calif., Aug. 5, 1946; d. Walter Max and Harriet Loveland Gordon; m. William Walter Wittmann, June 29, 1968; children: Emily Harriet Wittmann Gaskill, Gordon Thomas. BA in English, U. Calif., Davis, 1968. Mem. Shasta County Devel. Std. Com, Redding, Calif., 1978—81, Shasta County-Wide Planning Adv. Com., Redding, Calif., 1981—82; forewoman Shasta County Grand Jury, Redding, Calif., 1983—84, chair pub. works com., 1984—85; Brownie leader Sierra Cascade Coun. Girl Scouts USA, 1978—80, jr. leader, 1980—83, cadette leader, 1983—86, sr. leader, 1986—90, svc. unit treas., 1982—90, Day Camp co.- coord., 1986—87, coun. bd. dirs., 1990—91, 1st v.p. coun. bd. dirs., 1991—92, pres. coun. bd. dirs., 1992—97, chair self-evaluation task group, 1991—92, chair performance assessment task force, 1997—98; sec. Pacheco Elem. Sch. Home and Sch. Assn., 1985—87; assoc. mem. bd. dirs. Shasta Cmty. Concert Assn., 1993—95, bd. dirs., 1995—2000, pres., 2000—; ch. sch. coord. 1st Presbyn. Ch., Redding, 1988—91, elder on session, 1991—93, elder, 1991—. Mem.: AAUW (bull. editor 1973—74, membership treas. 1974—75, rec. sec. 1975—76, pres.-elect 1976—77, pres. 1977—78, historian 1978—79, legis. chair 1979—84, cmty. area rep. 1984—85, audit com./newsletter ads 1997—98, audit com. 1998—99). Presbyterian. Avocations: family activities, handbell choir, singing. Home: 6396 Vista del Sierra Dr Anderson CA 96007

WITTMIER, DENISE DONELLE, elementary school educator; b. Jamestown, N.D., Dec. 27, 1956; d. Boyd H. and Judith Williams; m. Dale M. Wittmier, June 17, 1978; children: Austin, Barret, Christa. B, Valley City (N.D.) State U., 1979. Tchr. elem. edn. Streeter (N.D.) Pub. Sch., 1979—97, Gackle (N.D.) Streeter Pub. Sch., 1997—, volleyball coach, 1996—. Mem. Am. Legin Aux. (sec. 1990—), N.D. Reading Assn., Streeter Homemaker's Club. Democrat. Lutheran. Home: 235 Helen St S Streeter ND 58483-7012 Office: Gackle Sch Dist 14 PO Box 375 Gackle ND 58442-0375

WITTNEBEL, MELISSA EILEEN, elementary school educator, music educator; b. Baltimore; Tchr. music Harford County Pub. Schs., Bel Air, Md., 2003—.

WITTNER, LOIS, education educator; d. Rudy Wittner and Stella Knoop; m. Evarkiou Wittner; children: Adrian, Alex. BA in comms., SDSU, 1972; M in comms., Purdue, Lafayette, Ind., 1974; MEd, U. San Diego, 1990. Prof. San Diego Mesa Coll., 1980—. Avocations: travel, model building. Personal E-mail: lwittner@sdccd.ed.

WITTY, ELAINE P., retired dean, education educator; m. Jack P. Witty; children: Janeen, Jack P., Jr. BS, Jackson State U., 1956; MS, Vanderbilt U., 1961, EdD, 1965; postgrad., U. Ga., 1978. Tchr. English McCullough High Sch., Monticello, Miss., 1956-58; mid. sch. tchr. Jackson (Miss.) State U. Lab. Sch., 1958-59, asst. prin., 1963-65; libr. asst. Jackson State U., 1959-60, dir. student teaching and field svcs., 1965-69; head dept. elem. edn. Norfolk (Va.) State U., 1969-79, dean sch. edn., 1979—98, assoc. v.p. acad. affairs, 1998—99, dean emeritus, 1998—. Dir. Norfolk Tchr. Corps Project, 1970-74; mem. Norfolk U. Long Range Planning Com., 1976-79, numerous univ. coms., 1969—; dir. univ. self study for accreditation Nat. Coun. Accreditation in Tchr. Edn., 1970, 80, 91, bd. appeals, 1977-80, vis. com. mem., 1977-83; dir. univ. self study for accreditation So. Assn. Colls. and Schs., 1986-88, vis. com. mem., 1976—; bd. dirs. Am. Assn. Colls. in Tchr. Edn., 1977-80, 85-88, mem. com. multicultural edn., 1980-83, nat. adv. bd. for the study of minority tchr. edn. achievement, 1990; mem. Nat. Tchr. Examinations Policy Bd., 1985-87, advanced edn. com. for GRE, 1983-88; bd. dirs. Va. ASCD, 1985-86; lectr. in field. Contbr. articles to profl. jours. including The Gifted Child Qaurterly, Jour. Tchr. Edn., Jour. Negro Edn., Assn. Tchr. Educators Jour. and Essence; dir. video tapes, 1991; prodr. video tape, 1992. Trustee Presbyn. Sch. Christian Edn., 1974-76, Union Theol. Sem., 1979-82; mem. gen. assembly mission bd. Presbyn. Ch. (USA), 1982-87, exec. com. nat. coun. ch. and race, 1984-87; chair edn. com. Urban League of Hampton Roads, 1987-91, 93—; bd. dirs. Children's Camp Fund of Hampton Roads, 1985—, Tidewater Red Cross, 1992—; campaign mgr. Va. House of Dels.,

Va. State Senate, 1984-91. Recipient Lola Parker Nat. Achievement award Iota Lambda Sorority, 1989, Eula Glover Regional Achievement award Norfolk chpt. Alpha Kappa Alpha Sorority, 1991, Pemeroy award Am. Assn. Colls. and Tchr. Edn., 1994. Office: Norfolk State U 2401 Corprew Ave Norfolk VA 23504-3993

WITZ, GISELA, research scientist, educator; b. Breslau, Federal Republic of Germany, Mar. 16, 1939; came to U.S., 1955. d. Gerhardt Witz and Hildegard (Sufeida) Minzak. BA, NYU, 1962, MS, 1965, PhD, 1969. Assoc. rsch. scientist NYU Med. Ctr., N.Y.C., 1970-73, rsch. scientist, 1973-77, asst. prof., 1977-80, U. Medicine and Dentistry of N.J.-Robert Wood Johnson Med. Sch., Piscataway, NJ, 1980-86, 1986—93, prof., 1993—2000, prof. emeritus, 2001—. Dep. dir. Joint Grad. Program in Toxicology, Rutgers U./Univ. Medicine and Dentistry of N.J.-Robert Wood Johnson Med. Sch., 1988, assoc. dir. 1992-2000; cons. Nat. Rsch. Coun., Washington, 1982-83, 85-86. Recipient Dupont Teaching award, NYU, 1966, Univ. Scholar, Founders Day award, N.Y. U., 1969, Student Appreciation award Rutgers Assn. Toxicology Grad. Students, 1996; honoree 3d Ann. Women in Sci. Symposium, 2000. Fellow Oxygen Soc.; mem. Am. Assn. Cancer Rsch., Am. Chem. Soc., Soc. Toxicology, N.Y. Acad. Sci., Sigma Xi. Avocations: gardening, painting. Office: U Medicine and Dentistry NJ Robert Wood Johnson Med Sch Piscataway NJ 08854 E-mail: witz@eohsi.rutgers.edu.

WIXEN, JOAN SAUNDERS, journalist; b. Boston, Dec. 26, 1931; d. Harry Hyman and Sadye (Ginsburg) Saunders; m. Burton N. Wixen, Aug. 9, 1953; children: Randall, Warren, Bradford. BA, U. So. Calif., LA, 1952; MS, UCLA, 1953. West coast corr. Sunday Mag., Detroit News, 1972—78; journalist LA Times, Christian Sci. Monitor, Chgo. Sun Times, Miami Herald, Fla., San Francisco Chronicle, Washington Star, Buffalo Evening News, LA Daily News, Parade. Contbr. articles to mags. including Family Cir., New Woman, Pageant, Modern Maturity, Eve, to syndicates including United Features, LA Times-Washington Post, N.Am. Newspaper Alliance, Universal Press Syndicate, others. E-mail: saunderswixen@earthlink.net.

WOBBLETON, JUDY KAREN, artist, educator; b. Williamston, NC, Aug. 31, 1947; d. Lloyd Thomas and Lillian Edith (Hudson) Letchworth; m. Albert Virgil Wobbleton Jr., Apr. 7, 1968; children: Olivia Elizabeth Stowe, Virgil Alan. Clk. Beaufort County Hosp., Washington, N.C., 1965-68; ins. supr. Mercy Hosp., Sacramento, 1968-72; adminstrv. asst. hosp. svcs. Fairbanks (Alaska) Meml. Hosp., 1972-75; basketry artist Williamston, 1983—. Co-founder, instr. basketry NC Basketmakers, 1984—; instr. Wayne C.C., Goldsboro, NC, 1986-91. Contbg. artist: The Basket Book, 1988, Basketmaker's Baskets, 1990, Craft Works in The Home, 1990. Troop leader Girl Scouts U.S., Goldsboro, 1983-88, svc. unit mgr., 1987-91; v.p. Roanoke Arts and Crafts Guild, 1991-97, pres., 1998-2003, 05—; active Martin County Arts Coun., 2001—, treas., 2005—. Recipient 2d pl. Wilson Arts Coun., 1987, 3d pl. Martin County Arts Coun., 1992-. Mem. NC Basketmakers Assn. (hon., co-founder 1984, bd. dirs. 1984-94, treas. 1984-90, membership chmn. 1984-87, pres. 1990-94, conv. rev. com. 1994—, mem.-at-large 2000-03, conv. coord. 1987, 2005, bd. dir. 2005—, past pres. 2005—), Goldweavers Basketry Guild (hon.) Avocations: reading, cooking, painting. Home and Office: Baskets By Judy 1325 Oakview St Williamston NC 27892-8664 Office Phone: 252-792-4301. Business E-Mail: wobbleton@coastalnet.com.

WOERTZ, PATRICIA ANN, agricultural company executive, retired oil company executive; b. Pitts., Mar. 17, 1953; married; 3 children. BS in Acctg., Pa. State U., 1974; grad. Internat. Exec. Devel. Program, Columbia U., 1994. Acct. Ernst & Young, Pitts., 1974—77; with Gulf Oil Corp., Pitts., 1977-81, Houston, 1981-85; with debt. reduction process, merger of Gulf and Chevron, 1985-87; fin. mgr. Chevron Info. Tech. Co., 1989-91, strategic planning mgr., 1991-93; pres. Chevron Can. Ltd., Vancouver, B.C., 1993-96, Chevron Internat. Oil Co., 1996-98; v.p. logistics and trading Chevron Products Co., Chevron Corp., 1996-98, v.p., 1998—2001; pres. Chevron Products Co., 1998—2001; exec. v.p. Global Downstream ChevronTexaco Corp, San Francisco, 2001—06; pres., CEO Archer Daniels Midland Co., Decatur, Ill., 2006—. Bd. dirs. Archer Daniels Midland Co., 2006—. Bd. trustees U. San Diego; bd. visitors Pa. State U. Named a Disting. Alumna, Pa. State U., 2005; named one of Most Powerful Women in Bus., Fortune mag., 2005, 100 Most Powerful Women, Forbes Mag., 2006, 50 Most Powerful Women in Bus., Fortune mag., 2006; recipient Alumni Fellow award, 2002. Mem.: Calif. C. of C. (bd. mem. 1999—), Am. Petroleum Inst. (bd. dirs.). Office: Archer Daniels Midland Co 4666 Faries Pkwy Decatur IL 62526*

WOFFORD, CHLOE ANTHONY See MORRISON, TONI

WOHL, LAURIE, artist; b. Washington, Dec. 17, 1942; d. Elmer Philip and Betty T. Wohl; m. Stephen J. Schulhofer, May 28, 1975; children: Samuel A. Schulhofer-Wohl, Jonah B. Schulhofer-Wohl. BA, Sarah Lawrence Coll., 1965; LLB, Columbia U., 1968. Bar: N.Y. 1968. Clk. to Hon. Charles Metzner U.S. Dist. Ct. (so. dist.) N.Y., 1968-69; assoc. Debevoise, Plimpton, N.Y.C., 1969-71; asst. prof. U. Nairobi, Kenya, 1971-72, Northeastern U. Law Sch., Boston, 1972-73, U. Pa. Law Sch., Phila., 1973-75; artist, 1976—. Reporter com. on lawyers' role in securities transactions N.Y. City Bar Assn., 1975-76; lectr. in field. One-person shows include ARC Gallery, 1987, 89, 92, C.G. Jung Inst., Evanston, Ill., 1988, Two Ill. Ctr., Chgo., 1990, Barrington (Ill.) Area Arts Coun. Gallery, 1990, Carole Jones Gallery, Chgo., 1994, 95, 96, Cuneo Mus., Vernon Hills, Ill., 1995, Cath. Theol. Union, 1996; exhibited in group shows Galerie Taub, Phila., 1984, Univ. City Arts League, Phila., 1985, ARC on Tour, 1986-87, Countryside Art Ctr., Arlington Heights, Ill., 1987, Galerie Ten, Rockford, Ill., 1988, ARC Gallery, 1988, 91, 93, 94, Around the Coyote, Chgo., 1990, 91, Cross Currents Gallery, Chgo., 1991, 4th Presbyn. Ch., Chgo., 1992, No. Ind. Arts Assn., Munster, 1991, Schneider Gallery, Chgo., 1992, Tonalli Gallery, Centro Cultural Ollin Yolliztli, Mexico City, 1992, Rush-Presbyn.-St. Lukes Med. Ctr. Chgo., 1992, R.H. Love Contemporary, Chgo., 1993, Seebeck Gallery, Kenosha, Wis., 1993, Old Courthouse Art Ctr., Woodstock, Ill., 1994, Chgo. Sch. Profl. Psychology, Chgo., 1994, Arts Ctr., Iowa City, 1994, Billy Graham Ctr. Mus., Wheaton (Ill.) Coll., 1995, 2d Presbyn. Ch., Chgo., 1995, Guilford (Conn.) Handcraft Ctr., 1995, Cuneo Mus., Am. Craft Mus., N.Y.C., 1995, Gen. Media Fine Arts Exec. Gallery, N.Y.C., 1995; represented in mus. and pub. collections Am. Craft Mus., N.Y.C., Kenosha Hosp. Chapel; represented in pvt. collections throughout U.S. and abroad. Mem. Textile Soc. Am., ARC Gallery (affiliate, bd. dirs. 1989-93). Home: 126 E 35th St New York NY 10016-3807 Office Phone: 646-486-0586. Personal E-mail: lauriewohl@yahoo.com.

WOHLER, MARJORIE LYNN COULTER, medical/surgical nurse, health facility administrator; d. Cleo Sr. and Ima Neola (Dean) Coulter; m. Robert Frederick Jr., Mar. 9, 1979. Diploma, Bapt. Hosp. Sch. Nursing, 1970; BSN, McNeese State U., 1975; MS in Nursing, Tex. Woman's U., 1978; postgrad., Baylor Coll., 1981-82. Cert. breast self-examination. Dir. nursing svc. Beaumont (Tex.) Remedial Clinic; staff nurse/charge Bapt. Hosp., Beaumont; asst. prof. Lamar U., Beaumont; nurse mgr. St. Elizabeth Hosp., Beaumont; dir. med. surg. svcs. Chester St. Elizabeth Hosp., Beaumont, 2006—. Mem. ANA, Tex. Nursing Assn., Heart Failure Nursing Assn., Health Profl. Edn. Forum, Leadership Beaumont, Sigma Theta Tau. Home: 5655 Margaret Ln Beaumont TX 77708-2921

WOHLTMANN, HULDA JUSTINE, pediatrician, endocrinologist; b. Charleston, S.C., Apr. 10, 1923; d. John Diedrich and Emma Lucia (Mohrmann) W. BS, Coll. Charleston, 1944; MD, Med. U. S.C., 1949. Diplomate Am. Bd. Pediatrics. Intern Louisville Gen. Hosp., 1949-50; resident in pediatrics St. Louis Children's Hosp., 1950-53, 1953-65, instr., 1953-58, asst. prof., 1958-65, postdoctoral fellow biochemistry, 1961-63; assoc. prof. pediatrics, head pediatric endocrinology Med. U. S.C., Charleston, 1965-70, prof., 1970-90, prof. emeritus, 1990—. Bd. dirs. Franke Home, Charleston, 1975-97, treas., 1989-91; mem. adv. bd. for ethics ctr. Newberry (S.C.) Coll., 1989—; trustee Luth. Theol. So. Sem., 1991-97. Contbr. articles to sci. jours. Mem. Am. Pediatric Soc., Ambulatory Pediatric Assn., Endocrine Soc., Am. Diabetes Assn., Am. Acad. Pediatrics, Midwest Soc. Pediatric Rsch., So. Soc. Pediatric Rsch., S.C. Diabetes Assn. (bd. dirs. 1970-86, pres. 1970-73, 84-85, v.p. 1982-83, Profl. Svc. award 1977), Lawson Wilkins Endocrine Soc., Sugar Club; fell. Am. Acad. Pediatrics. Lutheran. Home: 3 46th Ave Isle Of Palms SC 29451-2607

WOHRLE, MARTA, publishing executive; b. Manchester, Eng. Ptnr., co-founder Informed Sources, 1993—2002; dir. Mercer Mgmt. Cons., 2002—06; v.p., dir. digital media Hachette Filipacchi Media U.S., NYC, 2006—. Office: Hachette Filipacchi Media US 1633 Broadway New York NY 10019 Office Phone: 212-767-6000.*

WOIKE, LYNNE ANN, computer scientist; b. Torrance, Calif., Oct. 20, 1960; d. Stephen J. and Virginia (Ursich) Shane; m. Thomas W. Woike, Feb. 13, 1988; 1 child, Karla. BSc in Computer Sci. cum laude, Calif. State U., Dominguez Hills, 1994. Computer cons. Unocal Oil Co., Wilmington, Calif., 1992-94; x-window/motif software developer Logican Inc., San Pedro, Calif., 1994-95; reticle engr. TRW, Inc., Redondo Beach, Calif., 1982-88, sr. mem. tech. staff product data mgmt. database adminstr., 1995-98, chmn. product data mgmt. change control bd., 1995—98, sr. Unix/NT system adminstr., 1999; tech. lead, subscriber database DIRECTV, Inc., El Segundo, Calif., 1999—2002; computer and network mgr. Northrop Grumman Mission Systems, Redondo Beach, Calif., 2002—. Mem. IEEE, IEEE Computer Sci., Assn. for Computing Machinery (chmn. student chpt. 1993-94), Calif. State U. Sci. Soc. (computer sci. rep. 1993-95). Office: Northrop Grumman Mission Sys One Space Park R5/B180 Redondo Beach CA 90278 Office Phone: 310-813-3360. Business E-Mail: lynne.woike@ngc.com.

WOIT, BONNIE FORD, artist; b. N.Y.C., Jan. 19, 1931; d. Gaylon Tracy and Geraldine Ida (Gillespie) Ford; m. Erik Peter Woit; children: Peter, Steven. BA, Allegheny Coll., 1953; postgrad., Harvard U. Extension Courses, 1954-55; student advanced seminars, Silvermine Sch. Art, 1970-72. One-woman shows include U.S. Embassy, Paris, 1969, Galerie La Palette Bleu, Paris, 1970, Silvermine Guild Gallery, New Canaan, Conn., 1974, New Canaan Soc. for Arts, 1978, Olympic Towers, N.Y.C., 1980, Ingber Gallery, N.Y.C., 1981, 84, New Canaan Nature Mus., 1987, Munson Gallery, New Haven, 1990, Gallery Bai, Barcelona, Spain, 1999, Bowman Gallery, 2002; group shows include Green Farms Invitational, Conn. (award), 1977, New Eng. Exhbn. at Silvermine (William Lowman award, New. Eng. award 1979), 1978, Conn. Painters and Sculptors Annual Stamford (Conn.) Mus., 1980, Arteder Exhbn. Bilbao, Spain, 1982, Artists invite Artists, Art Pl., Southport, Conn., 1988, P.S. 122 Ann. Show, 1990, Silvermine Guild Gallery, 1990; large scale acrylics on canvas in pvt. and pub. collections U.S., France, Denmark, Fed. Republic Germany, Spain. V.p. Silvermine Guild Arts Ctr., 1976-78; pres. Resources Ultd., Darien, Conn., 1970-76, later advisor painting class for handicapped adults. Mem. Inst. for Visual Artists (founder, chmn. 1984—). Democrat. Avocation: gardening. Studio: 55 W 16th St Apt 5 New York NY 10011-6305

WOJCIECHOWSKI, AMY JO, college official; b. Bay City, Mich., Nov. 17, 1958; d. Carl Theodore and Erma Mina (Kilgus) Rummel; m. Jim E. Wojciechowski, Mar. 2, 1984; children: Jason, Krista. BS, Cen. Mich. U., 1980; M in Occupational Edn., Ferris State U., 1993. Cert. secondary vocat. tchr., Mich. Foodsvc. mgr. trainee Saga Foodsvc. Mgmt. Corp., Menlo Park, Calif., 1980; tchr. vocat. edn. Manistee (Mich.) High Sch., 1987-88; instr., mgr. foodsvc. West Shore Community Coll., Scottville, Mich., 1980-86, prof., 1988—, prof. food svc., 1988—. Mem. curriculum devel. team Food/Lodging Tourism Cluster State of Mich., 1990. Mem. Nat. Restaurant Assn., Am. Sch. Food Svc. Assn., Mich. Restaurant Assn., Mich. Coun. Hotel, Restaurant and Instnl. Edn. Republican. Lutheran. Avocations: snowmobiling, cooking, children. Home: 11725 Morton Rd Manistee MI 49660-9530 Office: West Shore C C 3000 S Stiles Rd Scottville MI 49454-9791

WOJCIK, BARBARA ELZBIETA, statistician, researcher; d. Stanislaw and Stanislawa Marciniak; m. Zbigniew M. Wojcik, 1974; children: Martin R., Paulina M. BSEE, MSEE, Tech. U. Warsaw, 1973; PhD, Polish Acad. Scis., 1979. Supervisory statistician Ctr. for Healthcare Edn. and Studies, Fort Sam Houston, Tex., 1993—2001; dep. dir. Ctr. for AMEDD Strategic Studies, Fort Sam Houston, 2001—. Named one of the Top 25 Cancer Rschrs. in the U.S., Am. Cancer Soc., 1998. Mem.: APHA. Achievements include research in healthcare, epidemiology, statistics, rough sets. Office: Ctr for AMEDD Strategic Studies 1608 Stanley Rd Bldg 2268 Fort Sam Houston TX 78234 Office Phone: 210-221-9633. Business E-Mail: barbara.wojcik@amedd.army.mil.

WOJTKO, DONNAMARIE, music educator, director; d. Joseph Zwolinsky and Pauline Putnick; m. Edward John Wojtko; children: Maribeth, Matthew, Mark. BA, Glassboro State Coll., NJ, 1973; MA, Rider U., Lawrenceville, NJ, 1978. Lic. music tchr. State of NJ, 1973, tchr. nursery sch. State of NJ, 1985, elem. sch. tchr. State of NJ, 1986, cert. student personnel svcs. State of NJ, 1989, substance awareness coord. State of NJ, 1994, lic. profl. counselor State of NJ, 1999, supr. State of NJ, 2004. Instrumental and vocal music tchr. Mt. Holly Twp. Sch., NJ, 1973—78; choir dir. St. Nicholas Byzantine Ch., Roebling, NJ, 1979—2005; music tchr. Lumberton Twp. Sch., NJ, 1988—91, sch. counselor, substance awareness coord., 1991; instrumental music tchr. Tabernacle Twp. Sch., NJ, 1990—91; choir dir. Holy Trinity Byzantine Ch. Choir, Phila., 2005. Bd. mem. RCASA-Regional Mcpl. Alliance, Mt. Holly, 1991—. Musician: (musical composition and arrangements) Byzantine Church Hymns. Bd. mem. Adv. Bd. Burlington County Coun. on Alcohol, NJ, 2006. Mem.: Burlington County Sch. Counselors Assn. (membership chair 1999—2003, exec. bd. 2000—04, Counselor of Yr. 2003), NJ. Sch. Counselors Assn. Avocations: fossil hunting, singing, gardening. Home: 114 Kingsbridge Dr Lumberton NJ 08048 Office: Lumberton Twp Sch 33 Municipal Dr Lumberton NJ 08048 Office Phone: 609-518-0030. Business E-Mail: dwojtko@lumberton.k12.nj.us.

WOJTUSIK, MARYLOU, special education educator, consultant; b. New Britain, Conn., Apr. 10, 1937; d. Joseph Peter and Jane Elizabeth (Kolpak) W. BE, St. John Coll., Cleve., 1961; MEd, Marquette U., 1966, cert., 1975. Cert. gen. and spl. edn. tchr., Conn. Tchr. Immaculate Heart of Mary Sch., Cleve., 1961-65, Holy Cross Sch., New Britain, 1965-72, Consol. Schs. of New Britain, 1972-85, dist. cons., 1985—. Guest lectr. Ctrl. Conn. State U., New Britain, 1985—, St. Joseph Coll., West Hartford, Conn., 1991—; co-presenter early intervention Keene (N.H.) State Coll., 1989—; co-presenter collaboration Nat. Assn. Sch. Psychologists, Chgo., 1989—, N.Y.C. Schs. Conf., 1989—; presenter state and nat. EIP Confs., 1990— Mem. Conn. Citizens Action Group, Hartford, 1987—; tech. advisor Conn. Early Intervention Project. Recipient L.E.A.D. award State of Conn., 1990. Mem. Coun. for Exceptional Children, ASCD, Cen. Cons. in Conn., Collaboration Network. Avocations: cross country skiing, handwork, computers, interior decorating, woodworking. Office: Cons Special Edn Resource Ctr Middletown CT

WOLAHAN, CARYLE GOLDSACK, nursing educator, consultant; b. Somerville, N.J., July 27, 1942; d. Wilbur Wood and Jane (Hadley) Goldsack; m. Thomas Warren Hussey, June 26, 1965 (dec. Oct. 1970); 1 child, Timothy Stephen; m. William Kevin Wolahan, Sept. 30, 1983 (dec. Jan. 2001). BS, Wagner Coll., 1964; MEd, Columbia U., 1973, EdD, 1979. Sch. nurse, tchr. Malverne Pub. Schs., NY, 1966—67, Dover-Wingdale Pub. Schs., Dover Plains, NY, 1967—68; head nurse Harlem Valley State Hosp., Wingdale, NY, 1968—69; asst. prof., acting dir. div. nursing Trenton State Coll., NJ, 1973—77; assoc. prof., acting dir. Felician Coll., Lodi, NJ, 1979—80, dir. divsn. nursing, 1982—87; dir. nursing program Stern Coll., Yeshiva U., N.Y.C., 1980—82; assoc. dean Coll. Nursing SUNY Health Sci. Ctr., Bklyn., 1987—91, acting dean Coll. Nursing, 1991—92; dean sch. nursing Adelphi U., 1992—2000; prof. nursing Adelphi U. Sch. Nursing, 2000—05; ret., 2005; nursing edn. cons., 2005—. Contbr. articles to profl. jours., chpts. to books; editor Topics in Clin. Nursing, 1983. Trustee Cath. Med. Ctrs. Bklyn. and Queens, 1989-2000, chair continuous quality improvement com., 1998-2000; regional bd. St. Vincent's Cath. Med. Ctrs. Recipient NEAA award, Disting. Trustee award United Hosp. Fund, 2000; named Woman of Achievement Alpha Omicron Pi; named to Nursing Hall of Fame Tchrs. Coll. Columbia U., 1999. Mem. ANA (del. 1978-87), NJ State Nurses Assn. (coun. on edn. 1976-82, chmn. com. on ednl. preparation 1984-88), NY State Nurses Assn. (chair pub. rels. com. 1990-92, spkrs. bur., recruitment com. Dist. 14, 1990, chair coun. on edn.), Nat. League for Nursing (accreditation com. 1985-90, site visitor 1984-98), Am. Acad. Nursing, Nursing Edn. Alumni Assn. Tchrs. Coll. (pres. 1990-94. v.p. 2003-04, pres. 2004-06), Lake Hopatcong Yacht Club (fleet surgeon 2004—), Sigma Theta Tau. Episcopalian. Avocations: boating, reading, theater, hand crafts. Home and Office: 13 Ford Rd Landing NJ 07850 Personal E-mail: dublin@optonline.net. Business E-Mail: wolahan@adelphi.edu.

WOLANER, ROBIN PEGGY, internet and magazine publisher; b. Queens, NY, May 6, 1954; d. David H. and Harriet (Radlow) W.; children: Terry David, Bonnie Lee. BS in Indsl. and Labor Rels., Cornell U., 1975. Sr. editor Viva Mag., N.Y.C., 1975-76; editor Impact Mag., N.Y.C., 1976-77; circulation mgr. Runner's World Mag., Mountain View, Calif., 1977-79; cons. Ladd Assocs., San Francisco, 1979-80; gen. mgr. Mother Jones Mag., San Francisco, 1980-81, pub., 1981-85; founder, pub. Parenting Mag., San Francisco, 1985-91, pres., 1991-92; v.p. Time Pub. Ventures, 1990-96; pres., CEO Sunset Pub. Corp., 1992-95; exec. v.p. CNET, 1997—2002. Bd. dirs. Working Assets, Tides Found. Author: Naked in the Boardroom: A CEO Bares Her Secrets So You Can Transform Your Career, 2005. Jewish. Personal E-mail: robin_wolaner@yahoo.com.

WOLANIN, BARBARA ANN BOESE, curator, art historian; b. Dayton, Ohio, Dec. 12, 1943; d. William Carl and Elisabeth Cassell Boese; m. Thomas R. Wolanin, 1966 (div. 1980); children: Peter, Andrew; m. Phillip F. Brown, 2001. AB, Oberlin Coll., 1966, AM, 1969; MAT, Harvard U., 1967; PhD, U. Wis., 1981. Art tchr. Newton (Mass.) Pub. Schs., 1969-71; asst. prof. art history Trinity Coll., Washington, 1978-83, James Madison U., Harrisonburg, Va., 1983-85; curator U.S. Capitol, Arch. of the Capitol, Washington, 1985—. Author: (exhbn. catalog) Arthur B. Carles, 1983, 2000, Constantino Brumidi, 1998; contbr. articles to profl. jours. Recipient Faculty Devel. award, James Madison U., 1985; Woodrow Wilson fellow, 1967, Kress fellow, U. Wis., 1974, Smithsonian fellow, 1976. Mem.: Am. Inst. Conservation, Coll. Art Assn., ArtTable (bd. dirs. DC chpt. 2003—05), Women's Caucus Art (pres. DC chpt. 1998—2001, nat. bd. dirs. 2002—), Phi Beta Kappa (pres. Trinity Coll. 1982—83). Home: 7807 Hamilton Spring Rd Bethesda MD 20817 Office: US Capitol Office Architect Washington DC 20515-0001

WOLD, PATRICIA N., psychiatrist; b. Lincoln, Nebr., Jan. 1, 1927; d. John Marshall Neely and Edna Pessy; m. Aaron Wold, Dec. 3, 1957; children: Marshall B., Leo J., Miriam J. BA, U. Nebr., 1948, MD, 1952. Chief of svc. MMHC, Boston, 1956—57; med. dir. East Providence Mental Health Clin., RI, 1964—80; pvt. practice Providence, 1964—. Contbr. articles to profl. jours., chapters to books. Fellow: APA; mem.: Am. Soc. of Women Psychiatrists, RI Med. Soc. Physician's Health Com., RI Med. Soc., Alpha Omega Alpha. Office: 355 Thayer St Providence RI 02906-1550

WOLDEN, SUZANNE LEESA, pediatric radiation oncologist; b. West Covina, Calif., June 30, 1969; MD, U. Calif. San Francisco Sch. Medicine, 1994. Cert. Radiation Oncology. Intern Cornell Med. Ctr., NY, 1994—95; resident Stanford U. Med. Ctr., Calif., 1995—98; asst. attending Meml. Sloan-Kettering Cancer Ctr., NY, 1998—. Contbr. articles to profl. jours. Office: Meml Sloan-Kettering Cancer Ctr 1275 York Ave New York NY 10021 Office Phone: 212-639-5148.*

WOLEK, ANDREA DUGAS, special education educator; b. New Rochelle, N.Y., Feb. 26, 1958; d. Franklyn John and Faye (Thornton) Dugas; m. William Charles Wolek, July 13, 1991; children: Steven Frank, Christopher James. BS, So. Meth. U., 1979; MEd, U. Tex., 1983. Tchr. deaf multi-handicapped Dallas Ind. Sch. Dist., 1979-81, tchr. autism program, 1983—; rsch. asst. Pro-Ed, Austin, 1981-83. Leader Cub Scouts, 2004—06. Zeta Tau Alpha Crown Found. grad. scholar, 1981, 82. Mem.: Alliance Dallas Educators, Dau. of the Rep. Tex. Roman Catholic. Avocations: bicycling, crafts, reading. Home: 7306 Dalewood Ln Dallas TX 75214-1815 Office: L K Hall Sch 2120 Keats Dr Dallas TX 75211-8538

WOLF, ALICE KOERNER, state legislator, former mayor; b. Vienna, Dec. 24, 1933; d. Frederick Koerner and Renee (Engel) K.; m. Robert A. Wolf, 1955; children: Eric Jeffrey, Adam Nathaniel. BS, Simmons Coll., 1955; MPA, Harvard U., 1978; EdD (hon.), Wheelock Coll., 2001. Residence staff MIT, Lincoln Lab, 1955-62, Computer Corp Am., 1967-71, pers. dir., 1971-76; mem. Cambridge Sch. Com., 1974-81, vicechairwoman, 1976-77, 80-81; chairwoman Ward 7 Dem. Com., 1976-85; committeewoman Mass. State Dem. Com.; former vice mayor City of Cambridge, Mass., mayor Mass., 1990-91; mem. dist. 25 Middlesex Mass. Ho. of Reps., Boston. Del. Dem. Nat. Conv., 1980, 84, 88, 92, State Conv. Mem. NOW, Mass. Women's Polit. Caucas Cambridge Mental Health Assn., Am. for Dem. Action, Nat. Orgn. Women Am. Civil Liberties Union, Nat. Office: Mass Ho of Reps State House Rm 134 Boston MA 02133 Home: 48 Huron Ave Cambridge MA 02138-6706 Office Phone: 617-722-2400. Personal E-mail: alice@alicewolf.org. Business E-Mail: rep.alicewolf@hou.state.ma.us.

WOLF, ANN E., chemistry educator; b. Herkimer, NY, Nov. 17, 1952; d. Clyde Smith and Marjorie Barker Wolf; 1 child, Samira Ann Borey. MAT in Chemistry, Bridgewater State Coll., Mass., 1988. Tchr. sci. East Jr. High, Brockton, Mass., 1975—76; tchr. chemistry Notre Dame H.S., Fitchburg, 1976—77, Am. Sch. Kuwait, Shaab, 1977—81, Am. Cultural Assn. Turin, Italy, 1981—83, Plymouth South H.S., 1983. Advisor student coun. Plymouth South HS, 1993. Avocations: travel, swimming, photography. Home: 9 Handy Rd Pocasset MA 02559-2218 Office: Plymouth South High School 4990 Long Pond Rd Plymouth MA 02360 Office Phone: 508-224-7512. Home Fax: 508-224-6765; Office Fax: 508-224-6765. Personal E-mail: aworl@plymouth.k12.ma.us. E-mail: awolf@plymouth.k12.ma.us.

WOLF, CHERYL JEANE, surgical nurse; b. Palmerton, Pa., Jan. 2, 1951; d. Daniel and Helen (Bruszo) Torretta; 1 child, Christopher. BS, St. Joseph's Coll., 1989; diploma, Christ Hosp. Sch. Nursing, 1972. RN, N.J.; cert. oper. rm. nurse, nursing adminstr. Charge nurse St. Vincents Hosp., Montclair, NJ, 1972-79; staff nurse Columbus Hosp., Newark, 1979-80; supr. oper. rm. Riverside Hosp., Boonton, NJ, 1980-82; dir. nursing surg. svcs. St. Clare's Hosp., Denville, NJ, 1982—2001; dir. perioperative svcs. St. Barnabas Health Svcs., Irvington (NJ) Gen. Hosp., 2001—06; adminstrv. dir. Perioperative Svcs. Joint Barnabas Health Svcs., NJ, 2006—. Faculty Met. Laparoscopic Inst. Pres. Rockaway Bd. Health. Mem. Assn. Oper. Room Nurses, Orgn. Nurse Execs., Am. Coll. Healthcare Execs. Office Phone: 908-851-7394.

WOLF, CHRISTINE STRELOW, piano teacher; b. Rochester, Minn., Jan. 27, 1964; d. Donald Eugene and Arlene Audrey Strelow; m. Michael Joseph Wolf, Nov. 02, 1991; children: Elizabeth and Gregory. MusB cum laude, St. Cloud State U., 1986; postgrad. piano performance, Hartt Sch. Music, 1987—89. Nat. cert. tchr. music. Ind. music tchr. Music Tchrs'. Nat. Assn., Rochester, St. Cloud, and Hartford, 1982—89, Apple Valley, Minn., 1992—; music link tchr. Nat. Assn. Music Tchrs., 1999—. Chmn. Nat. Guild Auditions, Apple Valley, 1999—; contest judge coord. Minn. Assn. Music Tchrs., 1991-98; accompanist Mayo H.S., Redeemer Lutheran Ch., Rochester, 1979-82, St. Cloud State U. choirs, vocal dept., 1982-86; dir. children's choir Emanuel Lutheran Ch., Hartford, 1988-89; music dir. Lutheran Ch. Our Savior, Rosemount, Minn., 1994—; min. of music All St. Eugen, 2002-. Composer, arranger contemporary Christian songs; TV and radio appearances including Live From Landmark, 1972-82, 86, 88-89; composer (piano duet) Porcupine Polka, 2003, (piano duet) I Wanna Be a Spy, 2005, (piano solo) Monkey Business, 2005; inventor (music theory tchg. aid) Bag O' Blocks, 2005 Performer various nursing homes, Dakota county; organizer student performances nursing homes, malls, Dakota County. Recipient Hiawathaland 1st place Rochester Keyboard Club, 1981, Duet Competition 1st place Dorian Music Festival Luther Coll., Decorah, Iowa, 1982; Ruth Gant Meml. scholar,

St. Cloud State U., 1984-86. Mem.: Minn. Assn. Music Tchrs. (v.p. conv. 2002—05), Minn. Music Tchrs. Assn. (judge 1991—, contest judge coord. 1992—99, adjudication com. 2000—, conv. com. 2001—, Young Artist of 1986), Am. Coll. Musicians (adjucator, chmn. 1991—, judge 1999—, Paderewski Gold medal, Piano diploma 1982), Music Tchrs. Nat. Assn., Nat. Fedn. Music Clubs. E-mail: wolfpiano@prodigy.net.

WOLF, GERALYN, bishop; b. Apr. 30, 1947; BS, West Chester U., Pa., 1968; MA in Edn., Trenton State Coll., NJ, 1971; MDiv, Episcopal Div. Sch., Cambridge, Mass., 1977. Tchr. George Sch., Newtown, Pa., 1970—74; ordained deacon, 1977, priest, 1978; served several Phila. area congregations, 1977—81; vicar St. Mary's Episcopal Ch., Phila., 1981—87; dean Christ Ch. Cathedral, Louisville, 1987—95; consecrated bishop, 1996; bishop Episcopal Diocese of RI, 1996—. Retreat leader and spkr. for the homeless. Author: Down and Out in Providence, various hymn texts. Episcopalian. Achievements include serving as the first female Dean of a Cathedral; mem. US Field Hockey Touring Team, Argentina, 1973. Office: Episcopal Diocese of RI Diocesan House & Resource Ctr 275 N Main St Providence RI 02903-1298 Office Phone: 401-274-4500. Office Fax: 401-331-9430. Business E-Mail: beeplepeople@cox.net.

WOLF, HELEN, director; d. Frank and Klara Wolf. BA, Pace U., NY, 1989; MS in Edn., CUNY, 2000. Cert. Child Abuse Tng. and Recognition N.Y., 1989. Tchr. grade 5 St. Pius V Elem. Sch., Jamaica, NY, 1986—95; tchr., religion and social studies Bishop Loughlin Meml. H.S., Bklyn., 1995—2000; tchr./rel. dept. chair Nazareth Regional H.S., Bklyn., 2001—02; campus min. The Coll. of New Rochelle, 2000—01, dir. campus ministry, 2002—. Dir. music St. Pius V R.C. Ch., Jamaica, 1990—. Contbr. book; author: (article) Celebration; musician (leader of song): (singing/playing guitar) St. Matthias R.C. Ch. Mem.: Pax Christi USA. Office: The Coll of New Rochelle 29 Castle Pl New Rochelle NY 10805 Office Phone: 914-654-5357.

WOLF, IRNA LYNN, psychologist; b. Dunottar, South Africa, Aug. 30, 1949; came to U.S., 1977; d. John and Tolsa W.; m. Raymond Frank Shamos, Feb. 22, 1976; children: Lorin Iver, Richard Lance, Ilan Hiram, Troy Joseph. MFA cum laude, U. Witwatersrand, 1976; MA, U. Rochester, 1983; PhD, Ariz. State U., 1991, postgrad., 1997. Lic. psychologist, Ariz., diplomate Am. Bd. Psychology; cert. sch. psychologist. Rsch., tchg. asst. Ariz. State U., Tempe, 1984-89; ind. rsch., 1989-97; pvt. practice Phoenix, 1997—. Lectr. in field; cons. Human Info. Processing, 1997—. Contbr. articles to profl. jours. Recipient Certificate of Appreciation Paradise Valley Police Dept., 1992. Mem. APA, Am. Psychol. Soc., Nat. Assn. Sch. Psychologists, We. Psychol. Assn., Ariz. Psychol. Assn., Phi Kappa Phi. Republican. Avocations: painting, drawing, hiking, swimming. Home: 4516 E Onyx Ave Phoenix AZ 85028-4200

WOLF, JEAN D., educational consultant, writer; b. Norfolk, Va., Oct. 19, 1947; d. James Charles and Jean Audrey (Emanuel) Dempsey; m. Donald Marshall Wolf, Oct. 2, 1971; children: James; Andrew, Katharine, Jeffrey and John (quads). AB in Polit. Sci., Smith Coll., 1969; MEd, Harvard U., 1977. Analyst, edn. and pub. welfare divsn. Congl. Rsch. Svc./Libr. of Congress, Washington, 1969-73; cons. ABT, Cambridge, Mass., 1973-74, Dunbar Assocs., Washington, 1999—. Chmn. Phillips coun. The Phillips Collection, Washington, 1996-98; chmn. Washington docents Nat. Gallery of Art, 1988-90; bd. dirs., bd. of lady visitors Children's Hosp., Washington, 1994—. Roman Catholic. Avocations: writing, travel. Home: 1 E Kirke St Chevy Chase MD 20815-4216 also: 6 Rue Chanoinesse Paris 75004 France

WOLF, JOAN SILVERMAN, special education educator; b. Boston, Aug. 28, 1936; d. Isaac and Rose (Berman) Silverman; m. Harold H. Wolf, Aug. 11, 1957; children: Gary, David. BS, U. Utah, 1960; MA, Ohio State U., 1970, PhD, 1976. Nat. cert. sch. psychologist; cert. tchr. in regular and spl. edn. Grad. rsch. assoc. Ohio State U., Columbus, 1974-76; clin. asst. prof. dept. spl. edn. U. Utah, Salt Lake City, 1976-82, asst. prof. dept. spl. edn., 1982-87, assoc. prof. dept. spl. edn., 1987-94, prof. dept. spl. edn., 1994—. Cons. for sch. dists. on issues related to gifted edn., tng. of tchrs. and parents; coord. gifted program U. Utah, Salt Lake City, 1978. Contbr. articles on gifted edn. and the learning disabled to profl. jours.; co-author books. Mem. Am. Psychol. Assn., Nat. Assn. Sch. Psychologists, Utah Psychol. Assn., Western Psychol. Assn., Coun. for Exceptional Children, Nat. Assn. for Gifted Children. Office: U Utah Dept Spl Edn Salt Lake City UT 84112

WOLF, KATIE LOUISE, state legislator; b. Wolcott, Ind., July 9, 1925; d. John H. and Helen Munsterman; m. Charles W. Wolf, 1945; children: Mark, Marcia. Grad., Ind. Bus. Coll., 1944. Registration officer County of White, Ind., 1960, mgr. lic. bur. Ind., 1960-68; clk. 39th Jud. Cir. Ct., 1968-78; mem. Ind. Ho. of Reps., 1985-86, Ind. State Senate, 1987—. Mem. Dem. Nat. Com., 1968-90; del. Dem. nat. convs., 1972, 76, 80, 84. Named Woman of Yr., Bus. and Profl. Women's Club, 1984, Outstanding Freshman Legislator, 1985, Legislator of Yr., Ind. Conservation Offices Assn., Ind. Trial Lawyers Assn.; recipient award, Ind. Broadcasters Assn., 1985, Athen award, Monticello Greater C. of C., 1987, award, Nat. Fedn. Ind. Bus., 1998, Lifetime Achievement award, Monticello Greater C. of C., 2000, Sagamore of the Wabash award, Gov. O'Bannon, 2000, Dir.'s award, Purdue U., 2000, 4-Way Test award, Monticello Rotary, 2001, Child Case Devel. and Step Ahead award, White County. Lutheran.

WOLF, LINDA S., retired advertising executive; Grad., Ohio Wesleyan U. Asst. account exec. Leo Burnett Group, Chgo., 1978; exec. v.p. new bus., dir. worldwide, group pres. N.Am. Leo Burnett Co., Inc., Chgo., 1978-2000; CEO Leo Burnett USA, Chgo., 2000—01; chmn., CEO Leo Burnett Worldwide, Chgo., 2001—05; ret., 2005. Bd. dir. Field Mus. Natural History, Children's Meml. Hosp., The Off The Street Club, Chgo. Coun. Fgn. Rels, Econ. Club Chgo.; adv. bd. Univ. Ill., Com. 200. Recipient Advt. Woman Yr., Women's Advt. Club Chgo., 2000.

WOLF, MARTHA MARIN, nurse; b. Kansas City, Oct. 31, 1969; d. Robert A. and Delia (Moreno) Marin; m. Mark F. Wolf II, Mar. 25, 1988; children: Britany Delia, Mark F. III. Diploma, Kansas City AVTS, 1991; A in Gen. Studies, Kansas City C.C., 1994, AS cum laude, 1995; BSN, U. Kans., 2006. Cert. oper. rm. nurse. Staff nurse U. Kans. Med. Ctr., Kansas City, 1991—97, Bethany Med. Ctr., Kansas City, 1994—95; clin. resource nurse, eyes, ears, nose, throat, plastic surgery Saint Luke's Hosp. Kansas City. Mem. Assn. Perioperative RNs, Am. Soc. Plastic Surgery Nurses, Phi Theta Kappa, Sigma Theta Tau. E-mail: mwolf6@rr.com.

WOLF, MICHAEL ANN, announcer; m. Kurt Wolf, 2000; 1 child. BS, Emerson Coll. Anchor WLIG-TV, L.I., NY, WJAC-TV, Johnstown, Pa., WHTM-TV, Harrisburg, Pa., 1993—95; weekend morning anchor WDIV-TV, Detroit, 1995—. Office: WDIV-TV 550 W Lafayette Blvd Detroit MI 48226

WOLF, MURIEL HEBERT, soprano, educator, performing company executive; b. Boston, Nov. 15, 1925; d. Joseph Aurel and Gertrude May (Schellenger) Hebert; m. Anton Wolf, Feb. 5, 1949 (dec. Jan. 1989); m. Albert Paul Steger, Feb. 14, 1991. BMus in Voice with Distinction, New Eng. Conservatory of Music, 1949, MMus in Musical Rsch., 1950; Artist's Diploma with Highest Honors, Acad. of Music, Vienna, Austria, 1955; Postgrad. in Musicology, Brandeis U., 1956-57; Postgrad. in Opera, Ind. U., 1962-64. Instr. in music and theatre Verde Valley Sch., Sedona, Ariz., 1957-62; coord. of voice SUNY, Buffalo, 1979-84, prodr., dir. of opera, 1966-79, instr. of music, 1965-68, asst. prof. of music, 1968-71, assoc. prof. of music, 1971-84, prof. of music, 1984-93, prof. emeritus, 1993—. Guest lectr., dir. opera U. No. Ariz., Flagstaff, 1961—62; lectr., recitals Am. Psychiat. Assn., N.Y.C., Dallas, Montreal, 1979—88; co-chair Ctrl. Opera Svc. Nat. Conf. Met. Opera Auditions; founder Musictheater Advocates, Inc., Buffalo, 1974. Contbg. editor: Opera Quar., 1981—87; editor, archivalist: Anton Wolf Collection, 1989—; contbr. Internat. Dictionary of Opera, 1993. Founder, pres. The Anton and Muriel Wolf Found., Inc., 1999—. Grantee, N.Y. State Coun. of Arts, Buffalo, 1973, 1975, 1977, Cameron Baird Found., 1976, Polonia Cultural Inst., 1979; scholar Fulbright, Vienna and Salzburg, Austria, 1953—55. Mem.: Nat. Assn. Tchrs. Singing (conf. panelist, moderator and lectr.), Met. Opera Assn., Nat. Opera Assn. (conf. panelist, moderator and lectr., assoc. editor jour. 1962—82). Avocation: travel. E-mail: mhwolf@adelphia.net.

WOLF, NAOMI, writer; b. San Francisco, Nov. 12, 1962; d. Leonard and Deborah W.; m. David Shipley, Sept. 1993. BA, Yale U., 1984. Author: The Beauty Myth: How Images of Beauty Are Used Against Women, 1990, Fire With Fire: The New Female Power and How It Will Change the 21st Century, 1993, The Treehouse: Eccentric Wisdom from My Father on How to Live, Love and See, 2005; contbr. to periodicals including New Republic, N.Y. Times, Wall Street Journal. Rhodes scholar, 1986. Office: c/o John Brockman Inc 5 E 59th St New York NY 10022

WOLF, PATRICIA B., museum director; Dir., exec. dir. Anchorage Mus. History and Art, 1989—. Steering com. mem. Arctic Studies Ctr. Office: Anchorage Mus History & Art 121 W 7th Ave Anchorage AK 99501-3611

WOLF, SHARON ANN, psychotherapist; b. Dallas, May 13, 1951; d. Frank Allan and Ursula (Mohnblatt) W.; 1 child, Allan. BA in Psychology, New Eng. Coll., 1973; MA in Counseling Psychology, Antioch Grad. Sch., 1976; PhD in Clin. Psychology, Union Grad. Sch., 1989. Cert. Mental Health Counselor, 1997. Behavioral spl. ednl. planner Philbrook Children's Learning Ctr., Concord, N.H., 1972; asst. to spl. edn. cons. N.H. Hosp., Concord, 1972-73; spl. edn. planner Rochester (N.H.) Child Devel. Ctr., 1973; counseling practicum Morrill Sch., Concord, N.H., 1973, Contoocook Valley Mental Health Ctr., Henniker, N.H., 1973-74, counseling psychology intern, 1974-76; lab. instr. New Eng. Coll., Henniker, 1973; ednl. and guidance counselor asst. Hillsboro (N.H.)-Deering Sch. Dist., 1973-74; pediatric psychology intern parent-infant devel. program Ctrl. N.H. C.M.H. Ctr., Concord, 1986-87; assoc. psychologist Easter Seal Rehab. Ctr., Manchester, N.H., 1976-80, Ctrl. N.H. Community Mental Health Svcs., Concord, 1980-88; intern forensic psychology Concord Dist. Ct., 1987-88; pvt. practice Northfield, N.H., 1988—. Psychol. cons. children and youth program Twin Rivers Counseling Ctr., Franklin, N.H. 1980-83, therapist, 1984-86; therapist Ctrl. N.H. Comm. Mental Health Ctr., 1980-83, Parent-Infant Devel. Program, Concord, N.H., 1983-88. Fellow Am. Orthopsychiat. Assn.; mem. Am. Assn. Suicidology, Am. Assn. Counseling and Devel., New England Coun. on Crime and Delinquency, N.H. Assn. of the Deaf, N.H. Registry of Interpreters for the Deaf. Avocations: rug hooking, music, spending time with son. Office: PO Box 253 Tilton NH 03276-0253

WOLF, TERESA ANN, minister, educator, nun; b. McIntosh County, ND, Jan. 26, 1943; d. Matthias Wolf and Theresia Zahn Wolf. BA in History, Loretto Heights Coll., Denver, 1967; M Religious Edn., St. Meinrad Sch. Theology, Ind., 1977; D Ministry, Cath. Theol. Union, Chgo., 1998. Lic. joined Benedictine Sisters, Mother of God Monastery, 1964. Tchr. Cath. Indian Mission, Ft. Yates, ND, 1967—79; pastoral min. San Solano Missions, Papago Reservation, Ariz., 1979—84, Diocese of Izabal, Guatemala, 1985—87, Diocese of Chulucanas, Marropon, Peru, 1988—90; dir. Hispanic ministry Diocese of Crookston, Minn., 1991—2000, Diocese of Madison, Wis., 2000—03; coord. pastoral care Tri-Diocesan Migrant Ministry, Canton, Ohio, 2003—. Columnist Spanish newspaper La Voz Latina, Madison. Author bilingual pastoral resource booklets. Prison ministry to Spanish-speaking, Minn., Wis., Ohio; sec. Hartville Migrant Coun., Cath. Migrant Farmworker Network; mem. Pastoral Care for Migrants and Refugees Adv. Group. Roman Catholic. Avocations: reading, walking, travel. Home: 205 19th St NE # 2065 Canton OH 44714

WOLFE, BARBARA L., economics professor, researcher; b. Phila., Feb. 15, 1943; d. Manfred and Edith (Heimann) Kingshoff; m. Stanley R. Wolfe, Mar. 20, 1965 (div. Mar. 1978); m. Robert H. Haveman, July 29, 1983; children: Jennifer Ann Wolfe, Ari Michael Wolfe. BA, Cornell U., Ithaca, N.Y., 1965; MA, U. Pa., 1971; PhD, U Pa., 1973. Asst. prof. Bryn Mawr (Pa.) Coll., 1973-76; rsch. assoc. Inst. Rsch. on Poverty, Madison, Wis., 1976-77, dir., 1994—2000; from asst. prof. to assoc. prof. U. Wis., Madison, 1977-88, prof., 1988—, dir., LaFollette Sch. Pub. Affairs, 2006—. Adj. prof. Australian Nat. U., 2002-; resident scholar NIAS, Wassenear, Netherlands, 1984-85, 96-97; vis. scholar Russell Sage Found., N.Y., 1991-92. Co-author: Succeeding Generations, 1994; editor: (book) Role of Budgetary Policy in Demographic Transitions, 1994, contbr. articles to profl. jours. Mem. Commn. on Children with Disabilities, Washington 1994-95, Tech. Adv. Panel Social Security, Washington, 1994-95; vice chair bd. on children, youth and families IOM and NAS, 2005—. Recipient Best Article of Yr. award Rev. Income and Wealth, 1992, Fulbright award Coun. Internat. Exch. of Scholars, 1984. Mem.: Inst. of Medicine, Assn. Pub. Policy Mgmt. (policy coun. 2001—04), Internat. Inst. Pub. Fin. (bd. mgmt. 1994—2000, v.p. 2000—03), Am. Econ. Assn. (bd. com. 1989—92, exec. bd. 1996—99). Office: U Wis Inst Rsch on Poverty 1180 Observatory Dr Madison WI 53706-1320 Office Phone: 608-262-0662. E-mail: wolfe@LaFollette.wisc.edu, bwolfe@wisc.edu.

WOLFE, CLAIRE V., physiatrist; b. Bronx, N.Y., 1943; MD, Ohio State U., 1968. Diplomate Am. Bd. Phys. Medicine and Rehab. Intern L.A. County-U. So. Calif. Med. Ctr., 1968—69; resident Ohio State U. Hosps., Columbus, 1969—72; pvt. practice phys. med. and rehab. Columbus, 1972—. Staff physiatrist Mt. Carmel Med. Ctr., Columbus; clin. asst. prof. Ohio State U. Coll. Medicine. Mem.: AMA, Am. Acad. Phys. Medicine and Rehab. (v.p. 2002—), Ohio State Med. Assn. Office: 793 W State St Columbus OH 43222-1551

WOLFE, CLAUDETTE TOBIN, elementary school educator; b. St. Louis, Aug. 31, 1939; d. Morris A. and Ruth (Koppel) Tobin; m. David Joe Wolfe, July 22, 1972. AB in Edn., Washington U., St. Louis, 1961; MEd in Elem. Edn., North Tex. State U., 1974. Cert. elem. supr., Tex. Elem. tchr. Hazelwood (Mo.) Ind. Sch. Dist., Irving (Tex.) Ind. Sch. Dist., Richardson (Tex.) Ind. Sch. Dist., Hockaday Sch., Dallas. Rep. faculty Hockaday Bd. Trustees, 2001—04. Faculty rep. Hockaday Sch. Bd. Trustees, 2001—04. Recipient Outstanding Tchr. award North Dallas C. of C., 1985; Hockaday Assocs. grantee, 1982, 83, 85, 87, 91, 92, 93, 94, 2001, 2003. Mem. Internat. Reading Assn., Tex. Assn. for Improvement in Reading (corr. sec., chmn. literacy award com., social com., program co.).

WOLFE, DARLENE S., secondary school educator, consultant; b. Washington, June 4, 1944; d. Sol and Esther Rose (Sherman) Shnider; m. Lawrence E. Wolfe, March 23, 1975. BS, U. Md., 1966; MA, U. Iowa, 1972; PhD, Peabody-Vanderbilt U., 1979. Cert. tchr. Tenn., Fla. Neighborhood Resource Ctr. rep. Mayor's Office of Comm. Svc., Nashville, 1979-81; program dir. Jewish Cmty. Ctr., Tampa, Fla., 1981; tchr. River Ridge and Ridgewood High Sch., New Port Richey, Fla., 1982-98; t.v. prodn. tchr. Dr. Phillips High Sch., Orlando, Fla., 1998—2002; sci. and health tchr. Lee Middle Sch., Orlando, Fla., 2002—05, Ocoee HS, Fla., 2005—. Bd. mem. Parent Tchr. Student Assn., New Port Richey, 1991-98, v.p., 1997-98; RACES & edn. officer Sun Coast Amateur Radio, 1995-96; pub. rels. officer Sun Coast Amateur Radio Club, New Port Richey, 1996-98. Recipient Ann. Kronman award for Human Svcs., B'nai B'rith, 1962; Blakemore fellow Found. thru Peabody Coll., 1977; named Outstanding Adult, River Ridge Drama Program, New Port Richey, 1997, Outstanding TV Prodn. Tchr., Fox 13 Mag., 1998 Mem. AARP, Spl. Interest Group Graphics Radio Amateur Civil Emergency Svc., Assn. Computing Machinery, Fla. Electronic Media Edn. Consortium Steering Com, Digital Media Alliance of Fla., adv. bd. FMAC, Discovery Educators Network, Fla. Digital Media Edn. Consortium. Avocations: natural history, bridge, bass clarinet, consulting and facilitating. Office: Ocoee High Sch 1925 Crown Point Blvd Ocoee FL 34761 Office Phone: 407-905-3000. Business E-Mail: wolfed@ocps.net.

WOLFE, ETHYLE RENEE (MRS. COLEMAN HAMILTON BENEDICT), academic administrator; b. Burlington, Vt., Mar. 14, 1919; d. Max M. and Rose (Saiger) Wolfe; m. Coleman Hamilton Benedict, Dec. 4, 1954. BA, U. Vt., 1940, MA, 1942; postgrad., Bryn Mawr Coll., 1942—43; PhD, NYU, 1950; LHD (hon.), CUNY, 1989; LittD (hon.), Iona Coll., 1989. Tchg. fellow U. Vt., 1940—42; rsch. fellow Latin Bryn Mawr (Pa.) Coll., 1942—43; instr. classics Bklyn. Coll., 1947—49, instr. classical langs., 1949—54, asst. prof., 1954—59, assoc. prof., 1960—68, prof., 1968—, acting chmn. dept. classics and comparative lit., 1962—63, chmn. dept., 1967—72; dean Bklyn. Coll. Sch. Humanities, 1971—78; exec. officer Bklyn. Coll. Humanities Inst., 1980—89; provost and v.p. for acad. affairs Bklyn. Coll., 1982—88, provost emeritus, 1989. Exec. com., chmn. com. on undergrad. affairs, com. on univ.-wide programs CUNY; study group AAAS, 1987—89, pub., 1987—89; dir. Nat. Core Visitors Programs, 1985—89, Fund for Improvement of Postsecondary Edn.-funded Ctr. for Core Studies, 1987—88; co-chair senate report Chancellor's Coll. Prep. Initiative, 1991; exec. com The Liberal Art of Sci.: Agenda for Action. Mem. editl. bd.: Classical World, 1965—71; co-editor: The Am. Classical Rev., 1971—76; contbr. articles to profl. jours. Named Ethyle R. Wolfe Inst. for the Humanities Bklyn. Coll. in her honor, 1989; named to Hall of Honor, U. Vt., 1991, Disting. U. Faculty Sen. Emeritus, CUNY, 1992; recipient Kirby Flower Smith award, 1939, Goethe prize, U. Vt., 1940, Alumni Achievement award, 1985, Nat. Presdl. medal, NEH, Charles Frankel prize, 1990; grantee, 1971, 1982—84, Mellon Found., 1982—85, 1986—89, Exxon, 1986—89, Josiah Macy, 1986—90. Mem.: Am. Soc. Papyrologists, Classical Assn. Atlantic States (exec. com.), Vergilian Soc. Am., Archeol. Inst. Am., Am. Philol. Assn., N.Y. Classical Club (past pres., exec. com.), Phi Beta Kappa (pres. 1988—90, past pres. Rho of N.Y. chpt., Spl. Citation of Honor on Sesquicentennial U. Vt. 1998). Home: 360 W 22nd St New York NY 10011-2600 Office: care Ethyle R Wolfe Inst Humanities Bklyn Coll Bedford Ave # H Brooklyn NY 11222

WOLFE, GERALDINE, administrator; b. Monticello, Ark., Mar. 29, 1944; d. John Wesley and Hazeline (Daniels) Fisher; 1 child, Arin. BA, Keuka Coll., 1965; MA, Mt. Holyoke Coll., 1967; MSEd, Elmira Coll., 1981; cert. ednl. adminstrn. SUNY-Brockport, 1985; PhD Cornell U., 1988. Tchr. biology and health Corning Sch. Dist., N.Y., 1967-90; asst. prof. SUNY, Plattsburgh, 1990-93; adminstr. Saranac Lake Ctrl. Sch. Dist., 1993-96; asst. supt. Schenectady City Sch. Dist., 1996-99; supt. Catskill (N.Y.) Ctrl. Sch. Dist., 1999—. Mem. Mid. States Evaluation Team, 1985; chmn. bd. trustees Friendship Bapt. Ch., Corning, 1984-90; bd. dirs. Hamilton Hill Arts Ctr., 1996-99, Oslo scholar U. Oslo, 1964, Coop. Ext., Common Ground of Catkill, Workforce Investment Act, Youth Coun., Grene County Collubirative Community Partnership for Youth; Mem. N.Y. State Profl. Health Educators Assn., Women in Ednl. Adminstrn., LWV, Sigma Xi, Sigma Lambda Sigma. Club: Cosmopolitan (officer 1979-81) (Elmira). Mem. allocations com. United Way, 1982-90; mem. edn. com. Planned Parenthood, 1984-90. Mem. NAACP, ASCD, Nat. Assn. Sec. Sch. Prins., Am. Assn. Sch. Adminstrs., Nat. Alliance Black Sch. Educators, N.Y.S. Assn. for Computers and Technologies in Edn., N.Y.S. Assn. Compensatory Educators, N.Y. State Coun. Sch. Supts., Cornell Edn. Soc., Jr. League of Elmira, Rotary Club of Catskill, Capital District Assn. of Women Adminstrs., Delta Kappa Gamma, Phi Delta Kappa. Avocations: tennis; cross countryskiing; travel; piano; reading. Home: 7 Forest Hills Dr Elmira NY 14905-1141 Office: Catskill Ctrl Sch Dist 343 W Main St Catskill NY 12414-1621

WOLFE, JANICE KAY, oncological nurse; b. Cedar Rapids, Iowa, Sept. 13, 1942; d. Francis Demerlin Brown and Lora Elizabeth Miller; m. Lincoln Louis Marburger Jr., Oct. 4, 1960 (dec. Aug. 1972); children; Rhonda, Lora, Helen, Phillip, Carmen, Deborah M. (dec. May 1970); m. Clifford G. Wolfe, Apr. 11, 1992. Diploma in nursing, Kirkwood Coll., 1977, ADN, 1982. RN, Iowa, Ariz. Supr. staff nurses Long Term Care Ctr., Marion, Iowa, 1977-79; staff nurse ICU Mercy Hosp., Cedar Rapids, 1979-80; hematology/oncology nurse U. Iowa Hosp. and Clinics, Iowa City, 1982-92; clin. nurse Indian Health Svc., USPHS, Winslow, Ariz., 1992—, HIV-AIDS coord. and counselor, 1994—. Named PALS & ACLS cert. Nurse of the Yr., 1994. Lutheran. Avocations: horseback riding, piano. Home: HC 61 Box 27 Winslow AZ 86047-9301

WOLFE, KAREN ANN, music educator; b. Rochester, NY, Oct. 19, 1978; d. Norman Edward and Joanne Rose Wolfe. MusB in Edn., Nazareth Coll., Rochester, 2000, M in Music Edn., 2005. Cert. Kodaly methods Nazareth Coll., 2005. Elem. music tchr. Byron Bergen Cmty. Sch. Dist., Bergen, NY, 2000—. Pvt. lesson instr., Rochester, 2000—. Eucharistic ministry St. Jude's Ch., Rochester, 1994—96. Recipient Terry Taylor award, Spencerport Cmty. Sch. Dist., 1996, scholar Music Tchr. award, 1996, Nazareth Coll., 1997, Purple and Gold award, 1996—2000. Mem.: NY State Sch. Music Assn. Home: 124 Windsorshire Dr Apt E Rochester NY 14624 Office: Byron Bergen CSD 6917 W Bergen Rd Bergen NY 14416 Office Phone: 585-494-2220. Personal E-mail: kshaw@bbcs.k12.ny.us.

WOLFE, L. DIANE, writer, photographer; b. Eugene, Oreg., Feb. 16, 1966; d. Carl Wesley Wittmeyer and Joan Mirriam DeSantis; m. Craig Robert Wolfe, May 1, 1991. Grad., HS, Salem, Oreg. Adminstrv. asst. Acads. Plus Learning Ctr., Goldsboro, NC, 1998—99; owner Wolfe Rock Enterprises, Goldsboro, 1995—. Motivational spkr., 2004—. Author: (novels) Lori: The Circle of Friends, Book I, Sarah: The Circle of Friends, Book II, James: The Circle of Friends, Book III. Singles ministry asst. The Lord's Table, Goldsboro, 2005. Mem.: Britt World Wide (assoc.), Goldsboro Area Photography Club (assoc.). Republican. Avocations: reading, photography, rollercoaster riding, jogging, writing. Office Phone: 919-221-1689. Home Fax: 866-627-5887. Office Fax: 866-627-5887. Personal E-mail: wolferock@earthlink.net.

WOLFE, MARGARET RIPLEY, historian, educator, consultant; b. Kingsport, Tenn., Feb. 3, 1947; d. Clarence Estill and Gertrude Blessing Ripley; m. David Earley Wolfe, Dec. 17, 1966; 1 child, Stephanie Ripley. BS magna cum laude, East Tenn. State U., 1967, MA, 1969; PhD, U. Ky., 1974. Instr. history East Tenn. State U., 1969-73, asst. prof., 1973-77, assoc. prof., 1977-80, prof., 1980—, sr. rsch. prof. history, 1999—2004, prof. history emerita, sr. faculty affiliate, 2004—. Disting. vis. prof. in history Washington and Lee U., 2006. Author: Lucius Polk Brown and Progressive Food and Drug Control, Tennessee and New York City, 1908-1920, 1978, An Industrial History of Hawkins County, Tennessee, 1983, Kingsport, Tennessee: A Planned American City, 1987, Daughters of Canaan: A Saga of Southern Women, 1995; gen. editor: Women in Southern Culture Series, 1995-2004; contbg. author to books, also introductions to books; contbr. articles to profl. jours. Mem. Tenn. Com. for Humanities, 1985-85, exec. coun. mem., 1984-85; mem. Women's Symphony Com., Kingsport, 1990-95; exec. com. Tenn. Commemorative Woman's Suffrage Commn., 1994-95; mem. state rev. bd. Tenn. Hist. Commn., 1995—2005. Haggin fellow U. Ky., 1972-73; recipient Disting. Faculty award East Tenn. State U., 1977, East Tenn. State U. Found. rsch. award, 1979, Alumni cert. merit, 1984. Mem. AAUP, ACLU (exec. com. Tenn. 1991-92), NOW, Tenn. State Employees Assn., Am. Studies Assn. (John Hope Franklin Prize com. 1992), Am. Hist. Assn., Orgn. Am. Historians, So. Assn. Women Historians (pres. 1983-84, exec. com. 1984-86), So. Hist. Assn. (com. on status of women 1987, program com. 1988, interim chair program com. 1988, mem. com. 1993, 94, 95, nominating com. 1994, chair nominating com. 1995, chmn. mem. com. 1997, exec. coun. 1998-2000), Smithsonian Assocs, Tenn. Hist Commn. (state rev. bd. 1995-2005), Tenn. Hist. Soc. (editl. bd. 1995—2004), Coordinating Com. for Women in History, East Tenn. Hist. Soc. (mem. editl. bd. Jour. East Tenn. History 1995-2004), St. George Tucker Soc., Phi Kappa Phi. Office: ETSU at Kingsport Kingsport TN 37660 also: East Tenn State U Dept History Johnson City TN 37614 Personal E-mail: mrwolfe47@earthlink.net. Business E-Mail: wolfem@etsu.edu.

WOLFE, RINNA EVELYN, writer, retired secondary school educator; b. Bklyn., May 2, 1925; BBA, CCNY, 1957; MA in Creative Arts, San Francisco State U., 1966. With Charles Stores, N.Y.C., 1944—55, Raylass Dept. Stores, N.Y.C., 1955—59; tchr. Lompoc, Calif., 1959—60, Mt. Diablo Schs., Calif., 1960—66, Danville Schs., Calif., 1966—68; tchr. black studies resource Berkeley Schs., Calif., 1968—72, tchr. elem. sch., 1972—80. Faculty U. Calif. Ext., 1966—76. Author: From Children With Love, 1970, The Singing

Pope, 1980 (presented to Pope John Paul Apr. 1982), Charles Richard Drew, 1991 (Sci. & Films children's best books list 1991), Mary McLeod Bethune, 1992, The Calvin Simmons Story, 1994, Edmonia Lewis: Wildfire in Marble, 1998 (secondary level award in honor of Carter G. Woodson 1998, initiator of Negro History Week, 1926). Point Found. fellow, 1976; grantee Children With Love. Mem. Women's Nat. Book Assn., Bay Area Ind. Publs. Assn., Calif. Writers Club. Office Phone: 510-845-0507.

WOLFE, SANDRA JEAN, elementary school educator; d. Tommy Gene Lee and Luetta Leoma Mattney; m. David Clifton Wolfe, Mar. 12, 1979; children: Diana, Bryon, Wendy. AS, Murray State Coll., Tishamingo, Okla., 1993; BS, So. Okla. State U., Durant, 1997. Tchr. Kingston Mid. Sch., Okla., 1999—. Mem.: Loyal Order Moose. Office Phone: 580-564-2996.

WOLFE, SHEILA A., journalist; b. Chgo. d. Leonard M. and Rena (Karn) W. BA, Drake U. Reporter Chgo. Tribune, 1956-73, asst. city editor, 1973-75; day city editor Chgo. Tribune, 1975-79; city editor Chgo. Tribune, 1979-81, met. coordinator, 1981-83, adminstrv. asst. to mng. editor, 1983-2000. Pres. City News Bur. Chgo. 1986-88, 94-96. Recipient Beck award for outstanding profl. performance Chgo. Tribune, 1979; recipient Disting. Service award Drake U., 1982 Mem. Phi Beta Kappa. Home: 71 E Division St Chicago IL 60610-8307 E-mail: chicagoshe@aol.com.

WOLFE, SUSAN MCNEILL, elementary education educator, guidance counselor; b. Marlinton, W.Va., June 17, 1952; d. Daniel Addison and Teresa (Bingham) McNeill. BA, Furman U., 1974; MEd, Clemson U., 1978, postgrad., 2000. Tchr. phys. edn. Trinity Luth. Day Sch., Greenville, SC, 1974-77; instr. phys. edn. Furman U., 1977-78; tchr. phys. edn. and math., guidance counselor, tchr. gifted, social studies tchr. Wren Mid. Sch., Piedmont, SC, 1978—2001; instrl. facilitator Centerville Elem. Sch., Anderson, SC, 2001—. Coach Odyssey of Mind, 1991. Named Tchr. of Yr., Wren Mid. Sch., 1991. Mem. S.C. Coun. Tchrs. Math. (sec. 1986-90). Avocations: gardening, pets.

WOLFE, SUZANNE L., artist, educator; b. Chgo., Feb. 4, 1942; d. John Charles and Rosetta Wolfe; 1 child, Kalu Alexander Wolfe. BA in Anthropology, U. Mich., 1965, BFA, 1968, MFA, 1970. Prof. art U. Hawaii, Honolulu, 1971—. Dir., curator East-West Ceramics Collaboration Exhbn. and Workshop, Honolulu, 1995, 98, 2002, 06. Exhibited in solo shows at Contemporary Mus., Honolulu, 1988; group exhbns. at Francis Marion U., Florence, S.C., 2006, Balt. Clayworks, 2006, Kellogg Art Gallery, Pomona, Calif., 2005, Denver Internat. Airport, 2004, Eleanor Bliss Ctr. Arts, Steamboat, Colo., 2005, Pottery Workshop, Hong Kong, 2003, Taipei Yingke County Mus., 2002, Mint Mus., Charlotte, 2001, Honolulu Acad. Arts, 2001, Slusser Gallery U. Mich., Ann Arbor, 2000, Bechtold Gallery, Amsterdam, 1997, Duchamp Gallery, Taipei, 1995, Dinnerworks, Louisville, 1993. Mem. Nat. Coun. Edn. in the Ceramic Arts. Office: U Hawaii Art Dept 2535 McCarthy Mall Honolulu HI 96822-2233 Office Phone: 808-956-5264. E-mail: swolfe@hawaii.edu.

WOLFERSTEIG, ELOISE SMITH, retired music educator; b. Bklyn., Oct. 7, 1930; d. George Francis and Louise C. (Becker) Smith; m. Robert Frederick Wolfersteig; 1 child, Patricia Lynn Albritton. MusB, West Minster Choir Coll., Princeton, N.J., 1953; MusM, Jamestown Coll., ND, 1958; MEd, Ga. Coll., 1973. Choir dir. St. Francis Assisi Cath. Ch.; tchr. Jacob Tome Inst., Md., 1953—54, Bainbridge (Md.) Elem. Sch., 1954—55; dir. Officers' Wives Nursery Sch., Bermuda, 1955—56; music tchr. Baldwin City Schs., Milledgesville, Ga., 1965—75; gifted edn. tchr. Bibb City Sch., Macon, Ga., 1975—90; music tchr. Cherokee City Sch., Andrews, NC, 1990—91; gifted edn. tchr. Clay City Schs., Hayesville, NC, 1991—95; tech. cons. Andrews, NC, 1995—99; dir. sch. age choirs Blairsville, Ga., 1998—. Finalist Excellence in Singing, Met. Opera, 1958; recipient District Star Tchr., Macon, Ga., 1985, Tchr. of Yr., Spl. Edn., Macon, Ga., 1988. Mem.: DAR (pres., regent), Delta Kappa Gamma, Phi Delta Kappa, Sigma Alpha Iota. Avocations: poetry, art, writing, drawing. Home: 5316 Pine Crest Rd Young Harris GA 30582 Personal E-mail: rfwolfer@alltel.net.

WOLFERSTEIG, JEAN LOIS, medical association administrator, educator; b. Kingston, NY, July 13, 1950; d. Evelyn Anna Schupp and John Raymond Wolfersteig; life ptnr. William Edward Miller. AS in Liberal Arts, Ulster County CC, 1970; BA in Secondary Edn., State U. Coll., 1972; MS in Pub. Svc. Adminstrn., Russell Sage Coll., Albany, New York, 1983. Unit mgr. Wassaic Devel. Ctr., Wingdale, NY, 1972—75, staff devel. specialist, 1976—79; dir. of staff devel. and tng. Westchester Devel. Disabilities Svcs. Office, Tarrytown, NY, 1979—84, Hudson River Psychiat. Ctr., Poughkeepsie, NY, 1984—92, quality mgmt. dir., 1992—98, dir. for facility admin. svcs., 1998—2002, CEO, 2002—. Bd. mem. Cmty. Adv. Bd. for Marist Coll., Poughkeepsie, 1985—90; adj. faculty Westchester CC, Valhalla, 1981—84; bd. mem. Adv. Bd. for Orange County CC. Forensic Mental Health Program, Middletown, NY, 1985—85. Co-author: (international presentations) Balanced Scorecard and Performance Improvement. Chairperson of selection com. Herman B. Snow Scholarship Fund, Poughkeepsie, 1991—2001. Recipient Salute to Women in Industry, Dutchess County YWCA, 1992. Mem.: Nat. Assn. of State Mental Health Dirs., Phi Kappa Phi. Avocations: writing, sailing, travel, gardening. Office: Hudson River Psychiatric Center 10 Ross Cir Poughkeepsie NY 12601 Office Phone: 845-483-3400. Business E-Mail: hrqajlw@omh.state.ny.us.

WOLFF, CANDIDA (CANDI WOLFF), federal official; b. Sharon, Conn., June 9, 1964; m. Mark Roger Wolff; 2 children. BA in math & polit. sci., Mount Holyoke Coll., 1986; JD, George Washington U., 1989. Pub. policy lobbyist Akin, Gump, Strauss, Hauer & Feld, LLP, 1989—93; tax counsel Office of Senator Malcolm Wallop, 1993—95; legis. counsel Senate Steering Com. U.S. Senate, 1995—96, dep. staff dir. Senate Rep. Policy Com., 1997—2000; dep. asst. to v.p. for legis. affairs Office of Pres. of Senate (v.p. of U.S.), 2001—02, asst. to v.p. for legis. affairs., 2002—04; asst. to pres., dir. legis. affairs The White House, 2005—; ptnr. Washington Coun. Ernst & Young, 2004. Office: The White House 2nd Fl, West Wing 1600 Pennsylvania Ave NW Washington DC 20500 Office Phone: 202-456-2230. Office Fax: 202-456-0200.

WOLFF, CATHERINE ELIZABETH, opera company executive; b. Evanston, Ill., June 11, 1957; AB with honors, Vassar Coll., 1979; MA in Performing Arts Mgmt., Am. U., 1982. Adminstrv. asst. Opera Am., 1982-85; artistic adminstr. Pitts. Opera, 1985-94; exec. dir. Del. Symphony Orch., Wilmington, 1994-95; gen. dir. Syracuse (N.Y.) Opera Co., 1996—. Music panelist N.Y. State Coun. Arts, 2000—02, co-chair music panel, 2003. Mem. steering com. Arts and Culture Leadership Alliance Ctrl. NY, 2004—, founding pres., 2005—. McGuire fellow Vassar Coll., 1979. Mem. Opera Am., Am. Symphony Orch. League, Phi Beta Kappa. Office: Syracuse Opera Co PO Box 1223 Syracuse NY 13201-1223 E-mail: cwolff@syracuseopera.com.

WOLFF, DEBORAH H(OROWITZ), lawyer; b. Phila., Apr. 6, 1940; d. Samuel and Anne (Manstein) Horowitz; m. Morris H. Wolff, May 15, 1966 (div.); children: Michelle Lynn, Lesley Anne; m. Walter Allan Levy, June 7, 1987. BS, U. Pa., 1962, MS, 1966; postgrad., Sophia U., Tokyo, 1968; JD, Villanova U., 1979, LLM, 1988. Tchr. Overbrook H.S., Phila., 1962-68; homebound tchr. Lower Merior Twp., Mongomery County, 1968-71; asst. dean U. Pa., Phila., 1975-76; law clk. Stassen, Kostos and Mason, Phila., 1977-78; assoc. Spencer, Sherr, Moses and Zuckerman, Norristown, Pa., 1980-81; ptnr. Wolff Assocs., Phila., 1981—. Lectr. law and estate planning, Phila., 1980—. Founder Take a Brother Program; bd. dirs. Germantown Jewish Ctr.; h.s. sponsor World Affairs Club, Phila., 1962-68; mem. exec. com., sec. bd. Crime Prevention Assn., Phila., treas., bd. dirs., 1965—; v.p. bd. dirs. U. Pa. Alumnae Bd., Phila., 1965—, pres. bd. dirs., 1993—, v.p. organized classes, bd. crime prevention; chmn. urban conf. Boys Club Am., 1987, treas., 1999; active Hahnaman Brain Tumor Rsch. Bd.; v.p., bd. dirs. Crime Prevention; treas. Assn. of Alumnae ds.; mem. Alumni Class Leadership Counsel bd. U. Pa., 2001—, sec., 2006-. Recipient 3d Ann. Cmty. Svc. award Phila. Mayor's Com. for Women, 1984; named Pa. Heroine of Month, Ladies Home Jour., 1984. Mem.: Lions (pres. Germantown Club 1997—). Home and Office: 422 W Mermaid Ln Philadelphia PA 19118-4204 Personal E-mail: debbyw@comcast.net.

WOLFF, DIANE PATRICIA, writer, film and television producer; b. N.Y.C., Oct. 12, 1945; d. Irving Mark and Catherine Halkett (Grossman); m. Wallace Gorell (div.). BS, Columbia U., 1968; postgrad., U. Calif., Berkeley, 1977-78, Stanford U., 1978-79; student, Interuniv. Ctr., Tokyo. Prodr. Sta. KRON-TV, San Francisco, 1983-87; prodr. ind. films, 1990-92; prodr. CD-ROM Exec. Prodrs., 1994-96; contbg. editor New Asia Pacific Review, Westport, Conn., 1996-98; ind. prodr. The BioNRG Show Genghis Prodns., 2006—. Journalist Nat. Interest, N.Y. Times, San Francisco Chronicle, San Jose Mercury News, Orlando Sentinel Author: Chinese Writing: An Introduction, 1975, Gone with the Gator, 2001; project editor: A Sun-Herald Serial Novel, Sack of Baghdad and Other Stories of Muslims and Mongols, Pitless Measurement of History: China and Tibet. Nat. def. fgn. lang. fellow Columbia U., 1967; recipient Most Notable Book award Am. Libr. Assn., 1975. Mem. Author's Guild, Am. Soc. Journalists & Authors, Assn. For Asian Studies, Asia Soc. Avocations: sailing, swimming, fitness, cooking, gardening. Home: 1184 Green Oak Trail Port Charlotte FL 33948 Office Phone: 941-456-4805. E-mail: dianepwolff@comcast.net.

WOLFF, ELEANOR BLUNK, actress; b. Bklyn., July 10, 1931; d. Sol and Bessie (Schultz) Blunk; m. William Howard Wolff, June 19, 1955; children: Ellen Jill, Rebecca Louise. BA in Edn., Speech and Theatre, Bklyn. Coll., 1972, MS in Spl. Edn., 1975; postgrad., Adelphi U., Garden City, N.Y., 1980-81. Cert. tchr., N.Y. Fashion model Garment Ctr., N.Y.C., 1949—50; sec. to v.p. out-of-town/export sales Liebmann Breweries Inc., Bklyn., 1950—58; tchr. N.Y.C. Bd. Edn., Bklyn., 1971-76; sec. to dir. environ. programs, pub. affairs officers, speakers bur. project leader Power Authority State of N.Y., N.Y.C., 1976-85; tchr. Hewlett-Woodmere (N.Y.) Sch. Dist., 1986-89; instr. adult edn. County of Nassau, NY, 1986-97. Actress/model, N.Y.C., 1992—; mem. Love Creek Prodns. V.p. program devel. for youth ctr. Wavecrest Gardens Cmty. Assn., Far Rockaway, N.Y., 1959-63; teen leader Far Rockaway Jewish Ctr. Youth Coun., 1965-68; pres. Parents Assn. P.S. 215Q, Far Rockaway, 1966-67; tutor N.Y.C. Bd. Edn. Sch. Vol. Program, Far Rockaway, 1969-71, New Ground Inc., Mineola, NY, 2004—; chair civic affairs Dem. Club, Far Rockaway, 1961-63; committeewoman Dem. Ctrl. Com., Queens County, N.Y., 1963-64, Nassau County Dem. Party, 1998-; v.p. membership, mem. constn. com. Nassau County Dem. Women's Caucus, 1988, 89; awards com. Bklyn. Coll., 1993-97, chair theatre arts affiliate, 1990-94, 2001-; mem. comm. adv. com. Hewlett-Woodmere Sch. Dist. 14, 1996-97; press/media steward vol. Goodwill Games, 1998; vol. program presenter Child Abuse Prevention Svcs., Roslyn, N.Y., 2003-05; vol. income tax assistance IRS, 2004-. Named Mother of Yr. Congregation Shaaray Tefila, Far Rockaway, 1968; recipient Merit award Wavecrest Gardens Cmty. Assn., 1960, Theater Arts Trophy for disting. svc. Bklyn. Coll. Alumni, 1992. Mem.: SAG (awards nominating com. 2000—01, 2006—), AFTRA, Actors Equity Assn., Alumni Assn. Bklyn. Coll. (life), Cmty. Garden Club of North Woodmere Park (corr. sec. 2001—03). Avocations: painting, piano, gardening. Personal E-mail: eleanorwolff@cs.com.

WOLFF, FERIDA, author; b. Bklyn., July 7, 1946; d. Sam and Shirley J. (Gootrad) Mevorach; m. Michael L. Wolff, Feb. 3, 1965; children: Stephanie E., Russell S. BA, Queens Coll., Flushing, N.Y., 1967, MS in Edn., 1970; cert. holistic studies, Rosemont (Pa.) Coll., 1992. Tchr. N.Y.C. Bd. Edn., Queens, 1967-68; head tchr. Happy Time Nursery Sch., Queens, 1968-70; freelance writer, 1972-87; instr. yoga adult schs. Camden County (N.J.) Coll., 1990-95. Spkr., 1989—; panelist Phila Writer's Conf., 1990, workshop leader, 1993; workshop leader Teen Arts Festival, Camden, N.J., 1993. Author: Pink Slippers, Bat Mitzvah Blues, 1989 (Syndey Taylor honor book), The Woodcutter's Coat, 1992, Danish edit., 1993, French edit., 1993, Seven Loaves of Bread, 1993, The Emporer's Garden, 1994, A Weed is a Seed, 1996, (with Dolores Kozielski) The Toothless Vampire and 99 Other Howl-oween Riddles, 1992, The Halloween Grab Bag., 1993, On Halloween Night, 1994, Spitballs and Spaghetti, 1995, The Bald Beagle, 1996; contbr. articles to profl. jours. Bd. mem., v.p. Friends of the Cherry Hill (N.J.) Free Pub. Libr., 1991-92; scouting coord., troop com. mem. troop 167 Boy Scouts Am., Cherry Hill, 1985-90; libr. vol. coord. Jos. D. Sharp Elem. Sch., Cherry Hill, 1979-87. Mem. Authors Guild, Soc. Children's Book Writers and Illustrators, Penn Laurel Poets, Phila. Children's Reading Round Table (steering com.). Home: 21 Candlewyck Way Cherry Hill NJ 08003-1226

WOLFF, GRACE SUSAN, pediatric cardiologist; b. Rome, NY; BS, Le Moyne Coll., 1961; MD, Med. Coll. Wis., 1965. Diplomate Am. Bd. Pediatrics, Pediatric Cardiology. Intern St. Vincents Hosp., N.Y.C., 1965-66; pediat. resident Babies Hosp.-Columbia Presbyn., 1967-69; fellow in pediat. cardiology Childrens Hosp., Boston, 1969-71; chief divsn. pediat. cardiology U. Miami-Jackson Meml. Hosp., 1995—2005; prof. U. Miami, 1984; pediatrician, pediatric cardiologist U. Miami-Jackson Meml. Hosp., 1977—. Mem. Am. Acad. Pediats., Am. Bd. Pediats., NASPE, Am. Acad. Pediat., Am. Coll. Cardiology, Am. Heart Assn. Office: U Miami-Jackson Meml Hosp PO Box 016960-R76 Miami FL 33101 Office Phone: 305-585-6683. Business E-Mail: gwolff@med.miami.edu.

WOLFF, KAREN LIAS, music educator; BA in Music Edn., Morningside Coll., Iowa; MusM, U. Mich., PhD in Music. Faculty mem., Coll./Conservatory of Music U. Cin., 1978—87, acting dean, academic affairs, assoc. dean, academic affairs; dir. Sch. of Music U. Minn., 1987—91; dean, prof. music Oberlin Coll. Conservatory of Music, 1991—99; dean, Sch. of Music U. Minn., 2000, U. Mich., 2000—05, Paul C. Boylan Collegiate Prof. Music. Bd. mem. Minn. Orch., Minn. Opera, Minn. Composers Forum, Greater Twin Cities Youth Orch., Ohio Chamber Orch., U. Musical Soc., Mich. Shakespeare Festival, Interlochen Arts Acad., Ann Arbor Summer Festival; v.p. Nat. Assn. of Schools of Music; mem. Nat. Coun. on Arts Nat. Endowment for Arts, 2003—. Mailing: Nat Endowment for Arts 1100 Pennsylvania Ave NW Washington DC 20506*

WOLFF, MARGARET LOUISE, lawyer; b. Rochester, N.Y., Jan. 27, 1955; d. Harvey A. and Miriam W. (Weinstein) W. BA cum laude, Mt. Holyoke Coll., 1976; JD, Case Western Res. U., 1979. Bar: N.Y. 1980. Assoc. Skadden, Arps, Slate, Meagher & Flom, N.Y.C., 1979-87, ptnr., 1987—. Editor Case Western Res. U. Law Rev. Office: Skadden Arps Slate Meagher & Flom 919 3rd Ave New York NY 10022-3902

WOLFF, MARIANNE, retired pathologist; b. Berlin, July 2, 1928; arrived in U.S., 1945; d. Joe and Hedy Wolff; m. Herbert Schainholz (dec.); children: Jay David Schainholz, Daniel Curtis Schainholz. BA, CUNY, 1948; MD, Columbia U., N.Y.C., 1952. Diplomate Am. Bd. Pathology, 1958. Asst. in surgery Columbia U., 1958, prof. clin. surg. pathology, 1982—93. Editor: 14 books; contbr. chapters to books, articles to profl. jours. Named to Outstanding Scientists of 20th Century, 2000. Mem.: Arthur Prudy Stout Soc. Surg. Pathologists, U.S. Can. Acad. Pathology. Home: 3 London Ct Teaneck NJ 07666

WOLFF, MICKIAH ANN, artist, educator; b. Hartford, Wis., Feb. 17, 1977; d. Michael David and Mary Lynn Fellin; m. Jason Todd Wolff, Aug. 20, 2005. BA in Art Edn., Cardinal Stritch U., Fox Point, Wis., 2000. Art tchr. Wauwatotosa Sch. Dist., Wis., 2001—03, West Bend Sch. Dist., 2003—. Owner and artist Houses Ink, West Allis, Wis., 2004—. Organizer West Bend Mile of Art, 2003—. Mem.: Bay View Artists Guild. Office: Decorah Elem Sch 1225 Sylvan Way West Bend WI 53095

WOLFF, SHARON L., photographer, department chairman; d. Werner and Rhea Wolff; life ptnr. Bruce Kincaid, Oct. 18, 2003. MFA, U. of Ariz., 1986—89. Art tchr. Western H.S., Las Vegas, 1990—96; dept. chair Thomas Nelson C.C., Hampton, Va., 1996—. Commr. Hampton Art Commn.; dir. Natchel Blues Network, Norfolk, Va., 2003—05; bd. dirs. Hampton Arts Found. Sgt. USAF, 1973—2002, Various. Decorated Achievement medal USAF. Mem.: Soc. For Photographic Edn. Office: Thomas Nelson CC PO Box 9407 Hampton VA 23670 Office Phone: 757-825-2775.

WOLFF, SIDNEY CARNE, astronomer, science administrator; b. Sioux City, Iowa, June 6, 1941; d. George Albert and Ethel (Smith) Carne; m. Richard J. Wolff, Aug. 29, 1962 BA, Carleton Coll., 1962, DSc (hon.), 1985; PhD, U. Calif., Berkeley, 1966. Postgrad. research fellow Lick Obs, Santa Cruz, Calif., 1969; asst. astronomer U. Hawaii, Honolulu, 1967-71, assoc. astronomer, 1971-76; astronomer, assoc. dir. Inst. Astronomy, Honolulu, 1976-83, acting dir., 1983-84; dir. Kitt Peak Nat. Obs., Tucson, 1984-87, Nat. Optical Astronomy Observatories, 1987-2001; dir. Gemini Project Gemini 8-Meter Telescopes Project, 1992-94; astronomer, project scientist Large Synoptic Survey Telescope, 2001—04. Pres. SOAR Inc., 1999-2003; project scientist Large Synoptic Survey Telescope, 2002-04. treas. 2005; bd. mem. LSST Corp. Author: The A-Type Stars--Problems and Perspectives, 1983, (with others) Exploration of the Universe, 1987, Realm of the Universe, 1988, Frontiers of Astronomy, 1990, Voyages Through the Universe, 1996, 2nd edit., 2003, Voyages to the Planets, 1999, 2nd edit., 2003, Voyages to the Stars and Galaxies, 1999, 2nd edit., 2003; founding editor: Astronomy Edn. Rev., 2002; contbr. articles to profl. jours. Trustee Carleton Coll., 1989—, chair acad. affairs com., 1995-2005. Rsch. fellow Lick Obs. Santa Cruz, Calif., 1967; recipient Nat. Meritorious Svc. award NSF, 1994. Fellow Royal Astronical Soc.; mem. Astron. Soc. Pacific (pres. 1984-86, bd. dirs. 1979-85), Am. Astron. Soc. (coun. 1983-86, pres.-elect 1991, pres. 1992-94, Edn. prize 2006). Office: Nat Optical Astronomy Obs PO Box 26732 950 N Cherry Ave Tucson AZ 85719-4933 Business E-Mail: swolff@noao.edu.

WOLFF, VIRGINIA EUWER, writer; b. Portland, Oreg., Aug. 25, 1937; d. Eugene Courtney and Florence Evelyn (Craven) Euwer; m. Art Wolff, July 19, 1959 (div. July 1976); children: Anthony Richard, Juliet Dianne. AB, Smith Coll., 1959; postgrad., Goddard Coll., Warren Wilson Coll., L.I. U., Portland State U., Lewis & Clark Coll. Cert. tchr., Oreg. Tchr. The Miquon Sch., Phila., 1968-72, The Fiedel Sch., Glen Cove, NY, 1972-75, Hood River Valley (Oreg.) H.S., 1976-86, Mt. Hood Acad., Govt. Camp, Oreg., 1986-98. 2d violinist Quartet con brio, Portland, 1989-94, Parnassius Quintet, Portland, 1996—. Author: Probably Still Nick Swansen, 1988, The Mozart Season, 1991, Make Lemonade, 1993, Bat 6, 1998, True Believer (Nat. Book award, Michael L. Printz honor, Pacific N.W. Booksellers Assn. award, Jane Addams Book honor, 2002), 2001, represented US, honor book, Internat. Board on Books for Young People, 2004. Violinist Mid-Columbia Sinfonietta, Hood River, 1976—92, Oreg. Sinfonietta, Portland, 1988—, Parnassius Chamber Ensemble, 2000- . Recipient Young Adult Book award Internat. Reading Assn., 1989, PEN U.S.A. Ctr. West, 1989, Best Young Adult Book of Yr. award Mich. Libr. Assn., 1993, Child Study Children's Book award Bank Street Coll., 1994, Oreg. Book award Oreg. Lit. Arts, 1994, 2001, Jane Addams Children's Book award Jane Addams Peace Assn. and the Women's Internat. League for Peace and Freedom, 1999, Nat. Book award, 2001, Printz Honor Book award, 2002, Jane Addams Honor Plaque, 2002, Evelyn Sibley Lampman award for svc. to the children of Oreg., Oreg. Libr. Assn., 2005; named to Carnegie medal Shortlist, ALA, 2002. Mem. Soc. Children's Book Writers/Illustrators (Golden Kite 1994, 2002), Chamber Music Soc. Oreg. Avocations: chamber music, swimming, hiking, playing violin, gardening. Office: Curtis Brown Ltd care Elizabeth Harding 10 Astor Pl Fl 3 New York NY 10003-6982

WOLFGANG, CRYSTAL, secondary school educator; b. Dover, Del., May 30, 1973; d. Jerry and Carolyn Scott; m. Christopher Wolfgang, July 15, 1995; children: Cody, Carly. BA in Sports Medicine, Catawba Coll., Salisbury, N.C., 1991—95; tchg. cert., U. N.C., Charlotte, 2002. Tchr./athletic trainer Mt. Pleasant HS, NC, 1998—2002; 9th grade tchr. Jefferson HS, Shenandoah Junction, W.Va., 2002—03; tchr. Park View HS, Sterling, Va., 2003—. Sponsor Nat. Honor Soc., Parkview HS, 2005—. Mem.: Loudoun Edn. Assn. Avocations: children, autism research, music. Office: Park View HS 400 W Laurel Ave Sterling VA 20164 Business E-Mail: cwolfga1@loudoun.k12.va.us.

WOLFHAGEN, HELEN JANE, education educator; b. Salem, Oreg., July 28, 1921; d. Thomas and Mary Lydia (Cone) Acheson; m. Robert Sidney Stephey (dec. 1945); m. James Langdon Wolfhagen, Jan. 1948; children: Carl Frederick, Margaret Josephine Pease, Roger Charles Acker, James(dec.). BS, Willamette U., 1942; PhD in Chemistry, U. Calif., Berkely, 1948. Chemist Pabco Paint Co., Oakland, Calif., 1945; tchg. asst. U. Calif., Berkely, 1945—48; instr. Whitworth Coll., Spokane, Wash., 1949—52; lectr. U. Maine, 1964—86; ret., 1986. Avocations: painting, reading, crossword puzzles.

WOLFMAN, BRUNETTA REID, education educator; b. Clarksdale, Miss., Sept. 4, 1931; d. Willie Orlando and Belle Victoria (Allen) Reid Griffin; m. Burton Wolfman, Oct. 4, 1952; children: Andrea, Jeffrey. BA, U. Calif., Berkeley, 1957, MA, 1968, PhD, 1971; DHL (hon.), Boston U., 1983; DP (hon.), Northeastern U., 1983; DL (hon.), Regis Coll., 1984, Stonehill Coll., 1985; DHL, Suffolk U., 1985; DET (hon.), Wentworth Inst., 1987; AA (hon.), Roxbury Community Coll., 1988. Asst. dean faculty Dartmouth Coll., Hanover, N.H., 1972-74; asst. v.p. acad. affairs U. Mass., Boston, 1974-76; acad. dean Wheelock Coll., Boston, 1976-78; cons. Arthur D. Little, Cambridge, Mass., 1978; dir. policy planning Dept. Edn., Boston, 1978-82; pres. Roxbury C.C., Boston, 1983-88, ACE sr. assoc., 1988-94, NAWE sr. assoc., 1994-98; assoc. v.p. acad. affairs George Washington U., Washington, 1989-92, prof. edn., 1992-96, prof. edn. emeritus, 1996—. Mem. Accrediting Commn. on Edn. on Health Svcs. Adminstrn.; pres. bd. dirs. Literacy Vols. of Capitol Region; mem. comm. com. bd., pub. rels. com. LVA, Inc.; bd. dirs. Am. Coun. Edn., Harvard Cmty. Health Plan. Author: Roles, 1983; contbr. articles to profl. jours. Mem. bd. overseers Wellesley Coll., 1981, Boston Symphony Orch.; trustee Mus. Fine Arts, Boston; mem. Coun. on Edn. for Pub. Health; chair Provincetown bd. Coun. on Aging, 1999—2005; mem. Halocause meml. com. NCCJ; bd. dirs. Boston-Fenway Program, 1977, Freedom House, Boston, 1983, Boston Pvt. Industry Coun., 1983; bd. dirs., co-chmn. NCCJ, Boston, 1983; bd. dirs. Elder Svcs. Cape Cod and the Islands, 2003. Named Wolfman Courtyard in their honor, Evergreen Ctr., 2000; recipient Freedom award, NAACP No.Calif., 1971, Amelia Earhart award, Women's Edn. and Indsl. Union, Boston, 1983, Provincetown Sr. Citizen of Yr., 2004; scholar Nat. Assn. Women in Edn. Mem. AAUW, Am. Sociol. Assn., Assn. Black Women in Higher Edn., Greater Boston C. of C. (edn. com. 1982), Sierra Club, Mass. Audubon Soc., Cosmos Club (Washington), Provincetown Art Assn. (sec. bd. trustees, mus. sch. com., nominating com.), Alpha Kappa Alpha (Humanitarian award 1984), Phi Delta Kappa. Home: 657 Commercial St Provincetown MA 02657-1759 Personal E-mail: bruburt2@comcast.net.

WOLFORD, CAROL D., special education educator; b. Slanesville, W.Va., Nov. 29, 1935; d. Mervin Joseph and Opal Pearl (Hott) W. BA, Shepherd U., Shepherdstown, W.Va., 1958; MS, McDaniel U., 1988; postgrad., W.Va. U., 1962-63, 68, 87, Gallaudet U., Washington, 1973-74. Cert. permanent profl. tchr., W.Va.; cert. Coun. on Edn. of Deaf. Elem. tchr. Hampshire County Bd. Edn., Romney, W.Va.; tchr. social living W.Va. Schs. for Deaf and Blind, Romney; ret., 1993. Contbr. articles to newspaper, sch. publs. and parent newsletter. Vol. tchr. W.Va. Schs., 1974-75. Named Employee of Month, Elem.Dept. for Deaf, 4-H Alumni award Hampshire County; named one of All-Stars, Hampshire County 4-H, W.Va. 4-H.

WOLFORD, KATHRYN FRANCES, religious organization administrator; b. Reading, Pa., Dec. 12, 1957; d. Howard Francis Wolford and Katherine Eva (Auker) Carbaugh. BA in History, Gettysburg Coll., 1979; MA in Religious Studies, U. Chgo. Divinity Sch., 1980; MA in Pub. Policy, U. Chgo., 1981; PhD (hon.), Gettysburg Coll., 1995; PhD (hon.), Muhlenberg Coll., 2003. Country program rep. Ch. World Svc., Dominican Republic, 1983-85;

regional rep. Nat. Coun. Chs., U.S.A., N.Y.C., 1985-90; program dir. for L.Am., Luth. World Relief, Balt., 1991-93, pres., 1993—. Named Md. Top 100 Women, Md. Daily Record, 2002, 2004. Democrat. Lutheran. Avocation: sailing.

WOLFSON, BARBARA LIBENSPERGER, guidance counselor; b. Mar. 9, 1949; BS in Elem. Edn., Trenton State Coll., 1971, M in Student Pers. Svcs. Guidance, 1983. Elem. sch. tchr. Trenton (N.J.) Bd. Edn., 1971-83, guidance counselor, 1983—. Chmn. Raritan Township (N.J.) Zoning Bd. 1988-92; mem. Raritan Township Recreation Bd., 1992-93, Cable TV Bd., 1993-94, County com., 1986-2000. Mem. Daus. Am. Revoultion, Order of Ea. Star (Ashler chpt.), Trenton Edn Assn. (chief del.), Cedar Mar. Yacht Club. Avocations: skiing, sailing. Home: 15 Blackwell Rd Flemington NJ 08822-1955

WOLFZAHN, ANNABELLE FORSMITH, psychologist; b. NYC, Jan. 23, 1932; d. Paul Phillip and Addie (Glassman) Forsmith; m. Herbert Eytan Wolfzahn, Feb. 4, 1956; children: Risa, Felice, Orna. BA, Hunter Coll., NYC, 1953; MA in Counseling Psychology, Manhattan Coll., 1971; PhD in Clin. and Community Psychology, Union Inst., Cin., 1979. Cert. sch. psychologist, sch. counselor, N.Y. Counselor for handicapped children Bklyn. Tuberculosis Assn., 1952; social worker Child Placement Svcs., NYC, 1953-58; fellow in social and community psychiatry Albert Einstein Coll. Medicine, NY, 1977-79; intern Bronx Devel. Svcs., NY, 1977-79; intern head trauma program Rusk Inst., NYU Med. Ctr., 1979; psychologist Creedmore Psychiat. Ctr., 1980-82, Harlem Valley Psychiat. Ctr., 1982-87; clin. coord. of group homes Green Chimneys Children's Svcs., 1987-88; with Ulpan Akiva and Assaf Harofeh Med. Ctr., Tel Aviv U., Israel, 1988-89; nursing home cons., psychotherapist Bklyn. Ctr. for Psychotherapy, 1989-91; pres., coord. Westchester chpt. Vols. for Israel, 1992—; pres. Westchester region Zionist Orgn. Am., 2003—; freelance psychologist, counselor, 1994—; retired, 2001—. Mem. workshops in field; mem. staff Mother-Child Home Program of White Plains, N.Y., 1975-76; mem. curriculum com. Learning in Retirement Iona Coll. (LIRIC), 1994—2005; counselor with multiple sclerosis victims and their families. Photog. artist; juried solo and group exhibits include Wuchinich Gallery, Mt. Kisco Libr., 1998, Somers Gallery, Somers Libr., 1998, Greenberg Gallery, Greenberg Libr., 1998, Gallery at New Rochelle Libr., 1998, Woods Gallery, Burke Ctr., White Plains, N.Y., 1998, Levine Art Gallery, Putnam Arts coun., 1998, Mid-Rockland Arts Festival, 1998, The Bendheim Performing Arts Ctr., 1999, Reflection of Westchester Exhibit, 1999, Art on Main St., 1999, Open Studios, 2000, Westchester Arts Coun., 2000, Oresman Art Exhibit, Oresman Gallery, Larchmont, N.Y., 2002, Visions of Israel, 2003, Westchester Treasures, Westchester Land Trust, 2004, Town and Country, 2005, Upstream Gallery, 2004, Northwest Coun. Arts, 2005; contbr. articles to profl. jours. Vol. Vols. for Israel, 1988, 91-92, 2003—; mem. archaeol. dig Bet Shaan, Israel; arts amb. White Plains Arts Coun., 2000—; active Westchester Arts Coun., SHARE Project. Recipient Vol. award White Plains Hosp., 1974-76, John C. Klein Meml. Writing award Newspaper Inst. Am., 1965; Alvin Johnson scholar, 1953. Mem. APA (life), Westchester County Psychol. Assn., N.Y. Neuropsychology Assn., Am. Mental Health Affiliates of Israel, N.Y. Acad. Scis., Nat. Coun. Jewish Women, Am. Orthopsychiat. Assn., Zionist Orgn. Am. (pres. Westchester region 2003-06). Avocations: painting, lap swimming, writing, travel, photography. Home and Office: 34 Springdale Rd Scarsdale NY 10583-7329 Office Phone: 914-472-3836.

WOLITZER, HILMA, novelist, short story writer; b. Bklyn., Jan. 25, 1930; d. Abraham Victor and Rose (Goldberg) Liebman; m. Morton Wolitzer, Sept. 7, 1952; children: Nancy J., Margaret R. Student, Bklyn. Mus. Art Sch. Vis. lectr. Iowa U. Writers Workshop, spring, 1978, fall 1979, 83. Author: (novels) Ending, 1974 (Gt. Lakes Coll. Assn. Best New Novel award 1975), In the Flesh, 1977, Hearts, 1980, In the Palomar Arms, 1983, Silver, 1988, (novels for young readers) Introducing Shirley Braverman, 1975, Out of Love, 1976, Toby Lived Here, 1978, Wish You Were Here, 1985, The Doctor's Daughter, 2006; contbr. short stories, revs. to various periodicals. Recipient Lit. award Am. Acad. and Inst. Arts and Letters, 1981; Bread Loaf fellow, 1974; Guggenheim fellow, 1976-77; Nat. Endowment Arts fellow, 1978 Mem. PEN (exec. bd. 1984—), Authors Guild, Writers Guild Am. East. Address: 81 N Broadway Hicksville NY 11801-2920*

WOLLARD, LAURA RAYNAE, science educator; b. Bellvue, Wash., Feb. 17, 1968; d. James Earnest Coon and Theresa Alice Rhodes; m. William Lee Wollard, Nov. 6, 1969; children: Carlee Raynae, Kylee Jane, William Lee Jr. BA in Biology, Southwestern Coll., Winfield, Kans., 1998; MS in Biology, U. Nebr., Kearney, 2006. Cert. tchr. Kans., 1998. Tchr. sci. Ark. City H.S., Kans., 2001—04, Winfield Mid. Sch., Kans., 2004—. Mem. Christian edn. com. First Presbyn. Ch., Winfield, 2000—06. Mem.: KNEA. Office: Winfield Mid Sch USD #465 400 E 9th Winfield KS 67156 Office Phone: 620-221-5130.

WOLLERSHEIM, JANET PUCCINELLI, psychology professor; b. Anaconda, Mont., July 24, 1936; d. Nello J. and Inez Marie (Ungaretti) Puccinelli; m. David E. Wollersheim, Aug. 1, 1959 (div. June 1972); children: Danette Marie, Tod Neil; m. Daniel J. Smith, July 17, 1976. AB, Gonzaga U., 1958; MA, St. Louis U., 1960; PhD, U. Ill., 1968. Lic. psychologist Mont. Asst. prof. psychology, asst. dir. testing/counseling ctr. U. Mo., 1968-71; prof. psychology U. Mont., Missoula, 1971—, dir. chin. psychology, 1980-87; chair Mont. Bd. Psychologists, 1977-78; cons. Mont. State Prison, 1971-85, Trapper Creek Job Corps, 1973—2003; pvt. practice Missoula, 1971—. Author numerous rsch. articles. Bd. dir. Crisis Ctr., Missoula, 1972-73; mem. profl. adv. bd. Head Start, Missoula, 1972-79. Recipient Disting. scholar award, U. Mont., 1991. Fellow Am. Psychol. Assn. (bd. dirs. div. clin. psychology 1990-92); mem. Rocky Mountain Psychol. Assn. (pres. 1983-84), Nat. Coun. Univ. Dirs. Clin. Psychology (bd. dirs. 1982-88). Home and Office: 105 Greenwood Ln Missoula MT 59803-2401 Office Phone: 406-543-6946. E-mail: jpwoller2000@yahoo.com.

WOLPE, MARCY SHEAR, artist, educator; b. Iowa City, Feb. 14, 1949; d. Louis John and Selma (Lang) Shear; m. Robert Neil Wolpe, Oct. 1, 1971. BA in Speech Pathology, U. Md., 1970; postgrad. in speech pathology, U. Pitts., 1972; MFA in Printmaking, Design, George Washington U., 1982. Part-time lectr. dept. art George Washington U., Washington, 1981-83; artist, painter, printmaker, 1982—; part-time faculty dept. art Montgomery Coll., Rockville, Md., 1984; workshop instr. Acad. Arts, Easton, Md., 1992; part-time instr. dept. art Salisbury (Md.) State U., 1993-96. V.p. bd. dirs. Washington Printmakers' Gallery, 1987-89; editor WPG News, Washington, 1992-96. One-woman shows include Acad. Arts, Easton, Md., 1991; group exhbns. include George Washington U., 1982, Dimock Gallery, Washington, 1982, Washington Women's Arts Ctr., 1982, 83, 84, Va. Intermont Coll., Bristol, Va., 1983, Fairfax County Coun. Arts, Arlington, Va., 1983, Springville (Utah) Mus. Art, 1983, 86, Acad. Artists' Soc., Springfield, Mass., 1984, 86, Arts Club Washington, 1984, 85, Nat. Arts Club, N.Y., 1984, 86, A.A.O. Gallery, Buffalo, 1984, 85, 87, North Miami (Fla.) Mus. and Art Ctr., 1984, Yale U., 1984, Auburn (Ill.) Arts Assn., 1985, Hunterdon Art Ctr., Clinton, N.J., 1985, Rose Art Mus., Waltham, Mass., 1985, Montpelier Cultural Arts Ctr., Laurel, Md., 1985, Artists' Welfare Fund, Inc., N.Y.C., 1986, Weinberg Ctr. for Arts, Frederick, Md., 1986, Mt. St. Mary's Coll. Fine Arts Gallery, Santa Monica, Calif., 1986, Galerie Triangle, Washington, 1986, Dulin Gallery Art, Knoxville, Tenn., 1986, Columbia Fine Arts Gallery and Mus. Art and Arch., 1986, Abington Art Ctr., Jenkintown, Pa., 1986, Springville (Utah) Mus. Art, 1987, Art Barn, Washington, 1987, Silvermine Guild Galleries, New Canaan, Conn., 1987, 88, Montpelier Cultural Arts Ctr., 1987, Midtown Gallery, Washington, 1987, Germanow Gallery, Rochester, N.Y., 1987, Washington Printmakers' Gallery, 1987, 89, Parkersburg (W.Va.) Art Ctr., 1988, Knoxville Mus. Art, 1988, Hunterdon Art Ctr., Clinton, N.J., 1988, Trenton (N.J.) State Coll., 1988, Internat. Monetary Fund Art Soc. Gallery, Washington, 1988, Boston Printmakers', Brockton, Mass., 1988, Woodmere Art Mus., Phila., 1988, Washington Printmakers' Gallery, Washington, 1992, The Pushkin Mus., Moscow, 1992, Miriam Periman Gallery, Chgo., 1992, Atrium Gallery, Salisbury, Md., 1993, Balcony Gallery, Berlin, Md., 1993, Trenton State Coll., 1993, Erector Sq. Gallery, 1994, The Baltimore Life Gallery, 1995, Hunterdon Art Ctr., 1996, Nabisco Headquarters, East Hanover, N.J., 1997, Yale U., 1997, various others. Bd. dirs. Am. Cancer Soc., Silver Spring, Md., 1976-80. Mem. Soc. Am. Graphic Artists, Md. Printmakers, Boston Printmakers, Phila. Print Club. Avocations: writing, walking. Office: 8 Ocean E Marathon FL 33050-2508 E-mail: mswolpe@aol.com.

WOLPERT, ANN J., library director; BA, Boston U.; MLS, Simmons Coll., Boston. Libr. Boston Redevelopment Authority, 1967—76; with Arthur D. Little Inc., 1976—92, from tech. info. specialist, to mgr. Rsch. Libr., to dir. Cambridge Info. Ctr.; dir. Rsch. and Info. Svc. Harvard Bus. Sch., 1992—93, exec. dir. Libr. and Info. Svc., 1993—95; dir. Mass. Inst. Tech. Librs., 1996—. Mem. Strategic Planning Com. Mass. Bd. Libr. Commr., 1992—; cons. U. N.Mex., Cornell U., Adelphi U., NYC, INCAE campuses, Costa Rica, Nicaragua, League European Rsch. Librs., Amsterdam, Nat. Libr. China, Malaysia U. Sci. and Tech.; spkr. in field; chmn. mgmt. bd. Mass. Inst. Tech. Press; bd. dirs. Tech. Rev., Inc. Mem. edtl. bd. Libr. and Info. Sci. Rsch., The Jour. Libr. Adminstrn., mem. adv. com. Sci. and Engring. Indicators; contbr. libr. papers to various publs.; reviewer Tech. Rev. Advisor Publ. Com. Mass. Med. Soc.; bd. dir. Boston Libr. Consortium; hon. bd. trustees Simmons Coll.; mem. bd. dirs. Boston Libr. Consortium, NIH's Pub. Access Working Group, Steering Coms. Coalition Networked Info., Digital Libr. Fedn.; mem. Nat. Network Women Leaders Higher Edn. Am. Coun. Edn., Dean's Com., Pres.'s Acad. Coun., OpenCourseWare Faculty. Named to Nat. Network for Women Leaders in Higher Edn., Am. Coun. Edn. Mem.: Info. Tech. Strategic Planning and Resources Coordinating Coun., Coun. Ednl. Tech., Com. Intellectual Property, Assn. Rsch. Libr. (past pres. 2004—05, v.p. to pres., mem. intellectual property and copyright com.). Office: Building 14S-216 MIT 77 Massachusetts Ave Cambridge MA 02139-4307 Office Phone: 617-253-5297. Office Fax: 617-253-8894. E-mail: awolpert@mit.edu.

WOLPERT-DEFILIPPES, MARY K., science administrator; BS in Pharmacy cum laude, Creighton U., 1963; MS in Pharmacology, U. Mich., 1966, PhD in Pharmacology, 1969; postdoctoral student, Yale U., 1969—. Rsch. assoc. in pharmacology Yale U., New Haven, 1970-71; staff fellow lab. chem. pharmacology NIH, Bethesda, Md., 1971-75, pharmacologist drug evaluation br., 1976-81, supervisory pharmacologist drug evaluation br., 1981-82, dep. chief drug evaluation br., 1982-85, pharmacologist Office of Assoc. Dir., 1985-88, program dir. Grants and Contracts Ops. Br., 1988-97, chief Grants and Contracts Ops. Br., 1997—. Contbr. articles to profl. jours.; patentee in field. Mem. Gamma Pi Epsilon, Rho Chi. Office: Nat Cancer Inst Divsn Cancer Treatment and Diagnosis Exec Pla N Rm 8150 Bethesda MD 20892 Office Phone: 301-496-8783. Business E-Mail: wolpertm@exchange.nih.gov.

WOLPERT RICHARD, CHAVA, artist; b. Frankfurt, Germany, Feb. 26, 1933; arrived in Palestine, 1934, arrived in U.S., 1958; d. Ludwig Y. and Else (Ahrens) Wolpert; m. Henry A. Richard, 1959 (dec. 1971). Student, Bezalel Acad. Arts and Design, Jerusalem, 1954—56. Artist-in-residence The Jewish Mus., N.Y.C., 1958—88. Painter, designer/creator of contemporary style ceremonial Judaica such as candelabra, Passover sets, Torah ornaments, decorative Judaica in enamel, silver, other metals, glass, porcelain, wood, acrylics, fabrics and oil painting; represented in 11 mus. collections in U.S., Australia, Europe, Israel. Pvt. Israeli Army, 1951—53. Recipient 2 Merit awards Interfaith Forum on Religion, Art and Arch., 1980, 83, Jurors' Choice award Liturgical Art Guild, 1991, Best in Judaica award Liturgical Art Guild, 1997. Mem. Judaic Art Guild, Liturgical Art Guild. Avocations: reflexology, healing with herbs. Office Phone: 718-896-4451.

WOLSCHLEGER, SUSAN ELIZABETH, elementary school educator; b. Killeen, Tex., Oct. 30, 1954; d. Robert Eugene and Margaret Elizabeth (Kemper) Sheffer; m. Thomas Gerard Krepps, Dec. 30, 1971 (div. Mar. 1979); children: Angela Lynn, Stephanie Sue; m. James Edward Wolschleger, Feb. 14, 1981; 1 child, Laura Marie. BA in Secondary Edn., Shepherd Coll., 1991. Math. and computer programming tchr. Jefferson H.S., Shenandoah Junction, W.Va., 1992-93; gen. and vocal music tchr. South Jefferson Elem. Sch., Charles Town, W.Va., 1993—. Pianist, musical dir. Apollo Civic Theater, Martinsburg, W.Va., 1985—; youth and children's choir dir. Pikeside United Meth. Ch., Martinsburg, 1990—. McMuran scholar Shepherd Coll., 1990. Mem. W.Va. Music Educator's Nat. Conf. Democrat. Avocations: doll collecting, playing piano. Home: 2383 Slater Hill Ln E York PA 17406-7589

WOLYNIES, EVELYN See GRADO-WOLYNIES, EVELYN

WOMACK, LANA D., elementary school educator; d. Lancaster L. Davis and Martha M. Womack, Angela Womack (Stepmother). Assoc. degree, Del. County C.C., Media, Pa., 1992; Bachelor's degree, West Chester U., Pa., 1995; Master's degree, Widener U., Chester, Pa., 2002. Cert. tchr. elem. K-6 Pa. Dept. Edn., elem. sch. counselor Pa. Dept. Edn. Tchr. Eisenhower Mid. Sch., Norristown, Pa., 1996—. Athletic coord. Eisenhower Mid. Sch., 2004—. With USAR, 1989. Mem.: Norristown Area Alliance Black Educators (assoc.; bldg. rep. 2005—06). Office: Eisenhower Mid Sch 1601 Markley St Norristown PA 19401 Office Phone: 610-277-8720. Office Fax: 610-270-2901. Business E-Mail: lwomack@nasd.k12.pa.us.

WOMACK, LEE ANN, country musician; b. Jacksonville, TX, Aug. 19, 1966; married; 2 children. Singer: (albums) Lee Ann Womack, 1997, Some Things I Know, 1998, I Hope You Dance, 2000, The Season for Romance, 2002, Something Worth Leaving Behind, 2002, Greatest Hits, 2004, There's More Where That Came From, 2005 (Album of Yr., Country Music Assn., 2005), (singles) The Fool, 1997, Does My Ring Burn Your Finger, 2000 (USA Today song of yr., 2001), I Hope You Dance, 2000, I May Hate Myself in the Morning, 2005 (Single of Yr., Country Music Assn., 2005); with Willie Nelson (duet) Mendonceno County Line, 2002 (Country Music Assn. Vocal Event of Yr.). Studio: MCA Records Inc 60 Music Sq E Nashville TN 37203 Office: Richard De la Font Agency Inc Ste 505 4845 S Sheridan Rd Tulsa OK 74145 Office Phone: 615-244-8944, 918-665-6200.*

WOMMACK, JANICE MARIE, insurance company executive; b. Springfield, Mo., Aug. 5, 1939; d. Karl William and Mary Ida (Cotter) Engelking; m. Lewis Rick Stephenson, Oct. 23, 1964 (div. 1988); children: Lara G. Stephenson Cunningham, Lewis Arn; m. Francis L. Wommack, Dec. 26, 1988; stepchild, Jon Wommack. Dental asst. Dr. Pete Emily, Denver, 1960-64; claims sec. State Farm Mutual Auto Ins. Co., Tulsa, 1965-71, exec. sec. Springfield, 1971-73; with Am. Nat. Property & Casualty Co., Springfield, 1973—, liability supr., 1982-88, dir. divisional support, 1988-99, ret., 1999, part-time, 1999—. Mem. Springfield Claims Assn., Springfield C. of C. (pres. women's div. 1985), Greater Ozark Bus. and Profl. Women's Assn. (pres. elect. 1988—), Alliance, St. John's Health Styles. Avocations: reading, travel, walking. Office: Am Nat Property & Casualty 1949 E Sunshine St Springfield MO 65899-0001 Home: Winter 10719 WhiteNHN Rd Sun City AZ 85351-1536

WONDERLY, HELEN MARIETTA, elementary school educator; b. Mt. Clemens, Mich., Jan. 15, 1941; d. John and Marietta Grace (Johnson) Porter; m. Edward C. Wonderly, Aug. 5, 1961; children: Mark Edward, Michael Patrick, Regina Lynn. MA, U. Mo., 1991. Tchr. 3rd and 4th grade Holy Family Sch., Independence, Mo., 1977-81; tchr. 4th grade St. Charles Sch., Kansas City, Mo., 1981-85; kindergarten and elem. tchr. reading Kansas City (Mo.) Schs., 1985-93; tchr. Kindergarten Camdenton Pub. Schs., 1993—2003, P.A.S.S., 2003—. Mem. Mo. State Tchrs. Assn., Rotary (Excellence in Edn. to Swinney award 1989—, Nat. award presented by Pres. Bush to Swinney, 1991), Phi Lambda Theta. Avocation: painting. Office: Hurrican Deck Elem Sch PO Box 57 # 77 Sunrise Beach MO 65079-0057

WONDERS, PAMELA KIM, music educator; b. East Liverpool, Ohio, Aug. 3, 1955; d. Richard Daniel and Lila Lee Wonders. BS in music edn., Trevecca Nazarene U., 1978; MEd, Tenn. State U., 1991. Band dir. Hillsboro H.S., Nashville, 1978—79, DuPont Elem., Nashville, 1979—80; choral dir. Maplewood H.S., Nashville, 1980—86, Hunters Lane H.S., Nashville, 1986—. Regional mgmt. team Sweet Adelweiss Internat., Tulsa, Okla., 2000—03, dir. musical activities, 1986—89; dir. Metro Nashville Chorus, 1988—. Mem.: Mid. Tenn. Vocal Assn., Music Educators Nat. Conf., Nat. Edn. Assn. Home: 590 Thomas Jefferson Circle Madison TN 37115 Office: Hunters Lane HS 1150 Hunters Lane Nashville TN 37207 Personal E-mail: wondersk@aol.com.

WONDRA, JUDY ANN, librarian, director; d. Joseph John and Nothburga Bernadette Steiner; m. Jerome A. Wondra, Oct. 10, 1969; children: Jeffrey, John, Joseph, Jennifer, Julie. Student, Sacred Heart Coll., 1962—64, Ft. Hays State, 1964—65, Barton CC, 1990—91. Cert. Level 1-4 in libr. sci. Kan. State Libr., 1989. Libr. tchr. Independent Township Libr., Claflin, Kans., 1988—, dir. summer reading program, 1988—96. Libr. grant writer, 2002—05. CCD tchr. Holy Family Parish, Odin. Grantee, Golden Belt Found., Libr. Found. Mem.: Am. Libr. Assn., Kans. Libr. Assn., Altar Soc. (v.p., pres., treas.). Roman Catholic. Avocations: cooking, gardening, reading. Office: Independent Township Libr 108 Main Claflin KS 67525 Office Phone: 620-587-3488. Personal E-mail: jwondra@hbcomm.net.

WONG, ALICE, lawyer; Graduate, Univ. Calif., Berkeley; JD, Hastings Coll. Law, San Francisco. Dep., homicide unit Dist. Atty., Sacramento. Pub. safety liaison officer Coun. Asian Pacific Islanders Together for Advocacy and Leadership; past bd. pres. My Sister's House women's shelter. Named one of Best Lawyers Under 40, Nat. Asian Pacific Am. Bar Assn., 2004; recipient Cmty. Svc. award, Asian Pacific Bar Assn. Sacramento, 2003. Office: Community Prosecutor Ste 700 901 G St Sacramento CA 95814 Office Phone: 916-874-4978. Office Fax: 916-874-5340. Business E-Mail: alwong@saccounty.net.

WONG, ANDREA, broadcast executive; b. 1966; BS in Elec. Engring., MIT, 1988; MBA, Stanford Univ., 1993. Rschr. ABC News PrimeTime Live, 1993—94; exec. asst. pres. ABC TV Network, 1994—95, ABC, Inc., 1995, v.p., exec. asst. pres.; v.p. alt. series, spls. ABC Entertainment, 1998, exec. v.p. alt. programming, spls., late night, 2004—. Office: ABC 77 W 66th St New York NY 10023-6298*

WONG, ANN LAM, secondary school educator; b. Washington, Apr. 18, 1972; d. Jack and Grace Lam; m. Ryan Lee Wong, July 10, 1999; children: Brandon, Steven. BS, Va. Tech. U., Blacksburg, Va., 1994. Lic. tchr. Va., 1994. Tchr. sci. Glasgow Mid. Sch., Alexandria, Va., 1994—97; tchr. biology West Springfield (Va.) H.S., 1997—. Academic coord. advanced placement West Springfield (Va.) H.S., 2005—. Mem.: Nat. Assn. Biology Tchrs. Office: West Springfield High School 6100 Rolling Road Springfield VA 22152 Office Phone: 703-913-3800. Personal E-mail: ann.wong@fcps.edu.

WONG, CHERYL M., psychiatrist; b. Singapore, Jan. 9, 1967; BS in Medicine, Northwestern U., 1990, MD, 1992, Honors Program in Medical Edn., 1992. Diplomate psychiatry Am. Bd. Psychiatry, Neurology, Nat. Bd. Med. Examiners, lic. MD NJ, NY, Pa., registered DEA, NJ CDS. Residency in psychiatry Mt. Sinai Sch. Medicine, N.Y.C., 1992—96, assoc., Dept. Psychiatry, 1996—98, fellowship in rsch. psychiatry, 1997—98, asst. prof., Dept. Psychiatry, 1997—98, rsch. asst. prof., Dept. Psychiatry, 1998—99, asst. attending, Dept. Psychiatry, 1998—2002, co-founder, med. dir., Women's After Trauma Care, Health Program, 1999—2002, asst. prof., Dept. Psychiatry, 1999—2002; rsch. assoc., clin. Mt. Sinai Med. Ctr. Traumatic Stress Studies Divsn., 1998—99; attending physician, rsch. assoc., Dept. Psychiatry Bronx Vets. Affairs Med., 1998—2002, attending dept. psychiatry, 1998—99, rsch. assoc., clin., 1999—2002; med. expert witness Sall Myers Med. Assoc., 2002—. Contbr. articles various profl. jours. Recipient Marcel Heiman Meml. award Outstanding Rsch., Mt. Sinai Sch. Medicine Dept. Psychiatry, 1996, Fellowship award Clin. Neuropsychopharmacolgy, ACNP Glaxo Wellcome, 1996—97, Fellowship Rsch. award, APA Program Minority Rsch. Tng. Program, 1997—2000, Cert. Commendation, VFW, 2001, Rsch. Career Devel. award, Vets. Affairs, 1999—2002. Mem.: State Psychiatric Soc., Am. Psychiatric Assn. Home: 118 Falls Bridge Dr Totowa NJ 07512 Personal E-mail: cmw12343@aol.com.

WONG, CORINNE HONG SLING, minister, theologian; b. Hong Kong, China, Nov. 24, 1930; came to U.S., 1940; d. William Hong Sling and Clara Grace (Low) Shen; m. Howard Marn Yung Wong, Sept. 16, 1953; children: Alison Marie Wong Noto, Mark David, Martin John. BS with honors, Houghton Coll., 1951; MRE in Christian Edn., N.Y. Theol. Sem., 1954; MDiv, Princeton Theol. Sem., 1986; postgrad. in New Testament, U. Aberdeen, Scotland, 1995—98; fellow, Yale Divinity Sch., 1999; PhD with honors in New Testament Studies, U. Pretoria, S. Africa, 2006; attended, NYU, Fuller Theol. Seminary Extension, Hawaii, Chaminade U., U. Hawaii, Internat. Coll. Grad. Sch., Hawaii. ordained Am. Bapt. Chs., 1992. Asst. to pastor 1st Presbyn. Ch., Honolulu, 1986-87; min. Christian edn. Wahiawa Korean Christian Ch., Hawaii, 1988-89; interim lay pastor St. Elizabeth's Episc. Ch., Honolulu, 1989-90; min. adult ministries and outreach 1st Bapt. Ch. Honolulu, 1991-92; min. Christian edn. Korean Christian Ch., Honolulu, 1992—93; supply pastor Aberdeen Chinese Christian Ch., Scotland, 1995—98. Rsch. tech. Osborn Zoological Lab., Yale U., New Haven, 1950, Strong Meml. Hosp., U. Rochester, 1951—52; ch. sch. staff Christ Meth. Ch., N.Y.C., 1952—54; christian educator N.Y.C. Mission Soc., 1954—55; ch. staff Bethany Congregational Ch., Corona, NY, 1954—55; lectr. sci. and math. Our Redeemer Luth. Sch., Honolulu, 1961—65, Hawaii Sch. for Girls at La Pietra, Honolulu, 1969—72; math. tchr. St. Andrew's Priory Sch. for Girls, Honolulu, 1972—74; outreach min. Internat. Students Aberdeen U., 1996—98, Yale U., 1999—2000; adj. faculty Pacific Rim Bible Coll., Honolulu, 2006. Recipient grants for religious study Chinese Christian Assn., Honolulu, 1984-86, C.K. Ai Found., Honolulu, 1984-86, Presbyn. Ch. (U.S.A.), 1985-86; Regents scholarship NY State, 1947-51, scholarship Am. Legion, 1947, Arnold Constable, 1947, Houghton Coll., 1947-51.

WONG, DIANA SHUI IU, artist; Student, Chinese U., Hong Kong; BA, Acad. Fine Arts, Rome; postgrad., Royal Sch. Arts, London. Artist, Santa Monica, Calif., 1960—. Guest on CNBC-TV News Hong Kong, 1997. One-women shows include Galleria Fontanella, Rome, 1960, City Hall Gallery, Hong Kong, 1962, Chatham Galleries, Kowloon, Hong Kong, 1964, Nat. Mus. History, Taipei, Taiwan, 1969, L.A. Mission Coll., San Fernando, Calif, 1976, M.M. Shinno Gallery, L.A., 1977, 82, 85-87, Pacific Asia Mus., Pasadena, Calif, 1983, Silpakom U. Art Gallery, Bangkok, 1987, Alison Fine Arts Gallery, 1988, Gallery Q + 1, Tokyo, 1989, Filipin Gallery, Milan, 1992, LA Artcore Gallery, L.A., 1992, Seibu Art Gallery, Hong Kong, 1992, Merging One Gallery, Santa Monica, Calif., 1993, 96, Nat. Gallery, Beijing, 1994, Galleria Spazio Prospectiva, Milan, 1995, Trigram Gallery, Hong Kong, 1997, Robert V. Fullerton Art Mus., San Bernardino, Calif., 1997, Galleria Mazzocchi, Parma, Italy, 1998, LA.A. Artcore Brewery, 1999, 456 Gallery, N.Y.C., 2000; exhibited in group shows includeBrand Libr. Art Galleries, Glendale, Calif., 1976, UCLA Group Invitational, 1978, L.A. County Mus. Art, 1982, LA Artcore Gallery, 1984, U. Hilo, Hawaii, 1986, Howard Salon, Taiwan, 1987, LA Artcore, Glendale, 1989, Korean Cultural Svcs., L.A., 1989, Johnson-Humrick House Mus., Ohio, 1990, ART LA, L.A., 1992, LaLit Kala Acad., New Dehli, 1996, David Lawrence Gallery, Beverly Hills, Calif., 1997, Alisan Fine Arts, Hong Kong, 1997, Pyong Tack (Korea) Internat. Art Festival, 1997, 98, Pao Galleries, Hong Kong, 1997, Gallery of the Rim, San Francisco, 1997, L.A. Internat. Art Festival, 1997, Merging One Gallery, Santa Monica, 1998, Gallery Blu, 1998, RTKL, Architects Gallery, L.A., 1998, Space One Gallery, Izu, Japan, 2001, Hong Kong Cultural Ctr., 2002; represented in permanent collections Hong Kong Mus. Art, The Walker Art Collection, others. Recipient Black and White Composition award, Internat. Young Artists Competition, Gubbio, Italy, 1960, 66th Annual Juried Show, 3rd prize, N.J., 1970, 66th Nat. Orange Festival, 2nd place, San Bernardino, 1981. Mem. Am. I-Ching Soc. (pres.), Chinese Hist. Soc. So. Calif. (life). Home and Office: c/o Tang 1518 15th St Santa Monica CA 90404-3305

WONG, ELAINE DANG, foundation executive; b. Canton, China, June 3, 1936 (parents Am. citizens); d. Robert G. and Fung Heong (Woo) Dang; A.A. (Rotary scholar), Coalinga Coll., 1956; B.S. (AAUW scholar, Grad. Resident scholar), U. Calif., Berkeley, 1958, teaching credential, 1959; m. Philip Wong, Nov. 8, 1959; children— Elizabeth, Russell, Roger, Edith, Valerie. Tchr. acctg. San Mateo (Calif.) High Sch., 1959-60; acct., 1960-75; substitute tchr. Richmond County Schs., Augusta, Ga., 1975-77; comptroller Central Savannah River Area, United Way, Augusta, 1977-82; asst. controller Hammermill Hardwoods div. Hammermill Paper Co., Augusta, 1982-84; controller SFN Communications of Augusta, Inc. (WJBF-TV), 1984-85; acct. Med. Coll. Ga. Found., Inc., 1986-88, Nat. Sci Ctr. Found., Inc., 1988-89; cons. small bus.; pvt. tutor acctg. Mem. adv. bd. Richmond County Bd. Edn., 1985-87; bd. dirs. Cen. Savannah River chpt. Girl Scouts US, 1986-92. Panel judge Jr. Achievement Treas. award, 1980, 81; treas. Chinese Lang. Sch., 1973-75, Merry Neighborhood Sch., 1974-75. Recipient Achievement award Bank of Am., 1954. Mem. Nat. Assn. Accts. (dir. 1978-85, treas. 1982-84), Chinese Assn. Republican. Presbyterian.

WONG, FAYE LING, public health service officer; BS in Dietetics, U. Wash., 1972; MPH, U. Calif.-Berkeley, 1973. Registered dietitian, lic. Ga. Relief dietary supr. Va. Mason Hosp., Seattle, 1968—72; chief Bur. of Nutrition Coconino County Dept. Pub. Health, Flagstaff, Ariz., 1974—76; nutrition cons. Office of Cmty. Health Svcs., Oreg. State Health Divsn., Portland, 1976—81; dir. Sentinel Site project Detroit Health Dept., 1981—83; pub. health nutritionist field svcs. br. Ctr. for Health Promotion and Edn. CDC, Atlanta, 1983—89, program analyst Ctr. for Chronic Disease Prevention and Health Promotion, 1988—89, chief field svcs. br. divsn. nutrition, 1989—92, chief program ops., program svcs. br., 1992—94, asst. chief divsn. cancer prevention and control, 1994—95, asst. chief policy and devel., 1995—96, assoc. dir. diabetes edn., dir. nat. diabetes edn. program, 1996—2000, dir. Youth Media Campaign, 2001—. Contbr. numerous articles, abstracts to profl. jours., to resource manuals. Recipient Award for Disting. Svc., Dept. Health and Human Svcs., 2000, Questar Internat. award, 2000, Thoth award., Pub. Rels. Assn. Am., 2000, Aesculapius Awards for Excellence, Nat. Diabetes Edn. Program, 1999, 1998, Award for Excellence in recognition of outstanding leadership and dedicated svc., Assn. of State and Territorial Pub. Health Nutrition Dirs., 1991. Mem.: Am. Diabetes Assn. (mem. health profls. sect. 1996—), Am. Assn. Diabetes Educators (mem. pub. health specialty practice group 1996—), Am. Dietetic Assn. (mem. diabetes care and edn. practice group 1996—, mem. nominating com. 1999—), APHA (mem. food and nutrition sect. 1975—, mem. exec. bd. pub. policy rev. and devel. com. 1995—97, chair editl. bd. Am. Jour. Pub. Health 1997—2000, pres. 2001—02, co-chair task force on aging 2001—03, chair, exec. dir. search com. 2001—, Apple award 1991). Office: 4770 Buford Hwy NE lc 94 Atlanta GA 30341 Business E-Mail: fwong@cdc.gov.

WONG, LILIANE, architect, educator; BA, Vassar Coll., 1981—81; MA, Harvard U.,, 1985. Registered arch. Assoc. Perry Dean Rogers & Ptnrs., Boston, 1985—94; prin. Mahon Wong Assocs., Cambridge, Mass., 1994—; assoc. prof. RISD, Providence, 1998—. Furniture line, Kore libr. furnishings line, 1995. Named Bulfinch Arch Competition winner, Hist. Neighborhood Found., 1987. Mem.: AIA, Boston Soc. Archs. (Women in Architecture award 1994, Women in Design aard 2002).

WONG, LINDA YUNWAI, nurse; b. Kowloon, Hong Kong, Oct. 28, 1958; came to U.S., 1968, naturalized, 1974; d. Roland Po Sum and Jean Mankit (Hong) W. BSN, U. Calif.-San Francisco, 1980. RN, Calif. Nurse, Cedars-Sinai Med. Ctr., West Hollywood, Calif., 1981-82, On Lok Sr. Health Svcs., San Francisco, 1983-84, 85—. Vol. student adviser Nurses Christian Fellowship, Pasadena, Calif., 1981-82; vol. missionary Youth with a Mission, Sunland, Calif., 1983. Named one of Outstanding Young Women in Am., 1984. Avocation: running. Home: 14 Idora Ave San Francisco CA 94127-1045

WONG, MARGARET WAI, lawyer; b. Hong Kong, July 27, 1950; d. Mien Lin and Kuan Kuo (Kwan) Hwang; m. Kam M. Chan, Jan. 3, 1983. AA, Ottumwa Heights Coll. (Iowa), 1971; BSc in Chemistry-Biology, Western Ill. U., 1973; JD, SUNY-Buffalo, 1976. Bar: Ohio 1977, N.Y. 1977, D.C. 1980, U.S. Dist. Ct. 1980, U.S. Ct. Appeals (6th cir.) 1983. Instr. bus. law SUNY-Fredonia, 1977; mgmt. trainee Cen. Nat. Bank, Cleve., 1977-78; chief legal and fin. officer Buffalo City Govt., 1979-80; assoc. Berger & Kirchenbaum, Cleve., 1980-81; prin. Margaret W. Wong & Assocs., Cleve., 1981—; co-founder, co-owner Pearl of the Orient Restaurant, Cleve., 1978—; co-founder, cons. Richmond Apothe-Care, Inc. Pharmcy, Cleve., 1982-95, Cleve. Apothe-Care, Inc. Pharmacy, 1986—. Contbr. articles to legal jours. Trustee, Women Space, Cleve., 1982—, Fedn. Community Planning, Cleve., 1983-84, Women City Club, Cleve., 1983—, Orgn. Chinese Ams., Cleve., 1983—, Cleve. Coun. Human Relations, 1983—; secs., trustee Chinese Assn. Greater Cleve., 1980—; bd. dirs. Greater Cleve. Growth Assn., Inter-Mus. Conservation Assn., Notre Dame Coll., Greater Cleve. Roundtable, NCCJ. Named one of Top Ten Outstanding Young Women, Glamour mag., 1983; YWCA Career Woman of Yr., 1984. Mem. ABA (vice chmn. immigration, naturalization and aliens sect. 1993-94), Fed. Bar Assn. (pres.-elect 1993, pres. 1994), N.Y. State Bar Assn., D.C. Bar Assn., Cuyahoga County Bar Assn., Cleve. Bar Assn., Ohio Bar Assn., Cleve. Trial Lawyers Assn., Am. Assn. Immigration Lawyers. Club: Zonta (trustee 1983-84) (Cleve.). Office: Margaret W Wong & Assoc 3150 Chester Ave Cleveland OH 44114 Office Phone: 216-566-9908. Business E-Mail: wong@imwong.com.

WONG, MARTHA JEE, state representative; b. Houston, Jan. 20, 1939; d. J.T. Jee and B.S. Joe. BS, U. Tex., 1960, M, 1977; EdD, U. Houston, 1983. Tchr. Houston Ind. Sch. Dist., 1973-76, prin., 1978-82, mgr. III, 1982-87; assoc. prof. Baylor U., Waco, Tex., 1987-88; dir. resource and community devel. Southwest Coll. HCCS, 1991-93; mem. Houston City Coun., 1994—2002, Ho. of Reps., Tex., 2003—. Cons. Tex. Ednl. Agency, Austin, 1983-86, SW Tech. Asst., Nacadoches, Tex., 1985-86; mem. state affairs com., Tex. Ho. of Reps., vice chair urban affairs com., rules & resolutions com. Contbr. articles to profl. jours. Bd. dirs Leadership Houston, 1985-88, Meyerland Improvement Assn., Houston, 1987-88; chair of bd. Vocat. Giudanmce Ctr.; founder Asian-Am. Coalition; vol. Ctr. Bd. Friends of Libr. Bd.; bd. mem. Orgn. of chinese Ams., Houston Chinese Lions, Am. Leadership Forum, Asia Soc., Houston Eye Bank, Greater Houston Women' Foun., Houston Mcpl. Employees Pension Bd. Named Outstanding Woman of the Yr. in Edn., YWCA, 1991. Mem. Tex. Council Women Sch. Execs. (chmn. career opportunities), Inst. for Chinese Culture and Language (bd. dirs.), Tex. Assn. Sch. Adminstrs., U. Houston Coll. Ednl. Alumni Assn. (bd. dirs.), Delta Kappa Gamma (v.p. 1985-87, scholar), Phi Delta Kappa, Phi Kappa Phi Honor Soc. Baptist. Office: Tex Ho of Reps PO Box 2910 Austin TX 78768

WONG, MITALI R.P., language educator, consultant; arrived in U.S., 1982; d. Anil Kumar and Amita Ray Chaudhuri; m. Eugene Franklin Wong, Mar. 4, 1998; m. Uttam Kumar Pati (div.); children: Paramita Pati, Sumitra Pati. BA in English with honors, U. Calcutta, India, 1974; MA in English, Jadavpur U., India, 1977; PhD in English, U. Manitoba, Winnipeg, Can., 1990. Asst. prof. So. Conn. State U., New Haven, 1989—91, Paine Coll., Augusta, Ga., 1992—93; acting chair humanities Voorhees Coll., Denmark, SC, 1993—94, asst. prof. English, 1993—97, assoc. prof. English, 1997—98, Claflin U., Orangeburg, SC, 1998—2004, prof. English, 2004—. Cons. editor Go Tech Write, Orangeburg, 2005—. Author: (book) Politics and Tropes in Renaissance History Plays, 2006; co-author: South Asian Fiction in North America and the Caribbean, 2004. Hindu. Office: Claflin Univ 400 Magnolia St Orangeburg SC 29115 Business E-Mail: wong@claflin.edu.

WONG, NANCY L., artist, retired dermatologist; b. Chung King, China, Aug. 23, 1943; arrived in US, 1947; d. YinPao Harry and Alice Wang; m. Robert Lipshutz; children: Seth, Alison, David. BS magna cum laude, Pa. State U., 1963; MS in Physics, Columbia U., 1965; MD, Jefferson Med. Coll., Phila., 1971. Diplomate Am. Bd. Dermatology. Intern Wilmington Med. Ctr., Del., 1972; resident Jackson Meml. Hosp., Miami, Fla., 1977, Mount Sinai Med. Ctr., 1977; pvt. practice Palo Alto, Calif., 1987—. One-woman shows include San Jose City Hall, 2005, Borders, Santa Clara, 2006, Books, Inc., Mountain View, Calif., 2006. Woodrow Wilson fellow 1963-64, NSF fellow, 1963-64, AEC fellow, 1963-64; recipient 1st pl. award Palo Alto Photo Contest, Calif., 2006, 3d pl. award, 2006' 2d pl. award Moscone Ctr., San Francisco, 2006, 3r pl. award Pacific Art League, Palo Alto, Calif, 2006, 3d pl. award Convention Ctr., Washington. Fellow Am. Acad. Dermatology. Avocations: music, writing. Office Phone: 650-322-8800. E-mail: watercolorartwork@mindspring.com.

WONG, SUZANNE CRAWBUCK, librarian; b. Englewood, N.J., July 13, 1957; d. George Austin and Marion Elizabeth (Fournier) Crawbuck; m. Thomas Kay Wong, June 7, 1986; children: Jeremy Richard, Christina Elizabeth. BA in Humanities, St. Peter's Coll., Englewood Cliffs, N.J., 1980. Resources control clk. Ernst & Young (merged with Ernst & Whinney), N.Y.C., 1982-85, libr. asst., 1985—. Mem. Amateur Press Assns. (contbr. assn. jour. 1979-86) Democrat. Avocation: writing.

WONG, TOH-HENG LIM, retired pediatrician, physician; d. SiSin Lim and PoSio Kwa; m. Victor F. Wong, Sept. 18, 1971; children: Matthew, Elizabeth C., Esther M. MD, Inst. Medicine, Rangoon, Burma, 1967. Intern Swedish Covenant Hosp., Chgo., 1969—70; resident U. Ill. Hosp., 1970—72; pediatrician Chgo. Bd. Health, 1973—75; pediatrician, family physician Wong Med. Assocs., 1975—95, St. Elizabeth Hosp., 1994—99. Recipient Slawalowski Recognition award, Swedish Covenant Hosp., 1970; fellow, Mt. Sinai Hosp., Chgo., 1972—73. Fellow: Am. Acad. Family Physician (life); mem.: AMA (life), Chgo. Med. Soc. (life), Ill. Acad. Family Physician (life). Personal E-mail: tohheng@sbcglobal.net.

WONG, WANDA YUK-WA, graphics designer, educator; d. Nung and Fung-Mei Cheng; m. Kenneth K. Wong, Apr. 7, 1985; children: Norman James, Simon Jimmy, Cynthia Janice. BA, U. Calif., Berkeley, 1987; MBA, Calif. State U., Hayward, 1998. Academic award evaluator IBM Corp., Berkeley, Calif., 1985—87; ptnr. Photo Type, Oakland, Calif., 1988—; instr. Chabot Coll., Hayward, 2000—; lectr. Calif. State U., Hayward, 2000—01. Alumni scholar, U. Calif., Berkeley, 1981—82. Avocations: travel, reading, crafts. Office: Chabot Coll 25555 Hesperian Blvd Hayward CA 94545 Office Phone: 510-723-7465. E-mail: wwong@chabotcollege.edu.

WONSEWITZ, POM CHA, artist, horticulturist; b. Hong-Sung, Korea, June 15, 1944; arrived in U.S., 1971; d. Moo-Yong Pyon and Yun-Soon Kim; m. Raymond Dwight Wonsewitz, July 16, 1971; children: Paul E., David R. AA, Yuba Coll., 1972; BA cum laude, Cameron U., 1996. Mgr. Flowerama Inc., Palmer, Alaska, 1984—87; instr. arts and crafts Ft. Sill (Okla.) Mil. Installation, 1990—91; substitute tchr. Lawton (Okla.) Pub. Schs., 1999—2000; assn. mgr. Homeland Corp., Oklahoma City, 2000—02; freelance artist PC1Sewitz Art Studio, Lawton, 2002—. One-woman shows include Carnegie Libr. Hall, Lawton, 1994, Pride Gallery, 1995, Higher Edn. Ctr., Ducan, Okla., 1996. Chair, vice chair ARC, Lawton-Ft. Sill, 1981—84; chair ARC Dentac, Ft. Sill, 1982—83; vice chair ARC Reynold Army Hosp., Ft. Sill, 1981—82; vol. floral designer Hospice of Lawton Area, 1998—99; vol. ESL instr. Lawton-Ft. Sill Outreach, 1983—84. Nominee First Lady of Lawton, 1983; recipient Molly Pitcher award, Ft. Sill Mil., 1983; scholar, McMahon Found., 1991, 1992, 1993, Leslie Powell Found., 1994—95. Mem.: Sierra Pastel Soc. Home and Office: PC1Sewitz Arts 15 SW 50th St Lawton OK 73505 Office Phone: 888-528-5538. E-mail: pomcha@swb.net.

WOO, ALEX, jewelry designer; BA, Cornell Univ. Owner and designer Alex Woo Jewelry, NYC, 1999—. Named NY's Rising Star, Crain's Bus. 40 Under 40, 2005, Rising Star, JCK Show, Design Ctr., 2006; named to Elite Women, Hispanic Bus. Mag., 2005; recipient Design Award, Women's Jewelry Assn., 1998. Office: Alex Woo Inc 70 Bowery Ste 208 New York NY 10013 Office Phone: 212-226-1352. Office Fax: 212-226-5533.*

WOO, CAROLYN YAUYAN, dean; b. Hong Kong, Apr. 19, 1954; arrived in US, 1972; m. David Bartkus; children: Ryan, Justin. BS in economics, Purdue U., 1975, MS in indsl. adminstrn., 1976, PhD in strategic mgmt., 1979. Asst. prof. mgmt. Purdue U., 1981—85, assoc. to full prof., 1985—93, assoc. exec. v.p. acad. affairs, 1995—97; dir. profl. master's programs Purdue U. Krannert Sch. Mgmt., 1993—95; Martin J. Gillen dean Mendoza Sch. Bus., Notre Dame U., 1997—, Ray and Milann Siegfried chair entrepreneurial studies, 1997—. Bd. dirs. Aon Corp., 1998—, Nisource Industries Inc., 1998—, Circuit City Stores Inc., 2001—. Bd. dirs. Catholic Relief Services, 2004—; bd. regents U. Portland, 2004—. Recipient TIEM Found. Disting. Scholar award, Internat. Coun. Small Bus., 1987, Excellence award for edn., Asian Am. Alliance, 2002, John S. Day alumni academic svc. award, Krannert Sch. Mgmt., Purdue U., 2003. Mem.: Com. of 100, Assn. to Advance Collegiate Schools Bus. Internat. (bd. dirs. 1999—, vice chair 2002—03, chair 2003—04). Office: Notre Dame Univ 204 Mendoza Coll Bus Notre Dame IN 46556-5646 Office Phone: 574-631-7992. Business E-Mail: Carolyn.Y.Woo.5@nd.edu.

WOO, CATHY M., artist; b. Oakland, Calif., May 20, 1949; d. Robert F. and Mary Barber; m. Daniel D. Woo, Apr. 25, 1971; children: Elliott S., Travis D. BA in Psychology, U. Calif., Berkeley, 1971; JD, Seattle U., 1978. Exhibited in group shows at Kindred Gallery, Seattle, 1982, Mercer Island Visual Arts League, Wash., 1982, Edmonds Arts Festival, 1982, 6th Ann. Eastside Assn. Fine Arts Show, Peter Kirk Gallery, Kirkland, Wash., 1982 (3rd prize award), 42nd Ann. Exhbn. Northwest Watercolors, Bellevue Art Mus., Wash., 1982, Edmonds Art Festival, 1983, 7th Ann. Eastside Assn. Fine Arts Show, Peter Kirk Gallery, 1983, Fergus-Jean Gallery, Harbor Springs, Mich., 1983, exhibitions include 43rd Ann. Exhbn. Northwest Watercolors, Bellevue Art Mus., Wash., 1983, exhibited in group shows at Northwest Watercolor Soc. and Safeco Ins. Co., Seattle, 1984, Puget Sound Country Show, Louise Matzke Gallery, 1984, 8th Ann. Eastside Assn. Fine Arts Show, Peter Kirk Gallery, Kirkland, Wash., 1984 (Hon. Mention), Edmonds Art Festival, Wash., 1984 (cash prize award), Fergus-Jean Gallery, Harbor Springs, Mich., 1984, Mont. Inst. Arts, 1984 (Best of Show awar), exhibitions include 44th Ann. Exhbn. Northwest Watercolors, Bellevue Art Mus., Wash., 1984 (First prize best transparent watercolor), exhibited in group shows at Women Painters of Wash., Seattle, 1985, exhibitions include Pacific Marine Ins. Corp., 1985, exhibited in group shows at Allied Arts Group Show, 1985, Sander Gallery, 1985, Gallery Mack, 1985, 9th Ann. Eastside Assn. Fine Arts Show, Peter Kirk Gallery, Kirkland, Wash., 1985, exhibitions include 45th Ann. Exhbn. Northwest Watercolors, Bellevue Art Mus., Wash., 1985, 46th Ann. Exhbn. Northwest Watercolors, Bellevue Art Mus., 1987, Woodin Gallery and Chateau Ste. Michelle Winery, Woodinville, Wash., 1987, exhibited in group shows at Pacific Northwest Art Exposition, Seattle, 1987, one-woman shows include Northwest Art Exchg., Gaches Mansion, La Connor, Wash., 1987, exhibitions include 29th Ann. Puget Sound Area Exhbn., Frye Art Mus., Seattle, 1987, exhibited in group shows at Matzke-Runnings Gallery, 1987, 11th Ann. Eastside Assn. Fine Arts Show, Gallery Dubois, Bellevue, 1987, Mercer Island Visual Arts League, Wash., 1987 (Hon. Mention), 2d Pacific Northwest Art Exposition, Seattle, 1987, exhibitions include 47th Ann. Exhbn. Northwest Watercolors, Bellevue Art Mus., Wash., 1987, exhibited in group shows at Puget Sound Country Show, Stillwater Gallery, Inc., Seattle, 1987, exhibitions include Northwest Watercolor Soc. 51st Ann. Open Exhbn., Howard/Mandville Gallery, Kirkland, 1991 (Seattle Art/Schminchke award), exhibited in group shows at Peter Kirk Gallery, 1993 (Northwest Watercolor Soc. award), Chuck Webster 1st Ann. Invitational Art Show, Kirkland, 1995, Backstreet Frame and Art, Bellevue, 1995 (Best of Show award), Waterworks 95, Tolles Gallery, Mercer Island, 1995, exhibitions include A Celebration of Watercolor, Meydenbauer Conv. Ctr., Bellevue, 1996, exhibited in group shows at Images of Women, ArtsWest Gallery, Seattle, 1996, Heartworks, Whatcom Mus. of History and Art, Bellingham, Wash., 1996, Soundings South: An Exploration of Water Media on Paper, Wash. Ctr. Performing Arts, Olympia, 1996, Reaching for the Light, Blue Horse Gallery, Bellingham, 1996, Moss Bay Gallery, Kirkland, 1996, exhibitions include Northwest Watercolor Soc. 56th Ann. Open Exhbn., Howard/Mandville Gallery, 1996 (Dakota Art Store Merchandise award), exhibited in group shows at Waterworks 96, Tolles Gallery, Mercer Island, 1996 (Northwest Watercolor Soc. merit award), exhibitions include Nat. Watercolor Soc. 76th Ann. Exhbn., Muckenthaler Cultural Ctr., Fullerton, Calif., 1996, A Celebration of Watercolor, Maydenbauer Conv. Ctr., Bellevue, 1997, exhibited in group shows at Heartworks, Whatcom Mus. History and Art, Bellingham, 1997, Moss Bay Gallery, Kirkland, 1997, Waterworks 97, Tolles Gallery, Mercer Island, 1997 (Northwest Watercolor Soc. merit award), exhibitions include Intimate Views of Women, Janet Laurel-A Woman's Gallery, Seattle, 1998, exhibited in group shows at Heartworks, Whatcom Mus. History and Art, Bellingham, 1998, exhibitions include Watercolor Messages, Meydenbauer Conv. Ctr., Bellevue, 1998, exhibited in group shows at Waterworks 98, Tolles Gallery, Mercer Island, 1998 (NBBJ Architects award), Mus. Northwest Art Auction 99, La Conner, 1999, one-woman shows include Alki Bathhouse Art Studio, Seattle, 1999, exhibited in group shows at Fresh Air, Issaquah Gallery, Wash., 1999 (Eastside Assn. Fine Arts award), Mus. Northwest Art Auction 2000, La Conner, 2000, Millennium Images, Wash. State Conv. & Trade Ctr., Seattle, 2000, Beyond Beginnings, Edmonds C.C. Art Gallery, Lynnwood, Wash., 2000, exhibitions include Evergreen State Coll., Olympia, Wash., 2000 (F&W Pub. Merchandise award), exhibited in group shows at Frye Art Mus., Seattle, 2000, exhibitions include Nat. Watercolor Soc. 80th Ann. Exhbn., Muckenthaler Cultural Ctr., Fullerton, 2000 (Purchase award, 2000), exhibited in group shows at Mus. Northwest Art Auction 2001, La Conner, 2001, Starbucks Coffee House on Alki, Seattle, 2001, The Runnings Gallery, 2001, exhibitions include Nat. Watercolor Soc. 81st Ann. Exhbn., Brea, Calif., 2001. Mem.: Women Painters of Wash., Northwest Watercolor Soc. (pres., bd. dirs. 1997—98, Best Transparent Watercolor award 1984), Nat. Watercolor Soc. (Purchase award 2000). Home: 3328 59th Ave SW Seattle WA 98116 Office Phone: 206-250-9123. Personal E-mail: cmwoo@msn.com. E-mail: cathywoo1949@comcast.net.

WOOD, ANDRÉE ROBITAILLE, archaeologist, researcher; b. Chgo., Feb. 10, 1929; d. Andrew George and Alice Marie (Fortier) Robitaille; m. Richard Lawrence Wood, Jan. 14, 1956; children: Mary Wood Molo, Matthew William Wood, Melissa Irene Wood, Elizabeth Wood Wesel, John Andrew Wood. BA, No. Ill. Univ., DeKalb, 1977, MA, 1982. Freelance archaeologist, 1981—84; rsch. asst. Prehistoric Project Oriental Inst., Univ. Chgo., Ill., 1984—98. Rsch., discovery, removal, analysis and identification of ancient blood residues on lithic material excavated at ten millenium old site, Çayönü in Ergani, Turkey. Contbr. articles to profl. jours. Avocations: poetry, boating, tennis. Home: 356 Old Sutton Rd Barrington IL 60010-9113 also: 8735 Midnight Pass Rd Apt 604B Sarasota FL 34242-2892

WOOD, BARBARA LOUISE, psychologist; b. Staunton, Va., Nov. 28, 1949; d. William Earle and Caroline Estelle (Marks) W.; B.A. in Psychology, Carnegie-Mellon U., 1971; M.A. in Counseling (EDPA fellow), U. Minn., 1974; Ph.D. in Counseling, U. Md., 1979; student Assn. for Psychoanalytic Study, 1980-84; m. Philip Bond Ray, Aug. 2, 1981; 1 child, Christopher William Ray. Counselor Kenyon Coll., Gambier, Ohio, 1976-77; psychol. counselor Am. U., Washington, 1977; cons. Temple Hills (Md.) Counseling Center, 1977-79; profl. assoc. Univ. Counseling Center, U. Md., College Park, 1977-79, teaching asst., 1977, 79, instr., 1978-84, adj. asst. prof., 1985-87; dir. Greenbelt-College Park (Md.) Counseling Center, 1979-81; pvt. practice psychology, Chevy Chase, Md., 1982-86, Bethesda and Gaithersburg, Md., 1986—; co-founder Bethesda Psychol. Ctr. Author: Children of Alcoholism, 1987, Raising Healthy Children in an Alcoholic Home, 1992; contbr. articles to profl. jours Mem. APA, Phi Kappa Phi. Democrat. Roman Catholic. Home: 16704 Baederwood Ln Rockville MD 20855-2009 Office: 4915 Saint Elmo Ave Ste 404 Bethesda MD 20814-6052 Office Phone: 302-652-4147. E-mail: blwood@alcoholismandthefamily.com.

WOOD, BARBARA LYNN, elementary school educator; b. Syracuse, N.Y. d. Robert Hilton and Carol (Flynn) W. BS, Springfield (Mass.) Coll., 1974; Cert. in advanced study in adminstrn., Cortland Coll., 1990; MS, Tex. Woman's U., 1991. Tchr. phys. edn. Homer (N.Y.) Cen. Sch., 1974-87, 88—. Designed, produced and impmented A Home/Sch. Based Devel. Phys. Edn. Program K-2, 1989-91. Author: School Based Home Developmental P.E. Program, 1998; devel., pub. The Wood Motor Success Screening Tool, 1999. Recipient coaches award, Onondaga High Sch. League, 1984, Ofcls. team sportsmanship award field hockey, 2003. Mem. AAHPER and Dance, N.Y. State Assn. Health, Phys. Edn., Recreation and Dance (conf. spkr. 1990, spkr. adminstr. course phys. edn. K-12 2003, 05). Avocations: stained glass, woodworking, sailing. Home: 28 Abdallah Ave Cortland NY 13045-3303 Office Phone: 607-749-1250.

WOOD, BETTY JEAN, conceptual artist, art educator; b. Pitts., Ind., Mar. 2, 1942; d. Ralph Alphas and Mary Cordis Blanton; m. John E. Ayers, Aug. 25, 1963 (div. May 1987); children: Mark Ayers, Kristin Ayers Torres; m. Frederick Harrison Wood, Jr., Nov. 28, 1987 (dec. Jan. 2002); children: Andrew, Christopher. BA with honors, Pa. State U., 1984; MFA, U. Okla., 1992. Artist-in-residence Okla. Arts Coun., 1993—2003; asst. instr. Okla. Arts Inst., Okla. State U., Stillwater, 1998; guest lectr. Southwestern State U., Weatherford, Okla., 2001; instr. Oklahoma City Mus. of Art., 2002—; guest lectr. Goddard Art Ctr., Ardmore, Okla., 2003. Spl. project asst. ConservArt Assoc., Culver City, Calif., 1991—93; asst. preparator Fred Jones, Jr. Mus. of Art, U. Okla., 1992—2005, installation asst., 1992; co-coord. SummerWind Arts Festival, Norman, 1994—96; coord. SummerWind Arts Festival, Children's Events, 1995—; art cons. Dept. Edn., San Juan, 1986; bd. dirs. Children's Art Network, Norman, 1996—2001; coord./curator spl. exhbn. Ctrl. Pa. Festival of the Arts, State College, 1973—87; adj. prof. U. Okla., Norman, Okla., 1997—98, 2004—06; artist resident, Costa Rica, 2006. Author: (book reviews) Museologist, 1986—87, Community Based Art Education, 1995; one-woman shows include Bricktown Fin. Inst., Okla., numerous others, exhibited in group shows at 50th Anniversary Nat. Art Exhibit, Wind River Valley Artist's Guild, Wyo., Leslie Powell Gallery, Okla., IAO Gallery, Okla., Gallery on the Sq., Ky., Period Gallery, Nebr., Suite 2 Portfolio, Okla., Kirkpatrick Galleries of Omniplex, Okla., Goddard Art Ctr., Ardmore, Okla., East Ctrl. U., Ada, Okla., Purdue U., West Lafayette, Ind., Lamar U., Beaumont, Tex., Mus. Great Plains, Lawron, Okla., Soho Art Dist., NYC, Murray State Coll., Tishomingo, Okla., Mainsite Art Gallery, Norman, Okla., Internat. Print Exhbn., Barcelona, Spain, Taiwan, Ponca City Gallery, Okla., others, over 330 exhbns., Represented in permanent collections Sch. of Visual Arts, Pa. State U., Sch. of Art, U. Okla., Okla., Fred Jones, Jr. Mus. of Art, Okla. City Art Mus., Okla. Sch. of Arts and Scis., Okla. Visual Arts Coalition, Oklahoma City, pvt. collections U.S. and abroad. Recipient numerous awards for art. Mem.: Fred Jones Jr. Mus. Art, Oklahoma City Mus. Art, Mus. Women in Art, Nat. Mus. for Women in Art, Five to Nine Artists, Jacobson House Found., U. Okla. Art Alumni Assn. (pres. 1993), Pa. State U. Alumni Assn., Beta Sigma Phi Sorority (pres. 1983—84). Democrat. Avocations: children's/adult's workshops, reading, antiques, art. Home: 3316 Riviera Dr Norman OK 73072-7613 Office Phone: 405-850-2051. Business E-Mail: fredwood@ou.edu.

WOOD, BRENDA, newscaster; m. Keith Wood; children: Kristen, Kandis. BA in Speech Comm. and Mass Media summa cum laude, Loma Linda U. With Sta. WAAY-TV, Huntsville, Ala., 1977, anchor, 1979—80; gen. assignment reporter Sta. WSM-TV, Nashville, 1978; anchor Sta. WMC-TV, Memphis, 1980—88, Sta. WAGA-TV, 1988—97, Sta. WXIA-TV, Atlanta, 1997—. Spkr. in field. Named Phoenix award, NAACP, 1997, Best Local News Anchor, Atlanta Mag., 1998; recipient Atlanta Assn. Black Journalists award, News Personality of the Yr. award, Ga. Assn. Broadcasters, Excellence in Local Programming award, Women in Comm. award, Gabriel award, Ga. Psychol. Assn. Mem.: NATAS (Emmy award), Women in Film, Atlanta Assn. Black Journalists (award), Nat. Assn. Black Journalists (Cmty. Affairs Programming award 1998), Atlanta Press Club. Office: Sta WXIA-TV 1611 W Peachtree St Atlanta GA 30309

WOOD, BRENDA JEAN, pastor, evangelist; b. Patrick AFB, Fla., Sept. 24, 1961; d. Terry Robert Hubbard and Cherry Ann Redwine, James William Redwine (Stepfather); m. Ross Landan Wood, Apr. 11, 1981; children: Jared Ross, Dwight Adam Myers, Christopher Wayne Pitts, Leslie Anne. AA,

Weatherford Coll., Weatherford, Texas, 1981; BA Psychology, Calif. State U., San Bernardino, Calif., 1995; MS Marriage & Family Therapy, Fuller Theol. Sem., Pasadena, Calif., 1999, MA in Theology, 2002. Ordained min. Bethel Christian Ctr., 2004, lic. min. Assemblies of God, Calif., 1999. Youth pastor Full Gospel Assembly of God, Norco, Calif., 1995—97; intern counselor Turning Point Counseling, Diamond Bar, Calif., 1997—99; christian edn. dir. New Life Christian Fellowship, Riverside, Calif., 1998—98, youth pastor, 1998—98, sr. pastor, 1998—2004; pastor, founder Word of Life Ministries Internat., 2005—; evangelist Word of Life Ministries in Nigeria and India. Spkr. Religious and Civic Functions, 1995—; evangelist New Life Christian Fellowship, Mexico, 2002—, Nigeria, 2003, pastoral counselor, Calif., 1995—; parenting educator Safe Haven Program, Riverside, Calif., 2002—03. Chaplain Calif. Dept. of Forestry, Riverside, Calif., 2001—04; mem. Cops and Clergy, Riverside, Calif., 2002, bd. mem., 2002; mem. Jurupa C. of C., Riverside, Calif., 2003, Pastors Prayer Fellowship, Riverside, Calif., 2001. Scholar Music, Weatherford Coll., 1979. Assemblies Of God. Avocations: spending time with my family, gardening, travel. Home: 1804 Noah Dr Corona CA 92880 E-mail: pastorbrenda@theword.us.

WOOD, CAROLINE, secondary school educator; b. Fredonia, N.Y., Nov. 4, 1925; d. Fred Jacob and Mary (Hall) Wood. BA in Sci., Cornell U., 1947; BS in Edn., SUNY, Fredonia, 1948, MS in Edn., 1952. Cert. elem. edn. tchr., N.Y. Tchr. elem. S.G. Love Sch., Jamestown, N.Y., 1948-59, Fredonia Cen. Schs., 1959-82, ret., 1982. Mem. AARP, Nat. Grape Coop, N.Y. State Ret. Tchrs. Assn., Farm Bur., Affenpinscher Dog Club, Concord Grape Belt Heritage Assn., Chautauqua County Coop. Ext., Order Eastern Star, Women of Moose, Rebekah Lodge, Fredonia Grange #1, Sheridan Srs., United Srs., Share and Care Ctr. Republican. Methodist. Avocations: porcelain dolls, flower gardening, grape farming. Home: 3624 E Main Rd Fredonia NY 14063-1436

WOOD, CATHERINE T., special education educator; b. Mineola, N.Y., Jan. 17, 1950; d. Owen Joseph Sheehan and Dorothy Margaret Carnaghan; m. David Patrick Wood, Aug. 7, 1976; 1 child, Khalie Tamara. BS in Psychology, Spanish and Edn., Molloy Coll., Rockville Ctr., N.Y., 1971; MS in Spl. Edn., Hofstra U., 1975, postgrad. in Speech and Lang., 1975—; postgrad., Nov Southeastern U., 2005—. Cert. tchr. N.Y., in sign lang. Spl. edn. tchr. Malverne Sch. Dist., NY, 1971—80; spl. edn. math specialist Horizion Sch. for Perceptual Devel., Bayside, NY, 1980—84; spl. edn. tchr. Valley Stream Dist. 30, NY, 1984—. Pres. sch. bd. Our Lady of Peace Sch., Lynbrook, NY, 1995—97; mem. regional sch. bd. Region#24, Lynbrook, NY, 1995—97; religous edn. tchr. Our Lady of Peace, Lynbrook, NY, 1994—98. Vol. Full Cir., N.Y.C., 1969—73; tchr. vol. Vocat. Edn. Extension Bd., Hempstead, 1994—98. Recipient Master Tchrs. Award, Molloy Coll., N.Y., 1995. Mem.: ASCD, NY Student Speech Lang. Hearing Assn., Valley Stream Tchrs. Assn., Nassau Reading Coun., Nat. Coun. Tchrs. English, Nassau County Math Tchr. Assn., Kappa Delta Pi. Roman Catholic. Avocations: sewing, knitting, kayaking, music, pottery. Office: Forest Rd Sch 16 Forest Rd Valley Stream NY 11581

WOOD, CORINNE GIESEKE, former lieutenant governor; b. Barrington, Ill., May 28, 1954; m. Paul R. Wood; children: Ashley, Brandon, Courtney. BS, U. Ill., 1976; JD, Loyola U., 1979. Bar: Ill. 1979. Pvt. practice; counsel Ill. Savs. and Residential Fin. Bd.; atty. Hopkins & Sutter, Chgo.; gen. counsel Ill. Commr. of Banks and trusts; state rep. 59th dist. 90th Ill. Gen. Assembly, Springfield; rep. State of Ill., 1997—99, former lt. gov. Springfield, 1999—2003. Appointed spec. asst., Ill. Atty. Gen. Former co-capt. Shields Twp. Rep. Precinct; Lake Forest chmn. John E. Porter for Congress, 1994, 96; adv. mem. Coun. of Women Advisors to U.S. Congress; past 1st v.p., bd. dirs. Women's Rep. Club, past pres., bd. mem. 10th Congl. Dist. of Lake Forest/Lake Bluff chpt.; past pres. (fin. chmn.), mem. bd. govs. Lake County Rep. Fedn.; bd. dirs. Allendale Shelter Club, Allendale Assn.; adv. bd. A Safe Place; transition bd. dirs. Anne M. Kiley Ctr. for the Developmentally Disabled; mem. LWV of Lake Forest/Lake Bluff; mem. Lake Forest Open Lands Assn.; former Lake Forest chmn., sustaining mem. Jr. League of Chgo.; former new mems. chair, membership com., Sunday sch. tchr. First Presbyn. Ch. of Lake Forest; den leader Pack 43, Boy Scouts Am.; plan commr. City of Lake Forest, 1993-97, sr. housing commr., 1993-97, ad hoc com. on sr. housing bd. mem. Recipient City of Lake Forest Spl. Recognition of Pub. Svc. award. Mem. ABA, Ill. Bar Assn., Lake County Bar Assn., Chgo. Bar Assn., House Financial Insts. Comm., Comm. on Aging, Edn. Appropriations Comm., Labor and Commerce Comm., appointed mem., Legislative Rsch. Bureau, bd. mem. Republican.

WOOD, CYNTHIA WILDER, elementary school educator; b. West Point, NY, July 4, 1952; d. Robert Morse and Cynthia Rich Wood. AA in Early Childhood Edn., Centenary Coll., 1974; BS in Health Edn., U. Conn., 1984; MAT in Elem. Edn., U. Portland, 1989. Med. assoc. pvt. med. office, Greenwich, Conn., 1974—80; radiol. tech. United Hosp., Port Chester, NY, 1980—84, Providence Milw. Hosp., Clackamas, Oreg., 1985—88, Willamette Falls Hosp., Oregon City, 1988—90; tchr. elem. sch. Portland Pub. Schs., 1990—2003, mentor reading coach, 2003—. Mem. Consortium Ednl. Advancement and Devel., Portland, 1994—; presenter in field. Mem. Alameda Tuesday Club, Portland, 1992—2000. Mem.: ASCD, Alpha Delta Kappa. Democrat. Episcopalian. Avocations: reading, needlepoint, gardening. Home: 5022 NE Sumner St Portland OR 97218 Office: Whitman Elem Sch 7326 SE Flavel St Portland OR 97206 Office Phone: 503-916-6370. Business E-Mail: cwood@pps.k12.or.us.

WOOD, DIANE MARY, special education educator; b. Athol, Mass., Feb. 11, 1953; d. Harold Warren and Ann Theresa (Karluk) Wood. BS, So. Conn. State U., New Haven, 1974; MS, So. Conn. State U., 1975; PhD, SUNY-Albany, 1994. Reading clinician New London (Conn.) pub. schs., 1975-77; developmental reading specialist Marlborough (N.H.) Sch. Dist. 29, 1977-78; spl. edn. tchr. Keene (N.H.) Sch. Dist., 1978-84, Ravena-Coeymans-Selkirk (N.Y.) Sch. Dist., 1984-89; teaching asst. SUNY-Albany, 1989-90; cons. tchr. Ravena-Coeymans-Selkirk Sch. Dist., 1990—. Ednl. cons. Keene Sch. Dist., 1983—84; adj. faculty SUNY, Albany, 1990—2003; lectr. Coll. of St. Rose, 1990—. Dir. YMCA Day Camp, Cheshire County, Richmond, summer 1979; driver, vol. Albany Meals on Wheels, 1989-90; bd. dirs. Monadnock Task Force on Child Abuse and Neglect, Keene, N.H., 1982-84; active Big Bros./Big Sisters, Keene, 1982-84. Mem. Coun. for Exceptional Children, Am. Ednl. Rsch. Assn., Learning Disabilities Assn. Am. Avocations: reading, skiing. Office: AW Becker Elem Sch RR 9 # W Selkirk NY 12158

WOOD, DIANE PAMELA, federal judge; b. Plainfield, N.J., July 4, 1950; d. Kenneth Reed and Lucille (Padmore) Wood; m. Dennis James Hutchinson, Sept. 2, 1978 (div. May 1998); children: Kathryn Hutchinson, David Hutchinson, Jane Hutchinson. BA, U. Tex., 1971, JD, 1975; JD (hon.), Georgetown U., 2003, Ill. Inst. Tech., 2004. Bar: Tex. 1975, D.C. 1978, Ill. 1993. Law clk. U.S. Ct. Appeals (5th cir.), 1975—76, U.S. Supreme Ct., 1976—77; atty.-advisor U.S. Dept. State, Washington, 1977—78; assoc. Covington & Burling, Washington, 1978—80; asst. prof. law Georgetown U. Law Ctr., Washington, 1980—81, U. Chgo., 1981—88, prof. law, 1988—95, assoc. dean, 1989—92, Harold J. and Marion F. Green prof. internat. legal studies, 1990—95, sr. lectr. law, 1995—; spl. cons. antitrust divsn. internat. guide U.S. Dept. Justice, 1986—87, dep. asst. atty. gen. antitrust divsn., 1993—95; judge U.S. Ct. Appeals (7th cir.), 1995—. Contbr. articles to profl. jours.; bd. editors: Am. Jour. Internat. Law. Bd. dirs. Hyde Park-Kenwood Cmty. Health Ctr., 1983—85. Fellow: Am. Acad. Arts and Scis.; mem.: Am. Law Inst. (elected coun. mem. 2003), Am. Soc. Internat. Law, Phi Alpha Delta. Democrat. Office: US Courthouse 219 S Dearborn St Chicago IL 60604-1803*

WOOD, ELIZABETH ANN, special education educator; b. Pittsfield, Mass., Aug. 2, 1979; d. Dennis Roy Luczynski and Tami Lee Daley; m. Jason Richard Wood, Aug. 31, 2000. BA in Sociology, BA in Early Childhood Edn., Mass. Coll. Liberal Arts, 2001, MEd in Spl. Needs, 2003. Cert. early childhood and moderate disability tcur. Mass. Mgr. Subway, North Adams, Mass., 1996—2002; lead pre-kindergarten tchr. North Berkshire YMCA, North Adams, 2001—03; spl. needs tchr. Hillcrest Edn. Ctrs., Pittsfield, Mass., 2003—. Mem.: Nat. Honor Soc. Roman Catholic. Avocations: sewing, exercise, scrapbooks. Home: 2 Daniels Ct Adams MA 01220 Office: Hillcrest Ednl Ctrs 1450 W Housatanic St Pittsfield MA 01201 Business E-Mail: lwood@hillcrestec.org.

WOOD, EVAN RACHEL, actress; b. Raleigh, NC, Sept. 7, 1987; d. Ira David Wood and Sara Lynn Moore. Actor: (films) Digging to China, 1998, Practical Magic, 1998, Detour, 1999, Little Secrets, 2001, S1m0ne, 2002, Thirteen, 2003, The Missing, 2003, Down in the Valley, 2005, Pretty Persuasion, 2005, The Upside of Anger, 2005, Running with Scissors, 2006, (voice) Asterix and the Vikings, 2006, Shark Bait, 2006,: (TV films) In the Best of Families: Marriage, Pride & Madness, 1994, Search for Grace, 1994, A Father for Charlie, 1995, Death in Small Doses, 1995, Get to the Heart: The Barbara Mandrell Story, 1997, Down Will Come Baby, 1999; (TV series) Profiler, 1998—99, Once and Again, 1999—2002, (guest appearances) American Gothic, 1995—98, Touched by an Angel, 2000, The West Wing, 2002, CSI: Crime Scene Investigation, 2003.*

WOOD, FRANCES DIANE, medical secretary, artist; b. Caddo, Okla., Mar. 7, 1950; d. Clovis Lynn and Hilda Dee (Guthrie) Wood; m. Samuel Dante Wolfe, Aug. 20, 1990 (div. Mar. 1992). BA, Southea. Okla. State U., 1972; postgrad., Grayson County Coll., 1987, Rose State Coll., 2002, U. Ctrl. Okla., 2004. Ins. clk. Sherman Cmty. Hosp., Tex., 1973—74; med. sec. Essin Clinic, Sherman, 1980—83; med. transcriptionist Texoma Med. Ctr., Denison, Tex., 1983—88, Wilson N. Jones Meml. Hosp., Sherman, 1989—95; CEO Designs by Diane, Caddo, 1995—. Conv. del. Blue Cross-Blue Shield Tex., Dallas, 1980—83; v.p. Jett Transcription, Denison, 1988. Exhibitions include paintings in cmty. art shows, Represented in permanent collections Shamrock Bank, Caddo, Indian Terr. Mus., Caddo. Charter mem. Caddo Edn. Found., Okla., 1993-95; sponsor Save the Children, Philippines, 1995. Mem. ASPCA, Friends Internat. Fellowship of Christians and Jews, Physicians Com. for Responsible Medicine, Nat. Trust Hist. Preservation, Okla. Sheriffs Assn. (hon.), Arts Coun. Co-op (life), Nat. Arbor Day Found., Sierra Club, Sacred Heart Auto League, People for Ethical Treatment Animals, Urban League Greater Oklahoma City Democrat. Avocations: pet care and pet psychology, interior decorating, astronomy, holistic and naturopathic medicine, gardening.

WOOD, JANE ROBERTS, writer; m. Dub Wood. Author: The Train to Estelline, 1987, A Place Called Sweet Shrub, 1990, Dance a Little Longer, 1993, Grace, 2001, Roseborough, 2003, Mocha, 2004. Recipient Tex. Inst. Letters award for best short story, 1998; fellow NEA, NEH. Office: c/o U North Texas Press PO Box 311336 Denton TX 76203-1336

WOOD, JANE SEMPLE, editor, writer; b. Easton, Pa., June 23, 1940; d. Royer Daniel and Wilhelmina Annette (Weichel) Semple; m. James MacPherson Wood, Sept. 8, 1961; children: James MacPherson Jr., Robert Semple. BA in Journalism, U. Calif., Berkeley, 1961. Reporter San Jose (Calif.) Mercury News, 1962; asst. dir. pub. rels. Nat. Symphony Orch., Washington, 1963-65; free-lance writer and editor Adoption Listing Svc. of Ohio, Cleve., 1976; freelance writer and editor AIA, Cleve., 1977; free-lance writer and editor City of Bedford Heights, Ohio, 1980-81, City of Shaker Heights, Ohio, 1979-80, pub. info. officer, dir. publs., 1980—85, 1992—99; founding editor Shaker mag., Shaker Heights, Ohio, 1983—2003; free-lance writer Exec. Living, Cleve., 1990-91; contbg. editor Corp. Cleve., 1991-92; editor e-letter This Week in Shaker, 2003—; columnist Sun Press, 2003—. Pub. rels. cons. Cable TV Com., Shaker Heights, 1978-85, Oak Park Exch. Congress, Shaker Heights, 1981. Vol. editor, columnist Friends of Shaker Sq., Cleve., 1979-82; vol. pub. rels. com. Cleve. Ballet, 1980, Cleve. Orch., 1983; vol. contbg. editor Univ. Hosps., Cleve., 1990-92; mem. Calif. Ann. Fund Adv. Coun., 2000; vol. contbg. writer Heights Arts Collaborative, Cleve., 2004 Recipient Grand award City Hall Digest, 1983, 85, 87, Excellence in Journalism award Soc. Profl. Journalists, 1988, 92, 95, Woman of Profl. Excellence award Cleve. YWCA, 1986, Ace award of Merit, 1991, Hon. mention Blue Pencil Competition of Nat. Assn. Govt. Communicators, 1993, Ohioana James P. Barry Editl. Excellence award, 1999; Jane Wood Excellence in Journalism award named in her honor, 2003. Mem.: Daily Calif. Alumni Assn. (Midwest coord.), U. Calif. Alumni Assn. (permanent class sec. 1961). Avocations: cooking, swimming, reading, travel, concerts. Business E-Mail: thisweekinshaker@sbcglobal.net.

WOOD, JEAN CAROL, poet, lyricist; b. Oklahoma City, Apr. 6, 1940; d. Howard Melvin and Ethel Matillda (Carroll) Sage; m. Harold David Wood; children: Howard David, Troy Don, Kevin Dale, L'lana Cayé. Freelance writer, 1976—. Contbr. poems in collections; lyricist: songs As It Should Be, 2001—02, As It Should Be III, 2005; author: (poem) Rest On His Thumb, 2003, The Transport Of a Winged Being. Recipient trophy, Internat. Soc. Poets, 2003. Mem.: Internat. Soc. Poets. Avocations: writing, gardening, reading. Home: 1047 W Windsor Way Mustang OK 73064

WOOD, JEANNINE KAY, legislative staff member; b. Dalton, Nebr., Apr. 22, 1944; d. Grover L. and Elsie M. (Winkelman) Sanders; m. Charles S. Wood, Dec. 7, 1968; children: Craig C., Wendi L. Wood Weaver. Exec. sec. Idaho Hosp. Assn., Boise, 1966-71; com. sec. Idaho State Senate, Boise, 1976-81, jour. clk., 1981-85, asst. to sec. of senate, 1985-91, sec. of senate, 1991—2002; pvt. practice typing svc. Boise, 1979-86. Mem. Am. Soc. Legis. Clks. and Secs. Methodist. Home: 3505 S Linder Rd Meridian ID 83642-6837 Office: Idaho State Capitol PO Box 83720 Boise ID 83720-0081

WOOD, KIMBA M., federal judge; b. Port Townsend, Wash., Jan. 2, 1944. BA cum laude, Conn. Coll., 1965; MSc, London Sch. Econs., 1966; JD, Harvard U., 1969. Bar: U.S. Dist. Ct. D.C. 1969, U.S. Ct. Appeals D.C. 1969, N.Y. 1972, U.S. Dist. Ct. (ea. and so. dists.) N.Y. 1974, U.S. Ct. Appeals (2d cir.) 1975, U.S. Supreme Ct. 1980, U.S. Dist. Ct. (we. dist.) N.Y. 1981. Assoc. Steptoe & Johnson, Washington, 1969-70; with Office Spl. Counsel, OEO Legal Svcs., Washington, 1970-71; assoc., then ptnr. LeBoeuf, Lamb, Leiby & MacRae, N.Y.C., 1971-88; judge, U.S. Dist. Ct. (So. Dist.), NY, 1988—. Mem. ABA (chmn. civil practice, procedure com. 1982-85, mem. coun. 1985-88, jud. rep. 1989-91), N.Y. State Bar Assn. (chmn. antitrust sect. 1983-84), Fed. Bar Coun. (trustee from 1978, v.p., 1984-85), Am. Law Inst. Office: US Dist Ct US Courthouse 500 Pearl St Rm 1610 New York NY 10007-1316

WOOD, LARRY (MARY LAIRD), journalist, writer, public relations executive, educator, environmental consultant; b. Sandpoint, Idaho; d. Edward Hayes and Alice (McNeel) Small; children: Mary, Marcia, Barry. BA summa cum laude, U. Wash., 1939, MA summa cum laude, 1940; postgrad., Stanford U., 1940—43, U. Calif., Berkeley, 1946—47, U. Wis., 1971—72, U. Minn., 1971—72, U. Ga., 1972—73, U. Calif., Santa Cruz, 1974—76, Stanford Hopkins Marine Sta., 1977—80. Cert. secondary and jr. coll. tchr., Wash., Calif. Feature writer and columnist Oakland Tribune and San Francisco Chronicle, Calif., 1939—; archtl. and environ. feature and travel writer and columnist San Jose (Calif.) Mercury News (Knight Ridder), 1972-90; tchg. fellow Stanford U., 1940-43; dir. pub. rels. 2-counties, 65-park 100,000 acre East Bay Regional Park Dist., No. Calif., 1948-68; pres. Larry Wood Pub. Rels., 1946—; pub. rels. dir. Calif. Children's Home Soc., 1947-58. Prof. pub. rels., mag. writing, journalism, investigative reporting San Diego State U., 1974-75; disting. vis. prof. journalism San Jose State U., 1976; assoc. prof. journalism Calif. State U., Hayward, 1978; prof. sci. and environ. journalism U. Calif. Berkeley Ext. grad. divsn., 1979—; press del. nat. convs. Am. Geophys. Union Internat. Conf., 1986—, AAAS, 1989—, Nat. Park Svc. VIP Press Tour, Yellowstone after the fire, 1989—, Nat. Assn. Sci. Writers, 1989—, George Washington U./Am. Assn. Neurol. Surgeons Sci. Writers Conf., 1990, Am. Inst. Biol. Scis. Conf., 1990, Nat. Conf. Sci. Writers, Am. Heart Assn., 1995, Internat. Cardiologists Symposium for Med./Sci. Writers, 1995, Annenberg Program Electronic Media Symposium, Washington, 1995; EPA del. to USSR and Ea. Europe; expert witness on edn., pub. rels., journalism and copyright; cons. sci. writers interne project Stanford U., 1989—; spl. media guest Sigma Xi, 1990—; mem. numerous spl. press corps; selected White House Spl. Media, 1993—; selected mem. Duke U. 14th Ann. Sci. Reporters Conf., 1995; internat. press guest Can. Consulate Gen. Dateline Can., 1995—, French Govt. Tourist Office, 1996—, Ministerio delle Risorse Agricole Alimentarie Forestali and Assocs. Conf., 1995; appeared in TV documentary Larry Wood Covers Visit of Queen Elizabeth II. Contbr. over 5,500 articles to newspapers, nat. mags., nat. and internat. newspapers including L.A. Times-Mirror Syndicate, Knight-Ridder Syndicate, Washington Post, Phila. Inquirer, Chgo. Tribune, Miami Herald, Oakland Tribune, Seattle Times, San Francisco Chronicle, 36 Million Circulation Parade, San Jose Mercury News (Nat. Headliner award), Christian Sci. Monitor, L.A. Times/Christian Sci. Monitor Worldwide News Syndicate, Washington Post, Phila. Inquirer, Hawaiian Airlines In Paradise and other in-flight mags., MonitoRadio, Donnelly Pubs., Sports Illus., Life, Mechanix Illus., Popular Mechanics, Parents (contbg. editor), House Beautiful, Am. Home (awards 1988-89), Travelday, Better Homes and Gardens, Sunset, Archtl. Digest, National Geographic World, Travel & Leisure, Chevron USA/Odyssey (Calif. Pub.'s award 1984), Xerox Edn. Publs., Europe's Linguapress, PSA Mag., Off Duty, Oceans, Sea Frontiers, AAA Westways, AAA Via, Travelin', others; home and garden columnist, editor, 5-part series Pacific Coast Ports, 5-part series Railroads of the West, series Immigration, Youth Gangs, Endangered Species, Calif. Lighthouse Chain, Lighthouses of the World, Pacific Coast Wetlands, Elkhorn Slough Nat. Estuarine Res., Ebey's Landing Nat. Hist. Island Res., Calif. Water Wars, BLM's Adopt a Horse Program, Mt. St. Helen's Eruption, Oreg's Covered Bridges, Loma Prieta Earthquake, Oakland Firestorm, Missing Children, Calif. Prison Reform, Columbia-Alaska's Receding Glacier, Calif. Underwater Parks, and many others; author: Wonderful U.S.A.: A State-by-State Guide to Its Natural Resources, 1989; co-author: McGraw-Hill English for Social Living, 1944, Fawcett Boating Books, 1956-66, Fodor's San Francisco, Fodor's California, 1982-89, Bell and Howell/Charles Merrill Focus on Life Science, Focus on Physical Science, Focus on Earth Science, 1983, 2d edit. 1987, State of California's Golden State Travel Guide, 1998; contbr. Earth Science 1987; 8 works selected for use by Europe's Woltors-Nordoff-Longman English Language Texts, U.K., Netherlands, 1988; author: (with others) anthology West Winds, 1989; reviewer Charles Merrill texts, 1983-84; book reviewer Profl. Communicator, 1987—; selected writings in permanent collections Oakland Pub. Libr., U. Wash. Main Libr.; environ. works included in Dept. Edn. State of Md. textbook; contbr., author Journalism Quar.; author script PBS/AAA America series, 1992; contbg. editor: Parents, Fashion Showcase, Spokane Mag. Nat. chmn. travel writing contest Assn. for Edn. in Journalism and Mass Comm. Soc. Am. Travel Writers, 1979-83; judge writing contest for Nat. Assn. Real Estate Editors, 1982—; cons. S.C. Dept. Parks, Recreation and Tourism, 1999—; invited Nat. Park Svc. Nat. Conf. Sci. Writers, 1985, Postmaster Gen.'s 1992 Stamps, 1991, Internat. Geophys. Union Conf., 1982—, The Conf. Bd., 1995—, Corp. Comm. Conf., Calif. Inst. Tech. Media and Sci. Seminar, 1995—, Med. Writers Delegation to Russia and Estonia, 1997, N.Y. Times Opinion Rsch. Co. Corp. Image Conf., 1999, EPA and Dept. Energy Tech. Conf., 1992, Am. Soc. Photogrammetry and Remote Sensing Internat. Conv. Mapping Global Change, 1992, U.S. Conf. on Oceans, 1998, N.Y. Mus. Modern Art Matisse Retrospective Press Rev. and all media previews, 1992—, celebration 150th anniversary Oreg. Trail, 1993, Nat. Coun. Advancement Sci. Writing, 1977-2003, Sigma Xi Nat. Conf., 1988-2003, Nat. Sci. Writers Confs., 1977-2003, PRSA Travel and Tourism Conf., 1993—, Internat. Conf. Environment, 1994, 95, Quality Life Europe, Prague, 1994, Calif. Sesquicentennial, 1996, 14th Ann. Sci. Writers Conf., 1996, Picasso Retrospective, 1996, others; mem. Gov.'s Conf. Tourism N.C., 1993-2002, Calif., 1976—, Fla., 1987—, N.C. Govs. conf. on tourism and film, 2000-, U.C. Irvine Calif. Computer Sci. Symposium, 2000, Sea Grant's conf. on sci. in the news, 2000, N.Y. conf. bd. conf. on environ. journalism, 2000, on economics, 2001; press guest 14 U.S. states and 12 fgn. countries' Depts. Tourism, 1986—; chmn. New Com. for Sci./Journalism Curricula U. Wash., 2006-. Named to Broadway Hall of Fame, U. Wash., 1984; recipient Broadway Disting. Alumnus award, 1995; citations for environ. writing Nat. Park Svc., U.S. Forest Svc., Bur. Land Mgmt., Oakland Mus. Assn., Oakland C. of C., Chevron USA, USN plaque and citation, Best Mag. articles citation Calif. Pubs. Assn., 1984, U.S. Treasury award, 1946; co-recipient award for best Sunday newspaper mag. Nat. Headliners, citation for archtl. features Oakland Mus., 1983; honoree for achievements in journalism Nat. Mortar Bd., 1988, 89; named one of 10 V.I.P. press 1989; one of Calif.'s top 40 Contemporary Authors, 1989; nat. honoree Social Issues Resources Series, 1987; recipient, Gov.'s Calif. Women of Achievement award, 1988-90. Mem.: AAAS, Calif. Acad. Scis., Am. Bd. Forensic Examiners, Pub. Rels. Soc. Am. (charter mem. travel, tourism, environment and edn. divsns.), Nat. Sch. Pub. Rels. Assn., Environ. Cons. N.Am., Am. Assn. Edn. in Journalism and Comm. (exec. bd. nat. mag. divsn. 1978, panel chmn. 1979—80, author Journalism Quart. jour.), Women in Comm. (nat. bd. officer 1975—77, book reviewer Prof. Communicator), Soc. Profl. Journalists (nat. bd. for hist. sites 1980—), Nat. Press Photographers Assn. (Bay area internet project 1989—, hon. life, honoree 1995), Investigative Reporters and Editors (charter), Nat. Assn. Sci. Writers, Bay Area Advt. and Mktg. Assn., Internat. Assn. Bus. Communicators, Am. Assn. Med. Writers, Soc. Am. Travel Writers, Am. Film Inst., Soc. Environ. Journalists (charter), Calif. Acad. Environ. News Writers, Am. Mgmt. Assn., Nat. Soc. Environ. Journalists (charter), Calif. Environ. Leadership Roundtable, Am. Heritage Found. (citation 1986—88), Fine Arts Mus., San Francisco, Calif. State Parks Found., Purple and Gold Soc., Mortar Board Alumnae Assn. (life honoree 1988—89), Stanford Alumni (life), U. Calif., Berkeley Alumni (life; v.p., scholarship chmn. 1975—81), U. Wash. Com. (life; charter mem. ocean scis. alumni, dept. adv. sci. journalism, disting. alumni 1987), Nat. Parks and Conservation Assn., Calif. Environ. Leadership Roundtable (trustee), Nat. Wildlife Fedn., Oceanic Soc., Nature Conservancy, Smithsonian Audubon Soc., Internat. Oceanog. Found., Calif. Writers Club (state bd., Berkeley bd. 1989—, honoree ann. conv. Asilomar, Calif. 1990), Nat. Press Club, San Francisco Press Club, Seattle Advt. and Sales Club (former officer), Seattle Jr. Advt. Club (charter), Phi Beta Kappa (statewide chmn. scholarship awards 1975—81, v.p., bd. dirs. Calif. Alumni Assn.), Pi Lambda Theta (charter 1995—, planning com.), Theta Sigma Phi. Home and Office: Piedmont Pines 6161 Castle Dr Oakland CA 94611-2737 Office Phone: 510-531-0977.

WOOD, LINDA MAY, librarian; b. Ft. Dodge, Iowa, Nov. 6, 1942; d. John Albert and Beth Ida (Riggs) Wiley; m. C. James Wood, Sept. 15, 1964 (div. Oct. 1984). BA, Portland State U., 1964; M in Librarianship, U. Wash., 1965. Reference libr. Multnomah County Libr., Portland, Oreg., 1965-67, br. libr., 1967-72, adminstrv. asst. to libr., 1972-73, asst. libr., asst. dir., 1973-77; asst. city libr. L.A. Pub. Libr., 1977-80; libr. dir. Riverside (Calif.) City and County Pub. Libr., 1980-91; county libr. Alameda County Libr., Fremont, Calif., 1991—. Adminstrv. coun. mem. Bay Area Libr. and Info. Svcs., Oakland, Calif., 1991—. Chair combined charities campaign County of Alameda, Oakland, Calif., 1992; bd. dirs. Inland AIDS project, Riverside, 1990-91; vol. United Way of Inland Valleys, Riverside, 1986-87, Bicentennial Competition on the Constitution, 36th Congl. Dist., Colton, Calif., 1988-90. Mem. ALA (CLA chpt. councilor 1992-95), Calif. Libr. Assn. (pres. 1985, exec. com., ALA chpt. councilor 1992-95), Calif. County Librs. Assn. (pres. 1984), League of Calif. Cities (cmty. svcs. policy com. 1985-90), OCLC Users Coun. (Pacific Network del. 1986-89). Democrat. Avocations: dance, opera, reading. Office: Alameda County Libr 2450 Stevenson Blvd Fremont CA 94538-2326 Office Phone: 510-745-1536. E-mail: lwood@aclibrary.org.

WOOD, LISA GODBEY, prosecutor; b. Lexington, Ky., Jan. 28, 1963; married; 2 children. BA summa cum laude, U. Ga., 1985, JD summa cum laude, 1990. Bar: Ga. 1990. Law clk. to Hon. Anthony A. Alaimo US Dist. Ct. (so. dist.) Ga., 1990; assoc. Gilbert, Harrell, Summerford & Martin, Brunswick, Ga., 1991—2004, ptnr., 1995—2004; US atty. (so. dist.) Ga. US Dept. Justice, Savannah, Ga., 2004—. Adv. com. US Dist. Ct.; disciplinary review panel State Bar Ga.; mem. Ga. Bd. Pub. Safety. Mem.: ABA, Def. Rsch. Inst. Office: US Attys Office So Dist PO Box 8970 Savannah GA 31412*

WOOD, LORRAINE DELL, artist, consultant; b. Vancouver, Can., Mar. 7, 1928; arrived in U.S., 1928; d. David Albert Kramer and Helen Eleanor Spurgeon; m. Allen Kirkham Wood (dec.); 1 stepchild, Allene Kay. Student, U. So. Calif., LA, 1945—46. Painter, color mixer Columbia Screen Gems,

Hollywood, 1944—45; painter, asst. animator Paramount George Pal, Hollywood, 1946; asst. paymaster Hunt Stromberg Productions, Hollywood, 1947—49; paymaster Western Electric Sound, Hollywood, 1947—49; prodn. office coord. Monogram/United Artists, Hollywood, 1949—51; asst. prodr. Guild Films TV, Hollywood, 1954—56; cmty. rels. liaison CBS TV, Hollywood, 1981—82; owner, pres. Dellwood Enterprises Literary Agy., Beverly Hills, 1983—87; exec. dir. Internat. Visitors Council, Orlando, 1992—94; dir. spl. guests Fla. Film Festival, Maitland, 1994—97; pres. Film Cons. Internat., Winter Park, Fla., 1995—2003; artists Park Ave. Fine Arts, Winter Park, Fla., 2004—05, Grand Bohemian Gallery, Orlando, Fla., 2005, Orlando Marriott Downtown Hotel, 2006—, The King's Gallery, The Villagers, 2006—. Author: Add A Pinch of Pizazz, 1979. Mem. Fla. Film Entertainment Adv.Coun., Tallahassee, 2002—06. Recipient Woman of Yr. award, C. of C. (Calif.), 1961. Republican. Episcopalian. Avocation: ballroom dancing.

WOOD, MARGO, academic administrator; b. Boston, Aug. 15, 1939; d. William Barry and Mary Lee Wood; m. Joel Baker Stevens, June 6, 1959 (div. Jan. 1976); children: Joel Matthew, Mary Stacey, Katrina Ellen, Hannah Hutchins. BA, Vassar Coll., 1961; EdM, U. So. Maine, 1981; EdD, Boston U., 1986. Tchr. Boothbay Regional Elem. Sch., Boothbay Harbor, Maine, 1969—78, reading specialist, 1978—79; coord. Basic Skills Project U. So. Maine, Gorham, 1979—82, asst. prof. lit. edn., 1982—90, assoc. prof. lit. edn., 1990—93, prof. lit. edn. Portland/Gorham, 1993—, assoc. provost, dean grad. studies and rsch. Portland, 1999—2002, assoc. provost, dean grad. studies, 2002—. Prin. investigator Project Story Boost U. So. Maine/Portland Schs., Maine, 1993—; mem. early lit. work group Maine Dept. Edn., Augusta, 1998—2002. Author: Becoming a Reader, 1992, 2001, 2004, Teaching Elementary Lang. Arts, 1994, 1999. Adv. Portland Rape Crisis Ctr., 1991—93; bd. mem. Sexual Assault Response Ctr., Portland, 1993—95, Grantee, N.E.R.A., Nellie Mae Edn. Fund, Ctrl. N.Y. Cmty. Found., 1993—. Mem.: Coun. Grad. Schs., New Eng. Reading Assn., Internat. Reading Assn. Avocations: reading, hiking.

WOOD, MARIAN STARR, publishing executive; b. NYC, Mar. 30, 1938; d. Edward James and Betty (Starr) Markow; m. Anthony Stuart Wood, Mar. 21, 1963. BA, Barnard Coll., 1959; postgrad., Columbia U., 1959—64. Tchg. asst., lectr. Columbia U., N.Y.C., 1960-64; editor Praeger Pubs., N.Y.C., 1965-71; sr. editor Henry Holt & Co., N.Y.C., 1972-81, exec. editor, 1981-96, assoc. pub. Marian Wood Books, 1996-99; v.p. Marian Wood Books at G.P. Putnam's Sons, N.Y.C., 1999—. Recipient Roger Klein Found. award for career achievement, 2001. E-mail: marian.wood@us.penguingroup.com.

WOOD, MARY ELIZABETH, retired secondary school educator, church musician; b. Berwyn, Ill., Apr. 15, 1929; d. Ralph Jerome Compton and Dora Mary Langlois; m. Harvey Eugene Wood, Aug. 21, 1954 (dec.); children: Joseph, Ann, Kim, Lynn, Christopher, Curtis, Carol, John, Nicole. BA in English and Edn., Marycrest U., Davenport, Iowa, 1951; MA in English and Edn., Mich. State U., East Lansing, 1958; AA in Music summa cum laude, Lansing C.C., Mich., 1980. Cert. permanent tchr. Mich. Tchr. H.S. Oxford (Iowa) Schs., 1951—52; tchr. jr. and sr. H.S. Gobles (Mich.) Schs., 1952—55; tchr. Cement City H.S., 1957—58, Portland H.S., 1958—60, Dimondale H.S., 1960—62; tchr. H.S. completion adults Holt Pub. Schs., 1965—95. Cantor Immaculate Heart Mary Ch., Lansing, Mich., 1970—84; dir. music Holy Cross Ch., Lansing, 1983—88, St. Peter Cath. Ch., Eaton Rapids, Mich., 1989—91, St. Jude Cath. Ch., DeWitt, Mich., 1992—2002; painter religious iconography. Singer: (albums) Jesus Lives by Fr. Lucien Deiss; composer: (children's operettas) The Country Cousin, 1984, The Touch, 1994, (liturgical music) Dedication Mass of St. Peter, 1992. Mem.: Nat. Assn. Pastoral Musicians (co-chmn. Lansing chpt. 1995—). Roman Catholic. Avocations: sewing, reading, singing, music, writing. Home: 5102 Killarney Dr Holt MI 48842

WOOD, MELISSA ANN, music educator; b. Houston, July 18, 1974; d. John William and Ruth Lizcano Scott; m. Robert Bryan Wood, June 26, 2004. MusB, Sam Houston State U., Huntsville, Tex., 1999; MusM, Sam Houston State U., Huntsville, 2001; postgrad., Tex. State U., San Marcos, 2006—. Assoc. dir. bands Leander H.S., Tex., 2001—. Guest clinician, brass methods classes Sam Houston State U., Huntsville, 2002—; assoc. dir. performances St. Patrick's Cathedral. Musician: Phantom Regiment Drum and Bugle Corps., 1996. Named to Chancellor's list, Tex. State U., 2005—06. Mem.: Tex. Band Masters Assn., Tex. Music Educators Assn., Pi Kappa Lambda (life), Sigma Alpha Iota (life). Office: Leander High School Band 3301 S Bagdad Rd Leander TX 78641 Office Phone: 512-435-8000. Business E-Mail: melissa.wood@leanderisd.org.

WOOD, NANCY ELIZABETH, psychologist, educator; d. Donald Sterret and Orne Louise (Erwin) W. BS, Ohio U., 1943, MA, 1947; PhD, Northwestern U., 1952. Prof. Case We. Res. U., Cleve., 1952—60; specialist, expert HEW, Washington, 1960—62; chief rschr. USPHS, Washington, 1962—64; prof. U. So. Calif., L.A., 1965—. Learning disabilities cons., 1960-70; assoc. dir. Cleve. Hearing and Speech Ctr., 1952-60; dir. licensing program Brit. Nat. Trust, London. Author: Language Disorders, 1964, Language Development, 1970, Verbal Learning, 1975 (monograph) Auditory Disorders, 1978, Levity, 1980, Stoneskipping, 1989, Bird Cage, 1994, Out of Control, 1999. Pres. faculty senate U. So. Calif., 1987—88. Recipient Outstanding Faculty award, Trojan Fourth Estate, 1982, Pres.' Svc. award, U. So. Calif., 1992. Fellow APA (cert.), AAAS, Am. Speech and Hearing Assn. (legis. coun. 1965-68); mem. Internat. Assn. Scientists. Republican. Methodist. Office: U So Calif University Park Los Angeles CA 90089-0001 Personal E-mail: woodn@adelphia.net.

WOOD, NICOLA, artist; b. Gt. Crosby, Lancashire, Eng., Oct. 18, 1936; d. John Wood and Eva Wood Heyes; m. Theodore Cartan, Mar. 25, 1965 (dec. 1972); m. Emmet Baxter June 11, 1981 (dec. 1994). Diploma with 1st class honors, Manchester (Eng.) Coll. Art, 1959, Royal Coll. Art, London, 1960; postgrad. degree, Parsons Sch. Design, N.Y.C., 1963. Freelance textile designer, 1959-84; graphic designer N.Y.C., 1960-63; wallpaper designer Rasch Tapeten Fabric, Osnabruck, Germany, 1965-84. Lectr. Farnham (Eng.) Coll. Art. 1975, Ctrl. Coll. Art, London, 1976-78, Claremont (Calif.) Coll., 1992-93, 95. Represented in permanent collections Sherry Frumkin Gallery, Santa Monica, Calif., Bruce Lewin Gallery, N.Y.C., O.K. Harris/David Klein Art Gallery, Detroit; group shows include Jerry Silverman Gallery, L.A., 1987, Pebble Beach Concours d'Elegance, Carmel, Calif., 1987-95, Lancaster (Calif.) Mus., 1988, Butler Inst., Ohio, 1988, Harrahs Mus., Las Vegas, 1989, Krasle Art Ctr., Mich., 1991, The Automobile in Art Gallery, Long Beach, Calif., 1992, Bakersfield (Calif.) Mus. Art, 1994, Peterson Automotive Mus., L.A., 1994, Chalmers Gallery, Tustin, Calif., 1996, Automotive Fine Art Soc., Pebble Beach, Carmel, Calif., 1996. Work auctioned for charity Pebble Beach Concourse d'Elegance. Proctor Meml. Travel scholar, 1959, Fulbright scholar, 1960, Am. Travel scholar Royal Coll. Art, 1960; recipient Excellence award Pebble Beach Concours d'Elegance, 1992, Peter Helk award, 1993, Raymond E. Holland award, 1993. Mem. Automotive Fine Art Soc. Avocations: photography, aerobics, classic automobiles. Studio: 1728 S Bedford St Los Angeles CA 90035-4321

WOOD, PAMELA SHARON, music educator, soprano; b. San Francisco, Mar. 29, 1944; d. Clinton Barford and Pearl (Henderson) Wood; m. Eric Scott Fraley, Dec. 28, 1968 (div. 1981); children: Ayanna Fraley Moore, Amara Fraley; m. Stephen B. Ambush, July 25, 1982 (div. 1996). MusB Edn. summa cum laude, Howard U., 1967; Tchg. and Musicianship Cert., Kodaly Musical Tng. Inst., Inc., 1976; MusM in Vocal Performance, U. Mass., 1980; Advanced Assocs. Cert., Kodaly Ctr. Am., 2000. Music instr. and choral dir. Baccus and Hamilton Jr. High Schs., Wash., DC, 1967—69; music instr. and choral dir., elem. jr. high sch. music specialist pub. schs., Stoneham, Mass., 1969—70; mem. faculty, chmn. dept. music theory and edn. Elma Lewis Sch. of Fine Arts, Nat. Ctr. of Afro-American Artists, Inc., Boston, 1970—76; music tchr. Boston Pub. Schs. and Kodaly Ctr. of Am., 1981—82; voice tchr. Tufts U., Medford, Mass., 1982—87; music instr. Wheelock Coll., Boston, 1983—87, Roxbury CC, Boston, 1986—87; lectr. music MIT Sch. Humanities, Arts and Social Scis., Cambridge, Mass., 1987—96, sr. lectr. music, 1996—. Voice tchr. Pine Manor Coll., Chestnut Hill, Mass., 2002—05, condr., 2004—05, Women's Inn at Pine St., Boston, 1995—2001, Sisters St. Joseph Cmty. Chorus, Brighton, Mass., 1996—2004; faculty Kodály Music Inst., Boston, 1999—; presenter in field, 1971—. Singer (soprano soloist): Steve Reich & Musicians, 1974—88, NY and Israel Philharm., London, Boston, Chgo., San Francisco Symphonies, 1974—96; choral conductor: The Women's Inn at Pine St., 1995—2001, St. Joseph Cmty. Chorus, 1996—2004, Pine Manor Coll., 2004—05. Bd. overseers New Eng. Conservatory of Music, Boston, 1996—2004; assoc. bd. mem. Kodaly Ctr. Am., Wellesley, Mass., 1996—; bd. dirs. Boston Orch. & Chorale, 1991—94, Boston Children's Chorus, 2006—. Recipient Sponsors and Patrons award, Met. Opera Co., 1972, award, Nat. Assn. Tchrs. of Singing, 1981, Black Achiever, Greater Boston YMCA, 1994; honoree, Oberlin Black Musicians' Guild, Oberlin Conservatory of Music, 2003. Mem.: Orgn. Am. Kodaly Educators (nat. conf. team 2004—05), Nat. Assn. Study and Performance of African-Am. Music, Ctr. Black Music Rsch., Boston Area Kodaly Educators, Pi Kappa Lambda. Office: Mass Inst of Tech 77 Massachusetts Ave Cambridge MA 02139 Office Phone: 617-253-8778.

WOOD, PAULA DAVIDSON, lawyer; b. Oklahoma City, Dec. 20, 1952; d. Paul James and Anna Mae (Ferrero) Davidson; children: Michael Paul, John Roland. BS, Okla. State U., 1976; JD, Oklahoma City U., 1982. Bar: Okla. 1983, U.S. Dist. Ct. (we. dist.) Okla. 1983, U.S. Supreme Ct. 1995; cert. pub. mgr. Pvt. practice, Oklahoma City, 1984-85; ptnr. Davidson & Wood, Oklahoma City, 1985-87; child support enforcement counsel Okla. Dept. Human Svcs., Oklahoma City, 1987-92, child support adminstr. (IV-D dir.), 1992-96; pvt. practice Oklahoma City, 1997—2004; counsel Legal Aid Svcs. Okla., Inc., Oklahoma City, 2004—. Adj. instr. Tech. Inst. Okla. State U., Oklahoma City, 1985. Articles editor Oklahoma City U. Law Rev., 1982. Bd. dirs. Okla. Youth Symphony, 2000-01. Mem. Okla. Bar Assn. (sec. family law sect. 1987, Golden Gavel award 1987, Artist of the Yr. 1999), Nat. Child Support Enforcement Assn. (bd. dirs. 1995, sec. 1997), Okla. Child Support Enforcement Assn. (pres. 1992), S.W. Regional Child Assn. (pres. 1996), Western Interstate Child Support Enforcement Coun. (sec. 1995). Republican. Roman Catholic. Office: Legal Aid Svcs Okla Inc 2901 Classen Blvd Ste 112 Oklahoma City OK 73106 Office Phone: 405-488-6775. Business E-Mail: paula.wood@laok.org.

WOOD, PEGGY, secondary school educator; b. Oak Park, Ill., Sept. 1, 1940; d. Alvin R. and Clara A. (Wright) Volk; 1 child, Deirdre. MusB in Edn., So. Meth. U., Dallas, Tex., 1962, MusB in Piano Performance, 1963; MusM in Edn., U. North Tex., Denton, 1975. Cert. K-12 music tchr., secondary English tchr., Tex. Choral dir. DeWitt Perry Jr. H.S., Carrollton, Tex., 1974—77; mktg. sec. Storage Tech. Corp., Louisville, Colo., 1981—84; music dir. Woodhaven Presbyn., Irving, Tex., 1986—94; choral dir. Travis Jr. H.S., Irving, Tex., 1985—87, Hillcrest H.S., Dallas, 1987—94; tchr. music D.D. Rogers Elem. Sch., Dallas, 1995—97; head dept. English, The Alexander Sch., Richardson, Tex., 1997—. Dir. music Woodhaven Presbyn. Ch., Irving. Pres. Mu Phi Epsilon, Dallas, 1970—72; precinct chmn. Rep. Party, Boulder, Colo., 1980. Mem. Tex. Music Educators Assn., MENC, ACDA, TCDA, ATPE, NCTE. Republican. Episcopalian. Avocations: reading classics, gourmet cooking, church activities. Home: 10668 Pagewood Dr Dallas TX 75230 Office: The Alexander Sch 409 International Pky Richardson TX 75081 Office Phone: 972-690-9210. Fax: 214-361-8781. E-mail: peggytree@aol.com.

WOOD, PHOEBE A., food products executive; Grad., Smith Coll.; MBA, UCLA. With Atlantic Richfield Co.; v.p. CFO Propel, Inc. divsn. Motorola, Inc.; exec. v.p., CFO Brown-Forman Corp., Louisville, 2002—. Office: Brown-Forman Corp 850 Dixie Hwy Louisville KY 40210

WOOD, RHONDA GAILETTE, secondary school educator; b. Amity, Ark., Jan. 14, 1957; d. Huey Edmond and Edrese Christell (Francis) Cogburn; m. Alan Clift Wood, Mar. 1, 2006; children: Dustin Dale Brymer, Billy, Carl; 1 child, Amber Lemser. BEd, Henderson State U., Arkadelphia, Ark., 1988. Tchr. Murfreesboro HS, Ark., 1989—. Avocations: fishing, camping, hunting. Office: Murfreesboro High Sch Art Dept PO Box 339 Murfreesboro AR 71958

WOOD, RUTH LUNDGREN WILLIAMSON **See LUNDGREN, RUTH WILLIAMSON WOOD**

WOOD, STEPHANIE, mathematics educator; b. Midland, Tex., July 30, 1976; d. Rodney and Jan Faulk; m. Chris Wood, June 20, 1998; 1 child, McKenzie. BS in Multidisciplinary Studies in Elem. Edn., Tex. Tech U., Lubbock, 1998. Cert. Tex., 1998. 4th grade tchr. Ector County Ind. Sch. Dist., Odessa, Tex., 1998—2000, 6th grade math tchr., 2000—02; 7th grade advanced math tchr. Midland (Tex.) Ind. Sch. Dist., 2003—, 7th grade girls coach, 2003—04, 8th grade girls coach, 2004—05; 6th grade math and sci. tchr. Santa Rita Elem., Midland, 2006—. Counselor h.s. team Kelview Heights Bapt. Ch., Midland, 2005. Recipient Lighthouse award, San Jacinto Jr. H.S., 2005. Mem.: Tex. Classroom Tchs. Assn. Baptist. Avocations: sports, travel. Office: Santa Rita Elem 5306 Whitman St Midland TX 79705 Office Phone: 432-689-1350. Personal E-mail: stephttu@hotmail.com. E-mail: swood@esc18.net.

WOOD, VIVIAN POATES, mezzo soprano, educator; b. Washington, Aug. 19, 1923; d. Harold Poates and Mildred Georgette (Patterson) W. Studies with Walter Anderson, Antioch Coll., 1953-55; studies with Denise Restout, Saint-Leu-A-Forêt, France and Lakeville, Conn., 1960—62, studies with Denise Restout, 1964—70; studies with Paul A. Pisk, 1968—71; studies with Paul Ulanowsky, NYC, 1958—68; Elemer Nagy, 1965-68, Vyautas Marijosius, 1967-68; MusB, Hartt Coll. Music, 1968; postgrad. (fellow), Yale U., 1968; MusM (fellow), Washington U., St. Louis, 1971, PhD (fellow), 1973. Debut in recital series Internat. Jeunesse Musicals Arts Festival, 1953; solo fellowship Boston Symphony Orch., Berkshire Music Ctr., Tanglewood, 1964, St. Louis Symphony Orch., 1969, Washington Orch., 1949, Bach Cantata Series Berkshire Chamber Orch., 1964, Yale Symphony Orch., 1968. Appearances in U.S. and European recitals, oratorios, operas, radio and TV, 1953-68; soloist Landowska Ctr., Lakeville, 1969, Internat. Harpsichord Festival, Westminister Choir Coll., Princeton, N.J., 1973; prof. voice, head voice area Sch. of Music, U. So. Miss., Hattiesburg, 1971-2000, ret. 2000, prof. emerita, 2000—; asst. dean Coll. Fine Arts, 1974-76, acting dean, 1976-77; guest prof. Hochschüle für Musik, Munich, 1978-79; prof. Italian Internat. Studies Program, Rome, 1986; Miss. coord. Alliance for Arts Edn., Kennedy Ctr. Performing Arts, 1974—; mem. Miss. Gov.'s Adv. Panel for Gifted and Talented Children, 1974—, 1st Miss. Gov.'s Conf. on the Arts, 1974—. Author: Polenc's Songs: An Analysis of Style, 1971. Recipient Young Am. Artists Concert award N.Y.C., 1955; Wanda Landowska fellow 1961-68. Mem. Miss. Music Tchrs. Assn., Nat. Assn. Tchrs. of Singing, Music Tchrs. Nat. Assn., Am. Musicology Soc., Golden Key, Mu Phi Epsilon, Delta Kappa Gamma, Tau Beta Kappa (hon.), Pi Kappa Lambda. Democrat. Episcopalian.

WOODALL, ELAINE, psychotherapist; b. Wilmington, Del., Aug. 12, 1947; d. H. R. and Allison Darst Woodall. BA, U. Del., Newark, 1971; MA, Pa. State U., University Park, 1977; MS, New Sem., NYC, 1994, MD, 1995; PhD, Columbia State U., New Orleans, 1998. Ordained Minister The New Sem., NY, NY, 1994. Instr. art history U. South Ala., Mobile, 1977—78; psychotherapist, psychol. intuitive pvt. practice, NYC, 1983—2005, ind. curator, 1985—88, med. intuitive, 2000—. Author: Archibald J. Motley and the Art Institute of Chicago, (exhibition catalog) Revelations: Spiritual Art at the End of the Second Millennium, Visions of America: 1787-1987; contbr. exhibition catalog; editor: Minority Voices: An Interdisciplinary Journal of Literature and the Arts Jour.; translator: Tao Te Ching Jour. Fellow, CUNY, 1983—84; Helena Rubinstein fellow, Whitney Mus. Am. Art, 1985—86. Mem.: Inst. Noetic Scis., Internat. Soc. Study Subtle Energy and Energy Medicine. Avocations: travel, swimming, reading. Office: Dr Elaine Woodall 19 W 34 Street Penthouse New York NY 10001 Office Phone: 212-781-3600. E-mail: psi3600@msn.com.

WOODALL, RUTH ANN, educational consultant; b. Dyersburg, Tenn., Jan. 3, 1953; d. Billy Eugene Page and Sue Scobey Clark; m. Charles Warner Woodall Sr., Nov. 14, 1998. BS in Chemistry, Union U., 1977; MEd in Curriculum, U. Memphis, 1984. Tchr. Halls High Sch., Tenn., 1977—78, Dyer County Sch., Newbern, 1978—79; real estate sales Century 21, 1979—81; tchr. Germantown High Sch., Germantown, 1981—94, Collierville High Sch., 1994—97, Nashville Sch. Arts, 1998—2001; dir. Tenn. Scholars, Tenn. C. of C. and Industry, Nashville, 2002—. Named Tenn. Sci. Tchr. of Yr., Tenn. Acad. Sci., 1991, Disting. Tchr., Tenn. Edn. Assn., 1991; recipient Presdl. award in Math. and Sci., 1994, 2000. Mem.: United Tchg. Assn., Tenn. Sci. Tchrs. Assn. (past pres.), Am. Chem. Soc. (mem. cmty. activities com. 1994—, mem. pub. rels. com. 1998—, Nashville chair 2001, 2004, past chair). Office: Tenn C of C & Industry 611 Commerce St Ste 3030 Nashville TN 37203 Office Phone: 615-256-5141. E-mail: ruth.woodall@tnchamber.org.

WOODARD, ALFRE, actress; b. Tulsa, Nov. 8, 1953; m. Roderick Spencer, 1983; 2 children. Student, Boston U. Appeared in (films) Remember My Name, 1976, Health, Cross Creek, 1983 (Acad. award nomination), Extremities, 1986, Scrooged, 1988, Mandela, 1988, Miss Firecracker, 1989, Grand Canyon, 1991, The Gun in Betty Lou's Handbag, 1992, Passion Fish, 1992, Heart and Souls, 1993, Rich in Love, 1993, Bopha!, 1993, Blue Chips, 1994, Crooklyn, 1994, How to Make an American Quilt, 1995, Statistically Speaking, 1995, Primal Fear, 1996, A Step Toward Tomorrow, 1996, Stat Trek: First Contact, 1996, Follow Me Home, 1996, Down in the Delta, 1998, Brown Sugar, 1998, Mumford, 1999, What's Cooking, 2000, Love and Basketball, 2000, K-PAX, 2001, Baby of the Family, 2002, (voice) The Wild Thornberrys Movie, 2002, The Singing Detective, 2003, The Core, 2003, Radio, 2003, The Forgotten, 2004, Beauty Shop, 2005, Something New, 2006, (TV series) Tucker's Witch, 1982-83, Sara, 1985, St. Elsewhere, 1985-87, Hill Street Blues (Emmy award for guest appearance in drama series 1984), L.A. Law (Emmy award for guest appearance in drama series 1987), Desperate Housewives (Screen Actors Guild Award for outstanding performance by an ensemble in a comedy series, 2006), 2005-; (TV spls.) For Colored Girls Who Have Considered Suicide/When the Rainbow is Enuf, Trial of the Moke, Words by Heart, (TV films) A Mother's Courage: The Mary Thomas Story, Child Saver, Ambush Murder, Freedom Road, 1979, Sophisticated Gents, 1981, The Killing Floor, Unnatural Causes, 1986, Mandela, 1987, The Child Saver, Sweet Revenge, 1990, Blue Bayou, 1990, Race to Freedom: The Underground Railroad, 1994, Wizard of Oz in Concert, 1995, The Piano Lesson, 1995, Journey to Mars, 1996, Gulliver's Travels, 1996, Member of the Wedding, 1997, Miss Evers' Boys, 1997, Cadillac Desert (miniseries), 1997, Funny Valentines, 1999 (also exec. prodr.), Holiday Heart, 2000, A Wrinkle in Time (miniseries), 2003, The Water is Wide, 2005, others, (plays) For Colored Girls Who Have Considered Suicide, When the Rainbow is Enuf, (off-Broadway plays) A Map of the World, 1985, A Winter's Tale 1989, So Nice They Named Twice, Horatio, What's Cookin', 2000, Love and Basketball, 2000, Dinosaur, 2000. Recipient Emmy awards for guest appearance in drama series, Josephine Premice award for sustained excellence Classical Theatre of Harlem, 2006. Office: Touchstone TV 100 Universal Plz Bldg 2128 Ste G Universal City CA 91608*

WOODARD, ANITRA DENISE, elementary school educator; b. Hartford, Conn., Nov. 14, 1975; d. Herman and Annie Woodard. BS, Del. State U., 1999; MS, Ctrl. Conn. State U., 2004. Cert. elem. tchr., remedial reading specialist 2007, reading cons. Ctrl. Conn. State U. Elem. tchr. Hartford Pub. Schs., 1999—. Social studes lead tchr. Hartford Pub. Schs., 2000—. Recipient Milken Educator award, Michael Milken Found., 2004. Avocations: reading, walking, vacationing, basketball.

WOODARD, CAROL JANE, educational consultant; b. Buffalo, Jan. 19, 1929; d. Harold August and Violet Maybelle (Landsittel) Young; m. Ralph Arthur Woodard, Aug. 19, 1950; children: Camaron Jane, Carsen Jane, Cooper Ralph. BA, Hartwick Coll., 1950; MA, Syracuse U., 1952; PhD, SUNY, Buffalo, 1972; LHD (hon.), Hartwick Coll., 1991; postgrad., Bank St. Coll., Harvard U. Cert. tchr., NY State. Tchr., Orchard Park, NY, 1950-51, Danville, Ind., 1951-52, Akron, NY, 1952-54; dir. Garden Nursery Sch., Williamsville, NY, 1955-65; tchr. Amherst Coop. Nursery Sch., NY, 1967-69; asst. prof. early childhood edn. SUNY, Buffalo, 1969-72, lab. demonstration tchr. and student teaching supr., 1969-76, assoc. prof., 1972-79, prof., 1979-88, prof. emeritus, 1988—; dir. Consultants in Early Childhood, 1988—. Cons. Lutheran Ch. Am., Villa Maria Coll., Buffalo Pub. Sch., Buffalo Mus. Sci., Headstart Tng. Programs, Erie Cmty. Coll., NY State Dept. Edn., numerous workshops.; cons. sch. systems, indsl. firms, pub., civic orgns. in child devel.; vis. prof. The Netherlands and East China Univ., Shanghai, People's Republic of China; sci. trainer The Wright Group, 1995. Author 7 books for young children, 2 textbooks in field; co-author: Physical Science in Early Childhood, 1987; co-author nat. curriculum for ch. sch. for 3-yr.-olds; author: (booklet) You Can Help Your Baby Learn; author/coord. TAKE CARE child protection project, 1987; contbr. chpt. to books, articles to profl. jour. Trustee Hartwick Coll., Oneonta, NY, 1978-87, trustee emeritus, 2004-; cons. EPIC Birth to Three Program, 1992; design cons. indoor playground Noah's Ark Jewish Ctr., Buffalo, 1992; Sites Project coord., cons. Let's Talk project Buffalo Pub. Sch., 1994—2005; student tchg. supr. SUNY, Fredonia, 1994-2004. Mem. Nat. Assn. Edn. Young Children, Early Childhood Edn. Council Western NY, Assn. Childhood Edn. Internat., Phi Delta Kappa, Pi Lambda Theta. Home: 85 Ruskin Road East Aurora NY 14052-3028

WOODARD, CATHERINE, arts patron; m. Nelson Blitz Jr.; children: Perri Blitz, Allison Blitz. BA in History magna cum laude, Wake Forest Univ., 1981; MS in Journalism, Columbia Univ., 1982. Reporter Fort Worth Star-Telegram, Tex., 1982—84, NY Newsday, 1984—94; dep. editor Newsday Direct, 1994—95; news editor, iGuide News Corp., NYC, 1995—96. Named one of Top 200 Collectors, ARTnews Mag., 2004; recipient James Wright Brown Pub. Svc. award, Deadline Club, NY Newspaper Pub. award, Soc. of Silurians award. Mem.: Mus. Modern Art Print Associates, Artists Space (bd. dir., coord. new media), Phi Beta Kappa. Avocation: Collecting Viennese furniture, prints and works on paper, especially Much, Picasso, Kirchner and Johns.

WOODARD, NINA ELIZABETH, banker; b. L.A., Apr. 3, 1947; d. Alexander Rhodes and Harriette Jane (Powers) Matthews; divorced; children: Regina M., James. D. Grad., Pacific Coast Banking Sch., 1987; BS in Mgmt., Calif. Coast U., 1993; postgrad., Ctr. for Creative Leadership, 1994. Lifetime cert. sr. profl. in human resources. Dental asst. Donald R. Shire DDS, L.A., 1965-66; with Security Pacific Nat. Bank, Marina Del Rey, Calif., 1968-69, First Interstate Bank, Casper, Wyo., 1971—, adminstr. asst. pers., 1975-78, asst. v.p., asst. mgr. pers., 1978-82, v.p., dir. mktg. and pers., 1982-84, v.p., mgr. human resources, 1984-88; v.p., mgr. employee rels. First Interstate Bank Ltd., L.A., 1988-93; v.p., mgr. employee rels. Ams. region Standard Chartered Bank, 1993-95, sr. v.p. human resources, 1995-99, sr. v.p. advisor cultural integration and employee comm. Thailand, 1999-2000, sr. v.p. mgmt. cultural integration Dubai, UAE, 2000—. Instr. mktg. Am. Inst. Banking, 1983, Casper Coll., 1982; mng. dir. Aradhana Human Resources Consulting Pvt. Ltd., India, 2002-2003; dir. Western Region Performance Consulting Internat. India, 2003. Mem. Civil Svc. Commn., City of Casper, 1983-88; bd. dirs. YMCA, 1984-87, Downtown Devel. Assn.; pres. Downtown Casper Assn.; instr. St. Patrick's Parish Religious Edn., 1991-92, mem. parish coun., 1993-94; advisor to the parish coun. Parish of the Resurrection, Jersey City, 1999. Named Bus. Woman of Yr., Bus. and Profl. Women, 198, Young Career Woman, 1975. Mem. Nat. Assn. Bank Women, Bus. and Profl. Women (dist. dir.), Am. Soc. Pers. Adminstrn. (regional v.p., state coun. Wyo. 1987-88), Pers. and Indsl. Rels. Assn. (chmn. govt. affairs com. 1989-90, Fast Track award 1991, Pres.'s Achievement award 1993, conf. chmn. 1991, 92, dist. chair 1993, 2d v.p. 1994), Fin. Women Internat. (Wyo. state chair 1986, regional edn. and tng. chair 1987, dist. coord. L.A. 1993, L.A. group chair 1994, nat. bd. dirs.), Soc. Human Resource Mgmt. (area I v.p. 1996-99, N.Y. chpt., NEHRA chpt.), Am. Alumni Assn. India, Bombay Mgmt. Assn., Bombay Midtown Rotary Club. Republican. Roman Catholic.

WOODARD, SHARON M., secondary school educator; d. Thomas L. and Reva Faye Marler; children: Jason T., Amanda J. BA, Northeastern State U., Tahlequah, Okla., 1996. Cert. tchr. Okla. English, lang. arts tchr. Nowata (Okla.) HS, Okla., 1996—. Mem.: NEA. Avocations: yoga, aerobics, reading, walking. Office Phone: 918-273-2221.

WOODBURN, CYNTHIA J., mathematics professor; BS in Edn. summa cum laude, Pittsburg State U., Kans., 1986, MS, 1987; PhD, N.Mex. State U., 1994. Tchg. assoc. Cornell U., Ithaca, NY, 1993—94; asst. prof. Pittsburg State U., 1994—99, assoc. prof., 1999—2005, prof., 2006—. Mem. secondary math. adv. bd. Pittsburg State U., 1996—2006; invited plenary address 4th Internat. Conf. on Digital Signal Processing, Moscow, 2002. Recipient Outstanding Alumni award, Pittsburg State U., 2002, Excellence in Tchg. award, 2003, Collaboration in Basic Sci. and Engring. grant, Nat. Rsch. Coun., 2001. Mem.: Am. Math. Soc., Math. Assn. Am. (Web master Kans. sect. 1997—2006, Meritorious Svc. award 2002), Kappa Mu Epsilon (regional dir. 2001—06). Avocation: handbell soloist. Office: Pittsburg State U Math Dept 1701 S Broadway Pittsburg KS 66762 Office Phone: 620-235-4409. Business E-Mail: cwoodbur@pittstate.edu.

WOODBURY, MARDA LIGGETT, librarian, writer; b. NYC, Sept. 20, 1925; d. Walter W. and Edith F. (Fleischer) Liggett; m. Philip J. Evans, Sept. 1948 (div. 1950); 1 child, Mark W. Evans; m. Mark Lee Woodbury, 1956 (div. 1969); children: Brian, Heather. Student, Bklyn. Coll., 1942-44; BA in Chemistry and Polit. Sci., Bard Coll., 1946; BS in L.S., Columbia U., 1948; postgrad., U. Calif., Berkeley, 1955-56, 60-61, MJ, 1995. Cert. tchr. Libr. various spl., med. and pub. librs., San Francisco, 1946-60, Coll. Pk. High Sch., Mt. Diablo, Calif., 1962-67; elem. sch. libr. Oakland and Berkeley, Calif., 1967-69; libr. dir. Far West Lab. Ednl. Rsch. & Devel., San Francisco, 1969-73; libr., editor Gifted Resource Ctr., San Mateo, Calif., 1973-75; libr. cons. Rsch. Ventures, Berkeley, Calif., 1975—2003; libr. dir. Life Chiropractic Coll., San Lorenzo, Calif., 1980-95. Author: A Guide to Sources of Educational Information, 1976, 2d edit., 1982, Selecting Instructional Materials, 1978, Selecting Materials for Instruction, Vol. I: Issues and Policies, 1979, Vol. II: Media and the Curriculum, 1980, Vol. III: Subject Areas and Implementation, 1980, Childhood Information Resources, 1985 (Outstanding Ref. Work, Assn. Ref. Librs. 1985), Youth Information Resources, 1987, Stopping the Presses: The Murder of Walter W. Liggett, 1998; mem. editorial bd. Ref. Libr., 1980-95. Home: 145 Monte Cresta Ave Apt 402 Oakland CA 94611-4809 Office Phone: 510-653-5876. Personal E-mail: mardawood@peoplepc.com.

WOODCOCK, JANET, federal official; b. Washington, Pa., Aug. 29, 1948; d. John and Frances (Crocker) W.; m. Roger Henry Miller, Nov. 16, 1981; children: Kathleen Miller, Susanne Miller. BS cum laude, Bucknell U., 1970; MD, Northwestern U., Chgo., 1977. Diplomate Am. Bd. Internal Medicine. Intern Hershey Med. Ctr./Pa. State U., 1977-78, resident in internal medicine, 1978-80, chief resident in medicine, 1980-81; fellow in rheumatology U. Calif./VA Med. Ctr., San Francisco, 1982-84; instr. medicine divsn. rheumatology and immunology VA Med. Ctr., San Francisco, 1984-85; med. officer divsn. biol. investigational new drugs Ctr. for Biologics Evaluation and Rsch./FDA, Rockville, Md., 1986-87, group leader divsn. biol. investigational new drugs, 1987-88, dep. dir. divsn. biol. investigational new drugs, 1988, dir. divsn. biol. investigational new drugs, 1988-90; dir. office of therapeutics rsch. and rev. Ctr. for Biologics Evaluation and Rsch., FDA, Rockville, Md., 1992-94, acting dep. dir., 1990-92; dir. Ctr. for Drug Evaluation and Rsch., FDA, Rockville, Md., 1994—2003; dep. commr. ops. FDA, Rockville, Md., 2003—. Instr. medicine, asst. prof. divsn. gen. internal medicine Hershey Med. Ctr./Pa. State U., 1981; analytical chemist rsch. divsn. A.B. Dick Co., Niles, Ill., 1971-73. Nat. Merit scholar Bucknell U., 1966, Pa. State scholar, 1966; Rsch. fellow Am. Rheumatism Assn.; VA Investigator grantee, 1985. Mem. Alpha Omega Alpha, Alpha Lambda Delta. Office: Ctr Drug Evaluation & Rsch US Food & Drug Admin 5600 Fishers Lane Rockville MD 20857

WOODFORD, ANN MARGUERITE, social services administrator, social worker; b. Bklyn., Mar. 12, 1954; d. Nicholas Gonzaga and Lilly Marguerite (Nielson) W. BS cum laude, CUNY, Bklyn., 1976; MA, Fordham U., 1979, MSW, 1990. Cert. secondary edn. educator. Youth dir. tchr. Cath. Diocese Bklyn., 1976-88; therapist, social worker Angel Guardian Home, Bklyn., 1988-90; program coord. Talbot Perkins Childrens Svcs., N.Y.C., 1990-92; supr. Angel Guardian Home Intensive Med. Mgmt. Program, Bklyn., 1992-96; program coord., supr. Cardinal McCloskey Svcs., Therapeutic Foster Boarding Home, Bronx, N.Y., 1996-97; exec. dir. Amethyst House, S.I., N.Y., 1997—. Resident vol. staff Providence House, Bklyn., 1981-96, Women Helping Women, Flushing, N.Y., 1984-85; cons. Providence House, Bklyn., 1981-97, Angel Guardian Home, Bklyn., 1996—. Mem. Sisters of Charity, Halifax, 1977—; bd. dirs. Advs. for Svcs. for the Blind Multihandicapped, 1994—, S.I. Com. on Alcoholism and Substance Abuse, 1997, co-chair, 1999—; leader Girl Scouts Am., 1994—. Named Outstanding Leader, Girl Scouts Am., Greater N.Y. Coun., 1996. Mem. NASW. Democrat. Roman Catholic. Avocations: gardening, cooking, camping, arts and crafts, singing. Office: Amethyst House Inc 75 Vanderbilt Ave Staten Island NY 10304-2604 Office Phone: 718-448-9588. Personal E-mail: cacacsw@aol.com.

WOODFORD, DEBRA JANE, elementary school educator; b. Scottdale, Nov. 25, 1954; d. Robert Thomas and Viola Korns Reese; m. Melvin J. Woodford, Apr. 9, 1977; children: Melvin J., Johnathan W. BA in Music Edn., Thiel Coll., Greenville, Pa., 1976. Tchr. elem. vocal music Southington Local Schs., Ohio, 1976—77, Niles City Schs., 1977—81, Cherry Creek Sch. Dist., Aurora, Colo., 1988—90, McDonald Local Schs., Ohio, 1991—2006. Dir.: (musicals) McDonald Local Schs., 1992—2006; composer, performer: CD Relay the Message, 2003. Participant Am. Cancer Soc. & Forum Health, Warren, Ohio, 2004—05. Mem.: NEA, McDonald Edn. Assn., Ohio Edn. Assn. Republican. Methodist. Home: 5172 Nelson Mosier Rd Southington OH 44470 Office: McDonald Local Schs 600 Iowa Ave Mc Donald OH 44437

WOODHAM, PATRICIA H., accounting and business consultant; b. Dothan, Ala., June 7, 1950; d. Ralph and Willie Frances (Hodges) Harrison; m. Jerry Frank Parmer, July 12, 1968 (dec. June 1995); children: Latricia Lynne, Jerry Wayne; m. James Edward Woodham, June 27, 1998. Student, Broward C.C., Pompano Beach, Fla., 1988-89. Contr. Atlantic Oil Co., Fayette, Ala., 1974-78; personnel dir. Fayco, Fayette, 1978-80; controller SAC Cons., Birmingham, 1980-82, Yarborough Co., High Point, N.C., 1982-84, S.E. Med. Cons., Tucker, Ga., 1984-86, Golnick Advtsg., Ft. Lauderdale, Fla., 1986-87; paraprofl. Ernst & Young, Ft. Lauderdale, 1987-91, Eric Young CPA, Norcross, Ga., 1991-95, Tim Couch CPA, Lawrenceville, Ga., 1995-96; bus. cons. McDaniel & Assoc. P.C., Dothan, Ala., 1996—. Pres. Women's Aux., Fayette, 1976-80; acct. Republican Woemn, Dothan, 1998; mem. Flower PAC, Thomasville, Ga., 1970-95. Mem. Inst. Mgmt. Accts. (dir. 1999—). Republican. Baptist. Avocations: fishing, hiking, football, reading, gardening. Home: RR 2 Box 135 Headland AL 36345-9431

WOODHOUSE, ELIZABETH C., retired government agency administrator; b. Cin., Nov. 10, 1911; d. John Michael Hughes and Katherine Martha Berger; m. Elton Lee Woodhouse, Mar. 25, 1932 (dec. Feb. 8, 1970); children: Allan, Jerry, Carolyn, Margaret. BS, Urbana U., Ohio, 1979; Masters Degree, Cath. Distance U., 2002. Dir. Child Care Ctr., Springfield, Ohio, 1953—82. Mental Health Soc., Springfield, Ohio, 1955—70, USDA Food Svc., Columbus, Ohio, 1977—97. Author: Beginnings, 1987, Johnny Appleseed Poems, 2001. Pres. Child Care Assn., Springfield, 1960—65, Mental Health Assn., Springfield, 1966—70; county chair Ohioana Libr. Assn., Columbus, 1980—; pres. Friends of the Libr. Clark County Pub. Libr., Springfield, Ohio, 2001; pres. Springfield Symphony Orch., 1997—99; pres., sec., treas. Altrusa Internat., 1970, Federated Women's Clubs, 1945—2001. Recipient 3 awards, Clark County and Ohio State Mental Health Assns., Elizabeth Woodhouse award named in her honor, Wittenberg U., Springfield, 1997. Roman Catholic. Avocations: doll collecting, collecting teapots. Home: 508 Latimer Dr Springfield OH 45503 E-mail: equote@aol.com.

WOODHOUSE, GAY VANDERPOEL, former state attorney general, lawyer; b. Torrington, Wyo., Jan. 8, 1950; d. Wayne Gaylord and Sally (Rouse) Vanderpoel; m. Randy Woodhouse, Nov. 26, 1983; children: Dustin, Houston. BA with honors, U. Wyo., 1972, JD, 1977. Bar: Wyo. 1978, U.S. Dist. Ct. Wyo., U.S. Supreme Ct. Dir. student Legal Svcs., Laramie, Wyo., 1976—77; assoc. Donald Jones Law Offices, Torrington, 1977—78; asst. atty. gen. State of Wyo., Cheyenne, 1978—84, sr. asst. atty. gen., 1984—89, spl. U.S. atty., 1987—89, asst. U.S. atty., 1990—95, chief dept. atty. gen., 1995—98, atty. gen., 1998—2000. Chmn. Wyo. Tel. Consumer Panel, Casper, 1982—86; advisor Cheyenne Halfway House, 1984—93; chmn. Wyo. Silent Witness Initiative Zero Domestic Violence by 2010, 1997, Wyo. Domestic Violence Elimination Coun., 1999—2001; mem. State Bar Commn. First Dist., 2002—05; spl. projects cons. N.Am. Securities Adminstrs. Assn., 1987—89; Chmn. bd. Pathfinder, 1987; S.E. Wyo. Mental Health. Mem.: Federalist Soc. for Law and Pub.Policy Studies (v.p., Wyo. chpt. 2003—04), Prevent Child Abuse Wyo. (pres. 2004—05), Laramie County Bar Assn., Cheyenne (Wyo.) C. of C., Cheyenne Rotary (bd. dirs.), Toastmasters, Rotary. Republican. Avocations: inline speed skating, stained glass. Address: 211 W 19th St Fl 3 Cheyenne WY 82001 Office: 123 Capitol Bldg Cheyenne WY 82002-0001 Office Phone: 307-432-9399. Personal E-mail: gaywoodhouselaw@aol.com. Business E-Mail: gay@woodhouselawoffice.com.

WOODHULL, PATRICIA ANN, artist; b. Gary, Ind., Nov. 24, 1924; d. John Joseph and Georgia Mildred (Voorhis) Harding; m. Bradley Allen Woodhull, May 8, 1948; children: Leslie, Marcia, Clarisse. BS in Clothing Design, Purdue U., 1946; life teaching credential, Calif. State U., Fullerton, 1978. Social worker County Dept. Lake County and Bartholomew County, Gary and Columbus, Ind., 1946-50; home demonstrator Pub. Svc. Co. Ind., Columbus, 1950-53; substitute tchr. Fullerton (Calif.) H.S. Dist., 1968-73; children's art and drama tchr. Fullerton Cmty. Svcs., 1973-85; children's pvt. art tchr. Fullerton, 1990-93; art tchr. Montessori Sch., Fullerton, 1990-91; art/drama tchr. creative arts program Fullerton Pub. Schs., 1972-89. Founder, dir. Players Improv Theatre Group, Fullerton, Calif. One woman shows include Fullerton City Libr., 1992, William Carlos Gallery, Fullerton, 1992, 93, Whittier (Calif.) City Hall, 1993, Muckenthaler Ctr., Fullerton, 1993, Brookhurst Ctr., Anaheim, 1993, Whittier Libr. Show, 1994, L.A. Mcpl. Art Gallery, 1996, Orlando Gallery, 1996, Laguna Art Inst., 1996, Whittier Cmty. Theatre, 2004, Whittier City Hall, 2004, Eileen Kremen Gallery, 2004; exhibited in group shows at Whittier Art Gallery, 1991, Hillcrest (Calif.) Art Show (1st award in Graphics), Creative Arts Ctr., Burbank, Calif., 1991, Bridge Gallery City Hall, L.A., 1992, The Art Store, Fullerton, 1992, Women Painters West, 1993, New England Fine Arts Inst., Boston, 1993; represented in pvt. collections; featured artist Night in Fullerton, Apr. 1999; mem. acting group Dames At Tea; flutist Fullerton Coll. Cmty. Band. Recipient Spl. award Orange County Fair, Costa Mesa (Calif.) County Fair, 1985; 3rd pl. award Hillcrest Whittier (Calif.) Show, 1990, 2nd award West Coast Collage Show, Lancaster, Calif., 1989, Evelyn Nunn Miller award Women Painters West, Torrance, Calif., 1994. Recipient 1st Place, Anaheim Art Assn., 2004, Winsor and Newton Painting award. Mem. Nat. League Am. Pen Women (pres. Orange County 1993), Women Painters West, Pan Hellenic Orange County (pres. 1994), Alpha Chi Omega (pres. local chpt. 1993). Republican. Avocations: designing knitwear, reading, music, community theatre. Home: 1519 Harmony Ln Fullerton CA 92831-2015 E-mail: patnbradw@cs.com.

WOODLEE, CHERYL LYNN, music educator; b. Madison, SD, Apr. 19, 1957; d. Robert Alden Gatts and Gloria Faye Williams; m. Walter Edward Woodlee, Sept. 6, 1985; m. Steven Allen Paulson (div.); 1 child, Beau Alan Paulson. BSc, Dakota State U., 1985. Music tchr. Canova (S.D.) Elem.-Mid. Sch., 1980—81; dir. Singing Plainsman, Canova, SD, 1982—85; music tchr. Goshen Cmty. Schools, Ind., 1987—, music dept. chmn., 1990—. Mem.: NEA, Goshen Edn. Assn., Ind. State Teachers Assn., Music Educators Nat. Conf. Avocations: sewing, crafts, gardening, music. Home: 55325 C R 14 Bristol IN 46507 Office: Goshen Cmty Schools Chandler Elem 419 S 8th St Goshen IN 46526

WOODMAN, BETTY, sculptor; b. Norwalk, Conn., 1930; Attended, Alfred U., 1948—50. Exhibitions include Mus. Arts and Design, Boston Mus. Fine Arts, Carnegie-Mellon Inst., Cooper Hewitt Nat. Design Mus., Internat. Ceramic Mus., Faenza, LA County Mus. Art, Met. Mus. Art, Mint Mus. Craft and Design, Musee de Arts Decoratifs, Stejelijk Mus., Victoria and Albert Mus., World Ceramic Ctr., Ichon, Korea, others. Recipient Visionary award, Am. Crafts Mus., 1998; fellow Nat. Endowment for Arts, 1980, 1986, Rockefeller Found., 1995; hon. fellow, Nat. Coun. Educators in Ceramic Arts, 2000. Office: c/o Garth Clark Gallery 24 W 57th St Ste 305 New York NY 10019*

WOODMAN, LUCY RHODES, music educator; b. Tryon, NC, Aug. 16, 1940; d. William Clarence and Ramona Edna (Brock) Rhodes; m. James W. Woodman; children: Claudia Catherine, James Jefferson, Andrew Brock. AA, Mars Hill Coll., 1960; MusB, U. N.C., Greensboro, 1962; MusM, U. Colo., 1965. Cert. permanent profl. piano tchr. Music Tchrs. Nat. Assn. Tchr. piano pvt. practice, Wheatland & Cheyenne, Wyo., 1965—; instr. in pre-piano and adult piano Cheyenne Parks and Recreation Dept., 1999—; organist St. Christopher's Episcopal Ch., Cheyenne, 1994—99. Adj. tchr. piano U. Wyo., Laramie, 1970-74, staff accompanist, 1973-74; instr. Laramie County C.C.; performer/clinician Wyo. Artist Roster, 1992-99; pianist Cheyenne A.M.E. Ch., 1998—; frequent adjudicator for piano students' events; workshop provider for piano tchrs.; authorized provider The Listening Program for enhanced learning. Author: Keys For Me; composer: (piano) Wyoming Postcards, 1988, Prayer for Peace, 1990, Piano-Sonata, 1990, others, 2 operettas and chamber works. Presenter Diversity!, chamber concerts. Recipient Winner of New Music Contest, Wyo. Artcore, 1990, Hon. Mention in music composition, Wyo. Arts Coun. Performing Arts Fellowship Competition, 2001; fellow Wyo. Art Coun., 1990; grantee Individual Artist grantee, Wyo. Art Coun., 1995, Travel grantee, 1997. Mem. Wyo. Music Tchrs. Assn. (pres. Cheyenne chpt. 1970, 89), Nat. Guild Piano Tchrs. (faculty mem.), Am. Soc. Composers, Authors and Pubs., Music Tchrs. Nat. Assn., Cheyenne Music Tchrs. Assn. Avocations: art, gardening, decorating, walking, reading. Home and Office: The Musical Home 1409 E 21 St Cheyenne WY 82001-1405

WOODRING, MARGARET DALEY, architect, urban planner; b. N.Y.C., Mar. 29, 1933; d. Joseph Michael and Mary (Barron) Daley; m. Francis Woodring, Oct. 25, 1954 (div. 1962); m. Robert Bell, Dec. 20, 1971 (dec.); children: Ward, Gabrielle, Phaedra. Student, NYU, 1959-60; BArch, Columbia U., 1966; MArch, Princeton U., 1971. Registered arch., cert. planner. Architect, planner various firms, N.Y.C.; environ. design specialist Rutgers U., New Brunswick, NJ, 1966-68; programming cons. Davis & Brody, N.Y.C., 1968-71; planning cons. William H. Liskamm, San Francisco, 1971-74; mgr. planning Met. Transp. Commn., Oakland, Calif., 1974-81; dir. Internat. Program for Housing and Urban Devel. Ofcls. Ctr. for Environ. Design Rsch. U. Calif., Berkeley, 1981-89; prin. Woodring & Assocs., San Rafael, Calif., 1989—. Adj. lectr. dept. architecture U. Calif., Berkeley, 1974—84; founder New Horizons Savs. Assn., San Rafael, 1977—79; mem. faculty Dominican U., San Rafael, 2003—05; cons. U.S. Agy. Internat. Devel., Washington, 1981—89; mem. jury Nat. Endowments Arts, others. Chair Bicentennial Com., San Rafael, 1976; bd. dirs. Displaced Homemakers Ctr., Oakland, 1981—84; pres. Environ. Design Found., San Francisco, 1984—90. William Kinne Travel fellow, Columbia U., 1965—66, Richard King Mellon fellow, Princeton U., 1968—71. Mem.: AIA (chair urban design com. San Francisco chpt. 1980—81), Internat. Congress Land Policy, World Affairs Coun., Soc. Internat. Devel. (pres. San Francisco chpt. 1980—83), Urban Land Inst., Am. Inst. Cert. Planners. Avocations: hiking, gardening, reading, race walking. Office Phone: 415-454-6837. Personal E-mail: mdwoodring@woodring.com.

WOODROW, JENNIFER COLE, music educator; b. Richmond, Ind., Oct. 25, 1963; d. Bobby J. and Norma J. Cole; m. David Joseph Woodrow, Nov. 2, 2002. MusB in Edn., Murray State U., Ky., 1985. Tchr. choral music Covington (Ind.) Sch. Corp., 1986—98, Southmont Jr. and Sr. H.S., Crawfordsville, Ind., 1998—2002, Danville (Ill.) Dist. 118, 2002—. Dir. music Beef Ho. Dinner Theatre, Covington, 1995—. Mem.: DAR (nat. chmn. music 1999—, dir. All Am. Chorus Ill. chpt. 2003—, dir. Ill. State Chorus 1998—), Phi Delta Kappa, Delta Kappa Gamma, Sigma Alpha Iota. Home: 13 Swisher Danville IL 61832 Office: North Ridge Mid Sch 1619 N Jackson Danville IL 61832

WOODRUFF, DIANE CAREY, college president; b. San Jose, Calif., Dec. 5, 1942; d. Evan Dennis and Dorothy Elizabeth Jelcick; m. D. Thomas Woodruff, July 11, 1998. BA, U. Calif. Berkeley, 1964, EdD, 1979; postgrad. fellow, U. Calif. L.A., 1979. Asst. supt. State Dept. Edn., Sacramento, 1983; dean Sacramento City Coll., 1983-85; dir. comms. and edn. devel. Los Rios Dist., Sacramento, 1985-88; v.p. Napa Valley Coll., Napa, Calif., 1988-92, supt./pres., 1992—. Author: Motivating and Dissatisfying Factors in a Group Profl. Educators, 1979. Recipient Woman of Yr. award, Calif. legis., 1996; leadership award, Napa Valley Peace Table, 1999; named Woman of Distinction in Wine Country, 2000. Mem. Rotary Napa. Office: Napa Valley Coll 2277 Napa Vallejo Hwy Napa CA 94558-6236 E-mail: dwoodruff@campus.nvc.cc.ca.us.

WOODRUFF, JUDY CARLINE, broadcast journalist; b. Tulsa, Nov. 20, 1946; d. William Henry and Anna Lee (Payne) W.; m. Albert R. Hunt, Jr., Apr. 5, 1980; children: Jeffrey Woodruff, Benjamin Woodruff, Lauren Ann Lee. Student, Meredith Coll., 1964-66; BA, Duke U., 1968. News announcer, reporter Sta. WAGA-TV, Atlanta, 1970-75; news corr. NBC News, Atlanta, 1975-76, White House corr. Washington, 1977-83; anchor Frontline, PBS documentary series, 1984—90; corr. MacNeil-Lehrer News Hour, PBS, Washington, 1983-93; anchor, sr. corr. CNN, Washington, 1993—2005, prime anchor, sr. coord.; moderator Vice Presidential Debate, 1988, America Votes, 2003, 2004. Bd. advisors Henry Grady Sch. Journalism, U. Ga., 1979-82, Benton Fellowship in Broadcast Journalism, U. Chgo., 1984-90, Knight Fellowship in Journalism, Stanford U., 1985-99; bd. visitors Wake Forest U., 1982-89; trustee Duke U., 1985-97, emerita; founding bd. dirs. Internat. Women's Media Found.; vis. fellow, Joan Shorenstein Ctr.on the Press, Politics and Pub. Policy, Harvard U., 2005—; vis. prof. media and politics Duke U., 2006. Author: This is Judy Woodruff at the White House, 1982; corr: PBS Special Generation Next, 2006. Active Commn. on Women's Health, The Commonwealth Fund.; bd. trustee Freedom Forum, Urban Inst.; trustee Nat. Mus. Am. History, 2006—. Recipient award Leadership Atlanta, Class of 1974, Atlanta chpt. Women in Comms., 1975, Edward Weintal award for excellence in fgn. policy reporting, 1987, Joan Shorenstein Barone award for series on def. issues, 1987, Helen Bernstein award for excellence in journalism N.Y. Pub. Libr., 1989, Pres.'s 21st Century award Nat. Women's Hall of Fame, 1994, CableAce award for best newscaster, 1995, CableAce Best Anchor Team award, 1996, Allen H. Neuharth award for excellence in journalism, 1995, News and Documentary Emmy award, 1997, Internat. Matrix award, Assn. for Women in Comm., 2003, Leonard Zeidenberg First Amendment award, Radio-Television News Directors Assn. and Found., 2003; named to Ga. Assn. of Broadcasters Hall of Fame, 2003; grantee Pru Charitable Trust, 2006—. Mem. NATAS (Atlanta chpt. Emmy award 1975), White House Corrs. Assn.

WOODRUFF, KATHRYN ELAINE, literature and language professor; b. Ft. Stockton, Tex., Oct. 12, 1940; d. James Arthur and Catherine H. (Stevens) Borron; m. Thomas Charles Woodruff, May 18, 1969; children: Robert Borron, David Borron. BA, Our Lady of the Lake U., San Antonio, 1963; MFA, U. Alaska, 1969; PhD, U. Denver, 1987. Cert. tchr., Tex., Colo. English and journalism tchr. Owensboro (Ky.) Cath. High Sch., 1963-64, Grand Junction (Colo.) Dist. 12, 1964-66; English tchr. Monroe High Sch., Fairbanks, Alaska, 1966-67; teaching asst. U. Alaska, Fairbanks, 1967-69, instr., 1969-70, U. Colo., Boulder, 1979, Denver, 1988-89, Regis Coll., Denver, 1987-89; asst. prof. Econ. Inst., Boulder, 1989—92; prof. English Colo. Christian U., Lakewood, 1993—. Tchr. Upward Bound, Fairbanks, 1968; instr. ethnic and women writers course U. Colo., Denver, 1988-93; mem. Assoc. Writing Programs; soprano Boulder Chorale, Cantabile Singers, St. John's Cathedral Choir, Augustana Chamber Choir; mem. Women's Studies Delegation to South Africa, 1998; active in missionary work in Ecuador, 1998, European Singing Tour with Augustana Arts, 1998, 2000; presenter Cambridge U., Eng., 2005; participant Oxford Summer Writing Programme, 2006; poetry readings various cities. Author: (poetry) Before the Burning, 1994; author numerous poems. Friend Chautauqua Music Festival, Boulder, 1985-2000; dir. 12th Annual Arts Festival, Fairbanks, 1969; mem. Augustana Chamber Chorus, St. John's Cathedral Choir; bd. dirs. Denver Bach Soc. Recipient Poet's Choice award Internat. Soc. Poetry, 1997; named one of Outstanding Young Women Am., 1966; NEH grantee, 1996. Mem. AAUW, MLA, Am. Assn. Univ. Professors, Assoc. Writing Programs, Soc. Internat. Devel. UN Assn., Nat. Women's Hall of Fame, Acad. Am. Poets, Denver Bach Soc. (bd. dirs. 2003-05), Internat. Women's Writing Guild. Democrat. Mem. Christian Ch. Avocations: singing, tennis, skiing, volleyball, travel. Office: Colo Christian U 8787 W Alameda Ave Lakewood CO 80226-1053 Business E-Mail: ewoodruff@ccu.edu.

WOODRUFF, MARY BRENNAN, elementary school educator; d. John L. and Josephine Brennan; m. Paul R. Woodruff; children: Christopher, Jeffery. BS, SUNY, Brockport; MS, SUNY, Buffalo, 1987. Cert. elem. tchr. N.Y., 1968. Third grade tchr. Middleport (N.Y.) Elem., fifth grade tchr., 1979—2003, math specialist K-6, 2003—05, math specialist 5-8, 2005—. Sch. improvement presenter, mem., dist. curriculum guide, facilitator Social Studies curriculum, Royalton-Hartland Cen. Sch., Middleport, NY, 1989—, co-author mentor program for Royalton-Hartland District, Project "Deep" Elem. Econ. faciliator Contributing author Royalton-Hartland Curriculum Guide 1989; designer of spelling program 5th grade. Campaign mgr. Rep. Legislator, Orleans County, 1979-87. Mem.: ASCD, Royalton-Hartford Tchrs. Assn. (v.p., pres. 1998—, chmn. grievance com.), N.Y State United Tchrs. (v.p. exec. coun., Leadership award 1997, 2004), Delta Kappa Gamma, Delta Xi. Avocations: political action, writing, reading. Office Phone: 716-735-3722.

WOODRUFF, SANDRA ANITA, mathematics and science educator; d. William Halstead and Willie Opal Brown; m. Ronald Earl Woodruff, Jan. 24, 1969; 1 child, Shawn Patrick. BS, East Tex. State U., Commerce, 1994; MS, Tex. A&M U., Commerce, 2003. Cert. tchr. Tex. Sci./math tchr. Wolfe City ISD, Wolfe City, Tex., 1994—; adj. prof. Paris Jr. Coll., Commerce, Tex., 1994—96. Mem. tchr. adv. panel Tex. Instruments, Dallas, 2006—. Sponsor Wolfe City Mid. Sch. Student Coun., 2005—. Mem.: Classroom Tchrs. Assn. (sec. 1994—2006), Sci. Tchrs. Assn. Tex., Nat. Sci. Tchrs. Assn., Order Ea. Star (charter mem.). Avocations: reading, scrapbooks, travel, photography. Office: Wolfe City Independent Sch Dist PO Box L Wolfe City TX 75496-0616

WOODRUFF, VALERIE, state agency administrator; m. Frank Woodruff; 1 child, Scott 1 stepchild, Sheri. BEd in Secondary Edn., Alderson Broaddus Coll., W. Va.; MA in guidance and counseling, U. Del.; postgrad. studies in vocat. edn. and curriculum devel., Temple U., 1999—. From tchr. to prin. New Castle County, Del., Cecil County Md.; assoc. sec. for curriculum and instructional improvement Del. Dept. Edn., Dover, Del., 1992—99, acting sec., 1999—2000, sec, 2000—. Office: Del Dept Edn Townsend Bldg #279 401 Federal St Ste 2 Dover DE 19903-1402 Office Phone: 302-739-4601.

WOODRUFF, VIRGINIA, broadcast journalist, writer; b. Morrisville, Pa. d. Edwin Nichols and Louise (Meredith) W.; m. Raymond F. Beagle Jr. (div.); m. Albert Plaut II (div.); 1 child, Elise Meredith. Student, Rutgers U. News corr. Sta. WNEW-TV Metromedia, N.Y.C., 1967; nat., internat. critic-at-large Mut. Broadcasting System, 1968-75; lectr. Leigh Bur., 1969-71; byline columnist N.Y. Daily Mirror, N.Y.C., 1970-71; first Arts critic Teleprompter and Group W Cable TV, 1977-84; host/producer The First Nighter N.Y. Times primetime cable highlight program, 1977-84; pres., chief exec. officer Starpower, Inc., 1984-91; affiliate news corr. ABC Radio Network, N.Y.C., 1984-86; pres. Promarket People Inc., 1991-93; S.W. contbg. corr. Am. in the Morning, First

Light, Mut. Broadcasting System, 1992; S.W. freelance corr. Voice of Am., USIA, 1992—. Perennial critic Off-Off Broadway Short Play Festival, N.Y.C., 1984—; was 1st Woman on 10 O'Clock News, WNEW-TV, 1967. Contbg. feature writer Vis a Vis mag., 1988-91. Mem. celebrity panel Arthritis Telethon, N.Y.C., 1976. Selected episodes of First Nighter program in archives N.Y. Pub. Libr., Billy Rose Theatre Collection, Rodgers and Hammerstein Collection, Performing Arts Rsch.Ctr. Mem. Drama Desk. Clubs: National Arts, Dutch Treat. Presbyterian. Personal E-mail: vwoodruff50@yahoo.com.

WOODRUM, PATRICIA ANN, librarian; b. Hutchinson, Kans., Oct. 11, 1941; d. Donald Jewell and Ruby Pauline (Shuman) Hoffman; m. Clayton Eugene Woodrum, Mar. 31, 1962; 1 child, Clayton Eugene, II. BA, Kans. State Coll., Pittsburg, 1963; MLS, U. Okla., 1966. Br. libr. Tulsa City-County Libr. System, 1964-65, head brs., 1965-66, head reference dept., 1966-67, chief extension, chief pub. svc., 1967-73, asst. dir., 1973-76, exec. dir., 1976-96; owner Paradigm Mgmt. Cons. Svcs., 1997—. Active Leadership Tulsa Alumni; exec. dir. Bot. Garden/Edn. and Rsch. Ctr.; bd. dirs. Tulsa Garden Ctr. Recipient Disting. Libr. award Okla. Libr. Assn., 1982, Leadership Tulsa Paragon award, 1987, Women in Comm. Newsmaker award, 1989, Outstanding Alumnus award U. Okla. Sch. Libr. Info. Studies, 1989, Headliner award Tulsa Press Club, 1996, Disting. Alumnus Coll. Arts and Scis., U. Okla., 2000; inducted into Tulsa City-County Libr. Hall of Fame, 1989, Okla. Womens Hall of Fame, 1993. Mem. ALA, Pub. Libr. Assn. (pres. 1993-94), Okla. Libr. Assn. (pres. 1978-79, Disting. Libr. award 1982, Meritorious Svc. award 1996), Tulsa Press Club. Democrat. Episcopalian. Avocations: swimming, gardening. Office Phone: 918-728-2700. Business E-Mail: pwoodrum@tulsaconnect.com.

WOODS, BARBARA O., mathematics educator; d. Harry James and Myrtle Reardon Odlum; m. John Andrews Woods, Sept. 6, 1969; 1 child, Kathleen Anne. BA, Annhurst Coll., Woodstock, Conn., 1967; MA, U. Conn., Storrs, 1969. Tchr. math. East Hartford (Conn.) H.S., 1969—. Home: 347 Main St South Windsor CT 06074

WOODS, BETTY, insurance company executive; b. 1938; BA in Psychology, Seattle U., 1974. With Organizational Cons. of the Northwest, Seattle, 1974-76; pres., CEO Premera Blue Cross, 1976—2000; dir. Beckman Coulter Inc., Fullerton, Calif., 1994—, chmn., 2005—. Founding mem. Nat. Inst. Health Care Mgmt.; trustee Western Wash. Univ. Mem.: Seattle NW chpt., Nat. Assn. Corp. Directors. Office: Beckman Coulter Inc 4300 N Harbor Blvd PO Box 3100 Fullerton CA 92834-3100

WOODS, CAROL SMITH, private school educator; d. David E. and Margaret (Ballinger) Smith; m. William Kent Woods, Apr. 1, 1980; children: Stephen, Todd. BA, U. Iowa, Iowa City, 1967; MEd, Xavier U., 1997. Tchg. coord. Montessori Ctr. Rm., Cin., 1975—. Cons. Am. Montessori Soc., Cin., 1982—99; adj. prof. Xavier U., Cin., 1992—2000; master tchr. Scottish Rite Learning Ctr., Cin., 1998—; presenter in field. Author: Wood's Words, 2002, Early Literacy Handbook, 2003; contbr. articles to profl. jours. Mem.: Orton-Gillingham Acad. (cert. mem. 2001—), Am. Montessori Soc., Internat. Dyslexia Assn. Avocations: reading, crossword puzzles, fitness. Home: 3750 Broadview Dr Cincinnati OH 45208

WOODS, DAISY DENNIS, chemistry educator; b. Woodville, Mass., Jan. 14, 1959; BS in Chemistry, Alcorn State U., Mo., 1980; MEd, Alcorn State U., 1982. Lic. Chemistry Teacher 7-12, General Science Teacher 7-12, Physics Teacher 7-12. Diversified tech. tchr. Dr. Martin Luther King Career and Tech. Complex, 1986—97; chemistry and physics tchr. Natches Adams Sch. Dist., 1997—. Recipient Vocational Tchr. of Yr., 1989, 1991, Award of Tchg. Excellence, 1996, Natches H.S. Tchr. of Mo., 2002. Home: 203 Tupelo Dr Natchez MS 39120

WOODS, DEANNA GAEL, education educator, consultant; b. Lebanon, Oreg., Dec. 23, 1945; d. Arthur James and Norma Vera (Quaring) W. BA in Lang. Arts, Portland State U., 1968, cert., 1972. Cert. secondary edn. tchr., Oreg. Sec. North Bapt. Ch., Portland, Oreg., 1965-69; tchr. Portland Pub. Schs., 1968—. Local site coord. ednl. rsch. and dissemination program Am. Fedn. Tchrs., Portland and Washington, 1985-2000, asst. dir. edn. issues dept., 1994-96; mem. adv. panel New Am. Schs. Devel. Corp., Arlington, Va., 1991—; mem. adv. com. N.W. Regional Ednl. Lab., Portland, 1987-2000, Edn. Testing Svc., Princeton, N.J., 1989—; cons. 2005—. Author: Moving Forward, 2002, Leadership in a Collaborative School, 2005. Mem. Milw. First Bapt., 1996—, Citizens Adv. Com. to Legis. Edn., Oreg., 1986—87. Recipient Educator award Oreg. Dept. Edn./Milken Family Found., 1991. Mem. ASCD, Am. Ednl. Rsch. Assn., Oreg. Fedn. Tchrs. (lobbyist 1989, Outstanding Contbn. to Edn. Awareness 1992), Portland Fedn. Tchrs. (cert. field rep., exec. coun. 1974—). Democrat. Baptist. Avocations: reading, skiing, cooking, travel, lifelong learning. Home: 608 N Morgan St Portland OR 97217-1770

WOODS, DEBORAH LYNN, recruiter; b. Denison, Tex., July 14, 1956; d. Carlos D. and Jo Ellen Woods; m. Melvin Ward Nichols, July 8, 1977 (div. Oct. 8, 1996); 1 child, Joni Mae Nichols. Degree in med. asst., Tex. Coll. Med. and Dental Asst., 1983. Registered med. asst. Tex. Office nurse T. R. Sharp D.O., Mesquite, Tex., 1983—88; OP scheduler, phlebotomist Garland Cmty. Hosp., Garland, Tex., 1989—95; data entry clerk Home, Health, and Hospice Care, Wilson, NC, 2000—02; med. sec. Wilson Digestive Disease Ctr., Wilson, NC, 2002; recruiter Cystic Fibrosis Found., Wilson, NC, 2003—06. Author: (novels) Something Special, 2003, poems. Mem.: Phi Beta Kappa. Republican. Baptist. Avocations: computers, reading, writing. Home: 2403 St John Dr SW Wilson NC 27893 Personal E-mail: ncdebz714@aol.com.

WOODS, DEIRDRE, information technology executive; With Wharton Sch., U. Pa., Phila., 1987—, dir., Wharton Learning Lab, chief information officer, assoc. dean, 2004—. Created a model for information technology support where information technology staff are embedded within faculty departments to provide maximum support and user satisfaction. This best practice came to be implemented by other business schools. Office: Wharton Sch U Pa 1030 Steinberg Hall Dietrich Hall Philadelphia PA 19104

WOODS, ELEANOR C., music educator; b. Stamford, Conn., Oct. 30, 1939; d. Richard and Anna Marie (Feldtmose) Cunliffe; m. David R. Woods, Aug. 18, 1962; children: Richard, Laurie. BA, Smith Coll., 1961; MAT, Yale U., 1962. String tchr., music tchr. Kariat Jr. High Sch., Spring Valley, N.Y., 1962-65; musich tchr. Flint Hill Sch., Fairfax, Va., 1966-68; violin tchr. Am. U. Prep, Washington, 1972; pvt. instr. Washington, 1972—; violin tchr. Nat. Cathedral Sch., St. Albans, Washington, 1988—. Chmn. Washington Internat. Competition, 2001—. Named Tchr. of Yr., Am. String Tchrs. Assn. of Md., 1993. Mem. Md. State Music Tchrs. Assn. (chmn., judge of competitions 1976—), Wash. Music Tchrs. Assn. (judge of competitions 1976—), Suzuki Assn. Am., Suzuki Assn. Greater Washington Area.

WOODS, HARRIETT RUTH, political organization worker, retired state official; b. Cleve., June 2, 1927; d. Armin and Ruth (Wise) Friedman; m. James B. Woods, Jan. 2, 1953; children: Christopher, Peter, Andrew. Student, U. Chgo., 1945; BA, U. Mich., 1949; LLD (hon.), Webster U., 1988, U. Missouri, 2003. Reporter Chgo. Herald-Am., 1948, St. Louis Globe-Democrat, 1949-51; prodr. Star, KPLR-TV, St. Louis, 1964-74; moderator, writer Sta. KETC-TC, St. Louis, 1962-64; council mem. University City, Mo., 1967-74; mem. Mo. Hwy. Commn., 1974, Mo. Transp. Commn., 1974-76, Mo. Senate, 1976-84; lt. gov. State of Mo., 1985-89; pres. Inst. for Policy Leadership, U. Mo., St. Louis, 1989-91, lectr., 1995—; commentator KWMU Radio, 1985—. Pres. Nat. Women's Polit. Caucus, 1991-95; fellow inst. politics J.F. Kennedy Sch. Govt., Harvard U., 1988; adj. prof. U. Mo., St. Louis, 1995—, Hunter Coll., N.Y.C., 2004—, Pace U., 2006—. Author: Stepping Up to Power: The Political Journey of American Women, 2000. Bd. dirs. LWV of Mo., 1963, Nat. League of Cities, 1972-74; Dem. nominee for U.S. Senate, 1982, 86; commr. St. Louis Regional Conf. and Sports Complex Authority, 2000—. Jewish. Office Phone: 314-863-4055. Personal E-mail: hw1781@sbcglobal.net.

WOODS, JEAN FRAHM, science educator; b. Boise, Idaho, Oct. 24, 1931; d. Theodore Roosevelt and Bonnie Mae (Gross) Frahm; m. Lonnie Lee Woods, June 24, 1951 (dec. May 7, 1977); children: Jeffrey Lee, Nicholaus Lon, Karl Eugene. BS in Sci. Edn., Home Econs., U. Idaho, Moscow, 1954; MS in Zoology, U. Wis., 1960. Tchr. 4th grade Rapid City Schs., SD, 1954-55; tchr. 7th and 8th grades Lovelock Schs., Nev., 1956-57; tchr. biology, chemistry, home econs. Richfield HS, Idaho, 1957-59; dietitian U. Idaho, Moscow, 1961-62; tchr. sci., home econs. Eagle Jr. HS, Idaho, 1962-63; sci. tchr. 7th grade Meridian Schs., Idaho, 1981-97. Tchr. of Yr. Meridian Schs., 1987. Mem. AAUW, Nat. Sci. Tchrs. Assn., Idaho Sci. Tchrs. Assn., Boise Home Economists (treas. 1968, pres. 1969), Native Daus. of Idaho, Ret. Educators Assn., Delta Kappa Gamma (1st v.p.) 2001-03. Avocations: reading, birdwatching. Home: 3518 Catalina Rd Boise ID 83705-4604

WOODS, KRYSTYNA JANINA, artist, pharmacist; b. Warwick, Queensland, Australia, Jan. 28, 1961; arrived in U.S., 1998; d. Jan and Janina Dzierzanowski; m. Ross Maxwell Woods, Aug. 28, 1993; children: Harrison George Maxwell, Jack Henry Alexander. BPharm, U. Queensland, Brisbane, 1980. Registered pharmacist Pharmacy Bd. Queensland. Pre-registration pharmacist, asst. mgr. Payless Chemists, Brisbane, Queensland, 1980—81; pharmacist, mgr. Benowa Pharmacy, Gold Coast, Australia, 1981—83; chief pharmacist, asst. mgr. Sorrento Pharmacy, Gold Coast, Australia, 1983—85; chief pharmacist, mgr. Moses Edward St. Pharmacy, Brisbane, 1986—88; chief pharmacist, part-time mgr. Aspley Day & Night Pharmacy, Brisbane, 1988—93; locum pharmacist mgr. Auchenflower Pharmacy, Brisbane, 1993—95, Terry White Pharmacy, Brisbane, 1993—95, Transit Ctr. Pharmacy, Brisbane, 1993—95; owner, mgr., chief pharmacist Indooroopilly Day & Night Pharmacy, Brisbane, 1995—2000. Model, actress Viviens Model Agy., Brisbane and Sydney, 1985—93; actress, model print, TV, radio and stage Margo Mott/Buckinghams, Gold Coast, 1985—93, Queensland Theatre Co., Brisbane, 1985—93, Javeenbah Little Theatre, Gold Coast, 1985—93, Gold Coast Little Theatre, 1982—84; mentor Young Australian Profls. in Am., N.Y.C., 2003; represented Queensland, Australia in Miss World Pageant, 1985; lectr. Mt. Gravatt Tech. Coll. Further Edn., Brisbane, 1989; interviewed by mags. N.J. Monthly, 2001, Australian House and Garden Mag., 1999, Sunday Mail Mag., 1998, Matters Mag., 2005. One-woman shows include Natura Gallery, Heritage Hotel, Brisbane, 1995—97, Brisbane Herbsfest, 1995—97, one-woman shows and exhbns., Wentworth Gallery, Palm Beach, 1995—96, White Plains, 1995—96, Boston, 1995—96, Chgo., 1995—96, one-woman shows include Madison Studio Gallery, 2001, The Show Gallery, Chatham, 2002—03, Internat. Art Expo, N.Y.C., 2003, Solange Rabello Art Gallery, Miami, 2003, Australian Consulate, N.Y.C., 2003, Solange Rab Art Gallery, Miami, 2004, Arts Coun. of Morris Area, 2004, Happy Dog Gallery, Piermont, N.Y., 2004—06, Maplewood Open Studio Exhbn., 2005, South Orange and Maplewood Artist Studio Tour, 2005, exhibitions include Village Gallery, Laguna Beach, 2003, Maplewood/So. Orange Artist Study Tour, 2004—06, Artists Studio Tours, 2004—05, Happy Dog Gallery, Piermont, N.Y., 2004—06, Maplewood Open Studio Exhbn., 2006, executed murals, S. Orange/Maplewood, NJ, 2005. Rep. city for state visit by Queen Elizabeth II; asst. to pres. in presentation to MP regarding protection of pharmacy ownership Queensland Pharmacy Guild, Brisbane, 1997. Recipient Award of Merit for Outstanding Achievement, Manhattan Arts Internat., 1999, Art Show awards, city couns. and art assns., 1977—89, Adjudicator's Choice award, Warana Drama Festival and Arts, 1982. Mem.: Australian Am. Assn., Arts Coun. of Morris Area (invited spkr. art promotion 2002), Nat. Mus. Women in Arts, Maplewood Club, Internat. Friends Club, Catharine Lorillard Wolfe Art Club (assoc.). Episcopalian. Avocations: tennis, golf, interior decorating, reading, travel. Office: Krysia D Designs 422 Walton Rd Maplewood NJ 07040 E-mail: krysiadart@aol.com.

WOODS, LINDA W., literature and language educator; children: Kevin Michael, Kathleen Megan. BS, Sam Houston U., Huntsville, Tex., 1974; BS in English Sec. Edn., Sam Houston U., 1984. English tchr. Conroe Ind. Sch. Dist., The Woodlands, Tex., 1984—. Office Phone: 936-273-4837.

WOODS, MERILYN BARON, psychologist, consultant; b. Bklyn., July 8, 1927; d. David Theodore and Helen (Mintz) Baron; m. John Galloway Woods, Sept. 15, 1948; children: Anne Helen, Elizabeth Ruth. BS, Cornell U., 1948; MEd, Temple U., 1957; PhD, Bryn Mawr Coll., 1968. Lic. psychologist, Pa. Rsch. asst. psychiatry Temple U., Phila., 1958-59, instr., counselor students, 1960-64; clin. psychologist Gloucester County Guidance Ctr., Woodbury, N.J., 1959-60; seminar coord. Bryn Mawr Coll., 1966-67, lectr., 1968-70, asst. prof., 1970-73; dir. counseling and placement Jewish Employment and Vocat. Svc., 1973-75; assoc. dean students Rider Coll., 1975-77; dir. student svcs., clin. asst. prof. mental health scis. Hahnemann Med. U., Phila., 1978-83; dir. Ctr. for Pers. and Profl. Devel. Pa. Coll. Optometry, Phila., 1983-93; pvt. practice psychologist Phila., 1983-86; pres. pvt. practice, 1986—. Mem., pres. bd. mgrs. Sr. Employment and Edl. Svc., Phila., 1983-95; bd. dirs. Awbury Arboretum Assn., 1986—; mem. Mayor's Sci. and Tech. Adv. Coun. divsn. Urban Affairs City of Phila., 1973-76. Tuition scholar Bryn Mawr Coll. Fellow Nat. Vocat. Guidance Assn., Pa. Psychol. Assn., Behavior Therapy and Rsch. Soc. (clin.); mem. APA, Ea. Psychol. Assn., Am. Counseling Assn., Am. Coll. Pers. Assn., Phila. Soc. Clin. Psychologists (bd. dirs. 1981-91), Cornell Alumni Club of Phila. (co-chair 1989-91).

WOODS, MISTIE LYNN, secondary school educator; b. Grand Junction, Colo., Aug. 16, 1974; d. Jerrold Dwain and Charlotte Marie Bradford; married; children: Sidnee Regan Akens, Nathanel Dwain Akens. BA in English Lang. Arts, Mesa State Coll., Grand Junction, Colo., 1997. Cert. tchr. tech. Mesa County Valley Sch. Dist. #51, 2005. Tchr. Ctrl. H.S., Grand Junction, Colo., 2001—. Adv. yearbook Ctrl. H.S., 2001—04, adv., 2001—. Author: A Surrender to the Moon, 2005. Named Hon. Poet, Nat. Poetry Soc., 2005. Mem.: NEA. Avocations: writing, being outdoors. Home: 3017 1/2 Sequel Way Grand Junction CO 81504 Office: Central High School 550 Warrior Way Grand Junction CO 81504 Office Phone: 970-254-7298. Business E-Mail: makens@mesa.k12.co.us.

WOODS, NANCY FUGATE, dean, women's health nurse, educator; BS, Wis. State U., 1968; MSN, U. Wash., 1969; PhD, U. N.C., 1978. Staff nurse Sacred Heart Hosp., Wis., 1968, Univ. Hosp., Wis., 1969-70, St. Francis Cabrini Hosp., 1970; nurse clinician Yale-New Haven Hosp., 1970-71; instr. nursing Duke U., Durham, N.C., 1971-72, from instr. to assoc. prof., 1972-78; assoc. prof. physiology U. Wash., Seattle, 1978-82, prof. physiology, 1982-84, chairperson dept. parent and child nursing, 1984-90, prof. dept. parent and child nursing, 1990—, dean Sch. Nursing, 1998—; dir. Ctr. Women's Health Rsch., U. Wash., Seattle, 1989—. Pres. scholar U. Calif., San Francisco, 1985-86. Contbr. articles to profl. jours. Fellow ANA, Am. Acad. Nursing, Inst. Medicare, N.A.S.; mem. AAUP, APHA, Am. Coll. Epidemiology, Soc. Menstrual Cycle Rsch. (v.p. 1981-82, pres. 1983-85), Soc. Advancement Women's Health Rsch. Office: U Wash Sch Nursing PO Box 357260 Seattle WA 98195-7260

WOODS, PHYLLIS MICHALIK, librarian; b. New Orleans, Sept. 12, 1937; d. Philip John and Thelma Alice (Carey) Michalik; 1 child, Tara Lynn Woods. BA, Southea. La. U., 1967. Cert. in speech and English, libr. sci., secondary edn., La. Tchr. speech, English and drama St. Charles Parish Pub. Schs., Luling, La., elem. tchr., secondary tchr. remedial reading, Chpt. I reading specialist, Wicat tchr. coord., elem. sch. libr.; media specialist Jefferson Parish Pub. Sch. System. Tchr. cons. St. Charles parish writing project La. State U. Writing Project; tchr. gifted writing students in a summer writing workshop. Author: Egbert, the Egret, Egbert's Picnic, Egbert Visits Sammy, Angel Without Wings, The Necklace and Egbert's Calf, The Hurricane, The Cleanup Day, The Rainbow, The Fair, The Tornado; song-writer; musical compositions include The Fruits of the Spirit, Father's Day Song, Mother's Day Song; contbr. articles and poems to River Parish Guide, St. Charles Herald. Sch. rep. United Fund, St. Charles Parish Reading Assn.; parish com. mem. Young Authors, Tchrs. Who Write; active 4-H leader; bd. trustees Michalik Scholarship Trust. Mem. ASCD, Internat. Platform Assn., Internat. Reading Assn., Am. Fedn. Tchrs., St. Charles Parish Reading Coun., Newspaper in Edn. (chmn., historian), La. Assn. Newspapers in Edn. (state com.), Jefferson Parish Libr. Assn., Jefferson Parish Reading Assn., Jefferson Parish Tchrs. Union.

WOODS, SANDRA KAY, real estate executive; b. Loveland, Colo., Oct. 11, 1944; d. Ivan H. and florence L. (Betz) Harris; m. Gary A. Woods, June 11, 1967; children: Stephanie Michelle, Michael Harris. BA, U. Colo., 1966, MA, 1967. Personnel mgmt. specialist CSC, Denver, 1967; asst. to regional dir. HEW, Denver, 1968-69; urban renewal rep. HUD, Denver, 1970-73, dir. program analysis, 1974-75, asst. regional dir. cmty. planning and devel., 1976-77, regional dir. fair housing, 1978-79; mgr. ea. facility project Adolph Coors Co., Golden, Colo., 1980, dir. real estate, 1981, v.p. chief environ. health and safety officer, 1982-96, v.p. strategic selling initiatives, 1996—2000; pres. Woods Properties LLP, Golden, 2000—. Mem. Exec. Exch., The White House, 1980. Bd. dirs. Golden Local Devel. Corp., 1981-82; fundraising dir. Coll. Arts and Scis., U. Colo., boulder, 1982-89, U. Colo.found.; mem. exec. bd. NCCJ, Denver, 1982-94; v.p. women in bus. Inc., Denver, 1982-83; mem. steering com. 1984 Yr. for All Denver Women, 1983-84; mem. 10th dist. Denver br. Fed. Res. Bd., 1990-96, chmn. bd., 1995-96; bd. dirs. Nat. Jewish Hosp., 1994—; chmn. Greater Denver Corp., 1991—. Named one of Outstanding Young Women Am., U.S. Jaycees, 1974, 78, Fifty Women to Watch, Businessweek, 1987, 92, Woman of Achievement YWCA, 1988. Mem. Indsl. Devel. Resources Coun. (bd. dirs. 1986-89), Am. Mgmt. Assn., Denver C. of C. (bd. dirs. 1988-96, Disting. Young Exec. award 1974, mem. Leadership Denver, 1976-77), Colo. Women's Forum, Nat. Assn. Office and Indsl. Park Developers (sec. 1988, treas. 1989), Committee of 200 (v.p. 1994-95), Phi Beta Kappa, Pi Alpha Alpha, PEO Club (Loveland). Republican. Presbyterian. E-mail: sandrawoods@qwest.net.

WOODS, SUSANNE, academic administrator, educator; b. Honolulu, May 12, 1943; d. Samuel Ernest and Gertrude (Cullom) W. BA in Polit. Sci., UCLA, 1964, MA in English, 1965; PhD in English and Comparative Lit., Columbia U., 1970; MA (hon.), Brown U., 1978. Institute of Educational Management Harvard U., 1993. Staff Senator Daniel K. Inouye, 1963; asst. editor Rand Corp., Calif., 1963-65; instr. Ventura Coll., Calif., 1965-66; lectr. CUNY, 1967-69; asst. prof. U. Hawaii, 1969-72; asst. prof. English Brown U., Providence, 1972-77, assoc. prof., 1977-83, prof., 1983-93, dir. grad. studies, 1986-88, assoc. dean faculty, 1987-90; v.p., dean Franklin and Marshall Coll., Lancaster, Pa., 1991-95, prof. English, 1991—99; provost, prof. English Wheaton Coll., Norton, Mass., 1999—. Vis. assoc. prof. U. Calif., 1981-82; chair exec. bd. NEH-Brown Women Writers Project, 1988—. Author: Natural Emphasis, 1984; gen. editor: Women Writers in English, 1350-1850, 1992—; editor: The Poetry of Aemilia Lanyer, 1993; contbr. numerous articles to profl. jours. and scholarly books; reviewer for various profl. jours., including Renaissance Quar., Jour. of English and Germanic Philology; reader for PMLA Jour., SEL Jour., also others; editorial bd. Hunting Libr. Quar., 1987-90, Ben Jonson Jour., Duquesne U. Press. Pres. Cultural Coun. of Lancaster County, 1993-95, bd. dirs., 1990-95; bd. dirs. Lancaster Gen. Hosp. Found., 1992-95; active various polit. campaigns, 1960-64, 68-76, 84, 92. Bronson fellow, 1976, Huntington Library, 1979-80, 81, Clark Library, 1981, Huntington-NEH, 1984-85, Woodrow Wilson Found., 1968-70 Mem. Am. Council Edn. (R.I. women's coord. 1988-90), MLA (chmn. div. 17th Century English lit. 1982), N.E. MLA (chmn. English Renaissance sect. 1978, Milton sect. 1983), Am. Assn. Higher Edn., Nat. Women's Studies Assn., Renaissance Soc. Am., Milton Soc. (exec. com. 1987-89), Lyrica Soc. (pres. 1987-90), Alpha Gamma Delta. Democrat. Episcopalian. Episcopalian. Achievements include Founding Director, Brown University Women Writers Project (literary recovery and text encoding). Avocations: music, travel, boating, scuba.

WOODS COGGINS, ALMA, artist; b. Canton, Pa., May 24, 1924; d. Fred and Essica Ortha (Manahan) Woods; m. Jack B. Coggins, Jan. 15, 1948. Grad. h.s., New Albany, Pa., 1941. Exhibited in shows at Wyomissing Inst. Fine Arts, Reading Mus., Yellow Springs Art Show, Valley Forge Small Paintings Exhbn., Pa. State Delawre County Cmapus, MainlineArt Ctr. Ann. Exhbn., Chester County Art Assn. Shows, Small Paintings Nat. Exhbn./Ky. Highlands Mus., Pa. State U., Harrisburg, numerous others. Sec. zoning hearing bd. Zoning Commn., Pike Twp., 1965-99. Recipient awards for art. Mem. Berks Art Alliance, Chester County Art Assn., Pen and Brush. Avocation: gardening. Home: PO Box 57 Boyertown PA 19512-0057

WOODSIDE, CARLENE, art educator; MBA, Western Ill. U., Macomb. Cert. leadership instr. Phi Theta Kappa, 1998. Desktop pub. coord. Carl Sandburg Coll., Carthage, Ill., 1991—99; graphic comm. coord. Southeastern C.C., West Burlington, Iowa, 1999—; owner/trainer CompuTrain, Burlington, Iowa. Dir./advisor Phi Theta Kappa, West Burlington, Iowa, 1999—2006; dir. Bethany Youth Advisor, Burlington, Iowa, 1998—2006. Recipient Faculty Mem. of Yr. award, Ill. C.C. Trustee Assn., 1995. Mem.: Southeaster C.C. Found. Bd. (assoc.), Delta Kappa Gamma (assoc.; yearbook chair 2000—06). Avocation: gardening. Office: Southeastern CC 1500 W Agency Rd West Burlington IA 52655 Office Phone: 319-208-5201.

WOODSIDE, LISA NICOLE, humanities educator; b. Portland, Oreg., Sept. 7, 1944; d. Lee and Emma (Wenstrom) W. Student, Reed Coll., 1962—65; MA, U. Chgo., 1968; PhD, Bryn Mawr Coll., 1972; cert., Harvard U. Inst. Ednl. Mgmt., 1979; MA, West Chester U., 1994. Cert. tchr. ecstatic trance postures Cuyamungue Inst., N.Mex., 2003, wellness counseling, creative energy options. Mem. dean's staff Bryn Mawr Coll., 1970-72; asst. prof. Widener U., Chester, Pa., 1972-77, assoc. prof. humanities, 1978-83, asst. dean student svcs., 1972-76, assoc. dean, 1976-79, dean, 1979-83; acad. dean, prof. humanities Holy Family Coll., Phila., 1983—, v.p., dean acad. affairs, prof. humanities, 1990-98, prof. humanities, 1998—. Cons. State NJ Edn. Dept., 1990, Houghton-Mifflin for English reader, 2000; cons., reader Test of Spoken English Ednl. Testing Svc., 2002—; accreditor Commn. on Higher Edn., Mid. States Assn., 1977—83, 1994. Co-author: New Age Spirituality: An Assessment. City commr. for cmty. rels., Chester, 1980-83; mem. Adult Edn. Coun. Phila. Recipient Crasilneck award for best paper Am. Soc. Clin. Hypnosis; Am. Assn. Papyrology grantee Bryn Mawr Coll., S. Maude Kaemmerling fellow. Mem.: MLA, AAUW (univ. rep. 1975—83), APA, Pa. Coll. Tchrs. Assn., Mid. States Classics Assn., Audubon Soc., Psi Chi, Alpha Sigma Lambda, Phi Eta Sigma. Office: Humanities Dept Holy Family Univ Torresdale Philadelphia PA 19114 Office Phone: 215-637-7700. E-mail: woodside@holyfamily.edu.

WOODSON, GAYLE ELLEN, otolaryngologist; b. Galveston, Tex., June 9, 1950; d. Clinton Eldon and Nancy Jean (Stephens) W.; m. Kevin Thomas Robbins; children: Nicholas, Gregory, Sarah. BA, Rice U., 1972; MD, Baylor Coll. Medicine, 1975. Diplomate Am. Bd. Otolaryngology (bd. dirs., residency rev. com. for otolaryngology, exam. chair). Fellow Baylor Coll. Medicine, Houston, 1976, Inst. Laryngology & Otology, London, 1981-82; asst. prof. Baylor Coll. Medicine, 1982-87; asst. attending Harris County Hosp. Dist., Houston, 1982-86; with courtesy staff Saint Luke's Episcopal Hosp., Houston, 1982-87; assoc. attending The Methodist Hosp., Houston, 1982-87; asst. prof. U. Calif. Med. Sch., San Diego, 1987-89; chief otolaryngology VA Med. Ctr., San Diego, 1987-92; assoc. prof. U. Calif. Sch. Med., San Diego, 1989-92; prof. otolaryngology U. Tenn., Memphis, 1993—2000, So. Ill. U., 2003—. Numerous presentations and lectures in field. Contbr. numerous articles and abstracts to med. jours., also videotapes. Recipient deRoldes award, Am. Laryngol. Assn., 2003. Fellow ACS (bd. govs.), Royal Coll. Surgeons, Soc. Univ. Otolaryngologists (past pres.), Am. Soc. Head and Neck Surgery, Am. Laryngol. Assn. (pres.-elect de Roaldes award, 2003), Triological Soc.; mem. AMA, Am. Acad. Otolaryngology-Head and Neck Surgery (bd. dirs. 1993-96), Am. Med. Women's Assn. (past pres. Memphis br.), Soc. Head and Neck Oncologists Eng., Am. Physiol. Soc.,

Assn. Women Surgeons, Am. Soc. Head and Neck Surgeons, Johns Hopkins Soc. Scholars, Collegium OtoRhinolaryngolicum Amicus Sacrum. Office: Southern Illinois Univ PO Box 19662 Springfield IL 62794-9662 Business E-Mail: gwoodson@siumed.edu.

WOODSON, JACQUELINE, writer; b. Columbus, Ohio, Feb. 12, 1964; 1 child. Fellow MacDowell Colony and the Fine Arts Work Ctr., Provincetown, Mass. Author: (book) Last Summer With Maizon, 1990, Martin Luther King Jr., and His Birthday, 1990, The Dear One, 1991, Maizon at Blue Hill, 1992, I Hadn't Meant to Tell You This, 1994, Between Madison and Palmetto, 1995, Autobiography of a Family Photo, 1995, From the Notebooks of Melanin Sun, 1995, A Way Out of No Way, 1996, The House You Pass on the Way, 1997, We Had a Picnic this Past Sunday, 1997, If You Come Softly, 1998, Lena, 1998, Miracle's Boys, 2000, Sweet, Sweet Memory, 2000, The Other Side, 2001, Hush, 2002, Our Gracie Aunt, 2002, Visiting Day, 2002, Locomotion, 2003 (Nat. Book award nominee, 2003); author: (ill. by E.B. Lewis) Coming On Home Soon, 2004 (Caldecott award, 2005, Am. Libr. Assn. Notable Book, 2005, Child Mag. Best of 2004, Booklist Editor's Choice); author: (ill. by Hudson Talbott) Show Way, 2005 (Newbery Honor Book, 2006). Recipient Coretta Scott King Honors, 2001, Kenyon Review award for lit. excellence in fiction, 3 Am. Libr. Assn. awards, 2 Jane Adams Peace award honors, 3 Lambda Lit. awards.*

WOODSON, LINDA TOWNLEY, English educator, writer; b. Clifton, Tex., Oct. 14, 1943; d. Richmond Alyet and Gena Lee (Wade) Townley; m. James Charles Woodson, Sept. 6, 1963 (div. Dec. 1982); 1 child, Rachel Woodson Garrett; m. Richard Patrick Smith, Mar. 24, 1983. BS in Edn., Tex. Christian U., Fort Worth, 1964, PhD, 1977. Cert. tchr., Tex., Calif. Elem. tchr. Fort Worth Ind. Dist., 1964-65, Austin (Tex.) Ind. Sch. Dist., 1965-67, Fairfield (Calif.)-Suisun Unified Sch., 1969-71; instr. English So. Meth. U., Dallas, 1977-79; asst. prof. English Tex. Tech. U., Lubbock, 1979-81; prof. English U. Tex., San Antonio, 1981—. Author: A Handbook of Modern Rhetorical Terms, 1979, From Cases to Composition, 1982, The Writer's World, 1986; co-author: Writing in Three Dimensions, 1995; co-editor: Modes of Inquiry, 1998. Mem. Nat. Coun. Tchrs. English (commn. on composition 1980-82), Conf. Coll. Composition and Communication (nominating com. 1985, exec. coun. 1995-98), Cormac McCarthy Soc., South Ctrl. MLA. Avocations: reading philosophy, dogs, gardening. Home: 16519 Loma Lndg Helotes TX 78023-3438 Office: U Tex at San Antonio Dept English Classics & Philosophy San Antonio TX 78249 Business E-Mail: linda.woodson@utsa.edu.

WOODSON-GLENN, YOLANDA, social worker; b. L.A., July 29, 1958; d. Lewie B. and Clareece Woodson; children: James Glenn, Kimberly Glenn. BA cum laude in journalism, Bowie State, 1995; MA in counseling psychology, Bowie State U.; postgrad., Calif. Grad. Inst. Social worker Dept. Children and Family Svcs., Baltimore, MD, 1994-95; victim advocate State's Atty's Office, Annapolis, MD, 1995-96; social worker Children of the Village, Carson, CA, 1997-99, Dept. of Children and Family Svcs., Lakewood, CA, 1999—. Counselor City of Refuge Ch., Gardena, Calif., 2000—. Author: Suffering for Righteousness, 2001. Pentecostal. Avocations: cooking, crafts, museums, concerts. Home: 17125 Stark Ave Cerritos CA 90703 E-mail: ywoodsonglenn@aol.com.

WOODSON-HOWARD, MARLENE ERDLEY, former state legislator; b. Ford City, Pa., Mar. 8, 1937; d. James and Susie (Lettrich) Erdley; m. Francis M. Howard; children: George Woodson, Bert Woodson, Robert Woodson, Daniel Woodson, David Woodson. BS, Ind. U. of Pa., 1958; MA, U. South Fla., 1968; EdD, Nova U., 1981. Prof. math. Manatee Community Coll., 1970-82, dir., Inst. Advancement, 1982-86; exec. dir. Manatee Community Coll. Foundation, 1982-86; pres. Pegasus Enterprises, Inc., 1986—; state senator Fla., 1986-90. Candidate for gov. of Fla., 1990; past pres. New Coll. Libr. Assn.; past pres. Manatee Symphony; bd. dirs. Manatee Red Cross; bd. dirs. Manatee Players, Inc., v.p.; trustee Fla. Kiwanis Found. Mem. Manatee C. of C., Sarasota C. of C., Sarasota Kiwanis (bd. dirs., v.p., pres.), Bradenton Kiwanis. Republican. Roman Catholic. Home: 12 Tidy Island Blvd Bradenton FL 34210-3301 E-mail: marlenewhoward@aol.com.

WOODS-STELLMAN, DONNA SUE, education educator, consultant; b. Springhill, La., Jan. 15, 1954; children: Klaten A. Woods, Matthew M. Woods, Laura E. Woods, Gabriele E. Woods; m. Felix A. Stellman II, June 28, 1997; 1 stepchild, Kellie N. Stellman. BA, La. Tech U., 1975; MEd, La. State U., 1983; EdD, Okla. State U., 1992. Cert. English, social studies, gifted edn. tchr., La.; cert. English, gifted edn. and reading tchr., Okla. Tchr. English Grawood Christian Schs., La., 1979-80; tchr. English, lang. arts reading Gentry Jr. Sch., Goose Creek Consolidate Ind. Sch. Dist., 2004—; tchr. spl. edn. Bossier Parish Sch. Bd., Benton, La., 1981-83; tchr. gifted Curtis Elem. Sch., Bossier City, La., 1983-88; tchr. lang. arts Elm Grove Jr. HS, La., 1988-90; curriculum developer Bossier Parish Sch. Bd., 1990; tchg. asst., univ. rep. Okla. entry yr. assistance Okla. State U., Stillwater, 1990-92, co-dir., instr. 13th ann. reading workshop, 1991, instr. Coll. Vet. Medicine, 1991, developer, dir. student tchr. seminar, 1992; dir. reading and literacy Okla. State Dept. Edn., Oklahoma City, 1995-97; asst. prof. Coll. Edn. Northwestern Okla. State U., Alva, 1992-95; asst. prof. dept. urban edn. U. Houston-Downtown, 1997—2004, asst. chair dept. urban edn., 2001—04. Adj. instr. Oklahoma City C.C., 1991-92, U. Okla., 1995-97. Tutor YWCA, Shreveport, La., 1975; supt. youth Sun. schs. 1st Presbyn. Ch., Edmond, Okla., 1991, youth choir dir., 1994-97, youth handbells dir., 1995-97; mem. Greater Houston Area Reading Coun. Named Favorite Tchr. of Yr., Bossier C. of C., 1987, Outstanding Instr. FB Urban Educators, 1999; Centennial scholar Okla. State U. Coll. Edn. Alumni Assn., 1992. Mem.: Soc. Children's Book Writers and Illustrators, Okla. Early Childhood Tchrs. Assn. (conf. presenter 1991), Greater Houston Area Reading Coun., Okla. Reading Assn. (conf. presenter 1993—97), Internat. Reading Assn. (conf. presenter 1996, 2001), Phi Delta Kappa, Kappa Delta Pi, Alpha Upsilon Alpha (faculty sponsor 1994—95). Avocations: reading, sailing. Home: PO Box 1206 Seabrook TX 77586 Personal E-mail: dsws97@yahoo.com.

WOODS-TAYLOR, CLEORA LYNESIA, mathematics educator, consultant; d. Ray Clayton and Clara Lynn Woods; children: Lynesia Raychelle Taylor, Lanetria Taylor Christa. BS, Prairie View A&M U., Tex., 1991; MA, U. Mo., Kansas City, 2003. Cert. tchr. Mo., 2003. Adj. instr. algebra Houston C.C. (NW Campus), 1992; instr. algebra Houston Ind. Sch. Dist., 1992—93, Faith Acad., Kansas City, Mo., 1995—99, Lincoln Coll. Prep. Acad., Kansas City, Mo., 2001—. Math cons. Mo. Math Acad. Dir. of performing arts dept. Harvest Ch., Kansas City, Mo., 1995—2001. Mem.: Alpha Kappa Alpha. Office: Lincoln Coll Prep Acad 2012 E 23rd St Kansas City MO 64127 Office Phone: 816-418-3525. Office Fax: 816-418-3530.

WOODSWORTH, ANNE, retired academic administrator, librarian; came to U.S., 1983; d. Thorvald Ernst and Roma Yrsa Lindner; 1 child, Yrsa Anne. BFA, U. Man., 1962; BLS, U. Toronto, 1964, MLS, 1969; PhD, U. Pitts., 1987. Edn. libr. U. Man., 1964—65; reference libr. Winnipeg Pub. Libr., 1965—67; reference libr. sci. and medicine dept. U. Toronto, 1967—68; med. libr. Toronto We. Hosp., 1969—70; rsch. asst. to chief libr. U. Toronto, 1970—71, head reference dept., 1971—74; pers. dir. Toronto Pub. Libr., 1975—78; dir. librs. York U., Toronto, 1978—83; assoc. provost for librs. U. Pitts., 1983—88, assoc. prof., 1988—91; dean Palmer Sch. Libr. and Info. Sci., L.I. U., 1991—98; dean Sch. Edn. Dowling Coll., Oakdale, NY, 1999—2000; dean sch. info. and libr. sci. Pratt Inst., Bklyn., 2000—02, acting provost, 2002—03; provost Katherine Gibbs Sch., Melville, NY, 2003; learning sys. advisor Bklyn. Pub. Libr., 2004—. Pres. Anne Lindner Ltd., 1974—83; rsch. libraries adv. coun. OCLC, 1984—87. Author: The Alternative Press in Canada, 1972, Leadership and Research Libraries, 1988, Patterns and Options for Managing Information Technology on Campus, 1990, Library Cooperation and Networks, 1991, Managing the Economics of Leasing and Contracting Out Information Services, 1993, Reinvesting in the Information Job Family, 1993, The Future of Education for Librarianship: Looking Forward from the Past, 1994. Sec., mem. bd. trustees Katharine Gibbs Sch., L.I., 2003-04; dir. Sr. Fellows Inst., 1995-98; trustee L.I. Librs. Resources Coun., 1993-96; bd. dirs. Population Rsch. Found., Toronto, 1980-83. Grantee Can. Coun., 1974, Ont. Arts Coun., 1974, Coun. on Libr. Resources, 1986, 88, 91, 93; UCLA sr. fellow, 1985. Mem. ALA (com. on accreditation 1990-94, councillor 1993-97), Can. Assn. Rsch. Librs. (pres. 1981-83), Assn. Rsch. Librs. (bd. dirs. 1981-84, v.p. 1984-85, pres. 1985-86), Assn. Coll. and Rsch. Librs. (chair K.G. Saur award com. 1991-93), Assn. for Libr. and Info. Sci. Edn. (chair honors and awards com. 1995, bd. dirs. 1998-99, v.p. 1998-99), Am. Soc. Higher Edn., Internet Soc., Am. Soc. Info. Sci. (convenor 1999-2000), Archons of Colophon. Personal E-mail: alwoods@intergate.com.

WOODWARD, BETTY SHAW, retired music educator; b. Russellville, Ky., Jan. 15, 1932; d. John Daniel and Martha Margaret (Hutcheson) Shaw; m. James D. Woodward, Aug. 13, 1955; children: Julia Woodward Haley, James David, Jr. AA, Va. Intermont Coll., Bristol, 1952; MusB, U. Ky., 1954, MA, 1955. Tchr. elem. music Jefferson County, Louisville, 1955-56; children's choir dir. Vineville Bapt. Ch., Macon, Ga., 1956-59; children's choir dir., supr. First Bapt. Ch., Tulsa, 1959-66; children's choir dir. First Bapt. Ch., Shawnee, Okla., 1966—, state pres., 1987-89; mem. music faculty Okla. Bapt. U., Shawnee, 1966—94, assoc. prof. music, 1983—94; children's choir clinician, 1966—; children's choir cons. Crystal Cathedral, Garden Grove, Calif., 1981-83; curriculum writer Young Musicians, Music Leader mags. Ch. Music Dept., Nashville, 1968—. Author: The Singing Book, 1975, Exploring Music, 1980, Go Out With Joy, 1981, Teaching Harmony and Part Singing, 1982, Leading Younger Children's Choirs, 1985; creator video tape series, Developing Pre-schooler's Singing Skills, Developing Younger Children's Singing Skills, Developing Older Children's Singing Skills, Teaching Children to Sing Parts, 1986. Mem. Music Educators Nat. Conf., Am. Choral Dirs. Assn., Am. Orff Schulwerk Assn., Okla. Kodaly Educatoro, Hymn Soc. Am., So. Bapt. Ch. Music Conf. Avocations: needlework, gardening, reading. Home: 22 Sequoyah St Shawnee OK 74801-5570

WOODWARD, DEBBIE CAROL, special education educator; b. Lufkin, Tex., Mar. 1, 1953; d. Robert Charles and Peggy Jean Beddingfield; m. Allen Wiley, Aug. 15, 1975 (div. Aug. 1984); 1 child, Richard Charles Wiley; m. Lee George Woodward, July 24, 1998. BS, Stephen F. Austin State U., Nacogdoches, Tex., 1995. Tchr. 5th grade Lufkin Ind. Sch. Dist., Tex.; owner Wiley's Wee Wons Nursery, Bryan, Tex., Wiley's Wee Wons Day Sch. and Nursery, Lufkin; faculty Ctr. for Retarded, Houston; spl. edn. tchr. Galena Park Ind. Sch., Houston, Channelview Ind. Sch. Dist., Tex. Homebound spl. svcs. provider and cons. Galena Park Ind. Sch. Dist., Houston, Channelview Ind. sch. Dist.; salesperson Avon Products. Active Cystic Fybrosis Found., Susan G. Komen Breast Cancer Found., Shriners Hosps., Inc.; pvt. cons. for families and schs. of terminally children in Galena Park and Channelview. Mem.: Coun. for Exceptional Children, Order Ea. Star.

WOODWARD, JOAN B., science association director; BS magna cum laude, U. Mo.; MS in engrng. econ. systems, Stanford U.; PhD in mech. engrng., U. Calif. With Sandia Nat. Labs., Albuquerque, 1974, dir., Environ. Progs. Ctr., leader material support group, nat. security and weapons progs., mgr., Neutron Generator and Explosives Component Ctr., v.p., Energy, Info., and Infrastructure Tech. Div., currently exec. v.p., dep. dir. Chair lab. mgmt. coun. for Mission and Risk Mgmt. Oversight Sandia Nat. Labs., responsible for ind. assessment of weapons' safety, security, and reliability; bd. mem. Intelligence Sci. Bd (ISB), Congl. Commn. to assess vulnerabilities of US infrastructure to Electromagnetic Pulse; mem. Army Sci. Bd (ASB) study on Force Protection, Defense Sci. Bd. (DSB) study on Homeland Security; co-chair Nat. Reconnaissance Office Bd. (NRO) for Nat. Space Security (NSS); served Nat. Acad. Study on S&T for countering Terrorism. Mem. adv. coun. Kirtland Hon. Comdrs.; mem. bd. adv. Family Security Group, Ctr. for Security Policy; bd. dirs. Bosque Sch., Greater Albuquerque C. of C. Mem.: U. N.Mex Sch. Engring. Bd. of Visitors, U. Mo.-Rolla Dean's Bd. Visitors, N.Mex Women's Forum, Soc. Women Engrs. (life), Phi Kappa Phi. Office: Sandia Nat Labs PO Box 5800, Mail Stop 0102 Albuquerque NM 87185-0102

WOODWARD, JOANNE GIGNILLIAT, actress; b. Thomasville, Ga., Feb. 27, 1930; d. Wade and Elinor (Trimmier) W.; m. Paul Newman, Jan. 29, 1958; children: Elinor Terese, Melissa Stewart, Clea Olivia. Student, La. State U., 1947-49; grad., Neighborhood Playhouse Dramatic Sch., N.Y.C. First TV appearance in Penny, Robert Montgomery Presents, 1952; understudy broadway play Picnic, 1953; appeared in plays Baby Want a Kiss, 1964, Candida, 1982, The Glass Menagerie, Williamstown Theatré Festival, 1985, Sweet Bird of Youth, Toronto, 1988; motion pictures include Three Faces of Eve, 1957 (Acad. award Best Actress, Nat. Bd. Rev. award, Fgn. Press award), Count Three and Pray, 1955, Long Hot Summer, 1958, No Down Payment, 1957, Sound and the Fury, 1959, A Kiss Before Dying, 1956, Rally Round the Flag Boys, 1958, The Fugitive Kind, 1960, Paris Blues, 1961, The Stripper, 1963, A New Kind of Love, 1963, A Big Hand for the Little Lady, 1965, A Fine Madness, 1965, Rachel, Rachel, 1968, Winning, 1969, WUSA, 1970, They Might Be Giants, 1971, The Effect of Gamma Rays on Man-in-the-Moon Marigolds, 1972 (Cannes Film Festival award), Summer Wishes, Winter Dreams, 1973 (N.Y. Film Critics award), The Drowning Pool, 1975, The End, 1978, Harry and Son, 1984, Glass Menagerie, 1987, Mr. & Mrs. Bridge, 1990, Philadelphia, 1993, The Age of Innocence (voice), 1993, My Knees Were Jumping: Remembering the Kindertransports, (voice) 1998; TV appearances include All the Way Home; TV-film appearances in Sybil, 1976, Come Back, Little Sheba, 1977, See How She Runs, 1978 (Emmy award), Streets of L.A., 1979, The Shadow Box, 1980, Crisis at Central High, 1981, Do You Remember Love?, 1985 (Emmy award), Blind Spot, 1993 (Emmy nomination, Lead Actress - Miniseries, 1993), Breathing Lessons, 1994 (Emmy nomination, Lead Actress - Special, 1994, Golden Globe award, Best Actress), James Dean: A Portrait, 1996; narrator film documentary Angel Dust, TV documentary on Group Theatre, 1989. Co-recipient (with Paul Newman) Kennedy Ctr. Honors for Lifetime Achievement in the Performing Arts. Democrat. Episcopalian. Office: ICM 40 W 57th St Fl 16 New York NY 10019-4098

WOODWARD, JULIA WILSON, elementary school educator; b. Danville, Va., Sept. 10, 1978; d. Dabney Langhorne and Victoria Brown Wilson; 1 child, Benjamin Charles. MEd, Va. Poly. Inst. and State U., Blacksburg, 2001. Lic. tchr. Va., 2001. Civics and econ. tchr. Tuckahoe Mid. Sch., Richmond, Va., 2001—04; world history tchr. Dan River Mid. Sch., Ringgold, Va., 2004—. Mem.: Nat. Coun. for the Social Studies. Office: Dan River Middle School 5875 Kentuck Rd Ringgold VA 24586 Office Phone: 434-822-6027. Personal E-mail: vtjewels2001@yahoo.com. E-mail: julia.woodward@pcs.k12.va.us.

WOODWARD, LUCINDA EMILY, psychology professor; b. Tacoma, Feb. 20, 1964; d. Douglas George and Clarice Woodward; m. Peter Reppert Galvin, Dec. 28, 1986; children: Mason Woodward Galvin, Madeline Lisa Galvin. BA, La. State U., 1989; PhD, U. Louisville, 2002. Dir. media rels. Sager-Bell, Inc., Louisville, 1993—95; dir. interactive pub. rels. Creative Alliance, Louisville, 1995—96; pub. rels. mgr. Klier Comm., Louisville, 1996—97; therapist Ind. U. Health Ctr., Bloomington, 2002—03; asst. prof. Ball State U., Muncie, Ind., 2003—. Contbr. articles various profl. jours. Faculty supr. Ball State Chpt. ARC, Muncie, 2004—06; disaster mental health counselor ARC, Muncie, 2005—06; jr. dir. Ind. Acad. Social Scis., Kokomo, Ind., 2005—06. Full Academic scholarship, U. Louisville, 1997-2002, Rsch. grant, Grawemeyer Found., 2002, Hollis Rsch. Found., 2004-2005. Mem.: APA (assoc.), Assn. Psychol. Sci. (assoc.), Soc. Southeastern Social Psychologists (assoc.). D-Liberal. Achievements include research in mediational model of secondary traumatic stress symptomology. Avocations: travel, literature, interior decorating. Office: Ball State U Dept Psychol Sci Muncie IN 47306 Office Phone: 765-285-1693. Business E-Mail: lewoodward@bsu.edu.

WOODWARD, MARY LOU, retired elementary school educator; b. Vandalia, Mo., Sept. 9, 1931; d. Carl Wesley and Katy Jane (Williams) Lovelace; m. A. Leon Woodward, Aug. 17, 1954; children: Charles Leon, Paul Louis, Robert Lee, William Lawrence. BA, N.E. Mo. U., 1954; MA, Washington U., St. Louis, 1980. Cert. elem. and secondary tchr. Tchr. elem. edn. Vandalia Pub. Schs., 1950-52, Berkeley (Mo.) Pub. Schs., 1954-55, St. Louis Pub. Schs., 1959-95. Mem. St. Louis tchrs. ret. com., ad hoc com. St. Louis Pub. Schs. Retirement Sys., 1988-95; cons. affective domain, presenter workshops for Title I Ctr., Insvc. Ctr., 1976-79; cons. spl. projects St. Louis Pub. Schs., 1979-82. Mem. Grand Oak Hill Neighborhood Assn., 1959—, pub. newsletter, 1960-75; block co-chmn. Operation Brightside, 1970-95; mem., spokesperson Mo. State Found., Columbia, 1990-1997; mem. Concerned Citizens Against Govt. Waste, Nat. Right to Work, Mo. Bot. Gardens, St. Louis Art Mus., St. Louis Zoo, Mo. Hist. Soc., St. Louis Sci. Ctr., St. Louis Geneal. Soc. Leader caregiver support group Oak Hill Presbyn. Ch., 1998—; pub. Caregiver Corner, 1999—. Mem. Mo. State Tchrs. Assn. (state exec. bd. 1984-90, pres. local chpt. 1992-94, pres.-elect local chpt. 1990-92, pub. newsletter 1972-92, Outstanding Educator of Yr. 1994), Ret. Tchrs. St. Louis, Am. Assn. Ret. Persons. Avocations: reading, travel, word puzzles, drama, research, computers. Home: 4158 Arsenal St Saint Louis MO 63116-3923

WOODWARD, NATALIE E., social studies educator; b. St. Johnsbury, Vt., Jan. 27, 1951; d. James Franklin and Catherine Therese (Fleming) Edgerton; m. Gregory Russell Woodward, May 20, 1972; children: Justin Russell, Theresa Claire, Sean Gregory. BS in Polit. Sci./Edn., U. Houston, 1973. Cert. treas. Tex. Tchr., dept. chair Cypress-Fairbanks Ind. Sch. Dist., Houston. Mem.: Tex. Coun. for Social Studies (Social Studies Tchr. of Yr. 1997), Nat. Coun. for Social Studies. Avocations: golf, reading, cooking. Office: Cypress Falls H S 9811 Huffmeister Rd Houston TX 77095

WOODWARD, SANDRA S., literature and language educator; b. San Diego, Jan. 4, 1948; d. Harold Herbert Woodward and Grace LaVerne Woodward (Usher). BA in English, Brigham Young U., Provo, Utah, 1969; MEd, U. Utah, Salt Lake City. Tchr. English Kennedy Jr. High, Salt Lake City, 1969—75; tchr. English, Latin Granger H.S., West Valley City, 1976—. Mem. nat. Latin exam adv. com. Am. Classical League, 1998—; chair world langs. dept. Granger H.S., West Valley City, Utah, 2000—, advisor nat. honor soc., Granger chpt., 2000—. Recipient Utah Lang. Arts Tchr. Yr., Utah Coun. Tchrs., 1980, Nat. Merit Tchg. award, Nat. Merit Scholarship Orgn., 1988, Excel Educator Yr., Granite Sch. Dist., 1999. Mem.: Utah Classical Assn. (acl liaison), Am. Classical League (nat. latin exam adv. com., coun. mem.). Office: Granger High School 3690 S 3600 W West Valley City UT 84119 Office Phone: 1-801-646-5320. Office Fax: 1-801-646-5336. Personal E-mail: sandra.woodward@granite.k12.ut.us.

WOODY, CAROL CLAYMAN, data processing executive; b. Bristol, Va., May 20, 1949; d. George Neal and Ida Mae Clayman; m. Robert William Woody, Aug. 19, 1972. BS in Math., Coll. William and Mary, Williamsburg, Va., 1971; MBA with distinction, Wake Forest U., 1979; PhD in Info. Sys., Nova Southeastern U., 2004. Programmer trainee GSA, 1971-72; systems engr. Citizens Fidelity Bank & Trust Co., Louisville, 1972-75; programmer/analyst-tng. coord. Blue Bell, Inc., Greensboro, N.C., 1975-79; supr. programming and tech. svcs. J.E. Baker Co., York, Pa., 1979-82; fin. design supr. bus. systems Lycoming divsn. AVCO, Stratford, Conn., 1982-83; project mgr. Yale U., New Haven, 1984-97; cons. ImageWork Technologies Corp., 1998-2001; co-owner Sign of the Sycamore, antiques; sr. mem. tech staff Software Engring. Inst. Carnegie Mellon U., 2001—. Mem. Data Processing Standards Bd., 1977, CICS/VS Adv. Council, 1975; speaker Nat. Fuse Conf., 1989, Aion expert systems nat. conf., 1990, bus. sch. Coll. William & Mary, 1994. Author various manuals; contbr. articles to profl. jours. IBM Corp. fellow, 1978; Stephen Bufton Meml. Ednl. Found. grantee, 1978-79. Mem. IEEE (section editor, 2003-, disting. spkr., 2005-), Am. Bus. Woman's Assn. (chpt. v.p. 1978-79, Merit award 1978), NAFE (founder shoreline network 1993), Assn. for System Mgmt., Assn. for Image Info. Mgmt., Project Mgmt. Inst., Network Inc. of Conn. (treas. 1996-97), Delta Omicron (alumni pres. 1973-75, regional chmn. 1979-82). Republican. Presbyterian. Home: PO Box 344 Sewickley PA 15143-0344

WOODY, MARY FLORENCE, nursing educator, academic administrator; b. Chambers County, Ala., Mar. 31, 1926; d. Hugh Ernest and May Lillie (Gilliland) W. Diploma, Charity Hosp. Sch. Nursing, 1947; BS, Columbia U., 1953, MA, 1955. Staff nurse Wheeler Hosp., Lafayette, Ala., 1947-48; polio nurse Willard Parker Hosp., NYC, 1949; staff nurse, supr. VA Hosp., Montgomery, Ala., 1950-53; faculty, field supr. nursing dept. Columbia U. Tchrs. Coll., NYC, 1955-56; asst. dir. nursing Emory U. Hosp., Atlanta, assoc. dir., DON, 1984-93; clin. asst. prof. Emory U. Sch. Nursing, Atlanta, 1956-68, interim dean, 1992-93; asst. dir., DON Grady Meml. Hosp., Atlanta, 1968-79; founding dean, prof. Auburn U. Sch. Nursing, Ala., 1979-84; disting. emeritus prof. Emory U., 2003—. Chair Ga. Statewide Master Planning Com. for Nursing and Nursing Edn., 1971-75; faculty preceptor patient care adminstrn. Sch. Public Health, U. Minn., 1977-79; bd. dirs. Wesley Woods Found. & Long Term Hosp.; chair bd. dirs. Am. Jour. Nursing Co., 1978-83. Recipent Spl. Recognition award 5th Dist. and Ga. Nurses Assn., 1978, 93, Disting. Achievement in Nursing Svc. award Columbia U. Tchrs. Coll. Alumni Assn., 1992, Jane Van de Vrede Outstanding Svc. to Citizens Ga. award Ga. League Nursing, Cert. Spl. Recognition award Ga. Nurses Assn., 1993, Internat. Founders award Sigma Theta Tau, 1999, The Marie Hippensteel award, 1999, Disting. Prof. award Emeritus Coll. Emory U., 2003; named Ga. Women Pioneer in Health Care, Ga. Commn. on Women and Ga. Womens History Month Com., 1998, Hall of Fame Nursing, Tchrs. Coll., Columbia, U., N.Y Fellow Am. Acad. Nursing (charter, Living Legend 1997); mem. Am. Nurses Assn., Nat. League Nursing, Am. Heart Assn., Emory U. Nell Hodgson Woodruff Sch. Nursing Alumni Assn. (hon.), Sigma Theta Tau (Marie Hippensteel Lingemald award for excellence in nursing 1999); mem. Nursing Tchr.'s Coll. Columbia U. of Hall of Fame (charter). Democrat. Address: 19488 Veterans Memorial Pkwy Lafayette AL 36862

WOODYARD, E. DORLEE See COLLINS-BROWN, E.

WOOFTER, VIVIEN PERRINE, interior designer, consultant; d. Orie Ray and Hazel Lucille (Bostic) Perrine; m. Perry Wilson Woofter, Oct. 5, 1952; children: James Perry, Lori Evan Hugh. BS in Home Econ., W.Va. U., 1952, LHD (hon.), 1998. Lic. interior designer Va., 2003. Interior designer GSA, Washington, 1968—76; head interior design The White Ho., 1976—77, U.S. Dept. Health & Human Services, 1977—81; sr. interior designer U.S. Dept. of State, 1981—88; dir. interiors & furnishings divsn. Overseas Buildings Ops., U.S. Dept. of State, 1988—. Mem. W.Va. U. Alumni Bd., Morgantown, 1994—; vol. mem. designer renovation W.Va. U. President's Ho. Com., 1996—2003; mem. W.Va. U. Found. Bd., 1999—; pres. Coll. Creative Arts Vis. Com., 2001—. Author: Develop. Furniture Standards- Phys. Handicap (Written up in Congl. Record, 1977); interior design Interior Design Hdqs. Bldg. for HHS (Fed. Design Coun. of Excellence, 1979), Riyadh Embassy, Paris, Buenos Aires - (Meritorius Honor & Superior Honor, 1988). Restoration work Met. Theater, Morgantown, 2003. Mem.: Internat. Interior Design Assoc. Achievements include development of Art Programs for all new embassies; Culturally Significan Program for US State Dept. Overseas Ident; a Maintenance Manual for US State Dept. Culturally Significant Buildingsofp; Featured in Articles, in Architectural Digest, Southern Accents, Paris Match, Chicago Tribune, other newspapersnchi. Home: 4856 N 35th Rd Arlington VA 22207 Office: Interiors & Furnishings Div Overseas Buildings Ops US Dept State Washington DC 20520 Personal E-mail: vivienwoofter@erols.com. E-mail: wooftervp@state.gov.

WOO HO, DOREEN, investment banker; b. Australia; m. James Woo Ho; 3 children. B, Smith Coll.; MA in East Asian Studies & Chinese History, Columbia U. With Citibank, Taipei; corr. Time mag., Phnom Penh, Cambodia; with Citibank, 1972—98; pres. Wells Fargo, 1998—. Bd. dir. San Francisco Opera Assn., 2001—, v.p. treas., exec. com. mem., chair audit com., vice chair dir. & officers com., fin. adv. com. Recipient Fin. Woman of Yr., San Francisco Fin. Women's Assn., 2004. Mailing: San Francisco Opera Assn 301 Van Ness Ave San Francisco CA 94102 Office: Wells Fargo 420 Montgomery St San Francisco CA 94163

WOOLDRIDGE, SUE ELLEN, federal agency administrator, lawyer; b. Riverside, Calif. d. Robert and Patricia Wooldridge. BA, U. Calif. Davis, 1983; JD, Harvard U., 1987. Bar: Calif., U.S. Supreme Ct. Assoc. Diepenbrock, Wulff, Plant & Hannegan, Sacramento, 1987—94; spl. asst. atty. gen. State of Calif., Sacramento, 1994—98; founding ptnr. Riegles Campos & Kenyon LLP, Sacramento, 1999—2001; gen. counsel Calif. Fair Polit. Practices Com., 2000; dep. chief of staff US Dept. Interior, Washington, DC, 2001—04, solicitor, 2004—05; asst. atty. gen. Environment & Nat. Resources Divsn. US Dept. Justice, Washington, DC, 2005—. Office: US Dept Justice 950 Pennsylvania Ave NW Rm 2141 Washington DC 20530*

WOOLHANDLER, ANN, law educator; b. Shreveport, La., 1953; BA, Yale U., 1975; JD, Harvard U., 1978. Bar: La. 1978. Atty. pvt. practice, New Orleans, 1978—85, 1988—90; Bigelow Tchg. fellow & lectr. U. Chgo., 1985—86; asst. prof. U. Cin., 1986—88; vis. asst. prof. Loyola U., New Orleans, 1990; vis. assoc. prof. Tulane U., New Orleans, 1990—91, assoc. prof., 1991—97, prof., 1997—2002; vis. prof. Boston U., 1998, Harvard U., Cambridge, Mass., 1999; vis. assoc. prof. U. Va. Sch. Law, Charlottesville, 1994—95, vis. prof., 2001, prof., 2002—, now William Minor Lile prof. law, Class of 1948 prof. scholarly rsch. law. Bd. gov. La. State Bar Assn., 1993. Office: U Va Sch Law 580 Massie Rd Charlottesville VA 22903 Office Phone: 434-924-4411. E-mail: naw2b@virginia.edu.

WOOLLEY, DONNA PEARL, lumber company executive; b. Drain, Oreg., Jan. 3, 1926; d. Chester A. and Mona B. (Cheever) Rydell; m. Harold Woolley, Dec. 27, 1952 (dec. Sept. 1970); children: Daniel, Debra, Donald. Diploma, Drain High Sch. Sec. No. Life Ins. Co., Eugene, Oreg., 1943—44; sec., bookkeeper D & W Lumber Co., Sutherlin, Oreg., 1944, Woolley Logging Co. & Earl Harris Lumber Co., Drain, 1944—70; pres. Woolley Logging Co., 1970—, Smith River Lumber Co., 1970—, Mt. Baldy Mill, Drain, 1970—81, Drain Plywood Co., 1970—81, Woolley Enterprises, Inc., Drain, 1973—, Eagle's View Mgmt. Co., Inc., Eugene, 1981—. Bd. dirs. Wildlife Safari, Winston, 1991, Oreg. Cmty. Found., Portland, 1990-99, chair, 1997-99; bd. trustees Linfield Coll., McMinnville, U. Oreg. Found., Eugene, Oreg. Trl. coun. Boy Scouts Am., 1980—, World Forestry Ctr., Portland, 1990, Umpqua C.C. Fedn., 2001. Recipient Pioneer award, U. Oreg., 1982, Pres.'s medal, 2005, Econ. and Social Devel. award, Soroptimist Club, 1991, First Citizen of Eugene award, 2000, Aubrey Watzek award, Lewis & Clark Coll., 2001, Howard Vollum award, Associated Fund Raisers in Philanthropy Oreg. chpt., 2001, Pioneer award, Umpqua C.C., 2003, Hart Pioneer award, Wildlife Safari, 2003, Pres. medal, U. Oreg., 2005, Paul Harris fellow, Rotary, 2006. Mem. Oreg. Women's Forum, Pacific Internat. Trapshooting Assn., Amateur Trapshooting Assn., Eugene C. of C. (bd. dirs. 1989-92), Arlington Club, Town Club (bd. dirs., pres.), Sunnydale Grange, Cottage Grove/Eugene Rod & Gun Club. Republican. Avocations: golf, travel. Office: Eagle's View Mgmt Co Inc 1399 Franklin Blvd Eugene OR 97403-1979 Office Phone: 541-683-0771.

WOOLLEY, JEAN GIBSON, retired instructional designer, consultant; b. L.A., Oct. 13, 1939; d. Robert Everett and Marie Laura (Butler) G.; m. William Jon Woolley, July 29, 1961; children: William Allen, Pamela Jean, Stephen Douglas, Jennifer Lynn. BA, U. Colo., 1961; MS, Ind. U., 1966. Cert. supr./coord., curriculum specialist, English and social studies tchr., Wis. Tchr. grade 4 Plaza Elem. Sch., Virginia Beach, Va., 1961-63, East Elem. Sch., Martinsville, Ind., 1963-64; comm./social sci. inst. educator Moraine Park Tech. Coll., Fond du Lac, Wis., 1976-81; curriculum planner Moraine Park, Fond du Lac, 1981-86, dean gen. edn./instrnl. support, 1986-97; mgr. tng. and cons. Wis. Instrnl. Design Sys., Ripon, 1997—2005, ret., 2005. Gen. edn. task force Wis. tech. Coll. Sys., Madison, 1989-94, mem. bd. gen. edn. deans, 1986-97, chmn., 1996-97. Chpt. advisor Alpha Delta Pi at Ripon (Wis.) Coll., 1969-75, 89-95; Sunday sch. tchr., liturgist at local ch., Ripon, 1986—. Recipient Excellence in Vocat. Adminstrn. award Moraine Park Vocat. Assn., 1986, 94. Mem. Am. Vocat. Assn., Wis. Vocat. Assn. Methodist. Avocations: downhill skiing, biking, travel, opera. Home: 611 Hillside Ter Ripon WI 54971-1605 Office: WIDS Worldwide Instrnl Design Sys 203 Blackburn St PO Box 67 Ripon WI 54971-0067

WOOLLEY, MARGARET ANNE (MARGOT WOOLLEY), architect; b. Bangor, Maine, Feb. 4, 1946; d. George Walter and Anne Geneva (Collins) W.; m. Gerard F. Vasisko, June 22, 1985. BA, Vassar Coll., 1969; MArch, Columbia U., 1974. Registered arch. N.Y. Urban designer Mayor's Office Lower Manhattan Devel., 1974-76, Mayor's Office Devel., N.Y.C., 1976-78; project mgr. Office Econ. Devel., N.Y.C., 1978-81, dep. dir. design and engring., 1981-83; dep. dir. design. N.Y.C. Pub. Devel. Corp., 1983-85, asst. v.p. design, 1985—86; v.p design N.Y.C. Econ. Devel. Corp., 1986—94; dep. program dir. corrections program unit N.Y.C. Dept. Design and Constrn., 1996-97, program dir. cts. and juvenile justice units, 1997—2001, asst. commr. architecture and engring., 2001—. Mem. N.Y. State Licensing Bd. Architecture, 1994—2004; mem. archtl. registration exam. com. Nat. Coun. Archtl. Registration Bds., 1995—99, mem. practice analysis steering com., 1999—2001; chair archtl. registration exam. specifications task force, 2000—01; mem. archtl. registration exam. devel. task force, 2001—04, Integrated Scoring Task Force, 2004—05; chair Intern Devel. Program/Archl. Registration Examination Task Force, 2005—06; mem. com. exams Nat. Coun. Archtl. Registration Bds.s, 2005—06. Mem. assoc. bd. of regents L.I. Coll. Hosp., Bklyn., 1982—93, mem. planning and devel. com., 1983—93, pres. assoc. bd. of regents, 1988—89; bd. dirs. AIA Found., 2005—. William Kinne Fellows scholar, 1973. Mem. AIA (bd. dirs. N.Y.C. chpt. 1988-90, nat. pub. archs. steering com. 1993-95) N.Y. State Assn. Archs. (bd. dirs. 1990-92, 2006—), Heights Casino Club, Vassar Club, Jr. League. Home: 135 Willow St Brooklyn NY 11201-2255

WOOLLEY, MARY ELIZABETH, science administrator, advocate; b. Chgo., Mar. 16, 1947; John Joseph and Ellen Louise (Bakke) McEnerney; m. John Stuart Woolley, Dec. 6, 1969 (div. 1985); children: George Newsom, Nora Ellen; m. Michael Howland Campbell, Jan. 1, 1989 (div. 2004). BS, Stanford U., 1969; MA, San Francisco State U., 1972; postgrad., U. Calif., San Francisco and Berkeley, 1974-75. Assoc. dir. Inst. Epidemiology and Behavioral Medicine, San Francisco, 1979-81; adminstr. Med. Rsch. Inst. of San Francisco, 1981-82, v.p., adminstr., 1982-86, v.p., exec. dir., 1986-90; pres. Research! Am., Alexandria, Va., 1990—. Cons. in fin. and mgmt. NIH, Bethesda, Md., 1984—92; adj. faculty U. Calif. Sch. Pub. Health, Berkeley, 1983—92, mem. Dean's adv. coun., 1995—2002; founding mem. Whitehead Inst. Bd. Assocs., 1995—; bd. dirs. Lovelace Inst., Respiratory Rsch. Inst., vice chmn., 1999—2004; bd. dirs. Children's Rsch. Inst., Washington, 2003—; lectr. to profl. assns.; mem. bd. visitors Harvard U. Sch. Pub. Health, Cambridge, 2002—; mem. dean's coun. Johns Hopkins Sch. of Nursing, 2002—; mem. bd. advisors IBM Life Scis., 2003—. Editor Jour. of Soc. Rsch. Adminstrs., 1986-89, mem. editl. rev. bd., 1989-95; mem. editl. bd. Jour. Women's Health, 1992-2003, Sci. Comm., 1994—; contbr. articles and editls. to profl. jours. Bd. dirs. Kensington (Calif.) Edn. Found., 1986-89, Enterprise for H.S. Students, 1990-92; mem. capital campaign com. Calif. Shakespeare Festival, 1989-91, v.p. Med. Rsch. Assns. Am., 1993-95; bd. advisors Friends of Cancer Rsch., 1996—; bd. dirs. Nat. Patient Safety Found., 1998-2000, Friends of Nat. Inst. of Nursing Rsch., 2001—. Recipient Silver Touchstone award Am. Hosp. Assn., 1994, Disting. Svc. award Columbia Coll. Physicians and Surgeons, 1994, Advocacy award Fedn. Am. Socs. Exptl. Biology, 1998, Advocacy award Friends Nat. Inst. Nursing Rsch., 1999, Leadership award Coun. Scientific Soc. Pres.'s, 1999, Advocacy award Friends of Dental Rsch., 2002; honored Women of Vision Am. Com. Weizmann Inst. Sci., 2004, 05. Fellow AAAS; mem. Assn. Ind. Rsch. Insts. (pres.-elect 1987-89, pres. 1989-90), Inst. Medicine (elected), Soc. Rsch. Adminstrs. (bd. dirs. 1986-90, bd. advisors 1990-93, Hartford-Nicholson Svc. award 1990, Disting. Contbn. to Rsch. Adminstrn. award, 1993), Calif. Biomed. Rsch. Assn. (bd. govs. 1986-90), Nat. Press Club. Democrat. Office: Research! Am 1101 King St Ste 520 Alexandria VA 22314-3067 Office Phone: 703-739-2577. Business E-Mail: mwoolley@researchamerica.org.

WOOLLS, ESTHER BLANCHE, library science educator; b. Louisville, Mar. 30, 1935; d. Arthur William and Esther Lennie (Smith) Sutton; m. Donald Paul Woolls, Oct. 21, 1953 (div. Nov. 1982); 1 son, Arthur Paul AB in Fine Arts, Ind. U., 1958, MA in Libr. Sci., 1962, PhD in Libr. Sci., 1973. Elem. libr. Hammond (Ind.) Pub. Schs., 1958-65, libr. coord., 1965-67, Roswell (N.Mex.) Ind. Schs., 1967-70; prof. libr. sci. U. Pitts., 1973-97; prof., dir. Sch. Lib. and Info. Sci. San Jose (Calif.) State U., 1997—2005; consulting editor LibRs. Unlimited, Glendale, Calif., 2005—. Exec. dir. Beta Phi Mu, 1981-95. Author: The School Library Media Manager, 1995, 3d edit., 2004, So You're Going to Run a Library, 1995, Ideas for School Library Media Centers, 1996, Whole School Library Handbook, 2004; co-author: Information Literacy, 1999; editor: Continuing Professional Education and IFLA: Past, Present, and a Vision for the Future, 1993, Delivering Lifelong Continuing Professional Education Across Space and Time, 2001. Fulbright scholar, 1995-96; recipient Disting. Svc. award Pa. Sch. Librs. Assn., 1993. Mem. ALA (mem. coun. 1985-89, 95—2003), Am. Assn. Sch. Librs. (bd. dirs. 1983-88, pres. 1993-94, Disting. Svc. award 1997), Pa. Learning Resources Assn. (pres. 1984-85), Internat. Assn. Sch. Librs. (pres. 1998-2001), Internat. Fedn. Libr. Assns. (mem. standing com. sch. librs. sect. 1991-99, sec. Continuing Profl. Edn. Round Table 2000—). Home: 144 S 4th St # 637 San Jose CA 95112 Office: Libraries Unlimited 2040 Verdugo Blvd Glendale CA 91208

WOOLRIDGE, KAY ELLEN JONES, music educator; d. Roland Page and Vivian Mae Williams Jones; m. Thomas Cofer Woolridge, Jan. 25, 1992; 1 child, Robert Thomas. B in Mus. Edn., Longwood U., Farmville, Va, 1977. Music tchr. Colonial Heights (Va.) City Pub. Sch., 1977—. Named Tchr. of Yr., Tussing Elem. Sch., 2000—01. Mem.: Nat. Assn. Music Edn., Alpha Delta Kappa (chpt. president-elect, chpt. pres., dist. pres.), Sigma Alpha Iota (coll. chpt. treas.). Office: Tussing Elem Sch 5501 Conduit Rd Colonial Heights VA 23834 Office Phone: 804-524-3440. E-mail: kay_woolridge@colonialhts.net.

WOOLSEY, LYNN C., congresswoman; b. Seattle, Nov. 3, 1937; 4 children. BS, U. San Francisco, 1981. Mgr. human resources Harris Digital Telephone, 1969—80; owner Woolsey Personnel Svs., 1980—92; mem. U.S. Congress from 6th Calif. dist., 1993—, ranking mem. edn. reform subcom. ho. com. edn. and the workforce. Mem. Petaluma City Coun., 1984-92 Mem.: NOW, LWV, Sierra Club. Democrat. Office: US Ho Reps 2263 Rayburn Ho Office Bldg Washington DC 20515-0506 Address: Santa Rosa Dist Office Ste 200 1101 College Ave Santa Rosa CA 95404 also: San Rafael Dist Office Ste 354 1050 Northgate Dr San Rafael CA 94903*

WOOLSEY, PATRICIA JANE, secondary school educator; b. El Campo, Tex., May 11, 1949; d. Vencil Albert and Hattie Sophie Andel; m. Ronnie Wayne Woolsey, Sept. 6, 1969; children: Danny Wayne, Jon Joseph. BA, U. Houston, 1976. Cert. tchr. Tex. Tchr. Palacios (Tex.) Ind. Sch. Dist., 1997—. Home: 842 Cr 162 Bay City TX 77414

WOOLSON, GLORIA JEAN, education educator; b. Syracuse, NJ, Nov. 7, 1941; d. Glen James Manuel and Mattie Florence Turner. BA, SUNY, Oswego, 1965, MA in Curriculum Devel., 1985. 5th grade tchr. Auburn City Sch. Dist., NY, 1965—66; 6th grade tchr. Jordan-Elbridge Ctrl. Sch. Dist., Jordan, NY, 1966—70, 3d grade tchr., 1970—2002; adj. tchr. Cayuga CC, Auburn, 2004—. Dir. one-rm. sch. program Spafford Hist. Soc.; deacon, mem. choir, clk. trustee, moderator Plainville United Ch. of Christ, NY. Recipient Excellence in Tchg. award, Syracuse U. Sch. Edn., 1996, Spl. Svc. award, Onondaga County Tchrs. Assn., 1997. Mem.: NY State Ret. Tchrs., Jordan-Elbridge Edn. Assn. (sec., bldg. rep., social dir.). Avocations: antiques, exercise, reading, travel. Home: 7688 Tater Rd Memphis NY 13112-8755

WOOLSTON, CAROL ANN, elementary school educator; d. Grace Geraldine Schaap; m. William Oliver Woolston, Sept. 28, 2002; 1 child, Sean Joseph Loyd. BA, Calif. State U., Fullerton, 1985; MA, Concordia U., Irvine, Calif., 2006. Cert. tchr. Calif. Tchr. Aliso Viejo Mid. Sch., Calif., 1996—. Mem.: Nat. Sci. Tchr. Assn. Personal E-mail: carolloyd@cox.net.

WOOLSTON-CATLIN, MARIAN, psychiatrist; b. Seattle, Jan. 20, 1931; d. Howard Brown and Katharine Nichols (Dally) Woolston; m. Randolph Catlin Jr., July 5, 1959; children: Laura Louise, Jennifer Woolston, Randolph III. BA cum laude, Vassar Coll., 1951; MD, Harvard U., 1955. Diplomate Nat. Bd. Med. Examiners. Intern in pediatric medicine Children's Hosp., Boston, 1956, asst. resident in pediatric medicine, 1956; resident in psychiatry Mass. Mental Health Ctr., Boston, 1957-59; fellow in child psychiatry Tavistock Clin., London, 1960; Commonwealth fellow in child psychiatry Harvard U. at Gaebler Children's Unit, Waltham, Mass., 1975-78, clin. instr. psychiatry, 1978-79; pvt. practice Wellesley Hills, Mass., 1978-91, Medfield, Mass., 1991—. Clin. instr. psychiatry Harvard U. at Mass. Mental Health Ctr., Boston, 1957-59, 78-82, Tufts U. at Mass. Mental Health Ctr., 1957-59; mem. exec. bd. Parents' and Children's Svcs., Boston, 1983-86. Designer H.H. Hunnewell Meml. Garden for New Eng. Flower Show Mass. Hort. Soc., 1975 (Ames Cup award). Mem. exec. bd. Ext. Divsn. New Eng. Conservatory Music, 1972-75; charter mem. reuse com. Medfield State Hosp., 1992—; corporator Schepens Eye Rsch. Inst., 2005—; mem. adv. bd. Women's Eye Health Task Force, 2005—. Fellow Am. Acad. Child and Adolescent Psychiatry; mem. AMA, Am. Psychiat. Assn. (life), Mass. Psychiat. Assn., Mass. Med. Soc., New Eng. Coun. Child and Adolescent Psychiatry (hon.), Boston Vassar Club (exec. bd. 1963-75), Hills Garden Club Wellesley (exec. bd. and design chief 1973-75). Episcopalian. Avocations: landscape design, sculpting.

WOOLWORTH, SUSAN VALK, primary school educator; b. Toledo, Ohio, Apr. 24, 1954; d. Robert Earl and Alice (Melick) Valk; children: Alison Valk, Andrew Baker. BA, Pine Manor Jr. Coll., Chestnut Hill, Mass., 1974; BS, Boston U., 1976. Tchr. kindergarten Lancaster (Pa.) Country Day Sch., 1986—. Bd. dirs. YWCA, Lancaster, Pa.; past bd. dirs. Fulton Opera House, Planned Parenthood, Vis. Nurse Assn., Hands-On House. Mem.: Jr. League (sustainer), Sigma Gamma. Republican. Episcopalian. Avocations: walking, gardening, tennis, decorating.

WOOTEN, CAROL G., music educator, minister; MusB in Edn., Gordon Coll., 1987; student, Gordon-Conwell Theol. Sem., 1999. Cert. tchr. Mass. Music dir. Danvers Pub. Schs., Danvers, Mass., 1988—92; dir. of music Orange UMC, Chapel Hill, NC, 1992—96; dir. music and arts ministry Epworth United Meth. Ch., Durham, NC, 2000—05; founder and condr. Triangle Youth Music Chorus, Durham and Chapel Hill, NC, 2000; chaplain resident Hosps. U. N.C., Chapel Hill, NC, 2006—. Instr. pvt. lessons, 1976—96; adjudicator, 1998—; dir. various workshops, 1998—. Founding dir. Arts Ministry, Inc., Durham and Chapel Hill, 2002—. Recipient First Pl. award, Jubilate Choral Soc., 1987. Mem.: Am. Choral Dirs. Assn. (life), Chorister's Guild (chpt. pres. 1994—96), Worship List (advisor and chaplain 1998—2003). Independent. Avocations: outdoors, reading, travel.

WOOTEN, JOAN HEDRICH, minister; b. Washington, Jan. 4, 1953; d. Albert Louis Hedrich and Maxine Keller Smith; m. David Randall Wooten, Jan. 11, 1983; children: Michael, Sarah. BA, Coll. William and Mary, 1975; MA, Bryn Mawr Coll., Mass., 1978; MDiv, Gordon-Conwell Theol. Sem., 1981; ThM, Duke U. Div. Sch., Durham, N.C., 1987. Ordained 1982. Chaplain U.S. Navy, Oak Harbor, Wash., 1982—84, Yokosuka, Japan, 1984—86, Norfolk, Va., 1987—90, res. chaplain, 1990—, capt.; pastoral counselor Episcopal Diocese of So. Va., Norfolk, 1990—93; campus min. Presbytery of Ea. Va., Portsmouth, 1993—2001; interim and stated supply pastor Presbytery Fla., 2003—. Doctoral fellow Union Theol. Sem., Richmond, 2001—. Singer Va. Symphony Chorus, Norfolk, 1992—2001. Decorated Commendation medal U.S. Navy. Presbyterian. Avocations: music, languages, cooking. Personal E-mail: joanwooten@aol.com.

WOOTEN, JULIE, secondary school educator; b. Dallas, Dec. 26, 1970; m. Kenneth Wooten, July 23, 2000; 1 child, Ryan. BA, Sam Houston State U., Huntsville, Tex., 1993. Cert. tchr. secondary sch. Tex., 1997. Tchr. H.S. Brownsboro (Tex.) Ind. Sch. Dist., 1994—2001, Van (Tex.) Ind. Sch. Dist., 2002—. Tchr. Sunday Sch. Pruitt Bapt. Ch., Van, 2005—06. Avocations: reading, crossword puzzles, swimming, travel. Office: Van High School Po Box 697 N Maple Street Van TX 75790 Office Phone: 903-963-8623. Home Fax: 903-963-5591; Office Fax: 903-963-5591.

WORACHEK, SUSAN, music educator; m. James Allen Worachek, July, 1978; children: Jennifer Ann, Sarah Elizabeth. BS, Miami U., Oxford, Ohio, 1974; MEd, Xavier U., Cin., 1981. Cert. tchr., Ohio. Music educator Norwood (Ohio) Pub. Schs., 1974-85; gifted students educator P.A.G.E., Inc., Cin., 1992-94; coord. musical arts program Cin. Hills Christian Acad., 1995—, coord. laptop program, 1995—. Dist. chmn. cultural arts contest Valley Area Coun. PTA, Cin, 1990-93, advisor, 1990-91; chmn. bd. Christian edn. Messiah Luth. Ch., Cin., 1993-96; mem. supt.'s adv. coun. Princeton Bd. Edn., Cin., 1993-95; mem. bus. adv. com. Glendale Elem. Sch., Cin., 1993-95, pres. No. Hills Piano Tchr's. Forum, 1991-93, Glendale PTA, 1993-95; judge Ohio Fedn. Music Clubs, Cin., 1986-94. Mem. Glendale Lyceum, Village Gardeners, Delta Omicron. Avocations: tennis, bridge, music. Office: Cin Hills Christian Acad 11312 Snider Rd Cincinnati OH 45249-2222

WORBY, RACHAEL BETH, conductor; b. Nyack, N.Y., Apr. 21, 1949; d. Louis Lincoln and Diana (Zacharia) W.; m. David Obst, Sept. 7, 1986. BS in Music, Crane Sch. of Music, 1971; postgrad., Ind. U., 1971-72; ABD, Brandeis U., 1979. Music dir. N.H. Philharmonic, Manchester, 1979-82, New Eng. Conservatory Youth Orch., Boston, 1980-82; Exxon asst. conductor Spokane (Wash.) Symphony, 1982-84; asst. conductor L.A. Philharmonic, 1983-87; music dir. Carnegie Hall, N.Y.C., from 1984, Wheeling (W.Va.) Symphony, 1986—. Instr. New Eng. Conservatory of Music, Boston, 1979-82, MIT, Boston, 1980-82; lectr. N.Y. Philharmonic, N.Y.C., 1978-86. Rockefeller Found. grantee, 1981, Exxon/NEA grantee, 1982. Mailing: 87 N Raymond Ave Ste 500 Pasadena CA 91103

WORDEN, KATHARINE COLE, sculptor; b. NYC, May 4, 1925; d. Philip Gillette and Katharine (Pyle) Cole; m. Frederic G. Worden, Jan. 8, 1944; children: Fred, Dwight, Philip, Barbara, Katharine. Student, Potters Ch., Tucson, 1940-42, Sarah Lawrence Coll., 1942-44. Exhibited in group shows at Royce Galleries, Galerie Francoise Besnard, Paris, Cooling Gallery, London, Galerie Schumacher, Munich, Selected Artists Gallery, N.Y.C., Art Inst. Boston, Reid Gallery, Nashville, Weiner Gallery, N.Y.C., Boston Athanaeum, House of Humor and Satire, Gabrovo, Bulgaria, 1983, Newport Bay Club, 1984; pvt. collections Grand Palais, Paris, Dakar and Bathurst, Africa. Occupl. therapist psychopathic ward L.A. County Gen. Hosp., 1953-57; Headstart vol., Watts, Calif., 1965-67; tchr. sculpture Watts Towers Art Ctr., 1967-69; participant White House Women Doers Luncheon meeting, 1968; dir. Cambridgeport Problem Ctr., Cambridge, Mass., 1969-71; mem. Jud. Nominating Commn., 1976-79; bd. overseers Boston Mus. Fine Arts, 1980-83; bd. govs. Newport Seamens Ch. Inst., 1989-91; tustee Comm. Rsch., Miami, Fla., 1960-69, chmn. bd., 1966-69; trustee Newport Art Mus., 1984-86, 92-94, Jamestown Cmty. Theatre, 1994-97, 99-2005, 06—, Newport Health Found., 1986-91, Hawthorne Sea Fund, 1990-93; bd. dirs. Boston Ctr. for Arts, 1976-80, Child and Family Svcs. Newport County, 1983-97, 99-2005, 2006—. Mem. Common Cause (Mass adv. bd. 1971-72, dir. 1974-75), Mass. Civil Liberties Union (exec. bd. 1973-74, dir. 1976-77). Home: 9 Meadow Ln Jamestown RI 02835 Office Phone: 401-423-1758.

WORDEN, VIRGINIA HILL, academic administrator, lawyer; b. Florence, SC, Dec. 4, 1947; d. Albert Michael and Virginia Copeland Hill; m. Geoffrey Field Worden; children: Annette Field, Katherine Hill, Zachary Albert. BA in Econs., Randolph-Macon Woman's Coll., Lynchburg, Va., 1969; MA in Econs., Vanderbilt U., Nashville, Tenn., 1973; JD, NYU, NYC, 1975; postgrad., Union Theol. Sem., NYC, 1987—93. Assoc. Davis, Pock & Warwell, NYC, 1975—80; co-founder, pres. Bridges, Inc. homeless outreach orgn., 1988—95; interim pres. Randolph-Macon Woman's Coll., 2006—. Trustee Kent Pl. Sch., 1986—98, pres. bd. trustees, 1993—97, Randolph-Macon Woman's Coll., 1992—2002, 1997—2000; mem. poverty initiative Union Theol. Sem., 2005—; bd. dirs. NC Outward Bound Sch., 1983—94, vice-chmn., 1992—94; bd. dirs. Outward Bound USA, 2000—06, vice chmn. expeditionary learning, 1993—. Address: 890 Mountain Ave Ste 4 New Providence NJ 07974

WORELL, JUDITH P., psychologist, educator; b. N.Y.C. d. Moses and Dorothy Goldfarb; m. Leonard Worell, Aug. 11, 1947 (div.); children: Amy, Beth, Wendy; m. H.A. Smith, Mar. 23, 1985 BS magna cum laude, Queens Coll., 1950; MA, Ohio State U., 1952, PhD in Clin. Psychology, 1954; DHL (hon.), Colby-Sawyer Coll., 1993. Research assoc. Iowa Psychopathic Hosp., Iowa City, 1957-59; research assoc. Okla. State U., 1960-66; asst. prof. U. Ky., Lexington, 1969-71, assoc. prof., 1971-75, prof. ednl. and counseling psychology, 1976—, dir. counseling psychology tng. program, 1980-93, chairperson dept. ednl. and counseling psychology, 1993-97, prof. emerita, 1999—. Author: (with C.M. Nelson) Managing Instructional Problems, 1974; (with W.E. Stilwell) Psychology for Teachers and Students, 1981; Psychological Development in the Elementary Years, 1982; (with Fred Danner) The Adolescent as Decision-maker: Applications to Development and Education, 1989; (with Pam Remer) Feminist Perspectives in Therapy: An Empowerment Model for Women, 1992; (with N. Johnson) Shaping the Future of Feminist Psychology: Education, Research, and Practice, 1997, (with Norine Johnson & Michael Roberts) Beyond Appearance: A New Look at Adolescent Girls, 1999, Encyclopedia of Women and Gender: Sex Similarities and Differences and the Impact of Society on Gender, 2001, (with Pam Remer) Feminist Perspectives in Therapy: Empowering Diverse Women, 2003, (with Carol Goodheart) Oxford Handbook of Girls' and Women's Psychological Health, 2006; assoc. editor Jour. Cons. and Clin. Psychology, 1976-79, mem. editl. bd., 1984-89; assoc. editor Psychol. Women Quar., 1984-89, editor, 1989-95; mem. editorial bd. Sex Roles, 1984-2000, Psychol. Assessment, 1991-97, Clin. Psychology Rev., 1991-97, Women and Therapy, 1992-2000; cons., reviewer 10 jours.; contbr. articles to profl. jours. Named U. Ky. Campus Woman of Yr., 1976, Outstanding Univ. Grad. prof., 1991, Disting. Ky. psychologist, 1990; USPHS fellow, 1953; NIMH rsch. grantee, 1962-69. Fellow APA (pres. Clin. Psychology of Women 1986-88, chmn. com. state assn. rels. 1982-83, fellow selection divsn. 35 com. 1983-84, policy and planning bd. 1989-92, publs. and comm. bd. 1992-99, chair 1996-98, chair jours. com., pres. divsn. psychology of women 1997-98, Disting. Leader for Women in Psychology 1990, Carolyn Wood Sherif award, 2001, Psychology of Women Heritage award 2004, coun. rep. 2000-02, chair women's caucus 2002) Soc. Psychol. Study of Social Issues (chmn. fellow com. 2005-), Ky. Psychol. Assn. (pres. 1981-82, rep. at large 1995-97), Southeastern Psychol. Assn. (exec. coun. mem.-at-large, pres.-elect 1993-94 pres. 1994-95), Am. Women in Psychology, Phi Beta Kappa. Home: 3892 Gloucester Dr Lexington KY 40510-9729 Office: U Ky Dept Ednl and Counseling Psychology 245 Dickey Hl Lexington KY 40506-0017 E-mail: jworell@alltel.net.

WORK, JANE ALLEN, psychologist; b. Phila., May 17, 1916; d. Robert Louis and Lois (McKinney) Allen; m. Homer R. Allen (dec. 1963); children: Robert M., Emily Allen Berg, Homer G.; m. William McClean Work, 1979. BA, Westminster Coll., 1965; MA, Case Western Res. U., 1967, PhD, 1973. Lic. psychologist, Penn. Sch. psychologist City of Cleve., 1968-70; psychologist spl. edn. dist. Lake County, Ill., 1970-73, Coop. Ednl. Svc. Agy. 18, Burlington, Wis., 1974-76; dir. psychol. svcs. Marion (Ohio) Area Counseling Ctr., 1976-78; pvt. practice psychology Pitts., 1979—99; freelance writer Pittsburgh, 1987—. Instr. Loyola U., Chgo., Roosevelt U., Chgo., 1973-74, Nat. Sch. Edn., Evanston, Ill., 1974. Mem. Pa. Task Force for Women, Harrisburg, 1986. Mem. APA, Pa. Psychol. Assn., NOW (pres. South Hills chpt. 1987-88, membership dir. 1992-94), Soc. for the Sci. Study of Sexuality, Alumni Coun. Case Western Res. U., Sylvania Hills Hound and Hunt Club, Entre Nous Club. Democrat. Presbyterian. Home: Apt B305 1290 Boyce Rd Pittsburgh PA 15241-3933

WORK, JANE MAGRUDER, retired professional society administrator; b. Owensboro, Ky., Mar. 30, 1927; d. Orion Noel and Willie May (Stallings) Magruder; m. William Work, Nov. 26, 1960; children: Paul MacGregor, Jeffrey William. BA, Furman U., 1947; MA, U. Wis., 1948; PhD, Ohio State U., 1959. Dir. radio U. South Miss., Hattisburg, 1948-51; pub. rels. assoc. Ohio Fuel Gas Co./Columbia Gas, Columbus, 1952-62; adj. prof. comm. Pace U., N.Y.C., 1963-75; dir. speechmodule ERIC, Washington, 1975-76; mgr. orgn. liaison, dir. legis. analysis Nat. Assn. Mfgs., Washington, 1977-84, asst. v.p. legis. analysis, 1984-87, v.p. legis. analysis, 1987-93, v.p. mem. comm., 1993-2001, ret., 2001. Adv. bd. pub. affairs NYU Grad. Bus. Sch., 1983-87; adv. bd. Prodn. Mag., 1984-87; cons. IBM, Xerox, 1963-77. Contbr. articles to profl. jours. Mem. transition team Consumer Product Safety Commn., Washington, 1979—80; chair No. Va. Pvt. Industry Coun., Fairfax County, 1979—85; co-chair Va. Gov.'s Employment & Tng. Task Force, Richmond, 1983; bd. dirs. Alzheimer's Assn. Nat. Capital Area, 2002—. Named to Acad. Women Achievers YWCA, 1987. Mem.: World Future Soc. (steering network 1993 Gen. Assembly), The Planning Forum (bd. dirs. Capital chpt. 1990—93), Speech Comm. Assn. (sect. chmn. 1980—82), Am. Soc. Assn. Execs. (rsch. adv. com. 1989—97), Nat. Assn. Industry-Edn. Coop. (bd. dirs. 1983—2001), Issue Mgmt. Assn. (bd. dirs. 1985—88), Future Homemakers of Am. (bd. dirs. 1985—88), Pi Kappa Delta (hon.), Alpha Psi Omega (hon.). Republican. Unitarian Universalist. Avocations: gardening, volunteering. Home: 6245 Cheryl Dr Falls Church VA 22044-1809

WORK, JANICE RENÉ, pediatric dentist; b. Porterville, Calif., Aug. 22, 1944; d. Weldon and Vivian May (Campbell) W. AA, Porterville Jr. Coll., 1964; BA, Brigham Young U., 1967, MFA, 1978; DDS, Georgetown U., 1984; pediatric cert., U. Nebr. Med. Ctr., 1991. Diplomate Am. Bd. Pediatric Dentists, 1998. Dentist Dedicated Dental Svcs., Media, Pa., 1985, Lehigh Dental Assocs., Bethlehem, Pa., 1985-86, Grenfell Regional Health Svcs., Forteau, Labrador, Nfld., Canada, 1986-88, Temporary Dental Help, Manhattan Beach, Calif., 1991, Dr. Randall G. Turner, Torrance, Calif., 1991, United Health Ctr. San Juaquim Valley, Inc., Huron, Calif., 1991; pediatric dentist Sacramento, 1992—. Mem. cleft palate panel The Sutter Hosp., 1992—. Chair Prevent Abuse and Neglect through Dental Awareness (PANDA) com., Sacramento; mem. bd. Sacramento Dist. Dental Found., 1993-98, Sacramento Dist. Midwinter Com., 1994-98, Sacramento Dist. Health Com., 1995-98. Fellow Acad. Gen. Dentistry, Acad. Dentistry Internat. Avocations: scuba diving, skiing, biking, camping. Home: PO Box 582880 Elk Grove CA 95758-0049

WORKMAN, JULIA L., music educator; b. Washington; d. Robert and Winnifred Geweke; children: John, Paul, Peter. B Music Edn., Ind. U., Bloomington, 1973; postgrad., U. Wis., Madison. Cert. tchr. Minn., 1974. Orch. tchr. Rochester Ind. Sch. Dist., Minn., 1974—. Prin. 2nd and 1st violin Rochester Orch., 1974—95; dir. All City Orch., Rochester; coach, substitute condr. Southeastern Minn. Youth Orch.; orch., string quartet and soloist Autumn Ridge Ch., Rochester. Women's Bible study leader Autumn Ridge Ch., Rochester. Recipient Queen of Analogies award, John Marshall Orch. Mem.: MnSOTA, ASTA, Music Educators Nat. Conf. Dfl. Avocations: interior design, church music. Office: Century High School 2525 Viola Road NE Rochester MN 55906 Business E-Mail: juworkman@rochester.k12.mn.us.

WORKMAN, KAYLEEN MARIE, special education and adult education educator; b. Paola, Kans., Aug. 25, 1947; d. Ralph I. and Pearl Marie (Shults) Platz; m. John Edward Workman, Aug. 10, 1980; children: Andrew Ray, Craig Michael. BS in Edn., Emporia State U., 1969, MS in Edn., 1983. Tchr. English/speech Lincoln (Kans.) High Sch., 1969-70, substitute tchr., 1970-71, Hudson (Wis.) Sch. Dist., 1971-72; tchrs. aide learning disabilities Park Forest South (Ill) Jr. High Sch., 1978—97; learning disabilities/English instr. George York Sch., Osawatomie, Kans., 1978-97; adult edn. instr. Adult Edn. Ctr., Osawatomie State Hosp., 1997-2000; spl. edn. tchr. Ottawa (Kans.) H.S., 2000—02; math. and sci. tchr. spl. edn. George York Cmty. Sch., Osawatomie, Kans., 2003; Braille & written lang. instr. Alphapointe Ctr. Blindness & Low Vision, Kans. City, 2003—. Supr. Loose Ends Clown Troop, 1988-91; presenter in field. Author of poems. Com. mem., sec. Cub Scouts, Osawatomie, 1987-88, com. mem. Boy Scouts Am., 1988-91, sec., 1990-91; forensics judge Osawatomie H.S. Forensics Team, 1991-92; hunter's safety instr. Osawatomie Sportsman's Club, 1982-86; mem. Osawatomie Cmty. Band, 1990-92. Mem. Osawatomie-NEA (v.p. 1982-83, 93-94, pres. 1983-84, 94-95, sec. 1986), Kans.-NEA (Sunflower Uniserv adminstrv. bd. 1985, Sunflower Uniserv coord. coun.), Assn. for Edn. and Rehab. of the Blind Visually Impaired. Avocations: hunting, fishing, collecting Santa Clauses, poetry, shopping.

WORKMAN, SHARON JOY, journalist; b. Louisa, Ky., May 20, 1930; d. Charlie B. Workman and Jessie Virginia Beaire; children: Patrick Corsiglia, Joan Corsiglia, James Corsiglia, Cynthia Corsiglia. BA, Marshall Coll., 1952; MA in Lit., Oxford U., Eng., 1990; MA in Creative Writing, Dartmouth Coll., 1992. Feature writer The Herald-Advertiser, Huntington, W.Va., 1951—52; mil. intelligence analyst Hdqrs. US Armed Forces Far East, Psychol. Warfare Sect., Japan, 1952—54; reporter Life Mag., NYC, 1954—59, People Mag., NYC, 1974—88. Mem.: DAR, TIME-LIFE Alumni Assn., Dartmouth Club, Overseas Press Club, The Coll. Club of Boston, The Tokeneke Club. Republican. Meth. Avocations: travel, swimming, opera, museums, concerts. Home: 9 Hale Ln Darien CT 06820 Personal E-mail: sharonworkman@aol.com.

WORKMAN, VIRGINIA LANE, music educator; b. Marion, Ohio, Dec. 12, 1951; d. George Washburn and Elizabeth Fravel Lane; m. Don W. Workman, June 17, 1978; children: Abigail, Kathryn. B in Music Edn., Capital U., Columbus, Ohio, 1974. Orch. dir. Newark (Ohio) City Schs., 1974—2004; ret. State chair Ohio Music Educators Assn., 1993—94; Suzuki instr. Denison U., Granville, Ohio, 1990; pvt. violin instr., Newark, 1974—; adj. faculty Denison U., 2006—. Named String Tchr. of Yr., State of Ohio, 1997; recipient Leader for Learning award, 1995. Mem.: Music Educators Nat. Conf., Philanthropic Edn. Orgn. (chaplain, pres., sec. 1974—), Delta Kappa Gamma (chmn. 1998—). Avocations: sewing, gardening, remodeling. Home: PO Box 1141 Newark OH 43058

WORKS, MARGARET ELIZABETH, retired art educator; b. Akron, Ohio, Mar. 28, 1931; d. William Paul and Florence E. Neal; m. Robert Lee Works (dec.). BFA, Carnegie Mellon U., Pitts., Pa., 1951; MS, U. So. Calif., LA, 1957. Cert. tchr. elem. and secondary art Pa., 1951, life credential in art Calif., 1953, secondary life credential Calif., 1960. Tchr. LA Unified Sch. Dist., 1953—91; supr. art edn. fieldwork Calif. State U. Dominguez Hills, Carson, Calif., 1993—2004, instr. art, 1993—2004; ret., 2004. Mem. new tchr. com. LA Unified Sch. Dist., 1965—66, mem. review and revision art com., 1984—85, 1992—93; mem. com. Eveinings for Educators LA County Mus. Art, 1975—90; workshop leader in field; curatorial asst. Minges Folk Art Mus., La Jolla, Calif., 1980, San Diego, 2002; judge advanced placement Ednl. Testing Svc., Princeton, NJ, 1989; tchr. mentor LA County Schs., 1993—2001. Exhibitions include Scaife House Gallery, 1952 (2d Pl. award, 1952), LA County Mcpl. Art Gallery, 1983. Judge art shows So. Calif., 1965—2006; ofcl. election poll LA County Election Bd., 1991—2006. Mem.: Calif. Art Edn. Assn. (historian 2004—06, chmn. 2004—06, named Retired Educator of Yr. 2005), PVAC Paleteers. Avocations: printmaking, drawing, painting, travel, cooking. Studio: 27850 Longhill Dr Rancho Palos Verdes CA 90274

WORLEY, DEBERE, educational consultant; b. Toledo, Apr. 22, 1953; d. Thomas Daniel and Dorothy Mae Worley. BS in Edn., Bowling Green State U., 1976; MS in Edn., U. Toledo, 1990. Cert. tchr. Ohio. Tchr. Toledo Pub. Schs., 1977—; rehab. technician Lucas County, Toledo, summers 83-85; ednl. cons. State Tchrs. Ret. Sys., Columbus, Ohio, 96-98, 99—; mem. pres.'s coun. Avon Products, Inc., Atlanta, 1997-98. Grad. asst. U. Toledo, 1988—89, Bowling Green State U., 1995—96. Actor: Godmother: The Late Dr. Ella P. Stewart, Goodwill Ambassador United States of America 1950-60, (poems) Dreams Really Do Come Tru, 1999. Scholar, U. Toledo, 1988—89, Bowling Green State U., 1995—96. Avocations: crafts, home decorating, gardening, home repair, collecting collectibles and restoring antiques. Office Phone: 419-917-2380. E-mail: dlworley@buckeyeexpress.com.

WORLEY, JANIS AVEREAL, writer; b. Mayfield Heights, Ohio, July 3, 1960; d. Albert Lisle Rhea and Avereal Jean Adams; m. Mark Pierce Worley, June 14, 1986; children: Grant Pierce, Grace Avereal. BA, Wittenberg U., Springfield, Ohio, 1982; MBA, Pa. State U., State College, 1985. Writer Worleybird Productions Inc., Hudson, Ohio, 1988—; bus. unit mgr. Sherwin Williams, Cleve., 1988—99. Author, assoc. prodr. (PBS TV Spl.) Heart of a Nation: America's First Ladies (Gracie Allen award for best documentary, 2001), Act of Duty (Regional Emmy nomination, Axiem award, Telly award, Aurora award, Omni award, 2001); prodr.: (TV series) Room by Room on HGTV (Telly award, Aurora award, Communicator award, Videographer award, 1999). Auction chair Parent's Assn. Old Trail Sch., Bath, Ohio, 2005—06; bd. mem. First Congl. Ch., Hudson, 2005—06; v.p. cmty. Jr. League Akron, Ohio, 2006—; bd. mem. Summit County Hist. Soc., Akron, 2006—, Women's Bd. Children's Hosp. Med. Ctr. Akron, 2006—. Recipient Rookie of Yr. award, Jr. League Akron, 2003—04. Avocations: reading, sewing, jewelry beading. Office: Worleybird Productions 5623 Williamsburg Circle Hudson OH 44236 Office Phone: 330-714-2061. Business E-Mail: worleybird98@hotmail.com.

WORLEY, KATHRYN ANN, secondary school educator; b. Vallejo, Calif., July 23, 1960; d. Terry Baldridge and Wilma Anita (Wilson) W. BA Applied Arts and Scis., San Diego State U., 1982, MA, 1991. Cert. secondary sch. tchr., Calif., tech. writing. cert., Ednl. Specialist Pt. Loma Nazarene U., 1999. Adminstrv. asst. athletic dept. San Diego State U., 1984-86, asst. athletic dir., 1986-87; substitute math. tchr. Lakeside Middle Sch., Lakeside (Calif.) Sch. Dist., 1988; indsl. tech. tchr., dept. chmn., softball team coach Mt. Miguel High Sch., Spring Valley, Calif., 1988—; athletic dir. Grossmont Union HS Dist., La Mesa, Calif., 1999—. Vocat. site specialist Grossmont Union High Sch. Dist., La Mesa, Calif., 1991-92. Mem. Nat. Assn. Sports Ofcls., Soc. for Tech. Communication, Epsilon Pi Tau. Avocation: competitive slow-pitch softball. Office: Mount Miguel High Sch 8585 Blossom Ln Spring Valley CA 91977-3822

WORLEY, NANCY L., state official; b. Madison County, Ala., Nov. 7, 1951; d. Leonard O. and Lillian (Smith) W. BA magna cum laude, U. Montevallo, Ala., 1973; MA, Jacksonville (Ala.) State U., 1974; postgrad., U. Ala., Tuscaloosa and Huntsville, 1974, U. Edinburgh, Scotland, 1975. Cert. English, speech and Latin tchr., Ala. Instr. English, NE State Jr. Coll., Rainsville, Ala., Calhoun Community Coll., Decatur, Ala.; tchr. lang. arts Decatur City Schs.; sec. of state State of Ala., Montgomery, 2003—. Former mem. Governor's Task Force on Welfare Reform, Governor's Task Force on Education Reform. Contbr. articles to profl. jours. Named Ala.'s Outstanding Young Educator, Dist. Tchr. of Yr., Decatur City Schs.; grantee grantee UN. Mem. NEA, Ala. Edn. Assn. (pres., 1983-84, 95-97, legis. com.), Ala. Fgn. Lang. Tchrs. Assn. (past pres.), Ala. Classroom Tchrs. Assn. (past pres., bd. dirs.), Sigma Tau Delta, Kappa Delta Pi, Lambda Sigma Chi, Omicron Delta Kappa. Office: Office of Sec of State State House 600 Dexter Ave Montgomery AL 36104 Office Phone: 334-242-7205. Office Fax: 334-242-4993. E-mail: nworley@sos.al.gov.*

WORLEY, RUTH, secondary school educator; b. Plön, Germany, Dec. 31, 1949; came to U.S., 1951; d. Rudi Eric and Lina Hanusch Hammer; m. Ben Farrell Worley, Sept. 14, 1973 (dec. Apr. 1993). BA, Taylor U., 1972; postgrad., Ball State U., 1972-73, North Tex. State U., 1985. Mem. sales staff AA Job Search, Memphis, 1973-74, Belo Corp., Dallas, 1974-75; owner, mem. sales staff Colony Carpets, Garland, Tex., 1976-83; tchr. Kennedale (Tex.) Ind. Sch. Dist., 1985—. Cons. Timbercreek Inc., Chatham, Va., 1993—. Journalist Taylor News, 1968-72. Campaigner Young Dems., Muncie, Ind., 1968-72, Dems. of Dallas County, Garland, 1977-80; intern Sen. Phillip Hart, Washington, 1971; fundraiser scholarship com., Kennedale. Named Tchr. of Yr., Kennedale C. of C., 2000; recipient cert. of merit, Meadow's Found., Dallas, 1993, 1997, C. of C. Tchr. of Yr., 2004. Mem. Social Studies Orgn., Educators of Psychology. Baptist. Avocations: photography, crossword puzzles, painting, travel, crocheting. Office: Kennedale Ind Sch Dist PO Box 1208 Kennedale TX 76060-1208 Business E-Mail: worleyr@kisdtx.net.

WORMACK, KAREN ELISE, small business owner, poet; b. Newark, Sept. 6, 1962; d. John Wesley Wormack Jr. and Gloria Marlena (Erwin) Wormack-Davis. BA in English/Comms., Kean Coll., 1985; MPA, Marywood U., Scranton, Pa., 2000; student, Sanford Brown Inst., Landover, Md. Cert. hypnotherapist 1998, lic. real estate salesperson SEC, N.J., SEC, Pa., life ins. investment rep. SEC, Series 6, 1987, SEC, Series 53, 1990. Customer svc. agt. Piedmont Airlines, Newark, 1986-87; investment rep., life ins. rep. Investment Rop. First Investor's Corp., Piscataway, NJ, 1987-90; sales assoc. Weichert Realtors, Morristown, NJ, 1991-93; real estate salesperson Shawnee Resort, Shawnee-on-Delaware, Pa., 1995-96; owner The Pocono Love Basket, 1995—; clin. hypnotherapist The Hypnosis Inst. N.Y., 1998; quality assurance coord. Cmty. Access Unltd., Human Svc. Agy. for Devel. Disabled, Elizabeth, NJ, 1999-2000; team leader Home Based Waiver Program Servicing Children and Adults with devel. disability, Step-By-Step, Inc., 2000—; therapeutic staff support Colonial Intermediate Unit 20, Easton, Pa., 2001, Youth Advocate Program, 2001—02; owner The Fancy Cone, Stroudsburg, Pa., 2001—, Ho. Guilded Scribe, Stroudsburg, Pa., 2003; referral agt. Weichert Realtors, Morristown, 1996—; tchr. English, tutor Md. Learning Ctr., Gaithensburg, 2005; tchr. English, Alternatives Unltd., Washington, 2005—. Sec., counselor Hugh O'Brian Youth Found., North Brunswick, NJ, 1988—89. Author: A Voice Crying in the Wilderness, 1990, The Adventures of Prissy and Missy, 1993, Enchanted Seraphim!, 1999, Emmanuel's Accolades!, 2000, A Good Teacher's Love, 2003; contbg. author: Great Poems of the Western World, 1990, On Terrorism, 1990, Spirit of the Age, 1996, Sound of Poetry, 1996, Lyricist: songs My Name is in the Book of Life, 2001, Where You Are We Want to Be, 2001, The Manners Song, 2002, Worship Him, 2004. Mem. Pocono Mt. C of C, 2003. Recipient Outstanding Poet award, World of Poetry, 1990, Clearance C. and Elizabeth Walton Medal of Honor for Excellence in Pub. Adminstrn., Marywood U., 2000. Mem.: Nat. Bd. Realtors, Assn. for the Severely Handicapped, Support Your Local Poet=Hooray (chairperson Strindsburg, Pa. 2004—), Pocono Mountain C. of C., Alpha Epsilon Lambda, Pi Alpha Alpha. Avocations: poetry, song writing, modeling, philanthropy, exploring caves. Home: 2001 Randolph Rd Apt 201 Silver Spring MD 20902-1461 Office Phone: 570-677-0800. Personal E-mail: kewormack@aol.com.

WORMALD, KATHLEEN MARIE, elementary school educator; b. Moorhead, Minn., Apr. 5, 1950; d. Lloyd Kendal and Donna Marie (Erickson) Stein; m. Tracy Wood Wormald, Jan. 30, 1971; children: Karla, Jennifer, Timothy. BS in Spl. Edn., Ea. Mont. Coll., 1973; MA, Lesley Coll., 1999. Tchr. fourth grade Sunset Sch., Cody, Wyo., 1980-81; tchr. sixth grade Livingston Sch., Cody, 1981-89, tchr. fifth grade, 1989—. Recipient Arch Coal Tchr. Achievement award for Wyo., 2006. Mem. Stampede Parade Com., Cody Edn. Assn., Cody Sch. Credit Union (sec. 2000—), Beta Sigma Phi Xi Nu Chpt. (pres. 1981-82, v.p., sec. 1989-90). Presbyterian. Avocations: walking, reading, scrapbooks, travel. Home: 2308 Meadowlark Ct Cody WY 82414-9784 Office: Livingston Sch 2001 12th St Cody WY 82414-4606 Office Phone: 307-587-4271.

WORONOV, MARY PETER, actress; b. Bklyn., Dec. 8, 1946; d. Victor D. and Carol W.; m. Ted Gershuny, 1969 (div.); m. Ted Whitehead, 1979. Student, Cornell Univ., 1964—68. Actor: (films) The Chelsea Girls, 1967, Death Race 2000, 1975, Rock 'n' Roll High School, 1979, Eating Raoul, 1982, Black Widow, 1987, Warlock, 1989, Good Girls Don't, 1995, The Munster's Scary Little Christmas, 1996, Invisible Mom II, 1999, New Women, 2001; (TV series) Logan's Run, 1977, Sledge Hammer!, 1987; (TV films) Challenge of a Lifetime, 1985, (TV spl.) Cheech and Chong's Get Out of My Room, 1985, (stage prodns.) Kitchenette, 1968, Boom Boom Room, 1974; author: Wake for the Angels: Paintings and Stories, 1994, Swimming Underground: My Years in the Warhol Factory, 1995, Snake, 2000, Niagara, 2002, Eyewitness to Warhol, 2002, Blind Love, 2004; dir.: (TV show) Little Vampire, Blind Love, The Gigolo. Avocation: painting.

WORRALL, JUDITH RAE, health and welfare plan consultant; BA, Simpson Coll., Indianola, Iowa, 1984. Fin. planner IDS/Am. Express, West Des Moines, Iowa, 1987-89; client mgr. Haake Cos., Kansas City, Mo., 1993-95; asst. v.p. Aon Cons. Group, Kansas City, Mo., 1995—2000; sr. cons. Gallagher Benefit Svcs., Kansas City, 2000—03; v.p. Marsh USA, Kansas City, Mo., 2003—. Bd. dirs. Arthritis Found., Kansas City, 2000—. Named Woman of Yr., Leukemia Soc. Am., 1997. Mem.: Greater Kansas City Health Underwriters Assn. (pres. 2001—02). Office: Marsh USA 2405 Grand Blvd Ste 1500 Kansas City MO 64108

WORREL, CONNIE RAE, science educator; d. Virginia Marie and Robert George Ryerson; m. Rick Allen Worrel, June 11, 1988; children: Stacie Rae, Jacob Allen. BS, N.D. State U., Fargo, 1985—88. Cert. Tchr., Sci. 6-12 Tex. Dept. Edn., 2004. Lab supr. Gustafson, McKinney, 1988—2000. Office Phone: 469-742-6800.

WORRELL, AUDREY MARTINY, geriatric psychiatrist; b. Phila, Aug. 12, 1935; d. Francis Aloysius and Dorothy (Rawley) Martiny; m. Richard Vernon Worrell, June 14, 1958; children: Philip Vernon, Amy Elizabeth. MD, Meharry Med. Coll., 1960. Diplomate Am. Bd. Psychiatry and Neurology. Intern Misericordia Hosp., Phila., 1960-61; resident SUNY-Buffalo Affiliated Hosp., NY, 1961-63, Buffalo Psychiat. Ctr., NY, 1963-64; dir. capitol region Mental Health Ctr., Hartford, Conn., 1974-77; acting regional dir. Region IV State Dept. Mental Health, 1976-77; asst. chief psychiatry VA Med. Ctr., Newington, Conn., 1977-78, acting chief psychiatry, 1978-79, chief psychiatry, 1978-80; dir. Capitol Regional Mental Health Facilities, Hartford, Conn., 1980-87; clin. prof. psychiatry U. Conn., 1981-87; commr. State Dept. Mental Health, Hartford, 1981-86; CEO, med. dir. Vista Sandia Hosp., Albuquerque, 1986-88; dir. consultation liason Lovelace Med. Ctr., Albuquerque, 1988-89, geriatric psychiatry, 1989-93; dir. geriatric psychiatry Charter Hosp., Albuquerque, 1993-96, St. Joseph Med. Sys., Albuquerque, 1994—; pvt. practice, 1996—2003; part-time cons. Albuquerque VA Hosp., 2003—. Contbr. articles to profl. jour. Bd. dir. Transitional Svc., Buffalo, 1973-74, ARC, Buffalo, 1973-74, Child and Family Svc., Hartford, 1972-73; co-chmn. United Way/Combined Health Appeal, State of Conn., 1983, 84; active Child Welfare Inst. Adv. Bd., Hartford, 1983—, Conn. Prison Bd., Hartford, 1984-85; chmn. Gov. Task Force on Mental Health Policy, 1982-85; mem. Gov.Task Force on Homeless, 1983-85. Recipient Leadership award Conn. Coun. Mental Health Ctr., 1983, Outstanding Contbn. award to Health Svc., YWCA, Hartford, 1983. Mem. AMA, APHA, NASMHPD (sec., bd. dir. 1982-86), New Eng. Mental Health Commr. Assn., Am. Med. Women's Assn., Conn. Assn. Mental Health and Aging, Conn. Coalition for Homeless Inc., Conn. Rehab. Assn., Am. Assn. Psychiat. Adminstr., Am. Hosp. Assn., Am. Orthopsychiat. Assn., Assn. Mental Health Adminstr., Hosp. and Cmty. Psychiatry Svc., Corporators of Inst. of Living of Hartford, Am. Psychiat. Assn., Conn. Psychiat. Soc., Am. Coll. Psychiatrists, Am. Coll. Mental Health Adminstr. Office: Albuquerque VA Hosp Gibson & San Mateo Albuquerque NM 87107

WORRELL, CYNTHIA LEE, bank executive; b. Moncton, N.B., Can., May 27, 1957; came to U.S., 1979; d. Ronald William and Audrey Helen (Crothers) Jones; m. Geoffrey H. Worrell, Sept. 1, 1979; children: Lindsay Andrea, Geoffrey Andrew, Ashley Taylor. BA in Edn. with honors, U. New Brunswick, Fredericton, 1979. Lic. real estate broker, Mass., Pa., Calif. Instr. New Brunswick C.C., Fredericton, N.B., Canada, 1978-79, Massasoit C.C., Brockton, Mass., 1981-82, Brockton Cmty. Schs., 1981-82; regional mgr. and instr. Worldwide Ednl. Svcs., Clifton, NJ, program dir. Taunton, Mass., 1995; procedures and documentation analyst Capital Blue Cross, Harrisburg, Pa., 1985; v.p., br. mgr. Comfed Mortgage Co., Inc., Mass., 1985-90; sr. residential loan officer Bank of Am., Santa Clara, Calif., 1990-92; regional sales mgr., asst. v.p. Shearson Lehman Mortgage, San Jose, Calif., 1992-93; br. mgr. Cypress Fin., San Jose, 1993-94; area and ops. br. mgr. PNC Mortgage Corp. Am., San Jose, 1994—; program dir. worldwide Ednl. Svcs., Taunton, Mass., 1995; area prodn. mgr. Plymouth Mortgage Co., Foxborough, Mass., 1995-96, Ameriquest Mortgage, Hingham, Mass., 1996-97; br. mgr. Bank United of Tex. Commonwealth United Mortgage, West Bridgewater, Mass., 1996—; br. mgr. Nat. City Mortgage-Commonwealth United Mortgage, 1997-98, Family Choice Mortgage, West Bridgewater, 1998—2000, Orchard Mortgage, Raynham, Mass., 2000—06; asst. v.p., br. mgr. Sallie Mae Home Loans, West Wareham, Mass., 2006—. Guest spkr. numerous trade shows, real estate bd. seminars, cmty. workshops, stress mgmt. personal profiles, motivational speaking and workshops; instr. mortgage banking Calif. State U., Hayward, 1994—; mem. adv. bd., instr., outside cons. Calif. State U. Ext. divsn., 1993-95; cert. trainer Carlson Learning Co., 1993—; trainer in diversity, conflict resolution, sexual harassment, and time mgmt.; cmty. trainer WCR, BPW, Old Colony Vocat. Sch., Wareham H.S., Wareham Mid. and Elem. Schs., Wareham Supts. Office, Fall River Sch. Dist., Old Rochester Jr. and Sr. H.S., Bristol County Tng. Consortium, and Transitional Assistance, Bridgewater Cmty., Wareham Foster Parents, Wareham Decas Sch., 1996—. Mem. editl. bd. Mortgage Originator, 1995; contbr. articles to profl. jours. Vol. Handi Kids, Bridgewater, Mass., 1985—90, Fremont/Newark YMCA youth basketball and soccer; active Forest Park PTA, Self-Def. Inst. Tau Kwon Do Club; donor Berwick Boys Club; mem. adv. com. Wareham H.S., mem. coun.; alumni dir. U. New Brunswick, 1998—; bd. dirs. Wareham Childcare; trustee Le Lycee Internat. de la Nouvelle Angleterre, Inc., Boston, 1997; trustee, chair Tabor Acad., Marion, Mass. Named to IBC 200 Women of Achievement, 1991-92, ABI 2000 Notable Women, 1991-92,ABI Personalities of Am., 1992, Internat. Order of Merit, 1992, The World Found. of Successful Women, 1992, Outstanding Young Women in Am., 1984, 88. Mem. NAFE, Mass. Mortgage Bankers Assn., Data Entry Mgmt. Assn., Middleboro C. of C., Chief Exec. Officer Club Boston, Wareham Bus. and Profl. Women's Club (v.p. program dir.), Taunton Area C. of C., Toastmasters, Plymouth Bd. Realtors, Bristol County Bd. Realtors, Women's Coun. of Realtors, Bristol County C. of C. Republican. Avocations: swimming, golf, horseback riding, curling. Home: 2 Peter Cooper Dr Wareham MA 02571-2209 Office: Sallie Mae Home Loans 2360 Cranberry Hwy PO Box 237 West Wareham MA 02570 Office Phone: 508-930-1792. E-mail: clworrell@aol.com.

WORRELL, MARY THORA, loan officer; b. Montreal, Quebec, Can., July 8, 1932; came to U.S., 1974; d. Samuel R. and Rose E. Lewis; m. Henry G. Worrell, July 18, 1953 (div. Aug. 1974); children: Deborah, Geoffrey, John. BA, Sir George Williams U., Montreal, 1957. Lic. real estate agt., Mass. Lectr. Sir George Williams U., Montreal, Canada, 1963—74; rschr. Pvt. Stock, Palo Alto, Calif., 1979-90; loan officer Gt. We. Bank, Dublin, Calif., 1990-91, San Francisco Fed. Savs. Bank, 1991-92; residential loan specialist Eureka Bank, Foster City, Calif., 1992-93; residential loan officer First Interstate Bank, Oakland, Calif., 1993-94; loan officer First Nationwide Bank, Walnut Creek, Calif., 1994-95, Chase Manhattan Mortgage, San Francisco, 1995-96; sr. loan officer Pacific Bay Bank, San Pablo, Calif., 1996-97, Wausau Mortgage Corp., Pleasanton, Calif., 1997—. Speaker, mem. panel nat. prayer breakfast Ho. Commons, Ottawa, Can., 1972; speaker Wharton Sch. Human Resources, Phila., 1976; group leader Nat. Sci. Found. and George Washington U., 1976-77; mem. prison visitation com. Antioch Missionary Bapt. Ch., Oakland, Calif., 1992-98. Recipient Outstanding Svc. Conf. Speaker Pub. Rels. Student Soc. Am., 1976. Avocations: american jurisprudence, prison fellowship, eagle watching, golf, ballroom dancing. E-mail: mthora@yahoo.com.

WORRELL, SHARYN DIANNE, volunteer, retired flight attendant; b. Lynn, Mass., Feb. 23, 1948; d. Richard Allen Kelley and Norma Lovett (Gregory); m. Blaine Patten Worrell, Feb. 15, 1979 (div. Dec. 20, 1985); 1 child, Ryan Richard. Flight attendant United Airlines, Chgo., 1966—2002. Spkr. and co-founder Speakers' Bur. LA-based Flight Attendants. Author: (book) Ancestral Lines of Joseph Browne of Essex County, Massachusetts and Mary Brown (Joseph's wife) of Kensington, New Hampshire with Related Brown Lines, From Stewardess to Flight Attendant-The Changing Years; co-author: The History of the Auxiliary of Good Shepherd Hospital,

Barrington, Illinois; compiler (book) Illinois Court, National Society Women Descendants of the Ancient and Honorable Artillery Company, Celebrating 60 Years, (books) A Few of My Favorite E-Mails. Co-founder Young Women's League for Muscular Dystrophy Assn., LA, 1975; asst. supt. of Sunday sch.; summer Sunday sch. supt.; sch. bd. Immanuel Luth. Ch. and Sch., Palatine, Ill., 1990—93, pub. rels. chair, 1992—2002, bd. of human care ministry com. mem., 1999—2001, pres's. vol. svc. award chmn., 2000—04, bd. of trustees, sec. of congregation, 2001—03; bd. mem. Aux. Good Shepherd Hosp., Barrington, Ill., 2000—, pres., 2006—, mem. chair, 2000—02, chef fest bd. mem., 2003—06; founding mem. Immanuel Luth. Sch. Edn. Found., Palatine, 1998—2003; program chair Art in the Barn, bd. mem., founder sch. artwork project; reach for the stars event chairperson Immanuel Luth. Sch. Edn. Found., Palatine, Ill., 1998—2003. Recipient Vol. Recognition, YMCA, 1988, Servant of Youth award, Boy Scouts Am., Merit awards (3), United Air Lines, Pres.'s Vol. Svc. Lifetime award, George W. Bush, 2006. Mem.: Clipped Wings (ways and means com. 2002—), others, Continental Soc. Daus. Indian Wars (charter mem., cradle roll), Nat. Soc. U.S. Daus. 1812, Nat. Soc. Daus. of Union (#2 tent), Nat. Soc. Sons and Daus. Pilgrims (Ill. br. organizing gov.), Daus. Am. Colonists (state libr.), Ill. State Soc. Dames Ct. of Honor (parliamentarian), Nat. Soc. Colonial Dames XVII Century (charter mem. lac des Ill. chpt., historian lac des Ill. chpt., state chaplain, pres. lac des Ill. chpt., state chair heraldry and coat arms, libr. lac des Ill. chpt., chaplain lac des Ill. chpt.), Order Descs. Colonial Physicians and Chirugiens (life), Order First Families of Maine (life; corres. sec. gen., charter mem.), Family of Bruce Soc. Am. (life), Guild Colonial Artists and Tradesmen (life; charter mem.), Sons and Daus. Colonial and Antebellum Bench and Bar (life), Hereditary Order Descs. Loyalists and Patriots Am. Revolution (life), Order First Families Conn. (life; founding mem.), Nat. Soc. Descs. Early Quakers (life), Hereditary Order First Families Mass. (life; primary), Soc. Mayflower Descs. State of Ill. (life; chmn. jr. membership, elder), Soc. Descs. of Colonial Clergy (life), Nat. Soc. Women Descs. Ancient and Hon. Arty. Co. (life; first v.p., treas., hospitality chmn.), Assn. Daus. Early Am. Witches (life; nat. corr. sec. gen., guest spkr.), Daus. Union Vets. of Civil War 1861-1865 (life; chaplain), Nat. Sons and Daus. Antebellum Planters (life), Presdl. Families Am. (life), Order Crown of Charlemagne in U.S.A. (life), Soveriegn Soc. Ams. Royal Descent (life), Huguenot Soc. Ill. (registrar, guest spkr., dir.), Nat. Soc. Magna Carta Dames and Barons, Order First Families R.I. and Providence Plantations, N.H. Hist. Soc., New Eng. Historic Geneal. Soc., Essex Soc. Genealogists, Flagon and Trencher (life), Nat. Soc. New Eng. Women (life; 1st v.p. 2006, program spkr., Vol. Cmty. Svc. award 1995), Ill. Cameo Soc. (life), Piscataqua Pioneers (life). Lutheran. Achievements include Lobbied 3 years for exoneration of 6 women executed in 1692 as Salem witches during the Witch Hysteria. Acting Gov. Jane Swift signed the Bill on October 31, 2001 exonerating all 6. Avocations: genealogy, volunteering. Home: 269 Bluff Ct Barrington IL 60010-7312 Personal E-mail: sdworrell@aol.com.

WORTH, DIANE BERNICE, physical education educator; b. Cleve., July 14, 1966; d. John Howard and Josephine Anne Worth. BS in Phys. Edn., Plymouth State Coll., N.H., 1990; MSS in Sports Medicine, U.S. Sports Acad., Daphne, Ala., 1995; MA in Tchr., U. of the Incarnate Word, San Antonio, 2006. Cert. athletic trainer Nat. Athletic Tng. Assn., 1996. Athletic trainer/ rehab technician Fairview Hosp., Great Barrington, Mass., 1992—2000; coach/ trainer/ instr. Catamount Ski Area, South Egremont, Mass., 1999—2000; head athletic trainer/tchr. North Middlesex Regional H. S., Townsend, Mass., 2000—01; athletic dir./ phys. edn. tchr./sci. tchr., coach St. James Cath. Sch., Seguin, Tex., 2002—03; TAKS reading tchr./coach Gonzales Jr. H.S., Tex., 2003—04; athletic coord./phys. edn. tchr./coach Sch. of Excellence in Edn., San Antonio, 2004—06; phys. edn. tchr./coach E. T. Wrenn Mid. Sch., San Antonio, 2006—. Nutrition cons. First Pl. Christian Weight Loss Program, Luling, Tex., 2001—03; boy scout adult leader Outdoor Adventure Program, Pittsfield, Mass., 2000—01; athletic trainer/asst. coach South County Youth Soccer League, Sheffield, Mass., 1998—2000; coaching asst. Ashland H.S., NH, 1986—90; teacher's aide Pemigewassett Easter Seal Ctr., Plymouth, NH, 1986—90. 2d lt. USAR, 2001—04. Home: 11800 Braesview #4407 San Antonio TX 78213 Office: ET Wrenn Middle School 627 South Acme Rd San Antonio TX 78237 Personal E-mail: trainerdi2001@yahoo.com.

WORTH, DOROTHY WILLIAMSON, retired foreign language educator; b. Ga., Dec. 28, 1930; d. John Elbert and Ela Mae (Bagwell) Williamson; m. Roy Eugene Worth, Aug. 29, 1965; 1 child, John Eugene. BA, West Ga. Coll., 1967; MA, Ga. State U., 1975. Sec., paralegal aide pvt. legal office, Carrollton, Ga., 1954-63; French instr. Oak Mountain Acad., Carrollton, 1967-68; part-time Spanish instr. Ashdun Hall Sch., Atlanta, 1973-75; Spanish and Eng. instr. DeKalb Community Coll., Clarkston, Ga., 1975-77; Spanish and French instr. Ga. State U., Atlanta, 1977—97; ret. Editor: (poetry anthology) The Reach of Song, V., 1986, VIII, 1989, Harvest of Poetry, 1989, 92; (lit. mag.) The Village Writer, 1989-90; contbr. poems, articles, stories to profl. publs. Recipient numerous awards for poetry, fiction and articles, 1967—. Mem. MLA, Ga. State Poetry Soc. (pres. 1983-85, bd. dir 1983—), Atlanta Writers Resource Group (bd. dirs. 1988—), Atlanta Writers Club (Carolyn Wyatt Meml. award 1987, 90, 94), Village Writers Group (bd. dir. 1988—), Southeastern Writers Conf. (bd. dirs. 1983—), Ga. Coun. Internat. Visitors, United Daus. Confederacy. Methodist. Avocations: reading, hiking, travel. Home: 1399 Vista Leaf Dr Decatur GA 30033-2028

WORTH, KATHERINE MARIE, retired vocalist; b. Pleasantville, N.J., Dec. 26, 1925; d. Thedore John Philippi and Anna Gladys Weber; m. Melvin R. Worth, June 23, 1952 (dec.). Grad. H.S., Pleasantville, N.J. Profl. vocalist, Atlantic City, 1945—75; ret. Past mem., pres. Red Cedar Twig Cmty. Med. Ctr.; educator Elder Hostle Stockton Coll., ATlantic County; hon. mem. Antique Seekers Ocean County ARea, 1st pres., 1962; bd. mem. Red Cross, Toms River, NJ, 1958—61; v.p., program chair Ocean County Hist. Soc., 1962—97, pres., 1995—97; dir., curator Berkeley Hist. Mus., Bayville, NJ, 1982—92; historian Berkeley Twp., Bayville, 1982—94; bd. mem. Former N.J. State Police Edn. Fund, 1967—. Recipient Outstanding Civic Contbn. award, Berkely Twp., 1975, Berkeley Twp. Hidden Heroine award, 1989. Mem.: Am. Contract Bridge League. Avocations: antiques, bridge, golf, singing, travel. Home: 8 Sloop Creek Rd Box 7 Bayville NJ 08721

WORTH, LYNN HARRIS, writer; b. Flushing, Sept. 21, 1934; d. Andrew Lamar Harris and Jean Hofmann; m. Chauncey Merrill Smith, Jr., June 20, 1992. AA in Journalism, Vt. Coll., 1954; degree in Interior Design, NY Sch. Interior Design, 1971. Editl. asst. Time Mag., N.Y.C., 1954—56; pub. rels. asst. Silver Hill Found., New Canaan, Conn., 1958—61. Ptnr. Chameleon Interiors, Westport, Conn., 1972—84. Editor and pub.: Va. Gamebird Jour., editor, pub.: Magyar Vizsla News, mem. editl. staff: AKC Perspectives; contbr. articles to mags.; editor: Clarksville About Town, 2004—05. Publicity dir. Westport Young Woman's League, 1967—68; publicity/pub. rels. Girl Scouts Am., Dist. 2, Fairfield County, 1967—69, LWV, Westport; founding mem. Lake Country SPCA; pres. Vizsla Club of Am. Welfare Found.; co-chmn. Clarksville Revitalization Com., 2004—05; publicity/pub. rels. polit. campaign for Gov. Tom Meskill, Conn. Mem.: Magyar Vizsla Soc. (founding mem.), numerous regional dog clubs, Vizsla Club of Am. (Am. Kennel Club del., v.p., sec. 1980—). Home: PO Box 1755 Clarksville VA 23927 Personal E-mail: lynhar@verizon.net.

WORTH, MARY PAGE, mayor; b. Balt., Jan. 23, 1924; d. Christian Allen and Margaret Pennington (Holbein) Schwarzwaelder; m. William James Worth, Nov. 4, 1947 (dec. May 1986); children: Margaret Page, William Allen, John David III. Student, Ladycliff Coll., Highland Falls, N.Y., 1941-42, Abbott Sch. Art, Washington, 1942-44; grad., Packer Coll. Inst., Brooklyn. Selectman Town of Searsport, Maine, 1973-75; mayor City of Belfast, Maine, 1986-2000. Recreation chmn. Town of Searsport, 1970-72. Del. Rep. State Conv., Maine, 1970-94; pres. Searsport Reps., 1974-76; active ARC Overseas Assn., 1976—; pres. Searsport C. of C., 1976-79; mem. exec. bd. Waldo County Com. for Social Action, Belfast, 1986—; mem. Abnacki coun. Girl Scouts U.S.; tutor Literacy Vols. Am.; recreation specialist ARC, Camp Haugen, Japan, 1946-47; bd. dirs. RSVP-Waldo County, Heat Start Waldo County; vol. tchr. Sch. for Blind, Cholon, Republic Vietnam, 1959-61, Am. Sch. at Saigon, Republic Vietnam, 1959-61; club dir. USAF Spl. Svcs., Ft. Meyer, Va., 1962-63, U.S. Army Spl. Svcs., Ft. Belvoir, Va., 1963-64; mem. Congresswoman Olympia Snow's Mpcl. Adv. Bd.; town chair Rep. Party; mem. adv. Belfast History Project. Mem. Gibson Island Club, 1938-73, mem. DAR (officer Maine 1986—), Internat. Platform Assn., Ret. Officers Assn. (life), 11th Airborne Assn./511th Parachute Infantry Regiment Korea War Vets. Assn., Waldo County Humane Soc. (pres. 1990—), Waldo County Law Enforcement (v.p. 1990—), VFW Aux., Am. Legion Aux., Belfast Garden Club (parliamentarian 1984—), Rotary (bd. govs. com. Maine St. '90), ARC Overseas Assoc. Avocations: great dane breeding, antiques. Office: City of Belfast Mayor's Office 71 Church St Belfast ME 04915-6208 Home: 10 Shoreland Dr Apt 306 Belfast ME 04915-6062

WORTHAM, ANNE ESTELLE, education educator; b. Jackson, Tenn., Nov. 26, 1941; d. Johnny and Bernice Wortham. BS, Tuskegee Inst., 1959—63; PhD, Boston Coll., 1977—82. Rschr., asst. editor Esquire Mag., NYC, 1965—67; rsch. asst. Huntley-Brinkley Report, NBC News, NYC, 1967—69; rsch. libr. ABC Radio News, NYC, 1970—71; freelance writer-rschr. Ford Found., IBM World Trade Corp., NYC, 1971—72; rsch. assoc. Ednl. Policy Ctr., NYC, 1972—74; rsch. libr. King Features Syndicate, NYC, 1974—77; adj. asst. prof. of sociology Wellesley Coll., Mass., 1982—83; vis. asst. prof. of pub. policy Harvard U., 1983—86; asst. prof. of sociology Wash. and Lee U., Lexington, Va., 1989—91; assoc. prof. of sociology Ill. State U., 1991—. Cons. Nat. Endowment for the Humanities, Washington, 1985—92; vis. scholar Hoover Instn., Stanford, Calif., 1986—89; cons. Mass. Dept. of Edn., 1996, US Dept. of Edn., Washington, 1987, Nat. Endowment for the Humanities, Washington, 1991—92. Author: The Other Side of Racism: A Philosophical Study of Black Race Consciousness; contbr. chapters to books The Libertarian Alternative:Essays in Social and Political Philosophy, 1975, American Sociological Association Presidential Volume on Public Policy, 1990, Civil Wrongs: What Went Wrong with Affirmative Action, 1994, Opposing Viewpoints: Interracial America, 1998, Character and Identity: Sociological Foundations of Literary and Historical Perspectives, 2000, articles to jours. Student participant Operation Crossroads Africa, Ethiopia, 1962; vol. US Peace Corps, Tanzania, 1963—65. Inst. for Humane Studies fellowship, Inst. for Humane Studies, 1977—78, Earhart Grad. fellowship, Earhart Found., 1978, Danforth Grad. fellowship, Danforth Found., 1979—81, Seifert Grad. fellowship, The Found. for Econ. Edn., 1979—81, Ludwig von Mises Humanities fellowship, Ctr. for Libertarian Studies, 1982—83, Earhart Post-Graduate fellow, Earhart Found., 1983—84, John M. Olin Faculty fellowship, John M. Olin Found., 1985—86, Earhart Found. Rsch. grant, Earhart Found., 2000. Mem.: Am. Sociol. Assn. Office: Illinois State University Campus Box 4660 Normal IL 61790

WORTHAM, DEBORAH LYNNE, principal; b. Chgo., May 13, 1949; d. Leon Cabot and Bessie (Summers) Smith; m. Chester Hopes Wortham, Jan. 29, 1972; children: Shelley Sharon, Chester Hopes III. BS, U. Wis., 1972; MS, Morgan State U., 1981; EdD, Nova Southeastern U., 1997. Tchr., reading tchr., support tchr. Balt. City Pub. Schs., 1972-87, asst. prin., 1988-90, prin. Samuel Coleridge Taylor Sch., 1990-94, dir. efficacy, 1994-97, prin. K-8, 1997—, dir. profl. devel., 2000—, asst. supt., 2005—. Program facilitator Balt. Schs.-Johns Hopkins U., 1987-88; dean of edn. Higher Dimensions Learning Ctr., Balt., 1985—. Author: Teaching by Signs and Wonders, 1992. Recipient Mayor's Citation for Volunteerism, Balt., 1982, Am. Best Elem. Sch. for Significant Improvement award Redbook Mag., 1993, 95; cited Administrator's Class Act, Channel ll TV, Balt., 1991. Mem. ASCD (nat. faculty), Phi Delta Kappa, Alpha Kappa Alpha. Democrat. Pentecostal. Personal E-mail: drdworth@aol.com.

WORTHEN, NANCY SMITH, federal agency administrator; b. Pawtucket, RI, Jan. 11, 1951; d. Norman Everett and Olga Sophia Smith; 1 child, Margaret Lucia. BA in Sociology and Religion, Douglass Coll., New Brunswick, N.J., 1972. Program dir. Westerly Ctr. for Arts, RI, 1979—89; dir. vols., dir. visitor svcs., dir. ops. Americorps Providence Children's Mus., Providence, 1989—. Mem. profl. devel. com. Vol. Ctr. R.I., Providence, 1989—2006, chair profl. devel. com., 1995—2004. Recipient Points of Light Vol. Achievement award, 2004. Democrat. Unitarian. Avocations: gardening, contra dancing. Home: 51 Hammond St Providence RI 02903 Office: Ready to Learn Providence 945 Westminster St Providence RI 02903

WORTHING, CAROL MARIE, retired minister; b. Duluth, Minn., Dec. 27, 1934; d. Truman James and Helga Maria (Bolander) W.; children: Gregory Alan Beatty, Graydon Ernest Beatty. BS, U. Minn., 1965; MDiv, Northwestern Theol. Seminary, 1982; DMin, Grad. Theol. Found., Notre Dame, Ind., 1988; MBA in Ch. Mgmt., Grad. Theol. Found., Donaldson, Ind., 1993; cert., Austin Presbyn. Theol. Sem., 2001; PhD, Grad. Theol. Found., 2002. Cert. Episcopal Diocese of Tex., 2003. Secondary educator Ind. (Minn.) Sch. Dist., 1965-78; teaching fellow U. Minn., 1968-70; contract counselor Luth. Social Svc., Duluth, 1976-78; media cons. Luth. Media Svcs., St. Paul, 1978-80; asst. pastor Messiah Luth. Ch., Fargo, ND, 1982-83, vice pastor, 1983-84; assoc. editor Luth. Ch. Am. Ptnrs., Phila., 1982-84; editorial assoc. Luth. Ptnrs. Evang. Luth. Ch. Am., Phila. and Mpls., 1984—2004; parish pastor Resurrection Luth. Ch., Pierre, SD, 1984-89; assoc. pastor Bethlehem Luth. Ch., Cedar Falls, Iowa, 1989-90; exec. dir. Ill. Conf. Chs., Springfield, 1990-96, Tex. Conf. of Chs., 1996—2003; ret., 2003. Asst. pastor Messiah Luth. Ch., Fargo, N.D., 1982-84; mem. pub. rels. and interpretation com. Red River Valley Synod, Fargo, 1984-86, mem. ch. devel., Pierre, 1986-87; mem. mgmt. com. office comm. Luth. Ch. in Am., N.Y.C., Phila., 1984-88; mem. mission ptnrs. S.D. Synod, 1988, chmn. assembly resolutions com., 1988; mem. pre-assembly planning com., ecumenics com., chmn. resolutions com. N.E. Iowa Synod, 1989-90; mem. ch. and society com., 1990-96; ecumenical com., 1995-96; Luth. Ecumenical Rep. Network, 1995—2003; mem. Cen. and So. Ill. Synod, 1996; mem. S.W. Tex. Synod, 1996—2003, mem. ecumenical com., 1998-2001; mem. ecumenical com. Mpls. Area synod and St. Paul Area synod ELCA, 2004—; nat. edn. cons. Am. Film Inst., Washington, 1967-70; chaplain state legis. bodies, Pierre, 1984-89; mem. exec. bd. Luth. Ecumenical Rep. Network for Region 4, Evang. Luth. Ch. in Am., 2002-03; preacher Nat. Cathedral, Washington, 2002. Author: Cinematics and English, 1967, Peer Counseling, 1977, Tischrede Lexegete, 1986, 88, 90, Way of the Cross, Way of Justice Walk, 1987, Introducing Collaboration as a Leadership Stance and Style in an Established Statewide Conference of Churches, 1993, The Anointing of Jesus--A Christological Necessity, 2001. Co-facilitator Parents of Retarded Children, 1985; bd. dirs. Countryside Hospice, 1985; cons. to adminstrv. bd. Mo. Shores Women's Ctr., 1986. Named John Macquarrie fellow, Grad. Theol. Found., 2002, homilist, Tex. Day, Washington Nat. Cathedral, 2002. Mem. NAFE, Nat. Assn. Ecumenical Staff (chair of site selection com. 1991-92, chair of scholarship com. 1993-94, mem. profl. devel. com. 1993-94, chair program planning com. 1996, bd. dirs. 1995-96), Pierre-Ft. Pierre Ministerium (v.p. 1986-87, pres. 1987-88). Democrat. Avocations: writing prose and poetry, concerts, theater, art, photography. Home: 5555 Dewey Hill Rd # 106 Edina MN 55439 Personal E-mail: cworthi@winternet.com.

WORTHINGTON, JOAN MARIE, information technology executive; b. Balt., May 26, 1961; m. John B. Bartkowiak. AA, Villa Julie Coll., 1982; BS, U. Balt., 1984, MBA, 1991. Sys. analyst CSX Tech., 1988—92; pres. J. Worthington & Assocs. Inc., 1992—99; project mgr. CSX Tech., 1999—2000; faculty assoc. Johns Hopkins U., 1993—; dir. Internet svcs. Sys. Source, 2000—. Mem. Leadership Alliance, 1996—; mem. dean selection com. Johns Hopkins U. Sch. Bus. and Edn., 1999—2000; mem., former pres., bd. govs. U. Balt., 1994—; mem., pres.-elect Merrick Sch. Bus. Adv. Bd., U. Balt., 1996—; bd. dirs. Notre Dame H.S.; mem., former bd. chair Women's Inst., Coll. Notre Dame Md., 1995—2000; mem., former pres. St. Mary of the Assumption Parish Coun., 1990—92. Named one of 100 Women of Genius, Trinity Coll., 2000; recipient 8 Gallon Pin, ARC, 2000. Office: 338 Clubhouse Rd Cockeysville Hunt Valley MD 21031

WORTHY, PATRICIA MORRIS, lawyer, educator; b. Fort Benning, Ga., May 28, 1944; d. Walter and Ruby Mae (Lovett) Morris. AA, Queensborough C.C., 1964; BA, Bklyn. Coll., 1966; JD, Howard U., 1969. Bar: DC 1971. Trial atty. NLRB, Washington, 1969—71; dep. gen. counsel ACTION, Washington, 1971—74; assoc. Dolphin, Branton, Stafford & Webber, Washington, 1974—77; dep. asst. sec. for regulatory functions HUD, Washington, 1977—80; adj. prof. Howard U. Sch. Law, 1979—82; chmn. D.C. Pub. Svc. Commn., 1980—91, Washington Met. Area Transit Commn., 1980—91; chief of staff Office of Mayor Sharon Pratt Kelly, Washington, 1991—92; prof. law Howard U., Washington, 1992—2001; dean acad. affairs Howard U. Law Sch., Washington, 2001—02, 2003—04, interim dean, 2002—03; prof. law Howard U., Washington, 2004—. Chmn. D.C. Jud. Nomination Commn., 1992-2005, mem., 2005—. Bd. dirs. Nat. Black Child Devel. Inst., 1975-80, Anacostia Econ. Devel. Corp., 1970-74; chmn. Occupl. Safety and Health Bd., Washington, 1979-80; trustee WETA-TV Channel 26, 1984-94. Mem. ABA, Nat. Conf. Black Lawyers, Nat. Conf. Bar Examiners (multistate profl. responsibility com. 1986-89), World Peace Through Law (chairperson young lawyers sect. 1973-75). Office: Howard U Sch Law Van Ness & Connecticut Ave NW Washington DC 20001 Office Phone: 202-806-8061.

WORTMAN, MARLENE STEIN, historian; b. Vienna; d. Leon and Pauline (Lindenbaum) Stein; m. Richard S. Wortman, June 14, 1960; 1 child, Leonie. AB, Syracuse U., 1958; PhD, U. Chgo., 1966; postgrad. in law, Bklyn. Law Sch., 1988-92. Asst. prof. in Am. history Ill. Inst. Tech., Chgo., 1969-77; ind. scholar Inst. for Rsch. in History, N.Y.C., 1977-81, Princeton (N.J.) Rsch. Forum, 1981-87. Pres., v.p. Princeton Rsch. Forum, 1981-85; grants officer Inst. for Rsch. in History, N.Y.C., 1980; coord. Chgo. Met. Area Women's History Group, 1974-76. Editor: (book) Women in American Law, 1985; co-author: The Roads They Made: Women in Illinois History, 1977; contbr. articles to profl. jours; editor: (newsletter) Conf. Group in Women's History, 1975-77. Vice pres. ACLU, N.J., 1982-84, co-chair Women's Rights Com., 1983-87. Conf. grantee on housing N.J. Com. for Humanities, Princeton, 1983; grantee NEH, 1979-81; recipient travel fellowship Am. Philos. Soc., 1975, rsch. fellowship Ill. Inst. Tech., 1974. Mem. NOW, Planned Parenthood. Avocation: hiking. Home: 410 Riverside Dr Apt 91 New York NY 10025-7924

WORTMANN, DOROTHY WOODWARD, physician; b. Easton, Pa., Mar. 14, 1945; d. Robert Simpson III and Esther (Thomas) Woodward; m. Robert Lewis Wortmann, June 14, 1969; children: Jonathan Thomas, William Lewis. BA, Mount Holyoke Coll., 1967; MD, U. Kans. Sch. Medicine, 1971. Diplomate Am. Bd. Pediatrics, subspecialty pediat. rheumatology. Clin. instr. pediatrics Med. Coll. Wis., Milw., 1979-80, instr. pediatrics, 1980-82, asst. prof. pediatrics, 1982-92; assoc. clin. prof. pediatrics East Carolina U. Sch. Medicine, Greenville, N.C., 1993—. Med. dir. rheumatology Children's Hosp. Wis., Milw., 1980-92. Chair for juvenile arthritis and mem. pub. and patient svcs. com. Arthritis Found., Milw., 1981-92, bd. dirs. Carolinas chpt., 1997—; med. adv. bd. Lupus Found., Milw., 1983-92. Recipient Disting. Svc. award Arthritis Found., 1991. Fellow Am. Acad. Pediatrics (mem. exec. coun. for rheumatology 1993-98), Am. Coll. Rheumatology (mem. sect. pediat. rheumatology); mem. N.C. Med. Soc., N.C. Pediat. Soc. Home: 9849 S Winston Ave Tulsa OK 74137-4840

WOSK, MIRIAM, artist; b. Vancouver, B.C., Can., Aug. 17, 1947; d. Morris and Dena Wosk; 1 child, Adam. Student, U. B.C., 1966; AAS, Fashion Inst. Tech., N.Y.C., 1969; postgrad., Sch. Visual Arts, New Sch. Social Rsch., N.Y.C., 1969—74. Freelance illustrator 1st cover Ms mag., 30th ann. cover Ms mag., Mademoiselle, N.Y. Times, Esquire, Vogue, N.Y. Mag., Viva, McCalls, Saturday Rev., Sesame St., New West, Psychology Today, 1969—79; curator group show The Inner Lives of Women: Psyche, Spirit and Soul Spring St. Gallery, L.A., 1996. One woman shows include Transam. Ctr., L.A., 1983, West Beach, L.A., 1988, Wilshire Pacific Bldg., L.A., 1991, 2001, Robert Berman Gallery, Santa Monica, Calif., 1991, 2001., Billy Shire Fine Arts, Culver City, 2006, Santa Monica Mus. Art, 2006; group shows include Harkness House Gallery, N.Y.C., 1979-80, Dist. 1199 Cultural Ctr. Inc., N,. 1981, Smithsonian Inst., Washington, 1981, Transam. Pyramid, San Francisco, 1983, Barnsdall Art Gallery, L.A., 1983, Functional Art Gallery, L.A., 1985, One Market Plaza, San Francisco, 1986, Laforet Mus., Tokyo, 1986, Art et Industrie Gallery, N.Y.C., 1986, Otis Parsons Sch. Design, L.A., 1987, B1 Gallery, Santa Monica, 1987, Katharina Rich Perlow Gallery, N.Y.C., 1988, Sam Francis Studio, Santa Monica, 1988, Gallery Functional Art, Santa Monica, 1989, 91, Santa Monica Mus. Art, 1990, 99, 2000, Getty Mus., Malibu, Calif., 1990, James Corcoran Gallery, Santa Monica, 1990, Joan Robey Gallery, Denver, 1992, Cultural Ctr., Eureka, Calif., Calif. State U., Long Beach, 1992, Pacific Design Ctr., L.A., 1992, U. Art Mus., Long Beach, 1992, L.A. County Mus. Art, 1992, 96, Helander Gallery, Palm Beach, Fla., 1993, Spring St. Gallery, L.A., 1994, 96, Anderson Ranch Art Ctr., Aspen, Colo., 1995, Park Ave. Armory, N.Y.C., 1997, 98, 2000, Adam Baumgold Gallery, N.Y.C., 1997, Pub. Corp. Arts, Long Beach Arts, 1998, Boritzer Gray Hamano, Santa Monica, 1999, Santa Monica Fine Arts Studio, 1999, Jan Baum Gallery, L.A., 2000, Ricco/Maresca Gallery, N.Y.C., 2003, Rosamund Felsen Gallery, Santa Monica, 2003; pub. in nat. and internat. mags., books and newspapers including The Golden Age of Mag. Illustration: The Sixties and Seventies, New Feminist Criticism-Art-Identity Action, L.A. Times, Washington Post, O At Home, Casa Vogue, L'Express Paris and Idea Internat. (Japan); artist: (book) Sequins and Skeletons: The Art of Miriam Wosk, 2006; film subject: (by Terry Sanders) Language of the Soul: The Art of Miriam Wosk, 2006. Recipient Merit award Art Dirs. Club N.Y., cert. of merit Soc. Illustrators, cert. excellence Am. Inst. Graphic Artists; named guest editor Mademoiselle Mag. Personal E-mail: miriamwosk@hotmail.com.

WOTHERSPOON, MARY RUTH, artist, writer; b. Greenville, SC, Feb. 3, 1924; d. Sigmond and Margaret Heyn Sanger; m. William Wallace Wotherspoon, Dec. 28, 1985; m. Eugene Thomas Swigart, Jr. (dec.); children: Thomas John, Stephen Herrick, Margaret Elizabeth, Mary Catherine. BA, Toledo U., 1976. Bd. dirs. Conlon Svc. Ctr., Toledo, 1974—75, Child Daycare Ctr., Toledo, 1964—66. Editor (also illustrator): Poems and Prose by Margot Sanger, 1979; illustrator Johnny Bushytail, 1957; author (also publisher): So Here I Am: But Where Did I Come From?: An Adoptee's Search for Identity, 1994; one-man shows include Sanger Libr., Toledo, Ohio, 1994, The Scarab Club, Detroit, 1992, Monkey Tree Gallery, N. Mex., 2003. Founding sustainer emeritus Art Mus. Aides, Toledo, 1957—2006; mem. Jr. League of Toledo, 1946—2006; mem. women's com. Det. Inst. Arts, Mich., 1992—94. Mem.: Alliance Francaise of Toledo, Nat. Mus. Women Arts, Covenant Auxilliary (life; pres., v.p., mem. ways and means com., corr. sec., mem. scholarship com.), N.Mex. Women in Arts, United Meth. Woman (various positions), Waterloo Woman's Club (v.p.), Garden Club Mich., Santa Fe Garden Club. Republican. Episc. Avocations: art, skiing, golf, aerobics, reading. Home: 3101 Pecos Trail #691 Santa Fe NM 87505

WOTIPKA, CHRISTINE MIN, education educator; BA in Internat. Rels. and French, U. Minn., Twin Cities, 1993; MA in Sociology, Stanford U., 1999, PhD in Internat. Comparative Edn., 2001. Vol. U.S. Peace Corps, Thailand, 1993—95; econ. rschr., English editor 1st Econ. Rsch. Inst., 1995—96; rsch. asst. Comparative Sociology Workshop, 1996—2001; cons. MentorNet, 2001; asst. prof. edn., dir. master's program in internat. and comparative edn. Stanford (Calif.) U., 2001—03; global fellow, vis. asst. prof. internat. inst. UCLA, 2003—04; vis. scholar, acting asst. prof., sch. edn. Stanford Univ., 2004—. Faculty affiliate Expansion and Impact of World Human Rights Regime project, 2002—; MacArthur Consortium affiliate Ctr. for Internat. Security and Coop., 2000—; mem. adv. bd. sci. and tech. TV Digital Turbulence, 2002—. Office: Stanford U Sch Edn 485 Lasuen Mall Stanford CA 94305-3096

WOYSKI, MARGARET SKILLMAN, retired geology educator; b. West Chester, Pa., July 26, 1921; d. Willis Rowland and Clara Louise (Howson) Skillman; m. Mark M. Woyski, June 19, 1948; children: Nancy Elizabeth, William Bruno, Ronald David, Wendelin Jane. BA in Chemistry, Wellesley (Mass.) Coll., 1943; MS in Geology, U. Minn., 1945, PhD in Geology, 1946. Geologist Mo. Geol. Survey and Water Resources, Rolla, 1946-48; instr. U. Wis., Madison, 1948-52; lectr. Calif. State U., Long Beach, 1963-67, lectr. to prof. Fullerton, 1966-91, assoc. dean Sch. Natural Sci. and Math., 1981-91, emeritus prof., 1991—. Contbr. articles to profl. jours.; author lab. manuals;

editor guidebooks. Fellow Geol. Soc. Am. (program chmn. 1982); mem. South Coast Geol. Soc. (hon. pres. 1974), Mineral Soc. Am. Home: 880 Morningside Dr Apt M-320 Fullerton CA 92835-3577

WOZNIAK, JOYCE MARIE, sales executive; b. Detroit, Aug. 3, 1955; d. Edmund Frank and Bernice (Liske) W. BA, Mich. State U., 1976; MA, Nat. U., San Diego, 1988; postgrad., U.S. Internat. U., 1989-90. Probation officer San Diego County Probation, 1979-81; prodn. engr. Tuesday Prodns., Inc., San Diego, 1981-85; nat. sales mgr. Advance Rec. Products, San Diego, 1986-88; acct. exec. Joyce Enterprises, San Diego, 1986-95; sales exec. Audio-Video Supply Inc., San Diego, 1988-98; account exec. M.C.S.I. (formerly Consol. Media Sys., Inc.), San Diego, 2000—02; sys. integration specialist TV Magic, Inc., San Diego, 2002—03; sys. sales engr. Opticomm Corp., San Diego, 2003—04; realtor Century 21-Harbor Realty Team LLC, Rogers City, Mich., 2004—. Producer (video) Loving Yourself, 1987, southwest cable access program, 1986-95; registered marriage, family and child counselor-intern, Calif., 1989. Active Zool. Soc. San Diego. Mem.: Internat. TV Assn. (treas. San Diego chpt. 1990—91), NAFE, NATAS, Calif. Assn. Marriage and Family Therapists, Art Glass Assn. So. Calif., Nat. Assn. Broadcasters. Personal E-mail: joycewozniak@hotmail.com. Business E-Mail: joyce.wozniak@century21.com.

WRAE, NATASHA, lawyer; b. 1971; BS in Molecular and Cell Biology, U. Ariz., 1992; JD, U. Balt., 1999. Lic.: Ariz. 1999, Md. 1999, bar: Ariz. Worked for Mayo Clinic, Rochester, Minn.; atty. Law Office of Natasha Wrae, Tucson, 1999—. Former coach Cholla High Sch. Mock Trial Prog.; head coach U. Ariz. Mock Trial Prog.; vol. judge Tucson 4-H. Named one of 40 Under 40, Tucson Bus. Edge, 2006. Mem.: Am. Mock Trial Assn., Am. Civil. Liberties Union, Nat. Assn. Women Bus. Owners, Nat. Assn. Criminal Def. Lawyers, Ariz. Attorneys for Criminal Justice, ABA, Pima County Bar Assn. Office: Law Office of Natasha Wrae 100 N Stone Ave Ste 512 Tucson AZ 85701 Office Phone: 520-624-4224.*

WRANCHER, ELIZABETH ANN, music educator, opera singer; b. Indpls., Oct. 19, 1930; d. Charles Edwin and Evelyn Louise (Helck) W. MusB, Ind. U., 1955. Opera singer, Europe, 1955-68; asst. prof. music U. South Fla., Tampa, 1968-74; pvt. practice Winter Park, Fla., 1974—; assoc. prof. music U. Ctrl. Fla., Orlando, 1974—2003. Cons. Disney World, Orlando, 1987—; summer tchr. Music Theatre Bavaria, Oberandorf, Germany, 2001. Actress in 3 German movies, 1963-67; opera concert singer, 1968-91; recorded music of Thomas Beversdorf. Past bd. dirs., adv. bd. Orlando Opera Co. Recipient Life Achievement award, 1993, T.I.P. award U. Ctrl. Fla., 1996; Fulbright scholar, Germany, 1955; U. Ctrl. Fla. grantee, 1987. Mem.: Fla. State Music Tchrs. Assn., Fla. Vocal Assn., Nat. Assn. Tchrs. Singing (pres. Ctrl. Fla. chpt. 1996—), Nat. Arts and Letters, Nat. Federated Music Clubs (life), Wed. Music Club (1st v.p. 2004—05, pres. 2005—), Phi Kappa Lambda, Mu Phi Epsilon (life). Republican. Baptist. Achievements include concert recordings in Mozart Deim Archives, Salzburg, Austria, Augsburg Archives. Avocations: art, pastels, philosophy, religions. Home: 2630 Amsden Rd Winter Park FL 32792-3513 Office Phone: 407-678-1916. Personal E-mail: ewrancher@yahoo.com.

WRAY, BETTY BEASLEY, allergist, immunologist, pediatrician; b. Ga., 1935; MD, Med Coll. Ga., 1960. Diplomate Am. Bd. Allergy and Immunology, Am. Bd. Clin. Lab. Immunology. Intern Talmadge Meml. Hosp., Augusta, Ga., 1960-61, resident in pediatrics, 1962, 64-65, fellow in pediatric allergy, 1966-68; staff mem. Med. Coll. Ga., Augusta, 1979—, prof. pediat. medicine, interim dean Sch. Medicine, v.p. clin. activities, 2000—02, prof. emeritus, 2002—. Mem.: Am. Coll. Allergy, Asthma and Immunology, Am. Acad. Pediat., Am. Acad. Allergy and Immunology, Am. Pediatric Soc. Office: Med Coll Georgia BG 1009 Augusta GA 30912 Office Phone: 706-721-3531. E-mail: bettyw@mail.mcg.edu.

WRAY, GERALDINE SMITHERMAN (JERRY WRAY), artist; b. Shreveport, La., Dec. 15, 1925; d. David Ewart and Mary Virginia (Hoss) Smitherman; m. George Downing Wray, June 24, 1947; children: Mary Virginia Hill, Deanie Galloway, George D. Wray III, Nancy Armistead. BFA with honors, Newcomb Art Sch., Tulane U., 1946. Tchr. children's art. One woman shows include Don Batman Gallery, Kansas City, Mo., 1982, Gallery II, Baton Rouge, 1985, McNeese Coll., Lake Charles, La., 1987, Dragonfly Gallery, Shreveport, La., 1987, Barnwell Garden and Art Ctr., Shreveport, 1988, 95, Southdown Mus., Houma, La., 1989, La. State U., Shreveport, 1991, WTN Radio Station, Shreveport, 1993, The Cambridge Club, Shreveport, 1993, Centenary Coll., 1993, Northwestern State U., Natchitoches, La., 1995, Goddard Mus., Ardmore, Okla., 1996, Art Buyers Caravan, Atlanta, 1996, Lockhaven (Pa.) U., 1996, Billingsley Gallery, Pensacola, Fla., 1996, Casa D'Arte, Shreveport, La., 1996, N.E. State U., Monroe, La., 1997, Art Expo, N.Y.C., 1997, Palmer Gallery, Hot Springs Ark., 1998, Tower Art Gallery, Shreveport, La., 1999, Meadows Mus. Retrospective, Shreveport, 2003, Schumpert Hosp. Integrated Medicine, Shreveport, 2003, Midwestern Tex. U., 2003, Wichita Falls, Tex., 2003, Bistineau Art Gallery, Shreveport, La., 2004; group shows include Watercolor USA Springfield, Mo., 1988, Waddell's Gallery, Shreveport, 1988, 91, Water Works Gallery, Dallas, 1990, Southwestern Watercolor Show, 1991 (D'Arches award, Creative Artist award 1997), Masur Mus. Exhbn. (honorable mention 91, 92), Bossier Art Ctr., Bossier City, La., 1992, Irving Art Assn. (honorable mention), 1992, Leon Loard Gallery, Montgomery, Ala., 1993, Ward-Nasse Gallery, N.Y.C., 1993, 97, Soc. Experimental Artists Internat. (1st. place, honorable mention), 1993, Nat. Watercolor Soc. Ann., 1994-96, 98, 2003, Art Expo, N.Y.C., 1996, Casa D'Arte, Shreveport, 1996, Art Buyers Caravan, Atlanta, 1996, Off The Wall Gallery, Savannah, Ga., 1997, Art Effects Gallery, Merian, Pa., Boulevard Art Gallery, Macon, Ga., 1997, Visual Inspirations, Newton, N.J., 1997, Mossey Brake Gallery, Tex., 1997, Barnwell Ctr. (with children & grandchildren), Shreveport LA, 1998, Schumpert Imaging Ctr., 2000, Manhattan Arts Mag. Showcase Award, Nat. Assn. Women Artist Traveling Show, Northwestern U., La., 2004, Catherine Lollard Wolf Competitive Show, N.Y.C., 2005, Shreveport Regional Arts Coun. Show, 2005, 06, Meadows Mus., Shreveport, La., 2006; permanent collections include NAWA, Zimmerli Mus., Rutgers Univ., N.J.-Meir Mus., Lynchburg, Va., Goddard Mus. Ardmore, Okla., Bibl. Arts Ctr., Dallas, La. State Capitol Bldg., Lockhaven Univ. Penn., LSUS Med. Ctr., Shreveport, LA., Shacknow Mus., Plantation, Fla., Meadows Mus., Shreveport, La., 2003, Integrated Medicine Schumpert Wellness Ctr., Shreveport, 2003, Midwestern U., Tex., 2003, Northwestern U., Natchitoches, La., 2004, Catherine Lollard Wolfe Exhibit, N.Y.C. Art chmn. Jr. League, Shreveport, 1955-60; bd. dirs. Holiday-in-Dixie Cotillion, Shreveport, 1974-76. Inducted into Visual Artists Hall of Fame, Shreveport, La., 1998. Mem. Nat. Assn. Women Artists, Nat. Watercolor Soc. (signature mem. 1994, 96), Southwestern Watercolor Soc. (signature mem. 1991), La. Watercolor Soc. (signature mem. 1990), La. Artists Inc. (elected mem.), Internat. Soc. Exptl. Artists (signature mem.), Western Fedn. Soc. Artists (signature mem.), Watercolor Soc. Houston (signature mem.). Episcopalian. Avocation: tennis. Home: 573 Spring Lake Dr Shreveport LA 71106-4603 Personal E-mail: jerrywray@bellsouth.net.

WRAY, YANA, medical/surgical nurse; b. Ky., Nov. 26, 1957; d. Raymond H. and ruby N. (Stidham) Combs; children: Kevin S., Amanda P. ADN, S.E. Community Coll., Cumberland, Ky., 1987. Head nurse med./surg. St. Mary's Hosp., Norton, Va.; staff nurse Diabetic Treatment Ctr. Indian Path Med. Ctr., Kingsport, Tenn.; home health aid supr. Superior Health Care, Kingsport; staff nurse med.-surg. Holston Valley Hosp. and Med. Ctr. Mem. Tenn. Geriatric Soc., U. Ky. Alumni Assn., Phi Theta Kappa. Home: 3100 Glen Alpine Rd Kingsport TN 37660-7848

WREN, LEAH, theater educator, director; b. Katy, Tex., June 27, 1978; d. Carl Eugene and Karen Norfolk Hursman; m. David Scott Wren, Nov. 28, 2003; 1 child, Sarah Bethany. BA in Theatre Edn., Brigham Young U., Provo, Utah, 2000; MEd, So. Wesleyan U., Central, SC, 2004. Tchr. theatre Fairforest Mid. Sch., Spartanburg, SC, 2000—. Dir. Greer Children's Theatre, SC, 2003—, Spartanburg Youth Theatre, 2001—; tchr. Boys and Girls Club, 2005—. Singer and actor (traveling performance troupe) Spartanburg Little Theatre's Downstage Centre; dir.: (play production) Charlie and the Chocolate Factory, (choreographer) Schoolhouse Rock Live! Jr., Alice in Wonderland; actor, dancer, singer (play production) Joseph and the Amazing Technicolor Dreamcoat. Recipient Advisor Yr., Muse Machine Spartanburg County, 2002—03. Mem. Lds Ch. Avocations: piano, scrapbooks, dance. Office: Fairforest Middle School 4120 N Blackstock Rd Spartanburg SC 29301 Office Phone: 864-576-1270. E-mail: wrenlh@spart6.org.

WRIGHT, AMY RALYNN, athletic trainer, small business owner; b. Wheeling, W.Va., May 29, 1978; d. Donald and Phyllis Marie Zalenski. BS in Edn., Ohio State U., Columbus, 2000. Cert. athletic trainer Nat. Athletic Trainers Assn., Tex., 2004. Claims examiner Compensation Consultants, Inc., Dublin, Ohio, 2002—04; cert. athletic trainer Southeastern Ohio Regional Med. Ctr., Cambridge, 2004—; cert. athletic trainer and instr. Belmont Tech. Coll., St. Clairsville, 2005—. Ind. cons. Mary Kay Cosmetics, Wheeling, W.Va., 2003—. Mem.: Ohio Athletic Trainers Assn., Nat. Athletic Trainers Assn., Ohio Occupl. Therapy, Phys. Therapy and Athletic Trainers Bd. (licentiate). Roman Catholic. Avocations: travel, crafts, music, pets. Home: 3118 Eoff St Wheeling WV 26003-4116 Office: SEa Ohio Regional Med Ctr 10095 Brick Church Rd Cambridge OH 43725 Office Phone: 740-439-8977. E-mail: wrightbuckeyes@yahoo.com.

WRIGHT, ANN FOLLINGER, psychotherapist; b. Ft. Wayne, Feb. 17, 1927; d. Alfred Martin Follinger and Margery Aurelia (Moon) Ziegfeld; m. Dudley Kingsbury Wright, Sept. 24, 1947 (div. 1967); children: Margery Wright Barnhorst, Dudley K., Joan C., Polly C., Stacey Wright Renker. Student, U. Mich., 1945-47; BA, Chapman Coll., 1966; MSW, San Diego State U., 1969. Sr. social work supr. Dept. of Social Services, San Diego, 1969-76; nun Order of St. Helena, Vails Gate, N.Y., 1976-83; sr. social work supr. Dept. of Social Svcs., San Diego, 1983-87; clin. social worker U. Calif. Med. Ctr., San Diego, 1987—93; pvt. practice San Diego, 1993—2005. Bd. dirs. Big Sister League, San Diego, 1984-85, San Diego AIDS Project, 1984-87, San Diego AIDS Assistance Fund, 1988. Mem. Nat. Assn. of Social Workers. Democrat. Episcopalian. Home: 74992 Havasu Ct Indian Wells CA 92210 Personal E-mail: wowwow5@aol.com.

WRIGHT, ANTOINETTE D., museum administrator; Dep. dir. Donor's Forum Chgo., 1990—93, dir. fin./adminstrn., asst. treas., 1993—97; pres., CEO DuSable Mus. African Am. History, Chgo., 1997—. Office: DuSable Mus African Am History 740 E 56th Pl Chicago IL 60637

WRIGHT, APRIL MARIE, elementary school educator; d. David McWilliams Wright and Nora Kathleen Swigart. BS in Elem. Edn. and Early Childhood Edn., Edinboro U., Edinboro, Pa., 2001. Cert. tchr. Pa. Long term day-to-day substitute tchr. Pine Richland Mid. Sch., Gibsonia, Pa., 2001—04; tchr. 5th grade Hance Elem. Sch., Gibsonia, 2004—. Ram Rangers sponsor Pine Richland Sch. Dist., 2002—04, student coun. sponsor, 2002—03, dance team coach, 2003. Mem.: Pa. State Edn. Assn., Nat. Sci. Tchrs. Assn. Avocations: golf, reading, walking, cooking. Office: Hance Elementary School Molnar Dr Gibsonia PA 15044

WRIGHT, ARTHUREE ROSEMILLE MCLAUGHLIN, library director; d. Arthur Speigel and Iris McLaughlin; m. Obie Wright, June 25, 1972; 1 child, Joshua Kondwani. BA, Ind. U., Bloomington, 1967; MLS, Rutgers U., New Brunswick, N.J., 1969; PhD, U. of Md., College Park, 1984. Diaconal min. Wesley Theol. Sem., D.C., 1995. Asst. sci. libr. MIT, Cambridge, Mass., 1969—73, assoc. sci. libr., 1973—75; asst. libr. Meredith Coll., Raleigh, NC, 1975—76; assoc. libr. Howard U., Washington, 1982—83, supr. of reference, 1983—89, coord. collection devel., 1989—91, asst. dir. for collection mgmt. and br. libr. svcs., 1991—95, asst. dir. for info., rsch., and resource devel., 1996—98, assoc. dir. for info., instrn. and resource svcs., 1998—. Adj. lectr. U. of Md., College Park, 1986—2001; bd. dirs. Wesley Found., Howard U., Washington; chair comm. on higher edn. and campus ministry Balt. Wash. Conf. of the United Meth. Ch., Columbia, Md., 2004—; mentor Chesapeake Info. Rsch. Libr. Alliance, Washington, 2003—; mem. nat. adv. com. ERIC Clearinghouse on Tchg. and Tchr. Edn., Washington, 1999—2003; founder, dir. Howard U. Cybercamp, Washington, 1998—2002; bd. dirs., pres. Cambridge YWCA, 1973—75; field reviewer Inst. of Mus. and Libr. Svcs., Washington, 1998—2002. Contbr. bibliography. Mem. NAACP; chair children and poverty task force Balt. Wash. Conf. of the United Meth. Ch., Columbia, Md., 1998—2003. Recipient Youth Outreach grant, Morino Inst., 1998—99, doctoral fellowship, U. of Md., 1977—80. Mem.: ALA (external rev. panelist com. on accreditation 2002—03), Assn. Coll. and Rsch. Librs. (chair rsch. com. 1988—89), Diakonia of the Americas and the Caribbean, Reference and User Svcs. Assn., Ch. and Synagogue Libr. Assn., Nat. Coun. of Negro Women, Beta Phi Mu, Delta Sigma Theta. United Methodist. Avocations: singing, playing piano. Office: Howard Univ 500 Howard Pl NW Washington DC 20059 Office Phone: 202-806-7926. Home Fax: 866-421-0834; Office Fax: 202-806-5903. Personal E-mail: drawright2001@yahoo.com. Business E-Mail: arwright@howard.edu.

WRIGHT, BARBARA EVELYN, microbiologist, educator; b. Pasadena, Calif., Apr. 6, 1926; d. Gilbert Munger Wright and Leta Luella (Brown) Deery. AB, Stanford U., 1947, MA, 1948, PhD, 1951. Biologist NIH, Bethesda, Md., 1953-61; assoc. biochemist Mass. Gen. Hosp., Boston, 1961-69; asst. prof. microbiology Harvard Med. Sch., Boston, 1966-75, assoc. prof., 1975-82; rsch. dir. Boston Biomed. Rsch. Inst., 1967-82; rsch. prof. divsn. biol. scis. U. Mont., Missoula, 1982—. Spkr. in field; dir. Stella Duncan Rsch. Inst., Missoula, 1982—; cons. Miles Lab., Elkhart, Ind., 1980-84. Author: Critical Variables in Differentiation, 1973; editor: Control Mechanisms in Respiration and Fermentation, 1963; contbr. articles to profl. jours. Grantee NIH, NSF, 1961—. Mem. AAAS (pres. Pacific divsn. 1984-85), Am. Soc. for Microbiology (Nat. Found. for Microbiology lectr. 1970, divsnl. lectr. 1978), Am. Soc. Biol. Chemists. Avocations: board sailing, skiing, tennis. Office: U Mont Divsn Biol Scis 32 Campus Dr #4824 Missoula MT 59812-4824 Home: 9650 Obrien Creek Rd Missoula MT 59804-5880 Office Fax: 406-243-4184. E-mail: bewright@selway.umt.edu.

WRIGHT, BELINDA LEIGH, music educator; d. Donald Leon and Margaret Ann Wright; life ptnr. Pooie G. Cantrell; children: Lynli Noel Cantrell-Wright, Tucker Leigh Cantrell-Wright. Assoc. band dir. Daleville Schs., Daleville, 1982—83; band dir. Miller County H.S., Colquitt, Ga., 1983—86, Reeltown H.S., Notasulga, Ala., 1986—. Named WSFA Class Act, TV Sta. WSFA, 1998, Tchr. of Yr., Reeltown H.S., 1999. Mem.: Tallapoosa County Educator's Assn., Ala. Educator's Assn., Music Educator's Nat. Conf., Ala. Bandmasters Assn. (vice chmn. dist. VI 1999—2000). Office Phone: 334-257-4185. Personal E-mail: reeltownband2002@yahoo.com.

WRIGHT, BETTY REN, children's book writer; b. Wakefield, Mich., June 15, 1927; d. William and Revena Evelyn (Trezise) W.; m. George Albert Frederiksen, Oct. 9, 1976. BA, Milw.-Downer Coll., 1949. With Western Pub. Co., Inc., 1949-78, mng. editor Racine Editl., 1967-78. Author: The Doll House Murders, 1983, Christina's Ghost, 1985, The Summer of Mrs. MacGregor, 1986, A Ghost in the Window, 1987, The Pike River Phantom, 1988, Rosie and the Dance of the Dinosaurs, 1989, The Ghost of Ernie P., 1990, A Ghost in the House, 1991, The Scariest Night, 1991, The Ghosts of Mercy Manor, The Ghost of Popcorn Hill, 1993, The Ghost Witch, 1993, A Ghost Comes Calling, 1994, Out of the Dark, 1995, Haunted Summer, 1996, Too Many Secrets, 1997, The Ghost in Room 11, 1998, A Ghost in the Family, 1998, Pet Detectives, 1999, The Moonlight Man, 2000, The Wish Master, 2000, Crandalls' Castle, 2003, The Blizzard, 2003, Princess for a Week, 2006; contbr. articles to mags. Recipient Alumni Svc. award Lawrence U., 1973, Lynde and Harry Bradley Maj. Achievement award, 1997, numerous awards for books including Mo. Mark Twain award, 1986, 96, Tex. Bluebonnet award, 1986, 88, Young Readers award Pacific N.W. Libr. Assn., 1986, Reviewer's Choice Booklist, Ala. Young Readers award, 1987, Ga. Children's Choice award, 1988, Ind. Young Hoosier Book award, 1989, 96, Children's Choice Book/Internat. Reading Assn.—CBC, 1984, S.C. Children's Choice award, 1995, Okla. Sequoyah Children's Choice award, 1988, 95, award Fla. Sunshine State, 2001, Notable Wis. Author for Youth Lit. award, 2006. Mem.: Coun. Wis. Authors (Juvenile Book award 1985, 1996), Allied Authors, Phi Beta Kappa. Avocations: reading, travel. Home and Office: 6223 Hilltop Dr Racine WI 53406-3479

WRIGHT, BONNIE H., elementary school educator; b. Raleigh, NC, Sept. 30, 1960; d. William T. and Secunda P. Huxster; m. Tony T. Wright, Aug. 8, 1989 (dec.); 1 child, Josh Gordon. BA in Early Childhood Edn., U. NC, Charlotte, 1982, BA in Intermediate Edn., 1984, BA in Intermediate Edn., 2002. Cert. mentor N.C., 1989. 6th & 7th grade mid. sch. math tchr. Scotland County Schs., Laurinburg, NC, 1984—88; 5th grade elem. tchr. Charlotte-Mecklenburg Schs., NC, 1988—89, 6th grade elem. tchr., 1989—90; 7th grade mid. sch. math tchr. Wake County Pub. Schs., Raleigh, NC, 1991—92; elem. and mid. sch. math tchr. Charlotte-Mecklenburg Schs., NC, 1992—2000; 7th and 8th grade mid. sch. sci. tchr. Charlotte Christian Sch., NC, 2000—. Migrant edn. instr. Scotland County Schs., Laurinburg, NC, 1984—85, math/sci. fair coord., 1984—85, math dept. head, 1985—86, so. assn. creditation for schools, 1985—86, math field day coord., 1986—87, grade level chairperson, 1986—87, mid. sch. tv teen scene, 1987—88, refugee tutorial program, 1987—88; assistance and intervention team Charlotte-Mecklenburg Schs., NC, 1988—91; math counts coord. Wake County Pub. Schs., Raleigh, NC, 1991—92, Beta Club sponsor, 1991—92, sch. improvement com., 1991—92, staff devel. com., 1991—92, math dept. head, 1991—92, team leader, 1991—92; grade level chairperson Charlotte-Mecklenburg Schs., NC, 1992—2000, mentor, 1992—2000, math field day coord., 1992—93, pre-algebra acad. instr., 1993—95, minority achievement com., 1995—98, sci. fair coord., 1995—98, right moves coord., 1998—99; sci. dept. com. Charlotte Christian Sch., NC, 2000—04, grade chairperson/team leader, 2000—05, initially lic. tchr. (ILT) coord., 2000—06, math tutor, 2000—06, 8th grade trip coord., 2000—06. Summer sch. instr. Charlotte-Mecklenburg Schs., NC, 1988—98, Scotland County Schs., Laurinburg, NC, 1985—88, Wake County Pub. Schs., Raleigh, NC, 1991—92; vol. Operation Christmas Child, Charlotte Christian Schs., NC, 2000—06; Bible svc. project Charlotte Christian Sch., 2002—03; Sunday sch. tchr. U. City United Meth. Ch., Charlotte, 1994—98; partnership of mid. sch. students with pre-k students as mentors and to incorporate literacy Charlotte Christian Sch., NC, 2005—06. Finalist Joint Engring. Societies Award for Outstanding Math & Sci. Tchr., Engrs. of Am., 1993, Harris Y award, First Union Bank, 1995; recipient Tchr. of the Yr. award, Sycamore Ln. Mid. Sch. in Scotland County, 1987, Tchr. of the Yr. 1st Runner-up in Scotland County, Scotland County Schs., 1987, Unsung Am. Heroes award, ING, 2005. Fellow: N.C. Assn. of Educators (assoc.), Internat. Reading Assn. (assoc.), Parent, Tchr., Student Assn. (assoc.), Career Devel. Program (assoc.), PTO (assoc.), Assn. of Christian Schs. (assoc.), Assn. of Christian Schs. (assoc.); mem.: Parent Tchr. Fellowship (assoc.), PTA (assoc.), N.C. Coun. of Tchg. Math. (assoc.), N.C. Sci. Tchrs. Assn. (assoc.), Delta Zeta (life). Dc Statehood Party. Methodist. Avocations: travel, coin collector, piano, cross-stitching, scrapbooking. Home: 2845 Sharon View Rd Charlotte NC 28210 Office: Charlotte Christian Sch 7301 Sardis Rd Charlotte NC 28270 Office Phone: 704-366-5657. Office Fax: 704-366-5678. Business E-Mail: bonnie.wright@charchrist.com.

WRIGHT, BONNIE MCLEAN, psychology educator; b. Tampa, Fla., Apr. 20, 1956; d. Thaddeus W. and Elizabeth (Jones) McLean; m. Jerry E. Wright, June 18, 1983; children: Heather L. and Nicole V. (twins). BS in Psychology, North Ga. Coll., 1978; MS in Psychology, U. Ga., 1981, PhD, 1983. Asst. prof. psychology Bluefield (Va.) Coll., 1984-85; asst. prof. Gardner-Webb U., Boiling Springs, N.C., 1985-93, assoc. prof. psychology, 1993—, chair dept. psychology, 1996—. Adj. prof. psychology Tex. Women's U., Denton, 1992-93; cons. in field. Contbr. articles to profl. jours. Bd. dirs. Life Enrichment Ctr., Shelby, N.C., 1985-87, ACCES, Shelby, 1990-92; leader Girl Scouts U.S., Lewisville, Tex., 1992-93, Boiling Springs, 1993—, United Way. Mem. Assn. Women in Psychology, Psi Chi, Sigma Phi Omega. Baptist. Avocations: sewing, aerobics, guitar. Office: Gardner-Webb U Dept Psychology Boiling Springs NC 28017

WRIGHT, BONNIE SHANKLE, assistant principal, choir director; b. Jan. 16, 1960; d. Preston and Adeline Luttrell Shankle; m. James Barry Wright, June 9, 1984; children: Preston, David. B in Music Edn., Ind. U., 1983; MA in Tchg., Bethel Coll., 1990. Cert. ednl. specialist Union U., 2005. Tchr. Covington Elem., Tenn., 1986—99; chorus, drama tchr. Covington HS, 1999—2003; asst. prin. Covington Integrated Arts Acad., 2003—05. Instr. Red Cross, 1983—2004; pianist, bell choir dir. First United Methodist Ch., Covington, 1997—2005, choir dir., 2003—05. Mem.: Alpha Delta Kappa (pres. 2003). Republican. Methodist. Office: Covington Integrated Arts Acad 760 Bert Johnston Covington TN 38019

WRIGHT, BRENDA K., primary and elementary school educator; b. Batavia, N.Y., Sept. 12, 1970; d. Ronald Garry and Beverly Frances Rosenberg; m. Murray F. Wright III, July 2, 1994; children: Sarah Catherine, Murray F. BS in Edn., Roberts Wesleyan Coll., 1992; M in Music Edn., Mansfield U., 1996. Robert Pace piano pedagogy cert., Orff Schulwerk level cert. Music tchr. Haverling H.S., Bath, NY, 1992—94, Dana L. Lyon Elem. Sch., Bath, 1994—, Vernon E. Whitman Primary Sch., Bath, 2000—. Choral mem. Orch. Choir So. Fingerlakes, Elmira, NY, 1992—97; music edn. tutor Empire State U., Alfred, NY, 1997—. Mem. Arts So. Fingerlakes Arts Connection, Elmira, NY, 1997—; soloist various chs., 1992—; coord. Sunday Sch. 1st Presby. Ch., 2001—, mem. sr. bell choir, 2001—; bd. dirs. Arts Infusion Project-Haverling Ctrl., NY, 1999—. Mem.: Steuben Educators Music Assn., NY State Music Assn., Music Educators Nat. Conf. Avocations: walking, creative dance, travel, photography, skiing. Home: 9 Mcmaster St Bath NY 14810-1614

WRIGHT, CAROL JEAN, medical/surgical nurse; b. Greenville, Ky., June 30, 1953; d. Charles Keith Fitzhugh and Jeannine Fitzhugh Watkins; children: David, Anthony. AA, Purdue U. Calumet, Hammond, Ind., 1989, postgrad. Laborer Inland Steel Co., East Chicago, Ind.; nurse tech. Community Hosp., Munster, Ind.; grad. nurse St. Mary Med. Ctr., Gary, Ind.; staff nurse At Home Health Inc.; indep. contr., 1992—99; nurse Walnut Creek Nursing Home, 1999—2001; charge nurse midnights Dyer Nursing Home, 2001—04; cons. State of IN., 2004—06. Home: 441 141st St Hammond IN 46327-1246

WRIGHT, CAROLYN D. (C.D. WRIGHT), language educator, poet; b. Mountain Home, Ark., 1949; BA, U. Memphis, 1971; MFA, U. Ark., 1976. Lectr. poetry San Francisco State U., 1979—81; prof. English Brown U., Providence, 1983—. Vis. faculty Burren Sch. Art., Ireland, 1996, U. Iowa., 1997, U. Cin., 2004. Author: Terrorism, 1979, Translations of the Gospel Back into Tongues, 1981, Further Adventures With You, 1986, String Light, 1991 (Poetry Ctr. Book award), Just Whistle, 1993, The Lost Roads Project: A Walk-in Book of Arkansas, 1994, The Reader's Map of Arkansas, 1994, Tremble, 1996, Deepstep Come Shining, 1998, Steal Away: Selected and New Poems, 2002, One Big Self, 2003, Cooling Time: An American Poetry Vigil, 2005, numerous poems. Named State Poet RI, 1994—99; recipient Witter Bynner prize for poetry, 1986, Whiting Writers award, 1989, Gov. Award for Arts, RI, 1990, Lila Wallace award, 1992; fellow, Nat. Endowment for Arts, 1981, 1987; Guggenheim fellow, 1987, MacArthur Fellow, 2004. Fellow: Am. Acad. Arts and Scis. Office: Brown U Box 1923 Providence RI 02912 Business E-Mail: Carolyn_Wright@Brown.edu.

WRIGHT, CECILIA POWERS, gifted and talented educator; b. Phila., Sept. 30, 1946; d. Robert Francis and Rosemary (Redditt) Powers. BS, West Chester (Pa.) U., 1968; MS, Pa. State U., 1972; MA, Gratz Coll., Melrose Park, Pa., 1996. Tchr. Haverford Twp. Sch. Dist., Havertown, Pa., 1968—73; author/editor and instr. McGraw Hill, Paoli, Pa., 1973—78; tchr. Lower Merion Sch. Dist., Wynnewood, Pa., 1987—90; tchr. of gifted West Chester Area Sch. Dist., 1990—. Instr., cons. Regional Tng. Ctr., Gratz Coll., Randolph, NJ, 1996—; seminar presenter Coll. of N.J., Trenton, 1998—2000. Author (and editor): Careers: A Multicultural View, 1977 (Excellence award, 1977). Leader Girl Scouts U.S., Havertown, 1983—87; chairperson good citizens DAR, Chester County, Pa., 1996—. Named to Leaders in Am. Elem.

Edn., Haverford Twp. Sch. Dist., 1971; recipient award, Nat. Band Assn., 2000—01. Mem.: NEA, Band and Orch. Assn. (pres. 2000), Pa. State Edn. Assn. (rep. 1998—). Avocations: watercolor, travel, biking. Home: 15 E Wilmot Ave Havertown PA 19083

WRIGHT, CHELY, country singer; b. Kans. City, Mo., Oct. 25, 1970; Founder Reading, Writing and Rhythm Found. Singer: (songs) He's a Good Ole Boy, 1994, Love That We Lost, 1996, Shut Up and Drive, 1997, Jezebel, 2001, Bumper of My S.U.V., 2004, (albums) Woman in the Moon, 1994, Right in the Middle of It, 1996, Let Me In, 1997, Single White Female, 1991, Never Love You Enough, 2001; actor: (films) Max Keeble's Big Movie, 2001, (TV appearance) Another World, 1999. Recipient Top New Female Vocalist award, Acad. Country Music, 1994. Mailing: PO Box 627 Mokena IL 60448

WRIGHT, CONSTANCE STOREY, retired humanities educator; b. Boston, Mar. 3, 1928; d. Samuel Lame and Dorothy Storey Wright. BA, Scripps Coll., 1950; MA, U. Calif., Berkeley, 1959, PhD, 1965. Instr. English Grinnell Coll., Iowa, 1952—65; asst. prof. U. Colo., Boulder, 1965—69, assoc. prof., 1969—92, prof. emeritus, 1992—; ret., 1992. Adv. bd. Genders, Boulder, 1985—89, Medieval Assn., Rocky Mountain, Tempe, Ariz., 1987—92; rschr. Monterey (Calif.) Mus. Art, 1996—. Editor: Equally in God's Image, 1990; asst. editor: English Lang. Notes, 1965—2003; author (editor): Tales within Tales: Apuleius through Time, 2000. Sec., bd. dirs. Residents Assn., Carmel, Calif., 1993—2000, Preservation Found., Carmel, 2002—. Mem.: MLA, Dante Soc. Am., New Chaucer Soc. Avocations: Asian art, Asian antiques, Latin literature. Home: PO Box 2331 Carmel CA 93921

WRIGHT, DANA JACE, retired emergency nurse practitioner; b. Cleve., Apr. 20, 1952; d. William James and Murl Jean (White) Ewing; m. David Alan Samball, June 22, 1968 (div. Apr. 1971); 1 child, David; m. David M. Wright, July 11, 1981; children: William James, Karen Marie. A in Nursing, Valencia Community Coll., 1973, AA, 1973; BS in Respiratory Therapy, U. Cen. Fla., 1975; MEd, Auburn U., 1979; D in Nursing, Case Western Res. U., 1982. RN, Fla., Ohio, N.Y., Ga.; cert. emergency med. technician; cert. and registered respiratory therapist; cert. med.-surg. nurse; lic. real estate agt., N.Y. Nursing asst. Holiday Hosp., Orlando, Fla., 1970-71, staff nurse critical care unit, intensive care unit, 1973; pvt. duty nurse Med. Personnel Pool, Orlando, 1973-74; nurse critical care burn team Upjohn, Inc., Augusta, Ga., 1976-77; ednl. dir. dept. respiratory therapy U. Hosp., Augusta, 1975-76; mem. staff respiratory therapy VA Hosp., Augusta, 1976-77; clin. instr. respiratory therapy Med. Coll. Ga., Augusta, 1976-77, Columbus Coll., 1977-78; ednl. dir. respiratory therapy Med. Ctr. Hosp., Columbus, 1977-79; staff nurse, relief supr. Kelly Health Care, Beachwood, Ohio, 1979-81; staff nurse Med. Staff, Inc., Cleve., 1981-83; dir. nursing S.R.T. Med. Staff Inc., Cleve., 1983; pres. Wright Properties, Buffalo, 1987-94, Med. Ctr. Vending, 1994-97; ret. nurse, 1994. Part-time nurse Millard Fillmore Suburban Hosp., 1990-91. Treas. Ch. Women's Assn., Snyder, N.Y., 1985-86; mem. nursing resources panel North Ohio Lung Assn., 1981-82; mem. Profl. Parent Network, Buffalo, 1987—, Erie Co. Commn. on the Status of Women, 2000-, vol. Food Shuttle, 1996-; rep. of McLain found. to grantmakers, 2000-; com. reviewer Internat. Charity Project Grants, 2004-05; bd. dirs. Virginia Guildasterne Internat. Fund. Mem. ANA (alt. del. 1993-94), Am. Assn. Nurses Practicing Independently (assoc.), Nat. Nurses Bus., N.Y. State Nurses Assn. (nurse rsch. cons. 1991-92, 94, chair nurse entrepreneurs 1992-94, WNY regional review team 1992-94), Women's Dental Guild, Internat. FEdn. of u. Woman, AAUW (mem. at large 2003-) Republican. Home and Office: 49 Colony Ct Buffalo NY 14226-3507 Personal E-mail: dwright394@aol.com.

WRIGHT, DEBORAH C., bank executive; b. Bennetsville, SC, Jan. 30, 1958; BA, Radcliffe, 1979; MBA, JD, Harvard U., 1984. Assoc. corp. fin. First Boston Bank, 1984; dir. mktg. NYC Partnership, Harlem, 1987; apptd. Housing Authority Bd. NYC, 1992, commr., 1994—96; dir. Upper Manhattan Zone Devel. Corp., 1996—99; pres, CEO Carver Bancorp, Harlem, 1999—, chmn., 2005—. Bd. dirs. Carver Bancorp, Inc., Kraft Foods, Time Warner, 2005—. Bd. dirs. Harvard U., Meml. Sloan-Kettering Cancer Ctr., Partnership NYC, Ministers and Missionaries Benefit Bd. Am. Baptist Churches; founding mem. Lower Manhattan Develop. Corp. Named Community Banker of the Year, The Am. Banker, 2003. Office: Carver Bancorp 75 W 125th St New York NY 10027*

WRIGHT, DIANE, procurement manager; b. St. Louis, Jan. 11, 1956; d. Henderson and Ernestine Brady; m. Kevin Wright; children: Deidre Terrell, Samuel Terrell. BA in Mgmt., Webster U., St. Louis, MO, 1997. Dir. bus. affairs Harris-Stowe State Coll., St. Louis, 1998; mgr. procurement Bi-State Devel. Agy., St. Louis, 1998—. Recruiter vote registration St. Louis Job Corps Center, St. Louis, 1987—95. Recipient Silver Spike award, Bi-State Devel. Agy., 2000 and 2001. Mem.: Nat. Inst. Govt. Purchasing. Avocations: sewing, travel. Office: Bi-State Devel Agy 707 North First St Saint Louis MO 63102-2552 Office Fax: 314982-1558. Business E-Mail: dwright@bsda.org.

WRIGHT, DONNA LAKE, retired marketing professional, volunteer; b. Phila., Jan. 26, 1943; d. William Thomas Lake and Virginia Blair Tobert Lake Sigler; m. Kenneth Harriman Wright, Nov. 4, 1967. BA in Psychology magna cum laude, U. Rochester, 1964. Systems engr. IBM Corp., N.Y.C., NY, 1964—69, sr. mktg. tng. instr., 1969—75, sr. regional mktg. rep., 1976—77, cons. mktg. rep., account mgr. Cranford and West Orange, NJ, 1978—91; part-time adminstr. asst. to pres. Fund for Ednl. Excellence, Montclair, NJ, 1992—94, Asian Creative Corp., Montclair, 1992—98; ret., 1999. COBOL and data processing instr. Montclair Adult Sch., 1969—72. Mem., com. chair Jr. League Montclair-Newark, 1965—; sustaining mem. Jr. League Palm Beaches, West Palm Beach, 1994—; treas. Montclair Arts and Cultural Alliance, 1992—94; dir. Assn. Jr. Leagues Internat., N.Y.C., 1993—95; co-chair Downtown Saturday Night, Montclair, 1993; master gardener Rutgers U. Ext. Svc., Essex County, NJ, 1995. Named honoree, Day Nurseries, Inc., Vol. Ctr. Greater Essex County, 1996, Sustainer of Yr., Jr. League Montclair-Newark, 1997; named one of 50 Woman You Should Know, YWCA Montclair-No. Essex, 1997; recipient Pres. award, Jr. League Montclair-Newark, 1987. Mem.: Garden Club Shelter Island (horticulture chair), Garden Club Montclair (com. chairs), Shelter Island Yacht Club, Gardiner's Bay Country Club, Phi Beta Kappa. Republican. Presbyterian. Avocations: gardening, boating, golf, cooking, piano. Home (Winter): 712 Sandpiper Way North Palm Beach FL 33408 Home (Summer): PO Box 3031 24 E Brander Pkwy Shelter Island Heights NY 11965

WRIGHT, ELLEN S., elementary school educator; d. John H. and Ruby Eileen Myers; m. Donald M. Wright, Apr. 1, 1978; children: Jamie E., Michelle L. B in Elem. Edn., Ill. State U., Normal, 1978; M in Elem. Edn., Ea. Ill. U., Charleston, 2003. Lic. tchr. Ill., 1978. Various tchg. positions Danville Sch. Dist. #118, Ill., 1978—2006; 6th grade math tchr. North Ridge Mid. Sch., Danville, Ill., 1998—, team leader. Named Tchr. of Yr., Danville Commerce Com., 1998.

WRIGHT, EVELYN LOUISE, artist; b. Odessa, Mo., Aug. 2, 1913; d. Elmer Clarence and Anna Bell (Ford) Adams; m. Douglas P. Wright, July 19, 1934 (dec. Dec. 27, 1986); children: Annetta Louise, Judith Elaine, Duane Douglas. Student, Stockton Coll., Calif., 1958—60, U. of Pacific, Stockton, 1960—61, Merced Coll., Calif., 1962—64, Columbia Coll., 1962—64. Graphic artist, Independence, Mo., 1928—34; asst. mgr., bookkeeper Wrights, Stockton, 1945—86; owner, instr. Evelyn's Art Classes and Workshops, Stockton, 1980—; instr. Stockton Sch. Sys., 1945—, Ripona Sch., Calif., 1992—94. Recipient Best of Show award, Richard Yip Art Co., 1980, award, Sonora Nat. Festival, 1982, 1984, Lodi Grape Festival, 1986. Avocation: travel. Home and Studio: 508 W Morada Ln Stockton CA 95210

WRIGHT, FAITH-DORIAN, artist; b. Bklyn., Feb. 9, 1934; d. Abraham and Molly (Janoff) J.; children: Jordan Merritt, Igrid-beth. BS, NYU, 1955, MA, 1958; postgrad., Pratt and Parsons Sch. of Design. Works exhibited in Kathryn Markel Gallery, N.Y.C., 1981, 92, Cumberland Gallery, Nashville, 1981, 92, Barbara Gillman Gallery, Miami, 1982, Hand and Hand Gallery, 1985, 86, Suzanne Gross, Phila., 1986, 87, Gallery Four, Alexandria, Va., 1986, 87, 88, Henri Gallery, Washington, 1986, 87, 88, 89, 90, 91, 92, 93, 94, Benton Gallery, Southampton, 1986, 87, 88, 89, 91, 92, 93, King Stephen Mus., Hungary, 1987, Nat. Gallery Women in the Arts, 1987, 88, 90, 91, 92, Ruth Volid Gallery, Chgo., 1990, James Gallery, Pitts., 1990, Aart Vark Gallery, Phila., 1990, Merrill Chase Gallery, Chgo., 1990, 91, 92, Guild Hall Mus., East Hampton, N.Y., 1991, Joy Berman Gallery, Phila., 1992, Ctr. for Book Arts, N.Y.C., 1992, Barnard-Biederman Fine Arts, N.Y.C., 1994, Arlene Bujese Gallery, East Hampton, 1994, 95, 96, Stoney Brook U., 1994, Harper Collins Exhbn. Space, 1995, Ctr. for Book Arts, 1996, arlene bujese, 1997, Galerie Cargo, Paris, 1997, N.Y. State Mus., Albany, 1997, U. Mont., Missoula, 2002, Nat. Mus. Women in Arts, Washington, 2002, Arlene Bujese, East Hampton, N.Y., 1997-03, Seton Hall U., NJ, 2003, Arlene Bujese Gallery, East Hampton, N.Y. 2003—, Gayle Wilson Gallery, Southampton, N.Y., 2004-2005; permanent collections Nat. Postal Art Mus., Ottawa, Can., Nat. Inst. Design, Ahmedabad, India, Fine Arts Acad., New Delhi, India, Mus. Modern Art, N.Y.C., Nat. Mus. Women in the Arts, Washington, D.C., Israel Mus., Jerusalem, Brenau Coll., Grainsville, Ga. Blue Cross, Blue Shield, Phila., Mc Donald's, Oakbrook, Ill., The Hyatt Collection, Chgo., Guild Hall Mus., Saul, Ewing, Reineck & Saul, Phila., Shevick, Ravich, Koster, Tobin, Clark, N.J., Sidley & Austin, L.A., Catalano & Sparber, N.Y., Islip (N.Y.) Mus. of Art, NY Pet Rescue Orgn., Larchmont, Islip (NY) Mus.; contbr. critical essays to various periodicals. Mem. Women in Arts, Women's Caucus for Arts, Artists Equity, Visitation Bd. of Met. Mus.-Rockefeller Connection. Address: 300 E 74th St New York NY 10021-3712

WRIGHT, FAYE See DAYA MATA, SRI

WRIGHT, FRANCES JANE, educational psychologist; b. L.A., Dec. 22, 1943; d. step-father John David and Evelyn Jane (Dale) Brinegar. BA, Long Beach State U., 1965; MA, Brigham Young U., 1968, EdD, 1980; postgrad., U. Nev., 1970, U. Utah, 1972-73; postdoctoral, Utah State U., 1985-86. Cert. secondary tchr., adminstr., Utah. Asst. dir. Teenpost Project, San Pedro, Calif., 1966; caseworker Los Angeles County, 1966-67; self-care inservice dir. Utah State Tng. Sch., American Fork, Utah, 1968, vocat. project designer, 1968; tchr. mentally handicapped Santa Ana Unified Schs., Calif., 1968-69; state specialist intellectually handicapped State Office Edn., Salt Lake City, 1969-70; vocat. counselor Manpower, Salt Lake City, 1970-71; tchr. severely handicapped Davis County Schs., Farmington, Utah, 1971-73, diagnostician, 1973-74, resource elem. tchr., 1974-78; instr. Brigham Young U., Salt Lake City, 1976-83; resource tchr. jr. high Davis County Schs., Farmington, 1978-90; ednl. cons. Murray, Utah, 1973-90; chief ednl. diagnostician Ctr. for Evaluation of Learning and Devel., Layton, Utah, 1989-90. Clin. dir. assessment and observation program Idaho Youth Ranch, 1990-95, clin. dir. intake program, 1992-94, supr. family preservation svc./aftercare teams, 1993-95, co-ranch treatment dir. and placement officer, 1995; cons. juvenile correctional dist. 5, 1996-2000; cons., counselor address issues with youth and families, 2001—; clin. cons. Magic Hot Springs Youth Camp, 1996-97; mem. cmty. accountability bd. McNeil Assn., 1996-2000, Dist. 5 Juvenile Justice Coun., 1997—, parent project facilitator, 1998—; trainer Detour prison prevention programfor adolescents, 1997-2000; cons. Northstar Family Preservation, 1997-2001; mem. Juvenile Justice Coun., 1996—; acting chmn. Dist. 5 Juvenile Justice Coun., 1998-99, chmn. 1999-2001; mem. Idaho Juvenile Justice Commn., 1999-2001; adv. bd. So. Central Learning Ctr., 1999-2001; mem. oversight bd., evaluator Status Offender prog. 1997-2000; program dir. Liberty Care Svc.; clin. program mgr. Liberty Care Svcs., 2002-06; clinician Adult Behavior Health Dept. Health/Welfare, 2006—; lectr. in field; pvt. cons./counselor lic. in juvenile justice, youth, edn. and other related concerns. Named Profl. of Yr. Utah Assn. for Children with Learning Disabilities, 1985, Prol. of the Yr., Idaho Youth Ranch Treatment Ctrs., 1992, 1993. Mem. Assn. Children/Adults with Learning Disabilities (del. 1979-85, 81, nat. nominating com., 1985-86, nat. bd. dirs. 1988-91), Am. Counseling Assn., Idaho Mental Health Counselors Assn., Utah Assn. Children/Adults with Learning Disabilities (exec. bd. 1978-84, profl. adv. bd. 1985-90, coord. LDA orgn. Idaho 1991-2000), Coun. Learning Disabilities, ASCD (regional adv.), Nat. Wildlife Found., World Wildlife Fedn., Best Friends Animal Sanctuary, Job's Daughters. Democrat. Mem. Lds Ch. Avocations: genealogy, horseback riding, sketching, crafts, reading. Home: 2176 Julie Ln Twin Falls ID 83301-8361 Office: Liberty Care Svc Pvt Mental Health Clin 460 Main Ave S Ste C Twin Falls ID 83301-7972 Office Phone: 208-736-2177. Business E-Mail: libertycare@onewest.net.

WRIGHT, GEORGETTE L., science educator; b. Miami, Fla., Dec. 28, 1968; d. Debra Jane and Jake Conley. BS, Fla. So. Coll., Lakeland, 1991. Sci. tchr. Collier County Pub. Sch., Naples, Fla., 1998—.

WRIGHT, GLADYS STONE, music educator, writer, composer; b. Wasco, Oreg., Mar. 8, 1925; d. Murvel Stuart and Daisy Violet (Warren) Stone; m. Alfred George Wright, June 28, 1953. BS, U. Oreg., 1948, MS, 1953. Dir. bands Elmira (Oreg.) U-4 H.S., 1948-53, Otterbein (Ind.) H.S., 1954-61, Klondike H.S., West Lafayette, Ind., 1962-70, Harrison H.S., West Lafayette, 1970-84. Organizer, condr. Musical Friendship Tours, Ctrl. Am., 1967-79; v.p., condr. U.S. Collegiate Wind Band, 1975—; bd. dirs. John Philip Sousa Found., 1984—; chmn. Sudler Cup, 1986—, Sudler Flag, 1982; pres. Internat. Music Tours, 1984—, Key to the City, Taxco, Mex., 1975. Editor: Woman Conductor, 1986—; composer: marches Big Bowl and Trumpets and Tabards, 1987; contbg. editor: Informusica (Spain). Recipient Medal of the order John Philip Sousa Found., 1988, Star of Order, 1991, Internat. Contbrn. to Music award Phi Beta Mu, 2000; 1st woman guest condr. U.S. Navy Band, Washington, 1961, Goldman Band, NYC, 1958, Kneller Hall Band, London, 1975, Tri-State Music Festival Massed Orch., Band, Choir, 1985; elected to Women Bd. Dirs. Hall of Fame of Disting. Women Condrs., 1994; inductee Hall of Fame Disting. Condrs., Nat. Band Assn., 1999; named Ind.'s Sagamore of the Wabash, 2004. Mem. Am. Bandmasters Assn. (bd. dirs. 1993, 1st woman mem.), Women Band Dirs. Nat. Assn. (founding pres. 1967, sec. 1985, recipient Silver Baton 1974, Golden Rose 1990, Hall of Fame 1995), Am. Sch. Band Dirs. Assn., Nat. Band Assn. (Citation excellence 1970), Tippecanoe Arts Fedn. (bd. dirs. 1986-90), Tippecanoe Fife and Drum Corps. (bd. dirs. 1984), DAR, Col. Dames-Pre Quitanen Chpt., New Eng. Women, Tau Beta Sigma (Outstanding Svc. to Music award 1970), Phi Beta Mu (1st hon. woman mem. 1972), N.Am. Wildlife Park (Battleground, Ind., bd dirs. 1985, 1990—). Avocation: history.

WRIGHT, GWENDOLYN, writer, architecture educator, historian; b. Chgo., May 14, 1946; d. William Kemp and Mary Ruth (Brown) W.; m. Paul Rabinow, Nov. 18, 1980 (div. 1982); m. Thomas Bender, Jan. 14, 1984; children: David, Sophia. BA, NYU, 1969; MArch, U. Calif., Berkeley, 1974, PhD, 1980. Assoc. prof. Columbia U., N.Y.C., 1983—87, prof., 1988—; dir. Buell Ctr. for Study Am. Architecture, N.Y.C., 1988—92. Cons. Fulbright Scholars, Coun. Internat. Exch. Scholars, Washington, 1988-91, ArchNet, 1999—, Nat. Bldg. Mus., Washington, 2001—. Author: Building the Dream: A Social History of Housing in America, 1980, Moralism and the Model Home, 1981, The History of History in American Schools of Architecture, 1990, The Politics of Design in French Colonial Urbanism, 1991; writer N.Y. Times, 1999; presenter PBS TV series History Detectives, 2003—. Fellow, Ford Found., 1979—80, Stanford Inst. for Humanities, 1982—83, Mich. Inst. for Humanities, 1991, Getty Ctr. for History of Art and the Humanities, 1992—93, Guggenheim Found., 2004—05, Graham Found., 2004—05. Fellow: Soc. Am. Historians, NY Inst. for Humanities; mem.: Soc. Archtl. Historians, Coll. Art Assn., Am. Hist. Assn., Orgn. Am. Historians. Democrat. Home: 54 Washington Mews New York NY 10003-6608 Office: Columbia U Avery Hall New York NY 10027 Office Phone: 212-854-1587. Business E-Mail: gw8@columbia.edu.

WRIGHT, JANE COOKE, oncologist, educator, consultant; b. N.Y.C., Nov. 30, 1919; d. Louis T. and Corinne (Cooke) W.; m. David D. Jones. AB, Smith Coll., 1942; MD with honors, N.Y. Med. Coll., 1945; D in Med. Scis., Women's Med. Coll. Pa., 1965; ScD, Denison U., 1971. Intern Bellevue Hosp., N.Y.C., 1945-46, resident, 1946, mem. staff, 1955-67; resident Harlem Hosp., 1947, chief resident, 1948; clin. Cancer Rsch. Found., Harlem Hosp., 1949-52; dir., 1952-55; mem. staff Harlem Hosp., 1949-55; practice medicine specializing in clin. cancer chemotherapy N.Y.C.; mem. faculty dept. surgery Med. Ctr., N.Y. U., N.Y.C., 1955-67, adj. assoc. prof., 1961-67, also dir. cancer chemotherapy services research, 1955-67; prof. surgery N.Y. Med. Coll., N.Y.C., 1967-87, prof. surgery emeritus, 1987—, assoc. dean, 1967-75; mem. staff Manhattan VA Hosp., 1955-67, Midtown, Met., Bird S. Color, Flower-Fifth Ave. Hosps., all N.Y.C., 1967-79, Westchester County Med. Center, Valhalla, NY, 1971-87, Lincoln Hosp., Bronx, NY, 1979-87. Cons. Health Ins. Plan of Greater N.Y., 1962—94, Blvd. Hosp., 1963—, St. Luke's Hosp., Newburgh, NY, 1964—; pelvic malignancy rev. com. N.Y. Gynecol. Soc., 1965—66, St. Vincent's Hosp., N.Y.C., 1966—, Dept. Health, Edn. and Welfare, 1968—70, Wyckoff Heights Hosp., N.Y.C., 1969—, NIH, 1971—, others; adv. bd. Skin Cancer Found. Contbr. articles to profl. jours. Mem. Manhattan coun. State Commn. Human Rights, 1949—, Pres.'s Commn. Heart Disease, Cancer and Stroke, 1964-65, Nat. Adv. Cancer Coun. NIH, 1966-70, N.Y. State Women's Coun., 1970-72; bd. dirs. Medico-CARE, Health Svcs. Improvement Fund Inc.; trustee Smith Coll., Northampton, Mass., 1970-80. Recipient numerous awards, including; Mademoiselle mag. award, 1952; Lady Year award Harriet Beecher Stowe Jr. High Sch., 1958; Spirit Achievement award Albert Einstein Sch. Medicine, 1965; certificate Honor award George Gershwin Jr. High Sch., 1967; Myrtle Wreath award Hadassah, 1967; Smith medal Smith Coll., 1968; Outstanding Am. Women award Am. Mothers Com. Inc., 1970; honored as one of 150 Am. Women Physicians at exhbn. Changing the Face of Medicine at the Nat. Libr. Medicine, NIH, 2003; Golden Plate award Am. Acad. Achievement, 1971; Exceptional Black Scientists Poster Ciba Geigy, 1980. Fellow N.Y. Acad. Medicine; mem. Nat. Med. Assn. (edit. bd. jours.), Manhattan Ctrl. Med. Soc., N.Y. County Med. Soc. (nominating com.), AMA, AAAS, Am. Assn. Cancer Rsch. (dir. Rsch. Salute 1971-74, established Jane Cooke Wright lectureship 2006), N.Y. Acad. Scis., N.Y. Cancer Soc., Internat. Med. and Rsch. Found. (v.p.), Am. Cancer Soc. (dir. div.), N.Y. Cancer Soc. (pres. 1970-71), Am. Soc. Clin. Oncology (sec. treas. 1964-67, Spl. Appreciation award as a founding mem. 2004), Contin Soc., Sigma Xi, Lambda Kappa Mu, Alpha Omega Alpha. Clubs: The 400 (N.Y. Med. Coll.). Address: 7002 Kennedy Blvd East Apt 9C Guttenberg NJ 07093

WRIGHT, JEANNE ELIZABETH JASON, advertising executive; b. Washington, June 24, 1934; d. Robert Stewart and Elizabeth (Gaddis) Jason; m. Benjamin Hickman Wright, Oct. 30, 1965; stepchildren: Benjamin (dec.), Deborah, David, Patricia. BA, Radcliffe Coll., 1956; MA, U. Chgo., 1958. Psychiat. social worker Lake County Mental Health Clinic, Gary, Ind., Psychiat. and Psychosomatic Inst., Michael Reese Hosp., Chgo., Jewish Child Care Assn., N.Y.C., 1958-70; gen. mgr. Black Media, Inc. (advt. rep. co.), N.Y.C., 1970-74, pres., 1974-75; pres., exec. editor, syndicator weekly editorial features Black Resources, Inc., N.Y.C., 1975-99; ret., 1999. Mem. planning com. First Black Power Conf., Newark, 1966, Second Black Power Conf., Phila., 1967, First Internat. Black Cultural & Bus. Expn., N.Y.C., 1971; nat. bd. dirs. Afro-Am. Family & Community Svcs., Inc., Chgo., 1971-75; founding coun. mem. Nat. Assault on Illiteracy Program, 1980-99; pres. Metro-N.Y. chpt. Nat. Assn. Media Women, Inc., 1986-89. Recipient Pres.' award Nat. Assn. Black Women Attys., 1977, 2d ann. Freedom's Jour. award Journalism Students and Faculty of U. D.C. Dept. Communicative and Performing Arts, 1979, Communication award Harlem Svc. Ctr., ARC, 1988, Spl. award Beta Omicron chpt. Phi Delta Kappa, 1982; named Disting. Black Woman in Industry, Nat. Coun. Negro Women, 1981. Mem. AAAS, Nat. Assn. Social Workers, Acad. Cert. Social Workers, Nat. Assn. Media Women (pres. Met. N.Y. chpt. 1986-89, Nat. Media Woman of Yr. award 1984, 86, Founders award 1986), Newswomen's Club N.Y., U. Chgo. Alumni Assn., NAACP, Radcliffe Club, Harvard Club, Alpha Kappa Alpha Sorority Inc. (Gamma Zeta Omega Chpt.). Democrat. Home and Office: 1800 NW 187th St Opa Locka FL 33056-3317

WRIGHT, JO ANNE, priest; b. Wichita, Kans., May 31, 1935; d. Everett Joseph and Agnes Josephine (Ketchman) Steinheimer; m. John Cook Wright, June 25, 1955 (div. June 1976); children: Elizabeth, Jennifer, Melanie, Kennedy Weston. AB, Oberlin Coll., 1955; MDiv, Ch. Divinity Sch. of Pacific, Berkeley, Calif., 1987. Ordained deacon Episcopal Ch., 1987, ordained priest, 1987. Pre-sch. tchr. Children's Hour Headstart, Lawrence, Kans., 1977-79; reference libr. Lawrence (Kans.) Pub. Libr., 1979-84; rector St. Luke's Episcopal Ch., Wamego, Kans., 1987-98, St. John's Episcopal Ch., Vinita, Okla., 1999—2005; mem. diocesan coun. Diocese of Okla., 2000—01, dean NE region, 2001—05; ret. Youth officer Diocese of Kans., Topeka, 1987-92, rural missioner, 1992-98, mem. standing com., mem. diocesan coun., 1997-98; pres. Vinita Minsterial Alliance, 2001, sec., 2003. Writer monthly column Plenteous Harvest, 1987-92. Chair Wamego Coun. Chs., 1998, CROP walk organizer, 1988, 92, 95; tour leader Ednl. Opportunities, Israel, 1998; mem. bishop search com. Diocese Okla., 2005—. Roanridge grantee Episcopal Ch. U.S.A., 1995. Mem. Phi Beta Kappa. Democrat. Avocations: reading, travel. Home: 821 N Foreman Apt 222 Vinita OK 74301-1432 E-mail: jowright@junct.com.

WRIGHT, JOAN L., artist; d. William Henry and Elsie Christina (Motzer) Harrison; m. Barry Duane Wright; children: Stephen Craig, Michael Alan, Jeffrey Lynn. Student, Art League LA, 1964-68, Valley Coll., 1966-69. Designer, sculpture, glazer Al Hardy, Burbank, Calif., 1951-53; budget coord. Los Angeles County, North Hollywood, Calif., 1953; writer Intermountain Contractor, Salt Lake City, 1954-56; artist, instr. Art League LA, Van Nuys, Calif., 1966—, Sylmar, Calif., 1966—. Rep. for State of Calif. Presdl. Arts Program, Washington. Contbr. articles to art publs.; films, children's books, album covers; featured in many books and publs. western art; collector plates, Danbury Mint, Norwalk, Conn., 1995—, other pub. cos., installations of murals worldwide, exhibitions include Gene Autry Western Heritage Mus., LA, Lancaster Mus. Art, Ronald Reagan Libr., Simi, Calif., Las Vegas (Nev.) Art Mus., Learnin' Tree, Boulder, Colo., Scafa, other cos. Mem.: Wildlife Waystation, Oil Painters Am., Internat. Art and Culture Assn., Women Artists of West (bd. dirs. 1971—73, pres. 1974—77, v.p. 1978—). Avocations: birdwatching, environmental activities, sports, stained glass, stamp collecting/philately. Personal E-mail: jwartist1@aol.com.

WRIGHT, JOSEPHINE ROSA BEATRICE, musicologist; b. Detroit, Sept. 5, 1942; d. Joseph Le Vander and Eva Lee Garrison W.; Mus.B., U. Mo., Columbia, 1963, M.A., 1967; Mus.M., Pius XII Acad., Florence, Italy, 1964; Ph.D., N.Y.U., 1975. Instr. music York Coll., CUNY, 1972-75, asst. prof., 1975; asst. prof. Afro-Am. studies in musicology Harvard U., Cambridge, Mass., 1976-81; assoc. dir. integration of Afro-Am. folk arts with music project, Nat. Endowment Humanities, 1979-82; assoc. prof. music and Black studies Coll. of Wooster, 1981-90, prof. music and Black studies, 1991-2000, prof. Music and the Josephine Lincoln Morris prof. Black studies, 2000, prof. music and African studies, 2005—; panelist, cons. on music Mass. Coun. of Arts and Humanities, 1978-80; cons. Nat. Endowment Humanities, 1982-83, 87, 89, 90, Ohio Humanities Coun., 1986; apptd. mem. Nat. Artistic Directorate, Am. Classical Music Hall of Fame, Cin. Author: Ignatius Sancho (1729-1780), An Early African Composer in England: The Collected Edition of His Music in Facsimile, 1981; editor: Am. Music, 1993-97, Journal American Music, 1994-1994, Music in African Am. Culture series, 1995—2000; editor of new music: The Black Perspective in Music, 1979-91, (with Sam Floyd) New Perspectives on Music: Essays in Honor of Eileen Southern, 1992; co-editor: The Bicentennial Issue of The Black Perspective in Music, 1976, (with Eileen Southern) African-American Traditions in Song, Sermon, Tale and Dance, 1991, (with Eileen Southern) Images: Iconography of Music in African-American Culture, 2000; mem. editl. bd. Jour. Am. Musicol. Soc., 2003, Am. Music, 2004; contbr. articles to profl. jours. Mem. Am. Musicol. Soc. (dir.-at-large 1998-2000), Soc. Am. Music (bd. dirs.), Nat. Coun. for black studies, U. Mo. Faculty of Arts and Sci. Alumni Assn. (trustee 1982-85), Pi Kappa Lambda. Democrat. Anglican. Office Phone: 330-263-2044. Business E-Mail: jwright@wooster.edu.

WRIGHT, JUDITH DIANE, elementary school educator; b. San Angelo, Tex., Nov. 13, 1946; d. John Jackson and Marjorie Ellen (Blackerby) Bentley; m. David Allen Wright, Nov. 24, 1965; children: Wendy Lynn Sullivan, Beth

Ann Re, Mack David. BSc in Edn., Kennesaw State U., 1996; MA in Edn., Piedmont Coll., 2005. Reading tchr. Marietta City Sch., Ga., 1996—97, tchr., 1997—. Chair, staff develop. com. Dunleith Elem., Marietta, 1997—; mem. profl. learning adv. com. Marietta City Sch., 1997—; team leader Dunleith Elem., 2006—, mem. sch. coun., 2006—. Mem. white Christmas com. Burnt Hickory Ch. of Christ, Marietta, 2001—05. Recipient Outstanding Cert. Employee, Dunleith Elem., 1999—2000, Tchr. of Yr., 2002—03, Going the Extreme Mile (GEM) award, Kiwanis Club, 1998. Mem.: ASCD, Internat. Reading Assn. Independent. Christian. Avocations: computers, stitchery, cooking, dachsunds. Office: Dunleith Elem Sch 120 Saine Dr Marietta GA 30008

WRIGHT, JUDITH MARGARET, law librarian, educator, dean; b. Jackson, Tenn., Aug. 16, 1944; d. Joseph Clarence and Mary Catherine (Key) Wright; m. Mark A. Johnson, Apr. 17, 1976; children: Paul, Michael. BS, U. Memphis, 1966; MA, U. Chgo., 1971; JD, DePaul U., 1980. Bar: Ill. 1980. Librarian Oceanway Sch., Jacksonville, Fla., 1966-67; program dir. ARC, South Vietnam, 1967-68; documents and reference librarian D'Angelo Law Library, U. Chgo., 1970-74, reference librarian, 1974-77, dir., lectr. in law, 1980—2000, law libr., assoc. dean for libr. and info. svcs., lectr. in law, 2000—. Mem. adv. bd. Legal Reference Svcs. Quar., 1981—. Mem.: Chgo. Assn. Law Libraries, Am. Assn. Law Libraries, ABA. Democrat. Methodist. Office: U Chgo Law Sch D'Angelo Law Libr 1111 E 60th St Chicago IL 60637-2745 Office Phone: 773-702-9616. Office Fax: 773-702-2889. Business E-Mail: jm-wright@uchicago.edu.

WRIGHT, KATIE HARPER, educational administrator, journalist; b. Crawfordsville, Ark., Oct. 5, 1923; d. James Hale and Connie Mary (Locke) Harper; m. Marvin Wright, Mar. 21, 1952; 1 child, Virginia K. Jordan. BA, U. Ill., 1944, MEd, 1959; EdD, St. Louis U., 1979. Elem. and spl. edn. tchr. East St. Louis (Ill.) Pub. Schs., 1944-65, dir. Dist. 189 Instrnl. Materials Program, 1965-71, dir. spl. edn. Dists. 188, 189, 1971-77, asst. supt. programs, 1977-79; interim supt. East St. Louis Sch. Dist. 189, 1993-94. Adj. faculty Harris/Stowe State Coll., 1980, adj. prof. edn. emeritus; mem. staff St. Louis U., 1989—; interim supt. Dist. 189 Schs., 1994—; mem. Pres.'s Commn. on Excellence in Spl. Edn. Author: Delta Sigma Theta/East St. Louis Chapter History, 1992; contbr. articles to profl. jours.; feature writer St. Louis Argus Newspaper, 1979—. Mem. Ill. Commn. on Children, 1973-85, East St. Louis Bd. Election Comms., East St. Louis Fin. Adv. Authority, 1999—; pres. bd. dirs. St. Clair County Mental Health Ctr., 1970-72, 87—; bd. dirs. River Bluff coun. Girl Scouts USA, 1979—, nat. bd. dirs., 1981-84; bd. dirs. Jackie Joyner-Kersee Youth Ctr. Found., 1991—, United Way, 1979—, Urban League, 1979—, Provident Counseling Ctr., 1995-98; pres. bd. trustees East St. Louis Pub. Libr., 1972-77; pres., bd. dirs. St. Clair County Mental Health Ctrs., 1987; mem. adv. bd. Magna Bank; charter mem. Coalition of 100 Black Women; mem. coord. coun. ethnic affairs Synod of Mid-Am., Presbyn. Ch. U.S.A.; mem. Ill. Dept. Corrections Sch. Bd., 1995—; charter mem. Metro East Links Group, Gateway chpt. The Links, Inc.; mem. Ill. Minority/Female Bus. Coun., 1991—; mem. Pres.'s Commn. on Excellence in Spl. Edn., 2001--. Recipient of more than 150 awards including Lamp of Learning award East St. Louis Jr. Wednesday Club, 1965, Outstanding Working Woman award Downtown St. Louis, Inc., 1967, Ill. State citation for ednl. document Love is Not Enough, 1974, Delta Sigma Theta citation for document Good Works, 1979, Girl Scout Thanks badge, 1982, award Nat. Coun. Negro Women, 1983, Cmty. Svc. award Met. East Bar Assn., 1983, Journalist award Sigma Gamma Rho, Spelman Coll. Alumni award, 1990, A World of Difference award, 1990, 92, Edn. award St. Louis, YWCA, 1991, SIU-E-Kimmel award, 1991, St. Clair County Mental Health award, 1992, Gateway East Met. Ministry Dr. M.L. King award, 1993, Nat. Coun. Negro Women Black Leader of Yr., 1995, Disting. Alumni award U. Ill., 1996, Pioneer award Mosque 28B, 2000, Tri Del Globe award, 2001, Urban League Merit award, 2002, Ill. Office of Edn. award, 2002, Eugene B. Redmond Writers Club award, 2002, NFPW Quest award, 2004, Liberty Bell award St. Clair County Bar Assocs., 2005, St. Clair County Bar Assn. award, 2005; named Woman of Achievement, St. Louis Globe Democrat, 1974, Outstanding Adminstr. So. Region III Office Edn., 1975, Woman of Yr. in Edn. St. Clair County YWCA, 1987, Nat. Top Lady of Yr., 1988, Disting. Alumnus U. Ill., 1996, Citizen Amb., South Africa, 1996, sch. named after her East St. Louis Sch., 2005; named to Vashon H.S. Hall of Fame, 1989, Sr. Illinoisan Hall of Fame, 1997; East St. Louis Elem. Sch. named for Dr. Katie Harper Wright, 2005. Mem. Am. Librs. Trustees Assn. (regional v.p. 1978-79, 92, nat. sec. 1979-80), Ill. Commn. on Children, Mensa, Coun. for Exceptional Children (mem. pres.'s commn. excellence spl. edn.), Top Ladies of Distinction (pres. 1987-91, nat. editor 1991—, Journalism award 1992, Media award 1992), Delta Sigma Theta (chpt. pres. 1960-62, Letters award 2000), Kappa Delta Pi (pres. So. Ill. U. chpt. 1973-74), Phi Delta Kappa (Svc. Key award 1984, chpt. pres. 1984-85), Iota Phi Lambda, Phi Lambda Theta (chpt. pres. 1985-87), East St. Louis Women's Club (pres. 1973-75). Republican. Home: 733 N 40th St East Saint Louis IL 62205-2138

WRIGHT, LAURA L., air transportation executive; m. Randy Wright; children: Lindsay, Jeffrey. BSA, MSA, Univ. No. Tex., 1982. CPA Tex. Tax mgr. Arthur Young & Co., Dallas; dir. corp. taxation Southwest Airlines, Dallas, 1988—90, dir. corp. fin., 1990—95, asst. treas., 1995—98, treas., 1998—2001, v.p. fin. & treas., 2001—04, sr. v.p. fin. & CFO, 2004—. Named one of 50 Women to Watch, Wall St. Journal, 2005. Office: Southwest Airlines 2702 Love Field Dr PO Box 36611 Dallas TX 75235-1611 Office Phone: 214-792-7784. Office Fax: 214-792-4011.*

WRIGHT, LILYAN BOYD, physical education educator; b. Upland, Pa., May 11, 1920; d. Albert Verlenden and Mabel (Warburton) Boyd; m. Richard P. Wright, Oct. 23, 1942; 1 child, Nicki Wright Vanek. BS, Temple U., 1942, MEd, 1946; EdD, Rutgers U., 1972. Tchr. health and phys. edn. Woodbury (N.J.) High Sch., 1942-43, Glen-Nor High Sch., Glenolden, Pa., 1944-46, Chester (Pa.) High Sch., 1946-54; chmn. women's dept. health and phys. edn. Union (N.J.) High Sch., 1954-61; with Trenton State Coll., 1961-90, head women's program health and phys. edn., 1967-77, chmn. dept. health, phys. edn. and recreation, 1977-86, adj. faculty mem., 1990-92, prof. emeritus, 1991—. Mem. N.J. State Com. Div. Girls and Women's Sports, 1958-80; chmn. New Atlantic Field Hockey Sectional Umpiring, 1981-85; chmn. New Atlantic Field Hockey Assn., 1985-90; with recreation after sch. program Newport Counseling Ctrl., 1992-93; vol. coach field hockey Goshen-Lempster Coop. Sch., 1995—. Active Chester United Fund; water safety, first aid instr.; vestry Ch. Epiphany, Newport, N.H., 1992—, sr. warden, 1995-99; vestry St. Luke's Episcopal Ch., 1988-91, clk. of the vestry, 2000—; trustee Olive Pettis Libr., Goshen, 1992—, chair of trustees, 1998—, Goshen budget com., 1999—; dist. ednl. improvement team for Goshen-Lempster Sch. Dist., 1995—, mem. sch. bd., 2001—. Recipient U.S. Field Hockey Assn. award, 1989; ARC Scholarship in her honor N.J. Athletic Assn. Girls, 1971; named to Hall of Fame, Temple U., 1976; named Nat. Honorary and Emeritus Field Hockey Umpire. Mem. AAHPERD (chmn. Ea. Dist. Assn. Div. Girls and Women's Sports, sec. to coun. for svcs. Ea. Dist. Assn. 1979-80, chmn. 1980-81, chmn. com. on aging and adult devel. of ea. dist. 1993-97, 2001—, N.J. rep. to council for convs. 1984-85, Honor Fellow award 1986), N.J. AHPER (pres. 1974-75, past pres. 1975-76, v.p. phys. edn. div., parliamentarian 1990—, Disting. Service and Leadership award 1969, 93, Honor Fellow award 1977, Presdl. Citation award 1993, 95, 96, 97, 98, 99, Disting. Leadership award 1994), N.J. Women's Lacrosse Assn. (umpiring chmn. 1972-76), Nat. Assn. Phys. Edn. in Higher Edn., Eastern Assn. Phys. Edn. Coll. Women, North Jersey, Ctrl. Jersey bds. women's ofcls., Am., Pa. (v.p. 1953-54), Chester (pres. 1949-54) fedns. tchrs., U.S. Field Hockey Assn. (exec. com., chair honorary umpire award com. 1992), North Jersey Field Hockey Assn. (past pres.), N.H. Field Hockey Umpires' Assn., No. New Eng. Lacrosse Officials Bd., U.S. Women's Lacrosse Assn. (Honorary and Emeritus Umpiring Rating award), Kappa Delta Epsilon, Delta Psi Kappa (past pres. Phila. alumni chpt.), Kappa Delta Pi. Home: PO Box 239 Goshen NH 03752-0239

WRIGHT, LORI DUNKLE, musician, educator; b. Kettering, Ohio, Sept. 17, 1967; d. Robert Kean and Elaine Mary Dunkle; m. Douglas Allan Wright, Aug. 1, 1992; 1 child, Rebecca Ann. MusB in Edn., Ohio State U., 1989, MA, 2001. Tchg. Cert., K12 Music Ohio Dept. of Edn., 1989. Orch. dir. Kent City Schs., Ohio, 1990—91, Worthington City Schs., Columbus, Ohio, 1991—. Clinician Ministry of Edn., Santiago, Chile, 2002; cellist, asst. prin. Springfield Symphony Orch., Ohio, 1991—; state treas. Ohio Music Edn. Assn., 2004—. Mem.: NEA (assoc.), Am. Fedn. of Musicians (assoc.), Music Edn. Nat. Conf. (assoc.; treas., state of ohio 2004—), Am. String Tchrs. Assn. (assoc.), Ohio State U. Alumni Assn. (life), Phi Kappa Phi (life), Delta Omicron (life). Conservative-R. Christian. Avocations: travel, golf, camping, hiking, backpacking.

WRIGHT, MARGARET HAGEN, computer scientist, administrator; b. San Francisco, Feb. 18, 1944; m. 1965; 1 child. BS in Mat., Stanford U., 1964, MS in Computer Sci., 1965, PhD in Computer Sci., 1976. Devel. engr. Sylvania Electronic System, 1965-71; sr. rsch. assoc., Systems Optimization Lab., Dept. Ops. Rsch. Stanford U., Palo Alto, Calif., 1976-88; with Computing Sci. Rsch. Ctr. Bell Lab., Lucent Tech., 1988, disting. mem. tech. staff, 1993, head Sci. Computing Rsch. Dept., 1997; prof. Dept. Computer Sci. Courant Inst. Math. Sci., NYU, 2005—, chair, Dept. Computer Sci., 2005—. Adv. com. Directorate Math. and Physical Sci., Nat. Sci. Found., 1994—98, chair., 1997—98; sci. adv. com. Math. Sciences Rsch. Inst., Berkeley, Calif. Assoc. editor Jour. Sci. Stats. Computer Programming, Math. Programming, Soc. Indsl. and Applied Math. Jour. on Sci. Computing, editor-in-chief Soc. Indsl. and Applied Math. Rev., Soc. Indsl. and Applied Math. Jour. on Optmization. Mem. Am. Acad. Arts and Sciences, NAE, NAS, Assn. Computing Machinery (bd. dirs. numerical analysis assn. spl. interest group), Soc. Indsl. and Applied Math. (pres. 1995-96, Award for Disting. Svc. to Profession 2001), Math. Programming Soc. Achievements include research contributing to enlarged knowledge of methods for nonlinear programming, particularly unconstrained; linearly constrained and nonlinearly constrained optimization; mathematical software, numerical linear algebra; software library development. Office: Computer Sci Dept Warren Wearver Hall Rm 405 251 Mercer St New York NY 10012 Office Fax: 212-995-4124. E-mail: mhw@cs.nyu.edu.*

WRIGHT, MARIE ANNE, management information systems educator; b. Albany, N.Y., Oct. 21, 1953; d. Arthur Irving and Ethel (Knickerbocker) W. BS, U. Mass., Boston, 1981; MBA, Clarkson U., 1984; PhD, U. Mass., Amherst, 1989. Cert. in homeland security. Grad. asst. Clarkson U., Potsdam, N.Y., 1982; sys. analyst St. Lawrence U., Canton, N.Y., 1983-84; instr. Bentley Coll., Waltham, Mass., 1984-85; tchg. asst. U. Mass., 1985, rsch. asst., 1986; computer cons. Amherst (Mass.) Police Dept., 1986-88; asst. prof. Elms Coll., Chicopee, Mass., 1986-89; assoc. prof. Western Conn. State U., Danbury, Conn., 1990—2002, prof., 2002—. Cons. Ctr. for Human Devel., Springfield, Mass., 1986-87, Early Childhood Ctr., 1986-87. Co-author: Information Security Casebook; contbr. articles to profl. jours. and mags. Recipient MIS award U. Mass., 1981. Mem. AAUW, IEEE, Assn. Computing Machinery, Internat. Computer Security Assn., Info. Sys. Security Assn., Am. Soc. Indsl. Security, Computer Security Inst., Assn. Info. Sys., Am. Coll. Forensic Examiners Internat., InfraGard, Beta Gamma Sigma. Democrat. Avocations: cross country skiing, swimming, reading. Office: Western Conn State U MIS Dept Danbury CT 06810 Office Phone: 203-837-9344. E-mail: wrightm@wcsu.edu.

WRIGHT, MARY E. (MARY E. GUEN), clinical psychologist; b. Rochester, Minn., Jan. 3, 1951; d. Robert George and Rosemarie Celine (Nowicki) Tompkins; m. Scotty Kane Wright, Mar. 17, 1977 (div. May 1984); children: Drew Robert, Rosemary Elizabeth. BA, U. South Ala., 1985; MA, U. Mo., 1989, PhD, 1993. Lic. psychologist, Calif., Ark. Family therapist Boone County Juvenile Ct. Svcs., Columbia, Mo., 1986—87; psychology extern, adolescent dept. Charter Hosp. of Columbia, Columbia, 1987; psychology clk. Psychology Clinic, Columbia, 1987—88, Mid-Mo. Mental Health Ctr., Columbia, 1988—89, Biggs Forensic Ctr./Fulton (Mo.) State Hosp. Sex Offender Program, 1989—90; psychology intern Atascadero (Calif) State Hosp., 1990—91; psychologist, program coord., team leader Fulton State Forensic Hosp. Sex Offender Program, 1991—93; primary therapist coord. Boone County Juvenile Sex Offender Project, Columbia, 1992—93; staff psychologist Atascadero State Hosp., 1993—96; staff adolescent psychologist team leader Wyo. State Hosp., Evanston, 1996—97, forensic psychologist, forensic examiner, 1996—98, core faculty psychologist, 1998—99; clin. psychologist, dir. psychol. svcs. Cornerstone Med. Group, Van Buren, Ark., 1999—2000; pvt. practice Ft. Smith, Ark., 1999—; clin. dir. RSVP program Ark. Dept. Corrections, 2002—. Author publs.; presenter in field. Mem. Crawford County Child Sexual Abuse Task Force, 1999-2002. Recipient awrds and grants. Mem. APA, Nat. Alliance for Mentally Ill, Ark. Psychol. Assn., Children and Adults with Attention Deficit. Democrat. Roman Catholic. Avocations: horticulture, books, historic preservation, human rights, outdoors. Home: 21824 Carter Rd Winslow AR 72959-9021 E-mail: cheekypin@aol.com.

WRIGHT, MARY ELLEN, theater educator; b. Commerce, Tex. d. Joseph Perry and Ora Berniece Gentry; m. James Hatfield; children: Christopher Collin, Sarah Allison Wright Metzger. BA summa cum laude, U. Tex., Tyler, 1988, MAIS, 1991—91; PhD, Tex. Tech U., Lubbock, 2001. Lectr. U. Tex. at Tyler, 1994—95, 1996—2001, asst. prof., 2002—. Adjudicator Tex. U. Interscholastic League, 1993—, St. Gregory's Sch., Tyler, 1999—; conf. planner Assn. for Theatre in Higher Edn., 1994—98; presenter in field. Costume designer (musical) Annie, (play) The Mandrake; dir.: (play) A Small Family Business, Eleemosynary; costume designer (play) Oleanna (Citation for Excellence in Costume Design, 1992); author: (play) Maggie and Mac; author: (presenter) (workshop) Creative Drama in the Classroom; costume designer (play) Othello; dir.: (play) The King Stag; costume designer (musical) The Fantasticks; dir.: (play) Art; costume designer (musical) Sound of Music, (play) Comic Potential (Citation of Excellence for Costume Design, 2001); dir.: (play) Beauty Queen of Leenane, Pygmalion; contbr. articles to profl. publs. Recipient award, Assn. for Theatre in Higher Edn., 2002, Citation of Excellence for Festival Hosting, Kennedy Ctr./Am. Coll. Theatre Festival, 1999—2000; grantee Adrian Hall Del. Project, Tex. Commn. on the Arts, 2003. Mem.: Tex. Ednl. Theatre Assn., Assn. for Theatre in Higher Edn. (conf. planner 1994—98), Alpha Chi, Phi Kappa Phi, Alpha Psi Omega (advisor 1996—2003), Gamma Phi Beta (life). Home: 5404 Briar Cove Dr Tyler TX 75703 Office: U Tex at Tyler 3900 University Blvd Tyler TX 75799 E-mail: mwright@mail.uttyl.edu.

WRIGHT, MARY LEE, retired dietician; b. Boone, Iowa, Sept. 24, 1921; d. Anton Martin and Emma Sebring Rosengreen; m. Evan Leonard Wright (dec. 1992); children: Anne Schmidt, Sally Vaurck, Wendy Morgan; m. Henry William Kipp, June 22, 2002. BS in Foods and Nutrition, Iowa State U., 1943. Intern Med. Coll. Va., Richmond, Va., 1943—44; dietition St. Louis (Mo.) Children's Hosp., 1945—47, St. Luke's Hosp., St. Louis, 1953—58, Faith Hosp., St. Louis, 1960—65; cons. dietition Epworth Sch., St. Louis, 1972—74, ret., 1974. Vol. Meals On Wheels, St. Louis, Grace United Meth. Ch., St. Louis. Democrat. Meth. Home: 7618 N Sunset Dr Saint Louis MO 63121

WRIGHT, MARY P., counselor; b. NC; AAS with honors, Ctrl. Carolina CC, Sanford, NC, 1992; BAS, Campbell U., Buies Creek, NC, 1994; MA, Campbell U., 1999. Dep. clk. of ct. Adminstrv. Office of the Cts., Raleigh, NC, 1978-83; computer lab. asst., news reporter Campbell U., 1992-94, asst. to curriculum materials coord., 1994-95; tutorial coord. Ctrl. Carolina CC, 1995-96; data entry staff N.C. Dept. Environ. Health, Raleigh, 1997; counseling intern North Harnett Elem. Sch., Angier, NC, 1997-98. Interviewer, counselor Employment Security Commn., 1998-2000; admissions counselor Campbell U., 2000-01, sch. counselor, 2001—. Mem. Cape Fear Friends of the Fine Arts, Buies Creek, 1996—. Recipient All Am. Scholar award, award, U.S. Achievement Acad. Mem. Omicron Delta Kappa, Delta Kappa Pi. Democrat. Baptist. Avocations: reading, singing, horseback riding, photography, computers. Home: PO Box 234 Buies Creek NC 27506-0234 Personal E-mail: wright_m03@yahoo.com.

WRIGHT, MARY ROSE, retired state agency administrator; b. Hartford, Conn., Jan. 12, 1949; d. J. William and Eileen J. (Walsh) Bigoness; m. Roy C. Gunter III, June 24, 1972 (div. Feb. 1988); m. Kenneth Ross Wright, Dec. 1, 1988. BA, Marquette U., 1970; MS, U. Mo., 1972. Prgram analyst State Calif. Dept. Health, Sacramento, 1972-76; tng. ctr. dir. State Calif. Dept. Parks and Recreation, Pacific Grove, 1976-81, visitor svcs. mgr. Monterey, 1981-83, Monterey dist. supr., 1983-92, dep. dir., 1992-93; Monterey dist. supt. Calif. Dept. Parks and Recreation, 1993-99, chief dep. dir. Sacramento, 1999—2002. Hist. preservation commr. City of Monterey, 1984-92. Bd. dirs. Big Sur Health Ctr., 1993—; bd. govs. Santa Lucia Conservancy, 1995-99. Office: Calif Dept Parks and Recreation Chief Dep Dir 1416 9th St Rm 1405 Sacramento CA 95814-5511

WRIGHT, MICHELLE BETH, elementary school educator; b. Youngstown, Ohio, Aug. 14, 1960; d. William Samuel and Elizabeth (Grear) Kurtz; m. Edgar Vernell Wright, Aug. 29, 1987. BS in Edn., Kent State U., Ohio, 1983; M in Reading Edn., Fla. Internat. U., 1998. Cert. elem. tchr., Fla., Ohio, spl. edn. tchr., Fla., Ohio. Sci. tchr. Kirk Mid. Sch., East Cleveland, Ohio, 1983-87; elem. tchr. Miami Lakes (Fla.) Elem. Sch., 1987—, grade chairperson, 1992-93. Mem. Alpha Kappa Alpha. Democrat. Home: 1780 NE 172nd St Miami FL 33162-1534 Office: Miami Lakes Elem Sch 14250 NW 67th Ave Hialeah FL 33014-2993

WRIGHT, MILDRED ANNE (MILLY WRIGHT), conservator, researcher; b. Athens, Ala., Sept. 9, 1939; d. Thomas Howard and Anne Louise (Ashworth) Speegle; m. William Paul Wright, Nov. 20, 1965; children: Paul Howard, William Neal. BS in Physics, U. Ala., Tuscaloosa, 1963. Rschr. in acoustics Wyle Labs., Huntsville, Ala., 1963-64; tchr. physics, English Huntsville H.S., 1964-67; ptnr. Flying Carpet Oriental Rugs, Florence, Ala., 1974—. Adj. mem. faculty U. North Ala., Florence, 1988, lectr. Inst. for Learning in Retirement, 1991—. Columnist Times Daily, 1992—; photojournalist, writer River Views Mag., 1993—1997; contbr. articles to profl. jours. (1st pl. award 1986, 87). Pianist, organist Edgemont Meth. Ch., Florence, 1987-90 (Outstanding Svc. award 1990); mem. steering com. Melton Hollow Nature Ctr., Florence, Design Ala., Florence, 1991, River Heritage Discovery Camp, 1993-95; mem. River Heritage Com., Florence, 1991—; accompanist Shoals Boy Choir, Muscle Shoals, Ala., 1992-93; bd. dirs. Heritage Preservation, Inc., Capital award, 1992, pres., 1990-92, 96-97, treas., 1995-96, Tenn. Valley Hist. Soc., pres., 1991-95, Ala. Preservation Alliance, treas., 1992-97, Florence Main Street program, 1992-94, Maud Lindsay Free Kindergarten, Frank Lloyd Wright Rosenbaum House Found., Inc., 1992-98, Gen. Joseph Wheeler Home Found., 1994—, treas. 1995-97, newsletter editor, 1995-97; mem. adv. bd. Friends of the Ala. Archives, 1995-98, sec., 1996-98; mem. adv. coun. Human Environ. Scis. Dept., 1992-98; mem. Coby Hall steering com. U. North Ala., 1992-98, Kennedy-Douglas Ctr. Arts; adv. bd. Old Cahawba of Ala., 1996-97; adv. bd. Waterloo Mus., 1995—, Florence Children's Mus., 1995-96; mem. bd. Friends of the Florence-Lauderdale Pub. Libr., 2002—, newsletter editor, 2002—. Recipient Disting. Svc. award Ala. Hist. Commn., 1991, Merit award Ala. Preservation Alliance, 1995, Gen. Joseph Wheeler Home Found. Merit award, 1996. Mem. Ala. Writers' Conclave (Creative Works award 1986, 87), Ala. Hist. Assn., Ala. Archeol. Soc., Natchez Trace Geneal. Soc., Colbert County Hist. Landmarks Found., Nat. Trust for Hist. Preservation, Tennessee Valley Art Assn. (Florence film com. vice chmn. 2003-2004), La Grange Living History Assn., Trail of Tears Assn., Florence Film Com. (v.p. 2003-04), Firenze Club, Florence Study Club, Optimist Club, Sigma Pi Sigma. Avocations: bridge, photography, travel, discovering old buildings, gardening. Home: PO Box 279 Florence AL 35631-0279

WRIGHT, NANCY HOWELL, interior designer; b. Sept. 6, 1932; d. David Austin and Catherine Howell; m. Hastings Kemper Wright, June 19, 1954; children: Mark, Barbara; children: Kenneth, Donald. BFA, Ohio Wesleyan U., 1954; student, Parsons Sch. Design, 1977. Interior decorator Country Manor of Branford (Conn.), 1971-75; design mgr., 1976-97; pres., owner Nancy Wright Interiors, 1997—. Sec. Branford Art League, 1977; bd. dirs. Harrison House Hist. House, Branford, Conn., 1983-84; mem. Rep Town Com., Branford, 1990-92; recording sec. Branford Garden Club, 1991—. Mem. Am. Soc. Interior Designers (award for best Conn. retail store design, 1980, Conn. Coalition), Branford Garden Club (rec. sec. 1990-94, membership chmn. 1995, v.p. 1997-99, pres. 1999-2000), Delta Phi Delta. Republican. Episcopalian. Home and Office: 35 Wood Rd Branford CT 06405-4935

WRIGHT, PAULINE M., elementary school educator, consultant; d. Gladlstone Alston and Olga Louise Wright. BS, Medgar Evers Coll., Bklyn., N.Y., 1977; MS in Early Childhood Edn., Bank St. Coll. Edn., N.Y.C., 1979; MEd, Columbia U., N.Y.C., 1983; Edn. Specialist, Curriculum, Sarasota U., Fla., 2001, D of Edn. Curriculum Instrn., 2004. Cert. tchr. pre-k to 6th gr. N.Y. Dept. Edn., 1979, tchr. pre-k to 8th gr. Ga. Dept. Edn., 1981. Tchr. St. Benedict's Day Nursery, N.Y.C., 1974—83; adj. prof. Malcom King Coll., N.Y.C., 1980—81; tchr. Christ United Meth. Headstart, Bklyn., 1983—84, ednl. dir., 1984—85; tchr. Pub. Sch. 308, Bklyn., 1985—86; tchr., educator Meadowview Elem. Sch., Atlanta, 1986—. Ednl. dir., cons. Christ United Meth. Headstart, Bklyn., 1983—84; assoc. Assn. Supervision Curriculum Devel., Va., 2002—. Sponsor Nat. Beta Orgn., NC, 1992—. Recipient cert. for Academic Excellence, cert. of Appreciation, Nat. Jr. Beta Orgn., N.C., Outstanding Educator of Yr., Mt. Halibeth Zion Ch., Bklyn., N.Y., 1985, Tchr. of Yr., Meadowview Elem. Sch., Atlanta, 1989, PTA Tchr. of Yr., 1996; grantee Coll. Alumni Scholarship award, 1977. Mem.: Assn. Supervision, Curriculum Devel., Internat. Reading Assn., Kappa Delta Pi. Roman Catholic. Avocations: cooking, reading, gourmet cooking, poetry, writing. Home: 6173 Wurtenburg Ct Stone Mountain GA 30087

WRIGHT, PEGGY SUE ESPY, elementary school educator; b. Chattanooga, Dec. 27, 1929; d. Lavada Pilgrim Espy Newell; m. John Lawton Wright, Nov. 27, 1959; children: John Lawton III, Stephen Martin. BA, U. Chattanooga, 1951, MEd, 1976; spl. cert., Emory U., 1957. Cert. elem. tchr., K-12 reading tchr., adminstrv., supr., music tchr., Tenn. Tchr. Bright Sch., Chattanooga; tchr. summer reading program McCallie Sch., Chattanooga; tchr. Chpt. I reading Chattanooga Pub. Schs. Adj. prof. Chattanooga State Tech. C.C.; workshop leader; presenter in field. Violinist Chattanooga Symphony; active local ch.; pres. Chattanooga Sister City Assn.; chmn. Tenn. Literacy Com. Mem. NEA, Internat. Reading Assn., Tenn. Reading Assn. (pres.), Tenn. Edn. Assn., Chattanooga Edn. Assn., MCCAC (past pres.), Delta Kappa Gamma, Alpha Xi. Presbyterian.

WRIGHT, SABRA DELL, music educator; b. Abilene, Tex., Nov. 4, 1953; d. Clead Elman Stark and Dottie Dell Quickel Stark; m. Richard Patrick Wright, Nov. 13, 1987; children: Richard Steven, Jerrod Sterling. B in Music Edn., Tarleton State U., Stephenville, Tex., 1975; M in Elem. Edn., Ariz. State U., Flagstaff, 1993. Cert. all-level music edn. Tex. Bd. Edn., 1975, K-12 music edn. Ariz. State Bd. Edn., 1992. Owner/tchr. Pirouette Dancers Studio, Stephenville, Tex., 1971—75; elem. music tchr. Irving Ind. Sch. Dist., Tex., 1975—80; mgr., horse trainer Bar Nothing Quarter Horse and Thoroughbred Ranch, Arthur City, Tex., 1980—85; mgr. brood mare farm Karho Arabians, Scottsdale, Ariz., 1985—86; elem. music tchr. Paradise Valley Ind. Sch. Dist., Phoenix, 1986—96; jr. high choral dir. Wichita Falls Ind. Sch. Dist., Tex., 1996—97; elem. music tchr. Iowa Pk. Consol. Ind. Sch. Dist., Tex., 1997—. Dance, choreography cons. U.S. Bi-Centennial Celebration, Irving, Tex., 1975—76; adult leader/ mgr. Wichita Count 4-H Horse Club, Iowa Park, Tex., 1998—2004; horse trainer, riding instr. Ridin' Right Tng. Facility, Iowa Park, 1998—. Student aide Teens Aid the Retarded, Irving, 1968—71, STARS: Teens Aid the Retarded, Stephenville, Tex., 1971—75; adult den leader Boy Scouts Am., Wichita Falls, 1996—97, Iowa Park, Tex., 1997—2004; instr. Whispers of Hope Riding Facility, Wichita Falls, 1998—2004. Recipient Outstanding Leadership award, Wichita County 4-H Orgn., 2000—01; scholar, Tarleton State U., 1971—75, Tex. State Teens Aid the Retarded, 1975. Mem.:

Ariz. State Tchrs. Assn. (site rep., tchr. adv. 1993—96), Tex. Assn.Choral Dir. (assoc.), Tex. Music Educators Assn. (assoc.), Assn. Tex. Profl. Educators (assoc.), Am. Quarter Horse Assn. (assoc.), Am. Paint Horse Assn. (assoc.). Non-Partisan. Christian. Avocations: reading, community theater, horseback riding. Office: Bradford Elem 809 Texowa Rd Iowa Park TX 76367 Office Phone: 940-592-5841. Business E-Mail: swright@ipcisd.net.

WRIGHT, SANDRA, science administrator; B in Acctg., Calif. State U., Long Beach. V.p., contr. Aerojet; with Litton; corp. v.p., contr. Northrop Grumman Corp., LA, 2001—. Office: Northrop Grumman Corp 1840 Century Park E Los Angeles CA 90067-2199

WRIGHT, SHANNON MARIE, psychotherapist, counselor; b. Syracuse, N.Y., Aug. 5, 1978; d. Steven Rae and Cindy Lou Phillips; m. Samuel Benjamin Wright, Apr. 7, 2002; children: Jayden Rain, Balyn Wind, Skylah Marie. MS Counseling and Psychology, Troy U., Fort Walton Beach, Fla., 2005. Registered Mental Health Counselor Intern Fla., 2005. Neuropsychometrist Pensacola Psychol. Clinic, Pensacola, Fla., 2004—; mental herALth counselor intern Pattison Profl. Counseling Ctr., Fort Walton Beach, Fla., 2005—. Advanced aftercare counselor U. W. Fla., Pensacola, Fla., 2003. Grantee Academic Award for single mothers, U. W. Fla., 2000-2002. Mem.: APA (corr.). Liberal. Native American. Office: Pensacola Psychol Clinic PA 3 W Garden St Ste 370 Pensacola FL 32501 Home: 1771 E Mallory St Pensacola FL 32503 Office Phone: 850-433-1656. Office Fax: 850-433-1656. Personal E-mail: sswright1@earthlink.net.

WRIGHT, SHEENA, not-for-profit developer; b. Bronx, NY; m. Gregg Walker; 2 children. BA, Columbia Coll., 1990; JD, Columbia Law, 1994. Former editl. asst., Washington Bureau NY Times; assoc. atty. Wachtell, Lipton, Rosen and Katz, 1994—99; sr. assoc. Reboul, MacMurray, Hewitt, Maynard and Kristol, 1999—2000; gen. coun., exec. v.p. bus. devel. Crave Technologies, 2000—02; pres., CEO Abyssinian Development Corp., 2002—. Spkr. in field; mem. Neighborhood Investment Advisory Panel, Fed. Reserve Bank of New York Advisory Bd.; bd. dir. Citizens Union Found.; chmn. SEA Corp. Named one of The Women Shaping the World, Essence Mag., 2006, 40 Under 40, Crain's NY Bus. Mag., 2006. Office: Abyssinian Devel Corp 4 W 125th St New York NY 10027*

WRIGHT, SHERRYL LEIGH, journalist; b. Washington, Sept. 18, 1950; d. John Hammett and Iris June (Tenney) W.; m. Dennis John Blair, Sept. 2, 1972. BA in Speech and Drama, Allegheny Coll., 1972; MS in Journalism, Kans. State U., 1987. Continuity dir. Sta. KMAN/KMKF, Manhattan, Kans., 1977-80; mil. corr. Manhattan Mercury, 1981-82; living editor Junction City (Kans.) Daily Union, 1982-83, features editor, 1983-84, asst. news editor, 1984-85; media specialist Kans. State U., Manhattan, 1985-88, guest lectr. internat. journalism manhattan, 1987—; fgn. expert, editing China Daily, Beijing, People's Republic of China, 1988-89; staff reporter Manhattan Mercury, 1989—. Frequent columnist and commentator on Chinese politics for media orgns., 1987—. Mem. Racial & Ethnic Harmony Com., Manhattan, 1989—. Selected for journalist's tour of People's Republic of China, Assn. Educators in Journalism and Mass Communications, 1987. Mem. Edn. Writers Am., Kans. Pres. Assn., Women in Comm., Inc., Phi Kappa Phi. Democrat. Methodist. Avocations: hiking, camping, photography. Office: USD 383 2031 Poyntz Ave Manhattan KS 66502-3898

WRIGHT, SUSAN WEBBER, federal judge; b. Texarkana, Ark., Aug. 22, 1948; d. Thomas Edward and Betty Jane (Gary) Webber; m. Robert Ross Wright, III, May 21, 1983; 1 child, Robin Elizabeth. BA, Randolph-Macon Woman's Coll., 1970; MPA, U. Ark., 1972, JD with high honors, 1975. Bar: Ark. 1975. Law clk. U.S. Ct. Appeals (8th Cir.), 1975-76; from asst. prof. to assoc. prof. law U. Ark., Little Rock, 1976—83, prof., 1983-90, asst. dean, 1976-78; dist. judge U.S. Dist. Ct. (ea. dist.) Ark., Little Rock, 1990—, chief judge, 1998—2005. Vis. assoc. prof. Ohio State U., Columbus, 1981, La. State U., Baton Rouge, 1982—83; mem. adv. com. U.S. Ct. Appeals (8th cir.), St. Louis, 1983—88. Author (with R. Wright): Land Use in a Nutshell, 1978, Land Use in a Nutshell, 2d edit., 1985; editor-in-chief: Ark. Law Rev., 1975; contbr. articles to profl. jours. Mem.: Am. Law Inst., Pulaski County Bar Assn., Ark. Bar Assn., Am. Judicature Soc., Ark. Women's Forum. Anglican. Office: US District Court 600 W Capitol Ave Ste 522 Little Rock AR 72201-3329 Office Phone: 501-604-5100. Business E-Mail: susan_wright@ared.uscourts.gov.

WRIGHT, SYLVIA, government agency administrator; b. Balt. BA, Temple U., 1963, MA, 1965. Group leader Sch. Improvement Program Office U.S. Dept. Edn., Washington, dir. Sch. Support and Tech. Programs, Office Elementary and Secondary Edn., 2001—. Office: US Dept Edn FB6 Rm 3E121 400 Maryland Ave SW Washington DC 20202

WRIGHT, TAMI LADONNA, pre-school educator; d. Joseph Edward and Eva LaVerne Wright; 1 child, William Marcus Reynolds. MusB, Bethany Coll., 1984; BS in Family & Child Devel., U. Ctrl. Okla., 2000, MS in Family & Child Svcs., 2002; MS in Reading, Okla. State U., 2004. Literacy mentor New Zealand Presch. Project, Auckland, 1986—90; lab. tchr. U. Va., Charlottesville, Va., 1990—92; lead tchr. Kinder Care, Okla. City, 1994; head start head tchr. Cmty. Action Program, Okla. City, 1994—2001; head start dir. CDI Temp. Grantee, Denver, 2002—03, Ponca Tribe Okla., 2003—05; child care tchr. Independence CC, Kans.; pre-sch. asst. St. Andrew's Catholic Sch., Independence, Kans. Mem. Success By Early Childhood Coun., Ponca City, 2003—; N.W. rep. Spirits Hope Domestic Violence Coalition, Okla. City, 2005—. Contbr. articles to profl. jours. Mem. troop coun. Boy Scout Am., Independence, 2006—. Mem.: Tri-State Indian Head Start Dirs. Assn., Nat. Assn. Edn. Young Children, Early Childhood Assn. Okla. (conf. co-chair 2000), Phi Kappa Phi. Democrat. Catholic. Avocations: cross stitch, reading. Home: 725 N 13th St Independence KS 67301-2740 Personal E-mail: ecteacher1@yahoo.com.

WRIGHT, TIFFANY ERIN, secondary school educator; b. Plainfield, NJ, Oct. 16, 1974; d. Charles O. and Juliette G. Wright. BA in English, Gettysburg Coll., 1993—97; M in edn., Millersville U., 2000—02; student, John Hopkins U., 2005—. Cert. Secondary English Edn. Pa., 1997, Emergency Secondary Math Edn. Pa., 1998. Ednl. supr./english instr./math instr. Cornell Abraxas, South Mountain, Pa., 1997—2000; softball coach Littlestown Area H.S., Littlestown, Pa., 1998—2000; edn. outreach coord. and summer camp dir. Penn Laurel Girl Scout Coun., Lancaster, Pa., 2001—02; english instr. York County Sch. of Tech., Pa., 2002—05, softball coach, 2003—06; asst. prin. C. Milton Wright HS, 2005—. Presenter Emerging Practices: Creating Learning Communities for the 21st Century, Tchr. Edn. Assembly, Grantville, Pa., 1997; mem. Assessment Com. of York County Sch. of Tech., Pa., 2002—05; powder puff football coach York County Sch. of Tech., Pa., 2002; accreditation team mem. Mid. States and Coun. of Occupl. Edn., Altoona, Pa., 2003; mem. student assistance program York County Sch. of Tech., Pa., 2002—05, vice chairperson, Renaissance Program, 2003—05. Chorus mem. Ctrl. Pa. Women's Chorus, Harrisburg, 2002—03, Unitarian Universalist Ch. of York. Recipient Fred D. Grist award, Adams County Literacy Coun., 2000; Meml. scholarship, Millersville U., 2002—03. Mem.: Assn. for Supervision and Curriculum Devel. (assoc.). Democrat. Unitarian Universalist. Avocations: travel, exercise, reading, outdoor activities. Office: C Milton Wright HS 1301 N Fountain Green Rd Bel Air MD 21014 Office Phone: 410-638-4110. Personal E-mail: tewright27@hotmail.com.

WRIGHT, VIRGINIA, art collector, curator; m. Bagley Wright; children: Merrill, Charles, Robin, Bing. BA, Barnard Coll., 1951. Asst. Sidney Janis Gallery; trustee Virginia Wright Fund, Seattle Art Mus. Curator Color Field Paintings and Related Abstractions, 2005. Named one of Top 200 Collectors, ARTnews Mag., 2004, 2006. Avocation: Collector of Contemporary Art; Japanese Art.*

WRIGHT-ELSON, LARISSA ANNE, literature and language educator; b. Anchorage, Alaska, July 23, 1971; d. Walter Caldwell Wright III and Leslie Erway Wright; m. Kevin Elson, July 7, 2000; 1 child, Cormac Walter Elson. BA in English, Ctrl. Conn. State U., New Britain, 1994; BS in Secondary Edn., U. Alaska, Anchorage, 1998. Cert. Nat. Bd. Profl. Tchg. Stds. English tchr. Anchorage Sch. Dist., 1998—. Scholar Horace Mann Educator Scholarship Program, 2004; Tech. Tchr. Leader grantee, ASD, 2006. Mem.: NEA, Nat. Coun. Tchrs. English, Pi Lambda Theta. Democrat. Quaker. Avocations: travel, art, writing, outdoor activities. Office: South Anchorage HS 13400 Elmore Anchorage AK 99516 Office Phone: 907-742-6200. E-mail: wright-elson_larissa@asdk12.org.

WRIGHT-EVERETT, ROSE MARY, elementary school educator; b. Columbus, Wis., Mar. 28, 1947; d. Jerome Edward Henderson and Edna Mary Beck-Henderson; children: Roseann Marie, Robyn Lynn, Renée Rose. BS, U. Wis., Oshkosh, 1976; 2-Yr. Tchg. Cert., Dodge County Tchrs. Coll., Mayville, Wis., 1967. Tchr. 3d grade Lincoln Elem. Sch., Hartford, Wis., 1967—68; tchr. adult basic edn. Moraine Park Tech. Coll., Beaver Dam, Wis., 1977—87; tchr. 4th grade St. Katharine Drexel Sch., Beaver Dam, 1987—. Lector St. Katharine Drexel Ch., Beaver Dam, 1986—. Mem.: Rock River Reading Coun. (treas. 1995—), Wis. State Reading Assn., Nat. Cath. Edn. Assn. Home: 306 E Mill St Beaver Dam WI 53916

WRIGHT PENN, ROBIN, actress; b. Dallas, Apr. 8, 1966; d. Fred Wright; m. Sean Penn, Apr. 27, 1996; children: Dylan Frances, Hopper Jack. Television appearances include The Yellow Rose, 1983-84, Santa Barbara, 1984-87 (Emmy awards Best Ingenue in a Daytime Drama series 1985-87); films include Hollywood Vice Squad, 1986, The Princess Bride, 1987, State of Grace, 1990, Denial, 1991, The Playboys, 1992, Toys, 1992, Forrest Gump, 1994, The Crossing Guard, 1995, Moll Flanders, 1995, Loved, 1996, She's so Lovely, 1997, Loved, 1997 (Seattle Film Festival Award for best actress, 1997), Hurly-Burly, 1998, Just to Be Together, 1999, Message in a Bottle, 1999, Unbreakable, 2000, The Pledge, 2001, The Last Castle, 2001, White Oleander, 2002, The Singing Detective, 2003, A Home at the End of the World, 2004, Nine Lives, 2005, Sorry Haters, 2005; actor, exec. prodr. (films) Virgin, 2003; (TV miniseries) Empire Falls, 2005. Office: United Talent Agy 9560 Wilshire Blvd Beverly Hills CA 90212

WRISTEN, NYALA COLLEEN, elementary school educator; b. Boise, Idaho, Nov. 30, 1953; d. William Nicholas and Joyce Catherine Hopkins; m. William Michael Wristen (dec. Sept. 3, 1994). AA, Chaffey Coll., Alta Loma, Calif., 1983; BA, Calif. Polytech. U., Pomona, Calif., 1986. Cert. tchr. Calif., 1986. Student tchr. Vista del Valle Elem. Sch., Clairmont, Calif., 1986—87; tchr. Ontario (Calif.) Montclair Sch. Dist., 1987—90, Puesta del Sol Elem. Sch., Victorville, Calif., 1990—92, Advocate Sch., Grand Terrace, Calif., 1993, Adelanto (Calif.) George Sch., 1993—94, Options for Youth, Victorville, 1994—99, Excelsior Edn. Ctr., Victorville, 1999—. Office: Excelsior Edn Ctr 7151 Svl Box Victorville CA 92395-5153

WRISTON, KATHRYN DINEEN, corporate director, consultant; b. Syracuse, N.Y. d. Robert Emmet and Carolyn (Bareham) Dineen; m. Walter B. Wriston, Mar. 14, 1968; 1 stepchild. Student, U. Geneva, 1958-59; BA cum laude, Smith Coll., 1960; LLB, U. Mich., 1963. Bar: N.Y. 1964, U.S. Ct. Appeals (2d cir.) 1964, U.S. Supreme Ct. 1968. Assoc. Shearman & Sterling, N.Y.C., 1963-68. Mem. audit com., corp. responsibility com., fin. com., 2003, Goodyear Tire and Rubber Co., 2002-03, mem. fin. com., 2003; bd. dirs. Northwestern Mut. Life Ins. Co., mem. ins. products and mktg. com., 1986-89, audit com., 1989-, chmn. audit com., 2001-05, investment and fin. policy com., 1989-95; dir. Santa Fe Snyder Corp., 1990-00, mem. audit com. 1990-93, 95-00, nominating com., 1990-99, compensation com., 1998-99, conceptual framework task force Indep. Standards Bd., 1998-00, dir. 1990-00; trustee Fin. Acctg. Found., 1992-97, selection com., 1992-97, audit com., 1992-96, chair, 1993-96, chair devel. com., 1996-97, fin. com., 1994-97. exec. com., 1996-97; task force on timely fin. reporting guidanace Fin. Acctg. Stds. Bd., 1982-83, mem. bd. agenda adv. com., 1981-85, process and structure com., 1981-85, chair, 1983-85, adv. coun., 1981-85; exec. com. CPR Inst. for Dispute Resolution, 1994-99; dir. The Stanley Works, 1996—, mem. fin. and pension coms., 1996-97, 02—, chair audit com., 1997-02, exec. com., 1997-05, mem. compensation com., 2004-. Mem. vis. com. U. Mich. Law Sch., 1973-2006; trustee Fordham U., Bronx, N.Y., 1971-81, vice-chair bd. trustees, 1980-81, student affairs com., 1971-77, chair, 1974-77, faculty affairs com., com. on law sch., 1978-81, grievance com., 1971-81; ea. region selection panel Pres. Commn. on White House Fellowships, 1981-83, chair, 1982-83; bus. com. Nat. Ctr. for State Cts., 1982-88; bd. overseers Rand Inst. for Civil Justice, 1985-93; trustee John A. Hartford Found., 1991—, pres., 2002-, grant com., 1991—, vice-chair, 1992—, chair evaluation com., 1998—, audit com., 1992-2002, chair, 1993-2002, sec., 1996-2002, ex-officio, 2002-; mem. Gov. Wilson's NY Little Hoover Commn., 1974; trustee Cath. Health Care Sys., NYC, 1999—2003. Mem. ABA, Nat. Assn. Accts., Practicing Law Inst. (exec. 1976—, programs and publs. com., chair 1979-04, membership com. 1976-79, chair 1977-79, nominating com. 1978, 81-85, v.p., 1985-05, mem. bar rev. courses 1978-79, fin. com. 1989—, mem. Am. Law Inst./ABA subcom. on Am. law network 1989-91), Fin. Women's Assn. N.Y., N.Y. County Lawyers Assn. (legal aid com. 1972-76), N.Y. State Bar Assn., Assn. of Bar of City of N.Y.

WRITER, SHARON LISLE, secondary school educator; b. L.A., Aug. 29, 1939; d. Harlan Lawerance and Emma Mae (Cordery) Lisle; m. Robert Vincent Writer, Dec. 30, 1961; children: Martin Carl, Cynthia Louise, Brian Robert, Scott Andrew. BS, Mt. St. Marys Coll., 1961; MS in Sci. Edn., Calif. State U., Fullerton, 1989; postgrad., U. Calif., Irvine, 1987, Colo. Sch. Mines, 1994. Cert. secondary tchr., Calif. Tchr. St. Mary's Acad., L.A., 1961-62, Escambia High Sch., Pensacola, Fla., 1962-63; rsch. asst. U. So. Calif., L.A., 1964-65, U. Calif., Irvine, 1965-66; tchr. aide Cerro Villa Jr. High Sch., Villa Park, Calif., 1975-76, tchr., 1976-88, Villa Park High Sch., 1988—98, mentor tchr., 1990—97; lectr. Calif. State Univ., Long Beach, 1999—; CA Dir. of Sci. Olympiad, Southern Section, 2000—. Tchr. of yr. com. Orange (Calif.) Unified Sch. Dist., 1992, supt. adv. coun., 1990-1998, curriculum sci. com., 1991-1997. Active Villa Park Womens League, 1975—, Assistance League of Orange, 1991—; project leader, county coord. Orange County 4-H Assn., Anaheim, Calif., 1975-84; bd. sec. Orange County Sci. Fair, 1986-91, awards chmn., 1991-94, pres., 1994—; mem. judging policy adv. com. Calif. State Sci. Fair, 1996-2001. Recipient Outstanding Sci. Tchr. award Orange County Sci. Tchrs. Assn., 1993; named Tchr. of Yr. Villa Park High Sch., 1990, 94, Outstanding Coach Orange County Sci. Olympiad, 1990, 92, 94, 96, Calif. State Sci. Olympiad, 1987. Mem. NSTA (conv. hospitality com. 1989, 90, hospitality co-chair 1994 nat. conv.), Am. Chem. Soc., Calif. Sci. Tchr. Assn., Orange County Sci. Educators Assn. (Disting. Sci. Tchr. award 1993). Roman Catholic. Avocations: tennis, swimming, water-skiing, needlepoint. Home: 18082 Rosanne Cir Villa Park CA 92861-6431 Office: CSULB Dept Sci Edn 1250 Bellflower Blvd Long Beach CA 90840-4501

WROBLE, LISA ANN, writer, educator; b. Dearborn, Mich., June 17, 1963; d. Robert Frank and Ruth Marie (Schiller) W. Diploma, Inst. Children's Lit., 1983; BA cum laude, Ea. Mich. U., Ypsilanti, 1985. Cert. ESL tchr., ltd. profl. class B, Libr. Mich. Asst. editor cmty. rels. Vets. Adminstrn., Ann Arbor, Mich., 1983-85; prodn. coord. Cmty. Crier Newspaper/COMMA Graphics, Plymouth, Mich., 1985-86; proofreader Valassis Inserts, Livonia, Mich., 1986-89; tech. writer Nat. TechTeam, Dearborn, Mich., 1989-90; freelance writer Plymouth, 1990—; libr. asst. Redford Dist. Libr., Mich., 1996—2002. Publicist Garden City Osteo. Hosp., Mich., 1990-91; creative writing instr. Cmty. Edn. Plymouth-Canton Schs., Mich., 1992-93, 97-2002, Collier County Schs., Fla., 2003—; instr. Inst. Children's Lit., 2000-06; spkr. in field. Author: (12 book series) Kids Throughout History, 1997, 98, The Oceans, 1998, How Things Work, Childcraft, vol. 9, 2000, The New Deal in American History, 2002, Danger on Ice, 2003, Nature Recovers, 2003, Firefighters!, 2003; contbg. editor Metroparent, 1991-93; contbg. tech. writer Cleaner Times, 1992-95, Facilities Planning News, 1993-96, FM Data Monthly, 1997-2000, Mich. Learning, 1998-2002, Wonder Years, Partnership for Learning, 2000—05; book rev. editor Parenting Today's Teens, 1998-2001; columnist Christian Libr. Jour., 1999-2002; book reviewer BookPage Promotions, 1997-2004, The ALAN Rev., 1993—, Christian Libr. Jour., 1997—, The Wonder Years, 2001-05; software reviewer Compute Publs., 1989-92, Falsoft Inc., 1991-94; contbr. articles to profl. jours., chpts. to books; contbg. writer Eye on the Web, 1998, Bridges CX, 1999-2000, Career Explorer, 1999-2000, Teach-Michigan Found., 1998-2000, Partnership for Learning, 2000-05, Learning through History, 2003—. Tutor Cmty. Literacy Coun., Plymouth, 1989-93. Recipient Reading Tutor award Cmty. Literacy Coun., 1991-93. Mem. ASCD, ACE of Fla., Soc. Childrens Book Writers and Illustrators (adv. com. Mich. chpt. 1993-94, 98-2003, workshop facilitator 1990, 97—, mentorship coord. 2000-03), Internat. Reading Assn., Nat. Writers Assn. (vol. critiquer 1989-93), Fla. Freelance Writers Assn., Fla. Reading Assn., Childrens Lit. Assn., Mich. Reading Assn., Womens Nat. Book Assn., Peninsula Writers, Livonia Writers Group Republican. Roman Catholic. Avocations: swimming, photography, crafting, cooking, rollerblading. Home and Office: 2638 Fountain View Cir #204 Naples FL 34109-1705 Personal E-mail: lwroble@lisawroble.com.

WROTTEN, MARYLEAN, medical coordinator, counselor; d. Evelyn Saxton and Perry Elmore; 1 child, Evelyn DeShawn Wroten. Student, Audrey Cohn Coll., 1984. Approved med. authorized pers. Fedn. Puerto Rican Orgns., 1991; strategist crisis intervention pers. Fedn. Puerto Rican Orgns., 1991, cert. CPR-First Aid Fedn. Puerto Rican Orgns., 2004. Resident therapist Audrey Cohen Coll., 1991—; med. coord. Agy. Fedn. Multicultural Orgns., NY, 1991—. Author: (poetry) I Love God (Editor's Choice award, 2004), Hope, 2004. Youth coord. Jackson Dem. Club, Bronx, 1995—99; Sunday sch. tchr. Praying Band of Faith, Bronx, 1985—89; proposal rev. com. Neighborhood Adv. Bd., Bronx, 1995—96; del. 1199 Nat. Health & Human Employees Union, NYC, 1996—2004. Mem.: Internat. Soc. Poets (disting.). Democrat. Pentecostal. Avocations: hiking, reading, volunteering, singing. Home: 1291 Union Ave Bronx NY 10459 Office: Federation Multicultural Organization 2 VanSinderen Ave Brooklyn NY 11207 Office Phone: 212-234-2268. Personal E-mail: Lynnmary10@yahoo.com.

WU, KATHLEEN J., lawyer; b. Great Neck, NY, 1960; BA, Columbia U., 1982; JD, George Washington U., 1985. Bar: NY 1986, Conn. 1986, Tex. 1987. Ptnr., Real Estate, Fin., Bus. Transactions Andrews Kurth LLP, Dallas, mem. mgmt. com. Contbr. articles to profl. jour.; lectr. in field. Mem. Dallas Assembly; bd. dir. Women's Leadership Exchange (Southwest), Tex. Cultural Trust Coun.; adv. bd. Turtle Creek Manor; bd. trustees Greenhill Sch. Named a Texas "super lawyer", Tex. Monthly Mag., 2003, 2004; named one of top 6 "go to" real estate lawyers in Tex., Tex. Lawyer Mag., 2003, best lawyers in Dallas, DMagazine, 2003. Mem.: Attys. Serving Cmty. (co-chmn. 2003), Nat. Asian Pacific ABA, State Bar Tex., ABA, Conn. Bar Assn., NY State Bar Assn., Dallas Bar Assn. Office: Andrews Kurth LLP 1717 Main St Ste 3700 Dallas TX 75201 Office Phone: 214-659-4448. Office Fax: 214-659-4401. Business E-Mail: kwu@andrewskurth.com.

WU, MIN, computer and electrical engineer; b. China; BA in Econs., Tshinghua U., 1996; BSE in Elec. Engring., Tsinghua U., 1996; MA in Elec. Engring., Princeton U., 1998, PhD in Elec. Engring., 2001. Asst. prof. dept. elec. and computer engring. U. Md., 2001—06, assoc. prof., 2006—. Author: Multimedia Fingerprinting Forensics for Traitor Tracing, 2005; co-author: Multimedia Data Hiding, 2003; contbr. articles to profl. jour. Named one of Top 100 Young Innovators, MIT Tech. Review, 2004; recipient Career award, NSF, 2002, Young Investigator award, US Dept. Defense, Office Naval Rsch., 2005, Best Paper award, IEEE, European Signal Processing Soc. Achievements include co-holder of 5 US patents. Business E-Mail: minwu@eng.umd.edu.

WU, NAN FAION, pediatrician; b. Malaysia, July 13, 1943; came to U.S., 1969; m. Chia F. Wu, June 22, 1969; children: Edwin, Karen. MD, Nat. Taiwan U., 1969. Diplomate Am. Bd. Pediatrics. Intern Atlantic City Med. Ctr., 1969-70; resident in pediatrics Martland Hosp. U. Medicine and Dentistry of N.J., N.J. Med. Sch., Newark, 1970-73; pvt. practice pediatrics West Orange, N.J., Farmingdale, NJ. Fellow Am. Acad. Pediatrics.

WUBBENA, TERESA R., music educator; b. Augusta, Ga., Nov. 16, 1952; d. Robert Basil and Wanda Lee (Harrison) Roper; m. Jan H. Wubbena, May 17, 1980; children: Robert, Mary. B of Music Edn., Sam Houston State U., 1973, MA, 1976; postgrad., U. North Tex., 1977—78. Cert. tchr. Tex., Ark. Prof. music John Brown U., Silcam Springs, Ark., 1976—, head dept. music, 1990—2002, chair divsn. lang. and arts, 1997—2006, chair divsn. comm. and fine arts, 2006—. Music tchr. Gentry (Ark.) Mid. Sch., 1985—86. Vol. receptionist St. Francis Clinic, Siloam Springs, 2003—. Mem.: Nat. Assn. Schs. Music, Coll. Music Soc., Music Educators Nat. Conf. (bd. dirs. 1989—91, 1999—2002), Choristers Guild. Episcopalian. Office: John Brown Univ 2000 W Univeristy Siloam Springs AR 72761

WUCHTE, MIA ANN, elementary school educator; b. Seoul, South Korea, Mar. 4, 1968; d. LeRoy Joseph and Myong Suk Johns; m. Gerald James Wuchte Jr, Feb. 23, 1990; children: Liana Danielle, Derik Levon, Shane Mitchell. BS, Augusta State U., Ga., 1998; MS, Augusta State U., 2002, Specialist, 2006. Tchr. Lakeside Mid. Sch., Evans, Ga., 2001—.

WU-CHU, STELLA CHWENYEA, nutritionist, consultant; b. Kaohsiung, Taiwan, Sept. 22, 1952; came to U.S., 1976; d. Jin-Shoui and Sue-Tuan (Ling) Wu; children: Christine, Whitney. BS, Fu-Jen Cath. U., Taiwan, 1974; MA, San Francisco State U., 1979. Registered dietitian. Intership U. Calif., Berkeley, 1978; food svc. supr. Calif. Surgery Hosp., Oakland, 1979—80; nutritionist, cons. Solano Napa Agy. on Aging, Vallejo, Calif., 1980—; nutrition cons. Marin County Div. of Aging, San Rafael, Calif., 1981—; nutritionist San Francisco Commn. on Aging, 1990—; nutrition cons. Contra Costa Office on Aging, 1995—. Mem. adv. bd. Staying Health project Am. Soc. on Aging, 1999—2000; nutritional advisor Veggie Life Mag., Walnut Creek, Calif., 1993, Salt Free Cooking Made Easy. Chief editor quar. publ. Taiwanese Assn. publ., 1991-94. Cmty. liaison East Bay Taiwanese Assn., Walnut Creek, 1992-93; v.p. No. Calif. Formosan Fedn., 1993; dist. supportive com. chair United Meth. Women, 1995-97, Bayview dist. social actions mission coord., 1997-98; adv. bd. Overseas Chinese Inst. on Aging, 2000—, Am. Soc. Aging, 2000. Mem. Am. Dietetic Assn., Am. Pub. Health Assn., Jacob Inst. of Women's Health, Nat. Assn. Nutrition and Aging Svcs., Formosan Assn. for Pub. Affairs, Am. Assn. of Meals on Wheels. Avocations: reading, concerts, dance, creative writing (in chinese). Home: 70 Seabreeze Dr Richmond CA 94804-7410 Office: San Francisco Commn Aging 25 Van Ness Ave Ste 650 San Francisco CA 94102-6057 E-mail: stellawc@aol.com.

WUENSTEL, KAREN L., elementary school educator; b. Wamego, Kans., Oct. 9, 1949; d. Albert J. and Lucille P. (Eagan) Fox; children: Christopher, Andrea, Mark. AA in Math., St. Mary's Coll., Leavenworth, Kans., 1971. Tchr. Assumption Sch., Topeka, 1971—74; G.E.D. instr. Topeka, Garan City, 1974—79; bookkeeper Assumption Sch./Parish, Topeka, 1979—84; tchr. Most Pure Heart of Mary Sch., Topeka, 1983—. Com. mem. Archdiocesan Curriculum Team, North Ctrl. Team, Kans. Assessment Team. Named Outstanding Elem. Tchr., 1973. Mem.: NEA, Kans. Assn. Tchrs. Math. Democrat. Catholic. Avocations: bicycling, racquetball, reading, cross stitch. Office: Most Pure Heart of Mary Sch 1750 SW Stone Ave Topeka KS 66604 Business E-Mail: kwuenstel@mphm.com.

WULF, SHARON ANN, management consultant; b. New Bedford, Mass., Aug. 23, 1954; d. Daniel Thomas and Norma Dorothy (McCabe) Vieira; m. Stanley A. Wulf, 1983. BS in Acctg. cum laude, Providence Coll., 1976; MBA, Northeastern U., 1977; PhD, Columbia Pacific U., 1984. Staff acct., intern Laventhol & Horwath, Providence, 1977; jr. fin. analyst Polaroid Corp., Waltham, Mass., 1977-78, fin. analyst Freetown, Mass., 1978-79, Cambridge, Mass., 1979-81; sr. fin. cons., mktg. strategic planner Digital Equipment Corp., Stow, Mass., 1981-82, Maynard, Mass., 1982-83, mgr. fin. devel. program, 1983-84, strategic fin. cons. engring. divsn., 1984-86, group mgr. planning & strategic ops. Hudson, Mass., 1986-87, group mgr. strategic bus.

planning, 1987-89; mktg. planning mgr. Diigital Equipment Corp., Marlboro, Mass., 1989-90; new ventures bus. devel. mgr. Digital Equipment Corp., Marlboro, Mass., 1990—93; pres. Enterprise Sytems, Framingham, Mass., 1993—; sr. instr. Cambridge Coll., 1997—, prof., 1998—; instr. strategic mktg. Boston U., 2005—. Lectr. fin. acctg. Southeastern Mass. U., 1979—81; adj. prof. acctg., mgmt. & fin., knowledge mgmt. strategies Northeastern U., Boston, 1980—; instr. Nat. Tech. U., 1991—95; instr., vis. asst. prof. mgmt. Framingham State Coll., 1999—; instr. Curry Coll., 2004—; instr. strategic mktg. Boston U., 2005; exec. com. enterprise forum MIT, 1987—92, lectr. network leadership workshop, 2003; prin. Work Sys. Assocs., Inc., Marlborough, Mass., 1992—93; bd. advisors Spaceball Tech., Inc., Lowell, Mass., Terasys., Inc.; sr. faculty advisor healthcare master's degree program Mass. Gen. Hosp., 2000—04; frequent keynote spkr.; cons. in field; keynote spkr. Internat. Facilities Mgmt. Assn. Conf., 2005; instr. Boston U., 2005—06; sr. faculty advisor, healthcare masters degree program Mass. Eye and Ear, 2006. Author: Building Performance Values, 1996, Customer Service Action Plans, 1997, Leadership in Action: The Way It Is Cersus The Way It Should Be, 1997, Secrets and Strategies for Effective Business Plans, 2004, The Strategy Guidebook, 2005 Chair pub. support and fund raising ARC, New Bedford, 1974-84; bd. dirs. Vets. Outreach Ctr., Metrowest, Framingham, 1989-93; v.p. MIT Leadership Found., Cambridge, 1991-93; mem. exec. com. MIT Enterprise Forum, also co-chair startup clinics, 1986-92. Recipient 25 Yr. Recognition award, Northeastern U., 2005. Mem. Black Alumni of MIT (bd. advisors 1989-92), Univ. Coll. Faculty Soc., Phi Sigma Tau. Home: 902 Salem End Rd Framingham MA 01702-5532 Office: Enterprise Systems 1257 Worcester Rd Ste 301 Framingham MA 01701-5217 Fax: 508-626-9038. Office Phone: 508-626-2233. Business E-Mail: sharonw@enters.com.

WULFEKUHLE, JENNY, pilates instructor, athletic trainer; b. Dubuque, Iowa, Sept. 10, 1977; d. Mark Joseph and Janet L. Wulfekuhle. BSc, Quincy U., Ill.; MA, San Jose State U., Calif. Cert. Pilates Instructor Polestar Pilates Education, 2005, Athletic Trainer Nat. Athletic Trainers Assn., 2001. Athletic trainer BaySport, Los Gatos, Calif., 2002—04, Physiotherapy Assoc., Cedar Rapids, Iowa, 2004—05; hostess Country Junction, Dyersville, Iowa, 2000—02, bartender, 2006—; athletic trainer Cascade H.S., Cascade, Iowa, 2006—; pilates instr. Rockwell Collins Recreation Ctr., Cedar Rapids, Iowa, 2005, Intelligent Movement, Peosta, Iowa, 2005—. Avocations: snowboarding, golf, reading. Home: 31158 Pin Oak Dyersville IA 52040 Office: Intelligent Movment Pilates Studio 742 Peosta St Ste2 P O Box 32 Peosta IA 52068

WULFF, LOIS YVONNE, librarian; b. Seattle, Nov. 23, 1940; d. Arthur Ray and Audrey June (Carpenter) Roark; B.S., Washington State U., 1962; M.L.S., U. Wash., 1963; postgrad. Syracuse U., 1969-70; m. Barry Kahn, Dec. 18, 1971 (dec. 1982). Intern, then head documents div. Ohio State U., 1963-67; spl. project investigator U. Wash., 1968-69; staff asst., head search unit Johns Hopkins Med. Instns., 1971-72; project coordinator, asst. to dir., coordinator health sci. libraries U. Minn., 1973-77; head librarian Alfred Taubman Med. Library, U. Mich., 1978-87, coordinator Med. and Sci./Tech. Libraries, 1981-87, asst. dir. for collection mgmt. Gaylord fellow, 1969-70. Mem. City Coun., Yachats, Oreg., 2002—. Mem. AAAS, Med. Library Assn., ALA, Mich. Library Assn., Assn. Coll. and Rsch. Libraries.

WULFF, VIRGINIA MCMILLAN, school system administrator; b. Glendale, Calif., May 27, 1958; d. Reginald Joseph and Virginia Ellen (Cavett) McMillan; m. Robert Reid Wulff, June 20, 1981; children: Kellyn Melissa, Katharine Cooper, Kyle Reid. BA in English with honors, Stanford U., 1980. Prodn. mgr. Addison Wesley/Benjamin Cummings Pub., Menlo Park, Calif., 1980-82; ways and means chair Oak Elem. PTA, Los Altos, Calif., 1988-89, pres., 1990-91, Los Altos/Mountain View PTA Coun., Los Altos, 1992-93; v.p. coms. Sixth Dist. PTA, San Jose, Calif., 1995-99, editor The Bell, 1995-99. Sec., mem. exec. bd. Peninsula Youth Theatre, Mountain View, Calif., 1994—; pres. San Juan Sensations Team, Los Altos, 1995—. Editor: The Bell, 1995-98. Oak chair Measure A Com., Los Altos, 1993, 95, 97; mem. parcel taxes bond measure coms. Los Altos Elem.; mem. Mountain View/Los Altos H.S. Dist. Bond Com., 1996, 97; lead parent rep. Castilleja Sch., 1998—; legislation chair Blach PTA, 1999—, Sixth Dist. PTA, San Jose, CA, 1995-98. Mem. AAUW. Home: 136 Waverly Pl Mountain View CA 94040-4573

WUNDER, HAROLDENE FOWLER, taxation and international accounting educator; b. Greenville, S.C., Nov. 16, 1944; d. Harold Eugene Fowler and Sarah Ann (Chaffin) Crooks. BS, U. Md., 1971; M Acctg., U. S.C., 1975, PhD, 1978. Vis. asst. prof. U. S.C., Columbia, 1977-78; asst. prof. U. Pa., Phila., 1978-81; vis. asst. prof. U. N.C., Chapel Hill, 1981-82; asst. prof. U. Mass., Boston, 1982-86; vis. assoc. prof. Suffolk U., Boston, 1986-87; assoc. prof. U. Toledo, 1987—93; prof. Calif. State U., Sacramento, 1993—. Contbr. articles to profl. and acad. jours. Fellow George Olson fellowship, 1975. Mem.: AICPA, Nat. Tax Assn., Am. Taxation Assn., Am. Acctg. Assn., Calif. Soc. CPAs, Beta Gamma Sigma. Avocation: reading. Office: Calif State U College of Bus Adminstrn Sacramento CA 95819-6088 Office Phone: 916-278-7134. Business E-Mail: wunderh@csus.edu.

WUNDERMAN, JAN DARCOURT, artist; b. Winnipeg, Man., Can., Jan. 22, 1921; d. Rene Paul and Georgette Marie (Guionet) Darcourt; m. Frank Joseph Malina, 1938 (div. 1945); m. Lester Wunderman (div. 1967); children: Marc, Geroge, Karen Renee. BFA, Otis Art Inst., L.A., 1942. One man shows include Easthampton Guild Hall, L.I., 1977, Denise Bibro Fine Art Gallery, N.Y.C., 1996-98, 2002, Roko Gallery, 1963, 66, 68, 71, 73, 76; represented in numerous permanent pub., corp. and pvt. collections including Zimmerli Mus., NYU Loeb Collection, Norfolk Mus., Health and Sci. Ctr., Salt Lake City, Alfred Kouri Collection, Skidmore Coll. Print Collection, Nat. Assn. of Women Artists, Rutgers U., 1994, Albright Knox Mus., 1998-99, Daimler Chrysler Coll., Germany, 2002, Northwest Airlines, Detroit, 2003, abstract-nonrepresentational. Recipient Ohashi award Pan Pacific Exhbn., Tokyo and Osaka, 1962, Emily Lowe award 1965, J.J. Akston Found. prize, 1965, Canaday Meml. prize, 1979, Marian De Solo Mendes prize, 1981, Charles Horman Meml. prize, 1983, Amelia Peabody award Nat. Assn. Women, 1991, Grumbacher Gold medal of honor, 1992, Doris Kreindler award 1992. Mem. Nat. Assn. Women Artists (medal of honor 1966, Marcia Brady Tucker award 1965, E. Holzinger prize 1966, Jane C. Stanley prize 1977, Marge Greenblatt award 1990, Amelia Peabody award 1991, Solveig Stomsoe Palmer prize 1997), Am. Soc. Contemporary Artists (corr. sec. 1977-78, Bocour award 1980, Elizabeth Erlanger Meml. award 1990, Kreindler award 1992, N. Ransom award 2002), Contemporary Artists Guild (Irwin Zlowe Meml. award 1998). Avocations: history, travel. Studio: 41 Union Sq W Rm 516 New York NY 10003-3208 Address: Denise Bibro Fine Art Gallery 529 West 20th St New York NY 10011

WUNNICKE, BROOKE, lawyer; b. Dallas, May 9, 1918; d. Rudolph von Falkenstein and Lulu Lenore Brooke; m. James M. Wunnicke, Apr. 11, 1940; (dec. 1977); 1 child, Diane B. BA, Stanford U., 1939; JD, U. Colo., 1945. Bar: Wyo. 1946, Colo. 1969, U.S. Dist. Ct. Wyo. 1947, U.S. Dist. Ct. Colo. 1970, U.S. Supreme Ct. 1958, U.S. Ct. Appeals (10th cir.) 1958. Pvt. practice law, 1946—56; ptnr. Williams & Wunnicke, Cheyenne, Wyo., 1956—69; counsel Calkins, Kramer, Grimshaw & Harring, Denver, 1969—73; chief appellate dep. atty. Dist. Atty's Office, Denver, 1973—86; counsel Hall & Evans L.L.C., Denver, 1986—. Adj. prof. law U. Denver Coll. Law, 1978-97, 1st Frank H. Ricketeen Jr. adj. prof., 2003; lectr. Internat. Practicum Inst. Denver, 1978-2003 Author: Ethics Compliance for Business Lawyers, 1987; co-author: Standby Letters of Credit, 1989, Corporate Financial Risk Management, 1992, UCP 500 and Standby Letters of Credit-Special Report, 1994, Standby and Commercial Letters of Credit, 2000, 2007, Legal Opinion Letters Formbook, 2002, 2007; contbr. articles to profl. jours. Pres. Laramie County Bar Assn., Cheyenne, 1967-68; Dir. Cheyenne C. of C., 1965-68 Recipient Outstanding Svc. award, Colo. Dist. Attys. Coun., 1979, 1982, 1986, Disting. Alumni awards, U. Colo. Sch. Law, 1986, 1993, William Lee Knous award, 1997, Lathrop Trailblazer award, Colo. Women's Bar Assn., 1997, Eleanor P. Williams award for Disting. Svc. to Legal Profession, 1997, Potter Lifetime Profl. Svc. award, 1999, Nat. award, Def. Rsch. Inst., 1999, Law Star award, Denver Coll. Law, 2003. Fellow Colo. Bar Found. (hon.), Am. Bar Found.; mem. ABA, Wyo. State Bar, Denver Bar Assn. (hon. life; trustee 1977-80, award of merit 2004), Colo. Bar Assn. (hon., life, Merit award 1999), Am. Arbitration Assn. (comml. panel), William E. Doyle Inn of Ct. (hon.), Order of Coif, Phi Beta Kappa. Republican. Avocations: reading, writing. Office: Hall & Evans LLC 1125 17th St Ste 600 Denver CO 80202-2037 Office Phone: 303-628-3300. Business E-Mail: wunnickeb@hallevans.com.

WURDINGER, VICTORIA, writer; b. Onedia, Wis., Apr. 16, 1957; d. John Lonewolf. BA, U. Wis., 1979; MA, Columbia U., 1983. Newswriter WHA Radio, Madison, Wis., 1979; editor Pivot Point Internat., Chgo., 1982, Harcourt, Brace, Jovanovich, N.Y.C., 1984; reporter L'Offical, Paris, 1986; author N.Y.C.; v.p. L.O.M.O. Internat., Cleve., 1987-91. Author: Competition, 1982, Conducting Your Own Photo Shoot, 1986, Soul Survivor, 1990, Home Haircutting Made Easy, 1993. Mem. Nat. Writers Union, L.O.M.O. Internat. Avocation: photography.

WURTH, PATSY ANN, geographic information systems specialist; b. Paducah, Ky., Dec. 5, 1947; d. James Edward and Olean Barbara (Sietz) W.; m. Jerry Leon Scarbrough, Aug. 7, 1965 (div. 1985); children: Tracy Ann, Ashli Michele, Scott Jeremy; m. Robert W. Luther, Feb. 25, 1995 (div. 1998). BS magna cum laude, Murray (Ky.) State U., 1988, MS, 1991. Cert. EMT. Instr. Ky. Cabinet for Human Resources, Frankfort, 1983-93, Vocat. Edn. Region I, Paducah, Ky., 1983-91, Murray State U., 1983-91, Calloway County Red Cross, Murray, 1985-89; exec. dir. Marshall County Red Cross, Benton, Ky., 1985-88; profl. intern Johnson Controls, Cadiz, Ky., 1986; grad. asst. Murray State U., 1988-91; fellow U.S. Dept. Energy/Oak Ridge (Tenn.) Nat. Lab., 1989-90; rsch. fellow U.S. Army Corps Engrs. Constrn. Engring. Rsch. Lab., Champaign, Ill., 1991-92, acting team leader spatial techs. support team, 1992-93; GIS facility mgr. environ. scis. divsn. Oak Ridge (Tenn.) Nat. Lab., 1993-95; mgr. GIS svcs. Solutions to Environ. Problems, Inc., Oak Ridge, 1995-96, Aegis Svcs. Corp., Clinton, Tenn., 1996-97; GIS program coord. Roane State C.C., Oak Ridge, 1996—; GIS program mgr. Sci. Applications Internat. Corp., Oak Ridge, Tenn., 1998—2001. Exec. dir. Marshall County Red Cross, Benton, Ky., 1985-88; first aid attendant Ohio River Steel, Calvert City, Ky., 1985-86. Troop leader Kentuckiana Girl Scouts, Benton, 1973-84, fund drive chair, 1973-84. Mem. LWV, Am. Soc. Safety Engrs., Ky. EMT Instrs. Assn. (instr.), Western Ky. EMT Assn., Am. Soc. Photogrametry and Remote Sensing (Western Great Lake region sec.-treas. 1992), Nat. Safety Coun. (cmty. health and emergency svcs. com.), Assn. Women in Sci., Women in Tech. and Sci. (chmn. 1997-98), Tenn. Geog. Info. Coun. (bd. dirs. 1997-2000), S.E. Regional ESRI Users Group (chair 1995), Nat. Assn. Environ. Profls., Oak Ridge Area ESRI Users Group (chmn. 1996-2000), Epsilon Pi Tau, Alpha Chi. Democrat. Roman Catholic. Home: 330 Melton Hill Dr Clinton TN 37716-7106 Office: Roane State CC 701 Briarcliff Ave Oak Ridge TN 37830

WUTHNOW, SARA MARGERY, retired nursing educator; b. Kansas City, Kans., Mar. 9, 1946; d. D. Ray and L. Elizabeth (Edgar) Wilcox; m. Robert Wuthnow, June 15, 1968; children: Robyn, Brooke, Joel. BSN, U. No. Colo., 1969; MSN, U. Calif., San Francisco, 1971; EdD, Rutgers U., 1982. Staff nurse Herrich Hosp., Berkeley, Calif., 1969-70; clin. supr. Samuel Merritt Hosp., Oakland, Calif., 1971-74; faculty U. Ariz., Tucson, 1975-76, Helene Fuld Sch. Nursing, Trenton, N.J., 1976-77, Trenton State Coll., 1977-78, 83-84, Holy Family Coll., Phila., 1984-93; chair dept. Nursing Eastern Coll., St. David's, Pa., 1993-99; acting MSN chair Holy Family Coll., Phila., 1999—2002; ret. Contbr. articles to profl. jours. Mem. Sigma Theta Tau.

WUTHRICK, EILEEN B., special education educator; b. Salem, Ohio, Aug. 29, 1949; d. Frederick Christian and Effie Marie Wuthrick. BA, Mt. Union Coll., 1973; EdM, Kent State U., 1996, EdS, 2003. Cert. tchg. Dept. Edn., Ohio, edn. handicapped K-12, learning disabled K-12, severe behavior handicapped K-12, reading K-12, visual art K-12, elem. 1-8, adminstrv. specialist. Art tchr. Carrollton (Ohio) Exempted Village Sch., 1975—77, West Br. Local Schs., Beloit, Ohio, 1977—78; spl. edn. tchr. Alliance (Ohio) City Schs., 1978—86, Marlington Local Schs., Alliance, 1986—. Spkr. in field. Contbr. articles to profl. jours. Grantee, Martha Holden Jennings Found., 2001—02, 2005—, Bank One, 2001—02, 2005—. Mem.: Coun. Exceptional Children, NEA, Ohio Edn. Assn., Phi Delta Kappa. Avocations: painting, drawing, music, gardening, skiing.

WYATT, CAROLYN J., psychologist; b. Fort Dodge, Iowa, July 4, 1946; d. Burt Eugene and Harriet Margaret (Gouge) W.; m. Jarrett W. Newbrey, Aug. 22, 1979 (dec. Aug., 1990). BS, Morningside Coll., 1968; MA, Wash. State U., 1979, PhD, 1982. Lic. psychologist, Wash., Idaho. Secondary sch. tchr. Jefferson City (Colo.) Schs., 1968-69; tchr. Mary Crest H.S., Denver, 1969-70, Aspen (Colo.) Pub. Schs., 1970-76; grad. rsch. and tchg. asst. Wash. State U., Pullman, 1976-81; staff counselor Wash. State U. Counseling Svcs., Pullman, 1981-82; pvt. practice, counselor, psychologist Moscow, Idaho, 1982—. Mem. APA, IPA. Office: Carolyn J Wyatt PhD 814 S Washington St Moscow ID 83843-3049

WYATT, EDITH ELIZABETH, elementary school educator; b. San Diego, Aug. 13, 1914; d. Jesse Wellington and Elizabeth (Fultz) Carne; m. Lee Ora Wyatt, Mar. 30, 1947 (dec. Jan. 1966); children: Glenn Stanley (dec.), David Allen. BA, San Diego State Coll., 1936. Elem. tchr. Nat. Sch. Dist., National City, Calif., 1938-76. Sec. San Diego County Parks Soc., 1986-96, sec.-treas., 1998—; librarian Congl. Ch. Women's Fellowship, Chula Vista, Calif., 1980—; active Boy Scouts Am. 1959—. Recipient Who award San Diego County Tchrs. Assn., 1968, Silver Fawn award Boy Scouts Am. Mem. AAUW (sec. 1978-80, pub. rels. 1985—), Calif. Ret. Tchrs. Assn. (scholarship com. 1985-90, 92-95, treas. South Shores divsn. # 60 1996-2004), Starlite Hiking Club (sec.-treas. 1979—). Avocation: hiking. Home: 165 E Millan St Chula Vista CA 91910-6255

WYATT, HELEN J., special education educator; b. Fayette, Miss., Jan. 1, 1948; d. Milton Louis and Hazel James; m. Dewitt Wyatt, Aug. 26, 1973; children: Derrick Dewayne, Carla Amaris. BS in Bus. Edn., Alcorn A & M Coll., Lorman, Miss., 1969; MS in Spl. Edn., Alcorn State U., Miss., 1979, MEd in Adminstrn and Supervision, 1994; EdD in Spl. Svcs. and Exceptional Edn., Nova Southeastern U., 2000. Lic. bus. edn. tchr. Miss. State Dept. Edn., spl. edn. tchr. La. Dept. Edn., child search coord. La. Dept. Edn., parish or city sch. supr. instrn. La. Dept. Edn., parish or city sch. supr.dir. spl. edn. La. Dept. Edn., supr. student tchg. La. Dept. Edn. Tchr. St. Joachim Cath. Elem. Sch., Chgo., 1970—71; counselor, employment and tng. instr. Fayette Pub. Svc. Careers Program, 1971—74; exec. sec. Alcorn State Admission Office, Lorman, 1975—78; spl. edn. tchr. Tensas Parish Sch. Dist., St. Joseph, La., 1978—86, Concordia Parish Sch. Dist., Vidalia, La., 1987—89, facilitator individual edn. plan, 1989—2000; assoc. prof., dir. Am. Reads-Miss. Alcorn State U., 2000—. Parish monitor Concordia Parish Spl. Edn. Dept., Vidalia, 1989—2000; state monitor La. State Dept. of Edn., Baton Rouge, 1995—2000; cons. automated individual edn. plan Region 6 parishes, Alexandria, La., 1998—2000; presenter for spl. edn. tngs. Concordia Spl. Edn. Dept., Vidalia, 1989—2000; adminstr. Alcorn State U., 2000—; trainer Americorps members Am. Reads-Miss., Alcorn State, 2000—; workshop presenter Multi-State Cross Program Tng. Conf., Nashville, 2005. Author: (practicum) Assisting Newly Hired Special Education Teachers to Function More Effectively Through Inservice Training and Mentoring; contbr., workshop presenter: 10th Nat. Svc. Orientation Life After AmeriCorps (Commendation, Gov. of Miss., 2003); writer (handbook) Guidebook for New Special Education Teachers (Commendation, Spl. Edn. Supr., 2000). Mentor for youth Zion Hill #1 Bapt. Ch., Natchez, Miss., 1995—2005. Recipient Cmty.-Based Tutorial Program grant, La. Dept. of Edn., 2000—06, Commendations for participating and moderating at several confs., Miss. Commn. for Vol. Svc., 2000—06, Commendation for judging reading and sci. fairs, Natchez-Adams Sch. Dist., 2001—04, Cert. of Excellence, SW Miss. Ctr. for Ednl. Tech., 2003, Read Across Am. Appreciation cert., NEA, 2006. Mem.: NAACP, CEC (assoc.), Alcorn Alumni Assn. (life), Phi Delta Kappa (assoc.; historian 1996—97, Cert. Appreciation 1997), Delta Sigma Theta (pres., v.p., treas. Vidalia Alumnae chpt. 1966—2006, Pres.'s award Vidalia Alumnae chpt. 2006). Democrat. Baptist. Avocations: travel, reading, completing puzzles, playing computer games. Home: 401 S Spruce St Vidalia LA 71373 Office: Alcorn State U 1000 ASU Dr 480 Alcorn State MS 39096 Office Phone: 601-877-6215. Office Fax: 601-877-6213. Personal E-mail: hjwyatt@bellsouth.net. E-mail: hwyatt@lorman.alcorn.edu.

WYATT, LENORE, civic worker; b. N.Y.C., June 12, 1929; d. Benedict S. Rosenfeld and Ora (Copel) Kanner; m. Bernard D. Copeland, May 17, 1953 (dec. March 1968); children: Harry (dec.), Robert (dec.); m. C. Wyatt Unger, Mar. 26, 1969 (dec. Feb. 1992); 1 child, Amy Unger; m. F. Lowry Wyatt, Sept. 12, 1992 (dec. Nov. 1996). Student, Mills Coll., 1946-48; BA, Stanford U., 1950, MA, 1952; postgrad., NYU, 1952-53. Instr. Stanford U., Palo Alto, Calif., 1952, Hunter Coll., N.Y.C., 1952-53, Calif. State U., Sacramento, 1956-60, U. Calif., Davis, 1965-69; property mgr. Unger, Demas & Markakis, Sacramento, 1974-83. Former actress and model; fin. com. Charles Wright Acad.; fin. mgr. several trusts. Pres. Sacramento Opera Assn., 1972—73; treas. Sacramento Children's Home, 1990—92, v.p., 1992—; former mem. bd. dirs. Sutter Hosp. Aux., Sutter Hosp. Med. Rsch. Found., Sacramento Symphony League, Temple B'nai Israel Sisterhood, Sacramento chpt. Hadassah, Sacramento Children's Home Guild; formerly active Sacramento Opera Assn., Crocker Soc. of Crocker Art Gallery, Sacramento Symphony Assn., Sacramento Reportory Theater Assn.; founding mem. Tacoma Cmtys. Art Sch.; past mem. bd. dirs. Charles Wright Acad.; past mem., bd. dirs. Tacoma Art Mus. Mem.: Century Orthop. Guild (pres. 2006—), Pathfinders of Palm Springs, Stanford U. Alumni Assn. (past bd. dirs. Sacramento), Am. Contract Bridge League, Sacramento Pioneer Assn., Del Paso Country Club (past capt. women's golf group, Sacramento), Thunderbird Country Club, Tacoma Club, Wash. Athletic Club, Maui Country Club, Tacoma Country and Golf Club, Sutter Club. Republican. Jewish. Avocations: golf, duplicate bridge, sculpting. Home: 70551 Placerville Rd Rancho Mirage CA 92270

WYATT, MARCIA JEAN, fine arts and speech educator, administrative assistant; b. Petersburg, Va., Nov. 2, 1959; d. Andrew Ezekiel and Lillian (Bonner) Wyatt; m. Nicholas Charles Cooper-Lewter, Nov. 29, 1986 (div. 1998). BS in Elem. Edn., Va. State U., Ettrick, 1984; MEd in Spl. Edn., 1993; Degree in Adminstrv. Ednl. Leadership, St. Mary's U., Mpls., 2000. Lic. minister, 1987; ordained to clergy, 1990. Tchr. Marion (Ind.) Community Schs., 1985-86, Inglewood (Calif.) Unified Schs., 1986-87; office mgr. C.R.A.V.E. Christ Counseling, Tustin, Calif., 1986—; asst. minister New Garden of Gethsemane B.C., L.A., 1987-90; assoc. minister New Hope Bapt. Ch., St. Paul, 1990—; assoc. pastor New Garden of Gethsemane B.C., L.A., 1990—; assoc. minister New Hope Bapt. Ch., 1990—, pulpit coord., 2002; pres. C.R.A.V.E. Christ Singers, L.A., 1987-90; adminstr. asst. Eldorado Bank, Orange, Calif., 1988-90; tchr. fine arts Broadway Cmty. Sch., Mpls., 1996—, Mpls. Sch. Dist., 1990—; assessment coord. Broadway Cmty. Sch., Mpls., 1999—; with Wyatt Consulting, Shoreview, Minn., 1986—; 4th grade tchr. Hall Cmty. Sch., Mpls. Founder, dir. Diversity in Motion program for A.A. students, 1992—; stage dir. Babu's Magic with dancer Chuck Davis, 1994; cons. Everyday Learning Corp., 1996—; assessment coord., curriculum writer Mpls. Pub. Schs., 1999—; 4th/5th grade curriculum instrn. assessment team lead Elizabeth Hall Elem. Sch., extended day coord., 2003; tchr. intermediate Spl. Program Emotional Needs Elizabeth Hall Sch., 2004-05. Nominated to Pres.'s Commn. White House Fellowships, 1993; mem. C.R.A.V.E. Christ Ministries (Relax in Christ, Affirm with Christ, Visualize Christ, Experience Christ); pulpit coord. New Hope Bapt. Ch.; 1st v.p. Minn. State Bapt. Conv. Women's Aux., 2006—. Finalist Minn. Tchr. of Yr., Edn. Minn., 2005; grantee, Star Tribune, 1994—96, African Studies, U. Wis., 1995—96, FASSE, U. Minn., 1996, Namibia, Fulbright (U.S. Govt.), 1996. Mem. NAFE, Alpha Kappa Alpha. Avocations: reading, music, fish breeding, travel. Office Phone: 612-668-2650.

WYATT, SUSAN SKINNER, education educator; m. Frank Lowell Wyatt. BS, Tex. Woman's U., Denton, 1971, MS, 1978, PhD, 1985. Tchr. Dallas Ind. Sch. Dist., 1972—85; exec. dir. Dallas Assn. Parent Edn., Richardson, Tex., 1987—93; prof., chmn. dept. Eastfield Coll., Mesquite, Tex., 1993—. Mem.: PTA (life hon.), Dallas Assn. for Edn. Young Children (pres., affiliate rep, nominating com. chair 1996—2006), Child Devel. Educator's Assn. (assoc.; pres. 1998—99), Tex. C.C. Teacher's Assn. (assoc.), Tex. Assn. for Edn. Young Children (assoc.; treas. 2005—06), So. Early Childhood Assn. (assoc.), Nat. Assn. Edn. Young Children (life; accreditation validator 1993—2006). Methodist. Avocations: travel, reading, singing. Office: Eastfield Coll 3737 Motley Dr Mesquite TX 75150 Office Phone: 972-860-7620. Home Fax: 972-860-8319; Office Fax: 972-860-8319. Business E-Mail: susanwyatt@dcccd.edu.

WYATT, WILLDA JEAN, elementary school educator; b. Ola, Ark., Nov. 5, 1933; d. William Edward and Mildred Lucille (Manning) Woodson; m. Oscar William Wyatt, May 26, 1956 (dec. Sept. 1992); children: Michael, Matthew (dec.), Cecilia, Margaret. BS in Edn., U. Cen. Ark., 1956; MA, U. Ark., 1960. Cert. life tchr.'s credential, Calif., Ark., Ariz. Tchr. pub. sch., Compton, Ark., 1952-53; tchr. Wilson Sch. Dist., Whitten, Ark., 1953-55, Whiteriver (Ariz.) Pub. Sch., 1956-57, Kingston (Ark.) Pub. Sch., 1957-59, Gustine (Calif.) Pub. Sch., 1961-63, William Burnett Elem. Sch., Milpitas, Calif., 1964-92; substitute tchr. Milpitas Unified Sch. Dist., 1992—. Developer: (study guide) California Missions, 1982 (grantee 1982). Publicity chair Milpitas Hist. Soc., 1995-97; mem. Milpitas Hist. Soc., 2004—. Mem. AAUW (fin. chair 1986-88, pres.-elect 1994-95, pres. 1995-96, past pres. 1996-97, parliamentarian 1997—, Grant Honoree 1986). Democrat. Episcopalian. Avocations: reading, travel, eating, visiting. Home: 181 Park Hill Dr Milpitas CA 95035-4607

WYATT-MAGALIAN, CATE, artist; d. James Larkin and Mary Ann Wyatt; married, Aug. 11, 1998; children: Jennifer Lynn Magalian, Natalie Blythe Woodward. BS, Fla. State U., 1980; BA, U. South Fla., 1986, MFA, 1990. Adj. instr. Eckerd Coll., St. Petersburg, Fla., 1992—95, Fla. State U., Tallahassee, 1995—2000, asst. art instr., 2000—06. Forum panelist Gt. Explorations Hands on Mus., St. Petersburg, 1993; artists' roundtable panelist Fla. Gulf Coast Art Ctr., Bellair, 1996; juror Cultural Resources Commn., Tallahassee, 2004. One-woman shows include U. South Fla. Tchg. Gallery, 1990, U. South Fla. Libr., 1991, Eckerd Coll., 1995, exhibitions include 2nd World Festival Art Paper, Bled, Slovenia, 2001, Art With Southern Drawl, So. US Regional, 1995, National Palace Culture, Sofia, Bulgaria, 2004, 2005, Lessedea Gallery, 2006, Gulf Coast Mus. Art, Largo, Fla., 2005. Bd. mem. 621 Gallery, Tallahassee, 1993—97, Cultural Resource Commn., Tallahassee, 1996—2002. Artists Resource Fund (ARF) grant, Pinellas County Arts Coun., Fla., 1994. Mem.: Tex. Fine Arts Assn., Tallahassee Mus. Art, Nat. Mus. Women in Arts. Personal E-mail: cwyattmagalian@yahoo.com.

WYCH, AMY, interpreter, educator; d. Eddie LaVan and Wanda Watts; m. Mark Wych; 1 child, Natalie. BS, Stephen F. Austin State U., 1984—87; MA, Gallaudet U., 1992—94. Level 3 Sign Language Interpreter Tex. Divsn. for Assistive and Rehabilitative Services, 1996, Professional Teacher Certification Coun. on Edn. for the Deaf, 1995, Provisional Texas Teacher Certification for the Hearing-Impaired State of Tex., 1987, Secondary American Sign Language Teacher State of Tex., 1998. Sign lang. interpreter/cons. Self-Employed, Huntington, Tex., 1996—; tchr. of the deaf and hard of hearing Lufkin Regional Day Sch. Program for the Deaf, Lufkin, Tex., 1988—2002; prevention specialist Gateway Prevention Services, Lufkin, Tex., 2002—. Charter mem. Deep East Tex. Interpreters for the Deaf, Lufkin, Tex., 1997—2003.

WYCKOFF, SUSAN, astronomy researcher; b. Santa Cruz, Calif., Mar. 18, 1941; d. Stephen and Jean (Taft) W.; m. Peter Augustus Wehinger, July 29, 1967. BA in Astronomy, Mount Holyoke, 1962; postgrad., Swarthmore Coll., 1962-63; PhD in Astronomy, Case Inst. Technology, 1967. Postdoctoral fellow U. Mich., Ann Arbor, 1967-68; asst. prof. Albion (Mich.) Coll., 1968-70; rsch. assoc. U. Kans., Lawrence, 1970-72; sr. lectr. Tel-Aviv U., Israel, 1972-75; prin. rsch. fellow Royal Greenwich Observatory, Sussex, Eng., 1975-78; vis. prof. Ohio State U., Columbus, 1978-79; assoc. prof. Ariz.

State U., Tempe, 1979-82, prof., 1982—, prof. emeritus, chair dept. physics and astronomy Tempe, 1991-94. Adj. prof. Sussex U., 1975-77, U. Heidelberg Theoretical Astrophysics Inst., 1980, U. Ariz., Tucson, 1984—; vis. astronomer Royal Greenwich Observatory, Sussex, Eng., 1983, Mt. Stromlo Observatory, Australian Nat. U., Canberra, 1987, Smith Coll., 1985; Shapley lectr., 1985-86; vis. com. Aura, Inc., Tucson, 1985-88; mem. Internat. Astron. Union Working Group High Resolution Spectra Comets, 1982—, space telescope working group key projects Extragalactic Astronomy, 1984-85. Contbr. articles profl. jours. Mem. Gov.'s Disease Control Commn., Phoenix, 1985-87; dir. Ariz. Collaborative for Excellence in Preparation of Tchrs., 1994-2000. Named Woman of Achievement Yr. Phoenix Jr. League, 1983. Fellow Royal Astron. Soc. (Eng.); mem. NSF adv. com. 1983—, Nat. Acad. Sci. space sci. bd. 1984—, Ariz. State U. Faculty Women's Assn. (pres. 1983-84, exec. bd. 1983—), Am. Astron. Soc. Coun. (A.J. Cannon award comm. 1982-87), Internat. Astron. Union, Mt. Graham Internat. Observatory (citizen's coun.), Internat. Halley Watch (dir. 1982-90), Am. Astron. Soc. (mem. coun. 1985-88). Avocations: jogging, swimming. Office: Ariz State U Physics Astronomy Dept Tempe AZ 85287-1504 Home: 5224 N Camino Escuela Tucson AZ 85718-5017 E-mail: wyckoff@asu.edu.

WYCKOFF, SYLVIA SPENCER, art educator, artist; b. Pitts., Nov. 14, 1915; d. Lynn Boyd Wyckoff and Bess Jeannette Hohes. BFA, Syracuse U., NY, 1937, MFA, 1944. Cert. art tchr. NY, 1987. Art tchr. various pub. schs., Homer and Cobleskill, NY, 1937—42; instr. Coll. Visual Arts, Syracuse U., 1942—81, asst. to full prof., chmn. freshman core program, 1971—72, chmn. London art program; ret., 1981. Adj. art instr. Cazenovia Coll.; judge arts recognition and talent search Nat. Found. Arts, Princeton, NJ, 1983. Exhibited in group shows, Cortland, NY, 1938, Syracuse Regional Show, 1942—45 (1st prize for watercolor, 1943), with Rick Wolff, Oneida, NY, exhibitions include Nat. League Am. Pen Women, NYC and Washington, DC, 1968 (1st prize for watercolor, 1945), Chancellor's Office, Syracuse U., 1976, St. Lawrence U., Munson William Proctor Mus. Art, Utica, NY, 1980—81, Cazenovia Watercolor Soc., 1981—95, Core Faculty-Wells Coll., one-woman shows include Coleman Hall, Cazenovia, NY, 1975, New Coll. Art Bldg., Cazenovia Coll., 2004. Dispatcher CAVAC (Cazenovia Area Vol. Corps., NY, 1974—91; vol. Stone Quarry Art Pk. Recipient 1st prize for watercolor, Onondaga Hist. Soc., 1945, Gordon Steele award for painting, Assoc. Artists of Syracuse, 1968, spl. award, NY State Tchrs. Assn., 1981. Mem.: Nat. Mus. Women in Arts (charter mem.), Stone Quarry Art Pk., Manson Williams Proctor Mus., Cazenovia Watercolor Soc. (founder 1976, first recipient Priscilla Hancock award 1992), Sigma Chi Alpha, Eta Phi Upsilon (hon.), Alpha Xi Delta (award to 10% Top Alumnae 1967). Presbyterian. Achievements include first woman on athletic bd., Syracuse U., 1974; named in honor of Spl. Sylvia Wyckoff Book award, Alpha Sigma Lambda, U. Coll. Syracuse, NY, 1981. Avocations: painting, drawing, bridge, knitting. Home: 4 Liberty St Cazenovia NY 13035

WYGANT, PATRICIA BRYANS, artist; b. Marion, Ohio, Nov. 10, 1926; d. Ralph Armond and Frances Annetta (Kilbury) Bryans. BFA, Syracuse U., 1950. Resident Millay Colony for Arts, Austerlitz, N.Y., 1979. Exhibited in 62 nat. juried exhbns. including Watercolor USA, Nat. Watercolor Soc., Watercolor Workshop Greek Islands Sifnos Amorgos, Paros, 1988; paintings publ. in A Gallery of Marine Art, 1988, 98, The Best of Watercolor, 1995 (1st Pl. award). Recipient Winsor Newton award Rochester Art Club, 1994. Mem. Am. Artists Profl. League, Ga. Watercolor Soc. (signature mem.), Niagara Frontier Watercolor Soc. (signature mem.). Avocation: travel. Office: Anderson Alley Artists 250 N Goodman St Rochester NY 14607

WYKES, MARY MAUSHAK, real estate agent; b. Elgin, Ill., May 13, 1925; d. William Frederick and Grace Stoxen Maushak; m. Arthur Albert Wykes, Oct. 13, 1956 (dec. Mar. 17, 2001); children: Pamela Wykes Armstrong, Paul Arthur. BS, U. Ill., Champaign, 1946; postgrad., Northwestern U., Chgo., 1950—52. Cert. tchr. Ill., realtor Md. Asst. office mgr. IBM Corp., Chgo., 1946—52; personnel asst. Internat. Minerals and Chem. Corp., Chgo., 1952—57; exec. asst. Hewitt Assocs., Libertyville, Ill., 1958—60; ch. sec. Deerfield Presbyn Ch., Ill., 1961—62; employee devel. specialist Nat. Bur. Stds., Gaithersburg, Md., 1970—87; realtor Shannon, Luchs & Weichert Realtors, Gaithersburg, Md., 1978—2003; adult evening sch. tchr. Montgomery County Schs. and Montgomery Coll., Gaithersburg, Md., 1970—85; realtor Weichert Realtors, 1978—. Mem. Grace United Meth. Ch., 1968—. Mem.: AAUW (program chmn. 2003—), Stds. Alumni Assn., Mortar Board Alumni Assn., Rockville-US Power Squadron (mem.-at-large 2002—03). Home: 18900 Diary Rd Montgomery Village MD 20886 Office: Weichert Realtors 19238 Montgomery Village Ave Montgomery Village MD 20886

WYLAN, BARBARA, artist; b. Providence, 1933; divorced; children: Andrea, Brock. BFA, R.I. Sch. of Design, Providence, 1955; studied with Donald Stoltenberg, Claude Croney, Murray Wentworth, Ruth Wynn, Charles Movalli, Dong Kingman. Tchr. watercolor workshops; juror various exhbns. One-woman shows include Sturgis Libr., Mass., 1974, 77, 83, Falmouth Artists' Guild, Mass., 1977, Skylight Gallery, Colo., 1979, Market Barn Gallery, Falmouth, Mass., 1981, 89, 91, Dom's Restaurant, Mass., 1981, Spectrum Am. Artists and Craftsmen, Brewster, Mass., 1983-88, 90, 92-93, 95, 2000, 03, Cape Cod Conservatory, Mass., 1984, 86, Cape Cod Mus. Nat. History, Brewster, Mass., 1987, Old Selectmens' Gallery, West Barnstable, Mass., 1995, Cahoon Mus. Am. Art, Cotuit, Mass., 1998; exhibited in group shows at Watercolor USA (Springfield award 1982), Nat. Soc. Painters in Casein and Acrylic 38th Ann., Nat. Arts club, NYC (Dr. David Soloway award 1991), Cahoon Mus. Art, Coteit, Mass., 1991, 97, 2003, 04, 06, Cape Cod Mus. Art, Dennis, Mass., 2002, 06; represented in permanent and pvt. collections Mobile (Ala.) Mus. Art, Cahoon Mus. Am. Art, Cotuit, Mass., Cape Cod Mus. of Art, Dennis, Mass., Springfield, Mo. Art Mus. Mem. Nat. Soc. Painters in Casein and Acrylic, Watercolor USA Honor Soc., New Eng. Watercolor Soc., Copley Soc. Art, and Twenty-one in Truro.

WYLDE, KATHRYN S., business organization executive; BA, St. Olaf Coll., 1968. With Lutheran Med. Ctr., 1968—79; pres., CEO, N.Y.C. Housing Partnership, 1982—96; founding pres., CEO, N.Y.C. Investment Fund, 1996—; pres., CEO Partnership for N.Y.C., 2000—. Chair Luth. Med. Ctr., Bklyn.; mem. bus. adv. bd. CUNY; bd. dirs. NYC Econ. Devel. Corp., Biomed. Rsch. Alliance N.Y., NYC Leadership Acad., Manhattan Inst. Policy Rsch. Recipient HBSCNY Bus. Statesman award. Office: Partnership for NYC One Battery Pk Plz 5th Fl New York NY 10004 Business E-Mail: kwylde@nycp.org.

WYLIE, JOAN BLOUT, real estate rehabilitator, ceramist, designer; b. Montgomery, Ala., Jan. 29, 1920; d. Jack Jonas and Ida (Lewis) Dreyfus; m. Elkan Rogers Blout, Aug. 27, 1939 (div. June 1981); children: James E. Blout, Susan B. Merry Lausch, William Blout; m. Laurence Wylie, Dec. 26, 1987 (dec. 1995). Student, Skidmore Coll., 1938—39; BA in Design, Finch Coll., N.Y.C., 1940. Owner, pres. YaYa Designs, Cambridge, Mass., 1977—; entrepreneur purchasing and revitalizing properties, Cambridge, 1978—; owner, mgr. rental housing, Cambridge, 1978—. Exhibited fountain, sculptures, tableware at University Place, Cambridge, 1991. Bd. dirs. Cambridge Cmty. Ctr., 1952-99; bd. dirs., treas. Riverside/Cambridgeport Cmty. Assn., 1983-93. Mem. Cambridge Art Assn. (bd. dirs. 1998—), Cambridge Boat Club, Cambridge Hist. Soc., Soc. Arts and Crafts, French Libr. and Cultural Ctr. Mem. Soc. Of Friends. Home: 1010 Memorial Dr Cambridge MA 02138-4866

WYLIE, TRISHA LYNN, principal; b. Chowchilla, Calif., June 7, 1965; d. Kenneth Lee and Karen Louise Sanders; m. Kevin Paul Wylie, June 26, 2000; 1 child, Thomas. BA in Social Sci., CSU Stanslaus, Turlock, Calif., 1987; MA, Chapman U., Orange, Calif., 1992. Cert. Clear Adminstrn. Calif., Clear Single Subject Calif., Clear Multple Subject. Tchr. Merced City Sch. Dist., Merced, Calif., 1988—95, asst. prin., 1995—2003, prin., 2003—. Mem. Rotary, Merced, 2002—03. Mem.: ASCD, Assn. Calif. Sch. Adminstrs. (treas. 2005—). Office: Wright Elem Sch 900 E 20th St Merced CA 95340

WYLLY, BARBARA BENTLEY, performing arts association administrator; b. Bala-Cynwyd, Pa., June 10, 1924; d. William Henry and Virginia (Barclay) Bentley; m. William Beck Wylly, Apr. 26, 1947; children: Virginia Wylly Johnson, Barbara Wylly Klausman, Thomas C. II. A, Briarcliff Jr. Coll., 1943. Pres. bd. dirs. Hillside Hosp. Inc., Atlanta, 1982, mem. adv. coun., 1982—; pres. Atlanta Symphony Assocs., 1975-76, mem. adv. bd., 1976—; chmn. bd. dirs. Ctr. for Puppetry Arts, Atlanta, 1988-2004, mem. exec. com., 1988—. Bd. dirs. Mountain Conservation Trust, Atlanta Opera Guild, 1999—; mem. bd. sponsors Georgian Chamber Players, 2000—. Republican. Episcopalian. Avocations: walking, reading, music. Home: 940 Foxcroft Rd NW Atlanta GA 30327-2622 Office: Ctr Puppetry Arts 1404 Spring St NW Atlanta GA 30309-2820

WYMAN, LOTTE ANN NOVAK, civic worker; b. Vienna, Austria, Aug. 15, 1925; d. Josef and Hertha (Wallnstorfer) Novak; B.A., Barnard Coll., 1947; 1 dau., Leslie Andrea. Grey Lady, ARC, 1947-55; treas. Women's Assn. First Presbyn. Ch., Greenwich, Conn., 1963-65, chmn. mission interpretation program, 1975-77; bd. dirs. Friends of Sunny Hill Sch. for Phys. and Emotionally Handicapped Children, Greenwich, 1960-78; bd. dirs. YWCA, Greenwich, 1963-78, 81-87, chmn. world fellowship, 1965, mem. bldg. com., 1965-70, pres., 1967-70; bd. dirs. Drug Liberation Program of Greater Stamford, 1970-74, Community Chest, Greenwich, 1967-70, Community Forum, Greenwich, 1970—; bd. dirs. Turtle Bay Music Sch., N.Y.C., 1970-80; bd. dirs. Greenwich Arts Council, 1974-79, pres., 1976-79; bd. dirs. Neuberger Mus., SUNY, 1979-85, M.I.T. Council for the Arts, 1980—, World Service Council YWCA, 1983—; mem. Met. Opera Assn., 1980—, adv. dir., 1982—; mem. Purchase Coll. Found., 1983—; cons. Nat. Exec. Service Corps, 1984—; elder 1st Presbyn. Ch. Greenwich, 1986-88; mem. Bd. Parks and Recreation, Greenwich, 1986—; vice chmn. bd. trustees Conn. Grand Opera and Orch., Greenwich, 1986-93; co-chair leadership divsn. United Way, 1994-95; bd. dirs. Parsonage Cottage, Greenwich, 1996—. Mem. Greenwich Country Club, Indian Harbor Yacht Club. Republican. Presbyterian. Home: Baldwin Farms North Greenwich CT 06831

WYMAN, PILAR, editor; b. Beirut, Nov. 14, 1964; d. Samuel Haynes and Laura Pilar (Garzon) W.; m. Peter John McMenamin, Nov. 4, 1991; children: Leith Maria, Hugh Haynes. BA, St. John's Coll., 1986. Typist Editl. Svcs., Annapolis, Md., 1983-86, assoc. indexer, 1989-93; chief indexer Wyman Indexing, Annapolis, 1990—. Instr. Basic Indexing and Applied Indexing USDA Grad. Sch., 1996—. Author: (booklet) Indexing FAQ, 1994; contbr. articles, letters, and indexes to profl. publs.; editor: Key Words, bull. of Am. Soc. Indexers, 2000—, Indexing Specialties: Medicine, 1999. Minority grad. fellow NSF, 1987. Mem. Soc. for Tech. Comm., Am. Med. Writers Assn., Am. Soc. Indexers (chair Washington chpt. 1995-96). Democrat. Avocations: gardening, reading, travel. Address: TA Wyman Indexing 1223 Mount Pleasant Dr Annapolis MD 21409-5237 Office Phone: 410-757-7119. Business E-Mail: pilarw@wymanindexing.com.

WYMER, BARBARA SUE, elementary school educator; b. Wood County, Ohio, Sept. 6, 1961; d. Robert Lee and Eileen Nettie (Snyder) Gore; m. Edward A. Wymer, Nov. 19, 1976; children: Graig, Larissa, Scott. BS in Edn., Bowling Green (Ohio) State U., 1981, postgrad., 1984—. Tchr. kindergarten North Baltimore (Ohio) Pub. Schs., 1982-84, tchr. 1st grade, 1984-88, 1998—. Penta sci. grantee. Mem. Kappa Delta Pi.

WYMER, DANIELLE MARIE, mathematics educator; b. Akron, Ohio, July 25, 1972; d. Barbara Ray and Walter Alan Burger; m. Michael Patrick Wymer, July 15, 1995; children: Luke Alan, McKayla Marie. Masters, Marygrove Coll., Mich., 2004. Cert. tchr. Ohio, 2003. Math. tchr. Manchester Local Schs., Ohio, 1995—. Ski club advisor Manchester HS, Akron, Ohio, 1995—, track coach, 1996—99. Named one of Top 10 Tchrs. award, Manchester Local Schs., 2000. Home: 2366 McGinty Rd North Canton OH 44720 Office: Manchester HS 437 W Nimisila Rd Akron OH 44319 Personal E-mail: danielle.wymer@mail.neonet.k12.oh.us.

WYMER, KELLYN LIN, biology and chemistry educator, coach; b. Elmhurst, Ill., Jan. 6, 1975; d. William Dixon and Linda Lee Andrews; m. Jason Matthew Wymer, Mar. 11, 1975; 1 child, Jason Matthew Jr. BS in Biology, State U. NY, Cortland, 1997. Biology, gen. sci. tchr. Park Hill HS, Kansas City, Mo., 1997—2001, soccer coach, 1997—2001; biology tchr. Kans. City Career Acad., 2001—02; biology, chemistry tchr. Bishop Ward HS, Kansas City, 2002—, softball, soccer coach, 2002—. Republican. Avocations: reading, sports, politics. Office: Bishop Ward High Sch 708 N 18th St Kansas City KS 66102 Office Phone: 913-371-1201. Business E-Mail: Kwymer@wardhigh.org. E-mail: jkwymer@everestkc.net.

WYMORE, LUANN COURTNEY, retired education educator; b. Kansas City, Mo., Feb. 22, 1942; d. Clifford Willis and Lola (Moore) Courtney; m. George Philip Wymore, Dec. 27, 1964; children: Courtney, Kristin, Ryan. BA, William Jewell Coll., 1964; MA, U. Mo., Kansas City, 1969; PhD, Mo. U., 1989. Cert. elem., biology, Englisy tchr., Mo. Elem. tchr. Sch. Dist. North Kansas City, Mo., 1964-69; assoc. prof. elem. edn. Mo. Valley Coll., Marshall, 1989—2004; ret., 2004. Presenter in field. Contbr. articles to profl. jours. Leader Girl Scouts U.S.A., Slater, Mo., 1980's, 4-H Club, Orearville, Mo., 1980's. Mem. ASCD, PEO, Internat. Reading Assn. Democrat. Avocations: reading, piano, organ, travel. Home: 820 Rich St Slater MO 65349-1258

WYNDEWICKE, KIONNE ANNETTE (ANNETTE JOHNSON MOORER), reading educator; b. Preston, Miss. d. Clifton Thomas and Missouria (Jackson) Johnson; m. Eugene C. Moorer, Sept. 23, 1961 (div.). BS, Ill. State U., 1961; postgrad., Williams Coll., 1972, Columbia Coll., 1972; MEd, Nat. Coll. Edn., 1982. Social worker Cook County Dept. Pub. Aid, 1961; tchr. reading Chgo. Bd. Edn., 1961—; asst. to news dir. Sta. WCIU-TV, 1972-74; asst. women's editor Chgo. Defender, 1970-72; social sec. Dr. William R. Clarke, 1972—77. Part-time photog. model, fashion commentator, pub. relations cons., pub. spkr. Contbr. articles to local newspapers. Co-chmn. installation Profl. Women's Aux., Provident Hosp., 1961, corr. sec., 1969, publicity chmn., 1969-72, 74-77. Selected as one of 13 persons in U.S. to attend Innovative Tchr. Tng. Seminar, funded by Henry Luce Found. at Williams Coll., 1972, Woman of the Day, WAIT Radio, 1978; one of 25 Black Women of Chgo. at receive Kizzy award, 1977; recipient Outstanding Cmty. Svc. award Beatrice Caffrey Youth Svc., Inc., 1978, 83, 85. Mem. Ill. Speech and Theatre Assn., Speech Comm. Assn. Am., Ret. Tchrs. Assn. Chgo., Art Inst. Chgo. Lutheran. Home: 2901 S King Dr Apt 1514 Chicago IL 60616-3314

WYNER, ETHEL SCHIFF, psychologist, director; b. NYC, May 22, 1929; d. Sidney and Esther Schiff; m. Jay S. Wyner (dec.); children: Shari Narva, Janis Sheinkopf. BA, Hunter Coll., 1948; MA, Syracuse U., 1950; EdD, Yeshiva U., 1961. Cert. psychologist, sch. psychologist NY. Head tchr. Sampson Coll. Nursery Sch., Geneva, NY, 1948—49; rsch. asst. reading lab. Syracuse (NY) U., 1949—50; tchr. Cicero (NY) Elem. Sch., 1950—51; psychologist League Sch. for Seriously Disturbed Children, NYC, 1957—59, Dry Leaning Industry, NYC, 1959—64; exec. dir. Lifeline Ctr. for Child Devel., NYC, 1959—2002; pvt. practice Port Washington, NY, 1959—.

WYNN, KAREN, psychologist, educator, researcher; b. Austin, Tex., Dec. 18, 1962; d. Lucy Shombert and William "Buddy" Wynn; m. Paul Bloom; children: Max Bloom, Zachary Bloom. BA, McGill U., Montreal, Que., Can., 1985; PhD, MIT, 1990. Asst. prof. psychology, asst. rsch. scientist in cognitive sci. U. Ariz., Tucson, 1990—96, assoc. prof. psychology, assoc. rsch. scientist in cognitive sci., dir. developmental psychology program, 1996—99; prof. psychology and cognitive sci. Yale U., New Haven, 1999—. Vis. assoc. rsch scientist, med. rsch. coun. cognitive develop. unit U. Coll. London, 1997—98; lectr. in field. Contbr. articles to profl. jours. and newspapers; participated in radio interviews. Recipient James McKeen Cattell Found. Sabbatical award, 1997, Disting. Sci. award for Early Career Contbn. to Psychology, APA, 2000, Troland Rsch. award, NAS, 2001; grantee, NIH, NSF, 1987—90. Mem.: Cognition (editl. bd. mem.), Trends in Cognitive Scis. (adv. editl. bd. mem. 1998), Soc. for Rsch. in Child Devel., Internat. Soc. Infant Studies. Avocation: dressage. Office: 2 Hillhouse Ave Yale Univ Dept Psychology Box 208205 New Haven CT 06520-8205 Office Phone: 203-436-1406. Office Fax: 203-436-1915. Business E-Mail: karen.wynn@yale.edu.

WYNN, KARLA WRAY, artist, agricultural products executive; b. Idaho Falls, Idaho, Oct. 1, 1943; d. Wiliam and Elma (McCowin) Lott; m. Russell D. Wynn, June 7, 1963 (div. 1996); children: Joseph, Jeffrey, Andrea. Student, Coll. of Holy Names, 1962-63, Providence Coll. Nursing, 1962-63; BFA, Idaho State U., 1989; postgrad., Alfred U., 1993. Co-owner R.D. Wynn Farms, American Falls, Idaho, 1963-96, office mgr., 1975-84; co-owner Redi-Gro Fertilizer Co., American Falls, 1970-96, office mgr., 1980-84; pres. Lakeside Farms, Inc. (name now Redi-Gro Fertilitzer Inc.), American Falls, 1975—96; artist, 1990—. Owner Blue Heron, Pocatello, Idaho, 1991-96. Exhibited in group shows at The Gallows, Pocatello, Idaho, 1989, Tara James Gallery, Pocatello, 1990, Carol Liber - Painted Apple Gallery, Victor, Idaho, 1990—94, Brown's Gallery, Boise, 1990—94, Pine Haven Pottery, Island Park, 1996—97, Samuel's Continental Imports, Jackson Hole, Wyo., 1995—97, Jackson, Wyo. Art Assn. Silent Auction, 2005, Idaho Watercolor Soc., 2005, Represented in permanent collections Am. Falls Pub. Libr., Am. Falls, Idaho, others, one-woman shows include Masks of the People, Boise Airport (award, 1993), artistic workshops, Christopher Shink Watercolor Workshop, Idaho Watercolor Soc., Boise, 1989, Katherine Hirsioux Porcelain Workshop, Haystack Mtn. Sch. of Arts and Crafts, Deer Isle, Maine, 1989, John Takahara Workshop at Idaho State U., 1989, Paul Dresong Porcelain Workshop, Arrowmont Sch. Arts and Crafts, U. Tenn., Gatlinburg, 1990. Recipient 2 awards, Ea. Idaho State Fair Art Show, 1987, award, Idaho Watercolor Soc. Exhibit, Boise, 1987, 1988, 1990, 2 awards, Art Ronderous, Montpelier, Idaho, 1988, Idaho Watercolor Soc. Traveling Exhibit award, Art des Refusé, Idaho State U. Transition Gallery, Earl Pond Student Union, 1989, award, Idaho State U. Biennial Exhibit, 1993, Cottages & Cranberries, Gingerbread Houses, Pocatello, Idaho, 1994, 1996, Festival of Trees, Gingerbread Houses, Boise, 1996; grantee scholarship, Idaho Watercolor Soc., 1987. Buddhist. E-mail: kwwynn@msn.com.

WYNN, MARY BETH, music educator; b. Indpls., Oct. 4, 1981; d. Lewie Lee and Jeanette Branscum; m. Cory Matthew Wynn, June 5, 2004. MusB in Music Edn., U. Indpls., 2004. Music tchr. MSD Warren Twp., Indpls., 2004—.

WYRSCH, MARTHA B., lawyer, energy executive; b. Laramie, Wyo., 1958; m. Gerry Wyrsch; 2 children. BA in Lit., U. Wyo., 1980; JD, George Washington U., 1986; graduate, Harvard Bus. Sch. Advanced Mgmt. Program, 2002. Legis. asst. to Sen. Alan K. Simpson of Wyo., 1980—83; assoc. Davis, Graham & Stubbs, 1986—91; v.p., gen. counsel and sec. KN Energy Inc. (now Kinder Morgan, Inc.), 1991—99; sr. v.p., gen. counsel, sec., Duke Energy Field Svcs. Duke Energy Corp., Charlotte, NC, 1999—2001, sr. v.p., gen. counsel, energy transmission and distbn., 2001—03, sr. v.p., legal affairs, 2003—04, group v.p., gen. counsel, sec., 2004—05; pres., CEO Duke Energy Gas Transmission, Houston, 2005—. Bd. advisors George Washington Law Sch.; bd. dirs. Inst. and Sch. for Environ. and Natural Resources, U. Wyo. Mem.: ABA (vice chair, pub. utility, comm. and transp. law sect.), Interstate Natural Gas Assn. Am., Edison Elec. Inst., Am. Gas Assn., Am. Corp. Counsel Assn., Colo. Bar Assn. Office: Duke Energy Gas Transmission 5400 Westheimer Ct Houston TX 77056

WYSCHOGROD, EDITH, philosophy educator; b. N.Y.C. d. Morris and Selma Shurer; m. Michael Wyschogrod, Mar. 6, 1955; children: Daniel, Tamar. AB, Hunter Coll., 1957; PhD, Columbia U., 1970. Prof. philosophy Queens Coll., Flushing, NY, 1967-92; J. Newton Rayzor prof. philosophy and religious thought Rice U., Houston, 1992—2003, emerita, 2003—. Vis. prof. philosophy Villanova U. 2003; Croghan vis. prof. religion Williams Coll. 2004. Author: Emmanuel Levinas: The Problem of Ethical Metaphysics, 1974, 2d edit., 2000, Spirit in Ashes, 1985, Saints and Postmodernism, 1990, An Ethics of Remembering: History, Heterology and the Nameless Others; co-editor: Lacan and Theological Discourse, 1989, The Enigma of Gift and Sacrifice, 2002, The Ethical, 2003, Crossover Queries: Dwelling with Negatives, Embodying Philosophy's Others, 2006. Nat. Humanities Ctr. fellow, 1981, Woodrow Wilson Ctr. fellow, 1987-88, Guggenheim fellow, 1995-96. Fellow Am. Acad. Arts and Scis.; mem. Am. Acad. Religion (pres. 1992-93). Home: Apt 9C 522 West End Ave New York NY 10024 E-mail: stedith@rice.edu.

WYSE, LOIS, advertising executive, writer; b. Cleve. d. Roy B. Wohlgemuth and Rose (Schwartz) Weisman; m. Marc Wyse (div. 1980); m. Lee Guber (dec. 1988). Pres. Wyse Advt. Inc., 1951—. Author: 60 books; syndicated columnist: Wyse Words; contbg. editor: (mag.) Good Housekeeping, 1983—98. Mem. bd. overseers Beth Israel Med. Ctr. Ctr. for Comms., N.Y.C.; trustees East Hampton Hist. Soc. Mem. Woman's Forum, PEN, Author's Guild, League of Profl. Theater Women. Office Phone: 631-324-3448. E-mail: lolowy@fastmail.fm.

WYSE-FEDERS, MARY, science educator; d. William and Grace Lorenz; m. Stephen M. Feders, Oct. 5, 2002; children: Kerri Wyse, Michael Wyse, Colleen Wyse. BE, Rider U., Lawrenceville, N.J., 1985—88, student. Cert. Elem. Edn. Tchr. N.J., Pa., Fla., Status of Eligibility, Biology 7-12. Tchr. Archdiocese of Phila.; biology tchr. Archbishop Ryan HS, Phila.; sci. lab. tchr. St. Gregory Sch., Plantation, Fla. Office: St Gregory Sch 200 N University Dr Plantation FL 33324-2018

WYSKOWSKI, BARBARA JEAN, lawyer; b. Jersey City, Feb. 20, 1967; d. Robert Louis and Barbara Joan (Dabrowski) W. BA, Rutgers U., New Brunswick, N.J., 1988; JD, Rutgers U., Camden, 1992; postgrad., Sch. Nursing, Muhlenberg Regional Med. Ctr., Plainfield, N.J. Bar: N.J., 1993, U.S. Dist. Ct. N.J., 1993. Law clk. Kevin William Kelly, Esq., Brick, N.J., 1989, Monke & Marriot, Sea Girt, N.J., 1990, Ann Segal, Esq., Voorhees, N.J., 1991; rsch. asst. Sch. Law Rutgers U., Camden, 1991-92; pro bono atty. Ocean-Monmouth Legal Svcs., Toms River, N.J., 1993-94; pvt. practice Manasquan, N.J., 1993—. Cons. in field; lectr. in field. Advocate Women Against Abuse, Phila., 1989-90; pres. Amnesty Internat., 1989-92. Mem. ABA, Am. Bankruptcy Inst., Nat. Assn. Consumer Bankruptcy Attys., IWIRC, INSOL Internat., N.J. State Bar Assn. (mem. lawyer to lawyer cons. network 1993-95), Ocean County Bar Assn., So. Monmouth Bd. Realtors. Avocations: surfing, running, skating.

WYSOCKI, SUSAN, women's health nurse practitioner; Grad., Boston Coll. Sch. Nursing; cert. as nurse practitioner, NJ Coll. Medicine and Dentistry and Planned Parenthood Fedn. Am. Cert. Women's Health nurse practitioner Nat. Certification Corp. Pres., CEO Nat. Assn. Nurse Practitioners in Women's Health. Spkr. and opinion leader in the field of women's health; mem. adv. bd., spkr. bur. Ortho-McNeil, Berlex, Pfizer (Parke-Davis), Wyeth, Pharmacia, Organon; mem. adv. bd. 3M Corp., Solvay, Novavax, Merck, Barr. Editor: Clinical Challenges in Women's Health: A Handbook for Nurse Practitioners, Women's Health Care: A Practical Journal for Nurse Practitioners, Conversations in Couseling; contbg. editor (and Washington DC bur. chief): Nurse Practitioner World News; mem. editl. bd. Am. Journal of Nurse Practitioners, Dialogues in Contraception, Contraceptive Tech. Update, Medscape Nurses, mem. adv. panel mem. Contraception Online; contbr. articles to nursing publications. Recipient Lifetime Achievement award, 2000, award for polit. activism, Nurse Practitioner Jour., 2003. Mem.: Am. Coll. Nurse Practitioners (founding pres., Cutting Edge award 2003), Nat. Alliance Nurse Practitioners (chair), Am. Acad. Nurse Practitioners (charter fellow). Office: Nat Assn Nurse Practitioners in Women's Health 505 C St NE Washington DC 20002 Office Phone: 202-543-9693. Office Fax: 202-543-9858.*

WYZIK, SUSAN ALDRICH, history professor; b. Barton, Vt., Apr. 5, 1948; d. Edwin John Aldrich and Marilyn Edith Aldrich-Meleleu; m. Ronald Walter Wyzik, July 4, 1969; children: Laurie, Kimberly, Ryan. Student, Springfield Tech. C.C., Mass., 1988; BA, Mount Holyoke Coll., South Hadley, Mass., 1991. History instr. Springfield Tech. C.C., 1992—. Advisor paraprofessionals update program Springfield Tech. C.C., 2000—02. Chairperson various fundraisers Springfield Tech. C.C., 1993—. Recipient Rosemarie Becker award, Springfield Tech. C.C., 2001. Mem.: Phi Theta Kappa. Avocations: martial arts, kayaking, reading, writing. Office: Springfield Tech CC One Armory Sq Springfield MA 01101 Business E-Mail: swyzik@stcc.edu.

XU, XIAOHONG NANCY, chemistry and biomedical science educator; came to U.S., 1989; d. Zhengqin Xu and Biyun Chen BS, Xiamen U., Fujian, 1985; PhD, U. Miss., 1992. Asst. prof. Nanjing Inst. Chem. Tech., China, 1985—87; rsch. asst. U. Miss., Oxford, 1989—92; postdoctoral fellow U. Tex., Austin, 1993—95, Ames Lab.-U.S. Dept. Energy/Iowa State U., 1995—98; asst. prof. dept. chemistry and biochemistry Old Dominion U., Norfolk, Va., 1998—2004, assoc. prof., 2004—. Presenter at nat. and internat. confs.; adj. asst. prof. Ea. Va. Med. Sch Contbr. numerous articles to profl. jours U. Miss. scholar, 1989-92 Mem. AAAS, Am. Chem. Soc., Electrochem. Soc., Soc. Applied Spectroscopy, Am. Acad. Nanomedicine, Women in Pub. Orgn., Chinese-Am. Chem. Soc., Xiamen U. Am. Alumni Assn Achievements include patent in field; research in single-molecule detection, single living cell imaging, nanobiotech, chromatography, capillary electrophoresis, electrogenerated chemiluminescence, electrochemistry. Office: Old Dominion U Dept Chemistry and Biochemistry Norfolk VA 23529

YABLON, HEATHER D., lawyer; b. LI, Jan. 14, 1970; BA, U. Mich., 1992; JD, St. John's U., 1995. Bar: NY 1996. Ptnr. Wilson, Elser, Moskowitz, Edelman & Dicker LLP, NYC. Mem.: Assn. of the Bar of the City of NY, NY State Bar Assn. Office: Wilson Elser Moskowitz Edelman & Dicker LLP 150 E 42nd St 23rd Fl New York NY 10017-5639 Office Phone: 212-490-3000 ext. 2578. Office Fax: 212-490-3038. Business E-Mail: yablonh@wemed.com.

YABLONSKAYA, OXANA, concert pianist; b. Moscow, Dec. 6, 1938; came to U.S., 1977; d. Michael Yablonski and Eugenia (Grozowsky) Yablonskaya; m. Albert Zajonz, Jan. 29, 1960 (div. 1976); 1 child, Dmitri Yablonsky. MusM, Moscow Conservatory, 1962, D of Musical Arts, 1965. Asst. to prof. piano Moscow Conservatory, 1965—75; piano tchr. Juilliard Sch. Music, N.Y.C., 1983—. Yamaha artist, artistic advisor Yamaha Master Classes; jury mem. Hamamatsu Horowitz, Leeds, Prokofer, Sendai. Concert performances include (world premiers) Sultan Zinzadze, Piano Concerto, Moscow, 1967, Revas Gabichevadze Piano Sonata (written & dedicated to her), Moscow, 1973; soloist for Dmitri Shostakovich anniversary concert, Kremlin, Moscow, 1971, Tchaikovsky 2d Piano Concerto, Moscow Stars Concert, Kremlin, 1972. Winner 2nd Grand Prix Long-Thibaud Internat. Competition, Paris, 1963, 1st prize Internat. Competition Rio de Janeiro, 1965, 2nd prize Beethoven Competition, Vienna, 1969; recipient Grand Prix du Disque for recording of Liszt Music, Internat. Liszt Soc., Budapest, 1981. Avocations: paintings, jewelry, ceramics. Home: 60 Eastern Dr Ardsley NY 10502-1704

YACOBIAN, SONIA SIMONE, metals company executive; b. Cairo, Egypt, Feb. 13, 1943; came to U.S., 1966, naturalized, 1971; d. Simon and Lucy (Guendimian) Samsonian; divorced; children: Tatiana, Richard. BS, Lycee of Cairo, 1962; BBA, U. Cairo, Egypt, 1965; student Pace U., 1978-80. Asst. mgr. new accounts Lincoln Savs. & Loan, Los Angeles, 1973-77; sr. acct. U.S. Industries, N.Y.C., 1977-81; dep. mgr. French C. of C., N.Y.C., 1981-82; mgr. mktg. Samancor Metals, New Rochelle, N.Y., 1982-84; pres. NIDDAM Inc., Huntington Sta., N.Y., 1984—; sales agency for Delachaux, France. Republican. Orthodox Christian. Home: 37 Wintergreen Dr Melville NY 11747-1812 Office: Niddam Inc PO Box 549 Huntington Station NY 11746-0435

YACOVONE, ELLEN ELAINE, banker; b. Aug. 4, 1951; d. Wilfred Elliott and Charlotte Frances (Fox) Drew; m. Richard Daniel Yacovone, June 2, 1979; stepchildren: Christopher Daniel, Kimberly Marie. Student, Broome C.C., 1973-80; cert., Inst. Fin. Edn., Chgo., 1974. Sec. to exec. v.p. Ithaca Savs., N.Y., 1968; mortgage clk. Citizens Savs. Bank, 1968-69; with Lincoln Bank, Van Nuys, Calif., 1970-71; asst. bookkeeper Henry's Jewelers, Binghamton, N.Y., 1971-74; teller, br. supt., br. mgr. 1st Fed. Savs., Binghamton, 1974-82, v.p., ctrl. regional sales mgr., 1982-86, dist. sales mgr., 1986-88; br. mgr. Gt. Western Bank, Pensacola, Fla., 1988-89, v.p., regional mgr. San Diego, 1989-95; br. v.p. Washington Mut. Bank (formerly Gateway Ctr.), San Diego, 1995—, Northpark, Calif., 1996—, fin. ctr. mgr. San Diego, Northpark; consumer lending mgr. Calif. Coast Credit Union, 2003. V.p., owner, operator EYE Shirts, 1995—. Vol. Sta. WSKG Pub. TV, Conklin, N.Y., 1974-88, United Way Broome County, Binghamton, 1976-88; mem. Gov.'s Commn. Domestic Violence, Albany, N.Y., 1983-87; mem. Found. State U. Ctr. Binghamton; bd. dirs. Interfaith Shelter Network, San Dieog, 1992-2002, Schs. Success and the San Diego Innovative Preschool Project, 1995-2000, San Diego Urban League, 1995—, Black Econ. Task Force, 1995—. Named Woman of Achievement Broome County Status Women Coun., 1981. Mem. Triple Cities Bus. and Prof. Women (pres. 1979-81, Young Careerist award 1977), Sales and Mktg. Execs., Inst. Fin. Edn. (bd. dirs. 1976-88, pres. 1984-85, winner N.Y. state speech contest 1984), Broome County C. of C., Broome County Bankers Assn. (bd. dirs. 1979-88, pres. 1983-84), Watercolor Soc., Catfish Club. Republican. Methodist. Avocations: exercise, hand painting wearables, woodworking, gardening, needlecrafts. Home: 602 Myra Ave Chula Vista CA 91910-6230 Office: Calif Coast Credit Union PO Box 502080 San Diego CA 92150

YAEGER, THERESE F., management professional; b. Chgo., 1955; d. Walter W. and Eileen O'Brien Bronson; m. Paul Alan Yaeger, 1975; children: Colleen Rose, Elizabeth Marie, Anne Therese, Julia Eileen. BA in Lit. and Comm. magna cum laude, Benedictine U., 1995, MS in Mgmt. and Orgnl. Behavior, 1996, PhD in Orgn. Devel., 2001. Gen. mgr. Bestway Carpeting Inc., Naperville, Ill., 1976—; assoc. dir. PhD dept. Orgn. Devel. Benedictine U., Lisle, 1995—. Mem. presenter Midwest Acad. Mgmt., 1996—, Orgn. Devel. Network, 1995—, Acad. Mgmt., 1996—, APA, Divsn. 13, 2001; adj. faculty Mgmt. & Orgnl. Behavior Benedictine U., 1996—; exec. bd. Midwest Acad. Mgmt. Author: (with others) Appreciative Inquiry: Rethinking Human Organization Toward a Positive Theory of Change, 1999, Appreciative Inquiry: An Emerging Direction for Organization Development, 2001, Global and International Organization Development, 2001, Organization Behavior and Change: Managing Human Resources, 2002; editor (mag.) DuPage Arts Life, 1995, 96; asst. editor (newsletter) rsch. O.D. Inst. OD Jour., 1996—; columnist Chgo. ASTD's Tng. Today, 1997—. Mem. ASTD, Chgo. Orgn. Devel. Inst. Chpt., Soc. Profl. Journalists, Nat. Acad. Mgmt. (exec. bd. mgmt. cons. divsn. 2003-). Roman Catholic.

YAES, JOYCE, musician, artist, educator; b. N.Y.C., July 18, 1944; m. Robert Yaes, Nov. 16, 1986. BA, Bklyn. Coll., 1966, MA, 1972; postgrad., Juilliard Sch., 1971-75, Mannes Coll., 1975, Manhattan Sch. Music, 1974-75, U. Neuchatel, Switzerland, 1967, U. San Miguel, Mex., 1969. Cert. tchr., N.Y., Ky. Tchr. art and music, N.Y.C., 1966-86; tchr. music Emerson Sch., N.Y.C., 1976-80; agt. ins. N.Y.C., 1982-87; tchr. Living Arts and Sci. Ctr., Lexington, Ky., 1987—. Pvt. tchr. music; violinist various orchs., N.Y., Ky.; dir. various art shows. Author: Humanities and Arts Perspectives, Microphishe Education Perspectives; one-woman show U. Ky. Ctr. for Arts, Arts Club Washington, 1994; 2-woman show Lexington Art League; exhibited in group shows Paula Insel Gallery, Harrison Gallery, N.Y.C., Aspen (Colo.) Gallery, Bklyn. Mus., Lincoln Ctr. Cork Gallery, Tchr. Group Show, N.Y.C., Lexington Art League, ArtsPlace, Lexington, Monserrat Gallery, N.Y.C., Accents Gallery, Lexington, Guild Hall, East Hampton, N.Y., West Hampton (N.Y.) Gallery, also others. Mem. United Fedn. Tchrs., Music Tchrs. Assn. (mem. exec. com.), Music Educators Nat. Conf., Port Educators Assn., Nat. Assn. Female Execs., Lexington Art League, Federated Music Club, U. Ky. Woman's Club. Avocations: horseback riding, ice skating, painting, travel, bicycle riding.

YAFFE, BARBARA MARLENE, journalist; b. Montreal, Que., Can., Mar. 4, 1953; d. Allan and Anne (Freedman) Yaffe; m. Wilson E. Russell, Aug. 30, 1985. Student, McGill U., 1970-73; BA, U. Toronto, 1974; B in Journalism, Carleton U., 1975. Reporter Montreal Gazette, 1975-76, Toronto Globe and Mail, 1976-79, reporter, columnist Halifax, N.S., 1979-81; chief nat. TV news bur. CBC, St. Johns, Nfld., Canada, 1981-84, Edmonton, Alta., Canada, 1983; reporter Toronto Globe and Mail, St. John's, 1984-86; editor Sunday Express, St. John's, 1987-88, Vancouver Sun, 1988-93, columnist, edit. bd. adv., 1993—. Recipient Gov. Gen.'s award, Roland Michener Found., 1977, Commentary award, Jack Webster Found., 2004, Animal Action award, Internat. Fund for Animal Welfare, 2004. Office: c/o Vancouver Sun Ste 1 200 Granville St Vancouver BC Canada V6C 3N3 Office Phone: 604-605-2189. E-mail: byaffe@png.canwest.com.

YAGER, AMANDA D., secondary school educator; d. Jim and Kathy Hughes; m. Jason J. Yager, Oct. 9, 1998; children: Maddison R., Olivia M. BS in Edn, Emporia State U., Emporia, Kans. Spl. edn. tchr. Andover H.S., Andover, Kans., 2000—; tchr. Emporia State Best Program, El Dorado, Kans., 2006—. Bd. dirs. Rainbows United, El Dorado, Kans., 2004. Mem.: Kans. Edn. Assn. Office: Andover High School 1744 N Andover Rd Andover KS 67002 Office Phone: 316-733-1335 203.

YAGER, PATRICIA LYNN, oceanographer, educator; d. Robert Davis and Janet L. Yager; m. Steven Matthew Holland; children: Zachary Yager Holland, Alexander Mark Holland. BS, Brown U., Providence, 1985—85; MS, U. Wash., Seattle, 1988, PhD, 1996. Fellow U. Wash., Sch. Oceanography, Seattle, 1991—96; U. Corp. Atmospheric Rsch. fellow U. Ga., Sch. Marine Programs, Athens, 1996; asst. prof. Fla. State U., Tallahassee, 1997—98, U. Ga., Sch. Marine Programs, Athens, 1998—. Contbr. articles to profl. jours. Fellow, Dept. of Energy, 1991—96; grantee, NSF, 1997—99, Nat. Oceanic and Atmospheric Adminstrn., 2002—05, Dept. of Energy, 2002—06. Mem.: Am. Geophys. Union, Am. Soc. Limnology and Oceanography. Office: Univ Ga Dept Marine Sci Athens GA 30602-3636 Office Phone: 706-542-6824. Office Fax: 706-542-5888. E-mail: pyager@uga.edu.

YAHN, MIMI, writer; b. NYC, June 16, 1954; d. Erle Brierly Yahn and Annette Norma Nagin; m. Vernon Marquez Cope, Jan. 27, 1993. Project coord. Agt. Orange Veterans Adv. Com., Berkeley, Calif., 1979—80; dir. Agt. Orange Info. Ctr., San Francisco, 1980—81; editor, pub. The Feminist Broadcast Quar. of Oreg., Portland, Oreg., 1992—94, The Swiftian Report, West Mifflin, Pa., 2003—. Writer, prodr. KBOO-FM, Portland, 1986—87; musical dir. Raging Grannnies, Pitts., 2003—; spkr., panelist, lectr. in field. Editor (graphic designer): The Feminist Broadcast Quarterly of Oregon; composer (singer): numerous political and satirical songs; prodr.(writer): (radio series) The American Chronicles: The Rise and Fall of Hollywood D.C.; author: Chloracne, Guide to Agent Orange, Annotated Bibliography of 2, 4-D, The Swiftian Report; columnist: Gulf War Revue. Steering com. mem. Nat. Veterans Task Force Agt. Orange, St. Louis, 1980—81; master gardener LSU Ext. Svc., New Orleans, 1998—2000, Pa., 2004—; brigade mem. Ben Linder Constrn. Brigade, Portland, 1989—91; steering com. mem. Californians Against Proposition 41, San Francisco, 1984—84; organizer, moderator town hall meetings The Feminist Broadcast Quar. Oreg., Portland, 1992—94; moderator at town halls meetings on the Balkans New Orleans, 1999—99; bd. dirs. Veterans Career Svcs., San Francisco, 1982—82, Portland Corinto Sister City Assn., Portland, 1991—91; legis. com. mem. Assn. Retarded Citizens, San Francisco, 1984—86. Achievements include development of objective methodology for determining and quantifying hate speech and bias language in the popular media; feminist theory of the Gender Minstrel Show; research in methodology for measuring gender statistics in Hollywood films; chloracne. Avocations: singing, gardening, cooking, photography, dance.

YAITES, LILLIANN, minister; b. Kansas City, Kans., Mar. 30, 1951; d. Irvin and Gladys Lovie Cushon; m. James Roy Yaites; children: James Brewer, Reginald Brewer, James, Natosha. AA in Bus. Adminstrn., Kansas City Cmty. Jr. Coll., 1971; BSBA, Emporia State U., 1973; postgrad., St. Paul Sch. Theology, 2004—, Brite Divinity Sch., 2005—. Mgr. info. tech. Sabre Inc., Ft. Worth, 1984—2000, GetThere Inc., Dallas, 2000—01; min., treas. Campus Dr. United Meth. Ch., Fort Worth, 2002—05; exec. dir. Tarrant County Restorative Justice Ctr., 2005—. Counselor Campus Dr. United Meth. Ch., Ft. Worth, 2000—; with life connections programs Fed. Bur. Prisons, Tex., 2002. Author: (book) I'm Saved, Now What?, 2001 (Book of the Month for Oct. Black Book Worm, 2001), 2005. Avocations: singing, writing. Office: Tarrant County Restorative Justice Ctr 1400 E Seminary Dr Fort Worth TX 76115 Office Phone: 817-921-4730. Business E-Mail: gimlmak@sbcglobal.net.

YAJIMA, HIROKO, violinist, music educator; b. Tokyo, Feb. 8, 1947; m. Samuel Rhodes, Dec. 30, 1968. Student, Juilliard Sch. Music, 1967. Mem. Galimir String Quartet, 1968—93, Mannes Trio, 1983—; mem. string faculty Mannes Coll. Music, NYC, 1980—, mem. chamber music faculty, 1981—, string dept. chair, 1998—. Mem. Young Concert Artists Roster, 1970-78; touring violinist Music from Marlboro; solo appearances Japan Philharmonic, St. Louis Little Symphony, Aspen Chamber Symphony, NY String Orchestra, Bergen Philharmonic, Brandenburg Ensemble; radio recital WQXR (NYC); TV appearance WRAR (Mich.); guest artist Chamber Music Soc. Lincoln Ctr., NY Sch. Concerts, 92nd St. Y, Bklyn. Acad. Chamber Music. Debut Town Hall, N.Y.C., 1971; rec. artist with Galimir String Quartet. Recipient numerous awards including Naumburg Internat. Chamber Music award, 1986. Office: care Mannes Coll Music 150 W 85th St New York NY 10024-4402

YALE (YELEYENIDE-YALE), MELPOMENE FOTINE, researcher, anthropologist, archaeologist, art historian, conservator; b. NYC, Mar. 31, 1963; d. John P. and Serina Yale (Yeleyenide-Yale). *Father John, a businessman, was one of the first to aid in the rebuilding of Europe after WWII sending medical relief to Greece without economic recompense. Mother Serina, born in 1924, in Moudros Lemnos, Greece to Adam Chiros is a philanthropist who served as president on various charity organizations and as NGO representative to the UN in 1992. One of first awarded the highest title of Archon of the Knights of St. Andrew from Patriarch Athenagoras for decades of selfless, important humanitarian work. Her name is inscribed in the rolls of the Knights of St. Andrew at the Patriarchate in Constantinople. She was awarded the Archdiocesan Medal of Saint Paul by Archbishop Iakovos.* BA in Art History, Columbia U., 1985, MA in Art History and Arch., 1998, MA in Anthropology, 2001; studied lithics and flint knapping with Prof. William Parry, CUNY Grad. Ctr., 2001; studied, Art Students League N.Y., 1987; studied fine art, Nat. Acad. Sch. Fine Arts, 1997—98; studied art history, painting, drawing, inorganic and organic chemistry, Lehman Coll., 1980—81, studied, 1987—88, studied, 1995, studied, 1996, Hunter Coll., 1983; studied with renowned iconographer Constantine Youssis, 1996—98. Sci. asst. dept. anthropology The Am. Mus. Natural History, N.Y.C., 1987—89, collections mgmt. asst. dept. anthropology, 1989—90; fieldwork archeologist (excavations) Brit. Sch. Arch., Palaikastro, Crete, 1990, 1991; fieldwork archeologist Fordham U., Rose Hill Excavations, NY, 2000; conservator The Benaki Mus., Athens, Greece, 1991, 1992, The Monastery of St. John the Theologian, Patmos, Greece, 1992, The Hispanic Soc. Am., N.Y.C., 1989—93, Brit. Sch. Archeol. Excavations, Palaikastro, Crete, 1990, 1991, Nat. Acad., 1997, Lilly Hollander Conservation Studio, NY, 1998—99, N.Y. Acad. Medicine, NY, 1999, Sherman Fairchild Ctr. Objects Conservation, Met. Mus. Art, NY, 2000; pvt. conservator, 1993—; rsch. asst. Ani project Columbia U.-World Monuments Found., NY, 1997; curatorial asst. Nat. Acad. N.Y., 1997; rsch. asst. to prof. emeritus Ralph Solecki and Dr. Rose Solecki Shanidar project Columbia U., 2001—03, coord. Ralph Holloway Endocast collection preservation and rsch. project, 2002—04, ind. rschr. prehistoric collection, 2003—. Designer (group fashion show) Chinese New Yr. Festival, Columbia Univ., 1984. Vol. Greek Orthodox Clergy Laity Congress, Greek Orthodox Archdiocese N.Am. and S.Am., NYC, 1984, NY Convocation for Peace in the Middle East, US Interreligious Com. for Peace in the Middle East, 1990. Recipient Cert. of merit Bd. Edn. Art Exhbn., N.Y. Daily News, Lever Ho., N.Y.C., 1981, Cert. of Achievement, N.Y. Acad. Medicine, 1999, Mcpl. hon., Moudros Lemnos Greece, 2004, Mcpl. award, 2005. Mem.: N.Y. State Archaeol. Assn., Archeol. Inst. Am., Registered Profl. Archaeologists, Am. Inst. Conservation (profl.), Am. Anthrop. Assn., The Prehistoric Soc. Achievements include research in emergence of human cognition in the Palaeolithic as indicated by stone tools and art; research on brain casting techniques; independent research towards a PhD on emergence of human cognition in Palaeolithic Period of Greece and Aegean based on Palaeontological-Palaeoanthropological data, stone tools, art, & their relation; to and their influence throughout the Palaeoanthropogeographic region of Europe and the World. Avocations: flintknapping, mosaics, painting, collecting art, archeł. material, and stone tools for study. Personal E-mail: mfy2@columbia.edu.

YALI, ANN MARIE, psychology professor; d. Al and Arlene Yali. BS, Eckerd Coll., St. Petersburg, Fla., 1992; PhD, SUNY, Stony Brook. Contbr. articles to profl. jours. Prayer chaplain Unity Ch. of NY. Recipient Madeline Fusco Dissertation award, 1998; grantee, Profl. Staff Congress of CUNY, 2001—02, Nat. Cancer Inst., 2002—04. Mem.: APA (grantee 2005—06), Soc. for Psychol. Study of Ethnic Minority Issues, Assn. Psychol. Sci. Office Phone: 212-650-5705.

YALIN, SERAP, biochemist, educator; b. Adona, Turkey, Sept. 27, 1969; d. Nureddin and Turkon Serin; m. Erdinc Yalin, Sept. 23, 1999; 1 child, Can. BS in Biology, Mid. East Tech. U., Ankara, Turkey, 1992; MS in Biochemistry, Gukurova U., Adona, 1996; PhD in Biochemistry, Gukerova U., Adona, 2001. Rsch. asst. Gukurova U., 1994—2001; asst. prof. Mersin (Turkey) U., 2001—. Vis. rsch. asst. Marmara Rsch. Ctr., Gebac, Turkey, 1997—99; vis. scientist Inst. Nazionale Tumori, Milan, 2002—03; mem. adv. bd. 1st Pharmaceutics Congress, Turkey, 2005—; mem. editl. bd. Jour. Sci. and Tech., Istanbul, Turkey, 2005—. Contbr. articles to profl. jours. Recipient Tech. Project award, Novartis Pharm.; postdoctoral fellow, Tubitak, Turkey, 2002, Govt. Planning Project grantee, Turkish Govt., 2003. Mem.: Turkish Biochem. Soc., European Assn. Cancer Rsch. (travel fellow 2002). Avocations: reading, swimming. Home: Cemalpaya St No 5 01122 Ankara Turkmenistan Office: Mersin U Pharmacy Faculty Yenisehir Campus 33169 Mersin Turkey

YALMAN, ANN, judge, lawyer; b. Boston, June 9, 1948; d. Richard George and Joan (Osterman) Yalman. BA, Antioch Coll., 1970; JD, NYU, 1973. Trial atty. Fla. Rural Legal Svcs., Immokalee, Fla., 1973-74; staff atty. EEO, Atlanta, 1974-76; pvt. practice Santa Fe, 1976—2005; probate judge Santa Fe County, 1999—2005; mcpl. judge Santa Fe, 2006—. Part time U.S. magistrate, N.Mex., 1988—96. Commr. Met. Water Bd., Santa Fe, 1986-88. Mem. N.Mex. Bar Assn. (commr. Santa Fe chpt. 1983-86). Home: 441 Calle La Paz Santa Fe NM 87505-2821 Office: 2511 Camino Entrada Santa Fe NM 87507 Office Phone: 505-955-5133. Business E-Mail: ayalman@santafenm.gov.

YALOW, ROSALYN SUSSMAN, biophysicist; b. NYC, July 19, 1921; d. Simon and Clara (Zipper) Sussman; m. Aaron Yalow, June 6, 1943; children: Benjamin, Elanna. AB, Hunter Coll., 1941; MS, U. Ill., Urbana, 1942, PhD, 1945; DSc (hon.), U. Ill., Chgo., 1974, Phila. Coll. Pharmacy and Sci., 1976, NY Med. Coll., 1976, Med. Coll. Wis., Milw., 1977, Yeshiva U., 1977, Southampton Coll., NY, 1978, Bucknell U., 1978, Princeton U., 1978, Jersey City State Coll., 1979, Med. Coll. Pa., 1979, Manhattan Coll., 1979, U. Vt., 1980, U. Hartford, 1980, Rutgers U., 1980, Rensselaer Poly. Inst., 1980, Colgate U., 1981, U. So. Calif., 1981, Clarkson Coll., 1982, U. Miami, 1983, Washington U., St. Louis, 1983, Adelphi U., 1983, U. Alta., 1983, SUNY, 1984, Tel Aviv U., 1985, Claremont U., Calif., 1986, Mills Coll., Oakland, Calif., 1986, Cedar Crest Coll., Allentown, Pa., 1988, Drew U., Madison, NJ, 1988, Lehigh U., 1988; LHD (hon.), Hunter Coll., 1978; DSc (hon.), San Francisco State U., 1989, Technion-Israel Inst. Tech., Haifa, 1989, Med. Coll. Ohio Toledo, 1991; LHD (hon.), Sacred Heart U., Conn., 1978, St. Michael's Coll., Winooski Park, Vt., 1979, Johns Hopkins U., 1979, Coll. St. Rose, 1988, Spertus Coll. Judaica, Chgo., 1988; DHC (hon.), U. Rosario, Argentina, 1980, U. Ghent, Belgium, 1984; D. Humanities and Letters (hon.), Columbia U., 1984; DSc (hon.), Fairleigh Dickinson U., 1992, Conn. Coll., 1992, Smith Coll., Northampton, Mass., 1994, Union Coll., Schenectady, 1994. Diplomate Am. Bd. Scis. Lectr., asst. prof. physics Hunter Coll., 1946-50; physicist, asst. chief radioisotope service VA Med. Ctr., Bronx, NY, 1950-70, acting chief nuclear medicine, 1970-80, acting chief radioisotope service, 1968-70, sr. med. investigator emeritus; research prof. Mt. Sinai Sch. Med., CUNY, 1968-74, Disting. Service prof., 1974-79, Solomon A. Berson Disting. prof.-at-large, 1986—; chmn. dept. clin. scis. Montefiore Med. Ctr., Bronx, 1980-85; Disting. prof.-at-large Albert Einstein Coll. Med., Yeshiva U., 1979-85, prof. emeritus, 1986. Cons. Lenox Hill Hosp., NYC, 1956—62, WHO, Bombay, 1978; sec. U.S. Nat. Com. on Med. Physics, 1963—67; mem. nat. com. Radiation Protection, subcom. 13, 1957, Pres.'s Study Group on Careers for Women, 1966—72; sr. med. investigator VA, 1972—92, sr. med. investigator emeritus, 1992—. Co-editor: Hormone and Metabolic Research, 1973—79; editl. adv. coun. Acta Diabetologica Latina, 1975—77, Ency. Universalis, 1978—, editl. bd. Mt. Sinai Jour. Medicine, 1976—79, Diabetes, 1976, Endocrinology, 1967—72, contbr. numerous articles to profl. jours. Bd. dirs. NY Diabetes Assn., 1974. Recipient VA William S. Middleton Med. Rsch. award, 1960, Eli Lilly award, Am. Diabetes Assn., 1961, Van Slyke award, NY met. sect. Am. Assn. Clin. Chemists, 1968, ACP award, 1971, Dickson prize, U. Pitts., 1971, Howard Taylor Ricketts award, U. Chgo., 1971, Gairdner Found. Internat. award, 1971, Commemorative medallion, Am. Diabetes Assn., 1972, Bernstein award, Med. Soc. State NY, 1974, Boehringer-Mannheim Corp. award, Am. Assn. Clin. Chemists, 1975, Sci. achievement award, AMA, 1975, Exceptional Svc. award, VA, 1975, A. Cressy Morrison award, NY Acad. Scis., 1975, sustaining membership award, Assn. Mil. Surgeons, 1975, Disting. Achievement award, Modern Medicine, 1976, Albert Lasker Basic Med. Rsch. award, 1976, La Madonnina Internat. prize, Milan, 1977, Golden Plate award, Am. Acad. Achievement, 1977, Nobel prize in physiology or medicine, 1977, citation of esteem, St. John's U., 1979, G. von Hevesy medal, 1978, Rosalyn S. Yalow R&D award established, Am. Diabetes Assn., 1978, Banting medal, 1978, Torch of Learning award, Am. Friends Hebrew U., 1978, Virchow Gold medal, Virchow-Pirquet Med. Soc., 1978, Gratum Genus Humanum Gold medal, World Fedn. Nuc. Medicine or Biology, 1978, Jacobi medallion, Assoc. Alumni Mt. Sinai Sch. Med., 1978, Jubilee medal, Coll. of New Rochelle, 1978, VA Exceptional Svc. award, 1978, Fed. Woman's award, 1961, Harvey lectr., 1966, Am. Gastroenterol. Assn. Meml. lectr., 1972, Joslin lectr., New Eng. Diabetes Assn., 1972, 1st Hagedorn Meml. lectr., Acta Endocrinologica Congress, 1973, Franklin I. Harris Meml. lectr., 1973, Sarasota Med. award for achievement and excellence, 1979, Gold medal, Phi Lambda Kappa, 1980, Achievement in Life award, Ency. Britannica, 1980, Theobald Smith award, 1982, Pres.'s Cabinet award, U. Detroit, 1982, John and Samuel Bard award in med. and sci., Bard Coll., 1982, Disting. Rsch. award, Dallas Assn. Retarded Citizens, 1982, Nat. medal of Sci., 1988, Abram L. Sachar Silver medallion, Brandeis U., 1989, Disting. Scientist of Yr. award, ARCS, NYC, 1989, Golden Scroll award, The Jewish Advocate, Boston, 1989, spl. award, Clin. Ligand Assay Soc., Washington, 1988, numerous others. Fellow: Clin. Soc. N.Y. Diabetes Assn., Am. Coll. Radiology (assoc. in physics), N.Y. Acad. Scis. (chmn. biophysics divsn. 1964—65); mem.: NAS, Am. Physiol. Soc., Endocrine Soc. (pres. 1978, Kocn award 1972), Soc. Nuc. Medicine, Soc. Nuc. Medicine (hon.), Am. Gastroenterol. Assn. (hon.), Am. Coll. Nuc. Physicians (hon.), Harvey soc. (hon.), Med. Assn. Argentina (hon.), Diabetes Soc. Argentina (hon.), The N.Y. Acad. Medicine (hon.), N.Y. Roentgen Soc. (hon.), Biophys. Soc., Am. Assn. Physicists in Medicine, Radiation Rsch. Soc., Am. Phys. Soc., Am. Acad. Arts and Scis., Tau Beta Pi, Sigma Delta Epsilon, Pi Mu Epsilon, Sigma Pi Sigma, Sigma Xi, Phi Beta Kappa. Office: Vet Affairs Med Ctr 130 W Kingsbridge Rd Bronx NY 10468-3904*

YAMAGUCHI, KRISTI TSUYA, ice skater; b. Hayward, Calif., July 12, 1971; d. Jim and Carole (Doi) Y.; m. Bret Hedican, July 8, 2000; children: Keara Kiyomi, Emma Yoshiko. Gold medalist, Figure Skating Albertville Olympic Games, 1992; U.S. Skating champion, 1992; World Skating champion, 1991, 1992; World Junior champion, 1988; world profl. figure skating champion, 1994. Founder Always Dream Found., 1996—; goodwill amb. Winter Olympics, Salt Lake City, 2002. Named Skater of the Yr., 1996, Favorite Female Athlete, Nickelodeon's Kid's Choice Awards, 1996—98,

Athlete of the Yr. for figure skating, US Olympic Com., 1989; named to World Figure Skating Hall of Fame, 1999, US Figure Skating Hall of Fame, 1998; recipient Women First award, YWCA, 1993, Make a Wish grantor recognition for the yr. award, 1999. Avocations: tennis, rollerblading, reading, dance.

YAMASHITA, ELIZABETH SWAYNE, university administrator, mass communications educator; b. Murrumburrah, New South Wales, Australia, Oct. 14, 1927; came to U.S., 1957; d. John B. Swayne; m. Donald M. Yamashita, Aug. 30, 1969. B.Ec., U. Sydney, 1948; MS in journalism, Northwestern U., 1959, PhD, 1969. Reporter, writer Australian Fin. Rev., Sydney, 1951-57; feature editor Haire Pub. Co., N.Y.C., 1959; reporter Fortune mag., N.Y.C., 1960-63; faculty mem. Northwestern U., Evanston, Ill., 1963-80, prof. journalism, 1975-80; chmn. Mich. State U. Sch. Journalism, East Lansing, 1980-82; prof. Sch. Journalism and Mass Communications U. Okla., Norman, 1982—. Mem. Assn. Edn. in Journalism and Mass Communications, Soc. Am. Bus. and Econ. Writers, Phi Kappa Phi Office: Sch Journalism and Mass Communication U Okla 860 Van Vleet Oval Norman OK 73019-2050

YANCEY, ELIZABETH STILPHEN, political scientist; b. Hempsted, N.Y., Nov. 22, 1945; d. Norris Williams and Gladys (Howgate) Stilphen; m. Thomas Erwin Yancey, July 31, 1971; children: Linda Siti, David Arthur, Karen Elaine. BA in Biology, Earth Sci., Marietta (Ohio) Coll., 1968; MA in Paleontology, U. Calif., Berkeley, 1971; postgrad., Blinn Coll., Bryan, Tex., 1999. Cert. secondary sch. tchr., Ohio, Idaho, Tex. Rsch. technician dept. bacteriology Harvard Med. Sch., Boston, 1968-69; tchg. lab. asst. paleontology dept. U. Calif., Berkeley, 1970-71; tchg. lab. asst. geology dept. U. Malaysia, Kuala Lumpur, 1971; substitute tchr. Pocatello (Idaho) pub. schs., 1976-77; lectr. night sch. Idaho State U., Pocatello, 1978; aliener AMI Computers, Pocatello, 1979; lab. technician Tex. A&M U., 1981-82; presch. tchr. A&M Meth. Nursery Sch., College Station, Tex., 1982-83; substitute tchr. College Sta. Ind. Sch. Dist., 1983-87; clk. Bur. Census U.S. Govt., College Station, 1990; interviewer Pub. Policy Rsch. Inst., Tex. A&M U., College Station, 1998—. Girl Scout leader Blue Bonnet coun. Peace Luth. Ch., 1984-85; Sunday Sch. tchr. Meth. Ch., 1979-83, Our Savior's Luth. Ch., 1984-85, Peace Luth. Ch., 1986-87. Lutheran. Avocations: crocheting lace, raising dogs, cavies and cats.

YANCEY, EMILY, secondary school educator; b. Wichita, Kans., Jan. 16, 1981; d. John and Margaret Yancey. B, Brigham Young U., Provo, Utah, 1999—2004. Cert. athletic trainer NATA, 2004. Athletic trainer Missionary Tng. Ctr., Provo, Utah, 2004—04, Kingman HS, Ariz., 2005—. Youth advisor Young Women, Kingman, 2005. Mem.: NATA. Latter Day Saints. Avocations: sports, travel, scrapbooking, music, piano. Office: Kingman HS 4182 N Bank St Kingman AZ 86409 Personal E-mail: emily_yancey@hotmail.com.

YANCEY, VICTORIA FRANCINE, education educator; d. Harold and Margaret Covington Ward; 1 child, Raina Ivy. BA, Pa. State U., Univ. Park, 1972; MEd, Antioch U., Seattle, 1976; postgrad., Temple U., Phila., 1980; EdD, Fielding Grad. U., Santa Barbara, Calif., 2002. Cert. counselor Pa., thought field therapist Calif., Pa., mediator Pa., therapist Pa., tchr. and adminstr. Pa., disaster first responder ARC, crisis therapist, crisis intervention 2005, pastoral crisis intervention 2005, response to weapons of mass destruction, disaster first responder. Tchr. Sch. Dist. Phila., 1972—76, counselor, 1976—2001, adminstr., 2001, coord., 2002, spl. rep., 2003; therapist Inst. Learning, Phila., 1987; tchr. Mentoring in Cyberspace, Oakland, Calif., 2005—. Therapist Inst. Learning, Phila., 1987; park ranger U.S. Dept. Interior, 1996; instr. U. Phoenix, 2003—05, Masters OnLine; bd. dir. Women's Heritage Soc.; presenter and keynote spkr. Author: Thought Field Therapy in Educational Settings, Creating Successful Telementoring Programs, 2005; featured in Phila. Inquirer and Christian Sci. Monitor; contbr. poems to religious publs. Mem. Women Making a Difference, Habitat for Humanity, Phila.; ordained deacon, ednl. rep. to Black clergy Presbyn. Ch.; bd. dirs. Salvation Army. Named Guardian Angel Children of Phila., subject cover feature story, Phila. Enquirer, 2005; recipient Movers and Shakers award, City of Phila., 2005; grantee, Internat. Woman Scholarship Pageant, 2000, Fielding Grad. Inst., 2001. Mem.: Bus. and Profl. Women, Coalition of 100 Women, Women's Heritage Soc., Nat. Assn. Univ. Women, TWIGS, Inc. (fin. sec. nat. chpt., pres.), Delta Sigma Theta (Paul Vallas Employee of Yr. Svc. award 2003). Avocations: travel, reading, dance, writing, public speaking.

YANCY, DOROTHY COWSER, college president; 1 child. BA in History and Social Sci., Johnson C. Smith U.; MA in History, U. Mass.; PhD in Polit. Sci., Atlanta U. Cert. MNGT, Harvard U. Tchr. Albany State Coll., Hampton U., Evanston (Ill.) Twp. H.S.; dir. Afro-Am. studies program Barat Coll., Lake Forest, Ill.; prof. Sch. History, Sch. Mgmt. Ga. Inst. Tech., Atlanta, 1972-94. Lectr. Acad. Pub. Adminstrn. and Social Studies of Small Hural and Ulan Bator, Mongolia, 1991; apptd. spl. master Fla. Pub. Employee Rels. Commn.; mem. labor del. to Soviet Union and Europe, 1988, 90; cons. to govt. agys., unions and cos., including GM, AT&T Bell Labs; arbitrator fed. mediation and conciliation svs. Am. Arbitration Assn. Contbr. over 40 articles to profl. jours. Bd. advisors USAR Historically Black Colls. and Univs./Minority Instn.; bd. dirs. College Fund/UNCF; past mem. N.C. Post-Secondary Eligibility Commn.; former bd. dirs. Opera Carolina, Charlotte Urban League, Charlotte C. of C. Fulbright scholar; named one of Six Best Tchrs. in U.S., Newsweek on Campus, 1988. Mem. Assn. Social and Behavioral Scientists (past pres., Torchbearer award, Belle Ringer Image award), Indsl. Rels. Rsch. Assn. (past pres. Atlanta chpt.), Ctrl. Intercollegiate Athletic Assn. (past pres.), Links, Inc. (past mem. exec coun.), Coun. Ind. Colls. (former mem. governing bd.), Assn. for Study of African-Am. Life and History (exec. coun.), Omega Psi Phi, Phi Kappa Phi, Alpha Kappa Mu, Sigma Rho Sigma, Omicron Delta Kappa, Phi Beta Kappa (mem. Delta Ga. chpt.). Episcopalian. Office: 100 Beatties Ford Rd Charlotte NC 28216-5302 Office Phone: 704-378-1007. Business E-Mail: dcyancy@jcsu.edu.

YANDA, CATHY L., small business owner, counselor, illustrator; b. Washington, Ohio, Dec. 5, 1959; d. Ronald K. Vaughan and Betty J. Plummer; 1 child, Micah B. Topping. AA in Liberal Arts, Chapman Coll., 1987; BS in Psychology, Wright State U., 1989. Sr. instr. USMC, 29 Palms, Calif., 1979—87; disease intervention specialist Combined Health Dist. of Montgomery County, Dayton, Ohio, 1990—, hiv educator/counselor, 1989—90; owner Sati, Dayton, 1998—; ho. mgr. Victoria Theatre, Dayton, Ohio, 2002—03; owner mykidstoo.com, Dayton, Ohio, 2003—. Cons. Children's Med. Ctr., Dayton, 2001—03; bd. dirs. Eristocrat, Inc. Contbg. illustrator Nuts & Bolts and Magic Wands: Children's Writing from the Bottom Up, 2001; contbg. author and pub.: newsletter Canal St. Tavern News, 2002. Point of dispensing mgr. Combined Health Dist. Montgomery CountyEmergency Response Team; bd. dirs. AIDS Found. Miami Valley, Dayton, 1993—95. Recipient Health Commr. award, Combined Health Dist. Montgomery County, 2005, Nat. Novel Writing Month winner, 2005. Buddhist. Office Phone: 937-496-7444. Business E-Mail: cyanda@gw.odh.ohio.gov.

YANDELL, CATHY MARLEEN, language educator; b. Anadarko, Okla., Dec. 27, 1949; d. Lloyd O. and Maurine (Dunn) Y.; m. Mark S. McNeil, Sept. 7, 1974; children: Elizabeth Yandell McNeil, Laura Yandell McNeil. Student, Inst. des Professeurs de Français à l'Etranger U. Sorbonne, Paris, 1970; BA, U. N.Mex., 1971; MA, U. Calif., Berkeley, 1973, PhD, 1977. Tchg. asst. U. Calif., Berkeley, 1971, acting instr., 1976—77; asst. prof. Carleton Coll., Northfield, Minn., 1977—83, assoc. prof., 1983—89, prof. French, 1989—. Chair commn. on the status of women Carleton Coll., Northfield, 1983-85, ednl. policy com., 1985-86, 96-97, romance langs. and lits., 1990-94, chair faculty affairs com., 2000-02, pres. of faculty, 1991-94, Bryn-Jones disting. tchg. prof. humanities, 1996-99, mentor to jr. faculty, 1996—, W.I. and Hulda F. Daniell prof. French lit., lang. and culture, 1999—; dir. Paris French Studies Program, 1998, 2004. Author: Carpe Corpus: Time and Gender in Early Modern France, 2000; co-author: Vagabondages: Initiation à la litt. d'expression française, 1996; contbr. to Art & Argumentation: The Sixteenth Century Dialogue, 1993, French Texts/American Contexts: French Women Writers, 1994, Montaigne: A Collection of Essays, Vol. 4, Language and Meaning, 1995, Reflexivity in Women Writers of the Ancien Régime, 1998, High Anxiety, 2002, Ronsard, figure de la variété, 2002, Lectrices d'Ancien Régime, 2003, Reflections on Teaching, 2004, Ecriture courante: Critical Perspectives on French and Francophone Women, 2005, Masculinities in the French Renaissance, 2006, Paysage et nature a La Renaissance, 2006; editor: Pontus de Tyard's Solitaire Second, ou prose de la musique, 1980; contbr. articles to profl. jours. Active exec. com., then mem. Amnesty Internat., Northfield, 1980—. Grantee Faculty Devel., Carleton Coll., 1988, 1991; Regents' Travelling fellow, U. Calif. Berkeley, 1975—76, NEH Rsch. fellow., 1994—95, Mellon Faculty fellow, 2003, Mellon New Directions grantee, 2006. Mem.: MLA (del. 1989—92, chair exec. com. French 16th Century lit. 2001—05), Phi Beta Kappa (pres. 2004—05). Democrat. Home: 514 5th St E Northfield MN 55057-2220 Office: Carleton College 1 N College St Northfield MN 55057-4044 Office Phone: 507-646-4245. Business E-Mail: cyandell@carleton.edu.

YANDELL, RUTH B., music educator; b. Cebu, Philippines; d. Alfredo A. and Susana L. Buot; m. David Palmer Yandell, June 29, 1966; children: Scott B., Eric L. BA, Silliman U., Dumaguete, Philippines, 1957; BA in Music, Philippine Womens U., Manila, 1962; MA in Music, Western Mich. U., 1966. Cert. Nat. Music. Tchrs. Assn. Mem. faculty Silliman U., 1962-64; music dir./accompanist Ariz. State U. Lyric Opera Theatre, Tempe, 1968-71; faculty/piano dept. coord. Mesa (Ariz.) C.C., 1971—. 2nd v.p. Young Artist com., Az., 1998-99. Author: (textbook) Introduction to Music Theory, 1995, Keyboard Technique, Level I, 1996, Keyboard Technique, Level II, 1997. Pres. Maricopa C.C. Dist. Asian Pacific Islander Assn., 2001—; scholarship chmn. Asian Pacific Islander Assn., 1999. Fulbright grantee, 1964-66; Western Mich. U. fellow, 1964-66; Aspen Music Festival scholar, 1965. Mem. Ariz. State Music Tchrs. Assn., Nat. Music Tchrs. Assn. Office: Mesa Cmty Coll 1833 W Southern Ave Mesa AZ 85202-4822 E-mail: ruth.yandell@mcmail.maricopa.edu.

YANERO, LISA JOYCE, medical and surgical nurse; b. Clarksburg, W.Va., May 13, 1970; d. Franklin Allen and Etheldean Joyce (Poe) Y. AS, Fairmont State Coll., 1991, BS in Psychology, 1994, BSBA, 1996. Cert. med./surg. nurse, qualified mental retardation profl., W.Va. Dept. Health and Human Resources, approved medication assistive pers. RN, Office of Health Facility Licensure and Cert. RN Monongalia Gen. Hosp., Morgantown, W.Va., 1991—2005, charge nurse, 1994-95; RN United Summit Ctr., Clarksburg, W.Va., 2005—. Mem.: ANA, W.Va. Acad. Med. Surg. Nurses, W.Va. Nurses Assn., Sigma Theta Tau, Pi Gamma Mu. Methodist. Avocation: piano. Office: United Summit Ctr #6 Hospital Plaza Clarksburg WV 26301 Office Phone: 304-623-5661 ext. 394. Personal E-mail: talktolisay@netzero.com.

YANG, DEBRA WONG, lawyer, former prosecutor; b. LA, 1959; 3 children. B, Pitzer Coll., 1981; JD, Boston Coll., 1985. Assoc. Haight Dickson Brown & Bonesteel, Santa Monica, Calif., 1985—87, Wildman Harrold Allen & Dixon, Chgo., 1987; law clk. to Dist. Judge Ronald Lew LA, 1988—89; atty. Greenberg Glusker, 1989; judge L.A. Mcpl. Ct., 1997—2000, L.A. Superior Ct., 2000—02; US atty. (ctrl. dist.) Calif. US Dept. Justice, LA, 2002—06; ptnr., co-chair crisis mgmt. practice group Gibson, Dunn & Crutcher LLP, LA, 2007—. Adj. prof. U. So. Calif. Law Sch. Mem.: Asian Pacific Bar Assn. (Pub. Svc. award 2003), Asian Am. Bar Assn., So. Calif. Chinese Lawyer Assn. Republican. Achievements include first to being the first Asian-American woman to serve as a US Attorney, 2002. Office: Gibson Dunn & Crutcher LLP 333 S Grand Ave Los Angeles CA 90071-3197*

YANG, SHU, materials scientist; b. China; BS in material sci., Fudan U., 1992; MS in chemistry and chemical biology, Cornell U., 1997, PhD in chemistry and chemical biology, 1999. Skirkanich asst. prof. in materials sci. and engring. U. Pa. Contbr. articles to profl. jour. Named one of Top 100 Young Innovators, MIT Tech. Review, 2004; recipient ICI award in applied polymer sci., ACS, 1999, Unilever award in polymer sci. and enring., 2001. Office: U Pa Dept Materials Sci and Engring 203 LRSM 3231 Walnut St Philadelphia PA 19104-6272

YANG, SUSAN XIA, real estate consultant, recreational therapist; b. Chuang De, China, Sept. 1, 1964; arrived in USA, 1989; d. Ming-Qi Yang and Chung-Zhen Cheng; m. Shide Hao, Jan. 5, 1988 (div. Apr. 1996); 1 child, Annie P. BA in Econs., Beijing Normal U., 1985; Diploma in Massage Therapy, Swedish Massage Inst., N.Y.C., 1998. Lic. massage therapist, N.Y., 1998. Rsch. asst. Econ. Rsch. Inst., State Planning Commn., Beijing, 1985—89; lobby asst., canvasser Conn. Citizen Action Group, West Hartford, Conn., 1989—92; export asst. Colt Mercantile Internat., N.Y.C., 1993—96; owner, dir. Miracle Touch Massage Therapy, P.C., Fresh Meadows, NY, 1998—; bus. cons. DermaRite Industries NJ, 2003—. Coach for women Alley Pond Strider Running Club, Queens Village, NY, 2001—; race dir. PS Q 178 Fun Run, Jamaica Estates, NY, 2002. Rep. in police dept. Utopia Civic Assn., Fresh Meadows, NY, 2001—. Recipient 5th place, female, Rocket City Marathon, Alabama, 1998, 1st place, female, Atlantic City Marathon, N.J., 1998, Treadmill Marathon, N.Y., 1995, N.Y.C. Marathon, 1996—97, Boston Marathon, 1997. Mem.: Am. Massage Coun., Am. Massage Therapy Assn., N.Y. Road Runners Club. Avocation: running, tennis, ping-pong, skiing, martial arts. Office: Miracle Touch Massage Therapy 75-20 188th St Fresh Meadows NY 11366 Office Phone: 718-454-6868.

YANIK, ELIZABETH GREENWELL, mathematics professor; d. Owen Clay and Catherine Elizabeth (Steinke) Greenwell; m. Joe Yanik; children: Elizabeth Lee, Mary Catherine. BS in Math. and Physics, Marshall U., Huntington, W.Va., 1974; MS in Math., U. Ky., Lexington, 1976, PhD in Math., 1982. Instr. La. State U., Baton Rouge, 1983—85; from asst. prof. to assoc. prof. Va. Commonwealth U., Richmond, 1985—90; prof. math. Emporia (Kans.) State U., 1990—. Co-dir. summer program for mid. sch. girls MASTER IT, Emporia, Kans.; co-dir. conf. for mid. sch. girls Expanding Your Horizons, Emporia, Kans.; co-dir. conf. for h.s. girls Sonia Kowalewsky Math. Day, Emporia, Kans. Recipient Presdl. award for excellence in sci., math., and engring. mentoring, Pres. Bush, 2004. Mem.: Women and Math. Network (dir. 1996—), Women in Math. Edn. (pres. 2005—07), Math. Assn. Am. (bd. dirs. 2003—06), Assn. for Women in Math. (exec. com.). Office: Emporia State U Dept Math Computer Sci and Econs Emporia KS 66801 Business E-Mail: eyanik@emporia.edu.

YANKEE, JULIE JO, elementary school educator; b. LaCrosse, Wis., Jan. 29, 1956; d. Donald Raymond and Evelyn Rose Kessel; m. David John Yankee, Oct. 15, 1983; 1 child, Jonathan. BS, North Ctrl. U., Mpls., 1978; BA, Concordia U., St. Paul, 1979. Sci. tchr. Dakar Acad., Senegal, 1979—80; 5th grade tchr. Alliance Christian Acad., Elk River, Minn., 1981—88; social studies tchr. Prince of Peace Sch., Lake Villa, Ill., 1990—. Jr. ch. leader CrossView Ch., Antioch, Ill., 1999—2001, libr. asst., 2001—04. Named to Nat. Honor Roll, Washington, 2006. Avocations: gardening, camping, fishing, reading, travel. Home: 22254 86th St Salem WI 53168 Office: Prince of Peace 135 S Milwaukee Lake Villa IL 60046

YANKOWSKI, KRISTIN LEANNE, mathematics educator; d. Richard Stanley and Janeen Carolyn Yankowski; life ptnr. Kathy Mary Varner; children: Courtney Marie Clark, Randall Joseph Clark. MS in Math. Edn., Nova Southeastern U., Ft. Lauderdale, Fla., 1999. Math. tchr. Charlotte HS, Punta Gorda, Fla., 1998—2001, Summit HS, Frisco, Colo., 2001—. Mem.: Nat. Tchrs. of Math. Democrat. Avocations: skiing, swimming, hiking, rugby. Home: PO Box 9666 Breckenridge CO 80424 Office: Summit HS PO Box 7 Frisco CO 80443 Office Phone: 970-547-2137.

YANNUZZI, ELAINE VICTORIA, food and home products executive; b. Summit, N.J. d. Emil and Alice (Vance) Y. BA, Seton Hall U., 1968. Pres. Expression Unltd., Warren, N.J., 1971-89; pvt. practice cons. pub. industry and bus. Bedminster, N.J., 1989—. Presenter seminar N.Y. Food and Wine Show, Splty. Food Show; lectr. NYU, Rutgers U.; moderator Am. Women's Econ. Devel., N.Y.C., 1985-87; spkr. Women Bus. Owners N.J., Princeton, 1986. Author: Gift Wrapping Food, 1985; editorial advisor Fancy Food mag., 1985—; editorial cons. Family Circle Gt. Ideas mag., 1987-89. Named Entrepreneur of Yr. N.J. Living mag., 1983, Woman of Yr. NYU, 1986. Mem. Roundtable for Women (bd. dirs. 1986-89, Pacesetter award 1985), Nat. Assn. for Splty. Food Trade (steering com. 1986). Home and Office: 612 Timberbrooke Dr Bedminster NJ 07921-2106 E-mail: eyannuzzi@aol.com.

YANOWITZ, JOYCE, nutritional counselor; d. Harry Horowitz and Sadie Cooper; m. Edwin J. Yanowitz, Oct. 19, 1958; children: Cindy Ann Newman, Nancy Ellen Powers. Grad. h.s., Bronx. Dir. Dietrition, Inc., Westfield, NJ, 1980—2005, Teledieting and Nutritional Counseling, Monroe Twp., NJ, 2005—. Spkr. in field. Columnist: health articles Union County Newspapers, 1990—93. Lifetime mem. Hadassah, bd. dirs.; purchasing agt. Temple Emanu-El, Westfield, 1974—2002; pres. Soroptomist Internat., Westfield, 1989. Office Phone: 908-789-3399.

YAO, FRANCES, music educator, small business owner; arrived in U.S., 1976; d. Ted Yao and Phuong Hue Chi; children: Christopher Y. Shi, Daniel H. Shi. BA, Nat. Conservatory, Saigon, Vietnam, 1973. Cert. tchr. Suzuki and piano performance Ga., 1973. Pianist Chinese Alliance Ch., Saigon, Vietnam, 1970—75; tchr. piano Hai Quang Music Sch., Saigon, Vietnam, 1973—75, Sandy Springs Music Sch., Roswell, Ga., 1976—78, Ephrata (Pa.) Music Acad., 1975—77, Frances Yao's Piano Studio, Alpharetta, Ga., 1980—. Mem. choir, leader sect. Johns Creek Bapt. Ch., Alpharetta, Ga., 2001—. Recipient Beethoven 200-yr. Piano Competition award, German Culture Inst., 1970. Mem.: Music Tchr. Nat. Assn., North Fulton Music Tchr. Assn., N.D. Music Tchrs. Assn. (chmn. auditions 1983—, v.p. 1992), Ga. Music Educators Assn. (assoc.), Ga. Music Teachers Assn. (assoc.). Avocations: swimming, travel, music, photography, reading.

YAO, JIANHUA, chemist, researcher; b. Suzhou, People's Republic of China, Feb. 26, 1962; d. Dawu Yao and Xiuzhen Lu; m. Youlu Yu, Mar. 21, 1987. BSc, Nanjing (China) U., 1982, MSc, 1985; PhD, Concordia U., Montreal, Can., 1992. Mem. tchg. and rsch. staff Nanjing U., 1985-87; postdoctoral fellow Concordia U., 1992-93; rsch. assoc. Nat. Rsch. Coun. Can., Ottawa, 1993-95; rsch. chemist Phillips Petroleum Co., Bartlesville, Okla., 1995—. Contbr. over 25 articles to profl. jours.; patentee in field. Mem. ACS. Home: 1532 Whitney Ln Bartlesville OK 74006-6037 Office: Phillips Petroleum Co 332 Pl Rsch Ctr Bartlesville OK 74004-0001

YARBOROUGH, JUDITH ANN, bookstore owner, librarian, academic administrator; b. Williamsport, Pa., Aug. 26, 1949; d. Fred Arlington and Ethel Mary (Parker) Bingaman; m. John Henry Yarborough, Aug. 24, 1972; 1 child, Wendy Renee. BA in English, U. Tex., Arlington, 1970; MLS, U. North Tex., 1973. Tchr. Parker Found., Dallas, 1971-72; saleswoman Sanger-Harris, Dallas, 1972; mgr. br. libr. Irving Pub. Libr. N.W., Tex., 1974-78; libr. cons. Vaughn & Yarborough Libr. Cons., Irving, 1980-81; owner, mgr. Young Ideas Bookstore, Irving, 1981—95; acad. adminstr. DeVry Inst. Tech., Irving, 1995—98; libr. Carrollton Pub. Library, Tex., 1998—. Bd. dirs. Irving Arts Reach Com., 1988; vol. coord. travelling exhbn. Smithsonian Instn., Irving, 1988. Mem. Am. Bookseller's Assn., Assn. Booksellers for Children (charter) AAUW (life, chmn. Ednl. Foudn. Irving br. 1987-88, v.p. programming 1988-89, 91—, v.p. mem. 1992-93), Belles-Lettres Book Discussion Club (pres. 1987-88, 91), Acad. Performing Arts (bd. dirs. 1992). Democrat. Methodist. Avocations: reading, sewing, travel, rollerblading, jogging. Office: Carrollton Pub Library 4220 N Josey Ln Carrollton TX 75010 Office Phone: 972-466-3364.

YARBOROUGH, NELLIE CONSTANCE, principal, minister; b. Cedar Groove, N.C. d. Anderson and Bessie Y. BA, Ea. Nazarene Coll., Quincy, Mass., 1978; MA, Antioch U./Cambridge (Mass.) Coll., 1979. Co-founder, exec. sec. Mt. Calvary Holy Ch., Boston, 1944—92, nat. youth pres., 1948—88, state sec. and treas., 1962—95; nat. missionary pres. Mt. Calvary Ch., Boston, 1960—90; founder, prin. Dr. Brumfield Johnson Acad., Boston, 1992—; founder, dean NCY Bible Inst., Boston, 1992—. Editor: (manual) YPHA Book, 1944; asst. editor: Jesus the Son of God, 1968, Spiritual Voice, 1948—72. Mem. adv. bd. Vision New Eng., Acton, Mass., 1998—; bd. dirs. Roxbury (Mass.) Multi-Svc. Ctr., 1970—85, Consumer's Credit, Boston, 1978—85, Project Right, Boston, 1991—, Blue Hill Task Force, Boston, 1995—. Named Pastor of the Yr., Vision New Eng., 1995, Woman of the Yr., Urban League of Ea. Mass., 1996; recipient Sojourner Truth award, Boston Profl. League, 1993. Democrat. Pentecostal. Avocations: reading, exercise, travel, motivational speaking. Home: 250 Seaver St Boston MA 02121 Office: Mt Calvary Holy Ch Am 9-19 Otisfield St Boston MA 02121

YARBROUGH, ALLYSON DEBRA, electrical engineer; b. Peterborough, England, Feb. 14, 1958; d. Freddy Dekhoma and Rosalind Mavis Y.; m. John Russell Scarpulla, May. 8, 1990. BSEE, N.Mex. State U., 1979; MSEE, Cornell U., 1985, PhD in Elec. Engring., 1988. Rsch. asst. Nat. Atmospheric and Ionospheric Ctr., Arecibo, P.R., 1979; microwave applications engr. Hewlett-Packard Co., Santa Rosa, Calif., 1979-82; assoc. prof. Calif. State U., L.A., 1988-89; tech. staff Aerospace Corp., El Segundo, Calif., 1989-93, sect. mgr., 1993-99, dept. dir., 1999—. Mem. IEEE, Microwave Theory and Techniques Soc., Alpha Kappa Alpha, Eta Kappa Nu. Democrat. Roman Catholic. Avocations: woodworking, sewing, collecting vintage radios. Home: 26821 Grays Lake Rd Palos Verdes Estates CA 90275 Office Phone: 310-375-9695. Personal E-mail: blue.onyx@verizon.net.

YARBROUGH, FRANCES CAROLE, music educator; b. Memphis, Aug. 28, 1938; d. Frank Chester Masserano and Iris Marcella Viehe; m. William Hugh Yarbrough Sr., Apr. 16; children: William Hugh Jr., Darrell Craig. B in Music Edn., McNeese State U., 1983; M in Sacred Music, Logos Grad. Sch., 2000. Music evangelist, Memphis, 1959—68, Christian Assemblies of God, Sherwood, Ark., 1968—76, Lake Area Worship Ctr., Westlake, La., 1979—2004, pastor; music tchr., music evangelist, 2004—. Mem.: Lake Charles Piano Tchrs. Assn., Nat. Music Tchrs. Assn., Sigma Alpha Iota. Address: PO Box 154 Westlake LA 70669 Office Phone: 337-912-9530.

YARBROUGH, ISABEL MILES, dentist, educator; b. Columbus, Ga., May 24, 1956; d. Wiley and Lillie Miles; m. David E. Yarbrough; children: Davida Elizabeth, David Earl Jr. BS in Zoology, Ala. A&M U., 1978; DDS, Loyola U., 1982. Instr. endodontics Howard U. Sch. Dentistry, Washington, 1989-91; asst. prof. biology Ala. A&M U., Normal, 1991-94; dentist Drs. David and Isabel Yarbrough, Huntsville, Ala., 1993—. Mem. NAACP, Huntsville, 1996. Capt. U.S. Army, 1986—89. Mem. North Ala. Med. Assn., Huntsville-Madison Dental Soc., Delta Sigma Theta, Psi Omega. Avocations: reading, swimming, jogging. Home: 204 Cheswick Dr Madison AL 35757-8720 Office: 4530 Bonnell Dr NW Ste A Huntsville AL 35816-2002 Office Phone: 256-430-3478.

YARBROUGH, JENNIFER GAY, science educator; b. Rogers, Tex., June 26, 1962; d. Marvin Joe and Beverly Arlene Ralston; m. Michael David Yarbrough, Jr., July 14, 1984; children: Amanda Leigh, Lauren Chérie. BS in Biology, U. Mary Hardin, Belton, Tex., 1984; BS in Med. Tech., S.W. Tex. State-Baylor, San Marcos, 1985. Cert. technologist & specialist in microbiology Am. Soc. Clin. Pathologists; tchr. Tex. Dept. Edn., 1995. Med. tech. Scott & White Hosp., Temple, Tex., 1985—95; sci. tchr. Rogers HS, 1995—98, Crawford HS, 1998—2001, Stony Point HS, Round Rock, 2001—06; edn. coord. Scott & White Hosp., 2006—. Recipient Outstanding Clin. Instr., CLS Program, Scott & White Hosp., 1994. Avocations: slalom waterskiing, running. Office: Scott & White Hosp 2401 S 31st St Temple TX 76508

YARBROUGH, KATHRYN DAVIS, public health nurse; b. Montrose, Colo., Aug. 31, 1947; d. L.O. and V. Jean (Dunn) Davis; m. James H. Yarbrough, Aug. 8, 1970; children: James, Jason. Diploma, Good Samaritan Hosp. Sch. Nursing, Phoenix, 1971; BSN, Kennesaw State Coll., 1996. RN, Ga.; cert. NAACOG. Supr. Cherokee County Health Dept., Canton, Ga., 1976-97. Den mother Boy Scouts Am., Canton, 1986-87; bd. dirs. Cancer soc., Canton, 1987—, Cherokee County Violence Ctr., 1990, First Steps Bd., 1993-97, Cherokee County Advocacy Ctr., 1994-97; HIV cons. ARC, Canton, 1988—, disaster vol., Cherokee County, 1993-99; co-chair Early Intervention Coun., Canton, 1991-93; mem. Leadership Cherokee, 1994, Interagy Coun., 1994; mem. Blue Ridge Jud. Cir. Domestic Violence Task Force, 1995. Mem.: ANA, Ga. Nurses Assn., Svc. League Cherokee County (hon.). Methodist. E-mail: Kyarbro216@aol.com.

YARBROUGH, MARTHA CORNELIA, music educator; b. Waycross, Ga., Feb. 8, 1940; d. Henry Elliott and Jessie (Sirmans) Y. BME, Stetson U., 1962; MME, Fla. State U., 1968, PhD, 1973. Choral dir. Ware County H.S., Waycross, 1962-64, Glynn Acad., Brunswick, Ga., 1964—70; asst. choral dir. Fla. State U., 1970-72; cons. in music Muscogee County Sch. Dist., Columbus, Ga., 1972-73; cons. in tchr. edn. Psycho-Edno. Cons., Inc., Tallahassee, 1972-73; asst. prof. music edn., dir. choruses and oratorio socs. Syracuse (NY) U., 1973-76; assoc. prof. music edn. Syracuse U., 1976-83, prof., 1983-86, acting asst. dean Coll. Visual and Performing Arts, 1980-82, acting dir. Sch. Music, 1980-82, chmn. music edn., 1982-86; prof. music La. State U., Baton Rouge, 1986—, coord. music edn., 1986—2000, Haymon prof. of music, 1995—, disting. rsch. master arts, humanities, social scis., 2004. Artist-in-residence Sch. Music U. Ala., Tuscaloosa, 1989-90, 98, 2002; chair exec. com. Music Edn. Rsch. Coun., 1992-94. Co-author: Competency-Based Music Education, 1980; mem. editl. com.: Jour. Rsch. in Music Edn., editor-in-chief:, 2000—; contbr. chapters to books, articles to profl. jours. Recipient Disting. Rsch. Master of Arts, Humanities and Social Scis. award, La. State U., 2004. Mem. Music Educators Nat. Conf. (Sr. Rschr. award 1996), La. State Music Assn., Am. Ednl. Rsch. Assn., Soc. Rsch. Music Edn. (mem. exec. com. 1988-90, program chair 1990-92, chair 1992-94). AAUP, Coll. Music Soc., Pi Kappa Lambda, Phi Beta, Kappa Delta Pi. Office: Sch Music La State U Baton Rouge LA 70803-2504 Office Phone: 225-578-2481. Business E-Mail: cyarbro@lsu.edu.

YARBROUGH, TRISHA MARIE, literature and language professor; d. George Morphy and Claudia Marie Ammons; m. M. Thomas Yarbrough, July 11, 1980. B.S., Okla. Bapt. U., Shawnee, OK, 1975—79; MA, Ariz. State U., 1982, PhD, 1987. Prof. English East Ctrl. U., Ada, Okla., 1987—, dir. honors program, 2006—. Collaborator (educational CD) Oklahoma Art in the '30s. Bible study tchr. First Bapt. Ch., Ada, Okla., 1987—2006. Recipient Tchg. Excellence award, East Ctrl. U., 1992, 1998, Disting. Svc. award, Alpha Chi, 2005. Mem.: South Ctrl. MLA, Conf. on Christianity and Lit. (sw region pres. 1999—2000). Office: East Ctrl U 1100 E 14th Ada OK 74820 Office Phone: 580-310-5454. Office Fax: 580-436-3329. Business E-Mail: trisha.yarbrough@ecok.edu.

YARES, RIVA, art dealer, writer, publishing executive; b. Tel-Aviv, Aug. 17, 1940; d. Fishel and Sala (Singer) Kilstok; single; children: Dennis, Shelli Yares Poulos. BA in Art and Psychology, U. Jerusalem. Art dealer Riva Yares Gallery, Scottsdale, Ariz., 1964—, Santa Fe, 1990—, Riva Yares Sculpture Pk., Ariz., 1985—. Pres. Pueblo Arts & Real Estate, Scottsdale, Ariz., 1970—. Author various books on artists. Recipient Archtl. award City of Scottsdale, 1972. Mem. Charter 100. Avocations: animals, dogs. Office: Riva Yares Gallery 3625 N Bishop Ln Scottsdale AZ 85251-5511

YARGER, RUTH ANKETELL, social worker; b. Detroit, Sept. 16, 1940; d. Thomas Jackson and Ruth LeRoux Anketell; m. Noel Henry Yarger, June 20, 1964; children: John Maurice, Christine Carol Yarger Weaver. BA, Mich. State U., 1962; MSW, Western Mich. U., 1980. LCSW Ind., Acad. Cert. Social Workers NASW. Lay therapist Child Abuse and Neglect Coordinating Orgn., Mishawaka, Ind., 1977—78; clin. social worker Madison Ctr., Inc., South Bend, Ind., 1980—. Dir. Madison Outpatient Svcs.; bd. mem. Planned Parenthood of N. Ctrl. Ind., South Bend, N.Am. Signs, Inc., South Bend. Bd. mem., past pres. Broadway Theater League, South Bend, 1989—; bd. mem. Morris Performing Arts Ctr., South Bend, 2000—. Mem.: Am. Assn. Sex Educators, Counselors and Therapists (cert. sex therapist), Jr. League South Bend. Methodist. Home: 17180 McErlain St South Bend IN 46635 Office Phone: 574-283-1370.

YARLOW, LORETTA, art museum director; b. NYC, Sept. 26, 1948; d. Albert and Sylvia (Seligsohn) Y.; m. Gregory Salzman, June 5, 1977; children: Nina, Alexander. BA, Sarah Lawrence Coll., 1970; EdM, Harvard U., 1971. Curator Inst. Contemporary Art, Boston, 1972-74; co-dir. Yarlow/Salzman Gallery, Toronto, Ont., Can., 1974-84; dir./curator Art Gallery York U., Toronto, 1988—2002; dir. exhibitions Pratt Inst., NYC, 2002—04; dir. Univ. Gallery, Univ. Mass., Amherst, Mass., 2004—. Commr. Can. Pavilion, 1997 Venice Biennale. Office Phone: 413-545-3670. Office Fax: 413-545-0218. Business E-Mail: lyarlow@pratt.edu, lyarlow@acad.umass.edu.

YARMO, FANNY F., not-for-profit fundraiser; b. Kansas City, Mo., Dec. 25, 1910; d. Sol and Della Fox; m. Al Yarmo (dec. Feb. 19, 1987); 1 child, Robert L.; m. Leo Sofnas, 1936 (dec. 1950). BS in Bus. summa cum laude, U. Kans., 1931. Ins. sec. Norman Hobart, Kansas City, 1931—32; Spanish translator Ismert Hincke Milling, Kansas City, 1932—35; pres. Fan-Ro Corp., Kansas City, 1954—75; regional treas. Sisterhood, Kansas City, 1989—90. Hon. fellow Truman Libr. Sch. for Democracy, Kansas City, 1992—; charter patron Spencer Libr.--Nelson-Atkins Mus., Kansas City, 1999; TZDA art patron Jewish Cmty. Ctr., Overland Park, Kans., 1999—; life mem. Hadassah Menorah Hosp., 1945—; mem. Kansas City Historic Found., 1999—; vol. Congregation Hesed Com.; charter patron Kemper Mus. Art; vol. Friends of O.P. Arts; mem. Nat. Wildlife Press, Friends of DAV; vice chmn. then life mem. chmn. NCJW, Kansas City; life mem. chmn. Brandeis U. Women, Kansas City, 1960; spl. gifts chmn. Fedn., Kansas City, 1965; mem. pres. coun. Art Inst., 1980—87; mem. nat. com. Kemper Art Mus., Kansas City, 2001—05; mem. univ. assocs. U. Mo., Kansas City, 1995—; active Habitat for Humanity, Prayerworks Group. Mem.: AAUW, Nelson-Atkins Mus. Art, Assn. Friends of Art, Mo. Reperatory Theatre Patron, Oakwood C.C., Native Sons of Kansas City, Smithsonian Inst., Jewish War Vets Assn., Phi Chi Theta. Jewish. Avocations: bridge, Mah Jongg, Bible study, computers. Home: 102 E Woodbridge Ln Kansas City MO 64145

YARNALL, SUSANNE LUSINK, elementary school educator; b. Rochester, NY, Sept. 6, 1945; d. George R. and Doris (Small) Lusink; m. Paul James Yarnall, Feb. 15, 1975. BS, Keuka Coll., 1967; MA, U. Rochester, 1973. Elem. sch. educator West Irondequoit Ctrl. Schs., Rochester, N.Y., 1967-68; instr. tchr. tng. US Peace Corps, Malawi, 1968-70; elem. sch. educator Brighton Ctrl. Schs., Rochester, 1970-2000; substitute tchr. Canandaigua Elem. Sch., 2000—. Sec., v.p., pres. Keuka Alumni Assn., 1978-84, pres.' adv. coun., 1988-98; bd. dirs. Preserve the Earth Through Edn., Rochester, N.Y., organizer area sch. programs, 1990—; spkr. on reef conservation, endangered marine animals local cmty. groups, schs., 1986—. Vol. conservation projects Cousteau Soc., Earthwatch, Conservation Edn. Diving Archeology and Mus. Internat., 1986—, AARP, Nature Conservancy, Nat. Edn. Assn. Retired, Nat. Wildlife Fedn., Oceana, Coral Reef Alliance, Humane Soc., Save the Manatee Club; bd. dirs. United Way Ontario County, Ontario County Red Cross, 1984-86, Nat. Assn. Returned Peace Corps. Vols., Friends of Malawi; contbr. devel. Canandaigua Airport. Recipient Svc. to Keuka award, 1986, Life Mem. award N.Y. State PTSA, 1989, Elem. Sch. Educator of the Yr. award Monroe County Environ. Mgmt. Coun., 1997. Mem. Tri County Women's Golf Assn. (pres. 1995-97), Rochester Women's Dist. Golf Assn. (sec. 1997-99, chair jr. girls 1999-2002, v.p. 2003-04, pres. 2004-06). Avocations: scuba diving, underwater photography, golf. Home: 5711 Thomas Rd Canandaigua NY 14424-7988

YARNELL, GAIL ELLEN, dentist, prosecutor; d. Marvin Edward and Gelene Louise Yarnell. BA in Biology (cum laude), Washington U., St. Louis, 1974; DMD, U. Pa., Phila., 1978; JD, Temple U., Phila., 2002. Bar: Pa., N.J.; lic. DMD, JD. Gen. practice resident U. N.C. Meml. Hosp., Chapel Hill, 1978—80; owner, mgr. pvt. practice, Waltham, Mass., 1983—91; staff dentist Greater Roslindale Med. Dental Ctr., Mass., 1992—94; asst. prof. U. Pa., Phila., 1994—98; reviewer dental cases for alleged dental malpractice St. Paul Fire and Marine Ins. Co., Plymouth Meeting, Pa., 1994—99; dentist pvt. practice, Phila., 1998—; dental expert Commonwealth of Pa., Harrisburg, Pa., 1998—; legal rschr., reviewer Medicaid provider contracts Columbia U. and Children's Health, NY, 2001; legal intern for pub. policy Ctr. for Social and Legal Rsch., Hackensack, NJ, 2001—02; judge at presentation of student appellate briefs and mock trials Temple U., Phila., 2003—; pvt. practice Phila., 2004—; bd. cons. N.J. State Bd. of Dentistry, Newark, 2005—. Mem.: Am. Assn. Dental Schs., Acad. General Dentistry, Am. Dental Assn., Women's Law Cacus, ABA. Avocations: sports, piano, water sports. Personal E-mail: gyarnell@verizon.net.

YARNO, WENDY, pharmaceutical executive; BS, Portland State U., 1982; MBA, Temple U., 1988. Profl. rep. U.S. Human Health, 1983—85, mktg. analyst, 1985—87, product mgr. pediatric vaccines, 1988, assoc. dir. econ. affaris, 1989, sr. dir. mktg. planning, 1990—91, nat. account exec., 1991, sr. dir. managed health care affairs, 1992, project leader for U.S. Health Care Reform, 1992—93; v.p. ctrl. region Merck-Medco, 1994; v.p. hypertension and heart failure therapeutic bus. group U.S. Human Health, 1994—97; v.p. Ortho McNeil Pharm., Johnson & Johnson, 1997—98; v.p. worldwide human health Merck & Co., Inc., Whitehouse Station, NJ, 1999, v.p. human resources, 1999, sr. v.p. human resources, 2000—, exec. v.p. worldwide human health mktg., 2003—. Bd. dirs. St. Jude Med. Ctr.; pres. bd. trustees Women's Health and Counseling Ctr., Somerville. Office: Merck and Co Inc One Merck Dr Whitehouse Station NJ 08889-0100 Office Phone: 908-423-6525.

YARRINGTON, PATRICIA, oil industry executive; b. Apr. 1956; B Polit. Sci., Pomona Coll., 1977; MBA, Northwestern U. With Chevron Corp., 1980—; sr. fin. analyst Chevron U.S.A. Inc., 1984—86, mgr. investor relations, 1986; various supervisory positions Chevron Products Co., Chevron U.S.A. Prodn. Co., Chevron Rsch. and Tech. Co.; mgr. credit card enterprises Chevron Products Co., 1995—97, comptr., 1997—98; pres. Chevron Can. Ltd., Vancouver, B.C., Canada, 1998—2000; v.p. strategic planning Chevron Corp., 2000—01; v.p. pub. and govt. affairs ChevronTexaco Corp., San Ramon, Calif., 2002—. Bd. dirs. Chevron Phillips Chem. Co. Bd. dirs. ChevronTexaco Found. Office: ChevronTexaco Corp 6001 Bollinger Canyon Rd San Ramon CA 94583-2324

YARYAN, RUBY BELL, psychologist; b. Toledo, Apr. 28, 1938; d. John Sturges and Susan (Bell) Y.; m. John Frederick Buenz, Jr., Dec. 15, 1962 (div. 1968). AB, Stanford U., 1960; PhD, U. London, 1968. Lic. clin. psychologist; diplomate Am. Bd. Psychology, Am. Acad. Experts in Traumatic Stess. Rsch. dir., univ. radio and TV, U. Calif., San Francisco, 1968-70; dir. delinquency coun. U.S. Dept. Justice, Washington, 1970-73; evaluation dir. Office Criminal Justice Planning, Sacramento, Calif., 1973-76; CAO project mgr. San Diego County, 1977-92; dir. devel. svcs. Childhelp USA, Woodland Hills, Calif., 1992-94; rsch. coord. Neuropsychiat. Inst. and Hosp., UCLA, 1986-87; exec. dir. Centinela Child Guidance Clinic, Inglewood, Calif., 1987-89; clin. dir. Nat. Found. Emotionally Handicapped, North Hills, Calif., 1990-93; pvt. practice, Beverly Hills, Calif., 1973—; supr. psychologist Los Angeles County Dept. Mental Health, 1998—. Psychologist Sr. Psychology Svcs., North L.A. County, 1994-98; cons. White House Conf. Children, Washington, 1970; mem. Nat. Adv. Com. Criminal Justice Standards and Goals, Washington, 1973; clin. affiliation UCLA Med. Ctr. Contbr. articles to profl. jours.; chpts. to books and monographs in field. Chair Human Svcs. Commn., City of West Hollywood, Calif., 1986; first vice-chair United Way/Western Region, L.A., 1988; mem. planning-allocations-rsch. coun. United Way, San Diego, 1980-82. Grantee numerous fed., state and local govt. orgns. Mem. Am. Psychol. Assn., Western Psychol. Assn., Calif. Psychol. Assn., Am. Orthopsychiat. Assn., Am. Profl. Soc. on Abuse of Children, Phi Beta Kappa. Episcopalian. Avocations: painting, music, theater, writing, reading. Office: 337 S Beverly Dr Ste 107 Beverly Hills CA 90212-4307 Office Phone: 310-271-3921.

YASTINE, BARBARA A., diversified financial services company executive; BA in Journalism, NYU, 1981, MBA in Finance, 1987. Various communications and investor-relations positions W.R. Grace & Co.; dir. investor relations, Primerica Citigroup, 1987—91, v.p. investor relations and fin. planning & analysis, Traveler's Group, 1991, exec. v.p. fin. and insurance, CitiFinancial, chief admin. officer, global consumer group, 1998, chief auditor, CFO, global corp. and investment bank, 2000—02; CFO Credit Suisse First Boston, 2002—. Office: Credit Suisse First Boston 11 Madison Ave New York NY 10010-3629 Office Phone: 212-325-2000. Office Fax: 212-325-6665.

YATES, ANNA MARIE, counselor, educator; b. Streator, Ill., July 2, 1940;. Andrew and Anna Frances (Vagasky) Bazik; m. June 28, 1969; children: Jane Bazik, Alice Meri, Ann Kirstine, Elizabeth Karen. BS, Ill. State U., 1962, MS, 1963; PhD, Northwestern U., 1969. Cert. supr., specialist-counselor, Ill. Counselor Arlington Heights (Ill.) High Sch. Dist. 214, 1963-64; asst. prof., counselor Harper Coll., Palatine, Ill., 1967-70; prof. Roosevelt U., Chgo., 1986; career counselor Harper Coll., Palatine, 1986; guidance counselor Elk Grove High Sch., Elk Grove Village, Ill., 1986—. Asst. prof. Nat. Louis U., 2002—. Home: 122 S Brighton Pl Arlington Heights IL 60004-6702 Office: Elk Grove High Sch 500 W Elk Grove Blvd Elk Grove Village IL 60007-4296 E-mail: amyates@starnetdial.net.

YATES, CHERYL ANN, home economist, educator; b. Cheyenne, Wyo., Oct. 11, 1945; d. Robert Watson and Harriette Julia (Oberg) Yates. BS, U. Wyo., 1968; MA, Ariz. State U., No. Ariz. U. Cert. home econ. tchr. Ariz. Tchr. Carson Jr. HS, Mesa, Ariz., 1968—69; tchr., chmn. home econs. dept. Powell Jr. HS, Mesa, 1970—80; tchr. Mountain View HS, Mesa, 1980—81, Dobson HS, Mesa, 1981—, dept. chair, 1981—. Contbr. articles to mags. in field. Active Friends of Channel 8. Mem.: NEA, Mesa Edn. Assn., Ariz. Edn. Assn. Republican. Office: 1502 W Guadalupe Rd Mesa AZ 85202

YATES, COLEEN DENISE, special education educator; b. Sacramento, Calif., Dec. 28, 1956; d. Kenneth Walter Brown and Edna Viola Pundt; children: James Jedidiah, Trista Denice, Devona Caryn. BS, Calif. State U., 1995. Substitute tchr. Roseville Union HS Dist., Roseville City Sch. Dist., Western Placer Unified Sch. Dist., Placer Union HS Dist., Eureka Union Sch. Dist., Calif., 1997; spl. edn. tchr. El Dorado HS, 1997, Chavez Elem. Sch., Davis Sr. HS, Calif., 1997—98, El Dorado HS, 1998, Mitchell Mid. Sch., Rancho Cordova, 1998—2000, Miles P. Richmond Sch., North Highlands, 2000—05, Rio Tierra Jr. HS, Sacramento, 2005—. Co-leader Girl Scouts Am., 1990—92, 1995—2000, parent vol., 1992—95; com. mem., parent vol. Boy Scouts Am., 1992—95; asst. biddy basketball coach Rocklin Parks & Recreation Dept., 1993—96; art docent vol. Rock Creek Elem. Sch., Auburn, 1990—92, Antelope Creek Elem. Sch., Rocklin, 1992—96; vol. classroom aide Rock Creek Elem. Sch., 1990—92, Antelope Creek Elem. Sch., 1992—96. Mem.: Calif. Assn. Health, Phys. Recreation, and Dance, Am. Alliance Health, Phys. Edn., Recreation and Dance, Golden Key. Home: 4900 2nd St Rocklin CA 95677

YATES, ELLA GAINES, librarian, consultant; b. Atlanta, June 14, 1927; d. Fred Douglas and Laura (Moore) Gaines; m. Joseph L. Sydnor (dec.); l child, Jerri Gaines Sydnor Lee; m. Clayton R. Yates (dec.). AB, Spelman Coll., Atlanta, 1949; MS in L.S, Atlanta U., 1951; JD, Atlanta Law Sch., 1979. 1954Asst. br. librarian Bklyn. Pub. Library, 1951; head children's dept. Orange (N.J.) Pub. Library, 1956—59; br. librarian East Orange (N.J.) Pub. Library, 1960—69; med. librarian Orange Meml. Hosp., 1967—69; asst. dir. Montclair (N.J.) Pub. Library, 1970—72, Atlanta-Fulton Pub. Library, 1972—76, dir., 1976—81; dir. learning resource ctr. Seattle Opportunities Industrialization Ctr., 1982—84; asst. dir. adminstrn. Friendship Force, Atlanta, 1984—86; state librarian Commonwealth of Va., 1986—90; library cons. Price Waterhouse, 1991; adv. bd. Library of Congress Center for the Book, 1977—85; interim dir. Atlanta-Fulton Pub. Libr., 1998—99; cons., dir. Woodruff Libr., Atlanta, 2000—02. Cons. in field; vis. lectr. U. Wash., Seattle, 1981-83; mem. Va. Records Adv. Bd., 1986-90; mem. Nagara Exec. Bd., 1987-91. Contbr. to profl. jours. Vice chmn. N.J. Women's Coun. on Human Rels., 1957-59; chmn. Friends Fulton County Jail, 1973-81; bd. dirs. United Cerebral Palsy Greater Atlanta, Inc., 1979-81 Coalition Against Censorship, Washington, 1981-84, YMCA Met. Atlanta, 1979-81, Exec. Women's Network, 1979-82, Freedom To Read Found., 1979-85, Va. Black History Mus., Richmond, 1990-91; sec., exec. dir. Va. Libr. Found. Bd., 1986-90; founder Coretta Scott King Book Award, Ala., 1968—. Recipient meritorious svc. award Atlanta U., 1977, Phoenix award City of Atlanta, 1980, Serwa award Nat. Coalition 100 Black Women, 1989, Black Caucus award, 1989, disting. svc. award Clark-Atlanta U., 1991, ednl. support svc. award Tuskegee Airmen, 1993, Alumnae Achievement award Spelman Coll., 1998, Annie McPheters award Atlanta-Fulton Pub. Libr., 1998, Disting. Alumnae award Clark Atlanta U., 2001; named profl. woman of yr. NAACP N.J., 1972, outstanding chum of yr., 1976; named outstanding alumni Spelman Coll., 1977, named to alumni hall of fame, 1995. Mem. ALA (exec. bd. 1977-83, commn. freedom of access to info., founder Coretta Scott King Book Award 1968), NAACP, Southeastern Libr. Assn., Nat. Assn. Govt. Archives and Records Adminstrn. (exec. bd. 1987-91), Delta Sigma Theta (Pinnacle leadership award 2001). Baptist. Home and Office: 1171 Oriole Dr SW Atlanta GA 30311-2424 E-mail: ellayates4@aol.com.

YATES, KIMBERLY NICOLE, school psychologist; b. St. Louis, Sept. 26, 1971; d. Clarenc and Odelia Yates. BA, Ala. A&M U., 1993; MEd, Howard U., 1995; EdD, Nova Southeastern U., 1999. Sch. psychologist Nat. Assn. Sch. Psychologists, 1994—. Mem. Alpha Kappa Alpha, Kappa Delta Pi. Democrat. Pentecostal. Avocations: aerobics, swimming. Personal E-mail: kny11@aol.com.

YATES, MARGARET MARLENE, psychologist; b. Sheridan, Wyo., Feb. 1, 1942; d. James H. and Dorothy H. (Weeks) Guy; m. Alan R. Yates, June 20, 1965 (div. 1978); stpchildren: Elizabeth, Samuel, LaDonna, Susan, Sally. AA, Sheridan Jr. Coll., 1962; BA, U. Wyo, 1964, PhD, 1974; EdS, MA, U. No. Colo., 1968. Lic. clin. psychologist, Wyo.; cert. nat. sch. psychologist, Calif. Caseworker, adminstrv. asst. Wyo. Dept. Health and Social Svcs., Cheyenne, 1964-68; counselor, psychometrist Gradenville Diagnostic Ctr., St. Louis, 1968-70; counselor, instr. Laramie County CC, Cheyenne, 1970-74; psychol. cons. div. mental health Wyo. Bd. Coop. Ednl. Svcs., Rock Springs, 1974-79; guidance counselor Colegio Karl C. Parrish, Barranquilla, Colombia, 1979-80; sch. psychologist Marin County Office Edn., San Rafael, Calif., 1981—. Cons. in field. Founder, pres., Sweetwater County Task Force on Sexual Abuse, Rock Springs, 1974-76; mem. adv. com. Open Day Care Ctr.,Rock Springs, 1974-76, Spl. Edn. Task Force, San Rafael, 1985-87; judge academic decathlon, Marin County Office Edn., 1984-87; founder Advocates for Health & Longevity, 1997. Mem. Nat. Assn. Sch. Psychologists, Phi Kappa Phi. Avocations: yoga, hiking, travel, piano, opera. Home: 269 Scenic Rd Fairfax CA 94930-1550 Office: Marin County Office Edn 1111 Las Gallinas Ave San Rafael CA 94903-1843

YATES, MARY CARLIN, former ambassador; b. Portland, Oreg., Dec. 1946; m. John Melvin Yates. BA in English, Oreg. State U.; M in Comparative East West Humanities, NYU, postgrad. Joined fgn. svc., 1980; press attaché for Amb. Pamela Harriman US Dept. State, sr. cultural attaché Am. Embassy Paris, U.S. amb. to Burundi Washington, 1999—2002, U.S. amb. to Ghana, 2002—05.

YATES, PATRICIA LAWRENCE, elementary school educator; b. Rockland, Maine, Feb. 5, 1947; d. Edward Mark and Helen Mattson Lawrence; m. George Radford Yates, Dec. 30, 1966; children: Michelle Thomas, Matthew, Amy Lally, Jeremy. BA in Edn., U. South Fla., 1969. Kindergarten tchr. Forest Heights Sch., Lakeland, Fla., 1972—81; sub.,tutor Strongsville City Sch., Ohio, 1982—85; fourth grade tchr. St. Joseph and John Sch., Strongsville, Ohio, 1985—. Sr. tchr. cons. Geographic Edn., 1992—. Author: (CD timeline) Timeline of Northeast Ohio 1620-1861, 2003. Mem.: Am. Guild of English Handbell Ringers, Nat. Coun. Geography, Nat. Coun. Social Studies. Republican. Cath. Avocations: piano, needlecrafts, travel, handbells. Home: 17045 Shurmer Rd Strongsville OH 44136 Office Phone: 440-238-4877. Business E-Mail: pyates@ameritech.net.

YATES, SHARON, artist; b. Rochester, NY, 1942; BFA, Syracuse Univ. Sch. Art, 1964; MFA, Tulane Univ., 1966. Faculty Md. Inst. Coll. Art, Balt., 1968—. One-woman shows include Fishbach Gallery, NYC, 1976, Univ. Maine, Macias, 1991, 1997, Maine Coast Artists Exec. Gallery, Rockport, 1993, exhibited in group shows at Turtle Gallery, Deer Isle, Maine, 1997, NAD Mus., NYC, 1997, Maine Coast Artists Gallery, Rockport, 1999, Va. Hist. Soc., Richmond, 2000, Bates Coll. Mus. Art, Maine, 2000, L.C. Bates Mus., Hinkley, Maine, 2000, Represented in permanent collections NAD, NYC, Bates Coll. Mus. Art, United Technologies, Conn., Lucent Technologies, Univ. Louisville, Okla. City Art Mus. Recipient Prix de Rome, 1972—74; grantee Ingram-Merrill Found. fellowship, France, 1977—78, Ludwig Vogelstein Found., 1996. Mem.: NAD (academician 1995—, Shatalov award). Office: Painting Drawing Found MICA 1300 Mount Royal Ave Baltimore MD 21217 Office Phone: 410-669-9200.

YATES, STELLA LOUISE, mathematics educator; b. Richlands, Va., Feb. 14, 1948; d. Wesley Harvey and Linda Francis Vandyke; m. Paul Robert Yates, Sept. 7, 1968; children: Christie Shantell Plymal, Coty Katrina Crigger. BS in Math., Pikeville Coll., Ky., 1970; MS, Radford U., Va., 2005. Cert. tchr. Va. HS tchr. math. and sci. Buchanan County Sch. Bd., Grundy, Va., 1970—; math. tchr. SW Va. C.C., Richlands, 1996—2006. Math. tchr. Va. Intermant Coll., Bristol, 2004—. Home: PO Box 588 Grundy VA 24614 Personal E-mail: syates@buc.k12.va.us.

YATES-WILLIAMS, LINDA SNOW, real estate broker; b. St. Louis, July 20, 1938; d. Robert Anthony Jerrue and June Alberta (Crowder) Armstrong; m. Charles Russell Snow, Nov. 26, 1958 (div. 1979); children: Cathryn Louise, Christopher Armstrong, Heather Highstone, Sean Webster; m. Alan Porter Yates, July 22, 1983 (dec.); m. John S. Williams, Mar. 10, 2006. BBA, Auburn U., 1973, MEd, 1975, EdD, 1998. Cert. profl. sec. Div. head placement div. Solutions Group, Atlanta, 1981-83; employment coord. Fulton Fed. Savs., Atlanta, 1983-84; owner, recruiter Data One, Inc., Atlanta, 1984-85; ops. mgr. Talent Tree Temporaries, Atlanta, 1985-87; legal asst., sec. Rice & Keene, Atlanta, 1987-90; legal word processing asst. Kilpatrick & Cody, Atlanta, 1990-94; pres., owner Power Comm., Cashiers, N.C., 1994-98; regional coord. S.E. region, regional mktg. rep. WorldConnect Comms., Tulsa; dir. mktg. electronic collection divsn. Am. Fin. and Credit Svcs., Inc.; area v.p., loan agent Enterprise Lenders, LLC; bd. dirs., corp. sec. The Hilltop Assocs. Inc., 1999—; real estate sales Exit Realty Beaufort; broker-in-charge Exit Island Realty, Bluffton, SC, 2006—. Adj. instr. DeKalb Coll., Atlanta, 1980-84, Mercer U., Atlanta, 1981-82; instr. bus. So. Union State Jr. Coll., Valley, Ala., 1974-75; radio advt. WAUD, Auburn, Ala., 1970-75, radio announcer Meet the Public; exec. legal sec. Swift, Currie, McGhee & Hiers, Atlanta, 1979-80, Samford, Torbert, Denson & Horsley, Opelika, Ala., 1969-71; dir. acad. planning, chmn. edn. divsn., mem. part-time faculty in ednl. adminstrn. CEU Grad. Coll., Nuevo Leon, Mex. Columnist Neon News Flash, 1995. Named Top Lister, Exit Island Realty, 2005; recipient Top Prodr. award, Exit Realty Beaufort, 2005. Mem. Paralegal Assn. Beaufort County (charter mem., sec. 1993-94), Women Bus. Owners, Nat. Assn. Pers. Cons., Internat. Soc. Poets (Disting. mem., Internat. Poet of Merit 1996, Internat. Poetry Hall of Fame 1996), Cashiers Writers Group, Phi Delta Kappa, Alpha Xi Delta. Republican. Episcopalian. Avocations: golf, writing poetry, international travel. Office: 91 N Boone Rd Saint Helena Island SC 29920 Office Phone: 843-252-4948. E-mail: lindayrealtor@aol.com, linday1000@yahoo.com.

YATSINKO, MARY ANN, elementary school educator; b. Dickson City, Pa., Mar. 26, 1942; d. Michael Vasil and Mary Celia (Solensky) Y. BS, U. Bridgeport, 1965; MA, So. Conn. State Coll., 1969, diploma advanced studies, 1986; PhD, LaSalle U., 1993. Cert. tchr., Conn. 2d and 3d grade tchr.

Bridgeport Bd. Edn., 1965-67, tchr. remedial reading, 1966, tchr. homebound for physically, mentally handicapped, 1967-69, 6th grade tchr., 1977—2002; tchr. presch. hearing impaired and physically handicapped Easter Seal Rehab. Ctr., Bridgeport, 1969-70; dir. med. social work Park City Hosp., Bridgeport, 1970-74; dir. admissions and med. social work Lord Chamberlain Skilled Nursing Facility, Stratford, Conn., 1976-77; ret., 2002. Guest lectr. U. Bridgeport, 1979; mem. clin. rev. patient's charts Vis. Nurses Assn., Bridgeport, 1973-76; tutor Title I program reading and math, 2002—; supr. students and tchrs. U. Bridgeport, 2005. Developer state cert. program for pre-sch. physically handicapped students. Fundraiser Am. Diabetes Assn., 1993. Mem. NEA, Conn. Edn. Assn., Bridgeport Edn. Assn. (med. ins. com. 1977—), Delta Tau Kappa. Roman Catholic. Avocations: reading, travel, tennis. Home: 202 Monroe St Milford CT 06460-5731

YATVIN, JOANNE INA, education educator; b. Newark, Apr. 17, 1931; d. John and Mary Edna (Cohen) Goldberg; m. Milton Brian Yatvin, June 8, 1952; children: Alan, Bruce, Lillian, Richard. Ba, Douglass Coll., 1952; MA, Rutgers U., 1962; PhD, U. Wis., 1974. Cert. sch. adminstr. Tchr. Hamburg Pub. Sch., NJ, 1952-53, New Brunswick Pub. Sch., NJ, 1953-55, Mayaguez Sch., PR, 1958-59, Milltown Pub. Sch., NJ, 1959-62, East Brunswick Pub. Sch., NJ, 1962-63; tchr., prin. Madison Met. Sch. Dist., Wis., 1963-88; supt. Cottrell Sch. Dist., Boring, Oreg., 1988-97, prin., 1997-2000; mem. faculty Portland State U., Oreg., 2000—. Adv. bd. mem. Big Books Mag., 1990—91; cons. various sch. dist.; apptd. to nat. reading panel Nat. Inst. of Child Health and Devel., 1998—2000. Author: Learning Language Through Communication, 1986, (monograph) A Whole Language Program for a Whole School, 1991, (monograph) Beginning a School Literacy Improvement Project: Some Words of Advice, Kdg Teachers Guide, Pegasus Reading Program, Kendall Hunt, 2000, A Room with a Differentiated View, 2004, Heinemann, 2004; contbr. chpts. in books and articles to profl. jour. Named Elem. Prin. of Yr., Wis. Dept. Edn., 1985, Wis. State Reading Assn., 1985; recipient Excellence in Print award, Washington Edpress, 1987, Disting. Elem. Edn. Alumni award, U. Wis., 1988, Kenneth S. Goodman In Def. of Good Tchg. award, Dept. Lang. and Learning U. Ariz., 2001. Mem.: ASCD, Oreg. Reading Assn., Nat. Coun. Tchrs. English (chair com. on ctrs. excellence 1986—89, mem. com. on curriculum 1999—2002, v.p. 2004—05, 2004—, pres.-elect 2005—06), Internat. Reading Assn. (pres. Portland coun. 2002—04, Portland Coun. Celebrate Literacy award 2002), Phi Delta Kappa. Home: 5226 SW Northwood Ave Portland OR 97239-2832 Office: Grad Sch Edn Portland State U PO Box 751 Portland OR 97207-0751

YAVORNIK, BARBARA ANN, pre-school educator; b. Olympia, Wash., July 12, 1957; d. Eugene Earl and Betty Ann Brown; m. Edward J. Yavornik, II, Jan. 11, 1980. BA, Cen. Wash. U., Ellensburg, 1981; MEd, West Tex. A&M U., 1990. Cert. adminstrn. Dir., tchr. Fifth Ave. Pres-Sch., Ellensburg, 1981—82; tchr. Coronado Acad., Albuquerque, 1985—86, N.W. Primary, Hereford, Tex., 1987—. Presenter I-Teach K West Tex. A&M U. Sci. Conf., 2000, 01, 05; presenter HISD Sci. Inservice, 2005. Greeter coord. St. Anthony's Parish Coun., 2004—, eucharistic minister, 2004—; bd. dirs. Campfire, Hereford, 1988—90. Named Tchr. of Yr., N.W. Primary, 2002; recipient Excel in Sci. Tchg. award, Tex. Sci. Assn., 2001, Golden Apple award, Hereford Ind. Sch. Dist., 2004. Mem.: Hereford C. of C. (v.p. women's divsn. 1987—89), Delta Kappa Gamma (pres. 2002—04, v.p., Achievement award 1999—2004). Republican. Roman Catholic. Avocations: gardening, reading, collecting bears, travel. Home: 201 N Texas Ave Hereford TX 79045 Office: NW Primary Sch 400 Moreman Ave Hereford TX 79045 Office Phone: 806-363-7660. E-mail: barbarayavornik@herefordisd.net.

YAWN, AMELIA LOU, adult education educator; b. McComb, Miss., Jan. 17, 1943; d. Lonnie L. and Frances McNeill Smith; m. Charles Larry Yawn, Nov. 23, 1975; children: Angela Nobert, Heidi Moore, Kandace McGinnis. AA, S.W. Miss. CC, Summit, 1973; BS, Miss. State, Starkville, 1975; M, So. Miss., Hattiesburg, 1990; student, Alcorn, Lorman, Miss., 1998. Clerical Fed. Res. Bank, Denver, 1962—63; bookkeeper E-J Newspaper, McComb, Miss., 1964—78; self-employed Yawn Svc. Co., McComb, 1979—88; biology instr. S.W. Miss. CC, Summit, 1989—2006. Girl's softball coach, 1968—96. Mem.: Phi Theta Kappa (adv. 1998—2006). Avocation: softball. Home: 3157 County Line Rd W Summit MS 39666

YAZDI, MAHVASH, utilities executive; BS in Indsl. Mgmt., Poly. U., Pomona; MBA, U. So. Calif.; grad. mgmt. info. tech. program, Harvard U. CIO Hughes Aircraft; joined Edison Internat., 1997, sr. v.p. bus. integration, CIO So. Calif. Edison subs., sr. v.p. bus. integration, CIO Rosemead, Calif. Bd. dirs. Claremont U. Consortium, Ptnrs. in Care Found., Columbus Newport Corp.; adv. dir. Lotus Corp., IBM Corp.; mem. So. Calif. Forum of the Trusteeship of the Internat. Women's Forum, 2003. Office: Edison Internat 2244 Walnut Grove Ave Rosemead CA 91770

YDE, JACQULYN RAE, interior designer, architectural colorist; b. Freeport, Ill. d. John Harrison and Ethlyn Roberta (Puckett) Groves; children: Michael, Michelle, Mark, Matthew, Gregory; m. Al Alschuler, 2000. Student, Harper C.C., Palatine, Ill., Chgo. Architecture Found.; degree, Harrington Inst. Interior Design, 1975. Lic. interior designer, NCIDQ cer. 1980-. Ptnr. Swedroe/Yde Design Assocs., Miami Beach, Fla., 1983—88; pres. Jacqulyn Yde Design, Inc., Miami, Fla., 1988—. Color design City of Miami Beach, 1986, South Beach hotels, 1987-, Fisher Island (original models) 1982-83, Suzanne's in the Grove Club and restaurant, 1986; mem. interior design adv. bd. Art Inst. Ft. Lauderdale, Fla., 1990-; public speaker, color/light/healing environ. Prin. works include North Shore Historic Homes, Miami Beach, 1988. Color designer North Miami Sr. H.S., 1987, Miami-Dade County Auditorium, Crescent and Sagamore Hotels, South Beach, Fla., Island Pointe Condominium, Bay Harbor, Fla. Named Designer of Yr., Art Deco Socs., Miami Style. Mem. Am. Soc. Interior Designers (bd. dirs. 2001—), The Color Assn. U.S. Avocations: writing, travel, reading, theater, opera. Office: Jacqulyn Yde Design Inc 2430 Brickell Ave Ste 104A Miami FL 33129 E-mail: jycolordesign@aol.com.

YEAGER, CAROLINE HALE, writer, retired radiologist, consultant; b. Little Rock, Sept. 5, 1946; d. George Glenn and Crenor Burnelle (Hale) Y.; m. William Berg Singer, July 8, 1978; children: Adina Atkinson Singer, Sarah Rose Singer. BA, Ind. U., Bloomington, 1968; MD, Ind. U., Indpls., 1971. Diplomate Am. Bd. Radiology; med. lic. State of Calif. Intern Good Samaritan Hosp., Los Angeles, 1971-72; resident in radiology King Drew Med. Ctr. UCLA, Los Angeles, 1972-76; dir. radiology Hubert Humphrey Health Ctr., Los Angeles, 1976-77; asst. prof. radiology UCLA, Los Angeles, 1977-84, King Drew Med. Ctr. UCLA, Los Angeles, 1977-85, dir. ultrasound, 1977-84; ptnr. pvt. practice Beverly Breast Ctr., Beverly Hills, Calif., 1984-87; cons. Clarity Communications, Pasadena, Calif., 1981—; pvt. practice radiology Claude Humphrey Health Ctr., 1991-93; dir. sonograms and mammograms Rancho Los Amigos Med. Ctr., 1993-94, ret., 1994. Trustee Assn. Teaching Physicians, L.A., 1976-81; cons. King Drew Med. Ctr., 1984, Gibraltar Savs., 1987, Cal Fed. Inc., 1986, Medical Faculty At Home Professions, 1989—, Mobil Diagnostics, 1991-92, Xerox Corp., 1990-91, Frozen Leopard, Inc., 1990-91; writer gen. med. answers pub. on internet, 1994-. Author: (with others) Infectious Disease, 1978, Anatomy and Physiology for Medical Transcriptionists, 1992; contbr. articles to profl. jours. Trustee U. Synagogue, Los Angeles, 1975-79; mem. Friends of Pasadena Playhouse, 1987-90. Grantee for innovative tng. Nat. Fund for Med. Edn., 1980-81. Mem. Am. Inst. Ultrasound in Medicine, L.A. Radiology Soc. (ultrasound sect.), Nat. Soc. Performance and Instrn. (chmn. conf. Database 1991, publs. L.A. chpt. 1990, info. systems L.A. chpt. 1991, dir. adminstrn. L.A. chpt. 1992, Outstanding Achievement in Performance Improvement award L.A. chpt. 1990, bd. dirs. 1990-93, Pres. award for Outstanding Chpt. 1992, v.p. programs 1993), Stanford Profl. Women L.A. Jewish. Avocations: writing, humor, design. Home and Office: 3520 Yorkshire Rd Pasadena CA 91107-5440 Personal E-mail: doccarrie@earthlink.net.

YEAGER, DEBRA LYN, science educator; b. St. Paul, Mar. 20, 1957; d. Lyle Milton and Grace Jeanette (Mitchell) Yeager, adopted d. Wilma Mitchell; life ptnr. Christopher Charles Pfannes. AS in Computer Sci., Mesa C.C., Ariz., 1982; student, Scottsdale C.C., Ariz., 1979—80. Ordained minister Order of Melchizedek, 1991. Investigator - profiler Elk River Sheriff's Dept., Minn., 1992—94; sensor sci. tchr. Open U. of Minn., Mpls., 1994—99; sensory sci. tchr. Yeager Consulting / Into the Mystic, Minnetonka, Minn., 1998—2005, Wis. Indianhead Tech. Coll., New Richmond, 2003—, West Ctrl. Cancer Symposium, Willmar, Minn., 2003, U. Alaska-Sitka, 2003—, U. Manitoba, 2004—, U. Coll. Dublin, Ireland, 2004—, Queens U.-Belfast, Ireland, 2004—; on the air talent, lectr. Kare 11 - NBC TV Mpls, 2002—03, WCCO 4 - CBS TV. Mpls., 2002, NW Mag. Cable Show, New Hope, Minn., 1996; sensory sci. specialist, prof. spirituality Park Hill, Okla., 2005—. Criminologist and profiler Crema Law Offices, Mpls., 1999—. Author: (novel) Encounters with the Sixth Dimension (Book in print), Intervention across time, Medium, Rare - the Bio of Debra Yeager, Karman from MU. Mem.: Delta Zeta (hon.). Achievements include research in Metaphysical Studies; development of Programs of Metaphysical Studies. Avocations: motorcycling, designing jewelry, horse training, running, travel. Home and Office: PO Box 310 Park Hill OK 74451 Personal E-mail: century30@aol.com.

YEAGER, NANCY ELLEN, literature and language educator; b. Reading, Pa., Sept. 28, 1960; d. Henry Burkhard Koehler and Helen Elizabeth Sattler; m. Conrad Charles Yeager III, May 31, 1997; m. Alan Antrim Beck (dec.); 1 child, Adrienne Marie Beck. BS in English and Secondary Edn. magna cum laude, Kutztown U., Pa., 1994, MEdn in English summa cum laude, 2001. Cert. tchr. English/Secondary Edn. Pa., 1995, lic. cosmetologist Pa., 1987, cert. aerobics instr. AAAI, 1990. Waitress and bartender The Inn at Redding (Pa.), 1978—80; freelance model, 1975—85; aerobics instr. Tri-Valley YMCA, Fleetwood, Pa., 1988—94; cosmetologist Randy Rick Salon, Leesport, 1987—94; tchr. English Brandywine Heights H.S., Topton, 1995—2000; tchr. gifted and talented Brandywine Heights Mid. Sch., Topton, 2000—01; tchr. English Brandywine Heights H.S., Topton, 2001—. Yearbook advisor Brandywine Heights H.S., Topton, Pa., 1995—2000, Sr. project advisor, 2000—, newspaper advisor, 2002—. Vol. organizer Berks Bards, Reading, Pa., Kutztown Arts Coun., Kutztown. Mem.: NEA, Pa. State Edn. Assn. Avocations: reading, writing, travel, fitness, kayaking. Home: 284 Forrest Rd Mertztown PA 19539 Office: Brandywine Heights HS 200 W Weis St Topton PA 19562

YEAGER, TONI LEE, special education educator, real estate manager; b. Los Angeles, Calif., Feb. 8, 1944; d. Nick Valestrino and Ione Elizabeth Nelson; m. Paul David Yeager; children: Patricia Elaine, Anne Marie. BA in Elem. Edn., UCLA, 1961; MA, Calif. State U., Long Beach, 1968. Cert. Reading Specialist, Elementary Education Ohio, Multi Handicapped Calif. Elem. tchr. Torrance Unified Sch., Calif., 1965, 1966—69, reading specialist, 1969—71, spl. edn. tchr., 1968; reading specialist Fairbanks Local Sch., Milford Ctr., Ohio, 1975—77, learning disabilities tchr., 1978—82, elem. tchr., 1983—98; reading specialist Spraings Acad., Layfavette, Calif., 1998—99, Clark County Sch., Las Vegas, 1999—2000. Sec. Fairbanks Edn. Assn., Milford Ctr., 1997. Mem. polit. campaign Nixonette, Los Angeles, 1960. Recipient Elem. Tchr. of Yr., Fairbanks Edn. Assn., 1995. Republican. Cath. Avocations: singing, travel, exercise, reading.

YEAGER-HALL, CARLI MARIE, biology educator; b. Wilkes-Barre, Pa. d. W. Brooke Yeager III and Dorothy Marie Wolff; m. Scott F. Hall. BS in Biology, Bloomsburg U., Pa., 1994, BS in Secondary Edn. Biology, 1995; MS in Cell & Molecular Biology, SUNY, Binghamton, 2002. Substitute tchr. Dallas Area H.S., 1995—96; tchr. sci. Conneaut Lake H.S., Pa., 1996—97, Epophany Sch., Sayre, 1997—98; substitute tchr. Sullivan County H.S., LaPorte, 1998—99; tchg. asst. SUNY, Binghamton, 1999—2002; tchr. biology Athens Area H.S., Pa., 2001—. Adj. faculty Luzerne County C.C., Nanticoke, Pa., 1999—2002; sec. Family Choice Charter Sch., Towanda, Pa. Mem.: Pa. Sci. Tchrs. Assn., Nat. Sci. Tchrs. Assn. Avocation: travel. Office: Athens Area High Sch 401 W Frederick St Athens PA 18810

YEAGLEY, JOAN HOWERTON, writer; b. Denver, Jan. 25, 1930; d. Harold Emery Howerton and Jeannette Louise Boule; m. Harold Arthur Yeagley, Apr. 14, 1951; children: Jan, Donn, Jeff, Jeanne. BSc in Edn., Kans. State U., 1984. Cons. N.E. Kans. Libr. Sys.; tchr. creative writing Mo. Southern State Coll., Joplin, Crowder Coll.; workshop leader in field. Author: Four Bookmark Poets, The Studs of McDonald County, 1987; contbr. articles and stories to mags. Great books coord. Kans. City Pub. Libr./Great Books Found., Chgo. Recipient Kans. City Star award, Kans. City Star, 1965—67, Gold Quill award, Crowder Coll., 1988, Sager Creek Arts Ctr. award, John Brown U., 1995—96. Home: 61 Tiffany Ln Stella MO 64867 Personal E-mail: jhyeagley@leru.net.

YEARWOOD, TRISHA, country music singer, songwriter; b. Monticello, Ga., 1964; m. Chris Latham (div.); m. Robert Reynolds, May 21, 1994 (div.); m. Garth Brooks, Dec. 10, 2005. Degree in Music Bus., Belmont U. Intern MTM Records, demo singer, commercial jingles singer; recording artist MCA Records. Albums include Trisha Yearwood, 1991 (double platinum), Hearts in Armor, 1992 (Grammy nomination: Best Country Female Vocal, 1994 for "Walkaway Joe"), The Song Remembers When, 1993, Thinkin' About You, 1995, Everybody Knows, 1996, (songbook) A Collection of Hits, 1997, Where Your Road Leads, 1998, Real Live Woman, 2000, Inside Out, 2001, Jasper County, 2005; back-up vocalist Garth Brooks albums; opening act Garth Brooks Tour, 1991; TV appearances on TNN American Music Shop, The Tonight Show, Late Night with David Letterman, Good Morning America, A&E Live By Request, 1998 Academy Awards, 1996 Summer Olympic Closing Ceremonies. Named Best New Country Artist by Am. Music Awards, 1992, Top New Female Vocalist by Acad. Country Music, 1992, Top Female Vocalist of Yr., 1998; Top Female Vocalist of Yr., Country Mus. Assn., 1997, 98; first female in country music history to have debut single reach #1 on charts with She's in Love with the Love, 1991; recipient Grammy awards for best female country vocal, 1998, best country vocal collaboration (with Aaron Neville) 1994, (with Garth Brooks), 1998.

YEATES, MARIE R., lawyer; b. New Orleans, Feb. 24, 1956; BS summa cum laude, La. State U., 1977, JD, 1980. Bar: La. 1980, U.S. Ct. Appeals (5th cir.) 1981, U.S. Ct. Appeals (11th cir.) 1981, Tex. 1982, Tex. Supreme Ct. 1982, U.S. Dist. Ct. (so. dist.) Tex. 1985, U.S. Supreme Ct. 1986, U.S. Ct. Appeals (9th cir.) 1998, U.S. Dist. Ct. (no. dist.) Tex. 2001, U.S. Ct. Appeals (10th cir.) 2002, U.S. Ct. Appeals (7th cir.) 2004. Ptnr., co-head Appellate Sect. Vinson & Elkins LLP, Houston, 1990—. Office: Vinson & Elkins LLP First City Tower 1001 Fannin St, Ste 2300 Houston TX 77002 Office Phone: 713-758-4576. E-mail: myeates@velaw.com.

YEATTS, SUSAN W., financial planner; b. Columbia, S.C., Jan. 4, 1973; d. George D. and Mary Genevieve Clark Wooldridge; m. Mark R. Yeatts, Feb. 2, 1964; children: Mary Morgan, Thomas George, Eleanor English. BA, Sweet Briar Coll., Sweet Briar, Va., 1995. CFP, The CFP Bd., 2006; chartered fin. cons. The Am. Coll., 2001. Office of supervisory jurisdiction mgr. Walnut St. Securities, Lexington, SC, 2000—06; chief compliance office and ops. mgr. Carolina Wealth Mgmt., LLC, Lexington, SC, 2005—. Sec. Unforgettable Angels, Inc., Columbia, SC, 2004—06. Conservative-R. Avocations: golf, travel. Home: 368 Presque Isle Rd Lexington SC 29072 Office: Carolina Wealth Management LLC 468 Old Cherokee Rd Lexington SC 29072 Office Phone: 803-808-0954. Home Fax: 803-996-0373; Office Fax: 803-808-0957. Personal E-mail: syeatts@sc.rr.com. E-mail: susan@susanyeatts.com.

YEAW, KIMBERLY A., secondary school educator; d. David Lee Gould and Kathleen Maryellen Thompson; m. Thomas Yeaw, Aug. 11, 1996; children: Sydney Ellen, Alexander Thomas. BS in Mktg., Plymouth State Coll., N.H., 1991; BA in Secondary Edn. in Math., R.I. Coll., Providence, 1995. Tchr. Attleboro Sch. Dept., Mass., 1995—98, Smithfield Sch. Dept., RI, 1998—. Office: Smithfield Sch Dept Pleasant View Rd Smithfield RI 02820 E-mail: kyeaw@smithfield-ps.org.

YEAZELL, RUTH BERNARD, English language educator; b. NYC, Apr. 4, 1947; d. Walter and Annabelle (Reich) Bernard; m. Stephen C. Yeazell, Aug. 14, 1969 (div. 1980). BA with high honors, Swarthmore Coll., 1967; MPhil, Yale U., 1970, PhD, 1971. Asst. prof. English Boston U., 1971-74, UCLA, 1975-77, assoc. prof., 1977-80, prof., 1980-91, Yale U., New Haven, 1991—, dir. grad. studies, 1993-98, Chace family prof., 1995—, chair, 2000—05. Author: Language and Knowledge in the Late Novels of Henry James, 1976, Death and Letters of Alice James, 1981, Fictions of Modesty: Women and Courtship in the English Novel, 1991, Harems of the Mind: Passages of Western Art and Literature, 2000; assoc. editor Nineteenth-Century Fiction, 1977-80; editor: Sex, Politics and Science in the 19th Century Novel, 1986, Henry James: A Collection of Critical Essays, 1994. Dir. Lewis Walpole Libr., 1996—. Woodrow Wilson fellow, 1967-68, Guggenheim fellow, 1979-80, NEH fellow, 1988-89, Pres.'s rsch. fellow U. Calif., 1988-89, Getty scholar, 2003-04 (declined), Bellagio Ctr. Residency scholar, 2005. Mem. MLA (exec. coun. 1985-88), English Inst. (supervising com. 1983-86). Office: Yale U Dept English New Haven CT 06520-8302 Office Phone: 203-432-2239.

YECKE, CHERI PIERSON, educational researcher, administrator, columnist, writer; b. St. Paul, Feb. 5, 1955; d. Leo Sylvester and Marceline Mae (Intihar) Pierson; m. Dennis Joseph Yecke, Dec. 22, 1973; children: Anastasia, Tiffany. BA, U. Hawaii, 1975; MST, U. Wis., River Falls, 1984; PhD, U. Va., 2001. Apptd. mem. State Bd. Edn., State of Va., 1995—98, dep. sec. edn., 1998—2001, sec. edn., 2001—02; dir. tchr. quality and pub. sch. choice US Dept. Edn., 2002—03; sr. adv. to White House on USA Freedom Corps., 2003; commr. edn. State of Minn., 2003—04; disting. sr. fellow for edn. and social policy Ctr. of the Am. Experiment, 2004—05; chancellor for K-12 edn. State of Fla., Tallahassee, 2005—. Author: The War Against Excellence: The Rising Tide of Mediocrity in America's Middle Schools, 2003, Mayhem in the Middle: How Middle Schools Have Failed America and How to Make Them Work, 2005. Mem.: Am. Coun. Trustees & Alumni, Nat. Assn. Scholars. Republican. Home: 1315 Peacefield Pl Tallahassee FL 32308-0844 Office Phone: 850-245-0509.

YEDVAB, LAUREN, health facility administrator; b. 1971; m. Joshua Y., May 1996. BS, SUNY Coll. Oneonta, 1992; MS, Cornell Univ., 1994. Asst. v.p. N.Y. Meth. Hosp., Brooklyn, 1995, sr. v.p., 2003—. Exec. bd. Sloan Coll. Cornell Univ. Alum. Assn., 2004—. Fellow N.Y. Meth. Hosp., 1995. Office: New York Meth Hosp 506 6th St Brooklyn NY 11215 Office Phone: 718-780-3301. Office Fax: 718-780-3770. E-mail: lyedvab@nyp.org.

YEE, NANCY W., travel consultant; b. Honolulu, Nov. 6, 1917; d. Sai Ho and Ah Oi Sen Wong; m. Ken Yee, Dec. 2, 1941; children: Roy Jensen, Sylvia Mei-ling McCaffrey, Carolyn Mei-en Lee, Susan Mei-jen. BA in Edn. Music and Dance, U. Hawaii, 1941. Sr. translator U.S. Postal Censorship, Honolulu, 1941-45; pvt. tchr. English and civics Honolulu, 1945-50; radio announcer Chinese KGMB Radio/TV, Honolulu, 1946-56; ptnr. Ken's Electric Motor Svc., Honolulu, 1949-65; travel cons. Royal Adventure/Quality, Honolulu, 1957—; sec., officer mgr. KEMS Inc., Honolulu, 1965-85. Radio announcer Chinese, KAHU, Honolulu, 1956; chmn. Small Bus. Adminstrn. Adv. Bd., Honolulu, 1967-68; advisor Jr. Achievement, Honolulu, 1970-71; pres. Women's Propeller Club U.S., Honolulu, 1977-78. Den mother Cub Scouts, 1948-50; mem., choir mem. First Chinese Ch. of Christ, 1950-99; chmn. fund raiser, den mother Pacific Girl Scouts Am., 1958-68; mem. Honolulu Youth Symphony, 1967-71; sec. Ctrl. Dist. PTA, Honolulu, 1968; vol. Hawaii Heart Assn., Honolulu, 1970-73; vol. tchr. Chinese song and dance Mun Lun Sch., 1970; mem., pres. Mun Lun Sch. PTA, 1970, Palolo Home Aux, Honolulu, 1977-78, Associated Chinese U. Women, 1978. Named Chinese Model Mother of the Yr., United Chinese Soc., Honolulu, 1986, Hawaii Chinese Living Treasure, Chinese Youth Hawaii, Honolulu, 1995. Avocations: playing chinese butterfly harp, singing chinese operas, travel, cruising, volunteer work.

YEE-MELICHAR, DARLENE, gerontological health educator; b. N.Y.C., Sept. 19, 1958; d. Jimmy Tow and Yuen Hing (Chin) Y.; m. Joseph F. Melichar. BA in Biology, Barnard Coll., 1980; MS in Gerontology, Coll. New Rochelle, 1981; MS in Health Edn., Columbia U., 1984, EdD in Health Edn., 1985. Cert. Nat. Commn. Health Edn. Asst. dir. biology lab. Barnard Coll., N.Y.C., 1980-83; rsch. assoc, safety rsch. and edn. project Columbia U. Tchrs. Coll., N.Y.C., 1983-85; asst. prof. health and phys. edn. York Coll., N.Y.C., 1985-88; cons. Transp. Rsch. Bd., NAS, Washington, 1987, N.Y. State Dept. Edn., Albany, 1987, U.S. Dept. Edn., Washington, 1991; assoc. prof. clin. gerontology, health edn. and promotion U. Tex. Med. Br., Galveston, 1988-90; assoc. prof. health edn. San Francisco State U., 1990-93; prof. health edn., 1994-95; dir., prof. gerontology San Francisco State U., 1995—. Contbr. articles to profl. jours. Mem. Am. Coll. Health Care Adminstrs., Gerontol. Soc. Am., Am. Soc. on Aging, Assn. for Advancement Health Edn., Nat. Coun. on Aging, Sigma Xi. Home: 1470 Tartan Trail Rd Hillsborough CA 94010-7220 Office Phone: 415-338-3558. E-mail: dyee@sfsu.edu.

YEH, HSIAO YEN C., artist; b. Chung-Qing, China, Mar. 4, 1942; arrived in U.S., 1963; d. Chien-Chung Chen and Gin-Ger Fan; m. Raymond W.H. Yeh, Sept. 16, 1967; children: Bryant P.Y., Clement C.Y., Emily S.Y. BA, U. Oreg., 1967; MEd, U. Minn., 1969. Owner, artist Art Inc., Oklahoma City, Honolulu, 1984—. Art instr. Firehouse Art Sta., Norman, Okla., Ctrl. State U., Edmond, Okla., 1989-91; art specialist U. Hawaii, Honolulu, 1993-95. Mem. AAUW (bd. mem.), Assn. Chinese U. Women (bd. mem. 1997-99), Nat. Assn. Art Educators. Home: 1821 Kumakani Pl Honolulu HI 96821-1327

YELENICK, MARY THERESE, lawyer; b. Denver, May 17, 1954; d. John Andrew and Maesel Joyce (Reed) Y. B.A. magna cum laude, Colo. Coll., 1976; J.D. cum laude, Georgetown U., 1979. Bar: D.C. 1979, U.S. Dist. Ct. D.C. 1980, U.S. Ct. Appeals (D.C. cir.) 1981, N.Y. 1982, U.S. Dist. Ct. (so. and ea. dists.) N.Y. 1982, U.S. Supreme Ct. 1992, U.S. Ct. Appeals (5th cir.) 1995. Law clk. to presiding justices Superior Ct. D.C., 1979-81; ptnr. Chadbourne & Parke, LLP, N.Y.C., 1981—. Editor Jour. of Law and Policy Internat. Bus., 1978-79.; mem. NETWORK, The Nat. Cath. Soc. Justice Lobby (bd. dirs., 2004—) Mem. Phi Beta Kappa. Democrat. Roman Catholic. Home: 310 E 46th St New York NY 10017-3002 Office: Chadbourne & Parke LLP 30 Rockefeller Plz Fl 31 Ste 3550 New York NY 10112-0129

YELICH, JANINE E., music educator; b. Buffalo, Dec. 19, 1965; d. William A. and Barbara C. Pirk; m. Michael J. Yelich, July 4, 1992; children: Allyson R., Nicholas M., Benjamin W. BS in Music Edn., Nazareth Coll., 1987; MA in Humanities, SUNY, Buffalo, 1992. Cert. Edn. K-12 Music NY. K-12 vocal music tchr. Christ The King Sch., Snyder, NY, 1987—88; k-12 instrumental, vocal itinerant tchr. Cattaragus, Allegany, Erie, Wyo. County Bd. Coop. Svcs., Olean, NY, 1988—89; 4-12 instrumental and vocal music tchr. Angelica Ctrl. Sch. Dist., NY, 1989—90; k-12 vocal, instrumental music Depew Union Free Sch. Dist., 1992—98, 5-6 instrumental music tchr., 1999—; 6-8 instrumental music tchr. Alden Ctrl. Sch. Dist., 1998—99. Original mem., co-creator Character Edn. Program, Depew, 1997—98; accompanist sch. chorus Depew (NY) Union Free Sch. Dist., 1992—, mem. orch. ann. musicals, 2000—, mentor, co-coordinator, co-creator, 2004—05; advisor Nat. Jr. Honor Soc., Depew, 2005—; mentor Depew (NY) Mentor Program, 2005—. Alumni Regional scholarship, Nazareth Coll. Rochester, 1983-1987, Music Dept. Competitive scholarship, 1983-1987. Mem.: Music Educators Nat. Conf., NY State Schs. Music Assn., Erie County Music Educators Assn., Depew Tchrs. Orgn. (bldg. rep. union 2003—04). Achievements include accompanist for All-County Women's Choir; dir. All-County Jazz Ensemble. Home: 11 Woodgate Dr Lancaster NY 14086 Office: Depew Union Free Sch Dist 5201 S Transit Rd Depew NY 14043 Office Phone: 716-686-2442. Personal E-mail: j9yelich@hotmail.com. Business E-Mail: jyelich@depew.wnyric.org.

YELLAND, MARY VIRGINIA, artist; b. Mason City, Iowa, Apr. 16, 1916; d. George Curtis and Gladys Adele (Richardson) Y. Student, Stephens Coll., 1935, U. Minn., 1936-37, Mills. Acad., 1938. Chief draftsman Northwest Airlines, St. Paul, 1941-45; drafting bus. owner Newport, Minn., 1947-85. Author: Unique Legacy of Red Rock and Newport, 1989; creator logo for

Newport Centennial, 1989. Bd. dirs. Newport Pub. Libr., 1955-80, 89—; chair Centennial Celebration, Newport, 1989; mem. Newport Hist. Preservation Commn., 1992—. Republican. Presbyterian. Avocation: photography. Home: 480 2nd Ave Newport MN 55055-1401

YELLEN, JANET LOUISE, bank executive; b. Bklyn., Aug. 13, 1946; d. Julius and Anna Ruth (Blumenthal) Y.; m. George Arthur Akerlof, July 8, 1978; 1 child, Robert Joseph. BA in Econs. summa cum laude, Brown U., 1967; PhD, Yale U., 1971; LLD (hon.), Brown U., 1998; LHD (hon.), Bard Coll., 2000. Asst. prof. econs. Harvard U., Cambridge, Mass., 1971-76; lectr. London Sch. Econs. and Polit. Sci., Washington, 1978-80; asst. prof. econs. Sch. Bus. Adminstrn., U. Calif., Berkeley, 1980-82, assoc. prof., 1982-85, prof. Haas Sch. Bus., 1985—, Bernard T. Rocca Jr. prof. internat. bus. and trade, 1992—, Eugene E. and Catherine M. Trefethem prof. bus., 1999—; cons. div. internat. fin., Fed. Res. Sys., Washington, 1974-75, economist trade and fin. studies sect., 1977-78, mem., 1994-97; chair, Coun. Econ. Advisors Exec. Office of the Pres., Washington, 1997-99; pres., CEO Fed. Res. Bank San Francisco, 2004—. Mem. adv. panel in economics NSF, 1977—78, 1991—92, com. visitors, economics program, 1996, 2004; adv. bd. Women's Econ. Round Table, 1999—, Ctr. Internat. Polit. Economy, 1999—, Jerome Levy Economics Inst., 2002—, Calif. Assembly Select Com. on Asian Trade, 2003; bd. dirs. Economists Allied for Arms Reduction, 2002—, Delta Dental of Calif., 2003—; mem. amb. adv. coun. for Marshall Scholarships, 1996—, OECD, High-Level Sustainable Devel. Group, 1999—2001, NAS Panel, Ensuring Best Presidential Sci. and Tech. Appointments, 2000; chair Pres. Interagency Com. on Women's Bus. Enterprise, 1997—99, Econ. Policy Com. Orgn. for Econ. Coop. and Devel., 1997—99; rsch. fellow MIT, Cambridge, 1974; cons. Congl. Budget Office, 1975—76, mem. panel econ. advisers, 1993—94; rsch. affiliate Yale U., 1976; fellow Yale Corp., 2000—; rsch. assoc. Nat. Bureau Econ. Rsch., 1999—; prin. investigator Russell Sage Found. Grant on Sustainable Employment, 2000; sr. adviser Macroeconomic Advisers, 2003—; mem. Brookings Panel on Econ. Activity, 1987—88, 1990—91, sr. adviser, 1989—94, adv. bd., 1999—; Yrjö Jahnsson Found. lectr. on macroecon. theory, Helsinki, 1977—78; mem. Coun. on Fgn. Rels, 1976—81. Author: (monograph) (with Arrow and Shavell) The Limits of the Market in Resource Allocation, 1977; assoc. editor Jour. Econ. Perspectives, 1987-91; contbr. articles to profl. jours. Hon. Woodrow Wilson fellow, 1967, grad. fellow NSF, 1967-71, Guggenheim fellow, 1986-87, fellow, Am. Academy Arts and Sciences, 2001; grantee NSF, 1975-77, 90-94; Maria and Sidney Rolfe award for Nat. Econ. Svc., Women's Econ. Round Table, 1997, Wilbur Lucius Cross Medal, Yale U., 1997; named one of 50 Women to Watch, Wall St. Journal, 2005. Mem. Am. Econ. Assn. (adv. com. to Pres. 1986-87, nominating com. 1988-90, v.p. 2004-), Western Econ. Assn. (pres., 2003-04), Phi Beta Kappa. Office: Fed Res Bank San Francisco 101 Market St San Francisco CA 94105-1579*

YELLIN, JUDITH, small business owner; b. Balt., Feb. 21; d. Jack and Sarah (Grebow) Levin; m. Sidney Yellin, Jan. 1; children: David, Paul, Tamar. Student, U. Md., Catonsville CC. Mgr. credit dept. Lincoln Co., Balt.; office mgr. Seaview Constrn. Co.; owner, operator Yellin Telephone Soliciting Agy.; mgr. Liberty Antique Shop; owner, mgr. Judith Yellin Electrology, 1973—. Creator jewelry; chief examiner Md. State Bd. Electrology, 1978-81; designer jewelry. Contbr. poetry: New American Poetry Anthology, 1988, Great Poems of the Western World, Vol. II, 1990. Mem. Am. Electrolysis Assn., Md. Assn. Profl. Electrologists. Avocations: writing, travel, collecting Haitian art, antique jewelry. Home: 6232 Blackstone Ave Baltimore MD 21209-3909

YELTON, DIANNE BURGESS, secondary school educator; b. Albuquerque, Nov. 23, 1954; d. Robert Allen and Elizabeth (Donnelly) B.; m. Steven John Yelton, Aug. 13, 1988. BS in Edn., Miami U., 1977, MEd, 1983; degree in Tchr. Leadership, No. Ky. U., 2003. Tchr. Defiance (Ohio) City Schs., 1977-78; jr. high devel. handicapped tchr. Princeton City Schs., Cin., 1978-79, Oak Hills Local Schs., Cin., 1979-82, tchr. primary developmentally handicapped, 1982-88; tchr. Ft. Thomas (Ky.) Ind. Schs., 1988—. Supr. student tchrs. various sch. dists., 1980—; spkr. convs. and inservice workshops, 1979—. Recipient Outstanding Woman of No. Ky., 1998, Golden Apple Achiever award Ashland Oil, 1998, Ky. Post Golden Apple award, 1997, Tchg. Excellence award Jiffy Lube, 1997. Mem. NEA, Internat. Reading Assn., Nat. Coun. Tchrs. English, PTA, Ky. Col. (hon.). Methodist. Avocations: aerobics, spectator sports, dining out. Office: Highlands Mid Sch 2350 Memorial Pkwy Fort Thomas KY 41075-1111 Office Phone: 859-441-5222 15303. E-mail: dbyelton@yahoo.com.

YENCHKO, SUZANNE, research and development company executive; b. Hazleton, Pa., Aug. 5, 1946; d. Joseph and Anna (Mital) Yenchko; m. Edward Jules Weintraub, Aug. 2, 1975 (div. Sept. 1993); stepchildren: Jessica Anne Lawrence, Morris Harry Weintraub. BA in English Lit., Susquehanna U., 1968; MBA, Mt. St. Mary's Coll., 1981. Legis. liaison Pa. Dept. Commerce, Harrisburg, 1969-71; asst. exec. dir. Pa. Assn. Retarded Children, Harrisburg, 1971-73; exec. dir. Pa. Joint Coun. Criminal Justice Sys., Harrisburg, 1973-76; dir. Adams County Office Aging, Gettysburg, Pa., 1976-83; dir. house consumer affairs com. Pa. Ho. of Reps., Harrisburg, 1983-85; dir. environ. resources Pa. Chamber Bus. and Industry, Harrisburg, 1985-95; dir. state govt. rels. AMP Inc., Harrisburg, 1995-99; regional pub. affairs mgr. Internat. Paper, Camp Hill, 1999—2002; v.p. Delta Devel. Group Inc., Mechanicsburg, Pa., 2003—. Mem. steering com. White Ho. Conf. Aging, Harrisburg, 1980—81; com. mem. Capitol Region Econ. Devel. Com., Harrisburg, 1990—97, bd. dirs., 2001—. Bd. dirs. Ctrl. Pa. Youth Ballet, Carlisle, 1994—2000, Theatre Harrisburg, 1995—2001, Whitaker Ctr. Sci. and Arts, 2001—; chair Pa. Commn. Women, Harrisburg, 1995—2001; chair lit. ho. tour West Shore Pub. Libr., Camp Hill, 1998; bd. dirs. Ctrl. Pa. Tech. Coun., chair govt. affairs com.; environ. com. chair Pa. Bus. Roundtable, 1999—2002. Named to Best Women in Bus. in Pa., 1999. Mem.: Soc. Women Environ. Profls., Women Pa. Govt. Rels., N.C. Citizens Bus. and Industry (com. 1996—99), Harrisburg Young Profls., Susquehanna U. Bd. (bd. dirs. 2002—). Republican. Lutheran. Avocations: photography, historic preservation, gardening, skiing, architecture.

YEO, KIM ENG, artist; b. Singapore, Apr. 24, 1947; came to U.S., 1978; d. Cheng Chye and Seok Kim (Chew) Lee; m. Bock Cheng Yeo; children: Beng Lin, Beng Jene. Student, Nanyang Acad. Fine Arts, Singapore, 1963; BSc with honors, U. Singapore, 1968. Watercolor demonstrator Flushing Art League, N.Y.C., 1980-84; art instr. Poppenhusen Inst., N.Y.C., 1984; substitute art tchr. UN Internat. Sch., N.Y.C., 1984-85; freelance paper product designer, 1981-87; textile designer J. Brown Designs, N.Y.C., 1987-91; tchg. artist Flushing (N.Y.) Town Hall, 1995—2002; artist-in-residence Pub. Sch. 214, 165, Francis Lewis H.S., Flushing, 1997-2001. Art cons. Corp. Art Directions, N.Y.C.; visual arts panelist, Flushing Coun., 1985-87, Queen's Coun., 1998-99, 2001-04. One person shows at Alliance Francais, 1975-77, Bhirasri Inst. Modern Art, Bangkok, Thailand, 1975-77, Flushing Coun. on Arts, 1995, 2000, Adirondack Lakes Ctr. for the Arts, N.Y., 2005, Synagogue For Arts Gallery, NY, 2006; exhibited Mallette Gallery, L.I., N.Y., 1998, 99, Artfolio Gallery, Singapore, 2000, Langston Hughes Cmty. Libr. and Cultural Ctr., N.Y., 2004; exhibited in group shows at Womanart Gallery, N.Y.C., 1979-80, Nat. Art League, Douglastown, N.Y., 1979-86, Flushing Coun. on Arts, 1984-88, 96-2004, Postcrypt Art Gallery, N.Y.C., 1997, Singapore Watercolor Soc., 1997-99, 2001-03; represented in corp. and pvt. collections; artist greeting cards UNICEF, 1997-98; featured on QPATV Artists Series, 1993, QPTV Queens Jour., 2000; featured in Watercolor Mag., 1997, Internat. Mag., 2004. Benefit show UN Devel. Fund for Women Singapore, 1999. Mem. Flushing Art League (bd. dirs., treas. 1979-85, award 1986), Flushing Coun. on Arts, Internat. Artists Mag. Buddhist. Avocations: gardening, bookmaking. Home: 16202 77th Ave Flushing NY 11366-1022 Fax: (718) 591-8483. E-mail: artist@kimengyeo.com.

YEO, PATRICIA, chef; Degree in Biochemistry, Princeton U. Line cook Miracle Grill, NYC; sous chef Mesa Grill, NYC, 1991, Bolo, NYC, 1993—95; chef China Moon; opened Hawthorne Lane, Calif.; owner, exec. chef AZ, NYC, 2000—, Pazo, NYC, Sapa, NYC. Author: Cooking from A to Z with Patricia Yeo, 2002. Office: Sapa 43 W 24th St New York NY 10010 Office Phone: 212-929-1800. Office Fax: 212-929-7070.*

YEOMANS, KATIE MORSE, writer; b. Ft. Collins, Colo. d. Charles W. Morse, III and Rea Elaine Morse; m. Robert John Yeomans, Sept. 6, 1996; 1 child, Robert John Jr. BA in English/Journalism cum laude, U. N.H., 1995; MFA in Creative Nonfiction, Goucher Coll., 1999. Boat capt. Coastal Discoveries, Newburyport, Mass., 1995—; assoc. editor Offshore Mag., Boston, 1995—99; sr. editor Nat. Fisherman, Portland, Maine, 1999—2000; freelance author, 2000—. Author: Dead Men Tapping, 2003. Recipient Writing award, Internat. Regional Mags. Assn., 2001, 2002. Mem.: Investigative Reporters and Editors (Writing awards 2001), Boating Writers Internat. (Writing awards 1998, 2000, 2002). Episcopalian. Avocations: boating, fishing, reading, travel, snowboarding. Home: 11 River St Byfield MA 01922-1201

YERG, BEVERLY JOHNSON, physical education educator, researcher; b. Warren, Pa., Nov. 11, 1938; d. C. Walter and Emma Josephine Erickson Johnson; m. Robert Robison Yerg, June 24, 1961; 1 child, David Robert. BS, Temple U., 1960, EdM, 1973; PhD, U. Pitts., 1977. Tchr., coach Manheim Ctrl. Schs., Pa., 1961—64; tchr. Lancaster City Schs., 1960—61; substitute and homebound tchr. Warren Area Schs., 1964—73; lectr. LaRoche Coll., 1973—74; tchg. fellow U. Pitts., 1974—77; asst. prof. Fla. State U., Tallahassee, 1977—82, assoc. prof., 1982—2001, dept. head, 1982—85, dir. acad. support programs student athletes, 1986—93, chair pres.'s com. intercollegiate athletics; ret. Editl. bd., reviewer Jour. Tchg. Physical Edn., Nat. Assn. Athletic Acad. Advisors Jour., reviewer Rsch. Quar. Exercise and Sport, Merrill Pub. Co., Mosby Book Co.; contbr. chapters to books, articles to profl. jours. Bd. dirs. Neighborhood Health Clinic, Tallahassee, 1986—88; bd. mem. North Fla. Fellow Christian Athletes, 1987—90; chair Fla. Cabinet for Campus Ministry, Presbyn. Ch. USA, Fla., 1996—; treas., interim bd. of dirs. Presbyn. Assn. for Collegiate and Higher Edn. Ministries, 2004—06, treas., bd. dirs., 2006—; leadership team Higher Edn. Ministries Presbyn. Ch. USA, Louisville, 2001—; mem., pres., com. chair Presbyn. U. Ctr., 1984—2000; elder Fellowship Presbyn. Ch., 1987—90, Christ Presbyn. Ch, 1994—97; permanent jud. commn. Fla. Presbyn., Panama City, Fla., 2002—05, com. on preparation for ministry, 1991—97; bd. mem. YWCA, Warren, Pa., 1965—67. Recipient Peter W. Everett Honor award, Fla. Assn. for Health, Phys. Edn., Recreation, and Dance, 2002; Rsch. Consortium fellow, Am. Alliance for Health, Phys. Edn., Recreation, and Dance, 1986 to present. Mem.: Am. Ednl. Rsch. Assn., Fla. Assn. for Health, Phys. Edn., Recreation, and Dance, Am. Alliance for Health, Phys. Edn., Recreation, and Dance (life), Delta Psi Kappa (life; pres. 1984—86, bd. dirs.). Presbyterian. Avocations: reading, handwork, gardening, woodworking. Home: 4121 Tralee Rd Tallahassee FL 32309-2822 Personal E-mail: yerg@coe.fsu.edu.

YERKES, SUSAN GAMBLE, newspaper columnist; b. Evanston, Ill., Sept. 5, 1959; d. Charles Anthony Yerkes and Darthea (Campbell) Higgins. BA in Liberal Arts (hon.), U. Austin, 1974; MA in Mass Comms., Wichita State U., 1976. Pub. affairs dir. anchor KAKE-TV, Wichita, Kans., 1977-81; freelance writer pub. rels. YS Comms. Global, 1981-84; metro columnist San Antonio Light, 1986-93; lifestyle columnist S.A. Express News, San Antonio, 1993—. Radio TV host WOAI-AM, San Antonio, 1993—; nat. assn. broadcast editls., Boston, 1978-81. Recipient 1st Place Column Writing Nat. Press Women, 1988, Tex. AP Mng. Editors, 1995, 97, Vivian Castelberry award Assn. for Women in Journalism, 1997, La Presna Hispanic Heroes award. Mem. Internat. Women's Forum, Women in Comm., Pub. Rel. Soc. Am., Rotary, Phi Beta Kappa. Episcopalian. Avocations: dance, horseback riding, travel, reading, computers. Home: 68 Granburg Cir San Antonio TX 78218-3011 Office Phone: 210-250-3455. E-mail: syerkes@express-news.net.

YERMAN, ANNE VERONICA, interior designer; d. Joseph Anthony and Eleanor Gallagher DeLue; m. Robert Neil Yerman, May 21, 1972; children: Brant Matthew Peace, Lesley Elizabeth Hope. Cert. completion, N.Y. Sch. Interior Design, 1966. Student/staff decorator, colorist Raymond Loewy/William Snaith, Inc., N.Y.C., 1965—69; dir. interior decoration Norwood Oliver Design Assocs., N.Y.C., 1970—75, Barnouw Design Assocs., Katonah, NY, 1982—94; prin., owner Anne V. Yerman Interiors, Potomac, Md., 1982—. Spkr. Show House with A Conscience, Washington, 2000. Mem. various coms., fundraiser Capital Children's Mus., Washington, 1982—88; bd. mem., trustee Round House Theatre, 2003—; treas., sec. Potomac Falls Homeowners Assn. Mem.: Potomac Book Club. Democrat. Roman Catholic. Avocations: tennis, reading, theater, art. Home: 9100 Falls Rd Potomac MD 20854

YERXA, JANE ANNE, artist; b. Wichita, Kans., July 3, 1933; d. Laurence Alan and Mary Jane (Nation) Figge; m. Jay Allen Yerxa, June 23, 1956; children: Jeffrey Todd, James Jay, Jonathan Alan. BA in Fine Arts and Comml. Arts, U. Kans., 1955. Fashion artist Wichita (Kans.) Beacon, 1955-56; freelance fashion artist Fall River, Mass., 1956-57; freelance artist agrl. extension dept. Wash. State U., Pullman, 1959; pub. rels. coord. Spokane (Wash.) Symphony, 1972. Docent Expo '76 Gallery, Spokane. Represented in pvt. collections in Kans., Tex., N.Mex., Ariz., Calif., Utah, and Wash. Vol. Spokane Art Sch., 1973-83, Corbin Art Ctr., Spokane, 1989-90. Mem. DAR, Spokane (Wash.) Watercolor Soc., Riverridge Fine Arts Assn. (v.p. 1994-95, pres. 1984, 85, 1st place watercolors 1986, Best of Show award 2002)), Stanek House Art Ctr. (charter mem.), Bible Study Fellowship, Gamma Alpha Chi, Alpha Delta Pi. Avocations: reading, cloth doll making, sewing, watching old movies.

YETT, SALLY PUGH, art educator, consultant; b. St. Louis, Feb. 15, 1935; d. John D. and Esther Ruth Pugh; m. Donald Edward Yett, June 19, 1964; children: Stephen Edward, John Harold. BFA, Washington U., St. Louis, 1956; tchg. credential, Calif. State U., L.A., 1989. Cert. gen. clear multiple subject and art supplementary Calif. Dept. Edn. Recreation therapist ARC, San Antonio, 1956-58; dir. recreation therapy dept. Jewish Hosp., St. Louis, 1958-64; tchr. art-gifted class Juan Cabrillo Elem., Malibu, Calif., 1975-78; educator pre-kindergarten Malibu Meth. Pre-Sch., 1979-81; spl. edn. educator grades 9-12 Santa Monica Sch. Dist., Calif., 1981-89; educator grades 1-6 art L.A. Unified Sch. Dist.-Visual and Performing Arts Magnet, 1990—2006; resource tchr., art edn. advisor Calif. State U., L.A., 2001—04, master tchr. Dominguez Hills, 2003—05. Judge Making History, L.A., 1998—2005; participant UCLA Tchrs. and Scholars Symposium, 1999—2003, 2005; state judge History Day in Calif., 2003; mem. art start curriculum com. Mus. Contemporary Art, 2005. Exhibitions include Malibu Art Festival, 1976 (3rd place award), Malibu Art Assn. Show, 1984 (3rd place award), Roberts Art Gallery, 1989, CAEA State Conv.-Calif. State Bakersfield Exhibit, 2001; contbr. articles to profl. jours. PTA pres. Juan Cabrillo Elem., Malibu, 1976—78, Malibu Park Jr. HS; pres. Santa Monica Jr. Programs, 1979—81; 2d, 3d, and 4th v.p. Santa Monica/Malibu PTA Coun., 1982—85; pres. Malibu Art Assn., 1992—93. Nominee Tchr. of Yr., Walt Disney Co.; recipient Honoree Bravo award, L.A. Music Ctr.; grantee, Calif. Cmty. Found., 2003. Mem.: Internat. Studies Overseas Program, Gene Autrey Mus., Calif. Art Edn. Assn., Soc. Calligraphy (pub. rels. 1987—91, bd. dirs.), Nat. Art Edn. Assn., Art Mus. Long Beach, Shakespeare Festival/L.A., S.W. Mus., UCLA Fowler Mus. Cultural History, L.A. County Art Mus., Mus. Contemporary Art (mem. curriculum com. 2005), Craft and Folk Mus., Mus. L.Am. Art, People to People Internat. (Indigenous Art del. to New Zealand, Australia 1998), Metro. Mus. Art, Kappa Alpha Theta. Avocations: travel, reading, calligraphy, hiking, gardening. Home: 2042 Hanscom Dr South Pasadena CA 91030-4012

YGLESIAS, HELEN BASSINE, author, educator; b. N.Y.C., Mar. 29, 1915; d. Solomon and Kate (Goldstein) Bassine; m. Bernard Cole, 1938 (div. 1950); children: Tamar Cole, Lewis Cole; m. Jose Yglesias, Aug. 19, 1950 (div. 1992); 1 child, Rafael. Student pub. schs.; LHD (hon.), U. Maine, 1996. Literary editor Nation Mag., 1965-70; adj. assoc. prof. writing Columbia Sch. Arts, N.Y.C., 1973—. Vis. prof. creative writing Writers Workshop, U. Iowa, Iowa City, 1980. Author: (novels) How She Died (Houghton Mifflin award), 1972, Family Feeling, 1976, Sweetsir, 1981, The Saviors, 1987, The Girls, 1999, (non-fiction) Starting: Early, Anew, Over and Late, 1978, Isabel Bishop, 1989. Home: Apt 1303 1261 5th Ave New York NY 10029-3866

YIH, ANN, writer, journalist; d. Roy Y. and Madeline Wu Yih. BA, Duke U., 1985; MS, Columbia U. Grad. Sch. of Journalism, 1987. Pub. rels. coord. Foote, Cone & Belding Advt., NYC, 1985—86; prodr./writer WCVB-TV, Boston, 1987—90; prodr. WCBS-TV, NYC, 1990—96; sr. prodr. CBS News Off Tenth, NYC, 1996—97; sr. broadcast prodr. CBS News Saturday Early Show, NYC, 1997—2002. Recipient Emmy award: Outstanding Single Newscast, NY Emmy Awards, 1994—95. Office Phone: 845-638-2898. Personal E-mail: annyih@aol.com.

YIH, MAE DUNN, state legislator; b. Shanghai, May 24, 1928; d. Chung Woo and Fung Wen (Feng) Dunn; m. Stephen W.H. Yih, 1953; children: Donald, Daniel. BA, Barnard Coll., 1951; postgrad., Columbia U., 1951-52. Asst. to bursar Barnard Coll., N.Y.C., 1952-54; mem. Oreg. Ho. Reps. from 36th dist., 1977-83, Oreg. Senate from 19th dist., 1983—. Mem. Clover Ridge Elem. Sch. Bd., Albany, Oreg., 1969-78, Albany Union H.S. Bd., 1975-79; mem. Joint Legis. Ways and Means Com., Senate Transp. Com., 1999, Senate pres. pro-temore, 1993. Episcopalian. Home: 34465 Yih Ln NE Albany OR 97322-9557 Office: Oreg Senate S 307 State Capitol Salem OR 97310-0001

YIN, BEATRICE WEI-TZE, medical researcher; b. Taipei, Taiwan, Mar. 9, 1959; came to U.S., 1970; d. Chuan Keun and Ming Hsien (Huang) Y. BS, CUNY, Flushing, 1982, MS, 1988. Rsch. asst. Meml. Sloan-Kettering Cancer Ctr., N.Y.C., 1982—. Inventor Monoclonal antibodies to human gastrointestinal cancers, 1992. Avocations: readings, travel, gardening. Office: Meml Sloan Kettering Cancer Ctr 1275 York Ave New York NY 10021-6094

YING, JACKIE, chemical engineer, educator; BE, The Cooper Union, 1987; MA, Princeton U., 1988, PhD, 1991. Prof. MIT, Cambridge, 1992—2005. Exec. dir. Inst. Bioengring. and Nanotech., Singapore, 2003—; mem. world economic forum Young Global Leaders, 2004. Mem. editl. bd. Jour. Metastable and Nanostructured Materials, Nanoparticle Sci. and Tech., Jour. Electroceramics, Jour. Porous Materials, Materials Today, Molecular and Supramolecular Sci., Jour. Exptl. Nanosciences, Jour. Nanomaterials, Materials for Tissue Engring. and Regenerative Medicine, Can. Jour. of Chem. Engring. Recipient Camille Dreyfus Tchr.-Scholar award, 1996, Exxon Solid-State Chemistry Fellowship award Am. Chem. Soc., 1997, Colburn award AIChE, 2000, TR100 Innovator award, 2000; David and Lucile Packard fellow, 1995. Mem.: German Acad. Natural Scientists. Office Phone: 65 6824 7100. Business E-Mail: jyying@ibn.a-star.edu.sg.

YINGER, EMILY M., lawyer; b. Bethesda, Md, Apr. 28, 1963; BA, U. Va., 1984; JD, UCLA, 1987. Bar: Md. 1987, D.C. 1988, U.S. Dist. Ct., D.C. 1989, bar: Va. 1999, U.S. Dist. Ct., Dist. Md. 1999, U.S. Dist. Ct., Ea. & We. Dist. Va. 1999, U.S. Ct. Appeals, D.C. Cir. 1999, U.S. Ct. Appeals, fourth cir. 1999. Joined Hogan & Hartson LLP, 1987, ptnr.-in-charge, Va. office, dir. litig. practice group. Mem.: Counsellors, Barristers, Fairfax County C. of C., Va. State Bar Assn. (gen. counsel, bd. dir.), Md. State Bar Assn., Va. State Bar, D.C. Bar. Office: Hogan & Hartson LLP 8300 Greensboro Dr Ste 1100 Mc Lean VA 22102 Office Phone: 703-610-6161. Office Fax: 703-610-6200. Business E-Mail: emyinger@hhlaw.com.

YINGLING, PHYLLIS STUCKEY, writer; b. Martinsburg, W.Va., May 22, 1931; d. Carlton Bennett and Virginia DeHaven Stuckey; m. Lewis Carroll Yingling, Jr., June 26, 1954; children: Deborah Beth, Lewis Carroll III. BA in Edn., Shepherd Coll. (now Shepherd U.), Shepherdstown, W.Va., 1952; MEd in Edn. of Deaf, Western Md. Coll., Westminster, 1979. Cert. tchr. of deaf State of Md., 1979. Tchr. of the deaf and hard of hearing Prince George's County Pub. Schools, Oxen Hill, Md., 1971—73, Balt. City Pub. Schs., 1973—86, Parkville, Md., 1986—92; ret., 1992. Author: (children's book) My Best Friend, Elena Pappas, 1986, My Best Friend, Tony Santos, 1988; co-author: (children's book for dyslexic learners) Adventures of Dan and Sam, 1997, The Fantastic Fan and 7 More Fantastic Stories, 1999, Dan and Sam and the RV Trip, 2000; contbr. articles and stories to mags. (Best Story Award, 1984). Docent Md. Hist. Soc. Mus.; pres. Women's Internat. League for Peace and Freedom, U.S. Sect., Phila., 1999—2002; co-chair Women's Internat. League for Peace and Freedom, Catonsville, Md., 1995—99. Mem.: United Meth. Women. United Methodist. Avocations: watercolor and oil painting, travel, hiking, poetry.

YIOTIS, GAYLE, archivist, researcher, anthropologist, writer; d. Pedro and Margarette Rionda; m. Christos Fotios Yiotis; children: Fotios Christos, Peter Wesley. MA, George Washington U., Washington, 1992. Mus. specialist anthropology Smithsonian Instn., Washington, 1995—2003, archivist Nat. Mus. of Am. Indian, 2003—. Student career alumni network Marquette U., Milw., 2000—; presenter in field. Contbr. articles to profl. jours. Mem.: Acad. Certified Archivists, Soc. of Am. Archivists. Avocations: historical research, writing, martial arts, collecting.

YIP, BETTINA W., lawyer; b. 1974; BA magna cum laude, Wellesley Coll., 1996; JD, Columbia Univ., 1999. Assoc., litig. Meadows, Ichter & Bowers; assoc., labor, employment law King & Spalding; corp. counsel, labor & human resources Cingular Wireless, Atlanta, 2003—. Mem. Ga. Supreme Ct. Commn. on Professionalism. Notes editor Jour. of Asian Law, Columbia. Founder People's Law Sch. for Asian Cmty., 2000; served on Ga. Commn. Asian Am. Affairs, 2002; bd. dir. Anti-Prejudice Consortium, 2001—02; graduate Diversity Leadership Acad., 2003; exec. bd. Ga. Lawyers for the Arts. Named a Harlan Fiske Stone Scholar; recipient Florence N. Shientag award, NY Women's Bar Assn. Fellow: Lawyers Found. Ga.; mem.: ABA, Ga. Assn. Women Lawyers, Multi-Bar Leadership Coun. (chair 2002—03), Atlanta Bar Assn., State Bar Ga. (bd. gov.), Nat. Asian Pacific Am. Bar Assn. (past southeast regional gov., named one of Best Lawyers Under 40 2004), Ga. Asian Pacific Am. Bar Assn. (pres. 2000—01, v.p. 2002). Office: Cingular Wireless Legal Dept Glenridge Highlands Two 5565 Glenridge Connector Atlanta GA 30342 Office Phone: 404-236-6265. Office Fax: 678-406-8122. Business E-Mail: bettina.yip@cingular.com.

YITTS, ROSE MARIE, nursery school executive; b. Bridgeport, Conn., Apr. 29, 1942; m. Richard Francis Yitts, Dec. 28, 1963; children: Anthony Michael, Jennifer Lisa, Heather Michelle. BS, So. Conn. State Coll., 1963; MS, So. Conn. State U., 1983. Tchr. Trumbull Bd. Edn., Conn., 1963-69; substitute tchr. Seymour and Oxford Bd. Edn., Conn., 1970-79; tchr. aide spl. edn. Oxford Bd. Edn., 1979-82; dir., founding ptnr., pres. and treas. Strawberry Tyme Nursery Sch. and Day Care Ctr. Ltd., Seymour, 1983—. Den leader, com. chmn. Boy Scouts Am., Seymour, 1973-77; troop leader Girl Scouts U.S., Seymour, 1978-80; chair fundraisers, coach George J. Hummel Little League, Seymour, 1982-86, 1st woman pres., 1987-88, player agt., 1990; tchr., spl. edn. curriculum developer Ch. of Good Shepherd, mem. parish coun., 1984-86; elected mem., corr. sec. Seymour Libr., bd. dirs., 1983-89; elected mem. Republican Town Com., 1996-, mem. exec. bd., 2000, GOP 5 State, 1998—2002; elected mem. Seymour Bd. Edn., 1999—, corr. sec., 2003-, chair curriculum com., 2003-, chair policy com., 2003-; bd. dirs. Seymour Hist. Soc., 2003-06. Recipient award of merit, honorable mention, Golden Poet award, World of Poetry, 1987, Editor's Choice award, Nat. Libr. Poetry, 1994, 1995, Joseph Gido award, Seymour Rep. Town. Com., 2001. Mem. Nat. Assn. for Edn. of Young Children, Oxford Bus. Assn. (membership com. 1993-95). Republican. Personal E-mail: michmax2@aol.com.

YMOORE, PAMELA GAY, music educator; b. Eugene, Oreg., Dec. 31, 1945; d. John Robert and Alta Rachel Wetzel; m. Glen Eugene Moore; children: Sean Eugene Moore, Connemara Heather Pursley. BA in Music, Seattle Pacific U., 1968; MA in Edn., U. Wash., Seattle, 1971. Cert. tchr. Wash., Yamaha Music Sch., Wash. Profl. musician, entertainer, Port Angeles and Seattle, Wash.; tchr.'s asst. Sharples Jr. HS, Seattle, 1971—72; preschool music tchr. Yamaha Music Sch., Seattle and Port Angeles, 1972—82; tchr. parent presch. coop. Peninsula Coll., Port Angeles, 1975—76; pvt. piano tchr.

Seattle and Port Angeles, 1973—85; elem. gen. music tchr. Port Angeles Pub. Schs., 1977—85, mid. sch. choral tchr. gen. music, 1985—97, k-5 elem. gen. music tchr., 1997—. Music entertainer, Oregon, Washington, Idaho, 1979—; choral dir. Holy Trinity Luth. Ch., Port Angeles, 1980—81; coord., dir. mid. sch. mass choir North Olympic Music Educators, Wash., 1986—88; music dir. musicals Port Angeles Cmty. Players, 1985—; site team mem. Franklin Elem. Sch., Port Angeles, 2003—. Composer scripts, musical arrangements, musicals for children, adult scripts, arrangements, songs; developer: curriculum in group music education, music composition. Women's retreat music dir. Holy Trinity Luth., Sequim Cmty. Ch., Port Angeles and Sequim, Wash., 1987—2006; mem. contemporary svc. worship team Sequim Cmty. Ch., 2002—06. Grantee, Port Angeles Pub. Schools, 1996; scholar, Seattle Pacific U., 1964. Mem.: Delta Kappa Gamma. Democrat. Avocations: painting, music synthesizers, reading, travel, sports. Office: Franklin Elem Sch 2505 S Washington St Port Angeles WA 98362

YNTEMA, MARY KATHERINE, retired mathematics educator; b. Urbana, Ill., Jan. 20, 1928; d. Leonard Francis and M. Jean (Busey) Y. BA in Math., Swarthmore Coll., 1950; MA in Math., U. Ill., 1961, PhD in Math., 1965. Tchr., secondary math. Am. Coll. for Girls, Istanbul, Turkey, 1950-54, Columbus (Ohio) Sch. for Girls, 1954-57; computer programmer MIT Lincoln Lab., Lexington, Mass., 1957-58; tchr., secondary math Roundup (Mont.) High Sch., 1959-60; asst. prof. math U. Ill., Chgo., 1965-67; asst. prof. computer sci. Pa. State U., University Park, 1967-71; assoc. prof. to prof. math. Sangamon State U. (now U. Ill. at Springfield), Springfield, Ill., 1971-91; ret., 1991. Avocation: enjoyment of nature.

YOCHEM, BARBARA JUNE (RUNYAN), sales executive, lecturer; b. Knox, Ind., Aug. 22, 1945; d. Harley Albert and Rosie (King) Runyan; m. Donald A. Yochem (div. 1979); 1 child, Morgan Lee; m. Don Heard, Dec. 12, 1987 (div. 1998). Grad. high school, Knox, Ind., 1963. Sales rep. Hunter Woodworks, Carson, Calif., 1979-84, sales mgr., 1984-87; sales rep. Comml. Lumber and Pallet, Industry, Calif., 1987-92; mgr. Desert Shadows Apts., Herperia, Calif., 1998—, Hesperia, Calif., 1998; real estate agt. Marina Properties, Victorville, Spring Valley Lake, 2000—01, Coldwell Banker Home Real Estate, 2001—. Owner By By Prodns., Glendora, Calif., 1976—. Author: Barbara Yochem's Inner Shooting; contbr. articles to profl. jours. Head coach NRA Jr. Olympic Shooting Camp, 1989-94, Recipient U.S. Bronze medal U.S. Olympic Com., 1976, World Bronze medal U.S. Olympic Com., 1980, Pres.'s Elite award, Coldwell Banker Internat., 2006, named Top One Percent, 2006; inductee Calif. Trapshooting Hall of Fame, 1998. Avocation: reading. Address: 9936 SVL Box Victorville CA 92395 Office Phone: 760-245-2227. E-mail: byochem@hotmail.com.

YOCK, NORMA IRIS, counselor, music educator; b. Pekin, Ill., Apr. 18, 1920; d. John Battista and Pauline (Gianessi) Lami; m. John Matthew Yock, June 1, 1946 (dec. July 1957); 1 child, Julie Ann. B. in Music Edn., Ill. Wesleyan U., 1941; M.A., Bradley U., Peoria, Ill., 1961; specialist cert. Ill. State U., 1961, 63; U. Louisville, 1965, U. Ill., 1975. Cert. sch. counselor. Supr. music, art High Sch., Venice, Ill., 1941-45; dir. vocal music Edison Jr. High Sch., Pekin, 1952-58; supr. music Pekin Pub. Schs., 1958-62; counselor Pekin Community High Sch., 1962-84; sales rep. Sutton Travel Services, 1984-90, ret. 1990. Pres., Pekin Jr. Women's Club, 1948-50; Pekin Civic Chorus, 1959—; bd. dirs. YWCA, Am. Cancer Soc., 1983—, Channel 47, Peoria, Ill., 1983—; pres. United Way, 1988—; mem. Dirksen Ctr. Guild, YWCA Adv. Panel, Cen. Ill. Wesleyan U. Bd. Cited for Outstanding Contbn. to Sch. and Community, Pekin Community High Sch. Bd. of Edn., 1984; chmn. United Way, 1985, pres. Pekin Civic Chours, 1953-2003. Recipient Outstanding Achievement award YWCA, 1982. Mem. Altrusa Internat., NEA, Ill. Edn. Assn., Tri-County Guidance, Federated Bus. and Profl. Women's Club (pres. 1970-75), Delta Kappa Gamma (pres. 1961-64), Sigma Alpha Iota (pres. 1940-44). Republican. Roman Catholic. Avocations: music; reading; travel. Home: 1314 State St Pekin IL 61554-3676

YODER, ANNA A., retired elementary school educator; b. Beach City, Ohio, Sept. 5, 1934; d. Abram J. and Barbara D. (Miller) Y. BS, Ea. Mennonite Coll., 1966; MEd, Frostburg State Coll., 1974. Cert. elem. tchr., Ohio, recreational leader. Tchr. Garrett County Schs., Oakland, Md., 1966-70, prin. elem. sch., 1970-74; tchr. E. Holmes Local Schs., Berlin, Ohio, 1974-98, ret., 1998. Chairperson edn. com. German Culture Mus., Berlin, Ohio, 1987-90; cons. bilingual edn. E. Holmes Local Schs., Berlin, Ohio, 1982-98, ret., 1998. Supporting mem. German Culture Mus., Berlin, Ohio, 1983—; mem. Killbuck (Ohio) Valley mus., 1988—, Holmes County Hist. Soc., Millersburg, Ohio, 1989—; life mem. Mennonite Info. Ctr., Berlin, Ohio, 1985—; sustaining mem. The Wilderness Ctr., Wilmot, Ohio, 1974—. Jennings scholar Martha Holden Jennings Found., 1983-84; Silver Poet award World of Poetry, 1986. Mem. AAUW (v.p. Holmes County chpt. 1994), Creative Arts Soc. (sec.-treas. 1987-89), Delta Kappa Gamma (sec. Beta Iota chpt. 1987-90, pres. 1990-92, pres. 1998-2000, chpt. v.p. 2002-04). Mennonite. Avocations: nature studies-birds and flowers, handcrafts. Home: 5229 State Route 39 Millersburg OH 44654-8408

YODER, MARY JANE WARWICK, psychotherapist; b. Corryton, Tenn., Nov. 20, 1933; d. Harry Alonzo and Mary Luzelle (Furches) Warwick; m. Edwin Milton Yoder, Jr., Nov. 1, 1958; children: Anne Daphne, Edwin Warwick. BA, U. N.C., Chapel Hill, 1956; MFA, U. N.C., Greensboro, 1969; MSW, Va. Commonwealth U., 1987; cert. individual psychotherapy, Smith Coll., 1991. Lic. ind. clin. social worker, D.C.; lic. clin. social worker, Va. Editorial asst. Harper & Bros., N.Y.C., 1956-57; flight attendant Pan Am. Airlines, N.Y.C., 1957-59; adj. faculty mem. in ballet Guilford Coll., Greensboro, 1961-64; ballet tchr., adminstr. Jane Yoder Sch. of Ballet, Greensboro, 1964-75; homilitics listener Va. Theol. Sem., Alexandria, 1978-80; social worker, dance therapist Woodbine Nursing Ctr., Alexandria, 1983-87; staff psychotherapist D.C. Inst. Mental Health, 1987-92; pvt. practice Capitol Hill Ctr. Individual and Family Therapy, 1992—. Ballet and book critic Greensboro Daily News, 1961-75. Dancer, choreographer Greensboro Civic Ballet, 1961-75. Mem. Nat. Assn. Social Workers, Greater Washington Soc. for Clin. Social Work, Inc., Washington Sch. Psychiatry, Washington Soc. for Jungian Psychology, Jungian Venture, Army-Navy Country Club, Phi Beta Kappa. Episcopalian. Avocations: ballet, modern dance, horseback riding, swimming, reading. Office: Capitol Hill Ctr Individual and Family Therapy 530 7th St SE Washington DC 20003-2768 Office Phone: 703-751-7836. Personal E-mail: janeyoder@att.net.

YODER, NANCI SUE, retired psychologist; b. Montpelier, Vt., June 2, 1936; d. Dayton Theodore and Dorothy Antoinette Badgley Yoder; m. Jim McKee Sears, Jan. 1, 1993; children: Olon Belcher, Shira Belcher. BA, Goddard Coll., Plainfield, Vt., 1959; MA, Putney Grad. Sch., Vt., 1963; PhD, Calif. Inst. Integral Studies, San Francisco, 1982. Registered Psychol. Assn. Calif., cert. hypnotherapist Am. Coun. Hypnotist Examiners. Rschr. in suicide San Francisco Gen. Hosp., 1969—71; predotoral intern Integral Counseling Ctr., San Francisco, 1978—79; child psychotherapist St. George Homes, Inc., Berkeley, Calif., 1982—83; hypnotherapist Wambach Rsch. and Therapy Assn., Berkeley, 1983—85; postdoctoral intern Profl. Comty. Svcs., El Cajon, Calif., 1985—86; psychotherapist Family Svc. Assn., San Jacinto, Calif., 1986—88, Hemet Counseling Ctr., Calif., 1988—93; ret. Contbr. short stories to popular publs. Bd. dirs. Com. for Nonviolent Action, Phila., 1963—78, Valley Restart Shelter, Hemet, 1988—93; stand-in Women in Black, Ft. Bragg, Calif., 1995—; mem. staff highlander Folk Sch., New Market, Tenn., 1962. Named to Wall of Tolerance, Nat. Campaign for Tolerance, 2005; recipient 1st prize art show, Goddard Coll., 1955. Mem.: ACLU, Women's Internat. League for Peace and Freedom, Am. Acad. Hypnoanalysts, Play Writer's Group. Society Of Friends. Avocations: sculpting, drawing, hiking, swimming.

YODER, PATRICIA DOHERTY, public relations executive; b. Pitts., Oct. 30, 1939; d. John Addison and Camella Grace (Conti) Doherty; children: Shari Lynn, Wendy Ann; m. James Ronald Wolfe, Oct. 30, 1999. BA, Duquesne U., 1961. Press sec. U.S. Ho. of Reps., 1965-69; dir. Office of Pub. Info., City of Ft. Wayne, 1973-76; asst. mgr. pub. and corp. comm. Mellon Bank N.A., Pitts., 1977-79; v.p. pub. affairs Am. Waterways Operators Inc., Washington, 1980-83, sr. v.p., gen. mgr., 1983-86, exec. v.p., dir. banking, 1989-91; exec. v.p., dir. internat. banking Hill and Knowlton Inc., Pitts.; sr. v.p. corp. and pub. affairs PNC Fin. Svcs. Group, Pitts., 1987-89; v.p., corp. pub. rels. and advt. GE Capital Svcs. Corp., Stamford, Conn., 1991-95; corp. v.p. pub. affairs and comm. GTE Corp., Stamford, 1995-96; sr. v.p. corp. comm. Avis Group Holdings, Garden City, NY, 1996-99; prin. PDY Assocs., 1999—. Trustee, exec. com. Duquesne U., Shadyside Hosp., Pressley Ridge Sch., Pitts., Ellis Sch.; bd. dirs. Children's Mus., Civic Light Opera, Pitts. Ballet Theatre, Jr. League of City of N.Y. Recipient Outstanding Woman Bus. and Industry, 1988, Disting. Alumni award Duquesne U., 1996. Mem. Pitts. Field Club, Duquesne Club, Indian Harbor Yacht Club, Boca Raton (Fla.) Resort and Country Club, Fox Hill Golf and Country Club. Roman Catholic. Home and Office: 500 SE 5th Ave Apt 601 Boca Raton FL 33432-5510 Address: 23 Wireless Way Southampton NY 10028 Personal E-mail: pdyoder@att.net.

YODER, SHARON KATHLEEN, educator; b. Wooster, Ohio, Sept. 16, 1942; d. John Thompson and Margaret Evelyn (Flanagan) Yoder; m. Theodore Cooley Burrowes, Aug. 7, 1965 (div. Apr. 1988); children: David, Bethanne, Scott, Bonnie; m. David G. Moursund, Oct. 19, 1989. BA, Coll Wooster, 1964; MAT, Oberlin Coll., 1965; PhD, U. Akron, 1983. Maths. tchr. Battle Creek (Mich.) Pub. Schs., 1965-66; Maths., Computer Sci., tchr., computer coord. Wooster City Schs., 1976-87; edn. specialist Logo Computer Systems Inc., N.Y., 1987-88; prof. computer edn. U. Oreg., Eugene, 1988—2002, ret., 2002. Cons. Ednl. Computers Consortium Ohio, 1985-86. Author: Introduction to Logo Programming Using LogoWriter, 1988, Introduction to Hyper Talk Programming, 1991, Introduction to Claris Works, 1994; editor Logo Exch., 1988—. Presbyterian. Avocations: reading, swimming, sewing, handwork, cats. Business E-Mail: skyoder@uoregon.edu.

YODER-GAGNON, PAMALA S., retired orthopedic nurse; b. Portage, Mich., Aug. 7, 1952; d. Jacob L. and Florence M. (Van Dommelen) Yoder; m. Georges Gagnon, July 3, 1982; children: Brianna Kay Marie, Garrett Patrick Antoine, Cameron Michael André. AAS, Kalamazoo Valley C.C., 1974, AAS in Nursing, 1975; BSN magna cum laude, Nazareth Coll., 1991. Staff nurse Borgess Med. Ctr., Kalamazoo, 1976-77, dept. dir. orthopedic/trauma unit, 1977-97, dept. dir. renal transplant, med. surgery unit, 1992-94, dir. and program coord. orthopedics, 1997-98, compiler HCFA orthopedic demonstration project, 1997-98; ret., 1998. Mem. Nat. Assn. Orthopedic Nurses (v.p. local chpt. 1986-89, pres.-elect 1990-91, pres. 1991-92). Home: 8362 Morning Dove Ln Kalamazoo MI 49009-0806

YODER-WISE, PATRICIA SNYDER, nursing educator; d. Belford Grant and Leona Cora (Mohler) Snyder; m. Robert Thomas Wise, Feb. 17, 1973; children: Doreen Ellen Wise, Deborah Ann Wise. BSN, Ohio State U., 1963; MSN, Wayne State U., 1968; EdD, Tex. Tech. U., 1984. RN Tex., CNAA. Interim assoc. dean practice program Tex. Tech. U. Health Sci. Ctr. Sch. Nursing, Lubbock, 1979—, interim dean, prof., 1991-93, dean, prof., 1993-2000; clin. prof. U. Tex. Health Sci. Ctr., San Antonio, 1993—2000; prof. Tex. Woman's U., 2004—. Mem. rev. panel Nursing Outlook, 1993—; mem. adv. com. GlaxoWellcome, 1996—2000; mem. Nat. Quality Forum Health Profls. Provide and Health Plans Panel, 2001—06. Author, editor: Leading and Managing in Nursing, 1994 (Book of Yr. award, 1996, 2003), 1998, 2002; co-author: Beyond Leading and Managing, 2006; peer reviewer Jour. Profl. Nursing, 1984—2003, mem. editl. bd. Jour. Continuing Edn. Nursing, 1978—; editor: Jour. Continuing Edn. Nursing, 1988—. Mem. Leadership Am., 1999—2000; participant Leadership Tex.-Found. Women's Resources, 1997—98; mem. Leadership Tex., 1998—99. Recipient Women of Excellence in Medicine, YWCA, Lubbock, 1996, Woman of Excellence in Medicine, 1996, Nurse of Yr. Fellow: Am. Acad. Nursing (chair Inst. for Nursing Leadership 1999—2002, mem. planning com. 2004); mem.: ANCC (pres. 2005—), ANA (del. 1995—2000, chair constituent assembly 1998—2000, sec. 2000—02, 1st v.p. 2002—05), Wise Group (pres.), Tex. Nurses Assn. (pres. 1995—99). Home: 7309 93d St Lubbock TX 79424 Office Phone: 806-866-9403. Personal E-mail: psywrn@aol.com.

YOFFA, ELLEN J., information technology executive; BS, PhD, MIT. Tech. asst. to dir. IBM Rsch. Divsn.; with IBM Microelectronics Divsn.; dir., emerging sys. technologies IBM T.J. Watson Rsch. Ctr., Hawthorne, NY, dir., next generation web. Gen. chair IEEE/Assn. Computing Machinery Design Automation Conf., 1997. Mem. external adv. bd. U. So. Calif. Electrical Engring. Dept., U. Mass Electrical and Computer Engring. Dept. Recipient Marie R. Pistilli Women in Electronic Design Automation award, Design Automation Conf., 2006. Fellow: IEEE (pres., circuits and systems soc. 2006—, mem. exec. com. and bd. gov., circuits and systems soc., editl. adv. bd., Spectrum mag.); mem.: Assn. for Computing Machinery, Sigma Xi, Phi Beta Kappa. Office: IBM TJ Watson Rsch Ctr Room 3N-C26 19 Skyline Dr Hawthorne NY 10532 Office Phone: 914-784-5222. Office Fax: 914-784-6324. Business E-Mail: yoffa@us.ibm.com.*

YOGEV, SARA, psychologist; b. Tel Aviv, May 23, 1946; came to U.S., 1975; d. Israel and Cila (Fink) Frankel; m. Ram Yogev, Oct. 2, 1967; children: Eldad, Shelly, Tomer. BA, Hebrew U., 1969, MA, 1973; PhD, Northwestern U., Evanston, Ill., 1979. Cert. clin. psychologist, Ill. Clin. experience dist. sch. psychologist Office Edn. and Culture, Jerusalem, 1968-71; intern. Beer Yaakov Psychiatric Hosp., Israel, 1971-72; asst. dir. Dept. Psychology, Hebrew U., Jerusalem, 1972-73; psychotherapist Mental Health Ctr., Hebrew U., Jerusalem; clin. psychologist Inst. Psychoanalysis, Jerusalem, 1973-75; psychotherapist, supr. Youth and Family Services, Ill., 1977-80; pvt. practice Skokie and Chgo., 1981—. Academic experience instr. counseling psychology, 1977-79, asst. prof., Northwestern U., 1979-82, research psychologist at the rank asst. prof., 1983-86, visiting scholar, Ctr. Urban Affairs and Policy Research, 1987. Author: For Better or Worse But Not for Lunch: Making Your Marriage Work in Retirement, 2001; contbr. articles to profl. jours., chpts. to books Mem. American Assn. for Marriage and Family Therapy, American Psyhological Assn., Nat. Register Health Service. Jewish. Office: # 32 5225 Old Orchard Rd Skokie IL 60077-1027 also: 500 1 East Superior St Chicago IL 60611 Office Phone: 847-470-1925. Business E-Mail: sarayogev@yahoo.com.

YOHE, LAURA KATHRYN, secondary school educator; b. Harrisburg, Pa., Mar. 7, 1979; d. T. Richard Yohe and Alanna Kathryn Berger. BS Computer Sci. magna cum laude, Millesville U., Pa., 2002; BSE Math., Millesville U.; 2002; postgrad. studies, Wilkes U., Wilkes-Barre, Pa., 2005—. Cert. Level 1 tchr. Pa. Tchr. Rose Tree Media Sch. Dist., Media, Pa., 2002—03, Conestoga Valley Sch. Dist., Lancaster, Pa., 2003—. Lab. asst., web designer Gov.'s Inst. for Math. Educators at Millesville U., Pa., 2000—; co-author and presenter of papers Sci. educators confs. and meetings, Pa., 2001—. Recipient Boyer award, Millesville U., 2001. Mem.: NEA, Pa. Edn. Assn. Democrat. Avocations: Celtic fiddler, travel. Office: Conestega Valley Sch Dist 2110 Horseshoe Rd Lancaster PA 17603 Office Phone: 717-397-5231 ext 2129. Personal E-mail: leorah3779@yahoo.com.

YOHE, ROBIN M., music educator; b. Richmond, Va., June 7, 1963; d. B. Franklin and Lorena L. Moore; m. David E. Yohe; children: Buffy, Chubby, Bailey. BS, Va. Commonwealth U., Richmond, 1986; studied, U. Va., Charlottesville, 2004—. Choral dir. Manchester HS, Richmond, Va., 1986—94; choral dir., chair fine art dept. James River HS, Midlothian, Va., 1994—98, Lee-Davis HS, Mechanicsville, Va., 1998—. Mem.: ACDA, Music Educators Nat. Conf. Office: Lee-Davis HS 7052 Mechanicsville Tpke Mechanicsville VA 23111

YOKLEY, KAREL, athletic trainer, educator; b. Phoenix, May 29, 1977; d. James Frederick and Sharon Elizabeth Drechsler; m. Kevin Shane Yokley, June 24, 2004. BS, No. Ariz. U., Flagstaff, 2000. Cert. tchr. Va., athletic trainer, tchr. Ariz. Athletic trainer Cactus Shadows HS, Cave Creek, Ariz., 2000—04, tchr., 2001—04, Bentsville Dist. HS, Nokesville, Va., 2004—05; athletic trainer Physiotherapy Assocs., Phoenix, 2005—06.

YOLANGO, MARLENE FANNING, special education educator; b. West Islip, NY, Aug. 5, 1975; d. James Jeffrey and Carol Cardarelli Fanning; m. Frank Yolango, July 16, 2005. BS in Edn. summa cum laude, SUNY, Geneseo, 1997; MS in Literary Studies, Hofstra U., Hempstead, N.Y., 2002. Cert. reading, spl. edn., elem. tchr. N.Y., biology tchr. Elem. tchr. Taylor Ave. Sch., Centerport, NY, 1997—98; tchr. spl. edn. N. Shore H.S., Glen Head, NY, 1998—99, Bellerose Ave. Sch., E. Northport, NY, 1999—. Coach Spl. Olympics; mem. N. Shore Pops Concert Band, 2006—. Mem.: Internat. Reading Assn. Avocations: music, hiking, travel. E-mail: mcfanning@optonline.net.

YOLEN, JANE, writer; b. NYC, Feb. 11, 1939; d. Will Hyatt and Isabelle (Berlin) Y.; m. David Wilber Stemple, Sept. 2, 1962; children: Heidi Elisabet, Adam Douglas, Jason Frederic. BA, Smith Coll., 1960; EdM, U. Mass., 1978, LLD (hon.), 2006, Coll. Our Lady of Elms, 1980, Smith Coll., Baypath Coll., Keene State Coll. Asst. editor This Week mag., 1960; mem. staff Saturday Rev., 1960; asst. editor Gold Medal Books, 1961, Rutledge Press, 1961—63; asst. juvenile editor A.A. Knopf, Inc., 1963—65; freelance writer, 1965—; lectr. dept. edn. Smith Coll., 1979—84; editor Jane Yolen books, imprint Harcourt Brace Jovanovich, 1988—97. Tchr. writers confs. Centrum, Cape Cod Writers Conf., Soc. Children's Book Writers, U. Mass.; mem. Mass. Coun. on Arts, 1974. Author: Pirates in Petticoats, 1963, The Witch Who Wasn't, 1964, The Emperor and the Kite, 1968, Writing Books for Children, 1973, The Girl Who Cried Flowers, 1974, The Hundredth Dove, 1978, The Dream Weaver, 1979, Commander Toad in Space, 1980, The Gift of Sarah Barker, 1981, Touch Magic, 1981, Dragon's Blood, 1982, Tales of Wonder, 1983, Heart's Blood, 1984, Cards of Grief, 1984, Dragonfield, 1985, Merlin's Booke, 1986, The Lullabye Songbook, 1986, Ring of Earth, 1986, Favorite Folktales From Around the World, 1986, Piggins, 1987, Owl Moon, 1987, Three Bears, 1987, A Sending of Dragons, 1987, The Devil's Arithmetic, 1988, Sister Light/Sister Dark, 1988, White Jenna, 1989, Dove Isabeau, 1989, Baby Bear's Bedtime Book, 1990, Tam Lin, 1990, Bird Watch, 1990, Sky Dogs, 1990, Wizard's Hall, 1991, All those Secrets of the World, 1991, Wings, 1991, Hark! A Christmas Sampler, 1991, Encounter, 1992, Briar Rose, 1992, Letting Swift River Go, 1992, What Rhymes with Moon, 1993, Welcome to the Greenhouse, 1993, Honkers, 1993, Here There Be Dragons, 1993, Grandad Bill's Song, 1994, Good Griselle, 1994, The Girl in the Golden Bower, 1994, Old Dame Counterpane, 1994, Old Macdonald's Songbook, 1994, Here There Be Unicorns, 1994, Beneath the Ghost Moon, 1994, The Wild Hunt, 1995, Ballad of the Pirate Queens, 1995, And Twelve Chinese Acrobats, 1995, Water Music, 1995, Among Angels, 1995, Here They Be Witches, 1995, O. Jerusalem, 1996, Welcome to the Sea of Sand, 1996, Passager, 1996, Hobby, 1996, Sacred Places, 1996, Here There Be Angels, 1996, Milk and Honey, 1996, Meet The Monsters, 1996, Once Upon Ice, 1997, Merlin, 1997, Child of Faerie, 1997, Twelve Impossible Things Before Breakfast, 1997, Miz Berlin Walks, 1997, Nocturne, 1997, Armageddon Summer, 1998, House/House, 1998, Prince of Egypt, 1998, Raising Yoder's Barn, 1998, The Wizard's Map, 1999, The Pictish Child, 1999, The Fairies' Ring, 1999, Moonball, 1999, Gray Heroes: Elder Tales From Around the World, 1999, How Does a Dinosaur Say Goodnight, 2000, Off We Go, 2000, Queen's Own Fool, 2000, Not One Damsel in Distress, 2000, Mirror/Mirror, 2000, Color Me a Rhyme, 2000, Welcome to the River of Grass, 2001, The Fish Prince and Other Merman Stories, 2001, Odysseus in the Serpent's Maze, 2001, Dear Mother/Dear Daughter, 2001, Hippolyta and the Curse of the Amazons, 2002, Wild Wings, 2002, Firebird, 2002, Horizons, 2002, Animal Train, 2002, Harvest Home, 2002, Girl in a Cage, 2002, Sword of the Rightful King, 2003, How Do Dinosaurs Get Well Soon, 2003, Take Joy, 2003, My Brothers' Flying Machine, 2003, Hoptoad, 2003, Mightier than the Sword, 2003, The Radiation Sonnets, 2003, The Flying Witch, 2003, Jason and the Gorgon's Blood, 2004, How Do Dinosaurs Clean their Rooms?, 2004, The Barefoot Book of Ballet Stories, 2004, Prince Across the Water, 2004, Grandma's Hurrying Child, 2005, Perfect Wizard, 2005, Pay the Piper, 2005, Apple for the Teacher, 2005, Meow, 2005, How Do Dinosaurs Eat Their Food?, 2005, Fairy Tale Feast, 2006, Troll Bridge, 2006, This Little Piggy, 2006, Dimity Duck, 2006, Baby Bear's Books, 2006, Count Me a Rhyme, 2006, over 200 others. Mass. del. Dem. Nat. Conv., 1972; town coord. Robert Drinan's campaign, 1970; chmn. bd. trustees Hatfield (Mass.) Libr., 1978-83. Mem. Soc. Children's Book Writers (bd. dirs. 1974—), Children's Lit. Assn. (bd. dirs. 1977-79), Sci. Fiction Writers Am. (pres. 1986-88), Mystery Writers Am., Authors Guild. Democrat. Jewish/Quaker. Home: PO Box 27 Hatfield MA 01038-0027 E-mail: janeyolen@aol.com.

YONKUS, JO MARIE MAIORANO, secondary school educator; b. Highland Park, Ill., Oct. 21, 1946; d. Louis Joseph and Eva Marie (Dinelli) Maiorano; m. Felix Dennis Yonkus, Apr. 17, 1971; children: Andrew Dennis, Eric Joseph. BA, Webster Coll., 1968; postgrad., Northeastern U., 1990—. Tchr., cons. Winnetka (Ill.) Pub. Schs., 1968-73; tchr. math. Dist. 214 High Schs., Arlington Heights, Ill., 1986-87, permanent substitute tchr., 1988-89; tchr. math. St. Viator High Sch., Arlington Heights, 1989—. Author elem. math. textbook, 1984. Mem. Lincolnshire Golf Club (pres. 1986-87). Roman Catholic. Avocations: golf, hand crafts, reading, travel. Office: St Viator High Sch 1213 E Oakton St Arlington Heights IL 60004-5099

YONTECK, ELIZABETH BARBARA, minister, health care consultant; b. Miami, Fla., Oct. 20, 1931; d. Frederick and Mary (Enyedy) Y. BS, U. Miami, 1953; MDiv, Columbia Theol. Sem., Decatur, Ga., 1971, D of Ministry, 1988. Ordained to ministry Presbyn. Ch. (U.S.A.), 1971. Ednl. missionary Presbyn. Ch. (U.S.A.), Japan, 1959-70; pastor various chs. W.Va. Presbytery, Presbyn. Ch. (U.S.A.), 1971-84; cons. surveys Cen. Pk. Lodges Inc., Sarasota, Fla., 1989—; coord. children's ministry 1st Presbyn. Ch., Sarasota, 1990—. Mem. Mission Gd. Gen. Assembly, Presbyn. Ch. (U.S.A.), Atlanta, 1974-78, chair standing com. Gen. Assembly, 1976; presenter women's issues and health care workshops, 1989—. Contbr. articles to profl. jours. Chair evaluation Planned Approach to Community Health, Sarasota County, 1987—; v.p. Adv. Commn. on Status of Women, Sarasota County, 1988-89. Mem. Acad. Parish Clergy (bd. dirs. 1986—), Assn. for Clin. Pastoral Edn., Nat. Coun. for Family Rels. (cert. family life educator), Bay Area Consortium for Women (sec. region 1988—). Office: 1st Presbyn Ch 501 Bowman Ct Sarasota FL 34237-7007

YOPCONKA, NATALIE ANN CATHERINE, executive secretary, computer specialist, educator, entrepreneur, small business owner; b. Taylor, Pa., July 21, 1942; d. Michael Joseph and Natalie Ann Lucille (Panek) Y. BS in Bus. Adminstrn., Pers. and Indsl. Rels. with high honors, U. Md., 1965; MBA, George Washington U., 1976, MA in Edn. and Human Devel., 1988; postgrad. in venture capital and entrepreneurship, U. Md., 1990—96. Mgmt. analyst, adminstrv. trainee, computer programmer U.S. Dept. Commerce, Maritime Adminstrn., Washington, 1965-67; computer programmer, computer specialist U.S. Dept. Labor, Washington, 1967-78; instr. computer sci. Assn. for Computing Machinery, Washington, 1978; instr. computer sci. and mgmt. tech. Montgomery Coll., Takoma Park and Rockville, Md., 1979; sr. programmer analyst Dynamic Data Processing, Inc., Silver Spring, Md., 1979; instr. Nat. Bus. Sch., Inc., Alexandria, Va., 1980; cons. McLeod Corp., Washington, 1980; lectr. computer sci., coop. coord. U. Md., College Park, 1980-81; sr. adminstrv. applications analyst programmer Data Transformation Corp., Washington, 1981; sr. sys. analyst Singer Link Simulation Sys. Divsn., Silver Spring, 1981-82; accessory designer Transart Corp., 1982-83; market rschr. Washington Fin. Svc., 1982-83; lectr. computer info. and sys. sci. U. D.C., Rockville, Md., 1983; prof. computer programming and mgmt. info. sys. Benjamin Franklin U., Washington, 1983; rschr. Info. U.S.A., Potomac, Md., 1983-85; admissions rep. Brook-Wein Bus. Inst., Washington, 1985; pvt. distbr. Hyattsville, Md., 1979—86; distbr. AMWAY Corp., 1979—93. Course developer, instr. Grad. Sch. USDA, Balt., 1986-87; field interviewer Nat. Drug Abuse Bur., 1989-90; chmn. Cert. for Computing Profls. Exam. Review Course for Balt. Washington, D.C. corridor, 1994-95; agent Kivex, Inc., 1996-97, 3COM Corp., 1997-99, Information Builders, Inc., 1997-2000; bus. owner, cons., computer specialist, application developer, educator, salesperson Sys. and Edn. Enterprises, 1979—. Mem. Takoma Park Disability Com., Mayor's Com. on Energy, Housing and Planning, 1980-81; mem. Vision 2030 Balt./Howard County, 2002-2003; mem. Missionary Oblates of Immaculate

Mary; choir Our Lady of Sorrows Cath. Ch., 1977-82, St. John the Evangelist Cath. Ch., eucharistic min. 1990-2003, internet com., 1996-97, lector, 2003-05; mem. Balt. Wash. Corridor C. of C., 1996-97, citizens adv. com. to Bd. Edn. Howard County, 1991-92, computer adv. com., 1993-95; chair Leukemia Soc. Md., 1996; active Suburban Md. High Tech. Coun., 1994-95, Howard County High Tech. Coun., 1994-95; sec., mem. T.R.I.A.D./S.A.L.T. for Howard County; mem. Howard County Council for the Arts. Recipient chmn./woman of the yr., Leukemia Soc. of Md., 1996. Mem. AARP, NAFE, IEEE (Balt. sect., earlier Washington sect., computer soc., commn. soc., tech. com. on software engrng., stds. coms. and groups, software standards assn.), ASCD, ASTD, IEEE, IEEE Computer Soc. (tech. com. on software engrng., software engrng. stds. coms. and groups), Software Stds. Assn., Info. Sys. Audit and Control Assn., Assn. Computing Machinery (DC chpt., edn. com., instr. 1978-79, edn. com. 1980-81, profl. devel. com. 1982-83), Data Processing Mgmt. Assn. (chmn. cert. for computing profls. exam. rev. course for Balt.-Washington corridor 1994-95), Balt. Washington Info. Sys. Educators (consortium com. 1984-85, program com. for 1986 regional tng. conf. 1985-86, vendor com. 1988-89), Fed. Automatic Data Processing Users Group (com. mem. 1976-1983), Armed Forces Comm. and Electronics Assn., Balt. Coun. Fgn. Affairs, Nat. Active and Ret. Fed. Employees Assn. (sec. Howard County chpt.), Nat. Bus. Edn. Assn., U. Md. Howard County Alumni Club (scholarship com. 1989), Columbia (Md.) Assn., Phi Delta Gamma (scholarship com. 1977-78, social com. 1980-81, hospitality com. 1982-83, sec. 1989-90). Achievements include first to write software engineering standards.

YOPPS, LINDA LEE, special education educator; d. Owen Gerald Jr. Hardy and Bernace Maria Francoeur; m. Roy Kenneth Yopps, Oct. 28, 1978; 1 child, Robert Owen. BS in Edn., U. Wis., Milw., 1976; MEd, Nat. Lewis U., Evanston, Ill., 1989. Spl. edn. tchr. Milw. Pub. Schs., 1976—85, Mukwonago Area Sch. Dist., Wis., 1985—. Contract negotiator Tchrs. Local Union, Mukwonago, 1996—. Bd. dirs. Mukwonago Choral Union, 2004—. Recipient Brass Lamp award, Lakewood Uniserv Coun., Brookfield, Wis., 1995. Lutheran. Home: 601A Hickory Hollow Rd Waterford WI 53185 Office: Clarendon Ave Elementary School 915 Clarendon Ave Mukwonago WI 53149-1248

YORBURG, BETTY (MRS. LEON YORBURG), sociology educator; b. Chgo., Aug. 27, 1926; d. Max and Hannay (Bernstein) Gitelman; m. Leon Yorburg, June 23, 1946; children: Harriet, Robert. PhB, U. Chgo., 1945, MA, 1948; PhD, New Sch. Social Rsch., 1968. Instr. Coll. New Rochelle, 1966-67; lectr. City Coll. and Grad. Ctr. CUNY, 1967-69, asst. prof. City Coll. and Grad. Ctr., 1969-73, prof. City Coll. and Grad. Ctr, 1978—2003, prof. emerita, 2003—. Rsch. asst. Prof. Clifford Shaw, Chto. Area Project, 1946-47. Author: Utopia and Reality, 1969, The Changing Family, 1973, Sexual Identity: Sex Roles and Social Change, 1974, The New Women, 1976, Introduction to Sociology, 1982, Families and Societies, 1983, Family Relationships, 1993, Sociological Reality, 1995, Family Realities A Global View, 2002 Mem. AAAS, Am. Sociol. Assn., Ea. Sociol. Assn., Am. Coun. Family Rels., N.Y. Acad. Scis. Home: 20 Earley St Bronx NY 10464-1512 Personal E-mail: byorburg@verizon.net.

YORINKS, ADRIENNE BERG, artist, illustrator; b. N.Y.C., May 25, 1956; d. Jerome Sydney and Helene Berg; m. Douglas Keith Schoenberg, June 8, 2003. BS Psychology Animal Behavior, U. Wis., 1977; M Dance Edn., NYU, 1982. Illustrator: Stand for Children, 1998, The Alphabet Atlas, 1999, The Last Will & Testament of an Extremely Distinguished Dog, 2000, Quack, 2003; illustrator My Travels with Capt. Lewis an Clark, 2004, writer, illustrator Quilt of States, 2005. Recipient Merit award, Ga. Coun. Arts. Mem.: Manhattan Quilters Guild. Avocations: hiking, tennis, dance. Home and Studio: 10 Edwards Pl Short Hills NJ 07078 Office Phone: 973-467-1001. Personal E-mail: adrienneyorinks@adrienneyorinks.com.

YORIO, KIMBERLY, public relations executive; married; 1 child. With Children's Television Workshop; dir. mktg. Tihany Internat.; account exec. Kratz & Co. Pub. Relations; dir. cookbook mktg., spl. sales mgr. William Morrow; dir. mktg. Artisan Books; publicity cons. Workman Publishing; cofounder (with Caitlin Friedman), prin. YC Media. Guest spkr. Cornell U., Harvard U., Warton Coll., The Mass. Governors Conf. for Women, The Phila. Conf. for Women. Co-author (with Caitlin Friedman): The Girl's Guide to Being the Boss (Without Being a Bitch): Valuable Lessons, Smart Suggestions and True Stories for Succeeding as the Chick-in-Charge, 2006 (Quills award business The Quills Literacy Found., 2006). Office: YC Media Ste 310 547 West 27th St New York NY 10001 Office Phone: 212-609-5009 ext. 1. Office Fax: 212-684-0059.*

YORK, CAROLYN PLEASANTS STEARNS, language educator; b. High Point, NC, Aug. 23, 1949; d. Frank Ellis and Jessie May (Pleasants) Stearns; m. Guy Aaron York, July 11, 1970; children: Adam Landon, Emily Pleasants, Jonathan Aaron. BA, U. N.C., Greensboro, 1971; MEd, U. N.C., Chapel Hill, 1985. Project Head Start asst. Forsyth County Schs., Winston-Salem, N.C., 1968; publicity dir. House in the Horseshoe Outdoor Drama, Southern Pines, N.C., 1975-76; chpt. I reading tchr. Lee County Schs., Sanford, N.C., 1977-86, English instr., 1987—. Reading instr. Ctrl. Carolina C.C., Sanford, 1985; reading chmn. So. Assn., Sanford, 1978; workshop dir., conf. spkr. N.C. Assn. Compensatory Educators, Raleigh, 1983; advisor, Internat. Thespian Soc., 2002-2003; writer-in-residence Peace Coll EDS Prog., 2003. Author: (poetry) Pleasantries, 1996, Weaver of Destiny, 1999; editor newsletter Creations, 1976; appeared on Friday Noon Poets Assn. Pub. TV Program, 1997, 2004-05; photographer Lee High Rev. lit. mag., 1998-99, Tarheel Tapestry, 2004; author numerous poems. Founding mem. Lee County Arts Coun., Sanford, 1975, v.p. 2004-05, pres., 2005; sec. Footlight Players, Lee County Recreation Dept., 2002, pres. 2005—; Sunday Sch. tchr., Bible sch. tchr. First Presbyn. Ch., Sanford, 1982, 86-89; bd. dir. Child Devel. Ctr., Sanford, 1980-82; adv. coun. Cmty. Playhouse of the Temple Theater, 1997-99; Builders Club sponsor Kiwanis Club of Lee County, Sanford, 1978-80. Recipient local and state prize, N.C. Reading Assn., 1995, 1st prize, Fields of Earth Poetry Symposium, 1996, Am. Scholastic Press Assn., 2000, Golden Pen award, Writers' Ink Guild, 2005. Mem. NC Poetry Soc. (bd. dir., 3d v.p. 1997-2005, workshop dir. 1993, 2d prize 1993, 1st prize 1999), San-Lee Writers (pres. 1993—, co-founder), Tri County English Alliance (coord., English Fair rep. 1995-2001), Lee County Reading Assn. (young authors' chmn. 1996-97; advisor lit. mag. Lee High Rev. 1998-2005), Guild Am. Papercutters, Poetry Coun. NC (contest judge 2003). Avocations: snorkeling, playing the dulcimer, weaving, collecting antique valentines, cutting schrenschnitte. Home: 315 N Steele St Sanford NC 27330-3956 E-mail: yorkshome@wave-net.net.

YORK, JOAN ELIZABETH SMITH, psychologist; b. Englewood, N.J., Jan. 18, 1940; s. Julius Freeman and Lottie Winfred (Mays) Smith; B.A., W.Va. State Coll., 1962; M.Ed., Trenton State Coll., 1980; postgrad. in counseling psychology Union Grad. Lic. drug and alcohol counselor. Sch. Counselor, Portsmouth (Va.) Child-Family Service, 1972-73; dir. Richmond (Va.) City Jail-Work Release Program, 1974-75; counselor Employee Adv. Service, Trenton, 1975—2002; part-time counselor Trenton State Prison Evening Sch., 1981-82; pvt. counselor Delaware Valley Psychol. Clinic, part-time 1982—; pvt. therapist Mercer Consultation Assn., 1986—; drug and alcoholism counselor, 1987—; pvt. practice 1980-. First v.p., mem. exec. bd. N.J. Task Force on Women and Alcohol. Mem. Assn. of Black Psychologists, Am. Assn. Counseling and Devel., Nat. Black Alcoholism Counselors, N.J. Alcoholism Assn. Democrat. Baptist. Office Phone: 609-396-4887. Personal E-mail: jesy138@comcast.net.

YORK, KAREN SUE, artist, historian; b. Wichita, Kans., Sept. 19, 1955; d. Jack Shannon and Pat Sue (Sittel) Compton; m. Kevin Blaine Hardin, June 1977 (div. 1981); 1 child, Kate; m. Robert Sterling York, Sept. 19, 1981. BFA, Tex. Woman's U., 1995; MA, Ind. U., 1998, PhD, 2003. Jr. art dir. Ackerman, Inc., Tulsa, Okla., 1977-78, Fred Davis & Assocs., Tulsa, 1977-78; graphic designer Tulsa, 1978-82; art dir. Advantage Advt., Tulsa, 1982-83; entertainment mgr. Tulsa, Houston, Denton, Tex., 1983-95. Art dir. Internat. Jugglers Assn., 1982-84; assoc. curator Ind. U., Bloomington, 2004-2005, assoc. curator, Montgomery Mus. Fine Arts, Ala., 2006. One-woman show includes Tex. Woman's U., 1995. Recipient Ben Keith award North Tex. Art League, 1995; fellow Ind. Art Mus., 2000-03; Metz fellow, Ind. U. Art Mus., Bloomington, 2000-2003. Mem. Phi Kappa Phi (Acad. Excellence award 1994, 95), Gamma Beta Phi, Alpha Chi, Ind. Univ. Art History Assn. (pres. 1998-99). Avocations: metalsmith, rockhound, scuba diver, golfer. Home: 1704 S Court St Montgomery AL 36104-5417

YORK, STAR LIANA, sculptor; b. Washington, Apr. 14, 1952; d. Robert Erastus and Adele York Northam; m. Rodney James Barker. Student, Prince Georges C.C.; BFA, U. Md.; postgrad., Balt. Inst. Art. Tchr., artist in residence CETA Program, Md., 1974-76. Subject of book and mags. articles; exhibited in group shows at Prince Georges Com Coll., 1970-72, U. of Md., 1972-74, Balt. Inst. Art, 1975, Artist in Residence at Prince Georges Com Coll, CETA, Medicine Man Gallery: Leading The West, 1997, Southwest Art Mag. traveling exhibit of all mag. cover artist, 1998; one person show at Gilcrease Mus., Tulsa, Okla., 1998; group mus. shows at Tuscon Fine Art, 1991, 92, 93, 94, Benineington Fie Art, Vermont, 1997, Wildlife Fine Art, Jackson, Wyo., 1997, Albuquerque Fine Art, N.M., 1992; AWA group shows at Total Arts Gallery, Taos, N.M., 1999, Trailside Gallery, Scottsdale, Ariz., 1998; one and two person shows at Zaplin Lampert, Sante Fe, N.M. 1994, 95, 98, 99, Dewey Gallery, Sante Fe, 1992, 93, Meyer Gallery, Scottsdale, Ariz., 1992, 93, Mountain Trails Gallery, Jackson, Wyo., 1997, Shriver Gallery, Taos, N.M., 1983, 84, 85, 86, 87, 88, 89, 90, 91, 92, 93, 94, 95, 96, 97, 98, 99, Pendragon Gallery, Annapolis, Md., 1980, 81, 82, 83, Squashblossom Gallery, Aspen, Colo., 1984, 85, 86, 87, 88, Cogswell Gallery, Vail, Colo., 1986, 87, 88, Dakota Gallery, Boca Raton, Fla., 1985, 86, 87, 88, 89, 90, Ton Atim Gallery, Durango, Colo., 1992, 94, 96, 98, Silverado Skies Gallery, Miami, 1989, 1990, Christi Lee Gallery, Basalt, Colo., 1997, Hawthorn Gallery, Branson, Mo., 1990. Recipient first place Lance Internat. award Nat. Sculpture Soc., N.Y.C., 1978-80, first place sculpture Catherine Lorillard Soc., N.Y.C. Mem. Am. Women Artists Assn. (chairperson 1996—), Am. Polocrosse Assn., Am. Quarter Horse Assn. Avocation: polocrosse. Home: 533 Onate Pl Santa Fe NM 87501-3676 Office: Star York Sculpture 1274 Calle De Comercio Ste 2 Santa Fe NM 87507-3117

YORK, TINA, painter; b. Germany, Feb. 9, 1951; Student, Sch. Mus. Fine Arts, Boston, 1967-71; studied with, George Dergalis, Wayland, Mass., 1967-75; BA cum laude, Brandeis U., 1978; postgrad., N.Y. Med. Coll., 1980-83. Contbr. works to numerous publs., 1987-2003; one woman shows include Gallery Contemporary Art, Provincetown, Mass., 1969, Springfield (Mass.) Art Assn., 1971, Copley Soc., Boston, 1972-73, Boston U., 1974, Mendler Gallery, Rockport, Mass., 1974, Cambridge (Mass.) Art Assn., 1975, Ames Gallery, N.Y.C., 1976, Gallery Seven, Boston, 1977, Brandeis U., Waltham, Mass., 1978, Rue Oker Gallery of Art, Sturbridge, Mass., 1979, Art Collectors Gallery, N.Y.C., 1981, 153 Gallery, Inc., N.Y.C., 1982, Creative Concepts, L.A., 1984, Alpha Contemporary Exhibits, L.A., 1985, Darraby Gallery, L.A., 1986, 8th St. Gallery, L.A., 1986, Koplin Gallery, L.A., 1987, Galerie Beverly Hills, Calif., 1988, Conv. Ctr., Rome, 1988, Merck, Sharpe & Dohme, Rahway, N.J., 1988, Erlgangen Kultur Borse, Germany, 1989, Arwell Gallery, Laguna, Calif., 1989, Deutsch-Amerikanisches Inst., Regensburg, Germany, 1990, Art in Pub. Bldgs., Nuremberg, Germany, 1990, Art Expo, N.Y.C., 1990, Amerikahaus, Nuremberg, 1990, Art 5, Nuremberg, 1990, Dresdner Bank, Nuremberg, 1990, Amer. Hosp. Assn., Washington, 1990, So. Med. Assn., Nashville, 1990, 94-95, Studio Gallery, North Hollywood, Calif., 1991-92, Galerie Lehman, Germany, Galerie Sud, Studio la Citta, Italy, Studio Gallery, Calif., 1991 La Foire Internat. d'Art Contemporain, Paris, 1992, 94, Med. Heritage Gall., Waco, Tex., 1991, Herbstmesse, Frankfurt, Germany, 1992-93, Kunstforum Internat., Aachen, Germany, 1993, Kunstlerhaus, Germany, 1993, Ambiente, Frankfurt, 1993-98, 2000-03, ART/LA, 1993-95, Internat. Art Fair, Czechoslovakia, 1993-2003, Art Fair, Seattle, 1993-94, Art Expo, Chgo., 1993-94, Frankfurter Buchmesse, Frankfurt, Germany, 1993, Art Expo, N.Y.C., 1993-96, Chgo. Trade Show, 1993, 95, 97, Toronto Trade Show, 1993, Art Cologne, Germany, 1993-94, 96, Centre d'Art Contemporain, Switzerland, Dresdner Bank, Germany, Galerie Littmann, Switzerland, Galerie Fischer, 1994, Art Asia, Hong Kong, 1994-96, Art Expo, Calif., 1994, 96, PPFA Toronto Trade Show, 1994-95, Limited Edit. Expo, New Orleans, 1994-95, Frankfurt Book Fair, 1994, 97-98, 2000, 03, Internat. Spring Fair, Birmingham, Eng., 1994, 95, Art Miami, 1994-95, Exposition of Art, Sydney, Australia, 1993, Art Taipei, Taiwan, 1993, 94, 95, Art Santa Fe, 1993-95, NASA Ames Rsch. Ctr., Moffett Field, Calif., 1994, NASA Johnson Space Ctr., Houston, 1995, Galerie Rudelko, Germany, Scheffler Galerie, Germany, 1995, Studio Gall., Ariz., 1996, Jahns House, Germany, 1996, Internat. Contemporary Art Fair, Madrid, 1995, West Valley Mus. Art, Phoenix, 1998, Las Vegas Art Mus., 2000, Paul Joseph Galleries, Las Vegas, 2002, Rio Decor, 2003, Tina York Studio, Naples, Fla., 2003, Marco Island Art Assn., Fla. 2004, Studio Gallery, Naples, 2004, 06, Area Arts Gallery, Naples, Fla., 2005, I.C. Fine Art 2000 Gallery, Las Vegas, 2005; group shows include Area Arts Gallery, Naples, NASA Art Programs, Washington, Mus. Fine Arts, Salt Lake City, Mus. Art, Las Vegas, Regional Mus. Art, Bautzen, Germany, Mus. Art, Downey, Calif., Carter Ctr., Atlanta; represented in permanent collections, Paul Joseph Galleries, Las Vegas, Rio Decor, Mus. of Art, Las Vegas, Downey (Calif.) Mus. Art, Mus. Fine Arts, Salt Lake City, Mcpl. Art Mus., Osaka, Japan, Regional Mus. Art, Bautzen, Germany, Carter Ctr., Atlanta, Kennedy Space Ctr., Fla., New Zealand Space Adminstrn., Auckland, NASA, Internat. Peace Acad., NY, USIA, BBC (Brit. Broadcasting Co.), Lagan Jute, Ltd., India, NIH, Universitet Kliment Orchridski, Bulgaria, Hiatt Internat., Beverly Hills, Calif., Paris, Gallery Dmovrosek, Yugoslavia, Columbia U., Nat. Cancer Inst., Md., Kulturamt der Stadt Nurnberg, Germany, Planetary Soc., Calif., Mayo Clin., Ariz., Nat. Air and Space Mus., Washington, Nat. Air and Space Mus., others; represented on Artrain USA; pub. NASA/Exploration of Space, 2004. First prize painting Arts Fest., Scituate, MA, 1969, Internatl. Show, Fall River, MA, 1971; third prize mixed media painting, De Cordova Mus., Lincoln, MA, 1972; second prize painting, Amer. Artists in Paris, Paris, 1975; first prize mixed media painting Inst. Contemporary Art, 1979; Gold medal painting, Spring Arts Fest., LA, 1985; first prize mixed media painting, One Fifty Three Gall., Inc., 1987. Mem.: Internat. High IQ Soc. Studio: Tina York Studio 754 Waterloo Ct Naples FL 34120 Office Phone: 239-659-2941. Business E-Mail: tinayorkstudio@aol.com.

YORKE, MARIANNE, lawyer, real estate executive; b. Nov. 4, 1948; d. Joseph George and Catherine Veronica (Friel) Y. BA, West Chester U., 1971; JD, Temple U., 1980; MS in Ognl. Dynamics, U. Pa., 1987; M in Corp. Real Estate, Internat. Assn. Corp. Real Estate Execs., 1996. Bar: Pa. 1981, N.Y. 1992. Mgr. CIGNA Corp., Phila., 1982-85, asst. dir., 1985-90; v.p. Chase Manhattan Bank, NYC, 1990-92; real estate dir. Johnson & Johnson, 1992—. Real estate atty. Garfinkel & Volpicelli, Phila., 1980-82; prin., mng. ptnr. Yorke & Eisenman, Real Estate, Phila., 1976-89, prin., mng. ptnr. Yorke & Mac Lachlin Real Estate, Phila., 1989-02; lectr. Women in the Arts, 1982-90; guest spkr. Wharton Sch. Bus. Class of 1989, U. Pa., grad. sch. arts and sci. Class of 1988; asst. prof. bus. law Rider U. Grad Sch., 2002-03, asst. prof. real estate law Rutgers U. Grad. Sch., 2003—. Contbr. articles to profl. jours. Solicitor Pa. Ballet, Phila., 1983-90, United Way, Phila., 1983-90; mem. steering com. U. Pa., 1986-90, dir. alumni assn., 1987-90; mem. adv. com. for econ. devel. Luth. Settlement House Adv., 1986-88; mem. Ctr. Adv. Bd., 2000—; bd. dirs. Hamilton Townhouse Assn., Phila., 1988-90, chmn. ins. com., 1989-90, 718 Broadway Inc., NYC, 1990-94, Johnson Health Care Svcs. Recipient Live for Life Mgmt., Johnson Health Mgmt., 1995, Pres. Quality Process Excellence award, EthiconEndo Surgery, 2000, Process Excellence award, Ethicon, Inc., 2001. Mem. ABA (forum on constrn. 1982-90), Pa. Bar Assn. (condominium and zoning com. 1982-90), Assn. of Bar of City of NY (sects. on internat. law and real property law 1992-94), Phila. Bar Assn., Phila. Women Real Estate Atty., CORENET, Nat. Assn. Corp. Real Estate Exec. (internat. coun. 1984-2002, comml. coun. 1984-2002), Internat. Atty., Roundtable, Women's Law Caucus, Phi Alpha Delta. Independent. Roman Catholic. Home: The Admiralty 55 Ocean Ave Monmouth Beach NJ 07750-1366 Office: Johnson & Johnson W H 7135 1 Johnson & Johnson Plz New Brunswick NJ 08933-0002 Office Phone: 732-524-3881. Business E-Mail: myorke@corus.jnj.com.

YOSHIMURA, YOSHIKO, librarian; b. Tokyo, Oct. 21, 1933; arrived in U.S., 1958; d. Shigeru and Jun Yoshimura. BA, Tsuda Coll., Tokyo, Japan, 1956; MSLS, Syracuse U, 1961; AM, Harvard U, 1971. Libr. asst. Toyo Bunko Libr., Tokyo, 1956—58; cadet, intern Syacuse (NY) U Libr., 1958—61; sr. cataloger Harvard-Yenching Libr., Cambridge, Mass., 1961—71; sr. Japanese cataloger Libr. of Congress, Washington, 1971—81, area specialist Japan, 1981—98. Author (compiler): Japanese Govt. Documents and Censored Pub., 1992, Censored Japanese Serials of the Pre-1946 Period, 1994, Pre 1956 Japanese Documents and Censored Materials, 2002—06. Home: 2311 Pimmit Dr No 1215 Falls Church VA 22043

YOSHIUCHI, ELLEN HAVEN, healthcare educator, clinical counselor; b. Newark, Apr. 15, 1949; d. Michael Joseph and Adeline V. (Lindblom) Haven; m. Takeshi Yoshiuchi, Dec. 1, 1973; children: Teri Takumi, Niki Noboru. BA summa cum laude, CUNY, 1980; M Profl. Studies in Human Rels., N.Y. Inst. Tech., 1991. Cert. bereavement svcs. counselor, cert. kidney early evaluation program. Pvt. practice childbirth edn., 1983—89; program asst. parent/family edn. St. Luke's/Roosevelt Hosp. Ctr., N.Y.C., 1989—93, mem. faculty parent/family edn. program, 1990—2002; mem. faculty Family Ctr. at Riverdale Neighborhood House, Bronx, 1991—96; faculty mem. The Greater N.Y. March of Dimes, N.Y.C., 1996—2001; mgr. patient svcs. N.Y.C. chpt. The Leukemia and Lymphoma Soc., 1998—2004; program dir. Nat. Kidney Found. of Greater N.Y., 2004—. Mem. perinatal bereavement com. St. Luke's/Roosevelt Hosp. Ctr., N.Y.C., 1989-95. Editor ASPO/N.Y.C. News, 1983-86; contbr. articles to profl. jours. Trustee Pan Asian Repertory Theatre, N.Y.C., 1996-2001. Fellow: Am. Coll. Childbirth Educators; mem.: NY Citizens' Com. on Health Care Decisions, Coun. Nephrology Social Workers, C.G. Jung Found. for Analytical Psychology, Lamaze Internat. (cert. tchr., pres. N.Y.C. chpt. 1987—91, nominating com. 1991—93, dir. ednl. program 1991—93). Office: 30 E 33d St New York NY 10016-6901 Office Phone: 212-889-2210. Personal E-mail: eenadoone@verizon.net.

YOSKEY, SYLVIA LYNN, surgical nurse; b. Waynesburg, Pa., Oct. 9, 1953; d. Walter John and Teresa (Matergan) Y. Diploma, Washington Hosp. Sch. Nursing, 1974; BSN, W.Va. U., 1979; MS in Nursing, Pa. State U., 1988. RN, Pa., W.Va. Staff nurse post anesthesia recovery, operating room W.Va. U. Hosps., Morgantown, nurse educator; staff nurse operating room AG Hosp., Pitts.; staff nurse ASC Shadyside Hosp., Pitts.; unit coord. oper. rm. Canonsburg (Pa.) Area Gen. Hosp.; ind. contractor, oper. rm. Ruby Meml. Hosp., Morgantown, W.Va.

YOST, BRANDY DIANA, secondary school educator; b. Connersville, Ind., Oct. 16, 1972; d. Carol Lucas; m. Corey Jacob Yost, Sept. 11, 2004. M in Edn., Ind. Wesleyan U., 2003; BS in Biology, Ind. U., Bloomington, 2006. Cert. Tchr. Ind. U. Purdue U., 1998. Secondary edn. Carmel HS, Ind., 1998—. Democrat. Avocation: jogging. Office: Carmel HS 520 East Main St Carmel IN 46032 Office Phone: 317-846-7721. Business E-Mail: byost@ccs.k12.in.us.

YOST, JEAN MARIE, administrative assistant; b. Washington, Aug. 8, 1928; d. John Joseph and Violet Jessica (Cusick) Werres; m. Meredith Loy Yost, June 11, 1955; children: Jean Marie Samuels, John Paul. Student, Loretto Hts. Coll., Denver, 1946-48. Sec. Marshal of the Supreme Ct. of U.S., Washington, 1946-58; exec. sec. Marriott Corp., Bethesda, Md., 1987-89, Bechtel Power Corp., Gaithersburg, Md., 1979-81; adminstrv. asst. Nat. Elec. Mfrs. Assn., Washington, 1989-95; legal sec. Glinsmann & Glinsmann, Gaithersburg, MD, 1995-96; profl. staff asst. York Internat., 1996-99; profl. staff asst. Dept. Juvenile Justice Washington County, Hagerstown, Md., 2000—. Contbr. (poetry) A Flood of Contentment Theater of The Mind, Today's Famous Poems, 2003, Letters from the Soul, 2003, The Colors of Life, 2003, CD reading listening, The Colors of Life, 2003. Pres. YWCA-Y Wives of Damascus, Md., 1976; sec. PTA, Damascus, 1976; 4-H leader, Damascus; active CCD, Silver Spring, Md., 1969. Mem.: AAUW, NAFE, Nat. Assn. Adminstrv. Assts. and Execs., Internat. Assn. Adminstrv. Profls. (sec. Toll Gate chpt.), Internat. Soc. Poets. Avocations: music, photography, travel, needlecrafts, plays and musicals.

YOST, KELLY LOU, pianist; b. Boise, Idaho, Aug. 10, 1940; d. Roy Daniel and Helen Roberta (Kingsbury) Frizzelle; m. Nicholas Peter Bond, Dec. 27, 1961 (div. 1973); 1 child, Brook Bernard; m. Samuel Joseph Yost, June 16, 1984. B.A. in Music, U. Idaho, 1962; postgrad., U. So. Calif., 1965-69. Pvt. tchr. classical piano, Twin Falls, Idaho, 1962-88; rec. artist, owner ind. record label Channel Prodns., Twin Falls, 1986—. Soloist U. Idaho Symphony Orch., Moscow, 1962; pianist, keyboardist Magic Valley Symphony Orch., Twin Falls, 1985, 86; touring guest piano soloist Vandaleer Concert Choir, Moscow, 1961. Recordings: Piano Reflection (excerpts included in Simple Abundance by Sarah Ban Breathnach), 1987, Quiet Colors, 1991, Roses and Solitude, 1996, Still.Still.Still, 1998, selectionssynchronized with Japanese film Gaia Symphony #4, 2001, Brand New Feel, 2002; recordings Dreams, Japan, 2003; recordings: 2 selections synchronized with Japanese film Gaia Symphony #5, 2004; appear and featured (films) Gaia Symphony #6, 2006. Mem. NARAS, Music Tchrs. Nat. Assn., Idaho Music Tchrs. Assn. (sec. 1981-82), Magic Valley Cmty. Concert Assn. (bd. dir. 1964-87), Phi Beta Kappa, Kappa Kappa Gamma (Alumnae Achievement award 1996). Avocations: skiing, hiking, philosophy. Office: Channel Prodns PO Box 454 Twin Falls ID 83303-0454 Office Phone: 208-734-8668. E-mail: chanpro@mindspring.com.

YOST, NANCY RUNYON, artist, small business owner; b. Eaton, Ohio, July 16, 1933; d. Stanley Everett and Treva (Geeting) Runyon; m. Kenneth John Yost, Aug. 17, 1952 (div. Dec. 1962); 1 child, Debra Colleen Yost Mayne. BS in Art Edn., Miami U., Oxford, Ohio, 1966, MEd in Art, 1970. Cert. profl. permanent tchr., Ohio. Sec. N.Am. Aircraft, Columbus, Ohio, 1957, Miami U., Oxford, 1957-61, textile instr., 1978, Living Arts Ctr., Dayton, Ohio, 1972-73; coord. art, music and phys. edn. Stewart Jr. High Sch., Oxford, 1981-86; art instr. Talawanda Sch. System, Oxford, 1965-90, dist. coord., 1986-90; owner, creator Allegro Adornments Bus., 1988—. Postgrad. Sem. Charles Jeffrey, Cleve., Inst. Art, Miami U., 1973, David Van Dommelen Penn State at U. Tenn., 1975, Bill Helwig, N.Y., 1975, Nik Krevitsky, N.Y., 1976, Tom Shafer, Columbus, Ohio, 1982; mem. curriculum coun. Talawanda Sch. Dist., 1982—; rep. Amway Corp., 1980-81, World Book Co., Chgo., 1986-88; lectr. Miami U., 1986; invited workshop speaker, presenter Nat. Art Edn. Assn. Conv., Phoenix, 1992. Contbg. artist Wall Hangings, 1971, Knotting, 1973; one-woman shows include Creative Fibers Studio, Buffalo, 1974, Fitton Ctr. for the Creative Arts, Hamilton, Ohio, 2003, one-woman retrospective, Preble County Art Ctr., 1998, exhibited in group shows at Dayton Art Inst., Invitational Fiber Artists Am., Ball State U., 1974, Christkindl Markt, Canton Art Inst., 1994 (hon. mention), Art All Over, Oxford, Ohio, 2002, Blue Heron Gallery, Liberty, Ind., 2003, Art on Symmes Gallery, Fairfield, Ohio, 2004, 2005, Blue Heron Gallery, 2005; one of two women artists (in exhibition of mixed media) Middletown Fine Arts Ctr., 2001, designer Oxford Bicentennial Calendar, 1976, guest jewelry designer Saks 5th Avenue, co-exhibitor (mixed media show exhibitions) Middletown Fine Arts Ctr.; exhibitions include Art on Symmes Gallery, 2003—, Blue Heron Gallery, 2003—, Sustainable Style Boutique, 2003—; author: The Pair Tree, 2006. Supr. Community Artworks, 1986; mem. adv. bd. Miami U. Summer Theatre, 1991-93; mem. spl. events planning com. Miami U. Art Mus., 1993—. Recipient Winner Most Creative Costume Ohio Mart, 1992, 93, First Pl. awards Community Photo Contest, 3d Pl. and Hon. Mention award Oxford Audubon Photo Show, 1994, 1st Pl. 3D Design, Greater Hamilton Art Exhibit at Fitton Ctr, 1995, Cash award ribbon and Purchase award Wyo. Art Show, 1996, Cash award ribbon Minnetrista Arts Fair, 1996, Best in Show Preble Co. Arts Assn. Juried Show, 1997, First Pl. Sculpture, 1997, 2d Pl Ribbon cash award Christ Kindl Markt, Canton Art Inst., 1999, 1st Pl. 3D Design award, Greater Hamilton Art Exhibit, 2000. Mem. Southwestern Art Edn. Assn., Ohio Art Edn. Assn., Ohio Edn. Assn.,

Talawanda Edn. Assn., Ohio Designer Craftsmen, Ohio Arts and Crafts Guild, Oxford Arts Club, Kappa Delta Pi. Avocations: commissioned artwork, sculpture, wearable art, fabric, metal collages, limited edition prints, painted wood furniture. Home: 6674 Fairfield Rd Oxford OH 45056-8813

YOUNATHAN, MARGARET TIMS, retired nutritionist, educator; b. Clinton, Miss., Apr. 25, 1926; d. Peter Asbury and Eula Lee (Tatum) Tims; m. Ezzat S. Younathan, Aug. 11, 1958; children: Janet Nadya, Carol Miriam. BA, U. So. Miss., 1946, BS, 1950; MS, U. Tenn., 1951; PhD, Fla. State U., 1958. Instr. food and nutrition Oreg. State U., 1951-55; postdoctoral rsch. assoc. Fla. State U., 1958-59; sr. nutritional cons. Ark. Dept. Health, Little Rock, 1962-68; instr. pediat. U. Ark. Sch. Medicine, Little Rock, 1962-65, asst. prof. pediat., 1965-68; assoc. prof. food and nutrition Sch. Human Ecology La. State U., 1971-79, prof., 1979-94; ret., 1994. Internat. nutrition work in Sierra Leone, 1984, Jamaica, 1987. Contbr. articles on food and nutrition rsch. to profl. jours. Summer faculty grantee La. State U. Coun. on Rsch., 1980, rsch. grantee Lou Ana Foods, Inc., 1987. Mem. Inst. Food Technologists, Am. Soc. for Nutritional Scis., Am. Dietetic Assn., Am. Assn. Family and Consumer Sci., La. Assn. Family and Consumer Sci. (pres. dist. D 1981-82, Disting. Home Economist award 1988), Sigma Xi, Phi Kappa Phi, Gamma Sigma Delta, Omicron Nu, Phi Upsilon Omicron. Mem. Christian Ch. (Disciples Of Christ). Home: 1048 Castle Kirk Dr Baton Rouge LA 70808-6023 Personal E-mail: eyounat@aol.com.

YOUNG, ALICE, lawyer; b. Washington, Apr. 7, 1950; d. John and Elizabeth (Jen) Y.; m. Thomas L. Shortall, Sept. 22, 1984; children: Amanda, Stephen. AB magna cum laude, Yale U., 1971; JD, Harvard U., 1974. Bar: N.Y. 1975. Assoc. Coudert Bros., NYC, 1974-81; mng. ptnr. Graham & James, NYC, 1981-87; ptnr. Milbank, Tweed, Hadley & McCloy, NYC, 1987-93; ptnr., chair Asia Pacific Practice Kaye, Scholer LLP, NYC, 1994—. Bd. dirs. Mizuho Trust and Banking Co., mem. examining com., 2003—; spkr. Traphagen Distinguished Alumni Speakers Forum, Harvard Law Sch., 2004; bd. dirs. Deloitte & Touche, adv. bd. diversity, 2005—. Contbr. articles to profl. jours. Bus. com. Nat. Com. on U.S.-China Rels., 1993—, U.S.-China Bus. Coun., 1993—, Com. of 100, 1993—, vice-chmn., 1999—; bd. overseers visitation com. to Law Sch. Harvard U., 1994—99, chair subcomm. on grad. program, 1996; trustee Lingnan Found., NYC, 1984—91, Pan-Asian Repertory Theatre, NYC, 1987—90, Aspen Inst., Colo., 1988—, Am. Assembly, 2000—; bus. com. Met. Mus. Art, NYC, 1989—94; active Coun. on Fgn. Rels., 1977—, Chmn.'s Forum, 2000—; trustee Asia Found., 2002—. Named one of Top 100 Minority Leaders, 1998, one of 40 Under 40 Crain's Bus., NYC, 1989; Bates fellow Yale U., 1970, NDFL fellow Harvard U., 1967-68; recipient Star award NY Women's Agenda, 1992, Justice in Action award, Asia Am. Legal Defense and Edn. Fund, 2004. Mem. ABA, NY State Bar Assn. (fgn. investment com.), Assn. Bar City NY (spl. com. on rels. with Japanese bar, Union Internat. des Avocats), Nat. Asian Pacific Am. Bar Assn., Asian Am. Bar Assn. NY, Harvard Law Sch. Assn. NYC (trustee 1990-94), Japan Soc. (sec. 1989-97), Asia Soc. (pres.'s coun. 1984-2002). Office: Kaye Scholer LLP 425 Park Ave New York NY 10022-3506 Office Phone: 212-836-8047. Business E-Mail: ayoung@kayescholer.com.

YOUNG, ALISON, music educator; d. Donald and Carol Young, Cynthia Frattesi-Young (Stepmother). BA in Music Edn., U. of Mass., Amherst, 2000. Provisional wtih advanced standing for music (5-12) Mass., provisional educator Conn. Music tchr. East Granby Mid. and H.S., Conn., 2000—. Mem.: NEA, Music Educators Nat. Conf., Conn. Edn. Assn., Nat. Band Assn., East Granby Edn. Assn., Conn. Music Educators Assn. Independent. Roman Catholic. Avocations: walking, reading, crafts, music. Office Phone: 860-653-2541 623.

YOUNG, ANN F., history professor; children: Michael Wade Kimmel, Maryanne. Master's degree, Fla. Internat. U., Miami, 1996. Adj. prof. of history Broward C.C., Ft. Lauderdale, Fla., 1996—. Cons. tchg. U.S. history grant program Broward County Pub. Schs., Ft. Lauderdale, 2002—04. Office: Broward C C 3501 SW Davie Rd Fort Lauderdale FL 33351 Office Phone: 954-201-6630.

YOUNG, ANNE B., neurologist, educator; AB, Vassar Coll., 1969; MD, Johns Hopkins U., 1973, PhD in Pharmacology, 1974. From asst. prof. to prof. chemistry Dept. Neurology, U. Mich., 1978-91; Julieanne Dorn prof. neurology Harvard Med. Sch., 1991—; chief neurology Mass. Gen. Hosp., 1991—. Fellow Scottish Rite Found., Lexington, 1973; med. intern Mt. Zion Hosp. & Med. Ctr., San Francisco; neurological resident Dept. Neurology U. Calif., San Francisco.; David Segal vis. prof. Columbia U., 1996; presdl. lectr. Am. Acad. Neurology, 1996. Contbr. numerous articles to profl. jours. Recipient Tchr./Investor Devel. award NIH, 1979-84, Facility Devel. award Merck, 1987-89, Milton Wexler award for Huntington's Rsch. Huntington's Dis. Soc. Am., 1989, Weinstein-Goldenson award United Cerebral Palsy Assn., Inc., 1990. Mem. Inst. Medicine-Nat. Acad. Science. Office: Dept Neurology Mass Gen 15 Parkman St Ste 835 Boston MA 02114-3117

YOUNG, BARBARA, psychiatrist, psychotherapist, educator, photographer; b. Chgo., Oct. 27, 1920; d. William Harvey and Blanche (DeBra) Y. AB, Knox Coll., 1942; MD, Johns Hopkins U., 1945; grad., Balt. Psychoanalytic Inst., 1953. Intern Univ. Hosps., Iowa City, 1945-46, asst. resident in neurology, 1946—47; asst. resident in psychiatry Phipps Clinic, Johns Hopkins U. Hosp., Balt., 1947-49; staff psychiatrist Perry Point (Md.) VA Hosp., 1949-51; practice medicine specializing in psychiatry/psychoanalysis Balt., 1951—; instr. Johns Hopkins U., 1953-69, asst. prof. psychiatry, 1969—, prof. emeritus, 1997—; freelance photographer, 1958—. Lectr. dept. psychiatry Johns Hopkins U.; lectr. Lucy Daniels Found., Carey, N.C., dept. humanities Yale U. Med. Sch., Boston Inst. for Psychotherapy, local psychiat. and social orgns. Works represented in Mus. Modern Art, N.Y.C., Balt. Mus. Art, Santa Barbara (Calif.) Mus. Art, Eastman House, Rochester, N.Y., Yale U. Gallery of Art; photographer: The Plop-A-Lop Tree, 1995, Tales of Courage: Recovering LIfe After Catastrophe, 2003; contbr. articles to profl. jours. Mem.: Am. Psychoanlytic Assn., Am. Psychiat. Assn., Balt.-Washington Ctr. for Psychoanalysis. Democrat. Address: 5307 Herring Run Dr Baltimore MD 21214-1937 Office Phone: 410-426-3583.

YOUNG, DEBORAH (DEBORAH AYLING YANOWITZ), social worker, librarian; b. Syracuse, NY, June 27, 1950; d. David and Jean (AyLing) Y. Student, Pa. State U., Wilkes-Barre and Altoona; postgrad., Pa. State U., Wilkes-Barre, 1988; BA magna cum laude, Wilmington Coll., 1972; MSW, Western Mich. U., 1979; postgrad., Elmira Coll, 1983-84; MLS, U. Pitts., 1994. Cert. social worker, Mich., Pa., NY, Va.; cert. pub. libr., NY, Va., Pa., Mich.; cert. homemaker-home health aide Found. Hospice and Homecare. Homeworker Kalamazoo Pub. Schs., 1974-76; group leader, project coord. Kalamazoo Parks-Recreation Dept.-Youth Conservation Corps, 1977, 78; dir. summer camp Huntington Family Ctrs., Inc., Syracuse, 1980-82; agy. dir. Schuyler Head Start-Day Care, Inc., Watkins Glen, Montour Falls, N.Y., 1982-87; pvt. practice child and elder care, NY, Mich., Pa., 1988—90; social worker, discharge planner VA Med. Ctr., Altoona, Pa., 1990-91; libr. worker U. Pitts. Sch. Libr. and Info. Scis., 1993-94; vocat. worker Laurelton (Pa.) Ctr., 1994-95; children-young adult svcs. coord., reference libr. Petersburg (Va.) Pub. Libr., 1996-97; libr. dir. Berwick (Pa.) Pub. Libr., 1997-98, Hollidaysburg (Pa.) Free Pub. Libr., 1999—2002; with Altoona (Pa.) Mirror Newspaper, 2003—04, Blair County Children and Youth Svcs., 2004, Alleghany Luth. Social Ministries, 2005; care mgr. Huntington-Bedford-Fulton Area Agy. on Aging, 2005—. Ref. and children's vol. helper Altoona Area Pub. Libr., 1992; caregiver Babysitter Heaven Referral Svc., Altoona, 1995—96; mem. Blair County Health and Welfare Coun., Altoona, 1990—95; help-line tel. worker Contact, Altoona, 1992; mem. choir, leader Blessed Sacrament Cathedral, Altoona, 1991—2001; mem., rotating chmn. Watkins Glen Human Svcs. Com., 1982—87; bd. dirs. Mental Health Assn. Human Svcs. Coalition, Columbia and Montour counties, Pa., 1997, 1998; mem., past camp staffer Cir. Pines Ctr., Delton, Mich., 1967—77. Scholar Wilmington Coll., 1968-72, Office Vocat. Rehab., Pa. Dept. Labor and Industry, 1993-94; Grad. fellow Western Mich. U., 1976. Mem. NASW, ALA, Religious Soc. Friends, Altoona YWCA, Hollidayburg YMCA, Green Key Honor Soc. Democrat. Roman Catholic. Avocations: swimming, travel, cooking, reading, writing. Personal E-mail: youngbaby@atlanticbb.net.

YOUNG, DELL, science educator; b. Franklin, Va., Nov. 4, 1951; d. Beale and Irene Edwards Young; m. Larry Horvath, Sept. 30, 1978. Degree in Biology, Va. Wesleyan Coll., Norfolk, 1974. Cert. secondary edn. Va. Tchr. Plz. Jr. H.S., Virginia Beach, Va., 1974—85, First Colonial H.S., Virginia Beach, 1985—; lead ap biology tchr. Va. Beach Pub. Sch., Virginia Beach, 1998—. Mem.: Va. Wesleyan Coll. Alumni (pres. bd. dirs. 1998—2000), Va. Assn. Sci. Tchrs. Democrat-Npl. Office: First Colonial High Sch 1272 Mill Dam Rd Virginia Beach VA 23454 Office Phone: 757 496 6711 77499. E-mail: dell.young@vbschools.com.

YOUNG, DONA DAVIS GAGLIANO, insurance company executive, lawyer; b. Bklyn., Jan. 8, 1954; BA and MA in Polit. Sci., Drew U., 1976; JD, U. Conn., 1980. Bar: Conn. 1980, U.S. Dist. Ct. Conn. 1980. Joined The Phoenix Cos., Hartford, Conn., 1980, asst. counsel, 1981—83, assoc. counsel, 1983, dir. reinsurance adminstrn., 1983—84, dir. and asst. v.p. reinsurance adminstrn., 1984—85, 2nd v.p., ins. counsel, 1985-87, v.p., asst. gen. counsel, 1987-89, sr. v.p. individual sales and mktg., gen. counsel, 1989-94, exec. v.p., gen. counsel, 1994—2000, pres., COO, 2000—02, pres., CEO, chmn., 2003—. Bd. dirs. Sonoco Products Co., 1995—, Wachovia Corp., 2000—, Foot Locker Inc. Chair United Way Capital Area Cmty. Campaign, 2003; bd. dirs. Hartford Hosp.; bd. trustees Goodspeed Opera House Found. Inc. Named Laura A. Johnson Woman of Yr., Hartford Coll. for Women, 2002; recipient Leadership Award for Women in Bus., New England Coun., 1994, Antoinette Bascetta Women's Career Devel. Award, Trust House, Hartford, Conn., 2000, Outstanding Alumni Award, Drew U., 2001, Disting. Grad. Award, U. Conn. Sch. Law, 2002, Human Rels. Award, Nat. Conf. Cmty. and Justice, 2002. Mem. ABA, Hartford County Bar Assn., Conn. Bar Assn., N.Y. Bar Assn. Office: The Phoenix Cos Inc 1 American Row Hartford CT 06102

YOUNG, ELIZABETH BELL, organization consultant; b. Franklinton, N.C., July 2, 1929; d. Joseph H. and Eulalia V. Bell; m. Charles A. Young, Nov. 27, 1964. BA, N.C. Cen. U., 1948, MA, 1950; PhD, Ohio State U., 1959. Cert. speech pathologist; cert. audiologist. Chairperson dept. English Barber Scotia Coll., Concord, NC, 1949-52; dir. speech area, prof. Talladega (Ala.) Coll., 1954-56; dir. speech clinic, prof. Va. State U., Petersburg, 1956-57; prof. Fla. A&M U., Tallahassee, 1959; chmn. dept. English Fayetteville (N.C.) State U., 1959-63; speech pathologist, rsch. assoc. Howard U. Sch. Dentistry, Washington, 1963-64; prof., chairperson dept. English U. Md.-East Shore, Princess Anne, Md., 1965-66; prof., supr. Speech Clinic Cath. U. Am., Washington, 1966-79; congl. staff aide U.S. Ho. of Reps., Washington, 1981-82, 88-90; prof. speech U. D.C., Washington, 1983-84; cons. nat. and local orgns. Washington, 1985-88, 90—. Lectr. over 250 speeches, seminars and workshops; speechwriter, cons. Nat. Assn. Equal Opportunity in Higher Edn., Washington, 1990. Contbr. articles to profl. jours. Fundraiser, pub. rels. polit. candidates, 1963-90; bd. dirs. United Negro Coll. Fund, 1970-80, D.C. Gen. Hosp. Handicapped Intervention Program, 1970-91. Recipient Citations and Certs. of Achievement community and nat. orgns., 1959-90. Fellow Am. Speech-Lang.-Hearing Assn.; mem. Pub. Mems. Assn. (bd. mem. 1980-91, 97-2003, 2003-04), Ohio State U. Alumni Assn., N.C. Cen. U. Alumni Assn. Democrat. Baptist. Avocations: reading, collecting sculpture of foreign countries, travel, writing, public speaking.

YOUNG, ESTELLE IRENE, dermatologist, educator; b. N.Y.C., Nov. 2, 1945; d. Sidney D. and Blanche (Krosney) Young. BA magna cum laude, Mt. Holyoke Coll., 1967; MD, Downstate Med. Ctr., 1971. Intern Lenox Hill Hosp., N.Y.C., 1971—72, resident in medicine, 1972—73; resident in dermatology Columbia Presbyn. Hosp., 1973—74, NYU Hosp., 1974—75, Boston U. Hosp., 1975—76; asst. dermatologist Harvard U. Health Svcs., Cambridge, 1975—76; assoc. staff mem. dermatology Boston U. Med. Ctr., 1975—76, 1976—77; pvt. practice medicine specializing in dermatology Petersburg, Va., 1976—97; mem. staff Poplar Springs Hosp., 1976—2002, Southside Regional Med. Ctr. (formerly Petersburg Gen. Hosp.), 1976—2002, Ctrl. State Hosp., 1984—. Clin. instr. dept. dermatology Med. Coll. Va., 1976-87, asst. clinic prof., 1988-94, assoc. clin. prof., 1994-2002; sec. med. staff Petersburg Gen. Hosp., 1982; dermatology cons. Cerebral Palsy Assn. N.Y. State, 1999-2005. Author: Visions of Mauna Kea; contbr. articles to profl. jours. Fellow: Am. Acad. Dermatology; mem.: Hawaii Dermatology Soc., Tidewater Dermatology Soc. (pres. 1982—83), Va. Dermatology Soc., Tidewater Physicians Social Responsibility (pres. 1990), Internat. Physicians Prevention of Nuclear War, Physicians Social Responsibility Soc., Sigma Xi. Home and Office: PO Box 20182 New York NY 10021-0063 Office Fax: 212-249-5948. Personal E-mail: eiy112@aol.com.

YOUNG, FREDDIE GILLIAM, principal, educator; b. Miami, Fla., Nov. 1, 1939; d. Thomas and Myrtle (Gibson) Gilliam. BS, Fla. A&M U., 1961; MS, Hunter Coll., 1970; postgrad., U. Ghana, 1970; EdD, Nova U., 1990. Cert. in supervision and adminstrn., African studies, elem. and jr. coll.; cert. asst. prin. Tchr. Collier County Pub. Schs., Naples, Fla., N.Y.C. Pub. Schs., Bronx, NY, Dade County Pub. Schs., Miami, prin.; adj. lead prof. Nova U. Presenter Am. Assn. Ethnic Studies Conf., Fla. Atlantic U., 1991, Assn. Carribean Studies Cairo, 1993, Georgetown, Guyana, 1994, Nat. Assn. African Am. Studies, Houston, 2000, Nat. Commn. on Educating the Black Child, others. Del. 19th congl. dist. Dem. conv., 1988; mem. Am. Jewish Com., African Am. Summitt, London, South Africa, Zimbabwe, West Africa, First Emancipation Independence Day, Ghanna, West Africa, 1998. Named Most Outstanding Black Woman, S. Fla., Women's C. of C., Educator of Yr. Zeta Phi Beta; recipient 50 outstanding svc. awards Prin. Ctr. Harvard U. Sch. Edn., 1989, Metro Dade County commendation for dedicated svc., Ida B. Wells Awd., Nat. Alliance of Black Sch. Educators; finalist for Adminstr. of Yr., 1991, DCSHA. Mem. AAUW, ASCD, Am. Jewish Com., Nat. Alliance Black Educators, S. Fla. Exec. Educators, Leadership Miami, Miami Alliance Black Educators, Nat. Black Women's Polit. Caucus, Dade County Adminstrs. Assn. (chair), Fla. Reading Assn., Dade Reading Coun., Fla. A&M U. Alumni Assn. (pres. Miami-Dade chpt.), Nova U. Alumni Assn. (sec. Miami chpt.), Phi Delta Kappa. Home: 12390 SW 144th Ter Miami FL 33186-7419

YOUNG, GENEVIEVE LEMAN, publishing executive, editor; b. Geneva, Sept. 25, 1930; came to U.S., 1945, naturalized, 1968; d. Clarence Kuangson and Juliana Helen (Yen) Y.; m. Cedric Sun, 1955 (div. 1972); m. Gordon Parks, Aug. 26, 1973 (div. 1979). BA (Wellesley Coll. scholar), Wellesley Coll., 1952. Asst. editor Harper & Row (pubs.), N.Y.C., 1960-62, editor, 1962-64, asst. mng. editor, 1964-66, mng. editor, 1966-70; exec. editor J.B. Lippincott Co., N.Y.C., 1970-77, v.p., 1972-77; sr. editor Little, Brown & Co., N.Y.C., 1977-85; editor-in-chief Lit. Guild Am., N.Y.C., 1985-88; v.p., editorial dir. Bantam Books, N.Y.C., 1988-92. Alumna trustee Phillips Acad., Andover, Mass., 1975-78, class agt., 1979-85; mem. Wellesley Bus. Leadership Coun., 1989-98; mem. Youth Counseling League, 1986-98, pres., 1989-96, mem. com. of 100, 1991-93; mem. Literacy Ptnrs., Inc., N.Y.C., 1992-2001, sec., 1996-2001; mem. Andover Devel. Bd., 1993-98; trustee Jewish Bd. Family and Children's Svcs., 1996-98. Recipient Alumna Achievement award Wellesley Coll., 1982, Matrix award, 1988. Mem. Assn. Am. Pubs. (exec. coun. gen. pub. div. 1975-78, 85-87, freedom to read com. 1972-75), Women's Media Group (pres. 1981-82, 2d v.p. 1994-95), Century Assn. Home: 30 Park Ave New York NY 10016-3801

YOUNG, GLADYS, business owner; m. H. Timothy Kuhn; 3 children. Pres. Young Pontiac Cadillac Dealership, Escondido, Calif. Dir. Downtown Escondido Redevel., Palomar Coll. Pres.'s Assn.; contbr. St. Clare's Home, The North County Interfaith Crisis Ctr., Palomar Pomerado Hosp. Health Found., EYE Counseling and Crisis Ctr., Calif. Ctr. Arts. Recipient Quality Dealer award Time Mag., 1996. Mem. New Car Dealers Assn. (San Diego county chpt. award), Escondido Auto Park Assn. (pres.), Escondido C. of C. (dir.). Office: Young Pontiac Cadillac Dealership 1515 Auto Park Way N Escondido CA 92029-2098

YOUNG, GWENDOLYN VAISEGA, federal agency administrator; b. Hawaii; BS in Elem. Edn., Brigham Young U., MS in Pub. Adminstrn. Intern Comptr. and Space Sta. Program Office NASA, Washington, with Office of Space Sta. Reston, Va., with Nat. Launch Sys. Joint Program Office L.A., with Stennis Space Ctr. Bay St. Louis, Miss., CFO Dryden Flight Rsch. Ctr. Edwards AFB, Calif., 1995—. Office: NASA Dryden Flight Rsch Ctr PO Box 273 MS 2007 Edwards AFB CA 93523-0273

YOUNG, GWYNNE A., lawyer; b. Durham, N.C., 1950; AB, Duke U., 1971; JD, U. Fla., 1974. Bar: Fla. 1974. Asst. state atty. 13th Judicial Cir., Fla.; mem. Carlton, Fields P.A., Tampa, Fla. Instr. U. Fla. Coll. Law, 1974. Exec. editor U. Fla. Law Review, 1973-74. Pres. Jr. League Tampa, Inc., 1985-86; bd. dirs. Assn. Jr. Leagues, Inc., 1987-89, Duke U. Nat. Alumni Assn., 1993—, pres., 1999-2000; trustee Duke U., 1999—2001, Tampa Bar Performing Arts Ctr. Fellow: Am. Bar Found.; mem.: U. Fla. Law Ctr. Assn. (trustee), Fla. Bar (bd. govs.). Office: Carlton Fields Corp Ctr Three at Internat Plaza 4221 W Boy Scout Blvd Tampa FL 33607-5736 Business E-Mail: gyoung@carltonfields.com.

YOUNG, HEATHER A., statistician, researcher; d. Thomas Andrew and Sandra Hope Young; m. James David Durick, June 2, 2001; 1 child, Zachary James Durick. BA, Colgate U., Hamilton, N.Y., 1995; MPH, George Washington U., Washington, 1998; PhD, George Washington U., 2002. Cert. health edn. tchr. Stats. cons. George Washington U., 1998—2002, asst. rsch. prof. dept. epidemiology/biostats., 2002—. Vis. lectr. Georgetown U., Washington, 1999—2001; stats. cons. NAS, Washington, 2003—; ad-hoc com. mem. FIFRA sci. adv. panel U.S. EPA, Washington, 2003—; cons., grant reviewer Anteron, 2003—; cons. editor Archives of Environ./Occupl. Health, 2005—. Contbr. articles to profl. jours. Judge Pa. Jr. Acad. Sci., 1996—2001; mem. cmty. svc. com. Colgate D.C. Alumni Bd. Dirs., 1996—98. Grantee Summer Rsch. grantee, NSF, 1994, Dissertation Rsch. grantee, Cosmos Club, 2000, Pub. Health traineeship, HRSA, 1995; scholar, Colgate U. Alumni Meml. scholar, 1991—95. Mem.: APHA (membership com. chair 1997—98), Internat. Soc. for Environ. Epidemiology, Soc. for Epidemiologic Rsch., Delta Omega, Phi Eta Sigma. Democrat. Presbyterian. Avocations: hiking, reading, running, spinning. Office: George Washington University 2300 Eye St NW Ross 120 Washington DC 20036

YOUNG, JACQUELINE EURN HAI, former state legislator, consultant; b. Honolulu, May 20, 1934; d. Paul Bai and Martha (Cho) Y.; m. Harry Valentine Daniels, Dec. 25, 1954 (div. 1978); children: Paula, Harry, Nani, Laura; m. Daniel Anderson, Sept. 25, 1978 (div. 1984); m. Everett Kleinjans, Sept. 4, 1988 (div. 1998). BS in Speech Pathology, Audiology, U. Hawaii, 1969; MS in Edn., Spl. Edn., Old Dominion U., 1972; advanced cert., Loyola Coll., 1977; PhD in Communication, Women's Studies, Union Inst., 1989. Dir. dept. speech and hearing Md. Sch. for the Blind, Balt., 1975-77; dir. deaf-blind project Easter Seal Soc. Oahu, Hawaii, 1977-78; project dir. equal ednl. opportunity programs Hawaii State Dept. Edn., Honolulu, 1978-85, state ednl. specialist, 1978-90; state rep. dist. 20 Hawaii State Legislature, Honolulu, 1990-92, state rep. dist. 51, 1992-94; vice-speaker Hawaii Ho. of Reps., Honolulu. Apptd. to U.S. Dept. Def. Adv. Commn. on Women in the Svc.; cons. spl. edn. U.S. Dept. Edn., dept. edn. Guam, Am. Samoa, Ponape, Palau, Marshall Islands, 1977-85; cons. to orgns. on issues relating to workplace diversity; adj. prof. commn., anthopology, mgmt. Hawaii Pacific U.; chief staff officer Am. Cancer Soc. Hawaii Pacific, 2004—. TV writer, host, producer, 1992—. 1st v.p. Nat. Women's Polit. Caucus, 1988-90; chair Hawaii Women's Polit. Caucus, 1987-89; bd. dirs. YWCA Oahu, Kalihi Palama Immigrant Svc. Ctr., Hawaii Dem. Movement, Family Peace Ctr.; appointee Honolulu County Com. on the Status of Women, 1986-87; founding bd. dirs. Windward Spouse Abuse Shelter, 1993—; campaign dir. Protect Our Constn., 1998; trustee St. Louis Sch., 1997-99; mem. nat. adv. coun. ACLU, 2004; nat. bd. dirs. Hawaiian Am. Coalition; mem. Asian and Pacific Islander Am. Health Assn.; mem. Hawaii State Adv. Com. on Civil Rights. Recipient Outstanding Woman Leader award YWCA of Oahu, 1994, Pres.'s award Union Inst., 1993, Fellow of the Pacific award Hawaii-Pacific U., 1993, Headliner award Honolulu chpt. Women in Commn., 1993, Korean Am. Alliance Washington Spl. Recognition award, 1998, Hawaii Women Lawyers Disting. Svc. award, 1999, Disting. Equity Adv. award Hawaii chpt. Nat. Coalition for Sex Equity in Edn., 1998, NEA Mary Hatwood Futrell for advancing women's rights award, 1999, Friend of Social Work award Hawaii chpt. NASW, 1998, Allan Saunders award Hawaii chpt. ACLU, 1999, Light of the Orient award Korean Am. Found., 2006; named one of Extraordinary Women Hawaii, Found. Hawaii Women's History, 2001. Home: 212 Luika Pl Kailua HI 96734-3237 Office Phone: 808-432-9142.

YOUNG, JANE ANN, special education educator; b. Evansville, Ind., Nov. 3, 1947; d. Ralph Harley and Rebecca Ann Freels; m. Rupert Stephen Young, Sept. 8, 1979. BSc in Spl. Edn., Ind. State U., 1969, MSc in Spl. Edn., 1973. Lic. spl. edn. educator Ind., Fla., real estate Fla. Tchr. spl. edn. Evansville (Ind.)-Vanderburgh Sch. Corp., 1969—79, Westlake Spl. Edn. Corp., Munster, Ind., 1979—83, Indian River County Schs., Vero Beach, Fla., 1984—87; dir. edn. Psychiatric Inst. Rivendell Hosp., Vero Beach, 1987—91; tchr. exceptional student edn. Brevard County Schs., Melbourne, Fla., 1992—. Dir. ednl. vocat. tng. Children's Psychiatric Ctr., Palm Bay, Fla., 1991—92; cons., revision writer Procedures for Residential Psychiatric Hospital, 1991. Coord. Columbia Elem. Keep Brevard (Fla.) Beautiful, 1996—. Grantee, Xeriscape Fund, 2000—01. Mem.: PTA (rep. 1999—), Audubon Soc., McKee Botanical Gardens, Brevard (Fla.) Fedn. Tchrs., Women of Moose. Avocations: cooking, crafts, theater, music, gardening. Home: 9797 Honeysuckle Dr Sebastian FL 32976 Office: Columbia Elementary Sch 1225 Waco Blvd SE Palm Bay FL 32909

YOUNG, JANET CHERYL, electrical engineer; b. Roanoke, Va., Oct. 3, 1960; d. Don Gordon and Barbara Hill (Mumpower) Y. BS in Physics, U. Tenn., Chattanooga, 1982; MSEE, Va. Tech. Inst., 1991. Engr. Sci. Applications Internat. Corp., Springfield, Va., 1982—91, United Telecom Coun., Washington, 1991—93, LCC, Internat., McLean, Va., 1993—2002, Sprint Nextel Corp., Reston, Va., 2002—. Active Cmty. Band, Vienna, Va., 1985; vol. Shakespeare Theatre Co., 1996—97; mem. Prince William County Dem. Com., Democracy for Am., 2004; active World Peace Mission Foundry United Meth. Ch., Washington, 1984. Mem. IEEE (mem. Electromagnetic Compatibility Soc. 1987-91, Comm. Soc. 1992—). Methodist. Avocations: gardening, travel, genealogy. Home: 4044 Chetham Way Woodbridge VA 22192 Office: 12000 Sunrise Valley Dr Reston VA 20191

YOUNG, JAYNE, recording industry executive; b. Houston, Dec. 6, 1961; d. James Nesbitt and Mary Frances Young. Student, Stephen F. Austin U., 1981-82, Belmont U., 1983-86. Mgr. prodn. MCA Records, Nashville, 1983-85, dir. mktg., 1985-90; pub. rels. dir. Hard Rock Cafe, Internat., N.Y.C., 1992-93; dir. product devel. RCA Records, Nashville, 1990-91; v.p. of artist repitorie W.& R. Group (divsn. Sony), N.Y.C., 1993—. Author: (series) What's a Girl to Do?; creator: (record series) Live at the Grand Old Opry, 1986—. Mem. transfer com. Jr. League Nashville, 1985-92, Jr. League N.Y., 1993—; bd. dirs. Arthritis Found., Nashville; mem. young com. N.Y. Hist. Soc., N.Y.C., 1995-97. Mem. NARAS. Republican. Baptist. Avocations: travel, collecting antiques, auctions, yoga, tennis. Office: W And R Group 7 Pratt Blvd Glen Cove NY 11542-2758

YOUNG, JEANNETTE ROSE, music educator; b. Columbus, Nebr., Feb. 19, 1949; d. Vladimir Joseph Hamata and Rose Elizabeth Stava; m. David Russell Young; 1 child, Angela Kroeger. MusM, U. Nebr., 1992, B in Music Edn., 1971; PhD in Adminstrn., U. Neb., 2002. Cert. Kodály method. Instr. vocal music Schuyler Ctrl. HS, Schuyler, Nebr., 1976—79; tchr. vocal music K - 9 Papillion-LaVista Sch. Dist., Papillion, Nebr., 1979—98; assoc. prof. music Nebr. Wesleyan U., Lincoln, Nebr., 1998—. Dir. Kodály cert. program Nebr. Wesleyan U., Lincoln, 1998—. Recipient Kodaly cert., 1991. Mem.: Nebr. Music Educators Assn., Music Educators Nat. Conf., Nebraska Choral Dirs. Assn., Am. Choral Dirs. Assn., Coll. Music Soc., Plains States Kodály Orgn. (pres. 1989—91), Orgn. Am. Kodály Educators, Internat. Kodaly Soc., Delta Kappa Gamma (Bernita Minkwitz Internat. scholarship 1997, Rho state scholarship, Alpha Alpha chpt. scholarship). Presbyterian. Avocations: bird-watching, architecture, gardening. Home: 8138 Wemsha St Lincoln NE 68507-3377 Office: Nebr Wesleyan U 5000 St Paul Ave Lincoln NE 68504-2794 Office Phone: 402-465-2290. Home Fax: 402-465-2179; Office Fax: 402-465-2179. Personal E-mail: dyoung1@neb.rr.com. Business E-Mail: jry@nebrwesleyan.edu.

YOUNG, JOYCE L., chemicals executive; Chief info. officer, v.p. info. tech. CP Kelco, 2003—. Named one of Premier 100 IT Leaders, Computerworld, 2005. Office: CP Kelco Ste 1000 1000 Parkwood Cir Atlanta GA 30339 Office Phone: 678-247-7300.

YOUNG, JUDITH ANNE, animal conservationist; b. LA, Feb. 11, 1953; d. John Mahlstedt Young and Cynthia Sheilds Tunnicciff. CEO Otter Conservation Ctr., Statesboro, Ga., 1983—. Copyright U.S. Govt., 1995. Avocations: gardening, agriculture. Office Phone: 912-839-2100. Personal E-mail: judy@g-net.net.

YOUNG, JUNE HURLEY, elementary school educator, writer; b. Cleve., Jan. 30, 1932; d. Albrd C. Ching and Helen M. Walker; m. John Robert Young, Feb. 17, 1977 (dec.); children: Sean K. Hurley, Kathleen Hurley Coker. BA in Edn. cum laude, Fla. State U., 1953; Master's, U. So. Fla., 1979. Cert. tchr. Fla. Tchr. grade 5 Norwood Elem. Sch.; tchr. grades 5 and 6 Pasadena Elem. Sch., tchr. grade 1; tchr. kindergarten Romper Room TV, Kindergarten Corners', WEDU-TV, 1985, Baypoint Elem. Sch.; tchr. gifted and talented 16th St. Mid. Sch., 1987; realtor Frank T. Hurley Assocs., Realtor, Inc., 1950—. Author: The Don CeSar Story, 1975, How to Be Your Child's Best Teacher, 1980, Florida's Pinellas Peninsula, 1985, updated, 1998, The Vinoy-Faded Glory Renewed, 1999; contbr. articles to newspapers. Pres. St. Petersburg Coterie, 1953—61, Pan Hellenic, St. Petersburg, 1965—67; chmn. Save the Don CeSar Hotel Com., St. Petersburg, 1971—72. Nominee Outstanding Tchr., 1957; recipient Outstanding Woman Vol. award, Eckerd Drug Co., 2000; grantee, Fla. Endowment of Arts, 1980—83. Mem.: Suntan Art Assn., Camp Farthest Out (sec.-leader 1980—2006), Pass-a-Grille Woman's Club (chorus mem. 1999—2005), Phi Kappa Phi. Republican. Methodist. Avocations: watercolor painting, designing glass jewelry. Home: 362 89th Ave NE Saint Petersburg FL 33702 Office Phone: 727-367-1949.

YOUNG, KATHLEEN MARIE, special education educator; b. Anchorage, July 29, 1953; BS in Spl. Edn., Ill. State U., 1975; MS in Spl. Edn., No. Ill. U., 1981; student, Concordia U., 1994. Cert. learning disabilities, EMH, elem., blind and visual impaired, social and emotional disorders, adminstrn. and supervision, Ill., 2005; nat. bd. cert. tchr.-exceptional needs specialist, 2005. Learning disabled/visually impaired tchr. St. Joseph (Ill.) Sch. Dist., 1975-78; learning disabilities resource tchr. Sch. Dist. # 300, West Dundee, Ill., 1978-81, Sch. Dist. # 102, Buffalo Grove, Ill., 1981—. Adj. faculty mem. Govs. State U., Univ. Park, Ill., 1988—; presenter in field Author: L.D. Simulation Materials, 1997, KidTips, 2003. Founder of Lambda Delta Fraternity, nat. recognized orgn. for successful people with learning disabilites. P. Buckley Moss Learning Disabled Tchr. of Yr. 2d place winner, 1994. Mem. Orton Dyslexia Soc. (pubs. chmn. 1987-90, tchr. trainer pres. 1991-94, v.p. 1992-94), Learning Disabilities Assn. (conf. com. 1994), Lions Club, Lioness Club, Delta Kappa Gamma (literacy com. 1991). Office: Meridian Mid Sch 2195 Brandywyn Ln Buffalo Grove IL 60089-6694

YOUNG, KIMBERLY S., finance educator, psychologist; m. James E. O'Mara, June 7, 1997. BS in Bus. and Fin., U. Buffalo, 1988; M in Clin. Psychology, Ind. U. Pa., 1992, PhD in Clin. Psychology, 1994. Lic. psychologist State Bd. Psychology, 1999. Clin. intern Cleve. Vets. Med. Ctr., 1993—94; post doctoral fellow Strong Meml. Hosp., Rochester, NY, 1994—95; CEO Ctr. for Online Addiction, Bradford, Pa., 1995—; prof. mgmt. scis. St. Bonaventure U., NY, 2000—. Author: Caught in the Net, Tangled in the Web; contbr. articles to profl. jours. Bd. dirs. Beacon Light Behavioral Health Sys., Bradford, Pa., 2004—05. Recipient Alumni award for Outstanding Achievement, Ind. U. of Pa., 2000. Fellow: Pa. Psychol. Assn. (Psychology in Media award 2001, 2004); mem.: APA, Internat. Soc. Mental Health Online, Employee Assistance Profls. Assn., Rotary. Office: St Bonaventure U Sch of Bus Saint Bonaventure NY 14778 Office Phone: 716-375-2076.

YOUNG, LAI-SANG, mathematician, educator; b. Hong Kong, 1952; BS, U. Wisconsin, 1973; MA, U. Berkeley, 1976, PhD, 1978. Prof. Northwestern U., 1978, U. Warwick, England, 1979—80, Michigan State U., 1980; prof. math. UCLA, 1981; visiting prof. Math. Sci. Rsch. Inst., Berkeley, 1983—84, U. Bielefeld, Germany, 1985—86, Inst. Advanced Study, Princeton, 1989; prof. math. NYU, Courant Inst. Math. Sci., NYC. Recipient Ruth Lyttle Math. prize Am. Math. Soc., 1993, Guggenheim Fellowship, 1997-98. Fellow: Am. Acad. Arts & Sci.

YOUNG, LAURA, dance educator, choreographer; b. Boston, Aug. 5, 1947; d. James Vincent and Adelaide Janet Young; m. Anthony Charles Catanzaro, Sept. 26, 1970 (div. Nov. 1981); m. Christopher Edward Mehl, Aug. 23, 1987. Grad. H.S., Cohasset, Mass. Dancer Met. Opera Ballet, N.Y.C., 1971-73, Boston Ballet Co., 1963-65, prin. dancer, 1965-71, 73-89, ballet mistress, 1989-91. Guest tchr. Dance Tchrs. Club Boston, 1978—82, Dance Masters Assn., 1979, 90, 92, 93, Walnut Hill Sch., Natick, Mass., 1984—87, Natick, 1990—91, Granite State Ballet, 1993, Portland Ballet, Maine, Nat. Dance Theatre Bermuda, 1993, Worcester Performing Arts Sch., Mass., 1994, Alwin Sch. Dance Summer Intensive, Albuquerque, 1994—95, Ashland Youth Ballet, Ky., 1995, N.E. Regional Festival, 1996, Okla. Summer Arts Inst., 2000, Pitts. Ballet Theater Summer Program, 2000; asst. dir. Boston Ballet II, 1984—86, tchr., dir., 1986—94, dir. Summer Dance Program, 1986—94; dir. DanceLab, 2001—; 1st hon. mem. Dance Masters Assn., Chpt. 5, 1992; mem. faculty Boston Conservatory, 1990—94, Boston Ballet Sch., 2004—, prin., 1993—2004. Choreographer (ballets) Occasional Waltzes, 1984, Albinoni Suite, 1986, Champ Dances, 1987, A Place of Sound and Mind, 1988, Deadlock, 1989, Rumpelstiltskin, 1989. Recipient Leadership award Greater Boston C. of C., 1987; named Disting. Bostonian Boston's 350th Jubilee Com., 1980. Mem. Am. Guild Mus. Artists, Dance Masters Am. (hon.). Office: Boston Ballet Co 19 Clarendon St Boston MA 02116-6100 Office Phone: 617-456-6250. Business E-Mail: lyoung@bostonballet.com.

YOUNG, LAURA ELIZABETH, artist; b. Glen Ridge, N.J., Apr. 1, 1941; d. Thomas Edward and Charlotte Elizabeth (Post) Y.; m. James Andrew Murphy, Jun. 15, 1963 (div. 1985); children: Kevin Thomas, Timothy James.; m. Thomas Raymond Aprile, May 20, 1995. BA, Skidmore Coll., 1963; MA, Montclair State Coll., 1978; MFA, Rutgers U., 1983. Cert. Fine Arts and English, K-12 tchr., N.J. Adj. faculty Fine Arts Dept. Kean Coll., Union, N.J., 1983-84, Montclair (N.J.) State Coll., 1983-92, Long Island U., Bklyn., 1994; cons., workshop leader The Lincoln Ctr. Inst., N.Y.C., 1983—96. Lectr. Mus. Modern Art, N.Y.C., 1990-96; visual arts cons., workshop leader The Nashville Inst. for the Arts, 1992-98—, Lincoln Ctr. Inst.; adj. faculty Fine Arts Dept. U. Iowa, 1996—' artist in residence Tyron Guthrie Ctr., Ireland, 2006. One person shows include: Interior Space Design, N.Y.C., 1991, Manhattenville Coll., N.Y., 1993, Cedar Rapids (Iowa) Mus. Art, 1998, Monmouth (Ill.) Coll., 2001; group shows Colgate U., Hamilton, N.Y., 1995, Vincennes (Ind.) U., 2003. Grantee fellow in painting N.J. State Coun. on the Arts, Trenton, 1985, Iowa Arts Coun., 1997, 2001, Va. Ctr. Creative Arts, Sweet Briar, Va., 1985, 86, 2001, 2002-03, 2004, Intermedia Performance grantee Sch. Fine and Performing Arts, Montclair, 1992, Pollock Krasner Found. grantee, 1994, fellow Tyrone Guthrie Ctr., Monaghan County, Ireland, 2006. Democrat. Avocations: nature walks, collecting folk art. Home: 50 Lakeview Pl NE Iowa City IA 52240-9162 E-mail: lauraelizabethyo@aol.com.

YOUNG, LORETTA ANN, auditor; b. Reading, Pa., Dec. 2, 1962; d. Milton and Delois Jean (Ridley) Y. BS, Towson U., 1985. CPA, cert. fin. svcs. auditor, internal auditor. Auditor Irving Burton Assocs., Inc., Washington, 1984-88; tax technician Gen. Bus. Svcs., Germantown, Md., 1989; auditor Montgomery County Govt., Rockville, Md., 1989-90; dir. membership devel. Nat. Forum for Black Pub. Adminstrs., Washington, 1990-91; sr. acct.-analyst Cox & Assocs. CPAs, P.C., Hyattsville, Md., 1992; mgr. ops. LKA Computer Cons., Inc., Hyattsville, 1992-94; supervisory auditor Office Specialists, Inc., Washington, 1994-97; sr. auditor Amtrak, Washington, 1997-2000; sr. mgr. Deloitte & Touche, 2000—05, Unisys, 2005—. Mem. AICPA, Inst. Internal Auditors, Md. Assn. CPAs., Assn. Govt. Accts. Home: PO Box 479 Germantown MD 20875-0479 Office: 11720 Plz Am Dr Reston VA 20190 Personal E-mail: lyoungcpa@aol.com. Business E-Mail: Loretta.Young@unisys.com.

YOUNG, LUCIA PATAT, psychotherapist; b. Charleston, SC, Aug. 19, 1947; d. Leon Philip and Amelia (Wallace) P.; m. David Michael Young, Sept. 2, 1972; children: David Michael II, Allison Amelia. BS, U. S.C., 1969; MEd, EdS, U. Fla., 1991, PhD, 1996. Lic. mental health counselor Nat. Bd. Cert. Counselors. Mental health assoc. Med. U. S.C., Charleston, 1969; exec. sec. Mass. Gen. Hosp., Boston, 1969-73, sr. biol. and biochem. technician dept. neurology, summer 1974; adminstrv. asst. Harvard U., Cambridge, Mass., 1973-74; tchr. biology, anatomy and physiology Brimmer & May Sch., Chestnut Hill, Mass., 1974-76; mng. editl. asst. Molecular and Cellular Biochemistry, Gainesville, Fla., 1982-86; adminstrv. asst. U. Fla. Found., Gainesville, Fla., 1986-89; addictions counselor Bridge House Residential Ctr., Gainesville, 1990-91; sch. guidance counselor Trenton (Fla.) Middle and H.S., 1991-92; mental health counselor, children's outpatient dept. Mental Health Svcs., Gainesville, 1992-93; children's bereavement counselor, family counselor Hospice of N. Ctrl. Fla., Gainesville, 1993-96; pvt. practice Gainesville, 1996—2000, Gloucester, Mass., 2000—01, Ellsworth, Maine, 2001—; trauma therapist Arbour Trauma Counseling Ctr., Allston, Mass., 2000—01. Mem. AAAS, Am. Assn. Marriage and Family Therapy, Internat. Assn. Eating Disorders Profls., Kappa Delta Pi, Chi Sigma Iota. Home: 29 Tenney Hl Blue Hill ME 04614-5948 Office: 114 State St Ellsworth ME 04605 Office Phone: 207-667-4334. Personal E-mail: luciayoungly@yahoo.com.

YOUNG, LUCY CLEAVER, retired physician; b. Aug. 8, 1943; d. Oliver B. and Ada (Smith) Cleaver; m. Lynn H. Young, Feb. 4, 1968 (div. 1977); m. Lynn H. Young, Apr. 2, 1986; 1 child, Clinton Oliver. BS in Chemistry, Wheaton Coll., Ill., 1965; MD, Ohio State U., 1969. Diplomate Am. Bd. Family Practice, Bd. Ins. Medicine. Rotating intern Riverside Meth. Hosp., Columbus, Ohio, 1969—70; resident Trumbull Meml. Hosp., Warren, Ohio, 1970—71; practice medicine specializing in family practice West Chicago, Ill., 1971—73, Paw Paw and Mendota, Ill., 1973—78; co-founder, med. dir. Wholistic Health Ctr. of Mendota, 1976—78; asst. med. dir. Gt. Lakes head office Met. Life Ins. Co., Aurora, Ill., 1979—80; med. dir. Commonwealth Life Ins. Co., Louisville, 1980—85; locum tenens family practice Kron Med. Corp. of Chapel Hill, NC, 1986—89; physician Red Bird Mission & Med. Ctr., Beverly, Ky., 1989—90; family practice floater Ochsner Clinic satellites, New Orleans, 1990—2006; ret. Assoc. prof. U. Ill. Abraham Lincoln Sch. Medicine, 1976-79; faculty monitor MacNeal Meml. Hosp. Family Practice Ctr. (Ill.), 1979-80; faculty preceptor U. Louisville Family Practice Dept., 1981-85; clin. faculty preceptor La. State U. Sch. Medicine, 1992-2006; mem. staffs Ctrl. DuPage Hosp., Winfield, Ill., 1971-73, Mendota Cmty. Hosp., 1973-80, Ochsner Found. Hosp., New Orleans, 1991-2006; musician La. Via de Cristo, 2003-05. Vol. Red Bird Med. Ctr., 1985—; part-time worship coord. Hosanna Luth. Ch., Mandeville, La., 1996-97; musician, lay preacher, nursing home visitor, 1990—. Fellow Am. Acad. Family Practice; mem. Christian Med. and Dental Assns. (del. to Ho. 1995-2000). Lutheran. Home: PO Box 0730 Madisonville LA 70447-0730

YOUNG, LYNN MARIE, psychotherapist, freelance artist; b. Mpls., Nov. 4, 1954; d. Vernon Earle and Shirley Ann (Mitchell) Mollan; m. Benjamin Brock Young, Dec. 22, 1979; children: Patrick Whiting, Megan Amanda. BS in Social Work magna cum laude, U. Minn., 1977; MA in Counseling and Human Svcs., Colo. U., 1996. Tng. asst. Planned Parenthood Minn., St. Paul, 1977-79; health educator Health Start, St. Paul, 1981-89; case mgr., regional affairs coord. Myron Stratton Home, Colorado Springs, Colo., 1990-91; adolescent outreach specialist Chrysalis, A Ctr. For Women, Mpls., 1994; sr. health educator Minn. Dept. of Health, Mpls., 1994-95; pregnancy counselor Luth. Family Svcs., Colorado Springs, 1996-98; pvt. practice psychotherapist Colorado Springs, 1996—. Co-author: Human Sexuality: Values and Choices, 1986, also video (Cert. of Merit, Chgo. Film Festival 1986, AMA 1989), Understanding Sexuality: Making Healthy Choices, 1988. Edn. program mgr. Planned Parenthood Rocky Mountains, 2003—. Sinclair scholar U. Minn., 1976. Mem. ACA, Colo. Counseling Assn. Democrat. Congregationalist. Avocations: spirituality, reading, cooking, skiing. Home: 10435 Marble Creek Cir Colorado Springs CO 80908-4501

YOUNG, MARGARET BUCKNER, civic worker, author; b. Campbellsville, Ky.; d. Frank W. and Eva (Carter) Buckner; m. Whitney M. Young, Jr., Jan. 2, 1944 (dec. Mar. 1971); children: Marcia Elaine, Lauren Lee. BA, Ky. State Coll., 1942, MA, U. Minn., 1946. Instr. Ky. State Coll., 1942-44; instr. edn. and psychology Spelman Coll., Atlanta, 1957-60; dir. emeritus N.Y. Life Ins. Co.; alt. del. UN Gen. Assembly, 1973. Mem. pub. policy com. Advt. Coun. Trustee emerita Lincoln Ctr. for Performing Arts; chmn. Whitney M. Young, Jr. Meml. Found., 1971-92; trustee Met. Mus. Art, 1976-90; bd. govs. UN Assn., 1975-82; bd. visitors U.S. Mil. Acad., 1978-80; dir. Philip Morris Cos., 1972-91. Author: The First Book of American Negroes, 1966, The Picture Life of Martin Luther King, Jr., 1968, The Picture Life of Ralph J. Bunche, 1968, Black American Leaders-Watts, 1969, The Picture Life of Thurgood Marshall, 1970, pub. affairs pamphlet.

YOUNG, MARGARET LABASH, librarian, information consultant, editor; b. Bridgeport, Conn., Aug. 17, 1926; d. George and Mary (Feltovic) Labash; m. Harold Chester Young, June 7, 1958 (div. July 1991); children: Jeffery Avery, Amy Margaret. BA, Cornell U., 1948; AMLS, U. Mich., 1959. Mktg. grader Harvard Bus. Sch., Boston, 1949-52; ops. rsch. sales asst. Arthur D. Little, Inc., Boston, 1953-57; reference libr. U. Mich., Dearborn, 1959-62; editor Gale Rsch., Detroit, 1964-74, Mpls., 1977-88; libr. Salzburg (Austria) Seminar, 1981-83; editor, info. cons. self employed, Hopkins, Minn., 1989—. Tax libr. cons. KPMG Peat Marwick, LLP, Mpls., 1991—; indexer Small Bus. Innovation Rsch., Minn. Project Innovation, Mpls., 1990-97. Co-editor: Directory of Special Libraries and Information Centers, edits. 3-6, 1974-81, Life Sciences Organizations and Agencies Directory, 1988; editor: Scientific and Technical Organizations and Agencies Directory, 1985, 2d edit., 1987. Host family Am. Field Svcs., 1979-80, 80-81; mem. steering com. Twin Cities Internat. Citizens Award, 1996-99. Mem. Spl. Librs. Assn. (internat. rels. chair Minn. chpt. 1994—2003, Quality in Action award, Minn. Chpt. Spl. Librs. Assn., 2003, Fannie Simon award Pub. divsn. 1989), Am. Soc. Indexers, Beta Phi Mu. Democrat. Episcopalian. Avocations: travel, gardening, classical music, dance, aerobics. Home: 313 Farmdale Rd W Hopkins MN 55343-7111

YOUNG, MARJORIE ANN, librarian; b. Ann Arbor, Mich., Jan. 30, 1945; d. Robert and Laura Kirstine (Larsen) Y. BA in French, Mich. State U., 1968; AMLS, U. Mich., 1969; MA in French Lang. and Lit., NYU, 1976. Asst. catalog libr. SUNY, New Paltz, 1969-73, asst. ref. libr., 1974-77, sr. asst. catalog libr., 1978-81, assoc. catalog libr., 1982-2000, catalog libr., 2000—. Chmn., bd. dirs. Adventist Sch., Poughkeepsie, NY; team leader Bibliographic Access, 2000—. Phi Beta Kappa. Avocations: singing, travel, languages, cooking, classical music. Home: PO Box 341 New Paltz NY 12561-0341 Business E-Mail: youngm@newpaltz.edu.

YOUNG, MARLENE ANNETTE, lawyer; b. Portland, Oreg., Mar. 3, 1946; d. Hardy Shelby and Eunice Jean (Gregory) Y.; m. Abdullah Samir Rifai, June 3, 1973 (div. May 1981); m. John Hollister Stein, Jan. 1, 1986. BS, Portland State U., 1967; PhD, Georgetown U., 1973; JD, Willamette U., 1975. Bar: Oreg. 1975. Dir. research Multnomah County Sheriff's Office, Portland, 1975-77; sole practice Wilsonville, Oreg., 1975-81; exec. dir. Applied Systems Research & Data, Wilsonville, 1976-81, Nat. Orgn. Victim Assistance, Washington, 1981—. Instr. Essex Community Coll., 1971-73, U. Utah, 1976-78, Portland State U., 1979; cons. U. Research Corp., Washington, 1979-83, ABT Assocs., Boston, 1984—. Author: Victim Service System, 1983; (manuals) Patrol Officers and Crime Victims, 1984, Prosecutors: Attorneys for the People, Advocates for the Victims, 1984; editor: Justice and Older Americans, 1977; contbr. articles to profl. jours. Mem. Ways and Means Com., Wilsonville City, 1977-79, planning commn., 1979-81; Bd. visitors Willamette Coll. Law, Salem, Oreg., 1981-83; bd. dirs. Chemeketa Community Coll., Salem, 1979. Recipient Presdl. award Nat. Orgn. Victim Assistance, Washington, 1981, 92, Pub.Policy award World Fedn. Mental Health, Washington, 1983, Found. for Improvementof Justice award, 1988. Mem. ABA (criminal justice sect., adv. bd. 1981-90), Am. Profl. Soc. Abuse of Children (bd. dirs. 1986—), Soc. Traumatic Stress Studies (bd. dirs. 1985—, treas.), World Soc. Victimology (adv. bd. 1979—, exec. com. 1986—, v.p., Hans Von Hentig award 1985). Democrat. Methodist. Avocations: piano, running, gardening, pets.

YOUNG, MARY DELORES, special education educator; b. Moulton, Ala., July 26, 1946; d. Roy Edgar Hood and Jimmie Florence Henson; children: Kristy Deanna Hawkins, Dawana Mechelle Long. BS in Psychology, Athens State U., Ala., 1980, BS in Elem. Edn., 1989; MS in Mental Retardation, U. N. Ala., Florence, 1991. Spl. edn. tchr. Hamilton H.S., Ala., 1986—. Sponsor S.A.D.D. Mem.: NEA, Ala. Edn. Assn. Democrat. Baptist. Avocations: horseback riding, genealogy. Home: PO Box 381 Hamilton AL 35570 Office: Hamilton HS 211 Aggie Ave Hamilton AL 35570 Office Phone: 205-921-3281. Personal E-mail: dyoung.hhh@emche.net.

YOUNG, MARY ELIZABETH, history professor; b. Utica, N.Y., Dec. 16, 1929; d. Clarence Whitford and Mary Tippit Y. BA, Oberlin Coll., 1950; PhD, Cornell U., 1955. Instr. dept. history Ohio State U., Columbus, 1955-58, asst. prof., 1958-63, assoc. prof., 1963-69, prof., 1969-73; prof. history U. Rochester, NY, 1973—2000, prof. emeritus, 2000—. Cons. in field. Author: Redskins, Ruffleshirts, and Rednecks: Indian Allotments in Alabama and Mississippi, 1830-1860, 1961; co-editor, contbr.: The Frontier in American Development: Essays in Honor of Paul Wallace Gates, 1969. Recipient Pelzer award Miss. Valley Hist. Assn., 1955, award Am. Studies Assn., 1982, Ray A. Billington award, 1982; Shalkenbach Found. grantee, 1951-55, Social Sci. Rsch. Coun. grantee, 1968-69; Ezra Cornell fellow Cornell U., 1951-55. Mem. Am. Hist. Assn., Orgn. Am. Historians, Soc. for Historians of the Early Am. Republic, Am. Antiquarian Soc. Home: 2230 Clover St Rochester NY 14618-4124 Office: U Rochester Dept History Rochester NY 14627 Office Phone: 585-275-2054. Business E-Mail: yngm@mail.rochester.edu.

YOUNG, MICHAEL COCHISE, academic administrator; b. Phila., Oct. 12, 1957; d. Donald Robert and Helene (Callahan) Y. BA in English, St. Joseph's U., Phila., 1976; MA in English, U. Pa., 1978, PhD in English, 1983. Asst. prof. Tulane U., New Orleans, 1981-86, health professions advisor, 1986-88, dir. honors program, 1986-90; dir. ednl. svcs. univ. honors coll. Ariz. State U., Tempe, 1990-91, assoc. dean, 1991—2001; dir. Flinn Found. Scholarship Program, LLC, Phoenix, 2001—. Contbr. articles to profl. jours. Mem. Nat. Collegiate Honors Coun. (exec. com. 1990-92), Nat. Assn. Fellowship Advisors. Avocations: music, theater, reading, cooking, hiking. Office: The Flinn Found 1802 N Central Ave Phoenix AZ 85004 Office Phone: 602-744-6800. Business E-Mail: myoung@flinn.org.

YOUNG, NANCY, lawyer; b. Washington, Dec. 3, 1954; d. John Young and Byounghye Chang; m. Paul Brendan Ford, Jr., May 28, 1983; children: Paul Brendan III, Ian A., Hunter Chang Young, Jade Augustine Young. BA, Yale U., 1975, MA, 1976; JD, Columbia U., 1979. Bar: N.Y. 1981. Assoc. Simpson Thacher & Bartlett, N.Y.C., 1979-82, Richards O'Neil & Allegaert, N.Y.C., 1982-86; ptnr., chair internat. practice group Richards & O'Neil, N.Y.C., 1986-2001, Bingham McCutchen LLP, N.Y.C. Lectr. Am. corp. and securities law Tokyo U. Faculty of Law, 1992. Author: Basic Business Japanese, 1998; contbr. articles to legal publs. Mem. Tribar Legal Opinion Com., 2001—. Named Internat. Woman of Yr., 1992-93. Mem. ABA (co-chmn. conf. minority ptnrs in corp. majority law firms 1992, mem. Triba legal opinion com. 2001-), Asian-Am. Bar Assn., Assn. Bar of City of N.Y., Am. Fgn. Law Assn., Coun. on Fgn. Rels., Fgn. Policy Assn. (bd. govs. 1995-2001), Yale U. Alumni Assn. (bd. govs. 1989-92), Columbia U. Law Sch. Assn. (bd. dirs. 1991-92), Columbia U. Alumni Assn. (bd. dirs. 1991-92), Yale Club N.Y. (bd. dirs. 1996-98), Asia Soc. Office: Bingham McCutchen LLP 399 Park Avenue New York NY 10022 Business E-Mail: nancy.young@bingham.com.

YOUNG, NANCY HENRIETTA MOE, retired elementary education educator; b. Athens, Ohio, June 25, 1936; d. Charles N. Moe and Mary E. (Sams) Moe-Oyler; m. Henry O. Young, May 13, 1956; children: Pamela Sue Young Paustenbach, Patrick H. BA in Elem. Edn., Ohio U., 1973, degree in elem. edn., 1983. Tchr. 3rd grade Berne Union Sch., Sugar Grove, Ohio, 1968-86, tchr. 4th grade, 1987-94, head dept., 1992-94; tchr. 8th grade English and reading Berne Union Mid. Sch., Sugar Grove, Ohio, 1995-96, 6th grade English, reading and sci. tchr., 1996-98. Music tchr. Fairfield Christian Acad., Lancaster, Ohio, 1999—. Jennings scholar Capital U., 1980-81. Mem. NEA, Ohio Edn. Assn., Berne Union Edn. Assn., Delta Kappa Gamma. Republican. Mem. 1st Ch. of God. Avocations: music, reading, travel. Home: 2410 Blue Valley Rd SE Lancaster OH 43130-9019

YOUNG, NANCY MAYER, retired secondary school educator, artist; b. Pensacola, Fla., May 24, 1933; d. Mark Bodenheimer Mayer and Elsie Nobles; m. Richard S. Young, June 7, 1955 (dec. Oct. 1996); children: Deeann, Sandra, Mark. BS, Fla. State U., 1955. Tchr. pub. schs., Athens, Ala., 1955—56; artist Sunnyvale, Calif., 1961—67; tchr. pub. schs., Arlington, Va., 1968—70; piano tchr. McLean, Va., 1968—75; salesperson art and pottery McLean and Annapolis, Md., 1975—81; salesperson Dee Real Estate, Bronxville, NY, 1981—83; travel agt. Travco, McLean, 1984—87. Mem. Beautification Bd., Cape Canaveral, Fla., 1989—96, Libr. Bd., Cape Canaveral, 1984—96. Avocation: watercolor painting. Home: 673 Heatherstone Dr Merritt Island FL 32953

YOUNG, NAOMI, lawyer; b. Bronx, NY; BA, Santa Clara U., 1971, JD, 1974. Bar: Calif. 1974, US Dist. Ct., Cent. Dist. Calif. 1978, US Ct. Appeals, Ninth Circuit 1978, US Dist. Ct., No. Dist. Calif. 1983, US Dist. Ct., So. Dist. Calif. 1985. Atty. Nat. Labor Rels. Bd.; founding prin. Gartner & Young; ptnr., labor, employment litig. Baker & Hostetler LLP, LA. Vol. referee Review Dept., Calif. State Bar Ct.; vol. mediator LA Superior Ct.; commr. Calif. Fair Employment and Housing Commn. Bd. dirs. Legal Aid Soc. San Francisco. Named So. Calif. Super Lawyer, Law & Politics, 2004; named one of Am. Top Black Lawyers, Black Enterprise Mag., 2003. Mem.: ABA, Calif. Women Lawyers (bd. dirs.), LA County Bar Assn. (exec. com. employment law section), Nat. Bar Assn., John M. Langston Assn., Black Women Lawyers' Assn. LA, Inc., Nat. Employment Law Coun. (founding mem.), Calif. Assn. Black Lawyers. Office: Baker & Hostetler LLP Ste 1800 333 S Grand Ave Los Angeles CA 90071-1523 Office Phone: 213-975-1600. Office Fax: 213-975-1740. Business E-Mail: nyoung@bakerlaw.com.

YOUNG, NATALIE JANE, elementary special education educator; b. Noel, Mo., Sept. 9, 1938; d. Steve E. and Iris Irene (Moseley) Brady; m. Ernest H. Young, Sept. 9, 1956; children: David E., Rebecca C. Boling, Karen J. Davis. AD, Crowder Coll., Neosho, Mo., 1973; BSE with honors, Mo. So. State U., Joplin, 1975; M in Spl. Edn., Pittsburg (Kans.) State U., 1979. Tchr. learning disabled, tchr. spl. edn. Gravette (Ark.) Elem. Sch., 1975—99; ret. Asst. leader 4-H Club, Noel, 1970s. Named Tchr. of Yr., Learning Disabilities Assn., Benton County, Ark., 1977. Mem. Ch. of Christ.

YOUNG, NORA JANE, actuary, consultant; b. Fargo, N.D., June 18, 1966; d. David Allan and Elaine Emily Young. BA in Math., Whitman Coll., Walla Walla, Wash., 1987. Cert. profl. ins. woman. Actuarial intern United Pacific Ins. Co., Federal Way, Wash., 1986, actuarial student, 1987, Milliman & Robertson, Seattle, 1988-89; actuarial cons., v.p. Marsh USA Inc., Seattle, 1989—. Mem. Ins. Profls. South King County (sec. 1995-97, v.p. 1997-98, pres. 1998-99, Most Valuable Mem. 1997, Rookie of Yr. 1996), Ins. Profls. of

South King County, Casualty Actuarial Soc. (assoc.), Am. Acad. Actuaries, Casualty Actuaries of the Northwest, Ins. Inst. of Am. (assoc. in risk mgmt.), Nat. Assn. Ins. Women (cert. profl.) Avocations: music, art, physical fitness. Office: Marsh USA Inc 1215 4th Ave Ste 2300 Seattle WA 98161-1086 E-mail: nora.young@marshmc.com.

YOUNG, OLIVIA KNOWLES, retired librarian; b. Benton, Ark., Sept. 3, 1922; d. Wesley Taylor and Med Belle (Crawford) Knowles; m. Calvin B. Young, Oct. 6, 1951; 1 child, Brigham Taylor. BA, Tenn. Tech. U., 1942, BS in Libr. Sci., 1946. Head periodicals and documents dept. Peabody Coll. Library, Nashville, 1946-49; area libr. U.S. Army, Austria, 1949-51; libr. Cairo Pub. Libr., Ga., 1955-57, Caney Fork Regional Libr., Sparta, Tenn., 1957-58; chief libr. Ft. Stewart (Ga.) U.S. Army, 1959-63; dir. Watauga Regional Libr., Johnson City, Tenn., 1963-70; dir. devel. and extension Tenn. State Libr. and Archives, Nashville, 1971-82, state libr. and archivist, 1982-85; ret., 1985. Mem. Tenn. Library Assn. (treas. 1970, Honor award 1985), Southeastern Library Assn., ALA, Boone Tree Library Assn. (pres. 1968), Altrusa Club (sec. 1967). Methodist. Home: 203 E Everett St Sparta TN 38583

YOUNG, PAMELA J., music educator; b. Westerly, R.I., Jan. 21, 1949; d. Robert W. and Jane C. Young. BA, Hobart and William Smith Colls., Geneva, N.Y., 1971; MusM, U. of R.I., Kingston, 1976. Dalcroze Eurhythmics Longy Sch. of Music, Cambridge, Mass. Music tchr. Stonington Pub. Schs., Conn., 1973—. Substitute organist Christ Ch., Westerly, RI, 1971—. Choir mem. Christ Episcopal Ch., Westerly, 1959—2006, vestry mem., 1985—88; pres. Chorus of Westerly, 1978—81. Episcopalian. Home: 14 E Stuart St Westerly RI 02891 Office: Deans Mill Sch 35 Deans Mill Rd Stonington CT 06378 Office Phone: 860-535-2235. Business E-Mail: pyoung@stoningtonschools.org.

YOUNG, PATRICIA ANNE, secondary school educator, writer; b. Missoula, Mont., Oct. 3, 1920; d. Dwight Newcomb and Lillian Rook Mason; m. William B. Burke (dec.); children: John Burke, Elizabeth Burke, Sean Burke; m. Willis Frederick Young, Aug. 13, 1997. BA, Ft. Lewis Coll., Durango, Colo.; MA, N.Mex. State U., 1972. Tchr. Farmington (N.Mex.) H.S., 1971—85, San Juan Coll. Founder, pres. S.W. Christian Writers Assn., 1979—2003. Author: Adventures from God's Word, 1983, The Big Missionary, 1997, China My Love, 1999. Recipient Appreciation Svc. plaque, S.W. Christian Writers Assn., 2003. Home and Office: 3204 N Coronado Ave Farmington NM 87401

YOUNG, PAULA EVA, animal shelter director; b. Caracas, Venezuela, May 11, 1958; arrived in U.S., 1962; d. James Francis and Fulvia (Guzzaloni) Y.; 1 child, Jonas Borra. Cert., Am. Acad. Dramatic Arts, N.Y.C., 1979; BA, CUNY, 1997. Lobbyist, facilitator East Bronx Coun. on Aging, N.Y.C., 1989—90; journalist N.Y. Newsday, N.Y.C., 1990—94; mng. editor, journalist City News, N.Y.C., 1994—95; dir. Office Comm. N.Y.C. Dept. Citywide Adminstrv. Svcs., 1995—98; asst. commr. pub. affairs N.Y.C. Dept. Sanitation, 1998—2001; owner, mgr. Between the Lines Restaurant, Westchester County, NY, 2001—03; dir. Mt. Vernon (NY) Animal Shelter, 2003—. Mem. animal cruelty task force Office of Dist. Atty., Westchester County, 2005—; bd. dirs. NY State Wildlife Rehab. Coun., 2003—. Democrat. Avocation: wildlife and animal rescue. Office: 600 Garden Ave Mount Vernon NY 10550 Home: 28 Colabaugh Pond Rd Croton On Hudson NY 10520-3313 Office Phone: 914-522-5945.

YOUNG, PHYLLIS CASSELMAN, music educator; b. Milan, Kans., Oct. 20, 1925; d. Phillip James and Velma (Stewart) Casselman; m. James M. Young, July 14, 1945 (dec. Sept. 1991). MusB with high honors, U. Tex., 1949, MusM, 1950. Tchr. string instruments Kansas City (Kans.) Pub. Schs., 1951-52; prof. cello and string pedagogy U. Tex., Austin, 1953—; dir. U. Tex. String Project, Austin, 1958-93; Parker C. Fielder Regents prof. music U. Tex., Austin, 1991—. Presenter numerous workshops and master classes, 1976—. Author: Playing the String Game, 1978, The String Play, 1986; also articles. Mem. Am. String Tchrs. Assn. (state pres. 1972-74, nat. pres. 1978-80, Nat. citation 1974, 82, Disting. Svc. award 1984, Paul Rolland Lifetime Achievement award 2002), European String Tchrs. Assn. (hon. mem. Brit. br.), Music Educators Nat. Conf., Suzuki Assn. Ams., Tex. Music Educators Assn. Home: 7304 W Rim Dr Austin TX 78731-2043 Office: Sch Music Univ Tex Austin TX 78712 Business E-Mail: phyllis@mail.utexas.edu.

YOUNG, REBECCA MARY CONRAD, retired state legislator; b. Clairton, Pa., Feb. 28, 1934; d. Walter Emerson and Harriet Averill (Colcord) Conrad; m. Merwin Crawford Young, Aug. 17, 1957; children: Eve, Louise, Estelle, Emily. BA, U. Mich., 1955; MA in Teaching, Harvard U., 1963; JD, U. Wis., 1983. Bar: Wis. 1983. Commr. State Hwy. Commn., Madison, Wis., 1974-76; dep. sec. Wis. Dept. of Adminstrn., Madison, 1976-77; assoc. Wadsack, Julian & Lawton, Madison, 1983-84; elected rep. Wis. State Assembly, Madison, 1985-99. Translator: Katanga Secession, 1966. Supr. Dane County Bd., Madison, 1970-74; mem. Madison Sch. Bd., 1979-85. Recipient Wis. NOW Feminist of Yr. award, 1996, Eunice Zoghlin Edgar Lifetime Achievement award ACLU, 1997, Outstanding Legislator award Wis. Counties Assn., 1998, Voice for Choice award Planned Parenthood Wis., 1998, Luan Gilbert award for outstanding activities in domestic violence intervention and prevention Domestic Violence Intervention Svc., 1998. Mem. LWV. Democrat. Avocations: board games, hiking. Home: 639 Crandall St Madison WI 53711-1836

YOUNG, ROBYN S., artist, historian, commentator; b. West Chester, Pa., Feb. 4, 1954; d. Edward Everett and Anna Marie (Murphy) Young; children: James, Harley. Cert.: Pa. State U. (paralegal) 1987. Owner and pres. Hera's House A Traveling History Show, West Chester, Pa., 1998—. Host women's history show WCHE 1520 AM Radio, West Chester, Pa., 2002—; co-founder Chester County Paralegal Assn., 1992, pres., 1992—96, chair pro bono com., 1992—96, v.p., 1995—96; founder, exec. dir. Pa. Women's History Project, 2005—06. Performer (and prodr.): (historic re-enactment) 1852 Women's Rights Conv., 1995—97; historic markers, Site of 1852 Women's Conv., 2003, Ida Ella Ruth Jones House, 2004, Ann Preston M.D. Home, 2005, Charlotte Moore Sitterly, PhD. Home, 2005, Mary Anne Shadd Cary Home, West Chester, Pa., 2005, Lynching of Zachariah Walker 1911, Coatesville, Pa., 2006. Recipient citation, Chester County Commrs., 2003, Pa. Hist. and Mus. Commn., 2004. Mem.: Nat. Collaborative of Women's History Sites, Orgn. Am. Historians, Chester County Art Assn. Republican. Mem. Soc. Of Friends. Avocation: reading. Home and Office: PO Box 157 Atglen PA 19310

YOUNG, SAMANTHA LEE, counselor; d. Leroy and Darlene Kay Preston. BS in Psychology, Mo. Bapt. U., St. Louis, 2000, MS in Edn., 2005. Bd. eligible. nat. cert. counselor Nat. Bd. Cert. Counselors, lic. counselor Md., cert. internal family sys. therapy. Staff counselor, therapist Castlewood Treatment Ctr., Ballwin, Mo., 2002—. Mem.: Am. Counseling Assn. Avocations: crocheting, painting, sculpting. Office: Castlewood Treatment Ctr 800 Holland Rd Ballwin MO 63021

YOUNG, SARAH MOSKOWITZ, educational and computer consultant, journalist; b. Galveston, Tex., June 10, 1947; d. Irving Leonard and Joyce (Schreiber) Moskowitz; children: Clement Clarke III, Leonard Arthur. B Tech. Edn., Nat. U., San Diego, 1984, postgrad., 1984; EdD, Calif. Coast U., San Diego, 1989, postgrad. Adult edn. and community coll. credentials, cert. vision and hearing tech., pers. cons., Calif.; cert. first aid and CPR instr. trainer. Tchr. Vista High Sch., San Diego, 1980-81; project dir. Robert Harrow Co., San Diego, 1981-82; instr. North County Coll., Eldorado Coll., San Diego County, 1982-84, Bangkok U., Kasesart U., 1985-86; assoc. dean, chmn. dept. edn. Phillips Coll., New Orleans, 1988-89; instr., radio performer Am. Lang. Tng., Jakarta, Indonesia, 1989-90; ednl. cons., journalist various mags. and newspapers, 1980—. Seminar speaker Sci. Rsch. Assocs., 1980; tng. officer Naval Sea Cadets, Monterey, Calif., 1988-89; mem. nat. curriculum com. Am. Assn. Med. Transcriptionists, 1978-88; med. instr. Kelsey-Jenney Coll., San Diego, 1990-91; founder Disabled Individuals Suggesting Computer Solutions. Mem., bd. dirs. Mira Mesa Town Coun., San Diego, 1980-84, sec., 1983-84; bd. dirs. Mira Mesa Community Coun., 1982-84; precinct chmn. San Diego Mayoral Election Com., 1982-84. Scholar Nat. U., 1984. Mem. NAFE, Leadership Edn. Awareness and Devel., San Diego Computer Soc., Mensa (chmn. mayor's adv. com. San Diego 1982-84, career day 1983), San Diego Press Club, Tetra Soc. San Diego (founder), Delta Omicron Epsilon. Avocations: artist, musician, world culturee, languages, animals. Home and Office: 10257 Trails End Cir San Diego CA 92126-3517

YOUNG, SHARON WISDOM, retired music educator; b. Newton, Iowa, Feb. 21, 1934; d. Albert Leslie Wisdom and Eudora Bishop McKee; m. Melvin Neely Young, Apr. 9, 1983; m. Glenn Allen Butler, July 30, 1960 (div. Apr. 15, 1981); 1 child, Kirsten Butler Sanderford. BA, Hanover Coll., Hanover, Ind., 1956; MA, St. Francis Coll., Ft. Wayne, Ind., 1966. Tchr. Dep. Grade Sch., Ind., 1956—57, Lone Tree Cmty. Sch., Iowa, 1957—58; sec. Allen Sharp Atty. at Law, Williamsport, Ind., 1958—59, Ransburg Electro-Cappting Corp., Indpls., 1959—60; tchr. Ft. Wayne Cmty Sch., Ft. Wayne, Ind., 1960—66, Des Plains Consol. Sch., Des Plains, Ill., 1966—69, Chesterfield County Sch., Chesterfield, Va., 1970—95; ret., 1995. Mentor program Chesterfield County Sch., Chesterfield, Va., 1995—99; cons. music Tuckahoe Elem. Sch., Henrico, Va., 2002—03; dir. music Bethel Bapt. Ch., Chesterfield, Va., 1980—83. Contbr. articles to profl. jour. Vol. mentor-breast cancer survivor Reach to Recovery, Richmond, Va., 1995—; del. Rep. Nat. Conv., Richmond, Va., 2001; worship com. chmn. Seventh St. Christian Ch., Richmond, Va., 1998—2000, choir; chmn. of dist. III Va. Music Educators Assn.; pres. Elem. Section of the Va. Music Educators Assn.; dir. Fine Arts Festival, Chesterfield and Henrico Counties, workshops on math and music. Mem.: Woman's Club of Bon Air (pres. 1998—2000, 2005—), Alpha Delta Pi, Alpha Delta Kappa (pres. Va. Fipelis Gamma chpt.). Republican. Avocations: beach, bridge, interior decorating, church choir. Home: 4411 W Grace St Richmond VA 23230 E-mail: sharon.notemi@aol.com.

YOUNG, SHERILYN BURNETT, lawyer; b. Providence, Nov. 7, 1953; d. Archie C. III and Hope (Westcott) Burnett; m. Gary Richard Young, Oct. 9, 1977; children: Garrett, Alanna, Valerie. BA, Cornell U., Ithaca, N.Y., 1975; JD, Franklin Pierce Law Ctr., 1982. Bar: N.H. 1982, U.S. Dist. Ct. N.H. 1982, U.S. Tax Ct. 1983. Assoc. Orr & Reno, P.A., Concord, N.H., 1982-87; ptnr. Rath, Young and Pignatelli, P.C., Concord, 1987—. Trustee U. Sys. N.H., Concord Hosp., 1991-98, N.H. Hist. Soc., 2001-, Franklin Pierce Law Ctr., 2005-; legis. counsel to Gov. Gregg, Concord, 1989-90; mem. adv. coun. to ins. commr., 1989-93; spkr. in field. Legal counsel Rudman for U.S. Senate campaign, Concord, 1984-93; bd. dirs. Concord chpt. ARC, 1988-91; mem. N.H. adv. bd. New Eng. Legal Found., 1991-97; pres. Concord Hosp. Assn., 1991-97, bd. dirs. Mem. ABA, NH Bar Assn., New Eng. Coun., Concord C. of C. (bd. dirs. 1988-91), NH Bus. and Industry Assn. (bd. dirs. 2004-), Cornell Club NH. Republican. Avocations: skiing, tennis. Office: One Capital Plz Concord NH 03302-1500 Office Phone: 603-226-2600.

YOUNG, STACY A., information technology manager; Knowledge officer Global Engine Manufacturing Alliance, DaimlerChrysler, Auburn Hills, Mich. Recipient Women of Color Tech. award, 2005. Office: Chrysler Group 1000 Chrysler Dr Auburn Hills MI 48326-2766*

YOUNG, SUSAN BABSON, retired library director; b. Boston, June 22, 1939; d. David Leaveau and Katherine Lockhart (Allen) Babson; m. Thomas Herbert Young III, June 17, 1961; children: Thomas Herbert IV, Nathaniel Allen. BA, Vassar Coll., 1961; MLS, SUNY, Albany, 1983. Cert. sch. media specialist, Mass. English and history tchr. St. Anthony's H.S., Long Beach, Calif., 1962-63; asst. dir. Geier Libr. Berkshire Sch., Sheffield, Mass., 1968-72, dir., 1972-95; ret., 1995. Contbr. articles to profl. jours. Chair Friends of the Bushnell-Sage Meml. Libr. Capital Fund, Sheffield, Mass., 1995—, trustee, 1994—; mem. Arts Coun., Sheffield, 1983-90, 95-2000; mem. So. Berkshire Regional Sch. Com., 1998-2004. Mem. Am. Needlepoint Guild (1st pl. Nat. Exhibit award 1980, 85, 2d Internat. Exhibit award 1982), Embroiders Guild Am., Sheffield Garden Club (pres. 1996-98), Phi Beta Mu. Republican.

YOUNG, SUSAN MARK, psychologist; b. Lancaster, Pa., May 18, 1955; d. John Thomas and Jean Annette (Hollinger) Mark; m. Curtis F. Young, June 22, 1996; 1 child, Jessica Selene. BA in Psychology, Shippensburg State Coll., Pa., 1977; MS in Sch. Psychology, U. Utah, Salt Lake City, 1986. Lic. sch. psychologist Oreg. Child care worker Primary Children's Med. Ctr., Salt Lake City; sch. psychologist Austin Schs., Tex.; tchr. emotionally disturbed youth Oaks Treatment Ctr., Austin; sch. psychologist Douglas Edn. Svc. Dist., Roseburg, Oreg. Mem.: Douglas Edn. Svc. Dist. Assn. (pres. 1991—97, 2005—06), Oreg. Sch. Psychologists Assn. Democrat. Avocations: kayaking, rafting, hiking, photography. Office: Douglas ESD 1871 NE Stephens St Roseburg OR 97470

YOUNG, SUZANNE M., music educator, director; b. SC; d. John Emil and Grace Addy McCoy; m. James L. Young, Dec. 19, 1981; children: Merrell M., Adrienne S. MusB, Converse Coll., Spartanburg, S.C., 1972; MusM, Univ. S.C., Columbia, S.C., 1974. Piano instr. Columbia Coll., Columbia, SC, 1973—79; tchr. Lexington County Sch. Dist, SC, 1979—80; ch. music dir St Peters Luth. Ch., Pawleys Island, SC, 1983—; tchr. Georgetown County Sch. Dist, SC, 1993—. H.s. com. SC. Music Educators Assn., SC, 2002—; all state chorus judge SCMEA, SC, 2000—. Dir.: (musical concert) WHS Annual Choral Festival, (choral, drama, dance) Renaissance Dinner Concert. Recipient Tchr. of the Yr., Georgetown County Sch. Dist., 1998. Lutheran. Avocations: tennis, travel. Office: Waccamaw HS 2412 Kings River Rd Pawleys Island SC 29585 Office Phone: 843-237-9899. Office Fax: 843-237-9883. Business E-Mail: syoung@wh.gcsd.k12.sc.us.

YOUNG, TERESA GAIL HILGER, retired adult education educator; b. Modesto, Calif., Mar. 4, 1948; d. Richard George and Jessie Dennie (Dennis) Long; m. Charles Ray Young, June 22, 1974; 1 child, Gregory Paul. BS in Edn., Abilene (Tex.) Christian U., 1970; MEd in Curriculum, Tarleton State U., Stephenville, Tex., 1976; postgrad., Tex. Tech U., 1990-92. Cert. supr., mid-mgmt., supt., Tex. Tchr. sci. Tex. Youth Coun., Gatesville, 1970-73, Gatesville Ind. Sch. Dist., 1973-81; coord. Edn. and Tng. Ctr., Cen. Tex. Coll., Gatesville, 1983; tchr. Tex. Dept. of Criminal Justice-ID, 1984—2002; ret., 2003. Conf. presenter. Trustee Jonesboro (Tex.) Ind. Sch. Dist., 1988-96. Teacher of the Year for Region II of Tex. Dept. of Criminal Justice, 1997-98. Mem. Am. Fedn. Tchrs., Assn. Tex. Profl. Educators. E-mail: tyoung@htcomp.net.

YOUNG, TERI ANN BUTLER, pharmacist; b. Littlefield, Tex., Aug. 22, 1958; d. Doyle Wayne and Bettie May (Lair) Butler; m. James Oren Young, Aug. 1, 1981; children: Andrew Wayne, Aaron Lee. BS in Pharmacy, Southwestern Okla. State U., 1981; Pharm D, Okla. State U., 2004. Staff pharmacist St. Mary of Plains Hosp., Lubbock, Tex., 1981-84, West Tex. Hosp., Lubbock, 1984-85, asst. dir. pharmacy, 1985-86; pharmacist cons. for nursing homes Billy D. Davis & Assocs., Lubbock, 1986—; relief pharmacist Prescription Lab., Med. Pharmacy and Foster Infusion Care, Lubbock, 1987-89; staff pharmacist Univ. Med. Ctr., 1990-96, diabetic teaching pharmacist, 1995-99; pharmacist Joe Arrington Cancer Ctr., 2000—. Pharmacist Home Health Preferred Infusion, Lubbock, 1994-98, now Covenant Home Infusion, 1998-2000, Covenent Health Care Sys., Joe Arrington Cancer Ctr. Pharmacy; relief pharmacist West Tex. Hosp., 1986-91, Highland Hosp., 1990-94, Med. Infusion Technology, 1992-94. Mem. Lubbock Area Soc. of Hosp. Pharmacists (sec., treas. 1982-83), Lubbock Area Pharm. Assn., West Tex. Pharm. Assn., Am. Soc. Hosp. Pharmacists, Pilot Internat., Lubbock Genealogical Soc. Lodges: Eastern Star. Republican. Baptist. Avocations: needlecrafts, reading, swimming, aerobics. Office: Joe Arrington Cancer Ctr Covenant Health Care Sys 4101 22nd Place Lubbock TX 79410-1130

YOUNG, VICTORIA, medical/surgical and oncology nurse; b. Pipestone, Minn., May 6, 1956; d. Alvin Edwin and Joyce Eileen (Jarl) Flint; m. Charles Young, Oct. 8, 1983; children: Deanna, Rebecca. BSN, Calif. State U., Chico, 1979. Staff nurse Huntington Meml. Hosp., Pasadena, Calif., 1979—. Mem. Oncology Nursing Soc. Home: 6017 N Kauffman Ave Temple City CA 91780-1742

YOUNG, VICTORIA E., occupational health nurse, lawyer; b. Concord, Mich., Apr. 20, 1933; d. Arthur Raymond and Edith Louise (Hands) Y. Diploma, Mercy Sch. Nursing, Jackson, Mich., 1954; BSN, UCLA, 1960, MPH in Adminstrn., 1966; JD, U. West LA, Culver City, 1973. Bar: Calif., U.S. Dist. Ct., Calif.; RN, Calif.; cert. pub. health nurse, pediatric nurse practitioner. Pub. health nurse L.A. City and Los Angeles County Health Dept.; exec. dir. Santa Monica (Calif.) Vis. Nurse Assn.; sch. nurse practitioner L.A. Unified Schs.; relief nurse L.A. Times. Vol. Moorpark City Hall, Moorpark Sr. Ctr; mem. Disaster Assistance Response Team, Moorpark. Ret. capt. USNR, Desert Storm. Mem. Nat. Assn. Pediatric Nurse Assocs. and Practitioners, Calif. Bar Assn., Fleet Res. Assn., Moorpark Woman's Fortnightly Club (treas. 1998-99). Home: 4359 Brookdale Ln Moorpark CA 93021-2302

YOUNG, VIRGINIA MCLAIN, information technology consulting executive; b. St. Louis, Jan. 31, 1954; d. John Robert and Virginia Elizabeth (Hauk) McL.; m. Gary Young, June 3, 1972; children: Justin, Jennifer, Julie. BA in Mgmt., Webster U., 1988, postgrad., 1988—. Dir. pub. rels. Sta. KWK, St. Louis, 1980-83; regional adminstr. CAP Gemini Am., St. Louis, 1983-86, profl. staffing specialist, 1987-89, regional mgr. staffing, 1989-91; pres. InTeCon, Inc., St. Louis, 1991-93; br. mgr. Programming Mgmt. Sys. Inc., 1993-98; reg. dir. Howard Sys. Internat. Inc., 1998; pres. G. Young and Assocs. Inc., 1998—. Mgr. campaign State Rep. 97th Dist., Webster Groves, Mo., 1990. Mem. Met. St. Louis Real Estate Bd., NAFE. Republican. Roman Catholic.

YOUNG, YVONNE DELEASE, elementary school educator; b. Welch, W.Va., Sept. 19, 1939; d. Albert Neal Sr. and Sylvia Claudine (Brooks) Baker; m. Thomas G. Young, June 9, 1973; 1 child, Tajauna D. Tims. BS in Edn., Wilberforce U., 1964; MEd in Adminstrn., Miami U., Oxford, Ohio, 1977. Tchr. Dayton (Ohio) Pub. Schs., 1964-95; retired, 1995. Coord. Careers in Schs., Dayton. Bd. dirs. Youth Engaged for Success, Dayton, 1973-88; vol tutor Right-to-Read, Dayton, 1970-73; vol. Feeding the Homeless, Dayton; pres. OptiMrs., Dayton, 1974—; nat. pres. Carrousels, Inc., 1999-2001. Jennings scholar U. Dayton, 1974-75. Mem. Carrousel's, Inc. (nat. pres.), Delta Sigma Theta (pres. Montgomery County alumnae chpt.), Phi Delta Kappa, Phi Delta Kappa. Avocations: reading, travel, dance, crossword puzzles, entertaining family. Home: 4224 Caylor Rd Dayton OH 45418-2406 E-mail: youngyvonne45418@aol.com.

YOUNGBLOOD, JULIETTE CAROLINA, lawyer; b. Lake Charles, La., Sept. 19, 1963; BA, BS summa cum laude, Fitchburg State Coll., 1984; MA with honors, U. Va., 1985; JD cum laude, Loyola U., 1990. Bar: Calif. 1990. Ptnr. Irell & Manella, LLP, LA, chair entertainment practice group. Mem. planning com. U. So. Calif. Law Sch. Beverly Hills Bar Assn. Inst. Entertainment Law; spkr. in field; mem. Beverly Hills roundtable group Mus. Radio and TV. Named Leading Lawyer in Entertainment, Chambers & Partners. Mem.: Women in Film, LA Copyright Soc., State Bar Calif., Alpha Sigma Nu, Order of Coif. Office: Irell & Manella LLP 1800 Ave of the Stars Century City Ste 900 Los Angeles CA 90067-4278 Office Phone: 310-203-7136. Office Fax: 310-203-7199. E-mail: jyoungblood@irell.com.

YOUNGER, DEIRDRE ANN, pharmacist; b. Washington, Oct. 17, 1958; d. Norman Sylvester Jr. and Doris Juanita (Smith) Coram; m. Michael Elmer Younger, May 22, 1982; children: Michael Elmer Jr., Brittney Ann. BS in Pharmacy, Duquesne U., 1981; MS in Health Care Adminstrn., Univ. Coll. Md. U., 2002. Registered pharmacist, D.C., Md. Pharmacy assoc. U.S. Pharmacopeial Conv., Inc., Rockville, Md., 1981-82; clin. pharmacist Children's Nat. Med. Ctr., Washington, 1983-84, clin. pharmacist supr., 1984-87, clin. pharmacist team leader, 1987-93; instr. Sch. Pharmacy U. Md., Balt., 1993-2000, clin. asst. prof., 2000—. Adj. asst. prof. Sch. Pharmacy, Howard U., Washington, 1990-93; pharmacy residency preceptor ASHP, Washington, 1984-93; prin. investigator Eutectic Mixture of Local Anesthetics; efficacy rsch. Children's Nat. Med. Ctr., 1993; coord. pharmacy and health svcs. Health Ctr. Pharmacy U. Md., College Park, 1993—. Editor: Children's Nat. Med. Ctr. Formulary, 1988-93. Sec. Evans' Ridge Home Owners' Assn., Bowie, Md., 1995-97. Mem.: Am. Coll. Health Assn., Am. Pharm. Assn. Avocations: reading, golf. Office: Health Ctr Pharmacy U Md Bldg 140 Campus Dr College Park MD 20742-0001 Office Phone: 301-314-9686. E-mail: younger@health.umd.edu.

YOUNGER, JENNIFER A., university librarian; BA in history, U. Wis.-Madison, MLA, PhD in info. studies. Various positions in libr. sys. U. Wis.-Madison, 1977—91; asst. dir. tech. svc. Ohio State U. libr., 1991—97; Edward H. Arnold dir. libraries U. Notre Dame, 1997—. Editor: (jour.) Library Resources & Technical Services. Mem.: ALA, Assn. Libr. Collections & Tech. Svc. (pres. 1993—94), Beta Phi Mu. Office: 221 Hesburgh Libr U Notre Dame Notre Dame IN 46556 Office Phone: 574-631-7790. Office Fax: 574-631-6772. E-mail: Jennifer.A.Younger@nd.edu.*

YOUNGER, JUDITH TESS, law educator; b. N.Y.C., Dec. 20, 1933; d. Sidney and Kate (Greenbaum) Weintraub; m. Irving Younger, Jan. 21, 1955; children: Rebecca, Abigail M. BS, Cornell U., 1954; JD, NYU, 1958; LLD (hon.), Hofstra U., 1974. Bar: N.Y. 1958, U.S. Supreme Ct 1962, D.C. 1983, Minn. 1985. Law clk. to judge U.S. Dist. Ct., 1958-60; assoc. firm Chadbourne, Parke, Whiteside & Wolff, N.Y.C., 1960-62; mem. firm Younger and Younger, and (successors), 1962-67; adj. asst. prof. NYU Sch. Law, 1967-69; asst. atty. gen. State of N.Y., 1969-70; assoc. prof. Hofstra U. Sch. Law, 1970-72, prof., assoc. dean, 1972-74; dean, prof. Syracuse Coll. Law, 1974-75; dep. dean, prof. law Cornell Law Sch., 1975-78, prof. law, 1975-85; vis. prof. U. Minn. Law Sch., Mpls., 1984-85, prof., 1985-91, Joseph E. Wargo Anoka County Bar Assn. prof. family law, 1991—. Of counsel Popham, Haik, Schnobrich & Kaufman, Ltd., Mpls., 1989-95; cons. NOW, 1972-74, Suffolk County for Revision of Its Real Property Tax Act, 1972-73; mem. N.Y. Gov.'s Panel To Screen Candidates of Ct. of Claims Judges, 1973-74; mem. Minn. Lawyers' Profl. Responsibility Bd., 1991-93. Contbr. articles to profl. jours. Trustee Cornell U., 1973-78. Mem.: AAUP (v.p. Cornell U. chpt. 1978—79), ABA (council legal edn. 1975—79), Minn. Bar Assn., Assn. of Bar of City of N.Y., Am. Law Inst. (adv. restatement property 1982—84). Home: 3520 W Calhoun Pkwy Minneapolis MN 55416-4657 Office: U Minn Law Sch Minneapolis MN 55455 Office Phone: 612-625-5844. Business E-Mail: young001@umn.edu.

YOUNGER, LAURIE, broadcast executive; BA in Comm., Queens Coll.; MBA, UCLA, 1983. Former dir. bus. affairs 20th Century Fox; dir. bus. affairs network TV divsn. The Walt Disney Co., 1985—86, v.p. bus. affairs, 1986—90; sr. v.p. bus. affairs and adminstrn. Walt Disney TV and Telecomm.; sr. v.p. ABC, Inc., 1996—98, sr. v.p., CFO, 1998—2003, exec. v.p., CFO, 2003—; exec. v.p. ABC TV Distbn., 2000—03; pres. Buena Vista Worldwide TV, 2003—. Named one of 100 Most Powerful Women in Hollywood, Hollywood Reporter, 2003, 2004, 2005. Office: ABC Inc 500 S Buena Vista St Burbank CA 91521-4775*

YOUNGERMAN, NAN GRONIK, elementary school educator; b. Milw., Oct. 27, 1948; d. Herbert Leon and Jeanne Louise (Capper) Gronik; m. James Nickoll Youngerman, June 20, 1971; children: Rebecca, Benjamin. BS in Edn., U. Wis., 1971, MS in Curriculum and Instrn., 1976. Cert. tchr. grades 1-8. Tchr. 3d grade Orchard Ridge Elem. Sch., Madison, 1971-73; tchr. 4th grade Falk Elem. Sch., Madison, 1974-78; tchr. 4th and 5th grades Crestwood Elem. Sch., Madison, 1978—. Presenter World Conf. Computers in Edn., Birmingham, U.K., 1995; spkr. Nat. Edn. Computing Conf., 1991-94; faculty Math.-Sci. Acad. (NSF project), Tufts U., Boston, 1994; planning com. mem., conf. planner Ednl. Development Ctr./Action Rsch. Ctr., Newton, Mass., 1992. Vol. various polit. campaigns, Madison, 1978—. Recipient Presdl. Award for Excellence in Math./Sci. Teaching, NSF, 1994, Logo Action Rsch. Site Leader, NSF/Edn. Development Ctr., 1990-91, Lois Gadd Nemec Disting. Alumni, U. Wis. Sch. Edn., 1995. Mem. ASCD, Phi Delta Kappa (Action Rsch. award 1992). Jewish. Avocations: biking, cross country skiing, travel, cooking. Home: 2445 Fox Ave Madison WI 53711-1924 Office: Crestwood Elem Sch 5930 Old Sauk Rd Madison WI 53705-2599

YOUNG-MALLIN, JUDITH, writer, archivist; b. Mt. Vernon, NY, Aug. 10, 1937; d. Milton and Marion Ethel (Peterfreund) Young; m. Joel Mallin, Aug. 8, 1957 (div. 1985); children: Jennifer Young, Adam Young, Noah Young. Student, Syracuse U., 1955, NYU, 1956, 86, 1956. Rschr. Conde-Nast, NYC, 1957-58; lectr. Am. Crafts Mus., NYC, 1986; ind. lectr. NYC, 1986—. Cons., innovator Surreal Eye Series, NYC, 1986-87; lectr. London-Courtauld Inst. Surrealism NY, 1991, Art Inst. Chgo., 1992, Sch. Visual Arts, NYC, 1992, Pollock-Krasner Found., 1997, Artists Talk Art, 1997, Guggenheim Mus., Venice, Italy, 1998; cons. Am. Masters, NYC, 1991; established Young-Mallin Archive; Surrealist Look New World, 1999-2000. Author: M.F.K. Fisher, Virgil Thomson, 1990, Juliet Man Ray, 1991, Surrealism and Women, Eileen Agar, 1991, View Anth. Index Edn., 1991, Edward James, 1991. Mem. James Beard Soc. (profl. mem.). Avocation: surrealism. Home: 719 Greenwich St New York NY 10014-2586

YOUNGMAN, LOLA JEANNE, music educator; b. Royal Oak, Mich., Mar. 18, 1951; d. Robert Edward Grant and Elaine Margaret Eddy; m. David Frederick Youngman, June 22, 2002; m. Richard Vincent Lewis, Apr. 9, 1977 (div. Sept. 30, 2001); children: Adam Ryan Lewis, Jessica Marie Lewis. BS in Edn., Ctrl. Mich. U., Mt. Pleasant, 1973; student, Wayne State U., Detroit, 1975—76. Cert. tchr. Yamaha Music Sch., Atlanta & L.A., lic. Real Estate N.C., 1987, cert. tchr. K-8, tchr. K-9 music. Elem. vocal music tchr. Lamphere Sch. Dist., Madison Heights, Mich., 1974—78; dir., tchr. Yamaha Music Sch., Raleigh, NC, 1985—95; pvt. piano tchr. Raleigh, 1985—97; real estate agent Doreen Silber & Co., Raleigh, 1987; elem. vocal music tchr. Wake County Schs., Raleigh, 1997—. Musician (pianist); singer: Dave Youngman Band, 2002—. Mem.: N.C. Assn. Educators, Black Horse Run Women's Club (pres. 1988, v.p.). Avocations: tennis, singing. Home: 4908 Boulder Creek Ln Raleigh NC 27613

YOUNG-POHLMAN, COLETTE LISA, music educator; b. Honolulu, July 20, 1952; d. Richard Ah On and Winifred Oi Chin Chang Young; m. Kurt I. Pohlman, Oct. 5, 1985; 1 child, Vinson Sterling Pohlman. EdB, U. Hawaii-Manoa, Honolulu, 1974, postgrad., 1975. Part-time tchr. dept. edn. Kalani High, Honolulu, 1978—79; chpt. 1 reading tchr. McKinley High, Honolulu, 1979—80, basic skills tchr., 1980—81; part-time tchg. asst. pvt. preschs., Honolulu, 1981—82; part-time tchr. dept. edn., chpt. 1 reading Ala Wai Elem. and Palolo Elem., 1982—83; classroom tchr. Heeia Elem., Kaneohe, Hawaii, 1990; part-time tchr. dept. edn. Wailupe Valley Elem., Honolulu, 1990—91; instrnl. resource augmentation tchr. Maemae Elem., Honolulu, 1991—92; project tchr. Title I reading Washington Intermediate, Honolulu, 1992—94; instrnl. resource augmentation tchr. Accelerated Gifted & Talented Performing Arts, Kailua, Hawaii, 1994—97; classroom tchr. Mokapu Elem., Kailua, 1997—2002, instrnl. resource augmentation music tchr., 2002—, Ann. Winter Concert and Talent Showcase, 2002—. Dir., choreographer, scripting/editing of musical play productions in elem. settings Windward Dist., Kalaheo Complex. Dir.(choreographer, writer): (multicultural musical plays) Little Firefly, the Rough-face Girl, Double Happiness, Souled Out; composer: There's Something About a Pet, 1998 (2d Pl. award, 1998); composer: (choreographer) (new sch. song dance) Enchantment of Mokapu, 2000, Reading Rap, 2003, (music video) Enchantment of Mokapu, 2006; prodr. (dir.): (weekly TV program Olelo Cablevision) Na Keiki Hauoli o Mokapu, The Happy Children of Mokapu. Mem., tchr. Boy Scouts Am. Troop 113, 1999—. Mem.: Hawaii State Tchrs. Assn., Hawaii Music Educators Assn., Hawaii Orff Schulwerk Assn. (bd. dirs. 2005—), Am. Orff Schulwerk Assn., Music Educators Nat. Conf., Nat. Educators Assn. Avocations: composing songs, poetry, singing, keyboard, storytelling. Home: 45-427 Loli'i St Kaneohe HI 96744-5911 Office Phone: 808-254-7964. Business E-Mail: colette-youngpohlman@notes.k12.hi.us.

YOUNGREN, DELVANA HOPE, secondary school educator; b. L.A., Apr. 13, 1941; d. Herman Melvin and Betty Floy (England) Ferguson; m. Allan Morse Youngren, June 17, 1961; children: Erik Allan, Deanna Marie. BA, Calif. State Coll., Long Beach, 1963; MA, Calif. State Coll., 1968. Cert. secondary tchr., Calif. Tchr. Long Beach (Calif.) Unified Sch. Dist., 1963-70, Faith Christian Acad., Pasadena, Tex., 1975-80, Cherry Valley (Calif.) Brethren Christian Sch., 1980-86, Arrowhead Christian Acad., Redlands, Calif., 1984—87, New Life Christian Acad., San Bernardino, Calif., 1987-90, Mt. View Jr. H.S., Beaumont, Calif., 1990—2002, Mt. View Mid. Sch., Beaumont, 2002—. Chmn. GATE, Gifted and Talented, Calif.; educator Drug, Alcohol & Tobacco Edn.; tech. computer tchr. On-Line Learning, Novanet. Head computer dept. San Gorgonio Pass Geneal. Soc., Banning, Calif., 1992-95; mem. Yucaipa Geneal. Soc., 1992-95. Mem. NEA, Calif. Tchrs. Assn., Beaumont Tchrs. Assn., Calif. Inland Area Math. Project, Soroptimists (Beaumont chpt.). Republican. Avocations: sports, cats. Home: 10640 Jonathan Ave Cherry Valley CA 92223-4974 Office: Beaumont United Sch Dist PO Box 187 Beaumont CA 92223-0187 Office Phone: 951-845-1627. E-mail: delvana@aol.com.

YOUNGS, DIANE CAMPFIELD, learning disabilities specialist, educator; b. Margaretville, NY, Feb. 16, 1954; d. Richard Maxwell and Charlotte June (Rickard) Campfield; m. William H. Youngs, June 30, 1984. BS in Edn., SUNY, Geneseo, 1976, MS in Edn., 1977. Professionally recognized spl. educator. Tchr. educable mentally retarded Tompkins-Seneca-Tioga Bd. Coop. Ednl. Svcs., Ithaca, NY, 1978-80; tchr. learning disabled Joint Svc. for Spl. Edn., Mishawaka, Ind., 1980-97; assoc. faculty Ind. U.-South Bend Grad. Sch. Edn., 1996-98. Vis. lectr. dept. edn. Ind. U., South Bend, 1998-2002, lectr., 2002—; mem. Task Force for Reorgn. Spl. Edn., Mishawaka, 1990-91; coord. Tiny Talkers Summer Speech/Lang. Camp, 1994—. Recipient Tchg. award, Ind. U. Trustees, 2005, 2006. Mem. AAUP, Coun. for Exceptional Children, Learning Disabilities Assn., Coun. for Learning Disabilities, Ind. Prof. Reading, Internat. Reading Assn., Nat. Coun. Tchrs. English, Kappa Delta Pi. E-mail: dyoungs@iusb.edu.

YOUNKER, KATHLEEN TEUBER, pianist, music educator; b. St. Cloud, Minn., Jan. 22, 1947; d. Hans Richard and Philomena (Hortsch) T.; m. Daniel William Younker, July 19, 1968; children: Laura, Jonathan. BA in History and Philosophy, St. Cloud State U., 1968; ARCT in Piano Performance, Royal Conservatory Toronto, Ont., Can., 1983; BA in Music, Bishop's U., Lennoxville, Que., Can., 1984; pvt. piano student, Rose Goldblatt, Montreal, 1985-95; MA in Spl. Studies, St. Cloud State U., 2002. Self-employed piano tchr., Lennoxville, 1978—97, St. Cloud, 1997—; sch. music tchr. Eastern Twps. Regional Sch. Bd., Lennoxville, 1982-86; ch. organist Peace United Ch. of Christ, St. Cloud, 1998-99; accompanist Sauk Rapids (Minn.) Rice HS, 1999—2000. Mem Music Tchrs. Nat Assn., Nat. Guild Piano Tchrs., Can. Fedn. Music Tcrs. Assns. (com. mem., ex officio nat. conv. 1997), Minn. Music Tchrs. Assn. (com. mem. state conv. 1999-01, com. mem. piano exam devel. com. 2002—), Eastern Twps. Music Tchrs. Assn. (pres. 1989-91), Que. Music Tchrs. Assn. (pres. provincial coun. 1993-97). Avocations: home restoration, pets, reading, gardening, cooking, entertaining.

YOUNKER, NANCY ELAINE, retired elementary school educator; b. Chambersburg, Pa., Oct. 17, 1948; d. Bruce O. and A. Virginia (Shutt) Bivens; m. Carl Thurman Younker, Nov. 22, 1969; children: Susan R. Younker, Carri L. BS, Shippensburg U., 1969, MEd, 1974. Elem. sch. tchr. Ctrl. Fulton Sch. Dist., McConnellsburg, Pa., 1969—2005; ret. Mem. supt.'s adv. com. Ctrl. Fulton Sch. Dist., McConnellsburg, 1990-94. Bd. dirs. Fulton County Med. Ctr. Mem. NEA, ASCD, Pa. Edn. Assn., Pa. Coun. Math. Tchrs., Beta Sigma Phi (past pres., v.p. Gamma Phi chpt., preceptor). Democrat. Presbyterian. Avocations: reading, travel, music. Home: 2182 Big Cove Tannery Rd Big Cove Tannery PA 17212-9605

YOUNKER, PAMELA GODFREY, business owner, consultant, accountant; b. Copperhill, Tenn., Apr. 5, 1955; d. Thomas Marvin and Betty Jean (Thomas) Godfrey; m. Ronald Joseph Younker, Nov. 18, 1978; children: David, John. AS, Young Harris Jr. Coll., 1975; BBA in Acctg., U. Ga., 1977. Mgmt. trainee Oxford Industries, Inc., Atlanta, 1977-78, divisional acct., 1978-79, sr. internal auditor, 1979-81, Lockheed Corp., Marietta, Ga., 1981-85; acctg. mgr. med. benefits dept. Lockheed Aero. Systems Co., Marietta, 1985-88; owner, cons. Pam Younker Acctg. & Tax Svc., Marietta, 1988—; v.p. Engring. Design Tech. Inc., Marietta, Ga., 2001—. Advisor U. Ga. Sch. Acctg., Athens, 1986-90; mem. benefits cons. Lockheed Aero. Systems Co., 1988-89. Vol. battered women program YWCA, Marietta, 1979-87, Hospice Jr. League of Cobb County, 1994-(praise team dir. 1998-2005); mem. Atlanta Hist. Soc., 1988-90; treas. Our House, Atlanta Area Hosp. House, 1988-90; pres., state conv. hmn. Women of Ga. Power, Canton, 1986-90, state treas., 1990—; sponsor FCA, 1994-2001; leadership com. Cobb County, 1999-. Recipient Cmty. Svc. award, 1998—99. Mem. Inst. Internal Auditors (pres. so. region 1984), Young Harris Coll. Alumni Assn. (coord. 1984-90), Alpha Chi Omega (province chmn. Tenn. 1988-91, pres. Atlanta chpt. 1985-87, Nat. Coun. award 1985, Continuing Excellence award 1986). Avocations: tennis, exercise. Home: 1001 Gentry Ln Marietta GA 30064-3882

YOUNT, GWENDOLYN AUDREY, humanities educator; b. Indpls., July 24, 1957; d. August de Alba and Hena Yount; 1 child, Clark. AA, L.A. City Coll., 1977; BA, UCLA, 1979, MA, 1982, Candidate in Philosophy, 1987. Cert. C.C. lifetime credential Calif., bilingual cert. competence. Ednl. aide Alexander Hamilton H.S., L.A., 1975—76; tchg. fellow UCLA, 1981—88; instr. L.A. Unified Sch. Dist., 1982—90; prof. Institut Franco-Americain de Mgmt., Paris, 1983—84; instr. Santa Monica Coll., Calif., 1987—88; lectr. U. Calif., Riverside, 1988—91; instr. Beverly Hills Adult Sch., Calif., 1986—88; assoc. prof. Riverside C.C., Calif., 1990—. Dir. RCC Study Abroad Program in Spain, Salamanca, Spain, 1998—2002, RCC Study Abroad Program in Costa Rica, San Jose, Costa Rica, 1993, UCLA Spanish Program in Mex., Guadalajara, Mexico, 1987. Dancer (ballet performance) Celebrate Dance, 2000; actor: (mus. theater) La Cage Aux Folles, 1998; singer: (vocal performance) Montreux Jazz Festival, 1993. Adminstr. G. Yount scholarship Riverside County Found., 1998—2003; sen. Acad. Senate, Riverside, 1997—2003; mem. Spanish lang. steering com. Riverside Pub. Libr., 1989—91; charter mem. Mus. of Tolerance, L.A., 1994—2003. Named Most Influential Instr., RCC Disabled Student Svcs., 1993, 1998, Tchr. of Distinction, LDS Ch., 1998, 2000, 2001, 2002, Tchr. of the Yr., Riverside C.C., 1999—2000, 2000—01, 2002—03; grantee Univ. grantee for grad. study, UCLA, 1979. Mem.: Philol Soc. of the Pacific Coast, Assn. for Tchrs. of Spanish, Sigma Tau Sigma, Alpha Mu Gamma (pres. 1977—78), Sigma Delta Pi (v.p. 1985—86). Liberal. Avocations: travel, reading, studying. Office: Riverside C C 4800 Magnolia Ave Riverside CA 92506 Business E-Mail: gwen.yount@rcc.edu.

YOUNT, SARA, academic administrator; b. Frankfort, Ky., July 11, 1972; d. Leonard Albert and Linda Allen (Dunavan) Y. BA in Comm., U. Ky., 1994; MPA, U. Louisville, 1997; postgrad., Bellarmine U., U. Louisville. Rep. Humana, Inc., Louisville, 1994-95; dep. clk. Henry County Clk.'s Office, New Castle, Ky., 1995-97; job developer City of Louisville, 1997-98; coord. part-time undergrad. recruitment Bellarmine U., Louisville, 1998—. Mem. Jefferson County home econs. adv. bd. U. Ky. Ext. Svc., Louisville, 1998—. Vol. Jr. Achievement Louisville, 1999, Arthritis Found.; officer Parkview Condominium Bd.; mem. Jr. League Louisville, 2001-. Mem. U. Ky. Young Alumni Assn., U. Louisville Alumni Assn., Louisville Athletic Club. Republican. Office: Bellarmine U 2001 Newburg Rd Louisville KY 40205-1863 Office Phone: 502-452-8401.

YOUSEF, MONA LEE, psychoanalytic psychotherapist; BS in Human Devel. and Family Studies, Cornell U.; MSW, NYU. Lic. clin. social worker NY, HIV counselor NY; credentialed alcoholism and substance abuse counselor NY, nat. cert. master addictions counselor. Psychotherapist pvt. practice, NYC, 1993—. Mem. NASW, Nat. Assn. Alcoholism and Drug Abuse Counselors-Assn. for Addiction Profls., Acad. Cert. Social Workers, Assn. Addiction Profls. of NY, Soc. Advancement Sexual Health, NY State Soc. for Clin. Social Work, Stuyvesant HS Alumni Assn., Psi Chi (life). Democrat. Avocations: dancing, writing, art/museums, shopping, restaurants/cuisine. Office: 19 W 34th St Penthouse New York NY 10001

YOVANOF, SILVANA, physician; b. Lubojno, Macedonia, Jan. 14, 1956; came to U.S., 1961; d. Peter and Nuna Yovanof. BS in Biology and Psychology, Loyola U., Chgo., 1978; MS, U. Ill., 1982; MD, Am. U. Caribbean, Montserrat, 1985. Diplomate Am. Bd. Internal Medicine. Intern Deaconess Hosp., St. Louis, 1986-87; resident in internal medicine St. Joseph Mercy Hosp., Pontiac, Mich., 1987-89, chief resident in medicine, 1989-90; fellow U. Ill. Med. Ctr., Chgo., 1990-92; chmn. dept. medicine Monongahela Valley Hosp., 2002—. Mem. adv. panel Internal Medicine for the Specialist, 1988—; affiliated with hosps. Jefferson Hosp., Pitts., 1991, MonValley Hosp., Monongahela, Pa., 1993, Mercy Hosp., Pitts., 1995. Contbr. articles to profl. jours. including Neurosci. Letters. Mem.: ACP, Am. Assn. Clin. Endocrinologists, Allegheny County Med. Soc. (med. legal com. 1996—), Pa. State Med. Soc., Am. Diabetes Assn. Office: Med and Endocrinology Assoc 420 W Main St Monongahela PA 15063-2552 Office Phone: 724-258-8680. E-mail: syovanof@peoplepc.com.

YOVANOVICH, ROBYN DOBSON, theater educator, department chairman; d. Robert Vernon and Gwendolyn Armstrong Dobson; m. Donald Yovanovich, Nov. 10, 1990; 1 child, Anna Clancey. BA, Cath. U. Am., Washington, DC, 1971—75. Editor Middleburg Life, Middleburg, Va., 1989—91; fine arts dept. chmn. Foxcroft Sch., Middleburg, 1997—. Chmn. of volunteers Va. Gold Cup/Internat. Gold Cup, The Plains, 1989—2006. Editor: (book) Middleburg and Nearby; contbr. color commentator; actor: (TV commercials) Soft and Dri/ Mountain Dew, (musical revue- ford's theatre) Uncle Funky's Mistletoe Revue; (Broadway plays, and Off Broadway), 1977—80. Com. mem. Am. Cancer Soc. Charity Polo Classic, The Plains, 1996, Range Rover Internat. Polo Classic, The Plains, 2002; bd. mem. The Middleburg Players, 1998—2002. Grantee Kenan Grant for Profl. Devel., Foxcroft Sch., 2006. Republican. Episcopalian. Avocation: interior design. Home: PO Box 1877 Middleburg VA 20118 Office: Foxcroft Sch PO Box 5555 Middleburg VA 20118 Office Phone: 540-687-4373. Personal E-mail: dony13@aol.com. Business E-Mail: ryovanovich@foxcroft.org.

YOW, AUDREY JO, artist, educator; A in Fine Arts, Sandhills C.C., 1994; BS in Art Edn., U. N.C., Pembroke, 1996; MA in Edn., East Carolina U., 2005. Cert. early and mid. childhood art Nat. Bd. Profl. Tchg. Standards, 2003, counter sketching Gemological Inst. Am., 2000. Art educator Philo Mid. Sch., Winston-Salem, NC, 1997, Kennedy Mid. Sch., Winston-Salem, NC, 1997, North Forsyth H.S., Winston-Salem, NC, 1997, Westfield Elem. Sch., Pilot Mountain, NC, 1998—, Shoals Elem. Sch., Pinnacle, NC, 1998—. Contbr. articles to profl. jours. Mem.: N.W. Artist League, Wilkes Art Gallery, N.C. Assn. Educators. Office Phone: 336-351-2745. Personal E-mail: mysticimages2003@yahoo.com.

YOWELL, NANCY T., photographer, retired elementary school educator; b. Compton, Calif., Apr. 30, 1934; d. Stanley Lawrence and Violet Beatrice Taufman; m. Don Arthur Yowell (dec. Mar. 1996); children: Paul Alan Yowell, Jack Leland Yowell. BA, Calif. State U., Fullerton, 1963; MA, Azusa Pacific U., 1975. Tchr. Rowland Unified Sch. Dist., Rowland Heights, Calif., 1963-80, Redlands (Calif.) Unified Sch. Dist., 1980-94; supr. interns Calif. State U., San Bernardino, 1994—. Exhibited photos in shows including Multi Media Mini show San Bernardino County Mus., 1996, 98, City of Redlands show, 1997, Redlands Camera Club Mus. Exhibit, 1998, others. Recipient awards for photos. Mem AAUW (pres. 1983-85), Redlands Camera Club, Redlands Arts Assn., Redlands Camera Club (pres. 1997-99), Delta Kappa Gamma (treas. 1992-94, pres. 1994-96, 97-98).

YRIZARRY, MAGDA N., communications executive; married; 2 children. Joined Bell Atlantic (predecessor to Verizon), 1991—; dir. cmty. affairs Bklyn. and S.I. Bell Atlantic; v.p. pub. policy and strategic affairs Verizon Comm., Washington, 2003—04, v.p., workforce culture and compliance, 2004—. Bd. mem. LULAC Nat. Edn. Svcs. Ctrs.; mem. corp. adv. bd. USHCC, Nat. Hispanic Caucus of State Legislators, Nat. Coun. LaRaza. Former trustee, pres. N.Y.C. Cmty. Sch. Bd. 9; former mem. Bd. Edn. Com. on Bilingual and Spl. Edn., NY; former vol. N.Y. State Mentoring Program, Sch.-Based Mgmt., Jr. Achievement. Recipient Pres. award, U.S. Hispanic C. of C. Found., Nat. Hispanic Corp. Achievers award, 1998, Corp. Rep. of the Yr. award, Am. GI Forum, 2003. Mem.: ASPIRA (chairperson N.Y., exec. bd. mem.), 100 Hispanic Women (founding mem.), Nat. Hispanic Leadership Inst. Office: Verizon 1095 Ave Americas New York NY 10036 Office Phone: 212-395-2121.

YSASI-DIAZ, GLORIA, wholesale distribution executive; BS in Chem. Engring., Univ. Rochester; MBA, Coll. William & Mary. Ops. positions GE Co., 1978—84; ops. positions to sr. v.p., process mgmt. R.R. Donnelley, Chgo., 1984—2005; v.p. operational excellence, US branch-based businesses WW Grainger Co., Chgo., 2005—. Named one of 50 Most Important Hispanics in Tech., Bus., Hispanic Engineer and Info. Tech. mag., 2005. Office: 100 Grainger Pkwy Lake Forest IL 60045-5201 Office Phone: 847-535-1000. Office Fax: 847-535-0878.

YSIKES, JUANITA LOU, art educator; b. Belen, N.Mex., Dec. 22, 1951; d. Melvin Vernette and Doris Marie (McArthur) Lovelady; m. James Carroll Fulcher, May 30, 1970 (div. Aug. 1988); children: Lee Collins Fulcher, Amy Laura Fulcher; m. Robert Harry Sikes, Dec. 26, 1990. BS in Edn., Ea. N.Mex. U., 1983. Cert. tchr., N.Mex. Bookkeeper J & L Auto Salvage, Socorro, N.Mex., 1970-72, Navajo Mobil, Truth or Consequences, N.Mex., 1972-75; subs. tchr. Portales (N.Mex.) Schs., 1977-78, art aide, 1988-91; tchr., aide spl. edn. Ft. Summer (N.Mex.) High Sch., 1978-83, tchr. spl. edn., 1983-86; tutor ESL and GED Ea. N.Mex. U. Clovis Campus, Ft. Summer, 1986-87; fashion illustrator Slyduds Clothing, Roswell and Ft. Summer, N.Mex., 1987-88; instr. drawing Ea. N.Mex. U., Portales, 1989-90; tchr. art Portales Jr. High Sch., 1991—. Supt. art dept. DeBaca County Fair Bd., Ft. Summer, 1979-87; advisor Portales Elem. Spl. Art Program, Portales, 1989-91; coord. Portales Jr. High Spl. Art Program, Portales, 1991-2001; sponsor art club Portales HS, 2001—; judge arts and crafts dept. Roosevelt County Fair, Portales, 1992. Exhibited in group shows Crafter's Crossing Gallery, Ft. Worth, numerous art fairs. Vol. Sierra County Rescue Squad, Truth or Consequences, 1973-75, Mayors Christmas Tree, Portales, 1989-90; coord., 1991—. Recipient Outstanding Citizenship award Sierra County Rescue Squad, 1974, 75; named Artist of Month Ft. Sumner Pub. Libr., 1987. Mem. NEA (pres. local chpt. 1992—), Nat. Art Edn. Assn., Gamma Zeta (pres. Beta Sigma Phi chpt. 1984-88). Democrat. Mem. Ch. of Christ. Avocations: painting, sewing, bowling, archery. Home: 2108 W Beech St Portales NM 88130-9303 Office: Portales Jr High Sch 300 E 5th St Portales NM 88130-6082

YU, PAULINE RUTH, former dean, educational association administrator; b. Rochester, NY, Mar. 5, 1949; d. Paul N. and Irene (Tang) Y.; m. Theodore D. Huters, Aug. 23, 1975 (div. Feb. 2000); children: Emily Elizabeth, Matthew Charles, Alexander David. BA in History and Lit. magna cum laude, Harvard U., 1971; MA in Comparative Lit., Stanford U., 1973, PhD in Comparative Lit., 1976. Asst. prof., then assoc. prof. U. Minn., Mpls., 1976-85; assoc. prof., then prof. Columbia U., N.Y.C., 1985-89; prof., founding chair dept. East Asian langs. and lit. U. Calif., Irvine, 1989-94; dean humanities UCLA, 1994—2003, prof. East Asian langs. and culture, 1994—2003; pres. Am. Coun. Learned Socs., N.Y.C., 2003—. Author: The Poetry of Wang Wei, 1980, The Reading of Imagery in the Chinese Poetic Tradition, 1987; editor and contbg. author: Voices of the Song Lyric in China, 1994, Culture and State in Chinese History: Conventions, Accommodations, and Critiques, 1997, Ways with Words: Writing about Reading Texts from Early China, 2000; editor, contbr.: The Longman Anthology of World Literature; mem. editl. bd. Tang Studies, Chinese Lit., Comparative Lit. Studies, 1993—. Mem. nat. adv. bd. Woodrow Wilson Found., 2004—; mem. internat. adv. bd. Asia Rsch. Inst., Nat. U. Singapore, 2002—; mem. western ctr. exec. coun. Am. Acad. Arts and Scis., 2000—03; bd. dirs. Am. Coun. Learned Socs., 1998—; trustee Nat. Humanities Ctr., 2000—, Asian Cultural Coun., 2006—; bd. dirs. The Teagle Found., 2003—; mem. adv. coun. dept. East Asian studies Princeton U., 2003—; bd. overseers Harvard U., 2003—; mem. adv. bd. Coun. for Internat. Exch. of Scholars, 2001—05. Guggenheim fellow, 1983-84, ACLS fellow, 1983-84; recipient Profl. Achievement award U. Calif. at Irvine Alumni Assn., 1993. Fellow Am. Acad. Arts and Scis.; mem. MLA, Assn. Asian Studies (mem. China and Inner Asia coun. 1982-85), Am. Comparative Lit. Assn., Am. Oriental Soc., Phi Beta Kappa Soc. (senator 1997—, exec. com. 2001—). Office: Am Coun Learned Societies 633 Third Ave New York NY 10017-6795 Office Phone: 212-697-1505 x 121. E-mail: paulineyu@acls.org.

YU, SUSAN C. (SUSAN CHUNG-MI YU), lawyer; BA, U. Calif., Berkeley, 1996; JD cum laude, Syracuse U., 1998. Bar: Calif. 1998. Ptnr. Collins, Mesereau, Reddock & Yu, LLP, LA, 1998—. Vol. St. James' Ch., First A.M.E. Ch. legal clinic; mem. panel of judges for annual student speech competition LA Olympic Lion's Club, 2000—. Dana Hinman Scholar. Mem.: ABA, Century City Bar Assn., Asian Pacific Am. Bar Assn., LA County Bar Assn., Justinian Hon. Law Soc. Office: Collins, Mesereau, Reddock & Yu LLP 1875 Century Park E 7th Fl Los Angeles CA 90067 Office Phone: 310-284-3120. Office Fax: 310-861-1007. E-mail: yu@cmrylaw.com.

YUASA, SHEILA THALASSA, literature and language educator; d. David James and Carol Ann Lee; m. Daijiro Yuasu, Nov. 11, 2000. BA in Edn./English, U. Findlay, Ohio, 1998; MEd, U. Hawaii, Honolulu, 2004. Asst. English tchr., Saitama, Japan, 1998—2000; tchr. English Mililani (Hawaii) H.S., 2000—. Sunday sch. tchr. 1st Presbyn. Ch., Honolulu, 2002—06. Mem.: Hawaii State Tchr. Assn. Avocations: travel, Japanese calligraphy. Home: # 191 95-1056 Kuauli St Mililani HI 96789

YUE, AGNES KAU-WAH, otolaryngologist; b. Shanghai, Peoples Republic China, Dec. 1, 1947; arrived in US, 1967; d. Chen Kia and Nee Yuan; m. Gerald Kumata, Sept. 25, 1982; children: Julie, Allison, Benjamin. BA, Wellesley Coll., 1970; MD, Med. Coll. Pa., 1974; postgrad., Yale U., 1974-78. Intern Yale-New Haven Hosp., 1974-75, resident, 1975-78; fellow U. Tex. M.D. Anderson Cancer Ctr., Houston, 1978-79; asst. prof. U. Wash., Seattle, 1979-82; physician Pacific Med. Ctr., Seattle, 1979-90; pvt. practice Seattle, 1991—. Fellow Am. Acad. Otolaryngology; mem. Northwest Acad. Otolaryngology. Avocations: sailing, opera, cooking. Office: 1801 NW Market St Ste 410 Seattle WA 98107-3909 Office Phone: 206-782-1090.

YUEN, ELLEN M., elementary school educator; d. Sydney Findel and Pearl Mait, Jerry Mait (Stepfather); m. Jeffrey Allen Yuen, Feb. 26, 1995; 1 child, Jonathan. BA magna cum laude, CUNY, Queens, 1974; cert., Neighborhood Playhouse Sch. of Theatre, NYC, 1979. Profl. clear multiple subject tchg. credential. Actress, NYC and LA, 1972—90; from account exec. to v.p. varous pub. rels. agys., NYC, San Francisco and LA, 1980—93; talent agt. LA, 1993—96; owner, voice/acting tchr Voiceovers One-On-One, LA, 1998—2001; substitute tchr. LA Unified Sch. Dist., 2001—04, tchr. 5th grade Calif., 2004—. Media trainer, San Francisco, NY and LA, 1989—90; crisis cons. Porter-Novelli for Allergan Med. Optics, LA, 1990—93. Founder Vocations for Social Change, Queens, 1970—74; vol. North Valley Jewish Cmty. Ctr., LA, 1999—2001, Darby Ave. Sch., LA, 2001—03. Recipient Compass award, Pub. Rels. Soc. Am., San Francisco, 1988; scholar, NY Bd. Regents, 1970. Mem.: UTLA, ASCD, Phi Kappa Phi. Democrat. Jewish. Avocations: writing children's books, cooking, travel, singing. Home: 11216 Chimineas Ave Northridge CA 91326 Office Phone: 818-348-2169. E-mail: nycwoman@socal.rr.com.

YULE, CAROLL JANE, real estate broker; b. Owatonna, Minn., Feb. 19, 1948; d. Leland R and Jean L Heiden; m. Dennis F Yule, June 6, 1969; 1 child, Tara K. Attended, Macalester Coll., 1966—68, U. Minn., 1968—69. Broker Calif., 1996. Owner All-U-Med, Temple, Tex., 1994—96; broker owner Shear Realty, Apple Valley, Calif., 1996—. Dir. Victor Valley Assn. of Realtors, Victorville, Calif., 2004—, Desert Cmty. Bank. Contbr. monthly column. Program com. Rotary Internat., Victorville, Calif., 2000—05; pres. Victorville C. of C., 2003—04; chmn. for ann. fundraiser Victor Valley Coll. Found., 2000—05; mem. chmn. Victor Valley Bd. of Realtors, 2004—05. Recipient Realtor of the Yr., Victor Valley Assn. of Realtors, 2003, Dir. of the Yr., Victorville C. of C., 2000—01, 2001—02, 2002—03. Avocations: golf, book club. Home: 13253 Country Club Dr Spring Valley Lake CA 92395 Office: Shear Realty 18564 Highway 18 Ste 205 Apple Valley CA 92307 Office Phone: 760-243-3803. Home Fax: 760-243-3804; Office Fax: 760-243-3804. Personal E-mail: cyule@mscomm.com.

YUNDT, BETTY BRANDENBURG, elementary school educator; b. Corydon, Ind., Sept. 23, 1957; d. Melvin Marion and Lena Beatrice (Blake) Brandenburg; m. Randall Gene Yundt, Apr. 2, 1978; 1 child, Cameron Blake. BS, Ind. U. SE, New Albany, 1981, MS with highest distinction, 1989. Cert. elem. tchr. Rank I, Ind., Ky. Tchr. pre-kindergarten Keneseth Israel Sch., Louisville; tchr. Dept. Def. Dependent Sch., Goppingen, Fed. Republic Germany; curriculum coord. Iroquois and West End Child Devel. Ctr., Louisville; elem. tchr. Ft. Knox (Ky.) Sch. Dist. KERA Fellows II cohort. Named Tchr. of Yr., Ft. Knox, Ky., 2003; named to, USA Today All Star Tchr. Team, 2003; recipient Campbellsville Coll. Excellence in Edn. award, 2003. Mem. NEA, ASCD, Internat. Reading Assn., Ind. Coun. Tchrs. Math., Louisville Assn. for Children Under Six, Kappa Delta Pi, Phi Lambda Theta, Alpha Chi. Home: 40 Springdale Rd Guston KY 40142-7151 Office Phone: 502-624-7835. Business E-Mail: betty.yundt@am.dodea.edu. E-mail: teechyundt@bbtel.com.

YUNG, PATSY P., lawyer; Grad., U. Tex., Austin; JD cum laude, South Tex. Coll. Law. Cert.: Tex. Bd. Legal Specialization (immigration and nationality law), bar: Tex. 1997. Ptnr., dir. Immigration Practice Grp. Lynn, Pham & Ross, L.L.P., Dallas. Named a Rising Star, Tex. Super Lawyers mag., 2006. Mem.: Dallas Asian Am. Bar Assn. (sec., exec. com. mem.), Tex. Young Lawyers Assn. (Pres.'s Award of Merit 2003, 2004), Am. Immigration Lawyers Assn. Office: Lynn Pham & Ross LLP 8080 N Ctrl Expressway Ste 400 Dallas TX 75206 Office Phone: 214-292-2830. E-mail: yung@laborcounsel.net.*

YUNGHANS, ELEANOR JANICE, social studies educator; b. Dayton, Ohio, July 13, 1946; d. Perrin Enos and Romaine Ann (Rideout) Steele; m. Howard O. Yunghans, July 1, 1972; children: Laura, David, Janet. BA, Bowling Green (Ohio) State U., 1968, MEd, 1974, Ohio U., 1969. Lic. tchr., social studies comprehensive, counselor, provisional. Tchr. Perkins High Sch. Perkins Local Sch. Dist., Sandusky, Ohio, 1969-75, tchr. Perkins Mid. Sch., 1976—. Mem. com. Ohio Ctr. for Law-Related Edn., Columbus, 1991-93; staff mem. Ohio Leadership Inst., Columbus, 1993—. Asst. leader Cub Scouts, Sandusky, 1985-88, Webelos leader, 1988-89; precinct leader Perkins Levy Campaign Com., Sandusky, 1990. Named Tchr. of Yr. Erie County Bd. Edn., Sandusky, 1992, Tchr. Nat. Winner History Day, Cleve., 1990, Tchr. Top 10 Am. Express, 1990, Model Tchr. Sports and Law Ohio Ctr. for Law-Related Edn., Columbus, 1990. Mem. Ohio Coun. Social Studies (sec. 1990—, exec. bd. 1986—, Tchr. of Yr. 1990), Firelands Coun. Social Studies (pres. 1986-89), Perkins Edn. Assn. (treas. 1971-75), Ohio Edn. Assn., Ohio Hist. Soc., Ohio Archaeol. Soc., Am. Hist. Assn., Orgn. Am. Historians, Phi Delta Kappa. Avocations: sewing, playing piano, reading historical fiction, flower gardening, crewel. Office: Perkins Local Schs Perkins Mid Sch 3700 South Ave Sandusky OH 44870-6913

YURACKO, KIMBERLY, law educator; BA with distinction, Stanford U., 1991, PhD in Polit. Sci., 1997, JD with distinction, 1998. Lectr. polit. sci. U. Calif., Irvine, 1999; vis. asst. prof. law Northwestern U. Sch. Law, Chgo., 2001—02, asst. prof., 2002—04, prof. law, 2005—. Law clk. to Hon. Gary L. Taylor US Dist. Ct. (ctrl. dist.) Calif., 1998—99; to Hon. Stanley Marcus US Ct. Appeals (11th cir.), 1999—2000; assoc. Paul, Hastings, Janofsky & Walker, LA, 2001. Author: Perfectionism and Contemporary Feminist Values, 2003; contbr. articles to profl. jours. Office: Northwestern U Sch Law 357 E Chicago Ave Chicago IL 60611 Office Phone: 312-503-3466. E-mail: k-yuracko@law.northwestern.edu.

YURCHENCO, HENRIETTA WEISS, musicologist, writer; b. New Haven, Mar. 22, 1916; d. Edward and Rebecca (Bernblum) Weiss; m. Basil Yurchenco, June 1936 (div. 1955); 1 child, Peter; m. Irving Levine, 1965 (div. 1979). Student, Yale U., 1935-36; student piano scholarship, Mannes Coll. Music, 1936-38. Radio prodr. Sta. WNYC, Sta. WBAI, others, 1939-69; writer, critic, tchr., folk music editor Am. Record Guide and Musical Am., 1959-70; radio prodr. Air Am., 2006. Prof. music CCNY, 1962—86, Bklyn. Coll., 1966—69, New Sch. Social Rsch., 1961—68; co-dir. project study women in music Grad. Ctr. CUNY; mem. exec. com. Panamerican Musical Rsch. Arts. Author: A Fiesta of Folk Songs from Spain and Latin America, 1967, A Mighty Hard Road: A Biography of Woody Guthrie, 1970, Hablamos! Puerto Ricans Speak, 1971, Around the World in 80 Years: A Memoir, 2003, in Spanish, 2004; contbr. articles to profl. jours.; field recs. issued by Libr. Congress, Folkways, Nonesuch, Folkways/Smithsonian, Global Village, Rounder Records, collections in Libr. Congress, Discoteca Hebrew U., Jerusalem, Arias Montana Inst., Madrid, Inst. Nacional Indigenista, Mexico City, Am. Sephardic Found., Instituto Cervantes (Spanish Cultural Inst.). Recipient award, Nat. Inst. Fine Arts, Mex., 2003; grants-in-aid, Am. Philos. Soc., 1954, 1956, 1957, 1965, 1967, 1989, CUNY Faculty Rsch. Fund, 1970, 1983, 1987, NEH grantee, 1964. Mem.: Am. Musicologists Soc., Internat. Assn. Study Popular Music, Soc. Am. Music, Soc. Asian Music, Soc. Ethnomusicology, Internat. Coun. Traditional Music (mem. com. women's studies). Home: 360 W 22d St New York NY 10011-2600 Office: 139th St And Convent Ave New York NY 10031 Personal E-mail: hyurchenco@verizon.net.

YURIKO, (YURIKO KIKUCHI), dancer, choreographer; b. San Jose, Calif., 1920; m. Charles Kikuchi, 1946. Student, UCLA, Martha Graham Sch. Mem. Martha Graham Dance Co., 1944-67; dance tchr. N.Y.C., 1945—; dir., founder Yuriko Dance Co., 1960—78; assoc. artistic dir. Martha Graham Dance Co., 1991—. Artistic dir. dance company Time and Talents Club, Bombay, 1974; organizer Modern Dance Sch., Ctr. Internat. de la Danse, Paris, 1975; resident guest tchr., modern dance cons. Ballet Nacional de Cuba, 1976; ind. modern dance choreographer Warsaw Weiklki Classic Ballet Co., 1977, 78, Australian Dance Theater's Concert at Adelaide Festival of the Arts, 1978; guest tchr., choreographer Akar Modern Dance Co., Switzerland, 1981; guest tchr. Nat. U. Costa Rica, Nat. Ballet of Mexico, Martha Graham Sch. Contemporary Dance; guest artist and tchr. various cities including London, Paris, Mexico City, Zurich, Tokyo and Cologne, Germany; founder & dir., The Arigato Project; founder Martha Graham Ensemble, 1983. Dancer premiere prodns. Appalachian Spring, Cave of the Heart, Dark Meadow, Embattled Garden, Clytemnestra; appeared on Broadway as Eliza in The King and I, 1951; performed feature role The Small House of Uncle Thomas, Sandhog, Flower Drug Song; dir., re-staged Broadway prodn. of The King and I, 1977, London prodn., 1979, dir. Toyko prodn., 1978; dir. Madame Butterfly. Recipient Bessie award NY Dance and Performance, 1991; Tribute NY/Japan Soc., 2004; Honor Saeko Ichinohe Dance Co., 2005; grantee NY State Arts Coun., Nat. Endowment for the Arts; Guggenheim fellow for choreography, 1968; commissioned to choreograph and perform Judith Symphony.

YURTH, HELENE LOUISE, librarian; b. Cleve., May 21, 1953; d. Joseph Alexander and Helen (Hegedus) Y.; m. William David Birskovich, June 14, 1975. BA in Botany, Kent State U., 1975; MS in Libr. Sci., Clarion U. Pa., 1998. Dir. Bemus Point (N.Y.) Libr., 1988-90, Smith Meml. Libr. at Chautauqua (N.Y.) Instn., 1991—. Avocations: gardening, pets, vegetarianism, reading, reiki. Office: Smith Meml Libr 21 Miller Ave Chautauqua NY 14722 Office Phone: 716-357-6296. Office Fax: 716-357-3657. Personal E-mail: hyurth@yahoo.com. Business E-Mail: hyurth@ciweb.org.

ZABEL, DIANNE DONNELLY, retired elementary school educator; b. Woodburn, Oreg., Jan. 11, 1944; d. Joseph Emmett Donnelly and Beatrice Anna Bailey, Walter Eugene Bailey (Stepfather); m. Alfred Anthony Zabel, June 11, 1972; children: Shane Allen, Jill Anne. BA in Elem. Edn., Mt. Marty Coll., Yankton, S.D., 1966. Cert. elem. edn. tchr. Fla., Mentally Handicapped (0-21 years) Fla. Tchr. 3d grade St. Joseph Sch., Pierre, SD, 1967—68, St. Anthony Parish, Tigard, Oreg., 1968—70; tchr. 2d gade Mohave County Sch. Dist., Peach Springs, Ariz., 1970—71; tchr. varying exceptionalities Brevard County Sch. Sys., Melbourne, Fla., 1986—2005. Editor: (exceptional children's cookbook) Cooking With Class (Achievement Excellence award, 2001). Vol. Habitat For Humanity, Melbourne, 2000—05. Mem.: Coun. Exceptional Children. Roman Catholic. Avocations: travel, crocheting. Home: 7730 Pine Lake Dr Melbourne FL 32904 Office: Croton Elem Sch 1449 Croton Rd Melbourne FL 32935 Personal E-mail: ajsz5260@earthlink.net.

ZABEL, VIVIAN ELLOUISE, writer, retired secondary school educator; b. Randolph AFB, Tex., July 28, 1943; d. Raymond Louis and Dolly Veneta (Lyles) Gilbert; m. Robert Lee Zabel, Feb. 18, 1962; children: René Lynne, Robert Lee Jr., Randel Louis, Regina Louise (dec.). BA in English and Speech, Panhandle State U., Goodwell, Okla., 1977; postgrad., U. Ctrl. Okla., Edmond, 1987-92. Cert. tchr. Okla. Tchr. English, drama, speech, debate Buffalo (Okla.) H.S., 1977-79; tchr. English, drama, speech Schulter (Okla.) H.S., 1979-80; tchr. English Morris (Okla.) H.S., 1980-81; tchr. speech, drama, debate Okla. Christian Schs., Edmond, 1981-82; tchr. English, drama, debate, speech/debate coach Braman (Okla.) H.S., 1982-83; debate coach Pawhuska (Okla.) H.S., 1983-84; tchr. English, French, drama, speech and debate coach Luther (Okla.) H.S., 1984-95; tchr. debate, forensics, yearbook, newspaper, mag., creative writing, competitive speech Deer Creek H.S., Edmond, Okla., 1995—2001; ret., 2001. Dir. drama Nazarene Youth Impact Team, Collinsville, Okla., 1979-81; tchr. h.s. Sun. sch. class Edmond Ch. of Nazarene, 1991-94; mem. cmty.-sch. rels. com. Luther Pub. Schs., 1991-92, supt.'s adv. com., 1992-94. Editor: Potpourri mag., 1975—77; author (as Vivian Gilbert Zabel): Reflected Images, 1999, Writing Poetry, 2000, The Base Stealers Club, 2006; author: Hidden Lies and Other Stories, 2005, Walking the Earth, 2005. Adult supr. Texas County 4-H, Adams, Okla., 1975-77; double diamond coach NFL; adjudicator and tournament dir. qualifying OSSAA Tournaments. Recipient Disting. Svc. award, NFL, 1994, Editor's Choice award for poetry, Nat. Poetry Assn., 1997—99, Outstanding Poet award, 1997—99, 2001, Tchr. of Excellence, 1996. Mem.: Nat. Debate Coaches Assn., Nat. Fedn. Interscholastic Speech and Debate Assn., Okla. Speech Theatre Comms. Assn., Okla. Tchrs. English. Republican. Nazarene. Home: 2912 Rankin Ter Edmond OK 73013-5344 Office Phone: 405-359-6365. Personal E-mail: vzabel@juno.com.

ZABLOCKI, ELAINE, writer; b. Bklyn., June 13, 1942; d. Harry and Anne Finkelstein; m. Benjamin D. Zablocki; 1 child, Abraham M. BA honors, Swarthmore Coll., 1963. Adminstr. Takilma Clinic, Oreg., 1973—80; freelance writer, polit. cons. Oreg., 1981—82; asst. com. adminstr. Oreg. Senate Com. on Human Svcs. and Aging, Salem, 1983; mgr. newsletter New Options, Inc., Washington, 1983—85; writer Craver, Mathews, Smith & Co., Falls Church, Va., 1985—86; freelance writer specializing in healthcare Corona Comm., Arlington, Va., 1986—98, Eugene, Oreg., 1999—. Reporter WebMD, 2000—01. Author: Changing Physician Practice Patterns, 1995—; editor Physician Mgr. Newsletter, 1994-95; contbg. editor The Quality Letter for Healthcare Leaders, 1994—; editor Alternative Medicine Business News, 1999; mng. editor CHRF News Files, 2002-05; contbr. numerous articles to profl. publs.

ZABROCKY, LOIS K., energy transportation executive; BS, U.S. Merchant Marine Acad. With Overseas Shipholding Group, Inc., NYC, 1992—, head Singapore chartering, 1995, v.p. comml. ops. Aframax Internat., v.p., head internat. product carrier strategic bus. unit, 2005—. Named one of 40 Under 40, Crain's NY Bus., 2006. Office: Overseas Shipholding Group Inc 666 Third Ave New York NY 10017 Office Phone: 212-953-4100. Office Fax: 212-578-1832.*

ZABUKOVEC, JAMIE JO, clinical psychologist; b. Waukegan, Ill., Oct. 27, 1954; d. John Joseph and Jennie Josephine (Zalaznik) Z. BA in Psychology and Math., Ea. Ill. U., 1976, MS, 1977; D in Psychology, Ill. Sch. Profl. Psychology, Chgo., 1988. Lic. psychologist, Ill. Family counselor Warren Twp. Youth Svcs., Gurnee, Ill., 1977-84; staff psychologist Stress Disorder Treatment Unit, VA Med. Ctr., North Chicago, Ill., 1988—92; psychologist Portland, Va., 1992—97, Dallas, Va., 1997—2003, Prescott Va. Med. Ctr., Prescott, Va., 2003—. Mem. adj. faculty Columbia Coll., Ft. Sheridan, Ill., 1989-1992, Ill. Sch. Profl. Psychology, 1990; co-trainer Eye Movement Desensitization and Reprocessing, 1991—. Mem. Lake County Sexual Abuse Task Force, Waukegan, 1984. Recipient Liaison award Gurnee Police Dept., 1984. Mem. APA. Avocations: running, Karate, volleyball, sailing, weightlifting. Office: Prescott Va Med Ctr 500 N Hwy 89 Prescott AZ 86313

ZACARÍAS, KAREN, playwright; m. Rett Zacarías; children: Nico, Kati. BA, Stanford U.; MA in Playwriting, Boston U., 1995. Cert. tchr. grades K-12 Washington, DC. Founding artistic dir. Young Playwrights Theater, Washington. Author: (plays) Blue Buick in My Driveway, The Thirteenth Summer of William and Pilar, The Barechested Man, 1995, The Sins of Sor Juana, 1998 (Hispanic Playwrights Project winner, 1998, Charles MacArthur award outstanding new play Helen Hayes awards, 2000), The Book Club Play, Mariela in the Desert, 2005 (AT&T First Stages award, 2004), (for children) Cinderella Eats Rice and Beans: A Salsa Musical, Ferdinand: The Bull, The Magical Pióata, Einstein Is A Dummy, 2004. Recipient Francesca Primus prize, The Francesca Ronnie Primus Found. and Am. Theatre Critics' Assn., 2006. Office: Young Playwrights Theatre 2437 15th St NW Washington DC 20009 Office Phone: 202-387-9173. Office Fax: 202-387-9176.*

ZACCHINO, NARDA, newspaper editor; b. San Diego, 1947; BA in english lit., UCLA. Assoc. editor L.A. Times, Calif. Office: Los Angeles Times Times Mirror Sq Los Angeles CA 90053

ZACCONE, SUZANNE MARIA, sales executive; b. Chgo., Oct. 23, 1957; d. Dominic Robert and Lorretta F. (Urban) Zaccone. Sales sec. Brookeridge Realty, Downers Grove, 1975-76; sales cons. Kafka Estates Inc., Downers Grove, 1975-76; adminstrv. asst. Chem. Dist., Inc., Oak Brook, Ill., 1976-77; sales rep., mgr. Anographics Corp., Burr Ridge, Ill., 1977-85; pres., owner Graphic Solutions, Inc., Burr Ridge, 1985—. Bd. dirs. Di Trolio Flexigraphic Inst. Curriculum adv. bd. mem. Sch. Dist. 99, 1997, 1998, 1999, 2000, 2001. Named Supplier of Yr. Through Preferred Supplied, Gen. Binding Corp., 1988—99; recipient Supplier Mem. award, Internat. Bottled Water Assn., 1987—88, Supplier award, SBA, 1990, Top Performer Supplier award, Cutler Hammer Westinghouse Divsn., 1993—99, Blue Chip Enterprise Initiative award, 1994. Mem.: NAFE, Ditrolio Flexographic Inst. (bd. dirs.), World Label Assn. (1st pl. in World Championship 1994—96, 2002—04), Women in Packaging (exec. bd.), Inst. Packaging Profls., Women Entrepreneurs DuPage County (past pres.), Tag and Label Mfrs. Inst. (chmn. pub. rels. and mktg. com., bd. dirs., pres. 1998—2000, Best Managed Co. award 1992, 1st place award in U.S. for Screen Printing 1994—97, 1999—2001, Best Managed Co. award 2001—03). Avocations: reading, sailing, cooking, needlepoint, scuba diving. Office: Graphic Solutions Inc 311 Shore Dr Burr Ridge IL 60521-5859 Office Phone: 630-325-8181. Business E-Mail: suzanne.zaccone@graphicsolutionsinc.com.

ZACHARY, JE'QUITA YVETTE, elementary school educator, singer; d. Jesse B. and Sharon Yvonne Zachary. AA in Music, Gordon Coll., 1997; BA in Music & Bus., Clayton Coll. and State U., 2000. Tchr. music Victory Charter Sch., East Point, Ga., 2002—04; music promoter Atlanta Internation Records, Atlanta, 1999—2001; tchr. Odyssey Charter Sch., Newnan, 2004—05; tchr. 5th grade reading tchr. KIPP WAYS Acad., New Birth South, Ga., 2004—05. Tchr. after sch. chorus Odyssey Charter Sch., Newnan, Ga., 2005—; children's choir helper New Birth South, New Birth South, Jonesboro, 2005—. Singer: (songs, plays and dances) Martin's Dream and Mine and Songs from His Heart. Ch. mem. New Birth South, New Birth South, Ga., 2004. Personal E-mail: jequitaz@yahoo.com.

ZACHARY, JEAN, personnel director; b. Atlanta, Nov. 7, 1945; d. Foye Mason and Cosma (Stacks) Zachary; m. James Robert Sturdevant, July 1966 (div. Aug. 1976); children: John Zachary Sturdevant, Richard Thomas Sturdevant. Student, U. Tex., 1963-66; BA, U. Houston, 1967; postgrad., Houston Bapt. U., 1976-78. Tchr. Johnston Jr. H.S./Houston Ind. Sch. Dist., 1967-71, 76-81; adminstrv. asst. Llano County Appraisal Dist., Llano, Tex., 1991-95; asst. treas. Llano County, 1995-97, grant coord., 1997-99; workforce specialist Lockheed Martin IMS, Johnson City, Tex., 1999—, Llano, 1999—. Mem. Blanco County Interagy. Coun., Johnson City, 1999—; mem. Capital Area TRACS, Austin, Tex., 1999; mem. CAPCO Criminal Justice Com., Austin, 1997-99. Author/developer seminars. Mem. Appraisal Rev. Bd., Llano County, 1989-91, chair, 1990-91; mem. Hill Country RC&D, Mason County, Tex., 1997-99; project SOS!2000, Llano, 1999; team mem. Hill Country Wellness Ctr., sec., 1998-99. Recipient Team Spirit award Easy Access, Inc., 1994., Mem. Preservation Tex. Inc. Avocations: reading, gardening, computers, historic preservation. Home: 106 Marschall Dr Llano TX 78643 Office: Tex Workforce Ctr for Llano County 119 W Main St Llano TX 78643-1931

ZACHERT, MARTHA JANE, retired librarian; b. York, Pa., Feb. 7, 1920; d. Paul Rodes and Elizabeth Agnes (Lau) Koontz; m. Edward G. Zachert, Aug. 25, 1946; 1 child, Lillian Elizabeth. AB, Lebanon Valley Coll., 1941; MLS, Emory U., 1953; DLS, Columbia U., 1968. Asst. Enoch Pratt Free Library, Balt., 1941-46; head librarian Wood Research Inst., Atlanta, 1947; sch. librarian DeKalb (Ga.) County Schs., 1950-52; head librarian, prof. history of pharmacy So. Coll. Pharmacy, Mercer U., Atlanta, 1952-63; instr. Ga. State Coll., 1962-63, Emory U., summers 1955-59, 1956-57, 59-60; mem. faculty Library Sch., Fla. State U., 1963-78, prof., 1973-78, Coll. Librarianship U. S.C., Columbia, 1974-78, 78-84. Vis. fellow Brit. Library, 1980; cons. So. Regional Med. Library, Emory U., 1976-77, Nat. Library Medicine, 1977, others. Author: Fine Printing in Georgia, 1950s-1990, 1994; assoc. editor Jour. Libr. History, 1966-71, 73-76; mng. editor, 1971-73; cons. editor Jour. Libr. Adminstrn., 1979-86; contbr. numerous articles to profl. jours. Fellow Med. Libr. Assn. (named among 100 Most Notables 1998); mem. ALA, Spl. Librs. Assn. (past pres. Fla. chpt., spl. citation 1977, Hall of Fame 1985), Am. Printing History Assn., Beta Phi Mu (pres. 1974-75). Home and Office: 4436 Meandering Way #108AG Tallahassee FL 32308-8705

ZACHERT, VIRGINIA, retired psychologist; b. Jacksonville, Ala., Mar. 1, 1920; d. R.E. and Cora H. (Massee) Z. Student, Norman Jr. Coll., 1937; AB, Ga. State Woman's Coll., 1940; MA, Emory U., 1947; PhD, Purdue U., 1949. Diplomate Am. Bd. Profl. Psychologists. Statistician Davison-Paxon Co., Atlanta, 1941-44; research psychologist Mil. Contracts, Auburn Research Found., Ala. Poly. Inst.; indsl. and research psychologist Sturm & O'Brien (cons. engrs.), 1958-59; research project dir. Western Design, Biloxi, Miss., 1960-61; self-employed cons. psychologist Norman Park, Ga., 1961-71, Good Hope, Ga., 1971-99; ret. Rsch. assoc. med. edn. Med. Coll. Ga., Augusta, 1963-65, assoc. prof., 1965-70, rsch. prof., 1970-84, rsch. prof. emeritus, 1984—, chief learning materials divsn., 1973-84, faculty senate, 1976-84, acad. coun., 1976-82, pres. acad. coun., 1983, sec., 1978; mem. Ga. Bd. Examiners Psychologists, 1974-79, v.p., 1977, pres. 1978; adv. bd. Comdr. Gen. ATC USAF, 1967-70; cons. Ga. Silver Haired Legislature, 1980-86, senator, 1987-93, pres. protem, 1987-88, pres., 1989-93, rep., spkr. protem, 1993-96, spkr., 1997-98, Nat. Silver-Haired Congress rep., 1995—, spkr. 1997-99; govs. appointee White House Conf. on Aging, 1971, 96, Ga. Coun. on Aging, 1988-96; U.S. Senate mem. Fed. Coun. on the Aging, 1990-93; senator appointee White House Conf. on Aging, 1995; Ga. Health Decision's appointee to Ga. Coalition for Health, 1996-98. Author: (with P.L. Wilds) Essentials of Gynecology-Oncology, 1967, Applications of Gynecology-Oncology, 1967. Del. White House Conf. on Aging, 1981, 95. Served as aerologist USN, 1944-46; aviation psychologist USAF, 1949-54. Recipient Jane Kennedy Excellence Aging award, 1999. Fellow AAAS, Am. Psychol. Assn.; mem. AAUP (chpt. pres. 1977-80), Sigma Xi. (chpt. pres. 1980-81) Baptist. Home: 4275 Owens Rd # 403 Evans GA 30809

ZACHMAN, KATHLEEN E., gifted and talented educator; b. Denver, Feb. 15, 1945; BA U. No. Colo., 1967; MA, U. No. Colo., 1969. Elem. music tchr. Jefferson Co. Pub. Schs., Golden, Colo., 1988—2001, Discover assessment observer, 2001—. Home: 13182 W Jewell Cir Lakewood CO 80228 Personal E-mail: zachmank@comcast.net.

ZACKHEIM, MICHELE, artist; b. Reno, May 5, 1941; d. Samuel and Elizabeth (Kamenetzky) Z.; m. Charles Ramsburg, May 29, 1980; children: Benjamin, Maggie. Student, U. Calif., Santa Barbara, 1959-60, Art Students League, 1960-62, New Sch. Social Rsch., 1963-64. Graphic designer NBC, N.Y.C., 1960-63; art dir. Metromedia, N.Y.C., 1963-65; creative dir. Advt. Design Assocs., N.Y.C., 1965-69; free-lance artist N.Y., N.Mex., 1969—. Artist-conceptor The Tent of Meeting, traveling exhibit of art and music, 1985—; one woman shows include Hill's Gallery of Contemporary Art, Santa Fe, 1980, Judah L. Magnes Meml. Mus., Berkeley, Calif., 1980, Bronfman Mus., Montreal, Can., 1981, Sarah Lawrence Coll., Bronxville, N.Y., 1981, Bryn Mawr Coll. Pa., 1981, 83, 85, N.Mex. Mus. Fine Arts, Santa Fe, 1985, Cathedral of St. John the Divine, 1985, Yale U., 1985, Mus. of Am. Jewish History, Phila., 1985, Art Mus. South Tex., Corpus Christi, 1986, Ufundi Gallery, Ottawa, Can., 1986, Landmark Ctr., St. Paul, Minn., 1986, Scottsdale (Ariz.) Ctr. for Arts, 1987, Bade Mus., Berkeley, Calif., 1988, St. Mary's Cathedral, San Francisco, 1988, City of Ottawa, 1986; exhibited in group shows Carlsbad Mus. Fine Arts, N.Mex., 1978, U. Calif.-Irvine Gallery, 1982, U. Toronto, 1983, Hebrew Union Coll. Skirball Mus., 1984; represented in numerous permanent collections; author: Violette's Embrace, 1996; Einstein's Daughter: The Search for Lieserl, 1999; contbr. articles in field. Recipient art awards Am. Inst. Graphic Arts, 1965, Art Dirs. Club N.Y., 1966, N.Mex. Advt. Assn., 1981, Graphic Arts/Printing Industries, 1967. Jewish. Home: 282 W 4th St New York NY 10014-2401 Personal E-mail: mszack447@aol.com.

ZAFFIRINI, JUDITH, state legislator, small business owner; b. Laredo, Tex., Feb. 13, 1946; d. George and Nieves Pappas; m. Carlos Zaffirini, 1965; 1 child, Carlos Jr. BS, U. Tex., 1967, MA, 1970, PhD, 1978. Committee-woman Tex. State Dem. Exec. Com., 1978-84; mem. Tex. State Senate, 1987—, pres. pro tempore, 1997; owner Zaffirini Comms., Laredo, 1998—. Del. Dem. Nat. Conv., 1980, 84. Recipient Medal of Excellence Nat. League United Latin Am. Citizens, 1987, Jose Maria Morelos y Pavon Medal of Merit for leadership in strengthening U.S.-Mex. rels., 1987; named Woman of Achievement Tex. Press Women, 1980, Gov. of Tex. for a Day, Apr. 19, 1997, Ten Best Legislators Tex. Monthly Mag., 1997, 2001, Disting. Alumnus U. Tex., 2003; inductee Nat. Hispanic Hal of Fame, 1987. Democrat. Roman Catholic. Home: PO Box 627 Laredo TX 78042-0627 Office: 1407 Washington St Laredo TX 78040-4411 Office Phone: 956-724-8379. E-mail: judith.zaffirini@senate.state.tx.us.

ZAGANO, PHYLLIS, religious studies educator; BA in English, Marymount Coll., Tarrytown, NY, 1969; MS in Pub. Rels., Boston U., 1970; MA in English, L.I.U., 1972; PhD in English, SUNY, Stony Brook, 1979; MA in Theology, St. John's U., Jamaica, N.Y., 1990. Program officer Nat. Humanities Ctr., N.Y.C., 1979—80; asst. prof. comms. Fordham U., Bronx, NY, 1980—84; rschr. Archdiocese of N.Y., 1984—86; ind. rschr. N.Y.C., 1986—88; assoc. prof. comm. Boston U., Comm. Theology Dem. Com., 1988—98; adj. assoc. prof. theology Boston U., 1988—98, dir. inst. for democratic comm., 1988—98; sr. rsch. assoc. in residence, spl. assoc. prof. religious studies Hofstra U., Hempstead, NY, 2002—. Vis. Aquinas chair St. Thomas Aquinas Coll., 2005; vis. assoc. prof. Cath. studies Yale Div. Sch.,

2005. Author: Religion and Public Affairs, 1987, Social Impact of the Mass Media, 1991, Woman to Woman, 1993, On Prayer, 1994, Ita Ford: Missionary Martyr, 1996, Twentieth Century Apostles, 1999, Things New and Old, 1999, Holy Saturday: An Argument for the Restoration of the Formale Diaconate in the Catholic Church, 2000 (Book award Catholic Press Assn. 2001, Coll. Theology Soc. 2002), Dorothy Day: In My Own Words, 2003, Called to Serve: A Spirituality for Deacons, 2004, The Dominican Tradition, 2006, Acerca de la Oracion: Una Carta a Mi Amijado (Book award Cath. Press Assn. 2003); monthly radio host Boston U. World of Ideas, 1992-97 Lector, lay min. Ch. St. Vincent Ferrer, N.Y.C., 1980—92, Our Lady of the Miraculous Medal Ch., 1996—, Newman Ctr., Boston U., 1992—96. Comdr. USNR, 1976—. Faculty Rsch. grantee Fordham U., 1983, Rsch. grantee Nat. Inst. Peace, 1989, Rsch. grantee Wabash Ctr., 2003; Coolidge fellow Episcopal Divinity Sch., 1987; recipient citation for heroism Nassau County (N.Y.) Fire Commn., 1995. Mem. Am. Acad. Religion (co-chair Roman Cath. Studies, 1991-2001), Am. Cath. Philos. Assn., Coll. Theology Soc., Cath. Theol. Soc. Am., Naval Res. Assn., Soc. for Study of Christian Spirituality. Roman Catholic. Office: 115 Hofstra Univ Hempstead NY 11549 Office Phone: 516-463-5612. Business E-Mail: phyllis.zagano@hofstra.edu.

ZAGAT, NINA, publishing executive; m. Tim Zagat, 1965; children: Ted, John. AB, Vassar Coll., 1963; LLB, Yale U.; attended, Le Cordon Bleu Ecole de Cuisine. Atty. Sherman and Sterling, N.Y.C., 1966—90; co-founder, co-pub. Zagat Survey, N.Y.C., 1979—; co-chair, co-founder Zagat.com, 1999—. Served on White House Conference on Travel and Tourism; mem. Who's Who of Food and Beverage in Am.; mem. of the corp. Culinary Institute of Am., 1994—, established lecture series, 2001. Office: Zagat Survey 4 Columbus Circle New York NY 10019

ZAGEL, MARGARET MAXWELL, lawyer; b. Centralia, Ill., Jan. 17, 1949; d. Francis Edgar and Joan (Beckmeyer) Maxwell; m. James Block Zagel, May 27, 1979. BA, Tulane U., 1970; JD, U. Ill., 1973. Bar: Ill. 1973, U.S. Ct. Appeals (7th cir.), U.S. Supreme Ct. Atty. Ill. Appellate Defender's Office, Chgo., 1973-75, law clk. to Hon. Seymour Simon, 1975-76; assoc., then ptnr. Schuyler Roche & Zwirner, Chgo., 1976-84; gen. counsel Grant Thornton LLP, Chgo., 1984-98, mng. prin. risk, regulatory & legal affairs, gen counsel, 2003; v.p., gen. counsel Tellabs, Inc., Lisle, Ill., 1998—99; sr. v.p., chief legal and admin. officer Organic, Inc., San Francisco, 1999—2001; spec. coun. litigation transactions Arthur Andersen LLP, 2002; practice lead, corp. governance, risk and crisis mgmt., co-gen. coun. Altheimer & Gray, 2002—03. Mem. planning com. Securities Inst. Northwestern U., Chgo., 1993—, mem. corp. counsel planning com., 1994-2000; mem. civil justice reform adv. com. U.S. Cir. Ct. (no. dist.) Ill., Chgo., 1994-95; mem. Ill. Commn. Regulatory Issues, mem. ACCA 1986, Nat. Assoc. Corp. Dir., 2002-2004, Economic Club Chgo. 2003-, Women Corp. Dirs. 2003-; mem. vis. com. Coll. Law U. Ill., 1997-2001.; bd. dirs. Atrion Corp. 2002-2003. Office: Grant Thornton LLP 175 W Jackson 20th Fl Chicago IL 60604 Office Phone: 312-602-8413.

ZAGER, DIANNE E., special education educator; b. Newark, Mar. 12, 1948; BS, Boston U., 1970, EdM, 1971; PhD, Hofstra U., Hempstead, N.Y., 1981. Tchr. Adams Sch., N.Y.C., 1970-72, Half Hollow Hills Sch. Dist., Dix Hills, N.Y., 1972-75, LD Specialist, 1975-76; program coord. tchr. training Northport Schs., Northport, N.Y., 1978-80; adminstr. Suffolk Child Devel. Ctr., Smithtown, N.Y., 1978-80; prof. L.I. U., 1981—2004, Pace U., N.Y.C., 2004—06, Michael C. Koffler prof. autism, 2006—, dir. Ctr. Tchg. and Rsch. Autism, 2006—. Dir. rsch. Ctr. Developmental Disabilities, Woodbury, N.Y., 1983-1997. Editor: Transition From School to Work, 1990, Autism, 1992, NERA Researcher newsletter, 1985-87. Scholar Project READDY, 1984-87, Personnel Preparation, 1992-96, Pers. Preparation Autism, 2005—, U.S. Dept. Edn. Mem. N.Y. State Coun. for Exceptional Children (pres., mental retardation div. bd. dirs.), Northeastern Ednl. Rsch. Assn. Office Phone: 212-346-1885. Business E-Mail: dzager@pace.edu.

ZAGON, LAURIE, artist; b. NYC, Feb. 4, 1950; d. Jerome and Janet (Rabinowitz) Z.; m. Joseph Sorrentino, Dec. 21, 1991. BFA, Md. Inst. Coll. Art, 1971; MFA, Syracuse U., 1973. Asst. prof. Art CUNY, NYC, 1973-87; color cons. Fieldcrest/Cannon, 1987-88. Spkr. Am. Soc. Interior Designers, Washington, 1993-97—; color, art therapit, Flagstaff, Ariz., 1996, Big Brothers/Big Sisters No. Ariz., 1996. Illustrator (book) It's Never Too Late To Have a Happy Childhood, 1989; one-woman shows include The Nat. Arts Club, NYC, 1989; group exhibits include John Szoke Gallery, NYC, Helio Galleries, NYC, CUNY Abstract Show of Shanghai, China, 1986, LA Mcpl. Gallery, 1993, The Brewery Artist Colony, 1996-2000; co-author: Power of Color, 1995. Color, art therapist for AIDS Children, LA Children's Hosp., 1994; Martin Luther Hosp., Anaheim, 1990; active painting workshops for the terminally ill, 1995—, City of Hope Nat. Cancer Ctr.; founder, dir. Art and Creativity for Healing, Inc., Laguna Niguel, Calif. Office: 26079 Getty Dr Laguna Niguel CA 92677-1233 Office Phone: 949-367-1902. E-mail: laurie@art4healing.org, lzagon@aol.com.

ZAGORIN, JANET SUSAN, legal firm administrator, marketing professional; b. Lakewood, NJ; d. Irving C. and Dorothy (Tarshish) Zagorin. BA, Douglass Coll., 1975; MLS, Rutgers U., 1977. Asst. law libr. N.J. Atty. Gen., Trenton, 1977-78; head of reference sect. Cardozo U. Law Sch., NYC, 1978-79; law and legis. svcs. libr. FTC, Washington, 1979-81; dir. of reference Paul Weiss Rifkind, NYC, 1981-82; libr. dir. Riker Danzig Scherer & Hyland, Morristown, NJ, 1982; libr., profl. devel. dir. Baker & McKenzie, NYC, 1982-96; dir. practice devel. and info. svcs. Stroock & Stroock & Lavan LLP, NYC, 1996-98; dir. practice devel. Cadwalader, Wickersham & Taft, NYC, 1998-99, Gibson, Dunn & Crutcher, NYC, 1999—2001; dir. mktg. Sidley Austin Brown & Wood, NYC, 2001—04; dir. practice devel. Sidley Austin LLP, NYC, 2004—. Bd. dirs. N.Y. Cares, 1998—. Mem.: ABA (vice chmn. standing com. Law Libr. Congress 1995—96, chmn. 1996—2001, law 2000 steering com. Libr. Congress), Am. Assn. Law Librs. (chair fgn. comparative internat. law com. 1990—91, vice chair pvt. law librs. 1990—91, chair com. on recruitment 1991, chair 1991—), Fin. Women's Assn. (bd. dirs. 1993—95, 1999—), Hadassah. Office: Sidley Austin LLP 787 Seventh Ave New York NY 10019-6018 Office Phone: 212-839-8797. Business E-Mail: jzagorin@sidley.com.

ZAHN, LAURA SUE NOYES, educational consultant, small business owner; b. Concord, N.H., Oct. 13, 1974; d. Douglas George and Susan Potter Noyes; m. Kenneth Edward Zahn, Aug. 18, 2000; children: Roy Anthony children: Susanna Kay. BA, Messiah Coll., Grantham, Pa., 1995; MA in Liberal Studies, Dartmouth Coll., Hanover, NH, 2004; MS in Ednl. Adminstrn., Nat. U., Sacramento, Calif., 2005. Cert. experienced educator English grades 5-12 N.H., 2006, preliminary single subject Calif., 2001, preliminary adminstrv. svcs. Calif., 2003. Tchr. English Concord Christian Schs., NH, 1995—96, Bishop Brady HS, Concord, 1996—97; tchr. Cardigan Mountain Sch., Canaan, NH, 1997—98; dir. Summerbridge Sacramento, 1998—2002; vice prin. Charles M. Goethe Mid. Sch., Sacramento City Unified Sch. Dist., 2002—04, interim prin., 2004; ednl. cons., small bus. owner Zahn Consulting, LLC, Bow, NH, 2005—. Bd. mem. Summerbridge Nat./The Breakthrough Collaborative, San Francisco, 2000—02, chair dir.'s coun., 2000—02; spkr. AmeriCorps, Sacramento, 2003—04; spkr. Passport to Success Parent Outreach Sacramento City Unified Sch. Dist., 2001. V.p. MOMS Club Greater Portsmouth Area, NH, 2006—. Recipient Excellence in Tchg. scholarship, Paul Douglas Tchg. Found., 1994, academic scholarship, Bow Rotary, 1994, Honors in Lang., Lit., and Comm., Messiah Coll., 1995, 1st pl. in Lincoln-Douglas Debate, Spkr. Points, and Extemporaneous Speaking, Nat. Forensic League-New Hampshire State Championship, 1992, Benjamin Russell Faculty Leadership award, Summerbridge, Manchester, 2006. Mem.: ASCD, MOMS Club (pres. 2006—, founder). Achievements include research in a formula for developing differentiated instruction curriculum in middle-school language arts. Avocations: writing, reading. Office Phone: 603-724-3708. Personal E-mail: lsnzahn@yahoo.com. Business E-Mail: zahnconsulting@gmail.com.

ZAHNER KRAEFT, DOROTHY SIMKIN, elementary school educator, school librarian; b. Chengdu, Szechuan, China, May 1, 1926; arrived in US, 1931; d. Robert Louis and Margaret Isadore (Timberlake) Simkin; m. Henry Zahner (div.); children: Mary De Avilan, Robert Louis; m. Norman John Kraeft, May 28, 2005. BA in Sociology, Whittier Coll., 1948; MLS, U. So. Calif., LA, 1952. Cert. tchr. Calif., Ariz. Tchr. LA and Pasadena Sch., Calif., 1969-93; dir., owner Betty Ingram Sch., North Hollywood, Calif., 1976-79; dir. Foothill Nursery Sch., La Crescenta, Calif., 1970s; tchr. L.A. Unified Sch. Dist.; guest tchr. Washington Unified Sch. Dist., Phoenix, 1994-97; ret., 2002. Guest tchr. Osborn Sch. Dist., 1998-2000, Madison Sch. Dist., Phoenix, 1999-2001. Author: poems pub. in U.S., Europe and China. Bd. dirs. Ariz. Tenants Assn., Phoenix, 1994, 95; vol. Am. Friends Svc. Com., Phila., Calif., 1985-, Common Cause, LA, 1990, Internat. Rescue Com.; domestic violence vol., Phoeniz, 1999-2000; vol. Dem. candidates, LA and Phoenix; poll marshall Election Bd., Phoenix. Recipient cert. appreciation, Project Hope, 2005. Mem.: Ariz. State Poetry Soc. (pres. 2002—, chmn. 2004), Alameda Writers Group, Phoenix Poetry Soc. (pres. 1998, anthology editl. co. 2001, featured reader 2005, com. mem., Poet of Yr. 2000, poetry awards 1995, 2000), Am. Assn. Ret. Persons, Phoenix Writers Club (sec. 1998). Democrat. Avocations: theater, films, music, swimming, reading.

ZAIDI, EMILY LOUISE, retired elementary school educator; b. Hoquiam, Wash., Apr. 20, 1924; d. Burdick Newton and Emily Caroline (Williams) Johnston; m. M. Baqar Abbas Zaidi, June 12, 1949 (dec. Dec. 1983). BA in Edn. and Social Studies, Ea. Wash. State U., 1948; MEd, U. Wash., 1964, EdD, 1974. Tchr. 4th grade Hoquiam Schs., 1948—49; tchr. grades 5-6 Lake Washington Sch. Dist., Kirkland, Wash., 1949—51; tchr. grades 2-3 Port Angeles Schs., Wash., 1951—54; tchr. grade 2 Seattle Schs., 1954—55; tchr., reading specialist Northshore Sch. Dist., Bothell, Wash., 1955—69, Sacramento City Schs., 1969—87; ret., 1987. Mem. Calif. State Instrnl. Materials Panel, Sacramento, 1975. Mem. Sacramento Opera Assn., 1986—, Sacramento Ballet Assn., 1987—2000. Fulbright Commn. Exch. Tchr., 1961—62. Democrat. Avocations: writing, children's literature, reading, travel. Home: 4230 N River Way Sacramento CA 95864-6055 Personal E-mail: louisezaidi@comcast.net.

ZAINELLI, GINA M., education educator; b. Chgo., Jan. 30, 1975; d. Roger N. and Susanne L. Zainelli. PhD in Molecular Biology, Loyola U. Stritch Sch. Medicine, Maywood, Ill., 2003; BS in Biology, Loyola U., Chgo., 1997. Postdoctoral fellow Nat. Eye Inst. Emory U., Atlanta, 2003—05; instr. Loyola U., Chgo., 2005—. Achievements include research in the involvement of the enzyme transglutaminase in neurodegenerative disease. Office: Loyola Univ 6525 N Sheridan Rd Chicago IL 60626 Office Phone: 773-508-3717. Business E-Mail: gzainel@luc.edu.

ZAININGER, LUCIE E., elementary school educator; d. Alex R. and Helen Gasick; m. Richard Harvey Zaininger; 1 child, Brittney Ashley. MEd, St. Xavier Coll., Chgo., 1998. Tchr. math. Still Mid. Sch., Aurora, Ill., 1994—. Cons. Packer Engring., Naperville, Ill., 2000. Mem. Naperville Christian Ch., 1993. Fellow, Packer Engring., Aurora U., 2000. Office: Still Middle School 780 Meadowridge Drive Aurora IL 60504 Office Phone: 630-375-3939.

ZAK, DOROTHY ZERYKIER, psychologist; b. Katowice, Poland, Jan. 11, 1950; came to U.S., 1969; d. Mieczystaw and Helena (Stahl) Zerykier; m. Jesse Cooper Brake (dec.); m. Sheldon Jerry Zak, July 6, 1986. BA, Queens Coll., 1973; MA, New Sch. Social Research, 1975. Clin. intern Bergen Pines Hosp., Paramus, NJ, 1976-77; psychologist State Sch. Mentally Retarded, Kinston, NC, 1977-78, Dorothea Dix Hosp., Raleigh, NC, 1978-83; pvt. practice cons. N.Y.C., 1983-84; psychologist Fed. Employment and Guidance Svcs., N.Y.C., 1984-85; vocat. counselor NY Assn. for New Ams. Inc., N.Y.C., 1985-88; ednl. counselor B'nai Brith Career and Counseling Svcs., N.Y.C., 1988-90; career acad. counselor Touro Coll., N.Y.C., 1990—97; continuing adult edn. counselor Bronx C.C., NY, 1997; counselor Jamaica Hosp. Med. Ctr., NY, 1999—. Part-time cons. St. John's Hosp.-Cath. Med. Ctr. Bklyn. and Queens Weight Loss Program, 1987-92. Mem. Am. Psychol. Assn., Polish Inst. Arts and Scis., Am. Assn. for Counseling and Devel., N.Y. Acad. Scis. Office: Jamaica Hosp Med Ctr 8900 Van Wyck Expy Jamaica NY 11418

ZAKEN, GRACE AMBROSE, project coordinator, educator; b. Pitts., Nov. 3, 1964; d. Stephen E. and Moira (Buckley) Ambrose; m. Benjamin Zaken; children: Ilana, Tal, Stephen. BA, U. New Orleans, 1986; MEd, U. Tex., 1993; EdD, Vanderbilt U., 1997. Tchr. students with visual disabilities St. Bernard Parish Sch. Bd., Arabi, La., 1987—90; play tutor for blind children Austin, Tex., 1990—92; pre-sch. tchr. students with visual disabilities Austin Ind. Sch. Dist., 1992—93; orientation and mobility specialist Tex. Commn. for the Blind, Austin, 1992—93; specialist orientation and mobility Nashville, 1993—97; project coord., lectr. Hunter Coll. CUNY, 1997—. Specialist orientation and mobility N.Y. State Commn. for the Blind and Visually Handicapped, N.Y.C., 1997—, N.Y. Duchess BOCES, 2005—; instr. spl. edn. on-line Internet Vanderbilt U., Nashville, 1996-97; asst. coord. Vision Rehab. program Lighthouse Internat., 1997-2002; coord. Access to Quality Vision Rehab. Svc., 2003-05 Contbr. articles to profl. jours. and conf. procs. Vol. surrogate parent Dept. Spl. Edn.-Cavert Br. Office Met., Nashville, 1997; vol. vision screener Prevent Blindness, Nashville, 1997; state coord. Nat. Agenda for Children and Youths with Visual Impairments Including Those with Multiple Disabilities, Nashville, 1997. Recipient Reading Program for At Risk Readers award Internat. Reading St. Bernard Parish La., 1990. Mem. Coun. Exceptional Children, Assn. for Edn. of Blind and Visually Impaired (cert. orientation and mobility specialist, chmn. O&M divsn. 2000-06), Assn. for Edn. and Rehab. of Blind and Visually Impaired. Avocations: mountain biking, cribbage. Address: Hunter Coll of CUNY 909W Park Ave New York NY 10021-0308 Fax: (212) 650-3542. E-mail: gambrose@hunter.cuny.edu.

ZALAZNICK, LAUREN, broadcast executive; married; 3 children. Grad., Brown U. With MTV Networks, USA Cable; sr. v.p. original programming & devel. VH1; exec. v.p. network enterprises NBC Universal Television Networks, pres. Trio Networks, 2002—05, pres. Bravo Network, 2004—. Office: NBC Universal Television Group 30 Rockefeller Plz New York NY 10112 Office Phone: 212-664-4444. Office Fax: 212-664-3720.*

ZALESKI, JEAN, artist; b. Birkirkara, Malta; d. John M. and Carolina (Micallef) Busuttil; children: Jeffrey, Philip, Susan. Student, Art Students League, N.Y.C., 1955—58, New Sch., 1967—69, Moore Coll. Art, Phila., 1970—71, Parsons Sch. Design, N.Y.C., 1974—75, Pratt Inst., 1976—77. Dir. art Studio 733, Great Neck, NY, 1963-67; sr. art instr. Hussian Coll. Art, Phila., 1970-71; dir. Naples (Italy) Art Studio, 1972-74; corp. sec. Women in The Arts, N.Y.C., 1974-75, exec. coord., 1976-78. Adj. lectr. Bklyn. Coll., 1974-75, Hofstra U., 1977-82, Cooper Union, 1986—. One-woman shows include Neikrug Gallery, NYC, 1970, Wallnuts Gallery, Phila., 1971, Il Gabbiano Gallery, Naples, Italy, 1973, Adelphi U., Garden City, NY, 1975, Women in Arts Gallery, NYC, 1975, Alonzo Gallery, 1979—80, Va. Ctr. for Creative Arts, Sweet Briar, 1981, Hodgell Galleries, Sarasota, Fla., 1982—83, Elaine Starkman Gallery, NYC, 1986, Romano Gallery, Barnegat Light, N.J., 1987—88, Citicorp Ctr., NYC, 1988—89, Z Gallery, 1991, Sweet Briar Coll., Va., 1993, Trinity Coll., Hartford, Conn., 1996, Myungsook Lee Gallery, NYC, 1997—98, Slater Mus., Norwich, Conn., 1999, Four Decades of Painting, Retrospective Westbeth Gallery, NYC, 2000, St. James Cavalier Contemporary Art Ctr., Valletta, Malta, 2002, exhibited in group shows at Art U.S.A., NYC, 1969, Internat. Art Exhbn., Cannes, France, 1969, Frick Mus., Pitts., 1970, NAD, NYC, 1970—71, Phila. Mus. Art, 1971, Am. Women Artists, Palazzo Vecchio, Florence, Italy, 1972, Internat. Women's Arts Festival, Milan, 1973 (Gold medal), Bklyn. Mus., 1975, Sweet Briar Coll., Va., 1977, CUNY, 1978, Va. Ctr., 1988, Mus. Hudson Highlands, 1982, Pace U. Gallery, NYC, 1982, Bayly Mus., Charlottesville, Va., 1986, Allbright Knox Mus., Buffalo, 1986, E. Starkman Gallery, NYC, 1987, Nabisco, 1989, Queens Coll., NY, 1991—92, Mus. City of N.Y., 1993, Nat. Mus. Fine Arts, Malta, 2000, Mediterranean Conf. Ctr., 2001, Westbeth Gallery, NYC, 2002—06, Represented in permanent collections N.Y. Pub. Libr., Met. Mus. Art, NYC, Va. Ctr. for Creative Arts, Nat. Mus. Women in Arts, Mus. City of NY, Nat. Mus. Malta; author: Winged Spirits, 1995; co-author: COW/LINES, 1983. Recipient Susan B. Anthony award NOW, 1986; MacDowell fellow, 1971—, Ragdale fellow, 1986—, Va. Ctr. for Creative Arts fellow, 1976—, Tyrone Guthrie Ctr. fellow, 1991; grantee NEA/Brown U., 1982, Artists Space, 1988; invited to White House by Pres. Carter, 1977. Mem. Artists Equity, Women in the Arts. Democrat. Roman Catholic. Achievements include represented Malta in UN art exhibition celebrating entry of 25 countries to E.U. 2004. Avocations: music, opera, writing. Office Phone: 212-929-4194. Personal E-mail: zaleskijean@aol.com.

ZALILA-MILI, RYM, computer scientist, educator; b. Tunis, Tunisia, Aug. 9, 1965; came to the U.S., 1995; d. Chedli and Melika (Amara) Zalila; m. Ali Mili, June 29, 1991 (div. Oct. 1998); 1 child, Noor. Pre-Engring. in Physics & Chemistry, U. Tunis, 1985, Engring. Degree in Computer Sci., 1989, Doctorat de Spécialité, 1991; PhD in Computer Sci., U. Ottawa, Ont., Can., 1997. Lectr. U. Ottawa, 1992-94, Inst. Informatics, Ottawa, 1994-95; asst. prof. U. Tex. Dallas, Richardson, 1995—. Cons. Philips, Surrey, Eng., 1998. Grantee Sandia Nat. Labs., N.Mex., 1998-99. Mem. IEEE Computer Soc., Assn. Computing Machinery. Achievements include An Effective Data Entry Method, A Cigarette Substitute.

ZALOZNIK, ARLENE JOYCE, retired oncologist, retired military officer; b. Pitts., Jan. 30, 1948; d. Ernest and Frances Elizabeth (Augustin) Z. BS, Carlow Coll., 1969; MS, Duquesne U., 1972; MD, Med. Coll. Pa., 1976. Diplomate Am. Bd. Internal Medicine, Am. Bd. Oncology. Commd. U.S. Army, 1976, advanced through grades to col.; intern then resident in internal medicine Madigan Army Med. Ctr., Tacoma, 1976-77; fellow in hematology and oncology Fitzsimons Army Med. Ctr., Aurora, Colo., 1979-81, staff oncology, 1981-82, asst. chief med. oncology, 1982-84, chief hematology and oncology, 1984-86, Brooke Army Med. Ctr., Ft. Sam Houston, Tex., 1986-90; assoc. prof., chief divsn. hematology/oncology divsn. Tex. Tech. U. Health Scis., El Paso, 1997—; ret. Clin. instr. dept. medicine U. Colo. Health Sci. Ctr., 1982-86. Contbr. articles to books and profl. jours. Active profl. edn. com. Aurora-Adams Unit Am. Cancer Soc., 1983-86, pres., 1983-86, active Colo. divsn., 1984-86. Fellow ACP; mem. Am. Soc. Clin. Oncology. Home: 324 Sharondale Dr El Paso TX 79912-4250

ZAMBONI-CUTTER, KATHRYN M., obstetrician, gynecologist, military officer; d. Floyd Frank and Janet Elaine Zamboni; m. Mark B. Zamboni-Cutter, Jan. 3, 1992; children: Kylie, Lindsey. Bachelor's, U. Colo., Denver, 1990, Master's, 1991; MD, Midwestern U., Chgo., 1999. Bd. cert. obstetrician, bd. cert. gynecologist. Resident ob/gyn St. Joseph Hosp., Ann Arbor, Mich., 2000—03; chief ob/gyn dept. Ob/Gyn Clinic Hosp. Ft. Polk, La., 2003—. Maj. U.S. Army, 1996—, Ft. Polk, La. Mem.: Am. Osteopath. Assn., Am. Coll. Ob/Gyn. Avocations: movies, mountain biking, aerobics. Home: 910 Charleston Pl Deridder LA 70634

ZAMBRANO, DEBRA KAY, community health nurse; b. Salida, Colo., Jan. 1, 1955; d. George and Kathleen Elizabeth (Davidoff) Argys; m. George Luis Zambrano, Mar. 11, 1978; children: George Jr., Jennifer. BSN, U. No. Colo., 1980; BS, Adams State Coll., Alamosa, Colo., 1977. RN, Colo. Sr. cmty. health nurse Alamosa County Nursing Svc., Alamosa, Colo., 1993—99; sch. nurse Alamosa Pub. Schs., 1999—2000; specialist communicable diseases Pueblo City-County Health Dept., Pueblo, Colo., 2000—03; nurse cons. Colo. Dept. Pub. Health and Environ., Pueblo, Colo., 2005—. Dist. commr. Cueno Verde dist. Boy Scouts Am., 2000—, dist. training chair, 2004—; booster club pres., Pride City Marching Band, Pueblo, 2004—; sec. to bd. dirs., Pueblo Choral Soc., Pueblo, 2006. Recipient Award of Merit, Boy Scouts of Am., 1998.

ZAMORA, MARJORIE DIXON, retired political science professor; b. Farm Randolph, N.Y., Nov. 8, 1933; d. Wendell Hadley and Jessie (Mercer) Dixon; m. Cornelio Raul Zamora, Dec. 20, 1969; 1 child, Daniel Cornelio. BA, Earlham Coll., 1956; MA, U. Ill., 1968; postgrad., U. Ill., Chgo., 1989—. Tchr. Ridge, Sch., Godsman Sch., Stenson Sch., various cities, 1956-62; with U.S. Peace Corps, tchr. Palmares High Sch., Costa Rica, 1963-64; reporter Lerner Newspaper, Chgo., 1965; dormitory counselor U. Ill., Urbana, 1966-68, 86; instr. Chgo. City Coll., 1968-69; prof. polit. sci. Moraine Valley C.C., Palos Hills, Ill., 1969-94, prof. emerita. Rschr. U. Ill., Chgo., 1985-88. Author short stories; contbr. articles on Costa Rican polit. bus. cycle and economy, land reform to publs. in U.S., Cen. Am.; contbr. short stories to mags. Dir., founder Dept. of Peace Coalition, 2000—05; rep. Beijing Plus Five Regional Steering Com., 1999; appointed to planning com. for a dept. of peace bill Rep. D. Kucinich; pub. speaker Dept. of Peace and Nonviolence & Peace in Space Bills in Congress, 2005—06; active Peace Alliance Orgn. Mem. AAUW (Western Spring area chpt. 1999, Ill. congressional liaison 2000—), Western Springs Band and Orch. Assn. (pres. 1990-91), Am. Assn. Ret. Persons, State Cmty. Coll. Retirees Assn. Mem. Soc. Of Friends. Avocations: skiing, swimming, writing fiction, nonfiction and filmscripts, symphonic music, scuba. Home: 3820 Lawn Ave Western Springs IL 60558-1141 Office Phone: 708-246-7363. E-mail: marjoriez@aol.com.

ZAMVIL, LINDA SUSAN, psychiatrist, educator; d. Louis and Stella Savage Zamvil; m. John Mott-Smith; m. John McNeil Angier II, Aug. 26, 1990; children: Lucas Angier, Robin Tucker Angier stepchildren: Katrina Meadville Angier, Judith Tegan Angier, John McNeil Angier III. BA cum laude, U. Calif., Berkeley, 1973; MD, U. Cinn., 1983. Lic. Mass., 1984, Calif., 1988, NH, 1990, Nat. Bd. Examiners, 1984, Am. Soc. Addiction Medicine, 1992, diplomate Am. Bd. of Psychiatry and Neurology, 1988, Am. Bd. of Psychiatry and Neurology, Am. Bd. Child and Adolescent Psychiatry, 1991, Am. Bd. of Adult Psychiatry. Counselor, med. asst. Santa Cruz Women's Health Ctr., Calif., 1977—78, Yolo County Rape Crisis and Womankind Health Ctr., Santa Cruz, 1978—79; clin. fellow in pediat. Harvard Med. Sch., 1983—84, clin. fellow in psychiatry, 1984—90, clin. instr. in psychiatry, 1990—98, asst. clin. prof. psychiatry, 1999—; intern, resident, psychiatrist Mass. Gen. Hosp., 1983—, intern in pediat., 1983—84, intern, resident Chelsea, 1983—85, resident in psychiatry Dept. Psychiatry, 1984—87, psychiatrist Revere Health Ctr. Mass., 1985—86, mem. women's com. Dept. Psychiatry, 1986—90, resident in child psychiatry, 1987—90, clin. assoc. in psychiatry, 1990—, psychiatrist, 2001; intern Med. Sch. Harvard U., Boston, 1983—84, resident Med. Sch., 1984—87, fellow child and adolescent psychiatry Med. Sch., 1987—90; with Pembroke Hosp., Mass., 1985—90, Westwood Lodge, Mass., 1985—90, Lynn and Union Hosps., Mass., 1988—90, The Cambridge (Mass.) Hosp., 1988—90, psychiatrist, 1988—90, 1997—, psychiatrist Ctr. St. Clinic Somerville, 1999—2002, dir. mental health and addictions, 1999—2000; with New Eng. Meml., Stoneham, Mass., 1989—90; staff psychiatrist Cath. Med. Ctr., Manchester, NH, 1990—94, with, 1990—95; staff psychiatrist Meml. Hosp., Nashua, 1990—94, with, 1990—96, McLean Hosp., Belmont, Mass., 1993—, attending child psychiatrist Child and Adolescent Program Dept. Psychiatry, 2002—; with Sts. Meml. Med. Ctr., Lowell, Mass., 1996—99, psychiatrist Teen Health/Pediatric Counseling Svcs., 1997—99; with St. Joseph Hosp., Nashua, 1997—99, Somerville Hosp., Mass., 1997—, Mt. Auburn Hosp., Cambridge, 1997—; med. dir. adolescent chem. dependency svcs. Brookside Hosp., Nashua, 1990—91, med. dir. child and adolescent psychiatry, 1990—94, mem. instnl. rev. bd. N.E. Psychiat. Assocs., 1990—94, mem. med. record and rev./utilization rev. com., 1990—94, with, 1990—99, med. dir. child and adolescent program svcs., 1991—94; intern, resident Chelsea Health Ctr., 1983—85, psychiatrist, 2001; psychiat. cons. STRAIGHT, Outpatient Adolescent Substance Abuse Treatment, Stoughton, Mass., 1986—87, McLean Hosp., Belmont, Mass., 1992—; psychiatrist Human Resource Inst., Malden and Franklin, Mass., 1986—87, Family Svc. Assn., Boston, 1988—90, Ctr. Mental Health and Retardation Svcs., Waltham, Mass., 1989—90, Stoneybrook Counseling Ctr., Chelmsford, Mass., 1989—90; staff psychiatrist Lahey Hitchcock Clinic, Nashua, 1994—96; med. dir. Northeast Psychiat. Assoc., Lowell, Mass., 1996—99, Charter Behavioral Health Sys. Brookside/New Eng., Lowell, 1996—99, Cambridge Psychiat. Svcs., Inc., Psychiat. Recruitment and Placement Svcs. (sub. North Charles, Inc.-affiliation with Harvard Med. Sch. Dept. Psychiatry Cambridge Hosp.), 1996—2000, Mass. Behavioral Health Partnership, Boston,

2000—01; dir. Ambulatory Psychiatry Svcs. The Cambridge Health Alliance, 1999—2000, Somerville, 1999—2000; mem. instnl. rev. bd. Dept. Psychiatry The Cambridge Health Alliance Cambridge Hosp., 1999—2000; dir. Child and Adolescent Psychiatry, Advs., Inc., Framingham, 2001—, Framingham/Marlborough, Mass., 2002—. Bd. dirs. New Eng. Coun. Psychiatrists, Waltham; mem. com. youth and children NH Coun. Child and Adolescent Psychiatry, 1992—94; mem. Psychiat. Adv. Panel Patient Care Assessment Com. Bd. Registration in Medicine Commonwealth Mass., 1997—; with New Eng. States Partnership Divsn. Med. Assistance Pediatric Psychoactive Medication Prescribing Workgroup Commonwealth Mass., 2001—; mem. adv. bd. Families Depression Awareness, Waltham, 2004—; invited spkr. in field; rschr. in field. Expert reviewer Bipolar Disorder and Depression, 1999; contbr. chapters to books, monographs in books, articles in newsletters. Organizer continuing edn. Ednl. Programs, N.E.; chair N.E. coms. Calif. Gov.'s scholar, Gov. Ronald Reagan, 1969. Mem.: Internat. Soc. Bipolar Disorders, Am. Soc. Addiction Medicine (spkr.), Am. Acad. Psychiatrists Alcoholism and Addictions, Am. Acad. Child and Adolescent Psychiatry, Mass. Med. Soc., Mass. Psychiat. Assn., New Eng. Coun. Child and Adolescent Psychiatry (mental health task force 2001—, mem. consortium New Eng. Coun. Child Psychiatry 2001—, mass. chpt. acad. pediat. com. access to mental health 2001—, mem. bd. 2002—05, spkr.), Am. Acad. Child and Adolescent Psychiatry (presenter 1992), Am. Psychiat. Assn. (mem. nat. com. psychiatrists 1985—86, leader pub. mental health programs 1985—86, spkr. 1986, 1991, Mead Johnson fellow 1985—86). Achievements include worked with Depakote/Valproate as both a principal investigator and as a co-investigator studying the effects of lithium on Bipolar Mood Disorder in adults, adolescents and children; contributed to neuroimaging studies with children and adolescents who are on the mood stabilizer lithium. Office: Advs Inc 27 Hollis St Framingham MA 01702 Office Phone: 508-935-0769.

ZANDER, JANET ADELE, psychiatrist; b. Miles City, Mont., Feb. 19, 1950; d. Adelbert William and Valborg Constance (Buckneberg) Z.; m. Mark Richard Ellenberger, Sept. 16, 1979; 1 child, Evan David Zander Ellenberger. BA, St. Olaf Coll., 1972; MD, U. Minn., 1976. Diplomate Am. Bd. Psychiatry and Neurology. Resident in psychiatry U. Minn., Mpls., 1976-79, fellow in psychiatry, 1979-80, asst. prof. psychiatry, 1981—; staff psychiatrist St. Paul Regions Hosp., 1980—, dir. edn. in psychiatry, 1980-94, dir. inpatient psychiatry, 1986—2005, vice chair dept. psychiatry, 1991-96, divsn. head behavioral health, 2002. Bd. dirs. Perry Assurance. Contbr. research articles to sci. jours. Sec. Concentus Musicus Bd. Dirs., St. Paul, 1981-89; mem. property com. St. Clement's Episcopal Ch., St. Paul, 1985. Mem. Am. Psychiat. Assn., Am. Med. Women's Assn., Minn. Psychiat. Soc. (ethics com. 1985-87, women's com. 1985-87, coun. 1994-96), Minn. Med. Assn., Ramsey County Med. Soc. (bd. dirs. 1994-96). Democrat. Avocations: singing, skiing. Home: 230 Crestway Ln West Saint Paul MN 55118-4424 Office: Regions Hosp 640 Jackson St Saint Paul MN 55101-2502 Office Phone: 651-254-2777. E-mail: janet.a.zander@healthpartners.com.

ZANDVAKILI, KATAYOON, writer; b. Tehran, Iran, Oct. 7, 1967; came to U.S., 1976; d. Amir Hossein and Nahid (Farzian) Z. BA, U. Calif., Berkeley, 1988; MFA, Sarah Lawrence Coll., 1992. Editl./oral history asst. McKinsey & Co., San Francisco, 1994-97; West Coast assoc. Pubs. Weekly, Woodacre, Calif., 1997-98. Contbr. poems to mags. and websites. Home: 6055 Fairlane Dr Oakland CA 94611-1849 Office Phone: 415-302-2889. Personal E-mail: kzawriter@mindspring.com.

ZANE, writer, publishing executive; Pub. Strebor Books Internat. LLC, Largo, Md., 1999—. Author: (novels) Addicted, 2001, Skyscraper, 2003, Nervous, 2003, The Heat Seekers, 2003, Afterburn, 2005; co-author Shame on it All, 2005; author: (short stories) (collection) The Sex Chronicles: Shattering the Myth, 2002, Gettin' Buck Wild: The Sex Chronicles, 2002; editor: Chocolate Flava, 2004, Breaking the Cycle, 2005 (NAACP Image award for outstanding lit. work-fiction, 2006). Office: Strebor Books PO Box 6505 Upper Marlboro MD 20792 Office Phone: 301-583-0616. Business E-Mail: zane@eroticanoir.com.*

ZANETTI, TERESA A., state representative; b. Columbus, Ga., Jan. 20, 1958; m. Gregory Zanetti; children: Daniel, Michael. BA, Harvard U., 1979; MA, St. John's Coll., 1987. Test adminstr. Army Edn. Ctrs., Augsburg, Germany, 1982—85; bur. chief N.Mex. State Dept. Regulation and Licensing, 1989—90; faculty Albuquerque Acad., 1990—97; columnist Albuquerque Tribune, 2000—02; state rep. dist. 15 N.Mex. Ho. of Reps., Santa Fe, 2002—. Mem. N.Mex. State. Bd. Edn., 2001—02. Named Rookie of the Yr., Greater Albuquerque C. of C., 2002; Coe fellow, Stanford U., 1995. Republican.

ZANJANI, SALLY, political science educator, author; b. San Francisco, Nov. 21, 1937; d. George and Sallie Maria (Ruperti) Springmeyer; m. Esmail D. Zanjani, May 31, 1963. BA magna cum laude, NYU, 1964, MA, 1967, PhD, 1974. Adj. prof. polit. sci. U. Nev., Reno, 1975—. Project dir. Jack Longstreet Country, touring art exhibit, Nev., 1990-92. Author: The Unspiked Rail, 1981, Jack Longstreet, 1988, Goldfield, 1992 (award Westerners Internat. 1992), Ghost Dance Winter and Other Tales of the Frontier, 1994, A Mine of Her Own, 1997, Sara Winnemucca, 2001 (Westerners Internat. award, 2001, Evans Biography award, 2001), Glory Days in Goldfield, 2002 Devils Will Reign, 2006; co-author: The Ignoble Conspiracy, 1986; tv interviewer hist. documentaries; contbr. numerous articles to profl. jours. Mem. Western Writers Am., Mining History Assn. (exec. coun. 1994-96, pres. 1998), Phi Beta Kappa. Democrat.

ZANK, MJ SUNNY, musician, department chair, educator; m. Jeremy P. Zank. MA in Music History, BA in Music History, U. Oreg., Eugene; ArtsD in Music Theory and Composition, U. No. Colo., Greeley, 1989; attended, German Music Ctr., Germany, Franz Liszt Acad., Budapest, Kodaly Sch., Kecskemet, Hungary, Orff Inst., Salzburg, Austria. Asst. prof. Bemidji State U., Minn., 1992—93; prof. music Ohio No. U., Ada, 1993—, vice chair coun., 2006—. Nat. chmn. scholarship com. The Nat. League Am. PEN Women, 2006. Composer: Judith, a choral work with piano accompaniment. Named Eleanor H. and Robert W. Biggs Endowed Chair in the Arts, Ohio No. U., 1999—2000; recipient Faculty Devel. Travel to Turkey award, World Affairs Coun. Greater Cin., 1998, Infusing Asian Studies into the Undergraduate Curriculum award, East West Ctr., 2001, Freeman Found. Summer Inst. on Japan award, Japan Studies Assn., 2004. Mem.: Coll. Music Soc. (assoc.; campus rep. 2002), Japan Studies Assn. (assoc.), Pi Kappa Lambda (life), Mu Phi Epsilon (life). Achievements include research in atonal music using set theory. Avocation: asian literature. Office: Ohio Northern University Presser Hall Ada OH 45810 Office Fax: 419-772-2488. Personal E-mail: m-zank@onu.edu.

ZANK, VIRGINIA, literature and language professor; b. Plainview, Ark., Apr. 29, 1942; d. Hayes Dale and Imogene Bridges; m. Martin J. Kugel (dec.); children: Cynthia Gail Kugel, Melissa Gene Kugel-Couch; m. Dale M. Zank, Nov. 25, 1995. BS in Secondary Edn., John Brown U., 1963; MA in English, Ctrl. Mo. State U., 1978. Lifetime cert. tchr. English Mo. Tchr. Higbee (Mo.) H.S., 1963—64; tchr. English Hallsville (Mo.) H.S., 1964—67, Marshall (Mo.) H.S., 1967—93; assoc. prof. English Mo. Valley Coll., Marshall, 1993—. Named Disting. Educator, Optimist Club, Marshall, 1997; recipient Gov.'s award for tchg. excellence, State of Mo., 1996. Mem.: Mo. State Tchrs. Assn., Nat. Coun. Tchrs. English, Mo. Assn. Tchrs. English (pres.). Home: PO Box 658 Marshall MO 65340 Office: Mo Valley Coll 500 E College Marshall MO 65340 Business E-Mail: zankv@moval.edu.

ZANNIERI, NINA, museum director; b. Summit, N.J., Feb. 1, 1955; d. Angelo Joseph and Louise Mary (Brumm) Z.; m. Douglas M. Vogel, Oct. 29, 1994. BA, Boston Coll., 1977; postgrad., Coll. of William & Mary, 1977-78; MA, Brown U., 1980. Curatorial asst. R.I. Hist. Soc., Providence, 1980-81, asst. curator, 1981-83, curator, 1983-86; dir. Paul Revere Meml. Assn., Boston, 1986—. Gen. editor: (exhbn. catalog) Paul Revere: The Man Behind the Myth, 1988; collaborator: A Most Magnificent Mansion; project dir.: (exhbn. catalog) Let Virtue Be A Guide To Thee, 1983 Mem. Am. Assn. Mus.'s (bd. dirs. 1999-02, vice-chair 2002-03), New Eng. Mus. Assn. (pres. 1998-02), Am. Assn. State and Local History (gov. coun. 2004-), Phi Beta Kappa. Office: Paul Revere Meml Assn The Paul Revere House 19 North Sq Boston MA 02113-2405

ZANUCK, LILI FINI, film director, producer; b. Leominster, Mass., Apr. 2, 1954; m. Richard Zanuck, Sept. 23, 1978. Rsch. asst. World Bank, Washington, 1970-78; office mgr. Carnation Co., L.A., 1977-78; rsch. and devel. Zanuck-Brown Co., 1978-89; co-founder, co-owner Zanuck Co., 1989—. Prodr. films Cocoon, 1985, Cocoon: The Return, 1988, Driving Miss Daisy, 1989 (Acad. award 1989), Rich in Love, 1993, Clean Slate, 1994, Wild Bill, 1995, Dvojnik, 1995, Mulholland Falls, 1996, True Crime, 1999, Reign of Fire, 2002; dir. film Rush, 1991, TV miniseries From the Earth to the Moon (Part 3), 1998. Mem.: Calif. Film Commn. Office: The Zanuck Company 9465 Wilshire Blvd Beverly Hills CA 90212-2612

ZAPATA, ANGELA L., counselor; b. Apr. 25, 1973; Student, Ariz. State U., Tempe, Ariz., 2001—. Rsch. asst. Ariz. State U., 2003—, tchg. asst., 2003—. Author: Handbook for counseling adolescent girls and women: A ten year study at Arizona State University, Development of Talent. Grantee, Grad. Divsn. Ariz. State U., 2005—06; scholar, Coca-Cola Found., 1991—95, Grad. Divsn. of Ariz. State U., 2003—04. Mem.: APA, ACA (student rep. to pubs. com.), Assn. Spiritual, Ethical and Religious Values in Counseling, Counselors Social Justice, Assn. Multicultural Counseling and Devel. (Mentee award 2005), Nat. Latino Psychol. Assn., Psi Chi, Golden Key Internat. Honor Soc. Office: Arizona State University PO Box 870611 Tempe AZ 85287-0611 Personal E-mail: angela.zapata@asu.edu.

ZAPFFE, NINA BYROM, retired elementary school educator; b. Independence, Mo., Aug. 17, 1925; d. Richmond Douglas and Nina Belle (Howell) Byrom; m. Robert Glenn Fessler, June 25, 1946 (dec. June 1947); 1 child, Robert Glenn Fessler Zapffe; m. Fred Zapffe, July 1, 1952 (dec. Dec. 1999); children: Paul Douglas, Carl Raymond. BA, So. Meth. U., Dallas, 1946. Fin. sec. Tyler St. Meth. Ch., Dallas, 1948-49; tchr. Dallas Ind. Sch. Dist., 1949-52, Norman (Okla.) Pub. Schs., 1966-74; chief reader for GED Writing Skills Test Part II GED Testing Svc., Am. Coun. on Edn., Washington, 1990—98; ret., 1998. Adv. com. Acad. Resource Ctr. Moore-Norman Tech. Ctr., 1988-2004. Adv. bd. Norman Salvation Army, 1978-90, chmn., 1986; organizer, historian Norman Salvation Army Womens Aux., 1983-2000, pres., 1985; organizer, past pres. Norman Literacy Coun., 1976—; organizing com., past pres. Norman Interfaith Coun., 1974-93; organizing com., past treas. Friends of the Norman Libr., 1979—; mem. McFarlin Meml. United Meth. Ch., historian 2-in-1 Sunday Sch. class, 1990-2002, lay leader, 1980-81, adminstrv. bd., 2001-2004. Named Woman of Yr., Norman Bus. and Profl. Women, 1999; named to Literacy Hall of Fame, Pioneer Libr. Sys., Norman, 1995; recipient medal of appreciation, SAR, 2002. Mem. DAR (regent Black Beaver chpt. 1998-2000, state literacy chmn. 2000-02, chpt. sec. 2003—), Nat. Soc. Daus. 1812 (pres. 1889er chpt. 1991-93, state treas. 1996-2000, chpt. sec. 2002—), Old Regime Study Club (pres. 1998-99), Coterie Club (pres. 1996, 2002), Delta Delta Delta Alumnae. Independent. Avocation: genealogy. Home: 2717 Walnut Rd Norman OK 73072-6940

ZAPICCHI, JOANNE FENITY, secondary school educator; b. Princeton, NJ, Apr. 20, 1960; d. Leo Wyatt Fenity and Mary Elizabeth Delatush; m. Michael Vincent Zapicchi, Feb. 14, 1987; children: Michael Leo, Alexa Philomena. BA, Coll. William and Mary, Williamsburg, Va., 1982, MEd, 1983. Cert. instr., CPR, first aid, AED ARC. Health and phys. edn. tchr. Hightstown HS, NJ, 1984—. Curriculum writer, cons. Washington Twp. Sch. Dist., Robbinsville, NJ, 2003—; instr. lifeguard tng. East Windsor Regional Sch. Dist. Cmty. Edn., Hightstown, 2006. Team leader Walk Am., March of Dimes, Hightstown, 1998—; legis. chmn. Robbinsville HS PTSA, 2005—; eucharistic min. St. Gregory of the Great Roman Cath. Ch., Hamilton Square, NJ. Named to, Hightstown HS Athletic Hall of Fame, 2004; grantee, Hightstown HS Parents Assn., 1999, East Windsor Edn. Found., 2004—05. Mem.: NH Alliance Health, Phys. Edn., Recreation and Dance, Nat. Athletic Trainers Assn., Mortar Bd. Honor Soc. Avocations: running, flea markets, reading, philanthropic activities. Home: 11 Chambers Ct Robbinsville NJ 08691 Office: Hightstown HS 25 Leshin Ln Hightstown NJ 08520

ZAPPA, GAIL, record producer; m. Frank Zappa (dec.); children: Moon, Dweezil, Ahmet, Diva. Recipient (with Frank Zappa) Best Recording Package-Boxed Grammy award for Frank Zappa's Civilization, Phaze III, 1996.

ZARAGOZA, RYLEE RENEE, elementary school educator; b. Ponca City, Okla., 1970; d. William Karrol and Janice Mae Ramsey; m. Dino Andreas Zaragoza, July 1993; children: Jaden Elliott, Micah Andreas, Eli Jamison. BS in Edn., Okla. Bapt. U., Shawnee, 1994; MS in Tchg., Learning and Leadership, Okla. State U., Tulsa, 2003. Cert. reading specialist Okla. Elem. tchr. Bartlesville (Okla.) Pub. Schs., 1997—2003; reading specialist Bixby (Okla.) Pub. Schs., 2003—. Mem.: Internat. Reading Assn. Democrat. Avocations: camping, scrapbooks, sports, travel. Personal E-mail: readingspecialist03@hotmail.com.

ZARDETTO-SMITH, ANDREA, medical educator; BS in Biology, Coll. of St. Elizabeth, 1978; MS in Physiology, Loyola U. of Chgo., 1983, PhD, 1990. Rsch. biologist G.D. Searle, Skokie, Ill., 1978—83; postdoctoral fellow dept. internal medicine U. Iowa, 1990—91; postdoctoral rschr. NIH, 1990—92; assoc. dept. anatomy U. Iowa, 1993—96; prof. phys. and occupl. therapy and pharm. sci. Creighton U., Omaha, 1996—2002; prof. biology and neuroscience U. Nebr., Omaha, 2002—. Prin. investigator Brains Rule! Nat. Neurosci. Expositions, a Sci. Edn. Drug Abuse Partnership Award Nat. Inst. on Drug Abuse. Grantee NSF, 1996—98. Mem.: AAAS, Assn. of Women in Sci. (pres. ea. Iowa chpt. 1994—96), Women in Neurosci. (past pres.), Am. Assn. Clin. Anatomists, Am. Assn. Anatomists, Soc. for Neurosci. (com. neuroscience literacy). Achievements include research in on the role of various neurotransmitters in brainstem and forebrain circuits that modulate body fluid balance and how they affect overall control of blood pressure; development of model program for improving neuroscience literacy. Office: Univ Nebraska 3001 Dodge St ASH 347 Omaha NE 68182

ZARGHAMI, CYMA, broadcast executive; b. Iran, 1962; d. Gorham and Catherine; m. George Obergfoll, 1994; children: Liam, Ethan. BA, U. of Vt., Burlington, 2000. Scheduling clerk, scheduling exec., programming exec. Nickelodeon, 1985—96, exec. v.p., gen. mgr., 1996—2004, pres., 2004—. Directs co. initiatives Big Help and Kids Pick the Pres. Campaign; launched Nick Jr., SNICK, Nicktoons. Office: Nickelodeon 1515 Broadway New York NY 10036*

ZARING, JANE THOMAS, retired editor, writer; b. Nelson, Wales, Dec. 26, 1936; arrived in U.S., 1962; d. Edward Thomas and Gwyneth Jennet Lewis; m. Philip Brewer Zaring; children: David, Noah. BA, U. Coll., London, 1959; diploma in edn., U. Cambridge, Eng., 1960; MA, Ind. U., Bloomington, 1966. Geography tchr. Putney Trust Sch., London, 1960—63; head geography Howell's Sch., Llandaff, Wales, 1965—67; lectr. Cardiff Coll. Edn., Wales, 1967—68; instr. earth sci. Iowa State U., Ames, 1968—75; editor Iowa State U. Press, Ames, 1985—98; ret., 1998. Mem. adv. bd. women's studies Iowa State U. Author: Return of the Dragon, 1980, Sharkes in the North Woods, 1982. Treas. Meadow Glen Rd. Assn., Iowa, 1972—. Mem.: Women's Dining Club. Democrat. Episcopalian. Avocations: reading, gardening, walking.

ZARRES, SHARON L., marriage and family therapist, health facility administrator; b. Altadena, Calif., June 11, 1947; d. Verne Ivan and Ruth Elizabeth Hatfield; m. Michael Paul Zarres, 1977; adopted children: Rebecca, Philip, Victor, Amber, James MacKenzie. BA, Azusa Pacific U., 2000, MA in Clin. Psychology, 2002, MA in Marriage and Family Therapy, 2003. Ordained to ministry Western Evang. Orgn. Dir. Jack & Jill Pre-Sch./Grade Sch., La Puente, Calif.; office mgr. World Vision Internat., Monrovia, Calif.; owner, mgr. Zarres Family Day Care, Covina, Calif., 1995—2005; adminstr., marriage and family therapist Father's Heart Ranch, Desert Hot Springs, Calif., 2003—. Mem. integration com. Azusa (Calif.) Pacific U., 2000—, tchg. and rsch. asst., 2001—02. Foster parent Koinonia Foster Homes, San Bernardino, Calif.; v.p., founder Lighthouse Prayer, Covina, lay counselor, 1980—90; bd. dirs. Prevailing Word, Azusa. Avocations: reading, travel, movies. Home and Office: 71-175 Aurora Rd Desert Hot Springs CA 92241

ZARRO, JANICE ANNE, lawyer; b. Newark, June 30, 1947; BA, Rutgers U., 1969; JD, IIT-Chgo.-Kent Coll. Law, 1973. Bar: Pa. 1974. Counsel jud. com. U.S. Ho. Reps., Washington, 1973-77; profl. staff mem. counsel labor and human resources com. U.S. Senate, Washington, 1977-80; dir. Avon Products, Inc., N.Y.C., 1980-81, Washington, 1982-86, v.p., 1986-90; pres. The Novus Group, Inc., 1990-92; dir. fed. affairs Mallinckrodt Med., 1992—, v.p., 1993-94; v.p. govt. affairs Worldwide Mallinckrodt Inc., 1994-2000; exec. dir. Women's Resource Ctr. Sarasota County, 2003—. Gen. counsel Nat. Italian-Am. Found., 1989-96, chair bd. trustees, 1996-99; mem. Bus. Govt. Rels. Coun., Washington, 1987—; past chair Women's Fgn. Policy Group. Past chmn. Nat. Capital chpt. Multiple Sclerosis Soc. Recipient Leadership Recognition award Nat. Women's Econ. Alliance, 1984. Office Phone: 341-366-1700. Business E-Mail: jzarro@thewomensresourcecenter.org.

ZASADA, MARY EILEEN, nursing administrator; b. Waterbury, Conn., July 23, 1957; d. Walter Francis and Elizabeth Ann (Doyle) Lewis; m. Peter Pilkington Zasada, Sept. 8, 1984; children: Kathleen, Andrew. Diploma in nursing, St. Vincent's Med. Ctr., 1978; BS in Mgmt., Tiekyo Post U., 1983; MSN, Sacred Heart U., 1997. RN, Conn. Staff New Britian (Conn.) Gen. Hosp., 1978-79, St. Mary's Hosp., Waterbury, Conn., 1980-84, nurse analyst, 1984-98, project leader clin. applications, 1998—. Bd. dirs. Conn. Healthcare Informatics Network. Mem. Rotary Internat. (bd. dirs. 1990-98, Paul Harris fellow), Girls Inc. of Waterbury (bd. dirs. 1996-2001), Sigma Theta Tau (Mu Delta chpt.). Home: 122 Terrell Farm Rd Bethlehem CT 06751-1408 Office: St Marys Hosp 56 Franklin St Waterbury CT 06706-1238

ZASTOCKI, DEBORAH K., health facility executive; Several exec. nursing positions in area hospitals; joined Chilton Meml. Hosp., Pompton Plains, NJ, 1990—, COO, chief nurse exec., pres., CEO, 2004—. Faculty, nursing adminstrn. William Paterson U., 1999—; spkr. in field. Co-author several books on home care and nursing, author on the topic of complexity. Bd. dir. Tri-County C. of C., Wayne, NJ, 2005—. Fellow: Am. Coll. Healthcare Executives NJ (former pres., Disting. Svc. 2005); mem.: NJ Hosp. Assn. (policy develop. com. mem. 2005—06). Office: Chilton Meml Hosp 97 W Parkway Pompton Plains NJ 07444*

ZATZ, ARLINE, writer, photographer; m. Joel Leon Zatz; children: Robert Jay, David Alan. BA in Journalism, Rutgers U., 1977. Asst. coord. N.J. Div. Consumer Affairs, Newark, 1972-75; writer, photographer A-Z Publs., Metuchen, N.J., 1977—. Author: 30 Bicycle Tours in New Jersey, 2003, New Jersey's Special Places, rev. edition 1994 (Best Book N.J. Press Women, Nat. Assn. Press Women), Best Hikes with Children in New Jersey, 2005, New Jersey's Great Gardens, 1999 (Best Book North Am. Travel Journalists Assn. 1999, Horsing Around in New Jersey: The Horse Lover's Guide to Everything Equine, 2004; contbr. articles to profl. jours. Bd. dirs. YMCA, Metuchen, 1984-86. Mem. Nat. Assn. Press Women, Outdoor Writers Assn. Am. Avocations: hiking, canoeing, horseback riding, sailing, reading. Home: 77 Woodside Ave Metuchen NJ 08840-1629 Office: A-Z Publs 77 Woodside Ave Metuchen NJ 08840-1629 Office Phone: 732-494-9258. E-mail: azatz@funtravels.com.

ZAUN, ANNE MARIE, lawyer; b. N.Y.C., Aug. 1, 1949; d. George F. and Clara J. (Varriale) Z.; m. Stephen A. Lokos, Oct. 17, 1987; children: Debra M., Anthony G. BS, Fordham U., 1970; JD cum laude, Seton Hall U., 1979. Assoc. mgr. Prudential Property and Casualty Ins. Co., Woodbridge, N.J., 1972-76; dep. atty. gen. State of N.J., Trenton, 1980-84; staff atty. Knapp & Blejwas, Edison, N.J., 1984-87; dir. legal writing program Law Sch. Seton Hall. U., Newark, 1987-89; prin. Anne M. Zaun, East Brunswick, N.J., 1989—. Adj. prof. paralegal program Middlesex County Coll., 1992—2002. Mem. N.J. Bar Assn. (elder law sect.), Middlesex County Bar Assn. (elder law sect.). Democrat. Avocations: reading, music, tennis, swimming. Office: G 12A Brier Hill Ct East Brunswick NJ 08816-3000 Office Phone: 732-613-3900. Personal E-mail: amzesq@earthlink.net.

ZAUSCH, JO FOUTS, literature and language professor, department chairman; d. Joseph William and May Hignite Fouts; married, Mar. 20, 1965; children: Walter W., Matthew W. BA in English, U. Evansville, Ind., 1964; MA in English Lit., Washington U., St. Louis, 1966; EdD in Ednl. Leadership, Spalding U., Louisville, 1996. Instr. English Ea. Ky. U., Richmond, 1966—69, U. Evansville, Ind., 1969—86, Henderson C.C., Ky., 1987—97; prof. English and humanities divsn. chair Jefferson Cmty. and Tech. Coll., Louisville, 1997—. Dir. Henderson Fine Arts Ctr., Ky., 1993—95; cons. bus. and tech. writing; theatre cons. Pres. Henderson Arts Coun., Ky., 1988—95. Office: Jefferson Cmty and Tech Coll 1000 Cmty Coll Dr Louisville KY 40272

ZAWADZKI-JANUSZ, STACY LYNN, music educator, performing arts educator; b. Buffalo, June 13, 1974; d. Michael Thomas Zawadzki and Diane Theresa Zawadzi; m. Robert Paul Janusz, Aug. 13. BA magna cum laude, U. Buffalo, N.Y., 1996, MA and Humanities magna cum laude, 2004. CPR, ARC; cert. tchr. N.Y. Substitute tchr. P.S. 139 Elem. Sch., 1999—2000; dance tchr. I.S. 232 Winthrop Intermediate Sch., 2000—00; choreographer, workshop tchr. West Seneca East H.S., NY, 2002—, Cheektowaga Ctrl. H.S., NY, 2002; tchr. art Arts in Edn., West Seneca, NY, 2002—; choreographer Walh's Performing Arts Studios, Orchard Park, NY, 2004—, Royal Acad. Ballet and Dance, Kenmore, NY, 2005—, Irish Classical Theatre, Buffalo, 2005—; prof. mus. theatre and dance Niagara U., Niagara Falls, NY, 2005—. Mem. Buffalo Contemporary Dance Co., Marie-Christine Giordano Dance Co., Alpha Omega Dance Co., New Dance Collective Dance Co., Zodiaque Dance Co.; dir. and founder ECNAD Dance Co.; dance educator, choreographer St. Margaret's Cath. Sch.; adjudicator dance competitions throughout U.S. Choreographer Music is Art Festival and Elmwood Art Festival, Zodiaque Dance Co., Am. Coll. Dance Festival, various musicals including Gypsy, Once on This Island, Pippin, Singin' the Rain, High Society, 42nd Street, Guys and Dolls, Hello Dolly, My Fair Lady, West Side Story, Oklahoma, Damn Yankees, Bye Bye Birdie, Anthing Goes, Jesus Christ Superstar and Grease, MTC Prodns., Lancaster Opera House, N.Y.c., dancer N.Y., Can., Conn., Mex., Brit. Virgin Islands. Recipient award for Choreography, N.Y. State Tannis Theatre Assn. Home: 145 Pierce St Buffalo NY 14206-3328 Office Phone: 716-435-1263. E-mail: dancestace@adelphia.net.

ZAWAIDEH, MONA A., pediatrician, endocrinologist, nephrologist, educator; b. Irbid, Jordan, May 4, 1974; d. Auni A. Zawaideh and Sylvia K. Ghishan; m. Nathaniel S. Wurthmann, May 28, 2005. MD, Jordan U. Sci. and Tech., 1997. Bd. cert. Am. Bd. Pediat., 2001, lic. Ariz. Med. Bd., 2005. Resident U. Ariz. Sch. Medicine, Tucson, 1998—2001, asst. prof. pediatric nephrology and endocrinology, 2005—. Med. dir. pediatric dialysis DCI/Desert Dialysis, Tucson, 2005—. Contbr. chapters to books. Fellow, Wash. U. Sch. Medicine, St. Louis, 2001—05; scholar, Jordanian Ministry Edn., 1991—97. Mem.: Am. Soc. Pediatric Nephrology (assoc.). Achievements include re-established the pediatric kidney transplant program in Tucson, Ariz. Office Phone: 520-626-6182.

ZBIKOWSKI, KRISTEN LYNN, education educator; d. Jacob Nathan Laakkonen and Bonita Rose Sutliff; m. Robert Paul Zbikowski, Aug. 6, 1993; 1 child, Benjamin Guy. BS in Psychology, Bemidji State U., Minn., 2000. Cert. CPhT Minn., 1995. Habilitation counselor CCP, St. Paul, 1990—95; pharm. technician United Children's Hosp., St. Paul, 1995—2000; coll. faculty State of Minn., Hibbing, Minn., 2000—06. Avocations: reading, gardening, cooking, musical instruments. Office: Hibbing CC 1515 E 25th St Hibbing MN 55746

ZEALEY, SHARON JANINE, lawyer; b. St. Paul, Aug. 30, 1959; d. Marion Edward and Freddie Zealey. BS, Xavier U. of La., 1981; JD, U. Cin., 1984. Bar: Ohio 1984; U.S. Dist. Ct. (so. dist.) Ohio 1985; U.S. Ct. Appeals (6th cir.) 1990; U.S. Supreme Ct. 1990. Law clk. U.S. Atty. for S. Dist. of Ohio, Cin., 1982; first adminstr. U.S. Bank (formerly First Nat. Bank), Cin., 1984-86; atty. UAW Legal Svcs., Cin., 1986-88; assoc. Manley, Burke, Lipton & Fischer, Cin., 1988-91; mng. atty. and dep. atty. gen. Ohio Atty. Gen. Office, Cin., 1991-95; asst. U.S. atty. criminal div. for So. Dist. Ohio U.S. Attys. Office, Cin., 1995-97; United States atty. So. Dist. Ohio, Cin., 1997—2001; ptnr. Blank Rome LLP, 2001—. Adj. instr. Coll. Law U. Cin., 1997—; mem. U.S. Atty. Gen.'s Adv. Com., 1999—2001, chair civil rights subcom., 2001; mem. merit selection com. Sixth Cir. Ct. of Appeals Bankruptcy Ct., 1992—96, 2003. Mem. commn. Cin. Cmty. Action Now, 2001—; commr. Tall Stacks Commn., City of Cin., 1990—94, Mayor's Commn. on Children, City of Cin., 1992—94; mem. equal employment adv. rev. panel City of Cin., 1989—91; bd. dirs. Nat. Inst. for Law and Equity, 2002—; trustee, bd. visitors U. Cin. Coll. Law, 1992—; trustee Legal Aid Soc. Cin., 1987—92; bd. dirs. Freestore Foodbank, 2003—, Playhouse in the Park, 2002—; co-chair Greater Cin. Minority Counsel Program, 2005—; mem. exec. bd. Cin. Youth Collaborative, 2005—. Named Career Woman of Achievement, Cin. YWCA, 1988; named one of Top Ten Women Attys., Women's Bus. Cin., 2005; named to Super Lawyers, Ohio, 2006; recipient Disting. Alumni award, Friends of Women's Studies, U. Cin., 2001, Theodore M. Berry award for outstanding achievement in politics and in svc. to cmty., Cin. chpt. NACCP, 1998, Nicholas Longworth III Alumni Achievement award for disting. pub. svc., U. Cin. Coll. Law, 1997. Mem. Black Lawyers Assn. of Cin. (pres. 1989-91, round table 1988-), Legal Aid Soc. (sec. 1991-92), ABA, Fed. Bar Assn., Ohio Bar Assn., Nat. Bar Assn. (bd. govs. 1988-1990, Mem. of Yr. region VI 1990), Cin. Bar Assn. (trustee 1989-94), Cin. CAN Commn. Democrat. Episcopalian. Office: Coca-Cola Co One Coca-Cola Plz NAT 2062 PO Box 1734 Atlanta GA 30301 Office Phone: 513-362-8700. Business E-Mail: zealey@blankRome.com.

ZEBI, SANDRA, artist; b. Sao Paulo, Brazil, Mar. 23, 1960; d. Fernando and Yvonne Landi (Visconti) Zeminian; children: Zebi Zeminian Birnbaum, Gabi Zeminian Birnbaum. BA, U. Mackenzie, Brazil, 1982; student in Architecture, Westminister Coll., London, Eng., 1983—84; student in Graphic Design, Santa Monica Coll. Artist Zebi Designs, L.A., 1990—. Prin. works include sculpture, Inglewood City Hall, Calif. Business E-Mail: sandrazebi@zebidesigns.com.

ZEBLEY, LISA CATHERINE, elementary school educator; b. Newport News, Va., July 28, 1961; d. Bobby O'Brien and Sylvia Jean (Jenkins) Dempsey; m. Douglas E. Zebley, June 14, 1984. BA, Christopher Newport U., 1984. Tchr. Newport News Pub. Schs., 1984-87, Virginia Beach (Va.) Pub. Schs., 1987—. Mem. Internat. Reading Assn., Va. State Reading Coun., Virginia Beach Reading Coun. (publicity com. 1997-98, bd. dirs.). Avocations: reading, walking, computers. Office: Christopher Farms Elem Sch 2828 Pleasant Acres Dr Virginia Beach VA 23453-7300

ZEE, PHYLLIS C., physician, educator, researcher; b. Hong Kong, June 27, 1954; came to U.S., 1973; d. William and King Di (Wong) Cheung; m. Benjamin Zee; children: David, Caroline, Alex. BA, Mills Coll., 1976; PhD, Chgo. Med. Sch., 1980, MD, 1983. Diplomate Am. Bd. Psychiatry and Neurology, Am. Bd. Med. Examiners, Am. Bd. Sleep Medicine. NIH postdoctoral fellow Northwestern U., Evanston, Ill., 1987-89, asst. prof. neurobiology and neurology Chgo., 1989-95, assoc. prof., 1996—2000, prof., 2001—; dir. Sleep Ctr. Northwestern Meml. Hosp., Chgo., 1991—. Mem. bd. advisors Jour. Biol. Rhythms, 1994—; bd. dirs. Nat. Sleep Found., 2003—; mem. NIH study sect. Contbr. articles to profl. jours. Fellow Buelher Ctr. on Aging, 1995—, Brookdale Found., 1994; grantee NIH, 1994—. Fellow: Am. Sleep Disorders Assn.; mem.: Am. Neurol. Assn., Soc. Biol. Rhythms, Soc. for Neuroscience, Am. Acad. Neurology. Office: Northwestern U 710 N Lake Shore Dr Chicago IL 60611-3006 Office Phone: 312-908-8549. Business E-Mail: p-zee@northwestern.edu.

ZEFFIRELLI, LUCIA, dance instructor, piano teacher, choreographer, director, dancer, actress; b. Michigan City, Ind., Mar. 18, 1961; d. Vincent J. and Lorraine May (Keen) Strangio; 1 child, Paolo Madden Zeffirelli; m. Scott Grady Madden, Mar. 4, 2000. BA in French and Music, U. Mich., 1984; student, Eastern Mich. U., Ypsilanti, 1986-87. Piano tchr. self employed, Tucson and Ann Arbor, Mich., 1985-86, 98—; dancer J. Parker Copley Repertory Co., Ann Arbor, 1986-88, Orts Theater of Dance, Tucson, 1994-95, dance instr., 1994—96, Dance Visions Studio, Tucson, 1996—2000, Dance Moves, Tucson, 2000—02, Flamenco Y Mas, 2002—03, Dance Rhapsody, 2003—05, Flor de Liz, 2005—; founder, artistic dir., choreographer Zeffirelli 8 Dance Co., Tucson, 1996—. Choreographer/dancer Neptune's Dream, No Exit, 8 of Swords, Night of the Gypsies, Stigmata, A Scream Got Lost, High Priestess, Longing, Sunnyside Up, True Camp, Still Life with Melancholy, Spleen; choreographer/dancer The 3 Marys, Vessels, Chess Game, Sisters, Too Busy, The Oldest Profession, Ashes, Ashes; choreographer/dancer others. Recipient 1st prize, Concerto Competition, LaPorte (Ind.) Symphony Orch., 1979, Individual Artist grant, Tucson/Pima Arts Coun., 2001, 2003. Democrat. Avocations: gardening, laying tile, remodeling, refinishing, Italian and French languages. Home: 4817 E Eastland St Tucson AZ 85711-4949

ZEGIOB-DEVEREAUX, LESLIE ELAINE, clinical psychologist; b. Cleve., Oct. 17, 1948; d. Charles G. and Elinore Lois (Jones) Zegiob; m. James Michael Devereaux, July 11, 1981. Student Allegheny Coll., 1966-68; BA, Am. U., 1971; MS, U. Ga., 1974, PhD, 1976. Lic. psychologist, Ariz., Ind. Asst. prof. dept. psychology Ariz. State U., Tempe, 1976-78, dir. psychology clinic, 1977-78; dir. childrens svcs. Dogwood Village, Memphis, 1978; adj. prof. dept. psychology Notre Dame (Ind.) U., 1979-80; clin. psychologist dept. psychology and psychiatry The Med. Group, Michigan City, Ind., 1978-2004, The Madison Ctr. for Children, 2005; cons. child protective svcs. LaPorte County Dept. Pub. Welfare, Headstart program, 1979-84, Michigan City schs., 1979-84; mem. adv. bd. Headstart, 1979-84. Contbr. articles to profl. jours. Ariz. State U. faculty grantee, 1978. Mem. APA, Assn. for Advancement Behavior Therapy, Sierra Club, Phi Kappa Phi, Phi Beta Kappa. Democrat. Office: The Madison Ctr for Children 701 N Niles Ave South Bend IN 46617

ZEHNPFENNIG, ELIZABETH FRANCES, secondary school educator; b. Milw., July 1, 1977; d. Frank and Marcy Vella; m. Elizabeth Frances Vella, Nov. 8, 2003. BS, Winona State U., Minn., 1999; EdM, St. Mary's U., Winona, 2005. Tchr. Richfield H.S., Minn., 2001—. Fellow Ctr. for German and European Studies, Mpls., 2006. Dfl. Avocations: tennis, travel, reading, running, camping. Home: 4734 Humboldt Ave N Minneapolis MN 55430 Office: Richfield Public Schs 7001 Harriet Ave S Richfield MN 55423 Office Phone: 612-798-6162. Home Fax: 612-798-6100; Office Fax: 612-798-6100. Personal E-mail: elizabeth.zehnpfennig. Business E-Mail: elizabeth.zehnpfennig@richfield.k12.mn.us.

ZEHR, CONNIE, sculptor, art educator; b. Ohio, 1938; BFA, Ohio State U. Artist Occidental Coll., 1977; visiting artist Calif. State U. Fullerton, 1978—80, Claremont Grad. Sch., 1981, UCLA, 1981, U. Calif. Irvine, 1981—82; prof. Claremont Grad. Sch., 1982—, chairperson dept. art. One-woman shows include Newspace, L.A., Calif., 2002, Harris Art Gallery, U. LaVerne, Calif., 1998, Weingart Gallery, Occidental Coll., 1991, Santa Monica (Calif.) Coll. Art Gallery Santa Monica (Calif.) Coll., 1989, West Gallery, Claremont Coll. Grad. Sch., 1988, Taipei (Taiwan) Fine Arts Mus., 1987, Calif. State U., Fullerton, Calif., Barnsdall Mcpl. Art Gallery, L.A., Calif. Mural Project Claremont Cmty. Found., 1999; Transit Ctr. Art Com. City Claremont, 1992; Visual Art Com. Claremont Cmty. Found., 1991—; Art Selection Panel for Grand Hope Park Cmty. Redevel. Agency, LA, 1986; Process Oriented Design Santa Ana Calif., 1987. Grantee Individual Artist Grant, Nat. Endowment Arts, 1975, Landmark Project, Art Collaboration, 1984, Individual Artist Grant, 1986, Mentor Grant, Lorser Feitelson & Helen Lundeberg-Feitelson Arts Found., 1987. Office: Art Dept Claremont Grad U 251 East 10th St Claremont CA 91711 Office Phone: 909-607-9292.

ZEIGLER, BEKKI LARISSA, biology professor; d. Barry L Zeigler and Barb A Boyer. BS, Ohio State U., Columbus, 1998; MS in Biology, Bowling Green State U., Ohio, 2005. Cert. basic and advanced tutor U. Findlay, Ohio, 1995. Prof. biology Pa. State U, Towson U., Gettysburg Coll., C.C. of Balt. County, Carroll C.C., Columbus State C.C., 2002—. Towson State U., Gettysburg Coll., C.C. of Baltimore County, Carroll C.C., Columbus State C.C. Recipient Acad. All-Am. scholar, USAA, 1996; scholar tchg. asst. in biology, Bowling Green State U., 1999—2001, Nancy Erme scholar, U. Findlay, 1994—95. Mem.: Aristos Ekletos, Tau Omega Pi, Sigma Kappa Upsilon (life; v.p. of scholarship 1995—97, Sigma Kappa Presidents Award & Sigma Kappa Violet Award 1995 & 1996). Achievements include research in field zoology, wetland ecology, marine biology. Personal E-mail: bzeigler@cscc.edu.

ZEIGLER, CARRIE ELIZABETH WATT, elementary school educator; b. Bklyn., 1947; d. William George Kitchener and Darlyn Watt; m. Robert Joel Zeigler; 1 child, Peter Kitchener. Student, Pratt Inst., Bklyn.; BS, MS, Elmira Coll., N.Y. Tchr. art Elmira Sch. Dist., 1985, Horseheads Ctrl. Sch. Dist., NY, 1986—. One-woman shows include Arnot Art Mus., 1974. Grantee for sculpture, Pratt Inst., 1973. Democrat. Episcopalian. Avocations: painting, photography, sewing, swimming, travel. Home: 74 Scott Ave Elmira NY 14905

ZEILIG, NANCY MEEKS, writer, editor; b. Nashville, Apr. 28, 1943; d. Edward Harvey and Nancy Evelyn (Self) Meeks; m. Lanny Kenneth Fielder, Aug. 20, 1964 (div. Dec. 1970); m. Charles Elliot Zeilig, Jan. 6, 1974 (div. Dec. 1989); 1 child, Sasha Rebecca. BA, Birmingham-So. Coll., 1964; postgrad., Vanderbilt U., 1971-73. Editorial asst. Reuben H. Donnelley, N.Y.C., 1969-70; asst. editor Vanderbilt U., Nashville, 1970-74; editor U. Minn., St. Paul, 1975; asst. editor McGraw-Hill Inc., Mpls., 1975-76; mng. editor Denver mag., 1976-80; editor Jour. Am. Water Works Assn., Denver, 1981—99; owner Nancy Zeilig Writing & Editing, Denver, 2000—. Editor, co-pub.: WomanSource, 1982, rev. edit., 1984; contbr. articles to trade and consumer mags. Co-chair arts adv. com. Denver Sch. Arts, 1994-96. Avocations: travel, reading, cooking. Office Phone: 303-758-7750. E-mail: nzeilig@earthlink.net.

ZEILINGER, ELNA RAE, elementary school educator, gifted and talented educator; b. Tempe, Ariz., Mar. 24, 1937; d. Clayborn Eddie and Ruby Elna (Laird) Simpson; m. Philip Thomas Zeilinger, June 13, 1970; children: Shari, Chris. BA in Edn., Ariz. State U., 1958, MA in Edn., 1966, EdS, 1980. Bookkeeper First Nat. Bank of Tempe, 1955-56; with registrar's office Ariz. State U., 1956-58; piano tchr., recreation dir. City of Tempe; tchr. Thew Sch., Tempe, 1958-61; elem. tchr. Mitchell Sch., Tempe, 1962-74, intern prin., 1976, personnel intern, 1977; specialist gifted edn. Tempe Elem. Schs., Tempe, 1977-86; elem. tchr. Holdeman Sch., Tempe, 1986-89; tchr. grades 1-12 and adult reading, lang. arts, English Zeilinger Tutoring Svc., 1991—. Grad. asst. ednl. adminstrn., Iota Workshop coordinator Ariz. State U., 1978; presenter Ariz. Gifted Conf., 1978-81; condr. survey of gifted programs, 1980; reporter pub. rels. Tempe Sch. Dist., 1978-80, Access com. for gifted programs, 1981-83. Author: Leadership Role of the Principal in Gifted Programs: A Handbook, 1980; Classified Personnel Handbook, 1977, also reports, monographs and paintings. Active Tempe Hist. Assn., liaison, 1975, Tempe Art League; freedom train com. Ariz. Bicentennial Commn., 1975-76; bd. dirs. Maple Property Owners Assn., 1994-2002; storyteller Tempe Hist. Mus., 1997—; dir. pagentry Daus. of the Nile, 2002-03. Named Outstanding Leader in Elem. and Secondary Schs., 1976' Ariz. Cattle Growers scholar, 1954-55; Elks scholar, 1954-55; recipient Judges award Tempe Art League, 1970, Best of Show, Scottsdale Art League, 1976. Mem.: Daus. of the Nile (dir. pageantry 2002—03). Independent. Congregationalist.

ZEILMAN, MICHELLE RENEE, counselor; d. Joseph Anthony Sr. and Pamela Jane Zeilman. BS in Psychology, George Mason U., 1997; MEd in Counseling, U. Mo., St. Louis, 2005, postgrad., 2005—. Cert. counselor Nat. Bd. Cert. Counselors, lic. profl. counselor. Tchr., counselor Pressley Ridge Schs., Pitts., 1997—99, therapeutic support staff mem., 1998—99; curriculum specialist Salvation Army Hope Ctr. for Children, St. Louis, 2000; family svc. worker Bringing Families Together, Hazelwood, Mo., 2000—03, adoption specialist, 2003—05, clin. services dir., ounselor, 2005—. Softball coach Spl. Olympics, Woodbridge, 1994; vol. fundraiser Am. Liver Found., St. Louis, 2005. Mem.: ACA (assoc.), Internat. Assn. Marriage and Family Counselors (assoc.), Mo. Mental Health Counselors Assn. (assoc.), Am. Mental Health Counselors Assn. (assoc.), George Mason U. Alumni Assn. (assoc.), U. Mo.-St. Louis Alumni Assn. (assoc.), Phi Kappa Phi. Avocation: softball. Office: Bringing Families Together 7151 N Lindbergh Blvd Hazelwood MO 63042 Office Phone: 314-731-3969. Business E-Mail: michellez@bringingfamiliestogether.com.

ZEITLIN, EUGENIA PAWLIK, librarian, educator, writer; b. N.Y.C., Jan. 29; d. Charles and Pauline (Klimowski) Pawlik; m. Herbert Zakary Zeitlin, July 3, 1949; children: Mark Clyde, Joyce Therese Zeitlin Harris, Ann Victoria, Clare Katherine. BA in English, Bklyn. Coll., 1945; MA in English, NYU, N.Y.C., 1951; MALS, Rosary Coll., 1968. Teaching credential N.Y., Ariz., Calif., Ill. English tchr., Sea Cliff, L.I., NY, 1945—47; English, math. tchr. Merrick (N.Y.) Sch. Dist., 1948—49; English tchr. Wilson Sch. Dist., Phoenix, 1949—50; counselor West Phoenix (Ariz.) High Sch., 1953—56; asst. prof. English Wright Coll., Chgo., 1965—66; asst. prof. English, asst. to v.p. curriculum and instrn. Oakton C.C., Des Plaines, Ill., 1970—76; libr. Pasadena City Coll., L.A., 1979—84, L.A. Pub. Libr., 1984—2004; ret., 2004. Contbr. articles to profl. jours. Named Northridge City Employee of Yr., 1986. Mem. AAUW (br. pres. Lancaster, Calif. 1959-60), Thoreau Soc. (life), Beta Phi Mu. Avocations: writing and editing, book collecting. Home: 20124 Phaeton Dr Woodland Hills CA 91364-5633 E-mail: epzeitlin2000@aol.com.

ZEITLIN, LAURIE, printing company executive, information technology executive; BA in Econs., Duke U., 1984; MBA in Fin., U. Pa., 1989. Rsch. asst. Touche Ross & Co., 1985—87; sr. mng. consulting Deloitte & Touche LLP, 1989—95; dir. info. tech., sr. mgr. application devel., v.p. info. tech. Home Depot, Inc., Atllanta, 1995—2003; sr. v.p., chief info. officer Kinko's Inc., Dallas, 2003—. Named one of Premier 100 IT Leaders, Computerworld, 2006. Office: Kinkos 13155 Noel Rd Ste 1600 Dallas TX 75240 Office Phone: 214-550-7020. E-mail: laurie.zeitlin@fedexkinkos.com.*

ZEITLIN, MARILYN AUDREY, museum director; b. Newark, July 14, 1941; d. Sidney M. and Theresa Feigenblatt) Litchfield; widowed; children: Charles C. Sweedler, Milo Sweedler. Student, Vanderbilt U., 1963-65; AB in Humanities, Harvard U., 1966, MA in Teaching of English, 1967; postgrad., Cornell U., 1971-74. Dir. Ctr. Gallery, Bucknell U., Lewisburg, Pa., 1975-78; Freedman Gallery, Albright Coll., Reading, Pa., 1978-81; Anderson Gallery, Va. Commonwealth U., Richmond, 1981-87; curator, acting co-dir. Contemporary Arts Mus., Houston, 1987-90; exec. dir. Washington Projects for the Arts, 1990-92; dir. Univ. Art Mus., Ariz. State U., Tempe, 1992—. Juror Dallas Mus. of Arts, McKnight Awards, Mpls.; grant evaluator IMS; grant evaluator, panelist NEH; lectr., cons. in field. Editor, contbr. essays to art publs. Bd. dirs. Cultural Alliance Washington; curator, commr. for U.S. for 1995 Venice Biennale. Samuel H. Kress fellow, 1972-73. Mem. Assn. Coll. and Univ. Mus. and Galleries (v.p. 1986-88), Am. Assn. Mus., Coll. Art Assn. (U.S. commr. Venice Biennale 1995). Office: Ariz State U Art Mus PO Box 872911 Tempe AZ 85287-2911

ZEKMAN, TERRI MARGARET, graphic designer; b. Chgo., Sept. 13, 1950; d. Theodore Nathan and Lois (Bernstein) Z.; m. Alan Daniels, Apr. 12, 1980; children: Jesse Logan, Dakota Caitlin. BFA, Washington U., St. Louis, 1971; postgrad, Art Inst. Chgo., 1974-75. Graphic designer (on retainer) greeting cards and related products Recycled Paper Products Co., Chgo., 1970—, Jillson Roberts, Inc., Calif.; apprenticed graphic designer Helmuth, Obata & Kassabaum, St. Louis, 1970-71; graphic designer Container Corp., Chgo., 1971; graphic designer, art dir., photographer Cuerden Advt. Design, Denver, 1971-74; art dir. D'Arcy, McManus & Masius Advt., Chgo., 1975-76; freelance graphic designer Chgo., 1976-77; art dir. Garfield Linn Advt., Chgo., 1977-78; graphic designer Keiser Design Group, Van Noy & Co., Los Angeles, 1978-79; owner and operator graphic design studio Los Angeles, 1979—. Art and photography tchr. Ctr. for Early Edn., L.A., 1996—, Buckley Sch., Sherman Oaks, 1996—; 3d grade tchr. asst., 1999—. Recipient cert. of merit St. Louis Outdoor Poster Contest, 1970, Denver Art Dirs. Club, 1973 Personal E-mail: redzek50@aol.com.

ZELBY, RACHEL, realtor; b. Sosnowiec, Poland, May 6, 1930; came to U.S., 1955; d. Herschel Kupfermintz and Sarah Rosenblatt; m. Leon W. Zelby, Dec. 28, 1954; children: Laurie Susan, Andrew Stephen. Student, U. Pa., 1955, Realtors' Inst., Norman, Okla., 1974; grad., Realtors Inst., Oklahoma City, 1978. Lic. realtor, broker, Okla.; cert. residential specialist, Okla. Realtor, broker, ptnr. Realty World Norman Heritage, 1973-81; realtor, broker Century 21 Elite Realty, Norman, 1981—, residential specialist, 1986—. Mem. Jr. Svc. League, Norman, 1980—; charter mem. Assistance League Norman, 1970—; bd. dirs. Juvenile Svcs., Inc., Norman, 1975-76; bd. viss. Coll. Fine Arts U. Okla., 1992—. Mem. Nat. Assn. Realtors, Norman Bd. Realtors, Women's Coun. Realtors (treas. 1985), U. Okla. Women's Assn. (past pres.), Norman C. of C., LWV. Avocations: aerobics, contract bridge, theater, music, travel. Home: 1009 Whispering Pines Dr Norman OK 73072-6912 Office: Century 21 Goodyear Green 223 N Interstate Dr Norman OK 73069 Office Phone: 405-366-1111. Personal E-mail: rachelz@telepath.com.

ZELDES, EDITH R., freelance journalist; b. NYC, Feb. 29, 1928; d. William Shakespeare and Harriet Edith (Pelikan) Herrmann; m. Benjamin Zeldes, July 4, 1948; children: Mildred R. Solomon, Hazel A., Beth E. Margulies, Ross E. BA in Fine Arts, U. Conn., 1948; MEd, Ctrl. Conn. State U., New Britain, 1970. Cert. advanced pilot New Britain Power Squadron chpt. U.S. Power Squadron. Freelance journalist. Writer features for Jour. Inquirer, Middletown Press, Imprint Publs., Life Publs. The (New Britain) Herald, The Hartford Courant. Sunday sch. tchr. Temple Sinai, Newington, Conn., Temple B'Nai Israel, New Britain, Conn.; producer, dir., publicist, booking agt., tchr. Newington Children's Theatre; dir., producer, actress, past pres. Theatre Newington On Stage; dir. Tri-Town Players, Vernon, Rockville, Conn.; dir. Aetna Players, Hartford, Conn. Mem. Theatre Newington On Stage (hon. life). Avocations: travel, boating, reading, theater. Home: 107 Lake Shore Blvd Stafford Springs CT 06076-3439

ZELDIN, KIM S., lawyer; b. Springfield, Pa., Nov. 24, 1961; d. Michael Herman and Saydean Zeldin. BA with highest honors, U. Calif., Santa Cruz, 1985; JD cum laude, U. Calif. Hastings Coll. Law, San Francisco, 1988. Bar: Calif. 1988, US Dist. Ct. (no. dist. Calif.) 1988, US Dist. Ct. (ctrl. and ea. dists. Calif.) 1990, US Dist. Ct. (so. dist. Calif.) 2000, Calif. Supreme Ct. 1988. Assoc., sr. counsel Pillsbury Winthrop LLP, San Francisco, 1988—2002; ptnr. Liner Yankelevitz, Sunshine & Regenstreif LLP, 2002—. Bd. mem. San Francisco Women Lawyers, 1994—97. Bd. mem. Pets are Wonderful Support, 2001—02, Breathe Calif., 2006—. Recipient Fair Housing Leadership award, Fair Housing of Marin, Calif., 2003, No. Calif. Super Lawyers award, Super Lawyers Mag., 2004—06. Mem.: ABA, Western Pension and Benefits Conf., French-Am. C. of C., Nat. Assn. Women Bus. Owners, Assn. Trial Lawyers Am., San Francisco Bar Assn., Order of the Coif. Office: Liner Yankelevitz Sunshine Regenstreif LLP 199 Fremont St 20th Fl San Francisco CA 94105 Office Phone: 415-489-7755. Office Fax: 415-489-7701.

ZELEI, RITA ANNETTE, retired educational administrator; b. Barberton, Ohio, Dec. 19, 1938; d. Joseph Emil and Kathryn (Novacic) Z.; m. Robert B. Brumbaugh (dec. Sept. 24, 2001); 1 child, Bernadette Veronica. BS, U. Akron, Ohio, 1960, MS, 1966, EdD, 1971. Music tchr. Hudson (Ohio) Local Schs., 1960, Akron Pub. Schs., 1960-68; staff Ohio Dept. of Edn., Columbus, 1968-69; spl. crew leader U.S. Bur. of Census, Washington, 1970; ednl. cons. N.J. Dept. Edn., Trenton, 1972; prin. Geneva (Ohio) Elem. Sch., 1972-91, ret., 1991. Adj. prof. Lake Erie Coll., Painesville, 1976-83; field ops. supr. U.S. Bur.Census, Washington, 2000, crew leader spl. census, Kansas City, 2006 Vice-pres. Geneva Civic Ctr. Bd., 1982-88, pres., 1983-91; pres. Geneva Area Grape JAMboree, pres., 1983-91, dedication, 1994; bd. dirs. Ashtabula County Scouts Coun., 1979, Geneva Area Human Svcs., 1982-89; mem. Gov.'s Travel and Tourism Bd., Ohio, 1987-91; del. to China, People to People Ohio Edn., 1986; v.p. Watermill Assn., Inc., 1992-93, pres., 1996-2000; vol. Fayetteville VA Hosp., 2004— Named Trendsetter New Cleve. Woman Mag., 1988; recipient Akron Crime Clinic, 1988. Mem. AAUW, Am. Assn. Sch. Adminstrs., Am. Ednl. Rsch. Assn., Geneva Area C. of C. (Citizen of Yr. 1987), Phi Delta Kappa (pres. 1986, Educator of Yr. 1992), Elks, Rural Builders and Quilters. Avocations: music, calligraphy, sewing, civic organizations. Home: PO Box 13 Goshen AR 72735-0013

ZELEK, CHERYL ANN, gifted and talented educator; d. Albert Peter Zebarah and Wilma Ruth Fite; m. Mark Clarence Zelek, Oct. 1, 1988. AA, Henry Ford C.C., Dearborn, MI, 1975; MusB, Wayne State U., Detroit, 1978; MLS, NC Ctrl. U., Durham, 2002. Cert. Teacher Dept. of Pub. Instrn., NC, 1990. Sub. tchr. Lincoln Pk. Pub. Sch. Sys., Mich., 1978—79, Wyandotte Pub. Schools, Mich., 1978—79; instrumental and vocal music tchr. St. Stephen Area Sch. - Diocese of Saginaw, Mich., 1979—80; salesperson Fitt-Well Shoes, Lincoln Park, Mich., 1981—85; sci., math. and religion tchr. Our Lady of Mt. Carmel Sch., Wyandotte, Mich., 1981—85; customer svc. TCI of Kingston, Kingston, NY, 1989; mail clk. Chrysler Corp., Highland Park, Mich., 1985—88. Parishioner Sacred Heart Cathedral, Raleigh, NC, 2000—05. Recipient Nat. Bd. Profl. Tchr. - Early Adolescent Sci., Nat. Bd. for Profl. Tchg. Standards, 2001—, Most Polite Tchr., Nat. League of Jr. Cotillons, 1994-1995, Tchr. of Yr., Fred J. Carnage GT Magnet Mid. Sch., 1994—95, Sci. Tchr. of Yr., 1995—96, Academically Gifted Tchr. of Yr., 1997—98; State of Mich. Competitive scholarships, State of Mich., 1973—77, Wayne State U. Bd. of Governors grant, Bd. of Governors, 1977—78. Mem.: Parents for the Advancement of Gifted Edn. , ALA, NSTA, Carolina Hurricanes Booster Club, Nat. DAR, Micajah Bullock Chpt., Delta Kappa Gamma (assoc.). Conservative. Roman Catholic. Avocations: genealogy, hockey, travel. Office: Fred J Carnage GT Magnet Mid Sch 1425 Carnage Dr Raleigh NC 27610-3909 Office Phone: 919-856-7618.

ZELEVANSKY, LYNN, curator; 2 children. Student in art history, NYU. Curator Mus. Modern Art, NYC, 1987—95; named assoc. curator dept. 20th century painting LA County Mus. Art, 1995, assoc. curator modern and contemporary art, curator, dept. head modern and contemporary art. Curator (exhibitions) Sense and Sensibility: Women Artists and Minimalism in the '90s, 1994, Love Forever: Yayoi Kusama 1958-68, 1998—99, Robert Therrian retrospective, 2000, Jasper Johns to Jeff Koons: Four Decades of Art from the Broad Collections, 2001, Keith Edmier and Farah Fawcett, 2002, Beyond Geometry: Experiments in Form, 1940s-70s, 2004 (Award for Best Thematic Mus. Show Nationally, Internat. Assn. Art Critics/USA, 2005), many others. Office: LACMA 5905 Wilshire Blvd Los Angeles CA 90036

ZELL, JOSEPHINE MAY, retired language educator; b. Harwood, Lancashire, England, Apr. 26, 1934; d. Joseph Henry Howe and Emily Emma Herod; m. Robert Zell, Apr. 17, 1968 (div. Oct. 2002); children: Rosemary, Philip. BA Honors English Lang. and Lit., U. Manchester, Eng., 1955; MA in Latin, U. Wis., 1989. Chair dept. English, Milham Ford Sch., Oxford, England, 1964—68; lectr. English, U. Wis., Milw., 1968—71; tchr. English, Madison (Wis) Met. Sch. Dist., 1977—97; tchr. Latin, West H.S., Madison Sch. Dist., 1992—97. Author: (poetry) The Curtain Rises, 1993. Mem.: AAUW. Methodist. Home: 7001 Havenswood Dr Madison WI 53718

ZELLER, MARILYNN KAY, retired librarian; b. Scottsbluff, Nebr., Mar. 1, 1940; d. William Harold and Dorothy Elizabeth (Wilkins) Richards; m. Robert Jerome Zeller, May 21, 1966; children: Kevin Jerome and Renae Kay. BS, Calvary Bible Coll., 1985; MLS, U. Mo., Columbia, 1989. Cert. libr. File clk. Waddell & Reed, Kansas City, Mo., 1962-65; payroll clk. Century Fin.

Co., Kansas City, Mo., 1965-67, Percy Kent Bag Co., Independence, Mo., 1968-70; accounts receivable Swansons on the Plaza, Kansas City, 1971-73; clk. casualty ins. Mill Mutuals, Kansas City, 1977-80; registrar's asst. Calvary Bible Coll., Kansas City, 1980-85, libr. asst., 1985-88, asst. libr., 1988-89, head libr., 1990—96. Chairperson libr. com. Calvary Bible Coll., Kansas City, 1990-96; libr. rep. Friends of the Hilda Kroeker Libr., Kansas City, 1990-96. Author: History of the Christian Librarian's Association, 1989. Mem. Christian Librs. Assn. Avocations: walking, reading, crocheting, sewing, swimming. Home: 401 13th Ave N Greenwood MO 64034-9750

ZELLIOT, ELEANOR MAE, history professor; b. Des Moines, Oct. 7, 1926; d. Ernest A. and Minnie (Hadley) Z. BA, William Penn Coll., 1948; MA, Bryn Mawr (Pa.) Coll., 1949; PhD, U. Pa., 1969. Assoc. editor The Am. Friend, Richmond, Iowa, 1950-58; tchr. Scattergood Sch., West Branch, Iowa, 1958-60; editor Pendle Hill Pubs., Wallingford, Pa., 1960-62; acting instr., asst. prof. U. Minn., Mpls., 1966-69; researcher South Asia Hist. Atlas, Mpls., 1966-69; from asst. prof. to assoc. prof. Carleton Coll., Northfield, Minn., 1969-79, prof., 1979-97, dept. chair, 1989-92, Laird Bell prof., 1993-97, prof. emerita, 1997—. Pres. Midwest Conf. on Asian Affairs, 1996-97. Author: From Untouchable to Dalit, 1992, 96, 2000; editor: Experience of Hinduism, 1988, Dr. Ambedkar and The Untouchable Movement, 2004, Untouchable Saints, 2005; editor jour. issue Marathi Sampler, 1982; contbr. articles to profl. jours. Mem. Dem. Farmer Labor Party, Minn., LWV. Fellowship NEH, 1987, Fulbright, 1992. Mem. Minn. Consortium South Asia, Am. Inst. Indian Studies (v.p. 1994-97, bd. trustees, fellowship 1975, 85, 89), Assn. Asian Studies (Disting. Svc. award 1999). Mem. Soc. Of Friends. Avocations: walking, cooking. Address: Carleton Coll Dept History Northfield MN 55057 Business E-Mail: ezelliot@carleton.edu.

ZELLWEGER, RENEE, actress; b. Katy, Tex., Apr. 25, 1969; d. Emil Erich Zellweger and Kjellfrid Irene Andreassen; m. Kenny Chesney, May 9, 2005 (annulled Dec. 20, 2005). BA in English, U. Tex., 1991. Actress feature films including Reality Bites, 1994, Love and a .45, 1994, 8 Seconds, 1994, The Low Life, 1995, Empire Records, 1995, The Whole Wide World, 1996, Jerry Maguire, 1996, Texas Chainsaw Massacre: The Next Generation, 1997, Deceiver, 1997, One True Thing, 1998, A Price Above Rubies, 1998, The Bachelor, 1999, Nurse Betty, 2000 (Golden Globe award for best actress in a comedy or musical 2000), Me, Myself & Irene, 2000, Bridget Jones's Diary, 2001 (nominee Best Actress SAG award, Broadcast Film Critics Assn. award, Brit. Acad. Award and Acad. award 2001; Golden Globe award nominee best actress in a comedy or musical, 2001), White Oleander, 2002, Chicago, 2002 (Golden Globe award for best supporting actress in a comedy or musical, 2002, SAG award for Best Actress, 2003, Academy award nominee Best Actress, 2003), Down With Love, 2003, Cold Mountain, 2003 (Golden Globe for best supporting actress, 2004, Screen Actors Guild Award for best supporting actress, 2004, Acad. Award for best supporting actress, 2004), (voice) Shark Tale, 2004, Bridget Jones: The Edge of Reason, 2004, Cinderella Man, 2005; (TV films) A Taste for Killing, 1992, Murder in the Heartland, 1993, Shake, Rattle and Rock 1994. Office: Byant Joel Creative Artists Agy 9830 Wilshire Blvd Beverly Hills CA 90212*

ZELMAN, SUSAN TAVE, school system administrator; DEd, U. Mich.; D in Pub. Edn. (hon.), U. Rio Grande, Ohio; D in Humanities (hon.), Youngstown U. Assoc. prof. edn. Emmanuel Coll., Boston, chair dept. edn.; assoc commr. ednl. dept. personnel Mo. Dept. Edn., Jefferson City, 1988—94; dep. commr. Mo. Dept. Elem. and Secondary Edn., Jefferson City, 1994—99; supt. pub. instrn. Ohio Dept Edn., Columbus, 1999—. Rschr. Edn. Tech. Ctr. Harvard Grad. Sch. Edn. Recipient Nat. Sci. Rsch. Opportunity award, Columbus Tchrs. Coll. Office: Ohio Dept Edn 25 S Front St Columbus OH 43215-4183

ZELON, LAURIE DEE, judge; b. Durham, NC, Nov. 15, 1952; d. Irving and Doris Miriam (Baker) Z.; m. David L. George, Dec. 30, 1979; children: Jeremy, Daniel. BA in English with distinction, Cornell U., 1974; JD, Harvard U., 1977. Bar: Calif. 1977, US Ct. Appeals (9th cir.) 1978, US Supreme Ct. 1989. Assoc. Beardsley, Hufstedler & Kemble, LA, 1977-81, Hufstedler, Miller, Carlson & Beardsley, LA, 1981-82, ptnr., 1983-88, Hufstedler, Miller, Kaus & Beardsley, LA, 1988-90, Hufstedler, Kaus & Ettinger, LA, 1990-91, Morrison & Foerster, LA, 1991-2000; judge LA Superior Ct., 2000—03; assoc. justice Calif. Ct. Appeal, LA, 2003—. Contbg. author: West's California Litigation Forms: Civil Procedure Before Trial, 1996; editor-in-chief Harvard Civil Rights and Civil Liberties Law Rev., 1976-77 Bd. dirs. NY Civil Liberties Union, 1973-74. Mem. ABA (chmn. young lawyers divsn. pro bono project 1981-83, delivery and pro bono projects com. 1983-85, subgrant competition-subgrant monitoring project 1985-86, chair standing com. on lawyers pub. svc. responsibility 1987-90, chair law firm pro bono project 1989-91, standing com. legal aid and indigent defendants 1991-97, chmn. 1993-97, mem. ho. dels. 1993—, state del. 1998-2006, commn. on ethics 2000 1997-2002, bd. govs. 2006—), Calif. Bar Assn. (bd. dirs. appellate project 1995-2000, chair commn. on access to justice 1997-99), LA County Bar Assn. (trustee 1989-91, v.p. 1992-93, sr. v.p. 1993-94, pres.-elect 1994-95, pres. 1995-96, fed. cts. and practices com. 1984-93, vice chmn. 1987-88, chmn. 1988-89, chmn. judiciary com. 1991-92, chmn. real estate litigation subsect. 1991-92), Women Lawyers Assn. LA, Calif. Women Lawyers Assn. Democrat. Office: Calif Ct of Appeal 2d Appellate Dist 300 S Spring St Los Angeles CA 90013 Business E-Mail: laurie.zelon@jud.ca.gov.

ZEMM, SANDRA PHYLLIS, lawyer; b. Chgo., Aug. 18, 1947; d. Walter Stanley and Bernice Phyllis (Churas) Z. BS, U. Ill., 1969; JD, Fla. State U., 1974. Bar: Fla. 74, Ill. 75. With fin. dept. Sinclair Oil, Chgo., 1969-70; indsl. rels. advisor Conco Inc., Mendota, Ill., 1970-72; assoc. Seyfarth, Shaw, Fairweather & Geraldson, Chgo., 1975-82, ptnr., 1982—. Mem. Art Inst. Alliance, Chgo., 1993—; bd. dirs. Chgo. Residential Inc., 1993—97, pres., 1995—97. Mem. Ill. State Bar Assn., Fla. State Bar Assn., Univ. Club Chgo. (bd. dirs. 1991-94); Nat. Coll. of Labor and Employment Lawyers. Office: Seyfarth Shaw LLP 55 E Monroe St Ste 4200 Chicago IL 60603-5863

ZENG, FANXING, chemist; arrived in U.S., 1999; d. Qingkai Zeng and Ruqin Shan; m. Yulong Li, Jan. 17, 1997; 1 child, Kevin Zeng Li. BS, Nanjing U. Sci. and Tech., 1993; PhD, Chinese Acad. Scis., 1999. Rsch. assoc. Shanghai (China) Inst. Materia Medica Chinese Acad. Scis., 1996—99; postdoc. fellow Purdue U., West Lafayette, Ind., 1999—2002, Ga. Inst. Tech., Atlanta, 2002—03; sr. rsch. assoc. Emory U., Atlanta, 2003—. Co-author: Handbook of Organopalladium Chemistry for Organic Synthesis, 2002, Encyclopedia of Reagents for Organic Synthesis, 2003; contbr. articles to profl. jours. Recipient Excellent Grad. Student award, Nanjing U. Sci. and Tech., 1996, P&G prize, Chinese Acad. Scis., 1999, Diao awards, 1998, 1999, Rsch. Accomplishments award, Purdue U., 2002. Mem.: Soc. Nuclear Medicine, Am. Chemical Soc., Am. Inst. Chemists, Am. Assn. Advancement Sci., Sigma Xi. Achievements include development of general method for the synthesis of conjugated oligoenes involving Pd-catalyzed cross coupling, and completed the synthesis of Vitamin A, beta Carotene, r-Carotene, and the polyene subunits; completed the synthesis and characterization of several chain-extended bismaleimides; completed the design, synthesis and pharmacological assay of several new types of AChE inhibitors-(+)-14-Fluorohuperzine A and Huperzine A-E2020 combined compound; development and evaluation of PET imaging agents for neurodegenerative diseases. Office: Dept Radiology Emory Univ 1364 Clifton Road NE Atlanta GA 30322 Home: 11155 Thames Ln Suwanee GA 30024 Office Phone: 404-727-1365. Personal E-mail: zengfanxing1@yahoo.com. Business E-Mail: fzeng@emory.edu.

ZENKOVSKY, BETTY JEAN, modern languages educator; b. Mankato, Minn., Mar. 6, 1927; d. William and Sarah (Cloyd) Bubbers; m. Serge A. Zenkovsky, May 10, 1952. AB in Russian, U. Mich., 1950; AM in Slavic Studies, Ind. U., 1954; postgrad., Radcliffe U., 1956—58. Instr. modern langs. Stetson U., DeLand, Fla., 1958—60, asst. prof., 1962—65; instr. fgn. langs. U. Colo., Boulder, 1960—62; vis. lectr. Russian, Vanderbilt U., Nashville, 1967—68; rsch. assoc., translator NEH, DeLand, 1978—82. Co-translator: The Nikonian Chronicle, (5 vols.), 1984, 86, 88, 89. Grace Hill fellow, Radcliffe Grad. Sch., 1957—58. Mem. AAUW (pres. DeLand chpr. 1982-84, sec. Daytona Beach chpt. 1984-86), DAR (chpt. James Ormond br, vice regent, 1988-89), Am. Assn. Advancement Slavic Studies, Am. Assn. Tchrs. Slavic and Ea. European Langs., UN Assn., So. Conf. Slavic Studies, Tiger Bay Club of Volusia County, St. Barbara's Philoptochos. Democrat. Greek Orthodox. Home: 1224 S Peninsula Dr Apt 507 Daytona Beach FL 32118-4861 Home Fax: 386-253-3540. Personal E-mail: bjzenk@aol.com.

ZENTZ, LAURIE FUNDERBURK, music educator; d. Charles Edward and Jean Sanders Funderburk; m. Donald Mark Zentz, June 29, 1985; children: Danielle Marie, Andrea Rose. MusB, Valdosta State Coll., Ga., 1984; MA, Jacksonville U., Fla., 1994. Cert. Orff Schulwerk Level III Am. Orff-Schulwerk Assn., 1993, Tchr. Fla., 1987, Nat. Bd. Cert. Tchr. Nat. Bd. for Profl. Tchg. Stds., 2005. Music specialist Cunningham Creek Elem. Sch., Jacksonville, 2000—. Music edn. cons., author Z&Z Publications, Jacksonville, 1990—. Author: (music edn. materials) Junior Jam Session, 1993, The Heart Chart, 1995, Note Name Nonsense, 2000, Percussion Playalongs, 2000. Children's music ministry Mandarin Presbyn. Ch., Jacksonville, 2001—06. Fellow Tchg. Fellowship, Nat. Endowment for the Arts, 1993. Mem.: North Fla. (pres., v.p. 1994—2006, pres. Orff chpt. 1994—98, v.p. 2004—06), Fla. Music Educators Assn. (dist. chmn. 1993—95). Avocations: running, music. Office Phone: 904-819-7860.

ZEPHIER, CAROL ANN, piano educator, retired organist; b. Huron, S.D., Sept. 21, 1937; d. William Arthur and Ida Isabelle Robbins; m. Richard Gene Zephier, Aug. 18, 1958; children: Kira Leigh Zephier LeCompte, Richard Donovan, Erin Dianne. BA, Yankton (S.D.) Coll., 1960. Nat. cert. tchr. piano. Elem. tchr. Aten (Nebr.) Sch. Dist., 1959-60; sec. nursing edn. Yankton State Hosp. (Human Svcs. Ctr.), 1960-62; tchr. music, K-12 Smee Sch. Dist., Wakpala, SD, 1963; piano tchr. pvt. studio McIntosh, SD, 1963-67; organist 1st Presbyn. Ch., McIntosh, 1963-67; tchr. 1st grade Northwestern Sch. Dist., Mellette, SD, 1967-71; pvt. piano tchr. Windsong Piano Studio, Mellette, SD, 1967—90, Aberdeen, SD, 1990—; organist St. Mark's Episcopal Ch., Aberdeen, 1990—2003. Author, editor: Windsong Piano Studio Notebook, 1979-. Mem. Nat. Guild Piano Tchrs. (local chairperson 1993—), Music Tchrs. Nat. Assn., S.D. Music Tchrs. Assn. (cert. piano tchr.), Aberdeen Music Tchrs. Assn. (treas., 2000-). Episcopalian. Avocations: reading, genealogy, travel, photography. Home: 401 19th Ave NE Aberdeen SD 57401-1350 Office: Windsong Piano Studio 401 19th Ave NE Aberdeen SD 57401-1350 Office Phone: 605-229-2663. E-mail: windsong@nvc.net.

ZEPHIER, JENNY RENEE, elementary school educator; children: Megan, Halley, Caleb. BA in Elem. Edn., Dakota Wesleyan U., Mithchell, S.D., 1993. Tchr. Andes Ctrl. Sch. Dist., Lake Andes, SD, 2001—. Mem.: Andes Ctrl. Tchrs. Assn. (pres. 2005—).

ZERBE, KATHRYN JANE, psychiatrist; b. Harrisburg, Pa., Oct. 17, 1951; d. Grover Franklin and Ethel (Schreckengaust) Z. BS with BA equivalent cum laude, Duke U., 1973; MD, Temple U., 1978. Diplomate Am. Bd. Psychiatry. Resident Karl Menninger Sch. Psychiatry, Topeka, 1982, dean, dir. edn. and rsch., 1992-97; staff psychiatrist Menninger Found., Topeka, 1982-2001; v.p. edn. and rsch. The Menninger Clinic, Topeka, 1993-97, prof., 1997-2001, Jack Aron chair in psychiat. edn., 1997-2001, apptd. tng. and supr. analyst, 1995—; prof. psychiatry, prof. ob-gyn. Oreg. Health Scis. Univ., Portland, 2001—; dir. behavioral medicine dept. Oreg. Health Scis. U., Portland, 2001—06; dir. outpatient clinic Oreg. Health Scis. Univ., Portland, 2003—, vice chair for psychotherapy, 2003—; tng. and supr. analyst Oreg. Psychoanalytic Inst., 2002—. Instr. numerous seminars and courses. Author: The Body Betrayed: Women, Eating Disorders and Treatment, 1993, Women's Mental Health in Primary Care, 1999, numerous articles profl. rsch. papers; editor: Womens Mental Health: Primary Care Clinics, 2001, Bull. of Menninger Clinic, 1998—2001; assoc. editor:, 1996—98, mem. editl. bd.: Eating Disorders Rev., Eating Disorders: The Jour. of Treatment and Prevention Postgrad. Medicine; editor (sect.): Current Women's Health; contbr. book revs. and articles to profl. jours. Probation officer Juvenile divsn. Dauphin County, Pa., 1973. Recipient Ann. Laughlin Merit award The Nat. Psychiat. Endowment Fund, 1982, Outstanding Paper of Profl. Programs award The Menninger Found. Alumni Assn., 1982, Writing award Topeka Inst. for Psychoanalysis, 1985, 90, Mentorship award, 1997, Women Helping Women award, 1995, Tchr. of Yr. award Psychiatry Residents, 1988, 96, 99, 03, 05, 06; named One of Outstanding Young Women in Am., 1986, 88; Seeley fellow, 1979-82; Hilde Bruch lectureship, 1996. Fellow Am. Psychiat. Assn. (Alexandra Symonds award 2005); mem. AMA, Am. Coll. Psychiatrists, Am. Med. Women's Assn., Oreg. Med. Assn., Oreg. Psychiat. Assn., Sigma Xi, Alpha Omega Alpha. Avocations: writing, reading, art history, travel. Office: Oreg Health and Scis U Adult Psychiatry 3181 SW Sam Jackson Park Rd Portland OR 97239-3098 Office Phone: 503-494-1009. Business E-Mail: zerbek@ohsu.edu.

ZERVOUDAKES, ANNETTE DIAN, reinsurance specialist; b. N.Y.C., Sept. 10, 1940; d. Abraham and Margaret (Roth) Dutchen; m. John W. Zervoudakes, June 17, 1966; children: Jason J., Alex R. Student, SUNY, Albany; grad., Career Blazers Inst., 2000. Underwriting asst. Aetna Life and Casualty, Garden City, NY, 1962—66; editor Rich Enterprises, Bellmore, NY, 1974—84; sr. reins. specialist William Penn Life, Garden City, 1984—99; human resources office assoc. Sears Roebuck & Co., Hicksville, NY, 1999—2001, Las Vegas, 2001—. Actor: (TV Comml.), 1981—83. Past pres. W.C. Mepham H.S. PTA, Saw Mill Rd. Sch. PTA, Bellmore-Merrick Ctr. H.S. Dist. Coun. PTAs, North Bellmore Coord. Coun. PTAs; assoc. dir. Nassau Co. Dist. PTA; hon. life mem. N.Y. State PTA; committeewoman Nassau County Dem. Party; election poll inspector Nassau County; elections clk. Clark County Elections, Nev.; sec. Mid Nassau Dem. Club. Recipient Disting. Svc. award, N.Y. State PTA, Bellmore-Merrick United Secondary Tchrs. Svc. award, 1991. Mem. W.C. Mepham Alumni Assn. (pres. 1995-99, adv., bd. dirs., class '58 rep. Meritorious Svc. award), N.Y. State PTA (hon., life). Democrat. Presbyterian. Avocations: poetry, music. Office: Sears Roebuck & Co 3450 S Maryland Pkwy Las Vegas NV 89109 E-mail: annetteZ910@msn.com.

ZETA-JONES, CATHERINE, actress; b. Swansea, Wales, Sept. 25, 1969; d. Dai and Pat Jones; m. Michael Douglas, Nov. 18, 2000; children: Dylan Michael, Carys Zeta. Film appearances include Les 1001 nuits (Italy), 1990, Christopher Columbus: The Discovery, 1992, Splitting Heirs, 1993, Blue Juice, 1995, The Phantom, 1996, The Mask of Zorro, 1998, Entrapment, 1999, The Haunting, 1999, High Fidelity, 2000, Traffic, 2000, America's Sweethearts, 2001, Chicago, 2002 (Best Sup. Actress Academy award, 2003, Best Actress in Sup. Role, British Acad. Film Award (BAFTA) 2003), Sinbad: Legend of the Seven Seas (voice only), 2003, Intolerable Cruelty, 2003, The Terminal, 2004, Ocean's Twelve, 2004, The Legend of Zorro, 2005; (T.V. films) Out of the Blue, 1991, The Cinder Path, 1994, The Return of the Native, 1994, Catherine the Great, 1995, Titanic, 1996,; (T.V. series) The Darling Buds of May, 1991; (T.V. appearances) The Adventures of Young Indiana Jones: Daredevils of the Desert, 1992.*

ZEVIAR-GEESE, GABRIOLE, stock market investor, lawyer; b. LA, Apr. 10, 1948; d. Harry Lindstedt and Josephine (Conrad) Blom; m. Stephan Otto Geese, Nov. 22, 1992. Diploma in Computer Programming and Analysis, Seneca Coll. Applied Arts and Tech., 1981; BA, York U., 1991; JD, Calif. Pacific Sch. Law, 1999. Data base cons., edn. specialist Bull Internat., Toronto, Canada, 1982—91; programmer Sparta, Laguna, Niguel, Calif., 1992; stock market investor, 1994—; small claims advisor County Counsel, 1998—2000; law clk. Kern County Superior Ct., 2000; pvt. practice Bakersfield, Calif., 2001—. Tech. educator, course developer, text book writer, data base adminstr. U.S. and Can. Contbr. articles to profl. jours. Mem.: Kern County Women Lawyers Assn., Kern County Bar Assn., Calif. Bar Assn. Avocations: piano, painting, Tae Kwon Do, Lightarian Reiki master, ballroom dancing. Office Phone: 661-859-1031. E-mail: geeselawoffice@aol.com.

ZEVNIK-SAWATZKY, DONNA DEE, retired litigation coordinator; b. Tulsa, Dec. 15, 1946; d. Robert Joseph and Dorothy Dee (Robertson) Zink; m. Kenneth Sawatzky, May 30, 1965; children: K. Brian Sawatzky, Kaira D. Sawatzky. Student, U. Ctrl. Okla., Edmond, 1977, Okla. State U., Oklahoma City, 1984. Cert. AIDS educator Okla. Sec. Farmers Ins. Co., Oklahoma City, 1974-80; office mgr. S.A.F.E., Inc., Oklahoma City, 1980-83; jr. acct. Southeast Exploration Corp., Oklahoma City, 1983-84; acct. Young Bros., Inc., Oklahoma City, 1984-88, The Denman Co., Inc., Oklahoma City, 1988-89; litig. coord. ACLU Okla., Oklahoma City, 1994—2003; ret., 2003; founder, owner, CEO Otherwhere Arts, 1999—2001. Author, illustrator: That Place--Otherwhere, 1994, Something for Otherwhere, 1995; author: At Our House, 1979—83; columnist: Putnam City-N.W. News, 1979—83; designer stage sets: Miss Warr Acres Pageant, 1971—88. Treas. ACLU Okla., 1995—2004, bd. dirs., 1994—2004, ACLU Okla. Found., 2005—; child welfare adv. Okla. State Dept. Human Svcs., Oklahoma City, 1987—89; coord. AIDS Clinic Triangle Assn., Oklahoma City, 1994—97; founder Cir. Friends with Arachnoiditis World Wide Web Chronic Pain Support Group, 1997; bd. dirs. Miss Warr Acres Pageant, 1984—88, Warr Acres C. of C., 1981—85. Named Hon. Mayor of Warr Acres, 1971, Super Citizen, 1973; recipient Oustanding Vol., Okla. State Dept. Human Svcs., 1988, Svc. award, Warr Acres C. of C., 1979, Legis. commendation, State of Okla., 1988, numerous Okla. Newspaper Column of the Month awards, Okla. Press Assn., 1981—82, Ten Yr. Vol. Svc. award, ACLU of Okla., 2005. Mem.: ACLU (Exec. Dir. Vol. Svc. award 1996), NAFE, Am. Inst. Profl. Bookkeepers, Nat. Notary Assn., Okla. Coalition to Abolish the Death Penalty, Amnesty Internat., Human Rights Campaign, Interfaith Alliance, Pflag. Democrat. Methodist. Avocations: painting, writing, photography. Office: 3000 Paseo Dr Oklahoma City OK 73103

ZEXTER, ELEANOR M., secondary school educator; b. Providence, R.I., Sept. 7, 1936; d. Morris and Anna Rae (Cantor) Marks; m. D. Ronald Zexter, Dec. 24, 1958; children: Francine Deborah, Judith Blair. BA, Brown U., 1958, MAT, 1962. Cert. tchr. R.I., Calif. Tchr. French and English Hope H.S., Providence, 1959—69, Nathan Bishop Mid. Sch., Providence, 1970—93; tchr. English and social studies Harkham Hillel Hebrew Acad., Beverly Hills, Calif., 1993—99. Mktg. dir. DRZ Sales; grant writer Nathan Bishop Mid. Sch., Providence, 1980-93, choral dir., 1985-93, founder Famous Authors, 1987-93; cons. substance abuse program, Brown U., 1987-93; ednl. cons. Vol. tutor Harkham Hillel Hebrew Acad., 1993-99, French club coord., Harkham Hillel Acad., 1993-99. Recipient Citizen Citation for outstanding efforts with Providence children, Mayor, 1990, McClorin award, 1991. Mem. Am. Assn. French Tchrs., Alliance Francaise, R.I. Assn. Foreign Language, Beverly Hills Country Club (tennis team capt.). Avocations: tennis, antique collecting, reading clubs, bridge, travel. Home: 8544 Burton Way Apt 401 Los Angeles CA 90048-3390

ZHANG, NIAN, engineering educator; d. Yiyu Xue and YouLing Zhang; m. Qiang Yao. BS, Wuhan U. Tech., China, 1996; MS, Huazhong U. Sci. and Tech., China, 1999; PhD, U. Mo., Rolla, 2004. From rsch. asst. to tchg. asst. U. Mo., Rolla, 2000—04; asst. prof. elec. and computer engring. dept. S.D. Sch. Mines and Tech., Rapid City, 2004. Contbr. articles to profl. jours. Mem.: IEEE, IEEE Computational Intelligence Soc., IEEE Women in Engring., IEEE Neural Networks Soc. Achievements include invention of subcircuit extraction using neural networks. Office: SD Sch Mines and Tech Elect and Computer Engring Dept 501 E St Joseph St Rapid City SD 57701 Home: 370 Denver St #303 Rapid City SD 57701 Office Phone: 605-394-2452. E-mail: nian.zhang@ieee.org.

ZHAO, JIA, lawyer; b. Shanghai, Sept. 23, 1940; came to U.S., 1980; BA, Beijing Fgn. Studies U., 1963; JD, Harvard U., 1983. Bar: Ill. 1985, D.C. 1986. U.S. desk officer dept. Am. and Oceanic Affairs, Fgn. Ministry People's Republic of China, 1972; atty. Arnold & Porter, Washington, Covington & Burling, Washington, Pillsbury, Madison & Sutro, San Francisco; 1st sec. dept. treaty and law, Am. and oceanic affairs Chinese Fgn. Ministry, 1986—88; with Baker & McKenzie, Chgo., 1988—, ptnr., 1994—. Mem. ABA, D.C. Bar, Chgo. Bar Assn., Beijing Fgn. Econ. Law Assn. Office: Baker and McKenzie One Prudential Plz 130 E Randolph Dr Chicago IL 60601

ZHONG, DAWN HE, materials engineer; b. Shanghai, Aug. 17, 1951; arrived in US, 1988; d. Qi Wei He and Yu Qin Shi; m. Kai Zhong, Jan. 20, 1987. BS, East China U. Chem. Tech., Shanghai, 1982; MS, Fla. Atlantic U., Boca Raton, 1992. Rsch. engr. Shanghai Fiber Reinforced Plastics Rsch. Inst., 1982-88; sr. analytical chemist Motorola, Inc., Boynton Beach, Fla., 1993-2001; sr. engr. Tyco Sensormatic, Boca Raton, Fla., 2001—. Contbr. articles to profl. jours. Mem. Am. Chem. Soc., Chinese Assn. Sci., Econs. and Culture South Fla. Achievements include patents in field. Avocations: travel, chinese cooking, singing, dance. Office: Tyco Sensormatic 6600 Congress Ave Boca Raton FL 33487 Business E-Mail: dzhong@tycoint.com.

ZHONG, MEI, music educator; came to U.S., 1990; d. Xiuming Wang and Huiping Zhong; m. Xiaoge Chu; 1 child, Bingbing. BA, Hunan Tchrs. U., China, 1981; Diploma, Shanghai CoOnservatory Music, China, 1986; MFA, UCLA, 1994; DMusical Arts, U. Ill., 1999. Asst. prof. dept. music Hunan Tchrs. U., 1982—87, Jiangshi, dept. music, 1987-90; asst. prof. dept. music Idaho State U., Pocatello, 1998—2002; assoc. prof. Sch. of Music Ball State U., Muncie, Ind., 2002—. Vis. prof. Wuhan (China) Conservatory of Music, 1999—, Hunan Tchrs. U., 1999—, Yueyang Tchrs. U., 1999—. Contbr. articles to ency. and profl. jours. Winner Idaho DIst. Nat. Vocal Competition, Am. Mothers Inc., 1999; Mimi Alpert Feldman scholar, 1993, 94; Atwater Kent scholar, 1993, 94; Phi Bet Kappa scholar, 1993. Mem. Coll. Music Soc., U. Ill. Alumni Assn., Phi Kappa Phi. Office: School of Music Ball State University Muncie IN 47306 Office Phone: 765-285-5431. Business E-Mail: mzhong@bsu.edu.

ZHOU, PING, physical engineer; b. Beijing; arrived in US, 1985; 1 child, Jie Yang. BA, Beijing U. Chem. Tech., 1964; postgrad., U. Sci. & Tech. China, 1978, Beijing U., 1982. Asst. prof. SUNY, Albany, 1985—87; engr. Chinese Acad. Scis., Beijing, 1970—90; rsch. engr. Stanford U., Calif., 1990—. Vis. porf. Stanford U., 1987-88. Mem. Am. Soc. Materials Internat., Materials Rsch. Soc., Am. Vacuum Soc., Am. Phys. Soc. Achievements include development of multilayer Ti-Cu thin films for gravity probe-B gyroscope housings, BSCCO thin films with Tc above 100K; development, manufacturing, and testing of the thin film coatings and the superconducting bearings for the accelerometer for the Satellite Test of Equivalence Principle (STEP) Project. Office: Stanford Univ Hansen Lab Stanford CA 94305 Office Phone: 650-725-5995. Business E-Mail: ping@relgyro.stanford.edu.

ZHOU, SOPHIA HUAI, biomedical engineering scientist; b. Huaiyin, Jiangsu, China, Dec. 6, 1953; MS, Dalhousie U., Halifax, Can., 1987, PhD, 1991. Profl. engr., Nova Scotia. Rsch. assoc. U. Alta., Edmonton, Canada, 1991-93, asst. prof., 1993-94, St. Louis U., 1994-95; engring. scientist Hewlett-Packard Co., Andover, Mass., 1995-99; prin. scientist Agilent Techs. Inc., Andover, Mass., 1999—2001; sr. rsch. mgr. Advanced Algorithm Rsch. Ctr.; prin. scientist Philips Med Sys., Thousand Oaks, Calif., 2001—. Contbr. articles to profl. jours.; editor: Jour. of Electrocardiology. Mem. editl. bd. Journ. of Electro Cardiology. Fellow Am. Coll. Cardiology; mem. NY Acad. Sci., Soc. Women Engrs., Internat. Soc. Electrocardiology, Internat. Soc. Computerized Electrocardiology, Am. Heart Assn., Assn. for Advancement of Med. Instrumentation, Internat. Electromagnetic Commn. (convener). Achievements include design of automated ECG interpretations. Office: Philips Med Sys 1525 Rancho Conejo Blvd Ste 100 Thousand Oaks CA 91320 Office Phone: 805-214-5111. Business E-Mail: sophia.zhou@philips.com.

ZHOU, YAN, chemist; b. Luobei, China, Jan. 23, 1963; came to U.S., 1989; d. Qingshun Zhou and Xi Chen; m. Tao Yuan, Nov. 11, 1987; 1 child, Karen. BS, Heilongjiang U., Harbin, China, 1983; MS, Ji Lin U., Changchun, China, 1986, Auburn U., 1993. Rsch. chemist Harbin Normal Univ., Harbin, China, 1986-89; grad. rsch. asst. Auburn (Ala.) U., 1990-93; prin. rsch. chemist

Unilever Rsch. U.S., Edgewater, N.J., 1993—. Contbr. articles to profl. jours., patentee in field. Mem. Am. Chemical Soc. Home: 6 Crest Ter Montville NJ 07045-9608 Office: 45 River Rd Edgewater NJ 07020-1017

ZHU, AI-LAN, opera singer; b. Nanjing, Jiang Su, Peoples Republic of China, Nov. 29, 1956; arrived in U.S., 1984; d. De-Chang Zhu and Shu-hua Tsao; m. Yuan Gong. MusB, Cen. Conservatory Music, Beijing, 1977; Artist Diploma in Opera, Hartt Sch of Music, U. Hartford, 1986. Appeared in leading opera houses of N.Am.; leading soprano in Tex. Opera Theater, Houston, 1987, 88, Va. Opera Assn., Norfolk, 1987, Met. Opera, 1988, Opera Theater St. Louis, 1989, PepsiCo Summerfare and European tour, N.Y., 1989, Lyric Opera of Boston, 1990, Glyndebourne Opera Festival, 1990, 91, Lyric Opera of Kansas City, 1990, Caramoor Festival, N.Y., 1990, Chautauqua Opera and Orch., 1990, Opera Pacific, L.A., 1991, 92, Dayton, Ohio, 1991, Minn. Opera, 1992, Opera Co. Phila., 1992, Mich. Opera Theater, 1993, Austin Lyric Opera, 1993, 94-99, Scottish Opera, 1994, Conn. Opera, 1995, Atlanta Opera, 1995, Conn. Opera, 1995, 96, 98, Shanghai Symphony, 1996, San Antonio Symphony, 1997, San Diego Opera, 1997, Conn. Opera, 1998, 99, William Hall Master Chorals, L.A., 1998, Opera Caroline, 1999, Opera de Quebec, Chattanooga, 2000, Orlando, Fla., 2000, Opera Regina, Can., 2000, Vancouver Opera, 2000, Opera Toledo, Ohio, 2000, Austin, Tex., 2000, 01, Orlando, Fla., 2001, Conn. Opera, 2001, Vancouver Opera, 2001, 03, Poughkeepsie, NY, 2002, Ariz. Opera, 2002, Montreal (Can.) Opera, 2002 Royal Albert Hall, London, 2003, San Diego Opera, 2004, Nat. Reissopera Netherlands, 2004, Concerts in China, 2004, Tulsa Opera, 2004, Ky. Opera, 2005; European tour Pellèas et Mèlisande, 1992-93; concert singer Chautauqua (N.Y.) Instn., 1987, Liederkranz Found., N.Y.C., 1989; recital The Theatre Musical de Paris, Chatelet, 1991; concert tour with Sherrill Milnes, Beijing, China, 1993. Finalist Luciano Pavarotti internat. vocal competition, Opera Cos. Phila., 1985; recipient 1st prize Sigma Alpha Iota vocal competition, Chautauqua, N.Y., 1986, 5th prize Liederkranz Found. vocal competition, N.Y.C., 1989. Mem. Am. Guild Mus. Artists. Office: John J Miller 889 9th Ave Ste 1 New York NY 10019-1781 Home: 14 Balmoral Crescent White Plains NY 10607 Office Phone: 212-397-7911. E-mail: ailanzhu@aol.com.

ZHU, HUA, biochemist, researcher; b. Xiaogan, Hubei, China, Nov. 5, 1965; came to U.S., 1994; d. Chaoqun Zhu and Yuanying Long; married, May 7, 1997; children: Jessica Xiaoman Yao, Stephanie Xiaoru Yao. BA in Agronomy, Hua Zhong Agrl. U., Wuhan, China, 1985; M in Botany, Northwestern Agrl. U., Yang Ling, China, 1991; PhD in Botany, Chinese Acad. Sci., Beijing, 1994; M in Biochemistry, U. Okla., 1997, PhD in Biochemistry, 2001. Rsch. asst. dept. botany and microbiology U. Okla., Norman, 1994-96, rsch. asst. dept. biochemistry and chemistry, 1996—2001; rsch. scientist Advanced Ctr. for Genome Tech., U. Okla., Norman, 2001—02; rsch. assoc. Civil Aerospace Med. Inst., FAA, Oklahoma City, 2002—04; rsch. assoc. NRC, NAS FAA, Oklahoma City, 2004—; assoc. rsch. scientist cardiovasc. biology dept. Okla. Med. Rsch. Found., Oklahoma City, 2004—. V.p. Soc. Chinese Scholar and Students of U. Okla., 1996-97. Mem. AAAS, Am. Chemistry Soc., Microscopy Soc. Am., Botanic Soc. China. Avocations: bedmington, swimming, travel, music, movies. Office: Cardiovasc Biology Dept Okla Med Rsch Found 825 13th NE St Oklahoma City OK 73104 E-mail: zhuhua9863@yahoo.com.

ZICH, SUE SCHAAB, nursing administrator, consultant; b. Buffalo, Oct. 18, 1946; d. Milan Harvey and Mary Margaret (Olmsted) Schaab; B.S. in Nursing, Villa Maria Coll., 1968; m. Timothy John Zich, Nov. 25, 1976; children— John Paul Trottman, Scott Francis Trottman. Staff nurse, charge nurse, team leader Children's Hosp., Buffalo, 1968-71; staff nurse plasmapheresis unit Roswell Park Meml. Inst., Buffalo, 1971-72, 73-75; staff devel. coordinator Episcopal Ch. Home, Buffalo, 1975-77; pediatric unit charge nurse Loudoun Meml. Hosp., Leesburg, Va., 1977; nursing instr. No. Va. Mental Health Inst., Falls Church, 1977-78; dir. nursing service Barcroft Inst., Falls Church, Va., 1978-89, Oakwood Health Care Ctr., 1989, Va. Dept. of Health Profl., 1992—; cons. nursing home design and remodeling systems, 1986-92, med. Legal Cons., 1994—. Troop com. mem. Troop 884, 1978—, den leader, 1980-85, den leader coach Pack 1982, 1983-88, dist. mem. Prince William Dist. Boy Scouts Am., day camp dir. Cub Scout Camp Tomahawk, 1983-87, asst. cub roundtable commr., 1986-98, Prince William Dist. tng. team, 1981-98, co-chmn., 1988-91, Exploring Training Chmn., 1993-95, vice chmn. membership, 1988; Bull Run Dist. Life to Eagle coord., 1998-, advancement chmn., 2001-; mem. Buckhall Fire Dept. Aux, EMT Buckhall Fire Dept., Rescue Lt., 1992-94, BVFD (life). Recipient Key Leader award Prince William dist. Boy Scouts Am., 1982, Den Leader Tng. award Boy Scouts Am., 1982, Dist. Merit award Boy Scouts Am., 1985, Den Leader Coach Tng. award Boy Scouts Am., 1986, Scouter's Tng. award Boy Scouts Am., 1984, commr. Training award Boy Scouts Am., 1989, Cubscout Trainer Wood Badge Beads, 1991, Exploring Training Award Boy Scouts Am., 1992, Explorer's Adv. key, 1995, dIST. com. tng. award, 1995, Dist. Com. key, 1998, James E. West award, 2001, Silver Beaver award, 2005. Mem. FMCA (life), Dir. Nurses Group No. Va. (sec.-treas. 1980-81, v.p. 1981-87), Nursing Soc. (hon.), Va. Emergency Svcs. Symposium (faculty appt. 2002), Sigma Theta Tau, Good Sam Club (life), Villa Maria Coll. Alumnae Assn. (life, past. pres. Buffalo chpt.), Mt. St. Mary Alumnae Assn. (life), St. Edmund's Ladies Guild (pres. 1972-73, advisor 1973-74), All Sts. Cath. Ch. (lector 1986—, lector coord. 1997-). Roman Catholic. Home: 6601 Deep Hollow Ln Manassas VA 20112-8621 Office: Enforcement Divsn Va Dept of Health Profl 6603 W Broad St Fl 5 Richmond VA 23230-1717 also: PO Box 10011 Manassas VA 20108-0596 Office Phone: 703-791-6297. Business E-Mail: sue.zich@dhp.virginia.gov.

ZIDOVEC, MIRTA ROSA, Spanish language professional; b. Tacanitas, Argentina, Mar. 28, 1945; d. Emilio Rodriguez Cereijo and Josefa (Mora) Rodriguez; m. Davor Felix Andres Zidovec, Dec. 30, 1969; children: Vladimir Rodrigo, Mariana Silvia, Liza Veronica. Grad., Nat. U. of La Plata, Argentina, 1974; MA in Spanish Lang. and Lit., SUNY, Buffalo, 1985, PhD in Spanish Lang. and Lit., 1991. Elem. tchr. La Plata (Argentina) Sch. Dist., 1966-70; social worker Escuela Diferencial Puerto Madryn, Argentina, 1977-80; tchr. in law Bus. High Sch., Puerto Madryn, 1976-80; tchng. asst. SUNY, Buffalo, 1983-87, rsch. asst. dept. critical langs., 1984-86; tchr. of Spanish lang. The Nichols Mid. Sch., 1985-86; tchr. of Spanish Niagara Falls (N.Y.) Sr. High Sch., 1987-88; Spanish instr. Millard Fillmore Coll., Buffalo, 1984-88; tchr. of Spanish La Salle Sr. High Sch., Niagara Falls, 1988-89; prof. Spanish Gaskill Middle Sch, Niagara Falls, 1989—90; Spanish instr. Millard Fillmore Coll., Buffalo. Adj. prof. Spanish, U. North Fla., 1990-91, Jacksonville U., 1992, Fla. C.C., Jacksonville, 1991, lang. lab. facilitator, 1995-96, prof Spanish FCCJ, 1996—; mem. Spanish grad. program admission com. SUNY, Buffalo, 1988-90; mem. local arrangements com. for III Congress of the Internat. Fedn. of Latin Am. and Caribbean Studies, Ctr. for Tomorrow, SUNY, Buffalo, 1987. Author essays in field., "Kismet", Published in Carrings in Stone, The National Library of Poetry and " Winter Leave", The Sounds of Poetry, 1996. Vol. ARC, Niagara Falls, 1981, Am. Cancer Soc., Niagara Falls, 1985, Am. Heart Assn., Jacksonville, 1994. Mem. ACTFL, AAUP, MLA, Am. Assn. Tchrs. of Spanish and Portuguese, Instituto Literario Cultural Hispánico. Office Phone: 904-646-2318. E-mail: mzidovec@fccj.edu.

ZIEGELMEIER, PATRICIA KAY, music educator, executive secretary; b. Colby, Kans., July 14, 1944; d. Lon Elmer and Mary Marie (Saddler) Sowers; m. Carl Ernest Ziegelmeier, June 9, 1963; children: Matt, Steve, Lisa, Amy, Lori. BA in Music Edn., U. Wyo., 1967; MS in Ednl. Adminstrn., Ft. Hays State U., 1991. Tchr. music, sub. tchr. Golden Plains Schs., Rexford, Kans., 1969-72; pvt. piano instr. Gem, Kans., 1972-87; ch. organist Gem and Colby, Kans., 1968—; instr. music Colby C.C., 1988—. Cmty. leader 4-H, Gem, 1980-88, 99-2005; bd. dirs. Thomas County Ext. Coun., Colby, 1982-86, 94-95. Mem. NEA, Music Tchrs. Nat. Assn., Kans. Music Tchrs. Assn. (bd. dirs. 1981—, exec. sec. 1987—, Outstanding Tchr. award 1994), Western Plains Arts Assn. (exec. dir. 1989—), Northwest Kans. Piano Assn. (clinic chair 1973—). Methodist. Avocations: reading, music listening, playing piano, walking. Office: Kans Music Tchrs Assn 2154 County Road 27 Gem KS 67734-9008 Office Phone: 785-462-3984 ext. 307. E-mail: patz@colbycc.edu.

ZIEGLER, ANN E., retail executive; b. 1958; BA, Coll. William and Mary; JD, U. Chgo. With Skadden, Arps, Slate, Meagher & Flom; asst. counsel Sara Lee Corp., 1993—94, exec. dir. corp. devel., 1994—2000, v.p., 1997—2000, sr. v.p. corp. devel., 2000—01, sr. v.p. mergers and acquisitions, 2001—, CFO bakery group, 2003—, sr. v.p. adminstrn. bakery group. Bd. dirs. Unitrin, Inc. Office: Sara Lee Corp 3 First Nat Plaza Chicago IL 60602-4260

ZIEGLER, DHYANA, broadcasting educator, academic administrator; b. NYC, May 5, 1949; d. Ernest and Alberta Allie (Guy) Z. BS cum laude, CUNY, 1981; MA in Radio and TV, So. Ill. U., 1983, PhD in Higher Edn., 1985. Freelance researcher Essence Mag., NYC, 1972-75; copywriter, radio producer Rosenfeld, Sirowitz & Lawson Advt. Agy., NYC, 1974-75; exec. v.p. Patten & Guest Prodns., NYC, 1976-79; prodn. intern Sta. WNEW TV, NYC, 1979-80; upward bound counselor Seton Hall U., South Orange, NY, 1979-81; prodn. intern Sta. WCBS TV, NYC, 1980-81; asst. prof. Jackson (Miss.) State U., 1984-85; assoc. dir. Diversity Resources and Ednl. Svcs. U. Tenn., Knoxville, 1995, prof. broadcasting, pres., faculty senate; Garth C. Reeves Eminent Scholar Chair of Excellence in Journalism Fla. A&M U., 1997, asst. v.p., instructional tech., asst. v.p. academic affairs, acting v.p. sponsored rsch., mem. Innovation Park bd., dir. U. planning, 2002. Bd. dirs. Knoxville Women's Ctr., 1989-92; bd. trustees East Tenn. Discovery Ctr., Knoxville, 1989-92; adv. bd. Bethel Love Kitchen, Knoxville, 1990-93; subject matter expert Gov.'s Digital Divide Coun. Author books; contbr. articles to profl. jours.; producer, dir. (video documentary) Single Parenting, 1988 (2d Pl. award), Rape is a Reality, 1982 (UPI Outstanding Achievement award 1982). Chmn. comms. Knoxville chpt. NAACP, 1990-91, chpt. advisor U. Tenn. student chpt., 1989—, chmn. chancellor's commn. for blacks, 1990-95, pres. faculty senate, 1995—; chmn. social action com. Delta Sigma Theta, Knoxville, 1986-89, mem. commn. on arts and letters, 1990-91; bd. dirs. East Tenn. regional Am. Heart Assn., 1990—; mem. athletics bd. U. Tenn., 1990—; regional devel. edn. coord. Delta Rsch. and Ednl. Found. (chairperson Rsch. and resource com.), v.p., bd. dirs.; mem. allocations com. United Way, Knoxville, 1990-91; bd. trustee Florida Virtual HS, 2002-04, 2004-; bd. dirs. Fla. Virtual Sch. So. Scholarship Found. Named one of Top 50 African-Ams. in Tech., U.S. Black Engring. Info. Tech. Mag. and Blackmoney.com, 2002, 2003, 2004; recipient Gov.'s Outstanding Faculty Mem. of the Yr., 1987—88, Rsch. award, 1992, Coll. of Comms., Outstanding Faculty award, Interfraternity Coun., 1992, YWCA Finalist in Edn., 1990, Consortium of Dr.'s award, 1991; fellow, Poynter Inst., 1992; grantee, FISPE, US Dept. of Edn., 1989—, Delta Rsch. & Ednl. Found., 1987, 1990; inductee, U. Tenn. African Am. Hall of Fame, 1994, Leadership Devel. Initiative scholar, Grad. Sch. Edn., Mgmt. and Leadership in Edn. Inst., Harvard U., 2000, Chosen Fulbright-Hays Spl. Seminar Participant, US Dept. Edn. and the Nat. Com. on US-China Rels., China, 2004. Mem. NAFE, Women in Comm. (pres. Knoxville chpt. 1990—), Broadcast Edn. Assn. (chair multicultural div. 1989-92, chair gender divsn. 1996—), Speech Comm. Assn., Soc. Profl. Journalists (Jane Pauley task force on mass comm. edn. 1995-96, co-author Jane Pauley Task Force Report 1996), Golden Key Nat. Honor Soc., Kappa Tau Alpha, Phi Delta Kappa, Delta Sigma Theta (Post-secondary Educators award 1992, Black Achievement award 1993), Phi Kappa Phi. Office: U Tenn 295 Communications Bldg Knoxville TN 37996-0001 also: Fla A&M U Academic Affairs I&R Program FHAC 301 Tallahassee FL 32307 Office Phone: 850-599-3460, 850-599-3461. Business E-Mail: dhyz@aol.com.

ZIEGLER, JANICE H., lawyer; b. Bklyn., Jan. 25, 1962; m. Karl Groskaufmanis. BS in Indsl. & Labor Rels., with honors, Cornell U., 1984; JD magna cum laude, Harvard U., 1987. Bar: Mass. 1987, DC 1989. Law clk. to Hon. John H. Pratt US Dist. Ct DC; assoc. to ptnr. Shaw Pittman LLP, Washington; ptnr., health care practice group Sonnenschein Nath & Rosenthal LLP, Washington, 2003—. Mem.: ABA (health law sect.), Am. Health Lawyers Assn., DC Bar Assn. (health law sect.). Office: Sonnenschein Nath & Rosenthal LLP Ste 600, E Tower 1301 K St NW Washington DC 20015 Office Phone: 202-408-9158. Office Fax: 202-408-6399. Business E-Mail: jziegler@sonnenschein.com.

ZIEGLER, ROCHELLE ELIZABETH, special education educator; b. Virginia Beach, Va., Dec. 21, 1974; d. Robert Herman and Elizabeth Ethiel Ziegler. BS in Interdisciplinary Studies /Mental Retardation, Norfolk State U., Norfolk, Va., 2003; M in Severe Disabilities, Norfolk State U., 2005. Tchr. asst. Southeastern Coop. Ednl. Programs, Norfolk, Va., 1995—2004; tchr. spl. edn. Portsmouth Pub. Schs., 2005—. Mentor Young Sister's In Christ, Virginia Beach, Va., 1996. Recipient Nat. Collegiate Edn. Awards, US Achievement Acad., 2000; scholar All-Am. Scholar at Large Divsn., 2000. Mem.: Coun. of Exceptional Children (assoc.). Democrat-Npl. Bapt. Avocations: reading, helping in the community/church, exercise. Home: 834 Tuition Dr Virginia Beach VA 23462 Personal E-mail: rez1221@msn.com.

ZIELINSKI, TERESA KRYSTYNA, music educator; b. Utica, N.Y., Aug. 24, 1978; d. Stephen Leonard and Janina Teresa Zielinski. BMus, Crane Sch. of Music, Potsdam, N.Y., 2002. Music tchr., Tupper Lake, NY, 2002—03; music tchr., dir. New York Mills Jr./Sr. H.S., 2003—. Sr. class advisor N.Y. Mills H.S., 2004—. Home: 245 Oxford Rd Apt 3D New Hartford NY 13413 Office: New York Mills CSD 1 Marauder Blvd New York Mills NY 13417 Office Phone: 315-768-8124. Business E-Mail: tzielinski@newyorkmillss.org.

ZIEMBA, KAREN, actress; Appeared in Broadway plays A Chorus Line, Teddy & Alice, 42nd Street, Crazy for You, Chicago, Contact (Drama Desk award, Outer Critics Cir. award, Tony award, 2000), Never Gonna Dance (Tony nom. best featured actress in a play, 2004); (off-Broadway) And the World Goes 'Round (Drama Desk award) I Do! I Do!; (musical) Steel Pier (Tony award nominee), The Pajama Game, Allegro, Leading Ladies, 2005; (tour) Crazy for You (Joseph Jefferson award), Chicago (1998-99); (regional plays) Much Ado About Nothing, House and Garden, The Foreigner, Fifth of July, Curtains, 2006; (opera) The Most Happy Fella, 110 in the Shade; singer Allegro, Grand Night for Singing; (TV show) Sondheim: A Celebration at Carnegie Hall, Evening at Pops, My Favorite Broadway: The Leading Ladies, Law and Order; (film) The Devil and Daniel Webster; (albums) And the World Goes 'Round, Fifty Million Frenchmen, Lost in Boston II, Shakespeare on Broadway, 110 In The Shade, The Most Happy Fella, Ziegfeld Follies of 1936.*

ZIENTARA, SUZANNAH DOCKSTADER, insurance agent; b. Wichita, Kans., Oct. 1, 1945; d. Ralph Walter and Patricia Ann (Harvey) Dockstader; m. Larry Henry Zientara, Oct. 18, 1975; 1 child, Jillian Sue Zientara Cox. Student, U. Kans., 1963-64; BS in Bus. Edn., Ft. Hays State U., 1968; MEd in Secondary Guidance and Counseling, U. Mo., St. Louis, 1973. CLU. Sec. to supt. Wichita Pub. Schs., 1968-69; tchr. bus. edn. Wichita Heights High Sch., 1969-71, Lindbergh High Sch., St. Louis, 1971-72, Holman Jr. High Sch., St. Louis, 1972-75; guidance counselor Pattonville Heights Jr. High Sch., St. Louis, 1975-79; tchr. data processing Lawrence (Kans.) High Sch., 1979-85; ins. agt. State Farm Ins. Cos., Lawrence, 1985-90, agy. mgr. Tulsa, 1990-95, agy. field exec. Topeka, 1995-98, agent, 1999—. Mem. Regional Mgr. Coun., Tulsa, 1992-93; participant Purdue Profl. Mgmt. Inst., West Lafayette, Ind., 1993. Author: Introduction to Data Processing, 1983. Mem. Williams Edn. Fund, U. Kans. Named Outstanding Young Woman of Am., 1974. Mem.: PEO, Soc. Fin. Svc. Profls., U. Kans. Alumni Assn., Mortar Bd., Pi Omega Pi. Republican. Episcopalian. Avocations: golf, skiing, music. Home: 3318 SE 23d Terrace Topeka KS 66605 Office Phone: 785-267-5090. Personal E-mail: agentz@cox.net. Business E-Mail: sue.zientara.icj6@statefarm.com.

ZIETLOW, RUTH ANN, reference librarian; b. Richland Center, Wis., Apr. 5, 1960; d. James Eldon and Dixie Ann (Doudna) Z.; m. David Robert Voigt, Aug. 22, 1992; children: Eleanor Ruth, Isabel Anna, Carl James. BA in English, U. Nebr., 1987; MA in Libr. Studies, U. Wis., 1990; cert. in info. sys., U. St. Thomas, St. Paul, 1995. English instr. Guangzhou (China) English Lang. Ctr. Zhongshan U., 1987-88; adminstrv. asst. Helm Group, Lincoln, Nebr., 1988-89; circulatio supr. Sch. Edn. U. Wis., Madison, 1990-91; libr. specialist St. Paul Pub. Libr., 1991-92; reference librarian coordinator extention library svcs. U. St. Thomas, 1991—. Author manual: Electronic Communication and Information Resources Manual, 1995. Mem. Minn. Libr. Assn. (chair Distance Learning Roundtable 1999-2000). Avocations: gardening, reading. Office: U St Thomas O'Shaughnessey-Frey Libr 2115 Summit Ave Saint Paul MN 55105-1048 E-mail: razietlow@stthomas.edu.

ZIGLER, MELISSA MAY, music educator; b. Mansfield, Ohio, Sept. 21, 1978; d. Stephen Alan and Anita Jane Ryan; m. Scott Alan Zigler, July 13, 2002. B in Music Edn., Ohio State U., Columbus, 2002. Music educator New Albany (Ohio) Mid. Sch., 2002—. Ops. mgr., asst. dir. Columbus Jr. Strings Orch., 2004—06. Mem.: Nat. Assn. for Music Edn., Ohio Music Edn. Assn., Sigma Alpha Iota (rec. sec. 2004—06, Sword of Honor award 2002).

ZIGRAY, DEBRA RENEE, elementary school educator; b. Brownsville, Pa., June 2, 1959; d. Tony Sr. and Iona Gertrude (Smith) Iacconi; m. m. Jeffrey John Zigray, Aug. 29, 1981; 1 child, Ethan John. BS, California (Pa.) State Coll., 1980; MA, W.Va. U., 1997. 1st grade tchr. Tunnelton (W.Va.)-Denver Elem., 1981-82, 2nd grade tchr., 1982-83, 3rd grade tchr., 1983-85; 4th grade tchr. Kingwood (W.Va.) Elem., 1985—. Cheerleader coach Varsity Coach for Ctrl. Preston Sr. H.S., Kingwood, 1985-91; competition dir. Jr. H.S. Cheerleader Competition, Preston County, 1987-2004; student coun. advisor Kingwood Elem., 1994—; editor sch. newspaper Kingwood Elem. Gazette, 1990-2005. Pub. affairs chmn. Kingwood Jr. Woman's Club, 1990-2000, corr. sec., 1996-99, edn. chmn., 1994-96; youth league cheerleader coord. Preston County Youth League, 1994-2004; children's ct. advisor Preston County Buckwheat Festival, 1993—; mem. W.Va. English Lang. Arts Coun., Kingwood Elem. PTA, 1987—, Nat. Youth League Sports Coaches Assn., 1996-2004; bd. dirs. Presbyn. Day Care, 1997-98; football cheerleader coach Preston County Mid. Sch., 2005; boys and girls cheerleader coach Ctrl. Preston Mid. Sch., 2005-06. Mem. Internat. Reading Coun., W.Va. State Reading Coun., Preston County Reading Coun. (pres. 1994-98), Nat. Youth Sports Coaches Assn., Kingwood Jr. Woman's Club (edn. chmn. 1994-98), Cheerleaders Assn, W.Va. Tchrs. Math., Delta Kappa Gamma Soc. Internat. Republican. Avocations: dance, horseback riding, shopping, vacationing, reading. Home: 123 Western Dr Kingwood WV 26537-1044 Office: Kingwood Elem 207 S Price St Kingwood WV 26537-1493 Business E-Mail: dzigray@atlanticbb.net.

ZIKMUND, BARBARA BROWN, minister, religious organization administrator, educator; b. Ann Arbor, Mich., Oct. 16, 1939; d. Henry Daniels and Helen Langworthy Brown; m. Joseph Zikmund II, Aug. 26, 1961; 1 child, Brian Joseph. BA, Beloit Coll., 1961; BDiv, Duke U., 1964, PhD, 1969; D in Div (hon.), Doane Coll., 1984, Chgo. Theol. Sem., 1985, Ursinus Coll., 1989; LHD, U. Hartford, 1998. Ordained to ministry United Ch. of Christ, 1964. Instr. Albright Coll., Reading, Pa., 1966-67, Temple U., Phila., 1967-68, Ursinus Coll., Collegeville, Pa., 1968-69; asst. prof. religious studies Albion Coll., Mich., 1970-75; asst. prof. ch. history, dir. studies Chgo. Theol. Sem., 1975-80; dean and assoc. prof. ch. history Pacific Sch. Religion, Berkeley, Calif., 1981-85, dean and prof. ch. history, 1985-90; pres. Hartford (Conn.) Sem., 1990-2000. Prof. grad. sch. am. studies Doshisha U., Kyoto, Japan, 2000-05; vis. Life Cycle Inst. scholar Cath. U. Am., 2005—; chmn. United Ch. of Christ Hist. Coun., 1983-85, mem. coun. for ecumenism, 1983-89; mem. Nat. Coun. Chs. Commn. on Faith and Order, 1979-87, World Coun. of Chs. Programme Theol. Edn., 1984-91, Nat. Coun. Chs. Working Group on Inter-Faith Rels., 1992-96, Nat. Coun. Chs. Commn. on Inter-faith Rels., 1996—, chair Commn. on Inter-faith Rels., 2000—, World Conf. Assns. for Theol. Instns., sec. treas., 1992-96, pres., 1996-2000. Author: Discovering the Church, 1983, Clergy Women: An Uphill Calling, 1998; editor: Hidden Histories in the UCC, 1984, vol. 2, 1987; (with Manschreck) American Religous Experiment, 1976; mem. edit. bd. Jour. Ecumenical Studies, 1987—, Mid-Stream, 1991—; series editor: Living Theological Heritage of the United Church of Christ, co-editor Vol. 7 United and Uniting, 2005; contbr. articles to profl. jours. Mem. City Coun., Albion, Mich., 1972-75; elector Wadsworth Atheneum, 1994-2000; corporator St. Francis Hosp., 1994-2000, Hartford Hosp., 1996-2000; pres. Greater Hartford Consortium for Higher Edn., 1994-96. Woodrow Wilson fellow, 1964-66; NEH grantee, 1974-75; vis. scholar Schlesinger Libr. Women's History, Radcliffe Coll., 1988-89, Disting. Alumna, Duke Divinity Sch., 1994; recipient Disting. Svc. Citation Beloit Coll., 1986; Antoinette Brown award, United Ch. of Christ, 2005. Mem. Assn. Theol. Schs. (v.p. 1984-86, pres. 1986-88, issues implementation grantee 1983-84, Disting. Svc. award 2004), Am. Soc. Ch. History (coun. 1983-85, pres. elect 1996-97, pres. 1997-98), Internat. Assn. Women Ministers (v.p. 1977-79), AAUW (v.p. 1973-75), Greater Hartford C. of C. (bd. dirs. 1992-95). Democrat. Office: Life Cycle Inst Cath U Am Washington DC 20064 Home: 4545 Connecticut Ave NW Apt 510 Washington DC 20008-6018 Business E-Mail: beebeezee@verizon.net. E-mail: zikmund@cua.edu.

ZILBERBERG, BARBARA, psychologist; b. Nairobi, Kenya, Sept. 15, 1943; came to U.S., 1950, naturalized, 1957; d. Isidore and Sophie (Werner) Zysman; BA cum laude, CUNY, 1964; MA, New Sch. Social Res., 1966; cert. in sch. psychology Montclair State Coll., 1979-81; m. Charles Zilberberg, Sept. 2, 1965; 1 child, Julie. Lic. profl. counselor, N.J.; lic. rehab. counselor, N.J. Intern in psychology Cen. Islip (N.Y.) State Hosp., 1965-66; sr. clin. psychologist Kings Park (N.Y.) State Hosp., 1966-68; psychologist Bonnie Brae Residential Treatment Ctr., Millington, N.J., 1977-78, Sayreville (N.J.) Pub. Schs., 1981-2004; ednl. support specialist U. Medicine and Dentistry, Piscataway, N.J., 2005-. Founder Women's Investment Partnership. Mem. Nat. Assn. Sch. Psychologists, N.J. Assn. Sch. Psychologists, Mensa, Psi Chi.

ZILCH, BRIANNA RAE, athletic trainer; b. Middleburg Hts., Ohio, June 9, 1981; d. David and Karla Zilch. BS in Athletic Tng., Mt. Union Coll., Alliance, Ohio, 2003; MEd in Exercise Sci., Cleve. State U., 2005. Cert. athletic trainer Nat. Athletic Tng. Assn., 2003. Cert. athletic trainer Cleve. Clinic Found., 2003—. Assoc. athletic trainer Cleve. Fusion, Cleveland, Ohio, 2003—06. Mem. St. Andrews Presbyn. Ch., Olmsted Falls, Ohio, 1991—2006. Mem.: Nat. Athletic Trainers Assn., Nat. Strength and Conditioning Assn. (assoc.), Alpha Delta Pi (new mem. coord. 2001—02). Presbyterian. Avocations: soccer, travel, baking. Home: 454 Cranston Dr Berea OH 44107 Office: Cleveland Clinic Foundation 9500 Euclid Ave Cleveland OH 44195 Office Phone: 216-378-6240. Office Fax: 216-378-6248.

ZILL, ANNE BRODERICK, foundation executive; b. Phila., Nov. 25, 1941; d. John Daniel and Mary Lynna (Flynn) Broderick; children: Katherine Zill, Persephone Zill, Oriana Valentina Zill, Lydia Daniel Dennett. BA in Govt., Barnard Coll., 1963; MA in Journalism, Am. Univ., 1970. Nat news prodr. Nat. Edn. Radio, Washington, 1969-71; congrl. fellow Am. Polit. Sci. Assn., Washington, 1972-73; project staff mem. Ralph Nader Congress Project Study, Washington, 1972; rep. Stewart R. Mott Charitable Trust, 1973—; founder Women's Campaign Fund, Washington, 1974; co-founder, pres. Fund Constitutional Govt., Washington, 1974—; co-founder Ctr. Consentual Democracy, Maine, 1991; founding cons., bd. dirs. Maine Women's Fund, 1989—. Washington rep. Women's Environ. and Devel. Orgn., 1994-96; project cons. China Strategic Inst., Washington, 1995—, Inter-Am. Devel. Bank Creator Women's Leadership Fund for LAC. Contbr. articles to profl. jours. Founder, dir. Ctr. for Ethics in Action, 1997—. Congrl. fellow Am. Polit. Sci. Assn., 1972-73. Office: Ctr for Ethics in Action 716 Stevens Ave Portland ME 04103-2670 also: 122 Maryland Ave NE Washington DC 20002-5610 E-mail: annebzill@aol.com.

ZILLMER, DEBRA ANN, orthopedist, sports medicine physician; b. Sept. 30, 1954; BS, Univ. Wis., LaCrosse, 1976; MD, Albert Einstein Coll. Med., NYC, 1984. Cert. Am. Bd. Orthopaedic Surgery. Physical therapist Columbia Presbyterian Med. Ctr., NYC, 1976—78, private practice, NYC, 1978—84; rsch. asst., dept. pathology Columbia Presbyterian Med. Ctr., NYC, 1978—80; internship Albert Einstein Coll. Med., Montefiore Med. Ctr., Bronx, NY, 1984—85, residency, 1985—89; fellowship, sports med. Univ. Iowa, 1989—90; orthopaedic surgeon Gundersen Lutheran Med. Ctr., La-Crosse, Wis., 1990—2001, med. dir., head sports med. sect., 1991—97, 2000—01; orthopaedic surgeon, sports med. physician M&M Orthopaedics, Downers Grove, Ill., 2001—. Adj. clinical prof. Univ. Wis., LaCrosse, 1991—2001; team physician U.S. Soccer Fedn. Fellow: Am. Acad. Orthopaedic Surgeons (chmn. task force family violence 2000); mem.: Am. Orthopaedic Soc. Sport Med., Ruth Jackson Orthopaedic Soc. (bd. mem. 1995—96, treas. 1996—98, v.p. 1998—99, pres. 1999—2000), Ill. Assn. Orthopaedic Surgeons. Office: M&M Orthopaedics 4115 Fairview Ave Downers Grove IL 60515*

ZIMBER, LISA MARIE, music educator; d. Daniel Dewey and Marie Jernigan; m. Scott Kiser Zimber, Mar. 4, 1989; children: Cameron Kiser, Brenna Marie, Mitch Kiser. M, Nat. Louis U., Ill., 2001—03. Music tchr. Nbcusd #200, Poplar Grove, Ill., 1995—. Music dir. 1st Presbyn. Ch., Belvidere, 2004—. Presbyterian. Avocation: bicycling. Office: Nbcusd #200 208 N State St Poplar Grove IL 61065 Office Phone: 815-765-3113.

ZIMMAN STETSON, NANCY See STUART, NANCY

ZIMMEL, TAMMY LYNN, psychologist; b. Mankato, Minn., June 9, 1963; d. James Harold Zimmel and Sheryl Rae Otten. BS, Bemidji State U., Minn., 1985; MSW, Loyola U. Chgo., 1990; D in Psychology, Ill. Sch. Profl. Psychology, Chgo., 1998. Lic. psychologist Wis., Ill. Therapist Family Svcs., McHenry, Ill., 1987—2001; psychologist Wis. Dept. Corrections, Racine, Wis., 1998—; pvt. practice Racine, 2000—. Mem.: Nat. Assn. Social Workers. Avocations: sports, reading, camping, dogs. Office: 3701 Durand Ave Ste 325 Racine WI 53405 Office Phone: 262-554-9846.

ZIMMER, AMELIA ELLEN, principal, educator; b. Benton Harbor, Mich., Sept. 4, 1959; d. Donald James and Johannah Marie Peterson; m. Ronald Zimmer, Dec. 15, 1984; children: Katherine E.L., Margaret J.J., Paul D.C., Joshua M.J. BA, Mich. State U., 1981; MA, Aurora U., Ill., 1993. Lic. tchr. 1-8 Wis. Dept. Pub. Instrn., cert. prin. Wis. Dept. Pub. Instrn., dir. curriculum and instrn. Wis. Dept. Pub. Instrn. Educator Apostles Luth. Sch., San Jose, Calif., 1981—85, St. Catherine of Siena Sch., Burlingame, Calif., 1985—89, Kenosha (Wis.) Unified Sch. Dist., 1989—95; educator, asst. adminstr. Lac du Flambeau (Wis.) Pub. Sch., 1995—. Educator U. Wis.-Parkside, Kenosha, 1990—94; adj. prof. Lac Courte Oreilles, Hayward, Wis., 2006—. Mem.: Nat. Sci. Tchrs. Assn., Soc. for Advancement of Chicanos and Native Ams. in Sci., Nat. Coun. Tchrs. Math., Assn. Supervision and Curriculum Devel. Lutheran. Avocations: volleyball coaching, travel. Office: Lac du Flambeau Pub Sch 2899 Hwy 47 Lac Du Flambeau WI 54538 Office Phone: 715-588-3800 406. Office Fax: 715-588-3243. E-mail: azimmer@ldf.k12.wi.us.

ZIMMER, ANNA HELD, social worker; b. Revere, Mass., Jan. 1, 1922; d. Morris and Sarah (Javits) Held; m. Fred Zimmer, Apr. 4, 1948; children: Harold, Sarah, Bonnie. BA, Bklyn. Coll., 1943; MSW, Smith Coll., 1944. Cert. social worker, N.Y. Caseworker New Haven Family Svc., 1944-46, Phila. Family Svc., 1946-48, United Svc. for New Ams., N.Y.C., 1948-49, Coun. Ctr. Sr. Citizens, Bklyn., 1957-69; caseworker, student supr. Community Svc. Soc. N.Y., N.Y.C., 1967-82; co-dir. Network Assocs., 1982-87; dir. media assistance to caregivers Brookdale Ctr. Aging/Hunter Coll., N.Y.C., 1985-87, dir. Inst. on Mut. Aid/Self Help in Field of Aging, 1986—2003. Mem. long term home health care com. Jewish Home and Hosp. for Aged; regional rep. Nat. Inst. on Community-Based Long-Term Care, Nat. Coun. on Aging, mem. adv. com. caregivers project, 1986; mem. adv. com. Ret. Sr. Vol. Program, N.Y.C. Editorial Bd. Jour. Gerontol. Social Work. Mem. NASW (Social Worker in Aging award N.Y.C. chpt. 1987, Walter Beattie award 1998), Aca.d Cert. Social Workers, Gerontol. Soc. Am., Am. Soc. Aging, N.Y. Soc. Aging. Home: 975 Massachusetts Ave Apt 305 Arlington MA 02476-4545

ZIMMER, ANNE FERN YOUNG, educator, researcher, administrator; b. Detroit, Dec. 19, 1920; d. Arthur Frederick and Jessie (Clements) Young; m. D. Robert Stewart, Oct. 3, 1942 (dec. July 1944); 1 child, Robert Arthur; m. Arnold Earnest Zimmer, Apr. 7, 1951; 1 child, Kathleen Anne (dec.). BS, Wayne State U., 1962, MA, 1964, PhD, 1966. With pers. dept. Standard Accident Ins. Co., Detroit, 1944-46, bond underwriter, 1946-52; part-time med. sec. various drs. and hosps. Detroit, 1955-59; instr. Wayne State U., Detroit, 1966-67, asst. prof., 1967, asst. prof., adminstr. grad. program, 1967-75, assoc. prof., 1976—, ret., 1986. Sec., treas. bicentennial com. Wayne State U., 1973-75, chmn., 1976. Author: (biography) Jonathan Boucher, Loyalist in Exile, 1978 (Ella V. Dobbs award 1979); contbr. articles to profl. jours. Initiator Citizens for Advanced Life Support, Grosse Pointe Woods (Mich.) Emergency Med. Svc., 1981, 83; founder Cass Assn. of Cass Tech. High Sch., Detroit. Wayne State U. fellow, 1962-64, scholar, 1959-62; recipient Colonial Dames award DAR, 1965. Mem. AAUW (chair ad hoc com. for emergency med. svcs. Grosse Pointe br. 1984-92, area rep. and bd. dirs. 1992-94), So. Assn. Women Historians, So. Hist. Assn. (membership com. 1974-75, chair nominating com. 1979-80, Francis Simkins award com. 1980-81, Green award com. 1976-78), Inst. Early Am. History, Smithsonian, Grosse Pointe Woman's Club. Avocations: travel, reading. Home: Lakepointe Towers 3309 Country Club Dr Saint Clair Shores MI 48082-1096

ZIMMER, BARBARA S., elementary school educator; b. McKeesport, Pa., May 20, 1955; d. Leo W. and Edity Buckley Stepansky; m. Charles D. Zimmer, Nov. 26, 1988; children: Danica L. Crawford, Devon M. Langham, Meaghan, Danae. BS in Elem. Edn., St. Petersburg Coll., 2004. Cert. tchr. Fla. Address: 406 Park Blvd Oldsmar FL 34677-3649

ZIMMER, GRETA GAY, secondary school educator; b. Goldthwaite, Tex., Mar. 19, 1941; d. Edwin John and Lillian (Elkins) Drueckhammer; m. Henry Junior Stagemeyer (div.); 1 child, Thomas David Dietrich; m. David LeRoy Zimmer, July 16, 1982. BA, Tex. Luth. U., Seguin, 1963; MS, Kearney (Nebr.) State U., 1969. Tchr. Channing (Tex.) Ind. Sch. Dist., 1963-64, Arapahoe (Nebr.) Ind. Sch. Dist., 1964-65, Loomis (Nebr.) Ind. Sch. Dist., 1965-68, Galena Park Ind. Sch. Dist., Houston, 1969-71, LaPorte (Tex.) Jr. High Sch., 1972-86; tchr. English and German, LaPorte High Sch., 1986-96; ret., 1996. Trainer N.J. Writing Inst. in Tex., LaPorte, 1990-93. Author short stories and poetry. Mem. NEA, Tex. State Tchrs. Assn., LaPorte Edn. Assn. (pres. 1990-91). Lutheran. Home: PO Box 175 Priddy TX 76870-0827 E-mail: ggzimmer@century.net.

ZIMMERER, KATHY LOUISE, museum director; b. Whittier, Calif., Dec. 9, 1951; BA cum laude, U. Calif., Berkeley, 1974; MA, Williams Coll., 1976. From tour guide to curatorial asst. Sterling and Francine Clark Inst., Williamstown, Mass., 1975-76; spl. asst. dept. modern art L.A. County Mus. Art, 1976-77; mus. edn. fellow Fine Arts Mus. San Francisco, 1977-78; dir. coll. art gallery SUNY, New Paltz, 1978-80; cons. in field, 1980-81; dir. univ. art gallery Calif. State U., Dominguez Hills, 1982—. Project dir. Painted Light: California Impressionist Paintings from the Gardena H.S./L.A. Unified Sch. Dist., 1996—. Mem. Internat. Assn. Art Critics, Art Table. Office: Univ Art Gallery Calif State U 1000 E Victoria St Carson CA 90747-0001 Office Phone: 310-243-3334. E-mail: kzimmerer@csudh.edu.

ZIMMERER, NANCY JEAN, elementary school educator, rancher; b. Torrington, Wyo., Jan. 10, 1951; d. George Frederick and Isabelle Brown Hill; m. David Lee Zimmerer, Aug. 9, 1975. AA, Ea. Wyo. Coll., Torrington, 1972; BS in Edn., Chadron State Coll., Nebr., 1974. Elem. tchr. Sch. Dist. # 44, Alliance, Nebr., 1974—75, Henry (Nebr.) Elem., 1975—79; tchr. grade 5 Platte County Sch. Dist. # 2, Guernsey, Wyo., tchr. grade 2, 1985—. Co-author: Let Your Light Shine, Vol. IV, 2002. Elder Lingle (Wyo.) Cmty. Presbyn. Ch., 1999—2002, tchr. Sunday sch., 2002—03, mem. choir. Recipient 3rd place Outstanding Tchr. Am. History, DAR, 1984, Nat. 3rd Place award for outstanding observance of Constitution Week, Washington DC, 1991. Mem.: DAR (state historian 1992—93, regent Elizabeth Ramsey chpt. 2001—03), Order Ea. Star (Torrington chpt. # 22), Delta Kappa Gamma (pres. Epsilon chpt. women tchrs. group 2002—04). Republican. Presbyterian. Avocations: genealogy, golf, photography, reading, crafts. Home: 2752 B Wyncote Rd Lingle WY 82223-8537 Office: Platte County Sch Dist #2 447 S Wyoming Ave Guernsey WY 82214-0189 Office Phone: 307-836-2733. Business E-Mail: nzimmerer@plt2.k12.wy.us.

ZIMMERMAN, ADRIA DAWN, composition educator; b. Tamuning, Guam, Mar. 28, 1975; d. John Craig Zimmerman and Laura Lynette Grimm. BA in English Lit. and Tchr. Preparation, Humboldt State U., Arcata, Calif., 1998, M in Tchg. Writing, 2001. Lectr. English dept. Humboldt State U., Arcata, 2001—; assoc. faculty English dept. Coll. of the Redwoods, Eureka, Calif., 2002—. Vol. Humboldt Literacy Project, Eureka, 2006—; presenter in field. Asst. coach Humboldt Youth Soccer League; active Coll. of the Redwoods Faculty Orgn., Eureka, 2006. Named Assoc. Faculty of Yr., Coll. of the Redwoods, 2006—. Mem.: NEA, Calif. Tchrs. Assn. Democrat. Avocations: soccer, travel. Office: College of the Redwoods 7351 Tompkins Hill Rd Eureka CA 95501-9300 Office Phone: 707-476-4300. Personal E-mail: adz1@humboldt.edu.

ZIMMERMAN, CONNIE ANN, public administrator; AA, Harrisburg Area CC, 1978; BS in Pub. Policy, Pa. State U., 2002. Exec. sec. DER, 1993—95, adminstrv. asst., 1995—99; adminstrv. mgr. PennDOT Bureau of Design, Harrisburg, 1999—. V.p. Women's Legis. Exchange, 2001—; chair legis. com. Ctrl. Pa. Female Execs., 2005—; bd. dirs. Ctrl. Pa. Women Execs., Harrisburg, Pa., 1997—2002, YWCA of Greater Harrisburg, 2002—. Recipient Sarah Wright award, YWCA, 2006. Mem.: NAFE, Am. Soc. Pub. Adminstrn., Nat. Women's History Mus. and Nat. Constl. Ctr. (charter), Hamburg Mannechor, Mitgleider Deutscher Verein, Pi Gamma Mu. Roman Catholic. Avocations: dance, music, gardening. Home: 933 Highland St Steelton PA 17113-1537

ZIMMERMAN, DIANE LEENHEER, law educator; b. Newton, N.J., Apr. 16, 1941; d. Adrian and Mildred Eleanor (Booth) Leenheer; m. Earl A. Zimmerman, Sept. 24, 1960 (div. Aug. 1982); m. Cavin P. Leeman, Feb. 18, 1984. BA, Beaver Coll., Glenside, Pa., 1963; JD, Columbia U., 1976. Bar: N.Y. 1977, US Supreme Ct. 1983. Reporter, Newsweek mag., N.Y.C., 1963-71; spl. features writer N.Y. Daily News, NYC, 1971-73; law clk. to Hon. Jack B. Weinstein US Dist. Ct. Ea. Dist. N.Y., 1976-77; asst. prof. law N.Y.U. Sch. Law, 1977-80, assoc. prof., 1980-82, prof., 1982—, now Samuel Tilden prof. law; mem. faculty Practicing Law Inst., N.Y.C., 1979, 84, 90, 92, 94, 96-02; Disting. Lee Vis. Prof. Constl. Law Coll. William and Mary, 1994; moderator justice and soc. program Aspen Inst., 1992, 99; Disting. Vis. Hosier Chair Intellectual Property, DePaul Coll. Law, Chgo., 2001; lectr. 17th Ann. Marques Lectr. Intellectual Property, 2004. Recipient citation of merit Columbia U. Sch. Journalism, 1972; Kent scholar and Stone scholar, 1973-76; Mem. ABA (vice chmn. tort liability study com. tort and ins. sect. 1986-87, chair 1st amendment rights com. 1989-94), Am. Law Inst., Assn. of Bar City of N.Y. (chairperson com. civil rights 1981-83), Copyright Soc. USA (trustee 1988-91, 2004—). Office: NYU Sch Law Vanderbilt Hall Rm 332 40 Washington Sq S New York NY 10012-1099 Office Phone: 212-998-6250. Business E-Mail: zimmermd@juris.law.nyu.edu.

ZIMMERMAN, ELYN, artist; b. Phila., Dec. 16, 1945; d. Louis B. and Sylvia (Snyder) Z.; m. Kirk Varnedoe, Oct. 8, 1983. BA in Psychology, UCLA, 1968, MFA in Painting, 1972. Apptd. mem. Commn. Fine Arts, 2003. One-man shows include Univ. Art Mus., Berkeley, Calif., 1974, P.S. 1, Long Island City, N.Y., 1977, Mus. Contemporary Art, Chgo., 1979, Hudson River Mus., Yonkers, N.Y., 1982, Joslyn Art Mus., Omaha, 1984, Wave Hill, Riverside, N.Y., Contemporary Art Mus. U. South Fla., Tampa, 1991, Gagosian Gallery, N.Y.C., 1993, 96, 98, 2001, 03, 04; exhibited in group shows at Whitney Mus. Am. Art, N.Y.C., 1975, Biennale of Sydney, Australia, 1976, Walker Art Ctr., Mpls., 1979, San Diego Mus. Art, 1980, Venice Biennale, USA Pavillion, Italy, 1980, Mus. Contemporary Art, Chgo., 1981, Newport Harbor Art Mus., Calif., 1982, Hirshhorn Mus., Washington, 1983, San Francisco Mus. Modern Art, 1984, Socrates Sculpture Park, N.Y.C., 1996, L.A. County Mus. Art, 1996, Addison Gallery, Andover, Mass., 1998, Marlborough Gallery, N.Y.C., 1998, Chesterwood, Stockbridge, Mass., Montclair Mus., N.J., 1999, Ctr. for Photography, Woodstock, N.Y., Witherspoon Gallery Durham, N.C., 2002; sculpture commns. include Nat. Geographic Soc., Washington, O'Hare Internat. Ctr., Rosemont, Ill., Dade County Justice Ctr., Miami, Fla., Moffit Rsch. Ctr./U. South Fla., Tampa, Market Plz., San Francisco, Birmingham Mus. Art, AT&T Hdqrs., N.J., World Trade Ctr. Meml., N.Y.C. Nat. Endowment for Arts grantee, 1976, 80, 83, Creative Artist Pub. Svc. grantee, 1980; NEA and Japan-U.S. Friendship Commn. fellow, 1982. Mem. Creative Time, Inc. (bd. dirs. 1984-90). Home: 140 Greene St New York NY 10012-3241 Office Phone: 212-219-3224. Business E-Mail: elynzimmerman@nyc.rr.com.

ZIMMERMAN, ERICKA POINT, academic administrator; d. James Nelson and Nancy Wilson Point; m. Steven Robert Zimmerman, Apr. 20, 1996; children: James Douglas, Alexandra Nadine. BA, St. Andrews Presbyn. Coll., Laurinburg, NC, 1993; MS, Ind. State U., Terre Haute, 1994. Cert. athletic trainer NATA Bd. Certification, 1993. Instr., asst. athletic trainer Union Coll., Barbourville, Ky., 1994—95; athletic trainer Lexington Sports Medicine Ctr., Ky., 1996—97; head athletic trainer Georgetown Coll., 1997—2002; instr., athletic trainer, dept. athletic trianing U. Charleston, W.Va., 2002—03, coord. clin. edn., dept. athletic tng., 2003—05, chair, program dir., dept. athletic tng., 2005—. Mem. BOC Regulatory Adv. Com., 2006—; vol. instr. Am. Heart Assn., 2003—, ARC, 1994—. Phys. tng. asst. Charleston City Police, 2005—06; tchr. Sunday sch. First Presbyterian Ch., Albans. Recipient Rollie Graves Tech. Staff award, Georgetown Coll., 2002, Outstanding Young Alumnus award, Ind. State U., Dept. Athletic Tng., 2006, Athletic Trainer Yr., W.Va. Athletic Trainers' Assn., 2006; grantee, U. Charleston, AAC&U, and Carnegie Found. Tchg., 2004, U. Charleston, U.S. Dept. Edn. Title III, 2005. Mem.: Nat. Athletic Trainers' Assn., W.Va. Athletic Trainers' Assn. (treas. 2003—06, rep. ethnic diversity com. 2003—06, rep. women athletic tng. com. 2004—06, strategic planning com. 2004—06). Avocations: piano, hiking, camping, reading. Office: U Charleston 2300 MacCorkle Ave SE Charleston WV 25304 Office Phone: 304-357-4828. Office Fax: 304-357-4965. Business E-Mail: erickazimmerman@ucwv.edu.

ZIMMERMAN, GAIL MARIE, medical foundation executive; b. Fort Wayne, Ind., June 23, 1945; d. Albert Douglas and Aina Dorothy (Johnson) Z. BA, U. Puget Sound, 1967. Intelligence analyst CIA, Washington, 1970-72; rsch. asst. Arthur Young & Co., Portland, Oreg., 1972-74; emergency med. service planner Marion-Polk-Yamhill Counties, Salem, Oreg., 1975-76; health cons. Freedman Assocs., Portland, Oreg., 1976-77; legis. asst. U.S. Senator Bob Packwood, Portland, Oreg., 1977-78; pres., CEO Nat. Psoriasis Found., Portland, 1979—. Mem. dermatology panel U.S. Parmacopoeial Conv., 1985-94; lay rep. Nat. Inst. Arthritis, Musculoskeletal and Skin Disease, NIH, 1990-94. Founding bd. dirs. Nat. Abortion Rights Action League, Portland, 1977; pres. bd. dirs. Oreg. Common Cause, Portland, 1977-78 Mem.: Internat. Fedn. Psoriasis Assn. (chair 1995—2001, vice chair 2001—). Avocations: tennis, flute. Office: Nat Psoriasis Found 6600 SW 92nd Ave Ste 300 Portland OR 97223-7195 Office Phone: 503-546-8366. Business E-Mail: gzimmerman@psoriasis.org.

ZIMMERMAN, HELENE LORETTA, retired business educator; b. Rochester, NY, Feb. 26, 1933; d. Henry Charles and Loretta Catherine (Hobert) Z. BS, SUNY, Albany, 1953, MS, 1959; PhD, U. N.D., 1969. Cert. records mgr. Bus. tchr., chmn. bus. dept. Williamson (N.Y.) Cen. Sch., 1953-69; asst. prof. U. Ky., Lexington, 1969-70; assoc. prof. bus. Cen. Mich. U., Mt. Pleasant, 1970-74, prof., 1974-98. Author General Business, 1977; contbg. author to records mgmt. text book, 1987. Sec. Isabella County Christmas Outreach, Mt. Pleasant, 1983-2004, internat. rels. com., 2003— Mem.: AAUW (pres. 1984—86), Mich. Bus. Edn. Assn. (bd. dirs. 1985—90, pres. 1988—89, bd. dirs. 1995—97), Nat. Bus. Edn. Assn., Internat. Soc. Bus. Edn. (internat. v.p. English speaking nations 1986—88, editor Internat. Rev. 1997—2006), Inst. Cert. Records Mgrs. (sec. 1985—89, exam. devel. com. 1993—2002), Assn. Records Mgmt. and Adminstrn., Gen. Fedn. Women's Clubs (pres. 2004—06, pres. Mt. Pleasant chpt. 2005—06), Delta Kappa Gamma (state pres. 1987—89, internat. fin. com. 1990—94, internat. ad hoc com. on tech. 1996—2000). Avocations: travel, crafts. Business E-Mail: zimme1hl@cmich.edu.

ZIMMERMAN, IRENA AGNES, nun, poet, educator; b. Westphalia, Iowa, Jan. 5, 1932; d. Emil John Zimmerman and Josephine Posch. BA, Alverno Coll., 1958; MA, U. Colo., 1966. Tchr. Pius XI H.S., Milw., 1957—77; moderator boarding sch. Singmaringen (Germany) Liebfrauenschule, 1978—81; archivist Sch. Sisters of St. Francis, Milw., 1981—88; sec. Alverno Coll., Milw., 1988—2002, editor, 1990—2002; poet-in-residence St. Joseph Retreat Ctr., Baileys Harbor, Wis., 2002—05, ret., 2005. Author: Convergence, 1983, For-Giving Ground, 1986, Woman Un-Bent, 1999, Incarnations: New & Co Heated Poems, 2004, (exhibition) poems for sculptures. Recipient 2d Pl. Poetry award, Cath. Press Assn., 1984, 1997, 1st Pl. Poets Clipica, Wisc. Fellowship Poetry, 2004. Democrat. Roman Cath. Home: 3035 O'Brien Rd Baileys Harbor WI 54202

ZIMMERMAN, JEAN, lawyer; b. Berkeley, Calif., Dec. 3, 1947; d. Donald Scheel Zimmerman and Phebe Jean (Reed) Doan; m. Gilson Berryman Gray III, Nov. 25, 1982; children: Charles Donald Buffum and Catherine Elisabeth Phebe (twins); stepchildren: Alison Travis, Laura Rebecca, Gilson Berryman. BSBA, U. Md., College Park, 1970; JD, Emory U., Atlanta, Ga., 1975. Bar: Ga. 1975, D.C. 1976, N.Y. 1980. Asst. mgr. investments FNMA, Washington, 1970-73; assoc. counsel Fuqua Industries Inc., Atlanta, 1976-79; assoc. Sage Gray Todd & Sims, N.Y.C., 1979-84; from assoc. counsel to sr. v.p., gen. counsel, sec. IBJ Whitehall Bank & Trust Co., N.Y.C., 1984—99; sr. v.p., gen. counsel, sec., bd. dirs. IBJ Schroder Bus. Credit Corp., N.Y.C., 1996-98, Innovest Capital Mgmt., Inc., N.Y.C., 1997-99; sr. v.p., gen. counsel, sec. Innovest Corp., N.Y.C., 1997-99; from gen. counsel, sec. to exec. v.p. ops. and legal ArrowSight, Inc. (formerly ParentWatch.com), Mt. Kisco, NY, 2001—. From asst. sec. to sr. v.p., gen. counsel, sec., bd. dirs. IBJ Whitehall Bus. Credit Corp., IBJ Whitehall Capital Corp., IBJ Whitehall Securities, Inc., Delphi Asset Mgmt., Inc., Innovest Asset Mgmt., Inc., N.Y.C., 1997-99; from asst. sec. to v.p., gen. counsel, sec. IBJ Schroder Internat. Bank, Miami, Fla., 1989-98; sr. v.p., gen. counsel, sec. Execution Svcs., N.Y.C., 1991-93. Founder, officer ERA Ga., Atlanta, 1977-79; bd. dirs. Ct. Apptd. Spl. Advs., 1988-94. Named one of Outstanding Atlantans, 1978-79; recipient Disting. Alumni award Emory U. Sch. Law, 1999. Mem.: ABA, LWV, Am. Soc. Corp. Secs., Inc., Ga. Assn. Women Lawyers (bd. dirs. 1977—79), Assn. Bar City N.Y., Assn. Emory Alumni (N.Y. pres. 1999—2003, bd. govs. 2001—05), DAR. E-mail: jzimmer642@aol.com, jean.zimmerman@arrowsight.com.

ZIMMERMAN, JO ANN, retired health science association administrator, educator, retired lieutenant governor; b. Van Buren County, Iowa, Dec. 24, 1936; d. Russell and Hazel (Ward) McIntosh; m. A. Tom Zimmerman, Aug. 26, 1956; children: Andrew, Lisa, Don and Ron (twins), Beth. Diploma, Broadlawns Sch. of Nursing, Des Moines, 1958; BA with honors, Drake U., 1973; postgrad., Iowa State U., 1973—75. RN, Iowa. Asst. head nurse maternity dept. Broadlawns Med. Ctr., Des Moines, 1958—59, weekend supr. nursing svcs., 1960—61, supr. maternity dept., 1966—68; instr. maternity nursing Broadlawns Sch. Nursing, 1968—71; health planner, community rels. assoc. Iowa Health Systems Agy., Des Moines, 1978—82; mem. Iowa Ho. Reps., 1982—86; lt. gov., pres. of Senate, State of Iowa, 1987—91; cons. health svcs., grant writing and continuing edn. Zimmerman & Assocs., Des Moines, 1991—2000; dir. patient care svcs. Nursing Svcs. Iowa, 1996—98; nurse case mgr. Olsten Health Svcs. (now Gentiva Health Svcs.), 1998—2004; founder JAZ Tours, 2002—04, ret., 2004, 2004. Ops. dir. Medlink Svcs., Inc., Des Moines, 1992-96. Contbr. articles to profl. jours. Mem. advanced registered nurse practioner task force on cert. nurse midwives Iowa Bd. Nursing, 1980-81, Waukee, Polk County, Iowa Health Edn. Coord. Coun., Iowa Women's Polit. Caucus, Dallas County Women's Polit. Caucus; chmn. Des Moines Area Maternity Nursing Conf. Group, 1969-70, task force on sch. health svcs. Iowa Dept. Health, 1982, task force health edn. Iowa Dept. Pub. Instruction, 1979, adv. com. health edn. assessment tool, 1980-81, Nat. Lt. Govs., chair com. on Agrl. and Rural Devel., 1989; Dallas County Dem. Ctrl. Com., 1972-84, 98—; bd. dirs. Waukee Cmty. Sch. Bd., 1976-79, pres. 1978-79; bd. dirs. Iowa PTA, 1979-83, chair Health Com., 1980-84; mem. steering com. ERA, Iowa, 1991-92; founder Dem. Activist Women's Network (DAWN), 1992; mem. Disciples of Christ Mission Group to El Salvadore, 2003, 04; founder health ministry First Christian Ch., Des Moines, Iowa, 2004. Named to Iowa Women's Hall of Fame, 2005; recipient Woman Achievement award, YWCA Greater Des Moines, 2005. Mem. ANA, LWV (health chmn. met. Des Moines chpt.), Iowa Nurses Assn., Iowa League for Nursing (bd. dirs. 1979-83), Family Centered Childbirth Edn. Assn. (childbirth instr., advisor), Iowa Cattleman's Assn., Am. Lung Assn. (bd. dirs. Iowa 1988-92), Dem. Activist Women's Network (founder 1992). Mem. Christian Ch. Avocations: gardening, sewing, reading, bridge.

ZIMMERMAN, KATHLEEN MARIE, artist; b. Floral Park, NY, Apr. 24, 1923; d. Harold G. and Evelyn M. (Andrade) Z.; m. Ralph S. Iwamoto, Nov. 23, 1963. Student, Art Students League, N.Y.C., 1942—44, Nat. Acad. Sch. Fine Arts, 1944—47, Nat. Acad. Sch. Fine Arts, 1950—54. Tchr. drawing and painting Midtown Sch. Art, N.Y.C., 1947-52. Illustrator (with Ralph S. Iwamoto) Diet for a Small Planet, 1971; one-woman shows include Westbeth Gallery, N.Y.C., 1973, 1974, St. Mary's Coll., St. Mary's City, Md., 1990, Broome St. Gallery, N.Y.C., 2002, Lecei Gallery, Concord, Mass., 2005, exhibited in group shows at Woodstock Art Gallery, N.Y., 1945, Nat. Arts Club, N.Y.C., 1948—56, 1984, Emily Lowe Award Show, 1951, Contemporary Arts Gallery, N.Y.C., 1952, 1960, Village Art Ctr., 1956—61, Allied Artists Ann., N.Y.C., 1956, 1978, 1980—91, 1993—2005, 2004, Studio Gallery, 1957—60, Nat. Assn. Women Artists, N.Y.C., 1957—85, 1987—98, 2000, 2003, Art USA, 1958, ACA Gallery, 1958—59, City Ctr. Gallery, 1960, Janet Nessler Gallery, N.Y.C., 1961, Silvermine Guild, Conn., 1962, Pioneer Gallery, Cooperstown, N.Y., 1962—63, Audubon Artists, N.Y.C., 1963—2005, NAD, 1969—2001, 2003, 2004, 2005, Women Artists Award Winners, N.Y.C., 1974, Am. Watercolor Soc., 1975—78, 1980, Cheyenne (Wyo.) Western Galleries, 1975—77, Edward-Dean Mus., Cherry Valley, Calif., 1975—77, Frye Mus., Seattle, 1975—76, 1997, Boise Gallery Art, 1975, Central Wyo. Mus. Art, 1975—76, Willamette U., 1975, Yellowstone Art Ctr., Billings, Mont., 1975, Utah State U., 1975, Applewood Art Gallery, Colo., 1976, Charleston Art Gallery, W.Va., 1976, Kent State U., 1976, Cin. Art Club, 1976, Martello Mus., Key West, Fla., 1976, Buecker Gallery, N.Y.C., 1976, Anchorage Fine Arts Mus., 1976, Davis and Long Gallery, N.Y.C., 1977, Butler Inst. Am. Art, 1978, 2000, Washington Square East Gallery, NYU, 1979, Internat. Festival Women Artists, Copenhagen, 1980, Westbeth Gallery, N.Y.C., 1980, 1983, 1999—2005, City Gallery, 1981, Bergen Cmty. Mus., Paramus, N.J., 1983, Kenkeleba Gallery, N.Y.C., 1985, Adelphi U., Garden City, N.Y., 1987, Lotos Club, N.Y.C., 1987, Temperance Hall Gallery, Bellport, N.Y., 1987, Monmouth Mus., Lincroft, N.J., 1987, Marbella Gallery, N.Y.C., 1989, Knickerbocker Artists, 1990, Brownstone Gallery, N.Y.C., 1993, Viridian Gallery, 1995, Sundance Gallery, Bridgehampton, N.Y., 1996, Mcpl. Art Ctr., Athens, Greece, 1996, ISE Art Found., N.Y.C., 1996, Nat. Soc. Painters in Casein & Acrylic, 1997-2001, 2004, Zimmerli Mus., Rutgers U., New Brunswick, N.J., 1998, Gallery OneTwentyEight, N.Y.C., 2001—03, Broome St. Gallery, 2002—03, Nat. Acad. Mus., 2003, Lecei Gallery, West Concord, Mass., 2003, 2004, 2005, Represented in permanent collections Butler Inst. Am. Art, Youngstown, Ohio, Sheldon Swope Art Gallery, Terre Haute, Ind., Lauren Rogers Mus. Art, Laurel, Miss., U. Wyo. Art Mus., Laramie, U. Miami Lowe Art Mus., Coral Gables, Fla., N.C. Mus. Art, Raleigh, Swarthmore Coll., Pa., Erie Art Mus., Nat. Acad. Design, N.Y.C., Zimmerli Mus., Rutgers U., New Brunswick, Nat. Mus. Women in the Arts, Washington; bibliography James Mellow, N.Y. Times Art Rev., 1973, Hilton Kramer, N.Y. Times Rev., 1977, Helen A. Harrison, N.Y.

Times Rev., 1987, William Zimmer, N.Y. Times Rev., 1999, Terry Teachout, Washington Post Review, 2003, Ken Johnson, N.Y. Times Rev., 2003, contbr. (bibliography) The Art of Collage, 1978, Mastering Color & Design in Watercolor, 1981, The Collage Handbook, 1985, Painting Without a Brush, 1992, Collage Techniques, 1994. John F. and Anna Lee Stacey scholar, 1954; recipient Nat. Soc. Painters in Casein and Acrylic award 1997, Liquitex Art award, 1999, Winsor & Newton award 2001, Howard Mandel Meml. award, 2004. Mem.: NAD (Henry Ward Ranger Fund purchase prize 1976, cert. of merit 1980, Henry Ward Ranger Fund purchase prize 1982, L.G. Sawyer prize 1988, Ogden Pleissner Meml. award 1991, William A. Paton prize 1993, 1997, Zellah W. Pike prize 2001), Nat. Acad. Design, N.Y. Artists Equity Assn. (Dr. Maury Leibovitz award 1985), Allied Artists Am. (Silver medal 1981, Jane Peterson award 1985, Creative Watercolor prize 1989, Silver medal 1991, Creative Watercolor prize 1997, Mary Lou Fitzgerald Meml. award 1998, John Young-Hunter Meml. award 2002, Pauline Law Meml. award 2003), Nat. Assn. Women Artists (14 prizes 1957—2003), Am. Watercolor Soc. (Barse Miller Meml. award 1976), Audubon Artists (John Wenger Meml. award 1978, Ralph Fabri medal 1981, J&E Liskin Meml. award 1987, Dick Blick award 1994, Gold Medal of Honor 2001, Art Students League award 2002, Giulia Palermo award 2005). Home: 463 West St Apt 1110A New York NY 10014-2040

ZIMMERMAN, LAURA ANN, biology educator; b. Buffalo, Sept. 8, 1957; d. Paul Thomas and Marjory Marie Zimmerman. BS in Cmty. Health Edn., Ea. Ky. U., Richmond, 1979, BS, 1987, MA in Biology Edn., 1995, cert. in sch. counseling, 2005. Biology educator Fayette County Sch., Lexington, 1992—. Mem. Fayette County Pub. Sch. Benefits, Lexington, Ky., 1993—; bd. dirs. Ky. Tchrs. Retirement Sys., Frankfort, 2003—. Named one of Tchrs. Who Make A Difference, U. Ky., 2001; recipient Second Mile award, Fayette County Pub. Sch., 1997—98; Auoobon scholar, 1991. Mem.: Alpha Delta Kappa. Democrat. Roman Catholic. Avocations: running, travel, photography. Office: Family Care Ctr 1135 Reo Mile Pl Lexington KY 40504 Office Phone: 859-288-4040. Office Fax: 859-288-4061. Business E-Mail: lzimmerm@fayette.k12.ky.us.

ZIMMERMAN, LISA A., music educator; b. Knox, Pa., June 6, 1975; d. Kenneth E. and Linda A. Mays; m. Kenneth D. Zimmerman, June 26, 1999; 1 child, Kaleb M. BS Elem. Edn., BS Music Edn., Clarion U. Pa., 1998; MusM Edn., West Chester U. Pa, 2001. Cert. Profl. Tchr. Pa., 1998. Tchr. elem. music Beaver Creek Elem., Downingtown, Pa., 1998—. Dir. chorus Beaver Creek Elem., Downingtown, Pa., 1998—; dean student activities Summer Inst. Gifted, Parsippany, NJ, 2004. Musician: (singer) Vocal Ensemble. Mem.: Pa. State Edn. Assn. Office: Downingtown Area School District 601 W Pa Ave Downingtown PA 17519 E-mail: lzimmerman@dasd.org.

ZIMMERMAN, MARY ALICE, performing arts educator; BA, MA, PhD, Northwestern U. Asst. prof. performance studies Northwestern U., Evanston, Ill.; artistic assoc. Goodman and Seattle Repertory Theater; mem. Lookingglass Theater Company, Chicago. Dir.: (plays) The Notebooks of Leonardo da Vinci, The Odyssey, Arabian Nights, Journey to the West, Metamorphoses (Tony award best dir., 2002), Secret in the Wings, Eleven Rooms of Proust, Measure for Measure, Henry VIII, A Midsummer Night's Dream, All's Well That Ends Well, Argonautika, 2006. Active Lookingglass Theatre Co. Recipient MacArthur Fellowship, 1998, 20 Joseph Jefferson Awards for best direction. Fellow: Am. Acad. Arts & Sci. Office: Dept Performance Studies Northwestern U 1920 Campus D Evanston IL 60208*

ZIMMERMAN, MELVA JEAN, journalist, retired audio-visual specialist; b. El Dorado, Ks., Mar. 3, 1941; d. Virgil Leroy Zimmerman and Aldena Berneice Tidball;m. Joe Hudson Yeaman, July 6, 1968 (divorced June 1980). BA, Kansas State U., 1963; MA, U. Colo., 1970, EdS, 1973. Tchr. Jefferson County Schs., Golden, Colo., 1963-71, libr. media splst., 1971-95. Co-chaired 1976 state Conv. Colo. Assn. Sch. Librs., 1976; mem. Colo. Assn. Sch. Librs., 1971-95 (v.p. 1979-80), Jefferson County Ed. Assn. (sec. 1980-82) Lakewood. Colo., 1968-95. Contbr. chpt. to book; columnist Insight, 1983-95. Docent Wichita (Kans.) Art Mus., 1996—, events chair, 2003-04, pres.-elect, 2006—, campaign treas. sch. bd. candidate, 1997, Kans. state legis. candidate, 1998, 2000, 04; mem. Sedgwick County Dem. Party; treas. Ambassadors' Polit. Action Com., 2000—. Recipient Lifetime Achievement award, Jefferson County Edn. Assn., Jeffey award for outstanding svc., Statewide Lion award, Colo. Edn. Assn. Mem. AAUW (treas. Wichita chpt. 2000-04), Sedgwick County Fedn. Dem. Women's Clubs (sec. 1998-2001, auditor 2001—). Home: 6704 Pepperwood Ct Wichita KS 67226-1609

ZIMMERMAN, NANCY PICCIANO, library and information scientist, educator; b. Jeannette, Pa., July 29, 1951; d. Daniel Joseph and Helen Elizabeth (Lipinski) Picciano; m. Lee W. Zimmerman, Aug. 10, 1974; children: Matthew, Renée. BA in English, Carlow Coll., Pitts., 1973; MLS in Libr. Sci., U. Pitts., 1974; MS in Computer Edn. and Cognitive Sys., U. North Tex., 1992; PhD in Libr. and Info. Studies, Tex. Woman's U., 1992. Lic. libr. media specialist, K-12, lang. arts/English 7-12. Libr. media specialist Fairfield (Calif.)-Suisun Sch. Dist., 1976-78; reference libr. Pikes Peak Libr. Dist., Colorado Springs, Colo., 1983; libr. media specialist North Pole (Alaska) H.S., 1984-85, Prince William County Schs., Woodbridge, Va., 1985-89; dir. info. retrieval lab. Tex. Woman's U., Denton, 1989-91; adj. prof., rsch. assoc. U. North Tex., Denton, 1991-92; from asst. to assoc. prof. Sch. Info. and Libr. Studies SUNY, Buffalo, 1993-99; assoc. prof. Sch. Libr. and Info. Scis. U. S.C., Columbia, 1999—. ALISE/OCLC rsch. grantee, 1994, 2004. Mem. ALA (coun. 2000—, chair Libr. Rsch. Round Table 1995-96, com. profl. ethics, 2006-), Am. Assn. Sch. Librs. (treas. 1996-99, pres. 2002-2003, exec. bd. 1996-99, 2001-04), Internat. Assn. Sch. Librs., N.Y. Libr. Assn. (pres. 1999), Nat. Bd. for Profl. Tchg. Stds. (sch. libr. media com. 1997-2000), Phi Delta Kappa, Beta Phi Mu (nat. exec. coun. 1994-99). Office: U SC Sch Libr and Info Scis 217 Davis Coll Columbia SC 29208-0001 Office Phone: 803-777-1215. Business E-Mail: nzimmerman@gwm.sc.edu.

ZIMMERMAN, PHYLLIS ELAINE, music educator, composer, director; b. Pitts., Feb. 22, 1934; d. William H. and Isabelle Anderson Zimmerman. BA in Sociology, Thiel Coll., 1956; BA in Vocal Performance, Concordia Coll., 1959; student in Voice, U. Colo., 1966; student in Choral Techniques and Voice, Meadowbrook Sch. Music, 1967; student in Music, Choral Conducting, Choral Technique & Voice, Occidental Coll., 1968—69. Dir. choral Wellsville (Ohio) H.S., 1959—63, Churchill Area H.S., Pitts., 1963—68; thr. music, dir. choral Santa Barbara (Calif.) H.S., 1969—95; founder, artistic dir. Canticle A Cappella Choir, Santa Barbara, 1995—. Dir. madrigal singers Santa Barbara H.S. Choir, 1969—95, dir. concert tours, 1972—92. Dir.(prodr.): (compact disc) Earth Chants, 1994, Canticle, 1996, My Song in the Night, 2000, O Wondrous Mystery, 2003, Phoenix (27 original compositions and arrangements), 2004, Every Time I Feel the Spirit, 2006; composer: (songs) Seasons of his Mercies, 2003, Four Songs of Concord, 2005, Four Lyrics of Sara Teasdale, 2006. Named Local Hero, Santa Barbara (Calif.) Ind., 1995; recipient Outstanding Contbn. to Cmty. award, Santa Barbara (Calif.) City Coun., 2004, Disting. Alumni award, Concordia Coll., 2006. Mem.: Am. Choral Dirs. Assn. (performer).

ZIMMERMAN, SHIRLEY LEE, family social science educator, researcher; b. Mpls., Nov. 23, 1925; m. Peter David Zimmerman, Aug. 3, 1947; children: Michael, Daniel, Kevin, Julie. BA in Sociology, U. Minn., 1947, MSW, PhD, U. Minn., 1977, postgrad., 1977-78. Social worker Hennepin County Dept. Pub. Welfare, Mpls., 1947-49; child welfare cons. Minn. Dept. Pub. Welfare, St. Paul, 1967-69; planner United Way, St. Paul, 1969-70; asst. dir.continuing edn. U. Minn., Mpls., 1970-84, prof. family social sci., 1984—2000, prof. emeritus, 2000—. Cons. Northstar Rsch. Inst., Mpls., 1969, Interstudy, Mpls., 1973-76. Author: Understanding Family Policy, 1988, Family Policies and Family Well-Being: The Role of Political Culture, 1992, Understanding Family Policy: Theories and Applications, 1995, Family Policy: Constructed Solutions To Family Problems, 2001; contbr. numerous articles to profl. jours. NIMH fellow, 1977-78. Mem. NASW, Nat. Coun. on Family Rels. (chmn., bd. dirs. family policy sect. 1989—, guest editor family rels. jours. 1990, program v.p. 1995-96), Policy Studies Orgn. Democrat. Avocations: music, theater, family, writing. Home: 3843 Glenhurst Ave Minneapolis MN 55416-4915 Office Phone: 612-625-5289.

ZIMMERMANN, BONNIE, physical and health education educator; d. Jack and Bette Tokar; m. Bill Zimmermann; 1 child, Eric. BS in Mktg., LaSalle U., Phila., 1982; BS in Exercise and Movement Sci., William Paterson U., Wayne, N.J., 2000. Fragrance buyer Abraham & Straus, Bklyn., 1982—86; ter. mgr. Calvin Klein Cosmetics, N.Y.C., 1986—89; tchr. phys. edn. and health Glen Rock H.S., NJ, 2000—. Named N.J. Gov. Tchr. of Yr., Glen Rock H.S., 2006; recipient Presdl. Scholarship award, Am. AAHPERD, 2000, Robert Pate Scholarship award, AAHPERD Ea. Dist. Assn., 2000.

ZIMMERMANN, ELÉONORE M., French and comparative literature educator; b. Oct. 2, 1931; came to U.S., 1949; d. Harry W. and Alice (Dreher) Z. BA, Swarthmore Coll., 1951; MA, Yale U., 1953, PhD, 1956. Mem. faculty Wellesley (Mass.) Coll., 1956-59, Brandeis U., Waltham, Mass., 1959-65, Rochester (N.Y.) U., 1966-72; prof. French and comparative lit. SUNY, Stony Brook, N.Y., 1972—, chmn., 1973-77, dir. grad. studies, 1973—78, 1980—83, 1985; ret., 1996. Author: Magies de Verlaine, 1967, 2d edit., 1981, La Liberté et le destin dans le théâtre de J. Racine, 1982, Poétiques de Baudelaize, dansles Fleurs du mal rythme, parfum, liquer, 1998; contbr. articles and book revs. to profl. publs. Decorated chevalier Palmes Académiques (France), 1977; Am. Coun. Learned Socs. fellow, 1963-64, Guggenheim Found. fellow 1971-72 Mem. AAUP, MLA, Am. Assn. Tchrs. French, Internat. Comparative Lit. Assn., Am. Comparative Lit. Assn., Assn. internat. des études françaises, N.Am. Soc. 17th Century Lit., Soc. des profs. français et francophone d'Amérique, Phi Beta Kappa. Office: SUNY Dept French Italian Stony Brook NY 11794-0001

ZIMMERN-REED, ANNETTE WACKS, psychologist; b. Exeter, Va., Feb. 7, 1933; d. Samuel Cleve and Zella Edith (Nelson) Wacks; m. James Robert Reed; children: Kenneth Zimmern, Ronald Zimmern stepchildren: Susan, Kathleen. RN, Sinai Hosp. Sch. Nursing, 1954; BA, U. Md., 1969, MA, 1971, PhD, 1975. RN Md.; lic. Family-Marriage Therapist Tex. Capt., dir. substance abuse, dir. mental health divsn. USPHS, Rockville, Md., 1976—96. Asst. prof. dept. psychiatry divsn. psychology U. Tex., Dallas, 1985. Author: Violence in America, 1986. Fellow: Am. Assn. Marriage and Family Therapists; mem.: Am. Counselors Assn. Avocations: swimming, reading, writing. Address: PO Box 5116 Johnson City TN 37602-5116

ZIMPHER, NANCY LUSK, academic administrator; b. Gallipolis, Ohio, Oct. 29, 1946; d. Aven Denzle and Elsie Gordon (Hammond) L.; 1 child from a previous marriage, William Fletcher Zimpher; m. Kenneth R. Howey, May 8, 1987. BS, Ohio State U., 1968, MA, 1971, PhD, 1976. Cert. K-12 Tchr., Ohio. English tchr. Montgomery County Schs., Md., 1968, Reynoldsburg (Ohio) Schs., 1970; substitute tchr. Rolla (Mo.) City Schs., 1970-71; tchr. Phelps County Schs., Mo., 1971-72; grad. teaching assoc. Coll. Edn. Ohio State U., Columbus, 1972-73; dir. Coll. of Edn. Ohio State U., Columbus, 1973-74, grad. adminstrn. asst. to dean, 1974-76, dir. field experiences alumni rels., 1976-80, coord. undergraduate programs, 1980-84; asst. prof. Ednl. Policy and Leadership Ohio State U., 1984-86, assoc. prof., 1986-91, full prof., 1991-98, assoc. dean, 1992, dean, 1993, exec. dean, 1994; chancellor, prof. curriculum and instrn. U. Wis., Milw., 1998—2003; pres. U. Cincinnati, 2003—. Prin. investigator U.S. Office Edn. Field Devel. Grant, 1981-83, 85-88; co-principal investigator Metro. Life Found. Grant. 1989—, 1992—; cons. The Holmes Group, Lansing, Mich., 1991—. Book rev., editor: Journal of Teacher Education, 1986-89; co-author: Book Profiles of Preservice Teacher Education, 1989, RATE Profiles, 1987-92. Chair Faculty Compensation and Benefits Commn., 1989-90, Fiscal Com., 1991-92, Spousal Equivalency Com., 1990-91, Search Com., v.p. for Fin., 1992, Ohio State U; pres., chair bd. dirs. Holmes Partnership, 1997; chair edn. vision coun. United Way Franklin County, 1997; chair bd. dirs. United Way Franklin County, 1998. Fellow Com. for Instnl. Coop., Acad. Leadership Program. 1989-90; recipient Disting. Rsch. award, Disting. Teacher Educator award Assn. Tchr. Educators, 1990, Adams Professorshi Coll. Edn. Ind. State U., 1990—, Alumni Disting. Tchg. award, The Ohio State U., 1992, Chief Exec. Leadership award Coun. for the Advancement and Support Edn., 2003, Career Woman of Achievement award YWCA, 2004, Profl. Achievement award Ohio State U., 2004; named YWCA Woman of Achievement, 1997. Mem. Am. Edn. Rsch. Assn., Am. Assn. Coll. Teacher Edn. Rsch. Comm., Assn. Tchr. Educators, ASCD, Phi Delta Kappa. Episcopalian. Avocations: watercolorist, golf, sewing. Office: Univ Cin 625 Univ Pavilion PO Box 210063 Cincinnati OH 45221-0063

ZINBERG, DOROTHY SHORE, sociologist, educator; b. Boston; m. Norman E Zinberg (dec.); children: Sarah Zinberg Mandel, Anne. BA, MA, Boston U.; PhD, Harvard U., 1966. Research chemist Lever Bros., Cambridge; sr. research assoc. Daniel Yankelovich, Inc., N.Y.C., and; Cambridge Center for Research in Behavioral Scis., 1966-68; NSF research sociologist dept. chemistry U. Coll. London, 1968-69; lectr. Harvard U., 1960—. Mem. adv. com. Office Sci. Pers. NRC, Washington, 1971—74, bd. on engring. edn., 1991; spl. adviser Aspen Inst.; cons. MacArthur Found., 1989—93; vis. scholar NAS, China, 1987, Nat. Inst. Sci. and Tech., Tokyo, 1991; vis. lectr. Inst. for Human Scis., Vienna, 1995; mem. adv. bd. Erik Erikson Inst. for Edn. and Rsch., 1996—; vis. prof. Imperial Coll., London, 2001—04; assoc. Whitehead Inst. Biomed. Rsch., MIT, 2004—; vis. sr. fellow U. Coll. London, 2006—. Columnist: London Times Higher Educ Supplement, 1993—2001, NY Times Syndication, 1994—96. Mem. internat. sci. exchs. NAS, 1994—96, mem comt int relations, 1977—80, mem comt int human resources; chmn adv coun int div NSF, 1978—81; mem coun Int Exchange Scholars, 1978—81; mem comt int exchange engrs NAE, 1987—88; mem adv panel Office Technology Assessment Educ and Employment Scientists and Engrs, 1986—88; trustee Simon's Rock Col, 1971—75; mem panel sci and tech policy NATO, 1995—99; bd. dirs. Fine Arts Workshop, Provincetown, Mass., 1970—86, Bill T. Jones Found for Dance Promotion, 1997—99; bd dirs Gen Scanning, Inc, 1998—99; bd dirs eng educ NRC, 1990—95. Fellow: AAAS (mem comt sci freedom and responsibility 1972—74, comt opportunities in sci 1973—76, comt sci, eng, and pub policy 1982—88, com. exch. scientists with Fed. Republic Germany 1987—91, 1991); mem.: NAS (com. to evaluate Internat. Sci. and Tech. Ctr. Moscow 1995—97), Int Sci Policy Found (adv. bd. 1988—2004), Coun Foreign Relations, Fedn. Am. Scientists (mem. coun. 1980—85, bd. talking sci.). Home: 3 Acacia St Cambridge MA 02138-4818 Office: Harvard U 79 JF Kennedy St Cambridge MA 02138 E-mail: dorothy_zinberg@harvard.edu.

ZINECKER, TRICIA JOLENE, music educator; b. Springfield, Mo., Aug. 3, 1966; d. Chesley Junior Wiggins and Jacquelyn Kay (Hamilton) Hamilton; m. James Paul Zinecker, Aug. 11, 1990. MusB, Drury U., 1988; MusM, Northwestern U., 1989. Cert. elem. tchr., Mo., Tex. Music tchr. Collins Intermediate Sch., The Woodlands, Tex., 1990—98, Republic (Mo.) Schs., 1998—. Soprano soloist, Tex., 1990—; pvt. voice tchr., Spring, Tex., 1990—; tchr. voice Drury U., 2000-03. Dir. choir Christ Episc. Ch., Springfield, Mo. Mem. Nat. Assn. Tchrs. of Singing, Mo. Music Educators Assn. (elem. honor choir dir. Tex. chpt. 1994), Mo. Choral Dir. Assn., Sigma Alpha Iota, Kappa Delta Pi. Democratic. Episcopalian. Avocations: dance, reading, antiques. Office: Republic Schools 517 E Hadley Republic MO 65738

ZINK, BRENDA LEE, biology professor; b. Denver, July 26, 1969; d. Thomas Eugene and Janice Lorraine Krieger; m. Paul Albert Zink, June 22, 1991; children: Austin, Adam. AS, Northeastern Jr. Coll., Sterling, Colo., 1989; BS in Biology, U. No. Colo., Greeley, 1991, MA in Biology, 1994. Tchr. Sterling Mid. Sch., 1991—96; assoc. prof., dept. chair Northeastern Jr. Coll., 1996—. Mem. adv. bd. Northeastern Jr. Coll., 2005—06. Coach Sterling Baseball Orgn., 2001—; active bible sch. classes United Ch. Christ, Crook, 2001—. Grantee, Northeastern Jr. Coll., 1996—. Mem.: Northeastern Jr. Coll. Faculty Assn. (pres., sec.), Colo. Assn. Biology Tchrs. Avocations: walking, reading, travel. Office: Northeastern Jr Coll 100 College Ave Sterling CO 80751

ZINNES, ALICE FICH, artist, educator; b. Norman, Okla., June 24, 1956; d. Irving I. and Harriet F. (Fich) Z BA Art History, Swarthmore Coll., 1977; cert. merit in painting, N.Y. Studio Sch., N.Y.C., 1977—80; postgrad., Skowhegan Sch. Art, Maine, 1980; MFA Painting, Queens Coll., CUNY, 1982. Tchr. Pratt Inst., Bklyn., 1999—. Tchr. N.Y.C. Tech. Coll., CUNY, Bklyn., 1983—88, Bklyn., 1997—, Baruch Coll., CUNY, N.Y.C., 1986, N.Y.C., 1988—97, Coll. S.I., CUNY, 1987—2001, Bklyn. Coll., 1998; guest lectr., vis. critic Millersville U., Pa., 1992, 93, 97, Dartmouth Coll., Hanover, NH, 1997; curator Frankel Pariser & Rudder, N.Y.C., 1994—97; vis. critic N.Y. Studio Sch., N.Y.C., 1997. One-woman shows include Queens Coll. Gallery, 1982, 2002, Swarthmore Coll., 1987, Frankel Pariser & Rudder, 1993, Dartmouth Coll., 1997, Tribes Gallery, N.Y.C., 1998, 2002, Hopper House, Nyack, N.Y., 2002, exhibited in group shows at Millersville U., 1992, Greenwich House, N.Y.C., 1992, Nat. Acad. Design, 1992, 1994, 1996, Tribeca 148 Gallery, 1992, 1996, 2000, N.Y. Studio Sch., 1993, 1995—2001, Bowery Gallery, N.Y.C., 1993, 1995, Salena Gallery-L.I. U., Bklyn., 1994, 1997, Art Showcase, The Bond Market, N.Y.C., 1998, Elsa Mott Ives Gallery, 1997, 1999, 2001, Grace Gallery, N.Y.C. Tech. Coll., Bklyn., 1999, Artist Space, N.Y.C., 1999, Simon Gallery, Morristown, N.J., 2000, 55 Mercer Gallery, N.Y.C., 2000, William Paterson U., N.J., 2000, Contemporary Mus., Balt., 2000, Key Span Corp. Galleries, Bklyn., 2000, Piergo, 2000—, Seton Hall U., Newark, 2000, NYU, 2000, Drawing Ctr. Registry, N.Y.C., 2001—, John Elder Gallery, 2001, Chelsea Pier 60, 2001, Exit Art, 2002, Sperone Westwater Gallery, 2002, Ayce de Roulet Williamson Gallery, Pasadena, Calif., 2002, Artisi Space, N.Y.C., 2004, Brent Sikkeme Gallery, 2004, Del. Arts Coun., Narrowsburg, N.Y., 2005, Times Square Lobby Gallery, N.Y.C., 2005, Pratt Inst., 2005, Painting Ctr., 2005, Lori Bookstein Fine Art, 2005. Named Barklie McKee Henry Meml. scholar, Skowhegan Sch. Art, 1980, Residency fellow, Va. Ctr. for the Creative Arts, Sweet Briar, 1992, 1997, 1999, 2001, Cummington (Mass.) Cmty. Arts, 1993; recipient Julius Hallgarten prize, Nat. Acad. Design, N.Y.C., 1988, 1990. Avocations: swimming, hiking. Home: 457 15th St Apt 5D Brooklyn NY 11215-5734 Office: NYC Tech Coll 300 Jay St Brooklyn NY 11201-1909

ZINNES, HARRIET FICH, poet, fiction writer, retired English educator, literary and art critic; b. Boston; d. Assir and Sarah (Goldberg) Fich; m. Irving I. Zinnes, Sept. 24, 1943 (dec. 1979); children: Clifford, Alice. BA cum laude, CUNY, 1939, MA, 1944; PhD, NYU, 1953. Editor publs. divsn. Raritan (N.J.) Arsenal, 1942-43; assoc. editor Harper's Bazaar, N.Y.C., 1944-46; tutor Hunter Coll. CUNY, N.Y.C., 1946-49; asst. prof. Queens Coll. CUNY, Flushing, 1949-53, assoc. prof., 1962-78, full prof., 1978-89, prof. emerita, 1989—; lectr. in English Rutgers U., New Brunswick, N.J., 1961-62. Vis. prof. Am. lit. U. Geneva, 1968. Author: Waiting and Other Poems, 1964, An Eye for an I, 1966, I Wanted to See Something Flying, 1976, Entropisms, 1978, Book of Ten, 1981, Lover: Short Stories, 1988, Book of Twenty, 1992, My, Haven't the Flowers Been?, 1995, The Radiant Absurdity of Desire, 1998, Plunge, 2001, Drawing on the Wall: Poems, 2002, Whither Nonstopping, 2005; editor: Ezra Pound and the Visual Arts, 1980; translator Blood and Feathers: Selected Poems of Jacques Prevert, 1988, rev. edit., 1993; contr. editor, Hollin's Critic, Denver Quarterly; contr. writer, N.Y. Arts Mag.; author numerous poems; contbr. articles to popular mags. MacDowell Art Colony fellow, 1972-74, 77, 2004, Yaddo fellow, 1978, 81, Va. Ctr. for Creative Arts fellow, 1975-76, 81-82, 84, 86, 88-93, resident fellow, Djerassi Found., 1990, La Napoul, 2002; Am. Coun. Learned Socs. grantee, 1978, CUNY summer grantee, 1979, 81, 86. Fellow Poets Editors & Novelists, Nat. Book Critics Circle, Acad. Am. Poets, Internat. Assn. Art Critics, Poetry Soc. Am.; mem. Phi Beta Kappa. Home: 25 W 54th St New York NY 10019-5404 Office: Dept English Queens Coll Flushing NY 11367 Office Phone: 212-582-8315. Personal E-mail: hzinnes@rcn.com.

ZINS, MARTHA LEE, elementary school educator, director; b. Mankato, Minn., Dec. 14, 1945; d. Hubert Joseph and Rose Marie (Johannes) Z. BS in History, Mankato State U., 1966, BA in English, 1967; MLS, Western Mich. U., 1971; postgrad., U. Minn. Tchr. history Worthington H.S., Minn., 1966-67; sch. media generalist Hopkins West Jr. H.S., Minn., 1967-83, Curren Elem. Sch., Hopkins, Minn., 1986—2005; dir. media svcs. Hopkins Sch. Dist., Minn., 2003—. Mem. Hopkins Dist. Tech. Com., 1986—; co-chair Hopkins Elem. Sci. Com., 1991—94; tchr. English, tchr. training (media portion) various tchg. groups, Thailand, 1998—. Contbr. articles to profl. jours.; presenter and speaker at confs. Pres. Saddlewood Patio Homes Assn. Inc., Minnetonka, 1991-95, bd. dirs., 1987-95, bd. dirs., 2003-; mem. various Minn. Gov.'s Task Forces; del. Ngo Forum 95, Beijing; mem. WILPF's Internat. Peace Train (Helsinki to Beijing), 1995; co-chair Minn. Metro WilPF, 1998-99; mem. Metronet Adv. Com., 1994-96; treas. Metro West Uniserv (Edn. Minn.), 1998—; organizer Hopkins Edn. Assn. Thailand Minn. Tchrs. Exch. Program, Minn. State U. Mem. NEA (bd. dirs. 1976-77, 91-97, Woman Educator of Yr. 1975), ALA, ACLU, Minn. Edn. Assn. (bd. dirs. 1975-86, 91-97, v.p. 1977-83, pres. 1983-86, Human Rels. award 1979), Minn. Civil Liberties Union (bd. dirs. 1982-95), State of Minn. Tchrs. Retirement Assn. (bd. dirs. 1989—, v.p. bd. 2003—), Minn. Ednl. Media Orgn. (co-founder, treas. 1990), Nat. Coun. Tchr. Retirement (trustee edn. com., 2005—), Delta Kappa Gamma (Beta Beta chpt., co-founder, chpt. treas.), Beta Phi Mu, Phi Alpha Theta. Mem. Dem. Farm Labor Party. Roman Catholic. Avocations: travel, reading, photography, volunteer work, environmental/hunger concerns. Home: 17509 Saddlewood Ln Minnetonka MN 55345-2663 Office: District Media Svcs 1001 State Hwy 7 Rm 96A Hopkins MN 55305 Personal E-mail: mzins@mn.rr.com. Business E-Mail: marti_zins@hopkins.k12.mn.us.

ZINSER, ELISABETH ANN, academic administrator; b. Meadville, Pa., Feb. 20, 1940; d. Merle and Fae Zinser. BS, Stanford U., 1964; MS, U. Calif., San Francisco, 1966, MIT, 1982; PhD, U. Calif., Berkeley, 1972. Nurse VA Hosp., Palo Alto, Calif., 1964-65, San Francisco, 1969-70; instr. Sch. Nursing U. Calif., San Francisco, 1966-69; pre-doctoral fellow Nat. Inst. Health, Edn. and Welfare, 1971-72; adminstr. Sch. Medicine U. Wash., Seattle, 1972-75, Coun. Higher Edn., State of Ky., 1975-77; prof., dean. Coll. Nursing U. N.D., Grand Forks, 1977-83; vice chancellor acad. affairs U. N.C., Greensboro, 1983-89; pres. Gallaudet U., Washington, 1988, U. Idaho, Moscow, 1989-95; chancellor U. Ky., Lexington, 1995—2001; pres. So. Oreg. Univ., Ashland, 2001—. Bd. dir. Assoc. Am. Coll. & Univ., 1999—, Am. Council Edn., Nat Assoc. State Univ. & Land Grant Coll.; bd. mem. Ctr. on Academic Integrity; past chmn. Commn. Outreach & Tech. Transfer. Primary author: (with others) Contemporary Issues in Higher Education, 1985, Higher Education Research, 1988; spkr. in field. Mem. Oreg. Women's Forum; bd. mem. Ashland C. of C., Oreg. Shakespeare Festival, Crater Lake Nat. Park Trust. Leadership fellow Bush Found., 1981-82. Office: So Oregon Univ 1250 Siskiyou Blvd Ashland OR 97520

ZIRBES, MARY KENNETH, retired minister; b. Melrose, Minn., Sept. 4, 1926; d. Joseph Louis and Clara Bernadine (Petermeier) Z. BA in History and Edn., Coll. St. Catherine, 1960; MA in Applied Theology, Sch. Applied Theology, Berkeley, Calif., 1976. Joined Order of St. Francis, Roman Cath. Ch., 1945. Tchr. Pub. Grade Sch., St. Nicholas, Minn., 1947-52; prin. Holy Spirit Grade Sch., St. Cloud, Minn., 1953-59, St. Mary's Jr. H.S., Morris, Minn., 1960-62; coord. Franciscan Mission Team, Peru, South America, 1962-67, Franciscan Missions, Little Falls, Minn., 1967-70; dir. St. Richard's Social Justice Ministry, Richfield, Minn., 1971-80, Parish Community Devel., St. Paul, Mpls., Minn., 1980-85; councillor gen. Franciscan Sisters of Little Falls, 1960-62, 67-70; asst. dir. Renew-Archdiocese of St. Paul-Mpls., 1986-89; coord. Parish Social Justice Ministry-Archdiocese of St. Paul-Mpls., 1990-93; min. Franciscan Assocs., 1993—2003; leader of team on evangelical life Franciscan Sisters of Little Falls, 1994-96; ret., 2003. Co-developer Assn. of Pastoral Ministers, Mpls., St. Paul, 1979-81, Compañeros/Sister Parishes-Minn. and Nicaragua, 1984-89, Minn. Interfaith Ecology Coalition, 1989-92. Author: Parish Social Ministry, 1985, (manual) Acting for Justice, 1992. Organizer Twin Cities Orgn., Mpls., 1979-80; bd. dirs. Franciscan Sisters Health Care, Inc., Little Falls, 1990-93, Rice-Marion Residents Assn., St. Paul, 1991-92. Named Outstanding chair Assn. Pastoral Ministers, 1981; recipient Five Yrs. of Outstanding Svc. award Companeros, 1989. Mem. Assn. Pastoral Ministers (chair 1979), Voices for Justice-Legis. Lobby,

Audubon Soc., Network, Minn. Call to Action, Com. on Peace, Justice and Integrity of Creation, Joint Religious Legislation Coalition. Avocations: water color painting, birding, golf, reading history and biography. E-mail: sebri02@charter.net.

ZIRINSKY, SUSAN, television producer; m. Joe Peyronnin; 1 child, Zoe. Grad., Am. U. Sr. prodr. CBS Evening News, 1986-91, sr. broadcast prodr., 1991-93; sr. prodr. Eye to Eye, 1993-94, exec. prodr., 1994-95, CBS News, 48 Hours, N.Y.C., 1996—. Sr. prodr. CBS News coverage of 1992 Olympic Winter Games, Campaign '96. Co-recipient Edward R. Murrow award, Overseas Press Club, 2006. Office: CBS News 48 Hours 524 W 57th St Fl 5 New York NY 10019-2924

ZIRNHELD, JENNIFER L., engineering educator, researcher; b. Buffalo, May 12, 1969; d. Mark D. McMahon and Carolyn V. Pfeil; m. Mark J. Zirnheld, May 22, 1993. BSEE, SUNY, Buffalo, 1993, MS, 1997, PhD, 2004. Lectr. SUNY, Buffalo, 1997—2004; co-prin., investigator, dep. dir. Energy Systems Inst., 2005—. Contbr. articles to profl. jours. Recipient Milton Plesur award, U. Buffalo Student Assn., 2000—01; Bergquist Doctoral fellow, SUNY, Buffalo, 1998—2002, James Clerk Maxwell Primex doctoral fellow, 2000—01. Mem.: IEEE (treas. 2000, newsletter editor 2000—, chair 2001—02), Am. Phys. Soc., Am. Soc. Engring. Edn., Eta Kappa Nu. Office: U Buffalo 312 Bonner Hall Buffalo NY 14260 Business E-Mail: zirnheld@eng.buffalo.edu.

ZISKIN, LAURA, television producer, film producer; Grad., USC, 1973. Asst. to Jon Peters; co-founder Frogwood Films, 1984; founder, pres. Fox 2000, Beverly Hills, Calif., 1994—99; founder Laura Ziskin Productions, 1999—. Films include: (assoc. prodr.) Eyes of Laura Mars, 1978; (prodr.) Murphy's Romance, 1985, No Way Out, 1987, D.O.A., 1988, Everybody's An American, 1988, The Rescue, 1988, What About Bob?, 1991, The Doctor, 1991, Hero, 1992, To Die For, 1995, Spider-Man, 2002, Spider-Man 2, 2004; (exec. prodr.) Pretty Woman, 1990, As Good As it Gets, 1997; (TV) Fail Safe, 2000, Dinner with Friends, 2001, 74th Ann. Acad. awards, 2002, Tarzan, 2003, The Spaces, 2003., prodr.(TV) How I Learned to Drive, 2001. Named one of 100 Most Powerful Women in Entertainment, Hollywood Reporter, 2004, 2005. Office: Laura Ziskin Prodns 10201 W Washington Blvd Astaire Bldg Culver City CA 90232 Office Phone: 310-244-7373. Office Fax: 310-244-0073.*

ZITO, RAE NANETTE, elementary school educator; b. Salt Lake, Utah, May 27; d. Grant Ludlow Cope and Mara Ardell Swain; m. Robert Waldemar Zito, Dec. 18, 1959; children: Penni Rae, Angela Dawne, Robert Grant. BSc cum laude, U. Utah, 1959, MS in Elem. Edn., 1987, cert. in Gerontology, 1989, MPhil in Health Edn., 1993. Tchr. Elem. Sch. Murray Dist. Schs., Salt Lake City, 1958—59, Salt Lake (Utah) Dist. Schs., 1959—61, Granite Dist. Schs., Salt Lake City, 1961—99. Vol. ARC, Salt Lake City, 1957—60; bd. dirs. Women's State Legis. Coun., 2001—05; specialist family history ctr. LDS Ch., Salt Lake City, 2003—05. Named Woman of Yr., Delta Kappa Gamma, 2004, Outstanding Vol., Retirement Inn, 1993; recipient award, Utah State Legis., 1994; scholar, PTA, 1955, Delta Kappa Gamma, 1985. Mem.: Learning Disabilities Assn. Utah (pres. 2002—05). Democrat. Mem. Lds Ch. Avocations: bicycling, golf, reading, knitting, marathon running.

ZITTEL, ANDREA, painter, sculptor; b. Escondido, Calif., 1965; BFA in Painting & Sculpture, San Diego State U., 1988; MFA in Sculpture, RI Sch. Design, 1990. Founder A-Z Adminstrv. Svcs., 1992—; co-organizer High Desert Test Sites. One-man shows include A-Z Living Units, Jack Hanley Gallery, San Francisco, 1993, A-Z Carpet Furniture, Christopher Grimes Gallery, Santa Monica, Calif., 1993, one-woman shows include Purity, Andrea Rosen Gallery, NY, 1993, Comfort, Anthony d'Offay Gallery, London, 1994, Three Living Systems, Carnegie Mus. Art, Pitts., 1994, A series of rotating installations, Andrea Rosen Gallery, NY, 1994, 1995, New Work, San Francisco Mus. Modern Art, 1995, Social Fictions, Barbara & Steven Grossman Gallery, Sch. Mus. Fine Arts, Boston, 1996, New Art 6, Cin. Art Mus., 1996, A-Z Travel Trailer Units, La. Mus. Modern Art, Humlebaek, Denmark, 1996, A-Z Escape Vehicles, Andrea Rosen Gallery, NY, 1996, RAUGH, 1998, A-Z Personal Panels, Sadie Coles HQ, London, 1999, Point of Interest, Public Art Fund, Central Park, NY, 1999, A-Z Time Trials: Free Running Rhythms, Regen Projects, LA, 2000, A-Z Sorting Trays, Susan Inglett, NY, 2001, Andrea Rosen Gallery, NY, 2002, Regen Projects, LA, 2002, Philomene Magers Projekte, Munich, Germany, 2003, Sammlung Goetz, Munich, Germany, 2003, Small Liberties, Whitney Mus. Am. Art, NYC, 2006, exhibited in group shows at Ornament: Ho Hum All Ye Faithfull, John Post Lee Gallery, NY, 1991, One Leading to Another, 303 Gallery, NY, 1992, Writing on the Wall, 1992, Radio Show, Artist's Space, NY, 1992, Add Hot Water, Sandra Gering Gallery, NY, 1993, Don't Look Now, Thread Waxing Space, NY, 1994, Sense & Sensibility, Mus. Modern Art, NY, 1994, Light for the Dark Days of Winter, A/D Gallery, NY, 1995, About Place: Recent Art of Am., Art Inst. Chgo., 1995, Whitney Biennial, Whitney Mus. Am. Art, NY, 1995, 2004, Just Past, Mus. Contemporary Art, LA, 1996, Staging Surrealism, Wexner Ctr. Arts, Ohio, 1997, Patrick Painter Editions, Lehmann-Maupin Gallery, NY, 1997, Travel & Leisure, Paula Cooper Gallery, NY, 1998, Inglenook, Feigen Contemporary, NY, 1998, Art in Pub. Places at Miami Design District, Dacra Companies, Miami Beach, 1999, Elysian Fields, Centre Georges Pompidou, Paris, 2000, Threshold: Invoking Domestic in Contemporary Art, Contemporary Art Ctr. Va., 2000, Drawings, Regen Projects, LA, 2001, Against Design, Mus. Contemporary Art, San Diego, Calif., 2001, Everything Can Be Different, Calif. Ctr. Arts, 2002, Tempo, Mus. Modern Art, NY, 2002, Just Love Me, Bergen Art Mus., 2003, Living Units, Triple Candie, Harlem, NY, 2003, and others. Recipient Distinction Art, San Diego State U., 1988, Award Excellence, RI Sch. Design, 1989, 1990, catalogue support prize, Alfried Krupp Von Bohlen und Halbach Found., 1999, Lucelia Artist Award, Smithsonian Am. Art Mus., 2005; Deutschen Akademischen Austauschdienst Grant, Berlin, Germany, 1995, Coutts Contemporary Arts Found., Zurich, Switzerland, 1996. Mailing: c/o Andrea Rosen Gallery 525 West 24th St New York NY 10011*

ZITTERMAN, JOLENE LAURET, mathematics educator; m. Richard Zitterman, Oct. 3, 1998. BA in Math. and Edn., Wagner Coll., 1995; MA in Sch. Adminstrn., Stony Brook U., NY, 1998. Cert. math. tchr. 7-12 State Edn. Dept. NY, 2001. Math tchr. Longwood Ctrl. Sch. Dist., Middle Island, NY, 1998—. Student govt./coun. advisor Longwood Ctrl. Sch. Dist., 2001—05, union rep., 2002—04, cooperating tchr., 2002—06, instrnl. support team, 2003—, mstp facilitator, 2003—, lap tchr., 2003—, mentor tchr., 2004. Recipient Staff Recognition award, Nat. Jr. Honor Soc., 2005; Smart Bd. grant, Longwood Ctrl. Sch. Dist., 2005. Mem.: Omicron Delta Pi, Alethea, Kappa Delta Pi. Avocations: reading, exercise, weightlifting. Office: Longwood Ctrl Sch Dist 198 Longwood Rd Middle Island NY 11953 Office Phone: 631-345-2745. Personal E-mail: jlauretz@aol.com. E-mail: jzitterman@longwoodcsd.com.

ZOBEL, LOUISE PURWIN, author, educator, lecturer, writing consultant; b. Laredo, Tex., Jan. 10, 1922; d. Leo Max and Ethel Catherine (Levy) Purwin; m. Jerome Fremont Zobel, Nov. 14, 1943; children: Lenore Zobel Harris, Janice A., Robert E., Audrey Zobel Dollinger. BA cum laude, Stanford U., 1943, MA, 1976. Cert. adult edn. and community coll. tchr., Calif. Freelance mag. writer and author, Palo Alto, Calif., 1942—; writer, editor, broadcastor UP Bur., San Francisco, 1943; lectr. on writing, history, travel No. Calif., 1964—; lectr., educator U. Calif. campuses, other colls. and univs., 1969—; writing cons. to pvt. clients, 1969—; editorial asst. Assn. Coll. Unions Internat., Palo Alto, 1972-73; acting asst. prof. journalism San Jose State U., 1976. Coord. TV shows; TV personality publicity and public rels. campaigns; tchr. corr. classes Writer's Digest Sch.; tchr. online writing classes for Writingschool.com, 1999—; spkr., presenter in field. Author: The Travel Writer's Handbook, 1980 (hard cover), 6th edit., 2006; author, narrator: (cassette) Let's Have Fun in Japan, 1982; contbr. articles to mags. and newspapers; writer advertorials. Bd. dirs., publicity chair Friends of Palo Alto Libr., 1985—; officer Santa Clara County Med. Aux., Esther Clark Aux., others; past pres. PTA. Recipient award for excellence in journalism Sigma Delta Chi, 1943, awards Writers Digest, 1967-95, Armed Forces Writers League, 1972, Nat. Writers Club, 1976, All Nippon Airways and Japanese Nat. Tourist Orgn., 1997. Mem. Am. Soc. Journalists and Authors, Travel Journalists Guild, Internat. Food, Wine and Travel Writers Assn., Pacific Asia Travel Assn., Calif. Writers Club (v.p. 1988-89), AAUW (v.p. 1955-57, Nat. writing award 1969), Stanford Alumni Assn., Phi Beta Kappa. Avocations: travel, reading, writing, photography. Home and Office: Unit 608 23600 via Esplendor Uni Cupertino CA 95014 Office Phone: 650-944-0200. Personal E-mail: lzobelwriter@cs.com.

ZOBEL, MARGARET RIETHMEIER, retired music educator; b. Saginaw, Mich., Jan. 23, 1939; d. Raymond Henry and Irma M. (Steuber) Riethmeier; m. Glen Fred Zobel, Aug. 12, 1962; children: Ann Simonet, Martin. MusB in Edn., Valparaiso U., 1960; MusM in Edn., Ctrl. Mich. U., Mt. Pleasant, Mich., 1976; postgrad., Eastman Sch. Music, Rochester, N.Y., 1962, U. Wis., 1973; cert. in Luth. tchr. colloquy, Concordia Coll., Bronxville, N.Y., 1992. Cert. MTNA piano tchr. Mich., Fla., 1978. Piano tchr., 1960—; dir. music Our Savior Luth. Ch., St. Petersburg, Fla., 1985—97; organist, choir dir. 1st Luth. Ch., Clearwater, 1982—85; tchr. music Trinity Luth. Ch., Port Huron, Mich., 1980—82, Holland Ave Mid. Sch., Port Huron, 1982; music dir. Messiah Luth. Ch., Saginaw, 1972—80; mem. prep. divsn. staff Delta Coll., Saginaw, 1976—80; band dir. Peace Luth. Sch., Saginaw, 1975—80; music tchr. Trinity Luth. Sch., Hicksville, NY, 1961-68, 70-72; tchr. music, English L.I. Luth. HS, Brookville, NY, 1960—62; dir. music, organist, dir. adult choir and men's ensemble Christ the King Luth. Ch., Largo, Fla., 1998—2004, ret., 2004. Achievement testing chmn. Saginaw Music Tchrs., 1978—80; mem. cert. bd. Mich. Music Tchrs., 1978—80; v.p., sec., treas. Upper Pinellas Music Tchrs., Fla., 1984—90, recording sec., 2003—05, v.p., 2005; mem. Fla., Ga. dist. music task force Luth. Ch. Mo. Synod, Fla., 1994—96; adult choir rehearsal accompanist Grace Luth. Ch., St. Petersburg, Fla., 2005—. Active Saginaw Symphony Women, 1975—80; accompanist Pinellas Luth. Choir, 1986—. Named Saginaw Piano Tchr. of the Yr., Saginaw Music Tchrs., 1979; named to Outstanding Young Women Am., 1970. Mem.: Valparaiso U. Guild (dir. Mich. area 1979—81, pres. Mich. state unit 1981—82, dir. S.E. area 1984—88, nat. v.p. 1994—96, nat. pres., bd.dirs. 1996—98, pres. St. Petersburg chpt. 2004—). Avocations: reading, travel, swimming. Home: 1913 Oakdale Ln S Clearwater FL 33764-6469 Office Phone: 727-535-6042. Personal E-mail: margzobe1@peoplepc.com, gmzobel@gmail.com.

ZOBEL, MELANIE CANNON, special education educator; b. Columbia, SC, Apr. 18, 1971; d. Roy Duman and Ann Brabham Cannon; m. Charlie Zobel, May 22, 1993; children: Katherine Leann, Tyler Alan. MEd, So. Wesleyan U., 2005. Cert. Spl. Edn. SC. Spl. edn. tchr. Saluda (SC) Elem. Sch., 1993—2000, Gallman Elem. Sch., Newberry, SC, 2000—. Girl scout leader Brownie Troop 1224, Chapin, SC, 2002—06. Mem.: Coun. Exceptional Children (assoc.). Office: Gallman Elem Sch 255 Hawkins Rd Newberry SC 29108 Office Phone: 803-321-2655.

ZOBEL, RYA WEICKERT, federal judge; b. Germany, Dec. 18, 1931; AB, Radcliffe Coll., 1953; LLB, Harvard U., 1956. Bar: Mass. 1956, U.S. Dist. Ct. Mass., 1956, U.S. Ct. Appeals (1st cir.) 1967. Assoc. Hill & Barlow, Boston, 1967-73, Goodwin, Procter & Hoar, Boston, 1973-76, ptnr., 1976-79; judge U.S. Dist. Ct. Mass., Boston, 1979—; dir. Fed. Jud. Ctr., Washington, 1995-99. Mem. Boston Bar Assn., Am. Bar Found., Mass. Bar Assn., Am. Law Inst. Office: US District Ct 1 Courthouse Way Boston MA 02210-3002

ZOCCO, PATRICIA ELIZABETH, human services manager, cardiac ultrasound technologist; b. Arlington, Va., Apr. 4, 1962; d. Natale Carmen and Barbara Elizabeth Zocco; children: Richard Natale Holloway, Matthew Tyler Holloway, Brianna Taylor Buckley. BSN, Thomas Edison State Coll., 1986, BSc, 1989; RN diploma, St. Luke's Sch. Nursing, 1983. Registered diagnostic cardiac sonographer Nat. ARDMS Allentown Hosp. Sch. Nursing. EKG tech. Lehigh Valley Hosp., Allentown, Pa., 1981—89, technologist cardiac ultrasound, 1989—96, clin. care coord./mgr. diagnostic care ctr., 1996—. Cardiac ultrasound instr. Lehigh Valley Hosp., Allentown, 1992—. Author: (tng. manual) Pediatric Training Manual for Cardiac Sonographers, 2000. Mem.: ReNew 2000-St. Catharine of Sienna Cathedral (facilitator 2000—). Roman Catholic. Achievements include development of the echo performance improvement program which is responsible for maintaining the highest level of Quality Assurance in the EchoLab at LVH; This is through biweekly continuing educational meetings that are teleconferenced nationally; These meetings have been also been approved for AMA cateogory I Type CMES for Echo technologists and physicians that attend. Avocations: dance, gardening, interior decorating, piano, cooking. Office: Lehigh Valley Hosp 1200 S Cedar Blvd Allentown PA 18105 E-mail: PatriciaZocco@aol.com

ZOFFER, RACHELLE, telecommunications industry executive; b. Pitts., 1967; BS, U. Mich.; MBA, U. NC Chapel Hill. Variuos mgmt. positions Oracle, The Walt Disney Co.; v.p. bus. devel. ShadowTV, Softel-USA; dir. interactive TV Verizon Comm. Inc., NYC, 2006—. Office: Verizon Comm Inc 140 West St New York NY 10036*

ZOFKIE, MARCIA MARY, music educator; d. Cletus Charles Zofkie and Beulah Anna Zint Zofkie. Student, Cin. Conservatory Music, 1947—49; BA in Music Edn. K-12, Mount Mary Coll., Milw., 1965; MMus, Mich. State U., 1971. Professed mem. Sch. Sisters of Notre Dame, 1961. Pvt. tchr. piano, violin, Wapakoneta, Ohio, 1948—61; tchr. Notre Dame H.S., Milw., 1964—65, West Cath. H.S., Grand Rapids, Mich., 1965—76; assoc. prof. music Mount Mary Coll., Milw., 1976—. Founder, performer Mount Mary String Quartet, 1992—. Author: Music Cultures of the World: A Feminine Perspective, 2006. Founder, coord. ann. Christmas Madrigal Dinner feast programs Mount Mary Coll., 1976—. Fellow, NEH, 1979, 1982; grantee Title VI grantee, U.S. dept. Edn., 2004. Mem.: Music Educators Nat. Conf., Soc. for Ethnomusicology. Roman Catholic. Avocations: gardening, photography, cooking, arranging string quartets and hymn accompaniments. Office: Mount Mary College 2900 N Menomonee R Pky Milwaukee WI 53222 Office Phone: 414-258-4810. Business E-Mail: zofkiem@mtmary.edu.

ZOGHBI, HUDA Y., neurologist, geneticist, educator; b. Beirut, June 29, 1955; BSc, Am. U. Beirut; MD, Meharry Med. Coll., 1979. Prof. pediat. neurology and geriatrics Baylor Coll. Medicine, Houston, 1994—; investigator Howard Hughes Med. Inst., 1996—; pediatrician Tex. Children's Hosp. and Ben Taub Gen. Hosp. Elected mem. Inst. of Medicine, 2000; sci. adv. bd. Internat. Rett Syndrome Assn.; med. rsch. adv. bd. Nat. Ataxia Found.; sci. issues com. Am. Acad. Neurology. Recipient Sidney Carter award, Acad. Neurobiology, Javits award, NIH, E. Mead Johnson award for pediat. rsch., Derek Denny-Brown Neurological Scholar award, Am. Neurol. Assn. Mem.: Am. Acad. Neurology (sci. issues com.), Inst. Medicine, NAS. Achievements include discovery (with others) of gene that causes spinocerebellar ataxia type 1; discovery of MECP2 gene that causes Rett syndrome; identifying Math1 gene that governs development of inner-ear hair cells. Office: Baylor College of Medicine T 807 1 Baylor Plz Houston TX 77030-3411 Office Phone: 713-798-6558. Office Fax: 713-798-8728. Business E-Mail: hzoghbi@bcm.tmc.edu.*

ZOLA, SHEILA FLEXER, retired elementary school educator; b. N.Y.C., May 1, 1935; d. Jack and Edna (Eagle) Flexer; children: Leslie Sheldon, Sharon Joanne. BA, BS, UCLA, 1957; MS, U. LaVerne, 1983. Cert. resource specialist, pupil personnel, Calif. Elem. tchr. L.A. Unified Sch. Dist., 1957-63, 1976-81, tchr. educationally handicapped, 1981-84, tchr. learning handicapped/severely handicapped, 1984-88, resource specialist, 1988—2003; ret. Mem. Spl. Edn. Commn., L.A., 1985-90; exec. bd. mem. Cedar-Sinai Hosp. Helping Hand Gift Shop, 2004—; bd. mem. U. Women, U. Judaism, 2005—. Mem. Assn. Ednl. Therapists, Coun. for Exceptional Children, UCLA Alumni Assn., Pi Lambda Theta. Avocations: reading, swimming, needlepoint. Home: 15455 Hamner Dr Los Angeles CA 90077-1802

ZOLAR, KAREN JANE, social services administrator; b. Cleve. Heights, Ohio; d. Frank Joseph and Lois Virginia Zolar. BA, Ohio State U., 1999. Speech writer Judge Donna Fitzsimmonds Rocky River (Ohio) Mcpl. Ct., 2000; liason Diabetes Assn. Greater Cleve., Beachwood, Ohio, 2000; program officer Employment and Family Svcs., Cleve., 2000—; mem. City of North Olmsted Civil Svcs. Commn., 2006—. Co-chmn. Harvest for Hunger Campaign Employment and Family Svcs. Mem. 5 Yr. Continuous Improvement Plan com. North Olmsted (Ohio) City Sch., 2004—, mem. adv. com. Cleve., 2003—; active Girl Scouts U.S.; del. Dem. Nat. Conv. Mem.: Ohio State Alumni Assn., Five Seasons Country Club, City Club Cleve., North Olmsted Dem. Club (corr. sec. 2000—03, rec. sec. 2000—, pres. 2006), Zeta Tau Alpha. Democrat. Roman Cath. Avocations: films, travel, politics, reading. Home: 5336 Evergreen Dr North Olmsted OH 44070 Office Phone: 216-987-8399. E-mail: kzolar@yahoo.com.

ZOLLAR, CAROLYN CATHERINE, lawyer; b. Evanston, Ill., July 5, 1947; d. Maurice Adam and Alice S. (Kelm) Z. BA, Smith Coll., Northampton, Mass., 1969; MA, Columbia U., 1970; JD, Am. U., Washington, 1976. Bar: D.C., Va. Legis. asst. Congressman William Anderson U.S. Ho. of Reps., Washington, 1970-72; planning cons. Nat. Inst. Edn., Washington, 1972, legal asst., 1973, asst. for govt. and external rels., 1973-75; assoc. Joe W. Fleming II, P.C., Washington, 1975-82; gen. counsel Nat. Assn. Rehab. Facilities, Washington, 1982-86, gen. counsel, dir. med. rehab., 1986-94; gen. counsel, v.p. policy Am. Rehab. Assn., Washington, 1994—97; v.p. govt. rels. and policy devel. Am Med. Rehab. Providers Assn., 1998—; v.p. Futures Rehab. Mgmt., 1998—. Sec. Am. Rehab. Svcs., Inc., Washington, 1988—94; mem. bd. advisors Ind. Living Mag., N.Y.C., 1988—97; mem. Joint Commn. Accreditation Health Care Orgns. Task Force on Rehab. Svcs., 1988; mem. various expert panels on postacute care and rehab. DHHS, 1999—. Sec. bd. dirs. Rock Creek Found., Silver Spring, Md., 1983-90; bd. dirs. Affiliated Sante Group, 1993-2002; chair Nat. Rehab. Caucus, 1991—. Mem. Am. Soc. Assn. Execs., Am. Health Lawyers Assn., Va. Bar Assn., D.C. Bar, Women in Govt. Rels. Episc. Avocations: skiing, golf, singing. Office: Am Med Rehab Providers Assn 1710 N St NW Washington DC 20036 Office Phone: 202-223-1920.

ZOLLAR, JAWOLE WILLA JO, artist, choreographer; b. Kansas City, Kans., Dec. 21, 1950; d. Alfred Jr. and Dorothy Delores Zollar; 1 child, Elizabeth Herron. BA in Dance, U. Mo., Kansas City, 1975; MFA in Dance, Fla. State U., 1979; PhD (hon.), Columbia Coll., Chgo., 2002. Faculty Fla. State U., Tallahassee, 1977-80, Nancy Smith Fichter prof. dance, 1997—; founding artistic dir. Urban Bush Women, Bklyn., 1984—; Worlds of Thought Resident Scholar Mankato State Univ., 1993—94; regents lectr., dept. dance, world arts and culture UCLA, 1995—96; vis. artist Ohio State Univ., 1996; Abramowitz Meml. lectr. MIT, 1998. Named Outstanding Alumni, U. Mo., 1993, Regent's lectr. dept. dance and worlds culture, UCLA, 1995—96, Alumna of Yr., U. Mo., 1993, Fla. State U., Tallahassee, 1997; recipient N.Y. Dance Performance award, 1992, Capezio award outstanding achievement in dance, 1994, Doris Duke awad, Am. Dance Festival, 1997; Choreography fellow, NEA, 1992, 1993, 1994, Worlds of Thought resident scholar, Mankato State U., 1994. Mem.: Internat. Assn. Blacks in Dance, Assn. Am. Cultures. Office: Urban Bush Women # 4B 138 S Oxford St Brooklyn NY 11217 also: care IMG Artists 420 W 45th St Fl 6 New York NY 10036-3503 Office: Artist in Residence Dept of Dance Florida State Univ Tallahassee FL 32306 Office Phone: 850-644-2525.

ZOLLER, KAREN ANN, library and art gallery director; b. East Cleveland, Ohio, May 16, 1956; d. Paul John and Sonia Ann Klodor. BA in Psychology summa cum laude, Case Western Res. U., 1978, MLS in Law Librarianship, 1981. Mgr. Booksellers, Beachwood, Ohio, 1982—87; cataloger, reference libr. Clara Fritzsche Libr., Notre Dame Coll., South Euclid, Ohio, 1988—92, interim libr. dir., 1992, libr. dir., 1993—, gallery dir., 1997—. Co-founder, bd. mem. Tolerance Resource Ctr. Notre Dame Coll., South Euclid, 1997—; presenter in field; established Eastern Ch. Resource Ctr., Notre Dame Coll., South Euclid, 1999—. Editor: On The Threshold of a New Century: The City of South Euclid, 1967-1999, 1999; compiler: source book Researching Grants on the Internet: A Resource Manual, 1999, mem. editl. bd.: Notre Dame Today, 2003—. Mem. steering com. Hillcrest Cmty. Connections, South Euclid, 2003—04; founding mem. South Euclid Cmty. Partnerships, 2005—. Recipient Ameritech Partnership award, Ameritech, 1999; N.E. Ohio Network grantee, Gund Found., 1998, mini-grant, Ohio Humanities Coun., 2005. Mem.: ALA, Cleve. Area Met. Libr. Sys., Ohio Libr. Coun., Phi Beta Kappa. Roman Catholic. Avocations: reading, hiking, antiques, movies, collecting shells. Office: Clara Fritzsche Libr Notre Dame Coll 4545 College Rd South Euclid OH 44121

ZOLOTH, LAURIE SUSAN, bioethicist; b. LA, June 15, 1950; d. Arthur and Helen (Cohen) Zoloth; m. Henry Levy (div. June 1980); m. Daniel Zoloth Dorfman, Aug. 17, 1986; children: Matthew, Noah, Benjamin, Joshua, Sarah. BA cum laude, U. Calif., Berkeley, 1974; BSN, SUNY, 1982; MA in English, San Francisco State U., 1991; MA, PhD in Theology and Jewish Studies, Grad. Theol. Union, 1993. Instr. adult edn. Jewish studies Lehrahaus Judaica, 1988-93; cons. ethicist Nat. Kaiser Permanente HMO, Berkeley, Calif., 1987; prof. ethics, dir. Jewish Studies prog. San Francisco State U., 1995—2003; dir. Ctr. Bioethics, Sci. and Soc. Northwestern U., Chgo., dir. bioethics Ctr. Genetic Medicine, Ctr. Regenerative Medicine and Inst. Nanotechnology; prof. med. ethics and humanities Northwestern U. Feinberg Sch. Medicine; prof. religion, mem Jewish Studies faculty Northwestern U. Weinberg Coll. Arts and Scis. Instr. ethics Chapman Coll., 1989; lectr. clin. bioethics prog. Stanford U. Grad. Theol. Union, 1991—92, instr. bioethics prog., 1994; asst. prof. Calif. State U., Sonoma, 1994; mem. Nat. Adv. Coun. NASA, mem. Planetary Protection Adv. Com., mem. Interagency Nat. Animal Care and Use Com.; chair bioethics adv. bd. Howard Hughes Med. Inst.; mem. data safety monitoring bd. NIH Asia AIDS Vaccine Trials. Mem. editl. bd.: Am. Jour. Law, Medicine and Ethics, Jour. Clin. Ethics, Am. Jour. Bioethics; author: Health Care and The Ethics of Encounter, 1999; co-editor: Notes From a Nattow Ridge: Religion and Bioethics, Riding on Faith: Religion, Popular Culture and the World of Disney, Margin of Error: The Ethics of Mistakes in Medicine, The Human Embryonic Stem Cell Debate: Ethics, Religion and Policy. Recipient NASA Nat. Pub. Svc. award, 2005. Mem.: Am. Acad. Religion (chair sect. on women), Soc. Women's Health Rsch. (bd. mem.), Soc. Neuroethics (bd. mem.), Soc. Scriptural Reasoning (bd. mem.), Internat. Soc. Stem Cell Rsch. (bd. mem.), Am. Soc. Bioethics and Humanities (pres. 2001). Jewish. Office: Ctr Bioethics Sci and Soc Northwestern U 676 N St Clair Rm 1260 Chicago IL 60611 E-mail: lzoloth@northwestern.edu.*

ZOLOTOW, CHARLOTTE SHAPIRO, retired author, editor; b. Norfolk, Va., June 26, 1915; d. Louis J. and Ella F. (Bernstein) Shapiro; m. Maurice Zolotow, Apr. 14, 1938 (div. 1969); children: Stephen, Ellen. Student, U. Wis., 1933-36. Editor children's book dept. Harper & Row, N.Y.C., 1938-44, sr. editor, 1962-70; v.p., assoc. pub. Harper Jr. Books, 1976-81; editorial cons., editorial dir. Charlotte Zolotow Books, 1982-90; pub. emerita, advisor Harper Collins Children's Books, 1991—. Tchr. U. Colo. Writers Conf. on Children's Books, U. Ind. Writers Conf.; also lectr. children's books. Author: The Park Book, 1944, Big Brother, 1960, The Sky Was Blue, 1963, The Magic Words, 1952, Indian Indian, 1952, The Bunny Who Found Easter, 1998, new edit., 1999, In My Garden, 1960, But Not Billy, 1947, 2d edit, 1983, Not a Little Monkey, 1957, 2d edit., 1989, The Man With The Purple Eyes, 1961, Mr. Rabbit and the Lovely Present, 1962, The White Marble, 1963, A Rose, A Bridge and A Wild Black Horse, 1964, 2d edit., 1987, Someday, 1965, When I Have a Little Girl, 1965, If It Weren't for You, 1966, 2d edit., 1987, Big Sister, Little Sister, 1966, All That Sunlight, 1967, When I Have A Son, 1967, My Friend John, 1968, new edit., 1999, Summer Is, 1968, Some Things Go Together, 1969, The Hating Book, 1969, The New Friend, 1969, River Winding, 1970, 79, Lateef and His World, 1970, Yani and His World, 1970, You and Me, 1971, Wake Up and Goodnight, 1971, William's Doll, 1972, Hold My Hand, 1972, 2d edit., 1987, The Beautiful Christmas Tree, 1972, new edit., 1999, Janie, 1973, My Grandson Lew, 1974, The Summer Night, 1974, 3d edit. 1991, The Unfriendly Book, 1975, It's Not Fair, 1976, 2d edit., 1987, Someone New, 1978, Say It, 1980, If You Listen,

1980, 2d edit. 1987, The New Friend, 1981, One Step, Two., 1981, The Song, 1982, I Know a Lady, 1984, Timothy Too!, 1986, Everything Glistens, Everything Sings, 1987, I Like to be Little, 1987, The Poodle Who Barked at the Wind, 1987, The Quiet Mother and the Noisy Little Boy, 1988, Something's Going to Happen, 1988, This Quiet Lady, 1992, The Seashore Book, 1992, Snippets, 1992, The Moon was the Best, 1993, Peter and the Pigeons, 1993, The Old Dog, 1995, When the Wind Stops, 1995, Who is Ben, 1997, Wake Up and Goodnight, Some Things Go Together, new edits., 1998, Do You Know What I'll Do?, new edit., 2000, When I Have a Little Girl When I Have a Little Boy, 2000, The Three Funny Friends, 2003; Overpraised Season, Early Sorrow. Recipient Harper Gold award for editorial excellence, 1974, Kerlan award U. Minn., 1986, Corp. award for children's books Lit. Market Pl., 1990, Silver medallion U. So. Miss., 1990, Tribute for Far Reaching Contbn. to Children's Lit., ALA, 1991, Otter award, 1997, Charlotte Zolotow award for text of disting. picture book U. Wis. named in her honor, 1998, Parent's Guide Children's Media outstanding achievement poetry books, 2002. Mem. PEN, Authors League. Home: 29 Elm Pl Hastings On Hudson NY 10706-1703 Office: 10 E 53d St New York NY 10022-5244

ZOMPARELLI, WENDY, newspaper publisher; b. Chgo., 1950; d. Rocco and Eileen Zomparelli; m. André Spies; 1 child, Samuel Z. Spies. BA, Cornell U., 1971. Staff writer Raleigh (N.C.) Times, 1978-80; writer, copy editor Raleigh (N.C.) News and Observer, 1982-84; staff writer Roanoke (Va.) Times, 1984-85, asst. features editor, 1985, features editor, 1985-92, asst. to pres. and pub., 1992-95, editor, 1995-98, v.p., gen. mgr., 1998-2000, pres., pub., 2000—. Mem. Pulitzer Prize journalism awards jury, 1998-99. Mem.: Soc. Profl. Journalists, Am. Soc. Newspaper Editors, Phi Beta Kappa. Office: The Roanoke Times PO Box 2491 201 Campbell Ave SW Roanoke VA 24011-1100 E-mail: wendy.zomparelli@roanoke.com.

ZOOK, MARTHA FRANCES HARRIS, retired nursing administrator; b. Topeka, Nov. 15, 1921; d. Dwight Thacher and Helen Muriel (Houston) Harris; m. Paul Warren Zook, July 2, 1948 (dec. 1995); children: Mark Warren (dec.), Mary Elizabeth Zook Hughey. Student nurses tng., 1944—47; RN, Meriden Hosp. and Yale U., Conn., 1947; student, U. Kans., 1948-49, Kans. State U., 1960-61, Barton County C.C., 1970-73; BA, Stephens Coll., 1977; postgrad., Ft. Hays State U., 1978-79. Staff nurse Stormont Hosp., Topeka, 1947-48, Watkins Meml. Hosp., Lawrence, Kans., 1948-49; nursing supr. Larned State Hosp., 1949-53, sect. supr., 1956-57, dir. nursing, 1958-61, 83-86; sect. nurse Sedgewick Sect., 1961-76, clin. instr. nursing edn., 1976-77, dir. nursing edn., 1977-83; sect. supr. Dillon Bldg., Larned, 1957-58; ret., 1986. Mem. DAR, Sacred Heart Altar Soc. Democrat. Roman Catholic. Home: 2526 Illinois Ave Joplin MO 64804-2221

ZOON, KATHRYN CHRISTINE, biochemist; b. Yonkers, NY, Nov. 6, 1948; d. August R. and Violet T. (Pollock) Egloff; m. Robert A. Zoon, Aug. 22, 1970; children: Christine K., Jennifer R. BS, Rensselaer Poly. Inst., 1970; PhD, Johns Hopkins U., 1976. Rsch. chemist divsn. biochem. biophys. Bur. Biologics FDA, Bethesda, Md., 1980-84, rsch. chemist divsn. virology, 1984-88, rsch. chemist divsn. cytokine biology Ctr. Biologics, 1988—92, divsn. dir., 1989-92; dir. Ctr. Biologics Evaluation and Rsch., 1992—2003; dep. dir. Ctr. for Cancer Rsch. Nat. Cancer Inst., NIH, 2003—04; dep. dir. planning and devel. divsn. intramural rsch. NIAID, NIH, 2004—06, dir. divsn. intramural rsch., 2006—. Chmn. expert com. on biol. standardization WHO, 1997-98, 99, 2000, 01; mem. adv. com. of CMR, 2000-03; dir. NIH, NIAID, DIR; lectr. in field. Contbr. articles to rsch. in biol. chemistry to sci. jours.; sect. editor Jour. Interferon and Cytokine Rsch., 1980—. Bd. dirs. Found. Advanced Edn. Scis., 1996-2004, 1st v.p., 1999-03; mem. adv. bd. Def. Advance Rsch. Projects Agy., 1998-00, Inst. Medicine Nat. Acad. Sci., 2002-. Recipient Person of the Yr. award Biopharm, 1992, Pub. Svc. and Genetic Engring. News award, 1995, Presdl. Meritorious Exec. Rank award, 1994, Grateful Patient award Nat. Assn. Cancer Patients, 1997, Rensselaer Alumni Assn. award, 1997, Sec.'s award for disting. svc. Dept. Health and Human Svcs., 2001, 03, Disting. Alumnus award Johns Hopkins U., 2003; NY State Regents fellow, 1970, Interferon rsch. fellow NIH, Bethesda, 1975-77, staff fellow, 1979-80. Mem. Am. Soc. Biochem. and Molecular Biology, Intenat. Soc. Interferon and Cytokine Rsch. (pres. elect 1998-99, pres. 2000-01), Internat. Assn. Biol. Standardization (mem. adv. coun. 2000—), Inst. of Medicine. Roman Catholic. Office: NIAID/NIH Bldg 10 Rm 4A30A 10 Center Dr Bethesda MD 20892 Office Phone: 301-496-3006. Personal E-mail: kzoon@comcast.net. Business E-Mail: kzoon@niaid.nih.gov.

ZOPF, EVELYN LANOEL MONTGOMERY, retired guidance counselor; b. Laurel, Miss., July 10, 1932; d. Arthur LaNoel and Ruby Lee (Lewis) Montgomery; m. Paul Edward Zopf, Aug. 5, 1956; 1 child, Eric Paul. MusB in Edn., U. So. Miss., 1953, MA, 1954. Guidance counselor U. So. Miss., 1953—54, U. Fla., 1954—56; tchr. New Orleans City Schs., 1956—57; pub. sch. music tchr., band dir., choral dir. Putnam County Schs., Fla., 1957—59; pvt. music tchr. voice, piano, clarinet and trumpet, 1953—61; substitute tchr. Guilford County Schs., 1959—93. Mem. arts series com. Guilford Coll., 1973—77; interim choir dir. New Garden Friends Meeting, 1961, chmn. music com., 1974—76; adviser to fgn. students, 1954—56, 1959—62; mem. First Internat. Congress on Quaker Edn. Com., 1987—88, Guilford Coll.'s Sesquicentennial Com., 1985—87; spkr. various religious and art groups. Vol. ARC, Boy Scouts Am.; mem. U. Fla. Union Bd., 1955—56; vol. com. worker NC dist. auditions Met. Opera, 1999—2001; precinct del. County Dem. Conv., 1977, 1979, precinct worker, 1980, campaign worker, 1980; bd. dirs. Greensboro Friends of Music, 1970—71; bd. dirs. Greensboro chpt. NC Symphony Bd., 1979—83; mem. feeder bd. The Guilford Coll. Friends of the Lib. Bd., 1993—94, mem. exec. bd., 1994—95. Mem.: United Soc. of Friends Women (pres. 1979—81), Internat. Fellowship Quaker Women, Guilford Coll. Cmty. Chorus, Women's Soc. (dir. 1978—82), Guilford Coll. Arts Appreciation (v.p. 1980—81, pres. 1981—82), Guilford Gourmet Club, Phi Mu. Home: 815 George White Rd Greensboro NC 27410-3317

ZOPFI, EMMA G., elementary school educator; arrived in U.S., 1961; d. Gilberto L. and Maria B. Garcia; m. Charles W. Zopfi, Dec. 2, 1975; children: Charles W. Jr., Catherine Marie. BS in Bilingual Elem. Edn., U. Tex., El Paso, 1989. 2d grade tchr. North Loop Elem., El Paso, 1989—2000, 3d grade tchr., 2001—02, 4th grade tchr., 2002—. Gifted & talented tchr. North Loop Elem., El Paso, 2003—06; grade level rep. CEIC-North Loop Elem., 2005—; tchr. rep. Bel Air area Sci. Scope & Seq. Revision Com., El Paso, 2005—06. Vol. Bel Air HS Theater, El Paso, 2001—02, Christo Rey Ch., El Paso, 2001—02. Named Tchr. of the Yr., YISD, 1998—99, 2002—03; grantee. Mem.: ATPE, State Tchr. Sci. Assn., Soc. Advancement Chirenas Math and Sci. Avocations: sewing, crafts. Office: North Loop Elem 412 Emerson El Paso TX 79915 Business E-Mail: ezopfi@yisd.net.

ZOPP, ANDREA LYNNE, lawyer, retail executive; b. Rochester, N.Y., Jan. 25, 1957; d. Reuben K. and P. Greta (Hurst) Davis; m. William E. Zopp, Jr., Oct. 7, 1989; children: Alyssa, Kelsey, William. BA cum laude, Harvard Coll., 1978; JD, Harvard U., 1981. Bar: Ill. 1981, U.S. Dist. Ct. (no. dist.) Ill. 1981, U.S. Ct. Appeals (7th cir.) 1982. Law clk. Hon. George N. Leighton, U.S. Dist. Ct., Chgo., 1981-83; asst. U.S. atty. U.S. Atty.'s Office, Chgo., 1983-86, dept. chief OCDETF, 1986-88, dep. chief criminal lit., 1988-90; ptnr. McDermott, Will & Emery, Chgo., 1990-91; chief narcotics prosecutions bur. Cook County State's Attys. Office, Chgo., 1991-92, first asst. state's atty., 1992—96; ptnr. Sonnenschein Nath & Rosenthal, 1997—2000; v.p., dep. gen. counsel Sara Lee Corp., 2000—03; sr. v.p., gen. counsel Sears, Roebuck & Co., Hoffman Estates, Ill., 2003—. Mem. Gov.'s Commn. on Capital Punishment, State of Illinois, 2000—. Bd. dirs. Aux. Bd., Art Inst. Chgo., 1987-2000; bd. dirs. Chgo. Regional Bd. of Jr. Achievement, 1991-95, Chgo. Area Project, 1992—. Fellow Leadership Greater Chgo., 1989-90; Kizzy Scholarship Fund award, 1991-92. Fellow Am. Bar Found., Am. Coll. Trial Lawyers; Mem. ABA, Chgo. Bar Assn., Chgo. Inn of Ct., Cook County Bar Assn., Black Women Lawyers Assn., Leadership Greater Chgo. (bd. dirs.). Avocations: running, music, theater. Office: Sears Roebuck & Co 3333 Beverly Rd Hoffman Estates IL 60179

ZORICK, NANCY LEE, artist, actress; b. Chgo., July 24, 1946; d. William Russel and Wilma Beatrice (Fithian) Noble; m. Peter Michael Zorick, Aug. 8, 1980. Student, Art Inst. Chgo., 1965-67, Second City Workshop, Chgo., 1967-68, Am. Acad. Art, 1971. Comml. artist Embosograph Display Co., Chgo., 1964-66, Stevens-Biondi-DiCiccio, Chgo., 1966-68. Illustrator: (book) Making Weight, 1991, The Little Acorn, 1996; exhibns. include Fontana (Calif.) Arts Assn., 1988, Riverside County Art Exhibnn., 1990; appeared in plays My Sweet Charlie, Chgo., 1968, Harold, Chgo., 1969, films include Medium Cool, 1968, Jackson County Jail, 1976, Outside Chance, 1978; appeared in commercial Tastee Freeze, 1969. Mem Des Arts, 1981, historian, 1983—85, parliamentarian, 1986—93, 1996—2006, pres., 1993—95, 2006—. Named to Taft Alumni Hall of Fame, Chgo., 2000; recipient 1st place in Fine Arts, Nat. Date Festival, 1983, 2d place, Riverside Nat. Date Festival, 1993, 1996, 2001, 3d place, 2004, Best of Show in Fine Arts, Des-Arts, 1988, 1st place, Des Arts, 1986, 1990, 1992—93, 1996—98, 2000—01, 2003—05, Best of Show in Fine Arts, Fontana (Calif.) Arts Assn., 1988. Avocations: teaching sunday school, ballet and art, volunteering. Home: 51-555 Monroe St #31 Indio CA 92201 Personal E-mail: noblezorick@aol.com.

ZORKIN, MELISSA WAGGENER, public relations executive; b. 1954; BA Eng., Lewis & Clark Coll. With Tektronix Inc., Beaverton, Oreg., 1975-80, Regis McKenna, Portland, 1980-83; founder Waggener Edstrom, Inc., 1983—, now pres. and CEO. Named Person of Yr., Media, Inc.; named one of 100 Most Influential People of the 20th Century in Pub. Rels., 50 Most Powerful Women in the Field, PR Week, 1999; recipient Alumni award, Lewis and Clark Coll. Office: Waggener Edstrom Inc 3 Centerpointe Dr Ste 300 Lake Oswego OR 97035-8663

ZORN, SARAH MARIE, secondary school educator; b. Sandusky, Ohio, Apr. 14, 1980; d. Mark Wallace and Teresa Ann Zorn. BS in Edn., Bowling Green State U., Ohio, 2002, M in Classroom Tech., 2006. Cert. integrated sci. tchr. 7-12 Ohio. Sci. tchr. Ottawa (Ohio)-Glandorf HS, 2002—05; tchr. Life Skills Ctr., Toledo, 2005—. Softball coach Ottawa-Glandorf Sch. Dist., 2003—05; summer softball coach Ottawa Pks. Dist., 2004—05. Vol. 4-H, Ohio, 1998—. Mem.: NEA, Nat. Sci. Tchrs. Assn. Lutheran. Avocations: travel, sewing, exercise. Home: 1500 Connell Ave Findlay OH 45840 Office: Life Skills Ctr 1500 Adams Toledo OH 43609 E-mail: poe14312@aol.com.

ZOSIKE, JOANIE FRITZ, theater director, actress; b. Bklyn., July 6, 1949; d. Nathan and Gloria S. (Greenberg) Hieger; m. Godson Zosike. BA in Theatre, NYU, 1980. Actor The Living Theatre, NYC, 1990—. Co-dir. DADAnewyork; co-founder and co-dir. Action Racket Theatre, N.Y.C., 1998—; artist-in-residence Living Theatre Workshops (USA) Author: (stage prodns.) You Told Me That the Carousel Was Crystal, Frames, Inside, 12 Steps to Murder; author: (with Hanon Reznikov) And Then The Heavens Closed; actress (stage prodns.) Chisciotte, Not in My Name, Mysteries and Smaller Pieces, Utopia, Anarchia, Humanity, Body of God, I and I, Midsummer Night's Dream, Mother Courage, Resistance, (solo performances) All Right So I AM the Earth, Harpies Complex, Ereshkigal's Peg, Fritzgabriel Cabaret, Alen Mak Festival (Bulgaria), Festival des Politisches Liedes (Germany), (films) Mass and Masses, Human Flesh; vocalist (radio show) Women on the Edge of Time; contbr. Between Ourselves: Letters Between Mothers and Daughters (edited by Karen Payne), Women in American Theatre (edited by Helen Krich Chinoy and Linda Walsh Jenkins); contbr. poetry and articles to artistic jours. Bd. dirs. N.Y.C. Peoples Life Fund; participating artist Theatres Against War. Mem. War Resisters League, New Yorkers Against the Death Penalty. Office: The Living Theatre 2565 Broadway 515 New York NY 10025

ZOSS, NANCY ALINE, psychotherapist, counseling administrator; b. LA, Dec. 15, 1943; d. Walter Burl Zoss and Jayne Frances Rush; m. Aaron Randolf Lalaian (div.); 1 child, Robert Randolf Lalaian. B English, Calif. State U., Northridge; M Clin. Psychology, Antioch U., LA. Cert. tchr. Calif., marriage and family therapist Calif. Claims examiner Occidental Life, LA; group ins. adminstr., comms. specialist Am. Honda Motor Co., Torrance, Calif.; human resources mgr. Eaton Corp., El Segundo, Calif.; sch. counselor Little Citizens Acad., LA; pvt. practice psychotherapy LA and Venice, Calif. Vol. therapist Women's Clinic, LA; vol. Beagles & Buddies Shelter, South El Monte, Calif.; visitor Chalet Convalescent Hosp., LA. Mem.: Calif. Assn. Marriage and Family Therapists. Avocation: tai chi chuan. Office: 1355 Westwood Blvd # 202 Los Angeles CA 90024

ZOU, CHANGPING, research scientist, educator; arrived in U.S., 1986; d. Daming Zou and Yidi Zhao; m. Sui Zhang; children: Aaron Tan Zou-Zhang, Philip Tigar Zou-Zhang. MD, Beijing Med. Coll., 1983; MPH, U Tex., Houston, 1990; PhD, U. Tex., Houston, 1994. Postdoctoral fellow U. Tex. MD Anderson Cancer Ctr., Houston, 1994—97, instr., 1997—98, asst. prof., 1998—2003; faculty mem. Grad. Sch. Biomed. Sci. U. Tex., Houston, 1998—2003; assoc. prof. U. Ariz., Tucson, 2003—. Grantee, Ovarian Cancer Rsch. Fund, 2004—05, Cervical Cancer Rsch., 2000—01, 2002—03; Cancer Prevention Grad. fellow, NCI, 1994—95. Mem.: Internat. Soc. Cancer Chemoprevention, Am. Soc. Preventive Oncology, Am. Assn. Cancer Rsch., Peking U. Alumni Assn. (bd. dirs. 2000—03). Achievements include patents pending for nutral products in cancer chemoprevention; research in Vitamin A derivatives in head and neck cancer chemoprevention; Vitamin A derivatives in bladder cancer chemoprevention. Office: U Ariz 1501 N Campbell Ave Tucson AZ 05078 Office Phone: 520-626-8883. Office Fax: 520-626-9287. Personal E-mail: zou@email.arizona.edu.

ZOUBAREFF, KATHY OLGA, administrative assistant; b. Hassalt, Belgium; d. Vladimir F. and Kataryna (Sarcov) Z. Grad. in TV acting, J.R. Powers Sch.-Model Agy.; BA in Polit. Sci., Wayne State U.; postgrad., Ann Parsley Sch. Dance, Clinton Twp., Mich., 1990-95, Mary Skiba Sch. Dance, 1995—; A in Gen. Studies, Drama, Macomb Community Coll.; fitness and nutrition cert., Internat. Corr. Schs. Ctr., Scranton, Pa.; voice studies, Ctr. for Creative Studies, Detroit, 1994—; drama studies, Wayne State U., 1994—; broadcasting studies, Macomb C.C., Warren, Mich., 2001. Acct./adminstrv. asst. Univ. Orthopaedic Assocs. Detroit, P.C., 1990-96, office mgr., 1996-98; with The Zoubareff Co., 1998—. Actress, dancer, fashion, TV comml. and photog. model/film screen extra, Hawaiian Tropic Pageants; fragrance model Coty Fragrances, Celion Dion; swimsuit model Ujena; nat. spokesperson Dryell, Physique, Pantene, Oil of O'Lay, Vidal Sassoon, Cover Girl, Coca Cola, Marlboro, Nascar, Indy 400, others; Mae West look-alike; beauty cons. Olay, Cover Girl, Rimmell, London, Lee Jeans. Mem. Renaissance Ctr. Fashion Panel, Detroit, 1989-91; rsch. bd. advisors Am. Biog. Inst.; mem. Internat. Biog. Centre Adv. Coun., 1992, St. Clair Shores Players; contbg. Am. Film Inst., L.A., 2006 Avocations: art, drawing, exercise. Home: 38579 Delta Dr Clinton Township MI 48036-1711 Office: Univ Orthopaedics 28800 Ryan Rd Warren MI 48092 Office Phone: 586-201-2903, 586-558-1290. Business E-Mail: kathy_zou@mclanemodels.com. E-mail: madonna48036@yahoo.com.

ZOULLAS, DEBORAH DECOTIS, investment company executive; b. Salem, Mass., Nov. 13, 1952; d. John and Marie (Mahoney) DeC.; m. Nicholas B. Zoullas, Aug. 15, 1987. BA, Smith Coll., 1974; MBA, Stanford U., 1978. Analyst Morgan Stanley & Co. Inc., N.Y.C., 1974-76, assoc., 1978-81, v.p. London, 1982-84, prin. N.Y.C., 1985-87, mng. dir., 1988-95, adv. dir., 1996—; exec. v.p. Sotheby's Holdings, N.Y.C., 1998—2000; dir. Sotheby's Holding Corp., N.Y.C., 2000, Armor Holdings Inc., 2002—. Co-chair spl. projects com. Meml. Sloan Kettering Cancer Ctr. Mem. adv. coun. Stanford Grad. Sch. Bus., 2003—; trustee Helena Rubinstein Found. Miller scholar Stanford U., 1978. Home: 160 E 72d St New York NY 10021

ZOVLUCK, ILEEN MARCY, music annotator; b. Englewood, NJ, Apr. 13, 1961; d. Arlene Carroll and Bernard Leonard Zovluck. MusB, Mannes Coll. Music, NY, 1986, MusM, 1987. Instr. of guitar and music theory Queensboro Inst. of Music, Queens, NY, 1986—87; instr. of music Classroom Recorder Arts, NYC, 1987—88, Queens NY Sch. of Music, Queens, 1988—89; asst. music libr. Boosey & Hawkes Music Pub., NYC, 1990—92; vis. fellow Clare Coll., Cambridge U., England, 1999; dir., artistic programming dept. Columbia Artists Mgmt. Inc., NYC, 1993—2001; pvt. instr. of guitar and music theory Self Employed, NY, 1979—, NJ, 1979—; chief music annotator, instrumental and vocal music IMZ Music Svcs., NYC, 2001—. Alto - choir Holy Trinity Luth. Ch., NYC, 1994—95, Concordia Choir, Trinity Luth. Ch., Bklyn., 2003—05. Achievements include Featured performer, Capital Rotunda in Washington DC at a celebratory festival for the 1976 US Bicentennial; Featured regular performance events (solo, duo and trio), Gracie Mansion, the administration of Mayor Edward I. Koch, New York, NY, 1985-87. Avocations: collecting rare musical instruments, needlepoint, cooking, poetry, bicycling. Home: 650 West 42nd St New York NY 10036 Office: IMZ Music Svcs 1 River Pl #1120 New York NY 10036 Office Phone: 212-868-0498. Personal E-mail: imz-vivace@att.net.

ZSCHAU, MARILYN, singer; b. Chgo., Feb. 9, 1944; d. Edwin Arthur Eugene and Helen Elizabeth (Kelly) Z. BA in Radio, TV and Motion Pictures, U. N.C., 1959; grad., Juilliard Sch. Music, 1965; studied opera theatre with Christopher West, studied voice with Florence Page Kimball, studied with John Lester. Toured with Met. Nat. Co., 1965-66; debut, Vienna Volksoper, in Die Tote Stadt, 1967, Vienna Staatsoper, in Ariadne auf Naxos, 1971; with N.Y.C. Opera in La Fanciulla del West, 1978; debut Royal Opera, covent Garden in La Boheme, 1982, Met. Opera, in La Boheme, 1985, La Scala, in Die Frau ohne Schatten, 1986; has toured and sung in many countries including S.Am., Japan, and Australia. Office: 4245 Wilshire Blvd Oakland CA 94602-3549 Office Phone: 510-484-7742. E-mail: marilynzschau@yahoo.com.

ZUBER, CATHERINE, costume designer; MFA, Yale Sch. Drama. Costume designer (plays) Brand, Frankenstein, Two Gentlemen of Verona, The Merchant of Venice, Silence, Cunning, Exile, Jack's Holiday, Troilus and Cressida, The Grey Zone, King Lear, Cowgirls, Nightmare Alley, Violet, Misalliance, The Primary English Class, Captains Courageous, The Musical, An Experiment with an Air Pump, Saturday Night, Time and Again, Servicemen, Othello, Andorra, Boys and Girls, Play Yourself, Far Away, The Mercy Seat, Julius Caesar, The Harlequin Studies, Beckett/Albee, The Beard of Avon (Lucille Lortel award, outstanding costume design, 2004), The Regard Evening, Frozen, Intimate Apparel (Lucille Lortel award, outstanding costume design, 2005), Engaged (Obie award, Village Voice, design, 2005), Last Easter, Five by Tenn, The Paris Letter, The House in Town, 2006, (Broadway plays) The Red Shoes, 1993, Philadelphia, Here I Come!, 1994, The Rose Tattoo, 1995, London Assurance, 1997, Triumph of Love, 1997, Ivanov, 1997, The Sound of Music, 1998, Twelfth Night, 1998, Dinner at Eight, 2002, Frozen, 2004, Dracula, the Musical, 2004, Little Women, 2005, Doubt, 2005, The Light in the Piazza, 2005 (Tony award, best costume design of a musical, 2005), Awake and Sing!, 2006 (Tony award, best costume design of play, 2006), Defiance, 2006. Recipient Obie award, sustained achievement in costume design, 1997, Henry Hewes award, outstanding costume design, 2003.*

ZUBER, MARIA T., geophysicist, educator; married; 2 children. BA in Astrophysics & Geology, U. Penn., 1980; SsM in Geophysics, Brown U., 1983, PhD in Geophysics, 1986. Rsch. asst. geological sciences Brown U., 1980—86; NRC rsch. assoc., Geodynamics Branch NASA/Goddard Space Flight Ctr., 1985—86, geophysicist, Geodynamics Branch, 1986—92, sr. rsch. scientist, Lab. for Terrestrial Physics, 1994—; assoc. rsch. prof. geophysics Johns Hopkins U., 1991—92, assoc. prof. geophysics, 1991—95, prof. geophysics, 1995; cons. aerospace div. MIT Lincoln Lab., 2002—; prof. geophysics & planetary sci. MIT, 1995—98, E.A. Griswold prof. geophysics, dept. earth, atmospheric & planetary scis., 1998—, head dept. earth, atmospheric & planetary sciences, 2003—. Visiting asst. prof. geophysics Johns Hopkins U., 1990; guest investigator Woods Hole Oceanographic Institution, 1996—2004; sr. sci. fellow Radcliffe Inst. for Advanced Study, 2002—03; visiting scholar Harvard U., 2002—03; bd. dirs. Planetary Soc., 2000—; mem. advisory council Jet Propulsion Lab., 2000—; mem. Independent Status Review Bd., NASA Mars Exploration Rover, 2003—, President's Commn. on Implementation of US Space Exploration Policy, 2004. Mem. bd. reviewing editors Science, 2000—. Recipient NASA Peer award, 1988, NASA Outstanding Performance award, 1988, 1989, 1990, 1991, 1992, NASA Exceptional Scientific Achievement medal, 1995, Scientific Achievement award, Am. Inst. of Aeronautics & Astronautics, 2002, NASA Disting. Public Service medal, 2004. Fellow: Am. Acad. Arts & Sciences, Am. Geophysical Union; mem.: NAS, Am. Astronomical Soc., AAAS. Office: MIT Dept Earth Atmospheric & Planetary Scis 54-518 77 Mass Ave Cambridge MA 02139 Business E-Mail: zuber@mit.edu.*

ZUBER, NORMA KEEN, career counselor, educator; b. Iuka, Miss., Sept. 27, 1934; d. William Harrington and Mary (Hebert) Keen; m. William Frederick Zuber, Sept. 14, 1958; children: William Frederick Jr., Michael, Kimberly, Karen. BS in Nursing, U. Southwestern La., 1956; MS in Counselling, Calif. Luth. U., 1984. Nat. cert. counselor, nat. cert. career counselor; registered profl. career counselor, Calif.; master career counselor. Intensive care nurse Ochsner Found. Hosp., New Orleans, 1956-59; career devel. counselor BFC Counseling Ctr., Ventura, Calif., 1984-87; founder, prin., counselor Career & Life Planning-Norma Zuber & Assocs., Ventura, 1987—. Instr. adult continuing edn. Ventura C.C., 1987—; instr. Calif. State U., Northridge, 1988-89; instr. U. Calif. Santa Barbara, Antioch U.; mem. adv. coun. on tchr. edn. Calif. Luth. U., Thousand Oaks, 1984-87; mem. adv. bd. for devel. of profl. career counseling cert. program U. Calif., San Diego, 2001-; fin. co-chair Calif. Coalition for Counselor Lisensure, 2003—, legis. com., fin. co-chair, 2004-; freelance writer Career Q&A, Ventura County Star, 2006. Co-author: The Nuts and Bolts of Career Counseling: How to Set Up and Succeed in Private Practice, 1992. Chmn. bd. dirs. women's ministries Missionary Ch., Ventura, 1987-90. Recipient profl. contbn. award H.B. McDaniel Found.-Stanford U. Sch. Edn., 1988, Govt. Rels. Com. Cert. of Appreciation, Am. Assn. for Counseling and Devel., Career Devel. Practitioner of the Year award Internat. Career Conf., 1998, Spirit of Networking award Ventura Profl. Women's Network, 2001; featured in Nat. Assn. of Women bus. Owners Bravo award, Ventura, Calif. Mem. NAFE, ACA, Nat. Career Devel. Assn. (western region trustee 1994-97, master career counselor 2002—), Calif. Assn. Couseling and Devel. (chmn. legis. task force 1987-89, Jim Saum govt. rels. award 1989), Internat. Platform Assn., Nat. Career Devel. Assn. (western regional trustee 1995-98), Internat. Career Conf. (Career Devel. Practitioner of Yr. 1998), Calif. Career Devel. Assn. (bd. dir. 1985-98, membership dir. 1991-92, pres. 1992-93, Leadership and Professionaliam award 1988, 89), Calif. Career Conf. (program chair 1993), Ventura County Profl. Women's Network (dir. membership 1990-91, pres. 1998-99), Calif. Registry Profl. Counselors and Paraprofls. (bd. dir. 1990-94, chair 1995-97), Chi Sigma Iota. Republican. Home: 927 Sentinel Cir Ventura CA 93003-1202 Office: Career and Life Planning Norma Zuber and Assocs 3585 Maple St Ste 237 Ventura CA 93003-9117 Office Phone: 805-656-6220. Business E-Mail: nzuberCDLP@msn.com.

ZUBERNIS, LYNN SMITH, psychologist, counselor; d. Kevlin Walter and Carol Luckins Smith; m. James J. Zubernis, June 25, 1983 (div. Mar. 1994); children: Emily Kevlin, Jeffrey James. BA in Psychology, Rosemont Coll., 1994; MA in Sch. Psychology, Bryn Mawr Coll., 1997, PhD in Clin., Devel. and Sch. Psychology, 2002. Cert. Sch. Psychologist Pa., 1997, lic. Psychologist Pa., 2005. Intern psychologist Marple Newtown Sch. Dist., Newtown Square, Pa., 1996—97, Child Study Inst., Bryn Mawr, Pa., 1996—98, St. Gabriel's Hall, Audubon, Pa., 1997—98; sch. psychologist Tower Hill Sch., Wilmington, Del., 1999—; intern psychologist Friends Hosp., Phila., 2000—01; therapist Penn Friends Behl Health, Phila., 2001—02; counselor St. Josephs U., Phila., 2002—, asst. dir., Counseling Ctr. Instr. West Chester State U., 1999, adj. prof., 2006; adj. Haverford Coll., 2000. Contbr. articles to profl. jours. Mem.: APA, Pa. Psychol. Assn., Delta Epsilon Sigma, Alpha Sigma Lambda. Avocations: writing, films. Office: St Josephs Univ Counseling Ctr 5600 City Ave Philadelphia PA 19131 Business E-Mail: lzuberni@sju.edu.

ZUCCO, RONDA KAY, planning and marketing professional; b. Peoria, Ill., Apr. 3, 1960; d. Richard Leon Zucco. BA, So. Ill. U., 1981; postgrad., Fla. So. Coll., 2005—. Cert. addictions profl.; cert. relapse prevention specialist. Addictions counselor Parkside at BroMenn, Bloomington, Ill., 1986-89; dir. continuing care/sr. counselor Fla. Hosp. (formerly Parkside), Orlando, Fla., 1989-95; addictions program mgr. Charter Behavioral Health Sys., Kissimmee, Fla., 1995-97; coord. outpatient svcs. Heart of Fla. Behavioral Ctr., Lakeland, Fla., 1997-99; bus. and industry rep., planning and mktg. dept. Lakeland Regional Med. Ctr., 1999—. Vol. ARC, Carbondale, Ill., 1978—81, Alliance for Mentally Ill of Greater Orlando, Fla., 1995—97, Coalition for Homeless, Orlando, 1995—97; crisis hotline vol. Jackson County Cmty. Mental Health Ctr., Carbondale, 1981; mem. AIDS spkrs. bur. BroMenn Healthcare, Bloomington, 1986—89; vol. Spl. Olympics, 1999—; adv. bd. Drug Prevention Resource Ctr., Lakeland, Fla., 1998—; sustainer Jr. League of Greater Lakeland, 2000—; torchbearer Salt Lake 2002 Olympics; bd. dirs. Imperial Symphony Orch., Lakeland, 2001—; adv. bd. Word Alive Ministries Cmty. Svc. Corp., 2006—. Named Outstanding Profl. of Yr., Fla. Sch. Addiction Studies, 1999; recipient State of Ill. scholar, Gen. Assembly, 1977—81, Leadership Lakeland XX, 2002—03. Mem. Am. Mktg. Assn., Am. Assn. for Counseling and Devel., Am. Mental Health Counselors Assn., Fla. Alcohol and Drug Abuse Assn., Fla. Prevention Assn., Nat. Businesswomen's Leadership Assn., Am. Bus. Women's Assn., C. of C. Greater Lakeland, Fla. Coun. on Crime and Delinquency, Kappa Delta Pi, Chi Sigma Iota. Avocations: reading, swimming, travel, the arts. Home: 1100 Oakbridge Pkwy Apt 296 Lakeland FL 33803-5964 Office Phone: 863-687-1055. Business E-Mail: Ronda.Zucco@LRMC.com.

ZUCK, ROSEMARY, social worker, educator; b. Rochester, NY, Sept. 11, 1948; d. George Philip and Laura Zuck. BA in Math., Nazareth Coll., Rochester, 1970; MA in Edn., U. Rochester, 1974; MSW, Syracuse U., N.Y., 1996. LCSW N.Y., 2005; cert. tchr. math. grades 7-12 N.Y., 1974. Tchr., coord. math. East Rochester Pub. Schs., NY, 1970—97; program coord./sr. social worker upstate N.Y. chpt. Nat. MS Soc., Rochester, 1997—2002, dir. programs, 2002—04; social worker Unity Health Sys. -Edna Tina Wilson Living Ctr., Rochester, 2004—; affiliate educator Aetna, 2001. MS support group facilitator, Rochester, 1997—; mem. Rochester Effectiveness Partnership Provider Tng. and Alumni Study Group Partnership, 2001—03. Contbr. book. Mem. City-County Coun. for People with Disabilities Accessibility Com., Rochester, 1998—2001; co-chair and com. mem. Women's Workshop Planning Com. - A Workshop for Women Living with Disabilities and Chronic Illnesses, Rochester, 2001—04; pastoral visitor Rochester Gen. Hosp., 1987—90. Mem.: NASW, Finger Lakes Choral Festival, Rochester Oratorio Soc. Avocations: singing, gardening, reading, antiques, journaling. Office Phone: 585-368-6107. Personal E-mail: rosemaryzuck@earthlink.net. Business E-Mail: rzuck@unityhealth.org.

ZUCKER, BARBARA J., artist, educator; b. Abington, Pa., Oct. 5, 1943; d. Martin J. Herbert and Jean Elizabeth (McCormick) Martin; m. F. Donald Zucker, Apr. 4, 1964. BA, Ursinus Coll., 1966; postgrad., Acad. Fine Arts, Florence, Italy, 1968-69; MEd, Temple U., 1971. Tchr. Ursinus Coll., 1982—99; gallery dir. ViewPoint LLC Arts and Events House, Lederach, Pa. One-woman shows include Bucknell U., Lewisburg, Pa., 1975, Phila. Art Alliance, 1975, Multiple Choice Gallery, Blue Bell, Pa., 1976, Ursinus Coll., 1977, 81, 85, Muhlenberg Coll., Allentown, Pa., 1979, Gwynedd-Mercy Coll., Gwynedd Valley, Pa., 1982, Glassboro (N.J.) State Coll., 1984, Gallery 1st Bapt. Ch. in Am., Providence, 1985, 2000, Univ. Gallery, St. Joseph's U., Phila., 1989, The Berman Mus. Art, Collegeville, 1990,2000, Moravian Coll., Bethlehem, Pa., 1992, Phila. Mus. Art, 1993, Widener U. Mus., Chester, Pa., 1994, 2000, Ocean Wood Gallery, Birch Harbor, Maine, 1995, Gloucester County Coll., Sewell, N.J., 1996, The Plastic Club, Phila., 1998, The Hahn Gallery, Phila., 2000, Hill Sch., Pottstown, Pa, 2004, Pfenninger Gallery, Lancaster, Pa., 2005; represented in collections at Berman Mus. Art, Reading (Pa.) Pub. Mus., Woodmere Art Mus., Phila., Rosemont (Pa.) Coll. Recipient Best of Show award Perkiomen Valley Art Ctr., 1993, 95, Open House Gallery award for excellence in water color, 1994, award in memory Ethel Sokolove, 1995, Fred D. Griffiths Printing Co. award, 1998, Friends of Artists Equity award Villanova U., 1998, 1st prize Phila./Tri State Artists Equity, 2002. Mem. Artists Equity Assn. (pres. Phila. chpt. 1993-94, exhibition chair 1993—, bd. dirs. 1992—, Golden Svc. award 1994), Phila. Water Color Club, Nat. League Am. Pen Women. Home: 10 Delphi Rd Schwenksville PA 19473-1713 Office Phone: 215-256-1444. Personal E-mail: bjzfdz@aol.com.

ZUCKER, BLANCHE MYRA, civic worker; b. Schenectady, NY, July 27, 1925; d. Cassius Alexander and Winifred Estelle (Davis) Millington; m. Nelson Marsh, July 7, 1947 (div. July 1967); children: Kay Patricia, Gary Nelson; m. Reuben Zucker, July 22, 1967 (dec. June 1987); m. Henry Bozarth, Feb. 13, 1994 (dec. Jan. 2005). Grad., Meth. Hosp. Sch. Nursing, Bklyn., 1946; BS in Nursing Edn., Columbia U., NYC, 1962; MEd, U. Nev., Las Vegas, 1975. RN, N.Y. Night shift head nurse Meth. Hosp., Bklyn., 1947; floor nurse Carle Meml. Hosp.Clinic, Urbana, Ill., 1947; med. librarian So. Nev. Meml. Hosp. (now Univ. Med. Ctr.), Las Vegas, 1963-66; librarian St. Viator Sch., Las Vegas, 1968-74. Del. Nev. Gov.'s Conf. on Library and Info. Services, 1978, publicity dir., 1978-79; alt. Nev. del. White House Conf. on Library and Info. Services, 1979. Mem. Univ. Med. Ctr. So. Nev. Aux, 1980—; trustee Univ. Libr. Soc., Las Vegas, 1985—2003; pres. We Can, 1985, 1986; mem. Nev. Com. for Protection of Children, 1985—2000, vice chmn., 1987—90, chmn., 1990—95; mem. Citizens Com. Victim Rights, 1986—90. Recipient Svc. award St. Viator Sch., 1975, Adminstrn. for Children, Youth and Families award U.S. Dept. Health and Human Svcs., 1985, Book of Golden Deeds award Las Vegas Exch. Club, 1986, Humanitarian award Las Vegas Women, 1986, Appreciation award We Can, Inc., 1987, Lifetime Achievement in Prevention award/20 Yr. Svc. to Children of Nev., 1994, Blanche Zucker Vol. award, 1990; named Vol. of Yr. Citizens Com. Victim Rights, 1989, Amb. of Courtesy, Las Vegas C. of C. and Las Vegas Conv. and Visitors Authority, 1998; named one of The Women Who Shaped Las Vegas, 2005 Mem. ALA, Nev. Libr. Assn. (publicity dir. 1979, appreciation award 1979), Friends So. Nev. Librs., Clark County Med. Soc. Aux. (pres. 1971-72), Gen. Fedn. Women's Clubs (chmn. Nev. chpt. child abuse project, 1984-90, mem. Past Pres.'s Club, pres. Mesquite Club 1980-81, mem. Nat. Child Care Action Campaign, 1st place Today's Women--the Vol. award 1986, 1st Place Nat. award photography, 1986, 94). Democrat. Avocations: swimming, photography, classical music, opera, creative arts. Home: 2520 Faiss Dr Las Vegas NV 89134-7241

ZUCKER, MAUREEN T., artist; b. Bisbee, Ariz., Dec. 1, 1961; d. Howard Boardman and Cathleen Diane Taylor; m. Barry Benjamin Zucker, Apr. 21, 1956. BFA, Cooper Union U., 1984. Graphic designer George Gerard Assocs., Roslyn, N.Y.; art dir. Ross & Jacobs, Woodbury, N.Y., CMP Media, Manhasset, N.Y., Virgo Publ., Scottsdale, Ariz.; creative svcs. art dir. CWP Publ., Phoenix. Avocations: hiking, walking, drawing, painting, teaching art.

ZUCKER-FRANKLIN, DOROTHEA, internist, educator; b. Berlin, Aug. 9, 1930; came to U.S., 1949; d. Julian J. and Gertrude Zucker; m. Edward C. Franklin (dec.); 1 child, Deborah Julie. BA, CUNY, 1952, PhD in Sci. (hon.), 1996; MD, N.Y. Med. Coll., 1956. Diplomate Am. Bd. Medicine. Intern Phila. Gen. Hosp., 1956-57; resident in internal medicine Montefiore Hosp., N.Y.C., 1957-59, postdoctoral fellow in hematology, 1959-61; postdoctoral fellow in electron microscopy NYU Sch. Medicine, N.Y.C., 1961-63, asst. prof. medicine, 1963-67, assoc. prof., 1968-74, prof. medicine, 1974—; assoc. attending physician Bellevue Hosp., 1968-74, attending physician, 1974—. Assoc. attending physician Univ. Hosp., Tisch Hosp., 1968—74, attending physician, 1974—; cons. physician Manhattan VA Hosp., 1970—; meml. editl. bd. numerous publs., including Blood, 1963—76, 1980—86, Am. Jour. Pathology, 1979—, Ultrastructure Pathology, 1979—, Blood Cells, 1980, Am. Jour. Medicine, 1981—87, Hematology Oncology, 1982—, Jour. AIDS Rsch., 1987—, Hematopathology and Molecular Hematology, 1987—, others; meml. bd. reviewing editors Jour. Lab. and Clin. Medicine, 1990—; mem. hematology panel Health Rsch. Coun. City of N.Y., 1971—74; mem. pathology tng. com. Nat. Inst. Med. Scis., 1971—74; mem. allergy and immunology rsch. com. Nat. Inst. Allergy and Infectious Diseases, 1974—81; mem. U.S.-Israel Binat. Sci. Found., 1980—; mem. ad hoc promotion com. Harvard Med. Sch., 1981, 83; mem. blood products adv. com. FDA, 1981—86; mem. sci. adv. bd. and sci. rev. panel Israel Cancer Rsch. Found., 1982—90; mem. grant rev. panel VA AIDS Ctr., 1988—89; vis. fellow Assn. Claude Bernard, 1974—75. Co-author: The Physiology and Pathology of Leukocytes, 1962, Amyloidosis, 1986, Atlas of Blood Cells: Function and Pathology, 2 vols., 1981, 3d edit., 2003, Thrombopoiesis and Thrombopoietins: Molecular, Cellular, Preclinical and Clinical Biology, 1996; contbr. over 300 articles to profl. jours. Bd. dirs. Henry M. and Lillian Stratton Found., Inc., 1987-95. Named to Hall of Fame, Hunter Coll., 1977, Internat. Profl. and Bus. Women, 1994. Fellow: AAAS, N.Y. Acad. Scis.; mem.: NTLV and Related Viruses, Internat. Retrovirology Assn., N.Y. Soc. Study of Blood (chair program com. 1976—80, pres. 1981—82), N.Y. Soc. Electron Microscopists (program chair 1984, pres. 1984—85), Am. Soc. Cell Biology (program com. internat. congress 1976), Am. Soc. Exptl. Pathology, Am. Assn. Immunologists, Am. Acad. Arts and Scis., Reticuloendothelial Soc. (life; program com. 1974—76, nominating com. 1976—78, pres. 1984—85), Am. Soc. Physiology, Federated Socs. Exptl. Biology and Medicine, Am. Soc. Hematology (program com. 1973, edn. com. 1974—78, chair subcom. on leukocyte physiology 1977, chair subcom. on immunohematology 1984, com. on advanced learning resources 1986—, exec. coun. 1987—91, pres.-elect 1992, v.p. 1993, pres. 1994—95, chair adv. bd. 1996, com. on govt. affairs 2001), Am. Soc. Clin. Investigation, Am. Fedn. Clin. Rsch., Am. Assn. Physicians, Inst. Medicine NAS, Alpha Omega Alpha, Phi Beta Kappa. Office: NYU Med Ctr 550 1st Ave New York NY 10016-6402 Office Phone: 212-263-5634. Business E-Mail: dorothea.zucker-franklin@med.nyu.edu.

ZUCKERMAN, DOROTHY ANN, elementary school educator; b. Bronx, N.Y., Aug. 26, 1932; d. Samuel and Rose (Rothbart) Sugarman; m. Jack Irwin Zuckerman, Aug. 14, 1955; children: Richard Karl, Geri Lynn. BA cum laude, Queens Coll., 1953; MLS, Stony Brook U., 1975. Cert. tchr. K-6, social studies 7-12; cert. advanced study in labor rels. Tchr. Bay Shore (N.Y.) Schs., 1953-58; 59tchr. Brentwood (N.Y.) Schs., 1958, 1969—91; retiree svcs. con. N.Y. State United Tchrs., 2000—. Pre-retirement coord. N.Y. State United Tchrs., Albany, 1980—, pres., 1999-2000; retirement cons. N.Y. State United Tchrs., Albany, 1990-2000; del. N.Y. State Retirement System, 1973-91; chmn. L.I. (N.Y.) Alliance Ret. Americans; pres. Retirees Barentwood Schs., 1991-2000, L.I. Retiree Dels. Coun., 1991-2000. Charter mem. Islip (N.Y.) Town League of Women Voters, 1961; v.p. Coalition of Labor Union Women, Massapequa, N.Y., 1982; officer, zone leader Dem. Com., Islip, 1984-88; trustee, sch. prin. Bnai Israel Reform Temple, Oakdale, N.Y., 1969-75; mediator Suffolk County Mediation Ctr., Coram, N.Y., 1985; pres. Bay Shore Tchrs., 1956-57. Mem. Am. Fedn. Tchrs. (del. 1981-2000), L.I. Fedn. of Labor (del. 1975-80), Brentwood Tchrs. Assn. (officer, negotiator 1972-80), Phi Beta Kappa. Avocations: gardening, needlecrafts, painting, orchids, travel. Office: 150 Vanderbilt Motor Pkwy Hauppauge NY 11788

ZUCKERMAN, HARRIET, sociologist, educator; b. NYC, July 19, 1937; d. Harry and Anne D. (Wiener) Z; m. Robert K. Merton, 1993. AB, Vassar Coll., 1958; PhD, Columbia U., 1965. Asst. prof. sociology Columbia U., 1965-72, assoc. prof., 1972-78, prof., 1978-92, prof. emerita, 1993—; sr. rsch. scholar, 1993—; chmn. dept. Columbia U., 1978-81; v.p. Andrew W. Mellon Found., 1991-98, sr. v.p., 1998—. Vis. scholar Russell Sage Found., 1971—72, 1985—87; mem. adv. bd. Social Sci. Citation Index Inst. Sci. Info., 1972—98; dir. Ann. Revs., Inc.; trustee Am. Savs. Bank, 1978—83. Author: Scientific Elite: Nobel Laureates in the United States, 1977, rev. edit., 1996; co-editor: Toward A Metric of Science: The Advent of Science Indictors, 1978, The Outer Circle: Women in the Scientific Community, 1991; mem. editorial bd. Scientometrics, 1977-, Am. Jour. Sociology, 1972-74, 77-79, Am. Sociol. Rev, 1972-74, 87-91, Sci., 1985-86; contbr. articles to profl. jours. Bd. dir. Social Sci. Rsch. Coun., 1974-76, AAAS, 1980-84, Women's Forum, 1989-91; trustee Ctr. for Advanced Study in Behavioral Scis., 1976-88, 89-2001, 03—; mem. ednl. adv. bd. John Simon Guggenheim Meml. Found., 1986-93, mem. com. on selection, 1989-91. Woodrow Wilson fellow, 1958-59; Ctr. for Advanced Study in Behavioral Scis. fellow, 1973-74; Guggenheim fellow, 1980-81; Phi Beta Kappa vis. scholar, 1982-83; recipient Dean's award for Disting. Achievement Columbia U. Grad. Sch., 1998. Mem. Am. Philos. Soc. (councillor 1997-03, 2005—, v.p. 2006-,chmn. Class III membership com. 2002-05), Am. Acad. Arts and Scis. (chmn. class III membership com. 1991-94), Soc. Social Studies Sci. (pres. 1989-91), The Century Assn., Coun. on Fgn. Rels.

ZUCKERMAN, NANCY ANN, writer, publicist, minister; b. Miami, Fla., Nov. 7, 1962; d. Harold and Gloria F. (Williams) Z. AAS, Suffolk Community Coll., 1985; BA, Hofstra U., 1987; Cert., Writer's Digest, Dana, Ohio, 1989; MDiv, Luth. Theol. So. Seminary, 2000. Sec. Town of Brookhaven Arts Coun., Yaphank, N.Y., 1981-84, writer, publicist, 1987—; sec. Accent Hardwood Flooring, Middle Island, N.Y., 1984-85; freelance writer Port Jefferson, N.Y., 1989—; cmty. rels. coord. Barnes & Noble Bookstore, Pembroke Pines, Fla., 1991-95; assoc. pastor Cmty. Ch. Midlands Columbia, SC, 2001—. Contbr. articles to profl. jours. Avocations: photography, record-collecting, reading.

ZUG, ELIZABETH E., concert pianist, educator; b. Phila., Oct. 8, 1907; d. Nathan Walter and Amelia Elizabeth (Nelson) Zug. BA in Music, Irving Coll., 1928. Mem. faculty Nat. Guild Piano Tchrs., 1949. Judge piano auditions Yr. in Music, Nat. Guild Piano Tchrs., 1949. Debut N.Y. Town Hall, 1938; concert pianist, S.Am. tour, 1941. Named Outstanding N.Y. Debut as Pianist, 1938, Judge of the Yr. Nat. Guild Piano Tchrs., 1949. Mem. Music Tchrs. Nat. Assn., Pa. Music Tchrs. Assn. United Ch. Christ. Avocations: writing, designing, landscaping. Studio: 12 N 4th St Reading PA 19601-3910

ZUK, CARMEN VEIGA, psychiatrist; b. Buenos Aires, Mar. 5, 1939; arrived in U.S., 1971; d. Carlos and Carmen Villella Veiga; m. Gerald Harvey, May 7, 1974; children: Cary Elizabeth and Gabrielle Ann (twins). MD, U. Buenos Aires, 1964, cert. psychiatry, 1969. Diplomate Am. Bd. Psychiatry and Neurology. Intern Med. Coll. Pa., Phila., 1974—75; resident in psychiatry Norristown State Hosp., Norristown, Pa., 1977—79; child psychiatry fellowship Med. Coll. Pa. and Ea. Pa. Psychiat. Inst., Phila., 1979—81; dir. child and adolescent unit Hosp. of Med. Coll. Ga., Augusta, 1981—83; dir. treatment team New Orleans Adolescent Hosp., 1983—85; assoc. Psychiatry Med. Group, Calif., 1985—86; mental health psychiatrist L.A. County Dept. Mental Health San Fernando Mental Health Svcs., 1986—88; psychiatrist-ptnr. So. Calif. Permanente Med. Group, Van Nuys, 1988—98, ptnr., 1988—98; staff psychiatrist Santa Clarita Child and Family Ctr., 1999—2002; ret., 2005. Asst. prof. dept. psychiatry Med. Coll. Ga., 1981-83; clin. asst. prof. dept. psychiatry and neurology Tulane U., 1983-85. Co-author: Psychology of Delusion, 2005; contbr. articles to profl. jours. Mem. AMA, Internat. Soc. for Adolescent Psychiatry. Avocations: reading, cooking, gardening, swimming, music. Home: 7620 Hollister Ave 219 Goleta CA 93117 Personal E-mail: carmenzuk@msn.com.

ZUK, JUDITH, retired botanist, director; b. Canandaigua, N.Y., Sept. 11, 1951; BA, Rutgers U., 1973; MS, U. Del., 1976. CEO, pres. Bklyn. Botanic Garden, 1990—2005; ret., 2005. Bd. dirs. Botanic Gardens Conservation Internat., Greenwood Cemetery; mem. regional adv. bd. JP Morgan Chase. Mem. Phi Beta Kappa.

ZULACK, MARY MARSH, law educator; BA, Smith Coll., 1965; JD, U. Mich., 1969. Clk. for Hon. Leonard H. Sandler; atty. MFY Legal Svcs., 1971—73, Bedford-Stuyvesant Cmty. Legal Svcs., Inc., 1973—80, Harlem Neighborhood Office of Legal Aid Soc., 1980—90; clin. prof. law Columbia Law Sch., 1990—. Bd. dirs. Welfare Law Ctr. Office: Columbia Law Sch 834 Jerome Greene Hall 435 W 116th St New York NY 10027 Office Phone: 212-854-8214. Office Fax: 212-854-3554. E-mail: mzulack@law.columbia.edu.

ZULAUF, MADELINE RUTH, photographer, artist; b. Neptune, N.J., Oct. 9, 1948; d. Everett Minor and Mary Elizabeth Slocum; m. Bateston Franklin Stoddard, Jr., Apr. 2, 1967 (div. July 1972); children: Michael, Mary Beth; m. Sander William Zulauf, May 26, 1979. AA, County Coll. of Morris, 1976; BA, Montclair State U., 1978. Photographer U.S. Army Rsch., Devel. & Engring. Ctr., Picatinny Arsenal, N.J., 1979-84, TV prodr., dir., 1984-87, visual info. specialist, 1987—96, multimedia specialist, 1996—2000, visual info. mgr., 2000—. Cons. phototech. program County Coll. of Morris, Randolph, N.J., 1983-88, mem. student co-op adv. bd., 1989-94; pres. federally employed women U.S. Army Rsch., Devel. & Engring. Ctr., Picatinny Arsenal, 1984-85, chairperson fed. women's program, 1987-89. Photographer: (mags.) Horns of Plenty, 1989, Jour. of NJ Poets, 2005, (book) Above the River, 1990; photo exhbns. include Sussex City Arts Coun., 1996-97, James Wright Poetry Festival, Martins Ferry, Ohio, 1999, McKeowns Gallery, Branchville, N.J., 1997, Tiger Gallery, Westerly, RI, 2005. Photographer Jersey Battered Women's Shelter, Morristown, N.J., 1985-88; dep. diocesan convs. Episcopal Diocese Newark, N.J. Recipient Humanitarian award Equal Opportunity Office, 1984. Mem. Acad. Am. Poets, Internat. Ctr. Photography. Episcopalian. Avocations: sailing, travel, hiking. Office: US Army Rsch Devel & Engring Ctr B-176 Picatinny Arsenal NJ 07806 Office Phone: 973-724-3839. Business E-Mail: mszulauf@msn.com.

ZULCH, JOAN CAROLYN, retired medical publishing company executive; b. Great Neck, N.Y., Apr. 10, 1931; d. Walter Howard and Edna Ruth (Howard) Z. BS in Biology, Allegheny Coll., 1952; postgrad., Hunter Coll., 1954. Med. sec. E.R. Squibb & Sons, N.Y.C., 1952; with Macmillan Pub. Co., N.Y.C., 1952-88, editorial asst. med. dept., 1952-56, asst. editor med. dept., 1956-58, editor med. dept., 1958-61, med. editor coll. and profl. div., 1961-75, sr. editor medicine, coll. and profl. div., 1975-78, exec. editor med. books, profl. books div., 1978-79, editor-in-chief, 1979-80, asst. v.p., editor-in-chief profl. books div., 1980-82, v.p., pub. med., nursing, health sci. dept., 1982-85, v.p., pub. med. books, sci., tech., med. dept., 1985-88. Recipient Best Illustrated Med. Book award Assn. Med. Illustrators, 1977, Outstanding Book in Health Sci. award Assn. Am. Pubs., 1982, Woman of Distinction award, 15th Dist. NYS Assembly, 2006. Mem. AAAS, Post Libr. Assn., L.I.U. (rec. sec. 1990-93, exec. coun. 1990—), Friends of Locust Valley Libr. (pres. 1991-93, 94-96, 98-2000, 2004—06, treas. 1993-94, 96-98, 2000-02, 1st v.p. 2002-04, 2006-), Locust Valley C. of C. (bd. dirs. 1997—), Alpha Gamma Delta, Delta Sigma Rho. Republican. Home: 36 Wood Ln Lattingtown PO Box 547 Locust Valley NY 11560-0547

ZUMBRUNNEN, ELIZABETH, artist, educator; m. David Zumbrunnen. BFA, U. Mich., 1971, MA, 1972. Cert. tchr. SC, Hirakata, Japan, 1974. Art tchr. Tri-Creek Sch., Sch. Dist. Oconee Country, Walhalla, SC, 1988—. Adjudicator violin SC Music Educators Assn. Musician (violinist): I Musici Del Piemonte. Mem.: NEA, Blue Ridge Art Assn., SC Arts Alliance, SC Art Edn. Assn., Nat. Art Edn. Assn., SC Edn. Assn. Business E-Mail: zliz@oconee.k12.sc.us.

ZUMO, BILLIE THOMAS, retired biologist; b. Cheyenne, Wyo., Sept. 25, 1936; d. Thomas Elias and Katherine A. (Pappas); m. Charles Vincent, Aug. 21, 1959; 1 child, Thomas J. BA, U. Wyo., Laramie, 1958; MA, U. No. Colo., Greeley, 1963. Cert. tchr. Tchr. Carey Jr. H.S., Cheyenne, 1958-61, 61-63; English lang. tchr. McCormick Jr. H.S., Cheyenne, 1961; biology tchr. Laramie County C.C., Cheyenne; tchr. Ctrl. H.S., Cheyenne, 1963—99; ret., 1999. Exec. bd. Sch. Dist. curriculum adv., 1982-85; chmn. sci. dept., 1990—; mem. faculty adv. com. Ctrl. H.S., 1988—, mem. prin. screening com., 1990-91. Editor: (newsletter) Philogramma. Football statistician Ctrl. Football Team, Cheyenne, 1976—; lay mem. rsch. com. of the Pharmacy Theraputics Com., 1985; judge sch. dist. sci. fair, Cheyenne, 1987-88; ch. choir dir., Cheyenne; judge Nat. Oratorical Contest, Greek Orthodox Archdiocese Am. Recipient Disting. Svc. award Sts. Constandine and Helen Orthodox Ch., 1979, Disting. Svc. award as choir dir. Archbishop Iakovas, NY, 1988, Disting. Svc. award as chior dir. Patriarch Athenagoras, 2006. Mem. Nat. Assn. Biology Tchrs. (state rep. 1992-99), NEA, Cheyenne Tchrs. Edn. Assn., Wyo. Edn. Assn., Nat. Forum of Greek Orthodox Musicians, Ladies Philoptochos Soc. of Denver Diocese (treas. 1989-93, 1st v.p. 1993-95, pres. 1995-99, diocese adv. 1999-2003, diocese philoptochos bd., 2003—, editor newsletter, 1997—, apptd. to nat. philoptochos bd. 1997-99, 2000—, ch. heritage com., nat. philoptochos chmn. Support A Mission Priest), AAUW, Phi Delta Kappa. Democrat. Ea. Greek Orthodox. Avocations: reading, walking, music, golf. Home: 900 Ranger Dr Cheyenne WY 82009-2535 Personal E-mail: bczoom2@att.net.

ZUMPE, DORIS, ethologist, researcher, educator; b. Berlin, May 18, 1940; came to U.S., 1972; d. Herman Frank and Eva (Wagner) Z. BSc, U. London, 1961, PhD, 1970. Asst. to K.Z. Lorenz, Max-Planck-Inst. für Verhaltensphysiologie, Seewiesen, Fed. Republic Germany, 1961-64; rsch. asst. and assoc., lectr. Inst. Psychiatry, U. London, 1965-72; rsch. assoc. Emory U. Sch. Medicine, Atlanta, 1972-74, asst. prof. psychiatry (ethology), 1974-77, assoc. prof., 1977-87, prof., 1987—. Reviewer NSF, 7 sci. jours. Contbr. over 150 articles to profl. jours. NIMH grantee, 1971-2000. Mem. AAAS, Internat. Soc. Psychoneuroendocrinology, Internat. Primatological Soc., Internat. Soc. for Human Ethology, Soc. Behavioral Neuroendocrinology, Am. Soc. Primatologists, N.Y. Acad. Scis., Earl Music Am., Viola da Gamba Soc. Am. Avocation: music. Office: Emory U Sch Medicine Dept Psychiatry Atlanta GA 30322-0001

ZUNICH, JANICE, pediatrician, geneticist, educator, health facility administrator; b. New Kensington, Pa., Sept. 2, 1953; d. Nick and Mary (Zivkovich) Z.; m. Milan Katic, June 20, 1981; children: Nikola Ilija, Milana. BS, Ohio State U., 1974, MD, 1978. Diplomate Am. Bd. Pediat., Nat. Bd. Med. Examiners, Am. Bd. Med. Genetics (clin. genetics, clin. cytogenetics). Intern, then resident in pediat. Columbus Children's Hosp., Ohio, 1978-81; genetics fellow Luth. Gen. Hosp., Park Ridge, Ill., 1981-83; asst. prof. pediat. W.Va. U. Med. Ctr., Morgantown, 1983-85, assoc. dir. cytogenetics, 1984-85; clin. assoc. prof. med. genetics, dir. Genetics Ctr. Ind. U. Sch. Medicine NW, Gary, 1985—. Genetics cons. Cmty. Hosp., Munster, Ind., Porter Meml. Hosp., Valparaiso, Ind., St. Anthony Med. Ctr., Crown Point, Ind., Meth. Hosp., Gary and Merrillville, Ind., St. Margaret Hosp., Hammond, Ind., St. Mary Med. Ctr., Hobart, Ind., LaPorte (Ind.) Hosp., Meml. Hosp., South Bend, Ind. Contbr. articles to profl. jours. Mem. med. com. Planned Parenthood, N.W.-N.E. Ind., Merrillville, 1987-99; mem. med. adv. com. Svcs. for Children with Spl. Health Care Needs, Indpls., 1989-92; chmn. Lake County Task Force on Teen Pregnancy, 1998-2000; mem. Lake County Child Fatality Rev. Com., 2003-; mem. Lake County Fetal and Infant Mortality Rev. Com., 2004—; mem. Lake County Child Protection Team, 2000—; treas. Mental Health Assn. Lake County, 1995-99, bd. dirs., 1991—. Named Person of Yr. Down Syndrome Assn. N.W. Ind., Highland, 1988; Charles F. Whitten fellow Sickle Cell Found. N.W. Ind., 1990. Fellow: AMA, Am. Coll. Med. Genetics (founding fellow), Am. Acad. Pediat.; mem.: Lake County Med. Soc., Ind. State Med. Assn., Am. Soc. Human Genetics, Great Lakes Regional Genetics Group (financing genetics svcs. sub-com. 1988—99), Alpha Epsilon Delta, Phi Beta Kappa. Eastern Orthodox. Avocations: piano, folk dancing, choral singing, travel. Office: Ind U Sch Medicine NW 3400 Broadway Gary IN 46408-1101 Office Phone: 219-980-6560. Business E-Mail: jzunich@iun.edu.

ZUNINO, NATALIA, psychologist; b. N.Y.C., Nov. 23, 1937; d. Frank Anthony and Elizabeth (Delafield) Zunino; m. Philip Puschel, June 29, 1974 (div. 1978). BA, Mt. Holyoke Coll., Mass., 1959; MA, Columbia U., 1962, NYU, 1975, PhD, 1982. Rschr. Time-Life Books, N.Y.C., 1962-67; sr. editor Harcourt Brace Jovanovich, N.Y.C., 1967-80; staff psychotherapist Met. Ctr. for Mental Health, N.Y.C., 1983-85; pvt. practice, 1984—; staff psychotherapist Washington Sq. Inst., N.Y.C., 1984-87; supr. Met. Inst. Tng. in Psychoanalytic Psychotherapy, N.Y.C., 1985—; supr., staff psychotherapist Eating Disorder Resource Ctr., N.Y.C., 1986—2004; mem. faculty Ctr. for Study of Anorexia and Bulimia, N.Y.C., 1987—, supr., 1987—; psychotherapist family and couple treatment Inst. Contemporary Psychotherapy, N.Y.C., 1988—90; participant intensive-extern program Family Inst. Westchester, Mt. Vernon, NY, 1990-94. Mem. intake com. Ctr. Study Anorexia and Bulimia, 1985—;

adj. asst. prof. Coll. S.I., NY, 1984—86. Editor: Psychology: Its Principles and Applications, 1969, 8th edit. 1984, Sociology: The Study of Human Relationships, 1972, 2nd edit. 1977; contbr. articles to profl. jours. Mem. APA, Acad. for Eating Disorders, Nat. Eating Disorders Assn., Ea. Group Pscyhotherapy Soc. (tng. program 1997-98). Avocations: horseback riding, gardening. Home: 115 4th Ave New York NY 10003-4909

ZUNKEL, GRETCHEN M., medical/surgical nurse, educator; children: Erica K., Mark D. BS, U. Colo., Denver; M in Nursing, UCLA; PhD, U. Wash., Seattle, 1996. Advanced practice nurse, Am. Nurses Credentialing Ctr., 1995. Advanced practice clin. nurse specialist Health Ptnrs. Med. Group, St. Paul, 2003—. Lectr. U. Minn., Mpls., 2002—, U. Wash., Bothell, Ariz. State U.; bd. dirs. Ctrl. Ctr. Mental Health, Spring Lake, Minn. Contbr. articles to profl. jours. Recipient Carol Lindeman Nursing Rsch. award, Western Inst. Nursing, 1998; Marilyn Sime fellow, U. Minn., Ctr. for Spirituality and Healing, 2004—06. Mem.: Nat. Orgn. Nurse Practitioner Faculties, Oncology Nursing Soc. (advanced nursing rsch. 2006—), Sigma Theta Tau. Home: 2120 Wellesley Ave Saint Paul MN 55105 Office: University of Minnesota 308 Harvard St SE Minneapolis MN 55455 Office Phone: 651-254-2752. Business E-Mail: zunke004@umn.edu.

ZUPKUS, ELLEN CICCONE, clinical psychologist, consultant; b. Passaic, N.J., Oct. 28, 1954; d. Joseph Condoluro and Emma (Gash) Ciccone; m. Edward Walter Zupkus Jr., July 29, 1984; children: Maureen, Erin, Emily, Lauren. BA, Kean Coll. N.J., 1976; MA, Seton Hall U., 1978, PhD, 1985. Cert. sch. psychologist N.J.; Nat. cert sch. psychologist, group psychotherapist; lic. psychologist, N.J., N.Y. Adj. instr. Seton Hall U., South Orange, N.J., 1979-84; chairperson child study team Bergen County Spl. Svcs. Sch. Dist., Paramus, N.J., 1983-85; pvt. practice Holmdel, N.J., 1985—; adj. instr. Rider Coll., Lawrenceville, N.J., 1986; prin. clin. psychologist Marlboro (N.J.) Psychiat. Hosp., 1986-88; cons. psychologist Arthur Brisbane Child Treatment Ctr., Farmingdale, N.J., 1988-89; adj. instr. Monmouth Coll., West Long Branch, N.J., 1989; cons. psychologist Cedar Grove (N.J.) Residential Ctr., 1989—. Cons. psychologist Adult Diagnostic and Treatment Ctr., Avenel, N.J., 1980-82; clin. psychologist Woodbridge Child Diagnostic Ctr., Avenel, 1980-83; presenter workshop on Million Adolescent Personality Inventories, 1989, Internat. Play Therapy Conf., The Netherlands, 1996. Author: (with others) Conference on the Millon Inventories, 1987; contbr. articles to profl. jours. Mem. Monmouth County Sexual Abuse Coalition, Monmouth County Child Sexual Abuse Com., Nat. Audubon Soc., Nat. Wildlife Fedn., Vienna, Va. Mem. APA (assoc.), N.J. Psychol. Assn., N.J. Assn. Sch. Psychologists, Monmouth Ocean County Psychol. Assn., Seton Hall U. Sch. Psychology Assn. (pres. 1981), N.J. Network for Treatment Sex Offenders, Am. Coll. Forensic Examiners. Avocations: running, bird watching, hiking. Office: 51 Main St Holmdel NJ 07733-2310

ZURAITIS, MARITA, insurance company executive; V.p. ceded-reins. USF&G Comml. Ins. Group, br. v.p., regional v.p., sr. v.p.; sr. v.p. U.S. ins. ops. The St. Paul Co., Inc., St. Paul, 1998—2001, exec. v.p. Comml. Lines Group, 2001—02, CEO Comml. Lines Group, 2003—. Office: The Saint Paul Cos Inc 385 Washington St Saint Paul MN 55102

ZURAW, KATHLEEN ANN, special education and physical education educator; b. Bay City, Mich., Sept. 29, 1960; d. John Luke and Clara Josephine (Kilian) Zuraw. AA with high honors, Delta Community Coll., 1980; BS with high honors, Mich. State U., 1984, MA, 1987. Cert. spl. edn., mentally impaired phys. edn. grade K-12, adaptive phys. edn. tchr., Mich. Summer water safety instr. Camp Midicha, Columbia, Mich., 1982, Bay Cliff Health Camp, Big Bay, Mich., 1983; summer spl. edn. tchr. Jefferson Orthopedic Sch., Honolulu, 1984, 85, 86, Ingham Intermediate Sch. Dist., Mason, Mich., 1987; spl. edn. tchr. Bay Arenac Intermediate Sch. Dist., Bay City, 1985-87, Berrien County Intermediate Sch. Dist., Berrien Springs, Mich., 1987—. Mem. citizen amb program fitness delegation People's Republic China, 1991. Area 17 coach Mich. Spl. Olympics, Berrien Springs, 1987—; mem. YMCA, St. Joseph, Mich., 1987—, Y-Ptnrs., 1989, Coun. Exceptional Children; participant Citizen Ambassador Delegation to People's Republic of China, 1991. Mem. Am. Alliance Health, Phys. Edn., Recreation and Dance, Phi Theta Kappa, Phi Kappa Phi, Phi Delta Kappa. Roman Catholic. Avocations: sports, crafts. Home: 7306 W S Saginaw Rd Bay City MI 48706 Office Phone: 269-473-2600.

ZURAW, LISA ANN, chemistry professor, department chairman; b. Worcester, Mass., July 25, 1960; d. Francis and Ann Frederico; m. Paul J. Zuraw. BA, St. Anselm Coll., Manchester, NH, 1982; PhD, Duke U., Durham, NC, 1988. Asst., assoc. prof. chemistry Citadel, Charleston, SC, 1992—, dept. head chemistry, 2006—. Mem. Coll. Bd. Advanced Placement Chemistry Test Devel. Com., 1997—2004, 2006—, chair, 2001—04. Vol. Girl Scouts Am., Mt. Pleasant, SC, 2004—06; exhibit guide SC Aquarium, 2002—06. Recipient Medbury Tchg. award, Citadel, 2002. Office: Citadel Chemistry Dept 171 Moultrie St Charleston SC 29409 Office Phone: 843-953-4976.

ZURBUCHEN, SUSAN JANE, arts consultant; b. Madison, Wis., June 28, 1949; d. Herbert August and Ruth Helen (Pfaffenbach) Z. BA in Speech and Theatre, Lakeland Coll., Sheboygan, Wis., 1970; MA in Theatre Arts, U. Minn., 1972. Regional coordinator Office Criminal Justice Programs, Traverse City, Mich., 1976-77; bus. mgr. Old Town Playhouse, Traverse City, 1978-81; dir. adminstrn. Ind. Arts Commn., Indpls., 1982-85; arts cons. 10th Pan Am. Games, Indpls., 1985-87; mem. faculty arts adminstrn. and theatre Butler U., Indpls., 1988—. Mng. dir. Indpls. Children's Choir, 1994—. Bd. dirs. Criminal Justice Adv. Council, Traverse City, 1976-82; pres. bd. dirs. Women's Resource Ctr., Traverse City, 1977-80; bd. dirs. Very Spl. Arts Ind., 1989-92, Fiesta Indpls., Ind. Assembly Local Arts Agys., 1995—. Mem. LWV (bd. dirs. 1981-82), Am. Theatre Assn. Mem. United Ch. of Christ.

ZURCHER, AMELIA ANNE, literature educator; b. N.Y.C., Feb. 16, 1965; d. Arnold John and Sarah Sykes Zurcher; children from previous marriage: Story Gresham Sandy, William Henry Sandy. BA, Yale U., New Haven, 1987; MPhil, Oxford U., England, 1989; PhD, Princeton, NJ, 1998. Asst. prof. English Marquette U., Milw., 1997—. Marshall scholarship, British Govt., 1987—89, Whiting fellowship, Mrs. Giles Whiting Found., 1992—93, Mellon fellowship, Newberry Libr., 2001—02. Mem.: Midern Lang. Assn. Office: Marquette U Dept English Milwaukee WI 53201 Office Phone: 414-288-3475. Business E-Mail: amelia.zurcher@mu.edu.

ZURENDA, DEB, biology educator; b. Pa. BS cum laude, Millersville U., Pa., 1986. Recipient Outstanding Tchr. award, Shippensburg U., 1995—96.

ZURFLUEH, LINDA JUNE, allergy and immunology nurse, educator; b. Passaic, N.J., June 22, 1948; d. Herman and Aline (Musterer) Morgner; m. Alfred Zurflueh, July 21, 1968; children: John P., Jennette E. Diploma, Hackensack Hosp. Sch. Nursing, 1969; BSN magna cum laude, Felician Coll., Lodi, N.J., 1985. Cert. asthma educator. Lactation cons. in pvt. practice, Waldwick, NJ; surg. staff nurse Hackensack Hosp.; office nurse Hohokus. Mem. Am. Acad. Allergy, Asthma and Immunology, Assn. Asthma Educators, Alumni Assn. Hackensack Hosp. Sch. Nursing, Sigma Theta Tau.

ZUSMAN, EDIE ELLEN, neurosurgeon; b. El Paso, Oct. 29, 1963; d. Sidney Harold and Sandra Phyllis Zusman; m. Stephen Roy Pratt, Feb. 17, 1991; children: Adam, Abby. BS, Northwestern U., 1985, MD, 1987. Diplomate Am. Bd. Neurol. Surgery, Nat. Bd. Med. Examiners. With U. Calif., San Francisco, 1993-94, clin. instr., 1994-97, molecular med. rsch. fellow, 1994-96; staff neurosurgeon Kaiser Permanent, Sacramento, 1997-99; asst. prof. U Calif. Davis Sch. Medicine, Sacramento, 1999—; dir. adult neurosurgery Sutter Neuroscience Inst., Sacramento. Mem. exec. com. Coun. State Neurol. Socs., 1997—; adj. asst. prof. neurol. surgery U. Calif., Davis; prin. investigator Ctr. for Biophotonics Sci. and Tech. Author: The Outcome Following Traumatic Spinal Cord Injuries, 1992; contbr. articles to profl. jours. Participant Habitat for Humanity, Oakland, Calif., 1997—. Mem. AMA, Am. Assn. Neurol. Surgeons (bd. dirs.), Congress Neurol. Surgeons, Calif. Assn. Neurol. Surgeons, Northwestern U. Alumni Assn., Women in Neurological Surgery (past pres.), Coun. of State Neurosurgical Soc., Am. Epilepsy Soc. Avocations: tennis, opera. Office: Sutter Neuroscience Med Group Ste 500 2800 L St Sacramento CA 95816 Office Phone: 916-454-6850. Business E-Mail: zusmane@sutterhealth.org. E-mail: eezusman@ucdavis.edu.

ZUSSY, NANCY LOUISE, librarian; b. Tampa, Fla., Mar. 4, 1947; d. John David and Patsy Ruth (Stone) Roche; m. R. Mark Allen, Dec. 20, 1986. BA in Edn., U. Fla., 1969; MLS, U. So. Fla., 1977, MS in Pub. Mgmt., 1980. Cert. librarian, Wash. Ednl. evaluator State of Ga., Atlanta, 1969-70; media specialist DeKalb County Schs., Decatur, Ga., 1970-71; researcher Ga. State Libr., Atlanta, 1971; asst. to dir. reference Clearwater (Fla.) Pub. Libr., 1972-78, dir. librs., 1978-81; dep. state libr. Wash. State Libr., Olympia, 1981-86, state libr., 1986—2002; owner Nancy Zussy Allen Massage Therapy, 2003—. Chmn. Consortium Automated Librs., Olympia, 1982-97; cons. various pub. librs., Wash. and other U.S. states, Uzbekistan, Russia, 1981—; exec. officer Wash. Libr. Network, 1986-90; v.p. WLN (non-profit orgn.), 1990-93. Contbr. articles to profl. jours. Treas. Thurston-Mason Community Mental Health Bd., Olympia, 1983-85, bd. dirs., 1982-85; mem. race com. Seafair Hydroplane Race, Seattle, 1986—, mem. milk carton derby team, 1994—, announcer, prodr. air show; co-chair Pub. Info. Access Policy Task Force, 1995-96; mem. Gov.'s Work Group on Comml. Access to Govt. Electronic Records, 1996-97; mem. K-20 Telecomms. Oversight and Policy Com., 1996-2002. Mem. ALA, Assn. Specialized and Coop. Libr. Agys. (legis. com. 1983-86, chmn. 1985-87, vice chmn. state libr. agys. sect. 1985-86, chmn. 1986-87, chmn. govt. affairs com. Libr. Adminstrn. and Mgmt. Assn., 1986-87), Freedom To Read Found. (bd. dirs. 1987-91), Chief Officers of State Libr. Agys. (bd. dirs.-at-large 1987-90, v.p., pres.-elect 1990-92, pres. 1992-94), Wash. Libr. Assn. (co-founder legis. planning com. 1982-2002, fed. rels. coord. 1984-2002), Fla. Libr. Assn. (legis. and planning com. 1978-81), Pacific N.W. Libr. Assn., Rotary (bd. dirs. 1995-96), Phi Kappa Phi, Phi Beta Mu. Avocations: hiking, barbershop quartets, boating, cross country skiing. Office: 1722 Harrison Ave NW Olympia WA 98502

ZWART-LUDEMAN, THERESA, graphics designer, artist; b. Tokyo, Sept. 26, 1953; arrived in U.S., 1955; m. Curtis D. Zwart, May 31, 1970 (div. 1983); 1 child, Justin C.; m. Clifford G. Ludeman, June 30, 1996. Student, Sch. Visual Arts, N.Y.C, 1978-81, Silvermine Sch. Arts, Conn., 1982-86. Asst. art dir. Arlington Pub., Westport, Conn., 1979-81; sr. art dir. Save The Children, Westport, 1981-86; art dir. MCA/Target Market Comm., Westport, 1986-87; creative/design cons. The Common Fund, Westport, 1987-93; prin. Zwart Design, Chester, Conn., 1988—; design cons. HEH Mktg., Wilton, 1990—, Pitney Bowes, Stamford, 1993—; owner Zwart-Ludeman Studio, Chester. Bd. dirs. Rowayton Art Ctr., Conn.; affiliate 18 Marshall St. Art Cooperative, Westport Art Ctr. One woman shows include: Solo Show at Studio 18, South Norwalk, Conn., 1998, Blood Root, 1999; 4 person shows include: Studio 3/On Location, 1992; group shows include: Studio 3, 1989, Nexus Gallery, N.Y.C., 1998; exhbns., juried shows include: Northeast Ann. Show at Silvermine, 1997, 98, New Britain (Conn.) Mus. Am. Art Fair, 1998, Nat. Acad. Mus. Design N.Y.C., 1998, Bridgeport U., Conn. Landscapes, 1999, New Art Ann. '99 Stamford Mus. Nature Ctr.; commd. Feb. window display Max's Art Supplies, Westport, conn., 1998; pub. in Apr. issue of Art Calendar (centerfold winner), 1999. Recipient Communicator award, Disting. award N.Y.C., 1997, award of Distinction, Zanders/Lindenmeyer, 1992, Silver award Advt. Club Fairfield County, 1983, DMA awards, 1983, 2d. prize Watercolors, Rowayton Art Ctr., 1999. Mem.: Lyme Art Assn., Essex Art Assn. Conservative Democrat. Unitarian. Home: 37 Pleasant St Chester CT 06412-1122 E-mail: zdes@aol.com.

ZWICKE, PAULA ANN, literature and language educator, communications educator; d. Warren Dean and Barbara Jane Bartels; m. Timothy David Zwicke, Oct. 30, 1982; children: Joseph Warren David, Tiffany Ann. BSc in English, Secondary Edn. magna cum laude, Northland Coll., 1998; EdM with Writing emphasis, St. Mary's U., Minn., 2005. Tchr. English Hayward H.S., Wis., 1999, Phillips H.S., 1999, Medford H.S., 1999—2000, Pk. Falls H.S., 2000—. Facilitator dist. writing plan Pk. Falls Sch. Dist., 2001—; adj. comm. instr. Northctrl. Tech. Coll., Wausau, 2004; adv. Nat. Honor Soc. Park Falls H.S., Park Falls, Wis., 2004—. Foster parent Price County Human Svcs., Phillips, 1990—2000, mentor, 1990—2000; Sunday sch. tchr. Peace Luth. Ch., Park Falls, 1990—2000, youth group leader, 1990—2000, lay reader, 2005. Recipient 10 Yr. Disting. Svc. award, Price County Human Svcs., 2000; Leadership and Svc. scholarship, Northland Coll., 1995. Mem.: Wis. Coun. Tchrs. of English and Lang. Arts (dist. dir. 2004), Nat. Coun. Tchrs. of English. Avocations: reading, writing, mountain biking, snowshoeing, hunting.

ZWICK-TAPLEY, SARAH LYNN, theater educator, director; b. Chgo., Sept. 7, 1969; d. Richard Philip and Carol Jean (Zwick) Tapley; m. Samuel Goodman (div.). BA, Ill.State U., Normal, 1991; MFA, Harvard U., Cambridge, Mass., 1999. Theater instr. Nebr. Scholars Inst., Lincoln, 2000; adj. theater prof. U. Northern Iowa, Cedar Falls, 2000, Coe Coll., Cedar Rapids, Iowa, 2000—01, U. Northern Iowa, 2001—02; theater dir. Newman U., Wichita, Kans., 2002—03; theater lectr. Iowa State U., Ames, 2003—; dept. chair Trollwood Performing Arts Sch., Fargo, ND, 2003—. Theater tutor Pvt. Practice, Ames, Iowa, 2004—; Irene Ryans acting judge Am. Coll.Theater Festival, Newton, Mass., 1999, 2006. Dir.: (plays) Once Upon a Mattress, 2002; actor: Tartufe, 2000, Snis of Sor Juana, 1998. Vol. dog walker Human Soc., Lincoln, Nebr., 2000; vol. Octagon Ctr. for the Arts, Ames, 2005; lic. foster care provider Iowa Youth and Shelter Services, 2006. Named to Metropolitan Who's Who, Deer Park, NY, 2006; recipient Who's Who in Fine Arts Edn., 2005. Mem.: AEA. Democrat. Unitarian Universalist. Avocations: gardening, animals, independent films. Office: Iowa State U 2238 Pearson Hall Ames IA 50011

ZWICKY, BARBARINA EXITA, humanities educator, researcher; d. Fritz and Anna Margaritha Zwicky; 1 child, Christian Alexander Fritz. Diploma in fashion design, Modeschule Brunn, Zurich, 1984; AS, Pasadena City Coll., 1999, AA, 2000; BA, Pacific Oaks Coll., 2002, MA, 2005. Cert. nursing asst. Calif., 1990. Mgr. Continental Enterprises, Pasadena, 1980—91; tchr. human devel. Pacific Oaks Coll., Pasadena, 2003—. Owner Barby's Baby Boutique, Monrovia, Calif., 1985—90. Bd. dirs. Arcadia Am. Little League, Calif., 2004, Fritz Zwicky Found., Switzerland; vol. Huntington Meml. Hosp., 1995, ARC, Pasadena, 2000; activist Rep. Party, Pasadena. Mem.: AAUW (chair pub. policy 2002—, mem. Evelyn Brandt Scholarship com. 2000—), Matterhorn Young Swiss Club, Swiss Ladies Soc., United Swiss Soc. So. Calif., Omicron Mu Delta, Alpha Gamma Sigma (hon. bd. 1999). Republican. Methodist. Avocations: skiing, art, literature, swimming. Home: 2065 Oakdale Ave Pasadena CA 91107 E-mail: barbarinaz@aol.com.

ZWIEBEL, MARIE BEE, retired librarian; b. Berea, W.Va., Apr. 4, 1934; d. Ernest Kay and Lillian Tallulah (Bottoms) Bee; m. Doyle Keith Zwiebel, Aug. 20, 1955 (dec.); children: Kevin Vaughn (dec.), Hans Kent (dec.), Veronica Ileen Zwiebel Sperry. BA cum laude, Salem Coll., 1955; MA, W.Va. U., 1978; postgrad., Marshall U., 1981-82. Cert. tchr., W.Va. English tchr. Canisteo (N.Y.) Cen. Sch., 1956-57; sci. and math. tchr. Richburg (N.Y.) Cen. Sch., 1957-60; dir. edn. W.Va. Indsl. Home for Youth, 1967-79; libr. Norwood Jr. High Sch., Nutter Fort, W.Va., 1979-81; libr., head tchr. Van Horn Elem. Sch., Salem, W.Va., 1981—. Mem. Elem. Classroom Instrn. Act Chpt. I Adv. Coun., Clarksburg, W.Va., 1980—; lead tchr. Cmty. Arts Partnership in Edn., 1995—. Author of poems; editor: Reference Skills (4-6), 1991; quilting artisan, Ft. New Salem, Salem, W.Va., 1989—. Sec. Camp Joy, Inc., Berea, 1990—; mem. Salem Bicentennial Com., 1991-95; mem. Christian Socal Action Com., Janesville, Wis., 1991-95, sec., 1993—; mem. Salem-Tiekyo U. Aux., Salem, 1991—; bd. dirs. Highland (W.Va.) Sch., 1981—; chmn. Harrison County Mini-Grant Com., Clarksburg, W.Va., 1988-95; mem. City of Salem Hist. Preservation Commn., 1992—. Grantee W.Va. Dept. Edn., 1990, Harrison County Bd. Edn., 1991. Mem. ALA, W.Va. Bus. and Profl. Women (pres. 1983-84, Woman of Yr. 1985), W.Va. Profl. Educators Assn., Harrison County Hist. Assn., Harrison County Cultural Found., Internat. Quilting Guild, Appalachian Folklife Found., Alpha Delta Kappa (historian 1990-92). Republican. Seventh Day Baptist. Avocations: reading, poetry, gardening, crafts. Home: 2788 Tysinger Rd Denton NC 27239-7049 Personal E-mail: mzwiebel@direcway.com. Business E-Mail: mzwiebel@hughes.net.

ZWILICH, ELLEN TAAFFE, composer; b. Miami, Fla., Apr. 30, 1939; d. Edward Porter and Ruth (Howard) Taaffe; m. Joseph Zwilich, June 22, 1969 (dec. June 1979). MusB, Fla. State U., 1960, MusM, 1962; D Mus. Arts, Juilliard Sch., 1975; studies with Roger Sessions and Elliott Carter; MusD (hon.), Oberlin Coll., 1987, Converse Coll., 1994; LHD (hon.), Manhattanville Coll., 1991, Marymount Manhattan Coll., 1994, N.Y. New Sch., Mannes, 1995, Mich. State U., 2006. Francis Eppes disting. prof. Fla. State U., Tallahassee, 1999—. Composer in residence Santa Fe Chamber Music Festival, 1990, Am. Acad. Rome, 1990; first Composer's Chair, Carnegie Hall, 1995-99, Saratoga Chamber Music Festival, 2004. Premiere, Symposium for Orch., Pierre Boulez, N.Y.C., 1975, Chamber Symphony and Passages, Boston Musica Viva, Richard Pittman, 1979, 82. Symphony 1, Gunther Schuller, Am. Composers Orch., 1982; violinist Am. Symphony, N.Y.C., 1965-73; composer: Sonata in Three Movements, 1973-74; String Quartet, 1974; Clarino Quartet, 1977; Chamber Symphony, 1979; Passages (for Soprano and Chamber Ensemble), 1981; String Trio, 1982; Symphony 1:3 Movements for Orch., 1982 (Grammy nomination New World Records, 1987); Divertimento, 1983; Einsame Nacht, 1971; Emlekezet, 1978; Im Nebel, 1972; Passages for Soprano and Orch., 1982; Trompeten, 1974; Fantasy for Harpsichord, 1983; Intrada, 1983; Prologue and Variations, 1983; Double Quartet for Strings, Chamber Music Soc. of Lincoln Ctr., 1984; Celebration for Orch., Indpls. Symphony, John Nelson, 1984; Symphony #2 (Cello Symphony) San Francisco Symphony, Edo De Waart, 1985, Symphony #2 Louisville Orch. recording, L.L. Smith (Grammy nomination 1991); Concerto Grosso 1985, Handel Festival Orch., Steven Simon, 1986; Concerto for Piano and Orch., Detroit Symphony, Gunther Herbig, Marc-André Hamelin, 1986; Images for 2 Pianos and Orch., Nat. Symphony Orch., F. Machetti, 1987; Tanzspiel, Peter Martins N.Y.C. Ballet, 1987; Praeludium Boston chpt. AGO, 1987; Trio for piano, violin and cello; Kalichstein, Laredo, Robinson trio, 1987; Symbolon, Zubin Mehta and the N.Y. Philharm., Leningrad and Moscow (USSR), N.Y.C. (Koussevitsky Internat. Rec. award nominee 1990), 1988; concerto for trombone and orch. J. Friedman, Sir Georg Solti, Chgo. Symphony, 1989, concerto for trombone and orch. Christian Lindberg, James De Priest, Malmö Symphony, concerto for flute and orch. D.A. Dwyer, Seija Ozawa, Boston Symphony, 1990, quintet for clarinet and string quartet David Schiffrin, Chamber Music N.W., Lincoln Ctr. Chamber Mus. Soc., 1990; concerto for oboe and orch. John Mack, Christoph von Dohnanyi, Cleve. Orch., 1991; concerto for bass trombone strings, timpani and cymbals Chgo. Symphony Orch. Ch. Vernon, Daniel Barenboim, 1991; concerto for violin, violoncello and orch. Jaime Laredo, Sharon Robinson, Louisville Orch., L. Smith, 1991; Immigrant Voices Peter Leonard, St. Lukes Orch., N.Y. Internat. Festival ot the Arts Chorus, Ellis Island, 1991, concerto for flute and orch, D.A. Dwyer, J. Sedares, London Symphony Orch., 1992, Symphony # 3 (Grammy nominee 1993), J. Ling, N.Y. Philharmonic, 1993, concerto for bassoon and orch., Nancy Goeres, Lorin Maazel, Pitts. Symphony, 1993, concerto for horn and string Orch., David Jolley, Rochester Philharm., L.L. Smith., 1993, Fantasy for Orch., JoAnn Falletta, Long Beach Symphony Orch., 1994, American Concerto Doc Severinsen, J. Falletta San Diego Symphony, 1994, A Simple Magnificat, 1994, Triple Concerto Kalichstein, Laredo, Robinson Trio Zdenek Macal, Minn. Orch., 1995, for piano and orch., Peanuts Gallery, 1996, violin concerto, Pamela Frank, H. Wolff, 1997; String Quartet # 2, 1998, Emerson Quartet; Upbeat! 1998, Nat. Symphony Orch., conducted by Anthony Aibel, Symphony # 4 (orch., chorus, children's chorus) Mich. State U., L. Gregorian 2000, Lament for solo piano Carnegie Hall, 2000, Millenium Fantasy for Piano & Orch., J. Biegel, J. Cobos-Lopez, Cin. Symphony, 2000, Lament for Cello & Piano, Met. Mus., N.Y.C., 2000, Partita for Violin & String Orch., Carnegie Hall, 2001, One Nation, 2002, Openings for Orch., 2002 JoAnn Falletta Va. Symphony, Clarinet Concerto, D. Shifrin, Chamber Music Soc. of Lincoln Ctr., Buffalo Philharm, 2002, Episodes for Violin & Piano, Itzhak Perlman, 2003, Quartet for Oboe & Strings, Saratoga Festival, 2004, Rituals for 5 Percussionists and Orchestra, Iris Orchestra, Nexus, 2004, LUVN BLM, Calif. Ear Unit, 2005, Naxos Am. Classics, Violin Concerto and Rituals, M.Stern, Frank, 2005; New World Records: Music By Ellen Taaffe Zwilich; N.Y. Philharm. conducted by Zubin Mehta. Bd. dir. Copland Fund. Named Martha Baird Rockefeller Fund rec. grantee, 1977, 1979, 1982, Guggenheim fellow, 1981; named to, Fla. Artists Hall of Fame, 1994; recipient Elizabeth Sprague Coolidge Chamber Music prize, 1974, Gold medal, G.B. Viotti, Vercelli, Italy, 1975, citation, Ernst von Dohnanyi, 1981, Pulitzer prize for music, 1983, Composers award, Lancaster Symphony Orch., Arturo Toscanini Music Critics award, 1987, Alfred I. DuPont award, 1991, Performing Arts award, Miami Ctr. Performing Arts, 2000, named, Musical Am. Composer of Yr., 1999, Key to the City Cinn., 2001. Fellow: Am. Acad. Arts & Sci.; mem.: AAAL (Acad. award 1984), Guggenheim Found. (bd. dirs.), MacDowell Colony (bd. dirs.), Am. Fedn. Musicians (hon.; life), BMI Found. (bd. dirs.), Am. Music Ctr. (v.p. 1982—84, bd. dirs.). Office: Coll Music Fla State Univ Tallahassee FL 32306-1180 Office Phone: 850-644-4744. Office Fax: 850-644-2033.

ZWIRGZDAS, SHIRLEY MARGARET, physical education educator; b. St. Louis, Mar. 6, 1954; d. Kenneth Wesley and Barbara Lee (Rea) Jones; children: Michael, Kristen. BSc, U. Wis., LaCrosse, 1976. Tchr. phys. edn. Westosha Ctrl. H.S., Salem, Wis., track coach, 1989—, cross country coach, 1979—82, 2005—. Office: Westosha Ctrl HS PO Box 38 Salem WI 53168 E-mail: margy@westosha.k12.wi.us.

ZYGLOCKE, ANN MADDING, elementary school educator; b. Ft. Benning, Ga., Mar. 9, 1950; d. Albert Scott and Dorothy (Peacock) Madding; m. Walter Frank Zyglocke, Jr., Dec. 27, 1969; children: Christopher David, Brian Michael. BA in Elem. Edn., Va. Commonwealth U., 1986. Tchr. Chesterfield County Pub. Schs., Richmond, Va., 1987—. Records chmn. Richmond Metro Aquatic League, 1989—; membership chmn. Monacan H.S. Athletic Boosters, 1988—. Recipient Presdl. award NSF, 1994, Tchg. Excellence award Greater Richmond Cmty. Found., 1989. Methodist. Office: Crestwood Elem Sch 7600 Whittington Dr Richmond VA 23225-2137 Home: 9007 Spyglass Hill Cres Chesterfield VA 23832-2592

ZYGOCKI, RHONDA I., oil industry executive; b. St. John's, Nfld., July 1957; B.Civil Engring., Meml. U. of Nfld., 1980. Petroleum engr. Chevron Can. Resources, Calgary, Canada, gen. mgr. strategic bus. svcs., 1993—94; profit ctr. mgr. Chevron U.S.A. Prodn. Co., Houston, 1994—97; CFO Chevron Can. Resources, Calgary, 1997—99; mgr. strategic planning Chevron Corp., San Ramon, Calif., 1999—2000, advisor to chmn. bd., 2000—01; mng. dir. ChevronTexaco Australia Pty. Ltd., Perth, Australia, 2001—03; v.p. health, environment and safety Chevron Texaco Corp., San Ramon, 2003—. Mem.: Engrs. Without Borders (bd. dirs.), Internat. Petroleum Industry Environ. Conservation Assn. (bd. dirs.), Internat. Assn. Oil and Gas Prodrs. (bd. dirs.). Office: Chevron Texaco Corp 6001 Bollinger Canyon Rd San Ramon CA 94583-2324

ZYROFF, ELLEN SLOTOROFF, information scientist, classicist, educator; b. Atlantic City, N.J., Aug. 1, 1946; d. Joseph George and Sylvia Beverly (Roth) Slotoroff; m. Jack Zyroff, June 21, 1970; children: Dena Rachel, David Aaron. AB, Barnard Coll., 1968; MA, The Johns Hopkins U., 1969, PhD, 1971; MS, Columbia U., 1973. Instr. The Johns Hopkins U., Balt., 1970-71, Yeshiva U., N.Y.C., 1971-72, Bklyn Coll., 1971-72; libr., instr. U. Calif., 1979, 81, 91, San Diego State U., 1981-85, 94; prof. San Diego Mesa Coll., 1981-95; dir. The Reference Desk Rsch. Svcs., La Jolla, Calif., 1983—; prin. libr. San Diego County Libr., 1985—. V.p. Archaeol. Soc. Am., Balt., 1970-71. Author: The Author's Apostrophe in Epic from Homer Through Lucan, 1971, Cooperative Library Instruction for Maximum Benefit, 1989; contbr. articles to profl. jours. Pres. Women's Am. ORT, San Diego, 1979-81, Zionist Orgn. of Am., San Diego dist., 1997-2000; mem. adv. bd. With Israel Now. Mem.: ALA (chair divsn. and roundtable coms. 1982—, coun. 2003—), Libr. Congress Cataloging in Publs. Adv. Group, Assn. Jewish Librs., Am.

Classical League, Calif. Libr. Assn. (assembly 1993—99, editor Calif. Librs. 1997—99, pres. mgmt. sect. 2000—01), Am. Philol. Assn., Toastmasters, Beta Phi Mu. E-mail: eszyroff@hotmail.com.

ZYSBERG, JANET GAIL, elementary school educator; d. Jerome and Esther Zeller; m. Jeffrey P. Zysberg, Nov. 4, 1989; 1 child, Zachary. BA, Bklyn. Coll., N.Y., 1990; MS, Bklyn. Coll., 1993, postgrad. Cert. tchr. NY, gifted edn. tchr. NY. 5th grade tchr. NYC Dept. Edn., Pub. Sch. 272, Bklyn., 1992—99; sci. facilitator NYC Dept. Edn. Pub. Sch. 272, Bklyn., 1999—. Grantee, Donors Choose, 2005—06. Mem.: NSTA, NY State Sci. Tchrs. Assn., Wildlife Conservation Soc., United Fedn. Tchrs. (chpt. leader 2000—06, Trachtenberg award 2004), NY State Union Tchrs. Office: Public Sch 272 101-24 Seaview Ave Brooklyn NY 11236 Office Phone: 718-241-1300. Office Fax: 718-241-5549. Business E-Mail: jzysber@nycenet.edu.

Geographic Index

UNITED STATES

ALABAMA

Alexander City
Chapman, Mary Kathryn *elementary school educator*
Towery, Sarah Carlisle *artist, retired educator*
Wheeles, Emily S. *biology educator*

Andalusia
Cross, Charlotte Lord *retired social worker, artist*

Anniston
Bragg, Cheryl *museum director*
Howell, Laura Clark *biologist, educator, small business owner*
Sparks, Telitha Elaine *music educator, director*

Athens
Gasbarro, Dottie Fuller *mathematics professor*
Kemp, Ann *retired librarian*
Lafevor, Kimberly Ann *human resources specialist, educator*
Newton, Janet Gail *office manager*
Page, Caroline Jane *social worker*
Smith, Patricia Crawford *elementary school educator*

Atmore
Smith, Debra L. *band director*

Attalla
Saffels, Anna Wayne Brothers *retired mathematician, educator*

Auburn
Clark, Janet Eileen *political science professor*
Galbraith, Ruth Legg *retired dean, home economist*
Turner, Louise (Lee) Kreher *retired dance educator*

Auburn University
Buchanan, Alice Moore *education educator*
Frieda-Siepmann, Elaina M. *psychology professor*
MacEwan, Bonnie *librarian, dean*
Sidler, Michelle Ann *literature and language professor*
Simmons, Karla Peavy *researcher, educator*

Bessemer
Collins, Patricia Ann *pastor, pastoral counselor*
Johnsey-Robertson, Anita Colleen *special education educator*
Miller, Carrie Sims *music educator*
Stevens, Elizabeth McCartha *secondary school educator*

Birmingham
Allen, Maryon Pittman *former senator, clothing designer, journalist*
Bonfield, Barbara Goldstein *non-profit organization administrator*
Booth, Rachel Zonelle *nursing educator*
Caffey, Linda Kaye *elementary school educator*
Carter, Frances Tunnell (Fran Carter) *fraternal organization administrator*
Clohan, Dexanne Bowers *physical medical rehabilitation physician*
Cohen-DeMarco, Gale Maureen *pharmaceutical executive*
Cooper, Karen René *health facility administrator, nursing administrator*
Corliss, Deane Kenworthy *lawyer*
Cormier, Loretta A. *anthropologist*
Crittenden, Martha A. *rehabilitation services professional*
Culpepper, Mary Kay *publishing executive*
Daniels-Rogers, LaTausha *social sciences educator, entrepreneur*
Davis, Gwendolyn Louise *military officer, literature educator*
Diasio, Ilse Wolfartsberger *volunteer*
Dryden, Susan Meredith *secondary school educator*
Elewski, Boni Elizabeth *dermatologist, educator*
Elgavish, Ada *molecular and cellular biologist*
Feldman, Jacqueline Maus *psychiatrist, educator*
Finley, Sara Crews *medical geneticist, educator*
Galloway, Catherine Black *writer, editor*
Garrison, Carol Z. *academic administrator*
Goldman, Renitta Librach *special education educator, consultant*
Hahn, Beatrice A. *education educator*
Henry, Ruth Swindle *dancer, educator*
Holmes, Suzanne McRae *nursing supervisor*
Hopkins, Martha Ann *sculptor*
Hullett, Sandral *hospital administrator, health facility administrator*
Jackson, Davida Janae *science educator*
Kapanka, Heidi *emergency physician*
Keller, Armor *artist, arts advocate*
Kent, Lysbeth Hawkins *artist*
Kirkley, D. Christine *not-for-profit developer*
Kluge, Janice *art educator*
Knight, Karen Chambers *nurse*
Laeger, Therese Roach *performing arts educator*
Long, Berneé E. *academic administrator, educator*
Long, Deborah Joyce *lawyer*
Long, Sheri Spaine *foreign language educator*
Lowery, Deborah Garrison *freelance writer, editor*
Maddox, Martha Lacey Gardner *artist*
Mohon, Earlene Mann *counselor*
Morgan, Kathryn Diane *criminology educator*
Morton, Marilyn Miller *retired genealogy educator, researcher, retired history professor, travel company executive*
Mueller, Dorothy Ann *university official*
Murrell, Susan DeBrecht *librarian*
Nikles, Jacqueline Amine *chemistry professor*
Odom, Mary E. (Libby Odom) *musician, educator*
Oparil, Suzanne *cardiologist, researcher, educator*
Ott, Victoria E. *history professor*
Perry, Helen *medical/surgical nurse, secondary school educator*
Pittman, Constance Shen *endocrinologist, educator*
Poole, Dorothea Veranetta *nursing educator*
Privett, Caryl Penney *judge*
Ritchie, Beth Bradley *elementary school educator*
Rivers, Sherry Diane *educational administrator, consultant*
Trechsel, Gail Andrews *museum director*
Tubbs, Cecilia Saulters *academic administrator, educator*
Turón, Mercedes *emeritus language professor*
Whitfield, Andrea Billingsley *elementary school educator*
Williams, Thomasyne Hill *speech pathology/audiology services professional*

Blountsville
Edwards, Sheila M. *banker, educator*
Owens, Teresa Gail *elementary school educator*

Boaz
Pierce, V. Renee *music educator*

Brewton
McDaniel, Miriam Lee McCain *anesthetist*

Centre
Ellis, Joanne Hammonds *computer consultant*

Chelsea
Alicea, Yvette *special education educator*

Cherokee
Daily, Freda Smith *superintendent*

Chickasaw
Erwin, Sandra Kay *music educator*

Citronelle
Black, Waynetta Grant *agricultural studies educator, retired counseling administrator*

Columbiana
Dobbs Black, Leah Faye *elementary school educator*

Crossville
Blessing, Maxine Lindsey *secondary school educator*

Cullman
Morris, Sylvia June Burbank *retired physician*
Thornton, Nancy Freebairn *psychotherapist, consultant, military officer*

Daphne
Henson, Pamela Taylor *secondary education educator*
Rush, Anne Kent *writer, illustrator*

Decatur
Blalock, Carmen *education educator*
Clark, Kathleen Vernon *special education educator*
Costello, Sheri Ann *primary school educator*
Howard, Sandra Dianne *secondary school educator*
Julich, Nancy C. *secondary school educator*
Keenum, Nancy Elizabeth *athletic director, coach*
Matherly, Virginia Williams *music educator*
Michelini, Sylvia Hamilton *auditor*
Smith, Trina *academic administrator*

Demopolis
Attaway, Amie Elizabeth *secondary school educator*
Reynolds, Louise Webb *retired volunteer, director*

Dothan
Benson, Marie Chapman *insurance agent*
Flowers, V. Anne *retired academic administrator*
Glanton, Jeraline Cain *retired language educator*
Jones, Sandra Lee *retired dean*
Kogelschatz, Joan Lee *psychologist, psychotherapist*
Williams, Claudia Baxter *retired media specialist, school librarian*

Double Springs
Slatton, Barbara *secondary school educator*

Eclectic
Rodi, Kathryn Kelly *elementary school educator*

Elmore
Williams, Glenda Carlene *writer*

Enterprise
Adkison, Charla S. *biology educator*

Eufaula
Conniff, Alexandra Acosta *secondary school educator*

Eutaw
Daniels, Benita Jean *special education educator*
Merritt, Edith Bradford *elementary school educator*

Eva
Hudson, Rhonda Ann *science educator*

Evergreen
Dailey, Marilyn *elementary school educator*
Lodge-Peters, Dianne Speed *writer, literature educator, researcher*

Fairhope
Norton, Margaret Sarah *retired insurance company executive*
Peck, Phyllis Hainline *educator*

Fayette
Burleson, Emily Jane *nursing educator*

Florence
Burkhead, Cynthia Anne *literature and language professor*
Foote, Dorothy Gargis *nursing educator*
Greenlee, Michelle Jayne Ory *science educator*
Knight, Karen Anne McGee *artist, educator, educational research administrator*
Linton, Phyllis Heflin *mathematics educator*
Schulman, Jean Ellen *artist, retired educator*
Williams, Joyce Hall *secondary school educator*
Wright, Mildred Anne (Milly Wright) *conservator, researcher*

Fort Payne
Beasley, Mary Catherine *retired secondary school educator, retired administrator*
Mitchell, Gwendolyn Ann *mathematics educator*
Wilbanks, Janice Peggy *special education educator*

Fultondale
Taylor, Patricia Nail *mathematics and science educator*

Gadsden
Coakley, Deirdre *columnist, writer*
Massaro, Traci Lynn *special education educator*
Montgomery, Constance O. *mathematics educator*
Murray, Harriet Johnson *secondary school educator*

Gardendale
Adams, Amanda Kelley *mathematics educator*

Geneva
Ellison, Cathy Walker *history educator, literature and language educator, educational consultant*

Gordo
Booth, Karen Lee *elementary school educator*

Grand Bay
Taylor, Anne Wilkerson *elementary school educator*

Greenville
Longmire, Venus DeLoyse *minister*
MacGuire, Nina Little *social worker*

Grove Hill
Clarke, Cheryl Crider *music educator*

Gurley
Patrick, Laura Daphene Layman *retired physicist*

Hamilton
Ray, Yvonne McCarley *elementary school educator*
Vinson, Leila Terry Walker *retired gerontological social worker*
Young, Mary Delores *special education educator*

Hanceville
Hazard, Lynn Marchetti *occupational therapist*
Hodge, Ida Lee *retired physical therapist assistant*
Holmes, Kristen Jones *academic administrator*

Hartselle
Coon, Elizabeth M. *artist*
Thompson, Wanda Dawson *music educator*

Harvest
Lasater, Jennifer A. *history educator, dance educator*

Hayden
Standridge, Jean *real estate company executive, broker*

Headland
Woodham, Patricia H. *accounting and business consultant*

Helena
Coulter, Fern Goshen *retired secondary school educator*

Homewood
Nance, Marione E. *biology educator*
Tucker, Rhonda Reneé *music educator*

Hoover
Fineburg, Amy C. *social studies educator*
Matherson, Rachael Akers *secondary school educator, dancer*
Slovensky, Deborah Wilbanks *secondary school educator*

Hueytown
Nelson, Susan Rhodes *media specialist, educator*

Huntsville
Bishop, Amy *biology professor*
Bledsoe, Adalene Hay *family counselor, retired elementary school educator*
Bounds, Sarah Etheline *historian*
Brightwell, Wendy Sue *biology educator*
Cruit, Wendy *mechanical engineer*
Freeman, Paula S. *social worker*
Gawronski, Elizabeth Ann *retired army officer, artist*
Gothart, Pamela Campbell *history educator*
Hall, Doris Spooner *music educator*
Hall, Elizabeth Murchie *retired special education educator, consultant*
Hancock, Jane Syers *music educator*
Hughes, Kaylene *historian, educator*
Ingram, Shirley Jean *social worker*
Lacy, Lucile C. *music educator*
McIntyre-Ivy, Joan Carol *data processing executive*
McNew, Jill Hasty *performing company executive, educator*
Moore, Ann Roy *school system administrator*
Morgan, Beverly Hammersley *elementary school educator, artist*
Neeley, Janet Meigs *surgical nurse*
Pearson, Susan *elementary school educator*
Pruitt, Alice Fay *mathematician, engineer*
Ratchford Merchant, Betty Jo *retired elementary school educator*
Reel, Heather W. *educational association administrator*
Richardson-Weninegar, Loretta Lynne *biologist, educator*
Simpson, Debra Brashear *artist*
Smothers, Deloris Rice *computer career educator*
Stephens, Connie E. *secondary school educator*
Stewart, Verlindsey Laquetta *accounting educator*
Tincher, Anne Harris *elementary school educator*
Turner, Mary Alice *curriculum specialist*
Wilksman, Karen Sonjia *secondary school educator*
Yarbrough, Isabel Miles *dentist, educator*

Irondale
Galamore, Shannon *mathematics educator*

Jacksonville
Chargois, Deborah Majeau *psychology professor, researcher*
Dunaway, Carolyn Bennett *retired sociology professor*
Eyre, Heidi L. *psychology professor*
Hutchinson, Francine Nelson *biology educator, consultant*
Lewis, Deborah Alice *tax company executive, writer*
McCrary, Judy Hale *education educator*
Merrill, Martha *library and information scientist*
Torgerson, Jennifer Ann *athletic trainer*

Jasper
Argo, Betty Earnest *business owner*

Jones
Tidwell, Betty Davenport *special education educator*

Kinston
Shaw, Sonya King *literature and language educator*

Lafayette
Woody, Mary Florence *nursing educator, academic administrator*

Lanett
Looser, Vickie Beard *secondary school educator*

Leeds
Denton, Joy Grigg *retired music educator*
Wilson, Maggie Isabelle Lovell *secondary school educator*

Lester
Matthews, Linda Nell *secondary school educator*

Lincoln
Wheelus, Elizabeth *mental health services professional*

Livingston
Duckworth, Tracy Wells *research scientist, educator, biotechnologist*

Loachapoka
Lishak, Lisa Anne *secondary school educator*
Schafer, Elizabeth Diane *historian, writer*

Madison
Bogard, Eileen Judith *investor, retired small business owner, retired education administrator*
Hellums, Lori Roberts *elementary school educator*
Johnson, Kathy Virginia Lockhart *art educator*

Mc Calla
Kes, Vicki *museum director*

Millbrook
Roberts, Lisa Dawn *elementary school educator*
Roy, Nancy Lou *science educator*

Mobile
Atkinson, Alanna Beth *music educator*
Bahr, Alice Harrison *librarian*
Bullard, Bettie Catherine Posey *adult education educator*

Clausell, Deborah Deloris *artist*
Crowell, Tangie Michelle *elementary school educator*
French, Elizabeth Irene *biology professor, musician*
Granade, Callie Virginia Smith *federal judge*
Nicholson, Yvette Renee *science educator*
Patten Starr, Barbara Sue Brummett *art educator, textile designer*
Rhodes, Deborah J. *prosecutor*
Scantlebury, Velma Patricia *surgeon*
Smith, Anne Sisson *private school educator*
Sumlin, Margaret Brown *special education educator*
Thompson, Nancy *art director*
Volkman, Beatrice Kramer *special education educator*
Wisner, Pamela L. *social worker*

Monroeville
Loyd, Martha Rose *forester*

Montevallo
Lumby, Betty Louise *music educator, organist, composer*
Payne, Tracy H. *academic director*
Stewart, Katherine Wood *middle school educator*

Montgomery
Baxley, Lucy *lieutenant governor*
Belt, Jean Rainer *art gallery owner*
Blackman, Kennette *secondary school educator*
Brock, Katrina Rae *music educator*
Brown, Jean Williams *former state supreme court justice*
Brown, June Iris *retired librarian, artist*
Bullard, Mary Ellen *retired religious organization administrator*
Campbell, Maria Bouchelle *lawyer, consultant*
Canary, Leura Garrett *prosecutor*
Chamberlain, Kathryn Burns Browning *retired military officer*
Copeland, Jacqueline Turner *music educator*
Farshee, Marlena W. *title company executive*
Fry, Donna Marie *military officer, educator*
Graham, Louvenia Dorsey *science educator*
Ivey, Kay Ellen *state official*
Jones, Kathy W. *research scientist, educator*
Kennedy, Kamela Denise *director*
Luna, Patricia Adele *marketing executive*
McClain, Juanita *library director*
McPherson, Vanzetta Penn *magistrate judge*
Moseley, Laurice Culp *small business owner*
Napier, Cameron Mayson Freeman *historic preservationist*
Phillips, Pamela B. *medical education coordinator*
Ray, Michelle L. *physical education educator*
Rose, Shirley Kelly *retired language educator*
Smith, Patricia M. (Patti Smith) *state supreme court justice*
Spear, Sarah G. *county administrator*
Stuart, Jacquelyn L. *state supreme court justice*
Uzzell-Baggett, Karon Lynette *career officer*
Wines, Lynne *bank executive*
Worley, Nancy L. *state official*
York, Karen Sue *artist, historian*

Montrose
Coffman, Elizabeth Thompson *retired language educator*
Haynie, Betty Jo Gillmore *personal property appraiser, antiques dealer*

Moody
Brasher, Terrie Walker *secondary school educator*

Morris
Murphy, Jennifer *elementary school educator*
Taylor, Brandy Miller *music educator*

Muscle Shoals
King, Amanda Wilhite *science educator*

New Hope
Loyd, Betsy Franklin *primary school educator*

Normal
Lane, Rosalie Middleton *extension specialist*

Opelika
Logan, Elizabeth *middle school educator*
Miller, Donna Kaye *mental health services professional, real estate investor*

Oxford
Flummer, Sandra Moon *elementary school educator*

Pell City
Dale, Sonia Ivette *principal*
Smith, Janet Newman *retired physical education educator*

Perdido
McDonald, Gerri Van Pelt *elementary school educator*

Piedmont
Kiser, Hazel Theresa *educational association administrator, lawyer*

Pleasant Grove
McCrary, Lori Sue *secondary school educator*
Robinson, Ella Garrett *editor, writer*

Point Clear
Englund, Gage Bush *dancer, educator*

Prattville
Lambert, Meg Stringer *construction executive, architect, interior designer*
Tutchtone, Sharon Sabrina *secondary school educator*

Ranburne
Thompson, Jacqueline *retired military officer*

Redstone Arsenal
Burrows, Shania Kay *civilian military employee*

Spanish Fort
Benjamin, Regina Marcia *physician, administrator*
Hollinger, Peggy Louise *elementary school counselor*
Wilkerson Walley, Hazel Sarah *music educator, lay worker*

Stevenson
Grider Watson, Mary Elizabeth *small business owner*

Sylacauga
Depew, Mae F. *director, educational consultant*
Scott, Arista V. *secondary school educator*

Talladega
McIlwain, Anna Keitt *elementary school educator, researcher*
Schwinghamer, Mary Denise *veterinarian*

Theodore
Hollis, Julia Ann Roshto *critical care, medical, and surgical nurse*
LeGros, Christy Callaghan *art educator*

Thomasville
Larrimore, Judith Rutledge *nurse*
Whitmire, Marilyn Therese *art educator*

Troy
Carpenter, Stacy *secondary school educator*

Tuscaloosa
Bonner, Judy L. *academic administrator*
Burry-Stock, Judith Anne (Anne Burry) *education educator*
Cartee, Karen Johnson *education educator, consultant*
Cook, Camille Wright *retired law educator*
Davis, Pam N. *literature and language professor*
Edgeworth, Emily *retired insurance agency executive, retired small business owner*
Fields, Ruth Kinniebrew *secondary and elementary educator, consultant*
Fish, Mary Martha *economics professor*
Gregory, Paula Elaine *gifted and talented educator*
Hendrix, Mary Elizabeth *language educator, researcher*
Jemison, Sandra J. *educational association administrator*
Nadine, Claudia *French language educator*
Orcutt, Ben Avis *retired social work educator*
Pass, Charlotte Louise *literature educator, consultant*
Ray, Nelda Howton *financial consultant*
Reinhart, Kellee Connely *journalist*

Tuscumbia
Linville, Kimberly E. *lawyer*
McWilliams, Elizabeth Ann *elementary school educator*
Mitchell, Joyce Faye *writer, editor*
Sutton, Wanda Lynne *language educator*

Tuskegee
Thomas, Elaine Freeman *artist, educator*
White, Mildred Virginia *secondary school educator, retired counseling administrator*

Tuskegee Institute
Cooley, Fannie Richardson *counselor, educator*
Gamble, Vanessa Northington *historian, healthcare educator, bioethicist*
Paris, Deidre Eileen *artificial intelligence researcher, educator*

Vance
Owenby, S. Diane *elementary school educator*

Vestavia Hills
Pierce, Kacy Jones *assistant principal*

Warrior
Johnson, Barbara L. *retired municipal official*

Wetumpka
Vilardi, Virginia Ann *secondary school educator, department chairman*

Woodville
Cook, Faye Hamlett *secondary school educator*

ALASKA

Anchorage
Andersen, Ellen Marie *social worker*
Bautista, Lina Judith *psychiatrist*
Baxley, Yvette *secondary school educator*
Britton, Emily Maddox *sales executive*
Burke, Marianne King *state agency administrator, finance company executive, consultant*
Comeau, Carol Smith *school system administrator*
Davis, Bettye Jean *school system administrator, state legislator*
DeLap, Miriam Anne *music educator*
Fabe, Dana Anderson *state supreme court justice*
Fortenberry, Nichole Audrey *paralegal, small business owner*
Foster, Rosemary Alice *lawyer, artist*
Gazaway, Barbara Ann *music educator, art educator*
Gottlieb, Katherine *health facility administrator*
Grahame, Heather H. *lawyer*
Habberstad, Amy Renae *secondary school educator*
Harvey, Elinor B. *child psychiatrist*
Hughes, Mary Katherine *lawyer*
Jones, Jewel *social services administrator*
Keffer, Maria Jean *environmental scientist*
Kelly, Maxine Ann *retired property developer*
Kincaid, Karen Owers *nursing educator*
Maimon, Elaine Plaskow *university chancellor*
McMorris, Cycelia A. *elementary school educator*
Nielsen, Jennifer Lee *molecular ecologist, researcher*
Obermeyer, Theresa Nangle *sociology educator*
Pendleton, Cynthia M. *art educator, artist*
Schmitt, Nancy Cain *retired public and corporate relations executive, writer*
Shadrach, Jean Hawkins (Martha Shadrach) *artist*
Skladal, Elizabeth Lee *retired elementary school educator*
Sturgulewski, Arliss *state legislator, director*
Thurber, Sharon Lee *elementary resource educator*
Underwood, Patricia Ford *elementary school educator*
Williams, Eleanor Joyce *retired government air traffic control specialist*
Wolf, Patricia B. *museum director*
Wright-Elson, Larissa Anne *literature and language educator*

Bethel
Owen, Lauri J. *lawyer*
Turner, Kathy Ann *special education educator*

Big Lake
Gillette, Muriel Delphine *nurse*

Chugiak
Nilsson, Annie *singer, music educator*
Stiehr, Lizette Estelle *special education educator, director*

Cordova
Bugbee-Jackson, Joan *sculptor, educator*

Eek
Fager, Heather Elaine *language educator*

Eielson Afb
Stoutenberg, Herminia Lilia *art educator*

Elmendorf Afb
Fassler, Kerin Irene *accountant*

Fairbanks
Alexander, Vera *dean, marine science educator*
Anderson, Jean Blanche *fiction writer*
Bodwell, Lori *lawyer*
Cahill, Catherine Frances *environmental scientist, educator*
Crawford, Sarah Carter (Sally Carter Crawford) *broadcast executive*
Heckman, Jyotsna (Jo) L. *bank executive*
Kessel, Brina *ornithologist, educator, researcher*
Krause, Marilyn Ruth *elementary school educator*
Mahurin Hadaway, Melanie L. *secondary school educator*
Mayer, Patricia E., Sr. *elementary school educator*
Mellish, Jo-Anne Elizabeth *marine biologist, researcher*
Nottingham, Juanita C. *medical/surgical nurse*
Shier, Juliet Marie *social studies educator*
Villano, Christine Pearsall *elementary school educator*

Juneau
Acres, Jo Devine *literature and language educator*
Albrecht, Bethany Jane *counselor*
McGuire, Lesil L. *state representative*
Rogers, Jean Clark *writer*
Waldrip, Karen Marie *career planning administrator*

Ketchikan
Kennedy, Peggy Boogaard *artist, writer*

Kodiak
Steffey, A Kay *accountant*

Nikiski
Thompson, Sharon Ruth *special education educator*

North Pole
James, Jeannette Adeline *state legislator, accountant, small business owner*
Martin, Dorothy Sue *secondary education educator, counselor*

Palmer
Hendrix, Dianne Roberson *artist, writer*
Lawler, Marita A. *addiction therapist*

Saint Marys
Alstrom, Gail *Native American tribal leader*

Saint Paul Island
Lestenkof, Aquilina Debbie *environmental advocate*

Salcha
Alsip, Cheryl Ann *small business owner*

Tanana
Marks, Stephanie I. *secondary school educator, biologist*

Togiak
Abington Alexie, Susan Edith *elementary school educator*

Wasilla
Brunke, Dawn Baumann *writer, editor*

Wrangell
Miller, Jennifer L. *elementary school educator, small business owner*
Smith, Kimmie Christine *small business owner*

ARIZONA

Avondale
Gillen, Katherine Elizabeth *librarian*
Sonmor, Marilyn Idelle *music educator*

Bisbee
Moreno, Patricia Frazier *lawyer*

Buckeye
Martinez, DiAnna *secondary school educator*
Privette, Louise Judith *school psychologist*

Camp Verde
Pastine, Maureen Diane *librarian*

Casa Grande
Landers, Patricia Glover *language educator*
McGillicuddy, Joan Marie *psychotherapist, consultant*

Cave Creek
Hatch, Barbara Jean *secondary school educator*
Metcalf, Amy Bolling *secondary school educator*

Chandler
Alvarado, Grace *elementary school educator*
Brunello-McCay, Rosanne *sales executive*
Casteel, Camille *school system administrator*
Chavez, Faith Coots *medical nurse*
Farenga, Justine-Louise Porter *music educator*
Miller, Patricia Ann *secondary school educator*
Moser, Teri *literature educator*
Newman, Phyllis *retired counselor, therapist, hypnotist*

Chinle
Quell, Margaret Anne *special education educator*

Chino Valley
Casey, Bonnie Mae *artist, educator*

Cibecue
Murphey, Margaret Janice *retired marriage and family counselor*

Clarkdale
Tod, Martha Ann *retired small business owner*

Congress
Scheall, Norma *writer, editor*

Coolidge
Pratt, Janice *hospitality and hotel services educator*

Cornville
Walsh, Arline Marie *retired alcohol/drug abuse services professional*

Cottonwood
Lay, Janice Amelia *special education educator*

Desert Hills
Evans, Carol Ann *reading specialist*

Douglas
Britton, Ruth Ann Wright *elementary school educator*
Murphy, Cathy Emily *photographer, educator, journalist*

Flagstaff
Barlow, Nadine Gail *planetary geoscientist*
Barnes, Charlotte Elizabeth *retired elementary school educator*
Copley, Edith Ann *music educator*
Cortner, Hanna Joan *retired research scientist, political scientist*
Hospodka, Lenka M. *hotel and restaurant management educator*
Larson, Ellen R. *health sciences instructor*
Lusk, Della S. *psychologist*
Marcus, Karen Melissa *language educator*
Poen, Kathryn Louise *music educator, performing arts association administrator*
Shoemaker, Carolyn Spellman *planetary astronomer*
Weeks, Edythe E. *writer, educator*
Wilcoxson-Ueckert, Catherine Ann *science educator, consultant*

Florence
Mosby Gnader, Nora Jane *music educator*

Fort Huachuca
Sleeper, Nancy JoAnn *mental health services professional*
Szymeczek, Peggy Lee *contract specialist*

Fountain Hills
Blatt, Melanie Judith *small business owner*
Sorenson, Gretchen Hartley *elementary school educator*

Gilbert
Hill, Maralyn Dennis *management consultant*

Glendale
Almstead, Sheila Louise *art gallery owner*
Avila, Lidia D. *principal*
Cacciatore, Joanne *social worker*
Carstens, Cyndy Louise *artist*
Connell-Allen, Elizabeth Ann *elementary school educator*
Cotton, Sally Jean *retired music educator*
Dixon-Nielsen, Judy E(arlene) *mortgage banker, marketing professional, consultant*
Eyres, Beth Kathleen *literature educator*
Fisher, Debra A. *communications executive, educator*
Louk, Donna Pat *elementary school educator, music educator*
Mahoney, Jill Elizabeth *music educator*
Milne, Karen Louise *science educator*
Scruggs, Elaine M. *mayor*
Sweat, Lynda Sue *cooking instructor, catering company owner, deaconess*
Thrasher, Jacqueline F. *elementary school educator*
Travis, Geraldine Washington *political organization worker*

Goodyear
McBride, Janet Marie *small business owner*
Molina, Tanya E. *school librarian*

Green Valley
Foley, Teresa A. *psychologist*
Forsyth, Garyfallia Lillian *nurse educator*
Fuer-Davis, Beverly Jean *retired elementary school educator*
Gilliam, Mary *travel company executive*

Shafer, Susan Wright *retired elementary school educator*

Kingman
Gragg, Julie Ann *music educator*
Jones, Barbara Christine *linguist, educator, creative arts designer*
Yancey, Emily *secondary school educator*

Lakeside
Mack, Ina Leah *secondary school educator, pre-school administrator*

Marana
Ruehle, Dianne Marie *retired elementary education educator*

Mesa
Adams, Heidi-Christa *counselor*
Ahearn, Geraldine *medical/surgical nurse, writer, poet*
Biggs, Kelly Kathleen *theater educator*
Bryant, Peggy Jean *editor, journalist*
Colledge, Deborah Gail *gifted and talented elementary educator*
David, Susan Holcombe *child and family therapist*
Duvall, Debra *school system administrator*
Ehlis, Kristine Marie *music educator*
Evans, Mary Magee *secondary school educator, language educator*
Jones, Linda L. *literature and language educator, department chairman*
Larson-Miller, Julie Kathleen *English educator*
Sarwar, Barbara Duce *educational consultant*
Seibert, Barbara *science educator*
Skoldberg, Phyllis Linnea *musician, educator*
Tacata, Felisa Padua *psychiatrist, researcher*
Taylor, Patti Ann *psychologist, educator*
Walter, Ann L. *special education educator*
Weber, Yvonne Roebuck *research administrator, educator*
Yandell, Ruth B. *music educator*
Yates, Cheryl Ann *home economist, educator*

Nogales
Boltjes, Connie Cloy *music educator*
Maxwell, Sonia L. *social worker*
Valdez, Wanda Daniel *county official*

Oro Valley
Baker, Veronica Ann *secondary school educator, writer*

Paradise Valley
Harnett, Lila *retired publishing executive*
Maxey, Diane Meadows *artist*
McCall, Louise Harrup *artist*
Targovnik, Selma E. Kaplan *retired dermatologist*

Payson
Lasys, Joan *medical/surgical nurse, educator*
Potvin, Barbara Dirks *librarian*
Salomon, Marilyn *artist*

Peoria
Bonner, Michelle *music educator*
Gould, Dorothy Mae *executive secretary, soprano*
Hagan, Judith Ann *social worker*
Nelson, Mary Kathryn *bilingual counselor, small business owner, real estate agent, artist, singer*
Paul, Melanie Frances *principal*
Willard, Garcia Lou *artist*

Phoenix
Adams, Gail Hayes *interior designer*
Aguiar, Elizabeth Joan *publishing executive, educator*
Allen, Janice Faye Clement *nursing administrator*
Altiere, Lauren M. *music educator, consultant*
Anderson, Vicki *retired librarian*
Beckman, Brenda Marshall *educational consultant*
Benjamin, M. Susan *special education educator*
Berch, Rebecca White *state supreme court justice, lawyer*
Brewer, Janice Kay *state official*
Chavez, Nelba R. *state agency administrator, former federal agency administrator*
Coyle, Linda Marie *elementary school educator*
Davey, Eleanor Ellen *science educator*
Davis, Darna Betts *elementary school educator*
Doto, Irene Louise *statistician*
Duyck, Kathleen Marie *poet, musician, retired social worker*
Erwin, Barbara F. *school system administrator*
Evans, Pamela H. *secondary school educator*
Fishgrab, Barbara Jeanne *school psychologist, mental health services professional*
Floyd, Pamela Kay *elementary school educator, artist*
Fontes, Bianca Michelle *social studies educator*
Forcier, Helene Francis *secondary school educator*
Frehner, Patricia Ann *education educator, consultant*
Gabaldon, Diana *writer*
Gillom, Jennifer *professional basketball player*
Grimwood, Helen Perry *lawyer*
Gwozdz, Kim Elizabeth *interior designer, furniture designer*
Hicks, Bethany Gribben *judge, lawyer*
Holaday, Barbara (Bobbie) Hayne *writer*
Hutchinson, Ann *management consultant*
James, Betty M. *secondary school educator*
Johnson, Elizabeth Misner *health services executive*
Johnson, Mystie L. *obstetrician, gynecologist, department chairman*
Jungbluth, Connie Carlson *banker*
Kane, Grace McNelly *retired women's health nurse, pediatrics nurse*
Karabatsos, Elizabeth Ann *career counseling services executive*
Kivlahan, Coleen *public health officer*
Klos, Siobhán Lydia *theater director*
Kohi, Susan *bilingual educator, translator*
Lawlis, Patricia Kite *military officer, computer consultant*
Laymon, Cynthia J. *artist, educator*
Le, Viet V. *lawyer*
Lee, Barbara S. *special education educator*
Loftin, Nancy Carol *lawyer, utilities executive*
Martinez, Maria Dolores *pediatrician*
Maxson, Barbara Jeanette *social worker, educator*
McBride, Melanie Grace *lawyer*
McCormick, Kathryn Ellen *prosecutor*
McGregor, Ruth Van Roekel *state supreme court justice*
McGuire, Maureen A. *artist*
McLendon, Kathleen Mary *elementary school educator*
McQuown, Kimberly Alyse *elementary school educator*
McWhorter, Ruth Alice *counselor, marriage and family therapist*
Meeks, Jacquelynn *city health department administrator*
Modny, Cynthia Jean *dermatologist*
Mogerman, Flora May *music educator, director*
Moriarty, Karen *state agency administrator*
Napolitano, Janet Ann *governor*
Nijinsky, Tamara *actress, puppeteer, author, librarian, educator*
Noone, Laura Palmer *academic administrator, lawyer*
Peterson, Patricia Mitchell *medical/surgical nurse*
Phanthourath, Anoma T. *lawyer*
Ralston, Barbara Jo *bank executive*
Rees, Sarah Lynn *school psychologist*
Refo, Patricia Lee *lawyer*
Richardson, Judy McEwen *investment banker, consultant, cartoonist*
Roof, Sally Jean-Marie *library and information scientist, educator*
Rosckowff, Carol Martha *pediatrician*
Schenkel, Barbara Ann *minister, nurse, social worker*
Schiffner, Adrienne Anita *art historian, educator*
Schrader, Susan Rae *elementary school educator*
Schroeder, Mary Murphy *federal judge*
Shelton, Rose E. *minister, retired tax specialist*
Siegenthaler, Denise L. *lawyer*
Silver, Roslyn Olson *federal judge*
Skinner, Nancy Jo *municipal recreation executive*
Smiley, Denisa Ann *music educator*
Smith, Barbara Gail *economist*
Steckler, Phyllis Betty *publishing consultant*
Steffey, Lela *state legislator, banker*
Stone, Hazel Anne Decker *artist*
Taurasi, Diana *college basketball player*
Thorne, Ann LaRayne *secondary school educator*
Turner, Doris Sewell *counselor, educator*
Udall, Vesta Hammond *special education educator*
Wells, GladysAnn *library director*
Wheaton, Marilyn *musician*
White, Annette Irene *marketing professional*
Wolf, Irna Lynn *psychologist*
Young, Michael Cochise *academic administrator*

Pinetop
Gilbert-Tiegs, Marion Ann *gifted and talented educator, consultant*

Prescott
Halvorson, Mary Ellen *education educator, writer*
Haverland, Muriel Jean *speaker, career management consultant*
Slominski, Elena Gregoryevna *mathematics educator*
Walker, Winnetta Dorrean *social studies educator*
Waterer, Bonnie Clausing *retired secondary school educator*
Zabukovec, Jamie Jo *clinical psychologist*

Prescott Valley
Decil, Stella Walters (Del Decil) *artist*

Queen Creek
Loss, Lynne Franklin *artist, volunteer*

Rio Rico
Coyle, Allison Brooke *director*

Sacaton
Howe, Anne Marie *director, educator*

Saddlebrooke
Schoepf, Virginia Anne *retired librarian*

Safford
Brady, Carole Ann *physical education teacher*

San Luis
Kryger, Jerri Renee *elementary school educator*

Scottsdale
Betts, Janet Gniadek *lawyer*
Blair, Karen Elaine *small business owner, social psychology researcher, psychiatric consultant*
Broe, Carolyn Waters *conductor, music educator, violist*
Brown, Shirley Margaret Kern (Peggy Brown) *interior designer*
Bullerdick, Kim H. *lawyer, petroleum executive*
Carpenter, Betty O. *writer*
Dalton, Phyllis Irene *library consultant*
Farney, Charlotte Eugenia *musician, educator*
Haas, Ingrid Elizabeth *physician*
Hadley, Jane Francis *family nurse practitioner*
Hokin, Jeanne *education educator*
Krane, Susan *museum director, curator*
Lavenson, Susan Barker *hotel corporate executive, consultant*
Lillestol, Jane Brush *educational consultant*
MacKinnon, Sally Anne *retired fast food company executive*
Manross, Mary *mayor*
McKay-Cox, Marianne *secondary school educator*
Meyer, Madeline Anna *librarian*
Meyers, Marlene O. *retired hospital administrator*
Milanovich, Norma JoAnne *training services executive*
Mohraz, Judy Jolley *foundation administrator*
Novak, Janice Elaine *pre-school educator*
O'Meara, Sara *non-profit organization executive*
Parsons, Cynthia *writer, consultant*
Phillips, Wanda Charity *secondary school educator, writer*
Prellberg, Joanne Marie *office manager*
Quayle, Marilyn Tucker *wife of former United States Vice President, lawyer*
Reid, Judith Solomon *elementary school educator*
Roberts, Joan Ila *psychologist, educator*
Shirk, Marianne Eileen *veterinarian*
Timmons, Evelyn Deering *pharmacist*
Vanier, Jerre Lynn *art director*
Weaver, Linda Marie *pharmacist, education educator*
Williams, Margaret M. (Meg Williams) *insurance company executive*
Williams-De Silva, Lisa Annette *small business owner, adult nurse practitioner*
Yares, Riva *art dealer, writer, publishing executive*

Sedona
Catterton, Marianne Rose *occupational therapist*
Copeland, Suzanne Johnson *real estate company executive*
Darrow, Jane *artist*
Richards, Wanda Jamie *retired education educator*

Sells
Juan-Saunders, Vivian *Native American tribal leader*

Shonto
Haviland, Marlita Christine *elementary school educator*

Sierra Vista
Boughan, Zanetta Louise *music educator*
Gignac, Judith Ann *retired utilities executive, land developer*
Smith, Barbara Jane *computer scientist, educator*
Spencer, Judith *retired secondary school educator, writer*

Sonoita
Browning, Sinclair *writer*
Sebert, Michelle Ann *school system network administrator*

Sun City
Crisman, Mary Frances Borden *librarian*
Davis, Virginia *trade show producer*
Duke, Ora Elizabeth *civic volunteer*
Keesling, Karen Ruth *lawyer*
Lopez, Jean Engebretsen *neuroscience nurse, researcher*
Peterson, Rebecca Thorine *retired voice educator, theater director*
Randall, Claire *retired religious organization administrator*
Thompson, Betty Jane *retired small business owner*
Wheeler, Janet Marilyn *retired special education educator*

Sun City West
Forti, Lenore Steimle *business consultant*
Holloway, Diane Elaine *psychotherapist, consultant, writer*
Ryan-Knuppel, Bette L. *nurse, educator*
Schrag, Adele Frisbie *business education educator*

Sun Lakes
Gersten, Shirley R. *elementary school educator*
Hall, Barbara Louise *interior designer, artist*
Johnson, Marian Ilene *education educator*

Surprise
Bradford, Mariah *elementary school educator, consultant*
Burns, Clare Marie *retired elementary school educator*
Eastman, Donna Kelly *composer*
Edwards, Gleita Kay *primary school educator*
Fennelly, Jane Corey *lawyer*
Lucchetti, Lynn L. *career officer*
Neuman, Isabel *mathematics educator*
Steimle, Jami P. *elementary school educator*
Stevenson, Norma Ann *elementary school educator, real estate agent, property manager*
Telban, Ethel *retired librarian*
Wargo, Andrea Ann *retired public health service officer*

Taylor
Kerr, Barbara Prosser *research scientist, educator*

Tempe
Anchie, Toby Levine *health facility administrator*
Arredondo, Patricia *educational association administrator*
Bartling, Sara *language educator*
Bowditch, Rachel Emily *theater educator*
Caterino, Linda Claire *psychologist*
Crawford, Susan Lee *health educator*
Dhillon, Janet L. *lawyer*
Dustman, Patricia (Jo) Allen *elementary school educator, consultant*
Essig, Linda *lighting designer, director*
Golden, Libby *artist*
Herald, Cherry Lou *medical researcher, educator*
Jefferson, Myra LaVerne Tull *sales executive*
Lemmon, Nicolette *small business owner, marketing professional*
Meissinger, Ellen Murray *artist, educator*
Menjivar, Cecilia *social sciences educator*
Milke, Linda Jean *elementary school educator*
Narayanan, Radha *chemist, researcher*
Papandreou-Suppappola, Antonia *electrical engineering educator*
Prom, M. Elaine *secondary school educator*
Rowley, Beverley Davies *sociologist*
Schilling, Amy Jo *private school educator*
Schmidt, Sherrie *library director, dean*
Thor, Linda M. *college president*
White, Patricia Denise *dean, law educator*
Wyckoff, Susan *astronomy researcher*
Zapata, Angela L. *counselor*
Zeitlin, Marilyn Audrey *museum director*

Thatcher
Jordahl, Patricia Ann *music educator, theater director*

Tsaile
Walters, Anna Lee *writer, educational association administrator*

Tuba City
Chang, Vivian K. *orthopedist, surgeon*

Tubac
Roseman, Kim *gallery director*

Tucson
Addis, Ilana Beth *obstetrician*
Altman, Ellen *librarian, educator*
Anderson, Dayna *medical researcher*
Arzoumanian, Linda Lee *school system administrator*
Barrette-Mozes, Susan Jean *counselor, psychotherapist*
Beaman, Colleen K. *education educator, choreographer*
Bernmúdez, Carmen *trust company executive*
Bernstein, Carol *molecular biologist*
Betteridge, Frances Carpenter *retired lawyer, mediator*
Bittel, Kirstin Alicia *science educator*
Bluemer, Bevan *acrobatics company executive*
Brennan, Carrie *principal*
Bryant, Marian Alanna *electric company consultant*
Burrows, Dorna B. *elementary school educator*
Carman, Mary Ann *realtor, writer, retired medical/surgical nurse*
Cisler, Theresa Ann *osteopath*
Click, Carrie *public relations executive*
Cooper, Corinne *communications consultant, lawyer*
Dailey, Lynne *secondary school educator*
Dale, Deborah *foundation executive*
Davenport, Sandra *cultural organization administrator*
Davis, Megan J. *consulting firm executive*
Denzler, Nancy J. *artist*
Dobyns, Susan Dianne *anthropologist, sociologist, educator*
Donnelly, Mavis J. *psychiatrist*
Dyer-Raffler, Joy Ann *retired special education diagnostician, educator*
Emerson, Kirk *government agency administrator*
Fajardo, Sarah Elizabeth Johnson *financial consultant*
Fay, Mary Anne *retail executive*
Flores, Candace *special events director*
Foley, Louise *medical educator, retired military officer*
Francesconi, Louise L. *defense equipment manufacturing company executive*
Froman, Sandra Sue *lawyer*
Gaines, Kendra Holly *language educator*
Glueck-Rambaldi, Mary Audrey *retired psychiatric and mental health nurse*
Goldberg, Charlotte Wyman *retired physical education educator, retired dean, retired counselor, retired travel company executive*
Gonzales, Sarah *women's organization director*
Graham, Anna Regina *pathologist, educator*
Griffen, Agnes Marthe *retired library administrator*
Hamner, Rome *social services administrator*
Hasselmo, Ann Hayes Die *executive recruiter, consultant, psychologist, educator, retired academic administrator*
Hayt, Therese D. *newspaper executive*
Healy, Stephanie Lemme *hospital organization administrator*
Hill, Jane H. *anthropologist, educator*
Hopper, Nancy Jane *author*
Ingram, Helen Moyer *political science professor*
James, Ruby May *retired librarian*
Janes, Raena *private school educator*
Jaramillo, Alba *community educator*
Johnson, Elissa Sarah *speech pathology/audiology services professional, writer*
Jolivet, Anna Mary *retired school system administrator, association executive*
Jones, Ronnell Andersen *lawyer, educator*
Karson, Catherine June *systems administrator*
Kennedy, Lydia *human resources specialist*
Koerber, Erica *photographer*
Kolchens, Silvia *science educator*
Kuklin, Susan Beverly *law librarian, lawyer*
Lai, LiWen *geneticist, educator*
Larwood, Laurie *psychologist*
LeCorgne, Lisette Mary *family practice nurse practitioner*
Ledin, Patricia Ann *nurse, legal consultant*
Lovejoy, Jean Hastings *social services counselor*
Macys, Sonja *science association director*
Márquez-Peterson, Lea *business broker*
Martin, June Johnson Caldwell *journalist*
McCabe, Monica Jane *oncological nurse*
Mercker, Mary Alice *aviation school administrator*
Miller, Elizabeth Rodriguez *city official*
Montero, Leticia *social studies educator*
Moran, Nancy A. *ecologist, educator*
Moten, Darlene *elementary school educator*
Neugebauer, Marcia *physicist, researcher*
Nord, Myrtle Selma *writer, researcher*
Norrander, Barbara *political science professor*
Parra, Elena Batriz-Guadalupe *psychologist, educator*
Pedersen, Arlene *web design company executive*
Pintozzi, Chestalene *librarian*
Porter, Jeanne Smith *civic worker*
Powell, Winona Kay *music educator*
Reinius, Michele Reed *executive recruiter*
Robles, Maricela *architect*
Roemer, Elizabeth *retired astronomer, educator*
Rose, Carol Marguerite *law educator*
Rufe, Laurie J. *museum director*
Samet, Dee-Dee *lawyer*
Sandoval, Arlene R. *elementary school educator*
Schulz, Renate Adele *German studies and second language acquisition educator*
Seagroves, Jean Franzen *secondary school educator*
Serido, Joyce *psychologist, researcher*
Sillman, Edlynne Mina *caseworker, consultant*
Simmons, Sarah R. *lawyer*
Smith, Kathy Wosnitzer *psychiatrist*
Sohnen-Moe, Cherie Marilyn *business consultant*
Spaeth, Jan Mills *jury consultant*
Sprague, Ann Louise *aerospace scientist*
Starkey, Shirley Condit *writer, artist*
Stein, Mary Katherine *photographer, communications executive*
Stitt, Mari Leipper *poet*
Stoffle, Carla Joy *university library dean*
Swerdlove, Dorothy Louise *librarian, consultant*

Tang, Esther Don *real estate developer, consultant, social worker*
Thompson, Kathleen Shambaugh *marriage and family counselor*
Tillman, Daisha A. *athletic trainer*
Treadwell-Rubin, Pamela A. *lawyer*
Underwood, Jane Hainline Hammons *anthropologist, educator*
Vandiver, Pamela Bowren *science educator*
Vernon, Ann *educator, therapist*
Vilas, Faith *aerospace scientist*
Villica—a, Taunya *corporate financial executive*
Waldt, Risa *psychotherapist, artist, writer*
Waterbury, Deborah Kay *minister*
Weeks, Wendy L. *chemistry professor, consultant*
Williams, Joy *writer*
Wolff, Sidney Carne *astronomer, science administrator*
Wrae, Natasha *lawyer*
Zeffirelli, Lucia *dance instructor, piano teacher, choreographer, director, dancer, actress*
Zou, Changping *research scientist, educator*

Vail
Denton-McGrew, Shela Iva *retired trade association administrator*

Wickenburg
Brooks, Donna Jean *counselor, educator*

Window Rock
Deschinny, Isabel *elementary school educator*

Winslow
Wolfe, Janice Kay *oncological nurse*

Yuma
Anderson, Stacey Ann *school psychologist*
Lineberry, Laurie Lawhorn *urban planner*
Lister, Patricia Ann *elementary school educator*
McCarthy, Sherri Nevada *psychologist, educator, educational consultant*
Morse, Kerry W. *elementary school educator*
Packard, Jennifer Ellen *music educator*
Rush, Dorie Mae *nursing educator*

ARKANSAS

Arkadelphia
Cornelius, Laura Elizabeth *music educator*
Pemberton, Barbara Butler *religious studies educator*
Sandford, Juanita Dadisman *sociologist, educator, writer*

Batesville
Beck, Martha Catherine *philosophy educator*
Bennett, Maria Beth *literature and language educator*

Beebe
Fletcher, Maris *literature educator*
Pillow-Price, Kathy *education educator*

Bella Vista
Anton, Cheryl L. *sales executive*
Jones, Jo Carol *pilot, educator*

Benton
Krueger, Marlo Bush *retired lawyer*

Bentonville
Chambers, Susan (M. Susan Chambers) *retail executive*
Curran, Patricia A. *retail executive*
Dillman, Linda M. *retail executive*
Nulty, Colleen M. *counseling administrator*
Swanson, Celia *retail executive*
Walton, Helen *philanthropist*
Watts, Claire A. *retail executive*
Weir, Rita Mary *retail executive*

Berryville
Brown, Frances Louise (Grandma Fran) *artist, art gallery director*

Bismarck
Trieschmann, Elizabeth Suzanne *elementary school educator*

Blytheville
Baker, Carlene Poff *real estate agent, reporter*
Estes, Pamela Jean *pastor*

Bryant
Kissire, Lisa Marie *learning specialist*

Cabot
Daugherty, Debra L. *science educator*

Cedarville
Whitaker, Ruth Reed *state legislator, retired newspaper editor*

Clarendon
Meacham, Dolores Ann (Sissy Meacham) *elementary librarian*

Clinton
Jevicky, Margo K. *secondary school educator*

Conway
Clanton, Kaye Reames *secondary school educator*
Fay, Samantha C. *mathematics educator*
Perry, Susan Nigemann *education educator, consultant*

Dardanelle
Wade, Amy Michelle *elementary school educator*

Dover
Kanady, Janet *science educator*

Dumas
Schexnayder, Charlotte Tillar *state legislator*

Earle
Swift, Peggy Lynette *elementary school educator*
Williams, Anita Jean *elementary school educator*

El Dorado
Cameron-Godsey, Melinda A. Brantley *artist*
Daymon, Joy Jones *school psychology specialist*
Jamerson, Sandra Mariea *music educator*

Elkins
Philip, Joan Mary *literature and language educator*

England
Wagoner, Johnna *elementary school educator*

Everton
Jones, Melba Kathryn *elementary school educator, librarian*

Fayetteville
Gann, Elizabeth Dianne *elementary school educator*
Henry, Ann Rainwater *retired education educator*
Kester, Cheryl L. *management consultant*
Musgnug, Kristin A. *art educator, artist*
Newgent, Rebecca Ann *counselor, educator*
Stephens, Wanda Brewer *social services administrator, investor*

Fort Smith
Ashley, Ella Jane (Ella Jane Rader) *medical technician*
Bricker, Carol Jean *biology educator*
Edwards, Cheryl L. *counselor*
Montgomery, M. Darlene *language educator*
Smith-Leins, Terri L. *mathematics instructor*

Goshen
Zelei, Rita Annette *retired educational administrator*

Gravette
Collins, Amy Lynn *music educator*
Duncan, Jean Marie *language educator*

Greenbrier
Brown, Lois Heffington *retired health facility administrator*

Guy
Ward, Sharon Dee *secondary school educator*

Harrison
Dodson, Leisa *music educator*
Hearn, Cynthia Ann *education educator*

Heber Springs
Stroud, Peggy *secondary school educator*

Helena
Stroope, Kay *mathematician, educator*

Hope
Chambless, Lori K. *secondary school educator*

Hot Springs
Gaither, Susan Anne *business education educator*

Hot Springs National Park
Stuber, Irene Zelinsky *writer, researcher*

Hot Springs Village
Lihs, Marilyn Louise *retired accountant*

Humphrey
Wilson, Victoria Jane Simpson *farmer, medical/surgical nurse*

Huntsville
Commerford, Patricia Bergman *elementary school educator*
Musick, Pat *artist*

Jacksonville
Johnson, Margo Faye *elementary school educator, nurse*

Jonesboro
Chrisman, Nancy Carol *city manager, director, small business owner*
Crecelius, Bridget Michelle *counselor*
Malinsky, Marci Ann *education educator*
Nelsen, Evelyn Rigsbee Seaton *retired secondary school educator*
Tims, Jane Moore *art educator*

Kirby
Mason, Brenda Kay *elementary school educator*

Little Rock
Abercrombie, Eydie L. *physiologist, consultant*
Adams, Rose Ann *nonprofit administrator*
Bass, Evelyn Elizabeth *elementary school educator*
Berry, Janet Claire *librarian*
Bourgeois, Sharon E. *mechanical engineer*
Brewer, Martha Johnston *gynecologist, educator*
Bright, Trina Lynn *secondary school educator*
Caldwell, Bettye McDonald *education educator, director*
Casey, Paula Jean *former prosecutor*
Cherry, Sandra Wilson *lawyer*
Coleman, Marshia Adams *social sciences educator*
Conger, Cynthia Lynne *financial planner*
Crisp, Sally Chandler *writing educator*
Dickey, Betty C. *state supreme court justice*
Dooley, Wendy Brooke *vocalist, music educator, administrative assistant*
Elders, Joycelyn (Minnie Jocelyn Elders, Minnie Joycelyn Lee) *public health service officer, endocrinologist, former Surgeon General of the United States*
Franks, Candace Ann *bank executive*
Gay, Agnolia Beatrice *actress, educator*
Geffken, Carolyn D. *special education educator*
Good, Mary Lowe (Mrs. Billy Jewel Good) *investment company executive, educator*
Greenwood, Sarah Elizabeth *lawyer*
Headley, Debbie Marcia *music educator*
Hochstetter, Sandra *state official*
Hodges, Jennefer Rae *sculptor*
Imber, Annabelle Clinton *state supreme court justice*
Johananoff, Pamela *jewelry designer, gemologist*
Johnson-Shockley, Willie Mae *retired academic administrator*
Lemke, Judith A. *lawyer*
Light, Jo Knight *stockbroker*
Mancino, Anne Rochelle *surgeon*
McCaleb, Annette Watts *executive secretary*
Mitchell, Jo Kathryn *retired hospital technical supervisor*
Moore, Helen Lucille *adult education educator, consultant*
Murray-Norman, Natasha J. *political science professor, pastor*
Nunn, Patarica Dian *poet*
O'Neal, Nell Self *retired principal*
Pennington, Melinda Snider *librarian*
Priest, Sharon Devlin *retired state official, not-for-profit developer*
Raney, Miriam Day *actress*
Smith, Mary Scott *elementary school and education educator*
Smith, Susan *bank executive*
Stockburger, Jean Dawson *lawyer*
Tarasenko, Olga *biologist, educator*
Thomas, Lestene *nurse*
Truex, Dorothy Adine *retired university administrator*
Waters, Zenobia Pettus *retired finance educator*
Wight, Patricia Anne *neuroscience educator*
Witherspoon, Carolyn Brack *lawyer*
Wright, Susan Webber *federal judge*

Magnolia
Hamilton, Barbara Denise *computer science educator*
Harrison, Betty Carolyn Cook *retired education educator, administrator*
Penick, Patricia Akins *art educator*

Malvern
Burks, Rebecca Ann *music educator*
Growney-Seals, Sharon Ann *literature and language professor, department chairman*

Marianna
Pruitt, Mary H. *social worker*

Marion
Logan, Sandra La Mastus *music educator*

Maynard
Stuart, Cynthia Hodge *literature and language educator*

Melbourne
Johnson, Ruby Diane *nursing educator, department chairman, nurse*

Monticello
Webster, Linda Jean *communications executive, media consultant*

Morrilton
Crawford-Larson, Kris *minister*

Mountainburg
Richmond, Daphne Kay *science educator*

Murfreesboro
Wood, Rhonda Gailette *secondary school educator*

Natural Dam
Butler, Paula Kay *elementary school educator*

Norman
Hokanson, Carol *speech therapist, special education educator*

North Little Rock
Betty-Singleton, Charmaine Elizabeth *lawyer, military officer*
Harrison, Angela Eve *manufacturing executive*
Kirchner, JoAnn Elaine *psychiatrist*
Valentine, Terri L. *secondary school educator, activities director*

Osceola
Landry, Sandra Denise *secondary school educator*

Palestine
Taylor, Barbara Mae Helm *artist, educator*

Paragould
Stallings, Phyllis Ann *music educator*
White, Sarah Elizabeth Sloan *elementary school educator*

Paris
Hawkins, Naomi Ruth *nurse*

Pine Bluff
Engle, Carole Ruth *aquaculture economics professor*
Teel, Gina A. *language educator*
Williams, Bettye Jean *language educator*

Pine Ridge
Hays, Annette Arlene *secondary school educator*

Pocahontas
Moss, Linda Elaine *science educator*
Rone, Monika Hiedi *mental health services professional, consultant*

Prairie Grove
Dunn, Anne Ewald Nefflen *retired elementary school educator*

Redfield
Wells, Linda Lee *retired elementary school educator*

Rose Bud
Spradley, Pamela Claire *art educator*

Russellville
Lake, Tina Selanders *artist, educator*
Morris, Lois Lawson *retired education educator*
Vance, Sue Ann *musician, educator*

Scranton
Uzman, Betty Ben Geren *retired pathologist*

Searcy
Coleman, Bobbie Ruth *literature and language educator*
Pruitt, Linda F. *elementary school educator*
Thompson, Linda Ruth *psychology educator, university administrator*
Watson, Betty Ann *early childhood education professor*

Sherwood
Eddy, Nancy C. *counselor*
Keaton, Frances Marlene *insurance sales representative*

Siloam Springs
Wubbena, Teresa R. *music educator*

Springdale
Beach, Jean Mrha *food products executive*
Davis, Deborah Ann St. Cyr *elementary school educator*
Dunn, Jeri R. *food products executive*
Durr, Tami Joleen *mathematics educator*
Earl, Heather Jo *food company professional*
Haseloff, Cynthia *fiction writer*
Holman, L. Charlene *elementary school educator*
Posey, Sandra Dalton *special education educator*

Stamps
Moore-Berry, Norma Jean *secondary school educator*

Stuttgart
Ashley-Iverson, Mary E. *retired librarian*

Texarkana
Beck, Tiffany *secondary school educator*
Walker, Barbara Ross *secondary school educator*

Tyronza
Debow, Bridgette M. *elementary school educator*

Van Buren
Kilgore, Mary Helen *mathematics educator*

Vanndale
Clark, Betty Susan *elementary school educator*

Walnut Ridge
Wheeless, Charlotte Ann *science educator*

Ward
Rudy, Janet Faye Walker *science educator*

Wasilla
Swanson, Carolyn Rae *news reporter, counselor*

West Fork
Higgins, Sarah Jean *literature and language professor*

West Memphis
Howell, Kathy Aileen *advertising executive*

Wheatley
Gehring, Elizabeth A. *social studies educator*

White Hall
Dumas, Sandra Kay *music educator*
Rushing, Annette *elementary school educator*

Wickes
Riley, Faith Lynch *retired historian, writer*

Winslow
Wright, Mary E. (Mary E. Guen) *clinical psychologist*

CALIFORNIA

Adin
Ellenberger, Kathleen Sue Bowman *special education educator*

Agoura Hills
Bach, Cynthia *educational program director, writer*
Piscitelli, Nancy L. *retired special education educator*

Alameda
Carter, Roberta Eccleston *counseling administrator*
Herrick, Sylvia Anne *health facility administrator*
Johnson, Beverly J. *lawyer, congressman*
LaRose, Katherine Stencel *music educator*
Leonard, Sheila Ann *former government agency executive, consultant*
Potash, Jeremy Warner *public relations executive*
Robinson, Joanne Adele *retired secondary school educator, volunteer*
Troll, Lillian Ellman *psychologist, educator*
Trufant, Carol Ann *psychologist, consultant*

Alamo
Pochmann, Virginia *retired artist, painter, draftsman*

Albany
Boris, Ruthanna *dancer, educator, choreographer, dance therapist*
Daniels, Lydia M. *health care administrator*
Ginzberg, Abigail *video producer*
Thomsen, Peggy Jean *mayor, educator*

Alhambra
Austin, Elizabeth Ruth *retired elementary school educator*
Birch, Tobeylynn *librarian*
Malonek, Jennie Sue *science educator*

Aliso Viejo
Cohen, Sasha (Alexandra Pauline Cohen) *ice skater*

Harder, Wendy Wetzel communications executive
Johanson, Wanda L. medical association administrator, critical care nurse

Alpine
Leyse-Wallace, Ruth Louise dietician, educator

Altadena
Hoskins, Cherise Lachelle elementary school educator
Klages, Karen Louise music educator, musician
Miller, Karen clinical psychologist, neuropsychologist
Mkryan, Sonya geophysicist, educator, research scientist
Rabe, Elizabeth Rozina hair stylist, horse breeder
Snortland, Ellen Barbara writer
Willans, Jean Stone bishop, religious organization administrator

Alturas
Johnson, Donna Marie elementary school educator

Anaheim
Barkemeijer de Wit, Jeanne Sandra graphic artist, illustrator, writer, multimedia consultant
Barry, Sandra school system administrator
Browne, Autumn Lee theater educator, actress, theater director
Goodspeed, Kathryn Ann pre-school educator
Lee, Donna Jean retired nurse
Miller, Jean Ruth retired librarian
Nelipovich, Sandra Grassi artist
Orlando, Valeria music educator, musician, artist
Pincombe, Jodi Doris health facility administrator
Vidergar, Teresa musician, educator

Anderson
Wittmann, Jane Gordon volunteer

Antioch
Adams, Liliana Osses music performer, harpist
Chan, Patty G. librarian
Stamm, Barbara Marie elementary school educator, interior designer
Thomson, Sondra K. secondary school educator

Apple Valley
Yule, Caroll Jane real estate broker

Aptos
Farhat-Holzman, Laina writer, editor
Hirsch, Bette G(ross) academic administrator, language educator
Miura, Masako Kusayanagi retired dermatologist
Pezzoni, Meri Kathryn music educator

Arcadia
Abramson, Leslie Hope lawyer
Anderson, Holly Geis health facility administrator, educator, commentator
Baltz, Patricia Ann (Pann Baltz) retired elementary school educator
Imbus, Sharon Haughey neuroscience nurse

Arcata
Green, Theresa Diane social worker
Land-Weber, Ellen photography professor

Arleta
Kelley, Frances A. occupational therapist, consultant

Armona
Vanderpool, Shawnee D. elementary school educator

Aromas
Anderson, Sara Shuttleworth artist, educator

Arroyo Grande
Oseguera, Palma Marie retired career officer

Atascadero
Colamarino, Katrin Belenky lawyer
Jones, Kathryn Cherie pastor
Locke, Virginia Otis writer
Rios, Evelyn Deerwester columnist, musician, artist, writer
Thacker, Stacy Leigh psychologist

Atwater
Duddy, Ethel Eileen (Eileen Duddy) accountant
Ryan, Kelli Lorraine ballerina, educator

Auburn
Larimore-Albrecht, Deni Denise social worker
Moore, Billie Jo minister
Rothwell, Elaine B. artist
Sanborn, Dorothy Chappell retired librarian

Azusa
Duskin, Kimberly J athletic trainer
Gahring, Sandra Ann secondary school educator, coach
Griesinger, Emily Ann literature and language professor
Lehman, Sharon Malani physical education educator
Miyake, Stephanie Ann psychology professor, director, marriage and family therapist

Bakersfield
Burns, Sarah Chloe historian, educator
Frazier, Jo Frances religious organization administrator, writer
Fuller, Jean school system administrator
Girga, Barbara psychotherapist, college counselor
Gong, Gloria Margaret lawyer, pharmacist
Granskog, Jane Ellen anthropologist, educator
Huerta, Dolores Fernandez labor union administrator
Johnson, Deborah Valerie Germaine parish administrator
Kegley, Jacquelyn Ann philosophy educator
Kelly, Diana Kay counselor, educator
Kemp, Donna Renee public administration educator, public policy educator, academic administrator
Kerr, Joan Lindsay supervisor, consultant
Kreber, Lisa Ann neuroscientist, psychologist
Martin, Maureen Frances medical educator
Osterkamp, Dalene May psychology educator, artist
Rienzi, Beth Ann Menees psychologist, educator, director
Smith, Cheryl Jan language educator

Banning
Finley, Margaret Mavis retired elementary school educator

Barstow
Gibbon, Mary-Lynn special education educator

Beaumont
Youngren, Delvana Hope secondary school educator

Belmont
Hollis, Mary Frances aerospace educator
Jacobson, Vera Lee secondary school educator

Belvedere
Crump, Ann artist
Doyle, Virginia Knepper artist
Hugenberg, Patricia Ellen Petrie product designer

Belvedere Tiburon
Dams, Jeanne M. writer

Berkeley
Agogino, Alice Merner computer scientist, mechanical engineer, educator
Arguedas, Cristina Claypoole lawyer
Azarpay, Guitty education educator
Bajcsy, Ruzena Kucerova computer science educator
Baumrind, Diana research psychologist
Bendix, Jane artist, writer, illustrator
Bissell, Mina J. lab administrator, biochemist
Bodenhausen, Judith Anne school system administrator
Buell, Evangeline Canonizado advocate
Buffler, Patricia Ann epidemiologist, educator, dean
Burch, Claire Rita writer
Burnside, Mary Beth biology professor, researcher
Canfield, Judy S. psychologist
Chen, Lu neurobiologist, biology professor
Chetin, Helen Campbell writer
Cochran, Myrtis librarian
Crawford, Charlotte Joanne psychologist, psychoanalyst, psychological anthropologist
Daly, Markate philosophical researcher, counselor
Day, Lucille Lang museum administrator, educator, writer
Diamond, Marian Cleeves anatomist, educator
Dong, Mabel H music educator
Doyle, Fiona Mary dean, metallurgical engineer, educator
Edelman, Lauren B. sociologist, law educator
Efimova, Alla curator
Ensign, Jacqueline social worker
Farina, Marianne theology studies educator, consultant
Felter, June Marie artist
Finnie, Joan adult education educator
Fleiszig, Suzanne Mariane Janete optometry educator
Freedman, Sarah Warshauer education educator
Fung, Inez Y. science educator
Gaillard, Mary Katharine physicist, educator
Gallagher, M. Catherine English literature educator
Genn, Nancy artist
Gibbs, Jewelle Taylor clinical psychologist
Ginger, Ann Fagan lawyer
Graham, Susan Lois computer scientist, consultant
Grimes, Ruth Elaine city planner
Grossman, Bonnie art gallery director
Grossman, Joan Delaney literature and language professor
Gumbs, Pam pharmacist
Hellman, Frances physics professor
Hill, Lorie Elizabeth psychotherapist
Hoffman, Darleane Christian chemistry professor
Hull, Glynda language educator
Ivey, Susan Lee health services researcher, emergency physician
Jones, Patricia Bengtson sculptor
Joseph, Anne M. lawyer, law educator
Josephian, Jenny Adele acupuncturist, artist
Joyce, Rosemary Alexandria anthropology educator, department chairman
Kay, Herma Hill law educator
King, Nicole molecular biologist, educator
Klinman, Judith Pollock biochemist, educator
Koehl, Mimi R. integrative biology professor
Kohwi-Shigematsu, Terumi research scientist
Korn, Claire Vedensky secondary school educator, writer
Kushner, Eve writer
Lark, Sylvia artist, educator
Lashof, Joyce Cohen public health service officer, educator
Lesser, Wendy editor, writer, consultant
Linn, Marcia Cyrog education educator
Little, Angela Capobianco nutritional science educator
Lovell, Margaretta M. art history educator, museum curator
Luker, Kristin sociology educator
Maslach, Christina psychology professor
Massie, Betsy McPherson clergywoman
Matsumura, Vera Yoshi pianist
Mavroudi, Maria philologist, educator
McBay, Ida LaVerne special education educator
McLaughlin, Sylvia Cranmer volunteer, environmentalist
McPhail-Geist, Karin Ruth secondary school educator, real estate agent, musician
Meyer, Roberta mediator, communication consultant
Minudri, Regina Ursula librarian, consultant
Moran, Rachel law educator
Mukherjee, Bharati (Mrs. Clark Blaise) writer, language educator
Nader, Laura anthropologist, educator
Nathanson, Marjorie Ann psychologist
Nemeth, Charlan Jeanne psychology educator
Petiet, Carole Anne psychologist
Pfeiffer, Phyllis Kramer publishing executive
Polos, Iris Stephanie artist
Ralston, Lenore Dale academic policy and program analyst
Rapoport, Sonya artist
Reid, Frances Evelyn Kroll freelance/self-employed cinematographer, film director, communications executive
Richards, Kyungnyun Kim Korean language educator, poet, translator
Samuelson, Pamela Ann law educator
Schild, Sylvia G. retired elementary school educator, realtor
Scott, Eugenie Carol science foundation director, anthropologist
Shapiro, Marjorie D. physics professor
Sher, Elizabeth artist, educator, filmmaker
Sherwood, Katherine D. artist, educator
Stewart, Patricia Rhodes former clinical psychologist, researcher
Stroup, Dorothy Anne author, educator
Susskind, Teresa Gabriel publishing executive
Torykian, Joan Marie archivist
Wake, Marvalee Hendricks biology professor
Watkins, Renee E. adult education educator

Bermuda Dunes
McCarthy, Kathleen Marie priest, nurse

Berry Creek
Montaño, Tiffany Dunhill aerospace production control specialist

Beverly Hills
Abdul, Paula (Paula Julie Abdul) singer, dancer, choreographer
Allen, Joan actress
Amado, Honey Kessler lawyer
Ambrose, Lauren (Lauren Anne D'Ambruoso) actress
Anderson, Pamela Denise actress
Ann-Margret, (Ann-Margret Olsson) actress, performer
Arquette, Patricia actress
Arutt, Cheryl clinical and forensic psychologist, educator
Azzara, Candice actress
Bao, Katherine Sung pediatric cardiologist
Barrymore, Drew actress
Barton, Mischa actress
Bates, Kathy actress
Bello, Maria Elana actress
Bening, Annette actress
Bergman, Nancy Palm real estate investment company executive
Biel, Jessica actress, model
Blakeley, Linda psychologist, speaker, consultant, writer
Blanchett, Cate (Catherine Elise Blanchett) actress
Bland, Janeese Myra editor
Bonham-Carter, Helena actress
Bosworth, Kate actress
Brenneman, Amy actress
Brockovich-Ellis, Erin legal researcher
Burnett, Carol actress, comedienne, singer
Burstyn, Ellen (Edna Rae Gillooly) actress
Bush, Sophia actress
Bymel, Suzan Yvette talent manager, film producer
Campbell, Neve actress
Capshaw, Kate (Kathy Sue Nail) actress
Carter, Lynda actress, entertainer
Casey, Sue (Suzanne Marguerite Philips) actress, real estate broker
Cattrall, Kim actress
Close, Glenn actress
Cloyde, Jan R. bank executive
Collette, Toni actress
Congdon, Amanda actress, web video blogger, writer
Connelly, Jennifer actress
Cox Arquette, Courteney actress
Cruz, Penelope actress
Curtis, Jamie Lee actress
Cusack, Joan actress
D'Abo, Olivia actress
Daly, Tyne actress
Davis, Geena (Virginia Davis) actress
DeGeneres, Ellen actress, comedienne, talk show host
Delaney, Kim actress
De Rosa, Ninon de Vere television producer
Drescher, Fran actress
Duke, Patty (Anna Marie Duke) actress
Eden, Barbara Jean actress
Eikenberry, Jill actress
Elfman, Jenna (Jennifer Mary Butala) actress
Evans, Louise investor, retired psychologist
Falco, Edie actress
Fey, Tina actress
Flockhart, Calista actress
Foch, Nina actress, creative consultant, film director, educator
Fonda, Jane actress
Gabler, Elizabeth Brand film company executive
Garofalo, Janeane actress, comedienne
Garr, Teri (Ann) actress
Gilpin, Peri actress
Gleason, Joanna actress
Graham, Heather actress
Graham, Lauren actress
Griffin, Kathy comedienne, actress
Gugino, Carla actress
Gyllenhaal, Maggie actress
Hamilton, Linda actress
Hamilton, Lisa Gay actress
Hannah, Daryl actress
Harden, Marcia Gay actress
Harmon, Angie (Angie Sehorn) actress
Hart, Melissa Joan Catherine actress
Hathaway, Anne actress
Hawn, Goldie actress
Hayek, Salma actress
Heaton, Patricia actress
Helmond, Katherine actress
Hershey, Barbara (Barbara Herzstein) actress
Hewitt, Jennifer Love actress, singer
Holmes, Katie (Katherine Noelle Holmes) actress
Hunt, Bonnie actress
Hunt, Linda actress
Hurd, Gale Anne film producer
Hurley, Elizabeth actress, model, film producer
Huston, Anjelica actress
Jackson, Janet (Janet Damita Jo Jackson) vocalist, dancer
Janseen, Famke actress
Jenkins, Patty film director, scriptwriter
Johansson, Scarlett actress
Jolie, Angelina actress
Jones, Cherry actress
Josephson, Nancy talent agency executive
Judd, Ashley actress
Kalawski, Eva lawyer
Keaton, Diane actress
Keener, Catherine actress
Kelly, Moira actress
Khan, Chaka (Yvette Marie Stevens) singer
Kidman, Nicole actress
Kingston, Alex (Alexandra Kingston) actress
Kleiner, Madeleine A. lawyer
Klum, Heidi model, actress
Lahti, Christine actress
Lake, Ricki (Ricki Pamela Lake) talk show host, actress
Lane, Diane actress
Lansbury, Angela Brigid actress
Leder, Mimi television director, film director, film producer
Leigh, Jennifer Jason (Jennifer Leigh Morrow) actress
Lewis, Juliette actress
Li, Linda (Linda Jian-Yuh Li) plastic surgeon
Linney, Laura actress
Liu, Lucy actress
Lohan, Lindsay actress
Lord, Marjorie actress
MacLaine, Shirley actress
Madigan, Amy actress
Malone, Jena actress
Manheim, Camryn television and film actress
Margulies, Julianna actress
Marshall, Penny (C. Marshall, Carole Penny Marshall) director, actress
Martin, Kellie (Noelle) actress
Martinson, Constance Frye television personality, television producer
Masterson, Mary Stuart actress
Mathis, Samantha actress
Mazar, Debi actress
McAdams, Rachel actress
McCarthy, Jenny actress
McDonnell, Mary actress
McKenzie-Swarts, Molly human resources specialist, hotel executive
Mendes, Eva actress
Messing, Debra actress
Meyers, Nancy Jane screenwriter, producer, director
Mol, Gretchen actress
Monaco, Kelly Marie actress
Moore, Julianne (Julie Anne Smith) actress
Moore, Mandy (Amanda Leigh Moore) actress, singer
Moore, Mary Tyler actress
Morton, Samantha actress
Moynahan, Bridget (Kathryn Bridget Moynahan) actress
Mullally, Megan actress
Najimy, Kathy actress
Nixon, Cynthia actress
Opri, Debra A. lawyer
Paltrow, Gwyneth actress
Parker, Mary-Louise actress
Parker, Sarah Jessica actress
Peet, Amanda actress
Perkins, Elizabeth Ann actress
Perlman, Rhea actress
Phillips, Debora Rothman psychotherapist
Pomeroy, Eleanor Lisa Beyea psychologist, psychoanalyst
Pompeo, Ellen actress
Portman, Natalie actress
Posey, Parker actress
Quinn, Patricia K. literary agent
Rai, Aishwarya actress
Ramser, Wanda Tene librarian, educator
Reese, Della (Deloreese Patricia Early) singer, actress
Ricci, Christina actress
Richardson, Patricia actress
Richie, Nicole television personality
Rinaldi, Renee Zaira physician
Ringwald, Molly actress
Roberts, Julia Fiona actress
Robinson Peete, Holly actress, writer
Rodkin, Loree jewelry artist
Rogers, Mimi actress
Rossellini, Isabella actress, model
Russell, Keri actress
Ryan, Meg (Margaret Mary Emily Ann Hyra) actress, film producer
Sagal, Katey actress
Scacchi, Greta actress
Scott-Thomas, Kristin actress
Sedgwick, Kyra actress
Seeger, Melinda Wayne realtor
Seidel, Joan Broude securities dealer, investment advisor
Seizer, Fern Victor retired mental health services administrator
Sellecca, Connie actress
Seymour, Jane actress
Shapiro-Mathes, Angela broadcast executive
Sherwood, Kehela (Karen Kehela Sherwood) broadcast executive
Shue, Elisabeth actress
Shuler Donner, Lauren film producer
Silverman, Sarah actress, comedian, writer
Simpson, Jessica Ann singer, actress
Smith, Jaclyn actress
Snyder, Liza actress
Sorvino, Mira actress
Spacek, Sissy (Mary Elizabeth Spacek) actress
Spelling, Tori (Victoria Davey Spelling) actress
Spheeris, Penelope film director
Steenburgen, Mary actress
Steinem, Gloria writer, editor, advocate
Stiles, Julia actress
Streep, Meryl (Mary Louise Streep) actress
Surface, Carol Price artist, educator
Suvari, Mena actress

Swank, Hilary Ann *actress*
Swofford, Beth *agent*
Sykes, Wanda *comedienne, actress*
Tamblyn, Amber Rose *actress*
Taylor, Christine *actress*
Taylor, Lili *actress*
Theron, Charlize *actress*
Thompson, Emma *actress*
Thurman, Uma Karuna *actress*
Tierney, Maura *actress*
Tilly, Jennifer *actress*
Tom, Lauren *actress, singer*
Tomei, Marisa *actress*
Travis, Nancy *actress*
Turner, Janine *actress*
Turner, Kathleen *actress*
Tyler, Liv *actress*
Utley, Nancy *film company executive*
Van Ark, Joan *actress*
Vardalos, Nia *actress, screenwriter*
Ward, Sela *actress*
Watts, Naomi *actress*
Weaver, Sigourney (Susan Alexandra Weaver) *actress*
Weisz, Rachel *actress*
White, Betty *actress, comedienne*
White, Meg (Megan Martha White) *musician, vocalist*
Williams, Michelle *actress*
Williams-Paisley, Kimberly *actress*
Witherspoon, Reese (Laura Jean Reese Witherspoon) *actress*
Wright Penn, Robin *actress*
Yaryan, Ruby Bell *psychologist*
Zanuck, Lili Fini *film director, producer*
Zellweger, Renee *actress*

Big Bear Lake
McCoy, Jennie Eileen *elementary school educator*
Mix, Jill Kaye *secondary school educator, artist*

Big Pine
Reynaud-Roepke, Suzanne *psychologist*

Bishop
Naso, Valerie Joan *automotive dealership executive, travel company executive*

Bodega Bay
Freeman, Donna Cook *small business owner*
Sorensen, Linda *lawyer*

Bonita
Deane, Debbe *psychologist, journalist, editor, consultant*

Bowman
Peppard, Jacqueline Jean *artist*

Brawley
King, Bonnie Bess Worline *writer, educator*

Brea
Ellis, Cynthia Bueker *musician, educator*
Missakian, Ilona Virginia *secondary school educator*

Brentwood
Fridley, Saundra Lynn *private investigator*
Groseclose, Wanda Westman *retired elementary school educator*
Lagano, Daneen Westphal *elementary school educator*
Paul, Yvonne C. *retired elementary school educator*

Brisbane
Baadh, Valerie *choreographer, movement educator, theater producer, production designer*
Daniels, Caroline *publishing executive*
Earl, Lois Marie *medical/surgical and home health nurse*

Burbank
Branch, Michelle *musician*
Brandis, Bernardine *lawyer*
Cher, (Cherilyn Sarkisian) *singer, actress*
Doud, Jacqueline Powers *academic administrator*
Fifield, Lillene H. *psychotherapist, educator*
Fleishman, Susan Nahley *entertainment company executive*
Frank, Amélie Lorraine *marketing professional*
Joseff, Joan Castle *manufacturing executive*
Jovovich, Milla (Natasha Militza Jovovich) *model, actress*
Kroll, Sue *broadcast executive*
Kwan-Rubinek, Veronika *broadcast executive*
Madison, Paula *broadcast executive*
Marinelli, Janice *broadcast executive*
Mc Govern, Maureen Therese *entertainer*
Mc Vie, Christine Perfect *musician*
Nelson, Diane W. *broadcast executive*
Neumann, Nancy Ruth *private school educator*
Nurik, Cindy Bunin *educational consultant, marriage and family therapist*
O'Dell, Nancy *television personality*
Remini, Leah *actress*
Rhimes, Shonda *producer, director, writer*
Ricketts, Amy Rene *elementary school educator, writer*
Rimes, LeAnn *country music singer*
Ruttan, Susan *actress*
Sherbert, Sharon Debra *financial services executive*
Sweeney, Anne M. *cable television company executive*
Taubin, Dawn *film company executive*
Ungerleider, Dorothy Fink *recreational therapist*
Weiskopf, Wanda *mezzo soprano, writer, poet*
Wise, Helena Sunny *lawyer*
Younger, Laurie *broadcast executive*

Burlingame
Stirm, Doris Elizabeth *artist*
Tirschwell-Newby, Kathy Ann *events production company executive*

Calabasas
Thompkins, Jennifer Eley *physician assistant, consultant*

Calexico
Ramirez, Elisa *mathematics educator*

Calistoga
Lochanko, Elizabeth Alexandra *communications executive*
Sassoon, Janet *ballerina, educator*

Camarillo
Arthington, Carol Ann *elementary school educator*
Cobb, Shirley Ann Dodson *public relations consultant, journalist*
Kaiman, Sarah *retired physician*
Meyer, Barbara *psychologist*
Truman, Ruth *administrator, writer, lecturer, consultant*

Cameron Park
Vorce-Tish, Helene R. *writer*

Canoga Park
Alexander, Sue *writer*
Lederer, Marion Irvine *cultural administrator*
Rosenfeld, Sarena Margaret *artist*

Canyon Country
Joseph, Michele Beth *special education educator, educational therapist*

Capitola
Baskerville, Elizabeth Bonham *pediatrician*
Hawes, Grace Maxcy *archivist, retired writer*

Carlsbad
Burns, Doris Eleanor *retired elementary school educator*
Crooke, Rosanne M. *pharmacologist*
Cuthbert, Emilie Ann (Emilie Winthrop) *interior designer*
Golden, Paula Englander *social work educator, consultant, addiction educator, consultant*
Lovell, Joan Ellen *mental health professional*
Parshall, B. Lynne *science administrator*
Ritchie, Doris Lee *executive secretary*
Rodak, Sharon Lorraine *elementary school educator, researcher*
Schmidt, Mary Louise Donnel *banker*
Sperling, Irene R. *publishing executive*

Carmel
de Vos, Paula Francesca *finance company executive, investment advisor, consultant*
Epstein-Shepherd, Bee *coach, hypnotist, educator*
Ferrari, Linda Gale *art educator*
Freed, Sharon Lou *retired principal*
Hamilton, Beverly Lannquist *investment executive*
Kleefeld, Carolyn Mary *artist, writer, poet*
Pasten, Laura Jean *veterinarian*
Reamy, Michaelin *marriage and family therapist, educator, consultant*
Wright, Constance Storey *retired humanities educator*

Carmel Valley
Heimann, Janet Barbara *volunteer trail consultant*

Carmichael
Betts, Barbara Lang *lawyer, real estate agent, rancher*
Friedman, Mary Kathleen *secondary school educator*
Money, Ruth Rowntree *retired infant development and care specialist, parent/infant programs consultant*
Moore, MaryLou *researcher*
Oprsal, Nancy Upshaw *retired elementary school educator*
Ryan, Gretchen Margarete Frieda *art educator*

Carpinteria
Rau, Margaret E. *writer*

Carson
Davis, Carylon Lee *mortgage company executive, real estate broker*
Hirsch, Gilah Yelin *artist, writer*
Hurtado-Ortiz, Maria T. *psychology professor*
Oropeza, Jenny *state official*
Paige, Dorothy Billiard *retired secondary school educator, educational consultant*
Palmer, Beverly Blazey *psychologist, educator*
Zimmerer, Kathy Louise *museum director*

Castro Valley
Mabee, Sandra Ivonne Noriega *musician, educator, clergy member*
Shoptaw, Shauna Lynn *middle school educator*

Cathedral City
Berry, Ester Lorée *vocational nurse*
Hoffman, Jetha L. *music educator, voice educator*
Karasik, Miriyam Beth *artist, writer*

Century City
Brazell, Tina Arning *actress, executive recruiter*

Ceres
Chamberlain, Candace Sue *music educator*

Cerritos
Woodson-Glenn, Yolanda *social worker*

Chatsworth
Stephenson, Irene Hamlen *biomedical researcher, consultant, editor, educator*
Strieby, B. Lorraine *artist*

Chico
Bernhardt, Victoria L. *director, researcher*
Dorsey-Tyler, April Melody *science educator*
Hyde, Geraldine Veola *retired secondary school educator*
Mathans, Sharron Hitt *retired librarian*
Mejia, Barbara Oviedo *retired chemistry professor*
Monges, Miriam M. *social studies educator*
Reinhardt, Deborah Ann *music educator*
Smith, Valene Lucy *anthropologist, educator*
Taylor, Carolyn Kay *music educator*
Transchel, Kate *social sciences educator*

China Lake
Bennett, Jean Louise McPherson *physicist, research scientist*

Chino
Alton, Colleen Edna *education educator*
Neal-Parker, Shirley Anita *obstetrician, gynecologist*
Wiegand, Penelope Tarleton *elementary school educator*

Chino Hills
Fisher, Teresa Marie *psychologist, forensic specialist*
Nash, Sylvia Dotseth *management consultant*
Sorenson, Sandra Louise *retired retail executive*

Chula Vista
Capehart, Bonnie *language educator*
Cohen, Elaine Helena *pediatrician, cardiologist, educator*
Greenway-August, Kristin Lee *dancer, educator*
Moreno-Ducheny, Denise *state senator*
Ryan, Candace I. *writer, director, editor*
Steele, Nancy Eden Rogers *nonprofit corporate executive, retired principal*
Weiss-Cornwell, Amy *interior designer*
Wyatt, Edith Elizabeth *elementary school educator*

Citrus Heights
Daves, Sandra Lynn *poet, lyricist*
Mart, Joann *social sciences educator*

City Of Industry
Cavanaugh, Janis Lynn *protective services official, educator*
Contreras-Sweet, Maria *bank executive*

Claremont
Albaum, Jean Stirling *psychologist, educator*
Bekavac, Nancy Yavor *academic administrator, lawyer*
Christian, Suzanne Hall *financial planner*
Deese, E(thel) Helen *retired literature and language professor*
Gann, Pamela Brooks *academic administrator*
Glass, Sandra Ann *foundation administrator, consultant*
Halpern, Diane F. *psychology educator, professional association executive*
Klawe, Maria Margaret *academic administrator, engineering educator, computer science educator*
Lipman-Blumen, Jean *public policy and organizational behavior educator*
Morgan, Ann Marie *psychologist*
Moss, Myra Ellen (Myra Moss Rolle) *philosophy educator*
O'Kelly, Crystal Kathleen *secondary school educator, television producer*
Phillips, Donna Rose *production artist, writer*
Rankaitis, Susan *artist*
Schroerlucke, Leslie Jean *music educator*
Skandera Trombley, Laura Elise *academic administrator, literature educator*
Stokes, Anne Dorothy *retired educational association administrator*
Vajk, Fiona *psychologist, educator*
Wheeler, Geraldine Hartshorn *historian, writer*
Zehr, Connie *sculptor, art educator*

Clayton
Bower, Fay Louise *academic administrator, nursing educator*

Clovis
Dixson, Judy Sue *retired elementary school educator*
Kawashima, Hope Nozomi *musician*
van der Paardt, Tamara Ann *music educator*
Von Prince, Kilulu Magdalene *retired occupational therapist, sculptor*

Coachella
Gonzales, Martha *elementary school educator*

Colton
Caseria, Carol Shuler *elementary school educator, researcher*

Colusa
Carter, Jane Foster *agricultural industry executive*

Compton
Drew, Sharon Lee *sociologist*
Gillette, Sister Joseph Ann *education educator, educator*

Concord
Broadbent, Amalia Sayo Castillo *graphic arts designer*

Copperopolis
White, Marnelle Rosalie *real estate broker*

Corcoran
Martines, Eugenia Belle *elementary school educator, special education educator*
Oliver, Patricia *physician assistant*

Corning
Brown, Betty J. *retired elementary school educator*

Corona
Hagmann, Lillian Sue *violin instructor*
Holt, Chifra *dancer, educator, choreographer, artist*
Snider, Jane Ann *retired elementary school educator*
White, Joy Mieko *retired communications executive*
Wood, Brenda Jean *pastor, evangelist*

Corona Del Mar
Dougherty, Jocelyn *retired neurologist*

Coronado
Akin, Lillie Violet *chemistry educator, writer, television personality, consultant*
Perry, Jantina *retired music educator*

Corte Madera
Andreini, Elizabeth B. *investment advisor, elementary school educator*
Dalpino, Ida Jane *retired secondary school educator*

Costa Mesa
Caldwell, Courtney Lynn *lawyer, real estate consultant*
Candelaria, Angie Mary *special education educator*
Epstein, Susan Baerg *librarian, consultant*
Fam, Hanaa *psychiatrist*
Graff, Cynthia Stamper *health facility administrator*
Grogan, Virginia S. *lawyer*
Marshall, Ellen Ruth *lawyer*
McCarthy, Mary Ann *counselor, educator*
Powers, Janet F. *special education educator*
Scheuneman, Christine A. *lawyer*
Stecker, Suzanne Louise *business executive*

Cotati
Hill, Debora Elizabeth *writer, journalist, screenwriter*

Cottonwood
Penrod, Rebecca Lorene Connelly *retired elementary school educator*
Pritchett, Lori L. *real estate broker, secondary school educator*

Covina
Cottrell, Janet Ann *controller*

Coyote
Keeshen, Kathleen Kearney *public relations consultant*

Crescent City
Swart, Bonnie Blount *artist*

Culver City
Bernstein, Diane *psychotherapist*
Boonshaft, Hope Judith *public relations executive*
Cole, Elaine Ann *marriage and family therapist, educator*
Finkelman Cox, Penney *film producer*
Fisher, Lucy *film producer*
Geiselman, LucyAnn *college president*
Grant, Joan Julien *artist*
Hall, Barbara *television producer*
Hoge, Geraldine Rajacich *elementary school educator*
Jacobs, Betty Jane Lazaroff *communications educator*
Maxwell-Brogdon, Florence Morency *school system administrator, educational consultant*
Muller, Jenny Helen *physician, psychiatrist*
Pascal, Amy Beth *film company executive*
Russell, Robin J. *broadcast executive*
Simmons, Kimora Lee *apparel designer, television personality, model*
Thomas, Marlo (Margaret Julia Thomas) *actress*
Van Galder, Valerie *marketing executive*
Vollack, Lia *broadcast executive*
Weil, Leah *lawyer*
Ziskin, Laura *television producer, film producer*

Cupertino
Fraser, Maida Lynn *director*
Johnson, Allison *corporate communications specialist, marketing executive*
Lyon, Mary Lou *retired secondary school educator*
Martin, Barbara Lynne *retired elementary school educator*
Starratt, Jeanette Ellen *elementary school educator*
Zobel, Louise Purwin *author, educator, lecturer, writing consultant*

Cypress
Armstrong, Sandra Rogers *secondary school educator, athletic trainer*
Bradaric, SuzAnne Joy *music educator, theater director*
Friess, Donna Lewis *children's rights advocate*
Garrett, Sharon *health services company executive*
Kosecoff, Jacqueline Barbara *health care company executive*

Daly City
Hargrave, Sarah Quesenberry *consulting company executive, public relations executive*
Kennedy, Gwendolyn Debra *artist, scriptwriter, playwright*

Danville
Gilcrist, Tracy Ann *science educator*
Henehan, Gina L. *history educator*
Spilker, Yvonne Wailes *mathematics educator*
Strohl, Elizabeth G. *banker*

Davis
Biggart, Nicole Woolsey *dean*
Blodgett, Harriet *retired language educator*
Bruch, Carol Sophie *law educator*
Cole, Kimberly Ree *music educator, musician*
DePaoli, Geri M. (Joan DePaoli) *artist, art historian*
Dickens, Janis *media services administrator*
Franco, Elaine Adele *librarian*
Ginosar, D. Elaine *elementary school educator*
Hinshaw, Virginia *academic administrator*
Horwitz, Barbara Ann *physiologist, educator, consultant*
Jensen, Hanne Margrete *pathologist, educator*
Keen, Susan Lynn *biology professor*
Keizer, Susan Jane *artist*
Kraft, Rosemarie *dean, educator*
Kuhl, Tonya L. *science educator*
Landau, Norma Beatrice *historian, educator*
MacGregor, Marilyn Elna *director*
McCutcheon, Jade Rosina *performing arts educator*
McPherson, Sandra Jean *poet, educator*
Meyer, Margaret Eleanor *retired microbiologist*
Powers, Gay Havens-Monteagle *artist, educator*

Robert, Ellen *university administrator*
Ronald, Pamela C. *plant pathologist, educator*
Savageau, Ann Elisa *artist*
Sharrow, Marilyn Jane *library administrator*
Silberstein, Allegra Jostad *retired elementary school educator*
Stern, Judith Schneider *nutritionist, researcher, educator*
Thompson, Abigail *mathematics professor*
Turnlund, Judith Rae *nutritionist*

Del Mar
Ceren, Sandra Levy *psychologist, writer*
Farquhar, Marilyn Gist *cell biologist, pathologist, educator*
Gray-Bussard, Dolly H. *energy company executive*
Quinn, Katherine Sarah *psychologist*
Rodger, Marion McGee *medical/surgical nurse, administrator*

Denair
Hale, Lois J. *retired mathematics educator*

Desert Hot Springs
Zarres, Sharon L. *marriage and family therapist, health facility administrator*

Diamond Bar
Mirisola, Lisa Heinemann *air quality engineer*

Dinuba
León, Rosemary Carrasco *gynecologist*

Downey
Achon, Raquel Andrea *music educator, consultant*
Brooks, Lillian Drilling Ashton (Lillian Hazel Church) *adult education educator*
Orange, Valerie *rehabilitation center executive*
Perry, Jacquelin *orthopedist, surgeon*
Ruecker, Martha Engels *retired special education educator*
Todd, Margaret Donnellan *librarian, director*

Dublin
Ingram, Judith Elizabeth *writer*

Earlimart
White, Kathleen *director*

East Palo Alto
Dillon, Carol K. *lawyer*

Edwards
Chacon, Maria *government agency administrator*
Losey, Lori *media specialist*
Regenie, Vicki *systems engineer*

Edwards AFB
Arevalo, Carmen *government agency administrator*
Meske, Sandy *government agency administrator*
Young, Gwendolyn Vaisega *federal agency administrator*

El Cajon
Haber, Susan C. *history professor*
Higginson, Jane *environmental educator, biologist, conservationist*
Kibble-Cacioppo, Maxine Lorraine *recording company executive*
Mapes, Gwenyth B. *humanities educator, writer*
Markarian, Alexia Mitrus *artist*
Thomas, Esther Merlene *elementary and adult education educator*

El Centro
Kussman, Eleanor (Ellie Kussman) *retired educational superintendent*
Roberts, Cristina Abeja *volunteer*

El Cerrito
Alldredge, Noreen S. *librarian*
Kao, Yasuko Watanabe *retired library director*
Tannenbaum, Judith Nettie *writer, educator*

El Dorado Hills
Moya, Marcia Tewksbury *director*

El Granada
Heere, Karen R. *astrophysicist*

El Monte
Last, Marian Helen *social services administrator*
Merrill Warner, Veronique *psychologist*

El Segundo
Buss, Jeanie *professional sports team executive*
Hsia, Irene Yee *electrical engineer*
Leslie, Lisa DeShaun *professional basketball player*
McCarty, Shirley Carolyn *consumer products company executive*
Milton-Jones, DeLisha *professional basketball player*
Toler, Penny *former professional basketball player, sports team executive*
Weatherspoon, Teresa Gaye *professional basketball player*
Willis, Judy Ann *lawyer*

Elizabeth Lake
Kozlow, Beverly Kay *retired physical therapist, psychologist, realtor*

Elk Grove
Moe, Janet Anne *elementary school educator, church organist*
Romano, Sheila June *telecommunications industry professional, writer, artist*
Work, Janice René *pediatric dentist*

Emeryville
Bartels, Ursula Brennan *lawyer*
Bibel, Debra Jan *public health scientist, editor*
Courtenaye, Catherine *artist*
Finney, Lee *retired social worker*
Hurst, Deborah *pediatric hematologist*

Encinitas
Litvin, Inessa Elizabeth *piano educator*
Lougeay, Denruth Colleen *clinical psychologist, educator*
Prodor, Leah Marie *secondary school educator*

Encino
Bond, Mary Llewellyn *movement education educator*
Davis, Berta *psychologist*
House, Karen Sue *nursing consultant*
Irmas, Audrey Menein *not-for-profit developer*
O'Riley, Karen E. *principal*
Smith, Selma Moidel *lawyer, composer*
Taylor, Renee *actress, writer*
Vogel, Susan Carol *nursing administrator*
Wald, Donna Gene *advertising executive*

Escondido
Carey, Catherine Anita *artist, educator*
Godone-Maresca, Lillian *lawyer*
Granet, Eileen *secondary school educator*
Linzey, Verna May *minister, writer*
McHenry, Anita Petei *historian, archaeologist*
Rockwell, Elizabeth Goode *dance company director, consultant, educator*
Sloan, Anne Elizabeth *food scientist, writer*
Young, Gladys *business owner*

Eureka
Zimmerman, Adria Dawn *composition educator*

Exeter
Pescosolido, Pamela Jane *graphics designer*

Fair Oaks
Dorf, Eve Buckle *artist*

Fairfield
Emmering, Adrienne Noelle *artist, graphics designer*
Forssell, Linda Lee *secondary school educator, illustrator*
Mary, Diane Bradley *elementary school educator, secondary school educator*
Schunke, Hildegard Heidel *accountant*

Fallbrook
Cordes, Kathleen Ann *retired physical education educator, director*

Folsom
Allaman, Kathryn Ann *vice principal, mathematician*
Sarraf, Shirley A. *secondary school educator*
Terranova, Elizabeth (Elisa) Jo *artist*

Fort Bragg
Dias, Michele C. *primary school educator*

Fountain Valley
Delisanti, Marilyn W. *medical/surgical and pediatrics nurse*
Kieu, Quynh Dinh *pediatrician, not-for-profit developer*
Mount, Cindy Kay *small business owner*
Smith, Marie Edmonds *real estate agent, property manager*
Treadway-Dillmon, Linda Lee *actress, stuntwoman, dancer, dispatcher, athletic trainer*

Frazier Park
Edwards, Sarah Anne *social worker, psychologist*

Fremont
Buswell, Debra Sue *small business owner, computer technician, financial analyst*
Horst, Barbara Lynn *primary school educator*
Hsu, Gloria *piano educator*
Lau, Michelle *mathematics educator*
Peebles, Lucretia Neal Drane *education educator*
Sahatjian, Manik *retired nurse, retired psychologist*
Sanchez, Marla Rena *communications executive*
Venturini, Judith Anne *education educator*
Willows, Mary Rose *special education educator*
Wilson, Judy *small business owner*
Wood, Linda May *librarian*

Fresno
Avants, Rebecca Maxine *biology educator*
Bundy-DeSoto, Teresa Mari *language educator, vocalist*
Corless, Dorothy Alice *nursing educator*
Cornish, Bonita Clark *retired secondary school educator*
Dale, Sharon Kay *real estate broker*
Dandoy, Maxima Antonio *retired education educator*
Diestelkamp, Dawn Lea *government agency administrator*
English, Erin *secondary school educator*
Fiester, Elizabeth Ann *secondary school educator*
Ganulin, Judy *public relations professional*
Garrison-Finderup, Ivadelle Dalton *writer, educator*
Girvin, Shirley Eppinette *retired elementary school educator, journalist*
Johnson, Ruth Anne *medical/surgical nurse*
Kuhn, Rose Marie *language educator*
Lanter, Lanore *writer, educator*
Lumbye, Betsy *editor*
McGough, MaryLee *marketing professional*
Monaghan, Kathleen M. *art museum director*
Ortiz, Christine E. *nursing educator*
Parker, Judith Elaine *retired language educator*
Raven, Patricia Elaine (Penny Raven) *real estate broker, developer, columnist, gas industry executive*
Riggs, Krista Dyonis *music educator, librarian*
Sargent, Molly Anne *literature and language educator*
Stewart, Deborah Claire *dean*
Stuart, Dorothy Mae *artist*
Tudman, Cathi Graves *elementary school educator*
Waters, Rosemary R. *biology professor*
Weymouth, Toni *social worker, writer, educator*

Fullerton
Bangerter, Renee Tanner *literature educator*
Breyer, Pamela Peterson *writer*
Connor, Danielle Broucqsault *secondary school educator*
Dickson, Kathryn *science educator*
Donoghue, Mildred Ransdorf *education educator*
Fearn, Heidi *physicist, researcher*
Ikeda, Nancy *mathematician, educator*
Johnson, Carolyn Elizabeth *librarian*
Renee (aka) Stevens, Rita *actor, theater educator, director*
Segal, Nancy Lee *psychology professor, researcher*
Tehrani, Fleur Taher *electrical engineer, educator, researcher*
Woodhull, Patricia Ann *artist*
Woods, Betty *insurance company executive*
Woyski, Margaret Skillman *retired geology educator*

Garberville
Nyokka, Suzette *artist, natural health educator*

Garden Grove
Cochrum, Ellen Joan *language educator*
Faust, Amy Kay *elementary school educator*
Greenslade, Cindy Louise *psychologist*
Ogata, Carolee Kimi *school system administrator*
Schwalm, Laura *school system administrator*

Gardena
Winn, Stephenie *senior program specialist*

Glendale
Blackwell, Linda Jane *elementary school educator*
Daly, Ann Michelle *broadcast executive*
Dudash, Linda Christine *insurance company executive*
Gibbons, Leeza *television and radio talk show host, entertainment reporter*
Halaby, Noelle M. *lawyer*
Kendrick, Katherine *lawyer*
MacDonald, Laurie *film company executive*
Michelson, Lillian *librarian, researcher*
O'Day, Anita Belle Colton *entertainer, musician, vocalist*
Phibbs, Mary Ellen *retired secondary school educator*
Shelburne, Merry Clare *public information officer, educator*
Shou, Sharon Louise Wikoff *vocational rehabilitation counselor*
Snider, Stacey *film company executive*
Spangler, Dianne Marie *physical education educator*
Stewart, Julia A. *food service executive*
Whalen, Lucille *retired academic administrator*
Woolls, Esther Blanche *library science educator*

Glendora
Acevedo, Elizabeth Morrison *special education educator*
Anderson, Annette Shirey *deaf education educator, educational consultant*

Gold River
Davidson, Diane (Marie Davidson) *publisher*
Reynolds, Marilyn Ann *writer*
Shaw, Eleanor Jane *newspaper editor*

Goleta
Koart, Nellie Hart *real estate investor, real estate company executive*
Nahra, Lynda *bank executive*
Robinson, Nancy A. *writer*
Zuk, Carmen Veiga *psychiatrist*

Granite Bay
Holtz, Sara *marketing consultant*
Kemper, Dorla Dean Eaton (Dorla Dean Eaton) *real estate broker*

Grass Valley
Dean, Barbara W. *elementary school educator*
Molitor, Kelley Marie *mathematics professor*
Phillips-Jones, Linda *consulting psychologist*

Gualala
Kelley, Barbara Elizabeth *artist*
Ring, Alice Ruth Bishop *retired preventive medicine physician*

Gustine
Ramirez, Nola Marie *librarian*

Hacienda Heights
Burkhart, Catherine Ray *secondary school educator*
Lee, Chieh-Chi *elementary school educator*

Half Moon Bay
Fennell, Diane Marie *marketing professional, process engineer*
Hinthorn, Micky Terzagian *retired executive secretary, volunteer*

Hanford
Harris, Mildred Staeger *retired broadcast executive*
Neos, Peri Fitch *small business owner*

Happy Camp
Black, Barbara Ann *publisher*

Hayward
Buchanan, Patricia O'Neill *retired social worker*
Fili, Patricia Kevena *social welfare administrator, poet, playwright*
Garcia, Melva Ybarra *counseling administrator, educator*
Jordahl, Kathleen Patricia (Kate Jordahl) *photographer, educator*
Meyer, Ann Jane *human development educator*
Pulliam, Glorious K. *elementary school educator*
Rees, Norma S. *academic administrator*
Wong, Wanda Yuk-Wa *graphics designer, educator*

Healdsburg
Castellini, Mary Mercer *author*

Helendale
Hoover, Linda Sue *elementary school educator, coach*

Hemet
Carr, Pamela *librarian*
Cook, Allyson Lea *secondary school educator*
Levine, Elaine Prado *psychologist, music educator, artist, small business owner*
Monk, Sharon Anne *special education educator*
Pumphrey, Bonnie Jean *music educator*

Hercules
Tyson, Kathleen Hayhurst *educational association administrator*

Hermosa Beach
Chi, Lois Wang *retired biology professor, research scientist*
LaBouff, Jackie Pearson *retired personal care industry executive*
Wickwire, Patricia Joanne Nellor *psychologist, educator*

Hesperia
Du Lac, Lois Arline *retired secondary school educator, writer*
May, Katherine Eleanor *art educator, photographer*

Highland
MacQueen, Cherie K. *interior designer, retired newscaster, sportscaster*

Hillsborough
Atwood, Mary Sanford *writer*
Yee-Melichar, Darlene *gerontological health educator*

Hollister
Grace, Bette Frances *certified public accountant*
Harris, Wendy Take *psychologist, educator*
Miller, Alisa Dorothy Norton *artist*
Twaddell, Karen Grace *elementary school educator*

Hollywood
Cummings, Joan *history educator*
Fergie, (Stacy Ann Ferguson) *singer*
Hoesli, Hanna *dentist*
Lynne, Shelby (Shelby Lynn Moorer) *country singer*
Miles, Joanna *actress, playwright, director*
Minnelli, Liza *singer, actress*
Pearlman, Alison *art educator*
Schuster, Peggy Lindner (Pravrajika Brahmaprana) *sister, nun*
Varner, Vicky Jo *actor, counselor*
Warren, Diane *lyricist*

Holtville
Macdonald, Andara *secondary school educator*

Homewood
Butler, Patricia *mental health nurse, educator, consultant*

Hughson
Hailey, Kathleen Wilson *elementary school educator*

Huntington Beach
Carey, Shirley Anne *nursing consultant*
Conrad, Janilyn McNees *special education educator*
De Massa, Jessie G. *media specialist*
Flakes, Susan *playwright, scriptwriter, theater director*
Garrels, Sherry Ann *lawyer*
Isabelle, Beatrice Margaret *artist*
Mazak, Arlene Patricia *marriage and family therapist*
McAlister, Chris *elementary school educator*
Ogata, Susan Naomi *psychologist*
Ramphal, Julie Frances *retired secondary school educator*
Silver, Lynn Ellen *music educator*
Sward, Andrea Jeanne *information and computer scientist, musician*

Huntington Park
Gaines-Page, Rena L. *science educator*

Idyllwild
Schneider, Margaret Perrin *scriptwriter*

Indian Wells
McGraw, Phyllis Mae *psychologist, geriatric specialist*
Wright, Ann Follinger *psychotherapist*

Indio
Zorick, Nancy Lee *artist, actress*

Inglewood
Cato, Gloria Maxine *retired secondary school educator*
Epstein, Marsha Ann *public health service officer, physician*
Lockhart, Claudia Jo *adult education educator, department chairman*
Logan, Lynda Dianne *elementary school educator*
Marks, Laura B. *psychologist*
Wakefield, Marie Cynthia *performing arts educator, playwright, poet*

Inverness
Ciani, Judith Elaine *retired lawyer*

Inyokern
Norris, Lois Ann *retired elementary school educator*

Irvine
Boyd, Carolyn Patricia *history professor*
Bryant, Susan V. *academic administrator*
Crawford, Denise F. *lawyer*
Dill, Laura Lee *athletic trainer, educator*
Feldman, Martha Sue *political scientist, educator*
Finlayson-Pitts, Barbara Jean *chemistry professor*
Freed, Judy Gayle *literature and language educator*
Gala, Debra Gail *elementary school educator*

Gilbert, Margaret P. *philosophy professor, researcher*
Greenberger, Ellen *psychologist, educator*
Harpen, Shawn M. *lawyer*
Hoheb, Camille E. *healthcare executive*
Hornig, Mady *psychiatrist, educator*
Huang, Wendy Wan-Juoh *lawyer*
Jitomirskaya, Svetlana *mathematics professor*
Keele, Lucy Anne McCandlish *communications executive, consultant*
Keller, Jennifer L. *lawyer*
Kluger, Ruth *German language educator, editor*
Langevin, Patricia Ann *mathematics educator*
Lee, Eva *medical educator*
Lesonsky, Rieva *editor-in-chief*
Lowe, Kathlene Winn *lawyer*
Maddy, Penelope Jo *philosopher, educator*
Myles, Margaret Jean *real estate appraiser*
Narayan, Ash *lawyer*
Nelson, June Lusk *music educator*
Riley, Sally Jean *science educator*
Ruttenberg, Susann I. *health sciences administrator*
Ruyter, Nancy Lee Chalfa *dance educator*
Treas, Judith Kay *sociology educator*
Tsao, Janie *information technology executive*

Joshua Tree
Goudelock, Carol V. *library consultant*

Kelseyville
Sandmeyer, E. E. *toxicologist, consultant*

Kentfield
Blum, Joan Kurley *not-for-profit fundraiser, marketing executive, consultant*
Buehler, Sally Salmen *clinical social worker*
Halprin, Anna Schuman (Mrs. Lawrence Halprin) *dancer*

La Canada Flintridge
Ciesniewski, Ann Marie *marriage and family therapist*
Rieger, Bin Hong *secondary school educator, elementary school educator*

La Crescenta
Purcell, Lee (Lee Jeune Williams) *actress, film producer*

La Habra
Enochs, Lori M. *science educator, department chairman*

La Habra Heights
Agajanian, Gilda *pianist*

La Jolla
Alvariño De Leira, Angeles (Angeles Alvariño) *biologist, oceanographer*
Antico-Pizzinat, Concetta K. *artist*
Baldridge, Kim *science educator*
Bardwick, Judith Marcia *management consultant*
Barrett-Conner, Elizabeth *physician, medical educator*
Barrett-Connor, Elizabeth Louise *epidemiologist, educator*
Beebe, Mary Livingstone *curator*
Burbidge, E. Margaret *astronomer, educator*
Chandler, Marsha *academic administrator, educator*
Coburn, Marjorie Foster *psychologist, educator*
Cohen, Barbara Ann *artist*
Covington, Stephanie Stewart *psychotherapist, writer, educator*
Cox, Barbara Joanne *psychologist, consultant*
Forsburg, Susan Louise *molecular geneticist*
Foxe, Marye Anne *academic administrator*
Fredman, Faiya Rubenstein *artist*
Hall, TennieBee M. *editor*
Hazzard, Mary Elizabeth *nursing educator*
Iddings, Kathleen *poet, editor, publisher, consultant*
Jennings, Jan Noreus *public relations executive, writer*
Johnson, Gayle Ann *cardiology nurse*
Jorgensen, Judith Ann *psychiatrist, educator*
Klonoff-Cohen, Hillary Sandra *epidemiologist*
Low, Mary Louise (Molly Low) *documentary photographer*
Lowe, Lisa *education educator, department chairman*
Mandler, Jean Matter *psychologist, educator*
Margolin, Frances Mongin *clinical psychologist, educator*
McDonald, Marianne *classicist*
Merrim, Louise Meyerowitz *artist, actress*
Miller, Carol *elementary school educator, counselor*
Mirsky, Phyllis Simon *librarian*
Moon, Mona McTaggart *activities educator, consultant*
North, Kathryn E. Keesey (Mrs. Eugene C. North) *retired music educator*
Oreskes, Naomi *science historian*
Rahman, Yueh-Erh *biologist*
Rearden, Carole Ann *clinical pathologist, educator*
Ride, Sally Kristen *physics professor, research scientist, retired astronaut*
Savoia, Maria Christina *vice dean*
Swain, Judith Lea *cardiologist, educator*
Taylor, Susan Serota *biochemist, researcher*
Terras, Audrey Anne *mathematics professor*
Thompson, Charlotte Ellis *pediatrician, educator, writer*
Thompson, Emily *historian*
White, Michelle Jo *economics professor*
Wilson, Bonnie Jean *lawyer, educator, investor*

La Mesa
Black, Eileen Mary *retired elementary school educator*
Charleton, Margaret Ann *child care administrator, consultant*
Lebeck, Carol E. *artist, educator*

La Puente
Ver Kuilen, Marion Jane *retired instructional aide*

La Quinta
Connerly, Dianna Jean *business official*
Eversole, Barbara Louise *administrative assistant*
Knoblauch, Mary Reilly (Mary Louise Reilly) *retired music educator, writer*
Puente, Maria Luz *bilingual educator*
Reordan, Beverly Jean *artist*

La Verne
Bentley, Donna Gale *school librarian*
Espinoza, Linda *elementary school educator*
Jalbert, Janelle Jennifer *executive recruiter, secondary school educator*

Ladera Ranch
Skidmore, Michelle Marie *elementary school educator, principal*

Lafayette
Shurtleff, Akiko Aoyagi *artist, consultant*

Laguna Beach
Bernstein, Jean Newman *retired public health information officer*
Heussenstamm, Frances Kovacs *psychologist, artist*
Jensen, Gloria Veronica *adult nurse practitioner*
Pories, Muriel H. *finance company executive*

Laguna Hills
Green, Millie Ann *mathematician, educator*
Reinglass, Michelle Annette *lawyer*
Schachter, Bernice *sculptor, educator, writer*
Widyolar, Sheila Gayle *dermatologist*

Laguna Niguel
André, Joy LaRae *elementary school educator, adult education educator, language educator*
Bauer, Barbara A. *financial consultant*
Greenberg, Lenore *public relations professional*
Gunning, Monica Olwen Minott *elementary school educator*
McClintock, Sandra Janise *writer, editor, book designer*
Rubinstein, Charlotte Streifer *writer, art historian, educator*
Tjandraswita, Maria C. Inawati *lawyer*
von Hutten, Gaia Theresa *performing company executive, choreographer, educator*
Zagon, Laurie *artist*

Lake Elsinore
Austin, Berit Synnove *retired small business owner, quality assurance professional*
Bouslog, Robbin Raye *performing arts educator, art educator*
Druskoff, Barbara Therese *elementary school educator*

Lake Forest
Boccia/Stacy, Judy Elaine *home health agency executive, consultant*
Smoot, Skipi Lundquist *psychologist*

Lake Hughes
La Mont, Tawana Faye *camera operator, video director, foundation administrator*

Lake Isabella
Fraser, Eleanor Ruth *radiologist, administrator*

Lake View Terrace
McCraven, Eva Stewart Mapes *health service administrator*

Lakeside
Koski, Donna Faith *poet*
Walker, Wanda Medora *retired elementary school educator, consultant*

Lakewood
Bogdan, Carolyn Louetta *financial specialist, retired small business owner*
White, Katherine Elizabeth *retired pediatrician*

Lancaster
Dalrymple, Marilyn Anita *small business owner, photographer*
Davison, Dawn Sherry *correctional administrator, educator*
Holley, Susan L. *psychologist*
Jones, Betty Ann *elementary school educator*

Lathrop
Daily, Diana Smith *music educator*

Lemon Grove
Robinson, Cheryl Jean *human services specialist, advocate*

Lincoln
Dorn, Mary Ann *retired auditor*
Johnson, Ursula Anne *artist*

Live Oak
Spilman, Janet Lynne *special education educator*

Livermore
Dutchover, Amy *mathematics educator*
Philipps, Julie Leighann *elementary school educator*

Lockeford
Walker, Nancy Anne *small business owner, history and art educator*

Lodi
Bishop-Graham, Barbara *secondary school educator, journalist*
McKelvey, Judy Eileen *language educator*
Puerta, Christy L. *construction executive*
Reinold, Christy Diane *school counselor, consultant*
Schulz, Laura Janet *writer, retired executive secretary*
Siler, Virginia Carlisle *retired elementary school educator*

Loleta
Schoenfeld, Diana Lindsay *photographer, educator*

Loma Linda
Behrens, Berel Lyn *physician, academic administrator, health facility administrator*
Coggin, Charlotte Joan *cardiologist, educator*
Condon, Vaneta Mabley *medical/surgical nurse*
Molnar, Violet *mental health nurse*

Lompoc
Barthel, Sarah Ann Moran *secondary school educator*
Jack, Morgann Tayllor *writer, artist*
Valla, Bree Butler *agricultural studies educator*
Wagner, Geraldine Marie *nursing educator, consultant*

Long Beach
Barron, (Mary Lou) Slater *artist, retired educator*
Beebe, Sandra E. *retired language educator, artist, writer*
Bowen, Fern Chambers *artist, educator*
Braunstein, Terry Malikin *artist*
Burton, Lucy *enterostomal therapy nurse*
Cobe-Ross, Lori *casting director*
Cone, Marla *environmentalist, writer*
Croteau, Patricia A. *nursing case manager*
Curry, Denise *women's college basketball coach*
Davies, Grace Lucille *real estate educator*
deAlbuquerque, Joan Marie *conductor, music educator*
Elftman, Susan Nancy *physician assistant, childbirth-lactation educator, research director*
Elston, Joan Wilma *adult education educator, real estate agent*
Fischler, Sandy Lynn *charitable and informational organization executive*
Fleming, Jane Williams *retired elementary school educator, writer*
Glenn, Constance White *art museum director, educator, consultant*
Gordon, Lynda L. *art educator*
Hansell, Susan *writer, educator*
Heggeness, Julie Fay *foundation administrator, lawyer*
Helwick, Christine *lawyer*
Karentte, Betty *state legislator*
Karnette, Betty *state representative*
Lofland, Patricia Lois *secondary school educator, travel company executive*
Magyar, Tina Michelle *physical education educator*
Mandarino, Candida Ann *education educator, consultant*
Mathieu, Susan Leifer *recreational therapist, educator*
Mieras, Elvia F. *dietician, educator*
Mullins Berg, Ruth Gladys *nurse*
Nguyen, Huong Tran *former elementary and secondary language educator, former district office administrator*
O'Neill, Beverly Lewis *mayor, former college president*
Proust, Joycelyn Ann *retired librarian*
Rosenberg, Jill *realtor, civic leader*
Rutherford, Vicky Lynn *special education educator*
Sanders, Joan Skogsberg *artist*
Sato, Eunice Noda *former mayor, consultant*
Sexauer, Roxanne Denise *artist, educator*
Shiffman, Leslie Brown *retired apparel executive*
Shoji, June Midori *import and export trading executive*
Solovei, Marion *clinical psychologist*
Springer, Wilma Marie *retired elementary school educator*
Writer, Sharon Lisle *secondary school educator*

Los Alamitos
Caplan, Karen B. *food products executive*
Njavro, E. Randelle *science educator*

Los Altos
Beer, Clara Louise Johnson *retired electronics executive*
Hickman, Martha Whitmore *writer*
Justice-Moore, Kathleen E. *lawyer*
Larson, Carol S. *foundation administrator, lawyer*
Orman, Nanette Hector *psychiatrist*
Orr, Susan Packard *small business owner, foundation administrator*
Rees, Marian Janet *librarian*
Roylance, Lynn Michelle *electrical engineer*
Sherwood, Patricia Waring *artist, educator*
Welsh, Doris McNeil *early childhood education specialist*

Los Altos Hills
Gibbs, Patricia Leigh *social sciences educator, researcher*

Los Angeles
Abell, Nancy L. *lawyer*
Akhavanhaidary, Sepideh *psychologist, educator*
Aldahl, Deborah Campbell *elementary school educator*
Alkon, Ellen Skillen *physician*
Allen, Sharon *accounting firm executive*
Allen, Suzanne *financial planning executive, insurance agent, writer, educator*
Allred, Gloria Rachel *lawyer*
Allums, Henriene *elementary school educator*
Alonso, Maria Conchita *actress, singer*
Anawalt, Patricia Rieff *anthropologist, researcher*
Anderson, Jane A. *scriptwriter*
Ansley, Julia E. *retired elementary school educator, poet, writer*
Apple, Jacki (Jacqueline B. Apple) *artist, educator, writer*
Appleby, Joyce Oldham *historian, educator*
Archer, Anne *actress*
Archuleta, Randi Lisa *psychologist*
Aronoff, Vera *law librarian*
Arora, Shirley Lease *Spanish language educator*
Ashwell, Rachel *entrepreneur, interior designer*
Atnip, Linda *writer*
Azad, Susan Stott *lawyer*
Balaski, Belinda L. *actress, educator, artist*
Banks, Tyra (Tyra Lynne Banks) *retired model, television personality*
Barberie, Jillian *newscaster, meteorologist*
Barone, Sherry Joy *test engineer*
Barrett, Jane Hayes *lawyer*
Barron, Stephanie *curator*
Barth, Uta *artist, educator*
Bates, Marcia Jeanne *information scientist educator*
Beckerman, Alyssa *gymnast*
Beezy, Miriam Claire *lawyer*
Bell, Lee Phillip *television personality, television producer*
Benatar, Pat (Pat Andrzejewski) *rock singer*
Bendix, Helen Irene *lawyer*
Bennett, Judith MacKenzie *historian*
Berger, Pat(ricia Eve) *artist, educator*
Bergman, Marilyn Keith *lyricist, writer*
Berman, Gail *film company executive*
Bernstein, Leslie *academic administrator, biostatistician, epidemiologist*
Bertero, Karen E. *lawyer*
Bianchi, Carisa *advertising company executive*
Blendell, Elizabeth A. *lawyer*
Bloom, Claire *actress*
Blumberg, Grace Ganz *lawyer, educator*
Bohle, Sue *public relations executive*
Boras, Kim *lawyer*
Boyle, Barbara Dorman *film company executive*
Brandon, Kathleen Alma *director*
Brown, Carol *make-up artist*
Brown, Deborah Ellen *gifted and talented educator, writer*
Brown, Kathleen *diversified financial services company executive*
Bryan, Karen Smith *lawyer*
Burbank, Lynda A. *painter*
Burke, Yvonne Watson Brathwaite (Mrs. William A. Burke) *lawyer*
Byers, Nina *physics professor*
Byrd, Christine Waterman Swent *lawyer*
Campanella, Yvette Lynn *cosmetics executive*
Campbell, Bebe Moore *writer*
Caram, Eve La Salle *language educator, writer*
Carlson, Jo Anne *nurse*
Caroompas, Carole Jean *artist, educator*
Carson, Margaret *human services administrator*
Caruso, Joanne E. *lawyer*
Cate, Jan Harris *lawyer*
Chang, Jane P. *chemical engineering educator*
Chapman, Carolyn *broadcasting director*
Chapman Collins, Janice *school system administrator*
Chapman Holley, Shawn Snider *lawyer*
Charen, Mona *columnist*
Cheeseboro, Margrit *retired economics educator*
Chen, Lynn *actress*
Cheung, Sheri T. *lawyer*
Christ, Roxanne E. *lawyer*
Chun, Jennifer *communications executive*
Chung, Christina *lawyer*
Ciccone, Amy Navratil *art librarian*
Clayburgh, Jill *actress*
Cohen, Cynthia Marylyn *lawyer*
Coker, Sybil Jane Thomas *counseling administrator*
Cole, K.C. *journalist, writer*
Coleman Smith, Salaam *communications executive*
Collier, Anna *photographer*
Collins, Audrey B. *judge*
Combs, Holly Marie *actress*
Compo, Susan Ann *writer, educator*
Comtois, Tiffany Lynn *academic advisor*
Connor-Dominguez, Billie Marie *science information professional*
Cook, Melanie K. *lawyer*
Coolbaugh, Carrie Weaver *librarian*
Coots, Laurie *advertising executive*
Cora, Cat *chef*
Cowan, Marie Jeanette *dean, nurse, medical educator*
Cox, Cathleen Ruth *zoologist, educator*
Craft, Cheryl Mae *neurobiologist, anatomist, researcher*
Crenshaw, Kimberle Williams *law educator*
Croson, Charlotte Joanne *retired language educator*
Currie, Janet M. *economics professor*
Dally, Lynn *choreographer, performing company executive, educator*
D'Angelo Melby, Donna Marie *lawyer*
Dantzscher, Jamie *gymnast*
Darby, Joanne Tyndale (Jaye Darby) *arts and humanities educator*
Davidson, Judi *public relations executive*
Davis-Fernandes, Tina Denise *secondary school educator, coach*
Dawson, Rosario *actress, singer*
Daya Mata, Sri (Faye Wright) *clergywoman*
Dee, Ruby (Ruby Dee Davis) *actress, writer, film director*
DeFrantz, Anita *sports association executive, lawyer*
De Larios, Dora *artist*
Demick, Barbara *journalist*
Dennis, Jessica Michele *psychology professor*
Diaz, Maria G. *lawyer*
Dickey, Teresa A. *secondary school educator*
Diehl, Dolores *performing company executive*
Dismukes, Valena Grace Broussard *photographer, retired physical education educator*
Dodd, Jan Eve *lawyer*
Doll, Lynne Marie *public relations agency executive*
Donahue, Ann M. *television producer*
Dragan, Alexandra *mechanical engineer, consultant, environmental engineer, researcher, engineering educator*
Drummy, Kathleen H. *lawyer*
Dudziak, Mary Louise *law educator*
Dunst, Kirsten *actress*
DuPuy, Pamela Marie *elementary school educator*
Edmonds, Tracey E. *film company executive*
Edmonson-Nelson, Gloria Jean *freelance writer*
Edwards, Kathryn Inez *educational consultant*
Elrod, Lu *retired music educator, actress*
Erdos, Joanna E. *school counselor, secondary school educator*
Farnham, Katherine A *music educator, vocalist*
Fenning, Lisa Hill *lawyer, mediator, retired judge*
Fernandez, Giselle *newscaster, journalist*
Firstenberg, Jean Picker *film institute executive*
Fischer, Dale Susan *judge*
Fitz-Carter, Aleane *retired elementary school educator, composer*

Flanagan, Fionnula Manon *actress, writer, theater director*
Fredericks, Beverly Magnuson *artist*
Gad, Simone *actress, performance artist, visual artist, writer*
Garrett, Betty *actress*
Garrett, Elizabeth *law educator, academic administrator*
Gasson, Judith C. *research scientist*
Gauff, Lisa *broadcast journalist*
Gelber, Danielle Arna *broadcast executive*
Geller, Debra F. *academic administrator, educator*
Ghez, Andrea Mia *astronomy educator, physics educator*
Giesser, Barbara Susan *neurologist, educator*
Giffin, Margaret Ethel (Peggy Giffin) *management consultant*
Gifford, Kathie Lee *television personality, vocalist*
Glasgow, Istiharoh *art administrator*
Good, Edith Elissa (Pearl Williams) *writer, lexicographer*
Graves, Anna Marie *lawyer*
Grinnan, Katie *artist*
Grode, Susan A. *lawyer*
Guarnieri, Roberta Jean *elementary school educator, consultant*
Gunn, Karen Sue *psychologist, educator*
Haines, Randa *film director*
Haley, Roslyn Trezevant *educational program director*
Hamilton, Patricia Rose *art dealer*
Handler, Carole Enid *lawyer, city planner*
Harkness, Nancy P. *lawyer*
Harrison, Gail G. *public health educator*
Hart, Mary *television talk show host*
Hartsough, Gayla Anne Kraetsch *management consultant*
Hecht, Susanna Bettina *adult education educator, writer*
Heigl, Katherine Marie *actress*
Hemminger, Pamela Lynn *lawyer*
Henderson, Florence *actress, singer*
Henkel, Kathy *composer*
Henriksen, Eva Hansine *retired anesthesiology educator*
Hernandez, Antonia *foundation administrator, lawyer*
Herrera, G. Shizuko *theater educator*
Hill, Bonnie Guiton *consulting company executive*
Hirano, Irene Ann Yasutake *museum director*
Hoffman, Margaret Ann Hovland *artist, activist*
Holly, Krisztina J. *entrepreneur, academic administrator*
Holmes, Fontayne *city librarian*
Horn, Cindy Harrell *environmental advocate*
Houston, Velina Hasu *education educator, writer*
Hoye, Maria Pilar *lawyer*
Hsu, Kylie *language educator, researcher, linguist*
Hufstedler, Shirley Mount *lawyer, former federal judge*
Hurt, Mary Beth *actress*
Husar, Linda S. *lawyer*
Hyman, Ursula H. *lawyer*
Ibarra, Irene M. *foundation administrator*
Im, Hyepin Christine *not-for-profit developer*
Iredale, Nancy Louise *lawyer*
Ireland, Kathy *actress, apparel designer*
Ivins, Molly (Mary Tyler Ivins) *columnist, writer*
Jacobs, Alicia Melvina *account executive*
Jalali, Behnaz *psychiatrist, educator*
Jeff, Gloria Jean *city official*
Jeffrey, Sheri *lawyer*
Johnston, Ynez *artist, educator*
Johnstone, Kathryn I. *lawyer*
Jordan, Martha B. *lawyer*
Kalish-Weiss, Beth Isaacs *psychologist, psychoanalyst, consultant*
Kamil, Elaine Scheiner *pediatric nephrologist, educator*
Kanoff, Mary Ellen *lawyer*
Kaplan, Nadia *writer*
Katzin, Carolyn Fernanda *nutritionist, consultant*
Kaufman, Francine R. *pediatric endocrinologist*
Keddie, Nikki R. *education educator*
Kellerman, Sally Claire *actress*
Kenyon, Geraldine Mona *psychologist, consultant*
Kessler, Joan Blumenstein *lawyer*
Keville, Terri Donna *lawyer*
Kiley, Katie *printmaker, painter*
Kim, Irene Jiyun *music professor, choral conductor*
Kim, Sabrina S. *lawyer*
Kirwan, Betty-Jane *lawyer*
Kivelson, Margaret Galland *physicist*
Klinger, Marilyn Sydney *lawyer*
Kobe, Lan *medical physicist*
Komaroff, Linda *curator*
Kozberg, Joanne Corday *public affairs consultant*
Krag, Olga *interior designer*
Kristof, Kathy M. *journalist*
Kupka, Nancy Elyse Wyatt *dance educator*
Kupper, Ketti *artist*
Landers, Audrey *actress, singer*
Larrubia, Evelyn *reporter*
Lawler, Jean Marie *lawyer*
Lear, Lyn Davis *psychologist*
Lee, Cecilia Hae-Jin *artist, writer*
Lee, Jeanette *professional pool player*
Lee, Joselyn C.R. *physician, researcher*
Leeves, Jane *actress*
Legohn, Lisa Marie *vocational school educator*
LeMaster, Susan M. *marketing executive, writer*
Lemlech, Johanna Kasin *education educator*
Leonard, Kandi *language educator*
Lesser, Joan L. *lawyer*
Levee, Barbara Poe *artist*
Levenson, Laurie L. *law educator*
Levin, Carol Arlene *adult education educator*
Levine, Pamela *film company executive*
Lew, Joycelyne Mae *actress*
Lewis, Marjorie Ehrich *lawyer*
Lewis, Samella Sanders *artist, educator*
Lhuillier, Monique (Diane Monique Lhuillier) *apparel designer*
Lipscomb-Brown, Edra Evadean *retired childhood educator*
Longval, Gloria *artist*
Looney, Claudia Arlene *health facility administrator*
Lozano, Monica Cecilia *publishing executive*
Lucoff, Kathy Ann *art advisor*
Lunden, Joan *television personality*
Lyles, Tracee *art association administrator, actress*
Lynch, Beverly Pfeifer *education and information studies educator*
Ma, Vivienne *dancer, educator*
Macalister, Kim Porter *advertising executive*
Macavinta-Tenazas, Gemorsita *physician*
Mahmoudi, Homa *psychologist*
Maker, Janet Anne *writer, retired literature educator*
Malkin, Michelle *syndicated columnist*
Maloney, Kristen *gymnast*
Manella, Nora Margaret *judge*
Marmorstein, Victoria E. *lawyer*
Marshall, Consuelo Bland *federal judge*
Marshall, Mary Jones *civic worker*
Marshall-Daniels, Meryl *mediator, executive coach*
Martinson, Deborah Ann *education educator, writer*
Massino, Laura Angela *small business owner*
Mataric, Maja J. *engineering educator*
Mathias, Alice Irene *business management consultant*
Mazes-Roque, Janet Maria *physician assistant*
McCormick, Carolyn *actress*
McFarling, Usha Lee *newswriter*
McGee, Lynda Plant *college counselor*
McKinney, Virginia Elaine Zuccaro *educational administrator*
Melby, Donna D. *lawyer*
Mentzer, Roslyn *academic administrator*
Mersel, Marjorie Kathryn Pedersen *lawyer*
Meyer, Catherine Dieffenbach *lawyer*
Miranda, M. Jeanne *psychiatrist*
Molina, Gloria *municipal official*
Montoya, Velma *economist, consultant*
Moreno, Rita (Rosita Dolores Alverio) *actress*
Morgan, Elizabeth *plastic surgeon*
Morris, Debbie Kay *director, educator*
Moss, Susan Hecht *artist, writer*
Muchnic, Suzanne *art writer, educator, lecturer*
Muldaur, Diana Charlton *actress*
Murphree, A. Linn *ophthalmologist*
Myrth, Judy G. *editor*
Neely, Sally Schultz *lawyer*
Nelson, Barbara J. *dean*
Neufeld, Elizabeth Fondal *biochemist, educator*
Neufeld, Naomi Das *endocrinologist*
Ng, Kim (Kimberly J. Ng) *professional sports team executive*
Nobumoto, Karen S. *prosecutor*
Norwood, Phyllis Katherene *director, educator*
O'Brien, Rosanne P. *corporate financial executive*
O'Connell, Taaffe Cannon *actress, publishing executive*
Oh, Angela E. *lawyer*
Olsen, Ashley Fuller *actress*
Olsen, Frances Elisabeth *law educator, theorist*
Olsen, Mary-Kate *actress*
Ordin, Andrea Sheridan *lawyer*
Ostroff, Dawn T. *broadcast executive*
Owens, Laura *painter*
Oyeyipo, Bolanle T. *geriatrician*
Palmer, Pamela S. *lawyer*
Patron, Susan Hall *librarian, writer*
Peña, Elizabeth *actress*
Perez, Edith R. *lawyer*
Perlmutter, Donna *music critic, dance critic*
Peters, Rita *university administrator*
Peterson, Linda S. *lawyer*
Petroff, Laura R. *lawyer*
Philbin, Ann *art facility director*
Phillips, Geneva Ficker *academic editor*
Phillips, Stacy D. *lawyer*
Pittman, Amanda Nelson *music educator*
Polk Gitlin, Mimi *film producer*
Porter, Verna Louise *lawyer*
Posner, Harriet S. *lawyer*
Postlethwaite, Alejandra *psychiatrist, researcher*
Prager, Susan Westerberg *academic administrator, law educator*
Prewitt, Jean *not-for-profit organization executive*
Pritzker, Jean *film producer*
Pruetz, Adrian Mary *lawyer*
Racklin, Barbara Cohen *fundraising consultant*
Rady, Elsa *artist*
Raeder, Myrna Sharon *lawyer, educator*
Reeves, Barbara Ann *lawyer*
Reisman, Ellen Kelly *lawyer*
Ressler, Alison S. *lawyer*
Reyes, Susana Marie *utilities executive, environmentalist*
Reznick, Charlotte *educational psychologist, consultant*
Rice, Constance LaMay *lawyer*
Rice, Regina Kelly *marketing executive*
Rich, Andrea Louise *museum administrator*
Rich, Caren *secondary school educator, hypnotherapist*
Richmond, Rocsan *television executive producer, small business owner*
Riffkind, Randi Jan *psychologist*
Robinson, Barbara Jon *librarian*
Rodriguez, Denise Rios *lawyer*
Rohrer, Susan Earley *film producer, film director, scriptwriter*
Rosenstock, Linda *dean, medical educator*
Ross, Marion *actress*
Rotell, Cynthia A. *lawyer*
Rowell, Victoria *actress*
Ruhl, Mary B. *lawyer*
Russo, Lisa Ann *registrar*
Russo, Rene *actress*
Rustand, Kay *lawyer*
Salmon, Beth Ann *magazine editor in chief*
Sanders, Kathryn A. *lawyer*
San Giacomo, Laura *actress*
Sawyer, Toni *actress*
Saxe, Deborah Crandall *lawyer*
Schuetze-Coburn, Marje *university librarian*
Sedaris, Amy *writer, actress*
See, Carolyn *English language educator, writer, book critic*
Sell, Ellen Jean *secondary school educator*
Serena, Monique *apparel executive*
Shanks, Patricia L. *lawyer*
Sheedy, Ally (Alexandra Elizabeth Sheedy) *actress*
Silverstein, Suzanne *art therapist*
Simmons, Ann Lorraine *actress, educator*
Simmons, Donna Marie *neuroscientist, histotechnologist, neuroendocrine anatomist, researcher*
Simun, Patricia Bates *education educator, consultant*
Singleton, Joan Vietor *publishing executive, writer, film producer*
Sloan, Judy Beckner *law educator*
Smith, Jean Webb (Mrs. William French Smith) *civic worker*
Smith-Meyer, Linda Helene (Linda Smith) *artist*
Spencer, Carole A. *medical association administrator, medical educator*
Stansfield, Claire *apparel designer*
Stapleton, Jean (Jeanne Murray) *actress*
Starrett, Lucinda *lawyer*
Stein, Sheryl E. *lawyer*
Stephens, Loren M. *publishing executive, writer*
Stern, Ruth Szold *artist*
Stern, Susan Toy *human resources specialist*
Stoll, Bobbi *art psychotherapist*
Streisand, Barbra Joan *singer, actress, film director*
Strickland, Julia B. *lawyer*
Sultan, Wafa *psychiatrist*
Swartz, Roslyn Holt *real estate company executive*
Swildens, Karin Johanna *sculptor*
Szego, Clara Marian *cell biologist, educator*
Tabrizi, Lili H. *electrical engineer, educator*
Tassler, Nina *broadcast executive*
Taylor, Shelley E. *psychology researcher, educator*
Tellem, Nancy Reiss *broadcast executive*
Telles, Cynthia Ann *psychologist*
Territo, Mary C. *health facility administrator, hematologist, educator*
Thompson, Anne Kathleen *entertainment journalist*
Thompson, Elizabeth *bank executive*
Thompson, Judith Kastrup *nursing researcher*
Thompson, Sada Carolyn *actress*
Tickner, Judith Ann *political science educator*
Title, Gail Migdal *lawyer*
Toffler, Heidi *author, futurist*
Toman, Mary Ann *federal official*
Tomlin, Lily *actress*
Tonick, Illene *clinical psychologist*
Torres, Cynthia Ann *marketing professional*
Trembly, Cristy *television executive*
Trenton, Patricia Jean *art historian*
Turner, Nancy Elizabeth *artist, designer*
Ullman, Tracey *actress, singer*
Utz, Sarah Winifred *nursing educator*
Van Buren, Abigail (Jeanne Phillips) *columnist, educator*
Van Tilburg, JoAnne *archaeologist, educator, foundation administrator*
Ver Steeg, Donna Lorraine Frank *nurse, sociologist, educator*
Von Eschen, Lisa A. *lawyer*
Vredevoe, Donna Lou *academic administrator, microbiologist, educator, biomedical researcher*
Wagner, Paula *film company executive, film producer*
Wagner, Ruth Joos *elementary school educator*
Walden, Dana *broadcast executive*
Walla, Catherine Anne *nursing administrator, educator*
Walter, Jessica *actress*
Warfel, Susan Leigh *editor*
Wasser, Laura Allison *lawyer*
Watson, Emily *actress*
Watson, Sharon Gitin *psychologist*
Wayne, June Claire *artist*
Weisberg, Ruth *artist*
Wellman, Marian C. *social worker*
Westhoff, Pamela Lynne *lawyer*
White, Daun Elois *professional society official*
Whitney, Constance Clein *psychologist, educator, consultant*
Wiggins, Marianne *writer*
Wilkerson, LuAnn *dean, medical educator*
Williams, Julie Ford *retired finance company executive, economist*
Wilson, Gayle Ann *civic worker*
Wilson, Miriam Geisendorfer *retired physician, educator*
Winters, Barbara Jo *musician*
Wood, Nancy Elizabeth *psychologist, educator*
Wood, Nicola *artist*
Wright, Sandra *science administrator*
Yang, Debra Wong *lawyer, former prosecutor*
Young, Naomi *lawyer*
Youngblood, Juliette Carolina *lawyer*
Yu, Susan C. (Susan Chung-Mi Yu) *lawyer*
Zacchino, Narda *newspaper editor*
Zelevansky, Lynn *curator*
Zelon, Laurie Dee *judge*
Zexter, Eleanor M. *secondary school educator*
Zola, Sheila Flexer *retired elementary school educator*
Zoss, Nancy Aline *psychotherapist, counseling administrator*

Los Banos
Ellington, Karen Renae *school system administrator*

Los Gatos
Benner, Patricia Ann *retired literacy educator*
Ferrari, L. Katherine *speech professional, consultant, entrepreneur*
Hartinger, Patricia Bernardine *retired elementary school educator*
Mintz, Marilyn D. *artist, writer*
Ohanjanian, Ruzanna *clinical psychologist*
Tinsley, Barbara Sher *historian, educator, writer*

Los Osos
Field-Haley, Betty *artist, art educator*
Van Ekeren, Ybi *artist*

Lower Lake
Garcia, Beatrice Maude *social worker, director*

Lynwood
Trousdale, Margaret Mary *science educator*

Madera
Angus, Gloria Michelle *elementary school educator*

Malibu
Barnett, Ola Wilma *psychology educator*
Clegg, Cyndia Susan *literature educator*
Field, Barbara Stephenson *small business owner*
Hunt, Valerie Virginia *electrophysiologist, educator*
LaChanze, (R. LaChanze Sapp, Rhonda Sapp) *actress*
Marvin, Barbara Joyce *writer*
Miller-Perrin, Cindy Lou *psychology professor*
Nettles, Jennifer *singer*
Palacio, June Rose Payne *nutritional science educator*
Raine, Melinda L. *academic librarian*
Ruse, Kathleen Diane *elementary school educator*
Tellem, Susan Mary *public relations executive*

Manhattan Beach
King, Sharon Marie *consulting company executive*
McMullen, Melinda Kae *public relations executive*

Marina
Mettee-McCutchon, Ila *municipal official, retired military officer*

Marina Del Rey
Gold, Carol Sapin *international management consultant, speaker, writer*
Heath, Berthann Jones *educational association administrator*

Mariposa
LeCocq, Karen Elizabeth *artist*

Martinez
Baird, Laurel Cohen *clinical nurse*
DeWolfe, Martha *singer, songwriter, publisher, producer*
Fein, Sylvia *painter, writer*
George, Julianne Mary *music educator, conductor*
Withrow, Sherrie Anne (Jimie Jean Pearl) *financial specialist*

Marysville
Day, Colien *retired secondary school educator*
Hurley, Allison Ruth *mentor coach specialist*

Mckinleyville
O'Dea, Suzanne Dores *author*
Sahlberg, Anne Kiszka *secondary school educator*

Mendocino
Alexander, Joyce Mary *illustrator*
Sharkey, Virginia Grace *artist*

Menifee
Levasseur, Janice Thoni *mathematician, educator*

Menlo Park
Baez, Joan Chandos *vocalist*
Collins, Nancy Whisnant *foundation administrator*
Drell, Persis *physicist*
Fisher, Ora T. *lawyer*
Gimon, Eleanor Hewlett *philanthropist*
Heller, Esther A. *writer, educator*
Hermle, Lynne C. *lawyer*
LaPorte, Kathleen Darken *venture capitalist*
Much, Kathleen *editor, publishing executive, consultant*
Perlman, Radia *communications engineer*
Steiger, Bettie Alexander *information industry specialist*

Merced
Tomlinson-Keasey, Carol Ann *academic administrator*
Wylie, Trisha Lynn *principal*

Midway City
Allen, Frances Michael *publisher*

Mill Valley
Adessa, Lori *music educator*
Coulter, Catherine *writer*
Kettunen Zegart, Mar(garet) Jean *artist, educator*
Mautner, Gabriella *writer, educator*
Newman, Nancy Marilyn *ophthalmologist, educator*
Owings, Alison June *writer, journalist*
Schiff, Jan Pedersen *conductor, voice educator*
Taylor, Rose Perrin *social worker*
Vaughan, Frances Elizabeth *psychologist*

Millbrae
Stamos, Kathryn Elizabeth *secondary school educator*

Milpitas
Allen, Irma M. *adult education educator*
Wyatt, Willda Jean *elementary school educator*

Mission Viejo
Burke, Kathleen J. *music director, writer*
Chattopadhyay, Collette Adele *art historian, critic*
Harris, Ruby Lee *realtor*
Hodge, Kathleen O'Connell *academic administrator*
Lake, Jane Burford *special education educator, hypnotherapist, small business owner*
Mc Afee, Margaret Anne *retired art educator*
Vergara, Lorenda *retired physician*

Modesto
Bucknam, Mary Olivia Caswell *artist, educator*
Holmboe, Susan Ann *elementary school educator*
Rogers, Wanda Faye *vocalist*
Stanley, Denise Yvonne *art educator*
Whiteside, Carol Gordon *foundation executive*
Wilde, Christine Bucey *secondary school educator*

Moffett Field
Bualat, Maria G. *computer engineer*
Clearwater, Yvonne A. *psychologist*
Hubbard, Kim *computer engineer*
Jackson, Lenore *computer technician*
Jarmann, Janet *systems administrator, systems analyst*
Luna, Bernadette *mechanical engineer*
Munoz, Christine *systems analyst*
Navarro, BJ *federal agency administrator*
O'Hara, Dee *medical/surgical nurse*

Monrovia
Brown, Gwendolyn Williams *music educator*
Salaman, Maureen Kennedy *writer, nutritionist*

Montara
Wall, Glennie Murray *historic preservation professional*

Montclair
Boyd, Mary H. (Mary H. Merrill) *social services administrator*

Montebello
Bucey, Constance Virginia Russell *retired elementary school educator, education educator*
Pasinato, Yvonne Louise *science educator*

Monterey
Blair, Cynthia *meteorologist, oceanographer, researcher*
Boger, Gail Lorraine Zivna *reading specialist*
Gaver, Frances Rouse *lawyer*
Packard, Julie *aquarium administrator*
Packard Burnett, Nancy *biologist*
Peet, Phyllis Irene *women's studies educator*
Reneker, Maxine Hohman *librarian*
Robinson, Marla Holbrook *community care nurse*

Monterey Park
Smith, Betty Denny *county official, administrator, fashion executive*
Stankevitz, Diane Lynn *athletic trainer*
Wilson, Linda *librarian*

Moorpark
Young, Victoria E. *occupational health nurse, lawyer*

Moraga
O'Brien, Bea Jae *artist*
Schwartz, Naomi J. *education educator*
Sestanovich, Molly Brown *writer*

Moreno Valley
Bajor, Renee Allyson *special education educator*
Calley, Tranquil Hudson *travel consultant, educator*
Guerrero, Donna Marie *sales executive*
Heacock, Lizbeth Lee *elementary school educator*
Marshall, Debra Lynn *secondary school educator*

Morgan Hill
Aranda, Sandra Louise *speech pathology/audiology services professional*
Haaser, Paula Marlene *language educator*

Moss Landing
McNutt, Marcia Kemper *geophysicist*
Parker, Joan M. *librarian*

Mount Shasta
Stienstra, Stephani Ann *editor, writer*

Mountain View
Abel, Elizabeth Ann *dermatologist*
Allen, Vicky *sales and marketing professional*
Baker, Mitchell *computer software development foundation administrator*
Brown, Shona *information technology executive*
Cabrol, Nathalie Agnes *research scientist*
Cassidy, Sukhinder Singh *information technology executive*
Craig, Joan Carmen *secondary school educator, performing arts educator*
Di Muccio, Mary-Jo *retired librarian*
Fuller, Jennifer L. *lawyer*
Lucas, Catherine *biotechnology company executive*
Mayer, Marissa Ann *information technology executive*
Rivera, Miriam *information technology executive, lawyer*
Sandberg, Sheryl *information technology executive*
Serebrennikova, Emiliya *musician, educator*
Singh, Sangita *information technology and marketing executive*
Tarter, Jill Cornell *science foundation director, astronomer, researcher*
Wildman, Iris J. *retired law librarian*
Wulff, Virginia McMillan *school system administrator*

Murrieta
Miller, Helen F. *music educator, musician*
Rose, Norma Louise *retired human services manager*

Napa
Barnes, Joy Vervene *retired literature and language educator*
Geca, Monique *psychologist*
Imbach, Janice Sprunger *marriage and family therapist, education educator*
Loar, Peggy Ann *foundation administrator, museum administrator*
Maas, Maxine Anna Adelaide Schumann *retired juvenile justice administrator*
Norman, Sheri Hanna *artist, educator, cartographer*
Renfrow, Patricia Anne *secondary school educator*
Woodruff, Diane Carey *college president*

National City
Quigley, Deborah Hewitt *adult education educator*

Nevada City
Clausen, Jeanne Lorraine *musician*

Newbury Park
Lindsey, Joanne M. *flight attendant, poet*
MacArthur, Marjorie Ellen Hottley *secondary school educator*

Newhall
Stone, Susan Foster *mental health services professional*

Newport Beach
Allen, Karen Alfstad *information technology executive*
Cano, Kristin Maria *lawyer*
Duvall, Florence Marie *software engineer*
Hancock, Ellen Marie *communications executive*
McManigal, Penny *artist*
Ortlund, Anne (Elizabeth Anne Ortlund) *writer, musician*
Spitz, Barbara Salomon *artist*
Wallis, Mary Camilla *civic leader*
Wentworth, Diana von Welanetz *author*

Nipomo
Aune, Alissa Marie *music educator*
Britton, Sandra Loucille Mary *artist, gallery owner*

Norco
McNeal, Phyllis Paulette *parole agent*

North Hollywood
Charis, Barbara *nutritionist, consultant, medical researcher*
Downey, Roma *actress*
Evans, Paula Lemmermann *educational association administrator*
Fanning, Dakota *actress*
Miller, Brenda *real estate investment analyst*
Newton-John, Olivia *singer, actress*
Reynolds, Debbie (Mary Frances Reynolds) *actress*
Stone, Sharon *actress*
Toplitt, Gloria H. *music educator, actress, vocalist*
Toussieng, Yolanda *make-up artist*

Northridge
Ackermann, Sue Ann *mathematics educator*
Boberg, Dorothy Kurth *author*
Butler, Karla *psychologist, educator*
Cartwright, Nancy *actress, television producer*
Curzon, Susan Carol *academic administrator*
Danin, Mary Ann *artist, designer, educator*
Duran, Karin Jeanine *librarian*
Koester, Jolene *academic administrator*
Reagan, Janet Thompson *psychologist, educator*
Rowlands, Kathleen Dudden *education educator*
Runquist, Lisa A. *lawyer*
Syms, Helen Maksym *educational administrator*
Weatherup, Wendy Gaines *graphic designer, writer*
Yuen, Ellen M. *elementary school educator*

Norwalk
Kiss, Boglarka *musician, educator*
Oliver, Susan *history professor, writer, consultant*

Novato
Codoner, Sheila Dowds *psychologist*
Conolly, Katharine Farnam *editor*
Criswell, Eleanor Camp *psychologist*
Farmer, Mary Bauder *artist*
Jaeger, Patsy Elaine *retired secondary school educator, artist*
Lane, Michele Jeanne *special education educator*
Miller, Emily Josephine *retired secondary school educator*
Podd, Marsha Dianne *small business owner, nurse*
Popovic, Bozena (Bo Popovic) *artist*
Weedn, Sonnee D. *psychologist*

Oakdale
Saletta, Mary Elizabeth (Betty Saletta) *sculptor*
Wharff, Julie Dawn *principal*

Oakhurst
Gyer, Jane E. *artist, educator*

Oakland
Alba, Benny *artist*
Banke, Kathy M. *lawyer*
Beeson, Montel Eileen *human services administrator, gerontologist*
Bobino, Rita Florencia *psychologist*
Boesing, Martha *theater artist*
Bouska Lee, Carla Ann *nursing and health care educator*
Brown, Oral Lee *real estate company executive, entrepreneur*
Cary, Alice Shepard *retired physician*
Caulfield, Carlota *education educator, researcher, poet*
Chetkovich, Carol *public policy educator*
Cole, Joan Hays *social worker, clinical psychologist*
Coleman-Perkins, Carolyn *retired medical/surgical nurse*
Cook, Lia *art educator*
Davies, Colleen T. *lawyer*
DeFazio, Lynette Stevens *dancer, educator, choreographer, violinist, actress*
DeMoro, Rose Ann *nursing administrator*
Diaz, Sharon *education administrator*
DiMaggio, Debbi *realtor*
Earle, Sylvia Alice *research biologist, oceanographer*
Erlich, Ruth L. *artist*
Fineman, Jeanette Krulevitz *retired artist*
Ford, Gail *library administrator*
Frady, Kisha *professional sports team executive*
Griffin, Betty Jo *elementary school educator*
Hafter, Ruth Anne *library director, educator*
Howatt, Sister Helen Clare *human services administrator, director, retired school librarian*
Hsu, Helen Hua *psychologist, consultant*
Isaac Nash, Eva Mae *secondary school educator*
Kane, Jacqueline *human resources specialist*
Killebrew, Ellen Jane (Mrs. Edward S. Graves) *cardiologist, educator*
King, Janet Carlson *nutrition educator, researcher*
Krause, Marcella Elizabeth Mason (Mrs. Eugene Fitch Krause) *retired secondary school educator*
Lake, Suzanne *singer, music educator*
Lee, Ella Louise *librarian, educator*
Linden, Margaret Joanne *librarian, foundation administrator*
Liveright, Betty Fouche *actress, writer*
Miller, Connie Joy *assistant real estate officer, real estate broker*
Neeley, Beverly Evon *sociologist, consultant*
Nelson, Shirley W. *bank executive*
Parker, Melissa Bernice *advertising executive*
Preston, Elizabeth A. *psychologist*
Randisi, Elaine Marie *accountant, educator, writer*
Reynolds, Kathleen Diane Foy (KDF Reynolds) *transportation executive*
Rubin, Rhea Joyce *library consultant*
Sandler, Marion Osher *bank executive*
Sargent, Arlene Anne *nursing educator*
Sartor, Vivian Juanita *nursing administrator*
Sims, Sandra *elementary school educator*
Slack, Vickie *human services administrator*
Sutter, Elouise C. *retired art educator*
Weaver, Pauline Anne *lawyer*
Widener, Mary Lee *non-profit financial executive*
Wilken, Claudia *judge*
Williams, Carol H. *advertising executive*
Wood, Larry (Mary Laird) *journalist, writer, public relations executive, educator, environmental consultant*
Woodbury, Marda Liggett *librarian, writer*
Zandvakili, Katayoon *writer*
Zschau, Marilyn *singer*

Oceanside
Beck, Marilyn Mohr *columnist*
Daniel, Susan Qualls *secondary school educator*
Freeman, Myrna Faye *county schools official*
Hertweck, Alma Louise *sociology and child development educator*
Johnson, Karen Elaine *secondary school educator, tax preparer*
McIntyre, Louise S. *income tax consultant*
Messner, Yvonne F. *physical education educator*
Mushinsky, Jane Marla *humanities educator, writer*
Villasenor, Barbara *book publisher*

Ontario
Chavez, Virginia *counselor*
Dastrup-Hamill, Faye Myers *city official*
Fangerow, Kay Elizabeth *nurse*
Hanner, Jean P. *retired nursing administrator, art gallery owner, religious organization administrator*
Kloepfer, Marguerite Fonnesbeck *writer*
Soto, Nell *state senator*

Orange
Banning, Donna Rose *art educator*
Busby, Nita June *small business owner*
Carson, Virginia Gottschall *academic administrator, biology educator*
Carty, Victoria Louise *sociologist, educator*
Christian-Brougham, Ruby Rosalie *education educator*
Felisky, Barbara Rosbe *artist*
Gibbons, Pamela R. *professional athletic trainer*
Hahn, Moira Elizabeth *artist, educator*
Hudson, Kelly Colleen Patrick *personal trainer, educator*
Karnes, Frances Rozelle *counselor, educator*
Matallana, Lynne *medical association administrator*
Morgan, Beverly Carver *pediatrician, educator*
Pickart, Caitlin Cahill *psychiatrist*
Ritman, Barbara Ellen *counselor*
Simjee, Aisha *ophthalmologist, educator*
Stevens, Cherita Wyman *social sciences educator, writer*
Williams, Danna Beth *reading specialist*
Williams, Patricia Sue *agricultural studies educator*

Orinda
Epperson, Stella Marie *artist*
Lorensen, Gunnhildur S. *librarian*
Strong, Susan Clancey *writer, communications executive, editor*

Oxnard
Neilson, Jane Scott *mathematics educator*
North, Michelle *mortgage broker*
Sands, Velma Ahda *lawyer*
Tolmach, Jane Louise *community activist, municipal official*

Pacific Grove
Flury, Jane Madawg *artist, educator*
O'Shaughnessy, Ellen Cassels *writer*
Penney, Beth *language educator, editor, writer*
Schapiro, Karen Lee *language educator*

Pacific Palisades
Helfgott, Gloria Vida *artist*
Holberg, Eva Maria *volunteer*
Jennings, Marcella Grady *rancher, investor*
Kamrany, Sajia *television producer*
Kaufer, Shirley Helen *artist, painter*
Kirkgaard, Valerie Anne *media group executive, radio host, writer, radio producer, consultant*
Love, Susan Margaret *surgeon, educator, writer*
Perloff, Marjorie Gabrielle *literature educator*
Snowhook, Ann Laferty *social services administrator*

Pacifica
Brooks-Korn, Lynne Vivian *artist*
Miller, Lynn Ruth *writer, artist, comedian*

Palm Desert
Adelman, Bayla Ann *occupational therapist*
Alpert, Shirley Marcia *librarian*
Bantz, Jody Lenore *psychologist*
Baxter, Betty Carpenter *academic administrator*
Carangelo, Lori *writer, not-for-profit developer, volunteer*
Heydman, Abby Maria *academic administrator*
Kaufman, Charlotte King *artist*
Owings, Thalia Kelley *elementary school educator*
Ponder, Catherine *clergywoman*
Sausman, Karen *zoological park administrator*

Palm Springs
Coffey, Nancy *real estate broker*
Hartman, Rosemary Jane *retired special education educator*
Hilb, Jeane Dyer *community volunteer*
Krans, Michelle M. *publishing executive*
Nelson, K. Bonita *literary agent*
Parks, Trina *dancer, educator*

Palmdale
Faulk, Betty Price *elementary school educator*
Phillips, Ruthanne *special education administrator*

Palo Alto
Berger-Granet, Nancy Sue *nursing researcher*
Blessing-Moore, Joann Catherine *allergist, pulmonologist*
Bystritsky, Marina *psychologist*
Chang, Carmen *lawyer*
Choy, Judy *secondary school educator*
Church, Katrina J. *pharmaceutical executive*
Chute, Deanna *mathematics educator*
Denzel, Nora *information technology executive*
Dugger, Marguerite J. *retired special education educator*
Dunn, Debra L. *computer company executive*
Estrin, Judith *computer company executive*
Fenney, Linda *pharmaceutical executive*
Fordis, Jean Burke *lawyer*
Frankle, Diane Holt *lawyer*
Goldstein, Mary Kane *physician*
Greene, Diane *information technology executive*
Gunther, Barbara *artist, educator*
Halloran, Jean M. *human resources specialist*
Hays, Marguerite Thompson *nuclear medicine physician, educator*
Heneveld-Story, Christy Jean *educational researcher*
Hubert, Helen Betty *epidemiologist*
Kaile, Davina K. *lawyer*
Kelsey, Edith Jeanine *psychotherapist, consultant*
Kincaid, Judith Wells *electronics company executive*
Kosacz, Barbara A. *lawyer*
Lewis, Virginia Marie *psychologist*
Lundy, Jackelyn Ruth *financial consultant, economist, researcher*
Lyons, Cathy *computer company executive*
McCall, Jennifer Jordan *lawyer*
Mommsen, Katharina *retired literature and language professor, foundation administrator*
Monroy, Gladys H. *lawyer*
Moore, Cassandra Chrones *real estate broker*
Park, Marina H. *lawyer*
Perez de Alonso, Marcela *human resources specialist, information technology executive*
Perl, Teri *computer educator*
Petkanics, Donna M. *lawyer*
Scitovsky, Anne Aickelin *economist, researcher*
Sherlock, Phyllis Krafft *psychologist*
Smith, Julie Ann *pharmaceutical executive*
Spohn, Nor Rae *computer company executive*
Sterling St. John, Vicki Lynn *lawyer*
Summers, Debra S. *lawyer*
Walker, Ann Yvonne *lawyer*

Palos Verdes Estates
Brigden, Ann Schwartz *mediator, educator*
Kingsley, Kathryn Alexis Krah *retired elementary school educator*
McNeill, Susan *marketing professional, real estate professional, sales professional*
Rogers, Rita Ruth *psychiatrist, political scientist*
Yarbrough, Allyson Debra *electrical engineer*

Palos Verdes Peninsula
Deveny, Charlotte Perry *musician, educator*
Julien, Gail Leslie *model, public relations professional*
Narasimhan, Padma Mandyam *physician*
Skorka, Darlene McDonald *psychologist*

Panorama City
Janis, Elinor Raiden *artist, educator*

Paramount
Kesten, Betty Lee *retired special education educator*
Landes, Geraldine Steinberg *psychologist*

Parlier
Manton, Linda Marie *academic administrator*

Pasadena
Arnold, Frances Hamilton *chemistry educator*
Avrech, Gloria May *psychotherapist*
Brogden-Stirbl, Shona Marie *writer, researcher*
Cepielik, Elizabeth Lindberg *elementary school educator*
Douglas, Kimberly *university librarian*
Effros, Michelle *electrical engineer, engineering educator*
Ellner, Carolyn Lipton *non-profit organization executive, dean, consultant*
Freedman, Wendy Laurel *astronomer, educator*
Hall, Cynthia Holcomb *federal judge*
Halsted, Margo *music educator, carillonneur*
Huang, Alice Shih-hou *biologist, educator, virologist*
Hunt, Hazel Analue Stanfield *retired accountant*
Kennard, Lydia H. *airport terminal executive*
Kilburn, Katherine Lynn (Kappy Kilburn) *theater director, theater producer*
Littke, Lael Jensen *author*
Lopes, Rosaly Mutel Crocce *astronomer, planetary geologist*
Matthews, Mildred Shapley *freelance/self-employed editor*
Mosher, Sally Ekenberg *lawyer, musician*
Muñoz Fernández, Michela *electrical engineer, researcher*
Nelson, Dorothy Wright (Mrs. James F. Nelson) *federal judge*
Newman, Marjorie Yospin *psychiatrist*
Olson, Diana Craft *image and etiquette consultant*
Pashgian, Margaret Helen *artist*
Rymer, Pamela Ann *federal judge*
Sanders, Jan W. *librarian*
Sargent, Anneila Isabel *astrophysicist*
Short, Elizabeth M. *internist, educator, retired federal agency administrator*
Smolke, Christina *chemical engineer*
Spilker, Linda Joyce *aerospace scientist*
Stroupe, Ashley W. *engineer*
Syvertson, Marguerite *geologist*
Trendler, Teresa Ann *science educator*
Wardlaw, Kim A. McLane *federal judge*
Wilson, Mary Ellen *retired project administrator*
Winbush, Olga Joyce *education educator, consultant*
Worby, Rachael Beth *conductor*
Yeager, Caroline Hale *writer, retired radiologist, consultant*

Zwicky, Barbarina Exita *humanities educator, researcher*

Paso Robles
Dabul, Barbara Lohman *speech pathologist*
Nelson, Bonnie Kay *elementary school educator*

Pebble Beach
Quick, Valerie Anne *sonographer*

Penn Valley
Collins, Linda L. *reading specialist, consultant*
Longan, Suzanne M. *retired elementary school educator*
Nix, Barbara Lois *real estate broker*
Sands, Sharon Louise *art director, publishing executive, artist*

Perris
Cavallaro, Judith *secondary school educator*

Petaluma
Ehret, Terry *writer*
Gervais, Cherie Nadine *small business owner*
Howell, Sharon L. *counseling administrator*
Sebold, Alice *writer*
Thomas, Nancy Hinckley *special education educator*
Tiedt, Iris McClellan *emeritus university dean*
Wilcoxson, Carol Ann *music educator*

Phelan
Erwin, Joan Lenore *artist, educator*

Pittsburg
Gustafson, Sally Ann *counselor, cosmetologist, educator*
Williams-Thomas, Elizabeth A. *financial planner, consultant*
Williscroft-Barcus, Beverly Ruth *retired lawyer*

Placentia
Cash, Jeanie Maritta *educational association administrator*

Placerville
Barber, Victoria *school system administrator, consultant*
Miller, Edna Rae Atkins *secondary school educator*
Wall, Sonja Eloise *nursing administrator*
Wessels-McCoy, Denise Wendy *pre-school administrator, consultant*
Wilkinson, Rosemary Regina Challoner *poet, writer*

Playa Del Rey
Reid, Jacqueline *lighting designer*

Pleasant Hill
Wapner, Donna *healthcare educator*

Pleasanton
Bieber, (Adda) Lynn *marriage, family and child counselor*
Fine, Marjorie Lynn *lawyer*
Foster, Bonnie Gayle *operating room nurse, real estate agent*
Novak, Randi Ruth *systems engineer, computer scientist*
Renda, Larree M. *retail executive*
Roshong, Dee Ann Daniels *dean, educator*

Pollock Pines
Rickard, Margaret Lynn *library director, consultant*

Pomona
Amaya-Thetford, Patricia *elementary school educator*
Bowlin, Stephanie D. *university dean*
Callaway, Linda Marie *special education educator*
Fetterly, Barbara Louise *artist*
Harms, Janet Berggren *music educator*
Maslow, Phyllis F. *retired educator*
Parrish, Joanna Faith *nursing consultant*
Podany, Amanda H. *history professor*
Saudek, Martha Folsom *artist, educator*
Starkey, Laurie Shaffer *chemistry professor*

Portola Valley
Nycum, Susan Hubbell *lawyer*

Poway
Conant, Kim Untiedt *retired elementary school educator*

Quartz Hill
Noble, Sunny A. *business owner*

Ramona
McAndrews, Shannon Marie *elementary school educator*
Newman, Malane L. *computer graphics designer, cartoonist, illustrator, computer graphics designer, educator*

Rancho Cordova
Hall-Barron, Deborah *lawyer*
Hendrickson, Elizabeth Ann *retired secondary school educator*
Kasch, Mary Courteol *occupational therapist*

Rancho Cucamonga
Decker, Catherine Helen *language educator*
Gavin, Mary Ellen *marketing professional, consultant*
Horsley, Paula Rosalie *accountant*

Rancho Mirage
Ballard, Kaye *actress*
Leydorf, Mary Malcolm *physician, writer*
Marsh, Betty June *retired education educator*
Wyatt, Lenore *civic worker*

Rancho Palos Verdes
Curtis, Carole Ortale *executive recruiter, consultant*
Sayers, Kari *literature and language professor, journalist*
Steiner, Frances Josephine *conductor, musician, educator*
Vanderlip, Elin Brekke *professional society administrator, volunteer*
Works, Margaret Elizabeth *retired art educator*

Rancho Santa Fe
Byrd, Betty Rantze *writer*
Land, Judy M. *real estate broker*

Rancho Santa Margarita
Berta, Melissa Rose *mathematics professor*
Hauser, Jean *theater educator, theater director*
Hoppe, Dorothe Anna *chemistry professor*
Newton, Michelle Marie *sales executive*

Red Bluff
Derk, Denise B. *nurse*

Redding
Bairrington, Ruth Ellen *retired secondary school educator, retired education educator*
Drake, Patricia Evelyn *psychologist*
Krupit, Alison *elementary school educator*
Matenaer, Tegwin A. *retired artist, educator, consultant*
Novo, Nieta R. *education educator*

Redlands
Auerbacher, Mary Jane *church organist*
Coleman, Arlene Florence *retired pediatrics nurse*
Goto, Toshiko *retired art educator*
Lewis, Victoria Ann *theater educator*
Tapia Parker, Carrie-Anne *massage therapist, healthcare educator*
Van Engelen, Debra Lynn *chemistry educator*
Wilson, Lois Fair *retired school system administrator*

Redondo Beach
Battles, Roxy Edith *novelist, consultant, educator*
Engstrom, Stephanie Cloes *artist, small business owner*
Mackenzie, Linda Alice *media company executive, radio personality, writer, hypnotherapist*
Martin, Melissa Carol *radiological physicist*
McWilliams, Margaret Ann *home economist, educator, writer*
Richards, Denise *actress*
Shellhorn, Ruth Patricia *landscape architect*
Woike, Lynne Ann *computer scientist*

Redwood City
Becker, Lindsey A. *art educator*
Catz, Safra *computer software company executive*
Chow, Irene A. *biopharmaceutical company executive*
Davidson, Mary Ann *information technology executive*
Minton, Jennifer *information technology executive*
Quartuccio, Maryann *insurance agent, home economist*
Sharpnack, Rayona *management consultant*
Smith, Nancy L. *information technology executive*
Spangler, Nita Reifschneider *volunteer*
Sullivan, Kathleen Marie *lawyer, educator, former dean*

Rescue
Ackerly, Wendy Saunders *construction company executive*

Reseda
Hoover, Pearl Rollings *nurse*

Rialto
Gilbert, Joanne Toone *director, educator*
Jackson, Betty Eileen *music and elementary school educator*
King, Muriel Eileen *secondary school educator*

Richmond
Corbin, Rosemary MacGowan *former mayor*
Poulos, Paige M. *public relations executive*

Ridgecrest
Miears-Cutsinger, Mary Ellen *artist, art gallery owner*
Swiridoff, Christine *literature and language professor*

Riverside
Alexander-Clarke, Marsia *artist*
Bell, Helen Lavin *artist*
Bridges, Lisa Jane *psychology educator*
Carney, Jane W. *lawyer*
Case, Janice Chang *naturopathic physician, psychologist, lawyer*
Chang, Sylvia Tan *health facility administrator, educator*
Clazie, Melissa A *literature and language educator*
Córdova, France Anne-Dominic *academic administrator, astrophysicist*
Dutton, Jo Sargent *education educator, researcher, consultant*
Fagundo, Ana Maria *language educator*
Fontana, Sandra Ellen Frankel *special education educator*
James, Etta (Jamesetta Hawkins) *recording artist*
Lobb, Cynthia Jean Hocking *lawyer*
Lyubomirsky, Sonja *psychology professor*
Macek, Pamela Kay *tax specialist, business executive*
Mancilla, Faustina Ramirez *retired psychologist*
Meadows, Joyce Katherine *nurse*
Murphy, Caroline Patricia *historian, writer*
Smith, Dorothy Ottinger *apparel designer, volunteer*
Staples, Karen Eleanor *special education educator*
Talbot, Prue *biology professor*
Tirabassi, Linda Sue *secondary school educator*
Warnke, Georgia C. *humanities educator*
Warren, Katherine Virginia *art gallery director*
White, Clara Jo *small business owner, consultant*
Winter, Patricia Lea *psychologist, researcher*
Witman, Laura Kathleen *writer, security professional*
Yount, Gwendolyn Audrey *humanities educator*

Rocklin
Blank, Lenore Kim *literature and language professor, consultant*
Yates, Coleen Denise *special education educator*

Rohnert Park
McKillop, Susan Regan *art educator*
Stetson, Nancy Emily *retired academic administrator*

Rolling Hills Estates
Corette, Deborah West *elementary school educator*
Marsh, Barbara Lynn *elementary school educator*

Rosemead
Collins, Jodi M. *utilities executive*
Featherstone, Diane L. *utilities executive*
Newton, Jo Ann Goddard *corporate financial executive*
Nishimoto, Alice Keiko *elementary school educator, consultant*
Parsky, Barbara *utilities executive*
Ryder, Beverly *utilities executive*
Yazdi, Mahvash *utilities executive*

Roseville
French, Leura Parker *secondary school educator*
Gambill, Cara Lee *physician assistant*
Grant, Barbara *venture capitalist*
Law, Jennifer *middle school educator, director*
Roberts, Angela Christine *audiologist*
Smith, Kaye Train *artist*

Ross
Godwin, Sara *writer*
Matan, Lillian Kathleen *secondary school educator, consultant, interior designer*

Rowland Heights
Smith, Barbara J. *music educator*

Sacramento
Adolphson, Vanessa *counseling administrator, educator, chemist*
Amezcua, Esther Hernandez *elementary school educator*
Artz, Ethel Angela Cleavenger *elementary school educator, consultant*
Boekhoudt-Cannon, Gloria Lydia *finance educator*
Callahan, Consuelo Maria *federal judge*
Chilton, Shirley R. *state agency administrator*
Chu, Judy May *assemblywoman*
Contreras, Dee (Dorothea Contreras) *municipal official, educator*
Doyel, Cindy M. *information technology specialist*
Elizabeth, Mary *science educator, consultant*
Fargo, Heather *mayor*
Gluckmann, Ema *science educator*
Gosfield, Margaret *secondary school educator, school system administrator, consultant, editor*
Griffith, Yolanda Evette *professional basketball player*
Grimes, Pamela Rae *retired elementary school educator*
Heaphy, Janis Besler *newspaper executive*
Henson, Glenda Maria *newswriter*
Hunter, Patricia Rae (Tricia Hunter) *state official*
Jones, Lial A. *museum director*
Krebs, Nina Boyd *psychologist*
Kuehl, Sheila James *state legislator, department chairman*
Lindahl, Kathleen Ann *archaeologist*
Liu, Carol *state representative*
Lundstrom, Marjie *editor*
Mattias, Mona Carol *elementary education educator, consultant*
McCann, Kim Lou M. *theater educator, director*
Melberg, Sharon Elaine *nurse*
Morison, Kathryn Diane *actor, consultant*
Nickless, Barbara A. *primary school educator*
Nisson, Mary *elementary school educator*
Opperman, Rosanna Resendez *vice principal*
Parker, Elizabeth Rindskopf *dean, law educator*
Pavley, Fran J. *state representative*
Piper, Jami Kathleen *music educator, composer, musician*
Piskoti, Carol Lee *art educator*
Pomeroy, Claire *dean*
Potter, Teresa Pearl *adult education educator*
Reed, Nancy Boyd *English language educator, elementary school educator*
Renforth, Dorothea Joyce *art educator, artist*
Robinson, Muriel Cox *psychiatrist*
Ross, Jean M. *think-tank executive*
Runfola, Sheila Kay *nurse*
Scholey, Diann Patricia *accountant*
Senna, Doborah Jean *psychology professor*
Shapiro, Lara Ruth *lawyer*
Shriver, Maria Owings *news correspondent*
Smith, Judith A. *legal analyst*
Speir, Marcia Ann *retired accountant*
Stolba, Soheir Sukkary *anthropologist, educator*
Thiltgen, Christine *law educator*
Totton, Gayle *professional sports team executive*
von Friederichs-Fitzwater, Marlene Marie *researcher*
Wicks, Debra S. *nursing educator*
Wilcox, Lynn E. *psychology educator*
Willis, Dawn Louise *legal assistant, small business owner*
Winney, Gayle Marie *music educator*
Wong, Alice *lawyer*
Wright, Mary Rose *retired state agency administrator*
Wunder, Haroldene Fowler *taxation and international accounting educator*
Zaidi, Emily Louise *retired elementary school educator*
Zusman, Edie Ellen *neurosurgeon*

Salinas
Chester, Lynne *foundation administrator, artist*
Slattery, Kathleen Milicent *language educator*
Sprude, Margaret *credit services company executive*

San Andreas
Buringrud, Lisa Marie *music educator*
Prema, Nitya *marriage and family therapist, artist*

San Anselmo
Ellenberger, Diane Marie *nurse, consultant*

San Bernardino
Brown, Marta Macías *legislative staff member, executive assistant*
Caballero, Sharon *academic administrator*
Ellis, Yvonne *mathematics professor*
Ereksen, Christa Ann *social worker, marriage and family therapist*
Evans, R. Marlene *county agency administrator*
Fong, Mary *ethnic studies educator*
Gilbert, Jennie *educator, consultant*
Griffiths, Barbara Lorraine *psychologist, writer, marriage and family therapist*
Hansen, Anne Katherine *poet*
Harlan, Shirley *protective services official, videographer*
Roberts, Katharine Adair *retired bookkeeper*

San Bruno
Bowman, Christine Diane *middle school educator*
Edwards, Kassandra Bennett *psychotherapist, consultant*
White, Frances LaVonne *academic administrator*

San Carlos
Oliver, Nancy Lebkicher *artist, retired elementary school educator*
Pollack, Betty Gillespie *retired health care services executive*
Sullivan, Shirley Ross (Shirley Ross Davis) *art appraiser*

San Clemente
Fox, Lorraine Esther *psychologist, human services consultant*
Geyser, Lynne M. *lawyer, writer*
Renk, Pamela Jean *counselor, psychotherapist, small business owner*

San Diego
Aaron, Cynthia G. *judge*
Adler, Louise DeCarl *judge*
Amos, Theresa Ann *marketing professional*
Amstadt, Nancy Hollis *retired language educator*
Astroth, Margo Foltz *mental health nurse, nurse psychotherapist*
Bates-Romeo, Delores Alvenia *music educator, consultant*
Blade, Melinda Kim *archaeologist, educator, research scientist*
Boesky, Lisa *child/adolescent psychologist, writer, speaker, consultant*
Brien, Lois Ann *psychologist, educator*
Brierton, Cheryl Lynn *lawyer*
Brooks, Juanita Rose *lawyer*
Brown, Barbara Sproul *retired librarian, consultant, writer*
Brown, Sandra Ann *psychology educator*
Buska, Sheila Mary *controller, writer, columnist*
Caldwell, Joan Marie *artist, educator*
Canales, Viola *management consulting executive, writer*
Cline, Stephanie E. *food service executive*
Cohn, Marjorie F. *law educator, legal association administrator*
Crill, Alice Eileen *music educator*
Crutchfield, Susan Ramsey *neurophysiologist*
Cummins, Patricia Ann *lawyer, educator*
Day, Valerie Marian *mechanical engineer*
Dollarhide, Mary C. *lawyer*
Donadey, Anne *humanities educator*
Drzewiecki, Darla Ruth *accountant*
Dunlop, Marianne *retired language educator*
Farmer, Janene Elizabeth *artist, educator*
Fernandes, Kathleen *scientist*
Flettner, Marianne *opera administrator*
Gillespie, Deirdre Y. *pharmaceutical executive*
Golding, Susan G. *former mayor*
Gonzalez, Irma Elsa *federal judge*
Graham, Ginger L. *pharmaceutical executive*
Haile, Lisa A. *lawyer*
Hammersmith, Nita Marie *writer*
Herriman, Darleen Ann *music educator*
Hoctor, Michanne *dean*
Hoston, Germaine Annette *political science professor*
Hunter, Anita J. *pediatric nurse practitioner, educator*
Idos, Rosalina Vejerano *secondary school educator*
Jacob, Dianne *county official*
Jaworski, Lisa *information technology executive*
Jellison, Beverly Irene *literature and language educator*
Jenkins, Adrienne *women's health nurse*
Kinsbruner Bush, Jennifer *lawyer*
Klamerus, Karen Jean *pharmacist, researcher*
Koppman, Mae Z. *writer, educator*
Kranz, Kathleen Nee *pianist, music educator*
Krupchak, Tamara *artist*
Lam, Carol C. *prosecutor, lawyer*
Lane, Gloria Julian *foundation administrator*
Lane, Sylvia *economist, educator*
Lang, Linda A. *food service executive*
Longenecker, Martha W. *museum director*
Lucas, Eloisa B. *tax consultant, management consultant*
Lyons, Mary E. *academic administrator*
Machi, Rita Mae *retired medical/surgical nurse, retired healthcare educator*
Maheu, Marlene Muriel *psychologist*
Maloney, Ellen Claire *elementary school educator*
McCoy, Lilys D. *lawyer*
McKeown, Mary Margaret *federal judge*
McNeely, Delores *banker*
Mebane, Julie S. *lawyer*
Miner, Allison Patrice *physical therapist*
Moore, Joyce West *social worker, psychotherapist*
Morris, Sandra Joan *lawyer*
Moss, Barbara Gae *education educator*
Mullins, Angela *lawyer*
Naughton, Gail K. *biomedical researcher, academic administrator*
Naughton, Pamela J. *lawyer*
Niedermeier, Mary B. *retired nutritionist*
Oldham, Maxine Jernigan *real estate broker*
Olson, Linda Ann Salmonson *minister*
Parthemore, Jacqueline Gail *internist, educator, hospital administrator*
Porter, Louisa S. *federal judge*

Rodenberg, Johanna Kristine *education educator, consultant*
Roeder, Phoebe Elizabeth *science educator*
Rovniak, Liza S. *research scientist, educator*
Ruth, Dianne *counselor*
Ryan, Sherry Lynn *executive administrator*
Saltman, Juliet A. *retired sociology educator*
Sanchez, Rita B. *humanities educator, writer*
Schwartz, Rhonda Alene *learning disabilities specialist*
Sheldon-Morris, Tiffini Anne *clinical psychologist, consultative examiner*
Shepard, Jean M. *city health department administrator*
Shields, Patricia Allene *retail executive*
Shippey, Sandra Lee *lawyer*
Sorrentino, Renate Maria *illustrator*
Sundayo, Judy *psychologist, educator*
Swanson, Ann Elizabeth *family counselor*
Swanson, Mary Catherine *educational association administrator*
Swenson, Christine Erica *microbiologist*
Swikard, Sandra J. *secondary school educator*
Tatár, Anna *library director*
Uribe, Jennie Ann *elementary school educator*
Vega, Carolyn Jane *elementary educator, consultant, writer*
Wagschal, Kathleen *education educator*
Wallace, Helen Margaret *pediatrician, preventive medicine physician, educator*
Winn, Jade G. *library science educator*
Winner, Karin E. *editor*
Withee, Diana Keeran *art historian, art dealer, educator*
Yacovone, Ellen Elaine *banker*
Young, Sarah Moskowitz *educational and computer consultant, journalist*

San Dimas
Cameron, Judith Lynne *secondary school educator*

San Fernando
Aguilar, Julia Elizabeth *real estate company executive*
Salkin, Barbara Ruth *social worker*

San Francisco
Ackerman, Arlene *school system administrator*
Ada, Alma Flor *education educator, writer*
Adamson, Mary Anne *geographer, systems engineer, consultant*
Alexis, Geraldine M. *lawyer*
Alioto, Angela Mia *lawyer*
Allecta, Julie *lawyer*
Allen, Lola *insurance agent*
Anastacia, (Anastacia Lyn Newkirk) *singer*
Archer, Cristina Lozej *meteorologist*
Arnold, Kathryn *artist, educator*
Arnold, Lauren *art historian, writer*
Asher, Shoshana Chana *mathematics professor*
Aslan, Madalyn *writer, educator*
August-deWilde, Katherine *banker*
Auwers, Linda S. *lawyer*
Bailey-Wells, Deborah *lawyer*
Bainton, Dorothy Ford *pathologist, educator*
Baker, Joy Doreen *art educator, artist*
Bancel, Marilyn *fund raising management consultant*
Bancroft, Rena Merritt *retired academic administrator*
Bargmann, Cornelia I. *neuroscientist, science educator*
Baxter-Lowe, Lee Ann *science educator*
Baysinger, Kara *lawyer*
Belaga, Debra S. *lawyer*
Berzon, Marsha S. *federal judge*
Bierly, Shirley Adelaide *communications executive*
Birnbaum, Lucia Chiavola *historian, educator*
Bitterman, Mary Gayle Foley *foundation executive*
Blackburn, Elizabeth Helen *molecular biologist*
Blake, Laura *architect*
Bocobo-Balunsat, Dalisay *librarian, journalist*
Boerste, Dorothy *psychotherapist*
Bonetti, Susanna *administrative director*
Bourne, JoAnn M. *bank executive*
Braasch, Barbara Lynn *banker, consultant*
Brady, Lauren Jean *corporate communications specialist*
Breschi, Karen Lee *artist, image consultant, educator*
Brindel, Jill Rachuy *cellist*
Broadway, Nancy Ruth *landscape company executive, consultant, model, actress*
Brothers, Lynda Lee *lawyer*
Brown, Bernice Leona Baynes *foundation administrator, secondary school educator, consultant*
Brown, Mehri I. *psychiatrist, educator*
Broyles, Deborah J. *lawyer*
Cabraser, Elizabeth Joan *lawyer*
Callahan, Patricia R. *bank executive*
Calvin, Dorothy Ver Strate *computer company executive*
Cameron, Heather Anne *publishing executive*
Campbell, Janet Coral *architect*
Capaldini, Lisa Claire *physician, educator*
Chang, Patti *foundation administrator*
Chase, Alexandra Nin *psychologist, writer*
Chin, Sue Soone Marian (Suchin Chin) *artist, photojournalist*
Chun, A. Marisa *lawyer*
Chung, Amy Teresa *lawyer, property manager*
Clever, Linda Hawes *physician*
Clifford, Geraldine Joncich (Mrs. William F. Clifford) *retired education educator*
Coleman, Kathryn Anne *lawyer*
Collins, Mary Ann *lawyer*
Corash, Michèle B. *lawyer*
Corrigan, Carol A. *state supreme court justice*
Cranston, Mary Bailey *lawyer*
Crawford, Carol Anne *marketing professional*
Cregan, Nora C. *lawyer*
Croughan, Mary *medical educator*
Davis, Joan Elan *artist*
Davis, Patricia Margaret Alice *psychology and religion educator*
Den Besten, Pamela Kay *biomedical researcher, dentist*
Dibble, Suzanne Louise *nurse, researcher*
Dickinson, Eleanor Creekmore *artist, educator*
Dracup, Kathleen Anne *dean, nursing educator*
Dunn, Patricia Cecile *investment company executive*
Dwyer, Carrie Elizabeth *lawyer*
Edmonson, Tracy K. *lawyer*
Edwards, Robin Morse *lawyer*
Egan, Patricia Jane *foundation administrator, retired director*
Eng, Catherine *health facility administrator, physician*
Estes, Carroll Lynn *sociologist, educator*
Etheridge, Melissa Lou *singer, lyricist*
Eurich, Judith *art appraiser, printmaker*
Everett-Thorp, Kate *digital marketing executive*
Felstiner, Mary Lowenthal *history professor*
Ferriero, Donna M. *pediatric neurologist*
Fields, Laurie *psychologist, educator*
Finocchiaro, Penny Morris *secondary school educator*
Fisher, Doris *retail executive*
Garchik, Leah Lieberman *journalist*
Garvey, Joanne Marie *lawyer*
Gibson, Virginia Lee *lawyer*
Gifford, Fereuza *retired military officer*
Gillette, Frankie Jacobs *retired savings and loan association executive, federal agency administrator, social worker*
Gillette, Patricia K. *lawyer*
Gimon, Juliette *foundation administrator, volunteer*
Giraudo, Suzanne McDonnell *psychologist*
Goldberg, Adele J. *computer scientist*
Goldstein, Sydney Rachel *photographer, writer, radio producer*
Goode, Erica Tucker *internist*
Gooding, Gretchen Ann Wagner *physician, educator*
Greenspan, Deborah *dental educator*
Gregory, Sara Susan (Sudie) *musician, singer, lyricist, poet, recording industry executive, sound recording engineer, archivist*
Guillermo, Tessie *foundation administrator*
Guo, Su *science educator*
Hale, Victoria G. *chemist, pharmaceutical executive*
Hall, Karen Janna *pediatrics nurse, critical care nurse*
Hamilton, Joan Nice *editor-in-chief*
Hane, Laurie S. *lawyer*
Hansen, Carol Louise *literature and language professor*
Harris, Kamala D. *prosecutor*
Harriss, Cynthia Therese (Cynthia Therese Clarke) *retail executive*
Henderson, Nancy Grace *marketing executive, technical documentation executive*
Hernandez, Aileen C(larke) *urban consultant*
Hewlett, Clothilde *lawyer*
Hirata, Rhonda Gay *advertising executive*
Hirst, Karen L. *theater educator*
Hudson, Patricia Ann Siegel *psychologist*
Hudson, Suncerray Ann *research and development company executive*
Hurst, Annette L. *lawyer*
Ikuta, Sandra Segal *federal judge*
Jimenez, Josephine Santos *portfolio manager*
Johnson, Abigail Ridley *tour/travel and performing arts executive*
Johnson, Michelle L. *lawyer*
Kahn, Linda McClure *actuary, consultant*
Kamkar, Rosemary *secondary school educator*
Kammerer, Ann Marie *geotechnical engineer*
Kane, Mary Kay *academic administrator, law educator*
Kennard, Joyce L. *state supreme court justice*
Kenyon, Cynthia J. *medical researcher*
Knutzen, Martha Lorraine *lawyer*
Koda-Kimble, Mary Anne *medical educator, pharmacologist, dean*
Krane, Hilary K. *lawyer*
Krevans, Rachel *lawyer*
Kunz, Heidi *healthcare company executive*
Lau, Jenny Kwok Wah *theater educator, consultant, film educator, consultant*
LeBlanc, Tina *dancer*
Lee, Pamela Anne *bank executive, accountant, financial analyst*
Leech, Marla Renée *media specialist, educator*
Levine, Alison *entrepreneur, leadership development consultant, adventurer*
Likova Mineva, Lora T. *research scientist*
Lim, Donna *music educator*
Loewy, Becky White *psychologist, educator*
Lord, Mia W. *advocate*
Lucia, Marilyn Reed *physician*
MacGowan, Eugenia *lawyer*
Mao, Dora *lawyer*
Marduel, Alix *venture capitalist*
Márquez-Magaña, Leticia Maria *biology professor*
Martinez, Belinda *health insurance company executive*
Martinez Tucker, Sara *educational association administrator*
Martin-O'Neill, Mary Evelyn *advertising executive, management consultant, marketing professional, consultant, educator*
Masaoka, Jan *not-for-profit executive*
McCollam, Sharon L. *retail executive*
McGuire, Kathleen Alison *conductor*
McQuown, Eloise *librarian*
Miller, Ann G. *lawyer*
Mimi, Haas *volunteer*
Mirabal, Nancy Raquel *social sciences educator, researcher*
Mirosevich, Toni *writer, educator*
Mitchell, Patricia Ann *education educator*
Modjtabai, Avid *bank executive*
Molland, Maria U. *Internet company executive*
Morris-Tyndall, Lucy *construction executive*
Muñoz, Calise I. *federal agency administrator*
Murphy, Kathleen Anne Foley *communications executive*
Neve, Victoria J. *music educator*
Newton, Nell Jessup *dean, law educator*
Nix, Katherine Jean *medical case manager*
O'Connor, Sheila Anne *freelance writer*
Parker, Diana Lynne *restaurant manager, special events director*
Paterson, Eva *legal association director, educator*
Pearlman, Amalia Cecile *artist, educator*
Pera, Renee Reijo *biology professor*
Peterson, Linda Lou *special education educator*
Pfaff, Laura King *auction house executive*
Pierce, Deborah Mary *educational administrator*
Pinsky, Charlotte Lee (Cherie Pinsky) *retired academic administrator*
Pope, Marcia L. *lawyer*
Pure, Pamela J. *information technology executive*
Raciti, Cherie *artist*
Ratum, Cecilia Bangloy *retired psychologist*
Reed, Pamela J. *lawyer*
Renstrom, Lisa *environmental organization administrator*
Rice, Dorothy Pechman (Mrs. John Donald Rice) *medical economist*
Richey, Ellen *credit card company executive*
Richey, Mary Ellen *lawyer*
Robertson, Dawn H. *retail executive*
Robertson, Merle Greene *art historian, academic administrator*
Romanello, Marguerite Marie *retired librarian*
Rosales, Suzanne Marie *hospital coordinator*
Rosenberg, Betsy *radio personality, environmentalist*
Rosenberg, Pamela *opera director, conductor*
Ross, Ivy *apparel executive, artist*
Roy, Beth *sociologist, mediator*
Royer, Kathleen Rose *pilot*
Sachs, Marilyn Stickle *writer, educator, editor*
Saeger, Rebecca *advertising executive*
Sage-Gavin, Eva Marie *retail executive*
Sanger, Priya Seshachari *lawyer*
Sano, Emily Joy *museum director*
Saunders, Virginia Fox *psychology educator*
Schechter, Lori A. *lawyer*
Schioldager, Amy Lee *investment company executive*
Schulze, Joan Theresa *artist*
Sedway, Lynn Massel *real estate economist*
Seebach, Lydia Marie *physician*
Seeger, Laureen E. *health products executive*
Shanahan, Lauri M. *lawyer*
Sherratt, Holly *art appraiser*
Shorenstein Hays, Carole *theater producer*
Smith, Jennie *artist*
Soberon, Presentacion Zablan *state bar administrator*
Soh, Chunghee Sarah *anthropology educator*
Solday, Alidra (Linda Brown) *psychotherapist, filmmaker*
Soler, Esta *foundation administrator*
Stahr, Celia Suzanne *art educator*
Steele, Shari *think-tank executive*
Stephens, Elisa *college president*
Stewart, Terry *lawyer*
Story, Joan H. *lawyer*
Studley, Jamienne Shayne *lawyer, educator*
Styles, Margretta Madden *nursing educator*
Sung, Audrey L. *lawyer*
Thacker-Estrada, Elizabeth Lorelei *librarian, historian*
Thornton, Ann Murphy *retired military officer*
Tlsty, Thea Dorothy *research scientist, educator*
Tolstedt, Carrie L. *bank executive*
Tom, Cynthia *sales executive, consultant*
Torme, Margaret Anne *public relations executive, management consultant*
Trott, Mena *application developer*
Tsoh, Janice Yusze *clinical psychologist, researcher*
Van Dyck, Wendy *dancer*
Van Hoesen, Beth Marie *artist, printmaker*
Veaco, Kristina *lawyer*
Ventura, Jacqueline N. *retired nurse*
Vidwans, Smruti Jayant *microbiologist*
Walsh, Joan *editor-in-chief*
Waltz, Judith A. *lawyer*
Wang, An-Yi (Anne) Chou *real estate broker*
Ward, Doris M. *county official*
Watkins, Elizabeth Siegel *history professor*
Weber, Paula M. *lawyer*
Welborn, Caryl Bartelman *lawyer*
Wells, Gertrude Beverly *psychologist*
Werdegar, Kathryn Mickle *state supreme court justice*
Wernick, Sandra Margot *advertising and public relations executive*
White, Wilda L. *lawyer*
Williams, Linda C. *lawyer*
Winblad, Ann *investment company executive*
Winkler, Agnieszka M. *marketing executive*
Winner, Sonya D. *lawyer*
Wirum, Andrea A. *lawyer*
Wong, Linda Yunwai *nurse*
Woo Ho, Doreen *investment banker*
Wu-Chu, Stella Chwenyea *nutritionist, consultant*
Yellen, Janet Louise *bank executive*
Zeldin, Kim S. *lawyer*

San Gabriel
Tomich-Bolognesi, Vera *education educator*

San Jacinto
Smith, Diane Jans *librarian, educator*
Stange, Sharon (Sherri) *science educator*

San Jose
Abbott, Barbara Louise *artist, educator*
Ammon, Carol Kay *social worker*
Boac, Thelma Blantucas *principal*
Bodensteiner, Lisa M. *utilities executive, lawyer*
Bostrom, Susan L. *marketing executive*
Burkhart, Sandra Marie *art dealer*
Connors, Mary Jean *communications executive*
Cottle, Karen Olson *lawyer*
Curtis, Ann B. *utilities executive*
Dalis, Irene *mezzo soprano, performing arts association administrator*
Duncan, Gloria Celestine *elementary school educator, consultant*
Fiedler, Lois Jean *psychologist, educator*
Gallo, Joan Rosenberg *lawyer*
Goldberg, Susan *editor*
Hernandez, Jo Farb *museum director, consultant*
Ho, Yinhsin *retired mathematician, artist*
Holyer, Erna Maria *adult education educator, writer, artist*
Lawrence, Deborah Jean *quality assurance professional*
Light, Jane Ellen *librarian*
Lobig, Janie Howell *special education educator*
Ma, Xing *optical engineer*
McDowell, Jennifer *sociologist, composer, playwright*
Mendoza, Martha *reporter*
Migielicz, Geralyn *photojournalist*
Monia, Joan *retired management consultant*
Moore, Melanie Ruth *medical technician*
Muller, Carol Blue *former academic administrator, nonprofit organization executive, consultant*
Nardi, Glen *publishing executive*
Okerlund, Arlene Naylor *academic administrator, writer*
Papalias, Tamara Ahrens *electrical engineer, educator*
Prestine, Joan Singleton *writer, educator, editor*
Purpura, Grace *artist, retired art educator*
Rose, Virginia Shottenhamer *secondary school educator*
Selinger, Patricia Griffiths *computer science professional*
Stapleton, Beverly Cooper *aerospace executive*
Stevens, Dorothy Frost *retired television producer*
Tabbut, Loreen M. *power industry executive*
Thaler-DeMers, Debra *clinical nurse*
Thompson, Jan Newstrom *art historian, educator*
Warner, Mary Louise *literature and language professor*
Weiss, Elizabeth *anthropologist, educator*
Whitman, Margaret C. (Meg Whitman) *Internet company executive*
Williams, Suzanne *writer, community volunteer*

San Juan Bautista
McGovern, Rebecca Maples *chamber of commerce executive*

San Juan Capistrano
Beemer, Margaret (Peggy) *history educator*
Ealy, Cynthia Pike *artist, real estate agent*
Larwood, Susan Elizabeth *elementary school educator*
White, Beverly Jane *cytogeneticist*

San Leandro
Chohlis, Dana Marie *school system administrator, theater director*

San Lorenzo
Olivier, Samara Lynn *music educator*

San Luis Obispo
Dalton, Linda Catherine *university administrator*
Dickerson, Colleen Bernice Patton *artist, educator*
Gardebring, Sandra S. *academic administrator*
Graham, Priscilla Mann *librarian*
Holder, Elaine Edith *psychologist, educator*
Kulp, Bette Joneve *retired educator, wallpaper installation business owner*
McQuaid, Patricia A. *information systems educator*
Nicholson, Bernice Loughran *art educator*
Waldo, Anna Lee *retired science educator, writer*

San Luis Rey
Williams, Elizabeth Yahn *writer, educator, lawyer*

San Marcos
Ball, Betty Jewel *retired social worker, consultant*
Ciurczak, Alexis *librarian*
Dowey, Ana L. *microbiologist, educator*
Fabry, Victoria Joan *biology professor*
Gilson, Susan Lee *performing arts educator*
Haynes, Karen Sue *academic administrator, educator*
Melcher, Trini Urtuzuastegui *retired finance educator*
Rolle-Rissetto, Silvia *foreign languages educator, writer, artist*
Watts, Jill Marie *history educator*
Winebrenner, Susan Kay *writer, consultant*

San Marino
Gouw, Julia Suryapranata *bank executive*
Martin, Olivia Jean *social studies educator*
Medici, Rochelle *psychologist, brain researcher*
Robertson, Mary Louise *archivist, historian*
Santoso, Michelle Jo *music educator, pianist*
Sherwood, Midge *writer*
Stefansson, Wanda Gae *language educator, literature educator*

San Mateo
Burzik, Catherine M. *pharmaceutical executive*
Huxley, Mary Atsuko *artist*
Infante, Beatriz V. *information technology executive*
Leong, Carol Jean *electrologist*
Mark, Lois Nora *psychotherapist, consultant*
Pileggi, Jennifer Wendy *transportation services executive*
Reider, Suzie *Internet company executive, marketing professional*
Trubow, Susan Elizabeth *visual artist, educator*

San Pablo
Maguire, Roberta Joan *elementary school educator, writer*

San Pedro
Bailey, Dorothy Jean *secondary school educator, consultant*
Ingerson, Nancy Nina Moore *special education educator*
Lowrey, Lida Miller *artist*
McMullen, Sharon Joy Abel *retired marriage and family therapist*
Parkhurst, Violet Kinney *artist*

San Rafael
Adcock, Muriel W. *special education educator*
Barker, Celeste Arlette *computer scientist*
Bartz, Carol A. *computer software company executive*
Blakeslee, Helen P. *columnist*
Gordon, Sharon J. *special education educator*
Keegan, Jane Ann *insurance executive, consultant*
Marcus, Adrianne Stuhl *writer*
Marsh, Marian E. *voice educator*
Sterling, Marcia Kemp *lawyer*
Thelen, Phyllis B. *artist*
Thomas, Mary Ann McCrary *counselor, school system administrator*
Tosti, Annette Brewer *artist*

Walker, Mary Alexander *writer*
Yates, Margaret Marlene *psychologist*

San Ramon
Cronin, Patricia Romero *computer company executive*
Jue, Susan Lynne *interior designer*
King Hauser, Ann Marie B. *retired controller, artist, realtor*
Yarrington, Patricia *oil industry executive*
Zygocki, Rhonda I. *oil industry executive*

San Ysidro
Schneider, Christine Lynn *customs inspector*

Santa Ana
Barry, Mary H. *college official*
Breeden, Carolyn Sullivan *dean, educator, interior designer, consultant*
Cohen-Strong, Elayne Barbara *director, educator*
Hope, Kathryn Mary *management consultant*
Katz, Tonnie *newspaper editor*
Klassen, Margreta *clinical psychologist, educator*
Lawson, Barbara Slade *elementary school educator, artist*
Martin, Felicia Dottore *mental health services professional, marriage and family therapist*
Mass, Sharon *social worker*
Moore, Eileen C. *judge, prosecutor*
Myers, Marilyn Gladys *pediatric hematologist, oncologist*
Oberstein, Marydale *geriatric specialist*
Prizio, Betty J. *volunteer, retired property manager*
Salem, Karen E. *information technology executive*
Stern, Sherry Ann *journalist*
Storer, Maryruth *law librarian*
Stotler, Alicemarie Huber *federal judge*
Torrez, Caroline Herminia *human resources specialist, director, actress, musician, singer, dancer*
Wilson, Beth A. *college official*

Santa Barbara
Behrens, June Adelle *writer*
Ben-Dor, Gisselle *conductor, musician*
Bischel, Margaret DeMeritt *physician, consultant*
Burns, Melinda *journalist*
Cathcart, Linda *art historian*
Cunningham, Julia Woolfolk *author*
Dirlam, Sharon Joan *writer*
Gallo, Marta Irene *retired language educator*
Gold, Calla Giselle *jewelry designer*
Göllner, Marie Louise *musicologist, retired educator*
Guerrini, Anita *historian, educator*
Harwick, Betty Corinne Burns *sociology educator*
Hayward, Jean *artist, musician, interior designer, performance artist*
Higgins, Isabelle Jeanette *retired librarian*
Horne, Marilyn Berneice *mezzo-soprano*
Jovanovic, Lois *medical researcher*
Kirkpatrick, Diane Yvonne *retired speech pathology/audiology services professional*
Larsen Hoeckley, Cheri Lin *language educator*
Larsgaard, Mary Lynette *librarian, writer*
Longo, Perie Jane *marriage and family therapist*
Mack, Judith Cole Schrim *retired political scientist*
Mahlendorf, Ursula Renate *literature educator*
Mathews, Barbara Edith *gynecologist*
McCaw, Wendy Petrak *publishing executive*
McCoy, Lois Clark *retired social services administrator, retired county official, editor*
McKee, Kathryn Dian Grant *human resources consultant*
Menkin, Eva L. *marriage and family therapist*
Mitchell, Shawne Maureen *author*
Molad, Clarisse Behar *writer, consultant*
Norris, Virginia Oakley *secondary school educator*
Nyborg, Vanessa Marie *psychologist, researcher, educator*
Obern, Vivian Marie *volunteer*
Rosen, Adele R. *interior designer*
Sebastian, Suzie *television producer*
Tettegah, Sharon Yvonne *secondary school educator*
Tucker, Shirley Lois Cotter *botanist, educator*
Weidemann, Celia Jean *social sciences educator, management consultant, financial consultant*

Santa Clara
Bell, Genevieve *anthropologist*
Chastain, Brandi Denise *professional soccer player*
Dai, Weili *information technology executive*
DeBartolo-York, Denise *sports team executive*
Dorchak, Glenda *electronics company executive*
Dunbar, Mary Judith *literature and language professor*
Gilbert, Lucia Albino *psychology professor*
Glancy, Dorothy Jean *lawyer, educator*
Hofstetter, Jane Robinson *artist, educator*
Hopkinson, Shirley Lois *library and information scientist, educator*
Jones, Kim *computer company executive*
Kiyota, Melodee Yoko *secondary school educator*
Lane, Holly Diana *artist*
Murray, Patricia *electronics company executive*
Peterson, Marissa *information technology executive*
Shavers, Cheryl L. *technology and business consultant*
Simmons, Janet Bryant *writer, publishing executive*
Stahl, Barbara E. *school counselor, consultant*
Talbot, Nyna Lucille *psychologist, writer*

Santa Clarita
Earnest-Rahman, Michelle L. *psychologist*
Sturges, Sherry Lynn *recording industry executive*

Santa Cruz
Bell, Clare Louise *writer, engineer*
Davis, Angela Yvonne *political activist, educator, writer*
Delaney, Margaret L. *academic administrator*
Faber, Sandra Moore *astronomer, educator*
Langenheim, Jean Harmon *biologist, educator*
Leites, Barbara L. (Ara Leites) *artist, educator*
Lenox, Catherine Corneau *volunteer*
Martinez, Alma R. *actress, theater director, educator*
Max, Claire Ellen *physicist*
Pletsch, Marie Eleanor *plastic surgeon*
Ripma, Mary *librarian*
Roby, Pamela Ann *sociologist, educator*
Sherman, Frieda Frances *writer*
Shorenstein, Rosalind Greenberg *internist*
Suckiel, Ellen Kappy *philosophy educator*
Welborn, Victoria Lee *science librarian, educator*

Santa Fe Springs
Pina, Martha Elaine *social worker, marriage and family therapist*

Santa Maria
Bowker, Margaret Sheard *artist*
Frith, Anna Barbara *artist*
Hoyt, Mary G(enevieve) *artist, educator*
Sparks, Jeanne *columnist, photographer, educator*

Santa Monica
Abarbanel, Gail *social services administrator, educator*
Aki, Angela *singer*
Amerian, Mary Lee *physician*
Anthony, Polly *broadcast executive*
Apple, Fiona (Fiona Apple Maggart) *singer, songwriter*
Archambault, Nicole Marie *speech pathology/audiology services professional, consultant*
Carr, Ruth Margaret *plastic surgeon*
Curran, Leigh *actress, playwright*
de La Vega, Dianne Winifred DeMarinis (Mrs. Jorge de La Vega) *government official*
Eizenberg, Julie *architect*
Ellickson, Phyllis Lynn *political scientist*
Eve, (Eve Jihan Jeffers) *rap artist, actress*
Feniger, Susan *chef, television personality, writer*
Fisher, Frances *actress*
Foley, Jane Deborah *foundation executive*
Frot-Coutaz, Cecile *television producer*
Gantley, Judy Ann *elementary school educator, retired music educator*
Gray, Laura B. *psychology professor, counselor*
Hannigan, Alyson *actress*
Haroon, Nasreen *artist*
Heimbuch, Babette E. *bank executive*
Huffington, Arianna (Arianna Stassinopoulos) *writer*
Intriligator, Devrie Shapiro *physicist*
Jeffers, Susan Jane *publishing executive, writer*
Jones, Janet Dulin *scriptwriter, film producer*
Katina, Elena Sergejevna *singer*
Kelley, Wendy Thue *fine arts advisor, curator*
Kennedy, Kathleen *film producer*
Kline, Margaret *chemistry professor*
Lee, Elizabeth Younju *apparel designer, design educator*
Lehman, Ellen J. *psychologist*
Louis-Dreyfus, Julia *actress*
Ly, Vi Kim *artist, educator*
Magnabosco-Bower, Jennifer Lynn *mental health services professional*
Malmstrom Lakeman, Dorothy E. *psychologist*
Marcil, Vanessa *actress*
McGlynn, Elizabeth A. *health policy analyst*
Meany, Angelina Marie *dancer, educator*
Milliken, Mary Sue *chef, television personality, writer*
Osbourne, Sharon Arden *music manager, television personality*
Rice, Pamela Ann *marriage and family therapist*
Roney, Alice Lorraine Mann *poet*
Shamban, Ava T. *dermatologist*
Shiffrin, Nancy *writer, educator*
Simpson, India.Arie *musician*
Snedaker, Catherine Raupagh (Kit Snedaker) *editor*
Sohaili, Monira *retired special education educator*
Soloff, Laura J. *academic administrator*
Spataro, Janie Dempsey Watts *freelance/self-employed writer*
Summer, Donna (La Donna Adrian Gaines) *singer, songwriter, actress*
Timmer, Barbara *state agency administrator*
Volkova, Julia Olegovna *singer*
Wong, Diana Shui Iu *artist*

Santa Paula
Broughton, Margaret Martha *mental health nurse*

Santa Rosa
Carlson-Sweet, Kim Lynette *dermatologist*
Cheung, Judy Hardin *retired special education educator*
Fields, Tina Rae *artist, ecopsychologist*
Foster, Lucille Caster *retired school system administrator*
Fruiht, Dolores Giustina *artist, educator, poet*
Jandrey, Becky Lee *psychologist*
Jones, Doris (Anna Doris Vogel) *retail buyer*
Monk, Diana Charla *small business owner*
Nickens, Catherine Arlene *retired nurse, freelance writer*
O'Donnell, Anne U. *dietician*
Rogers, Natalie *psychologist*
Smith, Fredrika Patchett *retired pediatrician*
Wartman, Mary Jane *family practice nurse practitioner*
Weare, Sally Spiegel *artist, educator*

Santee
Schenk, Susan Kirkpatrick *nursing educator, consultant, small business owner*

Saratoga
Barna, Lillian Carattini *school system administrator*
Chisholm, Margaret Elizabeth *retired library director*
deBarling, Ana Maria *language educator*
Stutzman, Gladys Blanche *retired secondary school educator, journalist*

Sausalito
Casals, Rosie *retired professional tennis player*
Groah, Linda Kay *nursing administrator, educator*

Seal Beach
Dunckley, Victoria Lynn *psychiatrist*

Seaside
Taylor, Lula Yvonne *music educator*

Sebastopol
Arnold, Marsha Diane *writer*
Filshie, Michele Ann *editor*
Grimmer, Margot *dancer, choreographer, director*
Marler, Joan *writer, educator*

Shasta Lake
Parsons, Debra Lea *elementary school educator*

Sherman Oaks
Alcott-Jardine, Susan *artist, writer*
Clark, Susan (Nora Goulding) *actress*
Endlich, Lili *psychotherapist*
Ferguson, Lisa Beryl *accountant*
Gross, Sharon Ruth *forensic psychologist, researcher*
Leighton, Carolyn *foundation administrator*
Levin, Evanne Lynn *lawyer, educator*
Levine, Allison *psychotherapist*
Norwood, Brandy Rayana (Brandy) *singer, actress*
Schlessinger, Laura *radio talk show host*
Stein, Kira D. *psychiatrist*
Taylor, Elizabeth (Dame Elizabeth Rosemond Taylor) *actress*

Signal Hill
James, Ann *physical therapist*

Simi Valley
Cirocco, Angela V. *adult education educator*
Eberhard-Neveaux, Christine *aviation executive, dispute resolution executive*
Erzinger, Kathy McClam *nursing educator*
Mikesell, Mary (Jane Mikesell) *psychotherapist*

Solana Beach
Culley, Deborah Anita *science educator*

Solvang
Rymer, Ilona Suto *artist, retired educator*

Somis
Premack, Ann J. *writer*

Sonoma
Fellows, Alice Combs *artist*
Fong, Edna M. *retired physician*
Hobart, Billie *education educator, consultant*
Huguenard, Joan *writer*
Kizer, Carolyn Ashley *poet, educator*
Minelli, Helene Marie *artist*
Pollack, Phyllis Addison *ballerina*
Racke, Anne Moller *winery executive*
Weinberger, Lilla Gilbrech *bookseller*

Sonora
Clarke, Paula Katherine *anthropologist, researcher, social studies educator*
Jones, Georgia Ann *publisher*
Mathias, Betty Jane *communications and community affairs consultant, editor, educator, writer*
McClymonds, Jean Ellen *marketing professional*
Padgett, Kathryn Ann Weiner *medical association administrator, special education educator*
Sonderman, Elizabeth Louise *literature and language educator, writer*

South Lake Tahoe
Nason, Rochelle *conservation organization administrator*

South Pasadena
Bernal, Harriet Jean Daniels *real estate agent*
Bishop, Carole C. *elementary school educator*
Bortell, Linda Lee *clinical psychologist*
Fuller, Kathy J. *special education educator, consultant, researcher*
Mantell, Suzanne Ruth *editor*
Yett, Sally Pugh *art educator, consultant*

South San Francisco
Desmond-Hellmann, Susan *medical products manufacturing executive*
Goldman, Barbara Bay *physical therapist*
Potter, Myrtle S. *research and development company executive*
Ruggles, Sandra Waugh *biophysicist*

Spring Valley
Heinecke, Margaret Theresa *librarian*
Roberts, Carolyn June *real estate broker*
Siddiqui, Razia Sultana *retired psychotherapisst, educator*
Soltero, Michelle Dolores *director*
Worley, Kathryn Ann *secondary school educator*

Stanford
Alexander, Janet Cooper *law educator*
Arvin, Ann Margaret *microbiology and immunology educator, researcher*
Babcock, Barbara Allen *lawyer, educator*
Ball, Arnetha *education educator*
Barron, Brigid *education educator*
Blau, Helen Margaret *pharmacology educator*
Boaler, Jo *education educator*
Bresnan, Joan W. *literature and language professor*
Brooks, Helen Bousky *literature and language professor, performing arts educator*
Corn, Wanda Marie *art educator*
Daily, Gretchen Cara *ecologist, environmental services administrator*
Derksen, Charlotte Ruth Meynink *librarian*
Donaldson, Sarah Susan *radiologist*
Francke, Uta *geneticist, educator*
Fried, Barbara H. *law educator*
Hensler, Deborah Rosenfield *law educator*
Jacobs, Charlotte De Croes *medical educator, oncologist*
Karlan, Pamela Susan *law educator*
Keren, Kinneret *biophysicist*
Koller, Daphne *computer scientist*
Kraemer, Helena Antoinette Chmura *psychiatry educator*
Loeb, Susanna *education educator*
Long, Sharon Rugel *dean, molecular biologist, educator*
Lotan, Rachel *education educator*
Maccoby, Eleanor Emmons *psychology professor*
Marsh, Martha H. *hospital administrator*
Martin, Joanne *social sciences educator*
Martinez, Jenny S. *lawyer*
Matson, Pamela Anne *environmental scientist, science educator*
Maxmin, Jody Lewis *art educator*
Mitchell, Beverly Shriver *hematologist, oncologist, educator*
Newman-Gordon, Pauline *French language and literature educator*
Paté-Cornell, Marie-Elisabeth Lucienne *finance educator, engineering educator*
Payne, Anita Hart *reproductive endocrinologist, researcher*
Polan, Mary Lake *obstetrics and gynecology educator*
Radin, Margaret Jane *law educator*
Rhode, Deborah Lynn *law educator*
Ricardo-Campbell, Rita *economist, educator*
Shapiro, Lucy *molecular biology educator*
Srikantiah, Jayashri *law educator*
Stipek, Deborah Jane *dean, education educator*
Strober, Myra Hoffenberg *education educator, consultant*
Suppes, Christine Johnson *publishing executive*
Theriot, Julie *microbiologist, medical educator*
Tomlin, Claire J. *aeronautical engineer, educator*
Traugott, Elizabeth Closs *linguist, educator, researcher*
Whittemore, Alice *biostatistician*
Wotipka, Christine Min *education educator*
Zhou, Ping *physical engineer*

Stinson Beach
Metz, Mary Seawell *retired foundation administrator, retired academic administrator*

Stockton
Acoba, Valerie Lee *performing arts educator*
Bickford, Melissa A. *computer scientist*
Blodgett, Elsie Grace *small business owner, property manager*
Cobb, Judy Lynn *elementary school educator*
Cooper, Iva Jean *special education educator*
Ford, Shirley Griffin *science educator, pharmacist*
Fung, Rosaline Lee *language educator*
Gottfried, Rosalind B. *humanities educator*
Hackley, Carol Ann *public relations educator, consultant*
Haines, Joybelle *retired elementary school educator*
Henderson, Elma Mae *singer, composer, educator, dancer, actress*
Hitchcock, Susan Y. *principal*
Jackson, Jewel *retired state agency administrator*
Jacobs, Marian *advertising executive*
Kizer, Nancy Anne *music educator, musician*
Lin-Cereghino, Joan *science educator*
Magness, Rhonda Ann *retired microbiologist*
Mann, Tori *secondary school educator*
Matuszak, Alice Jean Boyer *pharmacy educator*
McCarty, Lois Leone *retired sociologist*
Meissner, Katherine Gong *municipal official*
Niles, Joyce Lynn *writer, editor, consultant*
Norton, Linda Lee *pharmacist, educator*
Nusz, Phyllis Jane *not-for-profit fundraiser, consultant, educational consultant*
Roll, Renée F. *retired psychologist, publishing executive*
Sampson, Lynette Diane *secondary school educator*
Wilcox, Helena Marguerita (Rita) *music educator*
Wright, Evelyn Louise *artist*

Studio City
Basinger, Kim (Kimila Ann Basinger) *actress*
Boyett, Joan Reynolds *performing company executive*
Chambers, Clytia Montllor *retired public relations consultant*
Childs, Erin Therese *psychotherapist*
Gallardo, Sandra Silvana *television producer, actress*
King, Carole (Carole Klein) *lyricist, singer*
Lasarow, Marilyn Doris *artist, educator*
Manders, Susan Kay *artist*
Mc Donald, Meg *public relations executive*
Moseley, Chris Rosser *marketing executive*
Rogers, Suzanne C. *actress*
Weiner, Sandra Samuel *critical care nurse, consultant*
White, Julie *actress*
Wilson, Peta *actress*

Sugarloaf
Black, Victoria Lynn *writer, artist*

Suisun City
Altier, Judith Barrett *middle school educator*

Sun City
Schmoll, Edith Margaret *music educator*

Sun Valley
Gilmore, Dawn S. *music educator*

Sunnyvale
Briody, Lynn *municipal official*
Castro, Christine *Internet company executive*
Daltchev, Ana Ranguel *sculptor*
Decker, Sue (Susan L. Decker) *Internet company executive*
Dunaway, Cammie *marketing executive*
Garner, Shirley Imogene *retired music educator*
Lanaro, Clara Marrama *music educator, writer*
Merrill, Wendy Jane *financial services company executive*
Perdikou, Kim *information technology executive*
Sartain, Libby *human resources specialist*
Schneider, Hilary A. *Internet company executive*
Vettel, Cheryl Elynore *mathematics educator*
White, Christine A. *internist, oncologist, pharmaceutical executive*

Sunol
Rebello, Marlene Munson *speech pathologist*

Sutter Creek
Sanders, Elizabeth Anne Weaver (Betsy Sanders) *management consultant, writer*

Sylmar
Corry, Dalila Boudjellal *internist, educator*
Faye, Thalia Garin *retired microbiologist, educator*
Powers, Mala *actress*
Tully, Susan Balsley *pediatrician, educator*
Valdez, Denise *newscaster*

Taft
Lose, Cynthia A. *psychologist, educator*
Payne, Ruby Mae *secondary school educator*
Walters-Trapasso, Susan Diane *secondary school educator*

Tarzana
Easton, Sheena *rock vocalist, actress*
Neece, Olivia Helene Ernst *investment company executive, consultant*
Rinsch, Maryann Elizabeth *occupational therapist*

Tehachapi
Sprinkle, Martha Clare *elementary school educator*

Temecula
Arban, Diana Marie *social sciences educator*
Bathaee, Soussan *engineering technician*
Bauer, Judy Marie *minister*
Cherrington, Pamela Jo *special education educator*
Dolan-Jimenez, Mary F. *elementary school educator*
Hogerheiden, Lauren Michelle Valencia *secondary school educator*
Keenan, Retha Ellen Vornholt *retired nursing educator*
Lozosky, Lisa Lynn *music educator, elementary school educator*

Temple City
Young, Victoria *medical/surgical and oncology nurse*

Templeton
Foster-Wells, Karen Margaret *artist*

The Sea Ranch
Baas, Jacquelynn *museum director, art historian*

Thermal
Montoya, Leiala *assistant principal*

Thousand Oaks
Helton, Patricia Beth *realtor*
Herman, Joan Elizabeth *health insurance company executive*
Lieberman, Judith L. *retired special education educator*
Miller, Elizabeth Joan *artist, guidance counselor*
Mulkey, Sharon Renee *gerontology nurse*
Pakula, Anita Susan *dermatologist*
Scott, Mary Celine *pharmacologist*
Shannon, Barbara Helen *secondary school educator*
Shirley, Courtney Dymally *nurse*
Venable, Diane Dailey *retired elementary school educator*
Zhou, Sophia Huai *biomedical engineering scientist*

Toluca Lake
Ragan, Ann Talmadge *media and production consultant, actor*

Torrance
Birnbaumer, Diane Margaret *emergency physician, educator*
Blumenfeld, Anita *community relations consultant*
Brasel, Jo Anne *pediatrician, educator*
Brown, Adriane M. *aerospace transportation executive*
Ebeling, Vicki *marriage and family therapist, writer*
Enright, Stephanie Veselich *investment company executive, financial consultant*
Mesquita, Rosalyn *artist, educator*
Sorstokke, Susan Eileen *systems engineer*
Steckel, Julie Raskin *psychotherapist, lecturer, consultant*

Trabuco Canyon
Addy, Jo Alison Phears *economist*

Tracy
Kiggins, Mildred L. *marketing professional*
Raco, Ellen *secondary school educator*

Truckee
Otto, Christine Barnard *educational association administrator*
Todd, Linda Marie *nutrition researcher, circulation manager, financial consultant, pilot*

Tujunga
Pozzo, Mary Lou *retired librarian, writer*

Tulare
Hefflefinger, Clarice Thorpe *retired real estate broker*
Pinto, Marie Malania *academic administrator, consultant*
Vickrey, Herta M. *microbiologist*

Turlock
Antoniuk, Verda JoAnne *secondary school educator*

Tustin
Greene, Wendy Segal *retired special education educator*
Post, Shawn Marie *elementary school educator*

Ukiah
Newell, Barbara Ann *coatings company executive*
Niquette, Geraldine Norma *marriage and family therapist*

Union City
Baker, Vicki L. *science educator*
Fong, Elaine Susan *middle school educator*
Lockhart, Patsy Marie *secondary school educator, consultant*

Universal City
Bromstad, Angela *broadcast executive*
Cross, Marcia *actress*
Hammer, Bonnie *broadcast executive*
Hatcher, Teri *actress*
Huffman, Felicity (Flicka Huffman) *actress*
Langley, Donna *film company executive*
Longoria, Eva (Eva Jacqueline Longoria, Eva Longoria Christopher) *actress*
Menendez, Belinda *broadcast executive*
Merkerson, S. Epatha *actress*
Parent, Mary *film company executive*
Press, Terry *marketing executive*
Randall, Karen *film company executive*
Rocco, Nikki *film company executive*
Schulz, Diana *film company executive*
Sheridan, Nicolette *actress*
Woodard, Alfre *actress*

Upland
Barden, Shirley Ramsey *credit union executive*
Bast, Karolyn Anne (Kay Bast) *dance educator, choreographer*
Ford, Cheryl Anisia *elementary school educator*

Vacaville
Beals, Nancy Lunsford *photographer*

Valencia
Anguiano, Lupe *advocate*
Parks, Suzan Lori *playwright*

Vallejo
Murillo, Carol Ann *secondary school educator*
Toms, Kathleen Moore *nurse*
Wilson, Carrie Lee Stroud *principal*

Valley Center
Saffiote, Linda *secondary school educator*

Valley Glen
Corinblit, Nita Green *artist, educator*

Valley Village
Barkin, Elaine Radoff *composer*
Carabillo, Virginia Anne (Toni Carabillo) *writer, editor, graphic designer*
Diller, Phyllis (Phyllis Ada Driver Diller) *actress, writer*

Van Nuys
Boone, Deborah Ann (Debby Boone) *singer*
Cook, Jenik Esterm (Jenik Esterm Cook Simonian) *artist, educator*
Vasilyeva, Anna *artist, writer*

Vandenberg Afb
Huggins, Elaine Jacqueline *nurse, retired military officer*

Venice
Alf, Martha Joanne *artist*
Beery-Polglase, Penelope (Pixie) *education educator*
Greenfield, Patricia Ann Marks *psychology educator*
Rudnick, Pesha Eva *theater director*
Smith, Barbara T. *artist, educator*

Ventura
Armstrong, Dianne Owens *language educator*
Bircher, Andrea Ursula *psychiatric mental health clinical nurse specialist*
Cutler, Carole Marie *music educator*
Kreissman, Starrett *librarian*
White, Colleen Toy *judge*
Zuber, Norma Keen *career counselor, educator*

Victorville
Kildal, Lori Ann *dean*
McGulpin, Elizabeth Jane *nurse*
Moses, Gaye Anita *elementary school educator*
Polley-Shellcroft, Theresa Diane *art educator*
Wristen, Nyala Colleen *elementary school educator*
Yochem, Barbara June (Runyan) *sales executive, lecturer*

Visalia
Allstedt, Nora Marie *music educator*
Caldwell, Marcia Diane *nurse*
Porterfield-Pyatt, Chaumonde R. *music educator, advocate*
Taylor, Helen Shields *civic worker*

Vista
Cannon, Kathleen *lawyer, educator*
Ferguson, Margaret Ann *tax specialist, consultant*
Harper, Donna Marie *elementary education and performing arts educator, consultant, special education educator*
Linhart, Letty Lemon *editor*
Savage, Linda Eileen *psychologist*
Tadeo, Elvia *artist*

Volcano
Stone, Karen G. *writer*

Walnut
Anderson, Cynthia Boot *biological science educator*
Sholars, Joan Dianne *mathematics professor*
Tan, Colleen Woo *communications educator*

Walnut Creek
Alexandra, Allison Melissa *artist, writer, educator*
Ausenbaum, Helen Evelyn *social worker, psychologist*
Cannon, Grace Bert *retired immunologist*
Carver, Dorothy Lee Eskew (Mrs. John James Carver) *retired secondary school educator*
Elliott, Margaret S. *science educator*
Fielding, Elizabeth Brown *education educator*
Fowler, Carol W. *journalist, educator*
Grandi, Lois A. *theater director, choreographer, actor*
Lilly, Luella Jean *retired academic administrator*
Mackay, Patricia McIntosh *psychotherapist*
Reimann, Arline Lynn *artist*
Sheen, Portia Yunn-ling *retired physician*
Van Noy, Christine Ann *restaurateur*

Watsonville
McBride, Susan Alyse *interior designer, consultant*
West, Karrie L. *school psychologist*

Weed
Mann, Karen *consultant, educator*
Schaefer, M. Elaine *music educator, conductor*

West Covina
Adams, Sarah Virginia *psychotherapist, family counselor*
Kennelley, Rosario Catherine *secondary school educator*
Montooth, Sheila Christine *state agency administrator*

West Hills
Abdo, Lynda Lee *art director*
Cheney, Anna Marie Jangula *retired medical/surgical nurse*
Duzy, Merrilyn Jeanne *artist, educator*
Parisio, Tamara Lynn *marketing professional*
Todd, Katherine Laws *filmmaker, retired writer, human resources specialist*

West Hollywood
Bassett, Angela *actress*
Baxter, Meredith *actress*
Berry, Halle Maria *actress*
Cole, Natalie Maria *singer*
Dorn, Dolores *actress*
Franklyn, Audrey Pozen *talent promoter, television personality*
Geddes, Ann *talent agency director*
Goin, Suzanne *chef*
Harry, Deborah Ann *singer*
Kingsley, Patricia *public relations executive*
Mulgrew, Katherine Kiernan (Kate Mulgrew) *actress*
Peyton, Elizabeth Joy *writer, painter*
Presley, Priscilla (Pricilla Ann Wagner, Priscilla Beaulieu Presley) *actress*
Romijn, Rebecca *actress, model*
Shearmur, Alli *broadcast executive*

West Sacramento
Teel, Joyce Raley *retail executive*

Westchester
Capetillo, Charlene Vernelle *music educator, special education educator*

Westlake Village
Steadman, Lydia Duff *symphony violinist, retired elementary school educator*
Troxell, Lucy Davis *management consultant*
Weiss, Barbara G. *artist*

Westminster
Nguyen, Lan Thi Hoang *physician, educator*
Pitts-Cutler, Melissa Anne *counselor, social worker*

Whittier
Benavides, Greta Louise *elementary school educator, entrepreneur*
Harvey, Patricia Jean *retired special education services professional*
McKenna, Jeanette Ann *archaeologist*
Reid, Ivonne Figueroa *language educator*
Weismiller, Eleanor Kovacs *library director*
Williams, Jennifer Catherine *elementary school educator*

Williams
Knight, Katherine Ellen *science educator, mathematics educator*

Willits
Handley, Margie Lee *manufacturing executive*
Koliner, Frances Eloise *educational administrator*

Wilmington
Borell, Mary Putnam *language educator, playwright*
Smith, June Burlingame *English educator*

Wilton
Abraham, Bondi Corinne *artist*

Winchester
Ucmakli, Naciye Gunger *oncologist*

Windsor
Matkin, Judith Conway *product designer*

Winters
Paul, Sally Jones *secondary school educator, writer*

Woodland
Bauer, Cynthia Renae *nurse*

Woodland Hills
Berry, Carol Ann *insurance company executive*
Clarey, Patricia T. *health insurance company executive, former state official*
Goins, Jessica D. *editor*
Harris, Barbara S. *publishing executive, editor-in-chief*
Jason, Sonya *writer*
Mund, Geraldine *judge*
Pollock, Vicki Eileen *psychologist*
Rafter, Tracy *publishing executive*
Russell, Anne M. *editor-in-chief*
Stahlecker, Barbara Jean *marketing professional, consultant*
Thomsen, Mary Joan Margaret *psychology educator*
Zeitlin, Eugenia Pawlik *librarian, educator, writer*

Yorba Linda
Esparza, Karen Ann *history educator*
Lunde, Dolores Benitez *retired secondary school educator*
Stavropoulos, Rose Mary Grant *community activist, volunteer*

Yreka
Fiock, Shari Lee *marketing professional, consultant*

Yuba City
Leverett, Dawn R. *disability education consultant*
Myers, Nancy Elizabeth *education educator*

Yucaipa
deBaun, Linda Louise *performing arts educator*

COLORADO

Alamosa
Sanchez, Lupita A. *elementary school educator*

Arvada
Bair, Deborah Lynn *primary school educator*
Bert, Carol Lois *retired educational assistant*
Franklin, Tammy *performing arts educator*
Halley, Diane Esther *artist*
Meiklejohn, Mindy June (Lorraine Meiklejohn) *political organizer, realtor*
Moorhead, Jennifer Theresa *art educator*
Vanderkolk, Maria Elizabeth *city official*
Weitzel, Ginger M. *entrepreneur, critical care nurse*

Aspen
Bucksbaum, Melva *foundation administrator*
Newman, Ruth Gallert *psychologist*

Aurora
Berg, Karen Lynn Anderson *elementary school educator*
Bowdish, Colette Elizabeth *secondary school educator*
Brown, Anne Sherwin *speech pathologist, educator*
Churchill, Mair Elisa Annabelle *medical educator*
D'Amico, Sandra Hathaway *art educator*
Doze, Maureen Adele (Maureen Adele Mee) *social studies educator*
Dubuque, Amanda Sue *mental health services professional*
Hamrick, Eliza Carney *secondary school educator, consultant*
Hoffmaster, Nancy Jo Clement *retired social services professional*
Horwitz, Kathryn Bloch *molecular biologist, educator, breast cancer researcher*
Howard, Donna Jean *retired counselor*
Kellogg Fain, Karen *retired history educator*
Martinez-Nemnich, Maricela *realtor*
Miller, Dorothea Helen *librarian, educator*
Miller, Sarah Pearl *librarian*
Morrow, Caroline Donovan *retired social worker*
Muldrow, Elizabeth Smith *retired secondary school educator, minister*
Neville, Margaret Cobb *physiologist, educator*
Nora, Audrey Hart *physician*
Seslar, Tanya L. *music educator*
Seybert, Janet Rose *lawyer, military officer*
Sheffield, Nancy *city agency administrator*
Smith, Elaine Janet *social worker*
Sorenson, Katherine Ann *elementary school educator*
Spring, Kathleen Marie *musical program director, educator*
Suryanarayanan, Sowmya K. *endocrinologist*
Vitanza, Joanne Maria *allergist, pediatrician*
Waite, Cheryl Siebert *history professor, researcher*
Warnell, Rebecca E. *social studies educator*
Wessler, Mary Hraha *real estate company executive*

Bailey
Hoganson, Mary Margaret *librarian*

Basalt
Brune, Michelle L. *literature and language educator*
Stewart, Ann Burgess *elementary school educator*

Bayfield
Korns, Leota Elsie *writer, mountain land developer, insurance broker*

Bennett
Unger Young, Elizabeth (Betty) *hospital chaplain*

Black Hawk
Jones, Linda May *tour guide, writer*

Boulder
Anseth, Kristi S. *tissue engineer, educator*
Bergum, Lauren Jean *art educator*
Bintliff, Barbara Ann *law educator, library director*
Borko, Hilda *education educator*
Charteris, Frances A. *art educator, artist*
Coel, Margaret Speas *writer*
Davidson, Sara *writer*
deKieffer, Kitty *volunteer*
Doebele, Alexa C. *music educator, director*
Edwards, Donna Hohmann *psychologist*
El Mallakh, Dorothea Hendry *editor, publishing executive*
Evans, Claire (Mary Evans) *painter, educator*
Farsi, Carla Emilia *mathematics professor*
Fifkova, Eva *behavioral neuroscience educator*
Foland, Sara *geologist, association executive*
Hall, Joan Lord *language educator, literature educator*
Hayes, Deborah *musicology educator, college administrator*
Healy, Alice Fenvessy *psychology professor, researcher*
Heath, Josephine Ward *foundation administrator*
Hill, Mary C. *hydrologist*
Holdsworth, Janet Nott *women's health nurse*
Joyce, Janet S. *psychologist*

Kaye, Evelyn Patricia (Evelyn Patricia Sarson) *author, publisher, travel expert*
Kennedy, Teresa Jean *academic administrator, educator*
Kenney, Belinda Jill Forseman *information technology executive*
Kotter, Rita Joan *theatre educator, design consultant*
Lacy, Mary T. (Mary Keenan) *prosecutor*
LeMone, Margaret Anne *atmospheric scientist*
Meier, Beverly Joyce Loeffler *science educator, educational consultant*
Menken, Jane Ava *demographer, educator*
Middleton-Downing, Laura *psychiatric social worker, artist, small business owner*
Murnane, Margaret Mary *engineering and physics educator*
Pneuman, Linda Jackson *retired physician*
Princeton, Joy Carol *retired nursing educator*
Roberts, Pamela Ranger *secondary school educator*
Sable, Barbara Kinsey *retired music educator*
Schleiner, Anne-Marie *computer graphics designer*
Verdill, Elaine Denise *artisan*
Wallace, Stephanie Ann *music educator, conductor*
Wertheimer, Marilyn Lou *librarian, educator*

Brighton
Tyrrell-Meier, Cassandra B. *banker*

Broomfield
Flanders, Eleanor Carlson *community volunteer*
Lybarger, Marjorie Kathryn *nurse*

Canon City
Cochran, Susan Mills *research librarian*

Carbondale
Arnold, Kathleen Spelts *academic administrator*
Cowgill, Ursula Moser *biologist, educator, environmental consultant*
Williams, Natasha Bondareva *information scientist, educator*

Cascade
Seger, Linda Sue *script consultant, lecturer, writer*

Castle Rock
Broer, Eileen Dennery *management consultant*
Richardson, Suzanne Mays *communication consultant*
Wilcox, Bonita Diane *middle school educator*

Centennial
Dineen, Bonnie R. *social studies educator*
Galaznik, Judith Ann *elementary school educator*
Haskell, Cheryl Mona *telecommunications industry executive*
Heath, Jayne Marie *music educator*
Messer, Bonnie Jeanne *psychologist*
Wilks, Dana Lyn *protective services official, writer*
Williams, Julie Lynne *music educator*

Cherry Hills Village
Conroy, Mary Elizabeth *history professor*
Stapleton, Katharine Hall (Katie Stapleton) *commentator, writer*

Clifton
McCall, Ruby Elane *music educator*
Taddeo, Lexi-Anne *special education educator*

Colorado Springs
Abbott, Gina *municipal government executive*
Apodaca, Christy McCormick *exercise physiologist, athletic trainer*
Baldvins, Lynn Ann *medical/surgical nurse, army officer*
Barton, Ruth *language educator*
Beard, Amanda *swimmer, Olympic athlete*
Bennett, Brooke *Olympic athlete*
Biggs, Diana *elementary school educator*
Birtwistle, April Joy *layout artist*
Bobek, Nicole *professional figure skater*
Borgen, Irma R. *music educator*
Bowen, Clotilde Marion Dent *retired military officer, psychiatrist*
Bowers, Zella Zane *real estate broker*
Brierre, Micheline *artist*
Buehner, Andrea Ruth *small business owner*
Calvert, Susan Kadey *music educator*
Cash, Swin (Swintayla Marie Cash) *professional basketball player*
Comstock, Diane Elaine *science educator, consultant*
Coughlin, Natalie *Olympic athlete*
Coulter, Carolyn Kay *information technology executive*
Deiotte, Margaret Williams Tukey *nonprofit consultant, grants writer*
DeTurk, Pamela Elizabeth *retired special education educator, elementary school educator*
Farrer, Claire Anne Rafferty *anthropologist, educator*
Gifford, Marilyn Joyce *emergency physician, consultant*
Glenn, Shannon Lea *music educator*
Granato, Catherine (Cammi Granato) *Olympic athlete*
Hawley, Nanci Elizabeth *professional society administrator*
Hinkle, Betty Ruth *retired academic administrator*
Hughes, Sarah *figure skater*
Hyden, Dorothy Louise *consulting company owner*
Johnson, Stephanie L. B. *small business owner, office manager*
Kupets, Courtney *Olympic athlete*
Kwan, Michelle Wing *professional figure skater*
Lang, Naomi *ice skater*
Lang, Ping *former professional volleyball player; head coach Olympic volleyball team*
Leffingwell, Denise C. *social worker*
LeMieux, Linda Dailey *museum director*
Loo, Katherine Haughey *nonprofit organization consultant*
Lyddane, Anne Alexandra *retired writer*
Madsen, Karen F. *retired elementary school educator*
Mangone, JoEllen L. *retired hospital administrator*
May, Misty *Olympic athlete*
McCool, Courtney *Olympic athlete*
McDade, Roberta Clark *secondary school educator*
McDonough, Ann Patrice *ice skater*
Meese, Frances Mildred *library administrator*
Mery, Naomi Marie *music educator*
Miller, Zoya Dickins *civic worker, consultant*
Nikodinov, Angela *professional figure skater, Olympic athlete*
Orner, Linda Price *family therapist, counselor*
Papproth, Jodi Renee *theater educator*
Patterson, Carly *Olympic athlete*
Pfennigs, Kimberly Tucker *nurse*
Rowan, Cynthia L. Reeves *accountant*
Scott, Carla Anne *musician, educator*
Scott, Tiffany *ice skater*
Sherman, Louise Rinkob *special education educator*
Shockley-Zalabak, Pamela Sue *academic administrator*
Skadden, Vanda Sue *retired music educator*
Strickland, Sylvia Raye *social worker*
Swanson, Victoria Clare Heldman *lawyer*
Tabet, Renee' B. *voice educator, director*
Tesman, Laura Lynn *education educator*
Torres, Dara *Olympic athlete*
Tueting, Sarah *professional hockey player*
Varoglu, Mary *wholesale distribution executive*
Walsh, Kerri Lee *Olympic athlete*
Weir, Catherine Grant *psychology educator*
Weslin, Anna Therese *acute care nurse practitioner, dance consultant*
Williams, Ruth Lee *clinical social worker*
Young, Lynn Marie *psychotherapist, freelance artist*

Conifer
Boese, Michelle Lynne *accountant, consultant*

Cortez
Kristin, Karen *artist*

Creede
Gray, Johanna Jill *music educator*
Hague, Angela L. *artist, consultant, art gallery director*
Wintz, Marilyn Belle *retired elementary school educator*

Crested Butte
Baker, Ruth Mary *psychotherapist*

Denver
Albino, Judith Elaine Newsom *university president*
Alvarado, Linda G. *construction executive*
Anderson, Norma V. *retired state legislator*
Bahrych, Sharon *physician assistant*
Barber, Patricia Louise *clinical specialist*
Barr, Lois Faye *public relations executive, freelance/self-employed writer*
Binstock, Sonya (Toni) Katsh *social worker*
Brega, Kerry Elizabeth *physician, researcher*
Buckstein, Caryl Sue *writer*
Burrows, Bertha Jean *retired academic administrator*
Carroll, Kim Marie *nurse*
Chavez, Jeanette *editor*
Childears, Linda *foundation administrator*
Coan, Patricia A. *judge*
Coe, Judith Anne *music educator, composer, performer*
Cohen-Vader, Cheryl Denise *municipal official*
Corathers, Lorna Joan *artist*
Creamer, Deborah *library director, educator*
Dabbs Riley, Jeanne Kernodle *retired public relations executive*
Daley, Ann Scarlett *curator*
Dallas, Sandra *writer*
Dennis, Gigi (Ginette E. Dennis) *state official, former state legislator*
Dickerson, Cynthia Rowe *marketing executive, consultant*
Dicks, Patricia K. *legislative staff member*
Drake, Sylvie (Jurras Drake) *theater critic*
Dunham, Joan Roberts *administrative assistant*
Eckels, Mary Elizabeth *artist*
Ehret, Josephine Mary *microbiologist, researcher*
Enright, Cynthia Lee *illustrator*
Faatz, Jeanne Ryan *councilman*
Faigao, Wendy Kalayaan *musician, music company executive*
Fasel, Ida *literature and language professor, writer*
Fliss, Julia Wade *elementary school educator, poet*
Fogg, Janet *architectural firm executive*
Gabow, Patricia Anne *internist, health facility executive*
Gampel, Elaine Susan *investment company executive, consultant*
Garcia, June Marie *librarian*
Gibson, Elisabeth Jane *retired principal*
Gleason, Cynthia S. *public relations executive, educator*
Goldblatt, Barbara Janet *sex therapist, educator*
Gotlieb, Dorothy A. *deputy commissioner of education*
Gries, Robbie Rice *geologist, gas and petroleum company executive*
Hamm, Suzanne Margaret *psychologist*
Hammerman, Susan Frances Weissfeld *lawyer*
Hanna, Juliet Marie *lawyer*
Hays, Clare A. *veterinarian, biologist, educator*
Heitler, Susan McCrensky *clinical psychologist*
Heppler, Robin Lee *project manager*
Hirschfeld, Arlene *civic worker, former secondary school educator*
Hoffman, Elizabeth *economics professor*
Hotchkiss, Heather A. *social worker, consultant*
Howse, Cathy L. *writer, researcher, entrepreneur*
Huang, Linda Chen *plastic surgeon*
Jarles, Ruth Sewell *education educator*
Jennett, Shirley Shimmick *health facility administrator*
Johnson, Candice Elaine Brown *pediatrician, educator*
Johnson, Geraldine Esch *language specialist*
Johnston, Gwinavere Adams *public relations consultant*
Kaplan, Sandra Lee *artist*
Kendig, Lynne E. *physician*
Kourlis, Rebecca Love *director, former state supreme court justice*
Krendl, Cathy Stricklin *lawyer*
Krieger, Marcia Smith *federal judge*
Kruger, Paula *telecommunications industry executive*
Kundert, Judy A. *writer*
Kurtz, Maxine *personnel director, writer, lawyer*
Landon, Susan Melinda *petroleum geologist*
Langsley, Pauline Royal *psychiatrist*
Larsen, Letitia (Tish) Hoyt *history educator*
Lincoln, Sarah *social worker*
Linville, Susan Elizabeth *film studies educator*
Low, Merry Cook *civic worker*
Lundy, Barbara Jean *training services executive*
Mackey, Pamela Robillard *lawyer*
Marrack, Philippa Charlotte *immunologist, researcher*
Mathis, Karen J. *lawyer, legal association administrator*
Maul, Carol Elaine *small business owner*
McDowell, Karen Ann *lawyer*
Mencer, Sue (Constance Suzanne Mencer) *former federal agency administrator*
Meyer, Norma *secondary school educator*
Muja, Kathleen Ann *state official, consultant*
Mukherjee, Gopa *psychiatrist, educator*
Mullarkey, Mary J. *state supreme court chief justice*
Narey, Martha Adele Catherine *biomedical equipment technician, geography educator*
Nelson, Sarah Milledge *archaeology educator*
Nemiro, Beverly Mirium Anderson *author, educator*
Newberry, Elizabeth Carter *greenhouse and floral company owner*
Norton, Jane E. (Jane Bergman) *lieutenant governor*
Orullian, B. LaRae *bank executive*
O'Sullivan, Blythe Ann *marketing executive*
Payton, Cydney *museum director, curator*
Pegues, JoAnn *dietician*
Phillips, Dorothy Reid *retired medical library technician*
Plummer, Ora Beatrice *nursing educator, consultant*
Pollard, Marilyn Bergkamp *retired utility company executive*
Porter, Donna Jean *genealogist*
Post, Robin Dee *psychologist*
Regensteiner, Judith Gail *science educator, research scientist*
Rice, Nancy E. *state supreme court justice*
Robins, Judy Roselyn *interior designer*
Robinson, Cleo Parker *artistic director*
Rost, Christa VandeZande *graphics and product designer*
Rubin, Cathy Ann *retired secondary school educator*
Sather, Sylvia Carolyn *science educator, consultant*
Shaw, Priscilla *music educator, coach*
Shwayder, Elizabeth Yanish *sculptor*
Smith, Sallye Wrye *librarian*
Smith, Tara Michelle *counselor*
Stamm, Carol Ann *obstetrician, gynecologist*
Steigerwald-Clausen, Beverly *sculptor, educator*
Stephens, Kathryn J. *science educator*
Studevant, Laura *medical association administrator*
Sujansky, Eva Borska *pediatrician, geneticist, educator*
Swain, Nicole Falvo *psychologist*
Takis, Stephanie *retired state senator*
Taylor, Teresa *communications executive*
Thomas, Enolia *nutritionist, educator*
Tiner, Kathy Ann *special education educator*
Ullery, Patricia Anne *marketing professional*
Vosevich, Kathi Ann *writer, editor*
Waak, Patricia Ann *political organization administrator, environmental association executive*
Wagner, Judith Buck *investment firm executive*
Walcher, Jennifer Lynne *city official*
Walker, Joan H. *marketing and communications executive*
White, Joyce Louise *librarian*
White, Karen Jean *artist*
Williams, Marcia Putnam *human resources specialist*
Williams, Suzanne *state senator*
Witt, Catherine Lewis *neonatal nurse practitioner, writer*
Wunnicke, Brooke *lawyer*

Dolores
Betts, Dorothy Anne *retired elementary school educator*
Harper, Laura Lee *principal*
Robertson, Virginia Marie *small business owner, publisher*
Winterer-Schulz, Barbara Jean *graphics designer, writer*

Durango
Balas-Whitfield, Susan *artist*
Ballantine, Morley Cowles (Mrs. Arthur Atwood Ballantine) *editor*
Barter, Mary F. *academic administrator*
Erickson, Mary Ann *athletic trainer, educator*
Farrell, Kimberly H. *music educator*
Tischhauser, Katherine Jetter *music educator, cellist*

Eagle
Hunsaker, Jill Ann *public health official*
Sheaffer, Karen *county official, treasurer*

Edwards
Chambers, Joan Louise *retired librarian, retired dean*

Eldorado Springs
Lovins, L. Hunter *public policy institute executive, consultant, educator*

Englewood
Asarch, Elaine *interior designer, anthropologist*
Brown, Mary *nursing educator*
Graves, Nada Proctor *retired elementary school educator*
Keesling, Ruth Morris *foundation administrator*
Miles, Amy E. *recreational facility executive*
Rheney, Susan O. *paper company executive*
Spencer, Margaret Gilliam *lawyer*
Terakedis, Kathryn DeLee *mathematics educator*

Erie
Dilly, Marian Jeanette *humanities educator*
Nichols, Janet Hildreth *elementary school educator, childbirth and parenting educator*

Estes Park
Biehl, Julianne *art educator*
Gibbs, Dorothy Scott *retired Latin educator*
Varilek, Julie *music educator*

Evergreen
Ogle, Amanda McKibbin *music educator, theater educator, director*

Federal Heights
Fisher, Terri Lynn *emergency nurse practitioner*
Teigland, Brittany Paige *music educator*

Fleming
Nichols, LeeAnn *library media specialist*

Fort Collins
Clark, Claudia Ann *business development manager*
Colbert, Debora A. *director*
Eddy, Gladys Louise *educational administrator*
Grandin, Temple *industrial designer, science educator*
Honaker, Stevie Lee *career counselor, consultant*
Jensen, Margaret *real estate broker*
Ladanyi, Branka Maria *chemist, educator*
Menzel, Barbara Edwina *systems analyst*
Ricard, Virginia Belle *adult education educator*
Sedei Rodden, Pamela Jean *psychologist, director*
Sullivan, Patrice M. *artist, educator*
Thomas, Jeanette Mae *public accountant*
Tyler, Gail Madeleine *nurse*
Wallner, Melissa Kay *music and theater educator, director*
Wilber, Clare Marie *musician, educator*

Fort Garland
Taylor-Dunn, Corliss Leslie *marriage and family therapist*

Fort Morgan
Christensen, Cynthia L. *music educator*
Vogel, Sarah Elizabeth *music educator*

Fountain
Ortiz, Amy Mofford *surgical technologist*
Wilson, Roberta (Bobbi) Gail *performing arts educator*

Fowler
Giadone, Susan *livestock office manager*

Franktown
Kruse, Doris Evelyn *counselor*

Frisco
Yankowski, Kristin Leanne *mathematics educator*

Georgetown
Hildebrandt-Willard, Claudia Joan *banker*

Glenwood Springs
Candlin, Frances Ann *psychotherapist, social worker, educator*
Hauptli, Barbara Beatrice *foundation administrator*

Golden
Brainerd, Mary *small business owner*
Bullard, Christine Adele Doutt *retired physical education educator*
Cash, Kristy Rae *language educator*
Chouinard, Karen Reiko *elementary school educator*
Dickinson, Carol Rittgers *art historian, writer*
Fahey, Barbara Stewart Doe *public agency administrator*
Greenberg, Joanne *author, anthropologist*
Lott, Brenda Louise *insurance company executive*
Olson, Marian Katherine *management consultant*
Van Dusen, Donna Bayne *communications consultant, educator, researcher*

Grand Junction
Born, Frances Emmary Hollick *middle school art educator*
Burdick, Margaret Seale (Marge Burdick) *interior designer*
Childers, Margaret Anne *science educator*
Flick, Carol J. *middle school educator*
Fox, Carmen Alice *retired medical/surgical nurse*
Godsman, Katherine *retired psychologist, educator*
Hall, Kathryn H. *public relations executive*
Hoagland, Christina Gail *occupational therapist, industrial drafter*
Michels, Ruth Yvonne *retired cytologist*
Opsal, Pamela E. *music educator*
Pantenburg, Michel *health facility administrator, educator, holistic health coordinator*
Phillips, Ruth Amelia *retired music educator, artist*
Schmerler, Barbara Ann *social worker*
Wilson, Deborah Grim *music educator*
Woods, Mistie Lynn *secondary school educator*

Greeley
Ackerman, Joyce Shohet *psychologist*
Blake, Margaret Tate *psychologist, educator*
Green, Lynn Tesson *science educator, secondary school educator*
Hawthorne, Barbara L. *anthropologist, educator*
Jackson, Patricia Anne *primary school educator, consultant*
Meis, Jeanette Kay *elementary educator*
Miller, Diane Wilmarth *retired human resources director*
Ruyle, Lydia Miller *artist, writer, artist, educator*
Willis, Connie (Constance E. Willis) *writer*

Greenwood Village
Gold, Christina A. *data processing company executive*

Lesh-Laurie, Georgia Elizabeth *academic administrator, biology professor, medical researcher*
Wittman, Vanessa Ames *communications executive*

Guffey
Price, Faith Munford *retired psychiatrist, retired special education educator*

Henderson
Reibold, Dorothy Ann *accountant, researcher*

Highlands Ranch
Brennan, Deborah Dikeman *assistant principal*
Brierley, Corale L. *geological and biomining engineer*
Bublitz, Deborah Keirstead *pediatrician*
Erickson, Linda Rae *elementary school educator*
Torley, Margaret Jean *elementary school educator*

Holly
Sherwood, Louise Kay *literature and language educator*

Hotchkiss
Blackstock, Virginia Harriett *artist*

Jefferson
Maatsch, Deborah Joan *manufacturing executive*

Keenesburg
Vigil, Elizabeth Lee *music educator*

Lafayette
Elliott, Carolyn Elizabeth *educator, writer*
Hibbard, Christine *psychotherapist, educator, minister*

Lake George
Daniel, Deanna Alane *music educator*

Lakewood
Burry, Jennifer Wilborn *medical/surgical nurse*
Eikleberry, Lois Schillie *physician*
Finnie, Doris Gould *investment company executive*
Joy, Carla Marie *history educator*
Lautigar, Linda L. *lawyer*
Meyer, Lynn Nix *lawyer*
Nelson, Deborah Jane *family and consumer science educator*
Nichols, Vicki Anne *financial consultant, librarian*
Peters, Julie Anne *writer*
Reed, Joan-Marie *special education educator*
Stoloff, Carolyn Ruth *clinical psychologist*
Stromberg, Patricia Roberts *retired school librarian*
Wallisch, Carolyn E. *principal*
Woodruff, Kathryn Elaine *literature and language professor*
Zachman, Kathleen E. *gifted and talented educator*

Lamar
Tague, Vickie *music educator*

Laporte
iba, Shirley *artist*

Leadville
Brown, Jessi Eden *mental health services professional*

Limon
Huffman, Janet Faye *secondary school educator*
Richards, Ann Adair *psychologist*
Schmeiser, Melva Louise *history educator*

Littleton
Clark, Julie *consumer products company executive*
Davis, Betsy Rae *nurse*
Day, Susan Marie *music educator, composer*
Derjue, Rita *artist, educator*
Di Manna, Michelle Ann *mathematics educator*
Dinmore, Katherine *principal*
Early, Bonnie Sue *piano teacher, music educator*
Greenberg, Elinor Miller *director, consultant*
Hurt, Shanna L. *secondary school educator*
Johansson, Alicia Barbara *musician*
Keogh, Heidi Helen Dake *advocate*
King, Linda *musician, educator*
Lohman, Loretta Cecelia *social scientist, consultant*
Mosier, Cheryl Angeline *secondary school educator, consultant*
Mullarkey, Jill *secondary school educator*
Poduska, T. F. *artist*
Shepherd, Donna Lou *interior designer*
Strother, Cheri L. *secondary school educator*
Treybig, Edwina Hall *sales executive*
Walker, Louise Converse *obstetrician, gynecologist*

Longmont
Anderson-Kotts, Judith Anne *academic dean*
Blackwood, Lois Anne *elementary school educator*
Jones, Beverly Ann Miller *nursing administrator, retired patient services administrator*
Julien, Kristie *mathematics educator, department chairman*
Van Elsacker, Tulsa *health facility administrator*
Venrick, Kristie Lund *mathematics educator*
Walker, Kathleen Mae *health facility administrator*

Louisville
Bluestein, Eve *plastic surgeon*
Raymond, Dorothy Gill *lawyer*
Tyson, Charlotte Rose *software development manager*

Loveland
Ayers, Kris *secondary school educator*
Bierbaum, Janith Marie *artist*
Geisendorfer, Nancy Kay *mathematics educator*
Kasenberg, Darlene Frances *psychologist*
Lee, Evelyn Marie *elementary school educator, secondary school educator*
Nossaman, Marian Alecia *manufacturing engineering executive*

Patterson, Shirley Drury *genealogist, editor-in-chief*
Rodman, Sue A. *wholesale company executive, artist, writer*
Veach, Jennifer Jeanne *elementary school educator*

Mancos
Brown, Joy Alice *social services administrator*

Montrose
Berryman, Joan Eileen *elementary school educator*
Readout, Rosalee Joyce *retired education educator*

Monument
Engelman, Cylinda Anderson *elementary school educator*
McIver, Deborah Kay *tax specialist, entrepreneur, small business owner*

Morrison
Neumann, Stephanie Tower *retired librarian*

Nederland
Morrison, K. Jaydene *education counseling firm executive*

New Raymer
Williams, Doris W. *rancher*

Niwot
Farrington, Helen Agnes *personnel director*

Northglenn
BeVier Dill, Rene Lorraine *secondary school educator*
Hemlock, Roberta Leigh *veterinary technician*
Kappler, Karen L. *music educator, musician*
Nucci, Sunni Lynn *social studies educator*

Norwood
Brantingham, Andrya J. *special education educator*

Ouray
Rowe, Sherlie Jean *writer*

Pagosa Springs
Howard, Carole Margaret Munroe *retired public relations executive*

Palisade
Barnewall, Marilyn MacGruder *retired banker*

Parachute
Leonard, Betsy Ann *director, writer*

Placerville
Monferrato, Angela Maria *investor, writer*

Pueblo
Alt, Betty L. *sociology educator*
Barber, Margaret McAdow *education educator*
Deasy, Irene M. *retired protective services official*
Gardner, Tracy A. *social studies educator*
Ihm, Dana Elizabeth *music educator*
Jones, Donna Ruth *librarian*
Nimmo, Charlene *minister*
Puls, Elaine Allison *retired librarian*
Ramirez, Monica E. *education educator, consultant*
Van Etten, Nancy Kay *medical/surgical nurse, consultant*
Vest, Rosemarie Lynn Torres *secondary school educator*

Saguache
Marold, Judy L. *secondary school educator*
Sanchez, Karla Ann *language educator*

Sanford
Bond, Krista Suzette *secondary school educator*

Seibert
Sears, Joanne Carol *secondary school educator*

Snowmass Village
Tester-LaMar, Cynthia Coreyn *lawyer*

Steamboat Springs
Fenton, Monica *retired biomedical researcher*
Kiser-Miller, Kathy Joy *humanities educator*
Lykken, Christine Townley *social worker*

Sterling
Gumina, Pamela Ray *municipal government administrator*
Zink, Brenda Lee *biology professor*

Sugar City
McKee, Eleanor Swetnam *retired principal*

Superior
Forshee, Gladys Marie *insurance agent, writer*
Reagan, Melodie A. *communications executive*

Thornton
Bishop, Holly Ann *elementary school educator*
Johnson, Carole Jean *investment company executive*
McEachern, Susan Mary *physician assistant*

U S A F Academy
Born, Dana H. *dean, career military officer*
Caldwell, Jo Lynn *research psychologist*

Vail
Kelley Fitchett, Christine Ruth *business owner, consultant*
Logan, Vicki *art collector*

Walden
Ary, Bonnita Ellen *registrar, federal official*

Westminster
Bellino-Strickland, Roseanna *secondary school educator*
Dinkey, Laura Lee *literature and language educator*
Hallman, Janelle M. *psychotherapist, educator*

Kopperud, Marilyn Sue *music educator*
Mussehl, Peggy Ann *nurse*
Peterson, Candyce Leigh *music educator*
Rebuehr, Sage Lee *secondary school educator*
Shaeffer, Thelma Jean *primary school educator*
Stoian, Cristina *sales executive, real estate broker, mortgage company executive, tax specialist*
Vizyak, Lindy L. *retired elementary school educator*

Wheat Ridge
Blaschke, Rose Ann *elementary school educator*
Civish, Gayle Ann *psychologist*
Leino, Deanna Rose *business educator*
Wells, Karen Kay *medical librarian*
Wilcox, Mary Marks *retired Christian education consultant, educator*

Whitewater
Wheeler Russell, Gwendolyn Kay *education educator*

Wiggins
Kammerzell, Susan Jane *elementary school educator, music educator*
Midcap, Linda Luree *social studies educator*

Wolcott
Flacke, Joan Wareham *physician, anesthesiologist, educator*

Yuma
Sinclair, Lisa *science educator*

CONNECTICUT

Andover
Quint, Dawn Dunaway *personnel executive*

Avon
Kling, Phradie (Phradie Kling Gold) *small business owner, educator*
Levitz, I. S. *artist, educator, curator*

Baltic
Cipriani, Rebecca Michele *elementary school educator*

Bethel
Shepard, Jean Heck *retired publishing consultant*

Bloomfield
Baccus, R. Eileen Turner *retired academic administrator*
Bassett, Jean Williams *elementary school educator*
Nelson-Kauffman, Wendy *history educator*
Shimelman, Susan Fromm *state agency administrator*
Stravalle-Schmidt, Ann Roberta *lawyer*

Bolton
Toomey, Laura Carolyn *psychologist*

Branford
Abels, Gusta J. *artist, art and art history educator*
Anderson, Marjo Elizabeth *minister*
Johnson, Eva Jo *educational consultant*
Swofford, Sharon Ehlers *medical/surgical nurse*
Wright, Nancy Howell *interior designer*

Bridgeport
Anderson, Sheila K. *mathematics professor*
Berman, Renee Caggiano *lawyer*
Campbell, Stacey Lynne *music educator*
Coba-Loh, Claudine Jean *psychology professor*
Henry, Barbara Ann *finance company executive, director*
Johmann, Nancy *librarian*
King, Sister Eleace *special education services professional*
Macdonald, Karen Crane *occupational therapist, geriatrics services professional*
McAuliffe, Catherine A. *counselor, psychology educator, retired psychotherapist*
Orloski, Sharon *secondary school educator*
Psarras, Mary Auten *language educator, tax specialist*
Richard, Ellen *theater executive*
Sheridan, Eileen *librarian*
Simoneau, Cynthia Lambert *editor, educator*
Twist-Rudolph, Donna Joy *neurophysiology and neuropsychology researcher*

Bristol
DiCosimo, Patricia Shields *retired secondary school educator*
Donlin, Stephanie Dara Kalish *special education educator*
Driessen, Christine F. *broadcast executive*
LaGanga, Donna Brandeis *dean*
Larson, Audra *elementary school educator*
Morales, Mary E. *social worker*
Weaving, Christine A. *personal trainer*

Burlington
Jones, Phyllis Duyser *physical education educator*
Niehoff, Karissa L. *principal*

Chaplin
Bruckerhoff, Theresa *business owner, educational researcher*

Cheshire
Beitler, Karen Ann *biology professor, technologist*

Chester
Frost-Knappman, (Linda) Elizabeth *publishing executive, editor, writer*
Harwood, Eleanor Cash *retired librarian*
Stark, Evelyn Brill *poet, musician*
Zwart-Ludeman, Theresa *graphics designer, artist*

Clinton
Adler, Peggy Ann *writer, illustrator, consultant, protective services official*
McGinley, Marjorie *writer*

Colchester
Nikirk, (Silva) Susan *minister, writer, dancer*

Cos Cob
Leamy, Nancy M. *professional athletics coach*
McElwaine, Theresa Weedy *academic administrator, artist*
Wilson, Ruth Pester *elementary school educator, researcher*

Coventry
Dimmock, Virginia Ellen *literature and language educator, consultant*
Halvorson, Judith Anne (Judith Anne Devaud) *elementary school educator*
Hayes, Julia Moriarty *retired science educator*

Cromwell
Izzo, Lucille Anne *sales representative*

Danbury
Agoora, Lammia Hasson *mathematics educator*
Callaghan, Marjorie Seymour *music educator*
Good, Jennifer L. *pharmaceutical executive*
Hawkes, Carol Ann *academic administrator*
McCulloch, Angela Jean *theater educator, music educator*
Meyers, Abbey S. *foundation administrator*
Reynolds, Jean Edwards *publishing executive*
Skolan-Logue, Amanda Nicole *lawyer, consultant*
Wright, Marie Anne *management information systems educator*

Darien
Brooke, Avery Rogers *publisher, writer*
Gushée-Molkenthin, Allison *financial advisor*
Springer, Ruth Wiren *music educator*
Workman, Sharon Joy *journalist*

Deep River
Nidzgorski, Barbara Helen *gifted and talented educator, puppeteer*

Derby
Bonina, Sally Anne *principal*
Brassil, Jean Ella *psychologist*
McEvoy, Sharlene Ann *law educator*
Rinaldo, Sharon Ann *special education educator*

East Haddam
Clarke, Cordelia Kay Knight Mazuy *management consultant, artist*
Frost, Susan Beth *theater producer*

East Hampton
Klein, Gail Beth Marantz *freelance/self-employed writer, animal breeder*
Tucceri, Clive Knowles *writer, science educator, consultant*

East Hartford
Barredo, Rita M. *auditor*
Lautzenheiser, Barbara Jean *insurance company executive*

East Haven
Dayharsh, Virginia Fiengo *secondary school educator*
Gardner, Joan Andrews *artist educator*
Wallach, Carol Odile *elementary school educator*

Easton
Duffy, Natalie W. *retired physical education educator*
Meyer, Alice Virginia *state official*

Enfield
Reuter, Joan Copson *retired program director*

Essex
Hieatt, Constance Bartlett *English language educator*

Fairfield
Barone, Rose Marie Pace *writer, retired educator*
Bohrer, Jane Rothrock *controller*
Bryan, Barbara Day *retired librarian*
Cassidy, Katherine *energy executive*
Daley, Pamela *diversified services, technology and manufacturing company executive*
Earls, Christine Ross *biology professor*
Eigel, Marcia Duffy *editor*
Evans, Margaret A. *volunteer*
Fash, Victoria R. *business executive*
Ford, Maureen Morrissey *civic worker*
Howell, Karen Jane *private school educator*
Kelly, Colleen Adele *secondary school educator*
Mastrony, Sara Elizabeth *music educator, director*
Maxwell, Carole Ann *director*
Morehouse, Sarah McCally *retired political science professor*
Newton, Lisa Haenlein *philosopher, educator*
Orris-Modugno, Michele Marie *public relations, marketing and advertising consultant*
Peters, Susan P. *human resources specialist*
Reif, Deborah *manufacturing executive*
Rinaldi, Jacqueline Blanche *education educator, director*
Shaffer, Dorothy Browne *retired mathematician, educator*
Shelton, Carolyn Johnson *professional society administrator*
Spence, Barbara E. *former publishing company executive*
Turetsky, Judith *librarian, researcher*

Falls Village
Purcell, Mary Louise Gerlinger *retired adult education educator*
Toomey, Jeanne Elizabeth *animal activist*

Farmington
Comerford, Jane Deirdre *lawyer*
Ellis, Diane Deane *dental hygienist, educator*
Ford, Burch Tracy *headmaster*
Grunnet, Margaret Louise *retired pathologist, educator*
Nash, Judith Kluck *mathematics professor*
Osborn, Mary Jane Merten *biochemist, educator*
Rothfield, Naomi Fox *physician*

Runowicz, Carolyn Dilworth *physician*

Gaylordsville
Dunn, Virginia *artist*

Glastonbury
Cavanaugh, Marianne *secondary educator*
Googins, Sonya Forbes *state legislator, retired banker*
Ridgeway, Teresa Drivdahl *weaver, educator*
Snyder, Barbara Louise *language arts educator*

Granby
Gates, Joanne Ferry *counselor*

Greens Farms
St. Marie, Satenig *writer*

Greenwich
Bentley, Lissa Frances *elementary school educator*
Bjornson, Edith Cameron *foundation administrator, communications consultant*
Brown, Shannon Elizabeth *mathematics educator*
DeNigris, Carole Dell Cato *artist*
Farrell, Mary Cooney *securities analyst*
Gaudio, Maxine Diane *biofeedback therapist, stress management consultant*
Griggs, Nina M. *realtor*
Hershaft, Elinor *space planner, interior designer*
Hoberman, Mary Ann *author*
Kleinman, Noela MacGinn *family nurse practitioner*
Kovner, Kathleen Jane *civic worker, portrait artist*
Lacoff, Cheryl Klein *writer, artist*
Lewis, Audrey Gersh *marketing professional, public relations executive, consultant*
Marram, Ellen R. *investment company executive*
Perless, Ellen *advertising executive*
Rudy, Kathleen Vermeulen *small business owner*
Scott, Mariette A. *marketing executive*
Shimchick, Marie *music educator*
Wallach, Magdalena Falkenberg (Carla Wallach) *writer*
Welling, Kathryn Marie *editor*
Wyman, Lotte Ann Novak *civic worker*

Groton
Galbraith, Marian *elementary school educator*
Kennedy, Evelyn Siefert *foundation executive, textiles executive*
Payson, Herta Ruth *psychotherapist, theater educator, massage therapist*
Swindell, Dolores Holland *retired school librarian*

Guilford
Colish, Marcia Lillian *history professor*
Sharpe, Kathleen T. *secondary school educator*
Shelton, Darlene *psychologist, consultant*
Stevens, Lydia Hastings *community volunteer*

Hamden
Adair, Eleanor Reed *environmental biologist*
Balogh, Anne Marceline *personnel consultant*
Blumberg, Betty Lou *education educator*
Cole-Schiraldi, Marilyn Bush *occupational therapist, educator*
Davis, Lorraine Jensen *writer, editor*
Hill, Elizabeth Betty *retired secondary school educator*
Marino, Marissa A. *language educator*
Mulligan, Dana Mathews *assistant principal*
Oddi, Marie Caporale *educational administrator*
Robson, Carol Ann Shaffner *retired secondary school educator*

Hartford
Bidwell, Karen Rubino *mental health care clinician*
Brown, Nora M. *elementary school educator*
Brubeck, Marcia Ellen *psychotherapist*
Bysiewicz, Susan *state official*
Carey, Ellen *artist*
Carter, Annette Wheeler *state legislator*
Cross, Nadine Debra-Ann *pharmacist*
DeMarinis, Nancy A. *state legislator, educator*
Elliott, Eric S *insurance company executive*
Eshoo, Barbara Anne Rudolph *non-profit administrator*
Fahrbach, Ruth C. *state legislator*
Harkin, Ruth R. *lawyer*
Hassett, Patricia *university administrator*
Hedrick, Joan Doran *writer, university educator*
Humphreys, Karen Lynne *language educator*
Johnson, Bonnie *art educator*
Jung, Betty Chin *epidemiologist, educator, nurse*
Katz, Joette *state supreme court justice*
Kedderis, Pamela Jean *academic administrator*
Knott-Twine, Laura Mae *director*
Lumsden, Lynne Ann *publishing executive*
Martinez, Donna F. *federal judge*
Mills, Corinne C. *music educator*
Mushinsky, Mary M. *state legislator*
Nappier, Denise L. *state official*
O'Brien, Sally Nahas *special education educator, consultant*
Peters, Ellen Ash *retired judge*
Rell, M. Jodi *governor*
Souza, Diane D *corporate financial executive*
Sternberg, Betty J. *school system administrator*
Stuart, Ann *academic administrator, writer, educator*
Sullivan, Katherine McGurk *lawyer*
Valentine, Debra A. *lawyer*
Vertefeuille, Christine Siegrist *state supreme court justice*
Winter, Miriam Therese (Gloria Frances Winter) *nun, religious studies educator*
Young, Dona Davis Gagliano *insurance company executive, lawyer*

Higganum
de Brigard, Emilie *anthropologist, consultant*

Huntington
Richter, Elizabeth Lee *artist*

Kensington
Manning, Brenda Argosy *painter*

Kent
Friedman, Frances *public relations executive*

Lakeville
Kelly, Patricia Beyer *personal trainer*

Lebanon
Sola, Janet Elaine *retired secondary school educator*

Ledyard
McGrattan, Mary K. *state legislator*
O'Keefe, Kerry Ann *elementary school educator*

Lisbon
Powell, Diane Marie *psychologist*

Litchfield
Kennedy, Susan Orpha *physical education educator, consultant, sports official*
Mullins, Patty *artist*

Madison
Cappetta, Anna Maria *art educator*
Pauley, Barbara Anne *author, educator*

Manchester
Campbell, Katherine Marie Langrehr *elementary and secondary education educator*
Fitzgerald, Mary Irene *retired school psychologist*
Raffles, Linda N. *secondary school educator*
Randall, Frances J. *psychotherapist*

Marlborough
Garrett, Florence Rome *poet*

Meriden
Losada-Zarate, Gloria *psychologist*
Trotta, Marcia Marie *librarian, consultant, education educator*

Middletown
Blume, Ginger Elaine *psychologist*
Brown, Judith *academic administrator*
Corrao, Angela M. *psychologist*
Heimann-Hast, Sybil Dorothea *literature and language professor*
Henry, Lidia Agnieszka *elementary school educator*
Meyer, Priscilla Ann *literature and language professor*
Schwarcz, Vera *historian, educator, poet*
Winston, Krishna *foreign language professional*
Wojtusik, Marylou *special education educator, consultant*

Milford
Boyer, Carolyn Merwin *school psychologist*
Convertino, Charlene D. *language educator*
Krall, Vita *psychologist*
Siekierski, Kamilla Malgorzata *dental laboratory technician*
Sullivan, Christine Anne *secondary school educator*
Yatsinko, Mary Ann *elementary school educator*

Monroe
Kranyik, Elizabeth Ann *secondary school educator*
Morrison, Amanda Mary *music educator*

Mystic
Bobruff, Carole Marks *radio producer, radio personality*
Gilbert, Ellen Effman *music educator, conductor*
Hutchison, Dorris Jeannette *retired microbiologist, educator*
Spakoski, Marcia *insurance agent*

Naugatuck
Banner-Gray, Marion G. *secondary school educator*
Chrzanowski, Rose-Ann Cannizzo *art educator*
Mannweiler, Mary-Elizabeth *painter*
McLaughlin, Elaine M. *elementary school educator*
Sasso, Ruth Maryann *educator*

New Britain
Boyea, Ruthe W. *retired education educator*
Brancifort, Janet Marie *hospital administrator, respiratory therapist*
Fallon, Barbara G. *oncologist*
Margiotta, Mary-Lou Ann *application developer*
Munshi, Nalini Bhat *elementary school educator*
Pearl, Helen Zalkan *lawyer*
Sohn, Jeanne *librarian*
Stathos, Lifteria K. *retired educational association administrator*

New Canaan
Champion, Marge (Marjorie Celeste Champion) *actress, choreographer, dancer*
Despres, Louise Fay *secondary school educator*
Donnelly, Laura Jean *science educator*
Grace, Julianne Alice *retired biotechnologist*
Lione, Susan Garrett *consultant*
McKeough, Susan Anne *elementary school educator*
Thomas, Marianne Gregory *school psychologist*

New Fairfield
Lambrech, Régine M. *academic administrator, language educator*

New Haven
Ahern, Jo Ann *diabetes clinical nurse specialist*
Arterton, Janet Bond *federal judge*
Bartoshuk, Linda M. *otolaryngologist, educator*
Berland, Gretchen K. *medical educator, filmmaker*
Borroff, Marie *English language educator*
Brilmayer, R. Lea *lawyer, educator*
Burns, Ellen Bree *federal judge*
Chase, Linda (Lina Chase) *social worker, psychotherapist*
Chevalier, Judith A. *economics professor, finance professor*
Chua, Amy *law educator*
Clapp, Megan Elizabeth *art educator*
Cole, Elsa Kircher *lawyer*
Curran, Lisa M. *environmental scientist, educator*
Deamer, Peggy *architecture educator*
de Bretteville, Sheila Levrant *artist, art educator*
Degutis, Linda Christine *adult education educator, epidemiologist, researcher*
De Rose, Sandra Michele *psychotherapist, educator, administrator*
Dunleavy, Mara Anne *science educator*
Ember, Carol R. *anthropology educator, writer*
Feigenbaum, Joan *computer scientist, mathematician*
Ferholt, J. Deborah Lott *pediatrician*
Frank, Roberta *literature educator*
Garvey, Sheila Hickey *theater educator*
Glier, Ingeborg Johanna *German language and literature educator*
Greene, Liliane *literature and language educator, editor*
Grey, Margaret *nursing educator*
Hackman, (Mary) Judith Dozier *university administrator, researcher*
Hayden, Dolores *author, architecture educator*
Hostetter, Margaret K. *pediatrician, medical educator*
Hyman, Paula E(llen) *history professor*
Jackson, Sondi Elizabeth *language educator*
Jacob, Deirdre Ann Bradbury *manufacturing executive, finance educator, consultant*
Jolls, Christine Margaret *law educator*
Jones, Katherine R. *nursing educator*
Kane, Patricia Ellen *museum curator*
Kaufman, Nadeen Laurie *clinical psychology educator, writer*
Krauss, Judith Belliveau *nursing educator*
Lavik, Erin *chemical engineer*
Leo, Martha E. *advocate, counselor*
Lindroth, Linda (Linda Hammer) *artist, writer, curator*
Lord, Ruth *retired researcher, philanthropist, writer*
Lorimer, Linda Koch *university educator*
Lorkovic, Tatjana *librarian*
Marcus, Ruth Barcan *philosopher, educator, writer, lecturer*
McClain, Brenda C. *pain management physician*
McCorkle, Ruth *oncological nurse, educator, researcher*
McNamara, Julia Mary *academic administrator, foreign language educator*
Meyers, Amy *museum director*
Nelson, Alondra R. *social sciences educator*
Nolan, Victoria *theater director*
Norton, Cheryl J. *academic administrator*
Okerson, Ann Shumelda Lillian *librarian*
Patterson, Peyton R. *bank executive*
Peters, Jean Koh *law educator*
Peterson, Linda H. *English language educator*
Peterson, Sandra Kay *librarian*
Prochaska, Alice *historian, librarian*
Ramirez, Ainissa *materials scientist*
Resnik, Judith *law educator*
Robinson, Dorothy K. *lawyer*
Rose-Ackerman, Susan *law and political economy educator*
Scarf, Margaret (Maggie Scarf) *author*
Schepartz, Alanna *biochemist, educator*
Schirmeister, Pamela *dean, language educator*
Seashore, Margretta Reed *physician, educator*
Siegel, Reva *law educator*
Skinner, Helen Catherine Wild *biomineralogist*
Sommer, Miriam Goldstein (Mimi G. Sommer) *writer, photographer*
Sorkin, Jenni *curator, critic*
Speicher, Hilda *psychologist, educator*
Steitz, Joan Argetsinger *biochemistry professor*
Stith-Cabranes, Kate *law educator*
Tannenbaum, Rebecca Jo *historian, writer*
Titus, Julia Yeremina *Slavic languages educator, translator*
Vogel, Susan Mullin *museum director, art and archaeology professor*
Walbert, Kate *writer, educator*
Wynn, Karen *psychologist, educator, researcher*
Yeazell, Ruth Bernard *English language educator*

New London
Allen, Carol Marie *radiologic technologist*
Clarke, Florence Dorothy *minister, educator*
Daragan, Patricia Ann *librarian*
Johnson, Diana Atwood *business owner, innkeeper*
Martin, Lisa Marlene *language educator*
Tassinari, Melissa Sherman *reproductive toxicologist*
Wakeman, Martha Jane *artist, educator*

New Milford
Behan, Sandra Holloway *science educator*
Smith, Virginia *real estate broker*

Newington
Anderson, Kathryn Parks *music educator*
Cohen, Fern K. *music educator*
Foley, Patricia Jean *accountant*
Reynolds, Patricia Jean *psychiatric social worker, songwriter*

Newtown
Babbitt, Martha E. *science educator*

Niantic
Rigdon, Nancy Kenway *music educator*

Noank
Leeds, Robin Leigh *transportation executive*

Norfolk
O'Malley, Margaret Parlin *marketing administrator*

North Haven
Cofrancesco, Angela *insurance agent, coach*
Fuggi, Gretchen Miller *education educator*

Northford
Bonatti, Christine Anne *elementary school educator*
James, Virginia Stowell *retired elementary school educator, retired secondary school educator*

Norwalk
Babcock, Catherine Evans *artist, educator*
Freitag, Anna Carol *endocrinologist, internist*
McMahon, Elizabeth Mildred *educator*
Mintz, Lenore Chaice (Lea Mintz) *consultant*
Nelson, Paula Morrison Bronson *reading specialist*
Roman, Mary *city official*
Schaefer-Wicke, Elizabeth *reading consultant, educator*
Soper, Jeannine *real estate agent*
Timlin-Scalera, Rebecca Mary *neuropsychologist*

Norwich
Buddington, Olive Joyce *shop owner, retired education educator*
Thompson, Carrie Lorraine *volunteer*

Oakdale
Greenstein, Laura M. *education educator, department chairman*

Oakville
Carroll, Constance Marie *pianist, educator*
Moeller, Judith Stone *reading educator, consultant*

Old Greenwich
Parris, Sally Nye *real estate agent*
Whitlock, Veronica P. *interior designer, educator*

Old Lyme
LeBoutillier, Janet Ela *writer, real estate developer, minister*
Osborne, Judith Barbour *artist*
St. George, Judith Alexander *writer*

Old Mystic
Cassidy, Cindy Jane *secondary school educator*

Old Saybrook
Geer, Lois Margaret *music educator*

Oxford
Shupp, Karlen S. *language educator*

Plainville
Perkins- Banas, Melissa Veronica *psychologist*

Pomfret Center
Sweatt, Ermelinda Espinola *retired mathematics educator*

Preston
Gibson, Margaret Ferguson *poet, educator*

Putnam
Ames, Sandra Cutler *secondary school educator*
Leese, Jessica *language educator*

Ridgefield
Benton, Suzanne *sculptor, mask ritualist, printmaker, painter*
Johnson-Potok, Frieda T. *elementary school educator, consultant*
Lindsay, Dianna Marie *educational administrator*
Priest, Alexia Z. *purchasing agent*
Tamsett, Susan O. *architect, artist*

Riverside
Mallin, Jennifer *Internet company executive, writer*
Powers, Claudia McKenna *state legislator*

Rocky Hill
Kahn, Carolyn R. *biotechnology executive*
Wilson, Karen Lynn *esthetician*

Roxbury
Styron, Rose *human rights activist, poet, journalist*

Salisbury
Kilner, Ursula Blanche *genealogist, educator, writer*

Sandy Hook
Dakofsky, LaDonna Jung *medical counseling physician, radiation oncologist*

Shelton
Clark, Mary W. *biology educator*
Kaye, Jennifer A. *elementary school educator, dance educator*
Mariotti, Margaret *executive secretary*

Sherman
Cohn, Jane Shapiro *public relations executive*
Goodspeed, Barbara *artist*

Simsbury
Moran, Linda *management consultant, researcher*
Roberts, Celia Ann *librarian*
Roman, Robin *anesthesiologist*

South Windsor
Baretta, Marsha Motyl *elementary school physical education educator*
Woods, Barbara O. *mathematics educator*

Southbury
Bergen, Polly *actress*
Foxworth, Johnnie Hunter *retired state agency administrator*
Frost, Deborah E. *elementary school educator*

Southington
Bagwell, Carol Tessier *special education educator, consultant*
Carrington, Virginia Gail (Vee Carrington) *marketing professional, consultant*

Stafford Springs
Zeldes, Edith R. *freelance journalist*

Stamford
Aceto, Lisa M. *management consultant*
Aveni, Beverly A. *executive aide*
Babson, Jane Frances *artist, writer*
Berets, Eileen Tolkowsky *artist*
Burns, Ursula M. *printing company executive*
Dennies, Sandra Lee *city official*
Elizondo, Patricia *sales executive*
Goldsmith, Donna *sports association executive*

Goodkin, Deborah Gay *corporate financial executive*
Halligan, Fredrica Rose *clinical psychologist*
Handler, Evelyn *consultant, former university president*
Jason, J. Julie *portfolio manager, writer, lawyer*
Lane, Hana Umlauf *editor*
Mayes, Michele Coleman *lawyer*
McDonald, Cassandra Burns *lawyer*
McMahon, Linda E. *sports association executive*
Moggio, Barbara Jean *health education specialist*
Moore, Sharon Helen Scott *gerontological nurse*
Mulcahy, Anne Marie *printing company executive*
Nazemetz, Patricia *human resources specialist*
Ortner, Toni *language educator*
Pappas, Alceste Thetis *consulting company executive, educator*
Parrs, Marianne M. *paper and lumber company executive*
Perna, Janet *application developer*
Preiss-Harris, Patricia *music educator, composer, pianist*
Schiff, Jayne Nemerow *underwriter*
Staab, Diane D. *lawyer*
Stillings, Irene Ella Grace Cordiner *retired foundation executive*
Teeters, Nancy Hays *economist, director*
Vandebroek, Sophie Verdonckt *printing company executive*
Weinstein, Ruth Joseph *lawyer*
Wilderotter, Maggie (Mary Agnes Wilderotter) *software company executive, former cable television executive*
Williams, Reba White *corporate financial executive, writer, researcher*

Stonington
Elliott, Inger McCabe *apparel designer, consultant, textiles executive*
Stoddard, Alexandra *interior designer, educator, writer*
Thacher, Mary McGrath *historian, genealogist*
Young, Pamela J. *music educator*

Storrs Mansfield
Baldwin, Carlita Rose *minister*
Charters, Ann *literature educator*
Ford, Karrin Elizabeth *music educator, musician*
Kline, Nancy Mattoon *librarian*
Price, Glenda Delores *dean, college president*
Rimland, Lisa Phillip *writer, composer, lyricist*

Stratford
Blair, Sylvia H. *aerospace engineer*
DiCicco, Margaret C. *lawyer*
Monda, Marilyn *statistician, quality assurance professional*
Sahagian, Lucille Bedrosian *gasoline company executive*
Scott, Lorry Ann *elementary education music specialist*
Vlahac, Mary Ann Rita *marketing executive*

Suffield
Bianchi, Maria *critical care nurse, acute care nurse practitioner*
Hanzalek, Astrid Teicher *public information officer, consultant*

Taconic
Medvecky, Patricia *retired elementary school educator*

Terryville
Doughty-Jenkins, Bonnie-Marie *middle school educator*

Thomaston
Donohue, Diane Frances *artist*

Torrington
Bramble, Pamela Chace Leuba *artist, educator*
Di Russo, Terry *communications educator, writer*

Trumbull
D'Addario, Jody Ann *science educator*
Ewing, Anna M. *stock exchange executive*
Hochberg, Jennifer Anne *counselor*
Nevins, Lyn (Carolyn A. Nevins) *school disciplinarian*

Uncasville
Lobo, Rebecca *professional basketball player*

Unionville
Fantozzi, Janet Rosen *music educator*

Vernon Rockville
Davis, Nancy Costello *retired elementary school educator, retired vice principal, adult education coordinator*
Gallien, Sandra Jean *social worker*
Marmer, Ellen Lucille *pediatrician, cardiologist*

Voluntown
Thevenet, Patricia Confrey *social studies educator*

Wallingford
Lauttenbach, Carol *artist*
Lelas, Snjezana *pharmacologist, researcher*
Regueiro-Ren, Alicia *biomedical researcher*

Washington
Burton, Ann Mapes *historian, retired academic administrator*

Waterbury
Andonucci-Hill, Heather L. *psychologist*
Doback, Joan M. *physician assistant*
Donahue, Linda Wheeler *retired English educator, writer*
Lang, Christine JoAnn *elementary school educator*
Stella, Robin Lynn *psychologist*
Zasada, Mary Eileen *nursing administrator*

Waterford
Commire, Anne *playwright, writer, editor*
Hinkle, Janet *psychologist*
Hinkle, Muriel Ruth Nelson *naval warfare analysis company executive*

Pierson, Anne Bingham *physician*

West Hartford
Barry, Patricia Dowling *psychotherapist, consultant*
Butler, Kathleen A. *education educator, consultant*
Chase, Carol Johnson *mathematics educator*
Coleman, Winifred Ellen *academic administrator*
Collins, Alma Jones *language educator, writer*
Detmar-Pines, Gina Louise *business strategy and policy educator*
Dickie, Florence *science educator*
Gaumond, Lynn E. *elementary school educator*
Gebo, Susan Claire *consulting nutritionist*
Hornblow, Doris H. *retired nurse*
Karotkin, Rose A. *marketing professional*
Lawrence, Sarah Anne *social studies educator*
McAuliffe-Curnias, Susan Eileen *secondary school educator*
McGrory, Mary Kathleen *humanities educator, retired academic administrator*
Neisler, Otherine Johnson *education educator, consultant*
Rhinehart, Elizabeth D. *psychologist*
Salvatore, Nancy Baker *elementary school educator*
Washer, Barbara Mochrie *performing arts educator, director*

West Haven
Chavert, Georgia *nutritionist, educator*
Janeczek, Mary *secondary school educator, mathematician, department chairman*
Latham, Cynthia *elementary school educator*
Onton, Ann Louise Reuther *chemist*

West Redding
Wesselmann, Janine Carol *artist*

West Suffield
Jespersen, Wyn Cherie *music educator*

Westbrook
Fuller, Martha M. *poet*
Hall, Jane Anna *writer, model, artist*

Weston
Fredrik, Burry *theater producer, director*
Meyerson, Amy Lin *lawyer*

Westport
Boles, Lenore Utal *nurse psychotherapist, educator*
Campbell, Marta Smith *librarian*
Chernow, Ann Levy *artist, educator*
Davidson, JoAnn W. *retired elementary school educator*
Derr, Teresa Marie *social worker*
Freedman, Judith Greenberg *retired elementary school educator, state legislator*
Heyman, Ronnie Feuerstein *lawyer*
Huffman, Cathy Lilley *gifted and talented educator, special education educator*
Hunter, Gloria Eleanore *secondary school educator*
Lee, Janet Mentore *psychologist, educator*
Levy, Wendy *psychologist*
Lewis, Margaret Mary *marketing professional*
McCormack, Patricia Seger *editor, journalist*
McElroy, Abby Lucille Wolman *financial advisor*
Reilly, Nancy (Anne Caulfield Reilly) *painter*
Safran, Claire *writer, editor*
Siff, Marlene Ida *artist, designer*
Stewart, Martha Kostyra *entrepreneur, lecturer, author*
Warner, Kerstin Julianna *gifted and talented educator*

Wethersfield
Madigan, Rita Duffy *career planning administrator*

Willimantic
Clifford, Maryanne Theresa *economics professor, researcher*
Enggas, Grace Falcetta *academic administrator*
Free, Rhona Campbell *economics professor*

Wilton
Flesher, Margaret Covington *communications consultant, writer*
Holter, Patra Jo *artist, consultant*
Oberstar, Helen Elizabeth *retired cosmetics company executive*
Poundstone, Sally Hill *library director*
Reilly, Kathleen C. *director, retired secondary school educator*

Windsor
Simon, Dorothy Elaine *retired elementary school educator*

Winsted
Jassen, Alison P. *chemistry professor, biology professor*
Wilson, Mary Flynn *writer, educator*

Woodbridge
Cone, Virginia Williams *retired historian*
Ecklund, Constance Cryer *French language and literature educator*
Kleiner, Diana Elizabeth Edelman *art historian, educator, academic administrator*
Mahon, Anna Norgren *literature and language educator, coach*
O'Donnell, Janet Costa *secondary school educator*
Vasileff, Lili Alexandra *financial planner*

Woodbury
Bless, Martha M. *secondary school educator, department chairman*
O'Brien, Bonnie Jeanne *counseling administrator*

Woodstock
Ranta, Amy J. *music educator*

DELAWARE

Dagsboro
Davis, Marica Nanci Ella Riggin *retired artist*
Hanna, Anne Marie *artist*

Dover
Angstadt, Frances Virginia *language arts and theatre arts educator*
Bugglin, Carol Stephanie *clinical psychologist, psychotherapist*
Espadas, Elizabeth Anne *language educator*
Friedland, Billie Louise *former human services administrator, educator*
Guliana, Barbara Ann *retired director*
Haskins, Linda L. *language educator*
Jones, Geraldine Ann Johnson *secondary school educator*
Lott, Dawn Alisha *mathematics professor*
Minner, Ruth Ann *governor*
Perrine, Veronica Beader *music educator, director*
Royce, Christine Anne *primary school educator*
Rubino, Joelle L. *physical therapist, athletic trainer*
Sorenson, Liane Beth McDowell *director, state legislator*
Taylor, Suzonne Berry Stewart *real estate broker*
Windsor, Harriet Smith *state official*
Woodruff, Valerie *state agency administrator*

Frederica
Miller, Mary-Emily *history professor*

Georgetown
Nichols, M. Kathleen *therapist, educator*

Greenville
Reynolds Cooch, Nancy D. (Mrs. Edward W. Cooch Jr.) *sculptor*
Walker, Sally Barbara *retired glass company executive*

Hockessin
Croyle, Barbara Ann *health facility administrative executive*
Harris, Anne Eldredge *artist, educator*
Sawin, Nancy Churchman *educational consultant*

Lewes
Bala, Madeleine Jeanette *music educator*
Buchert, Stephanie Nicole *music educator*
Costigan, Constance Frances *artist, educator*
Spence, Sandra *retired trade association administrator*

Marydel
Whitaker, Susan LaVerne *retired secondary home economics educator*

Milford
Whitman, Ann Elizabeth *retired elementary school educator, education educator*

Millsboro
Price, Doris Coleen Davis *visual artist, printmaker*

Milton
Scott, Phyllis Wright *coach, music educator*

New Castle
Ainsworth, Elaine Marie *occupational therapist*
Bailey, Laurie Ruckert *music educator*
Keane, Marie Jeanette (Maria Keane) *art educator, artist*
Mullen, Regina Marie *lawyer*
Rolland, Kathy Ann *elementary school educator*
Williamson, Sandra Kaye *education educator*

Newark
Breslin, Wynn Boin *artist*
Cairns, Sara Albertson *retired physical education educator*
Carter, Mae Riedy *retired academic official, consultant*
Dean, Krysten *manufacturing engineer*
Friswell-Jacobs, Tracy *performing arts educator, dancer*
Gantzer, Mary Lou *medical products executive*
Gibson, Ann Eden *art historian, educator*
Isaacs, Diane Scharfeld *English educator*
Keppler, Mary Louise *elementary school educator*
McNeil, Sue *transportation system educator*
Talbert, Dorothy Georgie Burkett *social worker*
Wilson, Deborrah *physical education educator*

Rehoboth Beach
Giove, Susan Nancy *medical/surgical nurse, educator*

Seaford
Gandek, Jean Davis *secondary school educator*

Smyrna
McClellan, Stephanie Ann *speech pathology/audiology services professional*

Wilmington
Baron, Irene Jo *secondary school educator, artist, aerial photographer*
Baxter, Beverley Veloris *economic association administrator, educator*
Benson, Barbara Ellen *state agency administrator*
Berger, Carolyn *state supreme court justice*
Bounds-Seemans, Pamella J. *artist*
Breland, Elaine *webmaster, retired education specialist, special education educator, webmaster*
Butcher, Diane *chaplain, bereavement facilitator*
Carey, Frances Jane *elementary school educator*
Chagnon, Lucille Tessier *literacy acceleration consultant*
Cohen, Betsy Z. *bank executive*
Copeland, Tatiana Brandt *accountant*
Davis, Mary Kathryn *marketing professional*
Davis, Patricia Hewson *elementary school educator*
DeHart, Deborah Lee *private school educator, composer*
Dow, Lois Weyman *physician*
Doyle, Nancy Hazlett *artist*
Fleming, Blanche Miles *educational association administrator*
Freeman, Angela Y. *assistant principal*
Godfrey, Marion Ross *retired special education educator*

Graham, Frances Keesler (Mrs. David Tredway Graham) *psychologist, educator*
Gulyas, Diane H. *manufacturing executive*
Inselman, Laura Sue *pediatrician, educator*
Jolles, Janet K. Pilling *lawyer*
Kneavel, Ann Callanan *humanities educator, communications consultant*
Kullman, Ellen Jamison *chemicals executive*
Lagana, Laura A. *medical/surgical nurse, orthopedics nurse, volunteer*
Linderman, Jeanne Herron *priest*
Maley, Patricia Ann *preservation planner*
Marcali, Jean Gregory *retired chemist*
McIntyre, Megan D. *lawyer*
McLeer, Laureen Dorothy *drug development and pharmaceutical professional*
Meitner, Pamela *lawyer, educator*
Miranda-Evans, Valetta Lee *social worker, human services manager*
Petrilli, Michelle Leslie *lawyer*
Petrucci-Samija, Maria *chemist*
Robinson, Sue L(ewis) *federal judge*
Rogoski, Patricia Diana *corporate financial executive*
Roth, Jane Richards *federal judge*
Sippel-Wetmore, Frances Marie *microbiologist, retired business owner*
Stoker, Penny S. *human resources specialist*
Tjersland, Trina J. *performing arts educator*
Vary, Eva Maros *retired chemicals executive*
Weisenfeld, Carol Ann Trimble *marketing executive, consultant*
Winslow, Helen Littell *lawyer*
Witcher, Phyllis Herrmann *secondary school educator*

DISTRICT OF COLUMBIA

Washington
A-Baki, Ivonne *ambassador*
Abernathy, Kathleen Quinn *lawyer, former commissioner*
Abrecht, Mary Ellen Benson *lawyer*
Acker, Rose L. *elementary school educator*
Adams, Frances Grant, II, *lawyer*
Aikens, Martha Brunette *park service administrator*
Albrecht, Kathe Hicks *art historian, visual resources manager*
Albright, Madeleine Korbel *former secretary of state*
Allam, Hannah *journalist*
Allen, Bertrand-Marc *lawyer*
Altenhofen, Jane Ellen *federal agency administrator, auditor*
Altman, Beth Lee *social worker*
Alvillar-Speake, Theresa *federal agency administrator*
Alward, Ruth Rosendall *nursing consultant*
Amron, Cory M. *lawyer*
Anderson, M. Jean *lawyer*
Anderson, Mary Ann Grasso *theater association executive*
Angier, Natalie Marie *science journalist*
Anroman, Gilda Marie *college program director, lecturer, educator*
Anthony, Sheila Foster *government official*
Anthony, Virginia Quinn Bausch *medical association executive*
Appareddy, Vijaya L. *psychiatrist*
Apple, Daina Dravnieks *federal agency administrator*
Applebaum, Anne *journalist, writer*
Arana, Marie *editor, writer*
Aranoff, Shara L. *federal official*
Archibald, Jeanne S. *lawyer*
Arena, Kelli *news correspondent*
Armen, Margaret Meis *lawyer*
Armstrong, Alexandra *financial planner*
Arnez, Nancy Levi *educational leadership educator*
Arnold, Deborah J. *lawyer*
Arnwine, Barbara Ruth *lawyer*
Aron, Nan *lawyer, association executive*
Arrott, Elizabeth *journalist*
Aschenbrener, Carol Ann *pathologist, educator*
Ashmore-Hudson, Anne *psychologist, writer, consultant*
Atlas, Liane Wiener *writer*
Auberger, Marcia A. *lawyer*
Auerbach, Judith Diane *public health service officer*
Aviv, Diana L. *public policy analyst, psychotherapist*
Ayres, Margaret M. *lawyer*
Ayres, Mary Ellen *federal official*
Azcuenaga, Mary Laurie *government official*
Babby, Ellen Reisman *educational association executive*
Bachrach, Eve Elizabeth *lawyer*
Bacon, Sylvia *judge, law educator*
Baicker, Katherine (Kate Baicker) *federal official, economics professor*
Baigis, Judith Ann *nursing educator, academic administrator*
Bailey, Catherine Todd *ambassador*
Bailey, Judy Long *outreach and education specialist, social worker*
Bailey, Patricia Price *lawyer, former government official*
Bair, Sheila Colleen *federal agency administrator, former education educator*
Baker, P. Jean *lawyer, mediator*
Bakowski, Nancy *chemist*
Baldwin, Tammy *congresswoman, lawyer*
Bale, Judith R. *health science association administrator*
Balfour, Ana Maria *office manager*
Baran, Christine *systems analyst*
Barclay, Ellen S. *not-for-profit developer*
Barnett, Helaine M. *lawyer*
Barr, Joyce A. *ambassador*
Barron, Myra Hymovich *lawyer*
Barshefsky, Charlene *lawyer, former diplomat*
Bartnoff, Judith *judge*
Baskin, Roberta *television correspondent*
Batts, Alicia J. *lawyer*
Baum, Ingeborg Ruth *librarian*
Baumann, Linda Adriene *lawyer*
Baxter, Sandra L. *government agency administrator*

Bean, Melissa *congresswoman*
Bear, Dinah *lawyer*
Bea Roberts, Barbara Ann *legal secretary*
Beato, Cristina V. *government agency administrator*
Becker, Mary Louise *political scientist*
Bednash, Geraldine Polly *educational association administrator*
Behan, Kathleen A. (Kitty Behan) *lawyer*
Behrensmeyer, Anna K. *curator, research scientist*
Beiro Farabow, Sara *lawyer*
Bello, Judith Hippler *lawyer, trade association administrator*
Benitez, Brigida *lawyer*
Benoit, Marilyn B. *psychiatrist, consultant*
Berg, Gracia M. *lawyer*
Berg, Patricia Elene *molecular biologist*
Bergmann, Barbara Rose *economics professor*
Bergner, Jane Cohen *lawyer*
Berkley, Shelley (Rochelle Levine Berkley) *congresswoman, lawyer*
Berman, Ellen Sue *energy and telecommunications executive, theatre producer*
Berman, Louise Marguerite *education educator, writer*
Bernabei, Lynne Ann *lawyer*
Bertram, Connie N. *lawyer*
Bies, Susan Schmidt *bank executive*
Biggert, Judith Borg *congresswoman, lawyer*
Billauer, Barbara Pfeffer *lawyer, educator*
Birnbaum, S. Elizabeth *lawyer*
Blackburn, Marsha *congresswoman*
Blackburne-Rigsby, Anna *judge*
Blakey, Marion Clifton *federal agency administrator*
Blazek-White, Doris *lawyer*
Bloch, Susan Low *law educator*
Bloom-Feshbach, Sally *psychologist, educator*
Bloomfield, Sara J. *museum director*
Blumenthal, Susan Jane *psychiatrist, educator*
Bodine, Susan P. *federal agency administrator*
Bolton, Deborah A. *ambassador*
Bondareff, Joan M. *lawyer, retired government agency administrator*
Bondurant, Amy Laura *investment company executive*
Bono, Mary Whitaker *congresswoman*
Bonosaro, Carol Alessandra *professional society administrator, retired federal agency administrator*
Bordallo, Madeleine Mary (Mrs. Ricardo Jerome Bordallo) *congresswoman*
Born, Brooksley Elizabeth *retired lawyer*
Borra, Susan T. *dietician, medical association administrator*
Bosch, Michele C. *lawyer*
Bosco, Mary Beth *lawyer*
Bowes, Rosemary Tofalo *psychologist, consultant*
Bowman, Dorothy Louise *artist*
Boxer, Barbara *senator*
Boza, Clara Brizeida *marketing executive*
Bozarth, Stephanie Belle Mays *social worker*
Bradley, Barbra Bailey *musician, educator, accompanist*
Bradley, Mary Renee *research analyst*
Bradley Gardner, Janice *federal agency administrator*
Brand, Rachel L. *federal agency administrator, lawyer*
Brannan, Patricia A. *lawyer*
Brautigam, Deborah Anne *political science professor*
Brazeal, Aurelia Erskine *former ambassador*
Breathitt, Linda K. *energy advisor, former federal energy commissioner*
Bredhoff, Stacey Anne *curator*
Bresnahan, Pamela Anne *lawyer, mediator, arbitrator*
Bretzfelder, Deborah May *retired museum staff member*
Brice-O'Hara, Sally *career military officer*
Bridgeforth, Chrystl L. *former labor union administrator*
Bridgewater, Pamela E. *ambassador, former federal agency administrator*
Briggs, Ethel DeLoria *federal agency administrator*
Brobeck, Susan Williams *private school educator*
Broderick, Laura Anne *federal official*
Broering, Naomi Cordero *librarian*
Brooks, Jane K. *real estate agent, educator*
Brooks, Renana Esther *clinical psychologist, consultant, researcher*
Brooks, Sharon Diane *lawyer*
Brosnan, Carol Raphael Sarah *retired art association administrator*
Broun, Elizabeth *art historian, curator*
Brown, Ann W. *not-for-profit developer*
Brown, Barbara Berish *lawyer*
Brown, Corrine *congresswoman*
Brown, Dorothy M. *academic administrator*
Brown, Elizabeth Ann *foreign service officer*
Brown, Janice Rogers *federal judge, former state supreme court justice*
Brown, Pamela Wedd *artist*
Brown-Daniels, Patricia *budget analyst, wedding planner*
Browner, Carol M. *management consultant, former federal agency administrator*
Brown-Hruska, Sharon *federal agency administrator*
Brown Weiss, Edith *law educator*
Bruce, Carol Elder *lawyer*
Brueckner, Leslie A. *lawyer*
Bryan, Beth Ann *educational association administrator*
Buc, Nancy Lillian *lawyer*
Buhler, Leslie Lynn *museum director*
Bullett, Vicky *former professional basketball player*
Bumpus, Jeanne *lawyer*
Burger, Anna *labor union administrator*
Burk, Martha Gertrude *political psychologist*
Burke, Beverly J. *lawyer, utilities executive*
Burrous, Beth A. *lawyer*
Bush, Karen Lee *lawyer*
Bush, Laura Welch *First Lady of United States*
Bushnell, Prudence *diplomat, former management consultant, trainer*
Butcher, Karen A. *lawyer*
Butenis, Patricia A. *ambassador*
Butler, Mary K. *prosecutor*
Buto, Kathleen A. *health products executive*
Buzbee, Sally Streff *news correspondent*
Byrnes, Heidi *academic administrator, German language educator*
Cabaniss, Dale *government agency administrator*
Cafritz, Peggy Cooper *communications executive*
Callahan, Debra Jean *political organization worker*
Campbell, Nancy Duff *lawyer*
Campbell-Grothe, Ruth Ann *retired budget analyst*
Cantwell, Maria E. *senator*
Capito, Shelley Moore *congresswoman*
Capps, Lois Ragnhild Grimsrud *congresswoman, former school nurse*
Caproni, Valerie E. *lawyer, federal agency administrator*
Caputo, Anne Spencer *knowledge and learning programs director*
Carbonell, Josefina G. *federal agency administrator*
Carder-Thompson, Elizabeth B. *lawyer*
Carey, Sarah Collins *lawyer*
Carlisle, Linda Elizabeth *lawyer*
Carmody, Carol Jones *transportation executive, former federal agency administrator*
Carpenter, Sheila Jane *lawyer*
Carr, Carolyn Kinder *art gallery director*
Carr, Marie Pinak *book distribution company executive, publishing executive*
Carroll, M(argaret) Lizbeth Carr *art educator, graphics designer, photographer*
Carson, Julia M. *congresswoman*
Casey, Kathleen L. *commissioner*
Cashion, Ann *food service executive*
Catoe, Bette Lorrina *pediatrician, educator*
Cavalier, Gina M. *lawyer*
Cavendish, Elizabeth A. (Betsy Cavendish) *lawyer*
Chalk, Rosemary Anne *health science association administrator*
Chalkley, Jacqueline Ann *retail company executive*
Chammas, Judith Ann *diplomat*
Chan, Heng Chee *ambassador*
Chao, Elaine Lan (Hsiao Lan Chao) *secretary of labor*
Charytan, Lynn R. *lawyer*
Chavez-Thompson, Linda *labor union administrator*
Chen, Joie *news correspondent*
Cheney, Lynne Vincent *humanities educator, writer*
Chiechi, Carolyn Phyllis *federal judge*
Chin, Cecilia Hui-Hsin *librarian*
Chittum, Heather *chef*
Chotin, Elizabeth Ettlinger *science foundation director*
Christian, Betty Jo *lawyer*
Christian, Claudette Marie *lawyer*
Christian, Mary Jo Dinan *educational administrator, educator*
Christian-Christensen, Donna Marie *congresswoman*
Chun, Shinae *federal agency administrator*
Chute, Mary L. *library director*
Cinciotta, Linda Ann *lawyer*
Cino, Maria *federal agency administrator*
Clark, Kathryn *government agency administrator*
Clarke, Kathleen Burton *federal agency administrator*
Clayton, Carol A. *lawyer*
Cleave, Mary L. *environmental engineer, former astronaut*
Clift, Eleanor *news correspondent, writer*
Cline, Lynn F.H. *federal agency administrator*
Clinton, Hillary (Hillary Diane Rodham Clinton) *senator, lawyer, former First Lady of United States*
Cobb, Jane Overton *government official*
Cocco, Marie Elizabeth *journalist*
Coffield, Shirley Ann *lawyer, educator*
Cohen, Bonnie R. *government official*
Cohen, Mary Ann *federal judge*
Cole, Angela P. *psychologist, educator*
Collins, Susan Margaret *senator*
Colson, David A. *lawyer*
Colton Skolnick, Judith A. *artist*
Colvin, Carolyn W. *state agency administrator*
Combs, Linda Morrison *federal official*
Combs, Roberta *political organization administrator*
Comerford, Cristeta *chef*
Compton, Ann Woodruff *news correspondent*
Comstock, Amy L. *social services administrator*
Conlin, Linda Mysliwy *bank executive, former federal agency administrator*
Cook, Frances D. *management consultant*
Cooper, Constance Carter *academic administrator, education consultant, researcher*
Cooper, Ginnie *library director*
Cooper, Margaret J. *cultural organization administrator*
Cope, Jeannette Naylor *executive search consultant*
Corbett, Rebecca *editor*
Corrigan, Dara A. *lawyer, former federal agency administrator*
Corrigan, Janet M. *health science association administrator*
Coulter, Ann *writer, political columnist, lawyer*
Covington, Eileen Queen *secondary school educator*
Cowan, Joyce A. *lawyer*
Cox, M. Carolyn *lawyer*
Cranford, Judith *medical association administrator*
Crawford, Mary Louise Perri *career officer*
Crawford, Susan Jean *federal judge*
Crawford-Mason, Clare Wootten *television producer, journalist*
Crea, Vivien S. *career military officer*
Croser, Mary Doreen *educational association executive*
Cross, Meredith B. *lawyer*
Crowley, Juanita A. *lawyer*
Crown, Michele Fleurette *lawyer*
Cubin, Barbara Lynn *congresswoman*
Cunningham, Karen Lynn *social worker*
Curtiss, Catherine *lawyer*
Cushwa, Patricia K. *commissioner*
Daftary, Monika Neil *pharmacist, educator*
Dale, Adrianne Marie *information technology executive, consultant*
Dale, Shana L. *federal agency administrator*
Dana, Jane T. *lawyer*
Daniels, Diana M. *lawyer, publishing executive*
Dargan, Catherine Janine *lawyer*
Darling, Helen *health services consultant*
Darr, Carol C. *lawyer*
Davidson, Donetta Lea *federal official, former state official*
Davidson, Jo Ann *political organization executive, retired state legislator*
Davidson, Susan Bettina *editor, writer*
Davis, Jo Ann S. *congresswoman*
Davis, Michele A. *mortgage company executive, former federal agency administrator*
Davis, Susan A. *congresswoman*
Dawson, Jessica *art critic*
Day, Mary Louise *volunteer*
Deal, Jill B. *lawyer*
Dean, Lisa *foundation executive*
Deaton, Valerie L. *financial researcher, consultant*
Deeb, Mary-Jane *editor, educator*
Deese, Pamela McCarthy *lawyer*
DeFrancis, Suzy *federal agency administrator*
DeLauro, Rosa L. *congresswoman*
Delbanco, Suzanne F. *human services administrator*
de Leon, Sylvia A. *lawyer*
Delgado, Jane *health policy executive, writer, psychologist*
Denny, Judith Ann *retired lawyer*
DeParle, Nancy-Ann Min *former federal agency administrator, lawyer*
DePaul, Christina *dean, artist*
Dessaso, Deborah Ann *freelance/self-employed writer, corporate communications specialist*
DeSutter, Paula A. *federal agency administrator*
Devere, Amy Jo *physical education educator, director*
DeWaal, Caroline Smith *education and advocacy organization executive, lawyer*
Dewey, Elizabeth R. *lawyer*
Dhue, Stephanie *television producer, reporter*
Doan, Lurita Alexis *federal agency administrator*
Dobriansky, Paula Jon *federal agency administrator*
Dodge, Judith C. *musician*
Dole, Elizabeth Hanford (Liddy Dole) *senator, former federal agency administrator*
Dominguez, Cari M. *federal official*
Donley, Rosemary *university official*
Donlon, Claudette *performing company executive*
Donohoe, Cathryn Murray *journalist*
Donohue, Joyce Morrissey *biochemist, toxicologist, dietician, educator*
Dorfman, Cynthia Hearn *government agency administrator*
Doria, Marilyn L. *lawyer*
Dorn, Jennifer Lynn *federal official*
Dowd, Maureen *columnist*
Drake, Thelma Day *congresswoman*
Draper, Roberta Hornig *retired journalist*
Drew, Elizabeth *commentator, journalist, writer*
DuBelle, Molyneau *legal consultant*
DuCran, Claudette Deloris *retired financial analyst*
Duggan, Juanita D. *trade association administrator*
Dukert, Betty Cole *television producer*
Dunham, LizaMarie Bassiwa *medical technician*
Dunlop, Becky Norton *retired government agency administrator*
Dutton, Christina Parker *interior designer, event planner*
Duval, Sandra *director*
Duval-Pierrelouis, Jeanne-Marie *educational association executive*
Dwyer, Maureen Ellen *lawyer*
Dwyer Southern, Kathy *museum administrator*
Dye, Rebecca Feemster *commissioner*
Dyer, Susan Kristine *editor, librarian*
Earp, Naomi Churchill *federal official, lawyer*
Easterling, Barbara J. *labor union administrator*
Ebert, Carey Dalton *lawyer*
Edelman, Marian Wright *not-for-profit developer, lawyer*
Edlavitch, Susan T. *lawyer*
Efros, Ellen Ann *lawyer*
Egan, Michelle D. *social sciences educator*
Elcano, Mary S. *lawyer*
Elwood, Patricia Cowan *state official, political scientist, consultant, educational consultant*
Ely-Raphel, Nancy *diplomat*
Emerson, Jo Ann H. *congresswoman*
Engh, Anna P. *lawyer*
Engleman Connors, Ellen G. *federal agency administrator*
Epps, Roselyn Elizabeth Payne *pediatrician, educator*
Ericsson, Sally Claire *not-for-profit official*
Escobedo Cabral, Anna *federal official*
Esfandiary, Mary S. *physical scientist, operations consultant*
Eshoo, Anna Georges *congresswoman*
Espeut, Camille Cottrell *retired art educator*
Esserman, Susan Gayle *lawyer*
Etter, Delores M. *civilian military employee*
Evans, Joy *foundation administrator*
Fahmy Hudome, Randa *lawyer*
Faiks, Jan Ogozalek *lobbyist*
Fain, Cheryl Ann *translator, editor*
Fales, Lisa Jose *lawyer*
Falk, Diane M. *research information specialist, librarian, writer, editor, director*
Fall, Dorothy *artist, writer, art director, art association administrator*
Fallon, Sally *writer*
Farquhar, Michele C. *lawyer*
Farr, Judith Banzer *retired literature educator, writer*
Feder, Judith *dean*
Feinstein, Dianne *senator*
Feld, Karen Irma *columnist, journalist, commentator, speech professional*
Feldman, Clarice Rochelle *lawyer*
Fenton, Kathryn Marie *lawyer*
Ferrell, Elizabeth Ann *lawyer*
Field, Andrea Bear *lawyer*
Fields, Suzanne Bregman *syndicated columnist*
Fields, Wendy Lynn *lawyer*
Fifer Canby, Susan Melinda *library administrator*
Fingerhut, Marilyn Ann *federal agency administrator*
Fisher, Alice S. *federal agency administrator, lawyer*
Flannery, Ellen Joanne *lawyer*
Flattau, Pamela Ebert *research psychologist, consultant*
Fleming, Lee Virginia *art critic, writer, curator*
Fletcher, Keyana James *small business owner, performing company executive*
Flood, Sandra Wasko *artist, educator*
Flowe, Carol Connor *lawyer*
Foley, April H. *ambassador*
Fong, Phyllis Kamoi *federal agency administrator, lawyer*
Ford, Ann K. *lawyer*
Ford, Cecilia Sparks *federal agency administrator*
Fore, Henrietta Holsman *federal agency administrator*
Foreman, Carol Lee Tucker *consumer advocate*
Forkan, Patricia Ann *foundation executive*
Forrester, Patricia Tobacco *artist*
Foscarinis, Maria *lawyer*
Foster, Hope S. *lawyer*
Foster, Mercedes S. *curator, research scientist*
Foxwell, Elizabeth Marie *editor, writer*
Foxx, Virginia Ann *congresswoman, small business owner*
Francke, Rend Rahim *former ambassador*
Franklin, Barbara Hackman *former government official*
Frawley Bagley, Elizabeth *government advisor, ambassador*
Frazer, Jendayi Elizabeth *federal agency administrator, former ambassador*
Freeman, Sharee M. *federal agency administrator*
Fresh, Linda Lou *government official*
Freund, Deborah Miriam *transportation engineer*
Friday, Eleanor Sullivan *federal official*
Friedman, Elizabeth Ann *training services executive*
Friend, Patricia A. *trade association administrator*
Fries, Helen Sergeant Haynes *civic leader*
Fusco, Aurilla Marie *director*
Fusillo, Alice Elbert *retired sociologist, sculptor*
Gadson, Sandra L. *nephrologist, medical association administrator*
Gallagher, Patricia E. *government agency administrator*
Gallozzi, Marialuisa S. *lawyer*
Ganter, Susan Lynn *foundation administrator, retired mathematics professor*
Garfinkel, Renée Efra *psychologist*
Garr, Sally D. *lawyer*
Garrels, Anne *news correspondent*
Garrison, Gwen E. *educational researcher, consultant*
Garrison, LaTrease E. *association executive*
Garvey, Jane *public relations executive*
Gati, Toby T. *international advisor*
Gatons, Anna-Marie Kilmade *government official*
Gerber, Melanie K. *lawyer*
Gest, Kathryn Waters *public relations executive*
Geyer, Georgie Anne *columnist, educator, commentator, writer*
Gibson, Florence Anderson *talking book company executive, narrator*
Gilbert, Pamela *strategic services company executive*
Giles, Patricia Cecelia Parker *retired art educator, graphic designer*
Gilfoyle, Nathalie Floyd Preston *lawyer*
Gillan, Kayla J. *lawyer*
Gillen, Adrienne Kosciusko *librarian*
Gilligan, Courtney *lawyer*
Gilliom, Judith Carr *federal official*
Ginsburg, Ruth Bader (Joan Ruth Bader Ginsburg) *United States Supreme Court Justice*
Givhan, Robin Deneen *journalist*
Glasser, Susan Beth *journalist*
Glassman, Cynthia Aaron *federal agency administrator, former commissioner*
Gleason, Kathryn L. *lawyer*
Goldberg, Jolande Elisabeth *law librarian, lawyer*
Golden, Olivia Ann *human services administrator*
Goldstein, Doris Mueller *librarian, researcher*
Goldway, Ruth Y. *federal agency administrator*
Gonzalez, Cecelia *lawyer*
Gonzalez-Hermosillo, Brenda *economist, researcher*
Gordon, Dorothy K. *silversmith, goldsmith*
Gorelick, Jamie Shona *lawyer*
Gorman, Joyce J(ohanna) *lawyer*
Gorman, Patricia Jane *editor*
Gorn, Janet Marie *government official*
Grainger, Amanda R. *lawyer*
Granger, Kay *congresswoman*
Grant, Susan J. *federal agency administrator*
Grapin, Jacqueline G. *economist*
Graves, Ruth Elaine *minister, educator*
Gray, Carolyn Doppelt *lawyer*
Gray, Mary Wheat *statistician, lawyer*
Gray, Sheila Hafter *psychiatrist, researcher*
Grealy, Mary R. *medical association administrator*
Greaux, Cheryl Prejean *federal agency administrator*
Green, Joyce Hens *federal judge*
Green, Karen Ina Margulies *psychologist*
Green, Ricki Kutcher *television producer*
Greenberger, Marcia Devins *lawyer*
Greene, Marcia Slacum *editor*
Greenhill, Lisa Michelle *professional society administrator*
Greenhouse, Linda Joyce *journalist*
Griffin, Christine M. *commissioner*
Griffin, Kelly Ann *public relations executive, consultant*
Griggs, Linda L. *lawyer*
Grigsby, Sharlyn Ann *human resources specialist*
Grossman, Joanne Barbara *lawyer*
Gruman, Jessie Christine *not-for-profit developer*
Grunberg, Nancy R. *lawyer*
Guzy, Carol *photojournalist*
Hagen, Wendy W. *public relations executive*
Hager, Mary Hastings *nutritionist, educator, consultant*
Hahn, Lorna *political organization executive, author*
Haines, Martha Mahan *lawyer*
Hale, Suzanne K. *ambassador*
Hall, Oceola S. *federal agency administrator*
Halpern, Nora R. *museum director, curator*

Hamburg, Margaret Ann (Peggy Hamburg) *public health administrator*
Hanley, Allison Anne *federal agency administrator*
Harbert Mitchell, Karen (Karen Alderman Harbert Mitchell) *government agency administrator*
Harbour, Pamela Jones *commissioner, lawyer*
Harding, Fann *retired science administrator*
Hargrove, Linda *professional basketball coach*
Harlem, Susan Lynn *librarian*
Harling, Barbara Jean *social worker*
Harman, Jane *congresswoman*
Harpham, Virginia Ruth *violinist*
Harris, Katherine *congresswoman*
Harrison, Patricia de Stacy *broadcast executive, former federal agemcy administrator*
Hart, Melissa Anne *congresswoman*
Harvey, Eleanor Jones *museum curator*
Harvey, Jane Hull *church administrator*
Harvey, Sheila McCafferty *lawyer*
Haslach, Patricia M. *ambassador*
Hatfield, C. Maile *lobbyist*
Hayes, Allene Valerie Farmer *government executive*
Hayes, Paula Freda *federal agency administrator*
Headden, Susan M. *editor*
Hecht, Marjorie Mazel *editor*
Hedges, Kamla King *library director*
Hedges, Marietta *performing arts educator, actor*
Heichel, Paula *investment company executive, financial consultant*
Height, Dorothy I. *former foundation administrator*
Heinz Kerry, Teresa F. (Maria Teresa Thierstein Simoes-Ferreira) *foundation administrator*
Henderson, Frances J. *lawyer*
Henderson, Karen LeCraft *federal judge*
Hennessy, Ellen Anne *lawyer, financial analyst, educator*
Hentges, Harriet *not-for-profit developer*
Herbold, Patricia Louise *ambassador*
Herman, Andrea Maxine *newspaper editor*
Herridge, Catherine *political correspondent*
Herseth, Stephanie Marie *congresswoman, lawyer*
Hersman, Deborah A. P. *federal agency administrator*
Hewitt, Emily Clark *federal judge, minister*
Higgins, Kathryn O'Leary (Kitty O'Leary Higgins) *federal agency administrator, former consulting firm executive*
Hillman, Jennifer Anne *federal official*
Hills, Carla Anderson *lawyer, former secretary of housing and urban development*
Hillsman, Sally T. *sociologist*
Hinrichs, S. Jean *auditor*
Hirons, Jean Louise *librarian*
Hirshberg, Jennefer *public affairs executive*
Hobbs, Ann S. *lawyer*
Hodges, Heather M. *ambassador*
Hoffman, Ann Fleisher *labor union administrator, lawyer, consultant*
Hogan, Felicity *artist*
Holdsclaw, Chamique Shaunta *professional basketball player*
Holladay, Wilhelmina Cole *interior designer, museum director*
Hollis, Sheila Slocum *lawyer*
Hollman, K. Hollyn *lawyer*
Holt, Helen *librarian, consultant, former government official*
Hooley, Darlene *congresswoman*
Horn, Marian Blank *federal judge*
Horn, Sharon K. *government agency administrator*
Horner, Constance Joan *federal agency administrator*
Howell, Beryl A. *lawyer*
Howell, Deborah *editor*
Howland, Nina Davis *historian*
Hughes, Elizabeth R. (Beth) *lawyer*
Hughes, Karen Parfitt *federal agency administrator*
Hughes, Marija Matich *law librarian*
Huhtala, Marie Therese *federal agency administrator, former ambassador*
Hutchison, Kay Bailey *senator*
Hynson, Jan I. *federal ombudsman, artist*
Innis, Pauline *writer, publishing company executive*
Irving, Susan Jean *government executive*
Iverson, Kristine Ann *federal agency administrator*
Jackson, Jeanine E. *ambassador*
Jackson, Margaret Elizabeth *science educator*
Jackson Lee, Sheila *congresswoman*
Jacobs, Madeleine *professional society administrator, writer*
Jacobson, Sabina *library administrator*
Jacobson, Tracey Ann *ambassador*
Jarvis, Charlene Drew *academic administrator, former scientist*
Jecklin, Lois Underwood *art corporation executive, consultant*
Jenkins, Renee R. *medical educator, pediatrician*
Jennings, Deborah E. *lawyer*
Jewell, Linda L. *ambassador*
Johnson, Brenda LaGrange *ambassador*
Johnson, Eddie Bernice *congresswoman*
Johnson, Jennifer J. *federal official*
Johnson, Kelly A. *federal agency administrator*
Johnson, Nancy Lee *congresswoman*
Johnson, Sheila Crump *entrepreneur*
Jonas, Tina Westby *federal agency administrator*
Jones, A. Elizabeth *corporate communications specialist, former federal agency administrator*
Jones, Barbara Pendleton *psychologist, educator*
Jones, Coletta L. *senior pastor*
Jones, Erika Ziebarth *lawyer*
Jones, Judith Miller *director*
Jones, Stephanie Tubbs *congresswoman, lawyer, prosecutor*
Jones, Susan Dorfman *real estate broker, writer*
Jordan, Anne E. Dollerschell *journalist*
Jordan, Samantha Kristine *communications director*
Jordan, Sandra *public relations professional*
Joyce, Anne Raine *editor*
Kadis, Averil Jordan *retired librarian*
Kahlow, Barbara Fenvessy *statistician*
Kapikian, Catherine Andrews *artist*
Kaptur, Marcia Carolyn (Marcy Kaptur) *congresswoman*
Karle, Isabella L. *chemist*
Katzen, Sally *lawyer, educator*
Keenan, Nancy A. *pro-choice association executive*
Kelley, Colleen M. *labor union administrator*
Kelly, Holly Andrea *federal agency administrator, director, real estate developer*
Kelly, Sue W. *congresswoman*
Kelly, Suedeen G. *commissioner*
Kemnitz, D'Arcy *lawyer, gay lesbian association executive*
Kendrick, Kim *federal agency administrator*
Kennedy, Deborah *communications executive, writer, editor*
Kennelly, Barbara B. *retired congressman, federal agency administrator*
Kenney, Kristie Anne *ambassador*
Kent, Jill Elspeth *entrepreneur, art appraiser, lawyer*
Kessler, Gladys *federal judge*
Kiko, Colleen Duffy *lawyer*
Kilberg, Bobbie Greene *govenment official*
Kilpatrick, Carolyn Cheeks *congresswoman*
Kimble, Melinda Louise *environmental administrator*
King, Gwendolyn S. *retired utility company executive, retired federal official*
King, Patricia Ann *law educator*
Kirk, Artemis G. *university librarian*
Kirkien-Rzeszotarski, Alicja Maria *academic administrator, researcher, educator*
Kirkpatrick, Jeane Duane Jordan *political scientist, federal official*
Kiser, Chérie R. *lawyer*
Klee, Ann Renee *lawyer*
Knapp, Rosalind Ann *lawyer*
Knezo, Genevieve Johanna *science and technology policy researcher*
Knight, Athelia Wilhelmenia *journalist*
Kollar-Kotelly, Colleen *federal judge*
Kramer, Noël Anketell *judge*
Kraus, Margery *management consultant, communications company executive*
Kravis, Marie-Josee Drouin *economist*
Krokos, Kelley Joan *psychologist, consultant*
Kroupa, Diane Lynn *federal judge*
Krueger, Anne *economist*
Kruger, Leondra R. *lawyer*
Krulfeld, Ruth Marilyn *anthropologist, educator*
Kuh, Charlotte Virginia *economist*
Kuhn, Harriet Lurensky *school psychologist*
Kutler, Alison L. *lawyer*
Kybal, Elba Gómez del Rey *economist, not-for-profit developer*
Lajoux, Alexandra Reed *editor-in-chief, educator*
La Lime, Helen R. Meagher *ambassador*
Lambert, Deborah Ketchum *public relations executive*
Lamm, Carolyn Beth *lawyer*
Lampl, Peggy Ann *public information officer*
Landrieu, Mary Lorretta *senator*
Lardent, Esther Ferster *lawyer, consultant*
Larkin, Barbara Mills *state agency administrator*
Larson, Judy L. *museum director, curator*
LaSpada, Carmella *government agency administrator*
Lassen-Feldman, Wendy Anne *sales executive, lawyer*
Latham, Patricia Horan *lawyer*
Latimer, Allie B. *retired lawyer*
Latimer, Katharine Ruth *lawyer*
Lawson, Jennifer *broadcast executive*
Lawson, Kelli *communications executive*
Leckey, Dolores R. *religious organization administrator, writer*
Lederer, Laura J. *educational association administrator*
Lee, Barbara *congresswoman*
Lee, Debra Louise *cable television company executive*
Leff, Deborah *foundation administrator, former library director*
Legro, Patrice *museum director*
Lehrman, Margaret McBride *broadcast executive, television producer*
Leiter, Amanda C. *lawyer*
Lenn, Marjorie Peace *educational association administrator, consultant*
Levine, Felice *educational association administrator*
Levy, Ellen J. *writer, educator*
Levy, Leah Garrigan *federal official*
Lew, Ginger *lawyer*
Lewis, Anne McCutcheon *architect*
Lewis, Eleanor Roberts *lawyer*
Lewis, Prudence Fox *Christian science practitioner*
Liasson, Mara *news correspondent*
Lichtenbaum, Greta L.H. *lawyer*
Lichtenstein, Elissa Charlene *legal association executive*
Liebenson, Gloria Krasnow *interior design executive, freelance writer*
Liebman, Wilma B. *government agency administrator*
Lightman, Marjorie *historian*
Likins, Rose Marie *federal agency administrator, former ambassador*
Lim, Jeanette J. *federal agency administrator*
Lincoln, Blanche Lambert *senator*
Linehan, Lou Ann *political organization worker*
Lisboa-Farrow, Elizabeth Oliver *public and government relations consultant*
Little, Kathleen C. *lawyer*
Locke, Stephanie Frances *anesthesiologist, educator, consultant*
Locklear, Arlinda Faye *lawyer*
Loepere, Carol Colborn *lawyer*
Lofgren, Zoe *congresswoman*
Loo, Beverly Jane *publishing executive*
Lopatto, Mary A. *lawyer*
Lott, Cindy M. *lawyer*
Louison, Deborah Finley *global public affairs consultant*
Lovelace, Gail T. *human resources specialist*
Lowe, Mary Frances *federal official*
Lowey, Nita Melnikoff *congresswoman*
Lubic, Benita Joan Alk *travel company executive*
Lundsager, Margrethe (Meg Lundsager) *federal official*
Luque, Nancy *lawyer*
Lurensky, Marcia Adele *lawyer*
Luxton, Jane Charlotte *lawyer*
Lynn, Valerie Roemer *psychotherapist*
Lyons, Grace Jean *librarian*
Lyons, Mona *lawyer*
MacFarlane, Cathy M. *federal agency administrator*
Mack, Julia Cooper *retired judge*
Maddox, Lauren M. *federal agency administrator*
Madras, Bertha Kalifon *federal official, neuroscientist*
Majoras, Deborah Platt *commissioner*
Malcolm, Ellen Reighley *small business owner*
Malcom, Shirley Mahaley *science association executive*
Maloney, Carolyn Bosher *congresswoman*
Manley, Audrey Forbes *retired academic administrator, pediatrician, retired military officer*
Mantyla, Karen *distance learning consultant*
Marcoullis, Erato Kozakou *ambassador*
Marcum, Deanna Bowling *library administrator*
Marcus, Devra Joy Cohen *internist*
Marcuss, Rosemary Daly *economist*
Marlette, Cynthia *lawyer*
Marr, Phebe Ann *retired historian, educator*
Marshall, Maryann Chorba *executive secretary*
Martin, Kathleen Suzanne *librarian*
Martin, Linda Gaye *demographer, economist*
Martinez, Carmen Maria *ambassador*
Martinez, Herminia S. *economist, banker*
Martinez, Rose Marie *health science association administrator*
Marvel, L. Paige *federal judge*
Masekela, Barbara Joyce Mosima *ambassador*
Mason, Eileen B. *federal arts administrator*
Mason, Rosanna Marie *lawyer*
Matheis, Cheryl *not-for-profit developer*
Mathews, Jessica Tuchman *research executive, federal official, newswriter*
Matsui, Doris Okada *congresswoman*
Mays, Janice Ann *lawyer*
Mazzaferri, Katherine Aquino *lawyer, bar association executive*
McBee, Susanna Barnes *retired journalist*
McCaleb, Margaret Anne Sheehan *application developer*
McCarthy, Carolyn *congresswoman*
McCaul, Elizabeth *investment advisor, former state agency administrator*
McCaw, Susan Rasinski *ambassador*
McCollum, Betty *congresswoman*
McDavid, Janet Louise *lawyer*
McDowell, Barbara *lawyer*
McDowell, Heather L. *lawyer*
McDowell-Craig, Vanessa Dennise *supervisor, consultant*
McEldowney, Nancy *diplomat*
McElveen-Hunter, Bonnie *international relief organization executive*
McEntee, Christine W. *architecture association administrator, former medical association administrator*
McFeatters, Ann Carey *journalist*
McGervey, Teresa Ann *technical information specialist*
McGinnis, Patricia Gwaltney *non-profit organization executive*
McGoldrick, Jane R. *psychologist, writer, editor*
McGrath, Kathryn Bradley *lawyer*
McGreevey, Lisa S. *investment company executive*
McGuan, Kathleen H. *lawyer*
McGuirl, Marlene Dana Callis *law librarian, educator*
Mc Kay, Emily Gantz *civil rights and nonprofit professional*
McKay, Margo Marquita *federal agency administrator, lawyer*
McKee, Margaret Jean *federal agency administrator*
McKinney, Cynthia Ann *congresswoman*
McMeans, Sarah Dornin Wilkinson *communications regulatory specialist*
McMorris, Cathy *congresswoman*
McMurray, Claudia Anne *federal agency administrator, lawyer*
McSweeny, Dorothy Pierce *art association administrator*
Medaglia, Mary-Elizabeth *lawyer*
Mederos, Carolina Luisa *public policy consultant*
Medvidovich, Suzanne F. *human resources specialist*
Meers, Elizabeth Blossom *lawyer*
Meggers, Betty Jane *anthropologist, researcher*
Megginson, Elizabeth R. *legislative staff member, director, lawyer*
Mellan, Olivia Julie (Olivia Julie Shapiro) *psychotherapist*
Meloy, Sybil Piskur *retired lawyer*
Melton, Carol A. *communications executive*
Mendoza, Julie C. *lawyer*
Menkel-Meadow, Carrie Joan *law educator*
Merritt, Carolyn *government agency administrator*
Meshulam, Deborah R. *lawyer*
Meyer, Katherine Anne *lawyer*
Meyer, Lindsay Beardsworth *lawyer*
Meyer, Margaret Vaughan *librarian, educator*
Meyers, Linda Dee *non-profit administrator, researcher*
Mezoughem, Claire Virginia *economist*
Michaels, Jennifer *choreographer, dancer, educator*
Michnich, Marie E. *health policy analyst, consultant, educator*
Miers, Harriet Ellan *federal official, lawyer*
Mikel, Sarah Ann *librarian*
Mikulski, Barbara Ann *senator*
Millender-McDonald, Juanita *congresswoman*
Miller, Annie Christmas *secondary school educator*
Miller, Candice S. *congresswoman*
Miller, Christine Odell Cook *federal judge*
Miller, Jeanne-Marie Anderson (Mrs. Nathan J. Miller) *language educator, academic administrator*
Miller, Laura Jean *federal agency administrator*
Miller, Linda B. *administrator*
Miller, Margery *psychologist, educator, speech pathology/audiology services professional, mental health services professional*
Miller, Mary Rita *retired adult education educator*
Miller, Nicole *art columnist*
Miller, Susan M. *telecommunications industry executive*
Millman, Laura Diane *federal official*
Minardi, Ann Segura *lawyer, musician*
Mirvahabi, Farin *lawyer*
Mitchell, Andrea *journalist*
Mitchell, Ruthie Yvette *human services administrator, director*
Mock-Morgan, Mavera Elizabeth *artist, art educator*
Mohrman, Kathryn j. *academic administrator*
Moler, Elizabeth Anne *lawyer*
Molinari, Susan *former congresswoman*
Mondello, Lisette McSoud *federal agency administrator*
Monroe, Jane D. *federal agency administrator*
Monroe, Stephanie Johnson *federal agency administrator*
Montanez-Johner, Nancy *federal agency administrator*
Montoya, Regina T. *association executive, lawyer*
Mooney, Marilyn *lawyer*
Moore, Amy Norwood *lawyer*
Moore, Barbara C. *fraternal organization administrator*
Moore, Barbara C. *ambassador*
Moore, Gwendolynne S. (Gwen Moore) *congresswoman*
Moore, Jacquelyn Cornelia *retired labor union administrator, editor*
Moore, Kimberly Ann *federal judge, law educator*
Moran, Anne E. *lawyer*
Moriarty, Lauren *ambassador*
Morrissey, Patricia A. *federal agency administrator*
Moten, Sarah Elizabeth *federal agency administrator*
Moye, Sidley Andrea *lobbyist*
Mujica, Barbara Louise *language educator, writer*
Murguia, Janet *non-profit organization administrator*
Murkowski, Lisa Ann *senator*
Murphy, Betty Southard (Mrs. Cornelius F. Murphy) *lawyer*
Murphy, Caryle Marie *foreign correspondent*
Murphy, Frances M. *federal agency administrator*
Murphy, Joanne Becker *writer*
Murray, Patty (Patricia J. Murray) *senator*
Musgrave, Marilyn N. *congresswoman*
Myers, Julie L. *federal agency administrator*
Myrick, Sue Wilkins *congresswoman, former mayor*
Naegle, LaDawn *lawyer*
Napolitano, Grace F. *congresswoman*
Narasaki, Karen Keiko *advocate, lawyer*
Nardi Riddle, Clarine *chief of staff*
Nason, Nicole R. *federal agency administrator*
Nathan, Joan *cookbook author, freelance writer, lecturer*
Natividad, Irene *women's rights advocate*
Nazareth, Annette LaPorte *commissioner, lawyer*
Neal, Darwina Lee *federal agency administrator*
Neita, Marguerite Elaine *science educator*
Nesbitt, Veronica A. *program support analyst*
Newman, Pauline *federal judge*
Newman, Sherryl Hobbs *former district secretary*
Nielsen, Louisa Augusta *broadcast executive*
Nightingale, Elena Ottolenghi *pediatric geneticist, academic administrator, educator*
Noe, Adrianne *museum administrator*
Noonan, Norine Elizabeth *academic administrator, researcher*
Northup, Anne Meagher *congresswoman*
Norton, Eleanor Holmes *congresswoman, lawyer, educator*
Norwalk, Leslie V. *federal agency administrator*
Norwood, Deborah Anne *law librarian*
O'Brien, Soledad *news anchor*
O'Connor, Bridget *labor union administrator, lawyer*
O'Connor, Eileen J. *federal agency administrator*
O'Connor, Karen *political science professor, researcher, writer*
O'Day, Kathleen M. *federal official, lawyer*
Oertel, Yolanda Castillo *pathologist, educator*
Ohl, Joan Eschenbach *federal agency administrator*
O'Kane, Margaret E. *non-profit organization executive*
Okun, Deanna Tanner *federal official*
Oliphant, Martha Carmichael *civic worker*
Oliver-Simon, Gloria Craig *human resources advisor, consultant, lawyer*
Olsen, Jody (Josephine K. Olsen) *federal agency administrator*
Olson, Pamela Faith *lawyer, former federal agency administrator*
O'Malley, Susan *professional basketball team executive*
O'Neill, Catherine *cultural organization administrator*
O'Neill, Michelle *federal agency administrator*
Onel, Suzan *lawyer*
Ong, Laureen E. *broadcast executive*
Oran, Elaine Surick *physicist*
Orr, Bobette Kay *diplomat*
O'Sullivan, Stephanie L. *federal agency administrator*
Othello, Maryann Ceclilia *quality improvement specialist*
Otremba, Geraldine Marie *congressional and international relations executive*
Outlaw, Wanda Cecelia *priest*
Pack, Sandra L. *federal agency administrator*
Padgett, Nancy Weeks *law librarian, consultant, lawyer*
Palmer, Stacy Ella *periodical editor*
Parr, Carol Cunningham *academic administrator*
Patenaude, Pamela Hughes *federal agency administrator*
Patrick, Susan D. *federal agency administrator*
Patron, June Eileen *former government official*
Patterson, Anne Woods (Anne Brevard Woods Patterson) *federal agency administrator, former ambassador*
Patterson, Sally Jane *communications executive, consultant*
Patton, Sharon F. *museum director*
Payton, Sue C. *civilian military employee*
Pearce, Drue *federal official, former state legislator*

FLORIDA

Altamonte Springs

Apopka

Arcadia

Atlantic Beach

Auburndale

Aventura

Avon Park

Baker

Bal Harbour

Bartow

Bay Pines

Belleair

Belleair Beach

Belleair Bluffs

Boca Raton

Eisenberg, Robin Ledgin *religious education administrator*
Fabj, Valeria *education educator*
Fineman, Geraldine Gottesman *artist*
Fishenfeld, Grace *artist, educator*
Foreman, Barbara Blatt *healthcare facility administrator*
Goldstein, Shari *healthcare educator*
Innes-Brown, Georgette Meyer *real estate broker, insurance broker*
Jacobson, Susan Bogen *psychotherapist*
Jessup, Jan Amis *arts volunteer, writer*
Kewley, Sharon Lynn *systems analyst, consultant*
Klasfield, Ilene *psychologist*
Kramer, Cecile Edith *retired medical librarian*
Land, Judith Broten *stockbroker*
Levick, Myra Friedman *art psychotherapist, educator*
Mitchell, Carmencita C. *literature and language professor*
More, Kane Jean *science educator*
Morris, Jill Carole *psychotherapist*
Naples, Mary Cecilia *mental health services professional, health facility administrator*
Pajunen, Grazyna Anna *electrical engineer, educator*
Phelps, Annette Failla *realtor*
Price, Rita Fleischmann *artist, educator*
Rebel, Amy Louise *elementary school educator*
Reeves, Mary Jane W. *interior designer*
Robben, Tricia Elizabeth *protective services official*
Rosenthal, Marilyn *school librarian, educator*
Rothberg-Blackman, June Simmonds *retired nursing educator, psychotherapist*
Russ, Fenee L. *principal, consultant*
Shalom, Galit *psychologist*
Shepard, Colleen *elementary school educator*
Speer, Leona Bettina *secondary school educator*
Spencer, Angela *physician assistant*
Sterling, Lorraine *volunteer*
Turner, Lisa Phillips *human resources executive*
Vaccino, Alyce King *artist*
Yoder, Patricia Doherty *public relations executive*
Zhong, Dawn He *materials engineer*

Bonita Springs
Borchers, Janet Marise *elementary school educator, counselor*
Elliott, Donna Louise *artist*
Hastings, Vivien N. *lawyer*
Hauserman, Jacquita Knight *management consultant*
Liebman, Phyllis Janice *volunteer, educator*
McNamara-Ringewald, Mary Ann Thérèse *artist, educator*

Boynton Beach
Deling-Lewis, Elaine Marie *special education educator*
Jacobs, Wendy *editor, realtor*
Jones, Shirley Ellen *hearing impaired educator*
Moll, Lauretta Jane *guidance counselor*
Morris, Nancy Lois *elementary school educator*
Parsons, Mindy (Mindy Enos) *newsletter editor, publisher, non-profit organization executive*
Polinsky, Janet Naboicheck *retired state official, retired state legislator*
Ricks, Dallis Derrick Biehl *pianist*
Robinson, Brenda Kay *editor, public relations executive*
Srinath, Latha *physician*
Waldman, Gloria *art gallery owner, artist*
Wilner, Lois Annette *retired speech and language pathologist*

Bradenton
Bjorklund, Nancy Margarette Watts *music educator*
Driscoll, Constance Fitzgerald *education educator, writer, consultant*
Rahn, Saundra L. *councilman*
Vereb, Teresa B. *psychiatrist*
Woodson-Howard, Marlene Erdley *former state legislator*

Brandon
England, Lynne Lipton *lawyer, pathologist*
Richardson, Michelle Yvette *mathematics educator, mathematics professor*
Sanchez, Evelyn Ford *retired humanities educator*

Brooksville
Hartley-Lonabaugh, Karen Lee *critical care nurse*
McBride, Tamera Shawn Dew *geologist*
Saxe, Thelma Richards *secondary school educator, consultant*

Cantonment
Walker, Janie Suzanne *music educator*

Cape Canaveral
Roberts, Nancy Carolyn *retired counselor, elementary school educator*

Cape Coral
Andert, Darlene (Darlene Andert-Schmidt) *management consultant*
Bradley, Jean Irene *elementary school educator*
Covington, Patricia Ann *university administrator*
(Harrison) Flint, Nancy Elizabeth *retired medical association administrator*
Graff, Sherry *adult nurse practitioner*
Graham, Dorothy E. *elementary school educator*
Janssen, Janice Beaty *writer, educator*
Mac Master, Harriett Schuyler *retired elementary school educator*
Minich, Jacqueline Hutton *science educator*
Nightingale, Suzanne M. *management consultant*
Stoudt, Patricia Lupi *secondary school educator*
Wendel, Joan Audrey *music educator*

Casselberry
Jackowitz, Enid Duchin *psychotherapist*
Reiss, Deborah L. *elementary school educator*
Renee, Lisabeth Mary *small business owner, art designer*

Celebration
Renard, Meredith Anne *marketing and advertising professional*

Clearwater
Baker-Bowens, Helen L. *administrative assistant, genealogy researcher*
Barry, Joyce Alice *dietician, consultant*
Bazzone, Theresa (Terry) A. *sales executive*
Beeson, Mary *internist, endocrinologist, researcher*
Dougall-Sides, Leslie K. *lawyer*
Duncan, Holly H. *foundation executive*
Fenderson, Caroline Houston *psychotherapist*
Halsey, Jean Michele *nursing educator*
Henderson, Janet Lynn *small business owner*
Holbrook, Taryl Ann *psychological consultant*
Knoop, Maggie Pearson *language educator*
VanMeer, Mary Ann *publishing executive, writer, webmaster*
Werner, Elizabeth Helen *librarian, language educator*
Zobel, Margaret Riethmeier *retired music educator*

Clermont
Cox, Margaret Stewart *photographer*
Fox, Terri Jo *music educator*
Hicks, Debra Carter *biology professor*
Richardson, Dot (Dorothy Gay) *former Olympic softball player, physician*
Sides, I. Ruth S. *retired music educator*

Clewiston
Burroughs, Jeannette *elementary school educator*
Hamilton, Stefanie Marie *mathematics educator*
Mammen, Mary A. *elementary school educator*

Cocoa
Campbell, Kari Melissa *elementary school educator*
Valverde, Cheryl Lynn *secondary school educator*

Cocoa Beach
Herbstman, Loretta *sculptor, painter*
Taylor, Nancy Alice *mechandiser, buyer*
Weston, Janice Leah Colmer *librarian*
Wirtschafter, Irene Nerove *tax specialist, consultant, military officer*

Coconut Creek
Fait, Grace Wald *writer, retired language educator*

Cooper City
Birge, Beverly Harrington *secondary school educator*
Garrard, Patricia Renick *elementary school educator*

Coral Gables
Burini, Sonia Montes de Oca *apparel manufacturing executive, public relations executive*
Goldstein, Phyllis Ann *art historian, educator*
Gould, Taffy *Internet company executive, real estate executive*
Gustafson, Anne-Lise Dirks *lawyer, consul*
Harriell, Kysha *athletic trainer, educator*
Humphries, Joan Ropes *psychologist, educator*
Jackson, Yvonne Ruth *former pharmaceutical executive*
Koita, Saida Yahya *psychoanalyst, educator*
Lorber, Charlotte Laura *publisher*
Miller, Virginia Irene *fine art galleries executive*
Morales-Martin, Gisela *interior designer*
Perez, Josephine *psychiatrist, educator*
Shalala, Donna Edna *academic administrator, former secretary of health and human services*
Sola, Caridad Maria *architect*
Thomasson, Amie Lynn *philosopher, educator*
Touby, Kathleen Anita *lawyer*
Van Vliet, Carolyn Marina *physicist, researcher*
Welsh, Judith Schenck *communications educator*

Coral Springs
Kohl, Joan *not-for-profit developer, social worker*
Kroll, Lynne Francine *artist*
McFarlane, Dana B. *science educator, secondary school educator*
Rachlin Rubin, Joyce Linda *education educator*

Crestview
Howard, Kelli Michelle *science educator*

Crystal River
Keith, Carol Jean *writer, regional historian*

Dade City
Brown-Waite, Virginia (Ginny Brown-Waite) *congresswoman*
Lukacik, Denise Marie *dance studio owner, choreographer*

Dania
Quillen, Teresa *music educator*

Dania Beach
Satin, Claire Jeanine *sculptor, artist*

Davie
Bromante, Christina Garcia *mathematics educator*
Penhollow, Tina Marie *health science researcher, educator*
Ross, Kathryn Amie *psychologist*
Schwab, Judith *artist, educator, sculptor*
Sullivan, Kathryn Lynn *educational association administrator*
Walkinshaw, Nicole M. *performing arts educator*

Daytona Beach
Ahn, Shi Hyun *professional golfer*
Andrews, Donna L. *professional golfer*
Baena, Marisa *professional golfer*
Barrett, Tina *professional golfer*
Bivens, Carolyn Vesper *former advertising executive, golf association commissioner-elect*
Cool, Mary L. *education specialist*
Dalia, Vesta Mayo *artist*
David, Valentina S. *physics professor*
Davies, Laura *professional golfer*
DeLuca, Annette *professional golfer*
Doolan, Wendy *professional golfer*
Foushee-Higgs, Rosa *elementary school educator, artist*
Green, Betty Nielsen *education educator, consultant*
Han, Hee-Won *professional golfer*
Hastings, Mary Lynn *real estate broker*
Hurst, Patricia Ann *professional golfer*
Inkster, Juli *professional golfer*
Jang, Jeong *professional golfer*
Kane, Lorie *professional golfer*
Kennedy, Lesa France *professional sports team executive*
Kerr, Cristie *professional golfer*
Kim, Christina *professional golfer*
Kim, Mi Hyun *professional golfer*
Kruse, Marylin Lynn *retired language educator*
Kuehne, Kelli *professional golfer*
Kung, Candie *professional golfer*
Moodie, Janice *professional golfer*
Neumann, Liselotte *professional golfer*
Ochoa, Lorena *professional golfer*
Pak, Se Ri *professional golfer*
Park, Grace *professional golfer*
Park, Hee-Jung (Hee Jong Park) *professional golfer*
Poitier, Constance Rena *music specialist, educator*
Rosales, Jennifer *professional golfer*
Saiki, Kim *professional golfer*
Schandel, Susan *professional sports team executive*
Schauer, Catharine Guberman *public affairs specialist*
Sheehan, Patty *professional golfer*
Silverman, Beatrice Toltz *retired psychiatrist*
Sorenstam, Annika *professional golfer*
Steinhauer, Sherri *professional golfer*
Stupples, Karen *professional golfer*
Talley, Diane Yvonne *special education educator*
Teske, Rachel *professional golfer*
Voce, Joan A. Cifonelli *retired elementary school educator*
Webb, Karrie *professional golfer*
Whitwam, Eileen V. *adult nurse practitioner, educator*
Whitworth, Kathrynne Ann *professional golfer*
Wie, Michelle Sung *professional golfer*
Zenkovsky, Betty Jean *modern languages educator*

De Leon Springs
Price, Artis J. *retired secondary school educator*

Debary
Coble, Alicia Sharon *retired elementary school educator, retired secondary school educator*

Deerfield Beach
Berger, Barbara Paull *social worker, marriage and family therapist*
Bethel, Marilyn Joyce *librarian*
Moran, Patricia Genevieve *corporate financial executive*
O'Brien, Cindy *chemistry educator*
Wells, Bette Evans *psychotherapist*

Defuniak Springs
Brinson, Vida L. *counselor*

Deland
Caccamise, Genevra Louise Ball (Mrs. Alfred E. Caccamise) *retired librarian*
Carlin, Caty C. *artist, director*
Navarro, Lydia *language educator*
Sorensen, Jacki Faye *choreographer, aerobic dance company executive*

Delray Beach
Appel, Mindy R. *social worker*
Bishop, Kathleen Ann *customer service, education and communication consultant, professional speaker*
Campbell, Cynthia *retail executive*
Carter-Miller, Jocelyn *retail executive*
Ehrlich, Geraldine Elizabeth *management consultant*
Ellsweig, Phyllis Leah *retired psychotherapist*
Force, Elizabeth Elma *retired pharmaceutical executive*
Gilfilen, Teri *artist*
Hofman, Elizabeth Elveretta *retired mathematics educator, guidance counselor, dean*
Leeds, Susanne *special education educator, writer*
Luechtefeld, Monica *retail executive*
Mayer, Marilyn Goodwin *steel company executive*
McKay, Patricia A. *corporate financial executive*
Ross, Beatrice Brook *artist*
St. George, Elaine *art educator*
Schenkel, Suzanne Chance *retired natural resource specialist*
Scherer, Beverly *retired elementary school educator*
Snyder, Virginia Artrip *writer*
Stewart, Patricia Carry *foundation administrator*
Wells, Mary Elizabeth Thompson *deacon, chaplain, director*

Deltona
Bondinell, Stephanie *counselor, academic administrator*
Comeau, Heather Marie *dance instructor, administrator*
Drewry, Marcia Ann *physician*
Rossi, Jennifer Michelle *athletic trainer*

Destin
Deel, Frances Quinn *retired librarian*

Doral
Brioso-Mesa, Maureen Diane *mental health services professional*

Dunedin
Cappiello, Mimi *elementary school educator*
Foley, Briana *music educator, consultant*
Gamblin, Cynthia MacDonald *mathematics educator, lobbyist*
Pedretty, Catherine Partain *education educator*
Scott, Gwendolyn Lutz *internist*
Shaneyfelt, Patricia Tharin *elementary school educator*
Simmons, Patricia Ann *pharmacist, consultant*

Eatonville
Ebert, Tracy *science educator*

Edgewater
Lawson, Bonnie Hulsey *psychotherapist, consultant*
Schubert, Jeanne *artist*

Englewood
Catterlin, Cindy Lou *music educator, language educator*
Clark, Carolyn Chambers *nurse, educator, publishing executive*
Ness, Sharon L. *social studies educator, coach*

Estero
MacDougall, Frances Kay *marketing consultant*

Eustis
Falanga-Liverotti, Shauna Marie *secondary school educator*

Fernandina Beach
Barlow, Anne Louise *pediatrician, medical researcher*

Ferry Park
Seaver, Elizabeth Mary *music educator*

Fort Lauderdale
Adams, Nancy R. *nurse, retired military officer*
Ambrose, Judith Ann *wedding planner*
Bartelstone, Rona Sue *gerontologist*
Calloway, Carolyn *elementary school educator*
Carter, Marjorie Jackson *special education educator, consultant*
Carter Pereira, Claudine Renee *forensic specialist*
Castillo, Carmen *staffing company executive*
Cavendish, Kim L. Maher *museum administrator*
Coleman, Phyllis *law educator*
Donaldson, Lisa Miller *city administrator*
Durst, Kay Horres *physician*
Friedman, Marla Ilene *director, educator*
Gonzalez, Nancy Berger *healthcare professional, educator*
Guest, Suzanne Mary *adult education educator, artist*
Gunzburger, Suzanne Nathan *municipal official, social worker*
Haugen, Christine *plastic surgeon*
Hershenson, Miriam Hannah Ratner *librarian*
Hilburn, Dawn *special education educator*
Iglesias, Lisa G. *lawyer*
Jackson-Callandret, Shirley Lorraine *music educator*
Johnson, Mary Margaret Dickens *governmental and commercial researcher, consultant*
Kennedy, Beverly (Kleban) Burris *financial advisor, former television and radio personality*
Koch, Katherine Rose *communications executive*
Kornblau, Barbara L. *physical therapist, educator*
Labiner, Adria *psychotherapist*
LeRoy, Miss Joy *model, apparel designer*
Lilley, Mili Della *insurance company executive, entertainment management consultant*
Littman, Marlyn Kemper *information scientist, educator*
Loos, Roberta Alexis *advocate, artist, educator*
Mahan, Mary Hoyle *retired physical educator*
McCormick, Queen Esther Williams *clergyman*
McGreevy, Mary Sharron *former psychology educator*
Parker, Sasha Smilka *medical educator, nurse, consultant*
Parrish, Lori Nance *property appraiser*
Richmond, Gail Levin *law educator*
Sands, Roberta Alyse *real estate investor*
Schneider, Ursula Wilfriede *author*
Segal, Marilyn Mailman *psychologist, educator*
Sperling, Randi A. *pediatrician*
Spungin, Charlotte Isabelle *retired secondary school educator, writer*
Stewart, Linda Berenfield *librarian*
Swann, Elizabeth *director, personal trainer*
Van Alstyne, Judith Sturges *retired language educator*
Velez, Ines *oral pathologist, educator*
Wilbur, Colleen Patricia *elementary school educator, principal*
Young, Ann F. *history professor*

Fort Myers
Aron, Eve Glicka Serenson *personal care industry executive*
Brown, Jaclyn *elementary school educator*
Carney, Teryl Dawn *physician assistant*
Colgate, Doris Eleanor *sailing school owner, administrator*
Cummings, Rayann Burnham *minister*
Curtin, Constance O'Hara *language educator, writer*
Drushal, Mary Ellen *parish administrator, education educator, former academic administrator*
Elliot, Kathleen Ann *school system administrator*
Ellis, Maria Vanessa *dance educator*
Faith, Ruth L. *retired mathematician*
Goyak, Elizabeth Fairbairn *retired public relations executive*
Harmon, Elizabeth Oakwood *school system administrator*
Hugill, Chloe *artist, foundation administrator*
Jaye, Karen A. *human resources specialist*
Lewellen, Melissa Dawn *elementary school educator*
Lewton, Betsy *chemistry professor*
Lippens, Nancy Cobb *music educator*
Mendible, Myra *literature educator, researcher*
Robertson, Mary Amos *mathematics educator*
Thurman, Cynthia Denise *human services administrator*
Van Vleck, Pamela Kay *real estate company officer*
Varley, Elizabeth Gail *social worker*
Weiss, Susette Maré *technical and photographic consultant, mass communications and media relations specialist, investor*

Fort Pierce
Cassens, Susan Forget *artist*

Garde, Susan Reutershan *accountant*
Jefferson, Zanobia Bracy *art educator, artist*
Lindsay, Rita Carol *mathematics professor*
Peterson, Barbara Owecke *artist, retired nurse, retired real estate agent*
Rice, Mary Esther *biologist*
Swenson, Ada Perez *artist*
Widder, Edith Anne *biologist*

Fort Walton Beach
Bolt, Lynda Elaine *alcohol/drug abuse services professional*
Hart, Nancy Diane *family nurse practitioner, educator, consultant, writer, mental health nurse*
Hicks, Patricia J. *secondary school educator*
McDonald, Pamela Jane *educational media specialist*
Register, Annette Rowan *literature educator*
Williams, Bethtina Qubré *minister*

Gainesville
Abrams, Julie Marie *counseling psychologist*
Behnke, Marylou *pediatrician, educator*
Brown, Myra Suzanne *school librarian*
Canelas, Dale Brunelle *library director*
DesForges, Deborah Waln *music educator*
Dolan, Teresa A. *dean, educator, researcher*
Drummond, Willa Hendricks *neonatologist, educator, information technology executive*
Ellis, Laura Renee *music educator*
Fouke, Janie M. *academic administrator, educator*
Green, Eleanor Myers *veterinarian, educator*
Greenberg, Corinne Hunt *psychotherapist*
Grobman, Hulda Gross (Mrs. Arnold B. Grobman) *health science educator*
Hardt, Nancy Sisson *pathology and laboratory medicine educator*
Harley, Ruth *artist, educator*
Harrison, Faye Venetia *anthropologist, educator, writer*
Hartigan, Karelisa Voelker *classics educator*
Hasell, Mary Joyce (Jo) *architecture educator*
Hollien, Patricia Ann *small business owner, researcher*
Hoy, Marjorie Ann *entomology educator*
Kelly, Kathleen S(ue) *communications educator*
Kirkland, Nancy Childs *secondary school educator, consultant*
Kohen, Martha *architecture educator*
Korner, Barbara Oliver *academic administrator*
Limacher, Marian Cecile *cardiologist*
Linton, Kristy Ann *primary school educator*
Lockwood, Rhonda J. *mental health services professional*
Lucas, Michelle Denise *information technology manager*
MacLeod, Joan Ann *medical/surgical nurse, administrator*
Maple, Marilyn Jean *educational media coordinator*
Maurer, Virginia Gallaher *law educator*
Mendenhall, Nancy Price *radiologist, educator*
Navab, Aphrodite Desiree *artist, educator, writer*
Olsen, Maria Teresa *middle school educator*
Paul, Ouida Fay *music educator*
Peck, Carolyn *basketball coach*
Puckett, Ruby Parker *nutritionist, food service executive, writer*
Rosenberger, Margaret Adaline *retired elementary school educator, writer*
Sackellares, Dalma Kalogjera *psychologist*
Saucerman, Alvera Adeline *elementary school educator*
Schmidt-Nielsen, Bodil Mimi (Mrs. Roger G. Chagnon) *retired physiologist, educator*
Scott, Lynn Thomson *Spanish language and literature educator*
Small, Natalie Settimelli *retired pediatric mental health counselor*
Smith, Jo Anne *writer, retired communications educator*
Steffee, Nina Dean *publisher*
Stipek, Kathleen *reference librarian*
Taylor, Grace Elizabeth Woodall (Betty Taylor) *law educator, library administrator*
Wass, Hannelore Lina *educational psychology educator*
West, Robin Lea *psychology educator*
White, Susie Mae *school psychologist*
Wiggins-Rothwell, Jeanine Ellen *artist*

Glen Saint Mary
Bales, Mary Catherine *gifted and talented educator*
Richerson, Kristina Marie *social studies educator*

Goulds
Taylor, Millicent Ruth *elementary school educator*

Green Cove Springs
Davidson, Joy Elaine *retired mezzo soprano*

Gulf Stream
FitzSimons, Marjorie Kitchen *art consultant*

Gulfport
Davis, Ann Caldwell *history educator*
Morrison, Marlena *mathematics educator*

Hallandale Beach
Cooper, Joy Frances *mayor*
Engel, Tala *lawyer*
Geller, Bunny Zelda *poet, writer, publisher, sculptor, artist*

Harbour Heights
Nash, Ruth S. *foundation administrator*

Havana
Beare, Muriel Anita Nikki *public relations executive, author*

Hialeah
Engler, Eva Kay *dental and veterinary products company executive*
Jenkins, Dawn Paula *special education educator, dancer*
Wright, Michelle Beth *elementary school educator*

Hillsboro Beach
Marshall, Jo Taylor *social worker*

McGarry, Carmen Racine *historian, artist*

Hobe Sound
Haus, Judith Ann *elementary school educator*
Houser, Constance W. *writer, artist*
Mark, Marsha Yvonne Ismailoff *artistic director*

Holly Hill
Davis, Evangelyn S. *elementary school educator*

Hollywood
Berdich, Alla *psychiatrist*
Giulianti, Mara Selena *mayor*
King, Alma Jean *retired physical education educator, healthcare educator*
Lutchman, Eva *elementary school educator*
Mendez, Deborah *parochial school educator*
Pittarelli, Diana *entrepreneur*
Sadowski, Carol Johnson *artist*
Shane, Doris Jean *respiratory therapist, administrator*
Valdes, Jacqueline Chehebar *psychologist, consultant, researcher*
Wilson, Linda Edmiston *secondary school science educator*

Holmes Beach
Dunne, Nancy Anne *retired social services administrator*
Ehde, Ava Louise *librarian, educator*
Nevans, Laurel S. *rehabilitation counselor*

Homestead
Ferraro, Marie *dental hygienist*
Gray, Tonja Louise *literature and language educator*
Ireland, Patricia *lawyer*
Whitehorton, Thelma *educational administrator*

Homosassa
Frank, Elizabeth Ahls (Betsy Frank) *retired art educator*

Hudson
Bishop, Mildred Ann *literature and language educator*
Whatley, Yvonne Marie Tramontana *secondary school educator*
White-Myers, Barbara Jeanne *artist, retired educator*

Hutchinson Island
Welch, Martha Lynn *environmentalist, educator*

Immokalee
Foster, Lucille Stuart *music educator*

Indialantic
Claflin, Tracie Nadine *private school educator*
Pavlakos, Ellen Tsatiri *sculptor*

Indian Harbor Beach
Traylor, Angelika *stained glass artist*

Inverness
Hawk, Pauletta Browning *elementary school educator*
Kramer, Marlene Dixie *dietician*
Nichols, Sally Jo *geriatrics nurse*

Jacksonville
Ackerson, Becky Louise *literature and language educator*
Aleschus, Justine Lawrence *retired real estate broker*
Alexander, Edna M. DeVeaux *elementary school educator*
Bedell, Elizabeth Snyder (Betty Bedell) *editor-in-chief, marketing professional*
Blount, Yolanda Denise *social services administrator, psychologist*
Bodkin, Ruby Pate *real estate broker, educator*
Brady, Terrie *political organization executive*
Brown, Beverly Jean *retired elementary school educator*
Brown, Jerri Lynne *history educator*
Cagle, Margaret Broughton *retired parochial school educator*
Carson, Ellen Kathleen *biology professor*
Cohen, Kathleen Francis *librarian*
Collins, Carlita Raulerson *mathematician, educator*
Constantini, JoAnn M. *small business owner, systems administrator, consultant*
Crimmel, Cynthia Eileen *rail transportation executive*
Davis, Linda Lennon McConnell *critical care nurse*
Dundon, Margo Elaine *museum director*
Eden, F. Brown *artist*
Feber, Jane Boxer *elementary school educator*
Furdell, Elizabeth Lane *history professor*
Gubbin, Barbara Ashley Brendon *library director*
Halil, Susan Terrell *dental hygienist*
Hoffman, Helen Bacon *artist*
Hott, Peggy A. *mortgage banker*
Huber, Mary Susan *music educator*
Hughes, Carolyn Wright *elementary school educator, director*
Kelso, Linda Yayoi *lawyer*
Kinne, Frances Bartlett *academic administrator*
Longino, Theresa Childers *nurse*
Mack, Jeannette Ana *medical technician*
Main, Edna Dewey (June Main) *education educator*
Mauras, Nelly *pediatrics professor, department chairman, researcher*
Mueller, Cherone *religious organization administrator, writer, minister*
Murphy, Jeanne M. *science educator*
Nelson, Loraine Pratt *principal*
O'Donnell, Elisabeth Pallant *social studies educator*
Olin, Marilyn *secondary school educator*
Otto, Elizabeth Hall *education educator*
Pavlick, Pamela Kay *nurse, consultant*
Rider, Ruth Wheeler *elementary school educator*
Sanders, Marion Yvonne *retired geriatrics nurse*
ScarborougH, Marion Nichols *nutritionist, recreational facility executive*

Scheck, Elizabeth A. *sociologist, educator*
Schlette, Sharon Elizabeth *utility company executive*
Scott, Kamela Koon *psychologist, educator*
Stewart, Sandra Kay *music educator*
Vasana, Susan (Chun-Ye) *engineering educator*
Weaver, Dianne Jay *lawyer*

Jacksonville Beach
Hill, Joan Ann *retired university administrator*
Saltzman, Irene Cameron *consumer products company executive*

Jupiter
Colucci, Jacqueline Strupp *insurance agent, sculptor, management consultant*
Loper, Lucia Ann *retired elementary school educator*
Moseley, Karen Frances Flanigan *educational consultant, retired school system administrator, educator*
Szczesny, Marcia Linda *elementary school educator*

Kennedy Space Center
Alfonso, Berta *computer engineer*
Amos, Michelle *electronics engineer*

Key Biscayne
Cardozo, Arlene Rossen *writer*
Clay, Cynthia Joyce *writer, editor-in-chief*
de la Cruz, Carlos *wholesale distribution executive*
de la Cruz, Rosa *art collector*
Klarreich, Sue Friedman *education administrator, consultant*
Ross, Marilyn J. *language and communications educator*

Key Colony Beach
Crenshaw, Patricia Shryack *sales executive, consultant*

Key Largo
Kennedy, Mary Sussock *artist*

Key West
Armendariz, Alma Delia *small business owner, researcher*
Bradford, Judith Lynnell *journalist, artist*
Ersay, Molly Ann *counselor, consultant*
Pennington, Claudia *museum director*
Post-Gorden, Joan Carolyn *retired psychology educator*
Wisniewski, P. Michelle *retired obstetrician, gynecologist*

Kissimmee
Fahmie, Deborah *music educator*
King, Susan Marie *special education educator*
McCann, Jean Friedrichs *artist, educator*
Severance, Jeri-Lynne White *elementary school educator*
Toothe, Karen Lee *elementary and secondary school educator*
Wallace, Evelina Velvia Joetha *elementary school educator*

Lady Lake
Di Benedetto, Ann Louise *retired accounting administrator*
Whalen, Norma Jean *special education educator*

Lake City
Moore, Emma Sims *business educator*

Lake Mary
Reagan, Bettye Jean *artist*
Shanahan, Rebecca M. *lawyer*
Southward, Patricia C. *volunteer*

Lake Park
Heaton, Janet Nichols *artist, art gallery director*

Lake Placid
Post, Barbara Joan *elementary school educator*

Lake Wales
Butler, Susan *writer*
Dickey, Deena Lynne *music educator, vocalist*

Lake Worth
Asher, Kathleen May *communications educator*
Chittick, Elizabeth Lancaster *advocate*
Dilgen, Regina Marie *English educator*
Gilbert, Lisa Marie *social studies educator*
Heessel, Eleanor Lucille Lea *retired state agency administrator*
Palulis, Christine *biology educator, science educator*
Tracy, Ann Anderson *pediatrician*

Lakeland
Boulware, Carol Carter *retired music educator*
Chapman, Angela Marie *science educator*
Eskin, Catherine R. *language educator*
Garrott, Frances Carolyn *architectural engineer*
Jacobson, Barbara Dinger *music educator*
Markley, Kate *social worker, consultant*
Mason, Lois Ruth *retired elementary school educator*
Pospichal, Marcie W. *neuroscientist, psychologist, educator*
Rambaran, Sarah M. *music educator*
Spencer, Mary Miller *civic worker*
Stepp, Patricia Joann *middle school educator*
Varner, Marleen Allen *retired academic administrator*
Wilson, Micheline *small business owner*
Zucco, Ronda Kay *planning and marketing professional*

Land O Lakes
Mallon, Kellie Jane *special education educator*
O'Connell, Carmela Digristina *appraisal executive, consultant*
Webb, Mary Greenwald *cardiovascular clinical specialist, educator*
Wilkinson, Denise V. *psychologist*

Lantana
Gorman, Marcie Sothern *personal care industry executive*

Largo
Bush, Debra W. *occupational health nurse*
Schick, Alice Edith (Lisl Schick) *civic leader*
Szalkowski, Deborah *music educator*

Lecanto
Wheatley, Deborah A. *music educator*

Leesburg
Bolden, Kristin Elizabeth *secondary school educator*
Osborne, Glenna Jean *health facility administrator*
Smith, Kathy L. *elementary school educator, cosmetics executive, consultant*
Thompson, Mary B. *writer, illustrator*

Lithia
Kulkarni, Kavita-Vibha Arun *chemist*

Longboat Key
Hazan, Marcella Maddalena *writer, educator, consultant*

Longwood
Davis, Lisa *elementary school educator*
Gasperoni, Ellen Jean Lias *interior designer*
James, Kathleen Maria *music educator*
Sisselsky, Sharon Lee *travel company executive, secondary school educator*
Tomasulo, Virginia Merrills *retired lawyer*

Loxahatchee
Russell-Tyson, Pearl Leonie *elementary school educator*
Slygh, Carolyn V. *biologist, educator*

Lutz
Ellis, Leslie Elaine *psychologist*
Garcia, Sandra Joanne Anderson *law and psychology educator*
Miller, Bonnie Sewell *marketing professional, writer*
Saunders, Leslie *insurance company executive, marketing professional*
Smith, Marjorie *music educator, conductor*

Lynn Haven
Sheesley, Mary Frank *art educator*

MacDill AFB
Collins, Jessica Ann *military officer*

Macclenny
Hobbs, Brita Spence *science educator*

Madison
Hiss, Sheila Mary *librarian*

Maitland
Caston, Jane Pears *school nurse practitioner*
Mansson, Joan *librarian, consultant*
Stephens, Patricia Ann *marketing professional*
Vallee, Judith Delaney *environmentalist, writer, not-for-profit fundraiser*

Marathon
Giffen, Lois Key *artist, psychotherapist*
Vail, Elizabeth Forbus *volunteer*
Wolpe, Marcy Shear *artist, educator*

Marco Island
Henry, Sally *academic administrator*
Moore, Faye Halfacre *jewelry manufacturer*
Petry, Barbara Louise Cross *elementary educator*

Marianna
Speights, Lillie *elementary school educator*

Medley
O'Meara, Vicki A. *lawyer*

Melbourne
Greenblatt, Hellen Chaya *immunologist, microbiologist*
Helmstetter, Wendy Lee *librarian*
Hughes, A. N. *psychotherapist*
Jones, Elaine Hancock *humanities educator*
King, Virginia Shattuck *painter, retired school nurse, educator*
Scheuerer, Diane Thompson *home economics educator*
Storrs, Eleanor Emerett *science administrator, consultant*
Zabel, Dianne Donnelly *retired elementary school educator*

Merritt Island
Babcock, Hope Smith *counselor, educator, program designer*
Fischer, Linda DeMoss *small business owner*
Ocker, Debra Lynn *secondary school educator*
Young, Nancy Mayer *retired secondary school educator, artist*

Miami
Alvarez, Ofelia Amparo *pediatrician, hematologist*
Amos, Betty Giles *food service executive, accountant*
Arango, Penelope Corey *psychologist, consultant*
Arison, Marilyn Barbara (Lin Arison) *foundation administrator*
Arison, Shari *investment company executive*
Arrabal, Berta Isabel *radio producer*
Arsht, Adrienne *lawyer, broadcast executive, bank executive*
Auerbach, Ethel Louise *healthcare facility administrator*
Ayers, Mary Alice *writer, English educator*
Balmaseda, Liz *columnist*
Banas, Suzanne *middle school educator*
Barkett, Rosemary *federal judge*
Barreiro, Valerie *choreographer, educator*
Bass, Hilarie *lawyer*
Batson, Dawn Kirsten *music educator, cultural consultant*
Baugh, Cynthia *elementary school educator*

Borelli, Myriam *social worker, educator*
Brodsky, Beverly *artist*
Brooten, Dorothy *retired dean, nursing educator*
Bruel, Iris Barbara *psychologist*
Bunge, Mary Bartlett *medical educator*
Campos-Orrego, Nora Patricia *lawyer, consultant*
Carey-Shuler, Barbara *county commissioner*
Chambers, Elenora Strasel *artist*
Chisholm, Martha Maria *dietitian*
Chwat, Anne *food service executive*
Clemence, Cheryl Lynn *systems administrator*
Cooke, Marcia Gail *federal judge, lawyer*
Cortes, Carol Solis *school system administrator*
Coulter, Beverly Norton *singer, pianist, opera director*
Cubberley, Gayle Susan *band director*
Delehanty, Suzanne *museum director*
de Leon, Lidia Maria *magazine editor*
Dienstag, Cynthia Jill *lawyer*
Dimitriou, Dolores Ennis *computer consultant*
Ellner, Ruth H. *realtor*
Falco, Julia Faye *secondary school educator*
Faul, Maureen Patricia *health facility administrator*
Feinberg, Wendie *television producer*
Felton, Sandra Haley *special education educator*
Fichtner, Margaria *journalist*
Field, Julia Allen *futurist, strategist, environmentalist*
Fine, Rana Arnold *chemical and physical oceanographer*
Fleisher, Betty *artist, educator*
Floyd, Suzanne Elvira Izzo *music educator*
Galatas, Ruth Ann *musician, publishing executive, educator*
Gare, Fran *nutritionist*
Gimenes, Sonia Regina Rosendo *family therapist, psychologist*
Gonzalez, Ivette *biomedical engineer*
Goodman-Milone, Constance B. (Connie Goodman-Milone) *writer*
Gray, Frances Boone *minister*
Gyenizse, Debbie Linda *communications educator*
Harmon, Monica Renee *music educator*
Headley, Joanna Evonne *mental health services professional, researcher*
Heller, Ellen Distiller *gifted and talented educator*
Holifield, Marilyn J. *lawyer*
Hrinak, Donna Jean *lawyer, former ambassador*
Huysman, Arlene Weiss *psychologist, educator, writer*
Javier-Dejneka, Amelia Luisa *accountant*
Jones, Janice Cox *elementary school educator, writer*
Jones-Koch, Francena *school counselor, educator*
Kaelin, Jennifer Ann *secondary school educator*
Kaplan, Betsy Hess *retired school board member*
Kislak, Jean Hart *art director*
Knight Crane, Marjorie *foundation administrator*
Korchin, Judith Miriam *lawyer*
Kowalska, Maria Teresa *research scientist, educator*
Krissel, Susan Hinkle *transportation company executive*
Laje, Zilia L. *writer, publisher, translator*
Lando, Maxine Cohen *circuit judge*
Lawton, Thelma Cuttino *mathematics professor, consultant*
Leathers, Katherine Anne *education educator*
Leeder, Ellen Lismore *literature and language professor, literary critic*
Liebes, Raquel *retired import/export company executive*
Linoff-Thornton, Marian Gottlieb *retired psychologist*
Long, Maxine Master *lawyer*
Lynch, Catherine Gores *social services administrator*
Maggioni, Andrea *pediatrician*
Magrath, Kathleen Barry *retired municipal official*
Marsh, Sara Maria *music educator*
Mauch, Diane Farrell *music educator*
McLaughlin, Margaret Brown *adult education educator, writer*
McPhee, Penelope L. Ortner *foundation administrator, television producer, writer*
Mehta, Eileen Rose *lawyer*
Menendez Cambo, Patricia *lawyer*
Miliani, Lorenna *secondary school educator, social studies educator, writer*
Miller, Arlene *psychotherapist, mental health facility director*
Miller, Constance Johnson *elementary school educator*
Miller Udell, Bronwyn *judge*
Mischia, Marietta Cochran *retired principal*
Mitchell, Virginia Ann *investment company executive*
Moody, Jacqueline Elaine *music educator*
Moorman, Rose Drunell *county administrator, systems analyst*
Morgan, Dahlia *museum director, art educator*
Morgan, Marabel *writer*
Muniz, Diane Virginia *psychologist*
Mustelier, Alina Olga *travel consultant, music educator*
Nestor Castellano, Brenda Diana *real estate company executive*
O'Bryon, Linda Elizabeth *broadcast executive*
O'Connor, Kathleen Mary *lawyer*
Osman, Edith Gabriella *lawyer*
Parchment, Yvonne *nursing educator*
Parks, Arva Moore *historian*
Patrie, Cheryl Christine *elementary school educator*
Pelton, Margaret Marie Miller *retired art educator, academic administrator, artist*
Pfeiffer, Mary Louise *artist, educator*
Pierre-louis, Rosaire *elementary school educator, educator*
Pilafian, Audrey Kalenian *music educator*
Poston, Rebekah Jane *lawyer*
Potocky, Miriam *social worker, educator, writer*
Rawlings, Annette *painter*
Revis-Pyke, Robin Lynn *director*
Richards-Vital, Claudia *small business owner, recreational facility executive*
Rodriguez, Irmina Bestard *science educator*
Rodriguez, Joanne H. *literature and language educator, department chairman*
Rodriguez, Josefa Nieves *special education educator, language educator*
Rodriguez-Walling, Matilde Barcelo *special education educator*
Rourke, Diane McLaughlin *librarian*
Saland, Deborah *psychotherapist, educator*
Salinas, María Elena *newscaster, columnist*
Saralegui, Cristina Maria *Spanish language television personality, journalist*
Schumacher, Silvia C. *performing arts educator*
Seitz, Patricia Ann *judge*
Shipp, Theta Wanza *social service organization administrator, educator, consultant, minister*
Silverman, Wendy K. *psychologist, educator*
Skolnick, Holly R. *lawyer*
Spear, Laurinda Hope *architect*
Stanley, Sherry A. *lawyer*
Steinbaum, Bernice *art dealer*
Stiehm, Judith Hicks *director, political scientist, educator*
Stratos, Kimarie Rose *lawyer, sports association executive*
Tice, Dianne Lisa *social services administrator*
Vento, M. Thérèse *lawyer*
Vicente, Rachel *real estate agent*
Walkley, Mary L. *voice and music educator*
Weeks, Marta Joan *retired priest*
Weems, Lori K. *lawyer*
Weir-Soley, Donna Aza *language educator, writer*
Wolff, Grace Susan *pediatric cardiologist*
Yde, Jacqulyn Rae *interior designer, architectural colorist*
Young, Freddie Gilliam *principal, educator*

Miami Beach
Bredemeier, Mary Elizabeth *counselor, educator*
Camber, Diane Woolfe *museum director*
Danzis, Rose Marie *emeritus college president*
Foote, Gwendolyn Sue *middle school educator, artist*
Freshwater, Shawna Marie *neuropsychologist, clinical psychologist, cognitive neuroscientist*
Garbe-Morillo, Patricia Ann *preservationist*
Gardiner, Pamela Nan *performing company executive*
Gopman, Beth Alswanger *retired elementary school educator*
Kalsner-Silver, Lydia *psychologist*
Membiela, Roymi Victoria *marketing professional, consultant*
Ritvo, Eva Caroline *psychiatrist, educator*

Miami Shores
Diener, Betty Jane *business educator*
Konczal, Lisa *sociology educator, researcher*
Martino Maze, Claire Denise *nursing educator*

Miami Springs
Neasman, Annie Ruth *health facility administrator*

Micco
Christoph, Frances *painter*

Milton
Arnold, Margaret Morelock *music educator, soprano*
Coston, Brenda Maria Bone *language arts educator*

Miramar
Cooke, Honore Guilbeau *artist, educator*
Stephens, Sallie L. *retired assistant principal, commissioner*
Stewart Simpson, Donnamay Angela *interior designer*

Mount Dora
Kirton, Jennifer Myers *artist*
Mayek, Helen Cecilia *executive secretary*
Moreau, Patricia D. *science educator*

Mulberry
Bowman, Hazel Lois *retired English language educator*

Naples
Alty, Sally Joan *elementary school educator*
Ball, Kathleen M. *mathematics educator*
Bland, Iris C. *retired mathematics professor*
Blumenthal, Ronnie *lawyer*
Brooks, Joae Graham *psychiatrist*
Brown, Cindy Lynn *family practice nurse practitioner, critical care nurse*
Capelle-Frank, Jacqueline Aimee *writer*
Cotrone, Janice Lynne *nursing consultant*
Evans, Judith P. *music educator*
Fishbein, Estelle Ackerman *lawyer*
Gifford, Nancy (Mumtaz) *artist, poet*
Guerra, Mayra *insurance company executive*
Hall, Beverly Barton *librarian*
Hollenbeck, Karen Fern *foundation administrator, consultant*
Karkut, Bonnie Lee *retired dental office manager*
Kinder, Suzanne Fonay Wemple *retired historian, retired educator*
Maurides, Elaine *retired mental health services professional, retired social worker*
McCaffrey, Judith Elizabeth *lawyer*
McDonald, Jinx *interior designer*
Miles, Helen *oncological nurse*
Norton, Elizabeth Wychgel *lawyer*
Rawson, Marjorie Jean *lawyer*
Sekowski, Cynthia Jean *health products executive, medical consultant, contact lens specialist*
Watson, Dorothy Colette *real estate broker*
Wedel-Cowgill, Millie Redmond *secondary school educator, performing arts educator, communications educator, education educator*
Wroble, Lisa Ann *writer, educator*
York, Tina *painter*

Navarre
McLaughlin, Carolyn Lucile *elementary school educator*
Williams, Ella Owens *writer*

Neptune Beach
Chambers, Ruth Coe *writer*

New Port Richey
Cessna, Janice Lynn *systems administrator, information technology manager*
Charters, Karen Ann Elliott *critical care nurse, health facility administrator*
Sebring, Marjorie Marie Allison *former home furnishings company executive*

Niceville
Stallworth-Allen, Elizabeth Ann *business and computer science educator*

Nokomis
Gomber, Mary (Dee) *real estate broker*
Johns, Karen Jordan *music educator, small business owner*
Novak, Joyce Keen *artist, secondary school educator*
Robinson, Mary Catherine *artist*

North Fort Myers
Callanan, Kathleen Joan *Internet company executive, retired electrical engineer*
Carr-Carothers, Marcella Irene *medical surgical nurse*
Ranney, Mary Elizabeth *small business owner*

North Lauderdale
Dunham, Laura *elementary school educator*

North Miami
Kordalewski, Lydia Maria *news correspondent, municipal employee*

North Miami Beach
Girden, Ellen Robinson *retired psychology educator*
Rodriguez, Maria *social worker, counselor*
Sorosky, Jeri P. *academic administrator*

North Palm Beach
Kaplan, Muriel Sheerr *sculptor*
Wright, Donna Lake *retired marketing professional, volunteer*

North Port
Coe, Laurie Lynne Barker *photojournalist, artist*
Seiler, Charlotte Woody *retired elementary school educator, language educator*

Oakland Park
Krauser, Janice *special education educator*

Ocala
Blalock, Carol Douglass *psychologist, educator*
Booth, Jane Schuele *real estate company officer, real estate broker*
Brown, Sally Day *minister, literature and language educator, pre-school educator*
Delozier, Doris M. *retired secondary school educator*
Ettinger, Penny A. *medical/surgical nurse*
Fillion, Mary L. *history educator*
Haisten, Judy Aurich *language educator*
Hodges, Elizabeth Swanson *educational consultant, tutor*
Hornick, Susan Florence Stegmuller *secondary education educator, fine arts educator, curriculum specialist, artist*
Hudson, Ann Elizabeth *music educator*
Simon, Margaret Ballif *elementary school educator, writer*
Stickeler, Carl Ann Louise *legislator*
Westbrook, Rebecca Vollmer *secondary school educator*

Ocklawaha
Silagi, Barbara Weibler *corporate officer*

Ocoee
Davis, Elena Denise *accountant*
Wolfe, Darlene S. *secondary school educator, consultant*

Odessa
Diemer, Madeline Ann (Madeline DeMer) *psychology educator*

Okeechobee
Raulerson, Phoebe Hodges *school system administrator*

Oldsmar
Craft Davis, Audrey Ellen *writer, educator*
Hahn, Sharon Lee *city official*
Miller, Deborah *medical surgical nurse*
Zimmer, Barbara S. *elementary school educator*

Opa Locka
Robinson, Shirley S. *coach, educator*
Sample, Althea Merritt *secondary education educator, conductor*
Wright, Jeanne Elizabeth Jason *advertising executive*

Orange City
Kerben, Laura Sarah *middle and secondary school educator*

Orange Park
Combs, Diane Louise *elementary school educator, music educator*
Johns, Laurie Marie *dentist, hypnotherapist*

Orlando
Allison, Anne Marie *retired librarian*
Arlt, Devon Taylor *small business owner*
Ashe, Diane Davis *psychology professor, sport psychology consultant*
Baggott, Brenda Jane Lamb *elementary school educator*
Bauer, Maria Casanova *computer engineer*
Boyd, Be (Belinda) Carolyn *theater educator*
Brown, Diana L. *elementary school educator*
Chacon, Delia C. *secondary school educator*
Charles, Nancy Dufresne *reading educator, consultant*
Crabtree, Valleri Jayne *real estate company executive, educator, lawyer*
Davila - Madera, Maria L. *mathematics educator*
DeNoon, Patricia Y'Vette *science educator, consultant*
Eiffert, Crystal L. *lawyer*
Fawsett, Patricia Combs *federal judge*
Fine, Terri Susan *political science professor*
Flanagan, Marianne *music educator*
Foster-Hennighan, Shari M. *science educator*
Garavaglia, Jan C. *forensic pathologist, chief medical examiner*
Gouvellis, Mary C. *utilities executive*
Graham, Eleanore Davis *elementary school educator*
Griffith, Jeannette Teresa *elementary school educator, education educator*
Hall, Charlotte Hauch *editor*
Harris, Lani M. *theater educator*
Healy, Jane Elizabeth *newspaper editor*
Hom, Trudy A. *music educator*
Horning, Sheri *dietician, educator*
Houser, Ruth G. *corporate financial executive, accountant, municipal official*
Jacobs, Diane Margaret *academic administrator*
Johnson, Estelle Taylor *elementary school educator*
Jordan, Grace Carol *music educator*
Jung, Nicole P *psychologist*
Kilbourne, Krystal Hewett *retired rail transportation executive*
Klein, Jenny Lynn *neuroscientist, researcher*
Knowles, Patricia Marie *science educator*
Lee, Susan S. *mathematics educator*
Leuner, Jean D'Meza *nursing educator, director*
Lindner, Catherine Patricia *science educator*
Lloyd, Priscilla Ann *finance educator*
Magsino, Marissa Estiva *internist, pediatrician*
Maupin, Elizabeth Thatcher *theater critic*
Morrisey, Marena Grant *art museum administrator*
Moss, Kelly Anne *assistant principal*
Murphrey, Elizabeth Hobgood *history professor, librarian*
Murrah, Ann Ralls Freeman *historical association executive*
Pepper, Dottie *professional golfer*
Powell, Elaine Marie *writer, educator*
Radloff, Marie Ulrey *music educator*
Raffa, Jean Benedict *author, educator*
Raymond, Holly Cabrini *secondary school educator*
Rivera, Maira *elementary school educator*
Scarcella, Karyn Allee *staff developer, instructional coach*
Schultz, Victoria L. *music educator, entertainer*
Sharp, Christina Krieger *retired nursing educator*
Shives, Paula J. *lawyer*
Smetanka, Sally S. *small business owner*
Sourwine, Claire Elaine *retired music educator, conductor*
Thomas, Karen E. *elementary school educator*
Thorpe, Janet Claire *judge*
Vanderwerken, Sharon Lynn *nurse*
Waltz, Kathleen M. *publishing executive*
Wilson, Brenda Marie *secondary school educator*

Ormond Beach
Franchini, Roxanne *bank executive*
Graf, Dorothy Ann *human resources specialist*
Granville, Paulina *independent music scholar, educator*
Hoffman, Barbara Dianne *elementary school educator*
Logan, Sharon Brooks *lawyer*
Lynn, Evelyn Joan *state senator, consultant*
Smalbein, Dorothy Ann *guidance counselor*
von Fettweis, Yvonne Caché *archivist, historian*

Osprey
Holec, Anita Kathryn Van Tassel *civic worker*
Myers, Virginia Lou *education educator*

Palm Bay
Armstrong, Lillian M. *clinical counselor*
Boley, Andrea Gail *secondary school educator*
Downes, Patricia Ann *minister*
Hanna, Emma Harmon *architect, small business owner, mayor*
Kelley, Patricia *marketing representative*
Stone, Elaine Murray *writer, composer, television producer*
Young, Jane Ann *special education educator*

Palm Beach
Bagby, Martha L. Green *real estate holding company executive, writer, publishing executive*
Canary, Nancy Halliday *lawyer*
Coudert, Dale Hokin *real estate executive, marketing consultant*
Elson, Suzanne Goodman *social services administrator*
Floeckher, Louise Byrne Weldon *volunteer*
Harper, Mary Sadler *financial consultant*
Hope, Margaret Lauten *retired civic worker*
Javits, Joan (Zeeman) *writer, inventor*
Kay, Marcia Chellis *writer*
Krois, Audrey *artist*
Levine, Audrey Pearlstein *foundation administrator*
Whiteside, Patricia Lee *fine art antique and personal property appraiser*

Palm Beach Gardens
Burgeson, Joyce Ann *travel company executive*
Fiessinger, Bettina A. *mental health counselor, educator*
Peck, Maryly VanLeer *retired academic administrator, chemical engineer*
Schurtz, Ora Sears *hypnotist, educator*

Palm Coast
Barnes, Judith Ann *real estate company executive*
Boyer, Kaye Kittle *association management executive*
Franco, Annemarie Woletz *editor*
Jost, Kayren Prosser *accountant*

Palm Harbor
Diamond, Linda Mann *social studies educator*
Hewitt, Sarah Nichole *educational consultant, researcher*
Jones, Winona Nigels *retired media specialist*
Jordan, Patricia Colgan *physical education educator*

Katzen-Guthrie, Joy *performance artist, engineering executive*
Rivelli, Susan Veronica *nurse*

Panama City
Brown, Greta Kay *psychologist*
Carroll, Susan Victoria *lawyer*
Kline, Kelley Knapp *psychology professor*
Marino, Marion Lillian *health service administrator*
McArthur, Beth Golden *elementary school educator*
McCain, Lenda Haynes *librarian*
Rockhill, Marsha *special education educator*

Panama City Beach
Jenkins, Frances Owens *retired small business owner*

Parkland
Garcia, Laura Catherine *utilities executive*
Harris, Jacqueline Myers *speech pathology/audiology services professional*
Tharp, Karen Ann *insurance agent*

Parrish
Corey, Kay Janis *small business owner, apparel designer, nurse*

Pembroke Pines
Alber, Oro Linda *healthcare educator, consultant*
Allbee, Teresa Jo *elementary school educator*
Corbiere, Mary Louise Sambataro *music educator, musician*
Feldman, Jacqueline *retired small business owner*
Ferris, Rita Bernadette *social worker*
Hudson, Brenda Louise *soprano, opera singer, vocal coach*
Schaefer, Bonnie (E. Bonnie Schaefer) *retail executive*
Schaefer, Marla L. *retail executive*

Pensacola
Ables, Linda Bomberger *biology professor*
Burke-Fanning, Madeleine *artist*
Canady, Alexa Irene *pediatric neurosurgeon, educator*
Demars, Bonnie Macon *librarian*
Dettloff, Donna Jean *retired social worker*
Dorman, Jo-Anne *elementary school educator*
Galloway, Sharon Lynne *special education educator*
Gill, Becky Lorette *retired psychiatrist*
Holloway, Barbara Jean Chambers *retired secondary school educator*
Kuhl, Judith Annette *retired science educator*
Larson, Barbara Jean *art history professor*
Law, Carol Judith *medical psychotherapist*
Loesch, Mabel Lorraine *social worker*
Maki, Hope Marie *art educator*
Privette, P(atricia) Gayle *psychology educator, psychotherapist*
Roycroft, Elizabeth Anne *elementary school educator*
Shimmin, Margaret Ann *women's health nurse*
Sisk, Rebecca Benefield *retired secondary school educator, small business owner*
Stanny, Claudia J. *psychology professor*
Wernicke, Marian O'Shea *language educator*
Wilcox, Krysta *social studies educator*
Wright, Shannon Marie *psychotherapist, counselor*

Pinellas Park
Benedict, Gail Cleveland *music educator*

Plantation
Ackerman, Helen Ruth Penner *psychologist*
Ballantyne, Maree Anne Canine *artist*
Berger, Nancy *lawyer*
Najm, Tami Lynn *music educator*
Nickelson, Kim René *internist*
Tannen, Ricki Lewis *lawyer, psychologist, educator*
Wyse-Feders, Mary *science educator*

Pompano Beach
Brooker, Fern G. *healthcare educator*
Corsello, Lily Joann *minister, counselor, educator*
Endahl, Ethelwyn Mae *elementary education educator, consultant*
Gelske, Andrea Janna *psychologist*
Gross-Brein, Evelyn *counseling administrator, real estate broker*
Gude, Nancy Carlson *lawyer*
Henschel, Leonore Katherine *elementary educator*
Johnson, Dorothy Curfman *elementary school educator*
Kaskinen, Barbara Kay *writer, composer, lyricist, musician, educator*
Kory, Marianne Greene *lawyer*
Perkins, Lois Elaine *retired art educator*
Pigott, Melissa Ann *social psychologist*
Potash, Vella Rosenthal *lawyer, educator*
Silverman, Eileen R. *elementary school educator*

Ponte Vedra Beach
Millard, Jeri Killough *educational consultant*
Scott, Marie Claudine *ceramic artist, writer*
Simon, Lois Prem *interior designer, artist*
Soderberg, Nancy *former court official, writer*
Toker, Karen Harkavy *physician*

Port Charlotte
Reynolds, Helen Elizabeth *management consultant*
Wolff, Diane Patricia *writer, film and television producer*

Port Orange
Hensinger, Margaret Elizabeth *real estate, horticultural and agricultural advertising and marketing executive*
Johnson, Susan F. *elementary school educator*
Riegner, Elizabeth Jane *counselor, educator, mental health nurse*

Port Richey
Mueller, Lois M. *psychologist*

Port Saint John
Baumann, Patricia April *orthopedic surgery fellow*

Port Saint Lucie
Earley, Deborah Loraine *education educator, researcher*
Hogan, Roxanne Arnold *nursing consultant, risk management consultant, educator*
Hunt, Denyse *chemistry educator*
Mottram-Doss, Renée *corporate financial executive*

Punta Gorda
Clinton, Mariann Hancock *educational association administrator*
Gleason, Joyce Marie *educational consultant*
Hamel, Esther Veramae *author*
Hollinshead, Ariel Cahill *oncologist, educator, researcher*
Lynch, Constance *reading specialist*
Narrett, Carla Marie *university administrator*
Smith-Mooney, Marilyn Patricia *city government official, management consultant*
Stratas, Teresa (Anastasia Strataki) *soprano*
Van Pelt, Frances Evelyn *management consultant*

Quincy
Pinson, Margaret Ann *special education educator*

Reddick
Corwin, Joyce Elizabeth Stedman *construction company executive*
Romanski, Joyce Marie *secondary school educator, small business owner*

Redington Shores
McGhee, Kathryn Ann *foundation administrator*

Riviera Beach
Totten, Gloria Jean (Dolly Totten) *real estate company executive, financial consultant*

Rockledge
Ollie, Pearl Lynn *artist, singer, lyricist*
Passmore, Marian *mathematics educator*

Rotonda West
Broyles, Christine Anne *art educator*
Murnighan, Mary E. *elementary school educator*

Royal Palm Beach
MacEwan, Elizabeth Marie *pianist, vocalist*

Ruskin
Briscoe, Anne M. *retired science educator*
LaComb-Williams, Linda Lou *community health nurse*

Safety Harbor
Crafton-Masterson, Adrienne *real estate company executive*

Saint Augustine
Bishop, Claire DeArment *small business owner, retired librarian*
Couture, Sister Diane Rhea *sister, artist, educator*
Gutiérrez, Mary Carmen *artist*
Henderson, Hazel *economist, writer*
Jurgens, Julie Graham *mathematics professor*
Kehoe, Kathryn J. *science educator, researcher*
Oliver, Elizabeth Kimball *historian, writer*
Sappington, Sharon Anne *retired school librarian*
Wilson, Tamara Lee *English educator*

Saint Leo
Parrish, Patricia Anne *education educator*

Saint Petersburg
Anderson, Dawn Marie *elementary school educator*
Bairstow, Frances Kanevsky *arbitrator, mediator, educator*
Betzer, Susan Elizabeth Beers *physician, geriatrician*
Bryant, Laura Militzer *artist*
Carlson, Jeannie Ann *writer*
Clarke, Kit Hansen *radiologist*
Clijsters, Kim *professional tennis player*
Coetzer, Amanda *professional tennis player*
Coeyman, Emily Nollie Rogers *civic worker*
Cottrille, Patricia Anne *retired pediatrician*
Craybas, Jill *professional tennis player*
Dementieva, Elena *professional tennis player*
Despanza-Sprenger, Lynette Charlie *small business owner*
Dinsdale, Carol Ellen *special education educator*
Dokic, Jelena *professional tennis player*
Dunlap, Karen F. Brown *academic administrator*
Duval, Cynthia *art historian, museum administrator, consultant, curator*
Freeman, Corinne *financial analyst, retired mayor*
Frump, Stefanie L. *elementary school educator*
Geissler, Kristiana Andrea *secondary school educator*
Gordon-Harris, Cassandra I. *curator, educator*
Granville, Laura *professional tennis player*
Gregg, Kathy Kay *school system administrator*
Hantuchova, Daniela *professional tennis player*
Harkleroad, Ashley *professional tennis player*
Henin-Hardenne, Justine *professional tennis player*
Johnson, Edna Ruth *editor*
Keller, Natasha Matrina Leonidow *nursing administrator*
Kesler, Bonnie L. *psychology professor*
Khosh, Mary Sivert *psychologist*
Kuznetsova, Svetlana *professional tennis player*
Layton, Polly Kersker *mathematics educator, language educator*
Mauresmo, Amelie *professional tennis player*
McArdle, Barbara Virginia *elementary school educator*
McKeown, H. Mary *lawyer, law educator*
Metzger, Kathleen Ann *computer systems specialist*
Michael, Marilyn Corliss *music educator, mezzo soprano*
Moody, Lizabeth Ann *lawyer, educator*
Myskina, Anastasia *professional tennis player*
Nichols, Katie *investment company executive*
Peters, Susan *editor*
Petty, M. S. Marty *publisher*
Reeves, Samantha *professional tennis player*
Riley, Nancy J. *real estate broker*
Rosenblum, Zina Michelle Zarin *psychology professor, marketing professional, researcher*
Schefstad, Theresa *bank executive*
Sharapova, Maria *professional tennis player*
Shaughnessy, Meghann *professional tennis player*
Simpson, Lisa Ann *physician, educator*
Smith, Betty Robinson *retired elementary school educator*
Stevison, Wendy *personal trainer*
Thompson, Dayle Ann *small business owner, consultant*
Wasserman, Susan Valesky *accountant, artist, yoga instructor*
Weaver, F. Louise Beazley *curator, director*
Williams, Minnie Caldwell *retired special education educator*
Young, June Hurley *elementary school educator, writer*

San Antonio
Will, Betty *elementary school educator*

San Mateo
Pounds, Janice Jones *elementary school educator*

Sanford
Levings, Christine Romano *secondary school educator, real estate developer*
Mena, Michele M. *counselor, educator*
Scott, Mellouise Jacqueline *retired media specialist*
Tossi, Alice Louise *special education educator*

Sanibel
Allen, Patricia J. *library director*
Hamilton, Jeanne Marie *retired librarian*
Keogh, Mary Cudahy *artist*

Sarasota
Aull, Susan *physician*
Benowitz, June Melby *historian, educator*
Buchanowski, Teresa Lorraine *retired elementary school educator*
Burrell, Lynne *credit manager*
Byron, E. Lee *real estate broker*
Carstens, Charlene B. *composer, music educator*
Clark, Eugenie *zoologist, educator*
DiPirro, Joni Marie *artist*
Drake, Diana Ashley *retired financial planner*
Dungy, Kathryn R. *humanities educator*
Elmendorf-Landgraf, Mary Lindsay *retired anthropologist*
Feldhusen, Hazel Jeanette *elementary school educator*
Gassman, Stephanie Lynne *artist*
Goodacre, Glenna *sculptor*
Graham, Linda Ohlson *artist*
Hanson, Virginia A. *human services administrator*
Hapner, Joanna Sue *humanities educator*
Hentz, Susan Marie *private school educator, consultant*
Holcomb, Constance L. *sales and marketing management executive*
Honner Sutherland, B. Joan *advertising executive*
Hummel, Dana D. Mallett *librarian*
Jacobson, Jeanne McKee *humanities educator, writer*
Jelks, Mary Larson *retired pediatrician*
Jones, Sally Daviess Pickrell *writer*
Lee, Nancy Ranck *management consultant*
McFarlin, Diane Hooten *publisher*
Mohr, Victoria H. *obstetrician*
Noller, Ruth Brendel *retired education educator, consultant, researcher*
North, Marjorie Mary *columnist*
Randall, Vicky *artist, educator, sculptor, small business owner*
Retzer, Mary Elizabeth Helm *retired librarian*
St. John, Terri *secondary school educator*
Sanders, Coyetta Treshay *accountant*
Scanlon, Janice Lynn *retired gifted and talented educator*
Schafer, Amy Elisabeth *public relations executive*
Simons, Julio Merredith *psychotherapist, social worker*
Stevens, Elisabeth Goss (Mrs. Robert Schleussner Jr.) *journalist, writer, graphic artist*
Sturtevant, Ruthann Patterson *anatomist, educator*
Tachna, Ruth C. *retired lawyer*
Thompson, Annie Figueroa *retired academic administrator*
Towner, Margaret Ellen *retired minister*
Ward, Jacqueline Ann Beas *nurse, healthcare administrator*
Watson, Joyce Morrissa *forensic and clinical psychologist*
Wendlandt, Dorothea Schnepf *artist, writer*
Williams-Wetenhall, Tanya Dawn *art appraiser, consultant*
Winterhalter, Dolores (Dee) August *art educator*
Yonteck, Elizabeth Barbara *minister, health care consultant*

Satellite Beach
Miller, Susan Laura *real estate company executive, retired special education educator*
Molledo, Magdalena Ferreira *elementary school educator*
Osmundsen, Barbara Ann *sculptor*

Sebastian
Keaton, Jessica J. *secondary school educator*
Mauke, Leah Rachel *retired counselor*
Pieper, Patricia Rita *artist*

Sebring
Parrett, Janelle Swilley *secondary school educator*

Seminole
Schmitz, Dolores Jean *primary school educator*

Singer Island
Dixson, J. B. *communications executive*

Sneads
Scott, Brenda D. *writer*

South Daytona
Hollandsworth, Phyllis W. *marriage and family therapist*

South Miami
Villacian, Vanessa Luisa *psychologist*

Spring Hill
Del Toro-Politowicz, Lillian *medical association administrator, geriatrics services professional, consultant*
Pearson, Clara *elementary school educator, music educator*
Pedersen, Gladys del S. *volunteer*
Rothenberg, Linda Ann *science educator*

St Augustine
Cremona, Rachel Karen *political science professor*

Stuart
Cocoves, Anita Petzold *psychotherapist*
Donohue, Edith M. *human resources specialist, educator*
Kooluris, Hortense Dolan *performing arts educator, consultant, dancer*
Stimmell, Anne Krueger *special education educator*
Whichello, Carol *political scientist, educator, writer*

Sugarloaf
Greenberg, Linda Garrett *education educator, volunteer, singer*

Summerfield
Johnson, Charlene Rose *writer*
Lee, Ann McKeighan *curriculum specialist*

Sun City Center
King, Gladiola Tin *retired medical technician*
Mohin, Ann Marie *writer*
Petersen, Carolyn Ashcraft *psychologist*

Sunny Isles Beach
Buyanovsky, Sophia *linguist, educator*

Sunrise
Kolker, Sondra G. *not-for-profit fundraiser*
Rodriguez, Germaine *radiologist*

Tallahassee
Allen, Terice Diann *music educator*
Anderson, Theresa Ann *science educator*
Barlow, Margaret *editor, writer*
Barnett, Martha Walters *lawyer*
Bassett, Debra Lyn *lawyer, educator*
Blair, Maudine *psychotherapist, communications executive, management consultant*
Blanton, Faye Wester *legislative official*
Braswell, Jackie Boyd *state agency administrator*
Campbell, Frances Harvell *real estate developer*
Clayson, Carol Anne *meteorologist, educator*
Clifford, Dorothy Ring *journalist*
Cobb, Sue McCourt *state official, former ambassador*
Corzine, Jennifer Jean *music educator*
Crook, Wendy P. *management consultant, educator*
Ford, Ann Suter *family practice nurse practitioner, consultant*
Gilmer, Penny Jane *biochemist, educator*
Hanley, Deborah Elizabeth *meteorologist, wildland firefighter*
Harsanyi, Janice *retired soprano, educator*
Hernandez, Minerva Cuadrante *physician, consultant*
Hull, Elaine Mangelsdorf *psychology professor*
Humphrey, Louise Ireland *civic worker, equestrienne*
Hunt, Mary Alice *retired humanities educator*
Jennings, Toni *lieutenant governor*
Johnson, Kelly Overstreet *lawyer*
Johnson, Suzanne Bennett *psychologist*
Laird, Doris Anne Marley *retired humanities educator, musician*
Lisenby, Dorrece Edenfield *realtor*
Maguire, Charlotte Edwards *retired pediatrician*
Marshall, Elizabeth Annette *auditor*
Morgan, Lucy Ware *news correspondent, journalist*
Mortham, Sandra Barringer *former state official*
Moulton, Grace Charbonnet *retired physicist*
Palladino-Craig, Allys *museum director, educator*
Pariente, Barbara J. *state supreme court justice*
Porterfield, Amanda *religion educator*
Quince, Peggy A. *judge*
Reid, Sue Titus *law educator*
Spooner, Donna *management consultant*
Stebleton, Michelle Marie *musician, educator*
Thompson, Jean Tanner *retired librarian*
Waas, Harriet Issner *elementary school educator*
Walker, Karen D. *lawyer*
Wimberley, Cheryl Ann *choreographer, educator*
Yecke, Cheri Pierson *educational researcher, administrator, columnist, writer*
Yerg, Beverly Johnson *physical education educator, researcher*
Zachert, Martha Jane *retired librarian*
Zwilich, Ellen Taaffe *composer*

Tamarac
Baron-Malkin, Phyllis *artist, educator*
Brown Thomas, Rynn *elementary school educator*
Galipault, Lorraine D. *adult education educator*
Marged, Judith Michele *network technician, educator*
Toubes, Judith Esther *retired writer*

Tampa
Allison, Pamela A. *mathematics educator*
Andrews, Janice D. *elementary school educator*
Arfsten, Betty-Jane *nurse*
Bauwin, Roberta Elizabeth *counselor, director*
Berne, Patricia Higgins *psychologist, writer, educator*
Black, Caroline Kapusta *lawyer*
Boutros, Linda Nelene Wiley *medical/surgical nurse*
Branch, Mary Fletcher Cox *secondary school educator*
Cancio, Margarita R. *infectious disease physician*
Castellano, Josephine Massaro *medical records specialist*

Cimino, Cynthia R. *neuropsychologist, education educator*
Collins, Gwendolyn Beth *health facility administrator*
Cunningham, Kathleen Ann *researcher*
Davis, Helen Gordon *retired state senator*
DeVane, Mindy Klein *financial planner*
Diehr, Beverly Hunt *lawyer*
Eddy, Colette Ann *aerial photography studio owner, photographer*
Erickson, Linda E. *retired academic administrator*
Faulkner, Melanie E. *music educator*
Ferree, Patricia Ann *quality assurance professional*
Fosnaught, Patricia S. *art educator*
Freedman, Sandra Warshaw *former mayor*
Genshaft, Judy Lynn *psychologist, educator*
Ghiu, Silvana Melania Stefania *process and development engineer*
Gilbert-Barness, Enid F. *pathologist, educator*
Hanford, Grail Stevenson *writer*
Harkness, Mary Lou *librarian*
Henard, Elizabeth Ann *controller*
Hine, Betty Dixon *design consultant*
Hinsch, Gertrude Wilma *biology professor*
Huey, Peggy J. *communications educator, performing company executive*
Humphries, Celene *lawyer*
Iorio, Pam *county official*
Jacobus, Mary *publishing executive*
Jenkins, Elizabeth Ann *federal judge*
Kimmel, Ellen Bishop *psychologist, educator*
Lane, Robin *lawyer*
Lawson, Mary Carolyn *elementary school educator*
Loiselle, Joan Brenda *elementary school educator, art educator*
Luddington, Betty Walles *school library media specialist*
MacManus, Susan Ann *political science professor, researcher*
Matulich, Erika *marketing educator*
McCook, Kathleen de la Peña *librarian, educator*
McDevitt, Sheila Marie *lawyer, energy executive*
McGee, Nancy Pyle *college administrator, fashion designer, department chairman, artist*
Milito, Connie Marie *education administrator, government relations administrator*
Miller-Lachmann, Lyn *editor*
Mitchell, Mozella Gordon *language educator, minister*
Moore, Janet L.S. *music educator, dean*
Mulloy, Jean Marie *psychologist, human services administrator*
Musante, Linda *psychologist*
Nirmalani, Anjali *psychiatrist*
Novick, Cara D. *pediatric orthopedic surgeon*
Olson, Candy *school system administrator*
Palmer, Denise E. *publishing executive*
Pauly, Jennifer L. *director, graphics designer*
Pierantoni, Marlene Michelle *psychiatrist*
Pisaneschi, Dena Marie *science educator*
Platt, Jan Kaminis *former county official*
Powers, Pauline Smith *psychiatrist, educator, researcher*
Reed, Donna Marie *editor*
Ronson, Bonnie Whaley *literature educator*
Russell, Diane Elizabeth Henrikson *career counselor*
Schiefler, Karen Rosalie *artist, educator*
Schild, Nancy Lois *realtor, music educator*
Schultz, Barbara Marie *investment advisor*
Scialdo, Mary Ann *musician, educator*
Shedrick, Alberta Loretta *elementary school educator*
Sleeper, Cheri Acosta *music educator*
Sopher, Vicki Elaine *appraiser*
Stefanov, Ivanka *music educator*
Steiner, Sally Ann *psychiatric nurse practitioner*
Stiles, Mary Ann *lawyer, writer, lobbyist*
Tegarden, LoRetta Tudor *retired counselor*
Watkins, Joan Marie *osteopath, physician*
Weaver, Janet S. *editor*
Weisman, Diane Boyd *elementary school educator*
Young, Gwynne A. *lawyer*

Tarpon Springs
Browne, A. Pauline *accountant, writer*
Crismond, Linda Fry *public relations executive*
Keller-Augsbach, Linda Jean *elementary school educator*
Nothdurft, Donna Jean *occupational therapist*

Tavares
Livengood, Heather Jeanne *coach*
Spencer, Linda B. *painter*
Wilkins, Martha Ann *secondary school educator*

Tavernier
Engler, Deanna K. *science educator*

Temple Terrace
Kashdin, Gladys Shafran *painter, educator, volunteer*

Tequesta
Hires, Cheryl Lynn *literature and language educator*

Terra Ceia
Roehl, Nancy Leary *marketing professional, educator*

Titusville
Horn, Flora Leola *retired administrative assistant*
King, Sheila Sue *music educator, elementary school educator*
McDonald, Theresa Elizabeth *secondary school educator*
Rush, Patricia Anne *pastor, music educator*
Siegel, Judith S. *music educator*
Wilkinson, MaryE *mathematics educator*

Treasure Island
White, Donna Annette *retired secondary school educator*

Trinity
Akin, Donna Rae *retired elementary school educator*

University Park
Le Count, Virginia G. *communications company executive*

Valparaiso
Salsbury, Donna Denise *elementary school educator*
Williams, Betty *peace activist*

Valrico
Carlucci, Marie Ann *nursing administrator, consultant*
Straub, Susan Monica *special education educator*
Tirelli, Maria Del Carmen S. *retired realtor*

Venice
Barritt, Evelyn Ruth Berryman *nurse, educator, dean*
Belok, Carol Jean *nurse, alcohol/drug abuse services professional*
Bluhm, Barbara Jean *communications agency executive*
Crowe, Virginia Mary *retired librarian*
Felker, Ouida Jeanette Weissinger *special education educator*
Girman, Dee-Marie *artist, singer*
Kleinlein, Kathy Lynn *training and development executive*
Shaffer, Ethel Armstrong *volunteer speaker*

Vero Beach
Binney, Jan Jarrell *publishing executive, marketing professional*
Buker, Virginia Frances *elementary school educator*
Ferrell, Catherine K. *sculptor, painter*
Gedeon, Lucinda Heyel *museum director*
Haight, Carol Barbara *lawyer*
Harris, Nancy Lee *special education educator, behavior analyst*
Lange, Billie Carola *video specialist*
McCrystal, Ann Marie *community health nurse, administrator*
Murphy, Susan (Jane Murphy) *small business owner, real estate broker*
Wilson, Carol Perkins *principal*

Wauchula
Saddler, Peggy Chandler *counselor*

Wellington
Oser, Mary S. *music educator*
Pernezny, Lynn Anne *music educator*

Wesley Chapel
Grimes-Davis, Danna Elizabeth *elementary school educator, consultant*

West Melbourne
Chapman, DaLaine *music educator*

West Palm Beach
Baker, Dina Gustin *artist*
Bernhardt, Marcia Brenda *mental health counselor*
Blanchette, Beverly Beckman *dean, theater educator*
Brody, Carol Z. *artist, educator*
Browning, Sara Louise *science educator*
Cooper, Margaret Leslie *lawyer*
Hale, Marie Stoner *artistic director*
Iapaolo, Caterina A. *psychiatrist*
Kramer, Eleanor *retired real estate broker, tax specialist, financial consultant*
Marshall-Beasley, Elizabeth *landscape architect*
McKeen, Elisabeth Anne *oncologist*
Orr-Cahall, Anona Christina *museum director, art historian*
Vilchez, Victoria Anne *lawyer*
Waters, Lisa Lyle *airport administrator, consultant*

Weston
Adams-Sallustio, Patricia Jayne *elementary school educator*
Berry, Becky *music educator*
Deleuze, Margarita *artist*
Gordon, Lori Heyman *psychotherapist, author, educator*
Lazar, Marioara *psychiatrist*
Napp, Gudrun F. *artist*
Piken, Michele Reneé (Penn Piken) *artist, photographer*

Wewahitchka
de Abreu, Sue *elementary school educator*

Wilton Manors
Kaufmann, Vicki Marie *social services administrator*

Windermere
DeRubertis, Patricia Uhl *software company executive*
Rudzik, Lynne A. *musician, educator*

Winter Garden
Carter, Audrey E. *secondary school educator*
Ellis, Missie Lynne *music educator*
Gillet, Pamela Kipping *special education educator*

Winter Haven
Arens, Christine M. *musician, educator, composer*
Boully, LaJuan Bonnie *minister, religious studies educator*
Davis, Judith Lee *medical/surgical nurse*
Furnival, Patricia Anne *retired social worker*
Goodman, Karen Lacerte *financial services executive*

Winter Park
Bloodworth, Velda Jean *librarian, educator*
Bornstein, Rita *academic administrator*
Cook, Jo Ann Likins *psychologist*
Craig, Susan Lyons *library director*
DeMarco-Miller, Marie Lisa *lawyer*
Haendiges, Anne R. *marriage and family therapist*
Halladay, Laurie Ann *public relations consultant, food products executive*
Harvey, Joan Carol *psychologist*
Kaston, Lisa Marsha *social services administrator*
Rooks, Linda *writer*
Williams, Nan Parker *secondary school educator*
Wrancher, Elizabeth Ann *music educator, opera singer*

Winter Springs
Bevc, Carol-Lynn Anne *accountant*
Giuliano, Concetta *physician*
McNeal, Mary Kay *secondary school educator*

Zephyrhills
Anderson, Lisa D. *graphics designer, educator*
Barron, Ilona Eleanor *secondary school educator, consultant*
Summerhill, Elaine *music educator*
Walton, Shirley Dawn *retired medical technician*

GEORGIA

Acworth
Beale, Judith Ann *music educator*
Hussey, Shelley *graphic design company owner*
Johnson, Melissa Ann *special education educator*

Adairsville
Dobson, Suzanne *science educator*
Martin, Kristen Lacey *secondary school educator*

Albany
Adams-Cooper, Veronica Lynn *education educator, foundation administrator*
Buchanan, Valerie Russo *nursing administrator, critical care nurse, entrepreneur, consultant*
Forsyth, Rosalyn Moye *middle school educator*
Gates, Roberta Pecoraro *nursing educator*
Marshall, Cindy Lou *science educator, social studies educator*
Reece, Cheri Dodson *clinical nursing specialist, educator*
Shields, Portia Holmes *academic administrator*
Willis, Jakie Arleta *secondary school educator*

Alpharetta
Crider, Melinda Gray *artist*
DiFabio, Carol Anna *psychotherapist*
Filliat, Elizabeth Hartley *retired secondary school educator*
Greene, Melinda Jean *retail maintenance analyst*
Herbig, Joan E. *information technology executive*
Johnson, Sandra Bartlett *city official*
Lynn, Kristina *journalist, actress, writer, producer*
Mock, Melinda Smith *orthopedic nurse specialist, consultant*
Moore, Victoria Eberhard *elementary school educator*
Neff, Dianah L. *information technology executive*
Reed, Wendy *management consultant company executive, information technology executive*
Salay, Cindy Rolston *systems engineer*
Sirlin, Deanna Louise *artist*
Stalling, Janet Kitts *music educator*

Americus
Tietjen, Mildred Campbell *librarian, college official*

Athens
Allen, Sheila W. *dean*
Black, Marsha C. *environmental scientist*
David, Martha Lena Huffaker *retired music educator, retired sales executive*
Hill, Janet Elizabeth *lawyer*
Jacobsen, Karen Lee *educator, researcher, veterinarian*
Kurtz, Mary Denise Bates *secondary school educator*
McBee, Mary Louise *retired state legislator, retired academic administrator*
Meyer, Gail Barry *retired real estate broker*
Meyer, Judy L. *science educator, director*
Mullis, Rebecca *education educator, department chairman*
Puckett, Elizabeth Ann *law librarian, educator*
Smith, Susan Carlton *artist, illustrator*
West, Marsha *elementary school educator*
White, Rebecca Hanner *dean, law educator*
Yager, Patricia Lynn *oceanographer, educator*

Atlanta
Allen, Alana S. *not-for-profit developer*
Allen, Pinney L. *lawyer*
Amanpour, Christiane *news correspondent*
Ampola, Mary G. *pediatrician, geneticist*
Anderson, Barbara Allen *alcohol/drug abuse services professional, archivist*
Anderson, Gloria Long *chemistry professor*
Anderson, Marcie *communications executive*
Anthony, Barbara Cox *foundation administrator*
Arias, Ileana *psychiatrist, educator*
Austin, Jeannette Holland *genealogist, writer*
Bales, Virginia Shankle *health science association administrator*
Barnard, Patricia A. *human resources specialist*
Battista, Bobbie *public relations executive, former television news anchorperson*
Bawa, Avantika *artist, educator*
Becker, Jill *newscaster*
Bellamy, Ivory *elementary school educator, consultant*
Beres, Mary Elizabeth *religious organization administrator*
Bergeson, Donna Pottis *lawyer*
Berkelman, Ruth *medical educator*
Betts, Jennifer Leah *secondary school educator*
Biggins, J. Veronica *bank executive*
Bihary, Joyce *federal judge*
Birdsong, Alta Marie *volunteer*
Blum, Terry C. *dean*
Borders, Sarah Robinson *lawyer*
Braswell, Laura Day *periodontist*
Brice Ross, Carla Yvette *school counselor*
Bridges, Shirley Walton *air transportation executive*
Brown, Janine *lawyer*
Brown, Lorene B(yron) *retired library educator*
Brown-Olmstead, Amanda *public relations executive*
Butler, Gloria Singleton *state legislator*
Cahoon, Susan Alice *lawyer*
Calhoun, Sabrina *communications executive*
Camac, Margaret Victoria *construction company executive*
Carnes, Julie Elizabeth *judge*
Cavin, Kristine Smith *lawyer*
Chambers, Anne Cox *publishing executive, former diplomat*
Chang, Leng Kar *interior designer*
Charles, Sally Allen *financial analyst*
Chau, Pin Pin *bank executive*
Cilella, Mary Winifred *director*
Clark, Faye Louise *retired drama and speech educator*
Clark, Mary Elizabeth *medical/surgical nurse, diabetes specialist*
Clayton, Xernona *media executive*
Cleage, Pearl Michelle *writer, playwright, journalist*
Clearo, Kellie Anne *internist, pharmacist, psychiatrist*
Cohen, Lori G. *lawyer*
Collins, Janet L. *psychiatrist*
Cooper-Ruspoli, Annie Nataf *psychiatrist, director*
Corriher, Shirley *food writer*
Cox, Cathy *state official*
Cox, Kathy *school system administrator*
Cox, Nancy Jane *microbiologist*
Curtis, Lisa A. *accountant, administrator*
Davis, Aimee Slaughter *social studies educator*
Davis, Amanda *newscaster*
Day, Diane Elaine *science educator, researcher*
Day, Janet S. *academic administrator*
Dayhoff, Diane *retail executive*
Delaney-Lawrence, Ava Patrice *secondary school educator*
Deming, N. Karen *lawyer*
Dierickx, Constance Ricker *psychologist, management consultant*
DiSantis, Linda Katherine *lawyer*
Dobson, Bridget McColl Hursley *television executive, writer*
Domingo, Esther *music educator*
Dowling, Kathy *telecommunications industry executive*
Drennen, Eileen Moira *editor*
Dreyer, Susan *orthopedist, educator*
DuBose, Patricia Chapman *science educator, consultant*
Dukes, Deidra *newscaster*
Edson, Margaret *playwright*
Evans, Orinda D. *federal judge*
Falcones, Etta Z. *mathematician, math and computer science education and administration*
Farley, Wendy Lee *lay worker, educator*
Faulkner, Kristine *communications executive*
Feese, Suzanne *lawyer*
Fisher, Carlyn Feldman *artist, writer*
Fisher, Stephany *newscaster*
Fox-Genovese, Elizabeth Ann Teresa *humanities educator*
Francis, Julie *beverage company executive*
Franklin, Shirley Clarke *mayor*
Frazier, Emma L. *healthcare educator, researcher*
Frederick, Paula J. *lawyer*
Fuller, S(heri) Marce *energy executive*
Garland, LaRetta Matthews *psychologist, nursing educator*
Gayle, Helene D. *pediatrician, public health service officer*
Gerberding, Julie Louise *federal agency administrator*
Girth, Marjorie Louisa *lawyer, educator*
Glover, Lisa Marie *transportation executive, consultant*
Goetz, Betty Barrett *physicist*
Goizueta, Olga (Olga Casteleiro de Goizueta) *foundation administrator, philanthropist*
Goldsleger, Cheryl *artist, educator*
Good, Billie B. *sales executive, athletic trainer*
Gordon, Helen Tate *program assistant*
Gordon, Jasmine Rosetta *elementary school educator*
Grant, Susan *television executive*
Grumet, Priscilla Hecht *fashion specialist, consultant, writer*
Gundersen, Mary Lisa Kranitzky *finance company executive*
Hall, Beverly L. *school system administrator*
Hally, Jane Eloise *religious organization administrator, social worker*
Harper, Margaret Mills *educator*
Hayworth, Laura *banker, real estate analyst*
Heit, Marny *lawyer*
Hicks, Heraline Elaine *environmental health scientist, educator*
Higginbotham, Eve Juliet *ophthalmologist, educator, dean*
Hines, Alida N. *marketing professional, researcher*
Hogue, Carol Jane Rowland *epidemiologist, educator*
Huff, Sara Davis *nursing manager*
Hull, Frank Mays *federal judge*
Hunstein, Carol *state supreme court justice*
Isaac, Yvonne Renee *construction executive*
Jackson, Geraldine *entrepreneur*
James, Rose Victoria *sculptor, poet*
Jennings, Denise Elaine *art educator*
Jerden, Alison D. *human resources consultant*
Johnson, Carrie Clements *pharmaceutical executive*
Jones, Ingrid Saunders *food products executive*
Jordan, Katherine D. (Kate Jordan) *lawyer*
Kelley, Linda Elaine Spadafora *school psychologist, educator*
Kelly, Jean Slatter *healthcare administrator, nurse*
Kerr, Nancy Helen *psychology educator*
Khabbaz, Rima *government agency administrator*
King, Barbara Lewis *minister, lecturer*
King, Linda Orr *museum director, consultant*
Klein, Luella Voogd *obstetrics and gynecology educator*
Knowles, Marjorie Fine *law educator, dean*
Kravitch, Phyllis A. *federal judge*
Kropf, Nancy P. *social worker, educator, director*
Kuntz, Marion Lucile Leathers *classicist, educator, historian*
Lacy, Sheila Patricia *language educator*
LaDuke, Bettie *academic administrator*
Landers, Heather Renee *elementary school educator*
Landey, Faye Hite *small business owner*

Langston, Sheila Annette *special education educator, consultant*
Lattimore, Barbara *health facility administrator, consultant*
Lawson, Corliss Scroggins *lawyer*
Lemos, Gloria Elliott *soft drink company executive*
Lipstadt, Deborah E. *Jewish and Holocaust studies professor*
Lucas, M. Frances *university administrator*
Malcolm, Gloria J. *small business owner*
Mason, Karol V. *lawyer*
McClure, Teri Plummer *lawyer*
McDavid, Sara June *librarian*
McDonald, Kristen *lawyer*
McGill, Sylviette Delphine *editor*
McGowan, Angela Kay *government agency administrator, researcher*
McKenzie, Kay Branch *public relations executive*
McSwain, Georgia Haygood *educational program specialist, consultant*
Medows, Rhonda M. *state agency administrator, public health service officer*
Meshi, Alexis *psychiatrist*
Meyer, Ellen L. *academic administrator*
Miller, Patricia Hackney *psychology educator*
Miller, Rosalind Elaine *librarian, educator*
Miller, Sue *information technology executive*
Mills-Schreiber, Robin Kate *law librarian*
Minnick, Mary E. *beverage company executive*
Mogabgab, Rose-Warren Berryman *academic administrator, writer*
Morant, Brenda White *publishing executive, small business owner, investor*
Murray, Renee Logsdon *educational association administrator, consultant*
Noe, Elizabeth Hardy *lawyer*
Norman, Elaine Mitchell *information technology executive*
Oakley, Mary Ann Bryant *lawyer*
Ogden, Lydia Lee *government agency administrator*
Orrock, Nan *state legislator*
Ossewaarde, Anne Winkler *real estate company executive*
Owens, Laura Lewis *lawyer*
Palmer, Vicki R. *food products executive*
Parr, Sandra Hardy *small business owner*
Parrott, Janice Morton *medical/surgical nurse, nursing researcher*
Pelypenko, Elizabeth *lawyer*
Perez, Beatriz *marketing executive*
Polhamus, Barbara *nutritionist, educator*
Poston, Martha Anne *author, researcher*
Powers, Susan J. *information technology executive*
Price, Elizabeth Anne *lawyer*
Pritchett, Amy R. *aerospace engineer, educator*
Puckett, Susan *newspaper editor*
Rafuse, Nancy E. *lawyer, director*
Reese, Audrey Maria *music educator*
Reynolds, Paula Rosput *energy executive*
Rhodes, Lisa Diane *minister*
Richards, Jacqueline *artist, curator*
Robelot, Jane *anchor*
Roberts, Thomasene Blount *entrepreneur*
Rohr-Kirchgraber, Theresa M.B. *adolescent medicine*
Roseborough, Teresa Wynn *lawyer*
Rosenfeld, Rhoda Lynn *reading specialist*
Rouse, Sandra Howard *writer*
Salmon, Marla E. *nursing educator, dean*
Salo, Ann Sexton Distler *lawyer*
Sanger, Hazel A D *investment company executive*
Schuchat, Anne *health facility administrator*
Scott, Marian Alexis *journalist*
Sears, Leah Ward *state supreme court chief justice*
Senf, Carol Ann *literature educator*
Shelton, Elizabeth Colley *social worker*
Sloan, Mary Jean *retired media specialist*
Slocum, Susanne Tunno *medical/surgical nurse*
Smith, Marjorie Hagans *retired librarian*
Sorrells, Kristeen *violinist, music therapist*
Soupata, Lea N. *human resources specialist*
Speckhart, Dawn Seidner *bone marrow transplant/leukemia psychologist*
Spillett, Roxanne *social services administrator*
Stuart, Joan Martha *fund raising executive*
Thomas, Lizanne *lawyer*
Thoms, Jannet *rapid transit executive*
Thorpe, Jane Fugate *lawyer*
Tilley, Tana Marie *pharmaceutical executive*
Tome, Carol B. *consumer home products company executive*
Towslee, Janet L. *special education educator*
Tucker, Cynthia Anne *journalist*
Vadlamani, Suchita *newscaster*
Van Atta, Mary Carter *secondary school educator*
Varner, Chilton Davis *lawyer*
Venzer, Dolores *artist*
Vulgamore, Allison *performing arts association administrator*
Wallace, Gladys Baldwin *librarian*
Wallace, Julia Diane *newspaper editor*
Walton, Carole Lorraine *clinical social worker*
Waronker, Cecile C. *secondary school educator*
Weidman, Sheila *marketing professional*
Welsh, Melanie Millen *secondary school educator*
Wenger, Nanette Kass *cardiologist, researcher, educator*
White, Gayle Colquitt *writer, journalist*
Wilding, Diane *computer scientist, consultant*
Wilson, Debora J. *broadcast executive*
Wilson, Lori *newscaster*
Winkler, Rebecca B. *psychologist*
Winograd, Audrey Lesser *retired advertising executive*
Winslow, Anne Branan *artist*
Wong, Faye Ling *public health service officer*
Wood, Brenda *newscaster*
Wylly, Barbara Bentley *performing arts association administrator*
Yates, Ella Gaines *librarian, consultant*
Yip, Bettina W. *lawyer*
Young, Joyce L. *chemicals executive*
Zealey, Sharon Janine *lawyer*
Zeng, Fanxing *chemist*
Zumpe, Doris *ethologist, researcher, educator*

Auburn
Reuter, Helen Hyde *psychologist*

Augusta
Barab, Patsy Lee *nutritionist, realtor*
Craig, Cynthia Mae *mathematics professor*
Davis, Minnie P. *minister*
Drisko, Connie Lee Hastings *dean, dental educator*
Ellison, Lois Taylor *internist, educator, medical association administrator*
Fincher, Ruth Marie Edla *medical educator, dean*
Floyd, Rosalyn Wright *pianist, accompanist, educator*
Guill, Margaret Frank *pediatrician, educator, medical researcher*
Hand, Maryanne Kelly *artist, educator*
Jackson, Rosa M. *retired elementary school educator*
Johnson, Maria Elizabeth *psychiatrist, researcher*
Kutlar, Ferdane *genetics educator, researcher*
Lamb, M. Elizabeth *athletic trainer*
Lapp, Carol Anne *oral biology educator*
Logan, Betty Mulherin *human services specialist*
Narsavage, Georgia Roberts *nursing educator, researcher*
Nevins, Frances (Frankie) Rush *tourism professional*
Ottinger, Mary Louise *podiatrist*
Pryor, Carol Graham *obstetrician, gynecologist*
Schultz, Nancy Jansson *artist*
Wray, Betty Beasley *allergist, immunologist, pediatrician*

Austell
Lunaburg, Diane Gayle *chemistry educator*
Orr, Zellie *entrepreneur, educator, writer, researcher*
Vance, Sandra Johnson *secondary school educator*

Avondale Estates
Carroll, Jane Hammond *artist, writer, poet*

Bainbridge
Burkhalter, Myra Sheram *retired marketing professional*
Dixon, Lugenia *psychology educator*
Lucas, Tammi Michelle *music educator*
Palmer, Roslyn Wolffe *small business co-owner*

Ball Ground
Spare, Melanie Kim *management consultant*

Barnesville
Brown, Angelia *poet*

Blackshear
Vaughan, Mittie Kathleen *journalist*

Blairsville
Jones, Mary Emma B. *psychologist*
Stainback, Susan Bray *education educator*
Sterling, Colleen *artist*

Bonaire
James, Dianne *mathematics educator*

Bowdon
Donnell, Rebekah Jo *language educator, editor*
Sanders, Janet Ruth *elementary school educator*

Bowersville
Elrod, Joy Cheek *nurse*

Braselton
Romer, Denise Patrice *lawyer*

Brunswick
Essick, Carol Easterling *elementary school educator*
Gillis, Rhonda Radford *elementary school educator*
Herndon, Alice Patterson Latham *public health nurse*
Low, Anne Douglas *nurse*
Patrick, Connie L. *federal official*
Riner, Deborah Lillian *mental health services professional*

Buchanan
Vickie, Cash C. *elementary school educator*

Buena Vista
Jernigan, Melissa McGlaun *secondary school educator*

Buford
Smith, Rebecca L. *musician*

Byron
Chancellor, Elizabeth Ann *music educator*

Cairo
Oliver-Warren, Mary Elizabeth *retired library science educator, library and information scientist*

Calhoun
Haygood, Theresa *science educator, medical technician*

Camilla
Daniels, Deloria *elementary school educator*

Canton
Coleman, Sharon W. *elementary school educator*
Cudney, Amelia Harrison *medical/surgical nurse, obstetrics/gynecological nurse*
Frady, Rita R. *music educator, information technology manager*
Jones-Kelner, Barbara Teryl *music educator*
Lawrence, Karen K. *mathematics educator*
Lokey, Linda H. *music educator*
Taylor, Sue Ann *film and television producer*

Carrollton
Barr, Mary Jeanette *art educator*
Hill, Jane Bowers *English language educator, editor*
Holland, Laurel Long *sociologist, educator*
Insenga, Angela Suzanne *literature educator*
Lane, Pamela Lynn *language educator*
Sifton, Karen Marie *mathematics professor*
Stone, Sandra Smith *sociologist, researcher, academic administrator*
Williams, Mary Eleanor Nicole *writer*

Cartersville
Wheeler, Susie Weems *retired school system administrator*

Cataula
Averill, Ellen Corbett *retired secondary education science educator, administrator*

Cave Spring
Willis, Heather Nicole *science educator*

Cedartown
Renshaw, Judith Ann *special education educator, school system administrator*

Chamblee
Alexander, Dawn Jo *middle school educator*

Chatsworth
Bishop, Pamela June *elementary school educator*

Clarkston
Ehrlich, Margaret Isabella Gorley *systems engineer, mathematics professor, consultant*
Page, Anne Eichelberger *violinist*

Cleveland
Steele, Vicki Lynn *educator*
Swing, Amy Eileen *elementary school educator*

College Park
Bates, Carol Garrison *secondary school educator*
McDonald, Deborah Alyse *mathematics educator*

Columbus
Ballard, Laura Clay *small business owner*
Bryant, Mollie Annette *counselor*
Cook, Kate Sievert *lawyer*
Duncan, Frances Murphy *retired special education educator*
Gamber, Jamie Saddler *athletic trainer*
Hiatt, Florence Ellen *musician*
Hickson, Joyce Faye *counseling educator*
Hoyseth, Luann Rose *secondary school educator*
James, Elizabeth R. (Lee Lee James) *bank executive*
Norah, Patricia Ann *music educator*
Owens, Deborah *artist, writer*
Patrick, Cathy *music educator, administrative assistant*
Riggsby, Dutchie Sellers *education educator*
Siddall, Pam *publishing executive*
Simmons, Lynda Teel *nurse, healthcare executive*
Spenard, Patricia Ann *science educator*
Striblin, Lori Ann *critical care nurse, insurance agent*
Tidd, Joyce Carter *etiquette educator*

Conley
Grant, Lucille *hospital administrator, social worker*

Conyers
Averhart, Celestine *surgical nurse*
Greco, Mary Cebulski *elementary school educator*
Grider, Rhonda Patriece *elementary school educator, writer*
Henry, Lynn J. *youth church administrator*
Jattan, Lynette S. *pediatrician*
Jones, Cheryl E. *secondary school educator*
Smith-Porter, Suzanne Clare *mathematics educator*

Cordele
Lloyd, Amy L. *social worker*

Cornelia
Franks, Jane Woodall *science educator*

Covington
Harrington, Joan Kathryn *counselor*
Sauls Rains, Amy *elementary school educator*

Crawford
Spears, Louise Elizabeth *minister, secondary school educator*

Cumming
Beaty-Gunter, Sharon E. *music educator*
Pruitt-Streetman, Shirley Irene *small business owner*

Dahlonega
Bennett, Tanya Long *language educator, writer*
Williams, Linda Stallworth *literature and language professor*

Dallas
Dunton, Ouida Luedtke *secondary school educator, department chairman*
Hommick, Carol Mary *physical education educator*
Kinney, Bonnie Logan *retired music educator*

Dalton
Ford, Katherine Michelle *special education educator*
Kirkland, Cindy D. *paralegal*
Mahoney, Kelley K. *language educator*
Smith, Janet Susannah *literature and language educator, department chairman*
Tyl, Jennifer Amanda *special education educator*

Decatur
Barnett, Rebecca Lynn *communications executive*
Breckenridge, Betty Gayle *management development consultant*
Cravey, Pamela J. *librarian*
Daniel, Elinor Perkins (Perky Daniel) *clergywoman*
Farley, Monica M. *medical educator*
Freemont, Andria Shamona *lab administrator*
Groover, Lori Mobley *athletic trainer*
Hale, Cynthia Lynette *religious organization administrator*
Jones, Debbie Jo *finance educator*
Kelly, Karen Deloris *addiction counselor, administrator*
Kiss, Elizabeth *academic administrator, philosophy educator*
Majette, Denise *former congresswoman*
Marshall, Priscilla Jackson *elementary school educator*
Nease, Judith Allgood *marriage and family therapist*
Pharr, Paige Elizabeth *interior designer, real estate broker*
Pryce, Monica Elizabeth *music educator*
Ray, Amy *vocalist, guitarist*
Saliers, Emily *singer, musician*
Showers Johnson, Violet Mary-Ann Iyabo *history professor*
Strickland, Brenda B. *music educator*
Terry, Elizabeth Hudson *personal care industry executive, realtor*
Wheelan, Belle S. *educational association administrator*
Williams, Rita Tucker *lawyer*
Worth, Dorothy Williamson *retired foreign language educator*

Demorest
Rogers, Elizabeth (Betty) Carlisle *education educator, consultant*
Vance, Cynthia Lynn *psychology educator*

Douglas
Baars, Ella Jane *art educator*
Pugh, Joye Jeffries *educational association administrator, consultant, writer*
Tucker, Maureen Ann *musician*

Douglasville
Allen, Mia Florence *health and physical education educator*
Bronson, Carol E. *health facility administrator*
Howard, Karen S. *retail executive*
Jackson, Cynthia Williford *special education educator*
Smith, Stephanie Renae *middle school educator*
Waterman, Dianne Corrine *artist, educator, writer, religious organization administrator*

Dublin
Claxton, Harriett Maroy Jones *language educator*
McGruder, Tecia Adrienne *assistant principal*
Sapp, Peggy G. *pastor, editor, writer, speech professional*

Duluth
Cannon, Sherry Cloud *special education educator*
Gullickson, Nancy Ann *art association administrator*
Pickett, Christa Langford *elementary school counselor*
Pratt, Bonnie *science educator*

Dunwoody
Duvall, Marjorie L. *English and foreign language educator*

East Ellijay
Prince-Stokes, Cathy *neuro-orthopedic nurse administrator*

East Point
Jackson, Julie Ann *mathematics professor*
Renzi, Beth Paige *personal trainer*

Eastman
Hall, Lula *retired special education educator*

Eatonton
Digby, Pamela Annette *elementary school educator*

Elberton
McCarty, Dixie Rayle *science educator*

Ellijay
Mayfield, Katie Smith *music educator*

Evans
Feldman, Elaine Bossak *medical nutritionist, educator*
Lenox, Angela Cousineau *healthcare consultant*
McCorkle, Pamela Loveridge *elementary school educator*
Orlet, Veronica Lynne *secondary school educator*
Owen, Shaun Sonia *elementary school educator, small business owner, consultant*
Peebles, Betty Lea *secondary school educator*
Stout, Elva Carolyn Fraser *elementary school educator*
Zachert, Virginia *retired psychologist*

Fairburn
Bobo, Genelle Tant (Nell Bobo) *retired office administrator*
Johnston, Carolyn Judith *construction engineer*

Fayetteville
Eller, Karen Kreimann *elementary school educator*
Furbee, Amy H. *social studies educator*
Ward, Connie Michele *psychologist, educator, environmentalist*

Flowery Branch
Monroe, Melrose *retired bank executive*

Folkston
Crumbley, Esther Helen Kendrick *retired real estate agent, retired secondary school educator, councilman*

Forest Park
Grace-Crum, Phyllis Venetia *military officer*

Fort Benning
Astern, Laurie *psychotherapist, physician assistant*

Fort Gaines
Chaffin, LaVerne *music educator*

Fort Mcpherson
Emery, Carolyn Vera *civilian military employee, retired non-commissioned officer*
Karpinski, Janis Leigh *security manager*

Fort Oglethorpe
Lane, Darlene Kelley *history educator*
Mobley, Brooke Michelle *science educator*

Fort Stewart
McCarthy, Dorothy A. (Landers) *social studies educator*

Fort Valley
Monroe, Sandra Elaine *retired secondary art educator, minister*

Gainesville
Davis, Connie Waters *public relations executive, marketing professional*
Floyd, Hazel McConnell *special education educator*
Frank, Mary Lou Bryant *psychologist, educator*
Taylor, Mary Jane *artist, educator*

Glennville
Craft, Mary Faye *public relations executive, consultant, television producer, poet*

Greensboro
Copelan, Ann Hanson *artist, psychologist*

Griffin
Grant, Mary Alverson *music educator*
Nelson, Muriel Yvette *elementary school educator*
Shockley, Carol Frances *psychologist, psychotherapist*
Totman, Sharon Taylor *special education educator*

Hamilton
Hrncir, Jennifer Welch *elementary school educator*
Hubbard, Carla Dawn *secondary school educator*

Harlem
Huff, Amy M. *art educator, artist*

Hartwell
Royston, Pamela Jean *special education educator*
Rushing, Tonnie Austin Page *musician, educator*

Hiawassee
Brumbaugh, Melissa Beth *elementary school educator*
Davis, Nighta J. *photographer, artist*

Hinesville
Carter, Georgian L. *minister*

Hiram
Moyer, Dianna Kay *social studies educator*

Holly Springs
Neal, Teresa *school counselor, educator*

Homer
Dague, Teresa *elementary school educator, music educator*
Rylee, Gloria Genelle *music educator*

Hoschton
Jordan, Carol Morgan *music educator*
Keyes, Maria Vega *social studies educator*
Osburn, Ella Katherine *elementary school educator*

Ila
Greene, Sheree' Jeane *elementary school educator, consultant*

Jackson
Bomar, Laura Beth *music educator*
Rowe, Joyce *principal*

Jasper
Cagle, Glenda Johnston *elementary school educator*
Crotta, Annette Gunter *retired educator*
Ledford, Shirley Louise *practical nurse*

Jeffersonville
Hawthorne, Sarah Beck *reading educator*

Jekyll Island
Sennett, Patricia M. *artist, educator*

Jesup
Terradas, Shirley Arnold *clinical psychologist*

Jonesboro
Perez, Maritza E. *elementary school educator*

Kathleen
Talton, Karen Bryant *nurse*
Wills, Lois Elaine *art gallery owner, religious education educator*

Kennesaw
Cash, Stefanie Lynn *music educator, director*
Diaz, Anne Marie Theresa *music educator, musician*
Halwig, Nancy Diane *banker*
Kluka, Darlene Ann *human performance educator, researcher*
Lambert, Emily Jenkins *elementary school educator*
Mitchell, Judith Ann *education educator*
Rogers, Glenda Nelson *writer, photographer*
Siegel, Betty Lentz *university president*

Kingsland
Boyett, Linda Marie *music educator*

La Fayette
Roerdink, Lisa Marie *elementary school educator*

Lagrange
Ault, Ethyl Lorita *special education educator, consultant*
Greene, Annie Lucille *artist, retired art educator*
Hawkins, Frances Pam *business educator*
Merrill, Judith Allyn *small business owner*
Nixon, Juana Lynn Whitley *advertising executive*
Sankar, Lakshmi *special education educator*

Lake Park
Blanton, Vallye J. *elementary school educator*

Lawrenceville
Crain, Mary Ann *elementary school educator*
Edelberg, Mary *elementary school educator*
Harris, Melba Iris *elementary school educator, secondary school educator, state agency administrator*
Harsh, Alexis Goodsell *middle school educator*
Mayfield, Peggy Jordan *psychologist, minister*
Swanson, Lynnette Sue *special olympics coordinator, special education educator*

Leesburg
Hilley, Mary Kay *music educator*
Unger, Suzanne Everett *musician, educator*

Lilburn
Bendelius, Bonnie Sue *elementary school educator*
Cohorst, Lisa Moseley *elementary school educator*
Magnan, Sarah E. *court reporter*

Lindale
LeRoy, Judy Wright *middle school educator*

Lithia Springs
Kuncl, Kimberly A. *obstetrician, gynecologist*

Lithonia
Childs, Mattie Sue *mathematics educator*
Jones, Elizabeth Flanigan *literature and language educator*
Marion, Bernice Alexander *elementary school educator*

Locust Grove
Lloyd, Tracy Ann *secondary school educator*

Loganville
Jarrett, Benita V. *medical/surgical nurse, minister*
Morea, Michelle *performing arts educator*
Smelser, Thelma Ann *writer, tax specialist*

Lovejoy
Burchfield, Ella Loggins *science educator*

Mableton
Mounts, Kristi Lynn *personal trainer*
Reeves, Denise Moseley *dancer, educator*

Macon
Baima, Julie Martin *special education educator*
Brown, Nancy Childs *marriage and family therapist*
Cook, Charlotte C. *psychologist*
Dantzler, Deryl Daugherty *lawyer, educator, dean*
Dorsey, Donna Bagley *insurance agent*
Floyd, Daisy Hurst *dean, law educator*
Good, Estelle M. *minister*
Huffman, Joan Brewer *history professor*
Lengel, Elizabeth Hilscher *behavior specialist*
Lewis, Sandra Combs *research psychologist, writer*
McLemore, Ellen H. *music educator*
Pilcher, Christie W. *special education educator*
Quiroga, Alicia Espinosa *physiatrist*
Rigsby, Sheila Goree *accounting firm executive*
Scheetz, Allison Paige *medical educator*
Shomaker, Andrea Kay *secondary school educator*
Terry, Doris D. *music educator*

Madison
Short, Betsy Ann *elementary school educator*

Manchester
Gill, Kelley Henderson *elementary school educator*

Marietta
Biehle, Karen Jean *pharmacist*
Chase, Christa Joy *music educator*
Devigne, Karen Cooke *retired amateur athletics executive*
Dobrzyn, Janet Elaine *quality assurance professional*
Dunston-Thomas, Frances Johnson *pediatrician, public health service officer*
Eggersman, Denise *computer engineer, educator*
Guentner, Gail Marie *software engineer*
Henderson, Cynthia *medical librarian*
Hirsch, Kerri Ann *social studies educator*
Holland, Amy Jeanette *psychiatrist*
Hudson, Linda *health facility administrator*
Kellogg, Mary Marjorie *retired special education educator, supervisor*
Laframboise, Joan Carol *middle school educator*
Lahtinen, Silja Liisa *artist*
McEntire, Betty *health facility administrator*
Neff, Marilyn Lee *nursing consultant*
Overstreet, Regina Nix *mathematics educator*
Reid, Demetra Adams *insurance company executive*
Rivers, Alma Faye *secondary school educator*
Roach, Carole Hyde *music educator*
Roaché, Sylvia *social worker*
Robotham, Sattanya A. *private school educator*
Rogers, Gail Elizabeth *library director*
Rossbacher, Lisa Ann *academic administrator*
Rutherfoord, Rebecca Hudson *computer scientist, educator*
Shapiro, Abra Blair *real estate company executive*
Short-Mayfield, Patricia Ahlene *business owner*
Smith, Becky *charitable organizations consultant*
Smith, Irene Helen-Nordine *music educator*
Tucker, Rebecca Denise *science educator*
Veatch, Sheila Williamson *retired counselor*
Whitlock, Betty *retired secondary school educator*
Williamsen, Dannye Sue *publishing executive, writer*
Wright, Judith Diane *elementary school educator*
Younker, Pamela Godfrey *business owner, consultant, accountant*

Maysville
Herriman, Jean Ann *elementary school educator*

Mc Rae
Allen, Annette *minister*

Mcdonough
Brown, Joy Withers *music educator*
Brown, June Dyson *retired elementary school educator, principal*
Eskew, Dorothy *art educator*
Gale, Michelle Sue *retired clinical psychologist*
Mauney, Brandi Savage *special education diagnostician*
Norby, Rena Faye *science educator*
Riffel, Laura Ann *director, special education educator*

Milledgeville
Engerrand, Doris Dieskow *retired business educator*
Flory, Jennifer Morgan *conductor, educator*
Hill, Helen Marguerite Thacker *academic administrator*
Konersman, Elaine Reich *nursing administrator*
Leland, Dorothy *academic administrator*
Magoulick, Mary *literature and language professor*
Metzker, Julia *chemistry professor*
Moses, Catherine *political science professor*
Nunn, Cynthia S. *history educator*
Ragan, Charlotte Ann *music educator*
Sargent, Jane Diane Robertson *mathematician, educator*
Werts, Ruby Woodward *elementary school educator*

Morganton
Davis, Sarah C. *elementary school educator*

Morrow
Clark, Deborah J. *nursing administrator, educator*
Todebush, Patricia Metthe *chemistry professor*

Moultrie
Cox, Carol Yvonne *counselor*

Mount Airy
Sweatman, Wendy Leigh *secondary school educator*

Mount Vernon
Parker, Lisa E. *elementary school educator, gifted and talented educator*

Nashville
Cosson, Mary Gwendolyn *music educator*
Gaskins, Anne Carson *retired human resources specialist*

Newnan
Culbreth, Lucretia Joy *science educator*
Smith, Betty Ann Ingram *elementary school educator*

Norcross
Herron, Bonnie L. *management consulting company executive*
Holtzman, Mary *engineering company executive*
Mangum, Mylle Bell *information technology executive*
Montiel, Carol E. *health services administrator*
Moreno, Veronica *food products executive*
Robinson, Karen Ann *marketing executive*

Oakwood
Jondahl, Terri Elise *importing and distribution company executive*
Lindahl, Sarah Elizabeth *theater educator*

Ocilla
Busbin, Brenda C. *public health nurse*

Oxford
Archetto, Maria *music educator*

Peachtree City
Eichelberger, Lisa Wright *academic administrator, nursing educator*
Saulsbury, Glynis Elliott *elementary school educator*
Scott, Ann Marie *medical/surgical nurse*

Pearson
Delk, Charlotte Turley *elementary school educator*

Perry
Anderson, Denise Lynn *elementary school educator*
Jackson, Rutha Mae *pastor, military reserve officer, secondary school educator*

Pinehurst
Lowery, Laurie Blount *elementary school educator*

Powder Springs
Creighton, Peggy Milam *media specialist, writer*
Gaddy, Sarah Ann *elementary school educator*
Roberson-Brown, Linda Marie *social studies educator*

Rincon
Purcell, Ann Rushing *state legislator, human services manager*

Ringgold
Harper, Sandra Reynolds *music educator*
Hayes Gladson, Laura Joanna *psychologist*

Riverdale
Bean, Calandra LeShun *mathematics educator*
Warren, Barbara Denise *special education educator*
Wilson-Hunt, Simone Sonya Yevette *elementary school educator*

Robins Afb
Manley, Nancy Jane *environmental engineer*

Rockmart
West, Melanie Kim *elementary school educator*

Rome
Davis, Susan Lynn *music educator, musician*
Jones, Christa Walker *special education educator*
Knox, Barbara S. *education educator*
Mosley, Mary Mac *retired librarian*
Perdue, Judy Clark *academic administrator*
Potts, Glenda Rue *music educator*
Slack, Clemontene *education educator*
Stubblefield, Jenny Rebecca *educator*
Walker Vickers, Stephanie Carole *special education educator*
Watson, Mary Ann *marriage and family therapist*

Roopville
Huckeba, Emily Causey *retired elementary school educator*

Rossville
Anderson, Kristie *construction company executive*
Knight, Marsha Dianne *special education educator*

Roswell
Devine, Libby *art educator, consultant*
Herron, Harriette A. *retired occupational health nurse*
Hoskinson, Carol Rowe *middle school educator*
Lietch, Margie *insurance company administrator*
Maletta, Rose Helen *anesthesiologist*
Palermo, Barbara Kelly *health facility administrator*
Polatty, Rose Jackson *civic worker*
Stoffle, Sarah Elizabeth *theater educator*
Thibaudeau, Mary Frances *cultural organization administrator*
Vandiegriff, Vicki Alvinda *realtor*

Saint Marys
Hall, Lois Bremer *secondary school educator, volunteer*

Saint Simons Island
Brooks, Betty Ann *retired obstetrician, retired gynecologist*
Cedel, Melinda Irene *music educator, violinist*
Hall, Judith Ann *artist, printmaker*
Perry, Annette Owen *psychotherapist, educator*
Weinberg, Elisabeth H. *physical therapist, health facility administrator*

Sandersville
Dunn, Mary Ann *mathematics educator*

Savannah
Aja-Herrera, Marie *fashion designer, educator*
Aquadro, Jeana Lauren *graphic designer, educator*
Baker, Brinda Elizabeth Garrison *community health nurse*
Ball, Ardella Patricia *librarian, educator*
Borschel, Valerie Lynn *medical/surgical nurse*
DiClaudio, Janet Alberta *health information administrator*
Edeawo, Gale Sky *publishing company executive, writer*
Gabeler, Jo *artist*
Gentry, April Dawn *liberal arts professor*
Greene, Gail Purchase *medical/surgical nurse*
Hinson, Marvis Thedoria *education educator*
Honda, Sochiko *apparel designer, educator*
Joseph, Stefani Ann *art educator, painter*
LaSalle, Diana Margaret *consulting company executive, author*
Lesko, Diane *museum director, curator*
Marriott, Karla-Sue Camille *forensic specialist*
Martin, Grace Burkett *psychologist*
Murray, Mary A. *transportation executive*
Palanca, Terilyn *software industry analyst*
Polite, Evelyn C. *retired elementary school educator, evangelist*
Postell, Cindy Deborah *secondary school educator*
Rigelwood, Diane Colleen *insurance adjuster, administrator*
Rozantine, Gayle Stubbs *psychologist*
Runge, Linda Jacob *university administrator*
Smith, Elizabeth Mackey *retired financial consultant*
Thomson, Audrey Shire *volunteer*
Traylor, Jessica Stephens *psychologist*
Trittel, Rebecca B. *art historian, educator*
Vonschlegel, Patricia *artist*
Wallace, Paula S. *academic administrator*
Wood, Lisa Godbey *prosecutor*

Senoia
Griffin, Tammy Lynn *industrial engineer*

Sharpsburg
Crosby, Letitia Jordan *science educator*

Silver Creek
Boylan, Tonya R. *banker, consultant*
Edwards, Kandace Necole *secondary school educator*

Smyrna
English, Candace Allen *assistant principal*
Fitzner, Kathryn Ethridge *psychotherapist*
Rife, Elizabeth *musician, educator*
Stevenson, Mary Compher *pharmacist, educator*

Snellville
Blankenship, Colleen Marie-Krick *secondary school educator, writer*
Dodd, Violet M. *nursing educator, recreational therapist, counselor*
Sali, Amanda Leigh *choral director*

Social Circle
Archibald, Claudia Jane *parapsychologist, counselor, consultant*
Cannon, Constance Marie *literature and language educator*

Springfield
Hill, Lynda McSeveney *mathematics educator*

Statesboro
Bacon, Martha Brantley *small business owner*
Bartels, Jean Ellen *nursing educator*
Bryan, Carolyn J. *music educator, saxophonist*
Hamilton, Ann Hollingsworth *library director*
Lanier, Susie Mae *mathematics professor*
Leege, Lissa Maria *biology professor*
Lloyd, Margaret Ann *psychologist, educator*

Mitra, Aditi *mathematician, educator*
Nettles, Saundra R. Murray *psychologist, writer, educator*

Stockbridge
Seagraves, Karen Denise *elementary school educator*
Sprayberry, Roslyn Raye *retired secondary school educator*

Stone Mountain
Allen (Irvin M.N.), Georgianne Lydia Christian *writer, poet*
Antoine, Alissa Quiana *science educator*
Brown, Rhonda Jean *special education educator*
Bundy, Jane Bowden *artist, educator*
Farngalo, Rosemarie Merritt *school psychologist*
Gary, Julia Thomas *retired minister*
Gotlieb, Jaquelin Smith *pediatrician*
Jones, Ellen *elementary school educator*
Slaughter, Gloria Jean *elementary school educator*
Wright, Pauline M. *elementary school educator, consultant*

Summerville
Busby, Barbara Sue Hughes *geriatrics nurse*

Suwanee
Moras, Barbara J. *music educator*
Stanley, Gwen G. *elementary school educator*
Wing, Kerensa Shoemake *secondary school educator, assistant principal*

Temple
Elliott, Teri Michelle *elementary school educator*

Thomaston
Graham, Violet Joyce *writer*

Thomasville
Finland, Christine Elaine *school counselor*

Tifton
Hannon, Laura L. *accountant, educator*
Heidt, Amy R. *science educator*
Robinson, Kristina Parker *secondary school educator*

Tiger
Ring, Yvonne Ann *special education educator*

Toccoa
Slate, Mary Elizabeth *real estate agent, medical/surgical nurse*

Toccoa Falls
Brock, Dorothy Dixon *psychologist, psychology professor*
Gardner, Donna Rae (Diehl) *education educator*
Hoffman, Ruth Elaine *mathematics educator*

Tucker
Lacey, Ruthann P. *lawyer*
Stewart, Connie Ward *retired academic administrator*

Ty Ty
Howell, Eva Jane Wood *medical/surgical nurse*

Unadilla
Bartlett, Rhonda Woodward *library manager*

Union City
Drake-Hamilton, Lillie Belle *retired secondary school educator*
Riley, Francena *nurse, retired non-commissioned officer*

Valdosta
Burnette, Ada M. Puryear *program coordinator*
Byrd, Melanie Sue *history professor*
Coons-Long, Brittney Leigh *defender*
Corbin, Lynn Ann *music educator, conductor*
Moch, Peggy L. *mathematics professor*
Montgomery, Denise Lynne *librarian, researcher*

Vidalia
Hodge, Sharon Denise *mathematics educator*

Villa Rica
Abney, Martha McEachern *music educator*
Gaston, Barbara Lovell *elementary school educator*

Waleska
Farmer, Joy A. *literature educator*
Naylor, Susan Embry *music educator*

Warner Robins
Beck, Rhonda Joann *paramedic, educator, writer*
Coleman, Debbie L. *music educator*
Merk, P. Evelyn *librarian*

Washington
Tiller, Anna Frances *music educator*

Watkinsville
Smith, Vivian *elementary school educator*

Waycross
Copeland, Elizabeth Jane *special education educator*

West Point
Albarado, Rebecca Hill *elementary school educator*
Hart, Brenda Rebecca *retired gifted and talented educator*

Whitesburg
Nicholson, Diane M. *special education educator*

Winder
Michael, Claire Patricia *director*

Woodstock
Barthlow, Michelle Jones *political science educator*

Christmas, Bobbie Jaye *freelance.self-employed editor and writer*
Dowdy, Elizabeth Ann *mathematician, educator*
Ross, Jennifer Jo *science educator*

Wrens
Adams, Susan Seigler *music educator*

Young Harris
Wolfersteig, Eloise Smith *retired music educator*

Zebulon
Thomas, Joan E. *music educator*

HAWAII

Aiea
Chun, Cheryl *music educator*

Haleiwa
Shigemasa, Teresa *mental health services professional, educator*
Taylor, Kathryn Denise *music educator*

Hana
Stevens, Muriel Kauimaeole Lee *elementary school educator*

Hilo
Gersting, Judith Lee *computer scientist, educator, researcher*
golian-Lui, Linda Marie *librarian*
King, Codie Mary *art center director, artist*
Tseng, Rose *academic administrator*

Holualoa
Scarr, Sandra Wood *retired psychology educator, researcher*
Stoddard, Sandol *freelance/self-employed writer*

Honolulu
Abbott, Isabella Aiona *retired biology educator*
Akiba, Lorraine Hiroko *lawyer*
Baker, Helen Doyle Peil *realtor, contractor*
Baker, Rosalyn Hester *state senator*
Belknap, Jodi Parry *graphics designer, writer, small business owner*
Betts, Barbara Stoke *artist, educator*
Black, Cobey *journalist*
Blackfield, Cecilia Malik *civic volunteer, educator*
Bronster, Margery S. *retired state attorney general, lawyer*
Carson, Ellen Godbey *lawyer*
Chun Oakland, Suzanne Nyuk Jun *state legislator*
Finucane, Melissa Lucille *psychologist, researcher*
Flynn, Joan Mayhew *librarian*
Fok, Agnes Kwan *retired cell biologist, educator*
Fukino, Chiyome Leinaala *state agency administrator, public health service officer*
Gillmor, Helen *federal judge*
Gonsalves, Margaret Leboy *elementary school educator*
Grabowsky, Gail Leanne *education educator, consultant*
Hackler, Rhoda E. A. *retired historian*
Hamamoto, Patricia *school system administrator, educator*
Hatfield, Elaine Catherine *psychology professor*
Ingersoll, Caroline Yee *director*
Ishikawa-Fullmer, Janet Satomi *psychologist, educator*
Jensen, Barbara Wood *interior design business owner*
Kadohiro, Jane K. *nurse, educator, consultant*
Kadzielawa, Renata Maria *physician*
Kawakami, Bertha C. *state representative*
Kawamura, Georgina K. *finance company executive*
Kennedy, Reneau Charlene Ufford *forensic psychologist, consultant*
Keyes, Saundra Elise *newspaper editor*
Kong, Laura S. L. *geophysicist*
Kubo, Kimberly Annette *entrepreneur*
Lau, Constance H. (Connie Lau) *electric power industry executive*
Lee, Joelle L.K. *elementary school educator*
Lee, Yeu-Tsu Margaret *surgeon, educator*
Lingle, Linda *governor*
Loke, Joan Tso Fong *respiratory therapist*
Lu, Caixia *television director, language educator*
Lum, Jean Loui Jin *nursing educator*
Mau-Shimizu, Patricia Ann *lawyer*
Melcher, Kirsten Jegsen *physical therapist, consultant, small business owner*
Migimoto, Fumiyo Kodani *retired secondary school educator*
Nakayama, Paula Aiko *state supreme court justice*
Naughton, Noreen Kale *art educator, artist*
Niyekawa, Agnes Mitsue *foreign language professor*
Noe, Joyce M. *architecture educator*
O'Brien, Kendra Allen *psychologist, researcher*
Palumbo, Lorraine Reiko Minatoishi *architect, researcher*
Perushek, Diane *university librarian*
Pickens, Frances Jenkins *artist, educator*
Saiki, Patricia (Mrs. Stanley Mitsuo Saiki) *federal agency administrator, congressman*
Scanlan, Alicia Rae *music educator*
Schindler, Jo Ann *librarian, director*
Sharma, Santosh Devraj *obstetrician, gynecologist, educator*
Sheridan, Mary Stoebe *social worker*
Silva, Mary Barnes *retired elementary school educator*
Tanoue, Donna A. *bank executive, former federal agency administrator*
Thompson, Karen Marie *art educator*
Trahan, Ellen Vauneil *retired foundation administrator, public information officer*
Uchida, Janice Yukiko *plant pathologist/mycologist, researcher*
Udarbe, Christine *registrar*
Uejo, Colleen Misaye *elementary school educator*
Waslien, Carol Irene *educator, academic administrator*
Wee, Christine Dijos *elementary school educator*
Wellein, Marsha Diane Akau *military educator, director*

Wesselkamper, Sue *academic administrator*
Wolfe, Suzanne L. *artist, educator*
Yeh, Hsiao Yen C. *artist*

Kahului
Domingo, Cora Maria Corazon Encarnacion *minister*
Tolliver, Dorothy *librarian*

Kailua
Brown, Kaori Akamine *principal*
Carlisle, Darla Jean *elementary school educator, consultant*
Cooper, Louisa Sinclair *artist*
Fine, Virginia O. *psychologist*
Grimmer, Beverley Sue *consumer products company executive*
Ivey, Andi *special education educator*
Stamper, Ewa Szumotalska *psychologist*
Tavares, Samantha *psychologist, educator*
Tubbs, Mary S. *curriculum coordinator*
Young, Jacqueline Eurn Hai *former state legislator, consultant*

Kailua Kona
Iolana, Patricia Elvira *foundation administrator, consultant*
Leonardo, Ann Adamson *marketing and sales consultant*
Richardson, Mary L. *psychotherapist*
Spitze, Glenys Smith *retired teacher and counselor*

Kalaheo
Nakashima, Joanne Pumphrey *retired education administrator*

Kamuela
McDonough, Jean Whitney *personal trainer, sports medicine physician*
Richards, Phyllis Anderson *psychologist*
Stephenson, Nancy Louise *medical products company professional*

Kaneohe
Ashley, Elizabeth *dean, educator*
Coberly, Margaret *psychologist, educator*
Harner, Kathryn Denise *music educator*
LaMarchina, Marilynne May *elementary school educator*
Marineau, Michelle Lynn *nursing educator*
Young-Pohlman, Colette Lisa *music educator*

Kapaa
Caspillo, Carol A. *secondary school educator*
duPont, Nicole *artist*

Kapaau
Ralston, Joanne Smoot *public relations executive*

Kapolei
Moriyama, Karen Ito *educational association administrator*

Keaau
Kiefer, Cheryl Lynn *elementary school educator*

Kihei
Corell, Marcella Anne *community worker, retired educator*
Galesi, Deborah Lee *artist*
Palmer, Patricia G. *writer, retired psychologist*

Koloa
Cobb, Rowena Noelani Blake *real estate broker*

Kula
Mossman, Karolyn R. *elementary school educator*

Lahaina
Hill, Ruth Elaine *social studies educator, department chairman*
Percy, Helen Sylvia *physician*

Lihue
Ortiz, Joni Lynne *science educator*
Shigemoto, April Fumie *language educator*

Makawao
Huff, Harriet *art educator, artist*

Mililani
Carrillo, Linda Marie *counselor*
Gardner, Sheryl Paige *gynecologist*
Olson, Holly Louise *obstetrician, gynecologist*
Yuasa, Sheila Thalassa *literature and language educator*

Volcano
Nicholson, Marilyn Lee *arts administrator*

Wahiawa
Kiyota, Heide P. *psychologist*

Waialua
Pugliese Locke, Ranada Marie *nurse*

Waianae
Bourke-Faustina, Marlene Frances *music educator*
Holifield, Pearl Kam (Kam Holifield, Momi Kam Holifield) *poet*
Sakihara, Sandra I. *middle school educator*

Wailuku
Shimabukuro, Grace Kuo *mathematics educator*

Waimea
Merk, Elizabeth Thole *investment company executive*

IDAHO

Aberdeen
Krehbiel, Jennifer Nell *art educator*
Latsch, Nicole L. *elementary school educator*

Arco
Jardine, Cindy M. *music educator*

Bancroft
Rindlisbaker, Candace May *elementary school educator*

Bellevue
Jones, Krista Marie *elementary school educator*

Blackfoot
Law, Kathleen Sue *elementary school educator*

Boise
Brownson, Mary Louise *counselor, educator, artist*
Elg, Annette *food products executive*
Fanselow, Julie Ruth *writer*
Griffin, Sylvia Gail *reading specialist*
Herbert, Kathy J. *retail executive*
Holt, Isabel Rae *radio program producer*
Howard, Marilyn *state school system administrator*
Jones, Donna Marilyn *state agency administrator, former legislator*
Kendrick, Beverly Ann *medical/surgical nurse, small business owner*
Keough, Shawn *state legislator*
Lodge, Patti Anne *state senator*
McClain, Jennifer C. *middle school educator*
McKague, Shirley *state representative*
Miller, Sheila Diane *language educator*
Minnich, Diane Kay *legal association administrator*
Moen, Monica Balk *lawyer, real estate developer*
Peterson, Eileen M. *state agency administrator*
Pollard, Constance Jo *education educator*
Rearick, Anne *photographer, educator*
Richardson, Betty H. *lawyer, former prosecutor*
Scholl, Virginia May *retired plastic surgeon*
Silak, Cathy R. *lawyer, former state supreme court justice*
Sloan, Nina *language educator*
Smith, Marsha H. *state agency administrator, lawyer*
Sterling, Lisa Anne *psychologist*
Terteling-Payne, Carolyn Ann *city official*
Thornton, Felicia D. *food service company executive*
Trout, Linda Copple *state supreme court justice*
Wilde, Stephanie *artist*
Wood, Jeannine Kay *legislative staff member*
Woods, Jean Frahm *science educator*

Cocolalla
Groth-Marnat, Gabrielle *counselor*

Coeur D' Alene
Dahlgren, Dorothy *museum director*
Macey-Caloca, Patricia Ann *secondary school educator*
Shriner, Darlene Kay *professional athletics coach*

Craigmont
Niemela, April Joy *secondary school educator*

Eagle
Wickman, Patricia Ann *retired social worker*

Emmett
Richards, Vana Jean *elementary school educator*

Garden Valley
Bellamy, Joan Elizabeth *psychologist, consultant*

Glenns Ferry
Crum, Glenda M. *elementary school educator*
Dodge, Teresa Ann *elementary school educator*

Gooding
Larson, Lynn Wood *artist, musician*

Hailey
Liebich, Marcia Trathen *community volunteer*

Hayden
Morris, Mary Ann *bookkeeper*

Horseshoe Bend
Haley, Jenifer Jo *science educator*

Idaho Falls
Barbe, Betty Catherine *marketing professional, retired financial analyst*
Cannon, Mary Alice *literature and language educator*
Matthews, Janice C. *financial consultant*
Oe, Emily Norene *counselor, play therapist*
Robson-McCoy, Jeanie Ann *secondary school educator*
Rowberry, Connie *secondary school educator*
Rydalch, Ann *federal agency administrator*
Thorsen, Nancy Dain *real estate broker*

Jerome
Bell, Maxine Toolson *state legislator, librarian*
Rice, Melissa Ann *mathematics educator*
Ricketts, Virginia Lee *historian, researcher*

Kamiah
Mills, Carol Margaret *public relations executive, consultant*

Ketchum
Neely, Hilarie *dancer, educator*
Parry, Janet *retired health facility administrator*

Kimberly
Pack, Suzanne Christina *elementary school educator*

Lewiston
Finan, Jane *zoologist, educator*

Meridian
Greenspan, Valeda Clareen *nursing educator, consultant*
LeDoux, Patricia Renee *elementary school educator, science educator*
Oliver, Darla Deane *elementary school educator*
Pence, Linda Carol *mathematics educator*
Thorsted, V. Darleene *neonatal/perinatal nurse, community health nurse*
Vanderlaan, G. Anne *artist, educator*

Wilper, Kimberly Dawn *elementary school educator*

Middleton
Brown, Ilene De Lois *special education educator*

Midvale
Sutton, Lois Gene *elementary school educator*

Moscow
Sebald, Jama Lynn *academic administrator*
Shreeve, Jean'ne Marie *chemist, educator*
Wyatt, Carolyn J. *psychologist*

Mountain Home
Martin, Susan Jane *secondary school educator*

Nampa
Carrim, Rhonda Lynne *theology studies educator, priest*
Hopkins, Martha Jane *retired education educator*
Rau, Shirley A. *secondary school educator*

Pingree
Jackson, Sheila Benson *counselor*

Plummer
Harp, Diane Christine *librarian, educator*

Pocatello
Balls, Tedra Merrill *secondary school educator*
Bodily, Kim Gaylen *secondary school educator*
Crook, Lorraine Parker *secondary school educator*
Gebo, Emma Marie Joki *education educator*
Heberlein, Alice LaTourrette *healthcare educator, physical education educator, coach*
Hulet, Marjanna M. *literature educator*
Jacobsen, Bonnie Lee *artist, educational consultant*
McCune, Mary Joan Huxley *microbiology educator*
Robinson, Evelyn Etta *principal*

Ponderay
Nelson, Marcella May *volunteer*

Post Falls
Hasalone, Annette Leona *research and development company executive*
Mikles, Chris *secondary school educator*

Princeton
Severns, Karen S. *family court services administrator*

Rathdrum
Dickinson, Linda Mary *graphics designer, art educator*

Rexburg
Dick, Deborah Jean *elementary school educator*
Lankard Dewey, Judith Margaret *library director, lawyer*

Rigby
Hardyman, Lisa W. *music educator, elementary school educator*

Rogerson
Boss, Marylin Jeanette *elementary school educator*

Sandpoint
Bowne, Martha Hoke *editor, consultant*
Wills, Beth Louise *elementary school educator, social worker*

Shelley
Payne, Keri Tolman *dancer, educator*

Star
Miles, Michele Leslie *physician assistant*

Twin Falls
Callentine, Katherine Naomi *elementary school educator*
Cowger, Shari Ann *music educator*
Mathews, Donna Mae *special education educator*
McGregor, Wendolyn Suzanne *elementary school educator, mathematician*
Wright, Frances Jane *educational psychologist*
Yost, Kelly Lou *pianist*

ILLINOIS

Abbott Park
Burke, Sandra E. *information technology executive*
Flynn, Gary L. *pharmaceutical executive*

Addison
Christopher, Doris K. *consumer products company executive*
Evert, Margaret Jane *principal*
Leiber, Annette Perone *artist, art association administrator*

Algonquin
Lange-Connelly, Phyllis *musician, educator*
Weeks, Heidi K. *mathematics educator*

Alsip
Fournier, Maureen Mary *physical education educator*

Alton
Boyle, Ann M. *dean, dental educator*

Antioch
Dahl, Laurel Jean *human services administrator*

Argonne
Jonkouski, Jill Ellen *materials scientist, ceramics engineer, educator*

Arlington Heights
Biestek, Elizabeth Mary *forensic specialist*
Fields, Sara A. *travel company executive*
Giannini, Evelyn Louise *retired library consultant*
Greenburg, Sharon Louise *psychologist*
Griffin, Jean Latz *political strategist, writer, publisher*
Johnson, Margaret H. *welding company executive*
Kopielski, Camille Ann *counseling administrator, volunteer*
Kramer, Sybil Jean *elementary school educator, writer*
Lewin, Pearl Goldman *psychologist*
McEvers, Allison H. *psychologist*
Pasieka, Anne W. *elementary school educator*
Telleen, Judy *counselor*
Witt, Sally Eleanor *psychologist, educator*
Yonkus, Jo Marie Maiorano *secondary school educator*

Aurora
Belcher, La Jeune *automotive executive*
Císar, Margaret *special education educator*
Daugherty, Patricia Ann *retired elementary school educator*
Dillitzer, Dianne René *sales executive*
Easley, Pauline Marie *retired elementary school educator*
Elgar, Sharon Kay *science educator*
Franuik, Ranae *psychology professor*
Gudgeon, Valerie A. *school system administrator*
Herrera, Bethany Sara *social studies educator*
Lach, Elizabeth *science educator*
Lupei, Cynthia Therese *music educator*
Moore, Patricia Ann *alcohol/drug abuse services professional*
Pappas, Margene *retired music educator*
Powell, Kathryn A. *mathematics educator, athletic trainer*
Spencer, Kathryn Rose *secondary school educator*
Zaininger, Lucie E. *elementary school educator*

Bannockburn
Daube, Lorrie O. *sales executive*

Barrington
Amatangelo, Kathleen Driscoll *interior designer, educator*
Carter, Jeanie *performing company executive*
Roland, Regina E. *elementary school educator, educational consultant*
Sherman, Beth Marie *psychologist*
Stewart, Ann S. *music educator, director*
Wood, Andrée Robitaille *archaeologist, researcher*
Worrell, Sharyn Dianne *volunteer, retired flight attendant*

Bartlett
Lawrence, Madalena Joan Vignocchi *accountant*

Bartonville
Dina, Gwendolyn Judith *special education educator*

Batavia
Feuerborn, Rita Kazlauskas *music educator, musician*
Schulz, Jill Ann *elementary school educator*
Waranius Vass, Rosalie Jean *artist*

Beardstown
Vermillion, Julia Kathleen *music educator*

Belleville
Burch, Julie S. *science educator*
Mallette, Jennifer Denise *mathematics educator*
Megahy, Diane Alaire *physician*
Pounds, Regina Dorothea *writer*

Bellwood
Szilagyi-Hawkins, Elizabeth Maria *social services administrator*

Belvidere
Koch, Carol Sue *middle school educator*

Berwyn
Karasek, Mary Hapac *city treasurer, community volunteer*
Nicholson, Rosann *gifted and talented educator*

Bethalto
Sabaj, Nancy J. *secondary school educator*
Talbott, Janet K. *information technology executive*

Big Rock
Port, Ruth Elizabeth *literature and language professor*

Bismarck
Sellers-Evans, Cynthia *literature and language educator*

Bloomington
Beeler, Charlotte Jean *oil and supply company executive, interior design business executive*
Bryant, Deanne *music educator*
Campbell-Jackson, Carla Lanette *insurance company executive*
Daily, Jean A. *marketing executive*
Kennett, Christie Shih *lawyer*
Mosher, Donna Prescott *retired secondary school educator*
Olson, Rue Eileen *retired librarian*
Towner, Naomi Whiting *fiber artist, educator*

Blue Island
Hackenast, Sherri *race track owner, former race car driver*
Heckenast, Sherri *auto parts executive, sports association executive*

Bolingbrook
Day, Mary Ann *medical/surgical nurse*
Price, Theodora Hadzisteliou *individual, child and family therapist*
Sabau, Carmen Sybile *retired chemist*

Bourbonnais
Mills, Bethany S. *psychologist, educator*
Wilkey, Elmira Smith *illustrator, artist, writer, educator*

Bradley
Altenberger, Cynthia Ann *music educator*
Januski, Laurie A. *secondary school educator*
Mesengring, Tammie Lynn *elementary school educator*
White, Cheryl Louise *administrative assistant*

Brighton
Weinberg, Alexandrea *music educator*

Broadview
Bland, Pamela June *special education educator*

Buffalo Grove
Young, Kathleen Marie *special education educator*

Burbank
Parlin-McSharry, Barbara Ann *mathematics educator*

Burr Ridge
Daly-Gawenda, Debra *health facility administrator, nursing educator*
Jones, Shirley Joyce *small business owner, fashion designer*
Zaccone, Suzanne Maria *sales executive*

Byron
Schmitt, Diana Lynn *secondary school educator*

Cahokia
Butler, Donna Marcia *mathematics educator*
Williams, Cynthia Denise *secondary school educator*

Calumet City
Pickel, Joyce Kiley *psychologist*
Scullion, Annette Murphy *lawyer, educator*
Seifert, Suzanne Marie *physical education educator*

Canton
Hines, Daisy Marie *freelance/self-employed writer*

Carbondale
Achenbach, Laurie A. *science educator*
Bauner, Ruth Elizabeth *library director*
DiLalla, Lisabeth Anne Fisher *developmental psychology researcher, educator*
Fladeland, Betty *historian, educator*
Fuller, Janet McCray *anthropologist, educator*
Kawewe, Saliwe Moyo *social work educator, researcher*
Kim, Cheonae *artist, educator*
Koch, Loretta Peterson *librarian, educator*
Pinter, Susann Barbara *education educator*
Pohlmann, Mary Michaels *retired medical educator*
Quisenberry, Nancy Lou *academic administrator, educator*
Scott, Shirley Clay *dean*
Snyder, Carolyn Ann *education educator, librarian, director*

Carlinville
Bellm, Joan *civic worker*
Pride, Miriam R. *college president*

Carol Stream
Bemis, Mary Ferguson *magazine editor*
Franzen, Janice Marguerite Gosnell *magazine editor*

Carpentersville
Kozeva, Natalia *music educator*

Carterville
Minton, Jane Isabelle *education educator*

Cary
Irey, Robin Elizabeth *performing company executive, performing arts educator*
Monti, Laura Anne *psychology researcher, educator*

Caseyville
Dayton, Jean *principal*
Stanford, Diana L. *librarian*

Catlin
Asaad, Kolleen Joyce *special education educator*

Centralia
Davidson, Karen Sue *computer software designer*
Erwin, Nicole Renee *pharmacist*
Whitten, Mary Lou *nursing educator*

Champaign
Allen, Deborah Rudisill *clinical psychologist, educator*
Anthony, Kathryn Harriet *architecture educator*
Barrowman, Connie L. *investment advisor*
Dulany, Elizabeth Gjelsness *editor*
Follett, Deborah Elaine *sales executive, director, radio director*
Fosler, Norma Lorraine *counselor*
Hurd, Heidi M. *dean, humanities educator, law educator*
Jacobson, Elaine Zeporah *clinical psychologist*
Juraska, Janice Marie *psychology professor*
Kieffer, Gina Marie *history professor*
Loeb, Jane Rupley *academic administrator, educator*
May, Linda Karen Cardiff *occupational health nurse, safety engineer, consultant*
McCulloh, Judith Marie *editor*
Monda-Amaya, Lisa Ellen *education educator*
Osgood, Judy Kay *clinical psychologist, educator, consultant*
Pickard, Karen K. *parochial school educator*
Rooney, Gail Schields *academic administrator*
Stotler, Edith Ann *retired grain company executive*
Turquette, Frances Bond *editor*
Watts, Emily Stipes *retired English language educator*

Charleston
Ball-Saret, Jayne Adams *small business owner*
Coutant, Mary McElwee *retired editor*
Hedges, Edith Rittenhouse *retired nutrition and family and consumer sciences educator*
Ignazito, Madeline Dorothy *music educator, composer*
Price, Lee Ann *athletic trainer, educator*
Surles, Carol D. *academic administrator*

Chatham
Correll, Sally Ruth *elementary school educator*

Chicago
Acker, Ann E. *lawyer*
Adams, Lucille Joan *psychotherapist, health administrator*
Albright, Christine L. *lawyer*
Alden, Dawn Margarete *actor, choreographer, educator*
Alegre, Maria-Luisa *medical educator, researcher*
Alexander, Karen *museum staff member*
Allen, Belle *management consulting firm executive, communications executive*
Allen, Gemma B. *lawyer*
Allen, Julie O'Donnell *lawyer*
Anderson, Cathy C. *lawyer*
Andolino, Rosemarie S. *airport terminal executive*
Andreoli, Kathleen Gainor *nurse, educator, dean*
Apelbaum, Phyllis L. *delivery messenger service executive*
Appel, Nina Schick *law educator, dean, academic administrator*
Aronson, Virginia L. *lawyer*
Arvanitakis, Zoe *neurologist, researcher*
Aubin, Barbara Jean *artist*
Badel, Julie *lawyer*
Bae, Sue Hyun *psychologist, educator*
Bajich, Milena Tatic *psychologist*
Baker, Pamela *lawyer*
Baley, Joan Marie *elementary school educator*
Bancroft, Barbee N. *nursing educator*
Barbour, Claude Marie *minister, educator*
Barner, Sharon R. *lawyer*
Barnes, Brenda C. *food products executive*
Barney, Carol Ross *architect*
Barr, Emily L. *broadcast executive*
Barré, Laura *finance company executive*
Bart, Susan Therese *lawyer*
Basden, Cameron *ballet mistress, dancer*
Bates, Yasmin T. *bank executive*
Battrell, Ann *dental hygienist, educator, dental association administrator*
Bauer, Julie A. *lawyer*
Baum, Cynthia Gail *psychologist, educator, association administrator*
Beane, Marjorie Noterman *academic administrator*
Beaudet-Francès, Patricia Suzanne *photography editor*
Bellows, Laurel Gordon *business lawyer*
Benson, Irene M. *nurse*
Bentley, Carol Ligon *retired library and information scientist*
Bergstrom, Betty Howard *consulting executive, foundation administrator*
Berman, Debbie L. *lawyer*
Berman, Laura *sex therapist*
Bernstein, Gerda Meyer *artist*
Bernstein, Lisa E. *law educator*
Bertagnolli, Leslie A. *lawyer*
Bettman, Suzanne *lawyer*
Beugen, Joan Beth *communications executive*
Bienias, Julia Louise *medical researcher, statistician*
Blackshere, Margaret *labor union administrator*
Boggs, Catherine J. *lawyer*
Bomchill, Fern Cheryl *lawyer*
Bourdon, Cathleen Jane *professional society administrator*
Bowman, Barbara Taylor *early childhood educator*
Bowman, Cynthia Grant *law educator*
Bowman, Leah *fashion designer, consultant, photographer, educator*
Bradley, Vanessa Lynn *management consultant*
Brawner, Cynthia D. *elementary school educator*
Bregoli-Russo, Mauda Rita *language educator*
Brennan, Noelle C. *lawyer*
Bridges, Cynthia Elaine *music educator*
Bristo, Marca *human services administrator*
Bro, Ruth Hill *lawyer*
Brogan, Lisa S. *lawyer*
Brotman, Barbara Louise *journalist, writer*
Brown, Catherine Alletto *elementary school educator*
Brown, Elizabeth McCarthy *social services administrator*
Brown, Rosellen *writer*
Bucklo, Elaine Edwards *United States district court judge*
Burke, Anne M. *state supreme court justice*
Burke, Carol A. *lawyer*
Burke, Michelle C. *lawyer*
Burroughs, Margaret Taylor Goss *artist*
Burton, Cheryl *newscaster*
Busey, Roxane C. *lawyer*
Buss, Emily *law educator*
Butta, Deena Celeste *librarian*
Byther-Smith, Ida W. *social services administrator*
Cafferty, Pastora San Juan *education educator*
Canty, Dawn M. *lawyer*
Carnahan, Ellen *venture capitalist*
Carney, Jean Kathryn *psychologist*
Carr, Anne Elizabeth *theology studies educator*
Carroll, Margaret Kelly *education educator*
Carter, Christine *retired assistant principal*
Case, Mary Anne *law educator*
Casey, Linda Susan *school system administrator*
Ceko, Theresa C. *law educator, lawyer*
Chanyungco, Delly Yangco *dean*
Choldin, Marianna Tax *librarian, educator*
Christoffel, Katherine Kaufer *pediatrician, epidemiologist, educator*
Ciezadlo, Janina A. *art critic, educator*
Coffey, Susanna Jean *art educator, artist*
Cohen, Melanie Rovner *lawyer*
Collins, Michelle L. *venture capitalist*
Comella, Cynthia Louise *psychologist, neurologist, sociologist, educator*
Conant, Doris Kaplan *sculptor, civic worker, real estate developer*
Conlon, Suzanne B. *federal judge*
Connors, Mary Eileen *psychologist*
Cooper, Ilene Linda *magazine editor, author*
Cooper, Jo Marie *principal*
Cox, Julia Diamond *lawyer*
Cox-Hayley, Deon Melayne *geriatrics services professional*

Coyle, Dorothy *government agency administrator*
Crane, Barbara Bachmann *photographer, educator*
Crane, Charlotte *law educator*
Crone, Anna Lisa *Russian literature educator*
Cronin, Kathleen M. *lawyer*
Cueto, Rochelle E. *elementary school educator*
Cullina, Joanne Frances *medical/surgical nurse*
Culp, Kristine Ann *dean, theology studies educator*
Cummings, Andrea J. *lawyer*
Cummings, Maxine Gibson *elementary school educator*
Daley, Susan Jean *lawyer*
Dandridge, LeNor *paralegal*
Daniel, Elnora D. *academic administrator*
Danis, Julie Marie *writer, advertising executive*
Davis, Addie L. *mathematics educator*
Davis, Mary Ellen K. *library director*
Davlantes, Anna *newscaster*
Dawdy, Shannon Lee *archaeologist, historical anthropologist*
Deamant, Catherine D. *internist*
de Hoyos, Debora M. *lawyer*
Deli, Anne Tynion *retail executive*
Dempsey, Mary A. *commissioner, lawyer*
Desmond, Bevin *investment research company executive*
DeWoskin, Margaret Fogarty *real estate company executive*
Diamond, Shari Seidman *law professor, psychology professor*
Dickstein, Beth J. *lawyer, accountant*
Diederichs, Janet Wood *public relations executive*
DiMaggio, Lynette M. *physical education educator*
Dittmer, Frances R. *curator*
Doetsch, Virginia Lamb *former advertising executive, writer*
Doherty, Sister Barbara *religious institution administrator*
Dohrn, Bernardine *law educator, advocate*
Dooley, Sharon L. *obstetrician, gynecologist*
Douglas, Cynthia *academic administrator*
Dowling, Mary Kathleen *elementary school educator*
Dragonette, Rita Hoey *public relations executive*
Drake, Robyn Renée (Robyn Fielder) *writer, painter*
Drewry, June E. *information technology executive*
Dry, Judith Kallen *dental hygienist, cable producer, writer*
Dunlop, Karen Owen *lawyer*
Dunning, Jean *artist*
Dynek, Kathleen Marie *elementary school educator*
Easley, Cheryl Eileen *nursing educator, department chairman*
Easton, Lory Barsdate *lawyer*
Eaton, Maja Campbell *lawyer*
Edelman, Ruth Rozumoff *volunteer*
Edelstein, Teri J. *art educator, art director, consultant*
Eisner, Rebecca Suzanne *lawyer*
Elshtain, Jean Bethke *social sciences educator*
Epstein, Lee Joan *political science professor, law educator*
Eubanks-Pope, Sharon G. *real estate company executive, entrepreneur*
Evans, Thelma Jean Mathis *internist*
Ewert, Jennifer Kristin *counselor*
Fahnestock, Jean Howe *retired civil engineer*
Fawcett, Joy Lynn *retired professional soccer player*
Feig, Barbara Krane *elementary school educator, author*
Felden, Tamara *German language educator, translator*
Ferguson, Diana S. *food products executive*
Ferguson, Renee *news correspondent, reporter*
Ferrara, Annette *editor, educator*
Field, Karen Ann (Karen Ann Schaffner) *real estate broker*
Fontaine, Mary C. *lawyer*
Forbes, Dorsey Connors *commentator, journalist*
Foudy, Julie Maurine *retired professional soccer player, Olympic athlete*
Fox, Leslie B. *real estate company executive*
Frederiksen, Marilynn C. *physician*
Freedman, Joyce Beth *academic administrator*
Freeman, Susan Tax *anthropologist, educator, culinary historian*
Freidheim, Ladonna *dance company director*
Freund, Kristen P. *bank executive*
Friedlander, Patricia Ann *marketing professional, writer*
Friedli, Helen Russell *lawyer*
Friedman, Roselyn L. *lawyer, mediator*
Froetscher, Janet *social services administrator*
Funk, Carla Jean *library association director*
Furth, Yvonne *advertising executive*
Gabarra, Carin Leslie *professional soccer player, professional soccer coach*
Gadsby, Monica M. *marketing executive*
Gaines-Masak, Anne Farley *artist, art educator*
Gajic, Ranka Pejovic *secondary school educator*
Gand, Gale *chef, restaurateur*
Gannon, Sister Ann Ida *retired philosophy educator*
Gantz, Suzi Grahn *special education educator*
Garman, Rita B. *state supreme court justice*
Garza, Melita Marie *journalist*
Garzolini, Judith A. *information technology manager*
Gaters, Dorothy *basketball coach*
Geraghty, Diane C. *law educator*
Geraghty, Elizabeth *food products executive*
Gerber, Cecilia Elena *physics professor, researcher*
Gerske, Janet Fay *lawyer*
Getz, Bettina *lawyer*
Gewurz, Anita Tartell *physician, medical educator*
Gianos, Diane *lawyer*
Gibbons, Kathleen Marie *lawyer*
Gilbert, Debbie Rose *entrepreneur*
Gillis, Susan Fox *judge*
Goldsmith, Ethel Frank *medical social worker*
Gordon, Ellen Rubin *candy company executive*
Gorman, Maureen J. *lawyer*
Gottschall, Joan B. *judge*
Graber, Doris Appel *political scientist, writer, editor*
Gramer, Dorothy Anne *secondary school educator*
Grammer, Leslie Carroll *allergist*
Grange, Janet Lenore *lawyer, accountant, consultant*
Grant, Beatrice *underwriter, consultant*
Gray, Hanna Holborn *historian, educator*
Gray, Lucy *secondary school educator*
Green, RuthAnn *marketing and management consultant*
Gregory, Stephanie Ann *hematologist, educator*
Gulati, Martha *health facility administrator, cardiologist*
Gullikson, Rosemary *lawyer*
Guy, Sandra *journalist, telecommunications writer*
Haber, Catherine S. *medical/surgical nurse, nursing administrator*
Hablutzel, Nancy Zimmerman *lawyer, educator*
Hackett, Karen L. *medical association administrator*
Hambrick, Ernestine *retired colon and rectal surgeon*
Hamm, Mia (Mariel Margaret Hamm) *retired professional soccer player*
Hanrath, Linda Carol *librarian, archivist*
Harmon, Teresa Wilton *lawyer*
Harrington, Carol A. *lawyer*
Harris, Beth A. *lawyer*
Harris, Betty Jean *social sciences educator*
Harris, Joan White *foundation administrator*
Harris, Mildred Clopton *clergy member, educator*
Harris, Shirley *elementary school educator, secondary school educator, adult education educator*
Harris, Susan V. *lawyer*
Harrison, Holly A. *lawyer*
Hart, Pamela Heim *banker*
Harvey, Allison Charmaine *chemist*
Harvey, Katherine Abler *civic worker*
Hast, Adele *historian, editor, writer*
Hawkins, Loretta Ann *retired secondary school educator, playwright*
Hayes, Alice Bourke *academic administrator, biologist, researcher*
Healy, Sondra Anita *consumer products company executive*
Hefner, Christie Ann *publishing executive*
Heidkamp, Patricia Jean *librarian*
Heinrichs, April *soccer coach*
Henderson, Janet E. E. *lawyer*
Herting, Claireen LaVern *financial planner*
Herzenberg, Caroline Stuart Littlejohn *physicist*
Hesse, Carolyn Sue *lawyer*
Heydecker, Jeanne-Elise Marie *school district coordinator, traditional and web marketing executive*
Hibbard, Judith Usher *obstetrician*
Hightman, Carrie J. *telecommunications industry executive, lawyer*
Hill, Barbara Benton *healthcare executive*
Hill, Carlotta H. *physician*
Hilliard, Celia *cultural historian*
Hindman, Leslie Susan *auction company executive*
Hinkelman, Ruth Amidon *insurance company executive*
Hirt, Jane *editor*
Hitselberger, Carol A. *lawyer*
Hobor, Nancy Allen *communications executive*
Hobson, Mellody *investment company executive*
Hodge, Linda M. *former educational association administrator*
Hoffman, Valerie Jane *lawyer*
Hong, Ellee Pai *newscaster*
Hoogenboom, Carol Annette *clinical neuropsychologist*
Hsia, Sophie S. *language educator, researcher*
Hubbard, Elizabeth Louise *lawyer*
Huber, Anne Marrs *lawyer*
Hucles, Angela Khalia *professional soccer player*
Huggins, Lois M. *human resources specialist, consumer products company executive*
Hughes, Joyce Anne *law educator*
Hunt, Holly *small business owner*
Hunter Harris, Phyllis Irene *retired secondary school educator*
Idol, Anna Catherine *magazine editor*
Inan, Zabrin *psychiatrist*
Irvin-Mays, Vernita *medical educator*
Jachino, Daneen L. *legal administrator*
Jackson, Geraldine *literature and language educator*
Jacobs, Caryn Leslie *lawyer, former prosecutor*
Jacobson, Marian Slutz *lawyer*
Jacoby Hurd, Jennifer *foundation administrator*
James, Marie Moody *clergywoman, musician, vocal music educator*
Jarrett, Valerie Bowman *real estate company executive, stock exchange executive*
Jegen, Sister Carol Frances *religious studies educator*
Jibben, Laura Ann *state agency administrator*
Johnson, Janet Helen *literature educator*
Johnson, Raymonda Theodora Greene *retired humanities educator*
Jones, Cordia Cortez *minister*
Jones, Linda *communications educator*
Jones, Mary Laura *not-for-profit developer*
Julmy, Camille P. *real estate company executive*
Kalver, Gail Ellen *dance company executive, musician*
Kamerick, Eileen Ann *corporate financial executive, lawyer*
Kastiel, Elizabeth Maria *assistant principal*
Kataria, Tripti Caday *anesthesiologist*
Katz, Miriam Lesser *psychotherapist, educator*
Kaufman, Donna A. *elementary school educator*
Kaydanova, Yevgenya *neurologist*
Keenan, Barbara Byrd *professional society administrator*
Kehrer, Michele Ann *physical therapist, athleic trainer*
Kelley, Lydia R.B. *lawyer*
Kellman, Sandra Y. *lawyer*
Kenas-Heller, Jane Hamilton *musician*
Kerbis, Gertrude Lempp *architect*
King, Sharon Louise *lawyer*
Kinslow, Monica M. *forensic specialist*
Kirkpatrick, Anne Saunders *systems analyst*
Kirschner, Barbara Starrels *gastroenterologist*
Klaviter, Helen Lothrop *editor-in-chief, magazine editor*
Klimek, Kristen M. *physical therapist*
Klimley, Nancy E. *volunteer*
Kloss, Linda L. *medical association administrator*
Koehler, Irmgard Kilb *dermatologist, educator*
Koellner, Laurette *aerospace transportation executive*
Koenig, Bonnie *international non-profit organization consultant*
Korshak, Shelley J. *psychiatrist*
Kramer, Andrea S. *lawyer*
Krantz, Claire Wolf *artist, freelance critic, curator*
Krasny, Paula J. *lawyer*
Krueger, Bonnie Lee *editor, writer*
Kubistal, Patricia Bernice *educational consultant*
Kudo, Irma Setsuko *not-for-profit executive director*
Kumor, Michelle *special education educator*
Kurth, Jennifer Lynn *osteopath*
Lach, Alma Elizabeth *food and cooking writer, consultant*
Lake, Constance Williams *psychologist, public health administrator*
Landerholm, Elizabeth Jane *early childhood education educator*
Landow-Esser, Janine Marise *lawyer*
Landsberg, Jill Warren *lawyer, educator, arbitrator*
Larson, Nancy Celeste *information technology manager*
Lathon, Sheraine *clergyman*
LaVelle, Avis *consulting firm executive*
Lazar, Ludmila *concert pianist, music educator*
Leadbetter, Tiffany *hotel executive*
Lefco, Kathy Nan *law librarian*
Lefkow, Joan Humphrey *federal judge*
Legge Kemp, Diane *architect, landscape architect*
Leonard, Laura L. *lawyer*
Lerman, Zafra Margolin *science educator, public policy professor*
Lerner, Barbara *writer, researcher*
Levandowski, Barbara Sue *education educator*
Levenson, Carol A. *corporate bond research company executive*
Levy, Jerre Marie *psychobiology educator*
Lies, Valerie Sharp *foundation administrator*
Lilly, Aimee *radio personality*
Lilly, Kristine Marie *professional soccer player*
Lipinski, Ann Marie *publishing executive*
Loesch, Katharine Taylor *communications educator, theater educator*
Logemann, Jerilyn Ann *speech pathologist, educator*
Lona, Marie A. *lawyer*
Loo, Nancy *newscaster*
Lopez, Carolyn Catherine *physician*
Lorenz, Katherine Mary *bank executive*
Lowe, Sandra Elveta *psychologist*
Lurie, Ann LaSalle *investment company executive, foundation administrator*
Lusk, Peggy June *retired counseling administrator*
Macaulay, Susan Jane *lawyer, law educator*
Mach, Elyse *musician, music educator, writer*
MacMillan, Shannon Ann *professional soccer player*
Madigan, Lisa *state attorney general*
Madsen, Dorothy Louise (Meg Madsen) *writer*
Maehr, Kate *social services organization executive*
Mahaley-Johnson, Hosanna *school system administrator*
Majers, Elizabeth Louise *lawyer*
Malcolm, Christine Anne *university hospital administrator*
Mallow, Kathleen Kelly *accountant*
Manatt, Kathleen Gordon *publishing consultant*
Manning, Sylvia *language educator*
Mansfield, Karen Lee *lawyer*
Markey, Judy *radio personality, writer*
Marshall, Juli Wilson *lawyer*
Martin, Laura Keidan *lawyer*
Martinez, Natalie *newscaster*
Matlin, Susanne Summer *lawyer*
May, Aviva Rabinowitz *music educator, musician, linguist*
Mayer, Beatrice Cummings *civic worker*
Mayo, Cora Louise *educator*
Mazany, Terry *foundation administrator*
McBreen, Maura Ann *lawyer*
McCann, Renetta *advertising executive*
McClintock, Martha K. *biologist, educator*
McCue, Judith W. *lawyer*
McCurry, Margaret Irene *architect, educator, furniture designer, interior designer*
McDermott, Mary Ann *nursing educator*
McDonald, Theresa Beatrice Pierce (Mrs. Ollie McDonald) *church official, minister*
McGrail, Jeane Kathryn *artist*
McKay, Melinda *hotel executive*
McKinley, Anne C. *lawyer*
McMath, Lula Wray *retired elementary school educator, realtor*
Meares, Tracey Louise *law educator*
Mell, Patricia *dean*
Melnick, Jane Fisher *writer, educator, photographer*
Mendelson, Ellen B. *radiologist, educator*
Migala, Lucyna J. *journalist, broadcast executive, artistic director*
Mihelic, Tracey L. *lawyer*
Milbrett, Tiffeny Carleen *professional soccer player*
Mims, Joyce Elaine *lawyer*
Mindes, Gayle Dean *education educator*
Minow, Josephine Baskin *civic volunteer*
Morency, Paula J. *lawyer*
Morgan, Betsy Stelle *lawyer*
Morgan, Donna Evensen *lawyer*
Morris, Naomi Carolyn Minner *clinical pediatrician, medical researcher, educator, health facility administrator*
Morrison, Portia Owen *lawyer*
Mosley, Elaine Christian Savage *principal, consultant*
Mosley-McCall, Jeraldine *funeral director*
Moster, Mary Clare *public relations executive*
Mudd, Anne Chestney *mediator, law educator, real estate broker*
Muhammad, Ava *minister and national spokesperson for the Nation of Islam*
Murphy, Kathleen M. *lawyer*
Nadler, Judith *school librarian*
Nakamura, Kimiko *language educator*
Nash, Jessie Madeleine *journalist, science writer*
Neely, Ellen J. *lawyer*
Newman, Terry E. *lawyer*
Nicastro, Tracey A. *lawyer*
Nicklin, Emily *lawyer*
Nicolaides, Mary *lawyer*
Niehaus, Mary C. *lawyer*
Nijman, Jennifer T. *lawyer, department chairman*
Niro, Cheryl *lawyer*
Nissenson, Norma *clinical psychologist*
Noel, Carol Adele *music educator, opera singer*
Noesen, Darlene Dorothy *mathematics educator*
Nold, Lisa Marie *athletic trainer*
Odelbo, Catherine G. *publishing executive*
Odorizzi, Michele L. *lawyer*
Olopade, Olufunmilayo Falusi (Funmi Olopade) *geneticist, educator, oncologist, hematologist*
Olson, Sandra Forbes *neurologist*
O'Malley, Denise Margaret *judge*
O'Malley, Kathy *radio personality*
O'Meara, Anna M. *lawyer*
O'Neill, Bridget R. *lawyer*
O'Reilly, Heather Ann *Olympic athlete*
Overton, Jane Vincent Harper *biology professor*
Pacher, Nancy A. *real estate company executive*
Pallasch, Magdalena Helena (Mrs. Bernhard Michael Pallasch) *artist*
Pallmeyer, Rebecca Ruth *judge*
Panich, Danuta Bembenista *lawyer*
Parker, Bonita M. *civil rights organization executive*
Parkhurst, Beverly Susler *lawyer, administrative law judge*
Parlow, Cynthia Maria *professional soccer player*
Parr, Virginia Helen *retired librarian*
Paterakis, Angela Gregory *art educator, writer*
Pengra, R. Rene *lawyer*
Peres, Judith May *journalist*
Pesch, Ellen P. *lawyer*
Petrakos, Joan *elementary school educator*
Poethig, Eunice Blanchard *clergywoman*
Polaski, Anne Spencer *lawyer*
Ponder, Anita J. *lawyer*
Posner, Kathy Robin *retired communications executive*
Povsner, Laura Elizabeth *art educator, artist*
Powell, Enid Levinger *writer, educator*
Powell, Traci E. *psychiatrist*
Prather, Susan Lynn *public relations executive*
Pratt, Susan G. *architect*
Preciado, Pamela *artist*
Preece, Lynn Sylvia *lawyer*
Pritzker, Penny *investor*
Proctor, Millicent Carlé *social worker*
Purcell, Diane *addiction counselor*
Radomski, Robyn L. *marketing executive*
Raheja, Krishna Kumari *retired medical/surgical nurse*
Ramsey-Goldman, Rosalind *physician*
Ran, Shulamit *composer*
Rayner, Suzan L. *medical association administrator, physiatrist*
Rea, Anne E. *lawyer*
Reategui, Lisa J. *lawyer*
Reddick, Catherine Anne (Cat Reddick) *Olympic athlete*
Redmond, Andrea *executive recruiter*
Reece, Beth Pauley *chaplain*
Reed, Vastina Kathryn (Tina Reed) *child and adolescent psychotherapist*
Reis, Leslie Ann *law educator, lawyer*
Rhone, Elvie Sue *educational administrator*
Rice, Linda Johnson *publishing executive*
Rich, Nancy Jean *lawyer*
Rich, S. Judith *public relations executive*
Richardson-Lowry, Mary *lawyer*
Richman, Joan M. *lawyer*
Ridenour, Joey *medical association administrator, operations research specialist*
Roach, Kathleen Lynn *lawyer*
Robbins, Audrey *county official*
Robbins, Ellen Sue *lawyer*
Roberts, Dorothy E. *law educator*
Roberts, Jo Ann Wooden *school system administrator*
Roberts, Tiffany Marie *former soccer player*
Robertson, Donna Virginia *architect, educator, dean*
Robins, Judy Bess *sculptor*
Robinson, Jennifer Jean *lawyer*
Robinson, June Kerswell *dermatologist, educator*
Robinson, Robin *newscaster*
Rogalski, Carol Jean *clinical psychologist, educator*
Roin, Julie *law educator*
Romano-Magner, Patricia R. *English studies educator, researcher*
Rosenberg, Sheli Z. *investment company executive*
Rosenblum, Judith A. *law educator*
Rosenheim, Margaret Keeney *social welfare policy educator*
Rosenthal, Elizabeth Anne *writer, entrepreneur*
Ross, Lori *radio personality*
Ross, Nancy G. *lawyer*
Rothman-Denes, Lucia Beatriz *biology educator*
Rothstein, Ruth M. *county health official*
Rovner, Ilana Kara Diamond *federal judge*
Rowley, Janet Davison *physician*
Rudnick, Ellen Ava *health facility administrator*
Ruiz, Michele Ilene *lawyer*
Rupprecht, Elizabeth *art educator*
Ryan, Priscilla E. *lawyer*
Saltiel, Natalie *accountant*
Sampey, Debra A. *middle school principal*
Sanders, Doris Jean *mental health therapist*
Sanders, Jacquelyn Seevak *psychologist, educator*
Saracho, Tanya Selene *performing company executive, playwright*
Satish, Susany *biology educator*
Schanzenbach, Diane Whitmore *economist*
Scharf, Stephanie A. *lawyer*
Schiele, Michele M. *not-for-profit fundraiser, medical association administrator*
Schimberg, Barbara *organizational development consultant*
Schindler, Judi(th) (Judith Kay Schindler) *public relations executive, marketing professional, consultant*
Schwartzberg, Joanne Gilbert *physician*
Scott, Nancy L. *information technology manager, health facility administrator, consultant*
Scurry, Briana Collette *professional soccer player*
Seaman, Donna Jean *editor, writer*

Seebert, Kathleen Anne *international sales and marketing executive*
Seegers, Lori C. *lawyer*
Seeler, Ruth Andrea *pediatrician, educator*
Serlin, Marsha *waste management service administrator*
Sessions, Barbara C. *lawyer*
Sessions, Joan T. *director, educator*
Sexton, Brenda *film agency director*
Shanahan, Betty *professional society administrator*
Shannon, Iris Reed *health facility administrator, consultant*
Shapo, Helene S. *law educator*
Sheehy, Carolyn Aranka *curator*
Shen, Virginia Shiang-lan *Spanish and Chinese language educator*
Sher, Susan *lawyer*
Short, Marion Priscilla *neurogenetics educator*
Shoss, Deanna *theatre executive*
Shuman, Ann *investment company executive*
Simmons, Adele Smith *foundation executive, former educator*
Simons, Helen *school psychologist, psychotherapist, educator*
Singer, Emel *staffing industry executive*
Sive, Rebecca Anne *public relations executive*
Skinner, Mary Jacobs *lawyer*
Slaton, Danielle Victoria *professional soccer player*
Sledge, Carla Elissa *county official*
Smalley, Penny Judith *healthcare technology consultant*
Smith, Elizabeth Angele Taft *curator*
Smith, Leslie M. *lawyer*
Sobrero, Kate (Kathryn Michele Sobrero) *professional soccer player*
Sochen, June *history professor*
Sonderby, Susan Pierson *federal judge*
Spann-Cooper, Melody *broadcast executive*
Steinberg, Salme Elizabeth Harju *academic administrator, historian*
Steinhorn, Robin H. *neonatologist, educator*
Stevens, Linda K. *lawyer*
Stifler, Venetia Chakos *dancer, educator, choreographer*
Stillman, Nina Gidden *lawyer*
Stone, Susan A. *lawyer*
Storti, Pamela *elementary school educator*
Straus, Lorna Puttkammer *biology professor*
Strauss, Deborah *foundation administrator*
Strobel, Pamela B. *energy executive*
Strubel, Ella Doyle *advertising executive, public relations executive*
Sullivan, Marcia Waite *lawyer*
Sullivan, Peggy *librarian, consultant*
Swiger, Elinor Porter *lawyer*
Talbot, Pamela *public relations executive*
Tanzman, Mary *social worker*
Telfer, Margaret Clare *internist, hematologist, oncologist*
Terrassa, Jacqueline *museum director*
Tescher, Jennifer *bank executive*
Thistlethwaite, Susan Brooks *religious organization administrator*
Thomas, Barbara L. *not-for-profit executive*
Thomas, Cherryl T. *former federal agency administrator*
Thomas, Leona Marlene *healthcare educator*
Thompson, Jayne Carr *public relations and communications executive, lawyer*
Topinka, Judy Baar *state official, political organization worker*
Toriani, Denise Marie *hospital residency coordinator*
Treston, Sherry S. *lawyer*
Trogani, Monica *ballet dancer*
Trost, Eileen Bannon *lawyer*
True, Alison Cochran *newspaper editor*
Tryloff, Robin S. *food products executive*
Tsiang, Grace Renjuei *economist, educator*
Ullrich, Polly *art critic*
Utecht, Andrea E. *lawyer*
Van Demark, Ruth Elaine *lawyer*
VanderBeke, Patricia K. *architect*
Venturini, Tisha Lea *professional soccer player*
Vigen, Kathryn L. Voss *nursing administrator, educator, dean*
Villalon, Dalisay Manuel *nurse, real estate broker*
Vogelzang, Jeanne Marie *professional society administrator, lawyer*
Volgman, Annabelle Santos *cardiologist, educator*
Von Klan, Laurene *museum administrator*
Vowell, Sarah *writer, radio personality*
Wagner, Alyson Kay (Aly Wagner) *professional soccer player*
Walsh, Mary Caswell *psychotherapist*
Wambach, Abby (Mary Abigail Wambach) *Olympic athlete*
Watson, Easter Jean *psychotherapist, financial program consultant*
Waxler, Beverly Jean *anesthesiologist, physician*
Weber, Susan A. *lawyer*
Weed, Mary Theophilos *psychology educator*
Weinberg, Lila Shaffer *editor, writer*
Weinstein, Margo *lawyer*
Weselak, Anna Marie Schmidt *educational association administrator, media consultant*
Wharton, Margaret Agnes *artist*
White, Linda Diane *lawyer*
White, Linda Marie *former fraternal organization administrator*
Wiens, Ann *artist, writer, editor, art critic*
Wier, Patricia Ann *publishing executive, consultant*
Wille, Lois Jean *retired editor*
Williams, Ann Claire *federal judge*
Williams, Marsha C. *corporate financial executive*
Willis, Anna L. *commissioner*
Wilson, Cleo Francine *foundation administrator*
Wine-Banks, Jill Susan *lawyer*
Winfrey, Oprah *television talk show host, actress, television producer*
Winter, Jane *medical educator*
Wolfe, Sheila A. *journalist*
Wood, Diane Pamela *federal judge*
Wright, Antoinette D. *museum administrator*
Wright, Judith Margaret *law librarian, educator, dean*
Wyndewicke, Kionne Annette (Annette Johnson Moorer) *reading educator*
Yuracko, Kimberly *law educator*
Zagel, Margaret Maxwell *lawyer*
Zainelli, Gina M. *education educator*
Zee, Phyllis C. *physician, educator, researcher*
Zemm, Sandra Phyllis *lawyer*
Zhao, Jia *lawyer*
Ziegler, Ann E. *retail executive*
Zoloth, Laurie Susan *bioethicist*

Chicago Heights
Buishas, Kristin Maureen *elementary school educator*

Chicago Ridge
Socha, Maureen Patricia *elementary school educator*

Chillicothe
Griesbaum, Kamela Lee *music educator*

Clarendon Hills
Choice, Priscilla Kathryn Means (Penny Choice) *retired educational association administrator*

Clifton
Shifflet, Nicole R. *secondary school educator*

Coal City
DiGiusto, Elaine Bessie *science educator*
Major, Mary Jo *dance school artistic director*
O'Brien, Mary Kathleen *state legislator, lawyer*

Collinsville
Graebe, Annette Mulvany *retired university administrator, professor emeritus*
Kossina, Mary Helen *elementary school educator*
Massa, Martha Joann *retired elementary school educator*
Simon, Patricia Ann *art educator*

Columbia
Newell, Christel *music educator*

Country Club Hills
Crimmins-Snyder, Caroline Jean *secondary school educator, paralegal*
McClelland, Helen *music educator*

Countryside
Vondrak, Roberta G. *counselor*

Crystal Lake
Fleming, Marjorie Foster *freelance writer, artist*
Haas, Sheila Jean *secondary school educator*
Linklater, Isabelle Stanislawa Yarosh-Galazka (Lee Linklater) *foundation administrator*
Reed, Helen G. *poet*
Roehl, Kathleen Ann *financial executive*
Salvesen, B. Forbes *artist*
Thoms, Jeannine Aumond *lawyer*

Danville
Hiser, Paula J. *medical/surgical nurse*
Payne, Paula Marie *minister*
Woodrow, Jennifer Cole *music educator*

Decatur
Ewers, Marla Rouse *voice educator*
Loebl, Maragaret Margo *corporate financial executive*
Madding, Claudia *agricultural products executive*
Mancinelli, Judith *piano teacher, recitalist, chamber music performer*
Mayfield, Peggy Lee *counselor*
Woertz, Patricia Ann *agricultural company executive, retired oil company executive*

Deerfield
Adams, Jennifer *medical products executive*
Green, Dana I. *lawyer, human resources specialist*
Lezak, Carol Spielman *communications executive, editor, writer, design consultant, medical librarian*
Meyer, Mara Ellice *special education educator, consultant, academic administrator*
Parent, Miriam Stark *psychology educator*
Pearson, Louise S. *lawyer*
Persky, Marla Susan *lawyer*
Prete, Gayle Compton *advertising and marketing executive*

Dekalb
Crosser, Carmen Lynn *marriage and family therapist, social worker, consultant*
Folgate, Cynthia A. *social services administrator*
Jay, Danielle Mary *dancer, educator*
Koenig, Heidi O. *public administration professor*
McIntire, Penny A. Kendall *education educator*
Merritt, Helen Henry *retired art educator, sculptor, ceramist, art historian*
Rollman, Charlotte *artist, educator*
Simmons, Deborah Anne *environmental educator*
Sons, Linda Ruth *mathematician, educator*
Stewart, Mary R. *artist, educator*
Weisenthal, Rebecca G. *clinical psychologist*

Des Plaines
Clapper, Marie Anne *magazine publisher*
Drake, Ann M. *consumer products company executive*
Gold, Deidra D. *lawyer*
Korbel, Linda Anne *language educator, educator*
Lake, Noreen L. *retired accountant*
Lee, Margaret Burke *college president, language educator*
Pannke-Smith, Peggy *insurance company executive*
Pappas Parks, Katherine Louis *artist*
Wisz, Katherine *nurse*

Dixon
Anderson, Marion LeBlanc *history educator*
Ewers, Denise Yvonne *music educator*
Hansen, Linda Marie *small business owner*
Huber, Marianne Jeanne *art dealer, art appraiser*
Polascik, Mary Ann *ophthalmologist*
Vivian, Shirley Full *secondary educator*

Dolton
McNamara, Kimberly Diane *science educator, department chairman*

Dow
Schuler, Dorothy R. *education educator, consultant, retired elementary school educator*

Downers Grove
Blei, Laurie N. *counseling administrator*
Fugate, Kelly Anne *nurse*
LaRocca, Patricia Darlene McAleer *middle school educator*
MacArtney, Lisa Lani *science educator, consultant*
Ozog, Diane L. *allergist*
Poetzel, Susan Marie *elementary school educator*
Saricks, Joyce Goering *librarian*
Zillmer, Debra Ann *orthopedist, sports medicine physician*

Du Quoin
Ibendahl, Jean Ayres *retired elementary and secondary educator*

Dundee
Hernandez, Peggy Sue *science educator*
Weck Farrag, Kristin W. *bank executive*

Dunlap
Lueschow, Sarah Lynne *biology educator*
McCann, Louise A. *mathematics educator*
Pardieck, Sherrie Chan *education educator*
Traicoff, Sandra M. *lawyer*

Dupo
Kautzer, Susan Ann *science educator*

Dwight
Coulter, Carol Ann *retired secondary school educator*
Rosenbaum, Linda Jean *elementary school educator*

Earlville
Estell, Mary Esther *music educator, emergency medical technician, protective services official*

East Alton
DiPaolo, Marcella Kay *elementary school educator*

East Dundee
Simons, Gail S. *artist, educator, librarian*

East Saint Louis
Lane-Trent, Patricia Jean *social worker*
Roy, Darlene *human services administrator*
Thomas, Mary Lee *property manager*
Wright, Katie Harper *educational administrator, journalist*

Edwardsville
Anderson, Mary Jane *music educator*
Crowder, Barbara Lynn *judge*
Dietrich, Suzanne Claire *communications consultant, researcher*
Johnson, Charlotte Lee *librarian*
Kittrell, Ethel Jean *musician, retired literature and language professor*
Norris, Sandra Love *occupational therapist*
Stranc, Cathleen L. *music educator*

Effingham
Spelbring, Brandi D. *language educator, writer*
Van Ulft, Stephanie Ann *health facility administrator*
Whitlatch, Christine Lyn *music educator*

Elgin
Aydt, Mary I. *secondary school educator*
Barnett, Sue *nurse*
Colpitts, Gail Elizabeth *artist, educator*
Deichstetter, Peggy Ann *science educator*
Garcia, Donna M. *science educator*
Johnson, Jacquelyn Marie *elementary school educator*
Reimer, Judy Mills *pastor, religious executive*
Scherger, Nicole *mathematics educator*
Thompson, Phyllis Darlene *retired elementary school educator*

Elk Grove Village
Roberts, Verna Dean *music educator*
Sherwood, Barbara Jean *art educator*
Yates, Anna Marie *counselor, educator*

Elkhart
Cunningham, Donna Lynn *library director*

Elmhurst
Blain, Charlotte Marie *internist, educator*
Choyke, Phyllis May Ford (Mrs. Arthur Davis Choyke Jr.) *management executive, editor, poet*
Malo, Michele Lee *marketing professional*
Nedza, Sandra Louise *manufacturing executive*
Nega, Nancy Kawecki *middle school science educator*
Payne, Jan *medical/surgical nurse, educator*

Erie
Latham, LaVonne Marlys *physical education educator*
Orr, Kathleen Kayser *special education educator*

Evanston
Altman, Edith G. *sculptor*
Bjorncrantz, Leslie Benton *librarian*
Blair, Virginia Ann *public relations executive*
Cao, Hui *physics and astronomy professor*
Cates, Jo Ann *library director*
Crawford, Susan *library director, educator, editor, writer*
Eberley, Helen-Kay *opera singer, recording industry executive, poet*
Eisen, Marlene Ruth *psychologist, educator*
Enroth-Cugell, Christina Alma Elisabeth *neurophysiologist, educator*
Galvin, Kathleen Malone *communications educator*
Gentner, Dedre *psychology professor*
Godwin, Hilary A. *chemistry professor, research scientist*
Gordon, Julie Peyton *foundation administrator*
Hixson, Kathryn *art critic*
Holton, Lisa *writer, editor, researcher*
Hurd, Elizabeth Shakman *social studies educator*
Koenigsberg, Judy Z. Nulman *psychologist*
Lewis, Barbara-Ann Gamboa *chemistry educator*
McCoy, Marilyn *director*
McDonough, Bridget Ann *music theatre company director*
Mineka, Susan *psychology professor*
Mora, Dawn Ann *theater educator*
Odom, Teri Wang *chemist*
Persons, Fern *actress*
Peterson, Penelope Loraine *dean, education educator*
Pierrehumbert, Janet Breckenridge *language educator*
Power, Peggy Ann *elementary school educator*
Pritchard, Sarah Margaret *library director*
Rago-McNamara, Juliet Maggio *artist*
Reiss, Lenore Ann *language educator, retired secondary school educator*
Richeson, Jennifer Anne *psychology professor, researcher*
Sandor, Ellen Ruth *artist*
Schels, Margarete Theresa *secondary school educator*
Schwartz, Neena Betty *endocrinologist, educator*
Thompson, Leigh Lassiter *psychologist, educator*
Thrash, Patricia Ann *retired educational association administrator*
Wang, Sona *venture capitalist*
Weertman, Julia Randall *materials engineering educator*
Whiteley, Sandra Marie *librarian, editor*
Zimmerman, Mary Alice *performing arts educator*

Evansville
Walker, Cheryl A. *literature educator*

Evergreen Park
Arcieri, Sandy Lee *professional collector*
Prendergast, Carole Lisak *musician, educator*
Wigsmoen, Susan Catania *elementary school educator*

Ewing
Phelps, Elaine L. *special education educator*

Flossmoor
Backstein, Micki Lynn *social worker*
Micki, Backstein Lynn *social worker*

Forest Park
Poplawska, Anna *artist, educator, art critic*
Rozmus, Karen Janet *artist, porcelain doll maker*
Saiyed, Humaira *psychiatrist, director*

Frankfort
Halliman, Tina Lynette *special education educator*
Koesche, Aileen Mary *special education educator*

Freeport
Giglio, Emily Kristine *athletic trainer, educator*
Lestikow, Norma Jean *nursing educator*
Vogt, Lorna Corrine *retired librarian, small business owner*

Fulton
Specht, Lois Darlene *volunteer*

Galena
Alexander, Barbara Leah Shapiro *clinical social worker*

Galesburg
LaDage, Janet Lee *education educator*
Sunderland, Jacklyn Giles *retired writer*
Thenhaus, Paulette A. *artist, writer*
Wiegand, Julie Wilds *elementary school educator*

Gardner
Lutz, Betsy Ann *elementary school educator*

Geneseo
Brown, Mabel Welton *lawyer*

Geneva
Harmon Brown, Valarie Jean *hospital laboratory director, information systems executive*
Klenke, Deborah Ann *band and choral director, department chairman*
Mishina, Mizuho *artist*
Peterson, Rhonda Lynn *elementary school educator*
Stevens, Kristina Diane *art educator*

Glen Carbon
Adkerson, Donya Lynn *clinical counselor*

Glen Ellyn
Alberti, Jean Mae Claire *clinical psychologist*
Anderson, Barbara Jean *biology professor*
Benzies, Bonnie Jeanne *clinical and addictions psychologist*
Burkemper, Jennifer A. *secondary school educator*
Cook, Joann Catherine *computer professor*
Cummings, Joan E. *health facility administrator, educator*
Engelmann, Mary Lynn *nursing educator*
Gage, Nancy Elizabeth *academic administrator, accountant, educator*
Hoornbeek, Lynda Ruth Couch *librarian, educator*
King, Peggy Marsha *special education educator, researcher*
Marszalek, Elizabeth A. *computer graphics designer, educator*
McGovern, Meghan Marie *athletic trainer*
Neurauter, Elizabeth Strain *secondary school educator*
Nunamaker, Susan Sun *mathematics professor*
Persky, Karen Rae *biologist, educator*
Raymond, Amanda *chemistry educator*
Schmidt, Karen Lee *marketing professional, sales executive*

Glencoe
Siske, Regina *artist*

Glendale Heights
Cook, Doris Marie *retired accountant, educator*

Glenview
Bobay, Jennifer Ann *elementary school educator*
Casas, Laurie Ann *plastic surgeon*
Coulson, Elizabeth Anne *physical therapist, educator, state representative*
Epstein, Barbara Myrna Robbin *retired language educator*
Franklin, Lynne *corporate communications specialist, writer*
Halliday, Nancy Ruth *scientific illustrator*
King, Billie Jean Moffitt *retired professional tennis player*
Kohl, Dolores *museum director, educator*
Macsai, Marian Sue *ophthalmologist*
Rubin, Susan M. *neurologist*

Godfrey
McDowell, Angela Lorene *counselor*
Parton-Stanard, Susan *music educator, voice educator, musician*
Smith, Linda Jeane *allied health educator*

Granite City
Sullivan, Laura Ann *secondary school educator*

Grant Park
Koelling, Shirley M. *mathematics educator*

Grayslake
Craven, Deborah *performing arts educator*
Fout, Jeanine Marie *social studies educator*
Landry, Tracey Katherine *social studies educator*
Vaughn, Connie Marie *marketing professional, writer, consultant*

Grayville
Finkelstein, Honora Moore *writer, editor, consultant*

Greenfield
Weller, Robin Lea *elementary school educator*

Greenville
Weiss, Louise Annette *music educator*

Griggsville
Ratliff, Marguerite *special education educator*

Gurnee
Curns, Eileen Bohan *counselor, author, speaker*
Gertz, Suzanne C. *artist*
Hagins, Barbara J. *pharmaceutical consultant*
Hall, Terry *accountant*
Halsne-Baarda, Alana Michelle *secondary school educator*
Ullrich, Linda J. *medical technologist*

Hanover Park
Carter, Eleanor Elizabeth *account executive*

Harwood Heights
Rudel, Barbara Elizabeth *elementary school educator*

Hawthorn Woods
Gajda, Shirli Kubiak *literature and language educator*

Hazel Crest
Thies, Julie Ann *music educator*

Heyworth
Gregory, M. Christine *science educator*

Highland
Deets, Michelle Louise *secondary school educator*
Franklin, Patricia Lynn Powell *special education educator*

Highland Park
Axelrod, Leah Joy *tour company executive*
Burman, Diane Berger *career management and organization development consultant*
Greenblatt, Miriam *writer, editor, educator*
Hershenson, Martha Bradford *history educator*
Mervis, Bonnie Aaron *social worker*
Miller, Maureen Chertow *science educator*
Rutenberg-Rosenberg, Sharon Leslie *retired journalist*
Schindel, Alice *social worker*
Slavick, Ann Lillian *retired art educator*
Stein, Paula Jean Anne Barton *hotel real estate company executive, real estate broker*

Hillside
Kapsalis, Frances Hinos *psychologist, educator*

Hinsdale
Dillon, Jane Elizabeth *otolaryngologist*
Kim, Micaela *speech pathology/audiology services professional*
Mahmood, Samar *psychiatrist*
Migliorino, Caroline Milano *nursing consultant*
Szeremeta-Browar, Taisa Lydia *endodontist*
Unikel, Eva Taylor *interior designer*
Wachowski, Susan Marie *elementary school educator*

Hoffman Estates
Barraza, Lupe *retail executive*
Hays, Judy Meyer *music educator*
Koch, Carrie S. *mathematics educator*
Meads, Mindy *merchandising and design executive*
Schmitz, Alice J. *secondary school educator*
Wandro, Kathleen Mary *secondary school educator*
Zopp, Andrea Lynne *lawyer, retail executive*

Homer
Wascher, Deborah Lynn *elementary school educator*

Homewood
Chapman, Delores *elementary school educator*

Hoopeston
Hicks, Carol Ann *small business owner, educator*

Huntley
Johnson, Cheryl Lynn Hall *secondary education educator, website designer*

Indian Head Park
Beck, Ariadne Plumis *psychologist, psychotherapist, management consultant*

Indianhead Park
Johnson, Anita (Mary Anita Johnson) *physician, medical association administrator*

Itasca
Brazzle, Sara *publishing executive*
Constant, Anita Aurelia *publisher*
Porter, Ethel Mae *publishing executive*

Jacksonville
Beal, Deborah L. *environmental scientist, educator*
Curtis, Linda Kathryn *elementary school educator*
Humphries, Sherry Lynn *special education educator*
Johns, Beverley Anne Holden *special education administrator*
Moe-Fishback, Barbara Ann *counseling administrator*
Vaché, Martha Jo *retired special education educator*
Welch, Rhea Jo *special education educator*

Jerseyville
McCreary, Brenda Kay *elementary school educator*

Joliet
Bartow, Barbara Jené *university program administrator*
Doyle, Juanita *medical/surgical nurse*
Lynch, Priscilla A. *nursing educator, psychotherapist*
McMiller, Anita Williams *leasing company executive*
Schoonover, Melissa *music educator*
Starner, Barbara Kazmark *marketing, advertising and export sales executive*
Williams, Jennifer Ann *public relations executive*
Wilson, Bobbi Ellen *physical therapy assistant*

Justice
Casselle, Corene *elementary school educator*

Kankakee
Crady, Paula Gannon *secondary school educator*
Lingo, Shelley J. *social studies educator*

Kenilworth
Clary, Rosalie Brandon Stanton *timber farm executive, civic worker*
Owens, Donna Lee *small business owner, consultant*
Schneider-Criezis, Susan Marie *architect*
Weaver, Donna Rae *winery executive*

Kewanee
Grant, Linda Kay (Linda Kay Scott) *small business owner, sales executive*

Kildeer
Muffoletto, Mary Lu *retired educational association administrator, editor*

La Grange Park
Butler, Margaret Kampschaefer *retired computer scientist*
Johnson, Gertrude Coogan *educational consultant, elementary school educator*
Paliatka, Jeanne Therese *literature and language educator, department chairman*

Lake Barrington
Black, Kathryn N. *psychologist, educator*

Lake Bluff
Fletcher, Dorothy Jean *hospital administrator, educator*
Scott, Karen Bondurant *consumer catalog company executive*

Lake Forest
Birtman, Amy B. *secondary school educator*
Callan, Clair Marie *physician, consultant*
Chieger, Kathryn Jean *recreational facility executive*
Fetridge, Bonnie-Jean Clark (Mrs. William Harrison Fetridge) *civic volunteer*
Frederick, Virginia Fiester *state legislator*
Goldstein, Marsha Feder *tour company executive*
Krasnewich, Kathryn *water transportation executive*
McCaskey, Virginia Halas *professional sports team executive*
Murphy, Karen *sports association executive*
Palmer, Ann Therese Darin *lawyer*
Rand, Kathy Sue *public relations executive, consultant*
Stirling, Ellen Adair *retail executive*
Swanton, Virginia Lee *writer, publisher*
Szaksztylo, Kathee *design technologist*
Taylor, Barbara Ann Olin *writer, educational consultant*
Van Ella, Kathleen E. *fine art consultant*
Ysasi-Diaz, Gloria *wholesale distribution executive*

Lake Villa
Yankee, Julie Jo *elementary school educator*

Lake Zurich
Schwarz, Cheryl Marita *special education educator*

Lansing
Kaplan, Huette Myra *training services executive, consultant*

Lemont
Doebert, Sandra L. *school system administrator*

Liberty
Dickhut, Karen Sue *music educator*

Libertyville
Cunningham, Elizabeth Ann *librarian*
Devine, Barbara Armstrong *risk manager*
Hoyer, Mary Catherine *elementary school educator, director*
Peot, Deborah Lynn *music educator*
Pollina, Kristen Mittl *child and adolescent psychologist*
Stagge, Karen M. *elementary school educator*

Lincoln
Cook, Ruth Ellen *athletic trainer*
Freesmeier, Ruth Ann *music educator, director*
Gaddy, Stephanie Ann *director*

Lincolnshire
Rauch, Catherine Kerkes *secondary school educator*
Roler, Jo Anne Caruso *education educator, consultant*

Lindenhurst
Blumberg, Sherry Helene *Jewish education educator*
Eron, Madeline Marcus *psychologist*

Lisle
Bazik, Edna Frances *mathematician, educator*
Huffman, Louise Tolle *middle school educator*
Ruyle-Hullinger, Elizabeth Smith (Beth Ruyle) *municipal financial advisor, consultant*
Stephen, Doris Moyer *music educator*

Lombard
Blair, Teresa Tarallo *foreign language educator*
Bruzek, Patricia Ann *elementary school educator*
Egan, Karen Esther *elementary school educator*
Holgers-Awana, Rita Marie *electrodiagnosis specialist*
Kasprow, Barbara Anne *biomedical researcher, writer*
McCoy, Jeanie Shearer *analytical chemist, consultant*

Long Grove
Kile, Elizabeth Collier *art educator, artist*

Machesney Park
Brewer, Valerie D. *science educator, secondary school educator*
Vaughn, Linda Marie *municipal official*

Macomb
Barclay, Martha Jane *science educator, research scientist*
Barden, Laura Marie *science educator*
Gates, Janice Sue *management consultant, educator*
Goehner, Donna Marie *retired university dean*
Morton, Patsy Lou *social worker*
Sonnek, Bonnie Kay *education educator*

Madison
Purdes, Alice Marie *retired adult education educator*

Mahomet
Barger-Marcusiu, Eva *cardiovascular nurse*
Kennedy, Cheryl Lynn *museum director*
Lindley, Joyce E. *health facility administrator, consultant, real estate appraiser*
Thompson, Margaret M. *physical education educator*

Malta
Franklin, Nadine Karen *performing arts educator*

Manteno
Burlend, Virginia Ann *elementary school educator*
Bush, Dawn Marie *elementary school educator*

Maple Park
Carter, Ethel Ilene *secondary school educator*
Dripps-Paulson, Maria *music educator*

Mapleton
Forgason, Cheryl L. *secondary school educator*

Marion
Aikman, Elflora Anna K. *senior citizens center administrator*

Markham
Peacock, Marilyn Claire *primary school educator*

Marseilles
Bianchi, Gayle Ann *elementary school educator*

Marshall
Bolinger, Kay Lynn *literature and language educator*

Martinsville
Robinson, Sheila Frances *special education educator*

Maryville
Stark, Patricia Ann *psychologist*

Mascoutah
Roy, Elizabeth Mary *secondary school educator*
Setterlund, Tina A.M. *music educator*

Mattoon
Horton, Lucinda *biology professor*
Swartzbaugh, Dorothy Stoeppelwerth *middle school educator*

Maywood
Albain, Kathy S. *oncologist*
Gaynor, Ellen Rose *hematologist*
Hindle, Paula Alice *nursing administrator*
Nand, Sucha *medical educator*

Mc Gaw Park
Risen-White, Angela Lorri *systems analyst*

Mchenry
Carson, Linda Marie *elementary school educator*
Dam, Christina Malo *secondary school educator*

Melrose Park
Bernick, Carol Lavin *consumer products company executive*
Habel, Wendy Jo *elementary school educator*
Kloster, Carol Good *wholesale distribution executive*
Lavin, Bernice E. *cosmetics executive*
Wechter, Clari Ann *manufacturing executive*

Metamora
Greer, Renee Michelle *elementary school educator*
Rude, Debra Marie *music educator*

Midlothian
Griebel, Karen Ann *music educator*

Milford
Beall, Pamela Honn *psychologist, consultant*
Pyzek, Tamera Jean *music educator*

Minonk
Baumann, Barbara Jean *elementary school educator*

Minooka
Coclanes, Jacqueline Ann Fikes *elementary school educator*
Craig, Judith Marie *history educator*

Mokena
Vander Zanden, Marianne *music educator*
Wright, Chely *country singer*

Moline
Curry, Kathleen Bridget *retired librarian*
Johnson, Mary Lou *lay worker, educator*
Larson, Sandra B. *nursing educator*
Mitchell, Lucille Anne *retired elementary school educator*
Sausedo, Sasha A. *social studies educator*
Sierra, Dolores *communications educator*

Momence
Holland, Leslie Ann *special education educator*

Monmouth
Bruce, Mary Hanford *academic administrator, educator, writer*
Gossett, Barbara Jean *voice educator*

Morris
Wilson, Marcia Lee *secondary school educator*

Morton Grove
Hoffman, Joy Yu *harpist, pianist*
Johnson, Laura Stark *secondary school educator, administrator*
Smolyansky, Julie *consumer products company executive*

Mossville
Clary, Wendy Anne *principal*

Mount Prospect
Grossman, Barbara Anne *nurse*
Murray, Heidi Magdalena *secondary school educator*
O'Connor, Nan G. *social worker*

Mount Sterling
Bauer, Sarah L. *literature and language educator, coach*

Mount Vernon
Hall, Sharon Gay *retired language educator, artist*
Kendrick-Hopgood, Debra Jo *small business owner*

Mundelein
Berrong, Christine R. *music educator, voice educator*

Murphysboro
Berry, Alice Allen *retired music educator*

Naperville
Armstrong, Patricia Kay *ecologist*
Burken, Ruth Marie *utilities executive*
Corvino, Beth Byster *lawyer*
Cowlishaw, Mary Lou *government educator*
Ellingson, Mary
Fuhrer, Linda Larsen *social worker*
Gaeth, Roxanne *school psychologist*
Galvan, Mary Theresa *economics professor*
Gilmore, Brenda René *literature and language educator, theater director*
Harvard, Rita Grace *real estate agent, volunteer*
Knuckles, Barbara Miller *academic administrator*
Nicotra, Mary *health facility administrator, consultant*
Raccah, Dominique Marcelle *publisher*
Rebeck, Pamela Joan *psychologist*
Sherren, Anne Terry *chemistry professor*
Tan, Li-Su Lin *accountant, insurance company executive, consultant*

New Lenox
Heffernan, Debra Jane *administrator*

Niles
Schyvinck, Christine *electronics executive*

Normal
Davis, Janet R. Beach *science educator*
Deany, Donna Jean *radiology technologist*
Miller, Wilma Hildruth *education educator*
Musick, Marilyn Irene *retired secondary school educator*
O'Dell, Lisa A. *elementary school educator*
Rademacher, Betty Green *retired counselor, consultant*
Wortham, Anne Estelle *education educator*

North Aurora
Biggs, Jennifer M. *elementary school educator*

North Chicago
Loga, Sanda *physicist, researcher*

Northbrook
Brune, Catherine S. *insurance company executive*
Costello, Joan *psychologist*
Crockett, Joan M. *human resources executive*
Fettner, Marilyn *management consultant*
Garcia, Mary Frances *science educator*
Herrerias, Carla Trevette *epidemiologist, health science association administrator*
Heuer, Marilyn Patricia *operating room nurse, quality assurance nurse*
Kahn, Sandra S. *psychotherapist*
Mandel, Karyl Lynn *accountant*
McGinn, Mary J. *lawyer, insurance company executive*
Noeth, Carolyn Frances *speech and language pathologist*
Pesmen, Sandra (Mrs. Harold William Pesmen) *editor, educator*
Rosenberg, Auria Eleanor *secondary school educator*
Ross, Debra Benita *marketing executive, jewelry designer*
Silverman, Enid *painter, stained glass artist, muralist*
Sprieser, Judith A. *former software company executive*
Sudbrink, Jane Marie *sales and marketing executive*
Warchol, Judith Marie *small business owner*
Warren, Elizabeth Curran *retired political science professor*

Northfield
Grimes, Sally *marketing professional*
Lynch, Kirsten *food products executive*
Rosenfeld, Irene B. *food products company executive*
Sneed, Paula Ann *food products executive*
Vilim, Nancy Catherine *advertising executive*

O Fallon
Tiemann, Jeannine E. *music educator*

Oak Brook
Barnes, Karen Kay *lawyer*
Bower, Barbara Jean *nurse, consultant*
Congalton, Susan Tichenor *lawyer*
Fields, Janice L. *food service executive*
Fritzsche, Peggy J. *medical association administrator, radiologist*
Hoffmann, Joan Carol *retired academic dean*
Imran, Ayesha *internist*
Johnson, Shirley Elaine *management consultant*
Klinger, Gail Greaves *art educator, illustrator*
Marcus, Carol A. *information technology manager*
Santona, Gloria *lawyer*
Schultz, Karen Rose *clinical social worker, author, publisher, speaker*
Sherman, Jennifer L. *lawyer*
Sweeney, Patrice Ellen *health administration executive*
Vesely-Rice, Alison C. *theater director, actress, educator*

Oak Forest
Monaghan, M. Patricia *education educator, writer*

Oak Lawn
Laird, Jean Elouise Rydeski (Mrs. Jack E. Laird) *author, adult education educator*
Peczkowski, Kristin Marie *social sciences educator, coach*
Wiechert, Barbara Theresa *school nurse practitioner*

Oak Park
Bedrossian, Ursula Kay Kennedy *editor*
Brown, Mary Anne *childcare advocate*
Creed, Barbara Ellen *music educator*
Fleming, Margaret A. *adoption advocate, adoption service director*
Greer, Julianna Patterson *not-for-profit administrator*
Lare, Jane Cameron *school psychologist*
McLaren, Ruth *bank executive*
McMahon, Margot Ann *sculptor, art educator*
Pearson, Gayle Marlene *writer*
Schlesinger, Harriet Rose *retired psychiatrist*
Senese, Suzanne Marie *art and music educator, performance artist*
Venerable, Shirley Marie *retired gifted and talented educator*

Oakbrook Terrace
Cason, Marilynn Jean *academic administrator, lawyer*
Hegenderfer, Jonita Susan *public relations executive*

Oakland
Eriksen, Barbara Ann *writer, researcher*

Oglesby
Perez, Dorene Marie *computer-aided drafting and engineering educator*

Olympia Fields
Craig, Jessica Ann *secondary school educator*

Oneida
Furrow, Valerie *mathematics educator, coach*

Orion
Magee, Elizabeth Sherrard *civic organization volunteer*

Orland Park
Burfeind, Betty Ruth *science educator*
Knight, Eileen Quinn *education educator, consultant*
Ritchey, Lauretta Marie *secondary school educator*

Oswego
Johnson, Dawn Sundene *chemistry educator*
McBride, Sandra *secondary school educator*

Palatine
Bontempo, Elaine *language educator*
Keres, Karen Lynne *literature and language professor*
Leff, Rebecca A. *gifted and talented educator*
Scheid, Catherine Marie *elementary school educator*

Palos Heights
Ilangovan, Saroja *retired pathologist*
Powell, Patricia Lynn *education educator, educator, special education educator, educator*

Palos Hills
Lycardi, Joan C. *artist*
McGarel-Warkocki, Lynn M. *history educator*
Porter, Joyce Klowden *theater educator, director, actress*
Stratton, Pauline A. *retired elementary school educator, alderman*

Pana
Waddington, Irma Joann *music educator*

Paris
Essinger, Susan Jane *special education educator*
Hiddle, Susan K. *music educator, musician*

Park Forest
Billig, Etel Jewel *theater director, actress*
Cribbs, Maureen Ann *artist, educator*
Orr, Marcia *pre-school administrator, consultant*

Park Ridge
Albert, Elizabeth Franz (Mrs. Henry B. Albert) *investor, artist, conservationist*
Bateman, Andrea R. *insurance agent*
Chapman, Jacquelyn Sullivan *retired elementary school educator*
Culverwell, Rosemary Jean *principal, retired elementary school educator*
Naker, Mary Leslie *legal firm executive*
Palmer, Rose *humanities educator, writer*
Parilla, Barbara V. *medicine specialist*
Pippen, Jennifer Lynn *therapist, consultant*
Torosian, Sona *secondary school educator*

Paxton
Curry, Joan R. *medical/surgical nurse, emergency nurse*

Pekin
Herbstreith, Yvonne Mae *primary school educator*
Yock, Norma Iris *counselor, music educator*

Peoria
Adams-Curtis, Leah E. *academic administrator*
Frazier, Jan Elaine *literature and language educator, writer*
Frey, Yvonne Amar *librarian*
Grebner, Bernice Prill *author, astrological counselor*
Hojilla-Evangelista, Milagros Parker *research chemist, research scientist*
Kelly, Grace Dentino *secondary school educator*
Mariani, Theresa Lynn *sociologist, educator*
Martin, Coleen Marie *elementary school educator*
McCollum, Jean Hubble *medical technician*
Mitzelfelt, Connie J. *secondary school educator, principal*
Murphy, Sharon Margaret *retired communications educator*
Nunn, Carolyn M. *principal, speech pathology/audiology services professional*
Perrilles, Angela Terese *physical therapist*
Poteat, Thena G. *psychiatrist*
Rice, Monica Rochelle *elementary school educator*
Strauss, Wendy Eisenberg *music educator*
Watson, Ellen I. *academic administrator*

Peoria Heights
Haslett, Rhonda Lorraine *elementary school educator*

Plainfield
Alander, Virginia Nickerson *retired student assistance coordinator*
Bennett-Hammerberg, Janie Marie *small business owner, writer, consultant, administrative assistant*
Lalka, Monica Jean *music educator, consultant*
Matlock, B. Jane *science educator*
Vargo, Louise Ann *landscape artist, music educator*
Weis, Kristine Erica *secondary school educator*

Pleasant Plains
Thomas, Evelyn B. *agricultural products supplier*

Poplar Grove
Zimber, Lisa Marie *music educator*

Princeton
Collins, N. Dana *art gallery owner, consultant, retired art educator*

Prospect Heights
Derickson, Sandy *bank executive*

Quincy
Flinspach, Ursula R. *pharmacist, mathematics professor*
Gehrich, Leonora Suppan *artist, musician, German literature educator*
Reynolds, Judith Amy *nutritionist, consultant, animal scientist, educator*
Straub, Sunny L. *retired elementary school educator*
Taylor, Judith Caroline *entrepreneur*
Wemhoener, Dolores Lucille *cultural organization administrator, entertainer*

Rantoul
Holmes, Lois Rehder *composer, piano educator, voice educator*

Richmond
Schmidt, Sara Jean *special education educator*

Richton Park
Burt, Gwen Behrens *educational association administrator*
Morrissette, Danielle *biology educator*
Pierce, Mary E. *retired elementary school educator, public relations consultant*

Ringwood
Swanson, Marti *retired secondary educator, consultant*

River Forest
Bodi, Sonia Ellen *library director, educator*
Carroll, Donna M. *academic administrator*
Davlin, Mary Clemente *literature and language professor, sister*
Eisel, Jean Ellen *educational association administrator*
Helwig, Janet *computer science educator*
Sweeney, Mickey *literature and language professor*
Weedermann, Marion *mathematics professor*

River Grove
Dierking, Emilie M. *secondary school educator*
Gardner, Sandi B. *biology professor*
Hillert, Gloria Bonnin *anatomist, educator*
Jeans, Mary Millicent *educational association administrator*
LaGon, Cynthia Bostic *librarian*

Riverside
Van Cura, Joyce Bennett *librarian*

Robinson
Gangloff, Amber D. *music educator*
Mallard, Carrie Charlene *science educator*

Rochester
Petterchak, Janice A. *writer*

Rock Falls
Crebo, Mary Elizabeth *state agency official, assessor*
Julifs, Sandra Jean *community action agency executive*

Rock Island
Hand, Angela Rene *singer*
Johnson, Ruth Ann Craig Goswick *psychology educator*
Rafferty, Genevieve Kennedy *social service agency administrator*
Welling, Mary Ann *secondary school educator*

Rockford
Albert, Janyce Louise *human resources specialist, retired business educator, banker, consultant*
Fisher, Erin *psychology professor*
Gregory, Dola Bell *bishop, customer service administrator*
Heath, Alice Fairchild *retired mental health services professional*
Hendershott Love, Arles June *marketing professional*
Heuer, Beth Lee *music educator, composer*
Hughes, Carol Scelonge *retired secondary school educator*
Joachim, Peggy L. *secondary school educator*
Johnson, Elizabeth Ericson *retired educator*
Kaufman, Suzanne Dryer *art educator, artist, writer*
Schlub, Teresa Rae *minister*
Stromsdorfer, Deborah Ann *artist, educator*
Walhout, Justine Simon *chemistry professor*

Rolling Meadows
Bassi, Suzanne Howard *retired secondary school educator, volunteer*
Bauer, Lorain *art educator*
Burger, Mary Louise *psychologist, educator*
Nicol, Nancy J. *lawyer*
Strongin, Bonnie Lynn *language educator*

Romeoville
Hoppe, Elizabeth Anne *philosopher, educator*
Jones, Therese Margaret *language educator, editor*
Northrup, Rebecca Lynn *athletic trainer*
Rusnak, Martha Hendrick *reading education educator*
Simpson, Jayne Lou *retired academic administrator*
Vander Vliet, Valerie Jeanne *biology educator*

Rosemont
Le Menager, Lois M. *incentive merchandise and travel company executive*

Rushville
Burton, Sheila Belle *music educator*

Saint Charles
Abts, Gwyneth Hartmann *retired dietician*
Bull, Martha *artist, educator*
Freed, Karen Schmidt *elementary school educator*
Griffin, Sheila MB *strategic marketing excutive*
LaHood, Julie Ann *small business owner*
Leppert, Andrea *science educator*
Malinowski, Maryellen *photographer, artist*
O'Shea, Lynne Edeen *management consultant, educator*
Patten, Maurine Diane *psychologist*
Washkuhn, Erin Lynne *elementary school educator*

Saint Francisville
Harezi, Ilonka Jo *medical technology research executive*

Savoy
Bednar, Susan Gail *social worker, consultant, social sciences educator*

Schaumburg
Adrianopoli, Barbara Catherine *librarian*
Colberg, Linda *physical education educator*
Fattori, Ruth A. *human resources specialist, electronics executive*
Janssen, Carron Joyce *music educator*
Morrison, Patricia B. *information technology executive*
Tompson, Marian Leonard *professional society administrator*
Warrior, Padmasree *communications executive*
Westlund, Maribeth *secondary school educator*

Skokie
Anthony, Carolyn Additon *librarian*
Baehr, Elsa Telser *clinical psychologist, neurotherapist*
Breckel, Alvina Hefeli *librarian*
Brenner, Bonnie Sue *singer, artist, educator*
Guillermo, Linda *clinical social worker*
Langguth, Margaret Witty *health facility administrator*
Sheban, Lynne Rosenzweig *psychologist*
Yogev, Sara *psychologist*

Smithton
Hostetler, Elsie J. *musician, music educator*

South Barrington
Kissane, Sharon Florence *writer, consultant, educator*

South Elgin
Brhel, Karen Mollitor *elementary school educator, music educator*
Cebulski, Katherine K. *elementary school educator*

South Holland
Connolly, Carla Marie *librarian*
Ferrell, Marcie A. *elementary school educator*
Margosein, Carol Marie *secondary school educator*
Saltzman, Bobbie *theater educator*

Springfield
Clingan, Wanda Jacqueline *minister*
Collins, Annazette R. *state representative*
Collins, Jacqueline Y *state senator*
Currie, Barbara Flynn *state legislator*
Curry, Julie A. *state official*
Denham, Mary Washko *former college official, civic worker*
Duley, Margot Iris *historian, educator*
Franks, Amy Ann *healthcare educator, medical educator*
Jackson, Jacqueline Dougan *literature educator, writer*
Kaige, Alice Tubb *retired librarian*
Klingler, Gwendolyn Walbolt *state representative*
Kosel, Renée *state representative*
Kuhn, Kathleen Jo *accountant*
Martinez, Iris *state senator*
Morford, Lynn Ellen *state official*
Pankau, Carole *state senator*
Ramirez-Campbell, Christine M. *art council administrator*
Schroeder, Joyce Katherine *state agency administrator, research analyst*
Van Dyke, Annette Joy *university educator*
Witter, Karen Ackerman *museum administrator*
Woodson, Gayle Ellen *otolaryngologist*

Sterling
Albrecht, Beverly Jean *special education educator*
Moran, Joan Jensen *physical education educator, healthcare educator*

Sycamore
Hauser, Lynn Elizabeth *eye surgeon*
Johnson, Yvonne Amalia *elementary school educator, consultant*

Table Grove
Thomson, Helen Louise *retired artist*

Taylorville
Turner, Cynthia M. *science educator*

Tinley Park
Leeson, Janet Caroline Tollefson *cake specialties company executive*
Rubel, Lucia M. *music educator*

Tremont
Monk, Michelle L. *secondary school educator*
Sheehan, Donna Marie *reading educator*

Troy
Mallrich, Shannon Marie *secondary school educator*
Smargiassi, Rebecca Sue *secondary school educator*

Tuscola
Eskridge, Judith Ann *retired secondary school educator*
Henderson, E. Suzanne *elementary school educator*

University Park
Johnson, Elizabeth Jean *psychology professor*
Parin-Norris, Beth Lynn *art educator, researcher, artist*
Samson, Linda Forrest *nursing educator, nursing administrator*

Urbana
Berenbaum, May Roberta *entomology educator*
Caldwell-Colbert, A. Toy *academic administrator, psychology professor*
Davis, Elisabeth Bachman *librarian, library administration educator*
Dovring, Karin Elsa Ingeborg *writer, poet, playwright, media specialist*
Eddy-Johnson, Deanna M. *home health care advocate*
Goodrum, Shanda S. *science educator*
Kaufman, Paula T. *librarian*
Koenker, Diane P. *history professor*
Liebman, Judith Rae Stenzel *retired operations research specialist*
Makri, Nancy *chemistry professor*
Obermark, Sarah Marie *English educator*
O'Brien, Nancy Patricia *librarian, educator*
Prussing, Laurel Lunt *mayor, economist*
Ridgway, Marcella Davies *veterinarian*
Spence, Mary Lee *historian, educator*
Splittstoesser, Shirley O. *elementary school educator*
Vaughn, Linda F. *musician, educator*

Warren, Pamela A. *psychologist*
Watson, Paula D. *retired librarian*
Williams, Martha Ethelyn *information science educator*

Vandalia
Lawler, Crystal Ann *special education educator, consultant*

Varna
Rock, Beth Marie *voice educator, director*

Venice
Cunningham, Betty Jean De Bow *adult education educator*

Vermont
Datcu, Ioana *artist*

Vernon Hills
Bertermann, Laura Lynn *secondary school educator*
Kim, Sachiko O. *music educator*
Klein, Barbara A. *information technology executive*
Leahy, Christine A. *information technology executive*
Manchester, Kathleen A. *music educator*

Villa Grove
Olson, Rebecca Jane *special education educator*

Villa Park
Ellingsen, Barbara Joyce *music educator*
Fitzgerald, Christine Elizabeth *school psychologist*

Warren
Barker, Janice Marie *elementary school educator*

Warrenville
Smith, Michele *lawyer*

Waterloo
Freund, Elaine M. *literature and language educator*

Waterman
Arends, Ann M. *elementary school educator, pianist*

Wauconda
Gorski, Nancy Anne *retired elementary school educator*
Gotthardt, Mary Jane *religious studies educator*
Meehan, Jean Marie Ross *human resources, occupational health and safety management consultant*

Waukegan
Akouris, Dianne Frances *school system administrator*
Conolly-Wilson, Christina *psychologist*
Drapalik, Betty R. *volunteer, artist, educator*
Houle, Jeanne Larson *retired music educator*
Miller, Helen Elizabeth *art educator, adult education educator, artist*
Robinson, Georgia May *retired education educator*

Wayne
Chaudhry, Marie-Laurence *elementary school educator*

West Chicago
Deaver, Barbara Jean *manufacturing executive*
Noonan, Josette Marie *music educator*

West Dundee
Plunkett, Melba Kathleen *manufacturing executive*

West Frankfort
Holley-Gray, Margaret N. *minister*

Westchester
Abbinante, Vita *sales executive, administrator*
Castellano, Christine Marie *lawyer*
Doane, Marcia E. *lawyer, food products executive*
Lightford, Kimberly A. *state legislator*
Pudelek, Sherry Charlene *small business owner*
Webb, Emily *retired plant morphologist*

Western Springs
Zamora, Marjorie Dixon *retired political science professor*

Westmont
Harten, Ann M. *relocation services executive*
Lott, Kathy L. *language educator*
Nyien, Patricia *music educator*
Tricase, Elizabeth *gymnast*
Vitson, Robyn Stanko Hoye *singer, pianist, educator*
Volpe, Kathy A. *elementary school educator, consultant*

Westville
Delanois, Cynthia Sue *elementary school educator*

Wheaton
Elwell, Ellen Banks *music educator, writer*
LaFrancis, Nicole Marie *secondary school educator*
Martin, Marcia Gray *retired architecture educator, artist, designer*
Pape, Patricia Ann *social worker, consultant*
Riley, Betty Anne *psychologist, educator*
Tucker, Beverly Sowers *library and information scientist*

Wheeling
Long, Sarah Ann *librarian*

Wilmette
Boyle, Antonia Barnes *writer, editor*
Brindel, June Rachuy *writer*
Hass, Victoria Yusim *psychogeriatrics services professional, consultant*
Mandel, Judith Lynn *primary school educator*
McClure, Julie Anne *literature educator*
Merrier, Helen *actress, writer*
Miripol, Jerilyn Elise *poet, writer, writing therapist*
Shannon, Julie (Julie Geller) *musician, educator, composer, lyricist*
Smutny, Joan Franklin *academic director, educator*

Wilmington
Chappell, Elizabeth Irene *special education educator*

Winnetka
Cole, Kathleen Ann *advertising executive, social worker*
Huggins, Charlotte Susan Harrison *retired secondary school educator, writer, travel company executive*
Krueger, Deborah A. Blake *school psychologist, consultant*
McKee, Judith Nelson *elementary school educator, educational consultant*
Roush, Michelle Beason *secondary school educator*

Witt
Vollintine, Carol Louise *art educator*

Wood River
Hudson, Kimberly Lynn *music educator*

Woodridge
Rathke, Barbara Joanne Andrews *art educator*

Woodstock
Dorn, Diane M. *science educator*
Fain, Nicole M. *elementary school educator*
Koehler, Jane Ellen *librarian*
Totz, Sue Rosene *secondary school educator*
Wertheimer-Sexton, Willa Renee *clinical psychologist*

Yorkville
Freese, Carolyn Lee *art educator*
McEachern, Joan *medical association administrator*

Zion
Paulsen, Marsha E. *counselor*

INDIANA

Akron
Allen, Elizabeth Ann *writer*

Anderson
Bracken, Linda Darlene *medical/surgical nurse*
Chappell, Rebecca A. *music educator*
Harris, Tina *science educator*
Kratzner, Judith Evelyn *program manager*
Nicholson, Dorothy Nelis *retired pre-school educator*
Olson, Carol Lea *photographer*
Perry, Jane A. *customer service administrator*

Angola
Blaz, Deborah *secondary school educator, writer*
Deller, Rita Willennar *elementary school educator*

Atwood
Creamer, Kathy Jayne *writer*

Auburn
Chagnon, Marjorie Marie *retired elementary school educator*
Cupka, Nancy Irvine *artist, educator*

Avon
Lucas, Georgetta Marie Snell *retired educator, artist*
McKenzie, Ellen Porter *elementary school educator, consultant*

Bloomington
Anderson, Judith Helena *English language educator*
Austin, Joan Kessner *mental health nurse*
Baldner, Karen A. *artist, art educator*
Bornholdt, Laura Anna *academic administrator*
Brehm, Sharon Stephens *psychology professor, former academic administrator*
Brown, Mary Ellen *retired humanities educator*
Calinescu, Adriana Gabriela *curator, art historian*
Clevenger, Sarah *botanist, consultant*
Connally, Sandra Jane Oppy *retired art educator, freelance/self-employed artist*
Davis Deckard, Diane A. *art educator*
Easton, Susan Dawn *biochemist, educator*
Henson, Jane Elizabeth *information management professional, adult education educator*
Jagodzinski, Cecile Marie *librarian*
Ketterson, Ellen D. *biologist, educator*
Labovitz, Sarah Jane *musician, educator*
Lazerwitz, Katherine Christine *retired reading specialist, educator*
McClelland, Danielle *performing company executive*
Montgomery, Kathleen Rae *counselor*
Ochoa-Becker, Anna S. *education educator*
Ostrom, Elinor *political science professor, researcher*
Palmer, Judith Grace *university administrator*
Peterson, M. Jeanne *historian, educator*
Robel, Lauren *dean, law educator*
Spiro, Rosann Lee *marketing professional, educator*
Steele, Patricia Ann *dean, librarian*
Stines, Betty Irene Parham *artist*
Stirratt, Betsy *artist, gallery director*
Svetlova, Marina *ballerina, retired choreographer*
Thorelli, Sarah V. *economist, researcher*
Wells, Kimberly K. *not-for-profit organization executive*

Boonville
Clark, Linda Marie *music educator*

Burlington
Roussakis, Dorothy Ferguson *artist*

Cambridge City
Slonaker, Mary Joanna King *columnist*

Carmel
Brooks, Patricia Scott *principal*
Cohen, Marlene Lois *pharmacologist*
Dotzert, Jennifer Marie *special education educator*
Husman, Catherine Bigot *retired insurance company executive, consultant*
Kundrat, Virginia Lynn *science educator*
Mahoney, Margaret Ellis *accountant*
Pote, Gretta Lynn *music educator*
Slocum, Laura Elizabeth *chemistry educator*
Sterchi, Mary Elizabeth *social worker*
Sukapdjo, Wilma Irene *language educator*
Vargas-Williams, Traci Junelle *special education educator*
Yost, Brandy Diana *secondary school educator*

Chesterfield
Sellers, Angela *mathematics educator*

Columbus
Carter, Pamela Lynn *former state attorney general*
Farnsley, Gail *information technology executive*
Johnson, Jane *school psychologist*
Jorgensen, Virginia Dyer *antique dealer, museum consultant*
Rose, Marya Mernitz *lawyer*

Converse
Oatess, Janet Sue *language educator*

Crawfordsville
Everett, Cheryl Ann *music educator, pianist*
Karg, Thelma Aileen *writer*

Crown Point
Ciochina, Debra A. *secondary school educator*
Eisenhauer, Linda Ann *volunteer*
Shaffer, Peggy S. *music educator*

Culver
Warren, Stacey A. *music educator*

Danville
Baldwin, Patricia Ann *lawyer*
Dechert, Wendy Dawn *speech educator, literature and language educator, writer*

Delphi
Trueblood, Susan Ann *music educator*

Dyer
Crnkovich, Ruth Anne *art appraiser, museum director*

East Chicago
Fortenberry, Delores B. *dean*
Platis, Mary Lou *media specialist*
Psaltis, Helen *medical/surgical nurse*
Suhre, Edith Lavonne *adult education educator*

Elkhart
Burns, B(illye) Jane *museum director*
Eddy, Darlene Mathis *poet, educator*
Free, Helen Murray *chemist, consultant*
Strong, Nena L. *social studies educator*

Elwood
Toney, Brenda Sue *special education educator*

Evansville
Baker, Ann Long *language educator*
Baker, Gloria Marie *artist*
Blesch, K(athy) Suzann *small business owner*
Cliff, Karissa *consumer researcher, recruiter*
Hallock Morris, Mary Theresa *education educator*
Lawler, Zara Du Pont *musician, actor, dancer*
Litschgi, Barbara Nell *dietician*
Mohr, Doris Jean *mathematics professor*
Overton, Sharon Faye *elementary school educator*
Roth, Carolyn Louise *art educator*
Smith, Leslie Morrow *counselor*
Standley, Sherrianne Maddox *bank executive*
Tannenbaum, Karen Jean *library services supervisor*

Ferdinand
Wildeman, Rose A. *musician, educator*

Fishers
Marcus, Cynthia Ann *lawyer*
Moredock, Rebecca Juanette *psychiatrist*

Floyds Knobs
Berry, Dale M. *physical education specialist*
Egbert, Donna *elementary school educator*

Fort Wayne
Beam, Teresa Ann *biology professor*
Butler, Sally Kathryn *history educator*
Carroll, Betty Jean *retired application developer*
Cast, Anita Hursh *small business owner*
Cummins, Kathleen K. *retired elementary school educator*
Glick, Anna Margaret *real estate broker, consultant*
Goshert, Janet K. *dietitian*
Gutreuter, Jill Stallings *financial consultant, financial planner*
Hamrick, Linda L. *secondary school educator*
Harwood, Virginia Ann *retired nursing educator*
Holzmer, Sister Anita *nun, theology studies educator*
Jones, Louise Conley *drama and literature educator, academic administrator*
Langhinrichs, Ruth Imler *playwright, writer*
Neuman, Paula Anne Young *cultural organization administrator*
Raifsnider, Lauretta Jane *librarian*
Robinson, Wendy Y. *school system administrator*
Scheetz, Sister Mary JoEllen *English language educator*
Taritas, Karen Joyce *customer service administrator*
Ushenko, Audrey Andreyevna *artist, educator*

Fortville
Horner, Sylvia Ann *minister, real estate broker*

Frankfort
Borland, Kathryn Kilby *writer*
Sayers Butler, Patricia Ann *secondary school educator*

Franklin
Brailow, Norma Lipton *artist*
Moore, Beth A. *education educator*
Stone, Mary Ann *literature and language educator*

Frankton
Beck, Neva Ann *retired special education educator*

Gary
Beamer, Laura *women's health and genetic health nurse*
Hensley, Mary Kay *dietician*
Jones, Angela M. *secondary school educator, elementary school educator*
Knight, Harriette *secondary educator*
Pratt, Diane Ford *science educator*
Reed, Charlotte *education educator, consultant*
Steele, Beverly J. *elementary school educator*
Steinberg, Marilyn Marie *psychotherapist*
Zunich, Janice *pediatrician, geneticist, educator, health facility administrator*

Geneva
Roughia, Ginger Lou *elementary school educator*

Goshen
Roberts, Mary Lois *music educator*
Woodlee, Cheryl Lynn *music educator*

Granger
Harmelink, Ruth Irene *marriage and family therapist, writer*
Morgan, Ardys Nord *school improvement consultant*
Thomas, Debi (Debra J. Thomas) *ice skater*

Greencastle
Phang, May *music educator*
Rayce, Valerie Lynn *secondary school educator*

Greenfield
Kallman, Mary Jeanne *research scientist*

Greenwood
Knapp, Sylvia Clare *religious studies educator, language educator*
Tomlin, Jeanne Brannon *real estate broker, small business owner*

Griffith
Luetschwager, Mary Susan *educational consultant*

Hammond
Delph, Donna Jean (Donna Maroc) *education educator, consultant, academic administrator*
Florek, Michaeline *counselor*
Reinke, Frances Marylou *science educator*
Singer, Sandra Manes *university administrator*
Tazbir, Janice Elaine *nursing educator*
Wright, Carol Jean *medical/surgical nurse*

Hanover
Batchvarova, Madlen Todorova *music educator, conductor*
Nickels, Ruth Elizabeth *band director*

Haubstadt
Elpers, Kimberly Kay *science educator, consultant*

Hebron
Brooker, Nancy *literature and language educator*
Walker, Joyce L. *music educator*

Highland
DeVaney, Cynthia Ann *retired elementary school educator, real estate instructor*
Farag, Maureen Ann *assistant principal*
Feldman, Nancy E. *social worker*
Gregory, Marian Frances *retired elementary school educator, retired principal*
Mach, Michele R. *special education educator*

Howe
Bowerman, Ann Louise *writer, secondary school educator, genealogist*

Huntington
Lindsey, Jacquelyn Maria *editor*

Indianapolis
Adamak, M. Jeanelle *broadcast executive*
Adesiyan, Hattie Rose Olagbegi *education educator, consultant*
Austin, Terri Jo *state representative*
Ayars, Patti *human resources specialist, health products executive*
Barcus, Mary Evelyn *primary school educator*
Barker, Sarah Evans *judge*
Blanchfield, Kelly L. *adult education educator*
Braham, Delphine Doris *accountant, government official*
Braly, Angela F. *lawyer, insurance company executive*
Brooks, Susan W. *prosecutor*
Budniakiewicz, Therese *writer*
Burdine, Linda Sharon *secondary school educator, writer*
Caine, Virginia A. *city health department administrator*
Calvano, Linda Sue Ley *insurance company executive*
Cardwell, Sue Webb *psychology professor*
Carlini, Pat *newscaster*
Carlisle, Sheila A. *judge*
Catchings, Tamika Devonne *professional basketball player*
Chandler, Julie Light *secondary school educator*
Cliff, Johnnie Marie *mathematics and chemistry professor*
Connelly, Deirdre P. *pharmaceutical executive*
Connor, Ulla M. *linguistics educator*
Daniel, Ann Cummins *psychotherapist, consultant*
Dorr, Marjorie W. *healthcare insurance company executive*

Dragila, Stacy *track and field athlete*
Dumandan, Joy *newscaster*
Duncan-Ladd, Georgia Jones *elementary school educator*
Easter, Jeanmarie *conservator*
Fine, Pamela B. *newspaper editor*
Finley, Katherine Mandusic *professional society administrator*
Fischler, Barbara Brand *librarian*
Fortner, Nell *professional athletics coach*
Fox, Patricia Sain *academic administrator*
Fruehwald, Kristin Gail *lawyer*
Ganote, Angela *newscaster*
Garmel, Marion Bess Simon *retired arts journalist*
Gooldy, Patricia Alice *retired elementary school educator*
Gregory, Valiska *writer*
Hammontree, Marie Gertrude *writer*
Harcourt, Marion Goldthwaite *retired social worker*
Harden, Annette C. *recreation director*
Haverly, Pamela Sue *nursing administrator*
Hayes, Brenda Sue Nelson *artist*
Hearon, Holly Elizabeth *religious studies educator*
Hegel, Carolyn Marie *farm management extension agent*
Henry, Barbara Ann *publishing executive*
Hill, Beverly Ellen *medical educator*
Huehls, Frances A. *librarian*
Huffman, Cindy Kay *elementary school educator*
Huffman, Rosemary Adams *lawyer, corporate executive*
Israelov, Rhoda *financial planner, entrepreneur*
Jackson, Valerie Pascuzzi *radiologist, educator*
Jones, Marion *track and field athlete*
Keaton, Margaret-Ann Coleman *education educator*
Kinney, Eleanor De Arman *law educator*
Kleiman, Mary Margaret *lawyer*
Knoebel, Suzanne Buckner *cardiologist, educator*
Knox, Debby *newscaster*
Koch, Edna Mae *lawyer, nurse*
Koch, Linda Brown *utility administrator*
Lamkin, Martha Dampf *lawyer, foundation administrator*
Lisher, Mary Katherine *lawyer*
Lorell, Beverly H. *medical products executive*
Malone, Jean Hambidge *educational consultant*
McCall-Rodriguez, Leonor *healthcare services company executive, entrepreneur*
McClelland, Amy Kennard *elementary school educator*
McIntyre, Lola Mazza *music educator*
Mead, Susanah M. *dean*
Mesch, Debra J. *finance educator*
Moelhman, Amy Jo *social worker*
Monroe, Judith A. *state agency administrator, public health service officer*
Morehead, Andrea *newscaster*
Moser, Barbara Jo *elementary school educator*
Najjar, Diana *elementary school educator*
Nehez, Susan Springman *elementary school educator*
Niederberger, Jane *information technology executive*
Nnaemeka, Obioma Grace *French language and women's studies educator, consultant, researcher*
Onochie, Florence N. *accountant*
Orban, Kimberlie W. *elementary school educator*
Osborn, Kristy Lynn *elementary school educator*
Otero, Lettice Margarita *lawyer*
Pence, Linda Lee *lawyer*
Phelps, Jaycie *gymnast, Olympic athlete*
Pilgrim, Jill *lawyer, consultant*
Pitts, Beverley J. *academic administrator*
Plascak-Craig, Faye Dene *psychology educator, researcher*
Powers, Doris Hurt *retired engineering company executive*
Pruett, Lindy Newton *special education educator*
Pursley, Julie *newscaster*
Rankin, Jacqueline Annette *communications expert, educator*
Reed, Suellen Kinder *school system administrator*
Richter, Judith Anne *pharmacologist, educator*
Ritchie, Ingrid Maria *environmental scientist, educator*
Robinson, Rebecca Lynne *medical researcher*
Roger, Janice Lowenstein *cantor*
Rosenblatt, Alice F. *healthcare insurance company executive*
Rutledge, Joanne *artist, consultant*
Ryder, Anne *newscaster*
Sandberg, Marilyn Lee *special education educator*
Schilling, Emily Born *editor, professional society administrator*
Shuman, Lois Anna *educational coordinator*
Skillman, Becky Sue *lieutenant governor, former state legislator*
Smith, Christine Moore *literature and language professor, writer*
Solomon, Marilyn Kay *primary school educator, consultant, small business owner*
Strauss, Diane Jayne *retired elementary and secondary school educator, small business owner*
Sullender, Joy Sharon *retired elementary school educator*
Sykes, Linda Diane *elementary school educator, music educator*
Tandy, Kisha Renee *curator*
Tedesco, Kristi *newscaster*
Thiele, Michelle Renee *special education educator*
Thurston, Kathy Lynn *paralegal*
Trahan, Grace *newscaster*
Usher, Phyllis Land *state official*
Vann, Lora Jane *retired reading educator*
Warner, Joanne Rains *nursing educator, associate dean*
Watkins, Sherry Lynne *elementary school educator*
Waynick, Catherine Elizabeth Maples *bishop*
Weaver, Martha *newscaster*
Westenfelder, Harriet Ellen *retired elementary school educator*
Whitfield, Erica Sharon *director, career planning administrator*
Whitis, Cynthia M. *secondary school educator*
Williams, Judith Ellen *educational association administrator*
Williams, Luida K. *retired elementary school educator*
Wilson, Anne Marie *chemistry professor*
Winston, Robin Eugene *political party professional*

Jasonville
Collins, Katherine Louise *elementary school educator*

Jasper
Luebbehusen, Tina Marie *secondary school educator*
Wineinger, Barbara Ann *science educator*

Jeffersonville
Scholes, Janis Wolf *science educator*
Taylor, Andrea Reed *elementary school educator*

Kentland
Molter, Karen S *literature and language educator*

Knightstown
Richardson, Shirley Maxine *editor*
Ward, Sarah Frances *narcotic education consultant, counselor*

Kokomo
Baker, Janel Faith *music educator*
Cameron, Ann M. *language educator*
MacKay, Gail *librarian*
Weeks, Randi Lyn *performing arts and language educator*

Kouts
Miller, Sarabeth *secondary school educator*

La Porte
Hunter, Debora Ann Brobeck *secondary school educator*

Ladoga
Allen, Marilyn Kay *elementary school educator*

Lafayette
Luenz, Pamela Marie *educator*
McBride, Angela Barron *nursing educator*
McKowen, Dorothy Keeton *librarian, educator*
McLean, Cheryl L. *physics educator*
Mobley, Emily Ruth *library director, educator, dean*
Scaletta, Helen Marguerite *volunteer*

Lagrange
Glick, Cynthia Susan *lawyer*

Lanesville
Cleveland, Peggy Rose Richey *cytotechnologist*

Lawrenceburg
Edwards, Marie D. *social services administrator*

Lebanon
Beck, Denise Gail *secondary school educator*
Geisler, Kay *transportation executive*
Hedge, Christine Marle *science educator*

Lincoln City
Fischer, Deborah Lynn *school nurse practitioner*

Logansport
Howland, Bette *writer*
Walter, Patricia L. *psychotherapist, consultant*

Lowell
Myers, Charlotte *secondary educator*

Lynnville
Fulkerson, Jodi Lee *secondary school educator*

Madison
Bivens, Constance Ann *retired pre-school educator*
Grahn, Ann Wagoner *retired science administrator*

Marion
Henry, Michele Ferree *music educator, elementary school educator, language arts educator*
Personette, Louise Metzger (Sister Mary Roger Metzger) *mathematics professor*
Ransom, Peggy Elaine *retired education educator*
Vermilion, Marsha Renee *secondary school educator*

Martinsville
Palma, Kari Michelle *singer, actress, dancer, educator*

Maxwell
Proper, Kristine Suzanne *elementary school educator*

Merrillville
Brailey, Amy Lynora *secondary school educator, language educator*
Merrill-Washington, Victoria *elementary school educator, consultant*
Protho, Jessie *vocational school educator*
Wang, Josephine L. Fen *physician*

Michigan City
Varro, Barbara Joan *retired editor*
Wiegand, Elizabeth *musician, educator*

Milton
Wade, Deanna Jo *retired elementary school educator*

Mishawaka
Bays, June Marie *counselor, social worker*
Hossler, Elizabeth *psychology professor, department chairman, institutional researcher, director*
Rubenstein, Pamela Silver *manufacturing executive*
Stone, Cathy Jean *elementary school educator*
Wilson, Rebecca Jo *associate dean, education educator*

Monroeville
Lafrentz, Laverne B. *elementary school educator*
Sorgen, Elizabeth Ann *retired elementary school educator*

Monticello
Burkhardt, Mary Sue D. *secondary school educator*
Burns, Susan Kay *music educator*

Muncie
Amman, E(lizabeth) Jean *academic administrator*
Bade, Michelle L. *music educator, director*
Cantu, Sandra Lou *special education educator*
Farr, Barbara F. *minister*
Garringer, Barbara Lou *nurse*
Gora, JoAnn M. *academic administrator*
Hoffman, Mary Catherine *retired nurse, anesthetist*
Hunter, Miriam Eileen *artist, educator*
Klotz, Ann Marie *director*
Maine, Kathryn Lew *social studies educator*
Mjagkij, Nina *history professor*
Raleigh, Dawn Kristen *language educator*
Spencer, Anna Kathleen *mathematics educator*
Stewart, Rita Joan *academic administrator*
Woodward, Lucinda Emily *psychology professor*
Zhong, Mei *music educator*

Munster
Taylor, Gloria A. *minister, educator*

Nashville
Kriner, Sally Gladys Pearl *artist*

New Albany
Crump, Claudia *geographer, educator*
Orth, Susan Lynn *judge*
Rhodes, Betty Fleming *rehabilitation services professional, nurse*
Riehl, Jane Ellen *education educator*

New Castle
Pierce, Terry Jo *medical/surgical nurse*

New Harmony
Feiner, Arlene Marie *librarian, researcher, consultant*
Gray, Lois Mittino *biologist, educator*

New Haven
Moran, Donna Marie *school psychologist, counselor, educator*

Newburgh
McKown, Martha *minister, writer*
Saum, Elizabeth Pape *community volunteer*
Verley, Barbara Ann *music educator*

Noblesville
Poindexter, Beverly Kay *media and communications professional, real estate broker*

North Judson
Miller, Kimberly M. *social studies educator*

North Manchester
Switzer, Jo Young *college president*

Notre Dame
Davis, Stacy Nicole *religious studies educator*
Derakhshani, Mana *literature and language professor*
Dieckgrafe, Indi *performing arts educator, choreographer*
Doody, Margaret Anne *English language educator*
Feigl, Dorothy Marie *chemistry professor, academic administrator*
Hallinan, Maureen Theresa *sociologist, educator*
Johansen, Ruthann Knechel *education educator, writer*
Johnstone, Joyce Visintine *education educator*
Maurice, Patricia Ann *geochemist, educator*
Maziar, Christine M. *academic administrator*
O'Hara, Patricia Anne *dean, law educator*
Shrader-Frechette, Kristin *science educator*
Stevenson, Marsha Joan *librarian*
Woo, Carolyn Yauyan *dean*
Younger, Jennifer A. *university librarian*

Parker City
Cunningham, Kina Ann *media specialist, educator*
Lacy, Karen S. *special education educator*

Peru
McCaulley, Cynthia Jane *elementary art educator*
Nystrom, Tammy C. *elementary school educator, consultant*

Pittsboro
Swango, Colleen Jill *science educator*

Plainfield
Clark, Debra Elizabeth *music educator*

Plymouth
Cardinal-Cox, Shirley Mae *education educator*
Jurkiewicz, Margaret Joy Gommel *retired secondary school educator*

Portage
Schroeder, Marvis Lynn *accountant, artist*

Portland
Arnold, Beverly Sue *secondary school educator*
Bisel, Marsha McCune *elementary school educator*

Rensselaer
Slaby, Kristi Lynn *secondary school educator*

Richmond
Cooper, Jamie Lee *writer*
Robinson, Dixie Faye *elementary and secondary school educator*
Siatra, Eleni *English educator*
Tolliver, Lorraine *language educator, writer*

Rockport
Davis, Karen Sue *hospital nursing supervisor*

Rockville
Jones, Tamera Dawn *elementary school educator*

Rushville
Moore, Helen Elizabeth *reporter*

Saint Mary Of The Woods
Lescinski, Joan *higher education administrator, English educator*

San Pierre
Begley, Heidi Marie *nurse, entrepreneur*

Sandborn
Hartsburg, Judith Catherine *entrepreneur*

Schererville
Jarrett, Alexis *insurance agent, lawyer*

Scottsburg
Dockery, Linda *writer*
Kendall, Susan Carol *science educator*
Mosley, Sherry Jo *athletic trainer*

Seymour
Norrell, Mary Patricia *nursing educator*

Shelbyville
Clark, Rose Sharon *elementary school educator*
Jackson, Frances I. *music educator*
Lawler, Mary Lucille *secondary school educator*

South Bend
Bondi, Kathleen *social worker*
Davis, Kathryn Lyon *former lieutenant governor*
Hunt, Mary Reilly *organization executive*
Ivory, Goldie Lee *retired social worker, educator*
Knight, Ida Brown *retired elementary school educator*
Kuehner, Denise Ann *music educator, musician*
Martin, Debra Jane *assistant principal, basketball coach*
McDonnell, G. Darlene *retired business educator*
McElroy, Birdie Maria *artist, graphics designer*
Stelton, Susan Diane *nursing specialist, educator*
Tompsett, Lesley Ann *elementary school educator*
Yarger, Ruth Anketell *social worker*
Zegiob-Devereaux, Leslie Elaine *clinical psychologist*

Spencer
Coley, Brenda Ann *elementary school educator*

Spencerville
Clark, Donna M. *retired elementary school educator*

Straughn
Jordan, Lois Evelyn *retired educator*

Sullivan
Chavez, Mary Ann *osteopathic family physician*

Tell City
Arterberry, Patricia *retired elementary school educator*
Thrasher, Mary Ahlf Marcroft *educator, social worker*

Terre Haute
Anderson, Louise A. *public health service officer*
Anderson, Veanne Nixon *psychology educator, researcher*
Clouse, Bonnidell *psychology educator*
Daffron, Mitzi Lynnae *quality improvement specialist*
De Marr, Mary Jean *English language educator*
Flick, Connie Ruth *real estate agent, real estate broker*
Hare, Molly Kay *physical education educator*
Hunt, Effie Neva *retired dean, literature educator*
Montañez, Carmen Lydia *Spanish language educator, literature researcher, lawyer*
Nugent, Mary Katherine *elementary school educator*
Wisbey, Lou Ann *radiologist, department chairman*

Thorntown
Harris, Rebecca Sue *mathematics educator*

Trafalgar
Dyke, Brenda JoAnn *special education educator*

Upland
Collins, Jennifer L. *intercultural studies educator*
Harner, Cathy J. *social worker, educator*

Valparaiso
Corazzo, Michele *artist, educator*
Katich, Janet *librarian*
Maugans, Stacy *music educator, musician*
Taylor, Heather Marie *director*

Veedersburg
Dotson, Davina P. *music educator*

Wabash
Ward, Judith A. *elementary school educator*

West Lafayette
Andrews, Theodora Anne *retired librarian, educator*
Arns, Laura *research scientist*
Creech, Rebecca J. *science educator*
Gappa, Judith M. *academic administrator*
Hambrusch, Susanne *computer engineering educator*
Helton, Jane Marie *literature and language educator*
Jagacinski, Carolyn Mary *psychology professor*
Jamieson, Leah H. *engineering educator*
Katehi, Linda P.B. *engineering educator*
Kirksey, Avanelle *nutrition educator*
Lord, Victoria Lynn *artist*
Markee, Katherine Madigan *librarian, educator*
Mason, Sally Kay Frost *biology professor, academic administrator*

Moyars-Johnson, Mary Annis *retired history professor*
Nave, Pamela J. *music educator*
Nixon, Judith May *librarian*
Schneider, Lynette D. *secondary school educator, department chairman*
Scholer, Sue Wyant *retired state legislator*
Shackelford, Renae N. *literature educator, writer*
Taber, Margaret Ruth *retired engineering technology educator*

West Terre Haute
Adams, Diedre Shook *science educator*

Westfield
Bradbury, Betty Marie *history and music educator*

Wheatfield
Thornton, Debra Ann *special education educator*

Whiteland
Conrow, Ann E. *music educator*

Windfall
Cooper, Joyce Beatrice *medical/surgical nurse*

Winona Lake
McMunn, Nancy Lee *parochial school educator*

Woodburn
Stieglitz, Imogene L. *intravenous therapy nurse*

Yorktown
Murray, Stephanie Lynn *special education educator, consultant*

IOWA

Akron
Green, Carla Rae *music educator*

Albia
Caskey, Bethany Anne *artist*

Alden
Oliver, Kerryn Hinrichs *music educator, religious studies educator*

Allison
Reese, Susan Marie *elementary school educator*

Alta Vista
Sweeney, Eileen Mary *librarian, director*

Altoona
Berkenes, Joyce Marie Poore *social worker, director*

Ames
Alumbaugh, JoAnn McCalla *magazine editor*
Benson, Neala Lawrence *volunteer*
Berger, Kay Jackson *psychiatric social worker*
Blount, Jackie Marie *educator*
Bruene, Barbara Jane *artist, educator*
Crabtree, Beverly June *retired dean*
Flora, Cornelia Butler *sociologist, educator*
Goodwin, Tonja Trista *secondary school educator*
Hill, Fay Gish *retired librarian*
Hong, Mei *chemistry professor*
Mattila, Mary Jo Kalsem *elementary school educator, special education educator, art educator*
Maxwell Dial, Eleanore *foreign language educator*
Pohlman, Lynette *museum director, curator*
Roskey, Carol Boyd *social studies educator, dean, director*
Wendell, Barbara Taylor *retired real estate agent*
Zwick-Tapley, Sarah Lynn *theater educator, director*

Ankeny
Cowger, Karin R. *literature and language educator*
Goodin, Julia C. *forensic specialist, state official*
Sanders, Heather Jo *elementary school educator*
Tomb, Carol E. *retail executive*

Arlington
Turner, Jean Isabel *musician, educator*

Arthur
Votrobeck, Barbara Jan *music educator*

Atlantic
Johnson, Joan (Jan) Hope Voss *communications executive, photojournalist, public relations executive*
Van Ginkel, Marci Lou *education educator*

Aurelia
Winterhof, Suzanne *music educator*

Bettendorf
Brown, Lisa M. *academic administrator*
Collins, Kathleen Elizabeth *pharmaceutical company official*
Jacobsen, Barbara Ann *biology educator*
Ragan, Deborah Ann *music educator*
Schulz, Sally Ann *pastoral musician, conductor, educator*
Scupham, Carole Jean *elementary school educator*
Taylor, Paulette Ann *special education educator, educational consultant*

Burlington
Noll, Laurie Jane *secondary school educator*
Smith, Mona Riley *psychotherapist*
Trickler, Sally Jo *illustrator*

Calmar
Jarosh, Colleen Marie *nursing educator, consultant*

Carroll
Morlan, Joann G. *communications educator*

Cascade
Peryon, Charleen D. *education educator, consultant*

Casselman
Hansen, Micaela L. *assistant principal*

Cedar Falls
Balm-Demmel, Darline Dawn *retired minister*
Blakesley, Kimberly Kay *art educator, consultant*
Schulte, Jill Marie *elementary school educator*
Skaine, Rosemarie Keller *writer, consultant, publisher*

Cedar Rapids
Alderson, Karen Ann *librarian, private investigator*
Arnold-Olson, Helen B. *not-for-profit consultant*
Baermann, Donna Lee Roth *real estate property executive, retired insurance analyst*
Feuerhelm, Heather M. *language arts educator*
Knapp, Barbara Allison *financial planner, oncological nurse consultant*
Lewis, Rebecca Lee *medical/surgical nurse, educator*
Merritt, Sandra Lee *educational consultant*
Pike, Shirley *school psychologist*
Rohr, Carol Ann *composer, music educator*
Struthers, Eleanor Ann *writer, educator*
Tonsfeldt, Lori Ann *secondary school educator*
Wax, Nadine Virginia *retired bank executive*

Charles City
McCartney, Rhoda Huxsol *farm manager*

Charter Oak
Kutschinski, Dorothy Irene *elementary school educator*

Cherokee
Hankens, Deborah Jane *secondary school educator*

Clarinda
Vanden Bosch, Linda Kae Krull *elementary school educator*

Clear Lake
Bergvig, Chyrl Rae *counselor*

Clinton
Adkins, Catherine Irene *secondary school educator, department chairman*
Lowe, Flora Lester *librarian*

Coralville
Thomas, Carole Lesniak *retired music educator*

Corydon
Snook, Beverly Jean *elementary school educator*

Council Bluffs
Alley, Mary Lou Vande Woude *retired medical/surgical nurse*
Masker, Debera Ann *middle school educator*
Rachow, Cinda Lou *educational association administrator*

Creston
Dillenburg, Carolyn Eva Lauer *retired secondary school educator*
Fischer, Debra Lynne *music educator*

Dallas Center
Shepherd, Jean Marie *English educator*

Davenport
Beguhn, Sandra E. *poet, writer*
Currence, Glennda Kay *elementary school educator*
Davis, Pamela F. *orthopedist, surgeon*
Goudy, Josephine Gray *social worker*
Sheehey, Patricia Ann *secondary school educator*
Sievert, Mary Elizabeth *small business owner, retired secondary school educator*
Townsend, Julie Rae *artist, educator*
Van Dyke, Wendy Johanna *artist*
Wilson, Frances Edna *protective services official*

De Witt
Jackson, Lois Ann *special education educator*

Decorah
Wangsness, Harriet Ann *elementary school educator*

Delhi
Downs, Karla J. *secondary school educator*

Denison
Withhart, Carol Joyce *mathematician, educator*

Des Moines
Amendt, Marilyn Joan *personnel director*
Barnhart, Dorothy May Kohrs *small business owner*
Bennett, Virginia Cook *music educator, consultant*
Boettger, Nancy J. *state legislator*
Bremer, Celeste F. *judge*
Bukta, Polly *state representative*
Burn, Barbara Louise *literature and language educator*
Butler, Gayle *editor-in-chief*
Conlin, Roxanne Barton *lawyer*
Corning, Joy Cole *retired state official*
Dandekar, Swati *state representative*
DeWulf Nickell, Karol *editor-in-chief*
Dukes, Vanessa Johnson *dietician*
Ellis, Mary Louise Helgeson *information technology company executive*
Erickson, Elaine Mae *composer, educator, poet*
Fleagle, Cynthia Lynn *art educator*
Gaines, Ruth Ann *secondary school educator*
Getty, Amy C. *language educator, department chairman*
Green, Kelli Charnell *psychiatrist*
Hamilton, Elaine H. *retired nurse, artist*
Heiden, Cara *mortgage company executive*
Huser, Geri D. *state official*
Jacobs, Libby Swanson *state official*
Jeffrey, Judy *school system administrator*
Jochum, Pam *state representative*
Kramer, Mary Elizabeth *ambassador, former state legislator*
Lange, Lynn Marie *music educator*
Langholz, Rebecca Sue *music educator*
Mattsson, Lisa Miller *lawyer, social worker*
McGuire-Riggs, Sheila *Democratic party chairman*
Miller, Helen *state representative, lawyer*
Myers, Mary Kathleen *publishing executive*
Nelson, Charlotte Bowers *public administrator*
Paterik, Frances Sue *secondary school educator, actress*
Pederson, Sally *lieutenant governor*
Ragan, Amanda *state senator*
Ramsden, Mary Catherine *substance abuse specialist*
Rodgers Smith, Kimberly Jeanne *lawyer*
Runge, Kay Kretschmar *library director*
Shaff, Karen E. *lawyer, insurance company executive*
Smith, Diana Marie *business educator*
Snyder, Carolyn Swick (Carrie Snyder) *special education educator, vocational program administrator*
Spencer, Melissa Fischer *science educator*
Stier, Mary P. *publishing executive*
Szymoniak, Elaine Eisfelder *retired state senator*
Ternus, Marsha K. *state supreme court chief justice*
Van Zante, Shirley M(ae) *magazine editor*
Vaughan, Therese Michele *insurance educator*
Wattleworth, Roberta Ann *physician*
Weeks, Randi Montag *science educator*
Wilson, Sal *systems analyst*

Dubuque
Collins, Barbara Louise *retired elementary school educator*
Curoe, Bernadine Mary *counselor*
Hodge, Gail *dean, programming director, education educator*
Koch, Dianne M. *language educator, music educator*

Durant
Siebke, Loretta Belle *retired elementary school educator*

Eldon
Johnson, Lori Higinbotham *elementary school educator*

Eldridge
Hoyt, Kay Marie *elementary science specialist*
Schnekloth, Cindee J. *elementary school educator*

Elgin
Reierson, Carol Ann *elementary school educator*

Fairfield
Drees, Dorothy E. *small business owner, real estate manager*

Fayette
Kuker, Gina Joanne *education educator*
Leete, Angela Marie *athletic trainer, educator*

Fort Dodge
Lehman, Shari Joan *music educator*

Fort Madison
Sanford, Jane Agnes *music educator*
Sodey, Angela Ann *gifted and talented educator*

Garner
Duregger, Karen Marie *health facility administrator*

George
Symens, Maxine Brinkert Tanner *retired marketing professional*

Grinnell
Brand, Vicki L. *elementary school educator*
Gibson, Janet Marie *psychology educator*
Michaels, Jennifer Tonks *foreign language educator*

Hastings
Baird, Christine Mary *secondary school educator*

Holstein
Soseman, Eleanor Douglass *volunteer*

Hubbard
Reinert, Joy Ann *elementary school educator*

Indianola
Heinicke, Janet Louise *educator, artist*
Mace, Jerilee Marie *performing arts association administrator*

Iowa City
Andreasen, Nancy Coover *psychiatrist, educator, neuroscientist*
Baker, Nancy L. *university librarian, educator*
Chang, Lan Samantha *writer, educator*
Clark, Dianne Elizabeth *religious studies and reading educator*
DiPardo, Anne *English language educator*
Eichenberger Gilmore, Julie Mae *research scientist*
Gittler, Josephine *law educator*
Grant, Mary Lynn Johnson *academic administrator, literary scholar*
Hettmansperger, Sue *artist*
Jones, Carolyn *dean, law educator*
Jones, Catherine Clarissa *secondary school educator*
Kerber, Linda Kaufman *historian, educator*
Lopes, Lola Lynn *psychologist, educator*
Maxson, Linda Ellen *biologist, educator*
Muir, Ruth Brooks *alcohol/drug abuse services professional, consultant*
Niebyl, Jennifer Robinson *obstetrician, gynecologist, educator*
Packer, ZZ (Zuwena) *writer, literature educator*
Porter, Nancy Lefgren *reading recovery educator*
Preucil, Doris Bogen *music educator*
Solbrig, Ingeborg Hildegard *literature educator, writer*
Stay, Barbara *zoologist, educator*
Stratton, Margaret Mary *art educator*
Swensen, Cole *poet, educator*
Tsalikian, Eva *physician, educator*
Wing, Adrien Katherine *law educator*
Young, Laura Elizabeth *artist*

Jesup
Hover, Melissa Kaye *music educator*

Johnston
Heidbreder, Jessica Lou *music educator*
Poppe, Pamela J. *accountant*

Keokuk
Henoch, Reva *elementary school educator*
Mills, Sylvia Janet *secondary education educator*

Knoxville
Taylor, Mary Kay *medical, surgical nurse*

Le Claire
Mears, Joyce Lund *educational counselor*

Leon
Miller, Eleanora Genevieve *freelance/self-employed poet*

Lone Tree
Haack, Allison Kaye *music educator*

Long Grove
Holleran, Karen Elaine *literature and language professor*

Manchester
Cook, Sharon Lee Delancey *retired elementary school educator, musician*

Manilla
Smith, Fay G.N. *literature and language educator*
Stammer, Nancy A. *travel company executive*

Maquoketa
Krum, Dee *secondary school educator*

Marion
Van Nest, Ann Marie *science educator*

Marshalltown
Foote, Sherrill Lynne *retired manufacturing company technician*
Packer, Karen Gilliland *cancer patient educator, researcher*

Mason City
Iverson, Carol Jean *retired library media specialist*
Rodamaker, Marti Tomson *bank executive*
Sappenfield, Maedeane L. *piano and organ educator*

Mediapolis
Lerud-Chubb, DiAnne Kay *secondary school educator*

Morning Sun
Byers, Elizabeth *education educator*

Mount Vernon
Astley, Suzette Lynn *psychology educator, researcher*

New Hampton
Baltes, Sara Jayne *reading educator, elementary school educator*

New Providence
Reece, Marlene Williams *elementary school educator*

Newton
Graves, Margery A. *elementary school educator*
Ward, Doree Maxine *secondary school educator*

Nora Springs
Brockmeyer, Kristie Lee *secondary school educator*

Northwood
Schiltz, Polly Jo *special education educator*

Odebolt
Menage, Carolyn Lee *elementary school educator*
Swensen, Joan Linda *elementary school educator*

Oelwein
Flaucher-Falck, Velma Ruth *retired special education educator*
McFarlane, Beth Lucetta Troester *retired mayor*

Onawa
Hewitt, Lou *retired elementary school educator*

Orange City
Wielenga, Dixie Kay *music educator*

Oskaloosa
Anderson, Roxanna Marion *psychology professor*
Buresh, Laura Lynn *literature educator*
Burrow, Nancy Kay *special education educator*
DeBruin, Ruth Pearl *primary school educator*
Gleason, Carol Ann *mental health nurse, educator*
Robbins, Janet Linda *language educator*

Ottumwa
Dinsmore, Susan Marie *secondary school educator*
Krafka, Mary Baird *lawyer*
Lang, Janelle J. *accountant*
Mefford, Naomi Ruth Dolbeare *secondary school educator, elementary school educator*
Roberts, Sherrie Lynn *special education educator, secondary school educator*

Parkersburg
Lievens, Rebecca S.A. *science educator*

Pella
Baker-Roelofs, Mina Marie *retired home economist, educator*
Dout, Anne Jacqueline *manufacturing and sales company executive*
Hesselink, Ann Patrice *financial executive, lawyer*

Steele, Mildred Romedahl *educator*
Weber, Wendy A. *mathematics professor*

Peosta
Wulfekuhle, Jenny *pilates instructor, athletic trainer*

Pleasant Valley
Byrne, Margaret Ellen *voice educator*

Pocahontas
Jarvis, Sue Kay *science educator*

Postville
Heitland, Julie Ann *school librarian*

Prairie City
Hill, Pamela Jean *middle school educator*

Red Oak
Werner, Cecelia Marie *counselor*

Reinbeck
Koester, Lisa *principal*

Richland
Walter, Sandra S. *social worker*

Rock Rapids
Schram, Laureen Ann *reading specialist*

Rockwell City
Erkenbrack, Lori Jean *county official*

Sheffield
Hemm, Cynthia Jean *music educator*

Sioux City
Dillman, Kristin Wicker *elementary school educator, musician*
Dye, Lana L. *music educator*
Hatfield, Susan William *school psychologist*
Iverson, Ona Lee *retired elementary school educator*
Lewis, Arlene Jane Quiring *music educator*
Mounts, Nancy *secondary school educator*
Rants, Carolyn Jean *academic administrator, educator*

Sloan
Ullrich, Roxie Ann *special education educator*

Spencer
Hanthorne, Carol *elementary school educator*
Myers, Janis Marie *secondary school educator*

Springville
Beals, Karen Marie Downey *pastor*
Weber, Vickie Fey *secondary school educator*

Stanwood
Lehrman, Patricia Jayne *literature and language educator*

Story City
Dickson-Ferrell, Tamara L. *secondary school educator*

Stuart
King, Meghan Anne *secondary school educator*

Thornton
Jorgensen, Doris Jean *retired elementary school educator*

Toledo
Lyon, Norma Duffield *sculptor, agriculturist*

Urbandale
Hewitt, Lisa Carol (Lisa Carol Ver Hoef) *elementary school educator*

Vinton
Mulvaney, Lois *French, English educator*

Walford
Brooks, Debra L. *healthcare executive, neuromuscular therapist*

Waterloo
Alfrey, Marian Antoinette *retired education educator*
Gleason, Cindy S. *financial consultant, educator*
Green, Nancy Loughridge *publishing executive*
Kober, Arletta Refshauge (Mrs. Kay L. Kober) *supervisor*
Moore, Marilyn Ulfers *social worker*

Waverly
Ahrens, Mary Ann Painovich *small business owner*
Blair, Rebecca Sue *English educator*
Eick-Gamm, Kimberly Marie *social worker*
Koob, Kathryn Loraine *religious studies educator*
O'Konski, Marjorie Katherine *music educator*
Wade, Janice Elizabeth *musician, educator, conductor*

Webster City
Daniels, Karen S. *mathematics educator*
Hansen, Rae Lavone *secondary school educator*

West Branch
Mather, Mildred Eunice *retired archivist*

West Burlington
Woodside, Carlene *art educator*

West Des Moines
Goldsmith, Janet Jane *pediatric nurse practitioner*

West Point
Ortciger, Lisa Marie *history educator*

West Union
Hansen, Ruth Lucille Hofer *business owner, consultant*

Williamsburg
Sandersfeld, Lavonne Lucille *elementary school educator*

Winterset
Forsyth, Lacey Lynn *mathematics educator*
Silverthorn, Laura Lynne *secondary school educator*

Woodward
Jenkins, Alice Marie *secondary school educator*

KANSAS

Americus
Grimsley, Bessie Belle Gates *retired special education educator*

Andover
Reynolds, Charlene Jozina *music educator, composer*
Yager, Amanda D. *secondary school educator*

Arkansas City
Bruton, Rebecca Ann *mayor, commissioner*
Moscript, Barbara Ann *science educator*
Neal, Melinda K. *science educator*

Arma
Query, Lois A. *elementary school educator*

Atchison
Lane, Elizabeth Ann *genealogist, researcher*

Atwood
Girouard, Gail Patricia *family practice physician*

Auburn
Barr, Ginger *business owner, former state legislator*

Axtell
Broxterman, Lisa *secondary school educator*

Baldwin City
English, Evonne Kludas *artist*
Long, Patricia N. *academic administrator*

Bern
Dassel-Stuke, Donna Jane *psychologist, educator*

Berryton
Miller, Janeth Mauk *retired secondary education educator*

Burr Oak
Underwood, Deanna Kay *librarian*

Caldwell
Robinson, Alice Jean McDonnell *retired drama and speech educator*

Carbondale
Tubbs, Penny L. *art educator*

Chanute
Weilert, Mary E. *communications educator*

Chapman
Dawson, Joan Marie *elementary school educator*

Chase
Stull, Evalyn Marie *artist*

Claflin
Wondra, Judy Ann *librarian, director*

Clay Center
Bachand, Alice Jeanne *school library media specialist*

Clifton
Compton, Doris Martha *lay worker*

Coffeyville
Miller, Virginia Meredith *secondary school educator*

Colby
Baldwin, Irene S. *hotel executive, real estate developer*
Erickson, Patricia Ann *physical therapist, educator*

Coldwater
Adams, Elizabeth Herrington *banker*

Concordia
Hill, Judy Marie Zimmermont *mayor, secondary school educator*

Conway Springs
Lange, Karen R. *music educator*

Council Grove
Schroeder, Tracie Beth *secondary school educator*

Deerfield
Tackett, Gayle Enslow *medical/surgical nurse*

Denton
Scherer, Deanna *principal*

Dighton
Stanley, Ellen May *historian, consultant*

Dodge City
Chipman, Deborah J. *elementary school educator*
Ripple, Paula G. *literature and language educator*
Ross, Connie L. *music educator*
Sapp, Nancy L. *director*

Edwardsville
Boal, Marcia Anne Riley *clinical social worker*

El Dorado
Choate, Melody Lynn *mathematics professor*
Clarke, Linda Diane *mental health services professional, psychotherapist*
Mack, Valerie Lippoldt *music educator, performing arts educator, freelance/self-employed choreographer*

Ellsworth
Rathbun, Christina Sue *literature and language educator*

Emporia
Cookson, Linda Marie *retired elementary education educator*
Gerish, Deborah Elaine *history professor*
Hale, Martha Larsen *librarian*
Henry, Elaine Olafson *artist, educator*
Karr, Sharon Kay *psychology educator*
Mallein, Darla J. *social studies educator*
Thompson, Deborah K. *elementary school educator*
Yanik, Elizabeth Greenwell *mathematics professor*

Erie
Sherman, Nancy Kay Jackel *elementary school educator*

Fort Scott
Wassenberg, Evelyn M. *retired medical/surgical nurse, educator*
Weddle, Rebecca Rae *education educator*

Frankfort
Tilley, Diane *elementary school educator*

Garden City
Lisk, Martha Ann *rehabilitation services professional*

Garden Plain
Stovall, Carla Jo *former state attorney general*

Gem
Ziegelmeier, Patricia Kay *music educator, executive secretary*

Girard
Beezley, Sara Sue *lawyer*

Goddard
Molz, Carol Jean *elementary school educator*
Sandall, Joann Mary *mathematics educator*

Grantville
Hodges, Edna (Lee) Elizabeth *lawyer, educator*

Great Bend
Gunn, Mary Elizabeth *retired language educator*
Heidrick, Kathy Jo *medical technician, educator*
Rittenhouse, Nancy Carol *elementary school educator*
Siebert-Freund, Deborah Ann *public relations and marketing executive*

Hamilton
Ebberts, Deana Marie *mathematics educator*

Hays
Budig, Jeanette *special education educator*
Duffy, Cheryl Hofstetter *language educator*
Herl, Sonya *elementary school educator*

Holton
McDonald, Sharon Holliday *special education educator*

Hope
Hottman, Geneva Rae *elementary school educator*

Horton
Radford, Virginia Rodriguez *retired secondary school educator, librarian*

Hugoton
Stephens, Lindagrace *artist, educator*

Hutchinson
Baumer, Beverly Belle *journalist*
Graves, Kathryn Louise *dermatologist*
Rosenblad, Helen Viola *social services administrator*
Wendelburg, Norma Ruth *composer, educator, pianist*

Independence
Delacour, JoNell *music educator*
Randolph, Katrina J. *literature and language educator*
Wright, Tami LaDonna *pre-school educator*

Iola
Marsh, Alma Fern *retired music educator, director, organist*

Isabel
Brant, Dorris Ellen Stapleton *bacteriologist, music educator*

Kansas City
Atkinson, Barbara F. *dean, medical educator, executive vice chancellor*
Baggett, Kathleen M. *psychologist, research scientist*
Blythe, Mary Susan *retired elementary school educator*
Carlson-Jukes, Holly Ann *social studies educator*
Davis, Kathy E. *information analyst*
Hancock, Melinda Bowne *minister*
Hellings, Jessica Alice *psychiatrist, educator*
Hodison, Patricia Mary Kathleen *science educator*
Jerome, Norge Winifred *nutritionist, anthropologist, educator*
Johnson, Joy Ann *diagnostic radiologist*
Pettey, Patricia Huggins *county official*
Raab, Cecilia Marie *artist*
Vratil, Kathryn Hoefer *federal judge*
Wymer, Kellyn Lin *biology and chemistry educator, coach*

Kinsley
Burghart, Lynda R. *chemistry educator*

Kiowa
Brintnall, Charlene May *special education educator*

Lakin
Vieux, Carlee Annanette Noland *special education educator*

Larned
Hewson, Mary McDonald *civic volunteer*

Lawrence
Bangert, Colette Stuebe *artist*
Brasseur, Irma Faye *special education educator*
Briscoe, Mary Beck *federal judge*
Cienciala, Anna Maria *history professor*
Craig, Susan Virginia *librarian*
Dreschhoff, Gisela Auguste Marie *physicist, researcher*
Fredrickson, Karen Loraine *librarian*
Haines, Cynthia Weber Farah *photographer, publisher*
Hardy, Saralyn Reece *museum director*
Haricombe, Lorraine *library director, dean*
Henrickson, Bonnie *women's college basketball coach*
Kofler, Silvia Maria *writer, educator*
Loudon, Karen Lee *physical therapist*
Lyerla, Karen Dale *special education educator*
Norris, Andrea Spaulding *art museum director*
Peterson, Nancy *special education educator*
Tacha, Deanell Reece *federal judge*
Turnbull, Ann Patterson *special education educator, consultant, research director*
Wenger, Eleanor Lerner *retired science educator*

Leavenworth
Crow, Martha Ellen *lawyer*
Franklin, Shirley Marie *marketing consultant*
Heim, Dixie Sharp *family practice nurse practitioner*
Klemp, Nancy Jean *secondary school educator*

Leawood
Garwood, Julie *writer*
Joslin, Janine Elizabeth *preservationist, consultant*
King, Barbara Sackheim *travel company executive*
Pfingsten, Lynette M. *music educator*

Liberal
Boles, Sharon Isabelle O'Shields *mathematics educator*
Hicks, Linda Reona *elementary school educator*
Redd, Kathryn Elizabeth *education educator, department chairman*
Smothermon, Reba Maxine *elementary school educator*
Wilkerson, Rita Lynn *retired special education educator*

Logan
Manion, Kay Daureen *financial and office manager*

Louisburg
Best, Pamela LaFever *secondary school educator*

Lyndon
Fritz, Judith Ann *special education administrator, educator*

Maize
Van Arendonk, Susan Carole *elementary school educator*

Manhattan
Chance-Reay, Michaeline K. *educator, psychotherapist*
Garwick, Cynthia L. *elementary school educator*
Hahn, Joan L. *art educator, artist*
Kirkham, M. B. *plant physiologist, educator*
Mortenson, Kristin Oppenheim *musician*
Patterson, Deb *women's college basketball coach*
Shanklin, Carol W. *dietician, educator*
Stalheim-Smith, Ann *biology educator*
Wright, Sherryl Leigh *journalist*

Mc Louth
Cleavinger, Laurie A. *science educator*

Mcpherson
Coppock, Doris Ellen *retired physical education educator, retired music educator*
Tegethoff, Allece D. *elementary school educator, pharmacy technician*

Mission
Alexander, Anne A. *sales consultant*
McAleer, Ruth Bresnahan *priest*

Nashville
Huss, Bonnie Jean *intensive cardiac care nurse*

Neodesha
Campbell, Katherine Lucille *gifted and talented educator*

Newton
Barrett, Lois Yvonne *minister*
Morford, Marie Arlene *insurance company executive*

North Newton
Snider, Marie Anna *syndicated columnist*

Oakley
Oelke, Anita Jean *special education educator*

Olathe
Amborn, Jennifer *physical education educator*
Beacham, Janis Schlueter *educational consultant*
Colson, Judy C. *music educator*
Dennis, Patricia Lyon *adult education educator*
Goodwin, Becky K. *educational technology resource educator*
Henning, Lillian Joyce *special education educator*
Kamberg, Mary-Lane *writer, journalist*
Landon, Colleen *elementary school educator*
McCabe, Melissa Christine *music educator, researcher*

Olsen, Barbara Ann *music educator*
Stevens, Diana Lynn *elementary school educator*
Thompson, Kate Elaine *school librarian, educator*

Onaga
Dillinger, Susan Alice *reading specialist*

Osage City
Lieber, Joan Skonberg *special education educator*

Osawatomie
Baker, Kristi Ann *music educator, composer*

Overland Park
Amundson, Beverly Carden *artist*
Bronaugh, Deanne Rae *home health care administrator, consultant*
Carmack, Mona *library administrator*
Childers, Martha Patton *librarian*
Christian, Shirley Ann *journalist, author*
Daniel, Karen *engineering and design company executive*
Kempf, Andrea Caron *librarian, educator*
Liston, Helen J. *retired minister*
McCann, Vonya B. *federal agency administrator, telecommunications industry executive*
McKain, Maggie Marie *music educator*
Messmer, Melinda Ellen *elementary school educator*
Moulin, Linda Long *science educator*
Newman, Gayle JoAnn *elementary school educator*
Paulsen, Ruth Ann *French and Spanish language educator*
Regan, Patricia Lee *reading specialist*
Schmidt, Shelley Rae *cosmetics executive, educator*
Smith, Phyllis Elizabeth *community volunteer*
Strandjord, M. Jeannine *telecommunications industry executive*
Vandree, Elizabeth *secondary school educator*
Voska, Kathryn Caples *consultant, facilitator*
Walker, Kathryn A. *telecommunications industry executive*

Oxford
Patterson, Sandra May *school psychologist*

Parker
Gowing, Patricia M. *retired elementary school educator*

Peabody
Whiteman, Louise Ann *elementary school educator*

Pittsburg
Woodburn, Cynthia J. *mathematics professor*

Pomona
Gentry, Alberta Elizabeth *elementary school educator*

Prairie Village
Lyon, Joanne B. *psychologist*

Rossville
Marney, Sheila K. *science educator*

Russell
Branick, Terry Lynn *secondary school educator*

Saint John
Friesen, Cynthia DeAnn *elementary school educator*

Salina
Angell, Samantha *lawyer, educator*
Cleveland, Beverly K. *art educator, realtor*
Daniels, Tina Lynn *special education educator*
Webb, Debbie *elementary school educator*

Seneca
Eppich, Lois Kathleen *science educator*

Sharon Springs
North, Tricia A. *secondary school educator*

Shawnee
McPherson, Linda *music educator*
Scanlon, Vicki E. *secondary school educator*
Webb, Elaine Marie *reading specialist*

Shawnee Mission
Allen, Janet Lee *special education educator*
Barton, Betty Louise *school system administrator*
Bell, Deloris Wiley *physician*
Black, Lisa Zahn *elementary school educator*
Breen, Katherine Anne *speech and language pathologist*
Conry, Maura *pharmacist, social worker*
Gaar, Marilyn Audrey Wiegraffe *political scientist, educator, property manager*
Martin, Donna Lee *retired publishing company executive*
McLeod, Debra Ann *librarian, mail order book company executive*
Mindlin, Susan W. *small business owner, educator*
Sader, Carol Hope *former state legislator*
Stilwell, Connie Kay *retired elementary school educator*
Wallace, Sherry Lynn *speech-language pathologist*

Stilwell
Snodgrass, Connie Sue *secondary school educator*

Timken
Schwindt, Mary E. *retired secondary school educator*

Tonganoxie
Torneden, Connie Jean *banker*

Topeka
Altman, Joanne D. *psychology professor*
Altus, Deborah Elaine *social sciences educator*
Baldwin, Janet Sue *library media specialist*
Barnett, Mary Lorene *real estate manager*
Bartlett, Alice Brand *psychoanalyst, educator, researcher*
Barton, Janice Sweeny *chemistry professor*
Beier, Carol Ann *state supreme court justice*
Boydston, Resa Odette *mental health services professional*
Carlin, Sydney *state representative*
Cripe, Elizabeth Ann (Betty Cripe) *investment company executive*
Dick, Angela Dawn *elementary school educator*
Elrod, Linda Diane Henry *lawyer, educator*
Fink, Ruth Garvey *diversified financial services company executive*
Frahm, Sheila *association executive, academic administrator, former government official*
Gordon, Lana G. *state representative*
Greene, Jane *health educator*
Jenkins, Lynn M. *state official, former state legislator*
Knight, Billie-Renee *language educator*
Luckert, Marla Jo *state supreme court justice*
Lukert-Devoe, Linda Pauline *elementary school educator*
Marney, Brenda Joyce *minister, computer programmer*
Marquardt, Christel Elisabeth *judge*
Mc Candless, Barbara J. *financial consultant*
McFarland, Kay Eleanor *state supreme court chief justice*
Miller, Sharon Lea *art educator*
Monroe, Virginia Marie *library media specialist, educator*
Owsley, Tina Kathleen *special education educator*
Perry, Nancy *foundation administrator*
Peters, Barbara Waterman *artist, educator*
Petty, Marge D. *state senator*
Reymond, Patricia Ann *social worker*
Robinson, Julie Ann *judge*
Saville, Pat *state senate official*
Sebelius, Kathleen Gilligan *governor*
Sipes, Karen Kay *communications executive*
Smith, Linda S. *musician, educator*
Storm, Suzanne *state representative*
Varner, Charleen LaVerne McClanahan *nutritionist, educator, dietician*
Wagnon, Joan *retired banker, retired mayor*
Wuenstel, Karen L. *elementary school educator*
Zientara, Suzannah Dockstader *insurance agent*

Wathena
Elkins, Katherine Marie *elementary school educator*

Wellington
Tibbs, Kay *director*
White, Helen Lou *school nurse practitioner*

Wichita
Berner Harris, Cynthia Kay *librarian*
Bridge, Karen Sue *microbiologist, laboratory administrator*
Curry, Sherrie Donell *real estate agent*
Da'Luz Vieira-Jones, Lorraine Christine C. *acupuncturist, researcher*
Dill, Sheri *publishing executive*
Dorr, Stephanie Tilden *psychotherapist*
Ehrlich, Donna M. *director, educator*
Foulston, Nola Tedesco *lawyer*
Guthrie, Diana Fern *nursing educator*
Hawley, Suzanne *psychologist, researcher*
Hoefer, Gladys *lawyer*
Ines, Amy *elementary school educator*
Johnstone, Marva Jean (Jeanie Johnstone) *insurance agency executive*
Mitchell, Linda Marlene *education educator*
Moore, Peggy Sue *small business owner*
Myer, Cheryl Jo *music educator*
Palmer, Ada Margaret *systems analyst, consultant*
Pottorff, Jo Ann *state legislator*
Roach, Martha S. *art educator*
Rueb, Sheree A. *social services administrator*
Timmerman, Dora Mae *community volunteer, art advocate*
Wethington, Wilma Z. *artist, educator*
Zimmerman, Melva Jean *journalist, retired audio-visual specialist*

Winfield
Gray, Ina Turner *fraternal organization administrator*
Wollard, Laura Raynae *science educator*

KENTUCKY

Albany
Tallent, Brenda Colene *social worker, psychotherapist*
Thrasher, Allison *elementary school educator*

Bardstown
Carter, Carmen M. *elementary education educator, consultant*
Greenwell, Mary Jane *middle school educator*

Baxter
Ledford, Barbra Lynne *elementary school educator*

Benton
Brown, Sharon Webb *art educator*
Glass, Mary Jean *management executive*

Berea
Frazer, Joy A. *retired nurse*
Henthorn, Susan Kay *school librarian*
Howard, Jennifer Lee *not-for-profit fundraiser*
Lamb, Irene Hendricks *medical researcher*

Boston
Rosenbaum, Mary Heléne Pottker *writer, editor*

Bowling Green
Burch, Barbara G. *academic administrator*
Garrison, Geneva *retired administrative assistant*
Gilfillen, Rebecca *soil scientist, educator*
Groom, Mitzi D *music educator, department chairman*
Merryman-Marr, Melissa Jo *social studies educator*
Onyekwuluje, Anne Bernice *sociology educator*
Stuart, Flora Templeton *prosecutor*

Brandenburg
Bowen, Patricia Lederer *dental educator*

Brodhead
Bustle, Trina Gayle *gifted and talented educator*

Brooksville
Dorton, Truda Lou *medical/surgical nurse, geriatrics nurse*

Butler
Lustenberg, Michelle Williamson *gifted and talented educator*

Campbellsburg
Mitchell, Mary Ann Carrico *poet*

Campbellsville
Eastridge, Darlene F. *social worker, dean*
McArthur, Lisa R. *music educator, musician*
Miller, Janet Lutz *mathematics professor, department chairman*
Moore, Nevalyn *music educator*
Moore, Roberta York *secondary school educator, small business owner*
Skaggs, Karen Gayle *elementary school educator*

Carrollton
Plander, Susan Elaine *elementary school educator*

Catlettsburg
Nixon, Ronda Lynn *paralegal*
Selbee, Maxine Butcher *county clerk*

Cecilia
Thompson, Kathy Self *secondary school educator*

Cold Spring
Gooch, Deborah Ann Grimme *medical, surgical nurse, administrator*

Columbia
Boger, Cheryl Lynn *academic administrator, education educator*

Corbin
Barton-Collings, Nelda Ann *political organization worker, bank executive*
Bruce, Verna Lee Smith Hickey *media specialist, librarian*
Iley, Jenny Rebecca *elementary school educator*

Covington
Berg, Lorine McComis *retired guidance counselor*
Littleton, Nan Elizabeth Feldkamp *psychologist, educator*
McQueen, Regenia *writer*
Schaeffer, Andrew *lawyer*

Crestview Hills
Daoud, Julie Perry *literature and language professor*

Cumberland
Thomas, Katherine M. *humanities educator, department chairman*

Cynthiana
Bellis-Jones, Cynthia Axford *science educator*
Ellis, E. Susan *library director, lay minister*
Florence, Joyce Fritz *mathematics professor*

Danville
Holman, Deborah Young *art educator*
Kennan, Elizabeth Topham *academic administrator, retired historian*

Edmonton
Bunch, Kathy Lynn *secondary school educator*

Ekron
Hamilton, Amelia Wentz (Amy Wentz) *elementary school educator*

Elizabethtown
Sweat, Nora Ellen *home economics educator*

Ewing
Nichols, Joanie Mae *science educator*
Ramey, Susan Dorsey *elementary school educator*

Flemingsburg
Gossett, Linda Kelley *retired secondary school educator*

Florence
Gorman, Gayla Marlene Osborne *consumer affairs executive*

Fort Knox
Tucker, Brenda Brunette *elementary school educator*

Fort Mitchell
McQueen, Pamela *principal*
Webb, Diana Kay *music director*

Fort Thomas
Griggs, Rozellen *elementary school educator*
Skop, Kathy *art educator*
Slater, Rebecca Anne *music educator, director*
Yelton, Dianne Burgess *secondary school educator*

Fort Wright
Sullivan, Connie Castleberry *artist*

Frankfort
Fleming, Juanita Wilson *nursing educator, academic administrator*
Fletcher, Winona Lee *theater educator*
Marsh, Tiffany Nichelle *music educator*
McCarthy, Lynn Cowan *genealogist, researcher*
Palmore, Carol M. *state official*
Palumbo, Ruth Ann *state legislator*
Pullin, Tanya *state representative*
Sias, Mary *university president*
Stine, Katie Kratz *state legislator*

Franklin
Law, Jerriann Marcella *artist, poet, writer*

Garrison
Ruark, Sheila Gaye *elementary school educator*

Georgetown
Hall, Sara Y. *retired music educator*
Patton, Mary Ritchie *retired pediatric nurse practitioner, consultant*
White, Mary Ann *bank executive*

Glasgow
Duvo, Mechelle Louise *oil company executive, consultant*

Gray
Gaddis, Betty H. *retired elementary school educator*

Grayson
Adams, Briana Elizabeth *elementary school educator*
Hunt, Andrea Wheaton *nurse*

Greenville
Adams, Clara Webb *secondary school educator*

Grethel
Hughes, Cindi Baker *special education educator*

Guston
Yundt, Betty Brandenburg *elementary school educator*

Hanson
Duncan, Charlotte Diane *retired secondary school educator*

Harlan
Chitwood, Sharon Carmical *elementary school educator*
DeLong-Smith, Stephanie K. *secondary school educator*

Harrodsburg
Bradshaw, Phyllis Bowman *historian, historic site staff member*
Herman, Alice Gertrude *retired nursing educator*

Hartford
Stumpf, Christie Kell *retired music educator*

Hazard
Cory, Cynthia Strong *mathematics professor*
Feltner, Jeanne Lou *mathematics educator*

Highland Heights
Moss, Nancy Evans *nurse midwife, women's health nurse*
Short-Thompson, Cady W. *educator, director*

Hopkinsville
Lang, Colleen Anne *secondary school educator*
Soberal, Isabel M. *minister, music educator, social worker*

Horse Cave
Martin, Carmen Guinn *literature and language educator*

Hyden
Nienstadt, Jean E. (Jean E. Sullivan) *physician*

Inez
Cox, Rossalene Mullins *art educator*

Irvine
Moore, Kathy Lynn *elementary school educator*

Irvington
Miller, Jacquie Haynes *musician, educator*

Jackson
Guthery, Grace Maxine *retired secondary school educator*

Jeffersontown
Williams, Petra Schatz *antiquarian, director*

La Grange
Morgan, Mary Dan *librarian*

Lancaster
Montgomery, Betty Adams *elementary school educator*

Lexington
Birchfield, Martha *librarian*
Brock, Carolyn Pratt *chemist, educator*
Caldwell, Alethea Otti *health care systems executive*
Campbell, Zenita A. D. *environmental engineer, educator, safety engineer*
Canales, Denise Niles *software company executive*
Casey, Baretta A. *physician, educator*
Chandler, Sherry *writer, editor*
Coffman, Jennifer Burcham *judge*
Diedrichs, Carol Pitts *librarian, dean*
Elder, Donna Redd *real estate broker*
Farrar, Donna Beatrice *health facility administrator*
Gornik, Kathy *electronics executive*
Griffith, Gloria Jeanette *finance educator*
Hardin-Pierce, Melanie G. *nursing educator*
Hojahmat, Marhaba *research scientist*
Holley, Kay Moffitt *nutrition instructor, dietitian*
Hunt, Cathy Stevenson *academic administrator*
Isaac, Teresa Ann *mayor, lawyer*
Isenhour, Kathleen Chaney *special education educator, consultant*
Johnson, Jane Penelope *freelance/self-employed writer*
Jones, Bonnie Quantrell *automobile dealer*
Kewin, Cynthia McLendon *secondary school educator*
Logan, Joyce Polley *education educator*
Lowe, Jennifer Ruth *mental health services professional*

Marczinski, Cecile Anne *psychologist, researcher*
McQueen, Sharon *library and information scientist, educator*
Miller, Pamela Gundersen *retired mayor*
Norman, Charlene Wilson *secondary school educator*
Penn, Lynn Sharon *materials scientist, educator*
Perdue, Theda *history professor, writer*
Rogers, JoAnn Vedder *library and information science educator*
Rowe, Melinda Grace *public health service officer*
Shurling, Anne Marlowe *psychology educator, consultant*
Taylor, Angela Dawn *primary school educator*
Turner, Sharon P. *dean, dentist, educator*
Varellas, Sandra Motte *judge*
Wagner, Gretchen S. *dance educator*
Walsh-Piper, Kathleen A. *museum director*
Worell, Judith P. *psychologist, educator*
Zimmerman, Laura Ann *biology educator*

London
Bailey, Janna *mathematics educator*
Baker, Lori Lee *medical/surgical nurse*

Louisa
Jones Compton, Carol Ann *science educator*
Moran, Dara Elain *science educator*

Louisville
Ammon, Jennifer Tucker *orthopedist, surgeon*
Antoine, Janet Anne *social worker*
Ashby, Denise *medical/surgical nurse, director*
Ballew, Laurie K. *psychiatrist*
Becker, Gail Roselyn *museum director*
Boykin, Gladys *retired religious organization administrator*
Byerlein, Anne P. *human resources specialist, food products executive*
Cafaro, Debra A. *real estate company executive*
Cannon, Dannie Parker *special education educator*
Carranza, Jovita *delivery service executive*
Carroll, Jean Gray *mathematics educator*
Cherry, Sandra Osburn *mathematics educator*
Choi, Namok *education educator*
Dale, Judy Ries *religious organization administrator, consultant*
DeMunbrun-Harmon, Donne O'Donnell *retired family physician*
Dietrich, Ruth Robinson *chemist, researcher, genealogist*
Dunbar-Richman, Anne Cameron *pathologist*
Faller, Rhoda *lawyer*
Foster, Teresa E. *choral director, piano educator*
Goffner, Gwendolyn Denise *elementary school educator*
Gray, Joan S. *head of religious order*
Greaver, Joanne Hutchins *mathematics educator, writer*
Gulati, Geetanjali *psychologist*
Haddaway, Janice Lillian *psychotherapist, consultant*
Hathcock, Bonita Catherine (Bonnie Hathcock) *managed health care company executive*
Herron, Beckie Lee *health service executive*
Hixson, Allie Corbin *retired adult education educator, advocate*
Jenne, Sue Oak *secondary school educator*
Johnson, Adria Elaine *financial analyst, accountant*
Jolly, Barbara Lee *home healthcare professional*
Lee, Susan *dentist, microbiologist*
Leonard, Mona Freeman *communications educator*
Lyndrup, Peggy B. *lawyer*
Mahoney, Margaret H. *history professor*
Maloney, Stephanie Jernigan *art history educator, archaeologist*
Margulis, Heidi *health products executive*
Marsh, Virginia Jean *art educator*
Mather, Elizabeth Vivian *healthcare executive*
McKim, Ruth Ann *financial planner*
Musacchio, Marilyn Jean *nurse midwife, educator*
Nation, Pamela Grace *secondary school educator*
Newell, Elizabeth Carolyn *retired secondary school educator*
Poston, Janice Lynn *librarian*
Riedman, Mary Suzanne *lawyer*
Rothstein, Laura *dean, law educator*
Roubieu, Amanda Marcelle *elementary school educator*
Ruter, Ruth Evelyn *elementary school educator*
Sexton, Charlene Ann *education consultant*
Sherman, Mildred Mozelle *music educator, vocalist, actress, opera director*
Stoll, Shirley Gabriella *special education educator*
Thompson, Kathy C. *bank executive*
Titus, Donna G. *psychologist*
Todd, Cherie Clemons *elementary school educator*
Topcik, Deborah Fay *marketing executive*
Tuttle, Tara Marie *literature and language educator*
VanDiver, Betty J. *protective services professional*
Walker, Carol Ellen Burton *retired elementary school educator*
Weinberg, Elizabeth *education educator, researcher, retired small business owner*
White-Walker, Roxana *elementary school educator*
Wood, Phoebe A. *food products executive*
Yount, Sara *academic administrator*
Zausch, Jo Fouts *literature and language professor, department chairman*

Madisonville
Fugate, Sharon Jean *biology professor*
Moss, Susan P. *biology professor*
Parker, Faye C. *elementary school educator*
Peyton, Dianna Leah Davis *physical therapist, personal trainer*
Pruitt, Brenda Sue Branstetter *secondary school educator*
Veazey, Doris Anne *retired state agency administrator*

Manchester
Rowland, Vicki Diane *home health nurse*

Marion
Henley, Darl Heathcott *librarian, educator*

Masonic Home
Schweichler, Mary Ellen *childhood education educator, consultant*

Middlesboro
Miracle, Sheila Gibbs *science educator*

Middletown
Jones, Doris Moreland *minister, author*

Morehead
Miller, April D. *special education educator*
Nutter, Carol Angell *academic librarian*

Morning View
Harris, Tammy Dotson *elementary school educator*

Mount Sterling
Aileen-Donohew, Phyllis Augusta *educational consultant*

Murray
Boston, Betty Lee *investment company executive, financial consultant, financial planner*
Guy, Sallie T. *artist*
Neelon, Ann Marie *literature educator*
Russell, Mary Ann *secondary school educator*

New Haven
Hall, Martha Anne *elementary school educator*

Newport
Houghton, Barbara Jean *art educator, artist*
Taliaferro, Elizabeth W. *manufacturing executive*

Nicholasville
Armstrong, Marcy Lynn *literature and language educator, special education educator*
Bender, Betty Barbee *food service professional*
Midkiff, Dinah Lee *retired elementary and middle school educator*

Oil Springs
Robinson, Virginia Lynn *elementary school educator*

Owensboro
Hood, Mary Bryan *museum director, painter*
Mullikin, Sandra Marie *music educator*
Swystun-Rives, Bohdana Alexandra *dentist*
Thomas-Löwe, Christine L. *small business owner*

Owingsville
Little, Stephanie Jean *special education educator*

Paducah
Kirk, Charlotte Leidecker *director*
Machanic, Mindy Robin *artist, photographer, educator, consultant, writer*
Mittendorf, Kimberly Ann *secondary school educator, real estate consultant*
Selbe, Lisa Hancock *medical/surgical nurse*
Talbert, Debra Kaiser *elementary school educator, artist*

Paint Lick
Donaldson, Kathleen *special education educator*

Paintsville
Watson, Betty A. *mathematics educator*

Pendleton
Tribble, Joan Lucille (Joan Farnsley Tribble) *retired literature and language professor, writer*

Perry Park
Hess, Marcia Wanda *retired secondary school educator*

Pikeville
Hunter, Trudy Pearl *surgical nurse*
Mutter, Jennie *secondary school educator, artist*
Venters, Teresa Anne *elementary school educator*

Pineville
Hoskins, Barbara R(uth) Williams *retired elementary school educator, principal*

Prospect
Broaddus, Kristie Jones *elementary school educator*
Garner, Joyce Craig *artist*
McFerran, Debra Brady *parochial school educator*
Willenbrink, Rose Ann *retired lawyer*

Radcliff
Cole, Jessie Mae *nursing assistant, freelance/self-employed writer*
Froedge, Susan Janet *music educator*

Richmond
Adams, Constance Ewing *school psychologist, art therapist*
Beranek, Carla Tipton *music educator*
Callahan, Connie J. *psychologist, educator*
Dean, Margaret Justice *literature and language professor*
Hall, Kathy *health facility administrator*
Jackson, Cheryl Ann *music educator, director*
Kumoji, Ida *art educator*
Machado-Echezuria, Marianella Perpetua *composer, writer, educator*
Mercer, Dorothy L. *psychology educator, consultant*
Pogatshnik, Lee Wolfram *psychologist, educator*
Smith, Carla Anne *music educator*

Russell Springs
Spears, Angela Ray *science educator*

Russellville
Harper, Shirley Fay *nutritionist, educator, consultant, lecturer*
Ragland, Tera Denise *music educator*

Sadieville
Taylor-Hall, Mary Ann *writer*

Shelbyville
Miller, Mary Helen *retired state government administrator*
Scheidt, Rebecca Lynnell *psychologist, educator*

Shepherdsville
Carini, Karen Michelle *elementary school educator*

Somerset
Carter, Frances Ann *secondary school educator*

Stanton
Lockard, Dixie Davis *elementary school educator*

Verona
Blackburn, Patricia A. *elementary school educator*

Villa Hills
Wera, Suzy E. *science educator, golf and tennis coach*

Virgie
Martin, Melanie *music educator*

Waco
Hackman, Vicki Lou *physician*

Wickliffe
Frueh, Deborah K.A. (Debi Frueh) *artist, poet*

Williamsburg
Blackmore-Haus, Margaret Ann *athletic trainer, educator*
Weaver, Susan Jeanne *sociology educator*

Wilmore
Kuhn, Anne Naomi Wicker (Mrs. Harold B. Kuhn) *foreign language educator*
Pritchett, Rita Joyce *educator*

Winchester
Cantrell, Georgia Ann *realtor*
Jude, Cassandra Joy *music educator*
Snowden, Ruth O'Dell Gillespie *artist*

LOUISIANA

Abbeville
Hebert, Margaret Burns *social worker*
Hebert, Mona Milliman *elementary school educator*

Alexandria
Anderson, Rose Marie *insurance agent*
Brand-Buchanan, Michelle Cathy *elementary school educator*
Foster, Sally *interior designer*
Gill, Julie Franks *education educator*
Gootee, Christy Beck *minister, educator*
Maples, Mary Lou *elementary school educator*
Mathews, Peggy Anne *nurse*
Purifoy, Sandra Nabours *science educator*
Sneed, Ellouise Bruce *retired nursing administrator, educator*

Angie
Moses, Anice N. *elementary school educator, minister*

Baker
Baker, Yvonne Bell *elementary school educator*

Baton Rouge
Barron, Sherry *music educator*
Bennett, Toni Zimmer *special education educator*
Blanco, Kathleen Babineaux *governor*
Boulton, Bonnie Smith *assistant principal, special education educator*
Buchmann, Molly O'Banion *choreographer, educator*
Cargill, Jennifer S. *librarian, dean, educator*
Chatman, Dana (Pokey Chatman) *women's college basketball coach*
Doty, Gresdna Ann *theatre historian, educator*
Duval, Anne-Gwin *lawyer*
Emonet, Sheila LeBlanc *elementary school educator*
Eubanks, Sonia Melisa *education educator*
Floersch, Shirley Patten *dietician, consultant*
Garno, Jayne C. *chemistry professor*
Geiselman, Paula Jeanne *psychologist, educator*
Hackney, Marcella Wichser *biology professor*
Harper, Sandra Stecher *academic administrator*
Hayward, Olga Loretta Hines (Mrs. Samuel Ellsworth Hayward) *retired librarian*
Hillman, Christina Joy *mathematics educator*
Jonas, Jeanie Lynn *elementary school educator*
Kelley, Nanette Noland *business owner, entrepreneur*
Kimball, Dorothy Jean *retired foundation executive*
Lane, Margaret Beynon Taylor *librarian*
Litton, Nancy Joan *education educator*
Lusk, Glenna Rae Knight (Mrs. Edwin Bruce Lusk) *librarian*
Lusted, Dona Sanders *music educator, consultant, organist*
Malekian, Fatemeh *nursing educator*
Mathews, Sharon Walker *performing company executive, secondary school educator*
Morvant, Barbara L. *nursing administrator*
Mueller, Lisel *writer, poet*
Myers, Valerie Harwell *psychologist*
Noland, Christine A. *judge*
Orman, Evelyn Kay *music educator, consultant*
Ropers-Huilman, Becky Lynn *education and humanities educator*
Rutledge, Katherine Burck *artist*
Sanders, Mary Elizabeth *writer, historian*
Sasek, Gloria Burns *English language and literature educator*
Schechter, Lynn Renee *psychologist*
Spearman, Diane Negrotto *art/special education educator*
Stockwell, Mary Diamond *information technology manager*
Stubblefield, Luria Shaw *education educator*
Travis, Karen S. *clinical social worker*
Vigee, Kimberly Denise *anatomy and physiology educator*
Wald, Ingeborg *librarian, translator*
Wisbar, Rebecca Kittok *lawyer*

Yarbrough, Martha Cornelia *music educator*
Younathan, Margaret Tims *retired nutritionist, educator*

Bogalusa
Villarrubia, Glenda Boone *reading specialist, reading coordinator, educational consultant, educator*

Bossier City
Lim, Diana Magpayo *internist*
Paris, Norma Jean *psychologist, educator*
Phillips, Staci Davis *mathematics professor, director*
Rhoades, Paula K. *dietician, healthcare educator*

Boutte
Melancon, Wanda Lorie *secondary educator*

Boyce
Monroe, Nancy L. *secondary school educator*

Brusly
Theriot, Lisa Marie *social worker*

Chalmette
Crouchet, Kathleen Hunt *elementary school educator, reading educator*
Wheeler, Genevieve Stutes *library administrator, educator*

Chauvin
Chauvin, Cally Hebert *science educator, educational consultant*

Choudrant
Lofton, Brenda M. *middle school educator*

Covington
Burton, Barbara Able *psychotherapist*
Doody, Barbara Pettett *computer specialist*
Gilman-Anderson, Susan Ellen *real estate company executive, consultant*
Rohrbough, Elsa Claire Hartman *artist*
Stahr, Beth A. *librarian*

Crowley
Harris, Michelle Reneé *pastor*
Privat, Ruby (Ruby Thibodeaux) *elementary school educator*
Thibodeaux, Darla Faul *gifted and talented educator*

Denham Springs
Peacock, Mindy H. *music educator*

Dequincy
Cooper, Melonee V. *music educator*

Deridder
Franks, Cindi W. *supervisor*
Mallory, Patricia Jody *museum curator*
Zamboni-Cutter, Kathryn M. *obstetrician, gynecologist, military officer*

Destrehan
Blackwell, Karen Elaine *music educator*

Eunice
Hernandez, Gloria *mathematician, educator*

Ferriday
Bowman, Sarah *librarian*

Franklin
Fairchild, Phyllis Elaine *school counselor*
Rouly, Ellie Arceneaux *dancer, educator*

Franklinton
Wheeler, Gwen *medical, surgical, and critical care nurse*

Galliano
Orgeron, Rochelle Mary *secondary school educator*

Glenmora
Burns, Linda D. *elementary school educator*

Gonzales
Kidd, Ruth Price *retired secondary school educator*
Pierce, Carol *success strategist, writer*

Grambling
Warner, Neari Francois *university president*

Gretna
Doyle, Agnes J *minister*
Kennedy, Maydra Jane Penisson (J.P. Kennedy) *poet*

Hammond
Cook, Myrtle *special education educator, elementary school educator*
Day, Susan Brent *assistant principal, educator*
Huszar, Angelia *lawyer*
LaFargue, Melba Faye Fulmer *credit manager, realtor*
Nauman, Ann Keith *education educator*

Harvey
Henderson, Lillian Milbra *educator, librarian, clergyperson*

Houma
Bordelon, Dena Cox Yarbrough *retired special education educator, director*
Breaux, Monica LeBlanc *elementary school educator*
Eschete, Mary Louise *internist*

Iowa
Leonard, Linda Faye *secondary school educator*

Jeanerette
Garcia, Susan Breaux *multi-media specialist, consultant*

Jena
Smith, Robyn *secondary school educator*

Jennings
Benoit, Lillian Riquelmy *science educator, mathematics educator*

Kenner
Duplessis, Sandra Walsh *librarian, educator*

La Place
Blair, Ruth Reba *retired government official*
Fiffie Proctor, JoAnn *media and technology specialist*

Lafayette
Barry, Mildred Castille *artist*
Cain, Judith Sharp *mathematics professor, consultant*
Clark, Elsa Myriam *artist*
Colbert-Cormier, Patricia A. *secondary school educator*
Daniel, Margaret Hagen *music and voice educator*
Hail, Karen L. *bank executive*
LeBlanc, Dotsie L. *retired vocational school educator*
Lynch, Cheryl Stelly *psychology educator*
Marceaux, Linda d'Augereau *elementary school educator*
Menutis, Ruth Ann *small business owner*
Petry, Ruth Vidrine *retired principal*
Sherer, Wanda C. *secondary school educator*
Stravinska, Sarah *dance educator*
Willett, Anna Hart *composer, painter*

Lake Arthur
Dronet, Judy Lynn *elementary school educator, librarian*

Lake Charles
Andrus, Tiffany Shantel *mathematics professor*
Babin, Sally Wheeler *secondary school educator, consultant*
Batchelor, Karen Sue *music educator*
Curol, Helen Ruth *librarian, English language educator*
Dentler, Anne Lillian *artist*
Fields-Gold, Anita *retired dean*
Lee, Brandi Gremillion *elementary school educator*
Mount, Willie Landry *state legislator*

Leesville
Gutman, Lucy Toni *social worker, educator*
Kay-Atkins, Cheree' *elementary school educator*

Madisonville
Young, Lucy Cleaver *retired physician*

Mandeville
Arrowsmith, Marian Campbell *elementary school educator, supervisor, educator*
Colomb, Marjorie Monroe *investor, volunteer*
Dempsey, Margaret Theresa *psychologist*
Ewen, Pamela Binnings *retired lawyer*
Pittman, Jacquelyn *retired mental health nurse, nursing educator*
Treuting, Edna Gannon *retired nursing administrator, educator*

Metairie
Ales, Beverly Gloria Rushing *artist*
Blunt, Joyce Omega *special education educator*
Crosby, Deborah Berry *artist*
Crosby, Marena Lienhard *retired academic administrator*
deMoruelle, Charmaine *music educator*
Falco, Maria Josephine *political scientist*
Flake, Leone Elizabeth *special education educator*
Foucha, Laura Theresa *computer graphics designer, filmmaker, writer*
Friedman, Lynn Joseph *counselor*
Gereighty, Andrea Saunders *diversified financial services company executive, poet*
Grau, Shirley Ann (Mrs. James Kern Feibleman) *writer*
Myers, Iona Raymer *real estate property manager*
Nix, Linda Anne Bean *public relations executive*
Porter, Sheri Wagner *nursing administrator, educator*
Rice, Patricia Wegmann *counselor*
Sanderson, Christine Graves *literature and language educator*
Slattery, Michele G. *research scientist*
Travitzky McBride, Virginia Anne *administrator*

Monroe
Clayton-Dodd, Valera Jo *health facility administrator*
Fouts, Elizabeth Browne *psychologist, metals company executive*
LeBlanc, Melinda Anne *voice educator*
Puckett, Karen *communications executive*
Smith, Pamela LaTrice *school psychologist*

Napoleonville
Triche, Jane M. *lawyer*

Natchitoches
Egan, Shirley Anne *retired nursing educator*
Forsloff, Carol Marie *rehabilitation services professional, consultant*
Wells, Carol McConnell *genealogist, retired archivist*

New Iberia
Harrington, Chestee Marie *artist, sculptor*
Hockless, Mary Fontenot *educational consultant*
Romero, Traci Baudoin *science educator*

New Orleans
Adams, Ingrid G. *federal government intelligence specialist*
Beard, Elizabeth Letitia *physiologist, educator*
Benjamin, Adelaide Wisdom *retired lawyer, community volunteer and activist*
Berrigan, Helen Ginger *federal judge*
Brainard, Barbara *artist*
Butler, Shirley Ann *social worker*
Chessin, Cathy E. *lawyer*
Chetta, Holly Ann *transportation executive*
Clement, Edith Brown *federal judge*
Creppel, Claire Binet *hotel owner*
Davis, Pamela Marie *administrative analyst*
DeFelice, Frances Radosta *restaurateur*
Duncan, Margaret Caroline *physician*
Foundas, Anne Leigh *psychiatrist*
Fraiche, Donna DiMartino *lawyer*
Garcia, Patricia A. *lawyer*
Gatipon, Betty Becker *medical educator, consultant*
Hagedorn, Dorothy Louise *librarian*
Higgins, Oleda Jackson *retired medical and surgical nurse*
Hughes, Marvalene *academic administrator*
Irons, Paulette Riley *state legislator, lawyer*
Ivens, Mary Sue *microbiologist, medical mycologist*
Johnson, Bernette Joshua *state supreme court justice*
Jordan, Louise Herron *art educator*
Jumonville, Florence M. *librarian, historian*
Kimball, Catherine D. *state supreme court justice*
Knoll, Jeannette Theriot *state supreme court justice*
Landry, Sherry S. *lawyer*
Longwell, Kelly (A. Kelton Longwell) *lawyer*
McNeil, Vicki Laughter *student affairs administrator*
Mills, Cheryl E. *education educator*
Moely, Barbara E. *psychologist, educator*
Neff, Carole Cukell *lawyer*
O'Connor, Kim Claire *chemical engineering and biotechnology educator, researcher*
Orr, Margaret *newscaster*
Perlis, Sharon A. *lawyer*
Roberts, Louise Nisbet *philosopher, educator*
St. Julien, Thais Mary *soprano, musician*
Smith, Juanita Bérard *lawyer, artist*
Steinmetz, Deborah Susan *interior designer*
Strength, Catherine Bush *nursing educator*
Tahir, Mary Elizabeth (Liz Tahir) *marketing professional, consultant, writer*
Taylor, Phyllis Miller *energy executive*
Tesvich, Lisa Kay *industrial and organizational psychologist*
Weaver, Norma J. *medical/surgical nurse*
Wegmann, Mary Katherine *art director*

Newllano
Boren, Lynda Sue *gifted education educator*

Opelousas
LaBerteaux, Jennifer Claire *secondary school educator*

Pineville
Beall, Grace Carter *business educator*
Bolin, Julie Paul *secondary school educator*
Conway, Evelyn Atkinson *accountant, financial analyst*
Cummings, Karen Sue *retired corrections classification administrator*
DeLong, Lori Lynn *physical education educator, athletic trainer*
Lott, Johnnye Jo *elementary school educator, writer*
Smith, Mabel Hargis *retired secondary school educator, musician*

Plaquemine
Engolio, Elizabeth Ann *lawyer*

Ponchatoula
Warden, Waldia Ann *religious center administrator, director*

Port Allen
Kahao, Mary Jane *school librarian*

Prairieville
Biri, Toni Roppolo *elementary school educator*

Raceland
Cole, Anna Moore *chemistry educator*

Ruston
Bourgeois, Patricia McLin *academic administrator, women's health and pediatrics nurse, educator*
Carpenter, Jenna Price *mathematics professor, academic administrator*
Freasier, Aileen W. *special education educator*
Griffin, Susan *secondary school educator*
Johnson, Elaine Frances *mathematics educator*
Lewis, Doris Ann *principal*
Marbury, Virginia Lomax *insurance and investment executive*

Saint Martinville
Fournet, Patricia Sibley *retired secondary school educator*
Guilliot, Vickie Lee *secondary school educator*

Shreveport
Armstrong, Shelley N. *physical education educator, coach*
Brazile, Orella Ramsey *library director*
Delo, Lynda Jeanne *secondary school educator*
Easley, Linda Marie *education educator*
Finney, Lila D. *school system administrator*
Flournoy, Linda Wesley *minister, educator*
Foggin, Brenda Frazier *retired state agency administrator, volunteer*
Giles, Katharine Emily (J. K. Piper) *retired administrative assistant, writer*
Glasgow, Dianne Britt *education educator, writer, consultant*
Goodman, Sylvia Klumok *film center executive*
Hall, Amy Matthews *science educator*
Haughton, Mary L. *elementary school educator*
Hughes, Mary Sorrows *artist*
Leonard, Paula Leavy *school disciplinarian*
Mancini, Mary Catherine *cardiothoracic surgeon, researcher*
Morelock, Jasmine Crawford *artist*
Nelson, Meredith Gaffney *counselor, educator*
Pierson, Juanita (Nita Pierson) *secondary school educator*
Posey, Katye L. *retired school system administrator*
Pouncey, Annie Moore *retired secondary school educator*
Prunty, LeeAnn Marsiglia *gifted and talented educator*
Shepard, Emma Luster *elementary school educator*
Street, Jeanne *psychologist*
Wray, Geraldine Smitherman (Jerry Wray) *artist*

Simsboro
Talley, Dana Smith *principal*

Slidell
Fincher, Margaret Ann *retired secondary school educator*
Herron, Florine Pernell *retired music educator*
Jacob, Susan Marie *nurse*
Johnson, Lynn Marie Thornburg *parochial school educator*
Larson, Sandra Pauline *music educator*
Laurent, Lynn Margaret *nurse*
Lovell, Emily Kalled *retired journalist*
McBurney, Elizabeth Innes *dermatologist, physician, educator*
Risher, Mary Lou Bishop *artist*

Springfield
Smith, Keri A. *literature and language educator*

Stonewall
Jarquin, Theresa Binning *gifted and talented educator*

Sulphur
Fuller, Betty Stamps *music educator*
Toniette, Sallye Jean *physician*

Terrytown
Joyce, Marie Caldwell *medical, surgical, and mental health nurse*
Olson, Sandra Dittman *medical/surgical nurse*

Thibodaux
Carter, Iris Brown *pre-school educator*
Harris, Rose M. *academic administrator*
Smith, Victoria Weilepp *educator*
Tonn, Anke *library and information scientist, researcher*

Tickfaw
Bickham, Charlotte Marie *science educator*

Ville Platte
Patsicostas, Susan Joanna *mental health services professional, psychotherapist*

Walker
Michel, Jacqueline *geochemist*

Westlake
Yarbrough, Frances Carole *music educator*

Westwego
Brehm, Loretta Persohn *retired art educator, librarian, consultant*

White Castle
Williams, Ivory Lee *special education educator*

Zachary
Mills, Elizabeth Jennings *art educator*
Rogillio, Kathy June *musician, director, small business owner, educator*

MAINE

Acton
Cunningham, Joyce Wentworth *retired secondary school educator*

Alna
Beerits, Janet Penrose Robinson *sculptor*

Auburn
Bartlett, Elizabeth Louise *psychiatrist*
Van Deusen, Jenifer *educational consultant*

Augusta
Bowman, Esther Ruth-Kazian *music educator*
Bulba-Carvutto, Susan Dietz *rabbi*
Edmonds, Beth *state legislator, lieutenant governor*
Gendron, Susan Ann *school system administrator*
Jenkins, Pamela Lynn *music educator*
McCormick, Dale *state official*
Mills, Dora Anne *public health service officer*
Phillips, Gwethalyn *political organization administrator*
Rubinson, Jill Linda *literature and language professor*
Sheive, Doreen Laurel *fiscal administrator*
vonHerrlich, Phyllis Herrick *academic administrator*
Waldron, Janet E. *state commissioner*
Whitcomb, Lois Ann *retired academic administrator*

Bangor
Arps, Corabell Bennett *psychiatrist*
Ballesteros, Paula Mitchell *nurse*
Beaupain, Elaine Shapiro *psychiatric social worker*
Bickford, Meris J. *lawyer, bank executive*
King, Tabitha *author*
Merkel, Anne D. *science educator*
Rea, Ann W. *librarian*
Trask, Paula Elizabeth *mathematics educator*

Bar Harbor
Swazey, Judith Pound *academic administrator, science educator*

Bar Mills
Burns, Maryann Margaret *retired elementary school educator*

Bath
Galleher, Gay *psychologist*
Simone, Gail Elisabeth *manufacturing executive*

Belfast
Griffith, Patricia King *journalist*
Hughes, Helen Elizabeth *psychologist*
Worth, Mary Page *mayor*

Belgrade Lakes
Kany, Judy C(asperson) *retired state senator*

Bernard
Marchetti-Ponte, Karin *lawyer, land conservation consultant*

Boothbay
Watson, Caroline *secondary school educator*

Boothbay Harbor
Carpenter, Elizabeth Jane *mediator*

Bremen
Wilson, Linda Smith *retired academic administrator*

Brewer
Cote Robbins, Rhea Jeannine *writer, educator*

Brooklin
Schmidt, Lynda Wheelwright *psychotherapist*

Brunswick
Crandall, Elizabeth Walbert *retired home economics professor*
Karchov, Tatyana *psychiatrist*
Kline, Katy *museum director*
Peacher, Georgiana Melicent *poet, educator*
Pfeiffer, Sophia Douglass *retired state legislator, lawyer*

Canton
Parsons, Lorraine Leighton *nurse, pre-school administrator*

Cumberland
Carter, Gail Rae *history educator*
Jamison, Elizabeth Alease *drafting and design business owner*

Damariscotta
Swanson, Karin *hospital administrator, consultant*

Dresden
Haskell, Elizabeth McKnight *not-for-profit developer, educator*
Iserbyt, Charlotte Thomson *researcher, writer, educational consultant*
Kilkelly, Marjorie Lee *state legislator*

Edgecomb
Carlson, Suzanne Olive *architect*
Wait, Lea *writer, small business owner*

Eliot
Mahar, Carol *psychologist, consultant*

Ellsworth
Young, Lucia Patat *psychotherapist*

Fairfield
Joy, Suzanne Chauvin *language educator*

Falmouth
Boehmer, Raquel Davenport *newsletter editor*
Hathaway, Lynn McDonald *education advocate, administrator*
Winton, Linda *international trainer, consultant*

Farmington
Hiltz-Scerbo, Leiza Ann *apparel designer, photographer*
Kalikow, Theodora June *academic administrator*
Mathews, Linnea Koons *science educator, librarian*
Oliver, Diana Cloutier *elementary school educator*

Fort Fairfield
Shapiro, Joan Isabelle *lab administrator, medical/surgical nurse*

Fort Kent
Taggette, Deborah Jean *special education educator*

Gorham
Bearce, Jeana Dale *artist, educator*
Fall, Marijane Eaton *counselor educator*
Marasco, Rose C. *artist, educator*

Gouldsboro
Thayer, Cynthia A. *farmer, writer*

Hampden
Mahon, Julia *speech pathology/audiology services professional, educator*
Scroggins, M. Suzanne Paonessa *budget analyst*

Harpswell
Regan, Helen Brooks *education educator, educational consultant*

Hollis Center
Hodgdon, Paula Drake *retired physical education educator*

Houlton
Powers, Gloria Doody *mathematics educator*

Kennebunk
Boston, Lorraine *bank executive*

Kennebunkport
Chapman, Karina M. *elementary school educator*
Featherman, Sandra *retired academic administrator, political science professor*
Ray, Virginia H. S. *columnist, writer*

Kingfield
Clapp, Millicent Evans *real estate broker*
Silver, Sally *minister*

Lamoine
Schmidt, Christine Alice *art gallery owner*

Lee
Knapp, Lisa Marie *music educator*

Lewiston
Dodd, Anne Wescott *education educator*
Fatone, Gina Andrea *music educator*
Hansen, Elaine Tuttle *academic administrator*

Machias
Ball, Heather L. *special education educator, consultant*

Mount Desert
Weinberger, Jane Dalton *retired nurse, volunteer*

Naples
Byrne, Kelley Anne *special education educator*
McVety, Linda Dow *music educator*

North Yarmouth
Kuhrt, Sharon Lee *nursing administrator*

Oakland
Baker, Marshalyn Elaine *elementary school educator*
Osborne, Hannah Christine *school counselor, social worker*

Old Orchard Beach
Day, Marlene E. *elementary school educator*

Old Town
Alex, Joanne DeFilipp *elementary school educator*
Nelligan, Annette Frances *social worker*
Scribner, Princess Rose-Marie *not-for-profit developer*

Orono
Bartel, Lavon Lee *academic administrator, food scientist*
Billitteri, Carla *literature and language professor*
Marston-Scott, Mary Vesta *nurse, educator*
Szymanski, Edna Mora *dean*

Peaks Island
Stelk, Virginia Horn *retired language educator*

Pemaquid
Howell, Jeanette Helen *retired cultural organization administrator*

Poland
Herrick, Doris A. *elementary school educator*

Portland
Blair, Bonnie Kathleen *former professional speedskater, former Olympic athlete*
Calkins, Susan W. *state supreme court justice*
Chow, Amy *gymnast, Olympic athlete*
Glassman, Caroline Duby *state supreme court justice*
Khoury, Colleen A. *dean*
Knudsen, Chilton Abbie Richardson *bishop*
McDaniel, Sarah A. *lawyer*
Mitchell, Carol L. *lawyer*
Nectowak, Tillian *small business owner*
Reed, Maryann *nursing administrator*
Reid, Rosemary Anne *insurance agent*
Saufley, Leigh Ingalls *state supreme court chief justice*
Silsby, Paula D. *prosecutor*
Simpson, Nancy Ida *nursing educator*
Vincent, Christine *academic administrator*
Wilkinson, Barbara J. *pediatrician, educator*
Zill, Anne Broderick *foundation executive*

Presque Isle
Gardner, Julie Isabel *elementary school educator*
Gentile, Caroline D. *adult education educator*

Rangeley
Ruprecht, Susan Elizabeth *art educator*

Rockland
Anne, Lois *artist, educator*

Rockport
Goodwin, Doris Helen Kearns *historian, writer*

Rumford
Rouleau, Ann F. *retired elementary school educator*

Saco
Collins, Cynthia Jane *marriage and family therapist, priestess*
Mason, Nancy Tolman *retired state agency administrator*
Wilkinson, Anne *musician, educator*

Sanford
Field, Linda G. *secondary school educator*

Scarborough
Goulet, Christine Sweeney *elementary school educator*
Russo, Joan Mildred *special education educator*

South Bristol
Lasher, Esther Lu *minister*

South Paris
Johnson, Sarah N. *music educator*

Southwest Harbor
Goetze, Lydia B. *biology educator*

Standish
Gelzer, Lois Auge *foundation administrator*

Starks
Quimby, Janice Ann *minister*

Sullivan
Davis-Wexler, Ginia *singer, director*

Surry
Pickett, Betty Horenstein *psychologist*

Topsham
Arrington, Elisabeth Calvert *elementary education educator, artist*
Outhwaite, Lucille Conrad *ballerina, educator*
Palesky, Carol East *tax accountant*

Waterville
Cook, Susan Farwell *director*
Gilkes, Cheryl Louise Townsend *sociologist, educator, minister*
Paliyenko, Adrianna Maria *foreign language educator*

Wells
Lahar, Cindy J. *psychologist, educator*

West Baldwin
Simmonds, Rae Nichols *musician, composer, educator*

Wilton
Emerson, Kathy *writer*

Winslow
Bourgoin, Mary Beth Nivison *social studies educator*
Desrosiers, Muriel C. *music educator, retired nursing consultant*
Gillman, Karen Lee *clinical psychologist*

Woolwich
Clark, Joyce T. *piano teacher, church organist*

Yarmouth
McCoy, Carol P. *psychologist, training executive*
McHold, Sharon Lawrence *lawyer, mediator*
Northrup, Christiane *obstetrician, gynecologist*

York
Haley, Priscilla Jane *printmaker*
Hallam, Beverly (Beverly Linney) *artist*
Smart, Mary-Leigh Call (Mrs. J. Scott Smart) *civic worker*

MARYLAND

Aberdeen Proving Ground
Gibson, Annemarie *writer, editor*
Halstead, Rebecca S. *career military officer*

Adamstown
Church, Martha Eleanor *retired academic administrator*

Andrews Air Force Base
Hall, Molly J. *psychiatrist, educator*

Annapolis
Battaglia, Lynne Ann *judge*
Bowen, Linnell R. *director*
Brann, Eva Toni Helene *philosophy educator*
Byers, Meranda Faith *secondary school educator*
Carpenter, Marlene *retired philosopher, educator*
Clagett, Virginia Parker *state official*
Connolly, Janet Elizabeth *retired sociologist, retired criminal justice educator*
Doory, Ann Marie *legislator*
Farley, Dorothy Bieber *artist, educator*
Farmer, Martha Louise *retired academic administrator*
Flanagan, Susan Marie *special education educator*
Forehand, Jennie Meador *state senator*
Goldwater, Marilyn R(ubin) *medical/surgical nurse, state legislator*
Hollinger, Paula Colodny *state legislator*
Kane, Mary Deely *state official*
Kelley, Delores Goodwin *state legislator*
Klejnot, Getha Jean *school nurse practitioner, music educator*
Kopp, Nancy Kornblith *state official*
Lee, Susan C. *state legislator, lawyer*
Nolan, Theresa A. *retired judge, mediator, arbitrator*
Palmer, Laura Higgins *artist*
Powers, Eileen Elizabeth *lawyer, mediator*
Ruben, Ida Gass *state senator*
Ryan, Michele King *marketing professional*
Sagner, Dianne R. *lawyer*
Schleicher, Nora Elizabeth *bank executive, treasurer, accountant*
Seep, Dorothy M. *music educator*
Shapiro, Susan Stobbart *lawyer*
Snyder, Kathleen Theresa *state agency administrator*
Stern, Margaret Bassett *retired special education educator, author*
Thoms, Josephine Bowers *artist*
Wyman, Pilar *editor*

Arnold
Shatz, Jayne Eileen *artist, educator*
Shepard, Brandi R. *architecture educator*
Smith, Martha A. *academic administrator*
Walker, Martha M. *special education educator*

Baltimore
Abbey, Helen *science educator*
Abrams, Rosalie Silber *retired state agency official*
Adams, Clara I. *academic administrator*
Allen, Norma Ann *librarian, educator*
Alpern, Linda Lee Wevodau *retired health agency administrator*
Amos, Helen *hospital administrator*
Aneja, Alka *child psychiatrist*
Applefeld, Floraine B. *cultural organization administrator*
Apsel, Alyssa *electrical engineer, computer engineer*
Augustson, Edith *mental health clinician*
Aurelian, Laure *medical sciences educator*
Babb, Barbara A. *lawyer, educator*
Baker, Constance H. *lawyer*
Baker, Susan P. *public health educator*
Ball, Marion Jokl *academic administrator*
Baltzley, Patricia Creel *mathematics educator*
Barnes, Adrienne *public information officer*
Barnes, Janet Lynn *artist*
Barnhart, Jo Anne B. *federal agency administrator*
Blake, Catherine C. *judge*
Blakemore, Karin Jane *obstetrician, geneticist*
Bolger, Doreen *museum director*
Boyd, Amanda D. *elementary school educator*
Bradley, Wanda Louise *librarian*
Braggio, Sherryll Ann Morris *retired elementary school educator, volunteer*
Brennan, Janice M. *medical/surgical nurse, nursing educator*
Brewer, Nevada Nancy *elementary school educator*
Bright, Margaret *sociologist*
Brisbon, Ada Vanessa *assistant principal*
Brock, Roslyn McCallister *association executive*
Broda-Hydorn, Susan *entomologist*
Brodie, Angela M. *biomedical researcher, educator*
Brotman, Phyllis Block *advertising executive, public relations executive*
Brown, Florence S. *librarian, administrator*
Brown, Ruth Payne *retired elementary school educator, retired principal*
Bryn-Julson, Phyllis *soprano, music educator*
Busch-Vishniac, Ilene Joy *mechanical engineering educator, researcher*
Campbell, Jacquelyn C. *community health nurse*
Capute, Courtney G. *lawyer*
Carnell, Teresa Burt *lawyer*
Carper, Gertrude Esther *small business owner, real estate developer*
Chagnoni, Kathleen *energy executive*
Chapelle, Suzanne Ellery Greene *history professor*
Chaplin, Peggy Louie *lawyer*
Chesshire, Mary Claire *lawyer*
Chin, Katherine Moy *nutritionist, consultant*
Ciccolo, Angela *lawyer*
Clarizio, Lynda M. *advertising executive, lawyer*
Clements, Janice *science educator*
Coleman, Carolyn Quilloin *association executive*
Colomer, Veronica *medical educator, researcher*
Corley, Rose Ann McAfee *government official*
Crawford, Annette Lambson *elementary school educator*
Dawson, Valina L. *science educator*
DeAngelis, Catherine D. *pediatrics educator*
DeLateur, Barbara Jane *medical educator*
Delpit, Lisa D. *education educator, researcher, consultant*
de Soto, Lisa *lawyer*
Devan, Deborah Hunt *lawyer*
Dickinson, Jane W. *retired executive secretary, volunteer*
Ditz, Toby Lee *history professor*
Dixon, Sheila *municipal official*
Donovan, Dianne Francys *journalist*
Donovan, Sharon Ann *retired secondary school educator*
Eden-Fetzer, Dianne Toni *health facility administrator*
Edidin, Ruth Glicenstein *mathematics educator*
Edwards, Willarda V. *internist, medical association administrator*
Elias, Sarah Davis *retired English language educator*
Ensminger, Margaret E. *sociologist, researcher*
Eveleth, Janet Stidman *law association administrator*
Ferencz, Charlotte *pediatrician, epidemiologist, preventive medicine physician, educator*
Franklin, Paula Anne *artist, writer, psychologist*
Freischlag, Julie Ann *surgeon*
Fried, Linda P. *medical educator*
Friedman, Maria Andre *public relations executive*
Fulton, Judith P. *management consultant*
Gauvey, Susan Kathryn *judge*
Gilli, Lynne Marie *academic administrator*
Godenne, Ghislaine Dudley *physician, psychotherapist, educator*
Goldberg, Linda *utilities executive, professional society administrator*
Goldman, Lynn Rose *medical educator*
Gonzales, Louise Michaux *lawyer*
Gourley, Jacquelyn Elise *information technology manager, researcher*
Grant, Leslie Edwina *dentist, dental association administrator*
Grasmick, Nancy S. *school system administrator*
Greider, Carol Widney *molecular biology professor*
Guben, Jan K. *lawyer*
Haeri, Niloofar M. *linguist, educator*
Hall, Marian M. *retired music educator*
Hansen, Barbara Caleen *physiologist, science educator*
Harryman, Kathleen A. *board administrator*
Hayden, Carla Diane *library director, educator*
Heath, Emily B. *interior designer*
Hernandez, Iris N. *clinical specialist*
Hoffman, Barbara A. *state legislator*
Hofmann, Irene E. *art museum director*
Howard, Bettie Jean *surgical nurse*
Hsu, Cornelia Wang Mei-Chih *education educator*
Huggins, Amy Branum *music educator*
Jacobson, Katherine Louise *musician, music educator*
Jenkins, Lawanda W. *publishing executive*
Jenkins, Louise Sherman *nursing researcher, educator*
Jones, Hendree Evelyn *research scientist, psychologist*
Katz, Martha Lessman *lawyer*
Kemp, Suzanne Leppart *elementary school educator*
Kenney, Brigid E. *lawyer*
Kim, Lillian G. Lee *retired administrative assistant*
Kimbrough, Natalie *history and language educator*
Koch, Gretchen Ann *mathematics and computer science professor*
Koenig, Margaret Susanne *elementary school educator*
Kumin, Libby Barbara *speech language pathologist, educator*
Kyger, Brenda Sue *intravenous therapy nurse*
Lanier, Jacqueline Ruth *curator, artist*
Larch, Sara Margaret *healthcare executive*
Lee, Alice Inez *retired nurse*
Leffell, Mary Sue *educator*
Leonard, Angela Michele *librarian, educator*
Lidtke, Doris Keefe *retired computer science educator*
Litrenta, Frances Marie *psychiatrist*
Lucas, Barbara B. *electrical equipment manufacturing executive*
Lungaro Cid, Lisa *educational association administrator*
Lyles, Barbara Diggs *retired human development educator*
Magnuson, Nancy *librarian*
Massey, Allyn Francis *artist, educator*
Massey, Garnetta D. *bank executive*
Massie-Burrell, Terri L. *educational association administrator*
Matjasko, M. Jane *anesthesiologist, educator*
Matthews, Rondra J. *publishing executive*
Maumenee, Irene H. *ophthalmology educator*
McDaniel, Mildred Gage *elementary school educator*
McLaughlin, Patricia A. *social services administrator*
Mensh, Suzanne Cooper *state official*
Metzger, Delores Virginia *social services professional*
Migeon, Barbara Ruben *pediatrician, geneticist, educator*
Miser, Ann *retired government researcher*
Morton, Sandra Jorgensen *retired school librarian*
Motz, Diana Gribbon *federal judge*
Murphy, Frances Louise, II, *retired newspaper publisher*
Nelson, Betsy S. *association administrator*
Njie, Veronica P.S. *clinical nurse, educator*
Norris, Karen W. *grants specialist*
Novak, Donna Burnett *secondary school educator*
Nussbaum, Paul M. *lawyer*
Oji, Pauline E. *secondary school educator*
OReilly, Meaghan Kelly *art educator*
Orgelfinger, Gail *literature educator*
O'Toole, Tara Jeanne *medical educator, former federal agency administrator*
Ottesen, Bodil Bang *art educator*
Palka, Tamara *psychiatrist*
Park, Mary Woodfill *information consultant, librarian, writer*
Peirce, Carol Marshall *retired literature educator*
Phillips, Paula L. *foundation administrator, artist*
Pickett, Eugenia V. *social worker*
Pollak, Joanne Elizabeth *lawyer*
Puglisi, Mary Joanna *psychologist*
Ridenour, Deborah Hughes *elementary school educator*
Robinson, Carrie *pastor*
Robinson, Florine Samantha *marketing executive*
Robinson, Sally Shoemaker *lay associate*
Rose, Sara Margaret *English as a second language educator*
Rosen, Wendy Workman *advertising executive*
Rothenberg, Karen H. *dean, law educator*
Roup, Brenda Jacobs *nurse, retired military officer*
Rousuck, J. Wynn *theater critic*
Rusinko, Elaine *language educator*
Sadak, Diane Marie *director, performing arts educator*
Samuelson, Emily Meg *psychologist*
Scangarello, Danielle Lynn *music educator*
Schlaff, Barbara E. *lawyer*
Schmidt, Elizabeth Suzanne *history professor*
Schoenrich, Edyth Hull *internist, preventive medicine physician*
Schultheis, Patricia Ann *writer, editor*
Schumann, Jill *religious organization administrator*
Seurkamp, Mary Pat *college president*
Silbergeld, Ellen Kovner *epidemiologist, researcher, toxicologist*
Simpson, Mildred Kathleen *health facility administrator*
Skolnik, Sandra J. *educational association administrator*
Smith, E. Follin *corporate financial executive*
Somer-Greif, Penny Lynn *lawyer*
Starfield, Barbara Helen *pediatrician, educator*
Stewart, Doris Mae *biology professor*
Strachan, Nell B. *lawyer*
Streat, Karen Gray *community health and geriatrics nurse, adult nurse practitioner*
Terborg-Penn, Rosalyn Marian *historian, educator*
Thomas, Margaret Ann *not-for-profit developer*
Topper, Barbara MacNeal Blake *secondary school educator*
Tyler, Anne (Mrs. Taghi M. Modarressi) *writer*
Ushry, Roselyn *minister*
Uzarowski, Laura Helen *physical therapist*
Valentine, April Sue *elementary school educator, department chairman*
Warren, Melissa Allison *lawyer*
Washington, Earline *health facility administrator*
Wasik, Barbara Ann *psychologist, researcher*
Weldon, Linda Jean *psychology educator*
West, Virginia *artist, educator*
White, Libby Kramer *librarian*
White, Pamela Janice *lawyer*
Yates, Sharon *artist*
Yellin, Judith *small business owner*
Young, Barbara *psychiatrist, psychotherapist, educator, photographer*

Barnesville
Pearcy, Susan Beth Due *artist, printmaker*

Bel Air
Cash, LaVerne (Cynthia Cash) *physicist*
Miller, Dorothy Eloise *education educator*
Phillips, Bernice Cecile Golden *retired vocational education educator*
Sanders, Virginia Hinckley *music educator*
Webster, Colleen Michael *language educator*
Wright, Tiffany Erin *secondary school educator*

Bel Alton
Quesada-Embid, Mary Regina Chamberlain *library media specialist*

Belcamp
Tapp, Mamie Pearl *educational association administrator*

Beltsville
Andre, Pamela Q. J. *library director*

Collins, Anita Marguerite *research geneticist*
Frank, Robyn Claire *librarian*
Johnson, Phyllis Elaine *chemist, researcher*
Palm, Mary Egdahl *mycologist*

Berlin
Auxer, Cathy Joan *elementary school educator*
Passwater, Barbara Gayhart *real estate broker*
Smith, Gloria Young *retired graphics designer*

Bethesda
Abdoo, Elizabeth A. *lawyer*
Alving, Barbara *federal agency administrator, hematologist*
Anderson, Stasia Ann *medical researcher*
Barros, Colleen *federal agency administrator*
Benson, Elizabeth Polk *art specialist*
Black, Barbara Onderchek *retired physician*
Block, Marian S. *lawyer*
Brinton, Louise A. *cancer epidemiologist*
Burns, Drusilla Lorene *microbiologist*
Child-Olmsted, Gisèle Alexandra *retired language educator*
Christian, Michaele Chamblee *internist, oncologist*
Coe, Judith Lynn *retired automobile manufacturing company administrator*
Cohen, Lois Ruth Kushner *health research consultant*
Comiskey, Angela Picariello *accountant*
Conger, Lucinda *retired librarian*
de Vries, Margaret Garritsen *economist*
Dignac, Geny (Eugenia M. Bermudez) *sculptor*
Drazin, Lisa *investment banker, financial consultant*
Ehrenfeld, Ellie (Elvera Ehrenfeld) *biologist, researcher*
Fee, Elizabeth *medical historian, administrator*
Fleming, Patricia Stubbs (Patsy Fleming) *artist*
Fraser, Catriona Trafford *art gallery director, photographer*
Gaarder, Marie *speech pathologist*
Gorin, Susan *medical association administrator*
Gottesman, Susan *federal agency administrator*
Grady, Patricia A. *federal agency administrator*
Grais, Alexandra *art appraiser, director*
Greenberg, Judith Horovitz *geneticist*
Guttman, Helene Nathan *biomedical consultant, transpersonal counselor*
Hagberg, Viola Wilgus *lawyer*
Haseltine, Florence Pat *obstetrician, gynecologist, medical association administrator*
Haugan, Gertrude M. *clinical psychologist*
Helke, Cinda Jane *pharmacology and neuroscience educator, researcher, academic administrator*
Herman, Edith Carol *journalist*
Herman, Mary Margaret *neuropathologist*
Hoyer, Mary Louise *social worker, educator*
Hrynkow, Sharon Hemond *federal agency administrator, neuroscientist, researcher*
Humphreys, Betsy L. *librarian*
Jaffe, Elaine Sarkin *pathologist*
Johnson, Joyce Marie *psychiatrist, public health service officer, epidemiologist*
Joyce, Bernita Anne *retired federal agency administrator*
Kaplan, Marjorie *broadcast executive*
Kawazoe, Robin Inada *federal official*
Kelly, Kathleen *medical researcher*
Kelty, Miriam Carol *psychologist, health science administrator*
Kirschstein, Ruth Lillian *physician*
Klatzkin, Terri *real estate company executive*
Klee, Claude Blenc *medical researcher*
Koenig, Elizabeth Barbara *sculptor*
Landis, Story Cleland *federal agency administrator, neurobiologist*
Lannan, Maura Anne Kelly *reporter*
Larrabee, Barbara Princelau *retired intelligence officer*
Lipkin, Bernice Sacks *computer scientist, educator*
Lystad, Mary Hanemann (Mrs. Robert Lystad) *sociologist, writer*
Mackall, Crystal L. *medical researcher*
Maguire, Joanne M. *aerospace transportation executive*
Mancher, Rhoda Ross *federal agency administrator, financial planner*
McHale, Judith A. (Judith Ottalloran) *broadcast executive, lawyer*
Mock, Beverly A. *geneticist, researcher*
Nabel, Elizabeth G. *cardiologist, researcher*
Naylor, Phyllis Reynolds *writer*
Nelson, Ethelyn Barnett *civic worker*
Nieves, Josephine *federal agency administrator*
Obrams, Gunta Iris *clinical research administrator*
Ostrander, Elaine A. *federal agency administrator, geneticist*
Parron, Delores L. *federal agency administrator*
Pinn, Vivian W. *federal agency administrator, pathologist*
Polsby, Gail K. *psychotherapist*
Rapoport, Judith *psychiatrist*
Reed, Berenice Anne *cultural organization administrator, educator, artist*
Robinson, Sharon Beth *health science association administrator*
Romero, Jane Patricia *nursing administrator*
Rudolph, Carol Ann Greenberg *human resource education consultant*
Ruiz-Bravo, Norka *federal agency administrator*
Ruttenberg, Ruth A. *economist*
Saffiotti, Paola *retired music educator, performing arts association administrator*
Sarnoff, Lili-Charlotte (Lolo Sarnoff) *artist*
Singer, Dinah S. *federal agency administrator, immunologist, researcher*
Skirboll, Lana R. *federal health policy director*
Spector, Eleanor Ruth *manufacturing executive*
Springfield, Sanya A. *federal agency administrator*
Sternberg, Esther May *neuroendocrinologist, immunologist, hematologist*
Storz, Gisela T. *research scientist*
Stover, Ellen L. *health scientist, psychologist*
Tanzi, Elizabeth Lyn *dermatologist*
Tilley, Carolyn Bittner *information scientist*
Underwood, Brenda S. *information specialist, microbiologist, grants administrator*
Ungerleider, Leslie G. *neuroscientist*
Vaitukaitis, Judith Louise *medical researcher*
Vaughan, Martha *biochemist, educator*
Volkow, Nora Dolores *medical researcher, director*
Vonderhaar, Barbara K. *medical researcher*
Wagner, Cynthia Gail *editor, writer*
Wickner, Sue Hengren *biochemist*
Wolpert-DeFilippes, Mary K. *science administrator*
Wood, Barbara Louise *psychologist*
Zoon, Kathryn Christine *biochemist*

Boonsboro
Algood, Laurie *performing arts educator*
Butler, Naomi Witmer *librarian, educator*

Bowie
Baker, Marshina *physical education educator*
Bohrer, Terezie S. *human service consultant*
Dingle, Patricia A. *education educator, artist*
Gourdine-Tyson, Natachia *investment company executive, writer*
Hillsman, Joan Rucker *music educator*
LeCounte, Lola Houston *literature and language professor, educational consultant*
Lewis, Patricia Ann *music educator*
Parr-Corretjer, Polly *singer, music educator*
Stancil, Donielle LaVelle *nursing administrator*
Tesar, Patricia Marie *academic coordinator*
Wardrip, Elizabeth Jane *retired librarian*

Boyds
Carpenter, Dorothy Schenck *retired special education educator*

Brandywine
Guiffre, Jean Ellen *shopping service company executive*
Johnson, Madge Richards *business owner, fundraiser, consultant*

Brookeville
Rico, Stephanie Allcock *art educator*

Burtonsville
Kammeyer, Sonia Margaretha *real estate agent*

Cabin John
Bergfors, Constance Marie *artist, educator*

Cambridge
Brohawn, Virginia Bridgeman *retired music educator*
Rihanna, (Robyn Rihanna Fenty) *singer, actress*
Spahr, Elizabeth *environmental research administrator*
Tenanty, Jane Elizabeth *secondary school educator*

Capitol Heights
Johnson, Ruth Floyd *educational consultant*

Catonsville
Diggs, Carol Beth *marketing professional*
Drees, Dedree Ann *computer graphics designer, educator, artist*
Marlatt, Patricia Anne *secondary school educator*
Oden, Gloria *language educator, poet*
Smith, F. Louise *elementary school educator*

Centreville
Shoemaker, Anne Cunningham *retired mathematics educator*

Chestertown
Costella, Lorraine Adele *state agency administrator*
Docksteader, Karen Kemp *marketing professional*
Rather, Lucia Porcher Johnson *library administrator*

Chevy Chase
Allison, Adrienne Amelia *not-for-profit developer*
Basa, Enikö Molnár *retired librarian*
Cline, Ruth Eleanor Harwood *translator*
Darr, Clarissa McCudden *psychiatric clinical nurse specialist*
Diamond, Karen Waltzer *small business owner, educator*
Glaser, Vera Romans *journalist*
Greenspoon, Irma Naiman *travel company executive*
Groner, Beverly Anne *retired lawyer*
Kranking, Margaret Graham *retired artist, educator*
Kullen, Shirley Robinowitz *psychiatric epidemiologist, consultant*
Lynn, D. Joanne *physician, researcher*
Norwood, Janet Lippe *economist*
Rich, Doris L. *writer*
Spagnoli, Deborah Ann *commissioner*
Towsner, Cynthia Merle *academic administrator, educator*
Wolf, Jean D. *educational consultant, writer*

Chillum
Malbon, Louise *nursing educator, hypnotherapist*

Churchton
Miller, Sandra Ritchie *artist, art therapist*

Clinton
Cruz, Wilhelmina Mangahas *critical care physician, educator*

Cockeysville
Hager, Louise Alger *retired chaplain*

Cockeysville Hunt Valley
Elkin, Lois Shanman *business systems company executive*
Roeder Vaughan, Mimi *small business owner*
Worthington, Joan Marie *information technology executive*

College Park
Beasley, Maurine Hoffman *journalism educator, historian*
Beharry, Avalaura Gaither *healer*
Brazile, Donna *advocate*
Buggs, Elaine S. *financial analyst*
Dreher, Mariam Jean *education educator*
Fenselau, Catherine Clarke *chemistry professor*
Finkelstein, Barbara *education educator*
Flieger, Verlyn B. *literature educator*
Frese, Brenda *women's college basketball coach*
Gratz, Kim L. *psychologist, researcher*
Hage, Madeleine Cottenet *French language educator*
Hill, Clara Edith *psychologist, educator*
Ingold, Catherine White *academic administrator*
Lathan, Corinna Elisabeth *aerospace engineer*
Lowrey, Barbara R. *educator, former federal official*
Lubkin, Gloria Becker *physicist*
MacKenzie, Doris Layton *psychologist, educator, researcher, criminologist*
Murdoch, Amelia Clara *educational association administrator*
Orlando, Valerie *language educator*
Oster, Rose Marie Gunhild *foreign language professional, educator*
Presser, Harriet Betty *social studies educator*
Sandra, Charlene Greer *educator*
Sorenson, Georgia Lynn Jones *political science professor*
Struna, Nancy L. *social historian, American studies educator*
White, Marilyn Domas *information science educator*
Younger, Deirdre Ann *pharmacist*

Colmar Manor
Stallworth, Monica Lavaughn *geriatrician*

Columbia
Abel, Florence Catherine Harris *social worker*
Blackwell-Taffel, Camellia Ann *art educator, consultant*
Button, Katy *professional athletics manager*
Carter, Karen Zepp *music educator, elementary school educator*
Davis, Janet Marie Gorden *secondary school educator*
Duncan, Mary Ellen *academic administrator*
Gregorie, Corazon Arzalem *operations research specialist*
Greyson D'Otazzo, Meaghan Regina *literary critic*
Hafets, Claire M. *assistant principal*
Hale, Mignon S. Palmer-Flack *elementary school educator, educator*
Harris, Marion Hopkins *retired federal official, academic administrator*
Hartman, Lee Ann Walraff *secondary school educator, consultant*
Hyde, Rebecca Medwin *financial consultant*
Jani, Sushma Niranjan *pediatric psychiatrist*
Jones-Wilson, Faustine Clarisse *retired education educator*
Klein, Sami Weiner *librarian*
Knapp, Patricia Ann *psychologist, educator*
Lok, Joan Mei-Lok *community affairs specialist, artist*
Mills, Ianther Marie *minister*
Narvaez, Bernice Williams *process engineer, consultant*
Piou-Brewer, Magalie *psychotherapist, educator, small business owner*
Said, Naima *lawyer*
Scates, Alice Yeomans *retired federal official*
Scornaienchi, Joan Webb *supervisor, consultant*
Spicknall, Joan *music educator*
Warren, Rita Simpson *manufacturing executive*

Cooksville
Wells, Christine Valerie *music educator*

Crownsville
Sonde, Susan *writer*

Cumberland
Fuller, Mary Baker *chemistry educator*

Damascus
Styer, Joanne Louise *retired dietician*

Davidsonville
Blaxall, Martha Ossoff *economist*
Bowles, Liza K. *construction executive*

Denton
Nelligan, Gloria Jean *science educator*

Derwood
Bouvē, Janet Saar *secondary school educator*
Holloman, Marilyn Leona Davis *non profit administrator, new product developer*
Mizes, Maria Gabriela *cultural organization administrator, art historian*
Stadtman, Thressa Campbell *biochemist*

Easton
Bugg, Carol Donayre *interior designer*
Colton, Elizabeth Wishart *government agency administrator*
Velisek, Caryl Anne *journalist*
Whitten, Nancy Bimmerman *clinical social worker, marriage therapist*
Wilson, Laura Ann *newspaper editor*

Edgewater
Whaley, Beth Dowling *retired elementary school educator*

Edgewood
Fox, Jennifer Joy *artist, educator*

Elkridge
Matthews, Lois Marr *musician, music educator*

Elkton
Jasinski-Caldwell, Mary L. *insurance company executive*
Mayer, Margaret Ellen *medical coding specialist*

Ellicott City
Estin-Klein, Libbyada *advertising executive, writer*
Michel, Donna Tonty *education educator*
Robison, Susan Miller *psychologist, speaker, consultant*
Tolliver, Sheila Maureen *university administrator, alderman*

Finksburg
Galanakis, Patricia Sarigianis *special education resource educator*

Forest Hill
Klein, Shirley Snyderman *retail executive*

Forestville
Brooks, Marsinah L. *performing arts educator*
Kazimer, Denise *secondary school educator*

Fort Washington
Cameron, Rita Giovannetti *writer, publishing executive*
Fielding, Elizabeth M(ay) *public relations executive, writer*

Frederick
Barone, Kristen Therese *elementary school educator*
Byron, Beverly Butcher *retired congresswoman*
Cannon, Faye E. *bank executive*
Colburn, Nancy Hall *medical researcher*
Curtis Craney, Karen B. *reading specialist*
DeCarlo, Mary Kathleen *elementary school educator*
Gordon, Rita Simon *civic leader, former nurse, educator*
Henderson, Madeline Mary (Berry Henderson) *chemist, researcher, consultant*
Hoffman, Jean Lillian *parochial school educator*
Hogan, Ilona Modly *lawyer*
Hoyer, Phyllis Scarborough *retired elementary education educator*
Klein, Elaine Charlotte *school system administrator*
Randall, Frances *technical writer*
Schricker, Ethel Killingsworth *retired business management consultant*
Smith, Sharron Williams *chemistry professor*

Friendship
Clagett, Diana Wharton Sinkler *museum docent*

Frostburg
Coward, Patricia Ann *language educator*
Gira, Catherine Russell *retired academic administrator*
Lynch, Diane *volunteer*
Lyon, Linda M. *biology professor*
Weatherford, Hazel Alice *minister*

Gaithersburg
Bobka, Marlene S. *publishing executive*
Celotta, Beverly Kay *psychologist*
Ebinger, Mary Ritzman *pastoral counselor*
Gloyd, Rita A. *retired social worker*
Green, Shia Toby Riner *psychotherapist*
Hegyeli, Ruth Ingeborg Elisabeth Johnsson *pathologist, federal official*
Jacox, Marilyn Esther *chemist*
Kemmerer, Sharon Jean *computer systems analyst*
Kress, Jill Clancy *human resources professional, consultant*
Moquin, Barbara E. *psychotherapist*
Raffini, Renee Kathleen *foreign language professional, educator*
Raymond, Sandra Lynn *elementary school educator*
Rosenblatt, Joan Raup *mathematical statistician*
Sengers, Johanna M. H. Levelt *physicist*
Stroud, Nancy Iredell *retired secondary school educator, freelance writer, editor*
Wang, Josephine Jung-Shan *language educator, translator*

Gambrills
Trimnal, Wanda Lee *secondary school educator*

Garrett Park
Stembel, Margery Joan *elementary school educator*
Stites, M(ary) Elizabeth *architecture educator*
Vargas, Lena Bessette *nursing administrator*

Germantown
Brunett, Miranda Jo *systems administrator*
Foulke, Judith Diane *health physicist*
Isaacson, Elaine Marie *insurance agent*
Ritter, Nadine M. *research scientist*
Sourk, Catherine Cleary *educational consultant*
Weiner, Claire Muriel *freelance writer*

Gibson Island
Hyde, Diana Caroline *retired real estate agent*

Glen Burnie
Baillie, Miranda Lee *secondary school educator*
Barteet, Barbara Boyter *retired social worker*
Endres, Eleanor Estelle *speech pathology/audiology services professional*
Hofmann, Carole P. *bank executive*
Watts, Virginia Agnes *retired special education educator*

Goldsboro
Hutson Councell, Janet Kern *retired secondary school educator*

Grasonville
Ciotola, Linda Ann Miller *lifestyle counselor*

Great Mills
Gehring, Patti J. *principal*

Greenbelt
Amato, Deborah Douglass *aerospace engineer*
Cooper, Sharon Croft *aerospace engineer*
Ericsson, Aprille *aerospace engineer*
LaMarca, Mary Margaret *elementary school educator*
Maynard, Nancy Gray *biological oceanographer*
Moore, Virginia Bradley *librarian*
Obamogie, Mercy A. *physician*
Poland, Alison *artist*
Simpson, Joanne Malkus *meteorologist*
Wagner, Sally Sterrett *music educator*

Gwynn Oak
Hughes, Catherine L. (Cathy Hughes) *radio personality, broadcast executive*

Hagerstown
Corbett, Helen A. *chemist, chemical engineer*

Harrison, Lois Smith *hospital executive, educator*
Hatch, Sally Ruth *foundation administrator, writer, consultant*
Higgins, M. Eileen *management consultant, educator*

Hampstead
Holbrook, Jennifer Lynn *elementary school educator*
Howells, Martha Louise *secondary school educator*
Keogh, Molly Duffy *education educator, consultant*

Hanover
Henderson Hall, Brenda Ford *computer company executive*
Schmidt, Sandra Jean *secondary school educator*
Turner, Valarie English *electronics company administrator*

Harwood
Smith, Maria Lynn *school system administrator*

Havre De Grace
Reid, Susan G. *music educator*
Soldunias, Bernadette Louise *psychiatrist*
Wetter, Virginia Forwood Pate *broadcast executive*

Highland
Varga, Deborah Trigg *music educator, entertainment company owner*

Hollywood
Dietz, Laurel Patricia *music educator*

Hunt Valley
Downs, Mary Alane *lawyer*

Hurlock
Shively, Bonnie Lee *pastor*

Hyattsville
Dukes, Rebecca Weathers (Becky Dukes) *musician, singer, song writer*
Golden, Marita *English language educator, foundation executive*
Rodgers, Mary Columbro *literature educator, writer, academic administrator*
Shinolt, Eileen Thelma *artist*

Ijamsville
Thompson, Jaime Lynn *social studies educator*

Indian Head
Layton, Georgianna Vicik *mathematics educator*

Jefferson
Aughenbaugh, Deborah Ann *mayor, retired elementary school educator*
Ward, Susan Annette *music educator*

Joppa
Bates, Martha Copenhaver *elementary school educator*
Chase, Jaclyn Bosworth *secondary school educator*
Short, Judith Arduino *media specialist, educator*

Kensington
Mintz, Suzanne *association executive*

La Plata
Herdman-Fisher, Carolyn A. *music educator*
Mazzeo, Betty Teresa *music educator*
Stephanic, Barbara Jean *art historian, writer, curator, researcher*
Tubb, Elaine Ann *secondary school educator*

Landover
Frederick, Amy L. *science administrator*
Grasselli, Margaret Morgan *curator*

Landover Hills
Moreno, Renee Teresa *education educator*

Lanham
Eckard Vilardo, Linda J. *lawyer*
Godwin, Mary Jo *editor, librarian, consultant*

Lanham Seabrook
Barnes, Margaret Anderson *minister, statistician*
Corrothers, Helen Gladys *criminal justice official*
Moore, Erica *band director*
Ojinnaka, Becky *publishing executive*
Southall, Virginia Lawrence *retired artist*

Largo
Falkey, Mary E. *finance educator*
Ryan, Carol J. *educational administrator*

Laurel
Hammond, Deborah Lynn *lay worker*
Highman, Barbara *dermatologist*
Landis, Donna Marie *nursing administrator, women's health nurse*
Logsdon, Roslyn *artist, educator*

Laytonsville
Holland, Christie Anna *biochemist, virologist*

Lothian
Messenger, Barbara Beall *artist*

Lusby
Fialka, Deborah Ridgely *writer*

Lutherville
Goodman, Valerie Dawson *psychiatric social worker*
Smith, Michelle Sun *psychologist*
Weiss, Susan Forscher *musicologist, educator*

Lutherville Timonium
Brown, Ellyn L. *lawyer, consultant*
Krasevac, Esther *retired academic administrator*
Richmond, Lee Joyce *psychologist, educator*

Madison
Hoffman, Alicia Coro *retired federal executive*

Manokin
Miles, Elizabeth Jane *social worker*

McHenry
Biser, Elizabeth Grant *counselor, director*

Mcdaniel
Roth, Lisa Mae *writer*

Millersville
Culver, Catherine Marie *secondary school educator*
Liimatta, Janet Ann *mathematics educator*

Mitchellville
Chilman, Catherine Earles Street *social welfare educator, author*
Grier Wallen, Mary Elizabeth *retired psychologist*
Marsh, Caryl Amsterdam *retired curator, retired psychologist*

Montgomery Village
Wykes, Mary Maushak *real estate agent*

Mount Airy
Johnston, Josephine Rose *chemist*
Lemke, Jill *city planner*

Newburg
Mason, Christine Chapman *psychotherapist*

North East
Goldbach, Jennifer DeBerdine *bank executive*
Olsen, V. Beth Kuser *science educator*
Roney, Sarah Gordon *dancer, educator*

North Potomac
Menendez, Shirley Corbin *writer*

Ocean City
Showell, Ann Lockhart *small business owner*

Ocean Pines
Fullerton, Jean Leah *retired language educator, researcher, census researcher*

Odenton
Lambert, Vickie Ann *retired dean, nursing consultant*
Lundy, Sheila Edwards *lawyer*

Olney
Hails, Barbara Geldermann *artist*
Mardis, Linda Keiser *music educator, writer*
Sodetz, Carol Jean *aquatic fitness educator*
van den Berg, Elizabeth *actress, educator*

Owings
O'Neill, Patricia Tydings *performing arts educator, language educator*

Owings Mills
Adedeji, Sharon Lilly *literature and language educator*
Berg, Barbara Kirsner *health education specialist*
Fortuin, Diane Hay *historian, researcher*
Holdridge, Barbara *book editor, writer, consultant*
Johnson-Cohen, Yevonne B. *minister, counselor*
Oleisky, Deborah Fischer *elementary school educator*
Ryan, Judith W. *geriatrics nurse, educator*
Simmers, Andrea Jean *elementary school educator*
Smith, Katrina Diane *writer*

Pasadena
Bell, Patricia Wright *music educator*
De Pauw, Linda Grant *historian, educator, writer*
Kuhn, Jolyn *artist*

Perry Hall
Petchik, Marian *mathematics educator*

Perryville
Dunne, Judith Doyle *information scientist, educator*

Pikesville
Putzel, Constance Kellner *lawyer*
Sokol, Marian *medical association administrator*

Pocomoke City
Giles, Debra B. *gifted and talented educator*

Poolesville
Noble, Pamela Lee *primatologist*

Port Tobacco
Smith, Sheila Robertson *laboratory technician*

Potomac
Anfinsen, Libby Esther Shulman *social worker, clinical administrator*
Carper, Fern Gayle *small business owner, writer*
Dickerman, Serafina Poerio *real estate broker, consultant*
Eaves, Maria Perry *realtor*
Gaston, Marilyn Hughes *health facility administrator*
Hart, Betty Miller *artist*
Kuykendall, Crystal Arlene *educational consultant, lawyer*
Medin, Julia Adele *mathematics professor, researcher*
Murow, Christine *music educator*
Pastan, Linda Olenik *poet*
Peters, Carol Beattie Taylor (Mrs. Frank Albert Peters) *mathematician*
Roesser, Jean Wolberg *state official*
Rosenberg, Sarah Zacher *retired cultural organization administrator*
Rotberg, Iris Comens *social scientist*
Sceery, Beverly Davis *genealogist, writer, educator*
Sowalsky, Patti Lurie *author*
Sundick, Sherry Small *journalist, writer, poet*
Vadus, Gloria A. *scientific document examiner*

Yerman, Anne Veronica *interior designer*

Prince Frederick
Adams, Cheryl Palonis *secondary school educator, dancer, choreographer*
Galligan, Caitlin Maureen *elementary school educator*
Love, Margaret Wynn *physical education educator*

Princess Anne
Brockett, Ramona *criminologist, educator*
du Nord, Jeanne *writer, publishing executive*
Thompson, Thelma Barnaby *university president, classical languages educator*

Pylesville
Mullen, Lisa Caitlin *elementary school educator*

Reisterstown
Bart, Polly Turner *construction executive*
Besser, Sandra Herman *school nurse practitioner*
Goethe, Elizabeth Hogue *music educator*
Holley-Allen, Lauren Allana *psychologist*
Singer, Paula M. *management consultant*
Tirone, Barbara Jean *retired health insurance administrator*

Riverdale
Bernard, Cathy S. *management corporation executive*
Lippincott, Janet *artist, art educator*
Smith, Carmela Vito *administrator, counselor, educator*

Rock Hall
Mariner, Linda Ketterman *minister*

Rockville
Abron, Lilia A. *chemical engineer*
Boetticher, Helene *retired lawyer*
Cain, Karen Mirinda *musician, educator*
Cheston, Sheila Carol *lawyer*
Clancy, Carolyn M. *internist, federal agency administrator*
Cornelius, Maria G. *financial advisor*
Davis, Beverly Watts *federal agency administrator*
Duke, Elizabeth M. *federal agency administrator*
Fraser-Liggett, Claire M. *research scientist, science administrator*
Gray, Paulette Styles *federal agency administrator, biologist*
Haffner, Marlene Elisabeth *internist, public health administrator*
Hambleton, Betty Beall *public health administrator*
Hamilton, Parker *library director*
Hammond, Brenda Hines *elementary school educator*
Hodgson, Helen *writer*
Kiger, F. Louise *nursing administrator*
Kohlhorst, Gail Lewis *librarian*
Kopf, Randi *family and oncology nurse practitioner, lawyer*
Kurkul, Wen Wang *musician, educator, administrator*
MacArthur, Diana Taylor *advanced technology executive*
Marcuccio, Phyllis Rose *retired educational association administrator, editor*
Massie, Tammy Jeanne Parliment *statistician*
Messersmith, Stephanie Hunt *nursing administrator*
Miller, Claire Ellen *editor, educator, writer*
Moses, Cynthia Glass *realtor*
Mummaneni, Padmaja *research scientist, educator*
Murray, Mary Rose *securities regulation investigator*
Nay, Patricia Tomsko *medical association administrator*
Niewiaroski, Trudi Osmers (Gertrude Niewiaroski) *social studies educator*
O'Donnell, Duck Hee *cellist, music teacher*
Parham-Hopson, Deborah *health programs administrator*
Petzold, Carol Stoker *state legislator*
Power, A. Kathryn *federal agency administrator*
Pryor, Shannon Penick *otolaryngologist*
Raker, Irma S. *judge*
Rasmussen, Caren Nancy *health facility administrator*
Renninger, Mary Karen *retired librarian*
Robinson, Cheryl Jeffreys *special education educator*
Saljinska-Markovic, Olivera T. *oncology researcher, educator*
Schoenbrun, Lois *medical association administrator*
Scinto, Carol Murdock *writer, editor, social worker*
Shields, Julie Seligson *psychologist, entrepreneur*
Snyder, A. Michelle *federal agency administrator*
Solomon, Deborah *application developer, educator, lawyer*
Standing, Kimberly Anna *researcher*
Uhl, Kathleen *federal agency administrator*
Weinel, Pamela Jean *nurse administrator*
Woodcock, Janet *federal official*

Rosedale
Maskell, Kathleen Mary *English and reading educator*
Stearns, Ann Kaiser *psychologist, educator, writer*

Royal Oak
Israel, Lesley Lowe *retired political scientist*

Saint James
Duncan, Tanya Nicole *school athletic trainer*

Saint Marys City
Clifton, Lucille Thelma *author*
O'Brien, Jane Margaret *academic administrator*
Williams, Elizabeth Nutt *psychologist, educator*

Salisbury
Chen, Xingzhi Mara *science educator*
Loar, Sheila Rae *small business owner*
Shockley, Theresa Schisler *medical/surgical nurse*

Sandy Spring
Sinclair, Clara Mill *retired science educator*

Savage
Hicks, Karen T. *mathematician*

Severna Park
Hall, Marcia Joy *non-profit organization administrator*
Humphreys Troy, Patricia *communications executive*
Pumphrey, Janet Kay *editor, publishing executive*
Wade, Earline *elementary school educator*
Wilkins, Virginia Kathleen *government liason*
Windsor, Patricia (Katonah Summertree, Perrin Winters, Anna Seeling) *author, educator, lecturer*

Silver Spring
Adams, Diane Loretta *physician*
Altschul, B. J. *public relations counselor*
Aranya, Gwendalin Qi *painter, priest, educator*
Arvin, Linda Lee *counselor*
Baskerville, Lezli *educational association administrator*
Bate, Marilyn Anne *psychologist*
Beard, Lillian B. McLean *pediatrician, consultant*
Becker, Sandra Neiman Hammer *lawyer*
Bennett, Carol(ine) Elise *retired reporter, actress*
Blakeney, Barbara A. *public health service officer*
Bonner, Bester Davis *school system administrator*
Borkovec, Vera Z. *literature and language professor*
Brandt, Elsa Lund Erickson *music educator*
Brush, Julianna R. *marine biologist*
Bundy Farah, Santha Rarna Rau *science educator*
Burgos-Sasscer, Ruth *chancellor emeritus*
Burke, Margaret Ann *computer company executive, communications executive*
Carter-Johnson, Jean Evelyn *management consultant*
Clark, Julia L. Akins *labor union administrator, lawyer*
Clark, Mizzell Phillips (Mitzi Clark) *school librarian*
Coles, Anna Louise Bailey *retired dean, nurse*
Compton, Mary Beatrice Brown (Mrs. Ralph Theodore Compton) *public relations executive, writer*
Cooper, Nannie Coles *education educator, consultant*
de Zafra Atwell, Dorothea Elizabeth *retired government agency administrator*
Efron, Rosalyn Esther *special education educator*
Fay, Laurel Ann *marriage and family therapist*
Fickenscher, Dorothy (Debbie) E.B. *secondary school educator*
Fields, Daisy Bresley *human resources specialist, writer*
Foley, Mary E. *medical association administrator, nursing administrator*
Gandy, Kim Allison *feminist organization executive, lawyer*
Guzman, Martha Patricia *science educator*
Hay, Janisann *secondary school educator*
Hunt, Mary Elizabeth *religious studies educator*
Johnson, Cheryl L. *nursing administrator*
Kant, Gloria Jean *retired neuroscientist*
Kark, Victoria A. *open heart clinical specialist*
Kline, Syril Levin *writer, educator, educational consultant*
Lett, Cynthia Ellen Wein *customer service administrator*
Makris, Margaret Lubbe *elementary school educator*
Mashin, Jacqueline Ann Cook *health facility administrator, consultant*
Miller, Karla Patricia *elementary school educator*
Miller, Kendra Danette *art services business owner, consultant*
Mohr, Christina *retired economist*
Montalvo, Eileen *communications executive*
Moon, Marilyn Lee *economist*
Null, Elisabeth Higgins *librarian, editor*
O'Connell, Mary Ita *psychotherapist*
Oliver, Kimberly *Teacher of the Year*
Papas, Irene Kalandros *English language educator, poet, writer*
Ramsey, Priscilla R. *literature educator*
Rayburn, Carole Ann (Mary Aida) *psychologist, researcher, writer, consultant*
Rice, Michelle *communications executive*
Rivera-Sinclair, Elsa *psychologist, consultant, researcher*
Roth, Harriet Steinhorn *advocate, educator, public speaker*
Sammet, Jean E. *computer scientist*
Supanich, Barbara Ann *physician*
Vanzant, Iyanla *writer*
Wormack, Karen Elise *small business owner, poet*

Simpsonville
Altschuler, Ruth Phyllis *realtor, secondary school educator*

Sparks
Suarez-Murias, Marguerite C. *retired literature and language professor*

Springdale
Keith, Patricia *multi-media specialist*

Stevenson
Hyman, Mary Bloom *science education programs coordinator*

Sykesville
Crist, Gertrude H. *civic worker*
Perry, Nancy Trotter *retired telecommunications company executive*

Takoma Park
Conroy, Sarah Booth *columnist, writer, educator*
Gumaer, Amy Arnold *academic administrator*
von Hake, Margaret Joan *librarian*

Thurmont
Stitely, Karen Richardson *performing arts educator*

Towson
Ahearn, Elizabeth Lowe *performing arts educator*
Baker, Jean Harvey *history professor*

Boyle, Marcia *medical association administrator*
Chase, Jacquelyn Veronica *marketing professional*
Koetter, Cornelia M. *lawyer*
McCartney, Alison Rios Millett *political science professor*
Myers, Debra Taylor *elementary school educator, writer*
Nicolosi, Gianna Ruth *marketing professional*
Orlinsky, Diane Julie *dermatologist*
Pantzer, Mairee D. *music educator, director*
Tatman, Sandra L. *design educator*
Uhrich, Tabatha A. *education educator*
Williams, Tara Lyn *psychologist*

Trappe
Burns-Bowie, Maureen Elizabeth *sculptor*

Union Bridge
Hannah, Judy Challenger *private education tutor*

University Park
Holder, Sallie Lou *training and meeting management consultant, coach*

Upper Marlboro
Brown, Mary Louvinia *literature and language professor, lawyer*
Greene, Monica Lynn Banks *psychologist*
Hewlett, Elizabeth M. *county official*
Jones-Lukács, Elizabeth Lucille *physician*
Rough, Marianne Christina *librarian, educator*
Street, Patricia Lynn *retired secondary school educator*
Zane, *writer, publishing executive*

Waldorf
Alo, Theresa Reneé *secondary school educator, potter*
Bouchard, Lynne Katherine *music educator*
Raiman, Rosemary A. *advocate*
Robey, Sherie Gay Southall Gordon *secondary school educator, consultant*
Schwier, Patricia Branscome *science educator, department chairman*

West Bethesda
Vogelgesang, Sandra Louise *former ambassador, writer, consultant*

West River
Bower, Catherine Downes *management consultant*
Howl, Joanne Healey *veterinarian, writer*
Pratt, Katherine Merrick *environmental consulting company executive*

Westernport
Morgan, Sharon Lynn *principal*

Westminster
Coley, Joan Develin *education educator, academic administrator*
Erb, Betty Jane *retired real estate agent*
Mesta, Pamela Anne *supervisor, consultant*
Pappalardo, Faye *academic administrator*
Stoetzer, Kristen Gottleib *music educator*

Westover
Dougherty, Barbara Lee *artist, writer*

Wheaton
Folsom, Rose *calligrapher, writer, artist*
White, Martha Vetter *allergist, immunologist*

Woodbine
Nuss, Barbara Gough *artist*

MASSACHUSETTS

Abington
Delaplain, Laura Zuleme *psychologist*
Harrington, Joyce D. *music educator*

Agawam
Goodwin, Beverly Ann *elementary school educator*

Allston
FitzGibbon, Katherine Lenore *conductor, music educator*
Spencer, Lara *television personality, journalist*

Amesbury
Dowd, Frances Connelly *retired librarian*

Amherst
Aizen, Rachel K. *clinical psychologist*
Backes, Ruth Emerson *counseling psychologist*
Baker, Lynne Rudder *philosophy educator*
Barrett, Lora McNeece *art educator, artist*
Benson, Lucy Wilson *historian, consultant*
Brooks, A. Taeko *historian*
Deer Cloud, Susan Ann *writer*
Donohue, Therese Brady *artistic director, choreographer, costume and set designer*
Dunbar, Sue *music educator*
Elman, Naomi Geist *artist, theater producer*
Hopman, Ellen Evert *psychotherapist, author and herbalist*
Keen, Rachel *psychology professor*
Mac Donald, Marian Louise *psychologist, educator*
MacKnight, Carol Bernier *educational association administrator*
Margulis, Lynn (Lynn Alexander) *evolutionist, educator*
Mills, Patricia Jagentowicz *philosophy scholar, educator, writer*
Reed, Daphne Stevenson *artist*
Romney, Patricia Ann *psychologist, educator*
Rossi, Alice S. *sociology educator, writer*
Rudman, Masha Kabakow *education educator, author, consultant*
Sandweiss, Martha Ann *writer, history professor*
Seymour, Charlena *academic administrator*
Strickland, Bonnie Ruth *psychologist, educator*
Taubman, Jane Andelman *literature and language professor*
Whaples, Miriam Karpilow *music educator*

Andover
Braverman, Carole Gae *literature and language educator*
Nicolson, Christina Carrell *elementary school educator*

Arlington
Immanuel, Laura Amelia *dentist*
Samuelson, Joan Benoit *professional runner*
Stein, Miriam *social worker, training services executive*
Zimmer, Anna Held *social worker*

Ashfield
Leete, Elisabeth Bourquin *retired language educator*

Auburn
Allard, Marvel June *psychology educator, researcher*
Giannini, Antoinette Frances *music educator, researcher*
Mitchell, Karen Lee *special education educator, consultant*

Auburndale
Gulbrandsen, Natalie Webber *religious association administrator*
Kibrick, Anne *retired nursing educator, dean*

Babson Park
Lindsey-Mullikin, Joan *education educator, researcher*

Barnstable
Grodecki, Merrilyn *private school educator*
Lummus, Carol Travers *artist, printmaker*

Bedford
Herlihy, Maura Ann *medical technician*
Kampits, Eva *accrediting association administrator, educator*
Ryser, Carol Pierson *psychologist*

Belmont
Baddour, Anne Bridge *pilot*
Hanfling, Sue Carol (Suki Hanfling) *social worker*
Levine, Sarah Loewenberg *developmental psychologist, school director*
McEvoy, Frances Jane Coman *writer, editor*

Bernardston
Peoples, Marie D. *writer*

Beverly
Broderick, Jo Stewart *academic administrator*
Hart, Claire-Marie *secondary school educator*

Billerica
Barnes, Shirley Moore *retired psychiatric social worker, genealogist*

Bolton
Keane, Karen M. *auction house executive*

Boston
Abbott, Susan L. *lawyer*
Ablow, Roz Karol (Roselyn Karol Ablow) *painter, curator*
Abraham, Melissa E. *psychologist*
Abrahm, Janet Lee *hematologist, oncologist, educator, palliative care specialist*
Adams, Lisa *lawyer*
Agajanian, Anita Shakeh *lawyer*
Allen, Nancy Schuster *librarian, director information resources*
Allen, Rosemary M. *lawyer*
Allinson, Deborah Louise *economist*
Amatangel, Lisa *lawyer*
Anderson, Jewelle Lucille *musician, educator*
Andrews, Sally May *academic administrator*
Angell, Marcia *pathologist, editor-in-chief*
Angelou, Maya (Marguerite Annie Johnson) *writer, actress*
Antman, Karen H. *oncologist, educator, dean*
Appelbaum, Diana Karter *author*
Arrowood, Lisa Gayle *lawyer*
Asai, Susan Miyo *music educator, consultant*
Ash, Barbara Lee *education and human services educator*
Bachman, Katharine Elizabeth *lawyer*
Bacon, A. Smoki *television host*
Baker, Adrienne Marie *lawyer*
Baker, Hollie L. *lawyer*
Bakhshi, Nandita *bank executive*
Bapooji Ryan, Anita B. *lawyer*
Barnard, Deborah E. *lawyer*
Barnett, Jessica Vincent *lawyer*
Basil, Michelle L. *lawyer*
Bassil, Janice *lawyer*
Bavaria, Joan *finance company executive*
Beinfeld, Margery Cohen *neurobiology educator*
Bergstrom, Joan Margosian *education educator*
Berkman, Lisa F. *public health educator*
Berliner, Wendy Alissa *lawyer*
Bhatt, Manisha Hemendra *lawyer*
Bierman, Aimee Elizabeth *lawyer*
Bigby, JudyAnn *medical educator*
Bills, Jennifer Leah *lawyer*
Boehs, Sarah Teachworh *lawyer*
Bonauto, Mary *lawyer*
Bourque, Louise *film director, film instructor*
Bowler, Marianne Bianca *federal judge*
Browne, Marijane Leila Benner *lawyer*
Bruce, Maryann *bank executive*
Brugge, Joan S. *medical educator*
Bucci, Mary D. *lawyer*
Bunker, Beryl H. *retired insurance company executive, volunteer*
Burnett, Elizabeth B. *lawyer*
Burns, Catherine L. *lawyer*
Caldeira, Charlene A. *lawyer*
Caldwell, Ann Wickins *academic administrator*
Caldwell, Gail *book critic*
Canavan, Christine Estelle *state legislator*
Candela, Vanessa English *lawyer*
Cantor, Mira *artist, educator*
Caperna, Lisa Maria *lawyer*
Carr, Lisa Diane *lawyer*
Carroll, Jill *freelance journalist*
Carson, Jeniffer A.P. *lawyer*
Casal, Eileen *lawyer*
Cazabon, Rebecca Maria *lawyer*
Celestino-Arguinzoni, Wilma *academic administrator*
Chandler, Harriette Levy *state legislator, management consultant, educator*
Chandler, Robin Mary *artist, educator, writer*
Chang, Hemmie *lawyer*
Chapon, Eunice Kim *lawyer*
Chen, Ching-chih *information science educator, consultant*
Cherry, Sarah Kathryn *lawyer*
Christopher, Irene *librarian, consultant*
Chu, Sylvia *lawyer*
Chunias, Jennifer Lynn *lawyer*
Clendenning, Bonnie Ryon *college administrator*
Cohen, Rachelle Sharon *journalist*
Cone, Carol Lynn *public relations executive*
Connolly, Sarah Thiemann *lawyer*
Cornell, Deborah A. *artist, educator*
Costello, Katharine Pacella *lawyer*
Coville, Andrea *public relations executive*
Cowin, Judith Arnold *state supreme court judge*
Craig, Patricia *voice educator, opera singer*
Creedon, Geraldine *state legislator*
Creem, Cynthia Stone *state legislator, lawyer*
Crimlisk, Jane Therese *probation officer*
Cronin, Bonnie Kathryn Lamb *museum director*
Curran, Emily Katherine *museum director*
Daniels, Cara J. *lawyer*
Daum, Caryn Lynn *lawyer*
Deissler, Mary Alice *foundation executive*
DeJuneas, Patricia Ann *lawyer*
Delahanty, Linda Michele *dietician*
Del Sesto, Janice Mancini *opera company executive*
Desnoyers, Megan Floyd *archivist, educator*
Dimmitt, Cornelia *psychologist, educator*
Dluhy, Deborah Haigh *dean*
Dohoney, Michaela S. *lawyer*
Domini, Amy Lee *portfolio manager*
Donahoe, Patricia Kilroy *surgeon*
Donovan, Helen W. *newspaper editor*
Dreben, Raya Spiegel *judge*
Dujon, Diane Marie *director, advocate*
Duncan, Lyn M. *pathologist, educator*
Dwyer, Johanna Todd *nutritionist, educator*
Eckstein, Marlene R. *vascular radiologist*
Eder, Esther Garcia *artist*
Edwards, MJ *lawyer*
Egan, Jan Wenning *lawyer*
Emerson, Anne Devereux *museum administrator*
Epstein, Elaine May *lawyer*
Ericson, Elizabeth (Zibby) *architect*
Esper, Susan *diversified financial services company executive*
Feeney, Joan N. *judge*
Fergus, Katherine Young *lawyer*
Ferrera, Vinita *lawyer*
Fertitta, Angela *dean*
Fesko, Colleene *art appraiser*
Fiacco, Barbara A. *lawyer*
Finucane, Anne M. *communications executive, marketing executive*
Flaherty, Lois Talbot *editor, psychiatrist, educator*
Fleming, Darien K.S. *lawyer*
Fletcher, Carrie J. *lawyer*
Flynn, Gina Perez *lawyer*
Flynn-Poppey, Elissa *lawyer*
Fremont-Smith, Marion R. *lawyer*
Friedman, Paula Konowitch *dentist, academic administrator*
Furey, Jennifer B. *lawyer*
Furnald, Lisa Anne *lawyer*
Gagan, Sarah K. *lawyer*
Galligan, Lynda T. *lawyer*
Garcia, Grace V. Bacon *lawyer*
Garvin, Michele M. *lawyer*
Gerlovin, Samantha Leigh *lawyer*
Gibbs, Laura Elizabeth *lawyer*
Gilchrest, Barbara Ann *dermatologist*
Giner, A. Silvana *lawyer*
Gipson, Ilene Kay *ophthalmologist, educator*
Glasgow, Jordana Berkowitz *lawyer*
Gleason, Jean Berko *psychology professor*
Goldberg, Lena G. *lawyer, investment company executive*
Goldie, Sue J. *health service researcher*
Goldstein, Jane D. *lawyer*
Goody, Joan Edelman *architect*
Gordon, Cecelia T. *lawyer*
Gormley, Pamela D. *controller*
Gottlieb, Alice B. *dermatologist*
Goumnerova, Liliana Christova *physician, neurosurgeon, educator*
Greaney, Jennifer Ellen *lawyer*
Green, Karen F. *lawyer*
Grimes, Heilan Yvette *publishing executive*
Grossman, Frances Kaplan *psychologist*
Haddad, Lisa R. *lawyer*
Haight, Geri L. *lawyer*
Hamel, Suzanne Patrice *lawyer*
Hardy, Jennifer Beth *lawyer*
Hardy, Victoria Elizabeth *finance educator*
Harris, Gayle Elizabeth *bishop*
Harris, Kari K. *lawyer*
Harris, Maia H. *lawyer*
Harvey, Virginia Smith *psychologist, educator*
Hawley, Anne *museum director*
Hay, Elizabeth Dexter *embryologist, educator*
Healey, Kerry Murphy *lieutenant governor*
Hebard, Barbara Adams *conservator*
Hedges, Jessica Diane *lawyer*
Henry, Kathleen Cloherty *lawyer*
Herlihy, Jennifer Boyd *lawyer*
Herman, Kimberly B. *lawyer*
Hershey, Nona *artist, printmaker, educator*
Hertel, Jaime S. *lawyer*
Hertz, Jennifer L. *lawyer*
Herzlinger, Regina *economist, educator, writer*
Hesse, Julia Rush *lawyer*
Hills, Patricia Gorton Schulze *curator, art historian*
Hoey, Laura Gaffney *lawyer*
Hogan, Julie A. *lawyer*
Holt, Amanda C. *lawyer*
Howard, Sheryl Andrea *lawyer*
Howe, Janice W. *lawyer*
Howitt-Easton, Deborah *lawyer*
Iezzoni, Lisa I. *medical educator, healthcare educator, researcher*
Janos, Ellen L. *lawyer*
Jarrell, Brenda Herschbach *lawyer*
Jehlen, Patricia D. *state legislator*
Jochum, Veronica *pianist*
Johnson, Abigail Pierrepont *investment company executive*
Johnston, Susan A. *lawyer*
Jurgensen LaCivita, Mary R. *lawyer*
Kahn, Barbara B. *endocrinologist*
Katsoulomitis, Georgia *foundation administrator, lawyer*
Kaufman, Vicki *civil rights investigator*
Kay, Jane Holtz *writer*
Kearns, Ellen Cecelia *lawyer*
Kennedy, Louise Avery *theater critic, newspaper editor, writer*
Kessler, Diane Cooksey *religious organization administrator, minister*
Kim, Hazel *public relations executive*
Kindl, Patrice *writer*
King, Lynda Anne Whitlow *psychologist, educator*
Klieman, Rikki Jo *lawyer, legal analyst*
Kopell, Nancy *mathematician, education educator*
Krolewski, Bozena K. *molecular biologist, researcher, cell biologist*
LaForgia, Jeanne Ellen *performing arts educator*
Lahiri, Jhumpa (Nilanjana Sudeshna) *writer*
Lane, Kathy S. *information technology executive, consumer products company executive*
Lange, Maggie A. *lawyer*
Lawrence, Merloyd Ludington *editor*
LeBlanc, Marianne Camille *lawyer*
Lee, Grace H. *lawyer*
Leeman, Susan Epstein *neuroscientist, educator*
Lerner, Linda Joyce *human resources executive*
Liebergott, Jacqueline W. *academic administrator*
Ling, Chiew Sing *investment company executive*
Liotta, Jeanne *film director, film instructor*
Lowenstein, Arlene Jane *nursing educator, health facility administrator*
Lowry, Lois (Lois Hammersberg) *writer*
Lukey, Joan A. *lawyer*
Lynch, Sandra Lea *federal judge*
Manson, JoAnn Elisabeth *endocrinologist*
Marshall, Margaret Hilary *state supreme court chief justice*
Martin, Jacqueline Briggs *writer*
Masi, Dale A. *project director, social sciences educator, research and development company executive*
Mathis, Diane *cell biologist, educator*
McArdle, Patricia Anne *security company executive*
McChesney, S. Elaine *lawyer*
McColgan, Ellyn *investment company executive*
McCormick, Marie Clare *pediatrician, educator*
McDonald, Jane Theresa *athletic trainer, educator*
McGovern, Lore Harp *communications executive, philanthropist*
McIlvain, Isabel *sculptor, art educator*
McNamee, Linda Rose *broadcast executive*
McPhee, Joan *lawyer*
Medvedow, Jill *museum director*
Meisner, Mary Jo *foundation administrator, former newspaper editor*
Messing, Ellen Jean *lawyer*
Meyer, Fremonta Lee *psychiatrist*
Michon, Katherine J. *lawyer*
Miller, Michelle D. *lawyer*
Minehan, Cathy Elizabeth *bank executive*
Misra, Madhusmita *pediatric neuroendocrinologist, educator*
Montgomery, Susan Barbieri *lawyer*
Morby, Jacqueline *venture capitalist*
Morgan, Elise Feng-i *science educator*
Mulvey, Elizabeth N. *lawyer*
Murley, Susan W. *lawyer*
Nadelson, Carol Cooperman *psychiatrist, educator*
Nour, Nawal M. *obstetrician, gynecologist, health facility administrator*
Ocko, Stephanie *writer, journalist*
O'Connell, Mary-Kathleen *lawyer*
O'Donnell, Kathleen Marie *lawyer*
O'Hern, Jane Susan *psychologist, educator*
O'Rourke, Maureen A. *dean, law educator*
Ouellette, Eileen Marie *neurologist, consultant*
Paine, Lynn *academic administrator*
Painter, Pamela *writer, educator*
Parker, Olivia *photographer*
Peirce, Georgia Wilson *public relations executive*
Peisch, Alice Hanlon *state legislator*
Penney, Sherry Hood *academic administrator, consultant*
Pisa, Regina Marie *lawyer*
Piscatelli, Nancy Kelley *elementary school educator*
Plimpton, Leslie Kloville *lawyer*
Prothrow-Stith, Deborah *academic administrator, public health educator*
Ratner, Marcia *research scientist*
Reede, Joan Yvonne *academic administrator, medical educator, pediatrician*
Reinherz, Helen Zarsky *social worker, researcher*
Richmond, Alice Elenor *lawyer*
Robinson, Andrea J. *lawyer*
Rodman, Sarah *music critic*
Rogeness, Mary Speer *state legislator*
Ropple, Lisa M. *lawyer*
Rudavsky, Dahlia C. *lawyer*
Rupnick, Maria Ann *internist*
Saris, Patti Barbara *federal judge*
Scanlon, Dorothy Therese *history professor*
Schaller, Jane Green *pediatrician*
Schnitzer, Iris Taymore *diversified financial services company executive, lawyer, arbitrator, mediator*
Schotland, Judith *education educator*
Schribman, Shelley Iris *database engineer, consultant*
Scrimshaw, Susan Crosby *academic administrator*
Seddon, Johanna Margaret *ophthalmologist, epidemiologist*
Seidman, Christine E. *medical educator*
Shapiro, Sandra *lawyer*
Shatz, Carla J. *biology professor*
Shilepsky, Nancy Sue *lawyer*
Simmons, Sylvia Jeanne Quarles (Mrs. Herbert G. Simmons Jr.) *educator, academic administrator*
Sloan, Katherine (Kay Sloan) *college president*

Smith, Heather Clark *academic administrator*
Sosman, Martha B. *state supreme court justice*
Spencer, Renee A. *social worker, educator, researcher*
Spieler, Emily A. *dean, law educator*
Spiliotis, Joyce A. *state legislator*
Steinberg, Laura *lawyer*
Strothman, Wendy Jo *literary agent*
Sullivan Stemberg, Maureen *interior designer*
Swihart, Susannah M. *bank executive*
Tearney, Melissa Bayer *lawyer*
Tick, Judith *music historian, educator*
Tokunaga, Yasuko *performing company executive*
Tornow, Barbara *academic administrator*
Treadway, Jessica *writer, educator*
Tse, Marian A. *lawyer*
Van Marter, Linda Joanne *pediatrician, educator, neonatologist, researcher*
Vilker-Kuchment, Valeria *violinist*
Walrath, Patricia A. *state legislator*
Warren, Susan Hanke Murphy *international marketing business development executive*
Wedge, Carole C. *architectural firm executive*
White, Anne J. *lawyer*
Whitley, L. Tracee *lawyer*
Wiggleworth, Margaret *property manager*
Williams Gifford, Susan *state legislator*
Willock, Marcelle Monica *retired medical educator*
Wolf, Alice Koerner *state legislator, former mayor*
Yarborough, Nellie Constance *principal, minister*
Young, Anne B. *neurologist, educator*
Young, Laura *dance educator, choreographer*
Zannieri, Nina *museum director*
Zobel, Rya Weickert *federal judge*

Bourne
Fantozzi, Peggy Ryone *geologist, environmental planner*

Braintree
Hallenbeck, Rachel Kirsten *music educator, director*
Malloy, Ellen Ann *athletic trainer*
Salloway, Josephine Plovnick *psychologist, educator, marriage and family therapist, mental health counselor*
Watts, Kisha Mann *school system administrator, secondary school educator*

Bridgewater
Krauss, Jamie Gail *psychologist*
Laquale, Kathleen Marie *physical education educator*
McAlinden, Laura A. *humanities educator*
Minasian, Maureen *physical education educator*
Seide, Janet H. *psychologist*
Tinsley, Adrian *former college president*
Witherell, Nancy Louise *education educator*

Brockton
Belinsky, Ilene Beth *lawyer*
Carlson, Desiree Anice *pathologist*
Festin, Fe Erlita Diolazo *psychiatrist, director*
Moore, Mary Johnson *nurse*

Brookline
Assens, Nathalie *construction executive*
Barron, Ros *artist*
Baumrind, Lydia *psychologist*
Bourne, Katherine Day *journalist, educator*
Buchin, Jacqueline Chase *psychologist*
Cromwell, Adelaide M. *sociology educator*
Doherty, Patricia McGinn *psychologist*
Gewirtz, Mindy L. *organizational and leadership relations consultant*
Goodwin, Rhoda Sherman *psychologist*
Heilbrunn, Lorraine Judith *psychologist, educational administrator*
Jakab, Irene *psychiatrist*
Miller, Debra Lynn *political scientist*
Mountford, Alison Leigh *psychologist*
Rizzi, Marguerite Claire *music educator*
Rubin-Katz, Barbara *sculptor, human services manager*
Schiller, Sophie *artist, graphics designer*
Sethi, Chander Mohini *gynecologist, obstetrician, consultant*
Sho, Jennifer Yu-Fei *musician, educator*
Skeete, Helen Watkins *minister, counselor*

Bryantville
Peters, Marie T. *retired art educator*

Burlington
Greiner, Helen *mechanical engineer*
Rogers, Carol Rosenstein *social worker, educator*

Byfield
Densmore, Susan Elizabeth *secondary school educator, music educator*
Yeomans, Katie Morse *writer*

Cambridge
Bailyn, Lotte *psychologist, educator*
Baker, Tania Ann *biology professor, researcher*
Bane, Mary Jo *dean, political science professor*
Barnhart, Cynthia *engineering educator, researcher*
Bartholet, Elizabeth *law educator*
Bar-Yam, Miriam *psychologist, consultant, researcher*
Belcher, Angela *engineering educator*
Berlowitz, Leslie *cultural organization administrator*
Blake, Patricia *writer*
Bloom, Kathryn Ruth *public relations executive*
Boyce, Mary C. *mechanical engineer, educator*
Brackett, Prilla Smith *artist, educator*
Burns, Virginia *social worker*
Callahan, Barbara Ann *librarian*
Cazden, Courtney B(orden) *education educator*
Ceyer, Sylvia T. *chemistry professor, department chairman*
Chandler, Fay Martin *artist*
Chiles, Carol S. *architectural firm executive*
Chisholm, Sallie Watson *biological oceanography educator, researcher*
Chodorow, Nancy Julia *psychotherapist, educator*
Chvany, Catherine Vakar *foreign language educator*
Clifton, Anne Rutenber *psychotherapist, educator*
Cole, Heather Ellen *librarian*
Coleman, Sandra Sloan *librarian, academic dean*
Cooper, Mary Campbell *information services executive*
Daley, Barbara Sabin *clinical psychologist*
de Marneffe, Barbara Rowe *historic preservationist*
de Monteiro, Nadsa *chef*
Desan, Christine *law educator*
de Varon, Lorna Cooke *choral conductor*
DiCamillo, Kate *writer*
Dobson, Parrish *photographer, educator*
Drake, Elisabeth Mertz *chemical engineer, consultant*
Dresselhaus, Mildred Spiewak *physics professor, engineering educator*
Dulac, Catherine *biology professor, researcher*
Dunsire, Deborah *pharmaceutical executive*
Dunton, Susan Beth *academic administrator*
Eisenberg, Carola *psychiatrist, educator*
Elkins, Caroline M. *history professor, writer*
Eurich, Nell P. *education educator*
Faran, Ellen Webster *publishing executive*
Farver, Jane *museum director*
Faust, Drew Gilpin *historian, educator*
Field, Martha Amanda *law educator*
Fitzgerald-Huber, Louisa G. *education educator, researcher*
Flannery, Susan Marie *library administrator*
Forbes, Kristin J. *economics professor, former federal official*
Friend, Cynthia M. *chemist, educator*
Frisch, Rose Epstein *population sciences researcher*
Geller, Margaret Joan *astrophysicist, educator*
Glendon, Mary Ann *law educator*
Goldwasser, Shafrira *computer scientist*
Goodman, Ellen Holtz *journalist*
Graham, Jorie *writer, educator*
Graham, Patricia Albjerg *education educator*
Graybiel, Ann M. *medical educator*
Griffith, Linda G. (Linda Griffith-Cima) *biomedical engineer, chemical engineer, educator*
Guinier, Lani *law educator*
Halley, Janet E. *law educator*
Hamner, Suzanne Leath *retired history educator*
Hewitt, Jacqueline N. *astronomy educator*
Hockfield, Susan *academic administrator, medical educator*
Hopkins, Nancy H. *biology professor*
Hubbard, Ruth *retired biology professor*
Hughes, Libby *writer*
Hunt, Swanee G. *public policy educator, former ambassador*
Jacob, Wendy *artist, art educator*
Jeremijenko, Natalie H.M. *design engineer, educator, artist*
Johnson, Elvira Q. *dietician*
Johnson, Jennifer Toby *military officer*
Jonas, Joan (Joan Amerman Edwards) *artist*
Kagan, Elena *dean, law educator*
Keller, Evelyn Fox *philosophy of science professor*
Kellerman, Barbara *political science professor, writer*
Kilpatrick, Maureen *food service executive*
Kim, Josephine M. *education educator*
Koepp, Donna Pauline Petersen *librarian*
Kraus, Rozann B. *performing company executive*
Kujawa-Holbrook, Sheryl *theology studies educator, academic administrator*
Lagemann, Ellen Condliffe *history professor, education educator, dean*
Laiou, Angeliki Evangelos *history professor*
Langer, Ellen Jane *psychologist, educator, writer, artist*
Lawrence-Lightfoot, Sara *education educator, sociologist*
Lee, Barbara *political activist, foundation administrator*
Lepore, Jill *history professor, writer*
Lindblad-Toh, Kerstin *medical researcher*
Lindquist, Susan Lee *biology and microbiology professor*
Lipson, Pamela *information scientist*
Logan, Isabeall Talmadge *psychotherapist, writer*
Lynch, Nancy Ann *computer scientist, educator*
MacKinnon, Rebecca *media consultant, researcher*
Macrakis, A. Lily *academic administrator*
Maier, Pauline *historian, educator*
Mansbridge, Jane Jebb *political scientist, educator*
Marvin, Ursula Bailey *retired geologist*
Mathews, Joan Helene *pediatrician*
Matsui, Connie L. *pharmaceutical executive*
McCartney, Kathleen *dean, education educator*
McDonald, Christie Anne *literature and language professor, writer*
McKenna, Margaret Anne *academic administrator*
Merseth, Katherine K. *mathematician, education educator*
Meyer, Dorothy Virginia *retired education educator*
Minow, Martha Louise *law educator*
Mitchell, Barbara Anne *librarian*
Moore, Sally Falk *anthropology educator*
Murcott, Susan *civil and environmental engineer, lecturer, consultant*
Newman, Dava Jean *aerospace engineering educator, director*
Orfield, Antonia Marie *optometrist, researcher*
O'Shea, Erin K. *biomedical researcher*
Pardue, Mary-Lou *biology professor*
Parker, Lisa Frederick *music educator, Dalcroze specialist*
Parlee, Mary Brown *psychology educator*
Power, Samantha J. *public policy educator, writer*
Randall, Lisa *physics professor*
Rho, Yanni *psychiatrist*
Rhoda, Janice Tucker *writer, educator, musician*
Riley, Lynne F. *lawyer*
Ritvo, Harriet *historian*
Roberts, Nancy *computer scientist, educator*
Rorty, Amelie *philosopher, educator*
Rosenblum, Nancy Lipton *political science professor*
Rosenkrantz, Barbara Gutmann *science and medicine historian*
Ruggie, Mary *humanities educator*
Samson, Leona D. *biological engineering educator, research center director*
Santos, Adèle Naudé *architect, educator*
Schoon, Marion Else *librarian*
Schuessler Fiorenza, Elisabeth *theology studies educator*
Severin, Christina *public health service officer*
Shaheen, C. Jeanne *political organization administrator, former governor*
Shelemay, Kay Kaufman *music educator*
Slosburg-Ackerman, Jill Rose *artist, educator*
Smith, Amy B. *mechanical engineer, educator*
Sortun, Ana *food service executive*
Stathos, Anastasia *retired elementary school educator*
Steiker, Carol S. *law educator*
Toft, Monica Duffy *economics professor*
Torriani-Gorini, Annamaria *microbiologist, educator*
Ulrich, Laurel Thatcher *historian, educator*
Vandiver, Kathleen Mead *science educator*
Vendler, Helen Hennessy *literature educator, poetry critic*
von Deck, Mercedes Dina *orthopedist, surgeon*
Warren, Elizabeth A. *law educator*
Waters, Mary Catherine *sociology educator*
Watson, Rubie S. *museum director*
White, Lucie E. *law educator*
White, Shelby *art association administrator*
Widnall, Sheila Evans *aeronautical educator, former secretary of the airforce, former university official*
Wilcox, Maud *editor*
Wise, Virginia Jo *law educator, librarian*
Wolpert, Ann J. *library director*
Wood, Pamela Sharon *music educator, soprano*
Wylie, Joan Blout *real estate rehabilitator, ceramist, designer*
Zinberg, Dorothy Shore *sociologist, educator*
Zuber, Maria T. *geophysicist, educator*

Canton
Bentas, Lily Haseotes *retail executive*
Kelley, Irene W. *retired librarian, musician, artist*
Redmont, Joan *retired language educator*
Trupe, Mary-Ann *secondary school educator*

Carlisle
Friedman, Amy Lisa *social worker*

Carver
Tura, Carol Ann *medical/surgical and intravenous therapy nurse*

Cataumet
Murdock, Rosamond Louise *retired pediatrician*

Centerville
Condon, Ann Blunt *psychotherapist*
Williams, Ann Meagher *retired hospital administrator*

Chatham
Cogan, Mary Hart *community activist, educator*
Stout, Sharon Sparkes *elementary school educator, counselor*

Chelmsford
Cleven, Carol Chapman *retired state legislator*
Elwell, Barbara Lois Dow *foundation administrator*

Chelsea
Roman, Jane Sedgewick *nurse*

Chestnut Hill
Addis, Deborah Jane *management consultant*
Bando, Patricia Alice *academic administrator*
Boskin, Claire *psychotherapist, educator*
Burgess, Ann Wolbert *nursing educator*
Gottlieb, Marise Suss *epidemiologist*
Hawkins, Joellen Margaret Beck *nursing educator*
Kanin, Doris May *political scientist, consultant*
Kelley, Shana O. *biochemist*
Lyerly, Cynthia Lynn *history professor*
Monteila, Sharon Christine *dancer, educator, choreographer*
Munnell, Alicia Haydock *economist*
Munro, Barbara Hazard *nursing educator, dean, researcher*
Nemerowicz, Gloria *academic administrator*
Netzer, Nancy *museum director, art historian, educator*
Valette, Rebecca Marianne *Romance languages educator*

Chicopee
Chelte, Judith Segzdowicz *secondary school educator*
Costanzo, Nanci Joy *art educator*
Dame, Catherine Elaine *acupuncturist*

Cohasset
Chenault Minot, Marilyn *legal executive*

Concord
Giles, Kathleen C. *headmaster*

Cotuit
Crocker, Jean Hazelton *elementary school educator, consultant, environmental services administrator*

Danvers
Corkery, Antoinette Elizabeth *literature and language educator*

Dartmouth
Leandro, Patricia J. *mathematics educator*
Leclair, Susan Jean *hematologist, clinical laboratory scientist, educator*
Nieviedgal, Carol Belmarce *elementary school educator*
Sweeney, Shawna Elizabeth *political science professor, researcher*

Dedham
Kirby, Heather Suzanne *music educator*
Nichols, Nancy Ruth *elementary school educator*
Redstone, Shari E. *amusement company executive*

Dorchester
Lee, June Warren *dentist*
Medeiros, Jennifer Lynn *school psychologist, consultant*
Smith, Survilla Marie *social services administrator, artist, poet*
Wideman, Carol M. *accountant, consultant*

Douglas
Bachelder, Beverly Brandt *secondary school educator, assistant principal, director*
Socha, Cindy L. *secondary school educator*

Dover
Buyse, Marylou *pediatrician, geneticist, medical association administrator*

Duxbury
Thrasher, Dianne Elizabeth *mathematics educator, computer scientist, consultant*

East Boston
Crawford, Linda Sibery *lawyer, educator*

East Bridgewater
Heywood, Anne *artist, educator, author*

East Falmouth
Lincoln, Jane L. *artist, educator*

East Orleans
Natale, Barbara Gustafson *retired librarian*

Easthampton
Lake, Shelley *artist*

Edgartown
Gatting, Carlene J. *lawyer*
MacDonald, Duncan *broadcaster, writer, communications consultant*

Everett
Auger, Kimberly Ann *elementary school educator*

Fairhaven
Goes, Kathleen Ann *secondary school educator*
Lopes, Myra Amelia *writer*

Fall River
Andrade, Manuela Pestana *art educator*
Brion, Norma M. *real estate broker*
Grandchamp, Jeanne P. *literature educator*
Lynds, Lucinda *music educator*
Sullivan, Ruth Anne *librarian*
Wilner, Marion Leonard *art educator*

Falmouth
Fullerton, Davina *art historian, consultant, researcher*
Lamont, Rosette Clementine *language educator, journalist, translator*
Milkman, Marianne Friedenthal *retired city planner*
Studley, LaVada A. *music educator*

Fiskdale
Costello, Christine Ann *fine arts director, church organist*

Fitchburg
deDiego, Paula Dawn *education educator*
Levine, Sara Pollak *psychology professor*
Reed, Rosemary *learning specialist*
Scannell, Ann Elizabeth *nurse, educator*

Foxboro
Ferron, Jennifer *marketing executive*
Furtado-Lavoie, Julia *sales executive*
Kennedy, Susan Marie *music educator*

Framingham
Austin, Sandra Ikenberry *nursing educator, consultant*
Bogard, Carole Christine *soprano*
Coiner, Maryrose C. *psychologist*
Dawicki, Doloretta Diane *analytical chemist, research biochemist, educator*
Hagarty, Wendy L. *music educator*
Heineman, Helen L. *retired academic administrator*
Hillman, Carol Barbara *communications executive, consultant*
Komola, Christine T. *corporate financial executive*
Lindsay, Leslie *packaging engineer*
McCauley, Ann *lawyer*
McEntegart, Judy R. *gifted and talented educator*
Meyrowitz, Carol *retail executive*
Valakis, M. Lois *retired elementary school educator*
West, Doe *psychotherapist, educator*
Willinger, Rhonda Zwern *optometrist*
Wulf, Sharon Ann *management consultant*
Zamvil, Linda Susan *psychiatrist, educator*

Gardner
Herrnkind, Hilda Marie *writer, military volunteer*
Weitze, Teena *science educator*

Gloucester
Cheves, Vera Louisa *retired librarian*
Johnson, Anne Elisabeth *medical assistant*
Perry, Sarah Hollis *artist*
Swigart, Joan B. *artist, consultant*
White, Lucette Darby *painter, sculptor*

Great Barrington
Curtin, Phyllis *music educator, dean, vocalist*
Lewis, Karen Marie *human services administrator, writer*
Ryder, Lois Irene *artist*

Greenfield
Curtiss, Carol Perry *health facility administrator, consultant, nurse*
Jenks, Abigail *social worker, educator*

Groton
Anthony, Sylvia *social welfare organization executive*

Sawyer, Betsy (Rosemary) E. *elementary school educator*

Hadley
Friedman, D. Dina *writer, educator*
Rice, Rebecca Kynoch *writer, consultant, language educator*

Harwich
Caretti, Ann M. *school system administrator*
Medeiros, Donna *assistant principal*

Hatfield
Yolen, Jane *writer*

Haverhill
Kannan, Sandra Jean *elementary school educator, retired assistant principal*
Rubinstein, Nancy G. *social worker, consultant*

Hingham
Noel, Barbara Hughes McMurtry *retired music educator*
Richie, Margaret Bye *architectural historian*

Holden
Edson, Virginia Elizabeth *secondary school educator*

Holyoke
Dearborn, Maureen Markt *speech and language clinician*

Hopkinton
Moran, Wendy Jacqueline *music educator, musician*

Housatonic
Kelsey, Christine J. *innkeeper, chef*

Hubbardston
Marceau, Judith Marie *retired elementary school educator, small business owner*

Hudson
Ingano, Kathryn Marita *secondary school educator*
Opp, Nancy Jean Shiffler *visual artist, arts volunteer*

Hyannis
Devine, Nancy *retired postmaster*
Makkay, Maureen Ann *broadcast executive*
Nicholson, Ellen Ellis *clinical social worker*
O'Brien, Kathleen L. *special education educator*

Hyde Park
Harris, Emily Louise *special education educator*

Ipswich
Berry, Iris Elizabeth *academic administrator*
Lombardo, Ann Marie *special education educator, writer, artist*
Wilson, Doris H. *volunteer*

Jamaica Plain
Nambiar, Prabha *science educator*
White-Hammond, Gloria E. *pastor, pediatrician, human rights advocate*

Kingston
Scalese, Ellen Renee *hotel executive*

Lakeville
Ashley, Marjorie Lynn *intravenous therapy nurse*
Chase, Karen Humphrey *elementary school educator*

Lancaster
Dugan, Maureen *biology educator, consultant*

Lenox
Bruder, Judith *writer*
Hall, Frances Benn *writer, retired theater educator*
Lewis, Marianne H. *psychiatric nurse practitioner*
Smith, Elske Van Panhuys *retired academic administrator, astronomer*

Leominster
Lyons, Beryl Barton Anfindsen *advertising executive*
Suskind, Diana Lee *education educator*
Vogel, Gloria Jean Hilts *secondary school educator*

Leverett
Margolis, Nadia *language educator, translator, medievalist*

Lexington
Bombardieri, Merle Ann *psychotherapist*
Escott, Shoolah Hope *microbiologist*
Garing, Ione Davis *civic worker*
Jordan, Judith Victoria *clinical psychologist, educator*
Levine, Janice R. *clinical psychologist*
Miller, Inabeth *educational administrator, librarian, technology consultant*
Schafer, Alice Turner *retired mathematics professor*
Shapiro, Marian Kaplun *psychologist*
Tecca, Kimberly Ann *physician assistant*
Thernstrom, Abigail *federal agency administrator, writer*
Topalian, Naomi Getsoyan *writer*
Wilson, Wendy Scott *history educator*

Lincoln
Milan, Ellen Judith *artist*
Naiman, Adeline Lubell *educational administrator*

Littleton
Crory, Mary *town official*

Longmeadow
Donoghue, Linda *nursing administrator, community health nurse*
Frey, Mary Elizabeth *artist*
Katz, Barbara Stein *special education educator*
Leary, Carol Ann *academic administrator*

Schirmer-Smith, Sara Jane (Sally Schirmer-Smith) *director*
Teitz, Betty Beatrice Goldstein *retired interior designer*

Lowell
Clark, Kathyrn A. *elementary school educator*
Clark, Sharon Ann *educational consultant, music educator*
Galizzi, Monica *economics professor*
Greher, Gena R. *music production company executive*
Inco, Elizabeth Mary *nurse, consultant*
Klimczak, Janice Beverly *secondary school educator*
Lewis, Diane *educator*
McAfee, Noelle Claire *philosopher, educator*
Moore, Janet Lambert *artist, educator*
O'Donnell, Kathleen Marie *lawyer*

Ludlow
Marion, Elena Mendes *secondary school educator*

Lynn
Josephs, Judith *counseling administrator, educator*

Lynnfield
Kerrigan, Nancy *professional figure skater, retired Olympic athlete*

Malden
Darish, Bernice Steiman *realtor*
Hromada, Lauren Spada *athletic traniner*

Marblehead
DiCanio, Margaret Brien *freelance writer, former mental health agency administrator*
Heins, Esther *artist, illustrator*
Isaacson, Barbara Dorothy *retired elementary school educator, retired secondary school educator*
Kennedy, Elizabeth Mae *musician*
Tamaren, Michele Carol *spiritual director, writer, retired special education educator, personal coach, presenter*

Marion
McPartland, Patricia Ann *educational association administrator, health educator*

Marlborough
Bradley, Bonita Mae *psychotherapist*
Miotto, Mary Elizabeth G. *pediatrician*

Marshfield
Goode, Cynthia A. *social studies educator, secondary school educator*

Marstons Mills
Martin, Susan Katherine *librarian*

Mattapoisett
Bertram, Christine G. *artist, painter, graphics designer*
Guilbert, Frances *mathematics educator*

Maynard
Messina, Nance Ann *primary school educator*

Medfield
Nedder, Janet Marie *elementary school educator*
Phillips, Marion Grumman *civic volunteer, writer*

Medford
Abriola, Linda Marie *civil engineer, environmental engineer*
Ambady, Nalini *social psychologist, educator, researcher*
Ch'en, Li-li *literature and language educator, writer*
Goldberg, Pamela Winer *entrepreneur, educator*
Johnson, Virginia Bristol *costume designer, educator, small business owner*
Kanarek, Robin Beth *psychology educator, nutrition educator, researcher*
Michalak, Jo-Ann *library director*
Penick, Ann Clarisse *minister, counselor*
Perrone, Lisa *mathematics professor*
Romero, Christiane *German language educator*
Ruskai, Mary Beth *mathematics professor*
Schendan, Haline Elizabeth *cognitive neuroscience educator*
Weiler, Kathleen *education educator, researcher*

Medway
Montpelier, Pamela J. *bank executive*

Melrose
Desforges, Jane Fay *retired internist, hematologist, educator*
Sheerin, Margaret M. *elementary school educator*

Mendon
Bradley, Nancy Lovett *retired medical and surgical nurse, administrator*
Brewer, Justine Adrianne *zoological park administrator*
Thurber, Kirsten Nora *music educator*

Milford
Mancini, Joyce Katherine *family practice nurse practitioner*

Mill River
Jaffe, Katharine Weisman *retired librarian*

Milton
Raelin, Abby Phyllis *school psychologist*
Randall, Lilian Maria Charlotte *museum curator*
Robertson, Robin Alayne *headmaster, anthropologist*
Simon, Deborah Elizabeth *private school educator*

Nantucket
Bartlett, Cheryl Ann *public health service administrator*

Natick
Geller, Esther (Bailey Geller) *artist*
Lebowitz, Charlotte Meyersohn *social worker*

Ma, Jing-Heng Sheng *language educator*
Smith, Amanda R. *secondary school educator*
Stabin, Alice Marie *administrative assistant*
Strauss, Harlee Sue *environmentalist, consultant*
Taylor, Susan Garrett *academic administrator, school psychologist*
Walker, Kellye L. *lawyer*
Weber, Linda Horton *secondary school educator*

Needham
Boulding, Elise Marie *sociologist, educator*
Durbin, Kirsten Dahlman *academic administrator*
Kolb, Gloria Ro *medical products executive*
Kossuth, Joanne M. *academic administrator*
Lenehan, Pamela Farrell *financial executive*
Palmerio, Elvira Castano *art gallery director, art historian*
Ryan, Una Scully *health science association administrator, medical educator*
Shannon, Margaret Rita *retired education educator, retired college dean*
Silverstein, Judith Lynn *clinical psychologist*
Watt, Abby Naitove *elementary school educator*

Needham Heights
Salhany, Lucille S. (Lucy Salhany) *broadcast executive*

New Bedford
Cormier, Lorraine R. *secondary school educator*
Matsumoto, Carolee Setsuko *researcher, education developer and administrator*
Monteiro, Patricia M. *clinical social worker*
Stone, Anne Marie *elementary school educator*
Thomas, Sharon M. *city official*

Newbury
Hamond, Karen Marie Koch *secondary school educator*

Newburyport
Keller, Clare Graham Marrow *psychologist*
Krusemark, Janice Wells *physicial education educator*

Newton
Bassuk, Ellen Linda *psychiatrist*
Benner, Mary Wright *freelance/self-employed conference director*
Burlage, Dorothy Dawson *clinical psychologist*
Glick-Weil, Kathy *library director*
Havens, Candace Jean *urban planner, consultant*
Huber Warren, Gretchen *artist*
Hume, Ellen Hunsberger *media analyst, educator, journalist*
Isselbacher, Rhoda Solin *lawyer*
Jencks, Penelope *sculptor*
Krintzman, B. J. *lawyer, real estate broker, television show host*
LeRoux, Tessa *sociology professor, director*
Matteson, Carol J. *academic administrator*
Metzer, Patricia Ann *lawyer*
Mullen, Maureen Ann *social worker*
Pill, Cynthia Joan *social worker*
Rebelsky, Freda Ethel Gould *psychologist*
Reilly, Suzanne Sweeney *art historian, educator*
Stark, Martha *psychiatrist, environmental medicine physician*
Tannenwald, Leslie Keiter *rabbi, justice of peace, educational association administrator, chaplain*
Winston, Amy Danielle Picard *science educator, department chairman*

Newton Center
Lapierre, Katherine Ann *psychiatrist, educator*
Parker, Jacqueline Yvonne *lawyer, educator*
Veeder, Nancy Walker *social work educator*

Newton Highlands
Brant, Renee S. Tankenoff *psychiatrist*
Hummel, Margaret P. *state representative*

North Andover
Kimball, Virginia Marie *theology studies educator, writer*
Longsworth, Ellen Louise *art historian, consultant*

North Attleboro
Nicodemus, Emily Hulsizer *technology educator*

North Brookfield
Parker, Ann (Ann Parker Neal) *photographer, graphic artist, writer*

North Chelmsford
Erkkila-Ricker, Barbara Howell *writer, photographer*

North Dartmouth
Fair, Kathleen Margaret *elementary school educator*
Lilly, Emily L. *education educator*
Sitarz, Paula Gaj *writer*
Teboh, Bridget A. *history professor, researcher*

North Dighton
Patten, Brenda Anne *secondary school educator*

North Eastham
DeMuth, Vivienne Blake McCandless *artist, illustrator*

North Easton
Bundy, Annalee Marshall *library director*

Northampton
Anderson, Margaret Ellen (Margaret Ellen Anderson) *physiologist, educator*
Banerjee, Maria Nemcova *Russian language and literature educator*
Birdsall, Jeanne *writer, photographer*
Christ, Carol Tecla *academic administrator*
Dean, Dorothy G. *psychologist, social sciences educator, researcher*
Fabing, Suzannah *museum director*
Mahoney, Maureen A. *academic administrator*
Newman, Lesléa *writer*
Palser, Barbara F. *retired botanist*
Rupp, Sheron Adeline *photographer, educator*
Schuleit, Anna *artist*

Stinson, Susan Elizabeth *director, writer*

Northborough
Cradler, Judith A. *science educator*

Northfield
van Baaren, Margaret Miriam *learning disabilities educator*

Norwell
Brett, Jan Churchill *illustrator, author*
Porter, Marie Caroline *geriatrics nurse*

Norwood
Mallet, Kathleen W. *elementary school educator*
Rothauser, Florence Arax *artist*

Orange
Riddell, Tina Marie *secondary school educator*

Orleans
McDermott, Mary Ellen *insurance agent*
Patterson, Elizabeth C. *choir director*
Rappaport, Margaret Mary Williams Ewing *psychologist, physician, writer, pilot, consultant*

Osterville
McLean, Susan O'Brien *artist*
Weber, Adelheid Lisa *retired nurse, chemist*

Peabody
Birdsall, Melinda R. *gynecologist*
Dee, Pauline M. *artist*
Falkoff, Gail Goldstein *mathematics educator, department chairman*

Pepperell
Holmes, Jean Louise *real estate investor, humanities educator*
Jackson, Rebecca Lee *history educator, social studies educator*

Pittsfield
Begley, Charlene *electronics executive*
Boyd, Julianne Mamana *theater director, educator*
Fawcett, Gayle P. *bank executive*
Guzzo, Jessica Ann *music educator*
Norris, Jeannie *headmaster*
Wood, Elizabeth Ann *special education educator*

Plymouth
Flood, H. Gay (Hulda Gay Flood) *editor, consultant*
Lashley, Barbara Theresa *psychologist, educator, mental health counselor*
Leonard-Zabel, Ann Marie T. *psychologist, educator*
Paul, Carol Ann *retired academic administrator, biology educator*
Wolf, Ann E. *chemistry educator*

Provincetown
Oliver, Mary *poet*
Sturner, Lynda *performing company executive*
Wolfman, Brunetta Reid *education educator*

Quincy
Bunting, Carolyn Anne *writer*
Chung, Cynthia Norton *communications specialist*
Conley, Olga L. *retail executive*
Furtado, Beverly Ann *financial aid administrator*
Pratt, Mary *retired secondary school educator*
Wilson, Blenda Jacqueline *foundation administrator*

Reading
Frey, Joanne Alice Tupper *art educator*
Nordstrand, Nathalie Elizabeth Johnson *artist*

Rehoboth
McGee, Mary Alice *health science research administrator*

Revere
Ferrante, Olivia Ann *retired secondary school educator, consultant*
Recupero-Faiella, Anna Antonietta *poet*

Rockland
Blethen, Sandra Lee *pediatric endocrinologist*

Rockport
Eaton Adams, Elizabeth Susan *retired middle school educator, jazz musician*
Johnson, Janet Lou *real estate company executive, writer*
Olson, Mary Jane *elementary school educator*

Roslindale
Sullivan, Dorothy Rona *state official*

Roxbury
Alméstica, Johanna Lynnette *mental health counselor, administrator*
Cruthird, Brandy K. *gym owner and fitness instructor*
Simons, Elizabeth R(eiman) *biochemist, educator*

Roxbury Crossing
Berger, Ellen Tessman *psychologist*
Smith, Susie Irene *cytologist, histologist*

Salem
Gozemba, Patrica Andrea *women's studies and English language educator, writer*
Hewitt, Nancy Arlene *social worker*

Sandwich
Podbros, Linda Zoe *neuropsychologist, consultant*

Sharon
Berzon, Faye Clark *retired nursing educator*
Johnson, Addie Collins *secondary school educator, retired dietician*
Ross, Betsy R. *psychotherapist*

Shelburne Falls
Evelyn, Phyllis *minister*

Shrewsbury
DiGiorgio, Sara Ahern *assistant principal*
Kranich, Margaret Mansley *artist*
Smith, Carolyn J(ane) Hostetter *psychologist, educator*

Somerset
Lenz, Mary Lynn *bank executive*
Rapoza, Donna Lee *physical education educator*

Somerville
Corso, Susan Falk *minister*
Gurley, Rhonda Jean *special education educator, consultant*
Ragsdale, Katherine Hancock *Episcopal priest, political activist*

South Deerfield
Tarasuk, Penelope Antoinette *psychoanalyst, artist*

South Hadley
Creighton, Joanne Vanish *academic administrator*
Doezema, Marianne *art historian, museum director*
Elleman, Barbara *editor*
Ewing Browne, Sheila *chemistry professor, physical organic chemist*
Hall, Lee *artist, educator, writer*
Horsnell, Margaret Eileen *retired historian*
Tatum, Beverly Daniel *psychology and education educator*
Townsend, Jane Kaltenbach *biologist, educator*

South Hamilton
Kroeger, Catherine C. *writer, educator, editor*
Ray, Diane Marie Ayers *music educator*

South Harwich
Finn, Nita Ann *social worker*

South Natick
Cantor, Pamela Corliss *psychologist*

South Orleans
Hale, Margaret Smith *insurance company executive, educator*

South Yarmouth
Bowen, Alice Frances *retired school system administrator*

Southborough
Hill, Elsa N. *headmaster, literature and language educator, lawyer*

Southbridge
Vasey, Ann L. *pre-school administrator, counselor*

Spencer
Robinson, Evelyn Edna *secondary school educator*

Springfield
Bonemery, Anne M. *language educator*
Elam, Elizabeth L.R. *finance educator*
Garabedian-Urbanowski, Martha Ann *foreign language educator*
Harnois, Veronica *psychologist, educator*
Lucia, Mary Ann *elementary school educator*
Martorell, Claudia *infectious diseases physician*
Melconian, Linda Jean *state senator, lawyer, educator*
Modie, Christine M. *insurance company executive*
Murphy, Eileen Bridget *retired mathematics professor*
Price-Ware-Kabuti, Thelma *counselor*
Rooke, Michele A. *lawyer*
Saia, Diane Plevock DiPiero *nutritionist, educator, legal administrator*
Stack, May Elizabeth *retired library director*
Susse, Sandra Slone *lawyer*
Vincensi, Avis A. *sales executive, medical educator*
Winn, Janice Gail *food products administrator*
Wyzik, Susan Aldrich *history professor*

Sterling
Lundgren, Ruth Williamson Wood (Ruth Lundgren Williamson Wood) *public relations executive, writer*

Stockbridge
Fitzpatrick, Jane *entrepreneur*
MacDonald, Sharon Ethel *dancer, educator, choreographer, administrator*

Stoneham
Keenan, Carol *assistant principal*

Sudbury
Ames, Lois Winslow Sisson *social worker, educator, writer*
Deutsch, Judith *clergywoman*
Hillery, Mary Jane Larato *columnist, television personality, television producer, writer, military officer*
Pitman, Ursula Wall *curator, educator*
Thompson, Mary Lou *elementary school educator*

Taunton
Lopes, Maria Fernandina *commissioner*
Messaline, Wendy Jean *retail chain official*
Richardson, Marilyn Goff *small business owner, artist*

Tewksbury
Herlihy-Chevalier, Barbara Doyle *retired mental health nurse*

Townsend
Smith, Denise Groleau *data processing professional*

Truro
Chase, Naomi Feigelson *poet*
Kelley, Maryellen R. *economist, management consultant*

Turners Falls
Finley-Morin, Kimberley K. *secondary school educator*

Tyngsboro
Bomal, Cheryl Ann *secondary school educator*

Upton
DiNatale, Michelle *biology educator*

Vineyard Haven
Breuer, Joann Green *theater director*
Jacobs, Gretchen Huntley *psychiatrist*
Kimball, Julie Ellis *small press publisher, humorist, writer*

Waban
Etter, Faye Madalyn *interior design company executive*
Javitch, Anki Wolf (Ann Louise Wolf Javitch) *psychologist*

Wakefield
Singleton, Shirley *software development executive*

Waltham
Adams, Marilyn Jager *developmental psychologist*
Birren, Susan J. *medical educator*
Curnan, Susan P. *social policy and management educator, consultant*
Gray-Nix, Elizabeth Whitwell *occupational therapist*
Hale, Jane Alison *literature and language professor*
Heystee, Susan *information technology executive*
Hill, Anita Faye *law educator*
Kassman, Deborah Newman *university administrator, writer, editor*
Krauss, Marty Wyngaarden *academic administrator*
Lees, Marjorie Berman *biochemist, neuroscientist*
Marder, Eve Esther *neuroscientist, educator*
McCulloch, Rachel *economist, educator*
O'Donnell, Rhonda *software company executive*
Seiferle, Rebecca Ann *poet, editor, publisher*
Staves, Susan *humanities educator*
Thorne, Eva Treneice *political science professor*
Unger, Rhoda Kesler *psychology educator*
Wawrzaszek, Susan V. *university librarian*

Wareham
Gayoski, Kathleen Mary *counselor, minister*
Nolan, Marilyn Ann *health facility administrator*

Watertown
Mason, Linda Anne *daycare administrator*
Rivers, Wilga Marie *language educator*
Spivack, Kathleen Romola Drucker *writer, educator*
Weingarten, Kaethe *clinical psychologist*

Wayland
Caristo-Verrill, Janet Rose *international management consultant*
Humphrey, Diana Young *fundraiser*

Webster
Ducharme, Janice A. *secondary school educator*

Wellesley
Bailey, Susan McGee *educational administrator, researcher, educator*
Eappen, Deborah S. *ophthalmologist*
Heartt, Charlotte Beebe *university official*
Jacobs, Ruth Harriet *poet, playwright, sociologist, gerontologist*
Jacoff, Rachel *Italian language and literature educator*
Lacy, Ann Matthews *geneticist, educator, researcher*
Lefkowitz, Mary Rosenthal *ancient language educator*
Miller, Linda B. *political scientist*
Mistacco, Vicki E. *foreign language educator*
Pike, Judith Robyn *lawyer*
Putnam, Ruth Anna *philosopher, educator*
Walsh, Diana Chapman *academic administrator, sociologist, educator*

Wellesley Hills
Imbrescia, Marcia *landscape company executive*

Wellfleet
Piercy, Marge *poet, writer*

West Newbury
Dooley, Ann Elizabeth *freelance writers cooperative executive, editor*

West Newton
Logan, Georgiana Marie *psychotherapist*
Sarna, Helen Horowitz *retired librarian, educator*

West Roxbury
Barbosa, Tanya Marie *athletic trainer*

West Springfield
Anderson, Rita McKenzie *psychologist*
Barrientos, Jane Ellen *art educator*
Buckman, Lisa Pauline *psychotherapist*
Desai, Veena Balvantrai *obstetrician, gynecologist, educator*
McKenzie-Anderson, Rita Lynn *psychologist*
Moore, Kelly Ann *secondary school educator*

West Tisbury
Méras, Phyllis Leslie *journalist*

West Wareham
Worrell, Cynthia Lee *bank executive*

Westborough
Bok, Joan Toland *utilities executive*
Fenby, Barbara Lou *social worker*
Staffier, Pamela Moorman *psychologist*
Walker, Jeri A. *psychiatrist*

Westfield
Darling, Randi A. *science educator*
Dunphy, Maureen Milbier *literature educator*

Westford
Brady, Shelagh Ann *elementary school educator*
Geary, Marie Josephine *art association administrator*

Weston
Daly, Ellen M. *pediatrics nurse, educator*
Higgins, Sister Therese *literature educator, former college president*
Lin, Alice Lee Lan *physicist, researcher, educator*
Sanzone, Donna S. *publishing executive*
Tenney, Sarah G. *music educator*

Westwood
Philbrick, Margaret Elder *artist*

Weymouth
Atwater, Cynthia D. *English educator, secondary school educator*
Lamothe, Joanne Lewis *library director, consultant*

Williamstown
Blair, Phyllis E. *artist*
Conklin, Susan Joan *psychotherapist, educator, television personality, realtor*
Corrin, Lisa G. *museum director*
Cramer, Phebe *psychologist*
Driscoll, Genevieve Bosson (Jeanne Bosson Driscoll) *management and organization development consultant*
Graver, Suzanne Levy *English literature educator*
O'Brien, Elvy Setterqvist *art historian, educator, editor*

Wilmington
D'Alene, Alixandria Frances *human resources professional*
McLeod, Cheryl O'Halloran *artist, art educator*
Raven, Linda F. *mechanical engineer*

Winchester
Blackham, Ann Rosemary (Mrs. J. W. Blackham) *realtor*
Fitch, Blake *museum director, photographer, curator*
Harris, Carole Ruth *education educator, researcher, consultant*
Irving, Gitte Nielsen *secondary school educator*

Woburn
DeCrosta, Susan Elyse *graphic designer*
O'Doherty, Kathleen Marie *library director*
Preve, Roberta Jean *librarian, researcher*
Winson, Ellen-Marie (Macone) *school system administrator, reading specialist*

Woods Hole
Hart, Deborah Rachel *mathematical biologist, marine biologist*

Worcester
Byatt, Nancy *psychiatrist*
Cashman, Suzanne Boyer *health services administrator, educator*
Daley, Deborah Ann *assistant principal*
Dunlap, Ellen S. *library administrator*
Dwork, Debórah *history professor*
Dyer-Cole, Pauline *school psychologist, educator*
Falmagne, Rachel Joffe *psychologist, educator*
Hatfield, Renee S.J. *music educator*
Johnson, Penelope B. *librarian*
Kahn, AnnMarie *special education educator*
Kuklinski, Joan Lindsey *librarian*
Luna, Elizabeth (Jean) *cell biologist, educator, researcher*
Ott, Attiat Farag *economist, educator*
Plummer, Jeanine D. *engineering educator*
Pockwinse, Shirwin M. *research scientist, educator*
Selin, Lisa K. *physician*
Upshur, Carole Christof *psychologist, educator*

Worthington
Schrade, Rolande Maxwell Young *composer, pianist, educator*

Yarmouth Port
Jones, Marjorie Evelyn *retired special education educator*
McGill, Grace Anita *retired occupational health nurse*
St. Clair, Jane Elizabeth *health science association administrator, consultant*

MICHIGAN

Albion
Held, Nancy Jean *academic administrator, educator*
Lockyer, Judith *language educator*

Algonac
Bade, Sandra Lyne *secondary school educator*

Allen Park
Bizon, Emma Djafar *management consultant*

Allendale
Murray, Diane Elizabeth *librarian*
Thomas, Lorelle Otis *graphics designer, educator*

Alma
Kinkead, Verda Christine *non-profit organization executive, retired consultant*
Tracy, Saundra J. *academic administrator*

Ann Arbor
Agresta, Diane Marie *psychologist*
Akil, Huda *neuroscientist, educator, researcher*
Aller, Margo Friedel *astronomer*
Annchild, Cynthia *educational consultant*
Apperson, Jean *psychologist*
Arlinghaus, Sandra Judith Lach *mathematical geographer, educator*
Baler, Blanche Kimoto *retired child psychiatrist*
Ball, Deborah Loewenberg *dean, education educator*
Barbour, Carol Goodwin *psychoanalyst*
Beaubien, Anne Kathleen *librarian*
Beutler, Suzanne A. *retired secondary school educator, artist*
Bierbaum, Rosina M. *federal agency administrator*
Bloom, Jane Maginnis *emergency physician*
Bryant, Barbara Everitt *academic administrator, researcher, retired marketing professional, retired federal agency administrator*
Carpenter, Bogdana Maria Magdalena *language educator*
Chang, Annette M. *research scientist*
Chang, Hsueh-lun Shelley *historian, researcher, writer*
Clark, Noreen Morrison *behavioral science educator, researcher*
Conway, Lynn *computer scientist, electrical engineer, educator*
Curzan, Anne *linguist, educator*
Darlow, Julia Donovan *lawyer*
Daub, Peggy Ellen *library administrator*
Dede, Bonnie Aileen *librarian, educator*
Didier, Elaine K. *library director, educator*
Dominguez, Kathryn Mary *economist, educator*
Doyle, Constance Talcott Johnston *physician, educator, medical association administrator*
Dunlap, Connie *librarian*
Eccles, Jacquelynne S. *psychology educator*
Eisenstein, Elizabeth Lewisohn *historian, educator*
Ellsworth, Phoebe Clemencia *psychology professor*
Farmer, Cheryl Christine *internist, industrial hygienist*
Fleming, Suzanne Marie *academic administrator, freelance/self-employed writer*
Ford, Betty Ann (Elizabeth Ann Ford) *former First Lady of the United States, health facility executive*
Forsyth, Ilene Haering *art historian*
Garcia, Elisa Dolores *lawyer*
Gilbert, Anna *mathematics professor*
Green, Carmen R. *anesthesiologist, pain medicine physician*
Gregerson, Linda Karen *poet, language educator, critic*
Guardo, Carol J. *association executive*
Hanewich Duranczyk, Deborah A. *art therapist, educator*
Hinshaw, Ada Sue *nursing educator, former dean*
Holland, Jean Elinor *computer engineer, consultant*
Jackson, Trachette L. *biologist, educator*
Johnson, Brenda L. *university librarian*
Kalisch, Beatrice Jean *nursing educator, consultant*
Kaplan, Rachel *environmental psychologist, educator*
Katz, Ellen D. *law educator*
Kearfott, Kimberlee Jane *nuclear engineer, educator, health physicist*
Ketefian, Shaké *nursing educator*
Kramer, Barbara H. *lawyer*
Krauth, Laurie D. *psychotherapist, writer*
Leary, Margaret A. *law librarian, library director*
Lindsay, June Campbell McKee *communications executive*
Lozoff, Betsy *pediatrician, educator*
Ludwig, Martha *biochemist, educator*
MacKinnon, Catharine Alice *lawyer, educator, writer*
Marcus, Joyce (Joyce Marcus Flannery) *anthropology educator*
Markel, Geraldine *educational psychologist, consultant*
Matthews, Rowena Green *biological chemistry educator*
McCann, Peggy S. *physical education educator*
McLaughlin, Catherine G. *healthcare educator*
Mendelson, Nina *law educator*
Mitchell, Anna-Marie Rajala *quality/outcomes analyst*
Moore, Eleanor S. *retired elementary school educator*
Mouzon, Margaret Walker *information services executive*
Oakley, Deborah Jane *public health service officer, nursing educator*
Pascual, Mercedes *biology professor*
Payton, Sallyanne *law educator*
Perez, Laura R. *mathematics professor*
Porter, Amy *music educator*
Potempa, Kathleen M. *dean, nursing educator*
Powell, Linda Rae *educational healthcare consultant*
Ray, Elise *gymnast*
Reame, Nancy King *nursing educator*
Ross, Theresa Mae *secondary school educator*
Schmitt, Mary Elizabeth *retired postal supervisor*
Scott, Rebecca J. *law educator*
Shatz, Marilyn Joyce *psychologist, educator*
Sheldon, Ingrid Kristina *retired mayor, controller*
Sheon, Amy Ruth *biomedical researcher*
Shure, Patricia D. *mathematician, education educator*
Singer, Eleanor *sociologist, editor*
Sloat, Barbara Furin *cell biologist, educator*
Smith, Karen E. *mathematician, educator*
Strang, Ruth Hancock *pediatrician, educator, cardiologist, priest*
Sullivan, Teresa Ann *law and sociology educator, academic administrator*
Tice, Carol Hoff *intergenerational specialist, consultant*
Waltz, Susan *political scientist, educator*
Warren, Jane Carol *psychologist*
Whitesell, Patricia S. *academic administrator*
Whitman, Christina Brooks *law educator*
Whitman, Marina Von Neumann *economist, educator*
Wineman, Jean D. *architecture educator*

Armada
Price, Linda K. *small business owner*

Auburn Hills
Boyle, Olabisi Ariyo *manufacturing engineer*
Etefia, Florence Victoria *retired school psychologist*
Greenfield, Susan L. *lawyer*
Horiszny, Laurene Helen *lawyer*
Niekamp, Cynthia Ann *automotive executive*
Rae, Nancy A. *human resources specialist, automotive executive*
Suravajjala, Mamatha *information technology manager*

Unger, Susan J. *automotive executive*
Young, Stacy A. *information technology manager*

Bath
Wildt, Janeth Kae *small business owner*

Battle Creek
Baldwin, Susan Olin *commissioner, management consultant*
Banks, Donna Jo *food products executive*
Bowser, Shirley *volunteer*
Davis, Laura Arlene *retired foundation administrator*
Lincoln, Margaret *library media specialist*
Matthews, Wyhomme S. *retired music educator, academic administrator*
Siano, Jonna Teen *small business owner*
Stuever, Anita Carol *small business owner, secondary school educator*

Bay City
Frick, Kelly Adrian *editor*
Zuraw, Kathleen Ann *special education and physical education educator*

Belleville
Brown, Yvonne Theresa *retired writer*

Benton Harbor
Grove, Virginia A. *science educator*
Lundgren, Colleen Bowling *elementary school educator, consultant*
Tennant-Snyder, Nancy *appliance company executive*
Watkins, M(artha) Anne *family practice nurse practitioner*

Berkley
Leland, Janet K. *social work therapist*

Berrien Springs
Hamel, Lorie Ann *psychologist*
Rasmussen, Alice Call *retired nursing educator*
Summitt, April *history professor*

Beulah
Tanner, Helen Hornbeck *historian, consultant*

Beverly Hills
Harms, Deborah Gayle *psychologist*
Nawara, Lucille Procter *artist, educator*
Pardington, Mary Elizabeth *elementary school educator*

Bingham Farms
Krevsky, Margery Brown *talent agency executive*

Birch Run
Schluckebier, Carol J. *librarian*

Birmingham
Berman, Laura *journalist, writer*

Bloomfield
Tolmich, Andrea J. *music educator, department chairman*

Bloomfield Hills
Ball, Patricia Ann *physician*
Banas, C(hristine) Leslie *lawyer*
Bauser, Nancy *social worker, counselor*
Bogas, Kathleen Laura L. *lawyer*
Boulos, Nadia Ebid *medical/surgical nurse*
Haidostian, Alice Berberian *concert pianist, volunteer, not-for-profit fundraiser*
Jurkiewicz, Mary Louise *elementary school educator*
Katzman, Charlotte Phyllis *realtor*
Lapadot, Sonee Spinner *retired automobile manufacturing company official*
Levin, Carolyn Bible *volunteer*
Papai, Beverly Daffern *retired library director*
Simon, Evelyn *lawyer*
Starkman, Betty Provizer *genealogist, writer, educator*
Wermuth, Mary Louella *secondary school educator*

Bloomfield Township
Brown, Lynette Ralya *journalist, publicist*

Bloomingdale
Schultheis, Ann Lucia *curriculum specialist*

Bridgeport
Kushner, Aileen F. *elementary school educator*

Brighton
Jones, Marilyn Schlicher *conductor, retired music educator*

Brownstown
Slingerland, Mary Jo *writing educator*

Buchanan
Stromswold, Dorothy *retired secondary school educator*

Burton
Johnson-Brown, Linda Lee *music educator*

Cadillac
Mowrey, Corinne Ruth *secondary school educator*

Camden
Falls, Kathleene Joyce *photographer*

Canton
Schulz, Karen Alice *psychologist, medical psychotherapist, medical and vocational case manager*

Capac
Wagner, Dorothy Marie *retired senior creative designer, artist*

Carleton
Ely, Deborah D. *elementary school educator*

Caro
Galloway, Gladys *artist*
Hile, Michele Vera *middle school educator*
Ruckle, Barbara Ann *science educator*

Carrollton
Talik (Logan), Rebecca Lyn *chemistry professor*

Cass City
Kemp, Lori Ann *elementary school educator*

Charlotte
Coirolo, Christina *writer, author representative*
Walrath, Mary Therese *elementary school educator*

Cheboygan
Ostrowski, Stacey *athletic trainer, educator*

Chelsea
Kendall, Kay Lynn *interior designer, consultant*
Lipiec, Sherry Ann *art educator*

Chesterfield
Rodgers, Diana Lynn *elementary school educator*

Clarkston
Kovanis, Loukea Nakos *chemistry educator, researcher*
Snow, Sandra Inez *mortgage company executive*

Clawson
Smith, Paulette W. *secondary school educator*

Clifford
Staples, Lynne Livingston Mills *retired psychologist, educator, consultant*

Clinton
Anderson, Denice Anna *editor*
Scott, Sharon Ann *retired librarian, archivist*

Clinton Township
Fontanive, Lynn Marie *special education administrator*
Hage, Christine Lind *library administrator*

Commerce Township
Thibideau, Carolyn C. *musician, educator*

Davisburg
Forst, Catherine Phillips *library director*

Davison
West, Stacy Kathlena *athletic trainer*

Dearborn
Beauford, Sandra *nurse, data processing executive*
Berg, Nancy S. *science association director*
Buckingham, Lorie *automotive executive*
Fox, Stacy L. *lawyer*
Hansen, Barbara Sophie *elementary school educator*
Hess, Margaret Johnston *religious writer, educator*
Lee, Dorothy Ann *comparative literature educator*
Linnansalo, Vera *engineer*
MacLennan, Faith Alice *physical therapist, educator*
McKeage, Alice Jane *computer programmer*
Meyer, Lisa Marie *elementary school educator*
Wang, Liyan *product design engineer*

Dearborn Heights
Carter, Julia Marie *secondary school educator*
Chapper, Barbara Mae *retired pediatrician*

Detroit
Acton, Elizabeth S. *corporate financial executive*
Ashley, Lois A. *retired university reference librarian*
Audia, Christina *librarian*
Barclay, Kathleen S. *automotive executive*
Barrett, Nancy Smith *academic administrator*
Bassett, Tina *communications executive*
Bell Wilson, Carlotta A. *state official, consultant*
Bennett, Margaret Ethel Booker *psychotherapist*
Booth, Betty Jean *retired daycare administrator, poet*
Brown, Gloria Diane *elementary school educator*
Bully-Cummings, Ella M. *police chief*
Burnside, Wanda Jacqueline *elementary school educator*
Burzynski, Susan Marie *newspaper editor*
Chauderlot, Fabienne-Sophie *foreign language educator*
Colby, Joy Hakanson *critic*
Corbitt, Eumiller Mattie *special education educator*
Corrigan, Maura Denise *state supreme court justice*
Covensky, Edith *language educator, poet*
Crawford, Andrea Kirvene *business educator*
Dannin, Ellen Jean *lawyer*
Diehl, Nancy J. *lawyer*
Duensing, Dorothy Jean *music educator, vocalist*
Duncan-White, Dynah Naomi Juliette *marketing professional*
Edmunds, Nancy Garlock *federal judge*
Edwards, Lora Brunett *retired property manager*
Ellyn, Lynne *energy executive*
Engelhardt, Regina *cosmetologist, artist, small business owner*
Felt, Julia Kay *lawyer*
Field, Judith Judy *librarian*
Frenette, Geraldine Gloria *librarian*
Galovich, Beverly Lucille *psychologist*
Good, Amy *educational association administrator*
Hanks, Robin *rehabilitation nurse*
Harlan, Carmen *television journalist*
Heppner, Gloria Hill *health facility administrator, educator*
Ilitch, Marian *professional hockey team executive, food service executive*
Jackson, Linda Shorter *nutritionist, educator*
Jackson, Marion Elizabeth *art educator*
Jenkins-Anderson, Barbara Jeanne *pathologist, educator*
Kachalsky, Ellen *social worker*
Kantrowitz, Jean *health products executive*
Kelly, Marilyn *state supreme court justice*
Kempston Darkes, V. Maureen *automotive executive*
Kennedy, Cornelia Groefsema *federal judge*
Kline, Mable Cornelia Page *retired secondary school educator*
Klont, Barbara Anne *librarian*
Kruse, Ronia *information technology executive*
Lazarus, Lila *announcer*
Lee, Marcella *announcer*
Little, Laura Ann *elementary school educator, art educator*
Lusher, Jeanne Marie *pediatric hematologist, educator*
Madgett, Naomi Long *poet, editor, publisher, educator*
McCracken, Caron Francis *information technology consultant*
McCrae, Jocelyn Diane *psychologist*
McIntosh, Deborah V. *elementary school educator*
McKenzie, Diane M. *science educator*
McNichols, Mary Alice *humanities educator*
Moldenhauer, Judith A. *graphic design educator*
Morgan, Virginia Mattison *judge*
Morlan, Judith Jeannette *science eductor*
Morrow, Kathy Ann *psychologist, social worker*
Nabozny, Heather *professional sports team groundskeeper*
Owen, Karen Michelle *manufacturing executive*
Pacha, Melinda Jane *performing arts educator*
Parsons, Anne *performing company executive*
Redman, Barbara Klug *nursing educator*
Rozof, Phyllis Claire *lawyer*
Salter, Linda Lee *security officer*
Schlichting, Nancy Margaret *hospital administrator*
Shannon, Margaret Anne *lawyer*
Shorter, Michelle Anne *secondary educator*
Sikula, Christine Lynn *legal association administrator, education educator*
Sims, Veronica Gail *literature educator*
Skowronski, Nancy *library director*
Smith, Lillian Louise *biology educator, librarian*
Speegle, Laura Ann *elementary school educator*
Spencer, Ruth *announcer*
Taylor, Anna Diggs *federal judge*
Terry, Robin *museum director*
Thayer, Nancy J. *artist, educator*
Topacio, Angela *marketing executive*
Valentine, Cheryl Ann Whitney *music educator*
Walker, Rhonda Gillum *announcer*
Washington, Olivia Grace Mary *psychotherapist, educator, counselor, researcher*
White, Katherine E. *law educator*
Williams, Denise *academic administrator*
Wolf, Michael Ann *announcer*

Dexter
Hanamey, Rosemary T. *nursing educator*

Douglas
Karamas, Joyce Efthemia *art educator, consultant, artist*

Durand
Thorsen, Phyllis Lorane *middle school educator*

East Lansing
Bandes, Susan Jane *museum director, educator*
Bruno, Maria Frances *writing and cultural educator*
Crewe, Nancy Moe *retired psychologist*
Draper, Penny Kaye Pekrul *music educator*
Hine, Darlene Clark *history educator, administrator*
Kalof, Linda Henry *sociologist, educator*
Luecke, Eleanor Virginia Rohrbacher *civic volunteer*
McKinley, Camille Dombrowski *psychologist*
McMeekin, Dorothy *botanist, plant pathologist, educator*
Nickelson, Pamela Sue *music educator*
Noel, Mary Margaret *nutritionist, educator*
Patterson, Maria Jevitz *microbiology/pediatric infectious disease professor*
Rappley, Marsha D. *dean, physician, educator*
Reinhart, Mary Ann *medical board executive*
Rothert, Marilyn L. *dean, nursing educator*
Simon, Lou Anna Kimsey *academic administrator*
Sisk, Cheryl *neuroscientist, educator*
Tzitsikas, Helene *retired literature educator*
Wakoski, Diane *poet, educator*
Whiting Dobson, Lisa Lorraine *video production educator, producer, director*

Eastpointe
Patrick, Susanne *secondary school educator*

Elk Rapids
Kitchen, Barbette Louise *retired secondary school educator*

Erie
Jenne, Carole Seegert *minister, marriage and family therapist*

Escanaba
Bennett, Kathleen Mavourneen *elementary school educator*
Malenfant, Suzanne Marie *science educator*
Robinson, Laura Ann *music educator*

Farmington
Burns, Sister Elizabeth Mary *retired hospital administrator*
Cherem, Barbara Brown *education educator*
Purdy, Jan Rae *music educator*

Farmington Hills
Baughman, Leonora Knoblock *lawyer*
Dolan, Jan Clark *former state legislator*
Eisner, Gail Ann *artist, educator*
Ellmann, Sheila Frenkel *investment company executive*
Fershtman, Julie Ilene *lawyer*
Hurd, Mary K. *civil engineer, writer*
Robinson, Amorie Alexia *psychologist, educator*
Sparrow, Laura *secondary school educator*

Fenton
Hayes, Pamela M. *music educator*

Ferndale
Forkan, Eveleen *counselor, educator, researcher*

Flint
Alarie-Anderson, Peggy Sue *physician assistant*
Bobb, Carolyn Ruth *science writer*
Conyers, Jean Louise *chamber of commerce executive*
Heymoss, Jennifer Marie *librarian*
McClanahan, Connie Dea *pastoral minister*
Sharbaugh, Kathryn Kennedy *artist*
Thum, D. Maureen *language educator*
Williams, Veronica Myres *psychotherapist, social worker*

Flushing
Demankowski, Lisa Renee *architect, educator*

Fort Gratiot
Atkins, Cindy L. *elementary school educator*

Frankenmuth
Rau, Louise Billie *interior designer*

Franklin
Reinhart, Anne Christine *special education educator, consultant*
Sax, Mary Randolph *speech and language pathologist*

Fremont
Blamer, Beverly A. *elementary school educator*

Fruitport
Collier, Beverly Joanne *retired elementary school educator*

Gaylord
Magsig, Judith Anne *retired primary school educator*

Gladstone
Toutloff, Betty Jane *retired social worker*

Gladwin
Chartier, Mary Eileen *music educator*

Gobles
Jacus, Ann Margaret *secondary school educator*

Grand Blanc
McAlindon, Mary Naomi *retired nursing consultant*

Grand Haven
Cahalan, Amy K. *secondary school educator*

Grand Rapids
Bolhuis, Doreen *recreational facility executive, physical education educator*
Bolt, Eunice Mildred DeVries *artist*
Brent, Helen Teressa *school nurse*
Brink, Emily Ruth *music educator*
Chase, Sandra Lee *clinical pharmacist, consultant*
Chiara, Margaret M. *prosecutor, lawyer*
DeLapa, Judith Anne *business owner*
Gemmell-Akalis, Bonni Jean *psychotherapist*
Helder, Karen Fay *social worker*
Henry, Karen Lee *writer, educator*
Hollies, Linda Hall *pastor, educator, author*
Hoogenboom, Barbara Jo *physical therapist, educator*
Horn, Joyce Elaine *music educator*
Hoskins, Debbie Stewart *librarian, artist*
Hunt, Gladys Mae *writer*
Jackoboice, Sandra Kay *artist*
Jones, Ora McConner *retired foundation administrator*
Kramer, Carol Gertrude *marriage and family counselor*
Lewis Jackson, Wendy S. *social worker*
Maupin, Karin Louise *secondary school educator*
Paterson, Hattie P. *philanthropist*
Purchase-Owens, Francena *marketing professional, consultant, educator*
Saigal, Ashima *not-for-profit developer*
Stevenson, Jo Ann C. *federal bankruptcy judge*
Van Dyke, Michelle *bank executive*
Williams, Janice H. *business executive*

Grosse Ile
Smith, Veronica Latta *real estate company officer*
Stryker, Joan Copeland *retired obstetrician, retired gynecologist, educator*
Stump, M. Pamela *sculptor*

Grosse Pointe
Disanto, Carol L. (Carol La Chiusa) *artist*
Foust, Julie Ann *secondary school educator*
Whittaker, Jeanne Evans *retired journalist*

Grosse Pointe Farms
Couzens, Linda Lee Anderson *oncology nurse*
Kerns, Gertrude Yvonne *psychologist*
Obolensky, Marilyn Wall (Mrs. Serge Obolensky) *metals company executive*
Thibodeau, Virginia Durbin *artist*

Grosse Pointe Park
Harmon, Phyllis Darnell *mortgage banker*
Knapp, Mildred Florence *retired social worker*

Grosse Pointe Woods
McWhirter, Glenna Suzanne (Nickie McWhirter) *retired columnist*

Hale
Lixey, Elizabeth Voulgarakis *secondary school educator*

Hamtramck
LeVan, Deborah Jo *internist*

Hancock
Sampson, Susan Audrey *private school educator*
Tuisku, Mary Joan *volunteer, advocate*

Harbor Springs
Cappel, Constance *educational consultant, writer*

Harper Woods
Madeleine, Elizabeth Leigh *science educator*

Harris
Erva, Karen Therese *elementary school educator*

Harrison
Valentine, Anna Mae *retired nurse*

Hemlock
Wallace, Beatrice Leslie *secondary school educator*

Henderson
Miller, Kathleen Mae *educational association administrator*

Hillsdale
Robichaud, Donna Lynn *career planning administrator*
Stoyk, Kay Marie *special education educator*

Holland
Van Noord, Diane C. *artist, educator*

Holly
Evans Snowden, Audra Lynn *counselor*

Holt
Smith, Betty W. *librarian*
Thompson, Teresa Ackerman *special education educator*
Weinner, Brenda Lynne *director, education educator, special education educator*
Wood, Mary Elizabeth *retired secondary school educator, church musician*

Houghton
Beckwith, Mary Ann *art educator*
Bruch, Debra Lynn *theater educator*

Howell
Jagdfeld, Judy A. *coach, secondary school educator*
Schoendorff, Christine Joy *elementary school educator*

Ida
Griffith, Cathleen Ann *principal*

Imlay City
Kowalski, Kathleen Patricia *reporter, publishing executive*

Interlochen
Kamischke, Ellen Jane *mathematics educator, writer*
Tacke, Eleanor *archivist*

Ionia
Ulmer, Evonne Gail *health science association administrator*

Ishpeming
Hyttinen, Nicole Marie *elementary school educator*

Jackson
Feldmann, Judith Gail *language professional, educator*
Fifelski, Therese Yolande *microbiologist*
Genyk, Ruth Bel *psychotherapist*
Haglund, Bernice Marion *elementary school educator*
Livesay, Jacqueline Ryder *elementary school educator, music educator*
Riedel, Juanita Maxine *writing educator*
Stone, Marilyn Joanne *elementary school educator*
Wilcox, Charlene Deloris *retired elementary school educator*

Jenison
Frye, Della Mae *portrait artist*

Kalamazoo
Bailey, Judith Irene *academic administrator, educator, consultant*
Barth, Jessica L. *mathematics educator*
Bennett, Arlie Joyce *clinical social worker*
Brodbeck, Mary Lou *artist, furniture designer*
Buskirk, Phyllis Richardson *retired economist*
Chesak, Kristen *performing company executive*
Dahlinger, Martha Louise *elementary school educator*
Davison, Kim M. *elementary school educator*
Fredericks, Sharon Kay *nurse's aide*
Geerling, Falinda Sue *language educator*
Gordon, Alice Jeannette Irwin *retired secondary school educator, retired elementary school educator*
Grotzinger, Laurel Ann *librarian, educator*
Hollar, Susan Steffens *mathematics professor*
Howard-Wyne, Josie *elementary school educator*
Lander, Joyce Ann *retired nursing educator, retired medical/surgical nurse*
Lennon, Elizabeth Marie *retired special education educator*
Lester, Sandra Kay *social worker*
Moore, Stephanie LaFaye *advocate, director*
Morris, Martha Josephine *information services administrator*
Ortiz-Button, Olga *social worker*
Petersen, Anne C. (Cheryl Petersen) *foundation administrator, educator*
Pinkham, Eleanor Humphrey *retired university librarian*
Showalter, Shirley H. *academic administrator*
Walcott, Delores Deborah *psychologist, educator*
Wicklund, Karen Jean *voice and health professional, educator*
Yoder-Gagnon, Pamala S. *retired orthopedic nurse*

Keego Harbor
Gee, Sharon Lynn *funeral director, educator*

Kent City
Mulder, Susan Elizabeth *special education educator*

Kentwood
Thompson, Anne *music educator*

Laingsburg
Collins, Mary Alice *psychotherapist, social worker*

Lake Orion
Berger, Laura Ann *dance studio owner*
Leonard, Jacquelyn Ann *retired elementary school educator*

Lambertville
Korthuis, Kathleen Elizabeth *retired dean*

Lanse
Berggren-Moilanen, Bonnie Lee *education educator*
Butler, Patricia *protective services official*

Lansing
Blackwell, Dorothy Ruth *school system administrator*
Brendahl, Marcia *artist, illustrator*
Brown, Nancy Field *editor*
Chaney, Elizabeth Moncrief *state agency administrator*
Destrempes, Sandra Lee *elementary school educator*
Dickinson, Melinda S. *elementary school educator*
Granholm, Jennifer Mulhern *governor*
Land, Terri Lynn *state official*
Linder, Iris Kay *lawyer*
Marazita, Eleanor Marie Harmon *retired secondary school educator*
Nicholas, Caroline Jean *retired nurse, consultant*
Olszewski, Janet *state agency administrator*
Pollack, Lana *state senator*
Stanaway, Loretta Susan *small business owner*
Stein, Trisha *advocate*
Straus, Kathleen Nagler *academic administrator, educator*
Summitt, Alixandra Pablita *art educator*
Tombers, Evelyn Charlotte *lawyer, educator*
Torres-Dickson, Teresita Sancho *elementary school educator*
Winkler, Sue Elaine *art psychotherapist, social worker*

Lapeer
Gates, Penelope Kandis *obstetrical nurse*
McCauley, Betty Bailey *school system administrator*

Lathrup Village
Taylor, Alicia *art educator*

Lincoln Park
Russell, Harriet Shaw *social worker*

Linden
Tomaszewski, Kathleen Bernadette *social worker, educator*

Livonia
Baskin, Victoria *child and adolescent psychiatrist*
Gepford, Barbara Beebe *retired nutrition educator*
Holtzman, Roberta Lee *French and Spanish language educator*
Juenemann, Julie Ann *psychologist, educator*
Kujawa, Sister Rose Marie *academic administrator*
Needham, Kathleen Ann *gerontology educator, consultant*
Regner, Deborah Allyson *educator*
Thoms, Susan Stuckey *ophthalmologist*
Wilder, JaNell Lynn *music educator*

Lowell
Reid Jenkins, Debra L. *artist*

Macomb
Christopher, Kathy Lynn *secondary school educator*

Madison Heights
Uhlmann, Jamie A. *secondary school educator*

Manistee
Swan-Eagan, Cynthia J. *music educator*

Manistique
Jeffcott, Janet Bruhn *statistician, consultant*
LaLonde, Angela J. *primary school educator*

Marquette
Becker, Amy Salminen *librarian*
Coffey, Lauriann Gant *elementary school educator*
Earle, Mary Margaret *marketing executive*
Henderson, Roberta Marie *librarian, educator*
Kahler, Dorothy Stirling *psychotherapist*
Mahmood, Tallat *oncologist, hematologist*
Sherony, Cheryl Anne *dietician*

Marshall
Hammond, Jane Pamela *adult education educator*
Petrich, Kathryn *music educator*

Mecosta
Wenzel, Karen Marie *writer*

Merrill
Ellenwood, Heather Sky *music educator*

Midland
Barker, Nancy Lepard *university official*
Belton, Betty Kepka *retired art educator, artist*
Burns, Stephanie A. *chemicals executive*
Grzesiak, Katherine Ann *primary school educator*
Holder, Julie Fasone *chemicals executive*
Meinhardt, Carol Jean *education educator*
Messing, Carol Sue *communications educator*
Strange, Alice Marian *social worker*

Monroe
Bean, Lori J. *chemistry professor*
McCracken, Kathryn Angela *clinical social worker*
Siciliano, Elizabeth Marie *secondary school educator*
Sweat, Sara J. *secondary school educator*

Mount Pleasant
Louisell, Linda Kay *elementary education educator, musician*
Morrisroe, Julia Marie *art gallery director, artist*
Redman, Joann A. *medical/surgical nurse*
Seefelt, Nancy E. *academic administrator, educator*
Smallwood, Carol *writer*
Traines, Rose Wunderbaum *sculptor, educator*

Muskegon
Cirona, Jane Callahan *investment company executive*
Cusick Reimink, Ruth Elizabeth *community health nurse*
Ohst, Wendy Joan *government agency administrator, educator*
Ross, Annette Lee *educational consultant*
Swartz, Wilma Jeeanne *music educator*

Nashville
Pash, Teresa A. *piano teacher, performer*

New Baltimore
Sheldrick, Barbara England *music educator, consultant*

Niles
Wickham, Cindy Sue *principal*

North Branch
Forys, Linda R. *science educator*

North Muskegon
Heyen, Beatrice J. *psychotherapist*

Northville
Hansen, Jean Marie *mathematics educator, computer educator*
Long, Robin Jane Ellingsworth *elementary school educator, special education educator*

Norton Shores
Chichester, Faith Christine *elementary school educator*

Novi
Holforty, Pearl Martha *accountant*
Ligocki, Kathleen A. *auto parts company executive*
Myers, Lee Ann *accountant*
Serenson, Lynn Ann *mathematics educator*

Oak Park
Coleman, Dorothy Charmayne *nurse*
Rutherford, Guinevere Faye *surgeon*

Okemos
Behrens, Ellen Elizabeth Cox *writer, counselor, educator*
Berkman, Claire Fleet *psychologist*
Burnett, Jean B. (Mrs. James R. Burnett) *biochemist, educator*
Edwards, Caryn Louise *educational consultant, special education educator*
Herrick, Kathleen Magara *retired social worker*
Prout, Carolyn Ann *controller, personnel administrator*
Sliker, Shirley J. Brocker *bookseller*
Wager, Paula Jean *artist*

Oscoda
Shackleton, Mary Jane *small business owner*

Oshtemo
Arnold, Nancy Kay *writer*

Ossineke
Larson, Ilene Kay *elementary school educator*

Otisville
Morris, Valerie Lyn *secondary school educator*

Owosso
Bentley, Margaret Ann *librarian*
Reynolds, Pauline Phyllis *retired primary school educator*
Rugenstein, Carrie L. *secondary school educator*

Petoskey
Switzer, Carolyn Joan *artist, educator*

Pigeon
Jackson, Nancy Ellen *retired internist*

Pinckney
McNamara, Ann Dowd *medical technician*
Weatherbee, Ellen Gene Elliott *botanist, educator*

Plainwell
Flower, Jean Frances *art educator*
Tiefenthal, Marguerite Aurand *school social worker*

Plymouth
Berry, Charlene Helen *librarian, musician*
Melkvik, Jennifer Kent *retired mathematics educator*
Moore-Viculin, Charlotte Anne *artist, musician*
Whiteley, Kendra Leigh *secondary school educator*

Pontiac
Anderson, Anita A. *secondary school educator*
Hicks, Christy Ann *communications educator*
Riley, Mary Jane Stewart *secondary school educator*

Port Huron
Miller, Theresa L. *library director*
Rowark, Maureen *fine arts photographer*

Portage
Dobler, Janis Dolores *small business owner*
Farrand, Lois Barbara *pharmaceutical company administrator*
Kim, Sonja Chung *elementary school educator*
Poulsen, Daniall Rei *science educator*
Selden, Margery Juliet Stomne *music educator*

Powers
Kleikamp, Beverly *poet, writer, publisher*

Quinnesec
Opolka, Jayme Lyn *medical writer, researcher*

Redford
Karpinski, Huberta *library trustee*

River Rouge
Myhand, Cheryl *minister, educator*

Rochester
Cordes, Mary Kenrick *psychologist, retired*
Hughes, Rosemary A. *counselor, educator*
Kleimola, Sharon Leigh *retired elementary school educator*
Mullin, Norma Rose *psychotherapist*
Packard, Sandra Podolin *education educator, consultant*
Pope, Melissa Lopez *law educator*
Schimmelman, Janice G. *art historian*

Rochester Hills
Anjum, Uzma *pre-school educator*

Rockford
Irish, Diana Maria *wildlife rehabilitation agent*
Shutich, Tina Lynn *mathematics educator*

Romeo
Matthews Ellis, Bonnie *management consultant*

Roscommon
Balbach, Lisa Jean *information scientist, educator*

Royal Oak
Ernstoff, Raina Marcia *neurologist*
McCarroll, Kathleen Ann *radiologist, educator*
Thomson, Kathleen Kepner *retired state agency administrator*

Saginaw
Coughlin, Jeannine Marie *music educator*
Haynes, Iris Fitzgerald *music educator*
Killingbeck, Janice Lynelle (Mrs. Victor Lee Killingbeck) *journalist*
Markey, Leah Gene *elementary school educator*
Moyer, Genevieve J. *counselor*
Othersen-Khalifa, Cheryl Lee *insurance agent, realtor*
Shek, Eugenie Victoria *artist*
Strawter, Lee Anna *secondary school educator*
Venable, Sarah *art educator*

Saint Clair Shores
Kachman, Frances Guiducci *artist*
Kavadas-Pappas, Iphigenia Katherine *preschool administrator, educator, consultant*
Lapadot, Gayle K. *nursing administrator*
Skoney, Sophie Essa *educational administrator*
Vogel, Sally Thomas *psychologist, social worker, educator*
Zimmer, Anne Fern Young *educator, researcher, administrator*

Saline
Gannett, Diana Ruth *musician, educator*
Kittel, Pamela Rae *education educator*
Low, Louise Anderson *consulting company executive*

Scottville
Wojciechowski, Amy Jo *college official*

Shelby Township
Osuch, Debra K. *materials engineer*

Skandia
Johnson, Judy M. *artist, writer*

South Haven
Llorens, Merna Gee *elementary school educator, retired music educator*

South Lyon
Athey, Sarah Elizabeth-Marks *secondary school educator, social studies educator*

Southfield
Ali, Sandra *announcer*
Barnett, Marilyn *advertising executive*
Ben-Ami, Dorit Amalia *psychiatrist*
Bennett, Helen *psychotherapist*
Bingaman, Anne K. *lawyer*
Carman, Kam *announcer*
Centofanti, Deena *announcer*
Chudnov, Marlene Myra *elementary school educator, educational consultant*
Clifford, Carolyn *news correspondent, reporter*
Davis-Yancey, Gwendolyn *lawyer*
Giles, Lynda Fern *clinical psychologist*
Hartman-Abramson, Ilene *medical educator*
Hill, Juantonia NeKeshia *mathematics educator, consultant*
Hoffman, Susan Patricia Wary *special education educator, elementary school educator*
Hudson, Cheryl L. *communications executive*
Hupe, Pallas *announcer*
Lewis, Diane *announcer*
Makupson, Amyre Porter *broadcast executive*
Martin, Marcella Edric *retired community health nurse*
McDonald, Christy *newscaster*
Miller, Nancy Ellen *computer scientist, consultant*
Naber, Faith *retired librarian, educator*
Osborne, Marie-Angela *journalist*
Pickett, Sherry M. *social worker*
Primo, Joan Erwina *retail and real estate consulting business owner*
Purtan, JoAnne *announcer*
Quinlan, Patricia *retired art educator*
Sedler, Rozanne Friedlander *social worker, educator*
Siegel-Hinson, Robyn Lee *psychologist, consultant, clinic director*
Teska, Jane E. *science educator*
Timmons, Robbie *news anchor*
Torraco, Pamela Louise *psychotherapist*
Wagner, Muriel Ginsberg *nutrition therapist*

Weiner, Karen Colby (Karen Lynn Colby) *psychologist, lawyer*
Wheeland, Joyce A. *information technology executive*

Southgate
Gundick, Sinthea Marie *assistant principal*
Torok, Margaret Louise *insurance company executive*

Sparta
Bomhof, Robyn *artist, educator*
McDonald, Lois Alice *elementary school educator*
Miller, Barbara Jean *health facility administrator*

Spring Lake
Bussard, Janice Wingeier *retired secondary school educator*

Sterling Heights
Campbell, Nancy Jeanne *science educator*
Forche, Jennifer Roth *clinical psychologist*
Hammond-Kominsky, Cynthia Cecelia *optometrist*
McKinney, Theresa *secondary school educator*
Pericak, KrysAnna *biology educator*
Rotatchka, Janice Marie *medical/surgical and critical care nurse*

Sylvan Lake
Derdarian, Christine Anne *lawyer*

Taylor
Coleman, Fay *literature and language educator, director*
Crawford, Manette Sue *parochial school educator*

Tecumseh
Kane, Sue Ann *counselor, geriatrics nurse*
Sackett, Dianne Marie *city treasurer, accountant*

Three Rivers
Pierce, Sue *sales executive*

Traverse City
Anderson, Carol Lynn *social worker, educator*
Bullis, Jo Louise *social services administrator, educator*
Burton, Betty June *retired pastor*
Hale, Carol Jean *teacher, city commissioner*
Hogg, Cinda L.P. *elementary school educator*
Leuenberger, Betty Lou *psychologist, educator*
Lutes, Charlene Ann *academic administrator, director, consultant*
Tejkl, Pamela Marie *secondary school educator*
Weaver, Elizabeth A. *state supreme court justice*

Trenton
Beebe, Grace Ann *retired special education educator*

Troy
Austin, Karen *retail executive*
Elder, Irma *retail executive*
Healy, Karen *automotive executive*
Hodges, Michele *chamber of commerce executive*
Hucal, Michelle *editor*
Mahone, Barbara Jean *automotive executive*
Maierle, Bette Jean *director*
Majeske, Penelope Kantgias *education educator, educator*
Meyers, Christine Laine *marketing and media executive, consultant*
Navarro, Monica *lawyer*
Schafer, Sharon Marie *anesthesiologist*
Walker, Bette *automotive executive*

University Center
May, Margrethe *healthcare educator*
Rickey, Betty L. *nursing educator*

Walled Lake
Remer, Deborah Jane *elementary school educator*

Warren
Bell, Julie Marie *health facility administrator, consultant*
Henry, Julie L. *orthopedist, surgeon*
Kolakowski, Diana Jean *county commissioner*
Lavin, Sharon Renai *secondary school educator*
Pranger, Kathleen *computer science educator*
Shaw, Mary Joe *nurse*
Zoubareff, Kathy Olga *administrative assistant*

Washington
Gardner, Karen *mathematics educator, computer scientist, educator*

Waterford
Anderson, Francile Mary *secondary school educator*
Price, Kim Denise *counselor*
Pronovost, Amy Lynne *dancer, educator*

Watervliet
Kaiser, Susan J. *investment advisor*

Wayland
Stephenson-Bennett, Michelle Annette *music educator*

Wayne
Drake, Patricia Ann Glasscock *psychologist*

West Bloomfield
Beron, Gail Laskey *real estate analyst, real estate appraiser, consultant*
Lansaw, Traci Lynn *mathematics educator*
Mamut, Mary Catherine *retired entrepreneur*
Smith, Nancy Hohendorf *sales executive, marketing professional*
Williamson, Marilyn Lammert *literature educator, academic administrator*

Westland
Demonbruen, Tonya Rochelle *science educator*
Drews, Kristine Mae *secondary school educator*

Whitmore Lake
Kohler, Janet Sue *artist*
Wassilak, Janet Marian *choral director*

White, Susan Rochelle *psychologist, investor*

Wilson
Harris, Mary Lynn *science educator, consultant*

Wixom
Welch, Cherie Lynn *healthcare educator*

Wyandotte
Dunn, Gloria Jean *artist*

Wyoming
Couch, Katrina Denise *elementary school educator*

Ypsilanti
Beiting, Sarah Louise *library director*
Cantrell, Linda Maxine *counselor*
Fox, Diane Porretta *nursing educator*
Henderson, Maxine *writer*
Lewis-White, Linda Beth *elementary school educator*
Peoples, Alice Leigh *not-for-profit executive*
Pollock, Sandra Sue *retired elementary educator*
Stevens, Lizbeth Jane *special education educator, researcher*
Stuppard-Byars, Doris J. *minister*
Warner, Jo F. *mathematics instructor*

Zeeland
Pyle, Debra Lee *elementary school educator*

MINNESOTA

Afton
Robb, Babette *retired elementary school educator*

Anoka
Lindbergh, Reeve *writer, poet*

Apple Valley
Haaheim, Patricia Jane Dando *pastor, consultant*

Austin
Jelinek, Polly Madison *retired elementary school educator*

Baxter
Harmer, Nicole Christine *science educator*

Bemidji
Christenson, Eileen Esther *geriatrics nurse*
DeKrey, Petra Jean Hegstad *retired elementary school educator*
Martinson, Ida Marie *medical/surgical nurse, educator, physiologist*

Bloomington
Larson, Beverly Rolandson *retired elementary school educator*
Nichols, Donna Mardell *nurse anesthetist*
Taylor, Susan S. *performance consultant*
vanReken, Mary K. *psychologist*

Brainerd
Russell, Maxine *poet, writer*

Breezy Point
Anderson, Gail Marie *retired librarian*

Buffalo
Hemish, Carol Marie *liturgist/spiritual director, musician*

Caledonia
Lapham, Mary Ellen *elementary school educator*

Champlin
Lim, Joalin Peck-Kian *biomedical engineer, researcher*

Chaska
Affinito, Mona Gustafson *psychologist*

Circle Pines
Roden, Mary Jane *mathematician, educator*

Clara City
Jardine, Kathy Jo *science educator*

Cloquet
Belanger, Sharon Amling *special education educator*

Collegeville
Forman, Mary *dean*

Coon Rapids
Bordner, Patricia Anne *insurance agent, writer*
Boros, Deborah Theresa *elementary school educator*
Carlson, Linda Marie *language arts educator, consultant*
Goodstein-Shapiro, Florence (Florence Goodstein Walton) *artist, art historian*
Haij, Karla Marie *secondary school educator*
Wilson, Sylvia Alyce *musician, educator*

Cottage Grove
Glazebrook, Rita Susan *nursing educator*

Crystal
Stark, Janice Ann *elementary school educator*

Duluth
Amberg, Deborah Ann *lawyer*
Carlson, Helen Louise *educator*
Gruver, Nancy *publishing executive*
Heller, Lois Jane *physiologist, educator, researcher*
Jenkins, Virginia *artist, educator*
Martin, Kathryn A. *academic administrator*
Salmela, Lynn Marie *clinical nurse specialist*
Stauber-Johnson, Elizabeth Jane *retired elementary school educator*
Stoddard, Patricia Florence Coulter *retired psychologist*
Teich, Theresa Marie *educator*

Eagan
Bulger, Raymonde Albertine *French language educator*
Byrne, Roseanne *library director*
Dulas, DeAnne L. *lawyer*
Horvath, Betty Ferguson *writer*

East Grand Forks
Engel, Carol Louise *music educator*

Easton
Schrader, LuAnn Carol *art educator*

Eden Prairie
De Bono, Luella Elizabeth *music educator*
Feuss, Linda Anne Upsall *lawyer*
Knous, Pamela K. *wholesale distribution executive*
Petersen, Maureen Jeanette Miller *management information technology director, retired nurse*
Schaeffer, Brenda Mae *psychologist, author*

Edina
Davidson, Ann D. *lawyer, aerospace transportation executive*
Douglas, Marjorie Myers *writer*
Emmerich, Karol Denise *foundation executive, daylily hybridizer, former retail executive*
Holman, Iletta Marcella *retired art educator*
Kata, Marie L. *securities dealer, brokerage house executive*
Kirchner, Mary Katherine *musician, educator*
Nelson, Patricia Joan Pingenot *retired language educator*
Schaibley, Ann M. *lawyer*
Worthing, Carol Marie *retired minister*

Elbow Lake
Lohse, Susan Faye *county official, educator*

Elysian
Thayer, Edna Louise *health facility administrator*

Erskine
Wahlin, Shelly R. *voice educator*

Excelsior
Henke, Janice Carine *educational software developer, marketing professional*
Pfeifer, Polly Lee *elementary school educator*
Waterhouse, Beth Elaine *writer, editor, environmental educator*

Fairmont
Sadek, Noha *psychiatrist*

Faribault
Collins, Ruth Ann *principal*
Jensen, Annette M. *mental health nurse, administrator*

Fisher
Hanson, Tena Lorayn *finance educator*

Foley
Cross, Eunice D. *elementary school educator*

Forest Lake
Skrip, Cathy Lee *psychologist*

Fosston
Lohmeier, Lynda K. *secondary school educator*

Fridley
Larson, Marilyn J. *retired music educator*

Glencoe
Delagardelle, Linda *food executive*

Golden Valley
Leppik, Margaret White *municipal official*
Spake, Mary Barbara *music educator*

Goodridge
Hanson, Norma Lee *farmer*

Grand Marais
Napadensky, Hyla Sarane *engineering consultant*

Grand Meadow
Moe, Janet Kirsten *music educator*

Grand Rapids
King, Sheryl Jayne *secondary school educator, counselor*

Hackensack
Marquart, Petra A. *training consultant*

Hastings
Avent, Sharon L. Hoffman *manufacturing company executive*
Orr, Jennie Marie (Jennie Thomas) *family physician*

Hibbing
Langanki, Debra Lynn *secondary school educator*
Williams, Jojo Macasaet *office administrator*
Zbikowski, Kristen Lynn *education educator*

Hopkins
Young, Margaret Labash *librarian, information consultant, editor*
Zins, Martha Lee *elementary school educator, director*

Inver Grove Heights
Ochman, Janet *psychology professor*

Kenyon
Page, Amy Lynn *special education educator*

La Crescent
Moen, Cheryl A. *literature and language educator*

Lake Elmo
Tomljanovich, Esther M. *retired judge*

Lakeville
Schaefer, Elzbieta A. *music educator*

Lindstrom
Messin, Marlene Ann *plastics company executive*

Long Lake
Hofkin, Ann Ginsburgh *photographer, poet*
Lowthian, Petrena *academic administrator*
Priesz, Connie Joan *secondary school educator*

Mahtomedi
Nickleby, Kathe Jo Anne *assistant principal*

Mankato
Barber, Eddice Belle *retired education educator*
Fitzsimons, Nancy Marie *social work educator*
Haas, Gretchen *literature and language professor*
Joseph, Diana Jennifer *literature and language professor*
Korpal, Charyl Elaine *secondary school educator*
Manahan, Vanda Galen *social work educator, columnist*
Preska, Margaret Louise Robinson *historian, educational association administrator*
Purscell, Helen Duncan *sociologist, educator*

Maple Grove
Kirpes, Anne Irene *elementary school educator*
Leiseth, Patricia Schutz *educational technology specialist*
Nielsen, Diane Kay *music educator*
Ones, Deniz S. *psychologist, educator*
Shmidov, Anna *music educator*

Maplewood
St. Germain, Sharon Marie *writer*

Marshall
Tabaka, Sheila Marie *theater educator*

Medford
Cashman, Beverly J. *music educator*

Medina
McConnell, Mary Patricia *lawyer*

Menahga
Farnam, Jennifer M. *elementary school educator*

Mentor
Jerdee, Sylvia Ann *minister*

Minneapolis
Adlis, Susan Annette *biostatistician*
Ahlers, Linda L. *retail executive*
Anderson, Leslie J. *lawyer*
Ashton, Sister Mary Madonna *health facility administrator*
Augustus, Seimone *professional basketball player*
Bader, Kathleen M. *chemicals executive*
Bancroft, Ann E. *polar explorer*
Battle, Willa Lee Grant *clergywoman, educational administrator*
Beechem, Kathleen *bank executive*
Bell, Constance Conklin *child care association administrator*
Benson, Beverly J. *lawyer*
Berscheid, Ellen S. *psychology professor, writer, researcher*
Birk, Peggy J. *foundation administrator*
Boyer, Susan Elaine *psychotherapist, consultant, speaker*
Bretz, Kelly Jean Rydel *actuary, consultant*
Brooks, Gladys Sinclair *retired public affairs consultant*
Buckingham, Elizabeth C. *lawyer*
Campbell, Karlyn Kohrs *speech educator*
Carlson, Jennie Peaslack *bank executive*
Chavers, Blanche Marie *pediatrician, educator, researcher*
Chemberlin, Peg *minister, religious organization administrator*
Constantine, Katherine A. *lawyer*
Corcoran, Mary Elizabeth *educational psychology professor emeritus*
Corey, Candy Abramson *oncologist*
Crosby, Jacqueline Garton *newspaper editor, journalist*
Crosmer, Janie Lynn *insurance company executive*
Curry, Jane Anne *writer, educator, performer*
Dale, Candace L. *lawyer*
Deach, Jana Aune *lawyer*
deBruin Sample, Anne *human resources specialist*
Dengler, Eartha (Erdmuth) *librarian, archivist*
DeVries Smith, Kate *lawyer*
Durdahl, Carol Lavaun *psychiatric nurse*
Dworsky, Mary *interior designer*
Dyrud, Grace Beatrice *psychology professor*
Eng, Holly S.A. *lawyer*
Erdrich, Louise (Karen Erdrich) *writer, poet*
Feldman, Nancy Jane *insurance company executive*
Fergus, Patricia Marguerita *language educator, writer, editor*
Firchow, Evelyn Scherabon *German language and literature educator, writer*
Fisher, Michele Renee *lawyer*
Flanagan, Barbara *journalist*
Fleezanis, Jorja Kay *musician, educator*
Forneris, Jeanne M. *lawyer*
Fraser, Arvonne Skelton *retired diplomat*
Garner, Shirley Nelson *language educator*
Gerdner, Linda Ann *nursing researcher, educator*
Goldberg, Luella Gross *diversified financial services company executive*
Gralnek, Minda *retail executive*
Griffith, Sima Lynn *investment banker, consultant*
Gudmundson, Barbara Rohrke *ecologist*
Halbreich, Kathy *museum director*
Hand, Mary Jane *artist, poet, educator*
Hansen, Jo-Ida Charlotte *psychology professor, researcher*
Hansen, Robyn L. *lawyer*
Harper, Patricia Nelsen *psychiatrist*
Hauch, Valerie Catherine *historian, educator*
Heins, Dianne C. *lawyer*
Helsene, Amy L. *lawyer*
Henrickson, Martha Marie *trade association administrator*
Hill, Tessa *non profit environmental group executive*
Holden, Susan M. *lawyer*

Horton, Stephanie McNeill *psychologist*
Howland, Joan Sidney *law librarian, educator*
Hoyle, Karen Nelson *author, curator, educator*
Hunt, Kay Nord *lawyer*
Innmon, Arlene Katherine (Tara Innmon) *artist, writer, entertainer*
Jacobson, Carrie Isabelle *lawyer*
Jameson, Jennifer A. *lawyer*
Johnson, Lola Norine *retired advertising and public relations executive, educator*
Johnson, Margaret Ann (Peggy) *library administrator*
Jones, Stella Marie *retired school counselor*
Joseph, Marilyn Susan *gynecologist*
Kilbourne, Barbara Jean *health and housing executive*
King, Lyndel Irene Saunders *museum director*
Kirtley, Jane Elizabeth *law educator*
Kohlstedt, Sally Gregory *historian, educator*
Laing, Karel Ann *magazine publishing executive*
Leuchovius, Deborah *advocate, special education services professional, consultant*
Logan-Hudson, Veryle *retail executive, realtor*
Loucks, Kathleen Margaret *lawyer*
Lougee, Wendy Pradt *library director, educator*
Marinello, Kathryn V. *information technology executive*
Marling, Karal Ann *art history educator, social sciences educator, curator*
Marshall, Siri Swenson *lawyer*
Mathews, Kathleen Ann *social worker, psychotherapist*
May, Elaine Tyler *social sciences educator, history professor*
McConnell Serio, Suzie Theresa *former professional basketball player, professional basketball coach*
McDermott, Kathleen E. *lawyer*
Meier, Lisa M. *lawyer*
Meyers, Miriam Watkins *retired language educator*
Mondale, Joan Adams *wife of former Vice President of United States*
Montgomery, Ann D. *federal judge, educator*
Moore, Tanna Lynn *marketing professional*
Murphy, Diana E. *federal judge*
Murphy, Edrie Lee *laboratory administrator*
Nelson, Julie Loftus *lawyer*
Nortwen, Patricia Harman *music educator*
Olson, Cynthia Louise *dermatologist*
Ort, Shannon *lawyer*
Parent, Jill Cari-Stepanchak *elementary school educator*
Paul, Nora Marie *media studies educator*
Paulose, Rachel *prosecutor*
Perry, Julia Nichole *psychologist*
Platt, Nina *law librarian*
Pletcher, Carol H. *chemicals executive*
Porter, Jennifer Madeleine *film producer, film director*
Pour-El, Marian Boykan *mathematician, educator*
Powell, Deborah Elizabeth *pathologist, dean*
Ramalho-Ahrndt, Maria Gabriela *art educator*
Rasmussen, Teresa J. *lawyer, insurance company executive*
Reha, Rose Krivisky *retired finance educator*
Reichgott Junge, Ember Darlene *retired senator, lawyer, writer, broadcast commentator, radio personality*
Roth, Margaret Agnes *child development educator*
Saksena, Marian E. *lawyer*
Santana, Lymari Jeanette *lawyer*
Sayles Belton, Sharon *former mayor*
Schneider, Elaine Carol *lawyer, researcher, writer*
Schulkers, Joan M. *lawyer*
Serstock, Doris Shay *retired microbiologist, civic worker, educator*
Short, Marianne Dolores *lawyer*
Smetanka, Mary Jane *reporter*
Smith, Katie (Katherine May Smith) *professional basketball player*
Smith, Mary Hill *volunteer*
Solomonson, Katherine *architecture educator*
Steen-Hinderlie, Diane Evelyn *social worker, musician*
Struthers, Margo S. *lawyer*
Tatlock, Ann *writer*
Thormodsgard, Diane *bank executive*
Trout, Deborah Lee *clinical psychologist, healthcare executive, consultant, director*
Van Dyk, Suzanne B. *lawyer*
Veldey, Bonnie *special education educator*
Vollmar, Alice Mary *writer*
Voss, Melinda *health care association administrator*
Walker, Sally M. *writer*
Weber, Gail Mary *lawyer*
Wejcman, Linda *retired state legislator*
Wilhelm, Gretchen *retired secondary school educator, volunteer*
Wille, Karin L. *lawyer*
Williams, Carolyn Lillian *psychology educator*
Younger, Judith Tess *law educator*
Zimmerman, Shirley Lee *family social science educator, researcher*
Zunkel, Gretchen M. *medical/surgical nurse, educator*

Minnetonka

Anderson, Karen Jean *mayor, researcher, communications executive*
Cavanaugh, Margaret *aide*
Hartzler, Belinda Sue *social studies educator*
Morisato, Susan Cay *actuary*
Nelson, Marilyn Carlson *hotel executive, travel company executive*
Quam, Lois *healthcare company executive*
Rivet, Jeannine M. *insurance company executive*
Thomas, Heidi Janet Krueger *social studies educator*
Vanstrom, Marilyn June Christensen *retired elementary school educator*

Moorhead

Brekke, Kathrine Lydia *music educator*
Buckley, Joan N. *retired literature and language professor*
Kent, Jill *midwife*
Morrison, Barbara Sheffield *Japanese translator and interpreter, consultant, educator*
Strong, Judith Ann *chemist, educator*
Welken, Jan Denise *elementary school educator*

Morris

Benson, Katherine Alice *psychology educator*
Ordway, Ellen *biologist, educator, entomologist, researcher*

New Brighton

Carlson, Kaye Lilien *retired music educator*
Corey, Mara J. *language educator*
Kieffer, Kathleen Cecil *elementary school educator*
Matalamaki, Margaret Marie *health facility administrator, consultant*

Newport

Yelland, Mary Virginia *artist*

Northfield

Immel, Cynthia Luanne *medical sales specialist*
Lundergan, Barbara Keough *lawyer*
McKinsey, Elizabeth *humanities educator, consultant*
Steen, Mary Frost *literature and language professor*
Swanson, Judith Seleen *artist, graphics designer, advocate*
Yandell, Cathy Marleen *language educator*
Zelliot, Eleanor Mae *history professor*

Oakdale

Nagdimon, Ellen Tara *artist, educator*

Owatonna

Birk, Peg J. *lawyer*
Larson, Diane LaVerne Kusler *principal*

Palisade

Kilde, Sandra Jean *nurse anesthetist, educator*

Park Rapids

Miller, Tanya Joy *art educator*

Paynesville

Bungum, Cheryl Nancy *music educator, director*

Pelican Rapids

Hovland, Gladys Myhre *secondary school educator*

Pine Island

Blankenship, Carolyn Ann *elementary school educator, educator*

Pipestone

Ballou-Portz, Cynthia Celene *music educator*

Preston

Schommer, Trudy Marie *minister, religious studies educator*

Prinsburg

Mulder, Michelle Kay *music educator*

Redwood Falls

Mansour, Loretta Julia *retired medical and surgical nurse*

Richfield

Devlin, Barbara Jo *school district administrator*
Zehnpfennig, Elizabeth Frances *secondary school educator*

Robbinsdale

Maloney, Cheryl Ann *not-for-profit administrator, consultant*

Rochester

Dahlen, Tracy *music educator*
Destro, (Helen) Jane *artist, medical illustrator*
Gervais, Sister Generose *hospital consultant*
Grosset, Jessica Ariane *computer executive*
Hart, Dionne A. *physician*
Hiniker, LuAnn *management consultant, educator, researcher, grants consultant*
Hodgson, Harriet W. *health and wellness writer*
Kantarci, Kejal *radiologist, researcher*
Kummeth, Patricia Joan *nursing educator*
Lynch, Emily *elementary school educator*
Moertel, Cheryl Ann *science educator*
Shepard, Laura Ann *microbiologist, researcher*
Stelck, Mickie Joann *technologist*
Varkey, Prathibha *preventive medicine physician, medical educator*
Vitek, Carolyn Rohrer *geneticist, educator*
Workman, Julia L. *music educator*

Roseville

Fisher, Rebecca Rhoda *lawyer*
Fullerton, Denise S.S. *lawyer*
McMillan, Mary Bigelow *retired minister, volunteer*
Miller, Suzanne Marie *library director, educator*
Peterson, Jill Susan *retired elementary school educator*
Seagren, Alice *school system administrator, former state legislator*

Saginaw

Stauber, Marilyn Jean *retired elementary and secondary school educator*

Saint Cloud

Barth, M. Jane *secondary school educator*
Hoffman, Patricia Patrick *retired psychologist*
McKay, Joane Williams *dean*
Olson, Barbara Ford *physician*
Patton, Kristen Terese *music educator*
Supanvanij, Janikan *finance educator*

Saint Joseph

Wedl, Lois Catherine *counselor, educator*

Saint Louis Park

Frestedt, Joy Louise *research scientist, science administrator*
Husen, S. Aino Maria *retired elementary school educator*
Mills-Novoa, Beverly A. *psychologist, consultant*

Saint Paul

Archabal, Nina M(archetti) *historic site director*
Arnold, Valerie Downing *lawyer*
Barnwell, Adrienne Knox *pediatric psychologist*
Boudreau, Lynda L. *state agency administrator*
Bruhn, JoAnn Marie *radiologic technologist, writer, speaker*
Burke, Mary Griggs (Mrs. Jackson Burke) *art collector*
Clayton, Diane *education educator*
Cyr, Lisa Watson *lawyer*
Davis, Joy Lee *language educator*
Davis, Margaret Bryan *paleoecology researcher, educator*
Dybvig, Mary McIlvaine *educational consultant, psychologist*
Franey, Billie Nolan *political activist*
Frazee, Jane *music educator*
Gaskill, Gayle *literature and language professor*
Hall, Beverly Joy *police officer*
Hanna, Kathryn Lura *university administrator*
Harvey, Patricia A. *school system administrator*
Huber, Sister Alberta *academic administrator*
Huzar, Eleanor Goltz *historian, educator*
Johnson, Badri Nahvi *social studies educator, real estate company officer*
Kerr, Sylvia Joann *science educator*
Kiffmeyer, Mary *state official*
Kimberly, Susan Elizabeth *municipal official, writer*
Lancaster, Joan Ericksen *judge*
Lebedoff, Randy Miller *lawyer*
Lee, Andrea Jane *academic administrator, nun*
Lofquist, Vicki L. *journalist*
Mandernach, Dianne *state agency administrator*
Matteson, Clarice Chris *artist, educator*
McNamee, Sister Catherine *theology studies educator*
Meissner, Ann Loring *psychologist, educator*
Meyer, Helen M. *state supreme court justice*
Michels, Eileen Manning *retired art educator, curator, writer*
Molnau, Carol *lieutenant governor*
Monson, Dianne Lynn *literacy educator*
Nylander, Patricia Marie *pilot*
Olson, Bettye Johnson *artist, retired educator*
Oswald, Eva Sue Aden *retired insurance company executive*
Pappas, Sandra Lee *state senator*
Paulson, Patricia C. *science educator*
Pinke, Judith Ann *state official*
Rodríguez, Liliana Cristina *mathematics educator*
Rydell, Catherine M. *medical association administrator, former state legislator*
Sisson, Bernice Belair *advocate*
Skillingstad, Constance Yvonne *social services administrator, educator*
Sonday, Arlene W. *educational consultant*
Victor, Lorraine Carol *critical care nurse*
Wagner, Mary Margaret *library and information scientist, educator*
Wheelock, Pam *financial executive*
Zander, Janet Adele *psychiatrist*
Zietlow, Ruth Ann *reference librarian*
Zuraitis, Marita *insurance company executive*

Savage

Ottoson, Carol J. *literature and language educator*

Shakopee

Eliason, Arlene F. *mathematician, educator*

Stillwater

Asch, Susan McClellan *pediatrician*
Krentz, Jane *former state legislator, elementary school educator*

Thief River Falls

Fleischhaker, Karin *insurance agent*
Jauquet-Kalinoski, Barbara *library director*

Truman

Jones, Patricia Louise *elementary counselor*

Upsala

Cheney, Denise Kay *music educator*

Virginia

Wilcox, Sheila Maureen *music educator*

Wabasha

Brelsford, Mary J. *music educator*

Waconia

Aarsvold-Indrelie, Judith *psychologist*

Waite Park

Prins, LaVonne Kay *programmer analyst*

Waterville

Bennett, Jodi Lynn *music educator*
Pettis, Patricia Amanda *secondary school educator, farmer*

Waubun

Sullivan, Kathleen M. Skaro *secondary school educator*

White Bear Lake

Rogers, Megan Elizabeth *mental health therapist*

White Earth

Vizenor, Erma J. *Native American tribal leader*

Willmar

Aaker, Melissa B. *secondary school educator*
Crute, Beverly Jean *minister*

Winona

Heukeshoven, Janet Kay *music educator*
Holm, Joy Alice *goldsmith, psychology professor, artist, art educator*
Peterson, Nancy Kay *poet, editor, writer*
Sullivan, Kathryn Ann *librarian, educator*
Towers, Karen R. *education educator*
Wenzel, Ann Marie *music educator*
White, Marjorie Mary *retired elementary school educator*

Zumbrota

Post, Diana Constance *retired librarian*

MISSISSIPPI

Alcorn State

Wyatt, Helen J. *special education educator*

Ashland

Dillashaw, Eula Catherine *artist, graphics designer*

Bay Saint Louis

Foster, Willetta Jean *music educator*

Benton

Moore, Teresa L. *mathematics educator*

Biloxi

Brown, Sheba Ann *elementary school educator*
Manners, Pamela Jeanne *secondary school educator*
McCaughan, Della Marie *retired science educator*

Booneville

Scott, Brenda Sue *elementary school educator*

Brandon

Evans, Trese *psychometrist, psychotherapist*
Fargason, Patricia J. *psychologist*
Hall, Breda Faye Kimbrough Inman *counselor, educator*
Haralson, Keri Temple *prosecutor*
Hollis, June D. *secondary school educator*
Sparks, Pamela Shepherd *music educator*
Wallis, Haley Hickman *elementary school educator*
Wand, Kimberly Joanne *assistant principal*

Brooklyn

Gerald, Carolyn Aileen T. *emergency physician*

Byhalia

Tackett, Maresa D. *medical technician*

Carriere

Thompson, Catherine Lila *retired medical center nurse*

Centreville

Nelson, Janie Rish *health facility administrator*

Clarksdale

Walton, SuzAnne W. *elementary school educator*

Cleveland

Carlson, Lizabeth Len *nursing educator, dean*
Norris, Carolyn Sue *artist*
Odom, Maryann Bell *secondary school educator*

Clinton

Bigelow, Martha Mitchell *retired historian*
Gann, Melinda Denise *mathematics professor*
Jarmon, Jeanette *artist, educator*
Reynolds, Judith M. *secondary school educator*

Columbus

Barham, K. Dawn *music educator, lyricist*
Donat, Patricia Lyn *education educator, academic administrator*
Hall, Maxine P. *minister*
Hayes, Rebecca Everett *gifted and talented educator*
Jones, Carol A. *nutritionist, artist*
Kantack, Catherine Margaret *retired music educator, retired international broker*
Nawrocki, Susan Jean *librarian*
Rood, Cynthia Hooper *landscape architect, consultant*
Traynham, Lurene Jones *retired secondary school educator*

Crystal Springs

Bates, Lura Wheeler *retired trade association executive*
Nixon, Brenda Joyce *elementary school educator, small business owner*

Decatur

Pouncey, Alice Gertrude Moore *psychology professor, educator, home economics professor*

Diberville

Steuart, Sybil Jean *elementary school educator*

Dublin

Flowers, Judith Ann *marketing and public relations director*

Ellisville

Headrick, Lisa Hughes *biologist, educator*
Holifield, Patricia DiMiceli *educator*
McNair, Emma Louise *minister*
Ross, Lisa Sims *special education educator*

Florence

McLin-Mitchell, Velma Elaine *language educator, literature educator*

Fulton

Campbell, Beth B. *science educator*

Gallman

Henley, Rita Darby *biology educator*

Gautier

Parent, Tanya H. *dance educator, massage therapist*

Glen

Price, Tina Denise *music educator*

Goodman

King, Kathy Cooper *music educator*

Greenville

Carter, Tonya M. *science educator*

Greenwood
Jones, Carolyn Ellis *retired employment agency owner*

Grenada
Dugan, Cindy *music educator, organist*
Harville, Myra M. *psychologist, educator*
Howell, Sandra Stroud *assistant principal*
Jackson, Teresa Roberts *principal, consultant*

Gulfport
Egland, Katherine Tatum *educational consultant, director*
Phillips, Joy Lambert *lawyer, banker*

Hattiesburg
Bedenbaugh, Angela Lea Owen *chemistry educator, researcher*
D'Arpa, Josephine *music educator*
Davis, Doris Johnson *retired music educator*
Diket, Mary Read M. *academic administrator, educator*
Du Boise, Kim Rees *artist, photographer, art educator*
McRaney, Joan Katherine *artist*
Nicholson, Amber Shay *music educator*
Nicovich, Mary C. *medical/surgical nurse*
Odom, Janet Lynn *post-anesthesia nurse*
Price, Helen Hoggatt *counseling administrator*
Reinshagen, Yolanda P. *elementary school educator*

Heidelberg
Dewey, Linda L. *secondary school educator*

Holly Springs
Greer, Sarah Rolston Doxey *retired elementary school educator*

Itta Bena
Branton, Susan Camille *education educator, department chairman*
Washington, Barbara J. *language educator*

Iuka
Barnes, Betty Jean *educational administrator*

Jackson
Baird, Carol Lowry *elementary school educator*
Barnes, Andréa Reneé *lawyer*
Barron, Carol Ann *painter*
Begonia, Maria *biology professor*
Bounds, Renee P. *secondary school educator*
Bradley, Betsy *museum director*
Brewer, Cheryl Ann *obstetrics and gynecology educator*
Buckner-Brown, Joyce *allied health instructor*
Campbell-Duckworth, Terri Elaine *elementary school educator*
Carlisle, Peggy Jane *elementary school educator*
Carmichael, Sally W. *volunteer*
Channell, Linda Guynes *education educator*
Cobb, Kay Beevers *state supreme court justice, retired state senator*
Coleman, Mary H. *state legislator*
Collins, Deloris Williams *secondary school educator*
Creel, Sue Cloer *retired secondary school educator*
Dunaway, Charjean Laughlin *librarian*
Harrison, Esther M. *elementary school educator, state representative*
Hawkins, Mary Elizabeth *obstetrician, gynecologist, educator*
Hiatt, Jane Crater *arts agency administrator*
Holly, Ellistine Perkins *music educator*
Houston, Gerry Ann *oncologist*
Jones, Christy D. *lawyer*
Lawson, Patricia Bowman *physician, educator*
Lee, Lillian Aldridge *music educator*
Leonard, Pamela Dian *architect, artist*
Lofton, Susan Price *nursing educator, consultant*
Long, Kelly Tidwell *medical/surgical nurse, director*
Mayeaux, Anne Russell *education educator*
Mosley, Jessie Bryant *retired science educator*
Owens, Denise *judge*
Smith, Sharman Bridges *state librarian*
Stanton, Sylvia Doucet *artist, gallery owner*
Thompson, Judith Geoffriau *psychometrician, consultant*
Tuck, Amy *lieutenant governor*
Uzodinma, Minta LaVerne Smith *retired nursing administrator, nurse midwife*
Wasson, Catherine Church *education educator*

Kosciusko
Dorrill, Mary Sue Valentine *elementary school educator*

Lauderdale
Van Doren, Henrietta Lambert *nurse anesthetists*

Laurel
Asmar, Kathleen *educational association administrator*
Ladner, April C. *lawyer*
Stennett, Kathy Elaine *elementary school educator*

Leland
Stott, Barbara Paxton *volunteer*

Liberty
Filbert, Eleanor Jane *special education educator*

Louisville
Cunningham, Julie Kaye *music educator*
McMillin, Lisa Sullivan *education educator*

Lucedale
Nyman, Terri Ruffin *special education educator, director*

Madison
Crisler, Donna *music educator*
Fordice, Patricia Owens *civic leader, former state first lady*
Rupp, Naomi Nakano *science educator*

Mc Cool
Miller, Charlotte Faye *speech pathology/audiology services professional*

Mccomb
Everett, Katherine Milton *special education educator*

Meridian
Murphey, Jeannette Windham *psychology professor*
Russell, Joy R. *computer scientist, educator*

Minter City
Mitchell, Patsy Malier *religious school founder, administrator*

Mississippi State
Crudden, Adele Louise *social work research educator*
Delgado, Marica LaDonne *librarian, educator*
Este, Yolanda Denise *philosopher, educator*
Henington, Carlen *psychologist, educator*
Hopper, Peggy F. *education educator*
McLendon, Mary Kathryn *athletic trainer*
Wall, Diane Eve *political science professor*

Moorhead
Stone-Street, Nancy Harrington *art educator, painter, printmaker*

Moss Point
Bolton, Betty J. *medical/surgical nurse, poet*

Natchez
Anderson, Rose L. Dyess *elementary school educator, poet*
Butler, Aquetta Dennis *elementary school educator, social worker*
Foster, Evaline L. *education educator, researcher*
James, Lula Bonds *science educator, small business owner, apparel designer*
Marion, Ann *retired elementary school educator, psychologist*
McLemore, Joan Meadows *librarian, consultant*
Moore, Irma D. *alcohol and drug counselor, prevention specialist*
Woods, Daisy Dennis *chemistry educator*

Nettleton
Hairald, Mary Payne *retired secondary school educator*

Ocean Springs
Christman, Leslie Erin *music educator*

Oxford
Freeny, Sarah S. *science educator*

Pascagoula
Washington, Yvonne *surgical nurse*

Pass Christian
Henrion, Rosemary Provenza *psychotherapist, educator*

Picayune
Penton-Smith, Tammy L. *elementary school educator*

Port Gibson
Alford, Constance Keith *recreational facility executive, artist*

Puckett
Sanders, Barbara Boyles *secondary school educator*

Purvis
Walley, Vicky Cabaniss *medical/surgical consultant*

Raymond
Bee, Anna Cowden *dance educator*

Ridgeland
Adams, Betty Sue *mathematics educator*
Davis, Penni Tharp *science educator*

Rienzi
Price, Debbie F. *elementary school educator*

Rosedale
Bell, Carrie Ann *science educator, consultant*
Thomas, Aelicia *lawyer*

Saucier
Finley, Emma Rosemary *science educator*

Scooba
Penick, Catherine Tindal *literature and language professor*

Senatobia
Taylor, Janice Keith *elementary school educator*

Shaw
Garner, Mable Tecola *health facility administrator*

Southaven
Butler, Elizabeth Rosanne *music educator, director*
Wade, Tonya Sue *religious studies educator, small business owner*

Starkville
Dampier, Caryn *self-defense instructor*
Durst, Jo *artist, educator*
Pigg, Robin Clark *art educator, interior designer*

Summit
Yawn, Amelia Lou *adult education educator*

Sumrall
Graham, Barbara Anne *secondary school educator*
Parker, Edna Faye *special education educator*

Terry
Collins, Lynda B. *biology educator*

Tupelo
Botts, Lillian Sullivan *elementary school educator*
Fields-Jenkins, Deloris Jean *elementary school educator*
Randle, Barbara Ann *retired secondary school educator*

Tutwiler
Brooks, Sister Anne *osteopath*

Union
Feasel, Mandy Sessums *literature educator*

University
Wang, Diane *music educator*
Wiggers, Nancy Rhea *education educator*

Vardaman
Pettit, Melissa G. *special education educator*

Vicksburg
Keulegan, Emma Pauline *special education educator*
Pace, Carol Rebecca *elementary school educator*

Walls
Tharnish, Rose Maries Lehman *veterinarian*

Washington
Branyan, Cheryl Munyer *museum administrator*

Waveland
Pearce, Belinda Allen *elementary reading recovery educator*

Waynesboro
Crager, Ginny Lee *gifted and talented educator*

Wesson
Reid, Pamela Jones *humanities educator*

Whitfield
Swann, Melissa Lynne *psychologist*

MISSOURI

Anderson
Coble, Mary Gloria *protective services official, rancher*

Arnold
Porter, Kathy Lee *marriage and family therapist, minister*

Aurora
Gorman, Angela Sue *dental assistant*

Ballwin
Corno, Donna A. *retired public relations executive, consultant*
Humiston, Marilyn Koslov *music educator*
Pallozola, Christine *not-for-profit executive*
Rothermich, Gayla *music educator, director*
Young, Samantha Lee *counselor*

Belton
Daggett, Kathleen *special education educator*

Berkeley
Reynolds, Kara Stutsman *elementary school educator*

Bethel
Coonrod, Delberta Hollaway (Debbie Coonrod) *retired elementary school educator, consultant*

Blue Springs
Gard, Jean *music educator*
Hartford, Cathy Jeanette *elementary school educator*
Muir, Linda Ann *music educator, director*
Neff, Karla Sue *secondary school educator*
Poff, Sarah Ellen *art educator*
Powers, Cecile Lorraine *secondary school educator*
Washburn, Gladys Haase *retired church musician, educator, director*
Wasko, Deborah Ann *music educator*

Bolivar
Hill-Stanford, Holly *language educator*

Boonville
Burns, Elizabeth McMahon *dairy scientist, psychologist*
Lohr, Liberty Ann *biology educator*

Bosworth
Ireland, Betty Jean *retired principal, music educator*

Bourbon
Heitsch, Leona Mason *artist, writer*

Bowling Green
Bruce, Judith Esther *retired music educator, elementary school educator*
Eckhoff, Sarah Lynn *music educator*

Branson
Ford, Jean Elizabeth *retired language educator*
Meikle, Dora Quinn Arney *retired physical education educator*

Bridgeton
Adams, Mary Louise *education educator, archivist*
Hylla, Linda Kay *sister, social worker*

Bucklin
Payne, Flora Fern *real estate broker*

Butler
Baxter, Myrtle Mae (Bobbi Baxter) *artist*
Cochran, Beth *gifted and talented educator*
Turner, Vicky Jo *music educator*

Calhoun
Cook, Joni Leann *science educator*

Cameron
Goodwin Clark, Ann Elizabeth *music educator*

Campbell
Knapp, AnnaMaria Lois *music educator*

Cape Girardeau
Overbey, Gail Ann Urhahn *psychology professor*
Reinmann, Carol Sue *elementary school educator*
Stepenoff, Bonnie Marie *history professor*

Caruthersville
Burch, Paula Usery *special education educator*

Cassville
Byrd, Sharon Faye *medical/surgical nurse*

Catawissa
Strupp, Darlene Clara *special education educator*

Center
Casey, Theresa L. *science educator*

Chesterfield
Falk, Barbara Marie *psychologist*
Finley, Marlynn Holt *elementary educator consultant*
Goldman, Teri B. *lawyer*
Greene, Judith Orinda *theater educator, theater director*
Kohnen, Carol Ann *librarian*
Kruse, Margaret M. *art educator*
Landram, Christina Louella *librarian*
Lipman, Marilyn Lee *retired elementary school educator*
Morrison, Ann Hess *systems administrator*
Rifkind, Irene Glassman *legal secretary*
Stevens, Annie Bickett Parker *retired architect*

Columbia
Bank, Barbara J. *sociology educator*
Beedle, Dawn Danene *marketing professional*
Burgoyne, Suzanne *theater educator, writer*
Cameron, Brooke Bulovsky *art educator, artist*
Cunningham, Milamari Antoinella *retired anesthesiologist*
Dye, Laura *physical education educator*
Flournoy, Nancy *statistician, educator*
Hensley, Elizabeth Catherine *nutritionist, educator*
Horner, Winifred Bryan *humanities educator, researcher, consultant, writer*
James, Elizabeth Joan Plogsted *pediatrician, educator*
Keown, Linda Jane *language educator*
Libby, Wendy B. *academic administrator*
McGavock, Brenda Weishaar *clinical psychologist*
McVicker, Mary Ellen Harshbarger *museum director, art educator*
Nittler, Jessica Rae *psychiatrist*
Nolph, Georgia Bower *physician*
Northway, Wanda I. *real estate company executive*
Packard, Kerri Shannon *theater educator*
Pinkerton, Marjorie Jean *librarian, educator*
Plummer, Patricia Lynne Moore *chemist, educator*
Pringle, Norma Jean Poarch *translator, educator*
Ragland, Ellie *literature and language professor*
Randall, Linda Lea *biochemist, educator*
Sapp, Eva Jo *writer, editor, educator*
Tarnove, Lorraine *medical association executive*
Underdown, Joy *retired elementary school educator*
Vale, Janie Rhea *physician*
Vale, Patrice J. *musician, consultant*
Von Holt, Lael Powers *psychotherapist, psychiatric social worker*

Crane
Gipson, Pauline *special education educator*

Creve Coeur
Ehrlich, Martha Ann *elementary school educator*
Kemper, Christina *small business owner, respiratory therapist, elementary school educator*
Manne, Deborah Sue *dental hygienist, educator, oncological nurse*
Plankenhorn, Sharon A. *chaplain*

De Soto
Withinton, Nancy Kay *elementary school educator*

Defiance
LeMaster, Sherry Renee *not-for-profit fundraiser, foundation administrator, consultant*

Delta
Kidd, Mary Jane *literature and language educator*

Dixon
Pyatt, Lori *music educator*

Doniphan
Pigg, Brenda J. *music educator*

Earth City
Kiry-Ryan, Rita Irene *computer scientist, educator*

Edwards
Findley, Kathryn E.C. *psychologist*

El Dorado Springs
Hochstedler, Lisa Inez *educational association administrator*

Elsberry
Boley, Anna Marie *literature and language educator*
Talbot, Carla Renee *elementary school educator, veterinarian technician*

Eureka
Lindsey, Susan Lyndaker *zoologist*

Excelsior Springs
Hewitt, June Ann *elementary school educator*

Fair Grove
Piech, Mary Lou Rohling *medical psychotherapist, consultant*

Farmington
Betz-Bacon, Tina M. *communications educator*
Shaw, Betty Jane *medical/surgical nurse*

Fayette
Inman, Marianne Elizabeth *academic administrator*

Fenton
Hughes, Barbara Bradford *manufacturing executive, community health nurse*

Florissant
Ashhurst, Anna Wayne *foreign language educator*
Beckmann, Laura R. *healthcare educator*
Conrad, Mary Trench *elementary school educator*
James, Dorothy Louise King *special education educator*
Loraine, Sandra F. *secondary school educator*
Schutzius, Mary Jane *volunteer activist*
Shreves, Judy Rae *director*
Sikora, Diana Marie *elementary school educator*
Williams, Julie Marie *history educator*

Forsyth
Klinefelter, Sarah Stephens *retired dean, broadcast executive*

Fredericktown
Morris, Virginia Mary *retired minister*
Stephenson, Jane Phillips *librarian*
Sudmeyer, Alice Jean *art gallery owner*

Fulton
Bierdeman-Fike, Jane Elizabeth *social worker, educator*
Hartwell-Ivins, Vicky Rose *office manager, medical/surgical nurse*
McClain, Cindy Dunstan *music educator*
Robertson, Carol A. *science educator*
Windsor, Kendra Linnette *elementary school educator*

Gladstone
Eggleston, Rebecca Annette *maternal/women's health nurse, rehabilitation nurse*
Eldridge, Tamara Lynn *elementary school educator*
Lucas, Nancy Jean *elementary school educator*

Golden City
Smith, Karen Lynne *elementary school educator*

Greenwood
Zeller, Marilynn Kay *retired librarian*

Hannibal
St. Clair, Mary Ann Walker *secondary school educator, small business owner*
Snider, Lois A. Phillips *educator*
Webster, Carolyn Lucy *elementary school educator*

Harrisonville
Ellsworth, Tina Marie *elementary school educator, social studies educator*
Scavuzzo, Tracy Truesdell *mathematics educator, department chairman*

Hayti
Jones, Christine *language arts educator*

Hazelwood
O'Reilly, Mary Catherine *elementary school educator*
Zeilman, Michelle Renee *counselor*

Hermann
Lerbs, Leah Lynn *special education educator*
Mahoney, Catherine Ann *artist, educator*

High Ridge
Karll, Jo Ann *retired judge, lawyer*

Hillsboro
Leirer, Margaret (Peggy) L. *communications educator*

Holden
Martin, Laurabelle *property manager*
Pirch, Pamela Sue *elementary school educator*
Wagoner, Deborah Anne *social studies educator*

Hollister
Canfield, Cindy Sue *art educator*
Herron, Gayle Ann *health facility administrator, forensic psychotherapist, consultant*
Hopper, Ruby Lou *clergy member*

Holts Summit
Hewlett, Sandra Marie *clinical consultant*

Humansville
Richler, Zenia H. *naturopath educator, health facility administrator*

Imperial
Baxter, Judith A. *medical nurse*
Meloy, Patricia *vocational school educator, art educator*

Independence
Booz, Gretchen Arlene *marketing executive*
Bryan, Kay Marie *retired minister*
Coppenbarger, Cecelia Marie *special education educator*
Dorshow-Gordon, Ellen *epidemiologist*
Evans, Margaret Ann *human resources administrator, business owner*
Johnson, Sharon Elaine *elementary school educator*
Kilpatrick, Laura Shelby *music educator*
Lundy, Sadie Allen *small business owner*
Marlow, Lydia Lou *retired elementary school educator*
Mortimer, Anita Louise *minister*
Peake, Candice K. Loper *data processing executive*
Potts, Barbara Joyce *retired historic site director*
Ray, Nancy Roberta *retired secondary school educator*
Schultz, Janice Elaine *librarian*
Starks, Carol Elizabeth *retired principal*
Willett, Teri Kay *art educator*
Wishy, Shawna Nicole *special education educator*

Ironton
Pollock, Connie *mathematics educator*
Sebastian, Phylis Sue (Ingram) *real estate broker, appraiser, antique appraiser*

Jackson
Horst, Carol Berry *art educator*

Jamesport
Minnick, Sally Schaefer *director*

Jefferson City
Bussabarger, Mary Louise *retired mental health services professional*
Carnahan, Robin *state official*
Eckstein, Julie *state agency administrator*
Farmer, Nancy *state official*
Kuebler, Barbara Campbell *science educator*
Laden, Mary Ellen *literature and language educator*
Mahoney, Carolyn Ray *academic administrator*
McDaniel, Sue Powell *writer*
Milne, Jennifer Anne *literature and language educator*
Murray, Dana L. *state legislator*
Russell, Mary Rhodes *state supreme court justice*
Stith, Laura Denvir *state supreme court justice*
Tackett, Natalie Jane *state administrator*

Joplin
Chlanda, Suzanne Lea *secondary school educator*
Freeman, Catherine Elaine *education educator*
Huffman, Patricia Nell *entrepreneur*
Logsdon, Cindy Ann *small business owner*
McDonald, Laura Witek *science educator*
Murphy, Patricia *English educator*
Weber, Maryann *language educator*
Zook, Martha Frances Harris *retired nursing administrator*

Kahoka
Jones, Mary D. *court clerk*

Kansas City
Bakely, Lisa Meng *elementary school educator*
Baker, Sharlynn Ruth *livery and limousine service owner*
Barnes, Kay *mayor*
Belzer, Ellen J. *negotiations and communications trainer, consultant*
Benedict, Stephanie Michelle *purchasing agent, sales consultant*
Boysen, Melicent Pearl *finance company executive*
Busby, Marjean (Marjorie Jean Busby) *retired journalist*
Byers-Pevitts, Beverley *college administrator, educator*
Cannezzaro, Nikki Eckland *lawyer*
Caulfield, Joan *director, educator*
Clegg, Karen Kohler *lawyer*
Collins, Kathleen *academic administrator, art educator*
Courson, Marna B.P. *public relations executive*
Cozad, Rachael Blackburn *museum director*
Davis, Florea Jean *social worker*
Davis, Mary Bronaugh *music educator*
Donovan, Ann Burcham *medical office administrator*
Dumovich, Loretta *retired real estate company executive, retired transportation executive*
Epps, Mischa Buford *lawyer*
Farnan, Betty Lynne *secondary school educator*
Gallagher, Maggie *columnist*
Garner, Taralyn R. *secondary school educator*
Gray, Helen Theresa Gott *editor*
Guilliland, Martha W. *academic administrator*
Hebenstreit, Jean Estill Stark *religion educator, practitioner*
Hodges Morgan, Anne *historian*
Hoyland, Janet Louise *clergywoman*
Hutson, Betty Switzer *art educator, artist*
James, Claudia Ann *public speaker, corporate trainer, writer*
Jimenez, Bettie Eileen *retired small business owner*
Johnston, Lynn Beverley *animator*
Kloth, Carolyn *meteorologist*
Krieg, Nancy Kay *social worker, poet, musician*
Kuenn, Marjorie Asp *music educator*
Latza, Beverly Ann *accountant*
Lee, Margaret Norma *artist*
Leigh, Cheri J. *engineering consulting executive*
Levings, Theresa Lawrence *lawyer*
Lindsay, Twyla Lynn *music educator*
Lombard, Regina A. *elementary school educator*
Londré, Felicia Mae Hardison *theater educator*
Martin-Bowen, Lindsey *freelance writer*
Mast, Kande White *artist*
Meilink, Jacqueline Rae *music educator*
Minkoff, Jill S. *small business owner, educator, entrepreneur*
Mustard, Mary Carolyn *financial executive*
Nagle, Jean Susan Karabacz *retired sociologist, psychologist*
Nelson, Freda Nell Hein *librarian*
Nichols, Virginia Violet *independent insurance agent, accountant*
Nielson, Constance Jo *psychologist, educator*
Norris, Ruth Ann *social worker*
Olson, Elizabeth Ann *small business owner*
Phalp-Rathbun, Stephanie Dawn *music educator*
Plax, Karen Ann *lawyer*
Rhodes, Sandra Lavern *elementary school educator*
Rice, Levina Ruth (Sally) *alderman, retired government agency administrator*
Roush, Nancy Schmidt *lawyer*
Ruperd, Theresa *music educator*
Satterlee, Terry Jean *lawyer*
Schaffer, Sandra Sue *artist, educator*
Scott, Deborah Emont *curator*
Setser, Patricia A. *music educator*
Sexton, Jacqueline Madeline *lawyer*
Shomin, Janet L. *paralegal*
Solberg, Elizabeth Transou *public relations executive*
Stroup, Kala Mays *former education commissioner, educational alliance administrator*
Suni, Ellen Y. *dean, law educator*
Svadlenak, Jean Hayden *museum director, consultant*
Swaffar, Glenda Jean *director*
Thompson, Mary Elizabeth *application developer*
Ulrich, JoAnn D. *elementary school educator*
Vann-Hamilton, Joy *academic administrator*
Whittaker, Judith Ann Cameron *lawyer*
Willsie, Sandra Kay *provost, dean, internist, educator*
Wilson, Susan Bernadette *psychologist*
Woods-Taylor, Cleora Lynesia *mathematics educator, consultant*
Worrall, Judith Rae *health and welfare plan consultant*
Yarmo, Fanny F. *not-for-profit fundraiser*

Keytesville
McVeigh, Glenna Faye *minister*

Kirksville
Cox, Carolyn *healthcare educator*
McLane-Iles, Betty Louise *academic administrator, language educator, writer*
Newland, Cheyrl Marie *music educator*
Presley, Paula Lumpkin *retired editor*
Teter, Patricia Ann *librarian*

Kirkwood
Davis, Marilyn Jean *medical educator*
Feller, Candi P. *counselor*
Hoglen, Jewel Pamela *retired secondary school educator*
Muller, Nancy Hrdlicka *elementary school educator*
Pacheco, Jill *language educator*
Pierroutsakos, Sophia L. *psychology professor*
Wentzel, Karen Lynn *secondary school educator*

La Grange
Guilfoyle, Nancy Jean *biology educator*

Lamar
Landrum, Ann Louise *physical education educator*

Laurie
Reppert, Nancy Lue *retired municipal official, legal consultant*

Lebanon
Elsea, Christine E. *music educator*

Lees Summit
Cobbinah, Ingenue F. *obstetrician, gynecologist*
Linder, Beverly L. *elementary school educator*
Usher, Elizabeth Reuter (Mrs. William A. Scar) *retired librarian*

Lewistown
Terpening, Virginia Ann *artist*

Lexington
Ritchie, Kellie Wingate *lawyer*

Liberty
Asp, Janna C *healthcare educator*
Myers, Susan Marie *language educator*

Lockwood
Wehrman, Natalie Ann *retired music educator*

Madison
Hawkins, Diana Wendellin *elementary school educator*

Malden
Reaves, Marilynn *elementary school educator*

Malta Bend
Richtermeyer, Beverly Summers *special education consultant*

Marionville
Boaz, Bethany L. *secondary school educator*

Marshall
Howard, Tiffany *theater educator*
Zank, Virginia *literature and language professor*

Marshfield
Frame, Susan S. *special education educator*
Marlin, Elmeree McGoon *mathematics educator*

Maryland Heights
Wasserman, Abby Lois *child, adolescent and family psychiatrist*

Maryville
Dunnell, Rebecca *music educator*
Galbreath, Leslie M. *academic administrator*
Gorman, Karen Machmer *optometric physician*
Quinlin, Kelly LeAnn *physical education educator*
Schultz, Patricia Bowers *vocal music educator, conductor*
Strating, Sharon L. *elementary school educator, professional staff developer, educational consultant*
Tennihill, Sally Kay *writer, music educator*

Mc Fall
Gist, Rebecca Jane *special education educator*

Mexico
Teague, Deborah Gant *elementary school educator*

Moberly
Aulbur, Beth Anne *elementary school educator*
Helm, Dorothy Dawn *nurse*
Werner, Karen Elaine *music educator*

Mokane
Weber, Rita Faye *science educator*

Montrose
Talbot, Phyllis Mary *reading educator*

Mound City
Parker, Phyllis E. *mathematics educator*

Nelson
Humburg, Barbara Ann *elementary school educator*

Neosho
Allman, Margaret Ann Lowrance *counseling administrator*
Weber, Margaret Laura Jane *retired accountant*

Nevada
Callahan, Susan Lane *mathematics professor*

New Bloomfield
Melton, June Marie *nursing educator*

Norborne
Franklin, Susan Denise *science educator*

Oregon
Dudeck, Anne Lee *reading specialist*
Lynn, Brenda *physical education educator*

Osage Beach
DeShazo, Marjorie White *occupational therapist*
Troutwine, Gayle Leone *lawyer*

Overland
Clark, Maxine *retail executive*

Owensville
Leick, Carol Lynn *retired special education educator*

Pacific
Wilson, Jill Marie *elementary school educator*

Parkville
Mandernach, Beryl Jean *psychologist, educator*
Schultis, Gail Ann *library director*
Williams, Cynthia M. *literature and language professor*

Peculiar
Pierson, Linda Kay *music educator*

Platte City
Kalin, D. Jean (Dorothy Jean Kalin) *artist, educator*
Shier, Susan Lynne *music educator*

Poplar Bluff
Peick, Ann Lutzeier *surgeon*

Portageville
Booker, DeLois Fondon *art educator*

Prairie Home
Bacon, Sherri Leah *elementary school educator*

Reeds Spring
Brewer, Karen Elaine Lauterbach *secondary school educator*

Republic
Zinecker, Tricia Jolene *music educator*

Rich Hill
Laughlin, Jo Ann *retired elementary school educator*

Richmond
Bartlett, D. Jane *retired psychology educator*
Solomon, Patty Jo *elementary school educator*
Stoenner, Jessamine *music educator*

Rock Port
Ross, Becky L *social studies educator*

Rolla
Brewster, Louise Boone *artist, educator*
Sotiriou-Leventis, Chariklia *chemist, educator, researcher*

Saint Ann
Cook, Melissa Ann *elementary school educator*

Saint Charles
Baker, Mary Elizabeth *elementary school educator*
Brown, C. Alison *counselor*
Dorsey, Mary Elizabeth *lawyer*
Drury, Mildred Barbara *evangelist, music educator*
Green, Christina Marie *literature and language professor*
McDonnell, Kathleen A. *supervisor*
Purcell, Cheryl Linn *music educator*
Reed, Warlene Patricia *retired librarian*
Riley, Theresa Marie *elementary school educator*
Scofield, Nadine Renée *special education educator*
Tabaka, Sandra Lee *retired medical/surgical nurse*

Saint Clair
Jobe, Kimberly R. *art educator*

Saint James
Stevens, Helen Jean *music educator*

Saint Joseph
Beck, Christina Sue *music educator*
Brownell, Vickie Marie *elementary school educator*
Correu, Sandra Kay *special education educator*
Rachow, Sharon Dianne *realtor*
Sauls, Allison Houston *art educator*
Schneider, Julia *library director*
Schoenlaub, Elizabeth Mae *elementary school educator*
Smith, Patricia Laura *literature and language educator*
Wallace, Kathy Joan *secondary school educator*

Saint Louis
Atwood, Hollye Stolz *lawyer*
Baker, Shirley Kistler *academic administrator*

Bean, Joan Nona *merchant, consultant*
Beck, Lois Grant *anthropologist, educator, author*
Bell, Angela *music educator*
Bellville, Margaret (Maggie Bellville) *communications executive*
Bextermiller, Theresa Marie *architect, computer engineer*
Biby-Russina, Erika L. *counselor*
Blanton, Elizabeth Anne *secondary school educator*
Bockenkamp, Karen Ann *bank administrator*
Boggs, Beth Clemens *lawyer*
Bohan, Ruth Louise *art educator*
Bonacorsi, Ellen E. *lawyer*
Bonacorsi, Mary Catherine *lawyer*
Bradley, Marilynne Gail *advertising executive, educator*
Brauer, Camilla Thompson (Kimmy Thompson Brauer) *civic leader*
Brazell, Gloria Ruth *art educator, elementary school educator*
Briggs, Cynthia Anne *educational administrator, clinical psychologist*
Brown, Bettye *librarian, educator*
Brown, JoBeth Goode *food products executive, lawyer*
Bryant, Ruth Alyne *banker*
Burmeister, Virginia Elizabeth *retired secondary educator*
Burns, Kara Allyn *education educator*
Carleton, Patricia Ann *librarian*
Carson, Rebecca Ann *performing arts association administrator*
Case-Schmidt, Mary E. *pathologist, educator*
Chambliss, Linda R. *obstetrician, consultant*
Christiansen, Bernyce LeeAnn *librarian*
Cima, Cheryl Ann *medical/surgical nurse*
Corrigan, Meg M. *psychiatrist*
Covington, Ann K. *lawyer, former state supreme court justice*
Dawson, M. Susan *nursing educator, mental health services professional*
Deutsch, Jennifer Loren *mathematics professor*
De Voe, Pamela Ann *anthropologist, educator*
Dick, Danielle Marie *psychology professor, psychiatrist, educator*
Diekemper, Rita Garbs *landscape company executive*
Dodd, Kristen L *social studies educator*
Driemeyer, Mary Alice *elementary school educator*
Duhme, Carol McCarthy *civic worker*
Duke, Carolyn *medical/surgical and community health nurse*
Ehrlich, Ava *broadcast executive*
Eilers, Jennifer Ann *special education educator, counseling administrator*
Elgin, Sarah Carlisle Roberts *biology professor, researcher*
Elliott, Susan Spoehrer *information technology executive*
Eyerman, Charlotte *curator, art historian*
Ezenwa, Josephine Nwabuoku *social worker*
Filbert-Zacher, Laura Margaret *research and development company executive*
Finder, Joan Bornholdt *academic administrator*
Fisher-Bishop, Kelly Marie *literature educator, department chairman*
Fitch, Rachel Farr *health policy analyst*
Forbes, Karen Kay *science educator*
Frederiksen, Patricia Sullivan *elementary school educator*
Gibson, Marienne Antoinette *retired special education educator*
Gilligan, Sandra Kaye *private school director*
Goldberg, Anne Carol *physician, educator*
Gooch, Audrey Smith *retired education educator*
Goodman, Judith Ross *psychotherapist*
Grant, Michele Byrd *secondary school educator*
Green, Joyce *book publishing company executive*
Haley, Johnetta Randolph *music educator*
Hamilton, Jean Constance *judge*
Hanaway, Catherine Lucille *prosecutor*
Hicks, Shirley E. *director*
Hoare, Sister Mary Gabriel *nun, educator*
Holland, Sherry Lynn *elementary school educator*
Holmes, Nancy Elizabeth *pediatrician*
Holt, Leslie Edmonds *librarian*
Hood, Phyllis Ilene *special education educator*
Inman, Janice Elaine *special education educator*
Jackson, Carol E. *federal judge*
Jacob, Julie Ann *special education educator*
Johnson, Gloria Jean *counseling professional*
Johnson, Sandra Hanneken *law educator*
Joley, Lisa Annette *lawyer*
Joyner Kersee, Jackie (Jacqueline Joyner Kersee) *retired track and field athlete*
Karty, Karen S. *secondary school educator*
Kennelly, Sister Karen Margaret *retired academic administrator, church administrator, nun*
Kinney, Nancy Theresa *political science professor*
Knop, Ruth M. *mathematics educator*
Kolar, Janet Brostron *physician assistant, medical technologist*
Krause, Patricia Ann *elementary school educator*
Lauenstein, Ann Gail *librarian*
Lazio, Lisa Ann *psychotherapist*
Leavitt, Lynda *school system administrator, educator*
Leonard, Judith Price *educational advisor*
Loevinger, Jane *psychologist, educator*
Lupardus, S. Carol *education educator*
Martin, Lisa Demet *lawyer*
McDonald, Brenda Denise *librarian*
Medler, Mary Ann L. *federal judge*
Metcalfe, Elizabeth Brokaw *art educator*
Miller, Ellen Katherine *music educator*
Miller, Judith Braffman *writer*
Mitchell, Louise Tyndall *special education educator*
Monteleone, Patricia L. *dean*
Moore, Antoinette Mercedes *counselor*
Morgan, Jennifer *counselor*
Morrison, Liz *educational consultant*
Novak, Camille *small business owner, consultant*
Olsen, Tava Maryanne Lennon *industrial and operations engineering educator*
Ozawa, Martha Naoko *social work educator*
Perotti, Rose Norma *lawyer*
Petralli, Mary Jane *secondary school educator*
Petru, Marianne *mathematics educator*
Powell, Jill Kirsten *medical educator, obstetrician, gynecologist*
Powers, Margaret Pettey *counselor*
Pritchard, Nina Jean *communications educator*
Purkerson, Mabel Louise *physician, educator, physiologist*
Ramos-Voigt, Lisette D. *science educator*
Rava, Susan Roudebush *French language and literature educator, community volunteer*
Redington, Mary *music educator*
Reidy, Frances Ryan *language educator, editor, writer*
Rice, Patricia Jane *journalist*
Rice, Rose Ann M. *secondary school educator*
Richardson, Pollie *principal*
Robins, Lee Nelken *medical educator*
Romanowski, Sarah Rebecca *secondary school educator*
Rosen, Adrienne *artist, educator*
Rudd, Susan *retail executive*
Ryall, Jo-Ellyn M. *psychiatrist*
Ryan, Sister Mary Jean *health facility executive*
Sago, Janis Lynn *photography educator*
Saueressig-Riegel, Suzanne *veterinarian, writer, columnist*
Scheffing, Dianne Elizabeth *special education educator*
Schlafly, Phyllis Stewart *writer*
Searls, Eileen Haughey *retired lawyer, law librarian, educator*
She, Manjuan *chemical engineer, food research scientist*
Sherby, Kathleen Reilly *lawyer*
Shine, Katina Lynniece Wilbon *neuropsychologist, consultant*
Shodean, Lisa Diane *military officer*
Shrauner, Barbara Wayne Abraham *electrical engineer, educator*
Storandt, Martha *psychologist*
Stratman, Heather Marie *elementary school educator*
Stratmann, Gayle G. *lawyer, consumer products company executive*
Sutherland, Mary (Marcus) *composer, musician*
Sutter, Jane Elizabeth *conservationist, science educator*
Swearingen, Laura Colleen *music educator, director*
Swiener, Rita Rochelle *psychologist, educator*
Swinson, Sara Hope *writer*
Szwabo, Peggy Ann *social worker, educator, nurse, psychotherapist*
Telowitz, Marilyn Marie *English and social studies educator*
Tentschert, Cheryl Ann *middle school educator*
Ternberg, Jessie Lamoin *pediatric surgeon, educator*
Thomas, Pamela Adrienne *special education educator*
Thompson, Marie Kathlyn *middle school educator*
Todorova-Moreno, Ilina *psychologist, educator*
Topham, Suzanne Caston *journalist*
Ulmer, Donna K. *business educator, writer*
Van Fleet, Lisa A. *lawyer*
Van Trease, Sandra Ann *insurance company executive*
Waddington, Bette Hope (Elizabeth Crowder) *violinist, educator*
Walentik, Corinne Anne *pediatrician*
Walker Tucker, Dana *lawyer*
Wechter, Marilyn R. *psychotherapist*
Weldon, Virginia V. *retired food products executive, retired pediatrician*
Westhoff, Laura M. *history professor*
Wilkins, Addi L. *retired lay worker*
Williams, Nellie James Batt *secondary school educator, educator*
Wilson, Margaret Bush *lawyer*
Woodward, Mary Lou *retired elementary school educator*
Wright, Diane *procurement manager*
Wright, Mary Lee *retired dietician*

Saint Peters
Bond, Karla Jo *elementary school educator*
Caples, Linda Griffin *retired secondary school educator*
Dreyer, Shelly C. *lawyer, judge*
Poettker, Mary Therese *music educator*
Ranner, Shanna *music educator*

Sainte Genevieve
Fischer, Nancy *secondary school educator*

Salisbury
Royston, Ginger Knierim *secondary school educator*

Sedalia
Dedrick, Rebecca Ann *elementary school educator*
Frazelle, Rhonda J. *psychology professor, counselor*
Silvey, Marsha K. *elementary school educator*

Slater
Wymore, Luann Courtney *retired education educator*

Springfield
Blair, Starla Reneé *music educator*
Blake, Loretta L. *music educator*
Branstetter, Ann Dyche *psychology professor*
Brennan, Deborah Ann *artist*
Busch, Annie *library director*
Cavner, Nadia *investment company executive*
Champion, Norma Jean *communications educator, state legislator*
Corcoran, Deborah B. *geographer, educator*
Easley, June Ellen Price *genealogist*
Gammel, Gloria L. *secondary school educator*
Gholson, Martha Rachel *religious studies educator*
Gill, Angela Sue *clinical psychologist*
Greene, Janice Schnake *biology professor*
Groves, Sharon Sue *elementary school educator*
Hart, Nan Susan *counselor*
Hasty, Jennifer Eleanor *anthropologist, educator*
Herman, Mary Elizabeth *educator*
Holloway, Wanda Kaye *psychotherapist, consultant*
Horny, Karen Louise *library administrator*
Loomer, Manden Jane *elementary school educator*
Maples, Carol J. *director*
Shantz, Debra Mallonee *lawyer*
Sherman, Ruth Todd *counseling administrator, educator*
Traphagan, Helen Marie *voice educator*
Williams, Juanita (Tudie Williams) *home health care nurse, administrator*
Wilson, Judith Ann *secondary school educator*
Wommack, Janice Marie *insurance company executive*

Stella
Davidson, Cynthia Ann *elementary school educator*
Yeagley, Joan Howerton *writer*

Stockton
Jackson, Betty L. Deason *real estate developer*

Stover
Reynolds, Sallie Blackburn *artist, volunteer*

Sturgeon
Dawkins, Amy *artist*

Sunrise Beach
Wonderly, Helen Marietta *elementary school educator*

Trenton
Gentry, Shirley *music educator, writer*

Troy
McClellan, Betty *retired county official*
Mills, Marsha Lee *retired secondary school educator*

Union
Boehmer, Ann *mathematics professor*

Unionville
Stottlemyre, Donna Mae *retired small business owner*

University City
Collins, Nancy Lee *mathematician, educator*

Urbana
Frey, Lucille Pauline *social studies educator, consultant*

Vandalia
Berry, Rebecca Diane *artist, educator*

Warrensburg
Handly, Hilda Ann *gifted and talented educator*
McKee, Rhonda Louise *mathematics professor*
McLaughlin, Phoebe *mathematics professor*
Robbins, Dorothy Ann *foreign language educator*

Warsaw
Million, Charlene R. *music educator, church administrator*

Webb City
James, Kathryn A. *secondary school educator*

Webster Groves
Carr, Margaret *elementary school educator*
Gergeceff-Cooper, Lorraine *artist, consultant*
Mosley, Karen D. *retired elementary school educator*

Wentzville
Halliday, Kristen Lee *language educator*

West Plains
Elrod, Keri Lynn *athletic trainer*

Windyville
Blosser, Pamela Elizabeth *metaphysics educator, counselor, minister*
Condron, Barbara O'Guinn *philosopher, educator, academic administrator, writer*

Winona
Marshall, Lucille Ruth *retired mathematics professor*

MONTANA

Alberton
Jones, Maureen Gail *elementary school educator*

Anaconda
Ricci, Margaret Thea *music and piano educator, church organist*
Watt, Maureen R. *retired secondary school educator*

Belgrade
Dighans, Kay Marie *elementary school educator, education educator*

Bigfork
Brynie, Faith Hickman *writer, educator*
Remington, Michelle Ganiere *principal*
Wetzel, Betty Preat *writer*

Billings
Anderson, Janeil Eva *mental health services professional*
Deschner, Jane Waggoner *photo artist, arts in healthcare consultant*
Jones, Doris Logan *portrait painter, art educator*
Kerr, Shauna Gay *secondary school educator*
Paul, Bessie Margrette *retired weather forecaster*
Randall, Marilyn Kay *equine studies educator*
Scott, Linda Preston *psychologist, educator*
Stratton, Betty *realtor*

Bonner
Smith, Annick *writer*

Boulder
Schaef, Anne Wilson *writer, consultant*

Bozeman
Biegel, Debra Jeanne *music educator*
Buonamici, April Graham *elementary school educator, music educator*
Pape, Rebecca Hogan *lawyer*
VanDyken, Nancy A. *information technology executive, web site designer*
Warrick, Kimberley Kaye *language and social studies educator*

Browning
Doore, Cynthia May *elementary school educator*

Butte
Clark, Gloria A. *music educator*
Haugen, Margaret Ellen *daycare administrator*
Kohler, Nora Helen *music educator*
LaMiaux, Rita *pre-school educator, secondary school educator*
Ouellette, Debra Lee *administrative assistant, consultant*
Van Dyne, Michele Miley *information engineer*

Clancy
Ekanger, Laurie *retired state official, consultant*

Columbia Falls
Hanson, Marlene Kay *music educator*

Dixon
McMillan, Eileen Margaret *daycare administrator, educator*

Eureka
Kessler-Hodgson, Lee Gwendolyn *actress, performing company executive*

Floweree
Dawson, Dawn Louise *elementary school educator, church administrator*

Forsyth
Lincoln, Sharon Ann *retired county official*

Glendive
Kintz, Myrna Lutes *retired language educator*

Great Falls
Ledesma-Nicholson, Charmaine *psychotherapist*
Schmidt, Rita *librarian, retired media specialist*

Havre
Dolph, Sharon Jean *social worker*

Helena
Benyus, Janine M. *writer*
Cotter, Patricia O'Brien *state supreme court justice*
Craig, Mary Lauri *accountant*
Dance-Kaye, Pamela *equestrian educator, consultant*
Fitzpatrick, Lois Ann *library administrator*
Gray, Karla Marie *state supreme court justice*
Manuel, Vivian *public relations executive*
McCulloch, Linda *school system administrator*
Meadows, Judith Adams *law librarian, educator*
Miles, Joan *state agency administrator, former state legislator, lawyer*
Seiler, Karen Peake *organizational psychologist*
Stearns, Sheila MacDonald *academic administrator*
Toole, Joan Trimble *financial consultant*

Hinsdale
Mogan, Connie K. *secondary school educator, elementary school educator*

Kalispell
Gallagher-Dalton, Tonya Marie *family support specialist*
Kortum-Managhan, Santana Natasha *lawyer*

Libby
Comeau, Tracy Lynne *small business owner, tax specialist*

Lodge Grass
Rockabove, Magdalene M. *special education educator*

Lolo
Stewart, JoAnne *retired director*

Lustre
Herrin, Karen Patricia *secondary school educator, singer, musician*

Malta
Brewer, Lynne Orahood *elementary school educator*
Watts, Alice L. *nurse*

Martinsdale
Rostad, Lee B. *rancher, writer*

Medicine Lake
Nelson, Linda J. *state legislator*

Miles City
Martin, Brenda J. *science educator*
Welbes, Diane M. *literature and language educator*

Missoula
Ammons, Carol Hamrick *psychologist, editor*
Barnett, Mary Louise *elementary school educator*
Chin, Beverly Ann *language educator*
Cummings, Kelli Dawn *psychology professor*
Hulme, Janet A. *physical therapist, writer, small business owner*
McKeown, Ashley *biological anthropologist, educator*
Miller, Kathleen Elizabeth *college administrator*
Pahl, Laura E. *finance educator*
Wigfied-Phillip, Ruth Genivea *genealogist, writer*
Wilbur, Carol Anne *literature and language educator, researcher*
Wollersheim, Janet Puccinelli *psychology professor*

Wright, Barbara Evelyn *microbiologist, educator*

Red Lodge
Garrett, Maggie M. *retired literature educator*

Roundup
Stanfel, Jane Ellen *artist, adult education educator*

Seeley Lake
Sexton, Toni T *school system administrator, educator*

Thompson Falls
Pargeter, Fredericka Mae (Fredi Pargeter) *writer, publisher, insurance salesperson*

Troy
Arvish, Ellen Marie *elementary school educator*
Sherman, Signe Lidfeldt *portfolio manager, former research chemist*

NEBRASKA

Aurora
Miller, Shari Ann *art educator*

Bancroft
Ras, Ronda Sue *secondary school educator*

Bartley
Probasco, Gayla Rae *secondary school educator*

Bassett
Miner, Alice E. *medial/surgical, geriatric and charge nurse*

Bayard
Muhr, Sylvia Anne *elementary school educator*

Beatrice
Garrett, Amy J. *parks director, educational coordinator*
Henderson, Robyn Lee *health program executive director*

Bellevue
Hatfield, Stacie H. *professional pianist*
Ross, Sandra Rae *infection control practitioner, quality assessment manager*

Blair
Stensaas, Starla A. *education educator, artist*

Boys Town
DeSalvo, Catherine Gaston *principal*
DiBacco, Nadine Louise *retired library director, photographer, writer*

Brewster
Teahon, Jean Ann *county official*

Broken Bow
Bigbee, Darlene Mae *retired medical/surgical nurse*

Chadron
Buschkopf, Debora J. *court reporter*
Gaudet, Laura Latta *psychologist, educator*
Lecher, Belvadine (Belvadine Reeves) *museum curator*

Columbus
Micek, Isabelle *music educator*

Crete
Conway, Mary Margaret *social studies educator*
Holmes, Andrea *chemistry professor, researcher*

Fremont
Welstead, Jean Maudie *artist, educator*
Winfield, Joyce Helen *communications educator*

Fullerton
Blauhorn, Cathy A. *music educator*

Grand Island
Abernethy, Irene Margaret *civic worker, retired county official*
Fickes, Lynda LuRhae *elementary school educator*
Jobes, Janet Sue *elementary school educator*
Weseman, Vicki Lynne *elementary school educator*

Gretna
Druliner, Marcia Marie *education educator*

Hastings
Stalsberg, Geraldine McEwen *accountant*

Hay Springs
Raymer, Joan Kay *science educator*

Kearney
Bloomfield, Susanne George *language educator, writer*
Hoffman, M. Kathy *graphics designer, packaging designer*

Lincoln
Boyle, Anne C. *state commissioner*
Braymen-Lawyer, Rebecca Kay *psychologist*
Byrd, Lorelee *state treasurer*
Drullinger, Leona Pearl Blair *obstetrics nurse*
Fawcett-Yeske, Maxine Ann *music educator*
Fleharty, Mary Sue *government agency administrator*
Frobom, LeAnn Larson *lawyer*
Giesecke, Joan Ruth *librarian, dean*
Grew, Priscilla Croswell *academic administrator, geologist, educator*
Hansen-Daberkow, Michelle Len *elementary school art educator*
Hardin, Martha Love Wood *civic leader*
Hasselbalch, Marilyn Jean *retired state official*
Hawley, Kimra *computer company executive*
Katz, Wendy Jean *art historian*
Kern, Jeanne Rustemeyer Wood *retired secondary school educator*
Kilgarin, Karen *state official, public relations consultant*
Kunc, Karen *artist, educator*
Mach, Jan Ellen Walkenhorst *literature educator, editor*
Miller-Lerman, Lindsey *state supreme court justice*
Mulvaney, Mary Jean *retired physical education educator*
Nicoll, Gayle *chemistry educator*
Ogle, Robbin Sue *criminal justice educator*
Oman, Deborah Sue *health science facility administrator*
Rawley, Ann Keyser *small business owner, picture framer*
Raz, Hilda *editor-in-chief, language educator*
Redfield, Pamela A. *state legislator*
Robak, Kim M. *lawyer*
Rohren, Brenda Marie Anderson *therapist, educator*
Schaefer, Joann *public health service officer*
Schimek, DiAnna Ruth Rebman *state legislator*
Seng, Coleen Joy *mayor*
Simpson, Charlene Joan *elementary school educator*
Smith, Susan Louise *special educator*
Stuhr, Elaine Ruth *state legislator*
Sullivan, Mary Ann *retired school psychologist*
Summers, Jane Pfeifer *realtor*
Tegeler, Rebecca Sue *elementary school educator*
Vidaver, Anne Marie *plant pathology educator*
Wiegand, Sylvia Margaret *mathematician, educator*
Young, Jeannette Rose *music educator*

Macy
Klein, Crystal Shelayne *science educator, volleyball coach*

Madison
Westfall, Lois Lorene *retired minister, nurse*

Maywood
Schultz, Judy Kay *guidance counselor*

Mc Cook
Watts, Susan Helene *theater educator*

Newman Grove
Anderson, Joyce Lorraine *nurse*

Norfolk
Stewart, Marsha K. *science educator*
Timmer, Margaret Louise (Peg Timmer) *art educator*

Ogallala
Kennedy, Laurel R. *secondary school educator*

Omaha
Bang, Michele Alene *protective services official*
Batchelder, Anne Stuart *retired publishing executive, political organization worker*
Belck, Nancy Garrison *dean, educator*
Bouma, Lyn Ann Nichols *music educator*
Brown, Jennifer Leigh *music educator, musician*
Bruckner, Martha *academic administrator*
Burns, Erica Marie *orthopedist, surgeon*
Cappellano, Rosemarie Zaccone *small business owner*
Casper, Peggy Wiedman *court reporter*
Chesterman, Melany Sue *lawyer*
Collins, Susan Baer *theater director, actor, educator*
Coyne, Ann *social work educator*
Derrick, Deborah Ball *editor, writer*
De Santiago, Dena Kalene *investment company executive, writer*
Dufner, Donna Kane *management information systems, project management educator*
Faust, Diana Jean *religious studies educator*
Fyfe, Doris Mae *elementary school educator*
Gallagher, Paula Marie *real estate appraiser*
Ganzel, Linda Sue *secondary school educator*
Graves, Maureen Ann *self esteem and spirituality consultant*
Holian, Katherine Stover *administrator*
Jones-Thurman, Rosanna Marie *psychologist*
Kahn, Ronni M. *psychologist*
Kessinger, Margaret Anne *medical educator*
Koplow, Ellen *lawyer, brokerage house executive*
Kowal, Penny Hope *educational consultant*
Mactier, Ann Dickinson *state agency administrator*
Myers, Sara A. *research scientist*
Nabity, Cynthia Dawn *music educator*
Neal, Bonnie Jean *real estate agent*
Noble, Karyn Sue *elementary school educator*
O'Connell, Valerie Beth *finance educator*
Ranks, Anne Elizabeth *retired elementary and secondary education educator*
Ress, Patricia Colleen *editor, writer*
Rogan, Eleanor Groeniger *oncologist, educator*
Roland, Sally *music educator*
Rowley, Jan *secondary school educator*
Ryan, Sheila A. *retired dean, nursing educator*
Ryan, Shelli Ann *public relations executive*
Sands, Deanna *editor*
Saunders, Lucille Mae *elementary education educator, librarian*
Schinzel, Sue Madeline *nurse*
Seitz, Carole Jane *composer, educator*
Sinclair, Mary L. *science educator*
Squires, Sandra Kay *special education educator*
Swindells, Susan *HIV specialist*
Vieregger, Susan Waynette *marketing professional, educator*
Ward, Vanessa Gayle *religious organization administrator, minister, consultant*
Whitney, Tamora Ann *literature educator*
Zardetto-Smith, Andrea *medical educator*

Oneill
Hiebner, Aida Cecilia *secondary school educator, education educator*
Rolenc, Sister Anita *parochial school educator, archivist*

Plattsmouth
Toman, Barbara Katherine *renal, cardiac, vascular nurse*

Potter
Miller, Nancy Jo. *science educator*

Scottsbluff
Beard, Deborah A. *therapist, educator*
Salomon, Marylou Ann *elementary school educator*

Seward
Whitson, Janet Susan *biology professor*

Tekamah
Cooper, Velma J. *elementary school educator*

Utica
Merck, Gerry Elizabeth *counselor*

Whitney
Tejeda-Brown, Mary Louise *artist*

York
McNeese, Beverly Diane *language educator*

NEVADA

Baker
Koyle, Denys Marie *motel and restaurant executive*

Boulder City
Wiesenborn, Charlene M. *science educator*

Carson City
Agosti, Deborah Ann *retired senior justice*
Alexander, Judy Lynne *investor*
Ayres, Janice Ruth *social services administrator*
Bagley, Cynthia Elaine *writer*
Barbie, Cathy Therese *middle school educator*
Eftimoff, Anita Kendall *educational consultant*
Hunt, Lorraine T. *lieutenant governor*
Jones, Sara Sue Fisher *librarian*
McCarthy, Ann Price *lawyer*
Mielke, Nancy E. *music educator*
Molasky-Arman, Alice Anne *state commissioner*
Morgan, Elaine Ludlum *minister*
Stewart, Phillis *museum official*

Dayton
Bumgardner, Julie *music educator*
Hudgens, Sandra Lawler *retired state official*

Elko
Ballew, Kathy I. *controller*

Ely
Alderman, Minnis Amelia *psychologist, educator, small business owner*

Fallon
Lawson, Karen E. *mathematics educator*
Rhea, Mildred Louise *writer, poet*
Venturacci, Toni Marie *artist*

Fernley
Jergesen, Arvella G. *elementary school educator*

Genoa
Dix, Loraine H. *chemist*

Henderson
Absher, Robin Dawn *security firm executive, private investigator*
Andolina, Nancy Jean *middle school educator, dancer, English and language arts educator*
Bruno, Cathy Eileen *management consultant, former state official, social sciences educator*
Derner, Carol A. *retired librarian*
Drusedum, Kimberly Barclay *music educator*
Glazer, Lee Morrison (Lee Morrison) *writer, choreographer*
Hara-Isa, Nancy Jeanne *graphics designer*
Holmes, BarbaraAnn Krajkoski *retired secondary school educator*
Johnson, Joan Bray *insurance company consultant*
McKinney, Sally Vitkus *state official*
Tefani, Nancy Ann *music educator*

Incline Village
Neubauer, Antonia *educational association administrator*

Las Vegas
Adair, Irmalee Traylor *social worker*
Andersen, Nancy *music educator, director*
Anderson-Fintak, Heather *lawyer*
Ballance, Ann Elizabeth *elementary school educator, consultant*
Becker, Nancy Anne *state supreme court justice*
Benjamin, Jennifer *health educator*
Bernstein, Maureen Ann *theater educator, director*
Bersi, Ann *lawyer*
Blattner, Meera McCuaig *computer scientist, educator*
Borovicka, Marsha Lorraine *music educator*
Brock, Holly Melinda *marketing professional*
Cavnar, Margaret Mary (Peggy Cavnar) *researcher, retired state legislator*
Chung, Sue Fawn *educator, researcher*
Cole, Ann Harriet *psychologist, consultant*
Corbett, Susan *mathematics educator*
Cruz-Manrique, Diana Elizabeth *elementary school educator*
DeBusk, Lorraine *elementary school educator*
Dew, Joan King *freelance/self-employed writer*
Duncombe, Patricia Warburton *retired social worker*
Edmond, Pennie Anne *science educator*
Egidio, Martha L. *real estate broker and salesman*
Ekanger, Karin L. *educational consultant*
Ernst, Suzanne *academic administrator, educator*
Frances, Marie Cecilia *theater producer, television producer*
Freeman-Clark, J. P. Ladyhawk *vicar, underwater exploration, security and transportation executive, educator, model*
Frigard, Monique Denise *journalist*
Gafford, Mary May Grimes *retired humanities educator*
Gage, Miriam Betts *retired nutritionist*
Gardner, Grace Joely *writer, consultant, psychologist*
Goodwin, Nancy Lee *computer company executive*
Gordon, Lee Diane *school librarian, educator*
Granese, Judith Ann *secondary school educator*
Gray, Phyllis Anne *librarian*
Hair, Kittie Ellen *secondary school educator*
Hale, Marsha Bentley *journalist, photographer, real estate rehabilitator, song writer, mannequin historian*
Hansen, Janet M. *bank executive*
Harding, Nancy Elizabeth *language educator*
Harrison, Lizette Marie *language educator*
Harter, Carol Clancey *former academic administrator, English language educator*
Healy, Mary (Mrs. Peter Lind Hayes) *singer, actress*
Herridge, Elizabeth *museum director*
Hill, Judith Deegan *retired lawyer*
Honsa, Vlasta *retired librarian*
Huston, Joyce A. *web site design company executive*
Israel, Joan *social worker*
Ivy, Berrynell Baker *critical care nurse*
Johnson, Mary Elizabeth *retired elementary education educator*
Karl, Carol Yvonne *retired minister, religious studies educator, publisher*
Kennedy, Margaret Alexis *law educator, researcher*
Klein, Freda *retired state agency administrator*
Landau, Yvette E. *lawyer, resort company executive*
La Neve, Shannon Beth *healthcare educator*
Lerman, Hannah *psychologist*
Martinez, Adriana *political organization worker, photographer*
Mataseje, Veronica Julia *sales executive*
McNair-Styles, Kimberly René *secondary school educator*
Meiner, Sue Ellen Thompson *adult nurse practitioner, consultant, gerontologist*
Mercier, Linda Ann *secondary school educator*
Merrill, Lynda Mae *real estate broker*
Michel, Mary Ann Kedzuf *nursing educator*
Miller, Valerie Carol *journalist*
Nadelson, Sandra G. *nursing educator*
Palmer, Lynne *writer, astrologer*
Phillips, Karen *secondary school educator*
Pierce, Thresia Korte (Tish Pierce) *primary school educator*
Ramsey, Inez Linn *librarian, educator*
Rawlinson, Johnnie Blakeney *federal judge*
Rector, Mary Margaret *secondary school educator*
Richardson, Jane *retired librarian*
Roberts, Lia *investor, political organization worker*
Safford, Florence Viray Sunga *travel agent, consultant*
Shelton, Samantha *psychologist*
Shenassa, Cheryl Renée *psychologist, mediator*
Sherry, Krystal A. *real estate broker*
Shively, Judith Carolyn (Judy Shively) *administrative assistant*
Shriner, Joan Ward *secondary school educator*
Silver, Kathryn *health services executive*
Silverman, Elaine Ann *mathematics educator*
Slade, Barbara Ann *art educator*
Smith, Janice Alfreda *secondary school educator*
Spencer, Carol Brown *retired educational association administrator*
Stephen, Anne Marie DiIorio *music educator*
Stivers, Carol Urban *retired music educator, consultant*
Strahan, Julia Celestine *electronics company executive*
Tyler, Janet Irene *music educator*
Vilardo, Carole *retired small business owner, research association administrator*
Vlaming, Carrie *theater educator*
Walker, Gwendolyn Kaye *real estate agent*
Wiener, Valerie *state senator, writer, communications executive*
Williams, Mary Irene *business education educator*
Winters, Marjorie K. *retired writer, editor, researcher*
Zervoudakes, Annette Dian *reinsurance specialist*
Zucker, Blanche Myra *civic worker*

Mesquite
Frentz, Yvonne Elizabeth *science educator, sports official*

Nellis Afb
Malachowski, Nicole *pilot*

North Las Vegas
Maresso-Newell, Dee *arbitrator, educator*
Talley, Brenda S. *performing arts center director, theatrical light designer*

Owyhee
Shane, Virginia *tribal court judge, lawyer*

Reno
Baran, Shirley Walters *artist, sculptor*
Berger, Laura Patricia *psychologist*
Bramwell, Marvel Lynnette *nursing administrator, social worker*
Brennan, Susan Mallick *utilities executive*
Cafferata, Patricia Dillon *state official*
Cathey-Gibson, Sharon Sue Rinn *principal, academic administrator*
Collier, Helen Vandivort *psychologist*
Cornell, Annie Aiko *nurse, administrator, retired military officer*
Crowe, Jennifer *newspaper reporter*
Flowers, Marguerita Denise *banker, educator*
Ford, Victoria *retired public relations executive, writer, oral historian*
Frank, Lillian Gorman *human resources executive, management consultant*
Garcia, Katherine Lee *controller, accountant*
Geurden, Tammy Ann *education educator, counselor*
Graham, Margaret Katherine *retired secondary school educator*
Harsh, Antoinette Mollett *investor*
Hilts, Ruth *artist*
Hudson, Karen Ann Sampson *music educator*

Leland, Joy Hanson *retired anthropologist, researcher*
LoSasso, Vicki Rae *political organization worker, artist*
McLeod, Carolyn Louise *artist*
Middlebrooks, Deloris Jeanette *retired nursing educator*
Mullarkey, Maureen T. *game company executive*
Myers, Geraldine Ruth *special education educator, consultant*
Parsons, Cindy Michelle *special education educator*
Perry, Jean Louise *academic administrator*
Ragavan, Anpalaki Jeyabalasinkham *software developer, researcher*
Sheehan, Denise Lucille *alcohol/drug abuse services professional, writer*
Small, Elisabeth Chan *psychiatrist, educator*
Swanson, Dolores *special education educator, musician*
Verstegen, Deborah A. *finance educator*

Sandy Valley
Viscuglia, Jenny Lou *music educator*

Silver Springs
O'Malia, Mary Frances *special education educator*

Sparks
Boyer, Patricia W. *publishing executive, editor*
Bria, Janice *secondary school educator, sports official*
Rice, Jennifer Stacy *literature and language educator*

Wellington
Compston, Marion F. *small business owner*

Winnemucca
Hesse, Martha O. *gas industry executive*

Yerington
Scatena, Lorraine Borba *retired rancher, women's rights advocate, researcher*

Zephyr Cove
Wells, Cynthia *elementary school educator*

NEW HAMPSHIRE

Alstead
Beetle, Kate *artist, illustrator*
Boisvert-Buschbaum, M. Noella *music educator*

Alton
Corriveau, Heather M., II, *social studies educator*
Sweezy, Vicky Lynn *science educator, emergency medical technician*

Amherst
Johnson, Daryl Diane *painter*
Wilkins, Sally *writer*

Bedford
Collins, Diana Josephine *psychologist*
Hall, Pamela S. *environmental services administrator*
Miller, Christine Lee *psychotherapist*

Belmont
Donovan, Vicki Ann *elementary school teacher*

Berlin
Doherty, Katherine Mann *librarian, writer*
Lavertu, Monique Therese *music educator*

Brentwood
Boozer-Blasco, Claudia Ruth *family and consumer resources educator*
Micklos, Janet M. *state agency administrator, human services director*
Thompson, Eleanor Dumont *nurse*

Campton
Benton, Geraldine Ann *preschool owner, director*

Canaan
Conwell, Ruth Ingrid *assistant principal, educator*
Wilson, Kristin M. *mathematics educator*

Claremont
Liveston, Denise Anne *elementary school educator*

Concord
Ayotte, Kelly A. *state attorney general*
Birdsall, Lynne A. *academic administrator*
Bradley, Paula E. *former state legislator*
Clemons, Jane Andrea *state legislator*
Cooney, Mary Ann *public health service officer, community health nurse*
Ferland, Brenda L. *state representative*
Flora, Kathleen M. *retired state representative*
Foster, Linda Timberlake *state legislator*
Francoeur, Sheila T. *state representative*
Ginsburg, Ruth *state representative*
Hager, Elizabeth Sears *state legislator, social services administrator*
Kaen, Naida *state representative*
Larsen, Sylvia B. *state legislator*
Lowell, Janet Ann *nurse*
McCall, Junietta Baker *psychotherapist, minister*
Norelli, Terie Thompson *state legislator*
Raskin, Joy Lynn *art educator, silversmith*
Richardson, Barbara Hull *state legislator, social worker*
Scheckter, Stella Josephine *retired librarian*
Sprague, Marcia Scovel *small business owner*
Stickney, Nancy Carver *state legislator*
Young, Sherilyn Burnett *lawyer*

Conway
MacDonald, Christine *social worker*

Dover
Appel, Carole Stein *writer, political organizer*
Overbey, Susan J. *history educator*
Pelletier, Marsha Lynn *secondary school educator, poet*

Durham
Gold, Janet Nowakowski *Spanish language educator*
Kinner, Nancy E. *civil engineer, educator, environmental engineer, researcher*
Linden, Blanche Marie Gemrose *history professor*
Newman, J. Bonnie *academic administrator, former government official*
Wheeler, Katherine Wells *retired state legislator*

Etna
Picoult, Jodi *writer*

Exeter
McDonough, Cheryl York *principal, educational consultant*
Schubart, Caren Nelson *psychologist*
Thomas, Jacquelyn May *librarian*

Franklin
Trader, Patricia Annette *music educator*

Gilford
John, Lyvie Paige *music educator*

Gilsum
Henry, Maurine Dale *elementary school educator*

Goffstown
Holden, Carol Helen *county official*
Martel, Eva Leona *accountant*
Seastream, Doris *science educator*

Gorham
Langlois, Lori A. *human resources specialist*

Goshen
Wright, Lilyan Boyd *physical education educator*

Greenfield
Lewicke, Bette *psychologist, writer*

Hanover
Burchenal, Joan Riley *science educator*
Copenhaver, Marion Lamson *retired state legislator*
Crory, Elizabeth Lupien *retired state legislator*
Green, Mary Jean Matthews *foreign language educator*
Guerinot, Mary Lou *biology professor*
Kreiger, Barbara S. *writer, educator*
Otto, Margaret Amelia *librarian*
Spiegel, Evelyn Sclufer *biology professor*

Harrisville
Miller, Irene M. *physician assistant*

Henniker
Braiterman, Thea Gilda *economics professor, state legislator*

Hudson
Rosson, Elizabeth Hanle *artist, director*

Jackson
Baker, Mary Jane *social worker*

Jaffrey
Van Ness, Patricia Wood *religious studies educator*

Jefferson
Leiper Estabrooks, Esther *writer, artist, illustrator*

Keene
Bleam, Nancy Kay *physical education educator*
Frink, Helen Hiller *language educator*
Miller, Rita *die-casting company executive, personnel consultant*
Salcetti, Marianne *newswriter, educator*

Lancaster
Poekert, Rose A(nn) *elementary school educator*

Lebanon
Baker, Susan Chilton *health facility administrator, consultant*
Dillon Rydman, Linda Gay *nurse, consultant*
Emery, Virginia Olga Beattie *psychologist, researcher*
Galton, Valerie Anne *endocrinologist, educator*
Mc Cann, Frances Veronica *physiologist, educator*
Thompson, Pamela A. *nurse administrator*

Litchfield
Miller, Dawn Marie *retired meteorologist*

Littleton
Kelly, Dorothy Helen *pediatrician, educator*
Merritt, Mary Jane *community volunteer*

Londonderry
Ballard, Susan Doyon *library director*
Parten, Priscilla M. *medical and psychiatric social worker, educator*

Loudon
Moore, Beatrice *religious organization administrator*

Lyme
Wise, Joanne Herbert *art director*

Manchester
Ahern, Margaret Ann *nun, nursing educator*
Arnold, Barbara Eileen *state legislator*
Bois, Deborah Lynn *special education educator*
Bolduc, Diane Eileen Mary Buchholz *psychotherapist*
Bruno, Sherrie L. *science educator*
Cusson-Cail, Kathleen *consulting company executive*
Marchesseault, Anita *music educator*
Merideth, Susan Carol *business administration educator*
Mosher, Janet A. *counselor*
Naccach-Hoff, Selma *language educator*

Marlow
McCracken, Linda *artist, writer*

Melvin Village
Humphrey, Judith Poole *retired elementary school educator*

Meredith
Lane, Sophia *art gallery director*

Meriden
Ahlquist, Janet Sue *musician, music educator*
Brent, Patricia Lee *health facility administrator, writer*

Merrimack
Bruce, Rae Marie *retired language educator*
Cunningham, Patricia Ann Cahoy *band director, musician*
Gallup, Patricia *computer company executive*
Ross, Marie Elisa *elementary school educator*

Milford
Murphy, Sandra Ferguson *elementary school educator*
Queeney, Deborah Ann *special education educator*

Moultonborough
Patten, Betsey Leland *state legislator*

Nashua
Arthur, Rose Ann Horman *dean*
Brodeur, Esther Corinne *educator*
Descoteaux, Carol J. *health facility administrator*
Ferrigno, Helen Frances *librarian, educator*
Hansen, Michele Simone *communications executive*
Hayes, Maureen A. *psychotherapist, consultant*
Lerch, Carol M. *mathematics professor*
Matarazzo, Maria C. *finance educator, department chairman*
Najarian, Cheryl Ann *exercise physiology educator*
Pignatelli, Debora Becker *state official*
Provencher, Jeanne Stansfield *secondary school educator*
Williams, Paula Jo *nurse, educator*

Nelson
Kirk, Jane Seaver *municipal government administrator*

New Durham
Sullivan, Mary Ann *writer, marketing professional*

New London
Berlenbach-Coburn, Susan L. *elementary school educator*
DeLuca, Susan Rice *physical education educator*
Eckrich, Regina *physical education educator, department chairman*
Ponder, Anne *academic administrator*

Newfields
Buck-Bacon, Louise John *education educator*

Newport
Gayvoronsky, Ludmila *artist, educator*
Stamatakis, Carol Marie *lawyer, former state legislator*

North Hampton
Pazdon, Denise Joan *speech pathology/audiology services professional*

Ossipee
Bartlett, Diane Sue *counselor*

Pembroke
Poznanski, Margaret Mary *special education educator*

Peterborough
Eneguess, Ann Cavanaugh *social services administrator*
Gagnon, Nancy Spear *secondary school educator, consultant*
Thomas, Elizabeth Marshall *writer*

Plainfield
Brown, Judith Olans *retired lawyer, educator*

Plaistow
Senter, Merilyn P(atricia) *former state legislator, freelance/self-employed reporter*

Plymouth
DeCotis, Ruth Janice *career planning administrator, educator*
Vinogradova, Natalya *mathematician, educator*

Portsmouth
Brink, Marion Alice *retired human resources specialist*
Cunningham, Valerie S. *historic preservationist, researcher*
Day, Frances Ann *writer, educator*
Hopkins, Jeannette Ethel *book publisher, editor*
Nylander, Jane Louise *museum director, educator, writer*

Raymond
Gospodarek, Angela M *science educator*
Stathos, Donna Lee *mathematics educator*

Rochester
Hegger, Samantha Lynn *social studies educator*
Kumiski, Cheryl Marie *artist*

Rollinsford
Davis, Jewel Beth *literature and language professor, writer, actress*

Sanbornton
Weiant, Elizabeth Abbott *retired biology professor*

Sandown
Pajak, Louise Bears *music educator, musician*

Stark
Spaulding, Nancy Kelly *elementary school educator, small business owner*

Stratham
Wineberg, Danette *lawyer, apparel executive*

Temple
Weston, Priscilla Atwood *library director*

Tilton
Wolf, Sharon Ann *psychotherapist*

Walpole
Arnold, Jeanne Fessenden *retired physician*

Warner
Wingfield, Susan *energy executive*

Weare
White, Karen Ruth Jones *information systems executive*

Whitefield
Hicks, Erica C. *mathematics educator*

Winchester
Tandy, Jean Conkey *clay artist, potter, painter, retired educator*

Windham
Arndt, Janet S. *former state legislator, educator*

Wolfeboro
Bonin, Suzanne Jean *artist*
Hutchins, Carleen Maley *acoustical engineer, consultant*

NEW JERSEY

Absecon
Bean, Manya *psychotherapist, educator*
Paparone, Pamela Ann *nurse practitioner*

Allendale
Long, Jo-Nelle Desmond *editor, consultant, historian*
Repole, Maria *public relations executive*

Allenhurst
Tognoli, Era M. *performing company executive, artistic director*

Allenwood
Carbone, Diane M. *psychologist, consultant*

Andover
Mohammadi, Mina *physician, researcher*

Annandale
Baugh, Lisa Saunders (Lisa Saunders Boffa) *chemist, researcher*

Asbury Park
Sandberg-Morgan, Barbara *retired communication and women's studies educator*

Atco
DiAngelo, Linda Mary *secondary school educator, theater director*

Atlantic Highlands
Donoghue, Louise I. *retired language educator*

Audubon
McMichael, Maria Madelyn *publishing executive*

Avalon
Johnson, Adele Cunningham *small business owner*

Avenel
Hynes-Lasek, Nancy Ellen *secondary school educator*

Barnegat
Prisbell, Kathleen Frances *middle education educator, language arts*

Barrington
Florio, Maryanne J. *health and education research scientist*
Pawling, Patti J. *school system administrator*

Basking Ridge
Besch, Lorraine W. *special education educator*
Craven, Pamela F. *lawyer*
Helfant, Ann M. *history educator*
Moden, Joleen *communications executive*
Scites, Jan *business consulting services company executive*

Bayonne
Doyle, Enid *art educator*
Levin, Holly J. *science educator*

Bayville
Worth, Katherine Marie *retired vocalist*

Bedminster
Dabney, Michelle Sheila *administrative assistant*
Delehanty, Martha *human services administrator*
Flaherty, Kathleen Ruth *telecommunications industry executive*
Frediani, Diane Marie *graphics designer, interior designer, executive secretary*
Graddick-Weir, Mirian *human resources specialist*
Marrero, Teresa *lawyer*
Yannuzzi, Elaine Victoria *food and home products executive*

Belle Mead
Brown, Elizabeth Schmeck *fashion historian*
Thayer, Christina Sia *music educator*

Belmar
Farrell, Karen F. *school nurse practitioner*

Bergenfield
Aguado, Sandra *social studies educator*
Caramico, Lydia Frances *meeting planner*
Davidson, Marilyn Copeland *writer, music educator, musician*

Berkeley Heights
Hansburg, Freda B. *psychologist, mental health consultant*

Bernardsville
Boquist, Diana D. *mayor, real estate agent*
Robinson, Maureen Loretta *retired secondary school educator*
Spofford, Sally (Sally Hyslop) *artist*

Blackwood
Blume, Wendy M. *dean*
Perkins, Rita Wade *historian, educator*

Bloomfield
Glasser, Lynn Schreiber *publisher*
Kovacs, Christina Marie *music educator*
Mesuk, Elaine M. *music educator*

Bogota
Koshimitsu, Keiko *artist*
Livingston, Kathryn E. *writer*
Rogers, Alison M. *special education educator*

Boonton
Hanna, Annette A. *artist, art educator*
Ward, Solveig Maria *marketing professional*

Bordentown
Rasmuson, Lisa Marie *language educator*

Bound Brook
Blumberg, Adele Rosenberg *volunteer*

Brick
Bertoncin, Geraldine Johnnie *elementary school educator*
Herrmann, Elsa Marie *retired art educator*
Norgaard, Veronica R. *real estate lawyer*
White, Debra Ann *social worker, counseling administrator*

Bridgeton
Chanatry-Howell, Lorraine Marie *artist, educator*

Bridgewater
Bernson, Marcella S. *psychiatrist*
DeMaio, Donnalee A. *bank executive*
DeMatteo, Gloria Jean *banker*
Glesmann, Sylvia-Maria *artist*
Hart, Karen Jean *special education educator*
Simonds, Theresa M. Troegner *accountant*

Brigantine
Kickish, Margaret Elizabeth *elementary school educator*

Budd Lake
Rattner, Karlene Susan Katherine *special education educator*
Shepherd, Deborah Gulick *elementary school educator*

Burlington
Britt, Donna Marie *school nurse*
Cobb, Vanessa Wynvette *elementary school educator*
Hancock, Beverly J. *retired counseling consultant, secondary school educator*
Mustokoff, Henrietta M. *music educator*

Butler
Baskinger, Wilma *elementary school educator*

Caldwell
Alito, Martha-Ann B. *librarian*
Kearney, Sister Mary John *educator*
Palombo, Lisa *artist*
Ryan, Joanne Winona *art administrator, artist, consultant, educator*
Werner, Patrice (Patricia Ann Werner) *academic administrator*

Califon
Clipsham, Jacqueline Ann *artist*
Jeffers, Victoria Wilkinson *psychologist*
Rosen, Carol Mendes *artist*

Camden
Brooks, Gail Denise *school system administrator, consultant*
Coney, Stephné Reniá *communications educator*
Daniels, Albertina Diana *secondary school educator*
Kaden, Ellen Oran *lawyer, consumer products company executive*
Mazzoli, Linda Fabrizio *personal trainer, consultant, marketing professional*
O'Neal, Gwenelle Marine S. *mental health services administrator*
Reardon, Nancy Anne *food products executive*

Cape May
Byrnes, Christine Ann *internist*

Cape May Court House
Cohen, Susan Lois *writer*

Cape May Point
Chandler, Marguerite Nella *real estate company executive*

Carteret
John, Dolores *architect, consultant*

Cedar Grove
Helwig, Annette L. *retired elementary school educator*

Cedar Knolls
Van Wert, Linda *elementary school educator*

Cedarville
Marsella, Julia *music educator*

Chatham
Earle, Jean Buist *finance company executive, computer company executive*

Cherry Hill
Blakney, Juanita Mosley *psychotherapist*
Ciociola, Cecilia Mary *not-for-profit developer*
Collier-Evans, Demetra Frances *veterans benefits counselor*
Erdely, Diane Louise *educator*
Grado-Wolynies, Evelyn (Evelyn Wolynies) *nursing educator*
Gutin, Myra Gail *communications educator*
Mark, Susan A. *music educator*
Rose, Dori *real estate agent*
Solomon, Penny Goren *artist, designer*
Wolff, Ferida *author*

Chester
Gray, Pamela *gifted and talented educator*
Maddalena, Lucille Ann *management consultant*

Cinnaminson
Tosti, Susan Marie *reading specialist, educator*

Clark
Hasselman, San D. *secondary school educator*

Clarksburg
Gonyo, Marilyn E. *education educator*

Clementon
Albee, Gloria *playwright*

Cliffside Park
Brown, Shirley Ann *speech-language pathologist*
Chelariu, Ana Radu *library director*
de Gramont, Carol Carmel *writer*
Perhacs, Marylouise Helen *musician, educator*

Clifton
Bronkesh, Annette Cylia *public relations executive*
Dolinsky, Dianne Marie *secondary school educator*
Kalata, Mary Ann Catherine *architect*

Colonia
Wiesenfeld, Bess G. *interior designer*

Colts Neck
Crowder-Pagano, Linda Louise *special education educator*
Schmalz, Elizabeth Moody *cosmetics company executive*

Columbia
Timcenko, Lydia Teodora *secondary school educator, biochemist*

Cranbury
Burke, Laura Anne *elementary school educator*

Cranford
Boughner, Martha Reed *music educator*
Kardos, Amelia Marie Papetti *elementary school educator*

Dayton
Istafanous, Afifa W. *physician*

Delanco
Lane, Carrie Belle (Hairston) *retired music educator*

Delaware
Hill-Rosato, Jane Elizabeth *elementary school educator*

Denville
Buset, Joanna Lynn *counselor*
Doane, Eileen Maloney *learning disabilities teacher consultant*
Veech, Lynda Anne *musician, educator*

Deptford
Gigliotti, Amy Veronica *music educator*
Kelly, Barbara Sue *psychologist*
Shusterman, Linda *ceramist, educator*

Dover
Derr, Debra Hulse *advertising executive, writer*

East Brunswick
Dombrowski, Anne Wesseling *retired microbiologist*
Meningall, Evelyn L. *retired educational media specialist*
Rust, Mildred D. *retired psychiatrist*
Savio, Frances Margaret Cammarotta *music educator*
Schmidt, Michelle Moore *music educator*
Strapko, Irene *science educator*
Weiss, Judith Ann *music educator*
Zaun, Anne Marie *lawyer*

East Hanover
Nelson, Barbara Kasztan *marketing professional*
Nemecek, Georgina Marie *molecular pharmacologist*

East Orange
Amadei, Deborah Lisa *librarian*
Brundage, Gertrude Barnes *pediatrician*
Corbitt, Ann Marie *municipal official*
Fielo, Muriel Bryant *interior designer*
Hudson-Zonn, Eliza *nurse, psychologist*
Teetsell, Janice Marie Newman *business owner, lawyer*

East Rutherford
Cathey, Gertrude Brown *retired medical/surgical nurse*

East Windsor
Guarino, Danita Cronin *special education educator*

Eatontown
Priesand, Sally Jane *rabbi*

Edgewater
Berliner, Barbara *retired librarian, consultant*
Ellis, Carol Oster *rehabilitation physician*
Fletcher, Susann (Susann Renee Smith) *actress, playwright*
Paci, Ruth A. *freelance/self-employed writer*
Zhou, Yan *chemist*

Edison
Biunno, Theresa *physical education educator*
De Candido Kamin, Rosann Therese *secondary school educator*
De Siena-Rappa, Kelly Ann *principal*
Haberman, Louise Shelly *consulting company executive*
Kijowski, Rosemary Joan *small business owner, retired music educator*
Morse, Judith *music educator, conductor*
Pedescleaux-Muckle, Gail *retired business analyst, writer, artist*

Egg Harbor Township
Carney, Michelle Catherine *assistant principal*
Schreiber, Eileen Sher *artist*

Elizabeth
Blowe, Arnethia *religious studies educator*
de la Viña-Sierra, Diana Maria *music educator*
Fulmore, MaryAnn *state agency administrator*
Miller-Duffy, Merritt *insurance agent, camp director*
Pineros, Elizabeth *social services administrator, psychotherapist*

Elmer
Slavoff, Harriet Emonds *learning disabilities teacher, consultant*

Elmwood Park
Nadzick, Judith Ann *accountant*

Englewood
Choi, Namhong Lee *retired psychologist*
Fay, Toni Georgette *communications executive*
Frieden, Faith Joy *obstetrician*
Hurst, Wendy R(obin) *obstetrician*
Le Mée, Katharine Wilbur *author, educational consultant, educator*
Polk, Gene-Ann *retired pediatrician*

Englewood Cliffs
Chase-Brand, Julia *psychiatrist, researcher*
Dobrzynski, Judith Helen *journalist, commentator*
Farrell, Patricia Ann *psychologist, educator, writer*
Gurtman, Alejandra C. *epidemiologist, research scientist*
Saible, Stephanie Irene *magazine editor*

Erial
Browna, Jo McIntyre *nurse*

Essex Fells
Nevius, Janet Dryden *real estate company executive, government agency administrator*

Ewing
Chodoroff, Nancy Arlene *elementary school educator*
Gitenstein, Donna M. *academic administrator*
Kirnan, Jean Powell *psychology educator*

Fair Haven
Derchin, Dary Bret Ingham *writer, radio personality*

Fair Lawn
Bowman, Delores *medical cost management administrator*
Dadurian, Medina Diana *pediatric dentist, educator*
Wallace, Mary Monahan *elementary, secondary schools and university educator*

Fairfield
de Smet, Lorraine May *artist*
Sangiuliano, Barbara Ann *tax consultant*

Fanwood
Butler, Grace Caroline *medical researcher*

Far Hills
Burns, Amy Margaret *music educator*

Farmingdale
Jones, Elizabeth Harding *elementary school educator*

Flanders
Hilbert, Rita L. *librarian*

Flemington
Castelgrant, Elizabeth Ann Saylor *physical education educator, consultant*
Meagher, Deirdra M. *lawyer*
Salamon, Renay *real estate broker*
Van Ost, Lynn *physical therapist, Olympic team official*
Wolfson, Barbara Libensperger *guidance counselor*

Florham Park
Bauer, Jean Marie *accountant*
Brodkin, Adele Ruth Meyer *psychologist*
Fischer, Pamela Shadel *public relations executive*
Paulson, Sondra Lee *music educator*
Rexford, Jennifer *communications engineer*

Fort Lee
Baiul, Oksana *former figure skater, clothing designer*
Orman, Suze *news correspondent, writer*
Schirmer, Helga *retired chiropractor*
Sklar, Ethel (Dusty Sklar) *writer*
Stuart, Carole *publishing executive*
Weiss, Simona *retired paralegal*

Franklin Lakes
Baker, Cornelia Draves *artist*
Healy, Bridget M. *lawyer*
Pappas, Pamela A. *mathematics educator*
Reed, JoAnn A. *corporate financial executive*

Franklinville
Delia, Margaret M. *elementary school educator*

Freehold
Cheng, Grace Zheng-Ying *music educator*
Langan-Sattenspiel, F. Candy *medical/surgical nurse, writer*
Meckes, Kimberly Jo *music educator*
Wilson, Nancy Jeanne *laboratory consultant, medical technologist*

Gillette
Merkl, Elissa Frances *visual artist, editor, publishing executive*
Nathanson, Linda Sue *publishing executive, writer*
Pfafflin, Sheila Murphy *psychologist*

Gladstone
Kenny, Jane M. *management consulting executive*

Glassboro
Holdcraft, Janet Rulon *school system administrator*
Magnan, Ruthann *nurse, social worker*
McCabe, Mary Otillia Sorg *secondary school educator*
Murashima, Kumiko *artist, educator*
Willett, Holly Geneva *librarian, educator*

Glen Ridge
Roethlin, Mary Jane *science educator*

Glen Rock
Buchar, Karen *mathematics educator*
Plein, Beverly R. *elementary school educator*
Savoie, Brietta Dolores *retired librarian*

Glenwood
Greilich, Audrey *administrative assistant*

Green Brook
Balsamello, Melissa (Marley) *elementary school educator*

Guttenberg
Pozniakoff, Rita Oppenheim *education software consultant*
Wright, Jane Cooke *oncologist, educator, consultant*

Hackensack
Bronson, Meridith J. *lawyer*
Haines, Kathleen Ann *pediatrician, educator*
Hirsch, Elisabeth Schiff *education educator emeritus*
MacVicar, Lisa *music educator*
Phifer, Emily A. *elementary school educator*
Shapiro, Sylvia *psychotherapist*
Williamson, (Eulah) Elaine *elementary school educator*

Hackettstown
Coulson-Grigsby, Carolyn *theater educator*
Mulligan, Elinor Patterson *lawyer*

Haddon Heights
Weinberg, Ruthmarie Louise *special education educator, researcher*

Haddonfield
Chiulli, E. Antoinette *lawyer*

Haledon
Dougherty, June Eileen *librarian*

Hamburg
Hagin, Rosa A. *psychologist, educator*

Hamilton
Coccia, JoAnn *music educator, musician*
Sipski, Mary Leonide *physiatrist, health facility administrator*
Stuebe, Joanne *secondary school educator*

Hamilton Square
Ridolfi, Dorothy Porter Boulden *nurse, real estate broker*

Hammonton
Langston, Jessi Lea *music educator*

Harrington Park
Salmon, Margaret Belais *nutritionist, dietician*

Hasbrouck Heights
Savva, Andrea *financial advisor*

Haworth
Biesel, Diane Jane *editor, publishing executive*
Mango, Christina Rose *psychiatric art therapist*

Hazlet
Beaudry, Robin Sharkey *secondary school educator*
Citro, Janet *elementary school educator, coach, secondary school educator*
Van Pelt, Dara *mathematics educator*

Highland Park
Blum, Lisa Carrie *social worker, researcher*
Grady, Joyce (Marian Joyce Grady) *psychotherapist, consultant*
Kheel, Susan Talmadge *retired reference services manager*

Highlands
Dann, Emily *mathematics educator*
Lofstrom, Arlene Katherine *primary school educator*

Hightstown
Hull, Gretchen Gaebelein *lay worker, writer, lecturer*

Petri, Christine Ann *music educator*
Zapicchi, Joanne Fenity *secondary school educator*

Hillsborough
Butcher, Deborah *public relations and communications consultant*
Hasser, Julia M. *mathematics educator*

Hillsdale
Copeland, Lois Jacqueline *physician*

Hillside
Wilson, Bertina Iolia *retired music educator*

Hoboken
Capotorto, Rosette *small business owner, printing company executive, writer*
Frankenthal, Danielle *painter, sculptor*
Hakki, Ayesha *editor-in-chief*
Rose, Roslyn *artist*
Tardiff, Jill Alexandria *publishing executive, photographer*

Holmdel
Slovik, Sandra Lee *retired art educator*
Tambaro, Marie Grace *health specialist, nursing educator*
Zupkus, Ellen Ciccone *clinical psychologist, consultant*

Hopatcong
Hill, Linda Marie Palermo *elementary school educator*

Hopewell
Baeckler, Virginia Van Wynen *librarian*
Lester, Pamela Robin *lawyer*

Howell
Van Vliet, Heather Agnes Joan Devlin *elementary school educator*

Jackson
Carney, Rita J. *educational association administrator*
Gasparro, Madeline *retired banker*
Landau-Crawford, Dorothy Ruth *retired social services administrator*
Rickabaugh, Vicki *horse farm owner, mayor*
Rothman, Patricia Mary *elementary school educator*
Thomas, Doris Amelia *family practice nurse practitioner*

Jersey City
Barney, Christine J. *artist*
Curran, Barbara A. *superior court judge*
Downes, Marie Jean *music educator*
Dunham, Patricia Ann *elementary school educator*
Dupey, Michele Mary *communications specialist*
Eigen, Barbara Goldman *artist*
Gipson, Gloria Lorraine *social worker*
Girgis, Mary *counselor*
Golden, Amy Patrice *actress, performing company executive*
Graham, Susan Louise *religious studies educator, consultant*
Jennings, Sister Vivien *literature and language professor*
Katz, Colleen *publisher*
Kramer, Helene *banking executive*
Kuhn, Melanie R. *literature educator, consultant*
LeSiege, Annette *music educator, composer*
Mahood, Marie I. *counselor, educator*
Metallo, Frances Rosebell *mathematics professor*
Milton, Barbara Ella, II, *psychotherapist*
Mizzi, Charlotte H. *city director*
Poiani, Eileen Louise *mathematician, academic administrator*
Pratt, Minnie Bruce *writer, educator*
Queen Latifah, (Dana Elaine Owens) *actress, musician*
Stensgaard, Karen J. *brokerage house executive*
Urso, Ida *psychologist*
Warren, Maredia Delois *music educator*
West, Michelle *principal*
Windo, Pamela Ann *administrative assistant, writer*

Kenilworth
Cox, Carrie *pharmaceutical executive*
Kravec, Cynthia Vallen *microbiologist*

Lakewood
Burns, Ruth Ann Mary *television executive*
Daniels, Judith Wall *education educator, retired principal*
Doak, Nancy Ann *mathematics educator*
Herbert, Barbara Rae *librarian, educational media specialist*
Katz, Sally Norma *psychologist*
Pilgram, Suzanne *artist, art educator*
Williams, Barbara Anne *retired academic administrator*

Lambertville
Cusworth, Christyl J. *conservator, artist*

Landing
Wolahan, Caryle Goldsack *nursing educator, consultant*

Laurel Springs
Cleveland, Susan Elizabeth *library administrator, researcher*
Roma, Aida Clara *artist*

Lavallette
Donato, Michele Roseanne *lawyer, educator*

Lawrenceville
Cox, Teri Polack *public relations executive*
Jordan, Mildred Rice Loretta *education educator*
Oram, Fern Amy *editor-in-chief, director*
Stein, Sandra Lou *educational psychology professor*

Layton
Seely, Maribeth Walsh *elementary school educator*

Lebanon
Barto, Susan Carol *writer*
O'Neill, Elizabeth Sterling *trade association administrator*
Robertson, Tina Barbara *dancer, educator*
Wagner-Westbrook, Bonnie Joan *educational consultant, director*

Leonia
Deutsch, Nina *pianist, vocalist*
Luhrs, Joyce Ann *business owner, consultant, communications and management consultant, writer*
Pinsdorf, Marion Katheryn *diversified financial services company executive, educator, writer*
Thiesfeldt, Sheila M. *artist, educator, small business owner*

Lincroft
Benham, Helen *music educator*
Sidel, Enid Ruth *retired literature and language professor*
Sieben, Karen K. *philosopher, educator*
Ventola, Frances Ann *mathematics professor*

Linden
Bedrick, Bernice *retired principal, science educator*

Lindenwold
Clarke, Betty Ann *librarian, minister*

Linwood
Chernoff, Deborah Shelley *art educator*
Cohen, Diana Louise *psychologist, educator, consultant*
Harlan, Rebecca *secondary school educator, social sciences educator*

Little Falls
Shern, Stephanie Marie *investment company executive, accountant*
Varis, Agnes *pharmaceutical executive*

Little Ferry
Navarro-Steinel, Catherine A. *municipal official*

Little Silver
Marcus, Abir A. *psychiatrist*

Livingston
Feigen, Irene *artist, educator*
Hildenbrand, Joyce Pluhowski *social work professional, marketing specialist*
Saffer, Amy Beth *foreign language educator*
Scott, Jane Vicroy *microbiologist*
Sikora, Barbara Jean *library director*

Lodi
Arella, Ann Marietta *music educator, vocalist*

Long Branch
Janeczek, Terry Ann *director, science educator*
Klostreich, Eva Tricules *educational association administrator*
Lagowski, Barbara Jean *writer, editor*
Mindnich, Ellen *sales executive*
Stewart, Georgiana Liccione *writer*

Long Valley
Duane, Jeannine Morrissey *retired elementary school educator*
Falk, Barbara Higinbotham *music educator*

Lumberton
Campagnolo, Mary Frances *physician*
Losse, Catherine Ann *pediatrics nurse, critical care nurse, educator, family practice nurse practitioner*
Wojtko, Donnamarie *music educator, director*

Lyndhurst
Germann, JoAnn *mathematics educator*

Madison
Bull, Vivian Ann *retired academic administrator, educator*
Geehr, Patricia Bray *education educator*
Monte, Bonnie J. *performing arts company executive, director, educator*
O'Brien, Mary Devon *communications executive, consultant*

Magnolia
Finley, Charlene P. *elementary school educator*
Warden, Karen Barbara *special education educator*

Mahwah
Bello, Mary *physician*
Hailparn, Diana Finnegan *psychotherapist, writer*
Wagner, Susan Jane *sales and marketing consulting company executive*

Manahawkin
Barton, Noreen Duffy *secondary school educator*
Collins, Sarah Jane *secondary school educator*

Manalapan
Lin, Chiu-Tze *conductor, musician*
Reisman, Joan Ann *executive secretary*

Manasquan
Crowning, Lisa L. *secondary school educator, horticulturist, consultant*
Kelman, Marybeth *retired health care consultant, health policy analyst*
Robinson, Sarah Bonham *artist, educator, mental health services professional*

Manville
Spatz, Meagen Sorensen *music educator, director*

Maplewood
Hamburger, Mary Ann *management consultant*
Rabadeau, Mary Frances *protective services official*
Safian, Gail Robyn *public relations executive*
Woods, Krystyna Janina *artist, pharmacist*

Margate City
Pronesti, Rosa C. *artist*
Rose, Jodi *artistic director, film producer*

Marlboro
Francisco, Deborah Antosh *educational administrative professional*
Komisarczyk, Shirley Theresa *secondary school educator*

Marlton
Cheney, Eleanora Louise *retired secondary school educator*
Farwell, Nancy Larraine *public relations executive*
O'Connor, Genevieve *marketing executive*
Tuma, Michele *music educator*

Matawan
Liggett, Twila C. *academic administrator, broadcast executive, educator*

Mays Landing
Gross, Michelle Bayard *dancer, educator*
Parrish, Virginia Ellen *retired secondary school educator*
Reichert, Kathleen Evelyn *elementary school educator*
Risimini, Barbara Lynn *secondary school educator*

Medford
Isaacson, Edith L. *civic leader*
Mayer, Joyce Harris *artist*

Mendham
Bennett, Nancy Evans *secondary school educator*
Posunko, Linda Mary *retired elementary education educator*

Metuchen
Ackerson, Patricia Kathleen Freis *art educator, artist*
Arbeiter, Joan *artist, educator*
Kushinsky, Jeanne Alice *humanities educator*
Laguna, Asela Rodríguez *Spanish language and literature educator*
Macarin-Mara, Lynn *psychotherapist, consultant*
Zatz, Arline *writer, photographer*

Middlesex
Hilliard, Kathleen J. *costume designer*

Middletown
Heng, Siang Gek *communications executive*
Shields, Patricia Lynn *educational broker, consultant*

Milford
Hance, Laurie Ann *biology educator*

Millburn
O'Byrne, Elizabeth Milikin *retired pharmacologist*

Millville
Caldwell, Linda E. *critical care nurse*

Mine Hill
Gasperini, Elizabeth Carmela (Lisa Gasperini) *marketing professional*

Monroe Township
Cushman, Helen Merle Baker *retired management consultant*

Montclair
Barnes, Cynthia Lepre *university administrator*
Cass, Mary Louise *librarian*
Chemidlin, Michele Lynn *athletic trainer, consultant*
Cole, Susan A. *academic administrator, language educator*
Delbourgo, Joëlle Lily *publishing executive*
Dubrow, Marsha Ann *management consultant, musicologist*
Fabend, Firth Haring *writer*
Gill, Nia H. *state legislator*
Gogick, Kathleen Christine *magazine editor, publisher*
Gunthorpe, Karen Ann *elementary school educator*
Harayda, Janice *newspaper book editor, author*
Jones, Sylvia Calpurnia *investment company executive*
Kriftner, Gail Lyn *choreographer, educator*
Mason, Lucile Gertrude *not-for-profit fundraiser, consultant*
Murphy, Betty Jagoda *small business owner*
Nagorka, Stefanie *artist*
Peterson, Jane Temple *theater educator*
Phillips, Ann Y. *art advisor*
Reichslan, Michele B. *psychiatrist*

Montvale
Falk, Ellen Stein *media specialist, educator*
Gaeta, Michelle *mathematics educator*
Nachtigal, Patricia *lawyer*

Moorestown
Clark, Maryliz M. *retired minister*
Collins, Angelo *science educator*
Stine, Anna Mae *publishing company executive*

Morganville
Lechtanski, Cheryl Lee *chiropractor*
Marder, Carol *advertising specialist and premium firm executive*

Morristown
Armstrong, Diana Rose *financial consultant*
Blanchard, Mary Warner *historian, consultant*
Finkel, Marion Judith *internist, pharmaceutical administrator*
Flynn, Marie Cosgrove *portfolio manager, corporate financial executive*
Gorrell, Nancy S. *English language educator*
Hastings, Mary Jane *minister*
Martine, Cathy *telecommunications industry executive*
Mooney, Patricia Anne *secondary school educator*
Prince, Leah Fanchon *lab administrator, executive secretary*
Prisco, Dorothy DeSteno *academic administrator*

Rogachefsky, Arlene Sandra *dermatologist*
Sherman, Sandra Brown *lawyer*
Thomas, Nina K. *psychologist*

Mount Arlington
Davis, Dorinne Sue *audiologist*

Mount Holly
Kind, Rosalind Weintraub *special education educator*

Mount Laurel
Eiferman, Sharon Rees *language educator, poet*
Giampetro, Kathleen A. *school psychologist*
Jones, Marian C. *music educator*
Plye, Kelly Ann *nurse*

Mountain Lakes
Loomis, Rebecca C. *psychologist*
Shand, Kimberly *information technology consultant company executive*
Starger, Victoria Gondek *artist*
Wallace, MaryJean Elizabeth *science educator*

Mountainside
Bertsch, Patricia Ann *nature center director*
Lipton, Bronna Jane *marketing communications executive*
Vice, Susan F. *medicinal chemist*

Mullica Hill
Rose, Carol Ann *retired air transportation executive*

Murray Hill
Bruch, Ruth E. *information technology executive*
Christy, Cindy *telecommunications industry executive*
Davidson, Janet G. *telecommunications industry executive*

Neptune
Bediguian, Mariamig Jinx *operating room nurse*
Laraya-Cuasay, Lourdes Redublo *pediatrician, pulmonologist, educator*

Neshanic Station
Castellon, Christine New *information systems specialist, real estate agent*

New Brunswick
Adickes, Sandra Elaine *language educator, writer*
Bachmann, Gloria Ann *obstetrician, gynecologist, educator*
Bradley, Dondeena G. *consumer products company executive*
Bunch, Charlotte *advocate*
Clauss-Ehlers, Caroline S. *psychologist, educator, journalist*
Day-Salvatore, Debra Lynn *medical geneticist*
Formica, Palma Elizabeth *physician*
Foster-Cheek, Kaye I. *health products executive*
Gaunt, Marianne I. *university librarian*
Goggins, Colleen A. *health products executive*
Hartman, Mary Susan *historian, educator*
House, Renee S. *theological librarian, minister*
Leventhal, Elaine A. *internist*
Liao, Mei-June *pharmaceutical executive, researcher*
Mabb, Karen Terri *ornithologist*
Miller, Lynn Fieldman *lawyer*
Mills, Dorothy Allen *investor*
Poon, Christine A. *pharmaceutical company executive*
Russell, Louise Bennett *economist, educator*
Saidi, Parvin *hematologist, medical educator*
Saltz, Amy *theater educator, director*
Scanlon, Jane Cronin *mathematics professor*
Smoyak, Shirley Anne *psychiatric nurse practitioner, educator*
Snyder, Barbara K. *pediatrician, educator*
Strickland, Dorothy *education educator*
Todd, Mary Beth *oncologist, researcher*
Turock, Betty Jane *library and information science professor*
Weiss, Lynne S. *pediatrician, educator*
Yorke, Marianne *lawyer, real estate executive*

New Milford
McHenry, Esther Ann *artist*
Spiegel, Edna Z. *lawyer*

New Monmouth
Dickinson, Jeanne M. *secondary school educator*
Santos, Sharon Lee *parochial school educator*

New Providence
Barnes, Sandra Henley *retired publishing company executive*
Del Tiempo, Sandra Kay *sales executive*
Hackenson, Elizabeth *information technology executive, telecommunications industry executive*
Hirsch, Maxine K. *special education educator, councilman*
Reinsdorf, Judith A. *lawyer*
Rivo, Shirley Winthrope *artist*
Russo, Patricia F. *telecommunications company executive*
SanGiovanni, Mary Elizabeth *writer, freelance manager*
Sivco, Deborah Lee *materials scientist, researcher*
Spector, Magaly *telecommunications industry executive*
Worden, Virginia Hill *academic administrator, lawyer*

Newark
Adler, Freda Schaffer (Mrs. G. O. W. Mueller) *criminologist, educator*
Amalfe, Christine A. *lawyer*
Anderson, Gina Marie *obstetrician, gynecologist*
Arbuckle, Peggy Trawick *special education educator, consultant*
Ausley, Geneva Gardner *cosmetologist, foundation executive*
Baer, Susan M. *airport executive*
Banta, Vivian L. *insurance company executive*
Barry, Maryanne Trump *federal judge*
Bizub, Johanna Catherine *law librarian*

Cheng, Mei-Fang *psychobiology educator, neuroscientist*
Clowney, Mary L. *educational media specialist, librarian*
Cohen, Alice *hematologist*
Dauth, Frances Kutcher *journalist, editor*
Defeis, Elizabeth Frances *law educator, lawyer*
Ebenholtz, Jean Miriam *academic administrator*
Feldman, Cecile Arlene *dean, dental educator*
Ferris-Waks, Arlene Susan *compliance officer*
Fox, Jeanne Marie *lawyer*
Henry, Rolanne *law educator*
Hiltz, Starr Roxanne *sociologist, educator, writer, consultant, computer scientist*
Hochberg, Faith S. *US district court judge*
Koster, Barbara *insurance company executive*
Liu, Qinyue (Sherry Liu) *physician, consultant*
Mason, Joyce J. *lawyer, telecommunications industry executive*
Moore, Mattie H. *clergy, folk artist, retired educator*
Myers, Priscilla A. *insurance company executive*
Nash, Alicia *application developer, physicist*
Nutt, Amy Ellis *journalist*
Price, Mary Sue Sweeney *museum director*
Raveché, Elizabeth Scott *immunologist, educator*
Reynolds, Valrae *museum curator*
Rothschild, Gita F. *lawyer*
Sabio, Dorothy *elementary school educator*
Stephens, B. Consuela *minister, consultant*
Storch, Susan Borowski *lawyer*
Timko, Kathleen *communications executive*
Van Deusen, Lois M. *lawyer*
Varzegar, Minoo *literature educator, reading specialist*
Weis, Judith Shulman *biology professor*

Newfoundland
Divinsky, Miriam *psychotherapist*
Vandenburg, Mary Lou *psychologist*

Newton
Case, Tammy *bank executive*
Dougherty, Phyllis Marilyn *social worker*
Grodsky, Sheila Taylor *art educator, artist*
Hollander, Roslyn *artist, educator*
Koerber, Joan C. *retired elementary school educator*
MacMurren, Margaret Patricia *secondary school educator, consultant*
Naylis, Stephanie Anne *music educator*

North Arlington
Batshaw, Marilyn Seidner *education administrator*
Borowski, Jennifer Lucile *corporate administrator*

North Brunswick
Moon, Kathleen K. *language arts educator*
Shapiro, Marsha N. *social worker*
Shaw, Roslyn Lee *small business owner, retired elementary school educator*

North Haledon
Brenner, Betty Esther Bilgray *social worker*
Latner, Selma *psychoanalyst*

North Plainfield
Dunbar, Holly Jean *communications executive, public relations executive*
Irvine, Carol Stone *elementary school educator*

Northfield
McNeal, Jane Erskine *music educator, musician*

Nutley
Comune, Kathryn Ann *counselor*
Struble, Pamela Lynn *music educator*

Oakland
Farrell, Donna Marie *photographer, graphics designer*
Manheimer, Heidi *cosmetics company executive*
Schwager, Linda Helen *lawyer*

Oaklyn
Miranda, Minda *chemist, pharmacy technologist*

Ocean City
Culbertson, Jane Young *statistician*
Heist, Karen Gartland *elementary school educator*

Old Bridge
Luis, Belinda *graphic designer*

Old Tappan
Lovitch, Joan *science educator, coach*
Vella, April *mathematics educator*

Oradell
Carcich, Michele Leigh *biology educator*
Monticone, Diane Therese *French educator*
Struck, Norma Johansen *artist*

Palisades Park
McColl, Terrie Lee *library director*

Paramus
Atkins, Yvette *special education educator*
Boisits, Regina Marie *elementary school educator*
Crow, Lynne Campbell Smith *insurance company representative*
Fader, Shirley Sloan *writer*
Forman, Beth Rosalyne *specialty food trade executive*
Hershey, Lynne R. *elementary school educator*
Hochberg, Lois J. *school psychologist*
Jenkins, Elaine *middle school educator*
Marcel-Calderon, Linda *music educator*
Noguere, Suzanne *trade association executive, poet*
Perkins-Munn, Tiffany Sabrena *psychologist, researcher*
Satin, Elaine *educator*
Ward, Christine L. *elementary school educator*

Park Ridge
Ciannella, Joeen Moore *small business owner*

Parsippany
Albert, Susan *mathematics educator*
Anselmi, Elvira *psychologist, researcher*
Azzarone, Carol Ann *marketing executive*
Fletcher, Jean Stout *retired special education educator*
Langrana, Anita *financial analyst, personal trainer*
Puccio, Jane Anne *secondary school educator*
Solomon, Mary-Jo Kelleher *mathematics educator*
Timmins, Maryanne *real estate accountant, educator*

Passaic
Jakimowicz, Joan Marie *elementary school educator*
Johnson, Myrtle Alice Harris *elementary and secondary school educator*
Johnson, Sakinah *paralegal*

Paterson
Daniels, Cheryl Lynn *pediatrics nurse*
Kelder, Dorothy Mae *science educator*
Pou, Nellie *assemblywoman*
Schimpf, Kathleen *elementary school educator*
Tanis, Barbara Ann *science educator*

Pemberton
Bowker, Eileen Gunson *athletic trainer, educator*

Pennington
Czach, Gabriela Bozena *personal care industry executive*
Gundeck, Caroline Nyklewicz *investment company executive*
Palmisano, Hollie Leah *personal trainer, athletic trainer*

Pennsville
Latorre, Maria Joanne *health and physical education educator*

Perth Amboy
(Carlson)Reno, Arletta Lou *administrative assistant*
Daily, Anna Wilkins *science educator*
Dakelman, Rhonda Elyse *physical education educator*
Lavin-Pennyfeather, Rose *artist*
Reyes, Irma V. *adult education educator*
Richardson-Melech, Joyce Suzanne *music educator, singer*

Phillipsburg
Brown, Jerri L. *performing arts educator, choreographer*

Picatinny Arsenal
Zulauf, Madeline Ruth *photographer, artist*

Piscataway
Champe, Pamela Chambers *biochemistry professor, writer*
Coppola, Sarah Jane *special education educator*
Ferstandig Arnold, Gail *research scientist, educator*
Gelman, Rochel *psychology professor*
Goss, Mary E. Weber *sociology educator*
Gustafsson, Mary Beth *lawyer*
Lee, Barbara Anne *law educator, dean*
McCrady, Barbara Sachs *psychologist, educator*
Urban, Cathleen Andrea *graphics designer*
Volfson-Doubova, Elena *psychiatrist, researcher*
Witz, Gisela *research scientist, educator*

Pitman
Lohmann, Judith Leith *secondary school educator*

Pittsgrove
Chassier, Janice *elementary school educator, art educator*

Pittstown
Hierholzer, Joan *artist*

Plainfield
Clinton, Birdean R. *elementary school educator*

Plainsboro
Lansing, Martha Hempel *physician*
Spiegel, Phyllis *public relations consultant, journalist*

Pleasantville
London, Charlotte Isabella *secondary school educator*

Point Pleasant
Greene, Ellin *library service educator*

Point Pleasant Beach
McAllen, Regina K. *voice educator*

Pomona
Birdwhistell, Joanne (Anne) *retired education educator, researcher*
Bukowski, Elaine Louise *physical therapist, educator*
Dagavarian, Debra A. *college administrator, consultant*
Latourette, Audrey Wolfson *law educator*
Vaughn, Beverly Jean *music educator, mezzo soprano*
Vito, Marilyn Elaine *business educator*

Pompton Plains
Guida, Pat *information broker, literature chemist*
Zastocki, Deborah K. *health facility executive*

Port Monmouth
Pfennig, Jacqueline F. *elementary school educator*

Pottersville
Guerra, Jamee Elizabeth Rund *music educator*

Princeton
Altmann, Jeanne *zoologist, educator*
Bahcall, Neta Assaf *astrophysicist*
Beidler, Marsha Wolf *lawyer*
Bogan, Elizabeth Chapin *economist, educator*
Boretz, Naomi Messinger *artist, educator*
Boyer, M. Christine *architecture educator*
Browning, Charlotte Elisabeth *social studies educator*
Campbell, Mildred Corum *business owner, nurse*
Canright, Sarah Anne *artist, educator*
Cardaneo, Donna Marie *music educator, director*
Carter, Emily Ann *physical chemist, researcher, educator*
Chang, Sun-Yung Alice *mathematics professor*
Christian, Carole Ann *psychologist, academic administrator*
Contillo, Debbie B. *performing arts educator*
Crossley, Helen Martha *public opinion analyst, research consultant*
DeBardeleben, Martha Graves *counselor*
DeKlyen, Michelle *psychologist*
De Lung, Jane Solberger *independent sector executive*
Diller, Elizabeth E. *architect, educator, artist*
Drakeman, Lisa N. *biotechnologist*
Dubrovsky, Gertrude Wishnick *journalist, researcher*
Duncan, Dianne Walker *elementary school educator*
Finn, Frances Mary *biochemist, researcher*
Fisher, Heidi Alice *librarian*
Frenier, Diane M. *lawyer*
Frey, Julia Bloch *language educator, art historian, educator*
Girgus, Joan Stern *psychologist, educator, director*
Gmachl, Claire *electrical engineer, educator*
Graham, Nancy Love *music educator*
Grant, Barbara Rosemary *science educator, researcher*
Greenman, Jane Friedlieb *lawyer, human resources executive*
Hirschman, Sarah *educator*
Jeffers, Beverly Maynard *volunteer*
Jenson, Pauline Alvino *retired speech and hearing educator*
Johnson, Barbara Piasecka *volunteer, art historian, investor*
Kahn, Eiko Taniguchi *artist*
Kaplowitz, Karen (Jill) *lawyer, consultant*
Keller, Suzanne *sociologist, psychotherapist*
Krulewicz, Rita Gloria *special education educator*
Lavizzo-Mourey, Risa Juanita *medical foundation administrator, academic administrator*
Leonard, Naomi Ehrich *aerospace engineer, engineering educator*
Lincoln, Anna *publishing executive, language educator*
Logue, Judith Felton *psychoanalyst, educator*
Longenecker, LuAnn F. *music educator, department chairman*
Malkiel, Nancy Weiss *dean, historian, educator*
Marshall, Carol Joyce *science administrator*
McCauley, Elizabeth Anne *art educator*
McKaughan, Molly *writer, consultant*
Neimark, Edith Deborah *psychologist, educator*
Orphanides, Nora Charlotte *ballet educator*
Painter, Nell Irvin *historian, educator, writer*
Rose, Edith Sprung *retired lawyer*
Rubin, Dorothy Molly *language educator, writer*
Sayer, Ruth P. *realtor*
Scott, Joan Wallach *historian, educator*
Showalter, Elaine *humanities educator*
Siegel, Laurie *human resources specialist*
Slaughter, Anne-Marie *dean*
Sullivan, Diane P. *lawyer*
Taylor, Susan M. *museum director*
Tienda, Marta *demographer, educator*
Tilghman, Shirley Marie *academic administrator, biology professor*
Trainer, Karin A. *librarian*
Troyanskaya, Olga *biomedical researcher, computer scientist*
Vizzini, Carol Redfield *symphony musician, educator*
Ward, Bess B. *oceanographer, educator*
Weiss, Renée Karol *editor, musician*
Witkin, Evelyn Maisel *retired geneticist*

Princeton Junction
Rose, Peggy Jane *artist, educator, gifted education advocate*
Ruddiman, Joan *elementary school educator*

Prospect Park
Blair, Sherry Ann *psychotherapist, educator*

Rahway
Chen, Liya *chemist*
Dolinich-Matuska, Christine *artist*
Garcia, Maria Luisa *biochemist, researcher*
Strack, Alison Merwin *neurobiologist*

Randolph
Goldman, Phyllis E. *psychology educator*
Greenberger, Marsha Moses *sales executive*
Oliveira, Theresa Razzano *secondary school educator*
Rathore, Uma Pandey *utilities executive*
Sandidge, Kanita Durice *retired communications executive, consultant*
Whildin, Leonora Porreca *retired nursing educator*

Raritan
Weaver, Sylvia *information technology executive*

Red Bank
Brown, Valerie Anne *psychotherapist, social worker, educator*
Carmody, Margaret Jean *retired social worker*
Groves, Lizabeth A. *accountant, network administrator*
Gutentag, Patricia Richmond *social worker, family counselor, occupational therapist*
McWhinney, Madeline H. (Mrs. John Denny Dale) *economist, director*
Murray, Abby Darlington Boyd *psychiatric clinical specialist, educator*

Ridgefield
Campbell, Della Anne *nurse, researcher*
Riggs, Rory B. *pharmaceutical executive*

Ridgefield Park
Magdosko, Paula *school psychologist*

Ridgewood
Clements, Lynne Fleming *marriage and family therapist, application developer*
Fox, Ingrid *curator*
Friedrich, Margret Cohen *guidance and student assistance counselor*
Harris, Micalyn Shafer *lawyer, educator, arbitrator, consultant, mediator*
Kuiken, Diane (Dee) Marie *science educator*
Le May, Moira Kathleen *retired psychology educator*

Ringoes
Tema-Lyn, Laurie *management consultant*

Robbinsville
Muench, Debby S. *elementary school educator*

Rochelle Park
Donahoe, Maureen Alice *accounting consultant*
Olzerowicz, Sharon *information technology executive*
Sinis, Elaine M. *personnel director*

Rockaway
Karpack, Kimberlee June Rush *mental health counselor*
Steier, Audrey Keller *music educator*

Roseland
Graham, Patricia *information technology executive*
Steidl, Mary Catherine *food service executive*

Roselle
Di Marco, Barbaranne Yanus *principal*
Meister, Karen Olivia *secondary school educator*
Orlando, Ann Marie *educator*
Tanner-Oliphant, Karen M. *family and consumer science educator*

Roselle Park
Loredo, Linda S. *marketing executive*

Rumson
Swartz, Renee Becker *civic volunteer*
Topham, Sally Jane *performing arts educator*

Rutherford
Dahse, Linda Jewell *social studies educator*
Suarez, Sally Ann Tevis *health facility administrator, nurse, consultant*

Saddle Brook
Ballone, Eileen Marie *music educator, musician, organist*
Clifton, Nelida *social worker*
Luisi, Louisa *secondary school educator*
White, H. Katherine *lawyer*

Saddle River
Lasser, Gail Maria *psychologist, educator*

Scotch Plains
Johnsen, Karen Kennedy *marketing professional*
Levins, Mary Clare *science educator*
Marion, Sarah Elizabeth *elementary school educator*
Wagner, Brooke *secondary school educator*

Sea Girt
Herschel, Andrea B. *elementary school educator*
Hillman, Barbara Hall *retired elementary school educator*

Sea Isle City
Bruno, Carol Jeanette *library media specialist, gifted and talented education educator, innkeeper*
Tull, Theresa Anne *retired diplomat*

Seabrook
Nakai, Tanya B. *music educator*

Seaside Park
Golembeski, Beverly Long *artist, art educator*

Secaucus
Bay, Willow *news anchor*
Blackmon, Brenda *newscaster*
Crowley, Monica *political commentator*
Ferguson, Cathleen Michele *elementary school educator*
Grazioli, Margaret *librarian*
Sanders, Summer *Olympic athlete, news correspondent, newscaster*

Sewell
Crocker, Jane Lopes *library director*

Ship Bottom
Clark, Bonnie A. *small business owner, real estate agent*

Short Hills
Ogden, Maureen Black *retired state legislator*
Robbins-Wilf, Marcia *educational consultant*
Schaefer, Eleanor Montville *retired publishing executive*
Winter, Ruth Grosman (Mrs. Arthur Winter) *journalist*
Yorinks, Adrienne Berg *artist, illustrator*

Shrewsbury
Westerman, Liane Marie *research scientist executive*

Skillman
Brill, Yvonne Claeys *engineer, consultant*
Cummings, Peggy Ann *counseling administrator*
Diaz, Teresita Perez *chemist*

Somerdale
Botka, Betsy Jean *industrial arts and career awareness instructor*
Klenk, Christine *athletic trainer, educator*

Somers Point
Hagerthey, Gwendolyn Irene *retired music educator*
Hardy, Janice Audrey Neubert *elementary school educator, educator*

Clovis
Brown, Linda Currene *small business executive*
Crook, Anna Marie *legislator*
Kilian, Joy A. *pre-school educator*
Nigreville, Carrie Christopher *principal*
Shade, Marsha J. *elementary school educator*

Corrales
Campion, Kathleen Francis *lawyer, gifted and talented educator*
Eaton, Pauline *artist, educator*
Eisenstadt, Pauline Doreen Bauman *brokerage house executive, state legislator*

Deming
De Mott, Marianne *artist, educator, space designer, craftsperson*

Edgewood
Villagomez, Deborah Lynn *medical/surgical nurse, horse breeder*

El Prado
Reading, Margery Schrock *psychology professor, artist*

Elephant Butte
Anton, Carol J. *small business owner, writer*

Espanola
Jonker, Pamela Lynn *artist*
Montoya, Ruby *alcohol and drug abuse counselor*

Eunice
Gideon, Brenda K. *mathematics educator*

Farmington
Anderson, Evelyn Louise *elementary school educator*
Doig, Beverly Irene *retired systems specialist*
Espinosa, Nancy Sweet *artist, anthropologist*
Luttrell, Mary Lou *elementary school educator*
Ogilvie, Donna Lee *retired marketing professional, retired journalist*
Pepin, Fran *secondary school educator*
Peterson Gerstner, Janet *English professor*
Young, Patricia Anne *secondary school educator, writer*

Gallup
Cattaneo, Jacquelyn Annette Kammerer *artist, educator*
Fellin, Octavia Antoinette *retired librarian, historical researcher*
Mulligan, Erlinda Rita *medical/surgical nurse*

Grants
Barnes, Ina Jean *retired elementary educator*

Hagerman
McIntire, Linda Carole *mental health and substance abuse counselor*

Hobbs
Ayers, Dolores Elaine *literature and language educator*
Francke, Susan *elementary school educator*
Garey, Patricia Martin *artist*
Holladay, Kelly Gayle *dean*
Starling, Virginia R. *music educator, consultant*
Weldy, Lana Gail *secondary school educator*

Las Cruces
Amos, Shirleyann *mental health therapist, social worker*
Arnett, Rita Ann *business executive*
Bell, M. Joy Miller *financial planner, real estate agent*
Little, Karen J. *counselor*
Livermore, Fern Chrisman *retired artist*
Lopez, Carol Sue *artist*
Nelson, Antonya *writer*
Selden, Annie *mathematics professor*
Valdez, Michelle Liane *educator*

Las Vegas
Lopez, Clara M. *director*
Simpson, Dorothy Audrey *retired speech educator*
Wagner, Deborah Rae *musician, educator*

Lordsburg
Clem, Sarah Lynn *special education educator*
Moralez, Joselyn Hope *special education educator*

Los Alamos
Korber, Bette Tina Marie *chemist*
Lu, Ningping *environmental chemist*
Mendius, Patricia Dodd Winter *editor, educator, writer*
Ramsey, Margie *librarian*
Smith, Fredrica Emrich *rheumatologist, internist*
Thompson, Lois Jean Heidke Ore *psychologist*
Willerton, Beverly Kay *mathematics educator*

Lovington
Stuart, Lillian Mary *writer*

Mora
Abeyta, Jeanie *secondary school educator*

Moriarty
Cox, Darlene Beth *secondary school educator*
Moonwalker, Tu *minister, counselor, artist*

Penasco
Marx, Nicki Diane *sculptor, painter*

Placitas
Frantzve, Jerri Lyn *psychologist, educator, consultant*
McElhinney, Susan Kay (Kate Echeverria) (Kate McElhinney) *executive assistant*
Watson-Boone, Rebecca A. *dean, researcher, library and information scientist, educator*

Portales
Edwards, Carolyn Mullenax *public relations executive*
YSikes, Juanita Lou *art educator*

Prewitt
Droll, Ruth Lucille *missionary pastor*

Raton
Ahlm, Jo LaVonne *elementary school educator*

Rio Rancho
Duitman, Lois Robinson *artist*
Glaser, Kandace Kaye *elementary school educator*
Loiacono, Melissa Ann *athletic trainer*
Meyerson, Barbara Tobias *elementary school educator*
Severino, Sally K. *retired psychiatrist*
Weber, Alois Hughes *principal*

Roswell
Bailey, Sharon L. *history educator, literature and language educator*
Daugherty, Lynn Bayliss *psychologist, consultant*
Harvell, Gayle Marie *cardiovascular technologist*
Henry, Debbie Cheryl *elementary school educator*
Maley, Jean Carol *foreign language educator*
Martinez, Cheryl A. *mathematics professor*
Peterson, Dorothy Hawkins *artist, educator*
Watson, Marilyn Fern *writer*
Weikel, Sandra G. *music educator*

Ruidoso
Stover, Carolyn Nadine *middle school educator*

Ruidoso Downs
Templeton, Ann *artist, educator*

Sandia Park
Beffort, Sue Wilson *state legislator*
Weitz, Jeanne Stewart *artist, educator*

Santa Fe
Bergé, Carol *writer*
Caplan, Jessica Marie *small business owner, artist*
Carpenter, Carol Denise *writer, educator*
Chavez, Maria Lucinda *band director, educator*
Davis, Marcie L. *public health and human services consultant*
Dean, Nat *artist, designer, educator*
Denish, Diane D. *lieutenant governor*
Erdman, Barbara *visual artist*
Fisher, Lisa Gray *English language educator*
Garcia, Veronica *school system administrator*
Grisham, Michelle Lujan *state agency administrator*
Hanson, Linda N. *academic administrator, educator*
Harding, Marie *ecological executive, artist*
Harms, Cora Beenhouwer *music educator*
Howell, Vicky Sue *health data analyst*
Hyde, Pamela Suzon *housing and human services administrator*
Kahn, Margaret S. *social worker, language educator*
Kaman, Helen S. *retired aerospace engineer, artist*
Karp, Diane R. *art educator*
Kelly, Ruth *state agency administrator*
King, Ro *psychotherapist, educator*
Lichtenberg, Maggie Klee *publishing executive*
Madrid, Patricia A. *state attorney general*
Maes, Petra Jimenez *state supreme court justice*
Melnick, Alice Jean (AJ Melnick) *counselor*
Miller-Engel, Marjorie *foundation administrator, commissioner, small business owner*
Minzner, Pamela Burgy *state supreme court justice*
Moll, Deborah Adelaide *lawyer*
Moya, Rosemary Mercedes *mental health administrator*
Nixon, Sunny Jeanne *lawyer*
Perroni, Carol *artist*
Perry, Elisabeth Scherf *psychologist*
Peters, Margaret Annette *English language educator*
Pierson, Norah *artist*
Raeschild, Sheila *writer, humanities educator*
Reeve, Agnesa *writer*
Relkin, Michele Weston *artist*
Sakara, Marilyn Judith *retired social worker*
Sandoval, Isabelle Medina *education educator*
Sloan, Jeanette Pasin *artist*
Stieber, Tamar *journalist*
Tokheim, Sara Ann *writer, information technology professional*
Vaughn, Gloria C. *state representative*
Vázquez, Martha Alicia *federal judge*
Vigil-Giron, Rebecca *state official*
Vucinich, Janet *language educator*
Westbrook, Arlen Runzler *retired social worker*
White, Denise *mathematics professor, department chairman*
Wiese, Neva *critical care nurse*
Wilson, Avon W. *state representative*
Wilson, Laura Eleanor *landscape architect*
Wotherspoon, Mary Ruth *artist, writer*
Yalman, Ann *judge, lawyer*
York, Star Liana *sculptor*

Shiprock
Atcitty, Fannie L. *elementary school educator, education educator*

Silver City
Bettison, Cynthia Ann *museum director, archaeologist*
Gadberry, Vicki Lynn Himes *librarian*
Gilbert, Kathie Simon *economist, educator*
Lopez, Linda Carol *social sciences educator*
Paez, Carolyn Jean *secondary school educator*
Parent, Annette Richards *free lance writer, artist*

Socorro
Boston, Penelope J. *science educator, researcher*

Taos
Beck, Ursula *art educator, artist*
Bolls, Imogene Lamb *English language educator, poet*
Crespin, Leslie Ann *artist*
Garcia, Christine *academic administrator, educator, researcher*
Price, Brenda Chloè *artist, entrepreneur*
Winslow, Bette Killingsworth *dance studio owner*

Tesuque
MacGraw, Ali *actress*

Tohatchi
Tucker, Amanda Yeates *history educator*

Truth Or Consequences
Lyon, Diana *counselor, art educator, psychotherapist*

NEW YORK

Addison
Coombs, Joanne Dininny *kindergarten educator*
Haines, Caryl *retired medical/surgical nurse*

Albany
Branigan, Helen Marie *educational consultant, administrator*
Brewer, Aida M. *treasurer*
Capaldi, Elizabeth Ann Deutsch *psychological sciences professor*
Carson, JoAnne *art educator, artist*
Caruso, Aileen Smith *managed care consultant*
Clifford, Lisa Mary *marketing and sales professional*
Davis, Lydia *writer, educator*
Donohue, Mary *lieutenant governor*
Dushensky, Jacqueline Amelia *banker, educator*
Ebert, Loretta Caren *university librarian*
Hagan, Diana Lynn *elementary school educator*
Haig Nicol, Teresa Iminta *choreographer, educator*
Helmer, Nicole M. *lawyer*
Howard, Lyn Jennifer *medical educator*
Jacobs, Rhoda S. *state legislator*
Jonquières, Lynne *travel agent*
Kaye, Judith Smith *state appeals court judge*
Kruegler, Catherine A. *sister, parochial school educator*
Lagoy, Mary Elizabeth *sister*
Langer, Judith Ann *language educator*
Lawton, Nancy *artist*
Lepow, Martha Lipson *pediatric educator, consultant*
Lustenader, Barbara Diane *human resources specialist*
McCarthy, Denise Eileen *clinical psychologist*
McCarthy, Mary Lynn *social work educator*
McDade, Turina L. *principal*
Menges, Susan Debra Favreau *management consultant, retired protective services official*
Miles, Christine Marie *museum director*
Morris, Margretta Elizabeth *conservationist*
Mulholland, Nancy W. *state agency administrator*
Novello, Antonia Coello *state health commissioner, pediatric nephrologist, former Surgeon General of the United States*
Pezzulo, Jacqueline *psychologist, researcher*
Poleto, Mary Margaret *orthopedic nurse*
Read, Susan Phillips *state appeals court judge*
Roberson, Suzanne *librarian, researcher*
Rooney, Michele Lynn *music educator*
Sandhaas, Jill T. *lawyer*
Sharke, Ingrid *librarian*
Smith, Ada LaVerne *state legislator*
Stavisky, Toby Ann *state legislator*
Stewart, Margaret McBride *biology professor, researcher*

Albion
Allamon, Karen Henn *minister*

Alden
Bindemann, Lisa Marie *mathematics educator*

Alexandria Bay
Burris, Harriet Louise *emergency physician*

Alfred
Johnson, Carla Conrad *library dean*

Alfred Station
Knowlton, Sylvia Kelley *physician*

Almond
Olix-Anderson, Susan *music educator*

Amagansett
Fleetwood, M. Freile *psychiatrist, educator*
Seelbach, Anne Elizabeth *artist*

Amherst
Conner, Judith G. *elementary school educator*
Ifandis, Anastasia *lawyer*
Kester, Gunilla Theander *poet, literature educator, music educator*
Minklein, Sharon Elizabeth *elementary school educator*

Amity Harbor
O'Hanlon, Carol Ann *minister*

Amityville
Citrano-Cummiskey, Debra Moira *chemist, network technician*

Amsterdam
Tanguay, Janet *recreational therapist, writer, filmmaker*

Ancramdale
Weinstein, Joyce *artist*

Annandale On Hudson
Darrow, Emily M. *public relations executive, writer*
LÊ, An-My *photographer, educator*
Miyagawa, Chiori *theater educator, playwright*
Pfaff, Judy *artist*
Tower, Joan Peabody *composer, educator*

Apalachin
Linder, Fannie Ruth *psychotherapist, concert soprano*
Williams, Christin Michele *elementary school educator*

Ardsley
Silman, Roberta Karpel *writer, critic*
Sokolow, Isobel Folb *sculptor*
Yablonskaya, Oxana *concert pianist*

Armonk
Azua, Maria *computer company executive, computer engineer*
Kohnstamm, Abby E. *marketing executive*
Scotto, Renata *soprano*
Sydney, Doris S. *sports association executive, interior designer*
Villar, Maria *information technology executive*
Wago, Mildred Hogan *retired municipal official*

Astoria
Gibson, Deanna *actor*
Lekus, Diana Rose *librarian*
Matheson, Linda *retired social worker*
Sagiani, Frederica *science educator*
Sirignano, Monica Ann *performing company executive, playwright*
Unsal-Tunay, Nuran *geological engineer, researcher*

Attica
Allen, Susan Diane *educator*

Auburn
Coye, Judy *science educator*
Tennant, Bonnie W. *retired music educator*

Aurora
Greenwood, Pilar Fernández-Cañadas *language and literature educator*
Ryerson, Lisa M. *academic administrator*
Vargo, Jeri *librarian*
Wahl, Christina M. *biology professor, researcher*

Avon
Cole, Mary F. *music educator*

Babylon
DaSilva, Lynn Judith *special education educator*
Drance, Lisa Iacono *secondary school educator, department chairman*
Herbst, Jane Elizabeth *school librarian*
Meirowitz, Claire Cecile *publishing executive*
Schnepp, Angela J. *secondary school educator*
Schwarz, Barbara Ruth Ballou *elementary school educator*

Baldwin
Aliano, Joy Caryl *retired elementary school educator*
DeFilippis, Gladys Llanes *language educator*
Johnston, Kimberly Anne *social studies educator*
Parker, Arlene Sandra *social worker*

Baldwinsville
Lotano, Denise Arlene *mathematician, educator*

Ballston Spa
Brown, Ifigenia Theodore *lawyer*

Batavia
Dassinger, Kristine R. *literature and language professor*
Rigerman, Ruth Underhill *mathematics professor*
Taylor, Karen Marie *education educator*

Bath
Brautigan, June Marie *artist, poet*
Simonson, Donna Jeanne *accountant*
Wright, Brenda K. *primary and elementary school educator*

Bay Shore
Baradzi, Amelia *stained glass artist, restorationist*
Murphy, Kelly Ann *psychologist*
Shea, Melissa Gordon *biology educator*
Shreve, Sue Ann Gardner *retired health products company administrator*
Williams, Tonda *entrepreneur, consultant*

Bayside
Burton, Barbara Anne *plumbing and heating company executive*
Housman, B. Jane *secondary school educator*
Kennedy, Mary Theresa *mental health services professional*

Beacon
Rousseau, Christina Jeannie *elementary school educator*

Bearsville
Whitman, Karen *artist*

Bedford
Levin, Elizabeth *freelance/self-employed writer*

Beechhurst
Wingate, Constance Blandy *retired librarian*

Belle Harbor
Goldsmith, Cathy Ellen *retired special education educator*

Bellerose
Stecher, Pauline *painter, educator*

Belleville
Colby, Ann Julia *history educator*

Bellmore
Baer, Karen Faust *music educator, musician*
Dacek, Joanne Carole *psychologist*
Rosenstein, Elyse S. *secondary school educator*

Bellport
Hendrie, Elaine *public relations executive*
Moeller, Mary Ella *retired home economist, retired educator, radio personality*
Regalmuto, Nancy Marie *small business owner, consultant*
Townsend, Terry *publishing executive*

Belmont
Lasher, Sandra Lee *minister, artist*

Bemus Point
Rollinger, Mary Elizabeth *school counselor*

Bergen
Osborn, Nancyjean Marie *principal*
Penman, Loren Anne *academic administrator*
Stasko, Andrea Aloia *physical education instructor*
Wolfe, Karen Ann *music educator*

Bethpage
Leone, Michele Castaldo *secondary school educator*
Mahony, Sheila Anne *retired communications executive*

Binghamton
Collins, Mary Shaffer *community nursing educator*
DeFleur, Lois B. *academic administrator*
Gaddis Rose, Marilyn *literature educator, translator*
Lee-Whiting, Theresa A. *music educator, conductor*
Malin, Jo *college administrator*
Michael, Sandra Dale *biomedical educator, researcher*
Phelps, Susan Williams *secondary school educator*
Pierce, Lonna McKeon *school librarian*
Sauer, Karin *microbiology educator*
Sklar, Kathryn Kish *historian, educator*
Stewart, Ghislaine Lynne *music educator, conductor*
Swain, Mary Ann Price *university official*
Terriquez-Kasey, Laura Marie *emergency nurse*
Valencia, Melanie Laine *music educator, performer*
Weissman, Ann Paley *artist, educator, consultant*
Wildoner, Nancy Schamu *music educator, fine arts department chairman*

Blauvelt
Fox, Beth A. *music educator*

Bluff Point
Fitch, Linda Bauman *retired elementary school educator*

Bohemia
Fisher, Irene B. *lawyer*

Brainard
Johnsen, May Ann *artist, sculptor*

Brentwood
Couch, Miriam Knowles *retired special education educator*
Liebert, Lynn Langenbach *psychologist, educator*

Brewster
Bates, Barbara J. Neuner *retired municipal official*
Dahl, Linda M. *writer*
Dominicus, Adele Marilyn *mathematician, educator*
Sartori, Bridget Ann *home health care nurse*

Briarcliff Manor
Bernstein, Nadia Jacqueline *lawyer*
Kepcher, Carolyn *real estate company executive*

Bridgehampton
Kothera, Lynne Maxine *psychologist*
Weiner, Jennifer Agnes *writer*

Brightwaters
Kavanagh, Eileen J. *librarian*

Brockport
Anselm, Cherie Ann *social sciences educator*
Bowdler, Jane Maxon *mathematics educator*
McGhee, Diane Baumann *dance instructor, consultant*
McKeen, Catherine A. *humanities educator*
Safran, Franciska Kuharovits *retired librarian, curator*

Bronx
Adams, Alice *sculptor*
Afterman, Jean *professional sports team executive*
Ahmose, Nefertari A. *journalism educator*
Albrecht, Roberta J. *writer*
Bacarella, Flavia *artist, educator*
Bingham, June *playwright*
Block, Holly *museum director*
Brown, Lucy L. *neurology and neuroscience professor, researcher*
Bullaro, Grace Russo *literature, film and foreign language educator, critic*
Cammarata, Joan Frances *Spanish language and literature educator*
Carter, Majora *urban planner*
Cojuangco, Samantha Caballes *elementary school educator*
Coupey, Susan McGuire *pediatrician, educator*
Damico, Debra Lynn *academic administrator, language educator*
Dean, Nancy *literature educator, retired playwright*
Delaney, Sharon Elizabeth *elementary school educator*
De Luca, Eva *vocalist, writer, composer, entrepreneur, inventor*
Durglishvili, Nana Z. *psychologist, language educator*
Dutcher, Janice Jean Phillips *oncologist*
Glickman, Benita *language educator, writer, poet*
Gonzalez, Angela E. *obstetrician, gynecologist*
Hartil, Kirsten *research scientist*
Heagarty, Margaret Caroline *retired pediatrician*
Hilliard, Carol *nurse, educator, consultant, researcher*
Horwitz, Susan Band *pharmacologist*
Iannotta, Patricia N. *physician*
Iezza, Anita Kay *physician assistant*
Isaacman, Carrie Edel *actress, educator*
Kassoy, Hortense (Honey Kassoy) *artist, sculptor, painter*
Kirmse, Sister Anne-Marie Rose *nun, educator, researcher*
Kitt, Olga *artist*
Korman, Barbara *sculptor*
Lagares, Portia Octavia *music educator*
Leighton, Anne Renita *writer, educator*
Macklin, Ruth *bioethics educator*
Miller, Elizabeth J. *mathematician, educator*
Mittler, Diana (Diana Mittler-Battipaglia) *music educator, pianist*
Muller, Katherine Lynn *clinical psychologist*
O'Donnell, Angela Gina *literature and language professor, writer*
Ostrow, Rona Lynn *retired librarian, educator*
Pellowski, Anne Rose *writer, consultant, retired library director*
Prabhu, Vrunda P. *mathematics professor*
Procidano, Mary Elizabeth *psychologist, educator*
Radel, Eva *pediatrician, hematologist*
Ramsey, Doris Theresa *elementary school educator*
Rapin, Isabelle *physician*
Reeberg, Patricia Aldora *minister, entrepreneur*
Robinson, Gwendolyn Neina *elementary school educator*
Rongo, Lucille Lynn *medical center executive*
Ruffing, Janet Kathryn *spirituality educator*
Ryan, Theresa Ann Julia *accountant*
Salicrup, Madeline *nurse*
Sanchez-Silkman, Jennifer Christine *elementary school educator*
Satir, Birgit H. *medical educator, researcher*
Shanklin, Elizabeth E. *secondary school educator*
Shapiro, Nella Irene *surgeon, educator*
Sherman, Judith Dorothy *theater producer, engineer, recording industry executive*
Simpson-Jeff, Wilma *social worker*
Skurdenis, Julianna Veronica *librarian, educator, writer, editor*
Slade, Barbie Evette Delk *special education educator*
Stein, Ruth Elizabeth Klein *physician*
Tyler, Helene Renée *mathematics professor*
Velasquez, Rose *realtor*
Velazquez, Lyzette Eileen *neurologist*
Wertheim, Mary Danielle *educational coordinator*
Yalow, Rosalyn Sussman *biophysicist*
Yorburg, Betty (Mrs. Leon Yorburg) *sociology educator*

Bronxville
Doyle, Charlotte Lackner (Mrs. James J. Doyle) *psychology educator, writer*
Levitt, Miriam *pediatrician*
Myers, Michele Tolela *academic administrator*
Peters, Sarah Whitaker *art historian, writer*
Rosenthal, Lucy Gabrielle *writer, editor, educator*
Swann, Lois Lorraine *writer, editor, educator*

Brookhaven
Grucci Butler, Donna *fireworks company executive*

Brooklyn
Allotta, Joanne Mary *elementary school educator*
Altura, Bella T. *physiologist, educator*
Amon, Carol Bagley *federal judge*
Armstrong, L. C. *artist*
Avino-Barracato, Kathleen *construction executive, consultant*
Azrack, Joan M. *judge*
Bachmann, Karen Charlotte *artist, educator*
Bangs, Mary Constance (C Bangs) *artist, curator*
Belotserkovskaya, Yanina *internist*
Berger, Margaret Adlersberg *law educator*
Bhattacharya, Bhaswati *preventive medicine physician*
Biondi, Florence *freelance/self-employed artist*
Bossert, Jill Audrey *author*
Bucolo, Gail Ann *biotechnologist*
Cahill, Catherine M. *orchestra executive*
Carlile, Janet Louise *artist, educator*
Carswell, Lois Malakoff *botanical garden executive, consultant*
Casey, Joan Maureen *secondary school educator*
Clinton, Kisha *elementary school educator*
Coch, Dorrit Aria *obstetrician, gynecologist*
Cogan, Eva *education educator*
Cummings, Josephine Anna *writer, consultant, advertising executive*
Curtis-Tweed, Phyllis Marie *humanities educator*
Dantzic, Cynthia Maris *artist, educator*
De Lisi, Joanne *communications consultant, educator*
DeNicola, Michelle *mathematics educator*
Druett, Joan *writer, maritime historian*
Eisenberg, Karen Sue Byer *nurse*
Etkin, Alexandra *physician*
Evans-Tranumn, Shelia *commissioner, former literature and language educator*
Fairstein, Linda A. *prosecutor, writer*
Fischman, Myrna Leah *accountant, educator*
Fletcher, Donna Angella *secondary school educator*
Freis, Kathleen Marie *educational association administrator*
French, Margaret Diana *operating room nurse*
Gamble, Cahtina Robyne *elementary school educator*
Gershon, Nina *federal judge*
Gianlorenzi, Nona Elena *art dealer, painter*
Gilmore, Jennifer A.W. *computer specialist, educator*
Gioseffi, Daniela (Dorothy Daniela Gioseffi) *poet, writer, playwright, critic*
Gisolfi, Diana (Diana Gisolfi Pechukas) *art history educator*
Go, Marilyn Dolan *federal judge*
Gonsalves, Patricia E. *surgical nurse*
Greenwood, Monique *innkeeper, writer, restaurant owner*
Grinstein Richman, Louise Sonia *mathematics professor*
Gulstone, Jacqueline *nurse*
Hand, Joni Marie *art educator*
Hawkins, Vivian Agatha *mental health nurse, educator*
Hendra, Barbara Jane *public relations executive*
Henning, Roni *printmaker, artist*
Hill, Elizabeth Anne *academic administrator, lawyer*
Hill, Leda Katherine *librarian*
Hill, Victoria Ruth *librarian*
Hopkins, Karen Brooks *performing arts executive*
Horowitz, Sara *labor organizer*
Horvath, Annette *home care administrator*
Irizarry, Dora L. *federal judge*
Isaac-Emmons, Merlyn Hulda *academic administrator, educator*
Jacobson, Leslie Sari *biologist, educator*
Jaffe, Louise *literature and language professor, writer*
Jimenez, Kathryn Fisher *nurse, educator*
Jofen, Jean *foreign language educator*
Jones, Blanche *nursing administrator*
Jones, Susan Emily *fashion educator, administrator, educator emeritus*
Karmel, Roberta Segal *lawyer, educator*
Kerwick, Colleen *lawyer, artist*
Kilanko, Oyenike Eunice *obstetrician, gynecologist*
King, Margaret Leah *history professor*
Koppel, Audrey Feiler *electrologist, educator*
Lawrence, Deirdre Elizabeth *librarian*
Levy, Jill Sondra *educational association administrator*
Litto, Judith Cheryl *art educator*
Lobron, Barbara L. *speech educator, editor, photographer, writer*
Logan, Janet Artisam *mental health nurse*
Logan, Paula M. *entertainment company executive, accountant*
Lotringer, Sylvere *foreign language educator*
Luhrs, Carol *physician*
Mack-Harvin, Dionne *library director*
Mann, Roanne L. *federal judge*
Marino, Gena *speech educator*
Markgraf, Rosemarie *real estate broker*
Marsala-Cervasio, Kathleen Ann *medical/surgical nurse*
Matsumoto, Kiyo A. *federal judge*
Mauskopf, Roslynn R. *prosecutor*
McCormick, Mary F. *church administrator*
Meade, Dorothy Winifred *retired educational administrator*
Mirra, Suzanne Samuels *pathologist*
Mook, Sarah *retired chemist*
Moore, Anne Frances *art administrator, consultant, educator, art appraiser, dealer*
Moran, Marissa J. *law educator*
Morgan, Mary Louise Fitzsimmons *fund raising executive, lobbyist*
Moses Brown, Brenda Gene *elementary school educator*
Murillo-Rohde, Ildaura Maria *marriage and family therapist, consultant, educator, retired dean*
Murphy, Kathleen Mary *former law firm executive, alternative healing professional*
Nii, Yuko *artist*
Norstrand, Iris Fletcher *psychiatrist, neurologist, educator*
O'Connor, Sister George Aquin (Margaret M. O'Connor) *academic administrator, educator*
Ogunkoya, Andrea *marketing executive*
Peruggi, Regina S. *academic administrator*
Phillips, Gretchen *social worker*
Piene, Chloe *artist, filmmaker*
Pierre, Mirelle *physician, psychotherapist, health facility administrator*
Pine, Bessie Miriam *social worker, columnist*
Pines, Beverly Irene *retired clinical psychologist*
Plaut, Jane Margaret *art educator*
Pollak, Cheryl L. *federal judge*
Quamina, Joyce *management consultant*
Raggi, Reena *federal judge*
Reich, Olive Buerk *artist, educator*
Reinisch, June Machover *psychologist, educator*
Reynolds, Nancy Remick *writer, researcher, editor*
Rike, Susan *public relations executive*
Ross, Allyne R. *federal judge*
Roth, Pamela Susan *lawyer*
Rothenberg, Mira Kowarski *clinical psychologist, psychotherapist*
Sahlene, *singer*
Satterfield-Harris, Rita *financial analyst*
Schaefer, Marilyn Louise *artist, writer, educator*
Schwartz-Giblin, Susan Toby *neuroscientist, educator, dean*
Schweikert, Mary Lou *elementary school educator*
Sesin, Maria Carmen *psychologist, researcher*
Shahon, Laurie Meryl *investment company executive*
Shcherbakova, Estella *chemist, mathematician, educator*
Shechter, Laura Judith *artist*
Siegel, Stephanie S. *mathematics professor*
Somers, Marion *gerontologist, family therapist*
Sonnenfeld, Sandi *writer*
Stevenson, Gale *librarian*
Stukes, Geraldine Hargro *library and information scientist, educator*
Suarez, Maria C. *health care plan company executive*
Sullivan, Ann Catherine *health facility administrator*
Thacher, Barbara Burrall *psychologist, educator*
Thomas, Lucille Cole *librarian*
Townes, Sandra L. *federal judge*
Trice, Dorothy Louise *physician*
Twining, Lynne Dianne *psychotherapist, professional society administrator, writer*
Vidal, Maureen Eris *theater educator, actress*
Washington, Tyona *adult education educator*
Webber, Carolyn Ann (Mrs. Gerald E. Thomson) *pathologist, educator*
Weinstein, Marie Pastore *psychologist*
Weinstock, Deborah *psychologist*
Wexler, Joan G. *dean, law educator*
Wilson, Nancy Esther *social worker*
Wolfe, Ethyle Renee (Mrs. Coleman Hamilton Benedict) *academic administrator*
Woolley, Margaret Anne (Margot Woolley) *architect*
Wrotten, Marylean *medical coordinator, counselor*
Yedvab, Lauren *health facility administrator*
Zinnes, Alice Fich *artist, educator*
Zollar, Jawole Willa Jo *artist, choreographer*
Zysberg, Janet Gail *elementary school educator*

Buffalo
Amato, Rosalie *secondary school educator*
Ambrus, Clara Maria *physician*
Andersen, Martha S. *biophysicist, researcher*
Baer, Maria Renée *hematologist, researcher*
Bayles, Jennifer Lucene *museum program director, educator*
Busch, Susan Ellen *reading specialist*
Cajiao Salas, Teresa *language educator, educator*
Camhi, Rebecca Ann *librarian, writer*
Casper, Bernadette Marie *critical care nurse*
Cathey, Patrice Antoinette *secondary school educator, director*
Chopra-Sukumaran, Pratibha *secondary school educator*
Clarkson, Elisabeth Ann Hudnut *volunteer*
Daley, Ruth Margaret *advertising agency administrator*
DiFranco, Ani *music executive, musician*
Dudziak, Emma M. *cardiac sonographer*
Falk, Ursula Adler *psychotherapist*
Fischman, Jane Ann Vogel *retired secondary school educator*
Fitzgerald, Cathleen Marie *medical and surgical intensive care nurse*
Fox, Mary Hawkshaw *early childhood special education educator, consultant*
Freedman, Maryann Saccomando *lawyer*
Friedman, Gloria Landsman (Mrs. Daniel A. Roblin Jr.) *psychologist, educator*
Fuda, Siri Narayan K.K. (Elaine T. Barber) *director*
Garas-York, Keli Ann *reading specialist*
Gielow, Kathleen Louise *career planning administrator, consultant, special education educator*
Gingher, Merlene C. *occupational therapist, educator*
Hoffman, Faith Louise *social worker*
Hulicka, Irene M. *psychologist, educator*
Hunt, Jane Helfrich *volunteer*
Janiga, Mary Ann *art educator*
Jervis-Herbert, Gwendolyn Theresa *mental health services professional*
Kartha, Indira *retired pathologist*
Kessel, Joyce B. *English professor*
Kordinak, Irma L. *piano educator, musician*
Kreizman-Reczek, Karen Ingrid *librarian*
Lombardo Appleby, Linda Rose *music educator*
Macomber, Debbie *writer*
Marinaccio, Bridget C. *social sciences educator*
Mather, Lynn *law educator, political science professor*
Merini, Rafika *humanities educator, writer, language educator*
Mutton, Holly Beth *psychiatrist*
Myszka, Judith Anne *nurse*
Nielsen, Nancy H. *health organization executive*
Nowak, Carol Ann *city official*
O'Donnell, Denise Ellen *lawyer, former prosecutor*
O'Loughlin, Sandra S. *lawyer*
O'Quin, Karen *psychology professor, dean*
Overton, Nicole Yolanda *program analyst*
Payne, Frances Anne *literature educator, researcher*
Putnam, Susan K. *psychology educator*
Rodriguez, Gloria E. *science educator*
Saab, Maureen Wilson *social worker, consultant*
Seitz, Mary Lee *mathematics professor*
Slotkin, Alma Isobel *artist*
Smallwood, Sandra Denise *pastor, daycare administrator*
Smith, Barbara *camping administrator*
Sullivan, Margaret M. *editor*
Urdang, Nicole Severyna *holistic psychotherapist*
Veronica, Debra Clarisse *principal*
Virk, Subhdeep *psychiatrist*
Wactawski-Wende, Jean *epidemiologist, educator, researcher*
Wagner, Barbara Lee *musician*
Wright, Dana Jace *retired emergency nurse practitioner*
Zawadzki-Janusz, Stacy Lynn *music educator, performing arts educator*
Zirnheld, Jennifer L. *engineering educator, researcher*

Burnt Hills
Russell, Karen Sue *musician, educator*

Buskirk
Johanson, Patricia Maureen *artist, architect*

Cairo
Ludwig, Laura Lonshein *poet*

Camillus
Thompson, Mary Cecilia *nurse midwife*

Canandaigua
Blazak, Paige Gayle *psychotherapist, school counselor*
Chappelle, Lou Jo *physical therapist assistant*
Merrill, Trista Marie *literature and language professor, writer*
Ristuccia, Lavern K. Cole *psychologist, consultant*
Yarnall, Susanne Lusink *elementary school educator*

Canastota
Roth, Susan Betsy *artist*

Candor
Musgrave, Eva Mae *innkeeper, educator*

Canton
Auster, Nancy Eileen Ross *economics professor*
Bodensteiner, Karin Johanna *biology professor, researcher*
Goldberg, Rita Maria *foreign language educator*

Carle Place
Barnett, Emily *artist*

Carmel
Huckabee, Carol Brooks *psychologist*

Castleton On Hudson
Wagner, Mary Susan *academic administrator*

Catskill
Wolfe, Geraldine *academic administrator*

Cazenovia
Wyckoff, Sylvia Spencer *art educator, artist*

Cedarhurst
Lagnado, Jennifer M. *assistant principal*
Lipsky, Linda Ethel *health facility administrator*
Peel, Barbara Jean *science educator*
Solymosy, Hattie May *writer, educator*
Van Raalte, Polly Ann *reading and writing specialist, photojournalist*

Centereach
DuBarry, Jacqueline Anne *artist, educator*

Central Islip
Cyganowski, Melanie L. *bankruptcy judge*
Eisenberg, Dorothy *federal judge*
Feuerstein, Sandra Jeanne *judge*
James, Sharon Ann *elementary school educator*
Lindsay, Arlene Rosario *federal judge*
Seybert, Joanna *federal judge*
Wiggins, Gloria *not-for-profit developer, television producer*

Central Valley
Hafner, Catherine Courtney *retired physics educator*
Neyman, Paula *pediatrician*

Chappaqua
George, Jean Craighead *author, illustrator*
Hurford, Carol *retired lawyer*
Levine, Irene S. *journalist, psychologist*

Chatham
Squier, Rita Ann Holmberg *graphic designer*

Chautauqua
Campbell, Joan Brown *religious organization executive*
Yurth, Helene Louise *librarian*

Chazy
Ratner, Gayle *special education educator*

Cheektowaga
O'Brien, Nancy Marie (Meyer) *secondary school educator*
Rogers, Cheryl Ann *speech pathology services professional*

Chestnut Ridge
Orlando, Susan (Isadora) *academic administrator, educator*

Cicero
Pink, (Alecia B. Moore) *singer*
Schiess, Betty Bone *priest*

Clarence
Benz, Nancy Ann *music educator*
Furlano, Joanne Elizabeth *science educator*
Stringer, Gretchen Engstrom *consulting volunteer administrator*

Claverack
Vile, Sandra Jane *leadership training educator*

Clifton Park
Glasgow, Constance Lenore *pediatrician*
Kuhn, Audrey Grendahl *graphic designer, printmaker, fiber artist*
Murphy, Mary Patricia *elementary school educator*
Valenti, Laurie M. *elementary school educator*
Van Slyke, Rosemary *tax specialist*

Clifton Springs
DeRuyter, Marilyn *real estate broker*

Clinton
Havens, Pamela Ann *academic administrator*
Stewart, Joan Hinde *academic administrator*

Clinton Corners
McDermott, Patricia Ann *nursing administrator*
Rudolph, Nancy K. *photographer, writer*

Clyde
Barr, Marilyn G. *school system administrator*

Cobleskill
Colony, Pamela Cameron *medical researcher, educator*
Westervelt, Gayle Gaetano *physical education educator*

Cohoes
Kelly, Deanna M. *assistant principal*

Cold Spring
Battersby, Katherine Sue *elementary school educator*

Cold Spring Harbor
Maglione, Lili *artist, consultant*

Collins
Jackson, Jane *filmmaker, educator*

Commack
Berman, Patricia Karatsis *art director*
Capozzi, Suzanne *literature and language educator*
Cohen, Judith W. *retired academic administrator*
Nilson, Patricia *clinical psychologist*
Price, Amelia Ruth *not-for-profit foundation president, artist, small business owner*

Congers
Voce, Patricia Maria *medical/surgical nurse*

Copenhagen
O'Shaughnessy, Nadine M. *science educator*

Coram
Celella, Karen Ann *music educator, writer*
Mohanty, Christine Ann *retired language educator, actress*

Corning
Cicerchi, Eleanor Ann Tomb *not-for-profit fundraiser*
Hauselt, Denise Ann *lawyer*
Spillman, Jane Shadel *curator, writer, researcher*

Cornwall On Hudson
Abrams-Collens, Vivien *artist*
D'Alvia, Marlene *medical social worker, clinical social worker*
Lawrence, Sharon Lynn *director, educator*
Peirce, Karen Patricia *education educator*

Corona
Alfonso-Bica, Kristy Lynn *elementary school educator*
Maruca, Rita *real estate company executive, real estate broker*
Smith, Valerie *curator*

Cortland
Anderson, Donna Kay *musicologist, educator*
Brush, Florence Clapham *kinesiologist, exercise physiologist, physical education educator*
Masselink, Noralyn *literature educator*
McGuire, Mary Patricia *political science professor*
Summers, Pamela French *literature and language professor, consultant*
Wood, Barbara Lynn *elementary school educator*

Cortlandt Manor
Keating, Laura Lee M. *historian, records management professional*
Lupiani, Jennifer Lynne *school psychologist*
Rosenberg, Marilyn Rosenthal *artist, poet*
Traille, Joy Myra *microbiologist, eldercare service provider*

Cross River
Thorn, Susan Howe *interior designer*

Croton On Hudson
Wandel, Sharon Lee *sculptor*

Crugers
Norman, Jessye *soprano*

Cuba
Keough, Sandra J. *retired special education educator, retired principal, education educator*

De Ruyter
Jeschke, Carol T. *arts/theater consultant, real estate investor*

Deer Park
Grover, Penelope H. *singer, music educator*
Martone, Jeanette Rachele *artist*

Delhi
Townsend, Sue Joyce *retired air traffic controller*

Delmar
Button, Rena Pritsker *public relations executive*

Depew
Mercuri, Theresa B. *mathematician, educator*
Yelich, Janine E. *music educator*

Derby
Kieffer, Marcia S. *psychotherapist*

Dix Hills
Blumstein, Reneé J. *educational research and evaluation consultant*
Golden, Shawna *biomedical researcher*
Somerville, Daphine Holmes *retired elementary school educator*
Virostko, Joan *elementary school educator*

Dobbs Ferry
Fritz, Jean Guttery *writer*
Hotchkiss, Janet McCann *secondary school educator*
Kalvin-Stiefel, Judy *public relations executive*
Kraetzer, Mary C. *sociologist, educator, consultant*
Lesack, Beatriz Díaz *secondary school educator*
Maiocchi, Christine *lawyer*

Dryden
Morris, Carol E. *biologist, educator*

Dunkirk
Flaherty, Cynthia Mead *music educator*
Lewis, Amy Beth *newswriter, reporter, writer, photographer*

East Amherst
Kirdani, Esther May *retired school counselor*

East Aurora
Dohn, Julianne *child protective services specialist*
Hu, YuinSien Irene *obstetrician, gynecologist*
Woodard, Carol Jane *educational consultant*

East Chatham
Bues, Susan Denise Wildermuth *academic administrator*

East Greenbush
Van Alstyne, Ruth Beattie *elementary school educator*

East Hampton
Goldstein, Judith Shelley *director*
Hope, Judith H. *former political organization administrator*
Jaudon, Valerie *artist*
Riley, Cheryl *artist, educator*
Schetlin, Eleanor M. *retired associate dean*
Scott, Rosa Mae *art educator, artist*
Swerdlow, Amy *historian, educator, writer*
Vered, Ruth *art gallery director, owner*

East Islip
Cullen, Valerie Adelia *secondary school educator*
Donohue, Claire P. *retired school librarian*

East Moriches
Guthrie, Teresa Irene *pediatric nurse practitioner*

East Patchogue
Geller, Edith Harriet *elementary school educator*

East Quogue
Setlow, Neva Delihas *artist, research biologist*

East Setauket
Kefalas, Jessie Ae *visual merchandiser, artist*
Orlowski, Karel Ann *elementary school educator*
Tuttle, Anne Palmer *artist, education educator*

East Syracuse
DeSiato, Donna Jean *superintendent*
Duffy, Nancy Keogh *newscaster, broadcast executive*
Houde, Carmen Milagro *hotel executive*
Lamphere, Barbara L. *construction executive*
Simson, Renate Maria *English and African American studies professor*

Eastchester
Caine, Edye *social studies educator*
Weinberg, Dale Glaser *writer, consultant*

Eggertsville
Segalla, Mary Louise *elementary school educator*

Eldred
Campbell, Regina Farrell *literature and language educator*

Elmhurst
Hughes, Ann M. *medical/surgical nurse*
Prypchan, Lida D. *psychiatrist*
Staiano-Johannes, Barbara Ann *physician assistant, chiropractor*

Elmira
Barlow, Jo *psychotherapist*
Kerr-Nowlan, Donna Courtney *pre-school administrator*
Leveen, Pauline *retired history professor, government professor*
Miran, Patricia Marie *art educator*
Mitchell, Sharon *artist*
Pratt, Linda *language educator*
Wavle, Elizabeth Margaret *academic administrator*
Zeigler, Carrie Elizabeth Watt *elementary school educator*

Elmont
Butera, Ann Michele *consulting company executive*

Endicott
Carswell, Melissa J. *counselor, director*
Rittinger, Patricia Ann *secondary school educator, mathematician*

Erin
Locker, Cynthia Ann *elementary school educator*

Fairport
Fitch, Darlene *elementary school educator*
Holtzclaw, Diane Smith *elementary school educator*
Meck, J. Karen *retired elementary school educator*
Talty, Lorraine Caguioa *accountant*

Falconer
Halm, Nancye Studd *retired academic administrator*

Fallsburg
Biccum, Amanda *elementary school educator*

Far Rockaway
Mitchell, Lillian Adassa *principal*
Sussman, Laureen Glicklin *elementary school educator*

Farmingdale
Buzzell, Margaret *association adminstrator*
Colella, Cathleen *waste management administrator*
Issapour, Marjaneh *engineering educator, consultant*
Jacquette, Kathleen Marie *literature educator*
Lindsley, Michelle A. *theater educator, music educator*
Maurino, Paula San Millan *business educator, computer professor*
O'Brien, Joan Susan *lawyer, educator*
Segale, Althea Frances *music educator*
Shapiro, Ann R. *English educator*

Fayetteville
Hadyk-Wepf, Sonia Margaret *artist, real estate manager*

Fishkill
Colman, Jenny Meyer *psychiatrist*
Stein, Paula Nancy *psychologist, educator*

Floral Park
Curci, Paula *counseling administrator, poet, television personality*
Daloia, Rachel Rosemary *music educator*

Flushing
Anderson, Michelle J. *dean, law educator*
Baik-Han, Won H. *pediatrician, educator, consultant*
Bezrod, Norma R. *artist*
Bordoff, Sherri Beth *social worker*
Brooks, Helene Margaret *editorial consultant*
Capra, Linda Ann *elementary education educator*
Carlson, Cynthia Joanne *artist, educator*
Cooper, Marianne (Abonyi Cooper) *librarian, educator*
Evens, Lucie Ann *music educator*
Flechner, Roberta Fay *graphics designer*
Gomez, Pastora *medical/surgical nurse*
Jones, Tina Moreau *psychology educator*
Lee, Emily Lin *director, real estate company executive*
Matheis, Vickie Lynne *nurse*
Reuder, Mary E(ileen) *retired psychology professor, retired statistician*
Rivera, Jenny *law educator*
Rosenberg, Deborah A. *special education educator*
Rosen-Supnick, Elaine Renee *physical therapist*
Sanborn, Anna Lucille *pension fund administrator, consultant*
Schnall, Edith Lea *microbiologist, educator*
Schwartz, Estar Alma *lawyer*
Shen, Ronger *artist, educator*
Smith-Campbell, Charmaine *secondary school educator*
Torrence-Thompson, Juanita Lee *editor, public relations executive*
Yeo, Kim Eng *artist*
Zinnes, Harriet Fich *poet, fiction writer, retired English educator, literary and art critic*

Fly Creek
Steiner, Judith Marie *elementary school educator*

Forest Hills
Alsapiedi, Consuelo Veronica *psychoanalytic psychotherapist, consultant*
Dessylas, Ann Atsaves *human resources and office management executive*
Fernandez, Amy *artist, illustrator, writer, educator*
Flowers, Cynthia *investment company executive*
Hartig, Karen Joyce *psychotherapist, social worker*
Kortlander, Myrna *psychotherapist*
Kra, Pauline Skornicki *French language educator*
Lustgarten, Celia Sophie *freelance consultant, writer*
Mathieu Byers, Deborah Anne *performing company executive*
Morgan, Jacqui *illustrator, painter, art educator, writer*
Rhonda, Karol *dermatologist*
Spiegel, Andrea *marketing executive*

Forestville
Gier, Amy Louise *music educator*

Frankfort
Conigilaro, Phyllis Ann *retired elementary school educator*
Shuster, Donnalyn E. (Donalyn Eaton Shuster) *secondary school educator, artist*

Franklin Square
Bergen, Jeannine Evelyn *psychologist*
Henry, Clarice Ruth *librarian*

Franklinville
Schnell, Gertrude Helen *retired elementary school educator*

Fredonia
Holcomb, Paula Kae *conductor, educator*
Kenney, Dolores Theresa *home economist*
Marshall, Jill Galley *social studies educator*
Royal, Susan *classical musician, educator*
Smith, Claire Laremont *language educator*
Strada, Christina Bryson *retired humanities educator, librarian*
Wood, Caroline *secondary school educator*

Freeport
DiBenedetto, Michelle *finance company executive*
Ferentino, Sheila Connolly *psychologist, consultant*
Martorana, Barbara Joan *secondary school educator*
Mitchell, Alice Joyce *secondary school educator, dietician*

Fresh Meadows
Yang, Susan Xia *real estate consultant, recreational therapist*

Fulton
Dexter, Carol N. *mathematics educator*
Ludington, Janice Fay *speech pathology/audiology services professional*
Noel, Karen Ann *science educator*
Sisco, Melissa Ann *history educator*

Garden City
Amsler, Georgeann Lucille *publishing executive*
Berka, Marianne Guthrie *health and physical education educator*
Bouchard, Wendy Ann Borstel *language educator*
Burkett, Janice Mayo *science educator*
Caputo, Kathryn Mary *paralegal*
Cashin, Maura Dennehy *psychologist, music educator*
Doucette, Mary-Alyce *computer company executive*
Herzberg, Margaret Ann *orthopaedic nurse, researcher*
Klein, Kitty R. *counseling administrator*
McNair, Marcia L. *language educator, writer, editor*
Meng, M. Kathryn *lawyer*
Nelkin Miller, Cathy *hotel executive*
Podwall, Kathryn Stanley *biology professor*
Russell, Stella Pandell *artist, author, educator*
Steil, Janice M. *social psychology educator*
Ver Pault, Carolyn *science educator*
Wetherill-Smith, Linda Marie *musician, educator, performing arts association administrator*

Garnerville
Chapman, Margaret Elizabeth *elementary school educator*
Weaver, L. Karen *retired reading specialist*

Geneva
Best, Sharon Louise Peckham *retired college administrator*
Lucas, Karen *music educator*

Glen Cove
Rothberg, Judith *elementary school educator, researcher*
Young, Jayne *recording industry executive*

Glen Head
Heath-Psyd, Pamela B. Wasserman *psychologist*
Sewell, Laura J. Pollock *social worker*

Glen Oaks
Smith, Heather Lee *psychologist*

Glenmont
Haizlip, Viola *medical/surgical nurse*

Glens Falls
Rikhoff, Jean *writer*
Tucker, Bernadine *patient registrar*

Glenwood
Chambers, Denning Jessyca *middle school educator*

Goshen
DeMueller, Lucia *investment consultant*
Digby, Lynne A. *artist, writer*

Gouverneur
Stacy, Trudy L. *elementary school educator*

Grand Island
Kennedy, Magdalene Miller *secondary school educator*
Remson, Debra S. *music educator*

Granville
Baker, Donna Dougan *elementary school educator*
Halnon, Faith E. *elementary school educator*

Great Neck
Aronson, Margaret Rupp *school psychologist*
Burghardt, Linda Feuerberg *writer*
Fiel, Maxine Lucille *journalist, behavior analyst, educator*
Harris, Rosalie *psychotherapist, clinical counselor, Spanish language professional and multi-linguist, English as second language educator*
Helstein, Ivy Rae *communications executive, psychotherapist, writer*
Hurwitz, Johanna (Johanna Frank) *writer*
Kornahrens, Casey *elementary school educator*
Legatt, Hadassa *language educator*
Lieber, Constance E. *medical association administrator*
Mayer, Sondra *art educator*
Natalucci-Hall, Carla *psychologist*
Rieff, Harriet Lillian *librarian*
Roth, Gladys Thompson *retired special education educator*
Schoenholt, Helene M. *elementary school educator*
Seidler, Doris *artist*
Soleymani, Nancy *psychologist, researcher*

Great River
Edwards, Christine E. *artist*

Greenfield Center
Dittner, Deborah Marie *nurse practitioner in family health*
Nair, Laura *music educator*

Greenfield Park
Cosey Pulley, Bernice *volunteer*

Greenlawn
Lelyveld, Gail Annick *actress*
Roberts, Gloria Jean *writer*
Starost, Diane Joan *music educator*

Greenvale
Maillet, Lucienne *humanities educator*
Watt, Stephanie Denise *musician, educator, department chairman*

Greenville
Overbaugh, Maryanne W. *elementary school educator*

Greenwich
Edsforth, Maureen McGill *instructional technology specialist*

Guilderland
Escobar, Deborah Ann *gifted and talented educator*

Guilderland Center
Teeter, Rae Jean *music educator*

Halesite
Grey-Bethiel, Shari *artist, sculptor, apparel designer*

Hamburg
Dewey, Phyllis Keefer *counselor*
Haag, Jennifer Lynn *music educator*

Hamilton
Chopp, Rebecca S. *academic administrator*
Nakhimovsky, Alice Stone *foreign language educator*
Pagano, Jo Anne *education educator*
Staley, Lynn *literature educator*

Hampton Bays
Bucicchia, Carolanne Stephanie *elementary school educator*
Sherter, Selma *retired elementary school educator*

Harriman
Kay, Sandra Irene *special education educator, consultant*

Harrison
Krigsman, Naomi *psychologist, consultant, photographer*

Hartsdale
Fishman, Helene Beth *social worker*
Greenawalt, Peggy Freed Tomarkin *advertising executive*
Schweitzer, Caren S. *social worker*

Hastings On Hudson
Del Duca, Rita *language educator*

Hauppauge
Reid, Margaret Elizabeth *elementary school educator, secondary school educator*
Tublisky, Marcy *association administrator*
Zuckerman, Dorothy Ann *elementary school educator*

Haverstraw
Eidelman, Sharon (Sherry) R. *marriage and family therapist*

Hawthorne
Batstone, Joanna Louise *physicist*
Lieberman, Meryl Robin *lawyer*
Wen, Sheree *computer company executive*
Yoffa, Ellen J. *information technology executive*

Hempstead
Adams, Velma M. *assistant principal, consultant*
Ancrum, Cheryl Denise *dentist*
Bose, Meena *political science professor*
Connolly, Melissa Kane *public relations executive*
Fleming, Marion Parker *education educator*
Freese, Melanie Louise *librarian, educator*
Graffeo, Mary Thérèse *music educator, performer*
Heuermann-Nowik, Patricia Calhoun *theater director*
Levin, Phillis *education educator, writer*
Raney, Carolyn E. *educational consultant*
Roble, Carole Marcia *accountant*
Watford, Dolores *elementary school educator*
Zagano, Phyllis *religious studies educator*

Herkimer
Martin, Lorraine B. *humanities educator*

Hicksville
Appold, Cynthia *visual arts educator*
Kronowitz, Pamela Renee *music educator*
Noll, Amy *secondary educator*
Reedy, Catherine Irene *retired elementary school educator*
Svraka, Patti A. *elementary school educator*
Waxberg, Emily Steinhardt *special education educator, administrator*
Wolitzer, Hilma *novelist, short story writer*

Highland
Ratick, Randie H. *music educator, elementary school educator*

Highland Falls
Skibinski, Olga *artist, art conservator*
Smith, Cheryl Ann *secondary school educator*

Hillsdale
Kersten, Mary Lou *real estate broker*

Holbrook
Grenzig, Gail A. *school system administrator, consultant*

Holland
Hager, Maria Lynne *music educator*

Holley
Lepkowski, Suzanne Joy *language educator*
Ruck, Rosemarie Ulissa *retired social worker, freelance/self-employed writer*

Hoosick Falls
Benoit, Lois Elaine *director, retired music educator*

Hopewell Junction
Carey, Jacqueline Carter *retired elementary school educator*
Cznarty, Donna Mae *secondary school educator*
Lemy, Marie Edith *psychologist, educator*
Sellingsloh, Hulda Knipling *retired artist*

Hornell
Swift, Katharine I. *cytotechnologist*

Horseheads
Andrake, Nancy Carolyn *retired secondary school educator*
Clark, Judy Ann *elementary school educator*
Matejka, Tina Sochia *music educator*
Miller, Elaine Wolford *writer*

Howard Beach
Chwalek, Constance *real estate broker, mortgage broker*

Hudson
Miner, Jacqueline *political consultant*

Huntington
German, June Resnick *lawyer*
Kanner, Ellen Barbara *clinical psychologist*
Kirwin, Barbara Rosa *forensic specialist*
Munson, Nancy K. *lawyer*
Paul, Marianne *physician assistant*
Petersen, Patricia J. *real estate company executive*
Roberts, Elizabeth Anne Stephens *educational consultant*

Huntington Station
Cannistraci, Diane Frances *sales executive*
Devlin, Jean Theresa *education educator*
Haas, Terri Leigh *music educator*
Robins, Faye E. *principal, elementary school educator*
Stevens, Susan Seltenreich Cirillo *special education educator*
Williams, Una Joyce *psychiatric social worker*
Yacobian, Sonia Simone *metals company executive*

Hurley
Davila, Elisa *language educator, literature educator*
Petruski, Jennifer Andrea *speech and language pathologist*

Hyde Park
Beckmann, Kathleen Ann *music educator*
Blackman, Drusilla Denise *dean*
Koch, Cynthia M. *library director*

Ilion
Edwards, Christine Utley *social services administrator, consultant*
Nemyier, Margaret Gertrude *sales executive*

Inwood
Soffer, Grace Florey *retired elementary school educator, artist*

Irvington
Shapiro, Ellen M. *graphics designer, writer*

Islandia
Cooper, Nancy E. *computer software company executive*

Islip
Kacharaba, Nickolette Athanasia *vocalist*
Libert, Nancy Porta *retired elementary school educator*

Ithaca
Adkins-Regan, Elizabeth Kocher *biological psychology educator*
Arquit, Nora Harris *retired music educator, writer*
Assie-Lumumba, N'Dri T. *Africana studies educator*
Beneria, Lourdes *economist, educator*
Berkelman, Mary Hobbie *retired elementary school educator, adult education educator*
Blau, Francine Dee *economics professor*
Brazell, Karen Woodard *literature educator*
Clune, JoAnn Guardalibene *retired nurse*
Colby-Hall, Alice Mary *language educator*
DeLaurentis, Louise Budde *writer*
Dyckman, A(lice) Ann *retired academic administrator*
Firebaugh, Francille Maloch *academic administrator*
Garrison, Elizabeth Jane *artist*
Germain, Claire Madeleine *law librarian, educator, lawyer*
Grainger, Mary Maxon *civic volunteer*
Hardy, Jane Elizabeth *communications educator*
Henderson, Cynthia Anne *theater educator, actress*
Henry, Susan Armstrong *biology professor, dean*
Hockett, Shirley O. *mathematics professor, writer*
Howell, Debra Lynne *information technology executive*
Hughes, Diane L. Hicks *elementary school educator, secondary school educator*
Janowitz, Phyllis *poet, educator*
Johnson, Pam McAllister *newspaper publisher, consultant*
Kane, Marilyn A. *occupational therapist, educator*
Kaske, Carol Margaret Vonckx *educator*
Kittredge, Katharine Ottaway *literature and language professor*
Martin, Carolyn A. (Biddy Martin) *provost*
Mikus, Eleanore Ann *artist*
Mueller, Betty Jeanne *social work educator*
Nasrallah, June *plant pathologist, department chairman*
Norton, Mary Beth *history educator, writer*
Park, Dorothy Goodwin Dent (Mrs. Roy Hampton Park) *broadcast executive, publishing executive*
Pelto, Gretel H. *nutritional anthropologist, educator*
Perry, Margaret *librarian, writer*
Radzinowicz, Mary Ann *language educator*
Rasmussen, Kathleen Maher *nutritional sciences educator*
Schuler, Mary Callaghan *artist, educational association administrator*
Starer, Ruana Maxine *freelance/self-employed psychologist*
Stycos, Maria Nowakowska *adult education educator*
Thomas, Sarah E. *librarian*
Whitaker, Susanne Kanis *veterinary medical librarian*
Williams, Peggy Ryan *academic administrator*

Jackson Heights
Chang, Lydia Liang-Hwa *social worker, educator*
Gall, Lenore Rosalie *educational administrator*
Ryan, Judith Ann *dean*
Schuyler, Jane *fine arts educator*
Simeone, Helen Lilli *retired elementary school educator*
Stevenson, Amanda (Sandy Stevens) *librettist, composer, songwriter*

Jamaica
Becker, Nancy Jane *information science educator*
Brockway, Laurie Sue *editor-in-chief, journalist, writer, minister*
Cocchiarelli, Maria *artist, educator*
Daly, Mary C. *dean, law educator*
Davis-Jerome, Eileen George *educational consultant, principal*
DeBello, Joan Elizabeth *mathematics professor*
De La Paz, Lucia *social worker, consultant*
Edwards, Cynthia E. *principal*
Ekbatani, Glayol *language educator, director, writer*
Faust, Naomi Flowe *education educator*
Feldman, Arlene Butler *aviation industry executive*
Flink, Elisheva H. *orthopedic surgeon*
Geffner, Donna Sue *speech pathology/audiology services professional, audiologist, educator*
Jones, Cynthia Teresa Clarke *artist*
Kaplan, Carolyn Sue *elementary school educator*
Keizs, Marcia V. *academic administrator*
Kemeny, M. Margaret *oncologist, surgeon, educator, hospital administrator*
Lin, Shu-Fang Hsia *librarian*
Malewitz, Joan *elementary school educator, multi-media specialist*
Mohr, Iris *finance educator*
Ramos, Alice M. *education educator*
Wick, Erika Elisabeth *psychologist, educator, researcher*
Zak, Dorothy Zerykier *psychologist*

Jamestown
Disbro, Megan Benner *librarian*
Duncanson, Patricia Ann *mental health therapist*
Harms, Michele Gail *director*
Reale, Sara Jane *museum education director*
Thompson, Birgit Dolores *civic worker, writer*

Jamesville
DeCrow, Karen *lawyer, educator, writer*

Jeffersonville
Harms, Elizabeth Louise *artist*

Jericho
Beal, Carol Ann *lawyer*
Dore, Kathleen A. *broadcast executive*

Johnstown
Araldi, Mary-Jane Snyder *nurse, educator*
Winnie, Amy E. *music educator*

Katonah
Brownlee, Delphine *actress, musician*

Keene Valley
Butterworth, Nona Angel *artist, educator*

Kenmore
Gilham, Jennifer Erin *physical education educator, soccer coach*
Grant, Elaine Marion *music educator, voice educator*

Kew Gardens
Aldea, Patricia *architect*
Klein-Scheer, Cathy Ann *social worker*
Marshall, Helen M. *city manager*

Kings Park
LaFantano, Elizabeth *music educator*

Kingston
Bruck, Arlene Forte *secondary school educator*
Contrady, Erin Shaw *music educator*
Dougherty, Andrea M. *social studies educator*
Irvine, Rose Loretta Abernethy *retired communications educator, consultant*
Johnson, Marie-Louise Tully *dermatologist, educator*
Kolodziejski, Cynthia F. *secondary school educator*

Lagrangeville
Orlik, Dawn *mathematics and computer science educator*

Lake George
Nellis, Nora LaJoy *special education educator, writer*

Lake Huntington
Spafford, Suzanne Lee *biology educator*

Lake Katrine
Cariello, Kristine *music educator*

Lake Placid
Pappalardo, Rosa Gloria *secondary school educator*
Rickard, Anne Colton *art educator, artist*

Lakewood
McConnon, Virginia Fix *dietician*

Lancaster
Genewick, Tiffany Boquard *obstetrician, gynecologist*
Kappan, Sandra Jean *elementary school educator*
Meides, Holly Sue *music educator*
Otto, Tammy *author, poet, playwright*
Schunke, Crystal *physical education educator*

Larchmont
Greenwald, Carol Schiro *professional services marketing research executive*
Hinerfeld, Ruth G. *civic organization executive*

Latham
Catalano, Jane Donna *lawyer*
LeRoy, Beth Seperack *jazz musician, music educator*

Lawrence
Berman, Carol *retired commissioner*
Okos, Mildred *city manager*

Lewiston
LoTempio, Julia Matild *retired accountant*
Moraca-Sawicki, Anne Marie *oncology nurse*
Preston, Joan Muriel *psychology professor, communications educator*

Lindenhurst
Boltz, Mary Ann *aerospace materials company executive, travel company executive*
Kaufman, Susan Shiffman *psychologist*
Omeis, Lisa Marie *principal*
Scharf, Megan Jean *mathematics educator*
Sherrard, Jessica E. *mathematics educator*

Lisbon
Tyo Boscoe, Denise Marie *art educator*

Little Neck
Overton, Rosilyn Gay Hoffman *finance company executive*

Liverpool
Brooks, Janet Pfohl *social studies educator, department chairman*
Padula, Wanda Jean *secondary school educator*
Wightman, Sharon Leilani *librarian*

Lockport
Shaughnessy, Mary Ellen *educator*

Locust Valley
Hayduk, Sonna A.S. *secondary school educator, department chairman*
Zulch, Joan Carolyn *retired medical publishing company executive*

Long Island City
DeMaio, Barbara K. *principal*
Giaimo, Kathryn Ann *performing arts company executive*
Heiss, Alanna *museum director*
Hoffman, Merle Holly *advocate, psychologist, writer*

Jacobson, Sibyl C. *insurance company executive*
Lieberman, Janet Elaine *academic administrator*
Lloyd, Kenita *museum administrator*
Markus, Maura *bank executive*
McCoy, Ann *artist*
Rein, Catherine Amelia *insurance company executive, lawyer*
Roberts, Kathleen Joy Doty *secondary school educator*

Long Lake
Waagner, Sharon Flannery *library media specialist*

Loudonville
Burstein, Sharon Ann *corporate communications specialist, apparel designer*
Ribley-Borck, Joan Grace *medical/surgical rehabilitation nurse*

Lowville
Colton, Bonnie Myers *folklorist, writer*

Lynbrook
Cangemi, Lisa Lynne *art director, graphics designer*
Cline, Starr *elementary school educator, educator*

Mahopac
Castronovo, Bernadine Marro *music educator*
Greene, Geraldine Marie *family therapist, consultant*
McAvoy, Kathleen Fleming *mathematics educator*
Vigliotti, Patricia Noreen *metal products executive, sculptor*

Maine
Truex, Brenda *music educator*

Malone
Patterson, Valerie *art educator*

Malverne
Alesse, Judith *special education educator*

Mamaroneck
Lesser, Mimi Korach *artist*
McCormick, Margaret C. *science educator*
Merskey-Zeger, Marie Gertrude Fine *retired librarian*
Rosenthal, Elizabeth Robbins *physician*

Manchester
Wink, Laura A. *special education educator*

Manhasset
Kahn, Ellen Ida *physician, consultant*
Krim, Eileen Y. *physician*
Pitta, Patricia Joyce *psychologist*
Savage, Clare Leavy *school psychologist*
Seftel, Donna Selene *architect*
Siller, Pamela Pearl *psychiatrist*
Spetsieris, Phoebe George *physicist, application developer, researcher*

Manlius
der Boghosian, Paula *computer business consultant*
Gibson, Judith W. *psychotherapist*
Harriff, Suzanna Elizabeth Bahner *media consultant*
Koch, Catherine Ann *music educator, musician*
O'Reilly, Mary *environmental scientist, educator*

Margaretville
Brockway-Henson, Amie *producing artistic director*
Lewis-Ryder, Patricia A. *medical/surgical and community health nurse*

Maspeth
Dumitru, Mirela *accountant*

Massapequa
Batt, Alyse Schwartz *application developer*
Goldberg, Beth Sheba *artist, educator, art therapist*
Oliver, Danielle Michelle *special education educator, recreational therapist*
Pelkofsky, Janine Marie *special education educator*
Puleio, Ann Margaret *special education educator*
Turk, Elizabeth Ann *music educator*

Massena
Perez, Loretta Ann Bronchetti *secondary education educator, small business owner*

Mayville
Stacy, Ruth Clair *counselor, consultant*

Medford
Klement, Diane *retired educational assistant*

Medina
Chambers, Krista Ruth *mathematics educator*

Melville
Basile, Sheila *secondary school educator, consultant*
Drexel, Carolyn A. *bank executive*
Friedrich, Jennifer *lawyer*
Henley, Deborah S. *newspaper editor*
Krenek, Debby *newspaper editor*
McKane, Beatrix *accountant*
Richards, Carol Ann Rubright *retired editor, retired journalist*
Singer, Phyllis *editor-in-chief*
Sobol, Elise Schwarcz *music educator*
Stasi, Linda *writer, television producer, editor, scriptwriter*
Webber, Pamela D. *information technology executive*

Memphis
Woolson, Gloria Jean *education educator*

Merrick
Beckman, Judith Kalb *financial counselor and planner, educator, writer*

Fleischman, Francine D. *secondary school educator*
Glogau, Lillian Flatow Fleischer *educational administrator*
Howard, Joyce Anne *elementary school educator*
Kass-Johnson, Susan *artist*

Mexico
Deloff, Dola Louise *secondary school educator*

Middle Island
Andrews, Gaylen *public relations executive*
Clarke, Hughette Naomi *elementary school educator*
Curiale, Gina *secondary school educator, director*
Kanowsky, Janet Marie *secondary school educator*
Zitterman, Jolene Lauret *mathematics educator*

Middle Village
Fradella, Laura Toni *art educator, muralist*

Middleburgh
Mau, Lisa Anne *special education educator*

Middletown
Bedell, Barbara Lee *journalist*
Horler, Nichole *elementary school educator*
Lowe, Danielle Frances *elementary school educator*
McCord, Jean Ellen *art educator*

Millbrook
Duesberry, Joellyn Toler *artist*
Flexner, Josephine Moncure *musician, educator*
Hall, Penelope Coker *editor, writer*

Miller Place
Callahan, Jean M. *personnel administrator*

Millwood
Durst, Carol Goldsmith *food studies educator*

Mineola
Cardo, Marianne *lawyer*
Hammer, Deborah Marie *librarian, paralegal*
O'Connell, Maureen C. *county official, former state legislator*
Vogel, Jennifer Lyn *lawyer*

Mohegan Lake
Charney, Lena London *property manager, historian, poet*
Freeman, Sally Ann *writer, English language and literacy educator*

Monroe
Centeno-Dainty, Sonia Margarita *artist*
Santorelly, Annmarie *special education educator*
Shanley, Patricia Carolin *retired school media specialist*

Montauk
Hartsough, Cheryl Marie *recreation director, nutritionist*

Montgomery
Belgiovene, Melanie C. *science educator*
Moore, Virginia Lee Smith *elementary school educator*

Monticello
Stanton, Dorothy Marie *special education educator, tax specialist*

Montrose
Guadagno, Christine Ellen *social studies educator*
Miah, Jamila Sikander *social worker, researcher*
Paternoster, Kathleen A. *secondary school educator*

Mooers
Kokes, Kathleen A. *music educator, voice educator*

Moravia
Welch, Joan Minde *elementary school educator*

Morrisville
Cleland, Gladys Lee *academic administrator, adult education educator*

Mount Kisco
Bithoney, Carmen C. D'Amborsio *artistic director*
Hodara, Susan Mina *writer*
Keesee, Patricia Hartford *volunteer*

Mount Sinai
Lidstrom, Esther Marie *artist, photographer*
Sill, Linda DeHart *science educator*

Mount Vernon
Addesso, Angela Joyce *school system administrator*
NelsonWilliams, Cecelia Elaine *dietician, nutritionist*
Young, Paula Eva *animal shelter director*

Nanuet
Jelalian, Christine *elementary school educator, secondary school educator*

Narrowsburg
Krause, Gloria Rose *music educator*

Neponsit
Nicastri, Ann Gilbert *science educator*

Nesconset
Burns-Riviello, Michaela Aileen *social studies educator*
Goldstein, Joyce *special education educator*

New Hampton
Sinnard, Elaine Janice *painter, sculptor*

New Hartford
Battista, Diane Russo *elementary school educator, music educator, personal trainer*

New Hyde Park
Ashtari, Manzar *neuroscientist*
Haase, Lauren *mathematics educator*
Laudin, Riza Ann *elementary school educator*
Neal, Elaine Zirli *health products executive*
Seltzer, Vicki Lynn *obstetrician, gynecologist*

New Kingston
Chase, Linda *curator, writer*

New Paltz
Cheng, Amy *artist*
Emanuel-Smith, Robin Lesley *special education educator*
Flanagan Kelly, Anne Marie *academic administrator*
Freeman, Phyllis Risë *psychology educator*
Goodell, Kathy Susan *artist, educator*
Harris, Kristine *historian, educator*
List, Ilka Katherine *art educator, sculptor, writer, psychotherapist*
Nyquist, Corinne Elaine *librarian*
Young, Marjorie Ann *librarian*

New Rochelle
Adato, Linda Joy *artist, educator*
Black, Page Morton *civic worker, vocalist, musician*
Curry, Ellen R. *academic administrator, educator*
Fitch, Nancy Elizabeth *historian, educator*
Goodman, Joan Frances *avionics manufacturing executive*
Grimes, Tresmaine Judith Rubain *psychology educator*
Pérez-Bustillo, Mireya *language educator, writer, poet, translator*
Reddington, Mary Jane *retired secondary school educator*
Rutstein, Eleanor H. *psychologist*
Schreibman, Thelma Rabinowitz *psychotherapist, educator*
Swire, Edith Wypler *music educator, violist, violinist*
Tassone, Gelsomina (Gessie Tassone) *metal products executive*
Winstead, Melody *science educator*
Wolf, Helen *director*

New Windsor
Carson, Teresa Catherine *pediatrician*

New York
Abate, Catherine M. *retired state legislator*
Abatemarco, Tracy J. *lawyer*
Abish, Cecile *artist*
Abramovic, Marina *artist*
Abrams, Joyce D. *artist*
Abramson, Jill *newspaper publishing executive*
Aciman, Carole V. *lawyer*
Acra, Reem *apparel designer*
Adams, Cindy *journalist*
Adams, Jane *actress*
Adcroft, Patti (Patrice Gabriella Adcroft) *editor*
Addison, Anne Simone Pomex *television director, consultant, commentator*
Adler, Amy M. *law educator*
Adler, Margot Susanna *journalist, radio producer, radio correspondent, writer*
Adri, (Adri Steckling Coen) *fashion designer*
Adrian, Barbara (Mrs. Franklin C. Tramutola) *artist*
Agard, Emma Estornel *psychotherapist*
Aguilera, Christina *singer*
Aiello, Theresa *social sciences educator*
Aigen, Betsy Paula *psychotherapist*
Akabas, Sheila Helene *social work educator*
Albu, Jeanine Breazu *endocrinologist, educator*
Alemany, Ellen R. *bank executive*
Alex, Paula Ann *foundation administrator*
Alexander, Jane (Jane Quigley) *actress, theater educator, writer*
Ali, Laylah *artist*
Allen, Alice *communications and marketing executive*
Allen, Betty (Mrs. Ritten Edward Lee III) *mezzo-soprano*
Allen, Patricia Jean *graphics designer*
Allentuck, Marcia Epstein *English language educator, art history educator*
Almon, Lorie *lawyer*
Alston, Alyce *diamond company executive*
Alt, Carol A. *actress, model, entrepreneur, writer*
Alter, Eleanor Breitel *lawyer*
Altfest, Karen Caplan *diversified financial services company executive, director*
Alvarez, Julia *writer*
Amos, Tori *musician, singer*
Amster, Linda Evelyn *newspaper executive, consultant*
Andersen, Marianne Singer *psychologist*
Andersen, Susan Marie *psychologist, educator, director*
Anderson, Lisa *dean, political science professor, researcher*
Angelo, Bonnie *journalist*
Ansanelli, Alexandra *ballerina*
Antonacci, Lori (Loretta Marie Antonacci) *marketing executive, consultant*
Appel, Gloria *advertising executive*
Appelbaum, Ann Harriet *lawyer*
Apter, Emily *language educator*
Arabatzis, Constance Elaine *lawyer*
Aragno, Anna *psychoanalyst, author*
Armine, Cindy A. *bank executive*
Armitage, Karole *dancer*
Arms, Anneli (Anna Elizabeth Arms) *artist, educator*
Arndt, Carmen Gloria *secondary school educator*
Arndt, Cynthia *educational administrator*
Arnold, Ann *artist, illustrator*
Arts-Meyer, Katina *interior designer*
Asakawa, Takako *dancer, educator, choreographer, director*
Asbury, Carolyn *neuroscience researcher*
Ash, Karen Artz *lawyer*
Ashanti, (Ashanti Shequoiya Douglas) *vocalist*
Ashdown, Marie Matranga (Mrs. Cecil Spanton Ashdown Jr.) *writer, educator, cultural organization administrator*
Ashley, Elizabeth *actress*
Ashton, Dore *writer, educator*

Ashton, Jean Willoughby *library director*
Astley, Amy *editor-in-chief*
Atkins, Veronica *philanthropist*
Atwood, Margaret Eleanor *writer*
Axthelm, Nancy *advertising executive*
Azrielant, Aya *jewelry manufacturing executive*
Bacall, Lauren (Betty Joan Perske) *actress*
Bachant, Janet Lee *psychologist*
Bachrach, Nancy *retired advertising executive*
Backstedt, Roseanne Joan *artist*
Baglivo, Mary L. *advertising executive*
Bahr, Lauren S. *publishing executive*
Bains, Leslie Elizabeth *banker*
Baird, Lisa P. *marketing executive*
Baird, Penny Drue *interior designer*
Baird, Zoë *lawyer*
Baker, Deborah *editor, writer*
Balderston, Jean Merrill *marriage and family therapist, poet, writer*
Balmori, Diana *landscape designer*
Balogh, Mary *writer*
Balter, Bernice *religious organization administrator*
Bancroft, Margaret Armstrong *lawyer*
Bank, Melissa S. *writer*
Bansal, Preeta D. *lawyer*
Barash, Susan Shapiro *writer, humanities educator*
Barbosa, Shameka Brown *copywriter*
Barbour, Catherine Jean *actress, set designer, director, mime*
Bardach, Joan Lucile *clinical psychologist*
Bardin, Mary Beth *telecommunications company executive*
Barker, Barbara Ann *ophthalmologist*
Barker, Sylvia Margaret *nurse*
Barlow, Barbara Ann *surgeon*
Barnes, Jhane Elizabeth *fashion design company executive, designer*
Barnett, Amy DuBois *editor-in-chief*
Barnett, Vivian Endicott *curator*
Barnum, Barbara Stevens *retired nursing educator, writer*
Barolini, Teodolinda *literary critic*
Baron, Sheri *advertising agency executive*
Baron, Susan *publishing executive*
Barrett, Elizabeth Ann Manhart *psychotherapist, consultant, nursing educator*
Barrett, Susan Iris *actor, educator*
Barrish, Carol Lampert *psychologist*
Barron, Marlene *education educator*
Barry, Nancy Marie *bank executive*
Bartlett, Jennifer Losch *artist*
Bartow, Diane Grace *marketing professional, sales executive*
Barzilay, Judith Morgenstern *federal judge*
Baslaw-Finger, Annette *education educator, consultant*
Basquin, Mary Smyth (Kit Basquin) *museum administrator*
Bastianich, Lidia Matticchio *chef, food service executive*
Bateman, Maureen Scannell *lawyer*
Baten, Amanda Zoe *psychologist*
Batts, Deborah A. *federal judge*
Bauer, Marion Dane *writer*
Bauman, Susan *communications executive*
Baumrind, Rosalyn Muriel Greenwald *psychologist*
Bawden, Nina (Mary Bawden) *author*
Beattie, Ann *writer, educator*
Beausoleil, Doris Mae *retired federal agency housing specialist*
Beck, Martha Ann *curator, director*
Becker, Barbara Lynn *lawyer*
Becker, Helane Renée *financial analyst, finance company executive*
Becker, Susan Kaplan *management and marketing communication consultant, educator*
Beckman, Ericka *artist, filmmaker*
Been, Vicki Lynn *law educator*
Beerbower, Cynthia Gibson *lawyer*
Beers, Sydney (Sydney Davolos) *theater producer*
Beeson, Ann *lawyer*
Behar, Joy *television personality*
Beinecke, Candace Krugman *lawyer*
Beinecke, Frances G. *environmentalist*
Belag, Andrea Susan *artist*
Ben-Ami, Leora *lawyer*
Bender, Judith *journalist, editor*
Benedek, Melinda *television executive*
Benglis, Lynda *artist, sculptor, educator*
Bennett, Tina *literary agent*
Berentson, Jane *editor*
Berg, Elizabeth Ann *writer*
Berg, Madelaine R. *lawyer*
Berger, Pearl *library director*
Bergman, Arlene *lawyer*
Bergman, Michelle D. *lawyer*
Berkery, Rosemary T. *lawyer, investment company executive*
Berman, Ariane R. *artist*
Berman, Carol Wendy *psychiatrist*
Berman, Mira *advertising agency executive*
Berman, Rachel *dancer*
Berner, Mary *publisher*
Bernhard, Lisa *news correspondent*
Bernstein, Bonnie *sportscaster*
Bernstein, Phyllis J. *financial consultant*
Berresford, Susan Vail *foundation administrator*
Berrien, Jacqueline A. *lawyer*
Beshar, Christine *lawyer*
Beshar, Sarah E. *lawyer*
Best, Wanda *career planning consultant*
Bethel, Denise *art appraiser*
Beverley, Cordia Luvonne *gastroenterologist*
Bialler, Nancy *art appraiser*
Bibliowicz, Jessica M. *financial analyst*
Biddle, Flora Miller *art patron, museum administrator*
Binder, Susan A. *chemical company executive*
Bird, Sharlene *psychologist*
Birman, Ronnie Rathkopf *retired elementary school educator*
Birnbaum, Sheila L. *lawyer, educator*
Birstein, Ann *writer, educator*
Bischoff, Theresa Ann *not-for-profit association executive*
Bishopric, Susan Ehrlich *public relations executive*
Björk, (Björk Guðmundsdóttir) *singer, composer*
Bjorklund, Victoria B. *lawyer*
Black, Barbara Aronstein *legal history educator*

Black, Carole *broadcast executive*
Black, Cathleen Prunty *publishing executive*
Blalock, Sherrill *investment advisor*
Blanchard, Kimberly Staggers *lawyer, educator*
Blassberg, Franci J. *lawyer*
Blazejowski, Carol A. *professional sports team executive, retired professional basketball player*
Bledel, Alexis (Kimberly Alexis Bledel) *actress*
Block, Francesca Lia *writer*
Bloom, Lisa Read *lawyer*
Bloomgarden, Karenne Jo *elementary school educator, small business owner*
Bloomgarden, Kathy Finn *public relations executive*
Bluh, Bonnie *scriptwriter, actress, novelist, playwright*
Blum, Diane S. *human services manager*
Blume, Judy *author*
Blumenfeld, Joan *architect*
Boast, Molly Shryer *lawyer*
Boden, Katherine L. *utilities executive*
Bodini, Daniele Damaso *real estate company executive*
Bogen, Nancy *writer, English educator*
Boisseau, Jane *lawyer*
Bonfante, Larissa *classics educator*
Bonino, Fernanda *art dealer*
Booth, Barbara Ribman *civic worker*
Booth Corwin, Tami *publishing executive*
Borhi, Carol *data processing executive, finance company executive*
Boufford, Jo Ivey *health administrator, educator*
Bourgeois, Louise *sculptor*
Bowden, Linda *diversified financial services company executive*
Bowden, Sally Ann *choreographer, educator, dancer*
Bowen, Sharon Y. *lawyer*
Bowers, Patricia Eleanor Fritz *economist*
Boyer, Aurelia G. *information technology executive*
Boyer, Cheryl *finance company executive*
Boylan, Elizabeth Shippee *academic administrator, biologist, educator*
Brabeck, Mary Margaret *dean, psychology professor*
Bracco, Lorraine *actress*
Bradford, Barbara Taylor *writer, journalist*
Bradshaw, Dove *artist*
Brady, Adelaide Burks *public relations agency executive, giftware catalog executive*
Brashares, Ann *writer*
Bratten, Millie Martini *editor-in-chief*
Braudy, Susan Orr *writer*
Brenner, Beth Fuchs *publishing executive*
Breslow, Esther May Greenberg *biochemistry professor, researcher*
Breslow, Stephanie R. *lawyer*
Bressman, Susan Berliner *health facility administrator*
Brett, Nancy Heléne *artist*
Brewer, Karen *librarian*
Bricard, Yolanda Borras *music educator, music program administrator*
Brinkley, Christie *model, spokesperson, designer*
Brinson, Monica Evette *mental health specialist, pharmaceutical sales representative*
Brisman, Jennifer *event planning executive*
Bristah, Pamela Jean *librarian*
Bristor, Katherine M. *lawyer*
Britz Lotti, Diane Edward *investment company executive*
Brodie-Baldwin, Helen Sylvia *retired college and human services administrator*
Brody, Jane Ellen *journalist, researcher*
Brody-Lederman, Stephanie *artist*
Brooke, Linda Hundley *human resources specialist*
Brooks, Anita Helen *public relations executive*
Brooks, Diana B. *former auction house executive*
Brothers, Joyce Diane *television personality, psychologist*
Browar, Lisa Muriel *librarian*
Brown, Campbell *commentator*
Brown, Cecily *artist*
Brown, Helen Gurley *editor-in-chief*
Brown, Joyce F. *academic administrator*
Brown, Katie *columnist*
Brown, Renee *sports association executive*
Brown, Rita Mae *writer*
Brown, Tina *journalist, television personality*
Brown, Trisha *dancer*
Brown, Tyese Andrea *music educator*
Browne, Joy *psychologist, radio personality*
Brownell, Patricia Jane *social worker, educator*
Browning, Candace *corporate financial executive*
Brozman, Tina L. *federal judge*
Bruesewitz-LoPinto, Gail C. *marketing professional*
Bruning, Nancy Pauline *writer*
Bruno, Antoinette *food service executive*
Brunswick, Ann Finkenberg *social psychologist, health researcher*
Brychtova, Jaroslava *sculptor*
Bryson, Louise Henry *broadcast executive*
Brzezinski, Mika *TV news anchor*
Buchanan, Edna *writer, retired journalist*
Buchbinder, Ellen Maud *allergist*
Buchenhorner, Marianne *psychotherapist, psychoanalyst*
Buck, Louise Zierdt *psychologist*
Buckley, Nancy Margaret *retired research scientist*
Buckley, Priscilla Langford *magazine editor*
Buckley, Susan *lawyer*
Buckley, Virginia Laura *editor*
Buissonnière, Marine *international organization administrator; physician*
Bujold, Lois McMaster *writer*
Bundchen, Giselle *model*
Burbank, Jane Richardson *historian, educator*
Burgess, Clara Skipwith *retired principal*
Burgess, Lynne A *lawyer*
Burgman, Dierdre Ann *lawyer*
Burke, Delta *actress*
Burns, M. Michele *human resources company executive*
Burns, Red *academic administrator*
Burns, Robin *cosmetics company executive*
Burns, Sarah Ellen *law educator*
Burros, Marian Fox *writer*
Burt-Murray, Angela *editor-in-chief*
Burton, Eve B. *lawyer*
Burton, Peggy *advertising and marketing executive*
Buryk, Alexis *advertising executive*
Bush, Lauren *model*
Bushnell, Candace *columnist, writer*
Busquet, Anne M. *Internet company executive*
Butler, Carol Ann *psychotherapist, mediator*
Butler, Kerry *actress*
Butte, Amy S. *brokerage house executive*
Butterly, Kathy *sculptor*
Buttner, Jean Bernhard *diversified financial services company executive*
Byer, Diana *performing company executive*
Bynum, Sarah Shun-lien *writer, educator*
Byrd, Eva Wilson *communications executive*
Byrne, Jennie Louise *psychiatrist, researcher*
Caffrey, Patricia *diversified financial services company executive*
Cahan, Cora *not-for-profit developer*
Calabrese, Rosalie Sue *management consultant, writer*
Calame, Kathryn Lee *microbiologist, educator*
Caldwell, L. Scott *actress*
Caldwell, Leslie Ragon *lawyer, former prosecutor*
Caldwell, Paulette M. *law educator*
Calisher, Hortense (Mrs. Curtis Harnack) *writer*
Calvano, Phyllis *publishing executive*
Camp, Alida Diane *mediator, arbitrator, law educator*
Camp, Sharon L. *reproductive health organization administrator*
Campagnolo, Ann-Casey *retail executive*
Campbell, Judith E. *retired insurance company executive*
Campbell, Mary Schmidt *dean*
Canetti, Alexandra *psychiatrist*
Cannon, Elizabeth H. *dress and clothing designer, artist*
Canonero, Milena *costume designer*
Cantrell, Lana *actress, lawyer, singer*
Caploe, Roberta *magazine editor*
Caponnetto, Marianne *information technology executive*
Cappellazzo, Amy *art appraiser, writer*
Capriati, Jennifer Maria *professional tennis player*
Caputo, Lisa M. *finance company executive*
Cardinale, Kathleen Carmel *retired health facility administrator*
Carlson, Marian Bille *geneticist, researcher, educator*
Caroff, Phyllis M. *social work educator*
Carr, Claudia *art gallery director, artist, art gallery owner*
Carr, Gladys Justin *publishing executive, consultant, editor, writer*
Carter, Carolyn Houchin *advertising agency executive*
Caruso, Ann S. *fashion editor, stylist*
Case, Nan Barkin *psychologist*
Casella, Margaret Mary *artist*
Caserta, Jennifer *communications executive*
Cash, Rosanne *singer, songwriter*
Cassullo, Joanne Leonhardt *foundation administrator*
Castagna, Vanessa J. *retail executive*
Castoro, Rosemarie *sculptor*
Castro, Jan Garden *writer, art educator, consultant*
Castro, Rosa *drug counselor*
Catley-Carlson, Margaret *not-for-profit executive*
Cavallo, Jo Ann *language educator*
Caws, Mary Ann *literature and language professor*
Cazeaux, Isabelle Anne Marie *retired music educator*
Cedarbaum, Miriam Goldman *federal judge*
Cendali, Dale Margaret *lawyer*
Centrello, Gina *publishing executive*
Cerfolio, Nina Estelle *psychiatrist, educator*
Cesare, Christine B. *lawyer*
Chaitman, Helen Davis *lawyer*
Champion, Sara Stewart *lawyer*
Chamson, Sandra Potkorony *psychologist*
Chan, Janet *editorial director*
Chan, Siu-Wai *materials science educator*
Chang, Marian S. *filmmaker, composer*
Chang, Mona Mei-Hsuan *computer programmer, analyst*
Chang-Robbins, Joyce *diversified financial services company executive*
Channing, Stockard (Susan Antonia Williams Stockard) *actress*
Chao, Yu Chen *cellist, educator*
Chapman, Sally *chemistry professor*
Chase, Beverly Fanger *lawyer*
Chatfield-Taylor, Adele *historic site director*
Chell, Beverly C. *lawyer*
Chelstrom, Marilyn Ann *political science educator, consultant*
Chenoweth, Kristin *actress*
Cherryh, C. J. *writer*
Chesler, Gail *arts organization development executive*
Chesnutt, Jane *publishing executive*
Chestnut, Colette *broadcast executive*
Chichilnisky, Graciela *mathematician, educator, economist, writer*
Chierchia, Madeline Carmella *management consulting company executive*
Childs, Donna *finance company executive*
Chin, Sylvia Fung *lawyer*
Chira, Susan *editor*
Chirichella, Debra *publishing executive*
Choldenko, Gennifer *writer*
Christina, Sonja (Alisa Morris) *writer, poet*
Christodoulou, Marilena *investment banker, finance company executive*
Christopher, Maurine Brooks *foundation administrator, writer, editor*
Chromow, Sheri P. *lawyer*
Church, Pamela T. *lawyer*
Chu-Zhu, Janice Gail *social worker*
Chwatsky, Ann *photographer, educator*
Ciparick, Carmen Beauchamp *state appeals court judge*
Clamar, Aphrodite J. *psychologist*
Clark, Carolyn Cochran *lawyer*
Clark, Joan Hardy *retired journalist*
Clark, Mayree Carroll *investment banking executive*
Clark, Sheryl Diane *physician*
Clark, Victoria *actress*
Clarke, Pamela Jones *headmaster*
Clarkson, Kelly Brianne *singer*
Claster, Jill Nadell *academic administrator, history educator*
Cleary, Beverly Atlee (Mrs. Clarence T. Cleary) *writer*
Clemens, Rosemary A. *health facility administrator, foundation administrator*
Clinton, Chelsea Victoria *financial consultant, former first daughter*
Coan, Rachel B. *lawyer*
Coe, Sue *artist, journalist*
Coen, Jessica *blog writer, editor*
Cogger, Cassia Zamecki *painter*
Cohen, Abby Joseph *investment company executive*
Cohen, Betty L. *broadcast executive*
Cohen, Claire Gorham *investment company executive*
Cohen, Claudia *journalist, television reporter*
Cohen, Cora *artist*
Cohen, Lisa Janet *psychologist, educator*
Cohen, Madeleine L. *library and information scientist*
Cohen, Marsha R. *former diversified financial services company executive*
Cohen, Robin L. *lawyer*
Cohen, Selma *librarian, researcher*
Colburn, Martha *animator, filmmaker, artist*
Cole, Carolyn Jo *brokerage house executive*
Cole, Elma Phillipson (Mrs. John Strickler Cole) *social welfare executive*
Coleman, Jo-Ann S.E. *social worker*
Coles, Joanna *magazine editor-in-chief*
Collins, Gail *editor*
Collins, Jackie (Jacqueline Jill Collins) *writer*
Collins, Judy Marjorie *singer, songwriter*
Comfrey, Kathleen Marie *lawyer*
Comstock, Beth (Elizabeth J. Comstock) *marketing executive*
Conelli, Maria Ann *art educator, dean, architect*
Conley, Ellen Alexander *writer, educator*
Conlon, Peggy Eileen *publisher*
Conniff, Tamara *editor*
Connors, Cornelia Kathleen *marketing services company executive*
Consagra, Sophie Chandler *academic administrator*
Considine, Jill M. *securities trader*
Consolo, Faith Hope *real estate broker*
Cook, Blanche Wiesen *historian, educator, journalist*
Cook, Sarah Sheets *women's health nurse*
Cook, Traci *sports association executive*
Cooney, Joan Ganz *broadcast executive, director*
Cooper, Gloria *editor, press critic*
Cooper, Jennifer Royann *psychiatrist*
Cooper, Paula *art dealer*
Copeland, Michelle *plastic surgeon*
Corbet, Kathleen A. *financial information company executive*
Corcoran, Barbara *real estate company executive*
Corello, Sara A. *lawyer*
Corrales, Carmen Amalia *lawyer*
Corrigan, Maureen *book critic, English educator*
Cortina, Betty *magazine editor*
Cote, Denise Louise *federal judge*
Couric, Katie (Katherine Anne Couric) *newscaster, journalist*
Court, Kathryn Diana *editor*
Cox, Ana Marie *writer, former political blogger*
Cox, Mary Anthony *musician, educator*
Coyne, Judith *editor*
Cracauer, Cynthia Phifer *architectural firm executive*
Craft, Liz *artist*
Craig, Pamela J. *management consulting firm executive*
Crandell, Susan *magazine editor*
Creech, Sharon *children's author*
Creenan, Katherine Heras *lawyer*
Crier, Catherine *newscaster*
Crile, Susan *artist*
Crist, Judith *film and drama critic*
Crittenden, Danielle Ann *writer, journalist*
Croce, Arlene *critic*
Cronin, Doreen *writer, former lawyer*
Crost, Katharine I. *lawyer*
Crowley, Cynthia Wetmore *real estate broker*
Crown, Roberta *artist, educator*
Cruz, Zoe *diversified financial services company executive*
Cundiff, Victoria Anne *lawyer*
Curry, Ann *correspondent, anchor*
Curry, Jane Louise *writer*
Curtin, Jane Therese *actress, writer*
Curtis, Susan M. *lawyer*
Cutler, Amy *artist*
Cutler, Ronnie *artist*
Cuttner, Janet *hematologist, educator*
Czarniak, Julia A. *lawyer*
Daheim, Mary Rene Richardson *writer*
Dajani, Virginia *art association administrator*
Dakin, Christine Whitney *dancer, educator*
Daly, Cheryl *communications executive, broadcast executive*
Damrosch, Lori Fisler *law educator*
Dandonoli, Patricia A. *not-for-profit fundraiser*
Danielides, Joannie C. *public relations executive*
Daniels, Faith *former newscaster*
Danitz, Marilynn Patricia *choreographer, video specialist*
D'Antuono, Eleanor *ballet director, educator, coach*
Danziger, Lucy *editor*
Darrow, Jill E(llen) *lawyer*
Davarova, Elmira *musician*
Davenport, Margaret Andrews *lawyer*
Davidson, Nancy Brachman *artist, educator*
Davidson, Sheila Kearney *lawyer, insurance company executive*
Davis, D. Lavelda *dean, academic administrator*
Davis, Florence Ann *lawyer*
Davis, Jessica G. *geneticist*
Davis, Karen *insurance company executive, educator*
Davis, Kathryn Wasserman *foundation executive, educator, writer*
Davis, Lisa E. *lawyer*
Davis, Martha Frances *lawyer*
Davis, Peggy Cooper *law educator*
Dawson, Stephanie Elaine *city manager*
Dayson, Diane Harris *parks director, cultural organization administrator*
De Angelis, Judy *anchorwoman*
Deans, Patricia Herrmann *investment banker*
DeBeers, Sue *photographer*
DeCaro, Shana *lawyer*
deCoppet, Laura Louise *writer, editor*
Decter, Midge *writer*
Deen, Paula H. *television personality, restaurant owner, chef*
DeFelice, Laura A. *lawyer*
DeFord, Ruth I. *music educator*
Degener, Carol M. *lawyer*
Dehn, Cathleen Patterson *health facility administrator*
Deitz, Paula *magazine editor*
de Kretser, Michelle *writer*
de Lange, Titia *research scientist, educator*
De Lisi, Nancy *corporate financial executive*
DeLuccia, Paula *artist*
DeMasi, Karin A. *lawyer*
de Menil, Lois Pattison *historian, philanthropist*
DeMonte, Claudia Ann *artist, educator*
DeMonte, Cynthia Maria *investor relations and management consultant*
Denmark, Florence Harriet Levin *psychology professor*
Dennis, Diane Joy Milam *retired architect*
Dennis, Donna Frances *sculptor, art educator*
Dennison, Lisa *museum director*
Desai, Vishakha N. *museum director, professional society administrator*
DeVard, Jerri *marketing professional*
Deveraux, Jude (Jude Gilliam White) *writer*
Devi, Gayatri *physician*
DeVita, M. Christine *foundation administrator*
de Vries, Madeline *public relations executive*
DeWoody, Beth Rudin *film producer*
Diamond, Heidi Janice *marketing professional*
Diamonstein-Spielvogel, Barbaralee *writer*
Dias Griffin, Anne *investment advisor*
Diaz, Angela *pediatrician, educator*
Didion, Joan *writer*
Dienstag, Eleanor Foa *corporate communications consultant*
Dietz, Elizabeth Camilla *investment banker*
Difede, JoAnn *psychologist*
Dillard, Annie *writer*
Dimen, Muriel Vera *psychoanalyst*
Dinerman, Miriam *social work educator*
Disney, Anthea *publishing executive*
Dobrof, Rose Wiesman *gerontology educator*
Dodd, Lois *artist, art educator*
Dodge, Marcia Milgrom *director, choreographer*
Dolan, Regina A. *security firm executive*
Dole-Recio, Lecia *artist*
Donneson, Seena Sand *artist*
Donovan, Maureen Driscoll *lawyer*
Dorn, Sue Bricker *retired hospital administrator*
Doyle, Eugenie Fleri *pediatrician, cardiologist, educator*
Doyle, Kristene Anne *psychologist, educator*
Dozier, Kimberly *news correspondent*
Drago-Severson, Eleanor Elizabeth E. *developmental psychologist, educator, researcher*
Dratch, Rachel *comedienne, actress*
Drechsler, Beatrice Krain *lawyer*
Dreizen, Alison M. *lawyer*
Drew, Ina R. *bank executive*
Drexler, Joanne Lee *art appraiser*
Dreyfuss, Rochelle Cooper *law educator*
Driscoll, Karen *communications executive*
Driver, Martha Westcott *literature educator, researcher, writer*
Drum, Sydney Maria *artist*
Du Boff, Jill Bonnie Candise *sound effects artist*
Dubuc, Nancy *communications executive*
Duff, Hilary Ann *actress, singer*
Dufka, Corinne *human rights activist*
Dukakis, Olympia *actress*
Duke, Ellen (Bebe Duke) *bank executive*
Dunbar, Leila *antiques appraiser, auction house executive*
Duncan, Patricia *lawyer, broadcast executive*
Duncan, Pearl Rose *writer*
Dunkelman, Loretta *artist*
Duquesnay, Ann *actress, singer*
Durkin, Dorothy Angela *university official*
Durrant, M. Patricia *diplomat*
Dutchevici, Silvia M. *psychotherapist*
Eaker, Sherry Ellen *editor*
Earle, Eugenia *music educator*
Earling, Debra Magpie *writer, educator*
Ebersole, Christine *actress*
Eckhardt, Laurel Ann *biologist, researcher, educator*
Eckman, Fern Marja *journalist*
Economos, Katherine *oncologist*
Edelman, Judith H. *architect*
Edelson, Mary Beth *artist, educator*
Edelstein, Barbara A. *radiologist*
Egen, Maureen Mahon *publishing executive*
Einiger, Carol Blum *investment company executive*
Eisen, LizabethAnn R. *lawyer*
Eisenberg, Barbara Anne K. *lawyer*
Eisenberg, Sonja Miriam *artist*
Eisler, Susan Krawetz *advertising executive*
Eisner, Carole Swid *artist*
Elkin, Judith *lawyer*
Ellenbogen, Marjorie *retired elementary school educator*
Ellerbee, Linda (Linda Jane Smith) *reporter*
Ellingwood, Susan *editor*
Elliott, Eleanor Thomas *foundation executive, volunteer*
Elliott, Missy (Melissa Arnette Elliot) *musician*
Ellis, Loren Elizabeth *artist, educator*
Ellis, Rosemary *editor-in-chief*
Ellis, Ross *non-profit organization executive*
Elto, Erin K. *psychologist*
Emme, (Emme Aronson) *model, apparel designer*
Enders, Elizabeth McGuire *artist*
Engel, Amy J. *corporate financial executive*
Engelberg, Gail May *fine arts patron*
Ensler, Eve *playwright, actress*
Epstein, Cynthia Fuchs *sociology educator, writer*
Erdoes, Mary Callahan *investment banker*
Erlenmeyer-Kimling, L. *psychiatrist, researcher*
Eshleman, Diane Varrin *bank executive*

Essandoh, Hilda Brathwaite *primary school educator*
Estabrook, Alison *surgeon, educator*
Estlund, Cynthia *law educator*
Eterovich Maguire, Karen Ann *actress, writer*
Ethan, Carol Baehr *psychotherapist, psychoanalyst*
Etienne, Michele *financial consultant*
Evanovich, Janet *writer*
Evans, B. Paige *artistic director*
Evans, Faith *singer*
Evans, Julie Robin *lawyer*
Evans, Linda Kay *publishing executive*
Ewing-Mulligan, Mary *food products executive*
Fagin, Claire Mintzer *nursing educator, nursing administrator*
Fantasia, (Fantasia Monique Barrino) *singer*
Farinelli, Jean L. *management consultant*
Farley, Carole *soprano*
Farley, Katherine G. *real estate company executive*
Farley, Peggy Ann *finance company executive*
Fasnacht, Heide Ann *artist, educator*
Fears, Linda *editor-in-chief*
Felderman, Lenora I. *physician*
Feldman, Elise *lawyer*
Feldman, Helaine *editor, public relations associate*
Felious, Odetta *vocalist*
Fell, M. Ann *publishing executive*
Feltenstein, Martha *lawyer*
Fennell Robbins, Sally *writer*
Ferber, Linda S. *museum director*
Ferguson, Sarah *The Duchess of York*
Fernández, Teresita *sculptor*
Field, Patricia *apparel designer*
Fielding, Helen *writer*
Fields, C. Virginia *city manager*
Fields, Felicia P. *actress*
Filarski Hasselbeck, Elizabeth *television host/personality*
Fili-Krushel, Patricia *media company executive*
Finch, Sheila *writer*
Fine, Deborah *Internet company executive, former apparel executive*
Fiori, Pamela *publishing executive, writer*
Firestone, Susan Paul *artist*
Fischbach, Ruth Linda *ethics educator, social scientist, researcher*
Fischbarg, Zulema F. *pediatrician*
Fisher, Ann Bailen *lawyer*
Fisher, Joely *actress*
Fitch, Janet *writer*
Flack, Roberta *singer*
Flaherty, Pamela Potter *bank executive*
Flaherty, Tina Santi *corporate communications specialist, writer*
Flanagan, Deborah Mary *lawyer*
Fleesler, Faith B. *writer*
Fleming, Alice Carew Mulcahey *writer*
Fleming, Renée L. *opera singer*
Flesher, Gail A. *lawyer*
Fodor, Iris Elaine *clinical psychologist, educator, psychotherapist*
Fodor, Susanna Serena *lawyer*
Fogarassy, Helen Catherine *writer*
Foley, Ann *broadcast executive*
Forbes, Sally *researcher, editor, curator*
Forden, Diane Claire *magazine editor*
Forese, Laura Lee *hospital administrator, orthopedist*
Formenti, Silvia C. *radiation oncologist*
Forrest, Katherine B. *lawyer*
Fosler, Gail D. *economist*
Foster, Kim *art dealer, art gallery owner*
Fowler, Beth *actress*
Fowler, Karen Joy *writer*
Fox, Paula (Mrs. Martin Greenberg) *writer*
Frank, Elizabeth *writer, educator*
Franke, Katherine M. *law educator*
Frankenthaler, Helen *artist*
Franks, Lucinda Laura *journalist*
Freedman, Helen E. *judge*
Freeland, Chrystia *editor, director*
Freeman, Debra *federal judge*
Frehm, Lynne *painter*
Freilich, Joan Sherman *utilities executive*
Freyer, Dana Hartman *lawyer*
Freyre, Angela Mariana *lawyer*
Friedman, Adena T. *finance company executive*
Friedman, Caitlin *public relations executive*
Friedman, Debbie *singer, songwriter, religious studies educator*
Friedman, Elaine Florence *lawyer*
Friedman, Jane *publishing executive*
Friedman, Linda Weiser *operations researcher, educator*
Friedman, Rachelle *music retail executive*
Friedman, Sally *artist, educator*
Frost, Ellen Elizabeth *psychologist*
Fry, Elizabeth H. W. *lawyer*
Fuchs, Elaine V. *molecular biologist, educator*
Fudge, Ann Marie *advertising executive*
Fuentez, Tania Michele *journalist*
Fuhrman, Susan H. *academic administrator, education educator, researcher*
Fuller, Beverley Bozeman *dancer, singer, actress, choreographer, director*
Fuller, Bonnie *editor-in-chief*
Fullilove, Mindy Thompson *psychiatrist*
Fung, Mina Hsu *advertising executive*
Futter, Ellen Victoria *museum administrator*
Gage, Beau *artist*
Gallagher, Ellen *artist*
Gallegos, Deborah E. *pension fund administrator*
Gallo, Martha J. *diversified financial services company executive*
Garcia, Angela G. *lawyer*
Garcia, Minerva A.F. *microbiologist, research and clinical laboratory scientist*
Gardner, Janet Paxton *journalist, film producer*
Garland, Sylvia Dillof *lawyer*
Garrett, Celia Erica *human services administrator, consultant*
Garrett, Laurie *journalist, global health scholar*
Garrett, Margo *pianist, music educator*
Gath, Jean Marie *architectural firm executive*
Gaydos, Mary *writer, researcher, actress*
Geary, Hilary R. *society editor*
Gebbie, Kristine Moore *medical educator*
Geiser, Elizabeth Able *publishing company executive*
Gelb, Judith Anne *lawyer*
Geller, Ethell A. *consulting clinical psychologist*
Gendler, Ellen *dermatologist*
Geoghegan, Patricia *lawyer*
George, Elizabeth (Susan Elizabeth George) *writer*
Georgopoulos, Maria *architect, artist*
Gerard, Barbara *visual artist, educator*
Gerard-Sharp, Monica Fleur *communications executive*
Gerber, Gwendolyn Loretta *psychologist, educator*
Gerber, Jane Satlow *history professor*
Gerberg, Judith Levine *management consultant*
Geskin, Leah *foreign language educator*
Gewirtz-Friedman, Gerry *editor*
Ghaffari, Avideh Behrouz *interior designer*
Gharib, Susie *newscaster*
Gianinno, Susan McManama *advertising executive*
Gibbons, Kaye *writer*
Gibbs, Elsie Frances *social worker*
Gibson, Arlene Joy *headmaster*
Gibson, Sandra *painter, filmmaker*
Gill, E. Ann *lawyer*
Gill, Linda A. *advertising executive*
Gillespie, Donna Fay *novelist*
Gilligan, Carol *psychologist, writer*
Gilman, Dorothy (Dorothy Gilman Butters) *author*
Gilman, Susan Jane *writer*
Giordano, Marianne *not-for-profit developer*
Giral, Angela *librarian*
Girard, Andrea Eaton *communications executive, consultant*
Girard, Judy *broadcast executive*
Gittler, Wendy *artist, art historian, writer*
Giuliani, Judith *not-for-profit executive*
Glasberg, Lisa *radio personality*
Glass, Julia *writer*
Glassman, Debra *dentist*
Gleason, Barbara Jo *literature and language educator*
Glick, Anna H. *lawyer*
Glickstein, Eileen Agard *librarian, consultant*
Globus, Dorothy Twining *museum director*
Gluck, Abbe R. *lawyer*
Gluck, Carol *history professor*
Godoff, Ann *publishing executive*
Godridge, Leslie V. *bank executive*
Gold, Lois Meyer *artist*
Gold, Sharon Cecile *artist, educator*
Goldbard, Laura E. *lawyer*
Goldberg, Nieca *cardiologist, educator*
Golden, Thelma *curator*
Goldenberg, Elizabeth Leigh *finance company executive*
Goldsmith, Barbara *writer, historian*
Goldstein, Lisa Joy *writer*
Goldstein, Marcia Landweber *lawyer*
Goldstein, Sandra Cara *lawyer*
Goldwater, Edna M. *retired public relations executive*
Golici, Ana *artist*
Gonnerman, Jennifer *writer, journalist*
Gonzalez-Falla, Sondra Gilman *art collector*
Goodale, Toni Krissel *research and development company executive*
Goodkind, Joan Carol *librarian*
Goodman, Allegra *writer*
Goodman, Susan *curator*
Goodwin, Beatrice *nursing educator, consultant*
Gordon, Marsha L. *dermatologist*
Gordon, Mary Catherine *writer*
Gordon, Robbie *television producer*
Goreau, Angeline Wilson *writer*
Gotbaum, Betsy *municipal official*
Goto, Midori *classical violinist*
Gotti, Victoria *columnist, writer, actress*
Gould, Cheryl *broadcast executive*
Gould, Emily *editor*
Gourevitch, Jacqueline *artist*
Grace, Nancy A. *news correspondent, former prosecutor*
Graff, Randy *actress*
Grafstein, Bernice *physiology and neuroscience educator, researcher*
Grafton, Sue *novelist*
Graham, Alma Eleanor *editor, writer, educational consultant*
Grandizio, Lenore *social worker*
Grannan, Katy *photographer*
Granne, Regina *artist, educator*
Grant, Cynthia D. *writer*
Grant Goldman, Pamela *journalist, writer*
Grau, Marcy Beinish *real estate broker, former investment banker*
Gray, Deborah Dolia *business writing consultant*
Grayer, Elizabeth L. *lawyer*
Greene, Adele S. *management consultant*
Greene Oster, Selmaree *medical anthropologist, researcher*
Greenman, Paula S. *lawyer*
Greenthal, Jill A. *investment banker*
Greenwald, Julie *recording industry executive*
Greenwald, Sheila Ellen *writer, illustrator*
Greenzang, Katherine *lawyer, insurance company executive*
Gregory, Robin N. *lawyer*
Grifalconi, Ann *author, illustrator, producer*
Griffith, Nicola *writer*
Griffiths, Jem *singer*
Griffiths, Sylvia Preston *physician, educator*
Grillo, Janet *film producer*
Grimes, Martha *author*
Grimes, Suzanne *publishing executive*
Grody, Deborah *psychologist, director*
Gross, Amy *editor-in-chief*
Gross, Judy E. *publishing executive*
Gross, Karen Charal *lawyer*
Grossman, Elizabeth *lawyer*
Grossman, Melanie *dermatologist*
Grubin, Sharon Ellen *lawyer, former federal judge*
Guilfoyle Newsom, Kimberly Ann *legal commentator*
Gumpert, Lynn *gallery director*
Gund, Agnes *retired museum administrator*
Gure, Anna Valerie *retired social worker, consulting psychotherapist*
Gustafson, Judith *federal association administrator*
Guttmacher, Sally Jeanne *education educator*
Guzman, Kathleen McFadden *antiques appraiser, auctioneer*
Habachy, Suzan Salwa Saba *economist, not-for-profit developer*
Hadas, Rachel *poet, educator*
Haddad, Colleen *marketing executive*
Haegele, Patricia *publishing executive*
Hagberg, Karen L. *lawyer*
Hagin, Nancy *printmaker, painter*
Haigh, Jennifer *writer*
Halberstam, Malvina *law educator, lawyer*
Hall, Lisa Gersh *broadcast executive, lawyer*
Hall, Susan *author, film producer*
Hallingby, Jo Davis *arbitrator*
Halsband, Frances *architect*
Hamilton, Jane *writer*
Hamilton, Laurell K. *writer*
Hamilton, Linda Helen *psychologist*
Hamilton Jackson, Marilyn J. *dancer, educator, choreographer*
Hammond, Jane Rebecca *artist*
Hammond, Lou Rena Charlotte *public relations executive*
Hamoy, Carol *artist*
Hamura, Kaori *artist*
Handley, Siobhan A. *lawyer*
Hann, Lucy E. *radiologist, educator*
Hanson, Jane *newscaster*
Hanson, Jean Elizabeth *lawyer*
Hardwick, Elizabeth *writer*
Hargitay, Mariska Magdolina *actress*
Hariri, Gisue *architect, educator*
Harley, Naomi Hallden *radiologist, educator, environmental scientist*
Harlow, Ruth *lawyer*
Harmon, Jane *theater producer*
Harper, Karen *writer*
Harrington, E.B. *art dealer*
Harris, Arlene *lawyer*
Harris, Carla Ann *investment company executive*
Harris, Carolyn Louise *librarian*
Harris, Julie (Julie Ann Harris) *actress*
Harris, Katherine Safford *speech and hearing educator*
Harris, Rosemary Ann *actress*
Harris, Theresa *lawyer*
Harrison, Rachel *artist*
Harron, Phoebe Zaslove *investment banking executive*
Hart, Clare *information company executive*
Hart, Ellen *writer*
Hart, Mary T. *lawyer*
Hartman, Joan Edna *retired literature educator, provost*
Harvey, Julie L. *artist*
Haskell, Barbara *curator*
Hastings, Deborah *bass guitarist*
Hathaway, Robin *writer*
Haubegger, Christy *media consultant, publishing executive*
Hauser, Rita Eleanore Abrams *lawyer*
Hawkins, Katherine Ann *hematologist, educator, lawyer*
Hayman, Linda C. *lawyer*
Hazzard, Shirley *author*
Head, Elizabeth *lawyer, arbitrator, mediator*
Headley, Heather A. *actress*
Hedgpeth, Kim Roberts *trade association administrator*
Heinzelman, Kris F. *lawyer*
Henderson, Maxine Olive Book (Mrs. William Henderson III) *foundation executive*
Hengen, Nancy L. *lawyer*
Henriques, Diana Blackmon *journalist*
Henry, Sally McDonald *lawyer*
Henschke, Claudia Ingrid *physician, radiologist*
Henzel, Robyn Ellen *artist*
Herman, Dorothy *real estate broker*
Herman, Mindy *broadcast executive*
Hermann, Mildred L. *artist*
Hernstadt, Judith Filenbaum *city planner, real estate executive, broadcast executive*
Herrera, Carolina *fashion designer*
Herrera, Paloma *dancer*
Hershkoff, Helen *law educator*
Hertzig, Margaret E. *psychiatrist*
Herzeca, Lois Friedman *lawyer*
Herzig, Rita Wynne *critical care nurse, soprano*
Hesse, Karen (Karen Sue Hesse) *writer, educator*
Hesselbein, Frances Richards *foundation administrator, writer, editor*
Hewitt, Vivian Ann Davidson (Mrs. John Hamilton Hewitt Jr.) *retired librarian*
Heyde, Martha Bennett *psychologist*
Heyzer, Noeleen *international organization official*
Higgins, Tara A. *lawyer*
Hightower, Caroline Warner *arts management consultant*
Hill, Elizabeth Starr *writer*
Hill, Janine *think-tank associate*
Hill, Marjorie Jean *psychologist, association executive*
Hillenbrand, Laura *writer*
Himmel, Leslie Wohlman *real estate manager*
Hinz, Dorothy Elizabeth *writer, editor, corporate communications specialist*
Hirsch, Roseann Conte *publisher*
Hirschhorn, Rochelle *genetics educator*
Ho, Betty Juenyü Yülin *retired music educator, physiologist, educator*
Hoag, Tami *writer*
Hochlerin, Diane *pediatrician, educator*
Hodes, Martha *history professor, writer*
Hodges, Deborah *investment company executive*
Hoff, Margo *artist, printmaker, muralist*
Hoffman, Alice *writer*
Hoffman, Linda M. *chemist, educator*
Hoffman, Linda R. *social services administrator*
Hoffman, Nancy *art gallery director*
Hoffmann, Elinor R. *lawyer*
Hoffner, Marilyn *university administrator*
Hohauser, Marilyn *artist*
Holden, Sister Margaret Mary *sister*
Holland, Jimmie C. *psychiatrist, educator*
Holmes, Anna-Marie *ballerina*
Holmgren, Anna *psychiatrist*
Holton, Lisa *publishing executive*
Holtzman, Elizabeth *lawyer*
Hopkins, Deborah C. *diversified financial services company executive*
Horn, Karen Nicholson *investment company executive, former bank executive*
Horn, Roni *artist*
Horowitz, Frances Degen *academic administrator, psychology educator*
Hort, Susan *art collector*
Horvath, Polly *writer*
Hotchner, Holly *museum director, curator, conservator*
Hould-Ward, Ann *theatrical costume designer*
Howard, Bonnie *bank executive*
Howe, Florence *literature educator, writer, publisher*
Howe, Tina *playwright*
Howson, Tamar D. *pharmaceutical executive*
Hricik, Lorraine E. *bank executive*
Hrubec, Jane M. *advertising executive*
Hudes, Nana Brenda *marketing professional*
Hughes, Brigid *former editor*
Hughes, Julie *casting director, owner*
Hull, Cathy *artist, illustrator*
Humphreys, Josephine *writer*
Hunter, Patricia O. *psychologist*
Hurley, Cheryl Joyce *book publishing executive*
Huttner, Constance S. *lawyer*
Huxtable, Ada Louise *architecture critic*
Hynde, Chrissie *musician*
Hynes, Aedhmar *public relations executive*
Hynes, Patricia M. *lawyer*
Ibi, Keiko *film director*
Ilse-Neuman, Ursula *curator*
Iqbal, Syma U. *information technology executive*
Iskenderian, Mary Ellen *bank executive*
Istomin, Marta Casals *retired school president, performing company executive*
Ivanick, Carol W. Trencher *lawyer*
Jacker, Corinne Litvin *playwright, writer*
Jackson, Anne (Anne Jackson Wallach) *actress*
Jackson, Wynelle Redding *educational association administrator, accountant, tax specialist*
Jackson McCabe, Jewell *not-for-profit developer*
Jacob, Valerie Ford *lawyer*
Jacquette, Yvonne Helene *artist*
Jaffe, Helene D. *lawyer*
Jaffe, Irma Blumenthal *art educator*
Jaffe, Susan *ballerina*
Jamison, Jayne *publishing executive*
Jamison, Judith *dancer*
Jance, J.A. (Judith Ann Jance) *writer*
Jasso, Guillermina *sociologist, educator*
Jean-Baptiste, Tricia *public relations executive*
Jeanbart-Lorenzotti, Eva *retail executive*
Jefferson, Denise *dance school director*
Jefferson, Kristin Marie *art dealer, consultant, film producer, writer*
Jelinek, Vera *dean*
Jett, Joan (Joan Larkin) *musician*
Jeynes, Mary Kay *college dean*
Jhabvala, Ruth Prawer *writer*
Johansen, Iris *writer*
Johnson, Betsey Lee *fashion designer*
Johnson, Brooke Bailey *broadcast executive*
Johnson, Cecile Ryden (Mrs. Philip Johnson) *artist*
Johnson, Christine Toy *actress, writer*
Johnson, Suzanne M. Nora *diversified financial services company executive, lawyer*
Johnson, Verdia E. *marketing professional*
Johnson, Vickie *professional basketball player*
Jonas, Ruth Haber *psychologist*
Jones, Barbara S. *federal judge*
Jones, Diana Wynne *writer*
Jones, Laurie Lynn *magazine editor*
Jones, Sarah *actress, playwright, poet*
Jones Reynolds, Star (Starlet Marie Jones) *television host, lawyer, former prosecutor*
Jong, Erica Mann *writer*
Jordan, Nora Margaret *lawyer*
Josell, Jessica (Jessica Wechsler) *public relations executive*
Juliber, Lois D. *manufacturing executive*
Jung, Andrea *cosmetics company executive*
Jung, Doris *soprano*
Jurka, Edith Mila *psychiatrist, researcher*
Just, Gemma Rivoli *retired advertising executive*
Just, Julia Barnett *newspaper editor*
Kadohata, Cynthia *writer*
Kagan, Ilse Echt *librarian, researcher, historian*
Kagan, Julia Lee *magazine editor*
Kaggen, Lois Sheila *non-profit organization executive, advocate*
Kahan, Phyllis Irene *language educator, writer, editor, media consultant*
Kahn, Nancy Valerie *publishing and entertainment executive, consultant*
Kaish, Luise Clayborn *sculptor, painter, educator*
Kakutani, Michiko *critic*
Kalajian-Lagani, Donna *publishing executive*
Kalayjian, Anie *psychotherapist, educator, nurse, consultant*
Kalik, Mildred *lawyer*
Kalinich, Lila Joyce *psychiatrist, educator*
Kallir, Jane Katherine *art gallery director, author*
Kamali, Norma *fashion designer*
Kambour, Annaliese Spofford *lawyer, media company executive*
Kamen, Cheryl L. Heiberg *social worker*
Kamerman, Sheila Brody *social work educator*
Kamm, Linda Heller *lawyer*
Kan, Diana Artemis Mann Shu *painter, art educator, writer*
Kanakaredes, Melina *actress*
Kanick, Virginia *retired radiologist*
Kanter, Stacy J. *lawyer*
Kantor, Jodi M. *editor*
Kapelman, Barbara Ann *internist, hepatologist, gastroenterologist, educator*
Kaplan, Cathy M. *lawyer*
Kaplan, Jill Rebecca *publishing executive*
Kaplan, Madeline *legal administrator*
Kaplan, Roberta A. *lawyer*
Karan, Donna (Donna Faske) *fashion designer*
Kardish, Ruth *retired elementary school educator*
Kardon, Janet *museum director*
Karlin, Susan *design company executive*
Karmali, Rashida Alimahomed *lawyer*
Karon, Jan (Janice Meredith Wilson) *writer*
Karp, Roberta Schuhalter *retail executive, lawyer*
Karpen, Marian Joan *financial executive*
Karr, Kathleen *writer*
Karsen, Sonja Petra *retired literature educator*
Kasakove, Susan *interior designer*
Kasirer, Suri *lobbyist*
Kassel, Catherine M. *community, maternal, and women's health nurse, consultant*
Kassel, Terry *human resources specialist*

Kassel, Virginia Weltmer *television producer, scriptwriter*
Katz, Esther *historian, educator*
Katz, Jane *swimming educator*
Katz, Lois Anne *internist, nephrologist*
Katz, Sharon *lawyer*
Katz-Bearnot, Sherry P. *psychiatrist, educator*
Katzowitz Shenfield, Lauren *philanthropy consultant*
Kaufman, Amy *film company executive, film producer*
Kaufman, Bel *author, educator*
Kavaler, Rebecca *writer*
Kavaler-Adler, Susan *clinical psychologist, psychoanalyst*
Kearse, Amalya Lyle *federal judge*
Keating, Catherine *bank executive*
Keating, Isabel *actress*
Keefer, Elizabeth J. *lawyer*
Kehret, Peg *writer*
Kellar, Charlotte Avrutis *writer*
Keller, Marthe *artist, painter*
Kelley, Darcy B. *biology professor*
Kelley, Kitty *writer*
Kelly, Anastasia D. (Stasia Kelly) *telecommunications industry executive, lawyer*
Kelly, Mary *sculptor*
Keneally, Kathryn Marie *lawyer*
Kennedy, Adrienne Lita *playwright*
Kent, Julie *dancer, actress, model*
Kent, Linda Gail *dancer*
Kent, Susan *library director, consultant*
Kerz, Louise *historian*
Keys, Alicia (Alicia Augello Cook) *vocalist, musician, songwriter*
Keys, Elizabeth A. *accountant, director*
Khidekel, Regina P. *art historian, curator, educator*
Kim, Willa *costume designer*
Kim, Yunjim (Yun-jin Kim) *actress*
Kimber, Karen Beecher *law educator*
Kinberg, Judy *television producer, television director*
Kind, Susan J. *fundraiser*
King, Alison *lawyer*
King, Marcia Gygli *artist*
Kinney, Catherine R. *stock exchange executive*
Kirnos, Dina *technology support professional*
Kirschenbaum, Lisa L. *portfolio manager, financial advisor*
Kisch, Gloria *sculptor*
Kiser, Molly *musician*
Kitahata-Sporn, Amy *movement educator*
Klagsbrun, Francine *writer, editor*
Klein, Cynthia *art appraiser*
Klein, Laura Colin *publishing executive*
Klein, Nancy Lynn *fine jewelry company owner, consultant*
Knapp, Amy K. *insurance company executive*
Knapp, Ellen M. *financial company executive*
Kohlmann, Susan J. *lawyer*
Kolata, Gina *journalist*
Kolbert, Elizabeth Ruth *journalist*
Koopersmith, Kim *lawyer*
Kopenhaver, Patricia Ellsworth *podiatrist*
Koplovitz, Kay *television network executive*
Kopp, Wendy *educational association administrator*
Koppelman, Dorothy Myers *artist, consultant*
Korff, Phyllis G. *lawyer*
Korot, Beryl *artist*
Korry, Alexandra D. *lawyer*
Korsten, Susan Snyder *science educator*
Koster, Elaine *publishing executive*
Kostova, Elizabeth *writer*
Koteff, Ellen *periodical editor*
Kotuk, Andrea Mikotajuk *public relations executive, writer*
Kouffman, Paulette *psychologist*
Kourides, Ione Anne *endocrinologist, researcher, educator*
Kove, Miriam *psychotherapist*
Kozak, Harley Jane *actress, writer*
Kozik, Susan S. *information technology executive*
Kozloff, Joyce *artist*
Kozlowski, Cheryl M. *fixed income analyst*
Kraemer, Lillian Elizabeth *lawyer*
Kram, Shirley Wohl *federal judge*
Kramer, Elissa Lipcon *nuclear medicine physician, educator*
Kramer, Linda Konheim *curator, art historian*
Krantz, Judith Tarcher *novelist*
Kraus, Norma Jean *human resources executive*
Krawcheck, Sallie L. *bank executive*
Krawitz, Rhoda Nayor *clinical psychologist, psychoanalyst*
Kreek, Mary Jeanne *physician*
Krementz, Jill *photographer, author*
Krill, Kay (Katherine Lawther Krill) *apparel executive*
Krinsky, Carol Herselle *art historian, educator*
Krizer, Jodi *performing arts executive*
Kropf, Susan J. *retired cosmetics executive*
Kruger, Barbara *artist, art critic*
Kuck, Lea Haber *lawyer*
Kugelman, Stephanie *advertising executive*
Kujawski, Elizabeth Szancer *art curator, consultant*
Kunes, Ellen *magazine executive*
Kuo, Charlene *finance professional*
Kurli, Madhavi *ophthalmologist*
Kurman, Juta *music educator*
Kurz, Diana *artist, educator*
Kurzweil, Edith *social sciences educator, editor*
Kusmierski, Janet Louise *painter, graphics designer, illustrator*
Kutosh, Sue *artist*
Kuttler, Judith Esther *retired psychotherapist*
Kuyper, Joan Carolyn *foundation administrator*
Kyriakou, Linda Grace *communications executive*
LaBelle, Patti (Patricia Louise Holte) *singer, entertainer*
Lachman, Marguerite Leanne *real estate investment advisor*
Lambert, Judith A. Ungar *lawyer*
Landau, Annette Henkin *writer, librarian*
Landro, Laura *editor*
Lane, Nancy *advocate, editor*
Lang, Mary Ann *special education educator, administrator*
Lang, Pearl *dancer, choreographer*
Langan, Marie-Noelle Suzanne *cardiologist, educator*
Lange, Liz *apparel designer, director*
Langford, Laura Sue *corporate financial executive*
LaNicca Albanese, Ellen *public relations executive*
Lanpher, Katherine *radio personality, columnist*
Lanquetot, E. Roxanne *retired special education educator*
Lansner, Gabrielle *choreographer, dancer, performing company executive, actress*
Lanyon, Ellen (Mrs. Roland Ginzel) *artist, educator*
LaRose, Melba Lee *performing company executive, actress, playwright, theater director*
Larrick, Pamela Maphis *marketing executive*
Lassiter, Sheri L. *insurance company executive*
Lategno-Nicholas, Cristyne *travel company executive*
Lauber, Patricia Grace *writer*
Lauder, Aerin *cosmetics executive*
Lauder, Evelyn H. *cosmetics executive*
Lauder, Jo Carole *art association administrator*
Laughlin, Linda R. *psychoanalyst, psychotherapist*
Lauro, Shirley Mezvinsky *playwright, educator*
Lavori, Nora *real estate executive, lawyer*
Law, Sylvia A. *law educator*
Lawhon, Charla *editor*
Lawrence, Lauren *psychotherapist, writer*
Lawrence, Nina *publishing executive*
Laybourne, Geraldine B. *broadcast executive*
Lazarus, Adrienne *retail executive*
Lazarus, Shelly (Rochelle Braff Lazarus) *advertising executive*
Leahey, Lynn *editor-in-chief*
Lebenthal, Alexandra *investment firm executive*
Lederman, Sally Ann *nutritionist, researcher*
Lee, Amy *singer*
Lee, Catherine *sculptor, painter*
Lee, Frances Helen *editor*
Lee, Helie *writer*
Lee, Sally A. *editor-in-chief*
Lee, Vivian S. *radiologist*
Leech, Diane J. *publisher*
Leech, Katharine (Kitty Leech) *costume designer, educator*
Leeds, Dorothy *author, lecturer, consultant*
Leeman, Eve *psychiatrist*
Leet, Mildred Robbins *social welfare administrator, consultant*
Leff, Sandra H. *art gallery director, consultant*
Legato, Marianne *internist, medical educator*
Leibovitz, Annie *photographer*
Leiman, Joan Maisel *university administrator, hospital administrator*
Leive, Cynthia *editor-in-chief*
Lekberg, Barbara *sculptor*
Lemos, Margaret H. *lawyer*
L'Engle, Madeleine (Mrs. Hugh Franklin) *writer*
Lenox, Adriane *actress*
Lenz, Dolly (Idaliz Dolly Lenz) *real estate broker*
Lerner, Harriet Goldhor *psychologist, writer*
Lerner, Jill *architect*
Lerner, Sandra *artist*
Lesk, Ann Berger *lawyer*
Leven, Ann Ruth *financial consultant*
Levi, Vicki Gold *picture editor, historical consultant, writer, actress*
Levin, Gail *writer, educator, photographer*
Levin, Janna J. *physicist, educator*
Levine, Ellen R. *editor-in-chief*
Levine, Naomi Bronheim *academic administrator*
Levine, Sherrie *conceptual artist*
Levinson, Rascha *psychotherapist*
Lewin, Betsy R. *illustrator*
Lewis, Marcia *actress*
Lewyn, Ann Salfeld *retired English as a second language educator*
Liden, Hanna *photographer*
Lieberman, Nancy Ann *lawyer*
Liebman, Carol Bensinger *lawyer, educator*
Lil' Kim, (Kimberly Denise Jones) *rap artist, actress*
Lilly, Evangeline *actress*
Lindblom, Marjorie Press *lawyer*
Link, Nina Beth *publishing executive*
Lippman, Donna Robin *counselor*
Lippman, Laura *writer*
Lippman, Sharon Rochelle *art historian, filmmaker, art therapist*
Lipsky, Pat *artist*
Lipton, Jackie F. *artist, educator*
Lipton, Joan Elaine *advertising executive*
Lisle, Laurie *author*
Litwack, Arlene Debra *psychotherapist, psychoanalyst, educator, consultant*
Livingston, Debra A. *law educator*
Lloyd, Jean *retired early childhood educator*
Loeb, Lisa *singer, lyricist*
Løj, Ellen Margrethe *ambassador*
London, Nora Eleonor *foundation administrator*
Longley, Marjorie Watters *newspaper executive*
Loomis, Carol J. *journalist*
Lopez, Priscilla *actress*
Lorber, Barbara Heyman *communications executive, event producer*
Lorch, Maristella De Panizza *writer, educator*
Lord, M. G. *writer*
Loren, Pamela *telecommunications executive*
LoSchiavo, Linda Bosco *library director*
Loss, Margaret Ruth *lawyer*
Louizos, Anna Alexandra *set designer*
Love-Hassell, Esther Boyer *special education educator, consultant*
Lowry, Marcia Robinson *legal association administrator*
Lubetski, Edith Esther *librarian*
Lucci, Susan *actress*
Luckman, Sharon Gersten *arts administrator*
Lunardini, Christine Anne *writer, historian, school administrator*
LuPone, Patti *actress*
Luria, Mary Mercer *lawyer*
Lurie, Alison *writer*
Lyman, Peggy *artistic director, dancer, choreographer, educator*
Lynch, Florence *art gallery director*
Lynch, Loretta E. *lawyer, former prosecutor*
Lyne, Susan Markham *multi-media company executive, former broadcast executive*
Lynn, Judith *opera singer, artist, voice educator*
Lyons, Bridget Gellert *language educator*
MacBain, Louise T. Blouin *publishing executive*
Macer-Story, Eugenia Ann *writer*
MacGowan, Sandra Firelli *publishing executive, consultant*
Mack, Phyllis Green *retired librarian*
Mackey, Patricia Elaine *university librarian*
Mackler, Tina *artist*
Macklin, Elizabeth Jean *poet, editor*
MacLachlan, Patricia *author*
Madden-Lunsford, Kerry Elizabeth *writer*
Maddow, Rachel *radio personality, political activist*
Maffei, Susan Martin *artist, educator*
Magee-Egan, Pauline Cecilia *psychology professor, management educator*
Mahoney, Margaret Ellerbe *foundation executive*
Makowiecka, Maria Hanna *literature educator, educator*
Malamud, Deborah C. *law educator*
Maldonado-Bear, Rita Marinita *economist, educator*
Malfa, Frances *lawyer*
Malihan, Amie A. *physician*
Malman, Laurie L. *law educator*
Mamlok, Ursula *composer, educator*
Mandel, Carol *librarian*
Mandracchia, Violet Ann Palermo *psychotherapist, educator*
Mann, Aimee *singer, songwriter*
Marafioti, Kayalyn A. *lawyer*
Marcus, Maria Lenhoff *lawyer, educator*
Margalith, Helen Margaret *retired librarian*
Margolin, Jean Spielberg *artist*
Marks, Leah Ruth *judge*
Marks, Lillian Shapiro *retired secretarial studies educator, writer, editor*
Marshak, Hilary Wallach *psychotherapist, small business owner*
Marshall, Kathleen *choreographer, theater director*
Marshall, Sheila Hermes *lawyer*
Marshall, Simone Verniere *psychologist, psychoanalyst*
Martin, Judith Sylvia *journalist*
Martin, Leslie *performing arts association administrator*
Martin, Mary-Anne *art gallery owner*
Martínez-López, Carmen Leonor *management consultant, educator*
Martone, Patricia Ann *lawyer*
Maryles, Daisy *editor*
Maryschuk, Olga Yaroslava *artist, executive secretary*
Marzigliano, Tammy *lawyer*
Maslin, Janet *critic*
Mason, Bobbie Ann *writer*
Mason, Carol Ann *medical educator*
Mason, Linda *broadcast executive*
Massingale, Faith L. *bank executive*
Masterson, Ellen Hornberger *accountant*
Matera, Cristina *gynecologist, educator*
Matorin, Susan *social work administrator, educator*
Maxwell, Carla Lena *dancer, choreographer, educator*
May, Gita *literature educator*
Mayer, Eve Orlans *marketing professional, writer*
Mayer, Rosemary *artist*
Mayerson, Sandra Elaine *lawyer*
Mayes, Elaine *photographer, educator*
Mayleas, Ruth Rothschild *foundation administrator*
Maynard, Virginia Madden *foundation administrator*
Mayo-Johnston, Julia A. *psychiatry professor, psychotherapist*
Mays, Linda *performing arts association administrator*
Maysilles, Elizabeth *speech communication professional, educator*
Mazzenga, Carolyn *accountant*
Mazzo, Kay *ballet dancer, educator*
McAniff, Nora P. *publishing executive*
McAveney, Mary Susan *marketing executive*
McCabe, Mary F. *marketing professional*
McCaffrey, Carlyn Sundberg *lawyer*
McCarthy, Lisa *communications executive*
McCarthy, Pamela Maffei *magazine editor*
McCarty, V. K. *publishing executive, chaplain, librarian*
McCaslin, Teresa Eve *human resources specialist*
McCorduck, Pamela Ann *writer, educator*
McCormack, Patricia Marie *retired thoracic surgeon*
McCoy, Jennifer *artistic collaborator, educator*
McCrary, Eugenia Lester (Mrs. Dennis Daughtry McCrary) *civic worker, writer*
McDermott, Alice *writer*
McDonald, Audra Ann *actress, vocalist*
McFadden, Cynthia Graham *news correspondent, journalist*
McFadden, Mary Josephine *fashion industry executive*
McFarland, Kathleen Troia (KT McFarland) *government defense consultant*
McGarry, Martha E. *lawyer*
McGinn, Eileen *public health service officer, researcher*
McGowen, Lorraine S. *lawyer*
McGrady, Phyllis *television producer*
McGrath, Judy (Judith Ann McGrath) *broadcast executive*
McHale, Catherine A. *lawyer*
McHugh, Caril Eisenstein Dreyfuss *art dealer, art gallery director, consultant*
McKenzie, Mary Beth *artist*
McKerrow, Amanda *ballet dancer*
McLaurin, Toni Marie *orthopedist, surgeon, educator*
McNally, Michele *editor, photographer*
McNamara, Mary Ellen *not-for-profit executive*
McNaught, Judith *writer*
McNeely, Juanita *artist*
McNeil, Wendy Lawson-Johnston *foundation administrator*
McNutt, Edith Richards *psychiatrist*
McQuown, Judith Hershkowitz *writer, consultant, financial planner*
Meadow, Lynne (Carolyn Meadow) *theater producer*
Mechaneck, Ruth Sara *clinical psychologist*
Meed, Rita Goldwasser *clinical psychologist*
Meehan, Sandra Gotham *corporate financial executive, consultant, writer*
Meeker, Mary G. *brokerage house executive*
Meeropol, Rachel *lawyer*
Mehretu, Julie *artist*
Mehta, Linn Cary *literature educator*
Meili, Barbara *lawyer*
Meiselas, Susan Clay *photographer*
Mello, Dawn *retail executive*
Mendelson, Barbara R. *lawyer*
Menkes, Sheryl R. *lawyer*
Menton, Tanya Lia *lawyer, educator*
Merchant, Natalie Anne *musician, singer*
Merrill, Susan L. *lawyer*
Mertens, Joan R. *museum curator, art historian*
Metzger, Evelyn Borchard *artist*
Meyer, Janis M. *lawyer*
Meyer, Pearl *compensation executive consultant*
Meyers, Dale (Mrs. Mario Cooper) *artist*
Michelson, Gertrude Geraldine *retired retail executive*
Middlebrook, Diane Wood *English language educator, writer*
Mikumo, Akiko *lawyer*
Mildvan, Donna *infectious diseases physician*
Milford, Nancy Winston *writer, literature educator*
Miller, Barbara Kenton *retired librarian*
Miller, Beth McCarthy *television director*
Miller, Caroline *editor-in-chief*
Miller, Heidi G. *diversified financial company executive*
Miller, Lisa Friedman *psychology educator*
Miller, Nancy Suzanne *technology consultant, artist*
Miller, Nicole Jacqueline *fashion designer*
Miller, Ruby Sills *retired gerontologist*
Miller-Sydney, Audrey Yvonne *music educator*
Mills, Stephanie Ellen *writer*
Milman, Doris Hope *retired pediatrician, psychiatrist, educator*
Min, Janice Byung *editor-in-chief*
Minarik, Else Holmelund (Bigart Minarik) *author*
Mirrer, Louise *language educator, consultant*
Misher Stenzler, Shari *youth activities organization administrator*
Mitchell, Helen deRamus *public health administrator*
Mitchell, Mary Jenkins *public health service officer*
Mitchell, Patricia Edenfield *broadcast museum administrator*
Mogull, Kim *real estate company executive*
Mohler, Mary Gail *magazine editor*
Molholt, Pat *academic administrator, associate dean*
Mones, Joan Michele *pathologist*
Monk, Debra *actress*
Monk, Meredith Jane *artistic director, composer, choreographer, filmmaker*
Monk Kidd, Sue *writer*
Montero, Sylvia *pharmaceutical executive*
Moomjy, Maureen O'Brien *surgeon, educator*
Moore, Alma C. *publishing executive, consultant*
Moore, Ann S. *publishing executive*
Moore, Anne *physician*
Moore, Fay *artist*
Moore, Rachel Suzanne *performing company executive, dancer*
Moran, Juliette M. *retired chemicals executive*
Moran, Patricia *lawyer*
Morawetz, Cathleen Synge *mathematician*
Morgan, Florence Murdina *nurse*
Morgan, Mary E. *publishing executive*
Morgenson, Gretchen C. *reporter*
Morris, Valerie *news correspondent*
Morrison, Stacy Lynne *magazine editor*
Mortimer, Ann O. *executive secretary*
Mosbacher, Georgette Paulsin *cosmetics executive*
Moscatt, Angeline Alice *librarian*
Moskowitz, Randi Zucker *nurse*
Moss, Sara E. *delivery service executive, lawyer*
Moss-Salentijn, Letty (Aleida Moss-Salentijn) *anatomist, educator*
Moulton, Sara *chef, magazine editor*
Moyers, Judith Davidson *television producer*
Muller, Jennifer *choreographer, dancer*
Muller, Marcia *writer*
Mundinger, Mary O'Neil *nursing educator*
Munro, Alice *writer*
Munro, Eleanor *writer, lecturer*
Murney, Julia *actress*
Murphy, Carolyn *model*
Murphy, Catherine *painter*
Murphy, Donna *actress*
Murphy, Elva Glenn *executive assistant*
Murphy, Helen *recording industry executive*
Murphy, Patrice Ann (Pat Murphy) *writer*
Murphy, Rosemary *actress*
Murphy, Stacia *health service association executive*
Murray, Eileen K. *investment company executive*
Murray, Elizabeth *artist*
Murray, Judith *artist*
Muse, Martha Twitchell *foundation executive*
Myerberg, Marcia *investment banker*
Myers, Michelle *publishing executive*
Nadler-Hurvich, Hedda Carol *public relations executive*
Nafisi, Azar *humanities educator*
Nair, Mira *film director, film producer*
Nakhle, Djenane *psychologist*
Nascimento, Ana Paula *entrepreneur, food service executive*
Nass, Deanna Rose *counselor, professor*
Nass, Ruth *pediatric neurologist*
Natori, Josie Cruz (Josefina Almeda Cruz Natori) *apparel executive*
Naughton, Eileen *Internet company executive*
Navarra, Tova *writer*
Nazario, Sonia *reporter*
Nearing, Vivienne W. *lawyer*
Neidich, Brooke Garber *foundation administrator, art patron*
Nelson, Alison *food products executive*
Nelson, Anne *playwright, former reporter*
Nelson, Barbara Anne *judge*
Nelson, Joyce M. *medical association administrator*
Nelson, Kathy *broadcast executive*
Nelson, Sara *editor*
Nestle, Marion *nutritionist, educator*

Neugebauer, Cynthia A. *lawyer*
Neuner, Lynn K. *lawyer*
New, Maria Iandolo *pediatrician, educator*
Newberg, Esther *literary agent*
Newman, Geraldine Anne *advertising executive*
Newstead, Jennifer G. *lawyer*
Niccolini, Dianora *photographer*
Nichols, Carol D. *real estate professional*
Nichols, Edie Diane *real estate broker*
Nichols, Kyra *ballerina*
Noce, Donna *retail executive*
Nochlin, Linda *art history educator*
Noonan, Peggy *writer*
Norell, Judith Regina *small business owner, musician, political administrator*
Norman, Christina *broadcast executive*
North, Julie A. *lawyer*
Northup, Nancy Jean *lawyer*
Norville, Deborah Anne *news correspondent*
Novogrod, Nancy Gerstein *editor*
Nugent, Nelle *theater, film and television producer*
Nusbacher, Gloria Weinberg *lawyer*
Oates, Joyce Carol *writer*
Oberfield, Sharon Elefant *pediatric endocrinologist*
Oberlander, Eryn L. *psychiatrist, preventive medicine physician*
Oberly, Kathryn Anne *lawyer, diversified financial services company executive*
Obler, Geri *small business owner, artist, educator*
O'Brien, Catherine Louise *museum administrator*
O'Brien, Clare *lawyer*
O'Bryan, C. Jill *visual artist, writer*
Ochs, Carol Rebecca *theologian, writer, theology studies educator, philosopher*
O'Connor, Sandra Day *retired United States Supreme Court Justice*
O'Connor Vos, Lynn *healthcare group executive*
Ofri, Danielle *internist*
Ogden, Peggy A. *retired personnel director*
Ogut, Bilge Ayse *investment advisor*
Olds, Sharon *poet*
Olinger, Carla D(ragan) *medical advertising executive*
Olivier, Jeanne C. *lawyer*
O'Looney, Patricia Anne *medical association administrator*
Olsen, Tillie Lerner *author*
Olshan, Regina *lawyer*
O'Neil, Robyn *artist*
O'Neill, Judith D. *lawyer*
O'Neill, June Ellenoff *economist*
O'Neill McGivern, Diane *nursing educator*
Ono, Yoko *conceptual artist, singer, recording artist*
Openshaw, Jennifer *finance company executive*
Oppenheim, Sara E. *psychologist*
Orender, Donna *sports association executive*
Ortega, Melissa Lee *researcher*
Osborn, June Elaine *pediatrician, microbiologist, educator, foundation administrator*
Osborne, Mary Pope *writer*
O'Shea, Elizabeth Therese *counselor*
O'Toole, Patricia Ellen *writer, educator*
Ottombrino, Lois Kathryn *lawyer*
Owen, Sylvia *interior design executive*
Pakter, Jean *maternal and child health consultant*
Paladino, Jeannette E. *advertising executive, public relations executive*
Pall, Ellen Jane *writer*
Palma, Laura *lawyer*
Palmer, Catherine E. *lawyer*
Palmer, Jessica *diversified financial services company executive*
Pandolfi, Frances *health facility administrator*
Panken, Shirley *psychologist*
Papalia, Diane Ellen *humanities educator*
Pappas, Eva *psychologist, psychoanalyst*
Paretsky, Sara N. *writer*
Park, Barbara *writer*
Park, Cynthia *sociology educator, consultant*
Park, Linda Sue *writer*
Parker, Alice *composer*
Parker, Kelley D. *lawyer*
Parkes, Jacqueline *marketing executive*
Parkhurst, Carolyn *writer*
Parsons, Estelle *actress, director, theater producer*
Passlof, Pat *artist, educator*
Patchett, Ann *writer*
Paterson, Katherine Womeldorf *writer*
Payton-Wright, Pamela *actress*
Pearl, Mary Corliss *wildlife conservationist*
Peetz, Karen B. *bank executive*
Pennisi, Liz *women's health nurse*
Peretsman, Nancy B. *investment banker*
Perez, Wilma *microbiologist, researcher*
Persell, Caroline Hodges *sociologist, educator, author, researcher, consultant*
Peruo, Marsha Hope *artist*
Pesin, Ella Michele *journalist, public relations executive*
Pesner, Carole Manishin *art gallery owner*
Peters, Bernadette (Bernadette Lazzara) *actress*
Peters, Roberta *soprano*
Pfeifer, Tracy M. *plastic surgeon*
Pfeiffer, Jane Cahill *former broadcasting company executive, consultant*
Phair, Liz *vocalist*
Phillips, Karen A. *urban planner*
Phillips, Pamela Kim *lawyer*
Phillips, Reneé *writer*
Phillips, Tari *professional basketball player*
Picard, Leslie *publishing executive*
Piligian, Georgette A. *insurance company executive*
Pineda, Patricia Salas *lawyer*
Pines, Lori L. *lawyer*
Pinkwater, Julie *publishing executive*
Pistor, Katharina *law educator*
Pitt, Jane *medical educator*
Piven, Frances Fox *political scientist, educator*
Platzner, Linda *publisher*
Plavinskaya, Anna Dmitrievna *artist*
Plevan, Bettina B. *lawyer*
Podolsky, Andrea G. *lawyer*
Poehler, Amy *comedienne, actress*
Pogue, Velvie Anne *nephrologist, educator*
Polacco, Patricia *writer, illustrator*
Polenz, Joanna Magda *psychiatrist*
Polevoy, Nancy Tally *lawyer, social worker, genealogist*
Polin, Jane L. *foundation official*
Pollack, Jessica Glass *lawyer*
Pollard, Veronica *automotive executive*
Pollock-O'Brien, Louise Mary *public relations executive*
Polsky, Cynthia Hazen *artist, art collector, philanthropist*
Pomerantz, Charlotte *writer*
Pool, Mary Jane *writer, editor*
Porter, Liliana Alicia *artist, photographer, painter, printmaker, filmmaker*
Portnow, Marjorie *painter*
Posin, Kathryn Olive *choreographer*
Potash, Marlin Sue *psychologist, educator*
Poulet, Anne Litle *museum director, art historian*
Povlitz, Jennifer *investment company executive*
Powel, Jane C. *educational consultant, elementary school educator*
Powell, Julie *writer*
Poynor, Elizabeth Ann *surgeon, researcher*
Preska, Loretta A. *federal judge*
Press, Michelle *editor*
Preston, Frances Williams *music company executive*
Price, Leontyne (Mary Violet Leontyne Price) *retired concert and opera singer, soprano*
Prieto, Monique N. *artist*
Prives, Carol *biologist, educator*
Procope, Ernesta Gertrude *insurance company executive*
Proctor, Georganne C. *investment company executive*
Prutzman, Penelope Elizabeth *elementary school educator*
Pulos, Virginia Kate *actress, consultant*
Purcell, Karen Barlar *naturopathic physician, nutritionist, opera singer, writer*
Putnam, Keri *film company executive*
Pyle, Rolanda *social worker*
Quackenbush, Margery Clouser *psychoanalyst, researcher*
Queler, Eve *conductor*
Quiles, Esther *art educator*
Quilter, Deborah *writer, consultant, educator*
Quindlen, Anna *journalist, writer*
Quin-Harkin, Janet Elizabeth (Rhys Bowen) *writer*
Quinlan, Mary Lou *former advertising executive, consultant*
Quinn, Alice Freeman *literature educator*
Quinn, Christine Callaghan *councilwoman*
Quinn, Jane Bryant *journalist, writer*
Quinn, Yvonne Susan *lawyer*
Quiñones Keber, Eloise *art historian, educator*
Quisgard, Liz Whitney *artist, sculptor*
Quivers, Robin *radio personality*
Rabb, Harriet Schaffer *academic administrator, lawyer*
Rabiner, Susan *editor*
Rabinowitz, Dorothy *television critic*
Radin, Amy Janine *financial services company executive*
Rafferty, Emily Kernan *museum administrator*
Ramirez, Maria Fiorini *financial consultant*
Ramirez, Sara *actress*
Ramirez, Tina *artistic director*
Randel, Jane Ann *retail executive*
Ranney-Marinelli, Alesia *lawyer*
Rappaport, Linda Ellen *lawyer*
Rathmann, Peggy *writer, illustrator*
Ravdin, Lisa Dawn *neuropsychologist*
Raven, Abbe *broadcast executive*
Ravitch, Diane Silvers *historian, educator, writer, government official*
Ray, Rachael *chef, television personality*
Raymond, Dorothy Sarnoff *communications consultant, former actress, former singer*
Rchl, Beatrice Clair *editor, art historian*
Reals Ellig, Janice *marketing professional, human resources specialist*
Recanati, Dina *artist*
Redel, Victoria *writer, poet, educator*
Redgrave, Lynn *actress*
Redmond, Catherine *artist, educator*
Reese, Tracy *fashion designer*
Reeves, Dianne *singer*
Regan, Judith Terrance *publishing executive*
Reges, Marianna Alice *marketing executive*
Rehr, Helen *social worker*
Reichl, Ruth Molly *editor-in-chief*
Reichman, Bonnie S. *oncologist*
Reidy, Carolyn Kroll *publisher*
Reif Cohen, Jessica *broadcast executive*
Reig, June Wilson *scriptwriter, television director, television producer*
Reininghaus, Ruth *retired artist*
Reinking, Ann H. *dancer, actress*
Reisman, Sharyl A. *lawyer*
Reiss, Dale Anne *corporate financial executive*
Remington, Deborah Williams *artist*
Ren, Christine *surgeon*
Renna, Cathy *communications executive, activist*
Resnick, Rhoda Brodowsky *psychotherapist*
Resnick, Rosalind *multimedia executive*
Restani, Jane A. *federal judge*
Reuben, Gloria *actress, singer*
Reynard, Muriel Joyce *lawyer*
Rhoads, Geraldine Emeline *editor, consultant*
Rhodes, Randi *radio personality*
Rhone, Sylvia Marie Miller *recording industry executive*
Rice, Barbara Lynn *stage manager*
Rice, Luanne *writer*
Rich, Adrienne *poet*
Richard, Virginia Rynne *lawyer*
Richards, Cecile *healthcare network executive*
Richardson, Grace Elizabeth *consumer products company executive*
Riches, Wendy *magazine publishing executive*
Richman, Sophia *psychologist*
Ridgway, Delissa Anne *federal judge*
Rifka, Judy *artist, educator*
Rifkind, Arleen B. *pharmacologist, researcher, educator*
Rigg, Dame Diana *actress*
Ringgold, Faith *artist*
Ritch, Kathleen *diversified financial services company executive*
Ritter, Ann L. *lawyer*
Ritter, Jodi Gottesfeld *lawyer*
Rivera, Chita (Conchita del Rivero) *actress, singer, dancer*
Rizer, Maggie *model*
Roach, Margaret *editor-in-chief*
Robb, Kathy McCleskey *lawyer*
Robbins, Carrie Fishbein *costume designer, educator*
Robbins, Lillian Cukier *psychology educator*
Roberts, Nora *writer*
Robertson, Anne Ferratt *language educator, researcher*
Robfogel, Susan Salitan *lawyer*
Robinson, Barbara Paul *lawyer*
Robinson, Janet L. *publishing executive*
Robinson, Marilynne *writer*
Robinson, Roxana Barry *writer, art historian*
Robison, Paula Judith *flutist*
Rocchi, Robin Henning *financial executive, automotive company executive*
Rockas, Anastasia T. *lawyer*
Rockefeller, Allison Hall W. *conservationist*
Rocklen, Kathy Hellenbrand *lawyer*
Rodgers, Kathy *lawyer*
Rodin, Judith Seitz *foundation administrator, former academic administrator, psychologist, educator*
Rodin, Rita Angela *lawyer*
Roer, Ricki E. *lawyer*
Role, Lorna W. *medical educator*
Rollin, Betty *writer, television journalist*
Romano, Clare *artist*
Roney, Carley *wedding company executive, writer*
Ronstadt, Linda Marie *singer*
Root, Nina J. *librarian, writer*
Rosa, Margarita *agency executive director, lawyer*
Rose, Joanna Semel *volunteer*
Rose, Joanne W. *rating service executive*
Rose, Leatrice *artist, educator*
Rosenbaum, Joan Hannah *museum director*
Rosenberg, Ellen Y. *religious association administrator*
Rosenberg, Jill L. *lawyer*
Rosenberg, Tina *reporter*
Rosensaft, Jean Bloch *university administrator*
Rosenthal, Donna Myra *social worker*
Rosenthal, Jane *film company executive*
Rosenthal, Nan *curator, educator, author*
Rosenthal, Shirley Lord *cosmetics magazine executive, novelist*
Roskam, Catherine S. *bishop*
Rosman, Paula *anthropologist, educator*
Ross, Diana (Diana Ernestine Earle Ross) *singer, actress, entertainer, fashion designer*
Ross, Jo Ann *media buyer*
Ross, Karen *information technology executive*
Rossi, Norma M. *management consultant*
Roth, Daryl *theater producer*
Roth, Judith Shulman *lawyer*
Rothenberg, Eleanore *psychotherapist*
Rothenberg, Laraine S. *lawyer*
Rothman, Barbara Katz *sociology educator*
Rothman, Esther Pomeranz *social services administrator, psychologist*
Rothschild, Amalie Randolph *filmmaker, film producer, film director, photographer*
Rotolo, Susan (Suze) *artist*
Rovner, Michal *video artist, photographer*
Rowen, Ruth Halle *musicologist, educator*
Rowland, Esther E(delman) *retired dean*
Rozenberg, Lana *cosmetic dentist*
Rubell, Jennifer *writer, hotelier*
Rubenstein, Atoosa Behnegar *editor-in-chief*
Rubin, Judith O. *not-for-profit trustee*
Rubinstein, Rosalinda *allergist, medical association administrator*
Rubin-Vega, Daphne *actress*
Ruckert, Ann Johns *musician, singer*
Rudolph, Lisa Beth *news correspondent*
Ruesterholz, Virginia P. *telecommunications industry executive*
Ruhl, Sarah *playwright*
Russell, Charlotte Sananes *biochemistry professor, researcher*
Russell, Maryanne *photographer*
Rylant, Cynthia *writer*
Sabino, Catherine Ann *magazine editor*
Sackmann, Pamela Jayne *lawyer*
Sadik, Nafis *United Nations administrator*
Saeed, Faiza J. *lawyer*
Safro, Millicent *small business owner, decorative arts scholar, writer*
St. Germain, Jean Mary *medical physicist*
St. Jean, Catherine Avery *advertising executive*
St. Martin, Charlotte *trade association administrator*
Saint-Ouen Leung, Brigitte *art dealer, consultant*
Salembier, Valerie Birnbaum *publishing executive*
Salerno-Sonnenberg, Nadja *violinist*
Salonga, Lea *actress, singer*
Salter, Mary Jo *poet*
Saltzstein, Susan L. *lawyer*
Sanchez, Karla G. *lawyer*
Sanders, Gina Susan *publishing executive*
Sand Lee, Inger *artist, interior architect*
Sandler, Barbara S. *artist*
Sandler, Lucy Freeman *art history educator*
Sandy, Sandra V. *psychologist*
Sang, Barbara Ellen *psychologist*
Sanger, Carol *law educator*
Santaella, Irma Vidal *retired state supreme court justice*
Santos, Nadine *music director*
Sarachik, Myriam Paula Morgenstein *physics professor, condensed matter physicist*
Sarandon, Susan Abigail *actress*
Sard, Susannah Ellen *non-profit executive*
Sargent, Pamela *writer*
Sarnoff, Ann M. *publishing executive, former sports association executive*
Sasman, Irene Deak Handberg *publishing executive*
Saunders, Arlene *opera singer*
Sawyer, Diane (L. Diane Sawyer) *newscaster, journalist*
Saxton, Catherine Patricia *public relations executive*
Schaffner, Cynthia Van Allen *writer, educator, curator*
Schair, Robin A. *lawyer*
Schapiro, Miriam *artist*
Schatz, Barbara A. *law educator*
Scheindlin, Shira A. *federal judge*
Schenk, Deborah Huffman *law educator*
Schiller, Vivian *Internet company executive*
Schlain, Barbara Ellen *lawyer*
Schlossberg, Caroline Bouvier Kennedy (Caroline Kennedy) *writer, lawyer*
Schmertz, Mildred Floyd *editor-in-chief, writer*
Schneider, Jane Harris *sculptor*
Schneider, JoAnne *artist*
Schneider, Willys Hope *lawyer*
Schneirov, Allison R. *lawyer*
Schofield, Lorna Gail *lawyer*
Schoonover, Jean Way *public relations consultant*
Schorer, Suki *ballet teacher*
Schori, Katharine Jefferts *bishop*
Schorr, Collier *artist*
Schueneman, Diane L. *diversified financial services company executive*
Schulz, Susan *magazine editor*
Schuman, Patricia Glass *publishing company executive, educator*
Schuster, Carlotta Lief *psychiatrist*
Schwartz, Anna Jacobson *economist*
Schwartz, Carol Vivian *lawyer*
Schwartz, Renee Gerstler *lawyer*
Sclafani, Susan K. *educational consultant, former federal agency administrator*
Scott, Adrienne *social worker, psychotherapist*
Scott, Felicity Dale Elliston *architecture educator, editor*
Scott, Helen S. *law educator*
Scott, Karen Michele *television producer*
Scott, Mimi Koblenz *psychotherapist, actress, journalist, playwright*
Scott, Nancy Ellen *psychologist*
Scott, Susan Craig *plastic surgeon*
Scotti, R. A. *writer*
Scotto, Rosanna *newscaster*
Seaman, Barbara (Ann Rosner) *author*
Seele, Pernessa C. *immunologist, health science association administrator*
Seelig, Jill *publishing executive*
Segal, Lore *writer*
Seidenberg, Rita Nagler *education educator*
Selby, Cecily Cannan *dean, science educator*
Seldes, Marian *actress*
Semaya, Francine Levitt *lawyer*
Semlies, Lori R. *lawyer*
Serota, Susan Perlstadt *lawyer, educator*
Sevely, Maria *architect*
Sevilla-Sacasa, Frances Aldrich *bank executive*
Seymour, Karen Patton *lawyer, former prosecutor*
Seymour, Stephanie *model*
Shafrir, Doree *editor, journalist*
Shainwald, Sybil *lawyer*
Shallcross, Deanne J. *finance company executive*
Shamberg, Barbara A(nn) *psychologist*
Shane, Penny *lawyer*
Shapiro, Anna *microbiologist, researcher*
Shapiro, Judith R. *academic administrator, anthropology educator*
Shapiro, Myra Stein *poet*
Shapiro, Sandra M. *psychologist, psychoanalyst, educator*
Sharbel, Jean M. *editor*
Sharkey, Catherine Moira *law educator*
Shatter, Susan Louise *artist*
Shavin, Helene B. *venture capital company executive*
Sheehan, Susan *writer*
Sheldon, Eleanor Harriet Bernert *sociologist, writer*
Shell, (Peterson) Juanita *psychologist, educator*
Shelley, Carole *actress*
Shepard, Sarah *public relations company executive*
Sheridan, Virginia *public relations executive*
Sheridan LaBarge, Joan Ruth *publishing executive*
Sherin, Robin *artist*
Sherman, Cindy *artist*
Shientag, Florence Perlow *lawyer*
Shier, Shelley M. *production company executive*
Shohen, Saundra Anne *health facility administrator, public relations executive*
Shoss, Cynthia Renée *lawyer*
Shreve, Anita *writer*
Shriver, Lionel (Margaret Ann Shriver) *writer*
Shrouder, Hortense Eaileen *dietitian*
Shull, Mikki *media consultant*
Sidamon-Eristoff, Anne Phipps *not-for-profit developer*
Sidran, Miriam *retired physicist*
Siebert, Muriel (Mickie) *brokerage house executive, retired bank executive*
Siegel, Heidi Ellen *neurologist, researcher*
Siegel, Lucy Boswell *public relations executive*
Sigal-Ibsen, Rose *artist*
Sigmond, Carol Ann *lawyer*
Sikander, Shahzia *artist*
Silberman, Linda Joy *law educator*
Sills, Beverly (Mrs. Peter B. Greenough) *performing company executive, singer*
Silver, Joan Micklin *film director, screenwriter*
Silvers, Sally *choreographer, performing company executive*
Silvestri, Heather L. *psychologist*
Simmons, Sue *newscaster*
Simms, Marsha E. *lawyer*
Simon, Jacqueline Albert *political scientist, writer*
Simpson, Mary Michael *priest, psychotherapist*
Sims, Lowery Stokes *museum curator, museum administrator, writer, educator*
Sinclair, Daisy *communications executive*
Singer, Barbara Helen *photographer, radiographer*
Singer, Debra *curator*
Singer, Joy Daniels *journalist, consultant*
Singer, Niki *media consultant*
Sirgado, Jo Anne E. *lawyer*
Sisakian, Marina *psychiatrist*
Sischy, Ingrid Barbara *editor, art critic*
Sisto, Elena *artist, educator*
Sitarz, Anneliese Lotte *pediatrician, educator, physician*
Sitomer, Sheila Marie *television producer, television director*
Skaistis, Rachel G. *lawyer*
Skeeter, Sharyn Jeanne *literature educator, writer*
Skerl, Diana M. *stockbroker*
Sklyar, Adelina M. *lawyer*
Skoglund, Sandra Louise *artist, educator*
Sky, Alison *artist, designer*
Slavin, Arlene *artist*
Slavin, Rosanne Singer *textile converter*
Slawsky, Donna Susan *librarian, singer*

Sleigh, Sylvia *artist, educator*
Slitkin, Barbara Ann *artist*
Slutsky, Lorie A(nn) *foundation executive*
Smiley, Jane Graves *author, educator*
Smith, Barbara *food service executive, model*
Smith, Betty *writer, not-for-profit developer*
Smith, Clare *art appraiser*
Smith, Karen A. *lawyer*
Smith, Kiki *artist*
Smith, Liz (Mary Elizabeth Smith) *columnist, newscaster*
Smith, Mary-Ann Tirone *writer*
Smith, Shirley *artist*
Smith-Loeb, Margaret *marketing educator*
Snyder, Leslie Crocker *lawyer*
Snyderman, Selma Eleanore *pediatrician, educator*
Soave, Rosemary *internist*
Sochet, Mary Allen *psychotherapist, educator, writer*
Sokoloff, Audrey L. *lawyer*
Solanto, Mary Victoria *psychologist*
Solnit, Rebecca *writer, critic*
Solomon, Gail Ellen *physician*
Sonneman, Eve *artist*
Sorell Stehr, Deborah K. *lawyer*
Soriano, Nancy Mernit *editor-in-chief*
Sotomayor, Sonia *federal judge*
Soyster, Margaret Blair *lawyer*
Spade, Kate (Katherine Noel Spade) *apparel designer*
Spears, Britney *singer*
Spector, Johanna Lichtenberg *ethnomusicologist, former educator*
Spellman Sweet, Julia T. *lawyer*
Spence, Sique (Mary Stewart Spence) *art dealer*
Spencer, Ruth Albert *music educator*
Spencer-Fleming, Julia *writer*
Spero, Joan Edelman *foundation administrator*
Spikol, Eileen *artist*
Spinak, Jane M. *law educator*
Squire, Gilda N. *publishing executive, writer*
Stafford, Abi *ballerina*
Stanger, Ila *editor-in-chief*
Stanton, Amy *marketing executive*
Stark, Robin Caryl *psychotherapist, consultant*
Stautberg, Susan Schiffer *communications executive*
Steedman, Doria Lynne Silberberg *foundation administrator*
Steel, Danielle Fernande *author*
Steffe, Cynthia *fashion designer*
Steichen, Joanna T(aub) *psychotherapist, writer*
Stein, Jane Wallison *lawyer*
Stein, Zena A. *retired epidemiologist, educator*
Steinberg, Debra Brown *lawyer*
Steinherz, Laurel Judith *pediatric cardiologist*
Stern, Madeleine Bettina *rare book dealer, writer*
Stern, Roslyne Paige *magazine publisher*
Stern-Larosa, Caryl M. *advocate, educational association administrator*
Stevens, Risë *performing arts association administrator*
Stevens, Rosemary A. *medicine and public health historian, artist*
Steves, Gale C. *marketing professional, writer, editor-in-chief, publishing executive*
Stewart, Ellen D. *theater producer*
Stewart, Jennifer *advertising executive*
Stewart, Leora Klaymer *textile artist, educator*
Stewart, Ruth Ann *public policy educator*
Stimpson, Catharine Rosalind *literature educator, writer*
Stine, Catherine Morris *artist*
Stokes, Lori *newscaster*
Stone, Caroline Fleming *artist*
Stone, Shirley M. *pediatrician, educator*
Storm, Jackie *nutritionist*
Strachan, Dina Dawn *dermatologist, educator*
Strauss, Carolyn *broadcast executive*
Stroer, Rosemary Ann *real estate broker*
Stroman, Susan *choreographer, theater director*
Strossen, Nadine *legal association administrator, law educator*
Stuart, Alice Melissa *lawyer*
Stuart, Jill *apparel designer*
Stuart, Michelle Rae *artist*
Studin, Jan *publishing executive*
Sturm, Susan P. *law educator*
Subotnick, Ali *curator, writer*
Suk, Jeannie *lawyer*
Sullivan, Irene A. *lawyer*
Sullivan, Mary Brosnahan *advocate, social services administrator*
Sullivan, Trudy F. *apparel executive*
Sultan, Altoon *artist*
Summer, Sharon *marketing professional, former publisher*
Supino, Phyllis Gail *medical researcher, educator*
Sutherland, Susan J. *lawyer*
Sutton, Karen E. *museum director*
Suzuki, Wendy A. *neurology educator*
Swain, Laura Taylor *federal judge*
Swartz, Julianne *artist*
Sweed, Phyllis *publishing executive*
Swergold, Marcelle Miriam *sculptor*
Swittenberg, Michelle Minus *telecommunications industry executive*
Sykes, Plum *writer*
Symonette, Lys *foundation executive, musician, writer*
Szeto, Yvonne *architectural firm executive*
Tallmer, Margot Sallop *psychologist, gerontologist, psychoanalyst*
Tan, Amy Ruth *writer*
Tanaka, Patrice Aiko *public relations executive*
Tanenbaum, Judith Hertz *psychiatrist*
Tannenbaum, Bernice Salpeter *national religious organization executive*
Tarnofsky-Ostroff, Dawn *broadcast executive*
Taylor, Diana Lancaster *state official*
Taylor, Janie *ballerina*
Taylor, Jean Ellen *mathematics professor, researcher*
Taylor, Marilyn Jordan *architectural firm executive*
Taylor, Mildred D. *author*
Taylor, Regina *actress*
Taylor, Susan L. *magazine editor*
Taylor, Terry R. *editor, educator*
Tchoumak, Adelina *corporate financial executive*
Tenenbaum, Ann G. *art association administrator*
Tepper Madover, Arielle *theater producer*
Terris, Lillian Dick *psychologist, health facility administrator*
Tesori, Jeanine *composer*
Thaler, Linda Kaplan *advertising executive*
Thomas, Dorothy *indexing consultant, writer*
Thomas, Helen Amelia (Mrs. Douglas B. Cornell) *editor-in-chief, former White House correspondent*
Thompson, Jewel Taylor *music educator*
Thompson, Vicki Lewis *writer*
Thoyer, Judith Reinhardt *lawyer*
Thurston, Sally A. *lawyer*
Tiano, Linda V. *lawyer*
Tighe, Mary Ann *real estate company executive*
Tillman, Vickie A. *financial information company executive*
Tinsley, Jennifer *ballerina*
Tipton, Jennifer *lighting designer*
Tischler, Judith Blanche *retired publishing executive*
Tisch Sussman, Laurie *art gallery director*
Tobach, Ethel *retired curator*
Toben, Doreen A. *telecommunications industry executive*
Tober, Barbara D. (Mrs. Donald Gibbs Tober) *editor*
Toepfer, Susan Jill *editor-in-chief*
Tolchin, Joan Gubin *psychiatrist, educator*
Toll, Barbara Elizabeth *art gallery director*
Tong, Kaity *anchor*
Touby, Linda *artist*
Toulantis, Marie J. *retail executive*
Townsend, Alair Ane *publishing executive*
Townsend-Butterworth, Diana Barnard *educational consultant, educator*
Tracy, Janet Ruth *law educator, law librarian, director*
Traverse, Lyn D. *not-for-profit fundraiser, communications executive*
Travis, Sarah *orchestrator*
Tritch, Teresa *editor, writer*
Trombetta, Annamarie *artist*
Trump, Blaine (Martha Lindley Blaine Beard Trump) *philanthropist*
Tuccillo, Elaine *psychologist, educator*
Tuck, Lily *writer*
Turner, Alice Kennedy *editor*
Turner, Megan Whalen *author*
Turo, Joann K. *psychoanalyst, psychotherapist, consultant*
Tutwiler, Margaret DeBardeleben *stock exchange executive, former federal agency administrator*
Tyler, Dana *anchor*
Tyler, Wakenda Kachina *orthopedist, surgeon, researcher*
Uggams, Leslie *entertainer*
Ultra Violet, *artist*
Umansky, Diane *editor-in-chief*
Umeh, Marie Arlene *language educator*
Umlauf, Lynn Charlotte *art educator, sculptor*
Underwood, Carrie Marie *singer*
Underwood, Joanna DeHaven *environmental services administrator*
Ungaro, Susan Kelliher *foundation administrator, former magazine editor*
Updike, Helen Hill *financial advisor*
Upright, Diane Warner *art dealer*
Urban, Amanda (Binky Urban) *literary agent*
Urban, Nina B.L. *psychiatrist, psychotherapist, researcher*
Urda Kassis, Cynthia E. *lawyer*
Vale, Eleanor P. *lawyer*
Valenstein, Suzanne Gebhart *art historian*
Valletta, Amber *actress, model*
Van de Bovenkamp, Sue Erpf *foundation administrator*
Vanden Heuvel, Katrina *publishing executive*
Vander Heyden, Marsha Ann *business owner*
Van Goethem, Nancy Ann *painter, educator*
Van Susteren, Greta Conway *newscaster, lawyer*
Vargas, Elizabeth *newscaster*
Vass, Joan *apparel designer*
Vermeer, Maureen Dorothy *sales executive*
Vieira, Meredith *television personality*
Vigeant, Michele A. *mental health counselor*
Viladas, Pilar *editor*
Visser, Lesley *sports correspondent*
Vladeck, Judith Pomarlen *lawyer*
Volk, Kristin *advertising agency executive*
Vollweiler, Cheryl P. *lawyer*
von Baillou, Astrid *executive search consultant*
von Fraunhofer-Kosinski, Katherina *bank executive, advertising executive*
von Rydingsvard, Ursula Karoliszyn *sculptor*
Vyskocil, Mary Kay *lawyer*
Wachtell, Cynthia June *academic administrator, director, literature educator*
Wade, Estelle B. *psychologist, psychoanalyst*
Wainwright, Cynthia Crawford *banker*
Wajsfeld, Annie R. *volunteer*
Wald, Sylvia *artist*
Walker, Alice *writer*
Walker, Kara *artist*
Walker, Kim A. *lawyer*
Wallace, Nora Ann *lawyer*
Walters, Barbara Jill *broadcast journalist*
Walzer, Judith Borodovko *academic administrator, educator*
Wang, Vera *fashion designer*
Ward, Sarah M. *lawyer*
Waricha, Joan *publishing executive*
Warner, Jayne Lena *academic administrator*
Warshauer, Irene C. *lawyer*
Washburn, Joan Thomas *small business owner*
Watanabe, Nana *photographer*
Wattleton, Faye (Alyce Faye Wattleton) *educational association administrator, advocate*
Waxman, Anita *theater producer*
Waybourn, Kathleen Ann *lawyer, consultant*
Weber, Lisa M. *insurance company executive*
Webster, Catherine T. *telecommunications industry executive*
Webster, Lesley Daniels *bank executive*
Webster, Susan *lawyer*
Wedgeworth, Ann *actress*
Weiksner, Sandra S. *lawyer*
Weiler, Berenice *theater producer, consultant*
Weil-Garris Brandt, Kathleen (Kathleen Brandt) *art historian*
Weinberg, H. Barbara *art historian, educator, curator*
Weingarten, Rhonda (Randi Weingarten) *labor union administrator, lawyer*
Weinroth, Lois L. *lawyer*
Weinstein, Sharon Schlein *corporate communications executive, educator*
Weisberg-Samuels, Janet S. *psychologist*
Weiss, Carol Juliet *psychiatrist*
Weiss, Lisa Ann *lawyer*
Weiss, Marilyn Ackerman *artist*
Weiss, Myrna Grace *management consultant*
Weissler, Fran *theatrical producer*
Weissman, Myrna M. *epidemiologist, researcher, medical educator*
Welch, Martha Grace *physician, researcher*
Welker, Jennifer Carol Marie *artist*
Welkowitz, Joan *psychology educator*
Wells, Linda Ann *editor-in-chief*
Wells, Rebecca *writer*
Wells, Rosemary *writer*
Wender, Phyllis Bellows *literary agent*
Wenig, Cindy L. *lawyer*
Wesely, Marissa Celeste *lawyer*
Westheimer, Ruth Siegel (Karola Westheimer) *psychologist, television personality*
Wexler, Patricia Susan *dermatologist, surgeon*
Wheeler, Susan *poet, educator*
Whelchel, Betty Anne *lawyer*
White, Kate *editor-in-chief*
White, Lillias *actress*
White, Mary Jo *lawyer, former prosecutor*
Whitehouse, Anne Cherner *writer*
Whitney, Phyllis Ayame *author*
Whoriskey, Katherine Jane *theater director, educator*
Wijnberg, Sandra S. *professional services company executive*
Wile, Joan *composer, lyricist, singer*
Wilkins, Amy P. *publishing executive*
Willen, Liz *reporter*
Willett, Roslyn Leonore *public relations executive, food service consultant, writer, editor*
Williams, Diane *writer, editor*
Williams, Harriet Clarke *retired academic administrator*
Williams, Lena *sportswriter*
Williams, Marsha E. *broadcast executive*
Williams, Patricia J. *law educator*
Williams, Vanessa (Vanessa Lynn Williams) *recording artist, actress*
Williams, Wendy *radio personality, writer*
Willner, Judith P. *clinical geneticist, pediatrician, educator*
Wils, Madelyn *film company executive*
Wilson, Marie C. *foundation administrator*
Wilson, Pamela K. *corporate financial executive*
Winston, Mary A. *publishing executive*
Wintour, Anna *editor-in-chief*
Wiseman, Cynthia Sue *language educator*
Wohl, Laurie *artist*
Wohrle, Marta *publishing executive*
Woit, Bonnie Ford *artist*
Wolden, Suzanne Leesa *pediatric radiation oncologist*
Wolf, Naomi *writer*
Wolff, Margaret Louise *lawyer*
Wolff, Virginia Euwer *writer*
Wong, Andrea *broadcast executive*
Woo, Alex *jewelry designer*
Wood, Kimba M. *federal judge*
Woodall, Elaine *psychotherapist*
Woodman, Betty *sculptor*
Woodward, Joanne Gignilliat *actress*
Wortman, Marlene Stein *historian*
Wright, Deborah C. *bank executive*
Wright, Faith-dorian *artist*
Wright, Gwendolyn *writer, architecture educator, historian*
Wright, Margaret Hagen *computer scientist, administrator*
Wright, Sheena *not-for-profit developer*
Wunderman, Jan Darcourt *artist*
Wylde, Kathryn S. *business organization executive*
Wyschogrod, Edith *philosophy educator*
Yablon, Heather D. *lawyer*
Yajima, Hiroko *violinist, music educator*
Yastine, Barbara A. *diversified financial services company executive*
Yelenick, Mary Therese *lawyer*
Yeo, Patricia *chef*
Yglesias, Helen Bassine *author, educator*
Yin, Beatrice Wei-Tze *medical researcher*
Yorio, Kimberly *public relations executive*
Yoshiuchi, Ellen Haven *healthcare educator, clinical counselor*
Young, Alice *lawyer*
Young, Estelle Irene *dermatologist, educator*
Young, Genevieve Leman *publishing executive, editor*
Young, Nancy *lawyer*
Young-Mallin, Judith *writer, archivist*
Yousef, Mona Lee *psychoanalytic psychotherapist*
Yrizarry, Magda N. *communications executive*
Yu, Pauline Ruth *former dean, educational association administrator*
Yurchenco, Henrietta Weiss *musicologist, writer*
Zabrocky, Lois K. *energy transportation executive*
Zackheim, Michele *artist*
Zagat, Nina *publishing executive*
Zagorin, Janet Susan *legal firm administrator, marketing professional*
Zaken, Grace Ambrose *project coordinator, educator*
Zalaznick, Lauren *broadcast executive*
Zarghami, Cyma *broadcast executive*
Zhu, Ai-Lan *opera singer*
Zimmerman, Diane Leenheer *law educator*
Zimmerman, Elyn *artist*
Zimmerman, Kathleen Marie *artist*
Zirinsky, Susan *television producer*
Zittel, Andrea *painter, sculptor*
Zoffer, Rachelle *telecommunications industry executive*
Zolotow, Charlotte Shapiro *retired author, editor*
Zosike, Joanie Fritz *theater director, actress*
Zoullas, Deborah Decotis *investment company executive*
Zovluck, Ileen Marcy *music annotator*
Zucker-Franklin, Dorothea *internist, educator*
Zulack, Mary Marsh *law educator*
Zunino, Natalia *psychologist*

New York Mills
Zielinski, Teresa Krystyna *music educator*

Newark
Biddle, Jane Lammert *retired English educator*
Hemmings, Madeleine Blanchet *management consultant, not-for-profit administrator, media consultant*

Newburgh
Adams, Barbara *language educator, poet, writer*
Fallon, Rae Mary *psychology professor, educational consultant*
Garey, Velma Kay *science foundation director, educator*
Sabini, Barbara Dorothy *artist, educator*

Niagara Falls
DiVita-Frommert, Angela Marie *music educator*
Douglas, Frances Sonia *minister*
Gailie, Kristina Ann *music educator*
Jones, Suzanne P. *public relations executive*

Niagara University
Foote, Chandra Jeanet *education educator, writer, elementary school educator*

Niskayuna
Lavin, Linda K. *counselor*
Martin, Ruth C. (Ruth Martin Staff) *actress*
Quirion, Ramona Shaw *elementary school educator*
Steeley, Dolores Ann *music educator*

North Bellmore
Trigoboff, Sybelle *artist, educator*

North Collins
Brosnick, Lisa A. *science educator*

North Massapequa
Capone, Maryann *financial planner*

North Merrick
Rakas, Peggy Ann *music educator*

North Salem
Tompkins, Elizabeth J. *secondary school educator*

North Syracuse
Federico, Josephine A.M. *music educator*
Williamson, Donna Maria *pastoral counselor*

North Tonawanda
Insalaco, Lisa A. *reading specialist*
Strong, Audrey Farone *music educator*

North White Plains
Erla, Karen *artist, painter, collagist, printmaker*

Northport
Donenfeld, Sharon Etta *psychologist*
Hohenberger, Patricia Julie *fine arts and antique appraiser, consultant*
Johnson, Samira El-Chehabi *marketing professional*
McGarry, Frances Lorraine *education educator*
Russo, Christine Fiorella *language educator*

Northville
Fox, Patricia Ann *school librarian, media specialist*

Norwich
Dragoon, Valerie Baldwin *art educator*

Norwood
Musante, Patricia W. *library director*

Nyack
Carey, Lois J. *psychotherapist*
Cozart, Helen Ray *church administrator, educator*
Pease, Eleanor Jeanne *humanities educator*
Poston, Linda *dean, library director*
Scott-Battle, Gladys Natalie *retired social worker*

Oceanside
Kaikow, Rita Ellen *library media specialist*

Odessa
Stillman-Myers, Joyce L. *artist, educator, writer, illustrator, consultant*

Ogdensburg
Niederer, Marla Lee *special education educator*

Old Westbury
O'Brien, Adrienne Gratia *communications educator*
Tiscornia, Ana Maria *artist, educator, writer*

Olean
McGovern-Scaturo, Diane Joan *psychotherapist*

Olmstedville
LaPointe, Sabrina Ann *music educator*

Oneonta
Freckelton, Sondra *artist*
Holleran, Paula Rizzo *psychology and counseling educator, researcher, consultant*
Murphy, Susan Ryan *literature and language educator*

Ontario
Blackman, Lani Modica *copy editor*

Orangeburg
Dolgin, Ellen Ecker *English and gender studies professor*
Siegel, Carole Ethel *mathematician*

Orchard Park
Askew, Gloria Yarbrough *dietician*
Landrigan, Cynthia Scheer *mathematician, educator*
Lockwood, Deborah Jane *psychotherapist, consultant, educator*
Mosner, Ann L. *music educator*

Orser, Janet Christine *psychologist*
Urbanski, Jane F. *retired microbiologist*
Wiedl, Priscilla *music educator*

Orient
Cochran, Judy Anne *psychiatric nurse practitioner*

Oriskany
Jacobson, Karen *retired elementary school educator*

Ossining
Beard, Janet Marie *health facility administrator*
Galef, Sandra Risk *state legislator, educator*
Gilbert, Joan Stulman *retired public relations executive*
Poh-Fitzpatrick, Maureen B. *dermatologist, educator*
Reich, Susanna *children's book author, publicist*
Robinson, Karen Vajda *dietician*

Oswego
Loveridge-Sanbonmatsu, Joan Meredith *communication studies and women's studies educator, poet*
Rice, Brenda Jean *operating room nurse, educator*
Smiley, Marilynn Jean *musicologist*

Otego
Griffith, Roberta *art educator*

Ovid
Scoles, Marie Y. *elementary school educator*

Owego
Coppens, Laura Kathryn *special education educator*

Oxford
Hover, Dawn A. *director*

Oyster Bay
Landrón, Ana *school psychologist*
Prey, Barbara Ernst *artist*
Smith, Pamela Rosevear *air transportation executive*

Ozone Park
Bellamy, Renee Adele *secondary school educator*
Catalfo, Betty Marie *public health service officer, nutritionist, writer*
Scott, Vanessa Kathleen *writer*

Palisades
Balstad, Roberta *social scientist*
Davis, Dorothy Salisbury *writer*
Goddard, Lisa *meteorologist*
Knowlton, Grace Farrar *sculptor, photographer*

Parish
Campbell, Janet Schwagler *biology educator*

Patchogue
Franck CSJ, Suzanne Elizabeth *religious studies educator, minister*
McPherson, Sherry Lynn *social worker*
Tutino, Rosalie Jacqueline *college administrator*
Watkins, Linda Theresa *retired educational association administrator*

Pawling
Light, Sybil Elizabeth *executive secretary*
Peale, Ruth Stafford (Mrs. Norman Vincent Peale) *not-for-profit executive*

Peekskill
Jackson, Linda B. *social worker*
Mason, Rebecca Sussa *retired secondary school educator*
Wiggins, Ida Silver *elementary school educator*

Penfield
Dougherty, Janniese Marie *social services administrator, music educator*
Hamilton, Candis Lee *counselor*
Marbach, Donna Maureen *writer*

Perry
Hume, Linda Jean *music educator*

Piermont
Madawick, Paula Christian *artist, educator*

Pine Island
Rogowski, Cheryl *farmer*

Pittsford
Barker, Julie A. *school system administrator*
Clem, Kathy *artist*
Drake, Jill Leah *elementary school educator*

Plainview
Nichter, Rhoda Samuels *writer, educator*

Plattsburgh
Demers-Bourgeois, Aimee E. *physical therapist*
Fowler, Alyce Milton *health facility administrator*
Hughes, Nancy Copeland *early childhood education educator*
Rech, Susan Anita *obstetrician, gynecologist*

Pleasant Valley
Marshall, Natalie Junemann *economics professor*
Murthy, Padmini *physician*

Pleasantville
Graham, Paula Lee *intravenous nurse*
Leo, Jacqueline M. *editor-in-chief*
McEwen, Laura *publishing executive*
Palmer, Stephanie Teresa *elementary school educator*
Rockwood, Marcia *magazine editor*
Sachar, Emily M. *editor*

Pomona
DeMaio, Barbara Patricia *social worker*
Landau, Lauri Beth *accountant, consultant*

Port Chester
Aubry, Renée L. *secondary school educator*
Brescia, Alicia *science educator, vice principal*
Dessereau, April *art educator*
Oppenheimer, Suzi *state legislator*
Sayles, Eva *artist*

Port Jefferson
Block, Estell Lenora *educational consultant*
MacKinnon, Ann Laurie *retired elementary school educator*

Port Washington
Betensky, Rose Hart *artist*
Eagan, Marie T. (Ria Eagan) *chiropractor*
van Schenkhof, Carol Dougherty (Carol Dovan) *soprano, educator*
Weiner, Mina Rieur *museum consultant, civic worker*

Porter Corners
Manzi, Alice M. *artist, educator*

Potsdam
Downing, Caroline Jane *art historian, educator, archaeologist*
Regan, Marie Carbone *retired language educator*
Scott, Jean A. *university president*

Poughkeepsie
Brakas, Nora Jachym *education educator*
Carino, Aurora Lao *psychiatrist, health facility administrator*
Daniels, Elizabeth Adams *English language educator*
Deiters, Sister Joan Adele *psychoanalyst, nun, chemistry professor*
Hansen, Karen Thornley *accountant*
Hill, Carla Larsen *physical education educator, gymnastics judge*
Hill, Catharine Bond (Cappy Hill) *academic administrator, economics professor*
Hytier, Adrienne Doris *French language educator*
Jackson, Judy Faye *academic administrator*
Jacobi, Kerry Lee *information systems specialist*
LaGreca, Carla Irene *activist*
Peluse, Catherine Gina *artist*
Pisterzi, Candy *special education educator*
Saunders, Judith P. *literature and language professor, writer*
Teal, Arabella W. *lawyer, former state attorney general*
VanBuren, Denise Doring *corporate communications executive*
Willard, Nancy Margaret *writer, educator*
Wolfersteig, Jean Lois *medical association administrator, educator*

Pound Ridge
Schwebel, Renata Manasse *sculptor*

Pultneyville
Farrer-Bornarth, Sylvia *writer, artist*

Purchase
Ehrman, Lee *geneticist, educator*
Finnerty, Louise Hoppe *food products executive*
Frost, Elizabeth Ann McArthur *physician*
Hudson, Dawn Emily *food service company executive*
Moore, Margaret D. *human resources specialist*
Mullen, M. Denise *art educator, higher education administrator, photographer, artist*
Newton, Esther Mary *anthropologist, educator*
Nicholson, Cie (Cynthia Nicholson) *marketing executive, beverage company executive*
Nooyi, Indra K. *food products executive*
Phillips, Carly *writer*

Queens Village
Heckman, Lucy T. *librarian*
Megherian, Yefkin *sculptor*
Raines, Judi Belle *language educator, historian*

Red Hook
Beam, Deborah Ann *science educator*
Gudenzi-Ruess, Ida Carmen V. *music educator, artist*
Rovigo, Connie Brigitta *jewelry and fine arts retailer*
Turchetti, Celine Marie *elementary school educator*

Rego Park
Davidov, Ludmila G. *psychiatrist*
King, Deborah Irene *academic administrator*
Tsui, Soo Hing *educational research consultant*

Remsenburg
Hirsch, Ann Ullman *retired academic administrator*

Rensselaer
Whitney, Mary Ellen *not-for-profit developer, educator*

Rensselaerville
Hanson, Peg *gemstone dealer, psychic, graphic designer, writer*

Rexford
Schmitt, Claire Kunz *environmentalist, writer*

Rhinebeck
Ewald, Wendy Taylor *photographer, writer, educator*
Rabinovich, Raquel *painter, sculptor*
Sloane, Beverly LeBov *writer, consultant, writing instructor*

Richfield Springs
Walters, Marjorie Anne *interior designer, consultant*

Richmond Hill
Malhotra, Madhu Bala *psychiatrist*

Ridge
Carter, Sylvia *journalist*

Riverdale
Dytell, Rita Scher *health psychology educator, researcher, administra*
Greenberg, Arline Francine *artist*

Riverhead
Carpenter, Angie M. *small business owner, editor, county legislator*
Carr, Theresa *mathematics educator*
Molia, Denise F. *judge*
Passanante, Patricia Marie *middle school educator*

Rochester
Adams, Carol H. *dean*
Aydelotte, Myrtle Kitchell *retired nursing administrator*
Barone, Jessica Lynn *geology educator*
Berger, Audrey Marilyn *psychologist*
Blanda-Holtzberg, Marianne Lourdes *education educator, consultant*
Braley, Oleta Pearl *community health nurse, writer*
Bren, Kara L. *chemistry professor*
Buckbee, Malina *music educator*
Buckingham, Barbara Rae *social studies educator*
Campbell, Alma Jacqueline Porter *elementary school educator*
Chiverton, Patricia Ann *dean, nursing educator*
Christensen, Sonya Marie *school librarian*
Conwell, Esther Marly *physicist, researcher*
Danforth-Morningstar, Elizabeth *obstetrician, gynecologist*
Everett, Claudia Kellam *retired special education educator*
Follansbee, Patti A. *health educator, marriage and family therapist*
Fox, Donna Brink *music educator*
Frazee, Evelyn *lawyer, educator*
Frear, Lorrie *graphic designer, educator*
Freeman, Leslie Jean *neuropsychologist, researcher*
Friauf, Katherine Elizabeth *metal company executive*
Furness, Janet Elisabeth *social work educator*
Gong, Nancy Y. *artist, small business owner*
Gootnick, Margery Fischbein *lawyer*
Goyer, Virginia L. *accountant*
Grant, Marilynn Patterson *secondary school educator*
Grossi, Rose B. *director*
Guarnere, Joanne *protective services official*
Hanson, Karen Noble *financial holding company executive*
Harris, Diane Carol *merger and acquisition consulting firm executive*
Haynes, Linda Ann *health information management administrator*
Haywood, Anne Mowbray *pediatrician, educator*
Herminghouse, Patricia Anne *foreign language educator*
Herrera, Charlotte Mae *medical office administrator*
Hollis, Susan Tower *history professor*
Houde-Walter, Susan *optics scientist, educator*
John, Susan V. *state representative*
Jörgensen, Beth Ellen *Spanish language educator*
Kehoe, Jennifer Spungin *English language educator, writer, children's book editor*
Kelley, Lucille Knight *minister, retired neurology and special duty nurse*
Kirkebye, Amanda Stark *art educator*
Klinke, Louise Hoyt *volunteer*
Kuby, Patricia J. *mathematics professor*
Kunkel, Barbara J. *law firm executive*
Lacey, Dorothy Ellen *theology studies educator, religious organization administrator*
Lank, Edith Handleman *journalist, educator*
Lawrence, Ruth Anderson *pediatrician*
Lindsey, Margaret A. *psychiatrist*
Magnuson, Karen M. *editor*
Manley, Cathey Neracker *interior design executive*
Maquat, Lynne E. *biomedical researcher*
Marriott, Marcia Ann *business educator, economics professor, health facility administrator*
McAnarney, Elizabeth R. *pediatrician, educator*
McCreary, Jean Hutchinson *lawyer*
McDaniel, Susan Holmes *psychologist*
Mok, Carolyn Lee *physician*
Morrison, Patrice Burgert *lawyer*
Moss, Joy Folkman *elementary school educator*
Newport, Elissa L. *psychology professor*
Niznik, Carol Ann *electrical engineer, educator, consultant*
Parrinello, Diane Davies *retired pre-school educator*
Parrinello, Kathleen Ann Mulholland *nursing administrator, educator*
Patane, Joyce A. *secondary school educator*
Pavone, Jill Russell *special education educator*
Polowe-Aldersley, Stephanie Ruth *English language educator, educational association administrator, legislator*
Pratt, Alice S. *music educator*
Rehmani, Shahida *psychiatrist*
Robbins, Nancy Slinker *volunteer*
Roberts, Robyn Renay *elementary school educator, coach*
Rodgers, Suzanne Hooker *physiologist, consultant*
Routly, Tracey Laurene *elementary school educator*
Sammler, Anne Michelle *healthcare educator*
Satter, Mary Ann *literature and language educator*
Schneider, Sue R. *music educator*
Shedden-Coingill, Edythe B. *artist*
Shindelman, Marni *artist, educator*
Smith, Julia Ladd *oncologist, physician*
Spurrier, Mary Eileen *investment advisor, financial planner*
Stewart, Sue S. *lawyer*
Stiller, Sharon Paula *lawyer*
Swanton, Susan Irene *retired library director*
Tantillo, Mary Darlene *nurse*
Tobin, Barbara Kay *minister*
Toribara, Masako Ono *voice educator*
Truesdale, Carol A. *music educator*
VanderLinden, Camilla Denice Dunn *telecommunications industry executive*
VanGelder, Kim E. *information technology executive*
Wegman, Colleen *food service executive*
Wilson, Melissa Ann *athletic trainer*
Wygant, Patricia Bryans *artist*
Young, Mary Elizabeth *history professor*

Rockville Centre
Barkan-Clarke, Jacqueline Mia *artist, educator, art therapist, jewelry designer*
Beyer, Suzanne *advertising agency executive*
Epel, Lidia Marmurek *dentist*
Fitzgerald, Janet Anne *philosophy educator, academic administrator*
Honigsfeld, Andrea M. *education educator*
Mazzucelli, Colette Grace Celia *author, educator*
O'Brien, Donna M. *public health service officer*

Rocky Point
Tvelia, Carol Ann *principal, elementary school educator*

Rome
Anderson, Nora *nurse*
Hart, Margaret Rogene
Ramos, Maria *science educator*

Rosedale
Charrington, Karen Hillary *lawyer, consultant*

Rosendale
Kellner, Tatana *artist, art educator*

Roslyn
Hartman, Nancy Lee *physician*
Rosen, Sarah Perel *social worker*
Shubin, Joanna *science educator*
Siahpoosh, Farideh Tamaddon *librarian*

Roslyn Heights
Newmark, Marilyn *sculptor*
Rubrum, Erica Courtney *family therapist, school counselor*
Schwartzberg, Neala Spiegel *psychologist, writer*

Rotterdam Junction
Cox, Paulyn Mae *retired elementary school educator*

Roxbury
Green, Jean Hess *psychotherapist*

Ruby
Cole, Max *artist*

Rushville
Evans, Mary Melinda *special education educator*

Rye
Buchsbaum, Betty Cynthia *clinical psychologist*
Downer, Allison V. *adult, forensic, child and adolescent psychiatrist*
Harrington, Diane *librarian, writer*
Kaufman, Shirona *cantor, educator*
McDonnell, Mary Theresa *travel company executive*
Mickatavage, Jane Cline *director*
Nelson, Vita Joy *editor, publisher*
Olver, Ruth Carol *retired social worker*
O'Sullivan, Kerry *educational consultant*
Sales, Mitzi S. *science educator*
Walters, Carolyn Maria *secondary school educator*

Rye Brook
Goldberger, Blanche Rubin *sculptor, jeweler*
Lo Russo, Diane *radiologist*
Sarkodie-Mensah, Aimie *physical education educator*

Sabael
Morrill-Cummins, Carolyn *social worker, consultant*

Sag Harbor
Barry, Nada Davies *retail business owner*
Brody, Jacqueline *editor*
Deleski, Karen Margaret *athletic trainer*
Olson, Kryn Dacia *elementary school educator, artist*

Sagaponack
Cedering, Siv *poet, writer*

Saint Bonaventure
Donovan, Geraldine Ellen *sister*
Young, Kimberly S. *finance educator, psychologist*

Saint Johnsville
Schoff, Marcia Anne *elementary school educator*
Stock, Patricia D. *literature, language and history educator*

Salem
Duveen, Anneta *artist*

Salt Point
Botway, Jaclyn Cooper *antiques dealer, consultant*

Sanborn
Jeffords, Mary Margaret *community activist*
Nowak (Jarosz), Linda Therese *special education educator, consultant*
Robinson, Deborah J. *counselor, educator, consultant*

Sands Point
Cohen, Ida Bogin (Mrs. Savin Cohen) *import/export company executive*
Cullinan, Bernice Ellinger *education educator*
Olian, JoAnne Constance *curator, art historian*

Sandy Creek
Miller, Cheryl Marie *special education educator, small business owner*

Saratoga Springs
Caruso, Adrienne Iorio *retired language educator*
Miller, Anita Diane *psychologist*
Muller, Susan Marie *physician*
Ratzer, Mary Boyd *librarian, language educator*
Riley, Dawn C. *educational philosopher, researcher*

Turk, Jane Skouge *education educator*
Vernon, Lillian *mail order company executive*
Waterhouse, Lynette *mathematics educator*
Williams, Serena *professional tennis player, apparel designer*
Williams, Venus *professional tennis player*

Whitesboro
Campbell, Joann Cavo *social worker*

Willard
Covert, Sarah Jane (Sally) *elementary school educator*

Williamson
Thomason-Mussen, Janis Faye *human services administrator*

Williamsville
Ciprich, Paula Marie *lawyer, gas industry executive*
Fortunato, Pat Deakin *fine artist*
Krzyzan, Judy Lynn *automotive executive*

Willow
Bley, Carla Borg *composer*

Windsor
Meeker, Carol Louise *special education educator, consultant*
Warner, Roberta Arlene *retired accountant, financial services executive*

Wolcott
Wiggins, Dorothy L. *retired primary school educator*

Woodbury
Barnett, Rochelle *accountant*
Freedson, Grace Elizabeth *publishing executive*
Maltin, Marjorie Solomon *psychologist, psychoanalyst*

Woodhaven
Bolster, Jacqueline Neben (Mrs. John A. Bolster) *communications consultant*

Woodmere
Ronis, Gwendlyn *musician, educator*
Winick, Bernyce Alpert *artist, photographer*

Woodside
Sfiroudis, Gloria Tides *library and information scientist, educator*
Spain-Savage, Christi Lynn *secondary school educator*
Swift, Constance Redmond *special education educator*
VanArsdale, Diana Cort *social worker*

Woodstock
Banks, Rela *sculptor*
Godwin, Gail Kathleen *writer*
Hahne Hofsted, Janet Lorraine *artist*
Lieberman, Josefa Nina *psychologist, educator, writer*
Rissman, Barbara Susan Zimmer *psychotherapist*
Segal, Sabra Lee *artist, graphics designer, illustrator, actress*
Straight Arrow, Janet *holistic professional, educator*

Wyandanch
Hodges-Robinson, Chettina M. *nursing administrator*

Yaphank
Freund, Pepsi *artist, art educator*

Yonkers
Boveroux, Lorie Ann Hansen *secondary school educator, graphics designer*
Capodilupo, Elizabeth Jeanne Hatton *public relations executive*
Hough, Barbara *library media specialist, educator*
Lee, Claudia S. *retired elementary school educator*
Lieberman, Trudy *healthcare journalist*
Liggio, Jean Vincenza *adult education educator, artist*
Mayer, Heidi Marie *primary school educator*
Neal, Leora Louise Haskett *social services administrator*
Patton, Debra Ruth *elementary school educator*
Pickover, Betty Abravanel *retired executive legal secretary, civic volunteer*
Roberson, Doris Jean Herold *retired social worker*
Singer, Cecile Doris *bank executive, former state legislator*
Slade, Margot S. *editor*
Viola, Mary Jo *art history educator*
Weston, Francine Evans *secondary school educator*

Yorkshire
Friedhaber-Hard, Susan Margaret *library media educator*

Yorktown Heights
Braddock, Nonnie Clarke *religious organization administrator*
Jones, Lauretta Marie *artist, designer, computer science researcher*
Schiller, Barbara *retired special education educator*
Smith, Cheryl A. *science educator*

Youngstown
Askins, Nancy Ellen Paulsen *training services executive*
Mehr, Vicki Joyce *music educator*

Youngsville
Bracken, Lynda *physical education educator*

NORTH CAROLINA

Aberdeen
Sinclair, Ruth Spears Smith *music educator*

Advance
Cochrane, Betsy Lane *former state senator*
Jones, Jerry Lou Holbert *elementary school educator, rancher*

Ahoskie
Adams, Martha Jean Morris *art educator, artist*
Bracy, Cecelia Wiggins *primary school educator*

Albemarle
Adrian, Judy *healthcare educator*

Andrews
Marta, Dawn Reneé *psychologist*

Apex
Corn, Melissa Ann *secondary school educator*
Olson, Jean Lounsbury *social worker*
Sapp, Brenda *elementary school educator*

Arden
Cotsonas, Elena Catherine *music educator*

Asheboro
Buchanan, Elizabeth Spoon *assistant principal, language educator*
Menius, Joy Victoria *musician, music educator*
Ray, Juanita S. *secondary school educator*

Asheville
Allen-Swarttouw, Heather Lindsey *artist, art educator, writer*
Brooker, Lena Epps *human services administrator, consultant*
Cragnolin, Karen Zambella *real estate developer, lawyer*
Dotson, Elizabeth Quillen *speech pathology/audiology services professional*
Facciponti, Laura Lynne *theater educator*
Fedock, Barbara C. *primary school educator, consultant*
Hammett, Doris Bixby *retired pediatrician*
Korb, Elizabeth Grace *nurse midwife*
Letzig, Betty Jean *financial consultant*
Mack, Carole *financial consultant*
Plonka, Lavinia *performing arts educator*
Polite, Lettie Wilson *retired elementary school educator, retired school librarian*
Redmond, Glenis G. *performance poet*
Sgro, Beverly Huston *principal, elementary school educator, state official*
Sieber Johnson, Ruth E. *music educator*
Turcot, Marguerite Hogan *medical researcher*
Voigt, Ellen *literature educator*

Banner Elk
Persons, Marjorie AnnaBelle *publishing executive, writer*

Battleboro
Hardy, Linda Lea Sterlock *media specialist*

Belmont
Belli, Rebecca Sue *elementary school educator, music educator*
Cannon, Barbara Somers *secondary school educator*

Benson
Stewart, Kennette Nowell *music educator*

Bessemer City
Sellers, Laurie Jean *elementary school educator*

Black Mountain
Belue, Janie A. *music educator*
Blackwell, Anna Nelle *medical educator, medical technician*

Blowing Rock
Thomas-Bevington, Vera Ellen Ball *retired physical education educator*

Boiling Springs
Wright, Bonnie McLean *psychology educator*

Boone
McFadden, Margaret H. *education educator, writer*
Miller, Geraldine Alice *psychologist, educator*
Olin Zimmerman, Sara Jane *education educator*

Bostic
Hooper, Kay *writer*
Smith, Teresa Hunt *elementary school educator, counselor*

Brevard
Alcorn, Karen Zefting Hogan *artist, educator, journalist*
Dillon, Doris (Doris Dillon Kenofer) *artist, art historian, educator, interior designer*
Finnerty, Frances Martin *medical administrator*
Jones, Sandy (Sandra F. Jones) *writer, speaker, parenting expert*

Bryson City
Mason, Sonja *secondary school educator*

Buies Creek
Wright, Mary P. *counselor*

Burlington
Holt, Bertha Merrill *state legislator*
Moncure, Jane Belk *educator, author, consultant*
Phillips, Ruth Ann *retired secondary school educator*

Burnsville
Allen, Rosetta Rosetta *elementary school educator*

Butner
Crowell, Rosemary Elaine *social services administrator*

Canton
Dixon, Shirley Juanita *retired restaurant owner*

Carthage
Brady, Jean Vick *education educator*
Manning, Patricia Anne *small business owner*

Cary
Beals, Betsy Jones *elementary school educator*
Bruce, Brenda *pianist*
Bryant, Mynora Joyce *not-for-profit fundraiser*
Coderre, Nancy Adele *financial analyst*
Daniels, Astar *artist*
Gordon, Suzanne *information technology executive*
Kirk, Bonnie Longest *retired elementary school educator*

Chapel Hill
Bayen, Ute Johanna *psychology professor, researcher*
Berne, Suzanne *writer, educator*
Broad, Margaret Corbett (Molly Broad) *academic administrator*
Campbell, Frances Alexander *psychologist*
Davis, Sarah Irwin *retired language educator*
Dolan, Louise Ann *physicist*
Dolber, Carole Christoff *secondary school educator, music educator*
Farber, Rosann Alexander *geneticist, educator*
Fletcher, Suzanne Wright *epidemiologist, medical educator, editor*
Folkerts, Jean *dean, journalism educator*
Gasaway, Laura Nell *law librarian, educator*
Gervais-Gruen, Elizabeth *lawyer*
Gil, Karen M. *psychology professor*
Gordon-Larsen, Penny *nutritionist, educator, researcher*
Gray, Virginia Hickman *political science professor*
Gray-Little, Bernadette *psychologist, educator*
Harrison, Katherine Gordon *tennis coach*
Hill, Deborah Ann *special education educator*
Hunter, Brenda Ann *writer, psychologist*
Johnson, Lucie Jenkins *retired social worker*
Kagetsu, Naomi J. *dermatologist*
Kinnaird, Eleanor Gates *state legislator, lawyer*
Kytle, Caroline Elizabeth *writer*
Lauder, Valarie Anne *editor, educator*
Levine, Madeline Geltman *literature and language educator, translator*
Lucas, Carol Lee *biomedical engineer*
Martikainen, A(une) Helen *retired health specialist educator*
Michalak, Sarah C. *university librarian*
Moran, Barbara Burns *librarian, educator*
Mueller, Nancy Schneider *retired biology professor*
Peacock, Florence F. *professional musician, soprano, voice educator*
Pisano, Etta D. *radiologist, educator*
Prather, Donna Lynn *psychiatrist*
Ravenel, Shannon *book publishing professional*
Schoonover, Brenda B. *ambassador*
Sharpe, Karen L. *science association director*
Spencer, Elizabeth *writer*
Stevens, Phyllis A. *conceptual artist*
Vachudova, Milada Anna *political science professor*
Wasik, Barbara Hanna *psychologist, educator*
Wegner, Judith Welch *lawyer, educator, dean*
Weiss, Shirley F. *retired urban and regional planner, economist, educator*
Wilfert, Catherine M. *medical association administrator, pediatrician, epidemiologist, educator*
Willingham, Emagene Emanuel *social worker*

Charlotte
Barber, Martha Gayle *lawyer*
Bauroth, Nancy Ann *journalist, former marketing executive*
Benfield, Kimberly Joyce McFall *media specialist*
Bessant, Cathy (Catherine Pombier Bessant) *bank executive, marketing professional*
Bliss, Melissa Moore *chemistry educator*
Brazeal, Donna Smith *psychologist*
Brinkley, Amy Woods *bank executive*
Carino, Linda Susan *business consultant*
Cernyak-Spatz, Susan E. *retired language educator*
Clark, Ranjana B. *bank executive*
Crawford, Jenny Lynn Sluder *medical/surgical nurse, educator*
Crawford, Juanita Gatewood *nursing technician*
Davis, Jean E. *bank executive*
Desoer, Barbara J. *bank executive*
Dixon, Georgette (Gigi Dixon) *bank executive*
Dunn, Sandra E. *insurance agent*
Eppley, Frances Fielden *secondary school educator, writer*
Erwin, Betty *bank executive*
Finley, Glenna *writer*
Fornelli, Cynthia M. *bank executive*
Fretwell, Dorrie Shearer *retired psychologist*
Gambrell, Sarah Belk *retail executive*
Goode, Rebekah Evelyn *literature and language educator*
Goolkasian, Paula A. *psychologist, educator*
Graham, Sylvia Angelenia *wholesale distribution executive, retail buyer*
Gross, Patricia Louise *neuropsychologist*
Hayman, Helen Feeley *retired nursing director*
Hicks-Ray, Denyse *psychologist, commentator*
Higgins, Diane W. *music teacher*
Hill, Ruth Foell *language consultant*
Hinson, Jane Pardee Henderson *lactation consultant*
Hofmann, Noreen *elementary school educator, music educator*
Hoskie, Lorraine *consumer products representative, poet*
House, Robin Christine *real estate agent, art consultant*
Huss, Carol Berryhill *mathematics educator*
Iley, Martha Strawn *music educator*
Jain, Astrid Genda *obstetrician, gynecologist*
Kelley, Janet Godsey *lawyer*
Lacey, Trudi *professional athletics coach*
Locke, Elizabeth Hughes *retired foundation administrator*
Lyerly, Elaine Myrick *advertising executive*
McFayden, Shannon W. *bank holding company executive*
McKay-Wilkinson, Julie Ann *minister, marriage and family therapist*
McVicker, Melissa Quick *counseling administrator, educator*
Mercer, Evelyn Lois *retired counseling administrator*
Mickle, Deloris B. *retired credit manager, artist*
Moore, Bealer Gwen *transcription company executive*
Newcomb, Betty Lou Atkinson *retired mathematics educator*
Nichols, Debra *bank executive*
Pardee, Teresa Tansey *history educator*
Pearson, Gwendolyn Cureton *elementary school educator, singer*
Peterson, Evonne Stewart *elementary school educator*
Peterson, Teresa B. *educational consultant*
Ramminger, Shelly Lynn *elementary school educator*
Reese, Annette Evelyn *music educator*
Shappert, Gretchen C. F. (Gretchen Cecilia Frances Shappert) *prosecutor, lawyer*
Shaw, Ruth G. *energy company executive*
Simpson, Karen Crandall *artist, educator*
Staley, Dawn Michelle *professional basketball player*
Stinson, Andrea Maria *professional basketball player*
Stone, Katherine Smith *science educator*
Strawn, Martha Ann *art educator, photographer, writer*
Sutton, Cecilia (Cece Sutton) *bank executive*
Tobias, Dorothy Burton *retired music educator, consultant*
Tranquillo, Mary Dora *organization development consultant, educator*
Tyson, Cynthia Haldenby *academic administrator*
Vazquez Rivera, Ornela Amliv *psychologist*
Vowell, Evelene C. *retired real estate broker*
Wall, Audrey G. *secondary school educator*
Welch, Jeanie Maxine *librarian*
Withrow, Shawanna Nicole *paralegal, entrepreneur*
Wright, Bonnie H. *elementary school educator*
Yancy, Dorothy Cowser *college president*

Cherryville
Barger, Linda Kale *choral director*
Beam, Susan Putnam *elementary school educator*

Claremont
Elmore, Beth Robinson *science educator*

Clayton
Coates, Deborah Phillips *visual arts educator*

Clinton
Griffin, Betty Lou *not-for-profit developer, educator*

Colfax
Hodge, Katherine Rhodes *retired school guidance counselor*

Columbus
Sauvé, Carolyn Opal *writer, journalist, poet*
Wetherby, Ivor Lois *librarian*

Concord
DeVore, Leigh Ann *gifted and talented educator, elementary school educator*
Gardiner, Jill Kennon *secondary school educator*
Long, Amy E. *secondary school educator*
Sossamon, Nancy H. *city official*
Switalski, Joy Patricia *athletic trainer*

Conover
Williams, Nancy Carole *nursing researcher*

Cornelius
Lindenberger, Kathleen Marie *literature and language educator*

Cove City
Hawkins, Elinor Dixon (Mrs. Carroll Woodard Hawkins) *retired librarian*
Schiller, Pamela Ann *physical education educator*

Cullowhee
Armfield, Terri Elaine *music educator, musician*
Fenton, Mary Catherine *literature educator*
Schwiebert, Valerie L. *counselor*

Dallas
Brown, Pearlie Murray *school librarian*
McCullough, Alicia *English language educator*

Davidson
Cathey, Mary Ellen Jackson *religious studies educator*
Dixon, Stephanie Bell *elementary school educator*
Grosch, Laura Dudley *artist, educator*

Denton
Zwiebel, Marie Bee *retired librarian*

Denver
Gleasner, Diana Cottle *author*

Dobson
McNeil, Amy *language educator, web site designer*

Drexel
McCall, Maxine Cooper *publisher, minister, educator, writer*

Dunn
Hill, Susan Beasley *recreational therapist*
Norris, Wanda Payne *science educator*

Durham
Alden, Betsy Turecky *academic administrator, clergywoman*
Armstrong, Brenda Estelle *pediatrician, cardiologist*
Bartlett, Katharine Tiffany *dean, law educator*
Bernard, Pamela Jenks *lawyer*
Blissitt, Patricia Ann *medical/surgical nurse*
Bradford, Dolli Maria *music educator*
Buckley, Rebecca Hatcher *allergist, immunologist, pediatrician, educator*
Canada, Mary Whitfield *retired librarian*

Clayton, Marla Cooper *speech pathology/audiology services professional*
Demott, Deborah Ann *law educator*
Denlinger, Ann T. *school system administrator*
Fisk, Catherine Laura *law educator, lawyer*
Gilliss, Catherine Lynch *nursing educator*
Goestenkors, Gail *basketball coach*
Hankins, Sherlene LaSalle *mathematician, educator*
Hoffman, Jennifer Anne *vascular technician, director*
Hogan, Brigid L.M. *molecular biologist*
Holder, Angela Roddey *law educator*
Iarovici, Doris M *psychiatrist, writer*
Jakubs, Deborah *university librarian*
Jurgelski, Annette Elizabeth *academic administrator*
Kaprielian, Victoria Susan *medical educator*
Kerckhoff, Sylvia Stansbury *mayor*
King, Marjorie Jean *secondary school educator*
Krugman, Marian G. *retired librarian*
Kurtzberg, Joanne *pediatrician, educator*
Lewis, Margaret Shively *retired librarian*
McClain, Paula Denice *political scientist, educator*
Morris, Valerie L. *music educator*
Moss, Marcia Lynn *retired biochemist*
Nwosu, Veronica C. *microbiologist, science educator, medical researcher*
Nye, Mary Jane Love *pediatrician, educator*
Pericak-Vance, Margaret A. *health facility administrator*
Rorschach, Kimberly *museum director*
Rouse, Doris Jane *physiologist, research scientist*
Schiffman, Susan Stolte *medical psychologist, educator*
Stevens, Jane Sexton *psychologist*
Sylver, Donna *bank executive*
Van Duzer, Dory A. *translator*
Vick, Marsha Cook *writer, humanities educator*
Wald, Priscilla B. *language educator*
Watkins, Melynda *chemist, researcher*
Wilson, Ruby Leila *nursing educator*

Eden
Sanders, Barbara Fayne *artist, educator*

Edenton
Muro-Torres, Rosalita *elementary school educator*
Sams, Robin Dahl *artist*

Elizabeth City
Pierce, Dianne S. *city clerk*
Tomlinson, Susan K. *elementary school educator*

Elon
Smith, Carol Anne *retired physical education educator*
Wilmshurst, Linda Anne *psychologist, writer*

Emerald Isle
Mikkelsen, Nina Elizabeth Markowitz *writer, researcher*

Fairmont
Spencer, Melissa Johanna *psychotherapist, special education educator*

Fairview
Mullins, Diane Louise *dermatologist*

Fayetteville
Barnicle, Mary Anne *music educator, piano accompanist*
Batts, Dorothy Marie *clergywoman, educator, writer*
Carrasquillo, Katrina Beaufort *secondary school educator, consultant*
Curry, Virginia Frances *retired language educator*
Darnell, Michelle R. *philosophy educator*
Farrior, Helen Hooks *retired assistant principal*
Hagans, Valerie Mae Gee *special education educator*
Jordan, Karla Salge *retired primary school educator*
Kem, Katherine Frances *urban planner*
MacRae, Elizabeth (Elizabeth MacRae Halsey) *counselor, actor*
McMillan, Bettie Barney *language educator*
Miller, Bertha Hampton *history professor*
Mohn, Amy Elizabeth Brennan *special education educator, retail executive, consultant*
Parker, Ellen Koonce *retired secondary school educator*
Roe, Kathryn Jane *elementary school educator*
Smith, Mable Cogdell *retired county official*
Squire, Sheri Marie *science educator*
Widdows, Marianne Shuta *orchestra director*
Williams, Susan Bullard *music educator*

Fearrington Village
Cell, Gillian Townsend *retired historian, educator*

Flat Rock
Oliver, Ann Breeding *secondary school educator, art dealer*

Fort Bragg
Manning, Deborah Cothran *art educator*
Nichols, Carol-Lee *real estate broker, property manager*

Franklin
Berger, Lee Hollingsworth *secondary school educator*
Earhart, Eileen Magie *retired elementary school educator, retired child and family life educator*
Kinard, Cynthia Cochran *artist, writer*

Franklinton
Elmore, Cenieth Catherine *music educator*

Garner
Barbour, Charlene *management firm executive*
Retseck, Meghan Maerene *elementary school educator*

Gastonia
Burns, Judith O'Dell *library assistant, educator*
Evelyn, Ball Love *mathematics educator, department chairman*

Goldsboro
Cannon, Alice Grace *counselor*
Turlington, Patricia Renfrew *artist, educator*

Graham
Collins, Lucinda Varn *occupational therapist*

Greensboro
Abell, Nicole Forcht *secondary school educator*
Archibald, Brigitte Edith *language educator*
Bynum, Magnolia Virginia Wright *retired secondary school educator*
Chandler, Austin Grace *psychologist*
Chilton, Mary-Dell Matchett *chemical company executive*
Cole, Johnnetta Betsch *academic administrator, educator*
Gill, Diane Louise *psychology professor, dean*
Gill, Evalyn Pierpoint *editor, writer, publisher*
Green, Jill I. *dance educator, researcher*
Harris-Offutt, Rosalyn Marie *counselor, consultant, mental health nurse, writer*
Helms-VanStone, Mary Wallace *anthropology educator*
Hudgens, Jeanne Ellis *advocate*
Ingold, Jennifer Carrie *educator*
Kovacs, Beatrice *library studies educator*
Lloyd, Lila G. *business educator*
Nieman, Valerie Gail *language educator, journalist*
Oliver, Donna H. *academic administrator, secondary school educator*
Penninger, Frieda Elaine *retired literature educator*
Roerden, Chris (Claire Roerden) *editor, business owner, publishing consultant*
Russell, Anne Wrenn *property manager*
Russell, Peggy Taylor *soprano, educator*
Shaw, Linda Dare Owens *county commissioner*
Smith, Rebecca McCulloch *social sciences educator*
Spencer, Linda Anne *history professor*
Stone, Theresa M. *communications executive*
Styles, Teresa Jo *television producer, educator*
Sullivan, Patricia A. *academic administrator*
Tinsley, Karen Mccoy *psychology professor*
Wagoner, Anna Mills S. *prosecutor*
Wallace, Becky Whitley *protective services official*
Watson, Betty *artist*
Zopf, Evelyn LaNoel Montgomery *retired guidance counselor*

Greenville
Bauer, Margaret Donovan *literature and language professor, editor*
Bjorkman, Sylvia Johnson *psychologist*
Faircloth, Mary Williams *minister, educator*
Gilham, Hanna Kaltenbrunner *writer*
Honesty, Tara Marie *educational consultant, educator*
Johnson, Cynda Ann *physician, educator*
Khuri, Soumaya Makdissi *mathematics professor*
Mega, Lesly Tamarin *psychiatrist, educator*
Tripp, Linda A. Lynn *small business owner*
Turnage, Karen L. *medical technician*
Weatherington, LaVeta Hinson *visual arts specialist*
Weathers, Vivian Joy *physician administrator*

Hallsboro
Barefoot, Anne Farley *secondary education educator, consultant*

Havelock
Jacques, Paula G. *literature and language educator*

Hendersonville
Cochran, Linda Thornthwaite *psychotherapist, social worker, consultant*
Consilio, Barbara Ann *legal association administrator, management consultant*
Hamilton, Hilda Wingo *elementary school educator*
Houck, Amelia Ann *elementary school educator*
Jefferson, Letitia Gibson *rehabilitation counselor*
Kingsbury, Carolyn Ann *aerospace engineer, craftsman, writer*
Tatreau, (Dolores) Maxine *artist*
Tatsch, Jacki Lynn *music educator, diversified financial services company executive*

Hertford
Cole, Janice McKenzie *former prosecutor*

Hickory
Barnes, Sylvia *family practice physician*
Fisher, Kathryn Pattillo *education educator, department chairman*
Mason, Anne R. Hardin *municipal official*
Painter, Lorene Huffman *retired education educator, psychologist*
Samamra, Elizabeth Prestwood *literature educator*
Sherrill, Betty Pearson *retired elementary school educator*
Stokes, Betty *music educator*
Touchette, Collette W. *mathematics professor*
Whiteley, Emily C. *biology professor*

High Point
Draelos, Zoe Diana *dermatologist, consultant*
Ellis, Phyllis Simerly *elementary educator, reading specialist*
Howard, Lou Dean Graham *elementary school educator*
Palmer, Pamela Murrill *educator*
Scearse, Patricia Dotson *nursing educator, dean*

Highlands
DeWolf, Jane Evans *mathematics educator*

Hillsborough
Richmond, Donna *speech-language pathologist*
Roney, Sarah Davis *elementary school educator*
Stephens, Brenda Wilson *librarian*

Horse Shoe
Osby, Mary Ann Caroline *secondary school educator*

Hubert
Howell, Nelda Kay *commissioner*

Huntersville
Jagoe, Tonya Burr *elementary school educator*
Nowlin, Connie Blackwell *artist*
Taylor, Sylvia Dawn *music educator*

Jacksonville
Fischer, Violeta Pèrez Cubillas *Spanish literature and linguistics educator*
Harlow, Elizabeth Snell *physical education educator*

Jefferson
Maney, Lois Jean *postmaster*

Kannapolis
Wilson, Evelyn Gleen *retired language educator*

Kenly
Weaver, Ann Rogerson *art educator*

Kernersville
McGuire, Andrea Bullard *social studies educator*
Wallace, Stephanie Jean *language educator*
Webb, Ann Marie *literature and language educator, department chairman*

Kill Devil Hills
Blonder, Barbara Irene *biologist*

King
Hunter, Deborah H. *elementary school educator*
Shanahan, Elizabeth Anne *art educator*

Kings Mountain
Aderholdt, Traci Eaves *music educator*
Sellers, Elizabeth Ellison *special education educator*

Kinston
Baker-Gardner, Jewelle *interior designer, business consultant*
Matthis, Eva Mildred Boney *retired academic administrator*
Vernon, Jane Harper *music educator*

Kitty Hawk
Elliott, Candice K. *interior designer*

Knightdale
Rhodes, Rhonda Cockrell *science educator*

La Grange
Sasser, Brenda Glenn *elementary school educator*

Lake Toxaway
King, Carole Wayne *foundation administrator*
Raynolds, Elaine Spalding *sales executive, photojournalist*

Laurel Springs
Gilbert-Strawbridge, Anne Wieland *journalist*

Laurinburg
Hamby, Sherry Lynne *psychologist, researcher*
Key, Kristina Pope *literature and language professor*
Williams, Kathryn Vandervoort *science educator*

Leasburg
Treacy, Sandra Joanne Pratt *artist, educator*

Leicester
Entzi, Karen Russell *orchestra educator*

Lewisville
Gould, Anne Austin *special education educator*
Krier, Ann O. *product designer, writer*

Lexington
Carlton, Robbin Briley *elementary school educator*

Liberty
Coco, Donna A. W. *elementary school educator*

Lillington
O'Brien, Eileen Kathryn *art educator*

Littleton
Skinner, Sue Dossett *retired director*

Lumberton
Canonizado, Gloria M. *choreographer, educator*
Harris, Audra Brisson *education educator*
Johnson, Judy Van *minister, educator*
Tolar, Anne Melton *minister, music educator*

Manteo
Evans, Michelle T. *county official*

Marion
Pratt, Sarah Ellen *secondary school educator*
Weaver, Joe Le Ann *biology educator*

Mars Hill
Greene, Tena Lorraine *singer, educator, actor*

Matthews
Kocsis, Joan Bosco *elementary school educator*
McClanahan, Tina Annette *elementary school educator, consultant*
Rorie, Kathy Marie *artist*

Mebane
Fricke, Jill E. *elementary school educator*

Misenheimer
Kean, Barbara McSwain *education educator, department chairman*

Monroe
Rorie, Nancy Catherine *retired secondary school educator*
Wallace, Patricia Ellen *evangelist, minister*
Williams, Karen C. *elementary school educator*

Mooresboro
Goode, Elizabeth Ann *music educator*

Plummer, Doris Gochnauer *elementary school educator*

Mooresville
Dow, Leslie Wright *communications company executive, photographer, writer*
Münter, Leilani Maaja *race car driver*

Morehead City
Gross, Marjorie K. *education educator, educator, small business owner*

Morganton
Bailey-Day, Kay Lynn *psychotherapist*
Bivens, Marjorie Earley *retired nursing educator*
Pritchard, Michelle C. *lawyer*
Singleton, Stella Wood *nurse*

Mount Airy
Billings, Melanie Sparks *secondary school educator, department chairman*

Mount Holly
Whobrey, Virginia Jean *retired director*

Mount Olive
Damon, Sherri Marcia *music educator*
Day, Tyanna Yonkers *religious studies educator, minister*
Johnson, Josephine Powell *power and light company district manager*
Mason Foster, Angela Marie *biology professor*

Murfreesboro
Wallace, Dorothy Mae Adkins *educator*

Murphy
Brooks, Ellyn Hersh *retired special education educator*
Deslauriers, Suzanne Dawsey *secondary school educator, artist*
Holcomb, Linda Laine *elementary school educator, director*
Ricketson, Mary Alice *psychotherapist*
Russell, Margaret Jones (Peg Russell) *retired secondary school educator, writer*

Nashville
High, (Mary) Elizabeth Hilley *retired art educator*
Penick, Angela Lucas *elementary school educator*

New Bern
Harper, Elizabeth Scott *academic administrator, retired literature educator*
Linkonis, Suzanne Newbold *retired probation officer, retired counselor*
Phipps, Patsy Duncan *retired auditor*
White, Rhea Amelia *library and information scientist*

Newland
Campany, Kay Hudkins *biology educator, assistant principal*
Lustig, Susan Gardner *occupational therapist*

Newport
Mundine, Rachel Quinn *music educator*

North Topsail Beach
Kelley, Virginia Wiard (Judy Kelley) *dance educator*

North Wilkesboro
Parsons, Irene Adelaide *management consultant*
Shumaker, Tara L. *performing arts educator*

Otto
Harwell, Joanne Brindley *music educator*

Oxford
Hafner, Margot Annette *music educator, voice educator*
Harvey, Gloria-Stroud *physician assistant*

Pembroke
Jackson, B. Ellen Hursey *music educator*
Sexton, Jean Elizabeth *librarian*

Pfafftown
Johnson, Theresa M. *retired special education educator*

Pilot Mountain
Sawyers, Lorrie Brown *social studies educator*

Pine Knoll Shores
Graham, Gloria Flippin *dermatologist*

Pinehurst
Denton, Estelle Rosemary *retired federal agency administrator*

Pineville
Nemeth, Dian Jean *secondary school educator*

Pittsboro
Boyce, Emily Stewart *retired library and information science educator, retired library and information scientist*
Flowers, Helen Foote *librarian, educator*
Freehling, Brooke Ann *elementary school educator*

Raeford
Abreu, Sue Hudson *physician, retired military officer, health facility administrator, consultant*

Raleigh
Bailey, Mary Beatrice *retired health science association administrator*
Bar, Roselyn R. *legal association administrator, lawyer, executive secretary*
Bateman, Angela Anderson *anesthetist*
Bellamy, Kristi Michelle *prosecutor*
Brooks, Jackie Daniel *social studies educator*
Bykova, Marina F. *philosopher, educator*
Carter, Jean Gordon *lawyer*
Cauthen, Carmen Wimberley *legislative staff member, jewelry designer*

Davis, Janice *school system administrator*
Deihl, Susan Galyen *preservationist*
Dew, Carolyn Christine *health facility administrator, nurse*
Duncan, Allyson K. *federal judge*
Evans, Janet *publishing executive*
Fantz, Janet Nelsen *school psychologist*
Fincher, Norma Beeby *music educator, performer*
Freeman, Janet L. *librarian*
Garriss, Phyllis Weyer *music educator, performer*
Geller, Janice Grace *nurse*
Goldwasser, Shirley Whiteman *educational psychologist*
Gustafson, Sarah *elementary school educator*
Hardison, Cynthia Ann Stoltze *hematologist, retired oncologist*
Hartford, Maureen A. *academic administrator*
Henderson, Shirley Elizabeth *minister*
Hiday, Virginia Aldigé *sociologist, educator*
Hughes, Barbara Ann *dietician, public health administrator*
Jarrett, Polly Hawkins *retired secondary school educator*
Johnson, Mary Pauline (Polly Johnson) *nursing administrator*
Johnson, Melissa Ramirez *psychologist*
Jordan, Brenda Moore *artist*
Joyner, Lorinzo Little *commissioner*
Kauffman, Terry *broadcast and creative arts communication educator, artist*
Lamarque, Natalie Ghisslaine *psychologist*
Lenard, Mary Jane *finance educator*
Lilly, Nancy Cobb *civic worker*
Malling, Martha Hale Shackford *social worker, educator*
Marshall, Elaine Folk *state official*
McGee, Linda Mace *judge, lawyer*
McKinney, Carolyn *educational association administrator, educator*
McNish, Susan Kirk *retired lawyer*
Nelson, Brandy René *assistant principal*
Nelson, Cynthia Kaye *infrastructure security engineer*
Newhouse, Sherri France *elementary school educator*
Nutter, Susan K. *librarian, academic administrator*
Occhetti, Dianne *psychologist, writer*
Owen, Carolyn Trent *education educator*
Page, Anne Ruth *gifted and talented educator, education specialist*
Parker, Sarah Elizabeth *state supreme court chief justice*
Parramore, Barbara Mitchell *education educator*
Paschal, Beth Cummings *journalist, editor*
Pearsall, Mary Helen *retired counselor*
Perdue, Beverly Eaves *lieutenant governor, geriatric consultant*
Petteway, Diane Cashwell *music educator, musician*
Pope, Elizabeth Stephens *dance educator*
Rauch, Kathleen *computer executive*
Robinson, Charlotte Hill *artist*
Rudinger, Jennifer Irene *legal association administrator*
Rusher, Mary Nash Kelly *lawyer*
Sardi, Elaine Marie *special education educator*
Sill, Melanie *editor*
Steed, Michelle Elnora *special education educator, consultant*
Stevenson, Denise L. *diversified financial services company executive, consultant, realtor*
Susanka, Sarah Hills *architect*
Tally, Lura Self *state legislator*
Tucker, Helen Welch *writer*
Tyndall, Krystal Gwen *secondary school educator*
Webster, Debbie Ann *social worker*
Wilder, Lisa Yvette *dancer, educator*
Youngman, Lola Jeanne *music educator*
Zelek, Cheryl Ann *gifted and talented educator*

Randleman
Jordan, Lillian B. *judge*

Research Triangle Park
Bond, Enriqueta Carter *science administrator*
Bronstein, Lois Helene *marketing professional*
Campbell, Kay Nordan *nurse, health educator*
Fought, Lorianne *plant pathologist*
Haynes, Victoria F. *science administrator*
Karg, Rhonda Suzanne *psychologist, researcher*

Rockingham
Jackson, Anita Louise *otolaryngologist, editor-in-chief*

Rocky Mount
Davis, Barbara Judy *counselor, mental health educator*
Dickens, Alice McKnight *minister*
Edelman, Betsy A. (Elizabeth Edelman) *lawyer*

Rougemont
Holeman, Betty Jean *counseling administrator*
Nilsson, Mary Ann *music educator*

Roxboro
Broyles, Bonita Eileen *nursing educator*
Cowan, Amy Michelle *elementary school educator*
Hollingsworth, Brenda Jackson *employment consultant*

Rutherfordton
Crummie, Ann Vaughn *mental health services professional*

Salisbury
Hall, Telka Mowery Elium *retired assistant principal*
Julian, Rose Rich *music educator, director*
Troxler, Willie Thomasene *retired elementary school educator*
Ward, Brenda Robinson *social worker*

Sanford
Brown, Eva Everlean *business executive*
Lloyd, Jennifer Leigh *psychology professor*
York, Carolyn Pleasants Stearns *language educator*

Shallotte
Sabiston, Kelli Brewer *athletic trainer, consultant*
Weaver, Lyn Ann Simmons *psychologist*

Shelby
Edgar, Ruth R. *retired elementary school educator*

Sherrills Ford
Stynes, Barbara Bilello *integrative health professional, educator*

Smithfield
Harris, Patricia Ann Brady *principal, educational consultant*
Lamberson, Carolyn Jane Hinton *music educator*
Shumate, Donna Larsen *engineering educator, department chairman*
Wiggs, Shirley JoAnn *retired secondary school educator*

Snow Hill
Stevens, JoAnn A. *textile, political leader, author, minister*

Southern Pines
Cardwell, Nina Fern *special education educator*
Linsey, Elizabeth Arlline *primary school educator*

Southport
Kahai, Jugta *pediatrician*
Phelps, Mary Ann Bazemore *elementary school educator*
Pryor, Carolyn Gale Barnard *social work educator*

Spencer
Secreast, Patricia Lineberger *elementary school educator*

Spindale
Trautmann, Patricia Ann *communications educator, storyteller, art educator*

Stanley
Black, Saunders Proctor *special education educator*

Statesville
Crosby, Jane Watts *science educator*
Dacons, Gwendolyn Brown *educator*
Elliott, Carolyn Cole *secondary school educator, department chairman*
Gullett, Julia Shuping *judge*
Harris, Crystal Stone *science educator, coach*
Harris, Nancy Lewis *home economics educator*
Hoover, Lynn Horn *secondary school educator*
Johnston, Betty Parker *retired social service worker*

Swanquarter
Credle, Gina C. *mathematics educator*

Sylva
Clapp, Amanda Grace *elementary school educator*

Taylorsville
Johnston, April M. *elementary school educator*

Todd
Cole, Susan Stockbridge *retired theater educator*

Wadesboro
Hamby, Kristie Lynne *director*

Wake Forest
Kimrey, Karen Goss *secondary school educator*

Walstonburg
Beaman, Joyce Proctor *retired secondary and elementary school educator, writer*

Warrenton
Kearney, Irene Spruill *elementary school educator*
Weddington, Debralta Gardner (Liz Gardner) *actress*

Washington
Strayhorn Crump, Joretta Petrice *health educator, substance abuse consultant*

Waxhaw
Edwards, Irene Elizabeth (Libby Edwards) *dermatologist, educator, medical researcher*

Waynesville
Ingle, Marti Annette *protective services official, educator, chef*

Weaverville
Budhisetiawan, Barbara Crawford *music educator*
Chamberlain, Elizabeth Simmons *retired English language educator*

Wentworth
Lumpkin, Vicki G. *minister*

Wilkesboro
Anderson, Theresa A. *retail executive*
Dale, Brenda Stephens *gifted and talented educator*
Klark, Denise J. *special education educator, consultant*
Powell, Betty Crowder *artist, educator*

Williamston
Wobbleton, Judy Karen *artist, educator*

Willow Spring
Monahan, Sherry Ann *writer*
Valvo, Barbara-Ann *lawyer, surgeon*

Wilmington
Baehmann, Susan Elizabeth *artist*
Baldridge, Jane L. *graphic and fine artist*
Bomhan, Ruth Walker *social studies educator*
Cameron, Kay *conductor, composer*
Clinton, Lottie Dry Edwards *retired state agency administrator*
Coté, Debra Nan *surgical nurse*
DePaolo, Rosemary *academic administrator*
Desjardins, Betty Lee *histologist*
DeVos, Renee Nichole *personal trainer, elementary school educator*
Foglia, Michelle Lynn *psychologist*
Gray, Marilyn F. Grinwis *elementary school educator, music educator*
Israel, Margie Olanoff *psychotherapist*
Kelley, Patricia Hagelin *geology educator*
Kinney, Robin Smith *chemist, educator*
Maness, Eleanor Palmer *researcher*
Onufer, Nicole Holder *music educator*
Robinson, Robin Wicks *lawyer*
Seapker, Janet Kay *museum administrator, historic site director, consultant*
Stanfield-Maddox, Elizabeth *language educator, translator*
Stein, Joan Dorothy *nurse anesthetist*
Tallant, Carole E. *communications educator*
Walters, Doris Lavonne *retired religious organization administrator, human services manager*

Wilson
Howell, Maria DeLane *elementary school educator*
McCain, Betty Landon Ray (Mrs. John Lewis McCain) *political party official, state official*
Morris, Sharon Louise Stewart *emergency medical technician, paramedic*
Woods, Deborah Lynn *recruiter*

Wingate
Sunderland, Deborah P. *chemist, educator*

Winston Salem
Bottoms, Rebecca Lynn *literature and language educator*
Cahill, Eileen Mary *secondary school educator*
Caldwell, Toni Marie *religious organization administrator*
Cieszewski, Sandra Josephine *artist, retired manufacturing company manager*
Cook, Sharon Warren *social worker, educator*
Craven, Betty *educational association administrator*
Dalton, Mary M. *communications educator, documentary filmmaker*
Dixon, Patricia Abud *music educator*
Dykers, Carol Reese *communications educator*
Ferree, Carolyn Ruth *radiation oncologist, educator*
Gregg, Ellen M. *lawyer*
Handy, Danette Farmer *coach*
Hatcher, Beverly J. *pastor*
Hunt, Ellen *minister, evangelist*
Ivey, Susan M. *tobacco company executive*
Jarrell, Iris Bonds *elementary school educator, retired small business owner*
Jenkins, Barbara Alexander *pastor, overseer*
Lambeth, Judy (E. Julia Lambeth) *lawyer*
Ludolf, Marilyn Marie Keaton *lay worker*
Oliver, Patricia *lawyer*
Pubantz, Gloria Annunziata *elementary school educator*
Quick, Elizabeth L. *lawyer*
Saxton, Judith Ann *musician, educator*
Stewart, Gwendolyn Johns *music educator*
Sutton, Lynn Sorensen *librarian*
Weavil, Vicki Lemp *library director*

Winterville
Edwards, Sarah *biology educator*

Winton
Williams, Sue Darden *library director*

Wrightsville Beach
Marcolina, Kathryn Watkins *personal and professional success coach*

Youngsville
Burwell, Edith Brodie *retired elementary school educator*

Zebulon
McNair, Suzette Jordan *elementary school educator*
Privette, Janet Brown *elementary school educator*
Ruffing, Anne Elizabeth *artist*

NORTH DAKOTA

Belcourt
LaRocque, Geraldine Ann *literature educator*
Storey, Sandra Jean *emergency room nurse*

Beulah
Maize, Linda Lou *elementary school educator*

Bisbee
Keller, Michelle R. *science educator*

Bismarck
Evanson, Barbara Jean *middle school education educator*
Gray, Arlene *music educator, musician*
Joersz, Fran Woodmansee *secondary school educator*
Kapsner, Carol Ronning *state supreme court justice*
Ketterling, Debra M. *secondary school educator*
Knoll, Gloria Jean *music educator*
Maring, Mary Muehlen *state supreme court justice*
McCallum, Janet Ann Anderson *retired hardware store owner*
Moore, Sherry Mills *lawyer*
Nelson, Carolyn *state legislator*
Niksic, Gwen M. *biology professor*
Olson, Carol Hankins *occupational therapist, educator*
Ott, Doris Ann *librarian*
Reinert, Agnes Frances *chaplain, educator*
Schwartz, Judy Ellen *thoracic surgeon*
Solberg, Nellie Florence Coad *artist*
Stoller, Rose *think-tank executive*

Bottineau
Roemmich, Dalonnes Kay *music educator*

Devils Lake
Krogfoss, Kimberly Jean *elementary school educator*

Dickinson
Nelson, Debra L. *non-profit organization consultant*

Dunseith
Gladue, Irene *elementary school educator*

Edinburg
Myrdal, Rosemarie Caryle *state official, former state legislator*

Ellendale
Larson, Lavonne Fay *education educator*

Fargo
Ghazi, Stefanie Sara *obstetrician, gynecologist*
Herman, Sarah Andrews *lawyer*
Johnson Aldrich, Leslie Deborah *lawyer*
Lardy, Sister Susan Marie *academic administrator*
Lee, Judith *state legislator*
Meester, Holly *elementary school educator, music educator, sales executive*
Morey, Charlotte Ann *elementary school educator, music educator*
Richman, Rachel L. *food scientist, microbiologist, educator*
Schabert, Leah Christine *dance instructor*
Turka, Voleen Claire *surgeon*
Wachenheim, Cheryl J. *agricultural studies educator*

Fort Totten
Carlson, Eilene Theresa *counseling administrator*

Fort Yates
Chief Eagle, Joan *secondary school educator*

Gackle
Wittmier, Denise Donelle *elementary school educator*

Glenburn
Croonquist, Cheryl *music educator, realtor*

Golden Valley
Nordgren, Mary Kathleen (Kathy Nordgren) *secondary school educator*

Grand Forks
Ashe, Kathy Rae *special education educator*
Boesl, Beth Marie *music educator*
Caldwell, Mary Ellen *language educator*
DeMers, Judy Lee *retired state legislator, dean*
Heitkamp, Thomasine Lea *social work educator*
Hume, Wendelin M. *criminologist, educator*
Mikulak, Marcia Lee *anthropologist, educator*
Olson, Myrna Raye *education educator*
Page, Sally Jacquelyn *university official, management educator*
Popejoy, Melanie Ann *music educator*
Ryberg, Bridget Fay *literature and language educator*
Sobus, Kerstin MaryLouise *physician, physical therapist*
Swanson, Zona Luciel *retired elementary school educator*
Tiemann, Kathleen Anne *sociologist, educator*

Hettinger
Dunn, Jeri L. *literature and language educator*

Horace
Hajek, Melissa Dawn *elementary school educator*

Lisbon
Taylor, Ardis *science educator*

Mandan
Hossman, Rebecca Lynn *special education educator*

Mayville
Champion, Kathleen Ann *mathematics professor*
Karaim, Betty June *retired librarian*
LeClair, Elizabeth Jane *elementary school educator*

Minot
Moe, Vida Delores *civic worker*
Olson, Deborah J. *psychologist, educator*
Starr, Sandra Schjeldahl *music educator*
Watne, Darlene Claire *county official*

Ray
Anderson, Denise W. *psychologist, writer, musician*

Saint John
Haas, Judith *elementary school educator*

Stanley
Eliason, Bonnie Mae *county treasurer*

Trenton
Folkestad, Ruth L. *mathematics professor*

Valley City
Rogers, Patricia Louise *education educator, consultant*

Wahpeton
Dohman, Gloria Ann *librarian*
Donahe, Peggy Yvonne *gifted and talented educator, librarian*

West Fargo
Boutiette, Vickie Lynn *elementary school educator, reading specialist*
Morrison, Karen A. *music educator*
Simmons, Marti J. Johnson *gifted and talented education educator*
Ulrickson, Cheryl J. *elementary school educator*

Williston
Long, Amelia Rose *psychologist*

Slagle, Penny Lee *physical education educator*

Wishek
Dockter, Nancy Jean *principal, elementary school educator*

Zahl
Anfinson, Donna Mae *retired elementary school educator, home economics educator*

OHIO

Ada
Allison, Arlene Marie *elementary school educator*
Boger, Gail Green Parsons *educator*
Zank, MJ Sunny *musician, department chair, educator*

Akron
Beery, Amy Suzanne *music educator*
Bilgé-Johnson, Sumru A. *child psychiatrist*
Bishop, Christy B. *lawyer*
Collier, Alice Elizabeth Becker *retired social services administrator*
Dietz, Margaret Jane *retired public information director*
Donehey, Marilyn Moss *foundation administrator*
Evenski, Andrea Jean *orthopedist*
Franck, Ardath Amond *psychologist, educator*
Garbrandt, Gail Elaine *political science professor, consultant*
Geier, Kathleen T. *human resources specialist*
Graham, DeBorah Denise *minister, educator*
Houston, Alma Faye *psychiatrist*
Jones, Hedy Julie *retired secondary school educator*
Kazle, Elynmarie *theater producer, performing arts executive*
Keener, Polly Leonard *illustrator*
Korow, Elinore Maria *artist, educator*
Oldfield, Joy Malek *lawyer*
Piirma, Irja *chemist, educator*
Ramsey, Sally Judith Weine *chemist, research and development company executive*
Shane, Sandra Kuli *postal service administrator*
Shea-Stonum, Marilyn *federal bankruptcy judge*
Simmons, Debra Adams *editor*
Smith, Priscilla R. *social sciences educator*
Sparrow, Kathleen Gail *elementary school educator*
Stephens, Rachel De-Vore *finance company executive, educator*
Subich, Linda Mezydlo *counseling psychology educator*
Taylor, E. Jane *lawyer*
Usher, Ann L. *music educator*
Wymer, Danielle Marie *mathematics educator*

Alliance
Munford-Clark, Cenell Renea *healthcare educator, athletic trainer*
Smith Alder, Angela Grace *education educator*

Amelia
Hill, Diane L. *music educator*
Kahles, Cheryl Mary *elementary school educator*

Amherst
Gall, Simone Ellen *music educator*
Gerstenberger, Valerie *media specialist*
Von Kaenel, Michelle Lisa *elementary school educator*

Archbold
Guengerich, Ruth Lapp *counselor*

Ashland
Finnerty, Madeline Frances *consulting firm owner*
Ford, Lucille Garber *economist, educator*
Kodz, Irena Cheslavovna *internist*
Van Dresar, Vickie Janette *mathematician, educator*

Ashville
Beckman, Judith *art educator*

Athens
Cooper-Chen, Anne *journalism educator, researcher*
Harse, Constance Bradford *retired social worker*
Heaton, Jeanne Albronda *psychologist*
Miller, Peggy McLaren *retired management educator*
Purdy, Penny *music educator*
Safran, Joan Schulman *education educator, researcher*
Whealey, Lois Deimel *humanities scholar*

Aurora
Ross, Violet Bica *retired elementary school educator, retired psychologist*

Avon
Grmek, Dorothy Antonia *accountant*
Lahiff, Marilyn J. *nursing administrator*

Avon Lake
Parke, M(argaret) Jean *retired business owner, editor*
Shiba, Wendy C. *lawyer*

Bainbridge
Brizius, Janice Jane *producer, owner*

Barberton
Koch, Frances Didato *literature and language educator, writer*
Schrock, Ruth *elementary school educator*

Batavia
Campbell, Cheryl Gay *history educator*
Lewis, Joan Carol *chemist, educator*
Muskopf, Beth A. *supervisor*

Bath
Hoffer, Alma Jeanne *nursing educator*

Beachwood
Farley, Carolyn Juanita *music educator*
Fufuka, Natika Njeri Yaa *retail executive*

Beavercreek
Feller, Loretta Anne *elementary school educator*
Rinta, Christine Evelyn *nurse, air force officer*

Bedford
Pozz, Jennifer *art educator*

Bedford Heights
Golden, Virginia Ann *principal*

Bellbrook
Mann, Rebecca Ann *science educator, secondary school educator*
Requarth, Sherry Lorraine *special education services professional*

Berea
Bonds, Georgia Anna *writer, educator*
Sanders, Phyllis May *musician*
Tomlin-Houston, Lisa *higher education administrator, director*

Bergholz
Goddard, Sandra Kay *retired elementary school educator*

Berlin Center
Orevna, Nellie Lou *music educator*

Bethel
Weatherspoon, Mary Darlington *middle school educator*

Beverly
Foland-Bush, Terri *language educator, speech educator*
Spurr, Dawn M. *special education educator*

Bexley
Unverferth, Barbara Patten *small business owner*

Blacklick
Robinson, Bernice Joyce *secondary school educator*

Bolwing Green
Snavely, Deanne Lynn *chemistry professor*

Bowling Green
Baird, Alice Knar *retired education educator*
Clark, Eloise Elizabeth *biologist, educator*
Frederick, Janet Dennis *physical education educator*
Heckman, Carol A. *biology educator*
Krane, Vikki *psychology educator*
Krebs, Marjori Maddox *social studies educator, consultant*
McCutchan, Patricia Lynn *physician*

Brecksville
Pappas, Effie Vamis *language educator, finance educator, writer, poet, artist*

Broadview Heights
Jergens, Maribeth Joie *school counselor*

Brooklyn
Jaggard, Vicky Lynn *literature and language educator*

Brunswick
Harr, Gale Ann *school psychologist*
Kebberly, Dorene G. *elementary school educator, music educator*
Sadd, Wendy Marie *science educator*
Spirakus, Karen Ann *elementary school educator, researcher*
Timco, Melanie Suzanne *science educator*

Bryan
Nowak, Carol Lee *retired art educator*
Schroeder, Teresa Marie *athletic trainer*

Bucyrus
Cooper, April Helen *family practice nurse practitioner*

Cadiz
Thompson, Sandra Lee *library administrator*

Caldwell
Casto, Barbara L. *counselor*

Cambridge
Barzda, Susan Marie *special education educator, art educator*
Wright, Amy Ralynn *athletic trainer, small business owner*

Campbell
Peltz, Ruby *elementary school educator*

Canton
Bernstein, Penny L. *biologist, educator*
Cave, Yvonne S. *retired librarian*
Eshelman, Georgia Lee *music educator*
Fernandez, Kathleen M. *cultural organization administrator*
Kilcullen, Maureen *librarian, educator*
Klotz, Leora Nylee *retired music educator, vocalist*
Lowery-O'Connell, Susan Ellen *psychologist*
Moses, Marcia Swartz *artist*
Peters, Judy Gale *manufacturing executive, educator*
Ringley, Kathleen J. *director*
Swanson, Joyce Eileen *elementary school educator*
Torok, Tammy *mathematics educator*
Wolf, Teresa Ann *minister, educator, nun*

Cedarville
Anderson, Connie *music educator*
Haffey, Deborah Bush *communications educator*

Centerburg
Comstock-Jones, Janis Lou *business owner, consultant*

Centerville
Appelbaum, Bernardine *medical/surgical nurse*
Booth, Catherine Keener *music educator, director*
Coyle, Diane R. *artist, educator*
Geier, Sharon Lee *retired special education educator, realtor*
Kauffold, Ruth Elizabeth *psychologist*
Wasson, Carol R. *music educator*

Chagrin Falls
Boccardo-Dubey, Genny Mercedes *art dealer*
Brown, Jeanette Grasselli *retired director*
Cortese, Julia F. *retired elementary school educator*
Cox, Cynthia A. *art education specialist*
Held, Lila M. *art appraiser*
Kuby, Barbara Eleanor *personnel director, management consultant*
Ostendorf, Joan Donahue *fund raiser, volunteer*
Robertson, Linda F. *educational administrator*
Smith, Barbara Jean *lawyer*
Vail, Iris Jennings *civic worker*

Chandlersville
Herron, Janet Irene *retired industrial engineer*

Chardon
Clapsaddle, Patricia Lee *art educator*
Mihalik, Phyllis Ann *management consultant, systems analyst, educator*

Chesterland
Aster, Ruth Marie Rhydderch *business owner*
Cooey, Kathleen Marie *mathematics educator*
Witschi, Emily *art educator*

Chillicothe
Copley, Cynthia Sue Love *insurance adjuster*
Greene, Judy *secondary school educator*
Leedy, Emily L. Foster (Mrs. William N. Leedy) *retired education educator, consultant*
Matyi, Cindy Lou *psychology professor, consultant*
Metzger, Jamie B. *science educator*

Cincinnati
Abate, Anne Katherine *librarian, consultant, educator*
Anderson, Joan Balyeat *theology studies educator, minister*
Anstaett, Jennifer Griffin *lawyer*
Arnold, Susan E. *consumer products company executive*
Ashley, Lynn *social sciences educator, consultant*
Ates, Delories *retired counseling administrator*
Attee, Joyce Valerie Jungclas *artist*
Auttonberry, Sheri E. *lawyer*
Auyang, Grace Chao *education educator, consultant*
Aylesworth, Julie Ann *writer, personal care professional*
Barber-Foss, Kim Daneen *athletic trainer*
Bateman, Sharon Louise *public relations executive*
Beckwith, Barbara Jean *journalist*
Beckwith, Sandra Shank *federal judge*
Bell, Sandra Elizabeth *corporate financial executive*
Bestehorn, Ute Wiltrud *retired librarian*
Bluestein, Venus Weller *retired psychologist, educator*
Bollen, Sharon Kesterson *artist, educator*
Boyd, Deborah Ann *pediatrician*
Brady, Darlene Ann *artist, designer, architect*
Brestel, Mary Beth *librarian*
Bride, Nancy J. *lawyer*
Briskin, Madeleine *oceanographer, paleontologist*
Brown, Dale Patrick *retired advertising executive*
Brown, Lillie Harrison *music educator*
Bruvold, Kathleen Parker *retired lawyer*
Bryant, Irene Melba *retired elementary school educator, artist*
Burke, Rachel E. *lawyer*
Burklow, Kathleen Ann *psychologist*
Cain, Linda Joanne *retired academic administrator*
Chapman, Laura Hill *art education consultant*
Childs, Erin C. *lawyer*
Ching, Ho *surgeon*
Church, Sonia Jane Shutter *librarian*
Clark, Cathy Sue *special education educator*
Cook, Deborah L. *federal judge, former state supreme court justice*
Cors, Jeanne Marie *lawyer*
Curran, Mary Ann *chemical engineer*
Davis, Robin *publishing executive*
De Courten-Myers, Gabrielle Marguerite *neuropathologist*
Dember, Cynthia Fox *retired clinical psychologist*
De Witt, Jeanette Marie *physical therapist*
DeWitt, Katharine Cramer *museum administrator*
Dlott, Susan Judy *judge, lawyer*
Duffy, Virginia *minister*
Dunevant, Carol Dary *music educator, conductor*
Eckner, Shannon F. *lawyer*
Eckstein, Elaine Claire *theater educator*
Ellerman, Paige L. *lawyer*
Erhart, Sue A. *lawyer*
Everson, Jean Watkins Dolores *librarian, media consultant, educator*
Faller, Susan Grogan *lawyer*
Farrell, Pamela Christine *secondary school educator*
Faulkner, Laura R. *lawyer*
Fender, Kimber L. *library director*
Fitzsimmons, Becky Barlow *lawyer*
Flanagan, Martha Lang *publishing executive*
Florez, Mary A. *artist*
Galloway, Lillian Carroll *modeling agency executive, consultant*
Garfinkel, Jane E. *lawyer*
Gates, Katherine A. *accountant, writer*
Gaunt, Karen Kreider *lawyer*
Gehlert, Sally Oyler *healing touch practictioner*
Goodman, Phyllis L. *public relations executive*
Greenwald, Theresa McGowan *health services administrator, rehabilitation nurse*
Groppe, Elizabeth T. *education educator*
Hall, Madelon Carol Syverson *elementary school educator*
Halsall, Mary E. *biology educator*
Henretta, Deborah A. *consumer products company executive*
Hess, Evelyn Victorine *medical educator*
Hill-Cook, Patricia Ann *social services administrator*
Hinegardner, Laura A. *lawyer*
Hoguet, Karen M. *retail executive*
Holdren, Jamie Lynn *music educator*
Horrell, Karen Holley *insurance company executive, lawyer*
Hullinger, Charlotte M. *psychotherapist*
Hummel, Gayle Gillette *artist, poet*
Irwin, Miriam Dianne Owen *publishing executive, writer*
Isburgh, Anne Marie *engineering manager*
Kalfa, Theodosia Anastasios *pediatrician, educator*
Karle-Swails, Jeanine *neuroscience clinical nurse specialist*
Kendle, Candace *pharmaceutical executive*
King, Margaret Ann *communications educator*
Klein, Sophia H. *entrepreneur*
Kotchka, Claudia B. *consumer products company executive, accountant*
Kreps, Martha S. *elementary school educator*
Laney, Sandra Eileen *information technology executive*
Levin, Debbe Ann *lawyer*
Levy, Charlotte Lois *law librarian, educator, lawyer*
Levy, Helen E. *director*
Loggie, Jennifer Mary Hildreth *retired physician, educator*
Love, Lisa A. *lawyer*
Mason, Rachel J. *lawyer*
McCamley, Sherry Smith *entertainer, actor, vocalist, voice educator*
McMullin, Ruth Roney *retired publishing executive*
Meal, Larie *chemistry professor, researcher, consultant*
Meisner, Patricia Ann *assistant principal*
Meyers, Karen Diane *lawyer, educator*
Meyers, Pamela Sue *lawyer*
Monroe, Erin *psychiatric nurse practitioner*
Montavon, Victoria A. *university librarian, dean*
Morgan, Victoria *performing company executive, choreographer*
Morris, Margaret Elizabeth *marketing professional, small business owner*
Morrow, Ardythe Luxion *adult education educator, researcher*
Motch, Marjorie McCullough *service organization executive*
Murphy, Molly Ann *investment company executive*
Nagy, Donna M. *dean, law educator*
Narmoneva, Daria *engineering educator*
Otto, Charlotte R. *consumer products company executive*
Parker, Linda Bates *professional development organization administrator*
Patterson, Claire Ann *career technical educator*
Perna, Belinda A. *science educator*
Repka, Fran Ann, Sr. *psychologist*
St. John, Maria Ann *nurse anesthetist*
Schmidt, Leeanne *artist*
Schutzius, Lucy Jean *retired librarian*
Scott, Martha Ann *clinical social worker*
Sewell, Phyllis Shapiro *retail chain executive*
Shearer, Linda *museum director*
Spangenberg, Kristin Louise *curator*
Spohn, Dorothy M. *retired elementary school educator*
Steinberg, Janet Eckstein *journalist*
Stinson, Mary Florence *retired nursing educator*
Stoms, Donna Sue *librarian*
Swinford, Margaret Lynn Wright *medical/surgical nurse, educator*
Tankersley, Sarah *lawyer*
Teague, Carolyn Louise *daycare administrator*
Teeters, Linda Marie *retired secondary school educator*
Ten Eyck, Dorothea Fariss *real estate agent*
Thomas, Hannah H. *retired elementary school educator*
Timpano, Anne *museum director, art historian*
Trent, Judith Swanlund *communications educator*
Wall, Della *human resources specialist, manufacturing executive*
Walters, Bridget C. *science educator*
Weinstein, Anna *music educator*
Wellington, Jean Susorney *librarian*
Westbrook, Lynda A. *financial consultant*
Wilson, Wanda O. *nurse anesthetist, educator*
Winchell, Margaret J. *realtor*
Winfrey, Marcellene Sedetta *music educator, church musician*
Witschger, Mary Ann *medical/surgical nurse*
Woods, Carol Smith *private school educator*
Worachek, Susan *music educator*
Zimpher, Nancy Lusk *academic administrator*

Circleville
Southward, Patricia Ann *school psychologist*

Cleveland
Ainsworth, Joan Horsburgh *retired director*
Aldrich, Ann *judge*
Beall, Cynthia *anthropologist, educator*
Beamer, Yvonne Marie *psychotherapist, counselor*
Beard, Lydia Jean *research scientist, educator*
Bellamy, Gail Anne Ghetia *magazine editor, author, speaker*
Bersin, Susan Joyce-Heather (Reignbeaux Joyce-Heather Bersin) *critical care nurse, police officer*
Bixenstine, Kim Fenton *lawyer*
Borchert, Catherine Glennan *minister*
Boyle, Kammer *financial planner, investment advisor, research analyst, options trader*
Brennan, Maureen *lawyer*
Burke, Kathleen B. *lawyer*
Burke, Lillian Walker *retired judge*
Callesen-Gyorgak, Jan Elaine *special education educator*
Campbell, Jane Louise *former mayor*
Carrick, Kathleen Michele *law librarian*
Cook, Anda Suna *civil rights advocate*
Cook, Susan J. *human resources specialist, manufacturing executive*
Cudak, Gail Linda *lawyer*
Dancyger, Ruth *art historian*

Davis, Pamela Bowes *pediatric pulmonologist*
Denko, Joanne D. *psychiatrist, writer*
Dever, Joyce *materials engineer*
DiSilvio, Marilena *lawyer*
Dougherty, Ursel Thielbeule *communications executive, marketing executive*
Drake, Grace L. *retired state senator, cultural organization administrator*
Dunbar, Mary Asmundson *communications executive, public information officer, consultant, investor*
Dylag, Helen Marie *health facility administrator*
Eagleeye-Lord, Amy *writer, editor*
Eustis, Joanne D. *university librarian*
FallCreek, Stephanie Jean *non-profit organization executive*
Fischer, Michelle K. *lawyer*
Fugo, Denise Marie *small business executive*
Gapen, Delores Kaye *librarian, educator*
Goral, Judith Ann *language educator*
Hamilton, Nancy Beth *data processing executive*
Harf, Patricia Jean Kole *syndicated columnist, clinical and behavioral psychologist, educational consultant, marriage and family therapist, lecturer*
Hastings, Susan C. *lawyer*
Heintschel, Ruthann M. *school system administrator*
Hudak, Christine Angela *nursing informatics educator, specialist*
Jaffe, Marcia Weissman *elementary school educator*
Jensen, Kathryn Patricia (Kit) *broadcast executive*
Jindra, Christine *editor*
Jorgenson, Mary Ann *lawyer*
Kalina, Eunice Goldstein *human services director*
Kilbane, Catherine M. *lawyer*
Knieriem, Beulah White *retired elementary school educator, minister*
Kohn, Mary Louise Beatrice *nurse*
Kovel, Terry Horvitz *writer, antiques authority*
Kryshtalowych, Helen Zwenyslawa *lawyer*
Kwiatkowski, Tonia *former professional figure skater*
Lawrence, Estelene Yvonne *musician, transportation executive*
Leary, Mary Deborah *language educator*
Lennox, Heather *lawyer*
Leukart, Barbara J. J. *lawyer*
Lopez, Nancy *retired professional golfer*
Maloney, Mary D. *lawyer*
Manes, Andrea M. *science educator*
Mantzell, Betty Lou *school nurse practitioner, consultant*
Mast, Bernadette Mihalic *lawyer*
Mayne, Lucille Stringer *finance educator*
McCormick, Maureen Olivea *computer systems programmer*
Miller, Genevieve *retired medical historian*
Monihan, Mary Elizabeth *lawyer*
Mooney, Beth *bank executive*
Moore, Karen Nelson *judge*
Mucha, Mary Ann K. *quality assurance professional*
Nelson, Sue Grodsky *humanities educator, consultant*
Olness, Karen Norma *medical educator*
O'Malley, Kathleen M. *federal judge*
Penman, Robbie Mae *volunteer, political organization worker*
Pianalto, Sandra *bank executive*
Pierce, Mary *professional tennis player*
Pietrzen, Julie Lynn *lawyer*
Potter, Susan Kuniholm *bank executive*
Pujana, Maria Jose *neurologist*
Queen, Joyce *elementary school educator*
Quigney, Theresa Ann *special education educator*
Rawson, Rachel L. *lawyer*
Reveley, Mary *aeronautical engineer*
Rickert, Jeanne Martin M. *lawyer*
Roberts-Mamone, Lisa A. *lawyer*
Robinson, Alice Helene *language educator, administrative assistant*
Seifert, Shelley Jane *bank executive, human resources specialist*
Seles, Monica *professional tennis player*
Shrivastava, Sunita *secondary school educator*
Siess, Judith Ann *librarian*
Sila, Cathy Ann *neurologist*
Smith, Beverly Harriett *elementary school educator*
Snyder, Jill *museum director*
Soltis, Katherine *editor*
Spinner, Pamela Marie *special education educator*
Sposet, Barbara Ann *secondary school educator*
Striefsky, Linda A(nn) *lawyer*
Stupka, Renee C. *musician, educator*
Taylor, Margaret Wischmeyer *retired language educator*
Thimmig, Diana Marie *lawyer*
Thomas, Dynda A. *lawyer*
Trattner, Laura V. *middle school eductor*
Velasco, Esda Nury *speech and language professional*
Weir, Dame Gillian Constance *musician*
Wells, Lesley *federal judge*
Wertheim, Sally Harris *director, academic administrator, dean, education educator, consultant*
Wong, Margaret Wai *lawyer*
Zilch, Brianna Rae *athletic trainer*

Cleveland Heights
Challenger, Vicki Lee *elementary school educator*
Close, Carole Lynne *education educator, consultant*
Hefter, Shoshana *psychologist*
Riley, Sharon Lynn *elementary school educator*
Sandburg, Helga *author*
Weinbaum, Batya *artist, writer*

Columbia Station
Dadley, Arlene Jeanne *retired sleep technologist*

Columbus
Anderson, Carole Ann *nursing educator, academic administrator*
Arvia, Anne L. *bank executive*
Barrett, Catherine L. *state representative*
Bell, Karen A. *dean*
Benton-Borghi, Beatrice Hope *secondary school educator, consultant, writer*
Berndt, Ellen German *lawyer*
Bloomfield, Clara Derber *oncologist, educator, medical institute administrator*
Boyd, Hazel *minister*
Bradley, Betty Hunt *psychologist, consultant*
Bradley, Jennette B. *state official, former lieutenant governor*
Brewer, Marilynn B. *psychology professor*
Cambern, Andrea *newscaster, reporter*
Clancy, Patricia *state representative*
Clark, Babaa Ritah Annette *massage therapist*
Clark, Colleen Romick *academic administrator*
Codogni, Iwona M. *scientific information analyst, chemist*
Cottle, Deborah Ellen *elementary school educator*
Crowder, Marjorie Briggs *lawyer*
Cruz-Myers, Theresa *finance company executive*
Cuddihy, June Tuck *pediatrics nurse*
Daniels, Cassandra Diane *secondary school educator, choreographer*
Davis, Julia A. *lawyer, retail executive*
Dervin, Brenda Louise *communications educator*
Everhart, Velma Vizedom *retired home economics educator, retired real estate agent*
Foucht, Joan Lucille *retired elementary school educator, retired counseling administrator*
Gillmor, Karen Lako *state agency administrator*
Goorey, Nancy Jane *dentist*
Graham, Laurel Susan *elementary school educator*
Grant, Jean Terry *educational consultant*
Green, Lennis Harris *psychologist*
Grotenrath, Mary Jo *lawyer, writer*
Gruliow, Agnes Forrest *artist, educator*
Guglielmi, Rhonda E. *nursing administrator*
Gustina, Lori Lazenby *music educator*
Hailey, V. Ann *retail executive*
Hamilton, Ann Katherine *artist*
Hamper, Anietra *news anchor*
Haque, Malika Hakim *pediatrician*
Harris, Yolanda *newscaster*
Harwood, Sandra Stabile *lawyer, state representative*
Harzoff, Elizabeth Gail *special education educator*
Hatfield, Vicki D. *secondary school educator*
Hatler, Patricia Ruth *lawyer*
Henkin, Tina M. *science educator, researcher*
Herron, Holly Lynn *critical care nurse, educator*
Hill, Kathleen Blickenstaff *lawyer, nursing educator, mental health nurse*
Hill, Terri *diversified financial services company executive*
Holbrook, Karen Ann *academic administrator, biologist*
Hollingsworth, Holly *newscaster*
Hollis-Allbritton, Cheryl Dawn *retail paper supply store executive*
Holman-Rao, Marie *retail executive*
Holtz, Diane *retail executive*
Huber, Joan Althaus *sociology educator*
Huheey, Marilyn Jane *ophthalmologist, educator*
Hukill, Margaret Anne *physical therapist, rehabilitation services professional, educator*
James, Donna A. *diversified financial services company executive*
Janik, Melinda A. *real estate company executive*
Johnson, Martha (Marty) Junk (Marty Johnson) *psychology professor*
Johnson, Rebecca Grooms *music educator*
Julia, Maria C. *social worker, educator, consultant*
Kearns, Merle Grace *state agency administrator*
Kiecolt-Glaser, Janice Kay *psychologist*
King, Norah McCann *federal judge*
Knotts, Maureen Mary *science educator*
Koeppel, Holly Keller *electric power industry executive*
Krakoff, Diane Elizabeth Butts *medical/surgical nurse*
Kreager, Eileen Davis *financial consultant*
Lander, Ruth A. *medical association administrator*
Lanzinger, Judith Ann *state supreme court justice*
Lewis, Nina *social worker*
Long, Sarah Elizabeth Brackney *physician*
Long, Teresa C. *city health department administrator*
Marshall, Colleen *newscaster*
McDaniel, Helen Marie *retired social worker*
McGrath, Barbara Gates *city manager*
Meredith, Meri Hill *reference librarian, educator*
Mlawsky, Karen *hospital administrator*
Moncrief, Jacqueline C. *retired state agency administrator*
Montgomery, Betty Dee *state auditor, former state attorney general, former state legislator*
Morrison, Jacqueline Ann *social worker, psychologist*
Murnieks, Kimberly Ann *educational administrator*
Neill-Green, Teresa *art therapist, social worker, educator*
Newman, Diana S. *foundation administrator, consultant*
Nissl, Colleen Kaye *lawyer*
O'Connor, Maureen *state supreme court justice*
Olson, Carol Ann *retired librarian*
Oxley, Margaret Carolyn Stewart *elementary school educator*
Ozkan, Umit Sivrioglu *chemical engineering professor*
Pave, Angela *newscaster*
Peterson, Ruth D. *sociologist*
Pick, Heather *newscaster*
Prieto, Emily J. *small business owner, consultant*
Rector, Susan Darnell *lawyer*
Renshler, Rosemary P. *retired music educator*
Resnick, Alice Robie *state supreme court justice*
Ricord, Kathy *diversified financial services company executive*
Roeder, Rebecca Emily *software engineer*
Rogers, Nancy Hardin *dean, law educator*
Rosenstock, Susan Lynn *orchestra administrator*
Sawyers, Elizabeth Joan *librarian, director*
Seiling, Sharon Lee *family economics educator*
Selby, Diane Ray Miller *fraternal organization administrator*
Sellers, Barbara Jackson *federal judge*
Setzer, Arlene J. *state representative, retired secondary school educator*
Sevel, Francine *advocate, researcher*
Smith, Marcia J. *pastor*
Smith, Shirley A. *state legislator, state representative*
Snyder, Barbara Rook *academic administrator*
Sowald, Heather Gay *lawyer*
Stephens, Sheryl Lynne *physician*
Stratton, Evelyn Lundberg *state supreme court justice*
Sullivan, Terri *newscaster, reporter*
Taylor, Celianna Isley *information systems specialist*
Taylor, Mary *state representative*
Tomasky, Susan *electric power industry executive*
Turnbull, Cheryl Lankard *investment company executive*
Turney, Sharon Jester *retail executive*
Ware, Jane Orth *writer*
Webber, Sabra Jean *humanities educator, department chairman*
Wexner, Abigail *apparel executive*
Williams, Linda Dianne *music educator*
Williams, Susan Shidal *language educator*
Wolfe, Claire V. *physiatrist*
Zelman, Susan Tave *school system administrator*

Copley
Galang, Monica Lynn *science educator, department chairman*
Smith, Joan H. *retired women's health nurse, educator*

Coshocton
Freund, Carol Louise *social services consultant*

Cuyahoga Falls
Bultrowicz, Tara Lynn *school psychologist*
Hamilton, Priscilla *mathematics educator*
Kitska, Susan Ann *retired secondary school educator*
Walker, Suzannah Wolf *language educator*

Cuyahoga Heights
Holt Balis, Carolyn M. *secondary school educator*

Dayton
Alexander, Roberta Sue *history professor*
Barr, Ann Helen *director*
Boice, Martha Hibbert *writer, publishing executive*
Calhoun, Gloria Lynn *experimental psychologist*
Carrier, Rachel Esther *music educator, director*
Carson, Dora A. *secondary school educator*
Cobb, Cecelia Annette *retired counselor*
Cramblit, Miggie E. *lawyer*
Focht, Sandra Jean *retired elementary school educator*
Gillig, Paulette Marie *psychiatry educator, researcher*
Grant, Colleen *information systems specialist*
Hanna, Marsha L. *artistic director*
Harden, Oleta Elizabeth *literature educator, academic administrator*
Harris, Bonnie *psychological education specialist*
Heath, Mariwyn Dwyer *writer, legislative staff member*
Hitch, Melanie Audrey *orthopaedic nurse*
Hollebeke, Norma L. *biologist, educator*
Jagow, Shelley *music educator, musician*
Jelus, Susan Crum *writer, editor*
Jerome, Dolores *retired electronics executive*
Killian, Jerri *director, educator*
Klinck, Cynthia Anne *library director*
Leakas, Diana Brod *interior designer, educator*
Little, Tess (Teresa Fannin) *sculptor, fine arts educator*
Matheny, Ruth Ann *editor*
McCarrell, Lynette Marie *music educator, director*
McLin, Rhine Lana *mayor, former state legislator*
Monk, Susan Marie *pediatrician, educator*
Nanagas, Maria Teresita Cruz *pediatrician, educator*
O'Keefe, Linda Lee *physical education educator*
O'Malley, Patricia *nurse, researcher*
Reid, Marilyn Joanne *state legislator, lawyer*
Shaffer, Joanne Tyler *music educator*
Smith, Susan K. *director*
Smith, Vivian Blaine *elementary school educator*
Sowald, Debra Kay *psychologist*
Thomas, Marianna *volunteer community activist, writer, speaker*
Turner, Gladys Tressia *retired social worker*
Twale, Darla Jean *education educator*
Vaughn, Noel Wyandt *lawyer*
Versic, Linda Joan *nursing educator, research company executive*
Wasson, Barbara Hickam *music educator*
Wightman, Ann *lawyer*
Wikstrom, Loretta Wermerskirchen *artist*
Young, Yvonne Delease *elementary school educator*

Delaware
Fryer, Karen Helene *geologist, educator*
Gardner, Bonnie Milne *theater educator, playwright*
Lemke, Stacy J. *secondary school educator*
Schlichting, Catherine Fletcher Nicholson *librarian, educator*

Delta
Miller, Beverly White *former college president, educational consultant*

Dover
Haggis, Mary Ripley *nurse, genealogist*
Nign, Stacie Marie *secondary school educator*
Wenzel, Mary Joan *music educator*

Dublin
Anderson, Kerrii B. *food service executive*
Bird, Shelley *communications executive*
Bordelon, Carolyn Thew *elementary school educator*
Conrad, Marian Sue (Susan Conrad) *retired special education educator*
Davids, Jody R. *information technology executive*
Hugo, Jessica Lyn *physical education educator*
Laurence, Amy Rebecca *music educator, composer*
McGary, Daria L. *foreign languages educator*
Meek, Violet Imhof *retired dean*
Redman, Janis F. *special education educator, department chairman*
Souch, Mary Pauline *gifted and talented educator*
Tenuta, Luigia *lawyer*
Watkins, Carole S. *human resources specialist, medical products executive*

East Cleveland
Davis, Dianne *music educator*
Soule, Lucile Snyder *musician, educator*

Eaton
Kisling, Fanny *counselor, educator*

Elida
Oleson, Sarah Elizabeth *elementary school educator*

Elyria
Miller, Bridget A. *lawyer*
Nakoneczny, Nadia *marketing professional*
Pucko, Diane Bowles *public relations executive*
Thompson, Janis Grocock *biology professor*

Euclid
Adrine-Robinson, Kenyette *art educator, poet, artist, photographer*
Miller, Demetra Fay Pelat *elementary school educator, city official*

Fairfield
Crane, Debra K. *lawyer*
Goldberg, Bonita Williams *artist, consultant*
Jamison, Peggy Louise *elementary school educator*
Sheehan, Samantha *gymnast*
Templeton, Holly Jayne *elementary school educator*

Fairlawn
Brubaker, Karen Sue *small business owner*

Fairview Park
Flynn, Patricia M. *director, special education educator, gifted and talented educator*
Leickly, Portia Elaine *science educator*

Findlay
Drake, Jeanette Wenig *communications educator, writer, public relations consultant*
Gunda, Rajeswari *oncologist*
Irons, Sharon Lynn Erickson *elementary school educator, client relationship director*
McIntosh, Julie Dean *science educator*
Stephani, Nancy Jean *social worker, journalist*
Wickerham, Deborah Louise *elementary school educator*

Fostoria
Howard, Kathleen *computer company executive*

Fremont
Breidenbach, Tonya D. *educator*
Cruz-Weaver, Bonnie E. *elementary school educator*
Sattler, Nancy Joan *educational association administrator*

Galena
Latorre, Debi *medical/surgical nurse*

Galion
Harter, Lonna *city manager*

Gambier
Holdener, Judy Ann *mathematics professor, researcher*
Nugent, S. Georgia *academic administrator*
Payne, Tabitha Wynn *psychologist, educator, researcher*

Gates Mills
Fesler, Elizabeth *educator, psychologist*

Geneva
Arkkelin, Cora Rink *realtor*
Carrel, Marianne Eileen *music educator*
Chaundra, Gale Buckels *nursing administrator, writer*

Genoa
Hammoud, Catherine Louise *special education educator*

Granville
Buker, Eloise Ann *political science educator*
Hutson-Comeaux, Sarah Louise *psychology professor, department chairman*
Knox, Trudy *publisher, consultant, retired psychologist*
Sinsabaugh, Marie Elizabeth Diener *retired nurse, massage therapist*

Greenfield
Flora, Loretta Sue *music educator*

Greenville
Estes, Ruth Ann *art educator*
Foureman, Nancy Lee *artist*
Metzcar, Virginia Joyce *social worker*
Thieme, Jean Louise *art association administrator*

Groveport
Justice, Yvonne Horton *health facility administrator*

Hamilton
Colegate, Carol Ann *elementary school educator*
Fein, Linda Ann *nurse anesthetist, consultant*
Hornsby, Judith Elizabeth *special education educator*
Quay, Jacquelyn Sue *art educator, consultant*

Harrison
Beatty, Maria Lois *elementary school educator*
Kocher, Juanita Fay *retired auditor*

Heath
Brandt, Traci Lynn Keller *music educator, musician*

Hebron
Slater, Wanda Marie Worth *property manager*

Highland Hills
Kharina, Nina Yurievna *science educator, dental assistant*
Sender, Maryann *director*

Hilliard
McNutt, Suzanne Michaelene *music educator*

Holland
Beekley, Cynthia Xanthopoulos *school system administrator*

Howard
Dixon, Carmen Sue *science educator*

Hoytville
Shoemaker, Cynthia Louise *music educator*

Hubbard
Trucksis, Theresa A. *retired library director*

Hudson
Carducci, Judith Weeks Barker *artist, retired social worker*
Gauntner, Heidi Lynn *chemistry educator*
Gentile Sachs, Valerie Ann *lawyer*
Hallenbeck, Linda S. *elementary school educator*
Lambacher, Kathleen Hartwell *retired education educator*
Worley, Janis Avereal *writer*

Huron
Leser, Anne Elizabeth *education educator*
Strong, Kay Elaine *economics professor*

Independence
Slivka, Thomasina *secondary school educator*

Ironton
Curry, Estella Roberta *education educator, school psychologist, consultant*
Oakes, Maria Spachner *medical/surgical nurse*

Kent
Cartwright, Carol Ann *retired academic administrator*
Cielinski-Kessler, Audrey Ann *writer, publishing executive, small business owner*
Clawson, Judith Louise *middle school educator*
Fein, Susanna Greer *literature educator*
Iverson, Susan Van Deventer *education educator*
Khol, Charel L. *psychologist*
Ozanich, Ruth Shultz *artist, poet, retired elementary school educator*
Sonnhalter, Carolyn Therese *physical therapist, consultant*
Tuan, Debbie Fu-Tai *chemist, educator*

Kettering
Denlinger, Vicki Lee *secondary school educator, healthcare educator*
Hoffman, Sue Ellen *retired elementary school educator*
Martin, Margaret Gately *elementary school educator*

Kirtland
Asnien, Phyllis Arline *humanities educator, writer*

Lafayette
Spencer, Teresa Ann *music educator*

Lakeside
Stephens-Rich, Barbara E. *religious studies educator*

Lakewood
Ellis, Deborah Marie *art educator*
Hankins, Elizabeth Aylmer *orchestra director*
Hisey, Bernadette Anne *music educator*
McGlynn, Maureen Scalley *history educator*
Olson, Carol Joan *foundation administrator, consultant*

Lancaster
Huston, Susan Kay Myers *elementary school educator*
Shipley, Holly Rene *special education educator*
Young, Nancy Henrietta Moe *retired elementary education educator*

Lebanon
Bennett, Alison Mercedes *human resources specialist*
Davis, Barbara Ann Lane *retired elementary school educator, retired realtor*
Ruder, Diane G. *not-for-profit fundraiser*

Leetonia
Foreman, Gail Lynne *secondary school educator*

Lewis Center
Davison, Lesli Anne *elementary school educator*
Thomason, Sandra Lee *elementary school educator*

Liberty Center
Jones, Marlene Ann *retired education supervisor*

Liberty Township
Conditt, Margaret Karen *research scientist*

Lima
Bonifas, Jane Marie *psychologist*
Johnson, Patricia Joseph *librarian*
Smith, Heather Ann *elementary school educator*

Lisbon
Archer, Barrie W.S. *art educator*
Dailey, Coleen Hall *magistrate*
Danley, Linda Sharon *elementary school educator*

Lodi
Behrend, Kristel Nicole *music educator*

Logan
Price, Harlene Pamela *music educator*

London
Rosebrough, Catherine Marie *special education educator, consultant*

Londonderry
Lindsey, Bonnie Lou *minister*

Lorain
Comer, Brenda Warmee *elementary school educator, real estate company officer*
Gall-Iemma, Julie Jeannine *personal trainer*
Giannuzzi, Judy L. *psychologist*

Lucasville
Crotty, Ladonna Deane *librarian*

Lyndhurst
Carey, Reiko Marie *music educator*
Dellas, Marie C. *retired psychology educator, consultant*
Packer, Diana *retired reference librarian*
Ross, Sally Price *artist, painter*
Silver, Thelma *social worker*

Mansfield
Converse, Sandra *city finance director, financial planner*
Sturts, Donna Jean *music educator*

Mantua
Eslinger, Denise Marie *social worker*

Marietta
Francis, Lynne Ann *elementary school educator, music educator*
Fry, Mildred Covey *regional library executive director*

Marion
Blankenship, Betsy Lee *library director*
Rowe, Lisa Dawn *computer programmer/analyst, computer consultant*

Marshallville
Evert, Heather Lynn *dance instructor*

Mason
Cuff, Virginia Evelyn *architectural firm executive, consultant*
Solomon, Susanne Nina *podiatrist, surgeon*

Massillon
Hartline, Rebecca Sue *secondary school educator*

Maumee
McBride, Beverly Jean *lawyer*

Mayfield Heights
Vanderwist, Kathryn K. *lawyer*

Mc Donald
Daigle, Barbara Dianne *elementary school educator*
Woodford, Debra Jane *elementary school educator*

Medina
DeMars, Judith M. *elementary school educator*
Doyle, Heather Sue *psychologist*
Farver, Cindy L. *elementary school educator*
Jeffers, Lynette A. *anesthetist*
Moll, Sara H. *psychologist, volunteer*
Reichheld, Deborah Ann *retired secondary school educator, language educator*

Mentor
Blyth, Ann Marie *retired secondary school educator*
Priddy, Jean Marie *music educator, voice educator*

Miamisburg
Michaelis, Betty Jane *sculptor, retired small business owner*

Miamiville
Franz, Iris Vivian (Vivian Franz) *dean, director*

Middleburg Heights
Maciuszko, Kathleen Lynn *librarian, educator*

Middlefield
Archbold, Heather D. *personal trainer*
Jaite, Gail Ann *retired music educator*

Middleport
Cantrell, Carol Howe *municipal administrator*

Middletown
Gilmore, June Ellen *psychologist*
Marine, Susan Sonchik *analytical chemist, educator*

Milan
Jeffery, Suzanne *retired elementary school educator*
Kegarise, Carol Ann *primary school educator*
Wilbur, Dora Lynn *elementary school educator*

Milford
Parsons, Linda L. *art dealer*

Millersburg
Yoder, Anna A. *retired elementary school educator*

Mogadore
Kelly, Janice Helen *elementary school educator*

Monroeville
Lohmann, Gerry M. *elementary school educator*

Mount Gilead
Wells, Debra Elaine *parochial school educator*

Mount Vernon
Cameron, Virginia Anne *music educator*
Dessert, Kathryn Isobel *elementary school educator*
Koh-Baker, JoAnn Been *music educator*
Rice, Susan A. *elementary school educator*

Napoleon
Bevelhymer, Darlene Pearl *secondary school educator, lawyer*
Meekison, MaryFran *writer*

Nelsonville
Barrows, Roxane Renee *dean, mathematics professor*

New Albany
Page, Linda Kay *bank executive*
Partlow, Madeline *principal*

New Bremen
Wierwille, Marsha Louise *elementary school educator*

New Carlisle
Peters, Elizabeth Ann Hampton *retired nursing educator*

New Concord
Schumann, Laura Elaine *conductor*

New Holland
Reeves, Nancy Rapp *elementary school educator*

New Lexington
Raines, Martha Ann *elementary school educator*

New Matamoras
Brown, Blanche Y. *secondary school educator, genealogist, researcher*

New Philadelphia
Doughten, Mary Katherine (Molly Doughten) *retired secondary school educator*
Hendrix, Christine Janet *retired government agency administrator, retired small business owner, volunteer*
Mathias, Denise Susanne *music educator, music minister*
Smith, Shannon Diane *elementary school educator*

Newark
Mencer, Jetta *lawyer*
Paul, Rochelle Carole *special education educator*
Sharrock (Wrentmore), Anita Kay *information technology specialist*
Simpson, Linda Sue *elementary school educator*
Vaas, Lori Rhodes *music educator*
Wallace, Sarah Reese *banker*
Workman, Virginia Lane *music educator*

Niles
Linden, Carol Marie *special education educator*

North Canton
Cooney, Sondra Miley *literature and language educator*
Edwards, Sharon Marie *minister, educator*
Sebald, Carol June *retired secondary school educator*

North Olmsted
Rimm, Sylvia Barkan *psychologist, media personality educator*
Semple, Jane Frances *health facility director*
Zolar, Karen Jane *social services administrator*

Northfield
Sleeman, Mary (Mrs. John Paul Sleeman) *retired librarian*
Stavole, Janet M. *librarian, director*

Norwalk
Fresch, Marie Beth *court reporting company executive*
McGue, Rochelle Lee *music educator, rental manager*

Novelty
Cutujian, Paulette Sue *school psychologist*

Oak Harbor
Sievert, Vicki Lee *retired music educator*

Oberlin
Collins, Martha *English language educator, writer*
Dye, Nancy Schrom *academic administrator, historian, educator*
MacKay, Gladys Godfrey *retired adult education educator*
Moore, Jane Ross *librarian, educator*
Ramp, Marjorie Jean Sumerwell *civic worker*
Rutstein, Sedmara Zakarian *concert pianist, educator*

Okolona
Willeman, Florence Kay *secondary school educator, small business owner*

Oregon
Poad, Flora Virginia *retired librarian, retired elementary school educator*
Schwartz, Louise Marguerite *physical education educator*

Orrville
Harlan, M. Ann *lawyer*

Orwell
Strong, Marcella Lee *music specialist, educator*

Owensville
Seifert, Caroline Hamilton *community health nurse*

Oxford
Deines, Bethany A. *fraternal organization administrator*
Klosawska, Anna M. *literature and language professor*
Presnell, Jenny Lynn *librarian*
Sessions, Judith Ann *librarian, university library dean*
Thompson, Bertha Boya *retired education educator*
Thurston, Alice Janet *former college president*
Yost, Nancy Runyon *artist, small business owner*

Painesville
Davis, Barbara Snell *education educator*
Luhta, Caroline Naumann *airport manager, flight educator*

Parma
Feldman, Sari *library director*
Musat, Katherine Gadus *retired music educator*
Petrus, Sally A. *elementary school educator*
Romanovich, Patricia M. *parochial school educator*
Salzgeber, Karen A. *secondary school educator*
Scheffel, Donna Jean *elementary school educator*
Tener, Carol Joan *retired secondary school educator, consultant*
Tibbitts, Barbara J. *music educator*

Parma Heights
Monastero, Tina Marie *elementary school educator*

Pataskala
Honnold, Kathryn S. *real estate agent*
Thrasher, Rose Marie *critical care and community health nurse*

Patriot
Riggle, Patricia Carol *special education educator*

Paulding
Moore, Pamela Rae *elementary school educator*

Pepper Pike
Dunegan, Jennifer Lee *theater educator*
Helfand, Toby Scheintaub *retired dermatologist*
Oldenburg, Chloe Warner *performing arts association administrator, educator*
Seaton, Jean Robarts *psychology educator*
Stano, Sister Diana *academic administrator*
Wilkenfeld, Polly *librarian*

Perrysburg
Autry, Carolyn *artist, art history educator*
Billnitzer, Bonnie Jeanne *nurse, gerontologist*

Pickerington
Calderone, Jean Leslie *art educator, artist*
Callander, Kay Eileen Paisley *business owner, retired education educator, writer*
Collins, Arlene *secondary school educator*
Feesler, Molly J. *secondary school educator*
Kitsmiller, Myra Jordan *elementary school educator*
Lang, Lisa Ann *music educator*
Palmer, Noreen E. *psychotherapist*
Virden, Karen Frances *elementary school educator*

Piqua
Retman, Deborah W. *biology educator*

Plymouth
Hartman, Ruth Campbell *director, educator*

Port Clinton
Ewersen, Mary Virginia *retired school system administrator, poet*

Portsmouth
Johnson, Janice E. *education educator, writer*
Murphy, Pearl Marie *medical and surgical nurse*

Powell
Mitchell, Cathy (C.C.) Christine *art educator*

Quaker City
Morgan, Janet F. *elementary school educator*

Racine
Manuel, Jenny Lynn *elementary school educator*

Ravenna
O'Brien, Jane *special education educator*

Reynoldsburg
Boiman, Donna Rae *artist, art academy executive*
Maratta Snyder, Grace Elvira *volunteer*
Neal, Diane L. *retail executive*
Nichols, Grace A. *retail executive*

Richfield
Lewis, Sylvia Davidson *foundation executive*

Ridgeway
Moody, Loretta Jeanne *literature and language educator*

Rio Grande
Hatfield, Barbara Scott *academic administrator*

Rocky River
Briscar-Martel, Nancy Marie *agent, musician, educator*
Hartman, Kathryn Rose *elementary school educator*
Piper, Joann Lee Elliott *retired secondary school educator, swim coach*

Rootstown
Nora, Lois Margaret *neurologist, educator, academic administrator, dean*

Saint Clairsville
DeBertrand, Lynette Michele *clinical nurse specialist, educator*

Sandusky
Runner, Kathleen Kahle *secondary school educator*
Yunghans, Eleanor Janice *social studies educator*

Seaman
Cartaino, Carol Ann *editor*

Sebring
Kelley-Hall, Maryon Hoyle *retired social worker*

Seven Hills
Bowling, Rita Joan *medical/surgical nurse*
Giulivo, Cynthia Ann *secondary school educator*

Shadyside
DeBolt, Nanette C. *medical/surgical nurse*
Martin, Carol Jaye *retired elementary school educator*

Shaker Heights
Donnem, Sarah Lund *financial analyst, non-profit consultant, political organization consultant*
Freedman, Jacqueline Kahane *art educator*
Katz, Linda M. *social worker*
McBurney, Christine *performing arts educator, actress, director*
McKenna, Kathleen Kwasnik *artist*
Trefts, Joan Landenberger *retired principal*

Shiloh
Meyers, Pamela Sue *elementary school educator*

Sidney
Leffler, Carole Elizabeth *retired mental health nurse, women's health nurse*
Scott, Debra A. *special education educator*

Smithville
Sillman, Denise Marie *music educator, small business owner*

Solon
Bane, Glenice Gail *music educator*
Johnson, Madeline Mitchell *retired administrative assistant*
Robinson, Helene Susan *pharmacist*

Somerset
Green, Tammie *professional golfer*

South Euclid
Miller Schear, Annice Mara *music educator*
Zoller, Karen Ann *library and art gallery director*

Springfield
Pitzer, Betty Braun *retired social services administrator*
Stelzer, Patricia Jacobs *retired secondary school educator*
Woodhouse, Elizabeth C. *retired government agency administrator*

Stow
Castillo, Katherine Lynn *writer, translator, business owner*

Strongsville
Taghizadeh, Georgeanne Marie *medical/surgical nurse*
Webb, Tara Yvette *music educator*
Yates, Patricia Lawrence *elementary school educator*

Sylvania
Garrison, Linda *retired foundation administrator*
Heuschele, Sharon Jo *dean*
Parquette, Heather Ann *elementary school educator*
Sampson, Earldine Robison *education educator*
Verhesen, Anna Maria Hubertina *social worker*

Terrace Park
Fehl, Patricia Katherine *retired physical education educator*

Thornville
Coe, Linda Marlene Wolfe *retired marketing professional, freelance photographer*

Tiffin
Harner, Willa Jean *librarian*
Hillmer, Margaret Patricia *library director*
Holscher, Carol Ann *retired secondary school educator*

Tipp City
Ahmed, Gail R. *music educator*
Brewer, Traci Lynn *secondary school educator*
Tighe-Moore, Barbara Jeanne *electronics executive*

Toledo
Brickey, Suzanne M. *editor*
Dahl Reeves, Gretchen *occupational therapist, educator*
Danko-McGhee, Katherina Elaine *art educator, consultant*
Francis, Barbara Joan *nurse, paralegal*
Frank, Christine Marie *music educator*
Goldstein, Margaret Franks *special education educator*
Grant, Peggy (Margaret Mary Grant) *art gallery administrator, artist, consultant*
Grundish, Lee Anne *small business owner, writer*
Heintz, Carolinea Cabaniss *retired home economist, retired educator*
Knuth, Marya Danielle *special education educator*
Lyne, Janet Kay *music educator, director*
Mihura, Joni Lynn *psychologist, educator*
Overmyer, Janet Elaine *counselor*
Perz, Sally *academic administrator, former state legislator*
Rejent, Marian Magdalen *retired pediatrician*
Romanoff, Marjorie Reinwald *retired education educator*
Seubert, Lori A. *elementary school educator*
Wilde, Kerri Dawn *dance educator*
Wilson, Miriam S. *adult education educator*
Zorn, Sarah Marie *secondary school educator*

Tontogany
Baughman, Janine Kay *music educator*

Trenton
Crout, Elizabeth Roop *retired elementary school educator*

Trotwood
Staggs, Barbara J. *vice mayor*

Troy
DeHart, Karen Trautmann *artist, educator*

Tuscarawas
Lentz, Belinda Ann *elementary school educator*

Twinsburg
Murphy, Kathleen S. *science educator*
Washington, Annie Ruth *retired elementary school educator, minister*

University Heights
Seaton, Shirley Smith *academic administrator, consultant*
Starcher-Dell'Aquila, Judy Lynn *special education educator*

Upper Arlington
Walter, Jennie *elementary school educator*

Upper Sandusky
Miller, Angela Marie *elementary school educator*

Urbana
Meyers, Marsha Lynn *retired social worker*

Valley View
Miller, Susan Ann *retired school system administrator*

Van Wert
Huffman, Laura Christine *computer programmer, educator*

Vandalia
Korte, Genevieve L. *music educator*

Wadsworth
Aragon, Lynn D. *retired physician*
Ross, Jane Arlene *music educator*
Wilhelm, Cathy S. *elementary school educator*

Walbridge
Wiseman, Gretchen Renee *special education educator*

Wapakoneta
Lusk, Mary Margaret *music educator*
Wirth, Tamara L. *music educator*

Warren
Holt, Patricia Annette *retired music educator*
Landolfi, Jennie Louise *nursing administrator*
Ross, Karen Lee Hromyak *retired school psychologist*
Seachrist, Denise *music educator*
Thomas, Jane Ellen *elementary school educator*
VanAuker, Lana *recreational therapist, educator*

Washington Court House
Fichthorn, Fonda Gay *retired principal*

Wauseon
Stutzman, Donna J. *minister*

Waverly
Hartman, Mary Margaret *secondary school educator*

Waynesville
Doster, Susan Elizabeth *artist*

Wellston
Hockman, Lori Lynn *biologist, educator*
Loxley, Kathryn *retired elementary school educator*

West Carrollton
Bebout, Jennifer Lucille *science educator*

West Chester
Arnow, Jody L. *accountant*

West Farmington
Guyette, Diana *minister*
Smith, Agnes Monroe *history professor*

West Jefferson
Hepp, Jody *music educator*
Puckett, Helen Louise *retired tax consulting company executive*

West Unity
Heer, Carol Lynne *special education educator*

Westerville
Anderson, Judith Ann *artist, writer*
Diersing, Carolyn Virginia *educational administrator*
Lott, Vera Naomi *artist, educator*
Moss, Judith Dorothy *lawyer, consultant, lecturer*
Van Sant, Joanne Frances *academic administrator*
Volpe, Deborah L *mathematics educator*

Westfield Center
Bock, Carolyn A. *writer, consultant, small business owner*

Westlake
Bishop, Jeanne Emmons *director, science educator, researcher*
Coeling, Harriet Van Ess *nursing educator, editor*
Dechochrantraut, Leila L. *education educator*
Loehr, Marla *chaplain*
Schroth, Joyce Able *social worker*
Todd, Victoria L. *chlid psychoanalyst*

Whitehall
Falcon, Kimberly Sue *science educator*

Whitehouse
Gelsone, Amy J. *music educator*

Wickliffe
Barnes, Lili Darnelle *music educator, director*
Fisher, Nancy DeButts *library director*
Graves, Pamela Kay *music educator*
Krause, Marjorie N. *biochemist*
Wainio, Melody F. *registrar*

Wilberforce
Jones, LaShaunta' Lynn *athletic trainer, academic advisor*
Sanders, Augusta Carolyn *school librarian, educator*

Walker-Taylor, Yvonne *retired academic administrator*

Williamsburg
Hickey, Ena Varney *elementary school educator*

Willoughby
Corrigan, Faith *journalist, educator, historian*
Grossman, Mary Margaret *elementary school educator*
Linsenmeier, Carol Vincent *music educator*
Vokic, Heather Maureen *artist, educator*

Wilmington
Evans, Elizabeth Ann West *retired real estate agent*
Hamilton, Maxine Keiter *retired physician*
Mitchell, Angela D. *education educator*

Wooster
McClure, Carolyn F. *psychologist*
Saif, Linda J. *veterinary scientist, virologist, immunologist*
Schreiber, Clare Adel *journalist*

Worthington
Wade, Susan Prince *retired music educator*
Winston, Janet Margaret *real estate agent, volunteer*

Wyoming
Jablonsky, Atarah *retired music educator*

Xenia
Nutter, Zoe Dell Lantis *retired public relations executive*
Savard, Tamara Renee *music educator*
Vaughan, Doris Celestine Walker *retired librarian, educator*

Yellow Springs
Graham, Jewel Freeman *social worker, lawyer, educator*
Kadish, Katherine *artist, art educator*
Mercede, Nevin *art educator, artist*

Youngstown
Beasley-Martin, Monica Rachael *minister, director*
Bond, Christina M. *judge*
Bowers, Bege Kaye *literature educator, communications educator, academic administrator*
Camardese, Amy Hoffman *education educator*
Catoline-Ackerman, Pauline Dessie *small business owner*
Checcone, Iole Carlesimo *foreign language educator*
Clymer, Janis E. *physics professor*
Dunlap, Catherine Mary *clergywoman*
Itts, Elizabeth Ann Dunham *retired psychotherapist, consultant*
Kenner, Marilyn Sferra *civil engineer*
Robinson, Judith Adell *elementary school educator*
Thomas, Julie Elizabeth *clinical psychologist, educator*
Wells, Penny Whorton *gifted and talented educator, history educator*

Zanesville
Danford, Ardath Anne *retired librarian*
Jones, Jo Ann *retired elementary school educator*
Strahm, Mary Ellen *music educator*

OKLAHOMA

Ada
Baker, Judith Ann *retired computer technician*
Benson, Jade *science educator*
Dempsey, B. *artist*
Dennison, Ramona Pollan *special education educator*
Frye, Linda Beth (Linda Beth Hisle) *elementary school educator, secondary school educator*
Reese, Linda Williams *history professor*
Yarbrough, Trisha Marie *literature and language professor*

Altus
Purdue, Patricia *secondary school educator*

Alva
Almgren, Kandee Ann *language educator*
Cummings, Ramona *music educator*

Anadarko
Kidd, Lovetta Monza *music educator*

Ardmore
Fisher, Linda R. *science educator, department chairman*
Sadler, Marion Hanson *retired art educator*

Asher
Patterson, Lorie *literature and language educator*

Atwood
Perkins, Lorene K. *elementary school educator*

Bartlesville
Baker-Morris, Kay *special education educator*
Beech, Shelly Christine *dancer, educator, small business owner*
Chambers, Imogene Klutts *school system administrator, financial consultant*
Tupper, Becky Jean *registrar*
Wallace, Elizabeth Ann (Becky Wallace) *educator*
Yao, Jianhua *chemist, researcher*

Bethany
Cook, Wanda Reedy *music educator*
Garrett, Paula Kay *special education educator*

Bixby
McManus, Delana Ann *elementary school educator*
Wetzel, Marlene Reed *freelance/self-employed writer*

Blanchard
Kimbrough, Janie *library director*

Bristow
Caudle, Letha Grace *secondary school educator*

Broken Arrow
Baker, Bonnie Marie *real estate broker*
Barton/Strickland, Tammy Kay *elementary school educator, coach*
Biggs, Ruth Ann *social studies educator*
Hawkins, Pamela Kay *entertainer, writer*
Huff, Melinda Louise *art educator*
McManigal, Shirley Ann *retired dean*
Muller, Patricia Ann *nursing administrator, educator*
Roberts, Evelyn Smith *elementary school educator*
Strozier, Nancy Janelle *literature and language educator*
Swanson, Mary F. *education educator*

Calumet
Bradley, Nancy Elizabeth *elementary school educator*

Checotah
Cooper, Kathleen K. *music educator*

Chelsea
Geyer, Kathy Van Ness *retailer*

Chickasha
Critchfield, Tammy K. *elementary school educator*

Choctaw
Sendall, Paula *secondary school educator*
Warren-Billings, Janet Marie *language educator*

Claremore
Goff, Marilyn Russell McClain *counselor*
Hedge, Nancy *secondary school educator*
Heidlage, Patsy Jo *physical education educator*
Livingston, Sylvia Jean *art appraiser*

Cleveland
Henry, Kathleen Marie *marketing executive*

Clinton
Lewallen, Donna G. *elementary school educator*

Copan
Harsh, Mitzi Ann *language educator, coach*

Crescent
Lovett, Kristi Summer *art educator*

Cushing
Geyer, Karen Lea *writer*

Del City
Birdsong, Janet Louise *medical/surgical nurse*
Wallace, Fannie Margaret *minister, religious organization administrator*

Dewey
White, Joy Kathryn *retired claims consultant, artist*

Duncan
Dawkins, Barbara Elaine *retired secondary school educator*
Fike, Holly Renee *music educator*

Durant
Allen, Paula Smith *literature and language professor*
Dixon, Diane Marie *biology professor*

Edmond
Charoenwongse, Chindarat *pianist, music educator*
Danner, Julie A. *literature and language educator*
Dedmon, Angela Marie Maxine *psychologist*
Garrett, Kathryn Ann Byers (Kitty Garrett) *legislative clerk*
Haywood, B(etty) J(ean) *anesthesiologist*
Laughlin, Monique Myrtle Weant *mental health counselor*
Loman, Mary LaVerne *retired mathematics professor*
Loving, Susan Brimer *lawyer, former state official*
Necco, Edna Joanne *school psychologist*
Osgood, Virginia M. *vocational school educator*
Pydynkowsky, Joan Anne *journalist*
Sanchez, Cindi Asbury *physical education educator*
Thomas, Vicki Webb *theater educator*
Van Hemert, Phyllis Brown *counselor*
Wilson, Julia Ann Yother *lawyer*
Zabel, Vivian Ellouise *writer, retired secondary school educator*

El Reno
Grube, Deborah Jean *special education educator, science educator*

Elgin
McMasters, Glenetta G. *science educator*

Enid
Marquardt, Shirley Marie *retired management consultant*
Russell, Rhonda Cheryl *piano educator, recording artist, talent scout*
Seem, Evelyn Ashcraft *music educator*

Eufaula
Breon, Nancy G. *music educator*
Dawson, Cindy Marie *lawyer*
Flud, Sherrie Mae *science educator*

Forgan
Husted, Charlene E. *library media specialist, educator*

Fort Cobb
Rexroat, Vicki Lynn *occupational child development educator*

Frederick
Stone, Voye Lynne *women's health nurse practitioner*

Gore
Chair, Lisa *science educator*

Guthrie
Allen, Lori Ann *science educator*

Guymon
Gabel, Tera Christine *secondary school educator*

Hennessey
Fast, Naomi Mae *retired physician*

Hodgen
Brower, Janice Kathleen *library and information scientist*

Hollis
Stewart, Marcia Kathryn *music educator*

Inola
Mullen, Deborah W. *elementary school educator*

Jenks
Frazer, Janet Elizabeth *music educator*

Kremlin
Turner, LaWalta Dean *educator*

Lamont
Covalt, Edna Irene *retired medical/surgical nurse*

Langston
Haysbert, JoAnn Wright *academic administrator*

Lawton
Bonnell-Mihalis, Pamela Gay Scoggins *library director*
Ellenbrook, Carolyn Kay *religious organization administrator*
Gagliardi, Charlotte Marie *music educator, secondary school educator*
Garton, Janette *music educator*
Kroll, Connie Rae *librarian, information services consultant*
Reece, Juliette M. Stolper *community health and mental health nurse*
Underwood, Kirsten Fedje *musician, educator*
Wonsewitz, Pom Cha *artist, horticulturist*

Maramec
Blair, Marie Lenore *elementary school educator*

Mcalester
Burden, Sherri Lynn Erickson *secondary school educator*
Lutz, Marie Burns *retired secondary school educator*

Mcloud
Goats, Debbie *elementary school educator*

Miami
Koehler, Tammie *obstetrician, gynecologist*
Murphy, Carla M. *secondary school educator*

Midwest City
Cheek, Norma Jean *retired secondary school educator*
Mechling, Brenda L. *voice educator, director*
Robinson, Emily Sue *music educator*
Wier, Leanne M. *life sciences educator*

Moore
Chiles, Mary Jane *secondary school educator*
Sturch, Lois J. *elementary school educator*

Mounds
Fellows, Esther Elizabeth *musician, music educator*

Muskogee
Felts, Joan April *retired elementary school educator*
Heck, Jennifer Leigh *neonatal/perinatal nurse practitioner, educator*
Helwick, Amber *science educator*
Swanson, Jacqueline V. *academic administrator, educator, women's health nurse practitioner*

Mustang
Dunn, Karen S. *language educator*
Hutter, Teresa Ann *art educator*
Laurent, Jerry Suzanna *communications executive*
Wood, Jean Carol *poet, lyricist*

Newcastle
Howeth, Lynda Carol *small business owner*

Noble
Reynolds, Karen Ann *secondary school educator*

Norman
Affleck, Marilyn *retired sociology educator*
Bethel, Joann D. *computer programmer, analyst*
Biscoe, Belinda P. *academic administrator, psychologist*
Cochran, Gloria Grimes *retired pediatrician*
Dorrough, Vicki Lee *theater educator*
Harris, Carol Lynn *elementary school educator*
Jones, Charlotte *foundation administrator*
Lester, June *library and information scientist, educator*
Magrath, Jane *music educator*
Mergler, Nancy L. *academic administrator*
Michaud, Phyllis Carol *school counselor*
Nance, Starlynn R. *academic counselor*
Nelson, Donna Jean *chemistry educator, researcher*
Ogilvie, Marilyn Bailey *natural science educator, historian, writer, bibliographer*
Petersen, Catherine Holland *lawyer*
Price, Linda Rice *community development administrator*
Provine, Lorraine *retired mathematics educator*
Reedy, Mitsuno Ishii *artist, painter*
Sherman, Mary Angus *public library administrator*
Smith, Beulah Mae *music educator*
Tussing, Marilee Appleby *music educator*
Upchurch, Carol J. *elementary school educator*
Winters, Martha Patrice *history and language educator*
Wood, Betty Jean *conceptual artist, art educator*
Yamashita, Elizabeth Swayne *university administrator, mass communications educator*
Zapffe, Nina Byrom *retired elementary school educator*
Zelby, Rachel *realtor*

Okemah
DeShields, Elizabeth Peggy Bowen *artist, educator, poet*

Oklahoma City
Adams, Mary Lou *piano teacher*
Ainsworth, Sharie Lynn *athletic trainer, educator*
Alaupovic, Alexandra Vrbanic *artist, educator*
Allbright, Karan Elizabeth *psychologist, consultant*
Askins, Jari *lawyer, department chairman, state representative*
Bahr, Carman Bloedow *internist*
Bentley, Karen Gail *elementary school educator*
Beymer-Chapman, Brenda Marie *elementary school educator*
Binning, Bette Finese (Mrs. Gene Hedgcock Binning) *athletic association official*
Blackburn, Debbie *elementary school educator, state representative*
Boston, Billie *costume designer, costume history educator*
Brummett, Shirley Ann *art educator*
Campbell, Virginia Hopper *piano concert artist, composer, educator*
Cauthron, Robin J. *federal judge*
Douty, Sheila *softball player*
Easley, Mary *retired elementary school educator, state representative*
Fallin, Mary Copeland *lieutenant governor*
Fernandez, Lisa *softball player*
Fischer, Gayle *elementary school educator*
Forni, Patricia Rose *nursing educator*
Frates, Mex (Mrs. Clifford Leroy Frates) *civic worker*
Gabbard, Susan J. *art association administrator, educator*
Garrett, Sandy Langley *school system administrator*
Gilmore, Joan Elizabeth *small business owner, newspaper columnist*
Green, Vickie *music educator*
Gumerson, Jean Gilderhus *health foundation executive*
Hale, Sue A. *editor*
Halpin, Anna Marie *retired architect*
Hampton, Carol McDonald *priest, educator, historian*
Harrison-Bridgeman, Ann Marie *claims adjuster*
Herndon, Merri Kathleen *elementary school educator*
Hollingshead, Bonne Lou *fine art artist*
Hooper, Marie E. *history professor*
Iven, Marjorie L. *assistant principal*
Jones, Brenda Kaye *public relations executive*
Jones, Renee Kauerauf *health facility administrator*
Judge, Mary Kathleen *humanities educator*
Kauger, Yvonne *state supreme court justice*
Kerr, Lou C. *foundation administrator*
LaMotte, Janet Allison *retired management consultant*
Lester, Stacy A. *chemistry educator*
Lindenberg, Elanna Beth *communications educator, secondary school educator*
Marcussen, Carin Leigh *lawyer*
Mather, Stephanie June *lawyer*
McClellan, Mary Ann *pediatric nurse practitioner*
Miles-La Grange, Vicki *judge*
Mitchell, Ira Joan *nutritionist*
Morris, Phyllis *legislative staff member*
Noakes, Betty LaVonne *retired elementary school educator*
Ousley, Amy Michelle *science educator*
Pain, Betsy M. *lawyer*
Price, Donna J. *nurse*
Ragsdale, Jana Lynne *music educator*
Richardson, Jean Brooks *artist, printmaker*
Ridley, Betty Ann *theology studies educator*
Riley, Nancy C. *state legislator*
Rosenberg, Emily *psychiatrist*
Savage, Susan M. *state official, former mayor*
Shackleton, Jean L. *music educator*
Shuman-Miller, Nancy *education educator, department chairman*
Staggs, Barbara Annette *state representative*
Twyman, Nita (Venita Twyman) *music educator*
Wheeler, Jane Frances *protective services official*
Whitener, Carolyn Raye *artist*
Wilson, Francelia Latting *retired elementary school educator*
Wood, Paula Davidson *lawyer*
Zevnik-Sawatzky, Donna Dee *retired litigation coordinator*
Zhu, Hua *biochemist, researcher*

Owasso
Bettridge, Melinda Kae *secondary school educator, music educator, director*

Park Hill
Yeager, Debra Lyn *science educator*

Pauls Valley
McManus, Debra Lynne *secondary school educator*
Pesterfield, Linda Carol *retired principal*

Pawhuska
Adams, Jessica Tereace *music educator, director*

Perkins
Lewis, Mary May Smith *retired family practice nurse practitioner*

Pocola
Clouse, Nan *elementary school educator, musician*

Ponca City
Easley, Betsy Leabeth *secondary school educator*
Rice, Sue Ann *retired dean, psychologist*
Tatum, Betty Joyce *secondary school educator*

Poteau
Giles, Patty Dawn *school librarian*
Long, Sheila Joan *academic administrator*

Prague
Emery, Cecilia Ruth *learning disability educator*

Pryor
Dotson, Stella Marie *nurse*

Sayre
Haught, Judy C. *language educator*

Schulter
Ayres, Gwyneth Carol *elementary school educator*

Shawnee
Kappes, Marcia Ann *education educator*
McGuire, Anne C. *theology studies educator*
Woodward, Betty Shaw *retired music educator*

Skiatook
Dunham, Mary Helen *elementary school educator*
Meyer, Virginia Maurine *music educator*

Stillwater
Ferrell, Judy Ann *elementary school educator*

Stilwell
Doyle, Rhonda Gail *science educator*
Fourkiller, Diana Lynn *elementary school educator*

Tahlequah
Edwards, Terri Lyn Wilmoth *education educator*
Grant, Kay Lallier *early childhood education educator*

Tecumseh
Moser, Glenda Faye *media specialist*

Tinker Afb
Penn, Vernita Lynn *government agency administrator*
Scott, Carol Lee *child care educator*
Velasco, Jodi Marie *military lawyer*

Tulsa
Arrington, Rebecca Carol *occupational health nurse*
Barnes, Cynthia Lou *retired gifted and talented educator*
Blackstock, Virginia Lee Lowman (Mrs. LeRoy Blackstock) *civic worker*
Bransford-Young, Angharad Ann *counselor, educator*
Bridges, Mary Jo *music educator*
Buthod, Mary Clare *school administrator*
Candreia, Peggy Jo *medical educator*
Cardwell, Sandra Gayle Bavido *engineering company executive*
Carpenter, Nancy J. *health science association administrator*
Chew, Pamela Christine *language educator*
Clark, Marian Wilson *writer*
Clement, Evelyn Geer *librarian, educator*
Collins, Laura Jane *music educator, singer*
Dexter, Deirdre O'Neil Elizabeth *lawyer*
Fielding, Peggy Lou Moss *writer*
Frazier, Mary Ann *artist*
Gottschalk, Debbra J. *lawyer*
Gottschalk, Sister Mary Therese *nun, hospital administrator*
Gustavson, Cynthia Marie *social worker, writer*
Howerton, Helen F. *artist*
Hyland, Cheryl C. *health services administrator*
Jackson, Sandra Lee *health facility administrator*
Jurgensen, Monserrate *clinical nurse, consultant*
Lewis, Corinne Hemeter *psychotherapist, educator*
Lewis, Patricia Mohatt (Patty) *special education educator*
Marshall, Linda Lantow *pediatrics nurse*
Marshall-Chapman, Paula *food products executive*
Neal, Marilyn Young *librarian*
O'Sullivan, Cindy Marie *mathematics professor*
Owens, Jana Jae *entertainer*
Price, Alice Lindsay *writer*
Redfearn, Charlotte Marie *nursing administrator*
Saurer, Mary Marcelle *minister*
Seymour, Stephanie Kulp *federal judge*
Starr, Sharon Diane *elementary school educator*
Stewart, Mary Tomlinson *science educator, researcher*
Taylor, Kathy *mayor*
Troutman, Virginia E. *elementary school educator*
Undernehr, Laura Lee *elementary school educator*
Valero, Maria Teresa *photographer, art educator*
Vaniman, Vicki *lawyer*
Vaughan, Elizabeth L. *school nurse practitioner*
Vilar, Susan Ann *elementary school educator*
Vincent, Suzanne Sawyer *physiologist, educator*
Weinstock Rad, Katheryn Louise *music educator*
Werlla, Vanessa Lynn *psychiatrist*
Womack, Lee Ann *country musician*
Wortmann, Dorothy Woodward *physician*

Vici
White, Angela Pearl *literature and language educator*

Vinita
Johnston, Ruth Darrough *retired elementary school educator, counselor*
Wright, Jo Anne *priest*

Wagoner
Durham, Nancy Ruth *elementary school educator, music educator*
Hadley, Charline A. *protective services official*

Watts
Bell, Janice Lee *finance educator*

Weatherford
Craig, Viki Pettijohn *language educator*
Vanderslice, Ronna Jean *education educator*

Wilburton
Butler, Mary Edith *academic administrator, school librarian*
Carey, Levenia Marie *counselor*
Minshall, Dorothy Kathleen *music educator*

Woodward
Curtis, Kathryn Faye *medical laboratory technician*
Fisher, Deena Kaye *social studies education administrator*
Hurst, Tacy Marcella *literature and language educator*

Wynnewood
Parker, Lois W. *retired literature and language professor*
Powers, Shalia Jo *secondary school educator*
Watrous, Naoma Dickson *retired clinical psychologist*

Yukon
Griffin, Sharon Grass *elementary school educator*
Megli, Lisa L. *assistant principal*

OREGON

Albany
Haralson, Linda Jane *communications executive*
Oakley, Carolyn Le *state legislator, city manager, director*

Ashland
Burritt, Barbara *artist*
Cullinan, Mary Patricia *academic administrator, literature and language professor*
Titus, Karen J. *small business owner*
Zinser, Elisabeth Ann *academic administrator*

Astoria
West, Vanette Jane *secondary school educator*

Bandon
Handley, Louise Patricia *artist*

Beaverton
Burson-Dyer, Lorraine *library executive*
Dantas, Stella Marie *obstetrician, gynecologist*
DeBerry, Donna *retail executive*
de Sá e Silva, Elizabeth Anne *secondary school educator*
Mitchell, Bettie Phaenon *religious organization administrator*
Pepper, Floy Childers *educational consultant*
Pond, Patricia Brown *library and information scientist, educator*
Vardavas, Stephanie J. *lawyer*
Weygandt, Staci *mathematics educator*

Bend
Brooke, Sandra Lee *painter*
Evers-Williams, Myrlie Beasley *advocate, cultural organization administrator*
Forbes Johnson, Mary Gladys *retired secondary school educator*
McDermott, Mary Katheryn *science educator*
Moss, Patricia L. *bank executive*
Sabatella, Elizabeth Maria *clinical therapist, educator, mental health facility administrator*
Singletary, DeJuan Theresa *child and adolescent psychiatrist*
Wilbanks, Donna Mae *editor*

Brookings
Kucharski, Kathleen Martin *secondary school educator*

Canby
Sundquist, Leah Renata *military officer*
Walsh, Erin Kathleen *social studies educator*

Cannon Beach
Hellyer, Constance Anne (Connie Anne Conway) *writer, musician*
Wismer, Patricia Ann *retired secondary school educator*

Central Point
Ingraham, Laura *lawyer, political commentator*

Christmas Valley
Johnson, Mary Alice *magazine editor*

Clackamas
Agost, Dalene Beth *elementary school educator*
Love, Susan Denise *accountant, consultant, small business owner*

Corvallis
Achterman, Gail Louise *lawyer*
Aldwin, Carolyn Magdalen *behavioral science educator*
Cope, Rhian Brianna *toxicologist, educator*
Fucillo, Dawn M. *radiologic technologist*
Landers, Teresa Price *librarian*
McCormick, Stephanie L. Bell *music educator*
Nelson, Carol Gretchen *music educator*
Shoemaker, Clara Brink *retired chemistry professor, researcher*
Wilkins, Caroline Hanke *advocate, political organization worker*

Culver
Siebert, Diane Dolores *author, poet*

Depoe Bay
Fish, Barbara Joan *investor, small business owner*

Eagle Point
Blanchard, Shirley Lynn *primary school educator, consultant*
Lundgren, Karen Marie *disabilities professional*

Eugene
Aldave, Barbara Bader *lawyer, educator*
Arnaud, Velda *finance educator*
Bailey, Exine Margaret Anderson *soprano, educator*

Bascom, Ruth F. *retired mayor*
Bassett, Carol Ann *journalism educator, writer*
Beickel, Sharon Lynne *psychologist*
Benson, Joan *musician, educator*
Bossuat, Judy Weigert *music educator*
Cawood, Elizabeth Jean *public relations executive*
Dorn, Kathie Lee *medical/surgical nurse*
Freyd, Jennifer Joy *psychology professor*
Gillespie, Penny Hannig *business owner*
Gourley, Paula Marie *art educator, artist, writer, publishing executive*
Graziano, Margaret A. *chaplain, recreational therapist, educational consultant, volunteer*
Hunt, Elizabeth Hope *psychologist*
Lansdowne, Karen Myrtle *retired English language and literature educator*
Lary, Lynn M. *computer scientist, educator*
McCrea, Shaun S. *lawyer*
McMillan, Adell *retired academic administrator*
Metltzoff, Nancy Jean *education educator*
Peterson, Donna Rae *gerontologist*
Porter, Catherine (Kay Porter) *therapist, business consultant*
Richmond, Geraldine Lee *chemist, educator*
Sisley, Becky Lynn *physical education educator*
Smith, Vangy Edith *accountant, consultant, artist, writer*
Stirling, Isabel Ann *science librarian*
Taylor, Marjorie *psychology professor*
Theodoropoulos, Christine O. *architecture educator*
Utsey, Glenda Fravel *architecture educator*
Weiss, Marianna Shrenger *psychotherapist*
Wilhelm, Kate (Katy Gertrude) *author*
Woolley, Donna Pearl *lumber company executive*

Forest Grove
Fuiten, Helen Lorraine *small business owner*
Ginn, Sharon Patrick *mechanical engineer*
Valfre, Michelle Williams *nursing educator, administrator, writer*

Gladstone
Frank, Dee *artist, educator*

Grants Pass
Comeaux, Katharine Jeanne *realtor*
Murdock, Doris Dean *special education educator, program developer*

Gresham
Davidson, Joan Elizabeth Gather *psychologist*
Edwards, Julie Diane *women's health nurse*
Light, Betty Jensen Pritchett *retired dean*
Webb, Donna Louise *academic director, educator*

Hillsboro
Burke, Tara LeAnn *music educator*
Dubrulle, Françoise M. *architect, painter, interior designer*
Nelson, Heather M. *elementary school educator*
Porter, Roberta Ann *counseling administrator, educator, retired school system administrator*

Jacksonville
Beeler, Sherri *secondary school educator*

Jefferson
Varner, Helen *communications educator*

Keizer
Stevens, Sharon Cox *lawyer*

Klamath Falls
Crawford, Brenda R. *music educator*
Dow, Martha Anne *academic administrator, biology professor*
Koch, Margaret Rau *writer, artist, historian*
Payne, Tyana *psychotherapist*

La Grande
Ewing, Marilyn *English educator*
Thompson, Joan (Jo) *anthropologist*

Lafayette
Dow, Marla *counselor*

Lake Oswego
Finley, Patricia Ann *psychologist, artist*
Marietta, Elizabeth Ann *real estate broker*
McKay, Laura L. *bank executive, consultant*
Meltebeke, Renette *career counselor*
Rimerman, Janet Malaine *art educator, artist*
Zorkin, Melissa Waggener *public relations executive*

Lebanon
Griswold, Elaine C. *nurse, consultant*

Lincoln City
Casey, Darla Diann *elementary school educator*

Madras
Adams, Karen V. *elementary school educator*
Weires, Sally L. *paralegal*

Marylhurst
Roland, Meg *literature educator*

Mcminnville
Chappell, Annie-Dear *retired business manager*
Fread, Phyllis Jean *counselor, educator*
Nelson, Donna Gayle *state representative*

Medford
Bessey, Caroline A. *education educator*
Franklin, Darlene Kay *elementary school educator*
Hennion, Carolyn Laird (Lyn Hennion) *investment executive*
Linn, Carole Anne *dietician*
Maack, Jean Elizabeth *retired elementary school educator*
Morris, Judy *artist*
Schubert, Ruth Carol Hickok *artist, educator*

Milwaukie
Eichenger, Marilynne Katzen *museum administrator*

Monmouth
Strand, Cheryl Marie *Spanish language, literature educator*

Myrtle Creek
Kuk, Mary Halvorson *secondary school educator*

Newberg
Gathercoal, Kathleen Kleiner *psychology educator*
Keith, Pauline Mary *artist, illustrator, writer*
McGillivray, Karen *retired elementary school educator*
Warford, Patricia *psychologist*

Newport
Pavlish, Catherine Ann *language educator, writer*

Oceanside
Wadlow, Joan Krueger *retired academic administrator, retired construction executive*

Oregon City
White, Deborah Lee *psychologist*

Pendleton
Bedford, Amy Aldrich *public relations executive*
Blanc, Carol S. *biology educator*
Klepper, Elizabeth Lee *retired physiologist*

Phoenix
Dodd, Darlene Mae *retired nurse, retired military officer*

Pleasant Hill
Martin, Kelli Lynne *education educator*

Portland
Allan, Susan *public health service officer*
Baker, Barbara Jean *pediatrician, psychiatrist*
Baker, Diane R.H. *dermatologist*
Balkowiec, Agnieszka Zofia *science educator, researcher*
Bodin, Kate *dean*
Boutwell, Anne Dielschneider *artist, painter*
Boyle, Gertrude *sportswear company executive*
Bryant, Carmen Julia *missionary, educator*
Bunza, Linda Hathaway *editor, writer, composer, director*
Cady, Sherry L. *astrobiologist, educator*
Chan, Susan S. *music educator*
Chevis, Cheryl Ann *lawyer*
Collins, Maribeth Wilson *retired foundation administrator*
Cook, Nena *lawyer*
Corbett, Alice Catherine *investor*
Dailey, Dianne K. *lawyer*
Delcambre, Lois Marie Lundberg *academic administrator*
Dow, Mary Alexis *auditor*
Ebert, Leslie *artist*
Engelberg, Elaine A. *retired secondary school educator*
Farner, Darla A. *artist*
Fritz, Barbara Jean *occupational health nurse*
Frolick, Patricia Mary *retired elementary school educator*
Furse, Elizabeth *retired congressman, small business owner*
Gangle, Melanie Jean *counselor*
Gordly, Avel Louise *state legislator, political organization worker*
Graber, Susan P. *federal judge*
Harris, Cynthia Viola *principal*
Helmer, M(artha) Christie *lawyer*
Immergut, Karin J. *prosecutor*
Jacobson, Sig-Linda *obstetrician, educator*
Janovec, Madeline Meza *artist, educator*
Jensen, Marion Pauline *singer*
Johnson, Virginia Macpherson *secondary school educator, consultant*
Johnston, Virginia Evelyn *retired editor*
Kafoury, Ann Graham *psychotherapist*
Katz, Vera *former mayor, former college administrator, state legislator*
Kelly, Carol Rowden *psychologist*
Kirk, Jill *management consultant*
Kleim, E. Denise *city official*
Kohne, Heidi Ann *church musician*
Korb, Christine Ann *music therapist, researcher, educator*
Larson, Wanda Z. *writer, poet*
Leupp, Edythe Peterson *retired education educator*
Lorenz, Nancy *artist*
Massee, Judith Tyle *editor, educator*
Matarazzo, Ruth Gadbois *retired psychologist, educator*
Mendelson, Lottie M. *retired pediatric nurse practitioner, writer*
Merrill, Norma *video poducer, copy writer*
Mersereau, Susan S. *clinical psychologist*
Milton, Catherine Higgs *entrepreneur*
Mittelstaedt, Janet Rugen *music educator, composer*
Mullane, Jeanette Leslie *artist, educator*
Njoku, Scholastica Ibari *retired college librarian, writer*
Ozawa, Connie Patricia *science educator*
Parvin, RuthAnn *psychological services administrator*
Patterson, Beverly Ann Gross *not-for-profit fundraiser, consultant, social services administrator, writer*
Phillips, Vicki L. *school system administrator*
Porter, Elsa Allgood *writer, educator*
Robinson, Helene M. *retired music educator*
Robinson, Ruth Carleson *retired secondary school educator*
Rooks, Judith Pence *nurse midwife, consultant*
Rosenbaum, Lois Omenn *lawyer*
Rosenblum, Ellen F. *judge*
Rowe, Sandra Mims *editor*
Schumacher, Maria *biomedical researcher, educator*
Seymour, B(arbara) J(ean) *social worker*
Showalter, Marilyn Grace *trade association administrator, director*
Simmons, Laura *religious studies educator*
Solberg, Di Anne *retired secondary school educator*
Sonniksen, Janet W. *education educator*
Steinman, Lisa Malinowski *English literature educator, writer*
Stewart, Janice Mae *federal judge*
Street, Terri M. *artist, educator*
Swenson, Constance Rae *lawyer*
Taylor, J. Mary (Jocelyn Mary Taylor) *museum director, educator, zoologist*
Teller, Susan Elaine *lawyer*
Thompson, Terrie Lee *graphic designer*
Tower, Sue Warncke *artist*
Unger, Jane Ellen *performing company executive*
Vanderslice, Ellen *architect, composer*
White, Roberta Lee *financial analyst*
Wood, Cynthia Wilder *elementary school educator*
Woods, Deanna Gael *education educator, consultant*
Yatvin, Joanne Ina *education educator*
Zerbe, Kathryn Jane *psychiatrist*
Zimmerman, Gail Marie *medical foundation executive*

Prineville
Schulz, Suzon Louise *fine artist*

Redmond
Dey, Charlotte Jane *retired community health nurse*

Rhododendron
Williamson, Diana Jean *nurse*

Roseburg
Ball, Char Lee Frances *retired special education educator*
King, Lloyd JoAnn *music educator, volunteer*
Oleskowicz, Jeanette *physician*
Young, Susan Mark *psychologist*

Saint Helens
Morten, Ann Keane *nurse midwife*

Salem
Anderson, Laurie Monnes *state senator*
Beranek, Kim Marie *music educator*
Burdick, Ginny Marie *state senator*
Carter, Margaret L. *legislator*
Castillo, Susan *school system administrator*
Close, Betsy L. *state representative*
Gangle, Sandra Smith *arbitrator, mediator*
Hill, JoAnne Miller *special education educator, consultant*
Koch, Katrina M. *private school educator*
Marshall, Cak (Catherine Elaine Marshall) *music educator, composer*
Milbrath, Mary Merrill Lemke *quality assurance professional*
Minnis, Karen *state representative*
Page, Cheryl Miller *elementary school educator*
Qutub, Eileen *state legislator, real estate appraiser*
Robertson, Marian Ella (Marian Ella Hall) *small business owner, handwriting analyst*
Tomei, Carolyn *state representative*
Vernon, Olympia Flechet *writer*
Walker, Vicki L. *state senator*
Warnath, Maxine Ammer *psychologist, arbitrator*
Weide, Janice Lee *librarian*
Winters, Jackie F. *small business owner, foundation administrator*
Wirth, Kelley K. *state representative*
Yih, Mae Dunn *state legislator*

Sandy
Jensen, Judy Dianne *psychotherapist, consultant*
Thies, Lynn Wapinski *elementary school educator*

Silverton
Stone, Jane Buffington *artist, writer*

South Beach
Lick, Sue Fagalde *writer*

Stanfield
Durbin, Marilyn Ann Rafal *secondary school educator*

Sunriver
Seeger, Virginia Vincent *painter*

Sutherlin
Gugel, Merilynn Sue *artist*
Johnson, Barbara E. *adult education educator*
Littlejohn, Heather Sheri *music educator*

Talent
Meyers, Sharon May *sales executive*

The Dalles
Hayden, I. Jill *secondary school educator*

Veneta
Cotter, Roberta L. *elementary school educator*

Waldport
Abel, Laura Sorvetti *retired literature and language educator*

Wallowa
Hunter, Kathleen *writer, educator*

West Linn
Harris, Debra Coral *physical education educator*
Stoddard-Hayes, Marlana Kay *artist, educator*
Torsen, Marilyn Joanne *counselor, retired*

Woodburn
Anderson, Karen Mae *primary school educator*

Yamhill
Longton, Brenda Jo *music educator*

PENNSYLVANIA

Abington
Anderson, Valerie B. *actress, writer*
Goldfine, Beatrice *artist*
Lauck, Donna L. *mental health nurse*
Schuster, Ingeborg Ida *chemistry professor*

Acme
Babcock, Marguerite Lockwood *addictions treatment therapist, educator, writer*

Adrian
Hogg, Yvonne Marie *special education educator*

Akron
Dickinson, Margery Elsie *missionary, clinical psychologist*
Lapp, Alice Weber *secondary school educator, editor*

Aldan
Stegmuller, Agnes Leonore *physical education educator*

Aliquippa
Milanovich, Lynn Esther *counselor*

Allentown
Beltzner, Gail Ann *music educator*
Borger, Ann Work *communications professional, webmaster*
Brownback, Linda Mason *health company executive*
Ehritz, Marianne Louise *elementary school educator*
Franges, Gayle Louise *elementary school educator*
Glaessmann, Doris Ann *former county official, consultant*
Goodman, Pauline Rose *retired secondary school educator*
Martyska, Barbara *composer, performer, educator*
Moeller, MaryAnn *music educator*
Nippert, Carolyn Cochrane *academic administrator, information scientist*
Panfile, Patricia McCloskey *psychologist*
Pavelich, Judith *secondary school educator*
Pribanich, Cheryl Marie *music educator*
Rankin, Jean F. *lawyer*
Saab, Deanne Keltum *real estate broker, appraiser*
Sacks, Patricia Ann *librarian, consultant*
Shaffer-Shriver, Julie Renée *science educator*
Steinhauer, LuAnn *retired learning disabilities educator*
Teitsworth, Margaret Yvonne *nursing educator*
Tinsman-Schaffer, Patricia Joan *secondary school educator, artist*
Zocco, Patricia Elizabeth *human services manager, cardiac ultrasound technologist*

Allison Park
Bumblis, Kristin N. *music educator*
Hurst, Michele Lynn *elementary school educator*
Toerge, Lynn *athletic trainer*

Altoona
Anthony, Bertha M. *minister*
Damiano, Cathy *elementary school educator*
Love, Sharon RedHawk *education educator*
Vreeland-Flynn, Tracy Lynn *elementary school educator*

Ambler
Fiorito, Rebecca *elementary school educator*
Swansen, Donna Maloney *landscape designer, consultant*

Ambridge
Powell, Pamela Baker *education educator, minister*

Annville
Condran, Cynthia Marie *gospel musician*
Tezanos-Pinto, Rosa *Hispanic American literature educator*
Verhoek, Susan Elizabeth *botany educator*

Archbald
Cummings, Ellen Finan *special education educator*

Ardmore
Dagna, Jeanne Marie *special education educator*
Levy, Rochelle Feldman *artist*
Lockett-Egan, Marian Workman *advertising executive*
Schlegel, Gena Marie *paramedic*
Voegele, Karen E. *social worker*

Arnot
Ostrom, Brigette Dawn *special education educator*

Aston
Mirenda, Rosalie M. *academic administrator, nursing educator*

Atglen
Souders, Roberta Belshaw *literature and language educator*
Young, Robyn S. *artist, historian, commentator*

Athens
Luther-Lemmon, Carol Len *elementary school educator*
Yeager-Hall, Carli Marie *biology educator*

Avella
Blose, Ruth Elayne *language educator*

Bala Cynwyd
Armani, Aida Mary *small business owner*
Cohen, Rachel Rutstein *financial planner*
Culp, Dorie *marketing executive*
Dorwart, Bonnie Brice *historian, retired rheumatologist*
Kane-Vanni, Patricia Ruth *lawyer, paleontologist, educator*
Leibman, Faith H. *lawyer, psychologist*
Peret, Karen Krzyminski *health facility administrator*

Bangor
Pensack, Susan *elementary school educator*
Steele, Kathleen Patricia *science educator*

Barto
Kirk, Kathryn A. *science educator*

Beach Lake
Ash, Polly Gayenelle *secondary school educator, minister*

Beaver
Helmick, Gayle Johnston *retired elementary education educator*

Beaver Falls
Copeland, Deborah Gayle *education educator*
Miller, Kathleen S. *project engineer*
Thomas-Wright, Lisa Ann *elementary school educator*

Bedford
Weyant, Erin Kathleen Beegle *athletic trainer, small business owner*

Belle Vernon
Stimmell, Tamara *special education educator*

Bellefonte
Stevens-Sollman, Jeanne Lee *artist*

Bensalem
Bern, Dorrit J. *apparel executive*
Kline, Sharon Elaine *science educator*
Piscopio, Geraldine Anne *nurse anesthetist*

Bentleyville
Blasko, Barbara Ann *secondary school educator*

Benton
O'Brien, Lisa Anne *middle school educator*

Berwyn
Bluestone, Ellen Hope *literature, writing, and women's studies professor, writer*
Gingles, Marjorie Stanke *music educator*
Langford, Linda Kosmin *library consultant*

Bethel Park
Chmelynski, Donna *elementary school educator*
Douds, Virginia Lee *elementary school educator*
Menees, Katherine Determan *parochial school educator*

Bethlehem
Allen, Beatrice *music educator, pianist*
Corpora, Kathleen M. *middle school educator, technology integration specialist*
Del Cueto, S. E. *Spanish and English language educator*
Dorward, Judith A. *retired business ordering customer service representative*
Felix, Patricia Jean *retired steel company purchasing professional*
Fishbone, Vivian Manperl *artist*
Gast, Alice Petry *academic administrator, chemical engineering educator*
King, Jane Connell *mathematics professor*
Orr, Sandra Jane *civic worker, pharmacist*
Parmet, Harriet Abbey L. *literature educator*
Rambo, Kelly Clifford *lawyer*
Reilly, Suzette B. *counselor*
Schattschneider, Doris Jean *retired mathematics professor*
Simons, Audrey Kay *music educator*

Big Cove Tannery
Younker, Nancy Elaine *retired elementary school educator*

Biglerville
Hartlaub, Maxine Louise *literature educator*
Marks, Nora Maralea *retired secondary school educator*

Birdsboro
Dieffenbach, Lisa M. *music educator*

Blairsville
Stiffler, Erma Delores *minister, retired elementary school educator*

Bloomsburg
Holloway, Sybil Lymorise *psychologist, writer*
Kozloff, Jessica S. *academic administrator*
Trapane, Ruth *educator, artist*

Blue Bell
Deschaine, Barbara Ralph *retired real estate broker*
Edwards, Joselle Elizabeth *performing arts educator*
Gorby-Schmidt, Martha Louise *pharmacologist, researcher*
Halas, Cynthia Ann *business information specialist*
Haugen, Janet B. *corporate financial executive*
Martino, Robin Leigh *elementary school educator*
Roden, Carol Looney *retired language educator*
Sundheim, Nancy Straus *lawyer*
Welhan, Beverly Jean Lutz *nursing educator, administrator*

Bowmansville
Myers, Rose (Toni) A. *art educator*

Boyertown
Laskosky, Donna Marie *secondary school educator*
Woods Coggins, Alma *artist*

Bradford
Robbins, Andrea M. *science educator*
Thumpston, Kathleen Marie *music educator*

Breinigsville
Smith, Judith Lynn *physical education educator*

Bristol
Atkinson, Susan D. *producing artistic director, theatrical consultant*

Brodheadsville
Caines, Cheryl Lynne *supervisor*
Rissmiller, Carole *school system administrator*
Snyder, Nadine Eldora *music educator*

Brookville
Briggs, Carole A. *elementary school educator*

Broomall
Benner, Paula Roxanne *academic administrator, educator*
Puchalla, Mary Kay *elementary school educator*
Samans, Elaine Mae *education counselor, human services educator*
Saunders, Sally Love *poet, educator*

Bryn Mawr
Alter, Maria Pospischil *language educator*
Cooney, Patricia Ruth *civic worker*
Crawford, Maria Luisa Buse *geology educator*
Eiser, Barbara J.A. *management consultant*
Fellinger-Buzby, Linda *interior and industrial designer*
Fletcher, Marjorie Amos *librarian*
Gaisser, Julia Haig *classics educator*
Godinez, Marye H. *anesthesiologist*
Hirsh, Sharon Latchaw *academic administrator, art history educator*
Hughes, Rhonda J. *mathematics professor*
Lane, Barbara Miller (Barbara Miller-Lane) *humanities educator*
Lang, Mabel Louise *classics educator*
Porter, Judith Deborah Revitch *sociologist*
Riihimaki, Catherine Anne *geologist*
Salisbury, Helen Holland *education educator*
Smith, Nona Coates *academic administrator*
Vickers, Nancy J. *academic administrator*

Butler
Day, Margaret Ann *research librarian, information specialist*
Korn, Carol M. *retired elementary school educator*
Patterson, Patricia Lynne *artist, educator*

California
Schwerdt, Lisa Mary *language educator*
Twiss, Pamela *social worker, educator*

Cambridge Springs
Beltz, Sherree Lynne *music educator*

Camp Hill
Besch, Nancy Adams *county official*
Crist, Christine Myers *consulting executive*
McGeary, Barbara Joyce *artist, educator*
Parry-Solá, Cheryl Lee *critical care nurse*
Sammons, Mary F. *retail executive*
Stwalley, Diane Marie *pharmacist*
Sweeney, Susan Lynn *science educator*

Canonsburg
McMaster, Janet Lynn *psychologist*
Prost, Mary Jane *school nurse*

Canton
VanNoy, Vicki Lynne *mathematics educator, department chairman*

Carlisle
Berry, Karen S. *music educator*
Fendrich, Jean *elementary school educator*
Merrill, Heather Anne *geography and anthropology educator*
Nolt, Janelle *athletic trainer*
Ober, Jane Finley *career planning administrator*

Carnegie
Lear, Mary Catherine *music educator*
Whitfield, Tammy J. *elementary school educator, director*

Center Valley
Regnier, Sophie Anne Michelle *business research consultant*

Centre Hall
Fry, Theresa Eileen *therapeutic foster care aide*

Chadds Ford
Manogue, Caroline B. *lawyer*
Swensson, Evelyn Dickenson *conductor, composer, librettist*

Chalfont
Ashley, Kathleen Labonis *music educator*
Wilson, Jean Louise *retired state legislator*

Chambersburg
Bitner, Betty L. *education educator*
Hessler, Helen Stoeckel *social worker*
Petke, Beverly Ann *music educator*
Stillman, Mary Elizabeth *librarian, administrator, educator*

Charleroi
Carpenter, Heather L. *athletic trainer*
Kravec, Frances Mary *elementary school educator*
Strauser, Carol Ann *small business owner*

Cheltenham
Kuziemski, Naomi Elizabeth *educational consultant, counselor*

Chester
Graves, Maxine *medical and surgical nurse*
McJunkins, Kristin R. *academic administrator*

Chester Springs
Niggeman, Kimberly Supplee *medical nurse*

Cheyney
Bagley, Edythe Scott *theater educator*
Ellis-Scruggs, Jan *theater arts educator*

Clarion
Bonnett, Lou Ann Humphrey *education educator*
Dédé, Brenda Sanders *academic administrator*
Grejda, Gail Fulton *dean*
Hrisak, Cami Ann *mental health therapist*
Joslyn, Catherine Ruth *art educator, artist*
Miller, Andrea Lynn *library science educator*
Stearns, Ann Nicholson *education educator*

Clarks Summit
Gwillim, Allison Lee *conductor, music educator, department chairman*
Updyke, Rosemary Kathryn *writer*
Weiss, Tammy Lee *information technology manager*

Clearfield
Boykiw, Norma Severne *retired nutritionist, educator*
Krebs, Margaret Eloise *publishing executive*

Clifford
Elkins, Kathryn Marie *alcohol/drug abuse services professional, recreational therapist*

Clinton
Talbot, Mary Lee *minister*

Coatesville
Daigle, Sara Elizabeth *elementary school educator*
Petko, Patricia Ann *music educator*
Rodkey, Frances Theresa *elementary school educator*
Simmons, Barbara Ann *music educator*

Cochranton
Heltzel, Kathleen Lassalle *elementary school educator*

Collegeville
Barnes, Jo Anne *investment advisor*
Butz, Geneva Mae *pastor*
Maco, Teri Regan *accountant, engineer*
Shen, Hua-Qiong (Joan) *clinical research director*

Colmar
Weber-Roochvarg, Lynn *English as a second language educator, communications consultant*

Columbia
Jafri, Ayesha *family physician*
Steiner-Houck, Sandra Lynn *interior designer*

Connellsville
Brady, Marsha McCandless *secondary school educator*
Shearer, Linda Rae *English educator*

Conshohocken
Thompson, Pamela Padwick *public relations executive*

Coopersburg
Kohler, Deborah Diamond *dietitian, food service executive*

Coplay
Stockman, Kathleen Helen *elementary school educator*

Coraopolis
Stage, Ginger Rooks *psychologist*
Stevens, Paulette *daycare administrator*

Cornwall
Rovinski, Helen Thérèse *retired psychiatrist*

Cranberry Township
Tiller, Olive Marie *retired church worker*

Dallas
Albert, Rosalie Snow *secondary school educator, writer*
Baltimore, Ruth Betty *social worker*

Danielsville
Pagotto, Sarah Louise *retired library and information scientist*

Danville
Gubbiotti, Christine M. *lawyer*

Darby
Wardell, Lindy Constance *non-profit organization administrator*

Dayton
Patterson, Madge Lenore *elementary school educator*

Devon
Shurkin, Lorna Greene *writer, publicist*

Donora
Dillon, Susan *literature and language educator*
Todd, Norma Ross *retired government official*

Dover
Miller-Seda, Rhonda Grace *elementary school educator*
Spahr, Bertha E. *chemistry educator, department chairman*

Downingtown
Crescenz, Valerie J. *music educator*
Zimmerman, Lisa A. *music educator*

Doylestown
Borzio, Stephanie Jean *secondary school educator*
Dimond, Roberta Ralston *psychology and sociology educator*
Goldstein, Mary Wiseman *education educator*
McCafferty, Barbara Jean (BJ McCafferty) *sales executive*
Rodenbaugh, Marcia Louise *retired elementary school educator*
Taylor, Rosemary *artist*
Thomas, Ellen Louise *school system administrator*
Waite, Frances W. *librarian, genealogist*

Dresher
Levicoff, Valerie Ann *music educator*
Michael, Dorothy Ann *nursing administrator, military officer*

Drexel Hill
Turnbull, Mary Regina *secondary school educator*

Du Bois
Burkett, Julie Ann *science educator*
Morris, Trisha Ann *librarian*

Dunmore
Pencek, Carolyn Carlson *treasurer, finance educator*

East Petersburg
Kunkle, Mary Lou *counselor*
Walker, Sue Albertson *retired school system administrator, consultant*

East Stroudsburg
Baril, Nancy Ann *gerontological nurse practitioner, consultant*
Braithwaite, Barbara Jo *retired secondary school educator*
Hodge, Donna Lynn *psychologist, educator*
Miller, Edith Fisher *special education educator*
Shotwell, Colleen Aaron *personal trainer, educator*
Switzer, Sharon Cecile *language educator, researcher*

Easton
Bellissimo, Mary E. *art educator*
Byrd, Deborah Lea *literature and language professor*
Ciambrone, Cheryl C. *mathematics educator*
Kistler, Loretta M. *social worker, consultant*
Lombardozzi, Debra Ann *music educator*
Schlueter, June Mayer *literature educator, writer*
Stitt, Dorothy Jewett *journalist*
Teboh-Ewungkem, Miranda Ijang *education educator*

Ebensburg
Pereira, Melany *elementary school educator*

Eddystone
Fredrick, Susan Walker *tax company manager*

Edinboro
Burke, Rachael J. *art educator*
Curry-Carlburg, Joanne Jeanne *elementary school educator*
Kinch, Janet Carolyn Brozic *English and German language and literature educator, academic administrator*

Eighty Four
Magerko, Margaret Hardy (Maggie Magerko) *lumber company executive*

Elizabethtown
Bradley, Christine Owen *secondary school educator*
Chesbro, Karen E. Henise *nurse*
Marjorie, Reed L. *science educator*
Placeway, Joellen Peterson *elementary school educator*

Elkins Park
Burnley, June Williams *secondary school educator*
Erlebacher, Martha Mayer *artist, educator*
Pruce, Rhoda Posner *social worker, consultant*
Topper, Patricia Margaret *music educator*

Ellwood City
Windhorst, Jane Louise *elementary school educator*

Elverson
Colona, Frances Ann *elementary school educator*

Emlenton
Berg, Janice Carol *elementary school educator*

Emmaus
Favorule, Denise *publishing executive*
Long, Kathleen Anne *elementary school educator*
Vaccariello, Liz *editor-in-chief*

Erie
Azicri, Nicolette Maly *art educator, artist*
Bohman, Carol Elizabeth *secondary educator*
Brunner-Martinez, Kirstin Ellen *pediatrician, psychiatrist*
Burgoyne, Noel Jaeger *retired secondary school educator*
Chittister, Joan Daugherty *writer, educator*
Evanoff-McGeorge, Marnie Hubbell *elementary school educator*
Foltz, Katrina Marie *music educator*
Hess, Susan Irene *music educator*
Mackowski, Pamela Anne *science educator*
Mattis, Constance Marie *controller*
Nolan, Susan Marie *mathematics educator*
Pawlowski, Janet M. *psychologist*
Rosiak, Frances Ruth *elementary school educator*
Roth-Kauffman, Michele M. *dean*
Taylor, Margaret Uhrich *educational association administrator*
Voss, Margaret A. *biology professor*
Waldron, Allene *insurance group executive*

Etters
Steps, Barbara Jill *lawyer*

Everett
Whetstone, Joni Lee *music educator*

Exeter
Mudlock, Laura *athletic trainer*

Export
Carter, Linda Whitehead *oncological nurse, educator*

Exton
Segal, Jacqueline Gale *lawyer*
Webber, Helen *artist*

Factoryville
Elliott, Carolyn Sayre *librarian, educator*
Joyce, Janice Rose *supervisor, elementary school educator*

Fairfield
Ray, Lydia M. *nurse*

Fairless Hills
Glasheen, Gloria D. *secondary school educator*
Hess, Frances Elizabeth *retired secondary school educator, retired director*
Schmidt, Suzanne M. *music educator*

Fairview
Graziani, Linda Ann *secondary school educator*
Krider, Margaret Young *art educator*
Ruud, Ruth Marie *science educator*
Stern, Marilyn Jean *special education educator*

Farrell
Patton-Newell, Janet Lavelle *minister*
Pawluk, Annette Marie *secondary school educator*
Roberson, Deborah Lynn *special education educator*

Feasterville Trevose
Thee, Cynthia Urban *psychotherapist*

Flourtown
Cooke, Sara Mullin Graff *daycare provider, kindergarten educator, medical assistant*
Lambert, Joan Dorety *elementary school educator*

Fogelsville
Crooker, Barbara Ann *writer, educator*
Flores, Robin Ann *geriatric program and service consultant*

Fort Washington
Fulton, Cheryl L. *customer service administrator*

Fountainville
Brown, Madeline Morgan *internist*

Franklin
Sauer, Mary Julia *special education educator*

Friedens
Shaffer, Brenda Joyce *minister*

Friendsville
Bjick, Suzanne Carter *psychologist*

Galeton
Bull, Inez Stewart *retired music educator, curator, director, singer, writer, musician*

Gap
Beiler, Anne F. *food company executive*
Klinefelter, Hylda Catharine *retired obstetrician, retired gynecologist*

Gardners
Contento Covey, Nicki Ann *counselor*

Gettysburg
Bechtel, Kristen King *chemistry educator*
Gritsch, Ruth Christine Lisa *editor*
Jones, Gail Peters *music educator*
Nelson-Small, Kathy Ann *foundation administrator*
Schein, Virginia Ellen *psychologist, editor*
Will, Katherine Haley *academic administrator*

Gibsonia
Haas, Eileen Marie *homecare advocate*
Krause, Helen Fox *retired otolaryngologist*
Wright, April Marie *elementary school educator*

Gladwyne
Morrison, Gail *internist, nephrologist, educator*
Stick, Alyce Cushing *systems administrator, consultant*

Glen Mills
Collins, Rosemarie Marrocco *psychotherapist*
Shields, Martha Buckley *elementary school educator*
Turner, Janet Sullivan *painter, sculptor*

Glenmoore
Fix, Irene M. *music educator*
Humphreys-Heckler, Maureen Kelly *nursing home administrator*

Glenside
Crivelli-Kovach, Andrea *public health and nutrition consultant, educator*
Doman, Janet Joy *professional society administrator*
Jones, Elaine F. *psychologist, educator*
Medel, Rebecca Rosalie *artist*
Miserandino, Marianne *psychology educator*
Willig, Barbara Adele *music educator*

Grantham
Downing, Crystal L. *literature and language professor, writer*
Fieser, Cherie Rose *editor, curator*

Grantville
Sudor, Cynthia Ann *sales and marketing professional*

Greensburg
Conlin, Kathryn Marie *social studies educator*
Duck, Patricia Mary *librarian*
Elliott, Tammy Jo *chemistry educator*
Fajt, Karen Elaine *art educator*
Ferraco Redinger, Andrea *biology educator*
Kochman, Susan M. *language educator*
Kuznik, Rachelle Lee *science educator, writer*
Mann, Jacinta *academic administrator, mathematician, educator*
Neff, Mary Ellen Andre *retired elementary school educator*
Vissat, Maureen *art educator*

Grove City
Davidson, Heather Jean *gifted and talented educator*

Gwynedd
LeFevre, Carol Baumann *psychologist, educator*

Gwynedd Valley
Conaway, Cynthia Elizabeth *parochial school educator, department chairman*
Owens, Kathleen C. *academic administrator*

Halifax
Fasnacht, Judy Ann *science educator, small business owner*
Stauffer, Joanne Rogan *steel company official*

Hamburg
Schappell, Abigail Susan *retired speech, language and hearing specialist, massage therapist, Reiki master*

Hanover
Barnhart, Nikki Lynn Clark *elementary school educator*
Clark, Sandra Marie *school administrator*
Davis, Ruth Carol *pharmacist, educator*
Hartman, Carol Lee *art educator, reading specialist*

Hanover Township
Bannon, Desiree *mathematics educator*

Harleysville
Smagalski, Carolyn M. *publishing executive, webmaster, director*

Harmony
Fodi, Alison Elizabeth *mathematics educator*
Meredith, Joanne Cusick *special education educator, director*
Stephenson, Susan Marie *English educator*

Harrisburg
Adams, Barbara *lawyer*
Antoun, Annette Agnes *editor, publisher*
Bailey, Diandrea Michelle *rehabilitation services professional*
Baker Knoll, Catherine *lieutenant governor*
Batts, Barbara Jean *academic administrator, director*
Black, Shirley A. *healthcare educator*
Braun, Mary E. *elementary school educator*
Burns, Rebecca Ann *elementary school educator, librarian*
Butler, Jessie D. *community activist, retired educator, counselor*
Crahalla, Jacqueline R. *state representative*
Ellenbogen, Elisabeth Alice *retired accountant*
Fenstermacher, Joyce Doris *real estate agent, real estate appraiser*
Franco, Barbara Alice *museum director*
Fulmer, Deborah Lee *education educator, oncological nurse*
Gibson, Shere Capparella *foreign language educator*
Hafer, Barbara *state official*
Hample, Judy G. *academic administrator*
Hoffman, Mary Hills *literature educator, publishing executive*
Kane, Yvette *lawyer, judge*
Knackstedt, Mary V. *interior designer*
Meilton, Sandra L. *lawyer*
Miller, Leslie Anne *lawyer*
Miller, Sheila *state legislator*
O'Leary, Colleen Alison *counselor*
Pacuska, M. Abbegael *lawyer*
Pizzingrilli, Kim *state official*
Rambo, Sylvia H. *federal judge*
Ross, Ellyn N. *educational association administrator, consultant*
Schrader, Janet E. *music educator*
Vance, Patricia H. *state senator*
Weiser, Kathy M. *highway designer*
West, Eileen M. *caseworker*
Williams, Constance *state senator*
Wissler-Thomas, Carrie *professional society administrator, artist*

Hatboro
Carroll, Lucy Ellen *theater director, educator*

Hatfield
Madden, Theresa Marie *elementary school educator*
Reast, Deborah Stanek *small business owner*

Haverford
DiBerardino, Marie Antoinette *developmental biologist, educator*
Henle, Mary *retired psychology educator*
Jorden, Eleanor Harz *linguist, educator*
Miller, Geraldine B. *music educator*
Stiller, Jennifer Anne *lawyer*
Widseth, Jane Christina *psychologist, psychotherapist*

Havertown
Bobnak, Marsha Core *music educator*
Cox, Ruth Miller *music educator*
Evarts, Mary H. *mathematics educator*
Garrahan-Masters, Mary Patricia *retired social worker, writer*
Koenig, Norma Evans *retired religious studies educator*
Spicer, Jean Uhl *art educator*
Wright, Cecilia Powers *gifted and talented educator*

Hazleton
Dougherty, Jane *librarian*
Kraynak, Marcelle Georgeann *not-for-profit developer*

Hegins
Caulfield, Careen Anne *secondary school educator, biologist*

Hellertown
Kunkel-Christman, Debra Ann *secondary school educator*

Herminie
Sichok, Maryanne M. *art educator*

Hershey
Blosky, Elizabeth Anne *science educator*
Butterfield, Andrea Christine *psychology educator, educational association administrator*
Dellasega, Cheryl *humanities educator*
Derk, Patricia Keach *secondary school educator*
Eyster, Mary Elaine *hematologist, educator*
Hopper, Anita Klein *molecular genetics educator*
Kisthardt, Estelle A. *career planning administrator, educator*
Kreider, Susan B. *elementary school educator*
Ozereko-deCoen, Mary T. *therapeutic recreation specialist and therapist*
Schuller, Diane Ethel *allergist, immunologist, educator*
Thomas, Andrea B. *food products executive*
Thomas, Patricia Agnes *school system administrator*

Holland
Ryalls, Barbara Taylor *freelance/self-employed editor, critic*

Hollidaysburg
Mariano, Ana Virginia *retired pathologist*

Honey Brook
Johnson, Marjorie R. *special education educator*

Horsham
Christian, Mildred Stoehr *health products executive*

Hulmeville
Jackson, Mary L. *health services executive*

Huntingdon Valley
Freaney, Diane M. *financial executive*
McNemar, Robin M. *chemistry educator*

Immaculata
Fadden, Sister R. Patricia *academic administrator, nun*

Imperial
Boustead, Diane Dolores *secondary school educator, chemistry educator*
Meyers, Karen Evans *gifted and talented educator*

Indiana
Clark-Harley, Mary Dorcas *retired radiologist*
Jalongo, Mary Renck *educator*
Mabry, J. Beth *sociologist, educator*
Reynolds, Virginia Edith *sociologist, anthropologist, educator, artist*
Roumm, Phyllis Evelyn Gensbigler *retired literature educator, writer*
Ruddock, Ellen Sylves *management consultant*
Weber, Denise E. *retired history educator*

Jenkintown
Goldman, Janice Goldin *psychologist, educator*
Greenspan-Margolis, June E. *psychiatrist*
Hankin, Elaine Krieger *psychologist, researcher*
Lowry, Karen M. *biomedical research scientist, pharmacist*
Oh, Soojin Susan *elementary school educator*
Roediger, Janice Anne *artist, educator*
Sellers, Marlene *artist, educator*

Jessup
Karluk, Lori Jean *craft designer, copyeditor*

Johnstown
Arcurio, Jean Catherine *soprano, educator, director*
Borkow, Mary P. *small business owner, consultant*
Fisher, Connie Marie *physical therapist*
Grove, Nancy Carol *academic administrator*
Lynch, Alessandra Jacqueline *literature educator, poet*
McGarry-Corl, Kelly Jo *counselor, marriage and family therapist, consultant*
Puto, Anne-Marie *reading specialist*

Kennett Square
Coggins, Eileen M. *lawyer*
Harrington, Anne Wilson *medical librarian*
Landstrom, Elsie Hayes *retired editor*
Smith, Virginia Eleanore *psychologist, educator*

King Of Prussia
Goldsmith, Eleanor Jean *retired hospital administrator*
Hallman, Patricia L. *music educator, musician*
Helmetag, Diana *music educator*
McCairns, Regina Carfagno *pharmaceutical executive*
Musetti, Myrtle Jane Holt *clinical nurse specialist, community health nurse*
Phipps, Judith A. *social worker*
Schneider, Pam Horvitz *lawyer*
Schumann, Paula M. L. *writer*
Swank, Annette Marie *software designer*

Kingsley
McNabb, Corrine Radtke *librarian*

Kingston
Weisberger, Barbara *artistic director, advisor, educator*

Kintnersville
Sartori, Marilee A. *space designer*

Kittanning
Krzton, Nancy L. *lawyer, writer*

Knox
Rupert, Elizabeth Anastasia *retired dean*

Kutztown
Kuehne, Helenirene Anne *art educator*
Meyer, Susan Moon *speech pathologist, educator*
Nechas, Eileen Tucker *retired writer*
Vergereau Dewey, Sylvie Pascale *French and Spanish language educator*

La Plume
Fontana, Carol P. *education educator*

Owens, Kate A. *registrar*

Lafayette Hill
Klein, Carol Lynne *psychologist*
Miller, Nancy Lois *senior pastor*

Lancaster
Aronowicz, Annette *theology studies educator*
Best, Jane Evans *retired educator, historian*
Brunner, Lillian Sholtis *nurse, writer*
Burns, Erin Cathleen *lawyer*
Daugherty, Ruth Alice *religious association consultant*
Grube, Rebecca Sue *elementary school educator, consultant*
Hayward, Frances Crambert *retired dietician*
Hickle, Shalon R. *physical therapist*
Jordan, Lois Wenger *foundation official*
Kay, Margaret J. *psychologist*
McClellan, Joan C. Osmundson *art educator*
Miller, Erika Vittur *secondary school educator, language educator*
Polite, Karen E. *humanities educator*
Poser, Joan Rapps *artist, writer*
Saganich, Bonnie Sue *medical/surgical nurse*
Scranton, Megan Jennifer *speech therapist, educator*
Shenk, Lois Elaine Landis *writer*
Stewart, Arlene Jean Golden *art director*
Taylor, Ann *human resources specialist, educator*
Veri, Frances Gail *musician, educator*
Whare, Wanda Snyder *lawyer*
Yohe, Laura Kathryn *secondary school educator*

Landenberg
Lloyd, Nancy G. *language educator*

Langhorne
Dorfman, Lorraine M. *clinical psychologist, consultant*
Haimbach, Marjorie Anne *music educator*
Neff, Amy Hancock *elementary school educator*
Schadler, Florence *artist, educator*
Schoenstadt, Barbara Laison *special education educator*

Lansdowne
Karosas, Karen *social worker, quality assurance specialist*
Purcell, Mary Hamilton *speech educator*

Latrobe
Bates, Dawna Joyce *retired secondary school educator, department chairman*
Price, Peggy Reinecke *writer, researcher*
Snyder, Rebecca *literature and language educator*

Lebanon
Bybee, Deborah Ann *director, educator*
Hepler, Jane A. *secondary school educator*
Kopicki, Beth Ann *special education educator*
Kulikowski, Cheryl E. *music educator*

Lehman
Ruddy, Stacey Ann *literature and language educator*
Weyman, Sandra Lee *secondary school educator*

Lemont Furnace
Miller, Debbie Sue *special education educator*

Lemoyne
Hamme, Marta Denise *elementary school educator*

Leola
Puschak, Beth Anne *educational consultant*

Levittown
Camer, Mary Martha *retired secretary*
Perry, Beth Ann *elementary school educator*
Walker, Patricia Ann Dixon *retired elementary school educator, real estate rehabilitator*

Lewisburg
Brill, Marilyn *community-based collaboration consultant*
Huffines, Marion Lois *academic administrator, language and linguistics educator*
Lenhart, Lorraine Margaret *county official*
Morin, Karen M. *geographer, educator*
Morin, Karen Marie *education educator, researcher*
Muller, Riana Ricci *musician, educator*
Neuman, Nancy Adams Mosshammer *civic leader*
Pickering, Roberta Ann *language educator, gifted and talented educator*
Roberts, Ruth W. *retired elementary school educator*
Rote, Nelle Fairchild Hefty *management consultant*
Smith, Marguerite Irene *gifted and talented educator*

Lewistown
Wimsatt, Anne Mosher *retail bookstore owner*

Liberty
Morgan-Grala, Terry Lee *elementary school educator*

Lititz
Adair, Mary Roberts *special education educator*
Hudelson, Judith Giantomass *elementary school educator*
Weaver, Naomi M. *retired medical/surgical nurse, educator*

Lock Haven
Almes, June *retired education educator, librarian*
Story, Julie Ann *language educator*
Winters, Karen Crispell *educator*

Loretto
Clark, Rose Ann *chemist, educator*
Sackin, Claire *retired social work educator*

Loysburg
Stuckey, Ellen Mae *music educator*

Malvern
Gillespie, Mary Krempa *psychologist, consultant*
Hochberg, Marcia Gail *psychologist*

Manheim
Homan, Patricia Ann *counselor*

Mansfield
Dettwiler, Peggy Diane *music educator*
Donahue, Martha *retired librarian*
Loeschke, Maravene S. *academic administrator, theater educator*

Maple Glen
Jacobson, Bonnie Brown *writer, energy executive, statistician, researcher*
Weaver-Stroh, Joanne Mateer *education educator, consultant*

Maytown
Flanagan, Diane L. *property claims professional*

Mc Donald
Maurer, Karen Ann *special education educator*

Mc Keesport
Lodor, Marci Ann *dietitian*
Powroznik-Traeger, Rita *school counselor*
Preuss, Mary Herge *Spanish educator*
Ransil, Dorothy Mae *secondary school educator*

Mc Murray
Cmar, Janice Butko *home economist, educator*

Meadville
Stewart, Anne Williams *historian, writer, researcher*

Mechanicsburg
Blaisure, Terra Quinn *special education educator*
Gerstenlauer, Joyce Elaine *elementary school educator*
Harper, Diane Marie *retired corporate communications specialist*
Juditz, Lillian Mickley *retired communications educator*
Layton, Carol Eicherberger *dentist*
Ricedorf, Amy Elizabeth *mental health services professional*
Snider, Karen *human services administrator*

Media
Behbehanian, Mahin Fazeli *surgeon*
Diamond, Jacqlyn E. *health counselor*
Goldschmidt, Myra Margaret *literature and language professor*
Hanna, Carol Ann *nursing educator*
Steinhardt Gutman, Bertha *artist, educator*
Turner, Letitia Rhodes *artist*
Whittington, Cathy Dee *chemist*

Mercer
DaCosta, Caroline Lee *small business owner*

Merion Station
Littell, Marcia Sachs *Holocaust and genocide studies professor*

Middletown
Miller, Marilyn Jane *music educator*
Winch, Donna Gladhill *music educator*

Midland
Katich, Eleanor Patience *retired science educator*

Midway
Pierrard-Mutton, Mary V. *artist, educator*

Mifflintown
Sieber, Angela R. *social studies educator*

Milford
Le Guin, Ursula Kroeber *writer*

Milford Square
Sewell, Gloriana *music educator*

Mill Hall
Smith, Debra Farwell *school librarian*

Millersville
Bensur, Barbara Jean *art educator, researcher*
Hess, Patricia Ann *dietician*

Millheim
Horner, Mandy Sue *athletic trainer*

Milroy
Massa, Nancy G. *columnist*

Monaca
Marshall, Cynthia Louise *language educator*

Monessen
Smida, Mary Agnes *counselor*

Monongahela
Brown, Hilary Susanne *music educator, photographer*
Winkleblech, Shannan *music educator*
Yovanof, Silvana *physician*

Monroeville
Baker, Faith Mero *retired elementary education educator*
Emerick, Joyce Jean *elementary school educator*
Kennedy, Kathy Kay *library director*

Montrose
Cunningham, Mary Ann Michael *secondary school educator*

Moon Township
Mooney, Jennifer *literature educator*
Pociernicki, Janice Louise *artist*

Moscow
Grudeski, Jennifer Anne *elementary school educator*
Lisandrelli, Elaine Slivinski *secondary school educator*

Mount Bethel
LaRussa, Luann *small business owner*

Mount Gretna
Agudo, Mercedes Engracia *psychiatrist*
Warshaw, Roberta Sue *lawyer*

Mount Joy
Sater, Denise M. *journalist, editor*

Mount Pleasant
Morgan, Joyce Kaye *social worker*
Pyda, Dianne Sue *art educator*

Murrysville
Ferri, Karen Lynn *lawyer*

Myerstown
Robson, Barbara S. *elementary school educator*
Weaver, Patricia Ella *mathematics educator*

Nanticoke
Dalmas-Brown, Carmella Jean *special education educator*
Donohue, Patricia Carol *academic administrator*
Stchur, Mary Nanorta *literature and language professor*
Whitebread, Melanie Jo *language educator*

Narberth
Donohoe, Victoria *critic, art historian, researcher*
Pollack, Sonya A. *artist*

Natrona Heights
Becker, Rachel J. *biology educator*
Maleski, Cynthia Maria *lawyer*

Nazareth
Bartolacci, Paulette Marie *elementary school educator, aerobics instructor*
Brackbill, Nancy Lafferty *retired elementary school educator*
Ferraro, Margaret Louise (Peg Ferraro) *elementary school educator*

Nelson
Kyofski, Bonelyn Lugg *retired education educator*

New Alexandria
Sehring, Hope Hutchison *library science educator*

New Brighton
Ficca, Rhonda Lee *music educator*

New Castle
Palladino, Rosanne C. *music educator*
Sands, Christine Louise *retired English educator*
Schooley, Toni Ann *gifted and talented educator*

New Cumberland
Dunbar, Lorna J. *special education educator*

New Freedom
Sedlak, Valerie Frances *retired English language and literature educator, academic administrator*

New Holland
Fanus, Pauline Rife *librarian*

New Hope
Coyle, Diane Bonanomi *special education educator*
Freyer, Victoria C. *fashion and interior design executive*

New Oxford
Martin, Sandra Ann *special education educator, writer*

New Stanton
Tomajko, Kimberly Ann *mathematics and science educator*

New Tripoli
Hess, Darla Bakersmith *cardiologist, educator*

New Wilmington
Bolger, Dorita Yvonne Ferguson *librarian*
Cushman, Beverly White *religious studies educator*
Magyary, Cynthia Marie *retired elementary school educator, music educator*

Newtown
Finberg, Melinda C. *theater educator*
Kidd, Lynden Louise *healthcare consultant*
Somers, Anne Ramsay *retired medical educator*

Newtown Square
Bertolet, Caroline Lynne Georgeanne *special education educator, labor union administrator*
DeLuca, Jennie M. *English educator*
de Rivas, Carmela Foderaro *retired psychiatrist, retired health facility administrator*
LeDonne, Deborah Jane *secondary school educator*
Swing, Elizabeth Sherman *education educator*
Winter, Ruth *artist*

Norristown
Casale, Helen E. *lawyer*
Del Collo, Mary Anne Demetris *school administrator*
DeMedio, Kathleen Marie *chemistry educator*
Gold-Bikin, Lynne Z. *lawyer*
Magann, Joyce L. *music educator*
McGinnis, Patricia Anne *secondary school educator, biologist*
Raquet, Maureen Graham *protective services official, educator*
Rivera Matos, Carmen Lourdes *lawyer*
Weikert, Barbara Sliker *music educator*
Womack, Lana D. *elementary school educator*

North Huntingdon
Antolik, Elena Anne *performing company executive, choreographer*
Bryan, Peggy *mathematics educator*
Little, Jenifer Raye *music educator*

Northumberland
Collister, Nicole S. *counselor*

Oakdale
Feather, Nancy Joanne *lawyer, educator*

Oil City
Heckathorne, Deborah Kathryn *mathematics educator, supervisor*

Oley
Weller, Trudy A. *psychotherapist*

Olyphant
Paoloni, Virginia Ann *insurance company executive*
Turock, Jane Parsick *nutritionist*

Orefield
Eisenhard, Jennifer Lynn *elementary school educator*

Oreland
Perez, Patricia Streit *athletic trainer, small business owner*

Orwigsburg
Mason, Joan Ellen *nurse*

Paoli
Gotshall, Jan Doyle *financial planner*
Green, Mimi Theresa *social services administrator*
Laubenstein, Kathleen Marie *lawyer*
Whittington, Virginia Carolina *language educator, writer*

Patton
Pompa, Louise Elaine *secondary school educator*

Pennsauken
Ford, Mary Pat *art educator*

Pennsburg
Shuhler, Phyllis Marie *physician*

Perkasie
Ferry, Joan Evans *school counselor*
Vasoli, Glenna Isaac *elementary school educator, school system administrator*

Perryopolis
Kremposky, Vickey Darlene *secondary school educator*

Philadelphia
Abraham, Lynne M. *district attorney*
Ajzenberg-Selove, Fay *physicist, researcher*
Alaigh, Poonam *health facility administrator*
Allevi, Angela *pediatrician*
Angel, Marina *law educator*
Angell, Mary Faith *federal magistrate judge*
Austin, Regina *law educator*
Aversa, Dolores Sejda *educational administrator*
Baessler, Christina A. *medical/surgical nurse*
Bailey, Elizabeth Ellery *economics professor*
Bald, Diana *broadcast executive*
Ballard, Roberta A. *pediatrician, educator*
Barnett, Bonnie Allyn *lawyer*
Beck, Phyllis Whitman *lawyer, retired judge*
Bennett, Amanda *editor*
Bergmann, Renee F. *lawyer*
Berkley, Emily Carolan *lawyer*
Bernstein, Deborah *psychiatrist*
Berry, Mary Frances *history professor, former federal agency administrator*
Best, Kimberly Renee *psychiatrist*
Bibbo, Marluce *physician, educator*
Bilaniuk, Larissa Tetiana *neuroradiologist, educator*
Booth, Anna Belle *accountant*
Boss, Amelia Helen *lawyer, educator*
Bowman, Marjorie Ann *physician, educator*
Brandt, Jennifer Anne *lawyer*
Breslow, Tina *public relations executive*
Brier, Bonnie Susan *lawyer*
Brown, Delores Russell *health management company official*
Brown, Denise Scott *architect, urban planner*
Bryant, Jonanna Rochelle *registered nurse*
Burko, Diane *artist, educator*
Burns, Marian Law *human resources specialist, legal association administrator*
Cary, Lorene Emily *writer*
Cassel, Christine Karen *physician*
Castillo, Flora M. *health plan administrator, transportation executive*
Chambless, Dianne L. *psychology professor*
Chan, Ashely Michelle *lawyer*
Chapman, Judith Griffin *psychologist, educator, academic administrator*
Christman, Jolley Bruce *educational research executive, educator*
Ciszkowski, Grace Marie *art educator*
Coché, Judith *psychologist, educator*
Cohn, Mildred *retired biochemist, retired educator*
Collier, Charisse Audra *family service representative, greeting card designer*
Colson, Rosemary *music educator*
Comisky, Hope A. *lawyer*
Conlay, Lydia *anesthesiologist, educator, health science association administrator*
Connelly, Kori Ann *lawyer*
Coons, Helen L. *clinical psychologist*
Corprew, Helen Barbara *mental health services professional*
Coulson, Zoe Elizabeth *retired consumer marketing executive*
Cunningham, Jacqueline Lemmé *psychologist, educator, researcher*
Daly, Mary Beryl *health facility administrator*
Davidoff, Joanne Malatesta *multi-media specialist*
Dean-Zubritsky, Cynthia Marian *psychologist, researcher*
deBenedet, Rachel *actress*
Delaney, Anna T. *director*
Dennehy, Mary Nora *psychologist*
d'Harnoncourt, Anne *museum director, museum administrator*
DiMenna, Kathleen Polansky *special education educator*
Dougherty Buchholz, Karen *communications executive*
Drake, Jayne Kribbs *academic administrator, literature educator*
Duclow, Geraldine *historian, librarian*
Dunn, Linda Kay *physician*
Dunn, Mary Maples *academic administrator*
Eisenstein, Toby K. *microbiology professor*
Evans, Audrey Elizabeth *physician, educator*
Farren, Ann Louise *chemist, information scientist, educator*
Fauntleroy, Angela Colleen *music educator*
Fernandez, Happy Craven (Gladys Fernandez) *academic administrator*
Fickler, Arlene *lawyer*
Field, Charlotte *communications executive*
Finkelstein, Claire *law educator*
Finken, Tracy Ann *lawyer*
Foley, Regina M. *lawyer*
Fournaris, Christina Mesires *lawyer*
Fox, Renée Claire *sociology educator*
Frampton, J. Paige *lawyer*
Frankel, Francine Ruth *political science professor*
Fretz, Deborah McDermott *oil industry executive*
Gaillard, Margaret *communications executive*
Garonzik, Sara Ellen *stage producer*
Garvin, Vail Pryor *hospital administrator*
Gendron, Michèle Marguerite Madeleine *librarian*
Gershenfeld, Matti Kibrick *psychologist*
Givens, Janet Eaton *writer*
Glick, Jane Mills *biomedical researcher, educator*
Glickman, Sallie A. *professional society administrator*
Glusker, Jenny Pickworth *chemist*
Godley, Joanne *city health department administrator*
Gonglewski, Grace *actress*
Gordon, Anne Kathleen *editor*
Gordon, Sarah Barringer *law educator*
Goschke, Linda Fry *artist*
Gould, Claudia *museum director*
Gralik, Nancy Ellen *healthcare consultant*
Grimm, Melissa *sports association executive*
Gueson, Emerita Torres *obstetrician, gynecologist*
Gupta, Mona *lawyer*
Gur, Raquel E. *academic administrator*
Gussack, Nina M. *lawyer*
Gutmann, Amy *academic administrator, political science and philosophy educator*
Guyer, Hedy-Ann Klein *special education educator*
Harris, Judith E. *lawyer*
Hart, Ann Weaver *academic administrator*
Heller, Janet Seip *retired secondary school educator*
Henderson, Erin F. *lawyer*
Henry, Deborah Epstein *lawyer*
Hillgren, Sonja Dorothy *journalist*
Hobdy, Jerrilyn *nurse midwife*
Horwitz, Joy A. *foundation administrator*
Hughes Stanback, Francine *elementary school educator, school system administrator*
Hurlock, Joan Emma *physician*
Ingolfsson-Fassbind, Ursula G. *music educator*
James, Jennifer DuFault *lawyer*
Jemmott, Loretta Sweet *HIV/AIDS researcher, nursing educator*
Jones, Donna Lee *lawyer*
Jones, Kia Tanetta *daycare administrator*
Joseph, Rosaline Resnick *hematologist*
Josephs, Babette *legislator*
Junkerman, Denise Marie *secondary school educator*
Kaiser, Linda Susan *lawyer*
Kaji, Hideko *pharmacology educator*
Kane, Pamela *psychologist*
Kaplan, Barbara Jane *retired city planner*
Kim, Sangduk *biochemistry educator, researcher*
Klein, Julia Meredith *freelance journalist*
Koc, Lorraine K(iessling) *lawyer*
Kreider, Karen Beechy *secondary education educator, language professional*
Kumanyika, Shiriki K. *nutrition epidemiology researcher, educator*
Lasher, Lori L. *lawyer*
Laupheimer, Ann B. *lawyer*
Lee, Virginia M. -Y. *medical educator, health science association administrator*
Leister, Kelly M. *lawyer*
Lenhard, Sarah *advertising executive*
Lester, Marsha I. *chemistry professor*
Levering, Kathryn H. *lawyer*
Levin, Shanon S. (Shanon Levin Lehman) *lawyer*
Liebenberg, Roberta D. *lawyer*
Lillie, Charisse Ranielle *lawyer, educator*
Lippa, Carol Frances *neurologist*
Lipshutz, Laurel Sprung *psychiatrist*
Logue-Kinder, Joan *public relations consultant*
Long, Nina P. *library director, archivist*
Long, Sarah Sundborg *pediatrician, educator*
Lydick, Nancy M. *psychologist*
Maksymowicz, Virginia *art educator, writer, artist*
Mancall, Jacqueline Cooper *library and information scientist, educator*
Margo, Katherine Lane *family physician, educator*
Mariscotti, Janine M. *psychotherapist, educator*
Marple, Dorothy Jane *retired church executive*
Matus-Mendoza, Mariadelaluz *language educator, sociologist*
Maxman, Susan Abel *architect*
McDiarmid, Lucy *literature educator, writer*
McKee, Lynn B. *human resources specialist*
McKenna, Margaret Mary *foundation administrator*
Megerian, Talene *lawyer*
Melby, Barbara Murphy *lawyer*
Mellen, Joan *author*
Meredith, Lisa Ann Marie *social studies educator, consultant*
Miller, Arlyn Hochberg *psychologist*
Miller, Camille M. *lawyer*
Miller, Donna Reed *city official*
Miori, Virginia Marie *finance educator*
Mitchell, Brenda King *training services executive*
Miyamori, Keiko *artist*

Moss-Vreeland, Patricia Ellen *artist*
Mouzon, Thelma P. *retired elementary school educator*
Mueller, Jena Lynn *athletic trainer*
Mulé, Ann C. *oil industry executive*
Myers Brown, Joan *performing company executive*
Naylor, Mary D. *medical professor, director*
Newcombe, Nora *psychology professor*
Newman, Libby *painter, printmaker, curator*
Okoniewski, Lisa Anne *psychologist*
Onley, Sister Francesca *academic administrator*
Orne, Emily Carota *psychologist, researcher*
Orr, Nancy A. *educational psychologist*
Paglia, Camille *writer, humanities educator*
Pasternak, Jill Margot *radio producer, musician, educator*
Patrick, Ruth (Mrs. Ruth Hodge Van Dusen) *botany educator, curator*
Payne, Deborah Anne *retired medical company officer*
Payne, Jamila *retail executive, entrepreneur*
Peck, Julianne L. *lawyer*
Pedersen, Darlene Delcourt *publishing executive, writer, psychotherapist*
Porter, Jill *journalist*
Potter, Alice Catherine *medical technician*
Pratter, Gene E. K. *federal judge, lawyer*
Quann, Joan Louise *French language educator, real estate broker*
Ramsey, Natalie D. *lawyer*
Reed, Sally Gardner *cultural organization administrator*
Reid, Mary Wallace *retired secondary school educator*
Reisman, Fredricka Kauffman *education educator*
Rendell, Marjorie O. *federal judge*
Resnick, Stephanie *lawyer*
Rhodes, Alice Graham *lawyer, not-for-profit developer, consultant*
Rima, Ingrid Hahne *economics professor*
Ringpfeil, Franziska *dermatologist*
Roomberg, Lila Goldstein *lawyer*
Rorke-Adams, Lucy Balian *pathologist, educator*
Rosato, Jennifer L. *dean, law educator*
Rose, Jane A. *financial planner*
Rosen, Rhoda *obstetrician, gynecologist*
Russakoff, Nina L. *lawyer*
Russo, Irma Haydee Alvarez de *pathologist*
Safier, Regan S. *lawyer*
Schaeffer-Young, Judith *library director*
Schaff, Barbara Walley *artist*
Scheppele, Kim Lane *law educator*
Schneeberg, Helen Bassen *retired elementary school educator*
Schreur, Lynne Elizabeth *advertising executive*
Scott-Williams, Mildred P. *food service specialist*
Seaman, Tanya *urban planner*
Shapiro, Norma Sondra Levy *federal judge*
Shapiro, Paula *retired maternal/women's health nurse*
Shea, Judith *artist*
Shillingsburg, Cynthia Lynn *medical technician, educator*
Shoemaker, Innis Howe *art museum curator*
Shure, Myrna Beth *psychologist, educator*
Sibolski, Elizabeth Hawley *academic administrator*
Siegman, Marion Joyce *physiologist, educator*
Sigmund, Diane Weiss *judge*
Simms, Amy Lang *writer, educator*
Simpson, Carol Louise *investment company executive*
Sims-Nesmith, Carolyn Sandra *cultural arts association administrator*
Sklar, Gail Janice *special education educator*
Slaughter-Defoe, Diana Tresa *education educator, psychologist*
Sloviter, Dolores Korman *federal judge*
Smullens, SaraKay Cohen *psychotherapist, writer*
Sohn, Catherine Angell *pharmaceutical executive, pharmacist*
Solomon, Phyllis Linda *social work educator, researcher*
Spandorfer, Merle Sue *artist, educator, writer*
Stallings, Virginia A. *pediatric gastroenterologist*
Stern, Joan Naomi *lawyer*
Stevenson, Andrea J. (Andi Stevenson) *not-for-profit executive*
Stewart, Susan *writer*
Stuart, Marie Jean *physician, hematologist, researcher*
Summers, Anita Arrow *finance educator*
Thall, Letty Derman *social services administrator*
Thomas, Janet Y. *political science professor, researcher*
Tileston, Jackie *artist, educator*
Tran, Judith Thuha *psychiatrist*
Traynor, Tami Lee *lawyer*
Treichel, Monica Zimmerman *accountant, educator*
Tuttle, Karen Ann *violist, educator*
Velazquez, Omaida Caridad *vascular surgeon, researcher*
Vetter, Victoria L. *pediatric cardiologist, educator*
von Seldeneck, Judith Metcalfe *career planning administrator*
Vredenburgh, Judy *youth organization executive*
Wachter, Susan Melinda *finance educator*
Walker, Danielle *engineering executive*
Walker, Kathy Le Mons *history professor*
Wallowicz, Marcella Louise *mathematics professor*
Wax, Amy Laura *law educator*
Weller, Elizabeth Boghossian *child and adolescent psychiatrist*
Wilkinson, Signe *cartoonist*
Wilms, Anne M. *information technology executive*
Wolff, Deborah H(orowitz) *lawyer*
Woods, Deirdre *information technology executive*
Woodside, Lisa Nicole *humanities educator*
Yang, Shu *materials scientist*
Zubernis, Lynn Smith *psychologist, counselor*

Philipsburg
Genesi, Susan Petrovich *school system administrator*

Phoenixville
Gentile, Amber Leigh *assistant principal*
Hanlon, Barbara Jean *family and consumer sciences educator*
Harkin, Ann Winifred *elementary school educator, psychotherapist*
Nice, Katharine Anne *mathematics educator, music educator*
Smith-McLaughlin, Amy Elizabeth *psychologist*

Pittsburgh
Amara, Susan *neuroscientist*
Ambrose, Donetta W. *federal judge*
Anderson, Catherine M. *consulting company executive*
Anderson, Lea E. *lawyer*
Barack, Robin Sheffman *psychologist*
Barazzone, Esther Lynn *academic administrator, educator*
Bardyguine, Patricia Wilde *dancer, performing company executive*
Bates, Beverly Jo-Anne *artist, educator*
Bissoon, Cathy *lawyer*
Bleier, Carol Stein *writer, researcher*
Blum, Eva Tansky *lawyer*
Blum, Lenore *mathematician, computer scientist, educator*
Boyce, Doreen Elizabeth *foundation administrator, educator*
Buchanan, Mary Beth *prosecutor*
Cahouet, Ann P. *lawyer*
Candris, Laura A. *lawyer*
Carbo, Toni (Toni Carbo Bearman) *information scientist, educator*
Carney, Ann Vincent *retired secondary school educator*
Carr, Winifred Walker *artist, historian*
Caserio, Rebecca JoAnn *dermatologist, educator*
Castelluccio, Christia Marie *elementary school educator*
Chipman, Debra Decker *title insurance executive*
Choi, Sylvia Seung-Yun *pediatrician, educator*
Chorazy, Anna Julia Lyjak *retired pediatrician*
Clancey, Jeanne Katherine *neurosurgical nurse*
Coffey, Rosemary Klineberg *educator*
Collins, Rose Ann *minister*
Constantino-Bana, Rose Eva *nursing educator, researcher, lawyer*
Conti, Joy Flowers *judge*
Cunningham, Karla *political scientist, researcher*
Curry, Nancy Ellen *psychologist, psychoanalyst, educator*
Dana, Marie Immaculée *education educator, department chairman*
Dawson, Mary Ruth *curator, educator*
Donini, Dina A. *social studies educator*
Douglass, Nancy Ure *counselor*
Eckert, Jean Patricia *elementary school educator*
Eiler, Gertrude S. *writer*
Ellsworth, Laura E. *lawyer*
Feddersen Steward, Maryann Odilia *psychotherapist*
Fischer, Nora Barry *lawyer*
Fitzgerald, Judith Klaswick *federal judge*
Fogle, Jennifer Fox *elementary school educator*
Fox, Debra L. *educational association administrator, business owner*
Fredette, Barbara Wagner *art educator*
Frezza, Christine Anne *theater music composer*
Frost, Laura Lynn *microbiology educator*
Gaskey-Spear, Nancy Jane *nurse anesthetist*
Geibel, Sister Grace Ann *university president*
Gollin, Susanne Merle *cell biologist, researcher*
Granati, Diane Alane *retired ophthalmic nurse*
Gulley, Joan Long *banker*
Haas, Marlene Ringold *special education educator*
Hackett, Mary J. *lawyer*
Haggerty, Gretchen R. *accounting and finance executive*
Hajnik, Genevieve L. *accountant*
Harris, Ann Birgitta Sutherland *art historian*
Heinzl, Carolyn Barbara *school system administrator*
Heitzenroder, Wendy Roberta *elementary school educator*
Horowitz, Carole Spiegel *landscape contractor*
Ismail-Beigi, Judith Kaye *social worker*
Jaffe, Gwen Daner *museum program director, educator*
Jakub, Kathleen Ann *medical/surgical nurse*
Johnson, Florence Lester *retired elementary school educator*
Johnson-Houston, Debbie *librarian, educator*
Karenbauer, Jacalynn *science educator*
Karol, Meryl Helene *medical educator, researcher, health facility administrator, science educator*
Keairns, Yvonne Ewing *psychologist*
Keane, Margaret A. *lawyer*
Kikel, Suzanne *patent agent*
Kimmons, Cindy Lou *reading specialist*
King, Elaine A. *curator, art historian, critic*
Kitchens-Stephens, Evelyn H. *counselor, educator*
Knox, Lori Brickner *mathematician, educator*
Kreitzer, Tricia D. *chemistry educator*
Labriola Curran, Joanne Elizabeth *orthopedist*
Lave, Judith Rice *economics professor*
Li, Ying *dancer*
Litman, Roslyn Margolis *lawyer*
London-Gibbon, Mary Beth *elementary school educator*
Lowery, Willa Dean *obstetrician, gynecologist*
Lyjak Chorazy, Anna Julia *pediatrician, educator, retired health facility administrator*
Marano, Donna Inez *academic administrator*
Marazita, Mary Louise *genetics researcher*
Mason-Hipkins, Patricia *minister*
McCall, Dorothy Kay *social worker, psychotherapist*
McDaniel, Sharon Toliver *social welfare administrator, foundation administrator*
McKelway, Janet Barbara *music educator, retired*
Miller, Suzanne Evagash *education educator*
Monich, Marylou *music educator*
Moore, Pearl B. *nursing educator*
Muto, Susan Annette *theology studies educator, academic administrator*
Novelli, Katherine Anne *art educator*
Packard, Rochelle Sybil *elementary school educator*
Paugh, Patricia Lou *business consultant*
Paulston, Christina Bratt *linguistics educator*
Pease, Jennifer Kelley *sports medicine educator*
Peterman, Donna Cole *communications executive*
Petersen, Jean Snyder *educational association administrator*
Petro, Natalie Ann *secondary school educator*
Posvar, Mildred Miller *opera singer*
Pudlin, Helen Pomerantz *lawyer*
Puskar, Kathryn Rose *nurse, educator*
Rago, Ann D'Amico *academic administrator, public relations executive*
Rathke, Sheila Wells *marketing professional, consultant*
Rawski, Evelyn Sakakida *history professor*
Reichblum, Audrey Rosenthal *public relations executive, publishing executive*
Riley, Carole A. *music educator, religious institute director*
Rosnick, Kathy Conrad *mathematics educator*
Ross, Eunice Latshaw *retired judge*
Ross, Madelyn Ann *academic administrator, newspaper editor*
St. Clair, Gloriana Strange *librarian, dean*
Schaub, Marilyn McNamara *theology studies educator*
Scheuble, Kathryn Jean *social worker, family therapist*
Schorr-Ribera, Hilda Keren *psychologist*
Sensenich, Ila Jeanne *judge*
Shaw, Mary M. *computer scientist, educator*
Sikora, Gloria Jean *social studies educator, department chairman*
Spalding, Rita Lee *artist*
Stein, Laura *food products executive*
Strick, Sadie Elaine *psychologist*
Tsu, Susan *costume designer, educator*
Vergona, Kathleen Dobrosielski *biology educator, researcher*
Vetere, Kathleen Marie *athletic trainer*
Wagner, Cheryl Jean *elementary school educator*
Warner, Judith (Anne) Huss *elementary school educator*
Wilson, Frances Helen *retired occupational therapist*
Work, Jane Allen *psychologist*

Pittston
Pollick, Cynthia *lawyer*

Plymouth Meeting
Blessing, Carole Anne *human resources manager*
Sauer, Elizabeth Mason *school social worker*

Port Matilda
Holt, Frieda M. *nursing educator, retired academic administrator*
Ritti, Alyce Rae *artist*

Pottstown
Coulter, Kathleen Marie *psychotherapist, consultant*
Fillman, Michele Renee *nurse*
Nitsche, Linda *gifted and talented educator*

Pottsville
Stankavage, Amy L. *physical therapist, athletic trainer*

Presto
Moeller, Audrey Carolyn *retired energy company executive, retired corporate secretary*

Punxsutawney
Dinsmore, Roberta Joan Maier *library director*

Quakertown
Babb, Lisa Marie *physical education educator*
Emig, Carol A. *music educator, musician*

Quarryville
Braightmeyer, Janet Huber *elementary school educator, music educator*

Quincy
Gilbreath, Sarah Burkhart Gelbach *health facility administrator*

Radnor
Sicoli, Mary Louise Corbin *psychologist, educator*

Reading
Bell, Frances Louise *medical technologist*
Chinni, Rosemarie Catherine *science educator*
Dietrich, Renée Long *not-for-profit developer*
Forrer, Nan Louise *secondary school educator*
Gordon, Mildred Harriet Gross *hospital executive*
Hackenberg, Barbara Jean Collar *retired advertising and public relations executive*
Hamwi, Bonnie L. *education educator, consultant*
McCullough, Eileen (Eileen McCullough LePage, Elli McCullough) *financial consultant, writer, editor, educator*
McVey, Diane Elaine *accountant*
Peemoeller, Helen Carolyn *literature educator, department chairman*
Rodgers, Lana Loretta Lusch *retired elementary school educator*
Sauer, Elissa Swisher *nursing educator*
Shultz, Lois Frances Casho *nursing supervisor*
Ward, Joyce Dieckmann *nurse midwife*
Zug, Elizabeth E. *concert pianist, educator*

Richboro
Burtt, Larice Annadel Roseman *artist*

Riegelsville
Banko, Ruth Caroline *retired library director*

Robesonia
Kissling, Phleane M. *science educator*

Rochester
Wilkins, Arlene *social worker*

Royersford
Krell-Morris, Cheri Lee *psychologist*

Rydal
Fernberger, Marilyn Friedman *not-for-profit developer, consultant, volunteer*

Sadsburyville
Gellman, Gloria Gae Seeburger Schick *marketing professional*

Saegertown
Kopf, Nancy *special education educator*
Ralph, NancyJo *retired music educator*

Saint Davids
Boehne, Patricia Jeanne *foreign languages educator, department chairman*

Sayre
Bentley, Dianne H. Glover *minister, consultant*
Brittain, Nancy Hammond *accountant*
Smith, Robin L. *municipal official*

Schnecksville
Labbiento, Julianne Marie *mathematics professor*

Schwenksville
Zucker, Barbara J. *artist, educator*

Scottdale
Ware, Susan Joy *elementary school educator*

Scranton
Elvidge, Christina Marie *director*
Handley, Tillian Marie Rose *lawyer*
Lawhon, Patricia Patton *literature and language professor, writer educator*
Lemoncelli, Lorine Barbara *counselor, elementary school educator*
McKenna, Ann K. *nutritionist, educator*
Shiffer, Candice Caputo *retired special education educator, consultant*
Williams, Holly Thomas *retired business executive*

Selinsgrove
Barben, Sherry L. *music educator, choir director*
Martin, Valerie Gail *dean, music educator*
Pineno, Mariam Davis *retired music educator, poet*

Sewickley
Jackson, Velma Louise *lawyer*
Reilsono, Lynda Ann *elementary school educator*
Woody, Carol Clayman *data processing executive*

Sharon
Kovac, Shirley Ann *retired elementary school educator*

Shavertown
Fioti, Jean K. *pharmacist*
Motyka, Susanne Victoria *music educator*
Rockensies, Eileen Regina *retired nursing educator*

Shippensburg
Basler, Linda Gerber *retired elementary school educator*
Evans, Margaret Patsos *photographer, photography educator*
Miller, Linda Lou *education administrator, communications specialist*
Vaughan, Elizabeth Jean *education educator*

Shohola
Carlton, Heidi Lee *pianist, music educator*

Sidman
Cecere, Carol *secondary school educator*

Silverdale
Carney, Shannon Maureen *small business owner, educator*

Slippery Rock
McCollin, Michelle J. *special education educator*
Payne, Ursula Octavia *choreographer, educator*

Solebury
Gilleo, Sandra V. *elementary school educator*

Somerset
Koshewitz, Phyllis J. *elementary school educator*
Mayak, Jeannette M. *speech pathology/audiology services professional, educator*
Nicholson, Virginia Mae *retired elementary school educator*

Souderton
Rosenberger, Janet Thuma *retired elementary school educator*

South Park
Lotze, Barbara *retired physicist*

Southampton
Lenox, Gina Marie *music educator*

Spring City
Middleton, Dawn E. *education educator*

Springfield
Carter, Frances Moore *secondary school educator, personnel director, writer, foundation administrator*

State College
Coppersmith Fredman, Marian Ungar *magazine publisher*
Darnell, Doris Hastings *performance artist*
Erem, Suzan *writer*
Ferguson, Pamela Santavicca *language educator, department chairman*
Ione, Amy *artist, researcher*
Isenberg, Ann Marie *psychologist*
Johnson, Ruth *small business owner*
Kirchner, Elizabeth Parsons *clinical psychologist*
Koval, Donita R. *bank executive*
Link, Phoebe Forrest *education educator, writer, social worker, poet*
MacConnell-Davinroy, Irene J.H. *secondary education educator, consultant*
Mazza, Maralyn J. *director*
McKeel, Lillian Phillips *retired education educator*
Moore, Judy W. *music educator, musician*
Phillips, Janet Colleen *retired educational association administrator, editor*
Shakley, Heather *physical education educator*

Steelton
Zimmerman, Connie Ann *public administrator*

Stroudsburg
Aleman, Sheila B. *special education educator*
Brown, Carol Sue *minister*
Clogg, Katye Narise *music educator*
Finch, Alberta May *retired pediatrician*
Pope, Arlette Farrar *insurance company professional*
Rogers, Lisa Ann *music educator*

Summerdale
Pickel, Diane Dunn *education educator*

Sunbury
Maue, Leta Jo *instructional support teacher*

Swarthmore
Berger, Dianne Gwynne *family life educator, consultant*
Field, Dorothy Maslin *minister*
Kaufman, Antoinette Dolores *information technology manager*
Keith, Jennie *anthropology educator, academic administrator, writer*
Marecek, Jeanne *psychologist, educator*
Morgan, Kathryn Lawson *retired historian, educator*
Napoli, Donna Jo *linguistics educator, writer*
North, Helen Florence *classicist, educator*
Sawyers, Claire Elyce *arboretum administrator*
Valen, Nanine Elisabeth *psychotherapist, poet*

Telford
Boughter, Barbara B. *mathematics educator*
Nofziger, Karen Fae *elementary school educator*

Throop
Kozloski, Lisa Marie *psychologist, director*

Titusville
Altomare, Erica Von Scheven *psychologist*
Pilewski, Jennifer Marie *mathematics educator*

Topton
Yeager, Nancy Ellen *literature and language educator*

Towanda
Rockefeller, Shirley E. *court clerk*

Tower City
Adams, Susan L. *art educator*

Townville
Rudy, Elaine Kim *elementary school educator*

Trevose
Quinn, Holli Jo Bardo *social worker, educator, librarian*

Tunkhannock
Pugh, Melanie Sybil *elementary school educator*

Turbotville
Martine, Andrea Schultz *secondary school educator*

Uniontown
Wirick, Linda Jane *medical/surgical nurse*

Unionville
Benjamin, Angela M. *art educator*
Martin, Helen Elizabeth *educational consultant*

University Park
Amato, Michele Amateau *artist, educator*
Askov, Eunice May *adult education educator*
Brenchley, Jean Elnora *microbiologist, researcher, science administrator*
Cline, Nancy M. *librarian, department chairman*
Conway, Anne Marie *psychologist, social worker*
Eaton, Nancy Ruth Linton *librarian, dean*
Fedoroff, Nina Vsevolod *research scientist, consultant, educator*
Garrison, Barbara Jane *chemistry professor*
Grosholz, Emily Rolfe *philosopher, educator, poet*
Guthrie, Helen A. *nutritionist, educator, dietician*
Halsey, Martha Taliaferro *Spanish language educator*
Hamburger, Susan *librarian*
Heid, Mary Kathleen *mathematics educator*
Herrmann, Carol *university administrator*
Irwin, Mary Jane *engineering educator*
Kellerman, Lydia Suzanne (Sue) *librarian*
Muhlert, Jan Keene *art museum director*
Olian, Judy D. *dean*
Ross, A. Catharine *biochemist, educator*
Roy, Della Martin *materials science educator, researcher*
Stankiewicz, Mary Ann *art educator*
Todd Copley, Judith A. *engineering educator*

Upper Black Eddy
McIntyre, Linnea Andren *small business owner*

Upper Darby
Crouse, Carol K. Mavromatis *elementary school educator*
Pittman, Mia N. *educational association administrator, entrepreneur*

Upper Saint Clair
Smith, Gloria S. *local commissioner, educator*

Valley Forge
Miller, Betty Brown *freelance writer*

Vandergrift
Aikins, Candace Sue *music educator, consultant*

Verona
McWilliams, Betty Jane *science administrator, speech pathology/audiology services professional, educator*

Villanova
Fleischer, Amy *mechanical engineer, educator*
Gould, Lilian *writer*
Haynor, Patricia Manzi *nursing educator, consultant*
Olsen, Judith Johnson *reference librarian*
Reeder, Lindsay Erin *music educator*
Stefanowicz, Janus *costume designer*
Tinklepaugh, Valerie Marie *physical education educator*
Vander Veer, Suzanne *aupair business executive*

Wallingford
Adamiec, Jean Kraus *retired advertising executive*
Parker, Jennifer Ware *chemical engineer, researcher*
Shapiro, Roberta *secondary school educator*

Warminster
Chandler, Victoria Jane *elementary school educator, writer*
Ciabarra, Louise *secondary school educator, medical/surgical nurse*
Mull, Michelle Rachael *secondary school educator*
Vietri, Linda Smith *gifted and talented educator*
Winget, Dalores Loraine *educator, freelance writer*

Warrendale
Snyder, Linda Ann *editor*

Warrington
Pfeffer, Judith Stadlen *psychologist, consultant*

Warrior Run
Scott, Deborah Kathleen *private investigator*

Washington
Gregg, Cynthia Louise *music educator*
Knight, Sherry Ann *art educator*
Maloney, Patricia Diana *artist, educator*
Vande Kappelle, Susan Elizabeth *minister*

Washington Crossing
Roche, Gail Connor *editor*

Wayne
Annenberg, Leonore A. *foundation administrator*
Burton, Betty Jane (B.J. Burton) *playwright*
Fabbri, Anne R. *critic, curator*
Lynam, Beth *elementary school educator*
Miller, Marjorie Lyman *editor*
Rabii, Patricia Berg *church administrator*
Rubley, Carole A. *state legislator*
Thompson, Gloria Matthews *marketing and statistics educator*

Waynesboro
Mason, Susan Helen *mathematics educator*
Pflager, Ruth Wood *retired communications executive*

Waynesburg
Maguire, Mildred May *chemistry professor, researcher*

Weatherly
Moore, Cathleen Turner *retired psychology professor*

Wellsboro
Driskell, Lucile G. *artist*
Smithgall, Judy Lee *music educator, director*

West Chester
Abbott, Ann Augustine *social worker, educator*
Albert, Kristen Ann *music educator*
Baxter, Joan Anna Patten *technical writer*
Cinelli, Bethann *school health educator*
Flood, Dorothy Garnett *neuroscientist*
Gilbert, Sandee R. *art educator*
Hickman, Janet Susan *academic administrator, educator*
Keiser, Mary Ann Myers *special education educator*
Knuth Fischer, Cynthia Strout *environmental consultant*
McCullough, Mary W. *social work educator, therapist*
Pauly, Rebecca Mehl *foreign languages educator*
Schelling, Gloria Ann *art educator*
Staruch, Elizabeth *theater educator*
Strunk, Betsy Ann Whitenight *retired education educator*

West Conshohocken
Mullen, Eileen Anne *human resources executive*
Newman, Sandra Schultz *state supreme court justice*

West Grove
Loveland, Christine Frances *psychologist*

West Mifflin
Archey, Mary Frances Elaine (Onofaro) *academic administrator, educator*
Horvath (Selai), Cynthia M. *secondary school educator*
Rosko, Maryann A. *nurse*
Skonsky, Caroline Treschow *marriage and family therapist*
Vogel, Christy Rae *secondary school educator*

West Pittston
Gelb, Lesa S. *lawyer*

West Reading
Gyorky, Susan Meinig *medical/surgical nurse*
Kao, Winifred W. *otolaryngologist*
Spenier, Joanne B. *secondary school educator*

West Sunbury
Ferrere, Rita L. *band director, music educator*

Wexford
Kainaroi, Cynthia D. *assistant principal*
Osby, Larissa Geiss *artist*
Roy, Suzanne Scully *reading specialist*
Utay, Carol Mitnick *special education educator, computer consultant*

White Oak
Shaw, Renee S. *elementary school educator*

Whitehall
Tufton, Janie Lee (Jane Tufton) *dental hygienist, lobbyist*

Wilkes Barre
Baloga, Lucille Wujcik *psychologist*
Coffin, Joan M. *neuroscience educator*
Joyce, Ann Iannuzzo *art educator*
Pasonick, Kimberly Rose *elementary school educator*
Sweeney-Zamboni, Eileen T. *literature and language professor*

Williamsport
Buckman, Debra Ann *science educator*
Clarke, Louise Rigdon *gifted student program administrator, principal*
Gouldin, Judith Ann *nuclear medicine physician*
Jenkins, Gaye Ranck *adult education educator, consultant*
Lockcuff, Stacy Marie *personal trainer, pre-school educator*
Rosebrough, Carol Belville *cable television company executive*
Wittman, Brittany Lyn *design educator*

Willow Grove
Burtt, Anne Dampman *special education educator*
Moses, Bonnie Smith *lawyer, educator*
Windheim, Randi Mackler *literature educator*

Willow Hill
Dorand, Freda J. *music educator*

Willow Street
Eggers, Mary Lynn *elementary school educator*

Winfield
Wert, Barbara J. Yingling *special education consultant*

Wingate
Lomison, Marie Lucinda *mathematics educator*

Wrightsville
Huber, Cheryl S. *music educator*

Wyalusing
Goodman, Carol Hockenbury *retired elementary school educator, consultant*

Wyncote
Schaffner, Roberta Irene *retired medical/surgical nurse*
Weiss, Mili Dunn *artist, educator*

Wynnewood
Beck, Elaine Kushner *elementary and secondary school educator*
Bowes, Betty Miller *painter, art consultant*
Buffum, Kathleen D. *artist*
Camp, Kimberly N. *museum administrator, artist*
Frankl, Razelle *management educator*
Grenen, Judie Sann *librarian*
Koprowska, Irena *cytologist, medical researcher*
Meyers, Mary Ann *foundation administrator, consultant, writer*

Wyomissing
Genieser-DeRosa, Anya *psychologist*
Spatcher, Dianne Marie *finance executive*
Stevens, Anne L. *metal products executive, retired automotive executive*
Tarnoski, Lori M. *apparel executive*
Williams-Wennell, Kathi *human resources specialist*

Yardley
Millner, Rachel Erin *psychology educator, occupational therapist*
Newsom, Carolyn Cardall *management consultant*
Prato, Ellen C. *literature educator*
Setash, Kathleen Douglas *music educator*
Watson, Joyce Leslie *elementary school educator*

York
Alcon, Sonja L. *retired medical social worker*
Bitzer, Joan Louise *psychologist*
Cane, Susannah Richards *music educator*
Davis, Jane G. *lawyer*
Lindenmuth, Elise Bell *psychological consultant, educator*
Livingston, Pamela A. *corporate image and marketing management consultant*
Nusbaum, Candace Ann *elementary school educator*
Sebright, Melissa Marie *special education educator*
Snyder, Jan Louise *administrative aide*
Wiles, Lessley Decker *foundation administrator, preservationist*
Wolschleger, Susan Elizabeth *elementary school educator*

Youngsville
Pearson, Denise Anne *music educator*

Youngwood
Duvall, Hollie Jean *music educator*

RHODE ISLAND

Barrington
Henry, Kathleen Sue *minister*

Bristol
Grota, Barbara Lynn *academic administrator, educator*
Wexler, Roberta Vail *volunteer*

Central Falls
Bolandrina, Grethel Ramos *nurse*

Charlestown
Huetteman, Susan Bice *writer*

Chepachet
Jubinska, Patricia Ann *ballet instructor, choreographer, artist, anthropologist, archaeologist*

Cranston
Alston, Jametta O. *lawyer*
Lisi, Deborah Jeanne *nurse supervisor*
Livingston, Carolyn Harris *music educator*
Wilson, Valerie Petit *health science association director*

Cumberland
Murphy, Carolyn J. Mancini *secondary school educator*
Rush, Lee A. *marketing executive*

East Greenwich
Twardowski, Kristen M. *special education educator*

Glendale
Carlson, Jacqueline Ann *elementary school educator*

Greenville
Hopkins, Catherine Lee *music educator*

Jamestown
Logan, Nancy Allen *media specialist, consultant*
Worden, Katharine Cole *sculptor*

Johnston
Robinson, Marlene Theresa *special education educator*

Kingston
Caldwell, Naomi Rachel *library and information scientist, educator, writer*
Hufnagel, Linda Ann *biology professor, researcher*
Melanson, Kathleen Jean *nutritionist, educator*
Newman, Barbara Miller *psychologist, educator*
Schwartz, Marie Jenkins *historian, professor*

Lincoln
Marsden, Herci Ivana *classical ballet artistic director*

Middletown
Reed, Julia Constance *financial services executive*

Newport
Diamond, Deborah Lynn *psychotherapist*
Flowers, Sandra Joan *elementary school educator, educator*
French, Jae *theater producer, sculptor*
Hence, Jane Knight *interior designer*
Higgins, Harriet Pratt *investment advisor*
Liotus, Sandra Mary *lighting designer, small business owner, consultant*
Schneider, Carolyn Anne *educator, director*
Tinney, Harle Hope Hanson *museum administrator*
Wachs, Caryn Lee *psychologist, researcher*

North Kingstown
Kilguss, Elsie Schaich *small business owner, educator*
Mellor, Kathy *English as a second language educator*
Resch, Cynthia Fortes *secondary school educator*

North Providence
Bain, Marissa *social worker*
Maciel, Patricia Ann *not-for-profit developer, consultant*
Murray, Carol Anne *chemistry educator*

North Scituate
Angell, Jean E. *physical education educator, director*
Maynard, Joan Law *elementary school educator*

Pawtucket
Belliveau, Kathrin Pagonis *lawyer*
Boghossian, Joan Thompson *artist*
Ferland, Darlene Frances *management consultant*
Lepore, Lisa *principal*
McWilliams, Cheryl A. *music educator*
Moody, Marilyn Leavitt *special education educator*
Orson, Barbara Tuschner *actress*
Savella, Barbara Maria *educational association administrator*

Portsmouth
Dennis, Lorraine Bradt *psychology educator*
Fitzsimonds, Carol Strause *artist, art gallery director*
Parker, Nancy Knowles (Mrs. Cortlandt Parker) *publishing executive*

Providence
Ackerman, Felicia Nimue *philosophy educator, writer*
Ajello, Edith H. *state legislator*
Arant, Patricia *Slavic languages and literature educator*
Azarian, Anait *psychologist, researcher*
Barton, Alice *physician, educator*
Biron, Christine Anne *medical science educator, researcher*
Blasing, Mutlu Konuk *English language educator*
Bogan, Mary Flair *stockbroker*
Breton, Tracy Ann *journalist*
Coletta, Andria *lawyer*
Cox, Dawn Everlina *protective services official*
Farmer, Susan Lawson *retired broadcast executive, former secretary of state*
Farrell, Margaret Dawson *lawyer*
Gerbi, Susan Alexandra *biology professor*
Gibbs, June Nesbitt *state senator*
Gilmore, Judith Marie *physician*
Goldberg, Maureen McKenna *state supreme court justice*
Goldscheider, Frances K. *sociologist, educator*
Goulder, Caroljean Hempstead *retired psychologist, consultant*
Graziano, Catherine Elizabeth *state legislator, retired nursing educator*
Grossi, Linda Marie *elementary school educator*

Harleman, Ann *literature educator, writer*
Harman, Carole Moses *retired art educator, artist*
Hedlund, Ellen Louise *state agency administrator, educator*
Hemmasi, Harriette Ann *university librarian*
Howes, Lorraine de Wet *fashion designer, educator*
Jenness, Rebecca Estella *artist, educator*
Kagan, Marilyn D. *retired architect*
Kane, Agnes Brezak *pathologist, educator*
Killeen, Johanne *small business owner*
Leviten, Riva Shamray *artist*
Lisi, Mary M. *federal judge*
López-Morillas, Frances (Mapes) *translator*
McCann, Gail Elizabeth *lawyer*
Monteiro, Lois Ann *nursing educator*
O'Keefe, Beverly Disbrow *state official, federal official*
Olmsted, Audrey June *communications educator, department chairman*
Orabone, Joanne Christine *accountant, educator*
Recupero, Patricia Ryan *hospital president, psychiatrist, lawyer, health facility executive*
Rocha, Patricia Kennedy *lawyer*
Sapinsley, Lila Manfield *state official*
Schenck, Susan Jane *special education educator*
Schmitt, Johanna Marie *plant population biologist, educator*
Simmons, Ruth J. *academic administrator*
Spoolstra, Linda Carol *minister, educator, religious organization administrator*
Vogel, Paula Anne *playwright*
Waite-Franzen, Ellen Jane *academic administrator*
Waldrop, Rosmarie *writer*
Wetle, Terrie Fox *gerontologist, educator, dean*
Wold, Patricia N. *psychiatrist*
Wolf, Geralyn *bishop*
Worthen, Nancy Smith *federal agency administrator*
Wright, Carolyn D. (C.D. Wright) *language educator, poet*

Riverside
Lekas, Mary Despina *retired otolaryngologist*
Schwegler, Nancy Ann *librarian, writer*

Smithfield
Litoff, Judy Barrett *history professor*
Morahan-Martin, Janet May *psychologist, educator*
Weiss, Susan F. *accountant*
Yeaw, Kimberly A. *secondary school educator*

Wakefield
Alexander, Jacqueline Peterson *retired librarian*

Warwick
Brown-Duggan, Gloria Lorene *health facility administrator*
Charette, Sharon Juliette *library administrator*
DeCollibus, Paula (DiLuglio) *psychologist*
Richards, Priscilla Ann *medical/surgical nurse*

Westerly
Crowley, Cynthia Warner Johnson *secondary school educator*
Hindle, Marguerita Cecelia *textile chemist, consultant*
Saila, Colleen G. *special education educator*

Woonsocket
Carethers, Andrea *pharmacist*
Crowley, Rosa Quinonez *literature and language educator*
Frappier, Pearl Peters *retired bookkeeper*
Morris, Mary Elizabeth *pastor*
Walker, Suzanne Ross *mathematics and education educator*

SOUTH CAROLINA

Aiken
Clanton Harpine, Elaine *educational consultant, educator*
Hallman, Cecilia Ann *real estate consultant*
Hickey, Delina Rose *retired education educator*
Jefferson, Helen Butler *public health service officer*
Paviet-Hartmann, Patricia *chemist, researcher*
Rudnick, Irene Krugman *lawyer, educator, former state legislator*

Anderson
Broyles, Jennifer Kaye *elementary school educator*
Kaiser, Louise Martin *elementary school educator*
Moore, Priscilla W. *gerontological nurse*
Rhoe, Wilhelmina Robinson *retired science educator*
Roof, Cynthia White *special education educator*
Schiavi, Rosemary Filomena *secondary school educator*
Spigener, Susan Arnold *science educator*
Stowe, Jynne R. *athletic trainer*
Williford, Sandra Simmons *music educator*
Williford, Velma Jean *minister*
Wisler, Darla Lee *pastor*

Ballentine
Bayless, Alice Paige *psychologist*

Batesburg
Long, Drucilla *special education educator*

Beaufort
Eggen, Belinda Lay *education educator*
Guerry, Paula Mary *school nurse practitioner*
Hopkins, Ginger Allen *school system administrator*
Jones, Sarah Ann *science educator*
Moussatos, Martha Ann Tyree *librarian*

Bishopville
Miller, Blondell Stephenson *social worker, minister*
Roycroft, Cheryl *secondary school educator*

Blacksburg
Jones, Karen Faulkner *art educator*

Bluffton
Cann, Sharon Lee *retired health science librarian*
Scovel, Mary Alice *retired music therapy educator*
Windham, Melba B. *real estate broker*

Blythewood
Portee, Cassandra Smith *elementary school educator, music educator*

Boiling Springs
Rucker, Margaret Rickenbacker *psychologist, special education educator*

Camden
Koestner, Carol Ann *information technology manager, consultant*
Pierce, Janis Vaughn *insurance executive, consultant*

Catawba
Rankin, Betty Hill *retired special education educator*

Cayce
Bouknight, Fran Shoolbred *science educator*

Central
Bell, Gloria Jean *academic administrator, literature educator, dean*

Chapin
Bowers, Linda *educational association administrator*
Freitag, Carol Wilma *political scientist*

Charleston
Adelson, Gloria Ann *retired financial executive*
Austin, Linda S. *psychiatrist*
Ballard, Mary Melinda *corporate communications specialist, consumer products company executive*
Cordova, Maria Asuncion *dentist*
Doughty, Shannon Sue *behavior analyst*
Dupree, Nathalie *chef, television personality, writer*
Egelson, Pauline C. *director*
Garro-Bissette, Susan Ann *adult nurse practitioner*
Gupta, Monika *nephrologist, researcher*
Hampton, Marta Toruno *dermatologist, educator*
Jenkins, Pearl G. *retired elementary school educator, realtor*
Jones, Vivian Eilene *music educator*
Libet, Alice Quante *clinical psychologist*
Lovinger, Sophie Lehner *child psychologist*
Machowski, Liisa Ervin Sharpes *science educator*
McCann, Heather *orthopedic surgeon, physician*
Morris, Valerie Bonita *dean*
Nordquist, Sonya Lynn *information technology executive*
Suggars, Candice Louise *special education educator, consultant*
Swickert, Rhonda J. *psychology professor*
Wagoner, M. Deanna *advocate*
Williams, Barbara Stambaugh *editor*
Winter-Switz, Cheryl Donna *travel company executive*
Zuraw, Lisa Ann *chemistry professor, department chairman*

Chester
Mayhugh, Wanda E. *language educator*

Clemson
Caldwell, Judith *horticultural educator*
Hare, Eleanor O'Meara *computer scientist, educator*
Helms, Doris R. *academic administrator*
Minor, V. Christine Mahaffey *science educator*
Petzel, Florence Eloise *textiles educator*

Clinton
Donnan, Roxanne Marie *elementary school educator*

Columbia
Adcox, Seanna Michelle *reporter*
Aelion, C. Marjorie *science educator*
Barnum, Mary Ann Mook *information management manager*
Black, Rita Dutton *media specialist*
Boyce, Corrie Mosby *music educator*
Brosius, Karen *museum director*
Carter, Kathryn Gibson *education educator, consultant*
Chappell, Barbara Kelly *retired child welfare consultant*
Cofield, Virginia Riley *elementary school educator, piano teacher*
Davis, Michelle Marie *elementary school educator*
Della, Teresa Brisbon *social studies educator*
Dobrasko, Rebekah *cultural organization administrator, historian*
Duggan, Carol Cook *research and development company executive*
Elkins, Toni Marcus *artist, art association administrator*
Fields, Harriet Gardin *counseling administrator, educator*
Fowler, Linda McKeever *health facility administrator, educator*
Gasque, Diane Phillips *mortgage manager, marketing executive*
Gilbert, Katherine E. *literature and language professor*
Glad, Betty *political scientist, educator*
Gray, Elizabeth Van Doren *lawyer*
Greene, Claudia *education associate*
Gunter-Justice, Tracy D. *psychiatrist, educator*
Hudson, Carolyn Brauer *application developer, educator*
Logan, Sandra Jean *retired economics professor, retired business educator*
Manning, Sandra Chapman *psychologist, consultant*
McAlpine, Lisa K. *science educator*
McCaslin, Elizabeth Ann *athletic trainer*
McCoy, Dorothy Virginia *psychotherapist, consultant*
McCurdy, Paulette Quick *nurse anesthetist*
McLean, Jodie W. *investment company executive*
McNeely, Patricia Gantt *communications educator*
McWhorter, Elsie Jean *retired art educator, artist*
Newton, Rhonwen Leonard *writer, data processing executive, consultant*
Paschal, Rhoda Jones *voice educator*
Paulson-Crawford, Carol *conservator, educator*
Rawlinson, Helen Ann *librarian*
Resch, Mary Louise *town agency administrator*
Ruth, Deborah Ann *music educator*
Samuel, May Linda *environmental scientist*
Scott, Bernice G. *county official*
Seigler, Ruth Queen *college nursing administrator, educator, consultant, nurse*
Sepulveda, Sonja Marian Atkinson *choral director, accompanist*
Shea, Mary Elizabeth Craig *psychologist, educator*
Sinclair, Linda Drumwright *educational consultant*
Sloan, Saundra Jennings *real estate company executive*
Smith, Theresa Joanne *research scientist, educator*
Sproat, Ruth C. *retired director, consultant*
Stamps, Laura Anne *writer, poet*
Synnott, Marcia Graham *history professor*
Tenenbaum, Inez Moore *school system administrator*
Toal, Jean Hoefer *state supreme court chief justice*
Toth, Susan Helen *government agency administrator*
Waites, Candy Yaghjian *former state official*
Walters, Rebecca Russell Yarborough *medical technologist*
Wandersman, Lois Pall *psychologist*
Washington, Nancy Jane Hayes *librarian*
Wideman, Ida Devlin *science educator*
Wilson, Olive Fuller *librarian*
Zimmerman, Nancy Picciano *library and information scientist, educator*

Conway
Gilman, Sharon Larimer *biology professor*
Johnson-Leeson, Charleen Ann *retired elementary school educator, insurance agent, consultant, executive secretary*
Sinclair, Frances Teresa *music educator, musician*
Thompson, Sharon Howell *health educator*

Dillon
Chandler, Marcia Shaw Barnard *farmer*

Donalds
Hind, Elise Cromwell *music educator*

Dorchester
Taylor, Laney W. *mathematics educator*

Due West
Bruce, Chrystal Dawn *chemistry professor*

Duncan
Kelly, Loveta Brown *elementary school educator*

Easley
Howe, Linda Arlene *nursing educator, writer*
Sorrenti, Rushie Gowan *literature and language educator*

Edisto Island
Van Metre, Margaret Cheryl *performing company executive, dancer, educator*

Elgin
Pierce, Catherine Maynard *history educator*

Elloree
Stickles, Linda Cochran *elementary school educator*

Florence
Belissary, Karen *interior designer*
Chandler, Ann Rogers Tomlinson *music educator, director*
Chewning, Rangeley Bailey *lawyer*
Fisher, Christine S. *music educator*
Hanna, Wanda Simmons *secondary school educator*
Price, Stacy D. *science educator*
Singletary, Eloise *business educator*
Waddill, Cynthia Kay *nurse*

Fort Mill
Bowles, Crandall Close *textiles executive*
Honeycutt, Brenda *secondary school educator*
Pettus, Mildred Louise *retired history professor, writer*
Whitten, Jeanie G. *physics educator*

Gaffney
Edwards Duncan, Linda Kaye *elementary school educator*
Griffin, Penni Oncken *social worker, educator*
Ivey, Elizabeth Reeves *school system administrator*
Suttle, Helen Jayson *retired elementary school educator*
Whitt, Pamela P. *mathematics educator*

Georgetown
Bazemore, Trudy McConnell *librarian*

Goose Creek
Vogt, Kathleen Cunningham *musician, educator*

Gray Court
Smallwood, Rebecca Ruth *elementary school educator*

Green Sea
Donaldson, Robin Faulk *secondary school educator*

Greenville
Baker, Harriet Kugley *elementary school educator*
Beattie, Stephanie Shannon *human resources specialist*
Belanger, Laura Hewlette *environmental scientist, consultant*
Chickvary, Karin Elizabeth *literature educator*
Clarke, Jean Alderman *orchestra director*
Cureton, Claudette Hazel Chapman *biology professor*
Davis, Joan Carroll *retired museum director*
DeWeese, Anita Lynn *medical/surgical nurse*
Dreskin, Jeanet Steckler *painter, medical artist, educator*
Edwards, Ann Louise Corbin *elementary school educator*
Hancock, Donna *secondary school educator*
Harris-Lewis, Tamela Suzette *social studies educator, tax specialist*
Hendrix, Susan Clelia Derrick *civic worker*
Hill, Grace Lucile Garrison *education educator, consultant*
Kindall, Susan Carol *music educator*
Leavitt, Beth Meade *science educator, department chairman*
Lloyd, Wanda Smalls *newspaper editor*
Manly, Sarah Letitia *retired state legislator, ophthalmic photographer, angiographer*
McCune, Linda Williams *artist, educator*
Seibert, Lesa Marie *education educator*
Slough, Sandra Ollie *secondary school educator*
Steed, Connie Mantle *nurse*
Stoller, Patricia Sypher *structural engineer, executive*
Stratton, Sally G. (Sara) *retired school system administrator*
Westrope, Martha Randolph *psychologist, consultant*
Williams, Martha Garrison *lawyer*

Greenwood
Bateman, Carol Vaughan *pharmacist*
Bolen, Jane M. *music teacher, organist, choir director*
Boxx, Rita McCord *retired banker*
Lutz, Laura Elise *science educator*
Marino, Sheila Burris *education educator*
Psomas, Beverly T. *music educator, performing arts association administrator*

Greer
Gregg, Marie Byrd *retired farmer*

Hardeeville
Kadar, Karin Patricia *librarian*

Hartsville
McClerklin-Motley, Shirley *social sciences educator*

Hilton Head Island
Brock, Karena Diane *dancer, educator*
Davis, Mary Martha (Marty Davis) *small business owner, consultant*
Kearney-Nunnery, Rose *nursing administrator, educator, consultant*
Pustilnik, Jean Todd *elementary school educator, secondary school educator*
Reed, Frances Boogher *writer, actress*
Selvy, Barbara *dance instructor*
Stehle, Cheryl Diane French *language educator*

Holly Hill
Anderson, LaShawn Ecleasha *rehabilitation technician*

Hopkins
Daniels, Carla Lee *information technology specialist*
Garrett, Robin Scott *health facility administrator*

Irmo
Branham, Jennie Jones *artist*
Lee, Melinda Faye *mathematics educator*
Maybin, Jeannette Ergler *elementary school educator, art educator*

Isle Of Palms
McKinley, Debra Lynn McKinney *small business owner, dog show judge, real estate agent, artist*
Wohltmann, Hulda Justine *pediatrician, endocrinologist*

Iva
Riddle, Melanie Timms *secondary school educator*

Jackson
Abee, Rose Rooney *school guidance counselor*

Johns Island
Carter, Mary Andrews *paralegal*

Johnsonville
Davis, Aquilla *diversified financial services company executive*
Kelley, Patricia T. *music educator*

Kershaw
Wall, Kathy Elliott *secondary school educator*

Ladson
Groves, Charla M. *secondary school educator*
Stephens, Debra Young *elementary school educator*

Lake City
Hawkins, Linda Parrott *school system administrator*
Stone, Betty Frances *music educator*

Lamar
Greene, Michelle Renee *mathematics educator*

Lancaster
Garris, Annette D. Faile *medical, surgical, and rehabilitation nurse*

Laurens
Childers, Regina Wortman *counseling administrator*
Griffin, Mary Frances *retired media consultant*
Hair, Dina Marie *geriatrics services professional*
Henderson, Rita Beatrice *county official*

Lexington
Ferguson, Benetta N. *secondary school educator*
Floyd, Ann R. *elementary school educator*
Holland, Gene Grigsby (Scottie Holland) *artist*
Oswald, Leigh Heiting *counseling administrator*

Tunstall, Dorothy Fiebrich *retired pre-school administrator*
Yeatts, Susan W. *financial planner*

Manning
Boswell, Martha Lee *elementary school educator*

Marion
Sease, Susan G. *social worker*

Mauldin
Norris, Joan Clafette Hagood *retired assistant principal*

Mc Cormick
Clayton, Verna Lewis *retired state legislator*
Hofer, Ingrid *artist, educator*
Soni, Jayshri *science educator, director*

Moncks Corner
Hamilton, Marcella Laurette *social worker*
Robinson, Angela Regina *secondary school educator*

Moore
Darby, Shannon Smith *social studies educator*
King, Tamara Powers *music educator, musician*

Mount Pleasant
Abbott-Lyon, Frances Dowdle *journalist, civic worker*
Bernard, Caroline A. *lawyer*
Craven, Stella Maris *principal*
Falkowski, Brenda Lisle *retail buyer, director*
Gregory, Yvonne Elizabeth Heyning *interior designer*
Hill, Larkin Payne *jewelry designer, manufacturer*
Royall, Mary-Julia C. *church organist, historian*

Murrells Inlet
Howard, Joan Alice *artist*

Myrtle Beach
Gravely, Mary Jeane *volunteer*
Todd, Cheryl *art educator*

Newberry
Zobel, Melanie Cannon *special education educator*

North Augusta
Campbell, Helen R. *gifted and talented educator*
Rodriguez, Doris Jones *retired science educator*
Watson, Paula Sue *pre-school educator*

North Myrtle Beach
Cassidy, Dorothy Ann *special education educator*

Okatie
Matile, Madelon Elizabeth *secondary school educator*

Orangeburg
Dalton, Cheryl Renee *entrepreneur*
Deas, Alberta D. *educator, educational administrator*
Geslani, Gemma P. *health studies educator*
Hare, Ester Rose *physician*
Hemby, Tina Marie *elementary school educator*
Shuler, Caroletta Alexis *psychologist, educator*
Sibley, Rebecca Leigh Cardwell *dietician*
Stinchcomb, Audrey Thompson *respiratory care educator*
Thompson, Marguerite Myrtle Graming (Mrs. Ralph B. Thompson) *librarian*
Wong, Mitali R.P. *language educator, consultant*

Pageland
Simon, Kindra Lee *language educator, translator*

Pawleys Island
Ford, Anna Maria *language educator*
Matelic, Candace Tangorra *museum director, educator*
Young, Suzanne M. *music educator, director*

Pickens
Crowder, Heather Elizabeth *mental health services professional, consultant*
Denton, Jill B. *political science educator*
Hardin, Janet Becker *gifted and talented educator, music educator*

Piedmont
Hatcher, Carolyn Joyner *school nurse*

Prosperity
Hause, Edith Collins *retired academic administrator*

Ridgeville
Hill, Jacquelyn Louise Harrison *secondary school educator*

Rock Hill
Barbaree, Dorothy A. *secondary school educator*
Cramer, Lisa M. *elementary school educator*
Ford, Mary (Polly) Wylie *retired physical education educator*
Kedrowski, Karen Marie *political science professor*
Manetta, Ameda Avrill *social sciences educator*
Mintich, Mary R. *art educator, sculptor*
Wishert, Jo Ann Chappell *music educator, elementary and secondary school educator*

Roebuck
Baier, Susan Lovejoy *music educator*
Curry, Sheila Diane *secondary school educator, athletic trainer*
Mackenzie, Clara Childs *writer, editor*
McCraw, Kathy *elementary school educator, special education educator*

Ruffin
Lambright, Marilyn *elementary school educator*

Saint Helena Island
Tarr-Whelan, Linda *policy center executive*
Yates-Williams, Linda Snow *real estate broker*

Seneca
Sevic, Sybil Gibson *elementary school educator*
Strong-Tidman, Virginia Adele *marketing professional*

Simpsonville
Anderson, Martha Jean *retired media specialist*
Gilstrap, Leah Ann *media specialist*
Parrish, Cathy Waldron *elementary school educator*

Society Hill
King, Amanda Arnette *elementary school educator*

Spartanburg
Baker, Susan Himber *school psychologist*
Faulkner, Rebecca Clay *reading educator*
Foy, Patricia Solesbee *music educator*
Jenkins-Russ, Theresa Elizabeth *music educator*
Kennedy, Donna Chapman *counseling administrator*
Lucktenberg, Jerrie Čadek *music educator*
Newman, Barbara Tate *retired social studies educator*
Raquidel, Danielle Colette *language educator, researcher*
Sellars, Christi von Lehe *music educator*
Smithart-Oglesby, Debra Lynn *food service executive*
Steinmayer, Janet L. *food service executive, lawyer*
Wren, Leah *theater educator, director*

Summerville
Bratnely, Marcia J. *music educator*
Burke, Rhonda Williams *counselor*
Cook, Jurena Reneé *pastor*

Sumter
Barrow, Tawana Walker *psychiatrist, consultant*
Brown, Barbara Ann *county extension agent*
Dave', Anne Dupree *music educator*
Leavell, Elizabeth Boykin *retired pediatrician*
Moore, Verna *county official*
van Bulck, Margaret West *accountant, financial planner, educator*

Surfside Beach
Favaro, Mary Kaye Asperheim *pediatrician, writer*

Taylors
Hager, Beulah Elizabeth *lay worker*
Porter, Jean McRae *counselor*

Tigerville
Thompson, Becky Louise *English educator*

Ulmer
Mathias, Lynda Rowell *secondary school educator*

Walhalla
Duncan, Gwendolyn McCurry *elementary school educator*

Ware Shoals
Sullivan, Kelly Jones *critical care nurse, educator*

West Columbia
Byars, Merlene Hutto *accountant, artist, writer*
Carter, Saralee Lessman *immunologist, microbiologist*
Gates, Laura Love *physical education educator*
Moore, Shirley Throckmorton (Mrs. Elmer Lee Moore) *accountant*

Westminster
Holbrooks, Faye Griffin *elementary school educator*

Williamston
Hawkins-Sneed, Janet Lynn *school psychologist, human resources administrator, small business owner*

Woodruff
Baxley, Pamel W *secondary school educator*

York
Jonas, Cynthia *social studies educator*

SOUTH DAKOTA

Aberdeen
Anderson, Esther Elizabeth *retired pediatrician, educator*
Hornaman, Elaine Verna *librarian*
Omland, Jacqueline Leigh-Knute *secondary school educator, small business owner*
Paranto, Sharon *educator, consultant*
Pesicka, Harlene Neave *mental health services professional*
Seeklander, Marlene Kay *educational association administrator*
Zephier, Carol Ann *piano educator, retired organist*

Brandon
Chistenson, Rose Mary *elementary school educator*

Brookings
Eischen, Michelle Robin *art educator*
Fahrenwald, Nancy Lynn *nursing educator, researcher*
Hall, Teresa Joanne Keys *manufacturing engineer, educator*
McGee, Megan E. *coach, consultant*
Miller, Peggy Gordon Elliott *academic administrator*
Vanderpan, Norma *retired elementary school educator*
Williams, Elizabeth Evenson *writer*

Buffalo
Helms, Carol Dorothy *elementary school educator*

Canton
Kaufman, Angela J. *music educator*

Chamberlain
Gerlach, Amy Louise *physical education educator*

Eagle Butte
Webb, Yvonne M. *secondary school educator*

Florence
Black, Mary Kay *secondary school educator*

Freeman
Koller, Berneda Joleen *library administrator*

Hermosa
Hasselstrom, Linda Michele *writer, rancher*

Humboldt
Johnson, June Marilyn *music educator*

Kadoka
Stout, Maye Alma *secondary school educator*

Keystone
Harrison, Gloria Jean *retired music educator*

Madison
Johnson, Viki *sociology professor*

Miller
Morford, JoAnn (JoAnn Morford-Burg) *state senator, investment company executive*

Mission
MacKichan, Margaret Anna *artist, art educator*
Shabazz, Frances *lawyer*

Mitchell
Konechne, Ann M. *women's college basketball coach, director*
Langland, Laurie Lynne *archivist, director, educator*
Russell, Annika Renee *secondary school educator, financial consultant*

Mobridge
Hall, Jo(sephine) Marian *editor*

Mud Butte
Ingalls, Marie Cecelie *former state legislator, retail executive*

Parker
Christensen, Jill Renee *mathematics educator*

Pierre
Duhamel, Judith Reedu Olson *public information officer, former state senator*
Hollingsworth, Doneen *state agency administrator*
Johnson, Julie Marie *lawyer, lobbyist, judge*
Meierhenry, Judith Knittel *state supreme court justice*
Stiles, Doris D. *elementary school educator*
Weyer, Dianne Sue *health facility administrator*

Platte
Pennington, Beverly Melcher *financial services company executive*

Rapid City
Ball, Carol J. *elementary school educator*
Callahan, Susan Jane Whitney *accountant*
Chamberlain Hayman, Susan Denise *psychotherapist, physical therapist*
Geary, Laura Alma *mathematics professor*
Green, Sharon Vincentine *counselor, consultant*
Kennedy, Judith Mary *school psychologist*
Palmer, Sally Broadbent *language educator*
Schreier, Karen Elizabeth *judge*
Wishard, Della Mae *former newspaper editor*
Zhang, Nian *engineering educator*

Redfield
Schoen, Jill F. *psychologist, educator*

Roscoe
Flannery, Bernita L. *music educator*
Hettick, Sandra Ann *literature and language educator*

Saint Lawrence
Lockner, Vera Joanne *farmer, rancher, state legislator*

Scotland
Sunshower, Suzanne *freelance/self-employed journalist, poet, artist*

Sioux Falls
Ammann, Meladee *music educator*
Egan, Lora Rae *music educator*
Kuntz, Carol B. *psychologist, educator, marriage and family therapist*
Niemann, Patricia *nurse*
Richards, LaClaire Lissetta Jones (Mrs. George A. Richards) *social worker*
Tapken, Michelle G. *prosecutor*
Thompson, Ronelle Kay Hildebrandt *library director*
Volin, Suzanne *retired lab administrator*

Spearfish
Elsom, Margaret Striplin *elementary school educator*
Hubbard, Constance E. *language educator, piano teacher*
Shearer-Cremean, Christine Louise *literature educator*

Vermillion
Jacobs, Gera M. *early childhood educator*
Struck, Judy Kay *special education specialist*

Volin
Aiello, Judith A. *music educator*

Watertown
Lemke, Tracy A. *music educator*

White Lake
Munsen, Renee Lynn *music educator*

Yankton
Eisenhauer, Christine Marie *community health nurse, educator*
Muth, Jill *elementary school educator*
Tronvold, Linda Jean *occupational therapist*

TENNESSEE

Alamo
Finch, Evelyn Vorise *financial planner*

Alexandria
Thomas, Deona Lee *music educator*

Allardt
Copeland, Patricia Ruth *elementary school educator*

Allons
Reagan, Penny A. *elementary school educator*

Antioch
Housel, Natalie Rae Norman *physical therapist, educator*
Mattice, Debora J. *special education educator, consultant*

Athens
Brown, Sandra Lee *art association administrator, consultant, artist*
Higdon, Linda Hampton *congressional staff*

Bartlett
Ford, Nancy Leonard *retired special education educator*

Bells
Stephenson, Sylvia *elementary school educator*

Benton
Kingery, Alice L. *elementary school educator*

Birchwood
Lowrance, Rita Gale Hamrick *elementary school educator*

Blountville
Graybeal, Tracy Lynn *secondary school educator*

Bolivar
Traylor, Sharon Elain *writer, school food service staff member*

Brentwood
Berry, Kathryn-Grace *geriatrics nurse*
Bolton, Martha O. *writer*
Byars, Leisa *marketing professional, music company executive*
Ezell, Kimberly Hardison *educator*
Grant, Amy *singer, songwriter*
James, Elizabeth Jeanette Thompson *science educator*
Scurlock, Joy Shelton *elementary school educator*
Seifert, Rachel A. *lawyer*
Taylor, Nicole Renée (Niki Taylor) *model, shop owner*
Tucker, Tanya Denise *singer*
Vance, Kim *lawyer*
Walker Bonner, Linda Carol *music educator*

Bristol
Fey, Vicki Peterson *church musician*
Holler, Ann K. *music educator*

Brownsville
Wilson, Susan Rice *vice principal*

Burlison
German, Jennifer Elam *elementary school educator, music educator*

Butler
Stansberry, Joetta Lee *special education educator*

Camden
Jasper, Doris J. Berry *nurse*
Tippitt, Rhonda Clement *library director*

Chapel Hill
Miller, Betty *elementary school educator*

Charlotte
Rougemont, Denise *elementary school educator*

Chattanooga
Bechtel, Sherrell Jean *psychotherapist*
Bimrose, Heidi E. *human services administrator, director*
Cook, Charlene Lamar *elementary school educator, music educator*
Fouquet, Anne (Judy Fuqua) *musician, music educator*
Harrison (Ingle), Bettye (Bettye Ingle) *real estate company executive*
Kubic, M(arcia) Sylvia *elementary school educator*
McFarland, Jane Elizabeth *librarian*
McNeill-Murray, Joan Reagin *volunteer, consultant*
Mohney, Nell Webb *religion educator, speaker, author*
Nation, Samie Bowman *retired elementary and special education educator*
Norman, Mary Jo *education educator*
Pate, Lisa M. *transportation services executive, lawyer*
Steele, Shirley Sue *retired special resource educator*
Washburn, Sandra Paynter *art educator*

Church Hill
Bowers, Susan Bailey *secondary school educator*

Clarksville
Amstutz, Julie Denise *elementary school educator*
Clark, Janet Kaye *music educator*
Hoppe, Sherry Lee *academic administrator*
Johnson, Barbara Ella Jackson *city official*
Kincaid, Sarah Sanders *mathematics educator*

Staivisky, Jeanne Louise *counselor, alcohol/drug abuse services professional*

Cleveland
Hamid, Suzanne L *academic administrator*
Killen, Roseanne Marie *social worker*
Kraus, Ruby Jean *art educator*
Lockhart, Madge Clements *educational organization executive*
McDaniel, Kay *education educator, writer*

Clinton
Hutchens, Gail R. *chemist*
Price, Lori Jean *humanities educator*

Coalfield
Jackson, Vicki Annette *elementary school educator*

Collegedale
Bennett, Peggy Elizabeth *librarian, library director, educator*

Collierville
Hays, Louise Stovall *retail fashion executive*
Nichols, Christina R. *music educator*
O'Neill Tate, Frances *construction executive*
Smith, Vickie M. *chemicals executive*
Tesreau, Cynthia Lynn *elementary school educator*

Columbia
Cantrell, Sharron Caulk *principal*

Cookeville
Asanbe, Comfort Bola *psychologist, educator*
Reynolds, Barbara C. *retired mental health educator, dean*
Smolenski, Lisabeth Ann *physician*
Underwood, Lucinda Jean *poet, playwright, small business owner, researcher*

Cordova
Cheatham, Wanda M. *music educator*
Hatch, Margaret Oenone *secondary school educator*
Jacobs, M. Louise *secondary school educator*
Pugh, Dorothy Gunther *artistic director*

Corryton
Graves, Leslie Hill *secondary school educator*

Covington
Smith, Melody Kennon *mathematics professor*
Wright, Bonnie Shankle *assistant principal, choir director*

Crab Orchard
McBee, Christy Dawn *art educator, pre-school educator*

Crossville
Hyder, Deborah Jean *elementary school educator*
Ralstin, Betty Lou *religious organization administrator*
Ridge, Linda Kiser *secondary school educator*
Sower, Milene A. *nursing educator*

Cunningham
Mince, Carol Kirkham *history educator*

Dandridge
Coley, Jan Brumback *biology educator*
Evans, Sheila S. *secondary school educator*
Finchum, Sherry Sorrells *school system administrator*

Dayton
Bloxson, Phyllis Jane *art educator*
Luther, Sigrid *music educator*

Denmark
Lipscomb, Carol Matthews *science educator*

Dover
Cook-Elkins, Shana Free *elementary school educator*

Dunlap
Carr, Marsha Hamblen *elementary school principal*

Dyersburg
Rose, Wendy Michelle *science educator*

Enville
Campbell, Nell *mayor*

Etowah
Amos, Janette Garbee *retired secondary school educator*

Franklin
Brown, Gail *secondary school educator*
Daniel, Cathy Brooks *educational consultant*
Douglass, Dorris Callicott *librarian, historian, genealogist*
Horton, Rosalyn *underwriter*
Hughey, Brenda Joyce *supervisor*
Kemp, Nancy Martin *history educator*
McClellan, Dixie *secondary school educator*
Power, Elizabeth Henry *marketing professional, consultant*
Ward, Patricia S. *theater educator*
Wilharm, Sharon Lynette *religious studies educator, comedienne*

Gatlinburg
HcIntosh, Elaine Householder *physical education educator*

Germantown
Cohen, Diane A. *rabbi*
Mobley, Robin N. *nursing administrator*

Gleason
Freeman, Stacie Drerup *sociologist, educator*

Goodlettsville
Lanigan, Susan S. *lawyer*

Gray
Slagle, Lusetta *librarian*

Greenbrier
McClendon, Melinda White *medical/surgical nurse*

Greeneville
Breckenridge, Judith Watts *writer, educator*
Casteel, DiAnn Brown *education educator*
Parsons, Marcia Phillips *judge*
Wilhite, Nancy Jane *evangelist*

Greenfield
Engler, Sherrie Lee *artist, illustrator*

Hampton
Graham, Hilda Renae *mathematics educator*

Harrison
Sellers, Donna Northcutt *science educator*

Henderson
Elder, Jennifer Anne *music educator*

Hendersonville
Kinney, Betty Caudill *elementary school educator*
McPherson, Mona Sue *science educator, department chairman*
Spain, Mary Ann *realtor, educator, historian, writer*

Henry
Lowery, Dianne Armour *music educator*

Hermitage
Castner, Catherine S. *information technology administrator*
Lyle, Virginia Reavis *retired archivist, genealogist*
Reid, Donna Joyce *small business owner*
White, Mary Beth *counseling administrator, adult education educator*

Hickory Valley
Weaver, Peggy (Marguerite McKinnie Weaver) *plantation owner*

Hixson
O'Connor, Elizabeth Hill *elementary school educator*
Prichard, Lona Ann *retired elementary school educator*

Humboldt
Agee, Nelle Hulme *retired art history educator*

Huntingdon
King, Tracy Lynn *science educator*

Huntland
Burton, Janet Ruth Wisner *music educator*

Huntsville
Lewallen Reynolds, Cynthia Maire *city administrator, small business owner*

Jacksboro
King, Shelley B. *science educator*

Jackson
Gatwood, Dianne N. *music educator*
Golden, Christie M. *mathematics educator*
Hazlewood, Judith Evans *retired librarian*
Hearn, Beverly Jean *education educator*
Hoyle, Shetina Yevette *librarian*
Vantreese, Linda Fay Rainwater *retired medical/surgical nurse*
Wallace, Permelia Franklin *artist*

Jefferson City
Coffey, Kitty R. *dietician, healthcare educator*

Johnson City
Bonner, Patricia Jane *retired physical education and special education educator*
Corpening, Deborah Weems *dance educator*
Duncan, Corintha McKee *counselor*
Giorgadze, Tamar Alfred *pathologist, physician*
Pandian, Shantha G. *psychiatrist*
Rasch, Ellen Myrberg *cell biology educator*
Robertson, Laura Elizabeth *science educator*
Sell, Joan Isobel *mobile home company owner*
Snyder-Sowers, Mary Anne Sarah *performing arts educator, performing company executive, choreographer*
Taylor, Lesli Ann *pediatric surgeon, educator*
Zimmern-Reed, Annette Wacks *psychologist*

Kenton
Jenkins-Brady, Terri Lynn *publishing executive, journalist*

Kingsport
Abbott, Verna Ruth *social studies educator*
Egan, Martha Avaleen *history professor, archivist, consultant, music educator*
Fanslow, Mary Frances *information scientist*
Hart, Voleen Victoria *music educator*
Lee, Theresa K. *chemicals executive*
Rigsby, Mary Sue *retired elementary school educator, adult education educator*
Sass, Candace Elaine *chemist, researcher*
Wolfe, Margaret Ripley *historian, educator, consultant*
Wray, Yana *medical/surgical nurse*

Knoxville
Aguilar, Julia Shell *publishing executive*
Anderson, Ilse Janell *clinical geneticist*
Bateman, Veda Mae *industrial psychologist, management consultant*
Beeler, Sandra Gillespie *realtor*
Bell, Linda R. *writer, photographer*
Benson, Kathleen Sevier Kavanagh *retired counselor*
Billone, Amy Christine *education educator*
Bodenheimer, Sally Nelson *reading educator, retired*
Brown, Elizabeth *health science association administrator, educator*
Cottrell, Jeannette Elizabeth *retired librarian*
Cox, Anna Lee *retired administrative assistant*
Creasia, Joan Catherine *dean, nursing educator*
De Weerdt, Hilde Godelieve *humanities educator*
Dewey, Barbara I. *librarian, dean*
Drinnon, Janis Bolton *artist, poet, volunteer*
Drumheller, Janet Louise *librarian*
Dunn, Maureen H. *lawyer*
Earl, Martha Frances *librarian, researcher*
Felder-Hoehne, Felicia Harris *librarian, researcher*
Fender, Allison Jean *physical therapist, personal trainer*
Garrison, Arlene Allen *academic administrator, engineering educator*
Gaude, Emily Camp *elementary school educator*
Goforth, Cheryl Clewell *medical/surgical nurse*
Green, Linda Kay *retired dermatologist*
Harper, Janice *anthropologist, educator*
Harris, Diana Koffman *sociologist, educator*
Harris, Skila *government agency administrator*
Hatton, Barbara R. *academic administrator*
Herndon, Anne Harkness *sales executive*
Infante, Isa Maria *political scientist, educator, lawyer, writer*
Kennedy, Deseriee *law educator*
Landry, Mary Catherine *dance instructor, choreographer*
Lee, Jan Louise *nursing educator*
Lenhart, Suzanne *mathematician, education educator*
Markert, Cynthia Allin *artist*
Marshall-Hardin, Floy Jeanne *art educator*
Martin, Duy-Thu Phan-Dinh *obstetrician, gynecologist*
Matteson, Karla J. *health science association administrator*
McGuire, Sandra Lynn *nursing educator*
Moore, Louise Hill *surgical technologist*
Moore, Patricia Lynn Graves *school system administrator*
Owen, Angie D. *elementary school educator*
Pearman, Gwynn Taft *elementary school educator*
Penn, Dawn Tamara *entrepreneur*
Pirkle, Mänya Higdon *artist, craftsman*
Pulsipher, Lydia Mihelic *geographer, educator*
Reynolds, Marjorie Lavers *nutritionist, educator*
Roberts, Esther Lois *lawyer, music educator, composer, writer*
Rocha, Cynthia J. *social sciences educator, consultant*
Romeo, Joanne Josefa Marino *mathematics educator*
Rose, Terry Denise *secondary school educator*
Schumann, Jane Anne *education educator*
Thompson, Judy Ellen *elementary school educator*
Walsh, Joanne Elizabeth *retired elementary school educator, librarian*
Wilson, K. Shannon *psychologist*
Ziegler, Dhyana *broadcasting educator, academic administrator*

Lafayette
Carter, Anna Dean *volunteer*
Crowder, Bonnie Walton *small business owner, composer*
Oliver, Barbara Ann *retired apparel executive*

Lebanon
Lane, Nicole *dancer, educator*
Martin, Clair *academic administrator*

Lewisburg
Villines, Benita Curtis *language educator*

Lexington
Swatzell, Marilyn Louise *nurse*

Loudon
Hallstrand, Sarah Laymon *denomination executive*
Hicks, Betty Harris *real estate broker, real estate company executive*
Horst, Teresa Dale *music educator*
Llumbet, Patsi Lynn *pre-school educator*

Lynchburg
Gregory, Cheri B. *biology educator*

Madison
Cage, Allie M. *communications executive*
Collins, Joyce A.P. *minister, librarian, educator, realtor*

Manchester
Taylor, Linda Janelle Layne *secondary school educator*
Westberry, Anita Parrish *education educator*

Martin
Anderson, Pamela Susan *sports official, educator*
Cowser, Mary Ellen *literature and language professor*
Huse, Heidi Anne *language educator*
Moore, Earlene J. *school librarian*
Wade, Reba *musician, educator*

Maryville
Bratt, Peggy L. *personal trainer*
Briggs, Geraldine Hackworth *reading specialist eduator*
Davis, Vickie B. *pre-school educator, director*
Livesay, Tracie Lynn *paralegal*
McCord, Francine Nichole *elementary school educator*
Swann, Jerilyn Mitchell *science educator*

Maynardville
Collins, Sherrie Lynne *secondary school educator*

Mc Kenzie
Johnsonius, Jenny Ross *nursing administrator*
Swinea, Melissa Bailey *nursing educator*

Mc Minnville
Shockley, Penny Michelle *science educator*
Wilson, Debra Joanne *vice principal*

Memphis
Aaholm, Sherry A. *delivery service executive*
Anthony, Nakia Lacquers *healthcare educator*
Archer, Ruth Wallace *elementary school educator*
Bargagliotti, Lillian Antoinette *nursing educator*
Benstein, Barbara DuBray *cytotechnologist, educator*
Bollheimer, (Cecilia) Denise *marketing professional, finance company executive*
Bricker-Bone, Jennifer K. *athletic trainer*
Cook, Mary Phelps *chemistry professor*
Crane, Laura Jane *retired chemist*
Deutsch, Alleen Dimitroff *university administrator*
Dierkes, Judith Ann *art educator, artist*
Donahue, Joan Elizabeth *elementary school educator*
Donald, Bernice B. *judge*
Drescher, Judith Altman *library director*
Edwards, Doris Porter *computer specialist*
Feldman, Kaywin *museum director, curator*
Flood, Tamela Michelle *elementary school educator*
Geter, Jennifer L. *psychologist*
Gibbons, Julia Smith *federal judge*
Hardy, Grace Hervey *elementary guidance counselor, language arts eductor*
Harris, Cora Lee *science educator, small business owner*
Harris, Jenny Lou *elementary school counselor*
Helton, Kathleen Jacobson *neuroradiologist*
Holder, Janice Marie *state supreme court justice*
Howe, Martha Morgan *microbiologist, educator*
Jackson, Pamela Hall *school system administrator*
Jalenak, Peggy Eichenbaum *volunteer*
Jarvis, Daphne Eloise *laboratory administrator*
Johnson, Carol R. *school system administrator*
Johnson, Delores Gresham *retired counselor*
Joyner, Marguerite Austin *secondary school educator*
Kaste, Sue Creviston *pediatric radiologist, researcher*
Kelley, Linda Rose *human resources specialist*
Kelly, Aleda Mae *retired secondary education educator*
Landrum-Noe, Madeleine Elise *accountant*
Madlock, Yvonne *city health department administrator*
Mardis, Elma Hubbard *county administrator, consultant*
McGlown, Brenda Pryor *special education educator*
Morreim, E. Haavi *medical ethics educator*
Murphy, Margarette Celestine Evans *retired secondary school educator*
Newberry, Paula Anita *singer, music educator*
Philipp, Karla Ann *music educator, conductor, musician*
Phipps, Carolyn Sisk *secondary educator*
Piazza, Marguerite *opera singer, actress, entertainer*
Pourmotabbed, Tayebeh *biochemist*
Presley, Lisa Marie *singer*
Price, Hollister Anne Cawein *air transportation executive, interior designer, consultant*
Pruitt, Rosalyn Jolena *science educator*
Raines, Shirley Carol *academic administrator*
Ramsey, Gloria Rogers *elementary school educator*
Richards, Christine P. *transportation services executive*
Riely, Caroline Armistead *gastroenterologist, educator*
Russell, Judy D. *mathematics educator*
Sharon, Momany *retired elementary school and music educator*
Smith, Maura Abeln *lawyer, paper company executive*
Steinhauer, Gillian *lawyer*
Tibbs, Martha Jane Pullen *civic worker, retired social worker*
Turner, Bernice Hilburn *recording industry executive*
Watson, Sharon Diane *principal*

Millington
Fletchall, Sandra Kay *occupational therapist*
Gray, Barbara L. *assistant principal, tax specialist*
Thomas-Harris, Yvonne Anita *writer, poet*

Morristown
Johnson, Evelyn Bryan *airport terminal executive*
Ritter, Laura Lingerfelt *music educator*

Mountain City
DeGeorge, Gail *retired special education educator*
Gentry, Penny Michelle *elementary school educator*

Munford
King, Shirley Ann *middle school educator*

Murfreesboro
Doyle, Delores Marie *retired principal*
Garrison, Kathryn Ann *retired nutritionist*
Gilbert, Linda Arms *education educator, educational association administrator*
Hemby-Grubb, Virginia *education educator, consultant*
Jessie, Sarah Elrod *educational consultant*
Keel, Beverly J. *journalist, educator, director*
Kelker, Nancy Lee *art historian*
Kendrick, Kimpi King *lawyer*
Lewis, Brenda C. *secondary school educator*
Mock, Melanie Lynn *elementary school educator, music educator*
Reed, Angelica Denise *sculptor, writer, illustrator*
Rupprecht, Nancy Ellen *historian, educator*
Russell, Judith Kay *educator, researcher*
Schroeder, Kathleen Anne *secondary school educator*
Vesper, Virginia Ann *librarian*
Weller, Martha Riherd *physics and astronomy professor, consultant*

Nashville
Archibald, Chestina Mitchell *minister*
Ascencao, Erlete Malveira *psychologist, educator*
Bailey, Stephanie B.C. *city health department administrator*
Beach, Margaret Smith *retired language educator*
Benbow, Camilla Persson *dean, psychology professor*
Betts, Virginia Trotter *nursing educator, researcher*

Bigham, Wanda Durrett *religious organization administrator*
Bird, Caroline *author*
Blair, Margaret Mendenhall *economist, consultant, law educator*
Bramlett, Shirley Marie Wilhelm *interior designer, artist*
Brigham, Nicolette Bainbridge *educational consultant*
Brown, Tommie Florence *social work educator*
Brown, Wendy Weinstock *nephrologist, educator*
Butler, Carol Green *music educator*
Chandler, Nettie Johnson *artist*
Clark, Shari Jill *literature and language professor*
Clinton, Barbara Marie *director, social worker*
Collins, Joe Lena *retired secondary school educator*
Collins, Melanie Jean *elementary school educator*
Conway-Welch, Colleen *dean, nurse midwife*
Cook, Ann Jennalie *literature educator, cultural organization administrator*
Crittenden, Etta Marie *elementary school educator*
Crosswhite, Jeanette Elvira *art educator*
Cundiff, Lou Willie *artist, sculptor, writer*
Daughtrey, Martha Craig *federal judge*
Epps, Anna Cherrie *immunologist, educator, dean*
Etherington, Carol A. *medical association administrator*
Evans, Patti Renee *art director*
Evans, Sara *country singer, songwriter*
Fabian, Jane *former ballet company executive*
Fanning, Ellen *biology professor, research scientist*
Gore, Tipper (Mary Elizabeth Gore) *wife of the former vice president of the United States*
Green, Lisa Cannon *online editor*
Gusky, Diane Elizabeth *state agency administrator, planner*
Hammond, Marie S. *psychology educator, researcher, consultant*
Harper, Donna Waller *secondary school educator*
Harris, Emmylou *singer*
Hill, Faith *musician*
Ingram, Martha Rivers *publishing executive*
Irby, Jocelyn Adkins *language educator, consultant*
Jones, Evelyn Gloria *medical technologist, educator*
Kessler, Ingrid Anderson *musician, music educator*
Lake, Judith Ann *nurse*
Latendresse, Chessy Nakamoto *small business owner*
Maguire, Martie (Martha Elenor Erwin Maguire) *musician*
Maines, Natalie Louise *musician*
Martinez Bland, Veronica Kay *elementary school educator*
Mayden, Barbara Mendel *lawyer*
McBride, Martina *vocalist*
McKeel, Sheryl Wilson *pharmacist*
McMurray, Justine *elementary school educator*
McMurry, Idanelle Sam *educational consultant*
Melvin, Mary Belle *religious studies educator, director*
Moore, Elise Lucille *Christian Science practitioner, educator*
Morton, Linda June *academic administrator*
Morton-Young, Tommie *psychology professor, writer*
O'Leary, Hazel R. *academic administrator, retired federal official, lawyer*
Orgebin-Crist, Marie-Claire *retired biology professor, department chairman*
Perry, Glenda Lee *health science librarian*
Pierce, Patricia Ann *university administrator*
Radcliff, Joyce B. *librarian*
Reynolds, Doris Elizabeth *management consultant, poet*
Rhea, Karen Hendrix *health facility administrator*
Rhodes, Susan Elizabeth *secondary school educator*
Risko, Victoria J. *language educator*
Roberts, Margaret Reynolds *art educator*
Robison, Emily Burns *musician*
Schroeder, Joni Lynn *secondary school educator*
Seddon, Margaret Rhea *retired astronaut, physician, researcher*
Seivers, Lana C. *school system administrator*
Shaw, Carole *editor, publisher*
Sheffield, Stephanie S. *portfolio and marketing management consultant*
Short, Sallie Lee *physical plant service worker*
Skeen, Judy L. *religious studies educator*
Snyder, Barbara Lou *retired educational association administrator*
Stahlman, Mildred Thornton *pediatrician, pathologist, educator, medical researcher*
Tallon, Becky Jo *computer scientist, educator*
Thomas, Hazel Beatrice *state official*
Trauger, Aleta Arthur *judge*
Twain, Shania (Eilleen Regina Edwards) *musician*
Washington, JoAnn *elementary school educator*
Watkins, Sara *musician*
Whitten-Frickey, Wendy Elise *entertainer*
Willis, Eleanor Lawson *not-for-profit development director*
Wilson, Carolyn Taylor *librarian*
Wilson, Gretchen *vocalist*
Wisdom, Emma Nell Jackson *writer, educator*
Wonders, Pamela Kim *music educator*
Woodall, Ruth Ann *educational consultant*

New Tazewell
Leonard, Martha Gail *elementary school educator*

Newport
Dykeman, Wilma *writer, educator*
Gregg, Ella Mae *writer*
Hall, Mitzy Delaine *chemistry educator*
Williams, Stephanie Diane *music educator*

Oak Ridge
Cragle, Donna Lynne *medical researcher, director*
Foust, Donna Elaine Marshall *women's health nurse*
Holloway, Jacqueline *county commissioner*
Jones, Virginia McClurkin *retired social worker*
Regan-Stanton, Christa Maria *artist*
Silva, Joan Yvonne *writer*
Slusher, Kimberly Goode *researcher*
Wurth, Patsy Ann *geographic information systems specialist*

Old Hickory
Vivelo, Jacqueline Jean *writer, language educator*

Oliver Springs
Heacker, Thelma Weaks *retired elementary school educator*

Ooltewah
Farmer Ratz, Kathy Ann *secondary school educator*
Huston, Nancy Elizabeth *civic worker, educator*

Paris
Hawkins, Angela *music educator*
McFarlin, Shannon Dianne *writer, researcher*

Pigeon Forge
Parton, Dolly Rebecca *singer, composer, actress*
Puckett, Sandy Graves *elementary school educator*
Russell, Pamela Ruth *music and theater educator, singer, entertainer*

Pleasant Hill
Oldman, Martha Jeane *retired medical missionary*

Portland
Miller, Sandra Perry *middle school educator, department chair*

Ripley
Hartman, Joan Evans *educational consultant*

Robbins
Queener, Dana Brandon *elementary school educator*

Rogersville
Fairchild, Dorcas Sexton *language educator*

Savannah
Flanagan, Judy *director, special events consultant*

Selmer
Prather, Sophie S. *educational administrator*

Sevierville
Etherton, Jane *retired sales executive, marketing professional*
Heldman, Betty Lou Faulkner *retired health facility administrator*
Koff, Shirley Irene *writer*
O'Dell, Tonja Renee *primary school educator*
Rill, Vicki Lynn *healthcare educator, physical education educator*

Sewanee
Watson, Gail H. *retired librarian*

Smithville
Hinton, Susan Frazier *secondary school educator*

Smyrna
Campbell, Milbrey Anne *physical education educator*
Trea, Melissa Ann *mathematics educator*

Soddy Daisy
Bice, Edna Jewel *artist, educator*
Collins, Kathleen *mathematics educator*
May, Cathy June *elementary school educator*
Randall, Kay Temple *accountant, retired real estate agent*

Somerville
Macdonald, Sally Polk Bowers *retired addictions therapist*

South Pittsburg
Cloer, Jane *language educator*
Lawhorn, Shannon Hibbs *science educator*

Sparta
Keisling, Mary West *volunteer*
Klughart, Toni Anne *music educator, musician, singer*
Young, Olivia Knowles *retired librarian*

Springfield
Maddux, Sandra O'Kelly *retired language educator*

Strawberry Plains
Blanchard, Pamela Snyder *special education educator*
Snodderly, Louise Davis *librarian*

Townsend
Birdwell, Susan Elizabeth Smith *artist*

Trenton
Smith, Alice F. *medical/surgical, critical care, and home health nurse*

Tullahoma
Hazelwood, Christy Stamps *elementary school educator, small business owner*
Hill, Susan Sloan *safety engineer*
Majors, Betty-Joyce Moore *genealogist, writer*

Vonore
Riley, Betsy Lea *music educator*

Whitesburg
Seals, Kristi Dawn *elementary school educator*

TEXAS

Abilene
Alexander, Shirley Birdsall *retired librarian*
Bammel-Lee, Sharlyn D'Ann *elementary school educator, consultant*
Bertrand, Tina Louise *political science professor*
Crowell, Sherry Diegel *psychologist*
Durrington, Rose Colleen *education educator, director reading clinic, dean*
Flores, Kathryn Louise *mathematics educator*
Freeman, Carol Lyn *business administrator*
Hammer, Stephanie Ann *elementary school educator*
Kiel, Martha Guillet *art educator*
Konczak, Sandra M. *elementary school educator*
Lewis-Bradshaw, Mavis Latisha *healthcare educator*
Lloyd, Terry Lee *retired elementary school educator*
Pigott, Susan M. *religious studies educator*
Trimble, Celia Denise *lawyer*

Addison
Cotter, Ka *real estate company executive*
Epstein, Brooke C. *lawyer*
McKinney, Melissa A. *lawyer*
Ragusa, Elysia *real estate company executive*
Smith, Cece *venture capitalist*

Alice
Thomas, Katherine Carol *special education educator*

Allen
Screen, Robin Marie *secondary school educator*
Witt, Felicia Lestage *biology educator*

Alpine
Aldridge, Mary Nan *education educator*
Antrim, Nancy Mae *literature and language professor, consultant*
Fairlie, Carol Hunter *artist, art educator*
Moore, Zana Yvonne *secondary school educator, researcher*
Morgan, Mary Jane *retired mathematics educator*

Alvin
Orsak, Lisa Gayle *secondary school educator*

Alvord
King, Barbara Jean *nurse*

Amarillo
Barker, Sheila *chemist, educator*
Eimon, Pan Dodd *artist, writer*
Hicks, Ann Neuwirth *clinical social worker*
James, Linda Diane *media specialist*
Knutson, Bonnie Rae *secondary school educator, artist*
Mojtabai, Ann Grace *author, educator*
Parker, Lynda Michele *psychiatrist*
Robinson, Mary Lou *federal judge*
Robinson, Ola Mae *accountant*
Stovich, Joy *chemistry professor*

Andrews
Scarbrough, Glenda Judith *elementary school educator*

Angleton
Casey, Beth Mentelle *music educator*
Phillips, Nancy Chambers *social worker*
Williams, Tessa René *music educator*

Anson
Plank, Katrina Jean *secondary school educator*

Aransas Pass
Flores, Robin Kay *science educator*
Stehn, Lorraine Strelnick *physician*

Arlington
Aeschlimann, Sofia Lizbeth *psychiatrist*
Barkey, Debra Lynn *music educator*
Beaty, Barbara A. *secondary school educator*
Buckner, Joyce *psychologist, educator*
Butte, Norine *marketing executive*
Copeland, Anita Bob *director, retired elementary school educator, senior consultant*
Davidson, Martha W. *elementary school educator*
English, Marlene Cabral *management consultant*
Garrett, Stephanie Kay *history educator*
Hall, Anna Christene *retired government official*
Holley, Kathleen *secondary school educator*
Howell, Holly Lyn *athletic trainer*
Huse, Regina Marie *biologist, educator*
King, Teresa Howard *special education educator, consultant*
Kracht, Christina Marie *secondary school educator, coach*
McKeen, Sally Werst *volunteer*
Munoz, Celia Alvarez *artist*
Neaga Khayt, Angela *music educator*
Oehler, Judith Jane Moody *retired counselor*
Robinson, Mary Lu *retired accountant, artist*
Savage, Ruth Hudson *poet, writer, speaker*
Sawyer, Dolores *motel chain executive*
Scogno, Stacie Joy *financial services company executive*
Sierra, Regina Aurelia *science educator*
Stewart, Patricia Kimbriel *retired legal assistant*
Stripling, Betty Keith *artist, retired medical/surgical nurse*
Thomas, Lois C. *musician, educator, religious organization administrator, composer*
Willoughby, Sarah-Margaret C. *retired chemist, educator, chemical engineer, consultant*

Athens
Enger, Linda *mathematics educator, consultant*

Aubrey
Pizzamiglio, Nancy Alice *performing company executive*

Austin
Aguayo-Tabor, Maricruz Rocio *secondary school educator*
Alford, Frances Holliday *artist, retired special education educator*
Allen, Barbara Rothschild *retired psychology professor*
Anderson, Mo *real estate company executive*
Ardis, Susan Barber *librarian, educator*
Baltzer, Rebecca A. *musicologist, researcher, consultant*
Barnhill, Jane Cook *commissioner*
Barrera, Elvira Puig *retired counselor, academic administrator*
Bartoli, Catherine P. *legal assistant*
Bennett, Catherine Margaret *music educator*
Blackwell, Cara Lynn *printing company executive*
Bolm, Deborah Dell *elementary school educator, consultant*
Bost, Jane Morgan *psychologist*
Brannon-Peppas, Lisa *chemical engineer, researcher*
Brinkley, Edna *psychologist, consultant*
Brown, Vivian Anderson *retired government agency administrator*
Calfee, Laura Pickett *university administrator, photographer*
Cantú, Norma V. *law educator, former federal official*
Carroll, Yvette *voice educator*
Carter, Kimberly *obstetrician, gynecologist*
Case, Karen Elizabeth *theater educator*
Claflin, Janis Ann *psychotherapist, management consultant*
Combs, Susan *state agency administrator*
Conradt, Jody *basketball coach*
Cook, Kelli Brooke *elementary school educator*
Corcoran, Nancy Lee *retired elementary school educator*
Cunningham, Isabella Clara Mantovani *advertising executive, educator*
Cunningham, Judy Marie *lawyer*
Curle, Robin Lea *computer company executive*
Dahmus, Teresa A. *lawyer*
Davis, Merrill *public relations executive*
Dealey, Amanda Mayhew *former foundation administrator*
Denny, Mary Craver *state legislator, business owner*
DeWitt-Morette, Cécile *physicist*
Dolan, Jill S. *performing arts educator*
Dougherty, Molly Ireland *organization executive*
Drummond Borg, Lesley Margaret *geneticist*
Duke, Carol Michiels *health products executive*
Ehrenberg, Sara Jean *psychologist*
Eldredge, Linda *psychologist*
Engle, Sandra Louise *management consultant*
Fletcher, Robin Mary *health facility administrator*
Flowers, Betty Sue *library director, educator*
Fryxell, Greta Albrecht *marine botany educator, oceanographer*
Garcia, Sara Kruger *lawyer*
Gardner, Joan *medical, surgical nurse*
Gehm, Amy K. *lawyer*
Gerber, Kimberly Ann *music educator, singer*
Giblin, Pamela M. *lawyer*
Green, Shirley Moore *retired communications executive, public information officer*
Greer, Carolyn A. *guidance counselor*
Hall, Beverly Adele *nursing educator*
Hamilton, Dagmar Strandberg *lawyer, educator*
Hayes, Patricia Ann *health facility administrator*
Hitchcock, Joanna *publisher*
Hostetler, Lisa (Elizabeth) Marie *nursing consultant*
Hunter, Dorothy Evelyn *mathematician, educator*
Hutchins, Karen Leslie *psychotherapist*
Jensen, Julie Mae *educator*
Johnson, Jo-Ann Hunter *psychologist*
Johnson, Lady Bird (Mrs. Claudia Alta Taylor Johnson) *former First Lady of the United States*
Johnson, Sandra K. *electrical engineer*
Kallfelz, Tonya Leigh *secondary school educator*
Kirk, Lynda Pounds *biofeedback therapist, neurotherapist, counselor*
Kolar, Mary Jane *trade and professional association executive*
Lang, Roberta Lynn *food products company executive, lawyer*
Larkam, Beverley McCosham *social worker, marriage and family therapist*
Lehmann-Carssow, Nancy Beth *secondary school educator, coach*
Lenoir, Gloria Cisneros *secondary school educator, consultant*
Lindsay, Lynda *research scientist*
Long, Teresa Lozano *foundation administrator, educator*
Loo, Lynn (Yueh-Lin) *chemical engineer*
Lowry, Alaire Howard *psychologist*
MacLachlan, Patricia Lynn *political science professor*
Mathis, Marsha Debra *customer service administrator*
Mauzy, Martha Anne *retired deaf educator, audiologist*
McDaniel, Myra Atwell *lawyer, former state official*
McElroy, Mary M. (Mickie McElroy) *educational writer*
McKeown-Moak, Mary Park *educational consultant*
Meyers, Lauren Ancel *biologist*
Mikels, Jo *science educator*
Moore, Colleen *piano and voice instructor*
Morrow, Sandra Kay *librarian*
Mueller, Peggy Jean *dance educator, choreographer, rancher*
Mullenix, Linda Susan *law educator*
Neeley, Shirley *school system administrator*
Neuzil, Amy Reed *physician, entrepreneur*
O'Neill, Harriet *state supreme court justice*
Ossefort-Russell, Candyce *psychotherapist*
Owen, Priscilla Richman *federal judge, former state supreme court justice*
Owens, Margaret Alma *educational administrator*
Pickett, Sandra *information scientist*
Proctor, Carrie Ann *counseling administrator*
Qunell, Kerri Wynn *marketing professional*
Ramirez Garza, Elizabeth Ann *biology professor, researcher*
Rankin, Mary Ann *dean, biology professor*
Richards-Kortum, Rebecca Rae *biomedical engineering educator*
Robbins, Mary *concert pianist*
Rogers, Lorene Lane *university president emeritus*
Rostow, Elspeth Davies *political science professor*
Roueche, Suanne Davis *university administrator*
Ruiz, Cookie *performing company executive*
Sawyer, Margo Lucy *artist, educator*
Schloss, Hadassah *auditor*
Servantez, Melinda *elementary school educator*
Shapiro, Florence *state legislator, advertising executive, public relations executive*
Simon, Sandra Ruth Waldman *state agency administrator*
Simpson, Beryl Brintnall *botany educator*

Stout, Patricia A. *communications educator*
Strayhorn, Carole Keeton *comptroller*
Sutton, Beverly Jewell *psychiatrist*
Tankard, Elaine F. *editor, writing consultant*
Turner, Kathleen Kalin *musician, art director*
Vandel, Diana Geis *management consultant*
Varra, Dawn Renee *elementary school educator*
Walter, Virginia Lee *psychologist, educator*
Watson, Brenda Bennett *insurance company executive*
Weddington, Sarah Ragle *lawyer, educator*
Weinberg, Louise *law educator, writer*
Williams, Diane Elizabeth *architectural historian, photographer*
Williams, Mary Pearl *judge*
Wong, Martha Jee *state representative*
Young, Phyllis Casselman *music educator*

Bangs
Levisay, Joy Elice *art educator*

Bastrop
Clemons, Barbara Gail *history educator*

Bay City
Woolsey, Patricia Jane *secondary school educator*

Baytown
Soileau, Veronica Demoruelle *counselor, educator*

Beaumont
Alter, Shirley Jacobs *jewelry store owner*
Andes, Joan Keenen *tax specialist*
Baden, Sheri Louise *primary school educator*
Baker, Mary Alice *communications educator, consultant*
Brassard, Janice Aline *retired secondary school educator*
Compton, Valencia *pharmacist*
Davis, Gloria Whittie *educational association administrator*
Dousay, Linda Faye *academic administrator*
Gagne, Mary *academic administrator*
Hawkins, Emma B. *humanities educator*
Hickman, Matilda Coffey *principal*
Irons, Ellen Jane *educational leadership educator*
Lord, Evelyn Marlin *mayor*
McCray, Glenda Elaine *elementary school educator*
Meeks, Donna Marie *art educator*
Mueller, Lisa Maria *chemical engineer*
Phan, Tâm Thanh *medical educator, psychotherapist, consultant, researcher*
Prudhomme, Donna Powell *school counselor*
Wohler, Marjorie Lynn Coulter *medical/surgical nurse, health facility administrator*

Bedford
Deal, Marci Smith *social studies educator, consultant*
Hamstra, Christine Josephine *social worker*
Horvat, Vashti *online marketing consultant*
Newell, Karin Barnes *small business owner*
Swe, Ni Ni *psychiatrist*

Beeville
Freeman, Patsy L. *director*

Bellaire
Sperotto, Angela Diane *secondary school educator*

Bellville
Krueger, Betty Adel *county official*
Mann, Laura Susan *editor*

Belton
Anderson, Patricia Kay *social work educator*
Daniewicz, Susan Carney *education educator, social worker*
Fontaine-White, Barbara Frances *art educator*

Ben Bolt
Garza, Annabel *elementary school educator*

Bertram
Albert, Susan Wittig *writer*

Big Spring
Edgemon, Connie Kay *director, information management, hospital administrator*

Boerne
Daugherty, Linda Hagaman *real estate company executive*

Bogata
Lee, Leah Raynella *elementary school educator*

Booker
Doerrie, Bobette *educational consultant, secondary school educator*

Borger
Allen, Bessie Malvina *music educator, organist*

Bovina
Ayers, Kathy Venita Moore *librarian*

Brady
Dolberry, Jean Marie *nursing educator, supervisor*

Breckenridge
Jones, Karen Annette *civic volunteer*

Brenham
Anglin, Karen Locher *mathematics professor*
Brown, Marguerite Johnson *music educator*
Knebel, Rosemary *secondary school educator*
Lubbock, Mildred Marcelle (Midge Lubbock) *former small business owner*
Spears, Julia Buckner *psychologist*

Brooks City-Base
Miller, Carolyn Lyons *microbiologist, military officer*

Brookshire
Utley, Jane Beson *poet*

Brownsville
Ferráez-McKenzie, Marie Antoineta *literature and language professor, real estate agent*
Garcia, Juliet Villarreal *academic administrator*
Gorman, Margaret Norine *probation officer, chemical dependency counselor*
Halaby, Margarita Gonzalez *marketing professional, communications executive*
Rodriguez, Nora Hilda *social worker*
Trujillo, Anna *food company administrator, city official*

Brownwood
Campbell, Vicki F. *counseling administrator, educator*
Owens, Diane Dobray *music educator*
Wallace, Elizabeth A. *music educator*
Weeks, Patsy Ann Landry *librarian, educator*

Bryan
Beto, Donna L. *retired elementary school educator*
Emola, Shauna *athletic trainer*
Fields, Sheila Crain *elementary school educator*
Guitry, Loraine Dunn *community health nurse*
Kimbrough, Frances Harriett *psychologist*
Richmond, Dina Rae *retired secondary school educator*
Van Ouwerkerk, Anita Harrison *reading educator*
Voelkel, Jane Claudette *retired elementary school educator, home economist*

Buchanan Dam
Miloy, Leatha Faye *university program director*

Buda
Bagley Freels, Nancy Virginia *secondary school educator*
Hayden, Karen Boone *history educator*
Upton, Shelly Ann Vosburg *elementary school educator*

Bulverde
Lamoureux, Gloria Kathleen *nurse, consultant, retired military officer*

Burleson
Buford, Evelyn Claudene Shilling *retired consumer products company executive*
Hibben, Celia Lynn *psychiatric mental health nurse practitioner*

Calvert
Alemán, Marthanne Payne *environmental scientist, consultant*

Canyon
Bigham, Marsha Ellis *social studies educator, department chairman*
Brasher, Treasure Ann Kees *physics professor*
Casso, Rebecca Lynn *music educator*
Parker, Mary E. *educational psychology educator*
Rice, Lois *mayor*

Canyon Lake
Bowden, Virginia Massey *librarian*

Carrollton
Barland, Sarah Elizabeth *secondary school educator*
Bell, Laura Denise *music educator*
Boynton, Leigh Anne *secondary school educator*
Estilette, Kathleen C. *music educator*
Grimes, Terrie Lynn *elementary school educator*
Hart, Elizabeth Ann *foundation administrator*
Lieberman-Cline, Nancy *sports commentator, former professional basketball coach, former player*
Louie, Peggy C. *secondary school educator*
Mills, Patricia Lynn *theater director, educator*
Moellering, Charlotte Lareson *music educator*
Odem, Joyce Marie *human resources specialist*
Ratliff, Mary Jean Dougherty *fine arts educator*
Rejino, Mona *music educator, composer*
Rodriguez, Elaine Flud *lawyer*
Withrow, Lucille Monnot *nursing home administrator*
Yarborough, Judith Ann *bookstore owner, librarian, academic administrator*

Carthage
Cooke, Walta Pippen *automobile dealership owner*

Castroville
Nguyen-Poole, Mary *physician*

Cat Spring
Ramsey, Mary Catherine *mechanical engineer, consultant*

Cedar Hill
Findley, Milla Jean *nutritionist*
Hickman, Traphene Parramore *retired library director, consultant*
Moore, Jacquelyn *art educator*
Warren, Shirley M. *respiratory therapist*

Cedar Park
Gonzales, Elizabeth Betsy Barnes *elementary school educator, consultant*
Lam, Pauline Poha *library director*
Nader, Kathleen Olympia *psychotherapist, consultant in childhood trauma*
Serna, Jayne Elizabeth *history educator*

Center
Brazzel, Regina Gayle *secondary school educator*

Center Point
Turner, Brenda Gail *elementary school educator*

Channelview
Dishongh, Lisa Lynn *history educator*
Wallace, Betty Jean *retired elementary school educator, lay minister*

Channing
Brian, Mary H. *librarian*

Chillicothe
Brock, Helen Rachel McCoy *retired mental health and community health nurse*

China Spring
Hyatt, Anna Dale *music educator*
Smith, Laura Dossett *art dealer*
Weaver, Donna Kay *writer, genealogist, former actress, stuntwomam*

Chireno
Mayhar, Ardath Frances (Frank Cannon, John Killdeer, Frances Hurst) *writer*

Cibolo
Weaver, Melinda Yvonne *secondary school educator*

Clarksville
Smith, Roberta Hawkins *plant physiologist*

Cleburne
Arnold, Sandra Ruth Kouns *photographer*
Saul, Jennifer Ann *therapist*

Cleveland
Campbell, Selaura Joy *lawyer*

Clute
Patterson, Ronnye Williams *assistant principal*

Clyde
Pair, Marci Holt *secondary school educator*

Coleman
Smith, Eva Joyce *retired social worker*

College Station
Beaver, Bonnie Veryle *veterinarian, educator*
Butler-Purry, Karen L. *electrical engineer, educator*
Cook, C. Colleen *librarian, dean*
Cook, Violetta Burke *university administrator*
Dickey, Nancy Wilson *chancellor, physician*
Downing, Frances E. *architecture educator*
Ezell, Margaret M. *language educator*
Fechhelm, Janice *science educator, researcher, illustrator*
Foster, Andrea Susan *science educator*
Gangotena, Margarita *educator, consultant*
Kier, Ann B. Burnette *pathology educator*
Lu, Mi *computer engineer, educator*
Martin, Carol Jacquelyn *artist, educator*
Murano, Elsa A. *academic administrator, former federal agency administrator*
Ory, Marcia Gail *social science researcher*
Reinarz, Alice G. *academic administrator*
Unterberger, Betty Miller *history professor, writer*
Vandiver, Renee Lillian Aubry *interior designer, architectural preserver*
Wagner, Susan Alison *physical education educator*
Wilhelm, Vida Meadows *counselor*

Colleyville
Donnelly, Barbara Schettler *retired medical technologist*
Giesler, Karen Hofmann *elementary school educator*
Livaudais, Noel Elizabeth Dwyer *special education educator, secondary school educator*
Tigue, Virginia Beth (Ginny Tigue) *volunteer*

Comanche
Droke, Edna Faye *retired elementary school educator*

Commerce
Scott, Joyce Alaine *academic administrator*
Thompson, Jane Ann *elementary school educator, researcher*

Conroe
Cogdell, Paula L. *secondary school educator, real estate agent*
Covarrubias, Sherrie *nurse anesthetist*
Gray, Janet Ethel *elementary school educator*
Hinson, Cynthia Thomas *minister*
Judge, Dolores Barbara *real estate broker*
McNutt, Deborah Matoy *history educator*
Pitts, Holly Lea *elementary school educator*
Sharman, Diane Lee *mathematics professor*
Steed, Theresa Jean *manufacturing executive*

Coppell
McAlister, Michelle Nicole *mathematics educator*
Minyard, Liz *food products executive*
Owen, Cynthia Carol *sales executive*
Pitts, Jennifer Lynn *art educator*
Smothermon, Peggi Sterling *middle school educator*
Tabor, Lisa Ann *theater educator*
Williams, Gretchen Minyard *food store executive*

Copperas Cove
Barrick, Marla Caryn *music educator*
Townsend, Linda Ladd *mental health nurse*

Corpus Christi
Allison, Joan Kelly *music educator, pianist*
Bluntzer, Chispa Hernández *artist, educator*
Clark, Joyce Naomi Johnson *nurse, counselor*
Conwill, Linda Jill *enterostomal therapist*
Crane, Frances Hawkins *artist, educator*
French, Dorris Towers Bryan *volunteer*
Jack, Janis Graham *judge*
Marez, Rebecca Ann *literature and language educator*
McDowell, Barbara *artist*
Osborne-Kay, Trisha Ann *elementary school educator*
Sisley, Nina Mae *physician, public health service officer*
Stetina, Pamela Eleanor *nursing educator*

Corsicana
Hindman, Emily Ellen *counselor, director*
McSpadden, Jody Sodd *lawyer*

Crockett
Richards, Anita Henson *special education educator*

Cypress
Funk-Werblo, Dorothy *elementary school educator*
Gamber, Heather Anne *mathematics professor, statistician, consultant*
Hlozek, Carole Diane Quast *finance company executive*
Huss, Betty Jo *education educator*

Dallardsville
Oliver, Debbie Edge *elementary school educator*

Dallas
Ackerman, Deborah *lawyer*
Aldous, Charla G. *lawyer*
Alexander, Gail Susan *psychiatrist*
Anderson, Barbara McComas *lawyer*
Augur, Marilyn Hussman *distribution executive*
Austin-Thorn, Cynthia Kay *religious organization administrator, poet*
Baker, Jan E. *music educator*
Barnes, Madge Lou *physician*
Barnett, Patricia Ann *development professional*
Barrett, Colleen Crotty *air transportation executive*
Benson, BeLinda Lou *school system administrator*
Bergner, John F. *lawyer*
Betts, Dianne Connally *economist, educator*
Blanton, Patricia Louise *periodontal surgeon*
Blue, Lisa A. *lawyer, psychologist*
Blumenthal, Karen *newspaper executive*
Boyle, Jane J. *federal judge, lawyer*
Brainin, Stacy L. *lawyer*
Brandt, Carole *theater educator, department chairman*
Braswell, Mary Paul Gibson *elementary school educator*
Braun, Susan J. *foundation administrator*
Brinker, Nancy Goodman *social services administrator, former ambassador*
Burke, Carla Michelle *lawyer*
Burris, Kelly L. *lawyer*
Byas, Teresa Ann Uranga *customer service administrator, interior designer, consultant*
Byrne, Susan M. *investment company executive*
Casada, Hilaree A. *lawyer*
Castillo, Christine Lynn *pediatric neuropsychologist*
Castleberry, Vivian Lou Anderson (Mrs. Curtis Wales Castleberry) *free-lance writer, consultant, former newspaper editor*
Charriere, Suzanne *architectural firm executive*
Chawner, Lucia Martha *language educator*
Cirilo, Amelia Medina *educational consultant*
Clancy, Denyse Finn *lawyer*
Coggan, Patricia Conner *elementary school educator*
Comini, Alessandra *art historian, educator*
Coomer, Donna R. *communications executive*
Cottingham, Jennifer Jane *city official*
Crain, Gayla Campbell *lawyer*
Crockett, Dodee Frost *brokerage house executive*
Croskell, Madelon Byrd *music educator, classical vocalist*
Crossland, Mary Helen *language educator*
Daly, Gail M. *law librarian, educator*
Davis, Clarice McDonald *lawyer*
Davis, Daisy Sidney *history professor*
Dealey, Lynn Townsend *artist*
Dee, Ronda *poet, photographer, small business owner, journalist*
Dell, Susan *foundation administrator, apparel designer*
Demarest, Sylvia M. *lawyer*
Diaz Meyer, Cheryl *photojournalist*
Dinkins, Jane Poling *management consultant, application developer*
Donnell, Carolyn Faye *music educator*
Dutton, Diana Cheryl *lawyer*
Dykeman, Alice Marie *public relations executive*
Dykes, Virginia Chandler *occupational therapist, educator*
Elliott, Dorothy Gail *music educator, writer*
Evans, Laurie *library director*
Fairbairn, Ursula Farrell *human resources executive*
Farris, Erin Anderson *lawyer*
Fenner, Suzan Ellen *lawyer*
Fletcher, (Martha) Ann Messersmith *counseling administrator, educator*
Flood, Joan Moore *paralegal*
Fort, Wana Ann *retired pediatrician*
Frank, Paula Feldman *health facility administrator*
Franze, Laura Marie *lawyer*
Free, Mary Moore *biological and medical anthropologist*
Freiberger, Katherine Guion *composer, retired piano educator*
Freytag, Sharon Nelson *lawyer*
Gaiotti, Regina *civil engineer, educator*
Gibby, Diane Louise *physician, plastic surgeon*
Gibby, Mabel Enid Kunce *psychologist*
Glick, Gina Phillips Moran *retired physician*
Grable, Kristen Heather *psychiatrist*
Gray, Amy Castle *lawyer*
Gross, Harriet P. Marcus *religious studies and writing educator*
Harless, Katherine J. *telecommunications industry executive*
Harris, Hazel Lynn *medical/surgical nurse*
Hensley, Noel M. B. *lawyer*
Hester, Linda Hunt *retired dean, counseling administrator, sociology educator, health and physical education educator*
Hinkle, Bonnie *education educator*
Hirschman, Karen L. *lawyer*
Hobbs, Helen Haskell *medical geneticist*
Hoffman, Marguerite Steed *former art gallery director*
Howell, Bradley Sue *retired librarian*
Hoyt, Rosemary Ellen *trust advisor*
Huggins, Hollie Ann *athletic trainer, reporter*
Hurtwitz, Ann *lawyer*
Hurwitz, Ann *lawyer*
Huston, Angela C. *lawyer*
Jayson, Melinda Gayle *lawyer*
Jimenez, Mercy *corporate financial executive*
Johnson, Berit Bailey *psychologist, consultant*
Johnson, Mary Elizabeth *music educator, musician*
Johnson, Patricia Ann *music educator*
Kaiser, Fran Elizabeth *endocrinologist, gerontologist*

Key, Tara Ann *clinical social worker*
Knott, Jennifer W. *lawyer*
Kogan, Inna *psychiatrist, educator*
Kruse, Ann Gray *computer programmer*
Kutner, Janet *art critic, book reviewer*
Lafitte, Marissa B. *coach*
Landry, Jane Lorenz *architect*
Lang-Miers, Elizabeth Ann *judge*
Lesmes, Stephanie Brooks *lawyer*
Long, Sarah Holley *lawyer*
Loveless, Kathy Lynne *client services executive*
Lovett, Melendy *semiconductor company executive*
Madden, Teresa Darleen *insurance agency owner*
Madzik, Elizabeth May *hospital administrator*
Marlow, Patricia Bair Bond *realtor*
Mathis-Thorton, Dianna Dawn *protective services official, writer, publishing executive, not-for-profit developer*
McCurley, Mary Johanna *lawyer*
McDole, Sydney Bosworth *lawyer*
McInnis, Carolyn Crawford *real estate broker*
McKnight, Pamela Ann *art educator*
McPherson, Gail *publishing executive, real estate executive*
Melançon, Renée M. *lawyer*
Miller, Jo Carolyn Dendy *family and marriage counselor, educator*
Miller, Laura *mayor, journalist*
Moore, Cheryl Jerome (Cheryl Milkes Jerome) *lawyer*
Murphy, Kathryn J. *lawyer*
Nabors, Marion Carroll *retired English educator*
Nelson, Anna M. *elementary school educator, administrative assistant*
Nelson, Elaine Edwards *lawyer*
Nelson, Pamela Hudson *artist, educator*
Neumann, Luci *rehabilitation center executive*
Oualline, Viola Jackson *psychologist, consultant*
Palmer, Christine (Clelia Rose Venditti) *vocalist, educator, musician*
Parker, Emily *lawyer*
Patterson, Carole A. *psychologist, educator*
Pauley, Shirley Stewart *religious organization executive*
Pelletier, Sho-mei *musician, educator*
Penn, Linda *computer animator*
Pennington, Karen Harder *lawyer*
Phillips, Betty Lou (Elizabeth Louise Phillips) *writer, interior designer*
Poindexter, Barbara Glennon *secondary school educator*
Raggio, Louise Ballerstedt *lawyer*
Rice, Rebecca Dale *film producer, writer*
Richardson, Lynn *art educator*
Roberts, Lynne Jeanine *physician*
Robertson, Jane Ryding *marketing executive*
Robertson, Rose Marie *cardiologist, educator*
Robinson, Debra JoAnn *science educator*
Robles, Diana M *administrative assistant*
Russell-Love, Zelda M. *special education educator*
Sallee, Wanda Jean *music educator*
Sammons, Elaine D. *manufacturing executive*
Savannah, Mildred Thornhill *public school educator*
Schulz, Sandra E. *art educator*
Sengupta, Chaitali *computer engineer*
Sharry, Janice Vyn *lawyer*
Smith, Justine Townsend *recreational association executive*
Smith, Marsha Ann *literature and language educator*
Smith, Nancy Woolverton *journalist, real estate agent, antique appraiser*
Smith, Patsy Juanita *financial executive*
Smith, Sue Frances *newspaper editor*
Smith-Ingram, Karen Camille *reading specialist, educator*
Solomon, Risa Greenberg *clinical social worker, child and family therapist, former entertainment industry executive*
Stanfield, Margaret Helene *nursing educator, administrator*
Stearman, Sherri Lynn *physical education educator*
Stearns, Linda Brewster *sociologist, educator*
Stephens, Leonora *psychiatrist*
Stephenson, Jane Connell *artist, educator*
Stone, Karen *opera company director*
Stripling, Bettye Johnson *civic volunteer*
Sullivan, Judith Patrice *social worker*
Tanous, Melissa Lynn *science educator*
Thomas, Sarah Elaine *music educator*
Thompson, Tara D. *illustrator, writer, career planning administrator*
Tidwell, Trisha McIntosh *elementary school educator, department chairman*
Timpa, Vicki Ann *government health program administrator*
Turley, Linda *lawyer*
Turner, Ruth *academic administrator*
Tyson, Lisa N. *food products executive*
Villareal, Patricia J. *lawyer*
Villarreal, Christie M. *lawyer*
Vitetta, Ellen S. *microbiologist, educator, immunologist*
Wang, Cong *electrical engineer*
Wansbrough, Ann *legal assistant*
Warman, Lynnette R. *lawyer*
Wassenich, Linda Pilcher *retired health policy analyst*
West, Susan D. *lawyer*
West, Teresa L. (Terri West) *semiconductor company executive*
Whitaker, Elizabeth D. *lawyer*
Wilbur, Janis A. *financial consultant, sales professional*
Wilkerson, Patricia Helen *director*
Williams, Martha Spring *psychologist*
Winkley-Pikes, Sandra Kay *special education educator*
Wolek, Andrea Dugas *special education educator*
Wright, Laura L. *air transportation executive*
Wu, Kathleen J. *lawyer*
Yung, Patsy P. *lawyer*
Zeitlin, Laurie *printing company executive, information technology executive*

Decatur
Vaughan, Nancy King *school system administrator*

Deer Park
Guillory, Jennifer Lee *secondary school educator*
Lewis, Nancy L. *science educator*
Morse, Janice Lea *secondary school educator*

Del Valle
Titus, Alberta Christine *secondary school educator*

Denison
Arthur, Susan Helene *social studies educator*
Cameron, Frances Marilyn *elementary school educator*
Plunkett, Alexa *elementary school educator*
Rushing, Dorothy M. *retired historian, writer*

Denton
Bataille, Gretchen *academic administrator*
Bertine, Dorothy Wilmuth *artist, educator, accountant, genealogist, poet, writer*
Calabrese, Margaret Hoye *secondary school educator*
Cogan, Karen Diane *psychologist educator*
Coogan, Melinda Ann Strank *biology professor, chemistry professor*
Garcia, Rebekah *elementary school educator*
Gough, Georgia Belle *art educator*
Greenlaw, Marilyn Jean *retired adult education educator*
Hadsell, Nancy Ann *music educator*
Hays, Edith H. *mathematics professor*
Hughes, Deborah Bray *special education educator*
Jacobs, Bonita Cheryl *educational administrator*
Karr-Kidwell, P. J. *education educator, writer*
Keating, AnaLouise *educator, author*
Kooker, Jean L. *retired elementary school educator*
Lawhon, Tommie Collins Montgomery *humanities educator*
Mathes, Dorothy Jean Holden *occupational therapist*
McCoy, Amy L. *special education educator*
McMath, Elizabeth Moore *graphic artist*
McTee, Cindy *classical musician, educator*
Newell, Charldean *public administration educator*
Nichols, Margaret Irby *librarian, educator, library and information scientist*
Novak, Rynell Stiff *retired university official*
Odnoposoff, Berthe Huberman *musician*
Palermo, Judy Hancock *retired elementary school educator*
Poole, Eva Duraine *librarian*
Ring, Kristen M. *physical education educator*
Ryan, Melbagene T. *retired food service and nutrition director*
Saiyed, Seema *education educator, researcher*
Sánchez, Patsy Y. *bilingual educator*
Simpson, Carol Mann *librarian, educator, editor*
Snapp, Elizabeth *librarian, educator*
Surprise, Juanee *chiropractor, nutrition consultant*
Thompson, Frances McBroom *mathematics professor, writer*
Weller, Laurie June *artist, educator*
White, Nora Lizabeth *language educator*
Wilson, Angela K. *chemistry professor*
Wood, Jane Roberts *writer*

Detroit
Cates, Sue Sadler *special education counselor*

Devine
Whitaker, Ruth M. *newswriter, photographer, horse breeder*

Diboll
Tannery, Ginger *art educator*

Dickinson
Sawyer, Cheryl Lynne *foundation administrator, consultant*

Dripping Springs
DeLacretaz, Cheryl Diane *English educator*
Guess, Aundrea Kay *accounting educator*

Early
Ross-Parsons, Donna Michelle *counselor, small business owner*

Edinburg
Cardenas, Norma Alicia *music educator*
Farber, Roselee Cora *counselor*
García, Norma Garza *county treasurer*
Norman, Theresa J.C. *philosophy professor*
Selber, Kimberly Ann *communications educator, consultant*
Wedig, Cindy Martinez *director*

El Paso
Bartlett, Janet Sanford (Janet Walz) *school nurse practitioner*
Cancino, Nelly *language educator, adult education educator*
Casas, Martha *education educator*
Cuartas, Beatriz H. *humanities educator*
Deckert, Myrna Jean *nonprofit association administrator*
Dillon, Loretta Schoen *physical therapist, educator*
Edmonds, Velma McInnis *nursing educator*
Flores, Yolanda *speech pathology/audiology services professional, consultant*
Gardner, Kerry Ann *librarian*
Gladstein, Mimi Reisel *theater educator, literature educator*
Goodman, Gertrude Amelia *civic worker*
Gregory, Lynne Watson *oncology clinical nurse specialist, health facility administrator*
Guevara, Roxanna *elementary school educator, gifted and talented educator*
Herrera, Blanche Marie *elementary school educator*
Jordan, Shannon Colleen *medical/surgical nurse*
Korth, Charlotte Williams *retail executive*
Lincoln, Shelley *elementary school educator*
Martinez, Gloria Elena *elementary school educator*
Miller, Deane Guynes *salon and cosmetic studio owner*
Minney, Gloria Joan *massage therapist, holistic health practitioner*
Mitchelll, Paula Rae *nursing educator, dean*
Morales, Maria Cristina *social sciences educator*
Moya, Eva M. *health services executive*
Natalicio, Diana Siedhoff *academic administrator*
Pace, Diane Marie *elementary school educator*
Santiago, Irma *science educator, department chairman*
Silberg, Louise Barbara *physician, anesthesiologist*
Simon, Doris Marie Tyler *nurse*
Sloane, Brenda Sue *language educator*
Smith, Sarah Seelig *mathematics professor*
Smookler, Maurrissa *elementary school educator*
Talamantes, Claudia Liliana *secondary school educator*
Vojta-Oswald, Clarice Gertrude *educational diagnostician*
Zaloznik, Arlene Joyce *retired oncologist, retired military officer*
Zopfi, Emma G. *elementary school educator*

Elgin
Shelby, Nina Claire *special education educator*

Emory
Allen, G. Christy L. L. *physics educator*

Euless
Gibson, Karen Yvette *small business owner*
Kaufman, Susan Nanette Bland *secondary school educator*
McClure, Connie Diane *elementary school educator*
Traver, Sue Montgomery *secondary school educator*

Fairfield
Gooch, Nancy Eugenia South *retired secondary school educator, librarian*

Fairview
Hansen, Elizabeth (Beth) Stevens *human resources consultant*

Farmers Branch
Reyes, Czarina Suzanne *mathematics educator*
Walsh, Elizabeth Jameson *musician*

Farnsworth
Gramstorff, Jeanne B. *retired farmer*

Floresville
Tieken, Lisa Marie *science educator*

Flower Mound
Anderson, Deborah Lynn *music educator*
Marrs, Carol Faye *performing arts educator, writer*
Ross, Lesa Moore *quality assurance professional*
Sanders, Lisa Gail *mathematics educator*
Tillotson, Ellen Knieberg *communications educator*
West, Frances Lee *retired doll artist, freelance writer*

Flowermound
Furnas, Valerie Yvonne *secondary school educator*

Fluvanna
Jackson, Rebecca M. *elementary education educator, English as a second language educator*

Forestburg
Hayes, Audimarie *medical/surgical and critical care nurse*

Forney
Braden, Katie Elizabeth *elementary school educator*
Pick, Mary Frances *manufacturing executive*

Fort Hood
Anderson, Nanci Louise *computer analyst*
Reid, Sharon Lea *educational facilitator*

Fort Sam Houston
Gordon, Ella Dean *nursing educator, women's health nurse*
Williams, Pat L. *military officer*
Wojcik, Barbara Elzbieta *statistician, researcher*

Fort Worth
Adams, Lavonne Marilyn Beck *critical care nurse, educator*
Allison, Sarah Amanda *art educator, consultant*
Andrews, Jane Silvey *musician*
Austin, Linda LaRue *clergyperson*
Bailey, Susan Rudd *physician*
Behrens, Alisa D. *dancer, educator, performing company executive*
Brister, Gloria Nugent *small business owner, elementary school educator*
Bush, Jill Lobdill *artist*
Cagle, Karin Knowles *lawyer*
Case, Rachel *elementary school educator*
Colaluca, Beth *pediatric neurpsychologist*
Cox, Alma Tenney *retired language educator, retired science educator*
Danilow, Deborah Marie *realtor, vocalist, composer, musician, rancher*
Davis, Carol Lyn *museum administrator*
Dees, Sandra Kay Martin *psychologist, research scientist*
de Schweinitz, Jean Howard *biology professor*
Dilley, Carol *association administrator*
Dominiak, Geraldine Florence *retired accounting educator*
Dunleavy, Willa Gill *music educator, director*
Durham, Jo Ann Fanning *artist*
Engler, Jennifer A. *theater educator*
Ericson, Ruth Ann *retired psychiatrist*
Ford, Jeanette White *archivist, educator*
Fritz, Mary Ann *music educator*
Holcomb, Anna Louise *physical science educator*
Hollimon, Robyn Delyn *music director*
Hunt, Dianna *editor*
Ivy, Marilyn Atkinson *artist, educator, art director*
Johnson, Abbie Mae *language educator*
Keith, Courtney S. *lawyer*
Kowalski, Debra Atkisson *physician*
Loud, Patricia Cummings *curator*
Mays, Glenda Sue *retired education educator*
Miller, Carol Lynn *librarian*
Moore, Linda Sullivan *social work educator, dean*
Murph, Roxane Cohen *writer, researcher*
Newbern, Dianna J. *management consultant, educator*
Newsom, Douglas Ann Johnson *writer, journalism educator*
Ogle, Sarah J. *assistant principal*
Oliver, Susan M. *air transportation executive*
Pappas-Speairs, Nina *financial planner, educator*
Pelt, Judy Ann Lobdill *artist*
Phillips, Mary Ann *artist, writer, retired legal assistant*
Price, Marla *museum director, curator*
Procknow, Margot *artist*
Ray, Jessica B. *artist, poet, educator*
Reade, Kathleen Margaret *paralegal, author, educator*
Robin, Clara Nell (Claire Robin) *English language educator*
Robinson, Nell Bryant *nutrition educator*
Saenz, Nancy Elizabeth King (Mrs. Michael Saenz) *civic worker*
Scholl, Belinda K. *librarian*
Shehan, Geraldean Harrison *ESL educator*
Simmons, Jean Byers *academic administrator, director*
Sitterly, Connie S. *small business owner, writer, management consultant*
Stevenson, Ruth Carter *art patron*
Strother McKeown, Dora Dougherty *retired aviation psychologist, pilot*
Tarpenning, Emily *music educator*
Thompson, Sue Wanda *small business owner*
Wells, Edie Carol *artist, educator*
West, Sylvia Wandell *small business owner, director, educator, researcher*
Wilkins, Wanda Faye *retired publishing executive*
Wilson, Monica DeAnn *school guidance counselor*
Wilson-Webb, Nancy Lou *educational association administrator*
Yaites, LilliAnn *minister*

Franklin
Perry, Anne Marie Litchfield *secondary school educator*

Fredericksburg
Gibson, Frances Ernst *music educator*
Koym, Zala Cox *retired elementary school educator*
Manhart, Marcia Y(ockey) *art museum director*
Wahrmund, Peggy Stieler *artist, rancher*

Freeport
Gresham, Karen Renee *music educator, singer*

Freer
Blanton, Belia *secondary school educator*

Friendswood
Corley, Cathy F. *elementary school educator*
Overstreet-Goode, Janwin Gail *secondary school educator, music educator, director*
Sutter, Emily May Geeseman *retired psychologist, educator*

Frisco
Carlock, Rebecca Gail *biology educator, chemistry educator*
Coley, Donna S. *secondary school educator*
de Veritch, Nina *musician, educator*
Doone, Michele Marie *chiropractor*
Jackson, Rhonda Gail *secondary teacher*
Meadows, Patricia Blachly *curator, civic worker*
Penz, Roxanne Murray *elementary school educator*
Sexton, Karen Kay *music educator, actress*
Sisk, Kristin Carrington *secondary school educator*
Taylor, Teresa Marie *realtor*

Gainesville
McCormack, Lowell Ray *oil industry executive, corporate financial executive, consultant*

Galveston
Bertolino, Jennifer Ann *elementary school educator*
Chonmaitree, Tasnee *pediatrician, educator, epidemiologist*
Goodwin, Jean McClung *psychiatrist*
Goodwin, Sharon Ann *academic administrator*
Melton, Bengi Biber *psychiatrist, educator*
Rivaux, Lois Elaine *music educator*
Rosenthal, Susan Leslie *psychologist*

Garland
Albuquerque, Heather Lynne *biology educator*
Bjornson Pierce, Shauna *primary school educator*
Brumit, Jo Ann *sheet metal manufacturing executive*
Chenault, Sheryl Ann *elementary school educator*
Enaya, Maysaa Asad *chemistry educator, physics educator*
Fegraeus, Susie A. *principal*
Goheen, Debra Elaine *secondary school educator*
Hodges, Kathleen McGill *art educator*
LeDoux, Ellen G. *music educator*
Lord, Jacqueline Ward *accountant, photographer, artist*
Posey, Jan R. *music educator*
Quinn, Peggy Armstrong *elementary school educator, writer*
Rogers, Sharon *art educator*

Garrison
Cole, Luanna Cherry *literature and language educator, theater educator*

Gary
Coligan, Nerissa *secondary school educator*

Gatesville
Dossman, Virginia Gail *nurse*
Huntley, Barbara Nerine *secondary school educator*

Gause
Salcido, Debra Kay *elementary school educator*

Georgetown
Bencivenga, Alison R. *elementary school educator*
Russell, Eileen Meyer *music educator*
Shelby, Roselle Price *writer, retired special education educator*
Smitheram, Margaret Etheridge *health facility administrator, director*

Giddings
Dismukes, Carol Jaehne *county official*

Gilmer
Warden, Lenore Sponsler *physician*

Gladewater
Beaird, Dian Sanders *middle school educator*

Glenn Heights
Rowe, Nancie E. *director, minister*

Gonzales
Buesing, Leslie Marie *theater educator, director*
Ince, Laurel T. *music educator*

Gordonville
Van Arsdale, Marie Delvechio *artist*

Graham
Lovell, Lisa Inez *special education educator*

Granbury
Dyer, Dena Janan *writer*

Grand Prairie
Andrew, Kathryn Anderson *elementary school educator*
Bouliane, Mary Stephanie *elementary school educator*
Horak, Trish *city government worker*
Mathis, Prudence Marchman *realtor*
McMillan, Helen Berneice *sales executive*
Ritterhouse, Kathy Lee *librarian*

Grapevine
Hirsh, Cristy J. *principal*

Groves
Simon, Mary B. *primary school educator*

Hallsville
Goerner, Freda Ruth *secondary school educator*
Hutcherson, Donna Dean *retired music educator*

Hamilton
Keekley, Patricia Ann *counselor, psychologist*

Harker Heights
Rose, Doris Ann *elementary school educator*

Harlingen
Sandwell, Stephanie Annette *mathematics educator*

Hawkins
Holmes, Lorene Barnes *academic administrator*

Hempstead
Propst, Catherine Lamb *biotechnology company executive, pharmaceutical company executive*

Henderson
Knapp, Virginia Estella *retired secondary school educator*
Rhoades, Eva Yvonne *retired elementary school educator*

Hereford
Stewart, Tracy Flood *social studies educator*
Yavornik, Barbara Ann *pre-school educator*

Hewitt
rNix, Regina Leigh *performing arts educator, small business owner*

Hillsboro
Elkin, Carole Kaine *retired educational diagnostician*
Parks, Connie *elementary school educator*

Horseshoe Bay
Sommer, Alicia Pine *flight attendant, performing company executive*
Strang, Sandra Lee *airline official*

Houston
Adams, Joyce M. *retired academic administrator*
Adams, Yolanda Yvette *singer*
Addison, Linda Leuchter *lawyer, writer, commentator, columnist*
Aguirre, Sarah K. *lawyer*
Amador, Anne *architect, composer*
Anderson, Claire W. *gifted and talented educator*
Anderson, Doris Ehlinger *lawyer*
Andrews, Sally S. *lawyer*
Asselin, Heather E. *lawyer*
Atlas, Nancy Friedman *judge*
Auchter, Norma Holmes *musician, music educator*
Autry, Cheryl Renee *special education educator*
Avila, Susan Elizabeth *elementary school educator*
Backus, Marcia Ellen *lawyer*
Bailey, Kelley *foundation administrator*
Baker, Ellen Shulman *astronaut, physician*
Baldwin, Bonnie *physician*
Ball, Valdesha LeChante' *physician*
Ballard, Linda Christine *financial aid director*
Bankhead, Sherry L. *lawyer*
Barajas, Nancy Helen *assistant principal*
Bartling, Phyllis McGinness *oil company executive*
Bates, Gwen Lee *health facility administrator, consultant*
Bebis, Conchita Juban *mathematics educator*
Beckingham, Kathleen Mary *education educator, researcher*
Behan, Pamela S. *sociology professor*
Belk, Joan Pardue *language and literature educator*
Benefield, Janis Wilson *school librarian, media specialist*
Bennett, Olga Salowich *civic worker, graphic arts researcher, consultant*
Berg, Amie G. *lawyer*
Bethea, Louise Huffman *allergist*
Betts, Nicole Lavette *elementary school educator, consultant*
Beyoncé, (Beyoncé Giselle Knowles) *singer*
Biery, Evelyn Hudson *lawyer*
Bischoff, Susan Ann *newspaper editor*
Black, Donna Lord *psychologist*
Blackburn, Sadie Gwin Allen *conservation executive*
Bogan, Mary Ellen *draftsman, educator*
Bogle, Melissa Anne *dermatologist, educator*
Bourgeois, Patricia Ann *middle school educator*
Bourque, Peggy Sue *emergency nurse practitioner*
Boutwell, Sharon Marie *school system administrator, educator*
Boyce, Maria Wyckoff *lawyer*
Brandt, Astrid *elementary school educator*
Bridges, Margaret Elizabeth *physician*
Brown, Glenda Ann Walters *ballet director*
Brown, Jacqueline Elaine *obstetrician, gynecologist*
Brown, Karen Kennedy *judge*
Burks, Robin J. *psychologist*
Burnett, Susan Walk *personnel service company owner*
Buyse, Leone Karena *orchestral musician, educator*
Caldwell, Tracy Ellen *surface chemist, researcher*
Callender, Norma Anne *counselor, public relations executive*
Campbell, Eileen M. *oil industry executive*
Carnes, Tara Lea Barker *music educator*
Cash, Camille Geneva *physician*
Caskey, Caroline T. *lab administrator*
Cavitt, Rebecca Lynn *secondary school educator*
Chang, Helen T. *municipal official*
Chang, Nancy T. *pharmaceutical executive*
Chapman, Cynthia B. *lawyer*
Charnveja, Pat S. *civic leader, former oil and gas industry executive*
Clark, Janet F. *corporate financial executive*
Cline, Vivian Melinda *lawyer*
Cole, Eleanor Ophelia *retired medical/surgical nurse*
Condit, Linda Faulkner *retired economist*
Conner, Beverly T. *counseling administrator, educator*
Cooper, Valerie Gail *minister*
Cupp, Aneta Joan *music educator*
Curtis, Barbara *consumer products company professional*
Daniels, Davetta Mills *principal*
Darst, Mary Lou *elementary school educator*
Davis, Debra Ann *secondary school educator*
Davis, Marlece (Alice Marlece Davis) *secondary school educator, director*
Davis-Lewis, Bettye *nursing educator*
Day, Twila M. *food service executive*
Decker-Barnhill, Jennifer Grace *performing company executive, educator*
Demouy, Alyson M. *social studies educator*
Dent, Leanna Gail *art educator*
de Vries, Robbie Ray Parsons *writer, illustrator, management consultant*
Dinkins, Carol Eggert *lawyer*
Donnelly, Rosemarie *lawyer*
Downing, Margaret Mary *newspaper editor*
Drew, Katherine Fischer *history professor*
Durham, Susan K. *research scientist*
Dybell, Elizabeth Anne Sledden *psychologist*
Ehlig-Economides, Christine A. *petroleum engineer*
Ehrmann, Susanna *language educator, photographer, writer*
Eisner, Diana *pediatrician*
Ellis, Juliet S. *bank executive*
Estes, Mary K. *virologist*
Eugeni, Michelle L. *academic administrator*
Farenthold, Frances Tarlton *lawyer*
Farley, Barbara L. *elementary school educator*
Feigin, Judith Zobel *educational psychologist*
Feigon, Judith Tova *ophthalmologist, educator, surgeon*
Fenn, Sandra Ann *programmer, analyst*
Flagg, Mary Kay *mathematics educator*
Flaitz, Catherine M. *dean, dental educator*
Fleming, Gloria Elaine *retired physician*
Florian-Lacy, Dorothy *social worker, educator*
Floyd, Kristi *counseling administrator*
Foger, Frances Murchison *minister*
Foote, Jill *investment banker, educator*
Foronda, Lisa *newscaster*
Foss, Michelle Michot *think-tank executive, economist*
Frank, Hilda Rhea Kaplan *dancer*
Friday, Leah Rebecca *portfolio manager*
Fryer, Shara *newscaster*
Funk, Edith Kay *minister, consultant, social worker*
Galvin, Kerry A. *lawyer*
Garay, Dolores Lollie *science educator*
Garrett, Mary Jane *director*
Gaston, Gina *newscaster*
Gaucher, Jane Montgomery *retail executive*
Gentry, Tina *secondary school educator*
Gerhart, Glenna Lee *pharmacist*
Gibson, Kathleen Rita *anatomy and anthropology educator*
Gigli, Irma *dermatologist, educator, academic administrator*
Gillette, Estella Hernandez *government agency administrator*
Gillmore, Kathleen Cory *lawyer*
Girouard, Peggy Jo Fulcher *ballet educator*
Golan, Yvette Y. *consumer products company executive, lawyer*
Goode, Coralyn *lawyer*
Goodwin, Heather Marie *educational consultant*
Greco, Janice Teresa *psychology educator*
Green, Sharon Jordan *interior decorator*
Greenberg, Angela Barmby *lawyer*
Grossett, Deborah Lou *psychologist, consultant*
Gunn, Joan Marie *health facility administrator*
Gunsel, Selda *chemical engineer, researcher*
Gupta, Monesha *pediatrician, educator*
Haensly, Patricia Anastacia *psychology professor*
Halas, Naomi J. *nanoscale science and engineering educator*
Harris, Deborah Ann *science educator*
Harris, Venita Van Caspel *retired financial planner*
Hattab, Helen Nathalie *philosophy professor*
Hattaway, Karen Ann *literature and language professor*
Hawkins, Barbara Reed *mental health nurse*
Hawkins, Ida Faye *elementary school educator*
Hazelip, Linda Ann *musician, small business owner, executive assistant*
Heeg, Peggy A. *lawyer, former gas industry executive*
Hempfling, Linda Lee *nurse*
Henderson, (Ruejenuia) Secret *social worker*
Higginbotham, Joan E. *astronaut*
Higgins, Pauline Edwards *lawyer*
Hinton, Paula Weems *lawyer*
Hire, Kathryn P. (Kay) *astronaut, military officer*
Hollingsworth, Lara Hudgins *lawyer*
Holmes, Ann Hitchcock *journalist*
Hornak, Anna Frances *library administrator*
Hughes, Mary Katherine *nurse*
Innes, Debbie *bank executive*
Ivins, Marcia S. *astronaut*
Jacobs, Tonya A. *lawyer*
James, Virginia Lynn *contracts executive*
Jeevarajan, Judith A. *chemist*
Jemison, Mae Carol *physician, engineer, entrepreneur, philanthropist, educator, former astronaut*
Jimmar, D'Ann *elementary school educator, educational consultant*
Johnson, Alisa B. *lawyer, energy company executive*
Johnson, Marilyn *retired obstetrician, retired gynecologist*
Johnson, Sandra Ann *counselor, educator*
Johnson, Thelma Jean *secondary school educator*
Joiner, Jamie A. *lawyer*
Jones, Edith Hollan *federal judge*
Jones, Edith Irby *internist*
Jones, Florence M. *music educator*
Jones, Sonia Josephine *advertising executive*
Kasi, Leela Peshkar *pharmaceutical chemist*
Kavandi, Janet Lynn *aerospace power engineer, chemist*
Kavraki, Lydia *computer scientist, educator*
Keating, Sister Kevina *nun, education educator*
Kerr, Tonya *newscaster*
Kiang, Ching-Hwa *chemical engineering educator*
King, Carolyn Dineen *federal judge*
King, Kay Wander *academic administrator, design educator, fashion designer, consultant*
Kingsley, Ellen *publishing executive*
Kmiec Roberts, Helen Marie *middle school educator*
Kneese, Carolyn Calvin *retired education educator*
Knickel, Carin S. *oil industry executive*
Konefal, Margaret Moore *health facility administrator, critical care nurse, nursing consultant, educator*
Kornbleet, Lynda Mae *insulation, fireproofing and acoustical contractor*
Kripke, Margaret Louise *immunologist, health facility executive*
Krumrey, Carolyn *mechanical engineer*
Kupiec, Suzanne L. *utilities executive*
Lacy, Terri *lawyer*
Lake, Kathleen Cooper *lawyer*
Lamb, Teryana R. *secondary school educator*
Landers, Susan Mae *psychotherapist, professional counselor*
Lawrence, Wendy B. *astronaut*
Lawson, Melanie Cerise *newscaster*
Lawson, Rhea Brown *library director*
LeBoff, Barbara *elementary school educator*
Lee, Janie C. *curator*
Lemark, Noreen Anne *retired neurologist*
Leveille, Nancy Anne *mathematics professor*
Lewis, Martha Nell *Christian educator, lay minister, expressive arts therapist*
Liberato, Lynne *lawyer*
Long, Suzanne Lynn *apparel executive*
Looper, Marcia Lynn *elementary school educator, consultant*
Lorelle, Linda *journalist*
Lucid, Shannon W. *biochemist, astronaut*
Lukens, Susan Ackley *school system administrator*
Lutz, Danielle Renee *academic administrator*
Mallia, Marianne *medical writer*
Maloney, Marilyn C. *lawyer*
Mampre, Virginia Elizabeth *communications executive*
Marek, Joycelyn *publishing executive*
Mathers, Paula Janecek *lawyer*
Matthews, Kathleen Shive *biochemistry educator*
Mattox, Sharon M. *lawyer*
Mayo, Marti *museum director, curator*
McCleary, Beryl Nowlin *volunteer, travel company executive*
McCollam, Marion Andrus *consulting firm executive, educator*
McDonald, Marilyn A. *academic assistant*
McFarland, Marcie Allred *lawyer*
McGregor, Jacqueline Carinhas *psychiatrist*
McMahon, Catherine Driscoll *lawyer*
McMahon, Susanna Rosemary *clinical psychologist, author*
McPhail, JoAnn Winstead *writer, art dealer*
McPherson, Alice Ruth *ophthalmologist, educator*
Melroy, Pamela Ann *astronaut*
Mermelstein, Isabel Mae Rosenberg *financial consultant*
Merrill, Connie Lange *chemical company executive*
Miller, Janel Howell *psychologist*
Miller, Sabrina Wares *librarian*
Mintz-Hittner, Helen Ann *physician, researcher*
Mitcham, Carla J. *utilities executive*
Montgomery, Denise Karen *nurse*
Moore, Lois Jean *health science facility administrator*
Morgan, Barbara R. *astronaut*
Moroney, Linda L.S. (Muffie) *lawyer, educator*
Morris, Carolyn S. *elementary school educator*
Morrison, Stacey *information scientist*
Mukai, Chiaki *astronaut*
Nacol, Mae *lawyer*
Nelson, Joelle Grace Kenney *lawyer*
Nesbitt, DeEtte DuPree *small business owner, investor*
Nesbitt, Virginia *retired special education educator, poet*
Noland, Mary Richerson *retired management consultant*
Noonan, Shauna Gay *petroleum engineer*
Nowak, Lisa M. *astronaut, military officer*
Ochoa, Ellen *astronaut*
Oglesby, GeorgAnn Hedlesten *lawyer*
O'Neil, Sharon Lund *educator*
Orr, Carole *artist*
Ouellette, Jami *art educator*
Owen, Jane Dale *non-profit organization executive*
Pali, Jennifer Rochelle *language educator*
Parle, Bertha Ibarra *writer*
Parnas-Simpson, Marianna *chorus director, singer*
Peabody, Arlene L. Howland Bayar *retired enterostomal therapy nurse*
Pector, Michelle D. *lawyer*
Pennington, Lisa H. *lawyer*
Perkyns, Jane Elizabeth *music educator, composer*
Peterson, Terry Norris *lawyer*
Phelps, Cynthia L. *medical educator*
Pilibosian, Michele Mason *lawyer*
Pospisil, JoAnn *historian, archivist*
Ramirez, Mari Carmen *curator*
Randolph, Lynn Moore *artist*
Rapoport, Nancy B. *law educator*
Reed, Kathlyn Louise *occupational therapist, educator*
Reid, Katherine Louise *artist, educator, writer*
Reiff, Patricia Hofer *space physicist, educator*
Rhinehart, Peta-gay Chen *nurse, consultant*
Robbins, Susan Paula *social work educator*
Roberts, Janet Lynn Lekowski *science educator*
Rogers, Virginia Marie Buxton *industrial psychologist*
Romero, Annette Louise *multi-media specialist, educator*
Roos, Sybil Friedenthal *retired elementary school educator*
Rose, Beatrice Schroeder (Mrs. William H. Rose) *harpist, educator*
Ross, Patti Jayne *obstetrics and gynecology educator*
Rowland, Kelly (Kelendria Trene Rowland) *singer*
Rusnak, Cyndi Moss *lawyer*
Rustay, Jennifer Beth *lawyer*
Sachse, Dominique *newscaster*
Saizan, Paula Theresa *business consultant*
Salazar, Josephine M. *behavioral health specialist*
Salomon, Lauren Manning *psychologist*
Sanderson, Mary Louise *medical association administrator*
San Pedro, Sylvia P. *mathematics educator, department chairman*
Santi, Kristi L. *special education educator, researcher*
Sazama, Kathleen *pathologist, lawyer*
Scarbrough, Sara Eunice *librarian, archivist, consultant*
Schachtel-Green, Barbara Harriet Levin *retired epidemiologist*
Scharold, Mary Louise *psychoanalyst, psychiatrist, educator*
Schier, Mary Jane *science writer*
Schott, Sally Maria *music publisher, arts education consultant*
Schultz, Arlene Elaine *literature educator*
Schulz, Amanda Jean *real estate consultant, lawyer*
Seaton, Alberta Jones *biologist, educator, consultant*
Shannon, Margaret Barrett *lawyer*
Shapiro, Beth Janet *librarian*
Shuart, Carey Chenoweth *farmer, volunteer*
Sisson, Virginia Baker *geology educator*
Smeal, Janis Lea *psychiatrist*
Smiley, Cindy York *psychotherapist educator*
Smith, Alison Leigh *lawyer*
Smith, Joellen *dean, literature and language educator*
Smith, Martha Lee *lawyer*
Smith-Vallejo, Lora Lee *elementary school educator*
Snowden, Bernice Rives *former construction company executive*
Solomon, Marsha Harris *draftsman, artist*
Sondock, Ruby Kless *retired judge*
Sparks, Donna L. *school librarian*
Spikes, Patricia White *medical technologist*
Spitz, Margaret R. *epidemiologist, researcher*
Stanton, Vivian Brennan (Mrs. Ernest Stanton) *retired counseling administrator*
Stefanyshyn-Piper, Heidemarie M. *astronaut*
Steinhoff, Judith B. *art history educator*
Stockholder, Jessica *sculptor*
Stripling, Kaye *school system administrator*
Strong, Louise Connally *geneticist*
Sullivan-Szuts, Betty Anne *academic administrator, educator*
Supak, Cathy Poerner *athletic trainer, educator*
Sweet, Portia Ann *retired human resources specialist*
Swoopes, Sheryl Denise *professional basketball player*
Tervalon, Josephine M. *psychotherapist, social worker*
Thomas, M. Ann *bank executive*
Thompson, Ewa M. *foreign language educator*
Thompson, Sandra Guerra *lawyer, educator*
Thompson-Draper, Cheryl L. *electronics executive, real estate executive*
Tolley, Michelle Renee *secondary school educator*
Townsend, Elizabeth Kathleen *performing arts educator*
Trichel, Mary Lydia *middle school educator*
Tripp, Karen Bryant *lawyer*
Tucker, Anne Wilkes *curator, historian, photographer, critic*
Turnbach, Ann *publishing executive*
Vallbona, Rima-Gretel Rothe *retired foreign language educator, writer*
Vance, Vanessa L. *lawyer*
Vassilopoulou-Sellin, Rena *researcher*
Vogel, Jennifer *lawyer*
Wacker-B., Deborah *secondary Spanish and special education educator*
Wagner, Charlene Brook *secondary school educator*

Wagner, Leslie *lawyer*
Walls, Martha Ann Williams (Mrs. B. Carmage Walls) *publishing executive*
Walshak, Mary Lynn *academic librarian*
Webb, Marty Fox *principal*
Wejman, Janet P. *information technology executive, air transportation executive*
Whiting, Martha Countee *retired secondary school educator*
Whitson, Peggy Annette *astronaut, biochemist*
Wike, D. Elaine *small business owner*
Wilkenfeld, Johannah *labor union administrator*
Wilkin, Alana Zimmer *elementary school educator*
Williams, Michelle (Tenetria Michelle Williams) *singer*
Williams, Sunita L. *astronaut*
Wilson, Stephanie D. *astronaut*
Wilson-Lawson, Melanie *social worker, educator*
Wirz, Melody *lawyer*
Woodward, Natalie E. *social studies educator*
Wyrsch, Martha B. *lawyer, energy executive*
Yeates, Marie R. *lawyer*
Zoghbi, Huda Y. *neurologist, geneticist, educator*

Hubbard
Schronk, Patricia Lynn *secondary school educator*

Humble
Burns, Angela Kaye *secondary school educator*
Chevalier, Denise Ann *director*
Howsmon, Debra Sue *biology educator*
Schindler, Gail Lewis *psychologist*

Huntsville
Gratz, Cindy Carpenter *dance educator, choreographer*
Hickey, Lady Jane *librarian, minister*
McGee, Carol A. *retired elementary school educator*

Hurst
Baw, Cindy A. *literature and language professor*
Bowman, Karmien C. *art educator, artist, sculptor, ceramist*
Buinger, Mary Kay *history professor*
Cruze, Jennifer Lea *secondary school educator*
Harper, Jane Armstrong *college administrator, consultant*
Hoffman, Katherine Ann *education educator*
Jacaruso, Diana *biology professor*
Lindsey, Jerri Kay *biologist, educator*

Hutto
Sanders, Sarah Lynne *small business owner, director*

Idalou
Beeler, Bulah Ray *retired medical/surgical nurse*

Iowa Park
Wright, Sabra Dell *music educator*

Irving
Blankenship, Cynthia L. *bank executive*
Brown, Linda Harper *bookkeeping company executive*
Burton, Betsey (Mary Elizabeth Burton) *retail executive*
Cavanaugh, Lucille J. *oil industry executive*
Cherri, Mona Y. *computer scientist, educator, computer scientist, consultant*
Clifford, Lori Bevis *anesthesiologist*
Echols, Kari Elizabeth *music educator, elementary school educator*
Geisinger, Janice Allain *accountant*
Jorden, Yon Yoon *health services company executive*
Lang, Laura Smith *lawyer*
Massah, Cherilyn *auditor*
Molay, Hilary S. *lawyer*
Natour, Nahille I. *obstetrician, gynecologist*
Phares, Sharon C. *elementary school educator*
Rutledge, Deborah Jean *secondary school educator*
Sherlock, Jo Anne C. *librarian*
Snyder, Dolores Wilma *culinary educator*
Stapleton, Claudia Ann *academic administrator*
Wenetschlaeger, Patty Strader *lawyer*

Italy
Lawson, Diane Marie *counselor*

Jacksonville
Rich, Mary Ruth *music educator*

Jasper
Bennett-Greenleaf, Linda Fay *special education educator*
Edwards, Charlotte Ann *elementary school educator*
Nolen, Darlene Elizabeth *small business owner*

Joaquin
Gill, Madeline Kay *school and youth counselor*

Johnson City
Pollock, Margaret Landau Peggy *elementary school educator*

Joshua
Curlee, Carol Wynette *mathematics educator, science educator, small business owner, Internet company executive*

Junction
Evans, Jo Burt *communications executive, rancher*

Justin
Hearn, Robin Kim *secondary school educator*

Katy
Batten-Bishop, Ann Louise *theater educator*
Fruia, Carolyn Christine *hair designer, educator*
Gentry, Mary Jean Asher *music educator*
Haymond, Paula J. *psychologist, diagnostician, hypnotherapist*

Keene
Bittiker, Marjorie Joanne *principal*
Taroy-Valdez, Lolita B. *nursing educator, nurse*

Keller
Smith, Eleanor Jane *retired university chancellor, consultant*

Kenedy
Perez, Irene *music educator, director*

Kennedale
Worley, Ruth *secondary school educator*

Kerrville
Abney, Denise Ann Cardin *psychologist, researcher*
Gregory, Patrice D. *retired nurse, small business owner*
Love, Susan L. *music educator*

Kilgore
Johnson, Flora Mae *retired elementary school educator*

Killeen
Jenkins, Sharon Leigh *special education educator*
McPherson, Katharyn Ross *elementary school educator*
Peronto, Janice Lynn *principal*

Kingsland
Watson, Elizabeth Marion *protective services official*

Kingsville
Beach, Regina Lee *librarian*
Doughty, Pamela D. *education educator*
Hernandez, Thelma Quintanilla *secondary school educator*
Stanford, (Frances) Jane Herring *management consultant, educator, writer*

Kingwood
Foreman, Gini Diane *English educator*
Lard, Pamula D. *special education educator*
von Dohlen, Elizabeth K. *secondary school educator*

Klein
Thompson, Patricia Rather *literature educator, department chairman*

Kyle
Saunders, Patricia Gene Knight *freelance writer, editor*

La Grange
Ledwik, Gretchen Marie *elementary school educator, art educator*

La Marque
Matthews, Evelyn J. *nurse*

La Porte
Edwards, Kristina Nell *elementary school educator*

Lackland Afb
Neal-Walden, Tracy A. *psychologist*

Lago Vista
Angelo, Julie Crawford *performing arts association administrator*

Lake Jackson
Hill, Diane Louise *educator*

Lakehills
Spears, Diane Shields *art director, elementary school educator*

Laredo
Chavez, Mary Rose *counselor, educator*
Colón, Phyllis Janet *retired city manager*
Gómez, Angela González *art educator*
Goodman, N. Jane *law librarian*
Gutierrez, Yvonne Soliz *school system administrator*
Heimes, Charmaine Marie *elementary school educator, poet, writer*
Hinojosa, Sandra Joy *elementary special education educator*
Lozano, Araceli E. *foundation administrator, consultant*
Mendiola, Anna Maria G. *mathematics educator*
Paton, Lisa Dupree *elementary school educator*
Riggs, William W. *social sciences educator*
Sierra, Maria Patricia *special education educator*
Vargas, Sylvia Elia *dentist, small business owner*
Weber, Janice Ann *library director, grant writer*
Whitehawk, Ann *secondary school educator*
Zaffirini, Judith *state legislator, small business owner*

Leander
Almour, Vicki Lynn *elementary school educator*
Craddock, Catherine Todd *accountant*
Fraley, Linda Williams Darnell *music educator*
Witt, Doreen Marie *sales executive*
Wood, Melissa Ann *music educator*

Lewisville
Dumbravo, Cathy Crosby *primary school educator*
Jones, Pamela Walsh *science educator*
Mebane, Barbara Margot *artistic director, choreographer*
Netz, Deborah Rudder *psychologist*
Warburton, Shelly Jo *music educator*
Whitney, Sharry Jan *science educator*

Lexington
Baxter-Kegler, Demetra M. *principal*

Linn
MacMullen, Patricia Ellen *theater educator, theater director*

Littlefield
Muller, Janice Elaine *secondary school educator*

Livingston
Gordon, Pamela Ann Wence *pianist*

Llano
Alston, Debbie A. *instructional technologist, educator*
Zachary, Jean *personnel director*

Lockhart
White, Patricia Ann *chemistry educator, medical technician*

Longview
Berry, Keysha Roshawn *science educator*
Bolomey, Rose L. *secondary school educator*
Byrd, Carol Ann *music educator*
Cuba, Mattie Deneice *elementary school educator*
Modisette, Barbara Jane *education educator, psychologist*
Myers, Adrienne Celeste *assistant principal*
Udy, Rae *columnist, writer*
White, Jennifer Sullivan *secondary school educator*
Wilcox, Nancy Diane *nursing home administrator*

Lorena
Maricle, Robyn LuAnn (Ford) *band director*

Lubbock
Bredeson, Cheryl *elementary school educator*
Bronwell, Nancy Brooker *writer*
Edwards, Shannon J. *science educator*
Hawkins, Ann R. *educator, researcher*
Hollingsworth, Margie Ellen *counselor*
Hurley, Kristie DeLynn *primary school educator*
Hurst, Mary Jane *language educator*
Illner-Canizaro, Hana *physician, researcher, oral surgeon*
Kraft, Leah Michelle *art educator*
Livermore, Jane *foundation executive*
Lovering, Emma *secondary school educator*
McMillan, Tobi A. *career planning administrator*
Miller, Patricia Anne *speech and language pathologist*
Parks, Katie Mae *human services manager*
Pitcock, Michelle Marie *science educator*
Reed, Teresa F. *science educator, elementary school educator*
Roy, Juliana W. *music educator*
Sharp, Marsha *basketball coach*
Smith, JoBeth *elementary school educator*
Wall, Betty Jane *real estate consultant*
Yoder-Wise, Patricia Snyder *nursing educator*
Young, Teri Ann Butler *pharmacist*

Lufkin
Harmon, Jacqueline Baas *minister*
Randell, Stephanie McMillan *biology professor*
Standerford, Catherine Ann *school nurse practitioner, director*
Williams, Mary Hickman *social worker*

Luling
Collie, Paula Renea *secondary school educator*

Lytle
Cigarroa, Josie A. *psychiatrist*

Mabank
Lindsley, Catherine S. *voice educator, director*

Magnolia
Adams, Shirley A. *mathematics educator*
Bopp, Annette Lee *mathematics educator*
Tarver, Betty Gail *music educator*

Mansfield
Barnett, Bertha L. Strickland *elementary school educator*
McNairn, Peggi Jean *speech pathologist, educator*

Marfa
Allison, Amy S. *secondary school educator*
Chambers Tucker, Johnnie L. *elementary school educator, rancher*
Wimberly, Cynthia Diane *mathematics educator*

Marshall
Helton, Karen Johnson *college administrator*
Magrill, Rose Mary *library director*
Peterson, Cynthia Lynn *library director, educator*

Mc Kinney
Albano, Christine Grace *lawyer*
Anderson-Bruess, Judith *social studies educator*
Dorff, Barbara L. *elementary and secondary school educator*
Forte, Christina Kirby *financial analyst*
Hutchison, Monica Leigh *music educator*
Kirkley, Vicki *school system administrator, director*

Mcallen
Huber, Melba Stewart *dance educator, dance studio owner, historian, retailer*
Spyker, Leola Edith *missionary*

Mercedes
Alaniz, Theodora Villarreal *elementary school educator*
Rogers, Colette *counseling administrator*
Streicher, Georgina Rodriguez *special education educator*

Mesquite
Byrd, Kathryn Susan *psychologist, educator*
Caruthers, Tara M. *physics educator*
Dean, Sherry Lynn *language educator, speech professional*
Grant, Betty Ruth *retired elementary school educator*
Holt, Mildred Frances *special education educator*
Pecina, Kristianne *secondary school educator*
Turner, LaNell Daphene *physical education educator*
Tustin, Karen Gail *mathematics educator*
Wyatt, Susan Skinner *education educator*

Mexia
Chambers, Linda Dianne Thompson *social worker*

Midland
Faught, Brenda Dorman *health sciences educator*
Grover, Rosalind Redfern *oil and gas company executive*
Lindsey-Hicks, Glenda *literature and language professor*
McCracken, Terri *elementary school educator*
Rowe, Mary R. *lawyer*
Sherpa, Fran Magruder *geography educator*
Welch, Lisa Renea *biology professor*
Wood, Stephanie *mathematics educator*

Midlothian
Alderman, Amy Joy Spigel *elementary school educator*

Mineola
McCann, Evelyn Louise Johnson *retired minister, retired counselor*

Mineral Wells
Sherrill, Helen White *elementary school educator*

Mission
Eyre, Pamela Catherine *retired career officer*

Missouri City
de Kanter, Ellen Ann *retired English and foreign language educator*
Rathnau, Heather Hearn *music educator, writer*
Sturhan, Courtney *secondary school educator*
Watson, Loretta *medical/surgical nurse*
Weber, Katie *retired special education educator*

Montgomery
Dossey, Nancy Ruthstrom *elementary education educator, consultant*
Gooch, Carol Ann *psychotherapist, consultant*
Orr, Heather Michelle *music educator, vocalist*

Mount Pleasant
Geffers, Betty J. *secondary school educator*

Muleshoe
Logsdon, Judith Kay *merchandiser, small business owner, apparel designer*

Murchison
Taweel, Janice M. *artist, educator*

Nacogdoches
Ashley, Janelle Coleman *academic administrator*
Bacarisse, Angela *design educator, costume designer*
Carter, Evelyn *retired elementary school educator*
Cole, Sandra Sue *healthcare educator*
Long, Penny *mathematics educator*
Offield, Carol Jean Dubberly *elementary school educator*

Natalia
Chew, Lynda Casbeer *elementary school educator*

Navasota
Coffey, Sharon Marie *music educator*
Day, Kathryn Ann *history educator*

Nederland
Martin, Angela Denise *educator*
Rozell, Linda Joy *art educator*

New Braunfels
Alexander, Anna Margaret *artist, writer, educator*
Barragăn, Celia Silguero *elementary school educator*
Gray, Cari Laird *economics educator*
Jaroszewski, Lisa Elaine *literature and language educator*
Ortiz, Denise M. *science educator*
Pharis, Ruth McCalister *retired bank executive*

New Caney
Hayes, Ann Carson *computer company executive*
Slade-Redden, Debra Kay *biology educator*

New Deal
Howell, Allie Rhea *retired educator*

Normangee
Stork, Vera Lee *retired elementary school educator*

North Richland Hills
Moody, Mary Doyle *elementary school educator*
Shier, Elizabeth M. *music educator*

Odessa
Braswell, Jody Lynn *gifted and talented educator*
Forsyth, Beverly K. (Beverly K. Roy Davidson Forsyth) *language educator, writer*
Price, Pamela Champion *art educator*
Rasor, Doris Lee *retired secondary school educator*
Rocha, Osbelia Maria Juarez *librarian, principal*

Omaha
Moos, Verna Vivian *special education educator*

Orange
Hannegan, Rebecca Ann *retired elementary school educator*
Stuntz, Billie Williams *pediatrician*

Ore City
Hill, Margaret Janell *elementary school educator*

Palestine
Meyer, Darla Anne *accountant*

Palo Pinto
Blissitte, Karen Dawn *elementary school educator*

Pampa
Nava, Mary Margaret *secondary school educator*
Willingham, Jeanne Maggart *performing arts educator, performing company executive*

Paris
Cannon, Jenene *music educator*
Hines, Jaclyn Letta *counseling administrator*

Proctor, June *retired religious organization administrator, writer*

Pasadena
Kenagy, Cheri Lynn *nurse*
Kotecki, Dawn Marie *social studies educator*
Ruiz, Miriam *secondary school educator*

Pearland
Chung, Linda H. *obstetrician, gynecologist*
Dawson, Besse Malinda Barker *secondary school educator, department chairman*
Furnari, Rosemarie Ann *secondary school educator, real estate agent*
Hutsell, Janice *nurse midwife*

Pecos
Florez, Diane O. *county clerk*
Purcell, Bonnie Lou *librarian*

Perryton
Blasingame, Janet Lynn *primary school educator*

Pflugerville
Munzer, Annette Elizabeth *cultural affairs consultant*

Placedo
Rivera, Josie *elementary school educator*

Plainview
Dayton, Leah Jane *secondary school educator*
Pitts, Sharon Ann Gammage *nursing administrator*
Ticer, Terri Jean *sales executive*

Plano
Ansari, Anousheh *digital home and multimedia management technology company executive, first female civilian space traveler*
Becker, Doreen Doris *medical/surgical nurse*
Bober, Joanne L. *lawyer*
Boggan, Amy L. *secondary school educator, education educator*
Brown, Peggy Ann *language educator, writer*
Carver, Rita *not-for-profit fundraiser, consultant*
Dyer, Stephanie Jo *anesthesiologist*
Etheridge, Susan B. *social worker*
Evans, Pat *mayor*
Gallardo, Henrietta Castellanos *writer*
Gordon, Storrow Moss *information technology executive, lawyer*
Haggard, Geraldine Langford *primary school educator, adult education educator, consultant, writer*
Jacoby, Teresa Michelle *zoologist, consultant, small business owner, entrepreneur*
Kuddes, Kathryn M. *fine arts director*
Larsen, Paula Anne *operating room nurse*
Litwin, Ruth Ann Forbes *artist*
Newman, Deborah Rae *minister*
Reidling, Valerie Ann *secondary school educator*
Samford, Karen Elaine *small business owner, consultant*
Sivinski, Tina M. *human resources specialist*
Tucker, Ann *secondary school educator*
Verges, Marianne Murphree *writer*
Weeks, Tresi Lea *lawyer*
West, Catherine G. *retail executive*

Port Aransas
Beimers, Gertrude Hii *writer*
Turner, Elizabeth Adams Noble (Betty Turner) *real estate company executive*

Port Arthur
Wade, Ernestine *public health nurse*

Port Lavaca
Boyd, Ann Fisher *office administrator*
Fisher, Jewel Tanner (Mary Fisher) *retired construction company executive*

Portland
Culbertson, Deborah Jean *educational consultant*

Post
Neff, Marie Taylor *museum director, artist*

Pottsboro
Thomas, Ann Van Wynen *retired law educator*

Powell
Emerson, Harriett Anne *small business owner*

Prairie View
Barber-Freeman, Pamela Telia *mathematician, educator, researcher*
De Luna-Gonzalez, Elma *accountant, academic administrator*
Prestage, Jewel Limar *political science professor*

Priddy
Zimmer, Greta Gay *secondary school educator*

Quanah
Lee, Carol *lyricist, artist*

Quitman
Beverly, Kelly Dee Gray *elementary school educator*

Randolph Afb
Brennan-Bergmann, Bridget Catherine *special education educator*

Red Oak
Jones, Genia Kay *critical care nurse, consultant*
Kerzee, Beth Bumpas *music educator*
Shaw, Sue Ann *medical transcriptionist*

Richardson
Austin, Ann Sheree *lawyer*
Bray, Carolyn Scott *education educator*
Brooke, Melody *counselor, marriage and family therapist*
Carlson, Catherine Kossan *secondary school educator*
Dethrage, Debbie J *educational consultant*
Goodspeed, Linda A. *manufacturing executive*
Overall, Theresa Lynne *elementary school educator*
Salter, Elizabeth Mary *academic administrator*
Tipping, Sharon Rutledge *elementary school educator*
Unkenholz, Karla J. *elementary school educator*
White, Irene *insurance professional*
Whitt, Margaret Jean *educator*
Wood, Peggy *secondary school educator*

Richland Hills
Haynes, Ruth Elaine *accountant*

Richmond
Clark, Ruth Mae *music educator*
Rine, Patty Davis *music educator*

Rio Grande City
Lung, Auristela R. *music educator*

Rockdale
Estell, Dora Lucile *retired educational administrator*

Rockport
Acker, Virginia Margaret *nursing consultant*
Owen, Molly Jackson *music educator*

Rockwall
Anderson, Leslie Ann *secondary educator*
Johnston, Nicklett Rose *research nurse, clinical perfusionist*
Tucker, Kimberly Joan *music educator*

Rogers
Dolan, Andrea *secondary school educator*

Roscoe
Beeks, Cheryl Elaine *elementary school educator*

Rosenberg
Haygood, Eithel Marinella *artist, educator*
Lefler, Sherry LynettE *elementary school educator*
Slack, Molly Johanna *theater educator*
Trevino, Katherine Ann *elementary school educator*
Welch, Frances Suzanne *director*
White, Gretchen Nance *education educator, writer*

Rosharon
Lopez, Placida Ramos *elementary school educator*

Round Rock
Benford, Catherine S. *music educator*
Goodman, Kim *marketing professional, computer company executive*
Ledbetter, Sharon Faye Welch *retired educational consultant*
Mountain, Janet *foundation administrator, former computer company executive*
Nero, Molly Joanna *elementary school educator*
Sheskey, Susan E. *computer company executive*

Royse City
Atkins, Janet Necette *science educator, department chairman*

Rusk
Cook, Doris Adele *artist*
Hendrick, Zelwanda *performing arts educator, psychology educator*
Holder, Maxine E. *writer*

Sachse
Conoly, Kimberly Lane *dance studio owner*

San Angelo
Chatfield, Mary Van Abshoven *librarian*
Childress, Susan Lynette *retired elementary school educator*
Crenshaw, Rebecca Sue *physician*
Furlong, Ebba Von *science educator*

San Antonio
Accountius, Patricia L. *dietician, consultant*
Adcox, Mary Sandra *dietician, consultant*
Anderson, Anita L. *psychology professor*
Austin, Lola Houston *psychologist*
Avant, Patricia Kay *nursing educator*
Azzi, Jennifer L. *professional basketball player*
Bagin, Katherine *telecommunications industry executive*
Beauchamp, Francis Drake *real estate agent*
Beechinor, Diane Blanche *education educator*
Benavides, Deborah Ann *academic advisor*
Bennett, Sister Elsa Mary *retired secondary school educator*
Bivens, Lydia Ruth *librarian*
Bosquez, Joy Denise *elementary school educator*
Bowers, Kim *lawyer, energy executive*
Brown, Mary Rose *energy executive*
Burke, Betty Jane *retired real estate manager*
Callihan, D. Jeanne *psychologist, educator*
Carstensen, Maria Elena *academic administrator*
Case, Elizabeth Joy *psychology and educational assessment director*
Celmer, Virginia *psychologist*
Condos, Barbara Seale *real estate broker, developer, investor*
Condrill, Jo Ellaresa *freelance/self-employed small business owner, writer, consultant*
Corrigan, Helen González *retired cytologist*
Corrigan, Paula Ann *military officer, internist*
Crichton, Flora Cameron *volunteer, foundation administrator*
Cruz, Rosalina Sedillo *marriage and family therapist*
Cusack, Regina M. *psychology professor, lawyer*
Dacbert-Friese, Sharyn Varhely *social worker, evangelist*
Delaney, Maria Cissy *elementary school educator*
DeNice, Marcella Louise *counselor*
Donelson, Rosemarie Quiroz Carvajal *human services professional, state official*
Downing, Jane Katherine *psychiatric nurse practitioner, lawyer*
Dyas, Anna Marie *gifted and talented educator*
Edson, Marian Louise *communications executive*
Emery, Nancy Beth *lawyer*
Evans, Betty Vaughn *minister*
Faules, Barbara Ruth *retired elementary school educator*
Fischer, Marsha Leigh *retired civil engineer*
Flaherty, Sergina Maria *ophthalmic medical technologist*
Ford, Barbara G. *secondary school educator*
Foster, Nancy Haston *columnist, writer*
Funk, Charlotte Marie *art educator, artist*
Ghinaudo, Penny Alicia *science educator, department chairman*
Groos, April Cox *secondary school educator*
Gruenbeck, Laurie *librarian*
Hall, Denise *special education educator*
Hancock, Kathleen J. *political science professor*
Heloise, *columnist, writer*
Henderson, Connie Chorlton *retired city planner, artist, writer*
Hernandez, Adriana *athletic trainer*
Hoag, Rebecca Ebner *literature and language educator*
Hood, Sandra Dale *librarian*
Hudspeth, Almetra Kavanaugh *retired elementary school educator*
Hyman, Betty Harpole *technology executive*
Jary, Mary Canales *business owner*
Jennings, Karen *human resources specialist, telecommunications industry executive*
Johnson, Anne Stuckly *retired lawyer*
Johnson, Shannon *professional basketball player*
Keck, Judith Marie Burke *business owner, retired career officer*
Kosty, Carlita *secondary school educator*
Labenz-Hough, Marlene *mediator*
LeFevre, Geraldine *librarian*
Lenke, Joanne Marie *publishing executive*
Madrid, Olga Hilda Gonzalez *retired elementary school educator, school system administrator*
Marshall, Joyce Ramsey *secondary school educator*
Marvin, Catherine A. *financial consultant*
Masters, Bettie Sue Siler *biochemist, educator*
McCray, Nikki Kesangame *professional basketball player*
McSorley, Rita Elizabeth *adult education educator*
Moltz, Beverly Ann *elementary school educator*
Moss, Betty Harris *secondary education educator*
Murphy, Andra Brown *theater arts director, educator*
Myers, Ellen Howell *historian, educator*
Nance, Betty Love *librarian*
Nava, Carmen P. *communications executive*
Nelson, Glenda Kay *special education educator*
Newton, Virginia *archivist, historian, librarian*
Oleszkiewicz-Peralba, Malgorzata *Latin American literature and culture studies educator*
Oppenheim, Martha Kunkel *pianist, educator*
Patterson, Jan Evans *epidemiologist, educator*
Pawel, Nancy Emma Ray *oil industry executive, educator, artist*
Penrod, HazelL. L. *music educator*
Pitluk, Ellen Eidelbach *lawyer, mediator*
Potts, Martha Lou *elementary school educator*
Reed, Susan D. *prosecutor*
Rich, Melody M. *music educator, singer, conductor*
Robinson, Joyce Elaine *science educator*
Roy, Anuradha *statistician, educator, researcher*
Sanchez, Susie Riojas *elementary school educator*
Sarinana, Silvia *art educator*
Savala, Lindsay Kaye *athletic trainer*
Schuk, Linda Lee *legal assistant, business educator*
Spears, Sally *lawyer*
Stanson, Kay V. *elementary school educator, consultant*
Tackett, Susan J. *language educator*
Titzman, Donna M. *energy executive*
Todd, Jan Theresa *counselor*
Tschoepe, Deborah E. *special education educator*
Turner, Judy C. *research scientist*
Vargas-Tonsing, Tiffanye *medical educator*
Vinson, Audrey Lawson *retired literature and language professor*
von Raffler-Engel, Walburga (Walburga Engel) *retired language educator*
Wang, Yufeng *science educator*
Welch, Muriel Ruth *religious organization administrator*
White, Mary Ruth Wathen *social services administrator*
Williams, Docia Schultz *small business owner*
Williams-Perry, Brenda Lee *pre-school educator*
Wilson, F. Jill *real estate company executive, internet consultant*
Winstead, Antoinette Fay *performing arts educator*
Wise, Christina Renée *school disciplinarian*
Wiskocil, Angiolina *telecommunications industry executive*
Woodson, Linda Townley *English educator, writer*
Worth, Diane Bernice *physical education educator*
Yerkes, Susan Gamble *newspaper columnist*

San Marcos
Allsup, Roxane Cuellar *curriculum and instruction educator*
Carman, Mary Ann *retired special education educator*
Dowling, Catherine Lynn *secondary school educator*
Fischer, Joyce Faye *engineering educator*
Imel, Elizabeth Carmen *retired physical education educator*
Martin, Jerri Whan *public relations executive*
Taylor, Ruth Arleen Lesher *marketing educator*
Treanor, Betty McKee *interior design educator*

Sanger
Alexander, Vickie Lynn *music educator*

Santa Fe
Jernigan, Vicki Louise MacKechney *clinical nurse specialist*
Lambert, Willie Lee Bell *mobile equipment company owner, educator*
Paratore-Zarzana, Mary Gay *artist, art educator, lecturer*

Scurry
Newkirk, Trixie Darnell *family nurse practitioner*

Seabrook
Sterling, Shirley Frampton *artist, educator*
Woods-Stellman, Donna Sue *education educator, consultant*

Sealy
Stevens, Rhea Christina *lawyer*

Seguin
Miller, Bonnie Ruth *retired elementary school educator*

Selma
(Marbach) Miller, Amanda Joy *educator*
Sharp, Bridget Marie *science educator*

Seminole
Hill, Catherine Louise *secondary school educator*
Whitfield, Karen Kay *music educator*

Shamrock
Hervey, Nina Fern *retired church administrator, minister*

Shelbyville
Lifshutz, Melanie Janet Bell *patient education, medical, and surgical nurse*

Shepherd
Busteed, Diana Lynn *speech educator, theatre director*

Sherman
Carnes, La Zetta *retired secondary school educator*
Chavez-Hill, Tammy Lynn *elementary school educator*
Neathery, Cheryl Alissa *secondary school educator*
Williams, Ruby Jo *retired principal*

Smithville
Clark, LaVerne Harrell *writer*
Johnson, Melody Jean *special education educator*
Meyer, Donna W. *medical educator, director*
Scott, Mary Edith *special education educator*

Snyder
Barnes, Maggie Lue Shifflett (Mrs. Lawrence Barnes) *nurse*
Gray, Donna Lea *small business owner*

Somerville
Hairrell, Angela Renee *humanities educator, researcher*

Southlake
Arafat-Johnson, Danyah *secondary school educator, director*
Grosklos, Hollie Jo *music educator*
Peluso, Michelle *Internet company executive*
Sorge, Karen Lee *printing company executive, consultant*

Spring
Calabro, Joanna Joan Sondra *artist*
Jackson, Guida Myrl *writer, editor, literature educator*
Neill, Rebecca Anne *middle school educator*
Wasson, Kristi Byas *secondary school educator*
Westover, Diana Kay *interior designer, executive recruiter*
Wilbanks, Mary *artist*

Spurger
Gardner, Susan Kay *elementary school educator*

Stafford
Cahilly, Karen L. *quality assurance professional*
Hayes, Joyce Merriweather *retired secondary school educator*
Krenek, Mary Louise *political scientist, researcher*
Le, Duy-Loan *electrical engineer*
Wiersema, Donna Sanders *science educator*

Stephenville
Bane, Alma Lynn *computer scientist, educator, director*
McElroy, Linda Sue *retired elementary school educator*
Stricker, Mary Fran *music educator*

Sugar Land
Cleveland, Stephanie McDowell *secondary school educator*
Forbes, Sharon Elizabeth *software engineer*
Hall, Georganna Mae *elementary school educator*
Hosley, Marguerite Cyril *civic worker*
Keefe, Carolyn Joan *tax accountant*
Knight, Brenda Jean *mathematics educator*
Lankford, Janna Louise *social studies educator*
Matney, Judy McCaleb *secondary school educator*
Slack-Beard, Kay Lane *secondary school educator*
Waihman, Lisa Girard *mathematics educator*

Sulphur Springs
Alexander, Silvesta *elementary school educator*
Clayton, Pamela Sanders *special education educator*
Gibson, Jannette Poe *educational consultant*
Hadlow, Vivian Jean *elementary school educator, retired principal*

Sunnyvale
Parmenter, Kelli Denise *elementary school educator, small business owner*

Sweetwater
Taylor, Martha Sue *librarian*

Taylor Lake Village
Jenicek, Alicia Joanne *nursing consultant*

Temple
Cavanaugh, Rebecca Jo *medical nurse*
Frost, Juanita Corbitt *retired hospital foundation coordinator*
Hildebrand, Mary Sue *elementary school educator, principal*
Hoelscher, Margie Lynn *nurse*
Jackson, Karen *elementary school educator*

East Barre
Coughenour, Carrie Lee *music educator*

East Calais
Elliott, Susan Auguste *psychologist, psychotherapist, consultant*

East Dorset
Howe, Nancy *artist*

East Thetford
Cummings Rockwell, Patricia Guilbault *psychiatric nurse*

Essex Junction
Dietzel, Louise Alverta *psychologist*
Tedd, Monique Micheline *artist*

Hyde Park
Towle, Melissa Manchester *music educator*

Jacksonville
Hein, Karen Kramer *pediatrician, epidemiologist*

Johnson
Whitehill, Angela Elizabeth *artistic director*

Killington
Curtis, Sally Diane *educational consultant*

Lyndonville
Moore, Carol A. *academic administrator*
Werdenschlag, Lori B. *psychologist, educator*

Manchester Center
Sandler, Anita *singer, artist*
Waldinger Seff, Margaret *special elementary education educator*

Marshfield
Thomas, Susan Beth *writer*

Middlebury
Forman, Michele *secondary school educator*
Karnes, Elizabeth Helen *academic professional, television producer*
Lamberti, Marjorie *retired social studies educator*
Nuovo, Betty A. *state representative*
Spatafora, Grace Ann *biology professor*

Milton
Rivero, Marilyn Elaine Keith *state legislator*

Montgomery Center
Oktavec, Eileen M. *anthropologist, artist*

Montpelier
Blanchard, Margaret Moore *writer, educator*
Errecart, Joyce *lawyer*
Erskine, Kali (Wendy Colman) *psychoanalyst*
Johnson, Denise Reinka *state supreme court justice*
Markowitz, Deborah Lynn *state official*
Skoglund, Marilyn *state supreme court justice*
Talbot-Kelly, Samantha Rachel *artist*

Moretown
Hartshorn, Brenda Bean *elementary school educator*

Morrisville
Lechevalier, Mary Pfeil *retired microbiologist, educator*

North Bennington
Feidner, Mary P. *retired speech and language pathologist*

North Ferrisburg
Tulin, Marna *psychotherapist*

Norwich
Carlson, Elizabeth Borden *historian, educator*

Pittsfield
Wacker, Susan Regina *graphics designer, consultant*

Plainfield
Jervis, Jane Lise *academic administrator, historian*

Plymouth
Bittinger, Cynthia Douglas *foundation executive*

Poultney
Cooper, Charleen Frances *special and elementary education educator*
Keezer, Deborah Ann *elementary school educator*

Putney
Gill, Jane Roberts *retired psychotherapist, clinical social worker*
Loring, Honey *small business owner*

Randolph
French, Patsy *property manager, state representative*

Randolph Center
Murray, Nancy Jean *language educator, humanities educator*

Richmond
Fary, Sandra Suzanne *science educator*

Rutland
Calabrese, Eleanor Wallace *social worker*
Ferraro, Betty Ann *retired state senator*
Thompson, Marie Angela *computer engineer, consultant*

Saint Albans
Keenan, Kathleen *state legislator*

Saxtons River
Bosworth, Mary Jane *retired music educator*

South Duxbury
Villemaire, Diane Davis *science educator*

Stowe
Beach, Lisa Forster (Elizabeth Forster Beach) *artist, educator*

Swanton
Suitor, Dorcas P. *elementary school educator*

Thetford
Paley, Grace *author, educator*

West Burke
Van Vliet, Claire *artist*

White River Junction
Bohi, Lynn *state legislator*
Rutter, Frances Tompson *retired publisher*

Williston
Laskarzewski, Debra Sue *language educator*
Oakes, Jennifer Sharyl *physical education educator, athletic director, coach*

Winooski
Lemaire-Jenkins, Elizabeth Anne *psychotherapist*

Woodstock
Piccoli, Susan Elizabeth *secondary school educator*

VIRGINIA

Abingdon
Ball, Amy Catherine *education program manager*
Humphreys, Lois H. *retired realtor*
Jones, Mary Trent *endowment fund trustee*
Miller, Janice Brice *art educator*
Ramos-Cano, Hazel Balatero *caterer, chef, innkeeper, restaurateur, entrepreneur*
Williams, Barbara Kitty *nursing educator*

Afton
McCoy, Sue *retired surgeon, biochemist, bioethicist*

Alexandria
Bartlett, Elizabeth Susan *audio-visual specialist*
Berger, Patricia Wilson *retired librarian*
Blue, Catherine Anne *lawyer*
Brophy, Deborah Susan *secondary school educator*
Bryant, Anne Lincoln *educational association executive*
Budde, Mitzi Marie Jarrett *librarian*
Butler, Susan Lowell *educational association executive, writer*
Bynum, Gayela A. *public information officer*
Campagna, Dianna Gwin *real estate broker*
Ciofalo, Carol Ellen *obstetrician, gynecologist*
Collins, Cardiss *retired congresswoman*
Collins, Mary *writer, educator*
Connell, Mary Ellen *diplomat*
Coons, Barbara Lynn *public relations executive, librarian*
Cross, Dorothy Abigail *retired librarian*
Daly, Kay R. *public relations professional*
Davis, Ruth Margaret (Mrs. Benjamin Franklin Lohr) *information technology executive*
Drickey, Ruth Irene *elementary school educator*
Edgell, Karin Jane *special education educator, reading specialist*
Fisher, Colleen M. *trade association administrator*
Fitzgerald, Marilyn Hicks *health science association administrator*
Flippo, Karen Francine *social welfare administrator*
Fosdick, Cora Prifold (Cora Prifold Beebe) *management consultant*
Foster, Serrin Marie *non-profit organization executive*
Freeman-Wilson, Karen *retired state attorney general, prosecutor, educational association administrator*
Gallagher, Anne Porter *communications executive*
Ginsberg, Nina *lawyer*
Goodman, Sherri Wasserman *lawyer*
Grachek, Marianna Kern *healthcare administrator*
Greenstein, Ruth Louise *think-tank executive, lawyer*
Greer, Frances Ellen DuBois, Jr., (Nancy Greer Jr., Nancy Greer Hamilton) *retired statistician, volunteer*
Gurke, Sharon McCue *career officer*
Hallman, Linda D. *medical association administrator*
Haygood, Alma Jean *elementary school educator*
Higgins, Mary Celeste *lawyer, researcher*
Hughes, Grace-Flores *federal agency administrator*
Johnson, JoAnn Mardelle *federal agency administrator*
Johnson, Marlys Marlene *elementary school educator*
Kaye, Ruth Lincoln *historian*
Kelly, Nancy Frieda Wolicki *lawyer*
Kerger, Paula Arnold *broadcast executive*
Kim, Sook Cha *artist*
Kratovil, Jane Lindley *think tank associate, not-for-profit developer*
Lachance, Janice Rachel *professional association administrator, retired federal agency administrator, lawyer*
Lendsey, Jacquelyn L. *foundation administrator*
Leonhart, Michele Marie *federal agency administrator*
Lewin, Cynthia M. *lawyer*
Lightner, Candy (Candace Lynne Lightner) *non-profit management consultant, advocate*
Lipnick, Anne Ruth *advocate*
Lockett, Barbara Ann *librarian*
Lopatin, Carol Keesler *artist*
Lynn, Barbara Hoffman *music educator*
Maehara, Paulette V. *fundraising executive*
Matalin, Mary *political consultant*
Meisinger, Susan *human resources specialist*
Napier, Lisa Briggs *maternal/child health nurse*
Nesbitt, Wanda L. *ambassador*
Nicholas, Lynn B. *medical association administrator*
Nodeen, Janey Price *information technology executive*
Palma, Dolores Patricia *urban planner, consultant, writer*
Paulson, Gwen O. Gampel *government relations consultant, life and leadership coach*
Pearson, Lynda Ann *music educator*
Piecuch, Diane Marie *music educator*
Plitt, Jeanne Given *librarian*
Rae, Jeneanne *new product development and innovation development consultant, educator*
Rassai, Rassa *electrical engineering educator*
Richman, Arleen *professional society administrator*
Sampson, Jeanne Louise *retired special education educator*
Schmidt, Joan E. *educational association administrator*
Simonds, Marie Celeste *architect*
Slutsky, Bernice *agricultural products executive*
Stone, Ann Elizabeth *marketing agency executive, consultant, entrepreneur, volunteer*
Stone, Ann E.W. *marketing executive*
Sturtevant, Brereton *retired lawyer, retired federal official*
Tarr, Linda Haas *psychologist*
Tucker, Karen Sue *association executive*
Tyler, Cecilia Kay *retired military officer*
Vosbeck, Elizabeth Just *retired geneticist*
Wainscott, Cynthia *medical association administrator*
Whitson, Elizabeth Temple *graphics designer*
Winzer, P.J. *lawyer*
Woolley, Mary Elizabeth *science administrator, advocate*

Amelia Court House
Sampson, Mary Pond *special education educator*

Amissville
Hunter, Beverly Claire *research scientist, educator*

Annandale
Abdellah, Faye Glenn *retired public health service executive*
Carvalho, Julie Ann *psychologist*
Freeman, Baba Foster *editor*
Passut, Christine Diana *special education educator*
Seyler, Dorothy U. *literature and language professor, writer*
Somers, Janice A. *elementary school educator*
Wilhelmi, Mary Charlotte *education educator, academic administrator*

Appomattox
Pickrel, Felicia Renee *science educator*

Arlington
Askey, Thelma J. *federal agency administrator*
Baginski, Maureen A. *former federal agency administrator*
Beier, Anita P. *air transportation executive*
Binkowski, Sylvia Julia *water transportation executive, consultant*
Boesz, Christine C. *science foundation administrator*
Buchanan, Louise *political organization worker, consultant*
Bulkeley, Christy Claire *foundation administrator*
Bune, Karen Louise *state agency administrator*
Cehelsky, Marta *scientific organization executive*
Choksi, Mary *investment company executive*
Claussen, Eileen Barbara *environmental services administrator, former federal agency administrator*
Dalglish, Lucy Ann *lawyer, organization executive*
Davis, Lynn Etheridge *political scientist, educator*
Dorman, Janet Lee Vosper *elementary school educator*
Durham, Mary Sherrill *psychologist, writer*
Earl, Sister Patricia Helene *religious studies educator, director*
Ellinwood, Janice Greenberg *art educator*
Finta, Frances Mickna *secondary school educator*
Gramm, Wendy Lee *economics professor, retired government agency administrator*
Haggett, Rosemary Romanowski *academic administrator*
Harker, Victoria D. *electric power industry executive*
Harrison, Virginia M. *federal agency administrator*
Heivilin, Donna Mae *retired government executive*
Hickman, Elizabeth Podesta *retired counselor*
Highsmith, Wanda Law *retired medical association administrator*
Ifill, Gwen *moderator, political reporter*
Johnson, Rosemary Wrucke *personnel management specialist*
Klestzick, Barbara R. *social worker, educator*
Kline, Carol Marleigh *editor, writer*
Krusa-Dossin, Mary Ann *military officer*
Langley, Patricia Ann *lobbyist*
Lanier, Elizabeth K. *lawyer*
Lauderdale, Katherine Sue *lawyer*
Lieber, Carole Marguerite Renee *human resources specialist, consultant*
Lurie, Nicole *former health science association administrator*
Markessini, Joan *research scientist, psychologist*
McCarthy, Jane McGinnis *retired government agency administrator*
Mc Donald, Gail Faber *musician, educator*
Meadows, Vickers B. *federal agency administrator*
Mullett, Jennifer Anne *lawyer*
Nash, Cathy L. *meeting planner*
Neel, Barbara Anne Spiess *elementary school educator, artist*
Ochoa-Brillembourg, Hilda Margarita *investment banker*
Olsen, Kathie Lynn *science foundation director*
O'Sullivan, Lynda Troutman *lawyer*
Owen, Sarah-Katharine *language educator*
Pendleton, Mary Catherine *retired foreign service officer*
Pfister, Karstin Ann *human services administrator*
Porte, Barbara Ann *writer, librarian*
Rabbitt, Linda *construction executive*
Raizen, Senta Amon *educational association administrator, researcher*
Ramaley, Judith Aitken *retired academic administrator, endocrinologist*
Randolph, Carolyn *educational association administrator, educator*
Reiss, Susan Marie *editor, writer*
Rockefeller, Sharon Percy *broadcast executive*
Rogers, Sharon J. *education consultant*
Runkle, Beatriz Pamela *pediatrician, educator*
Siddayao, Corazón Morales *economist, educator, consultant*
Siegel, Laurie F. *accountant, painter*
Straus, Patricia W. *artist, retired educator*
Strelau, Renate *historical researcher, artist*
Sundquist, M. Alexandra (Alix Sundquist) *diplomat, consultant*
Swenson, Diane Kay *legal association administrator*
Thompson, Geraldine Kelleher Richter *retired orthopedist*
Vasquez, Jo Anne *retired science educator*
Wells, Christine *foundation executive*
Whitfield, Margaret Denny *retired music educator*
Whyte, Nancy Gooch *microbiologist*
Wilcox, Shirley Jean Langdon *genealogist*
Wise, Kathryn E *marketing professional*

Aroda
Nisly, Loretta Lynn *obstetrical nurse, geriatrics nurse*

Ashburn
Alison, Allison Merkle *secondary school educator, lawyer*
Bishop, Carol *oil industry executive*
Glick, Paula Florence *art historian, author, lecturer*
Gross, Linda Armani *social studies educator*
Newell, Rachel Pierce *music educator*
Trent, Grace Chen *communications executive*
Tribié, Amy Kathleen *music educator*

Ashland
Allen, Kimberly Ferrick *elementary school educator*
Polce-Lynch, Mary Elise *psychologist*

Assawoman
Holley, Pamela Spencer *retired librarian*

Barboursville
Slater, Valerie Periolat *volunteer*

Berryville
Martin, Alison Cady *interior designer*

Big Island
Durham, Betty Bethea *therapist*

Blacksburg
Blanchard, Dorothy Hardt *academic administrator, volunteer*
Bliznakov, Milka Tcherneva *architect, educator*
Campbell, Joan Virginia Loweke *secondary school educator, language educator*
Conrad, Sherry K. Lynch *counselor*
Gablik, Suzi *art educator, writer*
Hirt, Joan B. *education educator*
Hovakimyan, Naira *mathematician, educator*
Schmittmann, Beate *physics professor*
Weaver, Pamela Ann *education educator*

Bluemont
Johnson, Evelyn Porterfield *journalist, educator*

Boones Mill
Oyler, Amy Elizabeth *medical/surgical nurse*

Boyce
Bryant, Paula Jean *music educator*

Bristol
Cooper, Carlotta Arlene *writer, animal breeder*
Hagy, Teresa Jane *elementary school educator*
Wade, Thelma J. *lawyer, mental health nurse*

Bristow
Livengood, Carol Ann *elementary school educator*

Burke
Barrile, Judith *science educator, consultant*
Brant, Jacquelyn Lois *secondary school educator, history educator, department chairman*
Prieto, Nycthia Ophelia M. *realtor*

Callao
Freeman, Anne Hobson *language educator, writer*
Sisson, Jean Cralle *retired elementary school educator*

Capeville
Spady, Joanne Smith *secondary school educator*

Carrollton
Willard, Karen Walters *music educator*

Catawba
Bartizal, Denise *psychologist*

Centreville
De Gennaro, Eida Mendoza *interpreter, real estate agent*
Eisenberg, Sue Ann *music educator*
Hand, Antoinette Marie *accountant*

Chantilly
Austin, Wanda Murry *systems engineer*
Bergman, Nomi *communications executive*
Messinger, Holly Lynn *secondary school educator*
Sullivan, Penelope Dietz *computer software development company executive*

Charlottesville
Andrews, Minerva Wilson *retired lawyer*
Armacost, Barbara Ellen *law educator*
BeVier, Lillian Riemer *law educator*
Bishop, Ruth Ann *coloratura soprano, voice educator*
Bly-Monnen, April M. *quality assurance professional*
Brettschneider, Cathie I. *editor*
Brodrick, Sheri Mary-Ann *secondary school educator*

Brown, Rebecca Sue *director*
Buck, D. Ruth *legal research and writing educator*
Chase, Karen Susan *English literature educator*
Coughlin, Anne M. *law educator*
Dalton, Claudette Ellis Harloe *anesthesiologist, educator, dean*
DeGaynor, Elizabeth Anne *secondary school educator*
Dove, Rita Frances *poet, language educator*
Fitchett, Taylor *law librarian*
Forrest, Patricia Anne *publishing executive, editor*
Friedman, Susan Lynn Bell *economist*
Frye, LaToya Aisha Hortense *newswriter*
Gaskin, Felicia *biochemist, educator*
Greville, Florence Nusim *secondary school educator, mathematician*
Hanft, Ruth S. Samuels *economist, consultant*
Hartz, Jill *museum director*
Hetherington, Eileen Mavis *psychologist, educator*
Holmes, Carolyn Coggin *museum director*
Hurd, Nicole Farmer *director*
Hurwitz, Deena R. *law educator*
Johnson, Cornelia *city sheriff, small business owner*
Kaiserlian, Penelope Jane *publishing executive*
Lane, Ann Judith *history professor, women's studies educator*
Lanham, Betty Bailey *anthropologist, educator*
Long, Carolyn Evans *preschool special education educator*
MacIlwaine, Mary Jarratt *public relations executive*
Magill, M(ary) Elizabeth *law educator*
Mahoney, Julia Delong *law educator*
Miller, Margaret Alison *education educator*
Minehart, Jean Besse *tax accountant*
Moreno, Zerka Toeman *psychodrama educator*
Norcross, Barbara Breeden *retired educator*
Norment, Rachel Gobbel *artist, educator, writer*
Parshall, Karen Virginia Hunger *mathematician*
Pierce, Shayn *biomedical engineer, educator*
Rappaport, Yvonne Kindinger *educator*
Rehm, Patrice Koch *radiologist, educator*
Riley, Margaret Foster (Mimi Riley) *law educator*
Robinson, Mildred Wigfall *law educator*
Sanusi, Marina Theresia *retired psychiatrist*
Scott, Elizabeth S. *law educator*
Sibert, Polly Lou *conductor, music educator*
Soffa, Mary Lou *computer science and engineering educator*
Stanley, Courtenay Turner *secondary school educator*
Weinberger, Adrienne *artist, art appraiser*
Wittenborg, Karin *university librarian*
Woolhandler, Ann *law educator*

Charlottesvle
Walker, Beverly Ann *minister, health facility administrator*

Chesapeake
Beck-Hallenbeck, Debra Kay *music educator, musician*
Byrum, Edith Ward *retired music educator*
Gray, Margaret Edna *nursing educator, department chairman, dean*
Hayslett-Wallace, Jeanette *music educator*
Hill, Deborah Nixon *elementary school educator, minister*
Hoster-Burandt, Norma J. *musician, not-for-profit fundraiser*
Kelley, Sudha S. *operating room nurse*
Kringel, Deanna Lynn *music educator*
Lewter, Helen Clark *retired elementary school educator*
Notti, Donna Betts *special education educator*
Owens, Susan Elizabeth *realtor*
Potter, Cynthia M. *art educator, artist*
Skrip, Linda Jean *nurse*
Webb, Julia Jones *elementary school educator, minister*

Chester
Carr, Carol Elaine *biology professor*
Hoagland, Carolyn Markham *retired secondary school educator*
Smetana, Kristine Samaria *chemistry professor, consultant*

Chesterfield
Davis, Bonnie Christell *judge*
Wilczewski, Lynn Cheryl *social studies educator, department chairman*

Christiansburg
Burkhart, Katherine West *music educator, adult education educator*
Shelton, Sylvia Lawson *science educator*
Thorpe, Devoria D. *real estate agent*

Claremont
Seward, Troilen Gainey *retired psychologist*

Clarksville
Kyte, Susan Janet *lawyer, consultant*
Worth, Lynn Harris *writer*

Clifton
Hoffman, Karla Leigh *mathematician, educator*

Clifton Forge
Locher, Elizabeth Aiken *elementary education educator, reading specialist, library director*
Miller, Catherine H. *nursing administrator, property manager*

Cobbs Creek
Lawson, Janice Rae *retired elementary school educator*

Coeburn
Williams, Jo Karen Kobeck *artist, writer*

Colonial Heights
Grizzard-Barham, Barbara Lee *artist*
Huff, Rebecca Suzette *psychologist*
Woolridge, Kay Ellen Jones *music educator*

Covesville
Williams, Patricia Anne *philosopher, writer*

Covington
Spurlock, Evelyn Harvey *retired elementary school educator, minister*

Culpeper
Bahl-Moore, Elizabeth Ann *artist, educator*
Chaffee, Monica Weaver *primary school educator*
Pearson, Sarah Lynn *elementary school educator*
Sarah, Pearson Lynn *elementary school educator*
Thomson, Jane H. *elementary school educator*

Dale City
Baxter, Ruth Howell *educational administrator, psychologist*

Danville
Agnor, Kimberly Keatts *elementary school educator*
Moorefield, Jennifer Mary *legislative staff member*

Dinwiddie
McCray, Doris Raines *minister*

Draper
Whitehurst, Mary Tarr *artist, poet, writer*

Dry Fork
Poteat, Patsy *secondary school educator*
Robertson, Heather Anderson *musician, educator*

Dublin
Billaud, Louise Ann *musician, educator*
Clark, Shelia Roxanne *sports association executive, legislative analyst*
Lineberry, Rebecca J. *municipal official, treasurer*
Linzey, Juanita Bird *biology professor*
Spraker, Deanna King *biology educator*
Wall, Jennifer Grey *assistant principal*

Dulles
Balis, Janet *Internet company executive*
Gregus, Linda Anna *government official*
Jacobs, Janice Lee *ambassador*
Mathieu, Gail Dennise *ambassador*
Rollé, Janet Lydia *Internet company executive*

Dumfries
Thrall, Eileen Fowler *real estate broker*

Eastville
Lewis, Sandra B. *mathematics educator*
Williams, Ida Jones *consumer and home economics educator, writer*

Emporia
Butler, Tammy J. Wiley *medical, surgical, and pediatric nurse*

Ettrick
Davis, Minnie Louise *writer*

Fairfax
Bailey, Helen McShane *historian, consultant*
Best, Amy L. *education educator*
Bohan, Gloria *travel company executive*
Brown, Lorraine A. *literature educator*
Carr, Patricia Warren *adult education educator*
Crissey, Rebecca Lynn *special education educator*
Del Conte, L. Catherine *special education educator*
Given, Barbara (Barbara Knight) *secondary school educator*
Haskett, Dianne Louise *retired mayor, lawyer, consultant*
Kendall Hull, Margarida *art educator, painter*
Kitsantas, Anastasia *educational psychologist*
Knee, Ruth Irelan (Mrs. Junior K. Knee) *social worker, health care consultant*
Lavine, Thelma Zeno *philosophy educator*
Miller, Emilie F. *former state senator, consultant*
Miller, Patricia A. *music educator, opera and concert artist*
Monahan, Danielle Joan *renal nutritionist*
Mulvaney, Mary Frederica *systems analyst*
Price, Lois Ann *elementary school educator*
Siddons, Joy Garbee *music educator*
Solomon, Ellen Joan *business owner, consultant*
Susko, Carol Lynne *lawyer, accountant, educator*
Tolchin, Susan Jane *political science professor, writer*

Fairfax Station
Barringer, Joan Marie *counselor, educator, artist, writer*
Cantu, Jennifer St. John *gifted and talented educator*

Falls Church
Bankson, Marjory Zoet *former religious association administrator*
Barnes, Jennifer J. *lawyer*
Bryan, Billie Marie (Mrs. James A. Mackey) *retired biologist*
Calkins, Susannah Eby *retired economist*
Cazan, Sylvia Marie Buday (Mrs. Matthew John Cazan) *retired real estate executive*
Cianciolo-Carney, Rossana *investigative analyst*
Cooper, Jean Saralee *judge*
Dean-Pratt, Bridget *secondary school educator*
East, Mary Ann Hildegarde *vocalist*
Elderkin, Helaine Grace *lawyer*
Elliott, Virginia F. Harrison *retired anatomist, publisher, educator, investment advisor, kinesiologist, philanthropist*
Espenoza, Cecelia M. *lawyer, law educator*
Fink, Cathy DeVito *small business owner*
Gosnell, Nanci Little *information technology executive, nurse*
Honigberg, Carol Crossman *lawyer*
Inzana, Barbara Ann *musician, educator*
Jones, Linda R. Wolf *consulting company executive*
Keller, Mary Beth *lawyer*
Michelsen, Cleo *retired education educator, writer*
Miller, Martha Glenn *academic administrator, consultant*
Piccotti, Carolyn M. *lawyer*
Pomeranz, Sharon Jane *lawyer*
Rothwarf, Marta *lawyer*
Roussel, Lee Dennison *economist*
Ruskin, Ruth Zafren *social worker*
Seifert, Patricia Clark *cardiac surgery nurse, educator, consultant*
Simon, Deborah Blick *educational consultant, retired secondary school educator*
Smith, Barbara Rath *foundation executive*
Stratton, Dorothy E. *painter, printmaker*
Sveinsson, Linda Rodgers *engineering company executive*
Todd, Shirley Ann *school system administrator*
Van Cleve, Ruth Gill *retired lawyer*
Waylonis, Jean Lynnette *elementary school educator*
Webster, Mary Jo *music educator*
Work, Jane Magruder *retired professional society administrator*
Yoshimura, Yoshiko *librarian*

Farmville
Alvarez, Consuelo Jackeline *science educator, researcher*
Brock-Servais, Rhonda Lee *literature and language professor*
Cormier, Patricia Picard *academic executive*
Parry, Michelle *physics professor*

Ferrum
Grimes, Margaret Katherine *English educator*

Fincastle
Sprinkle, Denise L. *science educator*

Fishersville
Taylor, Donna Leona *advocate, writer*

Flint Hill
Forbush, Sandra M. *artist, educator*

Floyd
Bosniak, Kanta *artist*

Fort Belvoir
Clark, Trudy H. *career officer*
O'Kane, Barbara Lynn *research psychologist*
Smith, Margherita *writer, editor*

Fort Defiance
Floyd, Ruth Crummett *elementary school educator*

Franklin
Lamb, Julie Walsh *elementary school educator*

Franktown
Kellam, Caramine *volunteer*

Fredericksburg
Almond, Beverly McCullough *literature educator*
Chiang, Yuan Jen *mathematics professor*
Gill, Milvi Kosenkranius *artist, photographer*
Goss, Georgia Bulman *freelance/self-employed translator*
Harrod, Audrey Hunter *retired executive secretary*
Hickman, Margaret Capellini *advertising executive*
Holmes, Jacqueline Christobel Wright *art educator*
Nelson-Sargeant, Susan Marie *speech pathology professional*
Nidiffer, Sheri Lynn *medical/surgical nurse*
Potter, Sylvia *education educator*
Rampersad, Peggy A. Snellings *sociologist, consultant*
Ray, Margaret *education educator*
Westebbe, Barbara Liebst *writer, sculptor*

Front Royal
Call, Amy Lynn *music educator, director, classical singer*
Harrison, (Hilde) *artist*
Hrbek, Susan W. *school librarian*
Stevens, Loretta Marie *special education educator*

Gainesville
Bendig, Judith Joan *information systems specialist, computer company executive*
Burke, Marjorie Tisdale *retired special education educator*
French, Dorothy Marie *music educator*
Gorzka, Margaret Rose *retired elementary school educator*

Galax
Brooks, Sherry Moore *medical/surgical nurse*

Glen Allen
Alves, Constance Dillenger *special education educator*
Bosdell, Melony *special education educator*
Cornwell, Patricia Daniels *writer*
den Hartog, Grace Robinson *lawyer*
Weaver, Mollie Little *lawyer*

Gloucester
Pace, Sandra McMillen *science educator*

Gloucester Point
Bush, Elizabeth Olney *marine lab technician*

Great Falls
Castro-Klaren, Sara *Latin American literature professor*
Dinger, Ann Monroe *association executive, interior designer*
Ganley, Betty *artist*
Shay-Byrne, Olivia *lawyer*

Greenbackville
Lewis, Kay *interior designer, consultant*

Grundy
Yates, Stella Louise *mathematics educator*

Hampton
Andrews, Elizabeth Anne *human services and social work educator*
Carrington, Marian Denise *academic administrator, counselor, motivational speaker*
Daniels, Cindy Lou *aerospace transportation executive*
Duncan, Nancy Carol *psychology professor*
Goode, Constance Loper *elementary school principal*
Johnson, Leona Melissa *psychology professor, researcher*
Kelley, Mary E. *science educator*
Lawson, Donna Yvette *special education educator*
Manns, Helen Margaret *vice principal*
Martinez, Debbie *electronics engineer*
Murray, Jennifer Adams *music educator, musician*
Roe, Lesa B. *federal agency administrator*
Shaughnessy, Leslie Restaino *secondary educator*
Sypolt, Shirley Rae *elementary school educator*
Tominack, Debra Dillard *science educator*
Williams-Byrd, Julie *electronics engineer*
Wolff, Sharon L. *photographer, department chairman*

Harrisonburg
Comfort, Heather E. *education educator*
Davis, Melodie Miller *writer, editor*
Ferraiolo, Kathleen Mary *political science professor*
Finney, Sara Jane *psychologist, educator*
Gabbin, Joanne Veal *education educator*
Swope, Frances Alderson *retired librarian*
Theodore, Crystal *artist, retired educator*
Weaver, Jennefer Jean *musician, educator*

Heathsville
Stubbs, Susan Conklin *retired statistician*

Herndon
Alicudo, Lynda *management consultant*
Biely, Debra Marie *retired military officer*
Bobzien, Catherine Hardy *mathematics educator*
Harris, Shelley Follansbee *business development professional*
Hollis, Katherine Mary *information scientist, consultant*
Jones, Reba (Becki) Pestun *elementary school educator, music educator*
Kmetz, Leah E. *elementary school educator*
Lovejoy, Kristin Gallina *information technology executive*
Nolan, Leslie Marian *artist*
Simanski, Claire Dvorak *art educator*
Suess, Jennifer Lynn *elementary school educator*

Hillsville
Shelor, Vickie Poff *choir director*

Hollins
Brown-Black, Lillian (Rusty Brown-Black) *volunteer*

Hopewell
Arbogast, Sally S. *science educator*
Payne, Emily Mosley *music educator*
Vartanian, Isabel Sylvia *retired dietician*

Hudgins
Story, Martha vanBeuren *retired librarian*

Hurley
Blankenship, Linda Lou *education educator*

Independence
Davis, Carolyn Jean *music educator*

Ivor
Newby, Terrica Lee *elementary school educator*

Jonesville
Scott, Tammy Charlene *secondary school educator*

Kents Store
Brown, Nan Marie *retired minister*

Keswick
Nosanow, Barbara Shissler *museum program director, curator*

Keysville
Silver, Kyla Marie *music educator*

Lancaster
Beane, Judith Mae *retired psychologist*
Forrester, Alexis C.G. *elementary school educator*

Lansdowne
Miller, Dorothy Anne Smith *retired cytogenetics educator*
Stanley, Lila Gail *political science professor, art appraiser*

Lawrenceville
Hardy, Sandra Vanessa *elementary school educator*
Stransky, Maria Soledad *psychotherapist*

Leesburg
Abell, Johanna Mathis *music educator*
Brown, Toni *health and physical educator*
Carroll, Teresa Fiske *mathematics educator*
De Barbieri, Mary Ann *not-for-profit management consultant*
Green, May Clayman *elementary school educator, education administrator*

Lexington
Lyle, Katie Letcher *writer, educator*
Miller, Sherry Duncan *elementary school educator*
Parker, Phyllis R. *secondary school educator*
Rader, Angela Nichole *music educator*
Solod, Lisa *writer*

Locust Grove
Cordray-Van de Castle, Karen *elementary school educator*

Lorton
Celentano, Suzanne *movement educator*
Piskor, Susan Marie *secondary school educator*

Lovettsville
Ryan-Griffith, Mary Kate *special education educator*

Lynchburg
Bowman, Kathleen Gill *academic administrator*
Cash, Susan W. *career planning administrator*
Craddock, Mary Spencer Jack *volunteer*

DePew, Carol Ann *pharmaceutical sales representative*
Dodge, Lynn Louise *municipal official, librarian*
Foley, Ruth Iona *music educator*
Johnson, Kathie Carwile *education educator*
Law, Louise Disosway *education educator*
Massie, Anne Adams Robertson *artist*
Packert, G(ayla) Beth *retired lawyer*
Payne, Pauleta Polly *psychologist*
Schwedt, Rachel Elaine *librarian*

Manassas
Bahner, Sue (Florence Suzanna Bahner) *broadcast executive*
Boyles, Norma Jean *elementary school educator*
Casal, Laura C. *literature educator, consultant*
Dellinger, Mary *medical/surgical nurse*
Dommer, Susan Wampler *music educator*
Hermann, Sharon Beth Betsy *music educator*
Lawson, Nancy P. *retired county official*
Livingston, Jo Ellen Brooks *music educator*
Lytton, Linda Rountree *marriage and family therapist, consultant*
Smith, Margaret A. *secondary school educator*
Vance, Tanya Lee *music educator, director*

Marion
Elledge, Glenna Ellen Tuell *journalist*
Groseclose, Joanne Stowers *special education educator*
Lawrence, Evelyn Thompson *retired music educator, researcher*

Martinsville
Robertson, Margaret Moore *information technology educator*
Wade, Gayle Panagos *literature and language professor*

Mathews
Gillikin, Lynn *retired psychologist*

Mc Dowell
Harkleroad, Jo-Ann Decker *special education educator*

Mc Lean
Auerbach, Anita L. *psychologist*
Berdine, Linda *information technology executive*
Black, Ginger Elizabeth *elementary school educator*
Brown, Margaret Ann *lawyer*
Bullard, Marcia *publishing executive*
Burke, Sheila P. *federal agency administrator*
Clark-Johnson, Susan *publishing executive*
DeGiovanni-Donnelly, Rosalie Frances *biologist, educator*
Drew, K. *financial advisor, management consultant*
Feller, Mimi A. (Millicent Feller) *newspaper publishing executive*
Giallombardo, Leslie *publishing executive*
Glassman, M. Melissa *lawyer*
Goktepe, Janet Rose *retired financial analyst*
Harrison, Carol Love *fine art photographer*
Healy, Theresa Ann *retired ambassador*
LeSourd, Nancy Susan Oliver *lawyer, writer*
Lion, Linda N. *retired federal agency administrator*
Mars, Jacqueline Badger *food products executive*
Mars, Virginia Cretella *civic volunteer*
Martore, Gracia *publishing company executive*
Mathews, Linda McVeigh *newspaper editor*
McIlwain, Clara Evans *agricultural economist, consultant*
Neumann, Eva *information technology executive*
Pratt, Reyna Kushner *physics educator*
Price, Ilene Rosenberg *lawyer*
Reiff, Laura Foote *lawyer*
Rose, Susan Porter *management and governmental affairs consultant*
Saunders, Danielle *lawyer, telecommunications industry executive*
Scott, Concetta Ciotti *artist, educator*
Trout, Margie Marie Mueller *civic worker*
Wall, Barbara Wartelle *lawyer*
Wallace, Barbara Brooks *writer*
Walsh, Marie Leclerc *nurse*
Webber, Diana L. *management consultant executive, engineering educator*
Weiss, Susan *newspaper editor*
Yinger, Emily M. *lawyer*

Meadowview
Kingsolver, Barbara Ellen *writer*

Mechanicsville
McEntire, Jean Reynolds *music educator*
Wells, Mary Julia *psychologist*
Yohe, Robin M. *music educator*

Mechanicsvlle
Miles, Carole Harrison *artist*

Middleburg
Kaplan, Jean Gaither (Norma Kaplan) *retired reading specialist*
Larmore, Catherine Christine *university official*
vom Baur, Daphne de Blois *artist*
Yovanovich, Robyn Dobson *theater educator, department chairman*

Midlothian
Ameen, Betsy Harrison *science educator, department chairman*
Coats, Kathy Lynn *biology educator*
Lamont-Gordon, Melissa Lynne *orchestra director, music educator*
Mitchell, Biki-Ray *physical education educator*
Morse, Kimberly Deane *artist*
Stoodt, Barbara Dern *retired education educator, magazine editor*

Monterey
Akaike, Hiroko *music educator, conductor*

Natural Bridge Station
Compton, Mildred Lee *retired elementary school educator*
Randolph-Broughman, Mary Etta *music educator*

Newington
Clark-Bourne, Kathryn Orpha *consul*
Robertson, Jean Elizabeth *sociology educator*

Newport News
Behlmar, Cindy Lee *medical association administrator, management consultant*
Brunke, Kathleen Elizabeth *adult education educator*
Camp, Hazel Lee Burt *artist*
Carson, Denise Wilkinson *gifted and talented educator*
Dillon, Elizabeth Diggs *medical/surgical nurse*
Eanes, Janet Teresa *elementary school educator, music educator*
Forbes, Sarah Elizabeth *gynecologist, real estate company officer*
Hurst, Rebecca McNabb *language educator*
Keech, Ann Marie *training design and multimedia consultant*
Mazur, Rhoda Himmel *community volunteer*
Smith, Barbara Ruthjena Drucker *writer, educator*
Smith, Kelly McCoig *assistant principal*
Trachuk, Lillian Elizabeth *music educator*
Underwood, Lori J. *philosophy educator*
Williams, Cynthia Ann *small business owner, pediatrics nurse, writer*

Norfolk
Addis, Kay Tucker *newspaper editor*
Brower, Anne Clayton *radiologist*
Brown, Mary Wilkes *secondary school educator*
Diaz, Marla J. *lawyer*
Doumas, Judith *psychologist, educator*
Dryer, Barbara Ferrell *media specialist, educator*
Duncan, Cynthia Beryl *university library administrator*
Faulk, Tanya Williams *school disciplinarian*
Ferris, Ginger Leigh *education educator, consultant*
Finney, Fannie D. *minister, educator*
Gallagher, Carol Joy *bishop*
Heaton, Kathleen Hoge *realtor*
Herbert, Elizabeth Anne *elementary school educator*
Hilliard-Bradley, Yvonne *library administrator*
Hinsdale, Stephanie M. *social worker*
Hood, Antoinette Foote *dermatologist*
Hotaling, Diane Elizabeth Hickey *college administrator*
Huot, Rachel Irene *biomedical educator, research scientist, physician*
Jamison, Joi Nichole *media specialist, performing company executive, educator*
Leitch, Sally Lynn *social studies educator*
Lochen, Lynne Carol *cultural organization administrator*
Marshall, Deborah Kay *instructional technology resource specialist*
McDemmond, Marie Valentine *academic administrator, consultant*
Meyers, Carolyn Winstead *academic administrator, mechanical engineer, educator*
Miller, Yvonne Bond *state legislator, educator*
Musgrave, Thea *composer, conductor*
Nemara, Vanessa Anne *federal official*
Neumann, Serina Ann Louise *psychologist, researcher*
Newkirk, Ingrid *animal rights activist*
Poston, Anita Owings *lawyer*
Reynolds, Sheri *writer*
Rivera, Caroline Clark *biologist, educator*
Roth Taylor, Lynn E. *gifted and talented educator*
Runte, Roseann *academic administrator*
Shumadine, Anne Ballard *financial advisor, lawyer*
Spence, Fay Frances *lawyer, educator*
Stallings, Valerie A. *physician, state agency administrator*
Terzis, Julia Kallipolitou *plastic surgeon*
Warren, Ivory Jean *counselor, educator*
Winslow, Janet Lucas *elementary school educator*
Witty, Elaine P. *retired dean, education educator*
Xu, Xiaohong Nancy *chemistry and biomedical science educator*

Norton
Caruso, Carol Beverly *physical education educator*

Oak Hall
Kolbush, Elizabeth Ann Kuhns *secondary educator*

Oakton
Terzian, Grace Paine *communications executive*
Travis, Tracy Leigh *emergency physician*
Trifoli-Cunniff, Laura Catherine *psychologist, consultant*

Onancock
Fears, Belle DeCormis *retired physician*

Orange
Gore, Rebecca Estes *science educator*
Montgomery, Linda Boudreaux *artist*
Weaver, Karen Johnson *elementary school educator*

Petersburg
Abbott-Ryan, Pat *painter, writer*
Antunes, Marilyn Z. *mathematics educator*
Benn, Candace Marilea *elementary school educator*
Burns, Cassandra Stroud *prosecutor*
Dance, Gloria Fenderson *dance studio executive, ballet administrator*
Everitt, Alice Lubin *labor arbitrator*

Poquoson
Berg, Lillian Douglas *chemistry professor*
Tai, Elizabeth Shi-Jue Lee *library director*
Tuck, Carolyn Weaver *middle school educator*

Port Royal
Clarke-Hall, Deborah Renay *elementary school educator*

Portsmouth
Boshier, Maureen Louise *health facilities administrator*
Clary, Inez Harris *music educator*
Monroe, Evelyn Jones *retired librarian*
Ojeda, Ana Maria *therapist, clinical caseworker*
Rampersaud Lundy, Sheryll *special education educator*
Rhodes, Kendall Westbrook *language arts educator*
Smith, Martha Ann *retired special education educator*

Pound
Barnette, Nellie Marie *elementary school educator*

Powhatan
Pleasants, Glennis Jeter *music educator*

Prince George
Bishop, Stephanie Elizabeth *theater educator*

Prospect
Shield, Julie Marie Karst *artist, educator*

Purcellville
King, Tracey Groux *psychotherapist*
Taylor, Carolyn Roberts *small business owner, chef*

Quantico
Hodges, Adele E. *military officer*
Stout, Mary Webb *dean*

Radford
Carter, Edith Houston *statistician, educator*
Dunaway, Marsha Landrum *special education educator*
James, Clarity (Carolyne Faye James) *mezzo soprano*
Kessler, Kendall Seay Feriozi *artist*
Kirby, Susan Collins *literature and language professor, consultant*
Kyle, Penelope Ward *academic administrator*
Lips, Hilary Margaret *psychology educator, writer*
Parker, Jacqueline Kay *social work educator*
Salam, Halide *artist, educator*
Webb, Nancy Hutchinson *elementary school educator*

Rapidan
Knewstep, Nancy Coleman *secondary school educator*

Reedville
Smith, Monika Rose *researcher*

Reston
Aaron, Barbara Robinson *real estate broker*
Bredehoft, Elaine Charlson *lawyer*
Brennan, Norma Jean *professional society administrator, director*
Brooker, Susan Gay *employment consulting firm executive*
Brown, Della Hewett *elementary school educator*
Butler, Katherine E. *lawyer*
Di Trapani, Marcia A. *health facility administrator, community health nurse, educator*
Keler, Marianne Martha *lawyer*
Lynch, Monique Christine *mathematics educator*
Madry-Taylor, Jacquelyn Yvonne *educational association administrator*
Meyer, Patricia Hanes *social worker*
Miller, Lynne Marie *environmental services administrator*
Mitchell, Ellen Clabaugh *investment executive*
Mogge, Harriet Morgan *educational association executive*
Naeser, Nancy Dearien *geologist, researcher*
Norris, Susan Elizabeth *social worker*
Pappas, Virginia M. *medical association administrator*
Polemitou, Olga Andrea *accountant*
Posey, Ada Louise *human resources specialist*
Powell, Anne Elizabeth *editor-in-chief*
Pozun Watson, Heather Dawn *environmental scientist, educator*
Revesz, Kinga *chemist, isotope geochemist, researcher*
Sarreals, Sonia *data processing executive, consultant*
Spander, Deborah L. *lawyer*
Thayer, Joan Peregoy *ancient language educator*
Witt, Ruth Hutt *management consultant*
Young, Janet Cheryl *electrical engineer*
Young, Loretta Ann *auditor*

Richlands
Edgell, Judith Carol *theater educator*
Morris, Marilyn LaVonne *retired elementary school educator, minister*

Richmond
Aigner, Emily Burke *Christian lay minister*
Alewine, Betty *retired telecommunications executive*
Anderson, Bette (Bonnie) Ferguson *music educator*
Austin-Stephens, Ann-Marie *retail executive*
Baldwin, Billie Sue *principal*
Baskerville, Viola Osborne *state government official*
Blake, Miriam Snell *elementary school educator, choir director, organist, pianist*
Boadle-Biber, Margaret Clare *physiologist, educator*
Bohannon, Sarah Virginia *personnel professional*
Brackenridge, N. Lynn *not-for-profit developer*
Bray, Patricia Shannon *music educator, musician, small business owner*
Brissette, Martha Blevins *lawyer*
Brown, Marilyn Branch *retired educational administrator*
Brown, Patricia A. *customer service representative*
Bryant, Colleen Cannington *history educator*
Burner, Clara Miller *librarian*
Carpi, Janice E. *lawyer*
Casini, Jane Sloan *wholesale distribution executive*
Christenbury, Leila *education educator*
Cooper, Deborah Kay *forensic psychologist*
Davis, Phyllis J. *education educator*
DeMary, Jo Lynne *school system administrator, elementary school educator*
Devolites, Jeannemarie Aragona *state legislator*
Dias, Fiona P. *retail executive*
Dunn, Linda Baugh *elementary school educator*
Fierro, Marcella Farinelli *forensic pathologist, educator*
Frazer, Susan Hume *architectural firm executive*
Freund, Emma Frances *technologist*
Fullerton, Jessica Ann *music educator*
Girone, Joan Christine Cruse *realtor, former county official*
Gluck, Michelle H. *lawyer*
Gregory, Jean Winfrey *ecologist, educator*
Hackney, Virginia Howitz *lawyer*
Hammel, Alice Maxine *music educator*
Hanley, Katherine Keith *state official*
Harris, Grace E. *academic administrator*
Henderson, Harriet *librarian, director*
Hines, Linda Turner *health services administrator, nurse*
Humphrey, Mitzi Greene *artist*
Jewell-Sherman, Deborah *school system administrator*
Jones, Jeanne Pitts *pre-school administrator*
Joynes, Barbara Cole *marketing executive*
Keenan, Barbara Milano *state supreme court justice*
Kennedy, Patricia Berry *retired music educator*
Kiely, Christy E. *lawyer*
Kinnier, Emily P. *artist*
Kinser, Cynthia D. *state supreme court justice*
Koch, Aimee Helen *art gallery director, photographer*
Lacy, Elizabeth Bermingham *state supreme court justice*
Levit, Héloïse B. (Ginger Levit) *art historian, journalist, art dealer, consultant*
Liermann, Kelly *athletic trainer*
Martin, Ann McCarthy *library-media specialist*
Massenburg, Johnnye Smith *speech pathology/audiology services professional, minister*
McDermid, Margaret E. *information technology executive, engineer*
McQuigg, Michele Berger *state legislator*
Melcher, Elizabeth *musician*
Minor, Marian Thomas *educational consultant, retired elementary school educator, retired secondary school educator*
Morgan, Elizabeth Seydel *writer, educator, retired writer*
Moss, Princess Renai *elementary school educator*
Murray, Marian Selena *medical/surgical nurse*
Neal, Gail Fallon *physical therapist, educator*
Newton, Elizabeth Deane *music educator*
Ostrom, Kristina F. *academic administrator, optician*
Petera, Anne Pappas *state official*
Radecki, Catherine *psychologist*
Ragland, Ines Colom *principal*
Reid, Jodi Belinda Austin *music educator*
Rick, Roseleen P. *lawyer*
Rigsby, Linda Flory *lawyer*
Robertson, LaVerne *minister*
Robertson, Louise Wilkes *pediatrician, cardiologist*
Schaar, Susan Clarke *legislative staff member*
Schwarzschild, Jane L. *lawyer*
Seals, Margaret Louise Crumrine *managing editor*
Simmons, Martha R. *mortgage company executive*
Sood, Aradhana Avasthy *psychiatrist, director*
Stone, Jacquelyn Elois *lawyer*
Taggart, Barbara Ann *retired language educator*
Van Neste, Karen Lane *librarian, editor*
Wagner, Jody M. *treasurer*
Wallach, Kenya *mathematics educator*
Whitehurst, Lucinda Snyder *school librarian*
Williams, Amy McDaniel *lawyer*
Williams, Christine Alicia *lawyer*
Williams, Karen Johnson *federal judge*
Winslett, Stoner *artistic director*
Young, Sharon Wisdom *retired music educator*
Zich, Sue Schaab *nurse*
Zyglocke, Ann Madding *elementary school educator*

Ringgold
Woodward, Julia Wilson *elementary school educator*

Roanoke
Barnes, Sharon D. *director, music educator*
Gibson, Stella Eades *art educator, photographer*
Gray, Nancy Ann Oliver *academic administrator*
Hankla, Cathryn *language educator, writer*
Kinzie, Brenda Asburry *counselor*
Klein, Deborah Rae *nurse*
Manns, Essie Jeanette Delaney *advocate*
Schumm, Darla Yzonne *religious studies educator*
Taylor, Janet Droke *judicial assistant*
Tinsley, Shelia C. *nurse*
Vones, Cynthia Louise *art educator*
Wallace, Linda Kay *mathematics professor*
Zomparelli, Wendy *newspaper publisher*

Rose Hill
Lane, Mary Winston *secondary school educator*

Rosslyn
Agosta, Susan Marie *web site designer*

Round Hill
Chalifoux, Alice Ellen *harpist, educator*

Rural Retreat
Dutton, Sandra F. *music educator*

Saint Charles
Matlock, Anita Kay *family nurse practitioner*

Salem
Crowder, Rebecca Byrum *music educator, elementary school educator*
Gilpin, Jeanny *elementary school educator*
LaRocco, Theresa M. *social studies educator*
Secor, Margaret J. *science educator*

Sandston
Manson, Zynora Davis *music educator, minister*

Sandy Point
Douglas, Daisy Howard *retired elementary school educator, writer, consultant*

Scottsville
Griebenauw, Liza-Marie *secondary school educator*

Seaford
Jenkins, Margaret Bunting *human resources executive*

Smithfield
Newby Tynes, Denise J. *elementary school educator, secondary school educator*
Odom, Marsha McClelland *elementary school educator*

South Hill
Clay, Carol Ann *family nurse practitioner*
Evans, Cynthia Mae *music educator*
Taylor, Jean Mull *secondary school educator*

Spotsylvania
Hardy, Dorcas Ruth *business and government relations executive*
Peters, Joanna Eilene *music educator*
Pitts, Karen Colleen *art educator*
Thomas, Sue Ann Appleton *librarian, reading consultant*
Todd, Deborah Kathleen *library media specialist*

Springfield
Brown, Margaret Catherine *artist*
Dake, Marcia Allene *retired nursing educator, dean*
D'Elosua, Jennifer Dawn *music educator*
Dodson, Alicejean Leigh *nursing administrator*
Edwards-LeBoeuf, Renee Camille *public relations executive, protective services official*
Hairston, Geraldine *mathematics educator*
Heise, Dorothy Hilbert *retired librarian, retired government agency administrator*
Myers, Elissa Matulis *publishing executive, professional society administrator*
Ona, Caroline Jean *history educator*
Williams, Cecilia Lee Pursel *optometrist*
Wong, Ann Lam *secondary school educator*

Stafford
Gambaro, Retha Walden *artist*

Stanardsville
Anns, Arlene Eiserman *publishing company executive*

Staunton
Arnold, Ruth Southgate *librarian*
Cabe, Crista Ruth *academic administrator*
Firehock, Barbara A. *interior designer*
Grewe, Marjorie Jane *retired protective services official*
Jolloff, Nilda Elizabeth *art educator, artist*
Karaffa, Rebecca P. *elementary school educator*
Lembke, Janet *writer*
Sweetman, Beverly Yarroll *physical therapist*

Stephenson
Johnson, Eva Maria *retired translator*

Sterling
Austin, Lynne Hunzicker *secondary school educator*
Bartow, Nicole A. *secondary school educator*
Chavez, Linda *civil rights organization executive*
Gulden, Linda Lober *science educator*
Hill-Wagner, Aimee Elizabeth *social studies educator*
Naquin, Deborah Ann *humanities educator*
Newton, Cheryl Kay *music educator*
Skrzycki, Maryann *physics educator*
Wolfgang, Crystal *secondary school educator*

Stuart
Belcher, Lisa Roop *social studies educator*
Gregory, Jennifer Daryl *mathematics educator, small business owner*

Stuarts Draft
Mikell, Martha Simms *secondary school educator*

Suffolk
Brown, Alvenice Hortense Bryan *educator*
Burd, Joyce Ann *librarian*
Driggins, Elaine Eure *elementary school educator*
Harrell, Florence Louise *elementary school educator*
Noblitt, Nancy Anne *aerospace engineer*

Sumerduck
McCamy, Sharon Grove *English educator*

Sweet Briar
Kirkwood, Bessie Hershberger *mathematics professor*
Muhlenfeld, Elisabeth S. *academic administrator, literature educator, writer*

Tappahannock
McGuire, Lillian Hill (Lillian Elizabeth Hill McGuire) *historian, researcher, retired education educator, writer*

Tazewell
Thompson, Patricia DuBois *elementary school educator*

The Plains
O'Connor, Karen Lende *Olympic athlete, sports association administrator*

Upperville
Powell Gebhard, Joy Lee (Bok Sin Lee) *small business owner*

Verona
Grizzel, Patsy (Pat) Pauline *human services administrator*

Victoria
Bayne, Kathryn Ann *elementary school educator*
Sheffield, Elizabeth Rash *elementary school educator*

Vienna
Artz, Cherie B. *lawyer*
Beyer, Barbara Lynn *transportation executive, consultant*
Chin, May Lin *anesthesiologist*
Colón, Eugenia Valinda *development executive*
Davilis, Katrina Lyn *music educator*
Davis, Lauren Alexis *science educator*
Gardenier, Turkan Kumbaraci *statistician, researcher*
Higginbotham, Wendy Jacobson *legislative staff member, writer*
Kinsolving, Sylvia Crockett *musician, educator*
Lorfano, Pauline Davis *artist*
Maguire, Margaret Louise *lawyer*
Miller, Christine Marie *marketing executive, public relations executive*
Milton, Carol Lynne *artist*
Slowik, Sharon A. *real estate agent*

Virginia Beach
Ardison, Linda G. *author, writing educator*
Armstrong, Margaret *nursing administrator*
Boudreau, Sharon Kay *special education educator*
Cehelska, Olga M. *music educator, flight instructor*
Chalk, Barbara Ann *retired medical/surgical nurse*
Christiansen, Margaret Louise *law librarian, lawyer*
Costello, Stacy Ann *elementary school educator*
Cummings, Catherine T. *elementary school educator*
Dawson, Arleta M. *history educator*
DiCarlo, Susanne Helen *financial analyst*
Dickerson, Nancy Knewstep *language educator*
Dingman, Janet Simpson *counselor, educator*
DiTommaso, Phyllis Battis *special education educator*
Edwards, Cynthia (Cindy) Curtis *mathematics educator*
Fink, Eloise Bradley *art director*
Foster, Jeanne O'Cain *poet, fine arts educator*
Garcia, Sharon D. *elementary school educator*
Gardner, Karen High *special education educator*
Garvey, Dawn Elaine *elementary school educator*
Guckert, Nora Jane Gaskill *medical/surgical nurse, hospice nurse, holistic consultant*
Hague, Debbie Lou Tucker *secondary school educator*
Hodapp, Heidi Francine *middle school educator*
Hofler, Kay Robertson *secondary school educator, department chairman, artist*
Hunter, Anne Graves *counselor*
Hyman, Pamela Dronette *science educator*
Jacobson, Frances M. *history professor*
Jones, Felicia M. *director*
Keith, Barbara Ann *elementary school educator, educator*
Kiernan, Margaret M. *adult education educator*
Lawson, Beth Ann Reid *lawyer, strategic planner*
Lewis, Eleanor Adams *financial consultant*
Lutsyshyn, Oksana *concert pianist, organist*
McDonald, Linda L. *massage therapist*
Monroe, Katherine Diane Osborne *secondary school educator*
Oberndorf, Meyera E. *mayor*
Paqet, Shawna Lee *museum director*
Powell, Michele Hall *music educator*
Reece-Porter, Sharon Ann *international human rights educator*
Sears, Patricia Marie *elementary school educator, consultant*
Smith, Ruth Hodges *city clerk*
Smith, Thelma Cheryl *principal, minister*
Springstead, Martha Wyatt *voice educator*
Stanton, Pamela Freeman *interior designer, writer*
Talag, Trinidad Santos *educator*
Tuskey, Laura Jeanne *music educator, pharmacologist*
Von Mosch, Wanda Gail *middle school educator*
Walck, Camila Crockett *biology educator*
Waller, Neola Shultz *retired secondary school educator*
Watkins, Brenda L. *music educator*
Young, Dell *science educator*
Zebley, Lisa Catherine *elementary school educator*
Ziegler, Rochelle Elizabeth *special education educator*

Wachapreague
Rogers, Lynne Cary *artist, painter*

Wakefield
Nettles, Kathryn Chappell *visual artist, educator*

Warrenton
Gullace, Marlene Frances *systems engineer, consultant*
Harrison, Margie Ann *nursing educator, emergency nurse practitioner*

Washington
Arbelbide, C(indy) L(ea) *librarian, historian, author*

Waynesboro
Eary, Pamela Hall *obstetrics nurse, educator*
Phillips, Nancy Hopkins *elementary school educator*
Spilman, Patricia *artist, educator*

West Point
Trible, Martha Gregory *secondary school educator*

White Stone
Duer, Ellen Ann Dagon *anesthesiologist, general practitioner*
Graves, Pirkko Maija-Leena *clinical psychologist, psychoanalyst*

Wicomico Church
Kenna, Gail Ann *secondary and higher education educator*

Williamsburg
Bell, Christine Marie *secondary school educator*
Chandler, Kimberley Lynn *educational association administrator*
Christison, Muriel Branham *retired museum director, art history educator*
Drum, Joan Marie McFarland *federal agency administrator, educator*
Goldstein, Barbara Block *education educator, director*
Hawthorne, Shelby Myrick *reading specialist*
Hooker, Karen L. *mathematics educator*
Kerns, Virginia B. *anthropologist, writer*
Marcus, Becca Nimmer *psychotherapist*
McCarthy, Connie Kearns *university librarian*
McLennan, Barbara Nancy *tax specialist*
Myatt, Sue Henshaw *nursing home administrator*
Nettels, Elsa *English language educator*
Peterson, Susan *political science professor, dean*
Pyott, Caroline (Patty) *writer*
Richezza, Amanda *athletic trainer*
Ringlesbach, Dorothy Louise *retired nurse, writer*
Schwab, Nancy Jean *middle school educator*
Stanley, Shirley Davis *artist*
Turnage, Martha Allen *academic administrator*
Voorhess, Mary Louise *pediatric endocrinologist*
Wiley, Elizabeth Ann *theater educator, department chairman*

Winchester
Chen, Yvonne *economics professor*
Huddleston, Beth Simpson *middle school educator*
Orndoff, Betty Katherine (Betty Katherine Madagan) *secondary school educator*
Russell, Melinda Farrar *music educator*
Sposato, Aimé *music educator, opera singer*
Sproul, Joan Heeney *retired elementary school educator*
Tisinger, Catherine Anne *retired history professor*
Vaughan, Stephanie Ruth *water aerobics business owner, consultant*

Wirtz
Black, Cathy Turner *elementary school educator*

Wise
Collins, Susan V. *secondary school educator*

Woodbridge
Austin, Sandra J. *small business owner*
Butler, Leslie White *epidemiologist*
Denison, Cynthia Lee *accountant, tax specialist*
Donahue, Amy Stewart *early childhood education specialist*
Flori, Anna Marie DiBlasi *health facility administrator, nurse, anesthesiologist*
Gilmer, Staci Rose *special education educator*
Gilmore, Marjorie Havens *retired civic worker, lawyer*
Hayes, Linda Marie *coach*
Janik, Nicole Elizabeth *secondary school educator*
Ker, Lora Kay *elementary music educator*
Lee, Barbara Mahoney *career officer, educator*
McMahon, Janet Mankiewich *critical care nurse*
Peck, Dianne Kawecki *architect*
Phillips-LeSane, Fay M. *mental health professional*
Rethmel, Carol Ann *voice educator, director*
St. Clair, Miriam Macleod *biology professor*
Sullivan, Mia *special education educator*
Taylor, Jane Bartlett *biology professor, educational consultant*
Wallace, Fay Mary *columnist*

Woodstock
Maggiolo, Paulette Blanche *writer*

Yorktown
Butler, Katherine Ann *elementary school educator*
Pagels, Carrie Fancett *psychologist*

WASHINGTON

Aberdeen
Pieffer, Phyllis I. *music educator*

Anacortes
Holmes, Paula Ann *elementary school educator*

Arlington
Bullington, Gayle Rogers *writer, researcher*

Auburn
Sims, Marcie Lynne *language educator, writer*

Bainbridge Island
Burns, Shirley MacDonald *artist, educator*
Stewart, Kay Boone *writer, retired academic administrator*

Bellevue
Calinoiu, Ileana Nia *psychiatrist*
Foster, Linda Lee *artist*
Hackett, Carol Ann Hedden *physician*
Nowik, Dorothy Adam *medical equipment company executive*
Ostroff, Leslie Denise *elementary school educator*
Phillips, Zaiga Alksnis *pediatrician*
Pinney, Alesia L. *lawyer*
Porad, Francine Joy *poet, painter*
Rice, Kay Diane *elementary school educator, consultant*
Skredsvig, Janice B. *information technology executive*
Tee, Virginia *lawyer*
Van Natter, Gayl Price *residential construction company administrator*
Wallace, Mary Colette *architectural researcher, designer*
Wallentine, Mary Kathryn *secondary school educator*

Bellingham
Clark-Langager, Sarah Ann *curator, academic administrator*
Collamer, Barbara Ellen *social sciences educator*
Coss, Sharon Elizabeth *counselor*
Dooley, Kathleen Ann *elementary school educator*
Graves, Vicki Lloyd *retired mechanical engineer*
Hendricks, Marilyn Louise *small business owner*
Lois, Jennifer M. *sociologist, educator*
Morse, Karen Williams *academic administrator*
Ross, June Rosa Pitt *biologist, educator*
Stephens, H. Jeannette *mathematics educator*
Whyte, Nancy Marie *performing arts educator*

Benton City
Kromminga, An-Marie *special education educator*
Omel, June M. *elementary school educator*

Black Diamond
Walker, Minerva E. Gilara *poet, retail executive*

Bonney Lake
Wickizer, Cindy Louise *retired elementary school educator*

Bothell
Flynn-James, Stephanie *biologist, educator*
Jacobus, Elizabeth Loomis *volunteer*
Kraft, Elaine Joy *community relations and communications official*

Bow
Cole, Donna Kay *elementary school educator, science educator*

Bremerton
Burnett, Amy Louise *artist, art gallery owner*
Cottrell-Adkins, Leone *opera company director*
Fischer, Mary E. *special education educator*
Vondran, Janet Elise *physician*

Buckley
Hahn, Ellen R. *elementary school educator*

Camano Island
Hartley, Celia Love *nursing consultant, writer, retired nursing educator, nursing administrator*
Petrakis, Julia Ward *small business owner*

Camas
Liem, Annie *pediatrician*

Carlsborg
Scairpon, Sharon Cecilia *retired information scientist*

Carnation
Beshur, Jacqueline E. *animal trainer, farmer, writer*

Chehalis
Dennis, Linda Susan *not-for-profit developer*
Williams, Janelle Aust *literature and language educator*

Clarkston
Torgerson, Linda Belle *music educator*

Cle Elum
Galloway, Patricia Denese *civil engineer*

College Place
Gaskell, Carolyn Suzanne *librarian*

Colville
Culton, Sarah Alexander *psychologist, educator*
Rudd, Cheryl Kai *language educator*

Cosmopolis
Luark, Lillian *retired city clerk*

Coupeville
Martell, Maxine A. *artist*

East Wenatchee
Kissler, Cynthia Eloise *geologist, consultant*

Edgewood
Martin, Iris Weber *retired minister*

Edmonds
Deering, Anne-Lise *artist, retired real estate salesperson*
Johnson, d'Elaine Ann Herard *artist, consultant*
Morrison, Wynona Marvel *psychotherapist*
Rogers, Catherine Alice *obstetrician, gynecologist*

Ellensburg
Carrothers, Carol Ann *special education services professional, educator*
McIntyre, Jerilyn Sue *academic administrator*
Miller, Maxine Lynch *retired home economist, retired interior designer, educator*
Rosell, Sharon Lynn *physics and chemistry professor*
Schneider, Leslie Jean *elementary school educator*

Everett
Boschok, Jackie *labor union administrator*
Cappello, Laurie Sue *vocalist, educator*
Nelson, Carol Kobuke *bank executive*
O'Keefe, Kathleen Mary *state official*
Olsen-Estie, Jeanne Lindell *golf course owner*
Ostergaard, Joni Hammersla *lawyer*
Rimbach, Evangeline Lois *retired music educator*
Souza, Blase Camacho *librarian, educator*
Van Ry, Ginger Lee *school psychologist*

Federal Way
Ballard, Ernesta *lumber company executive*
Blywise, Barbara *mental health services professional*
Mersereau, Susan *information systems company executive, data processing executive*
Muzyka-McGuire, Amy *marketing professional, nutritionist, consultant*
Rossi, Ruth Harris *special education educator*
Ruddell, Alysa Ann *clinical psychologist*

Gig Harbor
Wissmann, Carol Reneé *sales executive*

Graham
Christensen, Doris Ann *antique dealer, researcher, writer*

Hansville
Blalock, Ann Bonar *evaluation researcher*

Hoquiam
Lamb, Isabelle Smith *manufacturing executive*

Issaquah
Cain, Coleen W. *writer, educator*
Drazdoff, Nola Gay *psychologist*
Newbill, Karen Margaret *elementary school educator, education educator*

Kelso
Spear, Patricia Ann *principal*

Kenmore
Montague, Deborah Marie *elementary school educator, music educator, consultant*
Sokol, Jennifer Marie *musician*

Kennewick
Fann, Margaret Ann *counselor*
Merkel, Patricia Mae *retired school system administrator*
Morris, Rusty Lee *architectural consulting firm executive*
Sullivan-Schwebke, Karen Jane *lawyer*

Kent
Dumitrescu, Cristina M. *intensive care nurse*

Kettle Falls
Pancoast, Brandy Elizabeth *music educator*

Kirkland
Barto, Deborah Ann *physician*
Sorenson, Lynette Evelyn *librarian*
Szablya, Helen Mary *writer, language educator*

La Center
Bryan, Sharon E. *literature and language educator*

Lacey
Van Leishout, Leslie Ann *theater educator, director*

Lakewood
Borgford, Norma Jeanne *minister*
Scannell, Vicki *humanities and language educator, consultant*

Langley
Cammermeyer, Margarethe *retired medical/surgical nurse*
Good, Linda Lee *music educator, musician*
Medlock, Ann *not-for-profit developer, writer*

Lilliwaup
McGrady, Corinne Young *design company executive*

Longview
Campbell, Kristine Koetting *academic administrator*

Lopez Island
Brownstein, Barbara Lavin *geneticist, educator, director*

Lummi Island
Hanson, Polly (Pauline) Mae Early *librarian*

Lynnwood
Floten, Barbara Jean *educational dean*
Tebbs, Carol Ann *secondary school educator, academic administrator*

Maple Valley
Aquino, Mary Ann *elementary school educator*

Marysville
Adams, Julie Karen *psychologist*

Medina
Ward, Marilyn Beeman *commissioner*

Mercer Island
Carey, Susan M. *psychologist*
Kessler, Gale Suzanne *psychologist, educator*
Langhout-Nix, Nelleke *artist*

Mill Creek
Dubois, Christine *writer, educator*
Latta, Diana Lennox *retired interior designer*

Monroe
Kirwan, Katharyn Grace (Mrs. Gerald Bourke Kirwan Jr.) *retired small business owner*

Montesano
Boyer, Carol A. *elementary school educator*

Moses Lake
Aur, Marina V. *choir conductor, music educator*
Irwin, Frances Darlene *nurse*

Naches
Assink, Nellie Grace *agricultural executive*

Newcastle
Rosa-Bray, Marilyn *physician*

Newport
Samson, Valerie J. *elementary school educator, consultant*

Nordland
Kepner, Rita Marie (Rita Marie Kramnicz) *communications educator, artist*
Kramnicz, Rosanne *freelance writer*

Normandy Park
Levack, Edna Bevan *music educator, choir director*

North Bend
Benyshek, Denita Maree *psychotherapist, educator, artist*

Oak Harbor
Lightbourne, Alesa M. *writer, educator*

Ocean Park
Lee, Martha *artist, writer*

Olympia
Anderson, Vicki Susan *legislative staff member, travel consultant*
Bergeson, Teresa *school system administrator*
Boland, Winnifred Joan *retired librarian*
Bridge, Bobbe Jean *state supreme court justice*
Coontz, Stephanie Jean *history professor, writer*
Fairhurst, Mary E. *state supreme court justice*
Fisher, Nancy Louise *pediatrician, geneticist, retired nurse*
Fleskes, Carol Lynn *environmental engineer*
Gregoire, Christine O. *governor, former state attorney general*
Haugen, Mary Margaret *state legislator*
Hayes, Maxine Delores *public health service officer, physician, pediatrician*
Humphrey, Camilla Marie *retired special education educator*
Hutchins, Diane Elizabeth Rider *librarian*
Isaki, Lucy Power Slyngstad *lawyer*
Jun, Heesoon *psychology professor*
Kessler, Lynn Elizabeth *state legislator*
Long, Jeanine Hundley *retired state legislator*
Macduff, Ilone Margaret *music educator*
Madsen, Barbara A. *state supreme court justice*
Myers, Sharon Diane *auditor*
Owens, Susan *state supreme court justice*
Randlett, Mary Willis *photographer*
Roach, Pam *state legislator*
Selecky, Mary C. *state agency administrator*
Spanel, Harriet *state legislator*
Tremblay, Gail Elizabeth *art educator*
Zussy, Nancy Louise *librarian*

Oysterville
Holway, Susan E. *writer*

Parkland
Johnson, LuAn K. *disaster management consultant*

Port Angeles
Lindberg, Judith Ann *retired elementary school educator*
McComb, Leann Marie *middle school educator*
McCormick, Karen Louise *savings and loan association executive*
Muller, Carolyn Bue *physical therapist, volunteer*
YMoore, Pamela Gay *music educator*

Port Ludlow
Pappas, Shirley Ann *sales executive*

Port Orchard
Albertus, Esther L. *vice principal*

Port Townsend
Buhler, Jill Lorie *editor, writer*
Miller, Maria B. *retired educator*

Poulsbo
Wayne, Kyra Petrovskaya *writer*

Pullman
Kelley, Margaret Mary *music educator, musician*
McSweeney, Frances Kaye *psychology professor*
Meier, Kathryn Elaine *pharmacologist, educator*
Paznokas, Lynda Sylvia *elementary school educator*
Sprunger, Leslie Karen *physiologist, educator*
Thomashow, Linda Suzanne *microbiologist*

Puyallup
Brittin, Marie E. *retired communications, psychology, speech-language and hearing science educator*
Phillips, Gail Susan *elementary school educator*
Sims, Darcie Dittberner *grief management specialist, psychotherapist, clinical hypnotherapist*

Redmond
Ambrose, Adele D. *communications executive*
Bottenberg, Joyce Harvey *writer, social services administrator*
Bradford, Joanne K. *computer software company executive*
Butler, Jannette Sue *human resources professional*
Doman, Margaret Horn *government policy consultant*
Oaks, Lucy Moberley *retired social worker*
Oliver, Nuria *computer scientist*

Renton
O'Dell, Patsy June *art gallery director*

Richland
Chou, Charissa J. *staff scientist*
Darby, Nancy *secondary school educator*
Ellis, Patricia *primary school educator*
Ristow, Gail Ross *art educator, paralegal, children's rights advocate*

Ridgefield
Potter, Debby *art educator*

Seattle
Allen, Judith Syma *art educator, artist*
Auer, Nancy Jane *emergency physician, medical association administrator*
Barnard, Kathryn Elaine *nursing educator, researcher*
Beaumonte, Phyllis Ilene *retired secondary school educator*
Beckmann, M. Patricia *biochemist*
Behler, Diana Ipsen *Germanic and comparative literature educator*
Berkowitz, Bobbie *medical educator*
Berni, Rosemarian Rauch *rehabilitation and oncology nurse*
Bibaud, Rene *artist, performer, consultant*
Bird, Sue (Suzanne Brigit Bird) *professional basketball player*
Bishop, Virginia Wakeman *retired librarian, retired humanities educator*
Blase, Nancy Gross *librarian*
Boersma, P. Dee *marine biologist, educator*
Boggs, Paula Elaine *lawyer*
Brandvold, Aurora Pauline *nursing researcher*
Burchfield, Susan *psychologist*
Burrows, Elizabeth MacDonald *religious organization executive, educator*
Byrd, Joann Kathleen *newswriter*
Chapman, Fay L. *lawyer*
Char, Patricia Helen *lawyer*
Clark, Dawn A. *architect*
Coffman, Sandra Jeanne *psychologist*
Coleman, Debra Lynn *electrical engineer*
Cote, Charlotte June *social sciences educator, consultant*
Covington, Germaine Ward *municipal agency administrator*
Cunningham, Janis Ann *lawyer*
Dawson, Patricia Lucille *surgeon*
Deming, Jody Wheeler *oceanography educator*
de Tornyay, Rheba *nursing educator, retired dean*
Dillard, Marilyn Dianne *property manager*
Dimmick, Carolyn Reaber *federal judge*
Dombro, Marcia Winters *nurse, academic administrator, educator*
El-Moslimany, Ann Paxton *paleoecologist, educator, writer*
Fetterly, Mary E. *counseling administrator*
Fidel, Raya *information science educator*
Fletcher, Betty Binns *federal judge*
Fluke, Lyla Schram (Mrs. John M. (Lyla) Fluke Sr.) *publisher*
Gates, Melinda French *foundation administrator*
Gates, Mimi Gardner *museum director*
Giblett, Eloise Rosalie *retired hematologist*
Gimbrère, Kathreen *psychiatrist, educator*
Glover, Karen Elaine *lawyer*
Godden, Jean W. *columnist*
Golston, Joan Carol *psychotherapist*
Gordon, Shirley Blom *college president*
Green, G. Dorsey *psychologist, author*
Grimley, Janet Elizabeth *newspaper editor*
Groshong, Laura Wolf *psychotherapist, researcher*
Gunter, Laurie M. *retired nurse educator*
Gwinn, Mary Ann *newspaper reporter*
Hampton, Shelley Lynn *hearing impaired educator*
Hannaford, Janet Kirtley *software administrative manager*
Harris, Kathryn A.Z. *internist*
Hayes, Camela Paige *psychologist*
Hazelton, Penny Ann *law librarian, educator*
Hellström, Ingegerd *medical researcher*
Henderson, Maureen McGrath *medical educator*
Herring, Susan Weller *dental educator, anatomist*
Hills, Regina J. *journalist*
Holcomb, Helen Lee *investor, interior designer*
Holmberg, Leona Ann *oncologist*
Jessen, Joel Anne *not-for-profit executive, art educator*
Johnsen, Lisa L. *lawyer*
Johnson, Mildred Grace Mash *investment company executive*
Jones, Susan Delanty *lawyer*
Kates, Carolyn Louise *physical therapist*
Katzman, Anita *writer*
Kelly, Carolyn Sue *newspaper executive*
Kelsey, Norma L. *labor union administrator*
Kennedy, Mary Virginia *retired diplomat*
King, Mary-Claire *geneticist, educator*
Kolbeson, Marilyn Hopf *holistic practitioner, artist, retired advertising executive, poet*
Kuhl, Patricia K. *science educator*
Kunkel, Georgie Bright *freelance writer, retired counselor*
Law, Marcia Elizabeth *rehabilitation services professional*
Leale, Olivia Mason *small business owner, import marketing executive*
Lee, Catherine Terri *psychiatrist*
Lidstrom, Mary E. *chemical engineering professor, microbiology professor*
Look, Janet K. *psychologist*
Mahdaviani, Miriam *choreographer, educator*
Marchese, Lisa Marie *lawyer, educator*
Martin, Joan Callaham *psychologist, educator*
Martínez, Yolanda R. *social services administrator*
Mason, Marilyn Gell *library administrator, writer, consultant*
Mathews, Sylvia Mary *foundation administrator*
McConney, Mary E. *information technology executive*
Miller, Leslie R. *obstetrician, gynecologist, educator*
Monsen, Elaine Ranker *nutritionist, educator, editor*
Murdock, Tullisse Antoinette (Toni Murdock) *academic administrator*
Nash, Cynthia Jeanne *journalist*
Nelson, Arleen Bruce *social worker*
Nelson, Karen Ann *lab administrator, director, immunologist, educator*
Niemi, Janice *retired lawyer, retired state legislator*
Niles, Nancy L. *endocrinologist*
Northen, Helen E. *retired social work educator, consultant*
Olmstead, Marjorie Ann *physics professor*
O'Neill, Maureen Anne *city administrator, arts administrator*
Osenbaugh, Kimberly W. *lawyer*
Ostrom, Katherine (Kate) Elma *retired secondary school educator*
Overstreet, Karen A. *federal bankruptcy judge*
Ozaki, Nancy Junko *performance artist, performing arts educator*
Pagon, Roberta Anderson *pediatrician, educator*
Papayannopoulou, Thalia *hematologist, oncologist, educator*
Parks, Patricia Jean *lawyer*
Patton, Jody *management company executive*
Perthou, Alison Chandler *interior designer*
Phillips, Cheryl *reporter*
Pizzorno, Lara Elise *medical writer, editor*
Punyon, Ellen *principal*
Reeves, Joan Hutchins *painter*
Reis, Jean Stevenson *administrative secretary*
Riddiford, Lynn Moorhead *biologist, educator*
Rivera, Bavi Edna (Nedi Rivera) *bishop*
Robinson, Nancy Mayer *psychology educator*
Ross, Joan Stuart *artist, art educator*
Rowe, Katherine L. *former computer company executive*
Ruffner, Ginny Martin *artist, glassblower*
Rule, Ann *author*
Russell, Francia *ballet director, educator*
Sandahl, Bonnie Beardsley *nursing administrator*
Sandstrom, Alice Wilhelmina *accountant*
Sas, Ellen *bank executive*
Schwartz, Pepper Judith *sociologist, educator*
Schwartz, Rosalye Ann *retired education educator*
Scott, Cheryl M. *foundation administrator, healthcare educator*
Snow-Smith, Joanne Inloes *art history educator*
Solchany, JoAnne Elizabeth *psychotherapist, nursing educator*
Somerman, Martha J. *dean, dental educator*
Stanovsky, Elaine J.W. *minister, church organization administrator*
Stearns, Susan Tracey *lighting design company executive, lawyer*
Stokke, Diane Rees *lawyer*
Stonesifer, Patty (Patricia Q. Stonesifer) *foundation administrator*
Strombom, Cathy Jean *transportation planner, consultant*
Szkody, Paula *astronomy educator, researcher*
Takenaka, Toshiko *lawyer, educator*
Teller, Davida Young *psychology, physiology and biophysics educator*
Testy, Kellye *dean*
Thomas, Karen P. *composer, conductor*
Tift, Mary Louise *artist*
Townsend, Wendy *retired marketing executive*
Trott, Nancy Roberts *editor*
Tunnell, Clida Diane *air transportation specialist*
Ullman, Joan Connelly *history professor, researcher*
VanArsdel, Rosemary Thorstenson *English studies educator*
Vestal, Josephine Burnet *lawyer*
Wasserman, Harriet M. *academic administrator*
Weaver, Lois Jean *physician, educator*
Wechsler, Mary Heyrman *lawyer*
Wight, Julia Helen *secondary school educator*
Wilke, Sabine *language educator*
Williams, Joan Elaine *podiatric surgeon, educator*
Williams, Nancy *lawyer*
Wilson, L. Michelle *lawyer*
Wilson, Lizabeth Anne *dean, library director*
Wilson-McNamara, Pamela *microbiologist, educator*
Woo, Cathy M. *artist*
Woods, Nancy Fugate *dean, women's health nurse, educator*
Young, Nora Jane *actuary, consultant*
Yue, Agnes Kau-Wah *otolaryngologist*

Sedro Woolley
Weaver, Diane Celeste *music educator*

Selah
Forbes, Jeanne C. *secondary school educator*
Ring, Lucile Wiley *lawyer*

Sequim
Guilmet, Glenda Jean *artist*
Kaps, Kay A. *physical education educator, coach*
McGee, Jane Marie *retired elementary school educator*

Shelton
Russman, Irene Karen *artist*
Thomas-John, Yvonne Maree *artist, interior designer*

Shoreline
Bailey, Sandra *secondary school educator, department chairman*
Dolacky, Susan K. *music educator*
Ladas-Gaskin, Carol *therapist, educator, artist*
Matesky, Nancy Lee *music educator*

Silverdale
Balcomb, Mary Nelson *small business owner*
Shaw, Annita Louise *art educator*

Snohomish
Litzenberger, Renee Claire *music educator, elementary school educator*
Tuengel, Lisa Marie *elementary school educator*

Soap Lake
Wesley, Susan Bray *psychotherapist, music educator*

Spanaway
Paris, Kathleen *secondary school educator*
Parker, Lynda Christine Rylander *secondary school educator*

Spokane
Bender, Betty Wion *librarian*
Bozo, Molly Catherine *elementary school educator*
Cadwallader, Fay Margaret *social worker*
Chamberlain, Barbara Kaye *small business owner, communications executive*
Clarke, Judy *lawyer*
Clayton, Katherine Gayle *elementary school educator*
Cope, Kathleen Adelaide *critical care nurse, parish nurse, educator*
Danke, Virginia *educational administrator, travel consultant*
Doty Sewall, Dana Lynne *choral director*
Dreis, Margaret K. *music educator, peer advisor*
Finley, Kathleen Marie *marriage and family therapist, educator*
Fritts, Anna Nicole *psychologist*
Gilpatrick, Janet *public relations executive, consultant*
Hood-Ryker, Joan Crandell *retired counselor*
Horton, Susan Pittman *bank executive*
Imbrogno, Cynthia *judge*
Lane, Iris Mary *retired elementary school educator*
Lee, Sun Myung *physician*
Linn, Diana Patricia *retired elementary school educator*
Martin, Janet Lynn *health facility administrator*
Metcalf, Ginger (Virginia) Arvan *psychotherapist, consultant*
Mobley, Karen Ruth *art director*
Murphy, Claire Rudolf *author, consultant*

Nemetz Mills, Patricia Louise *engineering educator*
Norell, Diane Marie *social worker, occupational therapist, educator*
Pfister, Terri *city official*
Powers, Theresa Mack *medical/surgical nurse, psychotherapist*
Rowley, Kathleen Dorothy *elementary school educator*
Stanley, Heidi *bank executive*
Steele, Karen Dorn *journalist*

Stanwood
Birkestol, Annabelle Mollie Elsie *retired elementary school educator*

Steilacoom
Norris, Laurie *secondary mathematics educator*

Sultan
Duffy, Anne M. *artist*

Tacoma
Bartlett, Norma Thyra *retired administrative assistant*
Baxter, Sheila R. *career military officer*
Brenner, Elizabeth (Betsy Brenner) *publishing executive*
Crotto, Denice *elementary school educator*
Don, Audrey *clinical psychologist, neuropsychologist, violist, artist*
Dressel, Melanie *bank executive*
Duchesne, Christina *secondary school educator*
Fischer, Karen A. *librarian*
Forrest, Kelly Alexandra *psychology professor*
Glick, R. Sara *music educator and performer, composer, writer*
Hacker, Colleen Marie *physical education educator, consultant, dean*
Harris, Marian S. *social work educator*
Hiller, Marsha Kay *physical therapist*
Lewis, Jan Patricia *education educator*
Pribble, Elizabeth J. *retired airline administrator*
Van Ry, Kimberly Anne *secondary school educator*
Wanwig, Annette Clare *nursing administrator*

Toppenish
Alexander, Judith Elaine *psychologist*
Ross, Kathleen Anne *academic administrator*

Tukwila
Carter, Pamela Jean *elementary school educator*

University Place
Pliskow, Vita Sari *anesthesiologist*

Vancouver
Engelker, Lynsey L. *athletic trainer, professional athletics manager*
Ernsberger, Phyllis W. *musician*
Hennum, Susanna Shelly *art history educator*
Hulburt, Lucille Hall *artist, educator*
Mabry, Linda S. *education educator*
Ogden, Valeria Munson *management consultant, state representative*
Perry, Daphne *social worker*
Raker, Emily Ellen *music educator*
Tuttle, Marcia *retired elementary school educator, music educator*
Vossler, Deborah J. *mathematics and science educator*

Vashon
Schwennesen, Carol Ann *artist, educator*

Walla Walla
Cooper, Sarah Jean *nursing educator*
Hagan, Dalia Lapatinskas *library director*
McIlvaine, Patricia Morrow *physician*
Rasmussen, Jo Anne Dickens *speech educator, theater director*
Rasmussen, Lisa Anne *art department administrator, art educator, art gallery director*
Ringhoffer, Winnifred Miriam *music educator, consultant*

Washougal
Semke-Fox, Suzanne Marie *elementary school educator*

Wenatchee
Marion, Sarah Kathleen *music educator*
Rappé, Teri Wahl *piano educator*

Woodway
Kent, Aimee Bernice Petersen *small business owner, interior designer, landscape architect, artist*

Yakima
Beehler, Tobi Lorraine *elementary school educator, education educator*
Newland, Ruth Laura *small business owner*
Savage, Carla Lee *insurance agent*
Scott, Ruth Ellen *music educator*
Walker, Lorene *retired elementary school educator*

WEST VIRGINIA

Alderson
Phipps, Meg Scott *former commissioner*

Barboursville
Parsons, Martha McGhee *rehabilitation nurse*

Beaver
White, Barbara Ann *technologist*

Beckley
Rhoades, Marye Frances *paralegal*

Bluefield
Brown, Sheri Lynn *artist, poet, educator*
Francis, Kerri Ann *athletic trainer*
Frazer, Teresa Elizabeth *pediatrician, endocrinologist*
Turnbull, Margaret Coombs *librarian*

Bridgeport
Jones, Mary Lou *real estate broker, real estate company executive*

Bunker Hill
Kifer, Brenda A. *medical/surgical and critical care nurse*

Charles Town
Fortney, Kimberly Benson *health and sports medicine educator*
Starks, Doris N. *retired nursing educator, administrator*
Wharton, Mary Merchant *secondary school educator*

Charleston
Arrington, Carolyn Ruth *school system administrator, consultant*
Betts, Rebecca A. *lawyer*
Brightbill, Janet M. *music educator*
Chilton, Elizabeth Easley Early *newspaper executive*
Davis, Robin Jean *state supreme court chief justice*
Higginbotham, Deborah Watts *social worker*
Ireland, Betty *state official*
King, Rebecca Jane *nursing administrator, educator*
Manning, Sherry Fischer *retired academic administrator, telecommunications industry executive*
Mellert, Lucie Anne *writer, photographer*
Meschke, Debra JoAnn *polymer chemist*
Offutt, Rebecca Sue *business and sales executive*
Oliver, Barbara Lynn *special education educator*
Richardson, Sally Keadle *academic administrator*
Smith, Stuart Lewis *community volunteer*
Stanley, Mary Elizabeth *judge*
Walker, Martha Yeager *state agency administrator, former state senator*
Zimmerman, Ericka Point *academic administrator*

Clarksburg
Keeley, Irene Patricia Murphy *federal judge*
Lapuz-De La Pena, Erlinda Laron *pathology professor*
Leuliette, Connie Jane *secondary school educator*
Yanero, Lisa Joyce *medical and surgical nurse*

Cross Lanes
Kinsolving, Ann Odene *elementary school educator, musician*

Davisville
Watts, Pamela Rae *elementary school educator*

Dunbar
Given, Melissa Ann *elementary school educator, educational consultant*

Elkins
Murphy, Patricia Ann *physician, otolaryngologist*
Payne, Gloria Marquette *business educator*

Elkview
Chambers-Ross, Charlotte Boyd *social worker, artist*

Fairmont
DeVito, Teresa Marie *artist*
Dudley-Eshbach, Janet *university president*
Martin, Evelyn G. *small business owner*
Swiger, Elizabeth Davis *chemist, educator*

Fayetteville
Seay-Bell, Margaretta *pastoral counselor*

Flemington
Miller, Patricia Anne *physician assistant*

Follansbee
Law, Phyllis Hampton *secondary school educator*

Frankford
Mazzio-Moore, Joan L. *retired radiology educator, physician*

Great Cacapon
Coe, Diana Ward (Dina Coe) *poet, writer*

Harpers Ferry
Cooley, Hilary Elizabeth *county official*

Hinton
Eagle, Karen Sue *special education educator*

Huntington
Engle, Jeannette Cranfill *medical technician*
Fannin, Josephine Jewell *social services administrator*
Fike, Dorothy Jean *science educator*
Howerton, Cheryl Alley *secondary school educator*
Joyce-Norris, Elaine Rozelle *elementary school educator*
Mayer, Lynne Supovitz *academic administrator*
Mills, Nina Rosalie *social worker*
Pratt, Mary Louise *librarian, writer*
Welch, Lynne Brodie *nursing school dean*

Kearneysville
Lotze, Evie Daniel *psychodramatist*

Keyser
Falkowski, Theresa Gae *chemistry educator*
Stephen, Tina Marie *elementary school educator*

Kingwood
Moyers, Sylvia Dean *retired medical librarian*
Zigray, Debra Renee *elementary school educator*

Logan
Baksh, Brenda J. *communications educator*

Marlinton
Sharp, Jane Price *retired editor*

Martinsburg
Ayers, Anne Louise *small business owner, consultant, counselor*
Braithwaite, Marilyn Jean *realtor*
Harkins, Ann M. *federal agency administrator*
Mauck, Elaine Carole *retired secondary education educator*

Monaville
Bell, Joann *nurse*

Morgantown
Albrink, Margaret Joralemon *medical educator*
Allamong, Betty Davis *retired academic administrator*
Ashenfelter, Helen Louise *elementary school educator*
Beattie, Diana Scott *biochemistry professor*
Bell, Dawn Marie *pharmacist, educator*
Blaydes, Sophia Boyatzies *English language educator*
DeFotis, Constance *choral conductor*
Drvar, Margaret Adams *vocational school educator*
Fergus, Victoria J. *art and education educator*
Jackson, Ruth Moore *academic administrator*
Janoo, Jabin *obstetrician, gynecologist*
Landreth, Barbara Bugg *librarian*
Peterson, Sophia *political scientist, educator*
Pinheiro, Germania Araujo *physician, researcher*
Scudiere, Debra Hodges *lawyer*
Sikora, Rosanna Dawn *emergency physician, educator*
Sturm, Connie Arrau *music and music education educator*
Waller, Stacey *psychologist*
Wenger, Sharon Louise *cytogeneticist, researcher, educator*
Wilson, Mary Alice *musician, educator*

New Martinsville
Francis, Elizabeth Romine *secondary school educator, theater director*

Parkersburg
Burdette, Jane Elizabeth *former nonprofit association executive, consultant*
Rowland, Angela Kay *education educator, consultant*
Wilson, Roberta Bush *retired psychotherapist, accountant*

Peterstown
Robertson, Connie Lynn *elementary school educator*

Princeton
Bolen, Bettye Sue *academic administrator*
Moody, Frances Marie *former performing arts educator, musician*
Vrinceanu, Alina Daniela *psychiatrist*

Ranson
Rudacille, Sharon Victoria *medical technician*

Ravenswood
Gouckenour, Sharon Craft *elementary school educator*

Ripley
Paxton, Julia Ann *music educator, director*

Ronceverte
Hooper, Anne Dodge *pathologist, educator*

Saint Albans
Alderson, Gloria Frances Dale *rehabilitation specialist*

Salem
Raad, Virginia *pianist, educator*

Shady Spring
Reed, Cathy Lorraine *elementary school educator*

Shepherdstown
Elliott, Jean Ann *retired library director*
Locke, Emma Mae *retired elementary school educator*
Spencer, Heidi Honnold *psychotherapist, writer, educator*
Valentine, Mary Ann *graphics designer*
Wilson, Rebecca Ann *retired English and special education educator*

Shinnston
Ford, Alma Regina *retired union official, educator*
Spears, Jae *state legislator*

South Charleston
Fishkin, Anne Sonya *retired special education educator*
Stedman, Molly Renee *special education educator, researcher*
Steinberg, Beth Aileen *employee assistance manager*

Spencer
Parker, Theresa Ann Boggs *special education educator, music educator*

Vienna
Acree, Wilma Katheryn *retired secondary school educator*
Arthur, Margaret Ferne *nurse, insurance paramedic*

Wayne
Davis, Paula May *music educator*

Webster Springs
Moore, Alma Merle *association executive*

Wellsburg
Viderman, Linda Jean *legal assistant, corporate financial executive*

West Columbia
Fowler, Sandra Lynn *poet*

Weston
Rastle, Maxine Shiflet Cole *retired elementary school educator*
Riddle, Anna Lee *retired elementary school educator, retired music educator*

Wheeling
Heceta, Estherbelle Aguilar *retired anesthesiologist*
Hickcox, Leslie Kay *health educator, consultant*
Matyskiela, Kristina L. *director*
Phillis, Marilyn Hughey *artist*
Poland, Michelle Lind *medical, surgical, and critical care nurse*
Thurston, Bonnie Bowman *religious studies educator, minister, poet*
Valdrini, Rita *prosecutor*

White Sulphur Springs
Spencer, Linda Lou *elementary school educator*

Williamsburg
Scott, Pamela Moyers *physician assistant*

Winfield
Barnett, Cheryl Jividen *elementary school educator*

WISCONSIN

Appleton
Amm, Sophia Jadwiga *artist, educator*
Beck, Jill *academic administrator, dancer, educator*
Malaney, Stephanie J. *reading specialist*
Meyer, Cheryl Lorraine *music educator*
Perrine, Colleen Fitzmartin *composer, educator*
Privatt, Kathy Lynne *theater educator, theater director, actor*

Auburndale
Fowler, Sue Ann *elementary school educator*

Baileys Harbor
Zimmerman, Irena Agnes *nun, poet, educator*

Balsam Lake
Mattson, Carol Linnette *social services administrator*

Baraboo
Gogue, Susan Diane *elementary school educator*
Mesmer, Karen Luann *elementary school educator*

Barron
Carley, Tamatha Lynn *music educator*
Kienbaum, Janice Mae *reading specialist*

Bayside
Topetzes, Fay Kalafat *retired school guidance counselor*

Beaver Dam
Brandenburg, Annabel June *retired small business owner*
Heffron, Judith Ann *music educator*
Wright-Everett, Rose Mary *elementary school educator*

Belleville
Alsteens, Susette Marie *English educator, athletic director*

Beloit
Doherty, Rhonda Sue *mental health services professional*
Licary, Cheryl Ann *retired music educator, church musician*

Blanchardville
Ryser, Robyn Carey *elementary school educator*

Bloomer
Kane, Lucile M. *retired archivist, historian*

Brookfield
Lavender, Cheryl Ann *music educator, composer, writer*
Pottebaum, Sharon Mitchell *health educator*
Rooney, Carol Bruns *dietician*

Cascade
Baumann, Carol Edler *retired political scientist*

Chippewa Falls
Anderson, Greta Mae *health facility administrator, educator*

Clintonville
Primmer, Lillian Juanda *science educator*

Columbus
Schellin, Patricia Marie Biddle *secondary school educator*

Conrath
Bentley, Linda Diane *application developer, artist*

Coon Valley
Nordstrom, Donna Olene *language educator*

Crivitz
Gerhart, Lorraine Pfeiffer *elementary school educator*

De Pere
Davis, Amanda Nicole *elementary school educator*
Frechette, Bonnie L. *secondary school educator*
Molnar, Kathleen Kay *management information systems educator*

Deerfield
Bazan, Angela Lynn *social studies educator*

Delafield
Haugner, Carolyn M. *elementary school educator*
Welsh, Christine Marie *small business owner, dance educator*

Delavan
Gauger, Michele Roberta *photographer*
Lepke, Charma Davies *musician, educator*

Dodgeville
Filardo, Tamra L. *social studies educator*

Dousman
Harris, Dorothy D. *residential treatment therapist*
Porter, Sally Louise *artist*

Drummond
Lintula, Margaret M. *elementary and secondary school educator*

Eagle
Kalnes, Donna M. Simondet *retired principal, alcohol and drug abuse education program director*

Eagle River
Weber, Lori Ann *elementary school educator*

Eau Claire
Biegel, Eileen Mae *retired hospital executive*
Hugo, Miriam Jeanne *counseling psychologist, educator*
Johnson, Eleanor Mae *education educator*
Kirkhorn, Lee-Ellen Charlotte *community health nurse, educator*
Klink, JoAnn Marie *clergywoman*
Lippold, Judith Rosenthal *retired occupational therapist*
McDougall-Gibbs, Mary Elizabeth (Betsy McDougall-Gibbs) *early childhood special education educator*
Sands, Dawn M. *lawyer*
See, Patti K. *humanities educator*
Tiefel, Virginia May *librarian*

Edgar
Olson, Rachel Ann *performing arts educator, director*

Elkhorn
Reinke, Doris Marie *retired elementary school educator*
Straz, Irene N. *special education educator*

Elm Grove
Rose, Darlene Joyce *speech pathology/audiology services professional*

Evansville
Finque, Susan Beth *theatre artist, theater director*

Fennimore
Croft, Candace Ann *psychology professor, academic administrator, small business owner*
Jahnke, Lisa Jo *secondary school educator*
Kopp, Carol Ann *special education educator*

Fitchburg
Schwenn, Kim Elizabeth *language educator*

Fond Du Lac
Christie, Jacqueline Ann *nurse*
Kuhls, Barbara Sue *medical/surgical nurse*

Fort Atkinson
Lorman, Barbara K. *retired state senator*
McDaniel, Kristen *secondary school educator*

Fox Point
Ellis, Nancy Kempton *adult education educator*
Froemming, Barbara G. *retired home economics educator*

Franklin
Resar, Laura A. *mathematics educator*
Stenzel, Mary Francis *social worker*

Franksville
Jensen, Dana G. *literature educator*

Glidden
Tunison, Dawn M. R. *music educator*

Goodman
Cummings, Toni Marie *language educator*

Gordon
La Liberte, Ann Gillis *graphics designer, educator*

Grafton
Kettling, Virginia *retired health facility administrator*

Green Bay
Capelle, Elaine M. *financial planner*
Domenoski, Ellen Marie *staff nurse*
Erickson, Ruth Alice *poet, artist*
LaViolette, Catherine Patricia *librarian*
McIntosh, Elaine Virginia *nutrition educator*
Salo, Patricia Ann *elementary school educator*
Schuecker, Amy K. *obstetrician, gynecologist*
Thill, Linda Susan *secondary school educator*

Green Lake
Mitchell, Tawnia Juanita *elementary school educator, music educator*

Greendale
Bousquet-Monk, Nancy Kathryn *elementary school educator*
Kaiser, Ann Christine *magazine editor*
Patterson, Amanda Margaret *music educator*
Pohl, Kathleen Sharon *editor*
Vinent-Cantoral, Aida R. *mediator*

Greenfield
Jirovec, Mary Ann *music educator*
McKillip, Patricia Claire *operatic soloist*
Redlinger, Melinda *secondary school educator*

Hales Corners
Case, Karen Ann *lawyer*
Holmes, Leigh Ann *web technician*

Hancock
Vroman, Barbara Fitz *writer, educator*

Hartford
Brandt, Pamela Ann *art educator, special education educator*
Karlus, Mary Teresa *elementary school educator*

Hartland
Judd, Diane Barbaa *literature and language educator*
Schabow, Nancy A. Dexter *music educator*
Stamsta, Jean F. *artist*

Horicon
Gasner, Renee *music educator*

Howards Grove
Bacigalupo, Sarah Elizabeth *literature and language educator*

Janesville
Davis, Paulette Jean Turner *secondary school educator, editor, consultant*
Detert-Moriarty, Judith Anne *graphic designer, educator, volunteer*
Thomas, Margaret Ann *principal*

Jefferson
Smith, Dena Michele *physical education educator*

Johnson Creek
Quest, Kristina Kay *art educator, small business owner*

Juda
Bredeson, Brenda Penniston *secondary school educator*

Juneau
Shramek, Erin Elizabeth *language educator*

Kaukauna
Brewster, Margaret Emelia *artist*

Kenosha
Cassiday, Karen Lynn *psychologist*
Gurnack, Anne Marie *healthcare educator, consultant*
Gustin, Brenda Sue *retired art educator, painter*
Helman, Iris Barca *elementary school educator, consultant*
Kolb, Vera M. *chemist, educator*
Kollatz, Rebecca Lynn *music educator*
Marrinan, Susan Faye *lawyer*
Persons, Kari Lynn *physical education educator, basketball coach*

Kewaskum
Blomquist, MaryLane Neubauer *secondary school educator*

Kimberly
Koll, Kathryn Jane *music educator*

Kohler
Kohler, Laura E. *human resources executive*
Reilly, Sharon *literature educator*

La Crosse
Anderson, Gwyn C. *computer company executive*
Birkle, Linda Jean *elementary school educator*
Eber, Laura Jean *personal trainer*
Gorman, Kathleen Jean *performing arts educator, choreographer*
Hatfield, Mary Lou *nurse, paramedic*
Johnson, Kim G. *medical/surgical nurse, consultant*
Oswalt, Sally Hundt *small business owner*
Poulton, Leslee *language educator*
Seebach, Elizabeth Emily *psychologist, educator*

Lac Du Flambeau
Zimmer, Amelia Ellen *principal, educator*

Lake Geneva
O'Reilly, Sarah M. *sales executive*

Lake Mills
Lazaris, Pamela Adriane *community planning and development consultant*

Laona
Sturzl, Alice A. *school library administrator*

Lomira
Olson, Ellen Jo *elementary school educator*

Luck
Wicklund, Judith K. *language educator, writer*

Madison
Abrahamson, Shirley Schlanger *state supreme court chief justice*
Albers, Sheryl Kay *state legislator*
Baldwin, Janice Murphy *lawyer*
Barnick, Helen *retired judicial clerk*
Bartley, Linda L. *musician, music educator*
Bauman, Susan Joan Mayer *mayor, lawyer, commissioner*
Behnke, Michelle A. *lawyer*
Beyer-Mears, Annette *physiologist*
Blankenburg, Julie J. *librarian*
Bochert, Linda H. *lawyer*
Braden, Betty Jane *legal association administrator*
Bradley, Ann Walsh *state supreme court justice*
Burmaster, Elizabeth *school system administrator*
Burns, Elizabeth Murphy *media executive*
Charo, Robin Alta *law educator*
Ciplijauskaite, Birute *humanities educator*
Coppersmith, Susan Nan *physicist*
Crabb, Barbara Brandriff *federal judge*
Darling, Alberta Helen *state legislator, art gallery director, marketing professional*
DeJoie, Carolyn Barnes Milanes *educator*
Deming, Joan *clergy*
Dierauf, Leslie Ann *wildlife veterinarian, conservation biologist, consultant*
Dubrow, Heather *literature educator*
Dunlavy, Colleen A. *historian*
Dunwoody, Sharon Lee *journalism and communications educator*
Engelman, Marjorie Jeckel *retired higher education administrator*
Faulkner, Julia Ellen *opera singer*
Foley, Ellen Madaline *journalist*
Gurkow, Helen J. *retired physician*
Handelsman, Jo *plant pathologist, educator*
Hansen, Sherri M. *psychiatrist*
Hawkinson, Lorraine A. *librarian*
Ivancic, Monika *director, research scientist*
Janson Heintz, Maureen *dancer, educator, choreographer*
Johnson, Jean Elaine *nursing educator*
Johnson, Maryl Rae *cardiologist*
Johnson, Sheri *state agency administrator, psychologist*
Knoll, Rose Ann *radiologist, technologist*
Kreilick, Marjorie Ellen *education educator*
Krusick, Margaret Ann *state legislator*
K-Turkel, Judith Leah Rosenthal (Judi K-Turkel) *writer, editor, publisher*
Lautenschlager, Peggy A. *state attorney general*
Lawton, Barbara *lieutenant governor*
Lucas, Patricia Whittlinger *small business owner*
Marlett, Judith Ann *nutritional sciences educator, researcher*
Marrett, Cora B. *science educator*
McCallum, Laurie Riach *state government lawyer*
McDonald, Susan B. *psychologist*
Melli, Marygold Shire *law educator*
Migas, Rosalie Ann *social worker*
Mitchell, Bryce Mahoney *psychotherapist, counselor*
Moore, Lorrie *writer, English professor*
Myers, Frances J. *artist*
Netzer, Lanore A(gnes) *retired educational administration educator*
Nicka, Betty Lou *secondary school educator*
Ossorio, Pilar Nicole *professional association administrator*
Pillaert, E(dna) Elizabeth *museum curator*
Rice, Joy Katharine *psychologist, education educator*
Riley, Jocelyn Carol *writer, television producer*
Roessler, Carol Ann *state legislator*
Roggensack, Patience Drake *state supreme court justice*
Rosser, Annetta Hamilton *composer*
Rowe, Marieli Dorothy *media literacy education consultant, organization executive, editor*
Sapiro, Virginia *academic administrator, political science professor*
Sherman, Julia Ann *psychologist*
Simone, Beverly Sue *academic administrator*
Sims, Terre Lynn *insurance company executive*
Sobkowicz, Hanna Maria *neurologist, researcher*
Sollenberger, Donna Kay Fitzpatrick *hospital and clinics executive*
Spencer, Cheryl L. *literature and language educator*
Steingass, Susan R. *lawyer*
Stites, Susan Kay *writer, human resources specialist*
Strier, Karen Barbara *anthropologist, educator*
Swan, Barbara J. *lawyer*
Thompson, Barbara Storck *state official*
Turner, Monica Goigel *ecologist*
Underwood, Julie K. *dean, former law educator*
Vandell, Deborah Lowe *educational psychology educator*
Whitney, Lori Ann *legislative staff member*
Wicklund, Gerri M. *finance educator*
Wolfe, Barbara L. *economics professor, researcher*
Young, Rebecca Mary Conrad *retired state legislator*
Youngerman, Nan Gronik *elementary school educator*
Zell, Josephine May *retired language educator*

Manitowoc
Schwarzenbart, Amy Jo *psychiatric nurse, case manager*
Shimek, Rosemary Geralyn *medical/surgical nurse*

Marinette
Malmstadt, Mary Jane *music educator*
Rice, Korlynn Kaye *elementary school educator*

Markesan
Chisnell, Debra Jean *special education educator*

Marshfield
Gardner, Ella Haines *artist*

Mc Farland
Deniston-Trochta, Grace Marie *educator, artist*

Medford
Wirkus, Carrie *elementary school educator*

Menasha
Streeter, Stephanie Anne *printing company executive*

Menomonee Falls
Diestelhorst, Amy Lea *obstetrician, gynecologist*
Hinnrichs-Dahms, Holly Beth *elementary school educator*
Janzen, Norine Madelyn Quinlan *clinical laboratory scientist*
Nelson, Mary Ellen Genevieve *adult education educator*

Menomonie
Cutnaw, Mary-Frances *retired communications educator, writer, editor*
Nyseth, Elizabeth Ann *retired secondary school educator*

Mequon
Denton, Peggy *occupational therapist, educator*
Kopfmann, Beverly Jean *small business owner*
Petersen, Dorothy Virginia *investment company executive*
Rice, Linda Lee *special education educator*
Tucholke, Christel-Anthony *artist, educator*
Wetzel, Karen J. *nurse*

Merrill
Goessl, Celine *head of religious order*

Middleton
Conaway, Jane Ellen *elementary school educator*
McDermott, Molly *lay minister*
Taylor, Fannie Turnbull *art association administrator, educator*

Milton
Parker, Letitia *secondary school educator*

Milwaukee
Babcock, Janice Beatrice *health facility administrator*
Ballman, Patricia Kling *lawyer*
Beaudry, Diane Fay *medical quality management executive*
Benfield, Linda E. *lawyer*
Carter, Charlene Ann *psychologist*
Davis, Susan F. *human resources specialist*
Delgado, Mary Louise *elementary school educator, secondary school educator, consultant, Internet company executive*
Eshetu, Gwendelbert Lewis *retired social worker*
Estrin, Alejandra Audrey *science educator*
Ferguson, Nancy L. *psychotherapist, social worker*
Fouad, Nadya A. *psychology professor*
Frank, Nancy *architecture educator*
Gallop, Jane (Jane Anne Gallop) *women's studies educator, writer*
Geske, Janine Patricia *law educator*
Gondek, Mary Jane (Mary Jane Suchorski) *property manager*
Grimes, Kristen *public health service officer*
Hamdani, Zubeda A. *elementary school educator*
Harris, Christine *dance company executive*
Hegerty, Nannette H. *police chief*
Heim, Kathryn Marie *psychiatric nurse*
Hidson, Patricia Diane *artist, educator*
Hubbard, Nancy *architecture educator*
Huston, Kathleen Marie *library administrator*
Keshvala, Seelpa H *secondary school educator*
Kessler, Joan F. *judge, lawyer*
Kiely, Paula *city librarian*
Kluthe, Kathleen A. *elementary school educator*
Kraut, Joanne Lenora *computer programmer, analyst*
Kupst, Mary Jo *psychologist, researcher*
Kwak, Eun-Joo *musician, educator*
Lea, Filomena *English language educator, writer*
Lenz, Debra Lynn *auditor*
Liebau, Catherine Annette *cardiac diagnostic nurse*
Lione, Gail Ann *lawyer*
Loehr, Stephanie Schmahl *psychotherapist, retired social worker*
McGinnity, Maureen Annell *lawyer*
McKinney, Venora Ware *librarian*
Mueller, Marylin *graphic supply company executive*
Murphy, Judith Chisholm *trust company executive*
Mykleby, Kathy *newscaster, reporter*
Neubauer, Lisa S. *lawyer*
Nielson, Kristy Ann *psychology educator, researcher*
Otto, Jean Hammond *journalist*
Peltz, Cissie Jean *art gallery director, cartoonist*
Piehler, Barbara F. *insurance company executive*
Pittman, Barbara N. *special education educator*
Poehlmann, JoAnna *artist, illustrator, book designer, educator*
Pugach, Marleen Carol *education educator*
Read, Sister Joel *academic administrator*
Rheams, Annie Elizabeth *education educator*
Rivera-Velazquez, Maria *marketing professional*
Sennett, Nancy J. *lawyer*
Shapiro, Mary Jo Farley *elementary school educator*
Shapiro, Robyn Sue *lawyer, educator*
Smith, Lois Ann *real estate company executive*
Sonnenberg, Linda L. *literacy educator*
Spann, Wilma Nadene *retired principal*
Stillman, Sharon J. *real estate broker*
Stokes, Kathleen Sarah *dermatologist, educator*
Sykes, Diane S. *federal judge, former state supreme court justice*
Taylor, Katherine *social services administrator*
Verhaalen, Marion *music educator*
Wake, Madeline Musante *academic administrator, nursing educator*
Waldbaum, Jane Cohn *art history educator*
Walsh, Kathleen *lawyer*
Weiner, Wendy L(ou) *elementary school educator, writer*
Wesner, Patricia *bank executive*
Williams, Maxine Eleanor *retired elementary school educator*
Zofkie, Marcia Mary *music educator*
Zurcher, Amelia Anne *literature educator*

Mishicot
Peters, Redebra Evyn *music educator*

Monona
Jensen, Jill Susan *music educator*

Monroe
Bean, Virginia Ann (Ginny Bean) *marketing executive*
Bennett, Judy A. *music educator*

Montello
Williams, Brenda Jeanne *literature and language educator*

Mukwonago
Koprowski, Suzanne Marie *educational diagnostician administrator, educator*
Yopps, Linda Lee *special education educator*

Neenah
Brehm-Gruber, Therese Frances *minister, consulting psychologist*
Orm, Sally S. *music educator, consultant*

Nekoosa
Ramirez, Mary Catherine *retired secondary school educator*

New Berlin
Belich, Kay S. *music educator*
Bielke, Patricia Ann *psychologist*
Duszynski-Waldbillig, Cynthia *piano educator, performer, adjudicator*
Gebhard, LaVerne Elizabeth *retired accounting educator*
Marsh, Clare Teitgen *retired school psychologist*
Winkler, Dolores Eugenia *retired health facility administrator*

New Franken
Tepe, Judith Mildred *vocal music teacher, choral director*

New Holstein
Frisch, Katherine Leigh *secondary school educator*

Oak Creek
Stroik, Marilyn L. *elementary school educator*
Weedman, Jean M. *secondary school educator*

Oconomowoc
Bleke, Diane K. *music educator, director*
Conrader, Constance Ruth *artist, writer*
Driscoll, Virgilyn Mae (Schaetzel) *retired art educator, artist, consultant*
Peebles, Allene Kay *manufactured housing company executive*
Reich, Rose Marie *retired art educator*

Oconto
Nichols, Diane Colleen *historian, retired municipal official*

Oregon
Glodowski, Shelley Jean *administrator, writer, musician*

Oshkosh
Buser, Rose M. *elementary school educator*
Cooper, Janelle Lunette *neurologist, educator*
Ristow, Thelma Frances *retired elementary school educator*
Smith, Merilyn Roberta *art educator*
Wells, Carolyn Cressy *social work educator*

Palmyra
Davis, Jaci Carroll *elementary school educator, musician*

Pelican Lake
Martin, Mary Wolf *newspaper editor*

Pembine
Mattison, Kathlene *secondary school educator*

Peshtigo
Prudhomme, Shirley Mae *small business owner*

Pewaukee
Farrow, Margaret Ann *former lieutenant governor*

Phelps
Christensen, Gloria Jean *secondary school educator*

Pittsville
Normington, Norma Shotwell *secretary*

Platteville
Armstrong, Amelia Luci *music educator*
Ressler, Amy June *theater educator, theater director*
Weber, Amelia Luci *music educator*

Plover
Kiefer, Kit Annette *editor*
Loteyro, Corazon Bigata *physician*

Plymouth
Groblewski, Jane (Jane Campbell) *secondary school educator*

Port Washington
Niffenegger, Tammie Jean *secondary school educator, science educator*

Racine
Baker, Joyce Mildred *medical/surgical nurse, volunteer*
Constantine, Margaret L(ouise) (Peggy Constantine) *newspaper reporter, freelance writer*
Johnson, Imogene Powers *foundation administrator*
Johnson-Leipold, Helen P. *outdoor recreation company executive*
Johnson-Marquart, Winnie *consumer products company executive*
Klein, Gabriella Sonja *retired communications executive*
Meyer, Alicia *special education educator*
Sahakian, Lillian Zarouhi *artist, designer*
Teegarden, Nicolee *artist, consultant, retired educator*
Walter, Barbara Sykes *reading educator*
Wright, Betty Ren *children's book writer*
Zimmel, Tammy Lynn *psychologist*

Redgranite
Borchardt, Betsy Olk *artist*

Reedsburg
Mockler, Jolee Marie *art educator*

Rhinelander
Wendt, Kristine Adams *librarian*

Rice Lake
Sampson, Zora J. *librarian*
Skrupky, Elaine Charlotte *art educator*
Strong, (Lin) Linda Louise *music educator*

Ripon
Dowdy, Harriet Brodhead *elementary school educator*
Prissel, Barbara Ann *paralegal, law educator*
Woolley, Jean Gibson *retired instructional designer, consultant*

River Falls
Crotty, Teri *education educator*
Krey, DeAn Marie *retired education educator*

Rudolph
Johnson, Ann Ruth *musician*

Salem
Zwirgzdas, Shirley Margaret *physical education educator*

Sauk City
Lins, Debra R. *bank executive*

Saukville
Gulan, Bonnie Marion *writer, researcher*

Seymour
Lentz, Cherie Lynn *nurse*

Sheboygan
Fritz, Kristine Rae *retired secondary school educator*
Ladiges, Lori Jean *learning disabilities specialist*

Sheboygan Falls
Deibert, Patricia J. *biology educator*

Shorewood
Bowers, Jane Meredith *retired music educator*

Sparta
Hagen, Joanne R. *elementary school educator*
Welch, Mary Rose Dwyer *secondary school educator*

Spring Green
Day, Sarah Jane *actor*

Stanley
Rasmussen, Dianne *English educator*

Stevens Point
Bunnell, Linda Hunt *academic administrator*
Doherty, Patricia Anne *psychologist*
Gott, Patricia A. *literature educator*

Stoughton
Ellickson, Judith A. *literature and language educator*
Winter, Shawne Nanisdilda *small business owner*

Sturgeon Bay
Korb, Joan *prosecutor*
Maher, Virginia Jones *art historian, educator*

Sturtevant
Brandes, Jo Anne *lawyer*

Sun Prairie
Jerg, Karen Leslie *elementary school educator*

Superior
Bowden, Laura Ann *retired secondary school educator, retired counselor*
Cheselski, Penny Lynn *special education educator*
McKnight, Patricia Gayle *musician, artist, writer, educator*
Robek, Mary Frances *business education educator*
Taylor, Winnifred Jane *psychologist*

Thiensville
Franciosi, L. Patt *psychologist, mental health services professional, consultant*

Three Lakes
Murphy, Erin Melissa *art educator*

Tomah
Neurohr, Shirley Ann *retired special education educator*

Two Rivers
Rank, Janet Carol *music educator*

Union Grove
Dawson, Rose Dorothy *elementary school educator*

Verona
Hawkins, Peggy Anne *veterinarian*
White, Carolyn Louise *music educator*

Viroqua
Banta, Vicki K. *mathematics educator*

Warrens
Potter, June Anita *small business owner*

Washburn
Krutsch, Phyllis *academic administrator*

Waterford
Hanson, Jody Elizabeth *special education educator*

Watertown
Burns, Noëlle Ann *art educator*

Waukesha
Bellovary, Cathy *social services administrator, volunteer*
Floeter, Valerie Ann *music educator*
Gustafson, Mardel Emma *secondary school educator, writer*
Leatherberry, Anne Knox Clark *architect*
Leekley, Marie Valpoon
Meyer, Debora Lynn *music educator*
Morris, Cathleen Ann *academic administrator*
Ness Marineau, Brenda L. *language educator*
Parsons, Virginia Mae *psychology educator*
Stringham, Phyllis Joan *retired music educator*

Waunakee
Simon, Sarah Marie *elementary school educator*

Waupaca
Hansen, Louise Hill *music educator, retired application developer*
Jahnke, Christiane Lynn *mathematics educator*

Wausau
Prey, Yvonne Mary *real estate broker*

Wauwatosa
Pomplun, Julie Ann *secondary school educator*

West Bend
Kogler, Donna Marie *elementary school educator*
Maskala, Kristen Lucy *orthopedic surgeon*
Roth, Kathleen C. *dentist*
VanBrunt-Kramer, Karen *business administration educator*
Wolff, Mickiah Ann *artist, educator*

Whitewater
Baica, Malvina Florica *mathematician, educator, researcher*
Busse, Eileen Elaine *special education educator*
Heidenreich, Lori Jean *music educator*
Kirst-Ashman, Karen Kay *social work educator*
Kumpaty, Hephzibah J. *chemistry professor*
Saunders, Martha Dunagin *academic administrator*

Wilmot
Volden, Stephanie Kay *science educator*

Winneconne
Gust, Joyce Jane *artist*

Wisconsin Dells
Kolumba, Kim Dale *elementary education educator, speech and language pathologist*

Wisconsin Rapids
Bilderback, Pamela Marie *elementary school educator*
Olson-Hellerud, Linda Kathryn *elementary school educator*

WYOMING

Basin
Gray, Lisa Marie *language educator*

Big Piney
Mitchell, Anne S. *music educator*

Casper
Boyes, Melanie Joan *secondary school educator*
Cotherman, Audrey Mathews *educational association administrator, management consultant*
Covert, Addey Elizabeth *art educator*
Davis, Lois Ann *computer specialist, educator*
Elliott, Marian Kay *real estate manager*
Foster, Vicki Anne *secondary school educator*
Graff, Cheryl L. *medical facility program administrator*
Hasely-Harshman, Tracy *nurse*
Jacobs, Carolyn Dianne Crouch *science educator*
Osborne, Gayle Ann *manufacturing executive*
Stoval, Linda *political party official*
True, Jean Durland *entrepreneur, oil industry executive, gas industry executive*
Underwood, Kristin Dana *elementary school educator*

Cheyenne
Carlson, Kathleen Bussart *law librarian*
Cornish, Nancy Lee *music educator*
Givens, Cynthia A. *educator*
Holden, Linda Kathleen *medical educator*
Kite, Marilyn S. *state supreme court justice, lawyer*
Kunz, April Brimmer *state legislator, lawyer*
LeBarron, Suzanne Jane *librarian*
Lee, Kristin H. *state agency administrator*
Lummis, Cynthia Marie *state official, lawyer*
Mockler, Esther Jayne *state senator*
Moore, Mary French (Muffy Moore) *potter, advocate*
Parrish, Denise Kay *regulatory accountant*
Thomson, Thyra Godfrey *former state official*
Woodhouse, Gay Vanderpoel *former state attorney general, lawyer*
Woodman, Lucy Rhodes *music educator*
Zumo, Billie Thomas *retired biologist*

Cody
Coe, Margaret Louise Shaw *community service volunteer*
Fees, Nancy Fardelius *special education educator*
Grimes, Daphne Buchanan *priest, artist*
Knaff, Rebecca E. *personal trainer*
Wormald, Kathleen Marie *elementary school educator*

Dubois
Glasser, Pamela Jean *musician, music educator*

Ethete
Tepper, Marcy Elizabeth *drug education director*

Evanston
Connelly, Diane *elementary school educator*

Green River
Albers, Dolores M. *secondary school educator*
Evans, Eileen *music educator*
Reinard, Kathleen Ann *elementary school educator*

Guernsey
Zimmerer, Nancy Jean *elementary school educator, rancher*

Jackson
Decker, Carol Arne *magazine publishing executive*
Hessel, Marieluise *art collector*
Law, Clarene Alta *small business owner, retired state legislator*

Lander
Alley, Nancy Corrin *elementary school educator*
Bakke, Luanne Kaye *music educator*
Nunley, Cynthia Ann *special education educator*

Laramie
Franks, Beverly Matthews *retired psychotherapist, consultant*
Hansen, Matilda *former state legislator*
Kinney, Lisa Frances *lawyer*
McBride, Judith *elementary school educator*
Moldenhauer, Susan *museum director, curator*
Schatz, Mona Claire Struhsaker *social worker, educator, consultant, researcher*
Schmitt, Diana Mae *elementary school educator*
Spiegelberg, Emma Jo *business education educator, academic administrator*
Thomas, Joi J. *personal trainer*
Williams, Martha Jane Shipe *psychologist, retired educator*

Moorcroft
McKillip, Mary *physical education educator*

Newcastle
Engle, Kathleen Faye *elementary education educator*
Hutchinson, Janet Lee Clark *elementary school educator*

Powell
Dean, Patricea Louise *lawyer, law educator, small business owner*

Rawlins
Rose, Kathleen Diane *elementary school educator*

Rock River
King, Corinne Michelle *music educator*

Rock Springs
Jackman Dabb, Holly Pieper *publisher*
Sheckler, Mindy Sue *elementary school educator*
Thompson, Josie *nurse*

Saratoga
Hileman, Linda Carol *elementary school educator*

Sheridan
Aguirre Batty, Mercedes *Spanish and English language educator, literature educator*
Pilch, Margaret L. *grant writer, researcher*
Robertson, Lisa Rae *music educator*

Sundance
Truchot, Janice Elaine *elementary school educator*

Thermopolis
Gear, Kathleen O'Neal *archaeologist, writer*

Torrington
Lewis, Mary Jane *retired elementary school educator*

Worland
Overcast, Vickie L. *librarian*

TERRITORIES OF THE UNITED STATES

AMERICAN SAMOA

Pago Pago
Fung-Chen-Pen, Emma Talauna Solaita *librarian, director*
Howland, Repeka Moata'a Isara *retired government community services administrator*
Varghese, Mary *secondary school educator*

GUAM

Agana Heights
Torres, Susie Apuron *special education educator*

Barrigada
McDonald Terlaje, Patricia *counselor*

Hagatna
Artero, Margaret T. *academic administrator, military officer*
Cruz, Teofila Perez *nursing administrator*
Flores, Christina Rosalie *art educator*
Tydingco-Gatewood, Frances Marie *judge*
Weeks, Janet Healy *retired supreme court justice*

Mangilao
Duenas, Laurent Flores *health and nursing consultant*

Tamuning
Cahinhinan, Nelia Agbada *retired public health nurse, health facility administrator*

NORTHERN MARIANA ISLANDS

Saipan
Gallardo, Sister Arsenia Pulumbarit *elementary school educator*
Inos, Rita Hocog *school system administrator*
Kaufer, Connie Tenorio *special education educator, researcher*
Lamkin, Celia Belocora *physician*
Post, Laura Leigh *psychiatrist*

PALAU ISLAND

Palau
Olkeriil, Lorenza *English language educator*

PUERTO RICO

Aguada
Ramírez-Ruiz, Doris M. *education educator*

Aguadilla
Cuebas Irizarry, Ana E. *director*
Jaramillo, Juana Segarra *chancellor*

Aguas Buenas
Melendez, Sonia Ivette *counselor*

Cabo Rojo
Rivera-Martinez, Socorro *retired elementary school educator, assistant principal*

Caguas
Agosto Rivera, Luz Esther *elementary school educator*

Carolina
Reyes-Hernández, Migdalia *counselor*

Fajardo
Colón, Nivia Enid *counseling administrator*

Guaynabo
Baquero, Maria Joaquina *elementary school educator*

Mayaguez
Ruiz-Vargas, Yolanda *finance educator*

Ponce
Smith, Maria Carmen *retired science educator*
Veray, Brunilda *psychologist, educator*

Rio Piedras
Gibbs Cruz, Katherine K. *science educator*

San German
Mojica, Agnes *academic administrator*

San Juan
Casiano, Kimberly *publishing executive*
Fiol Matta, Liana *judge*
Folch-Serrano, Karen D. *psychologist, consultant*
González Echevarria, Amelia L. *librarian, counseling administrator*
Luna Padilla, Nitza Enid *photography educator*
Marichal, Maria P. *physical education educator, soccer coach*
Mejia, Migdalia Teresa *psychologist, performing arts educator*
Muñoz-Solá, Haydeé Socorro *library administrator*
Roca de Torres, Irma Eneida *retired psychology professor*
Rodriguez, Annabelle *judge, former attorney general*
Rodriguez-Velez, Rosa *prosecutor*
Rosso de Irizarry, Carmen (Tutty Rosso de Irizarry) *finance executive*
Santos de Alvarez, Brunilda *lawyer*

Santa Isabel
Lugo-Paoli, Luz Minerva *counselor, educator*

Toa Baja
Almeida, Michelle Kathleen *psychologist, educator*

Trujillo Alto
Crespo de Sanabia, María Milagros *retired education educator*

VIRGIN ISLANDS

Charlotte Amalie
Stapleton, Marylyn Alecia *diplomat*

Christiansted
Christian, Cora L.E *health facility administrator, physician*

St Croix
Combie, Valerie Audrey *communications educator*

St Thomas
Berry, Lorraine Ledee *state senator*
DePass-Creque, Linda Ann *educational consultant association executive, former education commissioner*
Michael, Noreen *school system administrator*
Ragster, LaVerne E. *academic administrator*

MILITARY ADDRESSES OF THE UNITED STATES

ATLANTIC

APO
Sosa, Rita Sladen *social sciences educator*

EUROPE
Daly, Kathleen Ann *elementary school educator*
Hibben, Barbara Ann Pandzik *museum administrator, foreign service officer*
Morella, Constance Albanese *ambassador, former congresswoman*
Mungas, Andrea Marie *elementary school educator*
Simpson, Sandra Kay *operations research specialist*
Sokolowski, Denise Georgia *librarian, academic administrator*
Wagner, Ann Louise *ambassador, former political organization executive*
Wagner, Mary S. *education center administrator*

PACIFIC

Fpo
Tarpeh-Doe, Linda Diane *controller*

CANADA

ALBERTA

Edmonton
Hughes, Linda J. *newspaper publisher*

BRITISH COLUMBIA

Burnaby
Kimura, Doreen *psychology professor, researcher*

Coquitlam
Hainsworth, Melody May *library and information scientist, researcher*

Fernie
McFarlin-Kosiec, Barbara Ann *secondary school educator, literature and language professor, small business owner*

North Saanich
Saddlemyer, Ann (Eleanor Saddlemyer) *humanities educator, critic, theater historian*

Powell River
Carsten, Arlene Desmet *financial executive*

Prince George
Kerr, Nancy Karolyn *pastor, mental health services professional*

Salt Spring Island
Raginsky, Nina *artist*

Sidney
Bigelow, Margaret Elizabeth Barr (M.E. Barr) *retired botany educator*

Vancouver
Baird, Patricia Ann *physician, educator*
Beals, Jennifer *actress*
Bonifacho, Bratsa *artist*
Jones, Norah *vocalist, musician*
Krall, Diana *musician*
Lavigne, Avril *singer*
Levy, Julia *immunology educator, researcher*
Marchak, Maureen Patricia *anthropology and sociology educator, academic administrator*
McGeer, Edith Graef *retired neurological science educator*
McLachlan, Sarah *musician, composer*
Piternick, Anne Brearley *librarian, educator*
Salcudean, Martha Eva *mechanical engineer, educator*
Yaffe, Barbara Marlene *journalist*

NEW BRUNSWICK

Moncton
Robertson, Brenda *senator*

NEWFOUNDLAND AND LABRADOR

Torbay
Dabinett, Diana Frances *artist*

NORTHWEST TERRITORIES

Yellowknife
Blondin-Andrew, Ethel D. *Canadian government official*

NOVA SCOTIA

Bayfield
Blair, Rosemary Miles *retired art educator, environmentalist*

Chester Basin
Parr-Johnston, Elizabeth *economist, consultant*

Glasgow
Williams, Edna Aleta Theadora Johnston *journalist*

Halifax
Glube, Constance Rachelle *retired judge*
Kulyk, Karen Gay *artist*
LeValliant, Debbie *information technology executive*
Russell, Dawn Ann *dean*

Tatamagouche
Roach, Margot Ruth *retired biophysicist, educator*

ONTARIO

Callander
Haig, Susan *conductor*

Hamilton
Ryan, Ellen Bouchard *psychology professor, gerontologist*

London
Barfoot, Joan *writer*
Poole, Nancy Geddes *art gallery curator, writer*

North York
Gasparrini-Etheridge, Claudia *publishing executive, research scientist, writer*
Thomas, Clara McCandless *retired literature educator*

Ottawa
Adams, Gabrielle *biologist*
Bacon, Lise *Canadian senator*
Beare-Rogers, Joyce Louise *retired research and development executive*
Christensen, Ione *Canadian senator*
Cook, Joan *Canadian senator*
Cools, Anne C. *Canadian senator*
Copps, Sheila *former Canadian government official*
Cordy, Jane *Canadian senator*
Fairbairn, Joyce *Canadian government official*
Fraser, Sheila *government agency administrator*
Guarnieri, Albina *Canadian legislator*
Hervieux-Payette, Céline *Canadian senator*
Hubley, Elizabeth *Canadian senator*
Hylland, Sue *sports association executive*
Johnson, Janis G. *Canadian senator*
Labarge, Margaret Wade *medieval history professor, historian, writer*
Lay, Marion *sports association executive*
LeBreton, Marjory *senator*
Losier-Cool, Rose-Marie *Canadian senator*
Maxwell, Judith *think-tank executive, economist*
McLachlin, Beverley *Canadian supreme court chief justice*
Milne, Lorna *Canadian legislator*
Minna, Maria *member of Canadian Parliament*
Poy, Vivienne *Canadian senator, academic administrator, educator*
Roland, Anne *registrar Supreme Court of Canada*
St. Hilaire, Caroline *legislator*
Scott, Marianne Florence *retired librarian, educator*
Squire, Anne Marguerite *retired humanities educator*
Wendling, Louise *wholesale company executive*

Owen Sound
Jones, Phyllis Edith *nursing educator*

Toronto
Astman, Barbara Ann *artist, educator*
Augustine, Jean Magdalene *Canadian government official, former member of parliament*
Baxendale, Sonia A. *diversified financial services company executive*
Bolley, Andrea *artist*
Braswell, Paula Ann *artist*
Bryant, Josephine Harriet *library executive*
Clark, Maura J. *oil and gas industry executive*
Clarkson, Adrienne *former Governor General of Canada*
Dobson, Wendy Kathleen *economics professor*
Furtado, Nelly Kim *vocalist*
Goh, Chan Hon *ballerina*
Jaworska, Tamara *artist*
Kooluris Dobbs, Linda Kia *artist, photographer*
Lawson, Jane Elizabeth *retired bank executive*
McRae, Marion Eleanor *critical care nurse*
McWilliam, Joanne Elizabeth *retired theology studies educator*
Mercier, Eileen Ann *corporate financial executive*
Moore, Carole Irene *librarian*
Ostry, Sylvia *academic administrator, economist*
Packham, Marian Aitchison *biochemistry professor*
Peacock, Molly *poet, educator*
Taylor, Kathleen P. *hotel executive*
van Ginkel, Blanche Lemco *architect, educator*

QUEBEC

Montreal
Freeman, Carolyn Ruth *oncologist*
Gibbs, Sarah Preble *biologist, educator*
Ikawa-Smith, Fumiko *anthropologist, educator*
Jones, Barbara Ellen *neurologist, educator*
Messing, Karen *occupational health researcher*
Moss, David *music company executive*
Steinberg, Blema *political science professor*
Von Gencsy, Eva *dancer, choreographer, educator*

Pointe-Claire
Lapointe, Lucie *research institute executive*

Rosemere
Hopper, Carol *incentive program administrator, trade association administrator*

Saint-Adele
Rousseau-Vermette, Mariette *artist*

SASKATCHEWAN

Saskatoon
Kennedy, Marjorie Ellen *librarian*

Toronto
Patten, Rose *bank executive*
Stanley, Deirdre *lawyer*

Waterloo
Fréchette, Louise *international organization official*

Whistler
Rae, Barbara Joyce *employee placement company executive*

Windsor
Isajiw, Sophia O. *artist, educator, curator, writer*

AFGHANISTAN

Strongsville
Grumbach, Katherine Elizabeth *science educator*

AUSTRALIA

Altona
Daniel-Dreyfus, Susan B. Russe *information technology executive*

Darlinghurst
Davis, Judy *actress*

Double Bay
Peacock, Penne Korth *ambassador*

Melbourne
Bishop, Ruth Frances *microbiologist, research scientist, educator*

Redfern
Campion, Jane *film director, screenwriter*

Sydney
Rogers, Karen Beckstead *gifted studies educator, researcher, consultant*

AUSTRIA
Finley, Julie Hamm *ambassador, former political party official*

BELGIUM

Brussels
Nuland, Victoria *US permanent representative to NATO*

Genappe
Williams, Jody *political organization administrator*

BERMUDA

Saint Georges
Jackson, Hermoine Prestine *psychologist*

CHINA

Shanghai
Huang, Chang-yu *retired elementary school educator*
Lin, Maria C. H. *lawyer*

CZECH REPUBLIC

Prague
Love, Brenda Zejdl *writer*
Turková, Helga *librarian*

DENMARK

Copenhagen
Martin, Vivian *soprano*

EGYPT

Cairo
Lesch, Ann Mosely *political scientist, educator*

ENGLAND

Devon
Turner-Warwick, Margaret *physician, educator*

Essex
Collins, Joan Henrietta *actress*

Leeds
Ichino, Yoko *ballerina*

London
Arman Gelenbe, Deniz *concert pianist*
Atkins, Eileen *actress*
Bravo, Rose Marie *apparel executive*
Carroll, Cynthia B. *mining executive*
Clark, Cynthia Zang Facer *federal agency administrator*
Dial, Teresa *bank executive*
Duncan, Lindsay Vere *actress*
Edwards, Sylvia Ann *artist*
Elizabeth, , II, (Elizabeth Alexandra Mary) *By the Grace of God of the United Kingdom of Great Britain and Northern Ireland and of Her Other Realms and Territories Queen, Head of the Commonwealth, Defender of the Faith*
Fine, Anne *writer*
Galloway, Janice *writer, editor*
Goulekas, Karen *special effects supervisor*
Hewitt, Patricia Hope *English government official, political scientist, researcher, announcer*
Hite, Shere D. *writer, historian*
Holt, Thelma *theatrical producer*
Hunter Blair, Pauline Clarke *author*
Junz, Helen B. *economist*
McPhee, Katharine Hope *singer*
Osbourne, Kelly Lee *television personality, singer*
Paton Walsh, Jill *writer*
Rowling, J.K. (Joanne Kathleen Rowling) *writer*
Scardino, Dame Marjorie Morris *publishing executive*
Tyson, Laura D'Andrea *dean, finance educator*
Uchida, Mitsuko *pianist*
Wallace, Bonnie Ann *biochemist, biophysicist, educator*

Poole
Alsop, Marin *conductor, violinist, music director*

Richmond
Armfield, Diana Maxwell *artist, educator*
Ahrendts, Angela J. *apparel executive*

ETHIOPIA

Addis Ababa
Huddleston, Vicki Jean *ambassador*

FRANCE

Benerville-Sur-Mer
Feiler, Jo Alison *artist*

Draguignan
Frame, Nancy Davis *lawyer*

Lacoste
Strauss, Gwen B. *writer, editor*

Malaucene Vaucluse
Langenkamp, Mary Alice (M.A. Langenkamp) *artist, educator*

Normandy
Ndiaye, Marie *writer, playwright*

Paris
de Havilland, Olivia Mary *actress*
Deneuve, Catherine (Catherine Dorleac) *actress*
Lagarde, Christine *French government official, lawyer*
Oliver, Louise V. *ambassador*
Stoianovich, Marcelle Simone *artist*

GERMANY

Berlin
Piper, Adrian Margaret Smith *philosopher, artist, educator*

Frankfurt
Levin Baroness Von Gleichen, Tobe *language educator, editor, volunteer*

Mannheim
Flor, Herta *psychology professor*
Graf, Steffi *retired professional tennis player*

HONG KONG

Hong Kong
Podd, Ann *newspaper editor*

INDIA

Kollum
Devi, Amritanandamayi (Sri Mata Amritanandamayi Devi, Amma) *spiritual leader*

IRELAND

Dublin
O'Toole, Kathleen M. *protective services official*

ISRAEL

Jerusalem
Hazboun, Viveca *psychiatrist*
Singer, Suzanne Fried *editor*

ITALY

Milan
Versace, Donatella *fashion designer*

Rome
Masini, Eleonora Barbieri *futurist*

JAPAN

Kashiwara
Hori, Keiko *English literature educator*

Tokyo
Dixon, Bonnie Lynn *lawyer*

MEXICO

Ciudad Juarez
Tabuenca-Cordoba, Maria-Socorro *academic administrator*

Delegacion Miguel Hidalgo
de Fox, Marta Sahagun Jimenez *First Lady of Mexico*

Guadalajara Jalisco
Miranda-Diaz, Alejandra Guillermina *surgeon, medical educator, researcher*

Jalisco
Pordon, Grace *writer, poet, artist*

Mexico City
de Brun, Shauna Doyle *industrialist, investment banker*
De La Riva, Myriam Ann *artist*

MONGOLIA

Ulaanbaatar
Mandel, Leslie Ann *investment advisor, writer*

NETHERLANDS

The Hague
Cook, Linda Z. *utilities executive*
Hodge, Susan *oil industry executive*

NEW ZEALAND

Auckland
Swecker, Valerie Ann *accountant, consultant*

Wellington
Paquin, Anna *actress*

QATAR

Doha
Pedrosa, Veronica *journalist*

SAUDI ARABIA

Riyadh
Olayan, Lubna S. *finance company executive*

SCOTLAND

Saint Andrews
Tanner, Joanne Elizabeth *psychologist, researcher*

SINGAPORE

Singapore
Berkram, Patricia Clarke *religious studies educator*

SPAIN

Barcelona
Allende, Isabel Angelica *writer*

Canary Islands
Wells, Melissa Foelsch *retired ambassador*

Madrid
Sanona, Nuno Alexandre Fernandes Rorigues *financial consultant*

SWITZERLAND

Bern
Carlson, Dale Bick *writer*

Geneva
Kapp, Nathalie *obstetrician, educator, gynecologist*
McDougall, Gay *lawyer*

Kusnacht
Jones, Dame Gwyneth *soprano*

SYRIA

Damascus
Scobey, Margaret *ambassador*

THAILAND

Bangkok
McMillion, Margaret Kim *foreign service officer*

TURKEY

Mersin
Yalin, Serap *biochemist, educator*

WEST INDIES

Commonwealth Dominica
Sullivan, Marilyn Bobette *librarian, consultant*

ZAMBIA

Kitwe
Ryder, Elizabeth Godbey *psychiatric nurse consultant, missionary*

ADDRESS UNPUBLISHED

Aatrapi, Marjane *writer, illustrator*
Abajian, Wendy Elisse *broadcast executive, writer*
Abbe, Elfriede Martha *sculptor, graphics designer*
Abbey, Linda Rowe *artist, educator*
Abbott, Amy P. *design educator*
Abbott, Barbara Gayle *academic administrator*
Abbott, Linda Joy *stained glass artisan, educator, photographer*
Abbott, Rebecca Phillips *art historian, consultant, photographer, director*
Abbott, Regina A. *neurodiagnostic technologist, consultant, business owner*
Abboud, Sabra Natasha *psychotherapist, psychology professor*
Abdallah, Claude *anesthesiologist*
Abdoo, Rose Marie *actor*
Abel, Barbara Ellen *photographer*
Abeles, Kim Victoria *artist*
Abell, Anna Ellen *primary school educator*
Abell, Sara Nightingale *music educator, musician*
Aber, Ita *artist, conservator, historian*
Abernathy, Jennifer P. *music educator*
Abernethy, Sharron Gray *language educator*
Abey, Kathy Michele *district representative, congressional caseworker*
Abid, Ann B. *art librarian*
Aboussie, Marilyn *retired judge*
Abraham, Francine Dinneen *sales executive, banker*
Abrahamsen, Valerie *academic administrator*
Abramowicz, Janet *painter, print-maker*
Abrams, Roz *newscaster*
Abrams Finger, Iris Dale *retired elementary school educator*
Abramson, Stephanie W. *retired advertising executive, lawyer*
Absher, Donna Atkins *textile designer*
Abu-Lughod, Janet Lippman *sociologist, educator*
Ackerman, Diane *author, educator*
Ackerman, Valerie B. *former sports association executive*
Ackermann, Barbara Bogel *counselor*
Adam, Justine E. *psychologist*
Adams, Amy (Amanda Jessica Adams) *actress*
Adams, Betsy Anne *principal*
Adams, Cheryl *newscaster*
Adams, Eleanor June *medical/surgical nurse*
Adams, Joey Lauren *actress*
Adams, Leocadia Donat *secondary school educator, writer*
Adams, Margaret Bernice *retired museum official*
Adams, Patti Jean *literature and language educator*
AdamS, Sharon Butler *minister, philosopher, researcher*
Adams, Stephanie Lynn *elementary school educator*
Adams, Susan Lois *music educator*
Adams, Valencia I. *telecommunications industry executive*
Adamson, Jane Nan *retired elementary school educator*
Adamson, Lynda G. *literature educator, writer*
Adams-Passey, Suellen S. *retired elementary school educator*
Adang, Rosemary *humanities educator*
Adato, Perry Miller *documentary producer, director, writer*
Addicott, Beverly Jeanne *retired elementary school educator*
Addor, Lina Al Kaissy *science educator*
Adekson, Mary Olufunmilayo *counselor, educator*
Adiletta, Debra Jean Olson *mathematics professor*
Aehlert, Barbara June *health facility administrator*
Agee, Claudia *executive secretary, tax specialist*
Aghdashloo, Shohreh *actress*
Agne, Phyllis G. *artist, educator*
Agüero-Torres, Irene Beatriz *language educator*
Aguilar, Miriam Rebecca *technology project manager*
Ahearn, Holly Ande *music educator*
Ah Soon, Melanie Frances Kawamoto *science educator*
Aiello, Kimberly Jean *surgeon*
Aiello, Marcie Jeanne Gruener *secondary school educator*
Ailloni-Charas, Miriam Clara *interior designer, consultant*
Ain, Diantha *poet, artist, educator*
Aitchison, Anne Catherine *retired environmental activist*
Aitchison, Bridget Mary *theater educator, theater director*
Akbar, Shaakira Nadiya *elementary school educator*
Akin, Ann Foster *special education educator*
Akiyama, Karen N. *elementary school educator*
Alaimo, Terry M. *financial consultant*
Alanazi, Jessica Lane *science educator*
Alanis, Lorena *elementary school educator*
Alba, Jessica *actress*
Albagli, Louise Martha *psychologist*
Alberti-Chappell, Roxana Dearing *psychologist*
Albertson, Susan L. *retired federal government official*
Albrecht, Rebekah S. *mathematician, educator*
Alderman, Shirley M. *insurance agent*
Aldredge, Theoni Vachliotis *costume designer*
Aldrich, Patricia Anne Richardson *retired magazine editor*
Alexander, Alison F. *communication educator*
Alexander, Ascencion (Cency) H. *school psychologist, educator*
Alexander, Barbara Toll *financial consultant*
Alexander, Faith Dorothy *retired training services executive*
Alexander, Hope *actor, educator, theater director*
Alexander, Icie Mae *communications executive*
Alexander, Jessie Aronow *anesthesiologist*
Alexander, Marjorie Anne *artist, consultant*
Alexander, Nancy A. *information technology manager, consultant*
Alexiades-Armenakas, Macrene Renee *dermatologist, scientist, researcher, educator, consultant*
Alford, Renee Marie *speech pathology/audiology services professional, educator*
Aliga, Olivia R. *music educator, choral director*
Aligarbes, Sandra Lynne *nurse*
Alinder, Mary Street *writer, educator*
Allen, Denise Newbold *music educator*
Allen, Donna *mathematics educator*
Allen, Elizabeth Maresca *marketing executive, telecommunications industry executive*
Allen, Frances Elizabeth *computer scientist*
Allen, Gloria Ann *real estate broker, artist*
Allen, Jo Lynn *secondary school educator*
Allen, Leatrice Delorice *psychologist*
Allen, Linda S. *editor, writer*
Allen, Marilyn Myers Pool *theater director, video specialist*
Allen, Pamela Smith *retired psychologist, writer*
Allen, Renee Annette *application developer*
Allen, Roberta *writer, photographer, conceptual artist*
Allen, Toni K. *lawyer*
Allen, Victoria Taylor *archivist*
Allenson, Jennifer Leigh *elementary school educator*
Alley, Kirstie *actress*
Allred, Dawn Peterman *adult education educator*
Allston, Charita Capers *music educator*
Almore-Randle, Allie Louise *special education educator, academic administrator*
Aloff, Mindy *writer*
Alpert, Ann Sharon *retired insurance claims examiner*
Alston, Betty B. *retired elementary school educator*
Altekruse, Joan Morrissey *retired preventive medicine physician*
Altemara, Maria Christi Staley *anthropologist, sociologist, educator*
Altherr, Rita Jo *secondary school educator*
Altman, Adele Rosenhain *radiologist*
Altman, Sarah Busa *human services educator*
Altschuler, Marjorie *advertising executive*
Alvarez, Aida M. *former federal agency administrator*
Alvarez-Corona, Marti *school psychologist, educator*
Alward, Sarah Anne *mathematics educator*
Amadio, Bari Ann *metal fabrication executive, retired nurse*
Amano, Imelda *school librarian*
Amar, Paula Bram *psychologist, consultant*
Amara, Lucine *vocalist*
Amaro, Leticia *medical/surgical nurse*
Amato, Daria U. *critical care, medical, and surgical nurse*
Ambers, Ann *bishop, educator*
Amgott, Madeline *television producer, consultant*
Amick, Deborah Anne *medical/surgical and women's health nurse*
Amin, Farzana *psychiatrist, researcher*
Amos, Linda K. *academic administrator*
Amram, Laura *psychiatrist*
Amsterdam, Millicent *manufacturing executive*
Anania, Andrea *information technology executive*
Anastole, Dorothy Jean *retired electronics company executive*
Ancker-Johnson, Betsy *physicist, engineer, retired automotive executive*
Ancoli-Israel, Sonia *psychologist, researcher*
Anderegg, Karen Klok *business executive*
Anderson, Allamay Eudoris *health educator, home economist*
Anderson, Amy Lee *realtor*
Anderson, Cherine E. *television and film production manager, special events planner, marketing executive*
Anderson, Dorothy Fisher *social worker, psychotherapist*
Anderson, Elaine Janet *science educator*
Anderson, Geraldine Louise *medical researcher*
Anderson, Gillian *actress*
Anderson, Iris Anita *retired secondary school educator*
Anderson, Jennifer Ann *middle school educator*
Anderson, Kathryn M. *history educator*
Anderson, Linda Jean *critical care nurse, psychiatric nurse practitioner*
Anderson, Margaret Suzanne *elementary school educator, nurse*
Anderson, Mary Jane *library director, consultant*
Anderson, Melissa Ann *science educator*
Anderson, Monica Luffman *school librarian, educator, real estate broker*
Anderson, Nancy Odegard *medical/surgical nurse*
Anderson, Paulette Elizabeth *real estate developer, retired entrepreneur, retired elementary school educator*
Anderson, Peggy Rees *accountant*
Anderson, Rachael Keller (Rachael Keller) *retired library director*
Anderson, Rebecca Lynn *music educator*
Anderson, Rhoda *language educator*
Anderson-Spivy, Alexandra *news correspondent, editor, critic, writer, historian*
Andersson, Helen Demitrous *artist*
Andrade, Edna *artist, educator*
Andrau, Maya Hedda *physical therapist*
Andre, Angela Renee *science educator*
Andreason, Lee (Sharon Lee Andreason) *sculptor*
Andreassi, Kimberly Thompson *mathematics educator*
Andrew, Dolores Molcan *retired art educator, artist*
Andrews, Dame Julie (Julia Elizabeth Wells) *actress, singer*
Andrews, Pat R. *political science professor*
Andrews-McCall, Maxine R. *retired educational administration specialist*
Andrews-McCall, Maxine Ramseur *retired education educator*
Andrian-Ceciu, Roxanne R. *engineer, financial analyst*
Andrus, Sharon Arlene *electrical engineer, researcher*
Anisimova, Tanya *cellist, educator*
Aniston, Jennifer *actress*
Ankney, Rachel Blue *language educator*
Annis, Francesca *actress*
Ansevics, Nancy Leah *mental health services administrator*
Anshaw, Carol *writer*
Antaramian, Jacqueline *actress*
Anthony, Michele *former recording industry executive*
Anthony, Wilma Tylinda *retired customer service administrator*
Anthony-Perez, Bobbie Cotton Murphy *retired psychology professor*
Antignane, Diane Paquin *mathematics educator*
Antin, Eleanor *artist*
Antinone, Jo Ann Elliott *music educator*
Antolick, Lynn Ann *music educator*
Anton, Barbara *writer*
Apel, Marie U. *elementary school educator*
Apel-Brueggeman, Myrna L. *entrepreneur*
Aplin, Gina Suzette *secondary school educator, rancher*

Apogi, Evelyn *retired anesthesiologist*
Appelbaum, Marci Anne *theater director, educator*
Appell, Louise Sophia *retired consulting company executive*
Applegate, Christina *actress*
Applehans, Cynthia Diane *art educator, artist*
Apt, Joan Frank *volunteer*
Aranow, Ruth Lee Horwitz *academic advisor, chemist, researcher*
Arathuzik, Mary Diane *medical/surgical nurse*
Araujo, Ilka Vasconcelos *musicologist, educator*
Archbold, Ronna Rae *college administrator*
Archer, Lillian Patricia *academic administrator, dean*
Archer-Sorg, Karen S. *secondary school educator*
Arden, Sherry W. *publishing executive*
Areen, Judith Carol *law educator, dean*
Arenal, Julie (Mrs. Barry Primus) *choreographer*
Argers, Helen *writer, playwright*
Arifi, Fatana Baktash *artist, educator*
Arking, Lucille Musser *nurse, epidemiologist*
Armacost, Mary-Linda Sorber Merriam *retired academic administrator*
Armand, Margaret Mitchell *mental health services professional*
Armani, Donna *science educator*
Armatrading, Joan *singer, lyricist*
Armistead, Katherine Kelly (Mrs. Thomas B. Armistead III) *interior designer, travel consultant, civic worker*
Armstrong, Anne Legendre *retired ambassador*
Armstrong, Marsha Susan *elementary school educator*
Armstrong, Peg Jean *psychotherapist*
Armstrong Squall, Paula Estelle *executive secretary*
Arndt, Dianne Joy *artist, photographer*
Arndt, Laura Bodeen *mathematics educator*
Arnold, Alanna S. Welling *lawyer*
Arnold, Catherine Anderson *communications executive*
Arnold, Charlotte S. *criminal justice agency executive, activist*
Arnold, Janet Nina *health facility administrator, consultant*
Arnold, Karen Dorothy *education educator*
Arnold, Leslie Ann *special education educator*
Arnold, Mary Spears *retired music educator*
Arnold, Marygwen Suella *language educator, medical/surgical nurse*
Arnold-Rogers, Judy *education educator, language educator, coach*
Arnone, Mary Grace *radiologic technologist*
Arntz, Barbara C. *elementary school educator*
Arntzenius, Linda Galliard McArdle *writer*
Arp, Arlene *elementary school educator*
Arredondo, Adrianna Liza *secondary school educator*
Arrieta, Diane Marie *artist*
Arrigo, Jan Elizabeth *photographer, writer, artist*
Arrott, Patricia Graham *artist, educator*
Arrowood, Catharine Biggs *lawyer*
Arthur, Beatrice *actress*
Arthurs, Madeleine Hope *artist*
Artl, Karen Ann *business owner, author*
Arutyunyan, Emma *radio broadcaster*
Asadorian, Diana C. *electrical engineer, educator*
Ascherl, Amy M. *elementary school educator*
Aschheim, Eve Michele *artist, educator*
Ash, Dorothy Matthews *civic worker*
Ash, Jennifer Gertrude *writer, editor*
Ashimine, Tanya *biology educator*
Ashish-Mishra, Sonia *psychiatrist*
Ashkin, Roberta Ellen *lawyer*
Ashleigh, Caroline *art and antiques appraiser*
Ashley, Marjorie *retired secondary school educator*
Ashley, Renee *writer, creative writing educator, consultant*
Ashley, Sharon Anita *pediatric anesthesiologist*
Ashton, Betsy Finley *broadcast journalist, author, lecturer*
Ashworth, Bessie *benefits compensation analyst, writer*
Askew, Kim Juanita *lawyer*
Askew, Rilla *author*
Askine, Ruth Parse *elementary school educator*
Aslakson, Sarah *artist*
Assael, Alyce *artist*
Astaire, Carol Anne Taylor *artist, educator*
Astell, Christine Ann *school guidance counselor*
Astey, Tricia Anne *music educator*
Atamian, Susan *nurse*
Atchley, Nancy Faye *educator*
Atkins, Candi *management consultant, small business owner*
Atkins, Joanna Pang (Joanna Pang) *dancer, actress, choreographer, director*
Atkinson, Beth J. *music educator*
Atkinson, Holly Gail *physician, journalist, educator, human rights activist, writer*
Atkinson, Paula Mari *music educator*
Atkinson, Tracey Blake *artist, educator*
Atlee, Debbie Gayle *sales consultant, medical educator*
Atler, Vanessa *gymnast*
Atwater, Phyllis Y. *municipal official*
Atwood, Colleen *costume designer*
Atwood, Debra Smith *elementary school educator*
Atwood, Donna Elaine *retired financial manager*
Atwood, Sonya Elizabeth *music educator*
Augustine-Ascherl, Joan Michelle *music educator*
Aukofer, Clare Elizabeth *newspaper editor*
Aune, Debra Bjurquist *lawyer*
Aunio, Irene M. *artist*
Austin, Susannah Lyn *music educator*
Avery, Carolyn Elizabeth *artist*
Avery, Mary Ellen *pediatrician, educator*
Aviles, Alice Alers *psychologist*
Avrett, Roz (Rosalind Case) *writer*
Axner, Carol Christie *elementary school educator*
Ayers, Janet *technical college president*
Ayers, Janice R. *social service administrator*
Azarian, Mary *illustrator*
Azocar, Francisca *clinical psychologist*
Azpeitia, Lynne Marie *psychotherapist, educator, trainer, consultant*
Baba, Marietta Lynn *anthropologist, academic administrator*
Babao, Donna Marie *retired community health and psychiatric nurse, educator*
Babcock-Lumish, Terry Lynne *economic geographer*
Babitzke, Theresa Angeline *health facility administrator*
Babladelis, Georgia *retired psychology educator*
Babrowski, Claire Harbeck *retail executive*
Baca, Joy *science educator*
Bach, Mary Irene *music educator*
Bachelor, Malinda Mary *elementary school educator*
Back, Shannon Lee *music educator*
Bacon, Barbara McNutt *social worker*
Bacon, Caroline Sharfman *investor, consultant*
Bacon, Jeri Ann *music educator*
Bader, Lorraine Greenberg *textile stylist, designer, consultant, artist*
Badu, Erykah *singer, songwriter*
Baer, Diane Draper *artist*
Baghaei-Rad, Nancy Jane Bebb *elementary school educator*
Bahr, Christine Marie *special education educator*
Bahr, Gail G. *sportswriter*
Baier, Lucinda *corporate financial executive*
Bailar, Barbara Ann *retired statistician*
Bailey, Beverly Parker *secondary school educator*
Bailey, Carla Lynn *nursing administrator*
Bailey, Catherine Suzanne *psychologist*
Bailey, Janet Dee *publishing executive*
Bailey, Joy Hafner *counselor educator*
Bailey, Joy Y. *art educator*
Bailey, Keisha Ayanna *mathematics educator*
Bailey, Margaret Elizabeth *nurse, retired military officer*
Bailey, Rita Maria *investment advisor, psychologist*
Bailey, Shannon D. *elementary school educator*
Bailey, Vicky A. *lobbyist*
Baillos, Marianne Tkach *secondary school educator*
Baiman, Gail *real estate broker*
Bainbridge, Dona Bardelli *marketing professional*
Baird, Alison Elizabeth *neurologist*
Bajura, Rita A. *research scientist*
Baker, Amy Elaine *assistant principal*
Baker, Andrea J. *sociologist, educator*
Baker, Carolyn Simmons *library director, consultant, researcher*
Baker, Deborah *medical educator*
Baker, Jane E. *secondary school educator*
Baker, Katherine June *elementary school educator, minister, artist*
Baker, Kathy Whitton *actress*
Baker, Lesliegh *bank executive, lawyer*
Baker, Lucinda *writer*
Baker, Pamela Hudson *special education educator*
Baker, Patricia *health foundation administrator*
Baker, Paula Booker *secondary school educator*
Baker, Peggy Nell *retired secondary school educator*
Baker, Susan Marie Victoria *writer, artist, musician*
Baldassano, Corinne Leslie *radio executive*
Baldrige, Letitia *writer, management consultant*
Baldwin, Leah Zavin *minister, writer, interior designer, educator*
Baldwin, Marie Hunsucker *retired secondary school educator*
Balis, Jennifer Lynn *academic administrator, computer scientist, educator*
Ball, Brenda Joyce Sivils *retired secondary school educator*
Ball, Joyce *retired university librarian and dean*
Ball, Teresa Susan *secondary school educator*
Ballarian, Anna Nevarte *retired art educator*
Ballentine, Rosalie Simmonds *former attorney general*
Balter, Frances Sunstein *civic worker*
Baltimore, Pamela A. Grayson *social worker, consultant*
Balzer, Donna Carol *retired secondary school educator*
Bamberger, Phylis Skloot *lawyer, educator, retired judge*
Banaszynski, Carol Jean *secondary school educator*
Banbury, Demby Bowman *director*
Baney, Lori A. *medical technician, educator*
Banks, Carolyn Duty *retired history educator*
Banks, Deirdre Margaret *retired church organization administrator*
Banks, Sandra C. *retired elementary school educator*
Bankston, Sherri Renee *secondary school educator, director*
Barad, Jill Elikann *former family products company executive*
Baranowski, Mary Lou *elementary school educator*
Baranski, Christine *actress*
Barbeau, Adrienne *actress*
Barber, Elizabeth Jean *vocalist, educator, artist*
Barber, Joan Marie *artist*
Barbey, Adélaïde *publisher*
Barbo, Dorothy Marie *obstetrician, gynecologist, educator*
Barbour, Kelli D. *assistant principal, secondary school educator*
Barca, Kathleen *marketing executive*
Barcroft, Judith *artist, actress*
Bard, Ellen Marie *former state legislator, retired small business owner*
Bardole, Betty Jean *elementary school educator*
Barger, Barbara Elaine *medical and surgical nurse, nursing educator*
Barker, Virginia Lee *nursing educator*
Barlow, Jean *art educator, painter*
Barnes, Frances Johnson *retired secondary school educator*
Barnes, Suzanne Martin *speech pathology/audiology services professional*
Barnes-Kempton, Isabel Janet *retired microbiologist, dean*
Barnett-Evanson, Fila *artist, executive recruiter*
Barnhart, Cynthia Rogers *editor, writer*
Barnhill, Muriel *retired nurse*
Barone, Angela Maria *artist, researcher*
Barr, Marlene Joy *volunteer*
Barragan, Linda Diane *religious organization administrator*
Barranger, Milly Slater *theater educator, writer*
Barrett, Barbara McConnell *ranch owner, lawyer*
Barrett, Janet Tidd *academic administrator*
Barrett, Jessica (Donna Ann Nipert) *psychotherapist*
Barrett, Judith Ann *salon owner*
Barrett, Krista E. *psychotherapist, educator*
Barrett, Lida Kittrell *mathematics professor*
Barrett, Linda L. *real estate consultant*
Barrett, Paulette Singer *public relations executive*
Barrow, Dindria Cozette *elementary school educator, special education educator*
Bart, Muriel *library educator*
Bartel, Jeanine M. *actor*
Bartels, Marilynn Rae *education educator*
Bartenstein, Jeuli *federal agency administrator*
Barth, Carin Marcy *former federal agency administrator*
Barth, Frances *artist*
Bartholomew, Shirley Kathleen *municipal official*
Barthwell, Andrea Grubb *health care consultant, former federal official*
Bartlett, Dede Thompson *association executive*
Bartlett, Denise Margaret *science educator*
Bartlett, Shirley Anne *accountant*
Barto, Rebecca Lynn *systems analyst*
Bartoli, Cecilia *soprano*
Barton, Katie *music educator*
Bartz, Debra Ann *retired military officer, pilot*
Basham, Monnie *retired mental health services professional*
Basinger, Karen Lynn *renal dietitian*
Baskin, Barbara Holland *retired education educator, researcher*
Baskins, Ann O. *lawyer, former computer company executive*
Baskovitz, Diana *retired elementary school educator*
Bass, Lynda D. *retired medical/surgical nurse, nursing educator*
Bassett, Elizabeth Ewing (Libby Bassett) *writer, editor, consultant*
Batchelder, Alice M. *federal judge*
Bates, Margaret P. *historian*
Bates Appleton, Shirley Graves *music educator*
Bateson, Mary Catherine *retired anthropology educator*
Bates Stoklosa, Evelynne (Eve Bates Stoklosa) *educational consultant, educator*
Batory, Joan Anne *solid waste and environmental administrator*
Battin, Patricia Meyer *librarian*
Bauer, Barbara *information technology executive*
Bauer, Barbara Ann *marketing consultant*
Bauer, Irene Susan *elementary school educator*
Bauer, Jennifer Elizabeth *performing company executive*
Bauer, Mary Jane *lyricist*
Baugh, Terry *marketing professional*
Baum, Eleanor *electrical engineering educator*
Baum, Jeanne Ann *psychotherapist*
Bauman-Antoniello, Allison *special education educator*
Baxi, Laxmi V. *obstetrician, gynecologist, medical educator*
Baxter, Barbara Morgan *Internet service provider executive, educator*
Baxter, Kathleen Byrne *academic administrator*
Bayard, Susan Shapiro *adult education educator, small business owner*
Bayes, Beverley Joan *retired pediatrician*
Bayless, Betsey *state official*
Bayley, Suzanne Ludey *civic volunteer*
Baylor, Laurie Carol *emergency nurse practitioner*
Baym, Nina (Nina Baym Stillinger) *literature educator, researcher*
Baymiller, Lynda Doern *social worker*
Bays, Louise Marie *elementary school educator*
Beach, Nancy Ann Helen *special education educator*
Beals, Nancy Farwell *former state legislator*
Beard, Ann Southard *diplomat, oil industry executive*
Beard, Bernice Talbott *writer, publisher*
Bearden, Amy Jean *social studies educator, department chairman*
Beasley, Barbara Starin *sales executive, marketing professional*
Beaton, Meredith *enterostomal therapy clinical nurse specialist*
Beatts, Anne Patricia *writer*
Beatty, Frances *civic worker*
Beauchamp, Valdivia Vânia Siqueira *translator*
Beaver, Barbara Leann *elementary school educator, writer*
Beca, Monique *psychologist*
Beck, Irene Clare *educational consultant, writer*
Beck, Jane *dance educator, choreographer*
Beck, Pamela L. *realtor*
Beck, Susan Rebecca *voice educator, consultant*
Becker, Beverly June *educator*
Becker, Dorothy Loretta *education educator, librarian*
Becker, JoAnn Elizabeth *retired insurance company executive*
Becker, Karla Lynn *information technology manager, consultant*
Becker, Kathy Gail *medical/surgical nurse*
Becker, Kyra J. *neurologist, educator*
Becker, Nancy May *nursing educator*
Beckerman, Ellen *theater director*
Beckett, Faye Trumbo *school psychologist*
Beckett, Victoria Ling *physician*
Beckles, Ingrid *mortgage banker*
Beckstrand, Karin *music educator*
Bedelia, Bonnie *actress*
Bednar-Stanley, Monica Mary *science educator, educational consultant*
Beecher, Marguerite Ann *elementary school educator*
Beerman, Miriam *artist, educator*
Begley, Renee *history educator*
Begum, Momotaz *medical researcher, consultant, medical educator*
Behnke, Doleen *computer and environmental specialist, consultant*
Behr, Marion Ray *artist*
Behrmann, Joan Gail *editor*
Behrouz, Elizabeth Jean *service director*
Beider, Marlys Anna *hotel executive, writer*
Beiswinger, Virginia Graves *secondary school educator*
Belford, Roz *real estate broker*
Bel Geddes, Joan *writer*
Belkov, Meredith Ann *landmark administrator*
Bell, Anne Marie *music educator*
Bell, Elva Glenn *retired secondary school educator, retired counseling administrator, interpreter*
Bell, Felicia Renee *elementary school educator*
Bell, Kasey Ann *elementary school educator*
Bell, Kathy Dawn *medical/surgical nurse*
Bell, Linda Green *psychology educator, therapist*
Bell, Linda J. *broadcast executive*
Bell, Robinette N. *psychiatrist, educator*
Bell, Susan Jane *nurse*
Bellantoni, Maureen Blanchfield *manufacturing and retail executive*
Beller, Luanne Evelyn *retired accountant*
Bellon, Venetia Rochelle *retired financial consultant*
Bellospirito, Robyn Suzanne *artist, writer*
Bell-Rose, Stephanie *foundation administrator*
Beloff, Zoe *filmmaker, educator, photographer*
Belson, Abby Avin *writer*
Beluso, Karen Mae *performing company executive, music educator*
Belval, Josephine Antanette *retired elementary school educator*
Belyeu, Misty Lynn *elementary school educator*
Belzberg, Edet *filmmaker*
Bencini, Sara Haltiwanger *concert pianist*
Bencivengo, Cathy Ann *lawyer*
Bender, Janet Pines *artist*
Bender, Virginia Best *computer scientist, educator*
Benfield, Ann Kolb *retired lawyer*
Bennett, Janis M. *elementary school educator*
Bennett, Velma Jean *elementary school educator*
Benningfield, Carol Ann *lawyer*
Benoit, Jo *psychologist, consultant*
Benoit, Leilani *computer scientist, educator*
Benshoof, Janet Lee *lawyer, association executive*
Benson, Jeanne P. *music educator*
Benson, Joanne E. *retired lieutenant governor*
Bentley, Charmaine Clark O'Fallon *secondary school educator*
Bentley, Doris Broussard *retired educator, consultant*
Benton, Marjorie Craig *federal agency administrator*
Berenson, Abbey Belina *gynecologist, educator*
Berg, Darla Gaye *writer*
Berg, Teresa G. *elementary school educator*
Bergen, Candice *actress, writer, photojournalist*
Bergenfeld, Jennifer Rebekah Lynn *lawyer*
Berger, Barbara *special education educator, educational consultant*
Berger, Gisela Porsch *psychotherapist*
Berger, Joyce Muriel *foundation administrator, writer, editor*
Berger, Linda Fay *writer*
Berger, Miriam Roskin *dance therapist, educator*
Bergeron, Earleen Fournet *actress*
Bergeron, Patricia Ann *retired education educator, consultant*
Bergman, Janet Eisenstein *food industry executive*
Bergquist, Sandra Lee *claims consultant*
Berkley, Mary Corner *neurologist*
Berkwits, Gloria Kozin *psychiatrist*
Berlin, Beatrice Winn *artist, printmaker*
Berlin, Doris Ada *psychiatrist*
Berliner, Ruth Shirley *real estate company executive*
Berman, Cheryl R. *advertising company executive*
Berman, Eleanor *writer*
Berman, Jennifer R. *urologist*
Berman, Lori Beth *lawyer*
Berman, Miriam Naomi *librarian*
Berman, Sandra Rita *retired personnel director*
Berman, Shari Springer *film director, scriptwriter*
Berman Robinson, Sherry H. *science educator, consultant*
Bernard, Betsy J. *former telecommunications industry executive*
Bernard, Marcelle Thomasine *physician*
Berner, Judith *mental health nurse*
Bernhard, Sandra *actress, comedienne, singer*
Bernot, Jane Catherine *retired education educator*
Berns, Beverly J. *language educator*
Berns, Pamela Kari *artist, publisher*
Bernstein, Ellen *business owner*
Bernstein, Phyliss Louise *psychologist*
Bernstein, Sylvia *artist*
Berquist, Katherine Pauline *lawyer*
Berry, Gail W. *psychiatrist, educator*
Berry, Pamela C. *secondary school educator*
Berry, Sharon Elaine *interior designer*
Berryman, Mary Anne Pierce *elementary school educator*
Bersin, Mollie Klapper *physician*
Berson, Bella Zevitovsky *librarian*
Bert, Clara Virginia *retired secondary school educator, retired school system administrator*
Bertini, Catherine Ann *former international organization official*
Bertino, Patricia Nolan *science educator*
Bertram, Jean DeSales *writer*
Bertsch, Kelly Frances *mathematics educator*
Beseda, Amy Jo *special education educator*
Bess, Aimee Lynn *performing arts educator*
Best, Judith A. *political science professor*
Beston, Rose Marie *retired academic administrator*
Betancourt-Bryant, Sonia *music educator*
Bethea, Elizabeth *social sciences educator, psychologist, minister*
Bethune, Nikki *science educator*
Beuthien, Gayle Dawn *special education educator, swim coach*
Beyer, La Vonne Ann *special education educator*
Beyerle, Susan D. *retired elementary school educator*
Bhatia, Sonia Singh *psychologist*
Biberstine, Jolene Beth *medical/surgical nurse*
Bick, Jennie L *elementary school educator*
Bick, Katherine Livingstone *neuroscientist, educator, researcher*
Bickerstaff, Mina March Clark *retired academic administrator*
Bickford, Margaret Wyatt *minister*
Bier, Karla *manufacturing engineer, chemical engineer, educator*
Bierman, Sandra *artist*
Biesinger, Meghan Kathleen *secondary school educator*

Bigelow, Sharon Lee *elementary school educator*
Bigelow, Vivian Lou *elementary school educator, secondary school educator*
Biggers, Cornelia Anderson *musician*
Biles, Gloria C. *historian, educator*
Bilich, Marion Yellin *psychologist, writer*
Billingsley, Karen Joyce *music educator*
Bilstad, Sandra A. *medical/surgical nurse, home health care nurse*
Binder, Amy Finn *public relations company executive*
Binder, Madeline Dotti *retail executive*
Bingham, Jinsie Scott *broadcast company executive*
Bingham, Marian *artist, printmaker*
Binnie, Nancy Catherine *retired nurse, educator*
Binoche, Juliette *actress*
Binsfeld, Connie Berube *former state official*
Birchard, Catherine Suzanne Sieh *artist*
Bird, Mary Lynne Miller *professional society administrator*
Bird, Patricia Coleen *business owner*
Birdsall, Nancy *economist*
Birnbaum, Linda Shub *retired assistant principal*
Birr, Cynthia Ruth *special education educator*
Birtwistle, Monica Lynn *secondary school educator*
Bisconti, Ann Stouffer *public opinion research company executive*
Bishop, C. Diane *state agency administrator, educator*
Bishop, Delores Ann *artist, educator*
Bishop, Sue Marquis (Ina Sue Marquis Bishop) *retired dean*
Bistransky, Joyce Elaine *retired elementary school educator*
Bitman, Clara *writer, educator*
Bjornsrud, Marlene *professional athletics manager*
Black, Geneva Arlene *social services agency administrator*
Black, Julie L. *language educator*
Black, Lisa Hartman *actress, singer*
Black, Rebecca Leree *special education educator*
Black, Recca Marcele *elementary school educator*
Black, Ruth Idella *museum curator*
Black, Shirley Temple (Mrs. Charles A. Black) *retired ambassador, retired actress*
Black, Susan Harrell *federal judge*
Blackburn, Joy Martin *retired librarian*
Blackburn, Pamela M. *medical surgical nurse*
Blackman, Ghita Waucheta *natural energy consultant*
Blackmun, Barbara Winston *art historian, educator, academic administrator*
Blackstone, Dara *music educator, conductor*
Blackwell, Lois Moore *fashion designer, educator, visual artist*
Blagden, Susan Lowndes *retired small business owner*
Blais, Madeleine Helena *writer*
Blake, Kimberly Bosworth *pharmacist*
Blakeney, Karen Elizabeth *social service and community health program executive, consultant*
Blakeney, Kecia L. *disability examiner*
Blake Ramos, Debra Barbara *writer*
Blalock, Louise *librarian, public administrator*
Blanchard, Lou *school system administrator*
Blanchard, MaryAnn N. *state legislator*
Blanco, Laura *interior designer*
Bland, Deborah Elaine *science educator*
Bland, Deborah Shaffer *nurse*
Bland, Eveline Mae *real estate broker, musician, educator*
Blank, Rebecca Margaret *economist*
Blanken, Celeste S. *physician*
Blattner, Florence Anne *retired music educator*
Blatz, Kathleen Anne *former state supreme court justice*
Blatz, Lidia *music educator, elementary school educator*
Blatz, Linda Jeanne *sales manager*
Blauvelt, Barbara Louise *nutritionist*
Blazej, Penny Annette *clinical social worker, writer, artist*
Blazina, Janice Fay *pathologist*
Bleam, Laura Jane *pediatrics nurse, educator*
Bledsoe, Cynthia Wyrick *sales executive, consultant*
Blethyn, Brenda Anne *actress*
Blevins, Elaina Gwen *music educator, director*
Blige, Mary Jane *recording artist*
Blizard, Marjorie Claire *small business owner*
Bloch, Julia Chang *educational association administrator*
Blochowiak, Mary Ann *retired cultural organization administrator*
Block, Amanda Roth *artist*
Block, Lanise *secondary school educator*
Blom, Nicole Jan *magazine advertising executive*
Bloodworth, Gladys Leon *elementary school educator*
Blos, Joan W. *writer, critic, educator*
Blossom, Beverly *choreographer, educator*
Blue, Rose *writer, educator*
Bluitt, Karen *information technology executive*
Blum, Barbara Davis *investor*
Blum, Betty Ann *footwear company executive*
Blumberg, Barbara Salmanson (Mrs. Arnold G. Blumberg) *retired state housing official, housing consultant*
Blunt, Kathryn London *writer, scriptwriter*
Bluth, B. J. (Elizabeth Jean Catherine Bluth) *sociologist, aerospace technologist*
Blystone, Debra A. *social studies educator*
Blyth, Myrna Greenstein *publishing executive*
Boardman, Eunice *retired music educator*
Boatwright, Charlotte Jeanne *marketing professional, public relations executive*
Boberg, Laron Capbarat *importer, retailer*
Bock, Janine Schmelzer *music educator*
Bockhorst, Barbara Alice *retired secondary school educator*
Boda, Veronica Constance *lawyer*
Bodden, Lisa *theater educator*
Bodie, Phyllis Jean *art educator, watercolorist*
Bodnar-Balahutrak, Lydia *artist, educator*
Boeckman, Patricia Ellen *writer, educator*
Boepple, Bettie Ann *elementary school educator*
Boer, Linda Karen *medical/surgical nurse*
Bogacz, Dolores Rosalie Marie *retired elementary school educator, paralegal*
Bogard, Margaret Joan *nurse*
Bogdanowicz, Loretta Mae *artist, educator*
Boggess, Carol Brownscombe *language educator, writer*
Boggus, Tamara *elementary school educator*
Bogle, Kimberly Layng *physical education educator*
Bohanon, Kathleen Sue *neonatologist*
Bohen, Barbara Elizabeth *archaeologist, retired museum director*
Bohrman, Catherine Leuchs *sculptor*
Boise, Audrey Lorraine *retired special education educator*
Bok, Sissela *philosopher, writer*
Bokhari, Robina Maqbool *physician*
Boland, Deborah Catherine *music educator*
Bolding, Kandy Denese Mynear *special education educator*
Boldovitch, Gerri *art educator*
Boldt, Patricia C. *social worker*
Bolla, Karen Irene *neuropsychologist, educator*
Bolles, Susan *production designer*
Bollhofer-White, Joanne *pharmacist*
Bollinger, Sharon Moore *psychotherapist*
Bolognia, Jean Lynn *academic dermatologist*
Bolsterli, Margaret Jones *English professor, farmer*
Bolt, Dawn Maria *financial planner*
Bolton, Ann P. *music educator*
Boltuck, Mary A. *retired psychologist, educator*
Bomar, Gail Marie *language educator*
Bomboy, Jennifer Marie *social studies educator, coach*
Bonanni, Victoria *writer*
Bonassi, Jodi *artist, marketing professional, consultant*
Bonazzi, Elaine Claire *mezzo soprano*
Bond, Victoria Ellen *conductor, composer*
Bondy, Alison A. *music educator*
Boneau, Janne Marie *music educator*
Bonebrake, Tara Jane *elementary school educator*
Bonet, Lisa (Lilakoi Moon, Lisa Michelle Boney) *actress*
Bonn, Ethel May *psychiatrist, educator*
Bonneau, Wendy Sue *special education educator*
Bonnell, Victoria Eileen *sociologist, educator*
Bonney, Jo *theater director*
Bonsack, Rose Mary Hatem *state legislator, physician*
Bonzo, Deborah L. *dietician, educator*
Booher, Alice Ann *lawyer*
Booker, Nana Laurel *art gallery owner, honorary consul*
Bookman, Ann Edith *director*
Boone, Donna Clausen *physical therapist, statistician, researcher*
Booth, Ada Sokal *retired education educator*
Booth, Kortney Diana *music educator*
Booth, Susan *educational association administrator, product designer, marketing professional, researcher*
Borchers, Mary Amelia *middle school educator*
Bordelon, Suzanne Mackie *writing and rhetoric educator*
Borg, Ruth I. *home nursing care provider*
Born, Ethel Wolfe *religious writer*
Bornstein, Barbara Markey *psychologist*
Bornstein, Mimi *writer, social scientist*
Borysewicz, Mary Louise *editor*
Bose, Michelle Denise *secondary school educator*
Bosley, Valerie Lynne *elementary school educator*
Bosse, Margaret Fisher Ishler *education educator*
Boswell, Vivian Nicholson *protective services official*
Botsford, Mary Henrich *retired ophthalmologist*
Bott, Patricia Ann *medical/surgical nurse*
Bottari, Marianna Teresa *public relations executive*
Bottolfson, Wahnita Joan *parochial school educator*
Bottone, JoAnn *health services executive*
Bouchonville, Susan Joanne *public health service officer, medical technician*
Boughton, Lilian Elizabeth *secondary education educator, retired*
Boulanger, Carol Seabrook *lawyer*
Boumenot, Stacy Leah *school psychologist*
Bourguignon, Erika Eichhorn *anthropologist, educator*
Bouvier, Linda Fritts *publishing executive*
Boward, Diana Larson *medical/surgical nurse*
Bowe, Mary Ann *small business owner, art educator*
Bowen, Barbara Cherry *French and comparative literature educator*
Bowen, Ginger Ann *artist*
Bowen, Jean *retired librarian, consultant*
Bowens, Gloria Furr *educational administrator*
Bower, Janet Esther *writer, educator*
Bower, Jean Ramsay *lawyer, writer*
Bower, Laurel Lee *education educator, researcher*
Bowers, Andrea *artist*
Bowers, Christi C. *mediator, lawyer, educator, writer, poet*
Bowers, Madeline Katherine Jente *elementary school educator*
Bowick, Susan D. *retired computer company executive*
Bowles, Barbara Landers *investment company executive*
Bowles, Vicky Lynn Hill *elementary school educator*
Bowman, Lynne Barnett *medical librarian*
Bowman, Patricia Lynn *lawyer*
Bowne, Shirlee Pearson *credit manager*
Boyce, Martha Jo *artist, educator*
Boyce, Tiffany Marie *literature and language educator*
Boyd, Mary Frances *retired school nurse, pastor*
Boyd, Velena *retired community health nurse, consultant*
Boyer, Joan Sue *liberal arts educator, social sciences educator*
Boyer, Lisa *basketball coach*
Boyle, Lara Flynn *actress*
Boynton, Sandra Keith *illustrator, cartoonist, stationery products executive*
Boysen, Jonea Gene *marketing executive, copywriter*
Boyter, Judy B *music educator*
Boyum (Ball), Jennifer Marie *music educator*
Brabec, Rosemary Jean *retail executive*
Bracken, Peg *writer*
Braddy, Carolyn Morton *pastor*
Braden, Joan Kay *mental health counselor*
Bradford, Barbara Reed *retired lawyer*
Bradford, Louise Mathilde *social work administrator*
Bradford, Mary Rosen *lawyer*
Bradford, Susan Anne *management consultant, writer*
Bradley, Becky Sue *music educator*
Bradley, Carol Ann *nursing consultant, editor*
Bradley, Deborah J. *music educator*
Bradley, Deidra D. *elementary school educator*
Bradley, Janice Jeanenne *retired medical technician*
Bradley, Patricia Ellen *professional golfer*
Brady, Donna Elizabeth *sales executive, marketing executive, performing company executive*
Brady, Jean Stein *retired librarian*
Brady, M. Jane (Muriel Jane Brady) *judge, former state attorney general*
Brady, Mary Rolfes *music educator*
Brady-Borland, Karen *retired reporter, columnist*
Bragg, Lynn Munroe *trade association administrator, former federal commissioner*
Braggs, Patricia *account manager*
Brainard, Melissa *accountant*
Braisted, Madeline Charlotte *artist, retired financial planner, military officer*
Brakebill, Jean Newton *military officer, nurse, educator*
Bramhall, Debra A. *information technology manager, consultant*
Bramson, Phyllis Halperin *artist, educator*
Branch, Felecia Ann-Seldon *elementary school educator*
Branch, Laura Michelle *science educator*
Brand, Donna J. *career consultant, mental health counselor*
Brandler, Marcielle Y. *poet, educator*
Brandon, Kathryn Elizabeth Beck *pediatrician*
Brandon, Liane *filmmaker, educator*
Brandon, Michelle Marie *marketing executive*
Brandt, Leota Fay *medical/surgical nurse*
Brandt, Sara Jane *elementary school educator*
Brandt-Shapiro, Irene Hildegard *retired secondary school educator*
Branham, Regina Jeanette *elementary school educator*
Brannick, Ellen Marie *retired management consultant*
Brantley, Willa John *educational association administrator*
Brasoveanu Tarpy, Alexandra *mathematics professor*
Bratzler, Mary Kathryn *web services manager*
Brauer, Rhonda Lyn *publishing executive, lawyer*
Brault, G. Lorain *health facility administrator*
Braun, Lilian Jackson *writer*
Braxton, Toni *popular musician*
Brayer, Edith Marie *marriage and family therapist, consultant*
Brazil, Aine M. *engineering company executive*
Brdlik, Carola Emilie *retired accountant*
Breaux, Cheryl *counselor*
Brecht, Sally Ann *quality assurance executive*
Breitbart, Barbara Renee *psychologist, administrator, writer*
Brenken, Hanne Marie *artist*
Brennan, Donna Lesley *public relations company executive*
Brennen, Anna B. *theater producer, director, playwright, actor*
Breuning, Pamela *music educator*
Brevoort, Deborah B. *librettist*
Brewer, Angela Sue *middle school educator*
Brewer, Leslie Kay *elementary school educator*
Brewer, Lynn *energy executive*
Brewer, Rogenna Wynne *writer*
Brewster, Elizabeth Winifred *literature educator, poet, writer*
Brewster, Jamie Susan *theater educator*
Brewster, Mary Moorhead *retired educational association administrator*
Breyne, Michele K *mathematics educator*
Briand-Ryan, Donna Marie *artistic designer*
Brians, Michelle Suzanne *music educator, musician*
Brice, Jacqueline (Jackie Brice) *landscape artist*
Briceño, Candace Michele *artist*
Bricker, Ruth *national foundation administrator, real estate developer*
Bricker, Victoria Reifler *anthropologist, educator*
Bridges, Christine E. *elementary school educator*
Bridgewater, Dee Dee *jazz singer, diplomat*
Brienza, Paula Kenah *retired chemist*
Briggs, Bonnie Sue *school librarian, minister*
Briggs, Laura *education educator*
Bright, Sheryl Ann *special education educator*
Brightman, Carol *writer*
Brightman, Sarah *singer, actress*
Briles, Judith *writer, consultant*
Bringman, Debra Ann *music educator*
Brinkley, Glenda Willis *medical, surgical, and women's health nurse*
Briskin, Jacqueline Elizabeth *author*
Britt, Debra L. *medical/surgical nurse*
Britt, Julia Moody *secondary school educator*
Britton, Kim Barnett *medical/surgical nurse*
Broaddus, Andrea Lynn *environmental services administrator*
Brockington, Carolyn *neurologist*
Broderson, Thelma Sylvia *retired marketing professional*
Brodeur, Catherine Reckart *artist*
Brodie, Susan Gerrish *special education educator*
Brodowski, Debra Lee *consumer sciences educator*
Broers, Brenda Ann *chemistry professor*
Brogliatti, Barbara Spencer *retired television and motion picture executive*
Bromund, Alice A. *retired elementary school educator*
Bromwell, Linda Anne *librarian, writer*
Bronkar, Eunice Dunalee *artist, educator*
Bronzaft, Arline L. *psychology consultant*
Brooks, Andrée Aelion *journalist, educator, writer*
Brooks, Barbara Carrk *registered nurse, administrator*
Brooks, Deborah June *art educator*
Brooks, Geraldine *writer, reporter, news correspondent*
Brooks, Hillary Afton *social worker*
Brooks, Lorraine Elizabeth *retired music educator*
Brooks, Lynda Barbara *psychologist*
Brooks, Velma *entrepreneur, small business owner*
Brooks Shoemaker, Virginia Lee *librarian*
Brooks-Turner, Myra *music educator*
Bross, Kathleen *elementary school educator*
Broughton, Hazel Callen *rehabilitation counselor, consultant*
Broussard, Carol Madeline *writer, consultant, photographer*
Brown, Alice Elste *artist*
Brown, Amira Khalila *neuropsychologist, researcher*
Brown, Amy Christine *art educator*
Brown, Angela McHaney *editor*
Brown, Barbara June *hospital and nursing administrator*
Brown, Beulah Louise *retired elementary school educator*
Brown, Beverly Michelle *music educator*
Brown, Billye Jean *retired nursing educator*
Brown, Brenda Bernadine *education educator*
Brown, Carol Ann *librarian, director*
Brown, Carol Rose *artist*
Brown, Carolyn P. *retired librarian*
Brown, Crystal Jeanine *writer*
Brown, Dale Susan *retired federal agency administrator, academic administrator, consultant, writer*
Brown, Deborah Eleanor *priest*
Brown, Debra *elementary school educator*
Brown, Denise *poet*
Brown, Elmira Newsom *retired elementary school educator*
Brown, Fay *editor, writer*
Brown, Geraldine Reed *lawyer, management consultant*
Brown, Hollace Ann Holly *advertising executive*
Brown, Jennifer Kay *lawyer*
Brown, Joan Teresa *writer, retired language educator*
Brown, Julia *museum director*
Brown, June Gibbs *retired government official*
Brown, Kay (Mary Kathryn Brown) *retired state official, consultant, political organization worker*
Brown, L. Elizabeth *judge*
Brown, Laima Adomaitis *art therapist, artist, writer*
Brown, Linda Sue *elementary school educator*
Brown, Lora Alice *entertainment company executive, educator*
Brown, Marcia Joan *author, artist, photographer*
Brown, Margaret deBeers *lawyer*
Brown, Mary Ellen *former state legislator, accountant*
Brown, Mary Jane *history educator*
Brown, Maureen Jill *elementary school educator*
Brown, Melissa *secondary school educator*
Brown, Michelle Alise *elementary school educator*
Brown, Pamela S. *former attorney general*
Brown, Patricia Mary Clare *health facility administrator*
Brown, Rebecca *writer, educator*
Brown, Reni (Arlene Patricia Theresa Brown) *artist*
Brown, Rhonda Rochelle *chemist, health facility administrator, lawyer*
Brown, Sandra *writer*
Brown, Shari K. *special education educator*
Brown, Wilma Elaine *elementary school educator, artist*
Brown-Barton, Grace Olive *music educator*
Browne, Bonnie Esther *minister*
Brownell, Blanche P. *retired secondary school educator*
Brownell, Nora Mead *former commissioner*
Browning, Becky Beck *elementary school educator*
Browning, Emily Rose *science educator*
Browning, Jane Louise *social services administrator*
Brownlee, Paula Pimlott *higher education consultant*
Brownstein, Elizabeth Smith *writer*
Brown-Zekeri, Lolita Molanda *elementary school educator*
Brubach, Holly Beth *writer*
Bruce, Nadine Cecile *internist, educator*
Bruck, Connie Jane *reporter*
Bruckner, Matilda Tomaryn *romance language and literature educator*
Brundage, Marjorie Underwood *academic administrator*
Bruns, Christine *music educator*
Bruttomesso, Kathleen Ann *dean, nursing educator, researcher*
Bryan, Mary Jo W. *realtor, artist, art educator*
Bryant, Bertha Estelle *retired medical/surgical nurse*
Bryant, Betty Jean *bank executive*
Bryant, La Kesha Joy *physical education educator*
Bryjak, Jacqueline Mae *elementary school educator*
Brzozowy, Kandy Doris *behavioral health writer*
Bubeck, Margaret Ann *mathematics educator*
Buchanan, Carolee Horstman *special education educator, consultant*
Buchanan, Theresa Carroll *judge*
Bucheister, Patricia Louise (Patt Parrish) *writer, artist*
Buchner, Amanda Elizabeth *secondary school educator, coach, athletic trainer*
Buchwald, Emilie Daisy *publisher, editor*
Buchwald, Naomi Reice *federal judge*
Buck, Bernestine Bradford *retired counseling administrator*
Buck, Dorothy Cecelia *psychotherapist, writer*
Buck, Jane Louise *retired psychology professor*
Buck, Linda Dee *executive recruiting company executive*
Buckingham, Deidre Lyn *writer, musician*
Buckley, Eleanor Jane *retired elementary school educator*
Buckman, Tracey Ann *political finance director*
Budny, Lorraine *newspaper reporter, freelance writer*
Budoff, Penny Wise *retired physician, author, researcher*
Buechling, Linda *language educator*

Bugbee, Joan Barthelme *retired corporate communications executive*
Buhagiar, Marion *editor, writer*
Buhl, Cynthia Maureen *advocate, educator*
Buhro, Natalie Jo *mathematics educator*
Bullard, Cynthia L. *elementary school educator*
Bullard, Judith Eve *psychologist, systems engineer*
Buller, Carol H. *secondary school educator*
Bullin, Christine Neva *art association administrator*
Bullock, Mary Brown *former academic administrator*
Bullock, Molly *retired elementary school educator*
Bullock, Sandra (Sandra Annette Bullock) *actress*
Bulmer, Connie J. *film librarian*
Bumbry, Grace *soprano*
Bumbry-Bronson, Venetta *music educator*
Bump, Elizabeth Bertha *music educator*
Bundy, Barbara Korpan *former college president*
Bundy, Suzanne *human services administrator*
Bunte, Mandy Kay *principal, education educator*
Bunyan, Ellen Lackey Spotz *retired chemist*
Burau, Jennette Anne *music educator*
Burch, Lori Ann *obstetrics nurse*
Burch-Martinez, Berkeley Alison *primary school educator*
Burd, Barbara R. *mathematics educator*
Burdett, Barbra Elaine *biology professor*
Burdman, Jacqueline Bermel *retired special education educator*
Burge, Constance M. *television producer*
Burgess, Marjorie Laura *retired protective services official*
Burgher, Pauline Menefee *retired marriage and family therapist*
Burgio, Jane L. *pathologist, writer*
Burkard, Patricia *writer*
Burke, Brooke *actress, model*
Burke, Jan Helene *writer*
Burke, Karen A. *medical/surgical nurse*
Burke, Linda Beerbower *lawyer, mining executive, metal products executive*
Burkhardt, Joanna Marie *librarian*
Burkholder, Kelly Leann *elementary school educator*
Burks, Brenda Rounsaville *retired music educator, council member*
Burnett, Barbara Diane *retired social worker*
Burnett, Iris Jacobson *corporate communications specialist*
Burnett, Susan W. *academic administrator*
Burnham, Shannon L. *elementary school educator*
Burns, Barbara Belton *investment company executive*
Burns, Ellen Jean *distance education administrator*
Burns, Kathleen Adley *educational consultant*
Burns, Kitty *playwright*
Burns, Marcelline *retired psychologist, researcher*
Burns, Toni Anthony *artist*
Burnside, Mary Ardis *psychologist*
Burrell, Kimberly Meadows *assistant principal*
Burrell, Pamela *actress*
Burris-Schnur, Catherine *minister, pastoral psychotherapist, medical/surgical nurse, educator*
Bursley-Hamilton, Susan *secondary school educator*
Burton, Janis Elaine (Jan Burton) *retired writer, editor*
Burton, Kate *actress*
Burton, Kathleen T. *mental health services professional*
Busbea, Virginia Beth *mathematics educator*
Busby, Rebecca Ann *church musician, pianist*
Büsch, Annemarie *retired mental health nurse*
Busch, Joyce Ida *small business owner*
Bush, Barbara Pierce *former First Lady of the United States, volunteer*
Bush, Christine Gay *dental hygienist*
Bush, Lynn Jeanne *federal judge*
Bush, Rebecca R. *psychologist*
Bush, Sandi Tokoa *elementary school educator*
Bush, Sarah Lillian *historian*
Bush, Yvonne *writer, counselor*
Bushong Whitehead, Pat J. *science educator, consultant*
Bustreo, Flavia *epidemiologist*
Butler, Brett *comedienne, actress*
Butler, Debra Yvonne *special education educator, small business owner*
Butler, Linda Louise *elementary educator*
Butler Yank, Leslie Ann *artist, writer, editor*
Buttel, Stacey Jeanne *social studies educator*
Butter, Andrea *marketing executive, consultant*
Butterfield, Deborah Kay *sculptor*
Butterfield, Karen *educational association administrator*
Butts, Cherie LaVaughn *biomedical researcher*
Byars, Amanda *performing company executive, musician, educator*
Byars, Betsy Cromer *writer*
Bynes, Amanda *actress*
Byrd, Debra Ann *actor, theater producer, performing company executive*
Byrne-Dempsey, Cecelia (Cecelia Dempsey) *journalist*
Byrnes, Gail M. *endoscopy nurse*
Byrnes, Hope Huska *volunteer*
Bzdell, Susan Rosenblum *archivist, educator*
Cabaniss, Charlotte Jones *library services director*
Cable, Diane Lynne *marriage and family therapist, educator*
Cadwallader, Gwen Natalie *elementary school educator, music educator*
Cadwell, Courtney Bradshaw *elementary school educator*
Cafferty, Anita A. *music educator*
Cafiero, Jennifer Annette *academic administrator, educator*
Cager, Chezia Thompson *poet, literature educator*
Cahill, Verna Eleanore *writer*
Cai, Ming Zhi *chemist, researcher, film producer*
Cain, Wanda Neil *secondary school educator*
Cairns, Anne Marie *public relations executive*
Calabrese, Karen Ann *artist, educator*
Calamar, Gloria *artist*
Calder, Mary Alberta *elementary education educator, consultant*
Calderón, Sila Maria *former governor*
Caldicott, Helen *physician*
Caldwell, Cassandra Denise *education educator*
Caldwell, Eleanor *artist*
Caldwell, Judy Carol *advertising executive, consultant, writer*
Caldwell, Louise Phinney *historical researcher, community volunteer*
Caldwell, Patricia Ann *language educator*
Calegari, Maria *ballerina*
Caletti, Deb L. *writer*
Calhoun, Ramona *human services administrator, academic administrator, consultant*
Call, Whitney L. *paralegal*
Callahan, Vivian *broadcast executive*
Callis, Karen Denise *elementary school educator*
Calvin, Jamie Duif *retired interactive designer*
Cameron, Donna *artist, art educator*
Cameron, Lucille Wilson *retired dean*
Cameron, Stacey Rebecca *benefits compensation analyst*
Cammack, Ann *librarian, secondary school educator*
Camp, Alice W. *retired elementary education educator*
Campbell, Claire Patricia *nurse practitioner, educator*
Campbell, Judy *medical/surgical nurse, educator*
Campbell, Mary Stinecipher *retired chemist*
Campbell, Melissa Lynnsimmons *music educator*
Campbell, Naomi *model*
Campbell, Reginna Gladys *medical/surgical nurse*
Campbell, Sarah *elementary school educator, special education educator*
Campbell, Theresa Marie *mathematics educator*
Canelli, Jeanne *early childhood educator*
Canfield, Constance Dale *retired accountant, retired medical/surgical nurse, retired military officer*
Cannistraro, Carolyn Marie *financial recruiter*
Cannizzaro, Linda Ann *geneticist, researcher*
Cannon, Dyan *actress*
Cannon, Gayle Elizabeth *lawyer*
Cannon, Lena Ferrara (Lee) *retired education educator*
Cannon, Patricia Althen *librarian, writer*
Cano, Marta Mendendez *securities company executive, financial consultant*
Canobbio, Linda J. *elementary school educator*
Cantor, Susan *advertising executive*
Cantrell, Carol Whitaker *educational administrator*
Cantrell, Joyce Ann *mathematics educator*
Cantu, Delia *training services executive*
Capell, Cydney Lynn *editor*
Capello, Linda *artist*
Capes, Bonnie Heather *music educator*
Caplin, Jo Ann *communications company executive*
Caplin, Olga Yeryomina *psychiatrist*
Cappello, Eve *speaker, trainer, writer*
Capstick, Michelle *special education educator*
Carbone, Cassandra A. *theater educator*
Cardarelli, Lisa Monica *school system administrator*
Cardinale, Loretta Ann *educator*
Cardone, Bonnie Jean *freelance/self-employed photojournalist*
Cardwell, Nancy Lee *editor, writer*
Carey, Jana Howard *lawyer*
Carey, Kathryn Ann *retired foundation administrator, editor, consultant*
Carey, Mariah *vocalist, songwriter*
Carl, Susan Marie *photographer, photojournalist*
Carlin, Marian P. *secondary school educator*
Carlisle-Frank, Pamela L. *writer, researcher, consultant*
Carlock, Sandra Lynn *musician, educator*
Carls, Alice Catherine *history professor*
Carlsen, Mary Baird *clinical psychologist*
Carlson, Alyssa *literature and language educator*
Carlson, Cheryl Ann *literature and language educator*
Carlson, Janet Frances *psychologist, educator*
Carlson, Natalie Traylor *publisher*
Carlson, Nora *elementary school educator*
Carlson, Stacy C. *former motion picture association executive*
Carlson-Rukavina, Patricia Ann *small business owner*
Carlyle, Bobbie Kristine *sculptor*
Carmack, Mildred Jean *retired lawyer*
Carman, Susan Hufert *nurse coordinator*
Carnahan, Jean *former senator*
Caroleo, Linn E. *mathematician, writer*
Carolin, Kirstin Kerry *secondary school educator*
Carpenter, Candice *writer, former media executive*
Carpenter, Janella Ann *retired librarian*
Carpenter, Liz (Elizabeth Sutherland Carpenter) *journalist, writer, equal rights leader, lecturer*
Carpenter, Rosalie T. *education educator, consultant*
Carpenter, Susan Karen *defender*
Carpenter-Mason, Beverly Nadine *quality assurance professional, medical/surgical nurse, pediatric nurse practitioner, consultant, writer*
Carpentieri, Sarah C. *neuropsychologist, researcher, clinical psychologist*
Carper, Barbara Anne *nursing educator*
Carr, Bessie *retired elementary school educator*
Carr, E. Barbara *librarian*
Carraher, Mary Lou Carter *art educator*
Carr-DeRamus, Denise *mental health counselor*
Carrell, Jennifer Lee *writer*
Carrillo, Juanita *gerontological services consultant*
Carroll, Barbara *musician, composer, singer*
Carroll, Diahann *actress, singer*
Carroll, Marie-Jean Greve *retired art educator, artist*
Carroll, Mary Patricia *writer*
Carson, Regina E. *healthcare administrator, pharmacist, educator, geriatric specialist*
Carstairs, Sharon *legislator*
Carswell, Jane Triplett *retired family physician*
Carswell, Linda Gail *language educator, department chairman*
Carter, Barbara Dale *musician, educator, clinical counselor*
Carter, Betsy L. *editor, writer*
Carter, Cynthia (Cindy) Lynn *writer*
Carter, Dixie *actress*
Carter, Jaine M(arie) *human resources specialist, director*
Carter, Jeanne Wilmot *lawyer, publishing executive*
Carter, JoAnn Martin *retired education educator*
Carter, La Rae Dunn *music educator*
Carter, Melva Jean *retired medical technician*
Carter, Nanette Carolyn *artist*
Carter, Rebecca Gail *critical care nurse*
Carter, Rosalynn Smith (Eleanor Rosalynn Carter) *former First Lady of the United States*
Carter, Yvonne Pickering *art educator*
Carton, Lonnie Caming *educational psychologist*
Cartwright, Katharine Aileen *geologist*
Cartwright, Lillian *psychologist, researcher, artist*
Cartwright, Talula Elizabeth *management consultant, educator*
Carunchio, Florence Regina *financial planner*
Carver, Juanita Ash *inventor*
Cary, Emily Pritchard *columnist*
Casasanta, Mary Frances *medical/surgical nurse*
Casazza, Monica Kathryn *art educator*
Casei, Nedda *mezzo soprano*
Caseiras, Jo Ann Striga *artist, educator*
Cash, Deanna Gail *retired nursing educator*
Cash, Mary Frances *minister, retired civilian military employee*
Cason, Nica Virginia *nursing educator*
Cassell, Kay Ann *librarian*
Cassidy, Esther Christmas *retired government official*
Casson Madden, Chris *entrepreneur, interior designer*
Castellanos, Josephine Falcon *insurance agent, composer*
Castle, Nancy Margaret Timma *accountant, banker*
Castleman, Pamela Ann *assistant principal*
Castro, Maria Graciela *medical educator, geneticist, researcher*
Castro, Teresa Jacira *small business owner*
Castro-Pozo, Talía *dancer, educator*
Caswell, Dorothy Ann Cottrell *performing arts association administrator*
Caswell, Frances Pratt *retired language educator*
Cathcart, Sheila K. *athletic trainer*
Cathou, Renata Egone *chemist, consultant*
Caucia, Louisa B. *retired elementary school educator*
Caulfield, Kathleen Marie *medical health information administrator, geriatrics nurse*
Causey, Linda *secondary school educator*
Cauthorne-Burnette, Tamera Dianne *family practice nurse practitioner, consultant*
Cavallo-Best, Maria Isolina *language educator*
Cavanagh, Caitlin *music educator*
Cavanah, Sarah E. *music educator*
Cavender, Rebecca Ann *music educator*
Cavin, Jacinda Ann *music educator*
Cavin, Susan Elizabeth *sociologist, writer*
Cawley, Maureen E. *pharmacist*
Cawley, Patricia Blonts *secondary school educator*
Cazalas, Mary Rebecca Williams *lawyer, nurse*
Cecchini, Sonia Nathalie *speech and drama educator*
Cecil, Elizabeth Jean *writer*
Cerney, Angela Dawn *athletic trainer, health facility administrator*
Cerra, Wendy *psychotherapist*
Cervantez, Michelle *marketing professional*
Céspedes, Melinda Brown *elementary school educator, dancer*
Ceulemans, Sophia *biochemist*
Chadha, Gurinder *film director*
Chafel, Judith Ann *education educator*
Chafkin, Rita M. *retired dermatologist*
Chairsell, Christine *academic administrator*
Chait, Fay Klein *health administrator*
Chalcraft, Elena Marie *actress, singer*
Chalfant-Allen, Linda Kay *retired Spanish language educator*
Chalifoux, Thelma *Canadian senator*
Chamberlain, Diane *psychotherapist, writer, social worker*
Chamberlain, Jean Nash *consultant, former county government department director*
Chamberlain, Patricia Ann *retired land use planner, farmer*
Chambers, Marjorie Bell *historian*
Champey, Elaine *science foundation director*
Champion, Cheryl *educator*
Champion, Crystal *literature and language educator*
Chan, Elaine Elizabeth *elementary school educator*
Chan, Wilma *state legislator*
Chandler, Alice *retired academic administrator, educational consultant*
Chandler, Kathleen *retired executive secretary*
Chandler, Patricia Ann *retired special education educator*
Chang, Debbie I-Ju *health programs and research executive, director*
Chang, Sophia Ho Ying C. *pediatrician*
Chang, Yuan *neuropathologist, researcher, educator*
Chapman, Amy L. *religious studies educator*
Chapman, Elizabeth Nina *counselor*
Chapman, Geneva Joyce *entrepreneur, educator, writer*
Chapman, Hope Horan *psychologist*
Chapman, Linda Lee *computer company executive, consultant*
Chapman, Robyn Lemon *music educator*
Chappell, Annette M. *educational consultant, minister*
Chappell, Valerie *educational consultant*
Charette, Cecile M. *music educator*
Charles, Laura Jo *mathematics educator*
Charles, Marilyn Kay *secondary school educator*
Charlton, Shirley Marie *educational consultant*
Charnin, Jade Hobson *magazine executive*
Charnley, Cristen Marie *secondary school educator*
Charters, Cynthia Grace *artist, educator*
Chase, Dawn Eileen *language educator*
Chase, Doris Totten *sculptor, educator, filmmaker*
Chast, Roz *cartoonist*
Chatterji, Angana P. *anthropologist*
Chaudoir, Jean Hamilton (Jean Hamilton) *secondary school educator*
Chave, Carol *arbitrator, retired lawyer*
Chavis, Geneva Boone *retired dean*
Cheadle, Louise *music educator, musician*
Checinska, Bozena Teresa *media specialist*
Chee, Ann-Ping *music educator*
Cheever, Susan *freelance/self-employed writer*
Chen, Del-Min Amy *lawyer*
Chen, Lu *figure skater*
Cheney, Mary Claire *Internet company executive*
Chermayeff, Alexandra Sasha *artist*
Cherry, Kelley *secondary school educator*
Chesney, Margaret A. *medical educator, medical researcher*
Chesney, Susan Talmadge *writer, educational association administrator*
Chess, Sonia Mary *retired language educator*
Chiang, Alexis S. *orthopedist, surgeon*
Chiao, Christine Lynn *psychiatrist*
Chiavario, Nancy Anne *business and community relations executive*
Chicklis, Barbara Karen Burak *retired data processing executive*
Child, Abigail *filmmaker, educator*
Childs, Christine Manzo *language arts educator*
Childs, Wenetta Grybas *artist*
Chin, Janet Sau-Ying *data processing executive, consultant*
Chintella, Marilynn Anita *elementary school educator, department chairman*
Chirco, Jennifer B. *special education educator*
Chirico-Elkins, Ursula *retired librarian*
Chiu, Bella Chao *astrophysicist, writer*
Chiu, Dorothy *retired pediatrician*
Cholewka, Patricia Anne *health facility administrator*
Chou, Ruby *finance educator, real estate broker, consultant*
Chow, Rita Kathleen *nursing consultant*
Chretien, Carol Ann *chemical engineer*
Chretien, Jane Henkel *internist*
Christensen, Karen Kay *lawyer*
Christensen, Katharine Eleanor *retired education educator*
Christensen, Vickie J. *secondary school educator*
Christian, Pearl C. *musician*
Christiansen, Wendy Lynne *music educator*
Christie, Cheryl Ann *athletic trainer and physical therapist*
Christie, Pamela Sue *music educator*
Chu, Ellin Resnick *librarian, consultant*
Chu, Lili *jewelry designer, consultant*
Chu, Margaret S.Y. *former federal agency administrator*
Chubbuck, Linda J. *music educator, singer*
Chughtai, Raana Lynn *psychiatric nurse practitioner*
Chumley, Shannon Jackson *elementary school educator*
Chun, Jacqueline Clibbett *artist, educator*
Chung, Caroline *marketing professional*
Chung, Connie (Constance Yu-hwa Chung) *broadcast journalist*
Ciancio, Marilyn *television producer*
Cicero, Dianne *special education educator*
Cierpiot, Connie *former state legislator*
Cifolelli, Alberta Carmella *artist, educator*
Ciliberti, Ava Carol *artist*
Cimino, Ann Mary *education educator*
Ciocan, Eugenia *physicist, educator*
Citron, Beatrice Sally *law librarian, lawyer, educator*
Citron, Diane *lawyer*
Clabeaux-Fechter, Barbara Jean *artist, educator*
Claes, Gayla Christine *writer, editor, consultant*
Claiborne, Liz (Elisabeth Claiborne Ortenberg) *fashion designer*
Clarizio, Josephine Delores *retired foundation administrator, retired manufacturing executive, retired engineering company executive*
Clark, Alicia Garcia *political party official*
Clark, Barbara June *elementary school educator*
Clark, Beverly Ann *retired lawyer*
Clark, Candy *actress*
Clark, Christine W. *elementary school educator*
Clark, Eve Vivienne *linguist, educator*
Clark, Evelyn Jean *artist, educator*
Clark, Karen Heath *lawyer*
Clark, Margaret Ann-Cynthia *television producer, writer*
Clark, Marie *secondary school educator*
Clark, Mary Etta *science writing consultant*
Clark, Mary Higgins *writer, communications executive*
Clark, Nancy Lucinda Brown *retired music educator*
Clark, Patricia Sherbert *secondary school educator*
Clark, Patsy Vedder *retired educator and staff developer*
Clark, Paula Irene *elementary school educator, consultant*
Clark, Stephani Michelle Callahan *elementary school educator*
Clark, Terri *country singer*
Clarke, Janet Morrison *marketing executive*
Clarke, Victoria C. (Torie Clarke) *former federal agency administrator*
Clarkson, Patricia *actress*
Claus, Carol Jean *small business owner*
Clauser, Suzanne Phillips *author, screenwriter*
Clawson, Amy K. *music educator*
Claypool, Nancy *social worker*
Clayton, Heather Lynn *language educator*
Cleary, Manon Catherine *artist, retired art educator*
Clemens, Brenda *medical/surgical nurse, educator*
Clement, Betty Waidlich *retired literacy educator, consultant*
Clement, Hope Elizabeth Anna *retired librarian*
Clemetson, Cheryl Price *minister, consultant*
Clemons, Julie Payne *telephone company manager*
Cline, Ann *artist*
Cloud, Gary Lynn *food and nutrition services administrator*
Clugston, Bonnie Irene *nurse*
Clydesdale, Peggy *artist, medical/surgical nurse*
Coady, Mary Luz K. *pediatrician*
Coates, Shirley Jean *finance educator, secondary school educator*
Cobb, Delores Massey *science educator*
Cobb, Virginia Horton *artist, educator*
Cobey, Virginia Branum *artist, actress, art collector*
Coburn, Deborah Ann *elementary school educator*
Cochran, Kathy Holcombe *music educator, conductor*

Cockerham, Sherry L. *secondary school educator*
Cockram, Suzanne M. *elementary school educator*
Cockrell-Fleming, Shelia Yvette *public health nurse*
Code, Audrey B. *art educator*
Codo, Christina *securities executive*
Cody, Judith *composer, writer*
Coe, Jill *director, educator*
Coffey, Marilyn June *writer, educator*
Coffey, Sharon Thornton *chemistry educator*
Coffin, Bertha Louise *retired telecommunications industry executive*
Coffinas, Eleni *lawyer*
Cogen, Roberta *retired nursing administrator, medical/surgical nurse*
Cognetto, Anna M. *social worker*
Cohane, Heather Christina *publishing executive, editor*
Cohen, Carolyn A. *healthcare educator*
Cohen, Gloria Ernestine *elementary school educator*
Cohen, Lois Jean *developmental psychologist, retired*
Cohen, Marcia Friedlander *writer, editor-in-chief, journalist*
Cohen, Margaret Ann *artist, consultant*
Cohen, Miriam *writer, educator*
Cohen, Roberta Jane *think-tank associate*
Cohen, Sharleen Cooper *interior designer, writer*
Cohn, Marianne Winter Miller *civic activist*
Coker, Mary Shannon *perinatal and perioperative nurse*
Colage, Beatrice Elvira *education educator*
Colburn, Nancy Douglas *social worker, educator*
Colby, Marvelle Seitman *retired business management educator, administrator*
Cole, Carolyn *photojournalist*
Cole, Jean Anne *artist*
Cole, Lyn P. *tap dance instructor*
Cole, Rachel P. *science educator*
Coleman, Claire Kohn *public relations executive*
Coleman, Jean Black *nurse, physician assistant*
Coleman, Mary Sue *academic administrator*
Coleman, Patsy Ann *secondary school educator*
Colip, Olga Shearin *retired home economist, volunteer*
Collarini Schlossberg, Antoinette Marie *psychologist*
Collette, Frances Madelyn *retired tax specialist, lawyer, consultant, advocate*
Colline, Marguerite Richnavsky *maternal, women's health and pediatrics nurse*
Collins, Eileen Marie *astronaut*
Collins, Elizabeth Brooke *theater educator*
Collins, Irma Helen *music educator, consultant*
Collins, Jacqueline F. *nurse, case manager*
Collins, Jacqueline Wight *secondary school educator*
Collins, Jean Katherine *language educator*
Collins, Kathleen Anne *artistic director*
Collins, Sherri Smith *music educator*
Collins-Brown, E. Dorlee (E. Dorlee Woodyard) *registrar*
Collinson, Vivienne Ruth *education educator, researcher, consultant*
Collischan, Judy Kay *art gallery director, museum director, critic, artist*
Colmenares, Leticia *chemistry professor*
Colombo, Rose Marie *freelance/self-employed newswriter, television personality*
Colvin, Shawn *recording artist, songwriter*
Colvin, Tina Powell *elementary school educator*
Colwell, Heather Thorstad *secondary school educator*
Colwell, Rita Rossi *microbiologist, former federal agency administrator, medical educator*
Comar, Mary Alice *retired art educator, farmer*
Combs, Judy Diane *elementary school educator, civic association administrator*
Comerford, ShaLeigh Marie *dancer, educator, choreographer*
Compton, Diane Groat *professional counselor, researcher*
Compton, Norma Haynes *retired dean, artist*
Conaway, Margaret Grimes (Peggy Conaway) *library administrator*
Cone, Frances McFadden *data processing consultant*
Congdon, Sarah-Braeme Bird *medical equipment company executive*
Coniglio, Judith *music educator*
Conklin, Peggy Brown *history professor*
Conley, Ruth Irene *poet*
Conlon Khan, Lori Ellen *music educator*
Connell, Bonnie Bleier *mathematics educator*
Connell, Shirley Hudgins *public relations professional*
Connelly, Sharon Rudolph *lawyer*
Connolly, Michelle Marie *athletic trainer*
Connolly, Violette M. *small business owner*
Conover, Mona Lee *retired adult education educator*
Conover, Nancy Anderson *retired secondary school counselor, small business owner*
Conover, Pamela C. *cruise line executive*
Conover-Carson, Anne *writer*
Conquest, Claire M. *secondary school counselor*
Conrad-England, Roberta Lee *pathologist*
Conroy, Frances *actress*
Conroy, Tamara Boks *artist, special education educator, retired nurse*
Constantine, Jessica Lee *elementary school educator*
Constantinople, Alexandra *communications executive*
Conte, Jeanne L. *writer, photographer*
Conte, Julie Villa *nurse, administrator*
Conti, Joan Noel *social worker*
Contreras, Dawn Rachelle *performing arts educator*
Conway, Jaime J. *science educator*
Conway, Teresa J. *secondary school educator*
Conway-Langguth, Rebecca Joan *dance instructor, dance school owner*
Cook, Beth Marie *volunteer, poet*
Cook, Iva Dean *education educator*
Cook, Kimberly Sue *music educator*
Cook, Sister Mary Mercedes *school system administrator, director*
Cook, Rebecca McDowell *former state official*
Cook, Renay *elementary school educator*
Cooke, Chantelle Anne *writer*
Cooks, Pamala Aniece *insurance agent*
Coolidge, Martha *film director*
Cooper, Doris Jean *market research executive*
Cooper, Elva June *artist*
Cooper, Jeanne A. *retired pathologist*
Cooper, Josephine Smith *trade association and public affairs executive*
Cooper, Judith Kase *retired theater educator, playwright*
Cooper, Kathleen Bell *dean, former federal agency administrator*
Cooper, Lynne Marie *veterinarian, educator*
Cooper, Mary Ellen *writer*
Cooper, Nicole Robyn *writer*
Cooper, Rebecca *art dealer*
Cooper, Signe Skott *retired nursing educator*
Cope, Melba Darlene *volunteer, photographer*
Copeland, Bonnie S. *former school system administrator*
Coppola, Sofia Carmina *film director, scriptwriter, actress*
Copt, Phyllis Jean *secondary school educator*
Corbett, Lenora Meade *mathematician, community college educator*
Corbi, Lana *communications executive*
Corbin, Veronica L. *secondary school educator, information scientist, consultant*
Cordell, Joann Meredith *music educator*
Corkran, Virginia B. *retired real estate agent*
Cornelius, Tia Marie *physical education educator*
Cornell, Carole Anne Walcutt Arnold *nurse*
Cornish, Elizabeth Turverey *retired investment advisor*
Cornish, Jeannette Carter *lawyer*
Corno, Lyn *psychology educator*
Cornwell, Nancy Dunn *secondary school educator*
Cornwell, Susan *music educator*
Corradini, Deedee *real estate company executive, former mayor*
Corry, Aline Lahusen *art educator*
Corto, Diana Maria *coloratura soprano*
Corvini, Marguerite *social worker*
Corwin, Vera-Anne Versfelt *small business owner, consultant*
Cosgrove, Annmarie *special education educator*
Cosman, Francene Jen *former government official*
Costa, Mary *soprano*
Costantini, Mary Ann C. *writer, editor, adult education educator*
Coté, Kathryn Marie *psychotherapist, stress management educator*
Cothran, Anne Jennette *academic administrator*
Cothren, Evangeline (Mrs. J.C.) *retail store owner*
Cotmans, Sharon Jenkins *computer scientist, educator*
Cotten, Annie Laura *psychologist, educator*
Cotter, Emily Rexann *social worker, marriage and family therapist*
Cottingham, Martha Maxfield *journalist, volunteer*
Cottrell, Linda Billops *retired elementary school educator*
Cottrell, Mary-Patricia Tross *bank executive*
Couillard, Elizabeth L. *secondary school educator, department chairman*
Coulter, Cynthia Jean *artist, educator*
Coury, Kristen *theater director, theater producer*
Coutts, Linda Dale *elementary school educator, consultant*
Covassin, Tracey *athletic training educator*
Covey, Norma Scott *travel service executive*
Cowan, Rhonda Renee *nurse, social worker*
Cowen, Jean *employee benefits consultant*
Cowles, Elizabeth Hall *program consultant*
Cowles, Lois Anne Fort *social worker, educator, poet*
Cowles, Milly *education educator*
Cox, Beulah Elizabeth *violinist, music educator*
Cox, Christine K. *secondary school educator*
Cox, Joy Dean *small business owner*
Cox, Kathleen *broadcast executive, lawyer*
Cox, Lynne Craige *music educator, composer*
Coyle, Dorothy Sherin Behen *medical/surgical nurse*
Coyle, Marie Bridget *retired microbiologist, retired lab administrator*
Cozza, Helen Rock *art educator, artist*
Cozzens, Mimi *actress, director*
Crabb, Virginia Geany Ruth *librarian*
Crabtree, Davida Foy *minister*
Crahan, Elizabeth Schmidt *librarian*
Craig, Carol Mills *marriage, family and child counselor*
Craig, Linda (Teri) Carol *science educator*
Craik, Mary Bernice *artist, art gallery owner*
Crane, Kathleen Dickinson *elementary school educator, writer*
Crane, Rea Babcock *retired nurse*
Crawford, Carol Tallman *law educator*
Crawford, Cindy (Cynthia Ann Crawford) *model, actress*
Crawford, Helene Hope *elementary school principal*
Crawford, Mallory *counselor*
Crawford, Muriel Laura *lawyer, educator, writer*
Crawford, Sheila Jane *librarian, reading specialist*
Crawford, Vicky Charlene *perinatal clinical nurse specialist, nursing administrator*
Crenshaw, Marjorie Juaneta *retired music educator*
Creswell, Dorothy Anne *computer consultant*
Crewson, Wendy Jane *actress*
Crincoli, Tracy Anne *athletic trainer*
Crinklaw, Katherine Mary *artist*
Crino, Marjanne Helen *anesthesiologist*
Crisci, Pat Devita *retired psychology educator*
Criswell, Kimberly Ann *executive coach, communications consultant, performance artist*
Critelli, Nancy Barbara *music educator, cellist*
Crittendon, Donna Elizabeth *customer service administrator*
Crocker, Saone Baron *lawyer*
Crocker, Suzanne *painter*
Croft, Kathryn Delaine *social worker, consultant*
Crombie, Pamela Gasparin *restaurant and commercial property owner*
Cromwell, Florence Stevens *occupational therapist*
Cronholm, Lois S. *academic administrator*
Cronson, Mary Sharp *foundation administrator*
Crosby, Kathryn Grandstaff (Grant Crosby) *actress*
Cross, E. Ashley *special education educator*
Cross, Goldie K. *telecommunications engineer*
Cross, Joan Russin *medical technologist*
Cross, Kathryn Patricia *education educator*
Cross, Ruth Chaiken *retired educational administrator*
Cross, Wilda Sue *secondary school educator*
Crossley, Dolly Madena Johnston *retired elementary school educator*
Crossley, Nancy Ruth *retired federal agency administrator*
Crosthwaite, Diane Louise *secondary school educator*
Crow, Sheryl *singer, songwriter, musician*
Crown, Nancy Elizabeth *lawyer*
Crozier, Prudence Slitor *economist*
Crudup, Pamela Tracy Parham *science educator, writer*
Cruver, Suzanne Lee *communications executive, writer*
Cruz, Cassandra *elementary school educator*
Cruz-Connerton, Mayra *elementary school educator*
Cruz-Romo, Gilda *soprano*
Cryar, Rhonda Lynn *elementary school educator*
Cuenca, Carmen *piano teacher*
Culleeney, Maureen Ann *information technology executive, educator*
Cullingford, Hatice Sadan *chemical engineer*
Culliton, Barbara J. *publishing executive*
Culp, Faye Berry *state legislator*
Culp, Mildred Louise *corporate financial executive*
Culver, Mona Capricia *retired elementary school educator*
Cummings, Edith Jean *small business owner*
Cummings, Erika Helga *financial consultant*
Cummings, Mary Voigt *counselor*
Cummins, Nancyellen Heckeroth *electronics engineer*
Cummins, Wilma Jeanne *actress, comedienne*
Cunniff, Suzanne *surgical technician*
Cunningham, Alice Jeanne *chemistry educator, author, consultant*
Cunningham, Alice Norida *retired physician*
Cunningham, Alice Welt *law and mathematics educator*
Cunningham, Kathy *artist, educator*
Cunningham, Victoria L. *secondary school educator*
Cupp, Lucy Paschall *retired elementary school educator, minister*
Curl, Mackenzie Elizabeth *secondary school educator*
Curnutte, Mary E. *artist*
Curran, Emily K. *music educator*
Curran-Smith, Anita Stiles *retired public health medicine educator, dean*
Currier, Patty *physiologist*
Curry, Catharine Terrill *marketing executive, health facility administrator, sales executive*
Curry, Dale Blair *retired journalist*
Curry, Sadye Beatryce *gastroenterologist, educator*
Curry Scott, Shirley Goodman *retired director*
Curtin, Leigh *media consultant, writer*
Curtis, Dolores Rogers *writer*
Curtis, Katherine Lanae *pharmacist*
Curtis, Mary E. (Mary Curtis Horowitz) *publishing executive*
Curtis, Rachael Elizabeth *music educator*
Curtis, Susan Grace *lawyer*
Curtis, Susan Virginia *social worker*
Cushman, Oris Mildred *retired nurse, hospital education director*
Custureri, Mary Catherine Foca *literature educator*
Cutcher, Kresta King *photojournalist, educator*
Cutter Modlin, Beverly Wright *management consultant*
Cyford, Janet Irene *Spiritualist medium, meditation consultant*
Cyprus, Rhonda Reneé *marriage and family therapist, social worker*
Czesak, Linda Susan *secondary school educator, education educator*
Dable, Carol M. *primary school educator*
D'Abruzzo, Stephanie *actress*
Dacey, Kathleen Ryan *lawyer, former federal judge*
Daffron, MaryEllen *retired librarian*
Daglis, Lisa Genine *deputy attorney general*
D'Agusto, Karen Rose *lawyer*
Dahl, Marilyn Gail *psychotherapist*
Dahlin, Angela Denise *language educator*
Dahlmann, Mary Elsa *secondary school educator*
Dahlstrom, Becky Joanne *journalist*
Dahlstrom, Patricia Margaret *real estate appraiser*
Daie, Jaleh *investment company executive*
Daileader, Celia Rose *literature educator*
Dailey, Janet *writer*
D'Alessio, Valaida Corrine *artist, consultant*
Daley, Linda *lawyer*
Daley, Sandra *retired artist, filmmaker, photographer*
Dallas, Donna Ann *music educator*
Dallolio, Janelle K. *language educator, literature and language educator*
Dalphond-Guiral, Madeleine *member of Canadian parliament*
Dal Santo, Diane *retired judge, writer, arbitrator, mediator*
Dalton, Jeanne M. *musician, music educator*
Daly, Miriam Shamer *retired family physician*
Damon, Shirley Stockton *art gallery owner*
Damrosch, Shirley Patchel *social psychologist, educator*
Damsgaard, Patricia Rae *artist, educator*
Danaher, Mallory Millett (Mallory Jones) *actress, photographer, film and theater producer*
Danao-Salkin, Julie *actress*
Dandeneau, Billie Jo *retired data processing executive*
Danes, Claire *actress*
D'Angelo, Renée Young *special education educator*
Daniel, Beth *professional golfer*
Daniel, Marilyn S. *lawyer*
Daniel, Winifred Yvonne *elementary school educator*
Danielewski, Donna Krystyna *secondary school educator*
Daniels, Arlene Kaplan *sociology educator*
Daniels, Mary P. *academic administrator, technologist*
Daniels, Susanne *broadcast executive*
Danko, Cassandra Dawn *educational consultant, researcher*
Danner, Blythe *actress*
Danner, Patsy Ann *former congresswoman*
D'Antonio, Cynthia Maria *sales and marketing executive*
Danziger, Gertrude Seelig *retired metal fabricating executive*
D'Arbanville, Patti *actress*
D'Arcy, Paula *writer*
Darden, Lauretta *elementary school educator*
Daren, Sylvia *poet*
Dargan, Pamela Ann *systems engineer, consultant*
Darkovich, Sharon Marie *nursing administrator*
Darlington, Hilda Walker *real estate company officer*
Darnell, Susan Laura Browne *retired air force officer*
Darnley, Katherine E. *elementary school educator*
Darsch, Nancy *former professional basketball coach*
Darvarova, Elmira *musician, concertmaster*
DaSilva, Dina Patricia *science educator*
Date, Elaine Satomi *physiatrist, educator*
Dauphin, Sue *writer, producer*
Davenport, Donna Jeanne Swanson *elementary school educator*
Davidow, Jenny Jean *counselor, writer*
Davidson, Anne Stowell *lawyer*
Davidson, Bonnie Jean *gymnastics educator, sports management consultant*
Davidson, Jeannie *costume designer*
Davidson, Lisa Rae *physician*
Davidson, Sarah J. *educational consultant, healthcare educator*
Davidson, Tara Beth *secondary school educator*
Davies, Alma (Alma Rosita) *theater producer, composer, playwright, lyricist, sculptor*
Davies, Fonda Woodell *minister of music, music teacher*
Davies-McNair, Jane *retired educational consultant*
Davion, Ethel Johnson *school system superintendent, curriculum specialist*
Davis, Ada Romaine *nursing educator*
Davis, Anna Jane Ripley *elementary school educator*
Davis, Beth *elementary school educator*
Davis, Debra Greer *educational association administrator*
Davis, Diann Holmes *elementary school educator*
Davis, Doris Rosenbaum (Dee Davis) *artist, writer*
Davis, Elba Lucila *veterans affairs nurse*
Davis, Elizabeth Eileen *education educator*
Davis, Emmy Mae *school system administrator*
Davis, Joanne Fatse *lawyer*
Davis, Julia McBroom *college dean, speech pathology and audiology educator*
Davis, Karen Ann (Karen Ann Falconer) *special education educator*
Davis, Katherine Sarah *physical therapy educator*
Davis, Keigh Leigh *aerospace engineer*
Davis, Kristin *actress*
Davis, Lanita Irene *secondary school educator*
Davis, Lisa Rene *special education educator, consultant*
Davis, Mamie (Denise Davis) *writer*
Davis, Mary Byrd *conservationist, researcher*
Davis, Mary Helen *psychiatrist, educator*
Davis, Natalie Zemon *retired history professor*
Davis, Nicole D. *executive secretary, entrepreneur*
Davis, Sue Ellen H. *elementary and secondary music educator*
Davis, Suzanne Spiegel *retired information specialist*
Davis, Taylor *sculptor*
Davis, Teresann Weller *social worker*
Davis, Terri Myrl *theater educator*
Davis, Wanda Rose *lawyer*
Davis-Keith, Madelyn Michelle *elementary school educator*
Davis-Townsend, Helen Irene *retired art educator*
Dawkins, Teresa Gilliland *elementary school educator*
Dawson, Carol Gene *former commissioner, writer, consultant*
Dawson, Caron *medical and legal consultant*
Dawson, Geraldine *medical educator, social worker*
Dawson, Martha Bromley *retired software developer*
Dawson, Mary E. *lawyer*
Dawson, Suzanne Stockus *lawyer*
Dawson, Virginia Sue *retired editor*
Day, Anne White *retired nurse*
Day, Joyce Cerejo *school psychologist*
Dayton, Kathleen G. *nurse*
Dayton, Regina Laudi *secondary school educator*
Deal, Kate *language educator*
Deal, Rebecca L. *art educator*
Dean, Carole Lee *film company executive*
Dean, Diane (H.) Sweet *artist, retired credit manager*
Dean, Katherine S. *physical education educator, consultant*
DeAndrade, Kristy A. *elementary school educator*
Deane, Sally Jan *health facility administrator, consultant*
De Angelis, Rosemary Eleanor *actress*
DeAngelo, Judith *artist*
Deater, Eloise Elaine *mental health services professional*
Deaton, Fae Adams *social worker, consultant, artist, graphics designer*
Deats, Suzanne *writer, editor, artist*
Deats-O'Reilly, Diana Day *educator, journalist*
DeBakey, Lois *science administrator, educator*
DeBakey, Selma *communications educator, writer, editor*
De Both, Tanya *statistician*
DeBrincat, Susan Jeanne *nutritionist*
Debs, Barbara Knowles *former college president, consultant*
DeBuono, Barbara Ann *physician, state official*
deCastro, Cristina L. *secondary school educator*
Decatur, Raylene *former museum director*
Decker, Josephine I. *health clinic official*
Deeds, Virginia Williams *volunteer*

DeElejalde, Ana Levy *psychotherapist*
Deeves, Mary Ellen *medical/surgical nurse, nursing administrator*
Degann, Sona Irene *obstetrician, gynecologist, educator*
De Gette, Diana Louise *congresswoman, lawyer*
Dehle, Judy Jaye *education educator*
DeHoff, Valerie S. *music educator*
DeHority, Miriam Arnold Newman (Miriam Newman) *artist*
Deily, Linnet Frazier *former ambassador*
Deitz, Susan Rose *advice columnist, writer*
DeJack, Jacqueline Elvadeana *artist, educator*
DeJarnatt, Kitty M. *special education educator*
de Lacerda, Maria Assunção Escobar *retired social worker, consultant*
Delahanty, Rebecca Ann *school system administrator*
Delaney, Barbara Snow *retired editor*
Delaney, Marion Patricia *retail executive*
Delaney, Mary Anne *retired theology studies educator*
Delaney, Pamela DeLeo *foundation administrator*
DeLapp, Tina Davis *retired nursing educator*
de Limantour, Clarice Barr *food scientist*
Dell, Charlene Elizabeth *music educator*
Dell'Aringa, Yvonne Silvia Bozzini *elementary school educator*
De Long, Katharine *retired secondary school educator*
Del Papa, Frankie Sue *former state attorney general*
Delucia, Charlotte *psychotherapist*
Del Villar, Aurora *science educator*
Dema-ala, Relie L. *medical/surgical nurse*
Demant, Margaret H. *retired interior designer*
de Matteo, Drea *actress*
Dembeck, Mary Grace *artist, writer*
Dembrow, Dana Lee *lawyer*
Demetrakeas, Regina Cassar *social worker*
DeMitchell, Terri Ann *law educator*
De Mornay, Rebecca *actress*
Demou, Doris Beck *small business owner, civic leader*
Dempsey, Jane M. *nurse epidemiologist*
Denenberg, Katharine W. Hornberger (Tinka Denenberg) *artist, educator*
Denham, Carolyn Hunter *academic administrator, statistics educator*
Denham, Jill H. *bank executive*
Denious, Sharon Marie *retired publishing executive*
Dennany, Kelly *mechanical engineer, test engineer*
Dennick, Lori Ann (L. Anne Carrington) *publicist*
Dennis, Patricia Diaz *lawyer*
Denny, Terry Anne *elementary school educator*
Dent, Julie *executive director*
Denton, Judy Ann *art educator*
Denver, Eileen Ann *retired editor*
Deoul, Kathleen Boardsen *publishing executive*
De Palma-Iozzi, Frances M. *music educator, conductor*
de Planque, E. Gail *physicist*
Derber, Dana M. *graphic designer*
Dern, Laura *actress*
de Rossi, Portia *actress*
Derrick, Kathryn Thill *secondary school educator*
Desantis, Sherolyn Smith *foundation executive*
Deschamp, Gloria J. *retail liquor store owner*
DeShaw, Michele *principal*
Desio, Delores Jean *writer, artist, retired elementary school educator*
Desjardins, Judith Anne *psychotherapist*
Desjarlais, Georgia Kathrine *retired military officer*
Despot, Shirley Ann *artist*
D'Este, Mary Ernestine *investment group executive*
Detert, Miriam Anne *chemical analyst*
Deutschman, Louise Tolliver *curator*
Devany Serio, Catherine *clinical psychologist*
DeVaris, Jeannette Mary *psychologist*
de Varona, Donna *sports reporter, former Olympic swimmer*
DeVaughn, Tara Mary Lee *mathematics educator*
DeVault, Kathy *psychiatric consultant, liaison nurse*
DeVera, Gertrude Quenano *education educator*
deVille, Vicki Lynne *jewelry manufacturer, commercial real estate broker*
Devine, Katherine *environmental scientist, educator*
DeVivo, Ange *retired small business owner*
DeVore, Daun Aline *lawyer*
DeVore, Kimberly K. *healthcare executive*
DeVoueroix, Channing *interior designer, writer, educator*
DeVries, Linda Jane *music educator*
Dewar, Louise Helen *director*
DeWeese, Barb Oakley *secondary school educator*
Dewey, Ariane *artist, illustrator*
DeWolfe, Susan *elementary school educator*
Dey, Carol Ruth *secondary school educator*
de Zegher, Catherine *museum director, curator*
D'Haiti, Felicia Kathleen (Felicia Kathleen Messina) *fine arts educator*
Dial, Tamara Minique *secondary school educator*
Diamant, Anita *writer*
Diamond, Helen *arbitrator, freelance/self-employed mediator*
Diamond, Mary E(lizabeth) B(aldwin) *artist*
Diamond, Susan Zee *management consultant*
Dias, Mari Nardolillo *education educator, consultant*
Diaz, Cameron *actress*
Diaz, Laura O. *secondary school educator*
DiBattiste, Carol A. *military officer*
Dibelka, Charlene Fay Webster *secondary school educator*
Dibert, Rosalie *elementary school educator*
DiCiacco, Janis Annette *psychologist*
Dickens, Joyce Rebecca *addictions therapist, educator*
Dickerson, Betty *secondary school educator, consultant*
Dickerson, Claire Moore *lawyer, educator*
Dickinson, Gail Krepps *library science educator*
Dickinson, Marilynne Fay *elementary school educator*
Dickson, Andrea Rebecca *athletic trainer*
Dickson, Donna R. *medical/surgical nurse*
Dickson, Eva Mae *credit manager*
Diehl, Deborah Hilda *lawyer*
Diemer, Emma Lou *composer, educator*
Diercks, Elizabeth Gorman *elementary school educator*
Diggles, Patsy Ann *elementary school educator*
Di Giacomo, Fran *artist*
DiGiamarino, Marian Eleanor *retired realty administrator*
DiGiovanni, Joan Fimbel *psychology educator*
DiGregorio, Amanda Elizabeth *medical products executive*
Di Iorio, Daniela *oceanographer, researcher*
Dileone, Carmel Montano *retired dental hygienist*
DiLiberti, Lara Marie *music educator*
Dillard, Patricia Spratling *educational consultant*
Dillard, Teresa Mary *school counselor*
Dillenkoffer, Judith A. *music educator*
Dillon, Carolyn Fries *music educator*
Dillon, Joan Kent *civic worker, volunteer consultant*
Dillon, Kerris *social studies educator*
Dillon, Priscilla McAvoy *private school educator*
Dillon, Terri L. *consulting firm executive*
Dillon, Toni Ann *emotional support educator*
Dimaira, Ann B. *medical/surgical nurse*
Dimengo, Josephine *medical/surgical nurse*
Dimopoulos, Linda J. *food service executive*
Dincecco, Jennie Elizabeth Williams Swanson *healthcare administrator, mentor, educator, volunteer*
Ding, Ai-Yue *conductor, music educator*
Dion, Celine *musician*
Di Paolo, Maria Grazia *language educator, writer*
DiPaolo, Sonja Jean *retired nurse*
DiPasqua, Aimee Dora *physician*
Dishong, Linda S. *estate planner*
Dispensa-Rhoads, Jaclyn Marisa *environmental services administrator*
Dispenza, Mary Catherine *director, educator, photographer*
Diviney, Nancy Lynn *elementary school educator*
Dixon, Carrie J. *social studies educator*
Dixon, Kathryn A. *social worker*
Dixon, Mary *elementary school educator*
Dizzia, Maria Teresa *actress*
Djung-Wong, Ida I-Giai *retired pathologist*
Doan, Mary Frances *advertising executive*
Dobson, Dorothy Lynn Watts *retired elementary school educator*
Dockstader, Deborah Ruth *minister*
Dodds, Linda Carol *special education educator*
Doerksen, Mona Diane *music educator*
Doherty, Evelyn Marie *data processing consultant*
Doherty, Shannen *actress*
Dohmen, Mary Holgate *retired primary school educator*
Doligosa, Annie Lumampao *elementary school educator, researcher*
Doll, Patricia Marie *marketing professional, consultant*
Doman, Elvira *retired science administrator*
Dominguez, Andrea Hope *science educator*
Dominic, Magie *writer*
Domski, Mary Ann *philosopher, educator*
Donahue, Kathleen Frances *elementary school educator*
Donald, Aida DiPace *retired publishing executive*
Donaldson, Eva G. *chemist, writer*
Donaldson, Myrtle Norma *music educator, musician*
Donaldson, Wilma Crankshaw *elementary school educator*
Donat, Juliana Souther *elementary school educator*
Donath, Therese *artist, author*
Donberger, Karen Shepard *special education educator, elementary school educator*
Donegan, Teresa E. *pharmaceutical educator*
Donehew, Pamela K. *reading specialist*
Donick, Julie K *elementary school educator*
Donley, Corrine Russell *special education educator, educator*
Donnally, Patricia Broderick *writer*
Donoghue, Joan E. *lawyer*
Donohue, Anne Emlen *software engineer*
Donohue-Smith, Maureen A. *medical educator*
Donovan, Anne *professional basketball coach*
Donovan, Kierston Foley *science educator*
Donzell, Tara Elizabeth *secondary school educator*
Dore, Patricia Ann *psychologist*
Dorighi, Nancy S. *computer engineer*
Dorman, Stephanie *writer*
Dorr, Aimee *dean, education educator*
Dorsey, Dolores Florence *retired corporate treasurer, finance company executive*
Dorsey, Helen Danner (Johna Blinn) *writer, educator*
Doss, Delia L. *mathematics educator*
Doss, Jessica Yarina *financial analyst*
Dotterweich, Lisa Josette *political science professor, researcher*
Doucette, Betty *public and community health and geriatrics nurse*
Douglas, Mary Younge Riley *retired secondary school educator*
Douglas, Roxanne Grace *secondary school educator*
Douglas, Victoria Jean *marketing professional, communications executive, educator*
Douglass, Jane Dempsey *retired theology educator*
Douglass, Susan Daniel *communications engineer, consultant*
Dove, Judy Merryman *theater educator*
Doviak, Ingrid Ellinger *elementary school educator*
Dowben, Carla Lurie *lawyer, educator*
Dowdell, Donna Renea *nurse*
Dowdell, Sharonlyn Scott *accountant*
Dowdy, Joanne Kilgour *education educator*
Downey, Deborah Ann *systems specialist*
Downing, Kathryn M. *former newspaper publishing executive, lawyer*
Downing, Sarah Linn *application developer*
Downs, Dorothy Rieder *art historian, consultant, writer*
Downs, Kathleen Anne *health facility administrator*
Doyle, Christine Ellen *museum researcher, educator*
Doyle, Gillian *actress*
Doyle, Irene Elizabeth *electronic sales executive, nurse*
Dozier, Eleanor Cameron *computer company executive, writer*
Drahos, Sandra P. *retired chemist*
Drake, Carolyn A. *administrative assistant*
Drake, Evelyn Downie *retired secondary school educator*
Drake, Miriam Anna *retired librarian, educator, writer, consultant*
Drake, Patti Linn *retired consumer products company executive*
Drant, Sandra Elizabeth *court reporter, educator*
Drew, Donna Howell *elementary school educator*
Drew, Elizabeth Heineman *publishing executive*
Driscoll, Kimberlee Marie *lawyer*
Driver, Minnie *actress*
Drost, Marianne *lawyer*
Droste, Catherine Joseph *sister*
Droz, Elizabeth Jane *foundation administrator*
Druffel, Ann Bernice *researcher, writer*
Drum, Alice *academic administrator, educator*
Drummond, Carol Cramer *voice educator, lyricist, writer, artist*
Drummond, Pamela Johnson *mathematics educator*
Drummond, Sally Hazelet *artist*
Dryden, Mary Elizabeth *law librarian, writer, actress*
Dubin, Stacia *newscaster*
Dublon, Dina *former bank executive*
Dubner, Terye B. *secondary school educator*
Dubrow, Gail Lee *architecture educator*
Dubs, Gloria L. *artist, realtor*
Duckworth, Tara Ann *insurance company executive*
Ducote, Deborah M. *elementary school educator, reading specialist*
Dudash, Debra Ann *music educator*
Dudics-Dean, Susan Elaine *interior designer*
Dudley, Thora Louise *rehabilitation services professional*
Dufendach, Paula J. *elementary school educator*
Duff, Patricia *civic activist*
Duffey, Rosalie Ruth *elementary school educator*
DuFresne, Elizabeth Jamison *retired lawyer*
Duke, Betsy (Elizabeth A. Duke) *bank executive*
Duke, Robin Chandler Tippett *retired public relations executive, former ambassador*
Dumanoski, Dianne *journalist, writer*
Dumas, Rhetaugh Etheldra Graves *retired university official*
Dumas, Sandra Lee *medical technician, microbiologist*
Dumler, Patricia Ann *critical care nurse*
Dunaway, Faye (Dorothy Dunaway) *actress*
Dunbar, Bonnie J. *engineer, astronaut*
Dunbar, Diana L. (Diane L. Dunbar) *dancer, choreographer, educator, writer, storyteller, actress*
Dunbar, Shirley Eugenia-Doris *small business owner, writer*
Duncan, Kristina Yvonne *secondary school educator*
Duncan, Shirley A. *portfolio manager*
Duniphan, J. P. *state legislator, small business owner*
Dunkins, Betty *small business owner, publishing executive*
Dunlap, Martha McKinzie *retired middle school educator, small business owner*
Dunlap, Patricia C. *state legislator*
Dunmeyer, Sarah Louise Fisher *retired health care consultant*
Dunn, Audrey Christine *speech pathology/audiology services professional*
Dunn, Jennifer Blackburn *former congresswoman*
Dunn, Linda *special education educator*
Dunn, Nancy Marabella *artist, art educator*
Dunn, Rebecca M. *telecommunications industry executive*
Dunn Kelly, Ruth Emma *management consultant*
Dunst, Isabel Paula *lawyer*
Dunton-Downer, Leslie Linam *writer*
Duong, Anh *artist, actress*
Duplessis, Audrey Joseph *school system administrator*
Durek, Dorothy Mary *retired language educator*
Durell, Viviane G. *psychologist, small business owner*
Durgin, Diane *arbitrator, lawyer, mediator*
Durgom-Powers, Jane Ellyn *lawyer*
Durham Norman, Thena Monts *microbiologist, researcher, health facility administrator*
Durick, Joyce K. *elementary school educator*
Durkee, Dianna *medical/surgical nurse*
Durkin, Diane L. *retired nurse*
DuRocher, Frances A. *retired physician, educator*
Dusenbury, Ruth Ellen Cole *business owner*
Dussault, Nancy *actress, singer*
Dustman, Elizabeth *art educator, product designer*
Dworin, Micki (Maxine Dworin) *automobile dealership executive*
Dworin, Miriam Joy *occupational therapist, educator, advocate*
Dworkin, Irma-Theresa *school system administrator, researcher, secondary school educator*
Dwyer, Judith A. *marriage and family therapist*
Dwyer, Kelly *writer, educator*
Dyal, Edith Colvin *retired music educator*
Dyar, Kathryn Wilkin *pediatrician*
Dybowski, Jane *science educator*
Dycus, Patricia M. *education educator, chemical engineer*
Dye, Linda Kaye *elementary school educator*
Dye, Sharon Elizabeth Herndon *speech pathologist*
Dyer, Arlene Thelma *retail company owner*
Dykstra, Gretchen *former foundation administrator*
Dykstra Lynch, Mary Elizabeth *library and information scientist, educator*
Dyson, Esther *editor-in-chief*
Dziewanowska, Zofia Elizabeth *pharmaceutical executive*
Earles, Kathi Amille *pediatrician*
Earney, Mary K. *writer, educator*
East, Janette Diane *marketing consultant*
Easter, Wanda Denise *special education educator*
Eastman, Francesca Marlene *volunteer, art historian*
Easton, Michelle *foundation executive*
Eaton, Emma Parker *special education educator*
Eaton, Katherine Girton *retired library educator*
Eaton, Shirley M. *medical/surgical nurse*
Eberly, Raina Elaine *retired psychologist, educator*
Ebinger, Linda Ann *retired nurse*
Ebler, Marilyn Ann *graphic designer, educator*
Eby, Lois *artist*
Echols, Mary Evelyn *training services executive, writer*
Eck, Marla J. *special education educator*
Ecklar, Julia *freelance writer, novelist*
Ecton, Donna R. *business executive*
Eddy, Janet Elizabeth *retired elementary school educator*
Edelsberg, Sally Comins *retired physical therapist, educator*
Edelson, Zelda Sarah Toll *retired editor, artist*
Edelstein, Rosemarie (Rosemarie Hublou) *medical/surgical nurse, educator, geriatrics nurse*
Edens, Betty Joyce *reading recovery educator*
Edens, Rosemary Randall *secondary school educator*
Edmo, Jean Umiokalani *artist, poet*
Edmonds, Anne Carey *librarian*
Edmonds, Crystal D. *language educator, distance learning coordinator*
Edmonds, Slivy *corporate financial executive*
Edmunds, Jane Clara *media consultant*
Edmundson, Lorna Duphiney *academic administrator*
Edwards, Ann Concetta *human resources director*
Edwards, Annmarie Monica *language educator, career coach, entrepreneur*
Edwards, Julie Ann *science researcher*
Edwards, Kathleen *real estate broker, former educator*
Edwards, Lynn A. *retired school system administrator*
Edwards, Patricia Burr *small business owner, consultant*
Edwards, Sharon Jane *nurse*
Edwards, Tonya Green *elementary school educator*
Edwards, Virginia Davis *music educator, concert pianist*
Effel, Laura *lawyer*
Egan, Moira *poet, educator*
Egelston, Roberta Riethmiller *writer*
Egginton, Wynn Meagher *university administrator and program facilitator*
Ehlers, Joan *secondary school educator*
Ehlers, Kathryn Hawes (Mrs. James D. Gabler) *physician*
Ehlert, Nancy Lynne *elementary school educator*
Ehrenberg, Miriam Colbert *psychologist*
Ehrenreich, Barbara *writer*
Ehrlich, Amy *editor, writer*
Ehrlich, Risa Hirsch *artist, educator*
Eichenlaub, Rosemary Waring *retired music educator*
Eiklenborg, JoLeen *education educator, consultant*
Eimers, Jeri Anne *retired counselor*
Eisenberg, Patricia Lee *medical/surgical nurse*
Eisenberg, Phyllis Rose *author*
Eisenstein, Linda *playwright, composer*
Eisner, Edith C. *adult education educator*
Elbery, Kathleen Marie *lawyer, accountant, cartoonist*
Elcik, Elizabeth Mabie *fashion illustrator*
Elder, Mary Louise *librarian*
Electra, Carmen (Tara Leigh Patrick) *actress*
Elisha, Larisa *musician, performer, educator*
Elkins, Jeni L. McIntosh *systems support specialist*
Ellett, Linda Mick *special education educator*
Ellington, Jane Elizabeth *experimental psychologist*
Ellington, Mildred L. *librarian*
Elliot, Alexandra *special education educator, real estate agent*
Elliot, Janet Lee *occupational therapist*
Elliott, JoAnn Rose *retired elementary school educator*
Elliott, Meagan Byrne *elementary school educator*
Elliott-Zahorik, Bonnie *nurse, administrator*
Ellis, Anne Elizabeth *fundraiser*
Ellis, Carolyn Terry *lawyer*
Ellis, Harriette Rothstein *editor*
Ellis, Janice Rider *nursing educator, consultant*
Ellis, Joyce K. *writer, educator*
Ellis, Patricia Weathers *retired small business owner, computer technician*
Ellis, Rhonda Lyn *history educator*
Ellison, Betty D. *retired elementary school educator*
Ellstrom, Annette *research consultant*
Elmer, Marilyn Ann *education educator, author*
Elrod, Deborah Lee *special education educator*
Else, Carolyn Joan *retired library director*
Elwood-Akers, Virginia Edythe *librarian, retired archivist*
Emek, Sharon Helene *risk management consultant*
Emerling, Carol G. *management consultant*
Emerson, Alice Frey *political scientist, educator emerita*
Emerson, Claudia *poet, language professor*
Emmett, Rita *professional speaker*
Emmons, Mary K. *history educator*
Emrich, Jeanne Ann *poet, artist, publishing executive*
End, Laurel Jean *psychologist, educator*
Ender, Pauline Louise *painter*
Endicott, Jennifer Jane Reynolds *education educator*
Engel-Arieli, Susan Lee *physician*
Engelbreit, Mary *art licensing entrepreneur*
Engelman, Elizabeth *playwright, trade association administrator*
Engelman, Rosalyn Ackerman *artist, marketing executive*
Engels, Beatrice Ann *artist, poet, retired real estate company executive*
Engle, Jane *research nurse, artist, chaplain*
Engle, Mary Allen English *retired physician*
English, Mildred Oswalt *retired nurse supervisor*
Engstrom, Jean *medical/surgical nurse*
Ephron, Nora *writer*
Epp, Dianne Naomi *secondary school educator*
Eppolito, Mary *assistant principal, educator*
Erbacher, Kathy *writer, editor, marketing consultant*
Erbe, Chantell Van *artist*

Erickson, Carol Jean *literature and language professor*
Erickson, Donna Joy *writer*
Erlebacher, Arlene Cernik *retired lawyer*
Erler, Mary Frances *art educator*
Erlichson, Miriam *fundraiser, writer*
Erwin, Linda McIntosh *retired librarian*
Escallón, Ana María *writer*
Escarra, Vicki B. *retired airline company executive*
Eshel, Hanna M. *sculptor, painter, photographer*
Esparza, Kacie Lynne *military officer*
Espinosa, Carole Jo *counselor, educator*
Espiricueta, Sylvia *counseling administrator*
Espiritu, Antonina *economics professor*
Essa, Lisa Beth *elementary school educator*
Esselstein, Rachel *mathematician, educator*
Essig, Kathleen Susan *academic administrator, consultant, management consultant*
Estefan, Gloria Maria (Gloria Maria Milagrosa Fajardo) *singer, lyricist*
Esterly, Nancy Burton *retired physician*
Estés, Clarissa Pinkola *psychoanalyst, poet, writer*
Estes, Elaine Rose Graham *retired librarian*
Estevez, Anne-Marie *psychologist, lawyer*
Etheridge, Diana Carol *internet business executive*
Ettenger, Deborah Jean *music educator*
Etzel, Ruth Ann *pediatrician, epidemiologist, educator*
Etzkorn, Susan *elementary school educator, small business owner*
Eu, March Fong *ambassador*
Eubank, Piper *psychiatrist*
Eubanks, Sharon Y. *former federal agency administrator*
Eucharista, Sister Mary *sister, educational association administrator, secondary school educator*
Euster, Joanne Reed *retired librarian*
Evans, Barbara *art educator*
Evans, Bonita Dianne *education educator*
Evans, Carrie L. *state legislative lawyer*
Evans, Charlotte Mortimer *communications consultant, writer*
Evans, Helen Ruth *music educator, pianist*
Evans, Lara Adele *elementary school educator*
Evans, Margaret Utz *secondary school educator*
Evans, Marsha Johnson *former non-profit association administrator, retired military officer*
Evans, Meryl K. *writer*
Evans, Patricia Marie *sales executive*
Evans, Robyn V. *science educator*
Evans, Rosemary Hall *civic worker*
Evans, Sherrie Lea *secondary school educator*
Evans, Stephanie E. *theater producer*
Evans, Susan A. *chemist*
Evans, Zoe O'Quinn *elementary school educator*
Evdokimova, Eva *prima ballerina assoluta, director, producer, consultant, actress*
Everett, Donna Raney *finance educator*
Everett, Karen Joan *retired librarian, genealogist, educator*
Everhart, Angie *model*
Everhart, Gloria Elaine *music educator*
Eviatar, Lydia *pediatrician, neurologist*
Ewald, Roberta Grant *artist, writer*
Ewart, Claire Lynn *author, illustrator*
Ewing, Elisabeth Anne Rooney *priest*
Exum, Stephanie Roxanne *medical educator*
Eyring, Maxine Louise *small business owner, esthetician*
Ezaki-Yamaguchi, Joyce Yayoi *dietician*
Ezoe, Magdalena *music educator, composer, musician*
Fabian, Kelly Jean *physical therapist*
Fabre, Niza Elsie *African studies and Hispanic literature educator*
Fabricatore, Carol Diane *artist, educator*
Fabry, Marilyn Sue *mathematician, educator*
Fackler, Elizabeth *writer*
Fadiman, Anne *writer, educator*
Fadley, Ann Miller *language educator, literature educator*
Fagadau, Jeanne Malkoff *art dealer*
Fahringer, Catherine Hewson *retired savings and loan association executive*
Fair, Jean Everhard *retired education educator*
Fairbairn, Barbara Jean *university administrator*
Fairbanks, Cynthia *secondary school educator*
Fairfield, Paula Kathleen *sound recording engineer*
Faison, Lugenia Marion *special education educator*
Faiz, Alexandria *researcher, writer*
Fanos, Kathleen Hilaire *osteopathic physician, podiatrist*
Farber, Zulima V. *former state attorney general, lawyer*
Fardy, Lydia J. *educator*
Farkas, Rhonda Dawn *principal, education educator*
Farmer, Cornelia Griffin *lawyer, consultant, county hearings official*
Farmer, Laurel Ann *elementary school educator*
Farnham-Diggory, Sylvia *psychologist, educator*
Farnsworth, Elizabeth *broadcast journalist*
Faron, Fay Cheryl *private investigator, writer*
Farrar, Elaine Willardson *artist*
Farrell, Debbie L. *elementary school educator, media specialist*
Farrell, Elizabeth Ann *secondary school educator*
Farrell, Suzanne (Roberta Sue Ficker) *ballerina*
Farrigan, Julia Ann *retired small business owner, educator*
Farrington, Bertha Louise *retired nursing administrator*
Fasick, Adele Mongan *library and information scientist, educator*
Fasman, Marjorie Lesser *artist, writer*
Faucette, Merilon Cooper *retired secondary school educator*
Faulds, Roxanne M. *media and technology educator*
Faulkner, Frances Mayhew *retired federal agency administrator*
Faulkner, Martye Leanne *mathematician, educator*
Faunce, Sarah Cushing *retired curator*
Favero, Michele Maree *music educator, musician*
Favor-Hamilton, Suzanne Marie *track and field athlete, Olympian*
Fawcett, Farrah Leni *actress, model*
Fazio, Evelyn M. *publisher, writer, agent, editor*
Feal, Gisele Catherine *foreign language educator*
Fearon, Charlene O'Brien *special education educator*
Feathers, Gail M. Wratny *social worker*
Febrey, Theresa M. *assistant principal*
Fedeli, Shirley Ann Martignoni *retired secondary school educator*
Federman, Cindy B. *science educator, retail executive*
Feeback, Loreta Dotaline Kreeger *artist*
Feeney, Maryann McHugh *not-for profit professional*
Fehr, Lola Mae *health facility administrator*
Feigin, Barbara Sommer *marketing consultant*
Fein, Sheila Carol *artist*
Feinberg, Glenda Joyce *retail executive*
Feiner, Francine *art educator, photographer*
Feir, Dorothy Jean *entomologist, educator, physiologist*
Feisthammel, Audrey Marie *museum director, educator*
Feld, Carole Leslie *marketing executive*
Feldhamer, Thelma Leah *architect*
Feldman, Eva Lucille *neurology educator*
Feldman, Frances *retired social worker*
Feldman, Lillian Maltz *educational consultant*
Feldshuh, Tovah S. *actress*
Feldt, Gloria A. *social services administrator*
Fell, Elizabeth P. *education educator*
Fellenstein, Cora Ellen Mullikin *retired credit union executive*
Felsted, Carla Martindell *librarian, writer, editor*
Felton, Helen Martin *retired adult education educator, writer*
Fennell, Teresa Ann *psychologist*
Fenoglio-Preiser, Cecilia Mettler *retired pathologist, educator*
Ferguson, Margaret Geneva *writer, publisher, real estate broker*
Ferguson McGinnis, Kathryn Joan (Kathy Ferguson McGinnis) *flight attendant*
Ferguson-Whitehead, Wendy Sandra *elementary school educator, art educator, artist*
Fergusson, Frances Daly *former academic administrator*
Fernandes, Jane K. *academic administrator, educational consultant, sign language professional*
Fernandez, Suzanne Lyn *elementary school educator, music educator*
Ferraro, Geraldine Anne *lawyer, former congresswoman*
Ferringer-Burdick, Susan *elementary school educator*
Feshbach, Norma Deitch *psychologist, educator*
Feuerstein, Penny *artist*
Ficek, Debra L. *secondary school educator*
Fick, Denise *elementary school educator*
Fickes, Kelly Ann *personal trainer*
Fidler, Susan *recreation director*
Fidone, Laura Peebles *social worker*
Field, Sally Margaret *actress*
Fields, Emily Jill *secondary school educator*
Fields, Jerri Lynn *foundation administrator*
Fields, Velma Archie *medical/surgical nurse*
Fierman, Ella Yensen *retired psychotherapist*
Fiero-Maza, Lorraine Doris *music educator*
Filchock, Ethel *education educator*
Filer, Emily Symington Harkins *retired foundation administrator, writer, non-profit consultant*
Filer, Nalene Tai *literature and language educator*
Filewicz-Cochran, Renatta T. *parliamentarian*
Filippelli Marandola, Linda Patricia *school psychologist*
Finauri, Graciela Maria *foreign service official*
Finch, Julia Laura *counselor*
Fine, Jane Madeline *visual artist*
Fine, Sally Solfisburg *artist, educator*
Finestone, Sheila *senator, retired legislator*
Fink, Alma *retired elementary school educator*
Finley, Sarah Maude Merritt *retired social worker*
Finn, Charlotte Kaye *interior designer*
Finnberg, Elaine Agnes *psychologist, editor*
Finnegan, Jennifer Michelle *veterinarian*
Finnegan, Margaret Mary *school librarian*
Finnegan, Sara Anne (Sara F. Lycett) *publisher*
Finneran, Katie (Kathleen Finneran) *actress*
Finnerty, Isobel *Canadian senator*
Fiorina, Carly (Cara Carleton Sneed Fiorina) *former computer company executive*
Firestone, Nancy B. *federal judge*
Firmstone, Kristal *elementary school educator*
Fish, Janet Isobel *artist*
Fish, Jeanne Spencer *artist, retired lawyer*
Fishburn, Janet Forsythe *dean*
Fisher, Anita Jeanne (Kit Fisher) *retired language educator*
Fisher, Barbara A. *former broadcast executive*
Fisher, Carrie Frances *actress, writer*
Fisher, Janet Warner *secondary school educator*
Fisher, Jo Ann *television technical director*
Fisher, Kim *artist*
Fisher, Nancy *writer, producer, director*
Fisher, Sharon Sue *music educator*
Fisher, Sherry M. *secondary school educator*
Fisk, Lois L. *secondary school educator*
Fitts, Catherine Austin *investment advisor*
Fitzgerald, Adelaide Yvonne *occupational child care educator*
Fitzgerald, Angela Michelle *special education educator*
Fitzgerald, Joan V. *artist*
Fitzgerald, Kathy *health and physical education educator*
Fitzgerald-Verbonitz, Dianne Elizabeth *not-for-profit developer*
Fitzpatrick, Katrina S. *band director*
Fitzpatrick, Nancy Hecht *editor*
Fitzroy, Nancy deLoye *engineering executive, mechanical engineer*
FitzSimons, Sharon Russell *corporate financial executive*
Flanagan, Louise W. *federal judge*
Flannelly, Laura T. *mental health nurse, nursing educator, researcher*
Flannery, Rebecca R. *harpist*
Flato, Gwyndolynn Sue *fine art educator*
Flavin, Sonja *artist*
Fleksher, Cassandra C. *psychology and research rehabilitation professional*
Fleming, Cheryl Diane *realtor*
Fleming, Diane Price *academic administrator*
Fleming, Gina Marie *music educator*
Fleming, Rhonda *actress, singer*
Fletcher, Denise Koen *strategic and financial consultant*
Fletcher, Louise *actress*
Fletcher, Rita R. *social studies educator*
Flint, Laura A. *elementary school educator*
Florence, Melanie Anne *biologist, writer*
Flory, Evelyn Louise *educational administrator*
Flower, Renée Beville *artist*
Flowers-Schoen, Marylu Utley *art educator*
Floyd, Carol Ann *musician, recording artist, pianist, educator*
Flye, Carolyn Marie *minister*
Flynn, Pauline T. *retired speech pathologist, educator*
Foard, Susan Lee *editor*
Fodrea, Carolyn Wrobel *adult education educator, researcher*
Foerster, Jane A. *music educator*
Fogelman, Ann Florence *nutrition consultant, educator, researcher*
Foley, Virginia Sue Lashley *counselor, educational training consultant*
Follingstad, Carol C. *psychologist, consultant, educator*
Follit, Evelyn V. *former retail executive*
Folsom, Virginia Jean *music educator*
Fonda, Bridget *actress*
Fontaine, Jennifer Lynne *choreographer, educator*
Fontaine, Joan *actress*
Fontes, Patricia J. *psychologist*
Foosaner, Judith *artist, art educator*
Foote, Evelyn Patricia *retired military officer*
Forbes, Mary Allison *psychology educator, educator*
Ford, Barbara Jean *librarian, educator*
Ford, Carol *science educator*
Ford, Eileen Otte (Mrs. Gerard W. Ford) *modeling agency executive*
Ford, Faith *actress*
Ford, Irene Elaine *pastor*
Ford, Judith Ann Tudor *retired natural gas distribution company executive*
Ford, Loretta C. *retired dean, educator, consultant, nurse*
Ford, Maryestelle Beverly *piano educator, music researcher*
Ford, Nancy Louise *composer, scriptwriter*
Fordham, Beverly Surles *middle school educator*
Ford-Reed, Lillie Mae *geriatrics services professional*
Forero, Paula Juliana *academic administrator, artist*
Forest, Eva Brown *nursing home supervisor, composer*
Forester, Jean Martha Brouillette *retired librarian, educator, innkeeper*
Formato, Jonelle Nanette *secondary school educator*
Foronda, Monica F. *graphics designer*
Forrest, Linda Dotts *elementary school educator, social studies educator*
Foss, Linda Judd *banker, lawyer*
Foss, Valerie Ann *medical/surgical nurse*
Foster, Elaine Elizabeth *retired art educator*
Foster, Jodie (Alicia Christian Foster) *actress, film director, film producer*
Foster, Joy Via *retired library media specialist*
Foster, Mary Christine *film producer, writer*
Foster, Verna Lavonne *small business owner*
Fotopoulos, Sophia Stathopoulos *medical research scientist, administrator*
Fouché, Helen Strother *editorial design executive*
Fougerat, Karen Kay *mathematics educator*
Fountain, Karen Schueler *retired physician*
Fountain, Linda Kathleen *health science association executive*
Fountain, Ruth Anne *elementary school educator*
Fournet, Lisa Clark *music educator*
Fowler, Flora Daun *retired lawyer*
Fox, Betty *financial services executive*
Fox, Deborah Lee *elementary school educator*
Fox, Eleanor Mae Cohen *lawyer, educator, writer*
Fox, Kelly Diane *financial advisor*
Fox-Clarkson, Anne C. *fundraising company executive*
Foyouzi-Youssefi, Reyhaneh *pharmacologist*
Frackman, Noel *art critic*
Fralix Gold, Carolyn M. *medical/surgical nurse, educator, consultant*
Francis, Trina Michele *elementary school educator*
Francisco, Ana B. *medical/surgical nurse, legal nurse consultant*
Francke, Gloria Niemeyer *retired pharmacist, editor, writer*
Francke, Linda Bird *journalist*
Francoeur, Christina *special education educator*
Francois, Linda Jean *medical/surgical and psychiatric nurse*
Franey, Catherine T. *elementary school educator*
Frank, Jean Marie *educational association administrator, researcher*
Frank, Linda Maria *science educator*
Frankel, Jennie Louise *writer, composer, playwright*
Frankel, Judith Jennifer Mariasha *clinical psychologist, consultant*
Frankel, Terrie Maxine *writer, composer, playwright*
Franklin, Aretha Louise *singer*
Franklin, Bonnie Gail *actress*
Franklin, Bonnie Selinksy *retired federal agency administrator*
Franklin, Margery Bodansky *psychology professor, researcher*
Franklin, Rebecca *elementary school educator*
Franklin-Griffin, Cathy Lou Hinson *nursing educator*
Franks, Natalie Rose *music educator*
Frankson-Kendrick, Sarah Jane *publisher*
Frantz, Barbara M. *music educator*
Franz, Elizabeth *actress*
Franz, Judy R. *physics professor*
Franzetti, Lillian Angelina *former automobile dealership owner*
Franzoni, Delaina Day *special education educator, department chairman*
Frappia, Linda Ann *medical administrator*
Fraser, Kathleen Joy *poet, creative writing professor*
Fratkin, Leslie *photographer*
Frauenhoffer, Rose Marie *visual artist*
Frawley-O'Dea, Mary Gail *clinical psychologist, psychoanalyst, educator*
Frazier, Eloise M. *minister*
Frederick, Elizabeth Eleanor Tatum *watercolor artist, retired educator*
Frederick-Mairs, T(hyra) Julie *administrative health services official*
Frederickson, Christine Magnuson *reporter, researcher, editor, writer*
Freeman, Allison Browne *museum educator, researcher*
Freeman, Chanda *executive secretary, elementary school educator*
Freilicher, Jane *artist*
Freitas, Beatrice B(otty) *musician, educator*
French, Candace Lee *elementary secondary school educator, music educator*
French, Julia McAllister (Judy McAllister French) *environmental consultant*
French, Margo Ann *financial planner*
French, Marilyn *writer, critic, historian*
French, Stephanie Taylor *cultural organization administrator*
Frenning, Gineen F. *elementary school educator*
Frerk, Lori Ann *mathematics educator*
Frey, Margo Walther *career counselor, columnist*
Freyermuth, Virginia Karen *art educator*
Friars, Eileen M. *bank executive*
Fricker, Brenda *actress*
Frie, Dorothy Grace *retired physical education educator*
Friedman, Frances Wolf *political fund raiser*
Friedman, Fredrica Schwab *editor, publisher*
Friedman, Joan M. *retired accountant, educator*
Friedman, Kenni *health facility administrator, councilman*
Friedman, Mildred *architecture educator, design educator, curator*
Friedman, Nicole *psychologist, consultant*
Friedman, Sofia *social sciences educator, nutritionist, educator*
Friedman, Susan O. *retired academic administrator*
Frink, Jane Louise *literature and language educator*
Frontani, Heidi Glaesel *geographer, educator*
Frossard, Janice L. *science educator*
Frost, Amy Rosalie *choreographer, dancer, educator*
Frost, Ellen Louise *political economist*
Frost, Linda Gail *clergyman, hospital chaplain*
Fry, Hedy *Member of Parliament*
Fry, Jane Marie *secondary school educator*
Frye, Brandie Marie *personal trainer, educator*
Frye, Helen Jackson *federal judge*
Fuentes, June Toretta *language educator*
Fuerstner, Fiona Margaret Anne *ballet company executive, educator*
Fugett, Roberta Lynn *special education educator*
Fulbright, Harriet Mayor *educational association administrator*
Fullard, Henrietta *minister*
Fullenwider, Nancy Vrana *composer, dancer, musician, educator*
Fuller, Cassandra Miller *applications specialist*
Fuller, Kathryn Scott *former environmental services administrator*
Fullerton, Gail Jackson *retired academic administrator*
Fullwood, Altburg Marie *women's health nurse*
Fulmer, Amy M. *lawyer*
Fulton Ross, Gale *artist, actor*
Fumagalli, Barbara Merrill *artist, printmaker*
Funderburg, Jan *telecommunications industry executive*
Furman, Elise Hilary *middle school educator*
Furner, Bonita Baker *retired banker, consultant*
Furth, Karen J. *artist*
Fury, Sara Jo *social studies educator, coach*
Fuselier, Marilyn Monie *retired counselor*
Fusillo, Nancy Marie *medical/surgical, oncological, pediatric, community health and family nurse practitioner*
Gabel, Connie *chemist, educator*
Gabel, Katherine *retired academic administrator*
Gabor, Zsa Zsa (Sari Gabor) *actress, cosmetics executive*
Gabor-Hotchkiss, Magda *research scientist, librarian*
Gac-Artigas, Priscilla *foreign language educator*
Gadiesh, Orit *management consulting executive*
Gaggiano, Andrea Jean *secondary school educator*
Gahagen, Bonnie Knepp *elementary school educator*
Gainer, Leila J. *media relations executive, golf industry specialist*
Gaines, Brenda J. *retired financial services company executive*
Gaither, Ann Heafner *sales executive*
Gajl-Peczalska, Kazimiera J. *retired surgeon, pathologist, educator*
Galagan, Carol Anne *special education educator*
Galante, Jane Hohfeld *musician, music historian*
Galbraith, Marilyn Ann *secondary school educator*
Galindo, Karla Rae *retired secondary school educator*
Galitello-Wolfe, Jane Maryann *artist, writer*
Gall, Mary Sheila *former federal agency administrator*
Gallagher, Cynthia *artist, educator*
Gallagher, Lindy Allyn *banker, financial consultant*
Gallagher, Patricia Cecilia *author*
Gallarello, Josephine *performing arts educator, director*
Gallatin, Jennifer *music educator*
Gallaway, Marilyn *performing arts educator, communications educator*
Galloway, Eilene Marie *space and astronautics consultant*
Gallucci-Breithaupt, Adrianne *psychologist, social worker*
Gallup, Janet Louise *management consultant*
Gamache, Claudette Theresa *artist, nurse*
Gamble, Desirata *artist, poet*
Gambrell, Luck Flanders *corporate financial executive*
Gandhi, Purvi B. *psychologist*
Gansle, Marbry L. *physical education educator*

Garbacz, Patricia Frances *school social worker, therapist*
Garbecki, Ann M. *nurse*
Garber, Beth Carol *early childhood educator, music educator*
Garceau, Jo Mills *writer*
Garcia, Annette D'Urso *educational consultant*
Garcia, Emma Yvette *music educator*
Garcia, Julia Theresa *secondary school educator*
Garcia, Yvette *speech-language pathologist*
Garcia y Carrillo, Martha Xochitl *pharmacist*
Gardner, Elizabeth Ann Hunt *artist, poet, genealogist*
Gardner, Sonia Kay *writer*
Garfield-Woodbridge, Nancy *writer*
Garfinkle, Elaine Myra *writer*
Garity, Kathleen Mary *nurse coordinator, director*
Garmany, Catharine Doremus *astronomer*
Garner, Carlene Ann *not-for-profit fundraiser, consultant*
Garner, Jennifer Anne *actress*
Garnet, Eva Desca (Eva Desca) *dance educator, choreographer*
Garnett, Adrienne Wilma *art educator*
Garon, Phyllis S. *retired elementary school educator*
Garoogian, Rhoda *librarian*
Garrett, Shirley Gene *nuclear medicine technologist*
Garrison, Althea *government official*
Garvey, Arlene P. *media specialist, consultant*
Gary, Kathleen Noland *public relations executive*
Garzarelli, Elaine Marie *economist*
Gascoine-Molina, Jill Viola *actress, writer*
Gashaw-Gant, Gebaynesh Gelila *psychologist, consultant*
Gaskin-Butler, Vikki Twynette *clinical psychologist*
Gaskins, Karen D. *management consultant, research scientist*
Gasper, Jo Ann *social services administrator, consultant*
Gasper, Ruth Eileen *real estate executive*
Gates, Martina Marie *food products company executive*
Gates, Susan Inez *magazine publisher*
Gatison, Karen Ann *private school educator*
Gatria, America I *retired writer*
Gaulke, Mary Florence *retired library administrator*
Gault, Judith *piano educator*
Gaultiere, Kristi Southard *psychotherapist*
Gavin, Mary Jane *retired medical/surgical nurse*
Gavril, Jean (Jean Van Leeuwen) *writer*
Gavriloff, Katrina *writer*
Gawkowski, Spring Page *social sciences educator, social worker*
Gay, Faith E. *lawyer, educator*
Gaynor, Leah *radio personality, commentator*
Geary, Allyson *secondary school educator*
Gechtoff, Sonia *artist*
Geertz, Hildred Storey *anthropology educator*
Gegelmann, Sharon Fay *piano teacher*
Gehrke, Karen Marie *retired accountant*
Gehrman, Jody Elizabeth *writer*
Gelberg, Lillian *family medicine physician, educator*
Gelfand, Julia Maureen *librarian*
Gellar, Sarah Michelle *actress*
Geltzer, Sheila Simon *public relations executive*
Gemeinhardt, Judith M. (Judith Gamin) *writer, poet*
Genesoni, Jacqueline *mathematics educator*
Genest, Theresa Joan *lab technician*
Genét, Barbara Ann *accountant, travel company executive*
Genia, Vicky *psychologist*
Genieser, Nancy Branom *radiologist*
Genis, Alice Singer *psychologist*
Gennings, Kristen Ellen *music educator*
Gentilcore, Eileen Marie Belsito *principal*
George, Barbara Jean *literature and language educator, speech educator, communications educator*
George, Gay *lawyer*
George, Joyce Jackson *lawyer, writer, retired judge*
George, Katie *lawyer*
George, Linda Shumaker *freelance/self-employed writer*
George, Mary G. *health scientist*
George, Merrilou Kay *elementary school educator*
George, Sonya Carol *customer service administrator, educator*
Georges, Mara Stacy *lawyer*
Georgieff, Ellen *nurse*
Gerhardt, Carol *artist*
Gerlach, Jeanne Elaine *English language educator*
Gerlitzki, Ann L. *music educator*
Gerritsen, Mary Ellen *vascular and cell biologist*
Gerry, Debra Prue *psychotherapist, recording artist, writer*
Gersoni-Edelman, Diane Claire *author, editor*
Gerstein, Esther *sculptor*
Gersten, Elizabeth Welliver *education educator, researcher*
Gesualdo, Deborah Mary *music educator*
Gettinger, Susan Beth *literature and language educator*
Getty, Estelle (Estelle Scher) *actress*
Getzendanner, Susan *lawyer*
Ghebrhiwet, Freweiny Wendy *real estate broker, consultant*
Ghorayeb, Fay Elizabeth *nursing educator*
Gibb, Roberta Louise *lawyer, artist*
Gibbons, Mary Peyser *civic volunteer*
Gibbs, Johnie Elizabeth *information technology manager, educator, consultant*
Giberson, Joan Alyne *retired school nurse practitioner*
Gibson, Janice Thorne *developmental psychology educator, author, academic administrator*
Gibson, Jennifer Roseann *music educator*
Gibson, Kathy *secondary school educator, art educator*
Gibson, Lisette L. *elementary school educator, music educator*
Gibson, Melissa Upchurch *elementary school educator*
Gibson, Tracie M. *biology professor*
Giddens, Kathleen Colette *artist, art educator*
Gideon-Bradley, Anissa G. *voice educator*
Giebel, Miriam Catherine *librarian, genealogist*
Giele, Janet Zollinger *sociologist, educator*
Gieras, Angela Lee *theater manager*
Giffin, Marjie G. *writer*
Gifford, Heidi *writer, editor*
Gifford, Marjorie Fitting *mathematician, educator, consultant*
Gifford, Paula *elementary school educator*
Gilbert, Anita Rae *psychologist, educator*
Gilbert, Harriette Gurley *retired music educator*
Gilbert, Melissa *former actors guild executive, actress*
Gilbert, Ruth Elizabeth *inpatient obstetric nurse*
Gilbert, Sara *actress*
Gilberti, Shauna *music educator*
Gilchrist, E. Brenda *writer, freelance/self-employed editor*
Giles, Audrey Elizabeth *reference librarian*
Giles, Judith Margaret *minister, educator, real estate broker*
Gill, Libby *television executive*
Gillan, Rebecca Jane *music educator, composer*
Gillard, Beryl L. *mortgage company executive*
Gillenwater-Catron, Tashanna Shantay *elementary school educator*
Gillett, Mary Caperton *military historian*
Gillett, Patricia *family and acute care nurse practitioner, clinical nurse*
Gillette, Ethel Morrow *columnist*
Gilliland, Lucille Mary *artist, writer*
Gilmore, Connie Sue *director*
Gilmore, Kathi *former state treasurer*
Gilmore, Louisa Ruth *retired nurse*
Ginsberg-Fellner, Fredda *retired pediatric endocrinologist, researcher*
Ginsburg, Iona Horowitz *psychiatrist*
Giomi, Thelma Anne *clinical psychologist*
Giovanni, Nikki (Yolanda Cornelia Giovanni) *poet, educator*
Girouard, Shirley Ann *nurse, policy analyst*
Gish, Agnes Bridget *music educator*
Gisolo, Margaret *dancer, educator*
Gittman, Elizabeth *educational consultant*
Glacel, Barbara Pate *management consultant*
Gladden, Vivianne Cervantes *healthcare consultant, writer*
Glaser, Patricia L. *lawyer*
Glasgow, Karen *principal*
Glashan, Constance Elaine *retired nurse, volunteer*
Glasner, Cristin Anne *science educator*
Glass, Dorothea Daniels *physiatrist, educator*
Glassman, Judith Dale *chocolate company owner, realtor*
Gleason, Carol Ann *rehabilitation nurse*
Gleason, Kate *writer, educator, editor*
Gleim, Kathy Marie *music educator, performer, composer*
Glenn, Deborah Ann *economics educator, political science educator*
Glenn, Ethel Chappell *educator*
Glenn, Sara *religious studies educator, director*
Glenn, Violetta Colleen *retired secondary school educator*
Glick, Myrna Joan *psychologist*
Glick, Ruth Burtnick *literature educator, writer*
Glickman, Gladys *lawyer, writer*
Glimcher, Laurie H. *immunology educator*
Glismann, Clementine *retired elementary school educator*
Glover, Janet Briggs *artist*
Glück, Louise Elisabeth *poet, educator*
Glynn, Carlin (Carlin Masterson) *actress*
Gnezda, Nicole M. *art educator*
Gobler, Bina *assistant principal*
Godbille, Lara *museum director*
Goddess, Lynn Barbara *real estate investor*
Godwin, Carol *mathematics educator*
Goedken, Ann Mary *psychotherapist*
Goedken, Jennifer Lynn *mathematics educator*
Goeke, Lorise Ann *principal, elementary school educator*
Goetsch, Lara *marketing professional, director*
Goetzinger, Eleanor *special education educator*
Goff, Heather Elizabeth *psychiatrist*
Gofferje, Hadwig *retired language educator*
Gold, Alison Leslie *writer*
Gold, Betty Virginia *artist*
Gold, Judith Hammerling *psychiatrist*
Gold, Sarae R. *art educator*
Gold, Sylviane *editor, writer, film critic*
Goldberg, Lee Winicki *furniture company executive*
Goldberg, Lois D. *health facility administrator, disability analyst*
Goldberg, Nancy G. *business owner, community volunteer*
Goldberg, Whoopi (Caryn Elaine Johnson) *actress, comedienne*
Golden, Judith Greene *artist, educator*
Golden, Sheila S. *retired special education educator*
Goldfarb, Muriel Bernice *marketing consultant, advertising consultant*
Goldfarb, Ruth *poet, educator*
Goldie, Dorothy Roberta *retired counselor*
Golding, Carolyn May *former government senior executive, consultant*
Goldschmidt, Amanda (Amy) O'Connell *food service executive*
Goldschmidt, Eva *librarian*
Goldschmidt, Lynn Harvey *lawyer*
Goldsmith, Betty F. *counselor*
Goldstein, Debra Holly *judge*
Goldstein, Dora Benedict *pharmacologist, educator*
Goldstein, Joyce Esersky *restaurant owner*
Golomb, Claire *psychology educator*
Golub, Sharon Bramson *retired psychologist, educator*
Gomez, Margarita *language educator, researcher*
Gomez, Melissa Mordell *trial consultant*
Gonzalez, Mandy *actress*
Goodacre, Jill *model*
Goodall, Jane *zoologist*
Goodfellow, Robin Irene *surgeon*
Goodman, Elizabeth Ann *retired lawyer*
Goodman, Erika *dancer, actress*
Goodman, Gail Busman *small business owner*
Goodman, Jessica Mui Kwai *secondary school educator*
Goodrich Harwood, Gail Lee *management consultant*
Goodwin, Danielle Marie *mathematician*
Goodwin, Rebecca *literature and language educator*
Goodwyn, Betty Ruth *librarian*
Gora, Susannah Porter Martin *journalist, poet*
Gordon, Audrey Kramen *healthcare educator*
Gordon, Emmajean Elizabeth *farmer, entrepreneur, consultant*
Gordon, Fran *writer*
Gordon, Lisa M. *music educator*
Gordon, Marjorie *lyric-coloratura soprano, music educator, opera producer*
Gordon, Sharon Ann *mathematics educator, pre-school educator*
Gorelova, Linda M. *elementary school educator*
Goren, Judith Ann *retired psychologist*
Gorence, Patricia Josetta *judge*
Goron, Mara J. *social studies educator, assistant principal*
Goss, Martha Clark *consulting company executive*
Gossett, Janine Lee *middle school educator*
Gottlieb, Sherry Gershon *writer, editor*
Gottsegen, Gloria *psychologist, educator*
Gouker, Jane Ann *music educator*
Gould, Martha Bernice *retired librarian*
Gould, Mary Ann Carpenter *nephrology nurse consultant*
Goulet, Lorrie *sculptor*
Gouletas, Evangeline *investment executive*
Gourley, Sara J. *lawyer*
Gouskos, Lisa Marie *elementary school educator, music educator*
Gowler, Vicki Sue *newspaper editor, journalist*
Grace, L.A. *fine artist, designer*
Grace, Marcia Bell *advertising executive*
Grady, Sandra C. *minister, counselor*
Grafton, Beth P. *music educator*
Graham, Barbara J. *special education educator*
Graham, Cynthia Armstrong *banker*
Graham, K(athleen) M. (K. M. Graham) *artist*
Graham, Laurie *editor, writer*
Graham, Nancy G. *elementary school educator*
Graham, Olive Jane *retired medical/surgical nurse*
Graham, Sylvia Swords *retired secondary school educator*
Grames-Lyra, Judith Ellen *artist, educator, municipal official*
Gramling, Audrey *library media specialist, educator*
Grann, Phyllis E. *editor, former publisher executive*
Gransden, Charissa Sharron *music educator*
Grant, Carmen Hill *psychologist, psychotherapist*
Grant, Frances Bethea *editor*
Grant, Frances Elizabeth *retired educator*
Grant, Isabella Horton *retired judge*
Grant, Janett Ulrica *medical/surgical nurse*
Grant, Lee (Lyova Haskell Rosenthal) *actress, television and film director*
Grant, Nancy Marie *marketing professional, journalist*
Grant, Paula DiMeo *lawyer, nursing educator, mediator*
Grantham, Joyce Carol *small business owner, music educator*
Graser, Susan Vincent *physical education educator*
Grasham, Clara Langan *reading specialist*
Grasserbauer, Doris *computer scientist, mathematician, educator*
Graver, Mary Kathryn *medical/surgical nurse*
Graves, Lorraine Elizabeth *dancer, educator, coach*
Gray, Ann Maynard *broadcasting company executive*
Gray, Barbara May *artist*
Gray, Deborah Mary *wine importer*
Gray, Francine du Plessix *writer*
Gray, Gloria Meador *librarian*
Gray, Hazel Irene *retired special education educator, counselor, consultant*
Gray, LeAnn Marie *special education educator*
Gray, Linda Alyn *artist, educator*
Gray, Lisa Hart *secondary school educator*
Gray, Mary Jane *retired obstetrician, gynecologist*
Gray, Mary Margaret *nephrology and dialysis nurse*
Gray, Pamela *screenwriter, educator*
Gray, Patricia B. *retired librarian, information specialist*
Gray McCray, Rosalind *assistant principal*
Greaser, Constance Udean *retired automotive executive*
Green, Aimee Melissa *physical education educator*
Green, Andrea M. *college administrator*
Green, Barbara Marie *publisher, journalist, poet, writer*
Green, Carol H. *lawyer, educator*
Green, Carole L. *lawyer*
Green, Cheryl Faye *counseling administrator, educator*
Green, Karen Marie *science educator, gifted and talented educator*
Green, Kelly Allyson *gifted and talented educator, entrepreneur*
Green, Linda Gail *retired international healthcare and management consultant, nursing educator*
Green, Patricia Pataky *school system administrator, consultant*
Green, Rhonda Beverly *management consultant*
Green, Sonia Maria *automotive executive*
Greenberg, Bonnie Lynn *music industry executive*
Greenberg, Carolyn Phyllis *retired anesthesiologist*
Greenberg, Hinda Feige *library director*
Greene, Elaine D. G. *environmental science educator*
Greene, Janette Zaher *elementary school educator*
Greene, Jo *school system administrator*
Greene, Lynne Jeannette *wellness consultant, artist*
Greene, Margaret H. *telecommunications industry executive*
Greenfield, Linda Sue *nursing educator*
Greenwald, Alice Marian *museum director*
Greenwood, Anna Starbuck *librarian*
Greenwood, Jane *costume designer, educator*
Greenwood, Janet Kae Daly *psychologist, academic administrator, marketing professional*
Greer, Bonnie Beth *educator*
Greer, Carolyn Arlene *music educator, elementary school educator*
Greer, Cheryl L. *middle school educator*
Gregor, Dorothy Deborah *retired librarian*
Gregorius, Beverly June *retired obstetrician, gynecologist*
Gregory, Bettina Louise *retired journalist*
Gregory, J. L. *secondary school educator*
Gregory, Peggy J. *music educator*
Greiner, Nicole K. Hudak *physical education educator*
Gremmler, Margo Rowder *art director*
Grenz, M. Kay *manufacturing executive*
Grieb, Elizabeth *lawyer*
Griego, Angelic *marketing professional*
Griego, Linda *entrepreneur*
Griesemer, Carol J(oseph) *counselor*
Griffin, Laura Mae *retired elementary and secondary school educator*
Griffin, Sallie T. *artist, photographer, retired technologist*
Griffith, Melanie *actress*
Griffith, Patricia Browning *writer, educator*
Griffiths, Rachel *actress*
Griggs, Bobbie June *civic worker*
Griggs, Celia Josephine *music educator*
Grim, Ellen Townsend *retired art educator*
Grimaldi, Kathleen Galvin *literature and language educator, poet*
Grimes, Nancy Guerard *secondary school educator*
Grimme, A. Jeannette *retired elementary school educator, retired small business owner, volunteer*
Grindal, Mary Ann *former sales professional*
Griskey, Pauline Becker *education educator, researcher*
Grobstein, Ruth H. *health facility administrator*
Grodsky, Jamie Anne *law educator*
Grohskopf, Bernice *writer*
Gross, Amber Savage *social sciences educator*
Gross, Dorothy-Ellen *library director, educator*
Gross, Kathy Aldrich *mathematics professor*
Gross, Laura Ann *marketing and communications professional, herbalist, acupuncturist*
Gross, Leslie Pamela *sales executive, consultant*
Grossman, Carolyn Sylvia Cort *retired elementary school educator*
Grossman, Edith Marian *translator*
Grossman, Ginger Scheflin *advocate*
Grossman, Joyce Renee *pediatrician, internist*
Grossman, Patricia *writer*
Grosso, Camille M. *nurse*
Grosso, Doreen Elliott *management consultant*
Grove, Cherylee Vega *special education educator*
Grove, Myrna Jean *elementary school educator*
Groves, B. C. *educational consultant, writer*
Groves, Bernice Ann *retired elementary and secondary school coordinator, educator*
Gruebel, Barbara Jane *retired internist, pulmonologist*
Gruen, Margaret *actress*
Gruen, Shirley Schanen *artist*
Grutman, Jewel Humphrey *lawyer, writer*
Gudnitz, Ora M. Cofey *secondary school educator*
Guerra, Edna *pharmacist*
Guerrero, Lisa (Lisa Guerrero-Coles) *former sports reporter*
Guffey, Barbara Braden *retired elementary school educator*
Gugler, Mary Dugan *composer, music educator*
Guhl, Gabrielle V. *music educator*
Guichard, Susan Weil *dietician, consultant*
Guiliano, Mireille *consumer products company executive*
Guinn, Janet Martin *psychologist, consultant*
Guinther, Christine Louise *special education educator*
Gulbrandsen, Patricia Hughes *physician*
Gump, Abigail Michelle *music educator*
Gumpert, Carolyn L. *secondary school educator*
Gunderson, Judith Keefer *golf association executive*
Gunning, Carolyn Sue *dean, provost, nursing educator*
Gurvis, Sandra Jane *writer*
Gurwitz-Hall, Barbara Ann *artist*
Gussow, Sue Ferguson *artist, educator*
Gust, Anne Baldwin *former retail apparel company executive*
Gustafson, Sandra Lynne *retired secondary school educator*
Gustafson-Haigh, Marjorie Ann *retired librarian*
Guthrie, Janet *professional race car driver*
Gutowski, Kathleen Sullivan *special education educator*
Guy, Eleanor Bryenton *retired writer*
Guy, Jasmine *actress*
Guy, Mary (Penny) Whytlaw *secondary school educator, school librarian*
Guyett, Anne Elgar *performing arts educator*
Guze, Sandra Lee *secondary school educator*
Guzman, Carole L. *small business owner*
Gwalla-Ogisi, Nomsa *education educator*
Haagen, Elaine K. *psychiatrist*
Haake, Dorothy May *secondary school educator*
Haas, Beverly Jean *secondary school educator, coach*
Haas, Carolyn Buhai *elementary school educator, publisher, writer, consultant*
Haas, Suzanne Alberta *elementary school educator, secondary school educator*
Haberl, Valerie Elizabeth *physical education educator, small business owner*
Habermann, Helen Margaret *botanist, educator*
Hach, Phila Rawlings *small business owner, writer*
Hackel-Sims, Stella Bloomberg *lawyer, former government official*
Hackerman, Ann E. *psychotherapist*
Hackett, Molly Lynn *small business owner, consultant*
Hadda, Janet Ruth *language educator, lay psychoanalyst*
Haddady, Shirin *medical educator*
Haddy, Theresa Brey *pediatrician, educator, hematologist, oncologist*
Hadley, Leila Eliott-Burton (Mrs. Henry Luce III) *writer*
Haeberle, Rosamond Pauline *retired music educator*
Haeger, Gayle Mignon *biology educator*
Haerbig, Alaina Beth *elementary school educator*
Hafner-Eaton, Chris *medical researcher, educator*

Hoffman, Linda S. *science educator, special education educator*
Hoffman, Marian Ruth *singer, voice educator*
Hoffman, Sharon Lynn *adult education educator*
Hogaboom, Maurine Holbert *cultural organization administrator*
Hogensen, Margaret Hiner *retired librarian, consultant*
Hogg, Virginia Lee *retired medical educator*
Hoggatt, Clela Allphin *language educator*
Hogle, Ann Meilstrup *painter, art educator*
Hogue, Sharon Lea *music educator*
Hoke, Sheila Wilder *retired librarian*
Holbrook, Connie C. *lawyer*
Holbrow, Gwendolyn Jane *artist, writer*
Holcomb, Gene Ann *federal loan officer*
Holden, Betsy D. *former food products company executive*
Holden, Rebecca Lynn *artist*
Hollace, Barbara Jean *writer, property manager*
Holland, Beth *actress*
Holland, Branti Latessa *science educator*
Holland, Ellen C. *music educator*
Holland, Ruby Mae *social welfare administrator*
Hollander, Anne *writer*
Holleb, Doris B. *urban planner, economist*
Holleman, Marian Isabel *librarian, educator*
Holleman, Sandy Lee *religious organization administrator*
Hollenberg, Julia G. *music educator*
Holliday, Barbara Joyce *reference librarian, minister*
Hollie, Gladys Miriam *nurse*
Hollingsworth, Alison Berkeley *ballet dancer, educator*
Hollingworth, Beverly A. *former state legislator*
Hollis, Deborah D. *systems analyst, application developer*
Hollis, Robbie Smagula *marketing communications executive, advertising executive*
Holloway, Jennifer A. *elementary school educator, assistant principal*
Holloway, Judy Marie *music educator, minister*
Holm, Celeste *actress*
Holmes, Joan *retired social welfare administrator*
Holmes, Sandra *insurance underwriter*
Holmes, Serena Nicole *pre-school educator*
Holmes, Wilhelmina Kent *community health nurse*
Holmes, Willa B. *writer, former educator*
Holmes-Davis, Tina *music educator*
Holoman, Constance Currier *academic administrator*
Holsinger, Adena Seguine *music educator, community volunteer*
Holt, Marjorie Sewell *lawyer, retired congresswoman*
Holte, Debra Leah *investment company executive, financial analyst*
Holthausen, Martha Anne *interior designer*
Holtkamp, Susan Charlotte *elementary school educator*
Holton, Grace Holland *accountant*
Holton, Lesli Belflower *music educator*
Holyfield-Vega, Doretta Joyce *religious studies educator*
Holzer, Jenny *artist*
Hom, Mei Ling *artist, educator*
Homer, Melodie Antonette *oncological nurse, educator, consultant*
Homes, A. M. *writer*
Homestead, Susan E. (Susan Freedlender) *psychotherapist*
Honeycutt, Janice Louise *nurse*
Honig, Alice Sterling *psychologist*
Honour, Lynda Charmaine *research scientist, psychotherapist, educator*
Hood, Glenda E. *former state official, former mayor*
Hood, Katrina *pediatrician*
Hood, Luann Sandra *special education educator*
Hood, Patricia R. *music educator*
Hooper, Karen J. *music educator*
Hoopes, Margaret Howard *educator, psychologist, marriage and family therapist*
Hope, Carol J. *pharmacist, researcher, information technology manager*
Hopkins, Brenda Luvenia *social sciences educator, minister*
Hopkins, Cynthia *composer*
Hopkins, Jan *journalist, newscaster*
Hopkinson, Nicole Jean *elementary school educator*
Hopper, Bette Patricia *retired elementary school educator*
Hoppes, Laural Jean *elementary school educator*
Horai, Joann *psychologist*
Horlick, Ruth *photographer*
Hornbaker, Alice Joy *writer*
Hornby, Sara Ann *metallurgical engineer, marketing professional*
Horne, Kathryn Jennifer *elementary school educator*
Horne, Marjorie *production stage manager, event consultant*
Horner, Judith Anne *music educator*
Horner, Matina Souretis *retired academic administrator, corporate financial executive*
Horsch, Kathleen Joanne *social services administrator, educator, consultant*
Horsman, Lenore Lynde (Eleanora Lynde) *voice educator, soprano, actress*
Horstman, Suzanne Rucker *financial planner*
Horton, Deborah Jane *performing arts educator*
Horton, Joann *academic administrator*
Horton, Patricia Mathews *artist, violist and violinist*
Horton-Wright, Alma Irene *retired elementary school educator*
Horvath, Dolores Antionette *nurse*
Hosansky, Anne *writer*
Hosea, Julia Hiller *psychotherapist, communications executive, paralegal*
Hoskins, Lou Ann *art educator*
Hosman, Sharon Lee *retired music educator*
Hostler-Vaughan, ReBecca L. *educational consultant*
Hotaling, Carey *elementary school educator*
Houff, Bethany Dianne *music educator, conductor*
Houghtaling, Pamela Ann *communications professional, writer*
Houghton, Katharine *actress*
Houk, Irene Miller *dentist*
Hourani, Laurel Lockwood *epidemiologist*
House, Karen Elliott *former publishing executive, editor, journalist*
Houseknecht, Karen L. *research scientist, educator*
Houseman, Ann Elizabeth Lord *educational administrator*
Houser, Kyra Martin *counselor*
Houshiar, Bobbie Kay *retired language arts educator*
Houston, Gloria *author, educator, consultant*
Houston, Whitney *vocalist, recording artist*
Howard, Elena Calvillo *retired elementary school educator*
Howard, Wilma Parks *elementary school educator*
Howard-Peebles, Patricia Nell *clinical cytogeneticist*
Howell, Embry Martin *researcher*
Howell, Kimberly Lynne *science educator*
Howell, Mary Jean *artist, administrative assistant*
Howell, Saralee Fisher *retired pilot*
Howell, Teresa Christine Wallin *elementary school educator*
Howes, Sophia DuBose *writer*
Howze, Karen Aileen *newspaper editor, lawyer, multi-cultural communications consultant*
Hoye, Gwynne Sanders *retired mathematics educator*
Hricak, Hedvig *radiologist*
Hsieh, Tsui-Hsia *artist, educator*
Hsu, Apo (Ching Hsin Hsu) *conductor*
Hsu-Li, Magdalen *singer, poet, painter*
Htun, Mala *political science professor*
Hu, Hua-ling Wang *writer, historian*
Hubacz, Joan Rebecca *director, private school educator*
Hubbard, Elizabeth *actress*
Hubbard, Marguerite *retired elementary school educator*
Hubbs, Violet Elizabeth Shamblin *retired filmmaker, retired photographer*
Huckabee, Ebony *counselor, director*
Huckstead, Charlotte Van Horn *retired home economist, artist*
Hudachek-Buswell, Mary R. *mathematics professor*
Hudalla, Karen *dean, director, court reporter*
Hudson, Kate *actress*
Hudson, Katherine Mary *manufacturing executive*
Hudson, Sharon Marie *communications executive*
Huegel, Donna Marie *historian, writer, artist, archivist*
Huerta, Mary Zapata *English and foreign language educator*
Huey, Constance Anne Berner *mental health counselor*
Huffman, Amie Michelle Breaud *science educator*
Huffman, Cady (Catherine Elizabeth Huffman) *actress*
Huffman, Carol Cicolani *retired educational association administrator*
Huffman, Carol Koster *retired middle school educator*
Huffman, Melanie Diane *art educator*
Hughes, Ann Hightower *retired economist, trade association administrator*
Hughes, Cheryl Dempsey *theology studies educator*
Hughes, Deanna Elma *psychologist*
Hughes, Debra *writer, educator*
Hughes, Jennifer *utilities executive, photographer*
Hughes, Michaela Kelly *actress*
Hughes, Sue Margaret *retired librarian*
Hughes, Susan Michele *science educator, researcher*
Hughes, Teresa Mead *psychologist*
Hughes-Tebo, Jacqueline Emma *regional coordinator*
Huie, Carol P. *information science educator*
Hull, Jane Dee *former governor, former state legislator*
Hulstein, Mary Kathleen *music educator*
Humbach, Miriam Jane *publishing executive*
Hume, Susan Rachel *finance educator*
Humes, Elaine *mathematics educator*
Hummel, Marian *retired art educator, photographer*
Hummel, Marilyn Mae *retired elementary school educator*
Hummer-Sharpe, Elizabeth Anastasia *writer, genealogist, researcher*
Humphrey, Phyllis A. *writer*
Humphrey-Jefferson, Beverly C. *daycare administrator*
Humphreys, Lynne M. *secondary school educator*
Hundley, Carol Marie Beckquist *music educator*
Huning, Devon Gray *actress, audiologist, dancer, photographer*
Hunnicutt, Victoria Anne Wilson *educational consultant*
Hunt, L. Susan *publishing executive*
Hunt, Martha *sales executive, researcher*
Hunte, Beryl Eleanor *mathematics professor*
Hunter, Barbara Way *public relations consultant*
Hunter, Frances Ellen Croft *music educator*
Hunter, Georgia L. *clergywoman*
Hunter, Holly *actress*
Hunter, Juanita Walters *minister*
Hunter, Mattie Sue (Mattie Sue Moore) *health facility administrator*
Hunter, Sarah Ann *community health nurse*
Hunter-Gault, Charlayne *journalist*
Huntley-Wright, Joan Augusta (Joan Augusta Huntley) *musician*
Huntress, Betty Ann *retired small business owner, retired secondary school educator*
Hurley, Kathy Lee *mental health services professional, director*
Hurst, Anita Rose *social worker, counselor*
Hurst, Heather *illustrator*
Hurwitz, Ellen Stiskin *college president, historian*
Husky, Anrea Dalene *elementary school educator, director*
Huston, Margo *journalist*
Huszai, Kristen Renee *insurance agent*
Hutcheon, Linda Ann *English language educator*
Hutcherson, Rene Ridens *medical social services administrator*
Hutchinson, Edna M. *home care nurse*
Hutchinson, Glenda Dague *elementary school educator, small business owner*
Hutchison, Barbara Bailey *singer, songwriter*
Hutchison, Edna Ruth *artist*
Hutchison, Heather Nicole *secondary school educator*
Hutton, Carole Leigh *newspaper editor*
Hutton, Lauren (Mary Laurence Hutton) *model, actress*
Hyde, Alice Bach *artist*
Hyde, M. Deborah *neurosurgeon*
Hyland, Virginia Ling *small business owner*
Hyle-Worbets, Mary Elizabeth *nurse*
Hyman, Gayle M. *lawyer*
Hyman, Sylvia Gertrude *artist*
Hymes, Norma *internist*
Hyndman, Roberta *education educator*
Iannucci, Marilyn Butler *music educator*
Ibarra, Avelina C. *music educator*
Iceman, Sharon Lorraine *retired elementary school educator*
Idol, Lorna *education educator, writer*
Ignagni, Karen *healthcare association executive*
Ignatius, Nancy Weiser *foundation administrator*
Imai, Dorothy Kuniye *psychotherapist*
Iman, (Iman Abdulmajid) *model*
Impellizzeri, Anne Elmendorf *insurance company executive, non-profit executive*
Ina, Kyoko *professional figure skater*
Indenbaum, Dorothy *musician, researcher*
Infante-Ogbac, Daisy Inocentes *sales executive, real estate agent, marketing professional*
Ingberman, Sima *real estate company officer*
Ingebo, Marilyn Kay *human services manager, rehabilitation services professional*
Ingle, Beverly Dawn *elementary school educator*
Inglesi, Noreen Mary *music educator, poet, composer*
Ingram, Barbara Averett *minister*
Ingram, Tressia M. *mechanical engineer*
Innes, Laura *actress*
Insalaco-De Nigris, Anna Maria Theresa *middle school educator*
Inscho, Jean Anderson *retired social worker, landscape artist*
Intilli, Sharon Marie *television director, small business owner*
Intrater, Cheryl Watson Waylor *career management consultant*
Iovino, Pamela M. *federal agency administrator*
Iratene, Mary Susan *elementary school educator*
Ironbiter, Suzanne *writer, educator*
Irvan, Ashlee DeAnn *elementary school educator*
Irvin, Loretta Regan *elementary school educator*
Irving, Amy *actress*
Isaac, Susan Victoria *literature and language professor, department chairman*
Isaacs, Susan *writer, scriptwriter*
Isbell, Rita Anette *special education educator*
Isbin, Sharon *classical guitarist, guitar educator*
Isenberg, Jane Frances *writer, retired language educator*
Isidro, Rose Marie *physician*
Isom, Kawanya Kenyetta *assistant principal*
Ivanchenko, Lauren Margaret Dowd *pharmaceutical executive*
Ives, Colta Feller *museum curator, educator*
Ivey, Dana Robins *actress*
Ivey, Elizabeth Spencer *retired physicist, educator*
Ivey, Judith *actress*
Ivey, Mary Bradford *counselor*
Ivey, Sharon Dee *secondary school educator*
Izawa, Chizuko *psychologist, researcher*
Jabs, Aura Lee *minister, educator*
Jacir, Emily *photographer, conceptual artist*
Jack, Nancy Rayford *retired supplemental resource company executive, consultant*
Jackson, Clora Ellis *counseling administrator, psychologist, educator*
Jackson, Dana Lee *science educator*
Jackson, Dionne Broxton *chemist*
Jackson, Kate *actress*
Jackson, Katie J. *dancer, educator*
Jackson, Kelly Sue *social studies educator*
Jackson, Mary Alice *retired elementary school educator, retired realtor*
Jackson, Robbi Jo *agricultural products executive, lawyer*
Jackson, Tamra Lynn *literature and language educator*
Jackson, Valerie Lynnette *social worker*
Jackson, Victoria Lynn *actress, comedienne*
Jackson-Vanier, Linda M. *art educator*
Jackson Wright, Adrienne A. *educational consultant*
Jacob, Rosamond Tryon *librarian*
Jacober, Amy Elizabeth *theology studies educator*
Jacobowitz, Ellen Sue *curator, museum administrator*
Jacobs, Annette M. *music educator*
Jacobs, Eleanor *art consultant, retired art administrator*
Jacobs, Judith *county legislator*
Jacobs, Linda Rotroff *elementary school educator*
Jacobs, Marianne *anthropologist, educator, medical/surgical nurse*
Jacobs, Marion Kramer *psychologist*
Jacobs, Nancy Carolyn Baker *writer*
Jacobs, Patricia H. *social welfare organization executive*
Jacobs, Susan S. *ambassador*
Jacobs Gibson, Rose *alderman, not-for-profit developer*
Jacobson, Annette Moff *chemical engineer*
Jacobson, Joan Leiman *writer*
Jacobson, Nina R. *former film company executive*
Jacoby, Beverly Schreiber *art consultant*
Jacoby, Erika *social worker*
Jaeger, Ellen Louise *small business owner*
Jagdmann, Judith Williams *former state attorney general*
Jagerman, Adrienne *retired elementary school educator, nurse*
Jalbert, Amy *science educator*
Jalonen, Nancy Lee *academic administrator, educator*
Jamelli, Miriam H. *music educator, counseling administrator*
James, Estelle *economist, educator*
James, Kay Coles *former federal agency administrator*
James, Melissa Marie *religious studies educator*
James, Muriel Marshall *writer, educator, psychotherapist*
Jameson, Margaret Johnson *retired elementary school educator*
Jameson, Patricia Madoline *science librarian*
Jameson, Paula Ann *retired lawyer*
Janney, Allison *actress*
Janney, Kay Print *retired performing arts educator, theater director*
Jansen, Angela Bing *artist, educator*
Jappinen, Amy Jo *middle school educator*
Jaranilla, Sarah J. *critical care nurse, consultant*
Jarcho, Judith Lynn *artist*
Jarvis, Rebecca *financial reporter*
Jaska, Susan Park *retired radar systems engineer*
Javernick, Amy Sue *special education educator*
Jay, Norma Joyce *artist*
Jean, Claudette R. *retired elementary school educator*
Jean-Baptiste, Jean *minister*
Jeetah, Usha *Mauritius ambassador to the United States*
Jefferis, Bernice K. *education educator*
Jefferson, Kathleen Henderson *retired secondary school educator*
Jefferson, Marlene Rochelle *municipal official, director, minister*
Jefferson, Nanette Hawkins *special education educator*
Jeffery, Valerie *secondary school educator*
Jellison, Jenny Lynne *psychology professor*
Jelsma, Elizabeth Barbara *music educator*
Jenai, Marilyn *psychotherapist*
Jenkins, Billie Beasley *film company executive*
Jenkins, Brenda Gwenetta *pre-school administrator, special education educator*
Jenkins, Jill M. *gifted-talented education educator*
Jenkins, Lawanna *elementary school educator*
Jennings, Reba Maxine *retired critical care nurse*
Jensen, Eva Marie *medical/surgical nurse*
Jensen, Nancy Daggett *music educator*
Jensvold, Mary Lee Abshire *research scientist*
Jerger, Holly Anne *museum staff member, artist*
Jern, Donna L. *social studies educator*
Jernigan, Hilary Dawn *art educator, artist*
Jerome, Kathleen A. *writer, retired publishing executive*
Jerome, Marlene S. *nurse*
Jerviss, Joy J. (Joanne Jackson Jerviss) *artist, educator, small business owner*
Jessen, Shirley Agnes *artist*
Jessup, Catharine P. *retired medical/surgical nurse*
Jessup, Constance M. *music educator*
Jester, Nadine Anderson *music educator, elementary school educator*
Jewel, (Jewel Kilcher) *folk singer, songwriter*
Jewett, Mary (Betsy) Elizabeth *artist, conservationist*
Jirava, Carrie *music educator*
Joel, Katie (Katie Lee Joel, Katherine Lee) *television personality*
Joffe, Barbara Lynne *business transformation architect*
Johansen, Karen Lee *retired sales executive*
Johanyak, Debra L. *literature educator, consultant*
Johnsen, Barbara Parrish *writer, educator*
Johnson, Allyce A. *musician*
Johnson, Arica Reneé *elementary school educator*
Johnson, Barbara Elizabeth *lawyer*
Johnson, Betsie Ruth *pre-school educator*
Johnson, Camille *media executive*
Johnson, Carolyn M. *librarian, writer*
Johnson, Charlene Elizabeth *adult education educator, language educator, consultant*
Johnson, Crystal Duane *psychologist*
Johnson, Diane Lain *writer, critic*
Johnson, Dolores Estelle *retired small business owner*
Johnson, Doris Jean *social worker*
Johnson, Erma Jean *human services administrator*
Johnson, Everlene *materials engineer*
Johnson, Freda S. *financial analyst, consultant*
Johnson, Holly L. *elementary school educator*
Johnson, J(anet) Susan *psychologist*
Johnson, Jerrilyn Jenkins *academic administrator*
Johnson, Joyce *retired military officer*
Johnson, June Alexis *counselor, social worker*
Johnson, Karen *professional society administrator*
Johnson, Karen A. *legal association administrator*
Johnson, Karla Ann *county official*
Johnson, Kay Durbahn *real estate manager, consultant*
Johnson, Kirsten Denise *elementary school educator*
Johnson, Latonya *secondary school educator*
Johnson, Linda Arlene *transportation executive*
Johnson, Linda Sue *academic administrator, state agency administrator, retired state legislator*
Johnson, Lois Brooks *retired elementary guidance counselor*
Johnson, Margaret Heller *artist, educator*
Johnson, Marlene M. *nonprofit executive*
Johnson, Mary Elaine *interior designer, writer, counselor*
Johnson, Mary P. *freelance writer*
Johnson, Maryann Elaine *educational administrator*
Johnson, Meggan D. *school intervention specialist*
Johnson, Morgan Lea *artist, museum educator*
Johnson, Nichole Sharese *school nurse practitioner, basketball coach*
Johnson, Pam Clarene *radiographer, bone densitometrist, consultant*
Johnson, Patricia Diane *nurse anesthetist*
Johnson, Patricia Mary *writer*
Johnson, Ping Hu *nursing educator*
Johnson, Ruth Ann *music educator*
Johnson, Ruth Ann *literature and language educator*
Johnson, Sally A. *nurse, educator*
Johnson, Sandra Kay *music educator*
Johnson, Sheila Lynn *mathematician, educator*
Johnson, Sigrid *elementary school educator*
Johnson, Sylvia Sue *university administrator, educator*
Johnson, Trina Lynn *special education educator*
Johnson, Vera Lloyd *school system administrator*
Johnson, Yvonne Thomas *elementary school educator*
Johnson Holmes, SaBrina *music educator*

Johnson-MIller, Charleen V. educational coordinator
Johnston, Catherine Viscardi former magazine publisher
Johnston, Janis Clark psychologist, consultant
Johnston, Marguerite retired journalist
Johnston, Marilyn Frances-Meyers physician, educator
Johnston, Mary Hollis clinical psychologist
Jolly, Meenakshi rheumatologist
Jonas, Amy Joy music company executive
Jonas, Mary mental health counselor
Jones, Amanda Blakey actor
Jones, Anita Katherine computer scientist, educator
Jones, Ann writer, photographer
Jones, Anna elementary school educator
Jones, Carole A. elementary school educator
Jones, Carolyn Evans writer
Jones, Charlott Ann retired museum director, art educator
Jones, Christa M. secondary school educator
Jones, Christine Massey retired furniture company executive
Jones, Constance Coralie retired music educator
Jones, Cynthia R. social studies educator
Jones, Dale Cherner marketing executive, consultant
Jones, Elaine R. former legal association administrator, civil rights advocate
Jones, Elizabeth Jordan literature and language educator, art historian
Jones, Gwenyth Ellen information technology executive
Jones, Hettie Cohen writer, educator
Jones, Jane artist
Jones, Joan Megan anthropologist
Jones, Julie Ann elementary school educator, choreographer
Jones, Leonade Diane media publishing company executive
Jones, Lisa Maria Draper counselor
Jones, Martha Lee social worker, consultant
Jones, Mary Catherine medical/surgical nurse
Jones, Mary Ellen Snouffer language educator
Jones, Mary Gardiner lawyer, educator, consumer products company executive
Jones, Melissa Vincent secondary school educator
Jones, Phyllis Gene judge
Jones, Shirley actress, singer
Jones, Stacie Ann elementary school educator
Jones, Vivian Booker speech pathologist/audiology services professional
Jones-Eddy, Julie Margaret retired librarian
Jones-Ketner, Elizabeth Brown writer
Jones Tergeoglou, Beverly Gloria special education services professional
Jontz, Polly retired college official, museum director
Joosten, Kathryn (Kathryn Joostyn) actress
Jordan, Carrie Grayson (Carrie Grayson-Jordan) writer, poet, drama designer
Jordan, Crystal L. music educator
Jordan, Deovina Nasis nursing administrator
Jordan, Lisa Anne dancer, educator
Jordan, Mary Lucille commissioner
Jordan, Michelle Denise judge
Jordan, Phyllis C. Vaccaro special education educator
Jordan, Saskia A. lawyer
Joseph, Eleanor Ann health science association administrator, consultant
Joseph, Geri Mack (Geraldine Joseph) former ambassador, educator, journalist
Joseph, Kathie-Ann biomedical researcher
Josey, Donna Ashley accountant, educator
Joswiak, Ruth Ann retired dialysis nurse
Joyce, Diana psychologist, education educator
Joyce, Phyllis Norma principal
Joye, Afrie Songco minister
Joynes, Amelia C. art educator
Juarez, Maretta Liya Calimpong social worker
Judas, Ilse psychiatrist
Judd, Barbara Ann Eastwood financial management professional, union activist
Juffer, Kristin Ann researcher
Julian, Frances Bloch volunteer
Julien, JoElla L. educator
Junger, Patricia Carol nurse
Junker, Miriam M. music educator
Juodvalkis, Egle (Eglé Juodvalké) writer
Juran, Sylvia Louise retired editor
Jurgutis, Danguole artist
Jurman-Shulman, Claudia Lynne sales executive
Kabrich, Jeanine Renee broadcaster, educator
Kachur, Betty Rae elementary school educator
Kacines, Juliette Rosette behavior therapist
Kaczmarek, Jane actress
Kahana, Eva Frost sociology educator
Kahn, Cecily painter
Kahn, Herta Hess (Mrs. Howard Kahn) retired investment company executive
Kahn, Susan artist
Kahn, Victoria Elaine Hopkins special education educator
Kaiser, Bonnie L. science educator, educator
Kaiser, Karen Sue elementary school educator
Kaiser, Nina Irene healthcare consultant
Kalsow-Bernhard, Kathryn Marie retired music educator
Kamen, Paula journalist, playwright
Kamenske, Gloria L. retired psychologist
Kaminshine, Sarah Berne special education educator
Kaminski, Patricia Joyce lab administrator
Kaminsky, Alice Richkin retired literature educator
Kaminsky, Irene psychologist
Kamlay, Jane elementary school educator
Kamlet, Elizabeth Oseff elementary school educator
Kampen, Irene Blanche writer
Kan, Yue-Sai journalist, writer, television personality, entrepreneur, humanitarian
Kane, Carol actress
Kane, Heidi Baker secondary school educator
Kane, Karen Marie public affairs consultant
Kane, Margaret Brassler sculptor
Kane Hittner, Marcia Susan bank executive
Kang, Kyoung Sook retired special education educator
Kanich, Kelli Jo secondary school educator
Kanin, Fay screenwriter
Kannenstine, Margaret Lampe artist
Kantrowitz, Susan Lee lawyer
Kanuk, Leslie Lazar management consultant, educator
Kaplan, Alice humanities educator, writer
Kaplan, Elaine D. lawyer
Kaplan, Helene Lois lawyer
Kaplan, Phyllis artist, composer
Kapner, Lori marketing professional
Kapp, Gloria Jean retired academic program director
Kappner, Augusta Souza academic administrator
Kaps, Sydelle elementary school educator
Karabinus, Cynthia Julie Ann psychology and sociology educator
Karahalios, Sue M. Compton secondary school educator
Karalekas, Anne media executive
Karasick, Adeena Michelle literature and language professor, writer
Karayan, Ani A. psychologist, consultant
Karben, Shelley Valerie elementary and special education school educator
Karczewski, Lisa A. lawyer
Karfs, Tara Lynn elementary school educator
Karl, Kailah Marie military officer, small business owner
Karnowski, Maria A. special education educator
Karp, Naomi Katherine United States government administrator
Karp, Stephanie L. biology educator
Karpitskaya, Yekaterina orthopaedic surgeon
Karriem, Fatima real estate broker
Kartchner, Gayla L. elementary school educator
Kaslofsky, Wendy Anna special education educator
Kaslow, Florence Whiteman psychologist, educator, family business consultant
Kassewitz, Ruth Eileen Blower retired public relations executive
Kaster, Laura A. lawyer
Katen, Karen L. pharmaceutical company executive
Kates, Cheryl L. legal nursing consultant
Kathan, Joyce C. retired social worker, administrator
Katz, Anne Harris biologist, educator, writer
Katz, Phyllis Alberts developmental research psychologist
Katz, Susan Arons language arts specialist, writer, poet
Kauffman, Jenn band director
Kauffman, Marta producer, writer
Kaupa, Caroline Marqurite music educator
Kavanagh, Cornelia Kubler sculptor
Kavner, Julie actress
Kavovit, Barbara entrepreneur
Kay, Bonnie Kathryn management consultant
Kaye, Janet Miriam psychologist, educator
Kaye, Judy actress
Kazeminezhad, Zhabiz psychiatrist
Kazmarek, Linda Adams secondary school educator
Keala, Betty Ann Lyman computer scientist
Kearns, Ellen Veronica artist
Keat, Jane Blakely education educator
Keating, Regina G. computer analyst consultant
Keech, Elowyn Ann interior designer
Keegan, Catherine Ann medical/surgical nurse, endoscopy nurse
Keene, Sylvia White retired reading specialist
Keene-Burgess, Ruth Frances military official
Keener, Elizabeth Ann elementary school educator
Keeney, Marisa Gesina psychologist
Keeney, Virginia T. retired child psychiatrist
Keesee, Donna Christine retired elementary school educator
Keeter, Lynn Carpenter language educator
Keets, Elizabeth advocate, educator
Kehoe-Gadway, Nita L. art educator, art gallery director
Keim, Betty Lou actress, literary consultant
Keim, Katherine I. psychologist
Keiser, Nanette Marie research scientist
Keith, Katharine education educator
Keith Wagstaff, Mary Jane physician
Kelehear, Carole Marchbanks Spann legal assistant
Kellar, Marie Terese special education educator
Kelley, Kathryn B. actress
Kelley, Kathy literature and language educator
Kelley, Kristina Elizabeth secondary school educator
Kelley, Mary Elizabeth (Mary LaGrone) information technology specialist
Kelley, Sheila Seymour public relations consultant
Kelley, Wendy Rock academic administrator
Kellums, Karen J. psychologist
Kelly, Beverly Ann elementary school educator
Kelly, Carol A. travel company executive
Kelly, Christina editor
Kelly, Cleo Parker retired bank executive
Kelly, Sister Dorothy Ann academic administrator
Kelly, Judith Reese literature educator
Kelly, Lucie Stirm Young nursing educator
Kelly, Mary Kathryn special education administrator
Kelly, Nancy Folden art association administrator
Kelly, Pamela B. lawyer
Kelly, Susan writer, educator
Kelm, Bonnie G. art museum director, educator, art appraiser, consultant
Kelso, Charlotte Elizabeth elementary school educator, health and physical education specialist
Kemper Dietrich, Sheila educational association administrator
Kendall, Jacqueline A. social worker
Kendig, Florence Geertz (Bobbi Kendig) retired social worker
Kennedy, Barbara Ellen Perry art therapist
Kennedy, Debra Joyce marketing professional
Kennedy, Jerrie Ann Preston public relations executive
Kennedy, Joanie Tiska artist, painter
Kennedy, Karen Syence advertising agency executive
Kennedy, Leila accounting educator
Kennedy, Marla Catherine psychologist
Kennedy, Megan Catherine music educator
Kennedy, Muriel psychologist, consultant, educator
Kennedy, Sheryl J. elementary school educator
Kennedy, Virginia Frances retired education educator
Kenney, Estelle Koval artist, educator
Kenney, Marianne elementary school educator
Kenny, Deborah marketing professional, finance educator
Kent, Georgia L. obstetrician, gynecologist, healthcare executive, educator
Kent, Lisa Barnett marketing executive, small business owner
Keohane, Nannerl Overholser political scientist, academic administrator
Kepner, Jane Ellen psychotherapist, educator, minister
Kerby, Ramona Anne librarian
Kerkemeyer, Victoria Marie physical therapist
Kernan, Barbara Desind federal official
Kerr, Janet Spence physiologist, pharmacologist, researcher
Kerr Walker, Joi Mechelle literacy educator, consultant
Kerwin, Elizabeth Anderson retired anesthesiologist
Kerzmann, Olivia Lindsay music educator
Kesselring, Debbie Anne systems engineer
Kessler, Ann Michele dance educator, costume designer
Kessler, Jean S. clinical data manager
Kester, Helen Mary minister
Ketcham, Sally Ann historic site staff member, consultant
Ketchum, Irene Frances library supporter
Kewish, Sharon Patricia literature educator
Key, Rachel E. literature and language professor
Keyes, Joan Ross Rafter education educator, writer
Keywood, Kay Hill mathematics educator, small business owner
Kezlarian, Nancy Kay marriage and family therapist
Khan, Arfa radiologist, educator
Khatib, Kathy school administrator, educator
Khvost-Vostrikova, Natalia S. art educator, consultant
Kiefer, Rita Brady writer, educator
Kiel, Brenda Kay medical/surgical nurse
Kienitz, LaDonna Trapp lawyer, librarian, municipal official
Kierscht, Marcia Selland academic administrator, psychologist
Kilbane, Kathleen Ann stage manager
Kilcher, Q'Orianka (Q'orianka Waira Qoiana Kilcher) actress, singer, dancer
Kildee, Jennifer translator, editor
Kile, Patricia D. retired elementary school educator
Killebrew, Betty Rackley language educator
Killen, Kathleen Elizabeth systems engineer, retired military officer
Killian, Tiffany Noel secondary school educator
Killoran, Cynthia Lockhart retired elementary school educator
Kilpatrick, Jennifer M. counseling administrator
Kilpatrick, Judith Ann medical/surgical nurse, educator
Kimbriel-Eguia, Susan engineering planner, small business owner
Kimbrough, Lorelei retired elementary school educator, retired secondary school educator
Kimes, Beverly Rae editor, writer
Kindberg, Shirley Jane pediatrician
King, Amy Cathryne Patterson retired mathematics educator, researcher
King, Bonnie La Verne education educator
King, Cynthia Bregman writer
King, Elizabeth Ann writer
King, Imogene M. retired nursing educator
King, Jane Cudlip Coblentz volunteer educator
King, Joy Rainey poet, executive secretary
King, Joy Riemer art educator, linguist
King, Lindsay Brawner music educator
King, Lynda counselor
King, Molly Elizabeth Rutland elementary school educator
King, Regina actress
King, Rosalyn Mercita social sciences educator, researcher, psychologist
King, Susan Bennett retired glass company executive
King, Verna St. Clair retired school counselor
Kinget, G. Marian educator, psychologist
Kingsland, Grace Harvey retired medical/surgical nurse, artist
Kingston, Maxine Hong writer, educator
Kinley, Christine T. physician assistant
Kinney, Jeanne Kawelolani English studies educator, writer
Kinney, Joyce P. elementary school educator
Kinzie, Jeannie Jones radiation oncologist, nuclear medicine physician
Kinzler, Charissa D. special education educator
Kipniss MacDonald, Betty Ann artist, educator
Kipper, Barbara Levy wholesale distribution executive
Kirby, Marcia Karen library and information scientist
Kirby, Sheryl C. secondary school educator
Kirby, Vesta Ann artist
Kirchmeier, Emmalou Handford minister, writer
Kirchmeier-Boyes, Melanie Joan middle school educator
Kirchner, Lisa Beth actress, vocalist
Kirchner, Ursula Schwebs science educator
Kirchoff, Molly music educator
Kirk, Deborah piano educator
Kirk, Rea Helene (Rea Helene Glazer) special education educator
Kirkland, Rebecca Trent endocrinologist
Kirkpatrick, Alicia Ann elementary school educator, department chairman
Kirkpatrick, Edith Killgore music educator, volunteer
Kirkwood, Catherine artist
Kirschman, Ellen Freeman psychologist
Kirschner-Bromley, Victoria Ann clinical counselor
Kiser, Ruth Marguerite music educator
Kisiel, Ida Marie education educator, writer
Kistiakowsky, Vera physical researcher, educator
Kistler, Joyce Dianna secondary school educator
Kist-Tahmasian, Candace Lynee psychologist
Kisvarsanyi, Eva Bognar retired geologist
Kitch, Terri Lynn language educator
Kitt, Eartha Mae actress, singer
Kitzman, Mary Therese elementary school educator
Kivitter, Linda Jean medical nurse
Kjar, Nancy elementary school educator
Klages, Constance Warner management consultant
Klass, Phyllis Constance retired genetic counselor, psychotherapist
Klaw, Barbara Anne language educator
Klebanow, Barbara Elaine secondary school educator
Klein, Charlotte Conrad public relations executive
Klein, Charlotte Feuerstein art consultant
Klein, Cinthia Marie parochial school educator
Klein, Deborah Lynn art educator
Klein, Elayne Margery retired elementary school educator
Klein, Irma Molligan career planning administrator, consultant
Klein, Lynn Ellen artist
Klein, Mary Ann special education educator
Klein, Susan Elaine librarian
Kleiner, Heather Smith retired academic administrator
Kleinhenz, Nancy Alison medical/surgical nurse
Klement, Vera artist
Kleven, Laura science educator
Kleven, Marguerite state legislator
Kliebhan, Sister M(ary) Camille academic administrator
Kline, Leona Ruth nurse, volunteer
Kling, Jennifer Rae music educator
Klinger, Susan art educator, artist
Klinghoffer, Judith Apter historian, consultant
Klopfleisch, Stephanie Squance social services agency administrator
Klotter, Eleanor Irene retired social worker
Klutts, Rhonda Asbury music educator
Kmetz-McMillin, MArianne Denise secondary school educator
Knapp, Candace Louise sculptor
Knauer, Virginia Harrington (Mrs. Wilhelm F. Knauer) advocate, retired federal agency administrator
Knieser, Catherine music educator
Knight, Patricia Marie biomedical engineer, consultant
Knight, Rebecca Jean secondary school educator
Knight, Shirley actress
Knighten, Latrenda elementary school educator, consultant
Knightley, Keira actress
Knizeski, Justine Estelle insurance company executive
Knopf, Tana Darlene counselor, music educator
Knowles, Elizabeth Pringle museum director
Knowles, Marilyn Rae ballet company administrator
Knowlton, Marie retired special education educator
Knox, Deborah Carolyn state information systems administrator
Knox, Gertie R. compliance executive, accountant
Knudsen, Helen Ewing Zollars librarian
Ko, Christine J. dermatologist, educator
Koblick, Joan Lesser retired art educator, artist
Kocel, Katherine Merle psychology professor, researcher
Koch, Christine legislative aide
Koch, Dorothy Harriet artist
Koch, Molly Brown retired parent educator
Koch, Virginia Greenleaf (Virginia M. Greenleaf) painter
Kocheril, Sosa Varghese rheumatologist
Koehler, Charity Marie music educator
Koelmel, Lorna Lee data processing executive
Koenig, Maureen Catherine science educator
Koeppel, Mary Sue communications educator, writer
Koerber, Dolores Jean music educator, musician
Koerber, Marilynn Eleanor gerontology nursing educator, consultant, nurse
Koessel, Jeannine Carrol retired principal
Kohas, Artemis Diane guidance counselor
Kohler, Sheila M. humanities educator, writer
Kohn, Jean Gatewood retired health facility administrator, pediatrician
Kohn, Margaret Sherman music educator, pianist
Kokx, Sarah Lynn elementary school educator
Kolakoski, Dawn Laymond education educator, consultant, music educator
Kolasa, Kathryn Marianne food and nutrition educator, consultant
Kolb, Dorothy Gong elementary school educator
Kolbe, Stephanie Jill artist
Kolbert, Kathryn lawyer, educator
Kollmeyer, Carie Ann pediatrician
Komechak, Marilyn Gilbert psychologist, educator
Komins, Deborah psychotherapist
Konecky, Edith writer
Konigsburg, Elaine Lobl writer
Konner, Joan Weiner academic administrator, educator, television producer, writer, retired television executive
Konrad, Carol Joan secondary school educator
Kopec-Garnett, Linda nursing administrator, researcher
Koperski, Nanci Carol nursing consultant, women's health nurse
Koral, Marian writer
Koreman, Dorothy Goldstein physician, dermatologist
Korenic, Lynette Marie librarian
Korn, Jessica Susan research scientist, educator
Kornasky, Linda A. literature educator
Korn-Davis, Dottie artist, educator, consultant
Kornhaber, Donna Marie theater educator
Kornrich, Rhoda psychologist
Korologos, Ann McLaughlin communications executive
Korsgaard, Christine Marion philosophy educator
Korzenik, Diana art educator
Kos, Nirvana Gabriela psychologist
Kosisky, Shelley Ann psychologist

Koss, Mary Lyndon Pease *psychology educator, researcher*
Kostic, Dina *musician, music educator*
Kostick, Alexandra *ophthalmologist*
Kotcher, Shirley J.W. *lawyer*
Kott, Tama I. *music educator*
Kottler, Joan Lynn *counselor*
Kournikova, Anna *retired professional tennis player*
Kouzel, Mildred *artist*
Kowlessar, Muriel *retired pediatric educator*
Kozak, Karen S. *writer*
Kraft, Yvette *art educator*
Kraisosky, Alissa Jo *psychiatrist*
Kramer, Karen Sue *psychologist, educator*
Kramer, Lora L. *executive assistant*
Kramp, Suzan Marie *systems programmer*
Krane, Jessica (Aida Jessica Kohnop-Krane) *writer, educator*
Kranowitz, Carol Stock *pre-school educator, writer*
Kraus, Jill Gansman *former jewelry industry marketing executive*
Kraus, Lisa Marie Wasko *music educator, composer, musician*
Kraus, Naomi *retired biochemist*
Krause, Jennie Sue *athletic trainer, nutrition counselor*
Krauskopf, Nancy Kay *middle school educator, journalist*
Krauss, Diana S. *secondary school educator*
Kravitz, Ellen King *musicologist, educator*
Krebs, Martha *physicist, federal science agency administrator*
Krebs, Mary *art educator*
Krebsbach, Jennifer Susan *nurse*
Kregg, Helen Christine *foundation administrator*
Kreider, Louisa J. *biologist, librarian*
Kreindler, Marla J. *lawyer*
Kreitzburg, Marilyn June *academic librarian*
Krell, Rebecca Dawn *music educator*
Kremer, Honor Frances (Noreen Kremer) *real estate broker, small business owner*
Kretchmar, Leslie *medical/surgical nurse*
Kretzschmar, Angelina Genzer *small business owner, paralegal*
Krieger, Lois B. *retired state agency administrator*
Kriegsman, Sali Ann *performing arts executive, consultant, writer*
Krim, Mathilde *medical educator*
Krischer, Devora *writer, editor*
Krise, Patricia Love *automotive industry executive*
Krobath, Krista Ann *pharmacist*
Krohley-Gatt, Patricia Anne *marketing professional, sales executive*
Krominga, Lynn *cosmetics executive, lawyer*
Kronenberg, Mindy Ellen *psychologist, psychology professor*
Krotz, Janet M. Trahan *artist, former gallery owner, art educator*
Kroupa, Betty Jean *medical/surgical nurse*
Kruc, Antoinette Campion *family physician*
Krulik, Barbara S. *prodution manager, curator, art director, writer*
Krumholz, Mimi *human resources administrator*
Krupansky, Blanche Ethel *retired judge*
Krzykowski, Jamie Lee *education educator*
Kudrow, Lisa (Lisa Marie Diane Kudrow) *actress*
Kuehn, Lucille M. *retired humanities educator*
Kuehn, Mildred May *retired social worker*
Kuehn, Nancy Ann *retired secondary school educator*
Kuhfuss, Lisa A. *mathematics educator*
Kuhler, Deborah Gail *grief therapist, retired state legislator*
Kuhlmann-Wilsdorf, Doris *materials scientist, inventor, retired educator*
Kulik, Rosalyn Franta *food company executive, consultant*
Kulkarni, Shaila V. *secondary school educator*
Kumar, Faith *clinical professional counselor*
Kumar, Ramya *academic administrator*
Kumar, Rita *literature and language educator*
Kumin, Maxine Winokur *poet, writer*
Kunin, Jacqueline Barlow *retired art educator*
Kunstadter, Geraldine Sapolsky *foundation executive*
Kunz, Alexandra Cavitt *physician, anthropologist, researcher*
Kupelian, Louise Paulson *musician, educator*
Kuper, Daniela F. *writer*
Kupovits, Jene Irene *special education educator*
Kuriansky, Judy *television personality, radio personality, reporter, clinical psychologist, writer, educator*
Kurtz, Dolores May *civic worker*
Kurtz, Swoosie *actress*
Kussrow, Nancy Esther *educational association administrator*
Kuznetsova, Ekaterina G. *theater educator, dancer*
Kwik, Christine Irene *physician, retired military officer, retired foreign service officer*
Kwong, Eva *artist, educator*
Kyle, Gene Magerl *merchandise presentation artist*
Labbe-Webb, Elizabeth Geralyn *performing company executive*
LaBella, Janice Marie *peri-operative nurse*
Labiner, Caroline *architect*
LaCava, Laura L. *elementary school educator*
Lacher, Miriam Browner *neuropsychologist*
LaCroix, Sophia Marie *artist*
Ladd, Diane *actress*
Ladewig Goodman, Jeanne Margaret *artist*
Lafferty, Christine Elizabeth *science educator*
LaFlamme, Julie Lynn *secondary school educator*
LaGanke, Allyson Ann *psychologist*
Lagomasino, Maria Elena *retired bank executive*
LaHaye, Beverly *cultural organization administrator*
Lai, Feng-Qi *instructional designer, educator*
Laird, Cheryl F. *mental health services professional, paralegal*
Lake, Carol Lee *anesthesiologist, physician, educator*
Lamb, Darlis Carol *sculptor*
Lamb, Jo Ann P. *geriatrics nurse*
Lamb, Patsy (Pat) Lee *retired adult education educator, real estate broker*
Lambert, Christina *telecommunications executive*
Lamel, Linda Helen *professional society executive, retired insurance company executive, lawyer, arbitrator, retired college president*
LaMere, Melissa Jo *biomechanics educator*
Lami, Judith Irene *advertising executive*
Lamont, Lee *music company executive, communications executive*
Lamont, Marilyn Laree Claudel *reading specialist, accountant*
Lamontagne, Carole Hegland *retired art educator*
LaMorte, Joyce E. *music educator*
LaMotta, Connie Frances *public relations executive*
Lampert, Eleanor Verna *retired human resources specialist*
Lampl, Annie Wagner *psychotherapist*
Lanam, Linda Lee *lawyer*
Lancaster, Jeanette (Barbara Lancaster) *dean, nursing educator*
Lancaster, Karine R. *retired city health department administrator*
Lancaster, Kirsten Kezar *psychologist*
Lancaster, Sally Rhodus *retired non-profit executive, consultant*
Landau, Emily Fisher *art collector, foundation administrator*
Landgrebe, Marilyn Ann *nutritionist, chemicals executive*
Landon, Susan N. *humanitarian, arts and environmental advocate, poet*
Landovsky, Rosemary Reid *figure skating school director, coach*
Landrum, Beverly Hollowell *nurse, lawyer*
Landry, Abbie Vestal *librarian*
Landvogt, Penny Lucille *psychotherapist, educator*
Landy, Lisa Anne *lawyer*
Lane, Allyson C. *elementary school educator*
Lane, Colette Marie *writer*
Lane, Lilly Katherine *museum staff member*
Lane, Marsha K. *medical/surgical nurse*
Lane, Patricia Peyton *retired nursing consultant*
Lanes, Selma Gordon *critic, writer, editor*
Lane Stone, Nancy Ann *elementary school educator*
Lange, Jessica Phyllis *actress*
Lange, Mary Christine *music educator*
Lange, Natalie Lauren *social studies educator*
Langel, Teresa Lynn *music educator*
Langenkamp, Sandra Carroll *retired human services administrator*
Langham, Gail B. *writer*
Langmaid, Barbra Kay *elementary school educator*
Langton (Tomasiewicz), Dawn Theresa *literature and language educator*
Langum, Teresa Marie *elementary school educator*
Lanning, Yvonne Bradshaw *elementary school educator*
Lansing, Jewel Beck (Jewel Anne Beck) *writer, auditor*
Lansing, Sherry Lee *former film company executive*
Lantis, Donna Lea *retired banker, artist, art educator*
Lantz, Joanne Baldwin *retired academic administrator*
LaPalombara, Constance *artist*
LaParle, Paulette Gagnon *music educator*
LaPierre, Eileen Marie *technical services manager*
LaPolt, Margaret *librarian*
LaPorta, Sara *retail executive*
LaPorte, Adrienne Aroxie *nursing administrator*
Lapp, Kathryn S. *social studies educator*
Largent, Margie *retired architect*
Larkin, Joan *poet, literature and language educator*
Larkin, Mary Sue *financial planner*
LaRobardier, Genevieve Krause *lawyer*
La Rocca, Isabella *artist, educator*
LaRochelle, Wanda Carlene *science educator*
Larsdotter, Anna-Lisa *retired translator, artist*
Larsen, Brenda Joyce *elementary school educator*
Larsen, Kristina Ann *elementary school educator*
Larson, Amy F. *nurse*
Larson, Angela R. *secondary school educator*
Larson, Janece S. *elementary school educator*
Larson, Janice Talley *application developer*
Larson, Joan Isbell *musician, educator*
Larson, Vicki Lord *academic administrator, communication disorders educator*
LaRue, Eva Marie *actress*
Lasak, Janice Underhill *elementary school educator*
Lashley, Felissa Rose *dean, nursing educator, researcher*
Lass, Diane *counselor*
Lassaletta, Antonia Mir *language educator*
Lassmann, Marie Elizabeth *education educator, consultant*
Latendresse, Lanelle *financial services company executive*
Latham, Tamara Beryl *chemist, researcher*
Lathan, Monica J. *health science association administrator, epidemiologist*
Lathrop, Ann *retired librarian, educator*
Latimer, Helen *retired information resource manager, writer, researcher*
Latiolais, Minnie Fitzgerald *retired nurse, health facility administrator*
La Torre, Carissa Danitza *counselor*
Lattimore, Louise Joan *elementary school educator*
Lau, Christina Sielck *librarian*
Laudenklos, Terry Lynn *elementary school educator*
Laudone, Anita Helene *lawyer*
Lauer, Cassie Lynn *mathematics educator, department chairman*
Lauer, Jeanette Carol *dean, history educator, writer*
Lauper, Cyndi *musician*
Lautenschlager, Yetta Elizabeth *clinical social worker*
Lautzenhiser, Niann Kay *psychologist, real estate broker*
Lauzon, Laura M. *middle school educator*
LaVally, Rebecca Jean *research editor, journalist*
LaVerdiere, Claudette Marie *nun, head of religious order*
Lavery, Elizabeth J. *music educator*
Lavey, Sarah *assistant principal*
Lawer, Betsy *banker, small business owner, vintner, director*
Lawrence, Janice Fletcher *psychologist*
Lawrence, Kristine Guerra *project engineer*
Lawrence, Marilyn Edith (Marilyn Guthrie) *association executive*
Lawrence, Mary Josephine (Josie Lawrence) *artist, retired library official*
Lawrence, Sally Clark *retired academic administrator*
Lawrence, Sharon *actress*
Lawson, Carolina Donadio *language educator, translator*
Lawson, Sharianne Renee *political science educator*
Lawton, Violet *writer*
Layzell, Judy Kathleen *secondary school educator, writer*
Lazo, Caroline Evensen *writer*
Lazovsky, Lorna Deane *minister*
Lea, Karen *elementary education educator*
Leach, Janet C. *publishing executive*
Leachman, Cloris *actress*
Leaf, Ruth *artist*
Leafgren, Rita F. *education educator*
Leahy, Jeannette (Jeannette Oliver Leahy Tinen Kaehler) *actress*
Leak, Nancy Marie *artist*
Lean, Judith *physicist, researcher*
Learned, Michael *actress*
Leasor, Jane *religious studies educator, humanities educator, musician*
Leath, Cheryl Lynn *retired pre-school educator, poet, painter*
Leath, Mary Elizabeth *medical/surgical nurse*
Leather, Victoria Potts *college librarian*
Leavel, Beth *actress*
Leavell, Tausha Dawn *social studies educator*
Le Blanc, Alice Isabelle *academic administrator*
LeBlanc, Jean Eva *writer, poet, educator*
Leblanc, Jeanne Marie *psychologist, educator*
Lebowitz, Catharine Koch *state legislator*
Ledbetter, Merry W. *mathematics educator*
Ledet, Phyllis L. *assistant principal*
Lee, Anita Combs *writer, speaker, consultant*
Lee, Anne *music educator*
Lee, Carol Frances *lawyer*
Lee, Corinne Adams *retired English teacher*
Lee, Daphne Patrice *special events coordinator, academic administrator*
Lee, Donna A. *telecommunications industry executive*
Lee, Esther Bora *elementary school educator, gifted and talented educator*
Lee, Eunice *music educator*
Lee, Gwendolin Kuei *retired ballet educator*
Lee, Harper (Nelle Harper Lee) *writer*
Lee, Jeanne Kit Yew *retired administrative officer*
Lee, Katrina LaShawn *health insurance business consultant*
Lee, Krista *secondary school educator*
Lee, Linda M. *technical recruiter*
Lee, Marvina Sue *science educator*
Lee, Nelda S. *art appraiser, art dealer, film producer*
Lee, Tabia (T. Lee) *social studies educator*
Lee, Winnie Sita *dentist*
Leedom-Ackerman, Joanne *writer, educator*
Leeds, Nancy Brecker *sculptor, lyricist*
Leeper, Kathleen Marie *elementary school educator*
Leff, Ilene J(afnel) *corporate executive, federal official*
Lefranc, Margaret (Margaret Schoonover) *artist, illustrator, editor, writer*
Legace, Kathryn Jane *principal*
Legendre, Jaclyn *psychologist*
Léger, Viola *Canadian senator*
Legg, Hilda Gay *former federal agency administrator*
Leggett, Roberta Jean (Bobbi Leggett) *retired social services administrator*
Legington, Gloria R. *retired elementary school educator*
Lehman, Barbara Albu *foreign language educator, translator*
Lehman, Joan Alice *real estate company executive*
Lehner, Remy D. *publishing executive*
Lehner-Quam, Alison Lynn *library administrator*
Leibowitz, Bernice *artist, educator*
Leidel, Katherine *journalist, newscaster*
Leidig, Margot Helene *retired elementary school educator, retired secondary school educator*
Leighman, Marilyn Rust *school counselor*
Leinfellner, Ruth *strategic planner*
Leininger, Madeleine Monica *nursing educator, consultant, retired anthropologist, editor, writer, theorist*
Leistner, Mary Edna *retired secondary school educator*
Leith, Karen Pezza *psychologist, educator*
Leitzel, Joan Ruth *retired academic administrator*
LeMay, Gayla Denise *elementary school educator*
LeMay, Nancy *graphics designer, painter*
Lemieux, Annette Rose *artist*
Lemieux, Jaime Danielle *physical therapist*
Lemke, Carol Ann *music educator, pianist, accountant*
Lenhart, Cynthia Rae *conservation organization executive*
Leon, Nellie *health educator*
Leonard, Sister Anne C. *school system administrator*
Leonard, Carolyn Branch *editor, writer*
Leonard, Jo Ann Warner *social sciences educator*
Leonard, Kristi *education educator, director*
Leonard, Virginia Kathryn *financial manager*
Leone, Jeanne *artist*
Leoni, Tea (Elizabeth Tea Pantaleoni) *actress*
Leon Rivera, Aida I. *language educator*
Lepore, Dawn Gould *Internet company executive*
Leppard, Stephanie Jean *systems analyst, artist*
Lerner, Beth M. *non-profit consultant*
Lertora, Joanne Marie *psychologist*
Leslie, Maureen Heelan *university director*
Lesonsky, Paula Marlene *elementary school educator*
Lester, Alicia Louise *financial analyst*
Lester, Stephanie *elementary school educator, education educator*
Lester, Virginia Laudano *academic administrator*
Lesyinski, Diane M. *elementary school educator*
Letcher, Naomi Jewell *quality engineer, educator, counselor*
Leventer, Terri *psychologist*
Leventhal, Ruth *retired parasitology educator, university official*
Leventhal-Stern, Barbara Lynn *artist, marriage and family counselor*
Levermore, Monique A. *psychologist, educator*
Levey, Judith S. *lexicographer, publisher, editor*
Levi, Barbara Goss *physicist, editor*
Levi, Marina J. *language educator, theater educator*
Levine, Marilyn Markovich *lawyer, arbitrator*
Levine, Peggy Aylsworth *psychotherapist, poet, writer*
Levine, Ruth Hannah *retired sculptor*
Levinsky, Frieda Libby *language educator*
Levinson, Marina *information technology executive*
Levinson, Riki *art director*
Levitas, Miriam C. Strickman *documentary filmmaker*
Levitt, B. Blake *writer, medical writer*
Levy, Dara Michele *secondary school educator*
Levy, Leslie Ann *application developer*
Levy, Valery *publisher*
Lewie, Reva Goodwin *artist, educator*
Lewin, Nancy S. *actress*
Lewis, Kristen R. *mathematics educator*
Lewis, Mary-Frances *civic volunteer*
Lewis, Rita Hoffman *plastic products manufacturing company executive*
Lewis, Sharyn Lee *sculptor*
Lewis, Tommi *magazine editor*
Lewis-Gilchrist, Stephanie Kay *primary school educator*
Lewis-Griffith, Dorothy Ellen *music educator, pianist*
Lewis Riffle, Muriel Ann *retired secondary school educator*
Lewy, Helen Crosby *artist, writer, translator, painter*
Ley, Carmen B. *special education educator*
Leybourn, Carol *musician, educator*
Li, Lijuan *chemistry professor*
Li, Mary J. *scientist, educator*
Li, Qin *news anchor, reporter, television director, television producer*
Libbey, Darlene Hensley *artist, educator*
Libbin, Anne Edna *lawyer*
Liberati, Maria Theresa *lifestyle company executive, cooking expert, writer*
Liberman, Gail Jeanne *editor*
Libert, Cleo Patricia *computer scientist, consultant*
Lichtman, Judith L. *lawyer, organization administrator*
Liddell, Mary Louisa *elementary school educator, computers educator*
Liebeler, Susan Wittenberg *lawyer*
Lieberman, Gail Forman *investment company executive*
Liebman, Nina R. *economic developer*
Lief, Beth *educational association administrator*
Lien, Julie Ann *elementary school educator*
Light, Judith Ellen *actress*
Light, Marion Jessel *retired elementary school educator*
Lightbourne, Marva Henrietta *nurse*
Lightburn, Christa Pierpont *agricultural business manager*
Lightwood, Carol Wilson *writer*
Li-lan, *artist*
Liles, Virginia Rembert *retired art educator*
Lilly, Elizabeth Giles *small business owner*
Lilly, Elizabeth K. *art educator, artist*
Lilly-Hersley, Jane Anne Feeley *nursing researcher*
Liman, Ellen *art gallery owner, painter*
Limerick, Dianne A. *mathematics educator, athletic trainer*
Lin, Maya *architect, sculptor*
Lincoln, Rosamond Hadley *painter, photographer*
Lindbergh, Judith L. *writer, photographer*
Lindboe, Berit Roberg *retired language educator, literature educator*
Lindburg, Daytha Eileen *physician assistant*
Linde, Maxine Helen *lawyer, corporate financial executive, investor*
Lindeman, Carolynn Anderson *music educator*
Lindeman, Joyce Irene *university administrator*
Lindenfeld, Naomi *ceramic artist*
Lindenmayer, Elisabeth *international organization administrator*
Lindland, Marnetta *secondary school educator*
Lindley, Jolie Beth *choreographer, educator, actress*
Lindley, Suzanne Evers *biology professor, researcher*
Lindsey, Roberta Lewise *music researcher, historian*
Lindstrom, Rosetta Arline *retired medical technician*
Lingle, Marilyn Felkel *journalist, columnist*
Lingle, Sarah Elizabeth *research scientist*
Link, Phyllida Korman *artist, educator*
Lintner, Roberta Pompilio *art educator, artist*
Lippard, Lucy Rowland *writer, educator, critic, curator*
Lippman Salovesh, Dorothy *nurse practitioner*
Lipscomb, Laura *information architect*
Lipton, Nina Anne *healthcare executive*
Lipton, Susan Lytle *investment banker, lawyer*
Lisle, Janet Taylor *writer*
Little, Jennifer *performing arts educator, director, actress*
Little, Laura Janes *educational association administrator*
Little, Margaret F. Dixon Lesniak *electrical engineer, educator*
Litz, Claudia *science educator*
Litzenberger, Lesley Margaret *textiles executive*
Liu, Katherine Chang *artist, art educator*
Liu, Margaret C. *music educator*
Liu, Rhonda Louise *librarian*
Liu, Ruth Wang *retired academic administrator*
Liu, Te Hua *neuroradiologist, educator*
Livengood, Charlotte Louise *retired human resources specialist*
Liverman, Betty Jean *elementary school educator*

Livermore, Ann Martinelli *computer company executive*
Livingston, Gwendell Sheawanna *education educator*
Livingston, Margaret Gresham *civic leader*
Livingstone, Susan Morrisey *management consultant, former federal agency administrator*
Livingston-MacIrelan, Joan Persilla *artist*
Lloyd, Gwendolyn Monica *mathematics educator*
Lober, Irene Moss *educational consultant*
Lockhart, Julie A. *actor, consultant*
Lockhart, Sharon *artist*
Locklear, Heather *actress*
Locklear, Tina Michelle *science educator*
Locklin, Muriel Lucie *artist*
Lockney, Julianna Colleen *music educator*
Lockwood, Thelma Shirley *retired social worker*
Loeb, Debora Denise *music educator, vocalist, conductor*
Loewenstein, Lenore Cecile *retired school librarian*
Loewenthal, Nessa Parker *intercultural communications consultant*
Lofaro, Nanette *information services administrator*
Loftus, Kay Douglas Colgan *social worker*
Logstrom, Bridget A. *lawyer*
Loikkanen, Pirjo Tuulikki *music educator*
Loken, Barbara *marketing educator, social psychologist*
Lokmer, Stephanie Ann *international business development consultant*
Lombard, Marjorie Ann *financial officer*
Lombardi, Mary Luciana *musician, historian*
Lonchyna-Lisowsky, Maria *music educator*
Long, Elaine *writer, editor*
Long, Lisa Valk *communications company executive*
Long, Susie Ann *special education educator, consultant, writer*
Longaberger, Tami *home decor accessories company executive*
Longden, Claire Suzanne *retired financial planner, investment advisor*
Longman, Karen A. *higher education administrator*
Longobardo, Anna Kazanjian *engineering executive*
Longstreet, Wilma S. *retired education educator*
Longstreth-Brown, Kathryn *retired museum administrator*
Lonstein, Shoshanna *fashion designer*
Loomis, Janice Kaszczuk *artist*
Loop, Christine E. *elementary school educator*
Lopez, Annie Marie *artist*
Lopez, Jennifer *actress, singer, dancer*
Lopez, Patricia Nell *minister, educator*
Lopez, Soledad *actress*
Lopez Lysne, Robin *counselor, writer, artist*
Lopez-Munoz, Maria Rosa P. *real estate development company executive*
Lopo, Diana M. *lawyer*
Loredo, Doriselda *elementary school educator*
Lorelli, Elvira Mae *artist, art educator*
Loring, Gloria Jean *vocalist*
LoSchiavo, Francesca *set designer*
Lotas, Judith Patton *advertising executive*
Lotchin, Phyllis Morris *English language educator*
Loughlin, Ann Ursula *professional golfer, educator*
Love, Beverly Anne *retired elementary school educator*
Love, Courtney *singer, actress*
Love, Margaret Marks *business owner*
Love, Shirley Belle *psychotherapist*
Lovelace, Julianne *former library director*
Lovelace, Rose Marie Sniegon *federal space agency administrator*
Loveless, Patty (Patty Ramey) *country music singer*
Lovell, Michelle Paulette *physician's associate*
Loveman, Aurelia Leffler *psychologist, writer*
Lovett, Clara Maria *retired academic administrator, retired historian*
Lovick, Norma McGinnis *social studies educator*
Lovisone, Sylvia Ruth *lawyer*
Lovvorn, Audrey Marie *mental health therapist*
Low, Louise O. *volunteer*
Lowe, Carol Hill *social services director, management consultant*
Lowe, Patricia A. *psychologist, educator*
Lowe, Patricia McLaughlin *real estate company executive*
Lowell, Virginia Lee *retired librarian*
Lowenberg, Georgina Grace *retired elementary school educator*
Lowenthal, Constance *art historian, consultant*
Lower, Wendy Morgan *historian, educator*
Lowrie, Kathryn Yanacek *special education educator*
Lowry, Linda Eleanor *artist, educator*
Lowry, Marilyn Jean *horticultural retail company executive*
Loyd, Pamela Ann *academic administrator, educator*
Lozito, Lisa Carol *music educator, church musician*
Lu, May *psychologist, counselor, writer, watercolorist*
Luban, Naomi L. C. *hematologist*
Lubell, Ellen *writer*
Lubic, Ruth Watson *health facility administrator, nurse midwife*
Lucas, Karen Williams *controller*
Lucas, Michele Angelyn *learning consultant, special education educator*
Lucas, Teri Kathleen *elementary school educator*
Luce, Priscilla Mark *public relations executive*
Lucero, Anne *critical care nurse*
Luciano, Cara *mental health services professional*
Luciano, Roselle Patricia *advertising executive, editor*
Luckey, Doris Waring *civic volunteer*
Luckey, Norma Jean *music educator*
Luddy, Paula Scott *nursing educator*
Luderitz, Pamela Ann *secondary school educator*
Luebbe-Kemen, Kathy *music educator*
Luebke, Elizabeth Anne Silva *elementary school educator*
Lufkin, Martha B.G. *lawyer, legal writer, art law correspondent*
Luft, Cecile E. *music educator*
Lufty, JoyBeth *minister*
Luhrs, Caro Elise *internal medicine physician, administrator, educator*
Lukomsky, Vera *musicologist, music educator, pianist*
Lum, Viola Doris *music educator, personal financial analyst*
Lund, Rita Pollard *aerospace engineer, consultant*
Lundeen, Marga Laird *art educator*
Lustyk, Mary Kathleen *neuroscientist, educator*
Luttrell, Georgia Bena *musician*
Lyall, Katharine Culbert *former academic administrator, economist, educator*
Lynaugh, Barbara *judge*
Lynch, Charlotte Andrews *retired communications executive, consultant*
Lynch, Jessica *military officer*
Lynch, Patricia Gates *broadcast executive, consultant, ambassador*
Lynch-Stempfer, Tara Kathleen *physical therapist*
Lynds, Gayle Hallenbeck *writer*
Lyne, Dorothy-Arden *secondary school educator*
Lynn, Julia Carolyn *school nurse practitioner*
Lynn, Naomi B. *academic administrator*
Lynton, Sandra M. *psychologist*
Lyon, Barbara Kennedy *retired editor*
Lyon, Martha Sue *research engineer, retired military officer*
Lyons, Gloria Rogers *medical/surgical nurse, nursing educator*
Lyons, Natalie Beller *family counselor*
Lyshak-Stelzer, Frances *artist*
Maarbjerg, Mary Penzold *retired office equipment company executive*
MacCallum, Lorene (Edythe MacCallum) *pharmacist*
MacCarthy, Talbot Leland *civic volunteer*
MacCormack, Jean F. *academic administrator*
MacDowell, Andie (Rose Anderson MacDowell) *actress*
MacFarlane, Barbara Ann *secondary school educator*
Mack, Cheryl A. *principal*
Mackenzie, Sue *music educator, theater director*
Mackert, Rita Marie *elementary school educator*
MacKinnon, Nancy Williams *retired educator, state legislator*
Maclean, Rhonda *information technology executive*
MacLennan, Beryce Winifred *psychologist*
MacLeod, Normajean *writer*
Macpherson, Elle *model*
MacPherson, Shirley *clinical therapist*
MacWilliam, Barb *science educator*
Madariaga, Lourdes Mercedes *accountant*
Maddalena, Rosalie Anne *retired educator*
Madden, Glenda Gail *sales professional*
Maddock, Diana Gail *visual artist, educator*
Madejski, Rose Mary *pharmacist, educator*
Madison, Anne Conway *marketing professional, public relations professional*
Madison, Deborah Leafy *writer, chef*
Madison, Rachel Christine *science educator*
Madonna, (Madonna Louise Veronica Ciccone) *singer, actress, producer*
Madore, Teresa Sharon *secondary school educator*
Madsen, Virginia *actress*
Mady, Beatrice M. *artist*
Maeda, J. A. *data processing executive, consultant*
Maffia, Roma *actress*
Magana, Melanie G *psychologist, consultant*
Magee, Megan *elementary school educator*
Maglio, Gesomina V. *clinical social worker*
Magner, Marjorie *former bank executive*
Magoon, Nancy Amelia *art association administrator*
Maguire, Deirdre *federal community development management analyst*
Maher, Francesca Marciniak *lawyer, former air transportation executive*
Maher, Jan Colleen *writer, educator*
Maher, Lisa Krug *editor*
Mahmud, Shireen Dianne *photographer*
Mainella, Cindy L. *artist, researcher*
Mainella, Fran (Frances P. Mainella) *former federal agency administrator*
Mainor, Debra L. *elementary school educator*
Mains, Susan Jane *mathematics educator*
Mainwaring, Susan Adams *recreational facility executive*
Maio, Elsie Regina *communications consultant*
Maisner, Suzanne *technology consultant, educator*
Maitoza, Colleen *professional sports team executive*
Makepeace, Mary Lou *foundation administrator, former mayor*
Malberg, Melissa Dawn *music educator, dancer*
Maliff, Lori Christine *elementary school educator*
Malik, Josie M. Meza *psychologist*
Mallo-Garrido, Josephine Ann *advertising executive*
Mallory, Joan Matey *music educator, composer*
Malm, Mia *actress*
Malone, Claudine Berkeley *management consultant*
Malone, Nancy J. *librarian*
Maloney, Elizabeth Mary *mental health nurse, psychiatric health nurse*
Maloney, Therese Adele *insurance company executive*
Malouf, Pamela Bonnie *film editor, video editor*
Malvre, Maili *artist, educator, secondary school educator*
Manasc, Vivian *architect, consultant*
Manasse, Arlynn H. *pediatric nurse practitioner*
Mancini, Lorraine *science educator*
Mandel, Adrienne Abramson *state legislator*
Mandell, Gail Patricia *language educator*
Mandravelis, Patricia Jean *retired healthcare administrator*
Maneker, Roberta S(ue) *public relations executive*
Manglona, Ramona V. *judge, former attorney general*
Mangold, Sylvia Plimack *artist*
Manion, Bonnie J. *volunteer, poet, composer*
Manis, Laura Glance *retired psychology educator*
Manley, Joan A(dele) Daniels *retired publishing executive*
Manley, Judith L. *director*
Mann, Emily Betsy *writer, artistic director, theater director*
Mann, Joan Ellona *artist, editor*
Mann, Mary Anneeta *author*
Mann, Sally *photographer*
Mann-Bondat, Lydia Rachel *writer, researcher*
Manner, Jennifer Fouse *social worker*
Mannes, Elena Sabin *film and television producer, television director*
Manning, Janice *editor, writer*
Manning, Joan Elizabeth *health association administrator*
Manning, Nancy Christine *retired elementary school educator*
Manno, Rita *state agency administrator*
Mansfield, Lois Edna *mathematics professor, researcher*
Mantei, Lorraine E. *school system administrator*
Manuelian, Lucy Der *art historian, architecture educator*
Manville, Greta Craig *writer*
Maplesden, Carol Harper *marriage and family therapist, music educator*
Marcdante, Karen Jean *medical educator*
Marceau, Yvonne *ballroom dancer, educator*
March, Kathleen Patricia *judge*
Marchuk, Pamela Ann *retired elementary school educator*
Marcinek, Margaret Ann *nursing education administrator*
Marco, Patricia Louise *music educator*
Marcoux, Julia A. *midwife*
Marcus, Kelly Stein *psychologist, health science association administrator*
Marée, Kathleen Nancy *retired language educator*
Marenoff, Susan *professional athletics manager*
Marez, Trinnie Marie *marketing professional*
Margolis, Susan Ellen *psychiatric clinical nurse specialist, artist*
Margrave, Kathy Christine *nurse anesthetist*
Margules, Cecelia *composer, poet*
Mari, Dawn *composer, artist*
Marie, Shanti *artist*
Marino, Deirdre J. *science educator*
Marion, Marjorie Anne *English language educator, educational consultant*
Maris, Beth *clinical social worker, sex therapist*
Marisol, (Marisol Escobar) *sculptor*
Mark, Hon Fong Louie *cytogeneticist*
Mark, Judi *actress, choreographer*
Mark, Mary Ellen *photographer*
Marker, Rhonda Joyce *librarian*
Markle, Cheri Virginia Cummins *nurse*
Marko, Marlene *psychiatrist*
Markovich, Alexandria *assistant principal*
Markowitz, Phyllis Frances *retired mental health services professional, retired psychologist*
Marks, Martha Alford *writer*
Marks, Roberta Barbara *artist, educator*
Marks, Veronique *art educator*
Marlar, Janet Cummings *retired public relations officer*
Marlow, Marcia Marie *secondary school educator, publishing executive*
Marlowe, Willie *artist, fine arts educator*
Marmer, Nancy *editor*
Maroney, Jane Perkins *former state legislator, consultant*
Maroni, Donna Farolino *biologist, researcher*
Marotta, Gina *athletic trainer*
Marquand, Barbara K. *freelance writer*
Marquand, Jean MacMurtry *educational association administrator*
Marquis, Harriet Hill *social worker*
Marr, Carmel Carrington *retired state official*
Marrolli, Karen Lyn *conductor*
Mars, Cheri Higdon *science educator*
Marsee, Susanne Irene *vocalist*
Marsh, Frances Emily Francis *state agency administrator, set designer*
Marsh, Joan Knight *educational film company executive, video company executive, computer company executive, publishing executive*
Marsh, Lynn *elementary school educator*
Marsh, Merrilyn Delano *sculptor, artist, painter*
Marshall, Beverly Forrest *writer*
Marshall, Julie W. Gregovich *investor relations executive*
Marshall, Kathryn Sue *lawyer*
Marte-Bautista, Helen I. *retired performing arts educator*
Marth, Mary Ellen (Kim Martin) *entertainer*
Martin, Alice Howze *prosecutor*
Martin, Andrea Louise *actress, comedienne, writer*
Martin, Carolyn Stewart *retired school system administrator*
Martin, Christy *communications executive*
Martin, Colleen E. *nurse*
Martin, Dale *health facility administrator*
Martin, Helen Loene *minister*
Martin, Jean H. *retired interior designer*
Martin, Jeanine Kay *retired elementary school educator*
Martin, Kryssi Wyckoff *playwright, educator*
Martin, Lynn Morley *former secretary of labor*
Martin, Marcia D. *science educator*
Martin, Mariela *secondary school educator*
Martin, Marilyn Mann *retired media specialist*
Martin, Paula S. *principal*
Martin, Renee Cohen *forensic document examiner, author, expert witness*
Martin, Trisa *education and human development educator*
Martinez, Joanne O. *corporate executive*
Martinez, Veronica *special education educator*
Martin-Lowry, Beverly Anne *writer, columnist*
Martino, Cheryl Derby *insurance company executive*
Martyl, (Mrs. Alexander Langsdorf Jr.) *artist*
Martyn, Evi *music educator, musician*
Martz, Judy Helen *former governor*
Maruoka, Jo Ann Elizabeth *retired information systems manager*
Marvin, D. Jane *consumer products company executive*
Marvin, Freda Mary *art educator, nurse*
Marvin, Laura Lynn *art educator*
Mascheroni, Eleanor Earle *marketing communications executive*
Masi, Julia A. *elementary school educator*
Masiello, Lisa Anne *elementary school educator*
Mason, Connie Jeanne *writer*
Mason, Emily *painter*
Mason, Johanna Hendrika Anneke *retired secondary school educator*
Mason, Lois E. (J. Day Mason) *painter, poet, actress, educator*
Mason, Margaret Crather *elementary school educator*
Mason, Marsha *actress, theater director, writer*
Mason, Sara Smith *healthcare consultant*
Massagli, Jennifer Ann *science educator*
Massé, Michelle A. *language educator*
Masten, Jacqueline Gwendolyn *small business owner*
Masters, Ann Browning *education educator, poet*
Mastrian Bell, Samantha *music educator, vocalist*
Mata, Linda Sue Proctor *writer, consultant*
Matasar, Ann B. *retired dean, finance educator*
Matchette, Phyllis Lee *editor*
Mater, Maud *lawyer*
Matera, Frances Lorine *elementary school educator*
Materia, Kathleen Patricia Ayling *nurse*
Mates, Susan Onthank *physician, educator, musician, writer*
Mathews, E. Anne Jones *retired library educator, academic administrator*
Mathews, Jean Ann H. *political science educator*
Mathews, Mary Kathryn *retired government official*
Mathews-Mathena, Jennifer Kay *elementary school educator*
Mathias, Sharon A *secondary school educator*
Mathieu, Michele Suzanne *grant writer, computer scientist, consultant*
Matlin, Marlee *actress*
Matsa, Loula Zacharoula *social services administrator, educator*
Matson, Frances Shober *retired social worker*
Matterson, Joan McDevitt *physical therapist*
Matthew, Lyn *sales executive, consultant, marketing professional*
Matthews, Barbara Caridad *lawyer*
Matthews, Karen Sue *music educator*
Mattos Grell, Elizabeth *artist*
Mattrella, Anne Laura *secondary school educator*
Matyas, Cindy Susanne *psychologist, educator*
Matzkin, Elizabeth *orthopedic sports medicine surgeon*
Maurer, Marsha Kurs *art educator*
Maxfield, Brooke Davis *mathematics educator*
Maxfield, Louisa Fonda Gribble *executive secretary*
Maximciuc, Deborah Jean *special education educator*
Maxwell, Maureen Kay *media specialist, educator*
Maxwell, Ruth Elaine *artist, interior designer, painter*
May, Elaine *actress, film director, theater director*
May, Janet Sue *playwright, lyricist*
May, Phyllis Jean *financial executive*
Mayer, Anne Brestel *music educator*
Mayer, Kay Magnor *writer*
Mayer, Kristine I. *psychotherapist, writer*
Mayer, Susan Lee *nurse, educator*
Mayer, Susan Martin *art educator*
Mayes, Ila Laverne *minister*
Mayhugh, Tiffany *science educator*
Maynard, Mendy J. *secondary school educator*
Maynard, Natalie Ryshna *pianist, educator*
Mazzarelli, Debra Jean *real estate broker*
Mbadugha, Loretta Nkeiruka Akosa *social services administrator, consultant*
McAllister, Singleton Beryl *lawyer*
McAmis, Angie M. *elementary school educator*
McAteer, Deborah Grace *travel company executive*
McAuliffe, Maureen *science educator*
McBride, Mildred Maylea *retired elementary school educator*
McBride, Paula Brewer *chemistry educator, dean*
McBride, Sandra Teague *psychiatric nurse*
McCabe, Linda Jean *elementary school educator*
McCaffrey, Cindy *information technology executive*
McCain, Debbie M. *elementary school educator*
Mc Cain, Elizabeth Jean *elementary school educator*
McCall, Susan Elizabeth *small business owner*
McCalla, Sandra Ann *principal*
McCalley, Barbara Vaglia Dougherty *secondary school educator*
McCallion, Anne Dewey *finance executive, accountant*
McCandless, Carolyn Keller *retired human resources specialist*
Mc Cann, Cecile Nelken *writer, artist*
McCann, Diana Rae *secondary school educator*
McCann, Elizabeth Ireland *theater producer, television producer, motion picture producer*
McCann, Joyce Jeannine *retired elementary school educator*
McCann, Margaret Ann *sister, educator*
McCardel, Connie Shirley *music educator*
McCarey, Wilma Ruth *retired lawyer*
McCargar, Eleanor Barker *artist*
McCarthy, Aimee Lamar *science educator*
McCarthy, Carole Sullivan *retired special education educator, consultant, educational evaluator*
McCarthy, Karen P. *former congresswoman, former state legislator*
McCarthy, Kelli P. *music educator*
McCarthy, Mary Elizabeth (Beth) Constance *conductor, music educator*
McCarthy, Nobu *actress, performing company executive, educator*
McCarty, Diane Mary *education educator*
McCaslin, Kathleen Denise *child abuse educator*
McCaughey Ross, Elizabeth P. (Betsy McCaughey) *former lieutenant governor*
McClain, Lena Alexandria *protective services official*
McClain, Sylvia Nancy (Nancy Jo Grimm) *voice educator, vocalist*
McClain, Theresa L. *language educator*
McClanahan, Kay Marie *government official, lawyer*
McClanahan, Rue (Eddi-Rue McClanahan) *actress*
McClellan, Carole Ann *retired school nurse*
Mc Clellan, Catharine *anthropologist, educator*
McClellan, LeAnne *music educator*
McClennen, Miriam J. *former state official*

McClinton, Dorothy Hardaway *retired finance educator*
McCloskey, Dixie May *retired medical/surgical nurse*
McCloy, Shirley *physical education educator*
McClure, Erin E. *music educator*
McClure, Evelyn Susan *historian, photographer*
McClurg, Patricia A. *minister*
McCombs, Kelly Fritz *dietician*
McConnell, Mary Joan *civilian military employee*
McCord, Rita Rae *elementary school educator*
McCormick, Donna Lynn *social worker*
McCormick, Molly *elementary school educator*
McCormick, Susan Konn *retired publishing executive*
McCosham, Joyce L. *secondary school educator*
McCourt, Lisa *writer*
McCoy, Debra Marlene Black *sales executive*
McCoy, Diann L. *information technology acquisition executive*
McCoy, Dorothy Eloise *writer, educator*
McCoy, Mary Ann *state official*
McCoy, Mary Jane *retired principal*
McCoy, Mary Nell *music educator*
McCoy, Patricia A. *retired clinical special educator, art and culture critic, writer*
McCracken, Ursula E. *museum director*
McCrea, Melissa Lauren *elementary school educator*
McCubbin, Susan Brubeck *lawyer, advertising executive*
McCuistion, Peg Orem *retired health facility administrator*
McCully, Emily Arnold *illustrator, writer*
McDaniel, Anna S. *language educator*
McDaniel, Sara Sherwood (Sally McDaniel) *trainer, consultant*
McDarrah, Gloria Schoffel *editor, writer*
McDermott, Agnes Charlene Senape *philosophy educator*
McDermott, Lucinda Mary *ecumenical minister, educator, psychologist, poet, philosopher*
McDonald, Arlys Lorraine *retired librarian*
Mc Donald, Shirley Peterson *social worker*
McDonald, Vivian *minister*
McDonald-Pochiba, Elizabeth J. *secondary school educator*
McDormand, Frances *actress*
McDowell, Elaine *retired federal government executive, educator*
McDowell, Elizabeth Mary *retired pathology educator*
McDunn, Adrienne *human behavior consultant*
McElhannon, Nettie Marie *retired orthopaedic nurse*
McElhatten, Betty Shreve *writer, illustrator*
McElligott, Ann Theresa *accountant*
McElligott, Carroll A.A. *writer, horse breeder, rancher*
McElrath, Ah Quon *academic administrator*
McElwee, Doris Ryan *psychotherapist*
McElwreath, Sally Chin *corporate communications executive*
McEntire, Reba Nell *musician, actress*
McEvoy, Lorraine Katherine *oncology nurse*
McFadden, Cynthia Ann Bellville *middle school educator*
McFadden, Rosemary Theresa *retired lawyer, financial services executive*
McFall, Catherine Gardner *poet, critic, educator*
McFate, Patricia Ann *foundation executive, science educator*
McGann, Lisa B. Napoli *language educator*
McGarry, Marcia *retired community service coordinator*
McGarvey, Virginia Claire Lancaster *volunteer*
McGill, Carla Ann *language educator*
McGinn, Mary Lyn *real estate company executive*
McGinnis, Marcy Ann *broadcast executive*
McGinnis, Susan Pauliene *music teacher*
McGinn Miller, Janet Scrivner *retired elementary school educator, writer*
McGowan, Rose *actress*
McGowan, Susan *gifted and talented educator*
McGrath, Anna Fields *retired librarian*
McGrath, Mary Helena *plastic surgeon, educator*
McGraw, Lavinia Morgan *retired retail executive*
McGraw, Susan Catherine *interior designer*
McGuinness, Nanette Michele Cooper *singer, voice educator, writer, translator*
McGurk, Catherine S. *insurance adjuster, paralegal*
McHoes, Ann McIver *academic administrator, computer engineer*
McHugh, Annette S. *artist, educator, playwright, writer*
McHugh, Maura *professional basketball coach*
McIntosh, Kelli Lee *physics educator*
McIntosh, Kelli Marie *elementary school educator*
McIntosh, Terrie Tuckett *lawyer*
McIntyre, Elizabeth Jones *retired multi-media specialist, educator*
McIntyre, Judy *social worker, state representative*
McIntyre, Linda M. *healthcare risk analyst*
McIntyre, Virgie M. *elementary school educator*
McIver, Beverly Jean *art educator, artist*
McKay, Renee *artist*
McKay, Susan Bogart *social worker, consultant, artist*
McKee, Betty Davis *English language educator*
McKeown, Mary Elizabeth *retired educational association administrator*
McKinley, Ellen Bacon *priest*
McKinney, Cara Lynn *music educator*
McLaine, Barbara Bishop *counselor assistant*
McLaughlin, Ellen McGehee *playwright, educator, actor*
McLaughlin, Goldie Carter *music educator*
McLaughlin, Jean Wallace *art director, artist*
McLean, Julianne Drew *concert pianist, educator*
McLean, Katherine *artist, photographer*
McLellan, A. Anne *Canadian government official*
McLendon, Susan Michelle *lawyer*
McMahon Mastroddi, Marcia A. *secondary school educator, artist, writer*
McMaster, Belle Miller *religious organization administrator*
McMaster, Juliet Sylvia *English language educator*
McMillan, Terry L. *writer, educator*
McMillen, Elizabeth Cashin *artist*
McMinn, Virginia Ann *human resources consulting company executive*
McMorrow, Mary Ann Grohwin *retired state supreme court justice*
McMullen, Jennifer Anne *secondary school educator*
McNally, Connie Benson *magazine editor, publisher, antiques dealer*
McNeely, Bonnie L. (K.W. Rowe Jr.) *retired internist*
McNees, Pat (Patricia Ann McNees) *writer, editor*
McNulty, Kathleen Anne *social worker, consultant, psychotherapist*
McNutt, Margaret H. Honaker *secondary school educator*
McPeters, Sharon Jenise *artist, writer*
McPhearson, Geraldine June *retired medical/surgical nurse*
McPherson, JoAnne Frances *art educator, artist, special education educator*
McPherson, Mary E. *social studies educator*
McPherson, Renee *meteorologist*
McQuarrie, Megan *science educator*
McTague-Stock, Nancy A. *painter, printmaker*
McTyer-Clarke, Wanda Kathleen *interior designer*
McVeigh-Pettigrew, Sharon Christine *communications consultant*
McVey, Alice Lloyd *social worker*
McWeeny, Jen *philosopher, educator*
McWethy, Patricia Joan *educational association administrator*
McWhinney, Deborah *finance company executive*
McWhorter, Diane *writer*
Meade, Patricia Sue *marketing professional*
Meaders, Nobuko Yoshizawa *psychotherapist*
Meadows, Gwendolyn Joann *retired behavioral disorders educator*
Meara, Anne *actress, playwright, writer*
Medaglia, Elizabeth Ellen *small business owner*
Mederich, Amy Marie *social studies educator*
Medina, Janie *not-for-profit fundraiser*
Medina, Kathryn Bach *book editor*
Medina, Sandra *social worker, educator*
Medina-Hamilton, Ginny Evelyn *music educator*
Medwick, Debra Lou *special education services professional*
Meehan, Lil Euphrasia Therese *poet*
Meek, Amy Gertrude *retired elementary school educator*
Meek, Carrie P. *former congresswoman*
Meek, Carroll Lee Larson *psychologist, graphic designer*
Meers, Theresa Mary *nursing educator, science educator*
Mehltretter, Kathleen M. *former prosecutor*
Mehring, Nancy *medical/surgical nurse, administrator*
Meier, Enge *pre-school educator*
Meilan, Celia *food products executive*
Meis, Nancy Ruth *marketing executive*
Meit, Heather Tonia *psychologist*
Melamed, Carol Drescher *lawyer*
Melanson, Susan Chapman *small business owner*
Mele, Joanne Theresa *dentist*
Melicia, Kitty *human resources administrator, foundation administrator*
Melton, Amanda Louise *science educator*
Melton, Emma Alexander *educational consultant, retired elementary school educator*
Melton, Nancy Kerley *medical, surgical, and oncological nurse*
Melton, Stephanie Ann *music educator*
Meltzer, E. Alyne *elementary school educator, social worker, volunteer*
Menck, J Claire *chef, consultant*
Menconi, Marguerite L. *customer service logistics*
Mende, Maggie Sarah *elementary school educator*
Mendelsohn, Carol S. *television producer*
Mendelson, Joan Rintel *lawyer*
Mendon, Karen Jeanette *elementary school educator*
Mendoza, Karen Lynn *special education educator*
Menefee, Linnea-Norma *antique dealer*
Menlove, Frances Lee *psychologist*
Menna, Sári *artist, educator*
Menzel, Idina *actress, singer*
Menzel, Marybelle Proctor *volunteer*
Mercado, Mary Gonzales *cardiologist*
Mercer, Dorothy May *real estate company executive*
Mercer, Frances deCourcy *artist, educator*
Mercuri, Joan B. *museum administrator*
Mermelstein, Paula *broadcasting executive*
Merrill, Jean Fairbanks *writer*
Merritt, Nancy-Jo *lawyer*
Merritt, Susan Mary *computer science educator, dean*
Merriweather, Freda E. *education educator*
Merszei, Aimée Mörner *not-for-profit fundraiser*
Meserve, Marilyn Moses *retired pediatrician*
Mesrobian, Arpena Sachaklian *publishing executive, consultant, editor*
Mesrop, Alida Yolande *academic administrator*
Messé, Madelyn Renée *clinical psychologist, consultant*
Messerle, Judith Rose *retired medical librarian, retired public relations executive*
Messerly, Jennifer *science educator*
Mestel, Sherry Y. *social worker, school psychologist, art therapist*
Metcalf, Karen *retired foundation executive*
Metcalf, Pauline Cabot *architectural historian*
Metcalf, Susan Stimmel *community volunteer*
Metoyer, Pamela Paradis *scientific editor, writer*
Metz, Patricia A. *retired bank executive*
Metzler, Ruth Horton *genealogical educator*
Meyer, Carol Frances *retired pediatrician, allergist*
Meyer, Frances Margaret Anthony *educational consultant*
Meyer, Paula Jean *music educator*
Meyer, Pucci *editor*
Meyer, Rachel Abijah *foundation administrator, artist, poet*
Meyer, Ruth Krueger *museum director, educator, art historian*
Meyer, Ursula *retired library director*
Meyerink, Victoria Paige *film producer, actress*
Meyers, Elsie Flint *anesthesiologist*
Meyers, Jan *retired congresswoman*
Meyers, May Lou *retired psychologist, educational consultant*
Mezacapa, Edna S. *music educator, elementary school educator*
Michael, Jean *mathematics educator*
Michaelis, Gabrielle deMonceau *mathematics professor*
Michaels, Marion Cecelia *newswriter, editor, news syndicate executive*
Michalek, Tina A. *social studies educator*
Michel, Elizabeth Cheney *social reform consultant*
Michels, Mary Pat *music educator*
Mickelson, Rhoda Ann *speech pathology/audiology services professional*
Midler, Bette *singer, entertainer, actress*
Miekka, Jeanette Ann *retired science educator*
Miesle, Angela Denise *elementary school educator*
Miiller, Susan Diane *artist*
Mikiewicz, Anna Daniella *marketing and international business export manager*
Miksis, Christina Barbara *psychologist*
Milam, Melissa Gail *elementary school educator*
Milana Panopoulos, Maria *artist*
Milano, Alyssa *actress*
Milbourne, Melinda D. *elementary school educator, researcher*
Miles, Laveda Ann *advertising executive*
Miles, Mary Ellen *retired human resources specialist*
Milewski, Barbara Anne *pediatrics nurse, neonatal/perinatal nurse practitioner, critical care nurse*
Millane, Lynn *retired municipal official*
Miller, Angela *art educator*
Miller, Angela D. *secondary school educator*
Miller, Ann Clinton *communications educator*
Miller, Carolyn *secondary education educator, composer*
Miller, Cheryl DeAnn *former professional basketball coach, broadcaster*
Miller, Darcy M. *publishing executive*
Miller, Diane Faye *art education educator, business owner*
Miller, Ellen S. *marketing executive*
Miller, Eunice A. *marriage and family therapist, sex therapist, foundation administrator*
Miller, Geraldine *clinical psychologist*
Miller, Gwendolyn Doris *retired special education educator*
Miller, Jacqueline Winslow *library director*
Miller, Jenefer Ardell *elementary school educator, choreographer*
Miller, Judith A. (Judy Miller) *retired journalist*
Miller, Lillian May *psychologist*
Miller, Linda H. *accountant*
Miller, Linda Karen *retired secondary school educator, social studies educator, law educator*
Miller, Lisa Ann *lawyer*
Miller, Marian *professional society administrator*
Miller, Marilyn Lea *library and information scientist, educator*
Miller, Monica Lisa *social studies educator*
Miller, Nidi R. *artist, sculptor, educator*
Miller, Patricia Hoffman *human services administrator, finance educator*
Miller, Patricia Louise *state legislator, nurse*
Miller, Roberta Ann *gastroenterology nurse*
Miller, Ruth Ann *artist*
Miller, Sonja Glaaser *counselor*
Miller-Dreusicke, Connie Anne *special education educator*
Millett, Kate (Katherine Murray Millett) *political activist, sculptor, artist, writer*
Millican, Frances Kennedy *psychiatrist*
Milligan, Krista *drafting educator*
Milligan, Margaret Erin *science educator*
Milligan, Sister Mary *theology studies educator, consultant*
Millman, Amy J. *government official*
Millman, Marilyn Estelle *elementary school educator*
Mills, Celeste Louise *occupational therapist*
Mills, Dale Douglas *journalist*
Mills, Elizabeth Shown *historical writer, genealogist*
Mills, Gloria Adams *energy executive, consultant*
Mills, Helene Audrey *retired education educator*
Mills, Inga-Britta *artist*
Mills, Jean D. *education educator*
Mills, Melanie Marie *elementary school educator*
Millstein, Roberta L. *humanities educator*
Milner, Beverly Jane *retired medical/surgical nurse*
Milner, Joan W. *retired elementary school educator*
Milnor, Hazel *nurse*
Mims, Clarice Roberta *financial advisor*
Minahan, Janice Terry *science educator*
Minco, Debra Thompson *chemistry educator*
Mindt, Michele L.M. *music educator*
Ming, Jenny J. *former retail executive*
Ming-Na, *actress*
Mingus, Cherie Lynn *home economics educator*
Mingus, Lois Kagan *actor, dancer, singer, choreographer, playwright*
Minor, Addine E. *civic leader*
Mintz, Gwendolyn Joyce *writer, actress, comedian*
Mintz, Susan Ashinoff *apparel manufacturing company executive*
Miracle, Doris Jean *retired medical/surgical nurse*
Miranda-Morgart, Lynda Christine *elementary school educator*
Mirk, Judy Ann *retired elementary school educator*
Miscella, Maria Diana *humanities educator*
Miskill, Dee Shelton *graphics designer*
Miskimen, Theresa Marie *psychiatrist, educator*
Misner, Charlotte Blanche Ruckman *retired community organization administrator*
Misrack, Tana Marie *counselor, minister, writer*
Missele, Brenda Marie *secondary school educator*
Mitchard, Jacquelyn *writer*
Mitchell, Ada Mae Boyd *legal assistant*
Mitchell, Brenda Marie *humanities educator*
Mitchell, Carol Ann *nursing educator*
Mitchell, Carolyn Cochran *administrative assistant*
Mitchell, Kathleen *medical/surgical and geriatrics nurse*
Mitchell, M. Yvonne *paraprofessional*
Mitchell, Madeleine Enid *retired nutritionist*
Mitchell, Margaret Yvonne *forester*
Mitchell, Pamela Ann *airline pilot*
Mitchem, Cheryl E. *accounting educator*
Mittleider, Rebecca Ann *elementary school educator*
Mitty, Lizbeth *artist*
Mitzel, Brenda Renee *mathematics educator*
Mlay, Marian *retired government official*
Mockler, Anna *writer, ecologist*
Mockler, Jennifer Lynn *psychologist, education educator*
Moen, Margaret *editor*
Moevs, Maria Teresa Marabini *archaeologist*
Moffat, MaryBeth *consulting company executive*
Moffatt, Joyce Anne *performing company executive*
Moffatt, Katy (Katherine Louella Moffatt) *musician, lyricist, vocalist*
Mogy, Catherine Waddell *critical care nurse*
Mohr, Barbara Jeanne *elementary school educator*
Moistner, Mona Sue *adult education educator*
Molden, A(nna) Jane *counselor*
Molinari, Ana Maria *salon owner*
Molinari, Carol V. *writer, investment company executive, educator*
Molloy, Sylvia *language educator*
Molnar, Mary Anne *retired secondary school educator, consultant*
Molyneaux, Dorothy Munz *retired education educator, retired speech pathology/audiology services professional*
Molz, Redmond Kathleen *public affairs educator*
Monczewski, Maureen R. *art educator, visual artist*
Mongeon, Louise Bernadette *school nurse*
Mongiello, Christine *music educator*
Monheiser, Cheryl Ann *retired elementary school educator*
Montealegre, Eva Denise *artist, writer*
Monteilh, Yvette Marie *education educator*
Monteith, Tracy R. *music educator, lay worker*
Montgomery, Carolyn Williams *retired secondary school educator*
Montgomery, June C. *musician, composer*
Montgomery, Lani Lynn *art educator*
Montuori, Dona F. *retired elementary school educator*
Monzingo, Agnes Yvonne *veterinary technician*
Mood, Rosalyn Thomas *assistant principal*
Moody, Marilyn Dallas *retired librarian*
Moon, Gabrielle Marie *biology educator*
Moon, Jane Anderson *systems engineer, consultant*
Moon, Karen Robin *science educator*
Moon, Loretta Marie *recreational therapist*
Moon, Rose Ann *elementary school educator*
Moore, Alma Donst *writer, lyricist*
Moore, Betty Jo *legal assistant*
Moore, Beverly Ann *retired librarian*
Moore, Deana Daiello *art educator*
Moore, Erin M. *social studies educator*
Moore, Fay Linda *systems engineer*
Moore, Jean E. *social worker, academic administrator, educator, radio personality*
Moore, Juel Ann *retired elementary school educator*
Moore, Julia Gibert *retired educational administrator, priest*
Moore, Julie L. *bibliographer, librarian*
Moore, Marsha Lynn *retired elementary school educator, counseling administrator*
Moore, Mildred Thorpe *dietician*
Moore, Rosemary Kuulei *art gallery owner*
Moore, Ruth Johnston *retired medical center official*
Moore, Shanna La'Von *chemical company executive*
Moore, Wanda Sue *surgical nurse*
Moore-Wleklinski, Patricia Marie *secondary school educator*
Moorhead, Lucy Galpin *writer*
Moorhouse, Robbi Presswood *elementary school educator*
Mora, Maria *elementary school educator*
Mora, Pat *writer, speech professional*
Morales, Diane K. *former federal agency administrator*
Morales, Marcia Paulette Merry *language educator, archaeologist*
Moran, Sheila Kathleen *journalist*
Morang, Diane Judy *writer, television producer, entrepreneur*
Morelan, Paula Kay *choreographer*
Moreno, Jeanne Simonne *cardiac nurse*
Morey, Sharon Lynn *psychotherapist, mediator*
Morgan, Ann M. *artist, educator*
Morgan, Anne Marie G. *broadcast journalist, educator*
Morgan, Donna Jean *psychotherapist*
Morgan, Ellen Louise *elementary school educator*
Morgan, Evelyn Buck *retired nursing educator*
Morgan, Jane Hale *retired library director*
Morgan, Linda Gail *theater producer*
Morgan, Lynn *sports association executive*
Morgan, M. Jane *computer systems consultant*
Morgan, Marlene *education educator, consultant*
Morgan, Mary Lou *retired education educator, volunteer*
Morgan, Nicole Rae *theater director, educator*
Morgan, Patricia *financial consultant, former Republican party chairman*
Morgan, Robin Evonne *poet, writer, journalist, editor*
Morgan, Ruth Prouse *academic administrator, educator*
Morgan, Timi Sue *lawyer*
Mori, Mariko *artist*
Morin-Miller, Carmen Aline *writer*
Morissette, Alanis Nadine *singer*
Morphew, Dorothy Richards-Bassett *artist, real estate broker*
Morrill, Penny Chittim *art historian*
Morris, Greta N. *former ambassador*
Morris, Harriet R. *elementary school educator*
Morris, Holly *elementary school educator*
Morris, Laura *elementary school educator*
Morris, Lissa Camille *music educator*
Morris, Martha Marnel *music educator*
Morris, Maureen Sauter *banker*
Morris, Peggy Ann *elementary school educator, mathematics educator*
Morris, Sheila J. *elementary school educator*
Morris, Tammy Kay *bank executive*
Morrison, Amy Michele *secondary school educator*

Morrison, Margaret L. *artist, educator, consultant*
Morrison, Mary F. *psychiatrist, researcher*
Morrison, Nancy Jane *art educator*
Morrison, Sarah Lyddon *author*
Morrison, Shelley *actress*
Morrison, Toni (Chloe Anthony Wofford) *writer, educator, editor*
Morris-Robinson, Dorothy Kay *writer*
Morris-Wong, Beth *school librarian, educator*
Morrow, Susan Brind *writer*
Morse, Anne Bernadette *retired educational consultant*
Morse, Gayle Skawennio *psychologist, consultant*
Morse, Terri Fraser *mechanical engineer*
Morse-McNeely, Patricia *poet, writer, retired secondary school educator*
Mortensen-Say, Marlys *retired school system administrator*
Mortenson, Janice Gayle Mills *business owner, accountant*
Moseley, Carol June *security supervisor, small business owner*
Moseley, Julia W. *music educator, preservationist*
Mosely, Elaine W. *school librarian*
Moses, Sheila Johnson *nurse, bookkeeper*
Moses, Shelia P. *writer, poet, playwright, producer*
Moskovitz, Elisa McMillan *music educator, musician*
Moslak, Judith *retired music educator*
Mosquera, Zoila Bianca *social worker*
Moss, Lynda Bourque *museum director*
Moss, Susan *nurse, small business owner*
Mott, Mary Elizabeth *retired computer educator*
Motzkin, Judith E. *artist*
Moudy, Linda Ann *elementary school educator*
Mouledous, Pierrette Marie *music educator*
Moules, Deborah Ann *not-for-profit developer*
Mouttet, Jane Elizabeth *school librarian, educator*
Mowrer-Reynolds, Elizabeth Louise *educational psychology educator*
Moy, Audrey *retired retail buyer*
Moye, Alana Nicole *pre-school educator*
Moyers, Kelli R. *psychotherapist*
Moynahan, Karen Peeler *performing arts association administrator*
Mramor, Marti *engineer, linguist*
Muehl, Lois Baker *writer, retired language educator*
Mueller, Anita LaVonne *special education educator*
Mueller, Barbara Stewart (Bobbie Mueller) *alcohol/drug abuse services professional, volunteer*
Mueller, Paula Deutsch *retired music educator*
Muhammad, Claudette Marie *religious organization administrator*
Muhammad, Gholnecsa Eushena *elementary school educator*
Muhammad, LaTonja Walker *control engineer*
Muhn, Judy Ann *psychologist, genealogist, trainer*
Muir, Patricia Allen *professional association administrator*
Muir, Patty K. *special education educator*
Mulhall, Kimberly A. *business manager*
Mull, Beth A. *counseling educator*
Muller, Frederica Daniela *psychology educator*
Mullette, Julienne Patricia *health facility administrator*
Mulligan, Erin Leah *lawyer*
Mullins, Barbara J. *financial executive*
Mullins, Jane Compton *investment manager*
Mulryan, Lenore Hoag *art curator, writer*
Mulvihill, Maureen Esther *writer, educator*
Mundell, Susan Belle *special education educator*
Mundorff Shrestha, Sheila Ann *dental educator*
Munguia, Gay Yeager *retired elementary school educator, retired secondary school educator*
Munn, Polly *retired elementary school educator*
Munoz, Cheryl Ann *portfolio manager*
Muñoz Dones De Carrascal, Eloisa (Eloise Munoz Dones) *hospital administrator, pediatrician, educator*
Munroe, Mary Lou Schwarz (Mrs. Robert E. Munroe) *educational administrator*
Munsell, Elsie Louise *retired lawyer*
Munsterman, Ingrid Anita *assistant principal*
Munt, Janet Staples *state senator*
Murakane, Charleen *elementary school educator*
Murdock, Pamela Ervilla *travel and advertising company executive*
Murphey, Sheila Ann *infectious diseases physician, educator, researcher*
Murphy, Brittany *actress*
Murphy, Elisabeth Maria *physical design engineer, consultant*
Murphy, Evelyn Frances *economist*
Murphy, Lisa M. *primary school educator*
Murphy, Madeleine *literature educator*
Murphy, Mary Leigh *artist*
Murphy, Michelle Zick *special education educator*
Murphy, Sandra Robison *lawyer*
Murphy, Thelma Arabella *elementary school educator, photographer*
Murray, Amanda Kay *elementary school educator*
Murray, Carla Mary *sound effects artist, artist*
Murray, Catherine Mary Murphy *retired accountant*
Murray, Julia Kaoru (Mrs. Joseph E. Murray) *occupational therapist*
Murray, Kay *lawyer*
Murrell, Monica Lynn *personal trainer*
Muskopf, Margaret Rose *elementary school educator*
Musser, Cherri M. *information technology executive*
Muszynska, Agnieszka (Agnes Muszynska) *mechanical engineering researcher, consultant*
Myers, Angela Michelle *music educator, department chairman*
Myers, Dorothy Roatz *artist*
Myers, Libby Ann *retired medical/surgical nurse*
Myers, Margaret Jane (Dee Dee Myers) *television personality, editor*
Myers, Michelle E. *education educator, consultant*
Myers, Sue Bartley *artist*
Myers, Toby Millicent *advocate*
Myllymaki, Melanie Kaye *operating room nurse*
Myrick, Tana Shey *medical/surgical nurse, educator*
Nabuda, Janice Ann *social studies educator*
Nagra, Parminder *actress*
Nagy, Elizabeth Garver *artist*
Nagys, Elizabeth Ann *environmental services administrator, educator*
Nance, Mary Joe *retired secondary school educator*
Nankervis, Medora B. *artist*
Napoli, Mary *education educator*
Narbit, Heather Alyce *not-for-profit developer, writer*
Nash, Linda Kay *music educator*
Nason, Dolores Irene *computer company executive, social welfare administrator, minister*
Natarajan, Uma *mathematician, educator*
Nathanson, Barbara A. *painter, artist*
Natividad, Lisalinda Salas *health facility administrator*
Natsuyama, Harriet Hatsune Kagiwada *mathematician, educator*
Naughton, Margaret Mary *elementary school educator*
Naulty, Susan Louise *archivist*
Naumer, Carola *art historian, educator*
Naviaux, LaRee DeVee *retired psychologist, academic administrator, director*
Navratilova, Martina *professional tennis player*
Neagoy, Monica Maria Martha *mathematician, consultant*
Neal, Marietha Mae *primary school educator*
Neal, Teresa Schreibeis *secondary school educator*
Neary, Patricia Elinor *ballet director*
Neblett, Carol *soprano*
Neel, Judy Murphy *management consultant*
Neeley, Kathleen Louise *librarian*
Neff, Diane Irene *university administrator*
Neff, Jennifer Ellen *painter, artist*
Neibert, Betsy Lyn *psychologist*
Nelligan, Kate (Patricia Colleen Nelligan) *actress*
Nelson, Alice Carlstedt *retired nursing educator*
Nelson, Carol Evelyn *retired pre-school educator*
Nelson, Cynthia J. *city official*
Nelson, Deborah D. *music educator*
Nelson, Debra J. *dancer, educator, choreographer*
Nelson, Doreen Kae *mental health counselor, educator, reserve military officer*
Nelson, JoAnn *secondary school educator, educational consultant*
Nelson, Kimberly Terese *computer software company executive, former federal agency administrator*
Nelson, Kirsten Cigler *language educator*
Nelson, Lauren Kathryn *education educator*
Nelson, Lois Nadine *retired special education educator*
Nelson, Martha Jane *magazine editor*
Nelson, Martine Levy *mathematics professor*
Nelson, Nancy Eleanor *pediatrician, educator*
Nelson, Sandra E. *information technology executive*
Nelson, Susan Joy *nurse*
Nemiroff, Maxine Celia *small business owner, art historian*
Nereng, Linda Rae *elementary school educator*
Neroni, Jane Kessler *art educator*
Nesbit, Lynn *literary agent*
Nesbit, Melanie Ann *athletic trainer*
Neshyba, Monica Vasquez *language educator*
Ness, Bernice Hagie *retired music educator*
Ness, Susan *federal official*
Neu, Jennifer Elizabeth *music educator*
Neuerburg-Denzer, Ursula *theater director, educator, actress*
Neufeld, Maureen Patricia *elementary school educator*
Neuman, Linda Kinney *retired state supreme court justice, lawyer*
Neumann, Irma Wanda *musician, educator*
Neumark, Gertrude Fanny *materials science educator*
Neurath, Rachel *mathematics educator*
Neuvel, Melissa *secondary school educator*
Neuwirth, Bebe (Beatrice Neuwirth) *dancer, actress*
Neville, Elizabeth Egan *artist, educator*
Neville, Phoebe *choreographer, dancer, educator*
Nevin, Laura Jean *music educator*
Nevins, Sheila *television producer*
Nevins, Tracy Anne *elementary school educator*
New, Rosetta Holbrook *retired secondary school educator, retired department chairman, retired nutrition consultant*
Newbery, Ilse Sofie Magdalene *German language educator*
Newburg, Anne Colby *writer*
Newbury, Kirsten Rae *computer scientist, educator*
Newcomb, Rachel *anthropologist, educator*
Newdigger, Carrie *secondary school educator*
Newell, Ann Marie *music educator*
Newell, Shirley Ann Cecil *retired art dealer, artist*
Newhall, Barbara Falconer *writer, journalist*
Newhall, Edith Allerton *writer*
Newman, Barbara Mae *retired special education educator*
Newman, Carol L. *lawyer*
Newman, Constance Berry *federal agency administrator*
Newman, Gwill Linderme *volunteer*
Newman, Joan Meskiel *lawyer*
Newman, Margaret Ann *nursing educator, department chairman*
Newman, Muriel Kallis Steinberg *art collector*
Newman, Rachel *editor*
Newman, Suzanne Dinkes *web site design company executive*
Newport, L. Joan *retired social worker*
Newton, Elizabeth Purcell *counselor, consultant, writer*
Newton, Juanita *social worker, educator*
Newton, Niles Rumely *psychologist, educator*
Ney, Rhonda G. *elementary school educator*
Neziri, Maria G. De Lucia *elementary school educator*
Ng, Ming T. *psychologist*
Nguyen, Christal *personal trainer*
Nguyen, Mai (Mai Tuyet Nguyen) *writer*
Nicholas, Lynn Holman *historian, researcher, writer*
Nichols, Cherie L. *composer*
Nichols, Christine Carolyn *science educator*
Nichols, Elizabeth Grace *nursing educator, dean*
Nichols, Iris Jean *retired illustrator*
Nicholson, June Constance Daniels *retired speech pathologist*
Nickel, Janet Marlene Milton *retired geriatrics nurse*
Nickles-Murray, Elizabeth *advertising executive, writer*
Nickols, Marcia Lynn *retired art educator*
Nicks, Stevie (Stephanie Lynn Nicks) *singer, songwriter*
Nicols, Angela C. *software engineer, consultant*
Nielsen, Linda Miller *councilman*
Nielson, Alyce Mae *poet*
Nieto, Sonia Mary *retired education educator*
Niffenegger, Audrey Anne *artist, writer*
Nighswonger, Linda *science educator*
Niguidula, Kathleen Ann *music educator, musician*
Niles, Barbara Elliott *psychoanalyst*
Nipper, Christina Joy *music educator*
Nix, Patricia *artist*
Nix, Patricia Perry *retired librarian*
Nix, Rachel Ann Hackmann *science educator*
Nix, Sharon J. *principal*
Nixon, Marni *singer*
Nnadi, Eucharia E. *academic administrator*
Noah, Julia Jeanine *retired librarian*
Nobert, Frances *music educator*
Nochman, Lois Wood Kivi (Mrs. Marvin Nochman) *retired literature educator*
Noddings, Nel *education educator, writer*
Noddings, Sarah Ellen *lawyer*
Noe, Elnora (Ellie Noe) *retired chemicals executive*
Noel, Cheryl Elaine *artist, poet*
Noëldechen, Joan Marguerite *writer*
Noeldner-Weniger, Lisa Ann *music educator*
Noffsinger, Nancy Leigh *special education educator*
Nolan, Joan T. *elementary school educator*
Nold, Aurora Ramirez *finance company executive*
Nolen, Jeanada H. *retired state agency administrator, social worker, educator*
Nolff, Susan D. *web site designer, small business owner*
Noll, Jeanne C. *retired music educator*
Noonan, Jacqueline Anne *pediatrician, educator*
Noonan, Susan Abert *public relations executive*
Norbeck, Jane S. *retired nursing educator*
Norflus, Fran *biology professor*
Norkin, Cynthia Clair *retired physical therapist*
Norman, E. Gladys *retired finance educator, management consultant*
Normann, Margaret Ella *deacon, educator*
Norris, Mackie Lyvonne Harper *registered nurse, health care consultant*
Northcutt, Ora Beatrice *author*
Northern, Ernestine *gifted and talented educator*
Northup, Marie L. *music educator*
Norton, Gale Ann *former secretary of the interior*
Norton, Karen Ann *accountant*
Notley, Thelma A. *retired librarian, educator*
Novak, Barbara *art history educator*
Novetzke, Sally Johnson *former ambassador*
Novik, Yelena *oncologist, hematologist*
Novotna, Jana *retired professional tennis player*
Nowak, Judith Ann *psychiatrist*
Nowell, Linda Gail *not-for-profit executive*
Noziglia, Carla Miller *forensic scientist*
Nubel, Marianne Kunz *cultural organization administrator, writer, composer*
Nunes, Winifred O. *minister, educator*
Nuss, Joanne Ruth *artist*
Nussbaumer, Melany Hamilton *program director*
Nye, Dorothy Mae *freelance journalist, educator*
Nye, Jeni Hiatt *music educator*
Oakes, Ellen Ruth *psychotherapist, health facility administrator*
Oakes-Hall, Nancy Anne *artist, ski instructor*
O'Baire-Kark, Marika *nurse, educator, poet, writer*
Obert, Mary Ellen Newton *retired internist*
Oblinger, Jessica Marie *health facility administrator*
O'Boyle, Maureen *television show host*
O'Brien, Amy V. *apparel designer*
O'Brien, K. Patricia *product development engineer*
O'Brien, Kathleen Anne *science educator*
O'Brien, Odessa Louise *protective services official*
O'Brien, Orin Ynez *musician, educator*
Occhiogrosso, Mallay Barclay *psychiatrist*
Ocheskey, Elizabeth R. Bloom *theater director, educator*
Ochsner, Carol M. *science educator*
O'Connor, Betty Lou *retired hotel executive, food service executive*
O'Connor, Catherine Marie *music educator*
O'Connor, Doris Julia *not-for-profit fundraiser, consultant*
O'Dell, Joan Elizabeth *lawyer, mediator, consumer products company executive, educator*
Odom, Judy *software company executive*
O'Donnell, Elizabeth D. *music educator*
O'Donnell, Kathleen C. *artist*
O'Donnell, Rosie *television personality, actress, comedienne*
O'Donnell Rich, Dorothy Juanita *small business owner*
O'Dowd, Sarah A. *lawyer*
Oerter, Cynthia Lynn *medical technologist*
Oesterlin, Lovye Gwendolyn *retired chemist, educator, retired educational consultant*
O'Farrill, Marline Stabile *director*
Ofstad, Evelyn Larsen Boyl *retired primary school educator, radio personality, film producer*
O'Garden, Irene *writer, actress*
Ogilvie, Tamara A. *rancher, elementary school educator*
Oglesby, Elaine Sue *elementary school educator*
Oh, Sandra *actress*
O'Hagan, Denise Marie *physical therapist, personal trainer*
O'Hara, Maureen (Maureen FitzSimons) *actress*
O'Hara, Sabine U. *academic administrator, dean, economist, educator*
O'Hare, Virginia Lewis *human resources administrator*
O'Keefe-Hardy, Lee Marilyn *psychotherapist*
Okolski, Cynthia Antonia *psychotherapist, social worker*
Okonedo, Sophie *actress*
Okoshi-Mukai, Sumiye *artist*
Okouchi, Carla Ho'noa Higdon *music educator*
Oksas, Joan Kay *economist, educator*
Oksiloff, Christa *technologist, educator*
Okun, Barbara Frank *psychologist, educator*
Olds, Jacqueline *psychiatrist, educator*
O'Leary, Kathleen Ann *nonfiction writer*
Olesen, Carolyn McDonald *dance educator, choreographer*
Olin, Lena Maria Jonna *actress*
Olivos, Claudia *artist, educator*
O'Loughlin, Katie Eileen Bridget *poet*
Olsen, Virginia *human services manager*
Olson, Margaret Smith *retired foundation administrator*
Olson, Paula Sue *director*
Olson-Arenz, Barbara D. *chemistry educator*
O'Neil, Carolyn *cable network executive, cable television host*
O'Neill, Judith Jones *insurance agent*
O'Neill, Margaret E. *psychological counselor*
O'Neill, Mary Jane *not-for-profit administrator, consultant*
O'Neill Wotanowski, Eileen Mary *special education educator*
Ord, Linda Banks *artist*
Oritsky, Mimi *artist, educator*
Orlin, Karen J. *lawyer*
Orlowska-Warren, Lenore Alexandria *art educator, fiber artist*
Ormai-Buza, Ildiko *soprano, composer, music educator*
Ormond, Julia *actress*
Ornt, Jeanine Arden *lawyer*
O'Rork, Aimée *music educator, composer*
Orozco, Edith Dell *counselor, special education counselor*
Orr, Amy J. *sociologist, educator*
Orsborn, Mary Kay *school librarian, educator*
Ortego, Gilda Baeza *library director, educator*
Ortiz, Mayra Zoe *psychologist*
Ortiz-Walters, Rowena *management educator*
Osborn, Janie Dyson *early childhood education educator*
O'Shea, Anna Belle Marie *music educator, liturgy administrator*
Oskin, JoEllen Ross *special education educator, school librarian*
Oslak, Megan Kathleen *elementary school educator*
Osmer-McQuade, Margaret *broadcast executive, journalist*
Osmond, Marie *singer*
Osowiec, Darlene Ann *clinical psychologist, educator, consultant*
Ossana, Diana Lynn *author, screenwriter*
Ossello, Kristie *music educator*
Ossenberg, Hella Svetlana *psychoanalyst*
Oster, Terri *lawyer*
Ostriker, Alicia Suskin *poet*
O'Sullivan, Judith Roberta *lawyer, writer, artist*
Otani, Yuriko L. (Charko) *artist*
Otero-Smart, Ingrid Amarillys *advertising executive*
Otis, Lee (Sarah) Liberman *lawyer, educator*
Ott, Sharon *artistic director*
Ouradnik, Toni Kristin *elementary school educator*
Outt, Helen May *retired elementary school educator, psychologist*
Ouyang, Norma M. *psychologist*
Ovadiah, Janice *not-for-profit developer, cultural organization administrator*
Overcash, Shelia Ann *nurse*
Owen, Carol Thompson *artist, educator, writer*
Owens, Birdie Murphy *retired music educator*
Owens, Christine Claire *art educator, graphics designer*
Owens, Mary Bentley *science educator, mathematics educator*
Owen-Towle, Carolyn Sheets *clergywoman*
Owings, Anne Marie *counselor*
Oxell, Loie Gwendolyn *fashion and beauty educator, consultant, columnist*
Ozick, Cynthia *writer*
Pacecca, Andrea Leigh *mathematics educator*
Pacha-Guyot, Debra L. *forensic scientist*
Pacheco, Susan *automotive executive*
Pack, Susan Joan *writer*
Packard, Betty Jane *journalist, consultant*
Packard, Sophie S. *elementary school educator*
Packert, Ginger E. *social studies educator, education educator*
Padberg, Harriet Ann *mathematician, educator*
Paddock, Sandra Constance *music educator*
Padgett, Cynthia S. *artist*
Padian, Nancy *medical educator, epidemiologist*
Padilla, Rebecca Lynn *special education educator*
Padilla, Sarai Ramona *health facility administrator, psychologist*
Pagano, Michelina Olimpia *art director, consultant, writer, scriptwriter*
Page, Janet Louise *accountant*
Page, Patricia (Patty) Newton *real estate broker, real estate company executive*
Page, Stephanie *lawyer*
Pagels, Elaine Hiesey *theology studies educator, writer*
Paige, Vivian Jo-Ann *accountant*
Painter, Diana Jean *urban planner, artist, historian*
Pakenham, Rosalie Muller Wright *magazine and newspaper editor*
Pallas, Arlene Mary *elementary school educator*
Palmer, April Marie *social studies educator*
Palmer, Gracious Anne *small business owner*
Palmer, Irene Sabelberg *retired dean, retired nursing educator, genealogist*
Palmer, Jocelyn Beth *volunteer*
Palmer, Linda K. *psychology educator, writer, editor*
Palmer, Marilyn Joan *English composition educator*
Palmer, Martha H. *counseling educator, director*
Palmer, Rose Ann *television producer, writer, educator*
Palmieri, Dora Ann *retired language educator*
Palmquist, Carol Ann *educational association administrator*
Pancratz, Jeanette Diane *secondary school educator*
Panzer, Mary Caroline *historian, museum curator*
Paolucci, Anne Attura *playwright, poet, literature educator, educational consultant*
Papa, Phyllis Maryann *performing company executive, dancer, choreographer, educator*

Papaioannou, Evangelia-Lilly *psychologist, researcher*
Papathomas, Georgia Nikolakopoulou *technology executive*
Paradis-Kent, M. Robin *music educator*
Parchment, Robyn Renae *mathematics educator*
Parham, Ellen Speiden *nutrition educator*
Parham, Evelyn Lee *nurse*
Pariag, Haimwattie Ramkistodas *information management administrator*
Paris-De Monte, Ileana M. *assistant principal*
Parisi, Valerie Marie *former dean, medical educator*
Park, Nancy Marie *art director, illustrator, painter*
Parke, Janet Diane *interior designer*
Parker, Amy Lee *music educator*
Parker, Joel Louise *nursing administrator*
Parker, Marietta *prosecutor*
Parker, Sara Ann *librarian, consultant*
Parker, Susan Brooks *health facility administrator*
Parker, Suzanne Marie *physical education educator*
Parker, Towana D. *entrepreneur, director*
Parkinson, Dian *actress*
Parks, Grace Susan *bank executive*
Parks, Jean Anne *retired acute care nurse*
Parks, Margaret Laverne *secondary school educator, department chairman*
Parks, Tamara *elementary school educator*
Parode, Ann *lawyer*
Parpiani, Priya *obstetrician, retired gynecologist*
Parrish, Debra Marie *lawyer*
Parrish, Nancy Rebecca *elementary school educator*
Parrott, Annette Michele *science educator, consultant*
Parrott, Lois Anne Muyskens *humanities educator*
Parsons, Alexandra Clare *literature and language educator*
Parsons, Christina Anne *writer, photographer, educator*
Parsons, Marilee Benore *science educator*
Parulis, Cheryl *English, drama and speech educator*
Pascale, Jane Fay *pathologist*
Pascoe, Clara P. *public relations executive, property manager*
Pascoe, Patricia Hill *former state legislator*
Paskawicz, Jeanne Frances *pain specialist*
Paskman, Andrea *dance specialist*
Pastula, Leah Lynn *mental health services professional*
Patchin, Rebecca J. *anesthesiologist, educator, administrator*
Pate, Jacqueline Hail *retired data processing company executive*
Patino-Brandfon, Sylvia *retired psychologist*
Patrick, Danica Sue *race car driver*
Patrick, Pauline Margaret *secondary school educator*
Patten, Christine Taylor *artist*
Patterson, Elizabeth Johnston *retired congresswoman*
Patterson, Linda Darece *school disciplinarian*
Patterson, Mildred Lucas *retired teaching specialist*
Paul, Eve W. *retired lawyer*
Paul, Julia *ancient history researcher*
Pauley, Elsa P. *psychologist, educator*
Pauley, Jane *newscaster, journalist*
Payne, Barbara Ann *artist, educator*
Payne, Mary Libby *retired judge*
Payne, Peggy *writer*
Paysen, Bonnie B. *music educator, musician*
Peacock, Mary Willa *magazine editor, consultant*
Peacock, Virginia C. *artist*
Pearce, Karen Lee *elementary school educator*
Pearce, Serena Ray *performing arts educator, music director*
Pearce-Worthington, Carol *writer, editor*
Pearsall, Gloria W. *retired elementary school educator*
Pearson, Barbara Lee *social worker*
Pearson, Harriet D. *information technology executive*
Pearson, Landon *Canadian senator*
Pease-Pretty On Top, Janine B. *community college administrator*
Peaslee, Margaret Mae Hermanek *zoology educator*
Peattie, Lisa Redfield *retired urban anthropology educator*
Pedersen, Karen Sue *electrical engineer*
Pederson, Celine *secondary school educator, literature and language educator*
Pederson, Linda L. *music educator*
Pedini, Egle Damijonaitis *radiologist*
Peebles, Mary Lynn *nursing home administrator*
Peek, Stephanie *artist*
Peele, Tammy Sue *nurse*
Peeples, Mary Anne Baumann *science educator*
Pegs, Karen Rosamond *publishing executive, lawyer*
Peitsmeyer, Natalie Mary *science educator*
Peko, Linda D. *elementary school educator*
Pelcyger, Elaine *school psychologist*
Pelcyger, Gwynne Ellice *school psychologist*
Pellicciotto, Nicole Alyssa *special education services professional, consultant*
Peltz, Paulette Beatrice *corporate lawyer*
Pence, Jean Virginia (Jean Pence) *retired real estate broker*
Pencola, Annamaria Regina *elementary school educator*
Pendleton, Gail Ruth *newspaper editor, writer, educator*
Pendleton, Joan Marie *microprocessor designer*
Penniman, Linda Simmons *retired real estate agent*
Pennington, Valerie J. *biology professor, dancer*
Penny, Laura Jean *librarian*
Penrod, Marian Penuel *personnel consultant, retired school librarian*
Pentz, Anna Faye *nurse*
Penwell, Rebecca Ann *science educator*
Peper, Charlotte Ann *educational consultant*
Pepin-Wakefield, Yvonne Mary *artist, writer*
Pepper, Beverly *artist, sculptor*
Pepper, Dorothy Mae *nurse*
Pepper, Joline Romano *psychologist, educator*
Pepper, Pamela Poe *psychologist*
Peratoner, Heidi Esmeralda *marriage and family therapist intern*
Percoski, Kathryn Jean *secondary school educator*
Perdigó, Luisa Marina *foreign language and literature educator*
Peretti, Marilyn Gay Woerner *human services professional*
Peretti, Terri L. *political science professor, department chairman*
Perez, Barbara Sue *middle school educator*
Perez, Luz Lillian *psychologist*
Perez, Rosie *actress*
Perez-Orozco, Jacqueline *science educator*
Peri, Linda Carol *librarian*
Peringian, Lynda Ann *dietician, writer*
Perkins, Cheryl A. *paper company executive*
Perkins, Erma Young *English language educator*
Perkins, Nancy Jane *industrial designer*
Perkowski, Jennifer *music educator*
Perlingieri, Ilya Sandra *art history scholar, writer*
Perlmutter, Barbara S. *retired advertising executive*
Perlmutter, Diane F. *marketing executive*
Perlov, Dadie *management consultant*
Perniciaro, Alissa A. *dancer, educator*
Pero, Louise A. *elementary school educator*
Perraud, Pamela Brooks *human resources professional*
Perrin, Courtney Massey *history educator*
Perrin, Gail *editor*
Perry, Cynthia *social worker*
Perry, Diane Swaney *mathematics educator*
Perry, Misty J. *social studies educator*
Perry, Nancy Bland *accountant*
Perry-Camp, Jane *music educator, pianist*
Pervall, Stephanie Joy *management consultant*
Peters, Carol Ann Dudycha *counselor*
Peters, Eleanor White *retired mental health nurse*
Peters, Janice G. Spoth *elementary school educator*
Peters, Jennifer R. *music educator*
Petersen, Joyce Jean *retired elementary school educator*
Petersen, Shannyn Rae *music educator*
Peterson, Ann Sullivan *physician, consultant*
Peterson, Anne Elizabeth Wallace *music educator, composer*
Peterson, Betty W. *language educator, writer*
Peterson, Brandi Janell *elementary school educator*
Peterson, Clara Margaret *elementary school educator*
Peterson, Dawn Michelle *entrepreneur, writer*
Peterson, Ginger *secondary school educator*
Peterson, Jennifer Leigh *mathematics educator*
Peterson, Katherine H. *federal agency administrator, former ambassador*
Peterson, Kristin *artist*
Peterson, Martha *artist*
Peterson, Norma Jo *retired education educator*
Peterson, Rosetta Hicks *retired music educator*
Petree, Betty Chapman *anesthetist*
Petrelis, Stella Marsha *writer*
Petrie, Lois Ann *enterostomy therapy nurse*
Pettigrew, L. Eudora *retired academic administrator*
Pettine, Linda Faye *physical therapist*
Pettis-Roberson, Shirley McCumber *retired congresswoman*
Pevear, Roberta Charlotte *retired state legislator*
Pezeshk, Violet *psychologist, educator*
Pfanstiel Parr, Dorothea Ann *interior designer*
Pfeifer, Lola *mathematics educator*
Pfeiffer, Michelle *actress*
Pflum, Barbara Ann *retired allergist*
Pham, Lara Bach-Vien *small business owner*
Phan, Christina *electronic analog design executive*
Phelan, Mary Michenfelder *public relations executive, writer*
Phelan, Stephanie Ellen *artist, graphics designer*
Phelps, Mindy Shannon *communications consultant*
Phifer, Renita Y. *counselor, educator*
Phillips, Alys Swords *surgical nurse*
Phillips, Cynthia Ann *science educator*
Phillips, Dorothy K. *lawyer*
Phillips, Glynda Ann *editor*
Phillips, Jean Brown *public relations executive, consultant*
Phillips, Jill Meta *writer, critic, astrologer*
Phillips, Joyce Martha *human resources executive*
Phillips, Kathleen Gay *small business owner*
Phillips, Marjorie Ruth *retired elementary school educator*
Phillips, Peggy V. *former biotechnology company executive*
Phillips, Winifred Patricia *radio producer, composer*
Phipard, Nancy Midwood *retired special education educator, poet*
Piazza, Rosanna Joy *paralegal*
Pickle, Linda Williams *biostatistician*
Pieknik, Rebecca Anne *technologist, educator*
Pierce, Hilda (Hilda Herta Harmel) *painter*
Pierce, Linda Ann *nurse*
Pierce, Lisa Margaret *telecommunications industry executive, marketing professional, educator*
Pierce, Marian Marie *writer, educator*
Pierce, Ponchitta Ann *TV host, television producer, journalist, writer, consultant*
Pierce, Shaheeda Laura *nurse midwife, consultant*
Pierce, Susan Resneck *academic administrator, literature educator, consultant*
Pierik, Marilyn Anne *retired librarian, piano teacher*
Pierri, Mary Kathryn Madeline *cardiologist, emergency physician, educator*
Pilat, Jeanine Marie *medical researcher*
Pilgrim, Dianne Hauserman *retired museum director*
Pilous, Betty Scheibel *medical/surgical nurse*
Pincus, Nancy *architect, web site designer*
Ping-Robbins, Nancy Regan *musicologist, educator*
Pinkett-Smith, Jada *actress*
Pinkham, Lise Kutzman *humanities educator*
Pinkins, Tonya *actress*
Pinkus, Deborah Sue *special education educator*
Pinter, Elizabeth *retired communications educator*
Pinto, Marion *artist*
Piper, Margarita Sherertz *retired school system administrator*
Pipkin, Mary Margaret *artist*
Pirrone, Catherine Lynne *secondary school educator*
Pirsch, Carol McBride *retired county official, state senator, community relations manager*
Pisani, Margaret *elementary school educator*
Pisano, Carla Ann *mathematics educator, accountant*
Pisciotta, Vivian Virginia *retired psychotherapist*
Pisters, Katherine M.W. *internist, medical educator*
Pitter, Tracy Alana *athletic trainer*
Pittman, Rachel Doby *science educator*
Pitts, Amy Kathleen *science educator*
Pizzo, Pia *artist, educator*
Place, Janey *banking consultant, former bank executive*
Plaisted, Carole Anne *elementary school educator*
Plame, Valerie Elise *former intelligence agent*
Plank, Betsy (Mrs. Sherman V. Rosenfield) *public relations counsel*
Platek, Jennifer Bethany *voice educator*
Platt, Kathryn *special education educator*
Platzer, Cynthia Siemen *lawyer*
Player, Audrey Nell *research scientist*
Plaza, Eva M. *lawyer*
Plehaty, Phyllis Juliette *retired curator*
Pleshette, Suzanne *actress*
Plette, Sandra Lee *retired insurance company executive*
Plimpton, Peggy Lucas *trustee*
Pliska, Stephanie *history educator, special education educator*
Pliskin, Berenice Rita Chaplan *artist*
Ploeckelman, Amy Lynn *athletic trainer*
Plumb, Pamela Pelton *consulting company executive, retired mayor*
Plummer, Amanda *actress*
Plunket, Dolores *art educator, archaeology educator*
Pockrass, Marlene Morgan *retired literature educator*
Poe, Cheryl Toni *music educator*
Pogrebin, Letty Cottin *writer, educator*
Pohlmann, Evelyn Gawley *music educator, consultant*
Pohto, Susan Louise *secondary school educator*
Pokras, Sheila Frances *retired judge*
Poleshuk, Alicia L. *alcohol/drug abuse services professional*
Polfliet, Sarah Jean *physician*
Polimeni, Rebecca H. *special education educator*
Polite, Carlene Hatcher *writer, educator*
Polk, Emily DeSpain *conservationist, writer*
Pollack, Marsha *secondary school educator*
Pollack, Sylvia Byrne *retired science educator, researcher, counselor*
Pollitt, Katha *writer, educator, poet*
Pollock, Karen Anne *computer analyst*
Pomeroy, Heather Aline *sales executive, marketing executive*
Pomers, Tiffany Lee *mathematics educator*
Pompeo, Marie Antoinette *medical/surgical nurse, nursing educator*
Pond, Gloria Dibble *retired educator*
Pond, Peggy Ann *librarian*
Pond, Phyllis Joan Ruble *state legislator, educator*
Ponte, Jean Moore *artist, writer, actress*
Pont Marchese, Marisara *former Puerto Rican government official*
Poole, Katherine *government agency administrator*
Poorman, Christine K. *television producer*
Pope, Ingrid Bloomquist *sculptor, poet, painter*
Pope, Lena Elizabeth *human resources specialist*
Pope, Lillie *psychologist, educator, writer, consultant*
Pope, Mary Therese *retired elementary school educator*
Popian, Lucia *artist*
Popoff, Edna Spieler *psychologist, consultant*
Popp, Charlotte Louise *retired health facility administrator*
Poppe, Laurie Catherine *matrimonial lawyer, social worker, real estate executive*
Poppen, Marcella May *music educator*
Poppler, Doris Swords *lawyer*
Porch, Kathy M. *information technology executive, educator*
Porges, Lucie *apparel designer, educator*
Poritz, Deborah Tobias *retired state supreme court justice, former state attorney general*
Porter, Leah LeEarle *food products executive*
Porter, Margaret Evans *novelist, lecturer, historian*
Portnoy, Lynn Ann *fashion retailer*
Portnoy, Sara S. *lawyer*
Porto, Vicki A. *science educator*
Posner, Sylvie Pérez *lawyer*
Poster, Meryl *film company executive*
Poston, Ann Genevieve *psychotherapist, nurse*
Potok, Nancy Ann Fagenson *management consultant*
Potratz, Wendy Jean *athletic trainer, consultant*
Potsic, Amie Sharon *photographer, educator, artist*
Potter, Corinne Jean *retired librarian*
Potter, Patricia Rae *retired protective services official*
Potter, Polly Helene *elementary school educator*
Potts, Latonya G. *social studies educator*
Poulos, Clara Jean *nutritionist*
Poulson, Kristie M. *secondary school educator*
Poulton, Roberta Doris *nurse, consultant*
Povich, Lynn *journalist, internet executive*
Powell, Alma Johnson *writer, advocate, foundation administrator*
Powell, Cathy Gail *secondary school educator*
Powell, Lynnette *elementary school educator*
Powell, Ruth Aregood *music educator*
Powell, Sheryl Ann *elementary school educator*
Power, Mary Susan *political scientist, educator*
Powers, Debra Jean *medical/surgical nurse*
Powers, Elizabeth Whitmel *lawyer*
Prather, Lenore Loving *former State Supreme Court Chief Justice*
Pratt, Rachel C. *elementary school educator*
Pratt, Sandra Sowers *special education educator*
Prawdzik, Linda Condusta *mathematics educator, consultant, director*
Prazak, Bessmarie Lillian *science educator*
Prchal, Carol Louise *retired orthopedist*
Preer, Joan C. *retired assistant principal, retired science educator*
Preheim, Kathy Lynn *elementary school educator*
Prejean, Sister Helen Theresa *human rights advocate, writer, lecturer*
Prescott, Barbara Lodwich *educational association administrator*
Presmanes, Willa Summerour *behavioral health systems evaluator*
Press, Aida Kabatznick *retired editor, poet, writer*
Pressler, Ciara Nicole Frey *marketing executive, consultant*
Presto, Catherine Ann (Kay Presto) *media specialist, consultant*
Preston, Kelly *actress*
Preszler, Sharon Marie *psychiatric home health nurse*
Preudhomme, Marcia Denrique *finance company executive, writer*
Preysz, Sandra *music educator*
Pribble, Ghada Khoury *music educator, singer*
Price, Alicia Hemmalin *retired psychotherapist, alcohol/drug abuse services professional*
Price, Betty Jeanne *chimes musician*
Price, Helen Burdon (Helen Lois Burdon) *artist, retired nursing educator*
Price, Mary *elementary school educator*
Price, Myra B. *secondary school educator*
Price, Ruthe Payenson Geier *actress, writer, educator*
Prichard, Kathryn *adult education educator*
Priebe, Sue *retired secondary school educator, minister*
Priest, Jessie Shaw *media specialist*
Primack, Alice Lefler *retired librarian*
Prince, Anna Lou *composer, music publisher, construction executive*
Prince, Ginger Lee *actress, choreographer, educator*
Principal, Victoria (Victoria Ree Principale) *actress, film producer, writer*
Pringle, Ruth Evelyn *retired adult education educator*
Prinz, Kristie Dawn *lawyer*
Pritchard, Karri R. *chemistry educator*
Pritchard, Lucille Kramer *mathematics professor, department chairman*
Procter, Carol Ann *retired musician*
Proctor, Barbara Gardner *advertising agency executive, writer*
Proenza, Theresa Butler *adult education educator, writer*
Prokop, Susan *disability rights advocate*
Proulx, (Edna) Annie *writer*
Provensen, Alice *artist, writer*
Pruchnicki, Jennifer Ann *director*
Prucino, Diane L. *lawyer*
Pruett-Lawson, Jo Ann *marketing professional, special events coordinator*
Pruitt, Anne Loring *academic administrator, education educator*
Pruitt, Debra Marie *medical/surgical nurse*
Pruzan, Irene *musician, educator, public relations executive, art association administrator*
Pryce, Dana A. *special education educator*
Przybylski, Mercedes *retired medical and surgical nurse, health facility administrator*
Pugh, Ann Barham *writer, educator*
Pugh, Martha Greenewald *lawyer*
Pugh, Shante Camille *athletic trainer*
Puia, Mary Beth *educator*
Puleo, Jean Anne *music educator, musician*
Pulhamus, Marlene Louise *retired elementary school educator*
Pulitzer, Emily Rauh (Mrs. Joseph Pulitzer Jr.) *art historian, consultant*
Pullen, Penny Lynne *non-profit organization administrator, retired state legislator*
Pullium, Rita Marie *educational association administrator, director, psychologist*
Punnett, Audrey Frances *clinical psychologist, educator*
Purvis, Gail *elementary school educator*
Purvis, Rebecca C. *transportation executive*
Puster, Rebecca Lynn *music educator, director*
Putterman, Florence Grace *artist, printmaker*
Puttmann, Sara *mathematics educator*
Pyles, Carol DeLong *dean, consultant, educator*
Pytlewski, Laura Jean *chemistry professor*
Quade, Vicki *editor, writer, playwright, theater producer*
Quaife, Marjorie Clift *retired nursing educator*
Quast, Pearl Elizabeth Kolb *retired elementary school educator*
Quattrone-Carroll, Diane Rose *clinical social worker*
Quay, Joyce Crosby *writer*
Quick, Barbara *writer*
Quiles, Dolores *foreign language educator*
Quinn, Helen Rhoda Arnold *physicist*
Quinn, Maureen E. *ambassador*
Quintana-Allenson, Ana M. *media specialist*
Quirk, Kathleen L. *mining executive*
Quist, Jeanette Fitzgerald *television production educator, choreographer*
Raash, Kathleen Forecki *artist*
Rabkin, Peggy Ann *retired lawyer*
Raborn, Marcia MacArthur *primary school educator*
Rackin, Phyllis *retired English language educator*
Rada, Ruth Byers *retired dean*
Radcliffe, Redonia (Donnie Radcliffe) *journalist, writer*
Radell, Carol K. *elementary school educator*
Radkowsky, Karen *advertising research specialist*
Rae, Susanna-Judith *writer, retired marriage and family therapist*
Raes, Heather Rebecca *special education educator, consultant*
Raffo, Heather *playwright, actress*
Raffo, Susan Henney *retired elementary school educator*
Ragans, Rosalind Dorothy *writer, artist, retired educator*
Ragsdale, Sandra Russell *special education educator*
Rahming, Etta Lorraine *social worker, consultant, psychotherapist, counseling administrator*
Rail, Kathy Lynn Parish *accountant*
Railsback, Sherrie Lee *management consultant, educator*
Rain, Kathleen Marie *science educator*
Raines, Charlotte Austine Butler *artist*

Rainey, Pamela Leigh *dance educator*
Rainier, Ellen F. *nurse*
Rainwater, Joan Lucille Morse *investment company executive*
Raitt, Bonnie Lynn *singer, musician*
Raley, Beverly Spickelmier *systems administrator, educator, writer*
Ralston, Martha Jane *retired medical/surgical nurse*
Rambo, Domingo H. *elementary school educator*
Ramey, Eudora Malois *minister*
Ramirez, Leilani *music educator*
Ramirez, Maria C(oncepción) *retired educational association administrator*
Ramo, Virginia M. Smith *civic worker*
Rampone, Christie P. *professional soccer player*
Ramsay, Karin Kinsey *publisher, educator*
Ramsey, Emma Ruth *secondary school educator*
Ramsey, Lucie Avra *small business owner, consultant*
Ranada, Rose Marie *retired elementary school educator*
Rand, Joella Mae *retired nursing educator, counselor*
Randall, Catharine *French educator*
Rander, JoAnn Corpaci *musician, educator*
Randinelli, Tracey Anne *magazine editor*
Randle, Candace Latrice *government affairs consultant, political scientist*
Randolph, Nancy Adele *nutritionist, consultant*
Randolph, Virgella *retired federal official*
Ranney, Helen Margaret *retired internist, hematologist, educator*
Ransom, Nancy Alderman *sociology and women's studies educator, academic administrator*
Ransom, Tasha Elana *news production assistant, producer*
Rao-Remy, Yvonne Bernadette *special education educator*
Raoufi, Azadeh *music educator*
Raposo, Laura I. *music educator*
Rasberry, Dawn Yvette *counselor*
Rashad, Phylicia *actress, singer, dancer*
Rasor, Dina Lynn *journalist, private investigator*
Ratzlaff, Teresa *physical education educator*
Rauser, Connie Jean *athletic trainer*
Raval, Ma Florena Tenazas *retired pathologist*
Rawdon, Cheryl Ann *elementary school educator*
Ray, Carol Reneé *researcher*
Ray, Debra Ann *music educator*
Ray, Evelyn Lucille *art association administrator*
Ray, Jane Zimrude *retired machine shop executive*
Ray, Marjorie *retired financial planner*
Ray, Raegan L. *science educator*
Ray, Susan Davis *accountant*
Ray, Susan Elaine *principal*
Raymond, Jillynne *literature and language educator*
Raymond, Kristina Lynn *special education educator*
Razoharinoro, *archivist, historian, researcher*
Rea, Ann Hadley Kuehn *retired social services administrator, marketing professional*
Readie, Colleen Beth *microbiologist*
Reagan, Nancy Davis (Anne Francis Robbins) *former First Lady of the United States, volunteer*
Reams, Patricia Lynn *retired elementary school educator*
Reaves, Lisa Golden *science educator*
Reber, Cheryl Ann *consultant, social worker, trainer*
Reck, Elizabeth Torre *social worker, educator*
Recker, Stacy *social studies educator*
Reckers, Michele Yvonne *director, secondary school educator*
Reczek, Claire E. *reading specialist*
Redd, J. Diane *not-for-profit developer*
Reddick, Jacqueline Monique *social worker*
Redding-Lowder, Christine Arnita *elementary school educator*
Redgrave, Vanessa *actress*
Redican, Lois D. *small business owner*
Reece, Belynda M. *minister, consultant, military officer*
Reece, Julia Ruth *systems analyst, entrepreneur*
Reed, Anne F. Thomson *management consultant*
Reed, Brenda Kay *mathematics educator*
Reed, Cynthia Kay *minister*
Reed, Diane Marie *retired psychologist*
Reed, Georgia May *music educator*
Reed, Janel M. *music educator*
Reed, Mary Carolyn Camblin *retired music educator, retired county official*
Reed, Pamela *actress*
Reed, Susan J. *elementary school educator*
Reedy, Susan *painter*
Reese, Jacquelyn L. *elementary school educator*
Reese, Katherine Rose *music educator*
Reese, Linda Mae *elementary school educator*
Reeves, Barbara *writer, educator*
Reeves, Hallie Lawson *retired music educator, retired chaplain*
Reeves, Kathleen Walker *English language educator*
Reeves, Lucy Mary *retired elementary school educator*
Regan, Susan Wright *dance educator, small business owner, choreographer*
Regn Fraher, Bonnie *special education educator*
Rehnke, Mary Ann *academic administrator*
Rehth, Ann *counselor*
Reichmanis, Elsa *chemist*
Reichs, Kathy Joan *forensic anthropologist, educator, writer*
Reid, Dolores B. *retired social services administrator, consultant*
Reid, Geraldine Wold (Geraldine Reid Skjervold) *artist*
Reid, Helen Veronica *dean*
Reid, Joan Evangeline *lawyer, stockbroker*
Reid, Katharine Lee *museum director*
Reid, Katherine Lee *retired museum director, curator*
Reid, Orien *former medical association administrator*
Reid, Susan L. *conductor*
Reid, Tara *actress*
Reidy, Grace V. *retired music educator*
Reiff, Raychel Ann Haugrud *language educator*
Reilly, Ellen Jane *elementary school educator*
Reinhard, Diane L. *retired university president*
Reinike, Irma *retired writer, artist, poet, lyricist*
Reinke, Linda Jeanette *retired social worker*
Reisman, Judith Ann Gelernter *media communications executive, educator*
Reister, Ruth Alkema *lawyer, finance company executive*
Reitan, Ann *psychologist, writer*
Remes, Robin Eva *secondary school educator, cartographer*
Remkus, Connie Elaine *nutritional consultant*
Remley, Audrey Wright *retired academic administrator, psychologist*
Renaud, Bernadette Marie Elise *author*
Rench, Erin *elementary school educator*
Render, Arlene *former ambassador*
Rendich, Ana *painter, collage artist*
Rendl-Marcus, Mildred *artist, economist*
Renegar, Joan Ann *lawyer*
Renfro, Patricia Elise *library director, academic administrator*
Reno, Janet *former United States attorney general*
Reno Norton, Tabitha Dawn *music educator*
Renouf, Anne *corporate financial executive, consultant*
Rent, Clyda Stokes *academic administrator*
Repinski, Sara *library director*
Repko, Lisa *medical/surgical nurse*
Replogle, Jeanne Lonnquist *artist*
Resch, Rita Marie *retired music educator*
Resnick, Beth Elena *special education educator*
Resnick, Elaine Bette *psychotherapist, clinical social worker*
Retzlaff, Kay L. *literature educator, writer*
Revak, Claudia Anne *music educator*
Revere, Virginia Lehr *psychologist*
Reyes, Judy *actress*
Reynolds, Betty Ann *retired elementary school educator*
Reynolds, Charlotte N. *science educator*
Reynolds, Elizabeth Burson *social worker*
Reynolds, Louise Maxine Kruse *retired school nurse*
Reynolds, Rachelle Lynn *elementary school educator*
Reynolds, Wynetka Ann *academic administrator, educator*
Rez, Nancy Brubaker *nurse*
Rha, Lizette *social worker*
Rhode, Kim *Olympic athlete*
Rhodes, Karren *public information officer*
Rhodes, Linda Jane *psychiatrist*
Ribble, Judith Glenn *medical educator*
Riccio, Angela *science educator*
Rice, Anne *writer*
Rice, Cassandrea Rae *music educator*
Rice, Claretha Mayes *medical/surgical nurse, educator*
Rice, Donna S. *educational administrator*
Rice, Patricia Oppenheim Levin *special education educator, consultant*
Rice-Jones, Annie May *retired secondary school educator*
Richard, Candace L. *music educator*
Richard, Diana Marie *retired military officer*
Richards, Carmeleete A. *computer company executive, network administrator, consultant*
Richards, Lynn *company training executive, consultant*
Richards, Patricia Jones *artist, poet, musician, composer*
Richardson, Brownie F. *accountant*
Richardson, Elizabeth Wilson *middle school educator*
Richardson, Jean McGlenn *retired civil engineer*
Richardson, Joely *actress*
Richardson, Laurel Walum *sociology educator*
Richardson, Margaret Milner *retired lawyer*
Richardson, Natasha Jane *actress*
Richardson, Veta Teresa *professional society administrator, lawyer*
Richardson, Winifred *youth counselor, writer*
Richardson-Bowman, Lequetta Devera *finance company executive, consultant*
Richardson-Touson, F. Michelle *director*
Riche, Wendy *television producer*
Richstone, Beverly June *psychologist, writer*
Richter, Doris Louise *retired elementary school educator*
Rickard, Ruth David *retired history professor, retired political science professor*
Rickel, Annette Urso *psychology and psychiatry researcher, educator*
Ricketson, Mary E. *dean, lawyer, educator*
Rickson, Mary Jane *counseling administrator*
Ricks-Stanford, Hope Yvette *elementary school educator*
Riddle, Elsie Kathleen *elementary school educator, school librarian*
Ridenhour, Marilyn Housel *retired accountant*
Rider, Fae B. *freelance writer*
Ridgway, Rozanne LeJeanne *corporate director, retired ambassador*
Ridings, Dorothy Sattes *former association executive*
Ridlen, Judith Elaine *minister*
Ridley, Julie A. *biologist, educator*
Riehecky, Janet Ellen *writer*
Riehl, Lori Jo *art educator*
Rieselman, Deborah Sue *editor*
Rifman, Eileen *music educator*
Riggio, Kerry Kerstin *elementary school worker, researcher*
Righini, Marilou Mausteller *editor, consultant*
Riha, Janet M. *elementary school educator*
Riikonen, Charlene Boothe *international health administrator*
Riley, Cheryl M. *prosthodontist, military officer*
Riley, Pamela Janerico *artist*
Riley, Rebecca Michelle *music educator*
Riley-Davis, Shirley Merle *advertising agency executive, marketing consultant, writer*
Rimel, Rebecca Webster *foundation administrator*
Rimer, Beth A. *director*
Rimler, Anita A. *former state official*
Ring, Renee Etheline *lawyer*
Ringstead, Dee Ann *principal*
Rino, Barbara Elizabeth *music educator, musician*
Ripstein, Jacqueline *artist*
Rising, Catharine Clarke *author*
Riskin, Victoria *former trade association administrator*
Risser, Hilary S. *mathematician, educator*
Ritchie, Anna Spears *music educator*
Ritter, Heather Dawn *language educator*
Ritter, Renée *artist, educator*
Rivera, Georgina Pereira *mathematician, educator*
Rivera, Yelissa Marie *science educator, coach*
Rivero, Andria *education educator*
Rivers, Beverly D. *former district secretary*
Rivers, Lynn N. *former congresswoman*
Rivlin, Rachel *lawyer*
Riyaz, Najmun *psychiatrist*
Roark, Barbara Ann *librarian*
Roark, Mary Lou *educator, counselor*
Robb, Janet *secondary school educator*
Robbins, Jane Borsch *library and information science professor*
Robbins, Jane Lewis *retired elementary school educator*
Robbins, M. Joan *mental health services professional, sexual addictions therapist*
Robbins-O'Connell, Mindy *special education educator, consultant*
Roberson, Janet L. *manufacturing executive*
Roberson, Linda *lawyer*
Roberts, Anne Margaret *secondary school educator*
Roberts, Della *artist*
Roberts, Doris *actress*
Roberts, Holly Lynn *artist*
Roberts, Judith Marie *librarian, educator*
Roberts, Karlene Ann *education educator*
Roberts, Kathleen Anne *lawyer, former federal judge*
Roberts, Kathleen Mary *retired school system administrator*
Roberts, Kathy Desmond *executive director educational facility*
Roberts, Margaret Harold *editor, publisher*
Roberts, Margot Markels *art association administrator*
Roberts, Marie Dyer *retired computer systems specialist*
Roberts, Nancy Cohen *art dealer, marketing professional*
Roberts, Suzanne Catherine *artist*
Roberts, Toni *small business owner, jewelry designer*
Roberts, Victoria Lynn P. *antique expert*
Robertson, Kari Dawn *athletic trainer*
Robertson, Sara Stewart *private investigator, entrepreneur*
Robins, Cynthia Lou *journalist, jewelry designer*
Robins, Natalie *poet, writer*
Robinson, Aminah Brenda Lynn *artist, illustrator*
Robinson, Angela Tomei *clinical laboratory technologist, manager*
Robinson, Annettmarie *entrepreneur*
Robinson, Crystal *professional basketball player*
Robinson, Devette Lorraine *music educator*
Robinson, Elizabeth Leigh *special education educator*
Robinson, Gail Patricia *retired mental health counselor*
Robinson, Glenda Carole *pharmacist*
Robinson, Karen L. *music educator*
Robinson, Linda Gosden *communications executive*
Robinson, Linda Schultz *artist, educator*
Robinson, Lynda Hickox *artist*
Robinson, Marguerite Stern *anthropologist, educator, consultant*
Robinson, Mary Elizabeth Goff *retired historian, researcher*
Robinson, Molly Jahnige *statistician, educator*
Robinson, Nancy Nowakowski *academic administrator*
Robinson, Paula LeKatz *artist*
Robinson, Sandra Darlene *nursing educator*
Robinson, Sara Curtis *arts administrator*
Robinson, Stephanie Nicole *education educator*
Robinson, Verna Cotten *retired librarian, real estate manager*
Robison, June LeAnne *music educator*
Robison, Sylvia Potter *retired academic administrator*
Robles, Rosalie Miranda *elementary school educator*
Rocca, Christina B. *ambassador, former federal agency administrator*
Rochberg, Francesca *historian*
Roche, Barbara Anne *retired minister, editor*
Roche, Pauline Jennifer *artist*
Rochelle, Dorothy *educational consultant*
Rochelle, Lugenia *academic administrator*
Rochlin, Joyce Tretick *researcher*
Rock, Caro *publisher*
Rock, Jennifer Elizabeth *elementary school educator*
Rock, Mary Ann *artist, educator*
Rockburne, Dorothea Grace *artist*
Rockwell, Elizabeth Dennis *retirement specialist, financial planner*
Rode, Deborah Lynn *accountant*
Rodewald, Nancy Beal *history educator*
Rodgers, Betty Jo *mathematics educator*
Rodgers, Cheryl L. *elementary school educator, small business owner*
Rodgers, Lois Eve *secondary school educator*
Roditti, Esther C(laire) *lawyer, writer*
Rodriguez, Carolyn *lawyer*
Rodriguez, Gail Lee *music educator*
Rodriguez, Martha Jeanne *biology educator*
Rodriguez, Michelle (Mayte Michelle Rodriguez) *actress*
Rodriquez, Emily Kay *elementary school educator*
Roe, Wanda Jeraldean *artist, retired educator, lecturer*
Roebuck, Judith Lynn *retired secondary school educator*
Roeder, Gloria Jean *civil rights specialist, retired private investigator*
Roehlig, Nicole *elementary school educator*
Roemer, Carol Kaluga *art educator*
Roenicke, Norma Jean *music educator, pianist, organist, small business owner*
Roffé, Sarina *public relations executive*
Rog, Dorothy Ann *elementary school educator*
Rogaczewski, Sherrie Reece *small business owner, singer*
Rogalski, Lois Ann *speech and language pathologist*
Rogers, Audrey Patricia *social studies educator, consultant*
Rogers, Elaine P. *art educator*
Rogers, Elizabeth London *retired geriatrics services professional*
Rogers, Eva Marie VanLeuven *artist, poet*
Rogers, Kaaren Lea *music educator*
Rogers, Katharine Munzer *English literature educator*
Rogers, Kathie Anne *accountant*
Rogers, Margaret Ellen Jonsson *civic worker*
Rogers, Olivia Johnson *elementary school counselor*
Rogers, PJ *artist*
Rogers, Ruth Frances *retired microbiologist*
Rohlfing, Dorlee Clark *school system administrator, educator*
Rohlin, Diane Elizabeth *financial relations executive*
Rohne, Emily Hogan *medical nurse*
Rohner, Bonnie-Jean *small business owner, computer scientist, consultant*
Rohrbach, Heidi A. *lawyer*
Roitman, Judith *mathematician, educator*
Roles-Walter, Jennie Ruth *art educator, artist*
Rolland, Clara *pianist, educator*
Roller, Jeanne Keeney *education educator*
Roller, Marion *sculptor*
Roller, Pamela Jo *elementary school educator*
Rollins, Carole Ann *writer, artist*
Rollins, Diann Elizabeth *occupational health nurse, primary school educator*
Rollins, Doris Callela *music educator, pianist, performing accompanist*
Rollins, Margaret Ann *communications and theater educator*
Roman, Nancy Grace *astronomer, consultant*
Romana, Kathleen *writer*
Romano, Mena N. *artist, educator*
Romanucci-Ross, Lola *anthropologist, educator*
Romer, Ann Elizabeth *school psychologist*
Romer, Carole Joyce *volunteer*
Romero-Rainey, Rebeca *bank executive*
Rondeau, Doris Jean *entrepreneur, consultant*
Rook, Vicki Lynn *safety specialist*
Rook-Nykrin, Mary Carol *special education educator*
Roome, Kristine Ann *college administrator*
Roost, Alisa *theater educator*
Root, Janet Greenberg *private school educator*
Root, Phyllis Idalene *writer*
Rooth, Signe Alice *editor, consultant*
Rosales-Said, Marta Milagros *elementary school educator*
Rosander, Lynda Sue *elementary school educator*
Rose, Jolene Renee *music educator*
Rose, Nancy Joy *social worker*
Rose, Tessie E. *special education educator, consultant*
Rose, Tracey Anne *education educator*
Rosen, Ana Beatriz *electronics executive*
Rosen, Roberta *philosophy educator*
Rosenbaum, Belle Sara *religious studies educator, religious organization administrator*
Rosenberg, Alison P. *public policy officer*
Rosenberg, Jane *author, illustrator*
Rosenberg-Cortes, Stefanie Deanne *secondary school educator*
Rosenblum, Mindy Fleischer *pediatrician*
Rosenthal, Helen Nagelberg *county official, advocate*
Rosicki, Maria Trzetrzewinska-Trett *clinical psychologist*
Rosmus, Anna Elisabeth *writer*
Rosner, Sharon Ellen *actress, speech pathology/audiology services professional*
Rosof, Patricia J.F. *retired secondary school educator*
Ross, Donna Denice *elementary school educator*
Ross, Gloria Jean *artist*
Ross, Jeanne Nmi *psychologist*
Ross, Juliette *mathematics educator*
Ross, Molly Owings *jewelry designer, sculptor, small business owner*
Ross, Susan E. *elementary school educator*
Rossbach, Janet B. *art association administrator, not-for-profit fundraiser*
Rosseel-Jones, Mary Louise *lawyer*
Rossetti, Rosemarie *writer, publisher, speaker, consultant*
Rossi, Marianne *financial analyst*
Rossi, Mary Ann *classicist, researcher*
Rossi, Norma J. *retired not-for-profit developer, advocate*
Rossiter, Eileen *Canadian senator*
Rossman, Ruth Scharff *artist, educator*
Rostocil, Kelly Ann *secondary school educator, coach*
Roth, Aimee Elizabeth *secondary school educator, athletic trainer*
Roth, Pamela Jeanne *intellectual property asset management consultant*
Rothaar, Susanne Elisabeth *musician, educator*
Rothbard, Barbara *allergy and dermatology nurse*
Rothenberger, Dolores Jane *legal association administrator, actress, singer*
Rothermund, Cathy Lou *elementary school educator*
Rothman, Juliet Cassuto *social work educator, writer*
Rothman-Bernstein, Lisa J. *occupational health nurse*
Roths, Beverly Owen *municipal official*
Rothschild, Jennifer Ann *artist, educator*
Roukema, Margaret Scafati *congresswoman*
Roumbos, Maria K. *elementary school educator*
Rountree, Ruthann Louise *social worker, lecturer*
Routson, Mary A. *special education educator*
Rowe, Audrey *paralegal*
Rowe, Julie *theater educator, actress*
Rowell, Barbara Caballero *retired academic administrator*
Rowland, Pleasant T. *toy company executive, publisher*
Rowlands, Gena *actress*
Rozario Stewart, Gwendolyn Michelle *elementary school educator*
Rubin, Michele S. *radiologist*
Rubin, Phyllis Getz *health association executive*

Rubin, Sandra Mendelsohn *artist*
Rubin, Vera Cooper *astronomer, researcher*
Rubinstein, Eva (Anna) *photographer*
Rudd, Ann Talton *psychologist, artist*
Ruder, Tia L. *music educator*
Rudin, Anne *retired mayor, nursing educator*
Rudner, Sara *dancer*
Rudolph, Maya *actress, comedienne*
Rudy, Ruth Corman *former state legislator*
Ruehl, Mercedes *actress*
Ruemmler, Kathryn H. *prosecutor*
Ruffalo, Maria Therese *secondary school educator*
Ruhlig, Shelby Maria *secondary school educator*
Ruiz Diaz, Carolyn Ann *secondary school educator*
Rule, Molly McCorkle *music educator*
Rumfolo, Marilu *financial analyst, non-profit corporation executive*
Rundio, Joan Peters (Jo Rundio) *retired public information officer*
Rundquist, Elizabeth Ann *art therapist*
Runkle, Ethel Mona *artist*
Runolfson, Anne *soprano, actress*
Runyon, Melissa K. *psychologist, educator*
Rusaw, Sally Ellen *librarian*
Rush, Deborah *actress*
Rush, Julia Ann Halloran (Mrs. Richard Henry Rush) *artist, writer*
Rush, Kathryn Ann *psychotherapist*
Rush, Sophia *law educator*
Rushforth, Ann Fay *artist, educator*
Russ, Joanna *author*
Russell, Clara B. *information technology manager*
Russell, Deborah Louise *psychologist, researcher*
Russell, Elise Beckett *piano educator*
Russell, Florence L. *elementary school educator*
Russell, Jacqueline Annette *recreation director*
Russell, Joyce Ann *secondary school educator, librarian*
Russell, Louise *education educator*
Russell, Pamela Redford *scriptwriter, educator*
Russell, Sharon Lynn *educational consultant*
Russo, Gina Marie *music educator*
Russo, Judith A. *paralegal, writer*
Russo, Sabrina *architect*
Rustgi, Eileen Boyle *clinical psychologist*
Rutgard, Lorraine Levin *hearing impaired educator*
Rutherford, Doreen *artist, construction executive*
Rutledge, Mary Elizabeth *cultural organization administrator*
Rutledge, Patsy Leith *educational specialist*
Rutschke, Annamarie *artist*
Rutstein, Rebecca Anne *painter*
Rutter, Marie E. *music educator*
Ruviella-Knorr, Jeanne L. *music educator, consultant, clinician*
Ryan, Cynthia Rhoades *lawyer*
Ryan, Ione Jean Alohilani Rathburn *retired education educator, counselor*
Ryan, Jeanne Vanyo *music educator*
Ryan, Joyce Ethel *writer, artist*
Ryan, Marleigh Grayer *language educator*
Ryan, Rita Marie *science educator*
Ryan-Halley, Charlotte Muriel *oncology clinical specialist, family practice nurse practitioner*
Ryder, Tereasa Kai *retired protective services official*
Rypczyk, Candice Leigh *employee relations executive*
Sa, Lily *artist, educator*
Saari, Joy Ann *family practice nurse practitioner, geriatrics nurse, medical/surgical nurse*
Sabelhaus, Melanie R. *government agency administrator*
Saccoccio, Jacqueline *artist*
Sackett, Susan Deanna *writer*
Sacks, Temi J. *public relations executive*
Sade, (Helen Folasade Adu) *singer, lyricist*
Saegesser, Marguerite M. *artist*
Saenz, Cecilia Sonia *education educator*
Saenz, Silvia Patricia *special education educator*
Safian, Shelley Carole *advertising executive*
Safren, Cheryl *art educator, artist*
Sagawa, Shirley Sachi *lawyer*
Saidens, Susan M. *accountant, consultant*
Sainclivier, Annamaria Tambone *elementary school educator*
Saint, Eva Marie *actress*
St. Germain, Carol Ann *secondary educator*
St. Onge, Mary Frances Burkett *retired art education educator*
St. Pierre, Mary Sharon *literature educator*
Salamone-Kochowicz, Jean Gloria *retired bank executive*
Salat, Cristina *writer*
Saleh, Farida Yousry *chemistry professor*
Salerno, Cherie Ann (C. S. Mau) *artist*
Salerno, Laura Ann *elementary school educator*
Salerno, Sister Maria *advanced practice nurse, educator*
Sales, Catherine *special education educator*
Salier, Eva *artist, writer*
Salmi, Ellablanche *retired literature and language professor, artist, writer*
Salomon, Johanna *artist*
Salter, Phyllis Jean *counselor*
Salvatore, Diane J. *editor-in-chief*
Salzman, Anne Meyersburg *retired psychologist*
Samec, Diane Patricia *retired elementary school educator*
Samelson, Judy *editor*
Sammartino Frese, Jennifer M. *telecommunications industry executive*
Sampson, Donna Rene *mathematics educator*
Sampson, Martha Fray *portrait artist, educator*
Samson, Wanda Kay *retired secondary school educator, consultant*
Samuels, Linda S. *science administrator, consultant*
Samuelson, Linda J. *special education educator*
San Agustin, Mutya *pediatrician*
Sanchez, Alita Cassandra *physical education educator, personal trainer*
Sanchez, Marta *music educator*
Sandage-Mussey, Elizabeth Anthea *retired market research executive*
Sanders, Bessie Elaine *secondary school educator*
Sanders, Elizabeth Grey *English and history professor*
Sanders, Linda E. *psychologist, educator*
Sanders, Marlene *news correspondent, journalism educator*
Sanders, Patricia Smith *language educator, consultant*
Sanders, Robin Renee *former ambassador*
Sanderson, Janet A. *former ambassador*
Sandor, Jocelyn R. *artist*
Sandorsen, Cassiopeia *public health service officer*
Sandstead, Auriel J. *retired secondary school educator, researcher, historian*
Sandwell, Kristin Ann *special education educator*
Sandy, Catherine Ellen *librarian*
Sanford, Sarah J. *healthcare executive*
Sankoff, Tina M. *foundation administrator*
San Miguel, Lolita *artistic director*
Santamaria, Joanne C. *psychologist*
Santana, Niurka Maribel *neuropsychologist, educator*
Santina, Dalia *nutritionist, writer, skin care specialist*
Sapp, Gina Leann *music educator*
Sarana, Shiree *writer*
Saranac, Winnie B. *special education educator, educator*
Sarkisian, Pamela Outlaw *artist*
Sarofim, Louisa Stude *art patron, philanthropist*
Sarris, Jean Adams *retired psychologist*
Sarry, Christine *ballerina*
Sasko, Nancy Ann *insurance agent*
Sass, Mary Martha *freelance writer, artist*
Sassen, Saskia *urban planner, educator*
Sastrowardoyo, Teresita Manejar *nurse*
Sater, Beverly *music educator*
Satterthwaite, Helen Foster *retired state legislator*
Saucier, Guylaine *corporate financial executive*
Saunders, Antoinette Mercier *psychologist, educator*
Saunders, Donna M. *accountant*
Saunders, Lonna Jeanne *lawyer, newscaster*
Saunders, Mari Pittman *psychologist*
Savage, Kim I. *academic administrator*
Savage, Martha *art educator*
Savedra, Jeannine Evangeline *artist, educator*
Savenor, Betty Carmell *painter, printmaker*
Savercool, Susan Elisabeth *elementary school educator*
Savitz, Maxine Lazarus *aerospace transportation executive*
Savocchio, Joyce A. *former mayor*
Savoie, Allison Marie *secondary school educator*
Savory, Elaine *education educator*
Savoy, Suzanne Marie *nursing educator*
Sawai, Dahleen Emi *language educator*
Sawin, Therese Lynn *elementary school educator*
Sawyer, Diane Jane *education educator*
Sawyer, Lorraine McPherson *secondary school educator*
Sawyer-Morse, Mary Kaye *nutritionist, educator*
Scafuro, Lisa A. *writer, journalist, poet*
Scarborough, Ann Barlow *secondary school educator*
Scarbrough-Clay, Linda Kathleen *mathematician, educator*
Scarchuk, Lynn Nettleton *music educator*
Scarlett, Novlin Rose *occupational health nurse, educator*
Scarwid, Diana Elizabeth *actress*
Scego, Megan Elaine *music educator*
Schaal, Barbara Anna *evolutionary biologist, educator*
Schabacker, Betty Barchet *artist*
Schabner, Dawn Freeble *artist, educator*
Schadegg, Amy Rachelle *language educator*
Schadow, Karen E. *public speaking trainer, educator*
Schaefer, Lois Alma *special education educator*
Schaefer, Margaret F. *secondary school educator*
Schaeffer, Susan Fromberg *writer, educator*
Schafer, Jacqueline Ellen *federal agency administrator*
Schafer, Lorraine *psychologist, researcher*
Schaffer, Bonnie Lynn *psychologist*
Schaller, Christina C. *editor*
Schamburg, Tracy Marie *professional counselor*
Schanfield, Fannie Schwartz *community volunteer*
Schapira, Doris R. *UN observer*
Scharber, Susan Elizabeth *music educator, director*
Schardine, Heidi Fae *choral educator*
Schatz, Pauline *dietician, educator*
Schauf, Victoria *pediatrician, educator*
Schaupp, Joan Pomprowitz *trucking executive, writer*
Scheib, Rachel Theresa *psychiatrist*
Scheiberg, Susan L. *librarian*
Scheinman, Nancy Jane *psychologist*
Schell, Catherine Louise *physician*
Schendel, Kelly Ryan *literature educator, writer*
Scheps, Lynn Ruth *dancer, educator*
Schersten, Katherine Anne *volunteer*
Schiewe, Misti D. *secondary school educator*
Schiff, Molly Jeanette *artist, researcher*
Schiff, Stacy *writer*
Schiffer, Claudia *model*
Schinderling, Sandra *mathematics educator*
Schindler, Evelyn *medical/surgical nurse, educator*
Schindler, Holly Suzanne *freelance/self-employed writer*
Schlesinger, Deborah Lee *retired librarian*
Schless, Phyllis Ross *investment banker*
Schlitz, Stephanie Ann *adult education educator*
Schlosser, Anne Griffin *librarian*
Schmandt-Besserat, Denise *archaeologist, educator*
Schmeer, Arline Catherine *research scientist*
Schmeidler, Gertrude Raffel *psychology educator*
Schmid, Lynette Sue *child and adolescent psychiatrist*
Schmid, Michelle Louise *elementary school educator*
Schmider, Mary Ellen Heian *American studies educator, academic administrator*
Schmidt, Diane *retired elementary school educator*
Schmidt, Diane Joy *photographer, writer, creative arts educator*
Schmidt, Hildred Doris *music educator*
Schmidt, Ruth Ann *retired academic administrator*
Schmidtke, Suzanne de Fine *retired social worker*
Schmith, Rosalie LaVerne *special education educator*
Schmitz, Barbara *art preservationist*
Schnackenberg, Gjertrud Cecelia *poet*
Schneider, Catherine Chemin *occupational therapist, consultant*
Schneider, Gisela *art educator*
Schneider, Greta *economist, writer, speaker, efficiency expert, security consultant, public administration expert*
Schneider, Janet M. *museum administrator, painter, curator*
Schneider, Mary Etta *finance company executive*
Schneider, Mary Louise *retired elementary school educator*
Schneider, Phyllis Leah *writer, editor*
Schneider, Sherri *library clerk*
Schneider, Valerie Lois *retired speech educator*
Schneider Vaulman, Sharon Kay *neuropsychologist, educator*
Schnorr, Janet Kay *psychology educator, researcher*
Schoen, Carol Bronston *retired English language educator*
Schoeniger, Jane *music educator*
Schoettler, Gail Sinton *former ambassador*
Schon, Sandra Diane *elementary school educator*
Schoon, Doris Vivien *ophthalmologist*
Schoonmaker Powell, Thelma *film editor*
Schor, Laura Strumingher *historian*
Schor, Lynda *author, educator*
Schrage, Rose *retired academic administrator*
Schreck-Rosen, Ellen Elizabeth *special education educator*
Schremp, Faith Maryanne *writer*
Schroeder, Beth Ellan *school counselor*
Schroeder, LaVerne *medical/surgical nurse*
Schubert, Barbara Schuele *retired performing arts association administrator*
Schubert, Helen Celia *public relations executive*
Schuck, Joyce Haber *author*
Schucker, Veronica Jean *music educator*
Schudson, Ruth *actress*
Schultz, Dodi *writer, editor*
Schultz, Eileen Hedy *art director, advertising executive*
Schultz, Elizabeth Frances *elementary school educator*
Schultz, Janet W. *intelligence research analyst*
Schultz, Marian Starr *musician, educator*
Schultz, Susan D. *gifted and talented educator*
Schumacher, Cynthia Jo *retired elementary and secondary education educator*
Schumacher, Julie Alison *literature and language professor*
Schunk, Mae Gasparac *former state official*
Schur Kaufman, Susan *retired public affairs consultant*
Schuster, Carol Joyce *special education educator, consultant*
Schuster, Elaine *retired civil rights professional*
Schuster, Sylvia M. *education educator*
Schutt, Christine *writer, educator*
Schuur, Diane Joan *vocalist*
Schwab, Eileen Caulfield *lawyer, educator*
Schwartz, Ana Stella *art dealer, gallery owner*
Schwartz, Beth Meryl *psychology professor*
Schwartz, Carol Ann *investment company executive*
Schwartz, Carol Levitt *government official*
Schwartz, Eleanor Brantley *academic administrator*
Schwartz, Ilene *psychotherapist*
Schwartz, Lillian Feldman *artist, filmmaker, critic, nurse, writer*
Schwartz, Lisa M. (Lisa Shepard) *research and development chemist*
Schwartz, Lynne Sharon *freelance/self-employed writer*
Schwartz, Shirley E. *retired chemist, researcher*
Schwartz, Susan Evalyn *psychologist*
Schwarz, Rose Oberman *artist*
Schwarzkopf, Gloria A. *psychotherapist, educator*
Schweinhaut, Margaret Collins *state senator*
Schweitzer-Morris, Nancy N. *retired science educator, writer*
Schwendinger, Julia Rosalind Siegel *sociology researcher*
Sciacchetano, Gail Mary *lawyer*
Scialabba, Elmerinda Caccavo *retired pediatrician*
Sciolino, Elaine *reporter*
Sciorra, Annabella *actress*
Sciuva, Margaret W. *counselor*
Scoll, Eulalie Elizabeth *writer, researcher*
Scotland, Susan Jane *artist, educator*
Scott, Anne Byrd Firor *history professor*
Scott, Catherine Dorothy *librarian, library and information scientist, consultant*
Scott, Danelle Kay *secondary school educator*
Scott, Gloria Randle *former college president*
Scott, Jennifer Marie *special education educator*
Scott, Joyce *writer*
Scott, Juanita *elementary school educator*
Scott, Sherie René *actress*
Scott, Sue A. *music educator*
Scripture, Lois Jean *retired social services director*
Scrivner, B(arbara) E. *piano educator*
Scruggs, Sandra Nell *writer, former school teacher*
Scruggs, Teresa Eileen *science educator*
Scully, Susan *artist*
Seacat, Marian Louise *music educator*
Seagraves, Helen Leonard *librarian*
Searles, Edna Lowe *artist, illustrator, composer, poet*
Seaton, Joyah A. *nursing assistant*
Seckel, Carol Ann *Methodist minister*
Seddon, Priscilla Tingey *painter*
Sedgwick, Shannell Angela *elementary school educator, advocate*
Seeds, Sharon Lynn *bank processor*
Seely, Megan *activist, educator*
Segal, JoAn Smyth *library consultant, small business owner*
Segal, Linda Gale *retired insurance company executive*
Segal, Phyllis Nichamoff *mediator*
Segal, Rena Beth *artist*
Segall, Sarah Ostrovsky *psychoanalyst*
Segil, Laura Chipman *art dealer, consultant*
Segreto, Linda Mary Janeczek *special education educator*
Seidman, Ellen Shapiro *lawyer, government official*
Seiff, Gloria Louise *volunteer*
Seiger, Marilyn Sandra *public relations executive*
Seigler, Elizabeth Middleton *retired counseling administrator*
Seiler, Bonnie *academic administrator*
Selders, Jean E. *retired psychology professor*
Seldner, Betty Jane *environmental engineer, consultant, aerospace transportation executive*
Selig, Phyllis Sims *retired architect*
Seligman, Nicole K. *broadcast executive, lawyer*
Seligson, Judith *artist*
Sell, LeeLou *retired elementary school educator*
Sellers, Marjorie Stevenson *retired principal*
Seltzer, Vivian Center *psychologist, educator*
Seminara, Lynda Anne *editor*
Senechal, Alice R. *federal magistrate judge, lawyer*
Senerchia, Dorothy Sylvia *writer, urban planner*
Seneshen, Susan *music educator*
Senior Morandi, Grace Esther *mechanical engineer*
Seniors, Paula Marie *history professor, researcher*
Sentenne, Justine *corporate ombudsman consultant*
Seplowin, Judith *cantor*
Sergesketter, Sarah Kay Kuntz *elementary school educator*
Seroogy, Louise Amy *medical/surgical nurse*
Servedio, Maria R. *science educator*
Servidio, Barbara J. *mathematics educator, science educator*
Sessions, Bettye Jean *humanities educator*
Setser, Carole Sue *food scientist, educator*
Settles, Jeanne Dobson *retired librarian*
Sevick, Suzanne *secondary school educator*
Sevilla, Emerita Nepomuceno *writer*
Sewell, Amy J. *elementary school educator*
Sexton, Carol Burke *finance company executive, consultant*
Sexton, Charline *secondary school educator*
Sexton, Cheryl Booth *secondary school educator*
Seymour, Pearl M. *retired psychologist*
Shackelford, Lottie Holt *civic worker, former mayor*
Shackelford, Nancy Kay *retail executive*
Shaderowfsky, Eva Maria *photographer, writer, computer communications specialist*
Shafer, Beatrice R. *medical/surgical nurse, researcher*
Shafer-Kenney, Jolie E. *writer, columnist*
Shaffer, Dorothy Tien *clinical psychologist*
Shaffer, Judy Ann *retired data processing professional, educator*
Shaffer, Shirley Pollack *secondary school educator, sales executive*
Shafran, Faith *artist*
Shah, Muniza *psychiatrist*
Shanahan, Eileen Frances *retired secondary school educator*
Shands, Gail Maxine *environmental scientist*
Shane, Rita *opera singer, educator*
Shanks, Ann Zane *filmmaker, film producer, director, photographer, writer*
Shanks, Kathryn Mary *health facility administrator*
Shannon, Donna Lynne *physical education educator, real estate broker*
Shannon, Jonnie Lynn *nursing administrator*
Shannon, Marilyn McCusker *biologist, educator*
Shao Collins, Jeannine *magazine publisher*
Sharma, Jeanne Alexandra *artist, educator*
Sharma, Martha Bridges *geography educator*
Sharp, Angela Christine *dance educator*
Sharp, Anne Catherine *artist, educator*
Sharp, Kay Frances *psychologist*
Sharp, Stacy Lynn *media specialist*
Sharples, Ruth Lissak *communications executive*
Sharrow, Sheba Grossman *artist*
Shatin, Judith *composer, educator*
Shattuck, Cathie Ann *lawyer, former government official*
Shauers, Margaret Ann *author*
Shaughnessy, Marie Kaneko *artist*
Shavender, Marilyn Faye *retired elementary school educator*
Shaw, Cecelia *retired chef*
Shaw, Gloria Doris *art educator*
Shaw, Helen Lester Anderson *nutrition educator, researcher, retired dean*
Shaw, Judy Browder *engineer*
Shaw, Lisa Marie *secondary school educator*
Shaw, Nancy Rivard *museum curator, art historian, consultant*
Shaw, Nina L. *lawyer*
Shaw-Soderstrom, Katherine S. *retired anesthesiologist*
Shea, M. *psychology professor*
Shea, Rosanne Mary *artist, educator*
Shead, Mary Airthrlodios *elementary school educator*
Sheaffer, Suzanne Frances *geriatrics nurse*
Shearing, Miriam *retired state supreme court chief justice*
Sheckter, Bonnie *artist*
Sheehan, Cindy *anti war activist*
Sheehan, Sophia Ann *marriage and family therapist, director*
Sheffey, Ruthe T. *language educator*
Sheild, Carolyn Jean *science educator*
Sheindlin, Judith (Judge Judy) *television personality, judge*
Sheinin, Rose *biochemist, educator*
Sheldon, Beth Ann *music educator*
Sheldon, Brooke Earle *librarian, educator*
Sheldon, Edith Louise Thach *writer*
Sheldon, Louise Roberts *writer*
Shellman-Lucas, Elizabeth C. *special education educator, researcher*
Shelton, Margaret *counselor*
Shelton, Stephani *broadcast journalist, consultant*
Shepard, Christy J. *special education educator*
Shepard, Katherine *science educator, consultant*
Shepard, Suzanne V. *language educator*
Shepherd, Cybill Lynne *actress, singer*
Sheppard, Gayle Teresa *software executive*
Sheppard, Jennifer Modlin *genealogist*
Sheppard, Lenora Gertrude *mathematics professor*
Sherbell-Na, Rhoda *artist, sculptor*
Sherfinski, Kristina Leigh *performing arts educator*
Sheridan, Diane Frances *public policy facilitator*
Sheridan, Sonia Landy *artist, retired art educator*

Strachan, Linda Avery *federal agency administrator*
Strait, Viola Edwina Washington *librarian*
Strantz, Nancy Jean *law educator, consultant*
Stratton, Mariann *retired military nursing executive*
Straumanis, Joan *academic administrator, consultant*
Straus, A. Susan *volunteer*
Streck, Melissa Leigh *music educator*
Street, Lela Kathryn *retired secondary education educator*
Street, Picabo *Olympic athlete*
Streeter, Carol *technology marketing executive*
Strength, Janis Grace *retired management executive, educator*
Strevig, Janice Lee *music educator*
Strider, Marjorie Virginia *artist, educator*
Stried, Jessica Nicole *elementary school educator*
Striker, Susan Joan Glaser *art educator*
Stringer, C. Vivian *college basketball coach*
Stringer, Mary Evelyn *art historian, educator*
Stringfield, Sherry *actress*
Stringham, Amy *secondary school educator*
Stringham, Renée *physician*
Strom, Doris Marie *music educator*
Stromback, Mary Beth *secondary school educator*
Strong, Annsley Chapman *interior designer, volunteer*
Strong, Christina Cordaire *writer, artist*
Strong, Sara Dougherty *psychologist, family therapist, custody mediator*
Strong, Virginia Wilkerson *freelance writer, former special education educator*
Strong-Cuevas, Elizabeth *sculptor*
Stroud, Betsy Dillard *artist*
Strouse, Jean *writer*
Struble, Susan C. *recreational therapist*
Stuart, Nancy Rubin (Nancy Zimman Stetson) *journalist, writer, television producer*
Stuart, Sandra Joyce *computer information scientist*
Stuart, Sherry Blanchard *artist*
Studer, Kathy Lynn *music educator*
Studer-Rabeler, Karen Elizabeth *director*
Studley, Michelle *mathematics educator*
Stulpin, Cynthia Louise *mathematics professor, real estate appraiser*
Stupak, Mary Jo *psychotherapist, educator*
Sturtevant, Kristen Amy *science educator*
Stutzman, Misty Dawn *music educator*
Styer, Denise Marie *psychologist*
Suber, Dianne Boardley *educational administrator*
Suber, Robin Hall *former medical and surgical nurse*
Suberri, Keren Chansky *psychologist, educator, marriage and family therapist*
Subkowsky, Elizabeth *insurance company executive*
Subramanian, Laura Sita *public health service officer*
Sudanowicz, Elaine Marie *government executive*
Sugar, Sandra Lee *art consultant*
Sugra, Cynthia Mariel *marketing executive*
Suh, Eun Jung *psychologist, researcher*
Suhr, Geraldine M. *medical/surgical nurse*
Sulc, Jean Luena (Jean L. Mestres) *lobbyist, consultant*
Sullivan, Ann-Catherine *physical education educator*
Sullivan, Barbara Jean *artist*
Sullivan, Carley Hayden *political party executive*
Sullivan, Elizabeth Asmann *counselor*
Sullivan, Glenda Lee *secondary school educator*
Sullivan, Kathryn D. *geologist, former astronaut, former science association executive*
Sullivan, Kathryn Meara *telecommunications industry executive*
Sullivan, Margaret M. *biologist, educator*
Sullivan, Mary Ann *artist*
Sullivan, Mary Rose *retired English language educator*
Sullivan, Sister Sharon *education educator*
Sulzbach, Christi Rocovich *lawyer*
Summar, Sharon Kay *retired elementary school educator*
Summers, Cathleen *film producer*
Summers, Lorraine Dey Schaeffer *retired librarian*
Summitt, Patricia Head *college basketball coach*
Summors, Alma C. *principal*
Sumter, Joni Lynn *political science professor*
Sun, Nilaja *playwright, actress*
Sundvall, Sheila A. *lawyer*
Suppa-Friedman, Janice DeStefano *secondary school educator, consultant*
Surman, Susan (Susan Kramer) *writer, actress*
Sussman, Janet I. *social sciences educator*
Sutcliffe, Mary Ogden *clinical social worker*
Sutlin, Vivian *advertising executive*
Sutter, Dawn Marie *special education educator*
Sutter, Eleanor Bly *retired diplomat*
Sutton, Dolores *actress, writer*
Sutton, Julia *musicologist, dance historian*
Sutton, Julia Zeigler *retired special education educator*
Sutton, Nancy Thurmond *music educator*
Sutton-Creech, Donna Lynn *gifted and talented educator*
Svoboda, Janice June *nurse*
Swallum, Maryann *musician, educator*
Swan, Annalyn *writer*
Swan, Beth Ann *nursing administrator*
Swaner, Paula Margetts *clinical psychologist*
Swansinger, A. Jacqueline *history professor, academic administrator*
Swanson, Patricia Klick *retired academic administrator, retired foundation administrator*
Swearingen, Lucinda Ellen *retired psychologist*
Sweeney, Colleen Lauren *elementary school educator*
Sweeney, Kathleen P. *special education educator*
Swenson, Michele Ann *middle school educator*
Swift, Jane Maria *former governor*
Swift, Patricia Anne *school psychologist*
Swinburn, Carol Ditzler *retired state and municipal agency administrator*
Swing, Marce *film producer, director, writer*
Switzer, Toccoa *artist*
Swoap, Kristin Genty *marriage and family therapist*
Syjud, Laura Beth *music educator*
Symons, Barbara Adele Schalk *academic administrator, counselor*
Synnestvedt, Kirstin *musician, educator*
Sypolt, Diane Gilbert *retired judge*
Szczechowicz, Gretchen *medical/surgical nurse*
Szczublewski, Wendy Sue *small business owner, musician, freelance/self-employed writer*
Szeliga, Victoria I. *social studies educator*
Szentiranyi, Judith *physician, educator*
Tabandera, Kathlynn Rosemary *secondary school educator*
Tabazadeh, Azadeh *environmental scientist, researcher*
Tabor, Linda J. *performing arts educator*
Taddei, Lois Annette Magowan *artist, interior designer*
Tadlock, Anita Conner *volunteer*
Taetzsch, Lynne *writer, artist, educator*
Tafoya, Michele *sports reporter*
Taggart, Linda Diane *retired women's health nurse*
Taggett, Laura Kimberly *literature educator*
Tagiuri, Consuelo Keller *child psychiatrist, educator*
Tagliaferri, Rebecca Anne *mathematics educator*
Tagliente, Josephine Marlene *artist*
Taichert, Louise Cecile *retired psychiatrist*
Takanishi, Ruby *foundation administrator, researcher*
Takenaga, Diana Yayoi *elementary school educator*
Talbot-Elliott, Susan *artist*
Talbot-Ross, Tiffany Lyn *secondary school educator*
Talese, Nan Ahearn *freelance/self-employed publishing executive*
Tallett, Elizabeth Edith *biopharmaceutical company executive*
Tallman, Ann Marie *lawyer*
Tally, Paula Siniard *counselor*
Tamen, Harriet *lawyer*
Tane, Susan Jaffe *retired manufacturing company executive*
Tanner, Laurel Nan *education educator*
Tanner, Lynn *actress*
Tapia, Jo-Di Lynn *secondary school educator*
Taraki, Shirlee *librarian*
Taranto, Maria Antoinette *psychology researcher, educator*
Tarasiewicz, Tamara *painter*
Tarbuck, Barbara Joan *actress*
Tardos, Anne *artist, writer, composer*
Tarses, Jamie *television producer, former television network executive*
Tasman, Alice Lea Mast *not-for-profit fundraiser*
Tasse, Marie Jeanne *retired art educator*
Tassos, Alice Crowley *writer*
Tatelbaum, Linda *literature educator, writer*
Tatlock, Anne M. *trust company executive*
Tauber, Michele Ann *actress*
Tauber, Sonya Lynn *nurse*
Taulbee, Dianne R. *special education administrator*
Tauscher, Ellen O. *congresswoman*
Tavakoli, Sirpa Aulikki *physician*
Tavares, Marcia Lynn *mental health services professional*
Tayler, Irene *English literature educator*
Taylor, Charlotte Nicole *literature and language educator*
Taylor, Cora Hodge *social worker*
Taylor, Edna Jane *retired employment program counselor*
Taylor, Eleanor Ross *writer*
Taylor, Gina Adele *dermatologist*
Taylor, Holly Ann *music educator*
Taylor, June Ruth *retired minister*
Taylor, Karen Annette *mental health nurse*
Taylor, Kathleen (Christine Taylor) *physical chemist, researcher*
Taylor, Linda Rathbun *investment manager*
Taylor, Lyda Revoire Wing *artist, gallery owner*
Taylor, Margaret Turner *apparel designer, economist, writer, architectural designer*
Taylor, Mary Lee *retired college administrator*
Taylor, Michelle Y. *human resources consultant*
Taylor, Nathalee Britton *retired nutritionist, freelance/self-employed writer*
Taylor-Brown, Cameron Ann *artist, educator, consultant*
Taymor, Julie *theater, film and opera director and designer*
Teater, Dorothy Seath *retired county official*
Teater, Tricia L. *human resources specialist*
Tebedo, MaryAnne *state legislator*
Tebout, Wynta Barbara *elementary school educator*
Tegge, Patricia Ann *retired administrative assistant*
Tellers, Cheryl Lee *art association administrator, consultant*
Tellez, Laura Lynn *elementary school educator*
Telnaes, Ann *cartoonist*
Tempel, Jean Curtin *venture capitalist*
Tennant, Donna Kay *writer*
Tepe, Victoria *research psychologist, women's health care advocate*
Terada, Alice Masae *retired elementary school educator*
Tercero, Stephanie Tavarez *biology educator*
Terkel, Susan Neiburg *author*
Ternovitz, Ruth *mathematics and computer educator*
Terr, Lenore Cagen *psychiatrist, writer*
Terrell, Karenann *information technology executive*
Terris, Kathleen Elizabeth *social studies educator*
Terris, Susan *physician, cardiologist, researcher*
Terry, April Lynne *physical education educator*
Terry, Barbara L. *human services administrator*
Terry, Frances Jefferson *retired psychiatric nurse practitioner*
Terry, Mitzi H. *secondary school educator*
Terry, Rachel Marie *music educator*
Terry, Sandra Eleanor *visual artist*
Tersine, Brenda L. *funeral director*
Tesseneer-Street, Susan *photographer, artist, writer*
Tharp, Mary Therese *middle school educator*
Tharp, Twyla *dancer*
Thaxton, Jessie J. *elementary school educator*
Thayer, Jane Hillis *psychologist*
Thayer, Martha Ann *small business owner*
Thibideau, Regina *retail executive, social worker*
Thiede, Elena M. *elementary school educator*
Thiele, Gloria Day *librarian, small business owner*
Thomas, Angela M. *marketing professional*
Thomas, Audrey Corbin *music educator*
Thomas, Betty *director, actress*
Thomas, Beverly Irene *special education educator, counseling administrator, educational diagnostician*
Thomas, Beverly T. *education educator*
Thomas, Claudia Lynn *orthopedic surgeon*
Thomas, Denise M. *chemistry educator, director*
Thomas, Jo *journalist, educator*
Thomas, Lise-Marie *actress*
Thomas, Martha S. *secondary school educator*
Thomas, Maryellen *public relations executive*
Thomas, Matilda Ann *art educator*
Thomas, Patricia Anne *retired law librarian*
Thomas, Regena L. *former state official*
Thomas, Sara Alice Folger *school librarian, curator*
Thomas, Sherasa Malone *secondary school educator*
Thomas, Spring Ursula *not-for-profit developer, educator, photographer*
Thomas, Teresa Ann *microbiologist, educator*
Thomas-Graham, Pamela *apparel executive*
Thomason, Amy Lynn *history educator*
Thomason, Lynne *councilman, medical technician*
Thomas-Roots, Pamela M. *writer, educator*
Thompson, Carla Anne *literature and language educator*
Thompson, Deborah G. *secondary school educator*
Thompson, Diana Rosebud *poet, educator, history exhibit coordinator, marketing consultant, playwright*
Thompson, Holley Marker *lawyer, consultant, marketing professional*
Thompson, Joyce Lurine *retired information systems specialist*
Thompson, Lea *actress*
Thompson, Linda A. *art educator*
Thompson, Margie Ann *artist*
Thompson, Mari Hildenbrand *medico-legal and administrative consultant*
Thompson, Mary Eileen *chemistry professor*
Thompson, Mary Koleta *small business owner, not-for-profit developer*
Thompson, Ramona Kay *special education educator*
Thompson, Tina Marie *professional basketball player*
Thompson, Tracy Ann *mathematics educator*
Thompson, Vetta Lynn Sanders *psychologist, educator*
Thomson, Virginia Winbourn *humanities educator, writer*
Thon, Melanie Rae *writer*
Thornburg, Linda A. *writer*
Thorne, Rebecca Claire *ballet director, choreographer*
Thornton, Pauline Cecilia Eve Marie Suzanne *special education educator*
Thornton, Rita Louise *environmental scientist, lawyer*
Thornton, Yvonne Shirley *obstetrician, writer, musician*
Thornton-Artson, Linda Elizabeth *psychiatric nurse*
Thorsen, Marie Kristin *radiologist, educator*
Thorson, Connie Capers *library educator*
Thrift, Julianne Still *academic administrator*
Thurmaier, Mary Jean *educational association administrator*
Thurman, Karen L. *former congresswoman, lobbyist*
Thurner, Agnes H. *retired administrative secretary*
Ticotin, Rachel *actress*
Tidwell, Kathy *literature and language educator*
Tiedge-Lafranier, Jeanne Marie *editor*
Tiemann, Barbara Jean *special education educator*
Tiemann, Karen *elementary school educator*
Tiemann, Margaret Ann *health educator*
Tietze, Martha Katherine *secondary school educator*
Tigett-Parks, Elizabeth *arts administrator*
Tilghman, Elizabeth W. *retired medical/surgical nurse*
Tilley, Christine Lynn *secondary school educator*
Tillman, Mercia V. *musician*
Tillman, Shirley *retired military officer*
Tillotson, Mary *cable television host*
Timm, Nicolette Dee *special education educator*
Timmerman, Anne N. *retired public relations executive*
Timmons, Sharon L. *retired elementary school educator*
Timms, Michele *retired professional basketball player*
Tingey, JoAnna *secondary school educator, mathematician*
Tingler, Marlene Johannsen *music educator, insurance agent*
Tingstrum, Nancy Ash *dietitian*
Tinkelman, Joan *lawyer*
Tinner, Franziska Paula *social worker, artist, apparel designer, educator, entrepreneur*
Tipton, Melanie Carol *music educator*
Tirello, Maria Eugenia Duke *artist*
Tisch, Wilma Stein *foundation administrator*
Tishman, Lynn P. *psychoanalyst, psychologist*
Tison-Braun, Micheline Lucie *French language educator*
Toay, Thelma M. *columnist, poet*
Tobias, Judy *university development executive*
Tobias, Sheila *writer, educator*
Tobiassen, Barbara Sue *systems analyst, consultant, volunteer*
Todaro, Molly Ann *secondary school educator*
Todd, Catherine Jackson *writer*
Todd, Suzanne Marie *film producer*
Toensing, Victoria *lawyer*
Tögel, Cornelia (Conni) D. *artist*
Tolbert, Cornelia Emma *music educator*
Tolbert, Nina Dianne *library and information scientist*
Tolia, Vasundhara K. *pediatric gastroenterologist, educator*
Tollison, Courtney L. *history professor*
Tomkow, Gwen Adelle *artist*
Tompkins, Julie Lynberg *market research consultant*
Tonello-Stuart, Enrica Maria *political scientist, economist*
Tong, Rosemarie *humanities educator, philosopher*
Tonjes, Marian Jeannette Benton *education educator*
Tooker, Michelle *secondary school educator*
Toole, Christine R. *science educator*
Toomey, Paula Kathleen *special education educator, educational technologist, consultant*
Topolewski, Nancy Eleanor *minister*
Topolewski-Green, Mary Jo Therese *small business owner*
Topolski, Catherine *science educator*
Torgerson, Katherine P. *media consultant, corporate communications specialist*
Torkzadeh, Rita *health information scientist*
Torney-Purta, Judith Vollmar *developmental psychologist*
Toro-Gabrys, Patricia *secondary education educator, artist*
Torok, Sarah E. *psychology professor*
Torrence, Margaret Ann Johnson *data processing executive, writer*
Torres, Arelis *elementary school educator*
Torres-Mabasa, Virginia Maria *physician assistant*
Torresyap, Pearl Marie *surgical nurse*
Torrez, Michelle Marie *artist, educator*
Torrie, Jane Marie *chiropractor, secondary school educator*
Toshach, Clarice Oversby *real estate developer, retired computer company executive*
Toter, Kimberly Mrowiec *nurse*
Touhill, Blanche Marie *retired academic administrator, historian, educator*
Tovornik, Mary Rose *physical education educator*
Towe, A. Ruth *retired museum director*
Tower, Mollie Gregory *writer, educator, consultant*
Towler, Katherine *writer*
Town, Charlotte *artist, small business owner*
Towne, Monica Noelle *music educator*
Townsend, Katheryn Estelle *chemistry professor*
Townsend, Kathleen Kennedy *former lieutenant governor*
Tozzi, Deborah Frances *elementary school educator*
Trail, Margaret Ann *retired employee benefits company executive, rancher*
Traiman, Helen *school nurse practitioner*
Trainor, Sheena Marie *music educator*
Tralis-Levy, Despi *writer, painter*
Trammel, Denise *science educator*
Tran, Alice *automotive executive*
Trane, Leslie *science educator*
Transou, Lynda Lou *advertising art administrator*
Tranzor, Tina *elementary school educator*
Trapani, Gina *web programmer, writer*
Trapp, Angela Michele *counselor*
Trautman-Kuzma, Alta Louise *nurse, funeral director, writer*
Travaille, Madelaine *science educator*
Treiber, Susan *music educator*
Treitler, Rhoda Chaprack *artist*
Trejos, Charlotte Marie *humanities educator, consultant*
Treppler, Irene Esther *retired state senator*
Tresslar, Nola V. *artist, retired marketing professional, retired foundation administrator*
Trettin, Rosemary Elizabeth *secondary school educator*
Triana, Gladys *artist*
Triece, Anne Gallagher *magazine publisher*
Triipan, Maive *library director*
Triplett, Arlene Ann *management consultant*
Tripp, Aili Mari *political scientist, educator*
Tripp, Marian Barlow Loofe *retired public relations executive*
Tripple, Amy Colleen *elementary school educator*
Trobaugh, Tara Michelle *music educator*
Troiani, Maryann Victoria *psychologist*
Troiano, Marie *music educator*
Troll, Kitty *actress, writer*
Trow, Jo Anne Johnson *retired university official*
Truckenbrodt, Yolanda Bernabe *retired air force officer, consultant*
Trudel, Janice Cuevas *music educator*
Trujillo, Stephanie N. *social sciences educator*
Truman, Margaret *writer*
Trusdell, Mary Louise Cantrell *retired academic administrator*
Trutor, Genevieve Williamson *museum director*
Tryon, Elizabeth Anne *educational association administrator*
Tsai, Ruth Man-kam *nurse*
Tsoodle-Marcus, Charlene *education educator, school system administrator*
Tubb, Betty Freeze *music educator*
Tucker, Rochelle *special education educator*
Tucker-Keto, Claudia A. *academic administrator*
Tuckness, Amber Victoria *music educator*
Tudor, Brenda S. *retail company executive*
Tufano, Sylvia Hope *obstetrician, gynecologist*
Tufo Jarnagin, Kelli *social studies educator*
Tuft, Mary Ann *executive search firm executive*
Tuggle, Connie Kersey *biology educator, department chairman*
Tulbert, Carrie Ann *literature and language educator, gifted and talented educator*
Tullo, Barbara Ann *performing company executive*
Tully, Catherine L. *physical educator instructor*
Tumio, Vera Ann *Reiki master priest*
Turczyn, Christine Lilian *English literature and writing educator*
Turczyn-Toles, Doreen Marie *pharmaceutical consultant*
Turek, Sonia Fay *journalist*
Turk, Eleanor Louise *history professor*
Turk, Rosemary Eileen *mathematics educator*
Turley, Susan Gwen *minister*
Turnau, Vivian Williamson *retired literature and language educator*
Turner, Ann Marie *art therapist*
Turner, Belinda Engram *physical education educator, athletics coordintaor*
Turner, Bonese Collins *artist, educator*
Turner, Bracha *painter*
Turner, Camilla Ann *music educator*
Turner, Florence Frances *ceramist*
Turner, Madeline *elementary school educator*
Turner, Natalie A. *retired consultant*

Turner, Tina (Anna Mae Bullock) *singer*
Turner-Reid, Marsha Marie *science educator*
Turney, Virginia *writer*
Turturro, Aida *actress*
Tuttle, Martha Benedict *artist*
Tuttle, Mary Celia Putnam *retired social worker*
Twichell, Chase *poet*
Tydlacka, Patricia Ann *retired elementary school educator*
Tyler, Beverly Ott *medical/surgical nurse*
Tyler, Eiko Nakayama *mathematician, educator*
Tyng, Anne Griswold *architect*
Tyson, Cicely *actress*
Tyson, Lucille R. *health facility administrator, geriatrics nurse*
Tyszka, Cortney Marie *athletic trainer, educator*
Tytler, Linda Jean *science administrator, retired state legislator*
Ubel, Olive Jane *retired secondary school educator*
Ucko, Barbara Clark *writer*
Uehling, Barbara Staner *academic administrator*
Uken, Marcile Rena *music educator*
Ulen, Gene Eldridge *elementary school educator*
Ulgen, Ayse *statistical geneticist, educator*
Ullman, Nelly Szabo *statistician, educator*
Ulmen, Kathryn T. *neuroscience clinical nurse specialist*
Ulmer, Frances Ann *retired state official*
Uman, Sarah Dungey *editor*
Ungar, Roselva May *primary and elementary school educator*
Unger, Barbara *poet, retired educator*
Unitas Roos, Carolyn Ellen *music educator, voice instructor, classical singer*
Unithan, Dolly *visual artist*
Upbin, Shari *agent*
Upson, Helen Rena *retired history educator*
Upson, Jeannine Martin *retired academic administrator*
Urato, Barbra Casale *entrepreneur*
Urban, Carrie *computer specialist*
Uribe, Laura Beth *elementary school educator*
Usher, Nancy Spear *retired language arts educator*
Usinger, Martha Putnam *counselor, educator, dean*
Usman, Marion Wilma *retired medical/surgical and mental health nurse*
Ussery, Luanne *retired communications consultant*
Utley, Ebony A. *communications educator*
Vaccaro, Brenda *actress*
Vaccaro, Luella G. *painter, ceramist*
Vaerst, Wendy Karen *secondary school educator*
Vahlkamp, Marianne Hill *retired elementary school educator*
Vahradian, Melinda *fine artist*
Vail, Mary Beth *retired secondary school educator*
Vail, Nancy L. Scott *retired elementary school educator, artist*
Valentine, Jean *poet, educator, writer*
Valentine, Phyllis Louise *counseling administrator*
Valentini, Virginia Redd *audio-visual specialist, educator*
Valles, Judith V. *former mayor, retired academic administrator*
Vallianos, Carole Wagner *lawyer*
Vanaltenburg, Betty Marie *lumber company executive*
van Assendelft, Laura Anne *political science professor*
Van Ausdal, Vivian Garrison *retired language educator*
Vanbrocklin, Vicki M. *secondary school educator*
Van Bruggen, Coosje *artist, writer*
VanBuren, Carolyn Jean *special education educator*
VanBuren, Deborah Ann *health educator*
Van Buren, Kari *museum director*
Van Camp, Diana J. *music educator*
Van Cleave, Michelle Kim *former federal official*
Van Cleve, Barbara Page *photographer*
Van de Bogart, Debra Scherwerts *medical/surgical nurse, researcher*
Vandenburg, Kathy Helen *small business owner*
Vanderhost, Leonette Louise *psychologist*
Vander Naald Egenes, Joan Elizabeth *retired small business owner, educator*
Vandersypen, Rita DeBona *counseling and academic administrator*
VanDerTuuk-Perkins, Jennifer Elizabeth *counselor, psychologist*
Vandiver, Sara Elizabeth Sharp Rankin *retired postmaster*
Van Dover, Karen *elementary school educator, consultant*
Van Dyke, Debbie K. *special education services professional*
Van Dyken, Amy *Olympic athlete*
Van Gelder, Lydia M. *artist, educator*
Van Hooser, Patricia Lou Scott *art educator*
Van Houten, Elizabeth Ann *corporate communications executive, painter*
Vani, Anita H. *music and voice educator*
Vanica, Kristena L. *principal*
Van Landingham, Marian Amelia *retired state legislator, artist*
VanMeter, Vandelia L. *retired library director*
Vann, Esther Martinez *science educator*
Van Ness, Gretchen *lawyer*
Van Ness, Patricia Catheline *composer, violinist*
Van Orden, Phyllis Jeanne *librarian, educator*
Van Sickle, Barbara Ann *special education educator*
Van Slyke, Sherrie Marie *psychotherapist*
Van Wettering, Carolyn *elementary school educator*
Vanzura, Liz (Elizabeth K. Vanzura) *automotive executive*
Varner, Joyce Ehrhardt *retired librarian*
Varnum, Charis *writer, educator*
Vasulka, Steina (Steinunn Briem Bjarnadottir) *artist, educator*
Vauclair, Marguerite Renée *communications and sales promotion executive*
Vaughan, Nadine *psychologist*
Vaughn, Cynthia Stark *elementary school educator*
Vaughn, Pamela W. *music educator*
Vaughndorf, Betty Rachel *executive secretary, artist*
Vaz, Katherine Anne *language educator, writer*
Vedouras, Anna *federal lawyer*
Vega, Suzanne *singer, songwriter*
Veit, Clairice Gene Tipton *measurement psychologist*
Vella, Ruth Ann *real estate executive*
Vellenga, Kathleen Osborne *retired state legislator*
Venables, Norinne *administrative assistant, dancer, educator*
Vendela, *model*
Vergez, Sandra S. *retired secondary school educator*
Verlich, Jean Elaine *writer, public relations executive, consultant*
Vernazza, Trish Brown (Trish Eileen Brown) *visual artist, art therapist, sculptor*
Vernerder, Gloria Jean *retired librarian*
Vernon, Doris Schaller *retired newswriter, publishing executive*
Veronneau-Troutman, Suzanne *retired ophthalmologist*
Versch, Esther Marie *artist*
Vest, Gayle Southworth *obstetrician, gynecologist*
Veverka, Ruth Tonry *retired secondary school educator*
Vila, Adis Maria *lawyer, business government executive*
Villaire, Holly Hennen Hood *theater producer, director, actress, educator*
Villa-Komaroff, Lydia *molecular biologist, educator, academic administrator*
Villoch, Kelly Carney *art director*
Vinson, Deborah *secondary school educator, speaker*
Viorst, Judith Stahl *writer*
Viscelli, Therese Rauth *materials management consultant*
Visocki, Nancy Gayle *information services consultant*
Vittetoe, Marie Clare *retired clinical laboratory science educator*
Vittitow, Susan *librarian, writer*
Vitt-Maucher, Gisela Maria *German educator*
Vliet, Donna Love *education educator*
Voegtlin-Anderson, Mary Margaret *music educator, small business owner*
Voehringer, Heidi L. *history educator*
Vogel, H. Victoria *psychotherapist, educator, writer, stress disorder and addiction recovery counselor*
Vogt, Christy *music educator*
Voigt, Cynthia *writer*
Volk, Patricia Gay *writer, essayist*
Volkering, Mary Joe *retired special education educator*
Volpe, Eileen Rae *retired special education educator*
Volz, Annabelle Wekar *learning disabilities educator, consultant*
Von Brandenstein, Patrizia *production designer*
Von Braunsberg, Mary Jane *clinical psychologist*
von Furstenberg, Betsy *actress, writer*
von Furstenberg, Diane *fashion designer, writer, entrepreneur*
Von Gizycki, Alkistis Romanoff *research scientist, writer*
VonSchulze-Delitzsch, Marilyn Wandling (Lady VonSchulze-Delitzsch) *artist, writer*
Von Thurn, Jelena *health science specialist*
von Trotta, Tamara Jane *art educator*
Voytek, Mary Sullivan *sculptor*
Vozheiko Wheaton, Lena *musician, educator*
Vukoder, Velda Jane *social worker*
Vumbaco, Brenda J. *elementary school educator*
Vydareny, Kay Herzog *radiologist, medical educator*
Vyn, Eleanor Mears *physical therapist*
Wachner, Linda Joy *former apparel marketing and manufacturing executive*
Wachtell, Esther *non-profit management executive, consultant*
Wachtman, Jeanette Marie *art educator, artist, writer*
Waddell, Sarah Katherine *elementary school educator*
Wade, Allison Muia *orthopedic surgeon*
Waggoner, Kathleen Alice *psychotherapist*
Wagner, Angela Dawn *social studies educator*
Wagner, Cheri J. *business owner*
Wagner, Christina Irene *elementary school educator*
Wagner, Marilyn Faith *retired elementary school educator*
Wagner, Melinda *musician, composer*
Wagner Chappelear, Maria *director*
Wahlers, Jennifer Ann *art educator*
Wahweah, Linda McNeil *insurance agent, writer*
Waiss, Elaine Helen *retired physician*
Waites, Trina Sularin *history educator*
Wake, Judith Ann Van Buren *secondary school educator*
Wakeman, Olivia Van Horn *marketing professional*
Waksberg, Nomi *painter, photographer, artist*
Walk, Barbra Denise *customer service administrator, tutor*
Walker, Amal Khawam *elementary school educator*
Walker, Annette *retired counseling administrator*
Walker, Athena Marie *secondary school educator*
Walker, Bernice Baker *artist*
Walker, Carolyn Mae *retired secondary school educator*
Walker, Diane *assistant principal*
Walker, Dori *biology educator*
Walker, E. Ann *minister, writer, pastoral counselor, consultant*
Walker, Helen Smith *retired real estate broker*
Walker, Kelley *painter*
Walker, Linda Lee *lawyer*
Walker, Olene S. *former governor*
Walker, Pamela *mathematics educator*
Walker, Patricia Sines *elementary school educator*
Walker, Ruth Charlotta *language educator, real estate broker*
Walker-LaRose, Linda Waleska *elementary school educator*
Walkowski, Barbara A. *lawyer*
Wall, Sherry Hodges *elementary school educator*
Wallace, Ardelia Leslene *elementary school educator*
Wallace, Bertha *retired elementary school educator*
Wallace, Dee *actress*
Wallace, Jane House *retired geologist*
Wallace, Joyce Irene Malakoff *internist*
Wallace, Michele *writer, educator*
Wallace, Nicolle (Nicolle Devenish) *former federal official*
Wallace, Teresa Lynn *art educator*
Wallace-House, Mary Elaine *writer*
Wallach, Patricia *councilman, retired mayor*
Wallach-Levy, Wendee Esther *astronomer*
Wallack, Rina Evelyn *lawyer*
Wallen, Shelia Renee *counseling administrator, educator*
Wallentine, Kathie Jo *special education educator*
Waller, Eunice McLean *retired elementary school educator*
Wallerstein, Betty Cooper *clinical social worker, family therapist*
Wallingford, Anne *freelance/self-employed writer, marketing professional, consultant*
Wallington, Patricia McDevitt *computer company executive*
Wallis, Diana Lynn *artistic director*
Wallison, Frieda K. *lawyer*
Wallner, Amanda Ober *retired music educator*
Wallskog, Joyce Marie *nursing educator, retired psychologist*
Walsh, Alana Joy *science educator*
Walsh, Diane *pianist*
Walsh, Juanita *theater educator, actress*
Walsh, Merideth A. *secondary school educator, director*
Walsh, Nan *artist, painter, sculptor, consultant*
Waltemath, Joan M. *artist*
Walter, Carmel Monica *security firm executive, writer*
Walters, Bette Jean *lawyer, investor*
Walters, Erica Scheffler *special education educator*
Walton, Alice Louise *bank executive*
Walton, Ann Thorson *art historian, writer, curator, educator*
Walton, Jennifer Rebecca *middle school educator*
Walton, Kathleen Endres *librarian*
Wander-Perna, Lucy *film company executive*
Wang, Nancy *pathologist, educator*
Wangsness, Genna Stead *retired hotel executive, innkeeper*
Wanley, Patricia Ann *medical/surgical nurse*
Wantz, Kathy Lynn Zepp *school nurse*
Warberg, Willetta *concert pianist, music educator*
Ward, Anne Starr Minton *musician, educator*
Ward, Jeannette Poole *retired psychologist, educator*
Ward, Lakeysha Monique *alcohol/drug abuse services professional, special education services professional*
Ward, Nina Gillson *jewelry store executive*
Ware, Gwendolyn C. *retired counseling administrator*
Ware, Sandra Marie *minister, music educator, composer*
Warian, Christine Barbara *elementary school educator*
Waring, Mary Louise *retired social worker*
Warmack, Wanda Lucile *education educator*
Warman, Linda K. *retired language educator, retired art educator*
Warner, Emily Hanrahan Howell *retired pilot, writer*
Warner, Rosemarie *elementary school educator*
Warner, Susan *federal agency administrator*
Warnken, Paula Neuman *university library director, educator*
Warren, Alice Louise *artist*
Warren, Cindy Michelle *author*
Warren, Rosanna *poet*
Warres, Margie Black *retired social work administrator, human services manager*
Warrick, Lola June *management consultant*
Warrior, Della C. *academic administrator, art educator*
Wartella, Ellen Ann *communications educator, consultant*
Warwick, Dionne *singer*
Warwick, Margaret Ann *health science facility administrator, consultant*
Washburn, Harriet Caroline *secondary school educator*
Washburn, Nan *conductor*
Washburn, Patricia Cheyne *retired psychologist, environmental scientist, conservationist*
Washington, Kerry *actor*
Washington, Michele *educational consultant*
Wasnak, Diane Marie *comedian*
Wasow, Mona *social worker, educator*
Water, Linda Gail *public relations executive*
Waters, Betty Lou *newspaper reporter, writer*
Waters, Charlotte Ann *investment management company executive*
Waters, Jessica L. *elementary school educator, psychologist*
Waters, Mary Brice Kirtley *former federal agency administrator*
Waters, Sylvia *dance company artistic director*
Waters Barham, Treva Ruth *director*
Watkins, Ann Esther *mathematics professor*
Watkins, Cheryl Denise *special education educator*
Watkins, Daphne C. *entrepreneur, consultant, advocate*
Watkins, Esther Sherrod *secondary school educator, school librarian*
Watkins, Karen J. *librarian*
Watley, Natasha *Olympic athlete*
Watson, Catherine Elaine *journalist*
Watson, Patricia Pullums *school system administrator*
Watson, Patti Rae *counselor, psychologist*
Watson, Patty Jo *anthropology educator*
Watson, Rebecca Elaine *human resources specialist, consultant*
Watson, Renée *marketing professional, consultant*
Watson, Vera K. *music educator, pianist*
Wattoff, Elizabeth *special education educator*
Watton, Rhonda Kay *social studies educator*
Watts, Ginny (Virginia C. Watts) *artist*
Watts, Helena Roselle *military analyst*
Watts, Karen Young *mathematics educator*
Watts, Mary Ann *retired elementary school educator*
Watts, Vivian Edna *state legislator*
Watts, Wendy Hazel *wine consultant*
Way, Barbara Haight *retired dermatologist*
Wayne, Jane Ellen *author*
Wayne, Sharon H. *mathematics professor*
Wean, Karla Denise *secondary school educator*
Weaver, Barbara Frances *librarian, consultant*
Weaver, Donna L. *engraver*
Weaver, Karen Lynn *writer, performing arts educator, actress, poet*
Weaver, Kitra K. *sales and marketing executive*
Weaver, Sandra Kae *nurse anesthetist*
Weaver, Tanya Lea *elementary school educator*
Webb, Doris McIntosh *human resources specialist*
Webb, Linda Kay *elementary school educator*
Webb, Lucy Jane *actress, film producer, consultant*
Webber, Linda Judith Ritz *interior designer*
Weber, Christine Ruth *artist*
Weber, Elizabeth Ann *academic administrator, music educator*
Weber, Gloria Richie *retired minister, retired state legislator*
Weber, Grace T. *school system administrator*
Weber, Idelle *artist, educator*
Weber, Joan Geiger *music educator*
Weber, Marilyn Ann *history educator*
Wechsler, Susan Linda *business operations director, research and development software manager*
Weder, Natalie Danitza *psychiatrist*
Wedge, Barbara Jane *women's health nurse*
Weeks, Lori D. *elementary school educator*
Weeks, Skyla Gay *music educator*
Wegman, Doris Jean *retired nursing administrator*
Wegner, Darlene Joy *civic worker, event coordinator*
Wehn, Karen Swaney *education educator, consultant*
Weickert, Wanda Opal *child welfare and attendance counselor, psychotherapist, educator*
Weightman, Esther Lynn *emergency trauma nurse*
Weigle, Peggy *information technology executive*
Weihmuller, Patricia Ann *minister, artist, retired executive secretary*
Weikert, Barbara Ruth *librarian*
Weil, Lynne Amy *communications executive, writer*
Weiner, Anne Lee *social worker*
Weiner, Ferne *psychologist*
Weiner-Heuschkel, Sydell *theater educator*
Weingand, Darlene Erna *librarian, educator*
Weinkauf, Mary Louise Stanley *retired clergywoman, educator*
Weinstein, Deena *sociology professor*
Weis, Margaret Edith *writer, editor*
Weisbart, Jennifer Rachel *mathematician, educator*
Weisberg, Barbara *writer, editor*
Weisbrod, Tara Lynn *secondary school educator*
Weisburger, Elizabeth Kreiser *retired chemist*
Weisert, Mary Carol *language educator*
Weiss, Carol Ann *writer*
Weiss, Joan Oppenheimer *social worker, educator*
Weiss, Lyn Denise *physician*
Weiss, Nancy P. *artist*
Welch, Raquel *actress*
Weld, Alison Gordon *artist*
Weller, Debra Anne *elementary school educator*
Wells, Cathy Eckard *elementary school educator*
Wells, Kitty (Ellen Muriel Deason) *musician*
Wells, Toni Lynn *accountant*
Welna, Cecilia *retired mathematics professor, dean*
Welsh, Dorothy Dell *columnist, writer*
Welsh, Kathern Darlene *artist, writer*
Welsome, Eileen *journalist, writer*
Wen, Gwen GuoYao *music educator*
Wendelin, Denise Kay *performing arts educator, artist*
Wengerd, Carol Joyce *mathematics educator*
Wenglowski, Joyce *painter*
Wents, Doris Roberta *psychologist*
Wentworth, LaVerne Wellborn *university program coordinator*
Wentworth, Lynn A. *telecommunications industry executive*
Werkman, Rosemarie Anne *former public relations professional, volunteer*
Werley, Annmarie *secondary school educator*
Werley, Kelly *secondary school educator*
Werner-Jacobsen, Emmy Elisabeth *developmental psychologist*
Werra, Donna *elementary school educator*
Wershing, Julia M. *pediatrician*
Wesoloski, Deborah J. *music educator*
Wessner, Deborah Marie *telecommunications industry executive, consultant*
West, Betsy *broadcast executive*
West, Donna J. *language arts educator*
West, Karen Marie *musician, educator*
West, Marjorie Edith *former elementary education educator*
West, Nettie J.R. *music educator*
Westberry, Jenny Rebecca *elementary school educator*
Westberry, Paula I. *nursing administrator*
Westbie, Barbara Jane *retired graphics designer*
Westby, Marcia *language educator*
Westerberg, Mary L. *retired secondary school educator*
Westfall, Carol Ann *artist, educator*
Westheimer, Ruth Welling *retired management consultant*
Westmoreland, Barbara Fenn *neurologist, educator*
Weston, Joan Spencer *communications executive*
Weston, Rebecca Lynn *forensic specialist, educator*
Westrich, Kate Ann *web site editor, writer*
Westrich, Kathleen Maureen *science educator*
Westrick, Heidi Lynn *medical/surgical nurse*
Westwater, Martha Elizabeth *language educator*
Wetzel, Angela Denise *music educator*
Wexler, Sandra M. *artist, medical illustrator*
Weymouth, Elizabeth (Lally) Graham *editor, columnist*
Whalen, Loretta Theresa *educational association administrator*
Wharton, Margaret Mary *nun, educator*
Wheat, Margaret Ann *marriage and family therapist*
Wheat, Sheree Renee *elementary school educator*
Wheeler, Barbara J. *management consultant*
Wheeler, Elizabeth Darracott *volunteer*
Wheeler, Kathryn S. *editor*

Wheeler-Happ, Darra Anne *secondary school educator*
Whelan, Mary Jane *accountant, writer, photographer*
Whelan, Susan *former Canadian government official*
Whelchel, Sandra Jane *writer*
Whiley, Julia Helen *writer, actress*
Whipple, Judith Roy *retired editor*
Whitaker, Diana Marie *medical/surgical nurse*
Whitaker, Shirley Ann *retired communications executive*
White, Bonnie Yvonne *management consultant, retired educator*
White, Daphne Milbank *writer*
White, Dawn Marie *elementary school educator*
White, Florence May *retired special education educator*
White, Jill Carolyn *lawyer*
White, Katharine Stone *museum administrator*
White, Lani Nyla *real estate developer, real estate broker*
White, Leandres *history educator*
White, Melinda Elois *retired elementary school educator*
White, Othell *interior designer*
White, Pamela Jo *elementary school educator*
White, Pauline M. *interior decorator*
White, Rebecca E. *advocate*
White, Sarah Jowilliard *retired counselor*
White, Sharon LaRue *social worker, therapist*
White, Sonya Renee *music educator*
White, Yonsenia S. *artist, educator*
Whitehead, Jennifer Sue *choreographer*
Whitehead, Tanya Dianne Grubbs *psychologist, educator, researcher*
Whitehill, Mary Evelyn *artist, retired librarian*
Whitelo, Velma Holland *special education educator*
Whiteman Runs Him, Heather Daphne *prosecutor, artist*
Whiteside, Karen Sowards *mathematics educator*
Whitfield, Lynn *actress*
Whitfield, Rebecca Wavrin *art educator*
Whitman, Christine Todd *former federal agency administrator, former governor*
Whitmore, Menandra M. *librarian*
Whitney, Marilyn Louise *elementary school educator*
Whittaker, Lynn Marie *elementary school educator*
Whittell, Polly (Mary Kaye Whittell) *editor, journalist*
Whittington-Brown, Vanessa Elizabeth *secondary school educator*
Whitty, Mary Jane *counselor*
Whitworth, Peggy Agnes *special education educator, consultant*
Whyte, Bettina Marshall *financial crisis manager*
Wichman, Yvonne Beard *lighting designer, literature educator*
Wickham, Dianne *nursing administrator*
Wickiewicz, Jessica-Lauren Charlotte *academic administrator*
Widger, Tanya Marie *counselor*
Widner, Roberta Ann *accountant, artist*
Wiebenson, Dora Louise *architectural historian, editor, writer*
Wiehl, Lis W. *law educator, legal analyst*
Wiele, Patricia Giordano *interior decorator*
Wies, Barbara *publishing executive, editor*
Wiese, Denise Kay *music educator*
Wiesenberg, Jacqueline Leonardi *social sciences educator*
Wiest, Dianne *actress*
Wiggins, Karen Sue *education educator, counselor*
Wik, Jean Marie (Jean Marie Beck) *librarian, media specialist*
Wikarski, Nancy Susan *writer*
Wilbur, Marcia Kaoru *writer*
Wilcox, Diane Marie *educational psychologist, software designer*
Wilder, Janet Mary *performing company executive*
Wilhelm, Monica L. *music educator*
Wilhelmi, Cynthia Joy *information technology manager, information scientist, consultant*
Wilke Montemayor, Joanne Marie *nursing administrator*
Wilkening, Laurel Lynn *academic administrator, aerospace scientist*
Wilkey, Mary Huff *investor, writer, publisher*
Wilkins, Rita Denise *product development, research and technology director*
Wilkinson, Doris *medical sociology educator*
Wilkof, Marcia Valerie *finance educator*
Willeford, Pamela Pitzer *former ambassador*
Willenz, June Adele *writer, editor, playwright, scriptwriter, public relations executive*
Willett, Jane S. *biology educator*
Willett, Melissa Carol *art educator*
Willey, Frieda Anders *adult education educator*
Williams, Adella Judith *elementary education educator*
Williams, Alice Noel Tuckerman *retired foundation administrator*
Williams, Bobbretta M. *educational company executive*
Williams, Candice L. *special education educator*
Williams, Cecelia Peay *retired psychologist*
Williams, Charlotte Edwina *secondary school educator, real estate manager*
Williams, Cheryl A. *secondary school educator*
Williams, Darcel Patrice *writer, editor*
Williams, Dawn Monique *theater director, educator*
Williams, Dorothy Standridge *retired food products manager, civic worker*
Williams, Elizabeth *human services administrator*
Williams, Freda Berry *administrative assistant*
Williams, Freda Videll *speech pathology/audiology services professional*
Williams, Hazelyn Matthis *dancer, educator*
Williams, Helen Margaret *retired accountant*
Williams, Jeanne Elizabeth *music educator*
Williams, Jessica April *elementary school educator*
Williams, JoBeth *actress*
Williams, Leona Rae *small business owner, consultant*
Williams, Lisa A. *special education educator*
Williams, Lucinda *country musician*
Williams, Mildred Jane *librarian*
Williams, Monica Bernardette Ellen *jewelry designer*
Williams, Nettie *retired childcare facility administrator*
Williams, Patricia Badia *retired counseling administrator*
Williams, Phyllis Cutforth *retired realtor*
Williams, Shannon Renee *mental health services professional*
Williams, Sheila A.T. *elementary school educator, consultant*
Williams, Terrie Michelle *public relations executive*
Williams, Thelma B. *retired principal*
Williams, Tiffany N. *personal and athletic trainer*
Williams Ezell, Margaret (Peggy) *artist, educator*
Williams Maddox-Brown, Janice Helen *nurse*
Williamson, Brynne Amber *paralegal*
Williamson, Myrna Hennrich *retired career officer, lecturer, consultant*
Williman, Pauline *retired reporter, foundation administrator*
Willingham, Janice Ann *secondary school educator*
Willingham, Mary Maxine *fashion retailer*
Willis, Beverly Ann *architect*
Willis, Burdena *director*
Willis, Cheryl Mary *art educator*
Willis, Emma K. *mathematics educator*
Willis, Lani Tyler *elementary school educator*
Willis, Ruth *freelance/self-employed theater director, actress*
Willis, Selene Lowe *electrical engineer, application developer, consultant, information technology manager*
Willits, Eileen Marie *medical, surgical nurse, health facility administrator*
Willson, Doris *librarian*
Willson, Mary Frances *ecology researcher, educator*
Wilmot, Evelyn Miller *elementary school educator*
Wilson, Annette Sigrid *elementary school educator*
Wilson, Carolyn Ross *retired school system administrator*
Wilson, Cheryl Yvonne *elementary and secondary school educator*
Wilson, Donna Mae *academic administrator, language educator*
Wilson, Eleanor McElroy *county official*
Wilson, Frances C. *career military officer*
Wilson, Jane *artist*
Wilson, Karen Lee *museum staff member, researcher*
Wilson, Linda Lee *finance company executive*
Wilson, Lois M. *minister*
Wilson, Mary Elizabeth *epidemiologist, physician, educator*
Wilson, Michelle Lermond *internist*
Wilson, Mollie *retired music educator*
Wilson, Patricia Potter *library and information scientist, educator*
Wilson, Peggy Mayfield *retired chemist*
Wilson, Rita *actress*
Wilson, Roberta Louise *writer, editor, journalist, activist*
Wilson, Ruth Yvette *artist, educator*
Wilson, Shauna B. *psychologist, researcher*
Wilson-Jones, Linda *guidance counselor*
Wilson-Pleiness, Christine Joyce *writer, columnist, poet*
Wilson-Stewart, Marilyn Lucille *retired human resources leader*
Wimberly, Linda Roberts *music educator, artist*
Wimmer, Kathryn *retired elementary school educator*
Windsor, Margaret Eden *writer*
Windward, Shirley *secondary school educator, poet*
Wingate, Bettye Faye *librarian, educator*
Wingston-Jenkins, Mary Allyson *secondary school educator*
Winiecki, Alyssa *elementary school educator*
Winkie, Dusti Kai *director*
Winn, Nelroy Griffin *healthcare administrator*
Winokur, Marissa Jaret *actress*
Winston, Sandra *health sciences administrator*
Winter, Judy Elaine *freelance/self-employed journalist, speaker*
Winter, Kathryn *music educator, writer*
Winter, Nancy Fitz *retired media and public relations executive*
Winter-Neighbors, Gwen Carole *special education educator, art educator, consultant*
Wise, Patricia *opera singer, educator*
Wise, Sandra Casber *lawyer*
Wisehart, Mary Ruth *retired religious organization administrator*
Wisely, Donna *secondary school educator, athletic trainer*
Wish, LeslieBeth Berger *psychotherapist, writer, management consultant*
Wishnick, Marcia Margolis *pediatrician, educator, geneticist*
Wisniewski, Rosemary *mathematics educator*
Withrow, Mary Ellen *federal agency administrator*
Witoshynsky, Ruth Ellen *mathematics educator*
Witt, Alicia *actress*
Witt, Nancy Camden *artist*
Wittenstein, Shirley Ann *retired branch assistant*
Wittig, Rebecca C. *community health educator*
Wittnebel, Melissa Eileen *elementary school educator, music educator*
Wittner, Lois *education educator*
Wixen, Joan Saunders *journalist*
Wolaner, Robin Peggy *internet and magazine publisher*
Wolf, Cheryl Jeane *surgical nurse*
Wolf, Christine Strelow *piano teacher*
Wolf, Katie Louise *state legislator*
Wolf, Linda S. *retired advertising executive*
Wolf, Martha Marin *nurse*
Wolf, Muriel Hebert *soprano, educator, performing company executive*
Wolfe, Claudette Tobin *elementary school educator*
Wolfe, L. Diane *writer, photographer*
Wolfe, Rinna Evelyn *writer, retired secondary school educator*
Wolfe, Sandra Jean *elementary school educator*
Wolfe, Susan McNeill *elementary education educator, guidance counselor*
Wolff, Eleanor Blunk *actress*
Wolfhagen, Helen Jane *education educator*
Wolford, Carol D. *special education educator*
Wolford, Kathryn Frances *religious organization administrator*
Wolpert Richard, Chava *artist*
Wong, Corinne Hong Sling *minister, theologian*
Wong, Elaine Dang *foundation executive*
Wong, Liliane *architect, educator*
Wong, Nancy L. *artist, retired dermatologist*
Wong, Suzanne Crawbuck *librarian*
Wong, Toh-Heng Lim *retired pediatrician, physician*
Wood, Corinne Gieseke *former lieutenant governor*
Wood, Evan Rachel *actress*
Wood, Frances Diane *medical secretary, artist*
Wood, Jane Semple *editor, writer*
Wood, Lorraine Dell *artist, consultant*
Wood, Margo *academic administrator*
Wood, Marian Starr *publishing executive*
Wood, Vivian Poates *mezzo soprano, educator*
Woodard, Anitra Denise *elementary school educator*
Woodard, Catherine *arts patron*
Woodard, Nina Elizabeth *banker*
Woodard, Sharon M. *secondary school educator*
Woodring, Margaret Daley *architect, urban planner*
Woodruff, Judy Carline *broadcast journalist*
Woodruff, Mary Brennan *elementary school educator*
Woodruff, Virginia *broadcast journalist, writer*
Woodrum, Patricia Ann *librarian*
Woods, Eleanor C. *music educator*
Woods, Harriett Ruth *political organization worker, retired state official*
Woods, Linda W. *literature and language educator*
Woods, Merilyn Baron *psychologist, consultant*
Woods, Phyllis Michalik *librarian*
Woods, Sandra Kay *real estate executive*
Woods, Susanne *academic administrator, educator*
Woodson, Jacqueline *writer*
Woodsworth, Anne *retired academic administrator, librarian*
Woodward, Debbie Carol *special education educator*
Woolston, Carol Ann *elementary school educator*
Woolston-Catlin, Marian *psychiatrist*
Woolworth, Susan Valk *primary school educator*
Wooten, Carol G. *music educator, minister*
Wooten, Joan Hedrich *minister*
Workman, Kayleen Marie *special education and adult education educator*
Worley, Debere *educational consultant*
Woronov, Mary Peter *actress*
Worrel, Connie Rae *science educator*
Worrell, Mary Thora *loan officer*
Wortham, Deborah Lynne *principal*
Wosk, Miriam *artist*
Wozniak, Joyce Marie *sales executive*
Wright, Belinda Leigh *music educator*
Wright, Ellen S. *elementary school educator*
Wright, Georgette L. *science educator*
Wright, Gladys Stone *music educator, writer, composer*
Wright, Joan L. *artist*
Wright, Josephine Rosa Beatrice *musicologist, educator*
Wright, Lori Dunkle *musician, educator*
Wright, Peggy Sue Espy *elementary school educator*
Wright, Virginia *art collector, curator*
Wriston, Kathryn Dineen *corporate director, consultant*
Wu, Min *computer and electrical engineer*
Wu, Nan Faion *pediatrician*
Wuchte, Mia Ann *elementary school educator*
Wulff, Lois Yvonne *retired librarian*
Wurdinger, Victoria *writer*
Wuthnow, Sara Margery *retired nursing educator*
Wuthrick, Eileen B. *special education educator*
Wyatt, Marcia Jean *fine arts and speech educator, administrative assistant*
Wyatt-Magalian, Cate *artist*
Wych, Amy *interpreter, educator*
Wylan, Barbara *artist*
Wymer, Barbara Sue *elementary school educator*
Wyner, Ethel Schiff *psychologist, director*
Wynn, Karla Wray *artist, agricultural products executive*
Wynn, Mary Beth *music educator*
Wyse, Lois *advertising executive, writer*
Wyskowski, Barbara Jean *lawyer*
Yaeger, Therese F. *management professional*
Yaes, Joyce *musician, artist, educator*
Yahn, Mimi *writer*
Yale (Yeleyenide-Yale), Melpomene Fotine *researcher, anthropologist, archaeologist, art historian, conservator*
Yali, Ann Marie *psychology professor*
Yamaguchi, Kristi Tsuya *ice skater*
Yancey, Elizabeth Stilphen *political scientist*
Yancey, Victoria Francine *education educator*
Yanda, Cathy L. *small business owner, counselor, illustrator*
Yanowitz, Joyce *nutritional counselor*
Yao, Frances *music educator, small business owner*
Yarbrough, Kathryn Davis *public health nurse*
Yarlow, Loretta *art museum director*
Yarnell, Gail Ellen *dentist, prosecutor*
Yates, Kimberly Nicole *school psychologist*
Yates, Mary Carlin *former ambassador*
Yeager, Toni Lee *special education educator, real estate manager*
Yearwood, Trisha *country music singer, songwriter*
Yee, Nancy W. *travel consultant*
Yenchko, Suzanne *research and development company executive*
Yerxa, Jane Anne *artist*
Yih, Ann *writer, journalist*
Ying, Jackie *chemical engineer, educator*
Yingling, Phyllis Stuckey *writer*
Yiotis, Gayle *archivist, researcher, anthropologist, writer*
Yitts, Rose Marie *nursery school executive*
Yntema, Mary Katherine *retired mathematics educator*
Yoder, Nanci Sue *retired psychologist*
Yoder, Sharon Kathleen *educator*
Yokley, Karel *athletic trainer, educator*
Yolango, Marlene Fanning *special education educator*
Yopconka, Natalie Ann Catherine *executive secretary, computer specialist, educator, entrepreneur, small business owner*
York, Joan Elizabeth Smith *psychologist*
Yoskey, Sylvia Lynn *surgical nurse*
Yost, Jean Marie *administrative assistant*
Young, Alison *music educator*
Young, Deborah (Deborah Ayling Yanowitz) *social worker, librarian*
Young, Elizabeth Bell *organization consultant*
Young, Judith Anne *animal conservationist*
Young, Lai-Sang *mathematician, educator*
Young, Margaret Buckner *civic worker, author*
Young, Marlene Annette *lawyer*
Young, Natalie Jane *elementary special education educator*
Young, Susan Babson *retired library director*
Young, Teresa Gail Hilger *retired adult education educator*
Young, Virginia McLain *information technology consulting executive*
Youngs, Diane Campfield *learning disabilities specialist, educator*
Younker, Kathleen Teuber *pianist, music educator*
Yow, Audrey Jo *artist, educator*
Yowell, Nancy T. *photographer, retired elementary school educator*
Yuriko, (Yuriko Kikuchi) *dancer, choreographer*
Zablocki, Elaine *writer*
Zachary, Je'Quita Yvette *elementary school educator, singer*
Zager, Dianne E. *special education educator*
Zahn, Laura Sue Noyes *educational consultant, small business owner*
Zahner Kraeft, Dorothy Simkin *elementary school educator, school librarian*
Zaleski, Jean *artist*
Zalila-Mili, Rym *computer scientist, educator*
Zambrano, Debra Kay *community health nurse*
Zanetti, Teresa A. *state representative*
Zanjani, Sally *political science educator, author*
Zappa, Gail *record producer*
Zaragoza, Rylee Renee *elementary school educator*
Zaring, Jane Thomas *retired editor, writer*
Zarro, Janice Anne *lawyer*
Zawaideh, Mona A. *pediatrician, endocrinologist, nephrologist, educator*
Zebi, Sandra *artist*
Zeigler, Bekki LarissA *biology professor*
Zeilig, Nancy Meeks *writer, editor*
Zeilinger, Elna Rae *elementary school educator, gifted and talented educator*
Zekman, Terri Margaret *graphic designer*
Zentz, Laurie Funderburk *music educator*
Zephier, Jenny Renee *elementary school educator*
Zeta-Jones, Catherine *actress*
Zeviar-Geese, Gabriole *stock market investor, lawyer*
Zidovec, Mirta Rosa *Spanish language professional*
Ziemba, Karen *actress*
Zigler, Melissa May *music educator*
Zilberberg, Barbara *psychologist*
Zimmerman, Helene Loretta *retired business educator*
Zimmerman, Jean *lawyer*
Zimmerman, Jo Ann *retired health science association administrator, educator, retired lieutenant governor*
Zimmerman, Phyllis Elaine *music educator, composer, director*
Zimmermann, Bonnie *physical and health education educator*
Zirbes, Mary Kenneth *retired minister*
Zito, Rae Nanette *elementary school educator*
Zuber, Catherine *costume designer*
Zuck, Rosemary *social worker, educator*
Zucker, Maureen T. *artist*
Zuckerman, Harriet *sociologist, educator*
Zuckerman, Nancy Ann *writer, publicist, minister*
Zuk, Judith *retired botanist, director*
Zumbrunnen, Elizabeth *artist, educator*
Zurbuchen, Susan Jane *arts consultant*
Zurenda, Deb *biology educator*
Zurflueh, Linda June *allergy and immunology nurse, educator*
Zwicke, Paula Ann *literature and language educator, communications educator*
Zyroff, Ellen Slotoroff *information scientist, classicist, educator*

Professional Index

AGRICULTURE

UNITED STATES

ALABAMA

Citronelle
Black, Waynetta Grant *agricultural studies educator, retired counseling administrator*

ARKANSAS

Humphrey
Wilson, Victoria Jane Simpson *farmer, medical/surgical nurse*

CALIFORNIA

Lompoc
Valla, Bree Butler *agricultural studies educator*

Orange
Williams, Patricia Sue *agricultural studies educator*

Pacific Palisades
Jennings, Marcella Grady *rancher, investor*

Sonoma
Racke, Anne Moller *winery executive*

COLORADO

Fowler
Giadone, Susan *livestock office manager*

New Raymer
Williams, Doris W. *rancher*

ILLINOIS

Kenilworth
Clary, Rosalie Brandon Stanton *timber farm executive, civic worker*

Pleasant Plains
Thomas, Evelyn B. *agricultural products supplier*

INDIANA

Indianapolis
Hegel, Carolyn Marie *farm management extension agent*

IOWA

Charles City
McCartney, Rhoda Huxsol *farm manager*

MAINE

Gouldsboro
Thayer, Cynthia A. *farmer, writer*

MINNESOTA

Goodridge
Hanson, Norma Lee *farmer*

MONTANA

Martinsdale
Rostad, Lee B. *rancher, writer*

NEVADA

Yerington
Scatena, Lorraine Borba *retired rancher, women's rights advocate, researcher*

NEW JERSEY

Jackson
Rickabaugh, Vicki *horse farm owner, mayor*

NEW YORK

Pine Island
Rogowski, Cheryl *farmer*

NORTH DAKOTA

Fargo
Wachenheim, Cheryl J. *agricultural studies educator*

SOUTH CAROLINA

Clemson
Caldwell, Judith *horticultural educator*

Dillon
Chandler, Marcia Shaw Barnard *farmer*

Greer
Gregg, Marie Byrd *retired farmer*

SOUTH DAKOTA

Saint Lawrence
Lockner, Vera Joanne *farmer, rancher, state legislator*

TENNESSEE

Hickory Valley
Weaver, Peggy (Marguerite McKinnie Weaver) *plantation owner*

TEXAS

Farnsworth
Gramstorff, Jeanne B. *retired farmer*

Houston
Shuart, Carey Chenoweth *farmer, volunteer*

VIRGINIA

Mc Lean
McIlwain, Clara Evans *agricultural economist, consultant*

ADDRESS UNPUBLISHED

Barrett, Barbara McConnell *ranch owner, lawyer*
Gordon, Emmajean Elizabeth *farmer, entrepreneur, consultant*
Lightburn, Christa Pierpont *agricultural business manager*
Ogilvie, Tamara A. *rancher, elementary school educator*
Stanley, Marlyse Reed *horse breeder*

ARCHITECTURE & DESIGN

UNITED STATES

ARIZONA

Phoenix
Adams, Gail Hayes *interior designer*
Gwozdz, Kim Elizabeth *interior designer, furniture designer*

Scottsdale
Brown, Shirley Margaret Kern (Peggy Brown) *interior designer*

Tucson
Robles, Maricela *architect*

CALIFORNIA

Belvedere
Hugenberg, Patricia Ellen Petrie *product designer*

Carlsbad
Cuthbert, Emilie Ann (Emilie Winthrop) *interior designer*

Chula Vista
Weiss-Cornwell, Amy *interior designer*

Costa Mesa
Stecker, Suzanne Louise *business executive*

Highland
MacQueen, Cherie K. *interior designer, retired newscaster, sportscaster*

Los Angeles
Krag, Olga *interior designer*

Redondo Beach
Shellhorn, Ruth Patricia *landscape architect*

San Francisco
Blake, Laura *architect*
Campbell, Janet Coral *architect*

San Ramon
Jue, Susan Lynne *interior designer*

Santa Barbara
Rosen, Adele R. *interior designer*

Santa Monica
Eizenberg, Julie *architect*

Watsonville
McBride, Susan Alyse *interior designer, consultant*

Windsor
Matkin, Judith Conway *product designer*

COLORADO

Denver
Fogg, Janet *architectural firm executive*
Robins, Judy Roselyn *interior designer*

Englewood
Asarch, Elaine *interior designer, anthropologist*

Fort Collins
Grandin, Temple *industrial designer, science educator*

Grand Junction
Burdick, Margaret Seale (Marge Burdick) *interior designer*

Littleton
Shepherd, Donna Lou *interior designer*

CONNECTICUT

Branford
Wright, Nancy Howell *interior designer*

Greenwich
Hershaft, Elinor *space planner, interior designer*

New Haven
Deamer, Peggy *architecture educator*

Old Greenwich
Whitlock, Veronica P. *interior designer, educator*

Ridgefield
Tamsett, Susan O. *architect, artist*

Stonington
Stoddard, Alexandra *interior designer, educator, writer*

DISTRICT OF COLUMBIA

Washington
Dutton, Christina Parker *interior designer, event planner*
Holladay, Wilhelmina Cole *interior designer, museum director*
Lewis, Anne McCutcheon *architect*
Liebenson, Gloria Krasnow *interior design executive, freelance writer*
Woofter, Vivien Perrine *interior designer, consultant*

FLORIDA

Boca Raton
Reeves, Mary Jane W. *interior designer*

Coral Gables
Morales-Martin, Gisela *interior designer*
Sola, Caridad Maria *architect*

Gainesville
Hasell, Mary Joyce (Jo) *architecture educator*
Kohen, Martha *architecture educator*

Longwood
Gasperoni, Ellen Jean Lias *interior designer*

Miami
Spear, Laurinda Hope *architect*
Yde, Jacqulyn Rae *interior designer, architectural colorist*

Miramar
Stewart Simpson, Donnamay Angela *interior designer*

Naples
McDonald, Jinx *interior designer*

Palm Bay
Hanna, Emma Harmon *architect, small business owner, mayor*

Ponte Vedra Beach
Simon, Lois Prem *interior designer, artist*

West Palm Beach
Marshall-Beasley, Elizabeth *landscape architect*

GEORGIA

Atlanta
Chang, Leng Kar *interior designer*

Decatur
Pharr, Paige Elizabeth *interior designer, real estate broker*

HAWAII

Honolulu
Jensen, Barbara Wood *interior design business owner*
Noe, Joyce M. *architecture educator*
Palumbo, Lorraine Reiko Minatoishi *architect, researcher*

ILLINOIS

Barrington
Amatangelo, Kathleen Driscoll *interior designer, educator*

Champaign
Anthony, Kathryn Harriet *architecture educator*

Chicago
Barney, Carol Ross *architect*
Kerbis, Gertrude Lempp *architect*
Legge Kemp, Diane *architect, landscape architect*
McCurry, Margaret Irene *architect, educator, furniture designer, interior designer*
Pratt, Susan G. *architect*
Robertson, Donna Virginia *architect, educator, dean*
VanderBeke, Patricia K. *architect*

Hinsdale
Unikel, Eva Taylor *interior designer*

Kenilworth
Schneider-Criezis, Susan Marie *architect*

Plainfield
Vargo, Louise Ann *landscape artist, music educator*

Wheaton
Martin, Marcia Gray *retired architecture educator, artist, designer*

LOUISIANA

Alexandria
Foster, Sally *interior designer*

New Orleans
Steinmetz, Deborah Susan *interior designer*

MAINE

Edgecomb
Carlson, Suzanne Olive *architect*

MARYLAND

Arnold
Shepard, Brandi R. *architecture educator*

Baltimore
Heath, Emily B. *interior designer*

Easton
Bugg, Carol Donayre *interior designer*

Garrett Park
Stites, M(ary) Elizabeth *architecture educator*

Potomac
Yerman, Anne Veronica *interior designer*

Towson
Tatman, Sandra L. *design educator*

MASSACHUSETTS

Boston
Ericson, Elizabeth (Zibby) *architect*
Goody, Joan Edelman *architect*
Sullivan Stemberg, Maureen *interior designer*
Wedge, Carole C. *architectural firm executive*

Cambridge
Chiles, Carol S. *architectural firm executive*
Santos, Adèle Naudé *architect, educator*

Longmeadow
Teitz, Betty Beatrice Goldstein *retired interior designer*

Waban
Etter, Faye Madalyn *interior design company executive*

MICHIGAN

Ann Arbor
Wineman, Jean D. *architecture educator*

Chelsea
Kendall, Kay Lynn *interior designer, consultant*

Flushing
Demankowski, Lisa Renee *architect, educator*

Frankenmuth
Rau, Louise Billie *interior designer*

MINNESOTA

Minneapolis
Dworsky, Mary *interior designer*
Solomonson, Katherine *architecture educator*

MISSISSIPPI

Columbus
Rood, Cynthia Hooper *landscape architect, consultant*

Jackson
Leonard, Pamela Dian *architect, artist*

MISSOURI

Chesterfield
Stevens, Annie Bickett Parker *retired architect*

Saint Louis
Bextermiller, Theresa Marie *architect, computer engineer*

NEW JERSEY

Carteret
John, Dolores *architect, consultant*

Clifton
Kalata, Mary Ann Catherine *architect*

Colonia
Wiesenfeld, Bess G. *interior designer*

East Orange
Fielo, Muriel Bryant *interior designer*

Princeton
Boyer, M. Christine *architecture educator*
Diller, Elizabeth E. *architect, educator, artist*

Somerdale
Botka, Betsy Jean *industrial arts and career awareness instructor*

Trenton
Jones, Sophia LaShawn *architect*

NEW MEXICO

Albuquerque
Foster, Judi *interior designer, artist*
Gutierrez, Gabriella *architecture educator*
Gutierrez, Joni Marie *landscape architect, political organization worker*
Smith, Jean *interior design firm executive*

Santa Fe
Wilson, Laura Eleanor *landscape architect*

NEW YORK

Brooklyn
Woolley, Margaret Anne (Margot Woolley) *architect*

Cross River
Thorn, Susan Howe *interior designer*

Kew Gardens
Aldea, Patricia *architect*

Manhasset
Seftel, Donna Selene *architect*

New York
Arts-Meyer, Katina *interior designer*
Baird, Penny Drue *interior designer*
Balmori, Diana *landscape designer*
Blumenfeld, Joan *architect*
Cracauer, Cynthia Phifer *architectural firm executive*
Dennis, Diane Joy Milam *retired architect*
Edelman, Judith H. *architect*
Gath, Jean Marie *architectural firm executive*
Georgopoulos, Maria *architect, artist*
Ghaffari, Avideh Behrouz *interior designer*
Halsband, Frances *architect*
Hariri, Gisue *architect, educator*
Karlin, Susan *design company executive*
Kasakove, Susan *interior designer*
Lerner, Jill *architect*
Owen, Sylvia *interior design executive*
Scott, Felicity Dale Elliston *architecture educator, editor*
Sevely, Maria *architect*
Szeto, Yvonne *architectural firm executive*
Taylor, Marilyn Jordan *architectural firm executive*

Richfield Springs
Walters, Marjorie Anne *interior designer, consultant*

Rochester
Manley, Cathey Neracker *interior design executive*

Westhampton Beach
Flood, Angela *interior designer, artist*

NORTH CAROLINA

Kinston
Baker-Gardner, Jewelle *interior designer, business consultant*

Kitty Hawk
Elliott, Candice K. *interior designer*

Lewisville
Krier, Ann O. *product designer, writer*

Raleigh
Susanka, Sarah Hills *architect*

OHIO

Dayton
Leakas, Diana Brod *interior designer, educator*

Mason
Cuff, Virginia Evelyn *architectural firm executive, consultant*

OKLAHOMA

Oklahoma City
Halpin, Anna Marie *retired architect*

OREGON

Eugene
Theodoropoulos, Christine O. *architecture educator*
Utsey, Glenda Fravel *architecture educator*

Hillsboro
Dubrulle, Françoise M. *architect, painter, interior designer*

Portland
Vanderslice, Ellen *architect, composer*

PENNSYLVANIA

Ambler
Swansen, Donna Maloney *landscape designer, consultant*

Bryn Mawr
Fellinger-Buzby, Linda *interior and industrial designer*

Columbia
Steiner-Houck, Sandra Lynn *interior designer*

Harrisburg
Knackstedt, Mary V. *interior designer*
Weiser, Kathy M. *highway designer*

Kintnersville
Sartori, Marilee A. *space designer*

Philadelphia
Brown, Denise Scott *architect, urban planner*
Maxman, Susan Abel *architect*

Pittsburgh
Horowitz, Carole Spiegel *landscape contractor*

Williamsport
Wittman, Brittany Lyn *design educator*

RHODE ISLAND

Newport
Hence, Jane Knight *interior designer*

Providence
Kagan, Marilyn D. *retired architect*

SOUTH CAROLINA

Florence
Belissary, Karen *interior designer*

Mount Pleasant
Gregory, Yvonne Elizabeth Heyning *interior designer*
Hill, Larkin Payne *jewelry designer, manufacturer*

TENNESSEE

Nashville
Bramlett, Shirley Marie Wilhelm *interior designer, artist*

TEXAS

College Station
Downing, Frances E. *architecture educator*
Vandiver, Renee Lillian Aubry *interior designer, architectural preserver*

Dallas
Charriere, Suzanne *architectural firm executive*
Landry, Jane Lorenz *architect*

Houston
Amador, Anne *architect, composer*
Bogan, Mary Ellen *draftsman, educator*
Green, Sharon Jordan *interior decorator*
Solomon, Marsha Harris *draftsman, artist*

Katy
Fruia, Carolyn Christine *hair designer, educator*

Nacogdoches
Bacarisse, Angela *design educator, costume designer*

San Marcos
Treanor, Betty McKee *interior design educator*

Spring
Westover, Diana Kay *interior designer, executive recruiter*

UTAH

Salt Lake City
Jensen, Susan *design educator, multi-media specialist*

VIRGINIA

Alexandria
Simonds, Marie Celeste *architect*

Berryville
Martin, Alison Cady *interior designer*

Blacksburg
Bliznakov, Milka Tcherneva *architect, educator*

Greenbackville
Lewis, Kay *interior designer, consultant*

Richmond
Frazer, Susan Hume *architectural firm executive*

Staunton
Firehock, Barbara A. *interior designer*

Virginia Beach
Stanton, Pamela Freeman *interior designer, writer*

Woodbridge
Peck, Dianne Kawecki *architect*

WASHINGTON

Bellevue
Wallace, Mary Colette *architectural researcher, designer*

Kennewick
Morris, Rusty Lee *architectural consulting firm executive*

Mill Creek
Latta, Diana Lennox *retired interior designer*

Seattle
Clark, Dawn A. *architect*
Perthou, Alison Chandler *interior designer*

WISCONSIN

Milwaukee
Frank, Nancy *architecture educator*
Hubbard, Nancy *architecture educator*

Waukesha
Leatherberry, Anne Knox Clark *architect*

CANADA

ONTARIO

Toronto
van Ginkel, Blanche Lemco *architect, educator*

ADDRESS UNPUBLISHED

Abbott, Amy P. *design educator*
Ailloni-Charas, Miriam Clara *interior designer, consultant*
Armistead, Katherine Kelly (Mrs. Thomas B. Armistead III) *interior designer, travel consultant, civic worker*
Berry, Sharon Elaine *interior designer*
Blanco, Laura *interior designer*
Brice, Jacqueline (Jackie Brice) *landscape artist*
Cohen, Sharleen Cooper *interior designer, writer*
Demant, Margaret H. *retired interior designer*
DeVoueroix, Channing *interior designer, writer, educator*
Dubrow, Gail Lee *architecture educator*
Dudics-Dean, Susan Elaine *interior designer*
Feldhamer, Thelma Leah *architect*
Finn, Charlotte Kaye *interior designer*
Friedman, Mildred *architecture educator, design educator, curator*
Hardin, Mary L. *interior designer*
Hastings, L(ois) Jane *architect, educator*
Holthausen, Martha Anne *interior designer*
Joffe, Barbara Lynne *business transformation architect*
Johnson, Mary Elaine *interior designer, writer, counselor*
Keech, Elowyn Ann *interior designer*
Labiner, Caroline *architect*
Lai, Feng-Qi *instructional designer, educator*
Largent, Margie *retired architect*
Lin, Maya *architect, sculptor*
Lipscomb, Laura *information architect*
Manasc, Vivian *architect, consultant*
Martin, Jean H. *retired interior designer*
McGraw, Susan Catherine *interior designer*
McTyer-Clarke, Wanda Kathleen *interior designer*
Parke, Janet Diane *interior designer*
Perkins, Nancy Jane *industrial designer*
Pfanstiel Parr, Dorothea Ann *interior designer*
Pincus, Nancy *architect, web site designer*
Ross, Molly Owings *jewelry designer, sculptor, small business owner*
Russo, Sabrina *architect*
Selig, Phyllis Sims *retired architect*
Strong, Annsley Chapman *interior designer, volunteer*
Tyng, Anne Griswold *architect*
Webber, Linda Judith Ritz *interior designer*
White, Othell *interior designer*
White, Pauline M. *interior decorator*
Wiele, Patricia Giordano *interior decorator*
Willis, Beverly Ann *architect*
Wong, Liliane *architect, educator*
Woodring, Margaret Daley *architect, urban planner*

ARTS: LITERARY *See also* COMMUNICATIONS MEDIA

UNITED STATES

ALABAMA

Birmingham
Galloway, Catherine Black *writer, editor*
Lowery, Deborah Garrison *freelance writer, editor*

Daphne
Rush, Anne Kent *writer, illustrator*

Elmore
Williams, Glenda Carlene *writer*

Evergreen
Lodge-Peters, Dianne Speed *writer, literature educator, researcher*

Tuscumbia
Mitchell, Joyce Faye *writer, editor*

ALASKA

Fairbanks
Anderson, Jean Blanche *fiction writer*

Juneau
Rogers, Jean Clark *writer*

Wasilla
Brunke, Dawn Baumann *writer, editor*

ARIZONA

Congress
Scheall, Norma *writer, editor*

Flagstaff
Weeks, Edythe E. *writer, educator*

Phoenix
Duyck, Kathleen Marie *poet, musician, retired social worker*
Gabaldon, Diana *writer*
Holaday, Barbara (Bobbie) Hayne *writer*

Scottsdale
Carpenter, Betty O. *writer*
Parsons, Cynthia *writer, consultant*

Sonoita
Browning, Sinclair *writer*

Tsaile
Walters, Anna Lee *writer, educational association administrator*

Tucson
Hopper, Nancy Jane *author*
Nord, Myrtle Selma *writer, researcher*
Starkey, Shirley Condit *writer, artist*
Stitt, Mari Leipper *poet*
Williams, Joy *writer*

ARKANSAS

Hot Springs National Park
Stuber, Irene Zelinsky *writer, researcher*

Little Rock
Nunn, Patarica Dian *poet*

Springdale
Haseloff, Cynthia *fiction writer*

CALIFORNIA

Altadena
Snortland, Ellen Barbara *writer*

Aptos
Farhat-Holzman, Laina *writer, editor*

Atascadero
Locke, Virginia Otis *writer*

Belvedere Tiburon
Dams, Jeanne M. *writer*

Berkeley
Burch, Claire Rita *writer*
Chetin, Helen Campbell *writer*
Kushner, Eve *writer*
Mukherjee, Bharati (Mrs. Clark Blaise) *writer, language educator*
Stroup, Dorothy Anne *author, educator*

Beverly Hills
Meyers, Nancy Jane *screenwriter, producer, director*
Quinn, Patricia K. *literary agent*
Steinem, Gloria *writer, editor, advocate*

Brawley
King, Bonnie Bess Worline *writer, educator*

Camarillo
Truman, Ruth *administrator, writer, lecturer, consultant*

Cameron Park
Vorce-Tish, Helene R. *writer*

Canoga Park
Alexander, Sue *writer*

Carpinteria
Rau, Margaret E. *writer*

Chula Vista
Ryan, Candace I. *writer, director, editor*

Citrus Heights
Daves, Sandra Lynn *poet, lyricist*

Cotati
Hill, Debora Elizabeth *writer, journalist, screenwriter*

Cupertino
Zobel, Louise Purwin *author, educator, lecturer, writing consultant*

Davis
McPherson, Sandra Jean *poet, educator*

Dublin
Ingram, Judith Elizabeth *writer*

El Cerrito
Tannenbaum, Judith Nettie *writer, educator*

Fresno
Garrison-Finderup, Ivadelle Dalton *writer, educator*
Lanter, Lanore *writer, educator*

Fullerton
Breyer, Pamela Peterson *writer*

Gold River
Reynolds, Marilyn Ann *writer*

Goleta
Robinson, Nancy A. *writer*

Healdsburg
Castellini, Mary Mercer *author*

Hillsborough
Atwood, Mary Sanford *writer*

Huntington Beach
Flakes, Susan *playwright, scriptwriter, theater director*

Idyllwild
Schneider, Margaret Perrin *scriptwriter*

La Jolla
Iddings, Kathleen *poet, editor, publisher, consultant*

Laguna Niguel
McClintock, Sandra Janise *writer, editor, book designer*
Rubinstein, Charlotte Streifer *writer, art historian, educator*

Lakeside
Koski, Donna Faith *poet*

Lodi
Schulz, Laura Janet *writer, retired executive secretary*

Lompoc
Jack, Morgann Tayllor *writer, artist*

Long Beach
Hansell, Susan *writer, educator*

Los Altos
Hickman, Martha Whitmore *writer*

Los Angeles
Anderson, Jane A. *scriptwriter*
Atnip, Linda *writer*
Campbell, Bebe Moore *writer*
Compo, Susan Ann *writer, educator*
Edmonson-Nelson, Gloria Jean *freelance writer*
Good, Edith Elissa (Pearl Williams) *writer, lexicographer*
Kaplan, Nadia *writer*
Maker, Janet Anne *writer, retired literature educator*
Sedaris, Amy *writer, actress*
Toffler, Heidi *author, futurist*
Wiggins, Marianne *writer*

Malibu
Marvin, Barbara Joyce *writer*

Mckinleyville
O'Dea, Suzanne Dores *author*

Menlo Park
Heller, Esther A. *writer, educator*

Mill Valley
Coulter, Catherine *writer*
Mautner, Gabriella *writer, educator*
Owings, Alison June *writer, journalist*

Monrovia
Salaman, Maureen Kennedy *writer, nutritionist*

Moraga
Sestanovich, Molly Brown *writer*

Newport Beach
Wentworth, Diana von Welanetz *author*

Northridge
Boberg, Dorothy Kurth *author*

Oakland
Zandvakili, Katayoon *writer*

Ontario
Kloepfer, Marguerite Fonnesbeck *writer*

Orinda
Strong, Susan Clancey *writer, communications executive, editor*

Pacific Grove
O'Shaughnessy, Ellen Cassels *writer*

Pacifica
Miller, Lynn Ruth *writer, artist, comedian*

Palm Desert
Carangelo, Lori *writer, not-for-profit developer, volunteer*

Palm Springs
Nelson, K. Bonita *literary agent*

Pasadena
Brogden-Stirbl, Shona Marie *writer, researcher*
Littke, Lael Jensen *author*
Yeager, Caroline Hale *writer, retired radiologist, consultant*

Petaluma
Ehret, Terry *writer*
Sebold, Alice *writer*

Placerville
Wilkinson, Rosemary Regina Challoner *poet, writer*

Rancho Santa Fe
Byrd, Betty Rantze *writer*

Redondo Beach
Battles, Roxy Edith *novelist, consultant, educator*

Riverside
Witman, Laura Kathleen *writer, security professional*

Ross
Godwin, Sara *writer*

San Bernardino
Hansen, Anne Katherine *poet*

San Diego
Hammersmith, Nita Marie *writer*
Koppman, Mae Z. *writer, educator*

San Francisco
Aslan, Madalyn *writer, educator*
Mirosevich, Toni *writer, educator*
O'Connor, Sheila Anne *freelance writer*
Sachs, Marilyn Stickle *writer, educator, editor*

San Jose
Prestine, Joan Singleton *writer, educator, editor*
Williams, Suzanne *writer, community volunteer*

San Luis Rey
Williams, Elizabeth Yahn *writer, educator, lawyer*

San Marcos
Winebrenner, Susan Kay *writer, consultant*

San Marino
Sherwood, Midge *writer*

San Rafael
Marcus, Adrianne Stuhl *writer*
Walker, Mary Alexander *writer*

Santa Barbara
Behrens, June Adelle *writer*
Cunningham, Julia Woolfolk *author*
Dirlam, Sharon Joan *writer*
Mitchell, Shawne Maureen *author*
Molad, Clarisse Behar *writer, consultant*

Santa Clara
Simmons, Janet Bryant *writer, publishing executive*

Santa Cruz
Bell, Clare Louise *writer, engineer*
Davis, Angela Yvonne *political activist, educator, writer*
Sherman, Frieda Frances *writer*

Santa Monica
Huffington, Arianna (Arianna Stassinopoulos) *writer*
Jones, Janet Dulin *scriptwriter, film producer*
Roney, Alice Lorraine Mann *poet*
Shiffrin, Nancy *writer, educator*
Spataro, Janie Dempsey Watts *freelance/self-employed writer*

Sebastopol
Arnold, Marsha Diane *writer*
Marler, Joan *writer, educator*

Somis
Premack, Ann J. *writer*

Sonoma
Huguenard, Joan *writer*
Kizer, Carolyn Ashley *poet, educator*

Stockton
Niles, Joyce Lynn *writer, editor, consultant*

Sugarloaf
Black, Victoria Lynn *writer, artist*

Valencia
Parks, Suzan Lori *playwright*

Valley Village
Carabillo, Virginia Anne (Toni Carabillo) *writer, editor, graphic designer*

Volcano
Stone, Karen G. *writer*

West Hollywood
Peyton, Elizabeth Joy *writer, painter*

Woodland Hills
Jason, Sonya *writer*

COLORADO

Bayfield
Korns, Leota Elsie *writer, mountain land developer, insurance broker*

Boulder
Coel, Margaret Speas *writer*
Davidson, Sara *writer*
Kaye, Evelyn Patricia (Evelyn Patricia Sarson) *author, publisher, travel expert*

Cascade
Seger, Linda Sue *script consultant, lecturer, writer*

Colorado Springs
Lyddane, Anne Alexandra *retired writer*

Denver
Buckstein, Caryl Sue *writer*
Dallas, Sandra *writer*
Howse, Cathy L. *writer, researcher, entrepreneur*
Kundert, Judy A. *writer*
Nemiro, Beverly Mirium Anderson *author, educator*
Vosevich, Kathi Ann *writer, editor*

Golden
Greenberg, Joanne *author, anthropologist*

Greeley
Willis, Connie (Constance E. Willis) *writer*

Lakewood
Peters, Julie Anne *writer*

Ouray
Rowe, Sherlie Jean *writer*

CONNECTICUT

Chester
Stark, Evelyn Brill *poet, musician*

Clinton
Adler, Peggy Ann *writer, illustrator, consultant, protective services official*
McGinley, Marjorie *writer*

East Hampton
Klein, Gail Beth Marantz *freelance/self-employed writer, animal breeder*
Tucceri, Clive Knowles *writer, science educator, consultant*

Fairfield
Barone, Rose Marie Pace *writer, retired educator*

Greens Farms
St. Marie, Satenig *writer*

Greenwich
Hoberman, Mary Ann *author*
Lacoff, Cheryl Klein *writer, artist*
Wallach, Magdalena Falkenberg (Carla Wallach) *writer*

Hamden
Davis, Lorraine Jensen *writer, editor*

Hartford
Hedrick, Joan Doran *writer, university educator*

Madison
Pauley, Barbara Anne *author, educator*

Marlborough
Garrett, Florence Rome *poet*

New Haven
Hayden, Dolores *author, architecture educator*
Scarf, Margaret (Maggie Scarf) *author*
Sommer, Miriam Goldstein (Mimi G. Sommer) *writer, photographer*
Walbert, Kate *writer, educator*

Old Lyme
LeBoutillier, Janet Ela *writer, real estate developer, minister*
St. George, Judith Alexander *writer*

Preston
Gibson, Margaret Ferguson *poet, educator*

Storrs Mansfield
Rimland, Lisa Phillip *writer, composer, lyricist*

Waterford
Commire, Anne *playwright, writer, editor*

Westbrook
Fuller, Martha M. *poet*
Hall, Jane Anna *writer, model, artist*

Westport
Safran, Claire *writer, editor*

Winsted
Wilson, Mary Flynn *writer, educator*

DISTRICT OF COLUMBIA

Washington
Atlas, Liane Wiener *writer*
Coulter, Ann *writer, political columnist, lawyer*
Dessaso, Deborah Ann *freelance/self-employed writer, corporate communications specialist*
Fallon, Sally *writer*
Innis, Pauline *writer, publishing company executive*
Levy, Ellen J. *writer, educator*
Murphy, Joanne Becker *writer*
Nathan, Joan *cookbook author, freelance writer, lecturer*
Raloff, Janet *science writer*
Robb, Lynda Johnson *writer*
Tannen, Deborah Frances *writer*
Zacarías, Karen *playwright*

FLORIDA

Belleair Beach
Fuentes, Martha Ayers *playwright*

Cape Coral
Janssen, Janice Beaty *writer, educator*

Coconut Creek
Fait, Grace Wald *writer, retired language educator*

Crystal River
Keith, Carol Jean *writer, regional historian*

Delray Beach
Snyder, Virginia Artrip *writer*

Fort Lauderdale
Schneider, Ursula Wilfriede *author*

Gainesville
Smith, Jo Anne *writer, retired communications educator*

Hallandale Beach
Geller, Bunny Zelda *poet, writer, publisher, sculptor, artist*

Hobe Sound
Houser, Constance W. *writer, artist*

Key Biscayne
Cardozo, Arlene Rossen *writer*
Clay, Cynthia Joyce *writer, editor-in-chief*

Lake Wales
Butler, Susan *writer*

Leesburg
Thompson, Mary B. *writer, illustrator*

Longboat Key
Hazan, Marcella Maddalena *writer, educator, consultant*

Miami
Ayers, Mary Alice *writer, English educator*
Goodman-Milone, Constance B. (Connie Goodman-Milone) *writer*
Laje, Zilia L. *writer, publisher, translator*
Morgan, Marabel *writer*

Naples
Capelle-Frank, Jacqueline Aimee *writer*
Wroble, Lisa Ann *writer, educator*

Navarre
Williams, Ella Owens *writer*

Neptune Beach
Chambers, Ruth Coe *writer*

Oldsmar
Craft Davis, Audrey Ellen *writer, educator*

Orlando
Powell, Elaine Marie *writer, educator*
Raffa, Jean Benedict *author, educator*

Palm Bay
Stone, Elaine Murray *writer, composer, television producer*

Palm Beach
Javits, Joan (Zeeman) *writer, inventor*
Kay, Marcia Chellis *writer*

Pompano Beach
Kaskinen, Barbara Kay *writer, composer, lyricist, musician, educator*

Port Charlotte
Wolff, Diane Patricia *writer, film and television producer*

Punta Gorda
Hamel, Esther Veramae *author*

Saint Petersburg
Carlson, Jeannie Ann *writer*

Sarasota
Jones, Sally Daviess Pickrell *writer*

Sneads
Scott, Brenda D. *writer*

Summerfield
Johnson, Charlene Rose *writer*

Sun City Center
Mohin, Ann Marie *writer*

Tamarac
Toubes, Judith Esther *retired writer*

Tampa
Hanford, Grail Stevenson *writer*

Winter Park
Rooks, Linda *writer*

GEORGIA

Atlanta
Cleage, Pearl Michelle *writer, playwright, journalist*
Corriher, Shirley *food writer*
Edson, Margaret *playwright*
Poston, Martha Anne *author, researcher*
Rouse, Sandra Howard *writer*

Barnesville
Brown, Angelia *poet*

Carrollton
Williams, Mary Eleanor Nicole *writer*

Kennesaw
Rogers, Glenda Nelson *writer, photographer*

Loganville
Smelser, Thelma Ann *writer, tax specialist*

Stone Mountain
Allen (Irvin M.N.), Georgianne Lydia Christian *writer, poet*

Thomaston
Graham, Violet Joyce *writer*

Woodstock
Christmas, Bobbie Jaye *freelance.self-employed editor and writer*

HAWAII

Holualoa
Stoddard, Sandol *freelance/self-employed writer*

Kihei
Palmer, Patricia G. *writer, retired psychologist*

Waianae
Holifield, Pearl Kam (Kam Holifield, Momi Kam Holifield) *poet*

IDAHO

Boise
Fanselow, Julie Ruth *writer*

ILLINOIS

Belleville
Pounds, Regina Dorothea *writer*

Canton
Hines, Daisy Marie *freelance/self-employed writer*

Chicago
Brown, Rosellen *writer*
Danis, Julie Marie *writer, advertising executive*
Drake, Robyn Renée (Robyn Fielder) *writer, painter*
Lach, Alma Elizabeth *food and cooking writer, consultant*
Lerner, Barbara *writer, researcher*
Madsen, Dorothy Louise (Meg Madsen) *writer*
Melnick, Jane Fisher *writer, educator, photographer*
Powell, Enid Levinger *writer, educator*
Rosenthal, Elizabeth Anne *writer, entrepreneur*
Vowell, Sarah *writer, radio personality*

Crystal Lake
Fleming, Marjorie Foster *freelance writer, artist*
Reed, Helen G. *poet*

Evanston
Holton, Lisa *writer, editor, researcher*

Galesburg
Sunderland, Jacklyn Giles *retired writer*

Highland Park
Greenblatt, Miriam *writer, editor, educator*

Lake Forest
Swanton, Virginia Lee *writer, publisher*
Taylor, Barbara Ann Olin *writer, educational consultant*

Oak Lawn
Laird, Jean Elouise Rydeski (Mrs. Jack E. Laird) *author, adult education educator*

Oak Park
Pearson, Gayle Marlene *writer*

Oakland
Eriksen, Barbara Ann *writer, researcher*

Peoria
Grebner, Bernice Prill *author, astrological counselor*

Rochester
Petterchak, Janice A. *writer*

South Barrington
Kissane, Sharon Florence *writer, consultant, educator*

Urbana
Dovring, Karin Elsa Ingeborg *writer, poet, playwright, media specialist*

Wilmette
Brindel, June Rachuy *writer*
Miripol, Jerilyn Elise *poet, writer, writing therapist*

INDIANA

Akron
Allen, Elizabeth Ann *writer*

Atwood
Creamer, Kathy Jayne *writer*

Crawfordsville
Karg, Thelma Aileen *writer*

Elkhart
Eddy, Darlene Mathis *poet, educator*

Fort Wayne
Langhinrichs, Ruth Imler *playwright, writer*

Frankfort
Borland, Kathryn Kilby *writer*

Howe
Bowerman, Ann Louise *writer, secondary school educator, genealogist*

Indianapolis
Budniakiewicz, Therese *writer*
Gregory, Valiska *writer*
Hammontree, Marie Gertrude *writer*

Logansport
Howland, Bette *writer*

Richmond
Cooper, Jamie Lee *writer*

Scottsburg
Dockery, Linda *writer*

IOWA

Cedar Falls
Skaine, Rosemarie Keller *writer, consultant, publisher*

Cedar Rapids
Struthers, Eleanor Ann *writer, educator*

Davenport
Beguhn, Sandra E. *poet, writer*

Iowa City
Chang, Lan Samantha *writer, educator*
Packer, ZZ (Zuwena) *writer, literature educator*
Swensen, Cole *poet, educator*

Leon
Miller, Eleanora Genevieve *freelance/self-employed poet*

KANSAS

Lawrence
Kofler, Silvia Maria *writer, educator*

Leawood
Garwood, Julie *writer*

Olathe
Kamberg, Mary-Lane *writer, journalist*

KENTUCKY

Boston
Rosenbaum, Mary Heléne Pottker *writer, editor*

Campbellsburg
Mitchell, Mary Ann Carrico *poet*

Covington
McQueen, Regenia *writer*

Lexington
Chandler, Sherry *writer, editor*
Johnson, Jane Penelope *freelance/self-employed writer*

Sadieville
Taylor-Hall, Mary Ann *writer*

LOUISIANA

Baton Rouge
Mueller, Lisel *writer, poet*
Sanders, Mary Elizabeth *writer, historian*

Gretna
Kennedy, Maydra Jane Penisson (J.P. Kennedy) *poet*

Metairie
Grau, Shirley Ann (Mrs. James Kern Feibleman) *writer*

MAINE

Bangor
King, Tabitha *author*

Brewer
Cote Robbins, Rhea Jeannine *writer, educator*

Brunswick
Peacher, Georgiana Melicent *poet, educator*

Edgecomb
Wait, Lea *writer, small business owner*

Wilton
Emerson, Kathy *writer*

MARYLAND

Aberdeen Proving Ground
Gibson, Annemarie *writer, editor*

Baltimore
Schultheis, Patricia Ann *writer, editor*
Tyler, Anne (Mrs. Taghi M. Modarressi) *writer*

Bethesda
Naylor, Phyllis Reynolds *writer*

Chevy Chase
Rich, Doris L. *writer*

Crownsville
Sonde, Susan *writer*

Fort Washington
Cameron, Rita Giovannetti *writer, publishing executive*

Frederick
Randall, Frances *technical writer*

Germantown
Weiner, Claire Muriel *freelance writer*

Lusby
Fialka, Deborah Ridgely *writer*

Mcdaniel
Roth, Lisa Mae *writer*

North Potomac
Menendez, Shirley Corbin *writer*

Owings Mills
Smith, Katrina Diane *writer*

Potomac
Pastan, Linda Olenik *poet*
Sowalsky, Patti Lurie *author*

Princess Anne
du Nord, Jeanne *writer, publishing executive*

Rockville
Hodgson, Helen *writer*
Scinto, Carol Murdock *writer, editor, social worker*

Saint Marys City
Clifton, Lucille Thelma *author*

Severna Park
Windsor, Patricia (Katonah Summertree, Perrin Winters, Anna Seeling) *author, educator, lecturer*

Silver Spring
Kline, Syril Levin *writer, educator, educational consultant*
Vanzant, Iyanla *writer*

Upper Marlboro
Zane, *writer, publishing executive*

MASSACHUSETTS

Amherst
Deer Cloud, Susan Ann *writer*
Sandweiss, Martha Ann *writer, history professor*

Belmont
McEvoy, Frances Jane Coman *writer, editor*

Bernardston
Peoples, Marie D. *writer*

Boston
Angelou, Maya (Marguerite Annie Johnson) *writer, actress*
Appelbaum, Diana Karter *author*
Kay, Jane Holtz *writer*
Kindl, Patrice *writer*
Lahiri, Jhumpa (Nilanjana Sudeshna) *writer*
Lowry, Lois (Lois Hammersberg) *writer*
Martin, Jacqueline Briggs *writer*
Ocko, Stephanie *writer, journalist*
Painter, Pamela *writer, educator*
Strothman, Wendy Jo *literary agent*
Treadway, Jessica *writer, educator*

Byfield
Yeomans, Katie Morse *writer*

Cambridge
Blake, Patricia *writer*
DiCamillo, Kate *writer*
Graham, Jorie *writer, educator*
Hughes, Libby *writer*
Rhoda, Janice Tucker *writer, educator, musician*

Fairhaven
Lopes, Myra Amelia *writer*

Gardner
Hermkind, Hilda Marie *writer, military volunteer*

Hadley
Friedman, D. Dina *writer, educator*
Rice, Rebecca Kynoch *writer, consultant, language educator*

Hatfield
Yolen, Jane *writer*

Lenox
Bruder, Judith *writer*
Hall, Frances Benn *writer, retired theater educator*

Lexington
Topalian, Naomi Getsoyan *writer*

Marblehead
DiCanio, Margaret Brien *freelance writer, former mental health agency administrator*

North Chelmsford
Erkkila-Ricker, Barbara Howell *writer, photographer*

North Dartmouth
Sitarz, Paula Gaj *writer*

Northampton
Birdsall, Jeanne *writer, photographer*
Newman, Lesléa *writer*
Stinson, Susan Elizabeth *director, writer*

Provincetown
Oliver, Mary *poet*

Quincy
Bunting, Carolyn Anne *writer*

Revere
Recupero-Faiella, Anna Antonietta *poet*

South Hamilton
Kroeger, Catherine C. *writer, educator, editor*

Truro
Chase, Naomi Feigelson *poet*

Waltham
Seiferle, Rebecca Ann *poet, editor, publisher*

Watertown
Spivack, Kathleen Romola Drucker *writer, educator*

Wellesley
Jacobs, Ruth Harriet *poet, playwright, sociologist, gerontologist*

Wellfleet
Piercy, Marge *poet, writer*

West Newbury
Dooley, Ann Elizabeth *freelance writers cooperative executive, editor*

MICHIGAN

Ann Arbor
Gregerson, Linda Karen *poet, language educator, critic*

Belleville
Brown, Yvonne Theresa *retired writer*

Charlotte
Coirolo, Christina *writer, author representative*

Detroit
Madgett, Naomi Long *poet, editor, publisher, educator*

East Lansing
Wakoski, Diane *poet, educator*

Flint
Bobb, Carolyn Ruth *science writer*

Grand Rapids
Henry, Karen Lee *writer, educator*
Hunt, Gladys Mae *writer*

Imlay City
Kowalski, Kathleen Patricia *reporter, publishing executive*

Jackson
Riedel, Juanita Maxine *writing educator*

Mecosta
Wenzel, Karen Marie *writer*

Mount Pleasant
Smallwood, Carol *writer*

Okemos
Behrens, Ellen Elizabeth Cox *writer, counselor, educator*

Oshtemo
Arnold, Nancy Kay *writer*

Powers
Kleikamp, Beverly *poet, writer, publisher*

Quinnesec
Opolka, Jayme Lyn *medical writer, researcher*

Ypsilanti
Henderson, Maxine *writer*

MINNESOTA

Anoka
Lindbergh, Reeve *writer, poet*

Brainerd
Russell, Maxine *poet, writer*

Eagan
Horvath, Betty Ferguson *writer*

Edina
Douglas, Marjorie Myers *writer*

Excelsior
Waterhouse, Beth Elaine *writer, editor, environmental educator*

Maplewood
St. Germain, Sharon Marie *writer*

Minneapolis
Curry, Jane Anne *writer, educator, performer*
Erdrich, Louise (Karen Erdrich) *writer, poet*
Hoyle, Karen Nelson *author, curator, educator*
Tatlock, Ann *writer*
Vollmar, Alice Mary *writer*
Walker, Sally M. *writer*

Rochester
Hodgson, Harriet W. *health and wellness writer*

Winona
Peterson, Nancy Kay *poet, editor, writer*

MISSOURI

Columbia
Sapp, Eva Jo *writer, editor, educator*

Jefferson City
McDaniel, Sue Powell *writer*

Kansas City
Martin-Bowen, Lindsey *freelance writer*

Maryville
Tennihill, Sally Kay *writer, music educator*

Saint Louis
Miller, Judith Braffman *writer*
Schlafly, Phyllis Stewart *writer*
Swinson, Sara Hope *writer*

Stella
Yeagley, Joan Howerton *writer*

MONTANA

Bigfork
Brynie, Faith Hickman *writer, educator*
Wetzel, Betty Preat *writer*

Bonner
Smith, Annick *writer*

Boulder
Schaef, Anne Wilson *writer, consultant*

Helena
Benyus, Janine M. *writer*

Thompson Falls
Pargeter, Fredericka Mae (Fredi Pargeter) *writer, publisher, insurance salesperson*

NEVADA

Carson City
Bagley, Cynthia Elaine *writer*

Fallon
Rhea, Mildred Louise *writer, poet*

Henderson
Glazer, Lee Morrison (Lee Morrison) *writer, choreographer*

Las Vegas
Dew, Joan King *freelance/self-employed writer*
Gardner, Grace Joely *writer, consultant, psychologist*
Palmer, Lynne *writer, astrologer*
Winters, Marjorie K. *retired writer, editor, researcher*

NEW HAMPSHIRE

Amherst
Wilkins, Sally *writer*

Dover
Appel, Carole Stein *writer, political organizer*

Etna
Picoult, Jodi *writer*

Hanover
Kreiger, Barbara S. *writer, educator*

Jefferson
Leiper Estabrooks, Esther *writer, artist, illustrator*

New Durham
Sullivan, Mary Ann *writer, marketing professional*

Peterborough
Thomas, Elizabeth Marshall *writer*

Portsmouth
Day, Frances Ann *writer, educator*

NEW JERSEY

Bergenfield
Davidson, Marilyn Copeland *writer, music educator, musician*

Bogota
Livingston, Kathryn E. *writer*

Cape May Court House
Cohen, Susan Lois *writer*

Cherry Hill
Wolff, Ferida *author*

Clementon
Albee, Gloria *playwright*

Cliffside Park
de Gramont, Carol Carmel *writer*

Edgewater
Paci, Ruth A. *freelance/self-employed writer*

Englewood
Le Mée, Katharine Wilbur *author, educational consultant, educator*

Fair Haven
Derchin, Dary Bret Ingham *writer, radio personality*

Fort Lee
Sklar, Ethel (Dusty Sklar) *writer*

Jersey City
Pratt, Minnie Bruce *writer, educator*

Lebanon
Barto, Susan Carol *writer*

Long Branch
Lagowski, Barbara Jean *writer, editor*
Stewart, Georgiana Liccione *writer*

Metuchen
Zatz, Arline *writer, photographer*

Montclair
Fabend, Firth Haring *writer*

New Providence
SanGiovanni, Mary Elizabeth *writer, freelance manager*

Paramus
Fader, Shirley Sloan *writer*

Princeton
McKaughan, Molly *writer, consultant*

Teaneck
Hirschfelder, Arlene Phyllis *writer, educator*

Trenton
Obed, Leonora Rita Villegas *writer*

Warren
Baxter, Nancy *medical writer*

NEW MEXICO

Albuquerque
Gahala, Estella Marie *writer, consultant*
Harden, Neva Ninette *writer, consultant*
Kushlis, Patricia Hogin *foreign affairs writer, analyst*
Mulcahy, Lucille Burnett *freelance writer*
Putcamp, Luise, Jr. *writer, editor*

Las Cruces
Nelson, Antonya *writer*

Lovington
Stuart, Lillian Mary *writer*

Roswell
Watson, Marilyn Fern *writer*

Santa Fe
Bergé, Carol *writer*
Carpenter, Carol Denise *writer, educator*
Raeschild, Sheila *writer, humanities educator*
Reeve, Agnesa *writer*

Silver City
Parent, Annette Richards *free lance writer, artist*

NEW YORK

Albany
Davis, Lydia *writer, educator*

Amherst
Kester, Gunilla Theander *poet, literature educator, music educator*

Ardsley
Silman, Roberta Karpel *writer, critic*

Bedford
Levin, Elizabeth *freelance/self-employed writer*

Brewster
Dahl, Linda M. *writer*

Bridgehampton
Weiner, Jennifer Agnes *writer*

Bronx
Albrecht, Roberta J. *writer*
Bingham, June *playwright*
Leighton, Anne Renita *writer, educator*
Pellowski, Anne Rose *writer, consultant, retired library director*

Bronxville
Rosenthal, Lucy Gabrielle *writer, editor, educator*
Swann, Lois Lorraine *writer, editor, educator*

Brooklyn
Bossert, Jill Audrey *author*
Cummings, Josephine Anna *writer, consultant, advertising executive*
Druett, Joan *writer, maritime historian*
Gioseffi, Daniela (Dorothy Daniela Gioseffi) *poet, writer, playwright, critic*
Reynolds, Nancy Remick *writer, researcher, editor*
Sonnenfeld, Sandi *writer*

Buffalo
Macomber, Debbie *writer*

Cairo
Ludwig, Laura Lonshein *poet*

Cedarhurst
Solymosy, Hattie May *writer, educator*

Chappaqua
George, Jean Craighead *author, illustrator*

Dobbs Ferry
Fritz, Jean Guttery *writer*

Eastchester
Weinberg, Dale Glaser *writer, consultant*

Flushing
Zinnes, Harriet Fich *poet, fiction writer, retired English educator, literary and art critic*

Forest Hills
Lustgarten, Celia Sophie *freelance consultant, writer*

Glens Falls
Rikhoff, Jean *writer*

Great Neck
Burghardt, Linda Feuerberg *writer*
Hurwitz, Johanna (Johanna Frank) *writer*

Greenlawn
Roberts, Gloria Jean *writer*

Hicksville
Wolitzer, Hilma *novelist, short story writer*

Horseheads
Miller, Elaine Wolford *writer*

Ithaca
DeLaurentis, Louise Budde *writer*
Janowitz, Phyllis *poet, educator*

Lancaster
Otto, Tammy *author, poet, playwright*

Lowville
Colton, Bonnie Myers *folklorist, writer*

Melville
Stasi, Linda *writer, television producer, editor, scriptwriter*

Mohegan Lake
Freeman, Sally Ann *writer, English language and literacy educator*

Mount Kisco
Hodara, Susan Mina *writer*

New York
Alvarez, Julia *writer*
Ashdown, Marie Matranga (Mrs. Cecil Spanton Ashdown Jr.) *writer, educator, cultural organization administrator*
Ashton, Dore *writer, educator*
Atwood, Margaret Eleanor *writer*
Balogh, Mary *writer*
Bank, Melissa S. *writer*
Barash, Susan Shapiro *writer, humanities educator*
Bauer, Marion Dane *writer*
Bawden, Nina (Mary Bawden) *author*
Beattie, Ann *writer, educator*
Bennett, Tina *literary agent*
Berg, Elizabeth Ann *writer*
Birstein, Ann *writer, educator*
Block, Francesca Lia *writer*
Bluh, Bonnie *scriptwriter, actress, novelist, playwright*
Blume, Judy *author*
Bogen, Nancy *writer, English educator*
Bradford, Barbara Taylor *writer, journalist*
Brashares, Ann *writer*
Braudy, Susan Orr *writer*
Brown, Rita Mae *writer*
Bruning, Nancy Pauline *writer*
Buchanan, Edna *writer, retired journalist*
Bujold, Lois McMaster *writer*
Burros, Marian Fox *writer*
Bynum, Sarah Shun-lien *writer, educator*
Calisher, Hortense (Mrs. Curtis Harnack) *writer*
Castro, Jan Garden *writer, art educator, consultant*
Cherryh, C. J. *writer*
Choldenko, Gennifer *writer*
Christina, Sonja (Alisa Morris) *writer, poet*
Cleary, Beverly Atlee (Mrs. Clarence T. Cleary) *writer*
Collins, Jackie (Jacqueline Jill Collins) *writer*
Conley, Ellen Alexander *writer, educator*
Cox, Ana Marie *writer, former political blogger*
Creech, Sharon *children's author*
Crittenden, Danielle Ann *writer, journalist*
Cronin, Doreen *writer, former lawyer*
Curry, Jane Louise *writer*
Daheim, Mary Rene Richardson *writer*
deCoppet, Laura Louise *writer, editor*
Decter, Midge *writer*
de Kretser, Michelle *writer*
Deveraux, Jude (Jude Gilliam White) *writer*
Diamonstein-Spielvogel, Barbaralee *writer*
Didion, Joan *writer*
Dillard, Annie *writer*
Duncan, Pearl Rose *writer*
Earling, Debra Magpie *writer, educator*
Ensler, Eve *playwright, actress*
Evanovich, Janet *writer*
Fennell Robbins, Sally *writer*
Fielding, Helen *writer*
Finch, Sheila *writer*
Fitch, Janet *writer*
Fleesler, Faith B. *writer*
Fleming, Alice Carew Mulcahey *writer*
Fogarassy, Helen Catherine *writer*
Fowler, Karen Joy *writer*
Fox, Paula (Mrs. Martin Greenberg) *writer*
Frank, Elizabeth *writer, educator*
Gaydos, Mary *writer, researcher, actress*
George, Elizabeth (Susan Elizabeth George) *writer*
Gibbons, Kaye *writer*
Gillespie, Donna Fay *novelist*
Gilman, Dorothy (Dorothy Gilman Butters) *author*
Gilman, Susan Jane *writer*
Glass, Julia *writer*
Goldsmith, Barbara *writer, historian*
Goldstein, Lisa Joy *writer*
Gonnerman, Jennifer *writer, journalist*
Goodman, Allegra *writer*
Gordon, Mary Catherine *writer*
Goreau, Angeline Wilson *writer*
Grafton, Sue *novelist*
Grant, Cynthia D. *writer*
Gray, Deborah Dolia *business writing consultant*
Greenwald, Sheila Ellen *writer, illustrator*
Grifalconi, Ann *author, illustrator, producer*
Griffith, Nicola *writer*
Grimes, Martha *author*
Hadas, Rachel *poet, educator*
Haigh, Jennifer *writer*
Hall, Susan *author, film producer*
Hamilton, Jane *writer*
Hamilton, Laurell K. *writer*
Hardwick, Elizabeth *writer*
Harper, Karen *writer*
Hart, Ellen *writer*
Hathaway, Robin *writer*
Hazzard, Shirley *author*
Hesse, Karen (Karen Sue Hesse) *writer, educator*
Hill, Elizabeth Starr *writer*
Hillenbrand, Laura *writer*
Hinz, Dorothy Elizabeth *writer, editor, corporate communications specialist*
Hoag, Tami *writer*
Hoffman, Alice *writer*
Horvath, Polly *writer*
Howe, Tina *playwright*
Humphreys, Josephine *writer*
Jacker, Corinne Litvin *playwright, writer*
Jance, J.A. (Judith Ann Jance) *writer*
Jhabvala, Ruth Prawer *writer*
Johansen, Iris *writer*
Jones, Diana Wynne *writer*
Jong, Erica Mann *writer*
Kadohata, Cynthia *writer*
Karon, Jan (Janice Meredith Wilson) *writer*
Karr, Kathleen *writer*
Kaufman, Bel *author, educator*
Kavaler, Rebecca *writer*
Kehret, Peg *writer*
Kellar, Charlotte Avrutis *writer*
Kelley, Kitty *writer*
Kennedy, Adrienne Lita *playwright*
Klagsbrun, Francine *writer, editor*
Kostova, Elizabeth *writer*
Krantz, Judith Tarcher *novelist*
Landau, Annette Henkin *writer, librarian*
Lauber, Patricia Grace *writer*
Lauro, Shirley Mezvinsky *playwright, educator*
Lee, Helie *writer*
Leeds, Dorothy *author, lecturer, consultant*
L'Engle, Madeleine (Mrs. Hugh Franklin) *writer*
Levin, Gail *writer, educator, photographer*
Lippman, Laura *writer*
Lisle, Laurie *author*
Lorch, Maristella De Panizza *writer, educator*
Lord, M. G. *writer*
Lunardini, Christine Anne *writer, historian, school administrator*
Lurie, Alison *writer*
Macer-Story, Eugenia Ann *writer*
Macklin, Elizabeth Jean *poet, editor*
MacLachlan, Patricia *author*
Madden-Lunsford, Kerry Elizabeth *writer*
Mason, Bobbie Ann *writer*
McCorduck, Pamela Ann *writer, educator*
McDermott, Alice *writer*
McNaught, Judith *writer*
McQuown, Judith Hershkowitz *writer, consultant, financial planner*
Milford, Nancy Winston *writer, literature educator*
Mills, Stephanie Ellen *writer*
Minarik, Else Holmelund (Bigart Minarik) *author*
Monk Kidd, Sue *writer*
Muller, Marcia *writer*
Munro, Alice *writer*
Munro, Eleanor *writer, lecturer*
Murphy, Patrice Ann (Pat Murphy) *writer*
Navarra, Tova *writer*
Nelson, Anne *playwright, former reporter*
Newberg, Esther *literary agent*
Noonan, Peggy *writer*
Oates, Joyce Carol *writer*
Olds, Sharon *poet*
Olsen, Tillie Lerner *author*
Osborne, Mary Pope *writer*
O'Toole, Patricia Ellen *writer, educator*
Pall, Ellen Jane *writer*
Paretsky, Sara N. *writer*
Park, Barbara *writer*
Park, Linda Sue *writer*
Parkhurst, Carolyn *writer*
Patchett, Ann *writer*
Paterson, Katherine Womeldorf *writer*
Phillips, Reneé *writer*
Polacco, Patricia *writer, illustrator*
Pomerantz, Charlotte *writer*
Pool, Mary Jane *writer, editor*
Powell, Julie *writer*
Quilter, Deborah *writer, consultant, educator*
Quin-Harkin, Janet Elizabeth (Rhys Bowen) *writer*
Rathmann, Peggy *writer, illustrator*
Redel, Victoria *writer, poet, educator*
Reig, June Wilson *scriptwriter, television director, television producer*
Rice, Luanne *writer*
Rich, Adrienne *poet*
Roberts, Nora *writer*
Robinson, Marilynne *writer*
Robinson, Roxana Barry *writer, art historian*
Rollin, Betty *writer, television journalist*
Rubell, Jennifer *writer, hotelier*
Ruhl, Sarah *playwright*
Rylant, Cynthia *writer*
Salter, Mary Jo *poet*
Sargent, Pamela *writer*
Schaffner, Cynthia Van Allen *writer, educator, curator*

Schlossberg, Caroline Bouvier Kennedy (Caroline Kennedy) *writer, lawyer*
Scotti, R. A. *writer*
Seaman, Barbara (Ann Rosner) *author*
Segal, Lore *writer*
Shapiro, Myra Stein *poet*
Sheehan, Susan *writer*
Shreve, Anita *writer*
Shriver, Lionel (Margaret Ann Shriver) *writer*
Smiley, Jane Graves *author, educator*
Smith, Betty *writer, not-for-profit developer*
Smith, Mary-Ann Tirone *writer*
Solnit, Rebecca *writer, critic*
Spencer-Fleming, Julia *writer*
Steel, Danielle Fernande *author*
Sykes, Plum *writer*
Tan, Amy Ruth *writer*
Taylor, Mildred D. *author*
Thompson, Vicki Lewis *writer*
Tuck, Lily *writer*
Turner, Megan Whalen *author*
Urban, Amanda (Binky Urban) *literary agent*
Walker, Alice *writer*
Wells, Rebecca *writer*
Wells, Rosemary *writer*
Wender, Phyllis Bellows *literary agent*
Wheeler, Susan *poet, educator*
Whitehouse, Anne Cherner *writer*
Whitney, Phyllis Ayame *author*
Williams, Diane *writer, editor*
Wolf, Naomi *writer*
Wolff, Virginia Euwer *writer*
Wright, Gwendolyn *writer, architecture educator, historian*
Yglesias, Helen Bassine *author, educator*
Young-Mallin, Judith *writer, archivist*
Zolotow, Charlotte Shapiro *retired author, editor*

Ossining
Reich, Susanna *children's book author, publicist*

Ozone Park
Scott, Vanessa Kathleen *writer*

Palisades
Davis, Dorothy Salisbury *writer*

Penfield
Marbach, Donna Maureen *writer*

Plainview
Nichter, Rhoda Samuels *writer, educator*

Poughkeepsie
Willard, Nancy Margaret *writer, educator*

Pultneyville
Farrer-Bornarth, Sylvia *writer, artist*

Purchase
Phillips, Carly *writer*

Rhinebeck
Sloane, Beverly LeBov *writer, consultant, writing instructor*

Rockville Centre
Mazzucelli, Colette Grace Celia *author, educator*

Sagaponack
Cedering, Siv *poet, writer*

Sayville
Leuzzi, Linda *writer*

Sleepy Hollow
Stever, Margo Taft *poet*

Southampton
Jones, Kaylie Ann *writing educator, writer*

Southold
Small, Bertrice W. *writer*

Stow
Dunwich, Gerina *writer, editor*

Syracuse
Gaitskill, Mary Lawrence *writer, educator*
Keller, Johanna Beale *writer, editor*
Staples, Heidi L *poet, writer*

Tarrytown
Loxley, Alice A. *writer, educator*

Warwick
Linnéa, Sharon *writer, playwright*

Woodstock
Godwin, Gail Kathleen *writer*

NORTH CAROLINA

Asheville
Redmond, Glenis G. *performance poet*

Bostic
Hooper, Kay *writer*

Brevard
Jones, Sandy (Sandra F. Jones) *writer, speaker, parenting expert*

Chapel Hill
Berne, Suzanne *writer, educator*
Hunter, Brenda Ann *writer, psychologist*
Kytle, Caroline Elizabeth *writer*
Spencer, Elizabeth *writer*

Charlotte
Finley, Glenna *writer*

Columbus
Sauvé, Carolyn Opal *writer, journalist, poet*

Denver
Gleasner, Diana Cottle *author*

Durham
Vick, Marsha Cook *writer, humanities educator*

Emerald Isle
Mikkelsen, Nina Elizabeth Markowitz *writer, researcher*

Greenville
Gilham, Hanna Kaltenbrunner *writer*

Raleigh
Tucker, Helen Welch *writer*

Willow Spring
Monahan, Sherry Ann *writer*

OHIO

Berea
Bonds, Georgia Anna *writer, educator*

Cincinnati
Aylesworth, Julie Ann *writer, personal care professional*

Cleveland
Eagleeye-Lord, Amy *writer, editor*
Kovel, Terry Horvitz *writer, antiques authority*

Cleveland Heights
Sandburg, Helga *author*

Columbus
Ware, Jane Orth *writer*

Dayton
Boice, Martha Hibbert *writer, publishing executive*
Heath, Mariwyn Dwyer *writer, legislative staff member*
Jelus, Susan Crum *writer, editor*

Hudson
Worley, Janis Avereal *writer*

Kent
Cielinski-Kessler, Audrey Ann *writer, publishing executive, small business owner*

Napoleon
Meekison, MaryFran *writer*

Stow
Castillo, Katherine Lynn *writer, translator, business owner*

Westfield Center
Bock, Carolyn A. *writer, consultant, small business owner*

OKLAHOMA

Bixby
Wetzel, Marlene Reed *freelance/self-employed writer*

Cushing
Geyer, Karen Lea *writer*

Edmond
Zabel, Vivian Ellouise *writer, retired secondary school educator*

Mustang
Wood, Jean Carol *poet, lyricist*

Tulsa
Clark, Marian Wilson *writer*
Fielding, Peggy Lou Moss *writer*
Price, Alice Lindsay *writer*

OREGON

Cannon Beach
Hellyer, Constance Anne (Connie Anne Conway) *writer, musician*

Culver
Siebert, Diane Dolores *author, poet*

Eugene
Wilhelm, Kate (Katy Gertrude) *author*

Klamath Falls
Koch, Margaret Rau *writer, artist, historian*

Portland
Larson, Wanda Z. *writer, poet*
Porter, Elsa Allgood *writer, educator*

Salem
Vernon, Olympia Flechet *writer*

South Beach
Lick, Sue Fagalde *writer*

Wallowa
Hunter, Kathleen *writer, educator*

PENNSYLVANIA

Broomall
Saunders, Sally Love *poet, educator*

Clarks Summit
Updyke, Rosemary Kathryn *writer*

Devon
Shurkin, Lorna Greene *writer, publicist*

Erie
Chittister, Joan Daugherty *writer, educator*

Fogelsville
Crooker, Barbara Ann *writer, educator*

King Of Prussia
Schumann, Paula M. L. *writer*

Kutztown
Nechas, Eileen Tucker *retired writer*

Lancaster
Shenk, Lois Elaine Landis *writer*

Latrobe
Price, Peggy Reinecke *writer, researcher*

Maple Glen
Jacobson, Bonnie Brown *writer, energy executive, statistician, researcher*

Milford
Le Guin, Ursula Kroeber *writer*

Philadelphia
Cary, Lorene Emily *writer*
Givens, Janet Eaton *writer*
Mellen, Joan *author*
Paglia, Camille *writer, humanities educator*
Stewart, Susan *writer*

Pittsburgh
Bleier, Carol Stein *writer, researcher*
Eiler, Gertrude S. *writer*

State College
Erem, Suzan *writer*

Valley Forge
Miller, Betty Brown *freelance writer*

Villanova
Gould, Lilian *writer*

Wayne
Burton, Betty Jane (B.J. Burton) *playwright*

West Chester
Baxter, Joan Anna Patten *technical writer*

RHODE ISLAND

Charlestown
Huetteman, Susan Bice *writer*

Providence
López-Morillas, Frances (Mapes) *translator*
Vogel, Paula Anne *playwright*
Waldrop, Rosmarie *writer*

SOUTH CAROLINA

Columbia
Newton, Rhonwen Leonard *writer, data processing executive, consultant*
Stamps, Laura Anne *writer, poet*

Hilton Head Island
Reed, Frances Boogher *writer, actress*

Roebuck
Mackenzie, Clara Childs *writer, editor*

SOUTH DAKOTA

Brookings
Williams, Elizabeth Evenson *writer*

Hermosa
Hasselstrom, Linda Michele *writer, rancher*

TENNESSEE

Bolivar
Traylor, Sharon Elain *writer, school food service staff member*

Brentwood
Bolton, Martha O. *writer*

Cookeville
Underwood, Lucinda Jean *poet, playwright, small business owner, researcher*

Greeneville
Breckenridge, Judith Watts *writer, educator*

Knoxville
Bell, Linda R. *writer, photographer*

Millington
Thomas-Harris, Yvonne Anita *writer, poet*

Nashville
Bird, Caroline *author*
Wisdom, Emma Nell Jackson *writer, educator*

Newport
Dykeman, Wilma *writer, educator*
Gregg, Ella Mae *writer*

Oak Ridge
Silva, Joan Yvonne *writer*

Old Hickory
Vivelo, Jacqueline Jean *writer, language educator*

Paris
McFarlin, Shannon Dianne *writer, researcher*

Sevierville
Koff, Shirley Irene *writer*

TEXAS

Amarillo
Mojtabai, Ann Grace *author, educator*

Arlington
Savage, Ruth Hudson *poet, writer, speaker*

Austin
McElroy, Mary M. (Mickie McElroy) *educational writer*

Brookshire
Utley, Jane Beson *poet*

China Spring
Weaver, Donna Kay *writer, genealogist, former actress, stuntwomam*

Chireno
Mayhar, Ardath Frances (Frank Cannon, John Killdeer, Frances Hurst) *writer*

Dallas
Castleberry, Vivian Lou Anderson (Mrs. Curtis Wales Castleberry) *free-lance writer, consultant, former newspaper editor*
Dee, Ronda *poet, photographer, small business owner, journalist*
Phillips, Betty Lou (Elizabeth Louise Phillips) *writer, interior designer*

Denton
Keating, AnaLouise *educator, author*
Wood, Jane Roberts *writer*

Fort Worth
Murph, Roxane Cohen *writer, researcher*
Newsom, Douglas Ann Johnson *writer, journalism educator*

Georgetown
Shelby, Roselle Price *writer, retired special education educator*

Granbury
Dyer, Dena Janan *writer*

Houston
de Vries, Robbie Ray Parsons *writer, illustrator, management consultant*
Mallia, Marianne *medical writer*
McPhail, JoAnn Winstead *writer, art dealer*
Parle, Bertha Ibarra *writer*
Schier, Mary Jane *science writer*

Lubbock
Bronwell, Nancy Brooker *writer*

Plano
Gallardo, Henrietta Castellanos *writer*
Verges, Marianne Murphree *writer*

Port Aransas
Beimers, Gertrude Hii *writer*

Rusk
Holder, Maxine E. *writer*

Smithville
Clark, LaVerne Harrell *writer*

Spring
Jackson, Guida Myrl *writer, editor, literature educator*

UTAH

Bountiful
Flack, Dora Dutson *writer, performing artist, lecturer*

Saint George
Pearce, Carole Ann *poet*

Salt Lake City
Osherow, Jacqueline Sue *poet, English language educator*

VERMONT

Bennington
Bernard, April *poet, literature educator*
Feitlowitz, Marguerite *writer, literary translator*
Godwin, Rebecca Thompson *writer, educator, editor*

Brattleboro
Klaich, Dolores *writer, educator*

Burlington
Hearon, Shelby *writer, educator*

Marshfield
Thomas, Susan Beth *writer*

Montpelier
Blanchard, Margaret Moore *writer, educator*

Thetford
Paley, Grace *author, educator*

VIRGINIA

Alexandria
Collins, Mary *writer, educator*

Arlington
Porte, Barbara Ann *writer, librarian*

Bristol
Cooper, Carlotta Arlene *writer, animal breeder*

Charlottesville
Dove, Rita Frances *poet, language educator*

Clarksville
Worth, Lynn Harris *writer*

Ettrick
Davis, Minnie Louise *writer*

Fort Belvoir
Smith, Margherita *writer, editor*

Fredericksburg
Goss, Georgia Bulman *freelance/self-employed translator*
Westebbe, Barbara Liebst *writer, sculptor*

Glen Allen
Cornwell, Patricia Daniels *writer*

Harrisonburg
Davis, Melodie Miller *writer, editor*

Lexington
Lyle, Katie Letcher *writer, educator*
Solod, Lisa *writer*

Mc Lean
Wallace, Barbara Brooks *writer*

Meadowview
Kingsolver, Barbara Ellen *writer*

Newport News
Smith, Barbara Ruthjena Drucker *writer, educator*

Norfolk
Reynolds, Sheri *writer*

Reedville
Smith, Monika Rose *researcher*

Richmond
Morgan, Elizabeth Seydel *writer, educator, retired writer*

Staunton
Lembke, Janet *writer*

Stephenson
Johnson, Eva Maria *retired translator*

Virginia Beach
Ardison, Linda G. *author, writing educator*
Foster, Jeanne O'Cain *poet, fine arts educator*

Williamsburg
Pyott, Caroline (Patty) *writer*

Woodstock
Maggiolo, Paulette Blanche *writer*

WASHINGTON

Arlington
Bullington, Gayle Rogers *writer, researcher*

Bainbridge Island
Stewart, Kay Boone *writer, retired academic administrator*

Bellevue
Porad, Francine Joy *poet, painter*

Black Diamond
Walker, Minerva E. Gilara *poet, retail executive*

Issaquah
Cain, Coleen W. *writer, educator*

Kirkland
Szablya, Helen Mary *writer, language educator*

Mill Creek
Dubois, Christine *writer, educator*

Nordland
Kramnicz, Rosanne *freelance writer*

Oak Harbor
Lightbourne, Alesa M. *writer, educator*

Oysterville
Holway, Susan E. *writer*

Poulsbo
Wayne, Kyra Petrovskaya *writer*

Redmond
Bottenberg, Joyce Harvey *writer, social services administrator*

Seattle
Katzman, Anita *writer*
Kunkel, Georgie Bright *freelance writer, retired counselor*
Pizzorno, Lara Elise *medical writer, editor*
Rule, Ann *author*

Spokane
Murphy, Claire Rudolf *author, consultant*

WEST VIRGINIA

Charleston
Mellert, Lucie Anne *writer, photographer*

Great Cacapon
Coe, Diana Ward (Dina Coe) *poet, writer*

West Columbia
Fowler, Sandra Lynn *poet*

WISCONSIN

Green Bay
Erickson, Ruth Alice *poet, artist*

Hancock
Vroman, Barbara Fitz *writer, educator*

Madison
K-Turkel, Judith Leah Rosenthal (Judi K-Turkel) *writer, editor, publisher*
Moore, Lorrie *writer, English professor*
Riley, Jocelyn Carol *writer, television producer*
Stites, Susan Kay *writer, human resources specialist*

Racine
Wright, Betty Ren *children's book writer*

Saukville
Gulan, Bonnie Marion *writer, researcher*

CANADA

ONTARIO

London
Barfoot, Joan *writer*

Toronto
Peacock, Molly *poet, educator*

MEXICO

Jalisco
Pordon, Grace *writer, poet, artist*

CZECH REPUBLIC

Prague
Love, Brenda Zejdl *writer*

ENGLAND

London
Fine, Anne *writer*
Galloway, Janice *writer, editor*
Hite, Shere D. *writer, historian*
Hunter Blair, Pauline Clarke *author*
Paton Walsh, Jill *writer*
Rowling, J.K. (Joanne Kathleen Rowling) *writer*

FRANCE

Lacoste
Strauss, Gwen B. *writer, editor*

Normandy
Ndiaye, Marie *writer, playwright*

SPAIN

Barcelona
Allende, Isabel Angelica *writer*

SWITZERLAND

Bern
Carlson, Dale Bick *writer*

ADDRESS UNPUBLISHED

Aatrapi, Marjane *writer, illustrator*
Ackerman, Diane *author, educator*
Ain, Diantha *poet, artist, educator*
Alinder, Mary Street *writer, educator*
Allen, Roberta *writer, photographer, conceptual artist*
Aloff, Mindy *writer*
Anshaw, Carol *writer*
Anton, Barbara *writer*
Argers, Helen *writer, playwright*
Arntzenius, Linda Galliard McArdle *writer*
Ash, Jennifer Gertrude *writer, editor*
Ashley, Renee *writer, creative writing educator, consultant*
Askew, Rilla *author*
Baker, Lucinda *writer*
Baker, Susan Marie Victoria *writer, artist, musician*
Baldrige, Letitia *writer, management consultant*
Bassett, Elizabeth Ewing (Libby Bassett) *writer, editor, consultant*
Beard, Bernice Talbott *writer, publisher*
Beatts, Anne Patricia *writer*
Beauchamp, Valdivia Vânia Siqueira *translator*
Bel Geddes, Joan *writer*
Belson, Abby Avin *writer*
Berg, Darla Gaye *writer*
Berger, Linda Fay *writer*
Berman, Eleanor *writer*
Bertram, Jean DeSales *writer*
Bitman, Clara *writer, educator*
Blais, Madeleine Helena *writer*
Blake Ramos, Debra Barbara *writer*
Blos, Joan W. *writer, critic, educator*
Blue, Rose *writer, educator*
Blunt, Kathryn London *writer, scriptwriter*
Boeckman, Patricia Ellen *writer, educator*
Bonanni, Victoria *writer*
Bornstein, Mimi *writer, social scientist*
Bower, Janet Esther *writer, educator*
Bracken, Peg *writer*
Brandler, Marcielle Y. *poet, educator*
Braun, Lilian Jackson *writer*
Brewer, Rogenna Wynne *writer*
Brightman, Carol *writer*
Briles, Judith *writer, consultant*
Briskin, Jacqueline Elizabeth *author*
Brooks, Geraldine *writer, reporter, news correspondent*
Broussard, Carol Madeline *writer, consultant, photographer*
Brown, Crystal Jeanine *writer*
Brown, Denise *poet*
Brown, Joan Teresa *writer, retired language educator*
Brown, Marcia Joan *author, artist, photographer*
Brown, Rebecca *writer, educator*
Brown, Sandra *writer*
Brownstein, Elizabeth Smith *writer*
Brubach, Holly Beth *writer*
Brzozowy, Kandy Doris *behavioral health writer*
Bucheister, Patricia Louise (Patt Parrish) *writer, artist*
Buckingham, Deidre Lyn *writer, musician*
Burkard, Patricia *writer*
Burke, Jan Helene *writer*
Burns, Kitty *playwright*
Bush, Yvonne *writer, counselor*
Byars, Betsy Cromer *writer*
Cager, Chezia Thompson *poet, literature educator*
Cahill, Verna Eleanore *writer*
Caletti, Deb L. *writer*
Carlisle-Frank, Pamela L. *writer, researcher, consultant*
Carrell, Jennifer Lee *writer*
Carroll, Mary Patricia *writer*
Carter, Cynthia (Cindy) Lynn *writer*
Cecil, Elizabeth Jean *writer*
Cheever, Susan *freelance/self-employed writer*
Chesney, Susan Talmadge *writer, educational association administrator*
Claes, Gayla Christine *writer, editor, consultant*
Clark, Mary Higgins *writer, communications executive*
Clauser, Suzanne Phillips *author, screenwriter*
Coffey, Marilyn June *writer, educator*
Cohen, Marcia Friedlander *writer, editor-in-chief, journalist*
Cohen, Miriam *writer, educator*
Conley, Ruth Irene *poet*
Conover-Carson, Anne *writer*
Conte, Jeanne L. *writer, photographer*
Cooke, Chantelle Anne *writer*
Cooper, Mary Ellen *writer*
Cooper, Nicole Robyn *writer*
Costantini, Mary Ann C. *writer, editor, adult education educator*
Curtis, Dolores Rogers *writer*
Dailey, Janet *writer*
D'Arcy, Paula *writer*
Daren, Sylvia *poet*
Dauphin, Sue *writer, producer*
Davis, Mamie (Denise Davis) *writer*
Deats, Suzanne *writer, editor, artist*
Desio, Delores Jean *writer, artist, retired elementary school educator*
Diamant, Anita *writer*
Dominic, Magie *writer*
Donnally, Patricia Broderick *writer*
Dorman, Stephanie *writer*
Dorsey, Helen Danner (Johna Blinn) *writer, educator*
Druffel, Ann Bernice *researcher, writer*
Dunton-Downer, Leslie Linam *writer*
Dwyer, Kelly *writer, educator*
Earney, Mary K. *writer, educator*
Ecklar, Julia *freelance writer, novelist*
Egan, Moira *poet, educator*
Egelston, Roberta Riethmiller *writer*
Ehrenreich, Barbara *writer*
Eisenberg, Phyllis Rose *author*
Eisenstein, Linda *playwright, composer*
Ellis, Joyce K. *writer, educator*
Emerson, Claudia *poet, language professor*
Emrich, Jeanne Ann *poet, artist, publishing executive*
Engelman, Elizabeth *playwright, trade association administrator*
Ephron, Nora *writer*
Erbacher, Kathy *writer, editor, marketing consultant*
Erickson, Donna Joy *writer*
Escallón, Ana María *writer*
Evans, Meryl K. *writer*
Ewart, Claire Lynn *author, illustrator*
Fackler, Elizabeth *writer*
Fadiman, Anne *writer, educator*
Ferguson, Margaret Geneva *writer, publisher, real estate broker*
Fisher, Nancy *writer, producer, director*
Frankel, Jennie Louise *writer, composer, playwright*
Frankel, Terrie Maxine *writer, composer, playwright*
Fraser, Kathleen Joy *poet, creative writing professor*
French, Marilyn *writer, critic, historian*
Gallagher, Patricia Cecilia *author*
Garceau, Jo Mills *writer*
Gardner, Sonia Kay *writer*
Garfield-Woodbridge, Nancy *writer*
Garfinkle, Elaine Myra *writer*
Gatria, America I *retired writer*
Gavril, Jean (Jean Van Leeuwen) *writer*
Gavriloff, Katrina *writer*
Gehrman, Jody Elizabeth *writer*
Gemeinhardt, Judith M. (Judith Gamin) *writer, poet*
George, Linda Shumaker *freelance/self-employed writer*
Gersoni-Edelman, Diane Claire *author, editor*
Giffin, Marjie G. *writer*
Gifford, Heidi *writer, editor*
Gilchrist, E. Brenda *writer, freelance/self-employed editor*
Giovanni, Nikki (Yolanda Cornelia Giovanni) *poet, educator*
Gleason, Kate *writer, educator, editor*
Glück, Louise Elisabeth *poet, educator*
Gold, Alison Leslie *writer*
Goldfarb, Ruth *poet, educator*
Gordon, Fran *writer*
Gottlieb, Sherry Gershon *writer, editor*
Gray, Francine du Plessix *writer*
Griffith, Patricia Browning *writer, educator*
Grohskopf, Bernice *writer*
Grossman, Edith Marian *translator*
Grossman, Patricia *writer*
Gurvis, Sandra Jane *writer*
Guy, Eleanor Bryenton *retired writer*
Hadley, Leila Eliott-Burton (Mrs. Henry Luce III) *writer*
Hahn, Mary Downing *writer*
Hamby, Barbara Jean *writer, poet*
Hardwick, Melinda S. *writer*
Hart, Janet Marilyn *writer, lecturer*
Haskell, Molly *writer*
Hayes, Cynthia Ann (C.A. Hayes) *writer*
Herbert, Mary Katherine Atwell *writer*
Herman, Michelle *writer*
Heydron, Jo Ann *writer*
Higbee, Donna Good *writer, researcher*
Higdon, Pamela Leis *writer*
Hill, Donna Marie *writer, retired librarian*
Himmelfarb, Gertrude (Mrs. Irving Kristol) *writer, educator*
Hirschberg, Vera Hilda *writer*
Hitchcock, Jane Stanton *playwright, novelist*
Hockenbury, Sandra Ellen *writer*
Hoffman, Eva Alfreda *author, editor, educator*
Hollace, Barbara Jean *writer, property manager*
Hollander, Anne *writer*
Holmes, Willa B. *writer, former educator*
Homes, A. M. *writer*
Hornbaker, Alice Joy *writer*
Hosansky, Anne *writer*
Houston, Gloria *author, educator, consultant*
Howes, Sophia DuBose *writer*
Hu, Hua-ling Wang *writer, historian*
Hughes, Debra *writer, educator*
Hummer-Sharpe, Elizabeth Anastasia *writer, genealogist, researcher*
Humphrey, Phyllis A. *writer*
Ironbiter, Suzanne *writer, educator*
Isaacs, Susan *writer, scriptwriter*
Isenberg, Jane Frances *writer, retired language educator*
Jacobs, Nancy Carolyn Baker *writer*
Jacobson, Joan Leiman *writer*
James, Muriel Marshall *writer, educator, psychotherapist*
Jerome, Kathleen A. *writer, retired publishing executive*
Johnsen, Barbara Parrish *writer, educator*
Johnson, Diane Lain *writer, critic*
Johnson, Mary P. *freelance writer*
Johnson, Patricia Mary *writer*
Jones, Ann *writer, photographer*
Jones, Carolyn Evans *writer*
Jones, Hettie Cohen *writer, educator*
Jones-Ketner, Elizabeth Brown *writer*
Jordan, Carrie Grayson (Carrie Grayson-Jordan) *writer, poet, drama designer*
Juodvalkis, Egle (Eglé Juodvalké) *writer*
Kampen, Irene Blanche *writer*
Kanin, Fay *screenwriter*
Kelly, Susan *writer, educator*
Kiefer, Rita Brady *writer, educator*
Kildee, Jennifer *translator, editor*
King, Cynthia Bregman *writer*
King, Elizabeth Ann *writer*
King, Joy Rainey *poet, executive secretary*
Kingston, Maxine Hong *writer, educator*
Konecky, Edith *writer*
Konigsburg, Elaine Lobl *writer*
Koral, Marian *writer*
Kozak, Karen S. *writer*
Krane, Jessica (Aida Jessica Kohnop-Krane) *writer, educator*
Krischer, Devora *writer, editor*
Kumin, Maxine Winokur *poet, writer*
Kuper, Daniela F. *writer*
Lane, Colette Marie *writer*
Langham, Gail B. *writer*
Lansing, Jewel Beck (Jewel Anne Beck) *writer, auditor*
Larkin, Joan *poet, literature and language educator*
Larsdotter, Anna-Lisa *retired translator, artist*
Lawton, Violet *writer*
Lazo, Caroline Evensen *writer*
LeBlanc, Jean Eva *writer, poet, educator*
Lee, Harper (Nelle Harper Lee) *writer*
Leedom-Ackerman, Joanne *writer, educator*
Levey, Judith S. *lexicographer, publisher, editor*
Levitt, B. Blake *writer, medical writer*
Lightwood, Carol Wilson *writer*
Lindbergh, Judith L. *writer, photographer*
Lippard, Lucy Rowland *writer, educator, critic, curator*
Lisle, Janet Taylor *writer*
Long, Elaine *writer, editor*
Lubell, Ellen *writer*
Lynds, Gayle Hallenbeck *writer*
MacLeod, Normajean *writer*
Madison, Deborah Leafy *writer, chef*
Maher, Jan Colleen *writer, educator*
Mann, Emily Betsy *writer, artistic director, theater director*
Mann, Mary Anneeta *author*
Mann-Bondat, Lydia Rachel *writer, researcher*
Manville, Greta Craig *writer*
Marks, Martha Alford *writer*
Marquand, Barbara K. *freelance writer*
Marshall, Beverly Forrest *writer*
Martin, Kryssi Wyckoff *playwright, educator*
Martin-Lowry, Beverly Anne *writer, columnist*
Mason, Connie Jeanne *writer*
Mata, Linda Sue Proctor *writer, consultant*
Mathieu, Michele Suzanne *grant writer, computer scientist, consultant*
May, Janet Sue *playwright, lyricist*
Mayer, Kay Magnor *writer*
Mc Cann, Cecile Nelken *writer, artist*
McCourt, Lisa *writer*
McCoy, Dorothy Eloise *writer, educator*
McElhatten, Betty Shreve *writer, illustrator*
McElligott, Carroll A.A. *writer, horse breeder, rancher*
McFall, Catherine Gardner *poet, critic, educator*
McLaughlin, Ellen McGehee *playwright, educator, actor*
McMillan, Terry L. *writer, educator*

McNees, Pat (Patricia Ann McNees) *writer, editor*
McWhorter, Diane *writer*
Meehan, Lil Euphrasia Therese *poet*
Merrill, Jean Fairbanks *writer*
Mills, Elizabeth Shown *historical writer, genealogist*
Mintz, Gwendolyn Joyce *writer, actress, comedian*
Mitchard, Jacquelyn *writer*
Mockler, Anna *writer, ecologist*
Molinari, Carol V. *writer, investment company executive, educator*
Moorhead, Lucy Galpin *writer*
Mora, Pat *writer, speech professional*
Morang, Diane Judy *writer, television producer, entrepreneur*
Morgan, Robin Evonne *poet, writer, journalist, editor*
Morin-Miller, Carmen Aline *writer*
Morrison, Sarah Lyddon *author*
Morrison, Toni (Chloe Anthony Wofford) *writer, educator, editor*
Morris-Robinson, Dorothy Kay *writer*
Morrow, Susan Brind *writer*
Morse-McNeely, Patricia *poet, writer, retired secondary school educator*
Moses, Shelia P. *writer, poet, playwright, producer*
Muehl, Lois Baker *writer, retired language educator*
Mulvihill, Maureen Esther *writer, educator*
Nesbit, Lynn *literary agent*
Newburg, Anne Colby *writer*
Newhall, Barbara Falconer *writer, journalist*
Newhall, Edith Allerton *writer*
Nguyen, Mai (Mai Tuyet Nguyen) *writer*
Nielson, Alyce Mae *poet*
Noëldechen, Joan Marguerite *writer*
Northcutt, Ora Beatrice *author*
O'Garden, Irene *writer, actress*
O'Leary, Kathleen Ann *nonfiction writer*
O'Loughlin, Katie Eileen Bridget *poet*
Ossana, Diana Lynn *author, screenwriter*
Ostriker, Alicia Suskin *poet*
Ozick, Cynthia *writer*
Pack, Susan Joan *writer*
Paolucci, Anne Attura *playwright, poet, literature educator, educational consultant*
Parsons, Christina Anne *writer, photographer, educator*
Payne, Peggy *writer*
Pearce-Worthington, Carol *writer, editor*
Petrelis, Stella Marsha *writer*
Phillips, Jill Meta *writer, critic, astrologer*
Pierce, Marian Marie *writer, educator*
Pogrebin, Letty Cottin *writer, educator*
Polite, Carlene Hatcher *writer, educator*
Pollitt, Katha *writer, educator, poet*
Porter, Margaret Evans *novelist, lecturer, historian*
Powell, Alma Johnson *writer, advocate, foundation administrator*
Proulx, (Edna) Annie *writer*
Pugh, Ann Barham *writer, educator*
Quay, Joyce Crosby *writer*
Quick, Barbara *writer*
Rae, Susanna-Judith *writer, retired marriage and family therapist*
Raffo, Heather *playwright, actress*
Ragans, Rosalind Dorothy *writer, artist, retired educator*
Reeves, Barbara *writer, educator*
Reinike, Irma *retired writer, artist, poet, lyricist*
Renaud, Bernadette Marie Elise *author*
Rice, Anne *writer*
Rider, Fae B. *freelance writer*
Riehecky, Janet Ellen *writer*
Rising, Catharine Clarke *author*
Robins, Natalie *poet, writer*
Rollins, Carole Ann *writer, artist*
Romana, Kathleen *writer*
Root, Phyllis Idalene *writer*
Rosenberg, Jane *author, illustrator*
Rosmus, Anna Elisabeth *writer*
Russ, Joanna *author*
Russell, Pamela Redford *scriptwriter, educator*
Ryan, Joyce Ethel *writer, artist*
Sackett, Susan Deanna *writer*
Salat, Cristina *writer*
Sarana, Shiree *writer*
Scafuro, Lisa A. *writer, journalist, poet*
Schaeffer, Susan Fromberg *writer, educator*
Schiff, Stacy *writer*
Schindler, Holly Suzanne *freelance/self-employed writer*
Schnackenberg, Gjertrud Cecelia *poet*
Schneider, Phyllis Leah *writer, editor*
Schor, Lynda *author, educator*
Schremp, Faith Maryanne *writer*
Schuck, Joyce Haber *author*
Schultz, Dodi *writer, editor*
Schutt, Christine *writer, educator*
Schwartz, Lynne Sharon *freelance/self-employed writer*
Scoll, Eulalie Elizabeth *writer, researcher*
Scott, Joyce *writer*
Scruggs, Sandra Nell *writer, former school teacher*
Senerchia, Dorothy Sylvia *writer, urban planner*
Sevilla, Emerita Nepomuceno *writer*
Shafer-Kenney, Jolie E. *writer, columnist*
Shauers, Margaret Ann *author*
Sheldon, Edith Louise Thach *writer*
Sheldon, Louise Roberts *writer*
Shreve, Susan Richards *writer, educator*
Shulman, Alix Kates *writer*
Siddons, Anne Rivers (Sybil Anne Rivers Siddons) *writer*
Siefker, Judith Marie *writer*
Siegel, Mary Ann Garvin *writer*
Sims, Pamela Jan (Cerussi) *writer, minister*
Singer, Donna Lea *writer, editor, educator*
Sklar, Holly L. *writer, columnist*
Smith, Anne Day *writer*
Smith, Cora Adele *retired writer*
Smith, Jamesetta Delorise *author*
Smith, Marya Jean *writer*
Snow, Marina *writer*
Socolow, Elizabeth Anne *poet, educator, artist, writer*
Somerville, Diana Elizabeth *author*
Spencer, Tricia Jane *writer*
Standiford, Natalie Anne *writer*
Steele, Judith McConnell *writer*
Stevenson, Elizabeth *author, educator*
Stone, Bonnie Mae Domrose *writer*
Stone, Sandra *writer, artist*
Storey, Joyce R. *writer, actress*
Strong, Christina Cordaire *writer, artist*
Strong, Virginia Wilkerson *freelance writer, former special education educator*
Strouse, Jean *writer*
Sun, Nilaja *playwright, actress*
Surman, Susan (Susan Kramer) *writer, actress*
Swan, Annalyn *writer*
Taetzsch, Lynne *writer, artist, educator*
Tassos, Alice Crowley *writer*
Taylor, Eleanor Ross *writer*
Tennant, Donna Kay *writer*
Terkel, Susan Neiburg *author*
Thomas-Roots, Pamela M. *writer, educator*
Thompson, Diana Rosebud *poet, educator, history exhibit coordinator, marketing consultant, playwright*
Thon, Melanie Rae *writer*
Thornburg, Linda A. *writer*
Tobias, Sheila *writer, educator*
Todd, Catherine Jackson *writer*
Tower, Mollie Gregory *writer, educator, consultant*
Towler, Katherine *writer*
Tralis-Levy, Despi *writer, painter*
Truman, Margaret *writer*
Turney, Virginia *writer*
Twichell, Chase *poet*
Ucko, Barbara Clark *writer*
Unger, Barbara *poet, retired educator*
Valentine, Jean *poet, educator, writer*
Varnum, Charis *writer, educator*
Verlich, Jean Elaine *writer, public relations executive, consultant*
Viorst, Judith Stahl *writer*
Voigt, Cynthia *writer*
Volk, Patricia Gay *writer, essayist*
Wallace, Michele *writer, educator*
Wallingford, Anne *freelance/self-employed writer, marketing professional, consultant*
Warren, Cindy Michelle *author*
Warren, Rosanna *poet*
Wayne, Jane Ellen *author*
Weaver, Karen Lynn *writer, performing arts educator, actress, poet*
Weis, Margaret Edith *writer, editor*
Weisberg, Barbara *writer, editor*
Weiss, Carol Ann *writer*
Whelchel, Sandra Jane *writer*
Whiley, Julia Helen *writer, actress*
White, Daphne Milbank *writer*
Wikarski, Nancy Susan *writer*
Wilbur, Marcia Kaoru *writer*
Willenz, June Adele *writer, editor, playwright, scriptwriter, public relations executive*
Williams, Darcel Patrice *writer, editor*
Wilson, Roberta Louise *writer, editor, journalist, activist*
Wilson-Pleiness, Christine Joyce *writer, columnist, poet*
Windsor, Margaret Eden *writer*
Wolfe, L. Diane *writer, photographer*
Wolfe, Rinna Evelyn *writer, retired secondary school educator*
Woodson, Jacqueline *writer*
Wurdinger, Victoria *writer*
Yahn, Mimi *writer*
Yih, Ann *writer, journalist*
Yingling, Phyllis Stuckey *writer*
Zablocki, Elaine *writer*
Zeilig, Nancy Meeks *writer, editor*
Zuckerman, Nancy Ann *writer, publicist, minister*

ARTS: PERFORMING

UNITED STATES

ALABAMA

Anniston
Sparks, Telitha Elaine *music educator, director*

Atmore
Smith, Debra L. *band director*

Auburn
Turner, Louise (Lee) Kreher *retired dance educator*

Bessemer
Miller, Carrie Sims *music educator*

Birmingham
Henry, Ruth Swindle *dancer, educator*
Laeger, Therese Roach *performing arts educator*
Odom, Mary E. (Libby Odom) *musician, educator*

Boaz
Pierce, V. Renee *music educator*

Chickasaw
Erwin, Sandra Kay *music educator*

Decatur
Matherly, Virginia Williams *music educator*

Grove Hill
Clarke, Cheryl Crider *music educator*

Hartselle
Thompson, Wanda Dawson *music educator*

Homewood
Tucker, Rhonda Reneé *music educator*

Huntsville
Hall, Doris Spooner *music educator*
Hancock, Jane Syers *music educator*
Lacy, Lucile C. *music educator*
McNew, Jill Hasty *performing company executive, educator*

Leeds
Denton, Joy Grigg *retired music educator*

Mobile
Atkinson, Alanna Beth *music educator*

Montevallo
Lumby, Betty Louise *music educator, organist, composer*

Montgomery
Brock, Katrina Rae *music educator*
Copeland, Jacqueline Turner *music educator*

Morris
Taylor, Brandy Miller *music educator*

Point Clear
Englund, Gage Bush *dancer, educator*

Spanish Fort
Wilkerson Walley, Hazel Sarah *music educator, lay worker*

ALASKA

Anchorage
DeLap, Miriam Anne *music educator*
Gazaway, Barbara Ann *music educator, art educator*

Chugiak
Nilsson, Annie *singer, music educator*

ARIZONA

Avondale
Sonmor, Marilyn Idelle *music educator*

Chandler
Farenga, Justine-Louise Porter *music educator*

Flagstaff
Copley, Edith Ann *music educator*
Poen, Kathryn Louise *music educator, performing arts association administrator*

Florence
Mosby Gnader, Nora Jane *music educator*

Glendale
Cotton, Sally Jean *retired music educator*
Mahoney, Jill Elizabeth *music educator*

Kingman
Gragg, Julie Ann *music educator*

Mesa
Biggs, Kelly Kathleen *theater educator*
Ehlis, Kristine Marie *music educator*
Skoldberg, Phyllis Linnea *musician, educator*
Yandell, Ruth B. *music educator*

Nogales
Boltjes, Connie Cloy *music educator*

Peoria
Bonner, Michelle *music educator*

Phoenix
Altiere, Lauren M. *music educator, consultant*
Klos, Siobhán Lydia *theater director*
Mogerman, Flora May *music educator, director*
Nijinsky, Tamara *actress, puppeteer, author, librarian, educator*
Smiley, Denisa Ann *music educator*
Wheaton, Marilyn *musician*

Scottsdale
Broe, Carolyn Waters *conductor, music educator, violist*
Farney, Charlotte Eugenia *musician, educator*

Sierra Vista
Boughan, Zanetta Louise *music educator*

Sun City
Peterson, Rebecca Thorine *retired voice educator, theater director*

Surprise
Eastman, Donna Kelly *composer*

Tempe
Bowditch, Rachel Emily *theater educator*

Thatcher
Jordahl, Patricia Ann *music educator, theater director*

Tucson
Bluemer, Bevan *acrobatics company executive*
Powell, Winona Kay *music educator*
Zeffirelli, Lucia *dance instructor, piano teacher, choreographer, director, dancer, actress*

Yuma
Packard, Jennifer Ellen *music educator*

ARKANSAS

Arkadelphia
Cornelius, Laura Elizabeth *music educator*

El Dorado
Jamerson, Sandra Mariea *music educator*

Gravette
Collins, Amy Lynn *music educator*

Harrison
Dodson, Leisa *music educator*

Little Rock
Dooley, Wendy Brooke *vocalist, music educator, administrative assistant*
Gay, Agnolia Beatrice *actress, educator*
Headley, Debbie Marcia *music educator*
Raney, Miriam Day *actress*

Malvern
Burks, Rebecca Ann *music educator*

Marion
Logan, Sandra La Mastus *music educator*

Paragould
Stallings, Phyllis Ann *music educator*

Russellville
Vance, Sue Ann *musician, educator*

Siloam Springs
Wubbena, Teresa R. *music educator*

White Hall
Dumas, Sandra Kay *music educator*

CALIFORNIA

Alameda
LaRose, Katherine Stencel *music educator*

Albany
Boris, Ruthanna *dancer, educator, choreographer, dance therapist*
Ginzberg, Abigail *video producer*

Altadena
Klages, Karen Louise *music educator, musician*
Rabe, Elizabeth Rozina *hair stylist, horse breeder*

Anaheim
Browne, Autumn Lee *theater educator, actress, theater director*
Orlando, Valeria *music educator, musician, artist*
Vidergar, Teresa *musician, educator*

Antioch
Adams, Liliana Osses *music performer, harpist*

Aptos
Pezzoni, Meri Kathryn *music educator*

Atwater
Ryan, Kelli Lorraine *ballerina, educator*

Berkeley
Dong, Mabel H *music educator*
Matsumura, Vera Yoshi *pianist*
Reid, Frances Evelyn Kroll *freelance/self-employed cinematographer, film director, communications executive*

Beverly Hills
Abdul, Paula (Paula Julie Abdul) *singer, dancer, choreographer*
Allen, Joan *actress*
Ambrose, Lauren (Lauren Anne D'Ambruoso) *actress*
Anderson, Pamela Denise *actress*
Ann-Margret, (Ann-Margret Olsson) *actress, performer*
Arquette, Patricia *actress*
Azzara, Candice *actress*
Barrymore, Drew *actress*
Barton, Mischa *actress*
Bates, Kathy *actress*
Bello, Maria Elana *actress*
Bening, Annette *actress*
Biel, Jessica *actress, model*
Blanchett, Cate (Catherine Elise Blanchett) *actress*
Bonham-Carter, Helena *actress*
Bosworth, Kate *actress*
Brenneman, Amy *actress*
Burnett, Carol *actress, comedienne, singer*
Burstyn, Ellen (Edna Rae Gillooly) *actress*
Bush, Sophia *actress*
Bymel, Suzan Yvette *talent manager, film producer*
Campbell, Neve *actress*
Capshaw, Kate (Kathy Sue Nail) *actress*
Carter, Lynda *actress, entertainer*
Casey, Sue (Suzanne Marguerite Philips) *actress, real estate broker*
Cattrall, Kim *actress*
Close, Glenn *actress*
Collette, Toni *actress*
Congdon, Amanda *actress, web video blogger, writer*
Connelly, Jennifer *actress*
Cox Arquette, Courteney *actress*
Cruz, Penelope *actress*
Curtis, Jamie Lee *actress*
Cusack, Joan *actress*
D'Abo, Olivia *actress*
Daly, Tyne *actress*
Davis, Geena (Virginia Davis) *actress*
DeGeneres, Ellen *actress, comedienne, talk show host*
Delaney, Kim *actress*
De Rosa, Ninon de Vere *television producer*
Drescher, Fran *actress*
Duke, Patty (Anna Marie Duke) *actress*
Eden, Barbara Jean *actress*
Eikenberry, Jill *actress*
Elfman, Jenna (Jennifer Mary Butala) *actress*
Falco, Edie *actress*
Fey, Tina *actress*
Flockhart, Calista *actress*
Foch, Nina *actress, creative consultant, film director, educator*
Fonda, Jane *actress*
Garofalo, Janeane *actress, comedienne*
Garr, Teri (Ann) *actress*
Gilpin, Peri *actress*
Gleason, Joanna *actress*
Graham, Heather *actress*
Graham, Lauren *actress*
Griffin, Kathy *comedienne, actress*
Gugino, Carla *actress*

Gyllenhaal, Maggie *actress*
Hamilton, Linda *actress*
Hamilton, Lisa Gay *actress*
Hannah, Daryl *actress*
Harden, Marcia Gay *actress*
Harmon, Angie (Angie Sehorn) *actress*
Hart, Melissa Joan Catherine *actress*
Hathaway, Anne *actress*
Hawn, Goldie *actress*
Hayek, Salma *actress*
Heaton, Patricia *actress*
Helmond, Katherine *actress*
Hershey, Barbara (Barbara Herzstein) *actress*
Hewitt, Jennifer Love *actress, singer*
Holmes, Katie (Katherine Noelle Holmes) *actress*
Hunt, Bonnie *actress*
Hunt, Linda *actress*
Hurd, Gale Anne *film producer*
Hurley, Elizabeth *actress, model, film producer*
Huston, Anjelica *actress*
Jackson, Janet (Janet Damita Jo Jackson) *vocalist, dancer*
Janseen, Famke *actress*
Jenkins, Patty *film director, scriptwriter*
Johansson, Scarlett *actress*
Jolie, Angelina *actress*
Jones, Cherry *actress*
Josephson, Nancy *talent agency executive*
Judd, Ashley *actress*
Keaton, Diane *actress*
Keener, Catherine *actress*
Kelly, Moira *actress*
Khan, Chaka (Yvette Marie Stevens) *singer*
Kidman, Nicole *actress*
Kingston, Alex (Alexandra Kingston) *actress*
Klum, Heidi *model, actress*
Lahti, Christine *actress*
Lake, Ricki (Ricki Pamela Lake) *talk show host, actress*
Lane, Diane *actress*
Lansbury, Angela Brigid *actress*
Leder, Mimi *television director, film director, film producer*
Leigh, Jennifer Jason (Jennifer Leigh Morrow) *actress*
Lewis, Juliette *actress*
Linney, Laura *actress*
Liu, Lucy *actress*
Lohan, Lindsay *actress*
Lord, Marjorie *actress*
MacLaine, Shirley *actress*
Madigan, Amy *actress*
Malone, Jena *actress*
Manheim, Camryn *television and film actress*
Margulies, Julianna *actress*
Marshall, Penny (C. Marshall, Carole Penny Marshall) *director, actress*
Martin, Kellie (Noelle) *actress*
Martinson, Constance Frye *television personality, television producer*
Masterson, Mary Stuart *actress*
Mathis, Samantha *actress*
Mazar, Debi *actress*
McAdams, Rachel *actress*
McCarthy, Jenny *actress*
McDonnell, Mary *actress*
Mendes, Eva *actress*
Messing, Debra *actress*
Mol, Gretchen *actress*
Monaco, Kelly Marie *actress*
Moore, Julianne (Julie Anne Smith) *actress*
Moore, Mandy (Amanda Leigh Moore) *actress, singer*
Moore, Mary Tyler *actress*
Morton, Samantha *actress*
Moynahan, Bridget (Kathryn Bridget Moynahan) *actress*
Mullally, Megan *actress*
Najimy, Kathy *actress*
Nixon, Cynthia *actress*
Paltrow, Gwyneth *actress*
Parker, Mary-Louise *actress*
Parker, Sarah Jessica *actress*
Peet, Amanda *actress*
Perkins, Elizabeth Ann *actress*
Perlman, Rhea *actress*
Pompeo, Ellen *actress*
Portman, Natalie *actress*
Posey, Parker *actress*
Rai, Aishwarya *actress*
Reese, Della (Deloreese Patricia Early) *singer, actress*
Ricci, Christina *actress*
Richardson, Patricia *actress*
Richie, Nicole *television personality*
Ringwald, Molly *actress*
Roberts, Julia Fiona *actress*
Robinson Peete, Holly *actress, writer*
Rogers, Mimi *actress*
Rossellini, Isabella *actress, model*
Russell, Keri *actress*
Ryan, Meg (Margaret Mary Emily Ann Hyra) *actress, film producer*
Sagal, Katey *actress*
Scacchi, Greta *actress*
Scott-Thomas, Kristin *actress*
Sedgwick, Kyra *actress*
Sellecca, Connie *actress*
Seymour, Jane *actress*
Shue, Elisabeth *actress*
Shuler Donner, Lauren *film producer*
Silverman, Sarah *actress, comedian, writer*
Simpson, Jessica Ann *singer, actress*
Smith, Jaclyn *actress*
Snyder, Liza *actress*
Sorvino, Mira *actress*
Spacek, Sissy (Mary Elizabeth Spacek) *actress*
Spelling, Tori (Victoria Davey Spelling) *actress*
Spheeris, Penelope *film director*
Steenburgen, Mary *actress*
Stiles, Julia *actress*
Streep, Meryl (Mary Louise Streep) *actress*
Suvari, Mena *actress*
Swank, Hilary Ann *actress*
Swofford, Beth *agent*
Sykes, Wanda *comedienne, actress*
Tamblyn, Amber Rose *actress*
Taylor, Christine *actress*
Taylor, Lili *actress*
Theron, Charlize *actress*
Thompson, Emma *actress*
Thurman, Uma Karuna *actress*
Tierney, Maura *actress*
Tilly, Jennifer *actress*
Tom, Lauren *actress, singer*
Tomei, Marisa *actress*
Travis, Nancy *actress*
Turner, Janine *actress*
Turner, Kathleen *actress*
Tyler, Liv *actress*
Van Ark, Joan *actress*
Vardalos, Nia *actress, screenwriter*
Ward, Sela *actress*
Watts, Naomi *actress*
Weaver, Sigourney (Susan Alexandra Weaver) *actress*
Weisz, Rachel *actress*
White, Betty *actress, comedienne*
White, Meg (Megan Martha White) *musician, vocalist*
Williams, Michelle *actress*
Williams-Paisley, Kimberly *actress*
Witherspoon, Reese (Laura Jean Reese Witherspoon) *actress*
Wright Penn, Robin *actress*
Zanuck, Lili Fini *film director, producer*
Zellweger, Renee *actress*

Brea
Ellis, Cynthia Bueker *musician, educator*

Brisbane
Baadh, Valerie *choreographer, movement educator, theater producer, production designer*

Burbank
Branch, Michelle *musician*
Cher, (Cherilyn Sarkisian) *singer, actress*
Jovovich, Milla (Natasha Militza Jovovich) *model, actress*
Mc Govern, Maureen Therese *entertainer*
Mc Vie, Christine Perfect *musician*
O'Dell, Nancy *television personality*
Remini, Leah *actress*
Rhimes, Shonda *producer, director, writer*
Rimes, LeAnn *country music singer*
Ruttan, Susan *actress*
Weiskopf, Wanda *mezzo soprano, writer, poet*

Calistoga
Sassoon, Janet *ballerina, educator*

Castro Valley
Mabee, Sandra Ivonne Noriega *musician, educator, clergy member*

Cathedral City
Hoffman, Jetha L. *music educator, voice educator*

Century City
Brazell, Tina Arning *actress, executive recruiter*

Ceres
Chamberlain, Candace Sue *music educator*

Chico
Reinhardt, Deborah Ann *music educator*
Taylor, Carolyn Kay *music educator*

Chula Vista
Greenway-August, Kristin Lee *dancer, educator*

Claremont
Schroerlucke, Leslie Jean *music educator*

Clovis
Kawashima, Hope Nozomi *musician*
van der Paardt, Tamara Ann *music educator*

Corona
Hagmann, Lillian Sue *violin instructor*
Holt, Chifra *dancer, educator, choreographer, artist*

Coronado
Perry, Jantina *retired music educator*

Culver City
Finkelman Cox, Penney *film producer*
Fisher, Lucy *film producer*
Hall, Barbara *television producer*
Thomas, Marlo (Margaret Julia Thomas) *actress*
Ziskin, Laura *television producer, film producer*

Cypress
Bradaric, SuzAnne Joy *music educator, theater director*

Davis
Cole, Kimberly Ree *music educator, musician*
McCutcheon, Jade Rosina *performing arts educator*

Downey
Achon, Raquel Andrea *music educator, consultant*

El Cajon
Kibble-Cacioppo, Maxine Lorraine *recording company executive*

Encinitas
Litvin, Inessa Elizabeth *piano educator*

Encino
Taylor, Renee *actress, writer*

Escondido
Rockwell, Elizabeth Goode *dance company director, consultant, educator*

Fountain Valley
Treadway-Dillmon, Linda Lee *actress, stuntwoman, dancer, dispatcher, athletic trainer*

Fremont
Hsu, Gloria *piano educator*

Fresno
Riggs, Krista Dyonis *music educator, librarian*

Fullerton
Renee (aka) Stevens, Rita *actor, theater educator, director*

Glendale
Gibbons, Leeza *television and radio talk show host, entertainment reporter*
O'Day, Anita Belle Colton *entertainer, musician, vocalist*

Hemet
Pumphrey, Bonnie Jean *music educator*

Hollywood
Fergie, (Stacy Ann Ferguson) *singer*
Lynne, Shelby (Shelby Lynn Moorer) *country singer*
Miles, Joanna *actress, playwright, director*
Minnelli, Liza *singer, actress*
Varner, Vicky Jo *actor, counselor*
Warren, Diane *lyricist*

Huntington Beach
Silver, Lynn Ellen *music educator*

Inglewood
Wakefield, Marie Cynthia *performing arts educator, playwright, poet*

Irvine
Nelson, June Lusk *music educator*
Ruyter, Nancy Lee Chalfa *dance educator*

Kentfield
Halprin, Anna Schuman (Mrs. Lawrence Halprin) *dancer*

La Crescenta
Purcell, Lee (Lee Jeune Williams) *actress, film producer*

La Habra Heights
Agajanian, Gilda *pianist*

La Jolla
North, Kathryn E. Keesey (Mrs. Eugene C. North) *retired music educator*

La Quinta
Knoblauch, Mary Reilly (Mary Louise Reilly) *retired music educator, writer*

Laguna Niguel
von Hutten, Gaia Theresa *performing company executive, choreographer, educator*

Lake Elsinore
Bouslog, Robbin Raye *performing arts educator, art educator*

Lake Hughes
La Mont, Tawana Faye *camera operator, video director, foundation administrator*

Lathrop
Daily, Diana Smith *music educator*

Long Beach
Cobe-Ross, Lori *casting director*
deAlbuquerque, Joan Marie *conductor, music educator*

Los Angeles
Alonso, Maria Conchita *actress, singer*
Archer, Anne *actress*
Balaski, Belinda L. *actress, educator, artist*
Banks, Tyra (Tyra Lynne Banks) *retired model, television personality*
Bell, Lee Phillip *television personality, television producer*
Benatar, Pat (Pat Andrzejewski) *rock singer*
Bergman, Marilyn Keith *lyricist, writer*
Bloom, Claire *actress*
Brown, Carol *make-up artist*
Chapman, Carolyn *broadcasting director*
Chen, Lynn *actress*
Clayburgh, Jill *actress*
Combs, Holly Marie *actress*
Dally, Lynn *choreographer, performing company executive, educator*
Dawson, Rosario *actress, singer*
Dee, Ruby (Ruby Dee Davis) *actress, writer, film director*
Diehl, Dolores *performing company executive*
Donahue, Ann M. *television producer*
Dunst, Kirsten *actress*
Elrod, Lu *retired music educator, actress*
Farnham, Katherine A *music educator, vocalist*
Flanagan, Fionnula Manon *actress, writer, theater director*
Garrett, Betty *actress*
Gifford, Kathie Lee *television personality, vocalist*
Haines, Randa *film director*
Hart, Mary *television talk show host*
Heigl, Katherine Marie *actress*
Henderson, Florence *actress, singer*
Henkel, Kathy *composer*
Herrera, G. Shizuko *theater educator*
Hurt, Mary Beth *actress*
Ireland, Kathy *actress, apparel designer*
Kellerman, Sally Claire *actress*
Kim, Irene Jiyun *music professor, choral conductor*
Kupka, Nancy Elyse Wyatt *dance educator*
Landers, Audrey *actress, singer*
Leeves, Jane *actress*
Lew, Joycelyne Mae *actress*
Lunden, Joan *television personality*
Ma, Vivienne *dancer, educator*
McCormick, Carolyn *actress*
Moreno, Rita (Rosita Dolores Alverio) *actress*
Muldaur, Diana Charlton *actress*
O'Connell, Taaffe Cannon *actress, publishing executive*
Olsen, Ashley Fuller *actress*
Olsen, Mary-Kate *actress*
Peña, Elizabeth *actress*
Pittman, Amanda Nelson *music educator*
Polk Gitlin, Mimi *film producer*
Pritzker, Jean *film producer*
Richmond, Rocsan *television executive producer, small business owner*
Rohrer, Susan Earley *film producer, film director, scriptwriter*
Ross, Marion *actress*
Rowell, Victoria *actress*
Russo, Rene *actress*
San Giacomo, Laura *actress*
Sawyer, Toni *actress*
Sheedy, Ally (Alexandra Elizabeth Sheedy) *actress*
Simmons, Ann Lorraine *actress, educator*
Stapleton, Jean (Jeanne Murray) *actress*
Streisand, Barbra Joan *singer, actress, film director*
Thompson, Sada Carolyn *actress*
Tomlin, Lily *actress*
Ullman, Tracey *actress, singer*
Walter, Jessica *actress*
Watson, Emily *actress*
Winters, Barbara Jo *musician*

Malibu
LaChanze, (R. LaChanze Sapp, Rhonda Sapp) *actress*
Nettles, Jennifer *singer*

Martinez
DeWolfe, Martha *singer, songwriter, publisher, producer*
George, Julianne Mary *music educator, conductor*

Menlo Park
Baez, Joan Chandos *vocalist*

Mill Valley
Adessa, Lori *music educator*
Schiff, Jan Pedersen *conductor, voice educator*

Mission Viejo
Burke, Kathleen J. *music director, writer*

Modesto
Rogers, Wanda Faye *vocalist*

Monrovia
Brown, Gwendolyn Williams *music educator*

Mountain View
Serebrennikova, Emiliya *musician, educator*

Murrieta
Miller, Helen F. *music educator, musician*

Nevada City
Clausen, Jeanne Lorraine *musician*

Nipomo
Aune, Alissa Marie *music educator*

North Hollywood
Downey, Roma *actress*
Fanning, Dakota *actress*
Newton-John, Olivia *singer, actress*
Reynolds, Debbie (Mary Frances Reynolds) *actress*
Stone, Sharon *actress*
Toplitt, Gloria H. *music educator, actress, vocalist*
Toussieng, Yolanda *make-up artist*

Northridge
Cartwright, Nancy *actress, television producer*

Norwalk
Kiss, Boglarka *musician, educator*

Oakland
Boesing, Martha *theater artist*
DeFazio, Lynette Stevens *dancer, educator, choreographer, violinist, actress*
Lake, Suzanne *singer, music educator*
Liveright, Betty Fouche *actress, writer*
Zschau, Marilyn *singer*

Pacific Palisades
Kamrany, Sajia *television producer*

Palm Springs
Parks, Trina *dancer, educator*

Palos Verdes Peninsula
Deveny, Charlotte Perry *musician, educator*
Julien, Gail Leslie *model, public relations professional*

Pasadena
Halsted, Margo *music educator, carillonneur*
Kilburn, Katherine Lynn (Kappy Kilburn) *theater director, theater producer*
Worby, Rachael Beth *conductor*

Petaluma
Wilcoxson, Carol Ann *music educator*

Pomona
Harms, Janet Berggren *music educator*

Rancho Mirage
Ballard, Kaye *actress*

Rancho Palos Verdes
Steiner, Frances Josephine *conductor, musician, educator*

Rancho Santa Margarita
Hauser, Jean *theater educator, theater director*

Redlands
Auerbacher, Mary Jane *church organist*
Lewis, Victoria Ann *theater educator*

Redondo Beach
Richards, Denise *actress*

Rowland Heights
Smith, Barbara J. *music educator*

Sacramento
McCann, Kim Lou M. *theater educator, director*
Morison, Kathryn Diane *actor, consultant*

Piper, Jami Kathleen *music educator, composer, musician*
Winney, Gayle Marie *music educator*

San Andreas
Buringrud, Lisa Marie *music educator*

San Diego
Bates-Romeo, Delores Alvenia *music educator, consultant*
Crill, Alice Eileen *music educator*
Flettner, Marianne *opera administrator*
Herriman, Darleen Ann *music educator*
Kranz, Kathleen Nee *pianist, music educator*

San Francisco
Anastacia, (Anastacia Lyn Newkirk) *singer*
Brindel, Jill Rachuy *cellist*
Etheridge, Melissa Lou *singer, lyricist*
Gregory, Sara Susan (Sudie) *musician, singer, lyricist, poet, recording industry executive, sound recording engineer, archivist*
Hirst, Karen L. *theater educator*
Lau, Jenny Kwok Wah *theater educator, consultant, film educator, consultant*
LeBlanc, Tina *dancer*
Lim, Donna *music educator*
McGuire, Kathleen Alison *conductor*
Neve, Victoria J. *music educator*
Rosenberg, Betsy *radio personality, environmentalist*
Rosenberg, Pamela *opera director, conductor*
Shorenstein Hays, Carole *theater producer*
Van Dyck, Wendy *dancer*

San Jose
Dalis, Irene *mezzo soprano, performing arts association administrator*
Stevens, Dorothy Frost *retired television producer*

San Lorenzo
Olivier, Samara Lynn *music educator*

San Marcos
Gilson, Susan Lee *performing arts educator*

San Marino
Santoso, Michelle Jo *music educator, pianist*

San Rafael
Marsh, Marian E. *voice educator*

Santa Barbara
Ben-Dor, Gisselle *conductor, musician*
Horne, Marilyn Berneice *mezzo-soprano*
Sebastian, Suzie *television producer*

Santa Cruz
Martinez, Alma R. *actress, theater director, educator*

Santa Monica
Aki, Angela *singer*
Apple, Fiona (Fiona Apple Maggart) *singer, songwriter*
Curran, Leigh *actress, playwright*
Eve, (Eve Jihan Jeffers) *rap artist, actress*
Fisher, Frances *actress*
Frot-Coutaz, Cecile *television producer*
Hannigan, Alyson *actress*
Katina, Elena Sergejevna *singer*
Kennedy, Kathleen *film producer*
Louis-Dreyfus, Julia *actress*
Marcil, Vanessa *actress*
Meany, Angelina Marie *dancer, educator*
Simpson, India.Arie *musician*
Summer, Donna (La Donna Adrian Gaines) *singer, songwriter, actress*
Volkova, Julia Olegovna *singer*

Seaside
Taylor, Lula Yvonne *music educator*

Sebastopol
Grimmer, Margot *dancer, choreographer, director*

Sherman Oaks
Clark, Susan (Nora Goulding) *actress*
Norwood, Brandy Rayana (Brandy) *singer, actress*
Schlessinger, Laura *radio talk show host*
Taylor, Elizabeth (Dame Elizabeth Rosemond Taylor) *actress*

Sonoma
Pollack, Phyllis Addison *ballerina*

Stockton
Acoba, Valerie Lee *performing arts educator*
Henderson, Elma Mae *singer, composer, educator, dancer, actress*
Kizer, Nancy Anne *music educator, musician*
Wilcox, Helena Marguerita (Rita) *music educator*

Studio City
Basinger, Kim (Kimila Ann Basinger) *actress*
Boyett, Joan Reynolds *performing company executive*
Gallardo, Sandra Silvana *television producer, actress*
King, Carole (Carole Klein) *lyricist, singer*
Rogers, Suzanne C. *actress*
White, Julie *actress*
Wilson, Peta *actress*

Sun City
Schmoll, Edith Margaret *music educator*

Sun Valley
Gilmore, Dawn S. *music educator*

Sunnyvale
Garner, Shirley Imogene *retired music educator*
Lanaro, Clara Marrama *music educator, writer*

Sylmar
Powers, Mala *actress*

Tarzana
Easton, Sheena *rock vocalist, actress*

Temecula
Lozosky, Lisa Lynn *music educator, elementary school educator*

Universal City
Cross, Marcia *actress*
Hatcher, Teri *actress*
Huffman, Felicity (Flicka Huffman) *actress*
Longoria, Eva (Eva Jacqueline Longoria, Eva Longoria Christopher) *actress*
Merkerson, S. Epatha *actress*
Sheridan, Nicolette *actress*
Woodard, Alfre *actress*

Upland
Bast, Karolyn Anne (Kay Bast) *dance educator, choreographer*

Valley Village
Barkin, Elaine Radoff *composer*
Diller, Phyllis (Phyllis Ada Driver Diller) *actress, writer*

Van Nuys
Boone, Deborah Ann (Debby Boone) *singer*

Venice
Rudnick, Pesha Eva *theater director*

Ventura
Cutler, Carole Marie *music educator*

Visalia
Allstedt, Nora Marie *music educator*
Porterfield-Pyatt, Chaumonde R. *music educator, advocate*

Walnut Creek
Grandi, Lois A. *theater director, choreographer, actor*

Weed
Schaefer, M. Elaine *music educator, conductor*

West Hills
Todd, Katherine Laws *filmmaker, retired writer, human resources specialist*

West Hollywood
Bassett, Angela *actress*
Baxter, Meredith *actress*
Berry, Halle Maria *actress*
Cole, Natalie Maria *singer*
Dorn, Dolores *actress*
Franklyn, Audrey Pozen *talent promoter, television personality*
Harry, Deborah Ann *singer*
Mulgrew, Katherine Kiernan (Kate Mulgrew) *actress*
Presley, Priscilla (Pricilla Ann Wagner, Priscilla Beaulieu Presley) *actress*
Romijn, Rebecca *actress, model*

Westchester
Capetillo, Charlene Vernelle *music educator, special education educator*

Westlake Village
Steadman, Lydia Duff *symphony violinist, retired elementary school educator*

Yucaipa
deBaun, Linda Louise *performing arts educator*

COLORADO

Arvada
Franklin, Tammy *performing arts educator*

Aurora
Seslar, Tanya L. *music educator*
Spring, Kathleen Marie *musical program director, educator*

Boulder
Doebele, Alexa C. *music educator, director*
Hayes, Deborah *musicology educator, college administrator*
Kotter, Rita Joan *theatre educator, design consultant*
Sable, Barbara Kinsey *retired music educator*
Wallace, Stephanie Ann *music educator, conductor*

Centennial
Heath, Jayne Marie *music educator*
Williams, Julie Lynne *music educator*

Clifton
McCall, Ruby Elane *music educator*

Colorado Springs
Borgen, Irma R. *music educator*
Calvert, Susan Kadey *music educator*
Glenn, Shannon Lea *music educator*
Mery, Naomi Marie *music educator*
Papproth, Jodi Renee *theater educator*
Scott, Carla Anne *musician, educator*
Skadden, Vanda Sue *retired music educator*
Tabet, Renee' B. *voice educator, director*

Creede
Gray, Johanna Jill *music educator*

Denver
Coe, Judith Anne *music educator, composer, performer*
Faigao, Wendy Kalayaan *musician, music company executive*
Robinson, Cleo Parker *artistic director*
Shaw, Priscilla *music educator, coach*

Durango
Farrell, Kimberly H. *music educator*
Tischhauser, Katherine Jetter *music educator, cellist*

Estes Park
Varilek, Julie *music educator*

Evergreen
Ogle, Amanda McKibbin *music educator, theater educator, director*

Federal Heights
Teigland, Brittany Paige *music educator*

Fort Collins
Wallner, Melissa Kay *music and theater educator, director*
Wilber, Clare Marie *musician, educator*

Fort Morgan
Christensen, Cynthia L. *music educator*
Vogel, Sarah Elizabeth *music educator*

Fountain
Wilson, Roberta (Bobbi) Gail *performing arts educator*

Grand Junction
Opsal, Pamela E. *music educator*
Phillips, Ruth Amelia *retired music educator, artist*
Wilson, Deborah Grim *music educator*

Keenesburg
Vigil, Elizabeth Lee *music educator*

Lake George
Daniel, Deanna Alane *music educator*

Lamar
Tague, Vickie *music educator*

Littleton
Day, Susan Marie *music educator, composer*
Early, Bonnie Sue *piano teacher, music educator*
Johansson, Alicia Barbara *musician*
King, Linda *musician, educator*

Northglenn
Kappler, Karen L. *music educator, musician*

Pueblo
Ihm, Dana Elizabeth *music educator*

Westminster
Kopperud, Marilyn Sue *music educator*
Peterson, Candyce Leigh *music educator*

CONNECTICUT

Bridgeport
Campbell, Stacey Lynne *music educator*
Richard, Ellen *theater executive*

Danbury
Callaghan, Marjorie Seymour *music educator*
McCulloch, Angela Jean *theater educator, music educator*

Darien
Springer, Ruth Wiren *music educator*

East Haddam
Frost, Susan Beth *theater producer*

Fairfield
Mastrony, Sara Elizabeth *music educator, director*

Greenwich
Shimchick, Marie *music educator*

Hartford
Mills, Corinne C. *music educator*

Monroe
Morrison, Amanda Mary *music educator*

Mystic
Bobruff, Carole Marks *radio producer, radio personality*
Gilbert, Ellen Effman *music educator, conductor*

New Canaan
Champion, Marge (Marjorie Celeste Champion) *actress, choreographer, dancer*

New Haven
Garvey, Sheila Hickey *theater educator*
Nolan, Victoria *theater director*

Newington
Anderson, Kathryn Parks *music educator*
Cohen, Fern K. *music educator*

Niantic
Rigdon, Nancy Kenway *music educator*

Oakville
Carroll, Constance Marie *pianist, educator*

Old Saybrook
Geer, Lois Margaret *music educator*

Southbury
Bergen, Polly *actress*

Stamford
Preiss-Harris, Patricia *music educator, composer, pianist*

Stonington
Young, Pamela J. *music educator*

Storrs Mansfield
Ford, Karrin Elizabeth *music educator, musician*

Unionville
Fantozzi, Janet Rosen *music educator*

West Hartford
Washer, Barbara Mochrie *performing arts educator, director*

West Suffield
Jespersen, Wyn Cherie *music educator*

Weston
Fredrik, Burry *theater producer, director*

Woodstock
Ranta, Amy J. *music educator*

DELAWARE

Dover
Perrine, Veronica Beader *music educator, director*

Lewes
Bala, Madeleine Jeanette *music educator*
Buchert, Stephanie Nicole *music educator*

New Castle
Bailey, Laurie Ruckert *music educator*

Newark
Friswell-Jacobs, Tracy *performing arts educator, dancer*

Wilmington
Tjersland, Trina J. *performing arts educator*

DISTRICT OF COLUMBIA

Washington
Anderson, Mary Ann Grasso *theater association executive*
Bradley, Barbra Bailey *musician, educator, accompanist*
Crawford-Mason, Clare Wootten *television producer, journalist*
Dhue, Stephanie *television producer, reporter*
Dodge, Judith C. *musician*
Donlon, Claudette *performing company executive*
Dukert, Betty Cole *television producer*
Green, Ricki Kutcher *television producer*
Harpham, Virginia Ruth *violinist*
Hedges, Marietta *performing arts educator, actor*
Michaels, Jennifer *choreographer, dancer, educator*
Smith, Molly D. *theater director*
Stamberg, Susan Levitt *radio personality*
Stone, Florence Smith *film producer, consultant*
Weidenfeld, Sheila Rabb *television producer, writer*
Winans, Cece *gospel vocalist*
Wolff, Karen Lias *music educator*

FLORIDA

Auburndale
Rhinesmith, Heather Lynn *music educator*

Boca Raton
Dower Gold, Catherine Anne *music history educator*

Boynton Beach
Ricks, Dallis Derrick Biehl *pianist*

Bradenton
Bjorklund, Nancy Margarette Watts *music educator*

Cantonment
Walker, Janie Suzanne *music educator*

Cape Coral
Wendel, Joan Audrey *music educator*

Clearwater
Zobel, Margaret Riethmeier *retired music educator*

Clermont
Fox, Terri Jo *music educator*
Sides, I. Ruth S. *retired music educator*

Dade City
Lukacik, Denise Marie *dance studio owner, choreographer*

Dania
Quillen, Teresa *music educator*

Davie
Walkinshaw, Nicole M. *performing arts educator*

Daytona Beach
Poitier, Constance Rena *music specialist, educator*

Deland
Sorensen, Jacki Faye *choreographer, aerobic dance company executive*

Deltona
Comeau, Heather Marie *dance instructor, administrator*

Dunedin
Foley, Briana *music educator, consultant*

Englewood
Catterlin, Cindy Lou *music educator, language educator*

Ferry Park
Seaver, Elizabeth Mary *music educator*

Fort Lauderdale
Jackson-Callandret, Shirley Lorraine *music educator*
LeRoy, Miss Joy *model, apparel designer*

Fort Myers
Ellis, Maria Vanessa *dance educator*
Lippens, Nancy Cobb *music educator*

Gainesville
DesForges, Deborah Waln *music educator*
Ellis, Laura Renee *music educator*
Paul, Ouida Fay *music educator*

Green Cove Springs
Davidson, Joy Elaine *retired mezzo soprano*

Immokalee
Foster, Lucille Stuart *music educator*

Jacksonville
Huber, Mary Susan *music educator*
Stewart, Sandra Kay *music educator*

Kissimmee
Fahmie, Deborah *music educator*

Lake Wales
Dickey, Deena Lynne *music educator, vocalist*

Lakeland
Boulware, Carol Carter *retired music educator*
Jacobson, Barbara Dinger *music educator*
Rambaran, Sarah M. *music educator*

Largo
Szalkowski, Deborah *music educator*

Lecanto
Wheatley, Deborah A. *music educator*

Longwood
James, Kathleen Maria *music educator*

Lutz
Smith, Marjorie *music educator, conductor*

Miami
Arrabal, Berta Isabel *radio producer*
Barreiro, Valerie *choreographer, educator*
Batson, Dawn Kirsten *music educator, cultural consultant*
Coulter, Beverly Norton *singer, pianist, opera director*
Cubberley, Gayle Susan *band director*
Feinberg, Wendie *television producer*
Floyd, Suzanne Elvira Izzo *music educator*
Galatas, Ruth Ann *musician, publishing executive, educator*
Harmon, Monica Renee *music educator*
Marsh, Sara Maria *music educator*
Mauch, Diane Farrell *music educator*
Moody, Jacqueline Elaine *music educator*
Pilafian, Audrey Kalenian *music educator*
Saralegui, Cristina Maria *Spanish language television personality, journalist*
Schumacher, Silvia C. *performing arts educator*
Walkley, Mary L. *voice and music educator*

Miami Beach
Gardiner, Pamela Nan *performing company executive*

Milton
Arnold, Margaret Morelock *music educator, soprano*

Naples
Evans, Judith P. *music educator*

Nokomis
Johns, Karen Jordan *music educator, small business owner*

Ocala
Hudson, Ann Elizabeth *music educator*

Orlando
Boyd, Be (Belinda) Carolyn *theater educator*
Flanagan, Marianne *music educator*
Harris, Lani M. *theater educator*
Hom, Trudy A. *music educator*
Jordan, Grace Carol *music educator*
Radloff, Marie Ulrey *music educator*
Schultz, Victoria L. *music educator, entertainer*
Sourwine, Claire Elaine *retired music educator, conductor*

Ormond Beach
Granville, Paulina *independent music scholar, educator*

Palm Harbor
Katzen-Guthrie, Joy *performance artist, engineering executive*

Pembroke Pines
Corbiere, Mary Louise Sambataro *music educator, musician*
Hudson, Brenda Louise *soprano, opera singer, vocal coach*

Pinellas Park
Benedict, Gail Cleveland *music educator*

Plantation
Najm, Tami Lynn *music educator*

Punta Gorda
Stratas, Teresa (Anastasia Strataki) *soprano*

Royal Palm Beach
MacEwan, Elizabeth Marie *pianist, vocalist*

Saint Petersburg
Michael, Marilyn Corliss *music educator, mezzo soprano*

Sarasota
Carstens, Charlene B. *composer, music educator*

Stuart
Kooluris, Hortense Dolan *performing arts educator, consultant, dancer*

Tallahassee
Allen, Terice Diann *music educator*
Corzine, Jennifer Jean *music educator*
Harsanyi, Janice *retired soprano, educator*
Stebleton, Michelle Marie *musician, educator*
Wimberley, Cheryl Ann *choreographer, educator*
Zwilich, Ellen Taaffe *composer*

Tampa
Faulkner, Melanie E. *music educator*
Moore, Janet L.S. *music educator, dean*
Scialdo, Mary Ann *musician, educator*
Sleeper, Cheri Acosta *music educator*
Stefanov, Ivanka *music educator*

Titusville
King, Sheila Sue *music educator, elementary school educator*
Siegel, Judith S. *music educator*

Vero Beach
Lange, Billie Carola *video specialist*

Wellington
Oser, Mary S. *music educator*
Pernezny, Lynn Anne *music educator*

West Melbourne
Chapman, DaLaine *music educator*

West Palm Beach
Hale, Marie Stoner *artistic director*

Weston
Berry, Becky *music educator*

Windermere
Rudzik, Lynne A. *musician, educator*

Winter Garden
Ellis, Missie Lynne *music educator*

Winter Haven
Arens, Christine M. *musician, educator, composer*

Winter Park
Wrancher, Elizabeth Ann *music educator, opera singer*

Zephyrhills
Summerhill, Elaine *music educator*

GEORGIA

Acworth
Beale, Judith Ann *music educator*

Alpharetta
Stalling, Janet Kitts *music educator*

Athens
David, Martha Lena Huffaker *retired music educator, retired sales executive*

Atlanta
Clark, Faye Louise *retired drama and speech educator*
Domingo, Esther *music educator*
Grant, Susan *television executive*
Reese, Audrey Maria *music educator*
Vulgamore, Allison *performing arts association administrator*
Wylly, Barbara Bentley *performing arts association administrator*

Augusta
Floyd, Rosalyn Wright *pianist, accompanist, educator*

Bainbridge
Lucas, Tammi Michelle *music educator*

Buford
Smith, Rebecca L. *musician*

Byron
Chancellor, Elizabeth Ann *music educator*

Canton
Frady, Rita R. *music educator, information technology manager*
Jones-Kelner, Barbara Teryl *music educator*
Lokey, Linda H. *music educator*
Taylor, Sue Ann *film and television producer*

Clarkston
Page, Anne Eichelberger *violinist*

Columbus
Hiatt, Florence Ellen *musician*
Norah, Patricia Ann *music educator*
Patrick, Cathy *music educator, administrative assistant*

Cumming
Beaty-Gunter, Sharon E. *music educator*

Dallas
Kinney, Bonnie Logan *retired music educator*

Decatur
Pryce, Monica Elizabeth *music educator*
Ray, Amy *vocalist, guitarist*
Saliers, Emily *singer, musician*
Strickland, Brenda B. *music educator*

Douglas
Tucker, Maureen Ann *musician*

Ellijay
Mayfield, Katie Smith *music educator*

Fort Gaines
Chaffin, LaVerne *music educator*

Griffin
Grant, Mary Alverson *music educator*

Hartwell
Rushing, Tonnie Austin Page *musician, educator*

Homer
Rylee, Gloria Genelle *music educator*

Hoschton
Jordan, Carol Morgan *music educator*

Jackson
Bomar, Laura Beth *music educator*

Kennesaw
Cash, Stefanie Lynn *music educator, director*
Diaz, Anne Marie Theresa *music educator, musician*

Kingsland
Boyett, Linda Marie *music educator*

Leesburg
Hilley, Mary Kay *music educator*
Unger, Suzanne Everett *musician, educator*

Loganville
Morea, Michelle *performing arts educator*

Mableton
Reeves, Denise Moseley *dancer, educator*

Macon
McLemore, Ellen H. *music educator*
Terry, Doris D. *music educator*

Marietta
Chase, Christa Joy *music educator*
Roach, Carole Hyde *music educator*
Smith, Irene Helen-Nordine *music educator*

Mcdonough
Brown, Joy Withers *music educator*

Milledgeville
Flory, Jennifer Morgan *conductor, educator*
Ragan, Charlotte Ann *music educator*

Nashville
Cosson, Mary Gwendolyn *music educator*

Oakwood
Lindahl, Sarah Elizabeth *theater educator*

Oxford
Archetto, Maria *music educator*

Ringgold
Harper, Sandra Reynolds *music educator*

Rome
Davis, Susan Lynn *music educator, musician*
Potts, Glenda Rue *music educator*

Roswell
Stoffle, Sarah Elizabeth *theater educator*

Saint Simons Island
Cedel, Melinda Irene *music educator, violinist*

Smyrna
Rife, Elizabeth *musician, educator*

Snellville
Sali, Amanda Leigh *choral director*

Statesboro
Bryan, Carolyn J. *music educator, saxophonist*

Suwanee
Moras, Barbara J. *music educator*

Valdosta
Corbin, Lynn Ann *music educator, conductor*

Villa Rica
Abney, Martha McEachern *music educator*

Waleska
Naylor, Susan Embry *music educator*

Warner Robins
Coleman, Debbie L. *music educator*

Washington
Tiller, Anna Frances *music educator*

Wrens
Adams, Susan Seigler *music educator*

Young Harris
Wolfersteig, Eloise Smith *retired music educator*

Zebulon
Thomas, Joan E. *music educator*

HAWAII

Aiea
Chun, Cheryl *music educator*

Haleiwa
Taylor, Kathryn Denise *music educator*

Honolulu
Lu, Caixia *television director, language educator*
Scanlan, Alicia Rae *music educator*

Kaneohe
Harner, Kathryn Denise *music educator*
Young-Pohlman, Colette Lisa *music educator*

Waianae
Bourke-Faustina, Marlene Frances *music educator*

IDAHO

Arco
Jardine, Cindy M. *music educator*

Boise
Holt, Isabel Rae *radio program producer*

Ketchum
Neely, Hilarie *dancer, educator*

Rigby
Hardyman, Lisa W. *music educator, elementary school educator*

Shelley
Payne, Keri Tolman *dancer, educator*

Twin Falls
Cowger, Shari Ann *music educator*
Yost, Kelly Lou *pianist*

ILLINOIS

Algonquin
Lange-Connelly, Phyllis *musician, educator*

Aurora
Lupei, Cynthia Therese *music educator*
Pappas, Margene *retired music educator*

Barrington
Carter, Jeanie *performing company executive*
Stewart, Ann S. *music educator, director*

Batavia
Feuerborn, Rita Kazlauskas *music educator, musician*

Beardstown
Vermillion, Julia Kathleen *music educator*

Bloomington
Bryant, Deanne *music educator*

Bradley
Altenberger, Cynthia Ann *music educator*

Brighton
Weinberg, Alexandrea *music educator*

Carpentersville
Kozeva, Natalia *music educator*

Cary
Irey, Robin Elizabeth *performing company executive, performing arts educator*

Charleston
Ignazito, Madeline Dorothy *music educator, composer*

Chicago
Alden, Dawn Margarete *actor, choreographer, educator*
Basden, Cameron *ballet mistress, dancer*
Bridges, Cynthia Elaine *music educator*
Freidheim, Ladonna *dance company director*
Kalver, Gail Ellen *dance company executive, musician*
Kenas-Heller, Jane Hamilton *musician*
Lazar, Ludmila *concert pianist, music educator*
Lilly, Aimee *radio personality*
Mach, Elyse *musician, music educator, writer*
Markey, Judy *radio personality, writer*
May, Aviva Rabinowitz *music educator, musician, linguist*
Noel, Carol Adele *music educator, opera singer*
O'Malley, Kathy *radio personality*
Ran, Shulamit *composer*
Ross, Lori *radio personality*
Saracho, Tanya Selene *performing company executive, playwright*
Sexton, Brenda *film agency director*
Shoss, Deanna *theatre executive*
Stifler, Venetia Chakos *dancer, educator, choreographer*
Trogani, Monica *ballet dancer*
Winfrey, Oprah *television talk show host, actress, television producer*

Chillicothe
Griesbaum, Kamela Lee *music educator*

Coal City
Major, Mary Jo *dance school artistic director*

Columbia
Newell, Christel *music educator*

Country Club Hills
McClelland, Helen *music educator*

Danville
Woodrow, Jennifer Cole *music educator*

Decatur
Ewers, Marla Rouse *voice educator*
Mancinelli, Judith *piano teacher, recitalist, chamber music performer*

Dekalb
Jay, Danielle Mary *dancer, educator*

Dixon
Ewers, Denise Yvonne *music educator*

Earlville
Estell, Mary Esther *music educator, emergency medical technician, protective services official*

Edwardsville
Anderson, Mary Jane *music educator*
Kittrell, Ethel Jean *musician, retired literature and language professor*
Stranc, Cathleen L. *music educator*

Effingham
Whitlatch, Christine Lyn *music educator*

Elk Grove Village
Roberts, Verna Dean *music educator*

Evanston
Eberley, Helen-Kay *opera singer, recording industry executive, poet*

McDonough, Bridget Ann *music theatre company director*
Mora, Dawn Ann *theater educator*
Persons, Fern *actress*
Zimmerman, Mary Alice *performing arts educator*

Evergreen Park
Prendergast, Carole Lisak *musician, educator*

Geneva
Klenke, Deborah Ann *band and choral director, department chairman*

Godfrey
Parton-Stanard, Susan *music educator, voice educator, musician*

Grayslake
Craven, Deborah *performing arts educator*

Greenville
Weiss, Louise Annette *music educator*

Hazel Crest
Thies, Julie Ann *music educator*

Hoffman Estates
Hays, Judy Meyer *music educator*

Joliet
Schoonover, Melissa *music educator*

Liberty
Dickhut, Karen Sue *music educator*

Libertyville
Peot, Deborah Lynn *music educator*

Lincoln
Freesmeier, Ruth Ann *music educator, director*

Lisle
Stephen, Doris Moyer *music educator*

Malta
Franklin, Nadine Karen *performing arts educator*

Maple Park
Dripps-Paulson, Maria *music educator*

Mascoutah
Setterlund, Tina A.M. *music educator*

Metamora
Rude, Debra Marie *music educator*

Midlothian
Griebel, Karen Ann *music educator*

Milford
Pyzek, Tamera Jean *music educator*

Mokena
Vander Zanden, Marianne *music educator*
Wright, Chely *country singer*

Monmouth
Gossett, Barbara Jean *voice educator*

Morton Grove
Hoffman, Joy Yu *harpist, pianist*

Mundelein
Berrong, Christine R. *music educator, voice educator*

Murphysboro
Berry, Alice Allen *retired music educator*

O Fallon
Tiemann, Jeannine E. *music educator*

Oak Brook
Vesely-Rice, Alison C. *theater director, actress, educator*

Oak Park
Creed, Barbara Ellen *music educator*

Palos Hills
Porter, Joyce Klowden *theater educator, director, actress*

Pana
Waddington, Irma Joann *music educator*

Paris
Hiddle, Susan K. *music educator, musician*

Park Forest
Billig, Etel Jewel *theater director, actress*

Peoria
Strauss, Wendy Eisenberg *music educator*

Plainfield
Lalka, Monica Jean *music educator, consultant*

Poplar Grove
Zimber, Lisa Marie *music educator*

Rantoul
Holmes, Lois Rehder *composer, piano educator, voice educator*

Robinson
Gangloff, Amber D. *music educator*

Rock Island
Hand, Angela Rene *singer*

Rockford
Heuer, Beth Lee *music educator, composer*

Rushville
Burton, Sheila Belle *music educator*

Schaumburg
Janssen, Carron Joyce *music educator*

Skokie
Brenner, Bonnie Sue *singer, artist, educator*

Smithton
Hostetler, Elsie J. *musician, music educator*

South Holland
Saltzman, Bobbie *theater educator*

Tinley Park
Rubel, Lucia M. *music educator*

Urbana
Vaughn, Linda F. *musician, educator*

Varna
Rock, Beth Marie *voice educator, director*

Vernon Hills
Kim, Sachiko O. *music educator*
Manchester, Kathleen A. *music educator*

Villa Park
Ellingsen, Barbara Joyce *music educator*

Waukegan
Houle, Jeanne Larson *retired music educator*

West Chicago
Noonan, Josette Marie *music educator*

Westmont
Nyien, Patricia *music educator*
Vitson, Robyn Stanko Hoye *singer, pianist, educator*

Wheaton
Elwell, Ellen Banks *music educator, writer*

Wilmette
Merrier, Helen *actress, writer*
Shannon, Julie (Julie Geller) *musician, educator, composer, lyricist*

Wood River
Hudson, Kimberly Lynn *music educator*

INDIANA

Anderson
Chappell, Rebecca A. *music educator*

Bloomington
Labovitz, Sarah Jane *musician, educator*
McClelland, Danielle *performing company executive*
Svetlova, Marina *ballerina, retired choreographer*

Boonville
Clark, Linda Marie *music educator*

Carmel
Pote, Gretta Lynn *music educator*

Crawfordsville
Everett, Cheryl Ann *music educator, pianist*

Crown Point
Shaffer, Peggy S. *music educator*

Culver
Warren, Stacey A. *music educator*

Delphi
Trueblood, Susan Ann *music educator*

Evansville
Lawler, Zara Du Pont *musician, actor, dancer*

Ferdinand
Wildeman, Rose A. *musician, educator*

Goshen
Roberts, Mary Lois *music educator*
Woodlee, Cheryl Lynn *music educator*

Greencastle
Phang, May *music educator*

Hanover
Batchvarova, Madlen Todorova *music educator, conductor*
Nickels, Ruth Elizabeth *band director*

Hebron
Walker, Joyce L. *music educator*

Indianapolis
McIntyre, Lola Mazza *music educator*

Kokomo
Baker, Janel Faith *music educator*
Weeks, Randi Lyn *performing arts and language educator*

Marion
Henry, Michele Ferree *music educator, elementary school educator, language arts educator*

Martinsville
Palma, Kari Michelle *singer, actress, dancer, educator*

Michigan City
Wiegand, Elizabeth *musician, educator*

Monticello
Burns, Susan Kay *music educator*

Muncie
Bade, Michelle L. *music educator, director*
Zhong, Mei *music educator*

Newburgh
Verley, Barbara Ann *music educator*

Notre Dame
Dieckgrafe, Indi *performing arts educator, choreographer*

Plainfield
Clark, Debra Elizabeth *music educator*

Shelbyville
Jackson, Frances I. *music educator*

South Bend
Kuehner, Denise Ann *music educator, musician*

Valparaiso
Maugans, Stacy *music educator, musician*

Veedersburg
Dotson, Davina P. *music educator*

West Lafayette
Nave, Pamela J. *music educator*

Whiteland
Conrow, Ann E. *music educator*

IOWA

Akron
Green, Carla Rae *music educator*

Alden
Oliver, Kerryn Hinrichs *music educator, religious studies educator*

Ames
Zwick-Tapley, Sarah Lynn *theater educator, director*

Arlington
Turner, Jean Isabel *musician, educator*

Arthur
Votrobeck, Barbara Jan *music educator*

Aurelia
Winterhof, Suzanne *music educator*

Bettendorf
Ragan, Deborah Ann *music educator*
Schulz, Sally Ann *pastoral musician, conductor, educator*

Cedar Rapids
Rohr, Carol Ann *composer, music educator*

Coralville
Thomas, Carole Lesniak *retired music educator*

Creston
Fischer, Debra Lynne *music educator*

Des Moines
Bennett, Virginia Cook *music educator, consultant*
Erickson, Elaine Mae *composer, educator, poet*
Lange, Lynn Marie *music educator*
Langholz, Rebecca Sue *music educator*

Fort Dodge
Lehman, Shari Joan *music educator*

Fort Madison
Sanford, Jane Agnes *music educator*

Indianola
Mace, Jerilee Marie *performing arts association administrator*

Iowa City
Preucil, Doris Bogen *music educator*

Jesup
Hover, Melissa Kaye *music educator*

Johnston
Heidbreder, Jessica Lou *music educator*

Lone Tree
Haack, Allison Kaye *music educator*

Mason City
Sappenfield, Maedeane L. *piano and organ educator*

Orange City
Wielenga, Dixie Kay *music educator*

Pleasant Valley
Byrne, Margaret Ellen *voice educator*

Sheffield
Hemm, Cynthia Jean *music educator*

Sioux City
Dye, Lana L. *music educator*
Lewis, Arlene Jane Quiring *music educator*

Waverly
O'Konski, Marjorie Katherine *music educator*
Wade, Janice Elizabeth *musician, educator, conductor*

KANSAS

Andover
Reynolds, Charlene Jozina *music educator, composer*

Caldwell
Robinson, Alice Jean McDonnell *retired drama and speech educator*

Conway Springs
Lange, Karen R. *music educator*

Dodge City
Ross, Connie L. *music educator*

El Dorado
Mack, Valerie Lippoldt *music educator, performing arts educator, freelance/self-employed choreographer*

Gem
Ziegelmeier, Patricia Kay *music educator, executive secretary*

Hutchinson
Wendelburg, Norma Ruth *composer, educator, pianist*

Independence
Delacour, JoNell *music educator*

Iola
Marsh, Alma Fern *retired music educator, director, organist*

Leawood
Pfingsten, Lynette M. *music educator*

Manhattan
Mortenson, Kristin Oppenheim *musician*

Olathe
Colson, Judy C. *music educator*
McCabe, Melissa Christine *music educator, researcher*
Olsen, Barbara Ann *music educator*

Osawatomie
Baker, Kristi Ann *music educator, composer*

Overland Park
McKain, Maggie Marie *music educator*

Shawnee
McPherson, Linda *music educator*

Topeka
Smith, Linda S. *musician, educator*

Wichita
Myer, Cheryl Jo *music educator*

KENTUCKY

Bowling Green
Groom, Mitzi D *music educator, department chairman*

Campbellsville
McArthur, Lisa R. *music educator, musician*
Moore, Nevalyn *music educator*

Fort Mitchell
Webb, Diana Kay *music director*

Fort Thomas
Slater, Rebecca Anne *music educator, director*

Frankfort
Fletcher, Winona Lee *theater educator*
Marsh, Tiffany Nichelle *music educator*

Georgetown
Hall, Sara Y. *retired music educator*

Hartford
Stumpf, Christie Kell *retired music educator*

Irvington
Miller, Jacquie Haynes *musician, educator*

Lexington
Wagner, Gretchen S. *dance educator*

Louisville
Foster, Teresa E. *choral director, piano educator*
Sherman, Mildred Mozelle *music educator, vocalist, actress, opera director*

Owensboro
Mullikin, Sandra Marie *music educator*

Radcliff
Froedge, Susan Janet *music educator*

Richmond
Beranek, Carla Tipton *music educator*
Jackson, Cheryl Ann *music educator, director*
Machado-Echezuria, Marianella Perpetua *composer, writer, educator*
Smith, Carla Anne *music educator*

Russellville
Ragland, Tera Denise *music educator*

Virgie
Martin, Melanie *music educator*

Winchester
Jude, Cassandra Joy *music educator*

LOUISIANA

Baton Rouge
Barron, Sherry *music educator*
Buchmann, Molly O'Banion *choreographer, educator*
Lusted, Dona Sanders *music educator, consultant, organist*
Mathews, Sharon Walker *performing company executive, secondary school educator*
Orman, Evelyn Kay *music educator, consultant*
Yarbrough, Martha Cornelia *music educator*

Denham Springs
Peacock, Mindy H. *music educator*

Dequincy
Cooper, Melonee V. *music educator*

Destrehan
Blackwell, Karen Elaine *music educator*

Franklin
Rouly, Ellie Arceneaux *dancer, educator*

Lafayette
Daniel, Margaret Hagen *music and voice educator*
Stravinska, Sarah *dance educator*
Willett, Anna Hart *composer, painter*

Lake Charles
Batchelor, Karen Sue *music educator*

Metairie
deMoruelle, Charmaine *music educator*

Monroe
LeBlanc, Melinda Anne *voice educator*

New Orleans
St. Julien, Thais Mary *soprano, musician*

Slidell
Herron, Florine Pernell *retired music educator*
Larson, Sandra Pauline *music educator*

Sulphur
Fuller, Betty Stamps *music educator*

Westlake
Yarbrough, Frances Carole *music educator*

Zachary
Rogillio, Kathy June *musician, director, small business owner, educator*

MAINE

Augusta
Bowman, Esther Ruth-Kazian *music educator*
Jenkins, Pamela Lynn *music educator*

Lee
Knapp, Lisa Marie *music educator*

Lewiston
Fatone, Gina Andrea *music educator*

Naples
McVety, Linda Dow *music educator*

Saco
Wilkinson, Anne *musician, educator*

South Paris
Johnson, Sarah N. *music educator*

Sullivan
Davis-Wexler, Ginia *singer, director*

Topsham
Outhwaite, Lucille Conrad *ballerina, educator*

West Baldwin
Simmonds, Rae Nichols *musician, composer, educator*

Winslow
Desrosiers, Muriel C. *music educator, retired nursing consultant*

Woolwich
Clark, Joyce T. *piano teacher, church organist*

MARYLAND

Annapolis
Seep, Dorothy M. *music educator*

Baltimore
Bryn-Julson, Phyllis *soprano, music educator*
Hall, Marian M. *retired music educator*
Huggins, Amy Branum *music educator*
Jacobson, Katherine Louise *musician, music educator*
Scangarello, Danielle Lynn *music educator*

Bel Air
Sanders, Virginia Hinckley *music educator*

Bethesda
Saffiotti, Paola *retired music educator, performing arts association administrator*

Boonsboro
Algood, Laurie *performing arts educator*

Bowie
Hillsman, Joan Rucker *music educator*
Lewis, Patricia Ann *music educator*
Parr-Corretjer, Polly *singer, music educator*

Cambridge
Brohawn, Virginia Bridgeman *retired music educator*
Rihanna, (Robyn Rihanna Fenty) *singer, actress*

Columbia
Carter, Karen Zepp *music educator, elementary school educator*
Spicknall, Joan *music educator*

Cooksville
Wells, Christine Valerie *music educator*

Elkridge
Matthews, Lois Marr *musician, music educator*

Forestville
Brooks, Marsinah L. *performing arts educator*

Greenbelt
Wagner, Sally Sterrett *music educator*

Gwynn Oak
Hughes, Catherine L. (Cathy Hughes) *radio personality, broadcast executive*

Havre De Grace
Reid, Susan G. *music educator*

Highland
Varga, Deborah Trigg *music educator, entertainment company owner*

Hollywood
Dietz, Laurel Patricia *music educator*

Hyattsville
Dukes, Rebecca Weathers (Becky Dukes) *musician, singer, song writer*

Jefferson
Ward, Susan Annette *music educator*

La Plata
Herdman-Fisher, Carolyn A. *music educator*
Mazzeo, Betty Teresa *music educator*

Lanham Seabrook
Moore, Erica *band director*

North East
Roney, Sarah Gordon *dancer, educator*

Olney
Mardis, Linda Keiser *music educator, writer*
van den Berg, Elizabeth *actress, educator*

Owings
O'Neill, Patricia Tydings *performing arts educator, language educator*

Pasadena
Bell, Patricia Wright *music educator*

Potomac
Murow, Christine *music educator*

Reisterstown
Goethe, Elizabeth Hogue *music educator*

Rockville
Cain, Karen Mirinda *musician, educator*
Kurkul, Wen Wang *musician, educator, administrator*
O'Donnell, Duck Hee *cellist, music teacher*

Silver Spring
Brandt, Elsa Lund Erickson *music educator*

Thurmont
Stitely, Karen Richardson *performing arts educator*

Towson
Ahearn, Elizabeth Lowe *performing arts educator*
Pantzer, Mairee D. *music educator, director*

Waldorf
Bouchard, Lynne Katherine *music educator*

Westminster
Stoetzer, Kristen Gottleib *music educator*

MASSACHUSETTS

Abington
Harrington, Joyce D. *music educator*

Allston
FitzGibbon, Katherine Lenore *conductor, music educator*
Spencer, Lara *television personality, journalist*

Amherst
Donohue, Therese Brady *artistic director, choreographer, costume and set designer*
Dunbar, Sue *music educator*
Whaples, Miriam Karpilow *music educator*

Auburn
Giannini, Antoinette Frances *music educator, researcher*

Boston
Anderson, Jewelle Lucille *musician, educator*
Asai, Susan Miyo *music educator, consultant*
Bacon, A. Smoki *television host*
Bourque, Louise *film director, film instructor*
Craig, Patricia *voice educator, opera singer*
Del Sesto, Janice Mancini *opera company executive*
Jochum, Veronica *pianist*
LaForgia, Jeanne Ellen *performing arts educator*
Liotta, Jeanne *film director, film instructor*
Tokunaga, Yasuko *performing company executive*
Vilker-Kuchment, Valeria *violinist*
Young, Laura *dance educator, choreographer*

Braintree
Hallenbeck, Rachel Kirsten *music educator, director*

Brookline
Rizzi, Marguerite Claire *music educator*
Sho, Jennifer Yu-Fei *musician, educator*

Cambridge
de Varon, Lorna Cooke *choral conductor*
Kraus, Rozann B. *performing company executive*
Parker, Lisa Frederick *music educator, Dalcroze specialist*
Shelemay, Kay Kaufman *music educator*
Wood, Pamela Sharon *music educator, soprano*

Chestnut Hill
Monteila, Sharon Christine *dancer, educator, choreographer*

Dedham
Kirby, Heather Suzanne *music educator*

Fall River
Lynds, Lucinda *music educator*

Falmouth
Studley, LaVada A. *music educator*

Foxboro
Kennedy, Susan Marie *music educator*

Framingham
Bogard, Carole Christine *soprano*
Hagarty, Wendy L. *music educator*

Great Barrington
Curtin, Phyllis *music educator, dean, vocalist*

Hingham
Noel, Barbara Hughes McMurtry *retired music educator*

Hopkinton
Moran, Wendy Jacqueline *music educator, musician*

Lowell
Greher, Gena R. *music production company executive*

Marblehead
Kennedy, Elizabeth Mae *musician*

Mendon
Thurber, Kirsten Nora *music educator*

Orleans
Patterson, Elizabeth C. *choir director*

Pittsfield
Boyd, Julianne Mamana *theater director, educator*
Guzzo, Jessica Ann *music educator*

Provincetown
Sturner, Lynda *performing company executive*

South Hamilton
Ray, Diane Marie Ayers *music educator*

Stockbridge
MacDonald, Sharon Ethel *dancer, educator, choreographer, administrator*

Vineyard Haven
Breuer, Joann Green *theater director*

Weston
Tenney, Sarah G. *music educator*

Worcester
Hatfield, Renee S.J. *music educator*

Worthington
Schrade, Rolande Maxwell Young *composer, pianist, educator*

MICHIGAN

Ann Arbor
Porter, Amy *music educator*

Battle Creek
Matthews, Wyhomme S. *retired music educator, academic administrator*

Bloomfield
Tolmich, Andrea J. *music educator, department chairman*

Bloomfield Hills
Haidostian, Alice Berberian *concert pianist, volunteer, not-for-profit fundraiser*

Brighton
Jones, Marilyn Schlicher *conductor, retired music educator*

Burton
Johnson-Brown, Linda Lee *music educator*

Commerce Township
Thibideau, Carolyn C. *musician, educator*

Detroit
Duensing, Dorothy Jean *music educator, vocalist*
Engelhardt, Regina *cosmetologist, artist, small business owner*
Harlan, Carmen *television journalist*
Pacha, Melinda Jane *performing arts educator*
Parsons, Anne *performing company executive*
Valentine, Cheryl Ann Whitney *music educator*

East Lansing
Draper, Penny Kaye Pekrul *music educator*
Nickelson, Pamela Sue *music educator*
Whiting Dobson, Lisa Lorraine *video production educator, producer, director*

Escanaba
Robinson, Laura Ann *music educator*

Farmington
Purdy, Jan Rae *music educator*

Fenton
Hayes, Pamela M. *music educator*

Gladwin
Chartier, Mary Eileen *music educator*

Grand Rapids
Brink, Emily Ruth *music educator*
Horn, Joyce Elaine *music educator*

Houghton
Bruch, Debra Lynn *theater educator*

Kalamazoo
Chesak, Kristen *performing company executive*

Kentwood
Thompson, Anne *music educator*

Lake Orion
Berger, Laura Ann *dance studio owner*

Livonia
Wilder, JaNell Lynn *music educator*

Manistee
Swan-Eagan, Cynthia J. *music educator*

Marshall
Petrich, Kathryn *music educator*

Merrill
Ellenwood, Heather Sky *music educator*

Muskegon
Swartz, Wilma Jeeanne *music educator*

Nashville
Pash, Teresa A. *piano teacher, performer*

New Baltimore
Sheldrick, Barbara England *music educator, consultant*

Portage
Selden, Margery Juliet Stomne *music educator*

Saginaw
Coughlin, Jeannine Marie *music educator*
Haynes, Iris Fitzgerald *music educator*

Saline
Gannett, Diana Ruth *musician, educator*

Waterford
Pronovost, Amy Lynne *dancer, educator*

Wayland
Stephenson-Bennett, Michelle Annette *music educator*

Whitmore Lake
Wassilak, Janet Marian *choral director*

MINNESOTA

Coon Rapids
Wilson, Sylvia Alyce *musician, educator*

East Grand Forks
Engel, Carol Louise *music educator*

Eden Prairie
De Bono, Luella Elizabeth *music educator*

Edina
Kirchner, Mary Katherine *musician, educator*

Erskine
Wahlin, Shelly R. *voice educator*

Fridley
Larson, Marilyn J. *retired music educator*

Golden Valley
Spake, Mary Barbara *music educator*

Grand Meadow
Moe, Janet Kirsten *music educator*

Lakeville
Schaefer, Elzbieta A. *music educator*

Maple Grove
Nielsen, Diane Kay *music educator*
Shmidov, Anna *music educator*

Marshall
Tabaka, Sheila Marie *theater educator*

Medford
Cashman, Beverly J. *music educator*

Minneapolis
Fleezanis, Jorja Kay *musician, educator*
Nortwen, Patricia Harman *music educator*
Porter, Jennifer Madeleine *film producer, film director*

Moorhead
Brekke, Kathrine Lydia *music educator*

New Brighton
Carlson, Kaye Lilien *retired music educator*

Paynesville
Bungum, Cheryl Nancy *music educator, director*

Pipestone
Ballou-Portz, Cynthia Celene *music educator*

Prinsburg
Mulder, Michelle Kay *music educator*

Rochester
Dahlen, Tracy *music educator*
Workman, Julia L. *music educator*

Saint Cloud
Patton, Kristen Terese *music educator*

Saint Paul
Frazee, Jane *music educator*

Upsala
Cheney, Denise Kay *music educator*

Virginia
Wilcox, Sheila Maureen *music educator*

Wabasha
Brelsford, Mary J. *music educator*

Waterville
Bennett, Jodi Lynn *music educator*

Winona
Heukeshoven, Janet Kay *music educator*
Wenzel, Ann Marie *music educator*

MISSISSIPPI

Bay Saint Louis
Foster, Willetta Jean *music educator*

Brandon
Sparks, Pamela Shepherd *music educator*

Columbus
Barham, K. Dawn *music educator, lyricist*
Kantack, Catherine Margaret *retired music educator, retired international broker*

Gautier
Parent, Tanya H. *dance educator, massage therapist*

Glen
Price, Tina Denise *music educator*

Goodman
King, Kathy Cooper *music educator*

Grenada
Dugan, Cindy *music educator, organist*

Hattiesburg
D'Arpa, Josephine *music educator*
Davis, Doris Johnson *retired music educator*
Nicholson, Amber Shay *music educator*

Jackson
Holly, Ellistine Perkins *music educator*
Lee, Lillian Aldridge *music educator*

Louisville
Cunningham, Julie Kaye *music educator*

Madison
Crisler, Donna *music educator*

Ocean Springs
Christman, Leslie Erin *music educator*

Raymond
Bee, Anna Cowden *dance educator*

Southaven
Butler, Elizabeth Rosanne *music educator, director*

University
Wang, Diane *music educator*

MISSOURI

Ballwin
Humiston, Marilyn Koslov *music educator*
Rothermich, Gayla *music educator, director*

Blue Springs
Gard, Jean *music educator*
Muir, Linda Ann *music educator, director*
Washburn, Gladys Haase *retired church musician, educator, director*
Wasko, Deborah Ann *music educator*

Bowling Green
Bruce, Judith Esther *retired music educator, elementary school educator*
Eckhoff, Sarah Lynn *music educator*

Butler
Turner, Vicky Jo *music educator*

Cameron
Goodwin Clark, Ann Elizabeth *music educator*

Campbell
Knapp, AnnaMaria Lois *music educator*

Chesterfield
Greene, Judith Orinda *theater educator, theater director*

Columbia
Burgoyne, Suzanne *theater educator, writer*
Packard, Kerri Shannon *theater educator*
Vale, Patrice J. *musician, consultant*

Dixon
Pyatt, Lori *music educator*

Doniphan
Pigg, Brenda J. *music educator*

Fulton
McClain, Cindy Dunstan *music educator*

Independence
Kilpatrick, Laura Shelby *music educator*

Kansas City
Davis, Mary Bronaugh *music educator*
Kuenn, Marjorie Asp *music educator*
Lindsay, Twyla Lynn *music educator*
Londré, Felicia Mae Hardison *theater educator*
Meilink, Jacqueline Rae *music educator*
Phalp-Rathbun, Stephanie Dawn *music educator*
Ruperd, Theresa *music educator*
Setser, Patricia A. *music educator*

Kirksville
Newland, Cheyrl Marie *music educator*

Lebanon
Elsea, Christine E. *music educator*

Lockwood
Wehrman, Natalie Ann *retired music educator*

Marshall
Howard, Tiffany *theater educator*

Maryville
Dunnell, Rebecca *music educator*
Schultz, Patricia Bowers *vocal music educator, conductor*

Moberly
Werner, Karen Elaine *music educator*

Peculiar
Pierson, Linda Kay *music educator*

Platte City
Shier, Susan Lynne *music educator*

Republic
Zinecker, Tricia Jolene *music educator*

Richmond
Stoenner, Jessamine *music educator*

Saint Charles
Purcell, Cheryl Linn *music educator*

Saint James
Stevens, Helen Jean *music educator*

Saint Joseph
Beck, Christina Sue *music educator*

Saint Louis
Bell, Angela *music educator*
Carson, Rebecca Ann *performing arts association administrator*
Haley, Johnetta Randolph *music educator*
Miller, Ellen Katherine *music educator*
Redington, Mary *music educator*
Sutherland, Mary (Marcus) *composer, musician*
Swearingen, Laura Colleen *music educator, director*
Waddington, Bette Hope (Elizabeth Crowder) *violinist, educator*

Saint Peters
Poettker, Mary Therese *music educator*
Ranner, Shanna *music educator*

Springfield
Blair, Starla Reneé *music educator*
Blake, Loretta L. *music educator*
Traphagan, Helen Marie *voice educator*

Trenton
Gentry, Shirley *music educator, writer*

Warsaw
Million, Charlene R. *music educator, church administrator*

MONTANA

Anaconda
Ricci, Margaret Thea *music and piano educator, church organist*

Bozeman
Biegel, Debra Jeanne *music educator*

Butte
Clark, Gloria A. *music educator*
Kohler, Nora Helen *music educator*

Columbia Falls
Hanson, Marlene Kay *music educator*

Eureka
Kessler-Hodgson, Lee Gwendolyn *actress, performing company executive*

NEBRASKA

Bellevue
Hatfield, Stacie H. *professional pianist*

Columbus
Micek, Isabelle *music educator*

Fullerton
Blauhorn, Cathy A. *music educator*

Lincoln
Fawcett-Yeske, Maxine Ann *music educator*
Young, Jeannette Rose *music educator*

Mc Cook
Watts, Susan Helene *theater educator*

Omaha
Bouma, Lyn Ann Nichols *music educator*
Brown, Jennifer Leigh *music educator, musician*
Collins, Susan Baer *theater director, actor, educator*
Nabity, Cynthia Dawn *music educator*
Roland, Sally *music educator*
Seitz, Carole Jane *composer, educator*

NEVADA

Carson City
Mielke, Nancy E. *music educator*

Dayton
Bumgardner, Julie *music educator*

Henderson
Drusedum, Kimberly Barclay *music educator*
Tefani, Nancy Ann *music educator*

Las Vegas
Andersen, Nancy *music educator, director*
Bernstein, Maureen Ann *theater educator, director*
Borovicka, Marsha Lorraine *music educator*
Frances, Marie Cecilia *theater producer, television producer*
Healy, Mary (Mrs. Peter Lind Hayes) *singer, actress*
Stephen, Anne Marie DiIorio *music educator*
Stivers, Carol Urban *retired music educator, consultant*
Tyler, Janet Irene *music educator*
Vlaming, Carrie *theater educator*

North Las Vegas
Talley, Brenda S. *performing arts center director, theatrical light designer*

Reno
Hudson, Karen Ann Sampson *music educator*

Sandy Valley
Viscuglia, Jenny Lou *music educator*

NEW HAMPSHIRE

Alstead
Boisvert-Buschbaum, M. Noella *music educator*

Berlin
Lavertu, Monique Therese *music educator*

Franklin
Trader, Patricia Annette *music educator*

Gilford
John, Lyvie Paige *music educator*

Manchester
Marchesseault, Anita *music educator*

Meriden
Ahlquist, Janet Sue *musician, music educator*

Merrimack
Cunningham, Patricia Ann Cahoy *band director, musician*

Sandown
Pajak, Louise Bears *music educator, musician*

NEW JERSEY

Allenhurst
Tognoli, Era M. *performing company executive, artistic director*

Bayville
Worth, Katherine Marie *retired vocalist*

Belle Mead
Thayer, Christina Sia *music educator*

Bloomfield
Kovacs, Christina Marie *music educator*
Mesuk, Elaine M. *music educator*

Burlington
Mustokoff, Henrietta M. *music educator*

Cedarville
Marsella, Julia *music educator*

Cherry Hill
Mark, Susan A. *music educator*

Cliffside Park
Perhacs, Marylouise Helen *musician, educator*

Cranford
Boughner, Martha Reed *music educator*

Delanco
Lane, Carrie Belle (Hairston) *retired music educator*

Denville
Veech, Lynda Anne *musician, educator*

Deptford
Gigliotti, Amy Veronica *music educator*

East Brunswick
Savio, Frances Margaret Cammarotta *music educator*
Schmidt, Michelle Moore *music educator*
Weiss, Judith Ann *music educator*

Edgewater
Fletcher, Susann (Susann Renee Smith) *actress, playwright*

Edison
Morse, Judith *music educator, conductor*

Elizabeth
de la Viña-Sierra, Diana Maria *music educator*

Far Hills
Burns, Amy Margaret *music educator*

Florham Park
Paulson, Sondra Lee *music educator*

Freehold
Cheng, Grace Zheng-Ying *music educator*
Meckes, Kimberly Jo *music educator*

Hackensack
MacVicar, Lisa *music educator*

Hackettstown
Coulson-Grigsby, Carolyn *theater educator*

Hamilton
Coccia, JoAnn *music educator, musician*

Hammonton
Langston, Jessi Lea *music educator*

Hightstown
Petri, Christine Ann *music educator*

Hillside
Wilson, Bertina Iolia *retired music educator*

Jersey City
Downes, Marie Jean *music educator*
Golden, Amy Patrice *actress, performing company executive*
LeSiege, Annette *music educator, composer*
Queen Latifah, (Dana Elaine Owens) *actress, musician*
Warren, Maredia Delois *music educator*

Lebanon
Robertson, Tina Barbara *dancer, educator*

Leonia
Deutsch, Nina *pianist, vocalist*

Lincroft
Benham, Helen *music educator*

Lodi
Arella, Ann Marietta *music educator, vocalist*

Long Valley
Falk, Barbara Higinbotham *music educator*

Lumberton
Wojtko, Donnamarie *music educator, director*

Madison
Monte, Bonnie J. *performing arts company executive, director, educator*

Manalapan
Lin, Chiu-Tze *conductor, musician*

Manville
Spatz, Meagen Sorensen *music educator, director*

Margate City
Rose, Jodi *artistic director, film producer*

Marlton
Tuma, Michele *music educator*

Mays Landing
Gross, Michelle Bayard *dancer, educator*

Montclair
Kriftner, Gail Lyn *choreographer, educator*
Peterson, Jane Temple *theater educator*

Mount Laurel
Jones, Marian C. *music educator*

New Brunswick
Saltz, Amy *theater educator, director*

Newton
Naylis, Stephanie Anne *music educator*

Northfield
McNeal, Jane Erskine *music educator, musician*

Nutley
Struble, Pamela Lynn *music educator*

Paramus
Marcel-Calderon, Linda *music educator*

Perth Amboy
Richardson-Melech, Joyce Suzanne *music educator, singer*

Phillipsburg
Brown, Jerri L. *performing arts educator, choreographer*

Point Pleasant Beach
McAllen, Regina K. *voice educator*

Pomona
Vaughn, Beverly Jean *music educator, mezzo soprano*

Pottersville
Guerra, Jamee Elizabeth Rund *music educator*

Princeton
Cardaneo, Donna Marie *music educator, director*
Contillo, Debbie B. *performing arts educator*
Graham, Nancy Love *music educator*
Longenecker, LuAnn F. *music educator, department chairman*
Orphanides, Nora Charlotte *ballet educator*
Vizzini, Carol Redfield *symphony musician, educator*

Rockaway
Steier, Audrey Keller *music educator*

Rumson
Topham, Sally Jane *performing arts educator*

Saddle Brook
Ballone, Eileen Marie *music educator, musician, organist*

Seabrook
Nakai, Tanya B. *music educator*

Somers Point
Hagerthey, Gwendolyn Irene *retired music educator*

Southampton
Saltus, Phyllis Borzelliere *music educator*

Sparta
Cummings, Melva Andrews *music educator*
Jacobs-Quam, Vivien Marie *retired music educator*

Spotswood
Shaughnessy, Lauren Margaret *music educator*

Summit
Falletta, Jo Ann *conductor*

Teaneck
Carter, Regina *jazz violinist*
Graham, Janet Lorraine *music educator*

Tenafly
Tall, Susan Porter *music educator*

Toms River
Schwartz, Anna R. *musician, educator*

Trenton
Demitry, Elpis Hope *music educator*

Voorhees
Clarke, Sharon Elizabeth Borges *music educator*
Posey, Gail S *music educator*

Wayne
Demsey, Karen Boor *music educator*

Westampton
Welte, Linda Anne *music educator*

NEW MEXICO

Albuquerque
Ellen, Jane *composer, music educator, researcher*
Guerrant, Mary Thorington *music educator*
Mock, Joan Bodet *music educator*
Streng, Sarita B. *dancer, educator*

Hobbs
Starling, Virginia R. *music educator, consultant*

Las Vegas
Wagner, Deborah Rae *musician, educator*

Roswell
Weikel, Sandra G. *music educator*

Santa Fe
Chavez, Maria Lucinda *band director, educator*
Harms, Cora Beenhouwer *music educator*

Tesuque
MacGraw, Ali *actress*

NEW YORK

Albany
Haig Nicol, Teresa Iminta *choreographer, educator*
Rooney, Michele Lynn *music educator*

Almond
Olix-Anderson, Susan *music educator*

Annandale On Hudson
Miyagawa, Chiori *theater educator, playwright*
Tower, Joan Peabody *composer, educator*

Ardsley
Yablonskaya, Oxana *concert pianist*

Armonk
Scotto, Renata *soprano*

Astoria
Gibson, Deanna *actor*
Sirignano, Monica Ann *performing company executive, playwright*

Auburn
Tennant, Bonnie W. *retired music educator*

Avon
Cole, Mary F. *music educator*

Bellmore
Baer, Karen Faust *music educator, musician*

Bergen
Wolfe, Karen Ann *music educator*

Binghamton
Lee-Whiting, Theresa A. *music educator, conductor*
Stewart, Ghislaine Lynne *music educator, conductor*
Valencia, Melanie Laine *music educator, performer*
Wildoner, Nancy Schamu *music educator, fine arts department chairman*

Blauvelt
Fox, Beth A. *music educator*

Brockport
McGhee, Diane Baumann *dance instructor, consultant*

Bronx
De Luca, Eva *vocalist, writer, composer, entrepreneur, inventor*
Isaacman, Carrie Edel *actress, educator*
Lagares, Portia Octavia *music educator*
Mittler, Diana (Diana Mittler-Battipaglia) *music educator, pianist*
Sherman, Judith Dorothy *theater producer, engineer, recording industry executive*

Brooklyn
Cahill, Catherine M. *orchestra executive*
Hopkins, Karen Brooks *performing arts executive*
Sahlene, *singer*
Vidal, Maureen Eris *theater educator, actress*

Buffalo
DiFranco, Ani *music executive, musician*
Kordinak, Irma L. *piano educator, musician*
Lombardo Appleby, Linda Rose *music educator*
Wagner, Barbara Lee *musician*
Zawadzki-Janusz, Stacy Lynn *music educator, performing arts educator*

Burnt Hills
Russell, Karen Sue *musician, educator*

Cicero
Pink, (Alecia B. Moore) *singer*

Clarence
Benz, Nancy Ann *music educator*

Collins
Jackson, Jane *filmmaker, educator*

Coram
Celella, Karen Ann *music educator, writer*

Crugers
Norman, Jessye *soprano*

De Ruyter
Jeschke, Carol T. *arts/theater consultant, real estate investor*

Deer Park
Grover, Penelope H. *singer, music educator*

Depew
Yelich, Janine E. *music educator*

Dunkirk
Flaherty, Cynthia Mead *music educator*

Farmingdale
Lindsley, Michelle A. *theater educator, music educator*
Segale, Althea Frances *music educator*

Floral Park
Daloia, Rachel Rosemary *music educator*

Flushing
Evens, Lucie Ann *music educator*

Forest Hills
Mathieu Byers, Deborah Anne *performing company executive*

Forestville
Gier, Amy Louise *music educator*

Fredonia
Holcomb, Paula Kae *conductor, educator*
Royal, Susan *classical musician, educator*

Garden City
Wetherill-Smith, Linda Marie *musician, educator, performing arts association administrator*

Geneva
Lucas, Karen *music educator*

Grand Island
Remson, Debra S. *music educator*

Greenfield Center
Nair, Laura *music educator*

Greenlawn
Lelyveld, Gail Annick *actress*
Starost, Diane Joan *music educator*

Greenvale
Watt, Stephanie Denise *musician, educator, department chairman*

Guilderland Center
Teeter, Rae Jean *music educator*

Hamburg
Haag, Jennifer Lynn *music educator*

Hempstead
Graffeo, Mary Thérèse *music educator, performer*
Heuermann-Nowik, Patricia Calhoun *theater director*

Hicksville
Kronowitz, Pamela Renee *music educator*

Highland
Ratick, Randie H. *music educator, elementary school educator*

Holland
Hager, Maria Lynne *music educator*

Horseheads
Matejka, Tina Sochia *music educator*

Huntington Station
Haas, Terri Leigh *music educator*

Hyde Park
Beckmann, Kathleen Ann *music educator*

Islip
Kacharaba, Nickolette Athanasia *vocalist*

Ithaca
Arquit, Nora Harris *retired music educator, writer*
Henderson, Cynthia Anne *theater educator, actress*

Jackson Heights
Stevenson, Amanda (Sandy Stevens) *librettist, composer, songwriter*

Johnstown
Winnie, Amy E. *music educator*

Katonah
Brownlee, Delphine *actress, musician*

Kenmore
Grant, Elaine Marion *music educator, voice educator*

Kings Park
LaFantano, Elizabeth *music educator*

Kingston
Contrady, Erin Shaw *music educator*

Lake Katrine
Cariello, Kristine *music educator*

Lancaster
Meides, Holly Sue *music educator*

Latham
LeRoy, Beth Seperack *jazz musician, music educator*

Long Island City
Giaimo, Kathryn Ann *performing arts company executive*

Mahopac
Castronovo, Bernadine Marro *music educator*

Maine
Truex, Brenda *music educator*

Manlius
Koch, Catherine Ann *music educator, musician*

Margaretville
Brockway-Henson, Amie *producing artistic director*

Massapequa
Turk, Elizabeth Ann *music educator*

Melville
Sobol, Elise Schwarcz *music educator*

Millbrook
Flexner, Josephine Moncure *musician, educator*

Mooers
Kokes, Kathleen A. *music educator, voice educator*

Narrowsburg
Krause, Gloria Rose *music educator*

New Rochelle
Swire, Edith Wypler *music educator, violist, violinist*

New York
Adams, Jane *actress*
Addison, Anne Simone Pomex *television director, consultant, commentator*
Aguilera, Christina *singer*
Alexander, Jane (Jane Quigley) *actress, theater educator, writer*
Allen, Betty (Mrs. Ritten Edward Lee III) *mezzo-soprano*
Alt, Carol A. *actress, model, entrepreneur, writer*
Amos, Tori *musician, singer*
Ansanelli, Alexandra *ballerina*
Armitage, Karole *dancer*
Asakawa, Takako *dancer, educator, choreographer, director*
Ashanti, (Ashanti Shequoiya Douglas) *vocalist*
Ashley, Elizabeth *actress*
Bacall, Lauren (Betty Joan Perske) *actress*
Barbour, Catherine Jean *actress, set designer, director, mime*
Barrett, Susan Iris *actor, educator*
Beers, Sydney (Sydney Davolos) *theater producer*
Behar, Joy *television personality*
Berman, Rachel *dancer*
Björk, (Björk Guðmundsdóttir) *singer, composer*
Bledel, Alexis (Kimberly Alexis Bledel) *actress*
Bowden, Sally Ann *choreographer, educator, dancer*
Bracco, Lorraine *actress*
Bricard, Yolanda Borras *music educator, music program administrator*
Brinkley, Christie *model, spokesperson, designer*
Brothers, Joyce Diane *television personality, psychologist*
Brown, Trisha *dancer*
Brown, Tyese Andrea *music educator*
Brzezinski, Mika *TV news anchor*
Bundchen, Giselle *model*
Burke, Delta *actress*
Bush, Lauren *model*
Butler, Kerry *actress*
Byer, Diana *performing company executive*
Caldwell, L. Scott *actress*
Cantrell, Lana *actress, lawyer, singer*
Cash, Rosanne *singer, songwriter*
Cazeaux, Isabelle Anne Marie *retired music educator*
Chang, Marian S. *filmmaker, composer*
Channing, Stockard (Susan Antonia Williams Stockard) *actress*
Chao, Yu Chen *cellist, educator*
Chenoweth, Kristin *actress*
Clark, Victoria *actress*
Clarkson, Kelly Brianne *singer*
Collins, Judy Marjorie *singer, songwriter*
Cox, Mary Anthony *musician, educator*
Curtin, Jane Therese *actress, writer*
Dakin, Christine Whitney *dancer, educator*
Danitz, Marilynn Patricia *choreographer, video specialist*
D'Antuono, Eleanor *ballet director, educator, coach*
Davarova, Elmira *musician*
Deen, Paula H. *television personality, restaurant owner, chef*
DeFord, Ruth I. *music educator*
DeWoody, Beth Rudin *film producer*
Dodge, Marcia Milgrom *director, choreographer*
Dratch, Rachel *comedienne, actress*
Du Boff, Jill Bonnie Candise *sound effects artist*
Duff, Hilary Ann *actress, singer*
Dukakis, Olympia *actress*
Duquesnay, Ann *actress, singer*
Earle, Eugenia *music educator*
Ebersole, Christine *actress*
Elliott, Missy (Melissa Arnette Elliot) *musician*
Emme, (Emme Aronson) *model, apparel designer*
Eterovich Maguire, Karen Ann *actress, writer*
Evans, B. Paige *artistic director*
Evans, Faith *singer*
Fantasia, (Fantasia Monique Barrino) *singer*
Farley, Carole *soprano*
Felious, Odetta *vocalist*
Fields, Felicia P. *actress*
Filarski Hasselbeck, Elizabeth *television host/personality*
Fisher, Joely *actress*
Flack, Roberta *singer*
Fleming, Renée L. *opera singer*
Fowler, Beth *actress*
Friedman, Debbie *singer, songwriter, religious studies educator*
Fuller, Beverley Bozeman *dancer, singer, actress, choreographer, director*
Garrett, Margo *pianist, music educator*
Glasberg, Lisa *radio personality*
Gordon, Robbie *television producer*
Goto, Midori *classical violinist*
Graff, Randy *actress*
Griffiths, Jem *singer*
Grillo, Janet *film producer*
Hamilton Jackson, Marilyn J. *dancer, educator, choreographer*
Hargitay, Mariska Magdolina *actress*
Harmon, Jane *theater producer*
Harris, Julie (Julie Ann Harris) *actress*
Harris, Rosemary Ann *actress*
Hastings, Deborah *bass guitarist*
Headley, Heather A. *actress*
Herrera, Paloma *dancer*
Ho, Betty Juenyü Yülin *retired music educator, physiologist, educator*
Holmes, Anna-Marie *ballerina*
Hynde, Chrissie *musician*
Ibi, Keiko *film director*
Jackson, Anne (Anne Jackson Wallach) *actress*
Jaffe, Susan *ballerina*
Jamison, Judith *dancer*
Jefferson, Denise *dance school director*
Jett, Joan (Joan Larkin) *musician*
Johnson, Christine Toy *actress, writer*
Jones, Sarah *actress, playwright, poet*
Jung, Doris *soprano*
Kanakaredes, Melina *actress*
Kassel, Virginia Weltmer *television producer, scriptwriter*
Keating, Isabel *actress*
Kent, Julie *dancer, actress, model*
Kent, Linda Gail *dancer*
Keys, Alicia (Alicia Augello Cook) *vocalist, musician, songwriter*
Kim, Yunjim (Yun-jin Kim) *actress*
Kinberg, Judy *television producer, television director*
Kiser, Molly *musician*
Kitahata-Sporn, Amy *movement educator*
Kozak, Harley Jane *actress, writer*
Krizer, Jodi *performing arts executive*
Kurman, Juta *music educator*
LaBelle, Patti (Patricia Louise Holte) *singer, entertainer*
Lang, Pearl *dancer, choreographer*
Lanpher, Katherine *radio personality, columnist*
Lansner, Gabrielle *choreographer, dancer, performing company executive, actress*
LaRose, Melba Lee *performing company executive, actress, playwright, theater director*
Lee, Amy *singer*
Lenox, Adriane *actress*
Lewis, Marcia *actress*
Lil' Kim, (Kimberly Denise Jones) *rap artist, actress*
Lilly, Evangeline *actress*
Loeb, Lisa *singer, lyricist*
Lopez, Priscilla *actress*
Lucci, Susan *actress*
LuPone, Patti *actress*
Lyman, Peggy *artistic director, dancer, choreographer, educator*
Lynn, Judith *opera singer, artist, voice educator*
Maddow, Rachel *radio personality, political activist*
Mamlok, Ursula *composer, educator*
Mann, Aimee *singer, songwriter*
Marshall, Kathleen *choreographer, theater director*
Martin, Leslie *performing arts association administrator*
Maxwell, Carla Lena *dancer, choreographer, educator*
Mays, Linda *performing arts association administrator*
Mazzo, Kay *ballet dancer, educator*
McDonald, Audra Ann *actress, vocalist*
McGrady, Phyllis *television producer*
McKerrow, Amanda *ballet dancer*
Meadow, Lynne (Carolyn Meadow) *theater producer*
Merchant, Natalie Anne *musician, singer*
Miller, Beth McCarthy *television director*
Miller-Sydney, Audrey Yvonne *music educator*
Monk, Debra *actress*
Monk, Meredith Jane *artistic director, composer, choreographer, filmmaker*
Moore, Rachel Suzanne *performing company executive, dancer*
Moyers, Judith Davidson *television producer*
Muller, Jennifer *choreographer, dancer*
Murney, Julia *actress*
Murphy, Carolyn *model*
Murphy, Donna *actress*
Murphy, Rosemary *actress*
Nair, Mira *film director, film producer*
Nichols, Kyra *ballerina*
Nugent, Nelle *theater, film and television producer*
Parker, Alice *composer*
Parsons, Estelle *actress, director, theater producer*
Payton-Wright, Pamela *actress*
Peters, Bernadette (Bernadette Lazzara) *actress*
Peters, Roberta *soprano*
Phair, Liz *vocalist*
Poehler, Amy *comedienne, actress*
Posin, Kathryn Olive *choreographer*
Price, Leontyne (Mary Violet Leontyne Price) *retired concert and opera singer, soprano*
Pulos, Virginia Kate *actress, consultant*
Queler, Eve *conductor*
Quivers, Robin *radio personality*
Ramirez, Sara *actress*

Ramirez, Tina *artistic director*
Redgrave, Lynn *actress*
Reeves, Dianne *singer*
Reinking, Ann H. *dancer, actress*
Reuben, Gloria *actress, singer*
Rhodes, Randi *radio personality*
Rice, Barbara Lynn *stage manager*
Rigg, Dame Diana *actress*
Rivera, Chita (Conchita del Rivero) *actress, singer, dancer*
Rizer, Maggie *model*
Robison, Paula Judith *flutist*
Ronstadt, Linda Marie *singer*
Ross, Diana (Diana Ernestine Earle Ross) *singer, actress, entertainer, fashion designer*
Roth, Daryl *theater producer*
Rothschild, Amalie Randolph *filmmaker, film producer, film director, photographer*
Rubin-Vega, Daphne *actress*
Ruckert, Ann Johns *musician, singer*
Salerno-Sonnenberg, Nadja *violinist*
Salonga, Lea *actress, singer*
Santos, Nadine *music director*
Sarandon, Susan Abigail *actress*
Saunders, Arlene *opera singer*
Schorer, Suki *ballet teacher*
Scott, Karen Michele *television producer*
Seldes, Marian *actress*
Seymour, Stephanie *model*
Shelley, Carole *actress*
Sills, Beverly (Mrs. Peter B. Greenough) *performing company executive, singer*
Silver, Joan Micklin *film director, screenwriter*
Silvers, Sally *choreographer, performing company executive*
Sitomer, Sheila Marie *television producer, television director*
Spears, Britney *singer*
Spencer, Ruth Albert *music educator*
Stafford, Abi *ballerina*
Stevens, Risë *performing arts association administrator*
Stewart, Ellen D. *theater producer*
Stroman, Susan *choreographer, theater director*
Taylor, Janie *ballerina*
Taylor, Regina *actress*
Tepper Madover, Arielle *theater producer*
Tesori, Jeanine *composer*
Thompson, Jewel Taylor *music educator*
Tinsley, Jennifer *ballerina*
Travis, Sarah *orchestrator*
Uggams, Leslie *entertainer*
Underwood, Carrie Marie *singer*
Valletta, Amber *actress, model*
Vieira, Meredith *television personality*
Waxman, Anita *theater producer*
Wedgeworth, Ann *actress*
Weiler, Berenice *theater producer, consultant*
Weissler, Fran *theatrical producer*
White, Lillias *actress*
Whoriskey, Katherine Jane *theater director, educator*
Wile, Joan *composer, lyricist, singer*
Williams, Vanessa (Vanessa Lynn Williams) *recording artist, actress*
Williams, Wendy *radio personality, writer*
Woodward, Joanne Gignilliat *actress*
Yajima, Hiroko *violinist, music educator*
Zhu, Ai-Lan *opera singer*
Zirinsky, Susan *television producer*
Zosike, Joanie Fritz *theater director, actress*
Zovluck, Ileen Marcy *music annotator*

New York Mills
Zielinski, Teresa Krystyna *music educator*

Niagara Falls
DiVita-Frommert, Angela Marie *music educator*
Gailie, Kristina Ann *music educator*

Niskayuna
Martin, Ruth C. (Ruth Martin Staff) *actress*
Steeley, Dolores Ann *music educator*

North Merrick
Rakas, Peggy Ann *music educator*

North Syracuse
Federico, Josephine A.M. *music educator*

North Tonawanda
Strong, Audrey Farone *music educator*

Olmstedville
LaPointe, Sabrina Ann *music educator*

Orchard Park
Mosner, Ann L. *music educator*
Wiedl, Priscilla *music educator*

Perry
Hume, Linda Jean *music educator*

Port Washington
van Schenkhof, Carol Dougherty (Carol Dovan) *soprano, educator*

Red Hook
Gudenzi-Ruess, Ida Carmen V. *music educator, artist*

Rochester
Buckbee, Malina *music educator*
Fox, Donna Brink *music educator*
Pratt, Alice S. *music educator*
Schneider, Sue R. *music educator*
Toribara, Masako Ono *voice educator*
Truesdale, Carol A. *music educator*

Schenectady
Rice, Ruth Elaine *music educator*

Sea Cliff
Popova, Nina *dancer, choreographer, director*

Shrub Oak
Vaccaro, Annette Andréa *music educator*

Slingerlands
Jacobs, Karen Louise *musician, educator, medical technician*

Smithtown
McNeil, Jennifer Jayne *music educator*

South Kortright
Maeder-Chien, Rebecca L. *music educator*

Sparkill
Dahl, Arlene *actress, writer, designer, cosmetics executive*

Springville
Jurkowski, Karen Evans *music educator*

Staten Island
Shively, Sarah Elizabeth *actress*
Wachholtz, Andrea Marie *professional ballet dancer, choreographer*

Syracuse
Strempel, Eileen L. *singer, educator*
Wolff, Catherine Elizabeth *opera company executive*

Valley Stream
Cali, Mary Ann *music educator*

Verona
Carter, Linda Ann *music educator*

Vestal
O'Connell, Patricia Ellen *music educator, musician*

Wading River
Volonts, Marguente Louise *music educator, singer*

Walden
Murphy, Pamela Ann *music educator, actress, musician*
Thomas-Cappello, Elizabeth *performing arts association administrator*

White Plains
Chase, Jenny Wei-Lang Kao *singer, music educator*

Willow
Bley, Carla Borg *composer*

Woodmere
Ronis, Gwendlyn *musician, educator*

Youngstown
Mehr, Vicki Joyce *music educator*

NORTH CAROLINA

Aberdeen
Sinclair, Ruth Spears Smith *music educator*

Arden
Cotsonas, Elena Catherine *music educator*

Asheboro
Menius, Joy Victoria *musician, music educator*

Asheville
Facciponti, Laura Lynne *theater educator*
Plonka, Lavinia *performing arts educator*
Sieber Johnson, Ruth E. *music educator*

Benson
Stewart, Kennette Nowell *music educator*

Black Mountain
Belue, Janie A. *music educator*

Cary
Bruce, Brenda *pianist*

Chapel Hill
Peacock, Florence F. *professional musician, soprano, voice educator*

Charlotte
Higgins, Diane W. *music teacher*
Iley, Martha Strawn *music educator*
Reese, Annette Evelyn *music educator*
Tobias, Dorothy Burton *retired music educator, consultant*

Cherryville
Barger, Linda Kale *choral director*

Cullowhee
Armfield, Terri Elaine *music educator, musician*

Durham
Bradford, Dolli Maria *music educator*
Morris, Valerie L. *music educator*

Fayetteville
Barnicle, Mary Anne *music educator, piano accompanist*
Widdows, Marianne Shuta *orchestra director*
Williams, Susan Bullard *music educator*

Franklinton
Elmore, Cenieth Catherine *music educator*

Greensboro
Green, Jill I. *dance educator, researcher*
Russell, Peggy Taylor *soprano, educator*
Styles, Teresa Jo *television producer, educator*

Hendersonville
Tatsch, Jacki Lynn *music educator, diversified financial services company executive*

Hickory
Stokes, Betty *music educator*

Huntersville
Taylor, Sylvia Dawn *music educator*

Kings Mountain
Aderholdt, Traci Eaves *music educator*

Kinston
Vernon, Jane Harper *music educator*

Leicester
Entzi, Karen Russell *orchestra educator*

Lumberton
Canonizado, Gloria M. *choreographer, educator*

Mars Hill
Greene, Tena Lorraine *singer, educator, actor*

Mooresboro
Goode, Elizabeth Ann *music educator*

Mount Olive
Damon, Sherri Marcia *music educator*

Newport
Mundine, Rachel Quinn *music educator*

North Topsail Beach
Kelley, Virginia Wiard (Judy Kelley) *dance educator*

North Wilkesboro
Shumaker, Tara L. *performing arts educator*

Otto
Harwell, Joanne Brindley *music educator*

Oxford
Hafner, Margot Annette *music educator, voice educator*

Pembroke
Jackson, B. Ellen Hursey *music educator*

Raleigh
Fincher, Norma Beeby *music educator, elementary school educator*
Garriss, Phyllis Weyer *music educator, performer*
Petteway, Diane Cashwell *music educator, musician*
Pope, Elizabeth Stephens *dance educator*
Wilder, Lisa Yvette *dancer, educator*
Youngman, Lola Jeanne *music educator*

Rougemont
Nilsson, Mary Ann *music educator*

Salisbury
Julian, Rose Rich *music educator, director*

Smithfield
Lamberson, Carolyn Jane Hinton *music educator*

Todd
Cole, Susan Stockbridge *retired theater educator*

Warrenton
Weddington, Elizabeth Gardner (Liz Gardner) *actress*

Weaverville
Budhisetiawan, Barbara Crawford *music educator*

Wilmington
Cameron, Kay *conductor, composer*
Onufer, Nicole Holder *music educator*

Winston Salem
Dixon, Patricia Abud *music educator*
Saxton, Judith Ann *musician, educator*
Stewart, Gwendolyn Johns *music educator*

NORTH DAKOTA

Bismarck
Gray, Arlene *music educator, musician*
Knoll, Gloria Jean *music educator*

Bottineau
Roemmich, Dalonnes Kay *music educator*

Fargo
Schabert, Leah Christine *dance instructor*

Glenburn
Croonquist, Cheryl *music educator, realtor*

Grand Forks
Boesl, Beth Marie *music educator*
Popejoy, Melanie Ann *music educator*

Minot
Starr, Sandra Schjeldahl *music educator*

West Fargo
Morrison, Karen A. *music educator*

OHIO

Ada
Zank, MJ Sunny *musician, department chair, educator*

Akron
Beery, Amy Suzanne *music educator*
Kazle, Elynmarie *theater producer, performing arts executive*
Usher, Ann L. *music educator*

Amelia
Hill, Diane L. *music educator*

Amherst
Gall, Simone Ellen *music educator*

Athens
Purdy, Penny *music educator*

Beachwood
Farley, Carolyn Juanita *music educator*

Berea
Sanders, Phyllis May *musician*

Berlin Center
Orevna, Nellie Lou *music educator*

Canton
Eshelman, Georgia Lee *music educator*
Klotz, Leora Nylee *retired music educator, vocalist*

Cedarville
Anderson, Connie *music educator*

Centerville
Booth, Catherine Keener *music educator, director*
Wasson, Carol R. *music educator*

Cincinnati
Brown, Lillie Harrison *music educator*
Dunevant, Carol Dary *music educator, conductor*
Eckstein, Elaine Claire *theater educator*
Galloway, Lillian Carroll *modeling agency executive, consultant*
Holdren, Jamie Lynn *music educator*
McCamley, Sherry Smith *entertainer, actor, vocalist, voice educator*
Morgan, Victoria *performing company executive, choreographer*
Weinstein, Anna *music educator*
Winfrey, Marcellene Sedetta *music educator, church musician*
Worachek, Susan *music educator*

Cleveland
Lawrence, Estelene Yvonne *musician, transportation executive*
Stupka, Renee C. *musician, educator*
Weir, Dame Gillian Constance *musician*

Columbus
Gustina, Lori Lazenby *music educator*
Johnson, Rebecca Grooms *music educator*
Renshler, Rosemary P. *retired music educator*
Rosenstock, Susan Lynn *orchestra administrator*
Williams, Linda Dianne *music educator*

Dayton
Carrier, Rachel Esther *music educator, director*
Hanna, Marsha L. *artistic director*
Jagow, Shelley *music educator, musician*
McCarrell, Lynette Marie *music educator, director*
Shaffer, Joanne Tyler *music educator*
Wasson, Barbara Hickam *music educator*

Delaware
Gardner, Bonnie Milne *theater educator, playwright*

Dover
Wenzel, Mary Joan *music educator*

Dublin
Laurence, Amy Rebecca *music educator, composer*

East Cleveland
Davis, Dianne *music educator*
Soule, Lucile Snyder *musician, educator*

Geneva
Carrel, Marianne Eileen *music educator*

Greenfield
Flora, Loretta Sue *music educator*

Heath
Brandt, Traci Lynn Keller *music educator, musician*

Hilliard
McNutt, Suzanne Michaelene *music educator*

Hoytville
Shoemaker, Cynthia Louise *music educator*

Lafayette
Spencer, Teresa Ann *music educator*

Lakewood
Hankins, Elizabeth Aylmer *orchestra director*
Hisey, Bernadette Anne *music educator*

Lodi
Behrend, Kristel Nicole *music educator*

Logan
Price, Harlene Pamela *music educator*

Lyndhurst
Carey, Reiko Marie *music educator*

Mansfield
Sturts, Donna Jean *music educator*

Marshallville
Evert, Heather Lynn *dance instructor*

Mentor
Priddy, Jean Marie *music educator, voice educator*

Middlefield
Jaite, Gail Ann *retired music educator*

Mount Vernon
Cameron, Virginia Anne *music educator*
Koh-Baker, JoAnn Been *music educator*

New Concord
Schumann, Laura Elaine *conductor*

New Philadelphia
Mathias, Denise Susanne *music educator, music minister*

Newark
Vaas, Lori Rhodes *music educator*
Workman, Virginia Lane *music educator*

Norwalk
McGue, Rochelle Lee *music educator, rental manager*

Oak Harbor
Sievert, Vicki Lee *retired music educator*

Oberlin
Rutstein, Sedmara Zakarian *concert pianist, educator*

Parma
Musat, Katherine Gadus *retired music educator*
Tibbitts, Barbara J. *music educator*

Pepper Pike
Dunegan, Jennifer Lee *theater educator*
Oldenburg, Chloe Warner *performing arts association administrator, educator*

Pickerington
Lang, Lisa Ann *music educator*

Rocky River
Briscar-Martel, Nancy Marie *agent, musician, educator*

Shaker Heights
McBurney, Christine *performing arts educator, actress, director*

Smithville
Sillman, Denise Marie *music educator, small business owner*

Solon
Bane, Glenice Gail *music educator*

South Euclid
Miller Schear, Annice Mara *music educator*

Strongsville
Webb, Tara Yvette *music educator*

Tipp City
Ahmed, Gail R. *music educator*

Toledo
Frank, Christine Marie *music educator*
Lyne, Janet Kay *music educator, director*

Tontogany
Baughman, Janine Kay *music educator*

Vandalia
Korte, Genevieve L. *music educator*

Wadsworth
Ross, Jane Arlene *music educator*

Wapakoneta
Lusk, Mary Margaret *music educator*
Wirth, Tamara L. *music educator*

Warren
Holt, Patricia Annette *retired music educator*
Seachrist, Denise *music educator*

West Jefferson
Hepp, Jody *music educator*

Whitehouse
Gelsone, Amy J. *music educator*

Wickliffe
Barnes, Lili Darnelle *music educator, director*
Graves, Pamela Kay *music educator*

Willoughby
Linsenmeier, Carol Vincent *music educator*

Worthington
Wade, Susan Prince *retired music educator*

Wyoming
Jablonsky, Atarah *retired music educator*

Xenia
Savard, Tamara Renee *music educator*

Zanesville
Strahm, Mary Ellen *music educator*

OKLAHOMA

Alva
Cummings, Ramona *music educator*

Anadarko
Kidd, Lovetta Monza *music educator*

Bartlesville
Beech, Shelly Christine *dancer, educator, small business owner*

Bethany
Cook, Wanda Reedy *music educator*

Broken Arrow
Hawkins, Pamela Kay *entertainer, writer*

Checotah
Cooper, Kathleen K. *music educator*

Duncan
Fike, Holly Renee *music educator*

Edmond
Charoenwongse, Chindarat *pianist, music educator*
Thomas, Vicki Webb *theater educator*

Enid
Russell, Rhonda Cheryl *piano educator, recording artist, talent scout*
Seem, Evelyn Ashcraft *music educator*

Eufaula
Breon, Nancy G. *music educator*

Hollis
Stewart, Marcia Kathryn *music educator*

Jenks
Frazer, Janet Elizabeth *music educator*

Lawton
Gagliardi, Charlotte Marie *music educator, secondary school educator*
Garton, Janette *music educator*
Underwood, Kirsten Fedje *musician, educator*

Midwest City
Mechling, Brenda L. *voice educator, director*
Robinson, Emily Sue *music educator*

Mounds
Fellows, Esther Elizabeth *musician, music educator*

Norman
Dorrough, Vicki Lee *theater educator*
Magrath, Jane *music educator*
Smith, Beulah Mae *music educator*
Tussing, Marilee Appleby *music educator*

Oklahoma City
Adams, Mary Lou *piano teacher*
Campbell, Virginia Hopper *piano concert artist, composer, educator*
Green, Vickie *music educator*
Ragsdale, Jana Lynne *music educator*
Shackleton, Jean L. *music educator*
Twyman, Nita (Venita Twyman) *music educator*

Pawhuska
Adams, Jessica Tereace *music educator, director*

Shawnee
Woodward, Betty Shaw *retired music educator*

Skiatook
Meyer, Virginia Maurine *music educator*

Tulsa
Bridges, Mary Jo *music educator*
Collins, Laura Jane *music educator, singer*
Owens, Jana Jae *entertainer*
Weinstock Rad, Katheryn Louise *music educator*
Womack, Lee Ann *country musician*

Wilburton
Minshall, Dorothy Kathleen *music educator*

OREGON

Corvallis
McCormick, Stephanie L. Bell *music educator*
Nelson, Carol Gretchen *music educator*

Eugene
Bailey, Exine Margaret Anderson *soprano, educator*
Benson, Joan *musician, educator*
Bossuat, Judy Weigert *music educator*

Hillsboro
Burke, Tara LeAnn *music educator*

Klamath Falls
Crawford, Brenda R. *music educator*

Portland
Chan, Susan S. *music educator*
Jensen, Marion Pauline *singer*
Kohne, Heidi Ann *church musician*
Merrill, Norma *video poducer, copy writer*
Mittelstaedt, Janet Rugen *music educator, composer*
Robinson, Helene M. *retired music educator*
Unger, Jane Ellen *performing company executive*

Roseburg
King, Lloyd JoAnn *music educator, volunteer*

Salem
Beranek, Kim Marie *music educator*
Marshall, Cak (Catherine Elaine Marshall) *music educator, composer*

Sutherlin
Littlejohn, Heather Sheri *music educator*

Yamhill
Longton, Brenda Jo *music educator*

PENNSYLVANIA

Abington
Anderson, Valerie B. *actress, writer*

Allentown
Beltzner, Gail Ann *music educator*
Martyska, Barbara *composer, performer, educator*
Moeller, MaryAnn *music educator*
Pribanich, Cheryl Marie *music educator*

Allison Park
Bumblis, Kristin N. *music educator*

Annville
Condran, Cynthia Marie *gospel musician*

Berwyn
Gingles, Marjorie Stanke *music educator*

Bethlehem
Allen, Beatrice *music educator, pianist*
Simons, Audrey Kay *music educator*

Birdsboro
Dieffenbach, Lisa M. *music educator*

Blue Bell
Edwards, Joselle Elizabeth *performing arts educator*

Bradford
Thumpston, Kathleen Marie *music educator*

Bristol
Atkinson, Susan D. *producing artistic director, theatrical consultant*

Brodheadsville
Snyder, Nadine Eldora *music educator*

Cambridge Springs
Beltz, Sherree Lynne *music educator*

Carlisle
Berry, Karen S. *music educator*

Carnegie
Lear, Mary Catherine *music educator*

Chadds Ford
Swensson, Evelyn Dickenson *conductor, composer, librettist*

Chalfont
Ashley, Kathleen Labonis *music educator*

Chambersburg
Petke, Beverly Ann *music educator*

Cheyney
Bagley, Edythe Scott *theater educator*
Ellis-Scruggs, Jan *theater arts educator*

Clarks Summit
Gwillim, Allison Lee *conductor, music educator, department chairman*

Coatesville
Petko, Patricia Ann *music educator*
Simmons, Barbara Ann *music educator*

Downingtown
Crescenz, Valerie J. *music educator*
Zimmerman, Lisa A. *music educator*

Dresher
Levicoff, Valerie Ann *music educator*

Easton
Lombardozzi, Debra Ann *music educator*

Elkins Park
Topper, Patricia Margaret *music educator*

Erie
Foltz, Katrina Marie *music educator*
Hess, Susan Irene *music educator*

Everett
Whetstone, Joni Lee *music educator*

Fairless Hills
Schmidt, Suzanne M. *music educator*

Galeton
Bull, Inez Stewart *retired music educator, curator, director, singer, writer, musician*

Gettysburg
Jones, Gail Peters *music educator*

Glenmoore
Fix, Irene M. *music educator*

Glenside
Willig, Barbara Adele *music educator*

Harrisburg
Schrader, Janet E. *music educator*

Hatboro
Carroll, Lucy Ellen *theater director, educator*

Haverford
Miller, Geraldine B. *music educator*

Havertown
Bobnak, Marsha Core *music educator*
Cox, Ruth Miller *music educator*

Johnstown
Arcurio, Jean Catherine *soprano, educator, director*

King Of Prussia
Hallman, Patricia L. *music educator, musician*
Helmetag, Diana *music educator*

Kingston
Weisberger, Barbara *artistic director, advisor, educator*

Lancaster
Veri, Frances Gail *musician, educator*

Langhorne
Haimbach, Marjorie Anne *music educator*

Lebanon
Kulikowski, Cheryl E. *music educator*

Lewisburg
Muller, Riana Ricci *musician, educator*

Loysburg
Stuckey, Ellen Mae *music educator*

Mansfield
Dettwiler, Peggy Diane *music educator*

Middletown
Miller, Marilyn Jane *music educator*
Winch, Donna Gladhill *music educator*

Milford Square
Sewell, Gloriana *music educator*

Monongahela
Brown, Hilary Susanne *music educator, photographer*
Winkleblech, Shannan *music educator*

New Brighton
Ficca, Rhonda Lee *music educator*

New Castle
Palladino, Rosanne C. *music educator*

Newtown
Finberg, Melinda C. *theater educator*

Norristown
Magann, Joyce L. *music educator*
Weikert, Barbara Sliker *music educator*

North Huntingdon
Antolik, Elena Anne *performing company executive, choreographer*
Little, Jenifer Raye *music educator*

Philadelphia
Colson, Rosemary *music educator*
deBenedet, Rachel *actress*
Fauntleroy, Angela Colleen *music educator*
Garonzik, Sara Ellen *stage producer*
Gonglewski, Grace *actress*
Ingolfsson-Fassbind, Ursula G. *music educator*
Myers Brown, Joan *performing company executive*
Pasternak, Jill Margot *radio producer, musician, educator*
Tuttle, Karen Ann *violist, educator*

Pittsburgh
Bardyguine, Patricia Wilde *dancer, performing company executive*
Frezza, Christine Anne *theater music composer*
Li, Ying *dancer*
McKelway, Janet Barbara *music educator, retired*
Monich, Marylou *music educator*
Posvar, Mildred Miller *opera singer*
Riley, Carole A. *music educator, religious institute director*

Quakertown
Emig, Carol A. *music educator, musician*

Reading
Zug, Elizabeth E. *concert pianist, educator*

Saegertown
Ralph, NancyJo *retired music educator*

Selinsgrove
Barben, Sherry L. *music educator, choir director*
Pineno, Mariam Davis *retired music educator, poet*

Shavertown
Motyka, Susanne Victoria *music educator*

Shohola
Carlton, Heidi Lee *pianist, music educator*

Slippery Rock
Payne, Ursula Octavia *choreographer, educator*

Southampton
Lenox, Gina Marie *music educator*

State College
Darnell, Doris Hastings *performance artist*
Moore, Judy W. *music educator, musician*

Stroudsburg
Clogg, Katye Narise *music educator*
Rogers, Lisa Ann *music educator*

Vandergrift
Aikins, Candace Sue *music educator, consultant*

Villanova
Reeder, Lindsay Erin *music educator*

Washington
Gregg, Cynthia Louise *music educator*

Wellsboro
Smithgall, Judy Lee *music educator, director*

West Chester
Albert, Kristen Ann *music educator*
Staruch, Elizabeth *theater educator*

West Sunbury
Ferrere, Rita L. *band director, music educator*

Willow Hill
Dorand, Freda J. *music educator*

Wrightsville
Huber, Cheryl S. *music educator*

Yardley
Setash, Kathleen Douglas *music educator*

York
Cane, Susannah Richards *music educator*

Youngsville
Pearson, Denise Anne *music educator*

Youngwood
Duvall, Hollie Jean *music educator*

RHODE ISLAND

Chepachet
Jubinska, Patricia Ann *ballet instructor, choreographer, artist, anthropologist, archaeologist*

Cranston
Livingston, Carolyn Harris *music educator*

Greenville
Hopkins, Catherine Lee *music educator*

Lincoln
Marsden, Herci Ivana *classical ballet artistic director*

Newport
French, Jae *theater producer, sculptor*

Pawtucket
McWilliams, Cheryl A. *music educator*
Orson, Barbara Tuschner *actress*

SOUTH CAROLINA

Anderson
Williford, Sandra Simmons *music educator*

Charleston
Jones, Vivian Eilene *music educator*

Columbia
Boyce, Corrie Mosby *music educator*
Paschal, Rhoda Jones *voice educator*
Ruth, Deborah Ann *music educator*
Sepulveda, Sonja Marian Atkinson *choral director, accompanist*

Conway
Sinclair, Frances Teresa *music educator, musician*

Donalds
Hind, Elise Cromwell *music educator*

Edisto Island
Van Metre, Margaret Cheryl *performing company executive, dancer, educator*

Florence
Chandler, Ann Rogers Tomlinson *music educator, director*
Fisher, Christine S. *music educator*

Goose Creek
Vogt, Kathleen Cunningham *musician, educator*

Greenville
Clarke, Jean Alderman *orchestra director*
Kindall, Susan Carol *music educator*

Greenwood
Bolen, Jane M. *music teacher, organist, choir director*
Psomas, Beverly T. *music educator, performing arts association administrator*

Hilton Head Island
Brock, Karena Diane *dancer, educator*
Selvy, Barbara *dance instructor*

Johnsonville
Kelley, Patricia T. *music educator*

Lake City
Stone, Betty Frances *music educator*

Moore
King, Tamara Powers *music educator, musician*

Mount Pleasant
Royall, Mary-Julia C. *church organist, historian*

Pawleys Island
Young, Suzanne M. *music educator, director*

Rock Hill
Wishert, Jo Ann Chappell *music educator, elementary and secondary school educator*

Roebuck
Baier, Susan Lovejoy *music educator*

Spartanburg
Foy, Patricia Solesbee *music educator*
Jenkins-Russ, Theresa Elizabeth *music educator*
Lucktenberg, Jerrie Čadek *music educator*
Sellars, Christi von Lehe *music educator*
Wren, Leah *theater educator, director*

Summerville
Bratnely, Marcia J. *music educator*

Sumter
Dave', Anne Dupree *music educator*

SOUTH DAKOTA

Aberdeen
Zephier, Carol Ann *piano educator, retired organist*

Canton
Kaufman, Angela J. *music educator*

Humboldt
Johnson, June Marilyn *music educator*

Keystone
Harrison, Gloria Jean *retired music educator*

Roscoe
Flannery, Bernita L. *music educator*

Sioux Falls
Ammann, Meladee *music educator*
Egan, Lora Rae *music educator*

Volin
Aiello, Judith A. *music educator*

Watertown
Lemke, Tracy A. *music educator*

White Lake
Munsen, Renee Lynn *music educator*

TENNESSEE

Alexandria
Thomas, Deona Lee *music educator*

Brentwood
Grant, Amy *singer, songwriter*
Taylor, Nicole Renée (Niki Taylor) *model, shop owner*
Tucker, Tanya Denise *singer*
Walker Bonner, Linda Carol *music educator*

Bristol
Fey, Vicki Peterson *church musician*
Holler, Ann K. *music educator*

Chattanooga
Fouquet, Anne (Judy Fuqua) *musician, music educator*

Clarksville
Clark, Janet Kaye *music educator*

Collierville
Nichols, Christina R. *music educator*

Cordova
Cheatham, Wanda M. *music educator*
Pugh, Dorothy Gunther *artistic director*

Dayton
Luther, Sigrid *music educator*

Franklin
Ward, Patricia S. *theater educator*

Henderson
Elder, Jennifer Anne *music educator*

Henry
Lowery, Dianne Armour *music educator*

Huntland
Burton, Janet Ruth Wisner *music educator*

Jackson
Gatwood, Dianne N. *music educator*

Johnson City
Corpening, Deborah Weems *dance educator*
Snyder-Sowers, Mary Anne Sarah *performing arts educator, performing company executive, choreographer*

Kingsport
Hart, Voleen Victoria *music educator*

Knoxville
Landry, Mary Catherine *dance instructor, choreographer*

Lebanon
Lane, Nicole *dancer, educator*

Loudon
Horst, Teresa Dale *music educator*

Martin
Wade, Reba *musician, educator*

Memphis
Newberry, Paula Anita *singer, music educator*
Philipp, Karla Ann *music educator, conductor, musician*
Piazza, Marguerite *opera singer, actress, entertainer*
Presley, Lisa Marie *singer*

Morristown
Ritter, Laura Lingerfelt *music educator*

Nashville
Butler, Carol Green *music educator*
Evans, Sara *country singer, songwriter*
Fabian, Jane *former ballet company executive*
Harris, Emmylou *singer*
Hill, Faith *musician*
Kessler, Ingrid Anderson *musician, music educator*
Maguire, Martie (Martha Elenor Erwin Maguire) *musician*
Maines, Natalie Louise *musician*
McBride, Martina *vocalist*
Robison, Emily Burns *musician*
Twain, Shania (Eilleen Regina Edwards) *musician*
Watkins, Sara *musician*
Whitten-Frickey, Wendy Elise *entertainer*
Wilson, Gretchen *vocalist*
Wonders, Pamela Kim *music educator*

Newport
Williams, Stephanie Diane *music educator*

Paris
Hawkins, Angela *music educator*

Pigeon Forge
Parton, Dolly Rebecca *singer, composer, actress*
Russell, Pamela Ruth *music and theater educator, singer, entertainer*

Sparta
Klughart, Toni Anne *music educator, musician, singer*

Vonore
Riley, Betsy Lea *music educator*

TEXAS

Angleton
Casey, Beth Mentelle *music educator*
Williams, Tessa René *music educator*

Arlington
Barkey, Debra Lynn *music educator*
Neaga Khayt, Angela *music educator*
Thomas, Lois C. *musician, educator, religious organization administrator, composer*

Aubrey
Pizzamiglio, Nancy Alice *performing company executive*

Austin
Bennett, Catherine Margaret *music educator*
Carroll, Yvette *voice educator*
Case, Karen Elizabeth *theater educator*
Dolan, Jill S. *performing arts educator*
Gerber, Kimberly Ann *music educator, singer*
Moore, Colleen *piano and voice instructor*
Mueller, Peggy Jean *dance educator, choreographer, rancher*
Robbins, Mary *concert pianist*
Ruiz, Cookie *performing company executive*
Turner, Kathleen Kalin *musician, art director*
Young, Phyllis Casselman *music educator*

Borger
Allen, Bessie Malvina *music educator, organist*

Brenham
Brown, Marguerite Johnson *music educator*

Brownwood
Owens, Diane Dobray *music educator*
Wallace, Elizabeth A. *music educator*

Canyon
Casso, Rebecca Lynn *music educator*

Carrollton
Bell, Laura Denise *music educator*
Estilette, Kathleen C. *music educator*
Mills, Patricia Lynn *theater director, educator*
Moellering, Charlotte Lareson *music educator*
Rejino, Mona *music educator, composer*

China Spring
Hyatt, Anna Dale *music educator*

Coppell
Tabor, Lisa Ann *theater educator*

Copperas Cove
Barrick, Marla Caryn *music educator*

Corpus Christi
Allison, Joan Kelly *music educator, pianist*

Dallas
Baker, Jan E. *music educator*
Brandt, Carole *theater educator, department chairman*
Croskell, Madelon Byrd *music educator, classical vocalist*
Donnell, Carolyn Faye *music educator*
Elliott, Dorothy Gail *music educator, writer*
Freiberger, Katherine Guion *composer, retired piano educator*
Johnson, Mary Elizabeth *music educator, musician*
Johnson, Patricia Ann *music educator*
Palmer, Christine (Clelia Rose Venditti) *vocalist, educator, musician*
Pelletier, Sho-mei *musician, educator*
Rice, Rebecca Dale *film producer, writer*
Sallee, Wanda Jean *music educator*
Stone, Karen *opera company director*
Thomas, Sarah Elaine *music educator*

Denton
Hadsell, Nancy Ann *music educator*
McTee, Cindy *classical musician, educator*
Odnoposoff, Berthe Huberman *musician*

Edinburg
Cardenas, Norma Alicia *music educator*

El Paso
Gladstein, Mimi Reisel *theater educator, literature educator*

Farmers Branch
Walsh, Elizabeth Jameson *musician*

Flower Mound
Anderson, Deborah Lynn *music educator*
Marrs, Carol Faye *performing arts educator, writer*

Fort Worth
Andrews, Jane Silvey *musician*
Behrens, Alisa D. *dancer, educator, performing company executive*
Dunleavy, Willa Gill *music educator, director*
Engler, Jennifer A. *theater educator*
Fritz, Mary Ann *music educator*
Hollimon, Robyn Delyn *music director*
Tarpenning, Emily *music educator*

Fredericksburg
Gibson, Frances Ernst *music educator*

Freeport
Gresham, Karen Renee *music educator, singer*

Frisco
de Veritch, Nina *musician, educator*
Sexton, Karen Kay *music educator, actress*

Galveston
Rivaux, Lois Elaine *music educator*

Garland
LeDoux, Ellen G. *music educator*
Posey, Jan R. *music educator*

Georgetown
Russell, Eileen Meyer *music educator*

Gonzales
Buesing, Leslie Marie *theater educator, director*
Ince, Laurel T. *music educator*

Hallsville
Hutcherson, Donna Dean *retired music educator*

Hewitt
rNix, Regina Leigh *performing arts educator, small business owner*

Houston
Adams, Yolanda Yvette *singer*
Auchter, Norma Holmes *musician, music educator*
Beyoncé, (Beyoncé Giselle Knowles) *singer*
Brown, Glenda Ann Walters *ballet director*
Buyse, Leone Karena *orchestral musician, educator*
Carnes, Tara Lea Barker *music educator*
Cupp, Aneta Joan *music educator*
Decker-Barnhill, Jennifer Grace *performing company executive, educator*
Frank, Hilda Rhea Kaplan *dancer*
Girouard, Peggy Jo Fulcher *ballet educator*
Hazelip, Linda Ann *musician, small business owner, executive assistant*
Jones, Florence M. *music educator*
Perkyns, Jane Elizabeth *music educator, composer*
Rose, Beatrice Schroeder (Mrs. William H. Rose) *harpist, educator*
Rowland, Kelly (Kelendria Trene Rowland) *singer*
Townsend, Elizabeth Kathleen *performing arts educator*
Williams, Michelle (Tenetria Michelle Williams) *singer*

Huntsville
Gratz, Cindy Carpenter *dance educator, choreographer*

Iowa Park
Wright, Sabra Dell *music educator*

Irving
Echols, Kari Elizabeth *music educator, elementary school educator*

Jacksonville
Rich, Mary Ruth *music educator*

Katy
Batten-Bishop, Ann Louise *theater educator*
Gentry, Mary Jean Asher *music educator*

Kenedy
Perez, Irene *music educator, director*

Kerrville
Love, Susan L. *music educator*

Lago Vista
Angelo, Julie Crawford *performing arts association administrator*

Leander
Fraley, Linda Williams Darnell *music educator*
Wood, Melissa Ann *music educator*

Lewisville
Mebane, Barbara Margot *artistic director, choreographer*
Warburton, Shelly Jo *music educator*

Linn
MacMullen, Patricia Ellen *theater educator, theater director*

Livingston
Gordon, Pamela Ann Wence *pianist*

Longview
Byrd, Carol Ann *music educator*

Lorena
Maricle, Robyn LuAnn (Ford) *band director*

Lubbock
Roy, Juliana W. *music educator*

Mabank
Lindsley, Catherine S. *voice educator, director*

Magnolia
Tarver, Betty Gail *music educator*

Mc Kinney
Hutchison, Monica Leigh *music educator*

Mcallen
Huber, Melba Stewart *dance educator, dance studio owner, historian, retailer*

Missouri City
Rathnau, Heather Hearn *music educator, writer*

Montgomery
Orr, Heather Michelle *music educator, vocalist*

Navasota
Coffey, Sharon Marie *music educator*

North Richland Hills
Shier, Elizabeth M. *music educator*

Pampa
Willingham, Jeanne Maggart *performing arts educator, performing company executive*

Paris
Cannon, Jenene *music educator*

Quanah
Lee, Carol *lyricist, artist*

Red Oak
Kerzee, Beth Bumpas *music educator*

Richmond
Clark, Ruth Mae *music educator*
Rine, Patty Davis *music educator*

Rio Grande City
Lung, Auristela R. *music educator*

Rockport
Owen, Molly Jackson *music educator*

Rockwall
Tucker, Kimberly Joan *music educator*

Rosenberg
Slack, Molly Johanna *theater educator*

Round Rock
Benford, Catherine S. *music educator*

Rusk
Hendrick, Zelwanda *performing arts educator, psychology educator*

Sachse
Conoly, Kimberly Lane *dance studio owner*

San Antonio
Murphy, Andra Brown *theater arts director, educator*
Oppenheim, Martha Kunkel *pianist, educator*
Penrod, HazelL. L. *music educator*
Rich, Melody M. *music educator, singer, conductor*
Winstead, Antoinette Fay *performing arts educator*

Sanger
Alexander, Vickie Lynn *music educator*

Seminole
Whitfield, Karen Kay *music educator*

Southlake
Grosklos, Hollie Jo *music educator*

Stephenville
Stricker, Mary Fran *music educator*

Terlingua
Schell-Brady, G. Janelle *dancer, educator*

The Woodlands
Hall, Nancy Kay *music educator*
Lewis, Sandra Ann *music educator*

Tomball
Bates, Cheryl A *music educator*

Tyler
Baker, Rebecca Louise *musician, music educator, consultant*
Burns, Mary *performing arts educator*
Miller, Lara T. *dance educator*
Wright, Mary Ellen *theater educator*

Waco
Scattergood, Florence Gassler *music educator*

Webster
Stevens, Nicole Tanya *music educator*

Wharton
George, Lila Gene Plowe Kennedy *music educator*

UTAH

Draper
Newell, Charlene A *music educator*

Ephraim
McGarry, Rebecca A. *music educator*

Kaysville
Eads, Penni Daun *music educator*

Kearns
Player, Michelle *performing arts educator, choreographer*

Ogden
Stoker, Alexandra Iverson *musician, educator*

Orem
Riley, Dyanne Schrock *music professor*

Riverton
Willmore, LeAnna *music educator*

Roosevelt
Allred, Micki Kathleen *music educator*

Salt Lake City
Emerson, Norene Rogers *music educator*
Ewers, Anne *opera company director*
Kristensen, Kathleen Howard *music educator*
Romney-Manookin, Elaine Clive *retired music educator, composer*

Vernal
Kendall, Lynna Martin *music educator*

West Valley City
Lago, Adeena C. *performing arts educator*

VERMONT

Bellows Falls
Clark, Jodi D. *theater director, educator*

East Barre
Coughenour, Carrie Lee *music educator*

Hyde Park
Towle, Melissa Manchester *music educator*

Johnson
Whitehill, Angela Elizabeth *artistic director*

Manchester Center
Sandler, Anita *singer, artist*

Saxtons River
Bosworth, Mary Jane *retired music educator*

VIRGINIA

Alexandria
Lynn, Barbara Hoffman *music educator*
Pearson, Lynda Ann *music educator*
Piecuch, Diane Marie *music educator*

Arlington
Mc Donald, Gail Faber *musician, educator*
Whitfield, Margaret Denny *retired music educator*

Ashburn
Newell, Rachel Pierce *music educator*
Tribié, Amy Kathleen *music educator*

Boyce
Bryant, Paula Jean *music educator*

Carrollton
Willard, Karen Walters *music educator*

Centreville
Eisenberg, Sue Ann *music educator*

Charlottesville
Bishop, Ruth Ann *coloratura soprano, voice educator*
Sibert, Polly Lou *conductor, music educator*

Chesapeake
Beck-Hallenbeck, Debra Kay *music educator, musician*
Byrum, Edith Ward *retired music educator*
Hayslett-Wallace, Jeanette *music educator*
Hoster-Burandt, Norma J. *musician, not-for-profit fundraiser*
Kringel, Deanna Lynn *music educator*

Christiansburg
Burkhart, Katherine West *music educator, adult education educator*

Colonial Heights
Woolridge, Kay Ellen Jones *music educator*

Dry Fork
Robertson, Heather Anderson *musician, educator*

Dublin
Billaud, Louise Ann *musician, educator*

Fairfax
Miller, Patricia A. *music educator, opera and concert artist*
Siddons, Joy Garbee *music educator*

Falls Church
East, Mary Ann Hildegarde *vocalist*
Inzana, Barbara Ann *musician, educator*
Webster, Mary Jo *music educator*

Front Royal
Call, Amy Lynn *music educator, director, classical singer*

Gainesville
French, Dorothy Marie *music educator*

Hampton
Murray, Jennifer Adams *music educator, musician*

Harrisonburg
Weaver, Jennefer Jean *musician, educator*

Hillsville
Shelor, Vickie Poff *choir director*

Hopewell
Payne, Emily Mosley *music educator*

Independence
Davis, Carolyn Jean *music educator*

Keysville
Silver, Kyla Marie *music educator*

Leesburg
Abell, Johanna Mathis *music educator*

Lexington
Rader, Angela Nichole *music educator*

Lorton
Celentano, Suzanne *movement educator*

Lynchburg
Foley, Ruth Iona *music educator*

Manassas
Dommer, Susan Wampler *music educator*
Hermann, Sharon Beth Betsy *music educator*
Livingston, Jo Ellen Brooks *music educator*
Vance, Tanya Lee *music educator, director*

Marion
Lawrence, Evelyn Thompson *retired music educator, researcher*

Mechanicsville
McEntire, Jean Reynolds *music educator*
Yohe, Robin M. *music educator*

Middleburg
Yovanovich, Robyn Dobson *theater educator, department chairman*

Monterey
Akaike, Hiroko *music educator, conductor*

Natural Bridge Station
Randolph-Broughman, Mary Etta *music educator*

Newport News
Trachuk, Lillian Elizabeth *music educator*

Norfolk
Musgrave, Thea *composer, conductor*

Petersburg
Dance, Gloria Fenderson *dance studio executive, ballet administrator*

Portsmouth
Clary, Inez Harris *music educator*

Powhatan
Pleasants, Glennis Jeter *music educator*

Prince George
Bishop, Stephanie Elizabeth *theater educator*

Radford
James, Clarity (Carolyne Faye James) *mezzo soprano*

Richlands
Edgell, Judith Carol *theater educator*

Richmond
Anderson, Bette (Bonnie) Ferguson *music educator*
Bray, Patricia Shannon *music educator, musician, small business owner*
Fullerton, Jessica Ann *music educator*
Hammel, Alice Maxine *music educator*
Kennedy, Patricia Berry *retired music educator*
Melcher, Elizabeth *musician*
Newton, Elizabeth Deane *music educator*
Reid, Jodi Belinda Austin *music educator*
Winslett, Stoner *artistic director*
Young, Sharon Wisdom *retired music educator*

Round Hill
Chalifoux, Alice Ellen *harpist, educator*

Rural Retreat
Dutton, Sandra F. *music educator*

Salem
Crowder, Rebecca Byrum *music educator, elementary school educator*

Sandston
Manson, Zynora Davis *music educator, minister*

South Hill
Evans, Cynthia Mae *music educator*

Spotsylvania
Peters, Joanna Eilene *music educator*

Springfield
D'Elosua, Jennifer Dawn *music educator*

Sterling
Newton, Cheryl Kay *music educator*

Vienna
Davilis, Katrina Lyn *music educator*
Kinsolving, Sylvia Crockett *musician, educator*

Virginia Beach
Cehelska, Olga M. *music educator, flight instructor*
Lutsyshyn, Oksana *concert pianist, organist*
Powell, Michele Hall *music educator*
Springstead, Martha Wyatt *voice educator*
Tuskey, Laura Jeanne *music educator, pharmacologist*
Watkins, Brenda L. *music educator*

Williamsburg
Wiley, Elizabeth Ann *theater educator, department chairman*

Winchester
Russell, Melinda Farrar *music educator*
Sposato, Aimé *music educator, opera singer*

Woodbridge
Rethmel, Carol Ann *voice educator, director*

WASHINGTON

Aberdeen
Pieffer, Phyllis I. *music educator*

Bellingham
Whyte, Nancy Marie *performing arts educator*

Bremerton
Cottrell-Adkins, Leone *opera company director*

Clarkston
Torgerson, Linda Belle *music educator*

Everett
Cappello, Laurie Sue *vocalist, educator*
Rimbach, Evangeline Lois *retired music educator*

Kenmore
Sokol, Jennifer Marie *musician*

Kettle Falls
Pancoast, Brandy Elizabeth *music educator*

Lacey
Van Leishout, Leslie Ann *theater educator, director*

Langley
Good, Linda Lee *music educator, musician*

Moses Lake
Aur, Marina V. *choir conductor, music educator*

Normandy Park
Levack, Edna Bevan *music educator, choir director*

Olympia
Macduff, Ilone Margaret *music educator*

Port Angeles
YMoore, Pamela Gay *music educator*

Pullman
Kelley, Margaret Mary *music educator, musician*

Seattle
Mahdaviani, Miriam *choreographer, educator*
Ozaki, Nancy Junko *performance artist, performing arts educator*
Russell, Francia *ballet director, educator*
Thomas, Karen P. *composer, conductor*

Sedro Woolley
Weaver, Diane Celeste *music educator*

Shoreline
Dolacky, Susan K. *music educator*
Matesky, Nancy Lee *music educator*

Snohomish
Litzenberger, Renee Claire *music educator, elementary school educator*

Spokane
Doty Sewall, Dana Lynne *choral director*
Dreis, Margaret K. *music educator, peer advisor*

Tacoma
Glick, R. Sara *music educator and performer, composer, writer*

Vancouver
Ernsberger, Phyllis W. *musician*
Raker, Emily Ellen *music educator*

Walla Walla
Ringhoffer, Winnifred Miriam *music educator, consultant*

Wenatchee
Marion, Sarah Kathleen *music educator*
Rappé, Teri Wahl *piano educator*

Yakima
Scott, Ruth Ellen *music educator*

WEST VIRGINIA

Charleston
Brightbill, Janet M. *music educator*

Morgantown
DeFotis, Constance *choral conductor*
Sturm, Connie Arrau *music and music education educator*
Wilson, Mary Alice *musician, educator*

Princeton
Moody, Frances Marie *former performing arts educator, musician*

Ripley
Paxton, Julia Ann *music educator, director*

Salem
Raad, Virginia *pianist, educator*

Wayne
Davis, Paula May *music educator*

WISCONSIN

Appleton
Meyer, Cheryl Lorraine *music educator*
Perrine, Colleen Fitzmartin *composer, educator*
Privatt, Kathy Lynne *theater educator, theater director, actor*

Barron
Carley, Tamatha Lynn *music educator*

Beaver Dam
Heffron, Judith Ann *music educator*

Beloit
Licary, Cheryl Ann *retired music educator, church musician*

Brookfield
Lavender, Cheryl Ann *music educator, composer, writer*

Delavan
Lepke, Charma Davies *musician, educator*

Edgar
Olson, Rachel Ann *performing arts educator, director*

Evansville
Finque, Susan Beth *theatre artist, theater director*

Glidden
Tunison, Dawn M. R. *music educator*

Greendale
Patterson, Amanda Margaret *music educator*

Greenfield
Jirovec, Mary Ann *music educator*
McKillip, Patricia Claire *operatic soloist*

Hartland
Schabow, Nancy A. Dexter *music educator*

Horicon
Gasner, Renee *music educator*

Kenosha
Kollatz, Rebecca Lynn *music educator*

Kimberly
Koll, Kathryn Jane *music educator*

La Crosse
Gorman, Kathleen Jean *performing arts educator, choreographer*

Madison
Bartley, Linda L. *musician, music educator*
Faulkner, Julia Ellen *opera singer*
Janson Heintz, Maureen *dancer, educator, choreographer*
Rosser, Annetta Hamilton *composer*

Marinette
Malmstadt, Mary Jane *music educator*

Milwaukee
Harris, Christine *dance company executive*
Kwak, Eun-Joo *musician, educator*
Verhaalen, Marion *music educator*
Zofkie, Marcia Mary *music educator*

Mishicot
Peters, Redebra Evyn *music educator*

Monona
Jensen, Jill Susan *music educator*

Monroe
Bennett, Judy A. *music educator*

Neenah
Orm, Sally S. *music educator, consultant*

New Berlin
Belich, Kay S. *music educator*
Duszynski-Waldbillig, Cynthia *piano educator, performer, adjudicator*

New Franken
Tepe, Judith Mildred *vocal music teacher, choral director*

Oconomowoc
Bleke, Diane K. *music educator, director*

Platteville
Armstrong, Amelia Luci *music educator*
Ressler, Amy June *theater educator, theater director*
Weber, Amelia Luci *music educator*

Rice Lake
Strong, (Lin) Linda Louise *music educator*

Rudolph
Johnson, Ann Ruth *musician*

Shorewood
Bowers, Jane Meredith *retired music educator*

Spring Green
Day, Sarah Jane *actor*

Superior
McKnight, Patricia Gayle *musician, artist, writer, educator*

Two Rivers
Rank, Janet Carol *music educator*

Verona
White, Carolyn Louise *music educator*

Waukesha
Floeter, Valerie Ann *music educator*
Meyer, Debora Lynn *music educator*
Stringham, Phyllis Joan *retired music educator*

Waupaca
Hansen, Louise Hill *music educator, retired application developer*

Whitewater
Heidenreich, Lori Jean *music educator*

WYOMING

Big Piney
Mitchell, Anne S. *music educator*

Cheyenne
Cornish, Nancy Lee *music educator*
Woodman, Lucy Rhodes *music educator*

Dubois
Glasser, Pamela Jean *musician, music educator*

Green River
Evans, Eileen *music educator*

Lander
Bakke, Luanne Kaye *music educator*

Rock River
King, Corinne Michelle *music educator*

Sheridan
Robertson, Lisa Rae *music educator*

CANADA

BRITISH COLUMBIA

Vancouver
Beals, Jennifer *actress*
Jones, Norah *vocalist, musician*
Krall, Diana *musician*
Lavigne, Avril *singer*
McLachlan, Sarah *musician, composer*

ONTARIO

Callander
Haig, Susan *conductor*

Toronto
Furtado, Nelly Kim *vocalist*
Goh, Chan Hon *ballerina*

QUEBEC

Montreal
Von Gencsy, Eva *dancer, choreographer, educator*

AUSTRALIA

Darlinghurst
Davis, Judy *actress*

Redfern
Campion, Jane *film director, screenwriter*

DENMARK

Copenhagen
Martin, Vivian *soprano*

ENGLAND

Essex
Collins, Joan Henrietta *actress*

Leeds
Ichino, Yoko *ballerina*

London
Arman Gelenbe, Deniz *concert pianist*
Atkins, Eileen *actress*
Duncan, Lindsay Vere *actress*
Holt, Thelma *theatrical producer*
McPhee, Katharine Hope *singer*
Osbourne, Kelly Lee *television personality, singer*
Uchida, Mitsuko *pianist*

Poole
Alsop, Marin *conductor, violinist, music director*

FRANCE

Paris
de Havilland, Olivia Mary *actress*
Deneuve, Catherine (Catherine Dorleac) *actress*

NEW ZEALAND

Wellington
Paquin, Anna *actress*

SWITZERLAND

Kusnacht
Jones, Dame Gwyneth *soprano*

ADDRESS UNPUBLISHED

Abdoo, Rose Marie *actor*
Abell, Sara Nightingale *music educator, musician*
Abernathy, Jennifer P. *music educator*
Adams, Amy (Amanda Jessica Adams) *actress*
Adams, Joey Lauren *actress*
Adams, Susan Lois *music educator*
Adato, Perry Miller *documentary producer, director, writer*
Aghdashloo, Shohreh *actress*
Ahearn, Holly Ande *music educator*
Aitchison, Bridget Mary *theater educator, theater director*
Alba, Jessica *actress*
Alexander, Hope *actor, educator, theater director*
Aliga, Olivia R. *music educator, choral director*
Allen, Denise Newbold *music educator*
Allen, Marilyn Myers Pool *theater director, video specialist*
Alley, Kirstie *actress*
Allston, Charita Capers *music educator*
Amara, Lucine *vocalist*
Amgott, Madeline *television producer, consultant*
Anderson, Cherine E. *television and film production manager, special events planner, marketing executive*
Anderson, Gillian *actress*
Anderson, Rebecca Lynn *music educator*
Andrews, Dame Julie (Julia Elizabeth Wells) *actress, singer*
Anisimova, Tanya *cellist, educator*
Aniston, Jennifer *actress*
Annis, Francesca *actress*
Antaramian, Jacqueline *actress*
Antinone, Jo Ann Elliott *music educator*
Antolick, Lynn Ann *music educator*
Appelbaum, Marci Anne *theater director, educator*
Applegate, Christina *actress*
Arenal, Julie (Mrs. Barry Primus) *choreographer*
Armatrading, Joan *singer, lyricist*
Arnold, Mary Spears *retired music educator*
Arthur, Beatrice *actress*
Astey, Tricia Anne *music educator*
Atkins, Joanna Pang (Joanna Pang) *dancer, actress, choreographer, director*
Atkinson, Beth J. *music educator*
Atkinson, Paula Mari *music educator*
Atwood, Sonya Elizabeth *music educator*
Augustine-Ascherl, Joan Michelle *music educator*
Austin, Susannah Lyn *music educator*
Bach, Mary Irene *music educator*
Back, Shannon Lee *music educator*
Bacon, Jeri Ann *music educator*
Badu, Erykah *singer, songwriter*
Baker, Kathy Whitton *actress*
Baranski, Christine *actress*
Barbeau, Adrienne *actress*
Barber, Elizabeth Jean *vocalist, educator, artist*
Barranger, Milly Slater *theater educator, writer*
Bartel, Jeanine M. *actor*
Bartoli, Cecilia *soprano*
Barton, Katie *music educator*
Bates Appleton, Shirley Graves *music educator*
Bauer, Jennifer Elizabeth *performing company executive*
Bauer, Mary Jane *lyricist*
Beck, Jane *dance educator, choreographer*
Beck, Susan Rebecca *voice educator, consultant*
Beckerman, Ellen *theater director*
Beckstrand, Karin *music educator*
Bedelia, Bonnie *actress*
Bell, Anne Marie *music educator*
Beloff, Zoe *filmmaker, educator, photographer*
Beluso, Karen Mae *performing company executive, music educator*
Belzberg, Edet *filmmaker*
Bencini, Sara Haltiwanger *concert pianist*
Benson, Jeanne P. *music educator*
Bergen, Candice *actress, writer, photojournalist*
Bergeron, Earleen Fournet *actress*
Berman, Shari Springer *film director, scriptwriter*
Bernhard, Sandra *actress, comedienne, singer*
Bess, Aimee Lynn *performing arts educator*
Betancourt-Bryant, Sonia *music educator*
Biggers, Cornelia Anderson *musician*
Billingsley, Karen Joyce *music educator*
Binoche, Juliette *actress*
Black, Lisa Hartman *actress, singer*
Blackstone, Dara *music educator, conductor*
Blattner, Florence Anne *retired music educator*
Blatz, Lidia *music educator, elementary school educator*
Blethyn, Brenda Anne *actress*
Blevins, Elaina Gwen *music educator, director*
Blige, Mary Jane *recording artist*
Blossom, Beverly *choreographer, educator*
Boardman, Eunice *retired music educator*
Bock, Janine Schmelzer *music educator*
Bodden, Lisa *theater educator*
Boland, Deborah Catherine *music educator*
Bolles, Susan *production designer*
Bolton, Ann P. *music educator*
Bonazzi, Elaine Claire *mezzo soprano*
Bond, Victoria Ellen *conductor, composer*
Bondy, Alison A. *music educator*
Boneau, Janne Marie *music educator*
Bonet, Lisa (Lilakoi Moon, Lisa Michelle Boney) *actress*
Bonney, Jo *theater director*
Booth, Kortney Diana *music educator*
Boyle, Lara Flynn *actress*
Boyter, Judy B *music educator*
Boyum (Ball), Jennifer Marie *music educator*
Bradley, Becky Sue *music educator*
Bradley, Deborah J. *music educator*
Brady, Mary Rolfes *music educator*
Brandon, Liane *filmmaker, educator*
Braxton, Toni *popular musician*
Brennen, Anna B. *theater producer, director, playwright, actor*
Breuning, Pamela *music educator*
Brevoort, Deborah B. *librettist*
Brewster, Jamie Susan *theater educator*
Brians, Michelle Suzanne *music educator, musician*
Bridgewater, Dee Dee *jazz singer, diplomat*
Brightman, Sarah *singer, actress*
Bringman, Debra Ann *music educator*
Brooks, Lorraine Elizabeth *retired music educator*
Brooks-Turner, Myra *music educator*
Brown, Beverly Michelle *music educator*
Brown, Lora Alice *entertainment company executive, educator*
Brown-Barton, Grace Olive *music educator*
Bruns, Christine *music educator*
Bullock, Sandra (Sandra Annette Bullock) *actress*
Bumbry, Grace *soprano*
Bumbry-Bronson, Venetta *music educator*
Bump, Elizabeth Bertha *music educator*
Burau, Jennette Anne *music educator*
Burge, Constance M. *television producer*
Burke, Brooke *actress, model*
Burks, Brenda Rounsaville *retired music educator, council member*
Burrell, Pamela *actress*
Burton, Kate *actress*
Busby, Rebecca Ann *church musician, pianist*
Butler, Brett *comedienne, actress*
Byars, Amanda *performing company executive, musician, educator*
Bynes, Amanda *actress*
Byrd, Debra Ann *actor, theater producer, performing company executive*
Cafferty, Anita A. *music educator*
Calegari, Maria *ballerina*
Campbell, Melissa Lynnsimmons *music educator*
Campbell, Naomi *model*
Cannon, Dyan *actress*
Capes, Bonnie Heather *music educator*
Carbone, Cassandra A. *theater educator*
Carey, Mariah *vocalist, songwriter*
Carlock, Sandra Lynn *musician, educator*
Carroll, Barbara *musician, composer, singer*
Carroll, Diahann *actress, singer*
Carter, Barbara Dale *musician, educator, clinical counselor*
Carter, Dixie *actress*
Carter, La Rae Dunn *music educator*
Casei, Nedda *mezzo soprano*
Castro-Pozo, Talía *dancer, educator*
Caswell, Dorothy Ann Cottrell *performing arts association administrator*
Cavanagh, Caitlin *music educator*
Cavanah, Sarah E. *music educator*
Cavender, Rebecca Ann *music educator*
Cavin, Jacinda Ann *music educator*
Chadha, Gurinder *film director*
Chalcraft, Elena Marie *actress, singer*
Chapman, Robyn Lemon *music educator*
Charette, Cecile M. *music educator*
Cheadle, Louise *music educator, musician*
Chee, Ann-Ping *music educator*
Child, Abigail *filmmaker, educator*
Christian, Pearl C. *musician*
Christiansen, Wendy Lynne *music educator*
Christie, Pamela Sue *music educator*
Chubbuck, Linda J. *music educator, singer*
Ciancio, Marilyn *television producer*
Clark, Candy *actress*
Clark, Margaret Ann-Cynthia *television producer, writer*
Clark, Nancy Lucinda Brown *retired music educator*
Clark, Terri *country singer*
Clarkson, Patricia *actress*
Clawson, Amy K. *music educator*
Cochran, Kathy Holcombe *music educator, conductor*
Cody, Judith *composer, writer*
Cole, Lyn P. *tap dance instructor*
Collins, Elizabeth Brooke *theater educator*
Collins, Irma Helen *music educator, consultant*
Collins, Kathleen Anne *artistic director*
Collins, Sherri Smith *music educator*
Colvin, Shawn *recording artist, songwriter*
Comerford, ShaLeigh Marie *dancer, educator, choreographer*
Coniglio, Judith *music educator*
Conlon Khan, Lori Ellen *music educator*
Conroy, Frances *actress*
Contreras, Dawn Rachelle *performing arts educator*
Conway-Langguth, Rebecca Joan *dance instructor, dance school owner*
Cook, Kimberly Sue *music educator*
Coolidge, Martha *film director*
Cooper, Judith Kase *retired theater educator, playwright*
Coppola, Sofia Carmina *film director, scriptwriter, actress*
Cordell, Joann Meredith *music educator*
Cornwell, Susan *music educator*
Corto, Diana Maria *coloratura soprano*
Costa, Mary *soprano*
Coury, Kristen *theater director, theater producer*
Cox, Beulah Elizabeth *violinist, music educator*
Cox, Lynne Craige *music educator, composer*
Cozzens, Mimi *actress, director*
Crawford, Cindy (Cynthia Ann Crawford) *model, actress*
Crenshaw, Marjorie Juaneta *retired music educator*
Crewson, Wendy Jane *actress*
Critelli, Nancy Barbara *music educator, cellist*
Crosby, Kathryn Grandstaff (Grant Crosby) *actress*
Crow, Sheryl *singer, songwriter, musician*
Cruz-Romo, Gilda *soprano*
Cuenca, Carmen *piano teacher*
Cummins, Wilma Jeanne *actress, comedienne*
Curran, Emily K. *music educator*
Curtis, Rachael Elizabeth *music educator*
D'Abruzzo, Stephanie *actress*
Dallas, Donna Ann *music educator*
Dalton, Jeanne M. *musician, music educator*
Danaher, Mallory Millett (Mallory Jones) *actress, photographer, film and theater producer*
Danao-Salkin, Julie *actress*
Danes, Claire *actress*
Danner, Blythe *actress*
D'Arbanville, Patti *actress*
Darvarova, Elmira *musician, concertmaster*
Davies, Alma (Alma Rosita) *theater producer, composer, playwright, lyricist, sculptor*
Davies, Fonda Woodell *minister of music, music teacher*
Davis, Kristin *actress*
Davis, Terri Myrl *theater educator*
De Angelis, Rosemary Eleanor *actress*
DeHoff, Valerie S. *music educator*
Dell, Charlene Elizabeth *music educator*
de Matteo, Drea *actress*
De Mornay, Rebecca *actress*
De Palma-Iozzi, Frances M. *music educator, conductor*
Dern, Laura *actress*
de Rossi, Portia *actress*
DeVries, Linda Jane *music educator*
Diaz, Cameron *actress*
Diemer, Emma Lou *composer, educator*
DiLiberti, Lara Marie *music educator*
Dillenkoffer, Judith A. *music educator*
Dillon, Carolyn Fries *music educator*
Ding, Ai-Yue *conductor, music educator*
Dion, Celine *musician*
Dizzia, Maria Teresa *actress*
Doerksen, Mona Diane *music educator*
Doherty, Shannen *actress*
Donaldson, Myrtle Norma *music educator, musician*
Dove, Judy Merryman *theater educator*
Doyle, Gillian *actress*
Driver, Minnie *actress*
Drummond, Carol Cramer *voice educator, lyricist, writer, artist*
Dudash, Debra Ann *music educator*
Dunaway, Faye (Dorothy Dunaway) *actress*
Dunbar, Diana L. (Diane L. Dunbar) *dancer, choreographer, educator, writer, storyteller, actress*
Dussault, Nancy *actress, singer*
Dyal, Edith Colvin *retired music educator*
Edwards, Virginia Davis *music educator, concert pianist*
Eichenlaub, Rosemary Waring *retired music educator*
Electra, Carmen (Tara Leigh Patrick) *actress*
Elisha, Larisa *musician, performer, educator*
Estefan, Gloria Maria (Gloria Maria Milagrosa Fajardo) *singer, lyricist*
Ettenger, Deborah Jean *music educator*
Evans, Helen Ruth *music educator, pianist*
Evans, Stephanie E. *theater producer*
Evdokimova, Eva *prima ballerina assoluta, director, producer, consultant, actress*
Everhart, Angie *model*
Everhart, Gloria Elaine *music educator*
Ezoe, Magdalena *music educator, composer, musician*
Fairfield, Paula Kathleen *sound recording engineer*
Farrell, Suzanne (Roberta Sue Ficker) *ballerina*
Favero, Michele Maree *music educator, musician*
Fawcett, Farrah Leni *actress, model*
Feldshuh, Tovah S. *actress*
Field, Sally Margaret *actress*
Fiero-Maza, Lorraine Doris *music educator*
Finneran, Katie (Kathleen Finneran) *actress*
Fisher, Carrie Frances *actress, writer*
Fisher, Jo Ann *television technical director*
Fisher, Sharon Sue *music educator*
Fitzpatrick, Katrina S. *band director*
Flannery, Rebecca R. *harpist*
Fleming, Gina Marie *music educator*
Fleming, Rhonda *actress, singer*
Fletcher, Louise *actress*

Floyd, Carol Ann *musician, recording artist, pianist, educator*
Foerster, Jane A. *music educator*
Folsom, Virginia Jean *music educator*
Fonda, Bridget *actress*
Fontaine, Jennifer Lynne *choreographer, educator*
Fontaine, Joan *actress*
Ford, Eileen Otte (Mrs. Gerard W. Ford) *modeling agency executive*
Ford, Faith *actress*
Ford, Maryestelle Beverly *piano educator, music researcher*
Ford, Nancy Louise *composer, scriptwriter*
Foster, Jodie (Alicia Christian Foster) *actress, film director, film producer*
Foster, Mary Christine *film producer, writer*
Fournet, Lisa Clark *music educator*
Franklin, Aretha Louise *singer*
Franklin, Bonnie Gail *actress*
Franks, Natalie Rose *music educator*
Frantz, Barbara M. *music educator*
Franz, Elizabeth *actress*
Freitas, Beatrice B(otty) *musician, educator*
Fricker, Brenda *actress*
Frost, Amy Rosalie *choreographer, dancer, educator*
Fuerstner, Fiona Margaret Anne *ballet company executive, educator*
Fullenwider, Nancy Vrana *composer, dancer, musician, educator*
Gabor, Zsa Zsa (Sari Gabor) *actress, cosmetics executive*
Galante, Jane Hohfeld *musician, music historian*
Gallarello, Josephine *performing arts educator, director*
Gallatin, Jennifer *music educator*
Gallaway, Marilyn *performing arts educator, communications educator*
Garcia, Emma Yvette *music educator*
Garner, Jennifer Anne *actress*
Garnet, Eva Desca (Eva Desca) *dance educator, choreographer*
Gascoine-Molina, Jill Viola *actress, writer*
Gault, Judith *piano educator*
Gaynor, Leah *radio personality, commentator*
Gegelmann, Sharon Fay *piano teacher*
Gellar, Sarah Michelle *actress*
Gennings, Kristen Ellen *music educator*
Gerlitzki, Ann L. *music educator*
Gesualdo, Deborah Mary *music educator*
Getty, Estelle (Estelle Scher) *actress*
Gibson, Jennifer Roseann *music educator*
Gideon-Bradley, Anissa G. *voice educator*
Gieras, Angela Lee *theater manager*
Gilbert, Harriette Gurley *retired music educator*
Gilbert, Sara *actress*
Gilberti, Shauna *music educator*
Gillan, Rebecca Jane *music educator, composer*
Gish, Agnes Bridget *music educator*
Gisolo, Margaret *dancer, educator*
Gleim, Kathy Marie *music educator, performer, composer*
Glynn, Carlin (Carlin Masterson) *actress*
Goldberg, Whoopi (Caryn Elaine Johnson) *actress, comedienne*
Gonzalez, Mandy *actress*
Goodacre, Jill *model*
Goodman, Erika *dancer, actress*
Gordon, Lisa M. *music educator*
Gordon, Marjorie *lyric-coloratura soprano, music educator, opera producer*
Gouker, Jane Ann *music educator*
Grafton, Beth P. *music educator*
Gransden, Charissa Sharron *music educator*
Grant, Lee (Lyova Haskell Rosenthal) *actress, television and film director*
Graves, Lorraine Elizabeth *dancer, educator, coach*
Gray, Pamela *screenwriter, educator*
Greenberg, Bonnie Lynn *music industry executive*
Greer, Carolyn Arlene *music educator, elementary school educator*
Gregory, Peggy J. *music educator*
Griffith, Melanie *actress*
Griffiths, Rachel *actress*
Griggs, Celia Josephine *music educator*
Gruen, Margaret *actress*
Gugler, Mary Dugan *composer, music educator*
Guhl, Gabrielle V. *music educator*
Gump, Abigail Michelle *music educator*
Guy, Jasmine *actress*
Guyett, Anne Elgar *performing arts educator*
Haeberle, Rosamond Pauline *retired music educator*
Haldey, Olga *music educator*
Haley, Shirley Jean *piano educator, photographer*
Hall, Carol Ann *music educator*
Hall, Linda Kaye *music educator*
Halleck, Donna P. *piano educator*
Haney, Marlene Carol *music educator*
Hanover, Donna Ann (Donna Ann Kofnovec) *radio personality, actress, journalist*
Hans, Paula *television producer*
Hansen, Jeanne *music educator*
Hardwicke, Catherine Helen *film director, set designer*
Harold, Constance Cammille *theater educator, artist*
Harple, Erin H. *music educator*
Harriel, Marcy *actress*
Harris, Harriet *actress*
Harris, Lenna Rae *music educator*
Harris, Lucille Sawyer *retired music educator, musician, volunteer*
Hart, Cherie Ann *music educator*
Hart, Kitty Carlisle *performing arts association administrator*
Harvie, Jessica Granger *performing company executive*
Hasenjager, Tanya *music educator*
Hathorne, Gayle Gene *musician, family historian*
Haulenbeek, Andrea B. *music educator, farmer*
Hauser, Anne Lynn *music educator, director*
Hawkins, Alia Elaine *dancer, small business owner*
Hayes, Cynthia Ann *music educator*
Hayes, Patricia Thornton *music educator, retired director*
Head, Lori J. *performing arts educator*
Heche, Anne (Anne Celeste Heche) *actress*
Heinz, Lee *actress, educator*
Helgenberger, Marg *actress*
Henneberger, Judith Nolen *retired music educator*
Hergo, Jane Antoinette *music educator, composer*
Herold, Cassandra Ann *music educator*
Herson, Arlene *television producer, journalist, television personality, radio commentator*
Hertel, Suzanne Marie *musician*
Hess, Carol *music educator*
Heuer, Catherine Ann *music educator*
Higgins, Karen *television producer*
Hill, Laura Kerr *conductor, director, music educator*
Hill, Lauryn *vocalist, actress*
Hill, Valerie Komkov *dance educator, artist*
Hilton, Jean Bull *musician*
Hilton, Paris *actress*
Hines, Cheryl *actress*
Hirshtal, Edith *retired concert pianist, educator, chamber musician*
Hiscavich, Michelle *music educator, consultant*
Hislop, Kare Elizabeth *music director, educator*
Hodges, Ann *retired television editor, columnist*
Hodges, Ann *actress, singer, dancer*
Hoffman, Adria R. *music educator*
Hoffman, Marian Ruth *singer, voice educator*
Hogue, Sharon Lea *music educator*
Holland, Beth *actress*
Holland, Ellen C. *music educator*
Hollenberg, Julia G. *music educator*
Hollingsworth, Alison Berkeley *ballet dancer, educator*
Holloway, Judy Marie *music educator, minister*
Holm, Celeste *actress*
Holmes-Davis, Tina *music educator*
Holsinger, Adena Seguine *music educator, community volunteer*
Holton, Lesli Belflower *music educator*
Hood, Patricia R. *music educator*
Hooper, Karen J. *music educator*
Hopkins, Cynthia *composer*
Horne, Marjorie *production stage manager, event consultant*
Horner, Judith Anne *music educator*
Horsman, Lenore Lynde (Eleanora Lynde) *voice educator, soprano, actress*
Horton, Deborah Jane *performing arts educator*
Hosman, Sharon Lee *retired music educator*
Houff, Bethany Dianne *music educator, conductor*
Houghton, Katharine *actress*
Houston, Whitney *vocalist, recording artist*
Hsu, Apo (Ching Hsin Hsu) *conductor*
Hsu-Li, Magdalen *singer, poet, painter*
Hubbard, Elizabeth *actress*
Hubbs, Violet Elizabeth Shamblin *retired filmmaker, retired photographer*
Hudson, Kate *actress*
Huffman, Cady (Catherine Elizabeth Huffman) *actress*
Hughes, Michaela Kelly *actress*
Hulstein, Mary Kathleen *music educator*
Hundley, Carol Marie Beckquist *music educator*
Huning, Devon Gray *actress, audiologist, dancer, photographer*
Hunter, Frances Ellen Croft *music educator*
Hunter, Holly *actress*
Huntley-Wright, Joan Augusta (Joan Augusta Huntley) *musician*
Hutchison, Barbara Bailey *singer, songwriter*
Hutton, Lauren (Mary Laurence Hutton) *model, actress*
Iannucci, Marilyn Butler *music educator*
Ibarra, Avelina C. *music educator*
Iman, (Iman Abudulmajid) *model*
Indenbaum, Dorothy *musician, researcher*
Inglesi, Noreen Mary *music educator, poet, composer*
Innes, Laura *actress*
Intilli, Sharon Marie *television director, small business owner*
Irving, Amy *actress*
Isbin, Sharon *classical guitarist, guitar educator*
Ivey, Dana Robins *actress*
Ivey, Judith *actress*
Jackson, Kate *actress*
Jackson, Katie J. *dancer, educator*
Jackson, Victoria Lynn *actress, comedienne*
Jacobs, Annette M. *music educator*
Jamelli, Miriam H. *music educator, counseling administrator*
Janney, Allison *actress*
Janney, Kay Print *retired performing arts educator, theater director*
Jelsma, Elizabeth Barbara *music educator*
Jensen, Nancy Daggett *music educator*
Jessup, Constance M. *music educator*
Jester, Nadine Anderson *music educator, elementary school educator*
Jewel, (Jewel Kilcher) *folk singer, songwriter*
Jirava, Carrie *music educator*
Joel, Katie (Katie Lee Joel, Katherine Lee) *television personality*
Johnson, Allyce A. *musician*
Johnson, Ruth Ann *music educator*
Johnson, Sandra Kay *music educator*
Johnson Holmes, SaBrina *music educator*
Jones, Amanda Blakey *actor*
Jones, Constance Coralie *retired music educator*
Jones, Shirley *actress, singer*
Joosten, Kathryn (Kathryn Joostyn) *actress*
Jordan, Crystal L. *music educator*
Jordan, Lisa Anne *dancer, educator*
Junker, Miriam M. *music educator*
Kaczmarek, Jane *actress*
Kalsow-Bernhard, Kathryn Marie *retired music educator*
Kane, Carol *actress*
Kauffman, Jenn *band director*
Kauffman, Marta *producer, writer*
Kaupa, Caroline Marqurite *music educator*
Kavner, Julie *actress*
Kaye, Judy *actress*
Keim, Betty Lou *actress, literary consulant*
Kelley, Kathryn B. *actress*
Kennedy, Megan Catherine *music educator*
Kerzmann, Olivia Lindsay *music educator*
Kessler, Ann Michele *dance educator, costume designer*
Kilbane, Kathleen Ann *stage manager*
Kilcher, Q'Orianka (Q'orianka Waira Qoiana Kilcher) *actress, singer, dancer*
King, Lindsay Brawner *music educator*
King, Regina *actress*
Kirchner, Lisa Beth *actress, vocalist*
Kirchoff, Molly *music educator*
Kirk, Deborah *piano educator*
Kirkpatrick, Edith Killgore *music educator, volunteer*
Kiser, Ruth Marguerite *music educator*
Kitt, Eartha Mae *actress, singer*
Kling, Jennifer Rae *music educator*
Klutts, Rhonda Asbury *music educator*
Knieser, Catherine *music educator*
Knight, Shirley *actress*
Knightley, Keira *actress*
Knowles, Marilyn Rae *ballet company administrator*
Koehler, Charity Marie *music educator*
Koerber, Dolores Jean *music educator, musician*
Kohn, Margaret Sherman *music educator, pianist*
Kornhaber, Donna Marie *theater educator*
Kostic, Dina *musician, music educator*
Kott, Tama I. *music educator*
Kraus, Lisa Marie Wasko *music educator, composer, musician*
Krell, Rebecca Dawn *music educator*
Kriegsman, Sali Ann *performing arts executive, consultant, writer*
Kudrow, Lisa (Lisa Marie Diane Kudrow) *actress*
Kupelian, Louise Paulson *musician, educator*
Kuriansky, Judy *television personality, radio personality, reporter, clinical psychologist, writer, educator*
Kurtz, Swoosie *actress*
Kuznetsova, Ekaterina G. *theater educator, dancer*
Labbe-Webb, Elizabeth Geralyn *performing company executive*
Ladd, Diane *actress*
LaMorte, Joyce E. *music educator*
Lange, Jessica Phyllis *actress*
Lange, Mary Christine *music educator*
Langel, Teresa Lynn *music educator*
LaParle, Paulette Gagnon *music educator*
Larson, Joan Isbell *musician, educator*
LaRue, Eva Marie *actress*
Lauper, Cyndi *musician*
Lavery, Elizabeth J. *music educator*
Lawrence, Sharon *actress*
Leachman, Cloris *actress*
Leahy, Jeannette (Jeannette Oliver Leahy Tinen Kaehler) *actress*
Learned, Michael *actress*
Leavel, Beth *actress*
Lee, Anne *music educator*
Lee, Eunice *music educator*
Lee, Gwendolin Kuei *retired ballet educator*
Lemke, Carol Ann *music educator, pianist, accountant*
Leoni, Tea (Elizabeth Tea Pantaleoni) *actress*
Levitas, Miriam C. Strickman *documentary filmmaker*
Lewin, Nancy S. *actress*
Lewis-Griffith, Dorothy Ellen *music educator, pianist*
Leybourn, Carol *musician, educator*
Light, Judith Ellen *actress*
Lindeman, Carolynn Anderson *music educator*
Lindley, Jolie Beth *choreographer, educator, actress*
Lindsey, Roberta Lewise *music researcher, historian*
Little, Jennifer *performing arts educator, director, actress*
Liu, Margaret C. *music educator*
Lockhart, Julie A. *actor, consultant*
Locklear, Heather *actress*
Lockney, Julianna Colleen *music educator*
Loeb, Debora Denise *music educator, vocalist, conductor*
Loikkanen, Pirjo Tuulikki *music educator*
Lombardi, Mary Luciana *musician, historian*
Lonchyna-Lisowsky, Maria *music educator*
Lopez, Jennifer *actress, singer, dancer*
Lopez, Soledad *actress*
Loring, Gloria Jean *vocalist*
Love, Courtney *singer, actress*
Loveless, Patty (Patty Ramey) *country music singer*
Lozito, Lisa Carol *music educator, church musician*
Luckey, Norma Jean *music educator*
Luebbe-Kemen, Kathy *music educator*
Lum, Viola Doris *music educator, personal financial analyst*
Luttrell, Georgia Bena *musician*
MacDowell, Andie (Rose Anderson MacDowell) *actress*
Mackenzie, Sue *music educator, theater director*
Macpherson, Elle *model*
Madonna, (Madonna Louise Veronica Ciccone) *singer, actress, producer*
Madsen, Virginia *actress*
Maffia, Roma *actress*
Malberg, Melissa Dawn *music educator, dancer*
Mallory, Joan Matey *music educator, composer*
Malm, Mia *actress*
Malouf, Pamela Bonnie *film editor, video editor*
Mannes, Elena Sabin *film and television producer, television director*
Marceau, Yvonne *ballroom dancer, educator*
Marco, Patricia Louise *music educator*
Margules, Cecelia *composer, poet*
Mari, Dawn *composer, artist*
Mark, Judi *actress, choreographer*
Marrolli, Karen Lyn *conductor*
Marsee, Susanne Irene *vocalist*
Marte-Bautista, Helen I. *retired performing arts educator*
Marth, Mary Ellen (Kim Martin) *entertainer*
Martin, Andrea Louise *actress, comedienne, writer*
Martyn, Evi *music educator, musician*
Mason, Marsha *actress, theater director, writer*
Mastrian Bell, Samantha *music educator, vocalist*
Matlin, Marlee *actress*
Matthews, Karen Sue *music educator*
May, Elaine *actress, film director, theater director*
Mayer, Anne Brestel *music educator*
Maynard, Natalie Ryshna *pianist, educator*
McCann, Elizabeth Ireland *theater producer, television producer, motion picture producer*
McCardel, Connie Shirley *music educator*
McCarthy, Kelli P. *music educator*
McCarthy, Mary Elizabeth (Beth) Constance *conductor, music educator*
McCarthy, Nobu *actress, performing company executive, educator*
McClain, Sylvia Nancy (Nancy Jo Grimm) *voice educator, vocalist*
McClanahan, Rue (Eddi-Rue McClanahan) *actress*
McClellan, LeAnne *music educator*
McClure, Erin E. *music educator*
McCoy, Mary Nell *music educator*
McDormand, Frances *actress*
McEntire, Reba Nell *musician, actress*
McGinnis, Susan Pauliene *music teacher*
McGowan, Rose *actress*
McGuinness, Nanette Michele Cooper *singer, voice educator, writer, translator*
McKinney, Cara Lynn *music educator*
McLaughlin, Goldie Carter *music educator*
McLean, Julianne Drew *concert pianist, educator*
Meara, Anne *actress, playwright, writer*
Medina-Hamilton, Ginny Evelyn *music educator*
Melton, Stephanie Ann *music educator*
Mendelsohn, Carol S. *television producer*
Menzel, Idina *actress, singer*
Meyer, Paula Jean *music educator*
Meyerink, Victoria Paige *film producer, actress*
Mezacapa, Edna S. *music educator, elementary school educator*
Michels, Mary Pat *music educator*
Midler, Bette *singer, entertainer, actress*
Milano, Alyssa *actress*
Mindt, Michele L.M. *music educator*
Ming-Na, *actress*
Mingus, Lois Kagan *actor, dancer, singer, choreographer, playwright*
Moffatt, Joyce Anne *performing company executive*
Moffatt, Katy (Katherine Louella Moffatt) *musician, lyricist, vocalist*
Mongiello, Christine *music educator*
Monteith, Tracy R. *music educator, lay worker*
Montgomery, June C. *musician, composer*
Morelan, Paula Kay *choreographer*
Morgan, Linda Gail *theater producer*
Morgan, Nicole Rae *theater director, educator*
Morissette, Alanis Nadine *singer*
Morris, Lissa Camille *music educator*
Morris, Martha Marnel *music educator*
Morrison, Shelley *actress*
Moseley, Julia W. *music educator, preservationist*
Moskovitz, Elisa McMillan *music educator, musician*
Moslak, Judith *retired music educator*
Mouledous, Pierrette Marie *music educator*
Moynahan, Karen Peeler *performing arts association administrator*
Mueller, Paula Deutsch *retired music educator*
Murphy, Brittany *actress*
Murray, Carla Mary *sound effects artist, artist*
Myers, Angela Michelle *music educator, department chairman*
Myers, Margaret Jane (Dee Dee Myers) *television personality, editor*
Nagra, Parminder *actress*
Nash, Linda Kay *music educator*
Neary, Patricia Elinor *ballet director*
Neblett, Carol *soprano*
Nelligan, Kate (Patricia Colleen Nelligan) *actress*
Nelson, Deborah D. *music educator*
Nelson, Debra J. *dancer, educator, choreographer*
Ness, Bernice Hagie *retired music educator*
Neu, Jennifer Elizabeth *music educator*
Neuerburg-Denzer, Ursula *theater director, educator, actress*
Neumann, Irma Wanda *musician, educator*
Neuwirth, Bebe (Beatrice Neuwirth) *dancer, actress*
Neville, Phoebe *choreographer, dancer, educator*
Nevin, Laura Jean *music educator*
Nevins, Sheila *television producer*
Newell, Ann Marie *music educator*
Nichols, Cherie L. *composer*
Nicks, Stevie (Stephanie Lynn Nicks) *singer, songwriter*
Niguidula, Kathleen Ann *music educator, musician*
Nipper, Christina Joy *music educator*
Nixon, Marni *singer*
Nobert, Frances *music educator*
Noeldner-Weniger, Lisa Ann *music educator*
Noll, Jeanne C. *retired music educator*
Northup, Marie L. *music educator*
Nye, Jeni Hiatt *music educator*
O'Boyle, Maureen *television show host*
O'Brien, Orin Ynez *musician, educator*
Ocheskey, Elizabeth R. Bloom *theater director, educator*
O'Connor, Catherine Marie *music educator*
O'Donnell, Elizabeth D. *music educator*
O'Donnell, Rosie *television personality, actress, comedienne*
Oh, Sandra *actress*
O'Hara, Maureen (Maureen FitzSimons) *actress*
Okonedo, Sophie *actress*
Okouchi, Carla Ho'noa Higdon *music educator*
Olesen, Carolyn McDonald *dance educator, choreographer*
Olin, Lena Maria Jonna *actress*
Ormai-Buza, Ildiko *soprano, composer, music educator*
Ormond, Julia *actress*
O'Rork, Aimée *music educator, composer*
O'Shea, Anna Belle Marie *music educator, liturgy administrator*
Osmond, Marie *singer*
Ossello, Kristie *music educator*
Ott, Sharon *artistic director*
Owens, Birdie Murphy *retired music educator*
Paddock, Sandra Constance *music educator*
Palmer, Rose Ann *television producer, writer, educator*
Papa, Phyllis Maryann *performing company executive, dancer, choreographer, educator*
Paradis-Kent, M. Robin *music educator*
Parker, Amy Lee *music educator*
Parkinson, Dian *actress*
Paskman, Andrea *dance specialist*
Paysen, Bonnie B. *music educator, musician*
Pearce, Serena Ray *performing arts educator, music director*
Pederson, Linda L. *music educator*
Perez, Rosie *actress*

Perkowski, Jennifer *music educator*
Perniciaro, Alissa A. *dancer, educator*
Perry-Camp, Jane *music educator, pianist*
Peters, Jennifer R. *music educator*
Petersen, Shannyn Rae *music educator*
Peterson, Anne Elizabeth Wallace *music educator, composer*
Peterson, Rosetta Hicks *retired music educator*
Pfeiffer, Michelle *actress*
Phillips, Winifred Patricia *radio producer, composer*
Pierce, Ponchitta Ann *TV host, television producer, journalist, writer, consultant*
Pinkett-Smith, Jada *actress*
Pinkins, Tonya *actress*
Platek, Jennifer Bethany *voice educator*
Pleshette, Suzanne *actress*
Plimpton, Peggy Lucas *trustee*
Plummer, Amanda *actress*
Poe, Cheryl Toni *music educator*
Pohlmann, Evelyn Gawley *music educator, consultant*
Poorman, Christine K. *television producer*
Poppen, Marcella May *music educator*
Powell, Ruth Aregood *music educator*
Preston, Kelly *actress*
Preysz, Sandra *music educator*
Pribble, Ghada Khoury *music educator, singer*
Price, Betty Jeanne *chimes musician*
Price, Ruthe Payenson Geier *actress, writer, educator*
Prince, Anna Lou *composer, music publisher, construction executive*
Prince, Ginger Lee *actress, choreographer, educator*
Principal, Victoria (Victoria Ree Principale) *actress, film producer, writer*
Procter, Carol Ann *retired musician*
Pruzan, Irene *musician, educator, public relations executive, art association administrator*
Puleo, Jean Anne *music educator, musician*
Puster, Rebecca Lynn *music educator, director*
Quist, Jeanette Fitzgerald *television production educator, choreographer*
Rainey, Pamela Leigh *dance educator*
Raitt, Bonnie Lynn *singer, musician*
Ramirez, Leilani *music educator*
Rander, JoAnn Corpaci *musician, educator*
Ransom, Tasha Elana *news production assistant, producer*
Raoufi, Azadeh *music educator*
Raposo, Laura I. *music educator*
Rashad, Phylicia *actress, singer, dancer*
Ray, Debra Ann *music educator*
Redgrave, Vanessa *actress*
Reed, Georgia May *music educator*
Reed, Janel M. *music educator*
Reed, Mary Carolyn Camblin *retired music educator, retired county official*
Reed, Pamela *actress*
Reese, Katherine Rose *music educator*
Reeves, Hallie Lawson *retired music educator, retired chaplain*
Regan, Susan Wright *dance educator, small business owner, choreographer*
Reid, Susan L. *conductor*
Reid, Tara *actress*
Reidy, Grace V. *retired music educator*
Reno Norton, Tabitha Dawn *music educator*
Resch, Rita Marie *retired music educator*
Revak, Claudia Anne *music educator*
Reyes, Judy *actress*
Rice, Cassandrea Rae *music educator*
Richard, Candace L. *music educator*
Richardson, Joely *actress*
Richardson, Natasha Jane *actress*
Riche, Wendy *television producer*
Rifman, Eileen *music educator*
Riley, Rebecca Michelle *music educator*
Rino, Barbara Elizabeth *music educator, musician*
Ritchie, Anna Spears *music educator*
Roberts, Doris *actress*
Robinson, Devette Lorraine *music educator*
Robinson, Karen L. *music educator*
Robison, June LeAnne *music educator*
Rodriguez, Gail Lee *music educator*
Rodriguez, Michelle (Mayte Michelle Rodriguez) *actress*
Roenicke, Norma Jean *music educator, pianist, organist, small business owner*
Rogers, Kaaren Lea *music educator*
Rolland, Clara *pianist, educator*
Rollins, Doris Callela *music educator, pianist, performing accompanist*
Roost, Alisa *theater educator*
Rose, Jolene Renee *music educator*
Rosner, Sharon Ellen *actress, speech pathology/audiology services professional*
Rothaar, Susanne Elisabeth *musician, educator*
Rowe, Julie *theater educator, actress*
Rowlands, Gena *actress*
Ruder, Tia L. *music educator*
Rudner, Sara *dancer*
Rudolph, Maya *actress, comedienne*
Ruehl, Mercedes *actress*
Rule, Molly McCorkle *music educator*
Runolfson, Anne *soprano, vocal educator*
Rush, Deborah *actress*
Russell, Elise Beckett *piano educator*
Russo, Gina Marie *music educator*
Rutter, Marie E. *music educator*
Ruviella-Knorr, Jeanne L. *music educator, consultant, clinician*
Ryan, Jeanne Vanyo *music educator*
Sade, (Helen Folasade Adu) *singer, lyricist*
Saint, Eva Marie *actress*
Sanchez, Marta *music educator*
San Miguel, Lolita *artistic director*
Sapp, Gina Leann *music educator*
Sarry, Christine *ballerina*
Sater, Beverly *music educator*
Scarchuk, Lynn Nettleton *music educator*
Scarwid, Diana Elizabeth *actress*
Scego, Megan Elaine *music educator*
Scharber, Susan Elizabeth *music educator, director*
Schardine, Heidi Fae *choral educator*
Scheps, Lynn Ruth *dancer, educator*
Schiffer, Claudia *model*
Schmidt, Hildred Doris *music educator*
Schoeniger, Jane *music educator*
Schoonmaker Powell, Thelma *film editor*
Schubert, Barbara Schuele *retired performing arts association administrator*
Schucker, Veronica Jean *music educator*
Schudson, Ruth *actress*
Schultz, Marian Starr *musician, educator*
Schuur, Diane Joan *vocalist*
Sciorra, Annabella *actress*
Scott, Sherie René *actress*
Scott, Sue A. *music educator*
Scrivner, B(arbara) E. *piano educator*
Seacat, Marian Louise *music educator*
Seneshen, Susan *music educator*
Shane, Rita *opera singer, educator*
Shanks, Ann Zane *filmmaker, film producer, director, photographer, writer*
Sharp, Angela Christine *dance educator*
Shatin, Judith *composer, educator*
Sheindlin, Judith (Judge Judy) *television personality, judge*
Sheldon, Beth Ann *music educator*
Shepherd, Cybill Lynne *actress, singer*
Sherfinski, Kristina Leigh *performing arts educator*
Shields, Brooke Christa Camille *actress, model*
Shire, Talia Rose (Talia Rose Coppola) *actress*
Short, Sharon Holefelder *music educator*
Shull, Claire *documentary film producer, casting director*
Shwartz, Sima M. *music educator*
Sigler, Jamie-Lynn *actress*
Sikes, Cynthia Lee *actress, children's advocate, singer*
Silverstone, Alicia *actress*
Simmons, Deidre Warner *retired performing company executive, arts consultant*
Simon, Carly *singer, composer, author*
Simpson, Alfreda Gail *music educator*
Simpson, Ashlee Nicole *vocalist, actress*
Sisemore, Claudia *educational films and videos producer, director*
Skelton, Kristen Joy *music educator*
Skilling, Marie L. *music educator*
Skylar, Alayne *television producer, writer, educator, talent scout, agent*
Sloan, Carolyn *music educator, composer, lyricist*
Smart, Robin McDaniel *music educator*
Smith, Anna Nicole (Vickie Lynn Hogan) *television personality, model*
Smith, Betty Pauline *television producer*
Smith, Charlotte Reed *retired music educator*
Smith, Cheryl Diane *music educator*
Smith, Doris Irene *music educator*
Smith, Kathryn J. *music educator, conductor*
Smith, Lois Arlene *actress, writer*
Smith, Nina Marie *music educator*
Smith, Susan K. *musician, educator*
Smith, Yeardley *actress*
Snyder, Susan R. *music educator*
Soltes, Joann Margaret *retired music educator, realtor*
Somers, Suzanne Marie *actress, writer, singer*
Sonnemaker, Susan S. *music educator*
Sorrell, Rozlyn *singer, actress, educator, theater director*
Souther, Lisa *music educator*
Spanier, Deanne A. *music educator*
Spillman, Marjorie Rose *theater producer, dancer*
Sproul, Sarah Lee *conductor, musician, educator*
Staber, Judy White *retired performing arts association administrator, writer, director*
Stakoe, Lindsey Ann *actor, educator*
Stanley, Margaret King *performing arts association administrator*
Stanley, Martha Barbee *music educator*
Stearns, Marilyn Tarpy *music educator*
Stefani, Gwen Renee *singer*
Stein, Julie Esther *piano instructor*
Stephens, Tracy Lee *music educator*
Stephenson-Woolwine, Penny G. *music educator*
Sternhagen, Frances *actress*
Stevens, Christina Lea *film director, writer, film producer*
Stevenson, Cynthia *actress*
Stewart, Marsha Beach *performing arts educator*
Sticht, Miranda *music educator*
Stoddard, Erin *actress, artist*
Stone, Joss (Joscelyn Eve Stoker) *singer*
Stoneham, Sandra Lee *retired music educator*
Stoytcheva, Lilia Stefanova *concert pianist, educator*
Streck, Melissa Leigh *music educator*
Strevig, Janice Lee *music educator*
Stringfield, Sherry *actress*
Strom, Doris Marie *music educator*
Studer, Kathy Lynn *music educator*
Stutzman, Misty Dawn *music educator*
Summers, Cathleen *film producer*
Sutton, Dolores *actress, writer*
Sutton, Nancy Thurmond *music educator*
Swallum, Maryann *musician, educator*
Swing, Marce *film producer, director, writer*
Syjud, Laura Beth *music educator*
Synnestvedt, Kirstin *musician, educator*
Tabor, Linda J. *performing arts educator*
Tanner, Lynn *actress*
Tarbuck, Barbara Joan *actress*
Tarses, Jamie *television producer, former television network executive*
Tauber, Michele Ann *actress*
Taylor, Holly Ann *music educator*
Taymor, Julie *theater, film and opera director and designer*
Terry, Rachel Marie *music educator*
Tharp, Twyla *dancer*
Thomas, Audrey Corbin *music educator*
Thomas, Betty *director, actress*
Thomas, Lise-Marie *actress*
Thompson, Lea *actress*
Thorne, Rebecca Claire *ballet director, choreographer*
Ticotin, Rachel *actress*
Tillman, Mercia V. *musician*
Tillotson, Mary *cable television host*
Tingler, Marlene Johannsen *music educator, insurance agent*
Tipton, Melanie Carol *music educator*
Todd, Suzanne Marie *film producer*
Tolbert, Cornelia Emma *music educator*
Towne, Monica Noelle *music educator*
Trainor, Sheena Marie *music educator*
Treiber, Susan *music educator*
Trobaugh, Tara Michelle *music educator*
Troiano, Marie *music educator*
Troll, Kitty *actress, writer*
Trudel, Janice Cuevas *music educator*
Tubb, Betty Freeze *music educator*
Tuckness, Amber Victoria *music educator*
Tullo, Barbara Ann *performing company executive*
Turner, Camilla Ann *music educator*
Turner, Tina (Anna Mae Bullock) *singer*
Turturro, Aida *actress*
Tyson, Cicely *actress*
Uken, Marcile Rena *music educator*
Unitas Roos, Carolyn Ellen *music educator, voice instructor, classical singer*
Upbin, Shari *agent*
Vaccaro, Brenda *actress*
Van Camp, Diana J. *music educator*
Vani, Anita H. *music and voice educator*
Van Ness, Patricia Catheline *composer, violinist*
Vaughn, Pamela W. *music educator*
Vega, Suzanne *singer, songwriter*
Vendela, *model*
Villaire, Holly Hennen Hood *theater producer, director, actress, educator*
Voegtlin-Anderson, Mary Margaret *music educator, small business owner*
Vogt, Christy *music educator*
Von Brandenstein, Patrizia *production designer*
von Furstenberg, Betsy *actress, writer*
Vozheiko Wheaton, Lena *musician, educator*
Wagner, Melinda *musician, composer*
Wallace, Dee *actress*
Wallace-House, Mary Elaine *writer*
Wallis, Diana Lynn *artistic director*
Wallner, Amanda Ober *retired music educator*
Walsh, Diane *pianist*
Walsh, Juanita *theater educator, actress*
Warberg, Willetta *concert pianist, music educator*
Ward, Anne Starr Minton *musician, educator*
Warwick, Dionne *singer*
Washburn, Nan *conductor*
Washington, Kerry *actor*
Wasnak, Diane Marie *comedian*
Waters, Sylvia *dance company artistic director*
Watson, Vera K. *music educator, pianist*
Webb, Lucy Jane *actress, film producer, consultant*
Weber, Joan Geiger *music educator*
Weeks, Skyla Gay *music educator*
Weiner-Heuschkel, Sydell *theater educator*
Welch, Raquel *actress*
Wells, Kitty (Ellen Muriel Deason) *musician*
Wen, Gwen GuoYao *music educator*
Wendelin, Denise Kay *performing arts educator, artist*
Wesoloski, Deborah J. *music educator*
West, Karen Marie *musician, educator*
West, Nettie J.R. *music educator*
Wetzel, Angela Denise *music educator*
White, Sonya Renee *music educator*
Whitehead, Jennifer Sue *choreographer*
Whitfield, Lynn *actress*
Wiese, Denise Kay *music educator*
Wiest, Dianne *actress*
Wilder, Janet Mary *performing company executive*
Wilhelm, Monica L. *music educator*
Williams, Dawn Monique *theater director, educator*
Williams, Hazelyn Matthis *dancer, educator*
Williams, Jeanne Elizabeth *music educator*
Williams, JoBeth *actress*
Williams, Lucinda *country musician*
Willis, Ruth *freelance/self-employed theater director, actress*
Wilson, Mollie *retired music educator*
Wilson, Rita *actress*
Wimberly, Linda Roberts *music educator, artist*
Winokur, Marissa Jaret *actress*
Winter, Kathryn *music educator, writer*
Wise, Patricia *opera singer, educator*
Witt, Alicia *actress*
Wolf, Christine Strelow *piano teacher*
Wolf, Muriel Hebert *soprano, educator, performing company executive*
Wolff, Eleanor Blunk *actress*
Wood, Evan Rachel *actress*
Wood, Vivian Poates *mezzo soprano, educator*
Woods, Eleanor C. *music educator*
Wooten, Carol G. *music educator, minister*
Woronov, Mary Peter *actress*
Wright, Belinda Leigh *music educator*
Wright, Gladys Stone *music educator, writer, composer*
Wright, Lori Dunkle *musician, educator*
Wynn, Mary Beth *music educator*
Yaes, Joyce *musician, artist, educator*
Yao, Frances *music educator, small business owner*
Yearwood, Trisha *country music singer, songwriter*
Young, Alison *music educator*
Younker, Kathleen Teuber *pianist, music educator*
Yuriko, (Yuriko Kikuchi) *dancer, choreographer*
Zappa, Gail *record producer*
Zentz, Laurie Funderburk *music educator*
Zeta-Jones, Catherine *actress*
Ziemba, Karen *actress*
Zigler, Melissa May *music educator*
Zimmerman, Phyllis Elaine *music educator, composer, director*

ARTS: VISUAL

UNITED STATES

ALABAMA

Alexander City
Towery, Sarah Carlisle *artist, retired educator*

Birmingham
Hopkins, Martha Ann *sculptor*
Keller, Armor *artist, arts advocate*
Kent, Lysbeth Hawkins *artist*
Kluge, Janice *art educator*
Maddox, Martha Lacey Gardner *artist*

Florence
Knight, Karen Anne McGee *artist, educator, educational research administrator*
Schulman, Jean Ellen *artist, retired educator*

Hartselle
Coon, Elizabeth M. *artist*

Huntsville
Simpson, Debra Brashear *artist*

Madison
Johnson, Kathy Virginia Lockhart *art educator*

Mobile
Clausell, Deborah Deloris *artist*
Patten Starr, Barbara Sue Brummett *art educator, textile designer*
Thompson, Nancy *art director*

Montgomery
York, Karen Sue *artist, historian*

Theodore
LeGros, Christy Callaghan *art educator*

Thomasville
Whitmire, Marilyn Therese *art educator*

Tuskegee
Thomas, Elaine Freeman *artist, educator*

ALASKA

Anchorage
Pendleton, Cynthia M. *art educator, artist*
Shadrach, Jean Hawkins (Martha Shadrach) *artist*

Cordova
Bugbee-Jackson, Joan *sculptor, educator*

Eielson Afb
Stoutenberg, Herminia Lilia *art educator*

Ketchikan
Kennedy, Peggy Boogaard *artist, writer*

Palmer
Hendrix, Dianne Roberson *artist, writer*

ARIZONA

Chino Valley
Casey, Bonnie Mae *artist, educator*

Douglas
Murphy, Cathy Emily *photographer, educator, journalist*

Glendale
Carstens, Cyndy Louise *artist*

Paradise Valley
Maxey, Diane Meadows *artist*
McCall, Louise Harrup *artist*

Payson
Salomon, Marilyn *artist*

Peoria
Willard, Garcia Lou *artist*

Phoenix
Laymon, Cynthia J. *artist, educator*
McGuire, Maureen A. *artist*
Stone, Hazel Anne Decker *artist*

Prescott Valley
Decil, Stella Walters (Del Decil) *artist*

Queen Creek
Loss, Lynne Franklin *artist, volunteer*

Scottsdale
Vanier, Jerre Lynn *art director*
Yares, Riva *art dealer, writer, publishing executive*

Sedona
Darrow, Jane *artist*

Sun Lakes
Hall, Barbara Louise *interior designer, artist*

Tempe
Essig, Linda *lighting designer, director*
Golden, Libby *artist*
Meissinger, Ellen Murray *artist, educator*

Tucson
Denzler, Nancy J. *artist*
Koerber, Erica *photographer*

ARKANSAS

Berryville
Brown, Frances Louise (Grandma Fran) *artist, art gallery director*

El Dorado
Cameron-Godsey, Melinda A. Brantley *artist*

Fayetteville
Musgnug, Kristin A. *art educator, artist*

Huntsville
Musick, Pat *artist*

Jonesboro
Tims, Jane Moore *art educator*

Little Rock
Hodges, Jennefer Rae *sculptor*

Van Nuys
Cook, Jenik Esterm (Jenik Esterm Cook Simonian) *artist, educator*
Vasilyeva, Anna *artist, writer*

Venice
Alf, Martha Joanne *artist*
Smith, Barbara T. *artist, educator*

Victorville
Polley-Shellcroft, Theresa Diane *art educator*

Vista
Tadeo, Elvia *artist*

Walnut Creek
Alexandra, Allison Melissa *artist, writer, educator*
Reimann, Arline Lynn *artist*

West Hills
Abdo, Lynda Lee *art director*
Duzy, Merrilyn Jeanne *artist, educator*

Westlake Village
Weiss, Barbara G. *artist*

Wilton
Abraham, Bondi Corinne *artist*

COLORADO

Arvada
Halley, Diane Esther *artist*
Moorhead, Jennifer Theresa *art educator*

Aurora
D'Amico, Sandra Hathaway *art educator*

Boulder
Bergum, Lauren Jean *art educator*
Charteris, Frances A. *art educator, artist*
Evans, Claire (Mary Evans) *painter, educator*
Schleiner, Anne-Marie *computer graphics designer*
Verdill, Elaine Denise *artisan*

Colorado Springs
Birtwistle, April Joy *layout artist*
Brierre, Micheline *artist*

Cortez
Kristin, Karen *artist*

Creede
Hague, Angela L. *artist, consultant, art gallery director*

Denver
Corathers, Lorna Joan *artist*
Eckels, Mary Elizabeth *artist*
Enright, Cynthia Lee *illustrator*
Kaplan, Sandra Lee *artist*
Rost, Christa VandeZande *graphics and product designer*
Shwayder, Elizabeth Yanish *sculptor*
Steigerwald-Clausen, Beverly *sculptor, educator*
White, Karen Jean *artist*

Dolores
Winterer-Schulz, Barbara Jean *graphics designer, writer*

Durango
Balas-Whitfield, Susan *artist*

Estes Park
Biehl, Julianne *art educator*

Fort Collins
Sullivan, Patrice M. *artist, educator*

Greeley
Ruyle, Lydia Miller *artist, writer, artist, educator*

Hotchkiss
Blackstock, Virginia Harriett *artist*

Laporte
iba, Shirley *artist*

Littleton
Derjue, Rita *artist, educator*
Poduska, T. F. *artist*

Loveland
Bierbaum, Janith Marie *artist*

CONNECTICUT

Avon
Levitz, I. S. *artist, educator, curator*

Branford
Abels, Gusta J. *artist, art and art history educator*

Chester
Zwart-Ludeman, Theresa *graphics designer, artist*

East Haven
Gardner, Joan Andrews *artist educator*

Gaylordsville
Dunn, Virginia *artist*

Glastonbury
Ridgeway, Teresa Drivdahl *weaver, educator*

Greenwich
DeNigris, Carole Dell Cato *artist*

Hartford
Carey, Ellen *artist*
Johnson, Bonnie *art educator*

Huntington
Richter, Elizabeth Lee *artist*

Kensington
Manning, Brenda Argosy *painter*

Litchfield
Mullins, Patty *artist*

Madison
Cappetta, Anna Maria *art educator*

Naugatuck
Chrzanowski, Rose-Ann Cannizzo *art educator*
Mannweiler, Mary-Elizabeth *painter*

New Haven
Clapp, Megan Elizabeth *art educator*
de Bretteville, Sheila Levrant *artist, art educator*
Lindroth, Linda (Linda Hammer) *artist, writer, curator*

New London
Wakeman, Martha Jane *artist, educator*

Norwalk
Babcock, Catherine Evans *artist, educator*

Old Lyme
Osborne, Judith Barbour *artist*

Ridgefield
Benton, Suzanne *sculptor, mask ritualist, printmaker, painter*

Sherman
Goodspeed, Barbara *artist*

Stamford
Babson, Jane Frances *artist, writer*
Berets, Eileen Tolkowsky *artist*

Stonington
Elliott, Inger McCabe *apparel designer, consultant, textiles executive*

Thomaston
Donohue, Diane Frances *artist*

Torrington
Bramble, Pamela Chace Leuba *artist, educator*

Wallingford
Lauttenbach, Carol *artist*

West Redding
Wesselmann, Janine Carol *artist*

Westport
Chernow, Ann Levy *artist, educator*
Reilly, Nancy (Anne Caulfield Reilly) *painter*
Siff, Marlene Ida *artist, designer*

Wilton
Holter, Patra Jo *artist, consultant*

DELAWARE

Dagsboro
Davis, Marica Nanci Ella Riggin *retired artist*
Hanna, Anne Marie *artist*

Greenville
Reynolds Cooch, Nancy D. (Mrs. Edward W. Cooch Jr.) *sculptor*

Hockessin
Harris, Anne Eldredge *artist, educator*

Lewes
Costigan, Constance Frances *artist, educator*

Millsboro
Price, Doris Coleen Davis *visual artist, printmaker*

New Castle
Keane, Marie Jeanette (Maria Keane) *art educator, artist*

Newark
Breslin, Wynn Boin *artist*

Wilmington
Bounds-Seemans, Pamella J. *artist*
Doyle, Nancy Hazlett *artist*

DISTRICT OF COLUMBIA

Washington
Bowman, Dorothy Louise *artist*
Brown, Pamela Wedd *artist*
Carroll, M(argaret) Lizbeth Carr *art educator, graphics designer, photographer*
Colton Skolnick, Judith A. *artist*
Espeut, Camille Cottrell *retired art educator*
Fall, Dorothy *artist, writer, art director, art association administrator*
Flood, Sandra Wasko *artist, educator*
Forrester, Patricia Tobacco *artist*
Giles, Patricia Cecelia Parker *retired art educator, graphic designer*
Gordon, Dorothy K. *silversmith, goldsmith*
Hogan, Felicity *artist*
Jecklin, Lois Underwood *art corporation executive, consultant*
Kapikian, Catherine Andrews *artist*
Mock-Morgan, Mavera Elizabeth *artist, art educator*
Polan, Annette Lewis *artist, educator*
Ravenal, Carol Bird Myers *artist*
Rose, Deedie Potter *arts patron*
Tacha, Athena *sculptor, artist, educator*
Wasko-Flood, Sandra Jean *artist, educator*

FLORIDA

Bal Harbour
Bernay, Betti *artist*

Boca Raton
Fineman, Geraldine Gottesman *artist*
Fishenfeld, Grace *artist, educator*
Price, Rita Fleischmann *artist, educator*
Vaccino, Alyce King *artist*

Bonita Springs
Elliott, Donna Louise *artist*
McNamara-Ringewald, Mary Ann Thérèse *artist, educator*

Clermont
Cox, Margaret Stewart *photographer*

Cocoa Beach
Herbstman, Loretta *sculptor, painter*

Coral Springs
Kroll, Lynne Francine *artist*

Dania Beach
Satin, Claire Jeanine *sculptor, artist*

Davie
Schwab, Judith *artist, educator, sculptor*

Daytona Beach
Dalia, Vesta Mayo *artist*

Deland
Carlin, Caty C. *artist, director*

Delray Beach
Gilfilen, Teri *artist*
Ross, Beatrice Brook *artist*
St. George, Elaine *art educator*

Edgewater
Schubert, Jeanne *artist*

Fort Myers
Hugill, Chloe *artist, foundation administrator*
Weiss, Susette Maré *technical and photographic consultant, mass communications and media relations specialist, investor*

Fort Pierce
Cassens, Susan Forget *artist*
Jefferson, Zanobia Bracy *art educator, artist*
Peterson, Barbara Owecke *artist, retired nurse, retired real estate agent*
Swenson, Ada Perez *artist*

Gainesville
Harley, Ruth *artist, educator*
Navab, Aphrodite Desiree *artist, educator, writer*
Wiggins-Rothwell, Jeanine Ellen *artist*

Gulf Stream
FitzSimons, Marjorie Kitchen *art consultant*

Hobe Sound
Mark, Marsha Yvonne Ismailoff *artistic director*

Hollywood
Sadowski, Carol Johnson *artist*

Homosassa
Frank, Elizabeth Ahls (Betsy Frank) *retired art educator*

Hudson
White-Myers, Barbara Jeanne *artist, retired educator*

Indialantic
Pavlakos, Ellen Tsatiri *sculptor*

Indian Harbor Beach
Traylor, Angelika *stained glass artist*

Jacksonville
Eden, F. Brown *artist*
Hoffman, Helen Bacon *artist*

Key Biscayne
de la Cruz, Rosa *art collector*

Key Largo
Kennedy, Mary Sussock *artist*

Kissimmee
McCann, Jean Friedrichs *artist, educator*

Lake Mary
Reagan, Bettye Jean *artist*

Lake Park
Heaton, Janet Nichols *artist, art gallery director*

Land O Lakes
O'Connell, Carmela Digristina *appraisal executive, consultant*

Lynn Haven
Sheesley, Mary Frank *art educator*

Marathon
Giffen, Lois Key *artist, psychotherapist*
Wolpe, Marcy Shear *artist, educator*

Melbourne
King, Virginia Shattuck *painter, retired school nurse, educator*

Miami
Brodsky, Beverly *artist*
Chambers, Elenora Strasel *artist*
Fleisher, Betty *artist, educator*
Kislak, Jean Hart *art director*
Pelton, Margaret Marie Miller *retired art educator, academic administrator, artist*
Pfeiffer, Mary Louise *artist, educator*
Rawlings, Annette *painter*
Steinbaum, Bernice *art dealer*

Micco
Christoph, Frances *painter*

Miramar
Cooke, Honore Guilbeau *artist, educator*

Mount Dora
Kirton, Jennifer Myers *artist*

Naples
Gifford, Nancy (Mumtaz) *artist, poet*
York, Tina *painter*

Nokomis
Novak, Joyce Keen *artist, secondary school educator*
Robinson, Mary Catherine *artist*

North Palm Beach
Kaplan, Muriel Sheerr *sculptor*

Palm Beach
Krois, Audrey *artist*
Whiteside, Patricia Lee *fine art antique and personal property appraiser*

Pensacola
Burke-Fanning, Madeleine *artist*
Larson, Barbara Jean *art history professor*
Maki, Hope Marie *art educator*

Plantation
Ballantyne, Maree Anne Canine *artist*

Pompano Beach
Perkins, Lois Elaine *retired art educator*

Ponte Vedra Beach
Scott, Marie Claudine *ceramic artist, writer*

Rockledge
Ollie, Pearl Lynn *artist, singer, lyricist*

Rotonda West
Broyles, Christine Anne *art educator*

Saint Augustine
Gutiérrez, Mary Carmen *artist*

Saint Petersburg
Bryant, Laura Militzer *artist*

Sanibel
Keogh, Mary Cudahy *artist*

Sarasota
DiPirro, Joni Marie *artist*
Gassman, Stephanie Lynne *artist*
Goodacre, Glenna *sculptor*
Graham, Linda Ohlson *artist*
Randall, Vicky *artist, educator, sculptor, small business owner*
Wendlandt, Dorothea Schnepf *artist, writer*
Williams-Wetenhall, Tanya Dawn *art appraiser, consultant*
Winterhalter, Dolores (Dee) August *art educator*

Satellite Beach
Osmundsen, Barbara Ann *sculptor*

Sebastian
Pieper, Patricia Rita *artist*

Tamarac
Baron-Malkin, Phyllis *artist, educator*

Tampa
Fosnaught, Patricia S. *art educator*
Hine, Betty Dixon *design consultant*
Schiefler, Karen Rosalie *artist, educator*
Sopher, Vicki Elaine *appraiser*

Tavares
Spencer, Linda B. *painter*

Temple Terrace
Kashdin, Gladys Shafran *painter, educator, volunteer*

Venice
Girman, Dee-Marie *artist, singer*

Vero Beach
Ferrell, Catherine K. *sculptor, painter*

West Palm Beach
Baker, Dina Gustin *artist*
Brody, Carol Z. *artist, educator*

Weston
Deleuze, Margarita *artist*
Napp, Gudrun F. *artist*
Piken, Michele Reneé (Penn Piken) *artist, photographer*

Zephyrhills
Anderson, Lisa D. *graphics designer, educator*

GEORGIA

Alpharetta
Crider, Melinda Gray *artist*
Sirlin, Deanna Louise *artist*

Athens
Smith, Susan Carlton *artist, illustrator*

Atlanta
Bawa, Avantika *artist, educator*
Fisher, Carlyn Feldman *artist, writer*
Goldsleger, Cheryl *artist, educator*
Grumet, Priscilla Hecht *fashion specialist, consultant, writer*
James, Rose Victoria *sculptor, poet*
Jennings, Denise Elaine *art educator*
Richards, Jacqueline *artist, curator*
Venzer, Dolores *artist*
Winslow, Anne Branan *artist*

Farmington
Hiltz-Scerbo, Leiza Ann *apparel designer, photographer*

Gorham
Bearce, Jeana Dale *artist, educator*
Marasco, Rose C. *artist, educator*

Rangeley
Ruprecht, Susan Elizabeth *art educator*

Rockland
Anne, Lois *artist, educator*

York
Haley, Priscilla Jane *printmaker*
Hallam, Beverly (Beverly Linney) *artist*

MARYLAND

Annapolis
Farley, Dorothy Bieber *artist, educator*
Palmer, Laura Higgins *artist*
Thoms, Josephine Bowers *artist*

Arnold
Shatz, Jayne Eileen *artist, educator*

Baltimore
Barnes, Janet Lynn *artist*
Massey, Allyn Francis *artist, educator*
OReilly, Meaghan Kelly *art educator*
Ottesen, Bodil Bang *art educator*
West, Virginia *artist, educator*
Yates, Sharon *artist*

Barnesville
Pearcy, Susan Beth Due *artist, printmaker*

Berlin
Smith, Gloria Young *retired graphics designer*

Bethesda
Benson, Elizabeth Polk *art specialist*
Dignac, Geny (Eugenia M. Bermudez) *sculptor*
Fleming, Patricia Stubbs (Patsy Fleming) *artist*
Grais, Alexandra *art appraiser, director*
Koenig, Elizabeth Barbara *sculptor*
Sarnoff, Lili-Charlotte (Lolo Sarnoff) *artist*

Brookeville
Rico, Stephanie Allcock *art educator*

Cabin John
Bergfors, Constance Marie *artist, educator*

Catonsville
Drees, Dedree Ann *computer graphics designer, educator, artist*

Chevy Chase
Kranking, Margaret Graham *retired artist, educator*

Churchton
Miller, Sandra Ritchie *artist, art therapist*

Columbia
Blackwell-Taffel, Camellia Ann *art educator, consultant*

Edgewood
Fox, Jennifer Joy *artist, educator*

Greenbelt
Poland, Alison *artist*

Hyattsville
Shinolt, Eileen Thelma *artist*

Lanham Seabrook
Southall, Virginia Lawrence *retired artist*

Laurel
Logsdon, Roslyn *artist, educator*

Lothian
Messenger, Barbara Beall *artist*

Olney
Hails, Barbara Geldermann *artist*

Pasadena
Kuhn, Jolyn *artist*

Potomac
Hart, Betty Miller *artist*

Riverdale
Lippincott, Janet *artist, art educator*

Silver Spring
Aranya, Gwendalin Qi *painter, priest, educator*

Trappe
Burns-Bowie, Maureen Elizabeth *sculptor*

Westover
Dougherty, Barbara Lee *artist, writer*

Wheaton
Folsom, Rose *calligrapher, writer, artist*

Woodbine
Nuss, Barbara Gough *artist*

MASSACHUSETTS

Amherst
Barrett, Lora McNeece *art educator, artist*
Elman, Naomi Geist *artist, theater producer*
Reed, Daphne Stevenson *artist*

Barnstable
Lummus, Carol Travers *artist, printmaker*

Bolton
Keane, Karen M. *auction house executive*

Boston
Ablow, Roz Karol (Roselyn Karol Ablow) *painter, curator*
Cantor, Mira *artist, educator*
Chandler, Robin Mary *artist, educator, writer*
Cornell, Deborah A. *artist, educator*
Eder, Esther Garcia *artist*
Fesko, Colleene *art appraiser*
Hershey, Nona *artist, printmaker, educator*
McIlvain, Isabel *sculptor, art educator*
Parker, Olivia *photographer*

Brookline
Barron, Ros *artist*
Rubin-Katz, Barbara *sculptor, human services manager*
Schiller, Sophie *artist, graphics designer*

Bryantville
Peters, Marie T. *retired art educator*

Cambridge
Brackett, Prilla Smith *artist, educator*
Chandler, Fay Martin *artist*
Dobson, Parrish *photographer, educator*
Jacob, Wendy *artist, art educator*
Jonas, Joan (Joan Amerman Edwards) *artist*
Slosburg-Ackerman, Jill Rose *artist, educator*

Chicopee
Costanzo, Nanci Joy *art educator*

East Bridgewater
Heywood, Anne *artist, educator, author*

East Falmouth
Lincoln, Jane L. *artist, educator*

Easthampton
Lake, Shelley *artist*

Fall River
Andrade, Manuela Pestana *art educator*
Wilner, Marion Leonard *art educator*

Gloucester
Perry, Sarah Hollis *artist*
Swigart, Joan B. *artist, consultant*
White, Lucette Darby *painter, sculptor*

Great Barrington
Ryder, Lois Irene *artist*

Hudson
Opp, Nancy Jean Shiffler *visual artist, arts volunteer*

Lincoln
Milan, Ellen Judith *artist*

Longmeadow
Frey, Mary Elizabeth *artist*

Lowell
Moore, Janet Lambert *artist, educator*

Marblehead
Heins, Esther *artist, illustrator*

Mattapoisett
Bertram, Christine G. *artist, painter, graphics designer*

Medford
Johnson, Virginia Bristol *costume designer, educator, small business owner*

Natick
Geller, Esther (Bailey Geller) *artist*

Newton
Huber Warren, Gretchen *artist*
Jencks, Penelope *sculptor*

North Brookfield
Parker, Ann (Ann Parker Neal) *photographer, graphic artist, writer*

North Eastham
DeMuth, Vivienne Blake McCandless *artist, illustrator*

Northampton
Rupp, Sheron Adeline *photographer, educator*
Schuleit, Anna *artist*

Norwell
Brett, Jan Churchill *illustrator, author*

Norwood
Rothauser, Florence Arax *artist*

Osterville
McLean, Susan O'Brien *artist*

Peabody
Dee, Pauline M. *artist*

Reading
Frey, Joanne Alice Tupper *art educator*
Nordstrand, Nathalie Elizabeth Johnson *artist*

Shrewsbury
Kranich, Margaret Mansley *artist*

South Hadley
Hall, Lee *artist, educator, writer*

West Springfield
Barrientos, Jane Ellen *art educator*

Westwood
Philbrick, Margaret Elder *artist*

Williamstown
Blair, Phyllis E. *artist*

Wilmington
McLeod, Cheryl O'Halloran *artist, art educator*

Woburn
DeCrosta, Susan Elyse *graphic designer*

MICHIGAN

Allendale
Thomas, Lorelle Otis *graphics designer, educator*

Beverly Hills
Nawara, Lucille Procter *artist, educator*

Camden
Falls, Kathleene Joyce *photographer*

Capac
Wagner, Dorothy Marie *retired senior creative designer, artist*

Caro
Galloway, Gladys *artist*

Chelsea
Lipiec, Sherry Ann *art educator*

Detroit
Jackson, Marion Elizabeth *art educator*
Moldenhauer, Judith A. *graphic design educator*
Thayer, Nancy J. *artist, educator*

Douglas
Karamas, Joyce Efthemia *art educator, consultant, artist*

Farmington Hills
Eisner, Gail Ann *artist, educator*

Flint
Sharbaugh, Kathryn Kennedy *artist*

Grand Rapids
Bolt, Eunice Mildred DeVries *artist*
Jackoboice, Sandra Kay *artist*

Grosse Ile
Stump, M. Pamela *sculptor*

Grosse Pointe
Disanto, Carol L. (Carol La Chiusa) *artist*

Grosse Pointe Farms
Thibodeau, Virginia Durbin *artist*

Holland
Van Noord, Diane C. *artist, educator*

Houghton
Beckwith, Mary Ann *art educator*

Jenison
Frye, Della Mae *portrait artist*

Kalamazoo
Brodbeck, Mary Lou *artist, furniture designer*

Lansing
Brendahl, Marcia *artist, illustrator*
Summitt, Alixandra Pablita *art educator*

Lathrup Village
Taylor, Alicia *art educator*

Lowell
Reid Jenkins, Debra L. *artist*

Midland
Belton, Betty Kepka *retired art educator, artist*

Mount Pleasant
Morrisroe, Julia Marie *art gallery director, artist*
Traines, Rose Wunderbaum *sculptor, educator*

Okemos
Wager, Paula Jean *artist*

Petoskey
Switzer, Carolyn Joan *artist, educator*

Plainwell
Flower, Jean Frances *art educator*

Plymouth
Moore-Viculin, Charlotte Anne *artist, musician*

Port Huron
Rowark, Maureen *fine arts photographer*

Saginaw
Shek, Eugenie Victoria *artist*
Venable, Sarah *art educator*

Saint Clair Shores
Kachman, Frances Guiducci *artist*

Skandia
Johnson, Judy M. *artist, writer*

Southfield
Quinlan, Patricia *retired art educator*

Sparta
Bomhof, Robyn *artist, educator*

Whitmore Lake
Kohler, Janet Sue *artist*

Wyandotte
Dunn, Gloria Jean *artist*

MINNESOTA

Coon Rapids
Goodstein-Shapiro, Florence (Florence Goodstein Walton) *artist, art historian*

Duluth
Jenkins, Virginia *artist, educator*

Easton
Schrader, LuAnn Carol *art educator*

Edina
Holman, Iletta Marcella *retired art educator*

Long Lake
Hofkin, Ann Ginsburgh *photographer, poet*

Minneapolis
Hand, Mary Jane *artist, poet, educator*
Innmon, Arlene Katherine (Tara Innmon) *artist, writer, entertainer*
Marling, Karal Ann *art history educator, social sciences educator, curator*
Ramalho-Ahrndt, Maria Gabriela *art educator*

Newport
Yelland, Mary Virginia *artist*

Northfield
Swanson, Judith Seleen *artist, graphics designer, advocate*

Oakdale
Nagdimon, Ellen Tara *artist, educator*

Park Rapids
Miller, Tanya Joy *art educator*

Rochester
Destro, (Helen) Jane *artist, medical illustrator*

Saint Paul
Burke, Mary Griggs (Mrs. Jackson Burke) *art collector*
Matteson, Clarice Chris *artist, educator*
Michels, Eileen Manning *retired art educator, curator, writer*
Olson, Bettye Johnson *artist, retired educator*

MISSISSIPPI

Ashland
Dillashaw, Eula Catherine *artist, graphics designer*

Cleveland
Norris, Carolyn Sue *artist*

Clinton
Jarmon, Jeanette *artist, educator*

Hattiesburg
Du Boise, Kim Rees *artist, photographer, art educator*
McRaney, Joan Katherine *artist*

Jackson
Barron, Carol Ann *painter*
Stanton, Sylvia Doucet *artist, gallery owner*

Moorhead
Stone-Street, Nancy Harrington *art educator, painter, printmaker*

Starkville
Durst, Jo *artist, educator*
Pigg, Robin Clark *art educator, interior designer*

MISSOURI

Blue Springs
Poff, Sarah Ellen *art educator*

Bourbon
Heitsch, Leona Mason *artist, writer*

Butler
Baxter, Myrtle Mae (Bobbi Baxter) *artist*

Chesterfield
Kruse, Margaret M. *art educator*

Columbia
Cameron, Brooke Bulovsky *art educator, artist*

Hermann
Mahoney, Catherine Ann *artist, educator*

Hollister
Canfield, Cindy Sue *art educator*

Independence
Willett, Teri Kay *art educator*

Jackson
Horst, Carol Berry *art educator*

Kansas City
Hutson, Betty Switzer *art educator, artist*
Johnston, Lynn Beverley *animator*
Lee, Margaret Norma *artist*
Mast, Kande White *artist*
Schaffer, Sandra Sue *artist, educator*

Lewistown
Terpening, Virginia Ann *artist*

Platte City
Kalin, D. Jean (Dorothy Jean Kalin) *artist, educator*

Portageville
Booker, DeLois Fondon *art educator*

Rolla
Brewster, Louise Boone *artist, educator*

Saint Clair
Jobe, Kimberly R. *art educator*

Saint Joseph
Sauls, Allison Houston *art educator*

Saint Louis
Bohan, Ruth Louise *art educator*
Brazell, Gloria Ruth *art educator, elementary school educator*
Metcalfe, Elizabeth Brokaw *art educator*
Rosen, Adrienne *artist, educator*
Sago, Janis Lynn *photography educator*

Springfield
Brennan, Deborah Ann *artist*

Stover
Reynolds, Sallie Blackburn *artist, volunteer*

Sturgeon
Dawkins, Amy *artist*

Vandalia
Berry, Rebecca Diane *artist, educator*

Webster Groves
Gergeceff-Cooper, Lorraine *artist, consultant*

MONTANA

Billings
Deschner, Jane Waggoner *photo artist, arts in healthcare consultant*
Jones, Doris Logan *portrait painter, art educator*

Roundup
Stanfel, Jane Ellen *artist, adult education educator*

NEBRASKA

Aurora
Miller, Shari Ann *art educator*

Fremont
Welstead, Jean Maudie *artist, educator*

Kearney
Hoffman, M. Kathy *graphics designer, packaging designer*

Lincoln
Kunc, Karen *artist, educator*

Norfolk
Timmer, Margaret Louise (Peg Timmer) *art educator*

Whitney
Tejeda-Brown, Mary Louise *artist*

NEVADA

Fallon
Venturacci, Toni Marie *artist*

Henderson
Hara-Isa, Nancy Jeanne *graphics designer*

Las Vegas
Slade, Barbara Ann *art educator*

Reno
Baran, Shirley Walters *artist, sculptor*
Hilts, Ruth *artist*
McLeod, Carolyn Louise *artist*

NEW HAMPSHIRE

Alstead
Beetle, Kate *artist, illustrator*

Amherst
Johnson, Daryl Diane *painter*

Concord
Raskin, Joy Lynn *art educator, silversmith*

Hudson
Rosson, Elizabeth Hanle *artist, director*

Lyme
Wise, Joanne Herbert *art director*

Marlow
McCracken, Linda *artist, writer*

Newport
Gayvoronsky, Ludmila *artist, educator*

Rochester
Kumiski, Cheryl Marie *artist*

Winchester
Tandy, Jean Conkey *clay artist, potter, painter, retired educator*

Wolfeboro
Bonin, Suzanne Jean *artist*

NEW JERSEY

Bayonne
Doyle, Enid *art educator*

Bedminster
Frediani, Diane Marie *graphics designer, interior designer, executive secretary*

Bernardsville
Spofford, Sally (Sally Hyslop) *artist*

Bogota
Koshimitsu, Keiko *artist*

Boonton
Hanna, Annette A. *artist, art educator*

Brick
Herrmann, Elsa Marie *retired art educator*

Bridgeton
Chanatry-Howell, Lorraine Marie *artist, educator*

Bridgewater
Glesmann, Sylvia-Maria *artist*

Caldwell
Palombo, Lisa *artist*

Califon
Clipsham, Jacqueline Ann *artist*
Rosen, Carol Mendes *artist*

Cherry Hill
Solomon, Penny Goren *artist, designer*

Deptford
Shusterman, Linda *ceramist, educator*

Egg Harbor Township
Schreiber, Eileen Sher *artist*

Fairfield
de Smet, Lorraine May *artist*

Franklin Lakes
Baker, Cornelia Draves *artist*

Gillette
Merkl, Elissa Frances *visual artist, editor, publishing executive*

Glassboro
Murashima, Kumiko *artist, educator*

Hoboken
Frankenthal, Danielle *painter, sculptor*
Rose, Roslyn *artist*

Holmdel
Slovik, Sandra Lee *retired art educator*

Jersey City
Barney, Christine J. *artist*
Eigen, Barbara Goldman *artist*

Lakewood
Pilgram, Suzanne *artist, art educator*

Laurel Springs
Roma, Aida Clara *artist*

Leonia
Thiesfeldt, Sheila M. *artist, educator, small business owner*

Linwood
Chernoff, Deborah Shelley *art educator*

Livingston
Feigen, Irene *artist, educator*

Manasquan
Robinson, Sarah Bonham *artist, educator, mental health services professional*

Maplewood
Woods, Krystyna Janina *artist, pharmacist*

Margate City
Pronesti, Rosa C. *artist*

Medford
Mayer, Joyce Harris *artist*

Metuchen
Ackerson, Patricia Kathleen Freis *art educator, artist*
Arbeiter, Joan *artist, educator*

Middlesex
Hilliard, Kathleen J. *costume designer*

Montclair
Nagorka, Stefanie *artist*
Phillips, Ann Y. *art advisor*

Mountain Lakes
Starger, Victoria Gondek *artist*

New Milford
McHenry, Esther Ann *artist*

New Providence
Rivo, Shirley Winthrope *artist*

Newton
Grodsky, Sheila Taylor *art educator, artist*
Hollander, Roslyn *artist, educator*

Oakland
Farrell, Donna Marie *photographer, graphics designer*

Old Bridge
Luis, Belinda *graphic designer*

Oradell
Struck, Norma Johansen *artist*

Perth Amboy
Lavin-Pennyfeather, Rose *artist*

Picatinny Arsenal
Zulauf, Madeline Ruth *photographer, artist*

Piscataway
Urban, Cathleen Andrea *graphics designer*

Pittstown
Hierholzer, Joan *artist*

Princeton
Boretz, Naomi Messinger *artist, educator*
Canright, Sarah Anne *artist, educator*
Kahn, Eiko Taniguchi *artist*
McCauley, Elizabeth Anne *art educator*

Princeton Junction
Rose, Peggy Jane *artist, educator, gifted education advocate*

Rahway
Dolinich-Matuska, Christine *artist*

Seaside Park
Golembeski, Beverly Long *artist, art educator*

Short Hills
Yorinks, Adrienne Berg *artist, illustrator*

South Bound Brook
Weir, Sonja Ann *artist*

South River
Haller, Marcia Smith *art educator*

Springfield
DeVone, Denise *artist, educator*

Summit
Baker, Alden *artist*
Good, Joan Duffey *artist*
Rousseau, Irene Victoria *artist*

Surf City
Law, Jane Hinton *artist, small business owner*

Tenafly
Schoenberg, Coco *sculptor*

Trenton
Brearley, Candice *fashion designer*
Chavooshian, Marge *artist, educator*

Union
Whitelaw, Dolores Fahey *artist*

Ventnor City
Robbins, Hulda Dornblatt *artist, printmaker*

Waldwick
Samuelson, Billie Margaret *artist*

Wayne
Garcia, Ofelia *art educator, department chairman*

Westfield
King, Linda Marie *art educator, director*

Woodbridge
Nagy-Hartnack, Lois Ann *art educator*

NEW MEXICO

Alamogordo
Irving, Sara *art educator*

Albuquerque
Abrams, Jane Eldora *artist*
Baca, Vera Jennie Schulte *art educator*
Coleman, Barbara McReynolds *artist*
Culpepper, Mabel Claire *artist*
Duke, Wanda K. *artist*
Lampela, Laurel Ann *art educator*
Miera, Lucille Catherine Miera *artist, retired art educator*
Nelson, Mary Carroll *artist, writer*
Nevin, Jean Shaw *artist*
Steider, Doris *artist*
Truby, Betsy Kirby *artist, illustrator, photographer*
Williams, Juanita Rosalie *artist*

Belen
Chicago, Judy *artist*

Bernalillo
Pritchard, Betty Jean *retired art educator*

Caballo
Massengill, Barbara Daves *artist*

Capitan
Pekelsma, Judy Ann *artist, educator*

Carlsbad
Gwinn, Helen H. *artist, educator*

Corrales
Eaton, Pauline *artist, educator*

Deming
De Mott, Marianne *artist, educator, space designer, craftsperson*

Espanola
Jonker, Pamela Lynn *artist*

Farmington
Espinosa, Nancy Sweet *artist, anthropologist*

Gallup
Cattaneo, Jacquelyn Annette Kammerer *artist, educator*

Hobbs
Garey, Patricia Martin *artist*

Las Cruces
Livermore, Fern Chrisman *retired artist*
Lopez, Carol Sue *artist*

Penasco
Marx, Nicki Diane *sculptor, painter*

Portales
YSikes, Juanita Lou *art educator*

Rio Rancho
Duitman, Lois Robinson *artist*

Roswell
Peterson, Dorothy Hawkins *artist, educator*

Ruidoso Downs
Templeton, Ann *artist, educator*

Sandia Park
Weitz, Jeanne Stewart *artist, educator*

Santa Fe
Dean, Nat *artist, designer, educator*
Erdman, Barbara *visual artist*
Karp, Diane R. *art educator*
Perroni, Carol *artist*
Pierson, Norah *artist*
Relkin, Michele Weston *artist*
Sloan, Jeanette Pasin *artist*
Wotherspoon, Mary Ruth *artist, writer*
York, Star Liana *sculptor*

Taos
Beck, Ursula *art educator, artist*
Crespin, Leslie Ann *artist*
Price, Brenda Chloè *artist, entrepreneur*

NEW YORK

Albany
Carson, JoAnne *art educator, artist*
Lawton, Nancy *artist*

Amagansett
Seelbach, Anne Elizabeth *artist*

Ancramdale
Weinstein, Joyce *artist*

Annandale On Hudson
LÊ, An-My *photographer, educator*
Pfaff, Judy *artist*

Ardsley
Sokolow, Isobel Folb *sculptor*

Bath
Brautigan, June Marie *artist, poet*

Bay Shore
Baradzi, Amelia *stained glass artist, restorationist*

Bearsville
Whitman, Karen *artist*

Bellerose
Stecher, Pauline *painter, educator*

Binghamton
Weissman, Ann Paley *artist, educator, consultant*

Brainard
Johnsen, May Ann *artist, sculptor*

Bronx
Adams, Alice *sculptor*
Bacarella, Flavia *artist, educator*
Kassoy, Hortense (Honey Kassoy) *artist, sculptor, painter*
Kitt, Olga *artist*
Korman, Barbara *sculptor*

Brookhaven
Grucci Butler, Donna *fireworks company executive*

Brooklyn
Armstrong, L. C. *artist*
Bachmann, Karen Charlotte *artist, educator*
Bangs, Mary Constance (C Bangs) *artist, curator*
Biondi, Florence *freelance/self-employed artist*
Carlile, Janet Louise *artist, educator*
Dantzic, Cynthia Maris *artist, educator*
Gianlorenzi, Nona Elena *art dealer, painter*
Gisolfi, Diana (Diana Gisolfi Pechukas) *art history educator*
Hand, Joni Marie *art educator*
Henning, Roni Anita *printmaker, artist*
Jones, Susan Emily *fashion educator, administrator, educator emeritus*
Litto, Judith Cheryl *art educator*
Nii, Yuko *artist*
Piene, Chloe *artist, filmmaker*
Plaut, Jane Margaret *art educator*
Reich, Olive Buerk *artist, educator*
Schaefer, Marilyn Louise *artist, writer, educator*
Shechter, Laura Judith *artist*
Zinnes, Alice Fich *artist, educator*
Zollar, Jawole Willa Jo *artist, choreographer*

Buffalo
Janiga, Mary Ann *art educator*
Slotkin, Alma Isobel *artist*

Buskirk
Johanson, Patricia Maureen *artist, architect*

Canastota
Roth, Susan Betsy *artist*

Carle Place
Barnett, Emily *artist*

Cazenovia
Wyckoff, Sylvia Spencer *art educator, artist*

Centereach
DuBarry, Jacqueline Anne *artist, educator*

Chatham
Squier, Rita Ann Holmberg *graphic designer*

Clifton Park
Kuhn, Audrey Grendahl *graphic designer, printmaker, fiber artist*

Clinton Corners
Rudolph, Nancy K. *photographer, writer*

Cold Spring Harbor
Maglione, Lili *artist, consultant*

Commack
Berman, Patricia Karatsis *art director*

Cornwall On Hudson
Abrams-Collens, Vivien *artist*

Cortlandt Manor
Rosenberg, Marilyn Rosenthal *artist, poet*

Croton On Hudson
Wandel, Sharon Lee *sculptor*

Deer Park
Martone, Jeanette Rachele *artist*

East Hampton
Jaudon, Valerie *artist*
Riley, Cheryl *artist, educator*
Scott, Rosa Mae *art educator, artist*

East Quogue
Setlow, Neva Delihas *artist, research biologist*

East Setauket
Tuttle, Anne Palmer *artist, education educator*

Elmira
Miran, Patricia Marie *art educator*
Mitchell, Sharon *artist*

Fayetteville
Hadyk-Wepf, Sonia Margaret *artist, real estate manager*

Flushing
Bezrod, Norma R. *artist*
Carlson, Cynthia Joanne *artist, educator*
Flechner, Roberta Fay *graphics designer*
Shen, Ronger *artist, educator*
Yeo, Kim Eng *artist*

Forest Hills
Fernandez, Amy *artist, illustrator, writer, educator*
Morgan, Jacqui *illustrator, painter, art educator, writer*

Garden City
Russell, Stella Pandell *artist, author, educator*

Goshen
Digby, Lynne A. *artist, writer*

Great Neck
Mayer, Sondra *art educator*
Seidler, Doris *artist*

Great River
Edwards, Christine E. *artist*

Halesite
Grey-Bethiel, Shari *artist, sculptor, apparel designer*

Hicksville
Appold, Cynthia *visual arts educator*

Highland Falls
Skibinski, Olga *artist, art conservator*

Hopewell Junction
Sellingsloh, Hulda Knipling *retired artist*

Irvington
Shapiro, Ellen M. *graphics designer, writer*

Ithaca
Garrison, Elizabeth Jane *artist*
Mikus, Eleanore Ann *artist*
Schuler, Mary Callaghan *artist, educational association administrator*

Jackson Heights
Schuyler, Jane *fine arts educator*

Jamaica
Cocchiarelli, Maria *artist, educator*
Jones, Cynthia Teresa Clarke *artist*

Jeffersonville
Harms, Elizabeth Louise *artist*

Keene Valley
Butterworth, Nona Angel *artist, educator*

Lake Placid
Rickard, Anne Colton *art educator, artist*

Lisbon
Tyo Boscoe, Denise Marie *art educator*

Long Island City
McCoy, Ann *artist*

Lynbrook
Cangemi, Lisa Lynne *art director, graphics designer*

Malone
Patterson, Valerie *art educator*

Mamaroneck
Lesser, Mimi Korach *artist*

Massapequa
Goldberg, Beth Sheba *artist, educator, art therapist*

Merrick
Kass-Johnson, Susan *artist*

Middle Village
Fradella, Laura Toni *art educator, muralist*

Middletown
McCord, Jean Ellen *art educator*

Millbrook
Duesberry, Joellyn Toler *artist*

Monroe
Centeno-Dainty, Sonia Margarita *artist*

Mount Sinai
Lidstrom, Esther Marie *artist, photographer*

New Hampton
Sinnard, Elaine Janice *painter, sculptor*

New Paltz
Cheng, Amy *artist*
Goodell, Kathy Susan *artist, educator*
List, Ilka Katherine *art educator, sculptor, writer, psychotherapist*

New Rochelle
Adato, Linda Joy *artist, educator*

New York
Abish, Cecile *artist*
Abramovic, Marina *artist*
Abrams, Joyce D. *artist*
Acra, Reem *apparel designer*
Adri, (Adri Steckling Coen) *fashion designer*
Adrian, Barbara (Mrs. Franklin C. Tramutola) *artist*
Ali, Laylah *artist*
Allen, Patricia Jean *graphics designer*
Arms, Anneli (Anna Elizabeth Arms) *artist, educator*
Arnold, Ann *artist, illustrator*
Backstedt, Roseanne Joan *artist*
Bartlett, Jennifer Losch *artist*
Beckman, Ericka *artist, filmmaker*
Belag, Andrea Susan *artist*
Benglis, Lynda *artist, sculptor, educator*
Berman, Ariane R. *artist*
Bethel, Denise *art appraiser*
Bialler, Nancy *art appraiser*
Biddle, Flora Miller *art patron, museum administrator*
Bonino, Fernanda *art dealer*
Bourgeois, Louise *sculptor*
Bradshaw, Dove *artist*
Brett, Nancy Heléne *artist*
Brody-Lederman, Stephanie *artist*
Brown, Cecily *artist*
Brychtova, Jaroslava *sculptor*
Butterly, Kathy *sculptor*
Cannon, Elizabeth H. *dress and clothing designer, artist*
Canonero, Milena *costume designer*
Cappellazzo, Amy *art appraiser, writer*
Casella, Margaret Mary *artist*
Castoro, Rosemarie *sculptor*
Chwatsky, Ann *photographer, educator*
Coe, Sue *artist, journalist*
Cogger, Cassia Zamecki *painter*
Cohen, Cora *artist*
Colburn, Martha *animator, filmmaker, artist*
Conelli, Maria Ann *art educator, dean, architect*
Cooper, Paula *art dealer*
Craft, Liz *artist*
Crile, Susan *artist*
Crown, Roberta *artist, educator*
Cutler, Amy *artist*
Cutler, Ronnie *artist*
Davidson, Nancy Brachman *artist, educator*
DeBeers, Sue *photographer*
DeLuccia, Paula *artist*
DeMonte, Claudia Ann *artist, educator*
Dennis, Donna Frances *sculptor, art educator*
Dodd, Lois *artist, art educator*
Dole-Recio, Lecia *artist*
Donneson, Seena Sand *artist*
Drexler, Joanne Lee *art appraiser*
Drum, Sydney Maria *artist*
Dunbar, Leila *antiques appraiser, auction house executive*
Dunkelman, Loretta *artist*
Edelson, Mary Beth *artist, educator*
Eisenberg, Sonja Miriam *artist*
Eisner, Carole Swid *artist*
Ellis, Loren Elizabeth *artist, educator*
Enders, Elizabeth McGuire *artist*
Engelberg, Gail May *fine arts patron*
Fasnacht, Heide Ann *artist, educator*
Fernández, Teresita *sculptor*
Field, Patricia *apparel designer*
Firestone, Susan Paul *artist*
Foster, Kim *art dealer, art gallery owner*
Frankenthaler, Helen *artist*
Frehm, Lynne *painter*
Friedman, Sally *artist, educator*
Gage, Beau *artist*
Gallagher, Ellen *artist*
Gerard, Barbara *visual artist, educator*
Gibson, Sandra *painter, filmmaker*
Gittler, Wendy *artist, art historian, writer*
Gold, Lois Meyer *artist*
Gold, Sharon Cecile *artist, educator*
Golici, Ana *artist*
Gonzalez-Falla, Sondra Gilman *art collector*
Gourevitch, Jacqueline *artist*
Grannan, Katy *photographer*
Granne, Regina *artist, educator*
Guzman, Kathleen McFadden *antiques appraiser, auctioneer*
Hagin, Nancy *printmaker, painter*
Hammond, Jane Rebecca *artist*
Hamoy, Carol *artist*
Hamura, Kaori *artist*
Harrington, E.B. *art dealer*
Harrison, Rachel *artist*
Harvey, Julie L. *artist*
Henzel, Robyn Ellen *artist*
Hermann, Mildred L. *artist*
Herrera, Carolina *fashion designer*
Hightower, Caroline Warner *arts management consultant*
Hoff, Margo *artist, printmaker, muralist*
Hohauser, Marilyn *artist*
Horn, Roni *artist*
Hort, Susan *art collector*
Hould-Ward, Ann *theatrical costume designer*
Hull, Cathy *artist, illustrator*
Jacquette, Yvonne Helene *artist*
Jaffe, Irma Blumenthal *art educator*
Jefferson, Kristin Marie *art dealer, consultant, film producer, writer*
Johnson, Betsey Lee *fashion designer*
Johnson, Cecile Ryden (Mrs. Philip Johnson) *artist*
Kaish, Luise Clayborn *sculptor, painter, educator*
Kamali, Norma *fashion designer*
Kan, Diana Artemis Mann Shu *painter, art educator, writer*
Karan, Donna (Donna Faske) *fashion designer*
Keller, Marthe *artist, painter*
Kelly, Mary *sculptor*
Kim, Willa *costume designer*
King, Marcia Gygli *artist*
Kisch, Gloria *sculptor*
Klein, Cynthia *art appraiser*
Koppelman, Dorothy Myers *artist, consultant*
Korot, Beryl *artist*
Kozloff, Joyce *artist*
Krementz, Jill *photographer, author*
Kruger, Barbara *artist, art critic*
Kurz, Diana *artist, educator*
Kusmierski, Janet Louise *painter, graphics designer, illustrator*
Kutosh, Sue *artist*
Lange, Liz *apparel designer, director*
Lanyon, Ellen (Mrs. Roland Ginzel) *artist, educator*
Lee, Catherine *sculptor, painter*
Leech, Katharine (Kitty Leech) *costume designer, educator*
Leibovitz, Annie *photographer*
Lekberg, Barbara *sculptor*
Lerner, Sandra *artist*
Levine, Sherrie *conceptual artist*
Lewin, Betsy R. *illustrator*
Liden, Hanna *photographer*
Lipsky, Pat *artist*
Lipton, Jackie F. *artist, educator*
Louizos, Anna Alexandra *set designer*
Mackler, Tina *artist*
Maffei, Susan Martin *artist, educator*
Margolin, Jean Spielberg *artist*
Maryschuk, Olga Yaroslava *artist, executive secretary*
Mayer, Rosemary *artist*
Mayes, Elaine *photographer, educator*
McCoy, Jennifer *artistic collaborator, educator*
McHugh, Caril Eisenstein Dreyfuss *art dealer, art gallery director, consultant*
McKenzie, Mary Beth *artist*
McNeely, Juanita *artist*
Mehretu, Julie *artist*
Meiselas, Susan Clay *photographer*
Metzger, Evelyn Borchard *artist*
Meyers, Dale (Mrs. Mario Cooper) *artist*
Miller, Nancy Suzanne *technology consultant, artist*
Miller, Nicole Jacqueline *fashion designer*
Moore, Fay *artist*
Murphy, Catherine *painter*
Murray, Elizabeth *artist*
Murray, Judith *artist*
Niccolini, Dianora *photographer*
O'Bryan, C. Jill *visual artist, writer*
O'Neil, Robyn *artist*
Ono, Yoko *conceptual artist, singer, recording artist*
Passlof, Pat *artist, educator*
Peruo, Marsha Hope *artist*
Plavinskaya, Anna Dmitrievna *artist*
Polsky, Cynthia Hazen *artist, art collector, philanthropist*
Porter, Liliana Alicia *artist, photographer, painter, printmaker, filmmaker*
Portnow, Marjorie *painter*
Prieto, Monique N. *artist*
Quiles, Esther *art educator*
Quisgard, Liz Whitney *artist, sculptor*
Recanati, Dina *artist*
Redmond, Catherine *artist, educator*
Reese, Tracy *fashion designer*
Reininghaus, Ruth *retired artist*
Remington, Deborah Williams *artist*
Rifka, Judy *artist, educator*
Ringgold, Faith *artist*
Robbins, Carrie Fishbein *costume designer, educator*
Romano, Clare *artist*
Rose, Leatrice *artist, educator*
Rotolo, Susan (Suze) *artist*
Rovner, Michal *video artist, photographer*
Russell, Maryanne *photographer*
Saint-Ouen Leung, Brigitte *art dealer, consultant*
Sand Lee, Inger *artist, interior architect*
Sandler, Barbara S. *artist*
Sandler, Lucy Freeman *art history educator*
Schapiro, Miriam *artist*
Schneider, Jane Harris *sculptor*
Schneider, JoAnne *artist*
Schorr, Collier *artist*
Shatter, Susan Louise *artist*
Sherin, Robin *artist*
Sherman, Cindy *artist*
Sigal-Ibsen, Rose *artist*
Sikander, Shahzia *artist*
Singer, Barbara Helen *photographer, radiographer*
Sisto, Elena *artist, educator*
Skoglund, Sandra Louise *artist, educator*
Sky, Alison *artist, designer*
Slavin, Arlene *artist*
Sleigh, Sylvia *artist, educator*
Slitkin, Barbara Ann *artist*
Smith, Clare *art appraiser*
Smith, Kiki *artist*
Smith, Shirley *artist*
Sonneman, Eve *artist*
Spade, Kate (Katherine Noel Spade) *apparel designer*
Spence, Sique (Mary Stewart Spence) *art dealer*
Spikol, Eileen *artist*
Steffe, Cynthia *fashion designer*
Stewart, Leora Klaymer *textile artist, educator*
Stine, Catherine Morris *artist*
Stone, Caroline Fleming *artist*
Stuart, Jill *apparel designer*
Stuart, Michelle Rae *artist*
Sultan, Altoon *artist*
Swartz, Julianne *artist*
Swergold, Marcelle Miriam *sculptor*
Tipton, Jennifer *lighting designer*
Touby, Linda *artist*
Trombetta, Annamarie *artist*
Ultra Violet, *artist*
Umlauf, Lynn Charlotte *art educator, sculptor*
Upright, Diane Warner *art dealer*
Van Goethem, Nancy Ann *painter, educator*
Vass, Joan *apparel designer*
von Rydingsvard, Ursula Karoliszyn *sculptor*
Wald, Sylvia *artist*
Walker, Kara *artist*
Wang, Vera *fashion designer*
Watanabe, Nana *photographer*
Weiss, Marilyn Ackerman *artist*
Welker, Jennifer Carol Marie *artist*
Wohl, Laurie *artist*
Woit, Bonnie Ford *artist*
Woo, Alex *jewelry designer*
Woodman, Betty *sculptor*
Wright, Faith-dorian *artist*
Wunderman, Jan Darcourt *artist*
Zackheim, Michele *artist*
Zimmerman, Elyn *artist*
Zimmerman, Kathleen Marie *artist*
Zittel, Andrea *painter, sculptor*

Newburgh
Sabini, Barbara Dorothy *artist, educator*

North Bellmore
Trigoboff, Sybelle *artist, educator*

North White Plains
Erla, Karen *artist, painter, collagist, printmaker*

Northport
Hohenberger, Patricia Julie *fine arts and antique appraiser, consultant*

Norwich
Dragoon, Valerie Baldwin *art educator*

Odessa
Stillman-Myers, Joyce L. *artist, educator, writer, illustrator, consultant*

Old Westbury
Tiscornia, Ana Maria *artist, educator, writer*

Oneonta
Freckelton, Sondra *artist*

Otego
Griffith, Roberta *art educator*

Oyster Bay
Prey, Barbara Ernst *artist*

Palisades
Knowlton, Grace Farrar *sculptor, photographer*

Piermont
Madawick, Paula Christian *artist, educator*

Pittsford
Clem, Kathy *artist*

Port Chester
Dessereau, April *art educator*
Sayles, Eva *artist*

Port Washington
Betensky, Rose Hart *artist*

Porter Corners
Manzi, Alice M. *artist, educator*

Poughkeepsie
Peluse, Catherine Gina *artist*

Pound Ridge
Schwebel, Renata Manasse *sculptor*

Purchase
Mullen, M. Denise *art educator, higher education administrator, photographer, artist*

Queens Village
Megherian, Yefkin *sculptor*

Rhinebeck
Ewald, Wendy Taylor *photographer, writer, educator*
Rabinovich, Raquel *painter, sculptor*

Riverdale
Greenberg, Arline Francine *artist*

Rochester
Frear, Lorrie *graphic designer, educator*
Gong, Nancy Y. *artist, small business owner*
Kirkebye, Amanda Stark *art educator*
Shedden-Coingill, Edythe B. *artist*
Shindelman, Marni *artist, educator*
Wygant, Patricia Bryans *artist*

Rockville Centre
Barkan-Clarke, Jacqueline Mia *artist, educator, art therapist, jewelry designer*

Rosendale
Kellner, Tatana *artist, art educator*

Roslyn Heights
Newmark, Marilyn *sculptor*

Ruby
Cole, Max *artist*

Rye Brook
Goldberger, Blanche Rubin *sculptor, jeweler*

Salem
Duveen, Anneta *artist*

Salt Point
Botway, Jaclyn Cooper *antiques dealer, consultant*

Scarsdale
Goldenberg Abler, Mathilda Maslow *artist*
Newman, Stacey Clarfield *artist, curator*

Sharon Springs
Futerko, Suzanne *art educator*

Shelter Island Heights
Culbertson, Janet Lynn *artist*

Slingerlands
Carroll, Corlis Faith *artist, educator*

South Salem
Carpentieri, Carol Ellen *artist, educator*

Southampton
Freeman, Elaine Lavalle *sculptor*
Marinoff, Elaine *artist*
McLauchlen, Jennifer *art dealer*
Swift, Mary Lou *art dealer, financial consultant*

Stony Brook
Pindell, Howardena Doreen *artist*

Sugar Loaf
Endico, Mary Antoinette *artist*

Syosset
Greene, Christine Elizabeth *artist*

Syracuse
Darrow, Gretchen *costume designer*

Tonawanda
Peterson, Dorothy Lulu *artist*

Trumansburg
Day, Ann Elizabeth *artist, educator*
Kredell, Carol Ruth *artist*

Vestal
Adour, Colleen McNulty *artist, educator*

Walden
Hraniotis, Judith Beringer *artist*

West Islip
Burns, Kathleen DeMeo *art and photography educator*

Westernville
Hart, Pamela Walker *artist*

White Plains
Gabriele, Marguerite Ann (Margie St. John) *artist, nursing educator*

Williamsville
Fortunato, Pat Deakin *fine artist*

Woodmere
Winick, Bernyce Alpert *artist, photographer*

Woodstock
Banks, Rela *sculptor*
Hahne Hofsted, Janet Lorraine *artist*
Segal, Sabra Lee *artist, graphics designer, illustrator, actress*

Yaphank
Freund, Pepsi *artist, art educator*

Yonkers
Viola, Mary Jo *art history educator*

Yorktown Heights
Jones, Lauretta Marie *artist, designer, computer science researcher*

NORTH CAROLINA

Ahoskie
Adams, Martha Jean Morris *art educator, artist*

Asheville
Allen-Swarttouw, Heather Lindsey *artist, art educator, writer*

Brevard
Alcorn, Karen Zefting Hogan *artist, educator, journalist*
Dillon, Doris (Doris Dillon Kenofer) *artist, art historian, educator, interior designer*

Cary
Daniels, Astar *artist*

Chapel Hill
Stevens, Phyllis A. *conceptual artist*

Charlotte
Simpson, Karen Crandall *artist, educator*
Strawn, Martha Ann *art educator, photographer, writer*

Clayton
Coates, Deborah Phillips *visual arts educator*

Davidson
Grosch, Laura Dudley *artist, educator*

Eden
Sanders, Barbara Fayne *artist, educator*

Edenton
Sams, Robin Dahl *artist*

Fort Bragg
Manning, Deborah Cothran *art educator*

Franklin
Kinard, Cynthia Cochran *artist, writer*

Goldsboro
Turlington, Patricia Renfrew *artist, educator*

Greensboro
Watson, Betty *artist*

Greenville
Weatherington, LaVeta Hinson *visual arts specialist*

Hendersonville
Tatreau, (Dolores) Maxine *artist*

Huntersville
Nowlin, Connie Blackwell *artist*

Kenly
Weaver, Ann Rogerson *art educator*

King
Shanahan, Elizabeth Anne *art educator*

Leasburg
Treacy, Sandra Joanne Pratt *artist, educator*

Lillington
O'Brien, Eileen Kathryn *art educator*

Matthews
Rorie, Kathy Marie *artist*

Nashville
High, (Mary) Elizabeth Hilley *retired art educator*

Raleigh
Jordan, Brenda Moore *artist*
Robinson, Charlotte Hill *artist*

Wilkesboro
Powell, Betty Crowder *artist, educator*

Williamston
Wobbleton, Judy Karen *artist, educator*

Wilmington
Baehmann, Susan Elizabeth *artist*
Baldridge, Jane L. *graphic and fine artist*

Winston Salem
Cieszewski, Sandra Josephine *artist, retired manufacturing company manager*

Zebulon
Ruffing, Anne Elizabeth *artist*

NORTH DAKOTA

Bismarck
Solberg, Nellie Florence Coad *artist*

OHIO

Akron
Keener, Polly Leonard *illustrator*
Korow, Elinore Maria *artist, educator*

Ashville
Beckman, Judith *art educator*

Bedford
Pozz, Jennifer *art educator*

Bryan
Nowak, Carol Lee *retired art educator*

Canton
Moses, Marcia Swartz *artist*

Centerville
Coyle, Diane R. *artist, educator*

Chagrin Falls
Boccardo-Dubey, Genny Mercedes *art dealer*
Cox, Cynthia A. *art education specialist*
Held, Lila M. *art appraiser*

Chardon
Clapsaddle, Patricia Lee *art educator*

Chesterland
Witschi, Emily *art educator*

Cincinnati
Attee, Joyce Valerie Junglas *artist*
Bollen, Sharon Kesterson *artist, educator*
Brady, Darlene Ann *artist, designer, architect*
Chapman, Laura Hill *art education consultant*
Florez, Mary A. *artist*
Hummel, Gayle Gillette *artist, poet*
Schmidt, Leeanne *artist*

Cleveland Heights
Weinbaum, Batya *artist, writer*

Columbus
Gruliow, Agnes Forrest *artist, educator*
Hamilton, Ann Katherine *artist*

Dayton
Little, Tess (Teresa Fannin) *sculptor, fine arts educator*
Wikstrom, Loretta Wermerskirchen *artist*

Euclid
Adrine-Robinson, Kenyette *art educator, poet, artist, photographer*

Fairfield
Goldberg, Bonita Williams *artist, consultant*

Greenville
Estes, Ruth Ann *art educator*
Foureman, Nancy Lee *artist*

Hamilton
Quay, Jacquelyn Sue *art educator, consultant*

Hudson
Carducci, Judith Weeks Barker *artist, retired social worker*

Kent
Ozanich, Ruth Shultz *artist, poet, retired elementary school educator*

Lakewood
Ellis, Deborah Marie *art educator*

Lisbon
Archer, Barrie W.S. *art educator*

Lyndhurst
Ross, Sally Price *artist, painter*

Miamisburg
Michaelis, Betty Jane *sculptor, retired small business owner*

Milford
Parsons, Linda L. *art dealer*

Oxford
Yost, Nancy Runyon *artist, small business owner*

Perrysburg
Autry, Carolyn *artist, art history educator*

Pickerington
Calderone, Jean Leslie *art educator, artist*

Powell
Mitchell, Cathy (C.C.) Christine *art educator*

Reynoldsburg
Boiman, Donna Rae *artist, art academy executive*

Shaker Heights
Freedman, Jacqueline Kahane *art educator*
McKenna, Kathleen Kwasnik *artist*

Toledo
Danko-McGhee, Katherina Elaine *art educator, consultant*

Troy
DeHart, Karen Trautmann *artist, educator*

Waynesville
Doster, Susan Elizabeth *artist*

Westerville
Anderson, Judith Ann *artist, writer*
Lott, Vera Naomi *artist, educator*

Willoughby
Vokic, Heather Maureen *artist, educator*

Yellow Springs
Kadish, Katherine *artist, art educator*
Mercede, Nevin *art educator, artist*

OKLAHOMA

Ada
Dempsey, B. *artist*

Ardmore
Sadler, Marion Hanson *retired art educator*

Broken Arrow
Huff, Melinda Louise *art educator*

Claremore
Livingston, Sylvia Jean *art appraiser*

Crescent
Lovett, Kristi Summer *art educator*

Lawton
Wonsewitz, Pom Cha *artist, horticulturist*

Mustang
Hutter, Teresa Ann *art educator*

Norman
Reedy, Mitsuno Ishii *artist, painter*
Wood, Betty Jean *conceptual artist, art educator*

Okemah
DeShields, Elizabeth Peggy Bowen *artist, educator, poet*

Oklahoma City
Alaupovic, Alexandra Vrbanic *artist, educator*
Boston, Billie *costume designer, costume history educator*
Brummett, Shirley Ann *art educator*
Hollingshead, Bonne Lou *fine art artist*
Richardson, Jean Brooks *artist, printmaker*
Whitener, Carolyn Raye *artist*

Tulsa
Frazier, Mary Ann *artist*
Howerton, Helen F. *artist*
Valero, Maria Teresa *photographer, art educator*

OREGON

Ashland
Burritt, Barbara *artist*

Bandon
Handley, Louise Patricia *artist*

Bend
Brooke, Sandra Lee *painter*

Eugene
Gourley, Paula Marie *art educator, artist, writer, publishing executive*

Gladstone
Frank, Dee *artist, educator*

Lake Oswego
Rimerman, Janet Malaine *art educator, artist*

Medford
Morris, Judy *artist*
Schubert, Ruth Carol Hickok *artist, educator*

Newberg
Keith, Pauline Mary *artist, illustrator, writer*

Portland
Boutwell, Anne Dielschneider *artist, painter*
Ebert, Leslie *artist*
Farner, Darla A. *artist*
Janovec, Madeline Meza *artist, educator*
Lorenz, Nancy *artist*
Mullane, Jeanette Leslie *artist, educator*
Street, Terri M. *artist, educator*
Thompson, Terrie Lee *graphic designer*
Tower, Sue Warncke *artist*

Prineville
Schulz, Suzon Louise *fine artist*

Silverton
Stone, Jane Buffington *artist, writer*

Sunriver
Seeger, Virginia Vincent *painter*

Sutherlin
Gugel, Merilynn Sue *artist*

West Linn
Stoddard-Hayes, Marlana Kay *artist, educator*

PENNSYLVANIA

Abington
Goldfine, Beatrice *artist*

Ardmore
Levy, Rochelle Feldman *artist*

Atglen
Young, Robyn S. *artist, historian, commentator*

Bellefonte
Stevens-Sollman, Jeanne Lee *artist*

Bethlehem
Fishbone, Vivian Manperl *artist*

Bowmansville
Myers, Rose (Toni) A. *art educator*

Boyertown
Woods Coggins, Alma *artist*

Butler
Patterson, Patricia Lynne *artist, educator*

Camp Hill
McGeary, Barbara Joyce *artist, educator*

Clarion
Joslyn, Catherine Ruth *art educator, artist*

Doylestown
Taylor, Rosemary *artist*

Easton
Bellissimo, Mary E. *art educator*

Edinboro
Burke, Rachael J. *art educator*

Elkins Park
Erlebacher, Martha Mayer *artist, educator*

Erie
Azicri, Nicolette Maly *art educator, artist*

Exton
Webber, Helen *artist*

Fairview
Krider, Margaret Young *art educator*

Glen Mills
Turner, Janet Sullivan *painter, sculptor*

Glenside
Medel, Rebecca Rosalie *artist*

Greensburg
Fajt, Karen Elaine *art educator*
Vissat, Maureen *art educator*

Hanover
Hartman, Carol Lee *art educator, reading specialist*

Havertown
Spicer, Jean Uhl *art educator*

Herminie
Sichok, Maryanne M. *art educator*

Jenkintown
Roediger, Janice Anne *artist, educator*

Jessup
Karluk, Lori Jean *craft designer, copyeditor*

Kutztown
Kuehne, Helenirene Anne *art educator*

Lancaster
McClellan, Joan C. Osmundson *art educator*
Poser, Joan Rapps *artist, writer*
Stewart, Arlene Jean Golden *art director*

Langhorne
Schadler, Florence *artist, educator*

Media
Steinhardt Gutman, Bertha *artist, educator*
Turner, Letitia Rhodes *artist*

Midway
Pierrard-Mutton, Mary V. *artist, educator*

Millersville
Bensur, Barbara Jean *art educator, researcher*

Moon Township
Pociernicki, Janice Louise *artist*

Mount Pleasant
Pyda, Dianne Sue *art educator*

Narberth
Pollack, Sonya A. *artist*

New Hope
Freyer, Victoria C. *fashion and interior design executive*

Newtown Square
Winter, Ruth *artist*

Pennsauken
Ford, Mary Pat *art educator*

Philadelphia
Burko, Diane *artist, educator*
Ciszkowski, Grace Marie *art educator*
Goschke, Linda Fry *artist*
Maksymowicz, Virginia *art educator, writer, artist*
Miyamori, Keiko *artist*
Moss-Vreeland, Patricia Ellen *artist*
Newman, Libby *painter, printmaker, curator*
Schaff, Barbara Walley *artist*
Shea, Judith *artist*
Spandorfer, Merle Sue *artist, educator, writer*
Tileston, Jackie *artist, educator*

Pittsburgh
Bates, Beverly Jo-Anne *artist, educator*
Carr, Winifred Walker *artist, historian*
Fredette, Barbara Wagner *art educator*
Novelli, Katherine Anne *art educator*
Spalding, Rita Lee *artist*
Tsu, Susan *costume designer, educator*

Port Matilda
Ritti, Alyce Rae *artist*

Richboro
Burtt, Larice Annadel Roseman *artist*

Schwenksville
Zucker, Barbara J. *artist, educator*

Shippensburg
Evans, Margaret Patsos *photographer, photography educator*

State College
Ione, Amy *artist, researcher*

Tower City
Adams, Susan L. *art educator*

Unionville
Benjamin, Angela M. *art educator*

University Park
Amato, Michele Amateau *artist, educator*
Stankiewicz, Mary Ann *art educator*

Villanova
Stefanowicz, Janus *costume designer*

Washington
Knight, Sherry Ann *art educator*
Maloney, Patricia Diana *artist, educator*

Wellsboro
Driskell, Lucile G. *artist*

West Chester
Gilbert, Sandee R. *art educator*
Schelling, Gloria Ann *art educator*

Wexford
Osby, Larissa Geiss *artist*

Wilkes Barre
Joyce, Ann Iannuzzo *art educator*

Wyncote
Weiss, Mili Dunn *artist, educator*

Wynnewood
Bowes, Betty Miller *painter, art consultant*
Buffum, Kathleen D. *artist*

RHODE ISLAND

Jamestown
Worden, Katharine Cole *sculptor*

Newport
Liotus, Sandra Mary *lighting designer, small business owner, consultant*

Pawtucket
Boghossian, Joan Thompson *artist*

Portsmouth
Fitzsimonds, Carol Strause *artist, art gallery director*

Providence
Harman, Carole Moses *retired art educator, artist*
Howes, Lorraine de Wet *fashion designer, educator*
Jenness, Rebecca Estella *artist, educator*
Leviten, Riva Shamray *artist*

SOUTH CAROLINA

Blacksburg
Jones, Karen Faulkner *art educator*

Columbia
Elkins, Toni Marcus *artist, art association administrator*
McWhorter, Elsie Jean *retired art educator, artist*

Greenville
Dreskin, Jeanet Steckler *painter, medical artist, educator*
McCune, Linda Williams *artist, educator*

Irmo
Branham, Jennie Jones *artist*

Lexington
Holland, Gene Grigsby (Scottie Holland) *artist*

Mc Cormick
Hofer, Ingrid *artist, educator*

Murrells Inlet
Howard, Joan Alice *artist*

Myrtle Beach
Todd, Cheryl *art educator*

Rock Hill
Mintich, Mary R. *art educator, sculptor*

SOUTH DAKOTA

Brookings
Eischen, Michelle Robin *art educator*

Mission
MacKichan, Margaret Anna *artist, art educator*

TENNESSEE

Chattanooga
Washburn, Sandra Paynter *art educator*

Cleveland
Kraus, Ruby Jean *art educator*

Crab Orchard
McBee, Christy Dawn *art educator, pre-school educator*

Dayton
Bloxson, Phyllis Jane *art educator*

Greenfield
Engler, Sherrie Lee *artist, illustrator*

Humboldt
Agee, Nelle Hulme *retired art history educator*

Jackson
Wallace, Permelia Franklin *artist*

Knoxville
Drinnon, Janis Bolton *artist, poet, volunteer*
Markert, Cynthia Allin *artist*
Marshall-Hardin, Floy Jeanne *art educator*
Pirkle, Mänya Higdon *artist, craftsman*

Memphis
Dierkes, Judith Ann *art educator, artist*

Murfreesboro
Reed, Angelica Denise *sculptor, writer, illustrator*

Nashville
Chandler, Nettie Johnson *artist*
Crosswhite, Jeanette Elvira *art educator*
Cundiff, Lou Willie *artist, sculptor, writer*
Evans, Patti Renee *art director*
Roberts, Margaret Reynolds *art educator*

Oak Ridge
Regan-Stanton, Christa Maria *artist*

Soddy Daisy
Bice, Edna Jewel *artist, educator*

Townsend
Birdwell, Susan Elizabeth Smith *artist*

TEXAS

Abilene
Kiel, Martha Guillet *art educator*

Alpine
Fairlie, Carol Hunter *artist, art educator*

Amarillo
Eimon, Pan Dodd *artist, writer*

Arlington
Munoz, Celia Alvarez *artist*
Stripling, Betty Keith *artist, retired medical/surgical nurse*

Austin
Alford, Frances Holliday *artist, retired special education educator*
Sawyer, Margo Lucy *artist, educator*

Bangs
Levisay, Joy Elice *art educator*

Beaumont
Meeks, Donna Marie *art educator*

Belton
Fontaine-White, Barbara Frances *art educator*

Carrollton
Ratliff, Mary Jean Dougherty *fine arts educator*

Cedar Hill
Moore, Jacquelyn *art educator*

China Spring
Smith, Laura Dossett *art dealer*

Cleburne
Arnold, Sandra Ruth Kouns *photographer*

College Station
Martin, Carol Jacquelyn *artist, educator*

Coppell
Pitts, Jennifer Lynn *art educator*

Corpus Christi
Bluntzer, Chispa Hernández *artist, educator*
Crane, Frances Hawkins *artist, educator*
McDowell, Barbara *artist*

Dallas
Dealey, Lynn Townsend *artist*
McKnight, Pamela Ann *art educator*
Nelson, Pamela Hudson *artist, educator*
Penn, Linda *computer animator*
Richardson, Lynn *art educator*
Schulz, Sandra E. *art educator*
Stephenson, Jane Connell *artist, educator*
Thompson, Tara D. *illustrator, writer, career planning administrator*

Denton
Bertine, Dorothy Wilmuth *artist, educator, accountant, genealogist, poet, writer*
Gough, Georgia Belle *art educator*
McMath, Elizabeth Moore *graphic artist*
Weller, Laurie June *artist, educator*

Diboll
Tannery, Ginger *art educator*

Flower Mound
West, Frances Lee *retired doll artist, freelance writer*

Fort Worth
Allison, Sarah Amanda *art educator, consultant*
Bush, Jill Lobdill *artist*
Durham, Jo Ann Fanning *artist*
Ivy, Marilyn Atkinson *artist, educator, art director*
Pelt, Judy Ann Lobdill *artist*
Phillips, Mary Ann *artist, writer, retired legal assistant*
Procknow, Margot *artist*
Ray, Jessica B. *artist, poet, educator*
Stevenson, Ruth Carter *art patron*
Wells, Edie Carol *artist, educator*

Fredericksburg
Wahrmund, Peggy Stieler *artist, rancher*

Garland
Hodges, Kathleen McGill *art educator*
Rogers, Sharon *art educator*

Gordonville
Van Arsdale, Marie Delvechio *artist*

Houston
Dent, Leanna Gail *art educator*
Orr, Carole *artist*
Ouellette, Jami *art educator*
Randolph, Lynn Moore *artist*
Reid, Katherine Louise *artist, educator, writer*
Steinhoff, Judith B. *art history educator*
Stockholder, Jessica *sculptor*

Hurst
Bowman, Karmien C. *art educator, artist, sculptor, ceramist*

Lakehills
Spears, Diane Shields *art director, elementary school educator*

Laredo
Gómez, Angela González *art educator*

Lubbock
Kraft, Leah Michelle *art educator*

Murchison
Taweel, Janice M. *artist, educator*

Nederland
Rozell, Linda Joy *art educator*

New Braunfels
Alexander, Anna Margaret *artist, writer, educator*

Odessa
Price, Pamela Champion *art educator*

Plano
Kuddes, Kathryn M. *fine arts director*
Litwin, Ruth Ann Forbes *artist*

Rosenberg
Haygood, Eithel Marinella *artist, educator*

Rusk
Cook, Doris Adele *artist*

San Antonio
Funk, Charlotte Marie *art educator, artist*
Sarinana, Silvia *art educator*

Santa Fe
Paratore-Zarzana, Mary Gay *artist, art educator, lecturer*

Seabrook
Sterling, Shirley Frampton *artist, educator*

Spring
Calabro, Joanna Joan Sondra *artist*
Wilbanks, Mary *artist*

Watauga
Engisch, Tosca Marianne *artist, educator, social worker*

Wichita Falls
Rose, Carol Lee *artist, educator*

UTAH

Provo
Teeter, Lorna Madsen *art educator*

Salt Lake City
Clegg, Dixie Stallings *art educator, studio owner*
Huelskamp, Willamarie Ann *artist*

Stansbury Park
Moyer, Linda Lee *artist, educator, author*

VERMONT

Belvidere Center
Lipke, Kathryn *artist, educator*

Bennington
Lum, Mary *artist, art educator*

Brattleboro
Abrams, Jackie *artist, educator*

Burlington
Conant, Margaret Caney *art educator*
Gabriel, Diane Augusta *artist, educator*

Charlotte
Robinson, Sally Winston *artist*

Dorset
Marron, Pamela Anne *artist*

East Dorset
Howe, Nancy *artist*

Essex Junction
Tedd, Monique Micheline *artist*

Montpelier
Talbot-Kelly, Samantha Rachel *artist*

Pittsfield
Wacker, Susan Regina *graphics designer, consultant*

Stowe
Beach, Lisa Forster (Elizabeth Forster Beach) *artist, educator*

West Burke
Van Vliet, Claire *artist*

VIRGINIA

Abingdon
Miller, Janice Brice *art educator*

Alexandria
Kim, Sook Cha *artist*
Lopatin, Carol Keesler *artist*
Whitson, Elizabeth Temple *graphics designer*

Arlington
Ellinwood, Janice Greenberg *art educator*
Straus, Patricia W. *artist, retired educator*

Blacksburg
Gablik, Suzi *art educator, writer*

Charlottesville
Norment, Rachel Gobbel *artist, educator, writer*
Weinberger, Adrienne *artist, art appraiser*

Chesapeake
Potter, Cynthia M. *art educator, artist*

Coeburn
Williams, Jo Karen Kobeck *artist, writer*

Colonial Heights
Grizzard-Barham, Barbara Lee *artist*

Culpeper
Bahl-Moore, Elizabeth Ann *artist, educator*

Draper
Whitehurst, Mary Tarr *artist, poet, writer*

Fairfax
Kendall Hull, Margarida *art educator, painter*

Falls Church
Stratton, Dorothy E. *painter, printmaker*

Flint Hill
Forbush, Sandra M. *artist, educator*

Floyd
Bosniak, Kanta *artist*

Fredericksburg
Gill, Milvi Kosenkranius *artist, photographer*
Holmes, Jacqueline Christobel Wright *art educator*

Front Royal
Harrison, (Hilde) *artist*

Great Falls
Ganley, Betty *artist*

Hampton
Wolff, Sharon L. *photographer, department chairman*

Harrisonburg
Theodore, Crystal *artist, retired educator*

Herndon
Nolan, Leslie Marian *artist*
Simanski, Claire Dvorak *art educator*

Lynchburg
Massie, Anne Adams Robertson *artist*

Mc Lean
Harrison, Carol Love *fine art photographer*
Scott, Concetta Ciotti *artist, educator*

Mechanicsvlle
Miles, Carole Harrison *artist*

Middleburg
vom Baur, Daphne de Blois *artist*

Midlothian
Morse, Kimberly Deane *artist*

Newport News
Camp, Hazel Lee Burt *artist*
Keech, Ann Marie *training design and multimedia consultant*

Orange
Montgomery, Linda Boudreaux *artist*

Petersburg
Abbott-Ryan, Pat *painter, writer*

Prospect
Shield, Julie Marie Karst *artist, educator*

Radford
Kessler, Kendall Seay Feriozi *artist*
Salam, Halide *artist, educator*

Richmond
Humphrey, Mitzi Greene *artist*
Kinnier, Emily P. *artist*

Roanoke
Gibson, Stella Eades *art educator, photographer*
Vones, Cynthia Louise *art educator*

Spotsylvania
Pitts, Karen Colleen *art educator*

Springfield
Brown, Margaret Catherine *artist*

Stafford
Gambaro, Retha Walden *artist*

Staunton
Jolloff, Nilda Elizabeth *art educator, artist*

Vienna
Lorfano, Pauline Davis *artist*
Milton, Carol Lynne *artist*

Virginia Beach
Fink, Eloise Bradley *art director*

Wachapreague
Rogers, Lynne Cary *artist, painter*

Wakefield
Nettles, Kathryn Chappell *visual artist, educator*

Waynesboro
Spilman, Patricia *artist, educator*

Williamsburg
Stanley, Shirley Davis *artist*

WASHINGTON

Bainbridge Island
Burns, Shirley MacDonald *artist, educator*

Bellevue
Foster, Linda Lee *artist*

Bremerton
Burnett, Amy Louise *artist, art gallery owner*

Coupeville
Martell, Maxine A. *artist*

Edmonds
Deering, Anne-Lise *artist, retired real estate salesperson*
Johnson, d'Elaine Ann Herard *artist, consultant*

Lilliwaup
McGrady, Corinne Young *design company executive*

Mercer Island
Langhout-Nix, Nelleke *artist*

Ocean Park
Lee, Martha *artist, writer*

Olympia
Randlett, Mary Willis *photographer*
Tremblay, Gail Elizabeth *art educator*

Richland
Ristow, Gail Ross *art educator, paralegal, children's rights advocate*

Ridgefield
Potter, Debby *art educator*

Seattle
Allen, Judith Syma *art educator, artist*
Bibaud, Rene *artist, performer, consultant*
Reeves, Joan Hutchins *painter*
Ross, Joan Stuart *artist, art educator*
Ruffner, Ginny Martin *artist, glassblower*
Stearns, Susan Tracey *lighting design company executive, lawyer*
Tift, Mary Louise *artist*
Woo, Cathy M. *artist*

Sequim
Guilmet, Glenda Jean *artist*

Shelton
Russman, Irene Karen *artist*
Thomas-John, Yvonne Maree *artist, interior designer*

Silverdale
Shaw, Annita Louise *art educator*

Spokane
Mobley, Karen Ruth *art director*

Sultan
Duffy, Anne M. *artist*

Vancouver
Hennum, Susanna Shelly *art history educator*
Hulburt, Lucille Hall *artist, educator*

Vashon
Schwennesen, Carol Ann *artist, educator*

Walla Walla
Rasmussen, Lisa Anne *art department administrator, art educator, art gallery director*

WEST VIRGINIA

Bluefield
Brown, Sheri Lynn *artist, poet, educator*

Fairmont
DeVito, Teresa Marie *artist*

Morgantown
Fergus, Victoria J. *art and education educator*

Shepherdstown
Valentine, Mary Ann *graphics designer*

Wheeling
Phillis, Marilyn Hughey *artist*

WISCONSIN

Appleton
Amm, Sophia Jadwiga *artist, educator*

Delavan
Gauger, Michele Roberta *photographer*

Dousman
Porter, Sally Louise *artist*

Gordon
La Liberte, Ann Gillis *graphics designer, educator*

Hartford
Brandt, Pamela Ann *art educator, special education educator*

Hartland
Stamsta, Jean F. *artist*

Janesville
Detert-Moriarty, Judith Anne *graphic designer, educator, volunteer*

Johnson Creek
Quest, Kristina Kay *art educator, small business owner*

Kaukauna
Brewster, Margaret Emelia *artist*

Kenosha
Gustin, Brenda Sue *retired art educator, painter*

Madison
Myers, Frances J. *artist*

Marshfield
Gardner, Ella Haines *artist*

Mc Farland
Deniston-Trochta, Grace Marie *educator, artist*

Mequon
Tucholke, Christel-Anthony *artist, educator*

Milwaukee
Hidson, Patricia Diane *artist, educator*
Poehlmann, JoAnna *artist, illustrator, book designer, educator*
Waldbaum, Jane Cohn *art history educator*

Oconomowoc
Conrader, Constance Ruth *artist, writer*
Driscoll, Virgilyn Mae (Schaetzel) *retired art educator, artist, consultant*
Reich, Rose Marie *retired art educator*

Oshkosh
Smith, Merilyn Roberta *art educator*

Racine
Sahakian, Lillian Zarouhi *artist, designer*
Teegarden, Nicolee *artist, consultant, retired educator*

Redgranite
Borchardt, Betsy Olk *artist*

Reedsburg
Mockler, Jolee Marie *art educator*

Rice Lake
Skrupky, Elaine Charlotte *art educator*

Three Lakes
Murphy, Erin Melissa *art educator*

Watertown
Burns, Noëlle Ann *art educator*

West Bend
Wolff, Mickiah Ann *artist, educator*

Winneconne
Gust, Joyce Jane *artist*

WYOMING

Casper
Covert, Addey Elizabeth *art educator*

Cheyenne
Moore, Mary French (Muffy Moore) *potter, advocate*

Jackson
Hessel, Marieluise *art collector*

TERRITORIES OF THE UNITED STATES

GUAM

Hagatna
Flores, Christina Rosalie *art educator*

PUERTO RICO

San Juan
Luna Padilla, Nitza Enid *photography educator*

MILITARY ADDRESSES OF THE UNITED STATES

EUROPE

APO
Hibben, Barbara Ann Pandzik *museum administrator, foreign service officer*

CANADA

BRITISH COLUMBIA

Salt Spring Island
Raginsky, Nina *artist*

Vancouver
Bonifacho, Bratsa *artist*

NEWFOUNDLAND AND LABRADOR

Torbay
Dabinett, Diana Frances *artist*

NOVA SCOTIA

Bayfield
Blair, Rosemary Miles *retired art educator, environmentalist*

Halifax
Kulyk, Karen Gay *artist*

ONTARIO

Toronto
Astman, Barbara Ann *artist, educator*
Bolley, Andrea *artist*
Braswell, Paula Ann *artist*
Jaworska, Tamara *artist*
Kooluris Dobbs, Linda Kia *artist, photographer*

QUEBEC

Saint-Adele
Rousseau-Vermette, Mariette *artist*

Windsor
Isajiw, Sophia O. *artist, educator, curator, writer*

MEXICO

Mexico City
De La Riva, Myriam Ann *artist*

ENGLAND

London
Edwards, Sylvia Ann *artist*
Goulekas, Karen *special effects supervisor*

Richmond
Armfield, Diana Maxwell *artist, educator*

FRANCE

Benerville-Sur-Mer
Feiler, Jo Alison *artist*

Malaucene Vaucluse
Langenkamp, Mary Alice (M.A. Langenkamp) *artist, educator*

Paris
Stoianovich, Marcelle Simone *artist*

ITALY

Milan
Versace, Donatella *fashion designer*

ADDRESS UNPUBLISHED

Abbe, Elfriede Martha *sculptor, graphics designer*
Abbey, Linda Rowe *artist, educator*
Abbott, Linda Joy *stained glass artisan, educator, photographer*
Abel, Barbara Ellen *photographer*
Abeles, Kim Victoria *artist*
Aber, Ita *artist, conservator, historian*
Abramowicz, Janet *painter, print-maker*
Absher, Donna Atkins *textile designer*
Agne, Phyllis G. *artist, educator*
Aldredge, Theoni Vachliotis *costume designer*
Alexander, Marjorie Anne *artist, consultant*
Andersson, Helen Demitrous *artist*
Andrade, Edna *artist, educator*
Andreason, Lee (Sharon Lee Andreason) *sculptor*
Andrew, Dolores Molcan *retired art educator, artist*
Antin, Eleanor *artist*
Applehans, Cynthia Diane *art educator, artist*
Arifi, Fatana Baktash *artist, educator*
Arndt, Dianne Joy *artist, photographer*
Arrieta, Diane Marie *artist*
Arrigo, Jan Elizabeth *photographer, writer, artist*
Arrott, Patricia Graham *artist, educator*
Arthurs, Madeleine Hope *artist*
Aschheim, Eve Michele *artist, educator*
Ashleigh, Caroline *art and antiques appraiser*
Aslakson, Sarah *artist*
Assael, Alyce *artist*
Astaire, Carol Anne Taylor *artist, educator*
Atkinson, Tracey Blake *artist, educator*
Atwood, Colleen *costume designer*
Aunio, Irene M. *artist*
Avery, Carolyn Elizabeth *artist*
Azarian, Mary *illustrator*
Bader, Lorraine Greenberg *textile stylist, designer, consultant, artist*
Baer, Diane Draper *artist*
Bailey, Joy Y. *art educator*
Ballarian, Anna Nevarte *retired art educator*
Barber, Joan Marie *artist*
Barcroft, Judith *artist, actress*
Barlow, Jean *art educator, painter*
Barnett-Evanson, Fila *artist, executive recruiter*
Barone, Angela Maria *artist, researcher*
Barth, Frances *artist*
Beerman, Miriam *artist, educator*
Behr, Marion Ray *artist*
Bellospirito, Robyn Suzanne *artist, writer*
Bender, Janet Pines *artist*
Berlin, Beatrice Winn *artist, printmaker*
Berns, Pamela Kari *artist, publisher*
Bernstein, Sylvia *artist*
Bierman, Sandra *artist*
Bingham, Marian *artist, printmaker*
Birchard, Catherine Suzanne Sieh *artist*
Bishop, Delores Ann *artist, educator*
Blackwell, Lois Moore *fashion designer, educator, visual artist*
Block, Amanda Roth *artist*
Bodie, Phyllis Jean *art educator, watercolorist*
Bodnar-Balahutrak, Lydia *artist, educator*
Bogdanowicz, Loretta Mae *artist, educator*
Bohrman, Catherine Leuchs *sculptor*
Boldovitch, Gerri *art educator*
Bonassi, Jodi *artist, marketing professional, consultant*
Bowen, Ginger Ann *artist*
Bowers, Andrea *artist*
Boyce, Martha Jo *artist, educator*
Boynton, Sandra Keith *illustrator, cartoonist, stationery products executive*
Braisted, Madeline Charlotte *artist, retired financial planner, military officer*
Bramson, Phyllis Halperin *artist, educator*
Brenken, Hanne Marie *artist*
Briand-Ryan, Donna Marie *artistic designer*
Briceño, Candace Michele *artist*
Brodeur, Catherine Reckart *artist*
Bronkar, Eunice Dunalee *artist, educator*
Brooks, Deborah June *art educator*
Brown, Alice Elste *artist*
Brown, Amy Christine *art educator*
Brown, Carol Rose *artist*
Brown, Reni (Arlene Patricia Theresa Brown) *artist*
Burns, Toni Anthony *artist*
Butler Yank, Leslie Ann *artist, writer, editor*
Butterfield, Deborah Kay *sculptor*
Calabrese, Karen Ann *artist, educator*
Calamar, Gloria *artist*
Caldwell, Eleanor *artist*
Calvin, Jamie Duif *retired interactive designer*
Cameron, Donna *artist, art educator*
Capello, Linda *artist*
Carl, Susan Marie *photographer, photojournalist*
Carlyle, Bobbie Kristine *sculptor*
Carraher, Mary Lou Carter *art educator*
Carroll, Marie-Jean Greve *retired art educator, artist*
Carter, Nanette Carolyn *artist*
Carter, Yvonne Pickering *art educator*
Casazza, Monica Kathryn *art educator*
Caseiras, Jo Ann Striga *artist, educator*
Charters, Cynthia Grace *artist, educator*
Chase, Doris Totten *sculptor, educator, filmmaker*
Chermayeff, Alexandra Sasha *artist*
Childs, Wenetta Grybas *artist*
Chu, Lili *jewelry designer, consultant*
Chun, Jacqueline Clibbett *artist, educator*
Cifolelli, Alberta Carmella *artist, educator*
Ciliberti, Ava Carol *artist*
Clabeaux-Fechter, Barbara Jean *artist, educator*
Claiborne, Liz (Elisabeth Claiborne Ortenberg) *fashion designer*
Clark, Evelyn Jean *artist, educator*
Cleary, Manon Catherine *artist, retired art educator*
Cline, Ann *artist*
Clydesdale, Peggy *artist, medical/surgical nurse*
Cobb, Virginia Horton *artist, educator*
Cobey, Virginia Branum *artist, actress, art collector*

Code, Audrey B. *art educator*
Cohen, Margaret Ann *artist, consultant*
Cole, Jean Anne *artist*
Comar, Mary Alice *retired art educator, farmer*
Conroy, Tamara Boks *artist, special education educator, retired nurse*
Cooper, Elva June *artist*
Cooper, Rebecca *art dealer*
Corry, Aline Lahusen *art educator*
Coulter, Cynthia Jean *artist, educator*
Cozza, Helen Rock *art educator, artist*
Craik, Mary Bernice *artist, art gallery owner*
Crinklaw, Katherine Mary *artist*
Crocker, Suzanne *painter*
Cunningham, Kathy *artist, educator*
Curnutte, Mary E. *artist*
D'Alessio, Valaida Corrine *artist, consultant*
Daley, Sandra *retired artist, filmmaker, photographer*
Damsgaard, Patricia Rae *artist, educator*
Davidson, Jeannie *costume designer*
Davis, Doris Rosenbaum (Dee Davis) *artist, writer*
Davis, Taylor *sculptor*
Davis-Townsend, Helen Irene *retired art educator*
Deal, Rebecca L. *art educator*
Dean, Diane (H.) Sweet *artist, retired credit manager*
DeAngelo, Judith *artist*
DeHority, Miriam Arnold Newman (Miriam Newman) *artist*
DeJack, Jacqueline Elvadeana *artist, educator*
Dembeck, Mary Grace *artist, writer*
Denenberg, Katharine W. Hornberger (Tinka Denenberg) *artist, educator*
Denton, Judy Ann *art educator*
Derber, Dana M. *graphic designer*
Despot, Shirley Ann *artist*
Dewey, Ariane *artist, illustrator*
D'Haiti, Felicia Kathleen (Felicia Kathleen Messina) *fine arts educator*
Diamond, Mary E(lizabeth) B(aldwin) *artist*
Di Giacomo, Fran *artist*
Donath, Therese *artist, author*
Drummond, Sally Hazelet *artist*
Dubs, Gloria L. *artist, realtor*
Dunn, Nancy Marabella *artist, art educator*
Duong, Anh *artist, actress*
Dustman, Elizabeth *art educator, product designer*
Ebler, Marilyn Ann *graphic designer, educator*
Eby, Lois *artist*
Edmo, Jean Umiokalani *artist, poet*
Ehrlich, Risa Hirsch *artist, educator*
Elcik, Elizabeth Mabie *fashion illustrator*
Ender, Pauline Louise *painter*
Engelman, Rosalyn Ackerman *artist, marketing executive*
Engels, Beatrice Ann *artist, poet, retired real estate company executive*
Erbe, Chantell Van *artist*
Erler, Mary Frances *art educator*
Eshel, Hanna M. *sculptor, painter, photographer*
Evans, Barbara *art educator*
Ewald, Roberta Grant *artist, writer*
Fabricatore, Carol Diane *artist, educator*
Fagadau, Jeanne Malkoff *art dealer*
Farrar, Elaine Willardson *artist*
Fasman, Marjorie Lesser *artist, writer*
Feeback, Loreta Dotaline Kreeger *artist*
Fein, Sheila Carol *artist*
Feiner, Francine *art educator, photographer*
Feuerstein, Penny *artist*
Fine, Jane Madeline *visual artist*
Fine, Sally Solfisburg *artist, educator*
Fish, Janet Isobel *artist*
Fish, Jeanne Spencer *artist, retired lawyer*
Fisher, Kim *artist*
Fitzgerald, Joan V. *artist*
Flato, Gwyndolynn Sue *fine art educator*
Flavin, Sonja *artist*
Flower, Renée Beville *artist*
Flowers-Schoen, Marylu Utley *art educator*
Foosaner, Judith *artist, art educator*
Foronda, Monica F. *graphics designer*
Foster, Elaine Elizabeth *retired art educator*
Fouché, Helen Strother *editorial design executive*
Fratkin, Leslie *photographer*
Frauenhoffer, Rose Marie *visual artist*
Frederick, Elizabeth Eleanor Tatum *watercolor artist, retired educator*
Freilicher, Jane *artist*
Freyermuth, Virginia Karen *art educator*
Fulton Ross, Gale *artist, actor*
Fumagalli, Barbara Merrill *artist, printmaker*
Furth, Karen J. *artist*
Galitello-Wolfe, Jane Maryann *artist, writer*
Gallagher, Cynthia *artist, educator*
Gamache, Claudette Theresa *artist, nurse*
Gamble, Desirata *artist, poet*
Gardner, Elizabeth Ann Hunt *artist, poet, genealogist*
Garnett, Adrienne Wilma *art educator*
Gechtoff, Sonia *artist*
Gerhardt, Carol *artist*
Gerstein, Esther *sculptor*
Giddens, Kathleen Colette *artist, art educator*
Gilliland, Lucille Mary *artist, writer*
Glover, Janet Briggs *artist*
Gnezda, Nicole M. *art educator*
Gold, Betty Virginia *artist*
Gold, Sarae R. *art educator*
Golden, Judith Greene *artist, educator*
Goulet, Lorrie *sculptor*
Grace, L.A. *fine artist, designer*
Graham, K(athleen) M. (K. M. Graham) *artist*
Grames-Lyra, Judith Ellen *artist, educator, municipal official*
Gray, Barbara May *artist*
Gray, Linda Alyn *artist, educator*
Greenwood, Jane *costume designer, educator*
Gremmler, Margo Rowder *art director*
Griffin, Sallie T. *artist, photographer, retired technologist*
Grim, Ellen Townsend *retired art educator*
Gruen, Shirley Schanen *artist*
Gurwitz-Hall, Barbara Ann *artist*
Gussow, Sue Ferguson *artist, educator*
Hall, Susan Laurel *artist, educator, writer*
Hammond, Harmony *artist, educator*
Hancock, Patricia Ann *artist*
Handa, Eugenie Quan *graphic designer*
Hannaman, Alberta Anna *artist*
Hannon, Sherrill Ann *artist*
Hanson, Janice Crawford *artist*
Hanson, Jo *artist, educator, writer*
Harman, Maryann Whittemore *artist, educator*
Harmening, Gail Joan *craft pattern designer*
Harper, Gloria Janet *artist, educator*
Harrington, Michaele Mary *artist, educator*
Haskell, Jane Zirinsky *artist, educator*
Hauft, Amy Gilbert *artist*
Hawkins, Cynthia *artist, educator*
Head, Melva Ann *artist*
Heath, Audrey Mary *artist, jewelry designer*
Heath, Lia Kathryn *apparel designer*
Heath, Patti *art educator, musician*
Hector-Skinner, Vicki L. *artist*
Heiss, Mary Wynne *artist*
Heller, Mary Wheeler *photographer*
Hemmings, Dianne Smith *artist, educator*
Henes, Donna *artist, writer*
Henson Scales, Meg D(iane) *artist, writer, publisher*
Hepper, Carol *artist, educator*
Herley, Daveen Dorothy *art educator, artist*
Herman, Joni Marie-Victor *artist*
Hertel, Heather *artist*
Hessinger, Jill A. *art educator*
Hibel, Edna *artist*
Higgins, Larkin Maureen *artist, poet, educator*
Hillis, Catherine H. *artist*
Hillsmith, Fannie L. *artist*
Hilton, Nicky (Nicholai Olivia Hilton) *apparel designer*
Hinkle, Erica *art educator*
Hintzke, Teresa Anna *illustrator*
Hogle, Ann Meilstrup *painter, art educator*
Holbrow, Gwendolyn Jane *artist, writer*
Holden, Rebecca Lynn *artist*
Holzer, Jenny *artist*
Hom, Mei Ling *artist, educator*
Horlick, Ruth *photographer*
Horton, Patricia Mathews *artist, violist and violinist*
Hoskins, Lou Ann *art educator*
Howell, Mary Jean *artist, administrative assistant*
Hsieh, Tsui-Hsia *artist, educator*
Huffman, Melanie Diane *art educator*
Hummel, Marian *retired art educator, photographer*
Hurst, Heather *illustrator*
Hutchison, Edna Ruth *artist*
Hyde, Alice Bach *artist*
Hyman, Sylvia Gertrude *artist*
Jacir, Emily *photographer, conceptual artist*
Jackson-Vanier, Linda M. *art educator*
Jacobs, Eleanor *art consultant, retired art administrator*
Jacoby, Beverly Schreiber *art consultant*
Jansen, Angela Bing *artist, educator*
Jarcho, Judith Lynn *artist*
Jay, Norma Joyce *artist*
Jernigan, Hilary Dawn *art educator, artist*
Jerviss, Joy J. (Joanne Jackson Jerviss) *artist, educator, small business owner*
Jessen, Shirley Agnes *artist*
Jewett, Mary (Betsy) Elizabeth *artist, conservationist*
Johnson, Margaret Heller *artist, educator*
Johnson, Morgan Lea *artist, museum educator*
Jones, Jane *artist*
Joynes, Amelia C. *art educator*
Jurgutis, Danguole *artist*
Kahn, Cecily *painter*
Kahn, Susan *artist*
Kane, Margaret Brassler *sculptor*
Kannenstine, Margaret Lampe *artist*
Kaplan, Phyllis *artist, composer*
Kavanagh, Cornelia Kubler *sculptor*
Kearns, Ellen Veronica *artist*
Kehoe-Gadway, Nita L. *art educator, art gallery director*
Kennedy, Barbara Ellen Perry *art therapist*
Kennedy, Joanie Tiska *artist, painter*
Kenney, Estelle Koval *artist, educator*
Khvost-Vostrikova, Natalia S. *art educator, consultant*
King, Joy Riemer *art educator, linguist*
Kipniss MacDonald, Betty Ann *artist, educator*
Kirby, Vesta Ann *artist*
Kirkwood, Catherine *artist*
Klein, Charlotte Feuerstein *art consultant*
Klein, Deborah Lynn *art educator*
Klein, Lynn Ellen *artist*
Klement, Vera *artist*
Klinger, Susan *art educator, artist*
Knapp, Candace Louise *sculptor*
Koblick, Joan Lesser *retired art educator, artist*
Koch, Dorothy Harriet *artist*
Koch, Virginia Greenleaf (Virginia M. Greenleaf) *painter*
Kolbe, Stephanie Jill *artist*
Korn-Davis, Dottie *artist, educator, consultant*
Korzenik, Diana *art educator*
Kouzel, Mildred *artist*
Kraft, Yvette *art educator*
Krebs, Mary *art educator*
Krotz, Janet M. Trahan *artist, former gallery owner, art educator*
Krulik, Barbara S. *prodution manager, curator, art director, writer*
Kunin, Jacqueline Barlow *retired art educator*
Kwong, Eva *artist, educator*
Kyle, Gene Magerl *merchandise presentation artist*
LaCroix, Sophia Marie *artist*
Ladewig Goodman, Jeanne Margaret *artist*
Lamb, Darlis Carol *sculptor*
Lamontagne, Carole Hegland *retired art educator*
Landau, Emily Fisher *art collector, foundation administrator*
LaPalombara, Constance *artist*
La Rocca, Isabella *artist, educator*
Lawrence, Mary Josephine (Josie Lawrence) *artist, retired library official*
Leaf, Ruth *artist*
Leak, Nancy Marie *artist*
Lee, Nelda S. *art appraiser, art dealer, film producer*
Leeds, Nancy Brecker *sculptor, lyricist*
Lefranc, Margaret (Margaret Schoonover) *artist, illustrator, editor, writer*
Leibowitz, Bernice *artist, educator*
LeMay, Nancy *graphics designer, painter*
Lemieux, Annette Rose *artist*
Leone, Jeanne *artist*
Leventhal-Stern, Barbara Lynn *artist, marriage and family counselor*
Levine, Ruth Hannah *retired sculptor*
Levinson, Riki *art director*
Lewie, Reva Goodwin *artist, educator*
Lewis, Sharyn Lee *sculptor*
Lewy, Helen Crosby *artist, writer, translator, painter*
Libbey, Darlene Hensley *artist, educator*
Li-lan, *artist*
Liles, Virginia Rembert *retired art educator*
Lilly, Elizabeth K. *art educator, artist*
Lincoln, Rosamond Hadley *painter, photographer*
Lindenfeld, Naomi *ceramic artist*
Link, Phyllida Korman *artist, educator*
Lintner, Roberta Pompilio *art educator, artist*
Liu, Katherine Chang *artist, art educator*
Livingston-MacIrelan, Joan Persilla *artist*
Lockhart, Sharon *artist*
Locklin, Muriel Lucie *artist*
Lonstein, Shoshanna *fashion designer*
Loomis, Janice Kaszczuk *artist*
Lopez, Annie Marie *artist*
Lorelli, Elvira Mae *artist, art educator*
LoSchiavo, Francesca *set designer*
Lowry, Linda Eleanor *artist, educator*
Lundeen, Marga Laird *art educator*
Lyshak-Stelzer, Frances *artist*
Maddock, Diana Gail *visual artist, educator*
Mady, Beatrice M. *artist*
Mahmud, Shireen Dianne *photographer*
Mainella, Cindy L. *artist, researcher*
Malvre, Maili *artist, educator, secondary school educator*
Mangold, Sylvia Plimack *artist*
Mann, Joan Ellona *artist, editor*
Mann, Sally *photographer*
Marie, Shanti *artist*
Marisol, (Marisol Escobar) *sculptor*
Mark, Mary Ellen *photographer*
Marks, Roberta Barbara *artist, educator*
Marks, Veronique *art educator*
Marlowe, Willie *artist, fine arts educator*
Marsh, Merrilyn Delano *sculptor, artist, painter*
Martyl, (Mrs. Alexander Langsdorf Jr.) *artist*
Marvin, Freda Mary *art educator, nurse*
Marvin, Laura Lynn *art educator*
Mason, Emily *painter*
Mason, Lois E. (J. Day Mason) *painter, poet, actress, educator*
Mattos Grell, Elizabeth *artist*
Maurer, Marsha Kurs *art educator*
Maxwell, Ruth Elaine *artist, interior designer, painter*
Mayer, Susan Martin *art educator*
McCargar, Eleanor Barker *artist*
McCully, Emily Arnold *illustrator, writer*
McHugh, Annette S. *artist, educator, playwright, writer*
McIver, Beverly Jean *art educator, artist*
McKay, Renee *artist*
McLaughlin, Jean Wallace *art director, artist*
McLean, Katherine *artist, photographer*
McMillen, Elizabeth Cashin *artist*
McPeters, Sharon Jenise *artist, writer*
McPherson, JoAnne Frances *art educator, artist, special education educator*
McTague-Stock, Nancy A. *painter, printmaker*
Menefee, Linnea-Norma *antique dealer*
Menna, Sári *artist, educator*
Mercer, Frances deCourcy *artist, educator*
Miiller, Susan Diane *artist*
Milana Panopoulos, Maria *artist*
Miller, Angela *art educator*
Miller, Diane Faye *art education educator, business owner*
Miller, Nidi R. *artist, sculptor, educator*
Miller, Ruth Ann *artist*
Mills, Inga-Britta *artist*
Miskill, Dee Shelton *graphics designer*
Mitty, Lizbeth *artist*
Monczewski, Maureen R. *art educator, visual artist*
Montealegre, Eva Denise *artist, writer*
Montgomery, Lani Lynn *art educator*
Moore, Deana Daiello *art educator*
Morgan, Ann M. *artist, educator*
Mori, Mariko *artist*
Morphew, Dorothy Richards-Bassett *artist, real estate broker*
Morrison, Margaret L. *artist, educator, consultant*
Morrison, Nancy Jane *art educator*
Motzkin, Judith E. *artist*
Murphy, Mary Leigh *artist*
Myers, Dorothy Roatz *artist*
Myers, Sue Bartley *artist*
Nagy, Elizabeth Garver *artist*
Nankervis, Medora B. *artist*
Nathanson, Barbara A. *painter, artist*
Neff, Jennifer Ellen *painter, artist*
Neroni, Jane Kessler *art educator*
Neville, Elizabeth Egan *artist, educator*
Newell, Shirley Ann Cecil *retired art dealer, artist*
Newman, Muriel Kallis Steinberg *art collector*
Nichols, Iris Jean *retired illustrator*
Nickols, Marcia Lynn *retired art educator*
Niffenegger, Audrey Anne *artist, writer*
Nix, Patricia *artist*
Noel, Cheryl Elaine *artist, poet*
Novak, Barbara *art history educator*
Nuss, Joanne Ruth *artist*
Oakes-Hall, Nancy Anne *artist, ski instructor*
O'Brien, Amy V. *apparel designer*
O'Donnell, Kathleen C. *artist*
Okoshi-Mukai, Sumiye *artist*
Olivos, Claudia *artist, educator*
Ord, Linda Banks *artist*
Oritsky, Mimi *artist, educator*
Orlowska-Warren, Lenore Alexandria *art educator, fiber artist*
Otani, Yuriko L. (Charko) *artist*
Owen, Carol Thompson *artist, educator, writer*
Owens, Christine Claire *art educator, graphics designer*
Oxell, Loie Gwendolyn *fashion and beauty educator, consultant, columnist*
Padgett, Cynthia S. *artist*
Pagano, Michelina Olimpia *art director, consultant, writer, scriptwriter*
Park, Nancy Marie *art director, illustrator, painter*
Patten, Christine Taylor *artist*
Payne, Barbara Ann *artist, educator*
Peacock, Virginia C. *artist*
Peek, Stephanie *artist*
Pepin-Wakefield, Yvonne Mary *artist, writer*
Pepper, Beverly *artist, sculptor*
Peterson, Kristin *artist*
Peterson, Martha *artist*
Phelan, Stephanie Ellen *artist, graphics designer*
Pierce, Hilda (Hilda Herta Harmel) *painter*
Pinto, Marion *artist*
Pipkin, Mary Margaret *artist*
Pizzo, Pia *artist, educator*
Pliskin, Berenice Rita Chaplan *artist*
Plunket, Dolores *art educator, archaeology educator*
Ponte, Jean Moore *artist, writer, actress*
Pope, Ingrid Bloomquist *sculptor, poet, painter*
Popian, Lucia *artist*
Porges, Lucie *apparel designer, educator*
Potsic, Amie Sharon *photographer, educator, artist*
Price, Helen Burdon (Helen Lois Burdon) *artist, retired nursing educator*
Provensen, Alice *artist, writer*
Putterman, Florence Grace *artist, printmaker*
Raash, Kathleen Forecki *artist*
Raines, Charlotte Austine Butler *artist*
Reedy, Susan *painter*
Reid, Geraldine Wold (Geraldine Reid Skjervold) *artist*
Rendich, Ana *painter, collage artist*
Rendl-Marcus, Mildred *artist, economist*
Replogle, Jeanne Lonnquist *artist*
Richards, Patricia Jones *artist, poet, musician, composer*
Riehl, Lori Jo *art educator*
Riley, Pamela Janerico *artist*
Ripstein, Jacqueline *artist*
Ritter, Renée *artist, educator*
Roberts, Della *artist*
Roberts, Holly Lynn *artist*
Roberts, Nancy Cohen *art dealer, marketing professional*
Roberts, Suzanne Catherine *artist*
Roberts, Victoria Lynn P. *antique expert*
Robinson, Aminah Brenda Lynn *artist, illustrator*
Robinson, Linda Schultz *artist, educator*
Robinson, Lynda Hickox *artist*
Robinson, Paula LeKatz *artist*
Robinson, Sara Curtis *arts administrator*
Roche, Pauline Jennifer *artist*
Rock, Mary Ann *artist, educator*
Rockburne, Dorothea Grace *artist*
Roe, Wanda Jeraldean *artist, retired educator, lecturer*
Roemer, Carol Kaluga *art educator*
Rogers, Elaine P. *art educator*
Rogers, Eva Marie VanLeuven *artist, poet*
Rogers, PJ *artist*
Roles-Walter, Jennie Ruth *art educator, artist*
Roller, Marion *sculptor*
Romano, Mena N. *artist, educator*
Ross, Gloria Jean *artist*
Rossman, Ruth Scharff *artist, educator*
Rothschild, Jennifer Ann *artist, educator*
Rubin, Sandra Mendelsohn *artist*
Rubinstein, Eva (Anna) *photographer*
Runkle, Ethel Mona *artist*
Rush, Julia Ann Halloran (Mrs. Richard Henry Rush) *artist, writer*
Rushforth, Ann Fay *artist, educator*
Rutherford, Doreen *artist, construction executive*
Rutschke, Annamarie *artist*
Rutstein, Rebecca Anne *painter*
Sa, Lily *artist, educator*
Saccoccio, Jacqueline *artist*
Saegesser, Marguerite M. *artist*
Safren, Cheryl *art educator, artist*
St. Onge, Mary Frances Burkett *retired art education educator*
Salerno, Cherie Ann (C. S. Mau) *artist*
Salier, Eva *artist, writer*
Salomon, Johanna *artist*
Sampson, Martha Fray *portrait artist, educator*
Sandor, Jocelyn R. *artist*
Sarkisian, Pamela Outlaw *artist*
Sarofim, Louisa Stude *art patron, philanthropist*
Sass, Mary Martha *freelance writer, artist*
Savage, Martha *art educator*
Savedra, Jeannine Evangeline *artist, educator*
Savenor, Betty Carmell *painter, printmaker*
Schabacker, Betty Barchet *artist*
Schabner, Dawn Freeble *artist, educator*
Schiff, Molly Jeanette *artist, researcher*
Schmidt, Diane Joy *photographer, writer, creative arts educator*
Schmitz, Barbara *art preservationist*
Schneider, Gisela *art educator*
Schultz, Eileen Hedy *art director, advertising executive*
Schwartz, Ana Stella *art dealer, gallery owner*
Schwartz, Lillian Feldman *artist, filmmaker, critic, nurse, writer*
Schwarz, Rose Oberman *artist*
Scotland, Susan Jane *artist, educator*
Scully, Susan *artist*
Searles, Edna Lowe *artist, illustrator, composer, poet*
Seddon, Priscilla Tingey *painter*
Segal, Rena Beth *artist*
Segil, Laura Chipman *art dealer, consultant*
Seligson, Judith *artist*
Shaderowfsky, Eva Maria *photographer, writer, computer communications specialist*
Shafran, Faith *artist*
Sharma, Jeanne Alexandra *artist, educator*
Sharp, Anne Catherine *artist, educator*
Sharrow, Sheba Grossman *artist*
Shaughnessy, Marie Kaneko *artist*
Shaw, Gloria Doris *art educator*
Shea, Rosanne Mary *artist, educator*
Sheckter, Bonnie *artist*
Sherbell-Na, Rhoda *artist, sculptor*
Sheridan, Sonia Landy *artist, retired art educator*
Sherr, Sylvia *artist, educator*
Shiershke, Nancy Fay *artist, educator, real estate manager*
Shikashio, Hiroko *artist, interpreter, educator*

Shorr, Harriet *artist*
Shulman, Mildred *artist*
Shuss, Jane Margaret *artist*
Sillman, Amy *painter, art educator*
Silver, Shelly Andrea *artist*
Silvernell, Kerri Anne *artist, educator*
Sinclaire, Estelle Foster *appraiser, writer, former educator*
Sirna, Gail Carolyn *artist, educator, writer*
Smith, Gail Hunter *artist*
Smith, Karen Ann *visual artist*
Smith, Kathryn Lee *artist, educator*
Smith, Leila Hentzen *artist*
Smith, Leonore Rae *artist*
Smith, Margaret Ann *retired art educator*
Smith, Patricia Lynne *artist*
Smith, Zuleika *art educator*
Sniffen, Frances P. *artist*
Snowden, Ruth *artist, educator, executive secretary*
Snyder, Joan *artist*
Souders, Jean Swedell *artist, educator*
Sparrow, Alison Kidder *painter, sculptor*
Spero, Nancy *artist*
Spradlin, Rebecca L. *art educator*
Stack, Angela Johann *artist*
Steel, Claudia Williamson *artist*
Steinke, Carolyn Joyce *artist, educator*
Stelluto, Sharon Renee *apparel designer, painter*
Stern, Marilyn *photographer, editor, writer*
Stevens, May *artist*
Stewart, Heather Meri *painter, sculptor*
Stewart, Janet *artist*
Stinsmuehlen-Amend, Susan *artist*
Stockar, Helena Marie Magdalena *artist*
Stocks, Elizabeth Lunn *retired art educator*
Stone, Brenda Kershaw *art educator*
Storrs, Immi Casagrande *sculptor*
Strider, Marjorie Virginia *artist, educator*
Striker, Susan Joan Glaser *art educator*
Strong-Cuevas, Elizabeth *sculptor*
Stroud, Betsy Dillard *artist*
Stuart, Sherry Blanchard *artist*
Sugar, Sandra Lee *art consultant*
Sullivan, Barbara Jean *artist*
Sullivan, Mary Ann *artist*
Switzer, Toccoa *artist*
Taddei, Lois Annette Magowan *artist, interior designer*
Tagliente, Josephine Marlene *artist*
Talbot-Elliott, Susan *artist*
Tarasiewicz, Tamara *painter*
Tardos, Anne *artist, writer, composer*
Tasse, Marie Jeanne *retired art educator*
Taylor, Lyda Revoire Wing *artist, gallery owner*
Taylor, Margaret Turner *apparel designer, economist, writer, architectural designer*
Taylor-Brown, Cameron Ann *artist, educator, consultant*
Terry, Sandra Eleanor *visual artist*
Tesseneer-Street, Susan *photographer, artist, writer*
Thomas, Matilda Ann *art educator*
Thompson, Linda A. *art educator*
Thompson, Margie Ann *artist*
Tirello, Maria Eugenia Duke *artist*
Tögel, Cornelia (Conni) D. *artist*
Tomkow, Gwen Adelle *artist*
Torrez, Michelle Marie *artist, educator*
Town, Charlotte *artist, small business owner*
Treitler, Rhoda Chaprack *artist*
Tresslar, Nola V. *artist, retired marketing professional, retired foundation administrator*
Triana, Gladys *artist*
Turner, Bonese Collins *artist, educator*
Turner, Bracha *painter*
Turner, Florence Frances *ceramist*
Tuttle, Martha Benedict *artist*
Unithan, Dolly *visual artist*
Vaccaro, Luella G. *painter, ceramist*
Vahradian, Melinda *fine artist*
Van Bruggen, Coosje *artist, writer*
Van Cleve, Barbara Page *photographer*
Van Gelder, Lydia M. *artist, educator*
Van Hooser, Patricia Lou Scott *art educator*
Vasulka, Steina (Steinunn Briem Bjarnadottir) *artist, educator*
Vernazza, Trish Brown (Trish Eileen Brown) *visual artist, art therapist, sculptor*
Versch, Esther Marie *artist*
Villoch, Kelly Carney *art director*
von Furstenberg, Diane *fashion designer, writer, entrepreneur*
VonSchulze-Delitzsch, Marilyn Wandling (Lady VonSchulze-Delitzsch) *artist, writer*
von Trotta, Tamara Jane *art educator*
Voytek, Mary Sullivan *sculptor*
Wachtman, Jeanette Marie *art educator, artist, writer*
Wahlers, Jennifer Ann *art educator*
Waksberg, Nomi *painter, photographer, artist*
Walker, Bernice Baker *artist*
Walker, Kelley *painter*
Wallace, Teresa Lynn *art educator*
Walsh, Nan *artist, painter, sculptor, consultant*
Waltemath, Joan M. *artist*
Warren, Alice Louise *artist*
Watts, Ginny (Virginia C. Watts) *artist*
Weaver, Donna L. *engraver*
Weber, Christine Ruth *artist*
Weber, Idelle *artist, educator*
Weiss, Nancy P. *artist*
Weld, Alison Gordon *artist*
Welsh, Kathern Darlene *artist, writer*
Wenglowski, Joyce *painter*
Westbie, Barbara Jane *retired graphics designer*
Westfall, Carol Ann *artist, educator*
Wexler, Sandra M. *artist, medical illustrator*
White, Yonsenia S. *artist, educator*
Whitehill, Mary Evelyn *artist, retired librarian*
Whitfield, Rebecca Wavrin *art educator*
Wichman, Yvonne Beard *lighting designer, literature educator*
Willett, Melissa Carol *art educator*
Williams, Monica Bernardette Ellen *jewelry designer*
Williams Ezell, Margaret (Peggy) *artist, educator*
Willis, Cheryl Mary *art educator*
Wilson, Jane *artist*
Wilson, Ruth Yvette *artist, educator*
Witt, Nancy Camden *artist*
Wolpert Richard, Chava *artist*
Wong, Nancy L. *artist, retired dermatologist*
Wood, Lorraine Dell *artist, consultant*
Woodard, Catherine *arts patron*
Wosk, Miriam *artist*
Wright, Joan L. *artist*
Wright, Virginia *art collector, curator*
Wyatt, Marcia Jean *fine arts and speech educator, administrative assistant*
Wyatt-Magalian, Cate *artist*
Wylan, Barbara *artist*
Wynn, Karla Wray *artist, agricultural products executive*
Yerxa, Jane Anne *artist*
Yow, Audrey Jo *artist, educator*
Yowell, Nancy T. *photographer, retired elementary school educator*
Zaleski, Jean *artist*
Zebi, Sandra *artist*
Zekman, Terri Margaret *graphic designer*
Zuber, Catherine *costume designer*
Zucker, Maureen T. *artist*
Zumbrunnen, Elizabeth *artist, educator*
Zurbuchen, Susan Jane *arts consultant*

ASSOCIATIONS AND ORGANIZATIONS *See also specific fields*

UNITED STATES

ALABAMA

Birmingham
Bonfield, Barbara Goldstein *non-profit organization administrator*
Carter, Frances Tunnell (Fran Carter) *fraternal organization administrator*
Diasio, Ilse Wolfartsberger *volunteer*
Kirkley, D. Christine *not-for-profit developer*

Demopolis
Reynolds, Louise Webb *retired volunteer, director*

Huntsville
Reel, Heather W. *educational association administrator*

Montgomery
Phillips, Pamela B. *medical education coordinator*

Piedmont
Kiser, Hazel Theresa *educational association administrator, lawyer*

Tuscaloosa
Jemison, Sandra J. *educational association administrator*

ALASKA

Anchorage
Jones, Jewel *social services administrator*

Saint Marys
Alstrom, Gail *Native American tribal leader*

ARIZONA

Glendale
Travis, Geraldine Washington *political organization worker*

Scottsdale
Mohraz, Judy Jolley *foundation administrator*
O'Meara, Sara *non-profit organization executive*

Sells
Juan-Saunders, Vivian *Native American tribal leader*

Sun City
Duke, Ora Elizabeth *civic volunteer*

Tempe
Arredondo, Patricia *educational association administrator*

Tucson
Dale, Deborah *foundation executive*
Davenport, Sandra *cultural organization administrator*
Gonzales, Sarah *women's organization director*
Hamner, Rome *social services administrator*
Healy, Stephanie Lemme *hospital organization administrator*
Jaramillo, Alba *community educator*
Lovejoy, Jean Hastings *social services counselor*
Porter, Jeanne Smith *civic worker*

Vail
Denton-McGrew, Shela Iva *retired trade association administrator*

ARKANSAS

Bentonville
Walton, Helen *philanthropist*

Fayetteville
Stephens, Wanda Brewer *social services administrator, investor*

Little Rock
Adams, Rose Ann *nonprofit administrator*

CALIFORNIA

Anderson
Wittmann, Jane Gordon *volunteer*

Bakersfield
Huerta, Dolores Fernandez *labor union administrator*

Berkeley
Buell, Evangeline Canonizado *advocate*
McLaughlin, Sylvia Cranmer *volunteer, environmentalist*

Canoga Park
Lederer, Marion Irvine *cultural administrator*

Carmel Valley
Heimann, Janet Barbara *volunteer trail consultant*

Chula Vista
Steele, Nancy Eden Rogers *nonprofit corporate executive, retired principal*

Claremont
Glass, Sandra Ann *foundation administrator, consultant*
Stokes, Anne Dorothy *retired educational association administrator*

Cypress
Friess, Donna Lewis *children's rights advocate*

El Centro
Roberts, Cristina Abeja *volunteer*

El Monte
Last, Marian Helen *social services administrator*

Encino
Irmas, Audrey Menein *not-for-profit developer*

Hayward
Fili, Patricia Kevena *social welfare administrator, poet, playwright*

Hercules
Tyson, Kathleen Hayhurst *educational association administrator*

Kentfield
Blum, Joan Kurley *not-for-profit fundraiser, marketing executive, consultant*

Long Beach
Fischler, Sandy Lynn *charitable and informational organization executive*
Heggeness, Julie Fay *foundation administrator, lawyer*

Los Altos
Larson, Carol S. *foundation administrator, lawyer*

Los Angeles
Glasgow, Istiharoh *art administrator*
Hernandez, Antonia *foundation administrator, lawyer*
Ibarra, Irene M. *foundation administrator*
Im, Hyepin Christine *not-for-profit developer*
Lyles, Tracee *art association administrator, actress*
Marshall, Mary Jones *civic worker*
Prewitt, Jean *not-for-profit organization executive*
Racklin, Barbara Cohen *fundraising consultant*
Smith, Jean Webb (Mrs. William French Smith) *civic worker*
White, Daun Elois *professional society official*
Wilson, Gayle Ann *civic worker*

Marina Del Rey
Heath, Berthann Jones *educational association administrator*

Menlo Park
Collins, Nancy Whisnant *foundation administrator*
Gimon, Eleanor Hewlett *philanthropist*

Modesto
Whiteside, Carol Gordon *foundation executive*

Montclair
Boyd, Mary H. (Mary H. Merrill) *social services administrator*

Napa
Loar, Peggy Ann *foundation administrator, museum administrator*

Newport Beach
Wallis, Mary Camilla *civic leader*

North Hollywood
Evans, Paula Lemmermann *educational association administrator*

Oakland
Widener, Mary Lee *non-profit financial executive*

Oxnard
Tolmach, Jane Louise *community activist, municipal official*

Pacific Palisades
Holberg, Eva Maria *volunteer*
Snowhook, Ann Laferty *social services administrator*

Palm Springs
Hilb, Jeane Dyer *community volunteer*

Palmdale
Phillips, Ruthanne *special education administrator*

Pasadena
Ellner, Carolyn Lipton *non-profit organization executive, dean, consultant*

Placentia
Cash, Jeanie Maritta *educational association administrator*

Rancho Mirage
Wyatt, Lenore *civic worker*

Rancho Palos Verdes
Vanderlip, Elin Brekke *professional society administrator, volunteer*

Redwood City
Spangler, Nita Reifschneider *volunteer*

Sacramento
Ross, Jean M. *think-tank executive*

Salinas
Chester, Lynne *foundation administrator, artist*

San Diego
Lane, Gloria Julian *foundation administrator*
Swanson, Mary Catherine *educational association administrator*

San Francisco
Bitterman, Mary Gayle Foley *foundation executive*
Brown, Bernice Leona Baynes *foundation administrator, secondary school educator, consultant*
Chang, Patti *foundation administrator*
Egan, Patricia Jane *foundation administrator, retired director*
Gimon, Juliette *foundation administrator, volunteer*
Guillermo, Tessie *foundation administrator*
Lord, Mia W. *advocate*
Martinez Tucker, Sara *educational association administrator*
Masaoka, Jan *not-for-profit executive*
Mimi, Haas *volunteer*
Renstrom, Lisa *environmental organization administrator*
Soler, Esta *foundation administrator*
Steele, Shari *think-tank executive*

San Juan Bautista
McGovern, Rebecca Maples *chamber of commerce executive*

Santa Ana
Prizio, Betty J. *volunteer, retired property manager*

Santa Barbara
McCoy, Lois Clark *retired social services administrator, retired county official, editor*
Obern, Vivian Marie *volunteer*

Santa Cruz
Lenox, Catherine Corneau *volunteer*

Santa Monica
Abarbanel, Gail *social services administrator, educator*
Foley, Jane Deborah *foundation executive*

Sherman Oaks
Leighton, Carolyn *foundation administrator*

Stinson Beach
Metz, Mary Seawell *retired foundation administrator, retired academic administrator*

Stockton
Nusz, Phyllis Jane *not-for-profit fundraiser, consultant, educational consultant*

Torrance
Blumenfeld, Anita *community relations consultant*

Truckee
Otto, Christine Barnard *educational association administrator*

Valencia
Anguiano, Lupe *advocate*

Visalia
Taylor, Helen Shields *civic worker*

Weed
Mann, Karen *consultant, educator*

Yorba Linda
Stavropoulos, Rose Mary Grant *community activist, volunteer*

COLORADO

Arvada
Meiklejohn, Mindy June (Lorraine Meiklejohn) *political organizer, realtor*

Aspen
Bucksbaum, Melva *foundation administrator*

Aurora
Hoffmaster, Nancy Jo Clement *retired social services professional*

Boulder
deKieffer, Kitty *volunteer*
Heath, Josephine Ward *foundation administrator*

Broomfield
Flanders, Eleanor Carlson *community volunteer*

Colorado Springs
Deiotte, Margaret Williams Tukey *nonprofit consultant, grants writer*
Hawley, Nanci Elizabeth *professional society administrator*
Loo, Katherine Haughey *nonprofit organization consultant*
Miller, Zoya Dickins *civic worker, consultant*

Denver
Childears, Linda *foundation administrator*
Hirschfeld, Arlene *civic worker, former secondary school educator*
Low, Merry Cook *civic worker*

Waak, Patricia Ann *political organization administrator, environmental association executive*

Englewood
Keesling, Ruth Morris *foundation administrator*

Fort Collins
Eddy, Gladys Louise *educational administrator*

Glenwood Springs
Hauptli, Barbara Beatrice *foundation administrator*

Littleton
Keogh, Heidi Helen Dake *advocate*

Mancos
Brown, Joy Alice *social services administrator*

CONNECTICUT

Danbury
Meyers, Abbey S. *foundation administrator*

Fairfield
Evans, Margaret A. *volunteer*
Ford, Maureen Morrissey *civic worker*
Shelton, Carolyn Johnson *professional society administrator*

Falls Village
Toomey, Jeanne Elizabeth *animal activist*

Greenwich
Bjornson, Edith Cameron *foundation administrator, communications consultant*
Kovner, Kathleen Jane *civic worker, portrait artist*
Wyman, Lotte Ann Novak *civic worker*

Groton
Kennedy, Evelyn Siefert *foundation executive, textiles executive*

Guilford
Stevens, Lydia Hastings *community volunteer*

Hartford
Eshoo, Barbara Anne Rudolph *non-profit administrator*

New Britain
Stathos, Lifteria K. *retired educational association administrator*

New Haven
Leo, Martha E. *advocate, counselor*

Norwich
Thompson, Carrie Lorraine *volunteer*

Roxbury
Styron, Rose *human rights activist, poet, journalist*

Stamford
Stillings, Irene Ella Grace Cordiner *retired foundation executive*

DELAWARE

Dover
Friedland, Billie Louise *former human services administrator, educator*

Lewes
Spence, Sandra *retired trade association administrator*

Wilmington
Baxter, Beverley Veloris *economic association administrator, educator*
Chagnon, Lucille Tessier *literacy acceleration consultant*
Fleming, Blanche Miles *educational association administrator*

DISTRICT OF COLUMBIA

Washington
Aron, Nan *lawyer, association executive*
Aviv, Diana L. *public policy analyst, psychotherapist*
Babby, Ellen Reisman *educational association executive*
Barclay, Ellen S. *not-for-profit developer*
Bednash, Geraldine Polly *educational association administrator*
Bonosaro, Carol Alessandra *professional society administrator, retired federal agency administrator*
Bridgeforth, Chrystl L. *former labor union administrator*
Brosnan, Carol Raphael Sarah *retired art association administrator*
Brown, Ann W. *not-for-profit developer*
Bryan, Beth Ann *educational association administrator*
Burger, Anna *labor union administrator*
Callahan, Debra Jean *political organization worker*
Chavez-Thompson, Linda *labor union administrator*
Combs, Roberta *political organization administrator*
Comstock, Amy L. *social services administrator*
Cooper, Margaret J. *cultural organization administrator*
Croser, Mary Doreen *educational association executive*
Davidson, Jo Ann *political organization executive, retired state legislator*
Day, Mary Louise *volunteer*
Dean, Lisa *foundation executive*
DeWaal, Caroline Smith *education and advocacy organization executive, lawyer*
Duggan, Juanita D. *trade association administrator*
Duval-Pierrelouis, Jeanne-Marie *educational association executive*
Easterling, Barbara J. *labor union administrator*
Edelman, Marian Wright *not-for-profit developer, lawyer*
Ericsson, Sally Claire *not-for-profit official*
Evans, Joy *foundation administrator*
Faiks, Jan Ogozalek *lobbyist*
Foreman, Carol Lee Tucker *consumer advocate*
Forkan, Patricia Ann *foundation executive*
Friend, Patricia A. *trade association administrator*
Fries, Helen Sergeant Haynes *civic leader*
Ganter, Susan Lynn *foundation administrator, retired mathematics professor*
Garrison, LaTrease E. *association executive*
Greenhill, Lisa Michelle *professional society administrator*
Gruman, Jessie Christine *not-for-profit developer*
Hahn, Lorna *political organization executive, author*
Hatfield, C. Maile *lobbyist*
Height, Dorothy I. *former foundation administrator*
Heinz Kerry, Teresa F. (Maria Teresa Thierstein Simoes-Ferreira) *foundation administrator*
Hentges, Harriet *not-for-profit developer*
Hoffman, Ann Fleisher *labor union administrator, lawyer, consultant*
Jacobs, Madeleine *professional society administrator, writer*
Keenan, Nancy A. *pro-choice association executive*
Kelley, Colleen M. *labor union administrator*
Lederer, Laura J. *educational association administrator*
Leff, Deborah *foundation administrator, former library director*
Lenn, Marjorie Peace *educational association administrator, consultant*
Levine, Felice *educational association administrator*
Linehan, Lou Ann *political organization worker*
Mason, Eileen B. *federal arts administrator*
Matheis, Cheryl *not-for-profit developer*
McElveen-Hunter, Bonnie *international relief organization executive*
McEntee, Christine W. *architecture association administrator, former medical association administrator*
McGinnis, Patricia Gwaltney *non-profit organization executive*
Mc Kay, Emily Gantz *civil rights and nonprofit professional*
McSweeny, Dorothy Pierce *art association administrator*
Meyers, Linda Dee *non-profit administrator, researcher*
Montoya, Regina T. *association executive, lawyer*
Moore, Barbara C. *fraternal organization administrator*
Moore, Jacquelyn Cornelia *retired labor union administrator, editor*
Moye, Sidley Andrea *lobbyist*
Murguia, Janet *non-profit organization administrator*
Narasaki, Karen Keiko *advocate, lawyer*
Natividad, Irene *women's rights advocate*
O'Connor, Bridget *labor union administrator, lawyer*
O'Kane, Margaret E. *non-profit organization executive*
Oliphant, Martha Carmichael *civic worker*
O'Neill, Catherine *cultural organization administrator*
Otremba, Geraldine Marie *congressional and international relations executive*
Petito, Margaret L. *foundation president*
Ramphele, Mamphela A. *international organization administrator, physician, former academic administrator*
Rich, Dorothy Kovitz *educational association administrator, writer*
Richardson, Ann Bishop *foundation executive, lawyer*
Robinson, Jewell *arts and education administrator, actor*
Sanchez Mills, Peggy *women's association executive*
Sandler, Bernice Resnick *women's rights specialist*
Schneider, Carol Geary *educational association administrator*
Schroeder, Patricia Scott *trade association administrator, former congresswoman*
Shuy, Tanya Russell *educational association administrator*
Small, Sarah Mae *volunteer*
Smith, Elise Fiber *international non-profit development agency administrator*
Smith, Jessie P. Dowling *retired social services administrator*
Smith, Marie F. *lobbyist, small business owner, writer, retirement association executive*
Stich, Roberta Lynn *not-for-profit fundraiser, social worker*
Stockman, Jennifer Blei *political organization administrator*
Tosi, Gloria C. *labor union administrator*
Townsend, Ann Van Devanter *foundation administrator, art historian*
Tulo, Kellie J. *think-tank executive, director*
Turnbull, Susan *political organization worker*

FLORIDA

Boca Raton
Jessup, Jan Amis *arts volunteer, writer*
Sterling, Lorraine *volunteer*

Bonita Springs
Liebman, Phyllis Janice *volunteer, educator*

Clearwater
Duncan, Holly H. *foundation executive*

Coral Springs
Kohl, Joan *not-for-profit developer, social worker*

Davie
Sullivan, Kathryn Lynn *educational association administrator*

Delray Beach
Stewart, Patricia Carry *foundation administrator*

Fort Lauderdale
Loos, Roberta Alexis *advocate, artist, educator*

Harbour Heights
Nash, Ruth S. *foundation administrator*

Holmes Beach
Dunne, Nancy Anne *retired social services administrator*

Jacksonville
Blount, Yolanda Denise *social services administrator, psychologist*
Brady, Terrie *political organization executive*

Key Biscayne
Klarreich, Sue Friedman *education administrator, consultant*

Lake Mary
Southward, Patricia C. *volunteer*

Lake Worth
Chittick, Elizabeth Lancaster *advocate*

Lakeland
Spencer, Mary Miller *civic worker*

Largo
Schick, Alice Edith (Lisl Schick) *civic leader*

Marathon
Vail, Elizabeth Forbus *volunteer*

Miami
Arison, Marilyn Barbara (Lin Arison) *foundation administrator*
Knight Crane, Marjorie *foundation administrator*
Lynch, Catherine Gores *social services administrator*
McPhee, Penelope L. Ortner *foundation administrator, television producer, writer*
Shipp, Theta Wanza *social service organization administrator, educator, consultant, minister*
Tice, Dianne Lisa *social services administrator*

Naples
Hollenbeck, Karen Fern *foundation administrator, consultant*

Orlando
Murrah, Ann Ralls Freeman *historical association executive*

Osprey
Holec, Anita Kathryn Van Tassel *civic worker*

Palm Beach
Elson, Suzanne Goodman *social services administrator*
Floeckher, Louise Byrne Weldon *volunteer*
Hope, Margaret Lauten *retired civic worker*
Levine, Audrey Pearlstein *foundation administrator*

Palm Coast
Boyer, Kaye Kittle *association management executive*

Punta Gorda
Clinton, Mariann Hancock *educational association administrator*

Redington Shores
McGhee, Kathryn Ann *foundation administrator*

Saint Petersburg
Coeyman, Emily Nollie Rogers *civic worker*

Spring Hill
Pedersen, Gladys del S. *volunteer*

Sunrise
Kolker, Sondra G. *not-for-profit fundraiser*

Tallahassee
Humphrey, Louise Ireland *civic worker, equestrienne*
Yecke, Cheri Pierson *educational researcher, administrator, columnist, writer*

Tampa
Milito, Connie Marie *education administrator, government relations administrator*

Valparaiso
Williams, Betty *peace activist*

Venice
Shaffer, Ethel Armstrong *volunteer speaker*

Wilton Manors
Kaufmann, Vicki Marie *social services administrator*

Winter Park
Kaston, Lisa Marsha *social services administrator*

GEORGIA

Atlanta
Allen, Alana S. *not-for-profit developer*
Anthony, Barbara Cox *foundation administrator*
Birdsong, Alta Marie *volunteer*
Goizueta, Olga (Olga Casteleiro de Goizueta) *foundation administrator, philanthropist*
Murray, Renee Logsdon *educational association administrator, consultant*
Spillett, Roxanne *social services administrator*
Stuart, Joan Martha *fund raising executive*

Decatur
Wheelan, Belle S. *educational association administrator*

Douglas
Pugh, Joye Jeffries *educational association administrator, consultant, writer*

Duluth
Gullickson, Nancy Ann *art association administrator*

Marietta
Smith, Becky *charitable organizations consultant*

Roswell
Polatty, Rose Jackson *civic worker*
Thibaudeau, Mary Frances *cultural organization administrator*

Savannah
Thomson, Audrey Shire *volunteer*

HAWAII

Honolulu
Blackfield, Cecilia Malik *civic volunteer, educator*
Trahan, Ellen Vauneil *retired foundation administrator, public information officer*

Kailua Kona
Iolana, Patricia Elvira *foundation administrator, consultant*

Kapolei
Moriyama, Karen Ito *educational association administrator*

Kihei
Corell, Marcella Anne *community worker, retired educator*

Volcano
Nicholson, Marilyn Lee *arts administrator*

IDAHO

Hailey
Liebich, Marcia Trathen *community volunteer*

Ponderay
Nelson, Marcella May *volunteer*

ILLINOIS

Barrington
Worrell, Sharyn Dianne *volunteer, retired flight attendant*

Bellwood
Szilagyi-Hawkins, Elizabeth Maria *social services administrator*

Carlinville
Bellm, Joan *civic worker*

Chicago
Blackshere, Margaret *labor union administrator*
Bourdon, Cathleen Jane *professional society administrator*
Brown, Elizabeth McCarthy *social services administrator*
Byther-Smith, Ida W. *social services administrator*
Edelman, Ruth Rozumoff *volunteer*
Froetscher, Janet *social services administrator*
Harris, Joan White *foundation administrator*
Harvey, Katherine Abler *civic worker*
Hodge, Linda M. *former educational association administrator*
Jacoby Hurd, Jennifer *foundation administrator*
Jones, Mary Laura *not-for-profit developer*
Keenan, Barbara Byrd *professional society administrator*
Klimley, Nancy E. *volunteer*
Koenig, Bonnie *international non-profit organization consultant*
Kudo, Irma Setsuko *not-for-profit executive director*
Lies, Valerie Sharp *foundation administrator*
Maehr, Kate *social services organization executive*
Mayer, Beatrice Cummings *civic worker*
Mazany, Terry *foundation administrator*
Minow, Josephine Baskin *civic volunteer*
Parker, Bonita M. *civil rights organization executive*
Schiele, Michele M. *not-for-profit fundraiser, medical association administrator*
Schimberg, Barbara *organizational development consultant*
Shanahan, Betty *professional society administrator*
Simmons, Adele Smith *foundation executive, former educator*
Strauss, Deborah *foundation administrator*
Thomas, Barbara L. *not-for-profit executive*
Vogelzang, Jeanne Marie *professional society administrator, lawyer*
Weselak, Anna Marie Schmidt *educational association administrator, media consultant*
White, Linda Marie *former fraternal organization administrator*
Wilson, Cleo Francine *foundation administrator*

Clarendon Hills
Choice, Priscilla Kathryn Means (Penny Choice) *retired educational association administrator*

Crystal Lake
Linklater, Isabelle Stanislawa Yarosh-Galazka (Lee Linklater) *foundation administrator*

Dekalb
Folgate, Cynthia A. *social services administrator*

Evanston
Gordon, Julie Peyton *foundation administrator*

Thrash, Patricia Ann *retired educational association administrator*

Fulton
Specht, Lois Darlene *volunteer*

Kildeer
Muffoletto, Mary Lu *retired educational association administrator, editor*

Lake Forest
Fetridge, Bonnie-Jean Clark (Mrs. William Harrison Fetridge) *civic volunteer*

Marion
Aikman, Elflora Anna K. *senior citizens center administrator*

Oak Park
Brown, Mary Anne *childcare advocate*
Fleming, Margaret A. *adoption advocate, adoption service director*
Greer, Julianna Patterson *not-for-profit administrator*

Orion
Magee, Elizabeth Sherrard *civic organization volunteer*

Quincy
Wemhoener, Dolores Lucille *cultural organization administrator, entertainer*

Richton Park
Burt, Gwen Behrens *educational association administrator*

River Forest
Eisel, Jean Ellen *educational association administrator*

River Grove
Jeans, Mary Millicent *educational association administrator*

Rock Falls
Julifs, Sandra Jean *community action agency executive*

Rock Island
Rafferty, Genevieve Kennedy *social service agency administrator*

Schaumburg
Tompson, Marian Leonard *professional society administrator*

Springfield
Denham, Mary Washko *former college official, civic worker*
Ramirez-Campbell, Christine M. *art council administrator*

Waukegan
Drapalik, Betty R. *volunteer, artist, educator*

INDIANA

Bloomington
Wells, Kimberly K. *not-for-profit organization executive*

Crown Point
Eisenhauer, Linda Ann *volunteer*

Fort Wayne
Neuman, Paula Anne Young *cultural organization administrator*

Indianapolis
Finley, Katherine Mandusic *professional society administrator*
Williams, Judith Ellen *educational association administrator*
Winston, Robin Eugene *political party professional*

Lafayette
Scaletta, Helen Marguerite *volunteer*

Lawrenceburg
Edwards, Marie D. *social services administrator*

Newburgh
Saum, Elizabeth Pape *community volunteer*

South Bend
Hunt, Mary Reilly *organization executive*

IOWA

Ames
Benson, Neala Lawrence *volunteer*

Cedar Rapids
Arnold-Olson, Helen B. *not-for-profit consultant*

Council Bluffs
Rachow, Cinda Lou *educational association administrator*

Des Moines
McGuire-Riggs, Sheila *Democratic party chairman*

Holstein
Soseman, Eleanor Douglass *volunteer*

KANSAS

Hutchinson
Rosenblad, Helen Viola *social services administrator*

Larned
Hewson, Mary McDonald *civic volunteer*

Overland Park
Smith, Phyllis Elizabeth *community volunteer*

Topeka
Frahm, Sheila *association executive, academic administrator, former government official*
Perry, Nancy *foundation administrator*

Wichita
Rueb, Sheree A. *social services administrator*
Timmerman, Dora Mae *community volunteer, art advocate*

Winfield
Gray, Ina Turner *fraternal organization administrator*

KENTUCKY

Berea
Howard, Jennifer Lee *not-for-profit fundraiser*

Corbin
Barton-Collings, Nelda Ann *political organization worker, bank executive*

Florence
Gorman, Gayla Marlene Osborne *consumer affairs executive*

LOUISIANA

Baton Rouge
Kimball, Dorothy Jean *retired foundation executive*

MAINE

Augusta
Phillips, Gwethalyn *political organization administrator*

Dresden
Haskell, Elizabeth McKnight *not-for-profit developer, educator*

Falmouth
Hathaway, Lynn McDonald *education advocate, administrator*

Old Town
Scribner, Princess Rose-Marie *not-for-profit developer*

Pemaquid
Howell, Jeanette Helen *retired cultural organization administrator*

Portland
Zill, Anne Broderick *foundation executive*

Standish
Gelzer, Lois Auge *foundation administrator*

York
Smart, Mary-Leigh Call (Mrs. J. Scott Smart) *civic worker*

MARYLAND

Baltimore
Applefeld, Floraine B. *cultural organization administrator*
Brock, Roslyn McCallister *association executive*
Coleman, Carolyn Quilloin *association executive*
Lungaro Cid, Lisa *educational association administrator*
Massie-Burrell, Terri L. *educational association administrator*
McLaughlin, Patricia A. *social services administrator*
Metzger, Delores Virginia *social services professional*
Nelson, Betsy S. *association administrator*
Phillips, Paula L. *foundation administrator, artist*
Skolnik, Sandra J. *educational association administrator*
Thomas, Margaret Ann *not-for-profit developer*

Belcamp
Tapp, Mamie Pearl *educational association administrator*

Bethesda
Nelson, Ethelyn Barnett *civic worker*
Reed, Berenice Anne *cultural organization administrator, educator, artist*

Chevy Chase
Allison, Adrienne Amelia *not-for-profit developer*

College Park
Brazile, Donna *advocate*
Murdoch, Amelia Clara *educational association administrator*

Derwood
Mizes, Maria Gabriela *cultural organization administrator, art historian*

Frederick
Gordon, Rita Simon *civic leader, former nurse, educator*

Frostburg
Lynch, Diane *volunteer*

Hagerstown
Hatch, Sally Ruth *foundation administrator, writer, consultant*

Kensington
Mintz, Suzanne *association executive*

Largo
Ryan, Carol J. *educational administrator*

Potomac
Rosenberg, Sarah Zacher *retired cultural organization administrator*

Rockville
Marcuccio, Phyllis Rose *retired educational association administrator, editor*

Severna Park
Hall, Marcia Joy *non-profit organization administrator*

Silver Spring
Baskerville, Lezli *educational association administrator*
Clark, Julia L. Akins *labor union administrator, lawyer*
Gandy, Kim Allison *feminist organization executive, lawyer*
Roth, Harriet Steinhorn *advocate, educator, public speaker*

Sykesville
Crist, Gertrude H. *civic worker*

Waldorf
Raiman, Rosemary A. *advocate*

MASSACHUSETTS

Amherst
MacKnight, Carol Bernier *educational association administrator*

Bedford
Kampits, Eva *accrediting association administrator, educator*

Boston
Deissler, Mary Alice *foundation executive*
Katsoulomitis, Georgia *foundation administrator, lawyer*
Meisner, Mary Jo *foundation administrator, former newspaper editor*

Cambridge
Berlowitz, Leslie *cultural organization administrator*
Lee, Barbara *political activist, foundation administrator*
Shaheen, C. Jeanne *political organization administrator, former governor*
White, Shelby *art association administrator*

Chatham
Cogan, Mary Hart *community activist, educator*

Chelmsford
Elwell, Barbara Lois Dow *foundation administrator*

Dorchester
Smith, Survilla Marie *social services administrator, artist, poet*

Groton
Anthony, Sylvia *social welfare organization executive*

Ipswich
Wilson, Doris H. *volunteer*

Lexington
Garing, Ione Davis *civic worker*

Marion
McPartland, Patricia Ann *educational association administrator, health educator*

Medfield
Phillips, Marion Grumman *civic volunteer, writer*

Quincy
Wilson, Blenda Jacqueline *foundation administrator*

Wayland
Humphrey, Diana Young *fundraiser*

Westford
Geary, Marie Josephine *art association administrator*

MICHIGAN

Alma
Kinkead, Verda Christine *non-profit organization executive, retired consultant*

Ann Arbor
Guardo, Carol J. *association executive*

Battle Creek
Bowser, Shirley *volunteer*
Davis, Laura Arlene *retired foundation administrator*

Bloomfield Hills
Levin, Carolyn Bible *volunteer*

Detroit
Good, Amy *educational association administrator*

East Lansing
Luecke, Eleanor Virginia Rohrbacher *civic volunteer*

Grand Rapids
Jones, Ora McConner *retired foundation administrator*
Paterson, Hattie P. *philanthropist*
Saigal, Ashima *not-for-profit developer*

Hancock
Tuisku, Mary Joan *volunteer, advocate*

Henderson
Miller, Kathleen Mae *educational association administrator*

Kalamazoo
Moore, Stephanie LaFaye *advocate, director*
Petersen, Anne C. (Cheryl Petersen) *foundation administrator, educator*

Lansing
Stein, Trisha *advocate*

Traverse City
Bullis, Jo Louise *social services administrator, educator*

Troy
Hodges, Michele *chamber of commerce executive*

Ypsilanti
Peoples, Alice Leigh *not-for-profit executive*

MINNESOTA

Minneapolis
Bell, Constance Conklin *child care association administrator*
Birk, Peggy J. *foundation administrator*
Henrickson, Martha Marie *trade association administrator*
Leuchovius, Deborah *advocate, special education services professional, consultant*
Smith, Mary Hill *volunteer*
Voss, Melinda *health care association administrator*

Robbinsdale
Maloney, Cheryl Ann *not-for-profit administrator, consultant*

Saint Paul
Franey, Billie Nolan *political activist*
Sisson, Bernice Belair *advocate*
Skillingstad, Constance Yvonne *social services administrator, educator*

White Earth
Vizenor, Erma J. *Native American tribal leader*

MISSISSIPPI

Crystal Springs
Bates, Lura Wheeler *retired trade association executive*

Jackson
Carmichael, Sally W. *volunteer*
Hiatt, Jane Crater *arts agency administrator*

Laurel
Asmar, Kathleen *educational association administrator*

Leland
Stott, Barbara Paxton *volunteer*

Madison
Fordice, Patricia Owens *civic leader, former state first lady*

MISSOURI

Ballwin
Pallozola, Christine *not-for-profit executive*

Defiance
LeMaster, Sherry Renee *not-for-profit fundraiser, foundation administrator, consultant*

El Dorado Springs
Hochstedler, Lisa Inez *educational association administrator*

Florissant
Schutzius, Mary Jane *volunteer activist*

Kansas City
Yarmo, Fanny F. *not-for-profit fundraiser*

Saint Louis
Brauer, Camilla Thompson (Kimmy Thompson Brauer) *civic leader*
Duhme, Carol McCarthy *civic worker*

NEBRASKA

Grand Island
Abernethy, Irene Margaret *civic worker, retired county official*

Lincoln
Hardin, Martha Love Wood *civic leader*

NEVADA

Carson City
Ayres, Janice Ruth *social services administrator*

Incline Village
Neubauer, Antonia *educational association administrator*

Las Vegas
Martinez, Adriana *political organization worker, photographer*

Spencer, Carol Brown *retired educational association administrator*
Zucker, Blanche Myra *civic worker*

Reno
LoSasso, Vicki Rae *political organization worker, artist*

NEW HAMPSHIRE

Littleton
Merritt, Mary Jane *community volunteer*

Peterborough
Eneguess, Ann Cavanaugh *social services administrator*

NEW JERSEY

Bound Brook
Blumberg, Adele Rosenberg *volunteer*

Caldwell
Ryan, Joanne Winona *art administrator, artist, consultant, educator*

Cherry Hill
Ciociola, Cecilia Mary *not-for-profit developer*

Elizabeth
Pineros, Elizabeth *social services administrator, psychotherapist*

Jackson
Carney, Rita J. *educational association administrator*
Landau-Crawford, Dorothy Ruth *retired social services administrator*

Lebanon
O'Neill, Elizabeth Sterling *trade association administrator*

Long Branch
Klostreich, Eva Tricules *educational association administrator*

Medford
Isaacson, Edith L. *civic leader*

Montclair
Mason, Lucile Gertrude *not-for-profit fundraiser, consultant*

New Brunswick
Bunch, Charlotte *advocate*

Paramus
Noguere, Suzanne *trade association executive, poet*

Princeton
De Lung, Jane Solberger *independent sector executive*
Jeffers, Beverly Maynard *volunteer*
Johnson, Barbara Piasecka *volunteer, art historian, investor*

Rumson
Swartz, Renee Becker *civic volunteer*

Union Beach
Gilmartin, Clara T. *volunteer*

NEW MEXICO

Santa Fe
Miller-Engel, Marjorie *foundation administrator, commissioner, small business owner*

NEW YORK

Brooklyn
Freis, Kathleen Marie *educational association administrator*
Horowitz, Sara *labor organizer*
Levy, Jill Sondra *educational association administrator*
Moore, Anne Frances *art administrator, consultant, educator, art appraiser, dealer*
Morgan, Mary Louise Fitzsimmons *fund raising executive, lobbyist*

Buffalo
Clarkson, Elisabeth Ann Hudnut *volunteer*
Hunt, Jane Helfrich *volunteer*
Smith, Barbara *camping administrator*

Central Islip
Wiggins, Gloria *not-for-profit developer, television producer*

Clarence
Stringer, Gretchen Engstrom *consulting volunteer administrator*

Commack
Price, Amelia Ruth *not-for-profit foundation president, artist, small business owner*

Corning
Cicerchi, Eleanor Ann Tomb *not-for-profit fundraiser*

East Hampton
Hope, Judith H. *former political organization administrator*

Farmingdale
Buzzell, Margaret *association adminstrator*

Greenfield Park
Cosey Pulley, Bernice *volunteer*

Hauppauge
Tublisky, Marcy *association administrator*

Hudson
Miner, Jacqueline *political consultant*

Ilion
Edwards, Christine Utley *social services administrator, consultant*

Ithaca
Grainger, Mary Maxon *civic volunteer*

Jamestown
Thompson, Birgit Dolores *civic worker, writer*

Larchmont
Hinerfeld, Ruth G. *civic organization executive*

Long Island City
Hoffman, Merle Holly *advocate, psychologist, writer*

Mount Kisco
Keesee, Patricia Hartford *volunteer*

New Rochelle
Black, Page Morton *civic worker, vocalist, musician*

New York
Alex, Paula Ann *foundation administrator*
Atkins, Veronica *philanthropist*
Berresford, Susan Vail *foundation administrator*
Bischoff, Theresa Ann *not-for-profit association executive*
Booth, Barbara Ribman *civic worker*
Cahan, Cora *not-for-profit developer*
Cassullo, Joanne Leonhardt *foundation administrator*
Catley-Carlson, Margaret *not-for-profit executive*
Chesler, Gail *arts organization development executive*
Christopher, Maurine Brooks *foundation administrator, writer, editor*
Cole, Elma Phillipson (Mrs. John Strickler Cole) *social welfare executive*
Dajani, Virginia *art association administrator*
Dandonoli, Patricia A. *not-for-profit fundraiser*
Davis, Kathryn Wasserman *foundation executive, educator, writer*
DeVita, M. Christine *foundation administrator*
Elliott, Eleanor Thomas *foundation executive, volunteer*
Ellis, Ross *non-profit organization executive*
Giordano, Marianne *not-for-profit developer*
Giuliani, Judith *not-for-profit executive*
Hedgpeth, Kim Roberts *trade association administrator*
Henderson, Maxine Olive Book (Mrs. William Henderson III) *foundation executive*
Hesselbein, Frances Richards *foundation administrator, writer, editor*
Heyzer, Noeleen *international organization official*
Hill, Janine *think-tank associate*
Hoffman, Linda R. *social services administrator*
Jackson, Wynelle Redding *educational association administrator, accountant, tax specialist*
Jackson McCabe, Jewell *not-for-profit developer*
Kaggen, Lois Sheila *non-profit organization executive, advocate*
Kasirer, Suri *lobbyist*
Katzowitz Shenfield, Lauren *philanthropy consultant*
Kind, Susan J. *fundraiser*
Kopp, Wendy *educational association administrator*
Kuyper, Joan Carolyn *foundation administrator*
Lane, Nancy *advocate, editor*
Lauder, Jo Carole *art association administrator*
Leet, Mildred Robbins *social welfare administrator, consultant*
London, Nora Eleonor *foundation administrator*
Luckman, Sharon Gersten *arts administrator*
Mahoney, Margaret Ellerbe *foundation executive*
Mayleas, Ruth Rothschild *foundation administrator*
Maynard, Virginia Madden *foundation administrator*
McCrary, Eugenia Lester (Mrs. Dennis Daughtry McCrary) *civic worker, writer*
McNamara, Mary Ellen *not-for-profit executive*
McNeil, Wendy Lawson-Johnston *foundation administrator*
Muse, Martha Twitchell *foundation executive*
Neidich, Brooke Garber *foundation administrator, art patron*
Polin, Jane L. *foundation official*
Rodin, Judith Seitz *foundation administrator, former academic administrator, psychologist, educator*
Roney, Carley *wedding company executive, writer*
Rose, Joanna Semel *volunteer*
Rothman, Esther Pomeranz *social services administrator, psychologist*
Rubin, Judith O. *not-for-profit trustee*
St. Martin, Charlotte *trade association administrator*
Sard, Susannah Ellen *non-profit executive*
Sidamon-Eristoff, Anne Phipps *not-for-profit developer*
Slutsky, Lorie A(nn) *foundation executive*
Spero, Joan Edelman *foundation administrator*
Steedman, Doria Lynne Silberberg *foundation administrator*
Stern-Larosa, Caryl M. *advocate, educational association administrator*
Sullivan, Mary Brosnahan *advocate, social services administrator*
Symonette, Lys *foundation executive, musician, writer*
Tenenbaum, Ann G. *art association administrator*
Traverse, Lyn D. *not-for-profit fundraiser, communications executive*
Trump, Blaine (Martha Lindley Blaine Beard Trump) *philanthropist*
Ungaro, Susan Kelliher *foundation administrator, former magazine editor*
Van de Bovenkamp, Sue Erpf *foundation administrator*
Wajsfeld, Annie R. *volunteer*
Wattleton, Faye (Alyce Faye Wattleton) *educational association administrator, advocate*
Weingarten, Rhonda (Randi Weingarten) *labor union administrator, lawyer*
Wilson, Marie C. *foundation administrator*
Wright, Sheena *not-for-profit developer*
Wylde, Kathryn S. *business organization executive*

Patchogue
Watkins, Linda Theresa *retired educational association administrator*

Pawling
Peale, Ruth Stafford (Mrs. Norman Vincent Peale) *not-for-profit executive*

Penfield
Dougherty, Janniese Marie *social services administrator, music educator*

Port Washington
Weiner, Mina Rieur *museum consultant, civic worker*

Poughkeepsie
LaGreca, Carla Irene *activist*

Rensselaer
Whitney, Mary Ellen *not-for-profit developer, educator*

Rochester
Klinke, Louise Hoyt *volunteer*
Robbins, Nancy Slinker *volunteer*

Sanborn
Jeffords, Mary Margaret *community activist*

Scarsdale
Bruck Lieb Port, Lilly *retired advocate, columnist, commentator*
Paulin, Amy Ruth *civic activist, consultant*

Staten Island
Lutkenhouse, Anne *non-profit executive*
Woodford, Ann Marguerite *social services administrator, social worker*

Stony Brook
Rocchio, Gloria D. *cultural organization administrator*

Stony Creek
La Grasse, Carol Winter *property rights activist, retired civil engineer*

Tivoli
Cranna, Christina M. *social services specialist*

Tonawanda
Glickman, Marlene *non-profit organization administrator*

Wantagh
Maldonado, Judith Ann Batorski *art association administrator*

Watertown
Henderson, Gladys Edith *retired social welfare examiner*

White Plains
Howse, Jennifer Louise *foundation administrator*

Yonkers
Neal, Leora Louise Haskett *social services administrator*

NORTH CAROLINA

Butner
Crowell, Rosemary Elaine *social services administrator*

Cary
Bryant, Mynora Joyce *not-for-profit fundraiser*

Charlotte
Locke, Elizabeth Hughes *retired foundation administrator*

Clinton
Griffin, Betty Lou *not-for-profit developer, educator*

Greensboro
Hudgens, Jeanne Ellis *advocate*

Lake Toxaway
King, Carole Wayne *foundation administrator*

Raleigh
Lilly, Nancy Cobb *civic worker*
McKinney, Carolyn *educational association administrator, educator*

Statesville
Johnston, Betty Parker *retired social service worker*

Wilson
McCain, Betty Landon Ray (Mrs. John Lewis McCain) *political party official, state official*

Winston Salem
Craven, Betty *educational association administrator*

NORTH DAKOTA

Bismarck
Stoller, Rose *think-tank executive*

Minot
Moe, Vida Delores *civic worker*

OHIO

Akron
Collier, Alice Elizabeth Becker *retired social services administrator*
Donehey, Marilyn Moss *foundation administrator*

Canton
Fernandez, Kathleen M. *cultural organization administrator*

Chagrin Falls
Ostendorf, Joan Donahue *fund raiser, volunteer*
Vail, Iris Jennings *civic worker*

Cincinnati
Hill-Cook, Patricia Ann *social services administrator*
Motch, Marjorie McCullough *service organization executive*
Parker, Linda Bates *professional development organization administrator*

Cleveland
Cook, Anda Suna *civil rights advocate*
FallCreek, Stephanie Jean *non-profit organization executive*
Penman, Robbie Mae *volunteer, political organization worker*

Columbus
Newman, Diana S. *foundation administrator, consultant*
Selby, Diane Ray Miller *fraternal organization administrator*
Sevel, Francine *advocate, researcher*

Coshocton
Freund, Carol Louise *social services consultant*

Dayton
Thomas, Marianna *volunteer community activist, writer, speaker*

Fremont
Sattler, Nancy Joan *educational association administrator*

Greenville
Thieme, Jean Louise *art association administrator*

Lakewood
Olson, Carol Joan *foundation administrator, consultant*

Lebanon
Ruder, Diane G. *not-for-profit fundraiser*

North Olmsted
Zolar, Karen Jane *social services administrator*

Oberlin
Ramp, Marjorie Jean Sumerwell *civic worker*

Oxford
Deines, Bethany A. *fraternal organization administrator*

Reynoldsburg
Maratta Snyder, Grace Elvira *volunteer*

Richfield
Lewis, Sylvia Davidson *foundation executive*

Springfield
Pitzer, Betty Braun *retired social services administrator*

Sylvania
Garrison, Linda *retired foundation administrator*

OKLAHOMA

Norman
Jones, Charlotte *foundation administrator*

Oklahoma City
Frates, Mex (Mrs. Clifford Leroy Frates) *civic worker*
Gabbard, Susan J. *art association administrator, educator*
Gumerson, Jean Gilderhus *health foundation executive*
Kerr, Lou C. *foundation administrator*

Tulsa
Blackstock, Virginia Lee Lowman (Mrs. LeRoy Blackstock) *civic worker*

OREGON

Bend
Evers-Williams, Myrlie Beasley *advocate, cultural organization administrator*

Corvallis
Wilkins, Caroline Hanke *advocate, political organization worker*

Portland
Collins, Maribeth Wilson *retired foundation administrator*
Patterson, Beverly Ann Gross *not-for-profit fundraiser, consultant, social services administrator, writer*
Showalter, Marilyn Grace *trade association administrator, director*

PENNSYLVANIA

Bethlehem
Orr, Sandra Jane *civic worker, pharmacist*

Bryn Mawr
Cooney, Patricia Ruth *civic worker*

Darby
Wardell, Lindy Constance *non-profit organization administrator*

Erie
Taylor, Margaret Uhrich *educational association administrator*

Fogelsville
Flores, Robin Ann *geriatric program and service consultant*

Gettysburg
Nelson-Small, Kathy Ann *foundation administrator*

Gibsonia
Haas, Eileen Marie *homecare advocate*

Glenside
Doman, Janet Joy *professional society administrator*

Harrisburg
Butler, Jessie D. *community activist, retired educator, counselor*
Ross, Ellyn N. *educational association administrator, consultant*
Wissler-Thomas, Carrie *professional society administrator, artist*

Hazleton
Kraynak, Marcelle Georgeann *not-for-profit developer*

Lancaster
Jordan, Lois Wenger *foundation official*

Lewisburg
Neuman, Nancy Adams Mosshammer *civic leader*

Paoli
Green, Mimi Theresa *social services administrator*

Philadelphia
Glickman, Sallie A. *professional society administrator*
Horwitz, Joy A. *foundation administrator*
McKenna, Margaret Mary *foundation administrator*
Reed, Sally Gardner *cultural organization administrator*
Sims-Nesmith, Carolyn Sandra *cultural arts association administrator*
Stevenson, Andrea J. (Andi Stevenson) *not-for-profit executive*
Thall, Letty Derman *social services administrator*
Vredenburgh, Judy *youth organization executive*

Pittsburgh
Boyce, Doreen Elizabeth *foundation administrator, educator*
Fox, Debra L. *educational association administrator, business owner*
McDaniel, Sharon Toliver *social welfare administrator, foundation administrator*
Petersen, Jean Snyder *educational association administrator*

Reading
Dietrich, Renée Long *not-for-profit developer*

Rydal
Fernberger, Marilyn Friedman *not-for-profit developer, consultant, volunteer*

State College
Phillips, Janet Colleen *retired educational association administrator, editor*

Upper Darby
Pittman, Mia N. *educational association administrator, entrepreneur*

Wayne
Annenberg, Leonore A. *foundation administrator*

Wynnewood
Meyers, Mary Ann *foundation administrator, consultant, writer*

York
Wiles, Lesley Decker *foundation administrator, preservationist*

RHODE ISLAND

Bristol
Wexler, Roberta Vail *volunteer*

North Providence
Maciel, Patricia Ann *not-for-profit developer, consultant*

Pawtucket
Savella, Barbara Maria *educational association administrator*

SOUTH CAROLINA

Chapin
Bowers, Linda *educational association administrator*

Charleston
Wagoner, M. Deanna *advocate*

Columbia
Chappell, Barbara Kelly *retired child welfare consultant*
Dobrasko, Rebekah *cultural organization administrator, historian*

Greenville
Hendrix, Susan Clelia Derrick *civic worker*

Myrtle Beach
Gravely, Mary Jeane *volunteer*

Saint Helena Island
Tarr-Whelan, Linda *policy center executive*

SOUTH DAKOTA

Aberdeen
Seeklander, Marlene Kay *educational association administrator*

TENNESSEE

Athens
Brown, Sandra Lee *art association administrator, consultant, artist*

Chattanooga
McNeill-Murray, Joan Reagin *volunteer, consultant*

Lafayette
Carter, Anna Dean *volunteer*

Memphis
Jalenak, Peggy Eichenbaum *volunteer*
Tibbs, Martha Jane Pullen *civic worker, retired social worker*

Nashville
Snyder, Barbara Lou *retired educational association administrator*
Willis, Eleanor Lawson *not-for-profit development director*

Ooltewah
Huston, Nancy Elizabeth *civic worker, educator*

Sparta
Keisling, Mary West *volunteer*

TEXAS

Arlington
McKeen, Sally Werst *volunteer*

Austin
Dealey, Amanda Mayhew *former foundation administrator*
Dougherty, Molly Ireland *organization executive*
Kolar, Mary Jane *trade and professional association executive*
Long, Teresa Lozano *foundation administrator, educator*

Beaumont
Davis, Gloria Whittie *educational association administrator*

Breckenridge
Jones, Karen Annette *civic volunteer*

Carrollton
Hart, Elizabeth Ann *foundation administrator*

Colleyville
Tigue, Virginia Beth (Ginny Tigue) *volunteer*

Corpus Christi
French, Dorris Towers Bryan *volunteer*

Dallas
Braun, Susan J. *foundation administrator*
Brinker, Nancy Goodman *social services administrator, former ambassador*
Dell, Susan *foundation administrator, apparel designer*
Smith, Justine Townsend *recreational association executive*
Stripling, Bettye Johnson *civic volunteer*

Dickinson
Sawyer, Cheryl Lynne *foundation administrator, consultant*

El Paso
Deckert, Myrna Jean *nonprofit association administrator*
Goodman, Gertrude Amelia *civic worker*

Fort Worth
Dilley, Carol *association administrator*
Saenz, Nancy Elizabeth King (Mrs. Michael Saenz) *civic worker*
Wilson-Webb, Nancy Lou *educational association administrator*

Houston
Bailey, Kelley *foundation administrator*
Bennett, Olga Salowich *civic worker, graphic arts researcher, consultant*
Charnveja, Pat S. *civic leader, former oil and gas industry executive*
Foss, Michelle Michot *think-tank executive, economist*
McCleary, Beryl Nowlin *volunteer, travel company executive*
Owen, Jane Dale *non-profit organization executive*
Wilkenfeld, Johannah *labor union administrator*

Laredo
Lozano, Araceli E. *foundation administrator, consultant*

Lubbock
Livermore, Jane *foundation executive*

Mcallen
Spyker, Leola Edith *missionary*

Pflugerville
Munzer, Annette Elizabeth *cultural affairs consultant*

Plano
Carver, Rita *not-for-profit fundraiser, consultant*

Round Rock
Mountain, Janet *foundation administrator, former computer company executive*

San Antonio
Crichton, Flora Cameron *volunteer, foundation administrator*
White, Mary Ruth Wathen *social services administrator*

Sugar Land
Hosley, Marguerite Cyril *civic worker*

Texarkana
Malcolm, Molly Beth *political organization worker, counselor*

Tyler
Harrison, Marsha Yarberry *volunteer*

Weatherford
Bergman, Anne Newberry *civic leader*
Fisk, Doris Rosalie Scanlan *volunteer*

UTAH

Ogden
Davis, Lori *not-for-profit developer*

Salt Lake City
Clark, Deanna Dee *volunteer*
Julander, Paula Foil *foundation administrator*
Struhs, Rhoda Jeanette *civic and political worker*

Sandy
Littleton, Gaye Darlene *retired nonprofit executive director*

VERMONT

Brattleboro
Bellamy, Carol *international organization administrator*

Derby Line
Nelson, Beatrice Ruth *cultural organization administrator, artist*

Plymouth
Bittinger, Cynthia Douglas *foundation executive*

VIRGINIA

Alexandria
Bryant, Anne Lincoln *educational association executive*
Butler, Susan Lowell *educational association executive, writer*
Fisher, Colleen M. *trade association administrator*
Flippo, Karen Francine *social welfare administrator*
Foster, Serrin Marie *non-profit organization executive*
Greenstein, Ruth Louise *think-tank executive, lawyer*
Kratovil, Jane Lindley *think tank associate, not-for-profit developer*
Lachance, Janice Rachel *professional association administrator, retired federal agency administrator, lawyer*
Lendsey, Jacquelyn L. *foundation administrator*
Lipnick, Anne Ruth *advocate*
Maehara, Paulette V. *fundraising executive*
Richman, Arleen *professional society administrator*
Schmidt, Joan E. *educational association administrator*
Tucker, Karen Sue *association executive*

Arlington
Buchanan, Louise *political organization worker, consultant*
Bulkeley, Christy Claire *foundation administrator*
Langley, Patricia Ann *lobbyist*
Raizen, Senta Amon *educational association administrator, researcher*
Randolph, Carolyn *educational association administrator, educator*
Wells, Christine *foundation executive*

Barboursville
Slater, Valerie Periolat *volunteer*

Falls Church
Smith, Barbara Rath *foundation executive*
Work, Jane Magruder *retired professional society administrator*

Fishersville
Taylor, Donna Leona *advocate, writer*

Franktown
Kellam, Caramine *volunteer*

Great Falls
Dinger, Ann Monroe *association executive, interior designer*

Hollins
Brown-Black, Lillian (Rusty Brown-Black) *volunteer*

Leesburg
De Barbieri, Mary Ann *not-for-profit management consultant*

Lynchburg
Craddock, Mary Spencer Jack *volunteer*

Mc Lean
Mars, Virginia Cretella *civic volunteer*
Trout, Margie Marie Mueller *civic worker*

Newport News
Mazur, Rhoda Himmel *community volunteer*

Norfolk
Lochen, Lynne Carol *cultural organization administrator*
Newkirk, Ingrid *animal rights activist*

Reston
Brennan, Norma Jean *professional society administrator, director*
Madry-Taylor, Jacquelyn Yvonne *educational association administrator*
Mogge, Harriet Morgan *educational association executive*

Richmond
Brackenridge, N. Lynn *not-for-profit developer*

Roanoke
Manns, Essie Jeanette Delaney *advocate*

Sterling
Chavez, Linda *civil rights organization executive*

Vienna
Colón, Eugenia Valinda *development executive*

Williamsburg
Chandler, Kimberley Lynn *educational association administrator*

Woodbridge
Gilmore, Marjorie Havens *retired civic worker, lawyer*

WASHINGTON

Bothell
Jacobus, Elizabeth Loomis *volunteer*

Chehalis
Dennis, Linda Susan *not-for-profit developer*

Everett
Boschok, Jackie *labor union administrator*

Langley
Medlock, Ann *not-for-profit developer, writer*

Seattle
Gates, Melinda French *foundation administrator*
Jessen, Joel Anne *not-for-profit executive, art educator*
Kelsey, Norma L. *labor union administrator*
Martínez, Yolanda R. *social services administrator*
Mathews, Sylvia Mary *foundation administrator*
Scott, Cheryl M. *foundation administrator, healthcare educator*
Stonesifer, Patty (Patricia Q. Stonesifer) *foundation administrator*

WEST VIRGINIA

Charleston
Smith, Stuart Lewis *community volunteer*

Huntington
Fannin, Josephine Jewell *social services administrator*

Parkersburg
Burdette, Jane Elizabeth *former nonprofit association executive, consultant*

Shinnston
Ford, Alma Regina *retired union official, educator*

Webster Springs
Moore, Alma Merle *association executive*

WISCONSIN

Balsam Lake
Mattson, Carol Linnette *social services administrator*

Madison
Ossorio, Pilar Nicole *professional association administrator*

Middleton
Taylor, Fannie Turnbull *art association administrator, educator*

Milwaukee
Taylor, Katherine *social services administrator*

Mukwonago
Koprowski, Suzanne Marie *educational diagnostician administrator, educator*

Racine
Johnson, Imogene Powers *foundation administrator*

Waukesha
Bellovary, Cathy *social services administrator, volunteer*

WYOMING

Casper
Cotherman, Audrey Mathews *educational association administrator, management consultant*
Stoval, Linda *political party official*

Cody
Coe, Margaret Louise Shaw *community service volunteer*

MILITARY ADDRESSES OF THE UNITED STATES

EUROPE

APO
Wagner, Mary S. *education center administrator*

CANADA

ONTARIO

Ottawa
Maxwell, Judith *think-tank executive, economist*

Waterloo
Fréchette, Louise *international organization official*

BELGIUM

Genappe
Williams, Jody *political organization administrator*

ADDRESS UNPUBLISHED

Aitchison, Anne Catherine *retired environmental activist*
Apt, Joan Frank *volunteer*
Ash, Dorothy Matthews *civic worker*
Bailey, Vicky A. *lobbyist*
Baker, Patricia *health foundation administrator*
Balter, Frances Sunstein *civic worker*
Barr, Marlene Joy *volunteer*
Bartlett, Dede Thompson *association executive*
Bayley, Suzanne Ludey *civic volunteer*
Beatty, Frances *civic worker*
Bell-Rose, Stephanie *foundation administrator*
Berger, Joyce Muriel *foundation administrator, writer, editor*
Bertini, Catherine Ann *former international organization official*
Bird, Mary Lynne Miller *professional society administrator*
Black, Geneva Arlene *social services agency administrator*
Blakeney, Karen Elizabeth *social service and community health program executive, consultant*
Bloch, Julia Chang *educational association administrator*
Blochowiak, Mary Ann *retired cultural organization administrator*
Booth, Susan *educational association administrator, product designer, marketing professional, researcher*
Bradford, Louise Mathilde *social work administrator*
Bragg, Lynn Munroe *trade association administrator, former federal commissioner*
Brantley, Willa John *educational association administrator*
Brewster, Mary Moorhead *retired educational association administrator*
Bricker, Ruth *national foundation administrator, real estate developer*
Browning, Jane Louise *social services administrator*
Buckman, Tracey Ann *political finance director*
Buhl, Cynthia Maureen *advocate, educator*
Bullin, Christine Neva *art association administrator*
Butterfield, Karen *educational association administrator*
Byrnes, Hope Huska *volunteer*
Carey, Kathryn Ann *retired foundation administrator, editor, consultant*
Clarizio, Josephine Delores *retired foundation administrator, retired manufacturing executive, retired engineering company executive*
Clark, Alicia Garcia *political party official*
Cohen, Roberta Jane *think-tank associate*
Cohn, Marianne Winter Miller *civic activist*
Cook, Beth Marie *volunteer, poet*
Cooper, Josephine Smith *trade association and public affairs executive*
Cope, Melba Darlene *volunteer, photographer*
Cowles, Elizabeth Hall *program consultant*
Cronson, Mary Sharp *foundation administrator*
Davis, Debra Greer *educational association administrator*
Deeds, Virginia Williams *volunteer*
Delaney, Pamela DeLeo *foundation administrator*
Desantis, Sherolyn Smith *foundation executive*
Dillon, Joan Kent *civic worker, volunteer consultant*
Droz, Elizabeth Jane *foundation administrator*
Duff, Patricia *civic activist*
Dykstra, Gretchen *former foundation administrator*
Eastman, Francesca Marlene *volunteer, art historian*
Easton, Michelle *foundation executive*
Ellis, Anne Elizabeth *fundraiser*
Erlichson, Miriam *fundraiser, writer*
Evans, Marsha Johnson *former non-profit association administrator, retired military officer*
Evans, Rosemary Hall *civic worker*
Feeney, Maryann McHugh *not-for profit professional*
Feldt, Gloria A. *social services administrator*
Fields, Jerri Lynn *foundation administrator*
Filer, Emily Symington Harkins *retired foundation administrator, writer, non-profit consultant*
Fitzgerald-Verbonitz, Dianne Elizabeth *not-for-profit developer*
Fox-Clarkson, Anne C. *fundraising company executive*
Frank, Jean Marie *educational association administrator, researcher*
French, Stephanie Taylor *cultural organization administrator*
Friedman, Frances Wolf *political fund raiser*
Fulbright, Harriet Mayor *educational association administrator*
Garner, Carlene Ann *not-for-profit fundraiser, consultant*
Gasper, Jo Ann *social services administrator, consultant*
Gibbons, Mary Peyser *civic volunteer*
Gilbert, Melissa *former actors guild executive, actress*
Griggs, Bobbie June *civic worker*
Grossman, Ginger Scheflin *advocate*
Gunderson, Judith Keefer *golf association executive*
Hamilton, Wendy J. *foundation administrator*
Harris, Ellen Gandy (Mrs. J. Ramsay Harris) *civic worker*
Hawn, Molly Ker *not-for-profit developer*
Heiskell, Marian Sulzberger (Mrs. Andrew Heiskell) *newspaper executive, civic worker*
Henderson, Deirdre Healy *foundation administrator*
Herman, Alexis M. *retired labor union administrator*
Hinkley, Nancy Emily Engstrom *foundation administrator, educator*
Hodge, Mary Gretchen Farnam *trade association administrator*
Hoffheimer, Minette Goldsmith *community service volunteer*
Hoffman, Karen A. *foundation executive*
Hogaboom, Maurine Holbert *cultural organization administrator*
Holland, Ruby Mae *social welfare administrator*
Holmes, Joan *retired social welfare administrator*
Horsch, Kathleen Joanne *social services administrator, educator, consultant*
Huffman, Carol Cicolani *retired educational association administrator*
Ignatius, Nancy Weiser *foundation administrator*
Jacobs, Patricia H. *social welfare organization executive*
Johnson, Karen *professional society administrator*
Johnson, Marlene M. *nonprofit executive*
Julian, Frances Bloch *volunteer*
Keets, Elizabeth *advocate, educator*
Kelly, Nancy Folden *art association administrator*
Kemper Dietrich, Sheila *educational association administrator*
Khatib, Kathy *school administrator, educator*
King, Jane Cudlip Coblentz *volunteer educator*
Klopfleisch, Stephanie Squance *social services agency administrator*
Knauer, Virginia Harrington (Mrs. Wilhelm F. Knauer) *advocate, retired federal agency administrator*
Kregg, Helen Christine *foundation administrator*
Kunstadter, Geraldine Sapolsky *foundation executive*
Kurtz, Dolores May *civic worker*
Kussrow, Nancy Esther *educational association administrator*
LaHaye, Beverly *cultural organization administrator*
Lamel, Linda Helen *professional society executive, retired insurance company executive, lawyer, arbitrator, retired college president*
Lancaster, Sally Rhodus *retired non-profit executive, consultant*
Landon, Susan N. *humanitarian, arts and environmental advocate, poet*
Lawrence, Marilyn Edith (Marilyn Guthrie) *association executive*
Leggett, Roberta Jean (Bobbi Leggett) *retired social services administrator*
Lenhart, Cynthia Rae *conservation organization executive*
Lerner, Beth M. *non-profit consultant*
Lewis, Mary-Frances *civic volunteer*
Lichtman, Judith L. *lawyer, organization administrator*
Lief, Beth *educational association administrator*
Lindenmayer, Elisabeth *international organization administrator*
Little, Laura Janes *educational association administrator*
Livingston, Margaret Gresham *civic leader*
Low, Louise O. *volunteer*
Lowe, Carol Hill *social services director, management consultant*
Luckey, Doris Waring *civic volunteer*
MacCarthy, Talbot Leland *civic volunteer*
Magoon, Nancy Amelia *art association administrator*
Makepeace, Mary Lou *foundation administrator, former mayor*
Manion, Bonnie J. *volunteer, poet, composer*
Marquand, Jean MacMurtry *educational association administrator*
Matsa, Loula Zacharoula *social services administrator, educator*
Mbadugha, Loretta Nkeiruka Akosa *social services administrator, consultant*
McFate, Patricia Ann *foundation executive, science educator*
McGarry, Marcia *retired community service coordinator*
McGarvey, Virginia Claire Lancaster *volunteer*
McKeown, Mary Elizabeth *retired educational association administrator*
McWethy, Patricia Joan *educational association administrator*
Medina, Janie *not-for-profit fundraiser*
Menzel, Marybelle Proctor *volunteer*
Merszei, Aimée Mörner *not-for-profit fundraiser*
Metcalf, Karen *retired foundation executive*
Metcalf, Susan Stimmel *community volunteer*
Meyer, Rachel Abijah *foundation administrator, artist, poet*
Michel, Elizabeth Cheney *social reform consultant*
Miller, Marian *professional society administrator*
Millett, Kate (Katherine Murray Millett) *political activist, sculptor, artist, writer*
Minor, Addine E. *civic leader*
Misner, Charlotte Blanche Ruckman *retired community organization administrator*
Moore, Julia Gibert *retired educational administrator, priest*
Moules, Deborah Ann *not-for-profit developer*
Muir, Patricia Allen *professional association administrator*
Myers, Toby Millicent *advocate*
Narbit, Heather Alyce *not-for-profit developer, writer*
Newman, Gwill Linderme *volunteer*
Nowell, Linda Gail *not-for-profit executive*
Nubel, Marianne Kunz *cultural organization administrator, writer, composer*
O'Connor, Doris Julia *not-for-profit fundraiser, consultant*
Olson, Margaret Smith *retired foundation administrator*
O'Neill, Mary Jane *not-for-profit administrator, consultant*
Ovadiah, Janice *not-for-profit developer, cultural organization administrator*
Palmer, Jocelyn Beth *volunteer*
Palmquist, Carol Ann *educational association administrator*
Prejean, Sister Helen Theresa *human rights advocate, writer, lecturer*
Prescott, Barbara Lodwich *educational association administrator*
Prokop, Susan *disability rights advocate*
Pullen, Penny Lynne *non-profit organization administrator, retired state legislator*
Pullium, Rita Marie *educational association administrator, director, psychologist*
Ramirez, Maria C(oncepción) *retired educational association administrator*
Ramo, Virginia M. Smith *civic worker*
Ray, Evelyn Lucille *art association administrator*
Rea, Ann Hadley Kuehn *retired social services administrator, marketing professional*
Redd, J. Diane *not-for-profit developer*
Richardson, Veta Teresa *professional society administrator, lawyer*
Ridings, Dorothy Sattes *former association executive*
Rimel, Rebecca Webster *foundation administrator*
Riskin, Victoria *former trade association administrator*
Roberts, Margot Markels *art association administrator*
Roeder, Gloria Jean *civil rights specialist, retired private investigator*
Rogers, Margaret Ellen Jonsson *civic worker*
Romer, Carole Joyce *volunteer*
Rossbach, Janet B. *art association administrator, not-for-profit fundraiser*
Rossi, Norma J. *retired not-for-profit developer, advocate*
Rutledge, Mary Elizabeth *cultural organization administrator*
Sanford, Sarah J. *healthcare executive*
Sankoff, Tina M. *foundation administrator*
Schanfield, Fannie Schwartz *community volunteer*
Schapira, Doris R. *UN observer*
Schersten, Katherine Anne *volunteer*
Schuster, Elaine *retired civil rights professional*
Scripture, Lois Jean *retired social services director*
Seely, Megan *activist, educator*
Seiff, Gloria Louise *volunteer*
Shackelford, Lottie Holt *civic worker, former mayor*
Sheehan, Cindy *anti war activist*
Shriver, Eunice Mary Kennedy (Mrs. Robert Sargent Shriver Jr.) *foundation administrator, volunteer, social worker*
Smelser, Ruth Malone *volunteer*
Smith, Margaret Taylor *volunteer*
Smith, Wendy L. *foundation executive*
Snyder, Patricia *volunteer*
Solo, Joyce Rubenstein *volunteer*
Sorensen, Elizabeth Julia *retired cultural administrator*
Spaulding, Helen Bowdoin *former foundation administrator*
Spencer, Lonabelle (Kappie Spencer) *political agency administrator, lobbyist*
Stobb, Mary Jean *retired association administrator*
Straus, A. Susan *volunteer*
Sulc, Jean Luena (Jean L. Mestres) *lobbyist, consultant*
Sullivan, Carley Hayden *political party executive*
Tadlock, Anita Conner *volunteer*
Takanishi, Ruby *foundation administrator, researcher*
Tasman, Alice Lea Mast *not-for-profit fundraiser*
Tellers, Cheryl Lee *art association administrator, consultant*
Thomas, Spring Ursula *not-for-profit developer, educator, photographer*
Thurmaier, Mary Jean *educational association administrator*
Tigett-Parks, Elizabeth *arts administrator*
Tisch, Wilma Stein *foundation administrator*
Transou, Lynda Lou *advertising art administrator*
Tryon, Elizabeth Anne *educational association administrator*
Wachtell, Esther *non-profit management executive, consultant*
Wegner, Darlene Joy *civic worker, event coordinator*
Whalen, Loretta Theresa *educational association administrator*
Wheeler, Elizabeth Darracott *volunteer*
White, Rebecca E. *advocate*
Williams, Alice Noel Tuckerman *retired foundation administrator*
Wong, Elaine Dang *foundation executive*
Woods, Harriett Ruth *political organization worker, retired state official*
Young, Elizabeth Bell *organization consultant*
Young, Margaret Buckner *civic worker, author*

ATHLETICS

UNITED STATES

ALABAMA

Decatur
Keenum, Nancy Elizabeth *athletic director, coach*

Jacksonville
Torgerson, Jennifer Ann *athletic trainer*

Montgomery
Ray, Michelle L. *physical education educator*

Pell City
Smith, Janet Newman *retired physical education educator*

ARIZONA

Phoenix
Gillom, Jennifer *professional basketball player*
Taurasi, Diana *college basketball player*

Tucson
Goldberg, Charlotte Wyman *retired physical education educator, retired dean, retired counselor, retired travel company executive*
Tillman, Daisha A. *athletic trainer*

CALIFORNIA

Aliso Viejo
Cohen, Sasha (Alexandra Pauline Cohen) *ice skater*

Azusa
Duskin, Kimberly J *athletic trainer*
Lehman, Sharon Malani *physical education educator*

Carmel
Epstein-Shepherd, Bee *coach, hypnotist, educator*

El Segundo
Buss, Jeanie *professional sports team executive*
Leslie, Lisa DeShaun *professional basketball player*
Milton-Jones, DeLisha *professional basketball player*
Toler, Penny *former professional basketball player, sports team executive*
Weatherspoon, Teresa Gaye *professional basketball player*

Fallbrook
Cordes, Kathleen Ann *retired physical education educator, director*

Glendale
Spangler, Dianne Marie *physical education educator*

Irvine
Dill, Laura Lee *athletic trainer, educator*

Long Beach
Curry, Denise *women's college basketball coach*
Magyar, Tina Michelle *physical education educator*

Los Angeles
Beckerman, Alyssa *gymnast*
Dantzscher, Jamie *gymnast*
DeFrantz, Anita *sports association executive, lawyer*
Lee, Jeanette *professional pool player*
Maloney, Kristen *gymnast*
Ng, Kim (Kimberly J. Ng) *professional sports team executive*

Monterey Park
Stankevitz, Diane Lynn *athletic trainer*

Oakland
Frady, Kisha *professional sports team executive*

Oceanside
Messner, Yvonne F. *physical education educator*

Orange
Gibbons, Pamela R. *professional athletic trainer*
Hudson, Kelly Colleen Patrick *personal trainer, educator*

Sacramento
Griffith, Yolanda Evette *professional basketball player*
Totton, Gayle *professional sports team executive*

Santa Clara
Chastain, Brandi Denise *professional soccer player*
DeBartolo-York, Denise *sports team executive*

Sausalito
Casals, Rosie *retired professional tennis player*

COLORADO

Colorado Springs
Beard, Amanda *swimmer, Olympic athlete*
Bennett, Brooke *Olympic athlete*
Bobek, Nicole *professional figure skater*
Cash, Swin (Swintayla Marie Cash) *professional basketball player*
Coughlin, Natalie *Olympic athlete*
Granato, Catherine (Cammi Granato) *Olympic athlete*
Hughes, Sarah *figure skater*
Kupets, Courtney *Olympic athlete*
Kwan, Michelle Wing *professional figure skater*
Lang, Naomi *ice skater*
Lang, Ping *former professional volleyball player; head coach Olympic volleyball team*
May, Misty *Olympic athlete*
McCool, Courtney *Olympic athlete*
McDonough, Ann Patrice *ice skater*
Nikodinov, Angela *professional figure skater, Olympic athlete*
Patterson, Carly *Olympic athlete*
Scott, Tiffany *ice skater*
Torres, Dara *Olympic athlete*
Tueting, Sarah *professional hockey player*
Walsh, Kerri Lee *Olympic athlete*

Durango
Erickson, Mary Ann *athletic trainer, educator*

Golden
Bullard, Christine Adele Doutt *retired physical education educator*

CONNECTICUT

Bristol
Weaving, Christine A. *personal trainer*

Burlington
Jones, Phyllis Duyser *physical education educator*

Cos Cob
Leamy, Nancy M. *professional athletics coach*

Easton
Duffy, Natalie W. *retired physical education educator*

Lakeville
Kelly, Patricia Beyer *personal trainer*

Litchfield
Kennedy, Susan Orpha *physical education educator, consultant, sports official*

South Windsor
Baretta, Marsha Motyl *elementary school physical education educator*

Stamford
Goldsmith, Donna *sports association executive*
McMahon, Linda E. *sports association executive*

Uncasville
Lobo, Rebecca *professional basketball player*

DELAWARE

Milton
Scott, Phyllis Wright *coach, music educator*

Newark
Cairns, Sara Albertson *retired physical education educator*
Wilson, Deborrah *physical education educator*

DISTRICT OF COLUMBIA

Washington
Bullett, Vicky *former professional basketball player*
Devere, Amy Jo *physical education educator, director*
Hargrove, Linda *professional basketball coach*
Holdsclaw, Chamique Shaunta *professional basketball player*
O'Malley, Susan *professional basketball team executive*
Stanley, Marianne *professional athletics coach*

FLORIDA

Clermont
Richardson, Dot (Dorothy Gay) *former Olympic softball player, physician*

Coral Gables
Harriell, Kysha *athletic trainer, educator*

Daytona Beach
Ahn, Shi Hyun *professional golfer*
Andrews, Donna L. *professional golfer*
Baena, Marisa *professional golfer*
Barrett, Tina *professional golfer*
Davies, Laura *professional golfer*
DeLuca, Annette *professional golfer*
Doolan, Wendy *professional golfer*
Han, Hee-Won *professional golfer*
Hurst, Patricia Ann *professional golfer*
Inkster, Juli *professional golfer*
Jang, Jeong *professional golfer*
Kane, Lorie *professional golfer*
Kennedy, Lesa France *professional sports team executive*
Kerr, Cristie *professional golfer*
Kim, Christina *professional golfer*
Kim, Mi Hyun *professional golfer*
Kuehne, Kelli *professional golfer*
Kung, Candie *professional golfer*
Moodie, Janice *professional golfer*
Neumann, Liselotte *professional golfer*
Ochoa, Lorena *professional golfer*
Pak, Se Ri *professional golfer*
Park, Grace *professional golfer*
Park, Hee-Jung (Hee Jong Park) *professional golfer*
Rosales, Jennifer *professional golfer*
Saiki, Kim *professional golfer*
Schandel, Susan *professional sports team executive*
Sheehan, Patty *professional golfer*
Sorenstam, Annika *professional golfer*
Steinhauer, Sherri *professional golfer*
Stupples, Karen *professional golfer*
Teske, Rachel *professional golfer*
Webb, Karrie *professional golfer*
Whitworth, Kathrynne Ann *professional golfer*
Wie, Michelle Sung *professional golfer*

Deltona
Rossi, Jennifer Michelle *athletic trainer*

Fort Lauderdale
Mahan, Mary Hoyle *retired physical educator*

Gainesville
Peck, Carolyn *basketball coach*

Hollywood
King, Alma Jean *retired physical education educator, healthcare educator*

Opa Locka
Robinson, Shirley S. *coach, educator*

Orlando
Pepper, Dottie *professional golfer*

Palm Harbor
Jordan, Patricia Colgan *physical education educator*

Saint Petersburg
Clijsters, Kim *professional tennis player*
Coetzer, Amanda *professional tennis player*
Craybas, Jill *professional tennis player*
Dementieva, Elena *professional tennis player*
Dokic, Jelena *professional tennis player*
Granville, Laura *professional tennis player*
Hantuchova, Daniela *professional tennis player*
Harkleroad, Ashley *professional tennis player*
Henin-Hardenne, Justine *professional tennis player*
Kuznetsova, Svetlana *professional tennis player*
Mauresmo, Amelie *professional tennis player*
Myskina, Anastasia *professional tennis player*
Reeves, Samantha *professional tennis player*
Sharapova, Maria *professional tennis player*
Shaughnessy, Meghann *professional tennis player*
Stevison, Wendy *personal trainer*

Tallahassee
Yerg, Beverly Johnson *physical education educator, researcher*

Tavares
Livengood, Heather Jeanne *coach*

GEORGIA

Augusta
Lamb, M. Elizabeth *athletic trainer*

Columbus
Gamber, Jamie Saddler *athletic trainer*

Dallas
Hommick, Carol Mary *physical education educator*

Decatur
Groover, Lori Mobley *athletic trainer*

East Point
Renzi, Beth Paige *personal trainer*

Kennesaw
Kluka, Darlene Ann *human performance educator, researcher*

Mableton
Mounts, Kristi Lynn *personal trainer*

Marietta
Devigne, Karen Cooke *retired amateur athletics executive*

HAWAII

Kamuela
McDonough, Jean Whitney *personal trainer, sports medicine physician*

IDAHO

Coeur D' Alene
Shriner, Darlene Kay *professional athletics coach*

ILLINOIS

Alsip
Fournier, Maureen Mary *physical education educator*

Calumet City
Seifert, Suzanne Marie *physical education educator*

Charleston
Price, Lee Ann *athletic trainer, educator*

Chicago
DiMaggio, Lynette M. *physical education educator*
Fawcett, Joy Lynn *retired professional soccer player*
Foudy, Julie Maurine *retired professional soccer player, Olympic athlete*
Gabarra, Carin Leslie *professional soccer player, professional soccer coach*
Gaters, Dorothy *basketball coach*
Hamm, Mia (Mariel Margaret Hamm) *retired professional soccer player*
Heinrichs, April *soccer coach*
Hucles, Angela Khalia *professional soccer player*
Lilly, Kristine Marie *professional soccer player*
MacMillan, Shannon Ann *professional soccer player*
Milbrett, Tiffeny Carleen *professional soccer player*
Nold, Lisa Marie *athletic trainer*
O'Reilly, Heather Ann *Olympic athlete*
Parlow, Cynthia Maria *professional soccer player*
Reddick, Catherine Anne (Cat Reddick) *Olympic athlete*
Roberts, Tiffany Marie *former soccer player*
Scurry, Briana Collette *professional soccer player*
Slaton, Danielle Victoria *professional soccer player*
Sobrero, Kate (Kathryn Michele Sobrero) *professional soccer player*
Venturini, Tisha Lea *professional soccer player*
Wagner, Alyson Kay (Aly Wagner) *professional soccer player*
Wambach, Abby (Mary Abigail Wambach) *Olympic athlete*

Erie
Latham, LaVonne Marlys *physical education educator*

Freeport
Giglio, Emily Kristine *athletic trainer, educator*

Glen Ellyn
McGovern, Meghan Marie *athletic trainer*

Glenview
King, Billie Jean Moffitt *retired professional tennis player*

Lake Forest
McCaskey, Virginia Halas *professional sports team executive*
Murphy, Karen *sports association executive*

Lincoln
Cook, Ruth Ellen *athletic trainer*

Mahomet
Thompson, Margaret M. *physical education educator*

Romeoville
Northrup, Rebecca Lynn *athletic trainer*

Schaumburg
Colberg, Linda *physical education educator*

Sterling
Moran, Joan Jensen *physical education educator, healthcare educator*

Westmont
Tricase, Elizabeth *gymnast*

INDIANA

Granger
Thomas, Debi (Debra J. Thomas) *ice skater*

Indianapolis
Catchings, Tamika Devonne *professional basketball player*
Dragila, Stacy *track and field athlete*
Fortner, Nell *professional athletics coach*
Jones, Marion *track and field athlete*
Phelps, Jaycie *gymnast, Olympic athlete*

Scottsburg
Mosley, Sherry Jo *athletic trainer*

Terre Haute
Hare, Molly Kay *physical education educator*

IOWA

Fayette
Leete, Angela Marie *athletic trainer, educator*

Peosta
Wulfekuhle, Jenny *pilates instructor, athletic trainer*

KANSAS

Lawrence
Henrickson, Bonnie *women's college basketball coach*

Manhattan
Patterson, Deb *women's college basketball coach*

Mcpherson
Coppock, Doris Ellen *retired physical education educator, retired music educator*

Olathe
Amborn, Jennifer *physical education educator*

KENTUCKY

Williamsburg
Blackmore-Haus, Margaret Ann *athletic trainer, educator*

LOUISIANA

Baton Rouge
Chatman, Dana (Pokey Chatman) *women's college basketball coach*

Pineville
DeLong, Lori Lynn *physical education educator, athletic trainer*

Shreveport
Armstrong, Shelley N. *physical education educator, coach*

MAINE

Hollis Center
Hodgdon, Paula Drake *retired physical education educator*

Portland
Blair, Bonnie Kathleen *former professional speedskater, former Olympic athlete*
Chow, Amy *gymnast, Olympic athlete*

MARYLAND

Bowie
Baker, Marshina *physical education educator*

College Park
Frese, Brenda *women's college basketball coach*

Columbia
Button, Katy *professional athletics manager*

Olney
Sodetz, Carol Jean *aquatic fitness educator*

Saint James
Duncan, Tanya Nicole *school athletic trainer*

MASSACHUSETTS

Arlington
Samuelson, Joan Benoit *professional runner*

Boston
McDonald, Jane Theresa *athletic trainer, educator*

Braintree
Malloy, Ellen Ann *athletic trainer*

Bridgewater
Laquale, Kathleen Marie *physical education educator*
Minasian, Maureen *physical education educator*

Lynnfield
Kerrigan, Nancy *professional figure skater, retired Olympic athlete*

Malden
Hromada, Lauren Spada *athletic traniner*

Somerset
Rapoza, Donna Lee *physical education educator*

West Roxbury
Barbosa, Tanya Marie *athletic trainer*

MICHIGAN

Ann Arbor
McCann, Peggy S. *physical education educator*
Ray, Elise *gymnast*

Cheboygan
Ostrowski, Stacey *athletic trainer, educator*

Davison
West, Stacy Kathlena *athletic trainer*

Detroit
Ilitch, Marian *professional hockey team executive, food service executive*
Nabozny, Heather *professional sports team groundskeeper*

Howell
Jagdfeld, Judy A. *coach, secondary school educator*

MINNESOTA

Minneapolis
Augustus, Seimone *professional basketball player*
McConnell Serio, Suzie Theresa *former professional basketball player, professional basketball coach*
Smith, Katie (Katherine May Smith) *professional basketball player*

MISSISSIPPI

Mississippi State
McLendon, Mary Kathryn *athletic trainer*

MISSOURI

Branson
Meikle, Dora Quinn Arney *retired physical education educator*

Columbia
Dye, Laura *physical education educator*

Lamar
Landrum, Ann Louise *physical education educator*

Maryville
Quinlin, Kelly LeAnn *physical education educator*

Oregon
Lynn, Brenda *physical education educator*

Saint Louis
Joyner Kersee, Jackie (Jacqueline Joyner Kersee) *retired track and field athlete*

West Plains
Elrod, Keri Lynn *athletic trainer*

NEBRASKA

Lincoln
Mulvaney, Mary Jean *retired physical education educator*

NEVADA

Las Vegas
Benjamin, Jennifer *health educator*

NEW HAMPSHIRE

Goshen
Wright, Lilyan Boyd *physical education educator*

Keene
Bleam, Nancy Kay *physical education educator*

New London
Eckrich, Regina *physical education educator, department chairman*

NEW JERSEY

Camden
Mazzoli, Linda Fabrizio *personal trainer, consultant, marketing professional*

Flemington
Castelgrant, Elizabeth Ann Saylor *physical education educator, consultant*

Fort Lee
Baiul, Oksana *former figure skater, clothing designer*

Montclair
Chemidlin, Michele Lynn *athletic trainer, consultant*

Pemberton
Bowker, Eileen Gunson *athletic trainer, educator*

Pennington
Palmisano, Hollie Leah *personal trainer, athletic trainer*

Secaucus
Sanders, Summer *Olympic athlete, news correspondent, newscaster*

Somerdale
Klenk, Christine *athletic trainer, educator*

NEW MEXICO

Abiquiu
Howlett, Phyllis Lou *retired athletics conference administrator*

Rio Rancho
Loiacono, Melissa Ann *athletic trainer*

NEW YORK

Armonk
Sydney, Doris S. *sports association executive, interior designer*

Bronx
Afterman, Jean *professional sports team executive*

Cobleskill
Westervelt, Gayle Gaetano *physical education educator*

Garden City
Berka, Marianne Guthrie *health and physical education educator*

Kenmore
Gilham, Jennifer Erin *physical education educator, soccer coach*

New York
Blazejowski, Carol A. *professional sports team executive, retired professional basketball player*
Brown, Renee *sports association executive*
Capriati, Jennifer Maria *professional tennis player*
Cook, Traci *sports association executive*
Johnson, Vickie *professional basketball player*
Katz, Jane *swimming educator*
Orender, Donna *sports association executive*
Phillips, Tari *professional basketball player*

Poughkeepsie
Hill, Carla Larsen *physical education educator, gymnastics judge*

Rochester
Wilson, Melissa Ann *athletic trainer*

Sag Harbor
Deleski, Karen Margaret *athletic trainer*

South Salem
Schindler, Teri *sports association executive*

Syracuse
Duerr, Dianne Marie *sports medicine consultant, educator*

White Plains
Brandi, Kristina *professional tennis player*
Davenport, Lindsay *professional tennis player*
Frazier, Amy *professional tennis player*
Morariu, Corina *professional tennis player*
Raymond, Lisa *professional tennis player*
Rubin, Chanda *professional tennis player*
Tauziat, Nathalie *professional tennis player*
Williams, Serena *professional tennis player, apparel designer*
Williams, Venus *professional tennis player*

Youngsville
Bracken, Lynda *physical education educator*

NORTH CAROLINA

Blowing Rock
Thomas-Bevington, Vera Ellen Ball *retired physical education educator*

Chapel Hill
Harrison, Katherine Gordon *tennis coach*

Charlotte
Lacey, Trudi *professional athletics coach*
Staley, Dawn Michelle *professional basketball player*
Stinson, Andrea Maria *professional basketball player*

Concord
Switalski, Joy Patricia *athletic trainer*

Durham
Goestenkors, Gail *basketball coach*

Elon
Smith, Carol Anne *retired physical education educator*

Mooresville
Münter, Leilani Maaja *race car driver*

Shallotte
Sabiston, Kelli Brewer *athletic trainer, consultant*

Wilmington
DeVos, Renee Nichole *personal trainer, elementary school educator*

Winston Salem
Handy, Danette Farmer *coach*

Wrightsville Beach
Marcolina, Kathryn Watkins *personal and professional success coach*

NORTH DAKOTA

Williston
Slagle, Penny Lee *physical education educator*

OHIO

Bowling Green
Frederick, Janet Dennis *physical education educator*

Bryan
Schroeder, Teresa Marie *athletic trainer*

Cambridge
Wright, Amy Ralynn *athletic trainer, small business owner*

Cincinnati
Barber-Foss, Kim Daneen *athletic trainer*

Cleveland
Kwiatkowski, Tonia *former professional figure skater*
Lopez, Nancy *retired professional golfer*
Pierce, Mary *professional tennis player*
Seles, Monica *professional tennis player*
Zilch, Brianna Rae *athletic trainer*

Dayton
O'Keefe, Linda Lee *physical education educator*

Dublin
Hugo, Jessica Lyn *physical education educator*

Fairfield
Sheehan, Samantha *gymnast*

Lorain
Gall-Iemma, Julie Jeannine *personal trainer*

Middlefield
Archbold, Heather D. *personal trainer*

Somerset
Green, Tammie *professional golfer*

Terrace Park
Fehl, Patricia Katherine *retired physical education educator*

Wilberforce
Jones, LaShaunta' Lynn *athletic trainer, academic advisor*

OKLAHOMA

Edmond
Sanchez, Cindi Asbury *physical education educator*

Oklahoma City
Ainsworth, Sharie Lynn *athletic trainer, educator*
Binning, Bette Finese (Mrs. Gene Hedgcock Binning) *athletic association official*
Douty, Sheila *softball player*
Fernandez, Lisa *softball player*

OREGON

Eugene
Sisley, Becky Lynn *physical education educator*

West Linn
Harris, Debra Coral *physical education educator*

PENNSYLVANIA

Aldan
Stegmuller, Agnes Leonore *physical education educator*

Allison Park
Toerge, Lynn *athletic trainer*

Bedford
Weyant, Erin Kathleen Beegle *athletic trainer, small business owner*

Breinigsville
Smith, Judith Lynn *physical education educator*

Carlisle
Nolt, Janelle *athletic trainer*

Charleroi
Carpenter, Heather L. *athletic trainer*

East Stroudsburg
Shotwell, Colleen Aaron *personal trainer, educator*

Exeter
Mudlock, Laura *athletic trainer*

Millheim
Horner, Mandy Sue *athletic trainer*

Oreland
Perez, Patricia Streit *athletic trainer, small business owner*

Philadelphia
Grimm, Melissa *sports association executive*
Mueller, Jena Lynn *athletic trainer*

Pittsburgh
Pease, Jennifer Kelley *sports medicine educator*
Vetere, Kathleen Marie *athletic trainer*

Villanova
Tinklepaugh, Valerie Marie *physical education educator*

Williamsport
Lockcuff, Stacy Marie *personal trainer, pre-school educator*

RHODE ISLAND

North Scituate
Angell, Jean E. *physical education educator, director*

SOUTH CAROLINA

Anderson
Stowe, Jynne R. *athletic trainer*

Columbia
McCaslin, Elizabeth Ann *athletic trainer*

Rock Hill
Ford, Mary (Polly) Wylie *retired physical education educator*

West Columbia
Gates, Laura Love *physical education educator*

SOUTH DAKOTA

Brookings
McGee, Megan E. *coach, consultant*

Chamberlain
Gerlach, Amy Louise *physical education educator*

Mitchell
Konechne, Ann M. *women's college basketball coach, director*

TENNESSEE

Gatlinburg
McIntosh, Elaine Householder *physical education educator*

Martin
Anderson, Pamela Susan *sports official, educator*

Maryville
Bratt, Peggy L. *personal trainer*

Memphis
Bricker-Bone, Jennifer K. *athletic trainer*

Smyrna
Campbell, Milbrey Anne *physical education educator*

TEXAS

Arlington
Howell, Holly Lyn *athletic trainer*

Austin
Conradt, Jody *basketball coach*

Bryan
Emola, Shauna *athletic trainer*

Carrollton
Lieberman-Cline, Nancy *sports commentator, former professional basketball coach, former player*

College Station
Wagner, Susan Alison *physical education educator*

Dallas
Huggins, Hollie Ann *athletic trainer, reporter*
Lafitte, Marissa B. *coach*

Denton
Ring, Kristen M. *physical education educator*

Houston
Supak, Cathy Poerner *athletic trainer, educator*
Swoopes, Sheryl Denise *professional basketball player*

Lubbock
Sharp, Marsha *basketball coach*

San Antonio
Azzi, Jennifer L. *professional basketball player*
Hernandez, Adriana *athletic trainer*
Johnson, Shannon *professional basketball player*
McCray, Nikki Kesangame *professional basketball player*
Savala, Lindsay Kaye *athletic trainer*
Worth, Diane Bernice *physical education educator*

San Marcos
Imel, Elizabeth Carmen *retired physical education educator*

The Woodlands
Marr, Catherine Mary *physical education educator*

Wichita Falls
Lancaster, Jennifer Nicole *athletic trainer, educator*

UTAH

Park City
Mancuso, Julia *skier, Olympic athlete*
Stone, Nikki *motivational speaker, retired Olympic athlete*

Salt Lake City
Carver, Julia *retired physical education educator*

VERMONT

Williston
Oakes, Jennifer Sharyl *physical education educator, athletic director, coach*

VIRGINIA

Dublin
Clark, Shelia Roxanne *sports association executive, legislative analyst*

Midlothian
Mitchell, Biki-Ray *physical education educator*

Norton
Caruso, Carol Beverly *physical education educator*

Richmond
Liermann, Kelly *athletic trainer*

The Plains
O'Connor, Karen Lende *Olympic athlete, sports association administrator*

Williamsburg
Richezza, Amanda *athletic trainer*

Woodbridge
Hayes, Linda Marie *coach*

WASHINGTON

Carnation
Beshur, Jacqueline E. *animal trainer, farmer, writer*

Seattle
Bird, Sue (Suzanne Brigit Bird) *professional basketball player*

Sequim
Kaps, Kay A. *physical education educator, coach*

Tacoma
Hacker, Colleen Marie *physical education educator, consultant, dean*

Vancouver
Engelker, Lynsey L. *athletic trainer, professional athletics manager*

WEST VIRGINIA

Bluefield
Francis, Kerri Ann *athletic trainer*

WISCONSIN

Jefferson
Smith, Dena Michele *physical education educator*

Kenosha
Persons, Kari Lynn *physical education educator, basketball coach*

La Crosse
Eber, Laura Jean *personal trainer*

Salem
Zwirgzdas, Shirley Margaret *physical education educator*

WYOMING

Cody
Knaff, Rebecca E. *personal trainer*

Laramie
Thomas, Joi J. *personal trainer*

Moorcroft
McKillip, Mary *physical education educator*

Newcastle
Engle, Kathleen Faye *elementary education educator*

TERRITORIES OF THE UNITED STATES

PUERTO RICO

San Juan
Marichal, Maria P. *physical education educator, soccer coach*

CANADA

ONTARIO

Ottawa
Hylland, Sue *sports association executive*
Lay, Marion *sports association executive*

GERMANY

Mannheim
Graf, Steffi *retired professional tennis player*

ADDRESS UNPUBLISHED

Ackerman, Valerie B. *former sports association executive*
Atler, Vanessa *gymnast*
Bjornsrud, Marlene *professional athletics manager*
Bogle, Kimberly Layng *physical education educator*
Boyer, Lisa *basketball coach*
Bradley, Patricia Ellen *professional golfer*
Bryant, La Kesha Joy *physical education educator*
Cathcart, Sheila K. *athletic trainer*
Cerney, Angela Dawn *athletic trainer, health facility administrator*
Chen, Lu *figure skater*
Connolly, Michelle Marie *athletic trainer*
Cornelius, Tia Marie *physical education educator*
Covassin, Tracey *athletic training educator*
Crincoli, Tracy Anne *athletic trainer*
Daniel, Beth *professional golfer*
Darsch, Nancy *former professional basketball coach*
Davidson, Bonnie Jean *gymnastics educator, sports management consultant*
Dickson, Andrea Rebecca *athletic trainer*
Donovan, Anne *professional basketball coach*
Favor-Hamilton, Suzanne Marie *track and field athlete, Olympian*
Fickes, Kelly Ann *personal trainer*
Frie, Dorothy Grace *retired physical education educator*
Frye, Brandie Marie *personal trainer, educator*
Gansle, Marbry L. *physical education educator*
Graser, Susan Vincent *physical education educator*
Greiner, Nicole K. Hudak *physical education educator*
Guthrie, Janet *professional race car driver*
Haberl, Valerie Elizabeth *physical education educator, small business owner*
Hanson, Paula *sports association executive*
Hatchell, Sylvia *basketball coach*
Ina, Kyoko *professional figure skater*
Kournikova, Anna *retired professional tennis player*
Krause, Jennie Sue *athletic trainer, nutrition counselor*
Landovsky, Rosemary Reid *figure skating school director, coach*
Loughlin, Ann Ursula *professional golfer, educator*
Maitoza, Colleen *professional sports team executive*
Marenoff, Susan *professional athletics manager*
Marotta, Gina *athletic trainer*
McCloy, Shirley *physical education educator*
McHugh, Maura *professional basketball coach*
Miller, Cheryl DeAnn *former professional basketball coach, broadcaster*
Morgan, Lynn *sports association executive*
Murrell, Monica Lynn *personal trainer*
Navratilova, Martina *professional tennis player*
Nesbit, Melanie Ann *athletic trainer*
Nguyen, Christal *personal trainer*
Novotna, Jana *retired professional tennis player*
Patrick, Danica Sue *race car driver*
Pitter, Tracy Alana *athletic trainer*
Ploeckelman, Amy Lynn *athletic trainer*
Potratz, Wendy Jean *athletic trainer, consultant*
Pugh, Shante Camille *athletic trainer*
Rampone, Christie P. *professional soccer player*
Ratzlaff, Teresa *physical education educator*
Rauser, Connie Jean *athletic trainer*
Rhode, Kim *Olympic athlete*
Robertson, Kari Dawn *athletic trainer*
Robinson, Crystal *professional basketball player*
Shannon, Donna Lynne *physical education educator, real estate broker*
Smith, Janet Marie *sports executive*
Spearing, Karen Marie *retired physical education educator, coach*
Stevenson, Alexandra *professional tennis player*
Street, Picabo *Olympic athlete*
Stringer, C. Vivian *college basketball coach*
Sullivan, Ann-Catherine *physical education educator*
Summitt, Patricia Head *college basketball coach*
Terry, April Lynne *physical education educator*
Thompson, Tina Marie *professional basketball player*
Timms, Michele *retired professional basketball player*
Tovornik, Mary Rose *physical education educator*
Turner, Belinda Engram *physical education educator, athletics coordintaor*
Tyszka, Cortney Marie *athletic trainer, educator*
Van Dyken, Amy *Olympic athlete*
Watley, Natasha *Olympic athlete*
Williams, Tiffany N. *personal and athletic trainer*
Yamaguchi, Kristi Tsuya *ice skater*
Yokley, Karel *athletic trainer, educator*

BUSINESS *See* FINANCE: INDUSTRY

COMMUNICATIONS *See* COMMUNICATIONS MEDIA; INDUSTRY: SERVICE

COMMUNICATIONS MEDIA *See also* ARTS: LITERARY

UNITED STATES

ALABAMA

Birmingham
Culpepper, Mary Kay *publishing executive*

Dothan
Williams, Claudia Baxter *retired media specialist, school librarian*

Gadsden
Coakley, Deirdre *columnist, writer*

Hueytown
Nelson, Susan Rhodes *media specialist, educator*

Pleasant Grove
Robinson, Ella Garrett *editor, writer*

Tuscaloosa
Reinhart, Kellee Connely *journalist*

ALASKA

Fairbanks
Crawford, Sarah Carter (Sally Carter Crawford) *broadcast executive*

ARIZONA

Mesa
Bryant, Peggy Jean *editor, journalist*

Paradise Valley
Harnett, Lila *retired publishing executive*

Phoenix
Aguiar, Elizabeth Joan *publishing executive, educator*
Steckler, Phyllis Betty *publishing consultant*

Tucson
Hayt, Therese D. *newspaper executive*
Martin, June Johnson Caldwell *journalist*
Stein, Mary Katherine *photographer, communications executive*

ARKANSAS

Wasilla
Swanson, Carolyn Rae *news reporter, counselor*

CALIFORNIA

Atascadero
Rios, Evelyn Deerwester *columnist, musician, artist, writer*

Berkeley
Lesser, Wendy *editor, writer, consultant*
Pfeiffer, Phyllis Kramer *publishing executive*
Susskind, Teresa Gabriel *publishing executive*

Beverly Hills
Bland, Janeese Myra *editor*
Gabler, Elizabeth Brand *film company executive*
Shapiro-Mathes, Angela *broadcast executive*
Sherwood, Kehela (Karen Kehela Sherwood) *broadcast executive*
Utley, Nancy *film company executive*

Brisbane
Daniels, Caroline *publishing executive*

Burbank
Fleishman, Susan Nahley *entertainment company executive*
Kroll, Sue *broadcast executive*
Kwan-Rubinek, Veronika *broadcast executive*
Madison, Paula *broadcast executive*
Marinelli, Janice *broadcast executive*
Nelson, Diane W. *broadcast executive*
Sweeney, Anne M. *cable television company executive*
Taubin, Dawn *film company executive*
Younger, Laurie *broadcast executive*

Burlingame
Tirschwell-Newby, Kathy Ann *events production company executive*

Carlsbad
Sperling, Irene R. *publishing executive*

Culver City
Jacobs, Betty Jane Lazaroff *communications educator*
Pascal, Amy Beth *film company executive*
Russell, Robin J. *broadcast executive*
Vollack, Lia *broadcast executive*

Davis
Dickens, Janis *media services administrator*

Edwards
Losey, Lori *media specialist*

Fresno
Lumbye, Betsy *editor*

Glendale
Daly, Ann Michelle *broadcast executive*
MacDonald, Laurie *film company executive*
Snider, Stacey *film company executive*

Gold River
Shaw, Eleanor Jane *newspaper editor*

Hanford
Harris, Mildred Staeger *retired broadcast executive*

Huntington Beach
De Massa, Jessie G. *media specialist*

Irvine
Lesonsky, Rieva *editor-in-chief*

La Jolla
Hall, TennieBee M. *editor*

Los Angeles
Barberie, Jillian *newscaster, meteorologist*
Berman, Gail *film company executive*
Boyle, Barbara Dorman *film company executive*
Charen, Mona *columnist*
Cole, K.C. *journalist, writer*
Demick, Barbara *journalist*
Edmonds, Tracey E. *film company executive*
Fernandez, Giselle *newscaster, journalist*
Firstenberg, Jean Picker *film institute executive*
Gauff, Lisa *broadcast journalist*
Gelber, Danielle Arna *broadcast executive*
Ivins, Molly (Mary Tyler Ivins) *columnist, writer*
Kristof, Kathy M. *journalist*
Larrubia, Evelyn *reporter*
Levine, Pamela *film company executive*
Lozano, Monica Cecilia *publishing executive*
Malkin, Michelle *syndicated columnist*
McFarling, Usha Lee *newswriter*
Muchnic, Suzanne *art writer, educator, lecturer*
Myrth, Judy G. *editor*
Ostroff, Dawn T. *broadcast executive*
Perlmutter, Donna *music critic, dance critic*
Phillips, Geneva Ficker *academic editor*
Salmon, Beth Ann *magazine editor in chief*
Singleton, Joan Vietor *publishing executive, writer, film producer*
Stephens, Loren M. *publishing executive, writer*
Tassler, Nina *broadcast executive*
Tellem, Nancy Reiss *broadcast executive*
Thompson, Anne Kathleen *entertainment journalist*
Trembly, Cristy *television executive*
Van Buren, Abigail (Jeanne Phillips) *columnist, educator*
Wagner, Paula *film company executive, film producer*
Walden, Dana *broadcast executive*
Warfel, Susan Leigh *editor*
Zacchino, Narda *newspaper editor*

Menlo Park
Much, Kathleen *editor, publishing executive, consultant*

Mount Shasta
Stienstra, Stephani Ann *editor, writer*

Novato
Conolly, Katharine Farnam *editor*

Oakland
Wood, Larry (Mary Laird) *journalist, writer, public relations executive, educator, environmental consultant*

Oceanside
Beck, Marilyn Mohr *columnist*
Villasenor, Barbara *book publisher*

Pacific Palisades
Kirkgaard, Valerie Anne *media group executive, radio host, writer, radio producer, consultant*

Palm Springs
Krans, Michelle M. *publishing executive*

Pasadena
Matthews, Mildred Shapley *freelance/self-employed editor*

Riverside
James, Etta (Jamesetta Hawkins) *recording artist*

Sacramento
Heaphy, Janis Besler *newspaper executive*
Henson, Glenda Maria *newswriter*
Lundstrom, Marjie *editor*
Shriver, Maria Owings *news correspondent*

San Diego
Winner, Karin E. *editor*

San Francisco
Cameron, Heather Anne *publishing executive*
Garchik, Leah Lieberman *journalist*
Hamilton, Joan Nice *editor-in-chief*
Leech, Marla Renée *media specialist, educator*
Walsh, Joan *editor-in-chief*

San Jose
Goldberg, Susan *editor*
Mendoza, Martha *reporter*
Migielicz, Geralyn *photojournalist*
Nardi, Glen *publishing executive*

San Rafael
Blakeslee, Helen P. *columnist*

Santa Ana
Katz, Tonnie *newspaper editor*
Stern, Sherry Ann *journalist*

Santa Barbara
Burns, Melinda *journalist*
McCaw, Wendy Petrak *publishing executive*

Santa Clarita
Sturges, Sherry Lynn *recording industry executive*

Santa Maria
Sparks, Jeanne *columnist, photographer, educator*

Santa Monica
Anthony, Polly *broadcast executive*
Jeffers, Susan Jane *publishing executive, writer*
Osbourne, Sharon Arden *music manager, television personality*
Snedaker, Catherine Raupagh (Kit Snedaker) *editor*

Sebastopol
Filshie, Michele Ann *editor*

South Pasadena
Mantell, Suzanne Ruth *editor*

Stanford
Suppes, Christine Johnson *publishing executive*

Sylmar
Valdez, Denise *newscaster*

Toluca Lake
Ragan, Ann Talmadge *media and production consultant, actor*

Universal City
Bromstad, Angela *broadcast executive*
Hammer, Bonnie *broadcast executive*
Langley, Donna *film company executive*
Menendez, Belinda *broadcast executive*
Parent, Mary *film company executive*
Randall, Karen *film company executive*
Rocco, Nikki *film company executive*
Schulz, Diana *film company executive*

Vista
Linhart, Letty Lemon *editor*

Walnut
Tan, Colleen Woo *communications educator*

Walnut Creek
Fowler, Carol W. *journalist, educator*

West Hollywood
Shearmur, Alli *broadcast executive*

Woodland Hills
Goins, Jessica D. *editor*
Harris, Barbara S. *publishing executive, editor-in-chief*
Rafter, Tracy *publishing executive*
Russell, Anne M. *editor-in-chief*

COLORADO

Boulder
El Mallakh, Dorothea Hendry *editor, publishing executive*

Castle Rock
Richardson, Suzanne Mays *communication consultant*

Cherry Hills Village
Stapleton, Katharine Hall (Katie Stapleton) *commentator, writer*

Denver
Chavez, Jeanette *editor*
Drake, Sylvie (Jurras Drake) *theater critic*

Durango
Ballantine, Morley Cowles (Mrs. Arthur Atwood Ballantine) *editor*

Fleming
Nichols, LeeAnn *library media specialist*

CONNECTICUT

Bethel
Shepard, Jean Heck *retired publishing consultant*

Bridgeport
Simoneau, Cynthia Lambert *editor, educator*

Bristol
Driessen, Christine F. *broadcast executive*

Chester
Frost-Knappman, (Linda) Elizabeth *publishing executive, editor, writer*

Danbury
Reynolds, Jean Edwards *publishing executive*

Darien
Brooke, Avery Rogers *publisher, writer*
Workman, Sharon Joy *journalist*

Fairfield
Eigel, Marcia Duffy *editor*
Spence, Barbara E. *former publishing company executive*

Greenwich
Welling, Kathryn Marie *editor*

Hartford
Lumsden, Lynne Ann *publishing executive*

Stafford Springs
Zeldes, Edith R. *freelance journalist*

Stamford
Lane, Hana Umlauf *editor*

Torrington
Di Russo, Terry *communications educator, writer*

Westport
McCormack, Patricia Seger *editor, journalist*

DISTRICT OF COLUMBIA

Washington
Allam, Hannah *journalist*
Angier, Natalie Marie *science journalist*
Applebaum, Anne *journalist, writer*
Arana, Marie *editor, writer*
Arena, Kelli *news correspondent*
Arrott, Elizabeth *journalist*
Baskin, Roberta *television correspondent*
Buzbee, Sally Streff *news correspondent*
Chen, Joie *news correspondent*
Clift, Eleanor *news correspondent, writer*
Cocco, Marie Elizabeth *journalist*
Compton, Ann Woodruff *news correspondent*
Corbett, Rebecca *editor*
Davidson, Susan Bettina *editor, writer*
Dawson, Jessica *art critic*
Deeb, Mary-Jane *editor, educator*
Donohoe, Cathryn Murray *journalist*
Dowd, Maureen *columnist*
Draper, Roberta Hornig *retired journalist*
Drew, Elizabeth *commentator, journalist, writer*
Dyer, Susan Kristine *editor, librarian*
Feld, Karen Irma *columnist, journalist, commentator, speech professional*
Fields, Suzanne Bregman *syndicated columnist*
Fleming, Lee Virginia *art critic, writer, curator*
Foxwell, Elizabeth Marie *editor, writer*
Garrels, Anne *news correspondent*
Geyer, Georgie Anne *columnist, educator, commentator, writer*
Gibson, Florence Anderson *talking book company executive, narrator*
Givhan, Robin Deneen *journalist*
Glasser, Susan Beth *journalist*
Gorman, Patricia Jane *editor*
Greene, Marcia Slacum *editor*
Greenhouse, Linda Joyce *journalist*
Guzy, Carol *photojournalist*
Harrison, Patricia de Stacy *broadcast executive, former federal agency administrator*
Headden, Susan M. *editor*
Hecht, Marjorie Mazel *editor*
Herman, Andrea Maxine *newspaper editor*
Herridge, Catherine *political correspondent*
Howell, Deborah *editor*
Jordan, Anne E. Dollerschell *journalist*
Joyce, Anne Raine *editor*
Knight, Athelia Wilhelmenia *journalist*
Lajoux, Alexandra Reed *editor-in-chief, educator*
Lawson, Jennifer *broadcast executive*
Lee, Debra Louise *cable television company executive*
Lehrman, Margaret McBride *broadcast executive, television producer*
Liasson, Mara *news correspondent*
Loo, Beverly Jane *publishing executive*
McBee, Susanna Barnes *retired journalist*
McFeatters, Ann Carey *journalist*
Miller, Nicole *art columnist*
Mitchell, Andrea *journalist*
Murphy, Caryle Marie *foreign correspondent*
Nielsen, Louisa Augusta *broadcast executive*
O'Brien, Soledad *news anchor*
Ong, Laureen E. *broadcast executive*
Palmer, Stacy Ella *periodical editor*
Pelham, Ann *publishing executive, department chairman*
Pratt, Carin *television executive*
Priest, Dana *journalist*
Ratner, Ellen Faith *news analyst, news correspondent, writer*
Rice, Susan Elizabeth *foreign policy analyst, former federal agency administrator*
Riechmann, Deb *reporter*
Roberts, Cokie (Corinne Boggs Roberts) *newscaster*
Ross, Wendy Clucas *retired newspaper editor, retired journalist*
Schmidt, Susan *journalist*
Scholz, Jane *newspaper publisher*
Simons, Carol Lenore *magazine editor*
Stolberg, Sheryl Gay *journalist*
Totenberg, Nina *journalist*
Trafford, Abigail *columnist, editor, writer*
Waldman, Amy *journalist*

FLORIDA

Boynton Beach
Jacobs, Wendy *editor, realtor*
Parsons, Mindy (Mindy Enos) *newsletter editor, publisher, non-profit organization executive*
Robinson, Brenda Kay *editor, public relations executive*

Clearwater
VanMeer, Mary Ann *publishing executive, writer, webmaster*

Coral Gables
Welsh, Judith Schenck *communications educator*

Delray Beach
Bishop, Kathleen Ann *customer service, education and communication consultant, professional speaker*

Fort Walton Beach
McDonald, Pamela Jane *educational media specialist*

Gainesville
Kelly, Kathleen S(ue) *communications educator*

Jacksonville
Bedell, Elizabeth Snyder (Betty Bedell) *editor-in-chief, marketing professional*

Key West
Bradford, Judith Lynnell *journalist, artist*

Lake Worth
Asher, Kathleen May *communications educator*

Miami
Balmaseda, Liz *columnist*
de Leon, Lidia Maria *magazine editor*
Fichtner, Margaria *journalist*
Gyenizse, Debbie Linda *communications educator*
O'Bryon, Linda Elizabeth *broadcast executive*
Salinas, María Elena *newscaster, columnist*

North Miami
Kordalewski, Lydia Maria *news correspondent, municipal employee*

North Port
Coe, Laurie Lynne Barker *photojournalist, artist*

Orlando
Hall, Charlotte Hauch *editor*
Healy, Jane Elizabeth *newspaper editor*
Maupin, Elizabeth Thatcher *theater critic*
Waltz, Kathleen M. *publishing executive*

Palm Coast
Franco, Annemarie Woletz *editor*

Palm Harbor
Jones, Winona Nigels *retired media specialist*

Saint Petersburg
Johnson, Edna Ruth *editor*
Peters, Susan *editor*

Sanford
Scott, Mellouise Jacqueline *retired media specialist*

Sarasota
North, Marjorie Mary *columnist*
Stevens, Elisabeth Goss (Mrs. Robert Schleussner Jr.) *journalist, writer, graphic artist*

Tallahassee
Barlow, Margaret *editor, writer*
Clifford, Dorothy Ring *journalist*
Morgan, Lucy Ware *news correspondent, journalist*

Tampa
Huey, Peggy J. *communications educator, performing company executive*
Jacobus, Mary *publishing executive*
Miller-Lachmann, Lyn *editor*
Palmer, Denise E. *publishing executive*
Reed, Donna Marie *editor*
Weaver, Janet S. *editor*

Vero Beach
Binney, Jan Jarrell *publishing executive, marketing professional*

GEORGIA

Alpharetta
Lynn, Kristina *journalist, actress, writer, producer*

Atlanta
Amanpour, Christiane *news correspondent*
Becker, Jill *newscaster*
Chambers, Anne Cox *publishing executive, former diplomat*
Clayton, Xernona *media executive*
Davis, Amanda *newscaster*
Dobson, Bridget McColl Hursley *television executive, writer*
Drennen, Eileen Moira *editor*
Dukes, Deidra *newscaster*
Fisher, Stephany *newscaster*
McGill, Sylviette Delphine *editor*
Morant, Brenda White *publishing executive, small business owner, investor*
Puckett, Susan *newspaper editor*
Robelot, Jane *anchor*
Scott, Marian Alexis *journalist*
Sloan, Mary Jean *retired media specialist*
Tucker, Cynthia Anne *journalist*
Vadlamani, Suchita *newscaster*
Wallace, Julia Diane *newspaper editor*
Wilson, Debora J. *broadcast executive*
Wilson, Lori *newscaster*
Wood, Brenda *newscaster*

Blackshear
Vaughan, Mittie Kathleen *journalist*

Columbus
Siddall, Pam *publishing executive*

Marietta
Williamsen, Dannye Sue *publishing executive, writer*

Powder Springs
Creighton, Peggy Milam *media specialist, writer*

Savannah
Edeawo, Gale Sky *publishing company executive, writer*

HAWAII

Honolulu
Black, Cobey *journalist*
Keyes, Saundra Elise *newspaper editor*

IDAHO

Sandpoint
Bowne, Martha Hoke *editor, consultant*

ILLINOIS

Carol Stream
Bemis, Mary Ferguson *magazine editor*
Franzen, Janice Marguerite Gosnell *magazine editor*

Champaign
Dulany, Elizabeth Gjelsness *editor*
McCulloh, Judith Marie *editor*
Turquette, Frances Bond *editor*

Charleston
Coutant, Mary McElwee *retired editor*

Chicago
Barr, Emily L. *broadcast executive*
Beaudet-Francès, Patricia Suzanne *photography editor*
Brotman, Barbara Louise *journalist, writer*
Burton, Cheryl *newscaster*
Ciezadlo, Janina A. *art critic, educator*
Cooper, Ilene Linda *magazine editor, author*
Davlantes, Anna *newscaster*
Ferguson, Renee *news correspondent, reporter*
Ferrara, Annette *editor, educator*
Forbes, Dorsey Connors *commentator, journalist*
Garza, Melita Marie *journalist*
Guy, Sandra *journalist, telecommunications writer*
Hefner, Christie Ann *publishing executive*
Hirt, Jane *editor*
Hong, Ellee Pai *newscaster*
Idol, Anna Catherine *magazine editor*
Jones, Linda *communications educator*
Klaviter, Helen Lothrop *editor-in-chief, magazine editor*
Krueger, Bonnie Lee *editor, writer*
Lipinski, Ann Marie *publishing executive*
Loesch, Katharine Taylor *communications educator, theater educator*
Loo, Nancy *newscaster*
Manatt, Kathleen Gordon *publishing consultant*
Martinez, Natalie *newscaster*
Migala, Lucyna J. *journalist, broadcast executive, artistic director*
Nash, Jessie Madeleine *journalist, science writer*
Odelbo, Catherine G. *publishing executive*
Peres, Judith May *journalist*
Rice, Linda Johnson *publishing executive*
Robinson, Robin *newscaster*
Seaman, Donna Jean *editor, writer*
Spann-Cooper, Melody *broadcast executive*
True, Alison Cochran *newspaper editor*
Ullrich, Polly *art critic*
Weinberg, Lila Shaffer *editor, writer*
Wier, Patricia Ann *publishing executive, consultant*
Wille, Lois Jean *retired editor*
Wolfe, Sheila A. *journalist*

Des Plaines
Clapper, Marie Anne *magazine publisher*

Evanston
Galvin, Kathleen Malone *communications educator*
Hixson, Kathryn *art critic*

Grayville
Finkelstein, Honora Moore *writer, editor, consultant*

Highland Park
Rutenberg-Rosenberg, Sharon Leslie *retired journalist*

Itasca
Brazzle, Sara *publishing executive*
Porter, Ethel Mae *publishing executive*

Moline
Sierra, Dolores *communications educator*

Northbrook
Pesmen, Sandra (Mrs. Harold William Pesmen) *editor, educator*

Oak Park
Bedrossian, Ursula Kay Kennedy *editor*

Peoria
Murphy, Sharon Margaret *retired communications educator*

Wilmette
Boyle, Antonia Barnes *writer, editor*

INDIANA

Cambridge City
Slonaker, Mary Joanna King *columnist*

East Chicago
Platis, Mary Lou *media specialist*

Huntington
Lindsey, Jacquelyn Maria *editor*

Indianapolis
Adamak, M. Jeanelle *broadcast executive*
Carlini, Pat *newscaster*
Dumandan, Joy *newscaster*
Fine, Pamela B. *newspaper editor*
Ganote, Angela *newscaster*
Garmel, Marion Bess Simon *retired arts journalist*
Henry, Barbara Ann *publishing executive*
Knox, Debby *newscaster*
Morehead, Andrea *newscaster*
Pursley, Julie *newscaster*
Rankin, Jacqueline Annette *communications expert, educator*
Ryder, Anne *newscaster*
Schilling, Emily Born *editor, professional society administrator*
Tedesco, Kristi *newscaster*
Trahan, Grace *newscaster*
Weaver, Martha *newscaster*

Knightstown
Richardson, Shirley Maxine *editor*

Michigan City
Varro, Barbara Joan *retired editor*

Noblesville
Poindexter, Beverly Kay *media and communications professional, real estate broker*

Parker City
Cunningham, Kina Ann *media specialist, educator*

Rushville
Moore, Helen Elizabeth *reporter*

IOWA

Ames
Alumbaugh, JoAnn McCalla *magazine editor*

Carroll
Morlan, Joann G. *communications educator*

Des Moines
Butler, Gayle *editor-in-chief*
DeWulf Nickell, Karol *editor-in-chief*
Myers, Mary Kathleen *publishing executive*
Stier, Mary P. *publishing executive*
Van Zante, Shirley M(ae) *magazine editor*

Waterloo
Green, Nancy Loughridge *publishing executive*

KANSAS

Chanute
Weilert, Mary E. *communications educator*

Hutchinson
Baumer, Beverly Belle *journalist*

Manhattan
Wright, Sherryl Leigh *journalist*

North Newton
Snider, Marie Anna *syndicated columnist*

Overland Park
Christian, Shirley Ann *journalist, author*

Shawnee Mission
Martin, Donna Lee *retired publishing company executive*

Wichita
Dill, Sheri *publishing executive*
Zimmerman, Melva Jean *journalist, retired audio-visual specialist*

KENTUCKY

Louisville
Leonard, Mona Freeman *communications educator*

LOUISIANA

La Place
Fiffie Proctor, JoAnn *media and technology specialist*

New Orleans
Orr, Margaret *newscaster*

Slidell
Lovell, Emily Kalled *retired journalist*

MAINE

Belfast
Griffith, Patricia King *journalist*

Falmouth
Boehmer, Raquel Davenport *newsletter editor*

Kennebunkport
Ray, Virginia H. S. *columnist, writer*

MARYLAND

Annapolis
Wyman, Pilar *editor*

Baltimore
Donovan, Dianne Francys *journalist*
Jenkins, Lawanda W. *publishing executive*
Matthews, Rondra J. *publishing executive*
Murphy, Frances Louise, II, *retired newspaper publisher*
Rousuck, J. Wynn *theater critic*

Bethesda
Herman, Edith Carol *journalist*
Kaplan, Marjorie *broadcast executive*
Lannan, Maura Anne Kelly *reporter*
McHale, Judith A. (Judith Ottalloran) *broadcast executive, lawyer*
Wagner, Cynthia Gail *editor, writer*

Chevy Chase
Glaser, Vera Romans *journalist*

College Park
Beasley, Maurine Hoffman *journalism educator, historian*

Columbia
Greyson D'Otazzo, Meaghan Regina *literary critic*

Easton
Velisek, Caryl Anne *journalist*
Wilson, Laura Ann *newspaper editor*

Gaithersburg
Bobka, Marlene S. *publishing executive*

Havre De Grace
Wetter, Virginia Forwood Pate *broadcast executive*

Joppa
Short, Judith Arduino *media specialist, educator*

Lanham
Godwin, Mary Jo *editor, librarian, consultant*

Lanham Seabrook
Ojinnaka, Becky *publishing executive*

Owings Mills
Holdridge, Barbara *book editor, writer, consultant*

Potomac
Sundick, Sherry Small *journalist, writer, poet*

Rockville
Miller, Claire Ellen *editor, educator, writer*

Severna Park
Pumphrey, Janet Kay *editor, publishing executive*

Silver Spring
Bennett, Carol(ine) Elise *retired reporter, actress*

Takoma Park
Conroy, Sarah Booth *columnist, writer, educator*

MASSACHUSETTS

Boston
Caldwell, Gail *book critic*
Carroll, Jill *freelance journalist*
Cohen, Rachelle Sharon *journalist*
Donovan, Helen W. *newspaper editor*
Flaherty, Lois Talbot *editor, psychiatrist, educator*
Grimes, Heilan Yvette *publishing executive*
Kennedy, Louise Avery *theater critic, newspaper editor, writer*
Lawrence, Merloyd Ludington *editor*
McNamee, Linda Rose *broadcast executive*
Rodman, Sarah *music critic*

Brookline
Bourne, Katherine Day *journalist, educator*

Cambridge
Faran, Ellen Webster *publishing executive*
Goodman, Ellen Holtz *journalist*
MacKinnon, Rebecca *media consultant, researcher*
Wilcox, Maud *editor*

Edgartown
MacDonald, Duncan *broadcaster, writer, communications consultant*

Hyannis
Makkay, Maureen Ann *broadcast executive*

Needham Heights
Salhany, Lucille S. (Lucy Salhany) *broadcast executive*

Newton
Hume, Ellen Hunsberger *media analyst, educator, journalist*

Plymouth
Flood, H. Gay (Hulda Gay Flood) *editor, consultant*

Quincy
Chung, Cynthia Norton *communications specialist*

South Hadley
Elleman, Barbara *editor*

Sudbury
Hillery, Mary Jane Larato *columnist, television personality, television producer, writer, military officer*

West Tisbury
Méras, Phyllis Leslie *journalist*

Weston
Sanzone, Donna S. *publishing executive*

MICHIGAN

Bay City
Frick, Kelly Adrian *editor*

Birmingham
Berman, Laura *journalist, writer*

Bloomfield Township
Brown, Lynette Ralya *journalist, publicist*

Clinton
Anderson, Denice Anna *editor*

Detroit
Burzynski, Susan Marie *newspaper editor*
Colby, Joy Hakanson *critic*
Lazarus, Lila *announcer*
Lee, Marcella *announcer*
Spencer, Ruth *announcer*
Walker, Rhonda Gillum *announcer*
Wolf, Michael Ann *announcer*

Grosse Pointe
Whittaker, Jeanne Evans *retired journalist*

Grosse Pointe Woods
McWhirter, Glenna Suzanne (Nickie McWhirter) *retired columnist*

Lansing
Brown, Nancy Field *editor*

Midland
Messing, Carol Sue *communications educator*

Pontiac
Hicks, Christy Ann *communications educator*

Saginaw
Killingbeck, Janice Lynelle (Mrs. Victor Lee Killingbeck) *journalist*

Southfield
Ali, Sandra *announcer*
Carman, Kam *announcer*
Centofanti, Deena *announcer*
Clifford, Carolyn *news correspondent, reporter*
Hupe, Pallas *announcer*
Lewis, Diane *announcer*
Makupson, Amyre Porter *broadcast executive*
McDonald, Christy *newscaster*
Osborne, Marie-Angela *journalist*
Purtan, JoAnne *announcer*
Timmons, Robbie *news anchor*

Troy
Hucal, Michelle *editor*

MINNESOTA

Duluth
Gruver, Nancy *publishing executive*

Minneapolis
Crosby, Jacqueline Garton *newspaper editor, journalist*
Flanagan, Barbara *journalist*
Laing, Karel Ann *magazine publishing executive*
Paul, Nora Marie *media studies educator*
Smetanka, Mary Jane *reporter*

Saint Paul
Lofquist, Vicki L. *journalist*

MISSOURI

Farmington
Betz-Bacon, Tina M. *communications educator*

Hillsboro
Leirer, Margaret (Peggy) L. *communications educator*

Kansas City
Busby, Marjean (Marjorie Jean Busby) *retired journalist*
Gallagher, Maggie *columnist*
Gray, Helen Theresa Gott *editor*

Kirksville
Presley, Paula Lumpkin *retired editor*

Saint Louis
Ehrlich, Ava *broadcast executive*
Green, Joyce *book publishing company executive*
Pritchard, Nina Jean *communications educator*
Rice, Patricia Jane *journalist*
Topham, Suzanne Caston *journalist*

Springfield
Champion, Norma Jean *communications educator, state legislator*

NEBRASKA

Chadron
Buschkopf, Debora J. *court reporter*

Fremont
Winfield, Joyce Helen *communications educator*

Lincoln
Raz, Hilda *editor-in-chief, language educator*

Omaha
Batchelder, Anne Stuart *retired publishing executive, political organization worker*
Casper, Peggy Wiedman *court reporter*
Derrick, Deborah Ball *editor, writer*
Ress, Patricia Colleen *editor, writer*
Sands, Deanna *editor*

NEVADA

Las Vegas
Frigard, Monique Denise *journalist*
Hale, Marsha Bentley *journalist, photographer, real estate rehabilitator, song writer, mannequin historian*
Miller, Valerie Carol *journalist*

Reno
Crowe, Jennifer *newspaper reporter*

Sparks
Boyer, Patricia W. *publishing executive, editor*

NEW HAMPSHIRE

Keene
Salcetti, Marianne *newswriter, educator*

Portsmouth
Hopkins, Jeannette Ethel *book publisher, editor*

NEW JERSEY

Allendale
Long, Jo-Nelle Desmond *editor, consultant, historian*

Asbury Park
Sandberg-Morgan, Barbara *retired communication and women's studies educator*

Audubon
McMichael, Maria Madelyn *publishing executive*

Camden
Coney, Stephné Reniá *communications educator*

Cherry Hill
Gutin, Myra Gail *communications educator*

East Brunswick
Meningall, Evelyn L. *retired educational media specialist*

Englewood Cliffs
Dobrzynski, Judith Helen *journalist, commentator*
Saible, Stephanie Irene *magazine editor*

Fort Lee
Orman, Suze *news correspondent, writer*
Stuart, Carole *publishing executive*

Gillette
Nathanson, Linda Sue *publishing executive, writer*

Haworth
Biesel, Diane Jane *editor, publishing executive*

Hoboken
Hakki, Ayesha *editor-in-chief*
Tardiff, Jill Alexandria *publishing executive, photographer*

Lakewood
Burns, Ruth Ann Mary *television executive*

Lawrenceville
Oram, Fern Amy *editor-in-chief, director*

Montclair
Delbourgo, Joëlle Lily *publishing executive*
Gogick, Kathleen Christine *magazine editor, publisher*
Harayda, Janice *newspaper book editor, author*

Montvale
Falk, Ellen Stein *media specialist, educator*

Moorestown
Stine, Anna Mae *publishing company executive*

New Providence
Barnes, Sandra Henley *retired publishing company executive*

Newark
Clowney, Mary L. *educational media specialist, librarian*
Dauth, Frances Kutcher *journalist, editor*
Nutt, Amy Ellis *journalist*

Princeton
Dubrovsky, Gertrude Wishnick *journalist, researcher*
Lincoln, Anna *publishing executive, language educator*
Weiss, Renée Karol *editor, musician*

Sea Isle City
Bruno, Carol Jeanette *library media specialist, gifted and talented education educator, innkeeper*

Secaucus
Bay, Willow *news anchor*
Blackmon, Brenda *newscaster*
Crowley, Monica *political commentator*

Short Hills
Schaefer, Eleanor Montville *retired publishing executive*
Winter, Ruth Grosman (Mrs. Arthur Winter) *journalist*

Teaneck
Solá, Victoria M. *announcer, writer*

Trenton
Christopherson, Elizabeth Good *broadcast executive*

West New York
Knopf, Claire *editor, writer*

Woodbury
Jolis, Anne *journalist*

NEW MEXICO

Albuquerque
Blake, Renée *broadcast executive*
Hadas, Elizabeth Chamberlayne *editor*

Los Alamos
Mendius, Patricia Dodd Winter *editor, educator, writer*

Santa Fe
Lichtenberg, Maggie Klee *publishing executive*
Stieber, Tamar *journalist*

NEW YORK

Babylon
Meirowitz, Claire Cecile *publishing executive*

Bellport
Townsend, Terry *publishing executive*

Bronx
Ahmose, Nefertari A. *journalism educator*

Brooklyn
De Lisi, Joanne *communications consultant, educator*
Logan, Paula M. *entertainment company executive, accountant*

Buffalo
Sullivan, Margaret M. *editor*

Chappaqua
Levine, Irene S. *journalist, psychologist*

Dunkirk
Lewis, Amy Beth *newswriter, reporter, writer, photographer*

East Syracuse
Duffy, Nancy Keogh *newscaster, broadcast executive*

Flushing
Brooks, Helene Margaret *editorial consultant*
Torrence-Thompson, Juanita Lee *editor, public relations executive*

Garden City
Amsler, Georgeann Lucille *publishing executive*

Glen Cove
Young, Jayne *recording industry executive*

Great Neck
Fiel, Maxine Lucille *journalist, behavior analyst, educator*

Ithaca
Hardy, Jane Elizabeth *communications educator*
Johnson, Pam McAllister *newspaper publisher, consultant*
Park, Dorothy Goodwin Dent (Mrs. Roy Hampton Park) *broadcast executive, publishing executive*

Jamaica
Brockway, Laurie Sue *editor-in-chief, journalist, writer, minister*

Jericho
Dore, Kathleen A. *broadcast executive*

Kingston
Irvine, Rose Loretta Abernethy *retired communications educator, consultant*

Locust Valley
Zulch, Joan Carolyn *retired medical publishing company executive*

Manlius
Harriff, Suzanna Elizabeth Bahner *media consultant*

Melville
Henley, Deborah S. *newspaper editor*
Krenek, Debby *newspaper editor*
Richards, Carol Ann Rubright *retired editor, retired journalist*
Singer, Phyllis *editor-in-chief*

Middletown
Bedell, Barbara Lee *journalist*

Millbrook
Hall, Penelope Coker *editor, writer*

Monroe
Shanley, Patricia Carolin *retired school media specialist*

New York
Abramson, Jill *newspaper publishing executive*
Adams, Cindy *journalist*
Adcroft, Patti (Patrice Gabriella Adcroft) *editor*

Adler, Margot Susanna *journalist, radio producer, radio correspondent, writer*
Amster, Linda Evelyn *newspaper executive, consultant*
Angelo, Bonnie *journalist*
Astley, Amy *editor-in-chief*
Bahr, Lauren S. *publishing executive*
Baker, Deborah *editor, writer*
Barbosa, Shameka Brown *copywriter*
Barnett, Amy DuBois *editor-in-chief*
Barolini, Teodolinda *literary critic*
Baron, Susan *publishing executive*
Bender, Judith *journalist, editor*
Benedek, Melinda *television executive*
Berentson, Jane *editor*
Bernhard, Lisa *news correspondent*
Bernstein, Bonnie *sportscaster*
Black, Carole *broadcast executive*
Black, Cathleen Prunty *publishing executive*
Booth Corwin, Tami *publishing executive*
Bratten, Millie Martini *editor-in-chief*
Brenner, Beth Fuchs *publishing executive*
Brody, Jane Ellen *journalist, researcher*
Brown, Campbell *commentator*
Brown, Helen Gurley *editor-in-chief*
Brown, Katie *columnist*
Brown, Tina *journalist, television personality*
Bryson, Louise Henry *broadcast executive*
Buckley, Priscilla Langford *magazine editor*
Buckley, Virginia Laura *editor*
Burt-Murray, Angela *editor-in-chief*
Bushnell, Candace *columnist, writer*
Calvano, Phyllis *publishing executive*
Caploe, Roberta *magazine editor*
Carr, Gladys Justin *publishing executive, consultant, editor, writer*
Caruso, Ann S. *fashion editor, stylist*
Centrello, Gina *publishing executive*
Chan, Janet *editorial director*
Chesnutt, Jane *publishing executive*
Chestnut, Colette *broadcast executive*
Chira, Susan *editor*
Chirichella, Debra *publishing executive*
Clark, Joan Hardy *retired journalist*
Coen, Jessica *blog writer, editor*
Cohen, Betty L. *broadcast executive*
Cohen, Claudia *journalist, television reporter*
Coles, Joanna *magazine editor-in-chief*
Collins, Gail *editor*
Conniff, Tamara *editor*
Cooney, Joan Ganz *broadcast executive, director*
Cooper, Gloria *editor, press critic*
Corrigan, Maureen *book critic, English educator*
Cortina, Betty *magazine editor*
Couric, Katie (Katherine Anne Couric) *newscaster, journalist*
Court, Kathryn Diana *editor*
Coyne, Judith *editor*
Crandell, Susan *magazine editor*
Crier, Catherine *newscaster*
Crist, Judith *film and drama critic*
Croce, Arlene *critic*
Curry, Ann *correspondent, anchor*
Daniels, Faith *former newscaster*
Danziger, Lucy *editor*
De Angelis, Judy *anchorwoman*
Deitz, Paula *magazine editor*
Disney, Anthea *publishing executive*
Dozier, Kimberly *news correspondent*
Eaker, Sherry Ellen *editor*
Eckman, Fern Marja *journalist*
Egen, Maureen Mahon *publishing executive*
Ellerbee, Linda (Linda Jane Smith) *reporter*
Ellingwood, Susan *editor*
Ellis, Rosemary *editor-in-chief*
Evans, Linda Kay *publishing executive*
Fears, Linda *editor-in-chief*
Feldman, Helaine *editor, public relations associate*
Fell, M. Ann *publishing executive*
Fiori, Pamela *publishing executive, writer*
Foley, Ann *broadcast executive*
Forden, Diane Claire *magazine editor*
Franks, Lucinda Laura *journalist*
Freeland, Chrystia *editor, director*
Friedman, Jane *publishing executive*
Fuentez, Tania Michele *journalist*
Fuller, Bonnie *editor-in-chief*
Gardner, Janet Paxton *journalist, film producer*
Garrett, Laurie *journalist, global health scholar*
Geary, Hilary R. *society editor*
Geiser, Elizabeth Able *publishing company executive*
Gewirtz-Friedman, Gerry *editor*
Gharib, Susie *newscaster*
Girard, Judy *broadcast executive*
Godoff, Ann *publishing executive*
Gotti, Victoria *columnist, writer, actress*
Gould, Cheryl *broadcast executive*
Gould, Emily *editor*
Grace, Nancy A. *news correspondent, former prosecutor*
Graham, Alma Eleanor *editor, writer, educational consultant*
Grant Goldman, Pamela *journalist, writer*
Greenwald, Julie *recording industry executive*
Grimes, Suzanne *publishing executive*
Gross, Amy *editor-in-chief*
Gross, Judy E. *publishing executive*
Guilfoyle Newsom, Kimberly Ann *legal commentator*
Haegele, Patricia *publishing executive*
Hall, Lisa Gersh *broadcast executive, lawyer*
Hanson, Jane *newscaster*
Hart, Clare *information company executive*
Haubegger, Christy *media consultant, publishing executive*
Henriques, Diana Blackmon *journalist*
Herman, Mindy *broadcast executive*
Holton, Lisa *publishing executive*
Hughes, Brigid *former editor*
Hurley, Cheryl Joyce *book publishing executive*
Huxtable, Ada Louise *architecture critic*
Jamison, Jayne *publishing executive*
Johnson, Brooke Bailey *broadcast executive*
Jones, Laurie Lynn *magazine editor*
Jones Reynolds, Star (Starlet Marie Jones) *television host, lawyer, former prosecutor*
Just, Julia Barnett *newspaper editor*
Kagan, Julia Lee *magazine editor*
Kahn, Nancy Valerie *publishing and entertainment executive, consultant*
Kakutani, Michiko *critic*
Kalajian-Lagani, Donna *publishing executive*
Kantor, Jodi M. *editor*
Kaplan, Jill Rebecca *publishing executive*
Kaufman, Amy *film company executive, film producer*
Klein, Laura Colin *publishing executive*
Kolata, Gina *journalist*
Kolbert, Elizabeth Ruth *journalist*
Koplovitz, Kay *television network executive*
Koster, Elaine *publishing executive*
Koteff, Ellen *periodical editor*
Kunes, Ellen *magazine executive*
Landro, Laura *editor*
Lawhon, Charla *editor*
Lawrence, Nina *publishing executive*
Laybourne, Geraldine B. *broadcast executive*
Leahey, Lynn *editor-in-chief*
Lee, Frances Helen *editor*
Lee, Sally A. *editor-in-chief*
Leive, Cynthia *editor-in-chief*
Levi, Vicki Gold *picture editor, historical consultant, writer, actress*
Levine, Ellen R. *editor-in-chief*
Link, Nina Beth *publishing executive*
Longley, Marjorie Watters *newspaper executive*
Loomis, Carol J. *journalist*
Lyne, Susan Markham *multi-media company executive, former broadcast executive*
MacBain, Louise T. Blouin *publishing executive*
MacGowan, Sandra Firelli *publishing executive, consultant*
Martin, Judith Sylvia *journalist*
Maryles, Daisy *editor*
Maslin, Janet *critic*
Mason, Linda *broadcast executive*
McAniff, Nora P. *publishing executive*
McCarthy, Pamela Maffei *magazine editor*
McCarty, V. K. *publishing executive, chaplain, librarian*
McFadden, Cynthia Graham *news correspondent, journalist*
McGrath, Judy (Judith Ann McGrath) *broadcast executive*
McNally, Michele *editor, photographer*
Miller, Caroline *editor-in-chief*
Min, Janice Byung *editor-in-chief*
Mohler, Mary Gail *magazine editor*
Moore, Alma C. *publishing executive, consultant*
Moore, Ann S. *publishing executive*
Morgan, Mary E. *publishing executive*
Morgenson, Gretchen C. *reporter*
Morris, Valerie *news correspondent*
Morrison, Stacy Lynne *magazine editor*
Murphy, Helen *recording industry executive*
Myers, Michelle *publishing executive*
Nazario, Sonia *reporter*
Nelson, Kathy *broadcast executive*
Nelson, Sara *editor*
Norman, Christina *broadcast executive*
Norville, Deborah Anne *news correspondent*
Novogrod, Nancy Gerstein *editor*
Pesin, Ella Michele *journalist, public relations executive*
Pfeiffer, Jane Cahill *former broadcasting company executive, consultant*
Picard, Leslie *publishing executive*
Pinkwater, Julie *publishing executive*
Press, Michelle *editor*
Preston, Frances Williams *music company executive*
Putnam, Keri *film company executive*
Quindlen, Anna *journalist, writer*
Quinn, Jane Bryant *journalist, writer*
Rabiner, Susan *editor*
Rabinowitz, Dorothy *television critic*
Raven, Abbe *broadcast executive*
Rchl, Beatrice Clair *editor, art historian*
Regan, Judith Terrance *publishing executive*
Reichl, Ruth Molly *editor-in-chief*
Reif Cohen, Jessica *broadcast executive*
Resnick, Rosalind *multimedia executive*
Rhoads, Geraldine Emeline *editor, consultant*
Rhone, Sylvia Marie Miller *recording industry executive*
Riches, Wendy *magazine publishing executive*
Roach, Margaret *editor-in-chief*
Robinson, Janet L. *publishing executive*
Rosenberg, Tina *reporter*
Rosenthal, Jane *film company executive*
Rosenthal, Shirley Lord *cosmetics magazine executive, novelist*
Rubenstein, Atoosa Behnegar *editor-in-chief*
Rudolph, Lisa Beth *news correspondent*
Sabino, Catherine Ann *magazine editor*
Salembier, Valerie Birnbaum *publishing executive*
Sanders, Gina Susan *publishing executive*
Sarnoff, Ann M. *publishing executive, former sports association executive*
Sasman, Irene Deak Handberg *publishing executive*
Sawyer, Diane (L. Diane Sawyer) *newscaster, journalist*
Schmertz, Mildred Floyd *editor-in-chief, writer*
Schulz, Susan *magazine editor*
Schuman, Patricia Glass *publishing company executive, educator*
Scotto, Rosanna *newscaster*
Seelig, Jill *publishing executive*
Shafrir, Doree *editor, journalist*
Sharbel, Jean M. *editor*
Sheridan LaBarge, Joan Ruth *publishing executive*
Shier, Shelley M. *production company executive*
Shull, Mikki *media consultant*
Simmons, Sue *newscaster*
Singer, Joy Daniels *journalist, consultant*
Singer, Niki *media consultant*
Sischy, Ingrid Barbara *editor, art critic*
Smith, Liz (Mary Elizabeth Smith) *columnist, newscaster*
Soriano, Nancy Mernit *editor-in-chief*
Squire, Gilda N. *publishing executive, writer*
Stanger, Ila *editor-in-chief*
Stern, Roslyne Paige *magazine publisher*
Stokes, Lori *newscaster*
Strauss, Carolyn *broadcast executive*
Studin, Jan *publishing executive*
Sweed, Phyllis *publishing executive*
Tarnofsky-Ostroff, Dawn *broadcast executive*
Taylor, Susan L. *magazine editor*
Taylor, Terry R. *editor, educator*
Thomas, Helen Amelia (Mrs. Douglas B. Cornell) *editor-in-chief, former White House correspondent*
Tischler, Judith Blanche *retired publishing executive*
Tober, Barbara D. (Mrs. Donald Gibbs Tober) *editor*
Toepfer, Susan Jill *editor-in-chief*
Tong, Kaity *anchor*
Townsend, Alair Ane *publishing executive*
Tritch, Teresa *editor, writer*
Turner, Alice Kennedy *editor*
Tyler, Dana *anchor*
Umansky, Diane *editor-in-chief*
Vanden Heuvel, Katrina *publishing executive*
Van Susteren, Greta Conway *newscaster, lawyer*
Vargas, Elizabeth *newscaster*
Viladas, Pilar *editor*
Visser, Lesley *sports correspondent*
Walters, Barbara Jill *broadcast journalist*
Waricha, Joan *publishing executive*
Wells, Linda Ann *editor-in-chief*
White, Kate *editor-in-chief*
Wilkins, Amy P. *publishing executive*
Willen, Liz *reporter*
Williams, Lena *sportswriter*
Williams, Marsha E. *broadcast executive*
Wils, Madelyn *film company executive*
Winston, Mary A. *publishing executive*
Wintour, Anna *editor-in-chief*
Wohrle, Marta *publishing executive*
Wong, Andrea *broadcast executive*
Young, Genevieve Leman *publishing executive, editor*
Zagat, Nina *publishing executive*
Zalaznick, Lauren *broadcast executive*
Zarghami, Cyma *broadcast executive*

Old Westbury
O'Brien, Adrienne Gratia *communications educator*

Ontario
Blackman, Lani Modica *copy editor*

Oswego
Loveridge-Sanbonmatsu, Joan Meredith *communication studies and women's studies educator, poet*

Pleasantville
Leo, Jacqueline M. *editor-in-chief*
McEwen, Laura *publishing executive*
Rockwood, Marcia *magazine editor*
Sachar, Emily M. *editor*

Ridge
Carter, Sylvia *journalist*

Rochester
Lank, Edith Handleman *journalist, educator*
Magnuson, Karen M. *editor*

Rome
Hart, Margaret Rogene

Rye
Nelson, Vita Joy *editor, publisher*

Sag Harbor
Brody, Jacqueline *editor*

Scarsdale
Topping, Audrey Ronning *photojournalist*

Sleepy Hollow
Flynn-Connors, Elizabeth Kathryn *reporter, editor*

Staten Island
Dennery, Linda *newspaper publishing executive*

Stony Brook
Harvey, Christine Lynn *publishing executive*

Syracuse
Sharp, Nancy Weatherly *communications educator, dean*

Troy
Friedman, Sue Tyler *technical publications executive*

Warwick
Simon, Dolores Daly *copy editor*

Woodbury
Freedson, Grace Elizabeth *publishing executive*

Yonkers
Hough, Barbara *library media specialist, educator*
Lieberman, Trudy *healthcare journalist*
Slade, Margot S. *editor*

Yorkshire
Friedhaber-Hard, Susan Margaret *library media educator*

NORTH CAROLINA

Banner Elk
Persons, Marjorie AnnaBelle *publishing executive, writer*

Battleboro
Hardy, Linda Lea Sterlock *media specialist*

Chapel Hill
Lauder, Valarie Anne *editor, educator*
Ravenel, Shannon *book publishing professional*

Charlotte
Bauroth, Nancy Ann *journalist, former marketing executive*
Benfield, Kimberly Joyce McFall *media specialist*

Greensboro
Gill, Evalyn Pierpoint *editor, writer, publisher*
Roerden, Chris (Claire Roerden) *editor, business owner, publishing consultant*

Laurel Springs
Gilbert-Strawbridge, Anne Wieland *journalist*

Raleigh
Evans, Janet *publishing executive*
Kauffman, Terry *broadcast and creative arts communication educator, artist*
Paschal, Beth Cummings *journalist, editor*
Sill, Melanie *editor*

Spindale
Trautmann, Patricia Ann *communications educator, storyteller, art educator*

Wilmington
Tallant, Carole E. *communications educator*

Winston Salem
Dalton, Mary M. *communications educator, documentary filmmaker*
Dykers, Carol Reese *communications educator*

OHIO

Akron
Simmons, Debra Adams *editor*

Amherst
Gerstenberger, Valerie *media specialist*

Cedarville
Haffey, Deborah Bush *communications educator*

Cincinnati
Beckwith, Barbara Jean *journalist*
Davis, Robin *publishing executive*
Flanagan, Martha Lang *publishing executive*
Irwin, Miriam Dianne Owen *publishing executive, writer*
King, Margaret Ann *communications educator*
McMullin, Ruth Roney *retired publishing executive*
Steinberg, Janet Eckstein *journalist*
Trent, Judith Swanlund *communications educator*

Cleveland
Bellamy, Gail Anne Ghetia *magazine editor, author, speaker*
Harf, Patricia Jean Kole *syndicated columnist, clinical and behavioral psychologist, educational consultant, marriage and family therapist, lecturer*
Jensen, Kathryn Patricia (Kit) *broadcast executive*
Jindra, Christine *editor*
Soltis, Katherine *editor*

Columbus
Cambern, Andrea *newscaster, reporter*
Dervin, Brenda Louise *communications educator*
Hamper, Anietra *news anchor*
Harris, Yolanda *newscaster*
Hollingsworth, Holly *newscaster*
Marshall, Colleen *newscaster*
Pave, Angela *newscaster*
Pick, Heather *newscaster*
Sullivan, Terri *newscaster, reporter*

Dayton
Matheny, Ruth Ann *editor*

Findlay
Drake, Jeanette Wenig *communications educator, writer, public relations consultant*

Seaman
Cartaino, Carol Ann *editor*

Toledo
Brickey, Suzanne M. *editor*

Willoughby
Corrigan, Faith *journalist, educator, historian*

Wooster
Schreiber, Clare Adel *journalist*

OKLAHOMA

Edmond
Pydynkowsky, Joan Anne *journalist*

Forgan
Husted, Charlene E. *library media specialist, educator*

Oklahoma City
Hale, Sue A. *editor*
Lindenberg, Elanna Beth *communications educator, secondary school educator*

Tecumseh
Moser, Glenda Faye *media specialist*

OREGON

Bend
Wilbanks, Donna Mae *editor*

Christmas Valley
Johnson, Mary Alice *magazine editor*

Eugene
Bassett, Carol Ann *journalism educator, writer*

Jefferson
Varner, Helen *communications educator*

Portland
Bunza, Linda Hathaway *editor, writer, composer, director*
Johnston, Virginia Evelyn *retired editor*
Massee, Judith Tyle *editor, educator*

Brady-Borland, Karen *retired reporter, columnist*
Brauer, Rhonda Lyn *publishing executive, lawyer*
Brogliatti, Barbara Spencer *retired television and motion picture executive*
Brooks, Andrée Aelion *journalist, educator, writer*
Brown, Angela McHaney *editor*
Brown, Fay *editor, writer*
Bruck, Connie Jane *reporter*
Buchwald, Emilie Daisy *publisher, editor*
Budny, Lorraine *newspaper reporter, freelance writer*
Buhagiar, Marion *editor, writer*
Burton, Janis Elaine (Jan Burton) *retired writer, editor*
Byrne-Dempsey, Cecelia (Cecelia Dempsey) *journalist*
Callahan, Vivian *broadcast executive*
Capell, Cydney Lynn *editor*
Cardone, Bonnie Jean *freelance/self-employed photojournalist*
Cardwell, Nancy Lee *editor, writer*
Carlson, Stacy C. *former motion picture association executive*
Carpenter, Liz (Elizabeth Sutherland Carpenter) *journalist, writer, equal rights leader, lecturer*
Carter, Betsy L. *editor, writer*
Cary, Emily Pritchard *columnist*
Charnin, Jade Hobson *magazine executive*
Chast, Roz *cartoonist*
Checinska, Bozena Teresa *media specialist*
Chung, Connie (Constance Yu-hwa Chung) *broadcast journalist*
Cohane, Heather Christina *publishing executive, editor*
Cole, Carolyn *photojournalist*
Colombo, Rose Marie *freelance/self-employed newswriter, television personality*
Cottingham, Martha Maxfield *journalist, volunteer*
Cox, Kathleen *broadcast executive, lawyer*
Culliton, Barbara J. *publishing executive*
Curry, Dale Blair *retired journalist*
Curtin, Leigh *media consultant, writer*
Curtis, Mary E. (Mary Curtis Horowitz) *publishing executive*
Cutcher, Kresta King *photojournalist, educator*
Dahlstrom, Becky Joanne *journalist*
Daniels, Susanne *broadcast executive*
Dawson, Virginia Sue *retired editor*
Dean, Carole Lee *film company executive*
DeBakey, Selma *communications educator, writer, editor*
Deitz, Susan Rose *advice columnist, writer*
Delaney, Barbara Snow *retired editor*
Denious, Sharon Marie *retired publishing executive*
Denver, Eileen Ann *retired editor*
Deoul, Kathleen Boardsen *publishing executive*
de Varona, Donna *sports reporter, former Olympic swimmer*
Donald, Aida DiPace *retired publishing executive*
Downing, Kathryn M. *former newspaper publishing executive, lawyer*
Drant, Sandra Elizabeth *court reporter, educator*
Drew, Elizabeth Heineman *publishing executive*
Dubin, Stacia *newscaster*
Dumanoski, Dianne *journalist, writer*
Dyson, Esther *editor-in-chief*
Edelson, Zelda Sarah Toll *retired editor, artist*
Edmunds, Jane Clara *media consultant*
Ehrlich, Amy *editor, writer*
Ellis, Harriette Rothstein *editor*
Farnsworth, Elizabeth *broadcast journalist*
Fisher, Barbara A. *former broadcast executive*
Fitzpatrick, Nancy Hecht *editor*
Foard, Susan Lee *editor*
Frackman, Noel *art critic*
Francke, Linda Bird *journalist*
Frederickson, Christine Magnuson *reporter, researcher, editor, writer*
Friedman, Fredrica Schwab *editor, publisher*
Gainer, Leila J. *media relations executive, golf industry specialist*
Garvey, Arlene P. *media specialist, consultant*
Gates, Susan Inez *magazine publisher*
Gill, Libby *television executive*
Gillette, Ethel Morrow *columnist*
Gold, Sylviane *editor, writer, film critic*
Gora, Susannah Porter Martin *journalist, poet*
Gowler, Vicki Sue *newspaper editor, journalist*
Graham, Laurie *editor, writer*
Grann, Phyllis E. *editor, former publisher, executive*
Grant, Frances Bethea *editor*
Gray, Ann Maynard *broadcasting company executive*
Green, Barbara Marie *publisher, journalist, poet, writer*
Gregory, Bettina Louise *retired journalist*
Guerrero, Lisa (Lisa Guerrero-Coles) *former sports reporter*
Hahn, Helene B. *former motion picture company executive*
Hall, Teresa Ruth *publishing executive*
Hardcastle, Marcia E. (Marcia E. Temme) *retired journalist*
Harlan, Megan *journalist, poet*
Harvey, Lynne Cooper *broadcast executive, civic worker*
Harvey, Nancy Melissa *media specialist, art educator*
Hatfield, Julie Stockwell *journalist*
Hedin, Anne Miller *editor, writer, software marketing professional*
Heimbold, Margaret Byrne *publisher, educator, consultant, realtor*
Hemperly, Rebecca Sue *publishing manager*
Henry, Frances Ann *retired journalist, educator*
Hering, Doris Minnie *dance critic*
Herrera, Ana Luisa *news anchor, journalist, writer*
Hopkins, Jan *journalist, newscaster*
House, Karen Elliott *former publishing executive, editor, journalist*
Howze, Karen Aileen *newspaper editor, lawyer, multi-cultural communications consultant*
Humbach, Miriam Jane *publishing executive*
Hunt, L. Susan *publishing executive*
Hunter-Gault, Charlayne *journalist*
Huston, Margo *journalist*
Hutton, Carole Leigh *newspaper editor*
Jacobson, Nina R. *former film company executive*
Jenkins, Billie Beasley *film company executive*
Johnston, Catherine Viscardi *former magazine publisher*
Johnston, Marguerite *retired journalist*
Jonas, Amy Joy *music company executive*
Jones, Leonade Diane *media publishing company executive*
Juran, Sylvia Louise *retired editor*
Kabrich, Jeanine Renee *broadcaster, educator*
Kamen, Paula *journalist, playwright*
Kan, Yue-Sai *journalist, writer, television personality, entrepreneur, humanitarian*
Karalekas, Anne *media executive*
Kelly, Christina *editor*
Kimes, Beverly Rae *editor, writer*
Koeppel, Mary Sue *communications educator, writer*
Lamont, Lee *music company executive, communications executive*
Lanes, Selma Gordon *critic, writer, editor*
Lansing, Sherry Lee *former film company executive*
LaVally, Rebecca Jean *research editor, journalist*
Leach, Janet C. *publishing executive*
Lehner, Remy D. *publishing executive*
Leidel, Katherine *journalist, newscaster*
Leonard, Carolyn Branch *editor, writer*
Lewis, Tommi *magazine editor*
Li, Qin *news anchor, reporter, television director, television producer*
Liberman, Gail Jeanne *editor*
Lingle, Marilyn Felkel *journalist, columnist*
Long, Lisa Valk *communications company executive*
Lynch, Patricia Gates *broadcast executive, consultant, ambassador*
Lyon, Barbara Kennedy *retired editor*
Maher, Lisa Krug *editor*
Manley, Joan A(dele) Daniels *retired publishing executive*
Manning, Janice *editor, writer*
Marmer, Nancy *editor*
Marsh, Joan Knight *educational film company executive, video company executive, computer company executive, publishing executive*
Martin, Marilyn Mann *retired media specialist*
Martinez, Joanne O. *corporate executive*
Matchette, Phyllis Lee *editor*
Maxwell, Maureen Kay *media specialist, educator*
McCormick, Susan Konn *retired publishing executive*
McDarrah, Gloria Schoffel *editor, writer*
McGinnis, Marcy Ann *broadcast executive*
McNally, Connie Benson *magazine editor, publisher, antiques dealer*
Medina, Kathryn Bach *book editor*
Mermelstein, Paula *broadcasting executive*
Mesrobian, Arpena Sachaklian *publishing executive, consultant, editor*
Metoyer, Pamela Paradis *scientific editor, writer*
Meyer, Pucci *editor*
Michaels, Marion Cecelia *newswriter, editor, news syndicate executive*
Miller, Ann Clinton *communications educator*
Miller, Darcy M. *publishing executive*
Miller, Judith A. (Judy Miller) *retired journalist*
Mills, Dale Douglas *journalist*
Moen, Margaret *editor*
Moran, Sheila Kathleen *journalist*
Morgan, Anne Marie G. *broadcast journalist, educator*
Nelson, Martha Jane *magazine editor*
Newman, Rachel *editor*
Nye, Dorothy Mae *freelance journalist, educator*
O'Neil, Carolyn *cable network executive, cable television host*
Osmer-McQuade, Margaret *broadcast executive, journalist*
Packard, Betty Jane *journalist, consultant*
Pakenham, Rosalie Muller Wright *magazine and newspaper editor*
Pauley, Jane *newscaster, journalist*
Peacock, Mary Willa *magazine editor, consultant*
Pegs, Karen Rosamond *publishing executive, lawyer*
Pendleton, Gail Ruth *newspaper editor, writer, educator*
Perrin, Gail *editor*
Phelps, Mindy Shannon *communications consultant*
Phillips, Glynda Ann *editor*
Pinter, Elizabeth *retired communications educator*
Poster, Meryl *film company executive*
Povich, Lynn *journalist, internet executive*
Press, Aida Kabatznick *retired editor, poet, writer*
Presto, Catherine Ann (Kay Presto) *media specialist, consultant*
Priest, Jessie Shaw *media specialist*
Quade, Vicki *editor, writer, playwright, theater producer*
Quintana-Allenson, Ana M. *media specialist*
Radcliffe, Redonia (Donnie Radcliffe) *journalist, writer*
Ramsay, Karin Kinsey *publisher, educator*
Randinelli, Tracey Anne *magazine editor*
Rasor, Dina Lynn *journalist, private investigator*
Rieselman, Deborah Sue *editor*
Righini, Marilou Mausteller *editor, consultant*
Roberts, Margaret Harold *editor, publisher*
Robins, Cynthia Lou *journalist, jewelry designer*
Rollins, Margaret Ann *communications and theater educator*
Rooth, Signe Alice *editor, consultant*
Salvatore, Diane J. *editor-in-chief*
Samelson, Judy *editor*
Sanders, Marlene *news correspondent, journalism educator*
Schaller, Christina C. *editor*
Sciolino, Elaine *reporter*
Seligman, Nicole K. *broadcast executive, lawyer*
Seminara, Lynda Anne *editor*
Shao Collins, Jeannine *magazine publisher*
Sharp, Stacy Lynn *media specialist*
Shelton, Stephani *broadcast journalist, consultant*
Shuler, Sally Ann Smith *retired media consultant*
Shulgasser-Parker, Barbara *critic, writer*
Sidney, Corinne Entratter *retired journalist, actress*
Silvey, Anita Lynne *editor*
Sinclair, Carole *publishing executive, editor*
Soeteber, Ellen *journalist, editor*
Stahl, Lesley R. *news correspondent*
Steiner, Shari Yvonne *editor, journalist*
Stephenson, Toni Edwards *publishing executive, investment company executive, communications executive*
Steptoe, Sonja *journalist*
Stevens, Marilyn Ruth *editor*
Storm, Hannah *newscaster*
Stuart, Nancy Rubin (Nancy Zimman Stetson) *journalist, writer, television producer*
Tafoya, Michele *sports reporter*
Talese, Nan Ahearn *freelance/self-employed publishing executive*
Telnaes, Ann *cartoonist*
Thomas, Jo *journalist, educator*
Tiedge-Lafranier, Jeanne Marie *editor*
Toay, Thelma M. *columnist, poet*
Torgerson, Katherine P. *media consultant, corporate communications specialist*
Triece, Anne Gallagher *magazine publisher*
Turek, Sonia Fay *journalist*
Uman, Sarah Dungey *editor*
Utley, Ebony A. *communications educator*
Vernon, Doris Schaller *retired newswriter, publishing executive*
Wander-Perna, Lucy *film company executive*
Wartella, Ellen Ann *communications educator, consultant*
Waters, Betty Lou *newspaper reporter, writer*
Watson, Catherine Elaine *journalist*
Welsh, Dorothy Dell *columnist, writer*
Welsome, Eileen *journalist, writer*
West, Betsy *broadcast executive*
Weymouth, Elizabeth (Lally) Graham *editor, columnist*
Wheeler, Kathryn S. *editor*
Whipple, Judith Roy *retired editor*
Whittell, Polly (Mary Kaye Whittell) *editor, journalist*
Wies, Barbara *publishing executive, editor*
Williman, Pauline *retired reporter, foundation administrator*
Winter, Judy Elaine *freelance/self-employed journalist, speaker*
Wixen, Joan Saunders *journalist*
Wolaner, Robin Peggy *internet and magazine publisher*
Wood, Jane Semple *editor, writer*
Wood, Marian Starr *publishing executive*
Woodruff, Judy Carline *broadcast journalist*
Woodruff, Virginia *broadcast journalist, writer*
Zaring, Jane Thomas *retired editor, writer*

EDUCATION *See also* specific fields for postsecondary education

UNITED STATES

ALABAMA

Alexander City
Chapman, Mary Kathryn *elementary school educator*
Wheeles, Emily S. *biology educator*

Athens
Smith, Patricia Crawford *elementary school educator*

Auburn
Galbraith, Ruth Legg *retired dean, home economist*

Auburn University
Buchanan, Alice Moore *education educator*

Bessemer
Johnsey-Robertson, Anita Colleen *special education educator*
Stevens, Elizabeth McCartha *secondary school educator*

Birmingham
Caffey, Linda Kaye *elementary school educator*
Dryden, Susan Meredith *secondary school educator*
Garrison, Carol Z. *academic administrator*
Goldman, Renitta Librach *special education educator, consultant*
Hahn, Beatrice A. *education educator*
Long, Berneé E. *academic administrator, educator*
Morgan, Kathryn Diane *criminology educator*
Mueller, Dorothy Ann *university official*
Ritchie, Beth Bradley *elementary school educator*
Rivers, Sherry Diane *educational administrator, consultant*
Tubbs, Cecilia Saulters *academic administrator, educator*
Whitfield, Andrea Billingsley *elementary school educator*

Blountsville
Owens, Teresa Gail *elementary school educator*

Chelsea
Alicea, Yvette *special education educator*

Cherokee
Daily, Freda Smith *superintendent*

Columbiana
Dobbs Black, Leah Faye *elementary school educator*

Crossville
Blessing, Maxine Lindsey *secondary school educator*

Daphne
Henson, Pamela Taylor *secondary education educator*

Decatur
Blalock, Carmen *education educator*
Clark, Kathleen Vernon *special education educator*
Costello, Sheri Ann *primary school educator*
Howard, Sandra Dianne *secondary school educator*
Julich, Nancy C. *secondary school educator*
Smith, Trina *academic administrator*

Demopolis
Attaway, Amie Elizabeth *secondary school educator*

Dothan
Flowers, V. Anne *retired academic administrator*
Jones, Sandra Lee *retired dean*

Double Springs
Slatton, Barbara *secondary school educator*

Eclectic
Rodi, Kathryn Kelly *elementary school educator*

Enterprise
Adkison, Charla S. *biology educator*

Eufaula
Conniff, Alexandra Acosta *secondary school educator*

Eutaw
Daniels, Benita Jean *special education educator*
Merritt, Edith Bradford *elementary school educator*

Evergreen
Dailey, Marilyn *elementary school educator*

Fairhope
Peck, Phyllis Hainline *educator*

Florence
Linton, Phyllis Heflin *mathematics educator*
Williams, Joyce Hall *secondary school educator*

Fort Payne
Beasley, Mary Catherine *retired secondary school educator, retired administrator*
Mitchell, Gwendolyn Ann *mathematics educator*
Wilbanks, Janice Peggy *special education educator*

Fultondale
Taylor, Patricia Nail *mathematics and science educator*

Gadsden
Massaro, Traci Lynn *special education educator*
Montgomery, Constance O. *mathematics educator*
Murray, Harriet Johnson *secondary school educator*

Gardendale
Adams, Amanda Kelley *mathematics educator*

Geneva
Ellison, Cathy Walker *history educator, literature and language educator, educational consultant*

Gordo
Booth, Karen Lee *elementary school educator*

Grand Bay
Taylor, Anne Wilkerson *elementary school educator*

Hamilton
Ray, Yvonne McCarley *elementary school educator*
Young, Mary Delores *special education educator*

Hanceville
Holmes, Kristen Jones *academic administrator*

Harvest
Lasater, Jennifer A. *history educator, dance educator*

Helena
Coulter, Fern Goshen *retired secondary school educator*

Hoover
Matherson, Rachael Akers *secondary school educator, dancer*
Slovensky, Deborah Wilbanks *secondary school educator*

Huntsville
Brightwell, Wendy Sue *biology educator*
Gothart, Pamela Campbell *history educator*
Hall, Elizabeth Murchie *retired special education educator, consultant*
Moore, Ann Roy *school system administrator*
Morgan, Beverly Hammersley *elementary school educator, artist*
Pearson, Susan *elementary school educator*
Ratchford Merchant, Betty Jo *retired elementary school educator*
Smothers, Deloris Rice *computer career educator*
Stephens, Connie E. *secondary school educator*
Tincher, Anne Harris *elementary school educator*
Turner, Mary Alice *curriculum specialist*
Wilksman, Karen Sonjia *secondary school educator*

Irondale
Galamore, Shannon *mathematics educator*

Jacksonville
Hutchinson, Francine Nelson *biology educator, consultant*
McCrary, Judy Hale *education educator*

Jones
Tidwell, Betty Davenport *special education educator*

Kinston
Shaw, Sonya King *literature and language educator*

Lanett
Looser, Vickie Beard *secondary school educator*

Leeds
Wilson, Maggie Isabelle Lovell *secondary school educator*

Lester
Matthews, Linda Nell *secondary school educator*

Loachapoka
Lishak, Lisa Anne *secondary school educator*

Madison
Hellums, Lori Roberts *elementary school educator*

Millbrook
Roberts, Lisa Dawn *elementary school educator*

Mobile
Bullard, Bettie Catherine Posey *adult education educator*
Crowell, Tangie Michelle *elementary school educator*
Smith, Anne Sisson *private school educator*
Sumlin, Margaret Brown *special education educator*
Volkman, Beatrice Kramer *special education educator*

Montevallo
Payne, Tracy H. *academic director*
Stewart, Katherine Wood *middle school educator*

Montgomery
Blackman, Kennette *secondary school educator*
Kennedy, Kamela Denise *director*

Moody
Brasher, Terrie Walker *secondary school educator*

Morris
Murphy, Jennifer *elementary school educator*

New Hope
Loyd, Betsy Franklin *primary school educator*

Opelika
Logan, Elizabeth *middle school educator*

Oxford
Flummer, Sandra Moon *elementary school educator*

Pell City
Dale, Sonia Ivette *principal*

Perdido
McDonald, Gerri Van Pelt *elementary school educator*

Pleasant Grove
McCrary, Lori Sue *secondary school educator*

Prattville
Tutchtone, Sharon Sabrina *secondary school educator*

Sylacauga
Depew, Mae F. *director, educational consultant*
Scott, Arista V. *secondary school educator*

Talladega
McIlwain, Anna Keitt *elementary school educator, researcher*

Troy
Carpenter, Stacy *secondary school educator*

Tuscaloosa
Bonner, Judy L. *academic administrator*
Burry-Stock, Judith Anne (Anne Burry) *education educator*
Cartee, Karen Johnson *education educator, consultant*
Fields, Ruth Kinniebrew *secondary and elementary educator, consultant*
Gregory, Paula Elaine *gifted and talented educator*

Tuscumbia
McWilliams, Elizabeth Ann *elementary school educator*

Tuskegee
White, Mildred Virginia *secondary school educator, retired counseling administrator*

Vance
Owenby, S. Diane *elementary school educator*

Vestavia Hills
Pierce, Kacy Jones *assistant principal*

Wetumpka
Vilardi, Virginia Ann *secondary school educator, department chairman*

Woodville
Cook, Faye Hamlett *secondary school educator*

ALASKA

Anchorage
Baxley, Yvette *secondary school educator*
Comeau, Carol Smith *school system administrator*
Davis, Bettye Jean *school system administrator, state legislator*
Habberstad, Amy Renae *secondary school educator*
Maimon, Elaine Plaskow *university chancellor*
McMorris, Cycelia A. *elementary school educator*
Skladal, Elizabeth Lee *retired elementary school educator*
Thurber, Sharon Lee *elementary resource educator*
Underwood, Patricia Ford *elementary school educator*
Wright-Elson, Larissa Anne *literature and language educator*

Bethel
Turner, Kathy Ann *special education educator*

Chugiak
Stiehr, Lizette Estelle *special education educator, director*

Fairbanks
Alexander, Vera *dean, marine science educator*
Krause, Marilyn Ruth *elementary school educator*
Mahurin Hadaway, Melanie L. *secondary school educator*
Mayer, Patricia E., Sr. *elementary school educator*
Villano, Christine Pearsall *elementary school educator*

Juneau
Acres, Jo Devine *literature and language educator*
Waldrip, Karen Marie *career planning administrator*

Nikiski
Thompson, Sharon Ruth *special education educator*

North Pole
Martin, Dorothy Sue *secondary education educator, counselor*

Tanana
Marks, Stephanie I. *secondary school educator, biologist*

Togiak
Abington Alexie, Susan Edith *elementary school educator*

Wrangell
Miller, Jennifer L. *elementary school educator, small business owner*

ARIZONA

Buckeye
Martinez, DiAnna *secondary school educator*

Cave Creek
Hatch, Barbara Jean *secondary school educator*
Metcalf, Amy Bolling *secondary school educator*

Chandler
Alvarado, Grace *elementary school educator*
Casteel, Camille *school system administrator*
Miller, Patricia Ann *secondary school educator*

Chinle
Quell, Margaret Anne *special education educator*

Coolidge
Pratt, Janice *hospitality and hotel services educator*

Cottonwood
Lay, Janice Amelia *special education educator*

Desert Hills
Evans, Carol Ann *reading specialist*

Douglas
Britton, Ruth Ann Wright *elementary school educator*

Flagstaff
Barnes, Charlotte Elizabeth *retired elementary school educator*
Hospodka, Lenka M. *hotel and restaurant management educator*

Fountain Hills
Sorenson, Gretchen Hartley *elementary school educator*

Glendale
Avila, Lidia D. *principal*
Connell-Allen, Elizabeth Ann *elementary school educator*
Louk, Donna Pat *elementary school educator, music educator*
Sweat, Lynda Sue *cooking instructor, catering company owner, deaconess*
Thrasher, Jacqueline F. *elementary school educator*

Goodyear
Molina, Tanya E. *school librarian*

Green Valley
Fuer-Davis, Beverly Jean *retired elementary school educator*
Shafer, Susan Wright *retired elementary school educator*

Kingman
Yancey, Emily *secondary school educator*

Lakeside
Mack, Ina Leah *secondary school educator, pre-school administrator*

Marana
Ruehle, Dianne Marie *retired elementary education educator*

Mesa
Colledge, Deborah Gail *gifted and talented elementary educator*
Duvall, Debra *school system administrator*
Evans, Mary Magee *secondary school educator, language educator*
Jones, Linda L. *literature and language educator, department chairman*
Sarwar, Barbara Duce *educational consultant*
Walter, Ann L. *special education educator*
Weber, Yvonne Roebuck *research administrator, educator*

Oro Valley
Baker, Veronica Ann *secondary school educator, writer*

Peoria
Paul, Melanie Frances *principal*

Phoenix
Beckman, Brenda Marshall *educational consultant*
Benjamin, M. Susan *special education educator*
Coyle, Linda Marie *elementary school educator*
Davis, Darna Betts *elementary school educator*
Erwin, Barbara F. *school system administrator*
Evans, Pamela H. *secondary school educator*
Floyd, Pamela Kay *elementary school educator, artist*
Forcier, Helene Francis *secondary school educator*
Frehner, Patricia Ann *education educator, consultant*
James, Betty M. *secondary school educator*
Lee, Barbara S. *special education educator*
McLendon, Kathleen Mary *elementary school educator*
McQuown, Kimberly Alyse *elementary school educator*
Noone, Laura Palmer *academic administrator, lawyer*
Schrader, Susan Rae *elementary school educator*
Thorne, Ann LaRayne *secondary school educator*
Udall, Vesta Hammond *special education educator*
Young, Michael Cochise *academic administrator*

Pinetop
Gilbert-Tiegs, Marion Ann *gifted and talented educator, consultant*

Prescott
Halvorson, Mary Ellen *education educator, writer*
Slominski, Elena Gregoryevna *mathematics educator*
Waterer, Bonnie Clausing *retired secondary school educator*

Rio Rico
Coyle, Allison Brooke *director*

Sacaton
Howe, Anne Marie *director, educator*

Safford
Brady, Carole Ann *physical education teacher*

San Luis
Kryger, Jerri Renee *elementary school educator*

Scottsdale
Hokin, Jeanne *education educator*
Lillestol, Jane Brush *educational consultant*
McKay-Cox, Marianne *secondary school educator*
Novak, Janice Elaine *pre-school educator*
Phillips, Wanda Charity *secondary school educator, writer*
Reid, Judith Solomon *elementary school educator*

Sedona
Richards, Wanda Jamie *retired education educator*

Shonto
Haviland, Marlita Christine *elementary school educator*

Sierra Vista
Spencer, Judith *retired secondary school educator, writer*

Sonoita
Sebert, Michelle Ann *school system network administrator*

Sun City
Wheeler, Janet Marilyn *retired special education educator*

Sun Lakes
Gersten, Shirley R. *elementary school educator*
Johnson, Marian Ilene *education educator*

Surprise
Bradford, Mariah *elementary school educator, consultant*
Burns, Clare Marie *retired elementary school educator*
Edwards, Gleita Kay *primary school educator*
Neuman, Isabel *mathematics educator*
Steimle, Jami P. *elementary school educator*
Stevenson, Norma Ann *elementary school educator, real estate agent, property manager*

Tempe
Dustman, Patricia (Jo) Allen *elementary school educator, consultant*
Milke, Linda Jean *elementary school educator*
Prom, M. Elaine *secondary school educator*
Schilling, Amy Jo *private school educator*
Thor, Linda M. *college president*
White, Patricia Denise *dean, law educator*

Tucson
Arzoumanian, Linda Lee *school system administrator*
Beaman, Colleen K. *education educator, choreographer*
Brennan, Carrie *principal*
Burrows, Dorna B. *elementary school educator*
Dailey, Lynne *secondary school educator*
Janes, Raena *private school educator*
Jolivet, Anna Mary *retired school system administrator, association executive*
Moten, Darlene *elementary school educator*
Sandoval, Arlene R. *elementary school educator*
Seagroves, Jean Franzen *secondary school educator*
Stoffle, Carla Joy *university library dean*
Vernon, Ann *educator, therapist*

Window Rock
Deschinny, Isabel *elementary school educator*

Yuma
Lister, Patricia Ann *elementary school educator*

Morse, Kerry W. *elementary school educator*

ARKANSAS

Batesville
Beck, Martha Catherine *philosophy educator*
Bennett, Maria Beth *literature and language educator*

Beebe
Pillow-Price, Kathy *education educator*

Bentonville
Nulty, Colleen M. *counseling administrator*

Bismarck
Trieschmann, Elizabeth Suzanne *elementary school educator*

Bryant
Kissire, Lisa Marie *learning specialist*

Clinton
Jevicky, Margo K. *secondary school educator*

Conway
Clanton, Kaye Reames *secondary school educator*
Fay, Samantha C. *mathematics educator*
Perry, Susan Nigemann *education educator, consultant*

Dardanelle
Wade, Amy Michelle *elementary school educator*

Earle
Swift, Peggy Lynette *elementary school educator*
Williams, Anita Jean *elementary school educator*

El Dorado
Daymon, Joy Jones *school psychology specialist*

Elkins
Philip, Joan Mary *literature and language educator*

England
Wagoner, Johnna *elementary school educator*

Everton
Jones, Melba Kathryn *elementary school educator, librarian*

Fayetteville
Gann, Elizabeth Dianne *elementary school educator*
Henry, Ann Rainwater *retired education educator*

Fort Smith
Bricker, Carol Jean *biology educator*

Goshen
Zelei, Rita Annette *retired educational administrator*

Guy
Ward, Sharon Dee *secondary school educator*

Harrison
Hearn, Cynthia Ann *education educator*

Heber Springs
Stroud, Peggy *secondary school educator*

Hope
Chambless, Lori K. *secondary school educator*

Hot Springs
Gaither, Susan Anne *business education educator*

Huntsville
Commerford, Patricia Bergman *elementary school educator*

Jacksonville
Johnson, Margo Faye *elementary school educator, nurse*

Jonesboro
Malinsky, Marci Ann *education educator*
Nelsen, Evelyn Rigsbee Seaton *retired secondary school educator*

Kirby
Mason, Brenda Kay *elementary school educator*

Little Rock
Bass, Evelyn Elizabeth *elementary school educator*
Bright, Trina Lynn *secondary school educator*
Caldwell, Bettye McDonald *education educator, director*
Geffken, Carolyn D. *special education educator*
Johnson-Shockley, Willie Mae *retired academic administrator*
Moore, Helen Lucille *adult education educator, consultant*
O'Neal, Nell Self *retired principal*
Smith, Mary Scott *elementary school and education educator*
Truex, Dorothy Adine *retired university administrator*

Magnolia
Harrison, Betty Carolyn Cook *retired education educator, administrator*

Maynard
Stuart, Cynthia Hodge *literature and language educator*

Murfreesboro
Wood, Rhonda Gailette *secondary school educator*

Natural Dam
Butler, Paula Kay *elementary school educator*

North Little Rock
Valentine, Terri L. *secondary school educator, activities director*

Osceola
Landry, Sandra Denise *secondary school educator*

Paragould
White, Sarah Elizabeth Sloan *elementary school educator*

Pine Ridge
Hays, Annette Arlene *secondary school educator*

Prairie Grove
Dunn, Anne Ewald Nefflen *retired elementary school educator*

Redfield
Wells, Linda Lee *retired elementary school educator*

Russellville
Morris, Lois Lawson *retired education educator*

Searcy
Coleman, Bobbie Ruth *literature and language educator*
Pruitt, Linda F. *elementary school educator*
Watson, Betty Ann *early childhood education professor*

Springdale
Davis, Deborah Ann St. Cyr *elementary school educator*
Durr, Tami Joleen *mathematics educator*
Holman, L. Charlene *elementary school educator*
Posey, Sandra Dalton *special education educator*

Stamps
Moore-Berry, Norma Jean *secondary school educator*

Texarkana
Beck, Tiffany *secondary school educator*
Walker, Barbara Ross *secondary school educator*

Tyronza
Debow, Bridgette M. *elementary school educator*

Van Buren
Kilgore, Mary Helen *mathematics educator*

Vanndale
Clark, Betty Susan *elementary school educator*

White Hall
Rushing, Annette *elementary school educator*

CALIFORNIA

Adin
Ellenberger, Kathleen Sue Bowman *special education educator*

Agoura Hills
Bach, Cynthia *educational program director, writer*
Piscitelli, Nancy L. *retired special education educator*

Alameda
Carter, Roberta Eccleston *counseling administrator*
Robinson, Joanne Adele *retired secondary school educator, volunteer*

Alhambra
Austin, Elizabeth Ruth *retired elementary school educator*

Altadena
Hoskins, Cherise Lachelle *elementary school educator*

Alturas
Johnson, Donna Marie *elementary school educator*

Anaheim
Barry, Sandra *school system administrator*
Goodspeed, Kathryn Ann *pre-school educator*

Antioch
Stamm, Barbara Marie *elementary school educator, interior designer*
Thomson, Sondra K. *secondary school educator*

Aptos
Hirsch, Bette G(ross) *academic administrator, language educator*

Arcadia
Baltz, Patricia Ann (Pann Baltz) *retired elementary school educator*

Armona
Vanderpool, Shawnee D. *elementary school educator*

Azusa
Gahring, Sandra Ann *secondary school educator, coach*

Bakersfield
Fuller, Jean *school system administrator*
Kerr, Joan Lindsay *supervisor, consultant*

Banning
Finley, Margaret Mavis *retired elementary school educator*

Barstow
Gibbon, Mary-Lynn *special education educator*

Beaumont
Youngren, Delvana Hope *secondary school educator*

Belmont
Jacobson, Vera Lee *secondary school educator*

Berkeley
Azarpay, Guitty *education educator*
Bodenhausen, Judith Anne *school system administrator*
Doyle, Fiona Mary *dean, metallurgical engineer, educator*
Finnie, Joan *adult education educator*
Freedman, Sarah Warshauer *education educator*
Korn, Claire Vedensky *secondary school educator, writer*
Linn, Marcia Cyrog *education educator*
McBay, Ida LaVerne *special education educator*
McPhail-Geist, Karin Ruth *secondary school educator, real estate agent, musician*
Ralston, Lenore Dale *academic policy and program analyst*
Schild, Sylvia G. *retired elementary school educator, realtor*
Watkins, Renee E. *adult education educator*

Big Bear Lake
McCoy, Jennie Eileen *elementary school educator*
Mix, Jill Kaye *secondary school educator, artist*

Brea
Missakian, Ilona Virginia *secondary school educator*

Brentwood
Groseclose, Wanda Westman *retired elementary school educator*
Lagano, Daneen Westphal *elementary school educator*
Paul, Yvonne C. *retired elementary school educator*

Burbank
Doud, Jacqueline Powers *academic administrator*
Neumann, Nancy Ruth *private school educator*
Nurik, Cindy Bunin *educational consultant, marriage and family therapist*
Ricketts, Amy Rene *elementary school educator, writer*

Calexico
Ramirez, Elisa *mathematics educator*

Camarillo
Arthington, Carol Ann *elementary school educator*

Canyon Country
Joseph, Michele Beth *special education educator, educational therapist*

Carlsbad
Burns, Doris Eleanor *retired elementary school educator*
Golden, Paula Englander *social work educator, consultant, addiction educator, consultant*
Rodak, Sharon Lorraine *elementary school educator, researcher*

Carmel
Freed, Sharon Lou *retired principal*

Carmichael
Friedman, Mary Kathleen *secondary school educator*
Money, Ruth Rowntree *retired infant development and care specialist, parent/infant programs consultant*
Oprsal, Nancy Upshaw *retired elementary school educator*

Carson
Paige, Dorothy Billiard *retired secondary school educator, educational consultant*

Castro Valley
Shoptaw, Shauna Lynn *middle school educator*

Chico
Bernhardt, Victoria L. *director, researcher*
Hyde, Geraldine Veola *retired secondary school educator*

Chino
Alton, Colleen Edna *education educator*
Wiegand, Penelope Tarleton *elementary school educator*

Chula Vista
Wyatt, Edith Elizabeth *elementary school educator*

Claremont
Bekavac, Nancy Yavor *academic administrator, lawyer*
Gann, Pamela Brooks *academic administrator*
Klawe, Maria Margaret *academic administrator, engineering educator, computer science educator*
O'Kelly, Crystal Kathleen *secondary school educator, television producer*
Skandera Trombley, Laura Elise *academic administrator, literature educator*

Clayton
Bower, Fay Louise *academic administrator, nursing educator*

Clovis
Dixson, Judy Sue *retired elementary school educator*

Coachella
Gonzales, Martha *elementary school educator*

Colton
Caseria, Carol Shuler *elementary school educator, researcher*

Compton
Gillette, Sister Joseph Ann *education educator, educator*

Corcoran
Martines, Eugenia Belle *elementary school educator, special education educator*

Corning
Brown, Betty J. *retired elementary school educator*

Corona
Snider, Jane Ann *retired elementary school educator*

Coronado
Akin, Lillie Violet *chemistry educator, writer, television personality, consultant*

Corte Madera
Dalpino, Ida Jane *retired secondary school educator*

Costa Mesa
Candelaria, Angie Mary *special education educator*
Powers, Janet F. *special education educator*

Cottonwood
Penrod, Rebecca Lorene Connelly *retired elementary school educator*

Culver City
Geiselman, LucyAnn *college president*
Hoge, Geraldine Rajacich *elementary school educator*
Maxwell-Brogdon, Florence Morency *school system administrator, educational consultant*

Cupertino
Fraser, Maida Lynn *director*
Lyon, Mary Lou *retired secondary school educator*
Martin, Barbara Lynne *retired elementary school educator*
Starratt, Jeanette Ellen *elementary school educator*

Cypress
Armstrong, Sandra Rogers *secondary school educator, athletic trainer*

Danville
Henehan, Gina L. *history educator*
Spilker, Yvonne Wailes *mathematics educator*

Davis
Biggart, Nicole Woolsey *dean*
Ginosar, D. Elaine *elementary school educator*
Hinshaw, Virginia *academic administrator*
Kraft, Rosemarie *dean, educator*
MacGregor, Marilyn Elna *director*
Robert, Ellen *university administrator*
Silberstein, Allegra Jostad *retired elementary school educator*

Denair
Hale, Lois J. *retired mathematics educator*

Downey
Brooks, Lillian Drilling Ashton (Lillian Hazel Church) *adult education educator*
Ruecker, Martha Engels *retired special education educator*

Earlimart
White, Kathleen *director*

El Cajon
Thomas, Esther Merlene *elementary and adult education educator*

El Centro
Kussman, Eleanor (Ellie Kussman) *retired educational superintendent*

El Dorado Hills
Moya, Marcia Tewksbury *director*

Elk Grove
Moe, Janet Anne *elementary school educator, church organist*

Encinitas
Prodor, Leah Marie *secondary school educator*

Encino
Bond, Mary Llewellyn *movement education educator*
O'Riley, Karen E. *principal*

Escondido
Granet, Eileen *secondary school educator*

Fairfield
Forssell, Linda Lee *secondary school educator, illustrator*
Mary, Diane Bradley *elementary school educator, secondary school educator*

Folsom
Allaman, Kathryn Ann *vice principal, mathematician*
Sarraf, Shirley A. *secondary school educator*

Fort Bragg
Dias, Michele C. *primary school educator*

Fremont
Horst, Barbara Lynn *primary school educator*
Lau, Michelle *mathematics educator*
Peebles, Lucretia Neal Drane *education educator*
Venturini, Judith Anne *education educator*
Willows, Mary Rose *special education educator*

Fresno
Avants, Rebecca Maxine *biology educator*
Cornish, Bonita Clark *retired secondary school educator*
Dandoy, Maxima Antonio *retired education educator*
English, Erin *secondary school educator*
Fiester, Elizabeth Ann *secondary school educator*
Girvin, Shirley Eppinette *retired elementary school educator, journalist*
Sargent, Molly Anne *literature and language educator*
Stewart, Deborah Claire *dean*
Tudman, Cathi Graves *elementary school educator*

Fullerton
Connor, Danielle Broucqsault *secondary school educator*
Donoghue, Mildred Ransdorf *education educator*

Garden Grove
Faust, Amy Kay *elementary school educator*
Ogata, Carolee Kimi *school system administrator*
Schwalm, Laura *school system administrator*

Gardena
Winn, Stephenie *senior program specialist*

Glendale
Blackwell, Linda Jane *elementary school educator*
Phibbs, Mary Ellen *retired secondary school educator*
Whalen, Lucille *retired academic administrator*

Glendora
Acevedo, Elizabeth Morrison *special education educator*
Anderson, Annette Shirey *deaf education educator, educational consultant*

Grass Valley
Dean, Barbara W. *elementary school educator*

Hacienda Heights
Burkhart, Catherine Ray *secondary school educator*
Lee, Chieh-Chi *elementary school educator*

Hayward
Garcia, Melva Ybarra *counseling administrator, educator*
Pulliam, Glorious K. *elementary school educator*
Rees, Norma S. *academic administrator*

Helendale
Hoover, Linda Sue *elementary school educator, coach*

Hemet
Cook, Allyson Lea *secondary school educator*
Monk, Sharon Anne *special education educator*

Hesperia
Du Lac, Lois Arline *retired secondary school educator, writer*

Hollister
Twaddell, Karen Grace *elementary school educator*

Hollywood
Cummings, Joan *history educator*

Holtville
Macdonald, Andara *secondary school educator*

Hughson
Hailey, Kathleen Wilson *elementary school educator*

Huntington Beach
Conrad, Janilyn McNees *special education educator*
McAlister, Chris *elementary school educator*
Ramphal, Julie Frances *retired secondary school educator*

Inglewood
Cato, Gloria Maxine *retired secondary school educator*
Lockhart, Claudia Jo *adult education educator, department chairman*
Logan, Lynda Dianne *elementary school educator*

Inyokern
Norris, Lois Ann *retired elementary school educator*

Irvine
Bryant, Susan V. *academic administrator*
Freed, Judy Gayle *literature and language educator*
Gala, Debra Gail *elementary school educator*
Langevin, Patricia Ann *mathematics educator*

La Canada Flintridge
Rieger, Bin Hong *secondary school educator, elementary school educator*

La Jolla
Chandler, Marsha *academic administrator, educator*
Foxe, Marye Anne *academic administrator*
Lowe, Lisa *education educator, department chairman*
Miller, Carol *elementary school educator, counselor*
Moon, Mona McTaggart *activities educator, consultant*
Savoia, Maria Christina *vice dean*

La Mesa
Black, Eileen Mary *retired elementary school educator*
Charleton, Margaret Ann *child care administrator, consultant*

La Puente
Ver Kuilen, Marion Jane *retired instructional aide*

La Quinta
Puente, Maria Luz *bilingual educator*

La Verne
Bentley, Donna Gale *school librarian*
Espinoza, Linda *elementary school educator*

Ladera Ranch
Skidmore, Michelle Marie *elementary school educator, principal*

Laguna Niguel
André, Joy LaRae *elementary school educator, adult education educator, language educator*
Gunning, Monica Olwen Minott *elementary school educator*

Lake Elsinore
Druskoff, Barbara Therese *elementary school educator*

Lakeside
Walker, Wanda Medora *retired elementary school educator, consultant*

Lancaster
Jones, Betty Ann *elementary school educator*

Live Oak
Spilman, Janet Lynne *special education educator*

Livermore
Dutchover, Amy *mathematics educator*
Philipps, Julie Leighann *elementary school educator*

Lodi
Bishop-Graham, Barbara *secondary school educator, journalist*
Reinold, Christy Diane *school counselor, consultant*
Siler, Virginia Carlisle *retired elementary school educator*

Lompoc
Barthel, Sarah Ann Moran *secondary school educator*

Long Beach
Elston, Joan Wilma *adult education educator, real estate agent*
Fleming, Jane Williams *retired elementary school educator, writer*
Lofland, Patricia Lois *secondary school educator, travel company executive*
Mandarino, Candida Ann *education educator, consultant*
Rutherford, Vicky Lynn *special education educator*
Springer, Wilma Marie *retired elementary school educator*
Writer, Sharon Lisle *secondary school educator*

Los Altos
Welsh, Doris McNeil *early childhood education specialist*

Los Angeles
Aldahl, Deborah Campbell *elementary school educator*
Allums, Henriene *elementary school educator*
Ansley, Julia E. *retired elementary school educator, poet, writer*
Bernstein, Leslie *academic administrator, biostatistician, epidemiologist*
Brandon, Kathleen Alma *director*
Brown, Deborah Ellen *gifted and talented educator, writer*
Chapman Collins, Janice *school system administrator*
Cheeseboro, Margrit *retired economics educator*
Coker, Sybil Jane Thomas *counseling administrator*
Comtois, Tiffany Lynn *academic advisor*
Cowan, Marie Jeanette *dean, nurse, medical educator*
Davis-Fernandes, Tina Denise *secondary school educator, coach*
Dickey, Teresa A. *secondary school educator*
DuPuy, Pamela Marie *elementary school educator*
Edwards, Kathryn Inez *educational consultant*
Erdos, Joanna E. *school counselor, secondary school educator*
Fitz-Carter, Aleane *retired elementary school educator, composer*
Geller, Debra F. *academic administrator, educator*
Guarnieri, Roberta Jean *elementary school educator, consultant*
Haley, Roslyn Trezevant *educational program director*
Hecht, Susanna Bettina *adult education educator, writer*
Houston, Velina Hasu *education educator, writer*
Keddie, Nikki R. *education educator*
Legohn, Lisa Marie *vocational school educator*
Lemlech, Johanna Kasin *education educator*
Levin, Carol Arlene *adult education educator*
Lipscomb-Brown, Edra Evadean *retired childhood educator*
Lynch, Beverly Pfeifer *education and information studies educator*
Martinson, Deborah Ann *education educator, writer*
McGee, Lynda Plant *college counselor*
McKinney, Virginia Elaine Zuccaro *educational administrator*
Mentzer, Roslyn *academic administrator*
Morris, Debbie Kay *director, educator*
Nelson, Barbara J. *dean*
Norwood, Phyllis Katherene *director, educator*
Peters, Rita *university administrator*
Prager, Susan Westerberg *academic administrator, law educator*
Rich, Caren *secondary school educator, hypnotherapist*
Rosenstock, Linda *dean, medical educator*
Russo, Lisa Ann *registrar*
Schuetze-Coburn, Marje *university librarian*
Sell, Ellen Jean *secondary school educator*
Simun, Patricia Bates *education educator, consultant*
Vredevoe, Donna Lou *academic administrator, microbiologist, educator, biomedical researcher*
Wagner, Ruth Joos *elementary school educator*
Wilkerson, LuAnn *dean, medical educator*
Zexter, Eleanor M. *secondary school educator*
Zola, Sheila Flexer *retired elementary school educator*

Los Banos
Ellington, Karen Renae *school system administrator*

Los Gatos
Hartinger, Patricia Bernardine *retired elementary school educator*

Madera
Angus, Gloria Michelle *elementary school educator*

Malibu
Raine, Melinda L. *academic librarian*
Ruse, Kathleen Diane *elementary school educator*

Marysville
Day, Colien *retired secondary school educator*
Hurley, Allison Ruth *mentor coach specialist*

Mckinleyville
Sahlberg, Anne Kiszka *secondary school educator*

Merced
Tomlinson-Keasey, Carol Ann *academic administrator*
Wylie, Trisha Lynn *principal*

Millbrae
Stamos, Kathryn Elizabeth *secondary school educator*

Milpitas
Allen, Irma M. *adult education educator*
Wyatt, Willda Jean *elementary school educator*

Mission Viejo
Hodge, Kathleen O'Connell *academic administrator*
Lake, Jane Burford *special education educator, hypnotherapist, small business owner*

Modesto
Holmboe, Susan Ann *elementary school educator*
Wilde, Christine Bucey *secondary school educator*

Montebello
Bucey, Constance Virginia Russell *retired elementary school educator, education educator*

Monterey
Boger, Gail Lorraine Zivna *reading specialist*

Moraga
Schwartz, Naomi J. *education educator*

Moreno Valley
Bajor, Renee Allyson *special education educator*
Heacock, Lizbeth Lee *elementary school educator*
Marshall, Debra Lynn *secondary school educator*

Mountain View
Craig, Joan Carmen *secondary school educator, performing arts educator*
Wulff, Virginia McMillan *school system administrator*

Napa
Barnes, Joy Vervene *retired literature and language educator*
Renfrow, Patricia Anne *secondary school educator*
Woodruff, Diane Carey *college president*

National City
Quigley, Deborah Hewitt *adult education educator*

Newbury Park
MacArthur, Marjorie Ellen Hottley *secondary school educator*

Northridge
Ackermann, Sue Ann *mathematics educator*
Curzon, Susan Carol *academic administrator*
Koester, Jolene *academic administrator*
Rowlands, Kathleen Dudden *education educator*
Syms, Helen Maksym *educational administrator*
Yuen, Ellen M. *elementary school educator*

Novato
Jaeger, Patsy Elaine *retired secondary school educator, artist*
Lane, Michele Jeanne *special education educator*
Miller, Emily Josephine *retired secondary school educator*

Oakdale
Wharff, Julie Dawn *principal*

Oakland
Caulfield, Carlota *education educator, researcher, poet*
Chetkovich, Carol *public policy educator*
Diaz, Sharon *education administrator*
Griffin, Betty Jo *elementary school educator*
Isaac Nash, Eva Mae *secondary school educator*
Krause, Marcella Elizabeth Mason (Mrs. Eugene Fitch Krause) *retired secondary school educator*
Sims, Sandra *elementary school educator*

Oceanside
Daniel, Susan Qualls *secondary school educator*
Johnson, Karen Elaine *secondary school educator, tax preparer*

Orange
Carson, Virginia Gottschall *academic administrator, biology educator*
Christian-Brougham, Ruby Rosalie *education educator*

Oxnard
Neilson, Jane Scott *mathematics educator*

Palm Desert
Baxter, Betty Carpenter *academic administrator*
Heydman, Abby Maria *academic administrator*
Owings, Thalia Kelley *elementary school educator*

Palm Springs
Hartman, Rosemary Jane *retired special education educator*

Palmdale
Faulk, Betty Price *elementary school educator*

Palo Alto
Choy, Judy *secondary school educator*
Chute, Deanna *mathematics educator*
Dugger, Marguerite J. *retired special education educator*
Heneveld-Story, Christy Jean *educational researcher*
Perl, Teri *computer educator*

Palos Verdes Estates
Kingsley, Kathryn Alexis Krah *retired elementary school educator*

Paramount
Kesten, Betty Lee *retired special education educator*

Parlier
Manton, Linda Marie *academic administrator*

Pasadena
Arnold, Frances Hamilton *chemistry educator*
Cepielik, Elizabeth Lindberg *elementary school educator*
Douglas, Kimberly *university librarian*
Winbush, Olga Joyce *education educator, consultant*

Paso Robles
Nelson, Bonnie Kay *elementary school educator*

Penn Valley
Collins, Linda L. *reading specialist, consultant*
Longan, Suzanne M. *retired elementary school educator*

Perris
Cavallaro, Judith *secondary school educator*

Petaluma
Howell, Sharon L. *counseling administrator*
Thomas, Nancy Hinckley *special education educator*
Tiedt, Iris McClellan *emeritus university dean*

Placerville
Barber, Victoria *school system administrator, consultant*
Miller, Edna Rae Atkins *secondary school educator*
Wessels-McCoy, Denise Wendy *pre-school administrator, consultant*

Pleasanton
Roshong, Dee Ann Daniels *dean, educator*

Pomona
Amaya-Thetford, Patricia *elementary school educator*
Bowlin, Stephanie D. *university dean*
Callaway, Linda Marie *special education educator*
Maslow, Phyllis F. *retired educator*

Poway
Conant, Kim Untiedt *retired elementary school educator*

Ramona
McAndrews, Shannon Marie *elementary school educator*

Rancho Cordova
Hendrickson, Elizabeth Ann *retired secondary school educator*

Rancho Mirage
Marsh, Betty June *retired education educator*

Redding
Bairrington, Ruth Ellen *retired secondary school educator, retired education educator*
Krupit, Alison *elementary school educator*
Novo, Nieta R. *education educator*

Redlands
Wilson, Lois Fair *retired school system administrator*

Rialto
Gilbert, Joanne Toone *director, educator*
Jackson, Betty Eileen *music and elementary school educator*
King, Muriel Eileen *secondary school educator*

Riverside
Clazie, Melissa A *literature and language educator*
Córdova, France Anne-Dominic *academic administrator, astrophysicist*
Dutton, Jo Sargent *education educator, researcher, consultant*
Fontana, Sandra Ellen Frankel *special education educator*
Staples, Karen Eleanor *special education educator*
Tirabassi, Linda Sue *secondary school educator*

Rocklin
Yates, Coleen Denise *special education educator*

Rohnert Park
Stetson, Nancy Emily *retired academic administrator*

Rolling Hills Estates
Corette, Deborah West *elementary school educator*
Marsh, Barbara Lynn *elementary school educator*

Rosemead
Nishimoto, Alice Keiko *elementary school educator, consultant*

Roseville
French, Leura Parker *secondary school educator*
Law, Jennifer *middle school educator, director*

Ross
Matan, Lillian Kathleen *secondary school educator, consultant, interior designer*

Sacramento
Adolphson, Vanessa *counseling administrator, educator, chemist*
Amezcua, Esther Hernandez *elementary school educator*
Artz, Ethel Angela Cleavenger *elementary school educator, consultant*
Gosfield, Margaret *secondary school educator, school system administrator, consultant, editor*
Grimes, Pamela Rae *retired elementary school educator*
Mattias, Mona Carol *elementary education educator, consultant*
Nickless, Barbara A. *primary school educator*
Nisson, Mary *elementary school educator*
Opperman, Rosanna Resendez *vice principal*
Parker, Elizabeth Rindskopf *dean, law educator*
Pomeroy, Claire *dean*
Potter, Teresa Pearl *adult education educator*
Zaidi, Emily Louise *retired elementary school educator*

San Bernardino
Caballero, Sharon *academic administrator*
Gilbert, Jennie *educator, consultant*

San Bruno
Bowman, Christine Diane *middle school educator*
White, Frances LaVonne *academic administrator*

San Diego
Hoctor, Michanne *dean*
Idos, Rosalina Vejerano *secondary school educator*
Jellison, Beverly Irene *literature and language educator*
Lyons, Mary E. *academic administrator*
Maloney, Ellen Claire *elementary school educator*
Moss, Barbara Gae *education educator*
Rodenberg, Johanna Kristine *education educator, consultant*
Schwartz, Rhonda Alene *learning disabilities specialist*
Swikard, Sandra J. *secondary school educator*
Uribe, Jennie Ann *elementary school educator*
Vega, Carolyn Jane *elementary educator, consultant, writer*
Wagschal, Kathleen *education educator*
Young, Sarah Moskowitz *educational and computer consultant, journalist*

San Dimas
Cameron, Judith Lynne *secondary school educator*

San Francisco
Ackerman, Arlene *school system administrator*
Ada, Alma Flor *education educator, writer*
Bancroft, Rena Merritt *retired academic administrator*
Clifford, Geraldine Joncich (Mrs. William F. Clifford) *retired education educator*
Davis, Patricia Margaret Alice *psychology and religion educator*
Dracup, Kathleen Anne *dean, nursing educator*
Finocchiaro, Penny Morris *secondary school educator*
Kamkar, Rosemary *secondary school educator*
Kane, Mary Kay *academic administrator, law educator*
Mitchell, Patricia Ann *education educator*
Newton, Nell Jessup *dean, law educator*
Peterson, Linda Lou *special education educator*
Pierce, Deborah Mary *educational administrator*
Pinsky, Charlotte Lee (Cherie Pinsky) *retired academic administrator*
Robertson, Merle Greene *art historian, academic administrator*
Stephens, Elisa *college president*

San Gabriel
Tomich-Bolognesi, Vera *education educator*

San Jose
Boac, Thelma Blantucas *principal*
Duncan, Gloria Celestine *elementary school educator, consultant*
Holyer, Erna Maria *adult education educator, writer, artist*
Lobig, Janie Howell *special education educator*
Muller, Carol Blue *former academic administrator, nonprofit organization executive, consultant*
Okerlund, Arlene Naylor *academic administrator, writer*
Rose, Virginia Shottenhamer *secondary school educator*

San Juan Capistrano
Beemer, Margaret (Peggy) *history educator*
Larwood, Susan Elizabeth *elementary school educator*

San Leandro
Chohlis, Dana Marie *school system administrator, theater director*

San Luis Obispo
Dalton, Linda Catherine *university administrator*
Gardebring, Sandra S. *academic administrator*
Kulp, Bette Joneve *retired educator, wallpaper installation business owner*

San Marcos
Haynes, Karen Sue *academic administrator, educator*

San Pablo
Maguire, Roberta Joan *elementary school educator, writer*

San Pedro
Bailey, Dorothy Jean *secondary school educator, consultant*

Ingerson, Nancy Nina Moore *special education educator*

San Rafael
Adcock, Muriel W. *special education educator*
Gordon, Sharon J. *special education educator*
Thomas, Mary Ann McCrary *counselor, school system administrator*

Santa Ana
Barry, Mary H. *college official*
Breeden, Carolyn Sullivan *dean, educator, interior designer, consultant*
Cohen-Strong, Elayne Barbara *director, educator*
Lawson, Barbara Slade *elementary school educator, artist*
Wilson, Beth A. *college official*

Santa Barbara
Norris, Virginia Oakley *secondary school educator*
Tettegah, Sharon Yvonne *secondary school educator*

Santa Clara
Kiyota, Melodee Yoko *secondary school educator*
Stahl, Barbara E. *school counselor, consultant*

Santa Cruz
Delaney, Margaret L. *academic administrator*

Santa Monica
Gantley, Judy Ann *elementary school educator, retired music educator*
Sohaili, Monira *retired special education educator*
Soloff, Laura J. *academic administrator*

Santa Rosa
Cheung, Judy Hardin *retired special education educator*
Foster, Lucille Caster *retired school system administrator*

Saratoga
Barna, Lillian Carattini *school system administrator*
Stutzman, Gladys Blanche *retired secondary school educator, journalist*

Shasta Lake
Parsons, Debra Lea *elementary school educator*

Simi Valley
Cirocco, Angela V. *adult education educator*

Sonoma
Hobart, Billie *education educator, consultant*

Sonora
Sonderman, Elizabeth Louise *literature and language educator, writer*

South Pasadena
Bishop, Carole C. *elementary school educator*
Fuller, Kathy J. *special education educator, consultant, researcher*

Spring Valley
Soltero, Michelle Dolores *director*
Worley, Kathryn Ann *secondary school educator*

Stanford
Ball, Arnetha *education educator*
Barron, Brigid *education educator*
Boaler, Jo *education educator*
Loeb, Susanna *education educator*
Long, Sharon Rugel *dean, molecular biologist, educator*
Lotan, Rachel *education educator*
Stipek, Deborah Jane *dean, education educator*
Strober, Myra Hoffenberg *education educator, consultant*
Wotipka, Christine Min *education educator*

Stockton
Cobb, Judy Lynn *elementary school educator*
Cooper, Iva Jean *special education educator*
Haines, Joybelle *retired elementary school educator*
Hitchcock, Susan Y. *principal*
Mann, Tori *secondary school educator*
Sampson, Lynette Diane *secondary school educator*

Suisun City
Altier, Judith Barrett *middle school educator*

Sunnyvale
Vettel, Cheryl Elynore *mathematics educator*

Taft
Payne, Ruby Mae *secondary school educator*
Walters-Trapasso, Susan Diane *secondary school educator*

Tehachapi
Sprinkle, Martha Clare *elementary school educator*

Temecula
Cherrington, Pamela Jo *special education educator*
Dolan-Jimenez, Mary F. *elementary school educator*
Hogerheiden, Lauren Michelle Valencia *secondary school educator*

Thermal
Montoya, Leiala *assistant principal*

Thousand Oaks
Lieberman, Judith L. *retired special education educator*
Shannon, Barbara Helen *secondary school educator*
Venable, Diane Dailey *retired elementary school educator*

Tracy
Raco, Ellen *secondary school educator*

Tulare
Pinto, Marie Malania *academic administrator, consultant*

Turlock
Antoniuk, Verda JoAnne *secondary school educator*

Tustin
Greene, Wendy Segal *retired special education educator*
Post, Shawn Marie *elementary school educator*

Union City
Fong, Elaine Susan *middle school educator*
Lockhart, Patsy Marie *secondary school educator, consultant*

Upland
Ford, Cheryl Anisia *elementary school educator*

Vallejo
Murillo, Carol Ann *secondary school educator*
Wilson, Carrie Lee Stroud *principal*

Valley Center
Saffiote, Linda *secondary school educator*

Venice
Beery-Polglase, Penelope (Pixie) *education educator*

Victorville
Kildal, Lori Ann *dean*
Moses, Gaye Anita *elementary school educator*
Wristen, Nyala Colleen *elementary school educator*

Vista
Harper, Donna Marie *elementary education and performing arts educator, consultant, special education educator*

Walnut Creek
Carver, Dorothy Lee Eskew (Mrs. John James Carver) *retired secondary school educator*
Fielding, Elizabeth Brown *education educator*
Lilly, Luella Jean *retired academic administrator*

West Covina
Kennelley, Rosario Catherine *secondary school educator*

Whittier
Benavides, Greta Louise *elementary school educator, entrepreneur*
Williams, Jennifer Catherine *elementary school educator*

Willits
Koliner, Frances Eloise *educational administrator*

Winters
Paul, Sally Jones *secondary school educator, writer*

Yorba Linda
Esparza, Karen Ann *history educator*
Lunde, Dolores Benitez *retired secondary school educator*

Yuba City
Leverett, Dawn R. *disability education consultant*
Myers, Nancy Elizabeth *education educator*

COLORADO

Alamosa
Sanchez, Lupita A. *elementary school educator*

Arvada
Bair, Deborah Lynn *primary school educator*
Bert, Carol Lois *retired educational assistant*

Aurora
Berg, Karen Lynn Anderson *elementary school educator*
Bowdish, Colette Elizabeth *secondary school educator*
Hamrick, Eliza Carney *secondary school educator, consultant*
Kellogg Fain, Karen *retired history educator*
Muldrow, Elizabeth Smith *retired secondary school educator, minister*
Sorenson, Katherine Ann *elementary school educator*

Basalt
Brune, Michelle L. *literature and language educator*
Stewart, Ann Burgess *elementary school educator*

Boulder
Borko, Hilda *education educator*
Kennedy, Teresa Jean *academic administrator, educator*
Roberts, Pamela Ranger *secondary school educator*

Carbondale
Arnold, Kathleen Spelts *academic administrator*

Castle Rock
Wilcox, Bonita Diane *middle school educator*

Centennial
Galaznik, Judith Ann *elementary school educator*

Clifton
Taddeo, Lexi-Anne *special education educator*

Colorado Springs
Biggs, Diana *elementary school educator*
DeTurk, Pamela Elizabeth *retired special education educator, elementary school educator*
Hinkle, Betty Ruth *retired academic administrator*
Madsen, Karen F. *retired elementary school educator*

McDade, Roberta Clark *secondary school educator*
Sherman, Louise Rinkob *special education educator*
Shockley-Zalabak, Pamela Sue *academic administrator*
Tesman, Laura Lynn *education educator*

Creede
Wintz, Marilyn Belle *retired elementary school educator*

Denver
Albino, Judith Elaine Newsom *university president*
Burrows, Bertha Jean *retired academic administrator*
Fliss, Julia Wade *elementary school educator, poet*
Gibson, Elisabeth Jane *retired principal*
Jarles, Ruth Sewell *education educator*
Kourlis, Rebecca Love *director, former state supreme court justice*
Larsen, Letitia (Tish) Hoyt *history educator*
Linville, Susan Elizabeth *film studies educator*
Meyer, Norma *secondary school educator*
Rubin, Cathy Ann *retired secondary school educator*
Sather, Sylvia Carolyn *science educator, consultant*
Tiner, Kathy Ann *special education educator*

Dolores
Betts, Dorothy Anne *retired elementary school educator*
Harper, Laura Lee *principal*

Durango
Barter, Mary F. *academic administrator*

Englewood
Graves, Nada Proctor *retired elementary school educator*
Terakedis, Kathryn DeLee *mathematics educator*

Erie
Nichols, Janet Hildreth *elementary school educator, childbirth and parenting educator*

Fort Collins
Colbert, Debora A. *director*
Ricard, Virginia Belle *adult education educator*

Frisco
Yankowski, Kristin Leanne *mathematics educator*

Golden
Chouinard, Karen Reiko *elementary school educator*

Grand Junction
Born, Frances Emmary Hollick *middle school art educator*
Flick, Carol J. *middle school educator*
Woods, Mistie Lynn *secondary school educator*

Greeley
Jackson, Patricia Anne *primary school educator, consultant*
Meis, Jeanette Kay *elementary educator*

Greenwood Village
Lesh-Laurie, Georgia Elizabeth *academic administrator, biology professor, medical researcher*

Highlands Ranch
Brennan, Deborah Dikeman *assistant principal*
Erickson, Linda Rae *elementary school educator*
Torley, Margaret Jean *elementary school educator*

Holly
Sherwood, Louise Kay *literature and language educator*

Lafayette
Elliott, Carolyn Elizabeth *educator, writer*

Lakewood
Joy, Carla Marie *history educator*
Nelson, Deborah Jane *family and consumer science educator*
Reed, Joan-Marie *special education educator*
Stromberg, Patricia Roberts *retired school librarian*
Wallisch, Carolyn E. *principal*
Zachman, Kathleen E. *gifted and talented educator*

Limon
Huffman, Janet Faye *secondary school educator*
Schmeiser, Melva Louise *history educator*

Littleton
Di Manna, Michelle Ann *mathematics educator*
Dinmore, Katherine *principal*
Greenberg, Elinor Miller *director, consultant*
Hurt, Shanna L. *secondary school educator*
Mosier, Cheryl Angeline *secondary school educator, consultant*
Mullarkey, Jill *secondary school educator*
Strother, Cheri L. *secondary school educator*

Longmont
Anderson-Kotts, Judith Anne *academic dean*
Blackwood, Lois Anne *elementary school educator*
Julien, Kristie *mathematics educator, department chairman*
Venrick, Kristie Lund *mathematics educator*

Loveland
Ayers, Kris *secondary school educator*
Geisendorfer, Nancy Kay *mathematics educator*
Lee, Evelyn Marie *elementary school educator, secondary school educator*
Veach, Jennifer Jeanne *elementary school educator*

Montrose
Berryman, Joan Eileen *elementary school educator*
Readout, Rosalee Joyce *retired education educator*

Monument
Engelman, Cylinda Anderson *elementary school educator*

Nederland
Morrison, K. Jaydene *education counseling firm executive*

Northglenn
BeVier Dill, Rene Lorraine *secondary school educator*

Norwood
Brantingham, Andrya J. *special education educator*

Parachute
Leonard, Betsy Ann *director, writer*

Pueblo
Barber, Margaret McAdow *education educator*
Ramirez, Monica E. *education educator, consultant*
Vest, Rosemarie Lynn Torres *secondary school educator*

Saguache
Marold, Judy L. *secondary school educator*

Sanford
Bond, Krista Suzette *secondary school educator*

Seibert
Sears, Joanne Carol *secondary school educator*

Sugar City
McKee, Eleanor Swetnam *retired principal*

Thornton
Bishop, Holly Ann *elementary school educator*

U S A F Academy
Born, Dana H. *dean, career military officer*

Walden
Ary, Bonnita Ellen *registrar, federal official*

Westminster
Bellino-Strickland, Roseanna *secondary school educator*
Dinkey, Laura Lee *literature and language educator*
Rebuehr, Sage Lee *secondary school educator*
Shaeffer, Thelma Jean *primary school educator*
Vizyak, Lindy L. *retired elementary school educator*

Wheat Ridge
Blaschke, Rose Ann *elementary school educator*

Whitewater
Wheeler Russell, Gwendolyn Kay *education educator*

Wiggins
Kammerzell, Susan Jane *elementary school educator, music educator*

CONNECTICUT

Baltic
Cipriani, Rebecca Michele *elementary school educator*

Bloomfield
Baccus, R. Eileen Turner *retired academic administrator*
Bassett, Jean Williams *elementary school educator*
Nelson-Kauffman, Wendy *history educator*

Branford
Johnson, Eva Jo *educational consultant*

Bridgeport
McAuliffe, Catherine A. *counselor, psychology educator, retired psychotherapist*
Orloski, Sharon *secondary school educator*

Bristol
DiCosimo, Patricia Shields *retired secondary school educator*
Donlin, Stephanie Dara Kalish *special education educator*
LaGanga, Donna Brandeis *dean*
Larson, Audra *elementary school educator*

Burlington
Niehoff, Karissa L. *principal*

Cos Cob
McElwaine, Theresa Weedy *academic administrator, artist*
Wilson, Ruth Pester *elementary school educator, researcher*

Coventry
Dimmock, Virginia Ellen *literature and language educator, consultant*
Halvorson, Judith Anne (Judith Anne Devaud) *elementary school educator*

Danbury
Agoora, Lammia Hasson *mathematics educator*
Hawkes, Carol Ann *academic administrator*

Deep River
Nidzgorski, Barbara Helen *gifted and talented educator, puppeteer*

Derby
Bonina, Sally Anne *principal*
Rinaldo, Sharon Ann *special education educator*

East Haven
Dayharsh, Virginia Fiengo *secondary school educator*
Wallach, Carol Odile *elementary school educator*

Enfield
Reuter, Joan Copson *retired program director*

Fairfield
Howell, Karen Jane *private school educator*
Kelly, Colleen Adele *secondary school educator*
Maxwell, Carole Ann *director*
Rinaldi, Jacqueline Blanche *education educator, director*

Falls Village
Purcell, Mary Louise Gerlinger *retired adult education educator*

Farmington
Ford, Burch Tracy *headmaster*

Glastonbury
Cavanaugh, Marianne *secondary educator*
Snyder, Barbara Louise *language arts educator*

Greenwich
Bentley, Lissa Frances *elementary school educator*
Brown, Shannon Elizabeth *mathematics educator*

Groton
Galbraith, Marian *elementary school educator*
Swindell, Dolores Holland *retired school librarian*

Guilford
Sharpe, Kathleen T. *secondary school educator*

Hamden
Blumberg, Betty Lou *education educator*
Hill, Elizabeth Betty *retired secondary school educator*
Mulligan, Dana Mathews *assistant principal*
Oddi, Marie Caporale *educational administrator*
Robson, Carol Ann Shaffner *retired secondary school educator*

Hartford
Brown, Nora M. *elementary school educator*
Hassett, Patricia *university administrator*
Kedderis, Pamela Jean *academic administrator*
Knott-Twine, Laura Mae *director*
O'Brien, Sally Nahas *special education educator, consultant*
Sternberg, Betty J. *school system administrator*
Stuart, Ann *academic administrator, writer, educator*

Lebanon
Sola, Janet Elaine *retired secondary school educator*

Ledyard
O'Keefe, Kerry Ann *elementary school educator*

Manchester
Campbell, Katherine Marie Langrehr *elementary and secondary education educator*
Raffles, Linda N. *secondary school educator*

Middletown
Brown, Judith *academic administrator*
Henry, Lidia Agnieszka *elementary school educator*
Wojtusik, Marylou *special education educator, consultant*

Milford
Sullivan, Christine Anne *secondary school educator*
Yatsinko, Mary Ann *elementary school educator*

Monroe
Kranyik, Elizabeth Ann *secondary school educator*

Naugatuck
Banner-Gray, Marion G. *secondary school educator*
McLaughlin, Elaine M. *elementary school educator*
Sasso, Ruth Maryann *educator*

New Britain
Boyea, Ruthe W. *retired education educator*
Munshi, Nalini Bhat *elementary school educator*

New Canaan
Despres, Louise Fay *secondary school educator*
McKeough, Susan Anne *elementary school educator*

New Fairfield
Lambrech, Régine M. *academic administrator, language educator*

New Haven
Degutis, Linda Christine *adult education educator, epidemiologist, researcher*
Greene, Liliane *literature and language educator, editor*
Hackman, (Mary) Judith Dozier *university administrator, researcher*
Lorimer, Linda Koch *university educator*
McNamara, Julia Mary *academic administrator, foreign language educator*
Norton, Cheryl J. *academic administrator*
Schirmeister, Pamela *dean, language educator*

North Haven
Fuggi, Gretchen Miller *education educator*

Northford
Bonatti, Christine Anne *elementary school educator*
James, Virginia Stowell *retired elementary school educator, retired secondary school educator*

Norwalk
Schaefer-Wicke, Elizabeth *reading consultant, educator*

Oakdale
Greenstein, Laura M. *education educator, department chairman*

Oakville
Moeller, Judith Stone *reading educator, consultant*

Old Mystic
Cassidy, Cindy Jane *secondary school educator*

Pomfret Center
Sweatt, Ermelinda Espinola *retired mathematics educator*

Putnam
Ames, Sandra Cutler *secondary school educator*

Ridgefield
Johnson-Potok, Frieda T. *elementary school educator, consultant*
Lindsay, Dianna Marie *educational administrator*

Shelton
Clark, Mary W. *biology educator*
Kaye, Jennifer A. *elementary school educator, dance educator*

South Windsor
Woods, Barbara O. *mathematics educator*

Southbury
Frost, Deborah E. *elementary school educator*

Southington
Bagwell, Carol Tessier *special education educator, consultant*

Stamford
Handler, Evelyn *consultant, former university president*

Storrs Mansfield
Price, Glenda Delores *dean, college president*

Stratford
Scott, Lorry Ann *elementary education music specialist*

Taconic
Medvecky, Patricia *retired elementary school educator*

Terryville
Doughty-Jenkins, Bonnie-Marie *middle school educator*

Trumbull
Nevins, Lyn (Carolyn A. Nevins) *school disciplinarian*

Vernon Rockville
Davis, Nancy Costello *retired elementary school educator, retired vice principal, adult education coordinator*

Waterbury
Lang, Christine JoAnn *elementary school educator*

West Hartford
Butler, Kathleen A. *education educator, consultant*
Chase, Carol Johnson *mathematics educator*
Coleman, Winifred Ellen *academic administrator*
Gaumond, Lynn E. *elementary school educator*
McAuliffe-Curnias, Susan Eileen *secondary school educator*
Neisler, Otherine Johnson *education educator, consultant*
Salvatore, Nancy Baker *elementary school educator*

West Haven
Janeczek, Mary *secondary school educator, mathematician, department chairman*
Latham, Cynthia *elementary school educator*

Westport
Davidson, JoAnn W. *retired elementary school educator*
Freedman, Judith Greenberg *retired elementary school educator, state legislator*
Huffman, Cathy Lilley *gifted and talented educator, special education educator*
Hunter, Gloria Eleanore *secondary school educator*
Warner, Kerstin Julianna *gifted and talented educator*

Wethersfield
Madigan, Rita Duffy *career planning administrator*

Willimantic
Enggas, Grace Falcetta *academic administrator*

Wilton
Reilly, Kathleen C. *director, retired secondary school educator*

Windsor
Simon, Dorothy Elaine *retired elementary school educator*

Woodbridge
Mahon, Anna Norgren *literature and language educator, coach*
O'Donnell, Janet Costa *secondary school educator*

Woodbury
Bless, Martha M. *secondary school educator, department chairman*
O'Brien, Bonnie Jeanne *counseling administrator*

DELAWARE

Dover
Guliana, Barbara Ann *retired director*
Jones, Geraldine Ann Johnson *secondary school educator*
Royce, Christine Anne *primary school educator*
Sorenson, Liane Beth McDowell *director, state legislator*

Hockessin
Sawin, Nancy Churchman *educational consultant*

Marydel
Whitaker, Susan LaVerne *retired secondary home economics educator*

Milford
Whitman, Ann Elizabeth *retired elementary school educator, education educator*

New Castle
Rolland, Kathy Ann *elementary school educator*
Williamson, Sandra Kaye *education educator*

Newark
Carter, Mae Riedy *retired academic official, consultant*
Keppler, Mary Louise *elementary school educator*

Seaford
Gandek, Jean Davis *secondary school educator*

Wilmington
Baron, Irene Jo *secondary school educator, artist, aerial photographer*
Breland, Elaine *webmaster, retired education specialist, special education educator, webmaster*
Carey, Frances Jane *elementary school educator*
Davis, Patricia Hewson *elementary school educator*
DeHart, Deborah Lee *private school educator, composer*
Freeman, Angela Y. *assistant principal*
Godfrey, Marion Ross *retired special education educator*
Witcher, Phyllis Herrmann *secondary school educator*

DISTRICT OF COLUMBIA

Washington
Acker, Rose L. *elementary school educator*
Anroman, Gilda Marie *college program director, lecturer, educator*
Arnez, Nancy Levi *educational leadership educator*
Berman, Louise Marguerite *education educator, writer*
Bradley, Mary Renee *research analyst*
Brobeck, Susan Williams *private school educator*
Brown, Dorothy M. *academic administrator*
Byrnes, Heidi *academic administrator, German language educator*
Caputo, Anne Spencer *knowledge and learning programs director*
Christian, Mary Jo Dinan *educational administrator, educator*
Cooper, Constance Carter *academic administrator, education consultant, researcher*
Covington, Eileen Queen *secondary school educator*
DePaul, Christina *dean, artist*
Donley, Rosemary *university official*
Duval, Sandra *director*
Feder, Judith *dean*
Fusco, Aurilla Marie *director*
Garrison, Gwen E. *educational researcher, consultant*
Jarvis, Charlene Drew *academic administrator, former scientist*
Jones, Judith Miller *director*
Kirk, Artemis G. *university librarian*
Kirkien-Rzeszotarski, Alicja Maria *academic administrator, researcher, educator*
Manley, Audrey Forbes *retired academic administrator, pediatrician, retired military officer*
Mantyla, Karen *distance learning consultant*
McDowell-Craig, Vanessa Dennise *supervisor, consultant*
Miller, Annie Christmas *secondary school educator*
Miller, Mary Rita *retired adult education educator*
Mohrman, Kathryn j. *academic administrator*
Noonan, Norine Elizabeth *academic administrator, researcher*
Parr, Carol Cunningham *academic administrator*
Petty, Rachel *academic administrator*
Phillips, Susan Meredith *academic administrator, economist*
Ramos, Flavia Sales *education educator, consultant*
Roach, Hildred Elizabeth *education educator*
Smith, Abbie Oliver *college administrator, educator*
Smith-Smith, Peola *principal, not-for-profit executive*
Stewart, Debra Wehrle *academic administrator*
Strange, Sharon Louise *special education educator, musician*
Thomas, Romaine B. *principal, consultant*
Thompson, Bernida Lamerle *principal, consultant, educator*
Titus-Dillon, Pauline Yvonne *associate dean academic affairs, medical educator*
Van Ummersen, Claire A(nn) *academic administrator, biologist, educator*
Weingold, Marjorie Nassau *retired special education educator*

FLORIDA

Altamonte Springs
Keenan, Donna Hummel *elementary school educator*

Apopka
Bentley, Edith Louise *secondary school educator*
Golke-Bahnsen, Morna Raelynne Elsie *secondary school educator*
Nelund, Martha *secondary school educator*

Arcadia
Hardy, Sharon Arlene *elementary school educator, small business owner*

Atlantic Beach
Kelly, Candace Lee *secondary school educator*

Avon Park
Albritton, Evelyn McDonald *elementary school educator*

Bartow
Gano, Janet Anne *secondary school educator*

Boca Raton
Boykin, Anne Jane *dean*
Braisted, Mary Jo *elementary school educator*
Brehm, Patricia Christman *principal*
Comment, Anna Mae *retired principal*
Fabj, Valeria *education educator*
Rebel, Amy Louise *elementary school educator*
Rosenthal, Marilyn *school librarian, educator*
Russ, Fenee L. *principal, consultant*
Shepard, Colleen *elementary school educator*
Speer, Leona Bettina *secondary school educator*

Bonita Springs
Borchers, Janet Marise *elementary school educator, counselor*

Boynton Beach
Deling-Lewis, Elaine Marie *special education educator*
Jones, Shirley Ellen *hearing impaired educator*
Morris, Nancy Lois *elementary school educator*

Bradenton
Driscoll, Constance Fitzgerald *education educator, writer, consultant*

Brandon
Richardson, Michelle Yvette *mathematics educator, mathematics professor*

Brooksville
Saxe, Thelma Richards *secondary school educator, consultant*

Cape Coral
Bradley, Jean Irene *elementary school educator*
Covington, Patricia Ann *university administrator*
Graham, Dorothy E. *elementary school educator*
Mac Master, Harriett Schuyler *retired elementary school educator*
Stoudt, Patricia Lupi *secondary school educator*

Casselberry
Reiss, Deborah L. *elementary school educator*

Clewiston
Burroughs, Jeannette *elementary school educator*
Hamilton, Stefanie Marie *mathematics educator*
Mammen, Mary A. *elementary school educator*

Cocoa
Campbell, Kari Melissa *elementary school educator*
Valverde, Cheryl Lynn *secondary school educator*

Cooper City
Birge, Beverly Harrington *secondary school educator*
Garrard, Patricia Renick *elementary school educator*

Coral Gables
Shalala, Donna Edna *academic administrator, former secretary of health and human services*

Coral Springs
Rachlin Rubin, Joyce Linda *education educator*

Davie
Bromante, Christina Garcia *mathematics educator*

Daytona Beach
Cool, Mary L. *education specialist*
Foushee-Higgs, Rosa *elementary school educator, artist*
Green, Betty Nielsen *education educator, consultant*
Talley, Diane Yvonne *special education educator*
Voce, Joan A. Cifonelli *retired elementary school educator*

De Leon Springs
Price, Artis J. *retired secondary school educator*

Debary
Coble, Alicia Sharon *retired elementary school educator, retired secondary school educator*

Deerfield Beach
O'Brien, Cindy *chemistry educator*

Delray Beach
Hofman, Elizabeth Elveretta *retired mathematics educator, guidance counselor, dean*
Leeds, Susanne *special education educator, writer*
Scherer, Beverly *retired elementary school educator*

Dunedin
Cappiello, Mimi *elementary school educator*
Gamblin, Cynthia MacDonald *mathematics educator, lobbyist*
Pedretty, Catherine Partain *education educator*
Shaneyfelt, Patricia Tharin *elementary school educator*

Eustis
Falanga-Liverotti, Shauna Marie *secondary school educator*

Fort Lauderdale
Calloway, Carolyn *elementary school educator*
Carter, Marjorie Jackson *special education educator, consultant*
Friedman, Marla Ilene *director, educator*
Guest, Suzanne Mary *adult education educator, artist*
Hilburn, Dawn *special education educator*

Spungin, Charlotte Isabelle *retired secondary school educator, writer*
Swann, Elizabeth *director, personal trainer*
Wilbur, Colleen Patricia *elementary school educator, principal*

Fort Myers
Brown, Jaclyn *elementary school educator*
Colgate, Doris Eleanor *sailing school owner, administrator*
Elliot, Kathleen Ann *school system administrator*
Harmon, Elizabeth Oakwood *school system administrator*
Lewellen, Melissa Dawn *elementary school educator*
Robertson, Mary Amos *mathematics educator*

Fort Walton Beach
Hicks, Patricia J. *secondary school educator*

Gainesville
Brown, Myra Suzanne *school librarian*
Dolan, Teresa A. *dean, educator, researcher*
Fouke, Janie M. *academic administrator, educator*
Kirkland, Nancy Childs *secondary school educator, consultant*
Korner, Barbara Oliver *academic administrator*
Linton, Kristy Ann *primary school educator*
Maple, Marilyn Jean *educational media coordinator*
Olsen, Maria Teresa *middle school educator*
Rosenberger, Margaret Adaline *retired elementary school educator, writer*
Saucerman, Alvera Adeline *elementary school educator*

Glen Saint Mary
Bales, Mary Catherine *gifted and talented educator*

Goulds
Taylor, Millicent Ruth *elementary school educator*

Gulfport
Davis, Ann Caldwell *history educator*
Morrison, Marlena *mathematics educator*

Hialeah
Jenkins, Dawn Paula *special education educator, dancer*
Wright, Michelle Beth *elementary school educator*

Hobe Sound
Haus, Judith Ann *elementary school educator*

Holly Hill
Davis, Evangelyn S. *elementary school educator*

Hollywood
Lutchman, Eva *elementary school educator*
Mendez, Deborah *parochial school educator*
Wilson, Linda Edmiston *secondary school science educator*

Homestead
Gray, Tonja Louise *literature and language educator*
Whitehorton, Thelma *educational administrator*

Hudson
Bishop, Mildred Ann *literature and language educator*
Whatley, Yvonne Marie Tramontana *secondary school educator*

Indialantic
Claflin, Tracie Nadine *private school educator*

Inverness
Hawk, Pauletta Browning *elementary school educator*

Jacksonville
Ackerson, Becky Louise *literature and language educator*
Alexander, Edna M. DeVeaux *elementary school educator*
Brown, Beverly Jean *retired elementary school educator*
Brown, Jerri Lynne *history educator*
Cagle, Margaret Broughton *retired parochial school educator*
Feber, Jane Boxer *elementary school educator*
Hughes, Carolyn Wright *elementary school educator, director*
Kinne, Frances Bartlett *academic administrator*
Main, Edna Dewey (June Main) *education educator*
Nelson, Loraine Pratt *principal*
Olin, Marilyn *secondary school educator*
Otto, Elizabeth Hall *education educator*
Rider, Ruth Wheeler *elementary school educator*

Jacksonville Beach
Hill, Joan Ann *retired university administrator*

Jupiter
Loper, Lucia Ann *retired elementary school educator*
Moseley, Karen Frances Flanigan *educational consultant, retired school system administrator, educator*
Szczesny, Marcia Linda *elementary school educator*

Kissimmee
King, Susan Marie *special education educator*
Severance, Jeri-Lynne White *elementary school educator*
Toothe, Karen Lee *elementary and secondary school educator*
Wallace, Evelina Velvia Joetha *elementary school educator*

Lady Lake
Whalen, Norma Jean *special education educator*

Lake Placid
Post, Barbara Joan *elementary school educator*

Lake Worth
Palulis, Christine *biology educator, science educator*

Lakeland
Mason, Lois Ruth *retired elementary school educator*
Stepp, Patricia Joann *middle school educator*
Varner, Marleen Allen *retired academic administrator*

Land O Lakes
Mallon, Kellie Jane *special education educator*

Leesburg
Bolden, Kristin Elizabeth *secondary school educator*
Smith, Kathy L. *elementary school educator, cosmetics executive, consultant*

Longwood
Davis, Lisa *elementary school educator*

Loxahatchee
Russell-Tyson, Pearl Leonie *elementary school educator*

Marco Island
Henry, Sally *academic administrator*
Petry, Barbara Louise Cross *elementary educator*

Marianna
Speights, Lillie *elementary school educator*

Melbourne
Scheuerer, Diane Thompson *home economics educator*
Zabel, Dianne Donnelly *retired elementary school educator*

Merritt Island
Babcock, Hope Smith *counselor, educator, program designer*
Ocker, Debra Lynn *secondary school educator*
Young, Nancy Mayer *retired secondary school educator, artist*

Miami
Banas, Suzanne *middle school educator*
Baugh, Cynthia *elementary school educator*
Brooten, Dorothy *retired dean, nursing educator*
Cortes, Carol Solis *school system administrator*
Falco, Julia Faye *secondary school educator*
Felton, Sandra Haley *special education educator*
Heller, Ellen Distiller *gifted and talented educator*
Jones, Janice Cox *elementary school educator, writer*
Jones-Koch, Francena *school counselor, educator*
Kaelin, Jennifer Ann *secondary school educator*
Kaplan, Betsy Hess *retired school board member*
Leathers, Katherine Anne *education educator*
McLaughlin, Margaret Brown *adult education educator, writer*
Miliani, Lorenna *secondary school educator, social studies educator, writer*
Miller, Constance Johnson *elementary school educator*
Mischia, Marietta Cochran *retired principal*
Patrie, Cheryl Christine *elementary school educator*
Pierre-louis, Rosaire *elementary school educator, writer*
Revis-Pyke, Robin Lynn *director*
Rodriguez, Joanne H. *literature and language educator, department chairman*
Rodriguez, Josefa Nieves *special education educator, language educator*
Rodriguez-Walling, Matilde Barcelo *special education educator*
Stiehm, Judith Hicks *director, political scientist, educator*
Young, Freddie Gilliam *principal, educator*

Miami Beach
Danzis, Rose Marie *emeritus college president*
Foote, Gwendolyn Sue *middle school educator, artist*
Gopman, Beth Alswanger *retired elementary school educator*

Miami Shores
Konczal, Lisa *sociology educator, researcher*

Miramar
Stephens, Sallie L. *retired assistant principal, commissioner*

Naples
Alty, Sally Joan *elementary school educator*
Ball, Kathleen M. *mathematics educator*
Wedel-Cowgill, Millie Redmond *secondary school educator, performing arts educator, communications educator, education educator*

Navarre
McLaughlin, Carolyn Lucile *elementary school educator*

North Lauderdale
Dunham, Laura *elementary school educator*

North Miami Beach
Sorosky, Jeri P. *academic administrator*

North Port
Seiler, Charlotte Woody *retired elementary school educator, language educator*

Oakland Park
Krauser, Janice *special education educator*

Ocala
Delozier, Doris M. *retired secondary school educator*
Fillion, Mary L. *history educator*
Hodges, Elizabeth Swanson *educational consultant, tutor*
Hornick, Susan Florence Stegmuller *secondary education educator, fine arts educator, curriculum specialist, artist*

Simon, Margaret Ballif *elementary school educator, writer*
Westbrook, Rebecca Vollmer *secondary school educator*

Ocoee
Wolfe, Darlene S. *secondary school educator, consultant*

Okeechobee
Raulerson, Phoebe Hodges *school system administrator*

Oldsmar
Zimmer, Barbara S. *elementary school educator*

Opa Locka
Sample, Althea Merritt *secondary education educator, conductor*

Orange City
Kerben, Laura Sarah *middle and secondary school educator*

Orange Park
Combs, Diane Louise *elementary school educator, music educator*

Orlando
Baggott, Brenda Jane Lamb *elementary school educator*
Brown, Diana L. *elementary school educator*
Chacon, Delia C. *secondary school educator*
Charles, Nancy Dufresne *reading educator, consultant*
Davila - Madera, Maria L. *mathematics educator*
Graham, Eleanore Davis *elementary school educator*
Griffith, Jeannette Teresa *elementary school educator, education educator*
Jacobs, Diane Margaret *academic administrator*
Johnson, Estelle Taylor *elementary school educator*
Lee, Susan S. *mathematics educator*
Moss, Kelly Anne *assistant principal*
Raymond, Holly Cabrini *secondary school educator*
Rivera, Maira *elementary school educator*
Scarcella, Karyn Allee *staff developer, instructional coach*
Thomas, Karen E. *elementary school educator*
Wilson, Brenda Marie *secondary school educator*

Ormond Beach
Hoffman, Barbara Dianne *elementary school educator*

Osprey
Myers, Virginia Lou *education educator*

Palm Bay
Boley, Andrea Gail *secondary school educator*
Young, Jane Ann *special education educator*

Palm Beach Gardens
Peck, Maryly VanLeer *retired academic administrator, chemical engineer*

Palm Harbor
Hewitt, Sarah Nichole *educational consultant, researcher*

Panama City
McArthur, Beth Golden *elementary school educator*
Rockhill, Marsha *special education educator*

Pembroke Pines
Allbee, Teresa Jo *elementary school educator*

Pensacola
Dorman, Jo-Anne *elementary school educator*
Galloway, Sharon Lynne *special education educator*
Holloway, Barbara Jean Chambers *retired secondary school educator*
Roycroft, Elizabeth Anne *elementary school educator*
Sisk, Rebecca Benefield *retired secondary school educator, small business owner*

Pompano Beach
Endahl, Ethelwyn Mae *elementary education educator, consultant*
Gross-Brein, Evelyn *counseling administrator, real estate broker*
Henschel, Leonore Katherine *elementary educator*
Johnson, Dorothy Curfman *elementary school educator*
Silverman, Eileen R. *elementary school educator*

Ponte Vedra Beach
Millard, Jeri Killough *educational consultant*

Port Orange
Johnson, Susan F. *elementary school educator*

Port Saint Lucie
Earley, Deborah Loraine *education educator, researcher*
Hunt, Denyse *chemistry educator*

Punta Gorda
Gleason, Joyce Marie *educational consultant*
Lynch, Constance *reading specialist*
Narrett, Carla Marie *university administrator*

Quincy
Pinson, Margaret Ann *special education educator*

Reddick
Romanski, Joyce Marie *secondary school educator, small business owner*

Rockledge
Passmore, Marian *mathematics educator*

Rotonda West
Murnighan, Mary E. *elementary school educator*

Saint Augustine
Sappington, Sharon Anne *retired school librarian*

Saint Leo
Parrish, Patricia Anne *education educator*

Saint Petersburg
Anderson, Dawn Marie *elementary school educator*
Dinsdale, Carol Ellen *special education educator*
Dunlap, Karen F. Brown *academic administrator*
Frump, Stefanie L. *elementary school educator*
Geissler, Kristiana Andrea *secondary school educator*
Gregg, Kathy Kay *school system administrator*
Layton, Polly Kersker *mathematics educator, language educator*
McArdle, Barbara Virginia *elementary school educator*
Smith, Betty Robinson *retired elementary school educator*
Williams, Minnie Caldwell *retired special education educator*
Young, June Hurley *elementary school educator, writer*

San Antonio
Will, Betty *elementary school educator*

San Mateo
Pounds, Janice Jones *elementary school educator*

Sanford
Levings, Christine Romano *secondary school educator, real estate developer*
Tossi, Alice Louise *special education educator*

Sarasota
Buchanowski, Teresa Lorraine *retired elementary school educator*
Feldhusen, Hazel Jeanette *elementary school educator*
Hentz, Susan Marie *private school educator, consultant*
Noller, Ruth Brendel *retired education educator, consultant, researcher*
St. John, Terri *secondary school educator*
Scanlon, Janice Lynn *retired gifted and talented educator*
Thompson, Annie Figueroa *retired academic administrator*

Satellite Beach
Molledo, Magdalena Ferreira *elementary school educator*

Sebastian
Keaton, Jessica J. *secondary school educator*

Sebring
Parrett, Janelle Swilley *secondary school educator*

Seminole
Schmitz, Dolores Jean *primary school educator*

Spring Hill
Pearson, Clara *elementary school educator, music educator*

Stuart
Stimmell, Anne Krueger *special education educator*

Sugarloaf
Greenberg, Linda Garrett *education educator, volunteer, singer*

Summerfield
Lee, Ann McKeighan *curriculum specialist*

Tallahassee
Waas, Harriet Issner *elementary school educator*

Tamarac
Brown Thomas, Rynn *elementary school educator*
Galipault, Lorraine D. *adult education educator*

Tampa
Allison, Pamela A. *mathematics educator*
Andrews, Janice D. *elementary school educator*
Branch, Mary Fletcher Cox *secondary school educator*
Erickson, Linda E. *retired academic administrator*
Lawson, Mary Carolyn *elementary school educator*
Loiselle, Joan Brenda *elementary school educator, art educator*
Luddington, Betty Walles *school library media specialist*
McGee, Nancy Pyle *college administrator, fashion designer, department chairman, artist*
Olson, Candy *school system administrator*
Pauly, Jennifer L. *director, graphics designer*
Shedrick, Alberta Loretta *elementary school educator*
Weisman, Diane Boyd *elementary school educator*

Tarpon Springs
Keller-Augsbach, Linda Jean *elementary school educator*

Tavares
Wilkins, Martha Ann *secondary school educator*

Tequesta
Hires, Cheryl Lynn *literature and language educator*

Titusville
McDonald, Theresa Elizabeth *secondary school educator*

Treasure Island
White, Donna Annette *retired secondary school educator*

Trinity
Akin, Donna Rae *retired elementary school educator*

Valparaiso
Salsbury, Donna Denise *elementary school educator*

Valrico
Straub, Susan Monica *special education educator*

Venice
Felker, Ouida Jeanette Weissinger *special education educator*

Vero Beach
Buker, Virginia Frances *elementary school educator*
Harris, Nancy Lee *special education educator, behavior analyst*
Wilson, Carol Perkins *principal*

Wesley Chapel
Grimes-Davis, Danna Elizabeth *elementary school educator, consultant*

West Palm Beach
Blanchette, Beverly Beckman *dean, theater educator*

Weston
Adams-Sallustio, Patricia Jayne *elementary school educator*

Wewahitchka
de Abreu, Sue *elementary school educator*

Winter Garden
Carter, Audrey E. *secondary school educator*
Gillet, Pamela Kipping *special education educator*

Winter Park
Bornstein, Rita *academic administrator*
Williams, Nan Parker *secondary school educator*

Winter Springs
McNeal, Mary Kay *secondary school educator*

Zephyrhills
Barron, Ilona Eleanor *secondary school educator, consultant*

GEORGIA

Acworth
Johnson, Melissa Ann *special education educator*

Adairsville
Martin, Kristen Lacey *secondary school educator*

Albany
Adams-Cooper, Veronica Lynn *education educator, foundation administrator*
Forsyth, Rosalyn Moye *middle school educator*
Shields, Portia Holmes *academic administrator*
Willis, Jakie Arleta *secondary school educator*

Alpharetta
Filliat, Elizabeth Hartley *retired secondary school educator*
Moore, Victoria Eberhard *elementary school educator*

Athens
Allen, Sheila W. *dean*
Jacobsen, Karen Lee *educator, researcher, veterinarian*
Kurtz, Mary Denise Bates *secondary school educator*
Mullis, Rebecca *education educator, department chairman*
West, Marsha *elementary school educator*
White, Rebecca Hanner *dean, law educator*

Atlanta
Bellamy, Ivory *elementary school educator, consultant*
Betts, Jennifer Leah *secondary school educator*
Blum, Terry C. *dean*
Brice Ross, Carla Yvette *school counselor*
Cilella, Mary Winifred *director*
Cox, Kathy *school system administrator*
Day, Janet S. *academic administrator*
Delaney-Lawrence, Ava Patrice *secondary school educator*
Gordon, Jasmine Rosetta *elementary school educator*
Hall, Beverly L. *school system administrator*
Harper, Margaret Mills *educator*
LaDuke, Bettie *academic administrator*
Landers, Heather Renee *elementary school educator*
Langston, Sheila Annette *special education educator, consultant*
Lucas, M. Frances *university administrator*
McSwain, Georgia Haygood *educational program specialist, consultant*
Meyer, Ellen L. *academic administrator*
Mogabgab, Rose-Warren Berryman *academic administrator, writer*
Rosenfeld, Rhoda Lynn *reading specialist*
Towslee, Janet L. *special education educator*
Van Atta, Mary Carter *secondary school educator*
Waronker, Cecile C. *secondary school educator*
Welsh, Melanie Millen *secondary school educator*

Augusta
Drisko, Connie Lee Hastings *dean, dental educator*
Jackson, Rosa M. *retired elementary school educator*

Austell
Lunaburg, Diane Gayle *chemistry educator*
Vance, Sandra Johnson *secondary school educator*

Blairsville
Stainback, Susan Bray *education educator*

Bonaire
James, Dianne *mathematics educator*

Bowdon
Sanders, Janet Ruth *elementary school educator*

Brunswick
Essick, Carol Easterling *elementary school educator*
Gillis, Rhonda Radford *elementary school educator*

Buchanan
Vickie, Cash C. *elementary school educator*

Buena Vista
Jernigan, Melissa McGlaun *secondary school educator*

Camilla
Daniels, Deloria *elementary school educator*

Canton
Coleman, Sharon W. *elementary school educator*
Lawrence, Karen K. *mathematics educator*

Cartersville
Wheeler, Susie Weems *retired school system administrator*

Cataula
Averill, Ellen Corbett *retired secondary education science educator, administrator*

Cedartown
Renshaw, Judith Ann *special education educator, school system administrator*

Chamblee
Alexander, Dawn Jo *middle school educator*

Chatsworth
Bishop, Pamela June *elementary school educator*

Cleveland
Steele, Vicki Lynn *educator*
Swing, Amy Eileen *elementary school educator*

College Park
Bates, Carol Garrison *secondary school educator*
McDonald, Deborah Alyse *mathematics educator*

Columbus
Duncan, Frances Murphy *retired special education educator*
Hoyseth, Luann Rose *secondary school educator*
Riggsby, Dutchie Sellers *education educator*
Tidd, Joyce Carter *etiquette educator*

Conyers
Greco, Mary Cebulski *elementary school educator*
Grider, Rhonda Patriece *elementary school educator, writer*
Jones, Cheryl E. *secondary school educator*
Smith-Porter, Suzanne Clare *mathematics educator*

Covington
Sauls Rains, Amy *elementary school educator*

Dallas
Dunton, Ouida Luedtke *secondary school educator, department chairman*

Dalton
Ford, Katherine Michelle *special education educator*
Smith, Janet Susannah *literature and language educator, department chairman*
Tyl, Jennifer Amanda *special education educator*

Decatur
Kiss, Elizabeth *academic administrator, philosophy educator*
Marshall, Priscilla Jackson *elementary school educator*

Demorest
Rogers, Elizabeth (Betty) Carlisle *education educator, consultant*

Douglasville
Allen, Mia Florence *health and physical education educator*
Jackson, Cynthia Williford *special education educator*
Smith, Stephanie Renae *middle school educator*

Dublin
McGruder, Tecia Adrienne *assistant principal*

Duluth
Cannon, Sherry Cloud *special education educator*
Pickett, Christa Langford *elementary school counselor*

Eastman
Hall, Lula *retired special education educator*

Eatonton
Digby, Pamela Annette *elementary school educator*

Evans
McCorkle, Pamela Loveridge *elementary school educator*
Orlet, Veronica Lynne *secondary school educator*
Owen, Shaun Sonia *elementary school educator, small business owner, consultant*
Peebles, Betty Lea *secondary school educator*
Stout, Elva Carolyn Fraser *elementary school educator*

Fayetteville
Eller, Karen Kreimann *elementary school educator*

Fort Oglethorpe
Lane, Darlene Kelley *history educator*

Fort Valley
Monroe, Sandra Elaine *retired secondary art educator, minister*

Gainesville
Floyd, Hazel McConnell *special education educator*

Griffin
Nelson, Muriel Yvette *elementary school educator*
Totman, Sharon Taylor *special education educator*

Hamilton
Hrncir, Jennifer Welch *elementary school educator*
Hubbard, Carla Dawn *secondary school educator*

Hartwell
Royston, Pamela Jean *special education educator*

Hiawassee
Brumbaugh, Melissa Beth *elementary school educator*

Holly Springs
Neal, Teresa *school counselor, educator*

Homer
Dague, Teresa *elementary school educator, music educator*

Hoschton
Osburn, Ella Katherine *elementary school educator*

Ila
Greene, Sheree' Jeane *elementary school educator, consultant*

Jackson
Rowe, Joyce *principal*

Jasper
Cagle, Glenda Johnston *elementary school educator*
Crotta, Annette Gunter *retired educator*

Jeffersonville
Hawthorne, Sarah Beck *reading educator*

Jonesboro
Perez, Maritza E. *elementary school educator*

Kennesaw
Lambert, Emily Jenkins *elementary school educator*
Mitchell, Judith Ann *education educator*
Siegel, Betty Lentz *university president*

La Fayette
Roerdink, Lisa Marie *elementary school educator*

Lagrange
Ault, Ethyl Lorita *special education educator, consultant*
Sankar, Lakshmi *special education educator*

Lake Park
Blanton, Vallye J. *elementary school educator*

Lawrenceville
Crain, Mary Ann *elementary school educator*
Edelberg, Mary *elementary school educator*
Harris, Melba Iris *elementary school educator, secondary school educator, state agency administrator*
Harsh, Alexis Goodsell *middle school educator*

Lilburn
Bendelius, Bonnie Sue *elementary school educator*
Cohorst, Lisa Moseley *elementary school educator*

Lindale
LeRoy, Judy Wright *middle school educator*

Lithonia
Childs, Mattie Sue *mathematics educator*
Jones, Elizabeth Flanigan *literature and language educator*
Marion, Bernice Alexander *elementary school educator*

Locust Grove
Lloyd, Tracy Ann *secondary school educator*

Macon
Baima, Julie Martin *special education educator*
Floyd, Daisy Hurst *dean, law educator*
Lengel, Elizabeth Hilscher *behavior specialist*
Pilcher, Christie W. *special education educator*
Shomaker, Andrea Kay *secondary school educator*

Madison
Short, Betsy Ann *elementary school educator*

Manchester
Gill, Kelley Henderson *elementary school educator*

Marietta
Kellogg, Mary Marjorie *retired special education educator, supervisor*
Laframboise, Joan Carol *middle school educator*
Overstreet, Regina Nix *mathematics educator*
Rivers, Alma Faye *secondary school educator*
Robotham, Sattanya A. *private school educator*
Rossbacher, Lisa Ann *academic administrator*
Whitlock, Betty *retired secondary school educator*
Wright, Judith Diane *elementary school educator*

Maysville
Herriman, Jean Ann *elementary school educator*

Mcdonough
Brown, June Dyson *retired elementary school educator, principal*
Mauney, Brandi Savage *special education diagnostician*
Riffel, Laura Ann *director, special education educator*

Milledgeville
Hill, Helen Marguerite Thacker *academic administrator*

Leland, Dorothy *academic administrator*
Nunn, Cynthia S. *history educator*
Werts, Ruby Woodward *elementary school educator*

Morganton
Davis, Sarah C. *elementary school educator*

Mount Airy
Sweatman, Wendy Leigh *secondary school educator*

Mount Vernon
Parker, Lisa E. *elementary school educator, gifted and talented educator*

Newnan
Smith, Betty Ann Ingram *elementary school educator*

Peachtree City
Eichelberger, Lisa Wright *academic administrator, nursing educator*
Saulsbury, Glynis Elliott *elementary school educator*

Pearson
Delk, Charlotte Turley *elementary school educator*

Perry
Anderson, Denise Lynn *elementary school educator*

Pinehurst
Lowery, Laurie Blount *elementary school educator*

Powder Springs
Gaddy, Sarah Ann *elementary school educator*

Riverdale
Bean, Calandra LeShun *mathematics educator*
Warren, Barbara Denise *special education educator*
Wilson-Hunt, Simone Sonya Yevette *elementary school educator*

Rockmart
West, Melanie Kim *elementary school educator*

Rome
Jones, Christa Walker *special education educator*
Knox, Barbara S. *education educator*
Perdue, Judy Clark *academic administrator*
Slack, Clemontene *education educator*
Stubblefield, Jenny Rebecca *educator*
Walker Vickers, Stephanie Carole *special education educator*

Roopville
Huckeba, Emily Causey *retired elementary school educator*

Rossville
Knight, Marsha Dianne *special education educator*

Roswell
Hoskinson, Carol Rowe *middle school educator*

Saint Marys
Hall, Lois Bremer *secondary school educator, volunteer*

Sandersville
Dunn, Mary Ann *mathematics educator*

Savannah
Hinson, Marvis Thedoria *education educator*
Polite, Evelyn C. *retired elementary school educator, evangelist*
Postell, Cindy Deborah *secondary school educator*
Runge, Linda Jacob *university administrator*
Wallace, Paula S. *academic administrator*

Silver Creek
Edwards, Kandace Necole *secondary school educator*

Smyrna
English, Candace Allen *assistant principal*

Snellville
Blankenship, Colleen Marie-Krick *secondary school educator, writer*

Social Circle
Cannon, Constance Marie *literature and language educator*

Springfield
Hill, Lynda McSeveney *mathematics educator*

Stockbridge
Seagraves, Karen Denise *elementary school educator*
Sprayberry, Roslyn Raye *retired secondary school educator*

Stone Mountain
Brown, Rhonda Jean *special education educator*
Jones, Ellen *elementary school educator*
Slaughter, Gloria Jean *elementary school educator*
Wright, Pauline M. *elementary school educator, consultant*

Suwanee
Stanley, Gwen G. *elementary school educator*
Wing, Kerensa Shoemake *secondary school educator, assistant principal*

Temple
Elliott, Teri Michelle *elementary school educator*

Thomasville
Finland, Christine Elaine *school counselor*

Tifton
Robinson, Kristina Parker *secondary school educator*

Tiger
Ring, Yvonne Ann *special education educator*

Toccoa Falls
Gardner, Donna Rae (Diehl) *education educator*
Hoffman, Ruth Elaine *mathematics educator*

Tucker
Stewart, Connie Ward *retired academic administrator*

Union City
Drake-Hamilton, Lillie Belle *retired secondary school educator*

Valdosta
Burnette, Ada M. Puryear *program coordinator*

Vidalia
Hodge, Sharon Denise *mathematics educator*

Villa Rica
Gaston, Barbara Lovell *elementary school educator*

Watkinsville
Smith, Vivian *elementary school educator*

Waycross
Copeland, Elizabeth Jane *special education educator*

West Point
Albarado, Rebecca Hill *elementary school educator*
Hart, Brenda Rebecca *retired gifted and talented educator*

Whitesburg
Nicholson, Diane M. *special education educator*

Winder
Michael, Claire Patricia *director*

Woodstock
Barthlow, Michelle Jones *political science educator*
Ross, Jennifer Jo *science educator*

HAWAII

Hana
Stevens, Muriel Kauimaeole Lee *elementary school educator*

Hilo
Tseng, Rose *academic administrator*

Honolulu
Gonsalves, Margaret Leboy *elementary school educator*
Grabowsky, Gail Leanne *education educator, consultant*
Hamamoto, Patricia *school system administrator, educator*
Ingersoll, Caroline Yee *director*
Lee, Joelle L.K. *elementary school educator*
Migimoto, Fumiyo Kodani *retired secondary school educator*
Silva, Mary Barnes *retired elementary school educator*
Udarbe, Christine *registrar*
Uejo, Colleen Misaye *elementary school educator*
Waslien, Carol Irene *educator, academic administrator*
Wee, Christine Dijos *elementary school educator*
Wesselkamper, Sue *academic administrator*

Kailua
Brown, Kaori Akamine *principal*
Carlisle, Darla Jean *elementary school educator, consultant*
Ivey, Andi *special education educator*
Tubbs, Mary S. *curriculum coordinator*

Kailua Kona
Spitze, Glenys Smith *retired teacher and counselor*

Kalaheo
Nakashima, Joanne Pumphrey *retired education administrator*

Kaneohe
Ashley, Elizabeth *dean, educator*
LaMarchina, Marilynne May *elementary school educator*

Kapaa
Caspillo, Carol A. *secondary school educator*

Keaau
Kiefer, Cheryl Lynn *elementary school educator*

Kula
Mossman, Karolyn R. *elementary school educator*

Mililani
Yuasa, Sheila Thalassa *literature and language educator*

Waianae
Sakihara, Sandra I. *middle school educator*

Wailuku
Shimabukuro, Grace Kuo *mathematics educator*

IDAHO

Aberdeen
Latsch, Nicole L. *elementary school educator*

Bancroft
Rindlisbaker, Candace May *elementary school educator*

Bellevue
Jones, Krista Marie *elementary school educator*

Blackfoot
Law, Kathleen Sue *elementary school educator*

Boise
Griffin, Sylvia Gail *reading specialist*
Howard, Marilyn *state school system administrator*
McClain, Jennifer C. *middle school educator*
Pollard, Constance Jo *education educator*

Coeur D' Alene
Macey-Caloca, Patricia Ann *secondary school educator*

Craigmont
Niemela, April Joy *secondary school educator*

Emmett
Richards, Vana Jean *elementary school educator*

Glenns Ferry
Crum, Glenda M. *elementary school educator*
Dodge, Teresa Ann *elementary school educator*

Idaho Falls
Cannon, Mary Alice *literature and language educator*
Robson-McCoy, Jeanie Ann *secondary school educator*
Rowberry, Connie *secondary school educator*

Jerome
Rice, Melissa Ann *mathematics educator*

Kimberly
Pack, Suzanne Christina *elementary school educator*

Meridian
LeDoux, Patricia Renee *elementary school educator, science educator*
Oliver, Darla Deane *elementary school educator*
Pence, Linda Carol *mathematics educator*
Wilper, Kimberly Dawn *elementary school educator*

Middleton
Brown, Ilene De Lois *special education educator*

Midvale
Sutton, Lois Gene *elementary school educator*

Moscow
Sebald, Jama Lynn *academic administrator*

Mountain Home
Martin, Susan Jane *secondary school educator*

Nampa
Hopkins, Martha Jane *retired education educator*
Rau, Shirley A. *secondary school educator*

Pocatello
Balls, Tedra Merrill *secondary school educator*
Bodily, Kim Gaylen *secondary school educator*
Crook, Lorraine Parker *secondary school educator*
Gebo, Emma Marie Joki *education educator*
McCune, Mary Joan Huxley *microbiology educator*
Robinson, Evelyn Etta *principal*

Post Falls
Mikles, Chris *secondary school educator*

Rexburg
Dick, Deborah Jean *elementary school educator*

Rogerson
Boss, Marylin Jeanette *elementary school educator*

Sandpoint
Wills, Beth Louise *elementary school educator, social worker*

Twin Falls
Callentine, Katherine Naomi *elementary school educator*
Mathews, Donna Mae *special education educator*
McGregor, Wendolyn Suzanne *elementary school educator, mathematician*

ILLINOIS

Addison
Evert, Margaret Jane *principal*

Algonquin
Weeks, Heidi K. *mathematics educator*

Alton
Boyle, Ann M. *dean, dental educator*

Arlington Heights
Kopielski, Camille Ann *counseling administrator, volunteer*
Kramer, Sybil Jean *elementary school educator, writer*
Pasieka, Anne W. *elementary school educator*
Yonkus, Jo Marie Maiorano *secondary school educator*

Aurora
Cisar, Margaret *special education educator*
Daugherty, Patricia Ann *retired elementary school educator*
Easley, Pauline Marie *retired elementary school educator*
Gudgeon, Valerie A. *school system administrator*
Powell, Kathryn A. *mathematics educator, athletic trainer*
Spencer, Kathryn Rose *secondary school educator*
Zaininger, Lucie E. *elementary school educator*

Barrington
Roland, Regina E. *elementary school educator, educational consultant*

Bartonville
Dina, Gwendolyn Judith *special education educator*

Batavia
Schulz, Jill Ann *elementary school educator*

Belleville
Mallette, Jennifer Denise *mathematics educator*

Belvidere
Koch, Carol Sue *middle school educator*

Berwyn
Nicholson, Rosann *gifted and talented educator*

Bethalto
Sabaj, Nancy J. *secondary school educator*

Bismarck
Sellers-Evans, Cynthia *literature and language educator*

Bloomington
Mosher, Donna Prescott *retired secondary school educator*

Bradley
Januski, Laurie A. *secondary school educator*
Mesengring, Tammie Lynn *elementary school educator*

Broadview
Bland, Pamela June *special education educator*

Buffalo Grove
Young, Kathleen Marie *special education educator*

Burbank
Parlin-McSharry, Barbara Ann *mathematics educator*

Byron
Schmitt, Diana Lynn *secondary school educator*

Cahokia
Butler, Donna Marcia *mathematics educator*
Williams, Cynthia Denise *secondary school educator*

Carbondale
Pinter, Susann Barbara *education educator*
Quisenberry, Nancy Lou *academic administrator, educator*
Scott, Shirley Clay *dean*
Snyder, Carolyn Ann *education educator, librarian, director*

Carlinville
Pride, Miriam R. *college president*

Carterville
Minton, Jane Isabelle *education educator*

Caseyville
Dayton, Jean *principal*

Catlin
Asaad, Kolleen Joyce *special education educator*

Champaign
Hurd, Heidi M. *dean, humanities educator, law educator*
Loeb, Jane Rupley *academic administrator, educator*
Monda-Amaya, Lisa Ellen *education educator*
Pickard, Karen K. *parochial school educator*
Rooney, Gail Schields *academic administrator*

Charleston
Surles, Carol D. *academic administrator*

Chatham
Correll, Sally Ruth *elementary school educator*

Chicago
Baley, Joan Marie *elementary school educator*
Beane, Marjorie Noterman *academic administrator*
Bowman, Barbara Taylor *early childhood educator*
Brawner, Cynthia D. *elementary school educator*
Brown, Catherine Alletto *elementary school educator*
Cafferty, Pastora San Juan *education educator*
Carroll, Margaret Kelly *education educator*
Carter, Christine *retired assistant principal*
Casey, Linda Susan *school system administrator*
Chanyungco, Delly Yangco *dean*
Cooper, Jo Marie *principal*
Cueto, Rochelle E. *elementary school educator*
Culp, Kristine Ann *dean, theology studies educator*
Cummings, Maxine Gibson *elementary school educator*
Daniel, Elnora D. *academic administrator*
Davis, Addie L. *mathematics educator*
Douglas, Cynthia *academic administrator*
Dowling, Mary Kathleen *elementary school educator*
Dynek, Kathleen Marie *elementary school educator*
Feig, Barbara Krane *elementary school educator, author*
Freedman, Joyce Beth *academic administrator*
Gajic, Ranka Pejovic *secondary school educator*
Gantz, Suzi Grahn *special education educator*
Gramer, Dorothy Anne *secondary school educator*
Gray, Lucy *secondary school educator*
Harris, Shirley *elementary school educator, secondary school educator, adult education educator*
Hawkins, Loretta Ann *retired secondary school educator, playwright*
Hayes, Alice Bourke *academic administrator, biologist, researcher*
Heydecker, Jeanne-Elise Marie *school district coordinator, traditional and web marketing executive*
Hunter Harris, Phyllis Irene *retired secondary school educator*
Jackson, Geraldine *literature and language educator*
Kastiel, Elizabeth Maria *assistant principal*
Kaufman, Donna A. *elementary school educator*
Kubistal, Patricia Bernice *educational consultant*
Kumor, Michelle *special education educator*
Landerholm, Elizabeth Jane *early childhood education educator*
Levandowski, Barbara Sue *education educator*
Lusk, Peggy June *retired counseling administrator*
Mahaley-Johnson, Hosanna *school system administrator*
Malcolm, Christine Anne *university hospital administrator*
Mayo, Cora Louise *educator*
McMath, Lula Wray *retired elementary school educator, realtor*
Mell, Patricia *dean*
Mindes, Gayle Dean *education educator*
Mosley, Elaine Christian Savage *principal, consultant*
Nadler, Judith *school librarian*
Noesen, Darlene Dorothy *mathematics educator*
Petrakos, Joan *elementary school educator*
Rhone, Elvie Sue *educational administrator*
Roberts, Jo Ann Wooden *school system administrator*
Rothman-Denes, Lucia Beatriz *biology educator*
Sampey, Debra A. *middle school principal*
Satish, Susany *biology educator*
Sessions, Joan T. *director, educator*
Steinberg, Salme Elizabeth Harju *academic administrator, historian*
Storti, Pamela *elementary school educator*
Wyndewicke, Kionne Annette (Annette Johnson Moorer) *reading educator*
Zainelli, Gina M. *education educator*

Chicago Heights
Buishas, Kristin Maureen *elementary school educator*

Chicago Ridge
Socha, Maureen Patricia *elementary school educator*

Clifton
Shifflet, Nicole R. *secondary school educator*

Collinsville
Graebe, Annette Mulvany *retired university administrator, professor emeritus*
Kossina, Mary Helen *elementary school educator*
Massa, Martha Joann *retired elementary school educator*

Country Club Hills
Crimmins-Snyder, Caroline Jean *secondary school educator, paralegal*

Crystal Lake
Haas, Sheila Jean *secondary school educator*

Deerfield
Meyer, Mara Ellice *special education educator, consultant, academic administrator*

Dekalb
Koenig, Heidi O. *public administration professor*
McIntire, Penny A. Kendall *education educator*
Simmons, Deborah Anne *environmental educator*

Des Plaines
Lee, Margaret Burke *college president, language educator*

Dixon
Anderson, Marion LeBlanc *history educator*
Vivian, Shirley Full *secondary educator*

Dow
Schuler, Dorothy R. *education educator, consultant, retired elementary school educator*

Downers Grove
Blei, Laurie N. *counseling administrator*
LaRocca, Patricia Darlene McAleer *middle school educator*
Poetzel, Susan Marie *elementary school educator*

Du Quoin
Ibendahl, Jean Ayres *retired elementary and secondary educator*

Dunlap
Lueschow, Sarah Lynne *biology educator*
McCann, Louise A. *mathematics educator*
Pardieck, Sherrie Chan *education educator*

Dwight
Coulter, Carol Ann *retired secondary school educator*
Rosenbaum, Linda Jean *elementary school educator*

East Alton
DiPaolo, Marcella Kay *elementary school educator*

East Saint Louis
Wright, Katie Harper *educational administrator, journalist*

Elgin
Aydt, Mary I. *secondary school educator*
Johnson, Jacquelyn Marie *elementary school educator*
Scherger, Nicole *mathematics educator*
Thompson, Phyllis Darlene *retired elementary school educator*

Elmhurst
Nega, Nancy Kawecki *middle school science educator*

Winnetka
Huggins, Charlotte Susan Harrison *retired secondary school educator, writer, travel company executive*
McKee, Judith Nelson *elementary school educator, educational consultant*
Roush, Michelle Beason *secondary school educator*

Woodstock
Fain, Nicole M. *elementary school educator*
Totz, Sue Rosene *secondary school educator*

INDIANA

Anderson
Nicholson, Dorothy Nelis *retired pre-school educator*

Angola
Blaz, Deborah *secondary school educator, writer*
Deller, Rita Willennar *elementary school educator*

Auburn
Chagnon, Marjorie Marie *retired elementary school educator*

Avon
Lucas, Georgetta Marie Snell *retired educator, artist*
McKenzie, Ellen Porter *elementary school educator, consultant*

Bloomington
Bornholdt, Laura Anna *academic administrator*
Ochoa-Becker, Anna S. *education educator*
Palmer, Judith Grace *university administrator*
Robel, Lauren *dean, law educator*
Steele, Patricia Ann *dean, librarian*

Carmel
Brooks, Patricia Scott *principal*
Dotzert, Jennifer Marie *special education educator*
Slocum, Laura Elizabeth *chemistry educator*
Vargas-Williams, Traci Junelle *special education educator*
Yost, Brandy Diana *secondary school educator*

Chesterfield
Sellers, Angela *mathematics educator*

Crown Point
Ciochina, Debra A. *secondary school educator*

East Chicago
Fortenberry, Delores B. *dean*
Suhre, Edith Lavonne *adult education educator*

Elwood
Toney, Brenda Sue *special education educator*

Evansville
Hallock Morris, Mary Theresa *education educator*
Overton, Sharon Faye *elementary school educator*

Floyds Knobs
Berry, Dale M. *physical education specialist*
Egbert, Donna *elementary school educator*

Fort Wayne
Butler, Sally Kathryn *history educator*
Cummins, Kathleen K. *retired elementary school educator*
Hamrick, Linda L. *secondary school educator*
Robinson, Wendy Y. *school system administrator*

Frankfort
Sayers Butler, Patricia Ann *secondary school educator*

Franklin
Moore, Beth A. *education educator*
Stone, Mary Ann *literature and language educator*

Frankton
Beck, Neva Ann *retired special education educator*

Gary
Jones, Angela M. *secondary school educator, elementary school educator*
Knight, Harriette *secondary educator*
Reed, Charlotte *education educator, consultant*
Steele, Beverly J. *elementary school educator*

Geneva
Roughia, Ginger Lou *elementary school educator*

Granger
Morgan, Ardys Nord *school improvement consultant*

Greencastle
Rayce, Valerie Lynn *secondary school educator*

Griffith
Luetschwager, Mary Susan *educational consultant*

Hammond
Delph, Donna Jean (Donna Maroc) *education educator, consultant, academic administrator*
Singer, Sandra Manes *university administrator*

Hebron
Brooker, Nancy *literature and language educator*

Highland
DeVaney, Cynthia Ann *retired elementary school educator, real estate instructor*
Farag, Maureen Ann *assistant principal*
Gregory, Marian Frances *retired elementary school educator, retired principal*
Mach, Michele R. *special education educator*

Indianapolis
Adesiyan, Hattie Rose Olagbegi *education educator, consultant*
Barcus, Mary Evelyn *primary school educator*
Blanchfield, Kelly L. *adult education educator*
Burdine, Linda Sharon *secondary school educator, writer*
Chandler, Julie Light *secondary school educator*
Duncan-Ladd, Georgia Jones *elementary school educator*
Fox, Patricia Sain *academic administrator*
Gooldy, Patricia Alice *retired elementary school educator*
Huffman, Cindy Kay *elementary school educator*
Keaton, Margaret-Ann Coleman *education educator*
Malone, Jean Hambidge *educational consultant*
McClelland, Amy Kennard *elementary school educator*
Mead, Susanah M. *dean*
Moser, Barbara Jo *elementary school educator*
Najjar, Diana *elementary school educator*
Nehez, Susan Springman *elementary school educator*
Orban, Kimberlie W. *elementary school educator*
Osborn, Kristy Lynn *elementary school educator*
Pitts, Beverley J. *academic administrator*
Pruett, Lindy Newton *special education educator*
Reed, Suellen Kinder *school system administrator*
Sandberg, Marilyn Lee *special education educator*
Shuman, Lois Anna *educational coordinator*
Solomon, Marilyn Kay *primary school educator, consultant, small business owner*
Strauss, Diane Jayne *retired elementary and secondary school educator, small business owner*
Sullender, Joy Sharon *retired elementary school educator*
Sykes, Linda Diane *elementary school educator, music educator*
Thiele, Michelle Renee *special education educator*
Vann, Lora Jane *retired reading educator*
Watkins, Sherry Lynne *elementary school educator*
Westenfelder, Harriet Ellen *retired elementary school educator*
Whitfield, Erica Sharon *director, career planning administrator*
Whitis, Cynthia M. *secondary school educator*
Williams, Luida K. *retired elementary school educator*

Jasonville
Collins, Katherine Louise *elementary school educator*

Jasper
Luebbehusen, Tina Marie *secondary school educator*

Jeffersonville
Taylor, Andrea Reed *elementary school educator*

Kentland
Molter, Karen S *literature and language educator*

Kouts
Miller, Sarabeth *secondary school educator*

La Porte
Hunter, Debora Ann Brobeck *secondary school educator*

Ladoga
Allen, Marilyn Kay *elementary school educator*

Lafayette
Luenz, Pamela Marie *educator*
McLean, Cheryl L. *physics educator*

Lebanon
Beck, Denise Gail *secondary school educator*

Lowell
Myers, Charlotte *secondary educator*

Lynnville
Fulkerson, Jodi Lee *secondary school educator*

Madison
Bivens, Constance Ann *retired pre-school educator*

Marion
Ransom, Peggy Elaine *retired education educator*
Vermilion, Marsha Renee *secondary school educator*

Maxwell
Proper, Kristine Suzanne *elementary school educator*

Merrillville
Brailey, Amy Lynora *secondary school educator, language educator*
Merrill-Washington, Victoria *elementary school educator, consultant*
Protho, Jessie *vocational school educator*

Milton
Wade, Deanna Jo *retired elementary school educator*

Mishawaka
Stone, Cathy Jean *elementary school educator*
Wilson, Rebecca Jo *associate dean, education educator*

Monroeville
Lafrentz, Laverne B. *elementary school educator*
Sorgen, Elizabeth Ann *retired elementary school educator*

Monticello
Burkhardt, Mary Sue D. *secondary school educator*

Muncie
Amman, E(lizabeth) Jean *academic administrator*
Cantu, Sandra Lou *special education educator*
Gora, JoAnn M. *academic administrator*
Klotz, Ann Marie *director*
Spencer, Anna Kathleen *mathematics educator*
Stewart, Rita Joan *academic administrator*

New Albany
Riehl, Jane Ellen *education educator*

North Manchester
Switzer, Jo Young *college president*

Notre Dame
Johansen, Ruthann Knechel *education educator, writer*
Johnstone, Joyce Visintine *education educator*
Maziar, Christine M. *academic administrator*
O'Hara, Patricia Anne *dean, law educator*
Woo, Carolyn Yauyan *dean*
Younger, Jennifer A. *university librarian*

Parker City
Lacy, Karen S. *special education educator*

Peru
McCaulley, Cynthia Jane *elementary art educator*
Nystrom, Tammy C. *elementary school educator, consultant*

Plymouth
Cardinal-Cox, Shirley Mae *education educator*
Jurkiewicz, Margaret Joy Gommel *retired secondary school educator*

Portland
Arnold, Beverly Sue *secondary school educator*
Bisel, Marsha McCune *elementary school educator*

Rensselaer
Slaby, Kristi Lynn *secondary school educator*

Richmond
Robinson, Dixie Faye *elementary and secondary school educator*

Rockville
Jones, Tamera Dawn *elementary school educator*

Saint Mary Of The Woods
Lescinski, Joan *higher education administrator, English educator*

Shelbyville
Clark, Rose Sharon *elementary school educator*
Lawler, Mary Lucille *secondary school educator*

South Bend
Knight, Ida Brown *retired elementary school educator*
Martin, Debra Jane *assistant principal, basketball coach*
Tompsett, Lesley Ann *elementary school educator*

Spencer
Coley, Brenda Ann *elementary school educator*

Spencerville
Clark, Donna M. *retired elementary school educator*

Straughn
Jordan, Lois Evelyn *retired educator*

Tell City
Arterberry, Patricia *retired elementary school educator*

Terre Haute
Hunt, Effie Neva *retired dean, literature educator*
Nugent, Mary Katherine *elementary school educator*

Thorntown
Harris, Rebecca Sue *mathematics educator*

Trafalgar
Dyke, Brenda JoAnn *special education educator*

Valparaiso
Taylor, Heather Marie *director*

Wabash
Ward, Judith A. *elementary school educator*

West Lafayette
Gappa, Judith M. *academic administrator*
Helton, Jane Marie *literature and language educator*
Moyars-Johnson, Mary Annis *retired history professor*
Schneider, Lynette D. *secondary school educator, department chairman*

Westfield
Bradbury, Betty Marie *history and music educator*

Wheatfield
Thornton, Debra Ann *special education educator*

Winona Lake
McMunn, Nancy Lee *parochial school educator*

Yorktown
Murray, Stephanie Lynn *special education educator, consultant*

IOWA

Allison
Reese, Susan Marie *elementary school educator*

Ames
Blount, Jackie Marie *educator*
Crabtree, Beverly June *retired dean*
Goodwin, Tonja Trista *secondary school educator*
Mattila, Mary Jo Kalsem *elementary school educator, special education educator, art educator*

Ankeny
Cowger, Karin R. *literature and language educator*
Sanders, Heather Jo *elementary school educator*

Atlantic
Van Ginkel, Marci Lou *education educator*

Bettendorf
Brown, Lisa M. *academic administrator*
Jacobsen, Barbara Ann *biology educator*
Scupham, Carole Jean *elementary school educator*
Taylor, Paulette Ann *special education educator, educational consultant*

Burlington
Noll, Laurie Jane *secondary school educator*

Cascade
Peryon, Charleen D. *education educator, consultant*

Casselman
Hansen, Micaela L. *assistant principal*

Cedar Falls
Schulte, Jill Marie *elementary school educator*

Cedar Rapids
Merritt, Sandra Lee *educational consultant*
Tonsfeldt, Lori Ann *secondary school educator*

Charter Oak
Kutschinski, Dorothy Irene *elementary school educator*

Cherokee
Hankens, Deborah Jane *secondary school educator*

Clarinda
Vanden Bosch, Linda Kae Krull *elementary school educator*

Clinton
Adkins, Catherine Irene *secondary school educator, department chairman*

Corydon
Snook, Beverly Jean *elementary school educator*

Council Bluffs
Masker, Debera Ann *middle school educator*

Creston
Dillenburg, Carolyn Eva Lauer *retired secondary school educator*

Davenport
Currence, Glennda Kay *elementary school educator*
Sheehey, Patricia Ann *secondary school educator*

De Witt
Jackson, Lois Ann *special education educator*

Decorah
Wangsness, Harriet Ann *elementary school educator*

Delhi
Downs, Karla J. *secondary school educator*

Des Moines
Burn, Barbara Louise *literature and language educator*
Gaines, Ruth Ann *secondary school educator*
Jeffrey, Judy *school system administrator*
Paterik, Frances Sue *secondary school educator, actress*
Snyder, Carolyn Swick (Carrie Snyder) *special education educator, vocational program administrator*

Dubuque
Collins, Barbara Louise *retired elementary school educator*
Hodge, Gail *dean, programming director, education educator*

Durant
Siebke, Loretta Belle *retired elementary school educator*

Eldon
Johnson, Lori Higinbotham *elementary school educator*

Eldridge
Hoyt, Kay Marie *elementary science specialist*
Schnekloth, Cindee J. *elementary school educator*

Elgin
Reierson, Carol Ann *elementary school educator*

Fayette
Kuker, Gina Joanne *education educator*

Fort Madison
Sodey, Angela Ann *gifted and talented educator*

Grinnell
Brand, Vicki L. *elementary school educator*

Hastings
Baird, Christine Mary *secondary school educator*

Hubbard
Reinert, Joy Ann *elementary school educator*

Indianola
Heinicke, Janet Louise *educator, artist*

Iowa City
Grant, Mary Lynn Johnson *academic administrator, literary scholar*
Jones, Carolyn *dean, law educator*
Jones, Catherine Clarissa *secondary school educator*
Porter, Nancy Lefgren *reading recovery educator*

Keokuk
Henoch, Reva *elementary school educator*
Mills, Sylvia Janet *secondary education educator*

Manchester
Cook, Sharon Lee Delancey *retired elementary school educator, musician*

Manilla
Smith, Fay G.N. *literature and language educator*

Maquoketa
Krum, Dee *secondary school educator*

Mediapolis
Lerud-Chubb, DiAnne Kay *secondary school educator*

Morning Sun
Byers, Elizabeth *education educator*

New Providence
Reece, Marlene Williams *elementary school educator*

Newton
Graves, Margery A. *elementary school educator*
Ward, Doree Maxine *secondary school educator*

Nora Springs
Brockmeyer, Kristie Lee *secondary school educator*

Northwood
Schiltz, Polly Jo *special education educator*

Odebolt
Menage, Carolyn Lee *elementary school educator*
Swensen, Joan Linda *elementary school educator*

Oelwein
Flaucher-Falck, Velma Ruth *retired special education educator*

Onawa
Hewitt, Lou *retired elementary school educator*

Oskaloosa
Burrow, Nancy Kay *special education educator*
DeBruin, Ruth Pearl *primary school educator*

Ottumwa
Dinsmore, Susan Marie *secondary school educator*
Mefford, Naomi Ruth Dolbeare *secondary school educator, elementary school educator*
Roberts, Sherrie Lynn *special education educator, secondary school educator*

Pella
Steele, Mildred Romedahl *educator*

Postville
Heitland, Julie Ann *school librarian*

Prairie City
Hill, Pamela Jean *middle school educator*

Reinbeck
Koester, Lisa *principal*

Rock Rapids
Schram, Laureen Ann *reading specialist*

Sioux City
Dillman, Kristin Wicker *elementary school educator, musician*
Iverson, Ona Lee *retired elementary school educator*
Mounts, Nancy *secondary school educator*
Rants, Carolyn Jean *academic administrator, educator*

Sloan
Ullrich, Roxie Ann *special education educator*

Spencer
Hanthorne, Carol *elementary school educator*
Myers, Janis Marie *secondary school educator*

Springville
Weber, Vickie Fey *secondary school educator*

Stanwood
Lehrman, Patricia Jayne *literature and language educator*

Story City
Dickson-Ferrell, Tamara L. *secondary school educator*

Stuart
King, Meghan Anne *secondary school educator*

Thornton
Jorgensen, Doris Jean *retired elementary school educator*

Urbandale
Hewitt, Lisa Carol (Lisa Carol Ver Hoef) *elementary school educator*

Waterloo
Alfrey, Marian Antoinette *retired education educator*
Kober, Arletta Refshauge (Mrs. Kay L. Kober) *supervisor*

Webster City
Daniels, Karen S. *mathematics educator*
Hansen, Rae Lavone *secondary school educator*

West Point
Ortciger, Lisa Marie *history educator*

Williamsburg
Sandersfeld, Lavonne Lucille *elementary school educator*

Winterset
Forsyth, Lacey Lynn *mathematics educator*
Silverthorn, Laura Lynne *secondary school educator*

Woodward
Jenkins, Alice Marie *secondary school educator*

KANSAS

Americus
Grimsley, Bessie Belle Gates *retired special education educator*

Andover
Yager, Amanda D. *secondary school educator*

Arma
Query, Lois A. *elementary school educator*

Axtell
Broxterman, Lisa *secondary school educator*

Baldwin City
Long, Patricia N. *academic administrator*

Berryton
Miller, Janeth Mauk *retired secondary education educator*

Chapman
Dawson, Joan Marie *elementary school educator*

Coffeyville
Miller, Virginia Meredith *secondary school educator*

Council Grove
Schroeder, Tracie Beth *secondary school educator*

Denton
Scherer, Deanna *principal*

Dodge City
Chipman, Deborah J. *elementary school educator*
Ripple, Paula G. *literature and language educator*
Sapp, Nancy L. *director*

Ellsworth
Rathbun, Christina Sue *literature and language educator*

Emporia
Cookson, Linda Marie *retired elementary education educator*
Thompson, Deborah K. *elementary school educator*

Erie
Sherman, Nancy Kay Jackel *elementary school educator*

Fort Scott
Weddle, Rebecca Rae *education educator*

Frankfort
Tilley, Diane *elementary school educator*

Goddard
Molz, Carol Jean *elementary school educator*
Sandall, Joann Mary *mathematics educator*

Great Bend
Rittenhouse, Nancy Carol *elementary school educator*

Hamilton
Ebberts, Deana Marie *mathematics educator*

Hays
Budig, Jeanette *special education educator*
Herl, Sonya *elementary school educator*

Holton
McDonald, Sharon Holliday *special education educator*

Hope
Hottman, Geneva Rae *elementary school educator*

Horton
Radford, Virginia Rodriguez *retired secondary school educator, librarian*

Independence
Randolph, Katrina J. *literature and language educator*
Wright, Tami LaDonna *pre-school educator*

Kansas City
Atkinson, Barbara F. *dean, medical educator, executive vice chancellor*
Blythe, Mary Susan *retired elementary school educator*
Wymer, Kellyn Lin *biology and chemistry educator, coach*

Kinsley
Burghart, Lynda R. *chemistry educator*

Kiowa
Brintnall, Charlene May *special education educator*

Lakin
Vieux, Carlee Annanette Noland *special education educator*

Lawrence
Brasseur, Irma Faye *special education educator*
Lyerla, Karen Dale *special education educator*
Peterson, Nancy *special education educator*
Turnbull, Ann Patterson *special education educator, consultant, research director*

Leavenworth
Klemp, Nancy Jean *secondary school educator*

Liberal
Boles, Sharon Isabelle O'Shields *mathematics educator*
Hicks, Linda Reona *elementary school educator*
Redd, Kathryn Elizabeth *education educator, department chairman*
Smothermon, Reba Maxine *elementary school educator*
Wilkerson, Rita Lynn *retired special education educator*

Louisburg
Best, Pamela LaFever *secondary school educator*

Lyndon
Fritz, Judith Ann *special education administrator, educator*

Maize
Van Arendonk, Susan Carole *elementary school educator*

Manhattan
Garwick, Cynthia L. *elementary school educator*

Mcpherson
Tegethoff, Allece D. *elementary school educator, pharmacy technician*

Neodesha
Campbell, Katherine Lucille *gifted and talented educator*

Oakley
Oelke, Anita Jean *special education educator*

Olathe
Beacham, Janis Schlueter *educational consultant*
Dennis, Patricia Lyon *adult education educator*
Henning, Lillian Joyce *special education educator*
Landon, Colleen *elementary school educator*
Stevens, Diana Lynn *elementary school educator*
Thompson, Kate Elaine *school librarian, educator*

Osage City
Lieber, Joan Skonberg *special education educator*

Overland Park
Messmer, Melinda Ellen *elementary school educator*
Newman, Gayle JoAnn *elementary school educator*
Regan, Patricia Lee *reading specialist*
Vandree, Elizabeth *secondary school educator*
Voska, Kathryn Caples *consultant, facilitator*

Parker
Gowing, Patricia M. *retired elementary school educator*

Peabody
Whiteman, Louise Ann *elementary school educator*

Pomona
Gentry, Alberta Elizabeth *elementary school educator*

Russell
Branick, Terry Lynn *secondary school educator*

Saint John
Friesen, Cynthia DeAnn *elementary school educator*

Salina
Daniels, Tina Lynn *special education educator*
Webb, Debbie *elementary school educator*

Sharon Springs
North, Tricia A. *secondary school educator*

Shawnee
Scanlon, Vicki E. *secondary school educator*
Webb, Elaine Marie *reading specialist*

Shawnee Mission
Allen, Janet Lee *special education educator*
Barton, Betty Louise *school system administrator*
Black, Lisa Zahn *elementary school educator*
Stilwell, Connie Kay *retired elementary school educator*

Stilwell
Snodgrass, Connie Sue *secondary school educator*

Timken
Schwindt, Mary E. *retired secondary school educator*

Topeka
Dick, Angela Dawn *elementary school educator*
Lukert-Devoe, Linda Pauline *elementary school educator*
Owsley, Tina Kathleen *special education educator*
Wuenstel, Karen L. *elementary school educator*

Wathena
Elkins, Katherine Marie *elementary school educator*

Wellington
Tibbs, Kay *director*

Wichita
Ehrlich, Donna M. *director, educator*
Ines, Amy *elementary school educator*
Mitchell, Linda Marlene *education educator*

KENTUCKY

Albany
Thrasher, Allison *elementary school educator*

Bardstown
Carter, Carmen M. *elementary education educator, consultant*
Greenwell, Mary Jane *middle school educator*

Baxter
Ledford, Barbra Lynne *elementary school educator*

Berea
Henthorn, Susan Kay *school librarian*

Bowling Green
Burch, Barbara G. *academic administrator*

Brodhead
Bustle, Trina Gayle *gifted and talented educator*

Butler
Lustenberg, Michelle Williamson *gifted and talented educator*

Campbellsville
Moore, Roberta York *secondary school educator, small business owner*
Skaggs, Karen Gayle *elementary school educator*

Carrollton
Plander, Susan Elaine *elementary school educator*

Cecilia
Thompson, Kathy Self *secondary school educator*

Columbia
Boger, Cheryl Lynn *academic administrator, education educator*

Corbin
Iley, Jenny Rebecca *elementary school educator*

Covington
Berg, Lorine McComis *retired guidance counselor*

Danville
Kennan, Elizabeth Topham *academic administrator, retired historian*

Edmonton
Bunch, Kathy Lynn *secondary school educator*

Ekron
Hamilton, Amelia Wentz (Amy Wentz) *elementary school educator*

Elizabethtown
Sweat, Nora Ellen *home economics educator*

Ewing
Ramey, Susan Dorsey *elementary school educator*

Flemingsburg
Gossett, Linda Kelley *retired secondary school educator*

Fort Knox
Tucker, Brenda Brunette *elementary school educator*

Fort Mitchell
McQueen, Pamela *principal*

Fort Thomas
Griggs, Rozellen *elementary school educator*
Yelton, Dianne Burgess *secondary school educator*

Frankfort
Sias, Mary *university president*

Garrison
Ruark, Sheila Gaye *elementary school educator*

Gray
Gaddis, Betty H. *retired elementary school educator*

Grayson
Adams, Briana Elizabeth *elementary school educator*

Greenville
Adams, Clara Webb *secondary school educator*

Grethel
Hughes, Cindi Baker *special education educator*

Guston
Yundt, Betty Brandenburg *elementary school educator*

Hanson
Duncan, Charlotte Diane *retired secondary school educator*

Harlan
Chitwood, Sharon Carmical *elementary school educator*
DeLong-Smith, Stephanie K. *secondary school educator*

Hazard
Feltner, Jeanne Lou *mathematics educator*

Highland Heights
Short-Thompson, Cady W. *educator, director*

Hopkinsville
Lang, Colleen Anne *secondary school educator*

Horse Cave
Martin, Carmen Guinn *literature and language educator*

Irvine
Moore, Kathy Lynn *elementary school educator*

Jackson
Guthery, Grace Maxine *retired secondary school educator*

Lancaster
Montgomery, Betty Adams *elementary school educator*

Lexington
Hunt, Cathy Stevenson *academic administrator*
Isenhour, Kathleen Chaney *special education educator, consultant*

Kewin, Cynthia McLendon *secondary school educator*
Logan, Joyce Polley *education educator*
Norman, Charlene Wilson *secondary school educator*
Taylor, Angela Dawn *primary school educator*
Turner, Sharon P. *dean, dentist, educator*
Zimmerman, Laura Ann *biology educator*

London
Bailey, Janna *mathematics educator*

Louisville
Cannon, Dannie Parker *special education educator*
Carroll, Jean Gray *mathematics educator*
Cherry, Sandra Osburn *mathematics educator*
Choi, Namok *education educator*
Goffner, Gwendolyn Denise *elementary school educator*
Greaver, Joanne Hutchins *mathematics educator, writer*
Hixson, Allie Corbin *retired adult education educator, advocate*
Jenne, Sue Oak *secondary school educator*
Nation, Pamela Grace *secondary school educator*
Newell, Elizabeth Carolyn *retired secondary school educator*
Rothstein, Laura *dean, law educator*
Roubieu, Amanda Marcelle *elementary school educator*
Ruter, Ruth Evelyn *elementary school educator*
Sexton, Charlene Ann *education consultant*
Stoll, Shirley Gabriella *special education educator*
Todd, Cherie Clemons *elementary school educator*
Tuttle, Tara Marie *literature and language educator*
Walker, Carol Ellen Burton *retired elementary school educator*
Weinberg, Elizabeth *education educator, researcher, retired small business owner*
White-Walker, Roxana *elementary school educator*
Yount, Sara *academic administrator*

Madisonville
Parker, Faye C. *elementary school educator*
Pruitt, Brenda Sue Branstetter *secondary school educator*

Masonic Home
Schweichler, Mary Ellen *childhood education educator, consultant*

Morehead
Miller, April D. *special education educator*

Morning View
Harris, Tammy Dotson *elementary school educator*

Mount Sterling
Aileen-Donohew, Phyllis Augusta *educational consultant*

Murray
Russell, Mary Ann *secondary school educator*

New Haven
Hall, Martha Anne *elementary school educator*

Nicholasville
Armstrong, Marcy Lynn *literature and language educator, special education educator*
Midkiff, Dinah Lee *retired elementary and middle school educator*

Oil Springs
Robinson, Virginia Lynn *elementary school educator*

Owingsville
Little, Stephanie Jean *special education educator*

Paducah
Kirk, Charlotte Leidecker *director*
Mittendorf, Kimberly Ann *secondary school educator, real estate consultant*
Talbert, Debra Kaiser *elementary school educator, artist*

Paint Lick
Donaldson, Kathleen *special education educator*

Paintsville
Watson, Betty A. *mathematics educator*

Perry Park
Hess, Marcia Wanda *retired secondary school educator*

Pikeville
Mutter, Jennie *secondary school educator, artist*
Venters, Teresa Anne *elementary school educator*

Pineville
Hoskins, Barbara R(uth) Williams *retired elementary school educator, principal*

Prospect
Broaddus, Kristie Jones *elementary school educator*
McFerran, Debra Brady *parochial school educator*

Shepherdsville
Carini, Karen Michelle *elementary school educator*

Somerset
Carter, Frances Ann *secondary school educator*

Stanton
Lockard, Dixie Davis *elementary school educator*

Verona
Blackburn, Patricia A. *elementary school educator*

Wilmore
Pritchett, Rita Joyce *educator*

LOUISIANA

Abbeville
Hebert, Mona Milliman *elementary school educator*

Alexandria
Brand-Buchanan, Michelle Cathy *elementary school educator*
Gill, Julie Franks *education educator*
Maples, Mary Lou *elementary school educator*

Angie
Moses, Anice N. *elementary school educator, minister*

Baker
Baker, Yvonne Bell *elementary school educator*

Baton Rouge
Bennett, Toni Zimmer *special education educator*
Boulton, Bonnie Smith *assistant principal, special education educator*
Emonet, Sheila LeBlanc *elementary school educator*
Eubanks, Sonia Melisa *education educator*
Harper, Sandra Stecher *academic administrator*
Hillman, Christina Joy *mathematics educator*
Jonas, Jeanie Lynn *elementary school educator*
Litton, Nancy Joan *education educator*
Ropers-Huilman, Becky Lynn *education and humanities educator*
Spearman, Diane Negrotto *art/special education educator*
Stubblefield, Luria Shaw *education educator*

Boutte
Melancon, Wanda Lorie *secondary educator*

Boyce
Monroe, Nancy L. *secondary school educator*

Chalmette
Crouchet, Kathleen Hunt *elementary school educator, reading educator*

Choudrant
Lofton, Brenda M. *middle school educator*

Crowley
Privat, Ruby (Ruby Thibodeaux) *elementary school educator*
Thibodeaux, Darla Faul *gifted and talented educator*

Deridder
Franks, Cindi W. *supervisor*

Franklin
Fairchild, Phyllis Elaine *school counselor*

Galliano
Orgeron, Rochelle Mary *secondary school educator*

Glenmora
Burns, Linda D. *elementary school educator*

Gonzales
Kidd, Ruth Price *retired secondary school educator*

Grambling
Warner, Neari Francois *university president*

Hammond
Cook, Myrtle *special education educator, elementary school educator*
Day, Susan Brent *assistant principal, educator*
Nauman, Ann Keith *education educator*

Harvey
Henderson, Lillian Milbra *educator, librarian, clergyperson*

Houma
Bordelon, Dena Cox Yarbrough *retired special education educator, director*
Breaux, Monica LeBlanc *elementary school educator*

Iowa
Leonard, Linda Faye *secondary school educator*

Jena
Smith, Robyn *secondary school educator*

Lafayette
Colbert-Cormier, Patricia A. *secondary school educator*
LeBlanc, Dotsie L. *retired vocational school educator*
Marceaux, Linda d'Augereau *elementary school educator*
Petry, Ruth Vidrine *retired principal*
Sherer, Wanda C. *secondary school educator*

Lake Arthur
Dronet, Judy Lynn *elementary school educator, librarian*

Lake Charles
Babin, Sally Wheeler *secondary school educator, consultant*
Fields-Gold, Anita *retired dean*
Lee, Brandi Gremillion *elementary school educator*

Leesville
Kay-Atkins, Cheree' *elementary school educator*

Mandeville
Arrowsmith, Marian Campbell *elementary school educator, supervisor, educator*

Metairie
Blunt, Joyce Omega *special education educator*
Crosby, Marena Lienhard *retired academic administrator*
Flake, Leone Elizabeth *special education educator*
Sanderson, Christine Graves *literature and language educator*

New Iberia
Hockless, Mary Fontenot *educational consultant*

New Orleans
Hughes, Marvalene *academic administrator*
McNeil, Vicki Laughter *student affairs administrator*
Mills, Cheryl E. *education educator*

Newllano
Boren, Lynda Sue *gifted education educator*

Opelousas
LaBerteaux, Jennifer Claire *secondary school educator*

Pineville
Bolin, Julie Paul *secondary school educator*
Lott, Johnnye Jo *elementary school educator, writer*
Smith, Mabel Hargis *retired secondary school educator, musician*

Port Allen
Kahao, Mary Jane *school librarian*

Prairieville
Biri, Toni Roppolo *elementary school educator*

Raceland
Cole, Anna Moore *chemistry educator*

Ruston
Bourgeois, Patricia McLin *academic administrator, women's health and pediatrics nurse, educator*
Freasier, Aileen W. *special education educator*
Griffin, Susan *secondary school educator*
Johnson, Elaine Frances *mathematics educator*
Lewis, Doris Ann *principal*

Saint Martinville
Fournet, Patricia Sibley *retired secondary school educator*
Guilliot, Vickie Lee *secondary school educator*

Shreveport
Delo, Lynda Jeanne *secondary school educator*
Easley, Linda Marie *education educator*
Finney, Lila D. *school system administrator*
Glasgow, Dianne Britt *education educator, writer, consultant*
Haughton, Mary L. *elementary school educator*
Leonard, Paula Leavy *school disciplinarian*
Pierson, Juanita (Nita Pierson) *secondary school educator*
Posey, Katye L. *retired school system administrator*
Pouncey, Annie Moore *retired secondary school educator*
Prunty, LeeAnn Marsiglia *gifted and talented educator*
Shepard, Emma Luster *elementary school educator*

Simsboro
Talley, Dana Smith *principal*

Slidell
Fincher, Margaret Ann *retired secondary school educator*
Johnson, Lynn Marie Thornburg *parochial school educator*

Springfield
Smith, Keri A. *literature and language educator*

Stonewall
Jarquin, Theresa Binning *gifted and talented educator*

Thibodaux
Carter, Iris Brown *pre-school educator*
Harris, Rose M. *academic administrator*
Smith, Victoria Weilepp *educator*

White Castle
Williams, Ivory Lee *special education educator*

MAINE

Acton
Cunningham, Joyce Wentworth *retired secondary school educator*

Auburn
Van Deusen, Jenifer *educational consultant*

Augusta
Gendron, Susan Ann *school system administrator*
vonHerrlich, Phyllis Herrick *academic administrator*
Whitcomb, Lois Ann *retired academic administrator*

Bangor
Trask, Paula Elizabeth *mathematics educator*

Bar Harbor
Swazey, Judith Pound *academic administrator, science educator*

Bar Mills
Burns, Maryann Margaret *retired elementary school educator*

Boothbay
Watson, Caroline *secondary school educator*

Bremen
Wilson, Linda Smith *retired academic administrator*

Cumberland
Carter, Gail Rae *history educator*

Farmington
Kalikow, Theodora June *academic administrator*
Oliver, Diana Cloutier *elementary school educator*

Fort Kent
Taggette, Deborah Jean *special education educator*

Harpswell
Regan, Helen Brooks *education educator, educational consultant*

Houlton
Powers, Gloria Doody *mathematics educator*

Kennebunkport
Chapman, Karina M. *elementary school educator*
Featherman, Sandra *retired academic administrator, political science professor*

Lewiston
Dodd, Anne Wescott *education educator*
Hansen, Elaine Tuttle *academic administrator*

Machias
Ball, Heather L. *special education educator, consultant*

Naples
Byrne, Kelley Anne *special education educator*

Oakland
Baker, Marshalyn Elaine *elementary school educator*
Osborne, Hannah Christine *school counselor, social worker*

Old Orchard Beach
Day, Marlene E. *elementary school educator*

Old Town
Alex, Joanne DeFilipp *elementary school educator*

Orono
Bartel, Lavon Lee *academic administrator, food scientist*
Szymanski, Edna Mora *dean*

Poland
Herrick, Doris A. *elementary school educator*

Portland
Khoury, Colleen A. *dean*
Vincent, Christine *academic administrator*

Presque Isle
Gardner, Julie Isabel *elementary school educator*
Gentile, Caroline D. *adult education educator*

Rumford
Rouleau, Ann F. *retired elementary school educator*

Sanford
Field, Linda G. *secondary school educator*

Scarborough
Goulet, Christine Sweeney *elementary school educator*
Russo, Joan Mildred *special education educator*

Southwest Harbor
Goetze, Lydia B. *biology educator*

Topsham
Arrington, Elisabeth Calvert *elementary education educator, artist*

Waterville
Cook, Susan Farwell *director*

MARYLAND

Adamstown
Church, Martha Eleanor *retired academic administrator*

Annapolis
Bowen, Linnell R. *director*
Byers, Meranda Faith *secondary school educator*
Farmer, Martha Louise *retired academic administrator*
Flanagan, Susan Marie *special education educator*
Stern, Margaret Bassett *retired special education educator, author*

Arnold
Smith, Martha A. *academic administrator*
Walker, Martha M. *special education educator*

Baltimore
Adams, Clara I. *academic administrator*
Ball, Marion Jokl *academic administrator*
Baltzley, Patricia Creel *mathematics educator*
Boyd, Amanda D. *elementary school educator*
Braggio, Sherryll Ann Morris *retired elementary school educator, volunteer*
Brewer, Nevada Nancy *elementary school educator*
Brisbon, Ada Vanessa *assistant principal*
Brown, Ruth Payne *retired elementary school educator, retired principal*
Crawford, Annette Lambson *elementary school educator*
Delpit, Lisa D. *education educator, researcher, consultant*
Donovan, Sharon Ann *retired secondary school educator*
Edidin, Ruth Glicenstein *mathematics educator*
Elias, Sarah Davis *retired English language educator*
Gilli, Lynne Marie *academic administrator*
Grasmick, Nancy S. *school system administrator*
Hsu, Cornelia Wang Mei-Chih *education educator*
Kemp, Suzanne Leppart *elementary school educator*
Koenig, Margaret Susanne *elementary school educator*
Leffell, Mary Sue *educator*

McDaniel, Mildred Gage *elementary school educator*
Morton, Sandra Jorgensen *retired school librarian*
Norris, Karen W. *grants specialist*
Novak, Donna Burnett *secondary school educator*
Oji, Pauline E. *secondary school educator*
Ridenour, Deborah Hughes *elementary school educator*
Rose, Sara Margaret *English as a second language educator*
Rothenberg, Karen H. *dean, law educator*
Sadak, Diane Marie *director, performing arts educator*
Seurkamp, Mary Pat *college president*
Topper, Barbara MacNeal Blake *secondary school educator*
Valentine, April Sue *elementary school educator, department chairman*

Bel Air
Miller, Dorothy Eloise *education educator*
Phillips, Bernice Cecile Golden *retired vocational education educator*
Wright, Tiffany Erin *secondary school educator*

Berlin
Auxer, Cathy Joan *elementary school educator*

Bethesda
Rudolph, Carol Ann Greenberg *human resource education consultant*

Bowie
Dingle, Patricia A. *education educator, artist*
Tesar, Patricia Marie *academic coordinator*

Boyds
Carpenter, Dorothy Schenck *retired special education educator*

Cambridge
Tenanty, Jane Elizabeth *secondary school educator*

Capitol Heights
Johnson, Ruth Floyd *educational consultant*

Catonsville
Marlatt, Patricia Anne *secondary school educator*
Smith, F. Louise *elementary school educator*

Centreville
Shoemaker, Anne Cunningham *retired mathematics educator*

Chevy Chase
Diamond, Karen Waltzer *small business owner, educator*
Towsner, Cynthia Merle *academic administrator, educator*
Wolf, Jean D. *educational consultant, writer*

College Park
Dreher, Mariam Jean *education educator*
Finkelstein, Barbara *education educator*
Ingold, Catherine White *academic administrator*
Sandra, Charlene Greer *educator*

Columbia
Davis, Janet Marie Gorden *secondary school educator*
Duncan, Mary Ellen *academic administrator*
Hafets, Claire M. *assistant principal*
Hale, Mignon S. Palmer-Flack *elementary school educator, educator*
Hartman, Lee Ann Walraff *secondary school educator, consultant*
Jones-Wilson, Faustine Clarisse *retired education educator*
Scornaienchi, Joan Webb *supervisor, consultant*

Cumberland
Fuller, Mary Baker *chemistry educator*

Derwood
Bouvě, Janet Saar *secondary school educator*

Edgewater
Whaley, Beth Dowling *retired elementary school educator*

Ellicott City
Michel, Donna Tonty *education educator*
Tolliver, Sheila Maureen *university administrator, alderman*

Finksburg
Galanakis, Patricia Sarigianis *special education resource educator*

Forestville
Kazimer, Denise *secondary school educator*

Frederick
Barone, Kristen Therese *elementary school educator*
Curtis Craney, Karen B. *reading specialist*
DeCarlo, Mary Kathleen *elementary school educator*
Hoffman, Jean Lillian *parochial school educator*
Hoyer, Phyllis Scarborough *retired elementary education educator*
Klein, Elaine Charlotte *school system administrator*

Frostburg
Gira, Catherine Russell *retired academic administrator*

Gaithersburg
Raymond, Sandra Lynn *elementary school educator*
Stroud, Nancy Iredell *retired secondary school educator, freelance writer, editor*

Gambrills
Trimnal, Wanda Lee *secondary school educator*

Garrett Park
Stembel, Margery Joan *elementary school educator*

Germantown
Sourk, Catherine Cleary *educational consultant*

Glen Burnie
Baillie, Miranda Lee *secondary school educator*
Watts, Virginia Agnes *retired special education educator*

Goldsboro
Hutson Councell, Janet Kern *retired secondary school educator*

Great Mills
Gehring, Patti J. *principal*

Greenbelt
LaMarca, Mary Margaret *elementary school educator*

Hampstead
Holbrook, Jennifer Lynn *elementary school educator*
Howells, Martha Louise *secondary school educator*
Keogh, Molly Duffy *education educator, consultant*

Hanover
Schmidt, Sandra Jean *secondary school educator*

Harwood
Smith, Maria Lynn *school system administrator*

Indian Head
Layton, Georgianna Vicik *mathematics educator*

Joppa
Bates, Martha Copenhaver *elementary school educator*
Chase, Jaclyn Bosworth *secondary school educator*

La Plata
Tubb, Elaine Ann *secondary school educator*

Landover Hills
Moreno, Renee Teresa *education educator*

Lutherville Timonium
Krasevac, Esther *retired academic administrator*

Millersville
Culver, Catherine Marie *secondary school educator*
Liimatta, Janet Ann *mathematics educator*

Odenton
Lambert, Vickie Ann *retired dean, nursing consultant*

Owings Mills
Adedeji, Sharon Lilly *literature and language educator*
Oleisky, Deborah Fischer *elementary school educator*
Simmers, Andrea Jean *elementary school educator*

Perry Hall
Petchik, Marian *mathematics educator*

Pocomoke City
Giles, Debra B. *gifted and talented educator*

Potomac
Kuykendall, Crystal Arlene *educational consultant, lawyer*

Prince Frederick
Adams, Cheryl Palonis *secondary school educator, dancer, choreographer*
Galligan, Caitlin Maureen *elementary school educator*
Love, Margaret Wynn *physical education educator*

Princess Anne
Thompson, Thelma Barnaby *university president, classical languages educator*

Pylesville
Mullen, Lisa Caitlin *elementary school educator*

Rockville
Hammond, Brenda Hines *elementary school educator*
Robinson, Cheryl Jeffreys *special education educator*

Rosedale
Maskell, Kathleen Mary *English and reading educator*

Saint Marys City
O'Brien, Jane Margaret *academic administrator*

Severna Park
Wade, Earline *elementary school educator*

Silver Spring
Bonner, Bester Davis *school system administrator*
Burgos-Sasscer, Ruth *chancellor emeritus*
Clark, Mizzell Phillips (Mitzi Clark) *school librarian*
Coles, Anna Louise Bailey *retired dean, nurse*
Cooper, Nannie Coles *education educator, consultant*
Efron, Rosalyn Esther *special education educator*
Fickenscher, Dorothy (Debbie) E.B. *secondary school educator*
Hay, Janisann *secondary school educator*
Makris, Margaret Lubbe *elementary school educator*
Miller, Karla Patricia *elementary school educator*
Oliver, Kimberly *Teacher of the Year*

Stevenson
Hyman, Mary Bloom *science education programs coordinator*

Takoma Park
Gumaer, Amy Arnold *academic administrator*

Towson
Myers, Debra Taylor *elementary school educator, writer*
Uhrich, Tabatha A. *education educator*

Union Bridge
Hannah, Judy Challenger *private education tutor*

Upper Marlboro
Street, Patricia Lynn *retired secondary school educator*

Waldorf
Alo, Theresa Reneé *secondary school educator, potter*
Robey, Sherie Gay Southall Gordon *secondary school educator, consultant*

Westernport
Morgan, Sharon Lynn *principal*

Westminster
Coley, Joan Develin *education educator, academic administrator*
Mesta, Pamela Anne *supervisor, consultant*
Pappalardo, Faye *academic administrator*

MASSACHUSETTS

Agawam
Goodwin, Beverly Ann *elementary school educator*

Amherst
Rudman, Masha Kabakow *education educator, author, consultant*
Seymour, Charlena *academic administrator*

Andover
Braverman, Carole Gae *literature and language educator*
Nicolson, Christina Carrell *elementary school educator*

Auburn
Mitchell, Karen Lee *special education educator, consultant*

Babson Park
Lindsey-Mullikin, Joan *education educator, researcher*

Barnstable
Grodecki, Merrilyn *private school educator*

Beverly
Broderick, Jo Stewart *academic administrator*
Hart, Claire-Marie *secondary school educator*

Boston
Andrews, Sally May *academic administrator*
Ash, Barbara Lee *education and human services educator*
Bergstrom, Joan Margosian *education educator*
Caldwell, Ann Wickins *academic administrator*
Celestino-Arguinzoni, Wilma *academic administrator*
Clendenning, Bonnie Ryon *college administrator*
Dluhy, Deborah Haigh *dean*
Dujon, Diane Marie *director, advocate*
Fertitta, Angela *dean*
Liebergott, Jacqueline W. *academic administrator*
O'Rourke, Maureen A. *dean, law educator*
Paine, Lynn *academic administrator*
Penney, Sherry Hood *academic administrator, consultant*
Piscatelli, Nancy Kelley *elementary school educator*
Prothrow-Stith, Deborah *academic administrator, public health educator*
Reede, Joan Yvonne *academic administrator, medical educator, pediatrician*
Schotland, Judith *education educator*
Scrimshaw, Susan Crosby *academic administrator*
Simmons, Sylvia Jeanne Quarles (Mrs. Herbert G. Simmons Jr.) *academic administrator, educator*
Sloan, Katherine (Kay Sloan) *college president*
Smith, Heather Clark *academic administrator*
Spieler, Emily A. *dean, law educator*
Tornow, Barbara *academic administrator*
Yarborough, Nellie Constance *principal, minister*

Braintree
Watts, Kisha Mann *school system administrator, secondary school educator*

Bridgewater
Tinsley, Adrian *former college president*
Witherell, Nancy Louise *education educator*

Byfield
Densmore, Susan Elizabeth *secondary school educator, music educator*

Cambridge
Bane, Mary Jo *dean, political science professor*
Cazden, Courtney B(orden) *education educator*
Dunton, Susan Beth *academic administrator*
Eurich, Nell P. *education educator*
Fitzgerald-Huber, Louisa G. *education educator, researcher*
Graham, Patricia Albjerg *education educator*
Hockfield, Susan *academic administrator, medical educator*
Kagan, Elena *dean, law educator*
Kim, Josephine M. *education educator*
Lawrence-Lightfoot, Sara *education educator, sociologist*
Macrakis, A. Lily *academic administrator*
McCartney, Kathleen *dean, education educator*
McKenna, Margaret Anne *academic administrator*
Meyer, Dorothy Virginia *retired education educator*
Stathos, Anastasia *retired elementary school educator*

Canton
Trupe, Mary-Ann *secondary school educator*

Chatham
Stout, Sharon Sparkes *elementary school educator, counselor*

Chestnut Hill
Bando, Patricia Alice *academic administrator*
Nemerowicz, Gloria *academic administrator*

Chicopee
Chelte, Judith Segzdowicz *secondary school educator*

Concord
Giles, Kathleen C. *headmaster*

Cotuit
Crocker, Jean Hazelton *elementary school educator, consultant, environmental services administrator*

Danvers
Corkery, Antoinette Elizabeth *literature and language educator*

Dartmouth
Leandro, Patricia J. *mathematics educator*
Nieviedgal, Carol Belmarce *elementary school educator*

Dedham
Nichols, Nancy Ruth *elementary school educator*

Douglas
Bachelder, Beverly Brandt *secondary school educator, assistant principal, director*
Socha, Cindy L. *secondary school educator*

Duxbury
Thrasher, Dianne Elizabeth *mathematics educator, computer scientist, consultant*

Everett
Auger, Kimberly Ann *elementary school educator*

Fairhaven
Goes, Kathleen Ann *secondary school educator*

Fiskdale
Costello, Christine Ann *fine arts director, church organist*

Fitchburg
deDiego, Paula Dawn *education educator*
Reed, Rosemary *learning specialist*

Framingham
Heineman, Helen L. *retired academic administrator*
McEntegart, Judy R. *gifted and talented educator*
Valakis, M. Lois *retired elementary school educator*

Groton
Sawyer, Betsy (Rosemary) E. *elementary school educator*

Harwich
Caretti, Ann M. *school system administrator*
Medeiros, Donna *assistant principal*

Haverhill
Kannan, Sandra Jean *elementary school educator, retired assistant principal*

Holden
Edson, Virginia Elizabeth *secondary school educator*

Hubbardston
Marceau, Judith Marie *retired elementary school educator, small business owner*

Hudson
Ingano, Kathryn Marita *secondary school educator*

Hyannis
O'Brien, Kathleen L. *special education educator*

Hyde Park
Harris, Emily Louise *special education educator*

Ipswich
Berry, Iris Elizabeth *academic administrator*
Lombardo, Ann Marie *special education educator, writer, artist*

Lakeville
Chase, Karen Humphrey *elementary school educator*

Lancaster
Dugan, Maureen *biology educator, consultant*

Lenox
Smith, Elske Van Panhuys *retired academic administrator, astronomer*

Leominster
Suskind, Diana Lee *education educator*
Vogel, Gloria Jean Hilts *secondary school educator*

Lexington
Wilson, Wendy Scott *history educator*

Lincoln
Naiman, Adeline Lubell *educational administrator*

Longmeadow
Katz, Barbara Stein *special education educator*
Leary, Carol Ann *academic administrator*
Schirmer-Smith, Sara Jane (Sally Schirmer-Smith) *director*

Lowell
Clark, Kathyrn A. *elementary school educator*

Clark, Sharon Ann *educational consultant, music educator*
Klimczak, Janice Beverly *secondary school educator*
Lewis, Diane *educator*

Ludlow
Marion, Elena Mendes *secondary school educator*

Lynn
Josephs, Judith *counseling administrator, educator*

Marblehead
Isaacson, Barbara Dorothy *retired elementary school educator, retired secondary school educator*

Mattapoisett
Guilbert, Frances *mathematics educator*

Maynard
Messina, Nance Ann *primary school educator*

Medfield
Nedder, Janet Marie *elementary school educator*

Medford
Ch'en, Li-li *literature and language educator, writer*
Weiler, Kathleen *education educator, researcher*

Melrose
Sheerin, Margaret M. *elementary school educator*

Milton
Robertson, Robin Alayne *headmaster, anthropologist*
Simon, Deborah Elizabeth *private school educator*

Natick
Smith, Amanda R. *secondary school educator*
Taylor, Susan Garrett *academic administrator, school psychologist*
Weber, Linda Horton *secondary school educator*

Needham
Durbin, Kirsten Dahlman *academic administrator*
Kossuth, Joanne M. *academic administrator*
Shannon, Margaret Rita *retired education educator, retired college dean*
Watt, Abby Naitove *elementary school educator*

New Bedford
Cormier, Lorraine R. *secondary school educator*
Matsumoto, Carolee Setsuko *researcher, education developer and administrator*
Stone, Anne Marie *elementary school educator*

Newbury
Hamond, Karen Marie Koch *secondary school educator*

Newburyport
Krusemark, Janice Wells *physicial education educator*

Newton
LeRoux, Tessa *sociology professor, director*
Matteson, Carol J. *academic administrator*

North Attleboro
Nicodemus, Emily Hulsizer *technology educator*

North Dartmouth
Fair, Kathleen Margaret *elementary school educator*
Lilly, Emily L. *education educator*

North Dighton
Patten, Brenda Anne *secondary school educator*

Northampton
Christ, Carol Tecla *academic administrator*
Mahoney, Maureen A. *academic administrator*

Northborough
Cradler, Judith A. *science educator*

Northfield
van Baaren, Margaret Miriam *learning disabilities educator*

Norwood
Mallet, Kathleen W. *elementary school educator*

Orange
Riddell, Tina Marie *secondary school educator*

Peabody
Falkoff, Gail Goldstein *mathematics educator, department chairman*

Pepperell
Jackson, Rebecca Lee *history educator, social studies educator*

Pittsfield
Norris, Jeannie *headmaster*
Wood, Elizabeth Ann *special education educator*

Plymouth
Paul, Carol Ann *retired academic administrator, biology educator*
Wolf, Ann E. *chemistry educator*

Provincetown
Wolfman, Brunetta Reid *education educator*

Quincy
Furtado, Beverly Ann *financial aid administrator*
Pratt, Mary *retired secondary school educator*

Revere
Ferrante, Olivia Ann *retired secondary school educator, consultant*

Rockport
Eaton Adams, Elizabeth Susan *retired middle school educator, jazz musician*

Olson, Mary Jane *elementary school educator*

Sharon
Johnson, Addie Collins *secondary school educator, retired dietician*

Shrewsbury
DiGiorgio, Sara Ahern *assistant principal*

Somerville
Gurley, Rhonda Jean *special education educator, consultant*

South Hadley
Creighton, Joanne Vanish *academic administrator*

South Yarmouth
Bowen, Alice Frances *retired school system administrator*

Southborough
Hill, Elsa N. *headmaster, literature and language educator, lawyer*

Southbridge
Vasey, Ann L. *pre-school administrator, counselor*

Spencer
Robinson, Evelyn Edna *secondary school educator*

Springfield
Lucia, Mary Ann *elementary school educator*

Stoneham
Keenan, Carol *assistant principal*

Sudbury
Thompson, Mary Lou *elementary school educator*

Turners Falls
Finley-Morin, Kimberley K. *secondary school educator*

Tyngsboro
Bomal, Cheryl Ann *secondary school educator*

Upton
DiNatale, Michelle *biology educator*

Waltham
Kassman, Deborah Newman *university administrator, writer, editor*
Krauss, Marty Wyngaarden *academic administrator*
Wawrzaszek, Susan V. *university librarian*

Watertown
Mason, Linda Anne *daycare administrator*

Webster
Ducharme, Janice A. *secondary school educator*

Wellesley
Bailey, Susan McGee *educational administrator, researcher, educator*
Heartt, Charlotte Beebe *university official*
Walsh, Diana Chapman *academic administrator, sociologist, educator*

West Springfield
Moore, Kelly Ann *secondary school educator*

Westford
Brady, Shelagh Ann *elementary school educator*

Winchester
Harris, Carole Ruth *education educator, researcher, consultant*
Irving, Gitte Nielsen *secondary school educator*

Woburn
Winson, Ellen-Marie (Macone) *school system administrator, reading specialist*

Worcester
Daley, Deborah Ann *assistant principal*
Kahn, AnnMarie *special education educator*

Yarmouth Port
Jones, Marjorie Evelyn *retired special education educator*

MICHIGAN

Albion
Held, Nancy Jean *academic administrator, educator*

Algonac
Bade, Sandra Lyne *secondary school educator*

Alma
Tracy, Saundra J. *academic administrator*

Ann Arbor
Annchild, Cynthia *educational consultant*
Ball, Deborah Loewenberg *dean, education educator*
Beutler, Suzanne A. *retired secondary school educator, artist*
Bryant, Barbara Everitt *academic administrator, researcher, retired marketing professional, retired federal agency administrator*
Fleming, Suzanne Marie *academic administrator, freelance/self-employed writer*
Hanewich Duranczyk, Deborah A. *art therapist, educator*
Matthews, Rowena Green *biological chemistry educator*
Moore, Eleanor S. *retired elementary school educator*
Potempa, Kathleen M. *dean, nursing educator*
Ross, Theresa Mae *secondary school educator*
Tice, Carol Hoff *intergenerational specialist, consultant*
Whitesell, Patricia S. *academic administrator*

Bay City
Zuraw, Kathleen Ann *special education and physical education educator*

Benton Harbor
Lundgren, Colleen Bowling *elementary school educator, consultant*

Beverly Hills
Pardington, Mary Elizabeth *elementary school educator*

Bloomfield Hills
Jurkiewicz, Mary Louise *elementary school educator*
Wermuth, Mary Louella *secondary school educator*

Bloomingdale
Schultheis, Ann Lucia *curriculum specialist*

Bridgeport
Kushner, Aileen F. *elementary school educator*

Buchanan
Stromswold, Dorothy *retired secondary school educator*

Cadillac
Mowrey, Corinne Ruth *secondary school educator*

Carleton
Ely, Deborah D. *elementary school educator*

Caro
Hile, Michele Vera *middle school educator*

Cass City
Kemp, Lori Ann *elementary school educator*

Charlotte
Walrath, Mary Therese *elementary school educator*

Chesterfield
Rodgers, Diana Lynn *elementary school educator*

Clarkston
Kovanis, Loukea Nakos *chemistry educator, researcher*

Clawson
Smith, Paulette W. *secondary school educator*

Clinton Township
Fontanive, Lynn Marie *special education administrator*

Dearborn
Hansen, Barbara Sophie *elementary school educator*
Meyer, Lisa Marie *elementary school educator*

Dearborn Heights
Carter, Julia Marie *secondary school educator*

Detroit
Barrett, Nancy Smith *academic administrator*
Booth, Betty Jean *retired daycare administrator, poet*
Brown, Gloria Diane *elementary school educator*
Burnside, Wanda Jacqueline *elementary school educator*
Corbitt, Eumiller Mattie *special education educator*
Kline, Mable Cornelia Page *retired secondary school educator*
Little, Laura Ann *elementary school educator, art educator*
McIntosh, Deborah V. *elementary school educator*
Shorter, Michelle Anne *secondary educator*
Smith, Lillian Louise *biology educator, librarian*
Speegle, Laura Ann *elementary school educator*
Williams, Denise *academic administrator*

Durand
Thorsen, Phyllis Lorane *middle school educator*

East Lansing
Rappley, Marsha D. *dean, physician, educator*
Rothert, Marilyn L. *dean, nursing educator*
Simon, Lou Anna Kimsey *academic administrator*

Eastpointe
Patrick, Susanne *secondary school educator*

Elk Rapids
Kitchen, Barbette Louise *retired secondary school educator*

Escanaba
Bennett, Kathleen Mavourneen *elementary school educator*

Farmington
Cherem, Barbara Brown *education educator*

Farmington Hills
Sparrow, Laura *secondary school educator*

Fort Gratiot
Atkins, Cindy L. *elementary school educator*

Franklin
Reinhart, Anne Christine *special education educator, consultant*

Fremont
Blamer, Beverly A. *elementary school educator*

Fruitport
Collier, Beverly Joanne *retired elementary school educator*

Gaylord
Magsig, Judith Anne *retired primary school educator*

Gobles
Jacus, Ann Margaret *secondary school educator*

Grand Haven
Cahalan, Amy K. *secondary school educator*

Grand Rapids
Maupin, Karin Louise *secondary school educator*

Grosse Pointe
Foust, Julie Ann *secondary school educator*

Hale
Lixey, Elizabeth Voulgarakis *secondary school educator*

Hancock
Sampson, Susan Audrey *private school educator*

Harbor Springs
Cappel, Constance *educational consultant, writer*

Harris
Erva, Karen Therese *elementary school educator*

Hemlock
Wallace, Beatrice Leslie *secondary school educator*

Hillsdale
Robichaud, Donna Lynn *career planning administrator*
Stoyk, Kay Marie *special education educator*

Holt
Thompson, Teresa Ackerman *special education educator*
Weinner, Brenda Lynne *director, education educator, special education educator*
Wood, Mary Elizabeth *retired secondary school educator, church musician*

Howell
Schoendorff, Christine Joy *elementary school educator*

Ida
Griffith, Cathleen Ann *principal*

Interlochen
Kamischke, Ellen Jane *mathematics educator, writer*

Ishpeming
Hyttinen, Nicole Marie *elementary school educator*

Jackson
Haglund, Bernice Marion *elementary school educator*
Livesay, Jacqueline Ryder *elementary school educator, music educator*
Stone, Marilyn Joanne *elementary school educator*
Wilcox, Charlene Deloris *retired elementary school educator*

Kalamazoo
Bailey, Judith Irene *academic administrator, educator, consultant*
Barth, Jessica L. *mathematics educator*
Dahlinger, Martha Louise *elementary school educator*
Davison, Kim M. *elementary school educator*
Gordon, Alice Jeannette Irwin *retired secondary school educator, retired elementary school educator*
Howard-Wyne, Josie *elementary school educator*
Lennon, Elizabeth Marie *retired special education educator*
Showalter, Shirley H. *academic administrator*

Kent City
Mulder, Susan Elizabeth *special education educator*

Lake Orion
Leonard, Jacquelyn Ann *retired elementary school educator*

Lambertville
Korthuis, Kathleen Elizabeth *retired dean*

Lanse
Berggren-Moilanen, Bonnie Lee *education educator*

Lansing
Blackwell, Dorothy Ruth *school system administrator*
Destrempes, Sandra Lee *elementary school educator*
Dickinson, Melinda S. *elementary school educator*
Marazita, Eleanor Marie Harmon *retired secondary school educator*
Straus, Kathleen Nagler *academic administrator, educator*
Torres-Dickson, Teresita Sancho *elementary school educator*

Lapeer
McCauley, Betty Bailey *school system administrator*

Livonia
Kujawa, Sister Rose Marie *academic administrator*
Regner, Deborah Allyson *educator*

Macomb
Christopher, Kathy Lynn *secondary school educator*

Madison Heights
Uhlmann, Jamie A. *secondary school educator*

Manistique
LaLonde, Angela J. *primary school educator*

Marquette
Coffey, Lauriann Gant *elementary school educator*

Marshall
Hammond, Jane Pamela *adult education educator*

Midland
Barker, Nancy Lepard *university official*
Grzesiak, Katherine Ann *primary school educator*
Meinhardt, Carol Jean *education educator*

Monroe
Siciliano, Elizabeth Marie *secondary school educator*
Sweat, Sara J. *secondary school educator*

Mount Pleasant
Louisell, Linda Kay *elementary education educator, musician*
Seefelt, Nancy E. *academic administrator, educator*

Muskegon
Ross, Annette Lee *educational consultant*

Niles
Wickham, Cindy Sue *principal*

Northville
Hansen, Jean Marie *mathematics educator, computer educator*
Long, Robin Jane Ellingsworth *elementary school educator, special education educator*

Norton Shores
Chichester, Faith Christine *elementary school educator*

Novi
Serenson, Lynn Ann *mathematics educator*

Okemos
Edwards, Caryn Louise *educational consultant, special education educator*

Ossineke
Larson, Ilene Kay *elementary school educator*

Otisville
Morris, Valerie Lyn *secondary school educator*

Owosso
Reynolds, Pauline Phyllis *retired primary school educator*
Rugenstein, Carrie L. *secondary school educator*

Plymouth
Melkvik, Jennifer Kent *retired mathematics educator*
Whiteley, Kendra Leigh *secondary school educator*

Pontiac
Anderson, Anita A. *secondary school educator*
Riley, Mary Jane Stewart *secondary school educator*

Portage
Kim, Sonja Chung *elementary school educator*

Rochester
Kleimola, Sharon Leigh *retired elementary school educator*
Packard, Sandra Podolin *education educator, consultant*

Rochester Hills
Anjum, Uzma *pre-school educator*

Rockford
Shutich, Tina Lynn *mathematics educator*

Saginaw
Markey, Leah Gene *elementary school educator*
Strawter, Lee Anna *secondary school educator*

Saint Clair Shores
Kavadas-Pappas, Iphigenia Katherine *preschool administrator, educator, consultant*
Skoney, Sophie Essa *educational administrator*
Zimmer, Anne Fern Young *educator, researcher, administrator*

Saline
Kittel, Pamela Rae *education educator*

Scottville
Wojciechowski, Amy Jo *college official*

South Haven
Llorens, Merna Gee *elementary school educator, retired music educator*

South Lyon
Athey, Sarah Elizabeth-Marks *secondary school educator, social studies educator*

Southfield
Chudnov, Marlene Myra *elementary school educator, educational consultant*
Hill, Juantonia NeKeshia *mathematics educator, consultant*
Hoffman, Susan Patricia Wary *special education educator, elementary school educator*

Southgate
Gundick, Sinthea Marie *assistant principal*

Sparta
McDonald, Lois Alice *elementary school educator*

Spring Lake
Bussard, Janice Wingeier *retired secondary school educator*

Sterling Heights
McKinney, Theresa *secondary school educator*
Pericak, KrysAnna *biology educator*

Taylor
Coleman, Fay *literature and language educator, director*
Crawford, Manette Sue *parochial school educator*

Traverse City
Hale, Carol Jean *teacher, city commissioner*
Hogg, Cinda L.P. *elementary school educator*
Lutes, Charlene Ann *academic administrator, director, consultant*
Tejkl, Pamela Marie *secondary school educator*

Trenton
Beebe, Grace Ann *retired special education educator*

Troy
Maierle, Bette Jean *director*
Majeske, Penelope Kantgias *education educator, educator*

Walled Lake
Remer, Deborah Jane *elementary school educator*

Warren
Lavin, Sharon Renai *secondary school educator*
Pranger, Kathleen *computer science educator*

Washington
Gardner, Karen *mathematics educator, computer scientist, educator*

Waterford
Anderson, Francile Mary *secondary school educator*

West Bloomfield
Lansaw, Traci Lynn *mathematics educator*

Westland
Drews, Kristine Mae *secondary school educator*

Wyoming
Couch, Katrina Denise *elementary school educator*

Ypsilanti
Lewis-White, Linda Beth *elementary school educator*
Pollock, Sandra Sue *retired elementary school educator*
Stevens, Lizbeth Jane *special education educator, researcher*

Zeeland
Pyle, Debra Lee *elementary school educator*

MINNESOTA

Afton
Robb, Babette *retired elementary school educator*

Austin
Jelinek, Polly Madison *retired elementary school educator*

Bemidji
DeKrey, Petra Jean Hegstad *retired elementary school educator*

Bloomington
Larson, Beverly Rolandson *retired elementary school educator*

Caledonia
Lapham, Mary Ellen *elementary school educator*

Cloquet
Belanger, Sharon Amling *special education educator*

Collegeville
Forman, Mary *dean*

Coon Rapids
Boros, Deborah Theresa *elementary school educator*
Haij, Karla Marie *secondary school educator*

Crystal
Stark, Janice Ann *elementary school educator*

Duluth
Carlson, Helen Louise *educator*
Martin, Kathryn A. *academic administrator*
Stauber-Johnson, Elizabeth Jane *retired elementary school educator*
Teich, Theresa Marie *educator*

Excelsior
Pfeifer, Polly Lee *elementary school educator*

Faribault
Collins, Ruth Ann *principal*

Foley
Cross, Eunice D. *elementary school educator*

Fosston
Lohmeier, Lynda K. *secondary school educator*

Grand Rapids
King, Sheryl Jayne *secondary school educator, counselor*

Hackensack
Marquart, Petra A. *training consultant*

Hibbing
Langanki, Debra Lynn *secondary school educator*
Zbikowski, Kristen Lynn *education educator*

Hopkins
Zins, Martha Lee *elementary school educator, director*

Kenyon
Page, Amy Lynn *special education educator*

La Crescent
Moen, Cheryl A. *literature and language educator*

Long Lake
Lowthian, Petrena *academic administrator*
Priesz, Connie Joan *secondary school educator*

Mahtomedi
Nickleby, Kathe Jo Anne *assistant principal*

Mankato
Barber, Eddice Belle *retired education educator*
Fitzsimons, Nancy Marie *social work educator*
Korpal, Charyl Elaine *secondary school educator*

Maple Grove
Kirpes, Anne Irene *elementary school educator*
Leiseth, Patricia Schutz *educational technology specialist*

Menahga
Farnam, Jennifer M. *elementary school educator*

Minneapolis
Jones, Stella Marie *retired school counselor*
Parent, Jill Cari-Stepanchak *elementary school educator*
Roth, Margaret Agnes *child development educator*
Veldey, Bonnie *special education educator*
Wilhelm, Gretchen *retired secondary school educator, volunteer*

Minnetonka
Vanstrom, Marilyn June Christensen *retired elementary school educator*

Moorhead
Welken, Jan Denise *elementary school educator*

New Brighton
Kieffer, Kathleen Cecil *elementary school educator*

Owatonna
Larson, Diane LaVerne Kusler *principal*

Pelican Rapids
Hovland, Gladys Myhre *secondary school educator*

Pine Island
Blankenship, Carolyn Ann *elementary school educator, educator*

Richfield
Devlin, Barbara Jo *school district administrator*
Zehnpfennig, Elizabeth Frances *secondary school educator*

Rochester
Lynch, Emily *elementary school educator*

Roseville
Peterson, Jill Susan *retired elementary school educator*
Seagren, Alice *school system administrator, former state legislator*

Saginaw
Stauber, Marilyn Jean *retired elementary and secondary school educator*

Saint Cloud
Barth, M. Jane *secondary school educator*
McKay, Joane Williams *dean*

Saint Louis Park
Husen, S. Aino Maria *retired elementary school educator*

Saint Paul
Clayton, Diane *education educator*
Dybvig, Mary McIlvaine *educational consultant, psychologist*
Hanna, Kathryn Lura *university administrator*
Harvey, Patricia A. *school system administrator*
Huber, Sister Alberta *academic administrator*
Lee, Andrea Jane *academic administrator, nun*
Rodríguez, Liliana Cristina *mathematics educator*
Sonday, Arlene W. *educational consultant*

Savage
Ottoson, Carol J. *literature and language educator*

Truman
Jones, Patricia Louise *elementary counselor*

Waterville
Pettis, Patricia Amanda *secondary school educator, farmer*

Waubun
Sullivan, Kathleen M. Skaro *secondary school educator*

Willmar
Aaker, Melissa B. *secondary school educator*

Winona
Towers, Karen R. *education educator*
White, Marjorie Mary *retired elementary school educator*

MISSISSIPPI

Alcorn State
Wyatt, Helen J. *special education educator*

Benton
Moore, Teresa L. *mathematics educator*

Biloxi
Brown, Sheba Ann *elementary school educator*
Manners, Pamela Jeanne *secondary school educator*

Booneville
Scott, Brenda Sue *elementary school educator*

Brandon
Hollis, June D. *secondary school educator*
Wallis, Haley Hickman *elementary school educator*
Wand, Kimberly Joanne *assistant principal*

Clarksdale
Walton, SuzAnne W. *elementary school educator*

Cleveland
Odom, Maryann Bell *secondary school educator*

Clinton
Reynolds, Judith M. *secondary school educator*

Columbus
Donat, Patricia Lyn *education educator, academic administrator*
Hayes, Rebecca Everett *gifted and talented educator*
Traynham, Lurene Jones *retired secondary school educator*

Crystal Springs
Nixon, Brenda Joyce *elementary school educator, small business owner*

Diberville
Steuart, Sybil Jean *elementary school educator*

Ellisville
Holifield, Patricia DiMiceli *educator*
Ross, Lisa Sims *special education educator*

Gallman
Henley, Rita Darby *biology educator*

Grenada
Howell, Sandra Stroud *assistant principal*
Jackson, Teresa Roberts *principal, consultant*

Gulfport
Egland, Katherine Tatum *educational consultant, director*

Hattiesburg
Bedenbaugh, Angela Lea Owen *chemistry educator, researcher*
Diket, Mary Read M. *academic administrator, educator*
Price, Helen Hoggatt *counseling administrator*
Reinshagen, Yolanda P. *elementary school educator*

Heidelberg
Dewey, Linda L. *secondary school educator*

Holly Springs
Greer, Sarah Rolston Doxey *retired elementary school educator*

Itta Bena
Branton, Susan Camille *education educator, department chairman*

Iuka
Barnes, Betty Jean *educational administrator*

Jackson
Baird, Carol Lowry *elementary school educator*
Bounds, Renee P. *secondary school educator*
Campbell-Duckworth, Terri Elaine *elementary school educator*
Carlisle, Peggy Jane *elementary school educator*
Channell, Linda Guynes *education educator*
Collins, Deloris Williams *secondary school educator*
Creel, Sue Cloer *retired secondary school educator*
Harrison, Esther M. *elementary school educator, state representative*
Mayeaux, Anne Russell *education educator*
Wasson, Catherine Church *education educator*

Kosciusko
Dorrill, Mary Sue Valentine *elementary school educator*

Laurel
Stennett, Kathy Elaine *elementary school educator*

Liberty
Filbert, Eleanor Jane *special education educator*

Louisville
McMillin, Lisa Sullivan *education educator*

Lucedale
Nyman, Terri Ruffin *special education educator, director*

Mccomb
Everett, Katherine Milton *special education educator*

Minter City
Mitchell, Patsy Malier *religious school founder, administrator*

Mississippi State
Hopper, Peggy F. *education educator*

Natchez
Anderson, Rose L. Dyess *elementary school educator, poet*
Butler, Aquetta Dennis *elementary school educator, social worker*
Foster, Evaline L. *education educator, researcher*
Marion, Ann *retired elementary school educator, psychologist*
Woods, Daisy Dennis *chemistry educator*

Nettleton
Hairald, Mary Payne *retired secondary school educator*

Picayune
Penton-Smith, Tammy L. *elementary school educator*

Puckett
Sanders, Barbara Boyles *secondary school educator*

Ridgeland
Adams, Betty Sue *mathematics educator*

Rienzi
Price, Debbie F. *elementary school educator*

Senatobia
Taylor, Janice Keith *elementary school educator*

Starkville
Dampier, Caryn *self-defense instructor*

Summit
Yawn, Amelia Lou *adult education educator*

Sumrall
Graham, Barbara Anne *secondary school educator*
Parker, Edna Faye *special education educator*

Terry
Collins, Lynda B. *biology educator*

Tupelo
Botts, Lillian Sullivan *elementary school educator*
Fields-Jenkins, Deloris Jean *elementary school educator*
Randle, Barbara Ann *retired secondary school educator*

University
Wiggers, Nancy Rhea *education educator*

Vardaman
Pettit, Melissa G. *special education educator*

Vicksburg
Keulegan, Emma Pauline *special education educator*
Pace, Carol Rebecca *elementary school educator*

Waveland
Pearce, Belinda Allen *elementary reading recovery educator*

Waynesboro
Crager, Ginny Lee *gifted and talented educator*

MISSOURI

Belton
Daggett, Kathleen *special education educator*

Berkeley
Reynolds, Kara Stutsman *elementary school educator*

Bethel
Coonrod, Delberta Hollaway (Debbie Coonrod) *retired elementary school educator, consultant*

Blue Springs
Hartford, Cathy Jeanette *elementary school educator*
Neff, Karla Sue *secondary school educator*
Powers, Cecile Lorraine *secondary school educator*

Boonville
Lohr, Liberty Ann *biology educator*

Bosworth
Ireland, Betty Jean *retired principal, music educator*

Bridgeton
Adams, Mary Louise *education educator, archivist*

Butler
Cochran, Beth *gifted and talented educator*

Cape Girardeau
Reinmann, Carol Sue *elementary school educator*

Caruthersville
Burch, Paula Usery *special education educator*

Catawissa
Strupp, Darlene Clara *special education educator*

Chesterfield
Finley, Marlynn Holt *elementary educator consultant*
Lipman, Marilyn Lee *retired elementary school educator*

Columbia
Libby, Wendy B. *academic administrator*
Underdown, Joy *retired elementary school educator*

Crane
Gipson, Pauline *special education educator*

Creve Coeur
Ehrlich, Martha Ann *elementary school educator*

De Soto
Withinton, Nancy Kay *elementary school educator*

Delta
Kidd, Mary Jane *literature and language educator*

Elsberry
Boley, Anna Marie *literature and language educator*
Talbot, Carla Renee *elementary school educator, veterinarian technician*

Excelsior Springs
Hewitt, June Ann *elementary school educator*

Fayette
Inman, Marianne Elizabeth *academic administrator*

Florissant
Conrad, Mary Trench *elementary school educator*
James, Dorothy Louise King *special education educator*
Loraine, Sandra F. *secondary school educator*
Shreves, Judy Rae *director*
Sikora, Diana Marie *elementary school educator*
Williams, Julie Marie *history educator*

Forsyth
Klinefelter, Sarah Stephens *retired dean, broadcast executive*

Fulton
Windsor, Kendra Linnette *elementary school educator*

Gladstone
Eldridge, Tamara Lynn *elementary school educator*
Lucas, Nancy Jean *elementary school educator*

Golden City
Smith, Karen Lynne *elementary school educator*

Hannibal
St. Clair, Mary Ann Walker *secondary school educator, small business owner*
Snider, Lois A. Phillips *educator*
Webster, Carolyn Lucy *elementary school educator*

Harrisonville
Ellsworth, Tina Marie *elementary school educator, social studies educator*
Scavuzzo, Tracy Truesdell *mathematics educator, department chairman*

Hazelwood
O'Reilly, Mary Catherine *elementary school educator*

Hermann
Lerbs, Leah Lynn *special education educator*

Holden
Pirch, Pamela Sue *elementary school educator*

Humansville
Richler, Zenia H. *naturopath educator, health facility administrator*

Imperial
Meloy, Patricia *vocational school educator, art educator*

Independence
Coppenbarger, Cecelia Marie *special education educator*
Johnson, Sharon Elaine *elementary school educator*
Marlow, Lydia Lou *retired elementary school educator*
Ray, Nancy Roberta *retired secondary school educator*
Starks, Carol Elizabeth *retired principal*
Wishy, Shawna Nicole *special education educator*

Ironton
Pollock, Connie *mathematics educator*

Jamesport
Minnick, Sally Schaefer *director*

Jefferson City
Laden, Mary Ellen *literature and language educator*
Mahoney, Carolyn Ray *academic administrator*
Milne, Jennifer Anne *literature and language educator*

Joplin
Chlanda, Suzanne Lea *secondary school educator*
Freeman, Catherine Elaine *education educator*

Kansas City
Bakely, Lisa Meng *elementary school educator*
Byers-Pevitts, Beverley *college administrator, educator*
Caulfield, Joan *director, educator*
Collins, Kathleen *academic administrator, art educator*
Farnan, Betty Lynne *secondary school educator*
Garner, Taralyn R. *secondary school educator*
Guilliland, Martha W. *academic administrator*
Lombard, Regina A. *elementary school educator*
Rhodes, Sandra Lavern *elementary school educator*
Suni, Ellen Y. *dean, law educator*
Swaffar, Glenda Jean *director*
Ulrich, JoAnn D. *elementary school educator*
Vann-Hamilton, Joy *academic administrator*
Willsie, Sandra Kay *provost, dean, internist, educator*
Woods-Taylor, Cleora Lynesia *mathematics educator, consultant*

Kirksville
McLane-Iles, Betty Louise *academic administrator, language educator, writer*

Kirkwood
Hoglen, Jewel Pamela *retired secondary school educator*
Muller, Nancy Hrdlicka *elementary school educator*
Wentzel, Karen Lynn *secondary school educator*

La Grange
Guilfoyle, Nancy Jean *biology educator*

Lees Summit
Linder, Beverly L. *elementary school educator*

Madison
Hawkins, Diana Wendellin *elementary school educator*

Malden
Reaves, Marilynn *elementary school educator*

Malta Bend
Richtermeyer, Beverly Summers *special education consultant*

Marionville
Boaz, Bethany L. *secondary school educator*

Marshfield
Frame, Susan S. *special education educator*
Marlin, Elmeree McGoon *mathematics educator*

Maryville
Galbreath, Leslie M. *academic administrator*
Strating, Sharon L. *elementary school educator, professional staff developer, educational consultant*

Mc Fall
Gist, Rebecca Jane *special education educator*

Mexico
Teague, Deborah Gant *elementary school educator*

Moberly
Aulbur, Beth Anne *elementary school educator*

Mound City
Parker, Phyllis E. *mathematics educator*

Nelson
Humburg, Barbara Ann *elementary school educator*

Neosho
Allman, Margaret Ann Lowrance *counseling administrator*

Oregon
Dudeck, Anne Lee *reading specialist*

Owensville
Leick, Carol Lynn *retired special education educator*

Pacific
Wilson, Jill Marie *elementary school educator*

Prairie Home
Bacon, Sherri Leah *elementary school educator*

Reeds Spring
Brewer, Karen Elaine Lauterbach *secondary school educator*

Rich Hill
Laughlin, Jo Ann *retired elementary school educator*

Richmond
Solomon, Patty Jo *elementary school educator*

Saint Ann
Cook, Melissa Ann *elementary school educator*

Saint Charles
Baker, Mary Elizabeth *elementary school educator*
McDonnell, Kathleen A. *supervisor*
Riley, Theresa Marie *elementary school educator*
Scofield, Nadine Renée *special education educator*

Saint Joseph
Brownell, Vickie Marie *elementary school educator*
Correu, Sandra Kay *special education educator*
Schoenlaub, Elizabeth Mae *elementary school educator*
Smith, Patricia Laura *literature and language educator*
Wallace, Kathy Joan *secondary school educator*

Saint Louis
Baker, Shirley Kistler *academic administrator*
Blanton, Elizabeth Anne *secondary school educator*
Briggs, Cynthia Anne *educational administrator, clinical psychologist*
Burmeister, Virginia Elizabeth *retired secondary educator*
Burns, Kara Allyn *education educator*
Driemeyer, Mary Alice *elementary school educator*
Eilers, Jennifer Ann *special education educator, counseling administrator*
Finder, Joan Bornholdt *academic administrator*
Frederiksen, Patricia Sullivan *elementary school educator*
Gibson, Marienne Antoinette *retired special education educator*
Gilligan, Sandra Kaye *private school director*
Gooch, Audrey Smith *retired education educator*
Grant, Michele Byrd *secondary school educator*
Hicks, Shirley E. *director*
Holland, Sherry Lynn *elementary school educator*
Hood, Phyllis Ilene *special education educator*
Inman, Janice Elaine *special education educator*
Jacob, Julie Ann *special education educator*
Karty, Karen S. *secondary school educator*
Kennelly, Sister Karen Margaret *retired academic administrator, church administrator, nun*
Knop, Ruth M. *mathematics educator*
Krause, Patricia Ann *elementary school educator*
Leavitt, Lynda *school system administrator, educator*
Leonard, Judith Price *educational advisor*
Lupardus, S. Carol *education educator*
Mitchell, Louise Tyndall *special education educator*
Monteleone, Patricia L. *dean*
Morrison, Liz *educational consultant*
Petralli, Mary Jane *secondary school educator*
Petru, Marianne *mathematics educator*
Rice, Rose Ann M. *secondary school educator*
Richardson, Pollie *principal*
Romanowski, Sarah Rebecca *secondary school educator*
Scheffing, Dianne Elizabeth *special education educator*
Stratman, Heather Marie *elementary school educator*
Tentschert, Cheryl Ann *middle school educator*
Thomas, Pamela Adrienne *special education educator*
Thompson, Marie Kathlyn *middle school educator*
Williams, Nellie James Batt *secondary school educator, educator*
Woodward, Mary Lou *retired elementary school educator*

Saint Peters
Bond, Karla Jo *elementary school educator*
Caples, Linda Griffin *retired secondary school educator*

Sainte Genevieve
Fischer, Nancy *secondary school educator*

Salisbury
Royston, Ginger Knierim *secondary school educator*

Sedalia
Dedrick, Rebecca Ann *elementary school educator*
Silvey, Marsha K. *elementary school educator*

Slater
Wymore, Luann Courtney *retired education educator*

Springfield
Gammel, Gloria L. *secondary school educator*
Groves, Sharon Sue *elementary school educator*
Herman, Mary Elizabeth *educator*
Loomer, Manden Jane *elementary school educator*
Maples, Carol J. *director*
Sherman, Ruth Todd *counseling administrator, educator*
Wilson, Judith Ann *secondary school educator*

Stella
Davidson, Cynthia Ann *elementary school educator*

Sunrise Beach
Wonderly, Helen Marietta *elementary school educator*

Troy
Mills, Marsha Lee *retired secondary school educator*

Warrensburg
Handly, Hilda Ann *gifted and talented educator*

Webb City
James, Kathryn A. *secondary school educator*

Webster Groves
Carr, Margaret *elementary school educator*
Mosley, Karen D. *retired elementary school educator*

MONTANA

Alberton
Jones, Maureen Gail *elementary school educator*

Anaconda
Watt, Maureen R. *retired secondary school educator*

Belgrade
Dighans, Kay Marie *elementary school educator, education educator*

Bigfork
Remington, Michelle Ganiere *principal*

Billings
Kerr, Shauna Gay *secondary school educator*

Bozeman
Buonamici, April Graham *elementary school educator, music educator*

Browning
Doore, Cynthia May *elementary school educator*

Butte
Haugen, Margaret Ellen *daycare administrator*
LaMiaux, Rita *pre-school educator, secondary school educator*

Dixon
McMillan, Eileen Margaret *daycare administrator, educator*

Floweree
Dawson, Dawn Louise *elementary school educator, church administrator*

Helena
McCulloch, Linda *school system administrator*
Stearns, Sheila MacDonald *academic administrator*

Hinsdale
Mogan, Connie K. *secondary school educator, elementary school educator*

Lodge Grass
Rockabove, Magdalene M. *special education educator*

Lolo
Stewart, JoAnne *retired director*

Lustre
Herrin, Karen Patricia *secondary school educator, singer, musician*

Malta
Brewer, Lynne Orahood *elementary school educator*

Miles City
Welbes, Diane M. *literature and language educator*

Missoula
Barnett, Mary Louise *elementary school educator*
Miller, Kathleen Elizabeth *college administrator*
Wilbur, Carol Anne *literature and language educator, researcher*

Seeley Lake
Sexton, Toni T *school system administrator, educator*

Troy
Arvish, Ellen Marie *elementary school educator*

NEBRASKA

Bancroft
Ras, Ronda Sue *secondary school educator*

Bartley
Probasco, Gayla Rae *secondary school educator*

Bayard
Muhr, Sylvia Anne *elementary school educator*

Blair
Stensaas, Starla A. *education educator, artist*

Boys Town
DeSalvo, Catherine Gaston *principal*

Grand Island
Fickes, Lynda LuRhae *elementary school educator*
Jobes, Janet Sue *elementary school educator*
Weseman, Vicki Lynne *elementary school educator*

Gretna
Druliner, Marcia Marie *education educator*

Lincoln
Grew, Priscilla Croswell *academic administrator, geologist, educator*
Hansen-Daberkow, Michelle Len *elementary school art educator*
Kern, Jeanne Rustemeyer Wood *retired secondary school educator*
Nicoll, Gayle *chemistry educator*
Simpson, Charlene Joan *elementary school educator*
Smith, Susan Louise *special educator*
Tegeler, Rebecca Sue *elementary school educator*

Maywood
Schultz, Judy Kay *guidance counselor*

Ogallala
Kennedy, Laurel R. *secondary school educator*

Omaha
Belck, Nancy Garrison *dean, educator*
Bruckner, Martha *academic administrator*
Coyne, Ann *social work educator*
Fyfe, Doris Mae *elementary school educator*
Ganzel, Linda Sue *secondary school educator*
Holian, Katherine Stover *administrator*
Kowal, Penny Hope *educational consultant*
Noble, Karyn Sue *elementary school educator*
Ranks, Anne Elizabeth *retired elementary and secondary education educator*
Rowley, Jan *secondary school educator*
Ryan, Sheila A. *retired dean, nursing educator*
Saunders, Lucille Mae *elementary education educator, librarian*
Squires, Sandra Kay *special education educator*

Oneill
Hiebner, Aida Cecilia *secondary school educator, education educator*
Rolenc, Sister Anita *parochial school educator, archivist*

Scottsbluff
Salomon, Marylou Ann *elementary school educator*

Tekamah
Cooper, Velma J. *elementary school educator*

NEVADA

Carson City
Barbie, Cathy Therese *middle school educator*
Eftimoff, Anita Kendall *educational consultant*

Fallon
Lawson, Karen E. *mathematics educator*

Fernley
Jergesen, Arvella G. *elementary school educator*

Henderson
Andolina, Nancy Jean *middle school educator, dancer, English and language arts educator*
Holmes, BarbaraAnn Krajkoski *retired secondary school educator*

Las Vegas
Ballance, Ann Elizabeth *elementary school educator, consultant*
Chung, Sue Fawn *educator, researcher*
Corbett, Susan *mathematics educator*
Cruz-Manrique, Diana Elizabeth *elementary school educator*
DeBusk, Lorraine *elementary school educator*
Ekanger, Karin L. *educational consultant*
Ernst, Suzanne *academic administrator, educator*
Gordon, Lee Diane *school librarian, educator*
Granese, Judith Ann *secondary school educator*
Hair, Kittie Ellen *secondary school educator*
Harter, Carol Clancey *former academic administrator, English language educator*
Johnson, Mary Elizabeth *retired elementary education educator*
McNair-Styles, Kimberly René *secondary school educator*
Mercier, Linda Ann *secondary school educator*
Phillips, Karen *secondary school educator*
Pierce, Thresia Korte (Tish Pierce) *primary school educator*
Rector, Mary Margaret *secondary school educator*
Shriner, Joan Ward *secondary school educator*
Silverman, Elaine Ann *mathematics educator*
Smith, Janice Alfreda *secondary school educator*

Reno
Cathey-Gibson, Sharon Sue Rinn *principal, academic administrator*
Geurden, Tammy Ann *education educator, counselor*
Graham, Margaret Katherine *retired secondary school educator*
Myers, Geraldine Ruth *special education educator, consultant*
Parsons, Cindy Michelle *special education educator*
Perry, Jean Louise *academic administrator*
Swanson, Dolores *special education educator, musician*

Silver Springs
O'Malia, Mary Frances *special education educator*

Sparks
Bria, Janice *secondary school educator, sports official*
Rice, Jennifer Stacy *literature and language educator*

Zephyr Cove
Wells, Cynthia *elementary school educator*

NEW HAMPSHIRE

Belmont
Donovan, Vicki Ann *elementary school teacher*

Brentwood
Boozer-Blasco, Claudia Ruth *family and consumer resources educator*

Canaan
Conwell, Ruth Ingrid *assistant principal, educator*
Wilson, Kristin M. *mathematics educator*

Claremont
Liveston, Denise Anne *elementary school educator*

Concord
Birdsall, Lynne A. *academic administrator*

Dover
Overbey, Susan J. *history educator*
Pelletier, Marsha Lynn *secondary school educator, poet*

Durham
Newman, J. Bonnie *academic administrator, former government official*

Exeter
McDonough, Cheryl York *principal, educational consultant*

Gilsum
Henry, Maurine Dale *elementary school educator*

Lancaster
Poekert, Rose A(nn) *elementary school educator*

Manchester
Bois, Deborah Lynn *special education educator*

Melvin Village
Humphrey, Judith Poole *retired elementary school educator*

Merrimack
Ross, Marie Elisa *elementary school educator*

Milford
Murphy, Sandra Ferguson *elementary school educator*
Queeney, Deborah Ann *special education educator*

Nashua
Arthur, Rose Ann Horman *dean*
Brodeur, Esther Corinne *educator*
Provencher, Jeanne Stansfield *secondary school educator*

New London
Berlenbach-Coburn, Susan L. *elementary school educator*
DeLuca, Susan Rice *physical education educator*
Ponder, Anne *academic administrator*

Newfields
Buck-Bacon, Louise John *education educator*

Pembroke
Poznanski, Margaret Mary *special education educator*

Peterborough
Gagnon, Nancy Spear *secondary school educator, consultant*

Plymouth
DeCotis, Ruth Janice *career planning administrator, educator*

Raymond
Stathos, Donna Lee *mathematics educator*

Stark
Spaulding, Nancy Kelly *elementary school educator, small business owner*

Whitefield
Hicks, Erica C. *mathematics educator*

NEW JERSEY

Atco
DiAngelo, Linda Mary *secondary school educator, theater director*

Avenel
Hynes-Lasek, Nancy Ellen *secondary school educator*

Barnegat
Prisbell, Kathleen Frances *middle education educator, language arts*

Barrington
Pawling, Patti J. *school system administrator*

Basking Ridge
Besch, Lorraine W. *special education educator*
Helfant, Ann M. *history educator*

Bernardsville
Robinson, Maureen Loretta *retired secondary school educator*

Blackwood
Blume, Wendy M. *dean*

Bogota
Rogers, Alison M. *special education educator*

Brick
Bertoncin, Geraldine Johnnie *elementary school educator*

Bridgewater
Hart, Karen Jean *special education educator*

Brigantine
Kickish, Margaret Elizabeth *elementary school educator*

Budd Lake
Rattner, Karlene Susan Katherine *special education educator*
Shepherd, Deborah Gulick *elementary school educator*

Burlington
Cobb, Vanessa Wynvette *elementary school educator*
Hancock, Beverly J. *retired counseling consultant, secondary school educator*

Butler
Baskinger, Wilma *elementary school educator*

Caldwell
Kearney, Sister Mary John *educator*
Werner, Patrice (Patricia Ann Werner) *academic administrator*

Camden
Brooks, Gail Denise *school system administrator, consultant*
Daniels, Albertina Diana *secondary school educator*

Cedar Grove
Helwig, Annette L. *retired elementary school educator*

Cedar Knolls
Van Wert, Linda *elementary school educator*

Cherry Hill
Erdely, Diane Louise *educator*

Chester
Gray, Pamela *gifted and talented educator*

Cinnaminson
Tosti, Susan Marie *reading specialist, educator*

Clark
Hasselman, San D. *secondary school educator*

Clarksburg
Gonyo, Marilyn E. *education educator*

Clifton
Dolinsky, Dianne Marie *secondary school educator*

Colts Neck
Crowder-Pagano, Linda Louise *special education educator*

Columbia
Timcenko, Lydia Teodora *secondary school educator, biochemist*

Cranbury
Burke, Laura Anne *elementary school educator*

Cranford
Kardos, Amelia Marie Papetti *elementary school educator*

Delaware
Hill-Rosato, Jane Elizabeth *elementary school educator*

Denville
Doane, Eileen Maloney *learning disabilities teacher consultant*

East Windsor
Guarino, Danita Cronin *special education educator*

Edison
Biunno, Theresa *physical education educator*
De Candido Kamin, Rosann Therese *secondary school educator*
De Siena-Rappa, Kelly Ann *principal*

Egg Harbor Township
Carney, Michelle Catherine *assistant principal*

Elmer
Slavoff, Harriet Emonds *learning disabilities teacher, consultant*

Ewing
Chodoroff, Nancy Arlene *elementary school educator*
Gitenstein, Donna M. *academic administrator*

Fair Lawn
Wallace, Mary Monahan *elementary, secondary schools and university educator*

Farmingdale
Jones, Elizabeth Harding *elementary school educator*

Flemington
Wolfson, Barbara Libensperger *guidance counselor*

Franklin Lakes
Pappas, Pamela A. *mathematics educator*

Franklinville
Delia, Margaret M. *elementary school educator*

Glassboro
Holdcraft, Janet Rulon *school system administrator*
McCabe, Mary Otilia Sorg *secondary school educator*

Glen Rock
Buchar, Karen *mathematics educator*
Plein, Beverly R. *elementary school educator*

Green Brook
Balsamello, Melissa (Marley) *elementary school educator*

Hackensack
Hirsch, Elisabeth Schiff *education educator emeritus*
Phifer, Emily A. *elementary school educator*
Williamson, (Eulah) Elaine *elementary school educator*

Haddon Heights
Weinberg, Ruthmarie Louise *special education educator, researcher*

Hamilton
Stuebe, Joanne *secondary school educator*

Hazlet
Beaudry, Robin Sharkey *secondary school educator*
Citro, Janet *elementary school educator, coach, secondary school educator*
Van Pelt, Dara *mathematics educator*

Highlands
Lofstrom, Arlene Katherine *primary school educator*

Hightstown
Zapicchi, Joanne Fenity *secondary school educator*

Hillsborough
Hasser, Julia M. *mathematics educator*

Hopatcong
Hill, Linda Marie Palermo *elementary school educator*

Howell
Van Vliet, Heather Agnes Joan Devlin *elementary school educator*

Jackson
Rothman, Patricia Mary *elementary school educator*

Jersey City
Dunham, Patricia Ann *elementary school educator*
West, Michelle *principal*

Lakewood
Daniels, Judith Wall *education educator, retired principal*
Doak, Nancy Ann *mathematics educator*
Williams, Barbara Anne *retired academic administrator*

Lawrenceville
Jordan, Mildred Rice Loretta *education educator*

Layton
Seely, Maribeth Walsh *elementary school educator*

Lebanon
Wagner-Westbrook, Bonnie Joan *educational consultant, director*

Linden
Bedrick, Bernice *retired principal, science educator*

Linwood
Harlan, Rebecca *secondary school educator, social sciences educator*

Long Branch
Janeczek, Terry Ann *director, science educator*

Long Valley
Duane, Jeannine Morrissey *retired elementary school educator*

Lyndhurst
Germann, JoAnn *mathematics educator*

Madison
Bull, Vivian Ann *retired academic administrator, educator*
Geehr, Patricia Bray *education educator*

Magnolia
Finley, Charlene P. *elementary school educator*
Warden, Karen Barbara *special education educator*

Manahawkin
Barton, Noreen Duffy *secondary school educator*
Collins, Sarah Jane *secondary school educator*

Manasquan
Crowning, Lisa L. *secondary school educator, horticulturist, consultant*

Marlboro
Francisco, Deborah Antosh *educational administrative professional*
Komisarczyk, Shirley Theresa *secondary school educator*

Marlton
Cheney, Eleanora Louise *retired secondary school educator*

Matawan
Liggett, Twila C. *academic administrator, broadcast executive, educator*

Mays Landing
Parrish, Virginia Ellen *retired secondary school educator*
Reichert, Kathleen Evelyn *elementary school educator*
Risimini, Barbara Lynn *secondary school educator*

Mendham
Bennett, Nancy Evans *secondary school educator*
Posunko, Linda Mary *retired elementary education educator*

Middletown
Shields, Patricia Lynn *educational broker, consultant*

Milford
Hance, Laurie Ann *biology educator*

Montclair
Barnes, Cynthia Lepre *university administrator*
Cole, Susan A. *academic administrator, language educator*
Gunthorpe, Karen Ann *elementary school educator*

Montvale
Gaeta, Michelle *mathematics educator*

Morristown
Mooney, Patricia Anne *secondary school educator*
Prisco, Dorothy DeSteno *academic administrator*

Mount Holly
Kind, Rosalind Weintraub *special education educator*

New Brunswick
Strickland, Dorothy *education educator*

New Monmouth
Dickinson, Jeanne M. *secondary school educator*
Santos, Sharon Lee *parochial school educator*

New Providence
Hirsch, Maxine K. *special education educator, councilman*
Worden, Virginia Hill *academic administrator, lawyer*

Newark
Arbuckle, Peggy Trawick *special education educator, consultant*
Ebenholtz, Jean Miriam *academic administrator*
Feldman, Cecile Arlene *dean, dental educator*
Sabio, Dorothy *elementary school educator*

Newton
Koerber, Joan C. *retired elementary school educator*
MacMurren, Margaret Patricia *secondary school educator, consultant*

North Arlington
Batshaw, Marilyn Seidner *education administrator*

North Plainfield
Irvine, Carol Stone *elementary school educator*

Ocean City
Heist, Karen Gartland *elementary school educator*

Old Tappan
Vella, April *mathematics educator*

Oradell
Carcich, Michele Leigh *biology educator*

Paramus
Atkins, Yvette *special education educator*
Boisits, Regina Marie *elementary school educator*
Hershey, Lynne R. *elementary school educator*
Jenkins, Elaine *middle school educator*
Satin, Elaine *educator*
Ward, Christine L. *elementary school educator*

Parsippany
Albert, Susan *mathematics educator*
Fletcher, Jean Stout *retired special education educator*
Puccio, Jane Anne *secondary school educator*
Solomon, Mary-Jo Kelleher *mathematics educator*

Passaic
Jakimowicz, Joan Marie *elementary school educator*
Johnson, Myrtle Alice Harris *elementary and secondary school educator*

Paterson
Schimpf, Kathleen *elementary school educator*

Pennsville
Latorre, Maria Joanne *health and physical education educator*

Perth Amboy
Dakelman, Rhonda Elyse *physical education educator*
Reyes, Irma V. *adult education educator*

Piscataway
Coppola, Sarah Jane *special education educator*

Pitman
Lohmann, Judith Leith *secondary school educator*

Pittsgrove
Chassier, Janice *elementary school educator, art educator*

Plainfield
Clinton, Birdean R. *elementary school educator*

Pleasantville
London, Charlotte Isabella *secondary school educator*

Pomona
Birdwhistell, Joanne (Anne) *retired education educator, researcher*
Dagavarian, Debra A. *college administrator, consultant*

Port Monmouth
Pfennig, Jacqueline F. *elementary school educator*

Princeton
Duncan, Dianne Walker *elementary school educator*
Hirschman, Sarah *educator*
Krulewicz, Rita Gloria *special education educator*
Malkiel, Nancy Weiss *dean, historian, educator*
Slaughter, Anne-Marie *dean*
Tilghman, Shirley Marie *academic administrator, biology professor*

Princeton Junction
Ruddiman, Joan *elementary school educator*

Randolph
Oliveira, Theresa Razzano *secondary school educator*

Ridgewood
Friedrich, Margret Cohen *guidance and student assistance counselor*

Robbinsville
Muench, Debby S. *elementary school educator*

Roselle
Di Marco, Barbaranne Yanus *principal*
Meister, Karen Olivia *secondary school educator*
Orlando, Ann Marie *educator*

Saddle Brook
Luisi, Louisa *secondary school educator*

Scotch Plains
Marion, Sarah Elizabeth *elementary school educator*
Wagner, Brooke *secondary school educator*

Sea Girt
Herschel, Andrea B. *elementary school educator*
Hillman, Barbara Hall *retired elementary school educator*

Secaucus
Ferguson, Cathleen Michele *elementary school educator*

Short Hills
Robbins-Wilf, Marcia *educational consultant*

Skillman
Cummings, Peggy Ann *counseling administrator*

Somers Point
Hardy, Janice Audrey Neubert *elementary school educator, educator*

Somerset
Bruno, Phyllis *school system administrator*

Somerville
Gorton-Horan, Ann Hilbert *vice principal*
Weisblatt, Barbara Ann *secondary school educator*

South Hackensack
Wille, Rosanne Louise *educational consultant*

South Plainfield
Green, Angela Marie *biology educator*

Southampton
O'Connor, Sheryl Broderick *literature and language educator*

Stewartsville
DrakeoBrien, Constance Susan *elementary school educator*

Stratford
DeSanto, Grace L. *elementary school educator*

Succasunna
Heike, Melissa *secondary school educator*
Pellet, Carol *elementary school counselor*

Summit
Starks, Florence Elizabeth *retired special education educator*

Teaneck
Baldwin, Dorothy Leila *secondary school educator*
Bourne-Busby, Elise Bernadette *principal*
Lechman, Sharon Elizabeth *elementary school educator*
Smith, Susan Elizabeth *guidance director*
Walker, Lucy Doris *secondary school educator, writer*

Toms River
Casey, Margaret Ellen *elementary school educator, real estate agent*
Cebula, Mary Ann Antionette *special education educator, speech correctionist*
Hibbard, Susan Clayton *secondary school educator*

Township Of Washington
Suta, Deborah *secondary school educator*

Trenton
Brown, Peggy Lee *academic administrator, consultant, singer*
Catanese, Kathleen Smith *secondary school educator*
Jones, Sarah Lucille *principal, consultant*
Mendez, Miriam Roman *elementary school educator*
Plank, Helene Elizabeth *academic administrator*

Turnersville
Crone, Patricia Ann *gifted and talented educator*

Union
Lederman, Susan Sturc *public administration professor*

Union City
Bozoyan, Sylvia *elementary school educator*

Vernon
Maher, Jean Elizabeth *counseling administrator*
Struble, Suzanne R. *educator*

Verona
Sepcie, Christine *secondary school educator*

Vineland
Hesser, Lorraine M. *special education educator*

Voorhees
Carter, Catherine Louise *retired elementary school educator*

Waldwick
Lynch, Carol *special services director, psychologist*

Wall
Parsons, Susan Steele *secondary school educator*

Warren
Hennings, Dorothy Grant (Mrs. George Hennings) *education educator*

Wayne
Benedict, Theresa Marie *retired mathematics educator*
Goldstein, Marjorie Tunick *special education educator*

West Orange
Bojsza, Joan E. *elementary school educator*

Westville
Compo-Pratt, Paula Anita *secondary school educator*

Whippany
Vallee, Michelle Linda *pre-school educator*

Willingboro
Denslow, Deborah Pierson *primary school educator*
Franklin, Iris *elementary school educator*
Jenerette, Joyce Williams *elementary school educator, educational consultant*

Woodbine
Orlando-Spinelli, Josephine *gifted and talented educator, educational consultant*

Woodbridge
Paugh, Nancy Adele *secondary school educator, school system administrator*

Woodlyne
Vannais, Renae Michele *elementary school educator*

Woodstown
Tatnall, Ann Weslager *reading educator*

NEW MEXICO

Alamogordo
Hobson, Suellen Ann Weber *retired elementary school educator*
McFadin, Helen Lozetta *retired elementary school educator*

Albuquerque
Adams, Nancy D. *elementary school educator*
Beiler, Holly Anne *education educator*
Boivin, Carol Jane *retired secondary school educator*
DeNee, Lori S. *elementary school educator*
Draper, Dorothy E. *middle school mathematics educator*
Frias, Shirlee N. *elementary school educator*
Graff, Pat Stuever *secondary school educator*
Kirschman, Tammy Jean *literature and language educator*
Koester, Betty Jeannette *retired elementary school educator*
Long, Vonda Olson *educator, counselor*
Posey, Carolyn Ann *secondary school educator*
Scarnecchia, Suellyn *dean, law educator*
Wade, Gaylia Suzanne *secondary school educator*

Artesia
Flores, Sylvia A. *principal*
Taylor, Kathy Lynn *elementary school educator*

Carlsbad
Duarte, Rose Mary R. *elementary school educator*

Cerrillos
Lutz, Nancy Cole *educational consultant*

Clovis
Kilian, Joy A. *pre-school educator*
Nigreville, Carrie Christopher *principal*
Shade, Marsha J. *elementary school educator*

Eunice
Gideon, Brenda K. *mathematics educator*

Farmington
Anderson, Evelyn Louise *elementary school educator*
Luttrell, Mary Lou *elementary school educator*
Pepin, Fran *secondary school educator*
Young, Patricia Anne *secondary school educator, writer*

Grants
Barnes, Ina Jean *retired elementary educator*

Hobbs
Ayers, Dolores Elaine *literature and language educator*
Francke, Susan *elementary school educator*
Holladay, Kelly Gayle *dean*
Weldy, Lana Gail *secondary school educator*

Las Cruces
Valdez, Michelle Liane *educator*

Las Vegas
Lopez, Clara M. *director*

Lordsburg
Clem, Sarah Lynn *special education educator*
Moralez, Joselyn Hope *special education educator*

Los Alamos
Willerton, Beverly Kay *mathematics educator*

Mora
Abeyta, Jeanie *secondary school educator*

Moriarty
Cox, Darlene Beth *secondary school educator*

Placitas
Watson-Boone, Rebecca A. *dean, researcher, library and information scientist, educator*

Raton
Ahlm, Jo LaVonne *elementary school educator*

Rio Rancho
Glaser, Kandace Kaye *elementary school educator*
Meyerson, Barbara Tobias *elementary school educator*
Weber, Alois Hughes *principal*

Roswell
Bailey, Sharon L. *history educator, literature and language educator*
Henry, Debbie Cheryl *elementary school educator*

Ruidoso
Stover, Carolyn Nadine *middle school educator*

Santa Fe
Fisher, Lisa Gray *English language educator*
Garcia, Veronica *school system administrator*
Hanson, Linda N. *academic administrator, educator*
Sandoval, Isabelle Medina *education educator*

Shiprock
Atcitty, Fannie L. *elementary school educator, education educator*

Silver City
Paez, Carolyn Jean *secondary school educator*

Taos
Garcia, Christine *academic administrator, educator, researcher*

Tohatchi
Tucker, Amanda Yeates *history educator*

NEW YORK

Addison
Coombs, Joanne Dininny *kindergarten educator*

Albany
Branigan, Helen Marie *educational consultant, administrator*
Ebert, Loretta Caren *university librarian*
Hagan, Diana Lynn *elementary school educator*
McDade, Turina L. *principal*

Alden
Bindemann, Lisa Marie *mathematics educator*

Amherst
Conner, Judith G. *elementary school educator*
Minklein, Sharon Elizabeth *elementary school educator*

Apalachin
Williams, Christin Michele *elementary school educator*

Attica
Allen, Susan Diane *educator*

Aurora
Ryerson, Lisa M. *academic administrator*

Babylon
DaSilva, Lynn Judith *special education educator*
Drance, Lisa Iacono *secondary school educator, department chairman*
Herbst, Jane Elizabeth *school librarian*
Schnepp, Angela J. *secondary school educator*
Schwarz, Barbara Ruth Ballou *elementary school educator*

Baldwin
Aliano, Joy Caryl *retired elementary school educator*

Batavia
Taylor, Karen Marie *education educator*

Bath
Wright, Brenda K. *primary and elementary school educator*

Bay Shore
Shea, Melissa Gordon *biology educator*

Bayside
Housman, B. Jane *secondary school educator*

Beacon
Rousseau, Christina Jeannie *elementary school educator*

Belle Harbor
Goldsmith, Cathy Ellen *retired special education educator*

Belleville
Colby, Ann Julia *history educator*

Bellmore
Rosenstein, Elyse S. *secondary school educator*

Bemus Point
Rollinger, Mary Elizabeth *school counselor*

Bergen
Osborn, Nancyjean Marie *principal*
Penman, Loren Anne *academic administrator*
Stasko, Andrea Aloia *physical education instructor*

Bethpage
Leone, Michele Castaldo *secondary school educator*

Binghamton
DeFleur, Lois B. *academic administrator*
Malin, Jo *college administrator*
Phelps, Susan Williams *secondary school educator*
Pierce, Lonna McKeon *school librarian*
Sauer, Karin *microbiology educator*
Swain, Mary Ann Price *university official*

Bluff Point
Fitch, Linda Bauman *retired elementary school educator*

Brentwood
Couch, Miriam Knowles *retired special education educator*

Brockport
Bowdler, Jane Maxon *mathematics educator*

Bronx
Cojuangco, Samantha Caballes *elementary school educator*
Damico, Debra Lynn *academic administrator, language educator*
Delaney, Sharon Elizabeth *elementary school educator*
Ramsey, Doris Theresa *elementary school educator*
Robinson, Gwendolyn Neina *elementary school educator*
Sanchez-Silkman, Jennifer Christine *elementary school educator*
Shanklin, Elizabeth E. *secondary school educator*
Slade, Barbie Evette Delk *special education educator*
Wertheim, Mary Danielle *educational coordinator*

Bronxville
Myers, Michele Tolela *academic administrator*

Brooklyn
Allotta, Joanne Mary *elementary school educator*
Casey, Joan Maureen *secondary school educator*
Clinton, Kisha *elementary school educator*
Cogan, Eva *education educator*
DeNicola, Michelle *mathematics educator*
Fletcher, Donna Angella *secondary school educator*
Gamble, Cahtina Robyne *elementary school educator*
Hill, Elizabeth Anne *academic administrator, lawyer*
Isaac-Emmons, Merlyn Hulda *academic administrator, educator*
Meade, Dorothy Winifred *retired educational administrator*
Moses Brown, Brenda Gene *elementary school educator*
O'Connor, Sister George Aquin (Margaret M. O'Connor) *academic administrator, educator*
Peruggi, Regina S. *academic administrator*
Schweikert, Mary Lou *elementary school educator*
Washington, Tyona *adult education educator*
Wexler, Joan G. *dean, law educator*
Wolfe, Ethyle Renee (Mrs. Coleman Hamilton Benedict) *academic administrator*
Zysberg, Janet Gail *elementary school educator*

Buffalo
Amato, Rosalie *secondary school educator*
Cathey, Patrice Antoinette *secondary school educator, director*
Chopra-Sukumaran, Pratibha *secondary school educator*
Fischman, Jane Ann Vogel *retired secondary school educator*
Fox, Mary Hawkshaw *early childhood special education educator, consultant*
Fuda, Siri Narayan K.K. (Elaine T. Barber) *director*
Garas-York, Keli Ann *reading specialist*
Gielow, Kathleen Louise *career planning administrator, consultant, special education educator*
Putnam, Susan K. *psychology educator*
Veronica, Debra Clarisse *principal*

Canandaigua
Yarnall, Susanne Lusink *elementary school educator*

Castleton On Hudson
Wagner, Mary Susan *academic administrator*

Catskill
Wolfe, Geraldine *academic administrator*

Cedarhurst
Lagnado, Jennifer M. *assistant principal*
Van Raalte, Polly Ann *reading and writing specialist, photojournalist*

Central Islip
James, Sharon Ann *elementary school educator*

Central Valley
Hafner, Catherine Courtney *retired physics educator*

Chazy
Ratner, Gayle *special education educator*

Cheektowaga
O'Brien, Nancy Marie (Meyer) *secondary school educator*

Chestnut Ridge
Orlando, Susan (Isadora) *academic administrator, educator*

Clifton Park
Murphy, Mary Patricia *elementary school educator*
Valenti, Laurie M. *elementary school educator*

Clinton
Havens, Pamela Ann *academic administrator*
Stewart, Joan Hinde *academic administrator*

Clyde
Barr, Marilyn G. *school system administrator*

Cohoes
Kelly, Deanna M. *assistant principal*

Cold Spring
Battersby, Katherine Sue *elementary school educator*

Commack
Capozzi, Suzanne *literature and language educator*
Cohen, Judith W. *retired academic administrator*

Cornwall On Hudson
Lawrence, Sharon Lynn *director, educator*
Peirce, Karen Patricia *education educator*

Corona
Alfonso-Bica, Kristy Lynn *elementary school educator*

Cortland
Wood, Barbara Lynn *elementary school educator*

Cuba
Keough, Sandra J. *retired special education educator, retired principal, education educator*

Dix Hills
Somerville, Daphine Holmes *retired elementary school educator*
Virostko, Joan *elementary school educator*

Dobbs Ferry
Hotchkiss, Janet McCann *secondary school educator*
Lesack, Beatriz Díaz *secondary school educator*

East Amherst
Kirdani, Esther May *retired school counselor*

East Aurora
Woodard, Carol Jane *educational consultant*

East Chatham
Bues, Susan Denise Wildermuth *academic administrator*

East Greenbush
Van Alstyne, Ruth Beattie *elementary school educator*

East Hampton
Goldstein, Judith Shelley *director*
Schetlin, Eleanor M. *retired associate dean*

East Islip
Cullen, Valerie Adelia *secondary school educator*
Donohue, Claire P. *retired school librarian*

East Patchogue
Geller, Edith Harriet *elementary school educator*

East Setauket
Orlowski, Karel Ann *elementary school educator*

East Syracuse
DeSiato, Donna Jean *superintendent*

Eggertsville
Segalla, Mary Louise *elementary school educator*

Eldred
Campbell, Regina Farrell *literature and language educator*

Elmira
Kerr-Nowlan, Donna Courtney *pre-school administrator*
Wavle, Elizabeth Margaret *academic administrator*
Zeigler, Carrie Elizabeth Watt *elementary school educator*

Endicott
Rittinger, Patricia Ann *secondary school educator, mathematician*

Erin
Locker, Cynthia Ann *elementary school educator*

Fairport
Fitch, Darlene *elementary school educator*
Holtzclaw, Diane Smith *elementary school educator*
Meck, J. Karen *retired elementary school educator*

Falconer
Halm, Nancye Studd *retired academic administrator*

Fallsburg
Biccum, Amanda *elementary school educator*

Far Rockaway
Mitchell, Lillian Adassa *principal*
Sussman, Laureen Glicklin *elementary school educator*

Floral Park
Curci, Paula *counseling administrator, poet, television personality*

Flushing
Anderson, Michelle J. *dean, law educator*
Capra, Linda Ann *elementary education educator*
Lee, Emily Lin *director, real estate company executive*
Rosenberg, Deborah A. *special education educator*
Smith-Campbell, Charmaine *secondary school educator*

Fly Creek
Steiner, Judith Marie *elementary school educator*

Frankfort
Conigilaro, Phyllis Ann *retired elementary school educator*
Shuster, Donnalyn E. (Donalyn Eaton Shuster) *secondary school educator, artist*

Franklinville
Schnell, Gertrude Helen *retired elementary school educator*

Fredonia
Wood, Caroline *secondary school educator*

Freeport
Martorana, Barbara Joan *secondary school educator*
Mitchell, Alice Joyce *secondary school educator, dietician*

Fulton
Dexter, Carol N. *mathematics educator*
Sisco, Melissa Ann *history educator*

Garden City
Klein, Kitty R. *counseling administrator*

Garnerville
Chapman, Margaret Elizabeth *elementary school educator*
Weaver, L. Karen *retired reading specialist*

Geneva
Best, Sharon Louise Peckham *retired college administrator*

Glen Cove
Rothberg, Judith *elementary school educator, researcher*

Glenwood
Chambers, Denning Jessyca *middle school educator*

Gouverneur
Stacy, Trudy L. *elementary school educator*

Grand Island
Kennedy, Magdalene Miller *secondary school educator*

Granville
Baker, Donna Dougan *elementary school educator*
Halnon, Faith E. *elementary school educator*

Great Neck
Kornahrens, Casey *elementary school educator*
Roth, Gladys Thompson *retired special education educator*
Schoenholt, Helene M. *elementary school educator*

Greenville
Overbaugh, Maryanne W. *elementary school educator*

Guilderland
Escobar, Deborah Ann *gifted and talented educator*

Hamilton
Chopp, Rebecca S. *academic administrator*
Pagano, Jo Anne *education educator*

Hampton Bays
Bucicchia, Carolanne Stephanie *elementary school educator*
Sherter, Selma *retired elementary school educator*

Harriman
Kay, Sandra Irene *special education educator, consultant*

Hauppauge
Reid, Margaret Elizabeth *elementary school educator, secondary school educator*
Zuckerman, Dorothy Ann *elementary school educator*

Hempstead
Adams, Velma M. *assistant principal, consultant*
Fleming, Marion Parker *education educator*
Levin, Phillis *education educator, writer*
Raney, Carolyn E. *educational consultant*
Watford, Dolores *elementary school educator*

Hicksville
Noll, Amy *secondary educator*
Reedy, Catherine Irene *retired elementary school educator*
Svraka, Patti A. *elementary school educator*
Waxberg, Emily Steinhardt *special education educator, administrator*

Highland Falls
Smith, Cheryl Ann *secondary school educator*

Holbrook
Grenzig, Gail A. *school system administrator, consultant*

Hoosick Falls
Benoit, Lois Elaine *director, retired music educator*

Hopewell Junction
Carey, Jacqueline Carter *retired elementary school educator*
Cznarty, Donna Mae *secondary school educator*

Horseheads
Andrake, Nancy Carolyn *retired secondary school educator*
Clark, Judy Ann *elementary school educator*

Huntington
Roberts, Elizabeth Anne Stephens *educational consultant*

Huntington Station
Devlin, Jean Theresa *education educator*
Robins, Faye E. *principal, elementary school educator*
Stevens, Susan Seltenreich Cirillo *special education educator*

Hyde Park
Blackman, Drusilla Denise *dean*

Inwood
Soffer, Grace Florey *retired elementary school educator, artist*

Islip
Libert, Nancy Porta *retired elementary school educator*

Ithaca
Berkelman, Mary Hobbie *retired elementary school educator, adult education educator*
Dyckman, A(lice) Ann *retired academic administrator*
Firebaugh, Francille Maloch *academic administrator*
Hughes, Diane L. Hicks *elementary school educator, secondary school educator*
Kaske, Carol Margaret Vonckx *educator*
Martin, Carolyn A. (Biddy Martin) *provost*
Norton, Mary Beth *history educator, writer*
Stycos, Maria Nowakowska *adult education educator*
Williams, Peggy Ryan *academic administrator*

Jackson Heights
Gall, Lenore Rosalie *educational administrator*
Ryan, Judith Ann *dean*
Simeone, Helen Lilli *retired elementary school educator*

Jamaica
Daly, Mary C. *dean, law educator*
Davis-Jerome, Eileen George *educational consultant, principal*
Edwards, Cynthia E. *principal*
Faust, Naomi Flowe *education educator*
Kaplan, Carolyn Sue *elementary school educator*
Keizs, Marcia V. *academic administrator*
Malewitz, Joan *elementary school educator, multi-media specialist*
Ramos, Alice M. *education educator*

Jamestown
Harms, Michele Gail *director*

Kingston
Bruck, Arlene Forte *secondary school educator*
Kolodziejski, Cynthia F. *secondary school educator*

Lagrangeville
Orlik, Dawn *mathematics and computer science educator*

Lake George
Nellis, Nora LaJoy *special education educator, writer*

Lake Huntington
Spafford, Suzanne Lee *biology educator*

Lake Placid
Pappalardo, Rosa Gloria *secondary school educator*

Lancaster
Kappan, Sandra Jean *elementary school educator*
Schunke, Crystal *physical education educator*

Lindenhurst
Omeis, Lisa Marie *principal*
Scharf, Megan Jean *mathematics educator*
Sherrard, Jessica E. *mathematics educator*

Liverpool
Padula, Wanda Jean *secondary school educator*

Lockport
Shaughnessy, Mary Ellen *educator*

Locust Valley
Hayduk, Sonna A.S. *secondary school educator, department chairman*

Long Island City
DeMaio, Barbara K. *principal*
Lieberman, Janet Elaine *academic administrator*
Roberts, Kathleen Joy Doty *secondary school educator*

Lynbrook
Cline, Starr *elementary school educator, writer*

Mahopac
McAvoy, Kathleen Fleming *mathematics educator*

Malverne
Alesse, Judith *special education educator*

Manchester
Wink, Laura A. *special education educator*

Massapequa
Oliver, Danielle Michelle *special education educator, recreational therapist*
Pelkofsky, Janine Marie *special education educator*
Puleio, Ann Margaret *special education educator*

Massena
Perez, Loretta Ann Bronchetti *secondary education educator, small business owner*

Medford
Klement, Diane *retired educational assistant*

Medina
Chambers, Krista Ruth *mathematics educator*

Melville
Basile, Sheila *secondary school educator, consultant*

Memphis
Woolson, Gloria Jean *education educator*

Merrick
Fleischman, Francine D. *secondary school educator*
Glogau, Lillian Flatow Fleischer *educational administrator*
Howard, Joyce Anne *elementary school educator*

Mexico
Deloff, Dola Louise *secondary school educator*

Middle Island
Clarke, Hughette Naomi *elementary school educator*
Curiale, Gina *secondary school educator, director*
Kanowsky, Janet Marie *secondary school educator*
Zitterman, Jolene Lauret *mathematics educator*

Middleburgh
Mau, Lisa Anne *special education educator*

Middletown
Horler, Nichole *elementary school educator*
Lowe, Danielle Frances *elementary school educator*

Millwood
Durst, Carol Goldsmith *food studies educator*

Monroe
Santorelly, Annmarie *special education educator*

Montgomery
Moore, Virginia Lee Smith *elementary school educator*

Monticello
Stanton, Dorothy Marie *special education educator, tax specialist*

Montrose
Paternoster, Kathleen A. *secondary school educator*

Moravia
Welch, Joan Minde *elementary school educator*

Morrisville
Cleland, Gladys Lee *academic administrator, adult education educator*

Mount Vernon
Addesso, Angela Joyce *school system administrator*

Nanuet
Jelalian, Christine *elementary school educator, secondary school educator*

Nesconset
Goldstein, Joyce *special education educator*

New Hartford
Battista, Diane Russo *elementary school educator, music educator, personal trainer*

New Hyde Park
Haase, Lauren *mathematics educator*
Laudin, Riza Ann *elementary school educator*

New Paltz
Emanuel-Smith, Robin Lesley *special education educator*
Flanagan Kelly, Anne Marie *academic administrator*

New Rochelle
Curry, Ellen R. *academic administrator, educator*
Reddington, Mary Jane *retired secondary school educator*
Wolf, Helen *director*

New York
Anderson, Lisa *dean, political science professor, researcher*
Arndt, Carmen Gloria *secondary school educator*
Arndt, Cynthia *educational administrator*
Barron, Marlene *education educator*
Baslaw-Finger, Annette *education educator, consultant*
Best, Wanda *career planning consultant*
Birman, Ronnie Rathkopf *retired elementary school educator*
Bloomgarden, Karenne Jo *elementary school educator, small business owner*
Boylan, Elizabeth Shippee *academic administrator, biologist, educator*
Brabeck, Mary Margaret *dean, psychology professor*
Brown, Joyce F. *academic administrator*
Burgess, Clara Skipwith *retired principal*
Burns, Red *academic administrator*
Campbell, Mary Schmidt *dean*
Clarke, Pamela Jones *headmaster*
Claster, Jill Nadell *academic administrator, history educator*
Consagra, Sophie Chandler *academic administrator*
Davis, D. Lavelda *dean, academic administrator*
Durkin, Dorothy Angela *university official*
Ellenbogen, Marjorie *retired elementary school educator*
Essandoh, Hilda Brathwaite *primary school educator*
Fuhrman, Susan H. *academic administrator, education educator, researcher*
Gibson, Arlene Joy *headmaster*
Gleason, Barbara Jo *literature and language educator*
Guttmacher, Sally Jeanne *education educator*
Hoffner, Marilyn *university administrator*
Horowitz, Frances Degen *academic administrator, psychology educator*
Istomin, Marta Casals *retired school president, performing company executive*
Jelinek, Vera *dean*
Jeynes, Mary Kay *college dean*
Kardish, Ruth *retired elementary school educator*
Lang, Mary Ann *special education educator, administrator*
Lanquetot, E. Roxanne *retired special education educator*
Leiman, Joan Maisel *university administrator, hospital administrator*
Levine, Naomi Bronheim *academic administrator*
Lloyd, Jean *retired early childhood educator*
Love-Hassell, Esther Boyer *special education educator, consultant*
Misher Stenzler, Shari *youth activities organization administrator*
Molholt, Pat *academic administrator, associate dean*
Powel, Jane C. *educational consultant, elementary school educator*
Prutzman, Penelope Elizabeth *elementary school educator*
Rabb, Harriet Schaffer *academic administrator, lawyer*
Rosensaft, Jean Bloch *university administrator*
Rowland, Esther E(delman) *retired dean*
Sclafani, Susan K. *educational consultant, former federal agency administrator*
Seidenberg, Rita Nagler *education educator*
Selby, Cecily Cannan *dean, science educator*
Shapiro, Judith R. *academic administrator, anthropology educator*
Townsend-Butterworth, Diana Barnard *educational consultant, educator*
Wachtell, Cynthia June *academic administrator, director, literature educator*
Walzer, Judith Borodovko *academic administrator, educator*
Warner, Jayne Lena *academic administrator*
Williams, Harriet Clarke *retired academic administrator*
Yu, Pauline Ruth *former dean, educational association administrator*
Zaken, Grace Ambrose *project coordinator, educator*

Niagara University
Foote, Chandra Jeanet *education educator, writer, elementary school educator*

Niskayuna
Quirion, Ramona Shaw *elementary school educator*

North Salem
Tompkins, Elizabeth J. *secondary school educator*

North Tonawanda
Insalaco, Lisa A. *reading specialist*

Northport
McGarry, Frances Lorraine *education educator*

Nyack
Poston, Linda *dean, library director*

Ogdensburg
Niederer, Marla Lee *special education educator*

Oneonta
Murphy, Susan Ryan *literature and language educator*

Oriskany
Jacobson, Karen *retired elementary school educator*

Ovid
Scoles, Marie Y. *elementary school educator*

Owego
Coppens, Laura Kathryn *special education educator*

Oxford
Hover, Dawn A. *director*

Ozone Park
Bellamy, Renee Adele *secondary school educator*

Parish
Campbell, Janet Schwagler *biology educator*

Patchogue
Tutino, Rosalie Jacqueline *college administrator*

Peekskill
Mason, Rebecca Sussa *retired secondary school educator*
Wiggins, Ida Silver *elementary school educator*

Pittsford
Barker, Julie A. *school system administrator*
Drake, Jill Leah *elementary school educator*

Plattsburgh
Hughes, Nancy Copeland *early childhood education educator*

Pleasantville
Palmer, Stephanie Teresa *elementary school educator*

Port Chester
Aubry, Renée L. *secondary school educator*

Port Jefferson
Block, Estell Lenora *educational consultant*
MacKinnon, Ann Laurie *retired elementary school educator*

Potsdam
Scott, Jean A. *university president*

Poughkeepsie
Brakas, Nora Jachym *education educator*
Hill, Catharine Bond (Cappy Hill) *academic administrator, economics professor*
Jackson, Judy Faye *academic administrator*
Pisterzi, Candy *special education educator*

Red Hook
Turchetti, Celine Marie *elementary school educator*

Rego Park
King, Deborah Irene *academic administrator*
Tsui, Soo Hing *educational research consultant*

Remsenburg
Hirsch, Ann Ullman *retired academic administrator*

Riverhead
Carr, Theresa *mathematics educator*
Passanante, Patricia Marie *middle school educator*

Rochester
Adams, Carol H. *dean*
Barone, Jessica Lynn *geology educator*
Blanda-Holtzberg, Marianne Lourdes *education educator, consultant*
Campbell, Alma Jacqueline Porter *elementary school educator*
Chiverton, Patricia Ann *dean, nursing educator*
Christensen, Sonya Marie *school librarian*
Everett, Claudia Kellam *retired special education educator*
Grant, Marilynn Patterson *secondary school educator*
Moss, Joy Folkman *elementary school educator*
Parrinello, Diane Davies *retired pre-school educator*
Patane, Joyce A. *secondary school educator*
Pavone, Jill Russell *special education educator*
Roberts, Robyn Renay *elementary school educator, coach*
Routly, Tracey Laurene *elementary school educator*
Satter, Mary Ann *literature and language educator*

Rockville Centre
Honigsfeld, Andrea M. *education educator*

Rocky Point
Tvelia, Carol Ann *principal, elementary school educator*

Rotterdam Junction
Cox, Paulyn Mae *retired elementary school educator*

Rushville
Evans, Mary Melinda *special education educator*

Rye
Mickatavage, Jane Cline *director*
O'Sullivan, Kerry *educational consultant*
Walters, Carolyn Maria *secondary school educator*

Rye Brook
Sarkodie-Mensah, Aimie *physical education educator*

Sag Harbor
Olson, Kryn Dacia *elementary school educator, artist*

Saint Johnsville
Schoff, Marcia Anne *elementary school educator*
Stock, Patricia D. *literature, language and history educator*

Sanborn
Nowak (Jarosz), Linda Therese *special education educator, consultant*
Robinson, Deborah J. *counselor, educator, consultant*

Sands Point
Cullinan, Bernice Ellinger *education educator*

Sandy Creek
Miller, Cheryl Marie *special education educator, small business owner*

Saratoga Springs
Riley, Dawn C. *educational philosopher, researcher*

Saugerties
Falzano, Colleen *special education educator*

Schenevus
Peterson, Elizabeth *retired elementary school educator, advocate*

Seaford
Cupo, Janine *secondary school educator*

Selkirk
Wood, Diane Mary *special education educator*

Seneca Falls
Norman, Mary Marshall *academic administrator, alcohol/drug abuse services professional, educator*

Shortsville
King, Mary Esther *elementary school educator*

Shrub Oak
Semcken, Nancy *elementary school educator, singer*

Silver Creek
Cloud, Linda Beal *retired secondary school educator*

Skaneateles
Anderson, Ruth Liberty *retired special education educator*

Smithtown
Haskins, Debra May *academic administrator, educator*

Solvay
Miori-Merola, Doreen M. *literature and language educator*

South Ozone Park
Gallagher-Griffith, Victoria Alana *secondary school educator*

Southampton
Costa, Judith Ann *secondary school educator*

Sparkill
Boyd, Helen M. (S. Helen R. Boyd) *education educator*
Nelson, Marguerite Hansen *special education educator*

Spencerport
Clark, Kathleen Julia *mathematics educator*

Staten Island
Berci, Margaret Elizabeth *education educator*
Berman, Barbara *educational consultant*
Dobis, Joan Pauline *academic administrator*
Haupt, Carol Magdalene *retired elementary school educator*
Lockhart, Patricia Ann *elementary school educator*
Springer, Marlene *university administrator, educator*

Stillwater
Bourgeois, Kimberly Beth *mathematics educator*

Stony Brook
Flynn-Bisson, Kathleen Mary *school system administrator*
Kenny, Shirley Strum *academic administrator*

Sunnyside
O'Keefe, Katherine Patricia *elementary school educator*

Syracuse
Arterian, Hannah R. *dean, law educator*
Cantor, Nancy *academic administrator*
Custer, Mary Jo *university official*
Freund, Deborah A. *academic administrator*
Giacchi, Judith Adair *elementary school educator*
Macero, Jeanette DiRusso *academic administrator*
Neuburger, Jane *education educator*
Thorin, Suzanne E. *dean, university librarian*

Tonawanda
Vacanti, Mary Parisi *director, consultant*

Troy
Jackson, Shirley Ann *academic administrator, physicist*
Neff, Jeanne Henry *academic administrator*

Unadilla
Pagano, Alicia I. *education educator*

Utica
Bamberger, Sheila Lister *retired secondary school educator*

Valatie
Deily, Ann Beth *special education educator, consultant*

Valhalla
Jenks, Eileen A. *academic administrator, real estate agent*

Valley Stream
Wood, Catherine T. *special education educator*

Vestal
Harding, Linda Kristina *special education educator*

Wappingers Falls
Brusco, Teresa Eileen *special education educator*
Stabile, Patrice Christine *mathematics educator*

Webster
Bobb, Marie L. *mathematics educator*
Squires, Shelley Marx *retired special education educator*

West Babylon
Ford, Clara S. *retired secondary school educator*
Williams, Patricia Hill *retired academic administrator*

West Hempstead
Kayton-Courtney, Kathleen A. *elementary school educator*
Maus, Mary Ann Dillman *elementary school educator*

West Islip
D'Amour, Michelle Aline *principal*

West Nyack
Coffey, Kimberly E. *secondary school educator*

Westbury
Marks, Debra Jane *special education educator*

White Plains
High, Kemba M. *special education educator*
Turk, Jane Skouge *education educator*
Waterhouse, Lynette *mathematics educator*

Willard
Covert, Sarah Jane (Sally) *elementary school educator*

Windsor
Meeker, Carol Louise *special education educator, consultant*

Wolcott
Wiggins, Dorothy L. *retired primary school educator*

Woodside
Spain-Savage, Christi Lynn *secondary school educator*
Swift, Constance Redmond *special education educator*

Yonkers
Boveroux, Lorie Ann Hansen *secondary school educator, graphics designer*
Lee, Claudia S. *retired elementary school educator*
Liggio, Jean Vincenza *adult education educator, artist*
Mayer, Heidi Marie *primary school educator*
Patton, Debra Ruth *elementary school educator*
Weston, Francine Evans *secondary school educator*

Yorktown Heights
Schiller, Barbara *retired special education educator*

NORTH CAROLINA

Advance
Jones, Jerry Lou Holbert *elementary school educator, rancher*

Ahoskie
Bracy, Cecelia Wiggins *primary school educator*

Apex
Corn, Melissa Ann *secondary school educator*
Sapp, Brenda *elementary school educator*

Asheboro
Buchanan, Elizabeth Spoon *assistant principal, language educator*
Ray, Juanita S. *secondary school educator*

Asheville
Fedock, Barbara C. *primary school educator, consultant*
Polite, Lettie Wilson *retired elementary school educator, retired school librarian*
Sgro, Beverly Huston *principal, elementary school educator, state official*

Belmont
Belli, Rebecca Sue *elementary school educator, music educator*
Cannon, Barbara Somers *secondary school educator*

Bessemer City
Sellers, Laurie Jean *elementary school educator*

Boone
McFadden, Margaret H. *education educator, writer*
Olin Zimmerman, Sara Jane *education educator*

Bostic
Smith, Teresa Hunt *elementary school educator, counselor*

Bryson City
Mason, Sonja *secondary school educator*

Burlington
Moncure, Jane Belk *educator, author, consultant*
Phillips, Ruth Ann *retired secondary school educator*

Burnsville
Allen, Rosetta Rosetta *elementary school educator*

Carthage
Brady, Jean Vick *education educator*

Cary
Beals, Betsy Jones *elementary school educator*
Kirk, Bonnie Longest *retired elementary school educator*

Chapel Hill
Broad, Margaret Corbett (Molly Broad) *academic administrator*
Dolber, Carole Christoff *secondary school educator, music educator*
Folkerts, Jean *dean, journalism educator*
Hill, Deborah Ann *special education educator*
Levine, Madeline Geltman *literature and language educator, translator*
Michalak, Sarah C. *university librarian*

Charlotte
Bliss, Melissa Moore *chemistry educator*
Eppley, Frances Fielden *secondary school educator, writer*
Goode, Rebekah Evelyn *literature and language educator*
Hofmann, Noreen *elementary school educator, music educator*
Huss, Carol Berryhill *mathematics educator*
McVicker, Melissa Quick *counseling administrator, educator*
Mercer, Evelyn Lois *retired counseling administrator*
Newcomb, Betty Lou Atkinson *retired mathematics educator*
Pardee, Teresa Tansey *history educator*
Pearson, Gwendolyn Cureton *elementary school educator, singer*
Peterson, Evonne Stewart *elementary school educator*
Peterson, Teresa B. *educational consultant*
Ramminger, Shelly Lynn *elementary school educator*
Tranquillo, Mary Dora *organization development consultant, educator*
Tyson, Cynthia Haldenby *academic administrator*
Wall, Audrey G. *secondary school educator*
Wright, Bonnie H. *elementary school educator*
Yancy, Dorothy Cowser *college president*

Cherryville
Beam, Susan Putnam *elementary school educator*

Colfax
Hodge, Katherine Rhodes *retired school guidance counselor*

Concord
DeVore, Leigh Ann *gifted and talented educator, elementary school educator*
Gardiner, Jill Kennon *secondary school educator*
Long, Amy E. *secondary school educator*

Cornelius
Lindenberger, Kathleen Marie *literature and language educator*

Cove City
Schiller, Pamela Ann *physical education educator*

Dallas
Brown, Pearlie Murray *school librarian*

Davidson
Dixon, Stephanie Bell *elementary school educator*

Durham
Alden, Betsy Turecky *academic administrator, clergywoman*
Bartlett, Katharine Tiffany *dean, law educator*
Denlinger, Ann T. *school system administrator*
Jakubs, Deborah *university librarian*
Jurgelski, Annette Elizabeth *academic administrator*
King, Marjorie Jean *secondary school educator*

Edenton
Muro-Torres, Rosalita *elementary school educator*

Elizabeth City
Tomlinson, Susan K. *elementary school educator*

Fayetteville
Carrasquillo, Katrina Beaufort *secondary school educator, consultant*
Darnell, Michelle R. *philosophy educator*
Farrior, Helen Hooks *retired assistant principal*
Hagans, Valerie Mae Gee *special education educator*
Jordan, Karla Salge *retired primary school educator*
Mohn, Amy Elizabeth Brennan *special education educator, retail executive, consultant*
Parker, Ellen Koonce *retired secondary school educator*
Roe, Kathryn Jane *elementary school educator*

Flat Rock
Oliver, Ann Breeding *secondary school educator, art dealer*

Franklin
Berger, Lee Hollingsworth *secondary school educator*
Earhart, Eileen Magie *retired elementary school educator, retired child and family life educator*

Garner
Retseck, Meghan Maerene *elementary school educator*

Gastonia
Evelyn, Ball Love *mathematics educator, department chairman*

Greensboro
Abell, Nicole Forcht *secondary school educator*
Bynum, Magnolia Virginia Wright *retired secondary school educator*
Cole, Johnnetta Betsch *academic administrator, educator*
Ingold, Jennifer Carrie *educator*
Oliver, Donna H. *academic administrator, secondary school educator*
Sullivan, Patricia A. *academic administrator*
Zopf, Evelyn LaNoel Montgomery *retired guidance counselor*

Greenville
Honesty, Tara Marie *educational consultant, educator*

Hallsboro
Barefoot, Anne Farley *secondary education educator, consultant*

Havelock
Jacques, Paula G. *literature and language educator*

Hendersonville
Hamilton, Hilda Wingo *elementary school educator*
Houck, Amelia Ann *elementary school educator*

Hickory
Fisher, Kathryn Pattillo *education educator, department chairman*
Painter, Lorene Huffman *retired education educator, psychologist*
Sherrill, Betty Pearson *retired elementary school educator*

High Point
Ellis, Phyllis Simerly *elementary educator, reading specialist*
Howard, Lou Dean Graham *elementary school educator*
Palmer, Pamela Murrill *educator*

Highlands
DeWolf, Jane Evans *mathematics educator*

Hillsborough
Roney, Sarah Davis *elementary school educator*

Horse Shoe
Osby, Mary Ann Caroline *secondary school educator*

Huntersville
Jagoe, Tonya Burr *elementary school educator*

Jacksonville
Harlow, Elizabeth Snell *physical education educator*

Kernersville
Webb, Ann Marie *literature and language educator, department chairman*

King
Hunter, Deborah H. *elementary school educator*

Kings Mountain
Sellers, Elizabeth Ellison *special education educator*

Kinston
Matthis, Eva Mildred Boney *retired academic administrator*

La Grange
Sasser, Brenda Glenn *elementary school educator*

Lewisville
Gould, Anne Austin *special education educator*

Lexington
Carlton, Robbin Briley *elementary school educator*

Liberty
Coco, Donna A. W. *elementary school educator*

Littleton
Skinner, Sue Dossett *retired director*

Lumberton
Harris, Audra Brisson *education educator*

Marion
Pratt, Sarah Ellen *secondary school educator*
Weaver, Joe Le Ann *biology educator*

Matthews
Kocsis, Joan Bosco *elementary school educator*
McClanahan, Tina Annette *elementary school educator, consultant*

Mebane
Fricke, Jill E. *elementary school educator*

Misenheimer
Kean, Barbara McSwain *education educator, department chairman*

Monroe
Rorie, Nancy Catherine *retired secondary school educator*
Williams, Karen C. *elementary school educator*

Mooresboro
Plummer, Doris Gochnauer *elementary school educator*

Morehead City
Gross, Marjorie K. *education educator, educator, small business owner*

Mount Airy
Billings, Melanie Sparks *secondary school educator, department chairman*

Mount Holly
Whobrey, Virginia Jean *retired director*

Murfreesboro
Wallace, Dorothy Mae Adkins *educator*

Murphy
Brooks, Ellyn Hersh *retired special education educator*
Deslauriers, Suzanne Dawsey *secondary school educator, artist*
Holcomb, Linda Laine *elementary school educator, director*

Russell, Margaret Jones (Peg Russell) *retired secondary school educator, writer*

Nashville
Penick, Angela Lucas *elementary school educator*

New Bern
Harper, Elizabeth Scott *academic administrator, retired literature educator*

Newland
Campany, Kay Hudkins *biology educator, assistant principal*

Pfafftown
Johnson, Theresa M. *retired special education educator*

Pineville
Nemeth, Dian Jean *secondary school educator*

Pittsboro
Freehling, Brooke Ann *elementary school educator*

Raleigh
Davis, Janice *school system administrator*
Gustafson, Sarah *elementary school educator*
Hartford, Maureen A. *academic administrator*
Jarrett, Polly Hawkins *retired secondary school educator*
Nelson, Brandy René *assistant principal*
Newhouse, Sherri France *elementary school educator*
Owen, Carolyn Trent *education educator*
Page, Anne Ruth *gifted and talented educator, education specialist*
Parramore, Barbara Mitchell *education educator*
Sardi, Elaine Marie *special education educator*
Steed, Michelle Elnora *special education educator, consultant*
Tyndall, Krystal Gwen *secondary school educator*
Zelek, Cheryl Ann *gifted and talented educator*

Rougemont
Holeman, Betty Jean *counseling administrator*

Roxboro
Cowan, Amy Michelle *elementary school educator*

Salisbury
Hall, Telka Mowery Elium *retired assistant principal*
Troxler, Willie Thomasene *retired elementary school educator*

Shelby
Edgar, Ruth R. *retired elementary school educator*

Smithfield
Harris, Patricia Ann Brady *principal, educational consultant*
Wiggs, Shirley JoAnn *retired secondary school educator*

Southern Pines
Cardwell, Nina Fern *special education educator*
Linsey, Elizabeth Arlline *primary school educator*

Southport
Phelps, Mary Ann Bazemore *elementary school educator*

Spencer
Secreast, Patricia Lineberger *elementary school educator*

Stanley
Black, Saunders Proctor *special education educator*

Statesville
Dacons, Gwendolyn Brown *educator*
Elliott, Carolyn Cole *secondary school educator, department chairman*
Harris, Nancy Lewis *home economics educator*
Hoover, Lynn Horn *secondary school educator*

Swanquarter
Credle, Gina C. *mathematics educator*

Sylva
Clapp, Amanda Grace *elementary school educator*

Taylorsville
Johnston, April M. *elementary school educator*

Wadesboro
Hamby, Kristie Lynne *director*

Wake Forest
Kimrey, Karen Goss *secondary school educator*

Walstonburg
Beaman, Joyce Proctor *retired secondary and elementary school educator, writer*

Warrenton
Kearney, Irene Spruill *elementary school educator*

Wilkesboro
Dale, Brenda Stephens *gifted and talented educator*
Klark, Denise J. *special education educator, consultant*

Wilmington
DePaolo, Rosemary *academic administrator*
Gray, Marilyn F. Grinwis *elementary school educator, music educator*

Wilson
Howell, Maria DeLane *elementary school educator*

Winston Salem
Bottoms, Rebecca Lynn *literature and language educator*
Cahill, Eileen Mary *secondary school educator*

Jarrell, Iris Bonds *elementary school educator, retired small business owner*
Pubantz, Gloria Annunziata *elementary school educator*

Winterville
Edwards, Sarah *biology educator*

Youngsville
Burwell, Edith Brodie *retired elementary school educator*

Zebulon
McNair, Suzette Jordan *elementary school educator*
Privette, Janet Brown *elementary school educator*

NORTH DAKOTA

Beulah
Maize, Linda Lou *elementary school educator*

Bismarck
Evanson, Barbara Jean *middle school education educator*
Joersz, Fran Woodmansee *secondary school educator*
Ketterling, Debra M. *secondary school educator*

Devils Lake
Krogfoss, Kimberly Jean *elementary school educator*

Dunseith
Gladue, Irene *elementary school educator*

Ellendale
Larson, Lavonne Fay *education educator*

Fargo
Lardy, Sister Susan Marie *academic administrator*
Meester, Holly *elementary school educator, music educator, sales executive*
Morey, Charlotte Ann *elementary school educator, music educator*

Fort Totten
Carlson, Eilene Theresa *counseling administrator*

Fort Yates
Chief Eagle, Joan *secondary school educator*

Gackle
Wittmier, Denise Donelle *elementary school educator*

Golden Valley
Nordgren, Mary Kathleen (Kathy Nordgren) *secondary school educator*

Grand Forks
Ashe, Kathy Rae *special education educator*
Olson, Myrna Raye *education educator*
Page, Sally Jacquelyn *university official, management educator*
Ryberg, Bridget Fay *literature and language educator*
Swanson, Zona Luciel *retired elementary school educator*

Hettinger
Dunn, Jeri L. *literature and language educator*

Horace
Hajek, Melissa Dawn *elementary school educator*

Mandan
Hossman, Rebecca Lynn *special education educator*

Mayville
LeClair, Elizabeth Jane *elementary school educator*

Saint John
Haas, Judith *elementary school educator*

Valley City
Rogers, Patricia Louise *education educator, consultant*

Wahpeton
Donahe, Peggy Yvonne *gifted and talented educator, librarian*

West Fargo
Boutiette, Vickie Lynn *elementary school educator, reading specialist*
Simmons, Marti J. Johnson *gifted and talented education educator*
Ulrickson, Cheryl J. *elementary school educator*

Wishek
Dockter, Nancy Jean *principal, elementary school educator*

Zahl
Anfinson, Donna Mae *retired elementary school educator, home economics educator*

OHIO

Ada
Allison, Arlene Marie *elementary school educator*
Boger, Gail Green Parsons *educator*

Akron
Dietz, Margaret Jane *retired public information director*
Jones, Hedy Julie *retired secondary school educator*
Sparrow, Kathleen Gail *elementary school educator*
Wymer, Danielle Marie *mathematics educator*

Alliance
Smith Alder, Angela Grace *education educator*

Amelia
Kahles, Cheryl Mary *elementary school educator*

Amherst
Von Kaenel, Michelle Lisa *elementary school educator*

Athens
Cooper-Chen, Anne *journalism educator, researcher*
Safran, Joan Schulman *education educator, researcher*

Aurora
Ross, Violet Bica *retired elementary school educator, retired psychologist*

Barberton
Koch, Frances Didato *literature and language educator, writer*
Schrock, Ruth *elementary school educator*

Batavia
Campbell, Cheryl Gay *history educator*
Muskopf, Beth A. *supervisor*

Beavercreek
Feller, Loretta Anne *elementary school educator*

Bedford Heights
Golden, Virginia Ann *principal*

Berea
Tomlin-Houston, Lisa *higher education administrator, director*

Bergholz
Goddard, Sandra Kay *retired elementary school educator*

Bethel
Weatherspoon, Mary Darlington *middle school educator*

Beverly
Spurr, Dawn M. *special education educator*

Blacklick
Robinson, Bernice Joyce *secondary school educator*

Bowling Green
Baird, Alice Knar *retired education educator*
Heckman, Carol A. *biology educator*

Broadview Heights
Jergens, Maribeth Joie *school counselor*

Brooklyn
Jaggard, Vicky Lynn *literature and language educator*

Brunswick
Kebberly, Dorene G. *elementary school educator, music educator*
Spirakus, Karen Ann *elementary school educator, researcher*

Cambridge
Barzda, Susan Marie *special education educator, art educator*

Campbell
Peltz, Ruby *elementary school educator*

Canton
Ringley, Kathleen J. *director*
Swanson, Joyce Eileen *elementary school educator*
Torok, Tammy *mathematics educator*

Centerville
Geier, Sharon Lee *retired special education educator, realtor*

Chagrin Falls
Brown, Jeanette Grasselli *retired director*
Cortese, Julia F. *retired elementary school educator*
Robertson, Linda F. *educational administrator*

Chesterland
Cooey, Kathleen Marie *mathematics educator*

Chillicothe
Greene, Judy *secondary school educator*
Leedy, Emily L. Foster (Mrs. William N. Leedy) *retired education educator, consultant*

Cincinnati
Ates, Delories *retired counseling administrator*
Auyang, Grace Chao *education educator, consultant*
Bryant, Irene Melba *retired elementary school educator, artist*
Cain, Linda Joanne *retired academic administrator*
Clark, Cathy Sue *special education educator*
Farrell, Pamela Christine *secondary school educator*
Groppe, Elizabeth T. *education educator*
Hall, Madelon Carol Syverson *elementary school educator*
Halsall, Mary E. *biology educator*
Kreps, Martha S. *elementary school educator*
Levy, Helen E. *director*
Meisner, Patricia Ann *assistant principal*
Morrow, Ardythe Luxion *adult education educator, researcher*
Nagy, Donna M. *dean, law educator*
Patterson, Claire Ann *career technical educator*
Spohn, Dorothy M. *retired elementary school educator*
Teague, Carolyn Louise *daycare administrator*
Teeters, Linda Marie *retired secondary school educator*

Thomas, Hannah H. *retired elementary school educator*
Woods, Carol Smith *private school educator*
Zimpher, Nancy Lusk *academic administrator*

Cleveland
Ainsworth, Joan Horsburgh *retired director*
Callesen-Gyorgak, Jan Elaine *special education educator*
Eustis, Joanne D. *university librarian*
Heintschel, Ruthann M. *school system administrator*
Jaffe, Marcia Weissman *elementary school educator*
Knieriem, Beulah White *retired elementary school educator, minister*
Queen, Joyce *elementary school educator*
Quigney, Theresa Ann *special education educator*
Shrivastava, Sunita *secondary school educator*
Smith, Beverly Harriett *elementary school educator*
Spinner, Pamela Marie *special education educator*
Sposet, Barbara Ann *secondary school educator*
Trattner, Laura V. *middle school eductor*
Wertheim, Sally Harris *director, academic administrator, dean, education educator, consultant*

Cleveland Heights
Challenger, Vicki Lee *elementary school educator*
Close, Carole Lynne *education educator, consultant*
Riley, Sharon Lynn *elementary school educator*

Columbus
Bell, Karen A. *dean*
Benton-Borghi, Beatrice Hope *secondary school educator, consultant, writer*
Clark, Colleen Romick *academic administrator*
Cottle, Deborah Ellen *elementary school educator*
Daniels, Cassandra Diane *secondary school educator, choreographer*
Foucht, Joan Lucille *retired elementary school educator, retired counseling administrator*
Graham, Laurel Susan *elementary school educator*
Grant, Jean Terry *educational consultant*
Harzoff, Elizabeth Gail *special education educator*
Hatfield, Vicki D. *secondary school educator*
Holbrook, Karen Ann *academic administrator, biologist*
Murnieks, Kimberly Ann *educational administrator*
Oxley, Margaret Carolyn Stewart *elementary school educator*
Rogers, Nancy Hardin *dean, law educator*
Seiling, Sharon Lee *family economics educator*
Snyder, Barbara Rook *academic administrator*
Zelman, Susan Tave *school system administrator*

Cuyahoga Falls
Hamilton, Priscilla *mathematics educator*
Kitska, Susan Ann *retired secondary school educator*

Cuyahoga Heights
Holt Balis, Carolyn M. *secondary school educator*

Dayton
Barr, Ann Helen *director*
Carson, Dora A. *secondary school educator*
Focht, Sandra Jean *retired elementary school educator*
Harris, Bonnie *psychological education specialist*
Killian, Jerri *director, educator*
Smith, Susan K. *director*
Smith, Vivian Blaine *elementary school educator*
Twale, Darla Jean *education educator*
Young, Yvonne Delease *elementary school educator*

Delaware
Lemke, Stacy J. *secondary school educator*

Delta
Miller, Beverly White *former college president, educational consultant*

Dover
Nign, Stacie Marie *secondary school educator*

Dublin
Bordelon, Carolyn Thew *elementary school educator*
Conrad, Marian Sue (Susan Conrad) *retired special education educator*
Meek, Violet Imhof *retired dean*
Redman, Janis F. *special education educator, department chairman*
Souch, Mary Pauline *gifted and talented educator*

Elida
Oleson, Sarah Elizabeth *elementary school educator*

Euclid
Miller, Demetra Fay Pelat *elementary school educator, city official*

Fairfield
Jamison, Peggy Louise *elementary school educator*
Templeton, Holly Jayne *elementary school educator*

Fairview Park
Flynn, Patricia M. *director, special education educator, gifted and talented educator*

Findlay
Irons, Sharon Lynn Erickson *elementary school educator, client relationship director*
Wickerham, Deborah Louise *elementary school educator*

Fremont
Breidenbach, Tonya D. *educator*
Cruz-Weaver, Bonnie E. *elementary school educator*

Gambier
Nugent, S. Georgia *academic administrator*

Genoa
Hammond, Catherine Louise *special education educator*

Hamilton
Colegate, Carol Ann *elementary school educator*
Hornsby, Judith Elizabeth *special education educator*

Harrison
Beatty, Maria Lois *elementary school educator*

Highland Hills
Sender, Maryann *director*

Holland
Beekley, Cynthia Xanthopoulos *school system administrator*

Hudson
Gauntner, Heidi Lynn *chemistry educator*
Hallenbeck, Linda S. *elementary school educator*
Lambacher, Kathleen Hartwell *retired education educator*

Huron
Leser, Anne Elizabeth *education educator*

Independence
Slivka, Thomasina *secondary school educator*

Ironton
Curry, Estella Roberta *education educator, school psychologist, consultant*

Kent
Cartwright, Carol Ann *retired academic administrator*
Clawson, Judith Louise *middle school educator*
Iverson, Susan Van Deventer *education educator*

Kettering
Denlinger, Vicki Lee *secondary school educator, healthcare educator*
Hoffman, Sue Ellen *retired elementary school educator*
Martin, Margaret Gately *elementary school educator*

Lakewood
McGlynn, Maureen Scalley *history educator*

Lancaster
Huston, Susan Kay Myers *elementary school educator*
Shipley, Holly Rene *special education educator*
Young, Nancy Henrietta Moe *retired elementary education educator*

Lebanon
Davis, Barbara Ann Lane *retired elementary school educator, retired realtor*

Leetonia
Foreman, Gail Lynne *secondary school educator*

Lewis Center
Davison, Lesli Anne *elementary school educator*
Thomason, Sandra Lee *elementary school educator*

Liberty Center
Jones, Marlene Ann *retired education supervisor*

Lima
Smith, Heather Ann *elementary school educator*

Lisbon
Danley, Linda Sharon *elementary school educator*

London
Rosebrough, Catherine Marie *special education educator, consultant*

Lorain
Comer, Brenda Warmee *elementary school educator, real estate company officer*

Marietta
Francis, Lynne Ann *elementary school educator, music educator*

Massillon
Hartline, Rebecca Sue *secondary school educator*

Mc Donald
Daigle, Barbara Dianne *elementary school educator*
Woodford, Debra Jane *elementary school educator*

Medina
DeMars, Judith M. *elementary school educator*
Farver, Cindy L. *elementary school educator*
Reichheld, Deborah Ann *retired secondary school educator, language educator*

Mentor
Blyth, Ann Marie *retired secondary school educator*

Miamiville
Franz, Iris Vivian (Vivian Franz) *dean, director*

Milan
Jeffery, Suzanne *retired elementary school educator*
Kegarise, Carol Ann *primary school educator*
Wilbur, Dora Lynn *elementary school educator*

Millersburg
Yoder, Anna A. *retired elementary school educator*

Mogadore
Kelly, Janice Helen *elementary school educator*

Monroeville
Lohmann, Gerry M. *elementary school educator*

Mount Gilead
Wells, Debra Elaine *parochial school educator*

Mount Vernon
Dessert, Kathryn Isobel *elementary school educator*
Rice, Susan A. *elementary school educator*

Napoleon
Bevelhymer, Darlene Pearl *secondary school educator, lawyer*

Nelsonville
Barrows, Roxane Renee *dean, mathematics professor*

New Albany
Partlow, Madeline *principal*

New Bremen
Wierwille, Marsha Louise *elementary school educator*

New Holland
Reeves, Nancy Rapp *elementary school educator*

New Lexington
Raines, Martha Ann *elementary school educator*

New Matamoras
Brown, Blanche Y. *secondary school educator, genealogist, researcher*

New Philadelphia
Doughten, Mary Katherine (Molly Doughten) *retired secondary school educator*
Smith, Shannon Diane *elementary school educator*

Newark
Paul, Rochelle Carole *special education educator*
Simpson, Linda Sue *elementary school educator*

Niles
Linden, Carol Marie *special education educator*

North Canton
Cooney, Sondra Miley *literature and language educator*
Sebald, Carol June *retired secondary school educator*

Oberlin
Dye, Nancy Schrom *academic administrator, historian, educator*
MacKay, Gladys Godfrey *retired adult education educator*

Okolona
Willeman, Florence Kay *secondary school educator, small business owner*

Oregon
Schwartz, Louise Marguerite *physical education educator*

Orwell
Strong, Marcella Lee *music specialist, educator*

Oxford
Thompson, Bertha Boya *retired education educator*
Thurston, Alice Janet *former college president*

Painesville
Davis, Barbara Snell *education educator*

Parma
Petrus, Sally A. *elementary school educator*
Romanovich, Patricia M. *parochial school educator*
Salzgeber, Karen A. *secondary school educator*
Scheffel, Donna Jean *elementary school educator*
Tener, Carol Joan *retired secondary school educator, consultant*

Parma Heights
Monastero, Tina Marie *elementary school educator*

Patriot
Riggle, Patricia Carol *special education educator*

Paulding
Moore, Pamela Rae *elementary school educator*

Pepper Pike
Stano, Sister Diana *academic administrator*

Pickerington
Collins, Arlene *secondary school educator*
Feesler, Molly J. *secondary school educator*
Kitsmiller, Myra Jordan *elementary school educator*
Virden, Karen Frances *elementary school educator*

Piqua
Retman, Deborah W. *biology educator*

Plymouth
Hartman, Ruth Campbell *director, educator*

Port Clinton
Ewersen, Mary Virginia *retired school system administrator, poet*

Portsmouth
Johnson, Janice E. *education educator, writer*

Quaker City
Morgan, Janet F. *elementary school educator*

Racine
Manuel, Jenny Lynn *elementary school educator*

Ravenna
O'Brien, Jane *special education educator*

Ridgeway
Moody, Loretta Jeanne *literature and language educator*

Rio Grande
Hatfield, Barbara Scott *academic administrator*

Rocky River
Hartman, Kathryn Rose *elementary school educator*
Piper, Joann Lee Elliott *retired secondary school educator, swim coach*

Sandusky
Runner, Kathleen Kahle *secondary school educator*

Seven Hills
Giulivo, Cynthia Ann *secondary school educator*

Shadyside
Martin, Carol Jaye *retired elementary school educator*

Shaker Heights
Trefts, Joan Landenberger *retired principal*

Shiloh
Meyers, Pamela Sue *elementary school educator*

Sidney
Scott, Debra A. *special education educator*

Springfield
Stelzer, Patricia Jacobs *retired secondary school educator*

Strongsville
Yates, Patricia Lawrence *elementary school educator*

Sylvania
Heuschele, Sharon Jo *dean*
Parquette, Heather Ann *elementary school educator*
Sampson, Earldine Robison *education educator*

Tiffin
Holscher, Carol Ann *retired secondary school educator*

Tipp City
Brewer, Traci Lynn *secondary school educator*

Toledo
Goldstein, Margaret Franks *special education educator*
Knuth, Marya Danielle *special education educator*
Perz, Sally *academic administrator, former state legislator*
Romanoff, Marjorie Reinwald *retired education educator*
Seubert, Lori A. *elementary school educator*
Wilde, Kerri Dawn *dance educator*
Wilson, Miriam S. *adult education educator*
Zorn, Sarah Marie *secondary school educator*

Trenton
Crout, Elizabeth Roop *retired elementary school educator*

Tuscarawas
Lentz, Belinda Ann *elementary school educator*

Twinsburg
Washington, Annie Ruth *retired elementary school educator, minister*

University Heights
Seaton, Shirley Smith *academic administrator, consultant*
Starcher-Dell'Aquila, Judy Lynn *special education educator*

Upper Arlington
Walter, Jennie *elementary school educator*

Upper Sandusky
Miller, Angela Marie *elementary school educator*

Valley View
Miller, Susan Ann *retired school system administrator*

Wadsworth
Wilhelm, Cathy S. *elementary school educator*

Walbridge
Wiseman, Gretchen Renee *special education educator*

Warren
Thomas, Jane Ellen *elementary school educator*

Washington Court House
Fichthorn, Fonda Gay *retired principal*

Waverly
Hartman, Mary Margaret *secondary school educator*

Wellston
Loxley, Kathryn *retired elementary school educator*

West Unity
Heer, Carol Lynne *special education educator*

Westerville
Diersing, Carolyn Virginia *educational administrator*
Van Sant, Joanne Frances *academic administrator*
Volpe, Deborah L *mathematics educator*

Westlake
Bishop, Jeanne Emmons *director, science educator, researcher*
Dechochrantraut, Leila L. *education educator*

Wickliffe
Wainio, Melody F. *registrar*

Wilberforce
Sanders, Augusta Carolyn *school librarian, educator*
Walker-Taylor, Yvonne *retired academic administrator*

Williamsburg
Hickey, Ena Varney *elementary school educator*

Willoughby
Grossman, Mary Margaret *elementary school educator*

Wilmington
Mitchell, Angela D. *education educator*

Youngstown
Camardese, Amy Hoffman *education educator*
Robinson, Judith Adell *elementary school educator*
Wells, Penny Whorton *gifted and talented educator, history educator*

Zanesville
Jones, Jo Ann *retired elementary school educator*

OKLAHOMA

Ada
Dennison, Ramona Pollan *special education educator*
Frye, Linda Beth (Linda Beth Hisle) *elementary school educator, secondary school educator*

Altus
Purdue, Patricia *secondary school educator*

Asher
Patterson, Lorie *literature and language educator*

Atwood
Perkins, Lorene K. *elementary school educator*

Bartlesville
Baker-Morris, Kay *special education educator*
Chambers, Imogene Klutts *school system administrator, financial consultant*
Tupper, Becky Jean *registrar*
Wallace, Elizabeth Ann (Becky Wallace) *educator*

Bethany
Garrett, Paula Kay *special education educator*

Bixby
McManus, Delana Ann *elementary school educator*

Bristow
Caudle, Letha Grace *secondary school educator*

Broken Arrow
Barton/Strickland, Tammy Kay *elementary school educator, coach*
McManigal, Shirley Ann *retired dean*
Roberts, Evelyn Smith *elementary school educator*
Strozier, Nancy Janelle *literature and language educator*
Swanson, Mary F. *education educator*

Calumet
Bradley, Nancy Elizabeth *elementary school educator*

Chickasha
Critchfield, Tammy K. *elementary school educator*

Choctaw
Sendall, Paula *secondary school educator*

Claremore
Hedge, Nancy *secondary school educator*
Heidlage, Patsy Jo *physical education educator*

Clinton
Lewallen, Donna G. *elementary school educator*

Duncan
Dawkins, Barbara Elaine *retired secondary school educator*

Edmond
Danner, Julie A. *literature and language educator*
Osgood, Virginia M. *vocational school educator*

El Reno
Grube, Deborah Jean *special education educator, science educator*

Fort Cobb
Rexroat, Vicki Lynn *occupational child development educator*

Guymon
Gabel, Tera Christine *secondary school educator*

Inola
Mullen, Deborah W. *elementary school educator*

Kremlin
Turner, LaWalta Dean *educator*

Langston
Haysbert, JoAnn Wright *academic administrator*

Maramec
Blair, Marie Lenore *elementary school educator*

Mcalester
Burden, Sherri Lynn Erickson *secondary school educator*
Lutz, Marie Burns *retired secondary school educator*

Mcloud
Goats, Debbie *elementary school educator*

Miami
Murphy, Carla M. *secondary school educator*

Midwest City
Cheek, Norma Jean *retired secondary school educator*
Wier, Leanne M. *life sciences educator*

Moore
Chiles, Mary Jane *secondary school educator*
Sturch, Lois J. *elementary school educator*

Muskogee
Felts, Joan April *retired elementary school educator*
Swanson, Jacqueline V. *academic administrator, educator, women's health nurse practitioner*

Noble
Reynolds, Karen Ann *secondary school educator*

Norman
Biscoe, Belinda P. *academic administrator, psychologist*
Harris, Carol Lynn *elementary school educator*
Mergler, Nancy L. *academic administrator*
Michaud, Phyllis Carol *school counselor*
Nance, Starlynn R. *academic counselor*
Nelson, Donna Jean *chemistry educator, researcher*
Ogilvie, Marilyn Bailey *natural science eduator, historian, writer, bibliographer*
Provine, Lorraine *retired mathematics educator*
Upchurch, Carol J. *elementary school educator*
Winters, Martha Patrice *history and language educator*
Yamashita, Elizabeth Swayne *university administrator, mass communications educator*
Zapffe, Nina Byrom *retired elementary school educator*

Oklahoma City
Bentley, Karen Gail *elementary school educator*
Beymer-Chapman, Brenda Marie *elementary school educator*
Blackburn, Debbie *elementary school educator, state representative*
Easley, Mary *retired elementary school educator, state representative*
Fischer, Gayle *elementary school educator*
Garrett, Sandy Langley *school system administrator*
Herndon, Merri Kathleen *elementary school educator*
Iven, Marjorie L. *assistant principal*
Lester, Stacy A. *chemistry educator*
Noakes, Betty LaVonne *retired elementary school educator*
Shuman-Miller, Nancy *education educator, department chairman*
Wilson, Francelia Latting *retired elementary school educator*

Owasso
Bettridge, Melinda Kae *secondary school educator, music educator, director*

Pauls Valley
McManus, Debra Lynne *secondary school educator*
Pesterfield, Linda Carol *retired principal*

Pocola
Clouse, Nan *elementary school educator, musician*

Ponca City
Easley, Betsy Leabeth *secondary school educator*
Rice, Sue Ann *retired dean, psychologist*
Tatum, Betty Joyce *secondary school educator*

Poteau
Giles, Patty Dawn *school librarian*
Long, Sheila Joan *academic administrator*

Prague
Emery, Cecilia Ruth *learning disability educator*

Schulter
Ayres, Gwyneth Carol *elementary school educator*

Shawnee
Kappes, Marcia Ann *education educator*

Skiatook
Dunham, Mary Helen *elementary school educator*

Stillwater
Ferrell, Judy Ann *elementary school educator*

Stilwell
Fourkiller, Diana Lynn *elementary school educator*

Tahlequah
Edwards, Terri Lyn Wilmoth *education educator*
Grant, Kay Lallier *early childhood education educator*

Tinker Afb
Scott, Carol Lee *child care educator*

Tulsa
Barnes, Cynthia Lou *retired gifted and talented educator*
Buthod, Mary Clare *school administrator*
Lewis, Patricia Mohatt (Patty) *special education educator*
Starr, Sharon Diane *elementary school educator*
Troutman, Virginia E. *elementary school educator*
Undernehr, Laura Lee *elementary school educator*
Vilar, Susan Ann *elementary school educator*

Vici
White, Angela Pearl *literature and language educator*

Vinita
Johnston, Ruth Darrough *retired elementary school educator, counselor*

Wagoner
Durham, Nancy Ruth *elementary school educator, music educator*

Weatherford
Vanderslice, Ronna Jean *education educator*

Wilburton
Butler, Mary Edith *academic administrator, school librarian*

Woodward
Hurst, Tacy Marcella *literature and language educator*

Wynnewood
Powers, Shalia Jo *secondary school educator*

Yukon
Griffin, Sharon Grass *elementary school educator*
Megli, Lisa L. *assistant principal*

OREGON

Ashland
Cullinan, Mary Patricia *academic administrator, literature and language professor*
Zinser, Elisabeth Ann *academic administrator*

Astoria
West, Vanette Jane *secondary school educator*

Beaverton
de Sá e Silva, Elizabeth Anne *secondary school educator*
Pepper, Floy Childers *educational consultant*
Weygandt, Staci *mathematics educator*

Bend
Forbes Johnson, Mary Gladys *retired secondary school educator*

Brookings
Kucharski, Kathleen Martin *secondary school educator*

Cannon Beach
Wismer, Patricia Ann *retired secondary school educator*

Clackamas
Agost, Dalene Beth *elementary school educator*

Eagle Point
Blanchard, Shirley Lynn *primary school educator, consultant*

Eugene
McMillan, Adell *retired academic administrator*
Metltzoff, Nancy Jean *education educator*

Grants Pass
Murdock, Doris Dean *special education educator, program developer*

Gresham
Light, Betty Jensen Pritchett *retired dean*
Webb, Donna Louise *academic director, educator*

Hillsboro
Nelson, Heather M. *elementary school educator*
Porter, Roberta Ann *counseling administrator, educator, retired school system administrator*

Jacksonville
Beeler, Sherri *secondary school educator*

Klamath Falls
Dow, Martha Anne *academic administrator, biology professor*

Lincoln City
Casey, Darla Diann *elementary school educator*

Madras
Adams, Karen V. *elementary school educator*

Medford
Bessey, Caroline A. *education educator*
Franklin, Darlene Kay *elementary school educator*
Maack, Jean Elizabeth *retired elementary school educator*

Myrtle Creek
Kuk, Mary Halvorson *secondary school educator*

Newberg
McGillivray, Karen *retired elementary school educator*

Oceanside
Wadlow, Joan Krueger *retired academic administrator, retired construction executive*

Pendleton
Blanc, Carol S. *biology educator*

Pleasant Hill
Martin, Kelli Lynne *education educator*

Portland
Bodin, Kate *dean*
Delcambre, Lois Marie Lundberg *academic administrator*
Engelberg, Elaine A. *retired secondary school educator*
Frolick, Patricia Mary *retired elementary school educator*
Harris, Cynthia Viola *principal*
Johnson, Virginia Macpherson *secondary school educator, consultant*
Leupp, Edythe Peterson *retired education educator*
Njoku, Scholastica Ibari *retired college librarian, writer*
Phillips, Vicki L. *school system administrator*
Robinson, Ruth Carleson *retired secondary school educator*
Solberg, Di Anne *retired secondary school educator*
Sonniksen, Janet W. *education educator*
Wood, Cynthia Wilder *elementary school educator*
Woods, Deanna Gael *education educator, consultant*
Yatvin, Joanne Ina *education educator*

Roseburg
Ball, Char Lee Frances *retired special education educator*

Salem
Castillo, Susan *school system administrator*
Hill, JoAnne Miller *special education educator, consultant*
Koch, Katrina M. *private school educator*
Page, Cheryl Miller *elementary school educator*

Sandy
Thies, Lynn Wapinski *elementary school educator*

Stanfield
Durbin, Marilyn Ann Rafal *secondary school educator*

Sutherlin
Johnson, Barbara E. *adult education educator*

The Dalles
Hayden, I. Jill *secondary school educator*

Veneta
Cotter, Roberta L. *elementary school educator*

Waldport
Abel, Laura Sorvetti *retired literature and language educator*

Woodburn
Anderson, Karen Mae *primary school educator*

PENNSYLVANIA

Adrian
Hogg, Yvonne Marie *special education educator*

Akron
Lapp, Alice Weber *secondary school educator, editor*

Allentown
Ehritz, Marianne Louise *elementary school educator*
Franges, Gayle Louise *elementary school educator*
Goodman, Pauline Rose *retired secondary school educator*
Nippert, Carolyn Cochrane *academic administrator, information scientist*
Pavelich, Judith *secondary school educator*
Steinhauer, LuAnn *retired learning disabilities educator*
Tinsman-Schaffer, Patricia Joan *secondary school educator, artist*

Allison Park
Hurst, Michele Lynn *elementary school educator*

Altoona
Damiano, Cathy *elementary school educator*
Love, Sharon RedHawk *education educator*
Vreeland-Flynn, Tracy Lynn *elementary school educator*

Ambler
Fiorito, Rebecca *elementary school educator*

Ambridge
Powell, Pamela Baker *education educator, minister*

Archbald
Cummings, Ellen Finan *special education educator*

Ardmore
Dagna, Jeanne Marie *special education educator*

Arnot
Ostrom, Brigette Dawn *special education educator*

Aston
Mirenda, Rosalie M. *academic administrator, nursing educator*

Atglen
Souders, Roberta Belshaw *literature and language educator*

Athens
Luther-Lemmon, Carol Len *elementary school educator*
Yeager-Hall, Carli Marie *biology educator*

Bangor
Pensack, Susan *elementary school educator*

Beach Lake
Ash, Polly Gayenelle *secondary school educator, minister*

Beaver
Helmick, Gayle Johnston *retired elementary education educator*

Beaver Falls
Copeland, Deborah Gayle *education educator*
Thomas-Wright, Lisa Ann *elementary school educator*

Belle Vernon
Stimmell, Tamara *special education educator*

Bentleyville
Blasko, Barbara Ann *secondary school educator*

Benton
O'Brien, Lisa Anne *middle school educator*

Bethel Park
Chmelynski, Donna *elementary school educator*
Douds, Virginia Lee *elementary school educator*
Menees, Katherine Determan *parochial school educator*

Bethlehem
Corpora, Kathleen M. *middle school educator, technology integration specialist*
Del Cueto, S. E. *Spanish and English language educator*
Gast, Alice Petry *academic administrator, chemical engineering educator*

Big Cove Tannery
Younker, Nancy Elaine *retired elementary school educator*

Biglerville
Marks, Nora Maralea *retired secondary school educator*

Bloomsburg
Kozloff, Jessica S. *academic administrator*
Trapane, Ruth *educator, artist*

Blue Bell
Martino, Robin Leigh *elementary school educator*

Boyertown
Laskosky, Donna Marie *secondary school educator*

Brodheadsville
Caines, Cheryl Lynne *supervisor*
Rissmiller, Carole *school system administrator*

Brookville
Briggs, Carole A. *elementary school educator*

Broomall
Benner, Paula Roxanne *academic administrator, educator*
Puchalla, Mary Kay *elementary school educator*
Samans, Elaine Mae *education counselor, human services educator*

Bryn Mawr
Hirsh, Sharon Latchaw *academic administrator, art history educator*
Salisbury, Helen Holland *education educator*
Smith, Nona Coates *academic administrator*
Vickers, Nancy J. *academic administrator*

Butler
Korn, Carol M. *retired elementary school educator*

Canton
VanNoy, Vicki Lynne *mathematics educator, department chairman*

Carlisle
Fendrich, Jean *elementary school educator*
Merrill, Heather Anne *geography and anthropology educator*
Ober, Jane Finley *career planning administrator*

Carnegie
Whitfield, Tammy J. *elementary school educator, director*

Chambersburg
Bitner, Betty L. *education educator*

Charleroi
Kravec, Frances Mary *elementary school educator*

Cheltenham
Kuziemski, Naomi Elizabeth *educational consultant, counselor*

Chester
McJunkins, Kristin R. *academic administrator*

Clarion
Bonnett, Lou Ann Humphrey *education educator*
Dédé, Brenda Sanders *academic administrator*
Stearns, Ann Nicholson *education educator*

Coatesville
Daigle, Sara Elizabeth *elementary school educator*
Rodkey, Frances Theresa *elementary school educator*

Cochranton
Heltzel, Kathleen Lassalle *elementary school educator*

Connellsville
Brady, Marsha McCandless *secondary school educator*
Shearer, Linda Rae *English educator*

Coplay
Stockman, Kathleen Helen *elementary school educator*

Coraopolis
Stevens, Paulette *daycare administrator*

Dallas
Albert, Rosalie Snow *secondary school educator, writer*

Dayton
Patterson, Madge Lenore *elementary school educator*

Donora
Dillon, Susan *literature and language educator*

Dover
Miller-Seda, Rhonda Grace *elementary school educator*
Spahr, Bertha E. *chemistry educator, department chairman*

Doylestown
Borzio, Stephanie Jean *secondary school educator*
Goldstein, Mary Wiseman *education educator*
Rodenbaugh, Marcia Louise *retired elementary school educator*
Thomas, Ellen Louise *school system administrator*

Drexel Hill
Turnbull, Mary Regina *secondary school educator*

East Petersburg
Walker, Sue Albertson *retired school system administrator, consultant*

East Stroudsburg
Braithwaite, Barbara Jo *retired secondary school educator*
Miller, Edith Fisher *special education educator*

Easton
Ciambrone, Cheryl C. *mathematics educator*
Teboh-Ewungkem, Miranda Ijang *education educator*

Ebensburg
Pereira, Melany *elementary school educator*

Edinboro
Curry-Carlburg, Joanne Jeanne *elementary school educator*

Elizabethtown
Bradley, Christine Owen *secondary school educator*
Placeway, Joellen Peterson *elementary school educator*

Elkins Park
Burnley, June Williams *secondary school educator*

Ellwood City
Windhorst, Jane Louise *elementary school educator*

Elverson
Colona, Frances Ann *elementary school educator*

Emlenton
Berg, Janice Carol *elementary school educator*

Emmaus
Long, Kathleen Anne *elementary school educator*

Erie
Bohman, Carol Elizabeth *secondary school educator*
Burgoyne, Noel Jaeger *retired secondary school educator*
Evanoff-McGeorge, Marnie Hubbell *elementary school educator*
Nolan, Susan Marie *mathematics educator*
Rosiak, Frances Ruth *elementary school educator*
Roth-Kauffman, Michele M. *dean*

Factoryville
Joyce, Janice Rose *supervisor, elementary school educator*

Fairless Hills
Glasheen, Gloria D. *secondary school educator*
Hess, Frances Elizabeth *retired secondary school educator, retired director*

Fairview
Graziani, Linda Ann *secondary school educator*
Stern, Marilyn Jean *special education educator*

Farrell
Pawluk, Annette Marie *secondary school educator*
Roberson, Deborah Lynn *special education educator*

Flourtown
Cooke, Sara Mullin Graff *daycare provider, kindergarten educator, medical assistant*
Lambert, Joan Dorety *elementary school educator*

Franklin
Sauer, Mary Julia *special education educator*

Gettysburg
Bechtel, Kristen King *chemistry educator*
Will, Katherine Haley *academic administrator*

Gibsonia
Wright, April Marie *elementary school educator*

Glen Mills
Shields, Martha Buckley *elementary school educator*

Greensburg
Elliott, Tammy Jo *chemistry educator*
Ferraco Redinger, Andrea *biology educator*
Mann, Jacinta *academic administrator, mathematician, educator*
Neff, Mary Ellen Andre *retired elementary school educator*

Grove City
Davidson, Heather Jean *gifted and talented educator*

Gwynedd Valley
Conaway, Cynthia Elizabeth *parochial school educator, department chairman*
Owens, Kathleen C. *academic administrator*

Hanover
Barnhart, Nikki Lynn Clark *elementary school educator*
Clark, Sandra Marie *school administrator*

Hanover Township
Bannon, Desiree *mathematics educator*

Harmony
Fodi, Alison Elizabeth *mathematics educator*
Meredith, Joanne Cusick *special education educator, director*

Stephenson, Susan Marie *English educator*

Harrisburg
Batts, Barbara Jean *academic administrator, director*
Braun, Mary E. *elementary school educator*
Burns, Rebecca Ann *elementary school educator, librarian*
Fulmer, Deborah Lee *education educator, oncological nurse*
Hample, Judy G. *academic administrator*

Hatfield
Madden, Theresa Marie *elementary school educator*

Havertown
Evarts, Mary H. *mathematics educator*
Wright, Cecilia Powers *gifted and talented educator*

Hegins
Caulfield, Careen Anne *secondary school educator, biologist*

Hellertown
Kunkel-Christman, Debra Ann *secondary school educator*

Hershey
Derk, Patricia Keach *secondary school educator*
Kisthardt, Estelle A. *career planning administrator, educator*
Kreider, Susan B. *elementary school educator*
Thomas, Patricia Agnes *school system administrator*

Honey Brook
Johnson, Marjorie R. *special education educator*

Huntingdon Valley
McNemar, Robin M. *chemistry educator*

Immaculata
Fadden, Sister R. Patricia *academic administrator, nun*

Imperial
Boustead, Diane Dolores *secondary school educator, chemistry educator*
Meyers, Karen Evans *gifted and talented educator*

Indiana
Jalongo, Mary Renck *educator*
Weber, Denise E. *retired history educator*

Jenkintown
Oh, Soojin Susan *elementary school educator*
Sellers, Marlene *artist, educator*

Johnstown
Grove, Nancy Carol *academic administrator*
Puto, Anne-Marie *reading specialist*

Knox
Rupert, Elizabeth Anastasia *retired dean*

La Plume
Fontana, Carol P. *education educator*
Owens, Kate A. *registrar*

Lancaster
Best, Jane Evans *retired educator, historian*
Grube, Rebecca Sue *elementary school educator, consultant*
Miller, Erika Vittur *secondary school educator, language educator*
Yohe, Laura Kathryn *secondary school educator*

Langhorne
Neff, Amy Hancock *elementary school educator*
Schoenstadt, Barbara Laison *special education educator*

Latrobe
Bates, Dawna Joyce *retired secondary school educator, department chairman*
Snyder, Rebecca *literature and language educator*

Lebanon
Bybee, Deborah Ann *director, educator*
Hepler, Jane A. *secondary school educator*
Kopicki, Beth Ann *special education educator*

Lehman
Ruddy, Stacey Ann *literature and language educator*
Weyman, Sandra Lee *secondary school educator*

Lemont Furnace
Miller, Debbie Sue *special education educator*

Lemoyne
Hamme, Marta Denise *elementary school educator*

Leola
Puschak, Beth Anne *educational consultant*

Levittown
Perry, Beth Ann *elementary school educator*
Walker, Patricia Ann Dixon *retired elementary school educator, real estate rehabilitator*

Lewisburg
Huffines, Marion Lois *academic administrator, language and linguistics educator*
Morin, Karen Marie *education educator, researcher*
Roberts, Ruth W. *retired elementary school educator*
Smith, Marguerite Irene *gifted and talented educator*

Liberty
Morgan-Grala, Terry Lee *elementary school educator*

Lititz
Adair, Mary Roberts *special education educator*

Hudelson, Judith Giantomass *elementary school educator*

Lock Haven
Almes, June *retired education educator, librarian*
Winters, Karen Crispell *educator*

Mansfield
Loeschke, Maravene S. *academic administrator, theater educator*

Maple Glen
Weaver-Stroh, Joanne Mateer *education educator, consultant*

Mc Donald
Maurer, Karen Ann *special education educator*

Mc Keesport
Powroznik-Traeger, Rita *school counselor*
Ransil, Dorothy Mae *secondary school educator*

Mechanicsburg
Blaisure, Terra Quinn *special education educator*
Gerstenlauer, Joyce Elaine *elementary school educator*

Mill Hall
Smith, Debra Farwell *school librarian*

Monroeville
Baker, Faith Mero *retired elementary education educator*
Emerick, Joyce Jean *elementary school educator*

Montrose
Cunningham, Mary Ann Michael *secondary school educator*

Moscow
Grudeski, Jennifer Anne *elementary school educator*
Lisandrelli, Elaine Slivinski *secondary school educator*

Myerstown
Robson, Barbara S. *elementary school educator*
Weaver, Patricia Ella *mathematics educator*

Nanticoke
Dalmas-Brown, Carmella Jean *special education educator*
Donohue, Patricia Carol *academic administrator*

Natrona Heights
Becker, Rachel J. *biology educator*

Nazareth
Bartolacci, Paulette Marie *elementary school educator, aerobics instructor*
Brackbill, Nancy Lafferty *retired elementary school educator*
Ferraro, Margaret Louise (Peg Ferraro) *elementary school educator*

Nelson
Kyofski, Bonelyn Lugg *retired education educator*

New Castle
Schooley, Toni Ann *gifted and talented educator*

New Cumberland
Dunbar, Lorna J. *special education educator*

New Hope
Coyle, Diane Bonanomi *special education educator*

New Oxford
Martin, Sandra Ann *special education educator, writer*

New Stanton
Tomajko, Kimberly Ann *mathematics and science educator*

New Wilmington
Magyary, Cynthia Marie *retired elementary school educator, music educator*

Newtown Square
Bertolet, Caroline Lynne Georgeanne *special education educator, labor union administrator*
LeDonne, Deborah Jane *secondary school educator*
Swing, Elizabeth Sherman *education educator*

Norristown
Del Collo, Mary Anne Demetris *school administrator*
DeMedio, Kathleen Marie *chemistry educator*
McGinnis, Patricia Anne *secondary school educator, biologist*
Womack, Lana D. *elementary school educator*

North Huntingdon
Bryan, Peggy *mathematics educator*

Oil City
Heckathorne, Deborah Kathryn *mathematics educator, supervisor*

Orefield
Eisenhard, Jennifer Lynn *elementary school educator*

Patton
Pompa, Louise Elaine *secondary school educator*

Perkasie
Ferry, Joan Evans *school counselor*
Vasoli, Glenna Isaac *elementary school educator, school system administrator*

Perryopolis
Kremposky, Vickey Darlene *secondary school educator*

Philadelphia
Aversa, Dolores Sejda *educational administrator*
Christman, Jolley Bruce *educational research executive, educator*
Collier, Charisse Audra *family service representative, greeting card designer*
Delaney, Anna T. *director*
DiMenna, Kathleen Polansky *special education educator*
Drake, Jayne Kribbs *academic administrator, literature educator*
Dunn, Mary Maples *academic administrator*
Fernandez, Happy Craven (Gladys Fernandez) *academic administrator*
Gur, Raquel E. *academic administrator*
Gutmann, Amy *academic administrator, political science and philosophy educator*
Guyer, Hedy-Ann Klein *special education educator*
Hart, Ann Weaver *academic administrator*
Heller, Janet Seip *retired secondary school educator*
Hughes Stanback, Francine *elementary school educator, school system administrator*
Jones, Kia Tanetta *daycare administrator*
Junkerman, Denise Marie *secondary school educator*
Kim, Sangduk *biochemistry educator, researcher*
Kreider, Karen Beechy *secondary education educator, language professional*
Mouzon, Thelma P. *retired elementary school educator*
Onley, Sister Francesca *academic administrator*
Reid, Mary Wallace *retired secondary school educator*
Reisman, Fredricka Kauffman *education educator*
Rosato, Jennifer L. *dean, law educator*
Schneeberg, Helen Bassen *retired elementary school educator*
Sibolski, Elizabeth Hawley *academic administrator*
Simms, Amy Lang *writer, educator*
Sklar, Gail Janice *special education educator*
Slaughter-Defoe, Diana Tresa *education educator, psychologist*
von Seldeneck, Judith Metcalfe *career planning administrator*

Philipsburg
Genesi, Susan Petrovich *school system administrator*

Phoenixville
Gentile, Amber Leigh *assistant principal*
Harkin, Ann Winifred *elementary school educator, psychotherapist*
Nice, Katharine Anne *mathematics educator, music educator*

Pittsburgh
Barazzone, Esther Lynn *academic administrator, educator*
Carney, Ann Vincent *retired secondary school educator*
Castelluccio, Christia Marie *elementary school educator*
Coffey, Rosemary Klineberg *educator*
Dana, Marie Immaculée *education educator, department chairman*
Eckert, Jean Patricia *elementary school educator*
Fogle, Jennifer Fox *elementary school educator*
Geibel, Sister Grace Ann *university president*
Haas, Marlene Ringold *special education educator*
Heinzl, Carolyn Barbara *school system administrator*
Heitzenroder, Wendy Roberta *elementary school educator*
Johnson, Florence Lester *retired elementary school educator*
Kimmons, Cindy Lou *reading specialist*
Kreitzer, Tricia D. *chemistry educator*
London-Gibbon, Mary Beth *elementary school educator*
Marano, Donna Inez *academic administrator*
Miller, Suzanne Evagash *education educator*
Packard, Rochelle Sybil *elementary school educator*
Petro, Natalie Ann *secondary school educator*
Rago, Ann D'Amico *academic administrator, public relations executive*
Rosnick, Kathy Conrad *mathematics educator*
Ross, Madelyn Ann *academic administrator, newspaper editor*
Vergona, Kathleen Dobrosielski *biology educator, researcher*
Wagner, Cheryl Jean *elementary school educator*
Warner, Judith (Anne) Huss *elementary school educator*

Pottstown
Nitsche, Linda *gifted and talented educator*

Quakertown
Babb, Lisa Marie *physical education educator*

Quarryville
Braightmeyer, Janet Huber *elementary school educator, music educator*

Reading
Forrer, Nan Louise *secondary school educator*
Hamwi, Bonnie L. *education educator, consultant*
Rodgers, Lana Loretta Lusch *retired elementary school educator*

Saegertown
Kopf, Nancy *special education educator*

Scottdale
Ware, Susan Joy *elementary school educator*

Scranton
Elvidge, Christina Marie *director*
Shiffer, Candice Caputo *retired special education educator, consultant*

Selinsgrove
Martin, Valerie Gail *dean, music educator*

Sewickley
Reilsono, Lynda Ann *elementary school educator*

Sharon
Kovac, Shirley Ann *retired elementary school educator*

Shippensburg
Basler, Linda Gerber *retired elementary school educator*
Miller, Linda Lou *education administrator, communications specialist*
Vaughan, Elizabeth Jean *education educator*

Sidman
Cecere, Carol *secondary school educator*

Slippery Rock
McCollin, Michelle J. *special education educator*

Solebury
Gilleo, Sandra V. *elementary school educator*

Somerset
Koshewitz, Phyllis J. *elementary school educator*
Nicholson, Virginia Mae *retired elementary school educator*

Souderton
Rosenberger, Janet Thuma *retired elementary school educator*

Spring City
Middleton, Dawn E. *education educator*

Springfield
Carter, Frances Moore *secondary school educator, personnel director, writer, foundation administrator*

State College
Link, Phoebe Forrest *education educator, writer, social worker, poet*
MacConnell-Davinroy, Irene J.H. *secondary education educator, consultant*
Mazza, Maralyn J. *director*
McKeel, Lillian Phillips *retired education educator*
Shakley, Heather *physical education educator*

Stroudsburg
Aleman, Sheila B. *special education educator*

Summerdale
Pickel, Diane Dunn *education educator*

Sunbury
Maue, Leta Jo *instructional support teacher*

Telford
Boughter, Barbara B. *mathematics educator*
Nofziger, Karen Fae *elementary school educator*

Titusville
Pilewski, Jennifer Marie *mathematics educator*

Topton
Yeager, Nancy Ellen *literature and language educator*

Townville
Rudy, Elaine Kim *elementary school educator*

Tunkhannock
Pugh, Melanie Sybil *elementary school educator*

Turbotville
Martine, Andrea Schultz *secondary school educator*

Unionville
Martin, Helen Elizabeth *educational consultant*

University Park
Askov, Eunice May *adult education educator*
Heid, Mary Kathleen *mathematics educator*
Herrmann, Carol *university administrator*
Olian, Judy D. *dean*

Upper Darby
Crouse, Carol K. Mavromatis *elementary school educator*

Wallingford
Shapiro, Roberta *secondary school educator*

Warminster
Chandler, Victoria Jane *elementary school educator, writer*
Ciabarra, Louise *secondary school educator, medical/surgical nurse*
Mull, Michelle Rachael *secondary school educator*
Vietri, Linda Smith *gifted and talented educator*
Winget, Dalores Loraine *educator, freelance writer*

Wayne
Lynam, Beth *elementary school educator*

Waynesboro
Mason, Susan Helen *mathematics educator*

West Chester
Hickman, Janet Susan *academic administrator, educator*
Keiser, Mary Ann Myers *special education educator*
Strunk, Betsy Ann Whitenight *retired education educator*

West Mifflin
Archey, Mary Frances Elaine (Onofaro) *academic administrator, educator*
Horvath (Selai), Cynthia M. *secondary school educator*
Vogel, Christy Rae *secondary school educator*

West Reading
Spenier, Joanne B. *secondary school educator*

Wexford
Kainaroi, Cynthia D. *assistant principal*
Roy, Suzanne Scully *reading specialist*

Utay, Carol Mitnick *special education educator, computer consultant*

White Oak
Shaw, Renee S. *elementary school educator*

Wilkes Barre
Pasonick, Kimberly Rose *elementary school educator*

Williamsport
Clarke, Louise Rigdon *gifted student program administrator, principal*
Jenkins, Gaye Ranck *adult education educator, consultant*

Willow Grove
Burtt, Anne Dampman *special education educator*

Willow Street
Eggers, Mary Lynn *elementary school educator*

Wingate
Lomison, Marie Lucinda *mathematics educator*

Wyalusing
Goodman, Carol Hockenbury *retired elementary school educator, consultant*

Wynnewood
Beck, Elaine Kushner *elementary and secondary school educator*

Yardley
Millner, Rachel Erin *psychology educator, occupational therapist*
Watson, Joyce Leslie *elementary school educator*

York
Nusbaum, Candace Ann *elementary school educator*
Sebright, Melissa Marie *special education educator*
Wolschleger, Susan Elizabeth *elementary school educator*

RHODE ISLAND

Bristol
Grota, Barbara Lynn *academic administrator, educator*

Cumberland
Murphy, Carolyn J. Mancini *secondary school educator*

East Greenwich
Twardowski, Kristen M. *special education educator*

Glendale
Carlson, Jacqueline Ann *elementary school educator*

Johnston
Robinson, Marlene Theresa *special education educator*

Newport
Flowers, Sandra Joan *elementary school educator, educator*
Schneider, Carolyn Anne *educator, director*

North Kingstown
Resch, Cynthia Fortes *secondary school educator*

North Providence
Murray, Carol Anne *chemistry educator*

North Scituate
Maynard, Joan Law *elementary school educator*

Pawtucket
Lepore, Lisa *principal*
Moody, Marilyn Leavitt *special education educator*

Providence
Grossi, Linda Marie *elementary school educator*
Schenck, Susan Jane *special education educator*
Simmons, Ruth J. *academic administrator*
Waite-Franzen, Ellen Jane *academic administrator*

Smithfield
Yeaw, Kimberly A. *secondary school educator*

Westerly
Crowley, Cynthia Warner Johnson *secondary school educator*
Saila, Colleen G. *special education educator*

Woonsocket
Crowley, Rosa Quinonez *literature and language educator*
Walker, Suzanne Ross *mathematics and education educator*

SOUTH CAROLINA

Aiken
Clanton Harpine, Elaine *educational consultant, educator*
Hickey, Delina Rose *retired education educator*

Anderson
Broyles, Jennifer Kaye *elementary school educator*
Kaiser, Louise Martin *elementary school educator*
Roof, Cynthia White *special education educator*
Schiavi, Rosemary Filomena *secondary school educator*

Batesburg
Long, Drucilla *special education educator*

Beaufort
Eggen, Belinda Lay *education educator*
Hopkins, Ginger Allen *school system administrator*

Bishopville
Roycroft, Cheryl *secondary school educator*

Blythewood
Portee, Cassandra Smith *elementary school educator, music educator*

Catawba
Rankin, Betty Hill *retired special education educator*

Central
Bell, Gloria Jean *academic administrator, literature educator, dean*

Charleston
Egelson, Pauline C. *director*
Jenkins, Pearl G. *retired elementary school educator, realtor*
Morris, Valerie Bonita *dean*
Suggars, Candice Louise *special education educator, consultant*

Clemson
Helms, Doris R. *academic administrator*

Clinton
Donnan, Roxanne Marie *elementary school educator*

Columbia
Carter, Kathryn Gibson *education educator, consultant*
Cofield, Virginia Riley *elementary school educator, piano teacher*
Davis, Michelle Marie *elementary school educator*
Fields, Harriet Gardin *counseling administrator, educator*
Greene, Claudia *education associate*
Sinclair, Linda Drumwright *educational consultant*
Sproat, Ruth C. *retired director, consultant*
Tenenbaum, Inez Moore *school system administrator*

Conway
Johnson-Leeson, Charleen Ann *retired elementary school educator, insurance agent, consultant, executive secretary*
Thompson, Sharon Howell *health educator*

Dorchester
Taylor, Laney W. *mathematics educator*

Duncan
Kelly, Loveta Brown *elementary school educator*

Easley
Sorrenti, Rushie Gowan *literature and language educator*

Elgin
Pierce, Catherine Maynard *history educator*

Elloree
Stickles, Linda Cochran *elementary school educator*

Florence
Hanna, Wanda Simmons *secondary school educator*

Fort Mill
Honeycutt, Brenda *secondary school educator*
Whitten, Jeanie G. *physics educator*

Gaffney
Edwards Duncan, Linda Kaye *elementary school educator*
Ivey, Elizabeth Reeves *school system administrator*
Suttle, Helen Jayson *retired elementary school educator*
Whitt, Pamela P. *mathematics educator*

Gray Court
Smallwood, Rebecca Ruth *elementary school educator*

Green Sea
Donaldson, Robin Faulk *secondary school educator*

Greenville
Baker, Harriet Kugley *elementary school educator*
Edwards, Ann Louise Corbin *elementary school educator*
Hancock, Donna *secondary school educator*
Hill, Grace Lucile Garrison *education educator, consultant*
Seibert, Lesa Marie *education educator*
Slough, Sandra Ollie *secondary school educator*
Stratton, Sally G. (Sara) *retired school system administrator*

Greenwood
Marino, Sheila Burris *education educator*

Hilton Head Island
Pustilnik, Jean Todd *elementary school educator, secondary school educator*

Irmo
Lee, Melinda Faye *mathematics educator*
Maybin, Jeannette Ergler *elementary school educator, art educator*

Iva
Riddle, Melanie Timms *secondary school educator*

Kershaw
Wall, Kathy Elliott *secondary school educator*

Ladson
Groves, Charla M. *secondary school educator*

Stephens, Debra Young *elementary school educator*

Lake City
Hawkins, Linda Parrott *school system administrator*

Lamar
Greene, Michelle Renee *mathematics educator*

Laurens
Childers, Regina Wortman *counseling administrator*

Lexington
Ferguson, Benetta N. *secondary school educator*
Floyd, Ann R. *elementary school educator*
Oswald, Leigh Heiting *counseling administrator*
Tunstall, Dorothy Fiebrich *retired pre-school administrator*

Manning
Boswell, Martha Lee *elementary school educator*

Mauldin
Norris, Joan Clafette Hagood *retired assistant principal*

Moncks Corner
Robinson, Angela Regina *secondary school educator*

Mount Pleasant
Craven, Stella Maris *principal*

Newberry
Zobel, Melanie Cannon *special education educator*

North Augusta
Campbell, Helen R. *gifted and talented educator*
Watson, Paula Sue *pre-school educator*

North Myrtle Beach
Cassidy, Dorothy Ann *special education educator*

Okatie
Matile, Madelon Elizabeth *secondary school educator*

Orangeburg
Deas, Alberta D. *educator, educational administrator*
Hemby, Tina Marie *elementary school educator*

Pickens
Denton, Jill B. *political science educator*
Hardin, Janet Becker *gifted and talented educator, music educator*

Prosperity
Hause, Edith Collins *retired academic administrator*

Ridgeville
Hill, Jacquelyn Louise Harrison *secondary school educator*

Rock Hill
Barbaree, Dorothy A. *secondary school educator*
Cramer, Lisa M. *elementary school educator*

Roebuck
Curry, Sheila Diane *secondary school educator, athletic trainer*
McCraw, Kathy *elementary school educator, special education educator*

Ruffin
Lambright, Marilyn *elementary school educator*

Seneca
Sevic, Sybil Gibson *elementary school educator*

Simpsonville
Parrish, Cathy Waldron *elementary school educator*

Society Hill
King, Amanda Arnette *elementary school educator*

Spartanburg
Faulkner, Rebecca Clay *reading educator*
Kennedy, Donna Chapman *counseling administrator*

Taylors
Porter, Jean McRae *counselor*

Ulmer
Mathias, Lynda Rowell *secondary school educator*

Walhalla
Duncan, Gwendolyn McCurry *elementary school educator*

Westminster
Holbrooks, Faye Griffin *elementary school educator*

Woodruff
Baxley, Pamel W *secondary school educator*

SOUTH DAKOTA

Aberdeen
Omland, Jacqueline Leigh-Knute *secondary school educator, small business owner*
Paranto, Sharon *educator, consultant*

Brandon
Chistenson, Rose Mary *elementary school educator*

Brookings
Miller, Peggy Gordon Elliott *academic administrator*

Vanderpan, Norma *retired elementary school educator*

Buffalo
Helms, Carol Dorothy *elementary school educator*

Eagle Butte
Webb, Yvonne M. *secondary school educator*

Florence
Black, Mary Kay *secondary school educator*

Kadoka
Stout, Maye Alma *secondary school educator*

Mitchell
Russell, Annika Renee *secondary school educator, financial consultant*

Parker
Christensen, Jill Renee *mathematics educator*

Pierre
Stiles, Doris D. *elementary school educator*

Rapid City
Ball, Carol J. *elementary school educator*

Roscoe
Hettick, Sandra Ann *literature and language educator*

Spearfish
Elsom, Margaret Striplin *elementary school educator*

Vermillion
Jacobs, Gera M. *early childhood educator*
Struck, Judy Kay *special education specialist*

Yankton
Muth, Jill *elementary school educator*

TENNESSEE

Allardt
Copeland, Patricia Ruth *elementary school educator*

Allons
Reagan, Penny A. *elementary school educator*

Antioch
Mattice, Debora J. *special education educator, consultant*

Bartlett
Ford, Nancy Leonard *retired special education educator*

Bells
Stephenson, Sylvia *elementary school educator*

Benton
Kingery, Alice L. *elementary school educator*

Birchwood
Lowrance, Rita Gale Hamrick *elementary school educator*

Blountville
Graybeal, Tracy Lynn *secondary school educator*

Brentwood
Ezell, Kimberly Hardison *educator*
Scurlock, Joy Shelton *elementary school educator*

Brownsville
Wilson, Susan Rice *vice principal*

Burlison
German, Jennifer Elam *elementary school educator, music educator*

Butler
Stansberry, Joetta Lee *special education educator*

Chapel Hill
Miller, Betty *elementary school educator*

Charlotte
Rougemont, Denise *elementary school educator*

Chattanooga
Cook, Charlene Lamar *elementary school educator, music educator*
Kubic, M(arcia) Sylvia *elementary school educator*
Nation, Samie Bowman *retired elementary and special education educator*
Norman, Mary Jo *education educator*
Steele, Shirley Sue *retired special resource educator*

Church Hill
Bowers, Susan Bailey *secondary school educator*

Clarksville
Amstutz, Julie Denise *elementary school educator*
Hoppe, Sherry Lee *academic administrator*
Kincaid, Sarah Sanders *mathematics educator*

Cleveland
Hamid, Suzanne L *academic administrator*
Lockhart, Madge Clements *educational organization executive*
McDaniel, Kay *education educator, writer*

Coalfield
Jackson, Vicki Annette *elementary school educator*

Collierville
Tesreau, Cynthia Lynn *elementary school educator*

Columbia
Cantrell, Sharron Caulk *principal*

Cordova
Hatch, Margaret Oenone *secondary school educator*
Jacobs, M. Louise *secondary school educator*

Corryton
Graves, Leslie Hill *secondary school educator*

Covington
Wright, Bonnie Shankle *assistant principal, choir director*

Crossville
Hyder, Deborah Jean *elementary school educator*
Ridge, Linda Kiser *secondary school educator*

Cunningham
Mince, Carol Kirkham *history educator*

Dandridge
Coley, Jan Brumback *biology educator*
Evans, Sheila S. *secondary school educator*
Finchum, Sherry Sorrells *school system administrator*

Dover
Cook-Elkins, Shana Free *elementary school educator*

Dunlap
Carr, Marsha Hamblen *elementary school principal*

Etowah
Amos, Janette Garbee *retired secondary school educator*

Franklin
Brown, Gail *secondary school educator*
Daniel, Cathy Brooks *educational consultant*
Hughey, Brenda Joyce *supervisor*
Kemp, Nancy Martin *history educator*
McClellan, Dixie *secondary school educator*

Greeneville
Casteel, DiAnn Brown *education educator*

Hampton
Graham, Hilda Renae *mathematics educator*

Hendersonville
Kinney, Betty Caudill *elementary school educator*

Hermitage
White, Mary Beth *counseling administrator, adult education educator*

Hixson
O'Connor, Elizabeth Hill *elementary school educator*
Prichard, Lona Ann *retired elementary school educator*

Jackson
Golden, Christie M. *mathematics educator*
Hearn, Beverly Jean *education educator*

Johnson City
Bonner, Patricia Jane *retired physical education and special education educator*
Rasch, Ellen Myrberg *cell biology educator*

Kingsport
Rigsby, Mary Sue *retired elementary school educator, adult education educator*

Knoxville
Billone, Amy Christine *education educator*
Bodenheimer, Sally Nelson *reading educator, retired*
Creasia, Joan Catherine *dean, nursing educator*
Garrison, Arlene Allen *academic administrator, engineering educator*
Gaude, Emily Camp *elementary school educator*
Hatton, Barbara R. *academic administrator*
Moore, Patricia Lynn Graves *school system administrator*
Owen, Angie D. *elementary school educator*
Pearman, Gwynn Taft *elementary school educator*
Romeo, Joanne Josefa Marino *mathematics educator*
Rose, Terry Denise *secondary school educator*
Schumann, Jane Anne *education educator*
Thompson, Judy Ellen *elementary school educator*
Walsh, Joanne Elizabeth *retired elementary school educator, librarian*

Lebanon
Martin, Clair *academic administrator*

Loudon
Llumbet, Patsi Lynn *pre-school educator*

Lynchburg
Gregory, Cheri B. *biology educator*

Manchester
Taylor, Linda Janelle Layne *secondary school educator*
Westberry, Anita Parrish *education educator*

Martin
Moore, Earlene J. *school librarian*

Maryville
Briggs, Geraldine Hackworth *reading specialist eduator*
Davis, Vickie B. *pre-school educator, director*
McCord, Francine Nichole *elementary school educator*

Maynardville
Collins, Sherrie Lynne *secondary school educator*

Mc Minnville
Wilson, Debra Joanne *vice principal*

Memphis
Archer, Ruth Wallace *elementary school educator*
Deutsch, Alleen Dimitroff *university administrator*
Donahue, Joan Elizabeth *elementary school educator*
Flood, Tamela Michelle *elementary school educator*
Hardy, Grace Hervey *elementary guidance counselor, language arts eductor*
Jackson, Pamela Hall *school system administrator*
Johnson, Carol R. *school system administrator*
Joyner, Marguerite Austin *secondary school educator*
Kelly, Aleda Mae *retired secondary education educator*
McGlown, Brenda Pryor *special education educator*
Murphy, Margarette Celestine Evans *retired secondary school educator*
Phipps, Carolyn Sisk *secondary educator*
Raines, Shirley Carol *academic administrator*
Ramsey, Gloria Rogers *elementary school educator*
Russell, Judy D. *mathematics educator*
Sharon, Momany *retired elementary school and music educator*
Watson, Sharon Diane *principal*

Millington
Gray, Barbara L. *assistant principal, tax specialist*

Mountain City
DeGeorge, Gail *retired special education educator*
Gentry, Penny Michelle *elementary school educator*

Munford
King, Shirley Ann *middle school educator*

Murfreesboro
Doyle, Delores Marie *retired principal*
Gilbert, Linda Arms *education educator, educational association administrator*
Hemby-Grubb, Virginia *education educator, consultant*
Jessie, Sarah Elrod *educational consultant*
Lewis, Brenda C. *secondary school educator*
Mock, Melanie Lynn *elementary school educator, music educator*
Russell, Judith Kay *educator, researcher*
Schroeder, Kathleen Anne *secondary school educator*

Nashville
Benbow, Camilla Persson *dean, psychology professor*
Brigham, Nicolette Bainbridge *educational consultant*
Clinton, Barbara Marie *director, social worker*
Collins, Joe Lena *retired secondary school educator*
Collins, Melanie Jean *elementary school educator*
Conway-Welch, Colleen *dean, nurse midwife*
Crittenden, Etta Marie *elementary school educator*
Hammond, Marie S. *psychology educator, researcher, consultant*
Harper, Donna Waller *secondary school educator*
Martinez Bland, Veronica Kay *elementary school educator*
McMurray, Justine *elementary school educator*
McMurry, Idanelle Sam *educational consultant*
Morton, Linda June *academic administrator*
O'Leary, Hazel R. *academic administrator, retired federal official, lawyer*
Pierce, Patricia Ann *university administrator*
Rhodes, Susan Elizabeth *secondary school educator*
Schroeder, Joni Lynn *secondary school educator*
Seivers, Lana C. *school system administrator*
Washington, JoAnn *elementary school educator*
Woodall, Ruth Ann *educational consultant*

New Tazewell
Leonard, Martha Gail *elementary school educator*

Newport
Hall, Mitzy Delaine *chemistry educator*

Oliver Springs
Heacker, Thelma Weaks *retired elementary school educator*

Ooltewah
Farmer Ratz, Kathy Ann *secondary school educator*

Pigeon Forge
Puckett, Sandy Graves *elementary school educator*

Portland
Miller, Sandra Perry *middle school educator, department chair*

Ripley
Hartman, Joan Evans *educational consultant*

Robbins
Queener, Dana Brandon *elementary school educator*

Savannah
Flanagan, Judy *director, special events consultant*

Selmer
Prather, Sophie S. *educational administrator*

Sevierville
O'Dell, Tonja Renee *primary school educator*

Smithville
Hinton, Susan Frazier *secondary school educator*

Smyrna
Trea, Melissa Ann *mathematics educator*

Soddy Daisy
Collins, Kathleen *mathematics educator*
May, Cathy June *elementary school educator*

Strawberry Plains
Blanchard, Pamela Snyder *special education educator*

Tullahoma
Hazelwood, Christy Stamps *elementary school educator, small business owner*

Whitesburg
Seals, Kristi Dawn *elementary school educator*

TEXAS

Abilene
Bammel-Lee, Sharlyn D'Ann *elementary school educator, consultant*
Durrington, Rose Colleen *education educator, director reading clinic, dean*
Flores, Kathryn Louise *mathematics educator*
Hammer, Stephanie Ann *elementary school educator*
Konczak, Sandra M. *elementary school educator*
Lloyd, Terry Lee *retired elementary school educator*

Alice
Thomas, Katherine Carol *special education educator*

Allen
Screen, Robin Marie *secondary school educator*
Witt, Felicia Lestage *biology educator*

Alpine
Aldridge, Mary Nan *education educator*
Moore, Zana Yvonne *secondary school educator, researcher*
Morgan, Mary Jane *retired mathematics educator*

Alvin
Orsak, Lisa Gayle *secondary school educator*

Amarillo
Knutson, Bonnie Rae *secondary school educator, artist*

Andrews
Scarbrough, Glenda Judith *elementary school educator*

Anson
Plank, Katrina Jean *secondary school educator*

Arlington
Beaty, Barbara A. *secondary school educator*
Copeland, Anita Bob *director, retired elementary school educator, senior consultant*
Davidson, Martha W. *elementary school educator*
Garrett, Stephanie Kay *history educator*
Holley, Kathleen *secondary school educator*
King, Teresa Howard *special education educator, consultant*
Kracht, Christina Marie *secondary school educator, coach*

Athens
Enger, Linda *mathematics educator, consultant*

Austin
Aguayo-Tabor, Maricruz Rocio *secondary school educator*
Bolm, Deborah Dell *elementary school educator, consultant*
Calfee, Laura Pickett *university administrator, photographer*
Cook, Kelli Brooke *elementary school educator*
Corcoran, Nancy Lee *retired elementary school educator*
Greer, Carolyn A. *guidance counselor*
Jensen, Julie Mae *educator*
Kallfelz, Tonya Leigh *secondary school educator*
Lehmann-Carssow, Nancy Beth *secondary school educator, coach*
Lenoir, Gloria Cisneros *secondary school educator, consultant*
Mauzy, Martha Anne *retired deaf educator, audiologist*
McKeown-Moak, Mary Park *educational consultant*
Neeley, Shirley *school system administrator*
Owens, Margaret Alma *educational administrator*
Proctor, Carrie Ann *counseling administrator*
Rankin, Mary Ann *dean, biology professor*
Rogers, Lorene Lane *university president emeritus*
Roueche, Suanne Davis *university administrator*
Servantez, Melinda *elementary school educator*
Varra, Dawn Renee *elementary school educator*

Bastrop
Clemons, Barbara Gail *history educator*

Bay City
Woolsey, Patricia Jane *secondary school educator*

Beaumont
Baden, Sheri Louise *primary school educator*
Brassard, Janice Aline *retired secondary school educator*
Dousay, Linda Faye *academic administrator*
Gagne, Mary *academic administrator*
Hickman, Matilda Coffey *principal*
Irons, Ellen Jane *educational leadership educator*
McCray, Glenda Elaine *elementary school educator*
Prudhomme, Donna Powell *school counselor*

Beeville
Freeman, Patsy L. *director*

Bellaire
Sperotto, Angela Diane *secondary school educator*

Belton
Daniewicz, Susan Carney *education educator, social worker*

Ben Bolt
Garza, Annabel *elementary school educator*

Bogata
Lee, Leah Raynella *elementary school educator*

Booker
Doerrie, Bobette *educational consultant, secondary school educator*

Brenham
Knebel, Rosemary *secondary school educator*

Brownsville
Garcia, Juliet Villarreal *academic administrator*

Brownwood
Campbell, Vicki F. *counseling administrator, educator*

Bryan
Beto, Donna L. *retired elementary school educator*
Fields, Sheila Crain *elementary school educator*
Richmond, Dina Rae *retired secondary school educator*
Voelkel, Jane Claudette *retired elementary school educator, home economist*

Buchanan Dam
Miloy, Leatha Faye *university program director*

Buda
Bagley Freels, Nancy Virginia *secondary school educator*
Hayden, Karen Boone *history educator*
Upton, Shelly Ann Vosburg *elementary school educator*

Carrollton
Barland, Sarah Elizabeth *secondary school educator*
Boynton, Leigh Anne *secondary school educator*
Grimes, Terrie Lynn *elementary school educator*
Louie, Peggy C. *secondary school educator*

Cedar Park
Gonzales, Elizabeth Betsy Barnes *elementary school educator, consultant*
Serna, Jayne Elizabeth *history educator*

Center
Brazzel, Regina Gayle *secondary school educator*

Center Point
Turner, Brenda Gail *elementary school educator*

Channelview
Dishongh, Lisa Lynn *history educator*
Wallace, Betty Jean *retired elementary school educator, lay minister*

Cibolo
Weaver, Melinda Yvonne *secondary school educator*

Clute
Patterson, Ronnye Williams *assistant principal*

Clyde
Pair, Marci Holt *secondary school educator*

College Station
Cook, Violetta Burke *university administrator*
Dickey, Nancy Wilson *chancellor, physician*
Gangotena, Margarita *educator, consultant*
Murano, Elsa A. *academic administrator, former federal agency administrator*
Reinarz, Alice G. *academic administrator*

Colleyville
Giesler, Karen Hofmann *elementary school educator*
Livaudais, Noel Elizabeth Dwyer *special education educator, secondary school educator*

Comanche
Droke, Edna Faye *retired elementary school educator*

Commerce
Scott, Joyce Alaine *academic administrator*
Thompson, Jane Ann *elementary school educator, researcher*

Conroe
Cogdell, Paula L. *secondary school educator, real estate agent*
Gray, Janet Ethel *elementary school educator*
McNutt, Deborah Matoy *history educator*
Pitts, Holly Lea *elementary school educator*

Coppell
McAlister, Michelle Nicole *mathematics educator*
Smothermon, Peggi Sterling *middle school educator*

Corpus Christi
Marez, Rebecca Ann *literature and language educator*
Osborne-Kay, Trisha Ann *elementary school educator*

Crockett
Richards, Anita Henson *special education educator*

Cypress
Funk-Werblo, Dorothy *elementary school educator*
Huss, Betty Jo *education educator*

Dallardsville
Oliver, Debbie Edge *elementary school educator*

Dallas
Benson, BeLinda Lou *school system administrator*
Braswell, Mary Paul Gibson *elementary school educator*
Cirilo, Amelia Medina *educational consultant*
Coggan, Patricia Conner *elementary school educator*
Fletcher, (Martha) Ann Messersmith *counseling administrator, educator*
Hester, Linda Hunt *retired dean, counseling administrator, sociology educator, health and physical education educator*

Hinkle, Bonnie *education educator*
Nelson, Anna M. *elementary school educator, administrative assistant*
Poindexter, Barbara Glennon *secondary school educator*
Russell-Love, Zelda M. *special education educator*
Savannah, Mildred Thornhill *public school educator*
Smith, Marsha Ann *literature and language educator*
Smith-Ingram, Karen Camille *reading specialist, educator*
Stearman, Sherri Lynn *physical education educator*
Tidwell, Trisha McIntosh *elementary school educator, department chairman*
Turner, Ruth *academic administrator*
Wilkerson, Patricia Helen *director*
Winkley-Pikes, Sandra Kay *special education educator*
Wolek, Andrea Dugas *special education educator*

Decatur
Vaughan, Nancy King *school system administrator*

Deer Park
Guillory, Jennifer Lee *secondary school educator*
Lewis, Nancy L. *science educator*
Morse, Janice Lea *secondary school educator*

Del Valle
Titus, Alberta Christine *secondary school educator*

Denison
Cameron, Frances Marilyn *elementary school educator*
Plunkett, Alexa *elementary school educator*

Denton
Bataille, Gretchen *academic administrator*
Calabrese, Margaret Hoye *secondary school educator*
Garcia, Rebekah *elementary school educator*
Greenlaw, Marilyn Jean *retired adult education educator*
Hughes, Deborah Bray *special education educator*
Jacobs, Bonita Cheryl *educational administrator*
Karr-Kidwell, P. J. *education educator, writer*
Kooker, Jean L. *retired elementary school educator*
McCoy, Amy L. *special education educator*
Novak, Rynell Stiff *retired university official*
Palermo, Judy Hancock *retired elementary school educator*
Saiyed, Seema *education educator, researcher*

Detroit
Cates, Sue Sadler *special education counselor*

Edinburg
Norman, Theresa J.C. *philosophy professor*
Wedig, Cindy Martinez *director*

El Paso
Casas, Martha *education educator*
Guevara, Roxanna *elementary school educator, gifted and talented educator*
Herrera, Blanche Marie *elementary school educator*
Lincoln, Shelley *elementary school educator*
Martinez, Gloria Elena *elementary school educator*
Natalicio, Diana Siedhoff *academic administrator*
Pace, Diane Marie *elementary school educator*
Smookler, Maurrissa *elementary school educator*
Talamantes, Claudia Liliana *secondary school educator*
Vojta-Oswald, Clarice Gertrude *educational diagnostician*
Zopfi, Emma G. *elementary school educator*

Elgin
Shelby, Nina Claire *special education educator*

Emory
Allen, G. Christy L. L. *physics educator*

Euless
Kaufman, Susan Nanette Bland *secondary school educator*
McClure, Connie Diane *elementary school educator*
Traver, Sue Montgomery *secondary school educator*

Fairfield
Gooch, Nancy Eugenia South *retired secondary school educator, librarian*

Farmers Branch
Reyes, Czarina Suzanne *mathematics educator*

Flower Mound
Sanders, Lisa Gail *mathematics educator*

Flowermound
Furnas, Valerie Yvonne *secondary school educator*

Fluvanna
Jackson, Rebecca M. *elementary education educator, English as a second language educator*

Forney
Braden, Katie Elizabeth *elementary school educator*

Fort Hood
Reid, Sharon Lea *educational facilitator*

Fort Worth
Case, Rachel *elementary school educator*
Mays, Glenda Sue *retired education educator*
Ogle, Sarah J. *assistant principal*
Simmons, Jean Byers *academic administrator, director*
Wilson, Monica DeAnn *school guidance counselor*

Franklin
Perry, Anne Marie Litchfield *secondary school educator*

Fredericksburg
Koym, Zala Cox *retired elementary school educator*

Freer
Blanton, Belia *secondary school educator*

Friendswood
Corley, Cathy F. *elementary school educator*
Overstreet-Goode, Janwin Gail *secondary school educator, music educator, director*

Frisco
Carlock, Rebecca Gail *biology educator, chemistry educator*
Coley, Donna S. *secondary school educator*
Jackson, Rhonda Gail *secondary teacher*
Penz, Roxanne Murray *elementary school educator*
Sisk, Kristin Carrington *secondary school educator*

Galveston
Bertolino, Jennifer Ann *elementary school educator*
Goodwin, Sharon Ann *academic administrator*

Garland
Albuquerque, Heather Lynne *biology educator*
Bjornson Pierce, Shauna *primary school educator*
Chenault, Sheryl Ann *elementary school educator*
Enaya, Maysaa Asad *chemistry educator, physics educator*
Fegraeus, Susie A. *principal*
Goheen, Debra Elaine *secondary school educator*
Quinn, Peggy Armstrong *elementary school educator, writer*

Garrison
Cole, Luanna Cherry *literature and language educator, theater educator*

Gary
Coligan, Nerissa *secondary school educator*

Gatesville
Huntley, Barbara Nerine *secondary school educator*

Gause
Salcido, Debra Kay *elementary school educator*

Georgetown
Bencivenga, Alison R. *elementary school educator*

Gladewater
Beaird, Dian Sanders *middle school educator*

Glenn Heights
Rowe, Nancie E. *director, minister*

Graham
Lovell, Lisa Inez *special education educator*

Grand Prairie
Andrew, Kathryn Anderson *elementary school educator*
Bouliane, Mary Stephanie *elementary school educator*

Grapevine
Hirsh, Cristy J. *principal*

Groves
Simon, Mary B. *primary school educator*

Hallsville
Goerner, Freda Ruth *secondary school educator*

Harker Heights
Rose, Doris Ann *elementary school educator*

Harlingen
Sandwell, Stephanie Annette *mathematics educator*

Hawkins
Holmes, Lorene Barnes *academic administrator*

Henderson
Knapp, Virginia Estella *retired secondary school educator*
Rhoades, Eva Yvonne *retired elementary school educator*

Hereford
Yavornik, Barbara Ann *pre-school educator*

Hillsboro
Elkin, Carole Kaine *retired educational diagnostician*
Parks, Connie *elementary school educator*

Houston
Adams, Joyce M. *retired academic administrator*
Anderson, Claire W. *gifted and talented educator*
Autry, Cheryl Renee *special education educator*
Avila, Susan Elizabeth *elementary school educator*
Ballard, Linda Christine *financial aid director*
Barajas, Nancy Helen *assistant principal*
Bebis, Conchita Juban *mathematics educator*
Beckingham, Kathleen Mary *education educator, researcher*
Behan, Pamela S. *sociology professor*
Benefield, Janis Wilson *school librarian, media specialist*
Betts, Nicole Lavette *elementary school educator, consultant*
Bourgeois, Patricia Ann *middle school educator*
Boutwell, Sharon Marie *school system administrator, educator*
Brandt, Astrid *elementary school educator*
Cavitt, Rebecca Lynn *secondary school educator*
Conner, Beverly T. *counseling administrator, educator*
Daniels, Davetta Mills *principal*
Darst, Mary Lou *elementary school educator*
Davis, Debra Ann *secondary school educator*
Davis, Marlece (Alice Marlece Davis) *secondary school educator, director*
Eugeni, Michelle L. *academic administrator*
Farley, Barbara L. *elementary school educator*
Flagg, Mary Kay *mathematics educator*
Flaitz, Catherine M. *dean, dental educator*
Floyd, Kristi *counseling administrator*
Garrett, Mary Jane *director*
Gentry, Tina *secondary school educator*
Goodwin, Heather Marie *educational consultant*
Hattab, Helen Nathalie *philosophy professor*
Hawkins, Ida Faye *elementary school educator*
Jimmar, D'Ann *elementary school educator, educational consultant*
Johnson, Thelma Jean *secondary school educator*
King, Kay Wander *academic administrator, design educator, fashion designer, consultant*
Kmiec Roberts, Helen Marie *middle school educator*
Kneese, Carolyn Calvin *retired education educator*
Lamb, Teryana R. *secondary school educator*
LeBoff, Barbara *elementary school educator*
Looper, Marcia Lynn *elementary school educator, consultant*
Lukens, Susan Ackley *school system administrator*
Lutz, Danielle Renee *academic administrator*
Matthews, Kathleen Shive *biochemistry educator*
McDonald, Marilyn A. *academic assistant*
Morris, Carolyn S. *elementary school educator*
Nesbitt, Virginia *retired special education educator, poet*
O'Neil, Sharon Lund *educator*
Parnas-Simpson, Marianna *chorus director, singer*
Roos, Sybil Friedenthal *retired elementary school educator*
San Pedro, Sylvia P. *mathematics educator, department chairman*
Santi, Kristi L. *special education educator, researcher*
Smith, Joellen *dean, literature and language educator*
Smith-Vallejo, Lora Lee *elementary school educator*
Sparks, Donna L. *school librarian*
Stanton, Vivian Brennan (Mrs. Ernest Stanton) *retired counseling administrator*
Stripling, Kaye *school system administrator*
Sullivan-Szuts, Betty Anne *academic administrator, educator*
Tolley, Michelle Renee *secondary school educator*
Trichel, Mary Lydia *middle school educator*
Wacker-B., Deborah *secondary Spanish and special education educator*
Webb, Marty Fox *principal*
Whiting, Martha Countee *retired secondary school educator*
Wilkin, Alana Zimmer *elementary school educator*

Hubbard
Schronk, Patricia Lynn *secondary school educator*

Humble
Burns, Angela Kaye *secondary school educator*
Chevalier, Denise Ann *director*
Howsmon, Debra Sue *biology educator*

Huntsville
McGee, Carol A. *retired elementary school educator*

Hurst
Cruze, Jennifer Lea *secondary school educator*
Harper, Jane Armstrong *college administrator, consultant*
Hoffman, Katherine Ann *education educator*

Irving
Phares, Sharon C. *elementary school educator*
Rutledge, Deborah Jean *secondary school educator*
Snyder, Dolores Wilma *culinary educator*
Stapleton, Claudia Ann *academic administrator*

Jasper
Bennett-Greenleaf, Linda Fay *special education educator*
Edwards, Charlotte Ann *elementary school educator*

Joaquin
Gill, Madeline Kay *school and youth counselor*

Johnson City
Pollock, Margaret Landau Peggy *elementary school educator*

Joshua
Curlee, Carol Wynette *mathematics educator, science educator, small business owner, Internet company executive*

Justin
Hearn, Robin Kim *secondary school educator*

Keene
Bittiker, Marjorie Joanne *principal*

Keller
Smith, Eleanor Jane *retired university chancellor, consultant*

Kennedale
Worley, Ruth *secondary school educator*

Kilgore
Johnson, Flora Mae *retired elementary school educator*

Killeen
Jenkins, Sharon Leigh *special education educator*
McPherson, Katharyn Ross *elementary school educator*
Peronto, Janice Lynn *principal*

Kingsville
Doughty, Pamela D. *education educator*

Hernandez, Thelma Quintanilla *secondary school educator*

Kingwood
Foreman, Gini Diane *English educator*
Lard, Pamula D. *special education educator*
von Dohlen, Elizabeth K. *secondary school educator*

La Grange
Ledwik, Gretchen Marie *elementary school educator, art educator*

La Porte
Edwards, Kristina Nell *elementary school educator*

Lake Jackson
Hill, Diane Louise *educator*

Laredo
Gutierrez, Yvonne Soliz *school system administrator*
Heimes, Charmaine Marie *elementary school educator, poet, writer*
Hinojosa, Sandra Joy *elementary special education educator*
Mendiola, Anna Maria G. *mathematics educator*
Paton, Lisa Dupree *elementary school educator*
Sierra, Maria Patricia *special education educator*
Whitehawk, Ann *secondary school educator*

Leander
Almour, Vicki Lynn *elementary school educator*

Lewisville
Dumbravo, Cathy Crosby *primary school educator*

Lexington
Baxter-Kegler, Demetra M. *principal*

Littlefield
Muller, Janice Elaine *secondary school educator*

Lockhart
White, Patricia Ann *chemistry educator, medical technician*

Longview
Bolomey, Rose L. *secondary school educator*
Cuba, Mattie Deneice *elementary school educator*
Modisette, Barbara Jane *education educator, psychologist*
Myers, Adrienne Celeste *assistant principal*
White, Jennifer Sullivan *secondary school educator*

Lubbock
Bredeson, Cheryl *elementary school educator*
Hawkins, Ann R. *educator, researcher*
Hurley, Kristie DeLynn *primary school educator*
Lovering, Emma *secondary school educator*
McMillan, Tobi A. *career planning administrator*
Smith, JoBeth *elementary school educator*

Luling
Collie, Paula Renea *secondary school educator*

Magnolia
Adams, Shirley A. *mathematics educator*
Bopp, Annette Lee *mathematics educator*

Mansfield
Barnett, Bertha L. Strickland *elementary school educator*

Marfa
Allison, Amy S. *secondary school educator*
Chambers Tucker, Johnnie L. *elementary school educator, rancher*
Wimberly, Cynthia Diane *mathematics educator*

Marshall
Helton, Karen Johnson *college administrator*

Mc Kinney
Dorff, Barbara L. *elementary and secondary school educator*
Kirkley, Vicki *school system administrator, director*

Mercedes
Alaniz, Theodora Villarreal *elementary school educator*
Rogers, Colette *counseling administrator*
Streicher, Georgina Rodriguez *special education educator*

Mesquite
Caruthers, Tara M. *physics educator*
Grant, Betty Ruth *retired elementary school educator*
Holt, Mildred Frances *special education educator*
Pecina, Kristianne *secondary school educator*
Turner, LaNell Daphene *physical education educator*
Tustin, Karen Gail *mathematics educator*
Wyatt, Susan Skinner *education educator*

Midland
McCracken, Terri *elementary school educator*
Wood, Stephanie *mathematics educator*

Midlothian
Alderman, Amy Joy Spigel *elementary school educator*

Mineral Wells
Sherrill, Helen White *elementary school educator*

Missouri City
Sturhan, Courtney *secondary school educator*
Weber, Katie *retired special education educator*

Montgomery
Dossey, Nancy Ruthstrom *elementary education educator, consultant*

Mount Pleasant
Geffers, Betty J. *secondary school educator*

Nacogdoches
Ashley, Janelle Coleman *academic administrator*
Carter, Evelyn *retired elementary school educator*
Long, Penny *mathematics educator*
Offield, Carol Jean Dubberly *elementary school educator*

Natalia
Chew, Lynda Casbeer *elementary school educator*

Navasota
Day, Kathryn Ann *history educator*

Nederland
Martin, Angela Denise *educator*

New Braunfels
Barragān, Celia Silguero *elementary school educator*
Gray, Cari Laird *economics educator*
Jaroszewski, Lisa Elaine *literature and language educator*

New Caney
Slade-Redden, Debra Kay *biology educator*

New Deal
Howell, Allie Rhea *retired educator*

Normangee
Stork, Vera Lee *retired elementary school educator*

North Richland Hills
Moody, Mary Doyle *elementary school educator*

Odessa
Braswell, Jody Lynn *gifted and talented educator*
Rasor, Doris Lee *retired secondary school educator*

Omaha
Moos, Verna Vivian *special education educator*

Orange
Hannegan, Rebecca Ann *retired elementary school educator*

Ore City
Hill, Margaret Janell *elementary school educator*

Palo Pinto
Blissitte, Karen Dawn *elementary school educator*

Pampa
Nava, Mary Margaret *secondary school educator*

Paris
Hines, Jaclyn Letta *counseling administrator*

Pasadena
Ruiz, Miriam *secondary school educator*

Pearland
Dawson, Besse Malinda Barker *secondary school educator, department chairman*
Furnari, Rosemarie Ann *secondary school educator, real estate agent*

Perryton
Blasingame, Janet Lynn *primary school educator*

Placedo
Rivera, Josie *elementary school educator*

Plainview
Dayton, Leah Jane *secondary school educator*

Plano
Boggan, Amy L. *secondary school educator, education educator*
Haggard, Geraldine Langford *primary school educator, adult education educator, consultant, writer*
Reidling, Valerie Ann *secondary school educator*
Tucker, Ann *secondary school educator*

Portland
Culbertson, Deborah Jean *educational consultant*

Priddy
Zimmer, Greta Gay *secondary school educator*

Quitman
Beverly, Kelly Dee Gray *elementary school educator*

Randolph Afb
Brennan-Bergmann, Bridget Catherine *special education educator*

Richardson
Bray, Carolyn Scott *education educator*
Carlson, Catherine Kossan *secondary school educator*
Dethrage, Debbie J *educational consultant*
Overall, Theresa Lynne *elementary school educator*
Salter, Elizabeth Mary *academic administrator*
Tipping, Sharon Rutledge *elementary school educator*
Unkenholz, Karla J. *elementary school educator*
Whitt, Margaret Jean *educator*
Wood, Peggy *secondary school educator*

Rockdale
Estell, Dora Lucile *retired educational administrator*

Rockwall
Anderson, Leslie Ann *secondary educator*

Rogers
Dolan, Andrea *secondary school educator*

Roscoe
Beeks, Cheryl Elaine *elementary school educator*

Rosenberg
Lefler, Sherry LynettE *elementary school educator*
Trevino, Katherine Ann *elementary school educator*
Welch, Frances Suzanne *director*
White, Gretchen Nance *education educator, writer*

Rosharon
Lopez, Placida Ramos *elementary school educator*

Round Rock
Ledbetter, Sharon Faye Welch *retired educational consultant*
Nero, Molly Joanna *elementary school educator*

San Angelo
Childress, Susan Lynette *retired elementary school educator*

San Antonio
Beechinor, Diane Blanche *education educator*
Benavides, Deborah Ann *academic advisor*
Bennett, Sister Elsa Mary *retired secondary school educator*
Bosquez, Joy Denise *elementary school educator*
Carstensen, Maria Elena *academic administrator*
Delaney, Maria Cissy *elementary school educator*
Dyas, Anna Marie *gifted and talented educator*
Faules, Barbara Ruth *retired elementary school educator*
Ford, Barbara G. *secondary school educator*
Groos, April Cox *secondary school educator*
Hall, Denise *special education educator*
Hoag, Rebecca Ebner *literature and language educator*
Hudspeth, Almetra Kavanaugh *retired elementary school educator*
Kosty, Carlita *secondary school educator*
Madrid, Olga Hilda Gonzalez *retired elementary school educator, school system administrator*
Marshall, Joyce Ramsey *secondary school educator*
McSorley, Rita Elizabeth *adult education educator*
Moltz, Beverly Ann *elementary school educator*
Moss, Betty Harris *secondary education educator*
Nelson, Glenda Kay *special education educator*
Potts, Martha Lou *elementary school educator*
Sanchez, Susie Riojas *elementary school educator*
Stanson, Kay V. *elementary school educator, consultant*
Tschoepe, Deborah E. *special education educator*
Williams-Perry, Brenda Lee *pre-school educator*
Wise, Christina Renée *school disciplinarian*

San Marcos
Allsup, Roxane Cuellar *curriculum and instruction educator*
Carman, Mary Ann *retired special education educator*
Dowling, Catherine Lynn *secondary school educator*

Seabrook
Woods-Stellman, Donna Sue *education educator, consultant*

Seguin
Miller, Bonnie Ruth *retired elementary school educator*

Selma
(Marbach) Miller, Amanda Joy *educator*

Seminole
Hill, Catherine Louise *secondary school educator*

Shepherd
Busteed, Diana Lynn *speech educator, theatre director*

Sherman
Carnes, La Zetta *retired secondary school educator*
Chavez-Hill, Tammy Lynn *elementary school educator*
Neathery, Cheryl Alissa *secondary school educator*
Williams, Ruby Jo *retired principal*

Smithville
Johnson, Melody Jean *special education educator*
Scott, Mary Edith *special education educator*

Southlake
Arafat-Johnson, Danyah *secondary school educator, director*

Spring
Neill, Rebecca Anne *middle school educator*
Wasson, Kristi Byas *secondary school educator*

Spurger
Gardner, Susan Kay *elementary school educator*

Stafford
Hayes, Joyce Merriweather *retired secondary school educator*

Stephenville
McElroy, Linda Sue *retired elementary school educator*

Sugar Land
Cleveland, Stephanie McDowell *secondary school educator*
Hall, Georganna Mae *elementary school educator*
Knight, Brenda Jean *mathematics educator*
Matney, Judy McCaleb *secondary school educator*
Slack-Beard, Kay Lane *secondary school educator*
Waihman, Lisa Girard *mathematics educator*

Sulphur Springs
Alexander, Silvesta *elementary school educator*
Clayton, Pamela Sanders *special education educator*
Gibson, Jannette Poe *educational consultant*

Hadlow, Vivian Jean *elementary school educator, retired principal*

Sunnyvale
Parmenter, Kelli Denise *elementary school educator, small business owner*

Temple
Hildebrand, Mary Sue *elementary school educator, principal*
Jackson, Karen *elementary school educator*
Kreitz, Helen Marie *retired elementary school educator*
Staten, Donna Kay *elementary school educator*

Terrell
McCasland, Teresa *secondary school educator, director*

Texarkana
Griffis, Theresa A. *secondary school educator*

The Colony
Culver, Jennifer Lynn *secondary school educator*

Timpson
Samford, Sharon Annette *elementary school educator, researcher*

Tye
Hill, Emma Lee *education educator*

Tyler
Knox, Danielle Nicole *secondary school educator*
Oaxaca, Susan Renna *secondary school educator*
Waller, Wilma Ruth *retired secondary school educator, librarian*

Uvalde
Pollard, Honora Mae *elementary school educator*

Van
Wooten, Julie *secondary school educator*

Van Horn
Scott, Joy Marie *elementary school educator, educator*

Vernon
Black, Beverly Ann Marie Layton *secondary school educator, department chairman*

Victoria
Kendall, Dorothy Irene *secondary school educator*

Waco
Benedict, Helen Elizabeth *psychologist, university administrator*
Donnell, Gaylene Renee' *special education educator*
Emanuel, Gloria Page *retired secondary school educator*
Girouard, Tandy Denise *special education educator, psychology professor*
Hart, Maxine Barton *education educator*
Hollingsworth, Martha Lynette *secondary school educator*

Weatherford
Baker, Jacqueline Madden *special education educator*
Miller, Dixie Davis *elementary school educator*

Wharton
Wilkinson, Sharon Elizabeth Roberson *elementary school educator*

Whiteface
Lamb, Stacie Thompson *elementary school educator*

Wichita Falls
Hancock, Carole Patricia *academic administrator*
Lane, Sue Alison *literature and language educator*
Leishner, Jane Carlson *retired director*
Lowrance, Muriel Edwards *retired educational specialist*

Willis
Kercheval, Patricia *secondary school educator*

Winters
Moore, Donna Tipton *special education educator*

Woden
Fletcher, Martha Jane *elementary school educator*

Wolfe City
Woodruff, Sandra Anita *mathematics and science educator*

Wolfforth
LeMaster, Kathy Lynn *elementary school educator*

Wylie
Campbell, Sylvia June *secondary school educator*
Cheng, Pauline Shyh-yi *mathematics educator*
Milhoan, Susana *mathematics educator*

UTAH

Bountiful
Andersen, Julie B. *elementary school educator*
Bertelsen, Karyn *school system administrator, principal*

Cedar City
Williamson, Doris *business education educator*

Cedar Hills
Ashton, Dawne Belinda *retired secondary school educator*

Draper
Walz, Angela *retired secondary school educator*

Kaysville
Hunt, Rebecca R. *elementary school educator*

Le, Dai-Trang *mathematics educator*

Kearns
Glazier, Linda Hatch *mathematics educator*

Logan
Dennison, Elizabeth Cornelia *special education educator*
Minch, Donna Ruth Black *director*

Magna
Daraban, Vickie Leigh Plott *secondary school educator*
Richardson, Valerie *secondary school educator*

Manti
Schiffman, Karen Ashdown *secondary school educator*

Midvale
Smith, Mary Ellen *educational program facilitator*

Murray
Helms, Belva Elizabeth *secondary school educator, mathematician*
Lynes, BonnieJeane *mathematics educator, sales executive*

North Ogden
Heap, Joan S. *elementary school educator*

Ogden
Geide-Stevenson, Doris *adult education educator*
Millner, F. Ann *academic administrator*
Runolfson, Marilyn Dolores *special education educator*

Orem
Stevens, Lori Ann LaBeau *school librarian, educator*

Provo
Densley, Colleen T. *principal*

Riverton
Draper, Pamela Denkers *elementary school educator*

Roy
Tracy, Nadine Ruth *secondary school educator*

Salt Lake City
Harrington, Patti *school system administrator*
Huefner, Dixie Snow *special education educator*
Johnsen, Sheryl B. *secondary education educator, consultant*
Walton, Tyla Johnson *secondary school educator*
Wolf, Joan Silverman *special education educator*

Tooele
LaForge, Carol Anne *secondary school educator*

Tremonton
Clark, Ethelann P. *elementary school educator*

Vernal
Hall, Nanette H. *adult education educator*
Moulton, Mary E. *secondary school educator*

West Jordan
Betenson, Gaye Brinton *secondary school educator*
James, Linda Coates *elementary school educator*

West Valley City
Bandeka, Faun Ann *elementary school educator*
Woodward, Sandra S. *literature and language educator*

VERMONT

Bennington
Coleman, Elizabeth *college president*
McEwan, Dawn Marie *secondary school educator*

Bethel
Evans, Marcia K. *school system administrator*

Burlington
Allard, Judith Louise *secondary school educator*
Thompson, Ellen Ann *elementary school educator*

Castleton
Larrabee, Virginia Ann Stewart *education educator, department chairman*

Concord
Metzke, Linda Kuzan *education educator*

Dorset
Brophy-Antonez, Deborah Sue *special education educator*

Killington
Curtis, Sally Diane *educational consultant*

Lyndonville
Moore, Carol A. *academic administrator*

Manchester Center
Waldinger Seff, Margaret *special elementary education educator*

Middlebury
Forman, Michele *secondary school educator*
Karnes, Elizabeth Helen *academic professional, television producer*

Moretown
Hartshorn, Brenda Bean *elementary school educator*

Plainfield
Jervis, Jane Lise *academic administrator, historian*

Poultney
Cooper, Charleen Frances *special and elementary education educator*

Keezer, Deborah Ann *elementary school educator*

Swanton
Suitor, Dorcas P. *elementary school educator*

Woodstock
Piccoli, Susan Elizabeth *secondary school educator*

VIRGINIA

Abingdon
Ball, Amy Catherine *education program manager*

Alexandria
Bartlett, Elizabeth Susan *audio-visual specialist*
Brophy, Deborah Susan *secondary school educator*
Drickey, Ruth Irene *elementary school educator*
Edgell, Karin Jane *special education educator, reading specialist*
Haygood, Alma Jean *elementary school educator*
Johnson, Marlys Marlene *elementary school educator*
Rae, Jeneanne *new product development and innovation development consultant, educator*
Sampson, Jeanne Louise *retired special education educator*

Amelia Court House
Sampson, Mary Pond *special education educator*

Annandale
Passut, Christine Diana *special education educator*
Somers, Janice A. *elementary school educator*
Wilhelmi, Mary Charlotte *education educator, academic administrator*

Arlington
Dorman, Janet Lee Vosper *elementary school educator*
Finta, Frances Mickna *secondary school educator*
Haggett, Rosemary Romanowski *academic administrator*
Neel, Barbara Anne Spiess *elementary school educator, artist*
Ramaley, Judith Aitken *retired academic administrator, endocrinologist*
Rogers, Sharon J. *education consultant*

Ashburn
Alison, Allison Merkle *secondary school educator, lawyer*

Ashland
Allen, Kimberly Ferrick *elementary school educator*

Blacksburg
Blanchard, Dorothy Hardt *academic administrator, volunteer*
Campbell, Joan Virginia Loweke *secondary school educator, language educator*
Hirt, Joan B. *education educator*
Weaver, Pamela Ann *education educator*

Bristol
Hagy, Teresa Jane *elementary school educator*

Bristow
Livengood, Carol Ann *elementary school educator*

Burke
Brant, Jacquelyn Lois *secondary school educator, history educator, department chairman*

Callao
Sisson, Jean Cralle *retired elementary school educator*

Capeville
Spady, Joanne Smith *secondary school educator*

Chantilly
Messinger, Holly Lynn *secondary school educator*

Charlottesville
Brodrick, Sheri Mary-Ann *secondary school educator*
Brown, Rebecca Sue *director*
DeGaynor, Elizabeth Anne *secondary school educator*
Greville, Florence Nusim *secondary school educator, mathematician*
Hurd, Nicole Farmer *director*
Long, Carolyn Evans *preschool special education educator*
Miller, Margaret Alison *education educator*
Norcross, Barbara Breeden *retired educator*
Rappaport, Yvonne Kindinger *educator*
Stanley, Courtenay Turner *secondary school educator*
Wittenborg, Karin *university librarian*

Chesapeake
Hill, Deborah Nixon *elementary school educator, minister*
Lewter, Helen Clark *retired elementary school educator*
Notti, Donna Betts *special education educator*
Webb, Julia Jones *elementary school educator, minister*

Chester
Hoagland, Carolyn Markham *retired secondary school educator*

Clifton Forge
Locher, Elizabeth Aiken *elementary education educator, reading specialist, library director*

Cobbs Creek
Lawson, Janice Rae *retired elementary school educator*

Covington
Spurlock, Evelyn Harvey *retired elementary school educator, minister*

Culpeper
Chaffee, Monica Weaver *primary school educator*
Pearson, Sarah Lynn *elementary school educator*
Sarah, Pearson Lynn *elementary school educator*
Thomson, Jane H. *elementary school educator*

Dale City
Baxter, Ruth Howell *educational administrator, psychologist*

Danville
Agnor, Kimberly Keatts *elementary school educator*

Dry Fork
Poteat, Patsy *secondary school educator*

Dublin
Spraker, Deanna King *biology educator*
Wall, Jennifer Grey *assistant principal*

Eastville
Lewis, Sandra B. *mathematics educator*

Fairfax
Best, Amy L. *education educator*
Carr, Patricia Warren *adult education educator*
Crissey, Rebecca Lynn *special education educator*
Del Conte, L. Catherine *special education educator*
Given, Barbara (Barbara Knight) *secondary school educator*
Price, Lois Ann *elementary school educator*

Fairfax Station
Cantu, Jennifer St. John *gifted and talented educator*

Falls Church
Dean-Pratt, Bridget *secondary school educator*
Michelsen, Cleo *retired education educator, writer*
Miller, Martha Glenn *academic administrator, consultant*
Simon, Deborah Blick *educational consultant, retired secondary school educator*
Todd, Shirley Ann *school system administrator*
Waylonis, Jean Lynnette *elementary school educator*

Farmville
Cormier, Patricia Picard *academic executive*

Fort Defiance
Floyd, Ruth Crummett *elementary school educator*

Franklin
Lamb, Julie Walsh *elementary school educator*

Fredericksburg
Potter, Sylvia *education educator*
Ray, Margaret *education educator*

Front Royal
Hrbek, Susan W. *school librarian*
Stevens, Loretta Marie *special education educator*

Gainesville
Burke, Marjorie Tisdale *retired special education educator*
Gorzka, Margaret Rose *retired elementary school educator*

Glen Allen
Alves, Constance Dillenger *special education educator*
Bosdell, Melony *special education educator*

Grundy
Yates, Stella Louise *mathematics educator*

Hampton
Carrington, Marian Denise *academic administrator, counselor, motivational speaker*
Goode, Constance Loper *elementary school principal*
Lawson, Donna Yvette *special education educator*
Manns, Helen Margaret *vice principal*
Shaughnessy, Leslie Restaino *secondary educator*
Sypolt, Shirley Rae *elementary school educator*

Harrisonburg
Comfort, Heather E. *education educator*
Gabbin, Joanne Veal *education educator*

Herndon
Bobzien, Catherine Hardy *mathematics educator*
Jones, Reba (Becki) Pestun *elementary school educator, music educator*
Kmetz, Leah E. *elementary school educator*
Suess, Jennifer Lynn *elementary school educator*

Hurley
Blankenship, Linda Lou *education educator*

Ivor
Newby, Terrica Lee *elementary school educator*

Jonesville
Scott, Tammy Charlene *secondary school educator*

Lancaster
Forrester, Alexis C.G. *elementary school educator*

Lawrenceville
Hardy, Sandra Vanessa *elementary school educator*

Leesburg
Brown, Toni *health and physical educator*
Carroll, Teresa Fiske *mathematics educator*
Green, May Clayman *elementary school educator, education administrator*

Lexington
Miller, Sherry Duncan *elementary school educator*
Parker, Phyllis R. *secondary school educator*

Locust Grove
Cordray-Van de Castle, Karen *elementary school educator*

Lorton
Piskor, Susan Marie *secondary school educator*

Lovettsville
Ryan-Griffith, Mary Kate *special education educator*

Lynchburg
Bowman, Kathleen Gill *academic administrator*
Cash, Susan W. *career planning administrator*
Johnson, Kathie Carwile *education educator*
Law, Louise Disosway *education educator*

Manassas
Boyles, Norma Jean *elementary school educator*
Smith, Margaret A. *secondary school educator*

Marion
Groseclose, Joanne Stowers *special education educator*

Martinsville
Robertson, Margaret Moore *information technology educator*

Mc Dowell
Harkleroad, Jo-Ann Decker *special education educator*

Mc Lean
Black, Ginger Elizabeth *elementary school educator*
Pratt, Reyna Kushner *physics educator*

Middleburg
Kaplan, Jean Gaither (Norma Kaplan) *retired reading specialist*
Larmore, Catherine Christine *university official*

Midlothian
Coats, Kathy Lynn *biology educator*
Lamont-Gordon, Melissa Lynne *orchestra director, music educator*
Stoodt, Barbara Dern *retired education educator, magazine editor*

Natural Bridge Station
Compton, Mildred Lee *retired elementary school educator*

Newport News
Brunke, Kathleen Elizabeth *adult education educator*
Carson, Denise Wilkinson *gifted and talented educator*
Eanes, Janet Teresa *elementary school educator, music educator*
Smith, Kelly McCoig *assistant principal*
Underwood, Lori J. *philosophy educator*

Norfolk
Brown, Mary Wilkes *secondary school educator*
Faulk, Tanya Williams *school disciplinarian*
Ferris, Ginger Leigh *education educator, consultant*
Herbert, Elizabeth Anne *elementary school educator*
Hotaling, Diane Elizabeth Hickey *college administrator*
McDemmond, Marie Valentine *academic administrator, consultant*
Meyers, Carolyn Winstead *academic administrator, mechanical engineer, educator*
Roth Taylor, Lynn E. *gifted and talented educator*
Runte, Roseann *academic administrator*
Winslow, Janet Lucas *elementary school educator*
Witty, Elaine P. *retired dean, education educator*

Oak Hall
Kolbush, Elizabeth Ann Kuhns *secondary educator*

Orange
Weaver, Karen Johnson *elementary school educator*

Petersburg
Antunes, Marilyn Z. *mathematics educator*
Benn, Candace Marilea *elementary school educator*

Poquoson
Tuck, Carolyn Weaver *middle school educator*

Port Royal
Clarke-Hall, Deborah Renay *elementary school educator*

Portsmouth
Rampersaud Lundy, Sheryll *special education educator*
Rhodes, Kendall Westbrook *language arts educator*
Smith, Martha Ann *retired special education educator*

Pound
Barnette, Nellie Marie *elementary school educator*

Quantico
Stout, Mary Webb *dean*

Radford
Dunaway, Marsha Landrum *special education educator*
Kyle, Penelope Ward *academic administrator*
Webb, Nancy Hutchinson *elementary school educator*

Rapidan
Knewstep, Nancy Coleman *secondary school educator*

Reston
Brown, Della Hewett *elementary school educator*
Lynch, Monique Christine *mathematics educator*

Richlands
Morris, Marilyn LaVonne *retired elementary school educator, minister*

Richmond
Baldwin, Billie Sue *principal*
Blake, Miriam Snell *elementary school educator, choir director, organist, pianist*
Brown, Marilyn Branch *retired educational administrator*
Bryant, Colleen Cannington *history educator*
Christenbury, Leila *education educator*
Davis, Phyllis J. *education educator*
DeMary, Jo Lynne *school system administrator, elementary school educator*
Dunn, Linda Baugh *elementary school educator*
Harris, Grace E. *academic administrator*
Jewell-Sherman, Deborah *school system administrator*
Jones, Jeanne Pitts *pre-school administrator*
Minor, Marian Thomas *educational consultant, retired elementary school educator, retired secondary school educator*
Moss, Princess Renai *elementary school educator*
Ostrom, Kristina F. *academic administrator, optician*
Ragland, Ines Colom *principal*
Wallach, Kenya *mathematics educator*
Whitehurst, Lucinda Snyder *school librarian*
Zyglocke, Ann Madding *elementary school educator*

Ringgold
Woodward, Julia Wilson *elementary school educator*

Roanoke
Barnes, Sharon D. *director, music educator*
Gray, Nancy Ann Oliver *academic administrator*

Rose Hill
Lane, Mary Winston *secondary school educator*

Salem
Gilpin, Jeanny *elementary school educator*

Sandy Point
Douglas, Daisy Howard *retired elementary school educator, writer, consultant*

Scottsville
Griebenauw, Liza-Marie *secondary school educator*

Smithfield
Newby Tynes, Denise J. *elementary school educator, secondary school educator*
Odom, Marsha McClelland *elementary school educator*

South Hill
Taylor, Jean Mull *secondary school educator*

Springfield
Hairston, Geraldine *mathematics educator*
Ona, Caroline Jean *history educator*
Wong, Ann Lam *secondary school educator*

Staunton
Cabe, Crista Ruth *academic administrator*
Karaffa, Rebecca P. *elementary school educator*

Sterling
Austin, Lynne Hunzicker *secondary school educator*
Bartow, Nicole A. *secondary school educator*
Skrzycki, Maryann *physics educator*
Wolfgang, Crystal *secondary school educator*

Stuart
Gregory, Jennifer Daryl *mathematics educator, small business owner*

Stuarts Draft
Mikell, Martha Simms *secondary school educator*

Suffolk
Brown, Alvenice Hortense Bryan *educator*
Driggins, Elaine Eure *elementary school educator*
Harrell, Florence Louise *elementary school educator*

Sweet Briar
Muhlenfeld, Elisabeth S. *academic administrator, literature educator, writer*

Tazewell
Thompson, Patricia DuBois *elementary school educator*

Victoria
Bayne, Kathryn Ann *elementary school educator*
Sheffield, Elizabeth Rash *elementary school educator*

Virginia Beach
Boudreau, Sharon Kay *special education educator*
Costello, Stacy Ann *elementary school educator*
Cummings, Catherine T. *elementary school educator*
Dawson, Arleta M. *history educator*
DiTommaso, Phyllis Battis *special education educator*
Edwards, Cynthia (Cindy) Curtis *mathematics educator*
Garcia, Sharon D. *elementary school educator*
Gardner, Karen High *special education educator*
Garvey, Dawn Elaine *elementary school educator*
Hague, Debbie Lou Tucker *secondary school educator*
Hodapp, Heidi Francine *middle school educator*
Hofler, Kay Robertson *secondary school educator, department chairman, artist*
Jones, Felicia M. *director*
Keith, Barbara Ann *elementary school educator, educator*
Kiernan, Margaret M. *adult education educator*
Monroe, Katherine Diane Osborne *secondary school educator*

Sears, Patricia Marie *elementary school educator, consultant*
Smith, Thelma Cheryl *principal, minister*
Talag, Trinidad Santos *educator*
Von Mosch, Wanda Gail *middle school educator*
Walck, Camila Crockett *biology educator*
Waller, Neola Shultz *retired secondary school educator*
Zebley, Lisa Catherine *elementary school educator*
Ziegler, Rochelle Elizabeth *special education educator*

Waynesboro
Phillips, Nancy Hopkins *elementary school educator*

West Point
Trible, Martha Gregory *secondary school educator*

Wicomico Church
Kenna, Gail Ann *secondary and higher education educator*

Williamsburg
Bell, Christine Marie *secondary school educator*
Goldstein, Barbara Block *education educator, director*
Hawthorne, Shelby Myrick *reading specialist*
Hooker, Karen L. *mathematics educator*
McCarthy, Connie Kearns *university librarian*
Schwab, Nancy Jean *middle school educator*
Turnage, Martha Allen *academic administrator*

Winchester
Huddleston, Beth Simpson *middle school educator*
Orndoff, Betty Katherine (Betty Katherine Madagan) *secondary school educator*
Sproul, Joan Heeney *retired elementary school educator*

Wirtz
Black, Cathy Turner *elementary school educator*

Wise
Collins, Susan V. *secondary school educator*

Woodbridge
Donahue, Amy Stewart *early childhood education specialist*
Gilmer, Staci Rose *special education educator*
Janik, Nicole Elizabeth *secondary school educator*
Ker, Lora Kay *elementary music educator*
Sullivan, Mia *special education educator*

Yorktown
Butler, Katherine Ann *elementary school educator*

WASHINGTON

Anacortes
Holmes, Paula Ann *elementary school educator*

Bellevue
Ostroff, Leslie Denise *elementary school educator*
Rice, Kay Diane *elementary school educator, consultant*
Wallentine, Mary Kathryn *secondary educator*

Bellingham
Dooley, Kathleen Ann *elementary school educator*
Morse, Karen Williams *academic administrator*
Stephens, H. Jeannette *mathematics educator*

Benton City
Kromminga, An-Marie *special education educator*
Omel, June M. *elementary school educator*

Bonney Lake
Wickizer, Cindy Louise *retired elementary school educator*

Bow
Cole, Donna Kay *elementary school educator, science educator*

Bremerton
Fischer, Mary E. *special education educator*

Buckley
Hahn, Ellen R. *elementary school educator*

Chehalis
Williams, Janelle Aust *literature and language educator*

Ellensburg
McIntyre, Jerilyn Sue *academic administrator*
Schneider, Leslie Jean *elementary school educator*

Federal Way
Rossi, Ruth Harris *special education educator*

Issaquah
Newbill, Karen Margaret *elementary school educator, education educator*

Kelso
Spear, Patricia Ann *principal*

Kenmore
Montague, Deborah Marie *elementary school educator, music educator, consultant*

Kennewick
Merkel, Patricia Mae *retired school system administrator*

La Center
Bryan, Sharon E. *literature and language educator*

Longview
Campbell, Kristine Koetting *academic administrator*

Lynnwood
Floten, Barbara Jean *educational dean*
Tebbs, Carol Ann *secondary school educator, academic administrator*

Maple Valley
Aquino, Mary Ann *elementary school educator*

Montesano
Boyer, Carol A. *elementary school educator*

Newport
Samson, Valerie J. *elementary school educator, consultant*

Olympia
Bergeson, Teresa *school system administrator*
Humphrey, Camilla Marie *retired special education educator*

Port Angeles
Lindberg, Judith Ann *retired elementary school educator*
McComb, Leann Marie *middle school educator*

Port Orchard
Albertus, Esther L. *vice principal*

Port Townsend
Miller, Maria B. *retired educator*

Pullman
Paznokas, Lynda Sylvia *elementary school educator*

Puyallup
Phillips, Gail Susan *elementary school educator*

Richland
Darby, Nancy *secondary school educator*
Ellis, Patricia *primary school educator*

Seattle
Beaumonte, Phyllis Ilene *retired secondary school educator*
Fetterly, Mary E. *counseling administrator*
Gordon, Shirley Blom *college president*
Hampton, Shelley Lynn *hearing impaired educator*
Murdock, Tullisse Antoinette (Toni Murdock) *academic administrator*
Ostrom, Katherine (Kate) Elma *retired secondary school educator*
Punyon, Ellen *principal*
Schwartz, Rosalye Ann *retired education educator*
Somerman, Martha J. *dean, dental educator*
Testy, Kellye *dean*
Wasserman, Harriet M. *academic administrator*
Wight, Julia Helen *secondary school educator*
Wilson, Lizabeth Anne *dean, library director*
Woods, Nancy Fugate *dean, women's health nurse, educator*

Selah
Forbes, Jeanne C. *secondary school educator*

Sequim
McGee, Jane Marie *retired elementary school educator*

Shoreline
Bailey, Sandra *secondary school educator, department chairman*

Snohomish
Tuengel, Lisa Marie *elementary school educator*

Spanaway
Paris, Kathleen *secondary school educator*
Parker, Lynda Christine Rylander *secondary school educator*

Spokane
Bozo, Molly Catherine *elementary school educator*
Clayton, Katherine Gayle *elementary school educator*
Danke, Virginia *educational administrator, travel consultant*
Lane, Iris Mary *retired elementary school educator*
Linn, Diana Patricia *retired elementary school educator*
Rowley, Kathleen Dorothy *elementary school educator*

Stanwood
Birkestol, Annabelle Mollie Elsie *retired elementary school educator*

Steilacoom
Norris, Laurie *secondary mathematics educator*

Tacoma
Crotto, Denice *elementary school educator*
Duchesne, Christina *secondary school educator*
Lewis, Jan Patricia *education educator*
Van Ry, Kimberly Anne *secondary school educator*

Toppenish
Ross, Kathleen Anne *academic administrator*

Tukwila
Carter, Pamela Jean *elementary school educator*

Vancouver
Mabry, Linda S. *education educator*
Tuttle, Marcia *retired elementary school educator, music educator*
Vossler, Deborah J. *mathematics and science educator*

Washougal
Semke-Fox, Suzanne Marie *elementary school educator*

Yakima
Beehler, Tobi Lorraine *elementary school educator, education educator*
Walker, Lorene *retired elementary school educator*

WEST VIRGINIA

Charles Town
Fortney, Kimberly Benson *health and sports medicine educator*
Wharton, Mary Merchant *secondary school educator*

Charleston
Arrington, Carolyn Ruth *school system administrator, consultant*
Manning, Sherry Fischer *retired academic administrator, telecommunications industry executive*
Oliver, Barbara Lynn *special education educator*
Richardson, Sally Keadle *academic administrator*
Zimmerman, Ericka Point *academic administrator*

Clarksburg
Leuliette, Connie Jane *secondary school educator*

Cross Lanes
Kinsolving, Ann Odene *elementary school educator, musician*

Davisville
Watts, Pamela Rae *elementary school educator*

Dunbar
Given, Melissa Ann *elementary school educator, educational consultant*

Fairmont
Dudley-Eshbach, Janet *university president*

Follansbee
Law, Phyllis Hampton *secondary school educator*

Hinton
Eagle, Karen Sue *special education educator*

Huntington
Howerton, Cheryl Alley *secondary school educator*
Joyce-Norris, Elaine Rozelle *elementary school educator*
Mayer, Lynne Supovitz *academic administrator*
Welch, Lynne Brodie *nursing school dean*

Keyser
Falkowski, Theresa Gae *chemistry educator*
Stephen, Tina Marie *elementary school educator*

Kingwood
Zigray, Debra Renee *elementary school educator*

Martinsburg
Mauck, Elaine Carole *retired secondary education educator*

Morgantown
Allamong, Betty Davis *retired academic administrator*
Ashenfelter, Helen Louise *elementary school educator*
Drvar, Margaret Adams *vocational school educator*
Jackson, Ruth Moore *academic administrator*

New Martinsville
Francis, Elizabeth Romine *secondary school educator, theater director*

Parkersburg
Rowland, Angela Kay *education educator, consultant*

Peterstown
Robertson, Connie Lynn *elementary school educator*

Princeton
Bolen, Bettye Sue *academic administrator*

Ravenswood
Gouckenour, Sharon Craft *elementary school educator*

Shady Spring
Reed, Cathy Lorraine *elementary school educator*

Shepherdstown
Locke, Emma Mae *retired elementary school educator*
Wilson, Rebecca Ann *retired English and special education educator*

South Charleston
Fishkin, Anne Sonya *retired special education educator*
Stedman, Molly Renee *special education educator, researcher*

Spencer
Parker, Theresa Ann Boggs *special education educator, music educator*

Vienna
Acree, Wilma Katheryn *retired secondary school educator*

Weston
Rastle, Maxine Shiflet Cole *retired elementary school educator*
Riddle, Anna Lee *retired elementary school educator, retired music educator*

Wheeling
Matyskiela, Kristina L. *director*

White Sulphur Springs
Spencer, Linda Lou *elementary school educator*

Winfield
Barnett, Cheryl Jividen *elementary school educator*

WISCONSIN

Appleton
Beck, Jill *academic administrator, dancer, educator*

Auburndale
Fowler, Sue Ann *elementary school educator*

Baraboo
Gogue, Susan Diane *elementary school educator*
Mesmer, Karen Luann *elementary school educator*

Barron
Kienbaum, Janice Mae *reading specialist*

Bayside
Topetzes, Fay Kalafat *retired school guidance counselor*

Beaver Dam
Wright-Everett, Rose Mary *elementary school educator*

Belleville
Alsteens, Susette Marie *English educator, athletic director*

Blanchardville
Ryser, Robyn Carey *elementary school educator*

Columbus
Schellin, Patricia Marie Biddle *secondary school educator*

Crivitz
Gerhart, Lorraine Pfeiffer *elementary school educator*

De Pere
Davis, Amanda Nicole *elementary school educator*
Frechette, Bonnie L. *secondary school educator*

Delafield
Haugner, Carolyn M. *elementary school educator*

Drummond
Lintula, Margaret M. *elementary and secondary school educator*

Eagle
Kalnes, Donna M. Simondet *retired principal, alcohol and drug abuse education program director*

Eagle River
Weber, Lori Ann *elementary school educator*

Eau Claire
Johnson, Eleanor Mae *education educator*
McDougall-Gibbs, Mary Elizabeth (Betsy McDougall-Gibbs) *early childhood special education educator*

Elkhorn
Reinke, Doris Marie *retired elementary school educator*
Straz, Irene N. *special education educator*

Fennimore
Jahnke, Lisa Jo *secondary school educator*
Kopp, Carol Ann *special education educator*

Fort Atkinson
McDaniel, Kristen *secondary school educator*

Fox Point
Ellis, Nancy Kempton *adult education educator*
Froemming, Barbara G. *retired home economics educator*

Franklin
Resar, Laura A. *mathematics educator*

Green Bay
Salo, Patricia Ann *elementary school educator*
Thill, Linda Susan *secondary school educator*

Green Lake
Mitchell, Tawnia Juanita *elementary school educator, music educator*

Greendale
Bousquet-Monk, Nancy Kathryn *elementary school educator*

Greenfield
Redlinger, Melinda *secondary school educator*

Hartford
Karlus, Mary Teresa *elementary school educator*

Hartland
Judd, Diane Barbaa *literature and language educator*

Howards Grove
Bacigalupo, Sarah Elizabeth *literature and language educator*

Janesville
Davis, Paulette Jean Turner *secondary school educator, editor, consultant*
Thomas, Margaret Ann *principal*

Juda
Bredeson, Brenda Penniston *secondary school educator*

Kenosha
Helman, Iris Barca *elementary school educator, consultant*

Kewaskum
Blomquist, MaryLane Neubauer *secondary school educator*

La Crosse
Birkle, Linda Jean *elementary school educator*

Lac Du Flambeau
Zimmer, Amelia Ellen *principal, educator*

Lomira
Olson, Ellen Jo *elementary school educator*

Madison
Burmaster, Elizabeth *school system administrator*
DeJoie, Carolyn Barnes Milanes *educator*
Engelman, Marjorie Jeckel *retired higher education administrator*
Ivancic, Monika *director, research scientist*
Kreilick, Marjorie Ellen *education educator*
Netzer, Lanore A(gnes) *retired educational administration educator*
Nicka, Betty Lou *secondary school educator*
Sapiro, Virginia *academic administrator, political science professor*
Simone, Beverly Sue *academic administrator*
Spencer, Cheryl L. *literature and language educator*
Underwood, Julie K. *dean, former law educator*
Youngerman, Nan Gronik *elementary school educator*

Marinette
Rice, Karolyn Kaye *elementary school educator*

Markesan
Chisnell, Debra Jean *special education educator*

Medford
Wirkus, Carrie *elementary school educator*

Menomonee Falls
Hinnrichs-Dahms, Holly Beth *elementary school educator*
Nelson, Mary Ellen Genevieve *adult education educator*

Menomonie
Nyseth, Elizabeth Ann *retired secondary school educator*

Mequon
Rice, Linda Lee *special education educator*

Middleton
Conaway, Jane Ellen *elementary school educator*

Milton
Parker, Letitia *secondary school educator*

Milwaukee
Delgado, Mary Louise *elementary school educator, secondary school educator, consultant, Internet company executive*
Hamdani, Zubeda A. *elementary school educator*
Keshvala, Seelpa H *secondary school educator*
Kluthe, Kathleen A. *elementary school educator*
Pittman, Barbara N. *special education educator*
Pugach, Marleen Carol *education educator*
Read, Sister Joel *academic administrator*
Rheams, Annie Elizabeth *education educator*
Shapiro, Mary Jo Farley *elementary school educator*
Sonnenberg, Linda L. *literacy educator*
Spann, Wilma Nadene *retired principal*
Wake, Madeline Musante *academic administrator, nursing educator*
Weiner, Wendy L(ou) *elementary school educator, writer*
Williams, Maxine Eleanor *retired elementary school educator*

Montello
Williams, Brenda Jeanne *literature and language educator*

Mukwonago
Yopps, Linda Lee *special education educator*

Nekoosa
Ramirez, Mary Catherine *retired secondary school educator*

New Holstein
Frisch, Katherine Leigh *secondary school educator*

Oak Creek
Stroik, Marilyn L. *elementary school educator*
Weedman, Jean M. *secondary school educator*

Oshkosh
Buser, Rose M. *elementary school educator*
Ristow, Thelma Frances *retired elementary school educator*

Palmyra
Davis, Jaci Carroll *elementary school educator, musician*

Pembine
Mattison, Kathlene *secondary school educator*

Phelps
Christensen, Gloria Jean *secondary school educator*

Plymouth
Groblewski, Jane (Jane Campbell) *secondary school educator*

Port Washington
Niffenegger, Tammie Jean *secondary school educator, science educator*

Racine
Meyer, Alicia *special education educator*
Walter, Barbara Sykes *reading educator*

Ripon
Dowdy, Harriet Brodhead *elementary school educator*
Woolley, Jean Gibson *retired instructional designer, consultant*

River Falls
Crotty, Teri *education educator*
Krey, DeAn Marie *retired education educator*

Sheboygan
Fritz, Kristine Rae *retired secondary school educator*
Ladiges, Lori Jean *learning disabilities specialist*

Sheboygan Falls
Deibert, Patricia J. *biology educator*

Sparta
Hagen, Joanne R. *elementary school educator*
Welch, Mary Rose Dwyer *secondary school educator*

Stevens Point
Bunnell, Linda Hunt *academic administrator*

Stoughton
Ellickson, Judith A. *literature and language educator*

Sun Prairie
Jerg, Karen Leslie *elementary school educator*

Superior
Bowden, Laura Ann *retired secondary school educator, retired counselor*
Cheselski, Penny Lynn *special education educator*

Tomah
Neurohr, Shirley Ann *retired special education educator*

Union Grove
Dawson, Rose Dorothy *elementary school educator*

Viroqua
Banta, Vicki K. *mathematics educator*

Washburn
Krutsch, Phyllis *academic administrator*

Waterford
Hanson, Jody Elizabeth *special education educator*

Waukesha
Gustafson, Mardel Emma *secondary school educator, writer*
Leekley, Marie Valpoon
Morris, Cathleen Ann *academic administrator*

Waunakee
Simon, Sarah Marie *elementary school educator*

Waupaca
Jahnke, Christiane Lynn *mathematics educator*

Wauwatosa
Pomplun, Julie Ann *secondary school educator*

West Bend
Kogler, Donna Marie *elementary school educator*

Whitewater
Busse, Eileen Elaine *special education educator*
Saunders, Martha Dunagin *academic administrator*

Wisconsin Dells
Kolumba, Kim Dale *elementary education educator, speech and language pathologist*

Wisconsin Rapids
Bilderback, Pamela Marie *elementary school educator*
Olson-Hellerud, Linda Kathryn *elementary school educator*

WYOMING

Casper
Boyes, Melanie Joan *secondary school educator*
Foster, Vicki Anne *secondary school educator*
Underwood, Kristin Dana *elementary school educator*

Cheyenne
Givens, Cynthia A. *educator*

Cody
Fees, Nancy Fardelius *special education educator*
Wormald, Kathleen Marie *elementary school educator*

Evanston
Connelly, Diane *elementary school educator*

Green River
Albers, Dolores M. *secondary school educator*
Reinard, Kathleen Ann *elementary school educator*

Guernsey
Zimmerer, Nancy Jean *elementary school educator, rancher*

Lander
Alley, Nancy Corrin *elementary school educator*
Nunley, Cynthia Ann *special education educator*

Laramie
McBride, Judith *elementary school educator*
Schmitt, Diana Mae *elementary school educator*

Newcastle
Hutchinson, Janet Lee Clark *elementary school educator*

Rawlins
Rose, Kathleen Diane *elementary school educator*

Rock Springs
Sheckler, Mindy Sue *elementary school educator*

Saratoga
Hileman, Linda Carol *elementary school educator*

Sundance
Truchot, Janice Elaine *elementary school educator*

Torrington
Lewis, Mary Jane *retired elementary school educator*

TERRITORIES OF THE UNITED STATES

AMERICAN SAMOA

Pago Pago
Varghese, Mary *secondary school educator*

GUAM

Agana Heights
Torres, Susie Apuron *special education educator*

Barrigada
McDonald Terlaje, Patricia *counselor*

Hagatna
Artero, Margaret T. *academic administrator, military officer*

NORTHERN MARIANA ISLANDS

Saipan
Gallardo, Sister Arsenia Pulumbarit *elementary school educator*
Inos, Rita Hocog *school system administrator*
Kaufer, Cheryl Tenorio *special education educator, researcher*

PALAU ISLAND

Palau
Olkeriil, Lorenza *English language educator*

PUERTO RICO

Aguada
Ramírez-Ruiz, Doris M. *education educator*

Aguadilla
Cuebas Irizarry, Ana E. *director*
Jaramillo, Juana Segarra *chancellor*

Cabo Rojo
Rivera-Martinez, Socorro *retired elementary school educator, assistant principal*

Caguas
Agosto Rivera, Luz Esther *elementary school educator*

Fajardo
Colón, Nivia Enid *counseling administrator*

Guaynabo
Baquero, Maria Joaquina *elementary school educator*

Rio Piedras
Gibbs Cruz, Katherine K. *science educator*

San German
Mojica, Agnes *academic administrator*

Trujillo Alto
Crespo de Sanabia, María Milagros *retired education educator*

VIRGIN ISLANDS

St Thomas
DePass-Creque, Linda Ann *educational consultant association executive, former education commissioner*
Michael, Noreen *school system administrator*
Ragster, LaVerne E. *academic administrator*

MILITARY ADDRESSES OF THE UNITED STATES

EUROPE

APO
Daly, Kathleen Ann *elementary school educator*
Mungas, Andrea Marie *elementary school educator*

CANADA

BRITISH COLUMBIA

Fernie
McFarlin-Kosiec, Barbara Ann *secondary school educator, literature and language professor, small business owner*

NOVA SCOTIA

Halifax
Russell, Dawn Ann *dean*

ONTARIO

Toronto
Ostry, Sylvia *academic administrator, economist*

MEXICO

Ciudad Juarez
Tabuenca-Cordoba, Maria-Socorro *academic administrator*

AUSTRALIA

Sydney
Rogers, Karen Beckstead *gifted studies educator, researcher, consultant*

CHINA

Shanghai
Huang, Chang-yu *retired elementary school educator*

ENGLAND

London
Tyson, Laura D'Andrea *dean, finance educator*

ADDRESS UNPUBLISHED

Abbott, Barbara Gayle *academic administrator*
Abell, Anna Ellen *primary school educator*
Abrahamsen, Valerie *academic administrator*
Abrams Finger, Iris Dale *retired elementary school educator*
Adams, Betsy Anne *principal*
Adams, Leocadia Donat *secondary school educator, writer*
Adams, Patti Jean *literature and language educator*
Adams, Stephanie Lynn *elementary school educator*
Adamson, Jane Nan *retired elementary school educator*
Adams-Passey, Suellen S. *retired elementary school educator*
Addicott, Beverly Jeanne *retired elementary school educator*
Aiello, Marcie Jeanne Gruener *secondary school educator*
Akbar, Shaakira Nadiya *elementary school educator*
Akin, Ann Foster *special education educator*
Akiyama, Karen N. *elementary school educator*
Alanis, Lorena *elementary school educator*
Allen, Donna *mathematics educator*
Allen, Jo Lynn *secondary school educator*
Allenson, Jennifer Leigh *elementary school educator*
Allred, Dawn Peterman *adult education educator*
Almore-Randle, Allie Louise *special education educator, academic administrator*
Alston, Betty B. *retired elementary school educator*
Altherr, Rita Jo *secondary school educator*
Alward, Sarah Anne *mathematics educator*
Amano, Imelda *school librarian*
Amos, Linda K. *academic administrator*
Anderson, Iris Anita *retired secondary school educator*
Anderson, Jennifer Ann *middle school educator*
Anderson, Kathryn M. *history educator*
Anderson, Margaret Suzanne *elementary school educator, nurse*
Anderson, Monica Luffman *school librarian, educator, real estate broker*
Andreassi, Kimberly Thompson *mathematics educator*
Andrews-McCall, Maxine R. *retired educational administration specialist*
Andrews-McCall, Maxine Ramseur *retired education educator*
Antignane, Diane Paquin *mathematics educator*
Apel, Marie U. *elementary school educator*
Aplin, Gina Suzette *secondary school educator, rancher*
Aranow, Ruth Lee Horwitz *academic advisor, chemist, researcher*
Archbold, Ronna Rae *college administrator*
Archer, Lillian Patricia *academic administrator, dean*
Archer-Sorg, Karen S. *secondary school educator*
Armacost, Mary-Linda Sorber Merriam *retired academic administrator*
Armstrong, Marsha Susan *elementary school educator*
Arndt, Laura Bodeen *mathematics educator*
Arnold, Karen Dorothy *education educator*
Arnold, Leslie Ann *special education educator*
Arnold-Rogers, Judy *education educator, language educator, coach*
Arntz, Barbara C. *elementary school educator*
Arp, Arlene *elementary school educator*
Arredondo, Adrianna Liza *secondary school educator*
Ascherl, Amy M. *elementary school educator*
Ashimine, Tanya *biology educator*
Ashley, Marjorie *retired secondary school educator*
Askine, Ruth Parse *elementary school educator*
Astell, Christine Ann *school guidance counselor*
Atchley, Nancy Faye *educator*
Atwood, Debra Smith *elementary school educator*
Axner, Carol Christie *elementary school educator*
Ayers, Janet *technical college president*
Bachelor, Malinda Mary *elementary school educator*
Baghaei-Rad, Nancy Jane Bebb *elementary school educator*
Bahr, Christine Marie *special education educator*
Bailey, Beverly Parker *secondary school educator*

Bailey, Joy Hafner *counselor educator*
Bailey, Keisha Ayanna *mathematics educator*
Bailey, Shannon D. *elementary school educator*
Baillos, Marianne Tkach *secondary school educator*
Baker, Amy Elaine *assistant principal*
Baker, Jane E. *secondary school educator*
Baker, Katherine June *elementary school educator, minister, artist*
Baker, Pamela Hudson *special education educator*
Baker, Paula Booker *secondary school educator*
Baker, Peggy Nell *retired secondary school educator*
Baldwin, Marie Hunsucker *retired secondary school educator*
Balis, Jennifer Lynn *academic administrator, computer scientist, educator*
Ball, Brenda Joyce Sivils *retired secondary school educator*
Ball, Teresa Susan *secondary school educator*
Balzer, Donna Carol *retired secondary school educator*
Banaszynski, Carol Jean *secondary school educator*
Banbury, Demby Bowman *director*
Banks, Carolyn Duty *retired history educator*
Banks, Sandra C. *retired elementary school educator*
Bankston, Sherri Renee *secondary school educator, director*
Baranowski, Mary Lou *elementary school educator*
Barbour, Kelli D. *assistant principal, secondary school educator*
Bardole, Betty Jean *elementary school educator*
Barnes, Frances Johnson *retired secondary school educator*
Barrett, Janet Tidd *academic administrator*
Barrow, Dindria Cozette *elementary school educator, special education educator*
Bartels, Marilynn Rae *education educator*
Baskin, Barbara Holland *retired education educator, researcher*
Baskovitz, Diana *retired elementary school educator*
Bates Stoklosa, Evelynne (Eve Bates Stoklosa) *educational consultant, educator*
Bauer, Irene Susan *elementary school educator*
Bauman-Antoniello, Allison *special education educator*
Baxter, Kathleen Byrne *academic administrator*
Bayard, Susan Shapiro *adult education educator, small business owner*
Bays, Louise Marie *elementary school educator*
Beach, Nancy Ann Helen *special education educator*
Beaver, Barbara Leann *elementary school educator, writer*
Beck, Irene Clare *educational consultant, writer*
Becker, Beverly June *educator*
Becker, Dorothy Loretta *education educator, librarian*
Beecher, Marguerite Ann *elementary school educator*
Begley, Renee *history educator*
Beiswinger, Virginia Graves *secondary school educator*
Bell, Elva Glenn *retired secondary school educator, retired counseling administrator, interpreter*
Bell, Felicia Renee *elementary school educator*
Bell, Kasey Ann *elementary school educator*
Belval, Josephine Antanette *retired elementary school educator*
Belyeu, Misty Lynn *elementary school educator*
Bennett, Janis M. *elementary school educator*
Bennett, Velma Jean *elementary school educator*
Bentley, Charmaine Clark O'Fallon *secondary school educator*
Bentley, Doris Broussard *retired educator, consultant*
Berg, Teresa G. *elementary school educator*
Berger, Barbara *special education educator, educational consultant*
Bergeron, Patricia Ann *retired education educator, consultant*
Bernot, Jane Catherine *retired education educator*
Berry, Pamela C. *secondary school educator*
Berryman, Mary Anne Pierce *elementary school educator*
Bert, Clara Virginia *retired secondary school educator, retired school system administrator*
Bertsch, Kelly Frances *mathematics educator*
Beseda, Amy Jo *special education educator*
Beston, Rose Marie *retired academic administrator*
Beuthien, Gayle Dawn *special education educator, swim coach*
Beyer, La Vonne Ann *special education educator*
Beyerle, Susan D. *retired elementary school educator*
Bick, Jennie L *elementary school educator*
Bickerstaff, Mina March Clark *retired academic administrator*
Biesinger, Meghan Kathleen *secondary school educator*
Bigelow, Sharon Lee *elementary school educator*
Bigelow, Vivian Lou *elementary school educator, secondary school educator*
Birnbaum, Linda Shub *retired assistant principal*
Birr, Cynthia Ruth *special education educator*
Birtwistle, Monica Lynn *secondary school educator*
Bishop, Sue Marquis (Ina Sue Marquis Bishop) *retired dean*
Bistransky, Joyce Elaine *retired elementary school educator*
Black, Rebecca Leree *special education educator*
Black, Recca Marcele *elementary school educator*
Blanchard, Lou *school system administrator*
Block, Lanise *secondary school educator*
Bloodworth, Gladys Leon *elementary school educator*
Bockhorst, Barbara Alice *retired secondary school educator*
Boepple, Bettie Ann *elementary school educator*
Bogacz, Dolores Rosalie Marie *retired elementary school educator, paralegal*
Boggus, Tamara *elementary school educator*
Boise, Audrey Lorraine *retired special education educator*
Bolding, Kandy Denese Mynear *special education educator*
Bonebrake, Tara Jane *elementary school educator*
Bonneau, Wendy Sue *special education educator*
Bookman, Ann Edith *director*
Booth, Ada Sokal *retired education educator*
Borchers, Mary Amelia *middle school educator*
Bose, Michelle Denise *secondary school educator*
Bosley, Valerie Lynne *elementary school educator*
Bosse, Margaret Fisher Ishler *education educator*
Bottolfson, Wahnita Joan *parochial school educator*
Boughton, Lilian Elizabeth *secondary education educator, retired*
Bowens, Gloria Furr *educational administrator*
Bower, Laurel Lee *education educator, researcher*
Bowers, Madeline Katherine Jente *elementary school educator*
Bowles, Vicky Lynn Hill *elementary school educator*
Boyce, Tiffany Marie *literature and language educator*
Bradley, Deidra D. *elementary school educator*
Branch, Felecia Ann-Seldon *elementary school educator*
Brandt, Sara Jane *elementary school educator*
Brandt-Shapiro, Irene Hildegard *retired secondary school educator*
Branham, Regina Jeanette *elementary school educator*
Brewer, Angela Sue *middle school educator*
Brewer, Leslie Kay *elementary school educator*
Breyne, Michele K *mathematics educator*
Bridges, Christine E. *elementary school educator*
Briggs, Bonnie Sue *school librarian, minister*
Briggs, Laura *education educator*
Bright, Sheryl Ann *special education educator*
Britt, Julia Moody *secondary school educator*
Brodie, Susan Gerrish *special education educator*
Brodowski, Debra Lee *consumer sciences educator*
Bromund, Alice A. *retired elementary school educator*
Bross, Kathleen *elementary school educator*
Brown, Beulah Louise *retired elementary school educator*
Brown, Brenda Bernadine *education educator*
Brown, Debra *elementary school educator*
Brown, Elmira Newsom *retired elementary school educator*
Brown, Linda Sue *elementary school educator*
Brown, Mary Jane *history educator*
Brown, Maureen Jill *elementary school educator*
Brown, Melissa *secondary school educator*
Brown, Michelle Alise *elementary school educator*
Brown, Shari K. *special education educator*
Brown, Wilma Elaine *elementary school educator, artist*
Brownell, Blanche P. *retired secondary school educator*
Browning, Becky Beck *elementary school educator*
Brownlee, Paula Pimlott *higher education consultant*
Brown-Zekeri, Lolita Molanda *elementary school educator*
Brundage, Marjorie Underwood *academic administrator*
Bruttomesso, Kathleen Ann *dean, nursing educator, researcher*
Bryjak, Jacqueline Mae *elementary school educator*
Bubeck, Margaret Ann *mathematics educator*
Buchanan, Carolee Horstman *special education educator, consultant*
Buchner, Amanda Elizabeth *secondary school educator, coach, athletic trainer*
Buck, Bernestine Bradford *retired counseling administrator*
Buckley, Eleanor Jane *retired elementary school educator*
Buhro, Natalie Jo *mathematics educator*
Bullard, Cynthia L. *elementary school educator*
Buller, Carol H. *secondary school educator*
Bullock, Mary Brown *former academic administrator*
Bullock, Molly *retired elementary school educator*
Bundy, Barbara Korpan *former college president*
Bunte, Mandy Kay *principal, education educator*
Burch-Martinez, Berkeley Alison *primary school educator*
Burd, Barbara R. *mathematics educator*
Burdman, Jacqueline Bermel *retired special education educator*
Burkholder, Kelly Leann *elementary school educator*
Burnett, Susan W. *academic administrator*
Burnham, Shannon L. *elementary school educator*
Burns, Ellen Jean *distance education administrator*
Burns, Kathleen Adley *educational consultant*
Burrell, Kimberly Meadows *assistant principal*
Bursley-Hamilton, Susan *secondary school educator*
Busbea, Virginia Beth *mathematics educator*
Bush, Sandi Tokoa *elementary school educator*
Butler, Debra Yvonne *special education educator, small business owner*
Butler, Linda Louise *elementary educator*
Cadwallader, Gwen Natalie *elementary school educator, music educator*
Cadwell, Courtney Bradshaw *elementary school educator*
Cafiero, Jennifer Annette *academic administrator, educator*
Cain, Wanda Neil *secondary school educator*
Calder, Mary Alberta *elementary education educator, consultant*
Caldwell, Cassandra Denise *education educator*
Callis, Karen Denise *elementary school educator*
Cameron, Lucille Wilson *retired dean*
Camp, Alice W. *retired elementary education educator*
Campbell, Sarah *elementary school educator, special education educator*
Campbell, Theresa Marie *mathematics educator*
Canelli, Jeanne *early childhood educator*
Cannon, Lena Ferrara (Lee) *retired education educator*
Canobbio, Linda J. *elementary school educator*
Cantrell, Carol Whitaker *educational administrator*
Cantrell, Joyce Ann *mathematics educator*
Capstick, Michelle *special education educator*
Cardarelli, Lisa Monica *school system administrator*
Cardinale, Loretta Ann *educator*
Carlin, Marian P. *secondary school educator*
Carlson, Alyssa *literature and language educator*
Carlson, Cheryl Ann *literature and language educator*
Carlson, Nora *elementary school educator*
Carolin, Kirstin Kerry *secondary school educator*
Carpenter, Rosalie T. *education educator, consultant*
Carr, Bessie *retired elementary school educator*
Carter, JoAnn Martin *retired education educator*
Castleman, Pamela Ann *assistant principal*
Caucia, Louisa B. *retired elementary school educator*
Causey, Linda *secondary school educator*
Cawley, Patricia Blonts *secondary school educator*
Céspedes, Melinda Brown *elementary school educator, dancer*
Chafel, Judith Ann *education educator*
Chairsell, Christine *academic administrator*
Champion, Cheryl *educator*
Champion, Crystal *literature and language educator*
Chan, Elaine Elizabeth *elementary school educator*
Chandler, Alice *retired academic administrator, educational consultant*
Chandler, Patricia Ann *retired special education educator*
Chappell, Annette M. *educational consultant, minister*
Chappell, Valerie *educational consultant*
Charles, Laura Jo *mathematics educator*
Charles, Marilyn Kay *secondary school educator*
Charlton, Shirley Marie *educational consultant*
Charnley, Cristen Marie *secondary school educator*
Chaudoir, Jean Hamilton (Jean Hamilton) *secondary school educator*
Chavis, Geneva Boone *retired dean*
Cherry, Kelley *secondary school educator*
Chintella, Marilynn Anita *elementary school educator, department chairman*
Chirco, Jennifer B. *special education educator*
Christensen, Katharine Eleanor *retired education educator*
Christensen, Vickie J. *secondary school educator*
Christie, Cheryl Ann *athletic trainer and physical therapist*
Chumley, Shannon Jackson *elementary school educator*
Cicero, Dianne *special education educator*
Cimino, Ann Mary *education educator*
Clark, Barbara June *elementary school educator*
Clark, Christine W. *elementary school educator*
Clark, Marie *secondary school educator*
Clark, Patricia Sherbert *secondary school educator*
Clark, Patsy Vedder *retired educator and staff developer*
Clark, Paula Irene *elementary school educator, consultant*
Clark, Stephani Michelle Callahan *elementary school educator*
Clement, Betty Waidlich *retired literacy educator, consultant*
Coburn, Deborah Ann *elementary school educator*
Cockerham, Sherry L. *secondary school educator*
Cockram, Suzanne M. *elementary school educator*
Coe, Jill *director, educator*
Coffey, Sharon Thornton *chemistry educator*
Cohen, Gloria Ernestine *elementary school educator*
Colage, Beatrice Elvira *education educator*
Coleman, Mary Sue *academic administrator*
Coleman, Patsy Ann *secondary school educator*
Collins, Jacqueline Wight *secondary school educator*
Collins-Brown, E. Dorlee (E. Dorlee Woodyard) *registrar*
Collinson, Vivienne Ruth *education educator, researcher, consultant*
Colvin, Tina Powell *elementary school educator*
Colwell, Heather Thorstad *secondary school educator*
Combs, Judy Diane *elementary school educator, civic association administrator*
Compton, Norma Haynes *retired dean, artist*
Connell, Bonnie Bleier *mathematics educator*
Conover, Mona Lee *retired adult education educator*
Conover, Nancy Anderson *retired secondary school counselor, small business owner*
Conquest, Claire M. *secondary school counselor*
Constantine, Jessica Lee *elementary school educator*
Conway, Teresa J. *secondary school educator*
Cook, Iva Dean *education educator*
Cook, Sister Mary Mercedes *school system administrator, director*
Cook, Renay *elementary school educator*
Cooper, Kathleen Bell *dean, former federal agency administrator*
Copeland, Bonnie S. *former school system administrator*
Copt, Phyllis Jean *secondary school educator*
Corbin, Veronica L. *secondary school educator, information scientist, consultant*
Cornwell, Nancy Dunn *secondary school educator*
Cosgrove, Annmarie *special education educator*
Cothran, Anne Jennette *academic administrator*
Cottrell, Linda Billops *retired elementary school educator*
Couillard, Elizabeth L. *secondary school educator, department chairman*
Coutts, Linda Dale *elementary school educator, consultant*
Cowles, Milly *education educator*
Cox, Christine K. *secondary school educator*
Crane, Kathleen Dickinson *elementary school educator, writer*
Crawford, Helene Hope *elementary school principal*
Cronholm, Lois S. *academic administrator*
Cross, E. Ashley *special education educator*
Cross, Kathryn Patricia *education educator*
Cross, Ruth Chaiken *retired educational administrator*
Cross, Wilda Sue *secondary school educator*
Crossley, Dolly Madena Johnston *retired elementary school educator*
Crosthwaite, Diane Louise *secondary school educator*
Cruz, Cassandra *elementary school educator*
Cruz-Connerton, Mayra *elementary school educator*
Cryar, Rhonda Lynn *elementary school educator*
Culver, Mona Capricia *retired elementary school educator*
Cunningham, Alice Jeanne *chemistry educator, author, consultant*
Cunningham, Victoria L. *secondary school educator*
Cupp, Lucy Paschall *retired elementary school educator, minister*
Curl, Mackenzie Elizabeth *secondary school educator*
Curry Scott, Shirley Goodman *retired director*
Czesak, Linda Susan *secondary school educator, education educator*
Dable, Carol M. *primary school educator*
Dahlmann, Mary Elsa *secondary school educator*
D'Angelo, Renée Young *special education educator*
Daniel, Winifred Yvonne *elementary school educator*
Danielewski, Donna Krystyna *secondary school educator*
Daniels, Mary P. *academic administrator, technologist*
Danko, Cassandra Dawn *educational consultant, researcher*
Darden, Lauretta *elementary school educator*
Darnley, Katherine E. *elementary school educator*
Davenport, Donna Jeanne Swanson *elementary school educator*
Davidson, Sarah J. *educational consultant, healthcare educator*
Davidson, Tara Beth *secondary school educator*
Davies-McNair, Jane *retired educational consultant*
Davion, Ethel Johnson *school system superintendent, curriculum specialist*
Davis, Anna Jane Ripley *elementary school educator*
Davis, Beth *elementary school educator*
Davis, Diann Holmes *elementary school educator*
Davis, Elizabeth Eileen *education educator*
Davis, Emmy Mae *school system administrator*
Davis, Julia McBroom *college dean, speech pathology and audiology educator*
Davis, Karen Ann (Karen Ann Falconer) *special education educator*
Davis, Lanita Irene *secondary school educator*
Davis, Lisa Rene *special education educator, consultant*
Davis, Sue Ellen H. *elementary and secondary music educator*
Davis-Keith, Madelyn Michelle *elementary school educator*
Dawkins, Teresa Gilliland *elementary school educator*
Dayton, Regina Laudi *secondary school educator*
Dean, Katherine S. *physical education educator, consultant*
DeAndrade, Kristy A. *elementary school educator*
Deats-O'Reilly, Diana Day *educator, journalist*
Debs, Barbara Knowles *former college president, consultant*
deCastro, Cristina L. *secondary school educator*
Dehle, Judy Jaye *education educator*
DeJarnatt, Kitty M. *special education educator*
Delahanty, Rebecca Ann *school system administrator*
Dell'Aringa, Yvonne Silvia Bozzini *elementary school educator*
De Long, Katharine *retired secondary school educator*
Denham, Carolyn Hunter *academic administrator, statistics educator*
Denny, Terry Anne *elementary school educator*
Dent, Julie *executive director*
Derrick, Kathryn Thill *secondary school educator*
DeShaw, Michele *principal*
DeVaughn, Tara Mary Lee *mathematics educator*
DeVera, Gertrude Quenano *education educator*
Dewar, Louise Helen *director*
DeWeese, Barb Oakley *secondary school educator*
DeWolfe, Susan *elementary school educator*
Dey, Carol Ruth *secondary school educator*
Dial, Tamara Minique *secondary school educator*
Dias, Mari Nardolillo *education educator, consultant*
Diaz, Laura O. *secondary school educator*
Dibelka, Charlene Fay Webster *secondary school educator*
Dibert, Rosalie *elementary school educator*
Dickerson, Betty *secondary school educator, consultant*
Dickinson, Marilynne Fay *elementary school educator*
Diercks, Elizabeth Gorman *elementary school educator*
Diggles, Patsy Ann *elementary school educator*
Dillard, Patricia Spratling *educational consultant*
Dillard, Teresa Mary *school counselor*
Dillon, Priscilla McAvoy *private school educator*
Dillon, Toni Ann *emotional support educator*
Dispenza, Mary Catherine *director, educator, photographer*
Diviney, Nancy Lynn *elementary school educator*
Dixon, Mary *elementary school educator*
Dobson, Dorothy Lynn Watts *retired elementary school educator*
Dodds, Linda Carol *special education educator*
Dohmen, Mary Holgate *retired primary school educator*
Doligosa, Annie Lumampao *elementary school educator, researcher*
Donahue, Kathleen Frances *elementary school educator*
Donaldson, Wilma Crankshaw *elementary school educator*
Donat, Juliana Souther *elementary school educator*
Donberger, Karen Shepard *special education educator, elementary school educator*
Donehew, Pamela K. *reading specialist*
Donick, Julie K *elementary school educator*

Donley, Corrine Russell *special education educator, educator*
Donzell, Tara Elizabeth *secondary school educator*
Dorr, Aimee *dean, education educator*
Doss, Delia L. *mathematics educator*
Douglas, Mary Younge Riley *retired secondary school educator*
Douglas, Roxanne Grace *secondary school educator*
Doviak, Ingrid Ellinger *elementary school educator*
Dowdy, Joanne Kilgour *education educator*
Drake, Evelyn Downie *retired secondary school educator*
Drew, Donna Howell *elementary school educator*
Drum, Alice *academic administrator, educator*
Drummond, Pamela Johnson *mathematics educator*
Dubner, Terye B. *secondary school educator*
Ducote, Deborah M. *elementary school educator, reading specialist*
Dufendach, Paula J. *elementary school educator*
Duffey, Rosalie Ruth *elementary school educator*
Dumas, Rhetaugh Etheldra Graves *retired university official*
Duncan, Kristina Yvonne *secondary school educator*
Dunlap, Martha McKinzie *retired middle school educator, small business owner*
Dunn, Linda *special education educator*
Duplessis, Audrey Joseph *school system administrator*
Durick, Joyce K. *elementary school educator*
Dworkin, Irma-Theresa *school system administrator, researcher, secondary school educator*
Dycus, Patricia M. *education educator, chemical engineer*
Dye, Linda Kaye *elementary school educator*
Easter, Wanda Denise *special education educator*
Eaton, Emma Parker *special education educator*
Eck, Marla J. *special education educator*
Eddy, Janet Elizabeth *retired elementary school educator*
Edens, Rosemary Randall *secondary school educator*
Edmundson, Lorna Duphiney *academic administrator*
Edwards, Lynn A. *retired school system administrator*
Edwards, Tonya Green *elementary school educator*
Egginton, Wynn Meagher *university administrator and program facilitator*
Ehlers, Joan *secondary school educator*
Ehlert, Nancy Lynne *elementary school educator*
Eiklenborg, JoLeen *education educator, consultant*
Eisner, Edith C. *adult education educator*
Ellett, Linda Mick *special education educator*
Elliot, Alexandra *special education educator, real estate agent*
Elliott, JoAnn Rose *retired elementary school educator*
Elliott, Meagan Byrne *elementary school educator*
Ellis, Rhonda Lyn *history educator*
Ellison, Betty D. *retired elementary school educator*
Elmer, Marilyn Ann *education educator, author*
Elrod, Deborah Lee *special education educator*
Emmons, Mary K. *history educator*
Endicott, Jennifer Jane Reynolds *education educator*
Epp, Dianne Naomi *secondary school educator*
Eppolito, Mary *assistant principal, educator*
Espiricueta, Sylvia *counseling administrator*
Essa, Lisa Beth *elementary school educator*
Essig, Kathleen Susan *academic administrator, consultant, management consultant*
Etzkorn, Susan *elementary school educator, small business owner*
Evans, Bonita Dianne *education educator*
Evans, Lara Adele *elementary school educator*
Evans, Margaret Utz *secondary school educator*
Evans, Sherrie Lea *secondary school educator*
Evans, Zoe O'Quinn *elementary school educator*
Fair, Jean Everhard *retired education educator*
Fairbairn, Barbara Jean *university administrator*
Fairbanks, Cynthia *secondary school educator*
Faison, Lugenia Marion *special education educator*
Fardy, Lydia J. *educator*
Farkas, Rhonda Dawn *principal, education educator*
Farmer, Laurel Ann *elementary school educator*
Farrell, Debbie L. *elementary school educator, media specialist*
Farrell, Elizabeth Ann *secondary school educator*
Faucette, Merilon Cooper *retired secondary school educator*
Faulds, Roxanne M. *media and technology educator*
Fearon, Charlene O'Brien *special education educator*
Febrey, Theresa M. *assistant principal*
Fedeli, Shirley Ann Martignoni *retired secondary school educator*
Feldman, Lillian Maltz *educational consultant*
Fell, Elizabeth P. *education educator*
Felton, Helen Martin *retired adult education educator, writer*
Ferguson-Whitehead, Wendy Sandra *elementary school educator, art educator, artist*
Fergusson, Frances Daly *former academic administrator*
Fernandes, Jane K. *academic administrator, educational consultant, sign language professional*
Fernandez, Suzanne Lyn *elementary school educator, music educator*
Ferringer-Burdick, Susan *elementary school educator*
Ficek, Debra L. *secondary school educator*
Fick, Denise *elementary school educator*
Fields, Emily Jill *secondary school educator*
Filchock, Ethel *education educator*
Filer, Nalene Tai *literature and language educator*
Fink, Alma *retired elementary school educator*
Finnegan, Margaret Mary *school librarian*
Firmstone, Kristal *elementary school educator*
Fishburn, Janet Forsythe *dean*
Fisher, Janet Warner *secondary school educator*
Fisher, Sherry M. *secondary school educator*
Fisk, Lois L. *secondary school educator*
Fitzgerald, Adelaide Yvonne *occupational child care educator*
Fitzgerald, Angela Michelle *special education educator*
Fitzgerald, Kathy *health and physical education educator*
Fleming, Diane Price *academic administrator*
Flint, Laura A. *elementary school educator*
Flory, Evelyn Louise *educational administrator*
Fodrea, Carolyn Wrobel *adult education educator, researcher*
Forbes, Mary Allison *psychology educator, educator*
Ford, Loretta C. *retired dean, educator, consultant, nurse*
Fordham, Beverly Surles *middle school educator*
Forero, Paula Juliana *academic administrator, artist*
Formato, Jonelle Nanette *secondary school educator*
Forrest, Linda Dotts *elementary school educator, social studies educator*
Fougerat, Karen Kay *mathematics educator*
Fountain, Ruth Anne *elementary school educator*
Fox, Deborah Lee *elementary school educator*
Francis, Trina Michele *elementary school educator*
Francoeur, Christina *special education educator*
Franey, Catherine T. *elementary school educator*
Franklin, Rebecca *elementary school educator*
Franzoni, Delaina Day *special education educator, department chairman*
French, Candace Lee *elementary school educator, music educator*
Frenning, Gineen F. *elementary school educator*
Frerk, Lori Ann *mathematics educator*
Friedman, Susan O. *retired academic administrator*
Frink, Jane Louise *literature and language educator*
Fry, Jane Marie *secondary school educator*
Fugett, Roberta Lynn *special education educator*
Fullerton, Gail Jackson *retired academic administrator*
Furman, Elise Hilary *middle school educator*
Gabel, Katherine *retired academic administrator*
Gaggiano, Andrea Jean *secondary school educator*
Gahagen, Bonnie Knepp *elementary school educator*
Galagan, Carol Anne *special education educator*
Galbraith, Marilyn Ann *secondary school educator*
Galindo, Karla Rae *retired secondary school educator*
Garber, Beth Carol *early childhood educator, music educator*
Garcia, Annette D'Urso *educational consultant*
Garcia, Julia Theresa *secondary school educator*
Garon, Phyllis S. *retired elementary school educator*
Gatison, Karen Ann *private school educator*
Geary, Allyson *secondary school educator*
Genesoni, Jacqueline *mathematics educator*
Gentilcore, Eileen Marie Belsito *principal*
George, Barbara Jean *literature and language educator, speech educator, communications educator*
George, Merrilou Kay *elementary school educator*
Gersten, Elizabeth Welliver *education educator, researcher*
Gettinger, Susan Beth *literature and language educator*
Gibson, Kathy *secondary school educator, art educator*
Gibson, Lisette L. *elementary school educator, music educator*
Gibson, Melissa Upchurch *elementary school educator*
Gifford, Paula *elementary school educator*
Gillenwater-Catron, Tashanna Shantay *elementary school educator*
Gilmore, Connie Sue *director*
Gittman, Elizabeth *educational consultant*
Glasgow, Karen *principal*
Glenn, Deborah Ann *economics educator, political science educator*
Glenn, Ethel Chappell *educator*
Glenn, Violetta Colleen *retired secondary school educator*
Glismann, Clementine *retired elementary school educator*
Gobler, Bina *assistant principal*
Godwin, Carol *mathematics educator*
Goedken, Jennifer Lynn *mathematics educator*
Goeke, Lorise Ann *principal, elementary school educator*
Goetzinger, Eleanor *special education educator*
Golden, Sheila S. *retired special education educator*
Goodman, Jessica Mui Kwai *secondary school educator*
Goodwin, Rebecca *literature and language educator*
Gordon, Sharon Ann *mathematics educator, pre-school educator*
Gorelova, Linda M. *elementary school educator*
Gossett, Janine Lee *middle school educator*
Gouskos, Lisa Marie *elementary school educator, music educator*
Graham, Barbara J. *special education educator*
Graham, Nancy G. *elementary school educator*
Graham, Sylvia Swords *retired secondary school educator*
Grant, Frances Elizabeth *retired educator*
Grasham, Clara Langan *reading specialist*
Gray, Hazel Irene *retired special education educator, counselor, consultant*
Gray, LeAnn Marie *special education educator*
Gray, Lisa Hart *secondary school educator*
Gray McCray, Rosalind *assistant principal*
Green, Aimee Melissa *physical education educator*
Green, Andrea M. *college administrator*
Green, Cheryl Faye *counseling administrator, educator*
Green, Kelly Allyson *gifted and talented educator, entrepreneur*
Green, Patricia Pataky *school system administrator, consultant*
Greene, Elaine D. G. *environmental science educator*
Greene, Janette Zaher *elementary school educator*
Greene, Jo *school system administrator*
Greer, Bonnie Beth *educator*
Greer, Cheryl L. *middle school educator*
Gregory, J. L. *secondary school educator*
Griffin, Laura Mae *retired elementary and secondary school educator*
Grimaldi, Kathleen Galvin *literature and language educator, poet*
Grimes, Nancy Guerard *secondary school educator*
Grimme, A. Jeannette *retired elementary school educator, retired small business owner, volunteer*
Griskey, Pauline Becker *education educator, researcher*
Grossman, Carolyn Sylvia Cort *retired elementary school educator*
Grove, Cherylee Vega *special education educator*
Grove, Myrna Jean *elementary school educator*
Groves, B. C. *educational consultant, writer*
Groves, Bernice Ann *retired elementary and secondary school coordinator, educator*
Gudnitz, Ora M. Cofey *secondary school educator*
Guffey, Barbara Braden *retired elementary school educator*
Guinther, Christine Louise *special education educator*
Gumpert, Carolyn L. *secondary school educator*
Gunning, Carolyn Sue *dean, provost, nursing educator*
Gustafson, Sandra Lynne *retired secondary school educator*
Gutowski, Kathleen Sullivan *special education educator*
Guy, Mary (Penny) Whytlaw *secondary school educator, school librarian*
Guze, Sandra Lee *secondary school educator*
Gwalla-Ogisi, Nomsa *education educator*
Haake, Dorothy May *secondary school educator*
Haas, Beverly Jean *secondary school educator, coach*
Haas, Carolyn Buhai *elementary school educator, publisher, writer, consultant*
Haas, Suzanne Alberta *elementary school educator, secondary school educator*
Haeger, Gayle Mignon *biology educator*
Haerbig, Alaina Beth *elementary school educator*
Hagen, Linda Renee *secondary school educator*
Hagopian-Grantz, Holly Ann *elementary school educator*
Hahn, Margaret Catherine *secondary school educator*
Hales, Jacqueline A. *grant writer, elementary school educator*
Hale Singleton, Lori T. *special education educator*
Halfpap, Kayla Jean *special education educator*
Hall, Ami S. *elementary school educator, actress*
Hall, Kathryn Marie *elementary school educator*
Halloran-Barnes, Jill *secondary school educator*
Halter, Cassandra J. *elementary school educator*
Hamblin, Susan Annette *elementary school educator*
Hamecs, Francella Cheslock *secondary school educator*
Hamilton, Rhoda Lillian Rosén *retired guidance counselor, language educator, consultant*
Hamlin, Harriett E. *educational consultant*
Hammond, Ann P. *retired elementary, high school and college educator, poet*
Hamolsky, Tina Lorman *special education educator*
Hamtpton, Jacquelyn Dana *principal*
Hanna, Noreen Anelda *adult education educator, consultant*
Hansen, Carol Dianne *professor*
Hansen, Elizabeth Ann *education educator*
Hansen, Julia Ann *elementary school educator*
Hansen, Nancy C. Urdahl *retired special education educator, small business owner*
Hardage, Page Taylor *elementary school educator*
Hardy, Melanie Ann Walker *secondary school educator, science educator*
Hare, Norma Q. *retired school system administrator*
Harper, Janet Sutherlin Lane *retired educational administrator, writer*
Harrall, Neva Ann *elementary school educator*
Harrington, Jean Patrice *academic administrator*
Harrington, Terri Ann *retired elementary school educator*
Harris, Deanna Lynn *special education educator, writer*
Harris, Dolores M. *retired academic administrator, adult education educator*
Harris, Margaret T. *school system administrator*
Harris, Merle Wiener *college administrator, educator*
Harris-Barber, Daisy *elementary school educator*
Harrison, Diane B. *elementary school educator*
Harrison, Nicole Marie *special education educator*
Hartwig, Rhonda Dean *secondary school educator*
Harvey, Judith Gootkin *elementary school educator, real estate agent*
Hatfield, Stacey *elementary school educator*
Hatton, Laurie *elementary school educator*
Haupt, Patricia A. *principal*
Hawkins, Jacquelyn *elementary and secondary education educator*
Hawthorne, Terri *director*
Hayden, Jennifer B. *elementary school educator*
Hayes, Candace Ashmore *elementary school educator*
Hayes, Cynthia Lane *secondary school educator*
Hayes, Melanie *secondary school educator*
Haynie, Suzanna Kennedy *secondary school educator*
Hazel, Mary Belle *university administrator*
Hazelton, Catherine Lynette *elementary school educator*
Heald, Patricia Anne *middle school educator*
Hedges, Norma Ann *retired secondary education educator*
Hedricks, Phyllis *secondary school educator*
Heinzman, Barbara K. *educational consultant*
Hellwege, Nancy Carol *special education educator*
Helm, Monica M. *elementary school educator, psychotherapist, secondary school educator*
Helsel, Elsie Dressler *retired special education educator*
Hendershott, Anna Lorraine *educational director*
Hendricks, Shasaree *dean, music educator*
Henley, Patricia Joan *consultant, former superintendent*
Henning, Joan Denise *secondary school educator*
Henry, Donna Edwards *elementary school educator*
Hensel, Nancy H. *academic administrator*
Hensley, Patricia Drake *principal*
Henson, Joy Kay *special education educator*
Henson, Patricia Lou *elementary school educator*
Herder, Susan Hideko *secondary school educator*
Herge, Donna Carol *secondary school educator*
Hermance, Betty Jean *special education educator*
Herold, Rochelle Snyder *early childhood educator*
Herring, Joan Sanders *secondary school educator*
Herroon, Joan Geiger *secondary school educator*
Hess, Constance J. *mathematics educator*
Hess, Wendi Elizabeth *secondary school educator*
Heston, Bridget L. *vice principal, history educator*
Heymann, Jennifer Eden *elementary school educator*
Hibbs, Dawn Wilcox *elementary school educator*
Higgins, Dorothy Marie *dean, educator*
Hill, Alice Faye *secondary school educator*
Hill, Audrianne *English educator*
Hill, Cinnamon Michelle *secondary school educator, director*
Hill, Emita Brady *academic administrator, consultant*
Hill, Marion Thelma *elementary school educator*
Hillery, Susie Moore *retired elementary school educator*
Hines, Voncile *special education educator*
Hing, Barbara Lim *elementary school educator, assistant principal, data processing executive*
Hinkebein, Kathryn Ann *retired education educator*
Hinman, Eve Caison *retired academic administrator*
Hintz, Dawn M. *mathematics educator*
Hirai, Michiyo *education educator*
Hoberecht, Reynotta Jahnke *school system administrator, educator*
Hodge, Isa Ann *elementary school educator*
Hodges, Elizabeth C. *elementary school educator, principal*
Hodges, Shirley Marie *secondary school educator*
Hoering, Helen G. *elementary school educator*
Hoffman, Judy Greenblatt *preschool director*
Hoffman, Kathaleen May *biology educator*
Hoffman, Sharon Lynn *adult education educator*
Holloway, Jennifer A. *elementary school educator, assistant principal*
Holmes, Serena Nicole *pre-school educator*
Holoman, Constance Currier *academic administrator*
Holtkamp, Susan Charlotte *elementary school educator*
Hood, Luann Sandra *special education educator*
Hopkinson, Nicole Jean *elementary school educator*
Hopper, Bette Patricia *retired elementary school educator*
Hoppes, Laural Jean *elementary school educator*
Horne, Kathryn Jennifer *elementary school educator*
Horner, Matina Souretis *retired academic administrator, corporate financial executive*
Horton, Joann *academic administrator*
Horton-Wright, Alma Irene *retired elementary school educator*
Hostler-Vaughan, ReBecca L. *educational consultant*
Hotaling, Carey *elementary school educator*
Houseman, Ann Elizabeth Lord *educational administrator*
Howard, Elena Calvillo *retired elementary school educator*
Howard, Wilma Parks *elementary school educator*
Howell, Teresa Christine Wallin *elementary school educator*
Hoye, Gwynne Sanders *retired mathematics educator*
Hubacz, Joan Rebecca *director, private school educator*
Hubbard, Marguerite *retired elementary school educator*
Hudalla, Karen *dean, director, court reporter*
Huffman, Carol Koster *retired middle school educator*
Humes, Elaine *mathematics educator*
Hummel, Marilyn Mae *retired elementary school educator*
Humphrey-Jefferson, Beverly C. *daycare administrator*
Humphreys, Lynne M. *secondary school educator*
Hunnicutt, Victoria Anne Wilson *educational consultant*
Hurwitz, Ellen Stiskin *college president, historian*
Husky, Anrea Dalene *elementary school educator, director*
Hutchinson, Glenda Dague *elementary school educator, small business owner*
Hutchison, Heather Nicole *secondary school educator*
Hyndman, Roberta *education educator*
Iceman, Sharon Lorraine *retired elementary school educator*
Idol, Lorna *education educator, writer*
Ingle, Beverly Dawn *elementary school educator*
Insalaco-De Nigris, Anna Maria Theresa *middle school educator*
Intrater, Cheryl Watson Waylor *career management consultant*
Iratene, Mary Susan *elementary school educator*
Irvan, Ashlee DeAnn *elementary school educator*
Irvin, Loretta Regan *elementary school educator*
Isbell, Rita Anette *special education educator*
Isom, Kawanya Kenyetta *assistant principal*
Ivey, Sharon Dee *secondary school educator*
Jackson, Clora Ellis *counseling administrator, psychologist, educator*
Jackson, Mary Alice *retired elementary school educator, retired realtor*
Jackson, Tamra Lynn *literature and language educator*
Jackson Wright, Adrienne A. *educational consultant*
Jacobs, Linda Rotroff *elementary school educator*
Jagerman, Adrienne *retired elementary school educator, nurse*

Jalonen, Nancy Lee *academic administrator, educator*
Jameson, Margaret Johnson *retired elementary school educator*
Jappinen, Amy Jo *middle school educator*
Javernick, Amy Sue *special education educator*
Jean, Claudette R. *retired elementary school educator*
Jefferis, Bernice K. *education educator*
Jefferson, Kathleen Henderson *retired secondary school educator*
Jefferson, Nanette Hawkins *special education educator*
Jeffery, Valerie *secondary school educator*
Jenkins, Brenda Gwenetta *pre-school administrator, special education educator*
Jenkins, Jill M. *gifted-talented education educator*
Jenkins, Lawanna *elementary school educator*
Johnson, Arica Reneé *elementary school educator*
Johnson, Betsie Ruth *pre-school educator*
Johnson, Charlene Elizabeth *adult education educator, language educator, consultant*
Johnson, Holly L. *elementary school educator*
Johnson, Jerrilyn Jenkins *academic administrator*
Johnson, Kirsten Denise *elementary school educator*
Johnson, Latonya *secondary school educator*
Johnson, Linda Sue *academic administrator, state agency administrator, retired state legislator*
Johnson, Lois Brooks *retired elementary guidance counselor*
Johnson, Maryann Elaine *educational administrator*
Johnson, Meggan D. *school intervention specialist*
Johnson, Ruth Ann *literature and language educator*
Johnson, Sigrid *elementary school educator*
Johnson, Sylvia Sue *university administrator, educator*
Johnson, Trina Lynn *special education educator*
Johnson, Vera Lloyd *school system administrator*
Johnson, Yvonne Thomas *elementary school educator*
Johnson-MIller, Charleen V. *educational coordinator*
Jones, Anna *elementary school educator*
Jones, Carole A. *elementary school educator*
Jones, Christa M. *secondary school educator*
Jones, Elizabeth Jordan *literature and language educator, art historian*
Jones, Julie Ann *elementary school educator, choreographer*
Jones, Melissa Vincent *secondary school educator*
Jones, Stacie Ann *elementary school educator*
Jontz, Polly *retired college official, museum director*
Jordan, Phyllis C. Vaccaro *special education educator*
Joyce, Phyllis Norma *principal*
Julien, JoElla L. *educator*
Kachur, Betty Rae *elementary school educator*
Kahn, Victoria Elaine Hopkins *special education educator*
Kaiser, Karen Sue *elementary school educator*
Kaminshine, Sarah Berne *special education educator*
Kamlay, Jane *elementary school educator*
Kamlet, Elizabeth Oseff *elementary school educator*
Kane, Heidi Baker *secondary school educator*
Kang, Kyoung Sook *retired special education educator*
Kanich, Kelli Jo *secondary school educator*
Kapp, Gloria Jean *retired academic program director*
Kappner, Augusta Souza *academic administrator*
Kaps, Sydelle *elementary school educator*
Karahalios, Sue M. Compton *secondary school educator*
Karben, Shelley Valerie *elementary and special education school educator*
Karfs, Tara Lynn *elementary school educator*
Karnowski, Maria A. *special education educator*
Karp, Stephanie L. *biology educator*
Kartchner, Gayla L. *elementary school educator*
Kaslofsky, Wendy Anna *special education educator*
Kazmarek, Linda Adams *secondary school educator*
Keat, Jane Blakely *education educator*
Keene, Sylvia White *retired reading specialist*
Keener, Elizabeth Ann *elementary school educator*
Keesee, Donna Christine *retired elementary school educator*
Keith, Katharine *education educator*
Kellar, Marie Terese *special education educator*
Kelley, Kathy *literature and language educator*
Kelley, Kristina Elizabeth *secondary school educator*
Kelley, Wendy Rock *academic administrator*
Kelly, Beverly Ann *elementary school educator*
Kelly, Sister Dorothy Ann *academic administrator*
Kelly, Mary Kathryn *special education administrator*
Kelso, Charlotte Elizabeth *elementary school educator, health and physical education specialist*
Kennedy, Sheryl J. *elementary school educator*
Kennedy, Virginia Frances *retired education educator*
Kenney, Marianne *elementary school educator*
Kerr Walker, Joi Mechelle *literacy educator, consultant*
Keyes, Joan Ross Rafter *education educator, writer*
Keywood, Kay Hill *mathematics educator, small business owner*
Kierscht, Marcia Selland *academic administrator, psychologist*
Kile, Patricia D. *retired elementary school educator*
Killian, Tiffany Noel *secondary school educator*
Killoran, Cynthia Lockhart *retired elementary school educator*
Kilpatrick, Jennifer M. *counseling administrator*
Kimbrough, Lorelei *retired elementary school educator, retired secondary school educator*
King, Bonnie La Verne *education educator*
King, Molly Elizabeth Rutland *elementary school educator*
King, Verna St. Clair *retired school counselor*
Kinney, Joyce P. *elementary school educator*
Kinzler, Charissa D. *special education educator*
Kirby, Sheryl C. *secondary school educator*
Kirchmeier-Boyes, Melanie Joan *middle school educator*
Kirk, Rea Helene (Rea Helene Glazer) *special education educator*
Kirkpatrick, Alicia Ann *elementary school educator, department chairman*
Kisiel, Ida Marie *education educator, writer*
Kistler, Joyce Dianna *secondary school educator*
Kitzman, Mary Therese *elementary school educator*
Kjar, Nancy *elementary school educator*
Klebanow, Barbara Elaine *secondary school educator*
Klein, Cinthia Marie *parochial school educator*
Klein, Elayne Margery *retired elementary school educator*
Klein, Irma Molligan *career planning administrator, consultant*
Klein, Mary Ann *special education educator*
Kleiner, Heather Smith *retired academic administrator*
Kliebhan, Sister M(ary) Camille *academic administrator*
Kmetz-McMillin, MArianne Denise *secondary school educator*
Knight, Rebecca Jean *secondary school educator*
Knighten, Latrenda *elementary school educator, consultant*
Knowlton, Marie *retired special education educator*
Koch, Molly Brown *retired parent educator*
Koessel, Jeannine Carrol *retired principal*
Kohas, Artemis Diane *guidance counselor*
Kokx, Sarah Lynn *elementary school educator*
Kolakoski, Dawn Laymond *education educator, consultant, music educator*
Kolb, Dorothy Gong *elementary school educator*
Konner, Joan Weiner *academic administrator, educator, television producer, writer, retired television executive*
Konrad, Carol Joan *secondary school educator*
Kranowitz, Carol Stock *pre-school educator, writer*
Krauskopf, Nancy Kay *middle school educator, journalist*
Krauss, Diana S. *secondary school educator*
Krzykowski, Jamie Lee *education educator*
Kuehn, Nancy Ann *retired secondary school educator*
Kuhfuss, Lisa A. *mathematics educator*
Kulkarni, Shaila V. *secondary school educator*
Kumar, Ramya *academic administrator*
Kumar, Rita *literature and language educator*
Kupovits, Jene Irene *special education educator*
LaCava, Laura L. *elementary school educator*
LaFlamme, Julie Lynn *secondary school educator*
Lamb, Patsy (Pat) Lee *retired adult education educator, real estate broker*
Lamont, Marilyn Laree Claudel *reading specialist, accountant*
Lancaster, Jeanette (Barbara Lancaster) *dean, nursing educator*
Lane, Allyson C. *elementary school educator*
Lane Stone, Nancy Ann *elementary school educator*
Lange, Natalie Lauren *social studies educator*
Langmaid, Barbra Kay *elementary school educator*
Langton (Tomasiewicz), Dawn Theresa *literature and language educator*
Langum, Teresa Marie *elementary school educator*
Lanning, Yvonne Bradshaw *elementary school educator*
Lantz, Joanne Baldwin *retired academic administrator*
Larsen, Brenda Joyce *elementary school educator*
Larsen, Kristina Ann *elementary school educator*
Larson, Angela R. *secondary school educator*
Larson, Janece S. *elementary school educator*
Larson, Vicki Lord *academic administrator, communication disorders educator*
Lasak, Janice Underhill *elementary school educator*
Lashley, Felissa Rose *dean, nursing educator, researcher*
Lassmann, Marie Elizabeth *education educator, consultant*
Lattimore, Louise Joan *elementary school educator*
Laudenklos, Terry Lynn *elementary school educator*
Lauer, Cassie Lynn *mathematics educator, department chairman*
Lauer, Jeanette Carol *dean, history educator, writer*
Lauzon, Laura M. *middle school educator*
Lavey, Sarah *assistant principal*
Lawrence, Sally Clark *retired academic administrator*
Lawson, Sharianne Renee *political science educator*
Layzell, Judy Kathleen *secondary school educator, writer*
Lea, Karen *elementary education educator*
Leafgren, Rita F. *education educator*
Leath, Cheryl Lynn *retired pre-school educator, poet, painter*
Leather, Victoria Potts *college librarian*
Leavell, Tausha Dawn *social studies educator*
Le Blanc, Alice Isabelle *academic administrator*
Ledbetter, Merry W. *mathematics educator*
Ledet, Phyllis L. *assistant principal*
Lee, Anita Combs *writer, speaker, consultant*
Lee, Esther Bora *elementary school educator, gifted and talented educator*
Lee, Krista *secondary school educator*
Leeper, Kathleen Marie *elementary school educator*
Legace, Kathryn Jane *principal*
Legington, Gloria R. *retired elementary school educator*
Leidig, Margot Helene *retired elementary school educator, retired secondary school educator*
Leighman, Marilyn Rust *school counselor*
Leistner, Mary Edna *retired secondary school educator*
Leitzel, Joan Ruth *retired academic administrator*
LeMay, Gayla Denise *elementary school educator*
Leonard, Sister Anne C. *school system administrator*
Leonard, Kristi *education educator, director*
Leslie, Maureen Heelan *university director*
Lesonsky, Paula Marlene *elementary school educator*
Lester, Stephanie *elementary school educator, education educator*
Lester, Virginia Laudano *academic administrator*
Lesyinski, Diane M. *elementary school educator*
Levy, Dara Michele *secondary school educator*
Lewis, Kristen R. *mathematics educator*
Lewis-Gilchrist, Stephanie Kay *primary school educator*
Lewis Riffle, Muriel Ann *retired secondary school educator*
Ley, Carmen B. *special education educator*
Liddell, Mary Louisa *elementary school educator, computers educator*
Lien, Julie Ann *elementary school educator*
Light, Marion Jessel *retired elementary school educator*
Limerick, Dianne A. *mathematics educator, athletic trainer*
Lindeman, Joyce Irene *university administrator*
Lindland, Marnetta *secondary school educator*
Liu, Ruth Wang *retired academic administrator*
Liverman, Betty Jean *elementary school educator*
Livingston, Gwendell Sheawanna *education educator*
Lloyd, Gwendolyn Monica *mathematics educator*
Lober, Irene Moss *educational consultant*
Long, Susie Ann *special education educator, consultant, writer*
Longman, Karen A. *higher education administrator*
Longstreet, Wilma S. *retired education educator*
Loop, Christine E. *elementary school educator*
Loredo, Doriselda *elementary school educator*
Lotchin, Phyllis Morris *English language educator*
Love, Beverly Anne *retired elementary school educator*
Lovett, Clara Maria *retired academic administrator, retired historian*
Lowenberg, Georgina Grace *retired elementary school educator*
Lowrie, Kathryn Yanacek *special education educator*
Loyd, Pamela Ann *academic administrator, educator*
Lucas, Michele Angelyn *learning consultant, special education educator*
Lucas, Teri Kathleen *elementary school educator*
Luderitz, Pamela Ann *secondary school educator*
Luebke, Elizabeth Anne Silva *elementary school educator*
Luft, Cecile E. *music educator*
Lyall, Katharine Culbert *former academic administrator, economist, educator*
Lyne, Dorothy-Arden *secondary school educator*
Lynn, Naomi B. *academic administrator*
MacCormack, Jean F. *academic administrator*
MacFarlane, Barbara Ann *secondary school educator*
Mack, Cheryl A. *principal*
Mackert, Rita Marie *elementary school educator*
MacKinnon, Nancy Williams *retired educator, state legislator*
Maddalena, Rosalie Anne *retired educator*
Madore, Teresa Sharon *secondary school educator*
Magee, Megan *elementary school educator*
Mainor, Debra L. *elementary school educator*
Mains, Susan Jane *mathematics educator*
Maliff, Lori Christine *elementary school educator*
Manley, Judith L. *director*
Manning, Nancy Christine *retired elementary school educator*
Mantei, Lorraine E. *school system administrator*
Marchuk, Pamela Ann *retired elementary school educator*
Markovich, Alexandria *assistant principal*
Marlow, Marcia Marie *secondary school educator, publishing executive*
Marsh, Lynn *elementary school educator*
Martin, Carolyn Stewart *retired school system administrator*
Martin, Jeanine Kay *retired elementary school educator*
Martin, Mariela *secondary school educator*
Martin, Paula S. *principal*
Martinez, Veronica *special education educator*
Masi, Julia A. *elementary school educator*
Masiello, Lisa Anne *elementary school educator*
Mason, Johanna Hendrika Anneke *retired secondary school educator*
Mason, Margaret Crather *elementary school educator*
Masters, Ann Browning *education educator, poet*
Matasar, Ann B. *retired dean, finance educator*
Matera, Frances Lorine *elementary school educator*
Mathews, Jean Ann H. *political science educator*
Mathews-Mathena, Jennifer Kay *elementary school educator*
Mathias, Sharon A *secondary school educator*
Mattrella, Anne Laura *secondary school educator*
Maxfield, Brooke Davis *mathematics educator*
Maximciuc, Deborah Jean *special education educator*
Maynard, Mendy J. *secondary school educator*
McAmis, Angie M. *elementary school educator*
McBride, Mildred Maylea *retired elementary school educator*
McBride, Paula Brewer *chemistry educator, dean*
McCabe, Linda Jean *elementary school educator*
McCain, Debbie M. *elementary school educator*
Mc Cain, Elizabeth Jean *elementary school educator*
McCalla, Sandra Ann *principal*
McCalley, Barbara Vaglia Dougherty *secondary school educator*
McCann, Diana Rae *secondary school educator*
McCann, Joyce Jeannine *retired elementary school educator*
McCarthy, Carole Sullivan *retired special education educator, consultant, educational evaluator*
McCarty, Diane Mary *education educator*
McCord, Rita Rae *elementary school educator*
McCormick, Molly *elementary school educator*
McCosham, Joyce L. *secondary school educator*
McCoy, Mary Jane *retired principal*
McCoy, Patricia A. *retired clinical special educator, art and culture critic, writer*
McCrea, Melissa Lauren *elementary school educator*
McDaniel, Sara Sherwood (Sally McDaniel) *trainer, consultant*
McDonald-Pochiba, Elizabeth J. *secondary school educator*
McElrath, Ah Quon *academic administrator*
McFadden, Cynthia Ann Bellville *middle school educator*
McGinn Miller, Janet Scrivner *retired elementary school educator, writer*
McGowan, Susan *gifted and talented educator*
McHoes, Ann McIver *academic administrator, computer engineer*
McIntosh, Kelli Lee *physics educator*
McIntosh, Kelli Marie *elementary school educator*
McIntyre, Virgie M. *elementary school educator*
McMahon Mastroddi, Marcia A. *secondary school educator, artist, writer*
McMullen, Jennifer Anne *secondary school educator*
McNutt, Margaret H. Honaker *secondary school educator*
Meek, Amy Gertrude *retired elementary school educator*
Meier, Enge *pre-school educator*
Melton, Emma Alexander *educational consultant, retired elementary school educator*
Meltzer, E. Alyne *elementary school educator, social worker, volunteer*
Mende, Maggie Sarah *elementary school educator*
Mendon, Karen Jeanette *elementary school educator*
Mendoza, Karen Lynn *special education educator*
Merriweather, Freda E. *education educator*
Mesrop, Alida Yolande *academic administrator*
Metzler, Ruth Horton *genealogical educator*
Meyer, Frances Margaret Anthony *educational consultant*
Michael, Jean *mathematics educator*
Miesle, Angela Denise *elementary school educator*
Milam, Melissa Gail *elementary school educator*
Milbourne, Melinda D. *elementary school educator, researcher*
Miller, Angela D. *secondary school educator*
Miller, Carolyn *secondary education educator, composer*
Miller, Gwendolyn Doris *retired special education educator*
Miller, Jenefer Ardell *elementary school educator, choreographer*
Miller, Linda Karen *retired secondary school educator, social studies educator, law educator*
Miller-Dreusicke, Connie Anne *special education educator*
Milligan, Krista *drafting educator*
Millman, Marilyn Estelle *elementary school educator*
Mills, Helene Audrey *retired education educator*
Mills, Jean D. *education educator*
Mills, Melanie Marie *elementary school educator*
Milner, Joan W. *retired elementary school educator*
Minco, Debra Thompson *chemistry educator*
Mingus, Cherie Lynn *home economics educator*
Miranda-Morgart, Lynda Christine *elementary school educator*
Mirk, Judy Ann *retired elementary school educator*
Missele, Brenda Marie *secondary school educator*
Mittleider, Rebecca Ann *elementary school educator*
Mitzel, Brenda Renee *mathematics educator*
Mohr, Barbara Jeanne *elementary school educator*
Moistner, Mona Sue *adult education educator*
Molnar, Mary Anne *retired secondary school educator, consultant*
Molyneaux, Dorothy Munz *retired education educator, retired speech pathology/audiology services professional*
Monheiser, Cheryl Ann *retired elementary school educator*
Monteilh, Yvette Marie *education educator*
Montgomery, Carolyn Williams *retired secondary school educator*
Montuori, Dona F. *retired elementary school educator*
Mood, Rosalyn Thomas *assistant principal*
Moon, Gabrielle Marie *biology educator*
Moon, Rose Ann *elementary school educator*
Moore, Juel Ann *retired elementary school educator*
Moore, Marsha Lynn *retired elementary school educator, counseling administrator*
Moore-Wleklinski, Patricia Marie *secondary school educator*
Moorhouse, Robbi Presswood *elementary school educator*
Mora, Maria *elementary school educator*
Morgan, Ellen Louise *elementary school educator*
Morgan, Marlene *education educator, consultant*
Morgan, Mary Lou *retired education educator, volunteer*
Morgan, Ruth Prouse *academic administrator, educator*
Morris, Harriet R. *elementary school educator*
Morris, Holly *elementary school educator*
Morris, Laura *elementary school educator*
Morris, Peggy Ann *elementary school educator, mathematics educator*
Morris, Sheila J. *elementary school educator*
Morrison, Amy Michele *secondary school educator*
Morris-Wong, Beth *school librarian, educator*
Morse, Anne Bernadette *retired educational consultant*
Mortensen-Say, Marlys *retired school system administrator*
Mosely, Elaine W. *school librarian*
Mott, Mary Elizabeth *retired computer educator*
Moudy, Linda Ann *elementary school educator*
Mouttet, Jane Elizabeth *school librarian, educator*
Moye, Alana Nicole *pre-school educator*
Mueller, Anita LaVonne *special education educator*
Muhammad, Gholnecsa Eushena *elementary school educator*
Muir, Patty K. *special education educator*

Mull, Beth A. *counseling educator*
Mundell, Susan Belle *special education educator*
Munguia, Gay Yeager *retired elementary school educator, retired secondary school educator*
Munn, Polly *retired elementary school educator*
Munroe, Mary Lou Schwarz (Mrs. Robert E. Munroe) *educational administrator*
Munsterman, Ingrid Anita *assistant principal*
Murakane, Charleen *elementary school educator*
Murphy, Lisa M. *primary school educator*
Murphy, Michelle Zick *special education educator*
Murphy, Thelma Arabella *elementary school educator, photographer*
Murray, Amanda Kay *elementary school educator*
Muskopf, Margaret Rose *elementary school educator*
Myers, Michelle E. *education educator, consultant*
Nance, Mary Joe *retired secondary school educator*
Napoli, Mary *education educator*
Naughton, Margaret Mary *elementary school educator*
Neal, Marietha Mae *primary school educator*
Neal, Teresa Schreibeis *secondary school educator*
Neff, Diane Irene *university administrator*
Nelson, Carol Evelyn *retired pre-school educator*
Nelson, JoAnn *secondary school educator, educational consultant*
Nelson, Lauren Kathryn *education educator*
Nelson, Lois Nadine *retired special education educator*
Nereng, Linda Rae *elementary school educator*
Neufeld, Maureen Patricia *elementary school educator*
Neurath, Rachel *mathematics educator*
Neuvel, Melissa *secondary school educator*
Nevins, Tracy Anne *elementary school educator*
New, Rosetta Holbrock *retired secondary school educator, retired department chairman, retired nutrition consultant*
Newdigger, Carrrie *secondary school educator*
Newman, Barbara Mae *retired special education educator*
Ney, Rhonda G. *elementary school educator*
Neziri, Maria G. De Lucia *elementary school educator*
Nieto, Sonia Mary *retired education educator*
Nix, Sharon J. *principal*
Nnadi, Eucharia E. *academic administrator*
Noddings, Nel *education educator, writer*
Noffsinger, Nancy Leigh *special education educator*
Nolan, Joan T. *elementary school educator*
Northern, Ernestine *gifted and talented educator*
Nussbaumer, Melany Hamilton *program director*
O'Farrill, Marline Stabile *director*
Ofstad, Evelyn Larsen Boyl *retired primary school educator, radio personality, film producer*
Oglesby, Elaine Sue *elementary school educator*
O'Hara, Sabine U. *academic administrator, dean, economist, educator*
Olson, Paula Sue *director*
Olson-Arenz, Barbara D. *chemistry educator*
O'Neill Wotanowski, Eileen Mary *special education educator*
Orozco, Edith Dell *counselor, special education counselor*
Orsborn, Mary Kay *school librarian, educator*
Osborn, Janie Dyson *early childhood education education educator*
Oskin, JoEllen Ross *special education educator, school librarian*
Oslak, Megan Kathleen *elementary school educator*
Ouradnik, Toni Kristin *elementary school educator*
Outt, Helen May *retired elementary school educator, psychologist*
Pacecca, Andrea Leigh *mathematics educator*
Packard, Sophie S. *elementary school educator*
Padilla, Rebecca Lynn *special education educator*
Pallas, Arlene Mary *elementary school educator*
Palmer, Irene Sabelberg *retired dean, retired nursing educator, genealogist*
Pancratz, Jeanette Diane *secondary school educator*
Parchment, Robyn Renae *mathematics educator*
Paris-De Monte, Ileana M. *assistant principal*
Parisi, Valerie Marie *former dean, medical educator*
Parker, Suzanne Marie *physical education educator*
Parks, Margaret Laverne *secondary school educator, department chairman*
Parks, Tamara *elementary school educator*
Parrish, Nancy Rebecca *elementary school educator*
Parsons, Alexandra Clare *literature and language educator*
Patrick, Pauline Margaret *secondary school educator*
Patterson, Linda Darece *school disciplinarian*
Patterson, Mildred Lucas *retired teaching specialist*
Pearce, Karen Lee *elementary school educator*
Pearsall, Gloria W. *retired elementary school educator*
Pease-Pretty On Top, Janine B. *community college administrator*
Pederson, Celine *secondary school educator, literature and language educator*
Peko, Linda D. *elementary school educator*
Pencola, Annamaria Regina *elementary school educator*
Peper, Charlotte Ann *educational consultant*
Percoski, Kathryn Jean *secondary school educator*
Perez, Barbara Sue *middle school educator*
Perkins, Erma Young *English language educator*
Pero, Louise A. *elementary school educator*
Perrin, Courtney Massey *history educator*
Perry, Diane Swaney *mathematics educator*
Peters, Janice G. Spoth *elementary school educator*
Petersen, Joyce Jean *retired elementary school educator*
Peterson, Brandi Janell *elementary school educator*
Peterson, Clara Margaret *elementary school educator*
Peterson, Ginger *secondary school educator*
Peterson, Jennifer Leigh *mathematics educator*
Peterson, Norma Jo *retired education educator*
Pettigrew, L. Eudora *retired academic administrator*
Pfeifer, Lola *mathematics educator*
Phillips, Marjorie Ruth *retired elementary school educator*
Phipard, Nancy Midwood *retired special education educator, poet*
Pierce, Susan Resneck *academic administrator, literature educator, consultant*
Pinkus, Deborah Sue *special education educator*
Piper, Margarita Sherertz *retired school system administrator*
Pirrone, Catherine Lynne *secondary school educator*
Pisani, Margaret *elementary school educator*
Pisano, Carla Ann *mathematics educator, accountant*
Plaisted, Carole Anne *elementary school educator*
Platt, Kathryn *special education educator*
Pliska, Stephanie *history educator, special education educator*
Pohto, Susan Louise *secondary school educator*
Polimeni, Rebecca H. *special education educator*
Pollack, Marsha *secondary school educator*
Pomers, Tiffany Lee *mathematics educator*
Pond, Gloria Dibble *retired educator*
Pope, Mary Therese *retired elementary school educator*
Potter, Polly Helene *elementary school educator*
Poulson, Kristie M. *secondary school educator*
Powell, Cathy Gail *secondary school educator*
Powell, Lynnette *elementary school educator*
Powell, Sheryl Ann *elementary school educator*
Pratt, Rachel C. *elementary school educator*
Pratt, Sandra Sowers *special education educator*
Prawdzik, Linda Condusta *mathematics educator, consultant, director*
Preer, Joan C. *retired assistant principal, retired science educator*
Preheim, Kathy Lynn *elementary school educator*
Price, Mary *elementary school educator*
Price, Myra B. *secondary school educator*
Prichard, Kathryn *adult education educator*
Priebe, Sue *retired secondary school educator, minister*
Pringle, Ruth Evelyn *retired adult education educator*
Pritchard, Karri R. *chemistry educator*
Proenza, Theresa Butler *adult education educator, writer*
Pruchnicki, Jennifer Ann *director*
Pruitt, Anne Loring *academic administrator, education educator*
Pryce, Dana A. *special education educator*
Puia, Mary Beth *educator*
Pulhamus, Marlene Louise *retired elementary school educator*
Purvis, Gail *elementary school educator*
Puttmann, Sara *mathematics educator*
Pyles, Carol DeLong *dean, consultant, educator*
Quast, Pearl Elizabeth Kolb *retired elementary school educator*
Raborn, Marcia MacArthur *primary school educator*
Rada, Ruth Byers *retired dean*
Radell, Carol K. *elementary school educator*
Raes, Heather Rebecca *special education educator, consultant*
Raffo, Susan Henney *retired elementary school educator*
Ragsdale, Sandra Russell *special education educator*
Rambo, Domingo H. *elementary school educator*
Ramsey, Emma Ruth *secondary school educator*
Ranada, Rose Marie *retired elementary school educator*
Rao-Remy, Yvonne Bernadette *special education educator*
Rawdon, Cheryl Ann *elementary school educator*
Ray, Susan Elaine *principal*
Raymond, Jillynne *literature and language educator*
Raymond, Kristina Lynn *special education educator*
Reams, Patricia Lynn *retired elementary school educator*
Reckers, Michele Yvonne *director, secondary school educator*
Reczek, Claire E. *reading specialist*
Redding-Lowder, Christine Arnita *elementary school educator*
Reed, Brenda Kay *mathematics educator*
Reed, Susan J. *elementary school educator*
Reese, Jacquelyn L. *elementary school educator*
Reese, Linda Mae *elementary school educator*
Reeves, Lucy Mary *retired elementary school educator*
Regn Fraher, Bonnie *special education educator*
Rehnke, Mary Ann *academic administrator*
Reid, Helen Veronica *dean*
Reilly, Ellen Jane *elementary school educator*
Reinhard, Diane L. *retired university president*
Remes, Robin Eva *secondary school educator, cartographer*
Remley, Audrey Wright *retired academic administrator, psychologist*
Rench, Erin *elementary school educator*
Rent, Clyda Stokes *academic administrator*
Resnick, Beth Elena *special education educator*
Reynolds, Betty Ann *retired elementary school educator*
Reynolds, Rachelle Lynn *elementary school educator*
Reynolds, Wynetka Ann *academic administrator, educator*
Rice, Donna S. *educational administrator*
Rice, Patricia Oppenheim Levin *special education educator, consultant*
Rice-Jones, Annie May *retired secondary school educator*
Richardson, Elizabeth Wilson *middle school educator*
Richardson-Touson, F. Michelle *director*
Richter, Doris Louise *retired elementary school educator*
Ricketson, Mary E. *dean, lawyer, educator*
Rickson, Mary Jane *counseling administrator*
Ricks-Stanford, Hope Yvette *elementary school educator*
Riddle, Elsie Kathleen *elementary school educator, school librarian*
Riggio, Kerry Kerstin *elementary school worker, researcher*
Riha, Janet M. *elementary school educator*
Rimer, Beth A. *director*
Ringstead, Dee Ann *principal*
Rivero, Andria *education educator*
Roark, Mary Lou *educator, counselor*
Robb, Janet *secondary school educator*
Robbins, Jane Lewis *retired elementary school educator*
Robbins-O'Connell, Mindy *special education educator, consultant*
Roberts, Anne Margaret *secondary school educator*
Roberts, Karlene Ann *education educator*
Roberts, Kathleen Mary *retired school system administrator*
Roberts, Kathy Desmond *executive director educational facility*
Robinson, Elizabeth Leigh *special education educator*
Robinson, Nancy Nowakowski *academic administrator*
Robinson, Stephanie Nicole *education educator*
Robison, Sylvia Potter *retired academic administrator*
Robles, Rosalie Miranda *elementary school educator*
Rochelle, Dorothy *educational consultant*
Rochelle, Lugenia *academic administrator*
Rock, Jennifer Elizabeth *elementary school educator*
Rodewald, Nancy Beal *history educator*
Rodgers, Betty Jo *mathematics educator*
Rodgers, Cheryl L. *elementary school educator, small business owner*
Rodgers, Lois Eve *secondary school educator*
Rodriguez, Martha Jeanne *biology educator*
Rodriquez, Emily Kay *elementary school educator*
Roebuck, Judith Lynn *retired secondary school educator*
Roehlig, Nicole *elementary school educator*
Rog, Dorothy Ann *elementary school educator*
Rogers, Olivia Johnson *elementary school counselor*
Rohlfing, Dorlee Clark *school system administrator, educator*
Roller, Jeanne Keeney *education educator*
Roller, Pamela Jo *elementary school educator*
Rook-Nykrin, Mary Carol *special education educator*
Roome, Kristine Ann *college administrator*
Root, Janet Greenberg *private school educator*
Rosales-Said, Marta Milagros *elementary school educator*
Rosander, Lynda Sue *elementary school educator*
Rose, Tessie E. *special education educator, consultant*
Rose, Tracey Anne *education educator*
Rosenberg-Cortes, Stefanie Deanne *secondary school educator*
Rosof, Patricia J.F. *retired secondary school educator*
Ross, Donna Denice *elementary school educator*
Ross, Juliette *mathematics educator*
Ross, Susan E. *elementary school educator*
Rossetti, Rosemarie *writer, publisher, speaker, consultant*
Rostocil, Kelly Ann *secondary school educator, coach*
Roth, Aimee Elizabeth *secondary school educator, athletic trainer*
Rothermund, Cathy Lou *elementary school educator*
Roumbos, Maria K. *elementary school educator*
Routson, Mary A. *special education educator*
Rowell, Barbara Caballero *retired academic administrator*
Rozario Stewart, Gwendolyn Michelle *elementary school educator*
Ruffalo, Maria Therese *secondary school educator*
Ruhlig, Shelby Maria *secondary school educator*
Ruiz Diaz, Carolyn Ann *secondary school educator*
Russell, Florence L. *elementary school educator*
Russell, Joyce Ann *secondary school educator, librarian*
Russell, Louise *education educator*
Russell, Sharon Lynn *educational consultant*
Rutgard, Lorraine Levin *hearing impaired educator*
Rutledge, Patsy Leith *educational specialist*
Ryan, Ione Jean Alohilani Rathburn *retired education educator, counselor*
Saenz, Cecilia Sonia *education educator*
Saenz, Silvia Patricia *special education educator*
Sainclivier, Annamaria Tambone *elementary school educator*
St. Germain, Carol Ann *secondary educator*
Salerno, Laura Ann *elementary school educator*
Sales, Catherine *special education educator*
Samec, Diane Patricia *retired elementary school educator*
Sampson, Donna Rene *mathematics educator*
Samson, Wanda Kay *retired secondary school educator, consultant*
Samuelson, Linda J. *special education educator*
Sanchez, Alita Cassandra *physical education educator, personal trainer*
Sanders, Bessie Elaine *secondary school educator*
Sandstead, Auriel J. *retired secondary school educator, researcher, historian*
Sandwell, Kristin Ann *special education educator*
Saranac, Winnie B. *special education educator, educator*
Savage, Kim I. *academic administrator*
Savercool, Susan Elisabeth *elementary school educator*
Savoie, Allison Marie *secondary school educator*
Savory, Elaine *education educator*
Sawin, Therese Lynn *elementary school educator*
Sawyer, Diane Jane *education educator*
Sawyer, Lorraine McPherson *secondary school educator*
Scarborough, Ann Barlow *secondary school educator*
Schaefer, Lois Alma *special education educator*
Schaefer, Margaret F. *secondary school educator*
Schiewe, Misti D. *secondary school educator*
Schinderling, Sandra *mathematics educator*
Schlitz, Stephanie Ann *adult education educator*
Schmid, Michelle Louise *elementary school educator*
Schmidt, Diane *retired elementary school educator*
Schmidt, Ruth Ann *retired academic administrator*
Schmith, Rosalie LaVerne *special education educator*
Schneider, Mary Louise *retired elementary school educator*
Schon, Sandra Diane *elementary school educator*
Schrage, Rose *retired academic administrator*
Schreck-Rosen, Ellen Elizabeth *special education educator*
Schroeder, Beth Ellan *school counselor*
Schultz, Elizabeth Frances *elementary school educator*
Schultz, Susan D. *gifted and talented educator*
Schumacher, Cynthia Jo *retired elementary and secondary education educator*
Schuster, Carol Joyce *special education educator, consultant*
Schuster, Sylvia M. *education educator*
Schwartz, Eleanor Brantley *academic administrator*
Scott, Danelle Kay *secondary school educator*
Scott, Gloria Randle *former college president*
Scott, Jennifer Marie *special education educator*
Scott, Juanita *elementary school educator*
Sedgwick, Shannell Angela *elementary school educator, advocate*
Segreto, Linda Mary Janeczek *special education educator*
Seigler, Elizabeth Middleton *retired counseling administrator*
Seiler, Bonnie *academic administrator*
Sell, LeeLou *retired elementary school educator*
Sellers, Marjorie Stevenson *retired principal*
Sergesketter, Sarah Kay Kuntz *elementary school educator*
Servidio, Barbara J. *mathematics educator, science educator*
Sevick, Suzanne *secondary school educator*
Sewell, Amy J. *elementary school educator*
Sexton, Charline *secondary school educator*
Sexton, Cheryl Booth *secondary school educator*
Shaffer, Shirley Pollack *secondary school educator, sales executive*
Shanahan, Eileen Frances *retired secondary school educator*
Shavender, Marilyn Faye *retired elementary school educator*
Shaw, Lisa Marie *secondary school educator*
Shead, Mary Airthrlodios *elementary school educator*
Shellman-Lucas, Elizabeth C. *special education educator, researcher*
Shepard, Christy J. *special education educator*
Sherrick, Rebecca Louise *academic administrator*
Shiffer, Lorena Annette *secondary school educator, artist*
Shillingford, Pamela Lynn *mathematics educator*
Shin, Rose Yukino *elementary school educator*
Shore, Eleanor Gossard *retired medical school dean*
Shoun, Ellen Llewellyn *retired secondary school educator*
Showalter, Deanna Jo *secondary school educator*
Shugart, Jill *academic administrator*
Shutler, Mary Elizabeth *academic administrator*
Sibo, Elsa Lynette *secondary school educator*
Sich, Gloria Jean *elementary school educator*
Siddeeq, Baiyinah Nawal Rubye *secondary school educator*
Silverhart, Joy E. *retired elementary school educator*
Simmons, Barbara Louise *school system administrator, language educator*
Simmons, Lynda Merrill Mills *retired principal*
Simms, Adrienne Elaine *pre-school educator, consultant*
Simons, Lynn Osborn *educational consultant*
Singh-Knights, Doolarie *education educator*
Sirtak, Melissa Anne *mathematics educator*
Smallwood, Virginia N. *special education educator*
Smeltzer, Kathy Ann *mathematics educator*
Smith, Alice Davis *retired biology and art educator*
Smith, Carol C. *elementary school educator*
Smith, Debbie Ilee Randall *elementary school educator*
Smith, Lois C. *university administrator*
Smith, Martha Virginia Barnes *retired elementary school educator*
Smith, Sarah T. *educational specialist*
Smith Long, Caryn LeAnn *elementary school educator*
Smulyan, Lisa *educator*
Snell, Courtney Lynn *academic administrator*
Snell, Jennifer Lynn *literature and language educator*
Snell, Vicki L. *chemistry and physics educator*
Snider, Beverly Annette *mathematics educator*
Sobel, Faye Walton *elementary school educator*
Solberg, Amy Kathleen *director*
Somville, Marilyn F. *retired dean*
Southworth, Jamie MacIntyre *retired education educator*
Spallone, Sharon Lee *secondary school educator*
Spears, Gina Marie *elementary school educator*
Spellman, Elizabeth May *education administrator*
Spencer, JoAnn Nora *retired education educator*
Spencer, Lisa Ann *special education educator*
Spencer Chappell, Pinkie Mae *secondary school educator, actress*
Spillane, Barbara Ann *secondary school educator*
Spomer, Penny Sue *elementary school educator*
Spry, Barbara Diane *elementary school educator*
Stabinsky, Jean *elementary school educator*
Stacey, Susan Stephanie *education administrator*
Stafford, Rebecca *retired academic administrator, sociologist, consultant*
Stahl, Anne Louise *statistics educator, researcher*
Stalker, Jacqueline D'Aoust *academic administrator, educator*
Stalnaker, Judith Ann *education educator*
Stalvey, Cheryl B. *elementary school educator*
Stapleton, Romayne Huczek *secondary school educator*
Stark, Joan Scism *education educator*
Starnes, Susan Smith *elementary school educator*
Stea, Mary Lucille *secondary school educator*

Stearns, Susan A. *education educator*
Steele, Joan Dorothy *retired academic administrator*
Stefanek, Megan Lynn *elementary school educator*
Stein, Amy Renee *elementary school educator*
Steinberg, Joan Emily *retired secondary school educator*
Steiner, Janet Joy *educational consultant*
Stephansen, Stephanie *elementary school educator*
Stephens, Amy E. *middle school educator*
Stephens, Nichele Wiliams *elementary school educator, assistant principal*
Stephenson, Catherine *education educator*
Stepnick, Arlene Alice *nursing education administrator*
Stevens, Amy *history educator*
Stevens, Katherine *secondary school educator*
Stewart, Idalee Adel *educational administrator, consultant*
Stewart, Lucille Marie *retired special education coordinator, educator*
Stewart Tyler, Vivian DeLois *primary school educator*
Stickles, Paula Renee *mathematics educator*
Stilwell, Cynthia Ann *secondary school educator*
Stirl, Wilma Jean *mathematics educator*
Stockman, Carole Ann *elementary school educator*
Stout, Leeann Marie *secondary school educator*
Straumanis, Joan *academic administrator, consultant*
Street, Lela Kathryn *retired secondary education educator*
Stried, Jessica Nicole *elementary school educator*
Stringham, Amy *secondary school educator*
Stromback, Mary Beth *secondary school educator*
Studer-Rabeler, Karen Elizabeth *director*
Studley, Michelle *mathematics educator*
Suber, Dianne Boardley *educational administrator*
Sullivan, Glenda Lee *secondary school educator*
Sullivan, Sister Sharon *education educator*
Summar, Sharon Kay *retired elementary school educator*
Summors, Alma C. *principal*
Suppa-Friedman, Janice DeStefano *secondary school educator, consultant*
Sutter, Dawn Marie *special education educator*
Sutton, Julia Zeigler *retired special education educator*
Sutton-Creech, Donna Lynn *gifted and talented educator*
Swanson, Patricia Klick *retired academic administrator, retired foundation administrator*
Sweeney, Colleen Lauren *elementary school educator*
Sweeney, Kathleen P. *special education educator*
Swenson, Michele Ann *middle school educator*
Symons, Barbara Adele Schalk *academic administrator, counselor*
Tabandera, Kathlynn Rosemary *secondary school educator*
Tagliaferri, Rebecca Anne *mathematics educator*
Takenaga, Diana Yayoi *elementary school educator*
Talbot-Ross, Tiffany Lyn *secondary school educator*
Tanner, Laurel Nan *education educator*
Tapia, Jo-Di Lynn *secondary school educator*
Taulbee, Dianne R. *special education administrator*
Taylor, Charlotte Nicole *literature and language educator*
Taylor, Mary Lee *retired college administrator*
Tebout, Wynta Barbara *elementary school educator*
Tellez, Laura Lynn *elementary school educator*
Terada, Alice Masae *retired elementary school educator*
Tercero, Stephanie Tavarez *biology educator*
Terry, Mitzi H. *secondary school educator*
Tharp, Mary Therese *middle school educator*
Thaxton, Jessie J. *elementary school educator*
Thiede, Elena M. *elementary school educator*
Thomas, Beverly Irene *special education educator, counseling administrator, educational diagnostician*
Thomas, Beverly T. *education educator*
Thomas, Denise M. *chemistry educator, director*
Thomas, Martha S. *secondary school educator*
Thomas, Sara Alice Folger *school librarian, curator*
Thomas, Sherasa Malone *secondary school educator*
Thomason, Amy Lynn *history educator*
Thompson, Carla Anne *literature and language educator*
Thompson, Deborah G. *secondary school educator*
Thompson, Ramona Kay *special education educator*
Thompson, Tracy Ann *mathematics educator*
Thornton, Pauline Cecilia Eve Marie Suzanne *special education educator*
Thrift, Julianne Still *academic administrator*
Tidwell, Kathy *literature and language educator*
Tiemann, Barbara Jean *special education educator*
Tiemann, Karen *elementary school educator*
Tietze, Martha Katherine *secondary school educator*
Tilley, Christine Lynn *secondary school educator*
Timm, Nicolette Dee *special education educator*
Timmons, Sharon L. *retired elementary school educator*
Tingey, JoAnna *secondary school educator, mathematician*
Tobias, Judy *university development executive*
Todaro, Molly Ann *secondary school educator*
Tonjes, Marian Jeannette Benton *education educator*
Tooker, Michelle *secondary school educator*
Toomey, Paula Kathleen *special education educator, educational technologist, consultant*
Toro-Gabrys, Patricia *secondary education educator, artist*
Torres, Arelis *elementary school educator*
Touhill, Blanche Marie *retired academic administrator, historian, educator*
Tozzi, Deborah Frances *elementary school educator*
Tranzor, Tina *elementary school educator*
Trettin, Rosemary Elizabeth *secondary school educator*
Tripple, Amy Colleen *elementary school educator*
Trow, Jo Anne Johnson *retired university official*
Trusdell, Mary Louise Cantrell *retired academic administrator*
Tsoodle-Marcus, Charlene *education educator, school system administrator*
Tucker, Rochelle *special education educator*
Tucker-Keto, Claudia A. *academic administrator*
Tuggle, Connie Kersey *biology educator, department chairman*
Tulbert, Carrie Ann *literature and language educator, gifted and talented educator*
Tully, Catherine L. *physical educator instructor*
Turk, Rosemary Eileen *mathematics educator*
Turnau, Vivian Williamson *retired literature and language educator*
Turner, Madeline *elementary school educator*
Tydlacka, Patricia Ann *retired elementary school educator*
Ubel, Olive Jane *retired secondary school educator*
Uehling, Barbara Staner *academic administrator*
Ulen, Gene Eldridge *elementary school educator*
Ungar, Roselva May *primary and elementary school educator*
Upson, Jeannine Martin *retired academic administrator*
Uribe, Laura Beth *elementary school educator*
Usher, Nancy Spear *retired language arts educator*
Vaerst, Wendy Karen *secondary school educator*
Vahlkamp, Marianne Hill *retired elementary school educator*
Vail, Mary Beth *retired secondary school educator*
Vail, Nancy L. Scott *retired elementary school educator, artist*
Valentine, Phyllis Louise *counseling administrator*
Valentini, Virginia Redd *audio-visual specialist, educator*
Vanbrocklin, Vicki M. *secondary school educator*
VanBuren, Carolyn Jean *special education educator*
Vandersypen, Rita DeBona *counseling and academic administrator*
Van Dover, Karen *elementary school educator, consultant*
Vanica, Kristena L. *principal*
Van Sickle, Barbara Ann *special education educator*
Van Wettering, Carolyn *elementary school educator*
Vaughn, Cynthia Stark *elementary school educator*
Vergez, Sandra S. *retired secondary school educator*
Veverka, Ruth Tonry *retired secondary school educator*
Vinson, Deborah *secondary school educator, speaker*
Vliet, Donna Love *education educator*
Voehringer, Heidi L. *history educator*
Volkering, Mary Joe *retired special education educator*
Volpe, Eileen Rae *retired special education educator*
Volz, Annabelle Wekar *learning disabilities educator, consultant*
Vumbaco, Brenda J. *elementary school educator*
Waddell, Sarah Katherine *elementary school educator*
Wagner, Christina Irene *elementary school educator*
Wagner, Marilyn Faith *retired elementary school educator*
Wagner Chappelear, Maria *director*
Waites, Trina Sularin *history educator*
Wake, Judith Ann Van Buren *secondary school educator*
Walker, Amal Khawam *elementary school educator*
Walker, Annette *retired counseling administrator*
Walker, Athena Marie *secondary school educator*
Walker, Carolyn Mae *retired secondary school educator*
Walker, Diane *assistant principal*
Walker, Dori *biology educator*
Walker, Pamela *mathematics educator*
Walker, Patricia Sines *elementary school educator*
Walker-LaRose, Linda Waleska *elementary school educator*
Wall, Sherry Hodges *elementary school educator*
Wallace, Ardelia Leslene *elementary school educator*
Wallace, Bertha *retired elementary school educator*
Wallen, Shelia Renee *counseling administrator, educator*
Wallentine, Kathie Jo *special education educator*
Waller, Eunice McLean *retired elementary school educator*
Walsh, Merideth A. *secondary school educator, director*
Walters, Erica Scheffler *special education educator*
Walton, Jennifer Rebecca *middle school educator*
Ware, Gwendolyn C. *retired counseling administrator*
Warian, Christine Barbara *elementary school educator*
Warmack, Wanda Lucile *education educator*
Warner, Rosemarie *elementary school educator*
Warrior, Della C. *academic administrator, art educator*
Washburn, Harriet Caroline *secondary school educator*
Washington, Michele *educational consultant*
Waters, Jessica L. *elementary school educator, psychologist*
Waters Barham, Treva Ruth *director*
Watkins, Cheryl Denise *special education educator*
Watkins, Esther Sherrod *secondary school educator, school librarian*
Watson, Patricia Pullums *school system administrator*
Wattoff, Elizabeth *special education educator*
Watts, Karen Young *mathematics educator*
Watts, Mary Ann *retired elementary school educator*
Wean, Karla Denise *secondary school educator*
Weaver, Tanya Lea *elementary school educator*
Webb, Linda Kay *elementary school educator*
Weber, Elizabeth Ann *academic administrator, music educator*
Weber, Grace T. *school system administrator*
Weber, Marilyn Ann *history educator*
Weeks, Lori D. *elementary school educator*
Wehn, Karen Swaney *education educator, consultant*
Weinstein, Deena *sociology professor*
Weisbrod, Tara Lynn *secondary school educator*
Weller, Debra Anne *elementary school educator*
Wells, Cathy Eckard *elementary school educator*
Wengerd, Carol Joyce *mathematics educator*
Wentworth, LaVerne Wellborn *university program coordinator*
Werley, Annmarie *secondary school educator*
Werley, Kelly *secondary school educator*
Werra, Donna *elementary school educator*
West, Marjorie Edith *former elementary education educator*
Westberry, Jenny Rebecca *elementary school educator*
Westerberg, Mary L. *retired secondary school educator*
Wheat, Sheree Renee *elementary school educator*
Wheeler-Happ, Darra Anne *secondary school educator*
White, Dawn Marie *elementary school educator*
White, Florence May *retired special education educator*
White, Leandres *history educator*
White, Melinda Elois *retired elementary school educator*
White, Pamela Jo *elementary school educator*
Whitelo, Velma Holland *special education educator*
Whiteside, Karen Sowards *mathematics educator*
Whitney, Marilyn Louise *elementary school educator*
Whittaker, Lynn Marie *elementary school educator*
Whittington-Brown, Vanessa Elizabeth *secondary school educator*
Whitworth, Peggy Agnes *special education educator, consultant*
Wickiewicz, Jessica-Lauren Charlotte *academic administrator*
Wiggins, Karen Sue *education educator, counselor*
Wilkening, Laurel Lynn *academic administrator, aerospace scientist*
Willett, Jane S. *biology educator*
Willey, Frieda Anders *adult education educator*
Williams, Adella Judith *elementary education educator*
Williams, Bobbretta M. *educational company executive*
Williams, Candice L. *special education educator*
Williams, Charlotte Edwina *secondary school educator, real estate manager*
Williams, Cheryl A. *secondary school educator*
Williams, Jessica April *elementary school educator*
Williams, Lisa A. *special education educator*
Williams, Nettie *retired childcare facility administrator*
Williams, Patricia Badia *retired counseling administrator*
Williams, Sheila A.T. *elementary school educator, consultant*
Williams, Thelma B. *retired principal*
Willingham, Janice Ann *secondary school educator*
Willis, Burdena *director*
Willis, Emma K. *mathematics educator*
Willis, Lani Tyler *elementary school educator*
Wilmot, Evelyn Miller *elementary school educator*
Wilson, Annette Sigrid *elementary school educator*
Wilson, Carolyn Ross *retired school system administrator*
Wilson, Cheryl Yvonne *elementary and secondary school educator*
Wilson, Donna Mae *academic administrator, language educator*
Wilson-Jones, Linda *guidance counselor*
Wimmer, Kathryn *retired elementary school educator*
Windward, Shirley *secondary school educator, poet*
Wingston-Jenkins, Mary Allyson *secondary school educator*
Winiecki, Alyssa *elementary school educator*
Winkie, Dusti Kai *director*
Winter-Neighbors, Gwen Carole *special education educator, art educator, consultant*
Wisely, Donna *secondary school educator, athletic trainer*
Wisniewski, Rosemary *mathematics educator*
Witoshynsky, Ruth Ellen *mathematics educator*
Wittenstein, Shirley Ann *retired branch assistant*
Wittnebel, Melissa Eileen *elementary school educator, music educator*
Wittner, Lois *education educator*
Wolfe, Claudette Tobin *elementary school educator*
Wolfe, Sandra Jean *elementary school educator*
Wolfe, Susan McNeill *elementary education educator, guidance counselor*
Wolfhagen, Helen Jane *education educator*
Wolford, Carol D. *special education educator*
Wood, Margo *academic administrator*
Woodard, Anitra Denise *elementary school educator*
Woodard, Sharon M. *secondary school educator*
Woodruff, Mary Brennan *elementary school educator*
Woods, Linda W. *literature and language educator*
Woods, Susanne *academic administrator, educator*
Woodsworth, Anne *retired academic administrator, librarian*
Woodward, Debbie Carol *special education educator*
Woolston, Carol Ann *elementary school educator*
Woolworth, Susan Valk *primary school educator*
Workman, Kayleen Marie *special education and adult education educator*
Worley, Debere *educational consultant*
Wortham, Deborah Lynne *principal*
Wright, Ellen S. *elementary school educator*
Wright, Peggy Sue Espy *elementary school educator*
Wuchte, Mia Ann *elementary school educator*
Wuthrick, Eileen B. *special education educator*
Wymer, Barbara Sue *elementary school educator*
Yancey, Victoria Francine *education educator*
Yeager, Toni Lee *special education educator, real estate manager*
Yitts, Rose Marie *nursery school executive*
Yoder, Sharon Kathleen *educator*
Yolango, Marlene Fanning *special education educator*
Young, Natalie Jane *elementary special education educator*
Young, Teresa Gail Hilger *retired adult education educator*
Youngs, Diane Campfield *learning disabilities specialist, educator*
Zachary, Je'Quita Yvette *elementary school educator, singer*
Zager, Dianne E. *special education educator*
Zahn, Laura Sue Noyes *educational consultant, small business owner*
Zahner Kraeft, Dorothy Simkin *elementary school educator, school librarian*
Zaragoza, Rylee Renee *elementary school educator*
Zeilinger, Elna Rae *elementary school educator, gifted and talented educator*
Zephier, Jenny Renee *elementary school educator*
Zimmermann, Bonnie *physical and health education educator*
Zito, Rae Nanette *elementary school educator*
Zurenda, Deb *biology educator*
Zwicke, Paula Ann *literature and language educator, communications educator*

ENGINEERING

UNITED STATES

ALABAMA

Huntsville
Cruit, Wendy *mechanical engineer*

ARIZONA

Tempe
Papandreou-Suppappola, Antonia *electrical engineering educator*

ARKANSAS

Little Rock
Bourgeois, Sharon E. *mechanical engineer*

CALIFORNIA

Belmont
Hollis, Mary Frances *aerospace educator*

Diamond Bar
Mirisola, Lisa Heinemann *air quality engineer*

Edwards
Regenie, Vicki *systems engineer*

El Segundo
Hsia, Irene Yee *electrical engineer*

Fullerton
Tehrani, Fleur Taher *electrical engineer, educator, researcher*

Los Altos
Roylance, Lynn Michelle *electrical engineer*

Los Angeles
Barone, Sherry Joy *test engineer*
Chang, Jane P. *chemical engineering educator*
Dragan, Alexandra *mechanical engineer, consultant, environmental engineer, researcher, engineering educator*
Mataric, Maja J. *engineering educator*
Tabrizi, Lili H. *electrical engineer, educator*

Menlo Park
Perlman, Radia *communications engineer*

Moffett Field
Bualat, Maria G. *computer engineer*
Hubbard, Kim *computer engineer*
Luna, Bernadette *mechanical engineer*

Palos Verdes Estates
Yarbrough, Allyson Debra *electrical engineer*

Pasadena
Effros, Michelle *electrical engineer, engineering educator*
Muñoz Fernández, Michela *electrical engineer, researcher*
Smolke, Christina *chemical engineer*
Stroupe, Ashley W. *engineer*

Pleasanton
Novak, Randi Ruth *systems engineer, computer scientist*

San Diego
Day, Valerie Marian *mechanical engineer*

San Francisco
Kammerer, Ann Marie *geotechnical engineer*

San Jose
Ma, Xing *optical engineer*
Papalias, Tamara Ahrens *electrical engineer, educator*

Stanford
Tomlin, Claire J. *aeronautical engineer, educator*
Zhou, Ping *physical engineer*

Temecula
Bathaee, Soussan *engineering technician*

Thousand Oaks
Zhou, Sophia Huai *biomedical engineering scientist*

Torrance
Sorstokke, Susan Eileen *systems engineer*

COLORADO

Boulder
Anseth, Kristi S. *tissue engineer, educator*
Murnane, Margaret Mary *engineering and physics educator*

Highlands Ranch
Brierley, Corale L. *geological and biomining engineer*

Loveland
Nossaman, Marian Alecia *manufacturing engineering executive*

CONNECTICUT

New Haven
Lavik, Erin *chemical engineer*

Stratford
Blair, Sylvia H. *aerospace engineer*

DELAWARE

Newark
Dean, Krysten *manufacturing engineer*

DISTRICT OF COLUMBIA

Washington
Cleave, Mary L. *environmental engineer, former astronaut*
Freund, Deborah Miriam *transportation engineer*
Powell, Margaret Ann Simmons *computer engineer*
Townsend, Marjorie Rhodes *aerospace engineer, engineering executive*

FLORIDA

Boca Raton
Pajunen, Grazyna Anna *electrical engineer, educator*
Zhong, Dawn He *materials engineer*

Jacksonville
Vasana, Susan (Chun-Ye) *engineering educator*

Kennedy Space Center
Alfonso, Berta *computer engineer*
Amos, Michelle *electronics engineer*

Lakeland
Garrott, Frances Carolyn *architectural engineer*

Miami
Gonzalez, Ivette *biomedical engineer*

Orlando
Bauer, Maria Casanova *computer engineer*

Tampa
Ghiu, Silvana Melania Stefania *process and development engineer*

GEORGIA

Alpharetta
Salay, Cindy Rolston *systems engineer*

Atlanta
Pritchett, Amy R. *aerospace engineer, educator*

Clarkston
Ehrlich, Margaret Isabella Gorley *systems engineer, mathematics professor, consultant*

Fairburn
Johnston, Carolyn Judith *construction engineer*

Marietta
Eggersman, Denise *computer engineer, educator*

Norcross
Holtzman, Mary *engineering company executive*

Robins Afb
Manley, Nancy Jane *environmental engineer*

Senoia
Griffin, Tammy Lynn *industrial engineer*

ILLINOIS

Chicago
Fahnestock, Jean Howe *retired civil engineer*

Evanston
Weertman, Julia Randall *materials engineering educator*

INDIANA

Indianapolis
Powers, Doris Hurt *retired engineering company executive*

West Lafayette
Hambrusch, Susanne *computer engineering educator*
Jamieson, Leah H. *engineering educator*
Katehi, Linda P.B. *engineering educator*
Taber, Margaret Ruth *retired engineering technology educator*

KANSAS

Overland Park
Daniel, Karen *engineering and design company executive*

KENTUCKY

Lexington
Campbell, Zenita A. D. *environmental engineer, educator, safety engineer*

LOUISIANA

New Orleans
O'Connor, Kim Claire *chemical engineering and biotechnology educator, researcher*

MARYLAND

Baltimore
Apsel, Alyssa *electrical engineer, computer engineer*
Busch-Vishniac, Ilene Joy *mechanical engineering educator, researcher*

College Park
Lathan, Corinna Elisabeth *aerospace engineer*

Columbia
Narvaez, Bernice Williams *process engineer, consultant*

Greenbelt
Amato, Deborah Douglass *aerospace engineer*
Cooper, Sharon Croft *aerospace engineer*
Ericsson, Aprille *aerospace engineer*

Rockville
Abron, Lilia A. *chemical engineer*

MASSACHUSETTS

Burlington
Greiner, Helen *mechanical engineer*

Cambridge
Barnhart, Cynthia *engineering educator, researcher*
Belcher, Angela *engineering educator*
Boyce, Mary C. *mechanical engineer, educator*
Drake, Elisabeth Mertz *chemical engineer, consultant*
Griffith, Linda G. (Linda Griffith-Cima) *biomedical engineer, chemical engineer, educator*
Jeremijenko, Natalie H.M. *design engineer, educator, artist*
Newman, Dava Jean *aerospace engineering educator, director*
Samson, Leona D. *biological engineering educator, research center director*
Smith, Amy B. *mechanical engineer, educator*

Framingham
Lindsay, Leslie *packaging engineer*

Medford
Abriola, Linda Marie *civil engineer, environmental engineer*

Wilmington
Raven, Linda F. *mechanical engineer*

Worcester
Plummer, Jeanine D. *engineering educator*

MICHIGAN

Ann Arbor
Holland, Jean Elinor *computer engineer, consultant*
Kearfott, Kimberlee Jane *nuclear engineer, educator, health physicist*

Auburn Hills
Boyle, Olabisi Ariyo *manufacturing engineer*

Dearborn
Linnansalo, Vera *engineer*
Wang, Liyan *product design engineer*

Farmington Hills
Hurd, Mary K. *civil engineer, writer*

Shelby Township
Osuch, Debra K. *materials engineer*

MINNESOTA

Champlin
Lim, Joalin Peck-Kian *biomedical engineer, researcher*

Grand Marais
Napadensky, Hyla Sarane *engineering consultant*

MISSOURI

Kansas City
Leigh, Cheri J. *engineering consulting executive*

Saint Louis
Olsen, Tava Maryanne Lennon *industrial and operations engineering educator*
She, Manjuan *chemical engineer, food research scientist*
Shrauner, Barbara Wayne Abraham *electrical engineer, educator*

NEW HAMPSHIRE

Durham
Kinner, Nancy E. *civil engineer, educator, environmental engineer, researcher*

Wolfeboro
Hutchins, Carleen Maley *acoustical engineer, consultant*

NEW JERSEY

Florham Park
Rexford, Jennifer *communications engineer*

Princeton
Gmachl, Claire *electrical engineer, educator*
Leonard, Naomi Ehrich *aerospace engineer, engineering educator*

Skillman
Brill, Yvonne Claeys *engineer, consultant*

NEW MEXICO

Santa Fe
Kaman, Helen S. *retired aerospace engineer, artist*

NEW YORK

Astoria
Unsal-Tunay, Nuran *geological engineer, researcher*

Buffalo
Zirnheld, Jennifer L. *engineering educator, researcher*

Farmingdale
Issapour, Marjaneh *engineering educator, consultant*

Rochester
Niznik, Carol Ann *electrical engineer, educator, consultant*

South Bethlehem
Shirikian-Hesselton, Joan Lee *safety engineer*

Syracuse
Carrier, Terriruth *industrial engineer*

Utica
Dussault, Heather M.B. *electrical engineer, researcher*

NORTH CAROLINA

Chapel Hill
Lucas, Carol Lee *biomedical engineer*

Hendersonville
Kingsbury, Carolyn Ann *aerospace engineer, craftsman, writer*

Raleigh
Nelson, Cynthia Kaye *infrastructure security engineer*

Smithfield
Shumate, Donna Larsen *engineering educator, department chairman*

OHIO

Chandlersville
Herron, Janet Irene *retired industrial engineer*

Cincinnati
Curran, Mary Ann *chemical engineer*
Isburgh, Anne Marie *engineering manager*
Narmoneva, Daria *engineering educator*

Cleveland
Dever, Joyce *materials engineer*
Reveley, Mary *aeronautical engineer*

Columbus
Ozkan, Umit Sivrioglu *chemical engineering professor*

Youngstown
Kenner, Marilyn Sferra *civil engineer*

OKLAHOMA

Tulsa
Cardwell, Sandra Gayle Bavido *engineering company executive*

OREGON

Forest Grove
Ginn, Sharon Patrick *mechanical engineer*

PENNSYLVANIA

Beaver Falls
Miller, Kathleen S. *project engineer*

Philadelphia
Walker, Danielle *engineering executive*

University Park
Irwin, Mary Jane *engineering educator*
Todd Copley, Judith A. *engineering educator*

Villanova
Fleischer, Amy *mechanical engineer, educator*

Wallingford
Parker, Jennifer Ware *chemical engineer, researcher*

SOUTH CAROLINA

Greenville
Stoller, Patricia Sypher *structural engineer, executive*

SOUTH DAKOTA

Brookings
Hall, Teresa Joanne Keys *manufacturing engineer, educator*

Rapid City
Zhang, Nian *engineering educator*

TENNESSEE

Tullahoma
Hill, Susan Sloan *safety engineer*

TEXAS

Austin
Brannon-Peppas, Lisa *chemical engineer, researcher*
Johnson, Sandra K. *electrical engineer*
Loo, Lynn (Yueh-Lin) *chemical engineer*
Richards-Kortum, Rebecca Rae *biomedical engineering educator*

Beaumont
Mueller, Lisa Maria *chemical engineer*

Cat Spring
Ramsey, Mary Catherine *mechanical engineer, consultant*

College Station
Butler-Purry, Karen L. *electrical engineer, educator*
Lu, Mi *computer engineer, educator*

Dallas
Gaiotti, Regina *civil engineer, educator*
Sengupta, Chaitali *computer engineer*
Wang, Cong *electrical engineer*

Houston
Ehlig-Economides, Christine A. *petroleum engineer*
Gunsel, Selda *chemical engineer, researcher*
Halas, Naomi J. *nanoscale science and engineering educator*
Kavandi, Janet Lynn *aerospace power engineer, chemist*
Kiang, Ching-Hwa *chemical engineering educator*
Krumrey, Carolyn *mechanical engineer*
Noonan, Shauna Gay *petroleum engineer*

San Antonio
Fischer, Marsha Leigh *retired civil engineer*

San Marcos
Fischer, Joyce Faye *engineering educator*

Stafford
Le, Duy-Loan *electrical engineer*

Tyler
Walker, Alice R. *mechanical engineer*

UTAH

Brigham City
Tolle, Melinda Edith *engineer, researcher*

VERMONT

Rutland
Thompson, Marie Angela *computer engineer, consultant*

VIRGINIA

Alexandria
Rassai, Rassa *electrical engineering educator*

Chantilly
Austin, Wanda Murry *systems engineer*

Charlottesville
Pierce, Shayn *biomedical engineer, educator*
Soffa, Mary Lou *computer science and engineering educator*

Falls Church
Sveinsson, Linda Rodgers *engineering company executive*

Hampton
Martinez, Debbie *electronics engineer*
Williams-Byrd, Julie *electronics engineer*

Reston
Young, Janet Cheryl *electrical engineer*

Suffolk
Noblitt, Nancy Anne *aerospace engineer*

Warrenton
Gullace, Marlene Frances *systems engineer, consultant*

WASHINGTON

Bellingham
Graves, Vicki Lloyd *retired mechanical engineer*

Cle Elum
Galloway, Patricia Denese *civil engineer*

Olympia
Fleskes, Carol Lynn *environmental engineer*

Seattle
Coleman, Debra Lynn *electrical engineer*
Lidstrom, Mary E. *chemical engineering professor, microbiology professor*

Spokane
Nemetz Mills, Patricia Louise *engineering educator*

CANADA

BRITISH COLUMBIA

Vancouver
Salcudean, Martha Eva *mechanical engineer, educator*

ADDRESS UNPUBLISHED

Andrian-Ceciu, Roxanne R. *engineer, financial analyst*
Andrus, Sharon Arlene *electrical engineer, researcher*
Asadorian, Diana C. *electrical engineer, educator*
Baum, Eleanor *electrical engineering educator*
Bier, Karla *manufacturing engineer, chemical engineer, educator*
Brazil, Aine M. *engineering company executive*
Chretien, Carol Ann *chemical engineer*
Cross, Goldie K. *telecommunications engineer*
Cullingford, Hatice Sadan *chemical engineer*
Cummins, Nancyellen Heckeroth *electronics engineer*
Dargan, Pamela Ann *systems engineer, consultant*
Davis, Keigh Leigh *aerospace engineer*
Dennany, Kelly *mechanical engineer, test engineer*
Doríghi, Nancy S. *computer engineer*
Douglass, Susan Daniel *communications engineer, consultant*
Dunbar, Bonnie J. *engineer, astronaut*
Fitzroy, Nancy deLoye *engineering executive, mechanical engineer*
Harmon, Peggy W. *electronics engineer*
Hornby, Sara Ann *metallurgical engineer, marketing professional*
Ingram, Tressia M. *mechanical engineer*
Jacobson, Annette Moff *chemical engineer*
Jaska, Susan Park *retired radar systems engineer*
Johnson, Everlene *materials engineer*
Kesselring, Debbie Anne *systems engineer*
Killen, Kathleen Elizabeth *systems engineer, retired military officer*
Kimbriel-Eguia, Susan *engineering planner, small business owner*
Knight, Patricia Marie *biomedical engineer, consultant*
Lawrence, Kristine Guerra *project engineer*
Letcher, Naomi Jewell *quality engineer, educator, counselor*
Little, Margaret F. Dixon Lesniak *electrical engineer, educator*
Longobardo, Anna Kazanjian *engineering executive*
Lund, Rita Pollard *aerospace engineer, consultant*
Lyon, Martha Sue *research engineer, retired military officer*
Moon, Jane Anderson *systems engineer, consultant*
Moore, Fay Linda *systems engineer*
Morse, Terri Fraser *mechanical engineer*
Mramor, Marti *engineer, linguist*
Muhammad, LaTonja Walker *control engineer*
Murphy, Elisabeth Maria *physical design engineer, consultant*
Muszynska, Agnieszka (Agnes Muszynska) *mechanical engineering researcher, consultant*
O'Brien, K. Patricia *product development engineer*
Pedersen, Karen Sue *electrical engineer*
Phan, Christina *electronic analog design executive*
Richardson, Jean McGlenn *retired civil engineer*
Seldner, Betty Jane *environmental engineer, consultant, aerospace transportation executive*
Senior Morandi, Grace Esther *mechanical engineer*
Shaw, Judy Browder *engineer*
Siegal, Rita Goran *engineering company executive*
Sousa, Julie *biomedical engineer*
Stella, Marie Vita *retired engineer, consultant, homeland and information security*
Willis, Selene Lowe *electrical engineer, application developer, consultant, information technology manager*
Wu, Min *computer and electrical engineer*
Ying, Jackie *chemical engineer, educator*

FINANCE: BANKING SERVICES
See also **FINANCE: INVESTMENT SERVICES**

UNITED STATES

ALABAMA

Blountsville
Edwards, Sheila M. *banker, educator*

Montgomery
Wines, Lynne *bank executive*

ALASKA

Fairbanks
Heckman, Jyotsna (Jo) L. *bank executive*

ARIZONA

Glendale
Dixon-Nielsen, Judy E(arlene) *mortgage banker, marketing professional, consultant*

Phoenix
Jungbluth, Connie Carlson *banker*
Ralston, Barbara Jo *bank executive*
Richardson, Judy McEwen *investment banker, consultant, cartoonist*

Tucson
Bernmúdez, Carmen *trust company executive*

ARKANSAS

Little Rock
Franks, Candace Ann *bank executive*
Smith, Susan *bank executive*

CALIFORNIA

Beverly Hills
Cloyde, Jan R. *bank executive*

Carlsbad
Schmidt, Mary Louise Donnel *banker*

Carson
Davis, Carylon Lee *mortgage company executive, real estate broker*

City Of Industry
Contreras-Sweet, Maria *bank executive*

Danville
Strohl, Elizabeth G. *banker*

Goleta
Nahra, Lynda *bank executive*

Los Angeles
Thompson, Elizabeth *bank executive*

Oakland
Nelson, Shirley W. *bank executive*
Sandler, Marion Osher *bank executive*

Oxnard
North, Michelle *mortgage broker*

San Diego
McNeely, Delores *banker*
Yacovone, Ellen Elaine *banker*

San Francisco
August-deWilde, Katherine *banker*
Bourne, JoAnn M. *bank executive*
Braasch, Barbara Lynn *banker, consultant*
Callahan, Patricia R. *bank executive*
Gillette, Frankie Jacobs *retired savings and loan association executive, federal agency administrator, social worker*
Lee, Pamela Anne *bank executive, accountant, financial analyst*
Modjtabai, Avid *bank executive*
Tolstedt, Carrie L. *bank executive*
Woo Ho, Doreen *investment banker*
Yellen, Janet Louise *bank executive*

San Marino
Gouw, Julia Suryapranata *bank executive*

Santa Monica
Heimbuch, Babette E. *bank executive*

COLORADO

Brighton
Tyrrell-Meier, Cassandra B. *banker*

Denver
Orullian, B. LaRae *bank executive*

Georgetown
Hildebrandt-Willard, Claudia Joan *banker*

Palisade
Barnewall, Marilyn MacGruder *retired banker*

CONNECTICUT

New Haven
Patterson, Peyton R. *bank executive*

DELAWARE

Wilmington
Cohen, Betsy Z. *bank executive*

DISTRICT OF COLUMBIA

Washington
Bies, Susan Schmidt *bank executive*
Conlin, Linda Mysliwy *bank executive, former federal agency administrator*
Davis, Michele A. *mortgage company executive, former federal agency administrator*
St. John, Julie *mortgage company executive*

FLORIDA

Jacksonville
Hott, Peggy A. *mortgage banker*

Ormond Beach
Franchini, Roxanne *bank executive*

Saint Petersburg
Schefstad, Theresa *bank executive*

GEORGIA

Atlanta
Biggins, J. Veronica *bank executive*
Chau, Pin Pin *bank executive*
Hayworth, Laura *banker, real estate analyst*

Columbus
James, Elizabeth R. (Lee Lee James) *bank executive*

Flowery Branch
Monroe, Melrose *retired bank executive*

Kennesaw
Halwig, Nancy Diane *banker*

Silver Creek
Boylan, Tonya R. *banker, consultant*

HAWAII

Honolulu
Tanoue, Donna A. *bank executive, former federal agency administrator*

ILLINOIS

Chicago
Bates, Yasmin T. *bank executive*
Freund, Kristen P. *bank executive*
Hart, Pamela Heim *banker*
Lorenz, Katherine Mary *bank executive*
Tescher, Jennifer *bank executive*

Dundee
Weck Farrag, Kristin W. *bank executive*

Oak Park
McLaren, Ruth *bank executive*

Prospect Heights
Derickson, Sandy *bank executive*

INDIANA

Evansville
Standley, Sherrianne Maddox *bank executive*

IOWA

Cedar Rapids
Wax, Nadine Virginia *retired bank executive*

Des Moines
Heiden, Cara *mortgage company executive*

Mason City
Rodamaker, Marti Tomson *bank executive*

KANSAS

Coldwater
Adams, Elizabeth Herrington *banker*

Tonganoxie
Torneden, Connie Jean *banker*

Topeka
Wagnon, Joan *retired banker, retired mayor*

KENTUCKY

Georgetown
White, Mary Ann *bank executive*

Louisville
Thompson, Kathy C. *bank executive*

LOUISIANA

Lafayette
Hail, Karen L. *bank executive*

MAINE

Kennebunk
Boston, Lorraine *bank executive*

MARYLAND

Annapolis
Schleicher, Nora Elizabeth *bank executive, treasurer, accountant*

Baltimore
Massey, Garnetta D. *bank executive*

Bethesda
Drazin, Lisa *investment banker, financial consultant*

Frederick
Cannon, Faye E. *bank executive*

Glen Burnie
Hofmann, Carole P. *bank executive*

North East
Goldbach, Jennifer DeBerdine *bank executive*

MASSACHUSETTS

Boston
Bakhshi, Nandita *bank executive*
Bruce, Maryann *bank executive*
Minehan, Cathy Elizabeth *bank executive*
Swihart, Susannah M. *bank executive*

Medway
Montpelier, Pamela J. *bank executive*

Pittsfield
Fawcett, Gayle P. *bank executive*

Somerset
Lenz, Mary Lynn *bank executive*

West Wareham
Worrell, Cynthia Lee *bank executive*

MICHIGAN

Clarkston
Snow, Sandra Inez *mortgage company executive*

Grand Rapids
Van Dyke, Michelle *bank executive*

Grosse Pointe Park
Harmon, Phyllis Darnell *mortgage banker*

MINNESOTA

Minneapolis
Beechem, Kathleen *bank executive*
Carlson, Jennie Peaslack *bank executive*
Griffith, Sima Lynn *investment banker, consultant*
Thormodsgard, Diane *bank executive*

MISSOURI

Saint Louis
Bockenkamp, Karen Ann *bank administrator*
Bryant, Ruth Alyne *banker*

NEVADA

Las Vegas
Hansen, Janet M. *bank executive*

Reno
Flowers, Marguerita Denise *banker, educator*

NEW JERSEY

Bridgewater
DeMaio, Donnalee A. *bank executive*
DeMatteo, Gloria Jean *banker*

Jackson
Gasparro, Madeline *retired banker*

Jersey City
Kramer, Helene *banking executive*

Newton
Case, Tammy *bank executive*

Summit
Green, Meyra Jeanne *banker*

Trenton
Bakke, Holly C. *bank commission official*

NEW YORK

Albany
Dushensky, Jacqueline Amelia *banker, educator*

Long Island City
Markus, Maura *bank executive*

Melville
Drexel, Carolyn A. *bank executive*

New York
Alemany, Ellen R. *bank executive*
Armine, Cindy A. *bank executive*
Bains, Leslie Elizabeth *banker*
Barry, Nancy Marie *bank executive*
Christodoulou, Marilena *investment banker, finance company executive*
Deans, Patricia Herrmann *investment banker*
Dietz, Elizabeth Camilla *investment banker*
Drew, Ina R. *bank executive*
Duke, Ellen (Bebe Duke) *bank executive*
Erdoes, Mary Callahan *investment banker*
Eshleman, Diane Varrin *bank executive*
Flaherty, Pamela Potter *bank executive*
Godridge, Leslie V. *bank executive*
Greenthal, Jill A. *investment banker*
Howard, Bonnie *bank executive*
Hricik, Lorraine E. *bank executive*
Iskenderian, Mary Ellen *bank executive*
Keating, Catherine *bank executive*
Krawcheck, Sallie L. *bank executive*
Massingale, Faith L. *bank executive*
Myerberg, Marcia *investment banker*
Peetz, Karen B. *bank executive*
Peretsman, Nancy B. *investment banker*
Sevilla-Sacasa, Frances Aldrich *bank executive*
von Fraunhofer-Kosinski, Katherina *bank executive, advertising executive*
Wainwright, Cynthia Crawford *banker*
Webster, Lesley Daniels *bank executive*
Wright, Deborah C. *bank executive*

Rochester
Hanson, Karen Noble *financial holding company executive*

Yonkers
Singer, Cecile Doris *bank executive, former state legislator*

NORTH CAROLINA

Charlotte
Bessant, Cathy (Catherine Pombier Bessant) *bank executive, marketing professional*
Brinkley, Amy Woods *bank executive*
Clark, Ranjana B. *bank executive*
Davis, Jean E. *bank executive*
Desoer, Barbara J. *bank executive*
Dixon, Georgette (Gigi Dixon) *bank executive*
Erwin, Betty *bank executive*
Fornelli, Cynthia M. *bank executive*
McFayden, Shannon W. *bank holding company executive*
Nichols, Debra *bank executive*
Sutton, Cecilia (Cece Sutton) *bank executive*

Durham
Sylver, Donna *bank executive*

OHIO

Cleveland
Mooney, Beth *bank executive*
Pianalto, Sandra *bank executive*
Potter, Susan Kuniholm *bank executive*
Seifert, Shelley Jane *bank executive, human resources specialist*

Columbus
Arvia, Anne L. *bank executive*

New Albany
Page, Linda Kay *bank executive*

Newark
Wallace, Sarah Reese *banker*

OREGON

Bend
Moss, Patricia L. *bank executive*

Lake Oswego
McKay, Laura L. *bank executive, consultant*

PENNSYLVANIA

Pittsburgh
Gulley, Joan Long *banker*

State College
Koval, Donita R. *bank executive*

SOUTH CAROLINA

Columbia
Gasque, Diane Phillips *mortgage manager, marketing executive*

Greenwood
Boxx, Rita McCord *retired banker*

TEXAS

Houston
Ellis, Juliet S. *bank executive*
Foote, Jill *investment banker, educator*
Innes, Debbie *bank executive*
Thomas, M. Ann *bank executive*

Irving
Blankenship, Cynthia L. *bank executive*

New Braunfels
Pharis, Ruth McCalister *retired bank executive*

UTAH

Salt Lake City
Chillingworth, Lori *bank executive*
Kearns, Becky *bank executive*
Kirk, Diana E. *bank executive*
Linderman, LeeAnne B. *bank executive*

VIRGINIA

Arlington
Ochoa-Brillembourg, Hilda Margarita *investment banker*

Richmond
Simmons, Martha R. *mortgage company executive*

WASHINGTON

Everett
Nelson, Carol Kobuke *bank executive*

Port Angeles
McCormick, Karen Louise *savings and loan association executive*

Seattle
Sas, Ellen *bank executive*

Spokane
Horton, Susan Pittman *bank executive*
Stanley, Heidi *bank executive*

Tacoma
Dressel, Melanie *bank executive*

WISCONSIN

Milwaukee
Murphy, Judith Chisholm *trust company executive*
Wesner, Patricia *bank executive*

Sauk City
Lins, Debra R. *bank executive*

CANADA

ONTARIO

Toronto
Lawson, Jane Elizabeth *retired bank executive*
Patten, Rose *bank executive*

ENGLAND

London
Dial, Teresa *bank executive*

ADDRESS UNPUBLISHED

Baker, Lesliegh *bank executive, lawyer*
Beckles, Ingrid *mortgage banker*
Bryant, Betty Jean *bank executive*
Cottrell, Mary-Patricia Tross *bank executive*
Denham, Jill H. *bank executive*
Dublon, Dina *former bank executive*
Duke, Betsy (Elizabeth A. Duke) *bank executive*
Fahringer, Catherine Hewson *retired savings and loan association executive*
Fellenstein, Cora Ellen Mullikin *retired credit union executive*
Foss, Linda Judd *banker, lawyer*
Friars, Eileen M. *bank executive*
Furner, Bonita Baker *retired banker, consultant*
Gallagher, Lindy Allyn *banker, financial consultant*
Gillard, Beryl L. *mortgage company executive*
Graham, Cynthia Armstrong *banker*
Healy, Joyce Ann Kury *banker, marketing professional*
Helfer, Ricki Tigert *banking consultant*
Holcomb, Gene Ann *federal loan officer*
Kane Hittner, Marcia Susan *bank executive*
Kelly, Cleo Parker *retired bank executive*
Lagomasino, Maria Elena *retired bank executive*
Lantis, Donna Lea *retired banker, artist, art educator*
Lawer, Betsy *banker, small business owner, vintner, director*
Lipton, Susan Lytle *investment banker, lawyer*
Magner, Marjorie *former bank executive*
Metz, Patricia A. *retired bank executive*
Morris, Maureen Sauter *banker*
Morris, Tammy Kay *bank executive*
Parks, Grace Susan *bank executive*
Place, Janey *banking consultant, former bank executive*
Romero-Rainey, Rebeca *bank executive*
Salamone-Kochowicz, Jean Gloria *retired bank executive*
Schless, Phyllis Ross *investment banker*
Seeds, Sharon Lynn *bank processor*
Tatlock, Anne M. *trust company executive*
Walton, Alice Louise *bank executive*
Woodard, Nina Elizabeth *banker*
Worrell, Mary Thora *loan officer*

FINANCE: FINANCIAL SERVICES

UNITED STATES

ALABAMA

Decatur
Michelini, Sylvia Hamilton *auditor*

Headland
Woodham, Patricia H. *accounting and business consultant*

Huntsville
Stewart, Verlindsey Laquetta *accounting educator*

Jacksonville
Lewis, Deborah Alice *tax company executive, writer*

Tuscaloosa
Ray, Nelda Howton *financial consultant*

ALASKA

Elmendorf Afb
Fassler, Kerin Irene *accountant*

Kodiak
Steffey, A Kay *accountant*

ARIZONA

Sun City West
Schrag, Adele Frisbie *business education educator*

Tucson
Fajardo, Sarah Elizabeth Johnson *financial consultant*
Márquez-Peterson, Lea *business broker*
Villica—a, Taunya *corporate financial executive*

ARKANSAS

Hot Springs Village
Lihs, Marilyn Louise *retired accountant*

Little Rock
Conger, Cynthia Lynne *financial planner*
Waters, Zenobia Pettus *retired finance educator*

CALIFORNIA

Atwater
Duddy, Ethel Eileen (Eileen Duddy) *accountant*

Burbank
Sherbert, Sharon Debra *financial services executive*

Carmel
de Vos, Paula Francesca *finance company executive, investment advisor, consultant*

Claremont
Christian, Suzanne Hall *financial planner*

Covina
Cottrell, Janet Ann *controller*

Fairfield
Schunke, Hildegard Heidel *accountant*

Hollister
Grace, Bette Frances *certified public accountant*

Laguna Beach
Pories, Muriel H. *finance company executive*

Laguna Niguel
Bauer, Barbara A. *financial consultant*

Lakewood
Bogdan, Carolyn Louetta *financial specialist, retired small business owner*

Lincoln
Dorn, Mary Ann *retired auditor*

Los Angeles
Allen, Sharon *accounting firm executive*
Allen, Suzanne *financial planning executive, insurance agent, writer, educator*
Brown, Kathleen *diversified financial services company executive*
O'Brien, Rosanne P. *corporate financial executive*
Williams, Julie Ford *retired finance company executive, economist*

Martinez
Withrow, Sherrie Anne (Jimie Jean Pearl) *financial specialist*

Oakland
Randisi, Elaine Marie *accountant, educator, writer*

Oceanside
McIntyre, Louise S. *income tax consultant*

Palo Alto
Lundy, Jackelyn Ruth *financial consultant, economist, researcher*

Pasadena
Hunt, Hazel Analue Stanfield *retired accountant*

Pittsburg
Williams-Thomas, Elizabeth A. *financial planner, consultant*

Rancho Cucamonga
Horsley, Paula Rosalie *accountant*

Riverside
Macek, Pamela Kay *tax specialist, business executive*

Rosemead
Newton, Jo Ann Goddard *corporate financial executive*

Sacramento
Boekhoudt-Cannon, Gloria Lydia *finance educator*
Scholey, Diann Patricia *accountant*
Speir, Marcia Ann *retired accountant*
Wunder, Haroldene Fowler *taxation and international accounting educator*

Salinas
Sprude, Margaret *credit services company executive*

San Diego
Buska, Sheila Mary *controller, writer, columnist*
Drzewiecki, Darla Ruth *accountant*
Lucas, Eloisa B. *tax consultant, management consultant*

San Francisco
Jimenez, Josèphine Santos *portfolio manager*
Kahn, Linda McClure *actuary, consultant*
Richey, Ellen *credit card company executive*

San Marcos
Melcher, Trini Urtuzuastegui *retired finance educator*

San Ramon
King Hauser, Ann Marie B. *retired controller, artist, realtor*

Sherman Oaks
Ferguson, Lisa Beryl *accountant*

Stanford
Paté-Cornell, Marie-Elisabeth Lucienne *finance educator, engineering educator*

Sunnyvale
Merrill, Wendy Jane *financial services company executive*

Upland
Barden, Shirley Ramsey *credit union executive*

Vista
Ferguson, Margaret Ann *tax specialist, consultant*

COLORADO

Colorado Springs
Rowan, Cynthia L. Reeves *accountant*

Conifer
Boese, Michelle Lynne *accountant, consultant*

Fort Collins
Thomas, Jeanette Mae *public accountant*

Henderson
Reibold, Dorothy Ann *accountant, researcher*

Lakewood
Nichols, Vicki Anne *financial consultant, librarian*

Monument
McIver, Deborah Kay *tax specialist, entrepreneur, small business owner*

Wheat Ridge
Leino, Deanna Rose *business educator*

CONNECTICUT

Bridgeport
Henry, Barbara Ann *finance company executive, director*

Darien
Gushée-Molkenthin, Allison *financial advisor*

East Hartford
Barredo, Rita M. *auditor*

Fairfield
Bohrer, Jane Rothrock *controller*

Greenwich
Farrell, Mary Cooney *securities analyst*

Hartford
Souza, Diane D *corporate financial executive*

Newington
Foley, Patricia Jean *accountant*

Rocky Hill
Wilson, Karen Lynn *esthetician*

Stamford
Goodkin, Deborah Gay *corporate financial executive*
Jason, J. Julie *portfolio manager, writer, lawyer*
Williams, Reba White *corporate financial executive, writer, researcher*

Trumbull
Ewing, Anna M. *stock exchange executive*

West Hartford
Detmar-Pines, Gina Louise *business strategy and policy educator*

Westport
McElroy, Abby Lucille Wolman *financial advisor*

Woodbridge
Vasileff, Lili Alexandra *financial planner*

DELAWARE

Wilmington
Copeland, Tatiana Brandt *accountant*
Rogoski, Patricia Diana *corporate financial executive*

DISTRICT OF COLUMBIA

Washington
Armstrong, Alexandra *financial planner*
Brown-Daniels, Patricia *budget analyst, wedding planner*
Campbell-Grothe, Ruth Ann *retired budget analyst*
Deaton, Valerie L. *financial researcher, consultant*
DuCran, Claudette Deloris *retired financial analyst*
Hinrichs, S. Jean *auditor*
Schapiro, Mary L. *financial regulatory service executive*
Tolmachoff, Willadene *accountant, auditor*
White, Susan Colvin *finance educator*

FLORIDA

Cocoa Beach
Wirtschafter, Irene Nerove *tax specialist, consultant, military officer*

Deerfield Beach
Moran, Patricia Genevieve *corporate financial executive*

Delray Beach
McKay, Patricia A. *corporate financial executive*

Fort Lauderdale
Kennedy, Beverly (Kleban) Burris *financial advisor, former television and radio personality*

Fort Pierce
Garde, Susan Reutershan *accountant*

Lady Lake
Di Benedetto, Ann Louise *retired accounting administrator*

Lake City
Moore, Emma Sims *business educator*

Miami
Javier-Dejneka, Amelia Luisa *accountant*

Miami Shores
Diener, Betty Jane *business educator*

Ocklawaha
Silagi, Barbara Weibler *corporate officer*

Ocoee
Davis, Elena Denise *accountant*

Orlando
Houser, Ruth G. *corporate financial executive, accountant, municipal official*
Lloyd, Priscilla Ann *finance educator*

Palm Beach
Harper, Mary Sadler *financial consultant*

Palm Coast
Jost, Kayren Prosser *accountant*

Port Saint Lucie
Mottram-Doss, Renée *corporate financial executive*

Saint Petersburg
Freeman, Corinne *financial analyst, retired mayor*
Wasserman, Susan Valesky *accountant, artist, yoga instructor*

Sarasota
Drake, Diana Ashley *retired financial planner*
Sanders, Coyetta Treshay *accountant*

Tallahassee
Marshall, Elizabeth Annette *auditor*

Tampa
DeVane, Mindy Klein *financial planner*
Henard, Elizabeth Ann *controller*
Matulich, Erika *marketing educator*

Tarpon Springs
Browne, A. Pauline *accountant, writer*

Winter Haven
Goodman, Karen Lacerte *financial services executive*

Winter Springs
Bevc, Carol-Lynn Anne *accountant*

GEORGIA

Atlanta
Charles, Sally Allen *financial analyst*
Curtis, Lisa A. *accountant, administrator*
Gundersen, Mary Lisa Kranitzky *finance company executive*

Decatur
Jones, Debbie Jo *finance educator*

Lagrange
Hawkins, Frances Pam *business educator*

Macon
Rigsby, Sheila Goree *accounting firm executive*

Milledgeville
Engerrand, Doris Dieskow *retired business educator*

Savannah
Smith, Elizabeth Mackey *retired financial consultant*

Tifton
Hannon, Laura L. *accountant, educator*

HAWAII

Honolulu
Kawamura, Georgina K. *finance company executive*

IDAHO

Hayden
Morris, Mary Ann *bookkeeper*

Idaho Falls
Matthews, Janice C. *financial consultant*

ILLINOIS

Bartlett
Lawrence, Madalena Joan Vignocchi *accountant*

Chicago
Barré, Laura *finance company executive*
Herting, Claireen LaVern *financial planner*
Kamerick, Eileen Ann *corporate financial executive, lawyer*
Mallow, Kathleen Kelly *accountant*
Saltiel, Natalie *accountant*
Williams, Marsha C. *corporate financial executive*

Crystal Lake
Roehl, Kathleen Ann *financial executive*

Decatur
Loebl, Maragaret Margo *corporate financial executive*

Des Plaines
Lake, Noreen L. *retired accountant*

Elmhurst
Choyke, Phyllis May Ford (Mrs. Arthur Davis Choyke Jr.) *management executive, editor, poet*

Glendale Heights
Cook, Doris Marie *retired accountant, educator*

Gurnee
Hall, Terry *accountant*

Lisle
Ruyle-Hullinger, Elizabeth Smith (Beth Ruyle) *municipal financial advisor, consultant*

Naperville
Tan, Li-Su Lin *accountant, insurance company executive, consultant*

Northbrook
Mandel, Karyl Lynn *accountant*

Springfield
Kuhn, Kathleen Jo *accountant*

INDIANA

Carmel
Mahoney, Margaret Ellis *accountant*

Fort Wayne
Gutreuter, Jill Stallings *financial consultant, financial planner*

Indianapolis
Braham, Delphine Doris *accountant, government official*
Israelov, Rhoda *financial planner, entrepreneur*
Mesch, Debra J. *finance educator*
Onochie, Florence N. *accountant*

Portage
Schroeder, Marvis Lynn *accountant, artist*

South Bend
McDonnell, G. Darlene *retired business educator*

IOWA

Cedar Rapids
Knapp, Barbara Allison *financial planner, oncological nurse consultant*

Des Moines
Smith, Diana Marie *business educator*
Vaughan, Therese Michele *insurance educator*

Johnston
Poppe, Pamela J. *accountant*

Ottumwa
Lang, Janelle J. *accountant*

Pella
Hesselink, Ann Patrice *financial executive, lawyer*

Waterloo
Gleason, Cindy S. *financial consultant, educator*

KANSAS

Logan
Manion, Kay Daureen *financial and office manager*

Topeka
Fink, Ruth Garvey *diversified financial services company executive*
Mc Candless, Barbara J. *financial consultant*

KENTUCKY

Lexington
Griffith, Gloria Jeanette *finance educator*

Louisville
Johnson, Adria Elaine *financial analyst, accountant*
McKim, Ruth Ann *financial planner*

LOUISIANA

Hammond
LaFargue, Melba Faye Fulmer *credit manager, realtor*

Metairie
Gereighty, Andrea Saunders *diversified financial services company executive, poet*

Pineville
Beall, Grace Carter *business educator*
Conway, Evelyn Atkinson *accountant, financial analyst*

Shreveport
Goodman, Sylvia Klumok *film center executive*

MAINE

Augusta
Sheive, Doreen Laurel *fiscal administrator*

Hampden
Scroggins, M. Suzanne Paonessa *budget analyst*

Topsham
Palesky, Carol East *tax accountant*

MARYLAND

Baltimore
Smith, E. Follin *corporate financial executive*

Bethesda
Comiskey, Angela Picariello *accountant*

College Park
Buggs, Elaine S. *financial analyst*

Columbia
Hyde, Rebecca Medwin *financial consultant*

Largo
Falkey, Mary E. *finance educator*

Rockville
Cornelius, Maria G. *financial advisor*

MASSACHUSETTS

Boston
Bavaria, Joan *finance company executive*
Domini, Amy Lee *portfolio manager*
Esper, Susan *diversified financial services company executive*
Gormley, Pamela D. *controller*
Hardy, Victoria Elizabeth *finance educator*
Schnitzer, Iris Taymore *diversified financial services company executive, lawyer, arbitrator, mediator*

Dorchester
Wideman, Carol M. *accountant, consultant*

Framingham
Komola, Christine T. *corporate financial executive*

Needham
Lenehan, Pamela Farrell *financial executive*

Springfield
Elam, Elizabeth L.R. *finance educator*

Waltham
Curnan, Susan P. *social policy and management educator, consultant*

MICHIGAN

Detroit
Acton, Elizabeth S. *corporate financial executive*
Crawford, Andrea Kirvene *business educator*

Novi
Holforty, Pearl Martha *accountant*

Myers, Lee Ann *accountant*

Okemos
Prout, Carolyn Ann *controller, personnel administrator*

MINNESOTA

Fisher
Hanson, Tena Lorayn *finance educator*

Minneapolis
Bretz, Kelly Jean Rydel *actuary, consultant*
Goldberg, Luella Gross *diversified financial services company executive*
Reha, Rose Krivisky *retired finance educator*

Minnetonka
Morisato, Susan Cay *actuary*

Saint Cloud
Supanvanij, Janikan *finance educator*

Saint Paul
Wheelock, Pam *financial executive*

MISSOURI

Kansas City
Boysen, Melicent Pearl *finance company executive*
Latza, Beverly Ann *accountant*
Mustard, Mary Carolyn *financial executive*

Neosho
Weber, Margaret Laura Jane *retired accountant*

Saint Louis
Fitch, Rachel Farr *health policy analyst*
Ulmer, Donna K. *business educator, writer*

MONTANA

Helena
Craig, Mary Lauri *accountant*
Toole, Joan Trimble *financial consultant*

Missoula
Pahl, Laura E. *finance educator*

Troy
Sherman, Signe Lidfeldt *portfolio manager, former research chemist*

NEBRASKA

Hastings
Stalsberg, Geraldine McEwen *accountant*

Lincoln
Byrd, Lorelee *state treasurer*

Omaha
O'Connell, Valerie Beth *finance educator*

NEVADA

Elko
Ballew, Kathy I. *controller*

Las Vegas
Williams, Mary Irene *business education educator*

Reno
Garcia, Katherine Lee *controller, accountant*
Verstegen, Deborah A. *finance educator*

NEW HAMPSHIRE

Goffstown
Martel, Eva Leona *accountant*

Manchester
Merideth, Susan Carol *business administration educator*

Nashua
Matarazzo, Maria C. *finance educator, department chairman*

NEW JERSEY

Basking Ridge
Scites, Jan *business consulting services company executive*

Bridgewater
Simonds, Theresa M. Troegner *accountant*

Chatham
Earle, Jean Buist *finance company executive, computer company executive*

Edison
Pedescleaux-Muckle, Gail *retired business analyst, writer, artist*

Elmwood Park
Nadzick, Judith Ann *accountant*

Fairfield
Sangiuliano, Barbara Ann *tax accountant*

Florham Park
Bauer, Jean Marie *accountant*

Franklin Lakes
Reed, JoAnn A. *corporate financial executive*

Hasbrouck Heights
Savva, Andrea *financial advisor*

Leonia
Pinsdorf, Marion Katheryn *diversified financial services company executive, educator, writer*

Morristown
Armstrong, Diana Rose *financial consultant*
Flynn, Marie Cosgrove *portfolio manager, corporate financial executive*

Parsippany
Langrana, Anita *financial analyst, personal trainer*
Timmins, Maryanne *real estate accountant, educator*

Pomona
Vito, Marilyn Elaine *business educator*

Red Bank
Groves, Lizabeth A. *accountant, network administrator*

Rochelle Park
Donahoe, Maureen Alice *accounting consultant*

Trenton
Stefane, Clara Joan *finance educator*

NEW MEXICO

Albuquerque
Kaehele, Bettie Louise *accountant*

Las Cruces
Bell, M. Joy Miller *financial planner, real estate agent*

NEW YORK

Albany
Brewer, Aida M. *treasurer*

Bath
Simonson, Donna Jeanne *accountant*

Bronx
Ryan, Theresa Ann Julia *accountant*

Brooklyn
Fischman, Myrna Leah *accountant, educator*
Satterfield-Harris, Rita *financial analyst*

Claverack
Vile, Sandra Jane *leadership training educator*

Clifton Park
Van Slyke, Rosemary *tax specialist*

Fairport
Talty, Lorraine Caguioa *accountant*

Farmingdale
Maurino, Paula San Millan *business educator, computer professor*

Flushing
Sanborn, Anna Lucille *pension fund administrator, consultant*

Freeport
DiBenedetto, Michelle *finance company executive*

Hempstead
Roble, Carole Marcia *accountant*

Jamaica
Mohr, Iris *finance educator*

Lewiston
LoTempio, Julia Matild *retired accountant*

Little Neck
Overton, Rosilyn Gay Hoffman *finance company executive*

Maspeth
Dumitru, Mirela *accountant*

Melville
McKane, Beatrix *accountant*

Merrick
Beckman, Judith Kalb *financial counselor and planner, educator, writer*

New York
Altfest, Karen Caplan *diversified financial services company executive, director*
Becker, Helane Renée *financial analyst, finance company executive*
Bernstein, Phyllis J. *financial consultant*
Bibliowicz, Jessica M. *financial analyst*
Bowden, Linda *diversified financial services company executive*
Boyer, Cheryl *finance company executive*
Browning, Candace *corporate financial executive*
Buttner, Jean Bernhard *diversified financial services company executive*
Caffrey, Patricia *diversified financial services company executive*
Caputo, Lisa M. *finance company executive*
Chang-Robbins, Joyce *diversified financial services company executive*
Childs, Donna *finance company executive*
Clinton, Chelsea Victoria *financial consultant, former first daughter*
Cohen, Marsha R. *former diversified financial services company executive*
Corbet, Kathleen A. *financial information company executive*
Cruz, Zoe *diversified financial services company executive*
De Lisi, Nancy *corporate financial executive*
Engel, Amy J. *corporate financial executive*
Etienne, Michele *financial consultant*
Farley, Peggy Ann *finance company executive*
Friedman, Adena T. *finance company executive*
Gallegos, Deborah E. *pension fund administrator*
Gallo, Martha J. *diversified financial services company executive*
Goldenberg, Elizabeth Leigh *finance company executive*
Hopkins, Deborah C. *diversified financial services company executive*
Johnson, Suzanne M. Nora *diversified financial services company executive, lawyer*
Karpen, Marian Joan *financial executive*
Keys, Elizabeth A. *accountant, director*
Kirschenbaum, Lisa L. *portfolio manager, financial advisor*
Knapp, Ellen M. *financial company executive*
Kozlowski, Cheryl M. *fixed income analyst*
Kuo, Charlene *finance professional*
Langford, Laura Sue *corporate financial executive*
Leven, Ann Ruth *financial consultant*
Masterson, Ellen Hornberger *accountant*
Mazzenga, Carolyn *accountant*
Meehan, Sandra Gotham *corporate financial executive, consultant, writer*
Meyer, Pearl *compensation executive consultant*
Miller, Heidi G. *diversified financial company executive*
Openshaw, Jennifer *finance company executive*
Palmer, Jessica *diversified financial services company executive*
Radin, Amy Janine *financial services company executive*
Ramirez, Maria Fiorini *financial consultant*
Reiss, Dale Anne *corporate financial executive*
Ritch, Kathleen *diversified financial services company executive*
Rocchi, Robin Henning *financial executive, automotive company executive*
Schueneman, Diane L. *diversified financial services company executive*
Shallcross, Deanne J. *finance company executive*
Smith-Loeb, Margaret *marketing educator*
Tchoumak, Adelina *corporate financial executive*
Tillman, Vickie A. *financial information company executive*
Updike, Helen Hill *financial advisor*
Wilson, Pamela K. *corporate financial executive*
Yastine, Barbara A. *diversified financial services company executive*

North Massapequa
Capone, Maryann *financial planner*

Pomona
Landau, Lauri Beth *accountant, consultant*

Poughkeepsie
Hansen, Karen Thornley *accountant*

Rochester
Goyer, Virginia L. *accountant*
Marriott, Marcia Ann *business educator, economics professor, health facility administrator*

Saint Bonaventure
Young, Kimberly S. *finance educator, psychologist*

Somers
Gulick, Donna Marie *accountant*
Hall, Kathleen Yanarella *financial executive*

Valley Stream
Ellis, Bernice *financial planner, investment advisor*

Vestal
Lee, Michelle Anne *financial analyst*

Windsor
Warner, Roberta Arlene *retired accountant, financial services executive*

Woodbury
Barnett, Rochelle *accountant*

NORTH CAROLINA

Asheville
Letzig, Betty Jean *financial consultant*
Mack, Carole *financial consultant*

Cary
Coderre, Nancy Adele *financial analyst*

Greensboro
Lloyd, Lila G. *business educator*

New Bern
Phipps, Patsy Duncan *retired auditor*

Raleigh
Lenard, Mary Jane *finance educator*
Stevenson, Denise L. *diversified financial services company executive, consultant, realtor*

NORTH DAKOTA

Stanley
Eliason, Bonnie Mae *county treasurer*

OHIO

Akron
Stephens, Rachel De-Vore *finance company executive, educator*

Athens
Miller, Peggy McLaren *retired management educator*

Avon
Grmek, Dorothy Antonia *accountant*

Cincinnati
Bell, Sandra Elizabeth *corporate financial executive*
Gates, Katherine A. *accountant, writer*
Westbrook, Lynda A. *financial consultant*

Cleveland
Boyle, Kammer *financial planner, investment advisor, research analyst, options trader*
Mayne, Lucille Stringer *finance educator*

Columbus
Cruz-Myers, Theresa *finance company executive*
Hill, Terri *diversified financial services company executive*
James, Donna A. *diversified financial services company executive*
Kreager, Eileen Davis *financial consultant*
Ricord, Kathy *diversified financial services company executive*

Harrison
Kocher, Juanita Fay *retired auditor*

Shaker Heights
Donnem, Sarah Lund *financial analyst, non-profit consultant, political organization consultant*

West Chester
Arnow, Jody L. *accountant*

West Jefferson
Puckett, Helen Louise *retired tax consulting company executive*

OKLAHOMA

Watts
Bell, Janice Lee *finance educator*

OREGON

Clackamas
Love, Susan Denise *accountant, consultant, small business owner*

Eugene
Arnaud, Velda *finance educator*
Smith, Vangy Edith *accountant, consultant, artist, writer*

Mcminnville
Chappell, Annie-Dear *retired business manager*

Portland
Dow, Mary Alexis *auditor*
White, Roberta Lee *financial analyst*

PENNSYLVANIA

Bala Cynwyd
Cohen, Rachel Rutstein *financial planner*

Blue Bell
Haugen, Janet B. *corporate financial executive*

Collegeville
Maco, Teri Regan *accountant, engineer*

Dunmore
Pencek, Carolyn Carlson *treasurer, finance educator*

Eddystone
Fredrick, Susan Walker *tax company manager*

Erie
Mattis, Constance Marie *controller*

Harrisburg
Ellenbogen, Elisabeth Alice *retired accountant*

Huntingdon Valley
Freaney, Diane M. *financial executive*

Paoli
Gotshall, Jan Doyle *financial planner*

Philadelphia
Booth, Anna Belle *accountant*
Miori, Virginia Marie *finance educator*
Rose, Jane A. *financial planner*
Summers, Anita Arrow *finance educator*
Treichel, Monica Zimmerman *accountant, educator*
Wachter, Susan Melinda *finance educator*

Pittsburgh
Haggerty, Gretchen R. *accounting and finance executive*
Hajnik, Genevieve L. *accountant*

Reading
McCullough, Eileen (Eileen McCullough LePage, Elli McCullough) *financial consultant, writer, editor, educator*
McVey, Diane Elaine *accountant*

Sayre
Brittain, Nancy Hammond *accountant*

Wayne
Thompson, Gloria Matthews *marketing and statistics educator*

Wynnewood
Frankl, Razelle *management educator*

Wyomissing
Spatcher, Dianne Marie *finance executive*

RHODE ISLAND

Middletown
Reed, Julia Constance *financial services executive*

Providence
Orabone, Joanne Christine *accountant, educator*

Smithfield
Weiss, Susan F. *accountant*

SOUTH CAROLINA

Charleston
Adelson, Gloria Ann *retired financial executive*

Florence
Singletary, Eloise *business educator*

Johnsonville
Davis, Aquilla *diversified financial services company executive*

Lexington
Yeatts, Susan W. *financial planner*

Sumter
van Bulck, Margaret West *accountant, financial planner, educator*

West Columbia
Byars, Merlene Hutto *accountant, artist, writer*
Moore, Shirley Throckmorton (Mrs. Elmer Lee Moore) *accountant*

SOUTH DAKOTA

Platte
Pennington, Beverly Melcher *financial services company executive*

Rapid City
Callahan, Susan Jane Whitney *accountant*

TENNESSEE

Alamo
Finch, Evelyn Vorise *financial planner*

Memphis
Landrum-Noe, Madeleine Elise *accountant*

Soddy Daisy
Randall, Kay Temple *accountant, retired real estate agent*

TEXAS

Amarillo
Robinson, Ola Mae *accountant*

Arlington
Robinson, Mary Lu *retired accountant, artist*
Scogno, Stacie Joy *financial services company executive*

Austin
Schloss, Hadassah *auditor*
Strayhorn, Carole Keeton *comptroller*

Beaumont
Andes, Joan Keenen *tax specialist*

Cypress
Hlozek, Carole Diane Quast *finance company executive*

Dallas
Hoyt, Rosemary Ellen *trust advisor*
Jimenez, Mercy *corporate financial executive*
Smith, Patsy Juanita *financial executive*
Wilbur, Janis A. *financial consultant, sales professional*

Denton
Newell, Charldean *public administration educator*

Dripping Springs
Guess, Aundrea Kay *accounting educator*

Fort Worth
Dominiak, Geraldine Florence *retired accounting educator*
Pappas-Speairs, Nina *financial planner, educator*

Garland
Lord, Jacqueline Ward *accountant, photographer, artist*

Houston
Clark, Janet F. *corporate financial executive*
Friday, Leah Rebecca *portfolio manager*
Harris, Venita Van Caspel *retired financial planner*
Mermelstein, Isabel Mae Rosenberg *financial consultant*

Irving
Brown, Linda Harper *bookkeeping company executive*
Geisinger, Janice Allain *accountant*
Massah, Cherilyn *auditor*

Leander
Craddock, Catherine Todd *accountant*

Mc Kinney
Forte, Christina Kirby *financial analyst*

Palestine
Meyer, Darla Anne *accountant*

Prairie View
De Luna-Gonzalez, Elma *accountant, academic administrator*

Richland Hills
Haynes, Ruth Elaine *accountant*

San Antonio
Marvin, Catherine A. *financial consultant*

San Marcos
Taylor, Ruth Arleen Lesher *marketing educator*

Sugar Land
Keefe, Carolyn Joan *tax accountant*

UTAH

Salt Lake City
McAllister, Lynette J. *financial consultant*

VERMONT

Brandon
Aines, Linda Diane *financial consultant*

VIRGINIA

Abingdon
Jones, Mary Trent *endowment fund trustee*

Arlington
Siegel, Laurie F. *accountant, painter*

Centreville
Hand, Antoinette Marie *accountant*

Charlottesville
Minehart, Jean Besse *tax accountant*

Mc Lean
Drew, K. *financial advisor, management consultant*
Goktepe, Janet Rose *retired financial analyst*

Norfolk
Shumadine, Anne Ballard *financial advisor, lawyer*

Reston
Polemitou, Olga Andrea *accountant*
Young, Loretta Ann *auditor*

Richmond
Wagner, Jody M. *treasurer*

Virginia Beach
DiCarlo, Susanne Helen *financial analyst*
Lewis, Eleanor Adams *financial consultant*

Williamsburg
McLennan, Barbara Nancy *tax specialist*

Woodbridge
Denison, Cynthia Lee *accountant, tax specialist*

WASHINGTON

Olympia
Myers, Sharon Diane *auditor*

Seattle
Sandstrom, Alice Wilhelmina *accountant*
Young, Nora Jane *actuary, consultant*

WEST VIRGINIA

Elkins
Payne, Gloria Marquette *business educator*

WISCONSIN

Green Bay
Capelle, Elaine M. *financial planner*

Madison
Wicklund, Gerri M. *finance educator*

Milwaukee
Lenz, Debra Lynn *auditor*

New Berlin
Gebhard, LaVerne Elizabeth *retired accounting educator*

Superior
Robek, Mary Frances *business education educator*

West Bend
VanBrunt-Kramer, Karen *business administration educator*

WYOMING

Cheyenne
Parrish, Denise Kay *regulatory accountant*

Laramie
Spiegelberg, Emma Jo *business education educator, academic administrator*

Sheridan
Pilch, Margaret L. *grant writer, researcher*

TERRITORIES OF THE UNITED STATES

PUERTO RICO

Mayaguez
Ruiz-Vargas, Yolanda *finance educator*

San Juan
Rosso de Irizarry, Carmen (Tutty Rosso de Irizarry) *finance executive*

MILITARY ADDRESSES OF THE UNITED STATES

PACIFIC

Fpo
Tarpeh-Doe, Linda Diane *controller*

CANADA

BRITISH COLUMBIA

Powell River
Carsten, Arlene Desmet *financial executive*

ONTARIO

Toronto
Baxendale, Sonia A. *diversified financial services company executive*
Mercier, Eileen Ann *corporate financial executive*

NEW ZEALAND

Auckland
Swecker, Valerie Ann *accountant, consultant*

SAUDI ARABIA

Riyadh
Olayan, Lubna S. *finance company executive*

SPAIN

Madrid
Sanona, Nuno Alexandre Fernandes Rorigues *financial consultant*

ADDRESS UNPUBLISHED

Alaimo, Terry M. *financial consultant*
Alexander, Barbara Toll *financial consultant*
Anderson, Peggy Rees *accountant*
Ashworth, Bessie *benefits compensation analyst, writer*
Atwood, Donna Elaine *retired financial manager*
Baier, Lucinda *corporate financial executive*
Bartlett, Shirley Anne *accountant*
Beller, Luanne Evelyn *retired accountant*
Bellon, Venetia Rochelle *retired financial consultant*
Bolt, Dawn Maria *financial planner*
Bowne, Shirlee Pearson *credit manager*
Braggs, Patricia *account manager*
Brainard, Melissa *accountant*
Brdlik, Carola Emilie *retired accountant*
Cameron, Stacey Rebecca *benefits compensation analyst*
Canfield, Constance Dale *retired accountant, retired medical/surgical nurse, retired military officer*
Cannistraro, Carolyn Marie *financial recruiter*
Carunchio, Florence Regina *financial planner*
Castle, Nancy Margaret Timma *accountant, banker*
Chou, Ruby *finance educator, real estate broker, consultant*
Coates, Shirley Jean *finance educator, secondary school educator*
Colby, Marvelle Seitman *retired business management educator, administrator*
Collette, Frances Madelyn *retired tax specialist, lawyer, consultant, advocate*
Culp, Mildred Louise *corporate financial executive*
Cummings, Erika Helga *financial consultant*
Dickson, Eva Mae *credit manager*
Dorsey, Dolores Florence *retired corporate treasurer, finance company executive*
Doss, Jessica Yarina *financial analyst*
Dowdell, Sharonlyn Scott *accountant*
Duncan, Shirley A. *portfolio manager*
Edmonds, Slivy *corporate financial executive*
Everett, Donna Raney *finance educator*
FitzSimons, Sharon Russell *corporate financial executive*
Fletcher, Denise Koen *strategic and financial consultant*
Fox, Betty *financial services executive*
Fox, Kelly Diane *financial advisor*
French, Margo Ann *financial planner*
Friedman, Joan M. *retired accountant, educator*
Gaines, Brenda J. *retired financial services company executive*
Gambrell, Luck Flanders *corporate financial executive*
Gehrke, Karen Marie *retired accountant*
Genét, Barbara Ann *accountant, travel company executive*
Hamilton, Jean *financial services executive, software executive*
Hanson, Tamara W. *accountant*
Hargrove, Sandra Leigh *financial planner*
Hayek, Carolyn Jean *financial consultant, retired judge*
Holton, Grace Holland *accountant*
Horstman, Suzanne Rucker *financial planner*
Hume, Susan Rachel *finance educator*
Jarvis, Rebecca *financial reporter*
Johnson, Freda S. *financial analyst, consultant*
Josey, Donna Ashley *accountant, educator*
Judd, Barbara Ann Eastwood *financial management professional, union activist*
Kennedy, Leila *accounting educator*
Larkin, Mary Sue *financial planner*
Latendresse, Lanelle *financial services company executive*
Leonard, Virginia Kathryn *financial manager*
Lester, Alicia Louise *financial analyst*
Loken, Barbara *marketing educator, social psychologist*
Lombard, Marjorie Ann *financial officer*
Longden, Claire Suzanne *retired financial planner, investment advisor*
Lucas, Karen Williams *controller*
Madariaga, Lourdes Mercedes *accountant*
May, Phyllis Jean *financial executive*
McCallion, Anne Dewey *finance executive, accountant*
McClinton, Dorothy Hardaway *retired finance educator*
McElligott, Ann Theresa *accountant*
McWhinney, Deborah *finance company executive*
Miller, Linda H. *accountant*
Mims, Clarice Roberta *financial advisor*
Mitchell, M. Yvonne *paraprofessional*
Mitchem, Cheryl E. *accounting educator*
Morgan, Patricia *financial consultant, former Republican party chairman*
Mullins, Barbara J. *financial executive*
Munoz, Cheryl Ann *portfolio manager*
Murray, Catherine Mary Murphy *retired accountant*
Nold, Aurora Ramirez *finance company executive*
Norman, E. Gladys *retired finance educator, management consultant*
Norton, Karen Ann *accountant*
Ortiz-Walters, Rowena *management educator*
Page, Janet Louise *accountant*
Paige, Vivian Jo-Ann *accountant*
Perry, Nancy Bland *accountant*
Preudhomme, Marcia Denrique *finance company executive, writer*
Rail, Kathy Lynn Parish *accountant*
Ray, Marjorie *retired financial planner*
Ray, Susan Davis *accountant*
Renouf, Anne *corporate financial executive, consultant*
Richardson, Brownie F. *accountant*
Richardson-Bowman, Lequetta Devera *finance company executive, consultant*
Ridenhour, Marilyn Housel *retired accountant*
Rockwell, Elizabeth Dennis *retirement specialist, financial planner*
Rode, Deborah Lynn *accountant*
Rogers, Kathie Anne *accountant*
Rohlin, Diane Elizabeth *financial relations executive*
Rossi, Marianne *financial analyst*
Rumfolo, Marilu *financial analyst, non-profit corporation executive*
Saidens, Susan M. *accountant, consultant*
Saucier, Guylaine *corporate financial executive*
Saunders, Donna M. *accountant*
Schneider, Mary Etta *finance company executive*
Sexton, Carol Burke *finance company executive, consultant*
Sinclair, Carol Ann *accountant, consultant*
Smart, Jill Bellavia *financial consultant*
Smith, Linda Ann Glidewell *accountant*
Sonnier, Patricia Bennett *business management educator*
Stephens, Brooke *financial commentator, writer*
Trail, Margaret Ann *retired employee benefits company executive, rancher*
Wells, Toni Lynn *accountant*
Whelan, Mary Jane *accountant, writer, photographer*
Whyte, Bettina Marshall *financial crisis manager*
Widner, Roberta Ann *accountant, artist*
Wilkof, Marcia Valerie *finance educator*
Williams, Helen Margaret *retired accountant*
Wilson, Linda Lee *finance company executive*
Zimmerman, Helene Loretta *retired business educator*

FINANCE: INSURANCE

UNITED STATES

ALABAMA

Dothan
Benson, Marie Chapman *insurance agent*

Fairhope
Norton, Margaret Sarah *retired insurance company executive*

Tuscaloosa
Edgeworth, Emily *retired insurance agency executive, retired small business owner*

ARIZONA

Scottsdale
Williams, Margaret M. (Meg Williams) *insurance company executive*

ARKANSAS

Sherwood
Keaton, Frances Marlene *insurance sales representative*

CALIFORNIA

Fullerton
Woods, Betty *insurance company executive*

Glendale
Dudash, Linda Christine *insurance company executive*

Redwood City
Quartuccio, Maryann *insurance agent, home economist*

San Francisco
Allen, Lola *insurance agent*
Martinez, Belinda *health insurance company executive*

San Rafael
Keegan, Jane Ann *insurance executive, consultant*

Thousand Oaks
Herman, Joan Elizabeth *health insurance company executive*

Woodland Hills
Berry, Carol Ann *insurance company executive*
Clarey, Patricia T. *health insurance company executive, former state official*

COLORADO

Golden
Lott, Brenda Louise *insurance company executive*

Superior
Forshee, Gladys Marie *insurance agent, writer*

CONNECTICUT

East Hartford
Lautzenheiser, Barbara Jean *insurance company executive*

Hartford
Elliott, Eric S *insurance company executive*
Young, Dona Davis Gagliano *insurance company executive, lawyer*

Mystic
Spakoski, Marcia *insurance agent*

North Haven
Cofrancesco, Angela *insurance agent, coach*

Stamford
Schiff, Jayne Nemerow *underwriter*

DISTRICT OF COLUMBIA

Washington
Snider, Virginia L. *antitrust consultant*

FLORIDA

Fort Lauderdale
Lilley, Mili Della *insurance company executive, entertainment management consultant*

Jupiter
Colucci, Jacqueline Strupp *insurance agent, sculptor, management consultant*

Lutz
Saunders, Leslie *insurance company executive, marketing professional*

Naples
Guerra, Mayra *insurance company executive*

Parkland
Tharp, Karen Ann *insurance agent*

GEORGIA

Macon
Dorsey, Donna Bagley *insurance agent*

Marietta
Reid, Demetra Adams *insurance company executive*

Roswell
Lietch, Margie *insurance company administrator*

Savannah
Rigelwood, Diane Colleen *insurance adjuster, administrator*

ILLINOIS

Bloomington
Campbell-Jackson, Carla Lanette *insurance company executive*

Chicago
Grant, Beatrice *underwriter, consultant*
Hinkelman, Ruth Amidon *insurance company executive*

Des Plaines
Pannke-Smith, Peggy *insurance company executive*

Northbrook
Brune, Catherine S. *insurance company executive*

Park Ridge
Bateman, Andrea R. *insurance agent*

INDIANA

Carmel
Husman, Catherine Bigot *retired insurance company executive, consultant*

Indianapolis
Calvano, Linda Sue Ley *insurance company executive*
Dorr, Marjorie W. *healthcare insurance company executive*
Rosenblatt, Alice F. *healthcare insurance company executive*

Schererville
Jarrett, Alexis *insurance agent, lawyer*

KANSAS

Newton
Morford, Marie Arlene *insurance company executive*

Topeka
Zientara, Suzannah Dockstader *insurance agent*

Wichita
Johnstone, Marva Jean (Jeanie Johnstone) *insurance agency executive*

LOUISIANA

Alexandria
Anderson, Rose Marie *insurance agent*

MAINE

Portland
Reid, Rosemary Anne *insurance agent*

MARYLAND

Elkton
Jasinski-Caldwell, Mary L. *insurance company executive*

Germantown
Isaacson, Elaine Marie *insurance agent*

Reisterstown
Tirone, Barbara Jean *retired health insurance administrator*

MASSACHUSETTS

Boston
Bunker, Beryl H. *retired insurance company executive, volunteer*

Orleans
McDermott, Mary Ellen *insurance agent*

South Orleans
Hale, Margaret Smith *insurance company executive, educator*

Springfield
Modie, Christine M. *insurance company executive*

MICHIGAN

Saginaw
Othersen-Khalifa, Cheryl Lee *insurance agent, realtor*

Southgate
Torok, Margaret Louise *insurance company executive*

MINNESOTA

Coon Rapids
Bordner, Patricia Anne *insurance agent, writer*

Minneapolis
Crosmer, Janie Lynn *insurance company executive*
Feldman, Nancy Jane *insurance company executive*

Minnetonka
Rivet, Jeannine M. *insurance company executive*

Saint Paul
Oswald, Eva Sue Aden *retired insurance company executive*
Zuraitis, Marita *insurance company executive*

Thief River Falls
Fleischhaker, Karin *insurance agent*

MISSOURI

Kansas City
Nichols, Virginia Violet *independent insurance agent, accountant*

Saint Louis
Van Trease, Sandra Ann *insurance company executive*

Springfield
Wommack, Janice Marie *insurance company executive*

NEVADA

Henderson
Johnson, Joan Bray *insurance company consultant*

Las Vegas
Zervoudakes, Annette Dian *reinsurance specialist*

NEW JERSEY

Elizabeth
Miller-Duffy, Merritt *insurance agent, camp director*

Newark
Banta, Vivian L. *insurance company executive*
Koster, Barbara *insurance company executive*
Myers, Priscilla A. *insurance company executive*

Paramus
Crow, Lynne Campbell Smith *insurance company representative*

NEW YORK

Long Island City
Jacobson, Sibyl C. *insurance company executive*
Rein, Catherine Amelia *insurance company executive, lawyer*

New York
Campbell, Judith E. *retired insurance company executive*
Davis, Karen *insurance company executive, educator*
Knapp, Amy K. *insurance company executive*
Lassiter, Sheri L. *insurance company executive*
Piligian, Georgette A. *insurance company executive*
Procope, Ernesta Gertrude *insurance company executive*
Weber, Lisa M. *insurance company executive*

NORTH CAROLINA

Charlotte
Dunn, Sandra E. *insurance agent*

OHIO

Chillicothe
Copley, Cynthia Sue Love *insurance adjuster*

Cincinnati
Horrell, Karen Holley *insurance company executive, lawyer*

OKLAHOMA

Dewey
White, Joy Kathryn *retired claims consultant, artist*

Oklahoma City
Harrison-Bridgeman, Ann Marie *claims adjuster*

PENNSYLVANIA

Erie
Waldron, Allene *insurance group executive*

Maytown
Flanagan, Diane L. *property claims professional*

Olyphant
Paoloni, Virginia Ann *insurance company executive*

Pittsburgh
Chipman, Debra Decker *title insurance executive*

Stroudsburg
Pope, Arlette Farrar *insurance company professional*

SOUTH CAROLINA

Camden
Pierce, Janis Vaughn *insurance executive, consultant*

TENNESSEE

Franklin
Horton, Rosalyn *underwriter*

TEXAS

Austin
Watson, Brenda Bennett *insurance company executive*

Dallas
Madden, Teresa Darleen *insurance agency owner*

Richardson
White, Irene *insurance professional*

WASHINGTON

Yakima
Savage, Carla Lee *insurance agent*

WISCONSIN

Madison
Sims, Terre Lynn *insurance company executive*

Milwaukee
Piehler, Barbara F. *insurance company executive*

ADDRESS UNPUBLISHED

Alderman, Shirley M. *insurance agent*
Alpert, Ann Sharon *retired insurance claims examiner*
Becker, JoAnn Elizabeth *retired insurance company executive*
Bergquist, Sandra Lee *claims consultant*
Castellanos, Josephine Falcon *insurance agent, composer*
Cooks, Pamala Aniece *insurance agent*
Duckworth, Tara Ann *insurance company executive*
Emek, Sharon Helene *risk management consultant*
Henschel, Shirley Myra *licensing agent*
Hibner, Rae A. *risk management executive, medical/surgical nurse*
Hincks, Marcia Lockwood *retired insurance company executive*
Holmes, Sandra *insurance underwriter*
Huszai, Kristen Renee *insurance agent*
Impellizzeri, Anne Elmendorf *insurance company executive, non-profit executive*
Knizeski, Justine Estelle *insurance company executive*
Lee, Katrina LaShawn *health insurance business consultant*
Maloney, Therese Adele *insurance company executive*
Martino, Cheryl Derby *insurance company executive*
McGurk, Catherine S. *insurance adjuster, paralegal*
McIntyre, Linda M. *healthcare risk analyst*
O'Neill, Judith Jones *insurance agent*
Plette, Sandra Lee *retired insurance company executive*
Sasko, Nancy Ann *insurance agent*
Segal, Linda Gale *retired insurance company executive*
Smith, Jennifer C. *insurance company executive*
Soltz, Judith E. *insurance company executive, retired lawyer*
Subkowsky, Elizabeth *insurance company executive*
Wahweah, Linda McNeil *insurance agent, writer*

FINANCE: INVESTMENT SERVICES

UNITED STATES

ARKANSAS

Little Rock
Good, Mary Lowe (Mrs. Billy Jewel Good) *investment company executive, educator*
Light, Jo Knight *stockbroker*

CALIFORNIA

Beverly Hills
Evans, Louise *investor, retired psychologist*
Seidel, Joan Broude *securities dealer, investment advisor*

Carmel
Hamilton, Beverly Lannquist *investment executive*

Corte Madera
Andreini, Elizabeth B. *investment advisor, elementary school educator*

Los Angeles
Ashwell, Rachel *entrepreneur, interior designer*
Holly, Krisztina J. *entrepreneur, academic administrator*

Menlo Park
LaPorte, Kathleen Darken *venture capitalist*

North Hollywood
Miller, Brenda *real estate investment analyst*

Roseville
Grant, Barbara *venture capitalist*

San Francisco
Dunn, Patricia Cecile *investment company executive*
Levine, Alison *entrepreneur, leadership development consultant, adventurer*
Marduel, Alix *venture capitalist*
Schioldager, Amy Lee *investment company executive*
Winblad, Ann *investment company executive*

Tarzana
Neece, Olivia Helene Ernst *investment company executive, consultant*

Torrance
Enright, Stephanie Veselich *investment company executive, financial consultant*

COLORADO

Arvada
Weitzel, Ginger M. *entrepreneur, critical care nurse*

Denver
Gampel, Elaine Susan *investment company executive, consultant*
Wagner, Judith Buck *investment firm executive*

Lakewood
Finnie, Doris Gould *investment company executive*

Placerville
Monferrato, Angela Maria *investor, writer*

Thornton
Johnson, Carole Jean *investment company executive*

CONNECTICUT

Greenwich
Marram, Ellen R. *investment company executive*

New Canaan
Lione, Susan Garrett *consultant*

Westport
Stewart, Martha Kostyra *entrepreneur, lecturer, author*

DISTRICT OF COLUMBIA

Washington
Bondurant, Amy Laura *investment company executive*
Heichel, Paula *investment company executive, financial consultant*
Johnson, Sheila Crump *entrepreneur*
Kent, Jill Elspeth *entrepreneur, art appraiser, lawyer*
McCaul, Elizabeth *investment advisor, former state agency administrator*
McGreevey, Lisa S. *investment company executive*

FLORIDA

Boca Raton
Land, Judith Broten *stockbroker*

Fort Lauderdale
Sands, Roberta Alyse *real estate investor*

Hollywood
Pittarelli, Diana *entrepreneur*

Miami
Arison, Shari *investment company executive*
Mitchell, Virginia Ann *investment company executive*

Saint Petersburg
Nichols, Katie *investment company executive*

Tampa
Schultz, Barbara Marie *investment advisor*

GEORGIA

Atlanta
Jackson, Geraldine *entrepreneur*
Roberts, Thomasene Blount *entrepreneur*
Sanger, Hazel A D *investment company executive*

Austell
Orr, Zellie *entrepreneur, educator, writer, researcher*

HAWAII

Honolulu
Kubo, Kimberly Annette *entrepreneur*

Waimea
Merk, Elizabeth Thole *investment company executive*

ILLINOIS

Champaign
Barrowman, Connie L. *investment advisor*

Chicago
Carnahan, Ellen *venture capitalist*
Collins, Michelle L. *venture capitalist*
Desmond, Bevin *investment research company executive*
Gilbert, Debbie Rose *entrepreneur*
Hobson, Mellody *investment company executive*
Levenson, Carol A. *corporate bond research company executive*
Lurie, Ann LaSalle *investment company executive, foundation administrator*
Pritzker, Penny *investor*
Rosenberg, Sheli Z. *investment company executive*
Shuman, Ann *investment company executive*

Evanston
Wang, Sona *venture capitalist*

Park Ridge
Albert, Elizabeth Franz (Mrs. Henry B. Albert) *investor, artist, conservationist*

Quincy
Taylor, Judith Caroline *entrepreneur*

INDIANA

Sandborn
Hartsburg, Judith Catherine *entrepreneur*

KANSAS

Topeka
Cripe, Elizabeth Ann (Betty Cripe) *investment company executive*

KENTUCKY

Murray
Boston, Betty Lee *investment company executive, financial consultant, financial planner*

LOUISIANA

Mandeville
Colomb, Marjorie Monroe *investor, volunteer*

Ruston
Marbury, Virginia Lomax *insurance and investment executive*

MARYLAND

Bowie
Gourdine-Tyson, Natachia *investment company executive, writer*

Rockville
Murray, Mary Rose *securities regulation investigator*

MASSACHUSETTS

Boston
Johnson, Abigail Pierrepont *investment company executive*
Ling, Chiew Sing *investment company executive*
McColgan, Ellyn *investment company executive*
Morby, Jacqueline *venture capitalist*

Medford
Goldberg, Pamela Winer *entrepreneur, educator*

Pepperell
Holmes, Jean Louise *real estate investor, humanities educator*

Stockbridge
Fitzpatrick, Jane *entrepreneur*

MICHIGAN

Farmington Hills
Ellmann, Sheila Frenkel *investment company executive*

Muskegon
Cirona, Jane Callahan *investment company executive*

Watervliet
Kaiser, Susan J. *investment advisor*

West Bloomfield
Mamut, Mary Catherine *retired entrepreneur*

MINNESOTA

Edina
Kata, Marie L. *securities dealer, brokerage house executive*

MISSOURI

Joplin
Huffman, Patricia Nell *entrepreneur*

Springfield
Cavner, Nadia *investment company executive*

NEBRASKA

Omaha
De Santiago, Dena Kalene *investment company executive, writer*

NEVADA

Carson City
Alexander, Judy Lynne *investor*

Las Vegas
Roberts, Lia *investor, political organization worker*

Reno
Harsh, Antoinette Mollett *investor*

NEW JERSEY

Jersey City
Stensgaard, Karen J. *brokerage house executive*

Little Falls
Shern, Stephanie Marie *investment company executive, accountant*

Montclair
Jones, Sylvia Calpurnia *investment company executive*

New Brunswick
Mills, Dorothy Allen *investor*

Newark
Ferris-Waks, Arlene Susan *compliance officer*

Pennington
Gundeck, Caroline Nyklewicz *investment company executive*

NEW MEXICO

Corrales
Eisenstadt, Pauline Doreen Bauman *brokerage house executive, state legislator*

NEW YORK

Bay Shore
Williams, Tonda *entrepreneur, consultant*

Brooklyn
Shahon, Laurie Meryl *investment company executive*

Forest Hills
Flowers, Cynthia *investment company executive*

Goshen
DeMueller, Lucia *investment consultant*

New York
Blalock, Sherrill *investment advisor*
Britz Lotti, Diane Edward *investment company executive*
Butte, Amy S. *brokerage house executive*
Clark, Mayree Carroll *investment banking executive*
Cohen, Abby Joseph *investment company executive*
Cohen, Claire Gorham *investment company executive*
Cole, Carolyn Jo *brokerage house executive*
Considine, Jill M. *securities trader*
Dias Griffin, Anne *investment advisor*
Einiger, Carol Blum *investment company executive*
Harris, Carla Ann *investment company executive*
Harron, Phoebe Zaslove *investment banking executive*
Hodges, Deborah *investment company executive*
Horn, Karen Nicholson *investment company executive, former bank executive*
Kinney, Catherine R. *stock exchange executive*
Lebenthal, Alexandra *investment firm executive*
Meeker, Mary G. *brokerage house executive*
Murray, Eileen K. *investment company executive*
Nascimento, Ana Paula *entrepreneur, food service executive*
Nichols, Carol D. *real estate professional*
Ogut, Bilge Ayse *investment advisor*
Povlitz, Jennifer *investment company executive*
Proctor, Georganne C. *investment company executive*
Shavin, Helene B. *venture capital company executive*
Siebert, Muriel (Mickie) *brokerage house executive, retired bank executive*
Skerl, Diana M. *stockbroker*
Tutwiler, Margaret DeBardeleben *stock exchange executive, former federal agency administrator*
Zoullas, Deborah Decotis *investment company executive*

Rochester
Spurrier, Mary Eileen *investment advisor, financial planner*

OHIO

Cincinnati
Klein, Sophia H. *entrepreneur*
Murphy, Molly Ann *investment company executive*

Columbus
Turnbull, Cheryl Lankard *investment company executive*

OREGON

Depoe Bay
Fish, Barbara Joan *investor, small business owner*

Medford
Hennion, Carolyn Laird (Lyn Hennion) *investment executive*

Portland
Corbett, Alice Catherine *investor*
Milton, Catherine Higgs *entrepreneur*

PENNSYLVANIA

Collegeville
Barnes, Jo Anne *investment advisor*

Philadelphia
Simpson, Carol Louise *investment company executive*

RHODE ISLAND

Newport
Higgins, Harriet Pratt *investment advisor*

Providence
Bogan, Mary Flair *stockbroker*

SOUTH CAROLINA

Columbia
McLean, Jodie W. *investment company executive*

Orangeburg
Dalton, Cheryl Renee *entrepreneur*

TENNESSEE

Knoxville
Penn, Dawn Tamara *entrepreneur*

TEXAS

Addison
Smith, Cece *venture capitalist*

Dallas
Byrne, Susan M. *investment company executive*
Crockett, Dodee Frost *brokerage house executive*

VIRGINIA

Arlington
Choksi, Mary *investment company executive*

Reston
Mitchell, Ellen Clabaugh *investment executive*

WASHINGTON

Seattle
Holcomb, Helen Lee *investor, interior designer*
Johnson, Mildred Grace Mash *investment company executive*

WISCONSIN

Mequon
Petersen, Dorothy Virginia *investment company executive*

WYOMING

Casper
True, Jean Durland *entrepreneur, oil industry executive, gas industry executive*

MEXICO

Mexico City
de Brun, Shauna Doyle *industrialist, investment banker*

MONGOLIA

Ulaanbaatar
Mandel, Leslie Ann *investment advisor, writer*

ADDRESS UNPUBLISHED

Apel-Brueggeman, Myrna L. *entrepreneur*
Bacon, Caroline Sharfman *investor, consultant*
Bailey, Rita Maria *investment advisor, psychologist*
Blum, Barbara Davis *investor*
Bowles, Barbara Landers *investment company executive*
Brooks, Velma *entrepreneur, small business owner*
Burns, Barbara Belton *investment company executive*
Cano, Marta Mendendez *securities company executive, financial consultant*
Casson Madden, Chris *entrepreneur, interior designer*
Chapman, Geneva Joyce *entrepreneur, educator, writer*
Codo, Christina *securities executive*
Cornish, Elizabeth Turverey *retired investment advisor*
Daie, Jaleh *investment company executive*
D'Este, Mary Ernestine *investment group executive*
Engelbreit, Mary *art licensing entrepreneur*
Fitts, Catherine Austin *investment advisor*
Gouletas, Evangeline *investment executive*
Griego, Linda *entrepreneur*
Hapner, Mary Lou *securities trader, writer*
Harvey, Jane R. *retired investment company executive*
Holte, Debra Leah *investment company executive, financial analyst*
Kahn, Herta Hess (Mrs. Howard Kahn) *retired investment company executive*
Kavovit, Barbara *entrepreneur*
Lieberman, Gail Forman *investment company executive*
Marshall, Julie W. Gregovich *investor relations executive*
Mullins, Jane Compton *investment manager*
Parker, Towana D. *entrepreneur, director*
Peterson, Dawn Michelle *entrepreneur, writer*
Rainwater, Joan Lucille Morse *investment company executive*
Ridgway, Rozanne LeJeanne *corporate director, retired ambassador*
Robinson, Annettmarie *entrepreneur*
Rondeau, Doris Jean *entrepreneur, consultant*
Schwartz, Carol Ann *investment company executive*
Spivak, Carol *investment company executive, volunteer*
Squire, Beverly *entrepreneur, business owner*
Taylor, Linda Rathbun *investment manager*
Tempel, Jean Curtin *venture capitalist*
Urato, Barbra Casale *entrepreneur*
Waters, Charlotte Ann *investment management company executive*
Watkins, Daphne C. *entrepreneur, consultant, advocate*
Wilkey, Mary Huff *investor, writer, publisher*
Zeviar-Geese, Gabriole *stock market investor, lawyer*

GOVERNMENT: AGENCY ADMINISTRATION

UNITED STATES

ALASKA

Anchorage
Burke, Marianne King *state agency administrator, finance company executive, consultant*

ARIZONA

Phoenix
Chavez, Nelba R. *state agency administrator, former federal agency administrator*
Moriarty, Karen *state agency administrator*

Tucson
Emerson, Kirk *government agency administrator*

CALIFORNIA

City Of Industry
Cavanaugh, Janis Lynn *protective services official, educator*

Edwards
Chacon, Maria *government agency administrator*

Edwards AFB
Arevalo, Carmen *government agency administrator*
Meske, Sandy *government agency administrator*
Young, Gwendolyn Vaisega *federal agency administrator*

Fresno
Diestelkamp, Dawn Lea *government agency administrator*

Glendale
Shelburne, Merry Clare *public information officer, educator*

Lancaster
Davison, Dawn Sherry *correctional administrator, educator*

Moffett Field
Navarro, BJ *federal agency administrator*

Napa
Maas, Maxine Anna Adelaide Schumann *retired juvenile justice administrator*

Norco
McNeal, Phyllis Paulette *parole agent*

Sacramento
Chilton, Shirley R. *state agency administrator*
Wright, Mary Rose *retired state agency administrator*

San Bernardino
Harlan, Shirley *protective services official, videographer*

San Francisco
Muñoz, Calise I. *federal agency administrator*

San Ysidro
Schneider, Christine Lynn *customs inspector*

Santa Monica
Timmer, Barbara *state agency administrator*

Stockton
Jackson, Jewel *retired state agency administrator*

West Covina
Montooth, Sheila Christine *state agency administrator*

COLORADO

Centennial
Wilks, Dana Lyn *protective services official, writer*

Denver
Gotlieb, Dorothy A. *deputy commissioner of education*
Mencer, Sue (Constance Suzanne Mencer) *former federal agency administrator*

Eldorado Springs
Lovins, L. Hunter *public policy institute executive, consultant, educator*

Pueblo
Deasy, Irene M. *retired protective services official*

CONNECTICUT

Bloomfield
Shimelman, Susan Fromm *state agency administrator*

Southbury
Foxworth, Johnnie Hunter *retired state agency administrator*

Suffield
Hanzalek, Astrid Teicher *public information officer, consultant*

DELAWARE

Dover
Woodruff, Valerie *state agency administrator*

Wilmington
Benson, Barbara Ellen *state agency administrator*

DISTRICT OF COLUMBIA

Washington
Altenhofen, Jane Ellen *federal agency administrator, auditor*
Alvillar-Speake, Theresa *federal agency administrator*
Apple, Daina Dravnieks *federal agency administrator*
Bair, Sheila Colleen *federal agency administrator, former education educator*
Baxter, Sandra L. *government agency administrator*
Beato, Cristina V. *government agency administrator*
Blakey, Marion Clifton *federal agency administrator*
Bodine, Susan P. *federal agency administrator*
Bradley Gardner, Janice *federal agency administrator*
Brand, Rachel L. *federal agency administrator, lawyer*
Briggs, Ethel DeLoria *federal agency administrator*
Brown-Hruska, Sharon *federal agency administrator*
Cabaniss, Dale *government agency administrator*
Carbonell, Josefina G. *federal agency administrator*
Chun, Shinae *federal agency administrator*
Cino, Maria *federal agency administrator*
Clark, Kathryn *government agency administrator*
Clarke, Kathleen Burton *federal agency administrator*
Cline, Lynn F.H. *federal agency administrator*
Colvin, Carolyn W. *state agency administrator*
Dale, Shana L. *federal agency administrator*
DeFrancis, Suzy *federal agency administrator*
DeSutter, Paula A. *federal agency administrator*
Doan, Lurita Alexis *federal agency administrator*
Dobriansky, Paula Jon *federal agency administrator*
Dorfman, Cynthia Hearn *government agency administrator*
Dunlop, Becky Norton *retired government agency administrator*
Engleman Connors, Ellen G. *federal agency administrator*
Fingerhut, Marilyn Ann *federal agency administrator*
Fisher, Alice S. *federal agency administrator, lawyer*
Fong, Phyllis Kamoi *federal agency administrator, lawyer*
Ford, Cecilia Sparks *federal agency administrator*
Fore, Henrietta Holsman *federal agency administrator*
Frawley Bagley, Elizabeth *government advisor, ambassador*
Frazer, Jendayi Elizabeth *federal agency administrator, former ambassador*
Freeman, Sharee M. *federal agency administrator*
Fresh, Linda Lou *government official*
Gallagher, Patricia E. *government agency administrator*
Gatons, Anna-Marie Kilmade *government official*
Gilbert, Pamela *strategic services company executive*
Glassman, Cynthia Aaron *federal agency administrator, former commissioner*
Goldway, Ruth Y. *federal agency administrator*
Gorn, Janet Marie *government official*
Grant, Susan J. *federal agency administrator*
Greaux, Cheryl Prejean *federal agency administrator*
Hall, Oceola S. *federal agency administrator*
Hanley, Allison Anne *federal agency administrator*
Harbert Mitchell, Karen (Karen Alderman Harbert Mitchell) *government agency administrator*
Hayes, Paula Freda *federal agency administrator*
Hersman, Deborah A. P. *federal agency administrator*
Higgins, Kathryn O'Leary (Kitty O'Leary Higgins) *federal agency administrator, former consulting firm executive*
Horn, Sharon K. *government agency administrator*
Horner, Constance Joan *federal agency administrator*
Hughes, Karen Parfitt *federal agency administrator*
Huhtala, Marie Therese *federal agency administrator, former ambassador*
Iverson, Kristine Ann *federal agency administrator*
Johnson, Kelly A. *federal agency administrator*
Jonas, Tina Westby *federal agency administrator*
Kelly, Holly Andrea *federal agency administrator, director, real estate developer*
Kendrick, Kim *federal agency administrator*
Lampl, Peggy Ann *public information officer*
Larkin, Barbara Mills *state agency administrator*
LaSpada, Carmella *government agency administrator*
Liebman, Wilma B. *government agency administrator*
Likins, Rose Marie *federal agency administrator, former ambassador*
Lim, Jeanette J. *federal agency administrator*
MacFarlane, Cathy M. *federal agency administrator*
Maddox, Lauren M. *federal agency administrator*
McKay, Margo Marquita *federal agency administrator, lawyer*
McKee, Margaret Jean *federal agency administrator*
McMurray, Claudia Anne *federal agency administrator, lawyer*
Merritt, Carolyn *government agency administrator*
Miller, Laura Jean *federal agency administrator*
Mondello, Lisette McSoud *federal agency administrator*
Monroe, Jane D. *federal agency administrator*
Monroe, Stephanie Johnson *federal agency administrator*
Montanez-Johner, Nancy *federal agency administrator*
Morrissey, Patricia A. *federal agency administrator*
Moten, Sarah Elizabeth *federal agency administrator*
Murphy, Frances M. *federal agency administrator*
Myers, Julie L. *federal agency administrator*
Nason, Nicole R. *federal agency administrator*
Neal, Darwina Lee *federal agency administrator*
Norwalk, Leslie V. *federal agency administrator*
O'Connor, Eileen J. *federal agency administrator*
Ohl, Joan Eschenbach *federal agency administrator*
Olsen, Jody (Josephine K. Olsen) *federal agency administrator*
O'Neill, Michelle *federal agency administrator*
O'Sullivan, Stephanie L. *federal agency administrator*
Pack, Sandra L. *federal agency administrator*
Patenaude, Pamela Hughes *federal agency administrator*
Patrick, Susan D. *federal agency administrator*
Patterson, Anne Woods (Anne Brevard Woods Patterson) *federal agency administrator, former ambassador*
Ponticelli, Charlotte *federal agency administrator*
Pope, Anne B. *agency head, business executive, lawyer*
Powell, Dina Habib *federal agency administrator*
Powell, Marsha N. *federal program analyst*
Reef, Grace *government official*
Rees, Nina Shokraii *federal agency administrator*
Ressel, Teresa Mullett *federal agency administrator*
Richardson, Pamela F. *federal agency administrator*
Riggs, Barbara *federal agency administrator*
Rodley, Carol A. *federal agency administrator*
Russell, Judy C. *government agency administrator*
Sandberg, Annette M. *federal agency administrator*
Sauerbrey, Ellen Elaine Richmond *federal agency administrator, former ambassador*
Scarlett, Lynn (Patricia Lynn Scarlett) *federal agency administrator*
Scheinberg, Phyllis F. *federal agency administrator*
Schneider, Ann Imlah *federal agency administrator, education consultant*
Schoettle, Enid C.B. *federal agency administrator*
Schofield, Regina Brown *federal agency administrator*
Shiner, Josette Sheeran *federal agency administrator*
Sigal, Jill L. *federal agency administrator*
Silverberg, Kristen L. *federal agency administrator*
Steele, Ana Mercedes *retired federal agency administrator*
Stroup, Sally *federal agency administrator*
Thomsen, Linda Chatman *federal agency administrator*
Tinsley, Nikki Lee Rush *federal agency administrator*
Tomb, Diane Lenegan *former federal agency administrator*
Turner, Pamela Jayne *federal agency administrator*
Vargas Stidvent, Veronica *federal agency administrator*
Vaughn, Gladys Gary *federal agency administrator, researcher, not-for-profit executive*
Watson, Rebecca Wunder *federal agency administrator, lawyer*
Williams, Darlene F. *federal agency administrator*
Williams, Julie Lloyd *federal agency administrator, lawyer*
Wooldridge, Sue Ellen *federal agency administrator, lawyer*
Wright, Sylvia *government agency administrator*

FLORIDA

Boca Raton
Robben, Tricia Elizabeth *protective services official*

Delray Beach
Schenkel, Suzanne Chance *retired natural resource specialist*

Fort Lauderdale
Carter Pereira, Claudine Renee *forensic specialist*

Lake Worth
Heessel, Eleanor Lucille Lea *retired state agency administrator*

Orlando
Garavaglia, Jan C. *forensic pathologist, chief medical examiner*

Tallahassee
Braswell, Jackie Boyd *state agency administrator*

GEORGIA

Atlanta
Gerberding, Julie Louise *federal agency administrator*
Khabbaz, Rima *government agency administrator*
McGowan, Angela Kay *government agency administrator, researcher*
Medows, Rhonda M. *state agency administrator, public health service officer*
Ogden, Lydia Lee *government agency administrator*

Savannah
Marriott, Karla-Sue Camille *forensic specialist*

HAWAII

Honolulu
Fukino, Chiyome Leinaala *state agency administrator, public health service officer*
Saiki, Patricia (Mrs. Stanley Mitsuo Saiki) *federal agency administrator, congressman*

IDAHO

Boise
Jones, Donna Marilyn *state agency administrator, former legislator*
Peterson, Eileen M. *state agency administrator*
Smith, Marsha H. *state agency administrator, lawyer*

Idaho Falls
Rydalch, Ann *federal agency administrator*

ILLINOIS

Arlington Heights
Biestek, Elizabeth Mary *forensic specialist*

Chicago
Coyle, Dorothy *government agency administrator*
Jibben, Laura Ann *state agency administrator*
Kinslow, Monica M. *forensic specialist*
Thomas, Cherryl T. *former federal agency administrator*

Rock Falls
Crebo, Mary Elizabeth *state agency official, assessor*

Springfield
Schroeder, Joyce Katherine *state agency administrator, research analyst*

INDIANA

Indianapolis
Monroe, Judith A. *state agency administrator, public health service officer*

IOWA

Ankeny
Goodin, Julia C. *forensic specialist, state official*

Davenport
Wilson, Frances Edna *protective services official*

Des Moines
Nelson, Charlotte Bowers *public administrator*

KANSAS

Overland Park
McCann, Vonya B. *federal agency administrator, telecommunications industry executive*

KENTUCKY

Louisville
VanDiver, Betty J. *protective services professional*

Madisonville
Veazey, Doris Anne *retired state agency administrator*

LOUISIANA

New Orleans
Adams, Ingrid G. *federal government intelligence specialist*

Shreveport
Foggin, Brenda Frazier *retired state agency administrator, volunteer*

MAINE

Saco
Mason, Nancy Tolman *retired state agency administrator*

MARYLAND

Annapolis
Snyder, Kathleen Theresa *state agency administrator*

Baltimore
Abrams, Rosalie Silber *retired state agency official*
Barnes, Adrienne *public information officer*
Barnhart, Jo Anne B. *federal agency administrator*
Corley, Rose Ann McAfee *government official*
Harryman, Kathleen A. *board administrator*

Bethesda
Alving, Barbara *federal agency administrator, hematologist*
Barros, Colleen *federal agency administrator*
Gottesman, Susan *federal agency administrator*
Grady, Patricia A. *federal agency administrator*
Hrynkow, Sharon Hemond *federal agency administrator, neuroscientist, researcher*
Joyce, Bernita Anne *retired federal agency administrator*
Landis, Story Cleland *federal agency administrator, neurobiologist*
Larrabee, Barbara Princelau *retired intelligence officer*
Mancher, Rhoda Ross *federal agency administrator, financial planner*
Nieves, Josephine *federal agency administrator*
Ostrander, Elaine A. *federal agency administrator, geneticist*
Parron, Delores L. *federal agency administrator*
Pinn, Vivian W. *federal agency administrator, pathologist*
Ruiz-Bravo, Norka *federal agency administrator*
Singer, Dinah S. *federal agency administrator, immunologist, researcher*
Skirboll, Lana R. *federal health policy director*
Springfield, Sanya A. *federal agency administrator*

Chestertown
Costella, Lorraine Adele *state agency administrator*

Easton
Colton, Elizabeth Wishart *government agency administrator*

Madison
Hoffman, Alicia Coro *retired federal executive*

Rockville
Davis, Beverly Watts *federal agency administrator*
Duke, Elizabeth M. *federal agency administrator*
Gray, Paulette Styles *federal agency administrator, biologist*
Power, A. Kathryn *federal agency administrator*
Snyder, A. Michelle *federal agency administrator*
Uhl, Kathleen *federal agency administrator*

Silver Spring
de Zafra Atwell, Dorothea Elizabeth *retired government agency administrator*

MASSACHUSETTS

Boston
Crimlisk, Jane Therese *probation officer*
Kaufman, Vicki *civil rights investigator*

Cambridge
Hunt, Swanee G. *public policy educator, former ambassador*

Lexington
Thernstrom, Abigail *federal agency administrator, writer*

MICHIGAN

Ann Arbor
Bierbaum, Rosina M. *federal agency administrator*
Schmitt, Mary Elizabeth *retired postal supervisor*

Detroit
Bully-Cummings, Ella M. *police chief*

Lanse
Butler, Patricia *protective services official*

Lansing
Chaney, Elizabeth Moncrief *state agency administrator*
Olszewski, Janet *state agency administrator*

Muskegon
Ohst, Wendy Joan *government agency administrator, educator*

Royal Oak
Thomson, Kathleen Kepner *retired state agency administrator*

MINNESOTA

Saint Paul
Boudreau, Lynda L. *state agency administrator*
Hall, Beverly Joy *police officer*
Mandernach, Dianne *state agency administrator*

MISSOURI

Anderson
Coble, Mary Gloria *protective services official, rancher*

Jefferson City
Eckstein, Julie *state agency administrator*
Tackett, Natalie Jane *state administrator*

MONTANA

Helena
Miles, Joan *state agency administrator, former state legislator, lawyer*

NEBRASKA

Lincoln
Fleharty, Mary Sue *government agency administrator*
Kilgarin, Karen *state official, public relations consultant*

Omaha
Bang, Michele Alene *protective services official*
Mactier, Ann Dickinson *state agency administrator*

NEVADA

Las Vegas

Klein, Freda *retired state agency administrator*

NEW HAMPSHIRE

Brentwood

Micklos, Janet M. *state agency administrator, human services director*

NEW JERSEY

Barrington

Florio, Maryanne J. *health and education research scientist*

Elizabeth

Fulmore, MaryAnn *state agency administrator*

Maplewood

Rabadeau, Mary Frances *protective services official*

Trenton

Bauer, Virginia S. *state agency administrator*
Cardinali, Noreen Sadler *state agency administrator*

NEW MEXICO

Albuquerque

DeWitt, Mary Therese *forensic specialist, anthropologist, archaeologist, consultant*
Jaramillo, Mari-Luci *retired federal agency administrator*

Santa Fe

Grisham, Michelle Lujan *state agency administrator*
Kelly, Ruth *state agency administrator*

NEW YORK

Albany

Mulholland, Nancy W. *state agency administrator*

Huntington

Kirwin, Barbara Rosa *forensic specialist*

New York

Beausoleil, Doris Mae *retired federal agency housing specialist*
Gustafson, Judith *federal association administrator*
Rosa, Margarita *agency executive director, lawyer*
Stewart, Ruth Ann *public policy educator*

Rochester

Guarnere, Joanne *protective services official*

Springfield Gardens

Moore, Deborah Chantay *protective services official, psychotherapist*

NORTH CAROLINA

Greensboro

Wallace, Becky Whitley *protective services official*

Jefferson

Maney, Lois Jean *postmaster*

Pinehurst

Denton, Estelle Rosemary *retired federal agency administrator*

Waynesville

Ingle, Marti Annette *protective services official, educator, chef*

Wilmington

Clinton, Lottie Dry Edwards *retired state agency administrator*

OHIO

Akron

Shane, Sandra Kuli *postal service administrator*

Columbus

Gillmor, Karen Lako *state agency administrator*
Kearns, Merle Grace *state agency administrator*
Moncrief, Jacqueline C. *retired state agency administrator*

New Philadelphia

Hendrix, Christine Janet *retired government agency administrator, retired small business owner, volunteer*

Springfield

Woodhouse, Elizabeth C. *retired government agency administrator*

OKLAHOMA

Oklahoma City

Wheeler, Jane Frances *protective services official*

Tinker Afb

Penn, Vernita Lynn *government agency administrator*

Wagoner

Hadley, Charline A. *protective services official*

PENNSYLVANIA

Norristown

Raquet, Maureen Graham *protective services official, educator*

RHODE ISLAND

Providence

Cox, Dawn Everlina *protective services official*
Hedlund, Ellen Louise *state agency administrator, educator*
Worthen, Nancy Smith *federal agency administrator*

SOUTH CAROLINA

Columbia

Resch, Mary Louise *town agency administrator*
Toth, Susan Helen *government agency administrator*

SOUTH DAKOTA

Pierre

Duhamel, Judith Reedu Olson *public information officer, former state senator*
Hollingsworth, Doneen *state agency administrator*

TENNESSEE

Knoxville

Harris, Skila *government agency administrator*

Nashville

Gusky, Diane Elizabeth *state agency administrator, planner*

TEXAS

Austin

Brown, Vivian Anderson *retired government agency administrator*
Combs, Susan *state agency administrator*
Simon, Sandra Ruth Waldman *state agency administrator*

Brownsville

Gorman, Margaret Norine *probation officer, chemical dependency counselor*

Dallas

Barnett, Patricia Ann *development professional*
Mathis-Thorton, Dianna Dawn *protective services official, writer, publishing executive, not-for-profit developer*

Houston

Gillette, Estella Hernandez *government agency administrator*

Kingsland

Watson, Elizabeth Marion *protective services official*

Wharton

Maxfield, Rose Mary *retired government official*

UTAH

Salt Lake City

Sparks, Mildred Thomas *state agency administrator, educator*

VIRGINIA

Alexandria

Bynum, Gayela A. *public information officer*
Hughes, Grace-Flores *federal agency administrator*
Johnson, JoAnn Mardelle *federal agency administrator*
Leonhart, Michele Marie *federal agency administrator*

Arlington

Askey, Thelma J. *federal agency administrator*
Baginski, Maureen A. *former federal agency administrator*
Bune, Karen Louise *state agency administrator*
Harrison, Virginia M. *federal agency administrator*
McCarthy, Jane McGinnis *retired government agency administrator*
Meadows, Vickers B. *federal agency administrator*

Charlottesville

Johnson, Cornelia *city sheriff, small business owner*

Hampton

Roe, Lesa B. *federal agency administrator*

Mc Lean

Burke, Sheila P. *federal agency administrator*
Lion, Linda N. *retired federal agency administrator*

Richmond

Baskerville, Viola Osborne *state government official*

Staunton

Grewe, Marjorie Jane *retired protective services official*

Williamsburg

Drum, Joan Marie McFarland *federal agency administrator, educator*

WASHINGTON

Olympia

Selecky, Mary C. *state agency administrator*

WEST VIRGINIA

Charleston

Walker, Martha Yeager *state agency administrator, former state senator*

Martinsburg

Harkins, Ann M. *federal agency administrator*

WISCONSIN

Madison

Johnson, Sheri *state agency administrator, psychologist*

Milwaukee

Hegerty, Nannette H. *police chief*

WYOMING

Cheyenne

Lee, Kristin H. *state agency administrator*

TERRITORIES OF THE UNITED STATES

AMERICAN SAMOA

Pago Pago

Howland, Repeka Moata'a Isara *retired government community services administrator*

CANADA

ONTARIO

Ottawa

Fraser, Sheila *government agency administrator*

ENGLAND

London

Clark, Cynthia Zang Facer *federal agency administrator*

IRELAND

Dublin

O'Toole, Kathleen M. *protective services official*

ADDRESS UNPUBLISHED

Alvarez, Aida M. *former federal agency administrator*
Bartenstein, Jeuli *federal agency administrator*
Barth, Carin Marcy *former federal agency administrator*
Behrouz, Elizabeth Jean *service director*
Benton, Marjorie Craig *federal agency administrator*
Bishop, C. Diane *state agency administrator, educator*
Blakeney, Kecia L. *disability examiner*
Blumberg, Barbara Salmanson (Mrs. Arnold G. Blumberg) *retired state housing official, housing consultant*
Boswell, Vivian Nicholson *protective services official*
Brown, Dale Susan *retired federal agency administrator, academic administrator, consultant, writer*
Burgess, Marjorie Laura *retired protective services official*
Cassidy, Esther Christmas *retired government official*
Chu, Margaret S.Y. *former federal agency administrator*
Clarke, Victoria C. (Torie Clarke) *former federal agency administrator*
Crossley, Nancy Ruth *retired federal agency administrator*
Eubanks, Sharon Y. *former federal agency administrator*
Faulkner, Frances Mayhew *retired federal agency administrator*
Finauri, Graciela Maria *foreign service official*
Franklin, Bonnie Selinksy *retired federal agency administrator*
Gall, Mary Sheila *former federal agency administrator*
Golding, Carolyn May *former government senior executive, consultant*
Halpern, Cheryl F. *federal agency administrator*
Hamilton, Janet Renee *protective services official*
Henke, Tracy Ann *former federal agency administrator*
Iovino, Pamela M. *federal agency administrator*
James, Kay Coles *former federal agency administrator*
Karp, Naomi Katherine *United States government administrator*
Knox, Deborah Carolyn *state information systems administrator*
Krieger, Lois B. *retired state agency administrator*
Lancaster, Karine R. *retired city health department administrator*
Legg, Hilda Gay *former federal agency administrator*
Lokmer, Stephanie Ann *international business development consultant*
Lovelace, Rose Marie Sniegon *federal space agency administrator*
Mainella, Fran (Frances P. Mainella) *former federal agency administrator*
Manno, Rita *state agency administrator*
Marsh, Frances Emily Francis *state agency administrator, set designer*
McClain, Lena Alexandria *protective services official*
McDowell, Elaine *retired federal government executive, educator*
Millman, Amy J. *government official*
Mlay, Marian *retired government official*
Molz, Redmond Kathleen *public affairs educator*
Morales, Diane K. *former federal agency administrator*
Newman, Constance Berry *federal agency administrator*
Nolen, Jeanada H. *retired state agency administrator, social worker, educator*
Noziglia, Carla Miller *forensic scientist*
O'Brien, Odessa Louise *protective services official*
Peterson, Katherine H. *federal agency administrator, former ambassador*
Plame, Valerie Elise *former intelligence agent*
Poole, Katherine *government agency administrator*
Potter, Patricia Rae *retired protective services official*
Rhodes, Karren *public information officer*
Rosenberg, Alison P. *public policy officer*
Rundio, Joan Peters (Jo Rundio) *retired public information officer*
Ryder, Tereasa Kai *retired protective services official*
Sabelhaus, Melanie R. *government agency administrator*
Schafer, Jacqueline Ellen *federal agency administrator*
Schultz, Janet W. *intelligence research analyst*
Schur Kaufman, Susan *retired public affairs consultant*
Schwartz, Carol Levitt *government official*
Sheridan, Diane Frances *public policy facilitator*
Shows, Winnie M. *speaker, consultant, writer*
Simmons, Emmy B. *former federal agency administrator*
Slater, Cathryn Buford *former federal agency administrator*
Smith, Linda Wines *government official*
Smith, Nancy Angelynn *federal agency administrator*
Smith, Suzanne M. *federal agency administrator*
Smith, Wendy Haimes *federal agency administrator*
Steffy, Marion Nancy *state agency administrator*
Steuterman, Erika C. *government agency administrator*
Strachan, Linda Avery *federal agency administrator*
Swinburn, Carol Ditzler *retired state and municipal agency administrator*
Vandiver, Sara Elizabeth Sharp Rankin *retired postmaster*
Warner, Susan *federal agency administrator*
Waters, Mary Brice Kirtley *former federal agency administrator*
Werkman, Rosemarie Anne *former public relations professional, volunteer*
Weston, Rebecca Lynn *forensic specialist, educator*
Whitman, Christine Todd *former federal agency administrator, former governor*
Withrow, Mary Ellen *federal agency administrator*

GOVERNMENT: EXECUTIVE ADMINISTRATION

UNITED STATES

ALABAMA

Montgomery

Baxley, Lucy *lieutenant governor*
Ivey, Kay Ellen *state official*
Spear, Sarah G. *county administrator*
Worley, Nancy L. *state official*

Warrior

Johnson, Barbara L. *retired municipal official*

ARIZONA

Glendale

Scruggs, Elaine M. *mayor*

Nogales

Valdez, Wanda Daniel *county official*

Phoenix

Brewer, Janice Kay *state official*
Meeks, Jacquelynn *city health department administrator*
Napolitano, Janet Ann *governor*
Skinner, Nancy Jo *municipal recreation executive*

Scottsdale

Manross, Mary *mayor*
Quayle, Marilyn Tucker *wife of former United States Vice President, lawyer*

Tucson

Miller, Elizabeth Rodriguez *city official*

ARKANSAS

Jonesboro

Chrisman, Nancy Carol *city manager, director, small business owner*

Little Rock
Hochstetter, Sandra *state official*
Priest, Sharon Devlin *retired state official, not-for-profit developer*

CALIFORNIA

Alameda
Leonard, Sheila Ann *former government agency executive, consultant*

Albany
Thomsen, Peggy Jean *mayor, educator*

Carson
Oropeza, Jenny *state official*

Long Beach
O'Neill, Beverly Lewis *mayor, former college president*
Sato, Eunice Noda *former mayor, consultant*

Los Angeles
Jeff, Gloria Jean *city official*
Molina, Gloria *municipal official*
Toman, Mary Ann *federal official*

Marina
Mettee-McCutchon, Ila *municipal official, retired military officer*

Monterey Park
Smith, Betty Denny *county official, administrator, fashion executive*

Oceanside
Freeman, Myrna Faye *county schools official*

Ontario
Dastrup-Hamill, Faye Myers *city official*

Richmond
Corbin, Rosemary MacGowan *former mayor*

Sacramento
Contreras, Dee (Dorothea Contreras) *municipal official, educator*
Fargo, Heather *mayor*
Hunter, Patricia Rae (Tricia Hunter) *state official*

San Bernardino
Evans, R. Marlene *county agency administrator*

San Diego
Golding, Susan G. *former mayor*
Jacob, Dianne *county official*
Shepard, Jean M. *city health department administrator*

San Francisco
Ward, Doris M. *county official*

Santa Monica
de La Vega, Dianne Winifred DeMarinis (Mrs. Jorge de La Vega) *government official*

Stockton
Meissner, Katherine Gong *municipal official*

Sunnyvale
Briody, Lynn *municipal official*

COLORADO

Arvada
Vanderkolk, Maria Elizabeth *city official*

Aurora
Sheffield, Nancy *city agency administrator*

Colorado Springs
Abbott, Gina *municipal government executive*

Denver
Cohen-Vader, Cheryl Denise *municipal official*
Dennis, Gigi (Ginette E. Dennis) *state official, former state legislator*
Muja, Kathleen Ann *state official, consultant*
Norton, Jane E. (Jane Bergman) *lieutenant governor*
Walcher, Jennifer Lynne *city official*

Eagle
Sheaffer, Karen *county official, treasurer*

Golden
Fahey, Barbara Stewart Doe *public agency administrator*

Sterling
Gumina, Pamela Ray *municipal government administrator*

CONNECTICUT

Easton
Meyer, Alice Virginia *state official*

Hartford
Bysiewicz, Susan *state official*
Nappier, Denise L. *state official*
Rell, M. Jodi *governor*

Norwalk
Roman, Mary *city official*

Stamford
Dennies, Sandra Lee *city official*

DELAWARE

Dover
Minner, Ruth Ann *governor*
Windsor, Harriet Smith *state official*

DISTRICT OF COLUMBIA

Washington
A-Baki, Ivonne *ambassador*
Albright, Madeleine Korbel *former secretary of state*
Anthony, Sheila Foster *government official*
Aranoff, Shara L. *federal official*
Ayres, Mary Ellen *federal official*
Azcuenaga, Mary Laurie *government official*
Baicker, Katherine (Kate Baicker) *federal official, economics professor*
Bailey, Catherine Todd *ambassador*
Barr, Joyce A. *ambassador*
Bolton, Deborah A. *ambassador*
Brazeal, Aurelia Erskine *former ambassador*
Breathitt, Linda K. *energy advisor, former federal energy commissioner*
Bridgewater, Pamela E. *ambassador, former federal agency administrator*
Broderick, Laura Anne *federal official*
Brown, Elizabeth Ann *foreign service officer*
Bush, Laura Welch *First Lady of United States*
Bushnell, Prudence *diplomat, former management consultant, trainer*
Butenis, Patricia A. *ambassador*
Casey, Kathleen L. *commissioner*
Chammas, Judith Ann *diplomat*
Chan, Heng Chee *ambassador*
Chao, Elaine Lan (Hsiao Lan Chao) *secretary of labor*
Cobb, Jane Overton *government official*
Cohen, Bonnie R. *government official*
Combs, Linda Morrison *federal official*
Cushwa, Patricia K. *commissioner*
Davidson, Donetta Lea *federal official, former state official*
Dominguez, Cari M. *federal official*
Dorn, Jennifer Lynn *federal official*
Dye, Rebecca Feemster *commissioner*
Earp, Naomi Churchill *federal official, lawyer*
Elwood, Patricia Cowan *state official, political scientist, consultant, educational consultant*
Ely-Raphel, Nancy *diplomat*
Escobedo Cabral, Anna *federal official*
Foley, April H. *ambassador*
Francke, Rend Rahim *former ambassador*
Franklin, Barbara Hackman *former government official*
Friday, Eleanor Sullivan *federal official*
Gati, Toby T. *international advisor*
Gilliom, Judith Carr *federal official*
Griffin, Christine M. *commissioner*
Hale, Suzanne K. *ambassador*
Harbour, Pamela Jones *commissioner, lawyer*
Haslach, Patricia M. *ambassador*
Hayes, Allene Valerie Farmer *government executive*
Herbold, Patricia Louise *ambassador*
Hillman, Jennifer Anne *federal official*
Hodges, Heather M. *ambassador*
Hynson, Jan I. *federal ombudsman, artist*
Irving, Susan Jean *government executive*
Jackson, Jeanine E. *ambassador*
Jacobson, Tracey Ann *ambassador*
Jewell, Linda L. *ambassador*
Johnson, Brenda LaGrange *ambassador*
Johnson, Jennifer J. *federal official*
Kelly, Suedeen G. *commissioner*
Kenney, Kristie Anne *ambassador*
Kilberg, Bobbie Greene *government official*
La Lime, Helen R. Meagher *ambassador*
Levy, Leah Garrigan *federal official*
Lowe, Mary Frances *federal official*
Lundsager, Margrethe (Meg Lundsager) *federal official*
Madras, Bertha Kalifon *federal official, neuroscientist*
Majoras, Deborah Platt *commissioner*
Marcoullis, Erato Kozakou *ambassador*
Martinez, Carmen Maria *ambassador*
Masekela, Barbara Joyce Mosima *ambassador*
McCaw, Susan Rasinski *ambassador*
McEldowney, Nancy *diplomat*
Miers, Harriet Ellan *federal official, lawyer*
Millman, Laura Diane *federal official*
Moore, Barbara C. *ambassador*
Moriarty, Lauren *ambassador*
Nardi Riddle, Clarine *chief of staff*
Nazareth, Annette LaPorte *commissioner, lawyer*
Newman, Sherryl Hobbs *former district secretary*
O'Day, Kathleen M. *federal official, lawyer*
Okun, Deanna Tanner *federal official*
Orr, Bobette Kay *diplomat*
Patron, June Eileen *former government official*
Pearce, Drue *federal official, former state legislator*
Perino, Dana Marie *federal official*
Perry, June Carter *ambassador*
Peters, Mary Ann *ambassador*
Peters, Mary E. *secretary of transportation*
Powell, Nancy Jo *federal official, former ambassador*
Ragsdale, Marquerita D. *ambassador*
Rice, Condoleezza *secretary of state, former national security advisor*
Ries, Marcie Berman *ambassador*
Roe, Charlotte E. *diplomat*
Rogers, Thomasina Venese *federal commissioner*
Rose, Mary McNally *federal official*
Ruhe, Shirley Louise *government official*
Sanders, Jackie Wolcott *ambassador*
Schneider, Cynthia Perrin *former ambassador, political science professor*
Schwab, Susan Carroll *ambassador, former academic administrator*
Scott-Finan, Nancy Isabella *government administrator*
Sharpless, Mattie R. *ambassador*
Shaw, Theresa S. (Terri Shaw) *federal official*
Silverman, Leslie E. *commissioner*
Simmons, Anne L. *federal official*
Sison, Michele J. *ambassador*
Slutz, Pamela Jo Howell *ambassador*
Smith, Elaine Diana *foreign service officer*
Smith, Patricia Grace *federal official*
Solberg, Mary Ann *federal official*
Spellings, Margaret LaMontagne *secretary of education*
Springer, Linda M. *federal official*
Stock, Ann *federal official*
Suro-Bredie, Carmen Cecilia *federal official*
Tate, Deborah Taylor *commissioner*
Townsend, Fran (Frances Fragos Townsend) *federal official*
Van de Water, Read *federal official*
van Voorst, Carol *ambassador*
Varney, Christine A. *federal official*
Verville, Elizabeth Giavani *federal official*
Villarosa, Shari *ambassador*
Wang, Kim *commissioner, librarian*
Ware, Marilyn *ambassador, former utilities company executive*
Weintraub, Ellen L. *commissioner*
Wexler, Anne *government relations and public affairs consultant*
Wheatley, Katherine Holbrook *federal official, lawyer*
Wolff, Candida (Candi Wolff) *federal official*

FLORIDA

Boynton Beach
Polinsky, Janet Naboicheck *retired state official, retired state legislator*

Fort Lauderdale
Donaldson, Lisa Miller *city administrator*
Gunzburger, Suzanne Nathan *municipal official, social worker*
Johnson, Mary Margaret Dickens *governmental and commercial researcher, consultant*

Hallandale Beach
Cooper, Joy Frances *mayor*

Hollywood
Giulianti, Mara Selena *mayor*

Miami
Carey-Shuler, Barbara *county commissioner*
Magrath, Kathleen Barry *retired municipal official*
Moorman, Rose Drunell *county administrator, systems analyst*

Oldsmar
Hahn, Sharon Lee *city official*

Ponte Vedra Beach
Soderberg, Nancy *former court official, writer*

Punta Gorda
Smith-Mooney, Marilyn Patricia *city government official, management consultant*

Tallahassee
Cobb, Sue McCourt *state official, former ambassador*
Jennings, Toni *lieutenant governor*
Mortham, Sandra Barringer *former state official*

Tampa
Freedman, Sandra Warshaw *former mayor*
Iorio, Pam *county official*
Platt, Jan Kaminis *former county official*

GEORGIA

Alpharetta
Johnson, Sandra Bartlett *city official*

Atlanta
Cox, Cathy *state official*
Franklin, Shirley Clarke *mayor*

Brunswick
Patrick, Connie L. *federal official*

HAWAII

Honolulu
Bronster, Margery S. *retired state attorney general, lawyer*
Lingle, Linda *governor*

IDAHO

Boise
Terteling-Payne, Carolyn Ann *city official*

ILLINOIS

Berwyn
Karasek, Mary Hapac *city treasurer, community volunteer*

Chicago
Dempsey, Mary A. *commissioner, lawyer*
Madigan, Lisa *state attorney general*
Robbins, Audrey *county official*
Rothstein, Ruth M. *county health official*
Sledge, Carla Elissa *county official*
Topinka, Judy Baar *state official, political organization worker*
Willis, Anna L. *commissioner*

Machesney Park
Vaughn, Linda Marie *municipal official*

Springfield
Curry, Julie A. *state official*
Morford, Lynn Ellen *state official*

Urbana
Prussing, Laurel Lunt *mayor, economist*

INDIANA

Columbus
Carter, Pamela Lynn *former state attorney general*

Indianapolis
Caine, Virginia A. *city health department administrator*
Skillman, Becky Sue *lieutenant governor, former state legislator*
Usher, Phyllis Land *state official*

South Bend
Davis, Katherine Lyon *former lieutenant governor*

IOWA

Des Moines
Corning, Joy Cole *retired state official*
Huser, Geri D. *state official*
Jacobs, Libby Swanson *state official*
Kramer, Mary Elizabeth *ambassador, former state legislator*
Pederson, Sally *lieutenant governor*

Oelwein
McFarlane, Beth Lucetta Troester *retired mayor*

Rockwell City
Erkenbrack, Lori Jean *county official*

KANSAS

Arkansas City
Bruton, Rebecca Ann *mayor, commissioner*

Concordia
Hill, Judy Marie Zimmermont *mayor, secondary school educator*

Garden Plain
Stovall, Carla Jo *former state attorney general*

Kansas City
Pettey, Patricia Huggins *county official*

Topeka
Jenkins, Lynn M. *state official, former state legislator*
Sebelius, Kathleen Gilligan *governor*

KENTUCKY

Catlettsburg
Selbee, Maxine Butcher *county clerk*

Frankfort
Palmore, Carol M. *state official*

Lexington
Isaac, Teresa Ann *mayor, lawyer*
Miller, Pamela Gundersen *retired mayor*

LOUISIANA

Baton Rouge
Blanco, Kathleen Babineaux *governor*

La Place
Blair, Ruth Reba *retired government official*

MAINE

Augusta
McCormick, Dale *state official*
Waldron, Janet E. *state commissioner*

Belfast
Worth, Mary Page *mayor*

MARYLAND

Annapolis
Clagett, Virginia Parker *state official*
Kane, Mary Deely *state official*
Kopp, Nancy Kornblith *state official*

Baltimore
Dixon, Sheila *municipal official*
Mensh, Suzanne Cooper *state official*
Miser, Ann *retired government researcher*

Bethesda
Kawazoe, Robin Inada *federal official*

Chevy Chase
Spagnoli, Deborah Ann *commissioner*

College Park
Lowrey, Barbara R. *educator, former federal official*

Columbia
Harris, Marion Hopkins *retired federal official, academic administrator*
Lok, Joan Mei-Lok *community affairs specialist, artist*
Scates, Alice Yeomans *retired federal official*

Jefferson
Aughenbaugh, Deborah Ann *mayor, retired elementary school educator*

Potomac
Roesser, Jean Wolberg *state official*

Rockville
Woodcock, Janet *federal official*

Severna Park
Wilkins, Virginia Kathleen *government liason*

Upper Marlboro
Hewlett, Elizabeth M. *county official*

West Bethesda
Vogelgesang, Sandra Louise *former ambassador, writer, consultant*

MASSACHUSETTS

Boston
Healey, Kerry Murphy *lieutenant governor*

Hyannis
Devine, Nancy *retired postmaster*

Littleton
Crory, Mary *town official*

New Bedford
Thomas, Sharon M. *city official*

Roslindale
Sullivan, Dorothy Rona *state official*

Taunton
Lopes, Maria Fernandina *commissioner*

MICHIGAN

Ann Arbor
Ford, Betty Ann (Elizabeth Ann Ford) *former First Lady of the United States, health facility executive*
Sheldon, Ingrid Kristina *retired mayor, controller*

Battle Creek
Baldwin, Susan Olin *commissioner, management consultant*

Detroit
Bell Wilson, Carlotta A. *state official, consultant*

Flint
Conyers, Jean Louise *chamber of commerce executive*

Lansing
Granholm, Jennifer Mulhern *governor*
Land, Terri Lynn *state official*

Tecumseh
Sackett, Dianne Marie *city treasurer, accountant*

Warren
Kolakowski, Diana Jean *county commissioner*

MINNESOTA

Elbow Lake
Lohse, Susan Faye *county official, educator*

Golden Valley
Leppik, Margaret White *municipal official*

Minneapolis
Fraser, Arvonne Skelton *retired diplomat*
Mondale, Joan Adams *wife of former Vice President of United States*
Sayles Belton, Sharon *former mayor*

Minnetonka
Anderson, Karen Jean *mayor, researcher, communications executive*

Saint Paul
Kiffmeyer, Mary *state official*
Kimberly, Susan Elizabeth *municipal official, writer*
Molnau, Carol *lieutenant governor*
Pinke, Judith Ann *state official*

MISSISSIPPI

Jackson
Tuck, Amy *lieutenant governor*

MISSOURI

Jefferson City
Carnahan, Robin *state official*
Farmer, Nancy *state official*

Kansas City
Barnes, Kay *mayor*
Stroup, Kala Mays *former education commissioner, educational alliance administrator*

Laurie
Reppert, Nancy Lue *retired municipal official, legal consultant*

Troy
McClellan, Betty *retired county official*

MONTANA

Clancy
Ekanger, Laurie *retired state official, consultant*

Forsyth
Lincoln, Sharon Ann *retired county official*

NEBRASKA

Brewster
Teahon, Jean Ann *county official*

Lincoln
Boyle, Anne C. *state commissioner*
Hasselbalch, Marilyn Jean *retired state official*
Seng, Coleen Joy *mayor*

NEVADA

Carson City
Hunt, Lorraine T. *lieutenant governor*
Molasky-Arman, Alice Anne *state commissioner*

Dayton
Hudgens, Sandra Lawler *retired state official*

Henderson
McKinney, Sally Vitkus *state official*

Reno
Cafferata, Patricia Dillon *state official*

NEW HAMPSHIRE

Concord
Ayotte, Kelly A. *state attorney general*

Goffstown
Holden, Carol Helen *county official*

Nashua
Pignatelli, Debora Becker *state official*

Nelson
Kirk, Jane Seaver *municipal government administrator*

NEW JERSEY

Bernardsville
Boquist, Diana D. *mayor, real estate agent*

East Orange
Corbitt, Ann Marie *municipal official*

Jersey City
Mizzi, Charlotte H. *city director*

Little Ferry
Navarro-Steinel, Catherine A. *municipal official*

Sea Isle City
Tull, Theresa Anne *retired diplomat*

Trenton
Wells, Nina Mitchell *state official*

NEW MEXICO

Santa Fe
Denish, Diane D. *lieutenant governor*
Madrid, Patricia A. *state attorney general*
Vigil-Giron, Rebecca *state official*

NEW YORK

Albany
Donohue, Mary *lieutenant governor*
Novello, Antonia Coello *state health commissioner, pediatric nephrologist, former Surgeon General of the United States*

Armonk
Wago, Mildred Hogan *retired municipal official*

Brewster
Bates, Barbara J. Neuner *retired municipal official*

Brooklyn
Evans-Tranumn, Shelia *commissioner, former literature and language educator*

Buffalo
Nowak, Carol Ann *city official*

Kew Gardens
Marshall, Helen M. *city manager*

Lawrence
Berman, Carol *retired commissioner*
Okos, Mildred *city manager*

Mineola
O'Connell, Maureen C. *county official, former state legislator*

New York
Buissonnière, Marine *international organization administrator; physician*
Dawson, Stephanie Elaine *city manager*
Durrant, M. Patricia *diplomat*
Ferguson, Sarah *The Duchess of York*
Fields, C. Virginia *city manager*
Gotbaum, Betsy *municipal official*
Løj, Ellen Margrethe *ambassador*
McFarland, Kathleen Troia (KT McFarland) *government defense consultant*
Sadik, Nafis *United Nations administrator*
Taylor, Diana Lancaster *state official*

NORTH CAROLINA

Chapel Hill
Schoonover, Brenda B. *ambassador*

Concord
Sossamon, Nancy H. *city official*

Durham
Kerckhoff, Sylvia Stansbury *mayor*

Elizabeth City
Pierce, Dianne S. *city clerk*

Fayetteville
Smith, Mable Cogdell *retired county official*

Greensboro
Shaw, Linda Dare Owens *county commissioner*

Hickory
Mason, Anne R. Hardin *municipal official*

Hubert
Howell, Nelda Kay *commissioner*

Manteo
Evans, Michelle T. *county official*

New Bern
Linkonis, Suzanne Newbold *retired probation officer, retired counselor*

Raleigh
Joyner, Lorinzo Little *commissioner*
Marshall, Elaine Folk *state official*
Perdue, Beverly Eaves *lieutenant governor, geriatric consultant*

NORTH DAKOTA

Edinburg
Myrdal, Rosemarie Caryle *state official, former state legislator*

Minot
Watne, Darlene Claire *county official*

OHIO

Cleveland
Campbell, Jane Louise *former mayor*

Columbus
Bradley, Jennette B. *state official, former lieutenant governor*
Long, Teresa C. *city health department administrator*
McGrath, Barbara Gates *city manager*
Montgomery, Betty Dee *state auditor, former state attorney general, former state legislator*

Dayton
McLin, Rhine Lana *mayor, former state legislator*

Galion
Harter, Lonna *city manager*

Mansfield
Converse, Sandra *city finance director, financial planner*

Middleport
Cantrell, Carol Howe *municipal administrator*

Trotwood
Staggs, Barbara J. *vice mayor*

OKLAHOMA

Norman
Price, Linda Rice *community development administrator*

Oklahoma City
Fallin, Mary Copeland *lieutenant governor*
Savage, Susan M. *state official, former mayor*

Tulsa
Taylor, Kathy *mayor*

OREGON

Eugene
Bascom, Ruth F. *retired mayor*

Portland
Katz, Vera *former mayor, former college administrator, state legislator*
Kleim, E. Denise *city official*

PENNSYLVANIA

Allentown
Glaessmann, Doris Ann *former county official, consultant*

Camp Hill
Besch, Nancy Adams *county official*

Donora
Todd, Norma Ross *retired government official*

Harrisburg
Baker Knoll, Catherine *lieutenant governor*
Hafer, Barbara *state official*
Pizzingrilli, Kim *state official*

Lewisburg
Lenhart, Lorraine Margaret *county official*

Philadelphia
Godley, Joanne *city health department administrator*
Miller, Donna Reed *city official*

Sayre
Smith, Robin L. *municipal official*

Upper Saint Clair
Smith, Gloria S. *local commissioner, educator*

RHODE ISLAND

Providence
O'Keefe, Beverly Disbrow *state official, federal official*
Sapinsley, Lila Manfield *state official*

SOUTH CAROLINA

Columbia
Scott, Bernice G. *county official*
Waites, Candy Yaghjian *former state official*

Laurens
Henderson, Rita Beatrice *county official*

Sumter
Brown, Barbara Ann *county extension agent*
Moore, Verna *county official*

TENNESSEE

Clarksville
Johnson, Barbara Ella Jackson *city official*

Enville
Campbell, Nell *mayor*

Huntsville
Lewallen Reynolds, Cynthia Maire *city administrator, small business owner*

Memphis
Madlock, Yvonne *city health department administrator*
Mardis, Elma Hubbard *county administrator, consultant*

Nashville
Bailey, Stephanie B.C. *city health department administrator*
Gore, Tipper (Mary Elizabeth Gore) *wife of the former vice president of the United States*
Thomas, Hazel Beatrice *state official*

Oak Ridge
Holloway, Jacqueline *county commissioner*

TEXAS

Arlington
Hall, Anna Christene *retired government official*

Austin
Barnhill, Jane Cook *commissioner*
Johnson, Lady Bird (Mrs. Claudia Alta Taylor Johnson) *former First Lady of the United States*

Beaumont
Lord, Evelyn Marlin *mayor*

Bellville
Krueger, Betty Adel *county official*

Canyon
Rice, Lois *mayor*

Dallas
Cottingham, Jennifer Jane *city official*
Miller, Laura *mayor, journalist*

Edinburg
García, Norma Garza *county treasurer*

Giddings
Dismukes, Carol Jaehne *county official*

Grand Prairie
Horak, Trish *city government worker*

Houston
Chang, Helen T. *municipal official*

Laredo
Colón, Phyllis Janet *retired city manager*

Pecos
Florez, Diane O. *county clerk*

Plano
Evans, Pat *mayor*

San Antonio
Henderson, Connie Chorlton *retired city planner, artist, writer*

VERMONT

Burlington
Kunin, Madeleine May *former ambassador to Switzerland, former governor*

Montpelier
Markowitz, Deborah Lynn *state official*

VIRGINIA

Alexandria
Connell, Mary Ellen *diplomat*
Freeman-Wilson, Karen *retired state attorney general, prosecutor, educational association administrator*
Nesbitt, Wanda L. *ambassador*

Arlington
Heivilin, Donna Mae *retired government executive*
Pendleton, Mary Catherine *retired foreign service officer*
Sundquist, M. Alexandra (Alix Sundquist) *diplomat, consultant*

Dublin
Lineberry, Rebecca J. *municipal official, treasurer*

Dulles
Gregus, Linda Anna *government official*
Jacobs, Janice Lee *ambassador*
Mathieu, Gail Dennise *ambassador*

Fairfax
Haskett, Dianne Louise *retired mayor, lawyer, consultant*

Lynchburg
Dodge, Lynn Louise *municipal official, librarian*

Manassas
Lawson, Nancy P. *retired county official*

Mc Lean
Healy, Theresa Ann *retired ambassador*

Newington
Clark-Bourne, Kathryn Orpha *consul*

Norfolk
Nemara, Vanessa Anne *federal official*

Richmond
Hanley, Katherine Keith *state official*
Petera, Anne Pappas *state official*

Spotsylvania
Hardy, Dorcas Ruth *business and government relations executive*

Virginia Beach
Oberndorf, Meyera E. *mayor*
Smith, Ruth Hodges *city clerk*

WASHINGTON

Cosmopolis
Luark, Lillian *retired city clerk*

Everett
O'Keefe, Kathleen Mary *state official*

Medina
Ward, Marilyn Beeman *commissioner*

Olympia
Gregoire, Christine O. *governor, former state attorney general*

Redmond
Doman, Margaret Horn *government policy consultant*

Seattle
Covington, Germaine Ward *municipal agency administrator*
Kennedy, Mary Virginia *retired diplomat*
O'Neill, Maureen Anne *city administrator, arts administrator*

Spokane
Pfister, Terri *city official*

WEST VIRGINIA

Alderson
Phipps, Meg Scott *former commissioner*

Charleston
Ireland, Betty *state official*

Harpers Ferry
Cooley, Hilary Elizabeth *county official*

WISCONSIN

Madison
Bauman, Susan Joan Mayer *mayor, lawyer, commissioner*
Lautenschlager, Peggy A. *state attorney general*
Lawton, Barbara *lieutenant governor*
Thompson, Barbara Storck *state official*

Pewaukee
Farrow, Margaret Ann *former lieutenant governor*

WYOMING

Cheyenne
Lummis, Cynthia Marie *state official, lawyer*
Thomson, Thyra Godfrey *former state official*
Woodhouse, Gay Vanderpoel *former state attorney general, lawyer*

TERRITORIES OF THE UNITED STATES

VIRGIN ISLANDS

Charlotte Amalie
Stapleton, Marylyn Alecia *diplomat*

MILITARY ADDRESSES OF THE UNITED STATES

EUROPE

APO
Morella, Constance Albanese *ambassador, former congresswoman*
Wagner, Ann Louise *ambassador, former political organization executive*

CANADA

NORTHWEST TERRITORIES

Yellowknife
Blondin-Andrew, Ethel D. *Canadian government official*

ONTARIO

Ottawa
Copps, Sheila *former Canadian government official*
Fairbairn, Joyce *Canadian government official*
Guarnieri, Albina *Canadian legislator*
Hervieux-Payette, Céline *Canadian senator*
Johnson, Janis G. *Canadian senator*
Losier-Cool, Rose-Marie *Canadian senator*
Minna, Maria *member of Canadian Parliament*
Poy, Vivienne *Canadian senator, academic administrator, educator*
Roland, Anne *registrar Supreme Court of Canada*

Toronto
Augustine, Jean Magdalene *Canadian government official, former member of parliament*
Clarkson, Adrienne *former Governor General of Canada*

MEXICO

Delegacion Miguel Hidalgo
de Fox, Marta Sahagun Jimenez *First Lady of Mexico*

AUSTRALIA

Double Bay
Peacock, Penne Korth *ambassador*

AUSTRIA

Finley, Julie Hamm *ambassador, former political party official*

BELGIUM

Brussels
Nuland, Victoria *US permanent representative to NATO*

ENGLAND

London
Elizabeth, , II, (Elizabeth Alexandra Mary) *By the Grace of God of the United Kingdom of Great Britain and Northern Ireland and of Her Other Realms and Territories Queen, Head of the Commonwealth, Defender of the Faith*
Hewitt, Patricia Hope *English government official, political scientist, researcher, announcer*

ETHIOPIA

Addis Ababa
Huddleston, Vicki Jean *ambassador*

FRANCE

Paris
Lagarde, Christine *French government official, lawyer*
Oliver, Louise V. *ambassador*

SPAIN

Canary Islands
Wells, Melissa Foelsch *retired ambassador*

SYRIA

Damascus
Scobey, Margaret *ambassador*

THAILAND

Bangkok
McMillion, Margaret Kim *foreign service officer*

ADDRESS UNPUBLISHED

Albertson, Susan L. *retired federal government official*
Armstrong, Anne Legendre *retired ambassador*
Atwater, Phyllis Y. *municipal official*
Ballentine, Rosalie Simmonds *former attorney general*
Bartholomew, Shirley Kathleen *municipal official*
Bayless, Betsey *state official*
Beard, Ann Southard *diplomat, oil industry executive*
Benson, Joanne E. *retired lieutenant governor*
Binsfeld, Connie Berube *former state official*
Black, Shirley Temple (Mrs. Charles A. Black) *retired ambassador, retired actress*
Brown, June Gibbs *retired government official*
Brown, Kay (Mary Kathryn Brown) *retired state official, consultant, political organization worker*
Brown, Pamela S. *former attorney general*
Brownell, Nora Mead *former commissioner*
Bush, Barbara Pierce *former First Lady of the United States, volunteer*
Calderón, Sila Maria *former governor*
Carter, Rosalynn Smith (Eleanor Rosalynn Carter) *former First Lady of the United States*
Chamberlain, Jean Nash *consultant, former county government department director*
Cook, Rebecca McDowell *former state official*
Cosman, Francene Jen *former government official*
Daglis, Lisa Genine *deputy attorney general*
Dawson, Carol Gene *former commissioner, writer, consultant*
Deily, Linnet Frazier *former ambassador*
Del Papa, Frankie Sue *former state attorney general*
Eu, March Fong *ambassador*
Farber, Zulima V. *former state attorney general, lawyer*
Filewicz-Cochran, Renatta T. *parliamentarian*
Garrison, Althea *government official*
Gilmore, Kathi *former state treasurer*
Hamed, Martha Ellen *government administrator*
Hazeltine, Joyce *former state official*
Henry, Sherrye P. *political advisor, radio personality*
Hester, Nancy Elizabeth *county government official*
Hinds, Sallie Ann *retired township official*
Hirono, Mazie Keiko *former lieutenant governor*
Hood, Glenda E. *former state official, former mayor*
Hull, Jane Dee *former governor, former state legislator*
Jacobs, Judith *county legislator*
Jacobs, Susan S. *ambassador*
Jagdmann, Judith Williams *former state attorney general*
Jeetah, Usha *Mauritius ambassador to the United States*
Jefferson, Marlene Rochelle *municipal official, director, minister*
Johnson, Karla Ann *county official*
Jordan, Mary Lucille *commissioner*
Joseph, Geri Mack (Geraldine Joseph) *former ambassador, educator, journalist*
Kernan, Barbara Desind *federal official*
Maguire, Deirdre *federal community development management analyst*
Marr, Carmel Carrington *retired state official*
Martin, Lynn Morley *former secretary of labor*
Martz, Judy Helen *former governor*
Mathews, Mary Kathryn *retired government official*
McCaughey Ross, Elizabeth P. (Betsy McCaughey) *former lieutenant governor*
McClanahan, Kay Marie *government official, lawyer*
McClennen, Miriam J. *former state official*
McCoy, Mary Ann *state official*
McLellan, A. Anne *Canadian government official*
Millane, Lynn *retired municipal official*
Morris, Greta N. *former ambassador*
Nelson, Cynthia J. *city official*
Ness, Susan *federal official*
Norton, Gale Ann *former secretary of the interior*
Novetzke, Sally Johnson *former ambassador*
Pearson, Landon *Canadian senator*
Pirsch, Carol McBride *retired county official, state senator, community relations manager*
Pont Marchese, Marisara *former Puerto Rican government official*
Quinn, Maureen E. *ambassador*
Randle, Candace Latrice *government affairs consultant, political scientist*
Randolph, Virgella *retired federal official*
Reagan, Nancy Davis (Anne Francis Robbins) *former First Lady of the United States, volunteer*
Render, Arlene *former ambassador*
Reno, Janet *former United States attorney general*
Rimler, Anita A. *former state official*
Rivers, Beverly D. *former district secretary*
Rocca, Christina B. *ambassador, former federal agency administrator*
Rosenthal, Helen Nagelberg *county official, advocate*
Roths, Beverly Owen *municipal official*
Rudin, Anne *retired mayor, nursing educator*
Sanders, Robin Renee *former ambassador*
Sanderson, Janet A. *former ambassador*
Savocchio, Joyce A. *former mayor*
Schoettler, Gail Sinton *former ambassador*
Schunk, Mae Gasparac *former state official*
Sentenne, Justine *corporate ombudsman consultant*
Smith, Jean Kennedy *former ambassador*
Smith, Pamela Hyde *ambassador*
Sudanowicz, Elaine Marie *government executive*
Sutter, Eleanor Bly *retired diplomat*
Swift, Jane Maria *former governor*
Teater, Dorothy Seath *retired county official*
Thomas, Regena L. *former state official*
Townsend, Kathleen Kennedy *former lieutenant governor*
Ulmer, Frances Ann *retired state official*
Valles, Judith V. *former mayor, retired academic administrator*
Van Cleave, Michelle Kim *former federal official*
Walker, Olene S. *former governor*
Wallace, Nicolle (Nicolle Devenish) *former federal official*
Whelan, Susan *former Canadian government official*
Willeford, Pamela Pitzer *former ambassador*
Wilson, Eleanor McElroy *county official*
Wood, Corinne Gieseke *former lieutenant governor*
Yates, Mary Carlin *former ambassador*

GOVERNMENT: LEGISLATIVE ADMINISTRATION

UNITED STATES

ALABAMA

Birmingham
Allen, Maryon Pittman *former senator, clothing designer, journalist*

ALASKA

Anchorage
Sturgulewski, Arliss *state legislator, director*

Juneau
McGuire, Lesil L. *state representative*

North Pole
James, Jeannette Adeline *state legislator, accountant, small business owner*

ARIZONA

Phoenix
Steffey, Lela *state legislator, banker*

ARKANSAS

Cedarville
Whitaker, Ruth Reed *state legislator, retired newspaper editor*

Dumas
Schexnayder, Charlotte Tillar *state legislator*

CALIFORNIA

Chula Vista
Moreno-Ducheny, Denise *state senator*

Long Beach
Karentte, Betty *state legislator*
Karnette, Betty *state representative*

Ontario
Soto, Nell *state senator*

Sacramento
Chu, Judy May *assemblywoman*
Kuehl, Sheila James *state legislator, department chairman*
Liu, Carol *state representative*
Pavley, Fran J. *state representative*

San Bernardino
Brown, Marta Macías *legislative staff member, executive assistant*

COLORADO

Denver
Anderson, Norma V. *retired state legislator*
Dicks, Patricia K. *legislative staff member*
Faatz, Jeanne Ryan *councilman*
Takis, Stephanie *retired state senator*
Williams, Suzanne *state senator*

CONNECTICUT

Glastonbury
Googins, Sonya Forbes *state legislator, retired banker*

Hartford
Carter, Annette Wheeler *state legislator*
DeMarinis, Nancy A. *state legislator, educator*
Fahrbach, Ruth C. *state legislator*
Mushinsky, Mary M. *state legislator*

Ledyard
McGrattan, Mary K. *state legislator*

Riverside
Powers, Claudia McKenna *state legislator*

Stamford
Aveni, Beverly A. *executive aide*

DISTRICT OF COLUMBIA

Washington
Baldwin, Tammy *congresswoman, lawyer*
Bean, Melissa *congresswoman*
Berkley, Shelley (Rochelle Levine Berkley) *congresswoman, lawyer*
Biggert, Judith Borg *congresswoman, lawyer*
Blackburn, Marsha *congresswoman*
Bono, Mary Whitaker *congresswoman*
Bordallo, Madeleine Mary (Mrs. Ricardo Jerome Bordallo) *congresswoman*
Boxer, Barbara *senator*
Brown, Corrine *congresswoman*
Cantwell, Maria E. *senator*
Capito, Shelley Moore *congresswoman*
Capps, Lois Ragnhild Grimsrud *congresswoman, former school nurse*
Carson, Julia M. *congresswoman*

Christian-Christensen, Donna Marie *congresswoman*
Clinton, Hillary (Hillary Diane Rodham Clinton) *senator, lawyer, former First Lady of United States*
Collins, Susan Margaret *senator*
Cubin, Barbara Lynn *congresswoman*
Davis, Jo Ann S. *congresswoman*
Davis, Susan A. *congresswoman*
DeLauro, Rosa L. *congresswoman*
Dole, Elizabeth Hanford (Liddy Dole) *senator, former federal agency administrator*
Drake, Thelma Day *congresswoman*
Emerson, Jo Ann H. *congresswoman*
Eshoo, Anna Georges *congresswoman*
Feinstein, Dianne *senator*
Foxx, Virginia Ann *congresswoman, small business owner*
Granger, Kay *congresswoman*
Harman, Jane *congresswoman*
Harris, Katherine *congresswoman*
Hart, Melissa Anne *congresswoman*
Herseth, Stephanie Marie *congresswoman, lawyer*
Hooley, Darlene *congresswoman*
Hutchison, Kay Bailey *senator*
Jackson Lee, Sheila *congresswoman*
Johnson, Eddie Bernice *congresswoman*
Johnson, Nancy Lee *congresswoman*
Jones, Stephanie Tubbs *congresswoman, lawyer, prosecutor*
Kaptur, Marcia Carolyn (Marcy Kaptur) *congresswoman*
Kelly, Sue W. *congresswoman*
Kennelly, Barbara B. *retired congressman, federal agency administrator*
Kilpatrick, Carolyn Cheeks *congresswoman*
Landrieu, Mary Lorretta *senator*
Lee, Barbara *congresswoman*
Lincoln, Blanche Lambert *senator*
Lofgren, Zoe *congresswoman*
Lowey, Nita Melnikoff *congresswoman*
Maloney, Carolyn Bosher *congresswoman*
Matsui, Doris Okada *congresswoman*
McCarthy, Carolyn *congresswoman*
McCollum, Betty *congresswoman*
McKinney, Cynthia Ann *congresswoman*
McMorris, Cathy *congresswoman*
Megginson, Elizabeth R. *legislative staff member, director, lawyer*
Mikulski, Barbara Ann *senator*
Millender-McDonald, Juanita *congresswoman*
Miller, Candice S. *congresswoman*
Molinari, Susan *former congresswoman*
Moore, Gwendolynne S. (Gwen Moore) *congresswoman*
Murkowski, Lisa Ann *senator*
Murray, Patty (Patricia J. Murray) *senator*
Musgrave, Marilyn N. *congresswoman*
Myrick, Sue Wilkins *congresswoman, former mayor*
Napolitano, Grace F. *congresswoman*
Northup, Anne Meagher *congresswoman*
Norton, Eleanor Holmes *congresswoman, lawyer, educator*
Pelosi, Nancy Patricia *congresswoman*
Pendleton, Florence Howard *shadow senator*
Pryce, Deborah Denine *congresswoman*
Ros-Lehtinen, Ileana Carmen *congresswoman*
Roybal-Allard, Lucille *congresswoman*
Sanchez, Linda T. *congresswoman*
Sanchez, Loretta *congresswoman*
Schakowsky, Janice *congresswoman*
Schmidt, Jean *congresswoman*
Schwartz, Allyson Y. *congresswoman*
Slaughter, Louise McIntosh *congresswoman*
Snowe, Olympia J. *senator*
Solis, Hilda Lucia *congresswoman, educational administrator*
Stabenow, Deborah Ann *senator, former congresswoman*
Vazirani-Fales, Heea *legislative staff member, lawyer*
Velázquez, Nydia Margarita *congresswoman*
Wasserman-Schultz, Debbie *congresswoman*
Waters, Maxine *congresswoman*
Watson, Diane Edith *congresswoman*
Wilson, Heather Ann *congresswoman*
Woolsey, Lynn C. *congresswoman*

FLORIDA

Bradenton
Rahn, Saundra L. *councilman*
Woodson-Howard, Marlene Erdley *former state legislator*

Dade City
Brown-Waite, Virginia (Ginny Brown-Waite) *congresswoman*

Ocala
Stickeler, Carl Ann Louise *legislator*

Ormond Beach
Lynn, Evelyn Joan *state senator, consultant*

Tallahassee
Blanton, Faye Wester *legislative official*

Tampa
Davis, Helen Gordon *retired state senator*

GEORGIA

Athens
McBee, Mary Louise *retired state legislator, retired academic administrator*

Atlanta
Butler, Gloria Singleton *state legislator*
Orrock, Nan *state legislator*

Decatur
Majette, Denise *former congresswoman*

Rincon
Purcell, Ann Rushing *state legislator, human services manager*

HAWAII

Honolulu
Baker, Rosalyn Hester *state senator*
Chun Oakland, Suzanne Nyuk Jun *state legislator*
Kawakami, Bertha C. *state representative*

Kailua
Young, Jacqueline Eurn Hai *former state legislator, consultant*

IDAHO

Boise
Keough, Shawn *state legislator*
Lodge, Patti Anne *state senator*
McKague, Shirley *state representative*
Wood, Jeannine Kay *legislative staff member*

Jerome
Bell, Maxine Toolson *state legislator, librarian*

ILLINOIS

Coal City
O'Brien, Mary Kathleen *state legislator, lawyer*

Lake Forest
Frederick, Virginia Fiester *state legislator*

Springfield
Collins, Annazette R. *state representative*
Collins, Jacqueline Y *state senator*
Currie, Barbara Flynn *state legislator*
Klingler, Gwendolyn Walbolt *state representative*
Kosel, Renée *state representative*
Martinez, Iris *state senator*
Pankau, Carole *state senator*

Westchester
Lightford, Kimberly A. *state legislator*

INDIANA

Indianapolis
Austin, Terri Jo *state representative*

West Lafayette
Scholer, Sue Wyant *retired state legislator*

IOWA

Des Moines
Boettger, Nancy J. *state legislator*
Bukta, Polly *state representative*
Dandekar, Swati *state representative*
Jochum, Pam *state representative*
Miller, Helen *state representative, lawyer*
Ragan, Amanda *state senator*
Szymoniak, Elaine Eisfelder *retired state senator*

KANSAS

Shawnee Mission
Sader, Carol Hope *former state legislator*

Topeka
Carlin, Sydney *state representative*
Gordon, Lana G. *state representative*
Petty, Marge D. *state senator*
Saville, Pat *state senate official*
Storm, Suzanne *state representative*

Wichita
Pottorff, Jo Ann *state legislator*

KENTUCKY

Frankfort
Palumbo, Ruth Ann *state legislator*
Pullin, Tanya *state representative*
Stine, Katie Kratz *state legislator*

Shelbyville
Miller, Mary Helen *retired state government administrator*

LOUISIANA

Lake Charles
Mount, Willie Landry *state legislator*

New Orleans
Irons, Paulette Riley *state legislator, lawyer*

MAINE

Augusta
Edmonds, Beth *state legislator, lieutenant governor*

Belgrade Lakes
Kany, Judy C(asperson) *retired state senator*

Brunswick
Pfeiffer, Sophia Douglass *retired state legislator, lawyer*

Dresden
Kilkelly, Marjorie Lee *state legislator*

MARYLAND

Annapolis
Doory, Ann Marie *legislator*
Forehand, Jennie Meador *state senator*
Hollinger, Paula Colodny *state legislator*
Kelley, Delores Goodwin *state legislator*
Lee, Susan C. *state legislator, lawyer*
Ruben, Ida Gass *state senator*

Baltimore
Hoffman, Barbara A. *state legislator*

Frederick
Byron, Beverly Butcher *retired congresswoman*

Rockville
Petzold, Carol Stoker *state legislator*

MASSACHUSETTS

Boston
Canavan, Christine Estelle *state legislator*
Chandler, Harriette Levy *state legislator, management consultant, educator*
Creedon, Geraldine *state legislator*
Creem, Cynthia Stone *state legislator, lawyer*
Jehlen, Patricia D. *state legislator*
Peisch, Alice Hanlon *state legislator*
Rogeness, Mary Speer *state legislator*
Spiliotis, Joyce A. *state legislator*
Walrath, Patricia A. *state legislator*
Williams Gifford, Susan *state legislator*
Wolf, Alice Koerner *state legislator, former mayor*

Chelmsford
Cleven, Carol Chapman *retired state legislator*

Newton Highlands
Hummel, Margaret P. *state representative*

Springfield
Melconian, Linda Jean *state senator, lawyer, educator*

MICHIGAN

Farmington Hills
Dolan, Jan Clark *former state legislator*

Lansing
Pollack, Lana *state senator*

MINNESOTA

Minneapolis
Reichgott Junge, Ember Darlene *retired senator, lawyer, writer, broadcast commentator, radio personality*
Wejcman, Linda *retired state legislator*

Minnetonka
Cavanaugh, Margaret *aide*

Saint Paul
Pappas, Sandra Lee *state senator*

Stillwater
Krentz, Jane *former state legislator, elementary school educator*

MISSISSIPPI

Jackson
Coleman, Mary H. *state legislator*

MISSOURI

Jefferson City
Murray, Dana L. *state legislator*

Kansas City
Rice, Levina Ruth (Sally) *alderman, retired government agency administrator*

MONTANA

Medicine Lake
Nelson, Linda J. *state legislator*

NEBRASKA

Lincoln
Redfield, Pamela A. *state legislator*
Schimek, DiAnna Ruth Rebman *state legislator*
Stuhr, Elaine Ruth *state legislator*

NEVADA

Las Vegas
Wiener, Valerie *state senator, writer, communications executive*

NEW HAMPSHIRE

Concord
Bradley, Paula E. *former state legislator*
Clemons, Jane Andrea *state legislator*
Ferland, Brenda L. *state representative*
Flora, Kathleen M. *retired state representative*
Foster, Linda Timberlake *state legislator*
Francoeur, Sheila T. *state representative*
Ginsburg, Ruth *state representative*
Hager, Elizabeth Sears *state legislator, social services administrator*
Kaen, Naida *state representative*
Larsen, Sylvia B. *state legislator*
Norelli, Terie Thompson *state legislator*
Richardson, Barbara Hull *state legislator, social worker*
Stickney, Nancy Carver *state legislator*

Durham
Wheeler, Katherine Wells *retired state legislator*

Hanover
Copenhaver, Marion Lamson *retired state legislator*
Crory, Elizabeth Lupien *retired state legislator*

Manchester
Arnold, Barbara Eileen *state legislator*

Moultonborough
Patten, Betsey Leland *state legislator*

Plaistow
Senter, Merilyn P(atricia) *former state legislator, freelance/self-employed reporter*

Windham
Arndt, Janet S. *former state legislator, educator*

NEW JERSEY

Montclair
Gill, Nia H. *state legislator*

Paterson
Pou, Nellie *assemblywoman*

Short Hills
Ogden, Maureen Black *retired state legislator*

Teaneck
Weinberg, Loretta *state legislator*

Trenton
Allen, Diane Betzendahl *state legislator*

NEW MEXICO

Albuquerque
Stewart, Miriam Kay (Mimi Stewart) *state legislator, educator*

Clovis
Crook, Anna Marie *legislator*

Sandia Park
Beffort, Sue Wilson *state legislator*

Santa Fe
Vaughn, Gloria C. *state representative*
Wilson, Avon W. *state representative*

NEW YORK

Albany
Jacobs, Rhoda S. *state legislator*
Smith, Ada LaVerne *state legislator*
Stavisky, Toby Ann *state legislator*

New York
Abate, Catherine M. *retired state legislator*
Quinn, Christine Callaghan *councilwoman*

Ossining
Galef, Sandra Risk *state legislator, educator*

Port Chester
Oppenheimer, Suzi *state legislator*

Rochester
John, Susan V. *state representative*

NORTH CAROLINA

Advance
Cochrane, Betsy Lane *former state senator*

Burlington
Holt, Bertha Merrill *state legislator*

Chapel Hill
Kinnaird, Eleanor Gates *state legislator, lawyer*

Raleigh
Cauthen, Carmen Wimberley *legislative staff member, jewelry designer*
Tally, Lura Self *state legislator*

NORTH DAKOTA

Bismarck
Nelson, Carolyn *state legislator*

Fargo
Lee, Judith *state legislator*

Grand Forks
DeMers, Judy Lee *retired state legislator, dean*

OHIO

Cleveland
Drake, Grace L. *retired state senator, cultural organization administrator*

Columbus
Barrett, Catherine L. *state representative*
Clancy, Patricia *state representative*
Setzer, Arlene J. *state representative, retired secondary school educator*
Smith, Shirley A. *state legislator, state representative*
Taylor, Mary *state representative*

Dayton
Reid, Marilyn Joanne *state legislator, lawyer*

OKLAHOMA

Edmond
Garrett, Kathryn Ann Byers (Kitty Garrett) *legislative clerk*

Oklahoma City
Morris, Phyllis *legislative staff member*
Riley, Nancy C. *state legislator*
Staggs, Barbara Annette *state representative*

OREGON

Albany
Oakley, Carolyn Le *state legislator, city manager, director*

Mcminnville
Nelson, Donna Gayle *state representative*

Portland
Furse, Elizabeth *retired congressman, small business owner*
Gordly, Avel Louise *state legislator, political organization worker*

Salem
Anderson, Laurie Monnes *state senator*
Burdick, Ginny Marie *state senator*
Carter, Margaret L. *legislator*
Close, Betsy L. *state representative*
Minnis, Karen *state representative*
Qutub, Eileen *state legislator, real estate appraiser*
Tomei, Carolyn *state representative*
Walker, Vicki L. *state senator*
Wirth, Kelley K. *state representative*
Yih, Mae Dunn *state legislator*

PENNSYLVANIA

Chalfont
Wilson, Jean Louise *retired state legislator*

Harrisburg
Crahalla, Jacqueline R. *state representative*
Miller, Sheila *state legislator*
Vance, Patricia H. *state senator*
Williams, Constance *state senator*

Philadelphia
Josephs, Babette *legislator*

Wayne
Rubley, Carole A. *state legislator*

RHODE ISLAND

Providence
Ajello, Edith H. *state legislator*
Gibbs, June Nesbitt *state senator*
Graziano, Catherine Elizabeth *state legislator, retired nursing educator*

SOUTH CAROLINA

Greenville
Manly, Sarah Letitia *retired state legislator, ophthalmic photographer, angiographer*

Mc Cormick
Clayton, Verna Lewis *retired state legislator*

SOUTH DAKOTA

Miller
Morford, JoAnn (JoAnn Morford-Burg) *state senator, investment company executive*

Mud Butte
Ingalls, Marie Cecelie *former state legislator, retail executive*

TENNESSEE

Athens
Higdon, Linda Hampton *congressional staff*

TEXAS

Austin
Denny, Mary Craver *state legislator, business owner*
Shapiro, Florence *state legislator, advertising executive, public relations executive*
Wong, Martha Jee *state representative*

Laredo
Zaffirini, Judith *state legislator, small business owner*

UTAH

Salt Lake City
Moore, Annette B. *legislative staff member*
Shepherd, Karen *retired congresswoman*
Walker, Carlene Martin *state senator*

West Valley City
Peterson, Millie M. *state senator*

VERMONT

Brattleboro
Milkey, Virginia A. *state legislator*

Middlebury
Nuovo, Betty A. *state representative*

Milton
Rivero, Marilyn Elaine Keith *state legislator*

Rutland
Ferraro, Betty Ann *retired state senator*

Saint Albans
Keenan, Kathleen *state legislator*

White River Junction
Bohi, Lynn *state legislator*

VIRGINIA

Alexandria
Collins, Cardiss *retired congresswoman*

Danville
Moorefield, Jennifer Mary *legislative staff member*

Fairfax
Miller, Emilie F. *former state senator, consultant*

Norfolk
Miller, Yvonne Bond *state legislator, educator*

Richmond
Devolites, Jeannemarie Aragona *state legislator*
McQuigg, Michele Berger *state legislator*
Schaar, Susan Clarke *legislative staff member*

Vienna
Higginbotham, Wendy Jacobson *legislative staff member, writer*

WASHINGTON

Olympia
Anderson, Vicki Susan *legislative staff member, travel consultant*
Haugen, Mary Margaret *state legislator*
Kessler, Lynn Elizabeth *state legislator*
Long, Jeanine Hundley *retired state legislator*
Roach, Pam *state legislator*
Spanel, Harriet *state legislator*

WEST VIRGINIA

Shinnston
Spears, Jae *state legislator*

WISCONSIN

Fort Atkinson
Lorman, Barbara K. *retired state senator*

Madison
Albers, Sheryl Kay *state legislator*
Darling, Alberta Helen *state legislator, art gallery director, marketing professional*
Krusick, Margaret Ann *state legislator*
Roessler, Carol Ann *state legislator*
Whitney, Lori Ann *legislative staff member*
Young, Rebecca Mary Conrad *retired state legislator*

WYOMING

Cheyenne
Kunz, April Brimmer *state legislator, lawyer*
Mockler, Esther Jayne *state senator*

Laramie
Hansen, Matilda *former state legislator*

TERRITORIES OF THE UNITED STATES

VIRGIN ISLANDS

St Thomas
Berry, Lorraine Ledee *state senator*

CANADA

NEW BRUNSWICK

Moncton
Robertson, Brenda *senator*

ONTARIO

Ottawa
Bacon, Lise *Canadian senator*
Christensen, Ione *Canadian senator*
Cook, Joan *Canadian senator*
Cools, Anne C. *Canadian senator*
Cordy, Jane *Canadian senator*
Hubley, Elizabeth *Canadian senator*
LeBreton, Marjory *senator*
Milne, Lorna *Canadian legislator*
St. Hilaire, Caroline *legislator*

ADDRESS UNPUBLISHED

Abey, Kathy Michele *district representative, congressional caseworker*
Bard, Ellen Marie *former state legislator, retired small business owner*
Beals, Nancy Farwell *former state legislator*
Blanchard, MaryAnn N. *state legislator*
Bonsack, Rose Mary Hatem *state legislator, physician*
Brown, Mary Ellen *former state legislator, accountant*
Carnahan, Jean *former senator*
Carstairs, Sharon *legislator*
Chalifoux, Thelma *Canadian senator*
Chan, Wilma *state legislator*
Cierpiot, Connie *former state legislator*
Culp, Faye Berry *state legislator*
Dalphond-Guiral, Madeleine *member of Canadian parliament*
Danner, Patsy Ann *former congresswoman*
De Gette, Diana Louise *congresswoman, lawyer*
Duniphan, J. P. *state legislator, small business owner*
Dunlap, Patricia C. *state legislator*
Dunn, Jennifer Blackburn *former congresswoman*
Finestone, Sheila *senator, retired legislator*
Finnerty, Isobel *Canadian senator*
Hawkins, Mary Ellen Higgins (Mary Ellen Higgins) *retired state legislator, public relations executive*
Hearn, Joyce Camp *retired state legislator, educator, consultant*
Hickey, Win E(spy) *former state legislator, social worker*
Hollingworth, Beverly A. *former state legislator*
Jacobs Gibson, Rose *alderman, not-for-profit developer*
Kleven, Marguerite *state legislator*
Koch, Christine *legislative aide*
Lebowitz, Catharine Koch *state legislator*
Léger, Viola *Canadian senator*
Mandel, Adrienne Abramson *state legislator*
Maroney, Jane Perkins *former state legislator, consultant*
McCarthy, Karen P. *former congresswoman, former state legislator*
Meek, Carrie P. *former congresswoman*
Meyers, Jan *retired congresswoman*
Miller, Patricia Louise *state legislator, nurse*
Munt, Janet Staples *state senator*
Nielsen, Linda Miller *councilman*
Pascoe, Patricia Hill *former state legislator*
Patterson, Elizabeth Johnston *retired congresswoman*
Pettis-Roberson, Shirley McCumber *retired congresswoman*
Pevear, Roberta Charlotte *retired state legislator*
Pond, Phyllis Joan Ruble *state legislator, educator*
Rivers, Lynn N. *former congresswoman*
Rossiter, Eileen *Canadian senator*
Roukema, Margaret Scafati *congresswoman*
Rudy, Ruth Corman *former state legislator*
Satterthwaite, Helen Foster *retired state legislator*
Schweinhaut, Margaret Collins *state senator*
Skinner, Patricia Morag *state legislator*
Snelling, Barbara W. *retired state legislator*
Sorensen, Sheila *state legislator*
Stickney, Jessica *former state legislator*
Tauscher, Ellen O. *congresswoman*
Tebedo, MaryAnne *state legislator*
Thomason, Lynne *councilman, medical technician*
Thurman, Karen L. *former congresswoman, lobbyist*
Treppler, Irene Esther *retired state senator*
Van Landingham, Marian Amelia *retired state legislator, artist*
Vellenga, Kathleen Osborne *retired state legislator*
Wallach, Patricia *councilman, retired mayor*
Watts, Vivian Edna *state legislator*
Wolf, Katie Louise *state legislator*
Zanetti, Teresa A. *state representative*

HEALTHCARE: DENTISTRY

UNITED STATES

ALABAMA

Huntsville
Yarbrough, Isabel Miles *dentist, educator*

CALIFORNIA

Elk Grove
Work, Janice René *pediatric dentist*

Hollywood
Hoesli, Hanna *dentist*

San Francisco
Greenspan, Deborah *dental educator*

CONNECTICUT

Farmington
Ellis, Diane Deane *dental hygienist, educator*

Milford
Siekierski, Kamilla Malgorzata *dental laboratory technician*

FLORIDA

Homestead
Ferraro, Marie *dental hygienist*

Jacksonville
Halil, Susan Terrell *dental hygienist*

Orange Park
Johns, Laurie Marie *dentist, hypnotherapist*

GEORGIA

Atlanta
Braswell, Laura Day *periodontist*

Augusta
Lapp, Carol Anne *oral biology educator*

ILLINOIS

Chicago
Battrell, Ann *dental hygienist, educator, dental association administrator*
Dry, Judith Kallen *dental hygienist, cable producer, writer*

Hinsdale
Szeremeta-Browar, Taisa Lydia *endodontist*

KENTUCKY

Brandenburg
Bowen, Patricia Lederer *dental educator*

Louisville
Lee, Susan *dentist, microbiologist*

Owensboro
Swystun-Rives, Bohdana Alexandra *dentist*

MARYLAND

Baltimore
Grant, Leslie Edwina *dentist, dental association administrator*

MASSACHUSETTS

Arlington
Immanuel, Laura Amelia *dentist*

Boston
Friedman, Paula Konowitch *dentist, academic administrator*

Dorchester
Lee, June Warren *dentist*

MISSOURI

Aurora
Gorman, Angela Sue *dental assistant*

Creve Coeur
Manne, Deborah Sue *dental hygienist, educator, oncological nurse*

NEW JERSEY

Fair Lawn
Dadurian, Medina Diana *pediatric dentist, educator*

NEW YORK

Hempstead
Ancrum, Cheryl Denise *dentist*

New York
Glassman, Debra *dentist*
Rozenberg, Lana *cosmetic dentist*

Rockville Centre
Epel, Lidia Marmurek *dentist*

OHIO

Cincinnati
Gehlert, Sally Oyler *healing touch practictioner*

Columbus
Goorey, Nancy Jane *dentist*

PENNSYLVANIA

Mechanicsburg
Layton, Carol Eicherberger *dentist*

Whitehall
Tufton, Janie Lee (Jane Tufton) *dental hygienist, lobbyist*

SOUTH CAROLINA

Charleston
Cordova, Maria Asuncion *dentist*

TEXAS

Dallas
Blanton, Patricia Louise *periodontal surgeon*

Laredo
Vargas, Sylvia Elia *dentist, small business owner*

WASHINGTON

Seattle
Herring, Susan Weller *dental educator, anatomist*

WISCONSIN

West Bend
Roth, Kathleen C. *dentist*

ADDRESS UNPUBLISHED

Bush, Christine Gay *dental hygienist*
Dileone, Carmel Montano *retired dental hygienist*
Houk, Irene Miller *dentist*
Lee, Winnie Sita *dentist*
Mele, Joanne Theresa *dentist*
Mundorff Shrestha, Sheila Ann *dental educator*
Riley, Cheryl M. *prosthodontist, military officer*
Sinkford, Jeanne Craig *dental association administrator, retired dentist, dean, educator*
Yarnell, Gail Ellen *dentist, prosecutor*

HEALTHCARE: HEALTH SERVICES

UNITED STATES

ALABAMA

Andalusia
Cross, Charlotte Lord *retired social worker, artist*

Athens
Page, Caroline Jane *social worker*

Auburn University
Simmons, Karla Peavy *researcher, educator*

Birmingham
Booth, Rachel Zonelle *nursing educator*
Cooper, Karen René *health facility administrator, nursing administrator*
Crittenden, Martha A. *rehabilitation services professional*
Holmes, Suzanne McRae *nursing supervisor*
Hullett, Sandral *hospital administrator, health facility administrator*
Knight, Karen Chambers *nurse*
Mohon, Earlene Mann *counselor*
Perry, Helen *medical/surgical nurse, secondary school educator*
Poole, Dorothea Veranetta *nursing educator*
Williams, Thomasyne Hill *speech pathology/audiology services professional*

Brewton
McDaniel, Miriam Lee McCain *anesthetist*

Cullman
Thornton, Nancy Freebairn *psychotherapist, consultant, military officer*

Fayette
Burleson, Emily Jane *nursing educator*

Florence
Foote, Dorothy Gargis *nursing educator*

Greenville
MacGuire, Nina Little *social worker*

Hamilton
Vinson, Leila Terry Walker *retired gerontological social worker*

Hanceville
Hazard, Lynn Marchetti *occupational therapist*
Hodge, Ida Lee *retired physical therapist assistant*

Huntsville
Bledsoe, Adalene Hay *family counselor, retired elementary school educator*
Freeman, Paula S. *social worker*
Ingram, Shirley Jean *social worker*
Neeley, Janet Meigs *surgical nurse*

Lafayette
Woody, Mary Florence *nursing educator, academic administrator*

Lincoln
Wheelus, Elizabeth *mental health services professional*

Mobile
Wisner, Pamela L. *social worker*

Opelika
Miller, Donna Kaye *mental health services professional, real estate investor*

Spanish Fort
Hollinger, Peggy Louise *elementary school counselor*

Theodore
Hollis, Julia Ann Roshto *critical care, medical, and surgical nurse*

Thomasville
Larrimore, Judith Rutledge *nurse*

Tuscaloosa
Orcutt, Ben Avis *retired social work educator*

Tuskegee Institute
Cooley, Fannie Richardson *counselor, educator*
Paris, Deidre Eileen *artificial intelligence researcher, educator*

ALASKA

Anchorage
Andersen, Ellen Marie *social worker*
Gottlieb, Katherine *health facility administrator*
Kincaid, Karen Owers *nursing educator*

Big Lake
Gillette, Muriel Delphine *nurse*

Fairbanks
Nottingham, Juanita C. *medical/surgical nurse*

Juneau
Albrecht, Bethany Jane *counselor*

Palmer
Lawler, Marita A. *addiction therapist*

ARIZONA

Casa Grande
McGillicuddy, Joan Marie *psychotherapist, consultant*

Chandler
Chavez, Faith Coots *medical nurse*

Cibecue
Murphey, Margaret Janice *retired marriage and family counselor*

Cornville
Walsh, Arline Marie *retired alcohol/drug abuse services professional*

Flagstaff
Larson, Ellen R. *health sciences instructor*

Fort Huachuca
Sleeper, Nancy JoAnn *mental health services professional*

Glendale
Cacciatore, Joanne *social worker*

Mesa
Adams, Heidi-Christa *counselor*
Ahearn, Geraldine *medical/surgical nurse, writer, poet*
David, Susan Holcombe *child and family therapist*

Nogales
Maxwell, Sonia L. *social worker*

Payson
Lasys, Joan *medical/surgical nurse, educator*

Peoria
Hagan, Judith Ann *social worker*
Nelson, Mary Kathryn *bilingual counselor, small business owner, real estate agent, artist, singer*

Phoenix
Allen, Janice Faye Clement *nursing administrator*
Johnson, Elizabeth Misner *health services executive*
Kane, Grace McNelly *retired women's health nurse, pediatrics nurse*
Karabatsos, Elizabeth Ann *career counseling services executive*
Kivlahan, Coleen *public health officer*
Maxson, Barbara Jeanette *social worker, educator*
McWhorter, Ruth Alice *counselor, marriage and family therapist*
Peterson, Patricia Mitchell *medical/surgical nurse*
Turner, Doris Sewell *counselor, educator*

Scottsdale
Hadley, Jane Francis *family nurse practitioner*
Meyers, Marlene O. *retired hospital administrator*
Timmons, Evelyn Deering *pharmacist*
Weaver, Linda Marie *pharmacist, education educator*

Sedona
Catterton, Marianne Rose *occupational therapist*

Sun City
Lopez, Jean Engebretsen *neuroscience nurse, researcher*

Sun City West
Holloway, Diane Elaine *psychotherapist, consultant, writer*
Ryan-Knuppel, Bette L. *nurse, educator*

Surprise
Wargo, Andrea Ann *retired public health service officer*

Tempe
Anchie, Toby Levine *health facility administrator*
Zapata, Angela L. *counselor*

Tucson
Barrette-Mozes, Susan Jean *counselor, psychotherapist*
Dyer-Raffler, Joy Ann *retired special education diagnostician, educator*
Glueck-Rambaldi, Mary Audrey *retired psychiatric and mental health nurse*
Johnson, Elissa Sarah *speech pathology/audiology services professional, writer*
LeCorgne, Lisette Mary *family practice nurse practitioner*
Ledin, Patricia Ann *nurse, legal consultant*
McCabe, Monica Jane *oncological nurse*
Sillman, Edlynne Mina *caseworker, consultant*
Thompson, Kathleen Shambaugh *marriage and family counselor*
Waldt, Risa *psychotherapist, artist, writer*

Wickenburg
Brooks, Donna Jean *counselor, educator*

Winslow
Wolfe, Janice Kay *oncological nurse*

Yuma
Rush, Dorie Mae *nursing educator*

ARKANSAS

Fayetteville
Newgent, Rebecca Ann *counselor, educator*

Fort Smith
Ashley, Ella Jane (Ella Jane Rader) *medical technician*
Edwards, Cheryl L. *counselor*

Greenbrier
Brown, Lois Heffington *retired health facility administrator*

Jonesboro
Crecelius, Bridget Michelle *counselor*

Little Rock
Elders, Joycelyn (Minnie Jocelyn Elders, Minnie Joycelyn Lee) *public health service officer, endocrinologist, former Surgeon General of the United States*
Mitchell, Jo Kathryn *retired hospital technical supervisor*
Thomas, Lestene *nurse*

Marianna
Pruitt, Mary H. *social worker*

Melbourne
Johnson, Ruby Diane *nursing educator, department chairman, nurse*

Norman
Hokanson, Carol *speech therapist, special education educator*

Paris
Hawkins, Naomi Ruth *nurse*

Pocahontas
Rone, Monika Hiedi *mental health services professional, consultant*

Sherwood
Eddy, Nancy C. *counselor*

CALIFORNIA

Alameda
Herrick, Sylvia Anne *health facility administrator*

Albany
Daniels, Lydia M. *health care administrator*

Alpine
Leyse-Wallace, Ruth Louise *dietician, educator*

Anaheim
Lee, Donna Jean *retired nurse*
Pincombe, Jodi Doris *health facility administrator*

Arcadia
Anderson, Holly Geis *health facility administrator, educator, commentator*
Imbus, Sharon Haughey *neuroscience nurse*

Arcata
Green, Theresa Diane *social worker*

Arleta
Kelley, Frances A. *occupational therapist, consultant*

Auburn
Larimore-Albrecht, Deni Denise *social worker*

Bakersfield
Girga, Barbara *psychotherapist, college counselor*
Kelly, Diana Kay *counselor, educator*

Berkeley
Bissell, Mina J. *lab administrator, biochemist*
Daly, Markate *philosophical researcher, counselor*
Ensign, Jacqueline *social worker*
Gumbs, Pam *pharmacist*
Hill, Lorie Elizabeth *psychotherapist*
Lashof, Joyce Cohen *public health service officer, educator*
Little, Angela Capobianco *nutritional science educator*

Beverly Hills
Phillips, Debora Rothman *psychotherapist*
Seizer, Fern Victor *retired mental health services administrator*

Brisbane
Earl, Lois Marie *medical/surgical and home health nurse*

Burbank
Fifield, Lillene H. *psychotherapist, educator*
Ungerleider, Dorothy Fink *recreational therapist*

Carlsbad
Lovell, Joan Ellen *mental health professional*

Carmel
Reamy, Michaelin *marriage and family therapist, educator, consultant*

Carmichael
Moore, MaryLou *researcher*

Cathedral City
Berry, Ester Lorée *vocational nurse*

Cerritos
Woodson-Glenn, Yolanda *social worker*

Clovis
Von Prince, Kilulu Magdalene *retired occupational therapist, sculptor*

Corcoran
Oliver, Patricia *physician assistant*

Costa Mesa
Graff, Cynthia Stamper *health facility administrator*
McCarthy, Mary Ann *counselor, educator*

Culver City
Bernstein, Diane *psychotherapist*
Cole, Elaine Ann *marriage and family therapist, educator*

Davis
Stern, Judith Schneider *nutritionist, researcher, educator*
Turnlund, Judith Rae *nutritionist*

Del Mar
Rodger, Marion McGee *medical/surgical nurse, administrator*

Desert Hot Springs
Zarres, Sharon L. *marriage and family therapist, health facility administrator*

Downey
Orange, Valerie *rehabilitation center executive*

Elizabeth Lake
Kozlow, Beverly Kay *retired physical therapist, psychologist, realtor*

Emeryville
Finney, Lee *retired social worker*

Encino
House, Karen Sue *nursing consultant*
Vogel, Susan Carol *nursing administrator*

Fountain Valley
Delisanti, Marilyn W. *medical/surgical and pediatrics nurse*

Frazier Park
Edwards, Sarah Anne *social worker, psychologist*

Fremont
Sahatjian, Manik *retired nurse, retired psychologist*

Fresno
Corless, Dorothy Alice *nursing educator*
Johnson, Ruth Anne *medical/surgical nurse*
Ortiz, Christine E. *nursing educator*
Weymouth, Toni *social worker, writer, educator*

Glendale
Shou, Sharon Louise Wikoff *vocational rehabilitation counselor*

Hayward
Buchanan, Patricia O'Neill *retired social worker*

Hillsborough
Yee-Melichar, Darlene *gerontological health educator*

Homewood
Butler, Patricia *mental health nurse, educator, consultant*

Huntington Beach
Carey, Shirley Anne *nursing consultant*
Mazak, Arlene Patricia *marriage and family therapist*

Indian Wells
Wright, Ann Follinger *psychotherapist*

Inglewood
Epstein, Marsha Ann *public health service officer, physician*

Irvine
Hoheb, Camille E. *healthcare executive*
Ruttenberg, Susann I. *health sciences administrator*

Kentfield
Buehler, Sally Salmen *clinical social worker*

La Canada Flintridge
Ciesniewski, Ann Marie *marriage and family therapist*

La Jolla
Covington, Stephanie Stewart *psychotherapist, writer, educator*
Hazzard, Mary Elizabeth *nursing educator*
Johnson, Gayle Ann *cardiology nurse*

Laguna Beach
Bernstein, Jean Newman *retired public health information officer*
Jensen, Gloria Veronica *adult nurse practitioner*

Lake Forest
Boccia/Stacy, Judy Elaine *home health agency executive, consultant*

Lake View Terrace
McCraven, Eva Stewart Mapes *health service administrator*

Lemon Grove
Robinson, Cheryl Jean *human services specialist, advocate*

Loma Linda
Condon, Vaneta Mabley *medical/surgical nurse*
Molnar, Violet *mental health nurse*

Lompoc
Wagner, Geraldine Marie *nursing educator, consultant*

Long Beach
Burton, Lucy *enterostomal therapy nurse*
Croteau, Patricia A. *nursing case manager*
Elftman, Susan Nancy *physician assistant, childbirth-lactation educator, research director*

Mathieu, Susan Leifer *recreational therapist, educator*
Mieras, Elvia F. *dietician, educator*
Mullins Berg, Ruth Gladys *nurse*

Los Angeles
Carlson, Jo Anne *nurse*
Carson, Margaret *human services administrator*
Harrison, Gail G. *public health educator*
Katzin, Carolyn Fernanda *nutritionist, consultant*
Looney, Claudia Arlene *health facility administrator*
Mazes-Roque, Janet Maria *physician assistant*
Silverstein, Suzanne *art therapist*
Stoll, Bobbi *art psychotherapist*
Territo, Mary C. *health facility administrator, hematologist, educator*
Thompson, Judith Kastrup *nursing researcher*
Utz, Sarah Winifred *nursing educator*
Ver Steeg, Donna Lorraine Frank *nurse, sociologist, educator*
Walla, Catherine Anne *nursing administrator, educator*
Wellman, Marian C. *social worker*
Zoss, Nancy Aline *psychotherapist, counseling administrator*

Lower Lake
Garcia, Beatrice Maude *social worker, director*

Malibu
Palacio, June Rose Payne *nutritional science educator*

Martinez
Baird, Laurel Cohen *clinical nurse*

Mill Valley
Taylor, Rose Perrin *social worker*

Moffett Field
O'Hara, Dee *medical/surgical nurse*

Monterey
Robinson, Marla Holbrook *community care nurse*

Moorpark
Young, Victoria E. *occupational health nurse, lawyer*

Morgan Hill
Aranda, Sandra Louise *speech pathology/audiology services professional*

Murrieta
Rose, Norma Louise *retired human services manager*

Napa
Imbach, Janice Sprunger *marriage and family therapist, education educator*

Newhall
Stone, Susan Foster *mental health services professional*

North Hollywood
Charis, Barbara *nutritionist, consultant, medical researcher*

Oakland
Beeson, Montel Eileen *human services administrator, gerontologist*
Bouska Lee, Carla Ann *nursing and health care educator*
Cole, Joan Hays *social worker, clinical psychologist*
Coleman-Perkins, Carolyn *retired medical/surgical nurse*
DeMoro, Rose Ann *nursing administrator*
Howatt, Sister Helen Clare *human services administrator, director, retired school librarian*
King, Janet Carlson *nutrition educator, researcher*
Sargent, Arlene Anne *nursing educator*
Sartor, Vivian Juanita *nursing administrator*
Slack, Vickie *human services administrator*

Ontario
Chavez, Virginia *counselor*
Fangerow, Kay Elizabeth *nurse*
Hanner, Jean P. *retired nursing administrator, art gallery owner, religious organization administrator*

Orange
Karnes, Frances Rozelle *counselor, educator*
Ritman, Barbara Ellen *counselor*

Palm Desert
Adelman, Bayla Ann *occupational therapist*

Palo Alto
Berger-Granet, Nancy Sue *nursing researcher*
Kelsey, Edith Jeanine *psychotherapist, consultant*

Pasadena
Avrech, Gloria May *psychotherapist*

Paso Robles
Dabul, Barbara Lohman *speech pathologist*

Pebble Beach
Quick, Valerie Anne *sonographer*

Pittsburg
Gustafson, Sally Ann *counselor, cosmetologist, educator*

Placerville
Wall, Sonja Eloise *nursing administrator*

Pleasant Hill
Wapner, Donna *healthcare educator*

Pleasanton
Bieber, (Adda) Lynn *marriage, family and child counselor*
Foster, Bonnie Gayle *operating room nurse, real estate agent*

Pomona
Parrish, Joanna Faith *nursing consultant*

Rancho Cordova
Kasch, Mary Courteol *occupational therapist*

Red Bluff
Derk, Denise B. *nurse*

Redlands
Coleman, Arlene Florence *retired pediatrics nurse*
Tapia Parker, Carrie-Anne *massage therapist, healthcare educator*

Reseda
Hoover, Pearl Rollings *nurse*

Riverside
Chang, Sylvia Tan *health facility administrator, educator*
Meadows, Joyce Katherine *nurse*

Roseville
Gambill, Cara Lee *physician assistant*
Roberts, Angela Christine *audiologist*

Sacramento
Melberg, Sharon Elaine *nurse*
Runfola, Sheila Kay *nurse*
von Friederichs-Fitzwater, Marlene Marie *researcher*
Wicks, Debra S. *nursing educator*

San Andreas
Prema, Nitya *marriage and family therapist, artist*

San Anselmo
Ellenberger, Diane Marie *nurse, consultant*

San Bernardino
Ereksen, Christa Ann *social worker, marriage and family therapist*

San Bruno
Edwards, Kassandra Bennett *psychotherapist, consultant*

San Clemente
Renk, Pamela Jean *counselor, psychotherapist, small business owner*

San Diego
Astroth, Margo Foltz *mental health nurse, nurse psychotherapist*
Hunter, Anita J. *pediatric nurse practitioner, educator*
Jenkins, Adrienne *women's health nurse*
Klamerus, Karen Jean *pharmacist, researcher*
Machi, Rita Mae *retired medical/surgical nurse, retired healthcare educator*
Miner, Allison Patrice *physical therapist*
Moore, Joyce West *social worker, psychotherapist*
Niedermeier, Mary B. *retired nutritionist*
Ruth, Dianne *counselor*
Swanson, Ann Elizabeth *family counselor*

San Fernando
Salkin, Barbara Ruth *social worker*

San Francisco
Boerste, Dorothy *psychotherapist*
Dibble, Suzanne Louise *nurse, researcher*
Eng, Catherine *health facility administrator, physician*
Hall, Karen Janna *pediatrics nurse, critical care nurse*
Nix, Katherine Jean *medical case manager*
Rosales, Suzanne Marie *hospital coordinator*
Solday, Alidra (Linda Brown) *psychotherapist, filmmaker*
Styles, Margretta Madden *nursing educator*
Ventura, Jacqueline N. *retired nurse*
Wong, Linda Yunwai *nurse*
Wu-Chu, Stella Chwenyea *nutritionist, consultant*

San Jose
Ammon, Carol Kay *social worker*
Moore, Melanie Ruth *medical technician*
Thaler-DeMers, Debra *clinical nurse*

San Marcos
Ball, Betty Jewel *retired social worker, consultant*

San Mateo
Mark, Lois Nora *psychotherapist, consultant*

San Pedro
McMullen, Sharon Joy Abel *retired marriage and family therapist*

Santa Ana
Martin, Felicia Dottore *mental health services professional, marriage and family therapist*
Mass, Sharon *social worker*
Oberstein, Marydale *geriatric specialist*

Santa Barbara
Kirkpatrick, Diane Yvonne *retired speech pathology/audiology services professional*
Longo, Perie Jane *marriage and family therapist*
Menkin, Eva L. *marriage and family therapist*

Santa Fe Springs
Pina, Martha Elaine *social worker, marriage and family therapist*

Santa Monica
Archambault, Nicole Marie *speech pathology/audiology services professional, consultant*
Magnabosco-Bower, Jennifer Lynn *mental health services professional*
McGlynn, Elizabeth A. *health policy analyst*
Rice, Pamela Ann *marriage and family therapist*

Santa Paula
Broughton, Margaret Martha *mental health nurse*

Santa Rosa
Nickens, Catherine Arlene *retired nurse, freelance writer*
O'Donnell, Anne U. *dietician*
Wartman, Mary Jane *family practice nurse practitioner*

Santee
Schenk, Susan Kirkpatrick *nursing educator, consultant, small business owner*

Sausalito
Groah, Linda Kay *nursing administrator, educator*

Sherman Oaks
Endlich, Lili *psychotherapist*
Levine, Allison *psychotherapist*

Signal Hill
James, Ann *physical therapist*

Simi Valley
Erzinger, Kathy McClam *nursing educator*
Mikesell, Mary (Jane Mikesell) *psychotherapist*

South Pasadena
Bortell, Linda Lee *clinical psychologist*

South San Francisco
Goldman, Barbara Bay *physical therapist*

Spring Valley
Siddiqui, Razia Sultana *retired psychotherapist, educator*

Stanford
Marsh, Martha H. *hospital administrator*

Stockton
Norton, Linda Lee *pharmacist, educator*

Studio City
Childs, Erin Therese *psychotherapist*
Weiner, Sandra Samuel *critical care nurse, consultant*

Sunol
Rebello, Marlene Munson *speech pathologist*

Tarzana
Rinsch, Maryann Elizabeth *occupational therapist*

Temecula
Keenan, Retha Ellen Vornholt *retired nursing educator*

Temple City
Young, Victoria *medical/surgical and oncology nurse*

Thousand Oaks
Mulkey, Sharon Renee *gerontology nurse*
Shirley, Courtney Dymally *nurse*

Torrance
Ebeling, Vicki *marriage and family therapist, writer*
Steckel, Julie Raskin *psychotherapist, lecturer, consultant*

Truckee
Todd, Linda Marie *nutrition researcher, circulation manager, financial consultant, pilot*

Ukiah
Niquette, Geraldine Norma *marriage and family therapist*

Vallejo
Toms, Kathleen Moore *nurse*

Vandenberg Afb
Huggins, Elaine Jacqueline *nurse, retired military officer*

Ventura
Bircher, Andrea Ursula *psychiatric mental health clinical nurse specialist*
Zuber, Norma Keen *career counselor, educator*

Victorville
McGulpin, Elizabeth Jane *nurse*

Visalia
Caldwell, Marcia Diane *nurse*

Walnut Creek
Ausenbaum, Helen Evelyn *social worker, psychologist*
Mackay, Patricia McIntosh *psychotherapist*

West Covina
Adams, Sarah Virginia *psychotherapist, family counselor*

West Hills
Cheney, Anna Marie Jangula *retired medical/surgical nurse*

Westminster
Pitts-Cutler, Melissa Anne *counselor, social worker*

Whittier
Harvey, Patricia Jean *retired special education services professional*

Woodland
Bauer, Cynthia Renae *nurse*

COLORADO

Aurora
Brown, Anne Sherwin *speech pathologist, educator*
Dubuque, Amanda Sue *mental health services professional*
Howard, Donna Jean *retired counselor*
Morrow, Caroline Donovan *retired social worker*
Smith, Elaine Janet *social worker*

Boulder
Holdsworth, Janet Nott *women's health nurse*
Middleton-Downing, Laura *psychiatric social worker, artist, small business owner*
Princeton, Joy Carol *retired nursing educator*

Broomfield
Lybarger, Marjorie Kathryn *nurse*

Colorado Springs
Baldvins, Lynn Ann *medical/surgical nurse, army officer*
Leffingwell, Denise C. *social worker*
Mangone, JoEllen L. *retired hospital administrator*
Orner, Linda Price *family therapist, counselor*
Pfennigs, Kimberly Tucker *nurse*
Strickland, Sylvia Raye *social worker*
Weslin, Anna Therese *acute care nurse practitioner, dance consultant*
Williams, Ruth Lee *clinical social worker*
Young, Lynn Marie *psychotherapist, freelance artist*

Crested Butte
Baker, Ruth Mary *psychotherapist*

Denver
Bahrych, Sharon *physician assistant*
Binstock, Sonya (Toni) Katsh *social worker*
Carroll, Kim Marie *nurse*
Goldblatt, Barbara Janet *sex therapist, educator*
Hotchkiss, Heather A. *social worker, consultant*
Jennett, Shirley Shimmick *health facility administrator*
Lincoln, Sarah *social worker*
Narey, Martha Adele Catherine *biomedical equipment technician, geography educator*
Pegues, JoAnn *dietician*
Plummer, Ora Beatrice *nursing educator, consultant*
Smith, Tara Michelle *counselor*
Thomas, Enolia *nutritionist, educator*
Witt, Catherine Lewis *neonatal nurse practitioner, writer*

Eagle
Hunsaker, Jill Ann *public health official*

Englewood
Brown, Mary *nursing educator*

Federal Heights
Fisher, Terri Lynn *emergency nurse practitioner*

Fort Collins
Tyler, Gail Madeleine *nurse*

Fort Garland
Taylor-Dunn, Corliss Leslie *marriage and family therapist*

Fountain
Ortiz, Amy Mofford *surgical technologist*

Franktown
Kruse, Doris Evelyn *counselor*

Glenwood Springs
Candlin, Frances Ann *psychotherapist, social worker, educator*

Grand Junction
Fox, Carmen Alice *retired medical/surgical nurse*
Hoagland, Christina Gail *occupational therapist, industrial drafter*
Pantenburg, Michel *health facility administrator, educator, holistic health coordinator*
Schmerler, Barbara Ann *social worker*

Lafayette
Hibbard, Christine *psychotherapist, educator, minister*

Lakewood
Burry, Jennifer Wilborn *medical/surgical nurse*

Leadville
Brown, Jessi Eden *mental health services professional*

Littleton
Davis, Betsy Rae *nurse*

Longmont
Jones, Beverly Ann Miller *nursing administrator, retired patient services administrator*
Van Elsacker, Tulsa *health facility administrator*
Walker, Kathleen Mae *health facility administrator*

Pueblo
Van Etten, Nancy Kay *medical/surgical nurse, consultant*

Steamboat Springs
Lykken, Catherine Townley *social worker*

Thornton
McEachern, Susan Mary *physician assistant*

Westminster
Hallman, Janelle M. *psychotherapist, educator*
Mussehl, Peggy Ann *nurse*

CONNECTICUT

Branford
Swofford, Sharon Ehlers *medical/surgical nurse*

Bridgeport
King, Sister Eleace *special education services professional*
Macdonald, Karen Crane *occupational therapist, geriatrics services professional*

Bristol
Morales, Mary E. *social worker*

Granby
Gates, Joanne Ferry *counselor*

Greenwich
Gaudio, Maxine Diane *biofeedback therapist, stress management consultant*
Kleinman, Noela MacGinn *family nurse practitioner*

Groton
Payson, Herta Ruth *psychotherapist, theater educator, massage therapist*

Hamden
Cole-Schiraldi, Marilyn Bush *occupational therapist, educator*

Hartford
Bidwell, Karen Rubino *mental health care clinician*
Brubeck, Marcia Ellen *psychotherapist*
Cross, Nadine Debra-Ann *pharmacist*

Manchester
Randall, Frances J. *psychotherapist*

New Britain
Brancifort, Janet Marie *hospital administrator, respiratory therapist*

New Haven
Ahern, Jo Ann *diabetes clinical nurse specialist*
Chase, Linda (Lina Chase) *social worker, psychotherapist*
De Rose, Sandra Michele *psychotherapist, educator, administrator*
Grey, Margaret *nursing educator*
Jones, Katherine R. *nursing educator*
Krauss, Judith Belliveau *nursing educator*
Lord, Ruth *retired researcher, philanthropist, writer*
McCorkle, Ruth *oncological nurse, educator, researcher*

New London
Allen, Carol Marie *radiologic technologist*

Newington
Reynolds, Patricia Jean *psychiatric social worker, songwriter*

Norwalk
McMahon, Elizabeth Mildred *educator*

Stamford
Moggio, Barbara Jean *health education specialist*
Moore, Sharon Helen Scott *gerontological nurse*

Suffield
Bianchi, Maria *critical care nurse, acute care nurse practitioner*

Trumbull
Hochberg, Jennifer Anne *counselor*

Vernon Rockville
Gallien, Sandra Jean *social worker*

Waterbury
Doback, Joan M. *physician assistant*
Zasada, Mary Eileen *nursing administrator*

West Hartford
Barry, Patricia Dowling *psychotherapist, consultant*
Gebo, Susan Claire *consulting nutritionist*
Hornblow, Doris H. *retired nurse*

West Haven
Chavert, Georgia *nutritionist, educator*

Westport
Boles, Lenore Utal *nurse psychotherapist, educator*
Derr, Teresa Marie *social worker*

DELAWARE

Dover
Rubino, Joelle L. *physical therapist, athletic trainer*

Georgetown
Nichols, M. Kathleen *therapist, educator*

Hockessin
Croyle, Barbara Ann *health facility administrative executive*

New Castle
Ainsworth, Elaine Marie *occupational therapist*

Newark
Talbert, Dorothy Georgie Burkett *social worker*

Rehoboth Beach
Giove, Susan Nancy *medical/surgical nurse, educator*

Smyrna
McClellan, Stephanie Ann *speech pathology/audiology services professional*

Wilmington
Lagana, Laura A. *medical/surgical nurse, orthopedics nurse, volunteer*
Miranda-Evans, Valetta Lee *social worker, human services manager*

DISTRICT OF COLUMBIA

Washington
Altman, Beth Lee *social worker*
Alward, Ruth Rosendall *nursing consultant*
Auerbach, Judith Diane *public health service officer*
Baigis, Judith Ann *nursing educator, academic administrator*
Bale, Judith R. *health science association administrator*
Borra, Susan T. *dietician, medical association administrator*
Bozarth, Stephanie Belle Mays *social worker*
Chalk, Rosemary Anne *health science association administrator*
Corrigan, Janet M. *health science association administrator*
Cunningham, Karen Lynn *social worker*
Daftary, Monika Neil *pharmacist, educator*
Darling, Helen *health services consultant*
Delbanco, Suzanne F. *human services administrator*
Delgado, Jane *health policy executive, writer, psychologist*
DeParle, Nancy-Ann Min *former federal agency administrator, lawyer*
Dunham, LizaMarie Bassiwa *medical technician*
Golden, Olivia Ann *human services administrator*
Hager, Mary Hastings *nutritionist, educator, consultant*
Harling, Barbara Jean *social worker*
Lewis, Prudence Fox *Christian science practitioner*
Lynn, Valerie Roemer *psychotherapist*
Martinez, Rose Marie *health science association administrator*
Mellan, Olivia Julie (Olivia Julie Shapiro) *psychotherapist*
Michnich, Marie E. *health policy analyst, consultant, educator*
Miller, Linda B. *administrator*
Mitchell, Ruthie Yvette *human services administrator, director*
Penner, Alice Braeker *clinical social worker*
Rios, Elena *health association administrator*
Rouson, Vivian Reissland *alcohol/drug abuse services professional, journalist*
Rowland, Diane *health facility administrator, researcher*
Sanchez-Way, Ruth Dolores *public health administrator*
Stoiber, Susanne A. *health science organization administrator*
Theiss, Patricia Kelley *public health researcher, educator*
Turner, Brenda Lorraine *social worker*
Valentine, Nancy Marie *nursing administrator, educator*
Wager, Deborah Miller *researcher, consultant*
Walker, Audrey Thayer *social worker, psychotherapist*
Wesley, Ruby LaVerne *nursing educator, administrator, researcher*
Wysocki, Susan *women's health nurse practitioner*
Yoder, Mary Jane Warwick *psychotherapist*

FLORIDA

Altamonte Springs
Shapiro, Susan Janine *social worker, educator, consultant*

Avon Park
Cranfill, Virginia May *retired nursing administrator*

Boca Raton
Baumgarten, Diana Virginia *gerontological nurse*
Foreman, Barbara Blatt *healthcare facility administrator*
Goldstein, Shari *healthcare educator*
Jacobson, Susan Bogen *psychotherapist*
Levick, Myra Friedman *art psychotherapist, educator*
Morris, Jill Carole *psychotherapist*
Naples, Mary Cecilia *mental health services professional, health facility administrator*
Rothberg-Blackman, June Simmonds *retired nursing educator, psychotherapist*
Spencer, Angela *physician assistant*

Boynton Beach
Moll, Lauretta Jane *guidance counselor*
Wilner, Lois Annette *retired speech and language pathologist*

Brooksville
Hartley-Lonabaugh, Karen Lee *critical care nurse*

Cape Canaveral
Roberts, Nancy Carolyn *retired counselor, elementary educator*

Cape Coral
Graff, Sherry *adult nurse practitioner*

Casselberry
Jackowitz, Enid Duchin *psychotherapist*

Clearwater
Barry, Joyce Alice *dietician, consultant*
Fenderson, Caroline Houston *psychotherapist*
Halsey, Jean Michele *nursing educator*

Coral Gables
Koita, Saida Yahya *psychoanalyst, educator*

Daytona Beach
Whitwam, Eileen V. *adult nurse practitioner, educator*

Deerfield Beach
Berger, Barbara Paull *social worker, marriage and family therapist*
Wells, Bette Evans *psychotherapist*

Defuniak Springs
Brinson, Vida L. *counselor*

Delray Beach
Appel, Mindy R. *social worker*
Ellsweig, Phyllis Leah *retired psychotherapist*

Deltona
Bondinell, Stephanie *counselor, academic administrator*

Doral
Brioso-Mesa, Maureen Diane *mental health services professional*

Dunedin
Simmons, Patricia Ann *pharmacist, consultant*

Edgewater
Lawson, Bonnie Hulsey *psychotherapist, consultant*

Englewood
Clark, Carolyn Chambers *nurse, educator, publishing executive*

Fort Lauderdale
Adams, Nancy R. *nurse, retired military officer*
Gonzalez, Nancy Berger *healthcare professional, educator*
Kornblau, Barbara L. *physical therapist, educator*
Labiner, Adria *psychotherapist*

Fort Myers
Carney, Teryl Dawn *physician assistant*
Thurman, Cynthia Denise *human services administrator*
Varley, Elizabeth Gail *social worker*

Fort Walton Beach
Bolt, Lynda Elaine *alcohol/drug abuse services professional*
Hart, Nancy Diane *family nurse practitioner, educator, consultant, writer, mental health nurse*

Gainesville
Greenberg, Corinne Hunt *psychotherapist*
Lockwood, Rhonda J. *mental health services professional*
MacLeod, Joan Ann *medical/surgical nurse, administrator*
Puckett, Ruby Parker *nutritionist, food service executive, writer*
Small, Natalie Settimelli *retired pediatric mental health counselor*

Hillsboro Beach
Marshall, Jo Taylor *social worker*

Hollywood
Shane, Doris Jean *respiratory therapist, administrator*

Holmes Beach
Nevans, Laurel S. *rehabilitation counselor*

Inverness
Kramer, Marlene Dixie *dietician*
Nichols, Sally Jo *geriatrics nurse*

Jacksonville
Davis, Linda Lennon McConnell *critical care nurse*
Longino, Theresa Childers *nurse*
Mack, Jeannette Ana *medical technician*
Mauras, Nelly *pediatrics professor, department chairman, researcher*
Pavlick, Pamela Kay *nurse, consultant*
Sanders, Marion Yvonne *retired geriatrics nurse*
ScarboroughH, Marion Nichols *nutritionist, recreational facility executive*

Key West
Ersay, Molly Ann *counselor, consultant*

Lakeland
Markley, Kate *social worker, consultant*

Land O Lakes
Webb, Mary Greenwald *cardiovascular clinical specialist, educator*

Largo
Bush, Debra W. *occupational health nurse*

Leesburg
Osborne, Glenna Jean *health facility administrator*

Maitland
Caston, Jane Pears *school nurse practitioner*

Melbourne
Hughes, A. N. *psychotherapist*

Miami
Auerbach, Ethel Louise *healthcare facility administrator*
Borelli, Myriam *social worker, educator*
Chisholm, Martha Maria *dietitian*
Faul, Maureen Patricia *health facility administrator*
Gare, Fran *nutritionist*
Gimenes, Sonia Regina Rosendo *family therapist, psychologist*
Headley, Joanna Evonne *mental health services professional, researcher*
Miller, Arlene *psychotherapist, mental health facility director*
Parchment, Yvonne *nursing educator*
Potocky, Miriam *social worker, educator, writer*
Saland, Deborah *psychotherapist, educator*

Miami Beach
Bredemeier, Mary Elizabeth *counselor, educator*

Miami Shores
Martino Maze, Claire Denise *nursing educator*

Miami Springs
Neasman, Annie Ruth *health facility administrator*

Naples
Brown, Cindy Lynn *family practice nurse practitioner, critical care nurse*
Cotrone, Janice Lynne *nursing consultant*
Karkut, Bonnie Lee *retired dental office manager*
Maurides, Elaine *retired mental health services professional, retired social worker*
Miles, Helen *oncological nurse*

New Port Richey
Charters, Karen Ann Elliott *critical care nurse, health facility administrator*

North Fort Myers
Carr-Carothers, Marcella Irene *medical surgical nurse*

North Miami Beach
Rodriguez, Maria *social worker, counselor*

Ocala
Ettinger, Penny A. *medical/surgical nurse*

Oldsmar
Miller, Deborah *medical surgical nurse*

Orlando
Horning, Sheri *dietician, educator*
Leuner, Jean D'Meza *nursing educator, director*
Sharp, Christina Krieger *retired nursing educator*
Vanderwerken, Sharon Lynn *nurse*

Ormond Beach
Smalbein, Dorothy Ann *guidance counselor*

Palm Bay
Armstrong, Lillian M. *clinical counselor*

Palm Beach Gardens
Fiessinger, Bettina A. *mental health counselor, educator*
Schurtz, Ora Sears *hypnotist, educator*

Palm Harbor
Rivelli, Susan Veronica *nurse*

Panama City
Marino, Marion Lillian *health service administrator*

Parkland
Harris, Jacqueline Myers *speech pathology/audiology services professional*

Pembroke Pines
Alber, Oro Linda *healthcare educator, consultant*
Ferris, Rita Bernadette *social worker*

Pensacola
Dettloff, Donna Jean *retired social worker*
Law, Carol Judith *medical psychotherapist*
Loesch, Mabel Lorraine *social worker*
Shimmin, Margaret Ann *women's health nurse*
Wright, Shannon Marie *psychotherapist, counselor*

Pompano Beach
Brooker, Fern G. *healthcare educator*

Port Orange
Riegner, Elizabeth Jane *counselor, educator, mental health nurse*

Port Saint Lucie
Hogan, Roxanne Arnold *nursing consultant, risk management consultant, educator*

Ruskin
LaComb-Williams, Linda Lou *community health nurse*

Saint Petersburg
Keller, Natasha Matrina Leonidow *nursing administrator*

Sanford
Mena, Michele M. *counselor, educator*

Sarasota
Hanson, Virginia A. *human services administrator*
Simons, Julio Merredith *psychotherapist, social worker*
Ward, Jacqueline Ann Beas *nurse, healthcare administrator*

Sebastian
Mauke, Leah Rachel *retired counselor*

South Daytona
Hollandsworth, Phyllis W. *marriage and family therapist*

Stuart
Cocoves, Anita Petzold *psychotherapist*

Sun City Center
King, Gladiola Tin *retired medical technician*

Tallahassee
Blair, Maudine *psychotherapist, communications executive, management consultant*
Ford, Ann Suter *family practice nurse practitioner, consultant*

Tampa
Arfsten, Betty-Jane *nurse*
Bauwin, Roberta Elizabeth *counselor, director*
Boutros, Linda Nelene Wiley *medical/surgical nurse*
Castellano, Josephine Massaro *medical records specialist*
Collins, Gwendolyn Beth *health facility administrator*
Cunningham, Kathleen Ann *researcher*
Russell, Diane Elizabeth Henrikson *career counselor*
Steiner, Sally Ann *psychiatric nurse practitioner*
Tegarden, LoRetta Tudor *retired counselor*

Tarpon Springs
Nothdurft, Donna Jean *occupational therapist*

Valrico
Carlucci, Marie Ann *nursing administrator, consultant*

Venice
Barritt, Evelyn Ruth Berryman *nurse, educator, dean*
Belok, Carol Jean *nurse, alcohol/drug abuse services professional*

Vero Beach
McCrystal, Ann Marie *community health nurse, administrator*

Wauchula
Saddler, Peggy Chandler *counselor*

West Palm Beach
Bernhardt, Marcia Brenda *mental health counselor*

Weston
Gordon, Lori Heyman *psychotherapist, author, educator*

Winter Haven
Davis, Judith Lee *medical/surgical nurse*
Furnival, Patricia Anne *retired social worker*

Winter Park
Haendiges, Anne R. *marriage and family therapist*

Zephyrhills
Walton, Shirley Dawn *retired medical technician*

GEORGIA

Albany
Buchanan, Valerie Russo *nursing administrator, critical care nurse, entrepreneur, consultant*
Gates, Roberta Pecoraro *nursing educator*
Reece, Cheri Dodson *clinical nursing specialist, educator*

Alpharetta
DiFabio, Carol Anna *psychotherapist*
Mock, Melinda Smith *orthopedic nurse specialist, consultant*

Atlanta
Anderson, Barbara Allen *alcohol/drug abuse services professional, archivist*
Bales, Virginia Shankle *health science association administrator*
Clark, Mary Elizabeth *medical/surgical nurse, diabetes specialist*
Frazier, Emma L. *healthcare educator, researcher*
Huff, Sara Davis *nursing manager*
Kelly, Jean Slatter *healthcare administrator, nurse*
Kropf, Nancy P. *social worker, educator, director*
Lattimore, Barbara *health facility administrator, consultant*
Parrott, Janice Morton *medical/surgical nurse, nursing researcher*
Polhamus, Barbara *nutritionist, educator*
Salmon, Marla E. *nursing educator, dean*
Schuchat, Anne *health facility administrator*
Shelton, Elizabeth Colley *social worker*
Slocum, Susanne Tunno *medical/surgical nurse*
Sorrells, Kristeen *violinist, music therapist*
Walton, Carole Lorraine *clinical social worker*
Wong, Faye Ling *public health service officer*

Augusta
Barab, Patsy Lee *nutritionist, realtor*
Logan, Betty Mulherin *human services specialist*
Narsavage, Georgia Roberts *nursing educator, researcher*

Bowersville
Elrod, Joy Cheek *nurse*

Brunswick
Herndon, Alice Patterson Latham *public health nurse*
Low, Anne Douglas *nurse*
Riner, Deborah Lillian *mental health services professional*

Canton
Cudney, Amelia Harrison *medical/surgical nurse, obstetrics/gynecological nurse*

Columbus
Bryant, Mollie Annette *counselor*
Hickson, Joyce Faye *counseling educator*
Simmons, Lynda Teel *nurse, healthcare executive*
Striblin, Lori Ann *critical care nurse, insurance agent*

Conley
Grant, Lucille *hospital administrator, social worker*

Conyers
Averhart, Celestine *surgical nurse*

Cordele
Lloyd, Amy L. *social worker*

Covington
Harrington, Joan Kathryn *counselor*

Decatur
Freemont, Andria Shamona *lab administrator*
Kelly, Karen Deloris *addiction counselor, administrator*
Nease, Judith Allgood *marriage and family therapist*

Douglasville
Bronson, Carol E. *health facility administrator*

East Ellijay
Prince-Stokes, Cathy *neuro-orthopedic nurse administrator*

Evans
Feldman, Elaine Bossak *medical nutritionist, educator*
Lenox, Angela Cousineau *healthcare consultant*

Fort Benning
Astern, Laurie *psychotherapist, physician assistant*

Jasper
Ledford, Shirley Louise *practical nurse*

Kathleen
Talton, Karen Bryant *nurse*

Lawrenceville
Swanson, Lynnette Sue *special olympics coordinator, special education educator*

Loganville
Jarrett, Benita V. *medical/surgical nurse, minister*

Macon
Brown, Nancy Childs *marriage and family therapist*

Marietta
Biehle, Karen Jean *pharmacist*
Hudson, Linda *health facility administrator*
McEntire, Betty *health facility administrator*
Neff, Marilyn Lee *nursing consultant*
Roaché, Sylvia *social worker*
Veatch, Sheila Williamson *retired counselor*

Milledgeville
Konersman, Elaine Reich *nursing administrator*

Morrow
Clark, Deborah J. *nursing administrator, educator*

Moultrie
Cox, Carol Yvonne *counselor*

Norcross
Montiel, Carol E. *health services administrator*

Ocilla
Busbin, Brenda C. *public health nurse*

Peachtree City
Scott, Ann Marie *medical/surgical nurse*

Rome
Watson, Mary Ann *marriage and family therapist*

Roswell
Herron, Harriette A. *retired occupational health nurse*
Palermo, Barbara Kelly *health facility administrator*

Saint Simons Island
Perry, Annette Owen *psychotherapist, educator*
Weinberg, Elisabeth H. *physical therapist, health facility administrator*

Savannah
Baker, Brinda Elizabeth Garrison *community health nurse*
Borschel, Valerie Lynn *medical/surgical nurse*
DiClaudio, Janet Alberta *health information administrator*
Greene, Gail Purchase *medical/surgical nurse*

Smyrna
Fitzner, Kathryn Ethridge *psychotherapist*
Stevenson, Mary Compher *pharmacist, educator*

Snellville
Dodd, Violet M. *nursing educator, recreational therapist, counselor*

Statesboro
Bartels, Jean Ellen *nursing educator*

Summerville
Busby, Barbara Sue Hughes *geriatrics nurse*

Ty Ty
Howell, Eva Jane Wood *medical/surgical nurse*

Union City
Riley, Francena *nurse, retired non-commissioned officer*

Warner Robins
Beck, Rhonda Joann *paramedic, educator, writer*

HAWAII

Haleiwa
Shigemasa, Teresa *mental health services professional, educator*

Honolulu
Kadohiro, Jane K. *nurse, educator, consultant*
Loke, Joan Tso Fong *respiratory therapist*
Lum, Jean Loui Jin *nursing educator*
Melcher, Kirsten Jegsen *physical therapist, consultant, small business owner*
Sheridan, Mary Stoebe *social worker*

Kailua Kona
Richardson, Mary L. *psychotherapist*

Kaneohe
Marineau, Michelle Lynn *nursing educator*

Mililani
Carrillo, Linda Marie *counselor*

Waialua
Pugliese Locke, Ranada Marie *nurse*

IDAHO

Boise
Brownson, Mary Louise *counselor, educator, artist*
Kendrick, Beverly Ann *medical/surgical nurse, small business owner*

Cocolalla
Groth-Marnat, Gabrielle *counselor*

Eagle
Wickman, Patricia Ann *retired social worker*

Idaho Falls
Oe, Emily Norene *counselor, play therapist*

Ketchum
Parry, Janet *retired health facility administrator*

Meridian
Greenspan, Valeda Clareen *nursing educator, consultant*
Thorsted, V. Darleene *neonatal/perinatal nurse, community health nurse*

Pingree
Jackson, Sheila Benson *counselor*

Pocatello
Heberlein, Alice LaTourrette *healthcare educator, physical education educator, coach*

Star
Miles, Michele Leslie *physician assistant*

ILLINOIS

Antioch
Dahl, Laurel Jean *human services administrator*

Arlington Heights
Telleen, Judy *counselor*

Aurora
Moore, Patricia Ann *alcohol/drug abuse services professional*

Bolingbrook
Day, Mary Ann *medical/surgical nurse*
Price, Theodora Hadzistelliou *individual, child and family therapist*

Burr Ridge
Daly-Gawenda, Debra *health facility administrator, nursing educator*

Carbondale
Kawewe, Saliwe Moyo *social work educator, researcher*

Centralia
Erwin, Nicole Renee *pharmacist*
Whitten, Mary Lou *nursing educator*

Champaign
Fosler, Norma Lorraine *counselor*
May, Linda Karen Cardiff *occupational health nurse, safety engineer, consultant*

Charleston
Hedges, Edith Rittenhouse *retired nutrition and family and consumer sciences educator*

Chicago
Adams, Lucille Joan *psychotherapist, health administrator*
Andreoli, Kathleen Gainor *nurse, educator, dean*
Bancroft, Barbee N. *nursing educator*
Benson, Irene M. *nurse*
Berman, Laura *sex therapist*
Bristo, Marca *human services administrator*
Cox-Hayley, Deon Melayne *geriatrics services professional*
Cullina, Joanne Frances *medical/surgical nurse*
Easley, Cheryl Eileen *nursing educator, department chairman*
Ewert, Jennifer Kristin *counselor*
Goldsmith, Ethel Frank *medical social worker*
Gulati, Martha *health facility administrator, cardiologist*
Haber, Catherine S. *medical/surgical nurse, nursing administrator*
Hill, Barbara Benton *healthcare executive*
Katz, Miriam Lesser *psychotherapist, educator*
Kehrer, Michele Ann *physical therapist, athleic trainer*
Klimek, Kristen M. *physical therapist*
Logemann, Jerilyn Ann *speech pathologist, educator*
McDermott, Mary Ann *nursing educator*
Proctor, Millicent Carlé *social worker*
Purcell, Diane *addiction counselor*
Raheja, Krishna Kumari *retired medical/surgical nurse*
Reed, Vastina Kathryn (Tina Reed) *child and adolescent psychotherapist*
Rosenheim, Margaret Keeney *social welfare policy educator*
Rudnick, Ellen Ava *health facility administrator*
Sanders, Doris Jean *mental health therapist*
Shannon, Iris Reed *health facility administrator, consultant*
Smalley, Penny Judith *healthcare technology consultant*
Tanzman, Mary *social worker*
Thomas, Leona Marlene *healthcare educator*
Toriani, Denise Maria *hospital residency coordinator*
Vigen, Kathryn L. Voss *nursing administrator, educator, dean*
Villalon, Dalisay Manuel *nurse, real estate broker*
Walsh, Mary Caswell *psychotherapist*
Watson, Easter Jean *psychotherapist, financial program consultant*

Countryside
Vondrak, Roberta G. *counselor*

Danville
Hiser, Paula J. *medical/surgical nurse*

Decatur
Mayfield, Peggy Lee *counselor*

Dekalb
Crosser, Carmen Lynn *marriage and family therapist, social worker, consultant*

Des Plaines
Wisz, Katherine *nurse*

Downers Grove
Fugate, Kelly Anne *nurse*

East Saint Louis
Lane-Trent, Patricia Jean *social worker*
Roy, Darlene *human services administrator*

Edwardsville
Norris, Sandra Love *occupational therapist*

Effingham
Van Ulft, Stephanie Ann *health facility administrator*

Elgin
Barnett, Sue *nurse*

Elk Grove Village
Yates, Anna Marie *counselor, educator*

Elmhurst
Payne, Jan *medical/surgical nurse, educator*

Flossmoor
Backstein, Micki Lynn *social worker*
Micki, Backstein Lynn *social worker*

Freeport
Lestikow, Norma Jean *nursing educator*

Galena
Alexander, Barbara Leah Shapiro *clinical social worker*

Geneva
Harmon Brown, Valarie Jean *hospital laboratory director, information systems executive*

Glen Carbon
Adkerson, Donya Lynn *clinical counselor*

Glen Ellyn
Cummings, Joan E. *health facility administrator, educator*
Engelmann, Mary Lynn *nursing educator*

Glenview
Coulson, Elizabeth Anne *physical therapist, educator, state representative*

Godfrey
McDowell, Angela Lorene *counselor*
Smith, Linda Jeane *allied health educator*

Gurnee
Curns, Eileen Bohan *counselor, author, speaker*
Ullrich, Linda J. *medical technologist*

Highland Park
Mervis, Bonnie Aaron *social worker*
Schindel, Alice *social worker*

Hinsdale
Kim, Micaela *speech pathology/audiology services professional*
Migliorino, Caroline Milano *nursing consultant*

Joliet
Doyle, Juanita *medical/surgical nurse*
Lynch, Priscilla A. *nursing educator, psychotherapist*
Wilson, Bobbi Ellen *physical therapy assistant*

Lake Bluff
Fletcher, Dorothy Jean *hospital administrator, educator*

Lombard
Holgers-Awana, Rita Marie *electrodiagnosis specialist*

Macomb
Morton, Patsy Lou *social worker*

Mahomet
Barger-Marcusiu, Eva *cardiovascular nurse*
Lindley, Joyce E. *health facility administrator, consultant, real estate appraiser*

Maywood
Hindle, Paula Alice *nursing administrator*

Moline
Larson, Sandra B. *nursing educator*

Mount Prospect
Grossman, Barbara Anne *nurse*
O'Connor, Nan G. *social worker*

Naperville
Fuhrer, Linda Larsen *social worker*
Nicotra, Mary *health facility administrator, consultant*

Normal
Deany, Donna Jean *radiology technologist*
Rademacher, Betty Green *retired counselor, consultant*

Northbrook
Heuer, Marilyn Patricia *operating room nurse, quality assurance nurse*
Kahn, Sandra S. *psychotherapist*
Noeth, Carolyn Frances *speech and language pathologist*

Oak Brook
Bower, Barbara Jean *nurse, consultant*
Schultz, Karen Rose *clinical social worker, author, publisher, speaker*
Sweeney, Patrice Ellen *health administration executive*

Oak Lawn
Wiechert, Barbara Theresa *school nurse practitioner*

Park Ridge
Pippen, Jennifer Lynn *therapist, consultant*

Paxton
Curry, Joan R. *medical/surgical nurse, emergency nurse*

Pekin
Yock, Norma Iris *counselor, music educator*

Peoria
McCollum, Jean Hubble *medical technician*
Perrilles, Angela Terese *physical therapist*

Quincy
Flinspach, Ursula R. *pharmacist, mathematics professor*
Reynolds, Judith Amy *nutritionist, consultant, animal scientist, educator*

Rockford
Heath, Alice Fairchild *retired mental health services professional*

Saint Charles
Abts, Gwyneth Hartmann *retired dietician*

Savoy
Bednar, Susan Gail *social worker, consultant, social sciences educator*

Skokie
Guillermo, Linda *clinical social worker*
Langguth, Margaret Witty *health facility administrator*

Springfield
Franks, Amy Ann *healthcare educator, medical educator*

University Park
Samson, Linda Forrest *nursing educator, nursing administrator*

Urbana
Eddy-Johnson, Deanna M. *home health care advocate*

Wheaton
Pape, Patricia Ann *social worker, consultant*

Wilmette
Hass, Victoria Yusim *psychogeriatrics services professional, consultant*

Zion
Paulsen, Marsha E. *counselor*

INDIANA

Anderson
Bracken, Linda Darlene *medical/surgical nurse*
Kratzner, Judith Evelyn *program manager*

Bloomington
Austin, Joan Kessner *mental health nurse*
Montgomery, Kathleen Rae *counselor*

Carmel
Sterchi, Mary Elizabeth *social worker*

East Chicago
Psaltis, Helen *medical/surgical nurse*

Evansville
Litschgi, Barbara Nell *dietician*
Smith, Leslie Morrow *counselor*

Fort Wayne
Goshert, Janet K. *dietitian*
Harwood, Virginia Ann *retired nursing educator*

Gary
Beamer, Laura *women's health and genetic health nurse*
Hensley, Mary Kay *dietician*
Steinberg, Marilyn Marie *psychotherapist*

Granger
Harmelink, Ruth Irene *marriage and family therapist, writer*

Hammond
Florek, Michaeline *counselor*
Tazbir, Janice Elaine *nursing educator*
Wright, Carol Jean *medical/surgical nurse*

Highland
Feldman, Nancy E. *social worker*

Indianapolis
Daniel, Ann Cummins *psychotherapist, consultant*
Harcourt, Marion Goldthwaite *retired social worker*
Haverly, Pamela Sue *nursing administrator*
McCall-Rodriguez, Leonor *healthcare services company executive, entrepreneur*
Moelhman, Amy Jo *social worker*
Warner, Joanne Rains *nursing educator, associate dean*

Knightstown
Ward, Sarah Frances *narcotic education consultant, counselor*

Lafayette
McBride, Angela Barron *nursing educator*

Lincoln City
Fischer, Deborah Lynn *school nurse practitioner*

Logansport
Walter, Patricia L. *psychotherapist, consultant*

Mishawaka
Bays, June Marie *counselor, social worker*

Muncie
Garringer, Barbara Lou *nurse*
Hoffman, Mary Catherine *retired nurse, anesthetist*

New Albany
Rhodes, Betty Fleming *rehabilitation services professional, nurse*

New Castle
Pierce, Terry Jo *medical/surgical nurse*

Rockport
Davis, Karen Sue *hospital nursing supervisor*

San Pierre
Begley, Heidi Marie *nurse, entrepreneur*

Seymour
Norrell, Mary Patricia *nursing educator*

South Bend
Bondi, Kathleen *social worker*
Ivory, Goldie Lee *retired social worker, educator*
Stelton, Susan Diane *nursing specialist, educator*
Yarger, Ruth Anketell *social worker*

Tell City
Thrasher, Mary Ahlf Marcroft *educator, social worker*

Terre Haute
Anderson, Louise A. *public health service officer*
Daffron, Mitzi Lynnae *quality improvement specialist*

Upland
Harner, Cathy J. *social worker, educator*

West Lafayette
Kirksey, Avanelle *nutrition educator*

Windfall
Cooper, Joyce Beatrice *medical/surgical nurse*

Woodburn
Stieglitz, Imogene L. *intravenous therapy nurse*

IOWA

Altoona
Berkenes, Joyce Marie Poore *social worker, director*

Ames
Berger, Kay Jackson *psychiatric social worker*

Burlington
Smith, Mona Riley *psychotherapist*

Calmar
Jarosh, Colleen Marie *nursing educator, consultant*

Cedar Rapids
Lewis, Rebecca Lee *medical/surgical nurse, educator*

Clear Lake
Bergvig, Chyrl Rae *counselor*

Council Bluffs
Alley, Mary Lou Vande Woude *retired medical/surgical nurse*

Davenport
Goudy, Josephine Gray *social worker*

Des Moines
Dukes, Vanessa Johnson *dietician*
Hamilton, Elaine H. *retired nurse, artist*
Ramsden, Mary Catherine *substance abuse specialist*

Dubuque
Curoe, Bernadine Mary *counselor*

Garner
Duregger, Karen Marie *health facility administrator*

Iowa City
Muir, Ruth Brooks *alcohol/drug abuse services professional, consultant*

Knoxville
Taylor, Mary Kay *medical, surgical nurse*

Le Claire
Mears, Joyce Lund *educational counselor*

Oskaloosa
Gleason, Carol Ann *mental health nurse, educator*

Red Oak
Werner, Cecelia Marie *counselor*

Richland
Walter, Sandra S. *social worker*

Walford
Brooks, Debra L. *healthcare executive, neuromuscular therapist*

Waterloo
Moore, Marilyn Ulfers *social worker*

Waverly
Eick-Gamm, Kimberly Marie *social worker*

West Des Moines
Goldsmith, Janet Jane *pediatric nurse practitioner*

KANSAS

Colby
Erickson, Patricia Ann *physical therapist, educator*

Deerfield
Tackett, Gayle Enslow *medical/surgical nurse*

Edwardsville
Boal, Marcia Anne Riley *clinical social worker*

El Dorado
Clarke, Linda Diane *mental health services professional, psychotherapist*

Fort Scott
Wassenberg, Evelyn M. *retired medical/surgical nurse, educator*

Garden City
Lisk, Martha Ann *rehabilitation services professional*

Great Bend
Heidrick, Kathy Jo *medical technician, educator*

Kansas City
Jerome, Norge Winifred *nutritionist, anthropologist, educator*

Lawrence
Loudon, Karen Lee *physical therapist*

Leavenworth
Heim, Dixie Sharp *family practice nurse practitioner*

Manhattan
Chance-Reay, Michaeline K. *educator, psychotherapist*
Shanklin, Carol W. *dietician, educator*

Nashville
Huss, Bonnie Jean *intensive cardiac care nurse*

Overland Park
Bronaugh, Deanne Rae *home health care administrator, consultant*

Shawnee Mission
Breen, Katherine Anne *speech and language pathologist*
Conry, Maura *pharmacist, social worker*
Wallace, Sherry Lynn *speech-language pathologist*

Topeka
Bartlett, Alice Brand *psychoanalyst, educator, researcher*
Boydston, Resa Odette *mental health services professional*
Greene, Jane *health educator*
Reymond, Patricia Ann *social worker*
Varner, Charleen LaVerne McClanahan *nutritionist, educator, dietician*

Wellington
White, Helen Lou *school nurse practitioner*

Wichita
Da'Luz Vieira-Jones, Lorraine Christine C. *acupuncturist, researcher*
Dorr, Stephanie Tilden *psychotherapist*
Guthrie, Diana Fern *nursing educator*

KENTUCKY

Albany
Tallent, Brenda Colene *social worker, psychotherapist*

Berea
Frazer, Joy A. *retired nurse*

Brooksville
Dorton, Truda Lou *medical/surgical nurse, geriatrics nurse*

Campbellsville
Eastridge, Darlene F. *social worker, dean*

Cold Spring
Gooch, Deborah Ann Grimme *medical, surgical nurse, administrator*

Frankfort
Fleming, Juanita Wilson *nursing educator, academic administrator*

Georgetown
Patton, Mary Ritchie *retired pediatric nurse practitioner, consultant*

Grayson
Hunt, Andrea Wheaton *nurse*

Harrodsburg
Herman, Alice Gertrude *retired nursing educator*

Highland Heights
Moss, Nancy Evans *nurse midwife, women's health nurse*

Lexington
Caldwell, Alethea Otti *health care systems executive*
Farrar, Donna Beatrice *health facility administrator*
Hardin-Pierce, Melanie G. *nursing educator*
Holley, Kay Moffitt *nutrition instructor, dietitian*
Lowe, Jennifer Ruth *mental health services professional*
Rowe, Melinda Grace *public health service officer*

London
Baker, Lori Lee *medical/surgical nurse*

Louisville
Antoine, Janet Anne *social worker*
Ashby, Denise *medical/surgical nurse, director*
Haddaway, Janice Lillian *psychotherapist, consultant*
Hathcock, Bonita Catherine (Bonnie Hathcock) *managed health care company executive*
Jolly, Barbara Lee *home healthcare professional*
Mather, Elizabeth Vivian *healthcare executive*
Musacchio, Marilyn Jean *nurse midwife, educator*

Madisonville
Peyton, Dianna Leah Davis *physical therapist, personal trainer*

Manchester
Rowland, Vicki Diane *home health nurse*

Paducah
Selbe, Lisa Hancock *medical/surgical nurse*

Pikeville
Hunter, Trudy Pearl *surgical nurse*

Radcliff
Cole, Jessie Mae *nursing assistant, freelance/self-employed writer*

Richmond
Hall, Kathy *health facility administrator*

Russellville
Harper, Shirley Fay *nutritionist, educator, consultant, lecturer*

LOUISIANA

Abbeville
Hebert, Margaret Burns *social worker*

Alexandria
Mathews, Peggy Anne *nurse*
Sneed, Ellouise Bruce *retired nursing administrator, educator*

Baton Rouge
Floersch, Shirley Patten *dietician, consultant*
Malekian, Fatemeh *nursing educator*
Morvant, Barbara L. *nursing administrator*
Travis, Karen S. *clinical social worker*
Younathan, Margaret Tims *retired nutritionist, educator*

Bossier City
Rhoades, Paula K. *dietician, healthcare educator*

Brusly
Theriot, Lisa Marie *social worker*

Covington
Burton, Barbara Able *psychotherapist*

Franklinton
Wheeler, Gwen *medical, surgical, and critical care nurse*

Gonzales
Pierce, Carol *success strategist, writer*

Leesville
Gutman, Lucy Toni *social worker, educator*

Mandeville
Pittman, Jacquelyn *retired mental health nurse, nursing educator*
Treuting, Edna Gannon *retired nursing administrator, educator*

Metairie
Friedman, Lynn Joseph *counselor*
Porter, Sheri Wagner *nursing administrator, educator*
Rice, Patricia Wegmann *counselor*
Travitzky McBride, Virginia Anne *administrator*

Monroe
Clayton-Dodd, Valera Jo *health facility administrator*

Natchitoches
Egan, Shirley Anne *retired nursing educator*
Forsloff, Carol Marie *rehabilitation services professional, consultant*

New Orleans
Butler, Shirley Ann *social worker*
Higgins, Oleda Jackson *retired medical and surgical nurse*
Strength, Catherine Bush *nursing educator*
Weaver, Norma J. *medical/surgical nurse*

Shreveport
Nelson, Meredith Gaffney *counselor, educator*

Slidell
Jacob, Susan Marie *nurse*
Laurent, Lynn Margaret *nurse*

Terrytown
Joyce, Marie Caldwell *medical, surgical, and mental health nurse*
Olson, Sandra Dittman *medical/surgical nurse*

Ville Platte
Patsicostas, Susan Joanna *mental health services professional, psychotherapist*

MAINE

Augusta
Mills, Dora Anne *public health service officer*

Bangor
Ballesteros, Paula Mitchell *nurse*
Beaupain, Elaine Shapiro *psychiatric social worker*

Brooklin
Schmidt, Lynda Wheelwright *psychotherapist*

Canton
Parsons, Lorraine Leighton *nurse, pre-school administrator*

Damariscotta
Swanson, Karin *hospital administrator, consultant*

Dresden
Iserbyt, Charlotte Thomson *researcher, writer, educational consultant*

Ellsworth
Young, Lucia Patat *psychotherapist*

Fort Fairfield
Shapiro, Joan Isabelle *lab administrator, medical/surgical nurse*

Gorham
Fall, Marijane Eaton *counselor educator*

Hampden
Mahon, Julia *speech pathology/audiology services professional, educator*

Mount Desert
Weinberger, Jane Dalton *retired nurse, volunteer*

North Yarmouth
Kuhrt, Sharon Lee *nursing administrator*

Old Town
Nelligan, Annette Frances *social worker*

Orono
Marston-Scott, Mary Vesta *nurse, educator*

Portland
Reed, Maryann *nursing administrator*
Simpson, Nancy Ida *nursing educator*

Saco
Collins, Cynthia Jane *marriage and family therapist, priestess*

MARYLAND

Annapolis
Goldwater, Marilyn R(ubin) *medical/surgical nurse, state legislator*
Klejnot, Getha Jean *school nurse practitioner, music educator*

Baltimore
Amos, Helen *hospital administrator*
Augustson, Edith *mental health clinician*
Baker, Susan P. *public health educator*
Brennan, Janice M. *medical/surgical nurse, nursing educator*
Campbell, Jacquelyn C. *community health nurse*
Chin, Katherine Moy *nutritionist, consultant*
Eden-Fetzer, Dianne Toni *health facility administrator*
Hernandez, Iris N. *clinical specialist*
Howard, Bettie Jean *surgical nurse*
Jenkins, Louise Sherman *nursing researcher, educator*
Kumin, Libby Barbara *speech language pathologist, educator*
Kyger, Brenda Sue *intravenous therapy nurse*
Larch, Sara Margaret *healthcare executive*
Lee, Alice Inez *retired nurse*
Njie, Veronica P.S. *clinical nurse, educator*
Pickett, Eugenia V. *social worker*
Roup, Brenda Jacobs *nurse, retired military officer*
Simpson, Mildred Kathleen *health facility administrator*
Streat, Karen Gray *community health and geriatrics nurse, adult nurse practitioner*
Uzarowski, Laura Helen *physical therapist*
Washington, Earline *health facility administrator*

Bethesda
Cohen, Lois Ruth Kushner *health research consultant*
Gaarder, Marie *speech pathologist*
Hoyer, Mary Louise *social worker, educator*
Obrams, Gunta Iris *clinical research administrator*
Polsby, Gail K. *psychotherapist*
Robinson, Sharon Beth *health science association administrator*
Romero, Jane Patricia *nursing administrator*
Stover, Ellen L. *health scientist, psychologist*

Bowie
Bohrer, Terezie S. *human service consultant*
Stancil, Donielle LaVelle *nursing administrator*

Chevy Chase
Darr, Clarissa McCudden *psychiatric clinical nurse specialist*

Chillum
Malbon, Louise *nursing educator, hypnotherapist*

College Park
Younger, Deirdre Ann *pharmacist*

Columbia
Abel, Florence Catherine Harris *social worker*
Piou-Brewer, Magalie *psychotherapist, educator, small business owner*

Damascus
Styer, Joanne Louise *retired dietician*

Derwood
Holloman, Marilyn Leona Davis *non profit administrator, new product developer*

Easton
Whitten, Nancy Bimmerman *clinical social worker, marriage therapist*

Elkton
Mayer, Margaret Ellen *medical coding specialist*

Gaithersburg
Ebinger, Mary Ritzman *pastoral counselor*
Gloyd, Rita A. *retired social worker*
Green, Shia Toby Riner *psychotherapist*
Moquin, Barbara E. *psychotherapist*

Garrett Park
Vargas, Lena Bessette *nursing administrator*

Glen Burnie
Barteet, Barbara Boyter *retired social worker*
Endres, Eleanor Estelle *speech pathology/audiology services professional*

Grasonville
Ciotola, Linda Ann Miller *lifestyle counselor*

Hagerstown
Harrison, Lois Smith *hospital executive, educator*

Laurel
Landis, Donna Marie *nursing administrator, women's health nurse*

Lutherville
Goodman, Valerie Dawson *psychiatric social worker*

Manokin
Miles, Elizabeth Jane *social worker*

McHenry
Biser, Elizabeth Grant *counselor, director*

Mitchellville
Chilman, Catherine Earles Street *social welfare educator, author*

Newburg
Mason, Christine Chapman *psychotherapist*

Owings Mills
Berg, Barbara Kirsner *health education specialist*
Ryan, Judith W. *geriatrics nurse, educator*

Port Tobacco
Smith, Sheila Robertson *laboratory technician*

Potomac
Anfinsen, Libby Esther Shulman *social worker, clinical administrator*
Gaston, Marilyn Hughes *health facility administrator*

Reisterstown
Besser, Sandra Herman *school nurse practitioner*

Riverdale
Smith, Carmela Vito *administrator, counselor, educator*

Rockville
Hambleton, Betty Beall *public health administrator*
Kiger, F. Louise *nursing administrator*
Kopf, Randi *family and oncology nurse practitioner, lawyer*
Messersmith, Stephanie Hunt *nursing administrator*
Parham-Hopson, Deborah *health programs administrator*
Rasmussen, Caren Nancy *health facility administrator*
Standing, Kimberly Anna *researcher*
Weinel, Pamela Jean *nurse administrator*

Salisbury
Shockley, Theresa Schisler *medical/surgical nurse*

Silver Spring
Arvin, Linda Lee *counselor*
Blakeney, Barbara A. *public health service officer*
Fay, Laurel Ann *marriage and family therapist*
Johnson, Cheryl L. *nursing administrator*
Kark, Victoria A. *open heart clinical specialist*
Mashin, Jacqueline Ann Cook *health facility administrator, consultant*
O'Connell, Mary Ita *psychotherapist*

MASSACHUSETTS

Amherst
Backes, Ruth Emerson *counseling psychologist*
Hopman, Ellen Evert *psychotherapist, author and herbalist*

Arlington
Stein, Miriam *social worker, training services executive*
Zimmer, Anna Held *social worker*

Auburndale
Kibrick, Anne *retired nursing educator, dean*

Bedford
Herlihy, Maura Ann *medical technician*

Belmont
Hanfling, Sue Carol (Suki Hanfling) *social worker*

Billerica
Barnes, Shirley Moore *retired psychiatric social worker, genealogist*

Boston
Berkman, Lisa F. *public health educator*
Delahanty, Linda Michele *dietician*
Dwyer, Johanna Todd *nutritionist, educator*
Lowenstein, Arlene Jane *nursing educator, health facility administrator*
Reinherz, Helen Zarsky *social worker, researcher*
Spencer, Renee A. *social worker, educator, researcher*

Brockton
Moore, Mary Johnson *nurse*

Brookline
Gewirtz, Mindy L. *organizational and leadership relations consultant*
Heilbrunn, Lorraine Judith *psychologist, educational administrator*

Burlington
Rogers, Carol Rosenstein *social worker, educator*

Cambridge
Burns, Virginia *social worker*
Chodorow, Nancy Julia *psychotherapist, educator*
Clifton, Anne Rutenber *psychotherapist, educator*
Johnson, Elvira Q. *dietician*
Logan, Isabeall Talmadge *psychotherapist, writer*
Orfield, Antonia Marie *optometrist, researcher*
Severin, Christina *public health service officer*

Carlisle
Friedman, Amy Lisa *social worker*

Carver
Tura, Carol Ann *medical/surgical and intravenous therapy nurse*

Centerville
Condon, Ann Blunt *psychotherapist*
Williams, Ann Meagher *retired hospital administrator*

Chelsea
Roman, Jane Sedgewick *nurse*

Chestnut Hill
Boskin, Claire *psychotherapist, educator*
Burgess, Ann Wolbert *nursing educator*
Hawkins, Joellen Margaret Beck *nursing educator*
Munro, Barbara Hazard *nursing educator, dean, researcher*

Chicopee
Dame, Catherine Elaine *acupuncturist*

Fitchburg
Scannell, Ann Elizabeth *nurse, educator*

Framingham
Austin, Sandra Ikenberry *nursing educator, consultant*
West, Doe *psychotherapist, educator*
Willinger, Rhonda Zwern *optometrist*

Gloucester
Johnson, Anne Elisabeth *medical assistant*

Great Barrington
Lewis, Karen Marie *human services administrator, writer*

Greenfield
Curtiss, Carol Perry *health facility administrator, consultant, nurse*
Jenks, Abigail *social worker, educator*

Haverhill
Rubinstein, Nancy G. *social worker, consultant*

Holyoke
Dearborn, Maureen Markt *speech and language clinician*

Hyannis
Nicholson, Ellen Ellis *clinical social worker*

Lakeville
Ashley, Marjorie Lynn *intravenous therapy nurse*

Lenox
Lewis, Marianne H. *psychiatric nurse practitioner*

Lexington
Bombardieri, Merle Ann *psychotherapist*
Tecca, Kimberly Ann *physician assistant*

Longmeadow
Donoghue, Linda *nursing administrator, community health nurse*

Lowell
Inco, Elizabeth Mary *nurse, consultant*

Marlborough
Bradley, Bonita Mae *psychotherapist*

Mendon
Bradley, Nancy Lovett *retired medical and surgical nurse, administrator*

Milford
Mancini, Joyce Katherine *family practice nurse practitioner*

Nantucket
Bartlett, Cheryl Ann *public health service administrator*

Natick
Lebowitz, Charlotte Meyersohn *social worker*

Needham
Ryan, Una Scully *health science association administrator, medical educator*

New Bedford
Monteiro, Patricia M. *clinical social worker*

Newton
Mullen, Maureen Ann *social worker*
Pill, Cynthia Joan *social worker*

Newton Center
Veeder, Nancy Walker *social work educator*

Norwell
Porter, Marie Caroline *geriatrics nurse*

Osterville
Weber, Adelheid Lisa *retired nurse, chemist*

Rehoboth
McGee, Mary Alice *health science research administrator*

Roxbury
Alméstica, Johanna Lynnette *mental health counselor, administrator*

Salem
Hewitt, Nancy Arlene *social worker*

Sharon
Berzon, Faye Clark *retired nursing educator*
Ross, Betsy R. *psychotherapist*

South Deerfield
Tarasuk, Penelope Antoinette *psychoanalyst, artist*

South Harwich
Finn, Nita Ann *social worker*

Springfield
Price-Ware-Kabuti, Thelma *counselor*
Saia, Diane Plevock DiPiero *nutritionist, educator, legal administrator*

Sudbury
Ames, Lois Winslow Sisson *social worker, educator, writer*

Tewksbury
Herlihy-Chevalier, Barbara Doyle *retired mental health nurse*

Waltham
Gray-Nix, Elizabeth Whitwell *occupational therapist*

Wareham
Gayoski, Kathleen Mary *counselor, minister*
Nolan, Marilyn Ann *health facility administrator*

West Newton
Logan, Georgiana Marie *psychotherapist*

West Springfield
Buckman, Lisa Pauline *psychotherapist*

Westborough
Fenby, Barbara Lou *social worker*

Weston
Daly, Ellen M. *pediatrics nurse, educator*

Williamstown
Conklin, Susan Joan *psychotherapist, educator, television personality, realtor*

Worcester
Cashman, Suzanne Boyer *health services administrator, educator*

Yarmouth Port
McGill, Grace Anita *retired occupational health nurse*
St. Clair, Jane Elizabeth *health science association administrator, consultant*

MICHIGAN

Ann Arbor
Hinshaw, Ada Sue *nursing educator, former dean*
Kalisch, Beatrice Jean *nursing educator, consultant*
Ketefian, Shaké *nursing educator*
Krauth, Laurie D. *psychotherapist, writer*
McLaughlin, Catherine G. *healthcare educator*
Oakley, Deborah Jane *public health service officer, nursing educator*
Powell, Linda Rae *educational healthcare consultant*
Reame, Nancy King *nursing educator*

Benton Harbor
Watkins, M(artha) Anne *family practice nurse practitioner*

Berkley
Leland, Janet K. *social work therapist*

Berrien Springs
Rasmussen, Alice Call *retired nursing educator*

Bloomfield Hills
Bauser, Nancy *social worker, counselor*
Boulos, Nadia Ebid *medical/surgical nurse*

Dearborn
Beauford, Sandra *nurse, data processing executive*
MacLennan, Faith Alice *physical therapist, educator*

Detroit
Bennett, Margaret Ethel Booker *psychotherapist*
Hanks, Robin *rehabilitation nurse*
Heppner, Gloria Hill *health facility administrator, educator*
Jackson, Linda Shorter *nutritionist, educator*
Kachalsky, Ellen *social worker*
Redman, Barbara Klug *nursing educator*
Schlichting, Nancy Margaret *hospital administrator*
Washington, Olivia Grace Mary *psychotherapist, educator, counselor, researcher*

Dexter
Hanamey, Rosemary T. *nursing educator*

East Lansing
Noel, Mary Margaret *nutritionist, educator*

Farmington
Burns, Sister Elizabeth Mary *retired hospital administrator*

Ferndale
Forkan, Eveleen *counselor, educator, researcher*

Flint
Alarie-Anderson, Peggy Sue *physician assistant*
Williams, Veronica Myres *psychotherapist, social worker*

Franklin
Sax, Mary Randolph *speech and language pathologist*

Gladstone
Toutloff, Betty Jane *retired social worker*

Grand Blanc
McAlindon, Mary Naomi *retired nursing consultant*

Grand Rapids
Brent, Helen Teressa *school nurse*
Chase, Sandra Lee *clinical pharmacist, consultant*
Gemmell-Akalis, Bonni Jean *psychotherapist*
Helder, Karen Fay *social worker*
Hoogenboom, Barbara Jo *physical therapist, educator*
Kramer, Carol Gertrude *marriage and family counselor*
Lewis Jackson, Wendy S. *social worker*

Grosse Pointe Farms
Couzens, Linda Lee Anderson *oncology nurse*

Grosse Pointe Park
Knapp, Mildred Florence *retired social worker*

Harrison
Valentine, Anna Mae *retired nurse*

Holly
Evans Snowden, Audra Lynn *counselor*

Ionia
Ulmer, Evonne Gail *health science association administrator*

Jackson
Genyk, Ruth Bel *psychotherapist*

Kalamazoo
Bennett, Arlie Joyce *clinical social worker*
Fredericks, Sharon Kay *nurse's aide*
Lander, Joyce Ann *retired nursing educator, retired medical/surgical nurse*
Lester, Sandra Kay *social worker*
Ortiz-Button, Olga *social worker*
Yoder-Gagnon, Pamala S. *retired orthopedic nurse*

Laingsburg
Collins, Mary Alice *psychotherapist, social worker*

Lansing
Nicholas, Caroline Jean *retired nurse, consultant*
Winkler, Sue Elaine *art psychotherapist, social worker*

Lapeer
Gates, Penelope Kandis *obstetrical nurse*

Lincoln Park
Russell, Harriet Shaw *social worker*

Linden
Tomaszewski, Kathleen Bernadette *social worker, educator*

Livonia
Gepford, Barbara Beebe *retired nutrition educator*

Marquette
Kahler, Dorothy Stirling *psychotherapist*
Sherony, Cheryl Anne *dietician*

Midland
Strange, Alice Marian *social worker*

Monroe
McCracken, Kathryn Angela *clinical social worker*

Mount Pleasant
Redman, Joann A. *medical/surgical nurse*

Muskegon
Cusick Reimink, Ruth Elizabeth *community health nurse*

North Muskegon
Heyen, Beatrice J. *psychotherapist*

Oak Park
Coleman, Dorothy Charmayne *nurse*

Okemos
Herrick, Kathleen Magara *retired social worker*

Pinckney
McNamara, Ann Dowd *medical technician*

Plainwell
Tiefenthal, Marguerite Aurand *school social worker*

Rochester
Hughes, Rosemary A. *counselor, educator*
Mullin, Norma Rose *psychotherapist*

Saginaw
Moyer, Genevieve J. *counselor*

Saint Clair Shores
Lapadot, Gayle K. *nursing administrator*

Southfield
Bennett, Helen *psychotherapist*
Martin, Marcella Edric *retired community health nurse*
Pickett, Sherry M. *social worker*
Sedler, Rozanne Friedlander *social worker, educator*

Torraco, Pamela Louise *psychotherapist*
Wagner, Muriel Ginsberg *nutrition therapist*

Sparta
Miller, Barbara Jean *health facility administrator*

Sterling Heights
Hammond-Kominsky, Cynthia Cecelia *optometrist*
Rotatchka, Janice Marie *medical/surgical and critical care nurse*

Tecumseh
Kane, Sue Ann *counselor, geriatrics nurse*

Traverse City
Anderson, Carol Lynn *social worker, educator*

University Center
May, Margrethe *healthcare educator*
Rickey, Betty L. *nursing educator*

Warren
Bell, Julie Marie *health facility administrator, consultant*
Shaw, Mary Joe *nurse*

Waterford
Price, Kim Denise *counselor*

Wixom
Welch, Cherie Lynn *healthcare educator*

Ypsilanti
Cantrell, Linda Maxine *counselor*
Fox, Diane Porretta *nursing educator*

MINNESOTA

Bemidji
Christenson, Eileen Esther *geriatrics nurse*
Martinson, Ida Marie *medical/surgical nurse, educator, physiologist*

Bloomington
Nichols, Donna Mardell *nurse anesthetist*

Cottage Grove
Glazebrook, Rita Susan *nursing educator*

Duluth
Salmela, Lynn Marie *clinical nurse specialist*

Eden Prairie
Petersen, Maureen Jeanette Miller *management information technology director, retired nurse*

Elysian
Thayer, Edna Louise *health facility administrator*

Faribault
Jensen, Annette M. *mental health nurse, administrator*

Mankato
Manahan, Vanda Galen *social work educator, columnist*

Minneapolis
Ashton, Sister Mary Madonna *health facility administrator*
Boyer, Susan Elaine *psychotherapist, consultant, speaker*
Durdahl, Carol Lavaun *psychiatric nurse*
Gerdner, Linda Ann *nursing researcher, educator*
Kilbourne, Barbara Jean *health and housing executive*
Mathews, Kathleen Ann *social worker, psychotherapist*
Murphy, Edrie Lee *laboratory administrator*
Steen-Hinderlie, Diane Evelyn *social worker, musician*
Zimmerman, Shirley Lee *family social science educator, researcher*
Zunkel, Gretchen M. *medical/surgical nurse, educator*

Minnetonka
Quam, Lois *healthcare company executive*

Moorhead
Kent, Jill *midwife*

New Brighton
Matalamaki, Margaret Marie *health facility administrator, consultant*

Palisade
Kilde, Sandra Jean *nurse anesthetist, educator*

Redwood Falls
Mansoor, Loretta Julia *retired medical and surgical nurse*

Rochester
Gervais, Sister Generose *hospital consultant*
Kummeth, Patricia Joan *nursing educator*
Stelck, Mickie Joann *technologist*

Saint Joseph
Wedl, Lois Catherine *counselor, educator*

Saint Paul
Bruhn, JoAnn Marie *radiologic technologist, writer, speaker*
Victor, Lorraine Carol *critical care nurse*

White Bear Lake
Rogers, Megan Elizabeth *mental health therapist*

MISSISSIPPI

Brandon
Evans, Trese *psychometrist, psychotherapist*
Hall, Breda Faye Kimbrough Inman *counselor, educator*

Byhalia
Tackett, Maresa D. *medical technician*

Carriere
Thompson, Catherine Lila *retired medical center nurse*

Centreville
Nelson, Janie Rish *health facility administrator*

Cleveland
Carlson, Lizabeth Len *nursing educator, dean*

Columbus
Jones, Carol A. *nutritionist, artist*

Hattiesburg
Nicovich, Mary C. *medical/surgical nurse*
Odom, Janet Lynn *post-anesthesia nurse*

Jackson
Buckner-Brown, Joyce *allied health instructor*
Lofton, Susan Price *nursing educator, consultant*
Long, Kelly Tidwell *medical/surgical nurse, director*
Uzodinma, Minta LaVerne Smith *retired nursing administrator, nurse midwife*

Lauderdale
Van Doren, Henrietta Lambert *nurse anesthetists*

Mc Cool
Miller, Charlotte Faye *speech pathology/audiology services professional*

Mississippi State
Crudden, Adele Louise *social work research educator*

Moss Point
Bolton, Betty J. *medical/surgical nurse, poet*

Natchez
Moore, Irma D. *alcohol and drug counselor, prevention specialist*

Pascagoula
Washington, Yvonne *surgical nurse*

Pass Christian
Henrion, Rosemary Provenza *psychotherapist, educator*

Purvis
Walley, Vicky Cabaniss *medical/surgical consultant*

Shaw
Garner, Mable Tecola *health facility administrator*

MISSOURI

Arnold
Porter, Kathy Lee *marriage and family therapist, minister*

Ballwin
Young, Samantha Lee *counselor*

Cassville
Byrd, Sharon Faye *medical/surgical nurse*

Columbia
Hensley, Elizabeth Catherine *nutritionist, educator*
Von Holt, Lael Powers *psychotherapist, psychiatric social worker*

Fair Grove
Piech, Mary Lou Rohling *medical psychotherapist, consultant*

Farmington
Shaw, Betty Jane *medical/surgical nurse*

Florissant
Beckmann, Laura R. *healthcare educator*

Fulton
Bierdeman-Fike, Jane Elizabeth *social worker, educator*
Hartwell-Ivins, Vicky Rose *office manager, medical/surgical nurse*

Gladstone
Eggleston, Rebecca Annette *maternal/women's health nurse, rehabilitation nurse*

Hazelwood
Zeilman, Michelle Renee *counselor*

Hollister
Herron, Gayle Ann *health facility administrator, forensic psychotherapist, consultant*

Holts Summit
Hewlett, Sandra Marie *clinical consultant*

Imperial
Baxter, Judith A. *medical nurse*

Jefferson City
Bussabarger, Mary Louise *retired mental health services professional*

Joplin
Zook, Martha Frances Harris *retired nursing administrator*

Kansas City
Davis, Florea Jean *social worker*
Krieg, Nancy Kay *social worker, poet, musician*
Norris, Ruth Ann *social worker*
Worrall, Judith Rae *health and welfare plan consultant*

Kirksville
Cox, Carolyn *healthcare educator*

Kirkwood
Feller, Candi P. *counselor*

Liberty
Asp, Janna C *healthcare educator*

Maryville
Gorman, Karen Machmer *optometric physician*

Moberly
Helm, Dorothy Dawn *nurse*

New Bloomfield
Melton, June Marie *nursing educator*

Osage Beach
DeShazo, Marjorie White *occupational therapist*

Saint Charles
Brown, C. Alison *counselor*
Tabaka, Sandra Lee *retired medical/surgical nurse*

Saint Louis
Biby-Russina, Erika L. *counselor*
Cima, Cheryl Ann *medical/surgical nurse*
Dawson, M. Susan *nursing educator, mental health services professional*
Duke, Carolyn *medical/surgical and community health nurse*
Ezenwa, Josephine Nwabuoku *social worker*
Goodman, Judith Ross *psychotherapist*
Johnson, Gloria Jean *counseling professional*
Kolar, Janet Brostron *physician assistant, medical technologist*
Lazio, Lisa Ann *psychotherapist*
Moore, Antoinette Mercedes *counselor*
Morgan, Jennifer *counselor*
Powers, Margaret Pettey *counselor*
Ryan, Sister Mary Jean *health facility executive*
Szwabo, Peggy Ann *social worker, educator, nurse, psychotherapist*
Wechter, Marilyn R. *psychotherapist*
Wright, Mary Lee *retired dietician*

Springfield
Holloway, Wanda Kaye *psychotherapist, consultant*
Williams, Juanita (Tudie Williams) *home health care nurse, administrator*

MONTANA

Billings
Anderson, Janeil Eva *mental health services professional*

Great Falls
Ledesma-Nicholson, Charmaine *psychotherapist*

Havre
Dolph, Sharon Jean *social worker*

Helena
Dance-Kaye, Pamela *equestrian educator, consultant*

Malta
Watts, Alice L. *nurse*

Missoula
Hulme, Janet A. *physical therapist, writer, small business owner*

NEBRASKA

Bassett
Miner, Alice E. *medial/surgical, geriatric and charge nurse*

Beatrice
Henderson, Robyn Lee *health program executive director*

Bellevue
Ross, Sandra Rae *infection control practitioner, quality assessment manager*

Broken Bow
Bigbee, Darlene Mae *retired medical/surgical nurse*

Lincoln
Drullinger, Leona Pearl Blair *obstetrics nurse*
Oman, Deborah Sue *health science facility administrator*
Rohren, Brenda Marie Anderson *therapist, educator*
Schaefer, Joann *public health service officer*

Newman Grove
Anderson, Joyce Lorraine *nurse*

Omaha
Graves, Maureen Ann *self esteem and spirituality consultant*
Schinzel, Sue Madeline *nurse*

Plattsmouth
Toman, Barbara Katherine *renal, cardiac, vascular nurse*

Scottsbluff
Beard, Deborah A. *therapist, educator*

Utica
Merck, Gerry Elizabeth *counselor*

NEVADA

Las Vegas
Adair, Irmalee Traylor *social worker*
Cavnar, Margaret Mary (Peggy Cavnar) *researcher, retired state legislator*
Duncombe, Patricia Warburton *retired social worker*

Gage, Miriam Betts *retired nutritionist*
Israel, Joan *social worker*
Ivy, Berrynell Baker *critical care nurse*
La Neve, Shannon Beth *healthcare educator*
Meiner, Sue Ellen Thompson *adult nurse practitioner, consultant, gerontologist*
Michel, Mary Ann Kedzuf *nursing educator*
Nadelson, Sandra G. *nursing educator*
Silver, Kathryn *health services executive*

Reno
Bramwell, Marvel Lynnette *nursing administrator, social worker*
Cornell, Annie Aiko *nurse, administrator, retired military officer*
Middlebrooks, Deloris Jeanette *retired nursing educator*
Sheehan, Denise Lucille *alcohol/drug abuse services professional, writer*

NEW HAMPSHIRE

Bedford
Miller, Christine Lee *psychotherapist*

Brentwood
Thompson, Eleanor Dumont *nurse*

Concord
Cooney, Mary Ann *public health service officer, community health nurse*
Lowell, Janet Ann *nurse*
McCall, Junietta Baker *psychotherapist, minister*

Conway
MacDonald, Christine *social worker*

Harrisville
Miller, Irene M. *physician assistant*

Jackson
Baker, Mary Jane *social worker*

Lebanon
Baker, Susan Chilton *health facility administrator, consultant*
Dillon Rydman, Linda Gay *nurse, consultant*
Thompson, Pamela A. *nurse administrator*

Londonderry
Parten, Priscilla M. *medical and psychiatric social worker, educator*

Manchester
Bolduc, Diane Eileen Mary Buchholz *psychotherapist*
Mosher, Janet A. *counselor*

Meriden
Brent, Patricia Lee *health facility administrator, writer*

Nashua
Descoteaux, Carol J. *health facility administrator*
Hayes, Maureen A. *psychotherapist, consultant*
Najarian, Cheryl Ann *exercise physiology educator*
Williams, Paula Jo *nurse, educator*

North Hampton
Pazdon, Denise Joan *speech pathology/audiology services professional*

Ossipee
Bartlett, Diane Sue *counselor*

Tilton
Wolf, Sharon Ann *psychotherapist*

NEW JERSEY

Absecon
Bean, Manya *psychotherapist, educator*
Paparone, Pamela Ann *nurse practitioner*

Bedminster
Delehanty, Martha *human services administrator*

Belmar
Farrell, Karen F. *school nurse practitioner*

Brick
White, Debra Ann *social worker, counseling administrator*

Burlington
Britt, Donna Marie *school nurse*

Cherry Hill
Blakney, Juanita Mosley *psychotherapist*
Collier-Evans, Demetra Frances *veterans benefits counselor*
Grado-Wolynies, Evelyn (Evelyn Wolynies) *nursing educator*

Cliffside Park
Brown, Shirley Ann *speech-language pathologist*

Denville
Buset, Joanna Lynn *counselor*

East Orange
Hudson-Zonn, Eliza *nurse, psychologist*

East Rutherford
Cathey, Gertrude Brown *retired medical/surgical nurse*

Erial
Browna, Jo McIntyre *nurse*

Fair Lawn
Bowman, Delores *medical cost management administrator*

Flemington
Van Ost, Lynn *physical therapist, Olympic team official*

Fort Lee
Schirmer, Helga *retired chiropractor*

Freehold
Langan-Sattenspiel, F. Candy *medical/surgical nurse, writer*
Wilson, Nancy Jeanne *laboratory consultant, medical technologist*

Glassboro
Magnan, Ruthann *nurse, social worker*

Hackensack
Shapiro, Sylvia *psychotherapist*

Hamilton Square
Ridolfi, Dorothy Porter Boulden *nurse, real estate broker*

Harrington Park
Salmon, Margaret Belais *nutritionist, dietician*

Haworth
Mango, Christina Rose *psychiatric art therapist*

Highland Park
Blum, Lisa Carrie *social worker, researcher*
Grady, Joyce (Marian Joyce Grady) *psychotherapist, consultant*

Holmdel
Tambaro, Marie Grace *health specialist, nursing educator*

Jackson
Thomas, Doris Amelia *family practice nurse practitioner*

Jersey City
Gipson, Gloria Lorraine *social worker*
Girgis, Mary *counselor*
Mahood, Marie I. *counselor, educator*
Milton, Barbara Ella, II, *psychotherapist*

Landing
Wolahan, Caryle Goldsack *nursing educator, consultant*

Livingston
Hildenbrand, Joyce Pluhowski *social work professional, marketing specialist*

Lumberton
Losse, Catherine Ann *pediatrics nurse, critical care nurse, educator, family practice nurse practitioner*

Mahwah
Hailparn, Diana Finnegan *psychotherapist, writer*

Manasquan
Kelman, Marybeth *retired health care consultant, health policy analyst*

Metuchen
Macarin-Mara, Lynn *psychotherapist, consultant*

Millville
Caldwell, Linda E. *critical care nurse*

Morganville
Lechtanski, Cheryl Lee *chiropractor*

Morristown
Prince, Leah Fanchon *lab administrator, executive secretary*

Mount Arlington
Davis, Dorinne Sue *audiologist*

Mount Laurel
Plye, Kelly Ann *nurse*

Neptune
Bediguian, Mariamig Jinx *operating room nurse*

New Brunswick
Smoyak, Shirley Anne *psychiatric nurse practitioner, educator*

Newfoundland
Divinsky, Miriam *psychotherapist*

Newton
Dougherty, Phyllis Marilyn *social worker*

North Brunswick
Shapiro, Marsha N. *social worker*

North Haledon
Brenner, Betty Esther Bilgray *social worker*
Latner, Selma *psychoanalyst*

Nutley
Comune, Kathryn Ann *counselor*

Paterson
Daniels, Cheryl Lynn *pediatrics nurse*

Pomona
Bukowski, Elaine Louise *physical therapist, educator*

Pompton Plains
Zastocki, Deborah K. *health facility executive*

Princeton
DeBardeleben, Martha Graves *counselor*
Logue, Judith Felton *psychoanalyst, educator*

Prospect Park
Blair, Sherry Ann *psychotherapist, educator*

Randolph
Whildin, Leonora Porreca *retired nursing educator*

Red Bank
Brown, Valerie Anne *psychotherapist, social worker, educator*
Carmody, Margaret Jean *retired social worker*
Gutentag, Patricia Richmand *social worker, family counselor, occupational therapist*
Murray, Abby Darlington Boyd *psychiatric clinical specialist, educator*

Ridgefield
Campbell, Della Anne *nurse, researcher*

Ridgewood
Clements, Lynne Fleming *marriage and family therapist, application developer*

Rockaway
Karpack, Kimberlee June Rush *mental health counselor*

Rutherford
Suarez, Sally Ann Tevis *health facility administrator, nurse, consultant*

Saddle Brook
Clifton, Nelida *social worker*

Somerville
Klein, Virginia Sue *psychotherapist*

South Orange
Budin, Wendy C. *nursing educator, researcher*

Trenton
Muschal, Judith Ann *health facility administrator*

Union
Kuzan, Kathleen *speech pathology services professional, educator*
Williams, Carol Jorgensen *social work educator*

Vauxhall
Jacobs-Smith, Ruby Eudora *retired medical/surgical nurse, retired public health service officer*

Vineland
Santucci, L. Michelle *adult nurse practitioner, nutritionist, consultant*

Wanamassa
McTague-Dougherty, Amy Elizabeth *speech pathology/audiology services professional*

Warren
Kozberg, Donna Walters *rehabilitation services professional*

Wayne
D'Andrea, Kathleen Claire *speech therapist*
Gerber, Marlene *psychotherapist, health care administrator*

West Orange
Katz, Alix Martha *respiratory care practitioner*

Westfield
Roll, Marilyn Rita Brownlie *social worker*

Willingboro
Bevels, Esther Marie *medical technician, director*

Woodbury
O'Bryant, Cathy *retired social worker, evangelist*

NEW MEXICO

Alamogordo
Patch, Lisa E. *health services director, nurse*

Albuquerque
Auger, Tamara M. *psychotherapist*
Clark, Teresa Watkins *psychotherapist, clinical counselor*
Erickson, Sue Alice *health educator, consultant, nurse*
Free, Barbara A. *psychotherapist, writer*
Kroken, Patricia Ann *health science association administrator*
Maddoux, Barbara Tily *critical care nurse*
Madrid, Nancy Elizabeth *counselor, consultant, small business owner*
Maxson, Carol S. *health facility administrator*
Moody, Patricia Ann *psychiatric nurse, small business owner, artist*
Pasternacki, Linda Lea *critical care nurse*
Spinella, Judy Lynn *health facility administrator*

Carlsbad
Beal, Shannon *nursing educator*
Speed, Lynn Elizabeth *nurse practitioner*

Edgewood
Villagomez, Deborah Lynn *medical/surgical nurse, horse breeder*

Espanola
Montoya, Ruby *alcohol and drug abuse counselor*

Gallup
Mulligan, Erlinda Rita *medical/surgical nurse*

Hagerman
McIntire, Linda Carole *mental health and substance abuse counselor*

Las Cruces
Amos, Shirleyann *mental health therapist, social worker*
Little, Karen J. *counselor*

Roswell
Harvell, Gayle Marie *cardiovascular technologist*

Santa Fe
Davis, Marcie L. *public health and human services consultant*
Howell, Vicky Sue *health data analyst*

Hyde, Pamela Suzon *housing and human services administrator*
Kahn, Margaret S. *social worker, language educator*
King, Ro *psychotherapist, educator*
Melnick, Alice Jean (AJ Melnick) *counselor*
Moya, Rosemary Mercedes *mental health administrator*
Sakara, Marilyn Judith *retired social worker*
Westbrook, Arlen Runzler *retired social worker*
Wiese, Neva *critical care nurse*

Truth Or Consequences
Lyon, Diana *counselor, art educator, psychotherapist*

NEW YORK

Addison
Haines, Caryl *retired medical/surgical nurse*

Albany
Caruso, Aileen Smith *managed care consultant*
McCarthy, Mary Lynn *social work educator*
Poleto, Mary Margaret *orthopedic nurse*

Amsterdam
Tanguay, Janet *recreational therapist, writer, filmmaker*

Apalachin
Linder, Fannie Ruth *psychotherapist, concert soprano*

Astoria
Matheson, Linda *retired social worker*

Baldwin
Parker, Arlene Sandra *social worker*

Bayside
Kennedy, Mary Theresa *mental health services professional*

Binghamton
Collins, Mary Shaffer *community nursing educator*
Terriquez-Kasey, Laura Marie *emergency nurse*

Brewster
Sartori, Bridget Ann *home health care nurse*

Bronx
Hilliard, Carol *nurse, educator, consultant, researcher*
Iezza, Anita Kay *physician assistant*
Rongo, Lucille Lynn *medical center executive*
Salicrup, Madeline *nurse*
Simpson-Jeff, Wilma *social worker*

Brooklyn
Eisenberg, Karen Sue Byer *nurse*
French, Margaret Diana *operating room nurse*
Gonsalves, Patricia E. *surgical nurse*
Gulstone, Jacqueline *nurse*
Hawkins, Vivian Agatha *mental health nurse, educator*
Horvath, Annette *home care administrator*
Jimenez, Kathryn Fisher *nurse, educator*
Jones, Blanche *nursing administrator*
Koppel, Audrey Feiler *electrologist, educator*
Logan, Janet Artisam *mental health nurse*
Marsala-Cervasio, Kathleen Ann *medical/surgical nurse*
Murillo-Rohde, Ildaura Maria *marriage and family therapist, consultant, educator, retired dean*
Phillips, Gretchen *social worker*
Pine, Bessie Miriam *social worker, columnist*
Suarez, Maria C. *health care plan company executive*
Sullivan, Ann Catherine *health facility administrator*
Twining, Lynne Dianne *psychotherapist, professional society administrator, writer*
Wilson, Nancy Esther *social worker*
Wrotten, Marylean *medical coordinator, counselor*
Yedvab, Lauren *health facility administrator*

Buffalo
Casper, Bernadette Marie *critical care nurse*
Falk, Ursula Adler *psychotherapist*
Fitzgerald, Cathleen Marie *medical and surgical intensive care nurse*
Gingher, Merlene C. *occupational therapist, educator*
Hoffman, Faith Louise *social worker*
Jervis-Herbert, Gwendolyn Theresa *mental health services professional*
Myszka, Judith Anne *nurse*
Nielsen, Nancy H. *health organization executive*
Saab, Maureen Wilson *social worker, consultant*
Urdang, Nicole Severyna *holistic psychotherapist*
Wright, Dana Jace *retired emergency nurse practitioner*

Camillus
Thompson, Mary Cecilia *nurse midwife*

Canandaigua
Blazak, Paige Gayle *psychotherapist, school counselor*
Chappelle, Lou Jo *physical therapist assistant*

Cedarhurst
Lipsky, Linda Ethel *health facility administrator*

Cheektowaga
Rogers, Cheryl Ann *speech pathology services professional*

Clinton Corners
McDermott, Patricia Ann *nursing administrator*

Congers
Voce, Patricia Maria *medical/surgical nurse*

Cornwall On Hudson
D'Alvia, Marlene *medical social worker, clinical social worker*

Cortland
Brush, Florence Clapham *kinesiologist, exercise physiologist, physical education educator*

Derby
Kieffer, Marcia S. *psychotherapist*

East Aurora
Dohn, Julianne *child protective services specialist*

East Moriches
Guthrie, Teresa Irene *pediatric nurse practitioner*

Elmhurst
Hughes, Ann M. *medical/surgical nurse*
Staiano-Johannes, Barbara Ann *physician assistant, chiropractor*

Elmira
Barlow, Jo *psychotherapist*

Endicott
Carswell, Melissa J. *counselor, director*

Flushing
Bordoff, Sherri Beth *social worker*
Gomez, Pastora *medical/surgical nurse*
Matheis, Vickie Lynne *nurse*
Rosen-Supnick, Elaine Renee *physical therapist*

Forest Hills
Alsapiedi, Consuelo Veronica *psychoanalytic psychotherapist, consultant*
Hartig, Karen Joyce *psychotherapist, social worker*
Kortlander, Myrna *psychotherapist*

Fulton
Ludington, Janice Fay *speech pathology/audiology services professional*

Garden City
Herzberg, Margaret Ann *orthopaedic nurse, researcher*

Glen Head
Sewell, Laura J. Pollock *social worker*

Glenmont
Haizlip, Viola *medical/surgical nurse*

Glens Falls
Tucker, Bernadine *patient registrar*

Great Neck
Harris, Rosalie *psychotherapist, clinical counselor, Spanish language professional and multi-linguist, English as second language educator*

Greenfield Center
Dittner, Deborah Marie *nurse practitioner in family health*

Hamburg
Dewey, Phyllis Keefer *counselor*

Hartsdale
Fishman, Helene Beth *social worker*
Schweitzer, Caren S. *social worker*

Haverstraw
Eidelman, Sharon (Sherry) R. *marriage and family therapist*

Holley
Ruck, Rosemarie Ulissa *retired social worker, freelance/self-employed writer*

Hornell
Swift, Katharine I. *cytotechnologist*

Huntington
Paul, Marianne *physician assistant*

Huntington Station
Williams, Una Joyce *psychiatric social worker*

Hurley
Petruski, Jennifer Andrea *speech and language pathologist*

Ithaca
Clune, JoAnn Guardalibene *retired nurse*
Kane, Marilyn A. *occupational therapist, educator*
Rasmussen, Kathleen Maher *nutritional sciences educator*

Jackson Heights
Chang, Lydia Liang-Hwa *social worker, educator*

Jamaica
De La Paz, Lucia *social worker, consultant*
Geffner, Donna Sue *speech pathology/audiology services professional, audiologist, educator*

Jamestown
Duncanson, Patricia Ann *mental health therapist*

Johnstown
Araldi, Mary-Jane Snyder *nurse, educator*

Kew Gardens
Klein-Scheer, Cathy Ann *social worker*

Lakewood
McConnon, Virginia Fix *dietician*

Lewiston
Moraca-Sawicki, Anne Marie *oncology nurse*

Loudonville
Ribley-Borck, Joan Grace *medical/surgical rehabiliation nurse*

Mahopac
Greene, Geraldine Marie *family therapist, consultant*

Manlius
Gibson, Judith W. *psychotherapist*

Margaretville
Lewis-Ryder, Patricia A. *medical/surgical and community health nurse*

Mayville
Stacy, Ruth Clair *counselor, consultant*

Montrose
Miah, Jamila Sikander *social worker, researcher*

Mount Vernon
NelsonWilliams, Cecelia Elaine *dietician, nutritionist*

New Rochelle
Schreibman, Thelma Rabinowitz *psychotherapist, educator*

New York
Agard, Emma Estornel *psychotherapist*
Aigen, Betsy Paula *psychotherapist*
Akabas, Sheila Helene *social work educator*
Aragno, Anna *psychoanalyst, author*
Balderston, Jean Merrill *marriage and family therapist, poet, writer*
Barker, Sylvia Margaret *nurse*
Barnum, Barbara Stevens *retired nursing educator, writer*
Barrett, Elizabeth Ann Manhart *psychotherapist, consultant, nursing educator*
Blum, Diane S. *human services manager*
Boufford, Jo Ivey *health administrator, educator*
Bressman, Susan Berliner *health facility administrator*
Brinson, Monica Evette *mental health specialist, pharmaceutical sales representative*
Brodie-Baldwin, Helen Sylvia *retired college and human services administrator*
Brownell, Patricia Jane *social worker, educator*
Buchenhorner, Marianne *psychotherapist, psychoanalyst*
Burns, M. Michele *human resources company executive*
Butler, Carol Ann *psychotherapist, mediator*
Camp, Sharon L. *reproductive health organization administrator*
Cardinale, Kathleen Carmel *retired health facility administrator*
Caroff, Phyllis M. *social work educator*
Chu-Zhu, Janice Gail *social worker*
Clemens, Rosemary A. *health facility administrator, foundation administrator*
Coleman, Jo-Ann S.E. *social worker*
Cook, Sarah Sheets *women's health nurse*
Dehn, Cathleen Patterson *health facility administrator*
Dimen, Muriel Vera *psychoanalyst*
Dinerman, Miriam *social work educator*
Dorn, Sue Bricker *retired hospital administrator*
Dufka, Corinne *human rights activist*
Dutchevici, Silvia M. *psychotherapist*
Ethan, Carol Baehr *psychotherapist, psychoanalyst*
Fagin, Claire Mintzer *nursing educator, nursing administrator*
Forbes, Sally *researcher, editor, curator*
Forese, Laura Lee *hospital administrator, orthopedist*
Garrett, Celia Erica *human services administrator, consultant*
Gibbs, Elsie Frances *social worker*
Goodwin, Beatrice *nursing educator, consultant*
Grandizio, Lenore *social worker*
Gure, Anna Valerie *retired social worker, consulting psychotherapist*
Herzig, Rita Wynne *critical care nurse, soprano*
Kalayjian, Anie *psychotherapist, educator, nurse, consultant*
Kamen, Cheryl L. Heiberg *social worker*
Kamerman, Sheila Brody *social work educator*
Kassel, Catherine M. *community, maternal, and women's health nurse, consultant*
Kove, Miriam *psychotherapist*
Kuttler, Judith Esther *retired psychotherapist*
Lawrence, Lauren *psychotherapist, writer*
Lederman, Sally Ann *nutritionist, researcher*
Levinson, Rascha *psychotherapist*
Lippman, Donna Robin *counselor*
Litwack, Arlene Debra *psychotherapist, psychoanalyst, educator, consultant*
Mandracchia, Violet Ann Palermo *psychotherapist, educator*
Marshak, Hilary Wallach *psychotherapist, small business owner*
Matorin, Susan *social work administrator, educator*
McGinn, Eileen *public health service officer, researcher*
Mitchell, Helen deRamus *public health administrator*
Mitchell, Mary Jenkins *public health service officer*
Morgan, Florence Murdina *nurse*
Moskowitz, Randi Zucker *nurse*
Mundinger, Mary O'Neil *nursing educator*
Murphy, Stacia *health service association executive*
Nass, Deanna Rose *counselor, professor*
Nestle, Marion *nutritionist, educator*
O'Connor Vos, Lynn *healthcare group executive*
O'Neill McGivern, Diane *nursing educator*
Ortega, Melissa Lee *researcher*
O'Shea, Elizabeth Therese *counselor*
Pakter, Jean *maternal and child health consultant*
Pandolfi, Frances *health facility administrator*
Pennisi, Liz *women's health nurse*
Pyle, Rolanda *social worker*
Rehr, Helen *social worker*
Resnick, Rhoda Brodowsky *psychotherapist*
Richards, Cecile *healthcare network executive*
Rosenthal, Donna Myra *social worker*
Rothenberg, Eleanore *psychotherapist*
Scott, Adrienne *social worker, psychotherapist*
Scott, Mimi Koblenz *psychotherapist, actress, journalist, playwright*
Shohen, Saundra Anne *health facility administrator, public relations executive*
Shrouder, Hortense Eaileen *dietitian*
Sochet, Mary Allen *psychotherapist, educator, writer*
Stark, Robin Caryl *psychotherapist, consultant*
Steichen, Joanna T(aub) *psychotherapist, writer*
Storm, Jackie *nutritionist*
Turo, Joann K. *psychoanalyst, psychotherapist, consultant*
Vigeant, Michele A. *mental health counselor*
Woodall, Elaine *psychotherapist*
Yoshiuchi, Ellen Haven *healthcare educator, clinical counselor*
Yousef, Mona Lee *psychoanalytic psychotherapist*

Niskayuna
Lavin, Linda K. *counselor*

Nyack
Carey, Lois J. *psychotherapist*
Scott-Battle, Gladys Natalie *retired social worker*

Olean
McGovern-Scaturo, Diane Joan *psychotherapist*

Orchard Park
Askew, Gloria Yarbrough *dietician*
Lockwood, Deborah Jane *psychotherapist, consultant, educator*

Orient
Cochran, Judy Anne *psychiatric nurse practitioner*

Ossining
Beard, Janet Marie *health facility administrator*
Robinson, Karen Vajda *dietician*

Oswego
Rice, Brenda Jean *operating room nurse, educator*

Ozone Park
Catalfo, Betty Marie *public health service officer, nutritionist, writer*

Patchogue
McPherson, Sherry Lynn *social worker*

Peekskill
Jackson, Linda B. *social worker*

Penfield
Hamilton, Candis Lee *counselor*

Plattsburgh
Demers-Bourgeois, Aimee E. *physical therapist*
Fowler, Alyce Milton *health facility administrator*

Pleasantville
Graham, Paula Lee *intravenous nurse*

Pomona
DeMaio, Barbara Patricia *social worker*

Port Washington
Eagan, Marie T. (Ria Eagan) *chiropractor*

Poughkeepsie
Deiters, Sister Joan Adele *psychoanalyst, nun, chemistry professor*

Rochester
Aydelotte, Myrtle Kitchell *retired nursing administrator*
Braley, Oleta Pearl *community health nurse, writer*
Follansbee, Patti A. *health educator, marriage and family therapist*
Furness, Janet Elisabeth *social work educator*
Grossi, Rose B. *director*
Haynes, Linda Ann *health information management administrator*
Herrera, Charlotte Mae *medical office administrator*
Parrinello, Kathleen Ann Mulholland *nursing administrator, educator*
Sammler, Anne Michelle *healthcare educator*
Tantillo, Mary Darlene *nurse*

Rockville Centre
O'Brien, Donna M. *public health service officer*

Rome
Anderson, Nora *nurse*

Roslyn
Rosen, Sarah Perel *social worker*

Roslyn Heights
Rubrum, Erica Courtney *family therapist, school counselor*

Roxbury
Green, Jean Hess *psychotherapist*

Rye
Olver, Ruth Carol *retired social worker*

Sabael
Morrill-Cummins, Carolyn *social worker, consultant*

Scarsdale
Glickenhaus, Sarah Brody *speech therapist*

South Salem
Black, Devera Giges *psychotherapist*

Staten Island
Gaeta, Rosemarie *social worker*
Kennedy, Colleen Geralyn *nurse, social worker*
Lazzara, Margo Valentine *counselor, writer*
Martin, Frances Lee *nursing educator*
Morrison-Sasso, Patricia Blanche *nursing educator and practitioner*
Parente, Louise *social worker*

Stony Brook
Mueller, Jean Margaret *nursing consultant*

Suffern
Marsalisi, Patricia Dianne *nurse anesthetist*

Syracuse
Grégoire, Ida *nursing administrator*
Manley, Michelle S. *social worker, educator*
Walsh-Hunt, Linda Ann *social worker, consultant, poet*

Utica
De Iorio, Lucille Theresa *retired social worker*

Webster
Inzinga, Jacqueline Marie *counselor*

West Bloomfield
Charron, Helene Kay Shetler *retired nursing educator*

White Plains
Fowlkes, Nancy Lanetta Pinkard *social worker*
Hariton, Jo Rosenberg *psychotherapist, educator*

Whitesboro
Campbell, Joann Cavo *social worker*

Williamson
Thomason-Mussen, Janis Faye *human services administrator*

Woodside
VanArsdale, Diana Cort *social worker*

Woodstock
Rissman, Barbara Susan Zimmer *psychotherapist*
Straight Arrow, Janet *holistic professional, educator*

Wyandanch
Hodges-Robinson, Chettina M. *nursing administrator*

Yonkers
Roberson, Doris Jean Herold *retired social worker*

NORTH CAROLINA

Albemarle
Adrian, Judy *healthcare educator*

Apex
Olson, Jean Lounsbury *social worker*

Asheville
Brooker, Lena Epps *human services administrator, consultant*
Dotson, Elizabeth Quillen *speech pathology/audiology services professional*
Korb, Elizabeth Grace *nurse midwife*

Buies Creek
Wright, Mary P. *counselor*

Chapel Hill
Gordon-Larsen, Penny *nutritionist, educator, researcher*
Johnson, Lucie Jenkins *retired social worker*
Willingham, Emagene Emanuel *social worker*

Charlotte
Crawford, Jenny Lynn Sluder *medical/surgical nurse, educator*
Crawford, Juanita Gatewood *nursing technician*
Hayman, Helen Feeley *retired nursing director*
Hinson, Jane Pardee Henderson *lactation consultant*

Conover
Williams, Nancy Carole *nursing researcher*

Cullowhee
Schwiebert, Valerie L. *counselor*

Dunn
Hill, Susan Beasley *recreational therapist*

Durham
Blissitt, Patricia Ann *medical/surgical nurse*
Clayton, Marla Cooper *speech pathology/audiology services professional*
Gilliss, Catherine Lynch *nursing educator*
Hoffman, Jennifer Anne *vascular technician, director*
Pericak-Vance, Margaret A. *health facility administrator*
Wilson, Ruby Leila *nursing educator*

Fairmont
Spencer, Melissa Johanna *psychotherapist, special education educator*

Fayetteville
MacRae, Elizabeth (Elizabeth MacRae Halsey) *counselor, actor*

Goldsboro
Cannon, Alice Grace *counselor*

Graham
Collins, Lucinda Varn *occupational therapist*

Greensboro
Harris-Offutt, Rosalyn Marie *counselor, consultant, mental health nurse, writer*

Greenville
Turnage, Karen L. *medical technician*
Weathers, Vivian Joy *physician administrator*

Hendersonville
Cochran, Linda Thornthwaite *psychotherapist, social worker, consultant*
Jefferson, Letitia Gibson *rehabilitation counselor*

High Point
Scearse, Patricia Dotson *nursing educator, dean*

Hillsborough
Richmond, Donna *speech-language pathologist*

Morganton
Bailey-Day, Kay Lynn *psychotherapist*
Bivens, Marjorie Earley *retired nursing educator*
Singleton, Stella Wood *nurse*

Murphy
Ricketson, Mary Alice *psychotherapist*

Newland
Lustig, Susan Gardner *occupational therapist*

Oxford
Harvey, Gloria-Stroud *physician assistant*

Raleigh
Bailey, Mary Beatrice *retired health science association administrator*
Dew, Carolyn Christine *health facility administrator, nurse*
Geller, Janice Grace *nurse*
Hughes, Barbara Ann *dietician, public health administrator*
Johnson, Mary Pauline (Polly Johnson) *nursing administrator*
Malling, Martha Hale Shackford *social worker, educator*
Pearsall, Mary Helen *retired counselor*
Webster, Debbie Ann *social worker*

Research Triangle Park
Campbell, Kay Nordan *nurse, health educator*

Rocky Mount
Davis, Barbara Judy *counselor, mental health educator*

Roxboro
Broyles, Bonita Eileen *nursing educator*

Rutherfordton
Crummie, Ann Vaughn *mental health services professional*

Salisbury
Ward, Brenda Robinson *social worker*

Sherrills Ford
Stynes, Barbara Bilello *integrative health professional, educator*

Southport
Pryor, Carolyn Gale Barnard *social work educator*

Wilmington
Coté, Debra Nan *surgical nurse*
Israel, Margie Olanoff *psychotherapist*
Maness, Eleanor Palmer *researcher*
Stein, Joan Dorothy *nurse anesthetist*

Wilson
Morris, Sharon Louise Stewart *emergency medical technician, paramedic*

Winston Salem
Cook, Sharon Warren *social worker, educator*

NORTH DAKOTA

Belcourt
Storey, Sandra Jean *emergency room nurse*

Bismarck
Olson, Carol Hankins *occupational therapist, educator*

Grand Forks
Heitkamp, Thomasine Lea *social work educator*

OHIO

Alliance
Munford-Clark, Cenell Renea *healthcare educator, athletic trainer*

Archbold
Guengerich, Ruth Lapp *counselor*

Athens
Harse, Constance Bradford *retired social worker*

Avon
Lahiff, Marilyn J. *nursing administrator*

Bath
Hoffer, Alma Jeanne *nursing educator*

Beavercreek
Rinta, Christine Evelyn *nurse, air force officer*

Bellbrook
Requarth, Sherry Lorraine *special education services professional*

Bucyrus
Cooper, April Helen *family practice nurse practitioner*

Caldwell
Casto, Barbara L. *counselor*

Centerville
Appelbaum, Bernardine *medical/surgical nurse*

Cincinnati
De Witt, Jeanette Marie *physical therapist*
Greenwald, Theresa McGowan *health services administrator, rehabilitation nurse*
Hullinger, Charlotte M. *psychotherapist*
Karle-Swails, Jeanine *neuroscience clinical nurse specialist*
Monroe, Erin *psychiatric nurse practitioner*
St. John, Maria Ann *nurse anesthetist*
Scott, Martha Ann *clinical social worker*
Stinson, Mary Florence *retired nursing educator*
Swinford, Margaret Lynn Wright *medical/surgical nurse, educator*
Wilson, Wanda O. *nurse anesthetist, educator*
Witschger, Mary Ann *medical/surgical nurse*

Cleveland
Beamer, Yvonne Marie *psychotherapist, counselor*
Bersin, Susan Joyce-Heather (Reignbeaux Joyce-Heather Bersin) *critical care nurse, police officer*
Dylag, Helen Marie *health facility administrator*
Hudak, Christine Angela *nursing informatics educator, specialist*
Kalina, Eunice Goldstein *human services director*
Kohn, Mary Louise Beatrice *nurse*
Mantzell, Betty Lou *school nurse practitioner, consultant*

Columbia Station
Dadley, Arlene Jeanne *retired sleep technologist*

Columbus
Anderson, Carole Ann *nursing educator, academic administrator*
Clark, Babaa Ritah Annette *massage therapist*
Cuddihy, June Tuck *pediatrics nurse*
Guglielmi, Rhonda E. *nursing administrator*
Herron, Holly Lynn *critical care nurse, educator*
Hukill, Margaret Anne *physical therapist, rehabilitation services professional, educator*
Julia, Maria C. *social worker, educator, consultant*
Krakoff, Diane Elizabeth Butts *medical/surgical nurse*
Lewis, Nina *social worker*
McDaniel, Helen Marie *retired social worker*
Mlawsky, Karen *hospital administrator*
Morrison, Jacqueline Ann *social worker, psychologist*
Neill-Green, Teresa *art therapist, social worker, educator*

Copley
Smith, Joan H. *retired women's health nurse, educator*

Dayton
Cobb, Cecelia Annette *retired counselor*
Hitch, Melanie Audrey *orthopaedic nurse*
O'Malley, Patricia *nurse, researcher*
Turner, Gladys Tressia *retired social worker*
Versic, Linda Joan *nursing educator, research company executive*

Dover
Haggis, Mary Ripley *nurse, genealogist*

Eaton
Kisling, Fanny *counselor, educator*

Findlay
Stephani, Nancy Jean *social worker, journalist*

Galena
Latorre, Debi *medical/surgical nurse*

Geneva
Chaundra, Gale Buckels *nursing administrator, writer*

Granville
Sinsabaugh, Marie Elizabeth Diener *retired nurse, massage therapist*

Greenville
Metzcar, Virginia Joyce *social worker*

Groveport
Justice, Yvonne Horton *health facility administrator*

Hamilton
Fein, Linda Ann *nurse anesthetist, consultant*

Ironton
Oakes, Maria Spachner *medical/surgical nurse*

Kent
Sonnhalter, Carolyn Therese *physical therapist, consultant*

Lyndhurst
Silver, Thelma *social worker*

Mantua
Eslinger, Denise Marie *social worker*

New Carlisle
Peters, Elizabeth Ann Hampton *retired nursing educator*

North Olmsted
Semple, Jane Frances *health facility director*

Owensville
Seifert, Caroline Hamilton *community health nurse*

Pataskala
Thrasher, Rose Marie *critical care and community health nurse*

Perrysburg
Billnitzer, Bonnie Jeanne *nurse, gerontologist*

Pickerington
Palmer, Noreen E. *psychotherapist*

Portsmouth
Murphy, Pearl Marie *medical and surgical nurse*

Saint Clairsville
DeBertrand, Lynette Michele *clinical nurse specialist, educator*

Sebring
Kelley-Hall, Maryon Hoyle *retired social worker*

Seven Hills
Bowling, Rita Joan *medical/surgical nurse*

Shadyside
DeBolt, Nanette C. *medical/surgical nurse*

Shaker Heights
Katz, Linda M. *social worker*

Sidney
Leffler, Carole Elizabeth *retired mental health nurse, women's health nurse*

Solon
Robinson, Helene Susan *pharmacist*

Strongsville
Taghizadeh, Georgeanne Marie *medical/surgical nurse*

Sylvania
Verhesen, Anna Maria Hubertina *social worker*

Toledo
Dahl Reeves, Gretchen *occupational therapist, educator*
Francis, Barbara Joan *nurse, paralegal*
Overmyer, Janet Elaine *counselor*

Urbana
Meyers, Marsha Lynn *retired social worker*

Warren
Landolfi, Jennie Louise *nursing administrator*
VanAuker, Lana *recreational therapist, educator*

Westlake
Coeling, Harriet Van Ess *nursing educator, editor*
Schroth, Joyce Able *social worker*
Todd, Victoria L. *chlid psychoanalyst*

Yellow Springs
Graham, Jewel Freeman *social worker, lawyer, educator*

Youngstown
Itts, Elizabeth Ann Dunham *retired psychotherapist, consultant*

OKLAHOMA

Broken Arrow
Muller, Patricia Ann *nursing administrator, educator*

Claremore
Goff, Marilyn Russell McClain *counselor*

Del City
Birdsong, Janet Louise *medical/surgical nurse*

Edmond
Laughlin, Monique Myrtle Weant *mental health counselor*
Van Hemert, Phyllis Brown *counselor*

Frederick
Stone, Voye Lynne *women's health nurse practitioner*

Lamont
Covalt, Edna Irene *retired medical/surgical nurse*

Lawton
Reece, Juliette M. Stolper *community health and mental health nurse*

Muskogee
Heck, Jennifer Leigh *neonatal/perinatal nurse practitioner, educator*

Oklahoma City
Forni, Patricia Rose *nursing educator*
Jones, Renee Kauerauf *health facility administrator*
McClellan, Mary Ann *pediatric nurse practitioner*
Mitchell, Ira Joan *nutritionist*
Price, Donna J. *nurse*

Perkins
Lewis, Mary May Smith *retired family practice nurse practitioner*

Pryor
Dotson, Stella Marie *nurse*

Tulsa
Arrington, Rebecca Carol *occupational health nurse*
Bransford-Young, Angharad Ann *counselor, educator*
Carpenter, Nancy J. *health science association administrator*
Gustavson, Cynthia Marie *social worker, writer*
Hyland, Cheryl C. *health services administrator*
Jackson, Sandra Lee *health facility administrator*
Jurgensen, Monserrate *clinical nurse, consultant*
Lewis, Corinne Hemeter *psychotherapist, educator*
Marshall, Linda Lantow *pediatrics nurse*
Redfearn, Charlotte Marie *nursing administrator*
Vaughan, Elizabeth L. *school nurse practitioner*

Wilburton
Carey, Levenia Marie *counselor*

Woodward
Curtis, Kathryn Faye *medical laboratory technician*

OREGON

Bend
Sabatella, Elizabeth Maria *clinical therapist, educator, mental health facility administrator*

Corvallis
Fucillo, Dawn M. *radiologic technologist*

Eagle Point
Lundgren, Karen Marie *disabilities professional*

Eugene
Dorn, Kathie Lee *medical/surgical nurse*
Weiss, Marianna Shrenger *psychotherapist*

Forest Grove
Valfre, Michelle Williams *nursing educator, administrator, writer*

Gresham
Edwards, Julie Diane *women's health nurse*

Klamath Falls
Payne, Tyana *psychotherapist*

Lafayette
Dow, Marla *counselor*

Lake Oswego
Meltebeke, Renette *career counselor*

Lebanon
Griswold, Elaine C. *nurse, consultant*

Mcminnville
Fread, Phyllis Jean *counselor, educator*

Medford
Linn, Carole Anne *dietician*

Phoenix
Dodd, Darlene Mae *retired nurse, retired military officer*

Portland
Allan, Susan *public health service officer*
Fritz, Barbara Jean *occupational health nurse*
Gangle, Melanie Jean *counselor*
Kafoury, Ann Graham *psychotherapist*
Korb, Christine Ann *music therapist, researcher, educator*
Mendelson, Lottie M. *retired pediatric nurse practitioner, writer*
Parvin, RuthAnn *psychological services administrator*
Rooks, Judith Pence *nurse midwife, consultant*
Seymour, B(arbara) J(ean) *social worker*

Redmond
Dey, Charlotte Jane *retired community health nurse*

Rhododendron
Williamson, Diana Jean *nurse*

Saint Helens
Morten, Ann Keane *nurse midwife*

Sandy
Jensen, Judy Dianne *psychotherapist, consultant*

West Linn
Torsen, Marilyn Joanne *counselor, retired*

PENNSYLVANIA

Abington
Lauck, Donna L. *mental health nurse*

Acme
Babcock, Marguerite Lockwood *addictions treatment therapist, educator, writer*

Aliquippa
Milanovich, Lynn Esther *counselor*

Allentown
Brownback, Linda Mason *health company executive*
Teitsworth, Margaret Yvonne *nursing educator*
Zocco, Patricia Elizabeth *human services manager, cardiac ultrasound technologist*

Ardmore
Schlegel, Gena Marie *paramedic*
Voegele, Karen E. *social worker*

Bala Cynwyd
Peret, Karen Krzyminski *health facility administrator*

Bensalem
Piscopio, Geraldine Anne *nurse anesthetist*

Bethlehem
Reilly, Suzette B. *counselor*

Blue Bell
Welhan, Beverly Jean Lutz *nursing educator, administrator*

California
Twiss, Pamela *social worker, educator*

Camp Hill
Parry-Solá, Cheryl Lee *critical care nurse*
Stwalley, Diane Marie *pharmacist*

Canonsburg
Prost, Mary Jane *school nurse*

Centre Hall
Fry, Theresa Eileen *therapeutic foster care aide*

Chambersburg
Hessler, Helen Stoeckel *social worker*

Chester
Graves, Maxine *medical and surgical nurse*

Chester Springs
Niggeman, Kimberly Supplee *medical nurse*

Clarion
Hrisak, Cami Ann *mental health therapist*

Clearfield
Boykiw, Norma Severne *retired nutritionist, educator*

Clifford
Elkins, Kathryn Marie *alcohol/drug abuse services professional, recreational therapist*

Coopersburg
Kohler, Deborah Diamond *dietitian, food service executive*

Dallas
Baltimore, Ruth Betty *social worker*

Dresher
Michael, Dorothy Ann *nursing administrator, military officer*

East Petersburg
Kunkle, Mary Lou *counselor*

East Stroudsburg
Baril, Nancy Ann *gerontological nurse practitioner, consultant*

Easton
Kistler, Loretta M. *social worker, consultant*

Elizabethtown
Chesbro, Karen E. Henise *nurse*

Elkins Park
Pruce, Rhoda Posner *social worker, consultant*

Export
Carter, Linda Whitehead *oncological nurse, educator*

Fairfield
Ray, Lydia M. *nurse*

Feasterville Trevose
Thee, Cynthia Urban *psychotherapist*

Gardners
Contento Covey, Nicki Ann *counselor*

Glen Mills
Collins, Rosemarie Marrocco *psychotherapist*

Glenmoore
Humphreys-Heckler, Maureen Kelly *nursing home administrator*

Glenside
Crivelli-Kovach, Andrea *public health and nutrition consultant, educator*

Hamburg
Schappell, Abigail Susan *retired speech, language and hearing specialist, massage therapist, Reiki master*

Hanover
Davis, Ruth Carol *pharmacist, educator*

Harrisburg
Bailey, Diandrea Michelle *rehabilitation services professional*
Black, Shirley A. *healthcare educator*
O'Leary, Colleen Alison *counselor*
West, Eileen M. *caseworker*

Havertown
Garrahan-Masters, Mary Patricia *retired social worker, writer*

Hershey
Ozereko-deCoen, Mary T. *therapeutic recreation specialist and therapist*

Hulmeville
Jackson, Mary L. *health services executive*

Jenkintown
Lowry, Karen M. *biomedical research scientist, pharmacist*

Johnstown
Fisher, Connie Marie *physical therapist*
McGarry-Corl, Kelly Jo *counselor, marriage and family therapist, consultant*

King Of Prussia
Goldsmith, Eleanor Jean *retired hospital administrator*
Musetti, Myrtle Jane Holt *clinical nurse specialist, community health nurse*
Phipps, Judith A. *social worker*

Lancaster
Brunner, Lillian Sholtis *nurse, writer*
Hayward, Frances Crambert *retired dietician*
Hickle, Shalon R. *physical therapist*
Saganich, Bonnie Sue *medical/surgical nurse*
Scranton, Megan Jennifer *speech therapist, educator*

Lansdowne
Karosas, Karen *social worker, quality assurance specialist*

Lititz
Weaver, Naomi M. *retired medical/surgical nurse, educator*

Loretto
Sackin, Claire *retired social work educator*

Manheim
Homan, Patricia Ann *counselor*

Mc Keesport
Lodor, Marci Ann *dietitian*

Mechanicsburg
Ricedorf, Amy Elizabeth *mental health services professional*
Snider, Karen *human services administrator*

Media
Diamond, Jacqlyn E. *health counselor*
Hanna, Carol Ann *nursing educator*

Millersville
Hess, Patricia Ann *dietician*

Monessen
Smida, Mary Agnes *counselor*

Mount Pleasant
Morgan, Joyce Kaye *social worker*

Newtown
Kidd, Lynden Louise *healthcare consultant*

Northumberland
Collister, Nicole S. *counselor*

Oley
Weller, Trudy A. *psychotherapist*

Olyphant
Turock, Jane Parsick *nutritionist*

Orwigsburg
Mason, Joan Ellen *nurse*

Philadelphia
Alaigh, Poonam *health facility administrator*
Baessler, Christina A. *medical/surgical nurse*
Bryant, Jonanna Rochelle *registered nurse*
Castillo, Flora M. *health plan administrator, transportation executive*
Corprew, Helen Barbara *mental health services professional*
Daly, Mary Beryl *health facility administrator*
Garvin, Vail Pryor *hospital administrator*
Gralik, Nancy Ellen *healthcare consultant*
Hobdy, Jerrilyn *nurse midwife*
Kumanyika, Shiriki K. *nutrition epidemiology researcher, educator*
Mariscotti, Janine M. *psychotherapist, educator*
Potter, Alice Catherine *medical technician*
Shapiro, Paula *retired maternal/women's health nurse*
Shillingsburg, Cynthia Lynn *medical technician, educator*
Smullens, SaraKay Cohen *psychotherapist, writer*
Solomon, Phyllis Linda *social work educator, researcher*

Pittsburgh
Clancey, Jeanne Katherine *neurosurgical nurse*
Constantino-Bana, Rose Eva *nursing educator, researcher, lawyer*
Douglass, Nancy Ure *counselor*
Feddersen Steward, Maryann Odilia *psychotherapist*
Gaskey-Spear, Nancy Jane *nurse anesthetist*
Granati, Diane Alane *retired ophthalmic nurse*
Ismail-Beigi, Judith Kaye *social worker*
Jakub, Kathleen Ann *medical/surgical nurse*
Kitchens-Stephens, Evelyn H. *counselor, educator*
McCall, Dorothy Kay *social worker, psychotherapist*
Moore, Pearl B. *nursing educator*
Puskar, Kathryn Rose *nurse, educator*
Scheuble, Kathryn Jean *social worker, family therapist*
Wilson, Frances Helen *retired occupational therapist*

Plymouth Meeting
Sauer, Elizabeth Mason *school social worker*

Port Matilda
Holt, Frieda M. *nursing educator, retired academic administrator*

Pottstown
Coulter, Kathleen Marie *psychotherapist, consultant*
Fillman, Michele Renee *nurse*

Pottsville
Stankavage, Amy L. *physical therapist, athletic trainer*

Quincy
Gilbreath, Sarah Burkhart Gelbach *health facility administrator*

Reading
Bell, Frances Louise *medical technologist*
Gordon, Mildred Harriet Gross *hospital executive*
Sauer, Elissa Swisher *nursing educator*
Shultz, Lois Frances Casho *nursing supervisor*
Ward, Joyce Dieckmann *nurse midwife*

Rochester
Wilkins, Arlene *social worker*

Scranton
Lemoncelli, Lorine Barbara *counselor, elementary school educator*
McKenna, Ann K. *nutritionist, educator*

Shavertown
Fioti, Jean K. *pharmacist*
Rockensies, Eileen Regina *retired nursing educator*

Somerset
Mayak, Jeannette M. *speech pathology/audiology services professional, educator*

Swarthmore
Valen, Nanine Elisabeth *psychotherapist, poet*

Trevose
Quinn, Holli Jo Bardo *social worker, educator, librarian*

Uniontown
Wirick, Linda Jane *medical/surgical nurse*

University Park
Guthrie, Helen A. *nutritionist, educator, dietician*

Villanova
Haynor, Patricia Manzi *nursing educator, consultant*

West Chester
Abbott, Ann Augustine *social worker, educator*
Cinelli, Bethann *school health educator*
McCullough, Mary W. *social work educator, therapist*

West Mifflin
Rosko, Maryann A. *nurse*
Skonsky, Caroline Treschow *marriage and family therapist*

West Reading
Gyorky, Susan Meinig *medical/surgical nurse*

Winfield
Wert, Barbara J. Yingling *special education consultant*

Wyncote
Schaffner, Roberta Irene *retired medical/surgical nurse*

York
Alcon, Sonja L. *retired medical social worker*
Lindenmuth, Elise Bell *psychological consultant, educator*

RHODE ISLAND

Central Falls
Bolandrina, Grethel Ramos *nurse*

Cranston
Lisi, Deborah Jeanne *nurse supervisor*
Wilson, Valerie Petit *health science association director*

Kingston
Melanson, Kathleen Jean *nutritionist, educator*

Newport
Diamond, Deborah Lynn *psychotherapist*

North Providence
Bain, Marissa *social worker*

Providence
Monteiro, Lois Ann *nursing educator*
Recupero, Patricia Ryan *hospital president, psychiatrist, lawyer, health facility executive*

Warwick
Brown-Duggan, Gloria Lorene *health facility administrator*
Richards, Priscilla Ann *medical/surgical nurse*

Woonsocket
Carethers, Andrea *pharmacist*

SOUTH CAROLINA

Aiken
Jefferson, Helen Butler *public health service officer*

Anderson
Moore, Priscilla W. *gerontological nurse*

Beaufort
Guerry, Paula Mary *school nurse practitioner*

Bishopville
Miller, Blondell Stephenson *social worker, minister*

Bluffton
Scovel, Mary Alice *retired music therapy educator*

Charleston
Garro-Bissette, Susan Ann *adult nurse practitioner*

Columbia
Fowler, Linda McKeever *health facility administrator, educator*
McCoy, Dorothy Virginia *psychotherapist, consultant*
McCurdy, Paulette Quick *nurse anesthetist*
Seigler, Ruth Queen *college nursing administrator, educator, consultant, nurse*
Walters, Rebecca Russell Yarborough *medical technologist*

Easley
Howe, Linda Arlene *nursing educator, writer*

Florence
Waddill, Cynthia Kay *nurse*

Gaffney
Griffin, Penni Oncken *social worker, educator*

Greenville
DeWeese, Anita Lynn *medical/surgical nurse*
Steed, Connie Mantle *nurse*

Greenwood
Bateman, Carol Vaughan *pharmacist*

Hilton Head Island
Kearney-Nunnery, Rose *nursing administrator, educator, consultant*

Holly Hill
Anderson, LaShawn Ecleasha *rehabilitation technician*

Hopkins
Garrett, Robin Scott *health facility administrator*

Jackson
Abee, Rose Rooney *school guidance counselor*

Lancaster
Garris, Annette D. Faile *medical, surgical, and rehabilitation nurse*

Laurens
Hair, Dina Marie *geriatrics services professional*

Marion
Sease, Susan G. *social worker*

Moncks Corner
Hamilton, Marcella Laurette *social worker*

Orangeburg
Sibley, Rebecca Leigh Cardwell *dietician*
Stinchcomb, Audrey Thompson *respiratory care educator*

Pickens
Crowder, Heather Elizabeth *mental health services professional, consultant*

Piedmont
Hatcher, Carolyn Joyner *school nurse*

Summerville
Burke, Rhonda Williams *counselor*

Ware Shoals
Sullivan, Kelly Jones *critical care nurse, educator*

SOUTH DAKOTA

Aberdeen
Pesicka, Harlene Neave *mental health services professional*

Brookings
Fahrenwald, Nancy Lynn *nursing educator, researcher*

Pierre
Weyer, Dianne Sue *health facility administrator*

Rapid City
Chamberlain Hayman, Susan Denise *psychotherapist, physical therapist*
Green, Sharon Vincentine *counselor, consultant*

Sioux Falls
Niemann, Patricia *nurse*
Richards, LaClaire Lissetta Jones (Mrs. George A. Richards) *social worker*
Volin, Suzanne *retired lab administrator*

Yankton
Eisenhauer, Christine Marie *community health nurse, educator*
Tronvold, Linda Jean *occupational therapist*

TENNESSEE

Antioch
Housel, Natalie Rae Norman *physical therapist, educator*

Brentwood
Berry, Kathryn-Grace *geriatrics nurse*

Camden
Jasper, Doris J. Berry *nurse*

Chattanooga
Bechtel, Sherrell Jean *psychotherapist*
Bimrose, Heidi E. *human services administrator, director*

Clarksville
Staivisky, Jeanne Louise *counselor, alcohol/drug abuse services professional*

Cleveland
Killen, Roseanne Marie *social worker*

Cookeville
Reynolds, Barbara C. *retired mental health educator, dean*

Crossville
Sower, Milene A. *nursing educator*

Germantown
Mobley, Robin N. *nursing administrator*

Greenbrier
McClendon, Melinda White *medical/surgical nurse*

Jackson
Vantreese, Linda Fay Rainwater *retired medical/surgical nurse*

Jefferson City
Coffey, Kitty R. *dietician, healthcare educator*

Johnson City
Duncan, Corintha McKee *counselor*

Kingsport
Wray, Yana *medical/surgical nurse*

Knoxville
Benson, Kathleen Sevier Kavanagh *retired counselor*
Brown, Elizabeth *health science association administrator, educator*
Fender, Allison Jean *physical therapist, personal trainer*
Goforth, Cheryl Clewell *medical/surgical nurse*
Lee, Jan Louise *nursing educator*
Matteson, Karla J. *health science association administrator*
McGuire, Sandra Lynn *nursing educator*

Moore, Louise Hill *surgical technologist*
Reynolds, Marjorie Lavers *nutritionist, educator*

Lexington
Swatzell, Marilyn Louise *nurse*

Mc Kenzie
Johnsonius, Jenny Ross *nursing administrator*
Swinea, Melissa Bailey *nursing educator*

Memphis
Anthony, Nakia Lacquers *healthcare educator*
Bargagliotti, Lillian Antoinette *nursing educator*
Harris, Jenny Lou *elementary school counselor*
Jarvis, Daphne Eloise *laboratory administrator*
Johnson, Delores Gresham *retired counselor*

Millington
Fletchall, Sandra Kay *occupational therapist*

Murfreesboro
Garrison, Kathryn Ann *retired nutritionist*

Nashville
Betts, Virginia Trotter *nursing educator, researcher*
Brown, Tommie Florence *social work educator*
Jones, Evelyn Gloria *medical technologist, educator*
Lake, Judith Ann *nurse*
McKeel, Sheryl Wilson *pharmacist*
Rhea, Karen Hendrix *health facility administrator*

Oak Ridge
Foust, Donna Elaine Marshall *women's health nurse*
Jones, Virginia McClurkin *retired social worker*
Slusher, Kimberly Goode *researcher*

Sevierville
Heldman, Betty Lou Faulkner *retired health facility administrator*
Rill, Vicki Lynn *healthcare educator, physical education educator*

Somerville
Macdonald, Sally Polk Bowers *retired addictions therapist*

Trenton
Smith, Alice F. *medical/surgical, critical care, and home health nurse*

TEXAS

Abilene
Lewis-Bradshaw, Mavis Latisha *healthcare educator*

Alvord
King, Barbara Jean *nurse*

Amarillo
Hicks, Ann Neuwirth *clinical social worker*

Angleton
Phillips, Nancy Chambers *social worker*

Arlington
Oehler, Judith Jane Moody *retired counselor*

Austin
Barrera, Elvira Puig *retired counselor, academic administrator*
Claflin, Janis Ann *psychotherapist, management consultant*
Fletcher, Robin Mary *health facility administrator*
Gardner, Joan *medical, surgical nurse*
Hall, Beverly Adele *nursing educator*
Hayes, Patricia Ann *health facility administrator*
Hostetler, Lisa (Elizabeth) Marie *nursing consultant*
Hutchins, Karen Leslie *psychotherapist*
Kirk, Lynda Pounds *biofeedback therapist, neurotherapist, counselor*
Larkam, Beverley McCosham *social worker, marriage and family therapist*
Ossefort-Russell, Candyce *psychotherapist*

Baytown
Soileau, Veronica Demourelle *counselor, educator*

Beaumont
Compton, Valencia *pharmacist*
Wohler, Marjorie Lynn Coulter *medical/surgical nurse, health facility administrator*

Bedford
Hamstra, Christine Josephine *social worker*

Belton
Anderson, Patricia Kay *social work educator*

Brady
Dolberry, Jean Marie *nursing educator, supervisor*

Brownsville
Rodriguez, Nora Hilda *social worker*

Bryan
Guitry, Loraine Dunn *community health nurse*

Bulverde
Lamoureux, Gloria Kathleen *nurse, consultant, retired military officer*

Burleson
Hibben, Celia Lynn *psychiatric mental health nurse practitioner*

Carrollton
Withrow, Lucille Monnot *nursing home administrator*

Cedar Hill
Findley, Milla Jean *nutritionist*
Warren, Shirley M. *respiratory therapist*

Chillicothe
Brock, Helen Rachel McCoy *retired mental health and community health nurse*

Cleburne
Saul, Jennifer Ann *therapist*

Coleman
Smith, Eva Joyce *retired social worker*

College Station
Wilhelm, Vida Meadows *counselor*

Colleyville
Donnelly, Barbara Schettler *retired medical technologist*

Conroe
Covarrubias, Sherrie *nurse anesthetist*

Copperas Cove
Townsend, Linda Ladd *mental health nurse*

Corpus Christi
Clark, Joyce Naomi Johnson *nurse, counselor*
Conwill, Linda Jill *enterostomal therapist*
Stetina, Pamela Eleanor *nursing educator*

Corsicana
Hindman, Emily Ellen *counselor, director*

Dallas
Dykes, Virginia Chandler *occupational therapist, educator*
Frank, Paula Feldman *health facility administrator*
Harris, Hazel Lynn *medical/surgical nurse*
Key, Tara Ann *clinical social worker*
Madzik, Elizabeth May *hospital administrator*
Miller, Jo Carolyn Dendy *family and marriage counselor, educator*
Neumann, Luci *rehabilitation center executive*
Solomon, Risa Greenberg *clinical social worker, child and family therapist, former entertainment industry executive*
Stanfield, Margaret Helene *nursing educator, administrator*
Sullivan, Judith Patrice *social worker*
Timpa, Vicki Ann *government health program administrator*
Wassenich, Linda Pilcher *retired health policy analyst*

Denton
Mathes, Dorothy Jean Holden *occupational therapist*
Surprise, Juanee *chiropractor, nutrition consultant*

Early
Ross-Parsons, Donna Michelle *counselor, small business owner*

Edinburg
Farber, Roselee Cora *counselor*

El Paso
Bartlett, Janet Sanford (Janet Walz) *school nurse practitioner*
Dillon, Loretta Schoen *physical therapist, educator*
Edmonds, Velma McInnis *nursing educator*
Flores, Yolanda *speech pathology/audiology services professional, consultant*
Gregory, Lynne Watson *oncology clinical nurse specialist, health facility administrator*
Jordan, Shannon Colleen *medical/surgical nurse*
Minney, Gloria Joan *massage therapist, holistic health practitioner*
Mitchelll, Paula Rae *nursing educator, dean*
Moya, Eva M. *health services executive*
Simon, Doris Marie Tyler *nurse*

Forestburg
Hayes, Audimarie *medical/surgical and critical care nurse*

Fort Sam Houston
Gordon, Ella Dean *nursing educator, women's health nurse*

Fort Worth
Adams, Lavonne Marilyn Beck *critical care nurse, educator*
Moore, Linda Sullivan *social work educator, dean*
Robinson, Nell Bryant *nutrition educator*

Frisco
Doone, Michele Marie *chiropractor*

Gatesville
Dossman, Virginia Gail *nurse*

Georgetown
Smitheram, Margaret Etheridge *health facility administrator, director*

Hamilton
Keekley, Patricia Ann *counselor, psychologist*

Houston
Bates, Gwen Lee *health facility administrator, consultant*
Bourque, Peggy Sue *emergency nurse practitioner*
Callender, Norma Anne *counselor, public relations executive*
Caskey, Caroline T. *lab administrator*
Cole, Eleanor Ophelia *retired medical/surgical nurse*
Davis-Lewis, Bettye *nursing educator*
Florian-Lacy, Dorothy *social worker, educator*
Gerhart, Glenna Lee *pharmacist*
Gunn, Joan Marie *health facility administrator*
Hawkins, Barbara Reed *mental health nurse*
Hempfling, Linda Lee *nurse*
Henderson, (Ruejenuia) Secret *social worker*
Hughes, Mary Katherine *nurse*
Johnson, Sandra Ann *counselor, educator*
Konefal, Margaret Moore *health facility administrator, critical care nurse, nursing consultant, educator*
Montgomery, Denise Karen *nurse*
Moore, Lois Jean *health science facility administrator*
Peabody, Arlene L. Howland Bayar *retired enterostomal therapy nurse*
Reed, Kathlyn Louise *occupational therapist, educator*
Rhinehart, Peta-gay Chen *nurse, consultant*
Robbins, Susan Paula *social work educator*
Smiley, Cindy York *psychotherapist educator*
Spikes, Patricia White *medical technologist*
Tervalon, Josephine M. *psychotherapist, social worker*
Vassilopoulou-Sellin, Rena *researcher*
Wilson-Lawson, Melanie *social worker, educator*

Idalou
Beeler, Bulah Ray *retired medical/surgical nurse*

Irving
Jorden, Yon Yoon *health services company executive*

Italy
Lawson, Diane Marie *counselor*

Keene
Taroy-Valdez, Lolita B. *nursing educator, nurse*

Kerrville
Gregory, Patrice D. *retired nurse, small business owner*

La Marque
Matthews, Evelyn J. *nurse*

Laredo
Chavez, Mary Rose *counselor, educator*

Llano
Alston, Debbie A. *instructional technologist, educator*

Longview
Wilcox, Nancy Diane *nursing home administrator*

Lubbock
Hollingsworth, Margie Ellen *counselor*
Miller, Patricia Anne *speech and language pathologist*
Parks, Katie Mae *human services manager*
Yoder-Wise, Patricia Snyder *nursing educator*
Young, Teri Ann Butler *pharmacist*

Lufkin
Standerford, Catherine Ann *school nurse practitioner, director*
Williams, Mary Hickman *social worker*

Mansfield
McNairn, Peggi Jean *speech pathologist, educator*

Mexia
Chambers, Linda Dianne Thompson *social worker*

Missouri City
Watson, Loretta *medical/surgical nurse*

Montgomery
Gooch, Carol Ann *psychotherapist, consultant*

Nacogdoches
Cole, Sandra Sue *healthcare educator*

Pasadena
Kenagy, Cheri Lynn *nurse*

Pearland
Hutsell, Janice *nurse midwife*

Plainview
Pitts, Sharon Ann Gammage *nursing administrator*

Plano
Becker, Doreen Doris *medical/surgical nurse*
Etheridge, Susan B. *social worker*
Larsen, Paula Anne *operating room nurse*

Port Arthur
Wade, Ernestine *public health nurse*

Red Oak
Jones, Genia Kay *critical care nurse, consultant*

Richardson
Brooke, Melody *counselor, marriage and family therapist*

Rockport
Acker, Virginia Margaret *nursing consultant*

Rockwall
Johnston, Nicklett Rose *research nurse, clinical perfusionist*

San Antonio
Accountius, Patricia L. *dietician, consultant*
Adcox, Mary Sandra *dietician, consultant*
Avant, Patricia Kay *nursing educator*
Cruz, Rosalina Sedillo *marriage and family therapist*
Dacbert-Friese, Sharyn Varhely *social worker, evangelist*
DeNice, Marcella Louise *counselor*
Donelson, Rosemarie Quiroz Carvajal *human services professional, state official*
Downing, Jane Katherine *psychiatric nurse practitioner, lawyer*
Flaherty, Sergina Maria *ophthalmic medical technologist*
Todd, Jan Theresa *counselor*

Santa Fe
Jernigan, Vicki Louise MacKechney *clinical nurse specialist*

Scurry
Newkirk, Trixie Darnell *family nurse practitioner*

Shelbyville
Lifshutz, Melanie Janet Bell *patient education, medical, and surgical nurse*

Snyder
Barnes, Maggie Lue Shifflett (Mrs. Lawrence Barnes) *nurse*

Taylor Lake Village
Jenicek, Alicia Joanne *nursing consultant*

Temple
Cavanaugh, Rebecca Jo *medical nurse*
Frost, Juanita Corbitt *retired hospital foundation coordinator*
Hoelscher, Margie Lynn *nurse*
Tobin, Margaret Ann *clinical educator*
Whitis, Grace Ruth *retired nursing educator*

Texarkana
Bertrand, Betty Harleen *nurse*

The Woodlands
Mock, Cherry L. *marriage and family therapist*

Tomball
Burgoyne, Mojie Adler *clinical social worker*

Tyler
Coker, Melinda Louise *counselor*
Ebnet, Jeannie Marie *enterostomal therapist*

Universal City
White, Kathleen Mae *social worker, marriage and family therapist*

Waco
Hahn, Deborah Kay *nurse, consultant*

Waller
Evans, Nancy Peltier *behavioral specialist, educator*

Wichita Falls
Haynes, Linda Rose *medical/surgical nurse*
Rousey, Anne *social worker*

Woodway
Packard, Joyce Hornaday *retired counselor*

UTAH

Centerfield
Parkin, Fern Agnes Marvel *medical/surgical nurse, nursing educator*

Logan
Hepburn, Jeanette C. *family practice nurse practitioner*

Murray
Schutz, Roberta Maria (Bobbi Schutz) *social worker*

Ogden
Leggett, Diane *nurse, educator*

Orem
Takke, Karyn Coppock *social worker, educator*

Salt Lake City
Perkins, Nancy Ann *nurse*

VERMONT

Bradford
Boardman, Maureen Bell *community health nurse, educator*

Brattleboro
Bussino, Melinda Holden *human services administrator*
Smiley, Carol Anne *health facility administrator, sculptor*

East Thetford
Cummings Rockwell, Patricia Guilbault *psychiatric nurse*

Montpelier
Erskine, Kali (Wendy Colman) *psychoanalyst*

North Bennington
Feidner, Mary P. *retired speech and language pathologist*

North Ferrisburg
Tulin, Marna *psychotherapist*

Putney
Gill, Jane Roberts *retired psychotherapist, clinical social worker*

Rutland
Calabrese, Eleanor Wallace *social worker*

Winooski
Lemaire-Jenkins, Elizabeth Anne *psychotherapist*

VIRGINIA

Abingdon
Williams, Barbara Kitty *nursing educator*

Alexandria
Fitzgerald, Marilyn Hicks *health science association administrator*
Grachek, Marianna Kern *healthcare administrator*
Napier, Lisa Briggs *maternal/child health nurse*

Annandale
Abdellah, Faye Glenn *retired public health service executive*

Arlington
Hickman, Elizabeth Podesta *retired counselor*
Klestzick, Barbara R. *social worker, educator*
Lurie, Nicole *former health science association administrator*
Pfister, Karstin Ann *human services administrator*

Aroda
Nisly, Loretta Lynn *obstetrical nurse, geriatrics nurse*

Big Island
Durham, Betty Bethea *therapist*

Blacksburg
Conrad, Sherry K. Lynch *counselor*

Boones Mill
Oyler, Amy Elizabeth *medical/surgical nurse*

Chesapeake
Gray, Margaret Edna *nursing educator, department chairman, dean*
Kelley, Sudha S. *operating room nurse*
Skrip, Linda Jean *nurse*

Clifton Forge
Miller, Catherine H. *nursing administrator, property manager*

Emporia
Butler, Tammy J. Wiley *medical, surgical, and pediatric nurse*

Fairfax
Knee, Ruth Irelan (Mrs. Junior K. Knee) *social worker, health care consultant*
Monahan, Danielle Joan *renal nutritionist*

Fairfax Station
Barringer, Joan Marie *counselor, educator, artist, writer*

Falls Church
Ruskin, Ruth Zafren *social worker*
Seifert, Patricia Clark *cardiac surgery nurse, educator, consultant*

Fredericksburg
Nelson-Sargeant, Susan Marie *speech pathology professional*
Nidiffer, Sheri Lynn *medical/surgical nurse*

Galax
Brooks, Sherry Moore *medical/surgical nurse*

Hampton
Andrews, Elizabeth Anne *human services and social work educator*

Hopewell
Vartanian, Isabel Sylvia *retired dietician*

Lawrenceville
Stransky, Maria Soledad *psychotherapist*

Manassas
Dellinger, Mary *medical/surgical nurse*
Lytton, Linda Rountree *marriage and family therapist, consultant*

Mc Lean
Walsh, Marie Leclerc *nurse*

Newport News
Dillon, Elizabeth Diggs *medical/surgical nurse*

Norfolk
Hinsdale, Stephanie M. *social worker*
Warren, Ivory Jean *counselor, educator*

Portsmouth
Boshier, Maureen Louise *health facilities administrator*

Purcellville
King, Tracey Groux *psychotherapist*

Radford
Parker, Jacqueline Kay *social work educator*

Reston
Di Trapani, Marcia A. *health facility administrator, community health nurse, educator*
Meyer, Patricia Hanes *social worker*
Norris, Susan Elizabeth *social worker*

Richmond
Freund, Emma Frances *technologist*
Hines, Linda Turner *health services administrator, nurse*
Massenburg, Johnnye Smith *speech pathology/audiology services professional, minister*
Murray, Marian Selena *medical/surgical nurse*
Neal, Gail Fallon *physical therapist, educator*
Zich, Sue Schaab *nurse*

Roanoke
Kinzie, Brenda Asburry *counselor*
Klein, Deborah Rae *nurse*
Tinsley, Shelia C. *nurse*

Saint Charles
Matlock, Anita Kay *family nurse practitioner*

South Hill
Clay, Carol Ann *family nurse practitioner*

Springfield
Dake, Marcia Allene *retired nursing educator, dean*
Dodson, Alicejean Leigh *nursing administrator*
Williams, Cecilia Lee Pursel *optometrist*

Staunton
Sweetman, Beverly Yarroll *physical therapist*

Verona
Grizzel, Patsy (Pat) Pauline *human services administrator*

Virginia Beach
Armstrong, Margaret *nursing administrator*
Chalk, Barbara Ann *retired medical/surgical nurse*
Dingman, Janet Simpson *counselor, educator*
Guckert, Nora Jane Gaskill *medical/surgical nurse, hospice nurse, holistic consultant*
Hunter, Anne Graves *counselor*
McDonald, Linda L. *massage therapist*

Warrenton
Harrison, Margie Ann *nursing educator, emergency nurse practitioner*

Waynesboro
Eary, Pamela Hall *obstetrics nurse, educator*

Williamsburg
Marcus, Becca Nimmer *psychotherapist*
Myatt, Sue Henshaw *nursing home administrator*
Ringlesbach, Dorothy Louise *retired nurse, writer*

Woodbridge
Flori, Anna Marie DiBlasi *health facility administrator, nurse, anesthesiologist*
McMahon, Janet Mankiewich *critical care nurse*
Phillips-LeSane, Fay M. *mental health professional*

WASHINGTON

Bellingham
Coss, Sharon Elizabeth *counselor*

Camano Island
Hartley, Celia Love *nursing consultant, writer, retired nursing educator, nursing administrator*

Edmonds
Morrison, Wynona Marvel *psychotherapist*

Ellensburg
Carrothers, Carol Ann *special education services professional, educator*

Federal Way
Blywise, Barbara *mental health services professional*

Kennewick
Fann, Margaret Ann *counselor*

Kent
Dumitrescu, Cristina M. *intensive care nurse*

Langley
Cammermeyer, Margarethe *retired medical/surgical nurse*

Moses Lake
Irwin, Frances Darlene *nurse*

North Bend
Benyshek, Denita Maree *psychotherapist, educator, artist*

Olympia
Hayes, Maxine Delores *public health service officer, physician, pediatrician*

Port Angeles
Muller, Carolyn Bue *physical therapist, volunteer*

Puyallup
Sims, Darcie Dittberner *grief management specialist, psychotherapist, clinical hypnotherapist*

Redmond
Oaks, Lucy Moberley *retired social worker*

Seattle
Barnard, Kathryn Elaine *nursing educator, researcher*
Berni, Rosemarian Rauch *rehabilitation and oncology nurse*
Brandvold, Aurora Pauline *nursing researcher*
de Tornyay, Rheba *nursing educator, retired dean*
Dombro, Marcia Winters *nurse, academic administrator, educator*
Golston, Joan Carol *psychotherapist*
Groshong, Laura Wolf *psychotherapist, researcher*
Gunter, Laurie M. *retired nurse educator*
Kates, Carolyn Louise *physical therapist*
Kolbeson, Marilyn Hopf *holistic practitioner, artist, retired advertising executive, poet*
Law, Marcia Elizabeth *rehabilitation services professional*
Monsen, Elaine Ranker *nutritionist, educator, editor*
Nelson, Arleen Bruce *social worker*
Nelson, Karen Ann *lab administrator, director, immunologist, educator*
Northen, Helen E. *retired social work educator, consultant*
Sandahl, Bonnie Beardsley *nursing administrator*
Solchany, JoAnne Elizabeth *psychotherapist, nursing educator*

Shoreline
Ladas-Gaskin, Carol *therapist, educator, artist*

Soap Lake
Wesley, Susan Bray *psychotherapist, music educator*

Spokane
Cadwallader, Fay Margaret *social worker*
Cope, Kathleen Adelaide *critical care nurse, parish nurse, educator*
Finley, Kathleen Marie *marriage and family therapist, educator*
Hood-Ryker, Joan Crandell *retired counselor*
Martin, Janet Lynn *health facility administrator*
Metcalf, Ginger (Virginia) Arvan *psychotherapist, consultant*
Norell, Diane Marie *social worker, occupational therapist, educator*
Powers, Theresa Mack *medical/surgical nurse, psychotherapist*

Tacoma
Hiller, Marsha Kay *physical therapist*
Wanwig, Annette Clare *nursing administrator*

Vancouver
Perry, Daphne *social worker*

Walla Walla
Cooper, Sarah Jean *nursing educator*

WEST VIRGINIA

Barboursville
Parsons, Martha McGhee *rehabilitation nurse*

Beaver
White, Barbara Ann *technologist*

Bunker Hill
Kifer, Brenda A. *medical/surgical and critical care nurse*

Charles Town
Starks, Doris N. *retired nursing educator, administrator*

Charleston
Higginbotham, Deborah Watts *social worker*
King, Rebecca Jane *nursing administrator, educator*

Clarksburg
Yanero, Lisa Joyce *medical and surgical nurse*

Elkview
Chambers-Ross, Charlotte Boyd *social worker, artist*

Flemington
Miller, Patricia Anne *physician assistant*

Huntington
Engle, Jeannette Cranfill *medical technician*
Mills, Nina Rosalie *social worker*

Kearneysville
Lotze, Evie Daniel *psychodramatist*

Monaville
Bell, Joann *nurse*

Morgantown
Bell, Dawn Marie *pharmacist, educator*

Parkersburg
Wilson, Roberta Bush *retired psychotherapist, accountant*

Ranson
Rudacille, Sharon Victoria *medical technician*

Saint Albans
Alderson, Gloria Frances Dale *rehabilitation specialist*

Shepherdstown
Spencer, Heidi Honnold *psychotherapist, writer, educator*

Vienna
Arthur, Margaret Ferne *nurse, insurance paramedic*

Wheeling
Hickcox, Leslie Kay *health educator, consultant*
Poland, Michelle Lind *medical, surgical, and critical care nurse*

Williamsburg
Scott, Pamela Moyers *physician assistant*

WISCONSIN

Beloit
Doherty, Rhonda Sue *mental health services professional*

Brookfield
Pottebaum, Sharon Mitchell *health educator*
Rooney, Carol Bruns *dietician*

Chippewa Falls
Anderson, Greta Mae *health facility administrator, educator*

Dousman
Harris, Dorothy D. *residential treatment therapist*

Eau Claire
Biegel, Eileen Mae *retired hospital executive*
Kirkhorn, Lee-Ellen Charlotte *community health nurse, educator*
Lippold, Judith Rosenthal *retired occupational therapist*

Elm Grove
Rose, Darlene Joyce *speech pathology/audiology services professional*

Fond Du Lac
Christie, Jacqueline Ann *nurse*
Kuhls, Barbara Sue *medical/surgical nurse*

Franklin
Stenzel, Mary Francis *social worker*

Grafton
Kettling, Virginia *retired health facility administrator*

Green Bay
Domenoski, Ellen Marie *staff nurse*
McIntosh, Elaine Virginia *nutrition educator*

Kenosha
Gurnack, Anne Marie *healthcare educator, consultant*

La Crosse
Hatfield, Mary Lou *nurse, paramedic*
Johnson, Kim G. *medical/surgical nurse, consultant*

Madison
Johnson, Jean Elaine *nursing educator*
Marlett, Judith Ann *nutritional sciences educator, researcher*
Migas, Rosalie Ann *social worker*
Mitchell, Bryce Mahoney *psychotherapist, counselor*
Sollenberger, Donna Kay Fitzpatrick *hospital and clinics executive*

Manitowoc
Schwarzenbart, Amy Jo *psychiatric nurse, case manager*
Shimek, Rosemary Geralyn *medical/surgical nurse*

Mequon
Denton, Peggy *occupational therapist, educator*
Wetzel, Karen J. *nurse*

Milwaukee
Babcock, Janice Beatrice *health facility administrator*
Beaudry, Diane Fay *medical quality management executive*
Eshetu, Gwendelbert Lewis *retired social worker*
Ferguson, Nancy L. *psychotherapist, social worker*
Grimes, Kristen *public health service officer*
Heim, Kathryn Marie *psychiatric nurse*
Liebau, Catherine Annette *cardiac diagnostic nurse*
Loehr, Stephanie Schmahl *psychotherapist, retired social worker*

New Berlin
Winkler, Dolores Eugenia *retired health facility administrator*

Oshkosh
Wells, Carolyn Cressy *social work educator*

Racine
Baker, Joyce Mildred *medical/surgical nurse, volunteer*

Seymour
Lentz, Cherie Lynn *nurse*

Whitewater
Kirst-Ashman, Karen Kay *social work educator*

WYOMING

Casper
Graff, Cheryl L. *medical facility program administrator*
Hasely-Harshman, Tracy *nurse*

Ethete
Tepper, Marcy Elizabeth *drug education director*

Laramie
Franks, Beverly Matthews *retired psychotherapist, consultant*
Schatz, Mona Claire Struhsaker *social worker, educator, consultant, researcher*

Rock Springs
Thompson, Josie *nurse*

TERRITORIES OF THE UNITED STATES

GUAM

Hagatna
Cruz, Teofila Perez *nursing administrator*

Mangilao
Duenas, Laurent Flores *health and nursing consultant*

Tamuning
Cahinhinan, Nelia Agbada *retired public health nurse, health facility administrator*

PUERTO RICO

Aguas Buenas
Melendez, Sonia Ivette *counselor*

Carolina
Reyes-Hernández, Migdalia *counselor*

Santa Isabel
Lugo-Paoli, Luz Minerva *counselor, educator*

VIRGIN ISLANDS

Christiansted
Christian, Cora L.E *health facility administrator, physician*

CANADA

ONTARIO

Owen Sound
Jones, Phyllis Edith *nursing educator*

Toronto
McRae, Marion Eleanor *critical care nurse*

QUEBEC

Montreal
Messing, Karen *occupational health researcher*

ZAMBIA

Kitwe
Ryder, Elizabeth Godbey *psychiatric nurse consultant, missionary*

ADDRESS UNPUBLISHED

Abbott, Regina A. *neurodiagnostic technologist, consultant, business owner*
Abboud, Sabra Natasha *psychotherapist, psychology professor*
Ackermann, Barbara Bogel *counselor*
Adams, Eleanor June *medical/surgical nurse*
Adekson, Mary Olufunmilayo *counselor, educator*
Aehlert, Barbara June *health facility administrator*
Alford, Renee Marie *speech pathology/audiology services professional, educator*
Aligarbes, Sandra Lynne *nurse*
Amaro, Leticia *medical/surgical nurse*
Amato, Daria U. *critical care, medical, and surgical nurse*
Amick, Deborah Anne *medical/surgical and women's health nurse*
Anderson, Allamay Eudoris *health educator, home economist*
Anderson, Dorothy Fisher *social worker, psychotherapist*
Anderson, Linda Jean *critical care nurse, psychiatric nurse practitioner*
Anderson, Nancy Odegard *medical/surgical nurse*
Andrau, Maya Hedda *physical therapist*
Arathuzik, Mary Diane *medical/surgical nurse*
Arking, Lucille Musser *nurse, epidemiologist*
Armand, Margaret Mitchell *mental health services professional*
Armstrong, Peg Jean *psychotherapist*
Arnold, Janet Nina *health facility administrator, consultant*
Atamian, Susan *nurse*
Ayers, Janice R. *social service administrator*
Azocar, Francisca *clinical psychologist*
Azpeitia, Lynne Marie *psychotherapist, educator, trainer, consultant*
Babao, Donna Marie *retired community health and psychiatric nurse, educator*
Babitzke, Theresa Angeline *health facility administrator*
Bacon, Barbara McNutt *social worker*
Bailey, Carla Lynn *nursing administrator*
Bailey, Margaret Elizabeth *nurse, retired military officer*
Baltimore, Pamela A. Grayson *social worker, consultant*
Baney, Lori A. *medical technician, educator*
Barger, Barbara Elaine *medical and surgical nurse, nursing educator*
Barker, Virginia Lee *nursing educator*
Barnes, Suzanne Martin *speech pathology/audiology services professional*
Barnhill, Muriel *retired nurse*
Barrett, Jessica (Donna Ann Nipert) *psychotherapist*
Barrett, Krista E. *psychotherapist, educator*
Barthwell, Andrea Grubb *health care consultant, former federal official*
Basham, Monnie *retired mental health services professional*
Basinger, Karen Lynn *renal dietitian*
Bass, Lynda D. *retired medical/surgical nurse, nursing educator*
Baum, Jeanne Ann *psychotherapist*
Baylor, Laurie Carol *emergency nurse practitioner*
Baymiller, Lynda Doern *social worker*
Beaton, Meredith *enterostomal therapy clinical nurse specialist*
Becker, Kathy Gail *medical/surgical nurse*
Becker, Nancy May *nursing educator*
Bell, Kathy Dawn *medical/surgical nurse*
Bell, Susan Jane *nurse*
Berger, Gisela Porsch *psychotherapist*
Berger, Miriam Roskin *dance therapist, educator*
Berner, Judith *mental health nurse*
Biberstine, Jolene Beth *medical/surgical nurse*
Bilstad, Sandra A. *medical/surgical nurse, home health care nurse*
Binnie, Nancy Catherine *retired nurse, educator*
Blackburn, Pamela M. *medical surgical nurse*
Blake, Kimberly Bosworth *pharmacist*
Bland, Deborah Shaffer *nurse*
Blauvelt, Barbara Louise *nutritionist*
Blazej, Penny Annette *clinical social worker, writer, artist*
Bleam, Laura Jane *pediatrics nurse, educator*
Boer, Linda Karen *medical/surgical nurse*
Bogard, Margaret Joan *nurse*
Bohanon, Kathleen Sue *neonatologist*
Boldt, Patricia C. *social worker*
Bollhofer-White, Joanne *pharmacist*
Bollinger, Sharon Moore *psychotherapist*
Bonzo, Deborah L. *dietician, educator*
Boone, Donna Clausen *physical therapist, statistician, researcher*
Borg, Ruth I. *home nursing care provider*
Bott, Patricia Ann *medical/surgical nurse*
Bottone, JoAnn *health services executive*
Bouchonville, Susan Joanne *public health service officer, medical technician*
Boward, Diana Larson *medical/surgical nurse*
Boyd, Mary Frances *retired school nurse, pastor*
Boyd, Velena *retired community health nurse, consultant*
Braden, Joan Kay *mental health counselor*
Bradley, Carol Ann *nursing consultant, editor*
Bradley, Janice Jeanenne *retired medical technician*
Brandt, Leota Fay *medical/surgical nurse*
Brault, G. Lorain *health facility administrator*
Brayer, Edith Marie *marriage and family therapist, consultant*
Breaux, Cheryl *counselor*
Brinkley, Glenda Willis *medical, surgical, and women's health nurse*
Britt, Debra L. *medical/surgical nurse*
Britton, Kim Barnett *medical/surgical nurse*
Brooks, Barbara Carrk *registered nurse, administrator*
Brooks, Hillary Afton *social worker*
Broughton, Hazel Callen *rehabilitation counselor, consultant*
Brown, Barbara June *hospital and nursing administrator*
Brown, Billye Jean *retired nursing educator*
Brown, Laima Adomaitis *art therapist, artist, writer*
Brown, Patricia Mary Clare *health facility administrator*
Bryant, Bertha Estelle *retired medical/surgical nurse*
Buck, Dorothy Cecelia *psychotherapist, writer*
Bundy, Suzanne *human services administrator*
Burch, Lori Ann *obstetrics nurse*
Burgher, Pauline Menefee *retired marriage and family therapist*
Burke, Karen A. *medical/surgical nurse*
Burnett, Barbara Diane *retired social worker*
Burton, Kathleen T. *mental health services professional*
Büsch, Annemarie *retired mental health nurse*
Byrnes, Gail M. *endoscopy nurse*
Cable, Diane Lynne *marriage and family therapist, educator*
Calhoun, Ramona *human services administrator, academic administrator, consultant*
Campbell, Claire Patricia *nurse practitioner, educator*
Campbell, Judy *medical/surgical nurse, educator*
Campbell, Reginna Gladys *medical/surgical nurse*
Carman, Susan Hufert *nurse coordinator*
Carpentieri, Sarah C. *neuropsychologist, researcher, clinical psychologist*
Carper, Barbara Anne *nursing educator*
Carr-DeRamus, Denise *mental health counselor*
Carson, Regina E. *healthcare administrator, pharmacist, educator, geriatric specialist*
Carter, Melva Jean *retired medical technician*
Carter, Rebecca Gail *critical care nurse*
Casasanta, Mary Frances *medical/surgical nurse*
Cash, Deanna Gail *retired nursing educator*
Cason, Nica Virginia *nursing educator*
Caulfield, Kathleen Marie *medical health information administrator, geriatrics nurse*
Cauthorne-Burnette, Tamera Dianne *family practice nurse practitioner, consultant*
Cawley, Maureen E. *pharmacist*
Cerra, Wendy *psychotherapist*
Chait, Fay Klein *health administrator*
Chamberlain, Diane *psychotherapist, writer, social worker*
Chang, Debbie I-Ju *health programs and research executive, director*
Chapman, Elizabeth Nina *counselor*
Cholewka, Patricia Anne *health facility administrator*
Chow, Rita Kathleen *nursing consultant*
Chughtai, Raana Lynn *psychiatric nurse practitioner*
Claypool, Nancy *social worker*
Clemens, Brenda *medical/surgical nurse, educator*
Cloud, Gary Lynn *food and nutrition services administrator*
Clugston, Bonnie Irene *nurse*
Cockrell-Fleming, Shelia Yvette *public health nurse*
Cogen, Roberta *retired nursing administrator, medical/surgical nurse*
Cognetto, Anna M. *social worker*
Cohen, Carolyn A. *healthcare educator*
Coker, Mary Shannon *perinatal and perioperative nurse*
Colburn, Nancy Douglas *social worker, educator*
Coleman, Jean Black *nurse, physician assistant*
Colline, Marguerite Richnavsky *maternal, women's health and pediatrics nurse*
Collins, Jacqueline F. *nurse, case manager*
Compton, Diane Groat *professional counselor, researcher*
Conte, Julie Villa *nurse, administrator*
Conti, Joan Noel *social worker*
Cooper, Signe Skott *retired nursing educator*
Cornell, Carole Anne Walcutt Arnold *nurse*
Corvini, Marguerite *social worker*
Coté, Kathryn Marie *psychotherapist, stress management educator*
Cotter, Emily Rexann *social worker, marriage and family therapist*
Cowan, Rhonda Renee *nurse, social worker*
Cowles, Lois Anne Fort *social worker, educator, poet*
Coyle, Dorothy Sherin Behen *medical/surgical nurse*
Craig, Carol Mills *marriage, family and child counselor*
Crane, Rea Babcock *retired nurse*
Crawford, Mallory *counselor*
Crawford, Vicky Charlene *perinatal clinical nurse specialist, nursing administrator*
Croft, Kathryn Delaine *social worker, consultant*
Cromwell, Florence Stevens *occupational therapist*
Cross, Joan Russin *medical technologist*
Cummings, Mary Voigt *counselor*
Curran-Smith, Anita Stiles *retired public health medicine educator, dean*
Curtis, Katherine Lanae *pharmacist*
Curtis, Susan Virginia *social worker*
Cushman, Oris Mildred *retired nurse, hospital education director*
Cyprus, Rhonda Reneé *marriage and family therapist, social worker*
Dahl, Marilyn Gail *psychotherapist*
Darkovich, Sharon Marie *nursing administrator*
Davidow, Jenny Jean *counselor, writer*
Davis, Ada Romaine *nursing educator*
Davis, Elba Lucila *veterans affairs nurse*
Davis, Katherine Sarah *physical therapy educator*
Davis, Teresann Weller *social worker*
Dawson, Caron *medical and legal consultant*
Day, Anne White *retired nurse*
Dayton, Kathleen G. *nurse*
Deane, Sally Jan *health facility administrator, consultant*
Deater, Eloise Elaine *mental health services professional*
Deaton, Fae Adams *social worker, consultant, artist, graphics designer*
DeBrincat, Susan Jeanne *nutritionist*
Decker, Josephine I. *health clinic official*
DeElejalde, Ana Levy *psychotherapist*
Deeves, Mary Ellen *medical/surgical nurse, nursing administrator*
de Lacerda, Maria Assunçaõ Escobar *retired social worker, consultant*
DeLapp, Tina Davis *retired nursing educator*
Delucia, Charlotte *psychotherapist*
Dema-ala, Relie L. *medical/surgical nurse*
Demetrakeas, Regina Cassar *social worker*
Dempsey, Jane M. *nurse epidemiologist*
Desjardins, Judith Anne *psychotherapist*
DeVault, Kathy *psychiatric consultant, liaison nurse*
DeVore, Kimberly K. *healthcare executive*
Dickens, Joyce Rebecca *addictions therapist, educator*
Dickson, Donna R. *medical/surgical nurse*
Dimaira, Ann B. *medical/surgical nurse*
Dimengo, Josephine *medical/surgical nurse*
Dincecco, Jennie Elizabeth Williams Swanson *healthcare administrator, mentor, educator, volunteer*
DiPaolo, Sonja Jean *retired nurse*
Dixon, Kathryn A. *social worker*
Doucette, Betty *public and community health and geriatrics nurse*
Dowdell, Donna Renea *nurse*
Downs, Kathleen Anne *health facility administrator*
Dudley, Thora Louise *rehabilitation services professional*
Dumas, Sandra Lee *medical technician, microbiologist*
Dumler, Patricia Ann *critical care nurse*
Dunmeyer, Sarah Louise Fisher *retired health care consultant*
Dunn, Audrey Christine *speech pathology/audiology services professional*
Durkee, Dianna *medical/surgical nurse*
Durkin, Diane L. *retired nurse*
Dworin, Miriam Joy *occupational therapist, educator, advocate*
Dwyer, Judith A. *marriage and family therapist*
Dye, Sharon Elizabeth Herndon *speech pathologist*
Eaton, Shirley M. *medical/surgical nurse*
Ebinger, Linda Ann *retired nurse*
Edelsberg, Sally Comins *retired physical therapist, educator*
Edelstein, Rosemarie (Rosemarie Hublou) *medical/surgical nurse, educator, geriatrics nurse*
Edwards, Sharon Jane *nurse*
Eimers, Jeri Anne *retired counselor*
Eisenberg, Patricia Lee *medical/surgical nurse*
Elliot, Janet Lee *occupational therapist*
Elliott-Zahorik, Bonnie *nurse, administrator*
Ellis, Janice Rider *nursing educator, consultant*
Ellstrom, Annette *research consultant*
Engle, Jane *research nurse, artist, chaplain*
English, Mildred Oswalt *retired nurse supervisor*
Engstrom, Jean *medical/surgical nurse*
Espinosa, Carole Jo *counselor, educator*
Ezaki-Yamaguchi, Joyce Yayoi *dietician*
Fabian, Kelly Jean *physical therapist*
Faiz, Alexandria *researcher, writer*
Farrington, Bertha Louise *retired nursing administrator*
Feathers, Gail M. Wratny *social worker*
Fehr, Lola Mae *health facility administrator*
Feldman, Frances *retired social worker*
Fidone, Laura Peebles *social worker*
Fields, Velma Archie *medical/surgical nurse*
Fierman, Ella Yensen *retired psychotherapist*
Finch, Julia Laura *counselor*
Finley, Sarah Maude Merritt *retired social worker*
Flannelly, Laura T. *mental health nurse, nursing educator, researcher*
Fleksher, Cassandra C. *psychology and research rehabilitation professional*
Flynn, Pauline T. *retired speech pathologist, educator*
Fogelman, Ann Florence *nutrition consultant, educator, researcher*
Foley, Virginia Sue Lashley *counselor, educational training consultant*
Ford-Reed, Lillie Mae *geriatrics services professional*
Forest, Eva Brown *nursing home supervisor, composer*
Foss, Valerie Ann *medical/surgical nurse*
Fountain, Linda Kathleen *health science association executive*
Fralix Gold, Carolyn M. *medical/surgical nurse, educator, consultant*
Francisco, Ana B. *medical/surgical nurse, legal nurse consultant*
Francke, Gloria Niemeyer *retired pharmacist, editor, writer*
Francois, Linda Jean *medical/surgical and psychiatric nurse*
Franklin-Griffin, Cathy Lou Hinson *nursing educator*
Frederick-Mairs, T(hyra) Julie *administrative health services official*
Frey, Margo Walther *career counselor, columnist*
Friedman, Kenni *health facility administrator, councilman*
Fullwood, Altburg Marie *women's health nurse*
Fuselier, Marilyn Monie *retired counselor*
Fusillo, Nancy Marie *medical/surgical, oncological, pediatric, community health and family nurse practitioner*
Garbacz, Patricia Frances *school social worker, therapist*
Garbecki, Ann M. *nurse*
Garcia, Yvette *speech-language pathologist*
Garcia y Carrillo, Martha Xochitl *pharmacist*
Garity, Kathleen Mary *nurse coordinator, director*
Garrett, Shirley Gene *nuclear medicine technologist*
Gaultiere, Kristi Southard *psychotherapist*
Gavin, Mary Jane *retired medical/surgical nurse*
Genest, Theresa Joan *lab technician*
George, Mary G. *health scientist*
Georgieff, Ellen *nurse*
Gerry, Debra Prue *psychotherapist, recording artist, writer*
Ghorayeb, Fay Elizabeth *nursing educator*
Giberson, Joan Alyne *retired school nurse practitioner*
Gilbert, Ruth Elizabeth *inpatient obstetric nurse*
Gillett, Patricia *family and acute care nurse practitioner, clinical nurse*
Gilmore, Louisa Ruth *retired nurse*
Girouard, Shirley Ann *nurse, policy analyst*
Gladden, Vivianne Cervantes *healthcare consultant, writer*
Glashan, Constance Elaine *retired nurse, volunteer*
Gleason, Carol Ann *rehabilitation nurse*
Goedken, Ann Mary *psychotherapist*
Goldberg, Lois D. *health facility administrator, disability analyst*
Goldie, Dorothy Roberta *retired counselor*
Goldsmith, Betty F. *counselor*
Gordon, Audrey Kramen *healthcare educator*
Gould, Mary Ann Carpenter *nephrology nurse consultant*
Graham, Olive Jane *retired medical/surgical nurse*
Grant, Janett Ulrica *medical/surgical nurse*
Graver, Mary Kathryn *medical/surgical nurse*
Gray, Mary Margaret *nephrology and dialysis nurse*
Greene, Lynne Jeannette *wellness consultant, artist*
Greenfield, Linda Sue *nursing educator*
Griesemer, Carol J(oseph) *counselor*
Grobstein, Ruth H. *health facility administrator*
Grosso, Camille M. *nurse*
Guerra, Edna *pharmacist*
Guichard, Susan Weil *dietician, consultant*
Hackerman, Ann E. *psychotherapist*
Haley, Patricia Ann *psychiatric therapist, school counselor, administrator*
Hall, Wanda Jean *mental health professional, consultant*
Hampton, Margaret Frances *counselor*
Hanratty, Carin Gale *pediatric nurse practitioner*
Hansen-Kyle, Linda L *counselor, nursing educator*
Hanson, Margaret *social worker*
Harbaugh, Janice M. *counselor, consultant*
Hardin, Bridgette Everhart *educational research analyst*
Haren, Elizabeth Gaye *counselor*
Harms, Nancy Ann *nursing educator*
Harris, Deborah A. *psychotherapist, consultant*
Harris, Jewell Bachtler *social worker*
Hart-Duling, Jean Macaulay *clinical social worker*
Harter, Jacqueline A. *social worker, educator*
Harvey, Michelle Mauthe *researcher, consultant*
Harwell, Denise *researcher*
Harwell, Linda Waites *medical/surgical nurse*
Hass, Lisa M. *freelance/self-employed counselor*
Hathaway, Juanita *medical and surgical nurse*
Hatt, Joyce Lynn *peri-operative nurse*
Haviland, Kay Lynn (Kade Haviland) *mental health services professional*
Hawkins Blanchard, Kellee M. *mental health services professional*
Hay, Nancy Elizabeth *social worker*
Hayes, Danielle Dawn *counselor*
Hayes, Judith *psychotherapist, educator*
Haynes, Yvette *nurse, science educator*
Hearn, Melissa Pate *geriatric administrator*
Heifner, Carol Joan *social work educator*
Heim, Hazel *nurse*
Helms Guba, Lisa Marie *nursing administrator*
Henderson, Joann H. *social worker, consultant*
Henry, Muriel Boyd *retired social worker*
Herbert, Phyllis Sydney *social worker*
Hetu, Joan Lafford *nursing administrator, business executive*
Hibbard, Jennifer Sponhaltz *mental health services professional*
Higgins, Ruth Ann *social worker, family therapist*
Hill, Beverley Jane *physician assistant*
Hines, Colleen M. *clinical nurse specialist*
Hodnicak, Victoria Christine *pediatrics nurse*
Hoeffer, Beverly *nursing educator, researcher*
Hollie, Gladys Miriam *nurse*
Holmes, Wilhelmina Kent *community health nurse*
Homer, Melodie Antonette *oncological nurse, educator, consultant*
Homestead, Susan E. (Susan Freedlender) *psychotherapist*
Honeycutt, Janice Louise *nurse*
Hope, Carol J. *pharmacist, researcher, information technology manager*
Horvath, Dolores Antionette *nurse*
Hosea, Julia Hiller *psychotherapist, communications executive, paralegal*
Houser, Kyra Martin *counselor*
Howell, Embry Martin *researcher*
Huckabee, Ebony *counselor, director*
Huey, Constance Anne Berner *mental health counselor*
Hunter, Mattie Sue (Mattie Sue Moore) *health facility administrator*
Hunter, Sarah Ann *community health nurse*
Hurley, Kathy Lee *mental health services professional, director*
Hurst, Anita Rose *social worker, counselor*
Hutcherson, Rene Ridens *medical social services administrator*
Hutchinson, Edna M. *home care nurse*
Hyle-Worbets, Mary Elizabeth *nurse*
Ignagni, Karen *healthcare association executive*
Imai, Dorothy Kuniye *psychotherapist*
Ingebo, Marilyn Kay *human services manager, rehabilitation services professional*
Inscho, Jean Anderson *retired social worker, landscape artist*
Ivey, Mary Bradford *counselor*
Jackson, Valerie Lynnette *social worker*
Jacoby, Erika *social worker*

Jaranilla, Sarah J. *critical care nurse, consultant*
Jenai, Marilyn *psychotherapist*
Jennings, Reba Maxine *retired critical care nurse*
Jensen, Eva Marie *medical/surgical nurse*
Jerome, Marlene S. *nurse*
Jessup, Catharine P. *retired medical/surgical nurse*
Johnson, Doris Jean *social worker*
Johnson, Erma Jean *human services administrator*
Johnson, June Alexis *counselor, social worker*
Johnson, Nichole Sharese *school nurse practitioner, basketball coach*
Johnson, Patricia Diane *nurse anesthetist*
Johnson, Ping Hu *nursing educator*
Johnson, Sally A. *nurse, educator*
Jonas, Mary *mental health counselor*
Jones, Lisa Maria Draper *counselor*
Jones, Martha Lee *social worker, consultant*
Jones, Mary Catherine *medical/surgical nurse*
Jones, Vivian Booker *speech pathology/audiology services professional*
Jones Tergeoglou, Beverly Gloria *special education services professional*
Jordan, Deovina Nasis *nursing administrator*
Joseph, Eleanor Ann *health science association administrator, consultant*
Joswiak, Ruth Ann *retired dialysis nurse*
Juarez, Maretta Liya Calimpong *social worker*
Juffer, Kristin Ann *researcher*
Junger, Patricia Carol *nurse*
Kacines, Juliette Rosette *behavior therapist*
Kaiser, Nina Irene *healthcare consultant*
Kaminski, Patricia Joyce *lab administrator*
Kates, Cheryl L. *legal nursing consultant*
Kathan, Joyce C. *retired social worker, administrator*
Keegan, Catherine Ann *medical/surgical nurse, endoscopy nurse*
Kelly, Lucie Stirm Young *nursing educator*
Kendall, Jacqueline A. *social worker*
Kendig, Florence Geertz (Bobbi Kendig) *retired social worker*
Kepner, Jane Ellen *psychotherapist, educator, minister*
Kerkemeyer, Victoria Marie *physical therapist*
Kezlarian, Nancy Kay *marriage and family therapist*
Kiel, Brenda Kay *medical/surgical nurse*
Kilpatrick, Judith Ann *medical/surgical nurse, educator*
King, Imogene M. *retired nursing educator*
King, Lynda *counselor*
Kingsland, Grace Harvey *retired medical/surgical nurse, artist*
Kinley, Christine T. *physician assistant*
Kivitter, Linda Jean *medical nurse*
Klass, Phyllis Constance *retired genetic counselor, psychotherapist*
Kleinhenz, Nancy Alison *medical/surgical nurse*
Kline, Leona Ruth *nurse, volunteer*
Klotter, Eleanor Irene *retired social worker*
Knopf, Tana Darlene *counselor, music educator*
Koerber, Marilynn Eleanor *gerontology nursing educator, consultant, nurse*
Kohn, Jean Gatewood *retired health facility administrator, pediatrician*
Komins, Deborah *psychotherapist*
Kopec-Garnett, Linda *nursing administrator, researcher*
Koperski, Nanci Carol *nursing consultant, women's health nurse*
Kottler, Joan Lynn *counselor*
Krebsbach, Jennifer Susan *nurse*
Kretchmar, Leslie *medical/surgical nurse*
Krobath, Krista Ann *pharmacist*
Kroupa, Betty Jean *medical/surgical nurse*
Kuehn, Mildred May *retired social worker*
Kuhler, Deborah Gail *grief therapist, retired state legislator*
Kumar, Faith *clinical professional counselor*
LaBella, Janice Marie *peri-operative nurse*
Laird, Cheryl F. *mental health services professional, paralegal*
Lamb, Jo Ann P. *geriatrics nurse*
Lampl, Annie Wagner *psychotherapist*
Landgrebe, Marilyn Ann *nutritionist, chemicals executive*
Landrum, Beverly Hollowell *nurse, lawyer*
Lane, Marsha K. *medical/surgical nurse*
Lane, Patricia Peyton *retired nursing consultant*
Langenkamp, Sandra Carroll *retired human services administrator*
LaPorte, Adrienne Aroxie *nursing administrator*
Larson, Amy F. *nurse*
Lass, Diane *counselor*
Lathan, Monica J. *health science association administrator, epidemiologist*
Latiolais, Minnie Fitzgerald *retired nurse, health facility administrator*
La Torre, Carissa Danitza *counselor*
Lautenschlager, Yetta Elizabeth *clinical social worker*
Leath, Mary Elizabeth *medical/surgical nurse*
Leininger, Madeleine Monica *nursing educator, consultant, retired anthropologist, editor, writer, theorist*
Lemieux, Jaime Danielle *physical therapist*
Leon, Nellie *health educator*
Levine, Peggy Aylsworth *psychotherapist, poet, writer*
Lightbourne, Marva Henrietta *nurse*
Lilly-Hersley, Jane Anne Feeley *nursing researcher*
Lindburg, Daytha Eileen *physician assistant*
Lindstrom, Rosetta Arline *retired medical technician*
Lippman Salovesh, Dorothy *nurse practitioner*
Lipton, Nina Anne *healthcare executive*
Lockwood, Thelma Shirley *retired social worker*
Loftus, Kay Douglas Colgan *social worker*
Lopez Lysne, Robin *counselor, writer, artist*
Love, Shirley Belle *psychotherapist*
Lovvorn, Audrey Marie *mental health therapist*
Lubic, Ruth Watson *health facility administrator, nurse midwife*
Lucero, Anne *critical care nurse*
Luciano, Cara *mental health services professional*
Luddy, Paula Scott *nursing educator*
Lynch-Stempfer, Tara Kathleen *physical therapist*
Lynn, Julia Carolyn *school nurse practitioner*
Lyons, Gloria Rogers *medical/surgical nurse, nursing educator*
Lyons, Natalie Beller *family counselor*
MacCallum, Lorene (Edythe MacCallum) *pharmacist*
MacPherson, Shirley *clinical therapist*
Madejski, Rose Mary *pharmacist, educator*
Maglio, Gesomina V. *clinical social worker*
Maloney, Elizabeth Mary *mental health nurse, psychiatric health nurse*
Manasse, Arlynn H. *pediatric nurse practitioner*
Mandravelis, Patricia Jean *retired healthcare administrator*
Manner, Jennifer Fouse *social worker*
Manning, Joan Elizabeth *health association administrator*
Maplesden, Carol Harper *marriage and family therapist, music educator*
Marcinek, Margaret Ann *nursing education administrator*
Marcoux, Julia A. *midwife*
Margolis, Susan Ellen *psychiatric clinical nurse specialist, artist*
Margrave, Kathy Christine *nurse anesthetist*
Maris, Beth *clinical social worker, sex therapist*
Markle, Cheri Virginia Cummins *nurse*
Markowitz, Phyllis Frances *retired mental health services professional, retired psychologist*
Marquis, Harriet Hill *social worker*
Martin, Colleen E. *nurse*
Martin, Dale *health facility administrator*
Mason, Sara Smith *healthcare consultant*
Materia, Kathleen Patricia Ayling *nurse*
Matson, Frances Shober *retired social worker*
Matterson, Joan McDevitt *physical therapist*
Mayer, Kristine I. *psychotherapist, writer*
Mayer, Susan Lee *nurse, educator*
McBride, Sandra Teague *psychiatric nurse*
McCaslin, Kathleen Denise *child abuse educator*
McClellan, Carole Ann *retired school nurse*
McCloskey, Dixie May *retired medical/surgical nurse*
McCombs, Kelly Fritz *dietician*
McCormick, Donna Lynn *social worker*
McCuistion, Peg Orem *retired health facility administrator*
Mc Donald, Shirley Peterson *social worker*
McElhannon, Nettie Marie *retired orthopaedic nurse*
McElwee, Doris Ryan *psychotherapist*
McEvoy, Lorraine Katherine *oncology nurse*
McIntyre, Judy *social worker, state representative*
McKay, Susan Bogart *social worker, consultant, artist*
McLaine, Barbara Bishop *counselor assistant*
McNulty, Kathleen Anne *social worker, consultant, psychotherapist*
McPhearson, Geraldine June *retired medical/surgical nurse*
McVey, Alice Lloyd *social worker*
Meaders, Nobuko Yoshizawa *psychotherapist*
Medina, Sandra *social worker, educator*
Medwick, Debra Lou *special education services professional*
Meers, Theresa Mary *nursing educator, science educator*
Mehring, Nancy *medical/surgical nurse, administrator*
Melton, Nancy Kerley *medical, surgical, and oncological nurse*
Mestel, Sherry Y. *social worker, school psychologist, art therapist*
Mickelson, Rhoda Ann *speech pathology/audiology services professional*
Milewski, Barbara Anne *pediatrics nurse, neonatal/perinatal nurse practitioner, critical care nurse*
Miller, Eunice A. *marriage and family therapist, sex therapist, foundation administrator*
Miller, Patricia Hoffman *human services administrator, finance educator*
Miller, Roberta Ann *gastroenterology nurse*
Miller, Sonja Glaaser *counselor*
Mills, Celeste Louise *occupational therapist*
Milner, Beverly Jane *retired medical/surgical nurse*
Milnor, Hazel *nurse*
Miracle, Doris Jean *retired medical/surgical nurse*
Misrack, Tana Marie *counselor, minister, writer*
Mitchell, Carol Ann *nursing educator*
Mitchell, Kathleen *medical/surgical and geriatrics nurse*
Mitchell, Madeleine Enid *retired nutritionist*
Mogy, Catherine Waddell *critical care nurse*
Molden, A(nna) Jane *counselor*
Mongeon, Louise Bernadette *school nurse*
Moon, Loretta Marie *recreational therapist*
Moore, Jean E. *social worker, academic administrator, educator, radio personality*
Moore, Mildred Thorpe *dietician*
Moore, Ruth Johnston *retired medical center official*
Moore, Wanda Sue *surgical nurse*
Moreno, Jeanne Simonne *cardiac nurse*
Morey, Sharon Lynn *psychotherapist, mediator*
Morgan, Donna Jean *psychotherapist*
Morgan, Evelyn Buck *retired nursing educator*
Moses, Sheila Johnson *nurse, bookkeeper*
Mosquera, Zoila Bianca *social worker*
Moss, Susan *nurse, small business owner*
Moyers, Kelli R. *psychotherapist*
Mueller, Barbara Stewart (Bobbie Mueller) *alcohol/drug abuse services professional, volunteer*
Mulhall, Kimberly A. *business manager*
Mullette, Julienne Patricia *health facility administrator*
Muñoz Dones De Carrascal, Eloisa (Eloise Munoz Dones) *hospital administrator, pediatrician, educator*
Murray, Julia Kaoru (Mrs. Joseph E. Murray) *occupational therapist*
Myers, Libby Ann *retired medical/surgical nurse*
Myllymaki, Melanie Kaye *operating room nurse*
Myrick, Tana Shey *medical/surgical nurse, educator*
Natividad, Lisalinda Salas *health facility administrator*
Nelson, Alice Carlstedt *retired nursing educator*
Nelson, Doreen Kae *mental health counselor, educator, reserve military officer*
Nelson, Susan Joy *nurse*
Newman, Margaret Ann *nursing educator, department chairman*
Newport, L. Joan *retired social worker*
Newton, Elizabeth Purcell *counselor, consultant, writer*
Newton, Juanita *social worker, educator*
Nichols, Elizabeth Grace *nursing educator, dean*
Nicholson, June Constance Daniels *retired speech pathologist*
Nickel, Janet Marlene Milton *retired geriatrics nurse*
Niles, Barbara Elliott *psychoanalyst*
Norbeck, Jane S. *retired nursing educator*
Norkin, Cynthia Clair *retired physical therapist*
Norris, Mackie Lyvonne Harper *registered nurse, health care consultant*
Oakes, Ellen Ruth *psychotherapist, health facility administrator*
O'Baire-Kark, Marika *nurse, educator, poet, writer*
Oblinger, Jessica Marie *health facility administrator*
Oerter, Cynthia Lynn *medical technologist*
O'Hagan, Denise Marie *physical therapist, personal trainer*
O'Keefe-Hardy, Lee Marilyn *psychotherapist*
Okolski, Cynthia Antonia *psychotherapist, social worker*
Oksiloff, Christa *technologist, educator*
Olsen, Virginia *human services manager*
O'Neill, Margaret E. *psychological counselor*
Ossenberg, Hella Svetlana *psychoanalyst*
Overcash, Shelia Ann *nurse*
Owings, Anne Marie *counselor*
Pacha-Guyot, Debra L. *forensic scientist*
Padilla, Sarai Ramona *health facility administrator, psychologist*
Palmer, Martha H. *counseling educator, director*
Parham, Ellen Speiden *nutrition educator*
Parham, Evelyn Lee *nurse*
Parker, Joel Louise *nursing administrator*
Parker, Susan Brooks *health facility administrator*
Parks, Jean Anne *retired acute care nurse*
Paskawicz, Jeanne Frances *pain specialist*
Pastula, Leah Lynn *mental health services professional*
Pearson, Barbara Lee *social worker*
Peebles, Mary Lynn *nursing home administrator*
Peele, Tammy Sue *nurse*
Pellicciotto, Nicole Alyssa *special education services professional, consultant*
Pentz, Anna Faye *nurse*
Pepper, Dorothy Mae *nurse*
Peratoner, Heidi Esmeralda *marriage and family therapist intern*
Peringian, Lynda Ann *dietician, writer*
Perry, Cynthia *social worker*
Peters, Carol Ann Dudycha *counselor*
Peters, Eleanor White *retired mental health nurse*
Petree, Betty Chapman *anesthetist*
Petrie, Lois Ann *enterostomy therapy nurse*
Pettine, Linda Faye *physical therapist*
Phifer, Renita Y. *counselor, educator*
Phillips, Alys Swords *surgical nurse*
Pieknik, Rebecca Anne *technologist, educator*
Pierce, Linda Ann *nurse*
Pierce, Shaheeda Laura *nurse midwife, consultant*
Pilous, Betty Scheibel *medical/surgical nurse*
Pisciotta, Vivian Virginia *retired psychotherapist*
Poleshuk, Alicia L. *alcohol/drug abuse services professional*
Pompeo, Marie Antoinette *medical/surgical nurse, nursing educator*
Popp, Charlotte Louise *retired health facility administrator*
Poston, Ann Genevieve *psychotherapist, nurse*
Poulos, Clara Jean *nutritionist*
Poulton, Roberta Doris *nurse, consultant*
Powers, Debra Jean *medical/surgical nurse*
Presmanes, Willa Summerour *behavioral health systems evaluator*
Preszler, Sharon Marie *psychiatric home health nurse*
Price, Alicia Hemmalin *retired psychotherapist, alcohol/drug abuse services professional*
Pruitt, Debra Marie *medical/surgical nurse*
Przybylski, Mercedes *retired medical and surgical nurse, health facility administrator*
Quaife, Marjorie Clift *retired nursing educator*
Quattrone-Carroll, Diane Rose *clinical social worker*
Rahming, Etta Lorraine *social worker, consultant, psychotherapist, counseling administrator*
Rainier, Ellen F. *nurse*
Ralston, Martha Jane *retired medical/surgical nurse*
Rand, Joella Mae *retired nursing educator, counselor*
Randolph, Nancy Adele *nutritionist, consultant*
Rasberry, Dawn Yvette *counselor*
Ray, Carol Reneé *researcher*
Reber, Cheryl Ann *consultant, social worker, trainer*
Reck, Elizabeth Torre *social worker, educator*
Reddick, Jacqueline Monique *social worker*
Rehth, Ann *counselor*
Reid, Dolores B. *retired social services administrator, consultant*
Reinke, Linda Jeanette *retired social worker*
Remkus, Connie Elaine *nutritional consultant*
Repko, Lisa *medical/surgical nurse*
Resnick, Elaine Bette *psychotherapist, clinical social worker*
Reynolds, Elizabeth Burson *social worker*
Reynolds, Louise Maxine Kruse *retired school nurse*
Rez, Nancy Brubaker *nurse*
Rha, Lizette *social worker*
Rice, Claretha Mayes *medical/surgical nurse, educator*
Richardson, Winifred *youth counselor, writer*
Riikonen, Charlene Boothe *international health administrator*
Robbins, M. Joan *mental health services professional, sexual addictions therapist*
Robinson, Angela Tomei *clinical laboratory technologist, manager*
Robinson, Gail Patricia *retired mental health counselor*
Robinson, Glenda Carole *pharmacist*
Robinson, Sandra Darlene *nursing educator*
Rochlin, Joyce Tretick *researcher*
Rogalski, Lois Ann *speech and language pathologist*
Rogers, Elizabeth London *retired geriatrics services professional*
Rohne, Emily Hogan *medical nurse*
Rollins, Diann Elizabeth *occupational health nurse, primary school educator*
Rose, Nancy Joy *social worker*
Rothbard, Barbara *allergy and dermatology nurse*
Rothman, Juliet Cassuto *social work educator, writer*
Rothman-Bernstein, Lisa J. *occupational health nurse*
Rountree, Ruthann Louise *social worker, lecturer*
Rubin, Phyllis Getz *health association executive*
Rundquist, Elizabeth Ann *art therapist*
Rush, Kathryn Ann *psychotherapist*
Ryan-Halley, Charlotte Muriel *oncology clinical specialist, family practice nurse practitioner*
Saari, Joy Ann *family practice nurse practitioner, geriatrics nurse, medical/surgical nurse*
Salerno, Sister Maria *advanced practice nurse, educator*
Salter, Phyllis Jean *counselor*
Sandorsen, Cassiopeia *public health service officer*
Santina, Dalia *nutritionist, writer, skin care specialist*
Sastrowardoyo, Teresita Manejar *nurse*
Savoy, Suzanne Marie *nursing educator*
Sawyer-Morse, Mary Kaye *nutritionist, educator*
Scarlett, Novlin Rose *occupational health nurse, educator*
Schamburg, Tracy Marie *professional counselor*
Schatz, Pauline *dietician, educator*
Schindler, Evelyn *medical/surgical nurse, educator*
Schmidtke, Suzanne de Fine *retired social worker*
Schneider, Catherine Chemin *occupational therapist, consultant*
Schroeder, LaVerne *medical/surgical nurse*
Schwartz, Ilene *psychotherapist*
Schwarzkopf, Gloria A. *psychotherapist, educator*
Sciuva, Margaret W. *counselor*
Seaton, Joyah A. *nursing assistant*
Segall, Sarah Ostrovsky *psychoanalyst*
Seroogy, Louise Amy *medical/surgical nurse*
Shafer, Beatrice R. *medical/surgical nurse, researcher*
Shanks, Kathryn Mary *health facility administrator*
Shannon, Jonnie Lynn *nursing administrator*
Sheaffer, Suzanne Frances *geriatrics nurse*
Sheehan, Sophia Ann *marriage and family therapist, director*
Shelton, Margaret *counselor*
Sherry, Marilyn Morin *psychiatric social worker*
Sherwood-Fabre, Liese Anne *public health service officer*
Shinde, Patricia Suzann *special education services professional, educator*
Shirsat, Raakhee Nagesh *pharmacist*
Shores, Pearl Marie *health care company executive*
Siebenaler, Rita Reilly *clinical social worker, consultant*
Silver, Audrey Wilma *nurse, educator*
Silverman, Ellen-Marie *speech and language pathologist*
Silvers, Ann *peri-operative nurse, educator*
Simon, Bernece Kern *retired social worker*
Sinclair, Sara Voris *health facility administrator, nurse*
Sinconolfi, Deborah *medical/surgical nurse*
Slaven, Bettye DeJon *retired psychotherapist*
Smith, Barbara Anne *health facility administrator, consultant*
Smith, Cecilia May *hospital official*
Smith, Leonie C.R. *healthcare educator*
Snyder, Dorothy Z. *social worker*
Snyder (Mackley), Louise Marie *speech pathology/audiology services professional, consultant*
Sohonyay, Lisa Cella *orthopedic nurse*
Somes, Joan Marie *critical care nurse*
Sommerfeld, Marianna *retired social worker, writer*
Soper, Marsha Ann Paulson *counselor*
Soucy, Erin C. *nursing educator*
Spottswood, Lydia Carol *nurse, health facility administrator*
Spracher, Nancy A. *psychotherapist*
Sprungl, Janice Marie *nurse*
Stadler, Selise McNeill *laboratory and x-ray technician*
Stancil, Irene Mack *family counselor*
Stanley, Connie *medical/surgical nurse*
Stegge, Diane Faye *counselor*
Stein, Karen Lee *critical care nurse*
Stewart, Susan Hamilton *medical/surgical and oncological nurse*
Steytler, C. Anne Webster *clinical social worker*
Stocks, Mary Lee *social worker, social services administrator*
Storm, J. Reni *nurse, consultant*
Stratton, Mariann *retired military nursing executive*
Struble, Susan C. *recreational therapist*
Stupak, Mary Jo *psychotherapist, educator*
Suber, Robin Hall *former medical and surgical nurse*
Subramanian, Laura Sita *public health service officer*
Suhr, Geraldine M. *medical/surgical nurse*
Sullivan, Elizabeth Asmann *counselor*
Sutcliffe, Mary Ogden *clinical social worker*
Svoboda, Janice June *nurse*
Swan, Beth Ann *nursing administrator*
Swoap, Kristin Genty *marriage and family therapist*
Szczechowicz, Gretchen *medical/surgical nurse*
Taggart, Linda Diane *retired women's health nurse*
Tally, Paula Siniard *counselor*
Tauber, Sonya Lynn *nurse*
Tavares, Marcia Lynn *mental health services professional*
Taylor, Cora Hodge *social worker*
Taylor, Edna Jane *retired employment program counselor*
Taylor, Karen Annette *mental health nurse*
Taylor, Nathalee Britton *retired nutritionist, freelance/self-employed writer*
Terry, Barbara L. *human services administrator*

Terry, Frances Jefferson *retired psychiatric nurse practitioner*
Thompson, Mari Hildenbrand *medico-legal and administrative consultant*
Thornton-Artson, Linda Elizabeth *psychiatric nurse*
Tiemann, Margaret Ann *health educator*
Tilghman, Elizabeth W. *retired medical/surgical nurse*
Tingstrum, Nancy Ash *dietitian*
Tinner, Franziska Paula *social worker, artist, apparel designer, educator, entrepreneur*
Tishman, Lynn P. *psychoanalyst, psychologist*
Torres-Mabasa, Virginia Maria *physician assistant*
Torresyap, Pearl Marie *surgical nurse*
Torrie, Jane Marie *chiropractor, secondary school educator*
Toter, Kimberly Mrowiec *nurse*
Traiman, Helen *school nurse practitioner*
Trapp, Angela Michele *counselor*
Trautman-Kuzma, Alta Louise *nurse, funeral director, writer*
Tsai, Ruth Man-kam *nurse*
Turner, Ann Marie *art therapist*
Tuttle, Mary Celia Putnam *retired social worker*
Tyler, Beverly Ott *medical/surgical nurse*
Tyson, Lucille R. *health facility administrator, geriatrics nurse*
Ulmen, Kathryn T. *neuroscience clinical nurse specialist*
Usinger, Martha Putnam *counselor, educator, dean*
Usman, Marion Wilma *retired medical/surgical and mental health nurse*
VanBuren, Deborah Ann *health educator*
Van de Bogart, Debra Scherwerts *medical/surgical nurse, researcher*
VanDerTuuk-Perkins, Jennifer Elizabeth *counselor, psychologist*
Van Dyke, Debbie K. *special education services professional*
Van Slyke, Sherrie Marie *psychotherapist*
Vogel, H. Victoria *psychotherapist, educator, writer, stress disorder and addiction recovery counselor*
Von Thurn, Jelena *health science specialist*
Vukoder, Velda Jane *social worker*
Vyn, Eleanor Mears *physical therapist*
Waggoner, Kathleen Alice *psychotherapist*
Wallerstein, Betty Cooper *clinical social worker, family therapist*
Wallskog, Joyce Marie *nursing educator, retired psychologist*
Wanley, Patricia Ann *medical/surgical nurse*
Wantz, Kathy Lynn Zepp *school nurse*
Ward, Lakeysha Monique *alcohol/drug abuse services professional, special education services professional*
Waring, Mary Louise *retired social worker*
Warres, Margie Black *retired social work administrator, human services manager*
Warwick, Margaret Ann *health science facility administrator, consultant*
Wasow, Mona *social worker, educator*
Watson, Patti Rae *counselor, psychologist*
Weaver, Sandra Kae *nurse anesthetist*
Wedge, Barbara Jane *women's health nurse*
Wegman, Doris Jean *retired nursing administrator*
Weickert, Wanda Opal *child welfare and attendance counselor, psychotherapist, educator*
Weightman, Esther Lynn *emergency trauma nurse*
Weiner, Anne Lee *social worker*
Weiss, Joan Oppenheimer *social worker, educator*
Westberry, Paula I. *nursing administrator*
Westrick, Heidi Lynn *medical/surgical nurse*
Wheat, Margaret Ann *marriage and family therapist*
Whitaker, Diana Marie *medical/surgical nurse*
White, Sarah Jowilliard *retired counselor*
White, Sharon LaRue *social worker, therapist*
Whitty, Mary Jane *counselor*
Wickham, Dianne *nursing administrator*
Widger, Tanya Marie *counselor*
Wilke Montemayor, Joanne Marie *nursing administrator*
Williams, Elizabeth *human services administrator*
Williams, Freda Videll *speech pathology/audiology services professional*
Williams, Shannon Renee *mental health services professional*
Williams Maddox-Brown, Janice Helen *nurse*
Willits, Eileen Marie *medical, surgical nurse, health facility administrator*
Winn, Nelroy Griffin *healthcare administrator*
Winston, Sandra *health sciences administrator*
Wish, LeslieBeth Berger *psychotherapist, writer, management consultant*
Wittig, Rebecca C. *community health educator*
Wolf, Cheryl Jeane *surgical nurse*
Wolf, Martha Marin *nurse*
Wuthnow, Sara Margery *retired nursing educator*
Yale (Yeleyenide-Yale), Melpomene Fotine *researcher, anthropologist, archaeologist, art historian, conservator*
Yanowitz, Joyce *nutritional counselor*
Yarbrough, Kathryn Davis *public health nurse*
Yoskey, Sylvia Lynn *surgical nurse*
Young, Deborah (Deborah Ayling Yanowitz) *social worker, librarian*
Zambrano, Debra Kay *community health nurse*
Zimmerman, Jo Ann *retired health science association administrator, educator, retired lieutenant governor*
Zuck, Rosemary *social worker, educator*
Zurflueh, Linda June *allergy and immunology nurse, educator*

HEALTHCARE: MEDICINE

UNITED STATES

ALABAMA

Birmingham
Clohan, Dexanne Bowers *physical medical rehabilitation physician*
Elewski, Boni Elizabeth *dermatologist, educator*
Feldman, Jacqueline Maus *psychiatrist, educator*
Kapanka, Heidi *emergency physician*
Oparil, Suzanne *cardiologist, researcher, educator*
Pittman, Constance Shen *endocrinologist, educator*

Cullman
Morris, Sylvia June Burbank *retired physician*

Mobile
Scantlebury, Velma Patricia *surgeon*

Spanish Fort
Benjamin, Regina Marcia *physician, administrator*

ALASKA

Anchorage
Bautista, Lina Judith *psychiatrist*
Harvey, Elinor B. *child psychiatrist*

ARIZONA

Green Valley
Forsyth, Garyfallia Lillian *nurse educator*

Mesa
Tacata, Felisa Padua *psychiatrist, researcher*

Paradise Valley
Targovnik, Selma E. Kaplan *retired dermatologist*

Phoenix
Johnson, Mystie L. *obstetrician, gynecologist, department chairman*
Martinez, Maria Dolores *pediatrician*
Modny, Cynthia Jean *dermatologist*
Rosckowff, Carol Martha *pediatrician*

Scottsdale
Haas, Ingrid Elizabeth *physician*

Tempe
Crawford, Susan Lee *health educator*
Herald, Cherry Lou *medical researcher, educator*

Tuba City
Chang, Vivian K. *orthopedist, surgeon*

Tucson
Addis, Ilana Beth *obstetrician*
Anderson, Dayna *medical researcher*
Cisler, Theresa Ann *osteopath*
Donnelly, Mavis J. *psychiatrist*
Foley, Louise *medical educator, retired military officer*
Graham, Anna Regina *pathologist, educator*
Smith, Kathy Wosnitzer *psychiatrist*

ARKANSAS

Little Rock
Brewer, Martha Johnston *gynecologist, educator*
Mancino, Anne Rochelle *surgeon*

North Little Rock
Kirchner, JoAnn Elaine *psychiatrist*

Scranton
Uzman, Betty Ben Geren *retired pathologist*

CALIFORNIA

Aliso Viejo
Johanson, Wanda L. *medical association administrator, critical care nurse*

Aptos
Miura, Masako Kusayanagi *retired dermatologist*

Bakersfield
Martin, Maureen Frances *medical educator*

Berkeley
Buffler, Patricia Ann *epidemiologist, educator, dean*
Diamond, Marian Cleeves *anatomist, educator*
Ivey, Susan Lee *health services researcher, emergency physician*
Josephian, Jenny Adele *acupuncturist, artist*

Beverly Hills
Bao, Katherine Sung *pediatric cardiologist*
Li, Linda (Linda Jian-Yuh Li) *plastic surgeon*
Rinaldi, Renee Zaira *physician*

Calabasas
Thompkins, Jennifer Eley *physician assistant, consultant*

Camarillo
Kaiman, Sarah *retired physician*

Capitola
Baskerville, Elizabeth Bonham *pediatrician*

Carlsbad
Crooke, Rosanne M. *pharmacologist*

Chatsworth
Stephenson, Irene Hamlen *biomedical researcher, consultant, editor, educator*

Chino
Neal-Parker, Shirley Anita *obstetrician, gynecologist*

Chula Vista
Cohen, Elaine Helena *pediatrician, cardiologist, educator*

Corona Del Mar
Dougherty, Jocelyn *retired neurologist*

Costa Mesa
Fam, Hanaa *psychiatrist*

Culver City
Muller, Jenny Helen *physician, psychiatrist*

Davis
Jensen, Hanne Margrete *pathologist, educator*

Dinuba
León, Rosemary Carrasco *gynecologist*

Downey
Perry, Jacquelin *orthopedist, surgeon*

Emeryville
Hurst, Deborah *pediatric hematologist*

Fountain Valley
Kieu, Quynh Dinh *pediatrician, not-for-profit developer*

Goleta
Zuk, Carmen Veiga *psychiatrist*

Gualala
Ring, Alice Ruth Bishop *retired preventive medicine physician*

Irvine
Hornig, Mady *psychiatrist, educator*
Lee, Eva *medical educator*

La Jolla
Barrett-Conner, Elizabeth *physician, medical educator*
Barrett-Connor, Elizabeth Louise *epidemiologist, educator*
Jorgensen, Judith Ann *psychiatrist, educator*
Klonoff-Cohen, Hillary Sandra *epidemiologist*
Rearden, Carole Ann *clinical pathologist, educator*
Swain, Judith Lea *cardiologist, educator*
Thompson, Charlotte Ellis *pediatrician, educator, writer*

Laguna Hills
Widyolar, Sheila Gayle *dermatologist*

Lake Isabella
Fraser, Eleanor Ruth *radiologist, administrator*

Lakewood
White, Katherine Elizabeth *retired pediatrician*

Loma Linda
Behrens, Berel Lyn *physician, academic administrator, health facility administrator*
Coggin, Charlotte Joan *cardiologist, educator*

Los Altos
Orman, Nanette Hector *psychiatrist*

Los Angeles
Alkon, Ellen Skillen *physician*
Giesser, Barbara Susan *neurologist, educator*
Henriksen, Eva Hansine *retired anesthesiology educator*
Jalali, Behnaz *psychiatrist, educator*
Kamil, Elaine Scheiner *pediatric nephrologist, educator*
Kaufman, Francine R. *pediatric endocrinologist*
Lee, Joselyn C.R. *physician, researcher*
Macavinta-Tenazas, Gemorsita *physician*
Miranda, M. Jeanne *psychiatrist*
Morgan, Elizabeth *plastic surgeon*
Murphree, A. Linn *ophthalmologist*
Neufeld, Naomi Das *endocrinologist*
Oyeyipo, Bolanle T. *geriatrician*
Postlethwaite, Alejandra *psychiatrist, researcher*
Spencer, Carole A. *medical association administrator, medical educator*
Sultan, Wafa *psychiatrist*
Wilson, Miriam Geisendorfer *retired physician, educator*

Mill Valley
Newman, Nancy Marilyn *ophthalmologist, educator*

Mission Viejo
Vergara, Lorenda *retired physician*

Mountain View
Abel, Elizabeth Ann *dermatologist*

Oakland
Cary, Alice Shepard *retired physician*
Killebrew, Ellen Jane (Mrs. Edward S. Graves) *cardiologist, educator*

Orange
Matallana, Lynne *medical association administrator*
Morgan, Beverly Carver *pediatrician, educator*
Pickart, Caitlin Cahill *psychiatrist*
Simjee, Aisha *ophthalmologist, educator*

Pacific Palisades
Love, Susan Margaret *surgeon, educator, writer*

Palo Alto
Blessing-Moore, Joann Catherine *allergist, pulmonologist*
Goldstein, Mary Kane *physician*
Hays, Marguerite Thompson *nuclear medicine physician, educator*
Hubert, Helen Betty *epidemiologist*

Palos Verdes Estates
Rogers, Rita Ruth *psychiatrist, political scientist*

Palos Verdes Peninsula
Narasimhan, Padma Mandyam *physician*

Pasadena
Newman, Marjorie Yospin *psychiatrist*
Short, Elizabeth M. *internist, educator, retired federal agency administrator*

Rancho Mirage
Leydorf, Mary Malcolm *physician, writer*

Riverside
Case, Janice Chang *naturopathic physician, psychologist, lawyer*

Sacramento
Robinson, Muriel Cox *psychiatrist*
Zusman, Edie Ellen *neurosurgeon*

San Diego
Naughton, Gail K. *biomedical researcher, academic administrator*
Parthemore, Jacqueline Gail *internist, educator, hospital administrator*
Wallace, Helen Margaret *pediatrician, preventive medicine physician, educator*

San Francisco
Bainton, Dorothy Ford *pathologist, educator*
Brown, Mehri I. *psychiatrist, educator*
Capaldini, Lisa Claire *physician, educator*
Clever, Linda Hawes *physician*
Croughan, Mary *medical educator*
Den Besten, Pamela Kay *biomedical researcher, dentist*
Ferriero, Donna M. *pediatric neurologist*
Goode, Erica Tucker *internist*
Gooding, Gretchen Ann Wagner *physician, educator*
Kenyon, Cynthia J. *medical researcher*
Koda-Kimble, Mary Anne *medical educator, pharmacologist, dean*
Lucia, Marilyn Reed *physician*
Seebach, Lydia Marie *physician*

Santa Ana
Myers, Marilyn Gladys *pediatric hematologist, oncologist*

Santa Barbara
Bischel, Margaret DeMeritt *physician, consultant*
Jovanovic, Lois *medical researcher*
Mathews, Barbara Edith *gynecologist*

Santa Cruz
Pletsch, Marie Eleanor *plastic surgeon*
Shorenstein, Rosalind Greenberg *internist*

Santa Monica
Amerian, Mary Lee *physician*
Carr, Ruth Margaret *plastic surgeon*
Shamban, Ava T. *dermatologist*

Santa Rosa
Carlson-Sweet, Kim Lynette *dermatologist*
Smith, Fredrika Patchett *retired physician*

Seal Beach
Dunckley, Victoria Lynn *psychiatrist*

Sherman Oaks
Stein, Kira D. *psychiatrist*

Sonoma
Fong, Edna M. *retired physician*

Sonora
Padgett, Kathryn Ann Weiner *medical association administrator, special education educator*

Stanford
Blau, Helen Margaret *pharmacology educator*
Donaldson, Sarah Susan *radiologist*
Jacobs, Charlotte De Croes *medical educator, oncologist*
Kraemer, Helena Antoinette Chmura *psychiatry educator*
Mitchell, Beverly Shriver *hematologist, oncologist, educator*
Payne, Anita Hart *reproductive endocrinologist, researcher*
Polan, Mary Lake *obstetrics and gynecology educator*

Stockton
Matuszak, Alice Jean Boyer *pharmacy educator*

Sunnyvale
White, Christine A. *internist, oncologist, pharmaceutical executive*

Sylmar
Corry, Dalila Boudjellal *internist, educator*
Tully, Susan Balsley *pediatrician, educator*

Thousand Oaks
Pakula, Anita Susan *dermatologist*
Scott, Mary Celine *pharmacologist*

Torrance
Birnbaumer, Diane Margaret *emergency physician, educator*
Brasel, Jo Anne *pediatrician, educator*

Walnut Creek
Cannon, Grace Bert *retired immunologist*
Sheen, Portia Yunn-ling *retired physician*

Westminster
Nguyen, Lan Thi Hoang *physician, educator*

Winchester
Ucmakli, Naciye Gunger *oncologist*

COLORADO

Aurora
Churchill, Mair Elisa Annabelle *medical educator*
Nora, Audrey Hart *physician*
Suryanarayanan, Sowmya K. *endocrinologist*
Vitanza, Joanne Maria *allergist, pediatrician*

Boulder
Pneuman, Linda Jackson *retired physician*

Colorado Springs
Gifford, Marilyn Joyce *emergency physician, consultant*

Denver
Barber, Patricia Louise *clinical specialist*
Brega, Kerry Elizabeth *physician, researcher*
Gabow, Patricia Anne *internist, health facility executive*
Huang, Linda Chen *plastic surgeon*
Johnson, Candice Elaine Brown *pediatrician, educator*
Kendig, Lynne E. *physician*
Langsley, Pauline Royal *psychiatrist*
Marrack, Philippa Charlotte *immunologist, researcher*
Mukherjee, Gopa *psychiatrist, educator*
Stamm, Carol Ann *obstetrician, gynecologist*
Studevant, Laura *medical association administrator*
Sujansky, Eva Borska *pediatrician, geneticist, educator*

Grand Junction
Michels, Ruth Yvonne *retired cytologist*

Guffey
Price, Faith Munford *retired psychiatrist, retired special education educator*

Highlands Ranch
Bublitz, Deborah Keirstead *pediatrician*

Lakewood
Eikleberry, Lois Schillie *physician*

Littleton
Walker, Louise Converse *obstetrician, gynecologist*

Louisville
Bluestein, Eve *plastic surgeon*

Steamboat Springs
Fenton, Monica *retired biomedical researcher*

Wheat Ridge
Wells, Karen Kay *medical librarian*

Wolcott
Flacke, Joan Wareham *physician, anesthesiologist, educator*

CONNECTICUT

Bridgeport
Twist-Rudolph, Donna Joy *neurophysiology and neuropsychology researcher*

Farmington
Grunnet, Margaret Louise *retired pathologist, educator*
Rothfield, Naomi Fox *physician*
Runowicz, Carolyn Dilworth *physician*

Hartford
Jung, Betty Chin *epidemiologist, educator, nurse*

New Britain
Fallon, Barbara G. *oncologist*

New Haven
Bartoshuk, Linda M. *otolaryngologist, educator*
Berland, Gretchen K. *medical educator, filmmaker*
Ferholt, J. Deborah Lott *pediatrician*
Hostetter, Margaret K. *pediatrician, medical educator*
McClain, Brenda C. *pain management physician*
Seashore, Margretta Reed *physician, educator*

Norwalk
Freitag, Anna Carol *endocrinologist, internist*

Sandy Hook
Dakofsky, LaDonna Jung *medical counseling physician, radiation oncologist*

Simsbury
Roman, Robin *anesthesiologist*

Vernon Rockville
Marmer, Ellen Lucille *pediatrician, cardiologist*

Wallingford
Lelas, Snjezana *pharmacologist, researcher*
Regueiro-Ren, Alicia *biomedical researcher*

Waterford
Pierson, Anne Bingham *physician*

DELAWARE

Wilmington
Dow, Lois Weyman *physician*
Inselman, Laura Sue *pediatrician, educator*

DISTRICT OF COLUMBIA

Washington
Anthony, Virginia Quinn Bausch *medical association executive*
Appareddy, Vijaya L. *psychiatrist*
Aschenbrener, Carol Ann *pathologist, educator*
Benoit, Marilyn B. *psychiatrist, consultant*
Blumenthal, Susan Jane *psychiatrist, educator*
Catoe, Bette Lorrina *pediatrician, educator*
Cranford, Judith *medical association administrator*
Epps, Roselyn Elizabeth Payne *pediatrician, educator*
Gadson, Sandra L. *nephrologist, medical association administrator*
Gray, Sheila Hafter *psychiatrist, researcher*
Grealy, Mary R. *medical association administrator*
Hamburg, Margaret Ann (Peggy Hamburg) *public health administrator*
Jenkins, Renee R. *medical educator, pediatrician*
Locke, Stephanie Frances *anesthesiologist, educator, consultant*
Marcus, Devra Joy Cohen *internist*
Oertel, Yolanda Castillo *pathologist, educator*
Perez, Lucille C. Norville *medical association administrator, pediatrician*
Robinowitz, Carolyn Bauer *psychiatrist, educator, director*
Shanahan, Sheila Ann *pediatrician, educator*
Shrier, Diane Kesler *psychiatrist, educator*
Watkins, Deborah Karen *epidemiology investigator, educator*
Weinberg, Myrl *medical association administrator*

FLORIDA

Bay Pines
Jewell, Vanessa yoder *surgical physician's assistant*

Belleair
Dexter, Helen Louise *dermatologist, consultant*

Boca Raton
Kramer, Cecile Edith *retired medical librarian*

Boynton Beach
Srinath, Latha *physician*

Bradenton
Vereb, Teresa B. *psychiatrist*

Cape Coral
(Harrison) Flint, Nancy Elizabeth *retired medical association administrator*

Clearwater
Beeson, Mary *internist, endocrinologist, researcher*

Coral Gables
Perez, Josephine *psychiatrist, educator*

Davie
Penhollow, Tina Marie *health science researcher, educator*

Daytona Beach
Silverman, Beatrice Toltz *retired psychiatrist*

Deltona
Drewry, Marcia Ann *physician*

Dunedin
Scott, Gwendolyn Lutz *internist*

Fernandina Beach
Barlow, Anne Louise *pediatrician, medical researcher*

Fort Lauderdale
Durst, Kay Horres *physician*
Haugen, Christine *plastic surgeon*
Parker, Sasha Smilka *medical educator, nurse, consultant*
Sperling, Randi A. *pediatrician*
Velez, Ines *oral pathologist, educator*

Gainesville
Behnke, Marylou *pediatrician, educator*
Drummond, Willa Hendricks *neonatologist, educator, information technology executive*
Hardt, Nancy Sisson *pathology and laboratory medicine educator*
Limacher, Marian Cecile *cardiologist*
Mendenhall, Nancy Price *radiologist, educator*

Hollywood
Berdich, Alla *psychiatrist*

Key West
Wisniewski, P. Michelle *retired obstetrician, gynecologist*

Lake Worth
Tracy, Ann Anderson *pediatrician*

Melbourne
Greenblatt, Hellen Chaya *immunologist, microbiologist*

Miami
Alvarez, Ofelia Amparo *pediatrician, hematologist*
Bunge, Mary Bartlett *medical educator*
Maggioni, Andrea *pediatrician*
Wolff, Grace Susan *pediatric cardiologist*

Miami Beach
Ritvo, Eva Caroline *psychiatrist, educator*

Naples
Brooks, Joae Graham *psychiatrist*

Orlando
Magsino, Marissa Estiva *internist, pediatrician*

Pensacola
Canady, Alexa Irene *pediatric neurosurgeon, educator*
Gill, Becky Lorette *retired psychiatrist*

Plantation
Nickelson, Kim René *internist*

Ponte Vedra Beach
Toker, Karen Harkavy *physician*

Port Saint John
Baumann, Patricia April *orthopedic surgery fellow*

Punta Gorda
Hollinshead, Ariel Cahill *oncologist, educator, researcher*

Saint Petersburg
Betzer, Susan Elizabeth Beers *physician, geriatrician*
Clarke, Kit Hansen *radiologist*
Cottrille, Patricia Anne *retired pediatrician*
Simpson, Lisa Ann *physician, educator*

Sarasota
Aull, Susan *physician*
Jelks, Mary Larson *retired pediatrician*
Mohr, Victoria H. *obstetrician*
Sturtevant, Ruthann Patterson *anatomist, educator*

Spring Hill
Del Toro-Politowicz, Lillian *medical association administrator, geriatrics services professional, consultant*

Sunrise
Rodriguez, Germaine *radiologist*

Tallahassee
Hernandez, Minerva Cuadrante *physician, consultant*
Maguire, Charlotte Edwards *retired pediatrician*

Tampa
Cancio, Margarita R. *infectious disease physician*
Gilbert-Barness, Enid F. *pathologist, educator*
Nirmalani, Anjali *psychiatrist*
Novick, Cara D. *pediatric orthopedic surgeon*
Pierantoni, Marlene Michelle *psychiatrist*
Powers, Pauline Smith *psychiatrist, educator, researcher*
Watkins, Joan Marie *osteopath, physician*

West Palm Beach
Iapaolo, Caterina A. *psychiatrist*
McKeen, Elisabeth Anne *oncologist*

Weston
Lazar, Marioara *psychiatrist*

Winter Springs
Giuliano, Concetta *physician*

GEORGIA

Atlanta
Ampola, Mary G. *pediatrician, geneticist*
Arias, Ileana *psychiatrist, educator*
Berkelman, Ruth *medical educator*
Clearo, Kellie Anne *internist, pharmacist, psychiatrist*
Collins, Janet L. *psychiatrist*
Cooper-Ruspoli, Annie Nataf *psychiatrist, director*
Dreyer, Susan *orthopedist, educator*
Gayle, Helene D. *pediatrician, public health service officer*
Higginbotham, Eve Juliet *ophthalmologist, educator, dean*
Hogue, Carol Jane Rowland *epidemiologist, educator*
Klein, Luella Voogd *obstetrics and gynecology educator*
Meshi, Alexis *psychiatrist*
Rohr-Kirchgraber, Theresa M.B. *adolescent medicine*
Wenger, Nanette Kass *cardiologist, researcher, educator*
Zumpe, Doris *ethologist, researcher, educator*

Augusta
Ellison, Lois Taylor *internist, educator, medical association administrator*
Fincher, Ruth Marie Edla *medical educator, dean*
Guill, Margaret Frank *pediatrician, educator, medical researcher*
Johnson, Maria Elizabeth *psychiatrist, researcher*
Ottinger, Mary Louise *podiatrist*
Pryor, Carol Graham *obstetrician, gynecologist*
Wray, Betty Beasley *allergist, immunologist, pediatrician*

Conyers
Jattan, Lynette S. *pediatrician*

Decatur
Farley, Monica M. *medical educator*

Lithia Springs
Kuncl, Kimberly A. *obstetrician, gynecologist*

Macon
Quiroga, Alicia Espinosa *physiatrist*
Scheetz, Allison Paige *medical educator*

Marietta
Dunston-Thomas, Frances Johnson *pediatrician, public health service officer*
Henderson, Cynthia *medical librarian*
Holland, Amy Jeanette *psychiatrist*

Roswell
Maletta, Rose Helen *anesthesiologist*

Saint Simons Island
Brooks, Betty Ann *retired obstetrician, retired gynecologist*

Stone Mountain
Gotlieb, Jaquelin Smith *pediatrician*

HAWAII

Honolulu
Kadzielawa, Renata Maria *physician*
Lee, Yeu-Tsu Margaret *surgeon, educator*
Sharma, Santosh Devraj *obstetrician, gynecologist, educator*

Lahaina
Percy, Helen Sylvia *physician*

Mililani
Gardner, Sheryl Paige *gynecologist*
Olson, Holly Louise *obstetrician, gynecologist*

IDAHO

Boise
Scholl, Virginia May *retired plastic surgeon*

ILLINOIS

Belleville
Megahy, Diane Alaire *physician*

Carbondale
Pohlmann, Mary Michaels *retired medical educator*

Chicago
Alegre, Maria-Luisa *medical educator, researcher*
Arvanitakis, Zoe *neurologist, researcher*
Bienias, Julia Louise *medical researcher, statistician*
Christoffel, Katherine Kaufer *pediatrician, epidemiologist, educator*
Deamant, Catherine D. *internist*
Dooley, Sharon L. *obstetrician, gynecologist*
Evans, Thelma Jean Mathis *internist*
Frederiksen, Marilynn C. *physician*
Gewurz, Anita Tartell *physician, medical educator*
Grammer, Leslie Carroll *allergist*
Gregory, Stephanie Ann *hematologist, educator*
Hackett, Karen L. *medical association administrator*
Hambrick, Ernestine *retired colon and rectal surgeon*
Hibbard, Judith Usher *obstetrician*
Hill, Carlotta H. *physician*
Inan, Zabrin *psychiatrist*
Irvin-Mays, Vernita *medical educator*
Kataria, Tripti Caday *anesthesiologist*
Kaydanova, Yevgenya *neurologist*
Kirschner, Barbara Starrels *gastroenterologist*
Kloss, Linda L. *medical association administrator*
Koehler, Irmgard Kilb *dermatologist, educator*
Korshak, Shelley J. *psychiatrist*
Kurth, Jennifer Lynn *osteopath*
Lopez, Carolyn Catherine *physician*
Mendelson, Ellen B. *radiologist, educator*
Morris, Naomi Carolyn Minner *clinical pediatrician, medical researcher, educator, health facility administrator*
Olson, Sandra Forbes *neurologist*
Powell, Traci E. *psychiatrist*
Ramsey-Goldman, Rosalind *physician*
Rayner, Suzan L. *medical association administrator, physiatrist*
Ridenour, Joey *medical association administrator, operations research specialist*
Robinson, June Kerswell *dermatologist, educator*
Rowley, Janet Davison *physician*
Schwartzberg, Joanne Gilbert *physician*
Seeler, Ruth Andrea *pediatrician, educator*
Short, Marion Priscilla *neurogenetics educator*
Steinhorn, Robin H. *neonatologist, educator*
Telfer, Margaret Clare *internist, hematologist, oncologist*
Volgman, Annabelle Santos *cardiologist, educator*
Waxler, Beverly Jean *anesthesiologist, physician*
Winter, Jane *medical educator*
Zee, Phyllis C. *physician, educator, researcher*

Dixon
Polascik, Mary Ann *ophthalmologist*

Downers Grove
Ozog, Diane L. *allergist*
Zillmer, Debra Ann *orthopedist, sports medicine physician*

Elmhurst
Blain, Charlotte Marie *internist, educator*

Evanston
Schwartz, Neena Betty *endocrinologist, educator*

Forest Park
Saiyed, Humaira *psychiatrist, director*

Glenview
Casas, Laurie Ann *plastic surgeon*
Macsai, Marian Sue *ophthalmologist*
Rubin, Susan M. *neurologist*

Hinsdale
Dillon, Jane Elizabeth *otolaryngologist*
Mahmood, Samar *psychiatrist*

Indianhead Park
Johnson, Anita (Mary Anita Johnson) *physician, medical association administrator*

Lake Forest
Callan, Clair Marie *physician, consultant*

Lombard
Kasprow, Barbara Anne *biomedical researcher, writer*

Maywood
Albain, Kathy S. *oncologist*
Gaynor, Ellen Rose *hematologist*
Nand, Sucha *medical educator*

Northbrook
Herrerias, Carla Trevette *epidemiologist, health science association administrator*

Oak Brook
Fritzsche, Peggy J. *medical association administrator, radiologist*
Imran, Ayesha *internist*

Oak Park
Schlesinger, Harriet Rose *retired psychiatrist*

Palos Heights
Ilangovan, Saroja *retired pathologist*

Park Ridge
Parilla, Barbara V. *medicine specialist*

Peoria
Poteat, Thena G. *psychiatrist*

River Grove
Hillert, Gloria Bonnin *anatomist, educator*

Saint Francisville
Harezi, Ilonka Jo *medical technology research executive*

Springfield
Woodson, Gayle Ellen *otolaryngologist*

Sycamore
Hauser, Lynn Elizabeth *eye surgeon*

Yorkville
McEachern, Joan *medical association administrator*

INDIANA

Carmel
Cohen, Marlene Lois *pharmacologist*

Fishers
Moredock, Rebecca Juanette *psychiatrist*

Gary
Zunich, Janice *pediatrician, geneticist, educator, health facility administrator*

Indianapolis
Hill, Beverly Ellen *medical educator*
Jackson, Valerie Pascuzzi *radiologist, educator*
Knoebel, Suzanne Buckner *cardiologist, educator*
Richter, Judith Anne *pharmacologist, educator*
Robinson, Rebecca Lynne *medical researcher*

Merrillville
Wang, Josephine L. Fen *physician*

Sullivan
Chavez, Mary Ann *osteopathic family physician*

Terre Haute
Wisbey, Lou Ann *radiologist, department chairman*

IOWA

Davenport
Davis, Pamela F. *orthopedist, surgeon*

Des Moines
Green, Kelli Charnell *psychiatrist*
Wattleworth, Roberta Ann *physician*

Iowa City
Andreasen, Nancy Coover *psychiatrist, educator, neuroscientist*
Niebyl, Jennifer Robinson *obstetrician, gynecologist, educator*
Tsalikian, Eva *physician, educator*

Marshalltown
Packer, Karen Gilliland *cancer patient educator, researcher*

KANSAS

Atwood
Girouard, Gail Patricia *family practice physician*

Hutchinson
Graves, Kathryn Louise *dermatologist*

Kansas City
Hellings, Jessica Alice *psychiatrist, educator*
Johnson, Joy Ann *diagnostic radiologist*

Shawnee Mission
Bell, Deloris Wiley *physician*

KENTUCKY

Berea
Lamb, Irene Hendricks *medical researcher*

Hyden
Nienstadt, Jean E. (Jean E. Sullivan) *physician*

Lexington
Casey, Baretta A. *physician, educator*

Louisville
Ammon, Jennifer Tucker *orthopedist, surgeon*
Ballew, Laurie K. *psychiatrist*
DeMunbrun-Harmon, Donne O'Donnell *retired family physician*
Dunbar-Richman, Anne Cameron *pathologist*

Waco
Hackman, Vicki Lou *physician*

LOUISIANA

Bossier City
Lim, Diana Magpayo *internist*

Deridder
Zamboni-Cutter, Kathryn M. *obstetrician, gynecologist, military officer*

Houma
Eschete, Mary Louise *internist*

Madisonville
Young, Lucy Cleaver *retired physician*

New Orleans
Duncan, Margaret Caroline *physician*
Foundas, Anne Leigh *psychiatrist*
Gatipon, Betty Becker *medical educator, consultant*

Shreveport
Mancini, Mary Catherine *cardiothoracic surgeon, researcher*

Slidell
McBurney, Elizabeth Innes *dermatologist, physician, educator*

Sulphur
Toniette, Sallye Jean *physician*

MAINE

Auburn
Bartlett, Elizabeth Louise *psychiatrist*

Bangor
Arps, Corabell Bennett *psychiatrist*

Brunswick
Karchov, Tatyana *psychiatrist*

Portland
Wilkinson, Barbara J. *pediatrician, educator*

Yarmouth
Northrup, Christiane *obstetrician, gynecologist*

MARYLAND

Andrews Air Force Base
Hall, Molly J. *psychiatrist, educator*

Baltimore
Alpern, Linda Lee Wevodau *retired health agency administrator*
Aneja, Alka *child psychiatrist*
Aurelian, Laure *medical sciences educator*
Blakemore, Karin Jane *obstetrician, geneticist*
Brodie, Angela M. *biomedical researcher, educator*
Colomer, Veronica *medical educator, researcher*
DeAngelis, Catherine D. *pediatrics educator*
DeLateur, Barbara Jane *medical educator*
Edwards, Willarda V. *internist, medical association administrator*
Ferencz, Charlotte *pediatrician, epidemiologist, preventive medicine physician, educator*
Freischlag, Julie Ann *surgeon*
Fried, Linda P. *medical educator*
Godenne, Ghislaine Dudley *physician, psychotherapist, educator*
Goldman, Lynn Rose *medical educator*
Litrenta, Frances Marie *psychiatrist*
Matjasko, M. Jane *anesthesiologist, educator*
Maumenee, Irene H. *ophthalmology educator*
Migeon, Barbara Ruben *pediatrician, geneticist, educator*
O'Toole, Tara Jeanne *medical educator, former federal agency administrator*
Palka, Tamara *psychiatrist*
Schoenrich, Edyth Hull *internist, preventive medicine physician*
Silbergeld, Ellen Kovner *epidemiologist, researcher, toxicologist*
Starfield, Barbara Helen *pediatrician, educator*
Young, Barbara *psychiatrist, psychotherapist, educator, photographer*

Bethesda
Anderson, Stasia Ann *medical researcher*
Black, Barbara Onderchek *retired physician*
Brinton, Louise A. *cancer epidemiologist*
Christian, Michaele Chamblee *internist, oncologist*
Gorin, Susan *medical association administrator*
Guttman, Helene Nathan *biomedical consultant, transpersonal counselor*
Haseltine, Florence Pat *obstetrician, gynecologist, medical association administrator*
Herman, Mary Margaret *neuropathologist*
Jaffe, Elaine Sarkin *pathologist*
Johnson, Joyce Marie *psychiatrist, public health service officer, epidemiologist*
Kelly, Kathleen *medical researcher*
Kirschstein, Ruth Lillian *physician*
Klee, Claude Blenc *medical researcher*
Mackall, Crystal L. *medical researcher*
Nabel, Elizabeth G. *cardiologist, researcher*
Rapoport, Judith *psychiatrist*
Sternberg, Esther May *neuroendocrinologist, immunologist, hematologist*
Tanzi, Elizabeth Lyn *dermatologist*
Vaitukaitis, Judith Louise *medical researcher*
Volkow, Nora Dolores *medical researcher, director*
Vonderhaar, Barbara K. *medical researcher*

Chevy Chase
Kullen, Shirley Robinowitz *psychiatric epidemiologist, consultant*
Lynn, D. Joanne *physician, researcher*

Clinton
Cruz, Wilhelmina Mangahas *critical care physician, educator*

College Park
Beharry, Avalaura Gaither *healer*

Colmar Manor
Stallworth, Monica Lavaughn *geriatrician*

Columbia
Jani, Sushma Niranjan *pediatric psychiatrist*

Frederick
Colburn, Nancy Hall *medical researcher*

Gaithersburg
Hegyeli, Ruth Ingeborg Elisabeth Johnsson *pathologist, federal official*

Greenbelt
Obamogie, Mercy A. *physician*

Havre De Grace
Soldunias, Bernadette Louise *psychiatrist*

Laurel
Highman, Barbara *dermatologist*

Pikesville
Sokol, Marian *medical association administrator*

Rockville
Clancy, Carolyn M. *internist, federal agency administrator*
Haffner, Marlene Elisabeth *internist, public health administrator*
Nay, Patricia Tomsko *medical association administrator*
Pryor, Shannon Penick *otolaryngologist*
Saljinska-Markovic, Olivera T. *oncology researcher, educator*
Schoenbrun, Lois *medical association administrator*

Silver Spring
Adams, Diane Loretta *physician*
Beard, Lillian B. McLean *pediatrician, consultant*
Foley, Mary E. *medical association administrator, nursing administrator*
Supanich, Barbara Ann *physician*

Towson
Boyle, Marcia *medical association administrator*
Orlinsky, Diane Julie *dermatologist*

Upper Marlboro
Jones-Lukács, Elizabeth Lucille *physician*

Wheaton
White, Martha Vetter *allergist, immunologist*

MASSACHUSETTS

Boston
Abrahm, Janet Lee *hematologist, oncologist, educator, palliative care specialist*
Angell, Marcia *pathologist, editor-in-chief*
Antman, Karen H. *oncologist, educator, dean*
Bigby, JudyAnn *medical educator*
Brugge, Joan S. *medical educator*
Donahoe, Patricia Kilroy *surgeon*
Duncan, Lyn M. *pathologist, educator*
Eckstein, Marlene R. *vascular radiologist*
Gilchrest, Barbara Ann *dermatologist*
Gipson, Ilene Kay *ophthalmologist, educator*
Goldie, Sue J. *health service researcher*
Gottlieb, Alice B. *dermatologist*
Goumnerova, Liliana Christova *physician, neurosurgeon, educator*
Hay, Elizabeth Dexter *embryologist, educator*
Iezzoni, Lisa I. *medical educator, healthcare educator, researcher*
Kahn, Barbara B. *endocrinologist*
Manson, JoAnn Elisabeth *endocrinologist*
McCormick, Marie Clare *pediatrician, educator*
Meyer, Fremonta Lee *psychiatrist*
Misra, Madhusmita *pediatric neuroendocrinologist, educator*
Nadelson, Carol Cooperman *psychiatrist, educator*
Nour, Nawal M. *obstetrician, gynecologist, health facility administrator*
Ouellette, Eileen Marie *neurologist, consultant*
Rupnick, Maria Ann *internist*
Schaller, Jane Green *pediatrician*
Seddon, Johanna Margaret *ophthalmologist, epidemiologist*
Seidman, Christine E. *medical educator*
Van Marter, Linda Joanne *pediatrician, educator, neonatologist, researcher*
Willock, Marcelle Monica *retired medical educator*
Young, Anne B. *neurologist, educator*

Brockton
Carlson, Desiree Anice *pathologist*
Festin, Fe Erlita Diolazo *psychiatrist, director*

Brookline
Jakab, Irene *psychiatrist*
Sethi, Chander Mohini *gynecologist, obstetrician, consultant*

Cambridge
Eisenberg, Carola *psychiatrist, educator*
Graybiel, Ann M. *medical educator*
Lindblad-Toh, Kerstin *medical researcher*
Mathews, Joan Helene *pediatrician*
O'Shea, Erin K. *biomedical researcher*
Rho, Yanni *psychiatrist*
von Deck, Mercedes Dina *orthopedist, surgeon*

Cataumet
Murdock, Rosamond Louise *retired pediatrician*

Chestnut Hill
Gottlieb, Marise Suss *epidemiologist*

Dartmouth
Leclair, Susan Jean *hematologist, clinical laboratory scientist, educator*

Dover
Buyse, Marylou *pediatrician, geneticist, medical association administrator*

Framingham
Zamvil, Linda Susan *psychiatrist, educator*

Marlborough
Miotto, Mary Elizabeth G. *pediatrician*

Melrose
Desforges, Jane Fay *retired internist, hematologist, educator*

Newton
Bassuk, Ellen Linda *psychiatrist*
Stark, Martha *psychiatrist, environmental medicine physician*

Newton Center
Lapierre, Katherine Ann *psychiatrist, educator*

Newton Highlands
Brant, Renee S. Tankenoff *psychiatrist*

Peabody
Birdsall, Melinda R. *gynecologist*

Rockland
Blethen, Sandra Lee *pediatric endocrinologist*

Roxbury Crossing
Smith, Susie Irene *cytologist, histologist*

Springfield
Martorell, Claudia *infectious diseases physician*

Vineyard Haven
Jacobs, Gretchen Huntley *psychiatrist*

Waltham
Birren, Susan J. *medical educator*

Wellesley
Eappen, Deborah S. *ophthalmologist*

West Springfield
Desai, Veena Balvantrai *obstetrician, gynecologist, educator*

Westborough
Walker, Jeri A. *psychiatrist*

Worcester
Byatt, Nancy *psychiatrist*
Selin, Lisa K. *physician*

MICHIGAN

Ann Arbor
Baler, Blanche Kimoto *retired child psychiatrist*
Bloom, Jane Maginnis *emergency physician*
Doyle, Constance Talcott Johnston *physician, educator, medical association administrator*
Farmer, Cheryl Christine *internist, industrial hygienist*
Green, Carmen R. *anesthesiologist, pain medicine physician*
Lozoff, Betsy *pediatrician, educator*
Sheon, Amy Ruth *biomedical researcher*
Strang, Ruth Hancock *pediatrician, educator, cardiologist, priest*

Bloomfield Hills
Ball, Patricia Ann *physician*

Dearborn Heights
Chapper, Barbara Mae *retired pediatrician*

Detroit
Jenkins-Anderson, Barbara Jeanne *pathologist, educator*
Lusher, Jeanne Marie *pediatric hematologist, educator*

East Lansing
Reinhart, Mary Ann *medical board executive*

Grosse Ile
Stryker, Joan Copeland *retired obstetrician, retired gynecologist, educator*

Hamtramck
LeVan, Deborah Jo *internist*

Livonia
Baskin, Victoria *child and adolescent psychiatrist*
Thoms, Susan Stuckey *ophthalmologist*

Marquette
Mahmood, Tallat *oncologist, hematologist*

Oak Park
Rutherford, Guinevere Faye *surgeon*

Pigeon
Jackson, Nancy Ellen *retired internist*

Royal Oak
Ernstoff, Raina Marcia *neurologist*
McCarroll, Kathleen Ann *radiologist, educator*

Southfield
Ben-Ami, Dorit Amalia *psychiatrist*
Hartman-Abramson, Ilene *medical educator*

Troy
Schafer, Sharon Marie *anesthesiologist*

Warren
Henry, Julie L. *orthopedist, surgeon*

MINNESOTA

Fairmont
Sadek, Noha *psychiatrist*

Hastings
Orr, Jennie Marie (Jennie Thomas) *family physician*

Minneapolis
Chavers, Blanche Marie *pediatrician, educator, researcher*
Corey, Candy Abramson *oncologist*
Harper, Patricia Nelsen *psychiatrist*
Joseph, Marilyn Susan *gynecologist*
Olson, Cynthia Louise *dermatologist*
Powell, Deborah Elizabeth *pathologist, dean*

Rochester
Hart, Dionne A. *physician*
Kantarci, Kejal *radiologist, researcher*
Varkey, Prathibha *preventive medicine physician, medical educator*

Saint Cloud
Olson, Barbara Ford *physician*

Saint Paul
Rydell, Catherine M. *medical association administrator, former state legislator*
Zander, Janet Adele *psychiatrist*

Stillwater
Asch, Susan McClellan *pediatrician*

MISSISSIPPI

Brooklyn
Gerald, Carolyn Aileen T. *emergency physician*

Jackson
Brewer, Cheryl Ann *obstetrics and gynecology educator*
Hawkins, Mary Elizabeth *obstetrician, gynecologist, educator*
Houston, Gerry Ann *oncologist*
Lawson, Patricia Bowman *physician, educator*

Tutwiler
Brooks, Sister Anne *osteopath*

MISSOURI

Columbia
Cunningham, Milamari Antoinella *retired anesthesiologist*
James, Elizabeth Joan Plogsted *pediatrician, educator*
Nittler, Jessica Rae *psychiatrist*
Nolph, Georgia Bower *physician*
Tarnove, Lorraine *medical association executive*
Vale, Janie Rhea *physician*

Independence
Dorshow-Gordon, Ellen *epidemiologist*

Kirkwood
Davis, Marilyn Jean *medical educator*

Lees Summit
Cobbinah, Ingenue F. *obstetrician, gynecologist*

Maryland Heights
Wasserman, Abby Lois *child, adolescent and family psychiatrist*

Poplar Bluff
Peick, Ann Lutzeier *surgeon*

Saint Louis
Case-Schmidt, Mary E. *pathologist, educator*
Chambliss, Linda R. *obstetrician, consultant*
Corrigan, Meg M. *psychiatrist*
Goldberg, Anne Carol *physician, educator*
Holmes, Nancy Elizabeth *pediatrician*
Powell, Jill Kirsten *medical educator, obstetrician, gynecologist*
Purkerson, Mabel Louise *physician, educator, physiologist*
Robins, Lee Nelken *medical educator*
Ryall, Jo-Ellyn M. *psychiatrist*
Ternberg, Jessie Lamoin *pediatric surgeon, educator*
Walentik, Corinne Anne *pediatrician*

NEBRASKA

Omaha
Burns, Erica Marie *orthopedist, surgeon*
Kessinger, Margaret Anne *medical educator*
Rogan, Eleanor Groeniger *oncologist, educator*
Swindells, Susan *HIV specialist*
Zardetto-Smith, Andrea *medical educator*

NEVADA

Reno
Small, Elisabeth Chan *psychiatrist, educator*

NEW HAMPSHIRE

Lebanon
Galton, Valerie Anne *endocrinologist, educator*

Littleton
Kelly, Dorothy Helen *pediatrician, educator*

Walpole
Arnold, Jeanne Fessenden *retired physician*

NEW JERSEY

Andover
Mohammadi, Mina *physician, researcher*

Bridgewater
Bernson, Marcella S. *psychiatrist*

Camden
O'Neal, Gwenelle Marine S. *mental health services administrator*

Cape May
Byrnes, Christine Ann *internist*

Dayton
Istafanous, Afifa W. *physician*

East Brunswick
Rust, Mildred D. *retired psychiatrist*

East Hanover
Nemecek, Georgina Marie *molecular pharmacologist*

East Orange
Brundage, Gertrude Barnes *pediatrician*

Edgewater
Ellis, Carol Oster *rehabilitation physician*

Englewood
Frieden, Faith Joy *obstetrician*
Hurst, Wendy R(obin) *obstetrician*
Polk, Gene-Ann *retired pediatrician*

Englewood Cliffs
Chase-Brand, Julia *psychiatrist, researcher*
Gurtman, Alejandra C. *epidemiologist, research scientist*

Fanwood
Butler, Grace Caroline *medical researcher*

Guttenberg
Wright, Jane Cooke *oncologist, educator, consultant*

Hackensack
Haines, Kathleen Ann *pediatrician, educator*

Hamilton
Sipski, Mary Leonide *physiatrist, health facility administrator*

Hillsdale
Copeland, Lois Jacqueline *physician*

Little Silver
Marcus, Abir A. *psychiatrist*

Lumberton
Campagnolo, Mary Frances *physician*

Mahwah
Bello, Mary *physician*

Millburn
O'Byrne, Elizabeth Milikin *retired pharmacologist*

Montclair
Reichslan, Michele B. *psychiatrist*

Morristown
Finkel, Marion Judith *internist, pharmaceutical administrator*
Rogachefsky, Arlene Sandra *dermatologist*

Neptune
Laraya-Cuasay, Lourdes Redublo *pediatrician, pulmonologist, educator*

New Brunswick
Bachmann, Gloria Ann *obstetrician, gynecologist, educator*
Day-Salvatore, Debra Lynn *medical geneticist*
Formica, Palma Elizabeth *physician*
Leventhal, Elaine A. *internist*
Saidi, Parvin *hematologist, medical educator*
Snyder, Barbara K. *pediatrician, educator*
Todd, Mary Beth *oncologist, researcher*
Weiss, Lynne S. *pediatrician, educator*

Newark
Anderson, Gina Marie *obstetrician, gynecologist*
Cohen, Alice *hematologist*
Liu, Qinyue (Sherry Liu) *physician, consultant*
Raveché, Elizabeth Scott *immunologist, educator*

Piscataway
Volfson-Doubova, Elena *psychiatrist, researcher*

Plainsboro
Lansing, Martha Hempel *physician*

Princeton
Lavizzo-Mourey, Risa Juanita *medical foundation administrator, academic administrator*
Troyanskaya, Olga *biomedical researcher, computer scientist*

Stratford
Robinson, Mary Jo *pathologist*
Vitale, Patty A. *pediatrician, consultant, medical educator*

Summit
Greenberg, Rosalie *child psychiatrist*
Selinger, Sharon Eve *endocrinologist*

Teaneck
Halper, June *medical center director*
Wolff, Marianne *retired pathologist*

Totowa
Wong, Cheryl M. *psychiatrist*

Trenton
Paul, Sindy Michelle *preventive medicine physician*

Westwood
Fortunato, Julie Marianne *neurologist*

Wyckoff
Marcus, Linda Susan *dermatologist*

NEW MEXICO

Albuquerque
Chang, Barbara Karen *medical educator*
Clarke, Gray B. *psychiatrist*
Saland, Linda Carol *anatomist, educator, neuroscientist*
Worrell, Audrey Martiny *geriatric psychiatrist*

Los Alamos
Smith, Fredrica Emrich *rheumatologist, internist*

Rio Rancho
Severino, Sally K. *retired psychiatrist*

NEW YORK

Albany
Howard, Lyn Jennifer *medical educator*
Lepow, Martha Lipson *pediatric educator, consultant*

Alexandria Bay
Burris, Harriet Louise *emergency physician*

Alfred Station
Knowlton, Sylvia Kelley *physician*

Amagansett
Fleetwood, M. Freile *psychiatrist, educator*

Binghamton
Michael, Sandra Dale *biomedical educator, researcher*

Bronx
Coupey, Susan McGuire *pediatrician, educator*
Dutcher, Janice Jean Phillips *oncologist*
Gonzalez, Angela E. *obstetrician, gynecologist*
Heagarty, Margaret Caroline *retired pediatrician*
Horwitz, Susan Band *pharmacologist*
Iannotta, Patricia N. *physician*
Radel, Eva *pediatrician, hematologist*
Rapin, Isabelle *physician*
Satir, Birgit H. *medical educator, researcher*
Shapiro, Nella Irene *surgeon, educator*
Stein, Ruth Elizabeth Klein *physician*
Velazquez, Lyzette Eileen *neurologist*

Bronxville
Levitt, Miriam *pediatrician*

Brooklyn
Belotserkovskaya, Yanina *internist*
Bhattacharya, Bhaswati *preventive medicine physician*
Coch, Dorrit Aria *obstetrician, gynecologist*
Etkin, Alexandra *physician*
Kilanko, Oyenike Eunice *obstetrician, gynecologist*
Luhrs, Carol *physician*
Mirra, Suzanne Samuels *pathologist*
Norstrand, Iris Fletcher *psychiatrist, neurologist, educator*
Pierre, Mirelle *physician, psychotherapist, health facility administrator*
Trice, Dorothy Louise *physician*
Webber, Carolyn Ann (Mrs. Gerald E. Thomson) *pathologist, educator*

Buffalo
Ambrus, Clara Maria *physician*
Baer, Maria Renée *hematologist, researcher*
Dudziak, Emma M. *cardiac sonographer*
Kartha, Indira *retired pathologist*
Mutton, Holly Beth *psychiatrist*
Virk, Subhdeep *psychiatrist*
Wactawski-Wende, Jean *epidemiologist, educator, researcher*

Central Valley
Neyman, Paula *pediatrician*

Clifton Park
Glasgow, Constance Lenore *pediatrician*

Cobleskill
Colony, Pamela Cameron *medical researcher, educator*

Dix Hills
Golden, Shawna *biomedical researcher*

East Aurora
Hu, YuinSien Irene *obstetrician, gynecologist*

Elmhurst
Prypchan, Lida D. *psychiatrist*

Fishkill
Colman, Jenny Meyer *psychiatrist*

Flushing
Baik-Han, Won H. *pediatrician, educator, consultant*

Forest Hills
Rhonda, Karol *dermatologist*

Great Neck
Lieber, Constance E. *medical association administrator*

Ithaca
Whitaker, Susanne Kanis *veterinary medical librarian*

Jamaica
Flink, Elisheva H. *orthopedic surgeon*
Kemeny, M. Margaret *oncologist, surgeon, educator, hospital administrator*

Kingston
Johnson, Marie-Louise Tully *dermatologist, educator*

Lancaster
Genewick, Tiffany Boquard *obstetrician, gynecologist*

Mamaroneck
Rosenthal, Elizabeth Robbins *physician*

Manhasset
Kahn, Ellen Ida *physician, consultant*
Krim, Eileen Y. *physician*
Siller, Pamela Pearl *psychiatrist*

New Hyde Park
Seltzer, Vicki Lynn *obstetrician, gynecologist*

New Windsor
Carson, Teresa Catherine *pediatrician*

New York
Albu, Jeanine Breazu *endocrinologist, educator*
Asbury, Carolyn *neuroscience researcher*
Barker, Barbara Ann *ophthalmologist*
Barlow, Barbara Ann *surgeon*
Berman, Carol Wendy *psychiatrist*
Beverley, Cordia Luvonne *gastroenterologist*
Buchbinder, Ellen Maud *allergist*
Byrne, Jennie Louise *psychiatrist, researcher*
Canetti, Alexandra *psychiatrist*
Cerfolio, Nina Estelle *psychiatrist, educator*
Clark, Sheryl Diane *physician*
Cooper, Jennifer Royann *psychiatrist*
Copeland, Michelle *plastic surgeon*
Cuttner, Janet *hematologist, educator*
Devi, Gayatri *physician*
Diaz, Angela *pediatrician, educator*
Doyle, Eugenie Fleri *pediatrician, cardiologist, educator*
Economos, Katherine *oncologist*
Edelstein, Barbara A. *radiologist*
Erlenmeyer-Kimling, L. *psychiatrist, researcher*
Estabrook, Alison *surgeon, educator*
Felderman, Lenora I. *physician*
Fischbarg, Zulema F. *pediatrician*
Formenti, Silvia C. *radiation oncologist*
Fullilove, Mindy Thompson *psychiatrist*
Gebbie, Kristine Moore *medical educator*
Gendler, Ellen *dermatologist*
Goldberg, Nieca *cardiologist, educator*
Gordon, Marsha L. *dermatologist*
Grafstein, Bernice *physiology and neuroscience educator, researcher*
Griffiths, Sylvia Preston *physician, educator*
Grossman, Melanie *dermatologist*
Hann, Lucy E. *radiologist, educator*
Harley, Naomi Hallden *radiologist, educator, environmental scientist*
Hawkins, Katherine Ann *hematologist, educator, lawyer*
Henschke, Claudia Ingrid *physician, radiologist*
Hertzig, Margaret E. *psychiatrist*
Hochlerin, Diane *pediatrician, educator*
Holland, Jimmie C. *psychiatrist, educator*
Holmgren, Anna *psychiatrist*
Jurka, Edith Mila *psychiatrist, researcher*
Kalinich, Lila Joyce *psychiatrist, educator*
Kanick, Virginia *retired radiologist*
Kapelman, Barbara Ann *internist, hepatologist, gastroenterologist, educator*
Katz, Lois Anne *internist, nephrologist*
Katz-Bearnot, Sherry P. *psychiatrist, educator*
Kopenhaver, Patricia Ellsworth *podiatrist*
Kourides, Ione Anne *endocrinologist, researcher, educator*
Kramer, Elissa Lipcon *nuclear medicine physician, educator*
Kreek, Mary Jeanne *physician*
Kurli, Madhavi *ophthalmologist*
Langan, Marie-Noelle Suzanne *cardiologist, educator*
Lee, Vivian S. *radiologist*
Leeman, Eve *psychiatrist*
Legato, Marianne *internist, medical educator*
Malihan, Amie A. *physician*
Mason, Carol Ann *medical educator*
Matera, Cristina *gynecologist, educator*
Mayo-Johnston, Julia A. *psychiatry professor, psychotherapist*
McCormack, Patricia Marie *retired thoracic surgeon*
McLaurin, Toni Marie *orthopedist, surgeon, educator*
McNutt, Edith Richards *psychiatrist*
Mildvan, Donna *infectious diseases physician*
Milman, Doris Hope *retired pediatrician, psychiatrist, educator*
Mones, Joan Michele *pathologist*
Moomjy, Maureen O'Brien *surgeon, educator*
Moore, Anne *physician*
Moss-Salentijn, Letty (Aleida Moss-Salentijn) *anatomist, educator*
Nass, Ruth *pediatric neurologist*
Nelson, Joyce M. *medical association administrator*
New, Maria Iandolo *pediatrician, educator*
Oberfield, Sharon Elefant *pediatric endocrinologist*
Oberlander, Eryn L. *psychiatrist, preventive medicine physician*
Ofri, Danielle *internist*
O'Looney, Patricia Anne *medical association administrator*
Osborn, June Elaine *pediatrician, microbiologist, educator, foundation administrator*
Pfeifer, Tracy M. *plastic surgeon*
Pitt, Jane *medical educator*
Pogue, Velvie Anne *nephrologist, educator*
Polenz, Joanna Magda *psychiatrist*
Poynor, Elizabeth Ann *surgeon, researcher*
Purcell, Karen Barlar *naturopathic physician, nutritionist, opera singer, writer*
Quackenbush, Margery Clouser *psychoanalyst, researcher*
Reichman, Bonnie S. *oncologist*
Ren, Christine *surgeon*
Rifkind, Arleen B. *pharmacologist, researcher, educator*
Role, Lorna W. *medical educator*
Rubinstein, Rosalinda *allergist, medical association administrator*
Schuster, Carlotta Lief *psychiatrist*
Scott, Susan Craig *plastic surgeon*
Seele, Pernessa C. *immunologist, health science association administrator*
Siegel, Heidi Ellen *neurologist, researcher*
Sisakian, Marina *psychiatrist*
Sitarz, Anneliese Lotte *pediatrician, educator, physician*
Snyderman, Selma Eleanore *pediatrician, educator*
Soave, Rosemary *internist*
Solomon, Gail Ellen *physician*
Stein, Zena A. *retired epidemiologist, educator*
Steinherz, Laurel Judith *pediatric cardiologist*
Stone, Shirley M. *pediatrician, educator*
Strachan, Dina Dawn *dermatologist, educator*
Supino, Phyllis Gail *medical researcher, educator*
Suzuki, Wendy A. *neurology educator*
Tanenbaum, Judith Hertz *psychiatrist*
Tolchin, Joan Gubin *psychiatrist, educator*

Tyler, Wakenda Kachina *orthopedist, surgeon, researcher*
Urban, Nina B.L. *psychiatrist, psychotherapist, researcher*
Weiss, Carol Juliet *psychiatrist*
Weissman, Myrna M. *epidemiologist, researcher, medical educator*
Welch, Martha Grace *physician, researcher*
Wexler, Patricia Susan *dermatologist, surgeon*
Wolden, Suzanne Leesa *pediatric radiation oncologist*
Yin, Beatrice Wei-Tze *medical researcher*
Young, Estelle Irene *dermatologist, educator*
Zucker-Franklin, Dorothea *internist, educator*

Ossining
Poh-Fitzpatrick, Maureen B. *dermatologist, educator*

Plattsburgh
Rech, Susan Anita *obstetrician, gynecologist*

Pleasant Valley
Murthy, Padmini *physician*

Poughkeepsie
Carino, Aurora Lao *psychiatrist, health facility administrator*
Wolfersteig, Jean Lois *medical association administrator, educator*

Purchase
Frost, Elizabeth Ann McArthur *physician*

Rego Park
Davidov, Ludmila G. *psychiatrist*

Richmond Hill
Malhotra, Madhu Bala *psychiatrist*

Rochester
Danforth-Morningstar, Elizabeth *obstetrician, gynecologist*
Haywood, Anne Mowbray *pediatrician, educator*
Lawrence, Ruth Anderson *pediatrician*
Lindsey, Margaret A. *psychiatrist*
Maquat, Lynne E. *biomedical researcher*
McAnarney, Elizabeth R. *pediatrician, educator*
Mok, Carolyn Lee *physician*
Rehmani, Shahida *psychiatrist*
Smith, Julia Ladd *oncologist, physician*

Roslyn
Hartman, Nancy Lee *physician*

Rye
Downer, Allison V. *adult, forensic, child and adolescent psychiatrist*

Rye Brook
Lo Russo, Diane *radiologist*

Saratoga Springs
Muller, Susan Marie *physician*

Smithtown
Tuzel, Suzanne L. *psychiatrist*

Stony Brook
Lane, Dorothy Spiegel *preventive medicine physician*
Leske, M. Cristina *medical researcher, educator*
Steinberg, Amy Wishner *dermatologist*

Syosset
Rehm, Carolyn Agnes *pediatrician, educator*

Syracuse
Horst, Pamela Sue *medical educator, physician*
Numann, Patricia Joy *surgeon, educator*
Rogers, Sherry Anne *physician*
Streeten, Barbara Wiard *ophthalmologist, medical educator*

Tarrytown
Grant, Irene H. *epidemiologist*

Troy
Bruce, Melody Ann *obstetrician, gynecologist*

Tuxedo Park
Regan, Ellen Frances (Mrs. Walston Shepard Brown) *ophthalmologist, educator*

Valhalla
Kline, Susan Anderson *medical educator, internist*

Warsaw
Dy-Ang, Anita C. *pediatrician*

Water Mill
Chalif, Ronnie *medical association administrator, artist*

West Haverstraw
King, Marjorie Louise *cardiologist*

White Plains
Baran, Xiaolei Yu *physician, psychiatry professor*
Eil, Lois Helen *retired physician*
Kim, Jean *psychiatrist*
Monteferrante, Judith Catherine *cardiologist*
Pfeffer, Cynthia Roberta *psychiatrist, educator*
Silverman, Amy Jocelyn *psychiatrist*

NORTH CAROLINA

Asheville
Hammett, Doris Bixby *retired pediatrician*
Turcot, Marguerite Hogan *medical researcher*

Black Mountain
Blackwell, Anna Nelle *medical educator, medical technician*

Brevard
Finnerty, Frances Martin *medical administrator*

Chapel Hill
Fletcher, Suzanne Wright *epidemiologist, medical educator, editor*
Kagetsu, Naomi J. *dermatologist*
Martikainen, A(une) Helen *retired health specialist educator*
Pisano, Etta D. *radiologist, educator*
Prather, Donna Lynn *psychiatrist*
Wilfert, Catherine M. *medical association administrator, pediatrician, epidemiologist, educator*

Charlotte
Jain, Astrid Genda *obstetrician, gynecologist*

Durham
Armstrong, Brenda Estelle *pediatrician, cardiologist*
Buckley, Rebecca Hatcher *allergist, immunologist, pediatrician, educator*
Iarovici, Doris M *psychiatrist, writer*
Kaprielian, Victoria Susan *medical educator*
Kurtzberg, Joanne *pediatrician, educator*
Nye, Mary Jane Love *pediatrician, educator*

Fairview
Mullins, Diane Louise *dermatologist*

Greenville
Johnson, Cynda Ann *physician, educator*
Mega, Lesly Tamarin *psychiatrist, educator*

Hickory
Barnes, Sylvia *family practice physician*

High Point
Draelos, Zoe Diana *dermatologist, consultant*

Pine Knoll Shores
Graham, Gloria Flippin *dermatologist*

Raeford
Abreu, Sue Hudson *physician, retired military officer, health facility administrator, consultant*

Raleigh
Bateman, Angela Anderson *anesthetist*
Hardison, Cynthia Ann Stoltze *hematologist, retired oncologist*

Rockingham
Jackson, Anita Louise *otolaryngologist, editor-in-chief*

Southport
Kahai, Jugta *pediatrician*

Washington
Strayhorn Crump, Joretta Petrice *health educator, substance abuse consultant*

Waxhaw
Edwards, Irene Elizabeth (Libby Edwards) *dermatologist, educator, medical researcher*

Winston Salem
Ferree, Carolyn Ruth *radiation oncologist, educator*

NORTH DAKOTA

Bismarck
Schwartz, Judy Ellen *thoracic surgeon*

Fargo
Ghazi, Stefanie Sara *obstetrician, gynecologist*
Turka, Voleen Claire *surgeon*

Grand Forks
Sobus, Kerstin MaryLouise *physician, physical therapist*

OHIO

Akron
Bilgé-Johnson, Sumru A. *child psychiatrist*
Evenski, Andrea Jean *orthopedist*
Houston, Alma Faye *psychiatrist*

Ashland
Kodz, Irena Cheslavovna *internist*

Bowling Green
McCutchan, Patricia Lynn *physician*

Cincinnati
Boyd, Deborah Ann *pediatrician*
Ching, Ho *surgeon*
De Courten-Myers, Gabrielle Marguerite *neuropathologist*
Hess, Evelyn Victorine *medical educator*
Kalfa, Theodosia Anastasios *pediatrician, educator*
Loggie, Jennifer Mary Hildreth *retired physician, educator*

Cleveland
Davis, Pamela Bowes *pediatric pulmonologist*
Denko, Joanne D. *psychiatrist, writer*
Olness, Karen Norma *medical educator*
Pujana, Maria Jose *neurologist*
Sila, Cathy Ann *neurologist*

Columbus
Bloomfield, Clara Derber *oncologist, educator, medical institute administrator*
Codogni, Iwona M. *scientific information analyst, chemist*
Haque, Malika Hakim *pediatrician*
Huheey, Marilyn Jane *ophthalmologist, educator*
Lander, Ruth A. *medical association administrator*
Long, Sarah Elizabeth Brackney *physician*
Stephens, Sheryl Lynne *physician*
Wolfe, Claire V. *physiatrist*

Dayton
Gillig, Paulette Marie *psychiatry educator, researcher*
Monk, Susan Marie *pediatrician, educator*
Nanagas, Maria Teresita Cruz *pediatrician, educator*

Findlay
Gunda, Rajeswari *oncologist*

Mason
Solomon, Susanne Nina *podiatrist, surgeon*

Medina
Jeffers, Lynette A. *anesthetist*

Pepper Pike
Helfand, Toby Scheintaub *retired dermatologist*

Rootstown
Nora, Lois Margaret *neurologist, educator, academic administrator, dean*

Toledo
Rejent, Marian Magdalen *retired pediatrician*

Wadsworth
Aragon, Lynn D. *retired physician*

Wilmington
Hamilton, Maxine Keiter *retired physician*

OKLAHOMA

Edmond
Haywood, B(etty) J(ean) *anesthesiologist*

Hennessey
Fast, Naomi Mae *retired physician*

Miami
Koehler, Tammie *obstetrician, gynecologist*

Norman
Cochran, Gloria Grimes *retired pediatrician*

Oklahoma City
Bahr, Carman Bloedow *internist*
Rosenberg, Emily *psychiatrist*

Tulsa
Candreia, Peggy Jo *medical educator*
Werlla, Vanessa Lynn *psychiatrist*
Wortmann, Dorothy Woodward *physician*

OREGON

Beaverton
Dantas, Stella Marie *obstetrician, gynecologist*

Bend
Singletary, DeJuan Theresa *child and adolescent psychiatrist*

Portland
Baker, Barbara Jean *pediatrician, psychiatrist*
Baker, Diane R.H. *dermatologist*
Jacobson, Sig-Linda *obstetrician, educator*
Schumacher, Maria *biomedical researcher, educator*
Zerbe, Kathryn Jane *psychiatrist*
Zimmerman, Gail Marie *medical foundation executive*

Roseburg
Oleskowicz, Jeanette *physician*

PENNSYLVANIA

Blue Bell
Gorby-Schmidt, Martha Louise *pharmacologist, researcher*

Bryn Mawr
Godinez, Marye H. *anesthesiologist*

Collegeville
Shen, Hua-Qiong (Joan) *clinical research director*

Columbia
Jafri, Ayesha *family physician*

Cornwall
Rovinski, Helen Thérèse *retired psychiatrist*

Erie
Brunner-Martinez, Kirstin Ellen *pediatrician, psychiatrist*

Fountainville
Brown, Madeline Morgan *internist*

Gap
Klinefelter, Hylda Catharine *retired obstetrician, retired gynecologist*

Gibsonia
Krause, Helen Fox *retired otolaryngologist*

Gladwyne
Morrison, Gail *internist, nephrologist, educator*

Hershey
Eyster, Mary Elaine *hematologist, educator*
Schuller, Diane Ethel *allergist, immunologist, educator*

Hollidaysburg
Mariano, Ana Virginia *retired pathologist*

Indiana
Clark-Harley, Mary Dorcas *retired radiologist*

Jenkintown
Greenspan-Margolis, June E. *psychiatrist*

Kennett Square
Harrington, Anne Wilson *medical librarian*

Media
Behbehanian, Mahin Fazeli *surgeon*

Monongahela
Yovanof, Silvana *physician*

Mount Gretna
Agudo, Mercedes Engracia *psychiatrist*

New Tripoli
Hess, Darla Bakersmith *cardiologist, educator*

Newtown
Somers, Anne Ramsay *retired medical educator*

Newtown Square
de Rivas, Carmela Foderaro *retired psychiatrist, retired health facility administrator*

Pennsburg
Shuhler, Phyllis Marie *physician*

Philadelphia
Allevi, Angela *pediatrician*
Ballard, Roberta A. *pediatrician, educator*
Bernstein, Deborah *psychiatrist*
Best, Kimberly Renee *psychiatrist*
Bibbo, Marluce *physician, educator*
Bilaniuk, Larissa Tetiana *neuroradiologist, educator*
Bowman, Marjorie Ann *physician, educator*
Cassel, Christine Karen *physician*
Conlay, Lydia *anesthesiologist, educator, health science association administrator*
Dunn, Linda Kay *physician*
Evans, Audrey Elizabeth *physician, educator*
Glick, Jane Mills *biomedical researcher, educator*
Gueson, Emerita Torres *obstetrician, gynecologist*
Hurlock, Joan Emma *physician*
Joseph, Rosaline Resnick *hematologist*
Kaji, Hideko *pharmacology educator*
Lee, Virginia M. -Y. *medical educator, health science association administrator*
Lippa, Carol Frances *neurologist*
Lipshutz, Laurel Sprung *psychiatrist*
Long, Sarah Sundborg *pediatrician, educator*
Margo, Katherine Lane *family physician, educator*
Naylor, Mary D. *medical professor, director*
Ringpfeil, Franziska *dermatologist*
Rorke-Adams, Lucy Balian *pathologist, educator*
Rosen, Rhoda *obstetrician, gynecologist*
Russo, Irma Haydee Alvarez de *pathologist*
Stallings, Virginia A. *pediatric gastroenterologist*
Stuart, Marie Jean *physician, hematologist, researcher*
Tran, Judith Thuha *psychiatrist*
Velazquez, Omaida Caridad *vascular surgeon, researcher*
Vetter, Victoria L. *pediatric cardiologist, educator*
Weller, Elizabeth Boghossian *child and adolescent psychiatrist*

Pittsburgh
Caserio, Rebecca JoAnn *dermatologist, educator*
Choi, Sylvia Seung-Yun *pediatrician, educator*
Chorazy, Anna Julia Lyjak *retired pediatrician*
Karol, Meryl Helene *medical educator, researcher, health facility administrator, science educator*
Labriola Curran, Joanne Elizabeth *orthopedist*
Lowery, Willa Dean *obstetrician, gynecologist*
Lyjak Chorazy, Anna Julia *pediatrician, educator, retired health facility administrator*

Stroudsburg
Finch, Alberta May *retired pediatrician*

West Reading
Kao, Winifred W. *otolaryngologist*

Williamsport
Gouldin, Judith Ann *nuclear medicine physician*

Wynnewood
Koprowska, Irena *cytologist, medical researcher*

RHODE ISLAND

Providence
Barton, Alice *physician, educator*
Biron, Christine Anne *medical science educator, researcher*
Gilmore, Judith Marie *physician*
Kane, Agnes Brezak *pathologist, educator*
Wold, Patricia N. *psychiatrist*

Riverside
Lekas, Mary Despina *retired otolaryngologist*

SOUTH CAROLINA

Charleston
Austin, Linda S. *psychiatrist*
Gupta, Monika *nephrologist, researcher*
Hampton, Marta Toruno *dermatologist, educator*
McCann, Heather *orthopedic surgeon, physician*

Columbia
Gunter-Justice, Tracy D. *psychiatrist, educator*

Isle Of Palms
Wohltmann, Hulda Justine *pediatrician, endocrinologist*

Orangeburg
Geslani, Gemma P. *health studies educator*
Hare, Ester Rose *physician*

Sumter
Barrow, Tawana Walker *psychiatrist, consultant*
Leavell, Elizabeth Boykin *retired pediatrician*

Surfside Beach
Favaro, Mary Kaye Asperheim *pediatrician, writer*

West Columbia
Carter, Saralee Lessman *immunologist, microbiologist*

SOUTH DAKOTA

Aberdeen
Anderson, Esther Elizabeth *retired pediatrician, educator*

TENNESSEE

Cookeville
Smolenski, Lisabeth Ann *physician*

Johnson City
Giorgadze, Tamar Alfred *pathologist, physician*
Pandian, Shantha G. *psychiatrist*
Taylor, Lesli Ann *pediatric surgeon, educator*

Knoxville
Green, Linda Kay *retired dermatologist*
Martin, Duy-Thu Phan-Dinh *obstetrician, gynecologist*

Memphis
Helton, Kathleen Jacobson *neuroradiologist*
Kaste, Sue Creviston *pediatric radiologist, researcher*
Morreim, E. Haavi *medical ethics educator*
Riely, Caroline Armistead *gastroenterologist, educator*

Nashville
Brown, Wendy Weinstock *nephrologist, educator*
Epps, Anna Cherrie *immunologist, educator, dean*
Etherington, Carol A. *medical association administrator*
Stahlman, Mildred Thornton *pediatrician, pathologist, educator, medical researcher*

Oak Ridge
Cragle, Donna Lynne *medical researcher, director*

Pleasant Hill
Oldman, Martha Jeane *retired medical missionary*

TEXAS

Amarillo
Parker, Lynda Michele *psychiatrist*

Aransas Pass
Stehn, Lorraine Strelnick *physician*

Arlington
Aeschlimann, Sofia Lizbeth *psychiatrist*

Austin
Carter, Kimberly *obstetrician, gynecologist*
Neuzil, Amy Reed *physician, entrepreneur*
Sutton, Beverly Jewell *psychiatrist*

Beaumont
Phan, Tâm Thanh *medical educator, psychotherapist, consultant, researcher*

Bedford
Swe, Ni Ni *psychiatrist*

Castroville
Nguyen-Poole, Mary *physician*

College Station
Kier, Ann B. Burnette *pathology educator*

Corpus Christi
Sisley, Nina Mae *physician, public health service officer*

Dallas
Alexander, Gail Susan *psychiatrist*
Barnes, Madge Lou *physician*
Fort, Wana Ann *retired pediatrician*
Gibby, Diane Louise *physician, plastic surgeon*
Glick, Gina Phillips Moran *retired physician*
Grable, Kristen Heather *psychiatrist*
Hobbs, Helen Haskell *medical geneticist*
Kaiser, Fran Elizabeth *endocrinologist, gerontologist*
Kogan, Inna *psychiatrist, educator*
Roberts, Lynne Jeanine *physician*
Robertson, Rose Marie *cardiologist, educator*
Stephens, Leonora *psychiatrist*

El Paso
Silberg, Louise Barbara *physician, anesthesiologist*
Zaloznik, Arlene Joyce *retired oncologist, retired military officer*

Fort Worth
Bailey, Susan Rudd *physician*
Ericson, Ruth Ann *retired psychiatrist*
Kowalski, Debra Atkisson *physician*

Galveston
Chonmaitree, Tasnee *pediatrician, educator, epidemiologist*
Goodwin, Jean McClung *psychiatrist*
Melton, Bengi Biber *psychiatrist, educator*

Gilmer
Warden, Lenore Sponsler *physician*

Houston
Baldwin, Bonnie *physician*
Ball, Valdesha LeChante' *physician*
Bethea, Louise Huffman *allergist*
Bogle, Melissa Anne *dermatologist, educator*
Bridges, Margaret Elizabeth *physician*
Brown, Jacqueline Elaine *obstetrician, gynecologist*
Cash, Camille Geneva *physician*
Eisner, Diana *pediatrician*
Feigon, Judith Tova *ophthalmologist, educator, surgeon*
Fleming, Gloria Elaine *retired physician*
Gigli, Irma *dermatologist, educator, academic administrator*
Gupta, Monesha *pediatrician, educator*
Jemison, Mae Carol *physician, engineer, entrepreneur, philanthropist, educator, former astronaut*
Johnson, Marilyn *retired obstetrician, retired gynecologist*
Jones, Edith Irby *internist*
Kripke, Margaret Louise *immunologist, health facility executive*
Lemark, Noreen Anne *retired neurologist*
McGregor, Jacqueline Carinhas *psychiatrist*
McPherson, Alice Ruth *ophthalmologist, educator*
Mintz-Hittner, Helen Ann *physician, researcher*
Phelps, Cynthia L. *medical educator*
Ross, Patti Jayne *obstetrics and gynecology educator*
Salazar, Josephine M. *behavioral health specialist*
Sanderson, Mary Louise *medical association administrator*
Sazama, Kathleen *pathologist, lawyer*
Schachtel-Green, Barbara Harriet Levin *retired epidemiologist*
Scharold, Mary Louise *psychoanalyst, psychiatrist, educator*
Smeal, Janis Lea *psychiatrist*
Spitz, Margaret R. *epidemiologist, researcher*
Zoghbi, Huda Y. *neurologist, geneticist, educator*

Irving
Clifford, Lori Bevis *anesthesiologist*
Natour, Nahille I. *obstetrician, gynecologist*

Lubbock
Illner-Canizaro, Hana *physician, researcher, oral surgeon*

Lytle
Cigarroa, Josie A. *psychiatrist*

Orange
Stuntz, Billie Williams *pediatrician*

Pearland
Chung, Linda H. *obstetrician, gynecologist*

Plano
Dyer, Stephanie Jo *anesthesiologist*

Red Oak
Shaw, Sue Ann *medical transcriptionist*

San Angelo
Crenshaw, Rebecca Sue *physician*

San Antonio
Corrigan, Helen González *retired cytologist*
Patterson, Jan Evans *epidemiologist, educator*
Vargas-Tonsing, Tiffanye *medical educator*

Smithville
Meyer, Donna W. *medical educator, director*

Temple
Sulak, Patricia Jane *gynecologist, educator*

Webster
Farella, Angelina *pediatrician, educator*

UTAH

Salt Lake City
Carroll, Karen Colleen *pathologist, epidemiologist*
Howell, Elizabeth F. *psychiatrist, educator*
Meyers, Rebecka Louise *pediatric general surgeon*

VERMONT

Burlington
Hendley, Edith Di Pasquale *physiology and neuroscience educator*
Naylor, Magdalena Raczkowska *psychiatrist, educator*

Jacksonville
Hein, Karen Kramer *pediatrician, epidemiologist*

VIRGINIA

Afton
McCoy, Sue *retired surgeon, biochemist, bioethicist*

Alexandria
Ciofalo, Carol Ellen *obstetrician, gynecologist*
Hallman, Linda D. *medical association administrator*
Nicholas, Lynn B. *medical association administrator*
Wainscott, Cynthia *medical association administrator*

Arlington
Highsmith, Wanda Law *retired medical association administrator*
Runkle, Beatriz Pamela *pediatrician, educator*
Thompson, Geraldine Kelleher Richter *retired orthopedist*

Charlottesville
Dalton, Claudette Ellis Harloe *anesthesiologist, educator, dean*
Rehm, Patrice Koch *radiologist, educator*
Sanusi, Marina Theresia *retired psychiatrist*

Falls Church
Elliott, Virginia F. Harrison *retired anatomist, publisher, educator, investment advisor, kinesiologist, philanthropist*

Newport News
Behlmar, Cindy Lee *medical association administrator, management consultant*
Forbes, Sarah Elizabeth *gynecologist, real estate company officer*

Norfolk
Brower, Anne Clayton *radiologist*
Hood, Antoinette Foote *dermatologist*
Huot, Rachel Irene *biomedical educator, research scientist, physician*
Stallings, Valerie A. *physician, state agency administrator*
Terzis, Julia Kallipolitou *plastic surgeon*

Oakton
Travis, Tracy Leigh *emergency physician*

Onancock
Fears, Belle DeCormis *retired physician*

Reston
Pappas, Virginia M. *medical association administrator*

Richmond
Fierro, Marcella Farinelli *forensic pathologist, educator*
Robertson, Louise Wilkes *pediatrician, cardiologist*
Sood, Aradhana Avasthy *psychiatrist, director*

Vienna
Chin, May Lin *anesthesiologist*

White Stone
Duer, Ellen Ann Dagon *anesthesiologist, general practitioner*

Williamsburg
Voorhess, Mary Louise *pediatric endocrinologist*

Woodbridge
Butler, Leslie White *epidemiologist*

WASHINGTON

Bellevue
Calinoiu, Ileana Nia *psychiatrist*
Hackett, Carol Ann Hedden *physician*
Phillips, Zaiga Alksnis *pediatrician*

Bremerton
Vondran, Janet Elise *physician*

Camas
Liem, Annie *pediatrician*

Edmonds
Rogers, Catherine Alice *obstetrician, gynecologist*

Kirkland
Barto, Deborah Ann *physician*

Newcastle
Rosa-Bray, Marilyn *physician*

Olympia
Fisher, Nancy Louise *pediatrician, geneticist, retired nurse*

Pullman
Meier, Kathryn Elaine *pharmacologist, educator*

Seattle
Auer, Nancy Jane *emergency physician, medical association administrator*
Berkowitz, Bobbie *medical educator*
Dawson, Patricia Lucille *surgeon*
Giblett, Eloise Rosalie *retired hematologist*
Gimbrère, Kathreen *psychiatrist, educator*
Harris, Kathryn A.Z. *internist*
Hellström, Ingegerd *medical researcher*
Henderson, Maureen McGrath *medical educator*
Holmberg, Leona Ann *oncologist*
Lee, Catherine Terri *psychiatrist*
Miller, Leslie R. *obstetrician, gynecologist, educator*
Niles, Nancy L. *endocrinologist*
Pagon, Roberta Anderson *pediatrician, educator*
Papayannopoulou, Thalia *hematologist, oncologist, educator*
Weaver, Lois Jean *physician, educator*
Williams, Joan Elaine *podiatric surgeon, educator*
Yue, Agnes Kau-Wah *otolaryngologist*

Spokane
Lee, Sun Myung *physician*

University Place
Pliskow, Vita Sari *anesthesiologist*

Walla Walla
McIlvaine, Patricia Morrow *physician*

WEST VIRGINIA

Bluefield
Frazer, Teresa Elizabeth *pediatrician, endocrinologist*

Clarksburg
Lapuz-De La Pena, Erlinda Laron *pathology professor*

Elkins
Murphy, Patricia Ann *physician, otolaryngologist*

Frankford
Mazzio-Moore, Joan L. *retired radiology educator, physician*

Kingwood
Moyers, Sylvia Dean *retired medical librarian*

Morgantown
Albrink, Margaret Joralemon *medical educator*
Janoo, Jabin *obstetrician, gynecologist*
Pinheiro, Germania Araujo *physician, researcher*
Sikora, Rosanna Dawn *emergency physician, educator*

Princeton
Vrinceanu, Alina Daniela *psychiatrist*

Ronceverte
Hooper, Anne Dodge *pathologist, educator*

Wheeling
Heceta, Estherbelle Aguilar *retired anesthesiologist*

WISCONSIN

Green Bay
Schueckler, Amy K. *obstetrician, gynecologist*

Madison
Gurkow, Helen J. *retired physician*
Hansen, Sherri M. *psychiatrist*
Johnson, Maryl Rae *cardiologist*
Knoll, Rose Ann *radiologist, technologist*
Sobkowicz, Hanna Maria *neurologist, researcher*

Menomonee Falls
Diestelhorst, Amy Lea *obstetrician, gynecologist*

Milwaukee
Stokes, Kathleen Sarah *dermatologist, educator*

Oshkosh
Cooper, Janelle Lunette *neurologist, educator*

Plover
Loteyro, Corazon Bigata *physician*

West Bend
Maskala, Kristen Lucy *orthopedic surgeon*

WYOMING

Cheyenne
Holden, Linda Kathleen *medical educator*

TERRITORIES OF THE UNITED STATES

NORTHERN MARIANA ISLANDS

Saipan
Lamkin, Celia Belocora *physician*
Post, Laura Leigh *psychiatrist*

CANADA

BRITISH COLUMBIA

Vancouver
Baird, Patricia Ann *physician, educator*
Levy, Julia *immunology educator, researcher*
McGeer, Edith Graef *retired neurological science educator*

QUEBEC

Montreal
Freeman, Carolyn Ruth *oncologist*
Jones, Barbara Ellen *neurologist, educator*

MEXICO

Guadalajara Jalisco
Miranda-Diaz, Alejandra Guillermina *surgeon, medical educator, researcher*

ENGLAND

Devon
Turner-Warwick, Margaret *physician, educator*

ISRAEL

Jerusalem
Hazboun, Viveca *psychiatrist*

SWITZERLAND

Geneva
Kapp, Nathalie *obstetrician, educator, gynecologist*

ADDRESS UNPUBLISHED

Abdallah, Claude *anesthesiologist*
Aiello, Kimberly Jean *surgeon*
Alexander, Jessie Aronow *anesthesiologist*
Alexiades-Armenakas, Macrene Renee *dermatologist, scientist, researcher, educator, consultant*
Altekruse, Joan Morrissey *retired preventive medicine physician*
Altman, Adele Rosenhain *radiologist*
Amin, Farzana *psychiatrist, researcher*
Amram, Laura *psychiatrist*
Anderson, Geraldine Louise *medical researcher*

Apogi, Evelyn *retired anesthesiologist*
Arnone, Mary Grace *radiologic technologist*
Ashish-Mishra, Sonia *psychiatrist*
Ashley, Sharon Anita *pediatric anesthesiologist*
Atkinson, Holly Gail *physician, journalist, educator, human rights activist, writer*
Avery, Mary Ellen *pediatrician, educator*
Baird, Alison Elizabeth *neurologist*
Baker, Deborah *medical educator*
Barbo, Dorothy Marie *obstetrician, gynecologist, educator*
Baxi, Laxmi V. *obstetrician, gynecologist, medical educator*
Bayes, Beverley Joan *retired pediatrician*
Becker, Kyra J. *neurologist, educator*
Beckett, Victoria Ling *physician*
Begum, Momotaz *medical researcher, consultant, medical educator*
Bell, Robinette N. *psychiatrist, educator*
Berenson, Abbey Belina *gynecologist, educator*
Berkley, Mary Corner *neurologist*
Berkwits, Gloria Kozin *psychiatrist*
Berlin, Doris Ada *psychiatrist*
Berman, Jennifer R. *urologist*
Bernard, Marcelle Thomasine *physician*
Berry, Gail W. *psychiatrist, educator*
Bersin, Mollie Klapper *physician*
Blanken, Celeste S. *physician*
Blazina, Janice Fay *pathologist*
Bokhari, Robina Maqbool *physician*
Bolognia, Jean Lynn *academic dermatologist*
Bonn, Ethel May *psychiatrist, educator*
Botsford, Mary Henrich *retired ophthalmologist*
Bowman, Lynne Barnett *medical librarian*
Brandon, Kathryn Elizabeth Beck *pediatrician*
Brockington, Carolyn *neurologist*
Bruce, Nadine Cecile *internist, educator*
Budoff, Penny Wise *retired physician, author, researcher*
Burgio, Jane L. *pathologist, writer*
Bustreo, Flavia *epidemiologist*
Butts, Cherie LaVaughn *biomedical researcher*
Caldicott, Helen *physician*
Caplin, Olga Yeryomina *psychiatrist*
Carswell, Jane Triplett *retired family physician*
Castro, Maria Graciela *medical educator, geneticist, researcher*
Chafkin, Rita M. *retired dermatologist*
Chang, Sophia Ho Ying C. *pediatrician*
Chang, Yuan *neuropathologist, researcher, educator*
Chesney, Margaret A. *medical educator, medical researcher*
Chiang, Alexis S. *orthopedist, surgeon*
Chiao, Christine Lynn *psychiatrist*
Chiu, Dorothy *retired pediatrician*
Chretien, Jane Henkel *internist*
Coady, Mary Luz K. *pediatrician*
Conrad-England, Roberta Lee *pathologist*
Cooper, Jeanne A. *retired pathologist*
Crino, Marjanne Helen *anesthesiologist*
Cunniff, Suzanne *surgical technician*
Cunningham, Alice Norida *retired physician*
Curry, Sadye Beatryce *gastroenterologist, educator*
Daly, Miriam Shamer *retired family physician*
Date, Elaine Satomi *physiatrist, educator*
Davidson, Lisa Rae *physician*
Davis, Mary Helen *psychiatrist, educator*
Dawson, Geraldine *medical educator, social worker*
DeBuono, Barbara Ann *physician, state official*
Degann, Sona Irene *obstetrician, gynecologist, educator*
DiPasqua, Aimee Dora *physician*
Djung-Wong, Ida I-Giai *retired pathologist*
Donohue-Smith, Maureen A. *medical educator*
DuRocher, Frances A. *retired physician, educator*
Dyar, Kathryn Wilkin *pediatrician*
Dziewanowska, Zofia Elizabeth *pharmaceutical executive*
Earles, Kathi Amille *pediatrician*
Ehlers, Kathryn Hawes (Mrs. James D. Gabler) *physician*
Engel-Arieli, Susan Lee *physician*
Engle, Mary Allen English *retired physician*
Esterly, Nancy Burton *retired physician*
Etzel, Ruth Ann *pediatrician, epidemiologist, educator*
Eubank, Piper *psychiatrist*
Eviatar, Lydia *pediatrician, neurologist*
Exum, Stephanie Roxanne *medical educator*
Fanos, Kathleen Hilaire *osteopathic physician, podiatrist*
Feldman, Eva Lucille *neurology educator*
Fenoglio-Preiser, Cecilia Mettler *retired pathologist, educator*
Fountain, Karen Schueler *retired physician*
Foyouzi-Youssefi, Reyhaneh *pharmacologist*
Gajl-Peczalska, Kazimiera J. *retired surgeon, pathologist, educator*
Gelberg, Lillian *family medicine physician, educator*
Genieser, Nancy Branom *radiologist*
Ginsberg-Fellner, Fredda *retired pediatric endocrinologist, researcher*
Ginsburg, Iona Horowitz *psychiatrist*
Glass, Dorothea Daniels *physiatrist, educator*
Glimcher, Laurie H. *immunology educator*
Goff, Heather Elizabeth *psychiatrist*
Gold, Judith Hammerling *psychiatrist*
Goldstein, Dora Benedict *pharmacologist, educator*
Goodfellow, Robin Irene *surgeon*
Gray, Mary Jane *retired obstetrician, gynecologist*
Greenberg, Carolyn Phyllis *retired anesthesiologist*
Gregorius, Beverly June *retired obstetrician, gynecologist*
Grossman, Joyce Renee *pediatrician, internist*
Gruebel, Barbara Jane *retired internist, pulmonologist*
Gulbrandsen, Patricia Hughes *physician*
Haagen, Elaine K. *psychiatrist*
Haddady, Shirin *medical educator*
Haddy, Theresa Brey *pediatrician, educator, hematologist, oncologist*
Hafner-Eaton, Chris *medical researcher, educator*
Haft, Gail Klein *pediatrician*
Harmatuk, Frances A. *retired psychiatrist, anesthesiologist*
Harrigan, Rosanne Carol *medical educator*
Harris, Elaine K. *medical consultant*
Hartmeier, Gina Marie *psychiatrist*
Hasselmeyer, Eileen Grace *medical researcher*
Healy, Bernadine P. *physician, educator, former federal official*
Heestand, Diane Elissa *medical educator*
Heidelberger, Kathleen Patricia *physician*
Hendry, Jean Sharon *psychopharmacologist*
Henson, Anna Miriam *retired otolaryngologist, retired medical educator*
Hidaka, Chisa *medical researcher*
Higginbotham, Edith Arleane *radiologist, researcher*
Hoffman, Amy S. *internist*
Hogg, Virginia Lee *retired medical educator*
Hood, Katrina *pediatrician*
Hourani, Laurel Lockwood *epidemiologist*
Hricak, Hedvig *radiologist*
Hyde, M. Deborah *neurosurgeon*
Hymes, Norma *internist*
Isidro, Rose Marie *physician*
Johnson, Pam Clarene *radiographer, bone densitometrist, consultant*
Johnston, Marilyn Frances-Meyers *physician, educator*
Jolly, Meenakshi *rheumatologist*
Joseph, Kathie-Ann *biomedical researcher*
Judas, Ilse *psychiatrist*
Karpitskaya, Yekaterina *orthopaedic surgeon*
Kazeminezhad, Zhabiz *psychiatrist*
Keeney, Virginia T. *retired child psychiatrist*
Keith Wagstaff, Mary Jane *physician*
Kent, Georgia L. *obstetrician, gynecologist, healthcare executive, educator*
Kerwin, Elizabeth Anderson *retired anesthesiologist*
Khan, Arfa *radiologist, educator*
Kindberg, Shirley Jane *pediatrician*
Kinzie, Jeannie Jones *radiation oncologist, nuclear medicine physician*
Kirkland, Rebecca Trent *endocrinologist*
Ko, Christine J. *dermatologist, educator*
Kocheril, Sosa Varghese *rheumatologist*
Kollmeyer, Carie Ann *pediatrician*
Koreman, Dorothy Goldstein *physician, dermatologist*
Kostick, Alexandra *ophthalmologist*
Kowlessar, Muriel *retired pediatric educator*
Kraisosky, Alissa Jo *psychiatrist*
Krim, Mathilde *medical educator*
Kruc, Antoinette Campion *family physician*
Kunz, Alexandra Cavitt *physician, anthropologist, researcher*
Kwik, Christine Irene *physician, retired military officer, retired foreign service officer*
Lake, Carol Lee *anesthesiologist, physician, educator*
Liu, Te Hua *neuroradiologist, educator*
Lovell, Michelle Paulette *physician's associate*
Luban, Naomi L. C. *hematologist*
Luhrs, Caro Elise *internal medicine physician, administrator, educator*
Marcdante, Karen Jean *medical educator*
Marko, Marlene *psychiatrist*
Mates, Susan Onthank *physician, educator, musician, writer*
Matzkin, Elizabeth *orthopedic sports medicine surgeon*
McGrath, Mary Helena *plastic surgeon, educator*
McNeely, Bonnie L. (K.W. Rowe Jr.) *retired internist*
Meadows, Gwendolyn Joann *retired behavioral disorders educator*
Mercado, Mary Gonzales *cardiologist*
Meserve, Marilyn Moses *retired pediatrician*
Messerle, Judith Rose *retired medical librarian, retired public relations executive*
Meyer, Carol Frances *retired pediatrician, allergist*
Meyers, Elsie Flint *anesthesiologist*
Millican, Frances Kennedy *psychiatrist*
Miskimen, Theresa Marie *psychiatrist, educator*
Morrison, Mary F. *psychiatrist, researcher*
Murphey, Sheila Ann *infectious diseases physician, educator, researcher*
Nelson, Nancy Eleanor *pediatrician, educator*
Noonan, Jacqueline Anne *pediatrician, educator*
Novik, Yelena *oncologist, hematologist*
Nowak, Judith Ann *psychiatrist*
Obert, Mary Ellen Newton *retired internist*
Occhiogrosso, Mallay Barclay *psychiatrist*
Olds, Jacqueline *psychiatrist, educator*
Padian, Nancy *medical educator, epidemiologist*
Parpiani, Priya *obstetrician, retired gynecologist*
Pascale, Jane Fay *pathologist*
Patchin, Rebecca J. *anesthesiologist, educator, administrator*
Pedini, Egle Damijonaitis *radiologist*
Peterson, Ann Sullivan *physician, consultant*
Pflum, Barbara Ann *retired allergist*
Pierri, Mary Kathryn Madeline *cardiologist, emergency physician, educator*
Pilat, Jeanine Marie *medical researcher*
Pisters, Katherine M.W. *internist, medical educator*
Polfliet, Sarah Jean *physician*
Prchal, Carol Louise *retired orthopedist*
Ranney, Helen Margaret *retired internist, hematologist, educator*
Raval, Ma Florena Tenazas *retired pathologist*
Reid, Orien *former medical association administrator*
Rhodes, Linda Jane *psychiatrist*
Ribble, Judith Glenn *medical educator*
Riyaz, Najmun *psychiatrist*
Rosenblum, Mindy Fleischer *pediatrician*
Rubin, Michele S. *radiologist*
San Agustin, Mutya *pediatrician*
Schauf, Victoria *pediatrician, educator*
Scheib, Rachel Theresa *psychiatrist*
Schell, Catherine Louise *physician*
Schmid, Lynette Sue *child and adolescent psychiatrist*
Schoon, Doris Vivien *ophthalmologist*
Scialabba, Elmerinda Caccavo *retired pediatrician*
Shah, Muniza *psychiatrist*
Shaw-Soderstrom, Katherine S. *retired anesthesiologist*
Silberberg, Inga *dermatologist*
Silva, Omega Logan *physician*
Slater-Freedberg, Jill Rebecca *dermatologist*
Small, Joyce Graham *psychiatrist, educator*
Smits, Helen Lida *medical association administrator, educator*
Somburu, Zakiya Netifnet T. *physician*
Stabinsky, Susan *psychiatrist*
Steinbach, Lynne Susan *radiologist, educator*
Stillman, Belinda Ann *psychiatrist*
Stringham, Renée *physician*
Szentiranyi, Judith *physician, educator*
Tagiuri, Consuelo Keller *child psychiatrist, educator*
Taichert, Louise Cecile *retired psychiatrist*
Tavakoli, Sirpa Aulikki *physician*
Taylor, Gina Adele *dermatologist*
Terr, Lenore Cagen *psychiatrist, writer*
Terris, Susan *physician, cardiologist, researcher*
Thomas, Claudia Lynn *orthopedic surgeon*
Thornton, Yvonne Shirley *obstetrician, writer, musician*
Thorsen, Marie Kristin *radiologist, educator*
Tolia, Vasundhara K. *pediatric gastroenterologist, educator*
Tufano, Sylvia Hope *obstetrician, gynecologist*
Veronneau-Troutman, Suzanne *retired ophthalmologist*
Vest, Gayle Southworth *obstetrician, gynecologist*
Vittetoe, Marie Clare *retired clinical laboratory science educator*
Vydareny, Kay Herzog *radiologist, medical educator*
Wade, Allison Muia *orthopedic surgeon*
Waiss, Elaine Helen *retired physician*
Wallace, Joyce Irene Malakoff *internist*
Wang, Nancy *pathologist, educator*
Way, Barbara Haight *retired dermatologist*
Weder, Natalie Danitza *psychiatrist*
Weiss, Lyn Denise *physician*
Wershing, Julia M. *pediatrician*
Westmoreland, Barbara Fenn *neurologist, educator*
Wilson, Mary Elizabeth *epidemiologist, physician, educator*
Wilson, Michelle Lermond *internist*
Wishnick, Marcia Margolis *pediatrician, educator, geneticist*
Wong, Toh-Heng Lim *retired pediatrician, physician*
Woolston-Catlin, Marian *psychiatrist*
Wu, Nan Faion *pediatrician*
Zawaideh, Mona A. *pediatrician, endocrinologist, nephrologist, educator*

HUMANITIES: LIBERAL STUDIES

UNITED STATES

ALABAMA

Auburn University
Sidler, Michelle Ann *literature and language professor*

Birmingham
Long, Sheri Spaine *foreign language educator*
Morton, Marilyn Miller *retired genealogy educator, researcher, retired history professor, travel company executive*
Ott, Victoria E. *history professor*
Turón, Mercedes *emeritus language professor*

Dothan
Glanton, Jeraline Cain *retired language educator*

Florence
Burkhead, Cynthia Anne *literature and language professor*

Huntsville
Bounds, Sarah Etheline *historian*
Hughes, Kaylene *historian, educator*

Loachapoka
Schafer, Elizabeth Diane *historian, writer*

Montgomery
Napier, Cameron Mayson Freeman *historic preservationist*
Rose, Shirley Kelly *retired language educator*

Montrose
Coffman, Elizabeth Thompson *retired language educator*

Tuscaloosa
Davis, Pam N. *literature and language professor*
Hendrix, Mary Elizabeth *language educator, researcher*
Nadine, Claudia *French language educator*
Pass, Charlotte Louise *literature educator, consultant*

Tuscumbia
Sutton, Wanda Lynne *language educator*

Tuskegee Institute
Gamble, Vanessa Northington *historian, healthcare educator, bioethicist*

ALASKA

Eek
Fager, Heather Elaine *language educator*

ARIZONA

Casa Grande
Landers, Patricia Glover *language educator*

Chandler
Moser, Teri *literature educator*

Flagstaff
Marcus, Karen Melissa *language educator*

Glendale
Eyres, Beth Kathleen *literature educator*

Kingman
Jones, Barbara Christine *linguist, educator, creative arts designer*

Mesa
Larson-Miller, Julie Kathleen *English educator*

Phoenix
Kohi, Susan *bilingual educator, translator*
Schiffner, Adrienne Anita *art historian, educator*

Tempe
Bartling, Sara *language educator*

Tucson
Gaines, Kendra Holly *language educator*
Schulz, Renate Adele *German studies and second language acquisition educator*

ARKANSAS

Beebe
Fletcher, Maris *literature educator*

Fort Smith
Montgomery, M. Darlene *language educator*

Gravette
Duncan, Jean Marie *language educator*

Little Rock
Crisp, Sally Chandler *writing educator*

Malvern
Growney-Seals, Sharon Ann *literature and language professor, department chairman*

Pine Bluff
Teel, Gina A. *language educator*
Williams, Bettye Jean *language educator*

West Fork
Higgins, Sarah Jean *literature and language professor*

Wickes
Riley, Faith Lynch *retired historian, writer*

CALIFORNIA

Azusa
Griesinger, Emily Ann *literature and language professor*

Bakersfield
Burns, Sarah Chloe *historian, educator*
Kegley, Jacquelyn Ann *philosophy educator*
Smith, Cheryl Jan *language educator*

Berkeley
Gallagher, M. Catherine *English literature educator*
Grossman, Joan Delaney *literature and language professor*
Hull, Glynda *language educator*
Lovell, Margaretta M. *art history educator, museum curator*
Mavroudi, Maria *philologist, educator*
Richards, Kyungnyun Kim *Korean language educator, poet, translator*

Carmel
Wright, Constance Storey *retired humanities educator*

Chula Vista
Capehart, Bonnie *language educator*

Claremont
Deese, E(thel) Helen *retired literature and language professor*
Moss, Myra Ellen (Myra Moss Rolle) *philosophy educator*
Wheeler, Geraldine Hartshorn *historian, writer*

Davis
Blodgett, Harriet *retired language educator*
Landau, Norma Beatrice *historian, educator*

El Cajon
Haber, Susan C. *history professor*
Mapes, Gwenyth B. *humanities educator, writer*

Escondido
McHenry, Anita Petei *historian, archaeologist*

Eureka
Zimmerman, Adria Dawn *composition educator*

Fresno
Bundy-DeSoto, Teresa Mari *language educator, vocalist*
Kuhn, Rose Marie *language educator*
Parker, Judith Elaine *retired language educator*

Fullerton
Bangerter, Renee Tanner *literature educator*

Garden Grove
Cochrum, Ellen Joan *language educator*

Irvine
Boyd, Carolyn Patricia *history professor*
Gilbert, Margaret P. *philosophy professor, researcher*
Kluger, Ruth *German language educator, editor*
Maddy, Penelope Jo *philosopher, educator*

La Jolla
McDonald, Marianne *classicist*

Oreskes, Naomi *science historian*
Thompson, Emily *historian*

Lodi
McKelvey, Judy Eileen *language educator*

Long Beach
Beebe, Sandra E. *retired language educator, artist, writer*
Nguyen, Huong Tran *former elementary and secondary language educator, former district office administrator*

Los Angeles
Appleby, Joyce Oldham *historian, educator*
Arora, Shirley Lease *Spanish language educator*
Bennett, Judith MacKenzie *historian*
Caram, Eve La Salle *language educator, writer*
Croson, Charlotte Joanne *retired language educator*
Darby, Joanne Tyndale (Jaye Darby) *arts and humanities educator*
Hsu, Kylie *language educator, researcher, linguist*
Leonard, Kandi *language educator*
See, Carolyn *English language educator, writer, book critic*
Trenton, Patricia Jean *art historian*

Los Gatos
Benner, Patricia Ann *retired literacy educator*
Ferrari, L. Katherine *speech professional, consultant, entrepreneur*
Tinsley, Barbara Sher *historian, educator, writer*

Malibu
Clegg, Cyndia Susan *literature educator*

Mission Viejo
Chattopadhyay, Collette Adele *art historian, critic*

Monterey
Peet, Phyllis Irene *women's studies educator*

Morgan Hill
Haaser, Paula Marlene *language educator*

Norwalk
Oliver, Susan *history professor, writer, consultant*

Oceanside
Mushinsky, Jane Marla *humanities educator, writer*

Orange
Williams, Danna Beth *reading specialist*

Pacific Grove
Penney, Beth *language educator, editor, writer*
Schapiro, Karen Lee *language educator*

Pacific Palisades
Perloff, Marjorie Gabrielle *literature educator*

Palo Alto
Mommsen, Katharina *retired literature and language professor, foundation administrator*

Pasadena
Zwicky, Barbarina Exita *humanities educator, researcher*

Pomona
Podany, Amanda H. *history professor*

Rancho Cucamonga
Decker, Catherine Helen *language educator*

Rancho Palos Verdes
Sayers, Kari *literature and language professor, journalist*

Ridgecrest
Swiridoff, Christine *literature and language professor*

Riverside
Fagundo, Ana Maria *language educator*
Murphy, Caroline Patricia *historian, writer*
Warnke, Georgia C. *humanities educator*
Yount, Gwendolyn Audrey *humanities educator*

Rocklin
Blank, Lenore Kim *literature and language professor, consultant*

Sacramento
Reed, Nancy Boyd *English language educator, elementary school educator*

Salinas
Slattery, Kathleen Milicent *language educator*

San Bernardino
Fong, Mary *ethnic studies educator*

San Diego
Amstadt, Nancy Hollis *retired language educator*
Donadey, Anne *humanities educator*
Dunlop, Marianne *retired language educator*
Sanchez, Rita B. *humanities educator, writer*
Withee, Diana Keeran *art historian, art dealer, educator*

San Francisco
Arnold, Lauren *art historian, writer*
Birnbaum, Lucia Chiavola *historian, educator*
Felstiner, Mary Lowenthal *history professor*
Hansen, Carol Louise *literature and language professor*
Watkins, Elizabeth Siegel *history professor*

San Jose
Thompson, Jan Newstrom *art historian, educator*
Warner, Mary Louise *literature and language professor*

San Marcos
Rolle-Rissetto, Silvia *foreign languages educator, writer, artist*

Watts, Jill Marie *history educator*

San Marino
Stefansson, Wanda Gae *language educator, literature educator*

Santa Barbara
Cathcart, Linda *art historian*
Gallo, Marta Irene *retired language educator*
Göllner, Marie Louise *musicologist, retired educator*
Guerrini, Anita *historian, educator*
Larsen Hoeckley, Cheri Lin *language educator*
Mahlendorf, Ursula Renate *literature educator*

Santa Clara
Dunbar, Mary Judith *literature and language professor*

Santa Cruz
Suckiel, Ellen Kappy *philosophy educator*

Saratoga
deBarling, Ana Maria *language educator*

Stanford
Bresnan, Joan W. *literature and language professor*
Brooks, Helen Bousky *literature and language professor, performing arts educator*
Newman-Gordon, Pauline *French language and literature educator*
Traugott, Elizabeth Closs *linguist, educator, researcher*

Stockton
Fung, Rosaline Lee *language educator*
Gottfried, Rosalind B. *humanities educator*

Ventura
Armstrong, Dianne Owens *language educator*

Whittier
Reid, Ivonne Figueroa *language educator*

Wilmington
Borell, Mary Putnam *language educator, playwright*
Smith, June Burlingame *English educator*

COLORADO

Aurora
Waite, Cheryl Siebert *history professor, researcher*

Boulder
Hall, Joan Lord *language educator, literature educator*

Cherry Hills Village
Conroy, Mary Elizabeth *history professor*

Colorado Springs
Barton, Ruth *language educator*

Denver
Fasel, Ida *literature and language professor, writer*
Johnson, Geraldine Esch *language specialist*
Porter, Donna Jean *genealogist*

Erie
Dilly, Marian Jeanette *humanities educator*

Estes Park
Gibbs, Dorothy Scott *retired Latin educator*

Golden
Cash, Kristy Rae *language educator*
Dickinson, Carol Rittgers *art historian, writer*

Lakewood
Woodruff, Kathryn Elaine *literature and language professor*

Loveland
Patterson, Shirley Drury *genealogist, editor-in-chief*

Saguache
Sanchez, Karla Ann *language educator*

Steamboat Springs
Kiser-Miller, Kathy Joy *humanities educator*

CONNECTICUT

Bridgeport
Psarras, Mary Auten *language educator, tax specialist*

Essex
Hieatt, Constance Bartlett *English language educator*

Fairfield
Newton, Lisa Haenlein *philosopher, educator*

Guilford
Colish, Marcia Lillian *history professor*

Hamden
Marino, Marissa A. *language educator*

Hartford
Humphreys, Karen Lynne *language educator*

Middletown
Heimann-Hast, Sybil Dorothea *literature and language professor*
Meyer, Priscilla Ann *literature and language professor*
Schwarcz, Vera *historian, educator, poet*
Winston, Krishna *foreign language professional*

Milford
Convertino, Charlene D. *language educator*

New Haven
Borroff, Marie *English language educator*
Frank, Roberta *literature educator*
Glier, Ingeborg Johanna *German language and literature educator*
Hyman, Paula E(llen) *history professor*
Jackson, Sondi Elizabeth *language educator*
Marcus, Ruth Barcan *philosopher, educator, writer, lecturer*
Peterson, Linda H. *English language educator*
Prochaska, Alice *historian, librarian*
Tannenbaum, Rebecca Jo *historian, writer*
Titus, Julia Yeremina *Slavic languages educator, translator*
Yeazell, Ruth Bernard *English language educator*

New London
Martin, Lisa Marlene *language educator*

Norwalk
Nelson, Paula Morrison Bronson *reading specialist*

Oxford
Shupp, Karlen S. *language educator*

Putnam
Leese, Jessica *language educator*

Salisbury
Kilner, Ursula Blanche *genealogist, educator, writer*

Stamford
Ortner, Toni *language educator*

Stonington
Thacher, Mary McGrath *historian, genealogist*

Storrs Mansfield
Charters, Ann *literature educator*

Washington
Burton, Ann Mapes *historian, retired academic administrator*

Waterbury
Donahue, Linda Wheeler *retired English educator, writer*

West Hartford
Collins, Alma Jones *language educator, writer*
McGrory, Mary Kathleen *humanities educator, retired academic administrator*

Woodbridge
Cone, Virginia Williams *retired historian*
Ecklund, Constance Cryer *French language and literature educator*
Kleiner, Diana Elizabeth Edelman *art historian, educator, academic administrator*

DELAWARE

Dover
Angstadt, Frances Virginia *language arts and theatre arts educator*
Espadas, Elizabeth Anne *language educator*
Haskins, Linda L. *language educator*

Frederica
Miller, Mary-Emily *history professor*

Newark
Gibson, Ann Eden *art historian, educator*
Isaacs, Diane Scharfeld *English educator*

Wilmington
Kneavel, Ann Callanan *humanities educator, communications consultant*

DISTRICT OF COLUMBIA

Washington
Albrecht, Kathe Hicks *art historian, visual resources manager*
Broun, Elizabeth *art historian, curator*
Cheney, Lynne Vincent *humanities educator, writer*
Fain, Cheryl Ann *translator, editor*
Farr, Judith Banzer *retired literature educator, writer*
Howland, Nina Davis *historian*
Lightman, Marjorie *historian*
Marr, Phebe Ann *retired historian, educator*
Miller, Jeanne-Marie Anderson (Mrs. Nathan J. Miller) *language educator, academic administrator*
Mujica, Barbara Louise *language educator, writer*
Roberts, Jeanne Addison *retired literature educator*
Salamon, Linda Bradley *English literature educator*
Shih, J. Chung-wen *Chinese language educator*
Soltan, Margaret *literature and language professor*
Svoboda, Patricia Helen *art historian*
Taylor, Estelle Wormley *language educator, dean*

FLORIDA

Belleair Bluffs
Alexander, Christina Anamaria *translator, performing company executive*

Boca Raton
Mitchell, Carmencita C. *literature and language professor*

Brandon
Sanchez, Evelyn Ford *retired humanities educator*

Clearwater
Knoop, Maggie Pearson *language educator*

Coral Gables
Goldstein, Phyllis Ann *art historian, educator*

Thomasson, Amie Lynn *philosopher, educator*

Daytona Beach
Kruse, Marylin Lynn *retired language educator*
Zenkovsky, Betty Jean *modern languages educator*

Deland
Navarro, Lydia *language educator*

Fort Lauderdale
Van Alstyne, Judith Sturges *retired language educator*
Young, Ann F. *history professor*

Fort Myers
Curtin, Constance O'Hara *language educator, writer*
Mendible, Myra *literature educator, researcher*

Fort Walton Beach
Register, Annette Rowan *literature educator*

Gainesville
Hartigan, Karelisa Voelker *classics educator*
Scott, Lynn Thomson *Spanish language and literature educator*

Hillsboro Beach
McGarry, Carmen Racine *historian, artist*

Jacksonville
Furdell, Elizabeth Lane *history professor*

Key Biscayne
Ross, Marilyn J. *language and communications educator*

Lake Worth
Dilgen, Regina Marie *English educator*

Lakeland
Eskin, Catherine R. *language educator*

Melbourne
Jones, Elaine Hancock *humanities educator*

Miami
Leeder, Ellen Lismore *literature and language professor, literary critic*
Parks, Arva Moore *historian*
Weir-Soley, Donna Aza *language educator, writer*

Milton
Coston, Brenda Maria Bone *language arts educator*

Mulberry
Bowman, Hazel Lois *retired English language educator*

Naples
Kinder, Suzanne Fonay Wemple *retired historian, retired educator*

Ocala
Haisten, Judy Aurich *language educator*

Orlando
Murphrey, Elizabeth Hobgood *history professor, librarian*

Pensacola
Wernicke, Marian O'Shea *language educator*

Saint Augustine
Oliver, Elizabeth Kimball *historian, writer*
Wilson, Tamara Lee *English educator*

Saint Petersburg
Duval, Cynthia *art historian, museum administrator, consultant, curator*

Sarasota
Benowitz, June Melby *historian, educator*
Dungy, Kathryn R. *humanities educator*
Hapner, Joanna Sue *humanities educator*
Jacobson, Jeanne McKee *humanities educator, writer*

Sunny Isles Beach
Buyanovsky, Sophia *linguist, educator*

Tallahassee
Hunt, Mary Alice *retired humanities educator*
Laird, Doris Anne Marley *retired humanities educator, musician*

Tampa
Mitchell, Mozella Gordon *language educator, minister*
Ronson, Bonnie Whaley *literature educator*

GEORGIA

Atlanta
Austin, Jeannette Holland *genealogist, writer*
Brown, Lorene B(yron) *retired library educator*
Fox-Genovese, Elizabeth Ann Teresa *humanities educator*
Kuntz, Marion Lucile Leathers *classicist, educator, historian*
Lacy, Sheila Patricia *language educator*
Lipstadt, Deborah E. *Jewish and Holocaust studies professor*
Senf, Carol Ann *literature educator*

Bowdon
Donnell, Rebekah Jo *language educator, editor*

Cairo
Oliver-Warren, Mary Elizabeth *retired library science educator, library and information scientist*

Carrollton
Hill, Jane Bowers *English language educator, editor*

Insenga, Angela Suzanne *literature educator*
Lane, Pamela Lynn *language educator*

Dahlonega
Bennett, Tanya Long *language educator, writer*
Williams, Linda Stallworth *literature and language professor*

Dalton
Mahoney, Kelley K. *language educator*

Decatur
Showers Johnson, Violet Mary-Ann Iyabo *history professor*
Worth, Dorothy Williamson *retired foreign language educator*

Dublin
Claxton, Harriett Maroy Jones *language educator*

Dunwoody
Duvall, Marjorie L. *English and foreign language educator*

Macon
Huffman, Joan Brewer *history professor*

Milledgeville
Magoulick, Mary *literature and language professor*

Savannah
Gentry, April Dawn *liberal arts professor*
Trittel, Rebecca B. *art historian, educator*

Valdosta
Byrd, Melanie Sue *history professor*

Waleska
Farmer, Joy A. *literature educator*

HAWAII

Honolulu
Hackler, Rhoda E. A. *retired historian*
Niyekawa, Agnes Mitsue *foreign language professor*

Lihue
Shigemoto, April Fumie *language educator*

IDAHO

Boise
Miller, Sheila Diane *language educator*
Sloan, Nina *language educator*

Jerome
Ricketts, Virginia Lee *historian, researcher*

Pocatello
Hulet, Marjanna M. *literature educator*

ILLINOIS

Big Rock
Port, Ruth Elizabeth *literature and language professor*

Carbondale
Fladeland, Betty *historian, educator*

Champaign
Kieffer, Gina Marie *history professor*
Watts, Emily Stipes *retired English language educator*

Chicago
Bregoli-Russo, Mauda Rita *language educator*
Crone, Anna Lisa *Russian literature educator*
Felden, Tamara *German language educator, translator*
Gray, Hanna Holborn *historian, educator*
Hast, Adele *historian, editor, writer*
Hilliard, Celia *cultural historian*
Hsia, Sophie S. *language educator, researcher*
Johnson, Janet Helen *literature educator*
Johnson, Raymonda Theodora Greene *retired humanities educator*
Manning, Sylvia *language educator*
Nakamura, Kimiko *language educator*
Romano-Magner, Patricia R. *English studies educator, researcher*
Shen, Virginia Shiang-lan *Spanish and Chinese language educator*
Sochen, June *history professor*

Des Plaines
Korbel, Linda Anne *language educator, educator*

Effingham
Spelbring, Brandi D. *language educator, writer*

Evanston
Pierrehumbert, Janet Breckenridge *language educator*
Reiss, Lenore Ann *language educator, retired secondary school educator*

Evansville
Walker, Cheryl A. *literature educator*

Glenview
Epstein, Barbara Myrna Robbin *retired language educator*

Lombard
Blair, Teresa Tarallo *foreign language educator*

Mount Vernon
Hall, Sharon Gay *retired language educator, artist*

Palatine
Bontempo, Elaine *language educator*

Keres, Karen Lynne *literature and language professor*

Park Ridge
Palmer, Rose *humanities educator, writer*

River Forest
Davlin, Mary Clemente *literature and language professor, sister*
Sweeney, Mickey *literature and language professor*

Rolling Meadows
Strongin, Bonnie Lynn *language educator*

Romeoville
Hoppe, Elizabeth Anne *philosopher, educator*
Jones, Therese Margaret *language educator, editor*

Springfield
Duley, Margot Iris *historian, educator*
Jackson, Jacqueline Dougan *literature educator, writer*

Urbana
Koenker, Diane P. *history professor*
Spence, Mary Lee *historian, educator*

Westmont
Lott, Kathy L. *language educator*

Wilmette
McClure, Julie Anne *literature educator*

INDIANA

Bloomington
Anderson, Judith Helena *English language educator*
Brown, Mary Ellen *retired humanities educator*
Lazerwitz, Katherine Christine *retired reading specialist, educator*
Peterson, M. Jeanne *historian, educator*

Carmel
Sukapdjo, Wilma Irene *language educator*

Converse
Oatess, Janet Sue *language educator*

Danville
Dechert, Wendy Dawn *speech educator, literature and language educator, writer*

Evansville
Baker, Ann Long *language educator*

Fort Wayne
Jones, Louise Conley *drama and literature educator, academic administrator*
Scheetz, Sister Mary JoEllen *English language educator*

Indianapolis
Connor, Ulla M. *linguistics educator*
Nnaemeka, Obioma Grace *French language and women's studies educator, consultant, researcher*
Smith, Christine Moore *literature and language professor, writer*

Kokomo
Cameron, Ann M. *language educator*

Muncie
Mjagkij, Nina *history professor*
Raleigh, Dawn Kristen *language educator*

Notre Dame
Derakhshani, Mana *literature and language professor*
Doody, Margaret Anne *English language educator*

Richmond
Siatra, Eleni *English educator*
Tolliver, Lorraine *language educator, writer*

Terre Haute
De Marr, Mary Jean *English language educator*
Montañez, Carmen Lydia *Spanish language educator, literature researcher, lawyer*

Upland
Collins, Jennifer L. *intercultural studies educator*

West Lafayette
Shackelford, Renae N. *literature educator, writer*

IOWA

Ames
Maxwell Dial, Eleanore *foreign language educator*

Cedar Rapids
Feuerhelm, Heather M. *language arts educator*

Dallas Center
Shepherd, Jean Marie *English educator*

Des Moines
Getty, Amy C. *language educator, department chairman*

Dubuque
Koch, Dianne M. *language educator, music educator*

Grinnell
Michaels, Jennifer Tonks *foreign language educator*

Iowa City
DiPardo, Anne *English language educator*
Kerber, Linda Kaufman *historian, educator*
Solbrig, Ingeborg Hildegard *literature educator, writer*

Long Grove
Holleran, Karen Elaine *literature and language professor*

New Hampton
Baltes, Sara Jayne *reading educator, elementary school educator*

Oskaloosa
Buresh, Laura Lynn *literature educator*
Robbins, Janet Linda *language educator*

Vinton
Mulvaney, Lois *French, English educator*

Waverly
Blair, Rebecca Sue *English educator*

KANSAS

Atchison
Lane, Elizabeth Ann *genealogist, researcher*

Dighton
Stanley, Ellen May *historian, consultant*

Emporia
Gerish, Deborah Elaine *history professor*

Great Bend
Gunn, Mary Elizabeth *retired language educator*

Hays
Duffy, Cheryl Hofstetter *language educator*

Lawrence
Cienciala, Anna Maria *history professor*

Onaga
Dillinger, Susan Alice *reading specialist*

Overland Park
Paulsen, Ruth Ann *French and Spanish language educator*

Topeka
Knight, Billie-Renee *language educator*

KENTUCKY

Crestview Hills
Daoud, Julie Perry *literature and language professor*

Cumberland
Thomas, Katherine M. *humanities educator, department chairman*

Frankfort
McCarthy, Lynn Cowan *genealogist, researcher*

Harrodsburg
Bradshaw, Phyllis Bowman *historian, historic site staff member*

Lexington
Perdue, Theda *history professor, writer*

Louisville
Mahoney, Margaret H. *history professor*
Zausch, Jo Fouts *literature and language professor, department chairman*

Murray
Neelon, Ann Marie *literature educator*

Pendleton
Tribble, Joan Lucille (Joan Farnsley Tribble) *retired literature and language professor, writer*

Richmond
Dean, Margaret Justice *literature and language professor*

Wilmore
Kuhn, Anne Naomi Wicker (Mrs. Harold B. Kuhn) *foreign language educator*

LOUISIANA

Baton Rouge
Doty, Gresdna Ann *theatre historian, educator*
Sasek, Gloria Burns *English language and literature educator*

Bogalusa
Villarrubia, Glenda Boone *reading specialist, reading coordinator, educational consultant, educator*

Natchitoches
Wells, Carol McConnell *genealogist, retired archivist*

New Orleans
Roberts, Louise Nisbet *philosopher, educator*

MAINE

Augusta
Rubinson, Jill Linda *literature and language professor*

Brunswick
Crandall, Elizabeth Walbert *retired home economics professor*

Fairfield
Joy, Suzanne Chauvin *language educator*

Orono
Billitteri, Carla *literature and language professor*

Peaks Island
Stelk, Virginia Horn *retired language educator*

Rockport
Goodwin, Doris Helen Kearns *historian, writer*

Waterville
Paliyenko, Adrianna Maria *foreign language educator*

MARYLAND

Annapolis
Brann, Eva Toni Helene *philosophy educator*
Carpenter, Marlene *retired philosopher, educator*

Baltimore
Chapelle, Suzanne Ellery Greene *history professor*
Ditz, Toby Lee *history professor*
Haeri, Niloofar M. *linguist, educator*
Kimbrough, Natalie *history and language educator*
Orgelfinger, Gail *literature educator*
Peirce, Carol Marshall *retired literature educator*
Rusinko, Elaine *language educator*
Schmidt, Elizabeth Suzanne *history professor*
Terborg-Penn, Rosalyn Marian *historian, educator*

Bel Air
Webster, Colleen Michael *language educator*

Bethesda
Child-Olmsted, Gisèle Alexandra *retired language educator*
Fee, Elizabeth *medical historian, administrator*

Bowie
LeCounte, Lola Houston *literature and language professor, educational consultant*

Catonsville
Oden, Gloria *language educator, poet*

Chevy Chase
Cline, Ruth Eleanor Harwood *translator*

College Park
Flieger, Verlyn B. *literature educator*
Hage, Madeleine Cottenet *French language educator*
Orlando, Valerie *language educator*
Oster, Rose Marie Gunhild *foreign language professional, educator*
Struna, Nancy L. *social historian, American studies educator*

Frostburg
Coward, Patricia Ann *language educator*

Gaithersburg
Raffini, Renee Kathleen *foreign language professional, educator*
Wang, Josephine Jung-Shan *language educator, translator*

Hyattsville
Golden, Marita *English language educator, foundation executive*
Rodgers, Mary Columbro *literature educator, writer, academic administrator*

La Plata
Stephanic, Barbara Jean *art historian, writer, curator, researcher*

Lutherville
Weiss, Susan Forscher *musicologist, educator*

Ocean Pines
Fullerton, Jean Leah *retired language educator, researcher, census researcher*

Owings Mills
Fortuin, Diane Hay *historian, researcher*

Pasadena
De Pauw, Linda Grant *historian, educator, writer*

Potomac
Sceery, Beverly Davis *genealogist, writer, educator*

Silver Spring
Borkovec, Vera Z. *literature and language professor*
Papas, Irene Kalandros *English language educator, poet, writer*
Ramsey, Priscilla R. *literature educator*

Sparks
Suarez-Murias, Marguerite C. *retired literature and language professor*

Towson
Baker, Jean Harvey *history professor*

Upper Marlboro
Brown, Mary Louvinia *literature and language professor, lawyer*

MASSACHUSETTS

Amherst
Baker, Lynne Rudder *philosophy educator*
Benson, Lucy Wilson *historian, consultant*
Brooks, A. Taeko *historian*
Taubman, Jane Andelman *literature and language professor*

Ashfield
Leete, Elisabeth Bourquin *retired language educator*

Boston
Scanlon, Dorothy Therese *history professor*
Tick, Judith *music historian, educator*

Bridgewater
McAlinden, Laura A. *humanities educator*

Cambridge
Chvany, Catherine Vakar *foreign language educator*
Elkins, Caroline M. *history professor, writer*
Faust, Drew Gilpin *historian, educator*
Hamner, Suzanne Leath *retired history educator*
Keller, Evelyn Fox *philosophy of science professor*
Lagemann, Ellen Condliffe *history professor, education educator, dean*
Laiou, Angeliki Evangelos *history professor*
Lepore, Jill *history professor, writer*
Maier, Pauline *historian, educator*
McDonald, Christie Anne *literature and language professor, writer*
Ritvo, Harriet *historian*
Rorty, Amelie *philosopher, educator*
Rosenkrantz, Barbara Gutmann *science and medicine historian*
Ruggie, Mary *humanities educator*
Ulrich, Laurel Thatcher *historian, educator*
Vendler, Helen Hennessy *literature educator, poetry critic*

Canton
Redmont, Joan *retired language educator*

Chestnut Hill
Lyerly, Cynthia Lynn *history professor*
Valette, Rebecca Marianne *Romance languages educator*

Fall River
Grandchamp, Jeanne P. *literature educator*

Falmouth
Fullerton, Davina *art historian, consultant, researcher*
Lamont, Rosette Clementine *language educator, journalist, translator*

Hingham
Richie, Margaret Bye *architectural historian*

Leverett
Margolis, Nadia *language educator, translator, medievalist*

Lowell
McAfee, Noelle Claire *philosopher, educator*

Medford
Romero, Christiane *German language educator*

Natick
Ma, Jing-Heng Sheng *language educator*

Newton
Reilly, Suzanne Sweeney *art historian, educator*

North Andover
Longsworth, Ellen Louise *art historian, consultant*

North Dartmouth
Teboh, Bridget A. *history professor, researcher*

Northampton
Banerjee, Maria Nemcova *Russian language and literature educator*

Salem
Gozemba, Patrica Andrea *women's studies and English language educator, writer*

South Hadley
Doezema, Marianne *art historian, museum director*
Horsnell, Margaret Eileen *retired historian*

Springfield
Bonemery, Anne M. *language educator*
Garabedian-Urbanowski, Martha Ann *foreign language educator*
Wyzik, Susan Aldrich *history professor*

Waltham
Hale, Jane Alison *literature and language professor*
Staves, Susan *humanities educator*

Watertown
Rivers, Wilga Marie *language educator*

Wellesley
Jacoff, Rachel *Italian language and literature educator*
Lefkowitz, Mary Rosenthal *ancient language educator*
Mistacco, Vicki E. *foreign language educator*
Putnam, Ruth Anna *philosopher, educator*

Westfield
Dunphy, Maureen Milbier *literature educator*

Weston
Higgins, Sister Therese *literature educator, former college president*

Weymouth
Atwater, Cynthia D. *English educator, secondary school educator*

Williamstown
Graver, Suzanne Levy *English literature educator*
O'Brien, Elvy Setterqvist *art historian, educator, editor*

Worcester
Dwork, Debórah *history professor*

MICHIGAN

Albion
Lockyer, Judith *language educator*

Ann Arbor
Carpenter, Bogdana Maria Magdalena *language educator*
Chang, Hsueh-lun Shelley *historian, researcher, writer*
Curzan, Anne *linguist, educator*
Eisenstein, Elizabeth Lewisohn *historian, educator*
Forsyth, Ilene Haering *art historian*

Berrien Springs
Summitt, April *history professor*

Beulah
Tanner, Helen Hornbeck *historian, consultant*

Bloomfield Hills
Starkman, Betty Provizer *genealogist, writer, educator*

Brownstown
Slingerland, Mary Jo *writing educator*

Dearborn
Lee, Dorothy Ann *comparative literature educator*

Detroit
Chauderlot, Fabienne-Sophie *foreign language educator*
Covensky, Edith *language educator, poet*
McNichols, Mary Alice *humanities educator*
Sims, Veronica Gail *literature educator*

East Lansing
Bruno, Maria Frances *writing and cultural educator*
Hine, Darlene Clark *history educator, administrator*
Tzitsikas, Helene *retired literature educator*

Flint
Thum, D. Maureen *language educator*

Jackson
Feldmann, Judith Gail *language professional, educator*

Kalamazoo
Geerling, Falinda Sue *language educator*
Wicklund, Karen Jean *voice and health professional, educator*

Livonia
Holtzman, Roberta Lee *French and Spanish language educator*

Rochester
Schimmelman, Janice G. *art historian*

West Bloomfield
Williamson, Marilyn Lammert *literature educator, academic administrator*

MINNESOTA

Coon Rapids
Carlson, Linda Marie *language arts educator, consultant*

Eagan
Bulger, Raymonde Albertine *French language educator*

Edina
Nelson, Patricia Joan Pingenot *retired language educator*

Mankato
Haas, Gretchen *literature and language professor*
Joseph, Diana Jennifer *literature and language professor*
Preska, Margaret Louise Robinson *historian, educational association administrator*

Minneapolis
Campbell, Karlyn Kohrs *speech educator*
Fergus, Patricia Marguerita *language educator, writer, editor*
Firchow, Evelyn Scherabon *German language and literature educator, writer*
Garner, Shirley Nelson *language educator*
Hauch, Valerie Catherine *historian, educator*
Kohlstedt, Sally Gregory *historian, educator*
Meyers, Miriam Watkins *retired language educator*

Moorhead
Buckley, Joan N. *retired literature and language professor*
Morrison, Barbara Sheffield *Japanese translator and interpreter, consultant, educator*

New Brighton
Corey, Mara J. *language educator*

Northfield
McKinsey, Elizabeth *humanities educator, consultant*
Steen, Mary Frost *literature and language professor*
Yandell, Cathy Marleen *language educator*
Zelliot, Eleanor Mae *history professor*

Saint Paul
Davis, Joy Lee *language educator*
Gaskill, Gayle *literature and language professor*
Huzar, Eleanor Goltz *historian, educator*
Monson, Dianne Lynn *literacy educator*

MISSISSIPPI

Clinton
Bigelow, Martha Mitchell *retired historian*

Florence
McLin-Mitchell, Velma Elaine *language educator, literature educator*

Itta Bena
Washington, Barbara J. *language educator*

Mississippi State
Este, Yolanda Denise *philosopher, educator*

Scooba
Penick, Catherine Tindal *literature and language professor*

Union
Feasel, Mandy Sessums *literature educator*

Wesson
Reid, Pamela Jones *humanities educator*

MISSOURI

Bolivar
Hill-Stanford, Holly *language educator*

Branson
Ford, Jean Elizabeth *retired language educator*

Cape Girardeau
Stepenoff, Bonnie Marie *history professor*

Columbia
Horner, Winifred Bryan *humanities educator, researcher, consultant, writer*
Keown, Linda Jane *language educator*
Pringle, Norma Jean Poarch *translator, educator*
Ragland, Ellie *literature and language professor*

Florissant
Ashhurst, Anna Wayne *foreign language educator*

Hayti
Jones, Christine *language arts educator*

Joplin
Murphy, Patricia *English educator*
Weber, Maryann *language educator*

Kansas City
Hodges Morgan, Anne *historian*

Kirkwood
Pacheco, Jill *language educator*

Liberty
Myers, Susan Marie *language educator*

Marshall
Zank, Virginia *literature and language professor*

Montrose
Talbot, Phyllis Mary *reading educator*

Parkville
Williams, Cynthia M. *literature and language professor*

Saint Charles
Green, Christina Marie *literature and language professor*

Saint Louis
Fisher-Bishop, Kelly Marie *literature educator, department chairman*
Rava, Susan Roudebush *French language and literature educator, community volunteer*
Reidy, Frances Ryan *language educator, editor, writer*
Westhoff, Laura M. *history professor*

Springfield
Easley, June Ellen Price *genealogist*

Warrensburg
Robbins, Dorothy Ann *foreign language educator*

Wentzville
Halliday, Kristen Lee *language educator*

Windyville
Blosser, Pamela Elizabeth *metaphysics educator, counselor, minister*
Condron, Barbara O'Guinn *philosopher, educator, academic administrator, writer*

MONTANA

Bozeman
Warrick, Kimberley Kaye *language and social studies educator*

Glendive
Kintz, Myrna Lutes *retired language educator*

Missoula
Chin, Beverly Ann *language educator*
Wigfied-Phillip, Ruth Genivea *genealogist, writer*

Red Lodge
Garrett, Maggie M. *retired literature educator*

NEBRASKA

Kearney
Bloomfield, Susanne George *language educator, writer*

Lincoln
Katz, Wendy Jean *art historian*
Mach, Jan Ellen Walkenhorst *literature educator, editor*

Omaha
Whitney, Tamora Ann *literature educator*

York
McNeese, Beverly Diane *language educator*

NEVADA

Las Vegas
Gafford, Mary May Grimes *retired humanities educator*
Harding, Nancy Elizabeth *language educator*
Harrison, Lizette Marie *language educator*

NEW HAMPSHIRE

Durham
Gold, Janet Nowakowski *Spanish language educator*
Linden, Blanche Marie Gemrose *history professor*

Hanover
Green, Mary Jean Matthews *foreign language educator*

Keene
Frink, Helen Hiller *language educator*

Manchester
Naccach-Hoff, Selma *language educator*

Merrimack
Bruce, Rae Marie *retired language educator*

Rollinsford
Davis, Jewel Beth *literature and language professor, writer, actress*

NEW JERSEY

Atlantic Highlands
Donoghue, Louise I. *retired language educator*

Belle Mead
Brown, Elizabeth Schmeck *fashion historian*

Blackwood
Perkins, Rita Wade *historian, educator*

Bordentown
Rasmuson, Lisa Marie *language educator*

Jersey City
Jennings, Sister Vivien *literature and language professor*
Kuhn, Melanie R. *literature educator, consultant*

Lincroft
Sidel, Enid Ruth *retired literature and language professor*
Sieben, Karen K. *philosopher, educator*

Livingston
Saffer, Amy Beth *foreign language educator*

Metuchen
Kushinsky, Jeanne Alice *humanities educator*
Laguna, Asela Rodríguez *Spanish language and literature educator*

Morristown
Blanchard, Mary Warner *historian, consultant*
Gorrell, Nancy S. *English language educator*

Mount Laurel
Eiferman, Sharon Rees *language educator, poet*

New Brunswick
Adickes, Sandra Elaine *language educator, writer*
Hartman, Mary Susan *historian, educator*

Newark
Varzegar, Minoo *literature educator, reading specialist*

North Brunswick
Moon, Kathleen K. *language arts educator*

Oradell
Monticone, Diane Therese *French educator*

Princeton
Frey, Julia Bloch *language educator, art historian, educator*
Jenson, Pauline Alvino *retired speech and hearing educator*
Painter, Nell Irvin *historian, educator, writer*
Rubin, Dorothy Molly *language educator, writer*
Scott, Joan Wallach *historian, educator*
Showalter, Elaine *humanities educator*

Somerville
D'Alessio, Jacqueline Ann *English educator*
Dickens-Simon, Nicole Pearlene *language educator*

Teaneck
Czin, Felicia Tedeschi *Italian language and literature educator, small business owner*
Dowd, Janice Lee *foreign language educator*
Walensky, Dorothy Charlotte *language educator*

Toms River
Bosley, Karen Lee *language educator, communications educator*
Willetts, Elizabeth M. *humanities lecturer, actress*

Upper Saddle River
Altman, Dorothy Jewell *language educator*

Wall
Mudd, Mary Cordelia *historian*

Wayne
Avolio, Annette M. *language educator*

West Long Branch
Williams, Hettie V. *history professor*

NEW MEXICO

Albuquerque
Fuller, Anne Elizabeth Havens *English language and literature educator, consultant*
Houston, Gail Turley *English language educator*
Shigekuni, Julie Yuriko *language educator, writer*
Tyner, Barbara Jane *art historian, writer*
Valdez, Dianna Marie *language educator, consultant*

Farmington
Peterson Gerstner, Janet *English professor*

Las Vegas
Simpson, Dorothy Audrey *retired speech educator*

Roswell
Maley, Jean Carol *foreign language educator*

Santa Fe
Peters, Margaret Annette *English language educator*
Vucinich, Janet *language educator*

Taos
Bolls, Imogene Lamb *English language educator, poet*

NEW YORK

Albany
Langer, Judith Ann *language educator*

Aurora
Greenwood, Pilar Fernández-Cañadas *language and literature educator*

Baldwin
DeFilippis, Gladys Llanes *language educator*

Batavia
Dassinger, Kristine R. *literature and language professor*

Binghamton
Gaddis Rose, Marilyn *literature educator, translator*
Sklar, Kathryn Kish *historian, educator*

Brockport
McKeen, Catherine A. *humanities educator*

Bronx
Bullaro, Grace Russo *literature, film and foreign language educator, critic*
Cammarata, Joan Frances *Spanish language and literature educator*
Dean, Nancy *literature educator, retired playwright*
Glickman, Benita *language educator, writer, poet*
O'Donnell, Angela Gina *literature and language professor, writer*

Bronxville
Peters, Sarah Whitaker *art historian, writer*

Brooklyn
Curtis-Tweed, Phyllis Marie *humanities educator*
Jaffe, Louise *literature and language professor, writer*
Jofen, Jean *foreign language educator*
King, Margaret Leah *history professor*
Lobron, Barbara L. *speech educator, editor, photographer, writer*
Lotringer, Sylvere *foreign language educator*
Marino, Gena *speech educator*

Buffalo
Busch, Susan Ellen *reading specialist*
Cajiao Salas, Teresa *language educator, educator*
Kessel, Joyce B. *English professor*
Merini, Rafika *humanities educator, writer, language educator*
Payne, Frances Anne *literature educator, researcher*

Canandaigua
Merrill, Trista Marie *literature and language professor, writer*

Canton
Goldberg, Rita Maria *foreign language educator*

Coram
Mohanty, Christine Ann *retired language educator, actress*

Cortland
Anderson, Donna Kay *musicologist, educator*
Masselink, Noralyn *literature educator*
Summers, Pamela French *literature and language professor, consultant*

Cortlandt Manor
Keating, Laura Lee M. *historian, records management professional*

East Hampton
Swerdlow, Amy *historian, educator, writer*

East Syracuse
Simson, Renate Maria *English and African American studies professor*

Elmira
Leveen, Pauline *retired history professor, government professor*
Pratt, Linda *language educator*

Farmingdale
Jacquette, Kathleen Marie *literature educator*
Shapiro, Ann R. *English educator*

Forest Hills
Kra, Pauline Skornicki *French language educator*

Fredonia
Smith, Claire Laremont *language educator*
Strada, Christina Bryson *retired humanities educator, librarian*

Garden City
Bouchard, Wendy Ann Borstel *language educator*
McNair, Marcia L. *language educator, writer, editor*

Great Neck
Legatt, Hadassa *language educator*

Greenvale
Maillet, Lucienne *humanities educator*

Hamilton
Nakhimovsky, Alice Stone *foreign language educator*
Staley, Lynn *literature educator*

Hastings On Hudson
Del Duca, Rita *language educator*

Herkimer
Martin, Lorraine B. *humanities educator*

Holley
Lepkowski, Suzanne Joy *language educator*

Hurley
Davila, Elisa *language educator, literature educator*

Ithaca
Brazell, Karen Woodard *literature educator*
Colby-Hall, Alice Mary *language educator*
Kittredge, Katharine Ottaway *literature and language professor*
Radzinowicz, Mary Ann *language educator*

Jamaica
Ekbatani, Glayol *language educator, director, writer*

New Paltz
Harris, Kristine *historian, educator*

New Rochelle
Fitch, Nancy Elizabeth *historian, educator*
Pérez-Bustillo, Mireya *language educator, writer, poet, translator*

New York
Allentuck, Marcia Epstein *English language educator, art history educator*
Apter, Emily *language educator*
Bonfante, Larissa *classics educator*
Burbank, Jane Richardson *historian, educator*
Cavallo, Jo Ann *language educator*
Caws, Mary Ann *literature and language professor*
Cook, Blanche Wiesen *historian, educator, journalist*
de Menil, Lois Pattison *historian, philanthropist*
Driver, Martha Westcott *literature educator, researcher, writer*
Gerber, Jane Satlow *history professor*
Geskin, Leah *foreign language educator*
Gluck, Carol *history professor*
Harris, Katherine Safford *speech and hearing educator*
Hartman, Joan Edna *retired literature educator, provost*
Hodes, Martha *history professor, writer*
Howe, Florence *literature educator, writer, publisher*
Kahan, Phyllis Irene *language educator, writer, editor, media consultant*
Karsen, Sonja Petra *retired literature educator*
Katz, Esther *historian, educator*
Kerz, Louise *historian*
Khidekel, Regina P. *art historian, curator, educator*
Krinsky, Carol Herselle *art historian, educator*
Lewyn, Ann Salfeld *retired English as a second language educator*
Lippman, Sharon Rochelle *art historian, filmmaker, art therapist*
Lyons, Bridget Gellert *language educator*
Makowiecka, Maria Hanna *literature educator, educator*
May, Gita *literature educator*
Maysilles, Elizabeth *speech communication professional, educator*
Mehta, Linn Cary *literature educator*
Middlebrook, Diane Wood *English language educator, writer*
Mirrer, Louise *language educator, consultant*
Nafisi, Azar *humanities educator*
Nochlin, Linda *art history educator*
Papalia, Diane Ellen *humanities educator*
Quinn, Alice Freeman *literature educator*
Quiñones Keber, Eloise *art historian, educator*
Ravitch, Diane Silvers *historian, educator, writer, government official*
Raymond, Dorothy Sarnoff *communications consultant, former actress, former singer*
Robertson, Anne Ferratt *language educator, researcher*
Rowen, Ruth Halle *musicologist, educator*
Skeeter, Sharyn Jeanne *literature educator, writer*
Spector, Johanna Lichtenberg *ethnomusicologist, former educator*
Stevens, Rosemary A. *medicine and public health historian, artist*
Stimpson, Catharine Rosalind *literature educator, writer*
Umeh, Marie Arlene *language educator*
Valenstein, Suzanne Gebhart *art historian*
Weil-Garris Brandt, Kathleen (Kathleen Brandt) *art historian*
Weinberg, H. Barbara *art historian, educator, curator*
Wiseman, Cynthia Sue *language educator*
Wortman, Marlene Stein *historian*
Wyschogrod, Edith *philosophy educator*
Yurchenco, Henrietta Weiss *musicologist, writer*

Newark
Biddle, Jane Lammert *retired English educator*

Newburgh
Adams, Barbara *language educator, poet, writer*

Northport
Russo, Christine Fiorella *language educator*

Nyack
Pease, Eleanor Jeanne *humanities educator*

Orangeburg
Dolgin, Ellen Ecker *English and gender studies professor*

Oswego
Smiley, Marilynn Jean *musicologist*

Potsdam
Downing, Caroline Jane *art historian, educator, archaeologist*
Regan, Marie Carbone *retired language educator*

Poughkeepsie
Daniels, Elizabeth Adams *English language educator*
Hytier, Adrienne Doris *French language educator*
Saunders, Judith P. *literature and language professor, writer*

Queens Village
Raines, Judi Belle *language educator, historian*

Rochester
Herminghouse, Patricia Anne *foreign language educator*
Hollis, Susan Tower *history professor*
Jörgensen, Beth Ellen *Spanish language educator*
Kehoe, Jennifer Spungin *English language educator, writer, children's book editor*
Polowe-Aldersley, Stephanie Ruth *English language educator, educational association administrator, legislator*
Young, Mary Elizabeth *history professor*

Rockville Centre
Fitzgerald, Janet Anne *philosophy educator, academic administrator*

Saratoga Springs
Caruso, Adrienne Iorio *retired language educator*

Schenectady
Helmar-Salasoo, Ester Anette *language and literature educator, researcher*

South Fallsburg
Kalter, Eileen M. *retired language educator*

Stony Brook
Harris, Alice *linguist, educator*
Zimmermann, Eléonore M. *French and comparative literature educator*

Syracuse
Fish-Kalland, Yvonne J. *language educator*
Waddy, Patricia A. *historian, architecture educator*

Ticonderoga
Breitenbach, Deborah Jones *language educator*

Valley Stream
Lois, Dolores Carmen *literature educator*

Webster
Baden, Joan H. *retired language educator*

NORTH CAROLINA

Asheville
Voigt, Ellen *literature educator*

Chapel Hill
Davis, Sarah Irwin *retired language educator*

Charlotte
Cernyak-Spatz, Susan E. *retired language educator*
Hill, Ruth Foell *language consultant*

Cullowhee
Fenton, Mary Catherine *literature educator*

Dallas
McCullough, Alicia *English language educator*

Dobson
McNeil, Amy *language educator, web site designer*

Durham
Van Duzer, Dory A. *translator*
Wald, Priscilla B. *language educator*

Fayetteville
Curry, Virginia Frances *retired language educator*
McMillan, Bettie Barney *language educator*
Miller, Bertha Hampton *history professor*

Fearrington Village
Cell, Gillian Townsend *retired historian, educator*

Greensboro
Archibald, Brigitte Edith *language educator*
Nieman, Valerie Gail *language educator, journalist*
Penninger, Frieda Elaine *retired literature educator*
Spencer, Linda Anne *history professor*

Greenville
Bauer, Margaret Donovan *literature and language professor, editor*

Hickory
Samamra, Elizabeth Prestwood *literature educator*

Jacksonville
Fischer, Violeta Pèrez Cubillas *Spanish literature and linguistics educator*

Kannapolis
Wilson, Evelyn Gleen *retired language educator*

Kernersville
Wallace, Stephanie Jean *language educator*

Laurinburg
Key, Kristina Pope *literature and language professor*

Pittsboro
Boyce, Emily Stewart *retired library and information science educator, retired library and information scientist*

Raleigh
Bykova, Marina F. *philosopher, educator*

Sanford
York, Carolyn Pleasants Stearns *language educator*

Weaverville
Chamberlain, Elizabeth Simmons *retired English language educator*

Wilmington
Stanfield-Maddox, Elizabeth *language educator, translator*

NORTH DAKOTA

Belcourt
LaRocque, Geraldine Ann *literature educator*

Grand Forks
Caldwell, Mary Ellen *language educator*

OHIO

Athens
Whealey, Lois Deimel *humanities scholar*

Beverly
Foland-Bush, Terri *language educator, speech educator*

Brecksville
Pappas, Effie Vamis *language educator, finance educator, writer, poet, artist*

Cleveland
Dancyger, Ruth *art historian*
Goral, Judith Ann *language educator*
Leary, Mary Deborah *language educator*
Miller, Genevieve *retired medical historian*
Nelson, Sue Grodsky *humanities educator, consultant*
Robinson, Alice Helene *language educator, administrative assistant*
Taylor, Margaret Wischmeyer *retired language educator*
Velasco, Esda Nury *speech and language professional*

Columbus
Webber, Sabra Jean *humanities educator, department chairman*
Williams, Susan Shidal *language educator*

Cuyahoga Falls
Walker, Suzannah Wolf *language educator*

Dayton
Alexander, Roberta Sue *history professor*
Harden, Oleta Elizabeth *literature educator, academic administrator*

Dublin
McGary, Daria L. *foreign languages educator*

Kent
Fein, Susanna Greer *literature educator*

Kirtland
Asnien, Phyllis Arline *humanities educator, writer*

Oberlin
Collins, Martha *English language educator, writer*

Oxford
Klosawska, Anna M. *literature and language professor*

West Farmington
Smith, Agnes Monroe *history professor*

Youngstown
Bowers, Bege Kaye *literature educator, communications educator, academic administrator*
Checcone, Iole Carlesimo *foreign language educator*

OKLAHOMA

Ada
Reese, Linda Williams *history professor*
Yarbrough, Trisha Marie *literature and language professor*

Alva
Almgren, Kandee Ann *language educator*

Choctaw
Warren-Billings, Janet Marie *language educator*

Copan
Harsh, Mitzi Ann *language educator, coach*

Durant
Allen, Paula Smith *literature and language professor*

Mustang
Dunn, Karen S. *language educator*

Oklahoma City
Hooper, Marie E. *history professor*
Judge, Mary Kathleen *humanities educator*

Sayre
Haught, Judy C. *language educator*

Tulsa
Chew, Pamela Christine *language educator*

Weatherford
Craig, Viki Pettijohn *language educator*

Wynnewood
Parker, Lois W. *retired educator and language professor*

OREGON

Eugene
Lansdowne, Karen Myrtle *retired English language and literature educator*

La Grande
Ewing, Marilyn *English educator*

Marylhurst
Roland, Meg *literature educator*

Monmouth
Strand, Cheryl Marie *Spanish language, literature educator*

Newport
Pavlish, Catherine Ann *language educator, writer*

Portland
Steinman, Lisa Malinowski *English literature educator, writer*

PENNSYLVANIA

Annville
Tezanos-Pinto, Rosa *Hispanic American literature educator*

Avella
Blose, Ruth Elayne *language educator*

Bala Cynwyd
Dorwart, Bonnie Brice *historian, retired rheumatologist*

Berwyn
Bluestone, Ellen Hope *literature, writing, and women's studies professor, writer*

Bethlehem
Parmet, Harriet Abbey L. *literature educator*

Biglerville
Hartlaub, Maxine Louise *literature educator*

Blue Bell
Roden, Carol Looney *retired language educator*

Bryn Mawr
Alter, Maria Pospischil *language educator*
Gaisser, Julia Haig *classics educator*
Lane, Barbara Miller (Barbara Miller-Lane) *humanities educator*
Lang, Mabel Louise *classics educator*

California
Schwerdt, Lisa Mary *language educator*

Colmar
Weber-Roochvarg, Lynn *English as a second language educator, communications consultant*

East Stroudsburg
Switzer, Sharon Cecile *language educator, researcher*

Easton
Byrd, Deborah Lea *literature and language professor*
Schlueter, June Mayer *literature educator, writer*

Edinboro
Kinch, Janet Carolyn Brozic *English and German language and literature educator, academic administrator*

Grantham
Downing, Crystal L. *literature and language professor, writer*

Greensburg
Kochman, Susan M. *language educator*

Harrisburg
Gibson, Shere Capparella *foreign language educator*
Hoffman, Mary Hills *literature educator, publishing executive*

Haverford
Jorden, Eleanor Harz *linguist, educator*

Hershey
Dellasega, Cheryl *humanities educator*

Indiana
Roumm, Phyllis Evelyn Gensbigler *retired literature educator, writer*

Johnstown
Lynch, Alessandra Jacqueline *literature educator, poet*

Kutztown
Meyer, Susan Moon *speech pathologist, educator*
Vergereau Dewey, Sylvie Pascale *French and Spanish language educator*

Lancaster
Polite, Karen E. *humanities educator*

Landenberg
Lloyd, Nancy G. *language educator*

Lansdowne
Purcell, Mary Hamilton *speech educator*

Lewisburg
Pickering, Roberta Ann *language educator, gifted and talented educator*

Lock Haven
Story, Julie Ann *language educator*

Mc Keesport
Preuss, Mary Herge *Spanish educator*

Meadville
Stewart, Anne Williams *historian, writer, researcher*

Media
Goldschmidt, Myra Margaret *literature and language professor*

Merion Station
Littell, Marcia Sachs *Holocaust and genocide studies professor*

Monaca
Marshall, Cynthia Louise *language educator*

Moon Township
Mooney, Jennifer *literature educator*

Nanticoke
Stchur, Mary Nanorta *literature and language professor*
Whitebread, Melanie Jo *language educator*

New Castle
Sands, Christine Louise *retired English educator*

New Freedom
Sedlak, Valerie Frances *retired English language and literature educator, academic administrator*

Newtown Square
DeLuca, Jennie M. *English educator*

Paoli
Whittington, Virginia Carolina *language educator, writer*

Philadelphia
Berry, Mary Frances *history professor, former federal agency administrator*
Duclow, Geraldine *historian, librarian*
Matus-Mendoza, Mariadelaluz *language educator, sociologist*
McDiarmid, Lucy *literature educator, writer*
Quann, Joan Louise *French language educator, real estate broker*
Walker, Kathy Le Mons *history professor*
Woodside, Lisa Nicole *humanities educator*

Pittsburgh
Harris, Ann Birgitta Sutherland *art historian*
Paulston, Christina Bratt *linguistics educator*
Rawski, Evelyn Sakakida *history professor*

Reading
Peemoeller, Helen Carolyn *literature educator, department chairman*

Saint Davids
Boehne, Patricia Jeanne *foreign languages educator, department chairman*

Scranton
Lawhon, Patricia Patton *literature and language professor, writer educator*

State College
Ferguson, Pamela Santavicca *language educator, department chairman*

Swarthmore
Morgan, Kathryn Lawson *retired historian, educator*
Napoli, Donna Jo *linguistics educator, writer*
North, Helen Florence *classicist, educator*

University Park
Grosholz, Emily Rolfe *philosopher, educator, poet*
Halsey, Martha Taliaferro *Spanish language educator*

West Chester
Pauly, Rebecca Mehl *foreign languages educator*

Wilkes Barre
Sweeney-Zamboni, Eileen T. *literature and language professor*

Willow Grove
Windheim, Randi Mackler *literature educator*

Yardley
Prato, Ellen C. *literature educator*

RHODE ISLAND

Kingston
Schwartz, Marie Jenkins *historian, professor*

North Kingstown
Mellor, Kathy *English as a second language educator*

Providence
Ackerman, Felicia Nimue *philosophy educator, writer*
Arant, Patricia *Slavic languages and literature educator*
Blasing, Mutlu Konuk *English language educator*
Harleman, Ann *literature educator, writer*
Wright, Carolyn D. (C.D. Wright) *language educator, poet*

Smithfield
Litoff, Judy Barrett *history professor*

SOUTH CAROLINA

Chester
Mayhugh, Wanda E. *language educator*

Columbia
Gilbert, Katherine E. *literature and language professor*
Synnott, Marcia Graham *history professor*

Fort Mill
Pettus, Mildred Louise *retired history professor, writer*

Greenville
Chickvary, Karin Elizabeth *literature educator*

Hilton Head Island
Stehle, Cheryl Diane French *language educator*

Orangeburg
Wong, Mitali R.P. *language educator, consultant*

Pageland
Simon, Kindra Lee *language educator, translator*

Pawleys Island
Ford, Anna Maria *language educator*

Spartanburg
Raquidel, Danielle Colette *language educator, researcher*

Tigerville
Thompson, Becky Louise *English educator*

SOUTH DAKOTA

Rapid City
Palmer, Sally Broadbent *language educator*

Spearfish
Hubbard, Constance E. *language educator, piano teacher*
Shearer-Cremean, Christine Louise *literature educator*

TENNESSEE

Clinton
Price, Lori Jean *humanities educator*

Kingsport
Egan, Martha Avaleen *history professor, archivist, consultant, music educator*
Wolfe, Margaret Ripley *historian, educator, consultant*

Knoxville
De Weerdt, Hilde Godelieve *humanities educator*

Lewisburg
Villines, Benita Curtis *language educator*

Martin
Cowser, Mary Ellen *literature and language professor*
Huse, Heidi Anne *language educator*

Murfreesboro
Kelker, Nancy Lee *art historian*
Rupprecht, Nancy Ellen *historian, educator*

Nashville
Beach, Margaret Smith *retired language educator*
Clark, Shari Jill *literature and language professor*
Cook, Ann Jennalie *literature educator, cultural organization administrator*
Irby, Jocelyn Adkins *language educator, consultant*
Risko, Victoria J. *language educator*

Rogersville
Fairchild, Dorcas Sexton *language educator*

South Pittsburg
Cloer, Jane *language educator*

Springfield
Maddux, Sandra O'Kelly *retired language educator*

Tullahoma
Majors, Betty-Joyce Moore *genealogist, writer*

TEXAS

Alpine
Antrim, Nancy Mae *literature and language professor, consultant*

Austin
Baltzer, Rebecca A. *musicologist, researcher, consultant*
Williams, Diane Elizabeth *architectural historian, photographer*

Beaumont
Hawkins, Emma B. *humanities educator*

Bertram
Albert, Susan Wittig *writer*

Brownsville
Ferráez-McKenzie, Marie Antoineta *literature and language professor, real estate agent*

Bryan
Van Ouwerkerk, Anita Harrison *reading educator*

College Station
Ezell, Margaret M. *language educator*
Unterberger, Betty Miller *history professor, writer*

Dallas
Chawner, Lucia Martha *language educator*
Comini, Alessandra *art historian, educator*
Crossland, Mary Helen *language educator*
Davis, Daisy Sidney *history professor*
Nabors, Marion Carroll *retired English educator*

Denison
Rushing, Dorothy M. *retired historian, writer*

Denton
Lawhon, Tommie Collins Montgomery *humanities educator*
Sánchez, Patsy Y. *bilingual educator*
White, Nora Lizabeth *language educator*

Dripping Springs
DeLacretaz, Cheryl Diane *English educator*

El Paso
Cancino, Nelly *language educator, adult education educator*
Cuartas, Beatriz H. *humanities educator*
Sloane, Brenda Sue *language educator*

Fort Worth
Cox, Alma Tenney *retired language educator, retired science educator*
Johnson, Abbie Mae *language educator*
Robin, Clara Nell (Claire Robin) *English language educator*
Shehan, Geraldean Harrison *ESL educator*

Houston
Belk, Joan Pardue *language and literature educator*
Drew, Katherine Fischer *history professor*
Ehrmann, Susanna *language educator, photographer, writer*
Hattaway, Karen Ann *literature and language professor*
Pali, Jennifer Rochelle *language educator*
Pospisil, JoAnn *historian, archivist*
Schultz, Arlene Elaine *literature educator*
Thompson, Ewa M. *foreign language educator*
Vallbona, Rima-Gretel Rothe *retired foreign language educator, writer*

Hurst
Baw, Cindy A. *literature and language professor*
Buinger, Mary Kay *history professor*

Klein
Thompson, Patricia Rather *literature educator, department chairman*

Lubbock
Hurst, Mary Jane *language educator*

Mesquite
Dean, Sherry Lynn *language educator, speech professional*

Midland
Lindsey-Hicks, Glenda *literature and language professor*

Missouri City
de Kanter, Ellen Ann *retired English and foreign language educator*

Odessa
Forsyth, Beverly K. (Beverly K. Roy Davidson Forsyth) *language educator, writer*

Plano
Brown, Peggy Ann *language educator, writer*

San Antonio
Myers, Ellen Howell *historian, educator*
Oleszkiewicz-Peralba, Malgorzata *Latin American literature and culture studies educator*
Tackett, Susan J. *language educator*
Vinson, Audrey Lawson *retired literature and language professor*
von Raffler-Engel, Walburga (Walburga Engel) *retired language educator*
Woodson, Linda Townley *English educator, writer*

Somerville
Hairrell, Angela Renee *humanities educator, researcher*

Texas City
Allen, Shirley Jeanne *humanities educator*

Waco
McManness, Linda Marie *language educator*

UTAH

Logan
Funda, Evelyn *literature educator*

Provo
Adams, Linda Hunter *humanities educator*
Embry, Jessie L. *historian, researcher*

Salt Lake City
Arrington, Harriet Ann Horne *historian, biographer, researcher, writer*
Toscano, Margaret Merrill *humanities educator, writer*

South Jordan
Rowley, Maxine Lewis *retired home economics and consumer educator, retired department chairman*

VERMONT

Castleton
Keyes, Flo *language educator*
Meloy, Judith Marie *humanities educator*

Norwich
Carlson, Elizabeth Borden *historian, educator*

Randolph Center
Murray, Nancy Jean *language educator, humanities educator*

Williston
Laskarzewski, Debra Sue *language educator*

VIRGINIA

Alexandria
Kaye, Ruth Lincoln *historian*

Annandale
Seyler, Dorothy U. *literature and language professor, writer*

Arlington
Owen, Sarah-Katharine *language educator*
Strelau, Renate *historical researcher, artist*
Wilcox, Shirley Jean Langdon *genealogist*

Callao
Freeman, Anne Hobson *language educator, writer*

Centreville
De Gennaro, Eida Mendoza *interpreter, real estate agent*

Charlottesville
Chase, Karen Susan *English literature educator*
Lane, Ann Judith *history professor, women's studies educator*

Covesville
Williams, Patricia Anne *philosopher, writer*

Fairfax
Bailey, Helen McShane *historian, consultant*
Brown, Lorraine A. *literature educator*
Lavine, Thelma Zeno *philosophy educator*

Farmville
Brock-Servais, Rhonda Lee *literature and language professor*

Ferrum
Grimes, Margaret Katherine *English educator*

Fredericksburg
Almond, Beverly McCullough *literature educator*

Great Falls
Castro-Klaren, Sara *Latin American literature professor*

Manassas
Casal, Laura C. *literature educator, consultant*

Martinsville
Wade, Gayle Panagos *literature and language professor*

Newport News
Hurst, Rebecca McNabb *language educator*

Radford
Kirby, Susan Collins *literature and language professor, consultant*

Reston
Thayer, Joan Peregoy *ancient language educator*

Richmond
Levit, Héloïse B. (Ginger Levit) *art historian, journalist, art dealer, consultant*
Taggart, Barbara Ann *retired language educator*

Roanoke
Hankla, Cathryn *language educator, writer*

Sterling
Naquin, Deborah Ann *humanities educator*

Sumerduck
McCamy, Sharon Grove *English educator*

Tappahannock
McGuire, Lillian Hill (Lillian Elizabeth Hill McGuire) *historian, researcher, retired education educator, writer*

Virginia Beach
Dickerson, Nancy Knewstep *language educator*
Jacobson, Frances M. *history professor*
Reece-Porter, Sharon Ann *international human rights educator*

Williamsburg
Nettels, Elsa *English language educator*

Winchester
Tisinger, Catherine Anne *retired history professor*

WASHINGTON

Auburn
Sims, Marcie Lynne *language educator, writer*

Colville
Rudd, Cheryl Kai *language educator*

Lakewood
Scannell, Vicki *humanities and language educator, consultant*

Olympia
Coontz, Stephanie Jean *history professor, writer*

Puyallup
Brittin, Marie E. *retired communications, psychology, speech-language and hearing science educator*

Seattle
Behler, Diana Ipsen *Germanic and comparative literature educator*
Snow-Smith, Joanne Inloes *art history educator*
Ullman, Joan Connelly *history professor, researcher*
VanArsdel, Rosemary Thorstenson *English studies educator*
Wilke, Sabine *language educator*

Walla Walla
Rasmussen, Jo Anne Dickens *speech educator, theater director*

WEST VIRGINIA

Morgantown
Blaydes, Sophia Boyatzies *English language educator*

WISCONSIN

Coon Valley
Nordstrom, Donna Olene *language educator*

Eau Claire
See, Patti K. *humanities educator*

Fitchburg
Schwenn, Kim Elizabeth *language educator*

Franksville
Jensen, Dana G. *literature educator*

Goodman
Cummings, Toni Marie *language educator*

Juneau
Shramek, Erin Elizabeth *language educator*

Kohler
Reilly, Sharon *literature educator*

La Crosse
Poulton, Leslee *language educator*

Luck
Wicklund, Judith K. *language educator, writer*

Madison
Ciplijauskaite, Birute *humanities educator*
Dubrow, Heather *literature educator*
Dunlavy, Colleen A. *historian*
Zell, Josephine May *retired language educator*

Milwaukee
Gallop, Jane (Jane Anne Gallop) *women's studies educator, writer*
Lea, Filomena *English language educator, writer*
Zurcher, Amelia Anne *literature educator*

Oconto
Nichols, Diane Colleen *historian, retired municipal official*

Stanley
Rasmussen, Dianne *English educator*

Stevens Point
Gott, Patricia A. *literature educator*

Sturgeon Bay
Maher, Virginia Jones *art historian, educator*

Waukesha
Ness Marineau, Brenda L. *language educator*

WYOMING

Basin
Gray, Lisa Marie *language educator*

Sheridan
Aguirre Batty, Mercedes *Spanish and English language educator, literature educator*

CANADA

BRITISH COLUMBIA

North Saanich
Saddlemyer, Ann (Eleanor Saddlemyer) *humanities educator, critic, theater historian*

ONTARIO

North York
Thomas, Clara McCandless *retired literature educator*

Ottawa
Labarge, Margaret Wade *medieval history professor, historian, writer*
Squire, Anne Marguerite *retired humanities educator*

GERMANY

Berlin
Piper, Adrian Margaret Smith *philosopher, artist, educator*

Frankfurt
Levin Baroness Von Gleichen, Tobe *language educator, editor, volunteer*

JAPAN

Kashiwara
Hori, Keiko *English literature educator*

ADDRESS UNPUBLISHED

Abbott, Rebecca Phillips *art historian, consultant, photographer, director*
Abernethy, Sharron Gray *language educator*
Adamson, Lynda G. *literature educator, writer*
Adang, Rosemary *humanities educator*
Agüero-Torres, Irene Beatriz *language educator*
Alexander, Alison F. *communication educator*
Altman, Sarah Busa *human services educator*
Anderson, Rhoda *language educator*
Ankney, Rachel Blue *language educator*
Araujo, Ilka Vasconcelos *musicologist, educator*
Arnold, Marygwen Suella *language educator, medical/surgical nurse*
Bates, Margaret P. *historian*
Baym, Nina (Nina Baym Stillinger) *literature educator, researcher*
Berns, Beverly J. *language educator*
Biles, Gloria C. *historian, educator*
Black, Julie L. *language educator*
Blackmun, Barbara Winston *art historian, educator, academic administrator*
Boggess, Carol Brownscombe *language educator, writer*
Bok, Sissela *philosopher, writer*
Bolsterli, Margaret Jones *English professor, farmer*
Bomar, Gail Marie *language educator*
Bordelon, Suzanne Mackie *writing and rhetoric educator*
Bowen, Barbara Cherry *French and comparative literature educator*
Boyer, Joan Sue *liberal arts educator, social sciences educator*
Brewster, Elizabeth Winifred *literature educator, poet, writer*
Bruckner, Matilda Tomaryn *romance language and literature educator*
Buechling, Linda *language educator*
Bush, Sarah Lillian *historian*
Caldwell, Louise Phinney *historical researcher, community volunteer*
Caldwell, Patricia Ann *language educator*
Cappello, Eve *speaker, trainer, writer*
Carls, Alice Catherine *history professor*
Carswell, Linda Gail *language educator, department chairman*
Caswell, Frances Pratt *retired language educator*
Cavallo-Best, Maria Isolina *language educator*
Cecchini, Sonia Nathalie *speech and drama educator*
Chalfant-Allen, Linda Kay *retired Spanish language educator*
Chambers, Marjorie Bell *historian*
Chase, Dawn Eileen *language educator*
Chess, Sonia Mary *retired language educator*
Childs, Christine Manzo *language arts educator*
Clark, Eve Vivienne *linguist, educator*
Clayton, Heather Lynn *language educator*
Collins, Jean Katherine *language educator*
Conklin, Peggy Brown *history professor*
Custureri, Mary Catherine Foca *literature educator*
Dahlin, Angela Denise *language educator*
Daileader, Celia Rose *literature educator*
Dallolio, Janelle K. *language educator, literature and language educator*
Davis, Natalie Zemon *retired history professor*
Deal, Kate *language educator*
Di Paolo, Maria Grazia *language educator, writer*
Domski, Mary Ann *philosopher, educator*
Downs, Dorothy Rieder *art historian, consultant, writer*
Durek, Dorothy Mary *retired language educator*
Edens, Betty Joyce *reading recovery educator*
Edmonds, Crystal D. *language educator, distance learning coordinator*
Edwards, Annmarie Monica *language educator, career coach, entrepreneur*
Emmett, Rita *professional speaker*
Erickson, Carol Jean *literature and language professor*
Fabre, Niza Elsie *African studies and Hispanic literature educator*
Fadley, Ann Miller *language educator, literature educator*
Feal, Gisele Catherine *foreign language educator*
Fisher, Anita Jeanne (Kit Fisher) *retired language educator*
Freeman, Allison Browne *museum educator, researcher*
Fuentes, June Toretta *language educator*
Gac-Artigas, Priscilla *foreign language educator*
Gerlach, Jeanne Elaine *English language educator*
Gillett, Mary Caperton *military historian*
Glick, Ruth Burtnick *literature educator, writer*
Gofferje, Hadwig *retired language educator*
Gomez, Margarita *language educator, researcher*
Hadda, Janet Ruth *language educator, lay psychoanalyst*
Hamilton, Virginia Van der Veer *historian, educator*
Haring, Ellen Stone (Mrs. E. S. Haring) *philosophy educator*
Hartman, Marilyn D. *English and art educator*
Hegler, Ellen Marie *retired language educator, small business owner*
Hicks, Melinda M. *history professor*
Hiler, Monica Jean *reading educator, sociology educator*
Hoart, Gladys Gallagher *language educator*
Hoggatt, Clela Allphin *language educator*
Houshiar, Bobbie Kay *retired language arts educator*
Huegel, Donna Marie *historian, writer, artist, archivist*
Huerta, Mary Zapata *English and foreign language educator*
Hutcheon, Linda Ann *English language educator*
Isaac, Susan Victoria *literature and language professor, department chairman*
Johanyak, Debra L. *literature educator, consultant*
Jones, Mary Ellen Snouffer *language educator*
Kaminsky, Alice Richkin *retired literature educator*
Kaplan, Alice *humanities educator, writer*
Karasick, Adeena Michelle *literature and language professor, writer*
Katz, Susan Arons *language arts specialist, writer, poet*
Keeter, Lynn Carpenter *language educator*
Kelly, Judith Reese *literature educator*
Kewish, Sharon Patricia *literature educator*
Key, Rachel E. *literature and language professor*
Killebrew, Betty Rackley *language educator*
Kinney, Jeanne Kawelolani *English studies educator, writer*
Kitch, Terri Lynn *language educator*
Klaw, Barbara Anne *language educator*
Klinghoffer, Judith Apter *historian, consultant*
Kohler, Sheila M. *humanities educator, writer*
Kornasky, Linda A. *literature educator*
Korsgaard, Christine Marion *philosophy educator*
Kravitz, Ellen King *musicologist, educator*
Kuehn, Lucille M. *retired humanities educator*
Lassaletta, Antonia Mir *language educator*
Lawson, Carolina Donadio *language educator, translator*
Lee, Corinne Adams *retired English teacher*
Lehman, Barbara Albu *foreign language educator, translator*
Leon Rivera, Aida I. *language educator*
Levi, Marina J. *language educator, theater educator*
Levinsky, Frieda Libby *language educator*
Lindboe, Berit Roberg *retired language educator, literature educator*
Lowenthal, Constance *art historian, consultant*
Lower, Wendy Morgan *historian, educator*
Lukomsky, Vera *musicologist, music educator, pianist*
Mandell, Gail Patricia *language educator*
Manuelian, Lucy Der *art historian, architecture educator*
Marée, Kathleen Nancy *retired language educator*
Marion, Marjorie Anne *English language educator, educational consultant*
Martin, Trisa *education and human development educator*
Massé, Michelle A. *language educator*
Mathews, E. Anne Jones *retired library educator, academic administrator*
McClain, Theresa L. *language educator*
McClure, Evelyn Susan *historian, photographer*
McDaniel, Anna S. *language educator*
McDermott, Agnes Charlene Senape *philosophy educator*
McGann, Lisa B. Napoli *language educator*
McGill, Carla Ann *language educator*
McKee, Betty Davis *English language educator*
McMaster, Juliet Sylvia *English language educator*
McWeeny, Jen *philosopher, educator*
Metcalf, Pauline Cabot *architectural historian*
Millstein, Roberta L. *humanities educator*
Miscella, Maria Diana *humanities educator*
Mitchell, Brenda Marie *humanities educator*
Molloy, Sylvia *language educator*
Morales, Marcia Paulette Merry *language educator, archaeologist*
Morrill, Penny Chittim *art historian*
Murphy, Madeleine *literature educator*
Naumer, Carola *art historian, educator*
Nelson, Kirsten Cigler *language educator*
Neshyba, Monica Vasquez *language educator*
Newbery, Ilse Sofie Magdalene *German language educator*
Nicholas, Lynn Holman *historian, researcher, writer*
Nochman, Lois Wood Kivi (Mrs. Marvin Nochman) *retired literature educator*
Palmer, Marilyn Joan *English composition educator*
Palmieri, Dora Ann *retired language educator*
Panzer, Mary Caroline *historian, museum curator*
Parrott, Lois Anne Muyskens *humanities educator*
Parulis, Cheryl *English, drama and speech educator*
Paul, Julia *ancient history researcher*
Perdigó, Luisa Marina *foreign language and literature educator*
Perlingieri, Ilya Sandra *art history scholar, writer*
Peterson, Betty W. *language educator, writer*
Ping-Robbins, Nancy Regan *musicologist, educator*
Pinkham, Lise Kutzman *humanities educator*
Pockrass, Marlene Morgan *retired literature educator*
Pulitzer, Emily Rauh (Mrs. Joseph Pulitzer Jr.) *art historian, consultant*
Quiles, Dolores *foreign language educator*
Rackin, Phyllis *retired English language educator*
Randall, Catharine *French educator*
Ransom, Nancy Alderman *sociology and women's studies educator, academic administrator*
Reeves, Kathleen Walker *English language educator*
Reiff, Raychel Ann Haugrud *language educator*
Retzlaff, Kay L. *literature educator, writer*
Rickard, Ruth David *retired history professor, retired political science professor*
Ritter, Heather Dawn *language educator*
Robinson, Mary Elizabeth Goff *retired historian, researcher*
Rochberg, Francesca *historian*
Rogers, Katharine Munzer *English literature educator*
Rosen, Roberta *philosophy educator*
Rossi, Mary Ann *classicist, researcher*
Ryan, Marleigh Grayer *language educator*
St. Pierre, Mary Sharon *literature educator*
Salmi, Ellablanche *retired literature and language professor, artist, writer*
Sanders, Elizabeth Grey *English and history professor*
Sanders, Patricia Smith *language educator, consultant*
Sawai, Dahleen Emi *language educator*
Schadegg, Amy Rachelle *language educator*

Schadow, Karen E. *public speaking trainer, educator*
Schendel, Kelly Ryan *literature educator, writer*
Schmider, Mary Ellen Heian *American studies educator, academic administrator*
Schneider, Valerie Lois *retired speech educator*
Schoen, Carol Bronston *retired English language educator*
Schor, Laura Struminger *historian*
Schumacher, Julie Alison *literature and language professor*
Scott, Anne Byrd Firor *history professor*
Seniors, Paula Marie *history professor, researcher*
Sessions, Bettye Jean *humanities educator*
Sheffey, Ruthe T. *language educator*
Shepard, Suzanne V. *language educator*
Sheppard, Jennifer Modlin *genealogist*
Sherwin, Susan J. *retired language arts educator*
Shillingsburg, Miriam Jones *literature educator, academic administrator*
Shoebridge, Sylvia B. *retired historian, educator*
Shubert, Abby Noonan *language educator*
Silverman, Joan L. *historian, consultant*
Sinclair, Patricia White *literature educator*
Skory, Janel Lynn *English and speech educator*
Slagle, Judith Bailey *literature/language educator*
Smith, Betty Mallett *philosopher, educator*
Smith, Dolores T. *language educator, consultant*
Soleimanpour, Mojgan *language educator*
Speck, Heidi *philosopher, educator*
Stanberry, D(osi) Elaine *English literature educator, writer*
Stendahl, Brita Kristina *humanities educator, social studies educator*
Stocker, Christine Marie *language educator*
Stone, Marilyn *foreign language educator, consultant*
Stringer, Mary Evelyn *art historian, educator*
Sullivan, Mary Rose *retired English language educator*
Sutton, Julia *musicologist, dance historian*
Swansinger, A. Jacqueline *history professor, academic administrator*
Taggett, Laura Kimberly *literature educator*
Tatelbaum, Linda *literature educator, writer*
Tayler, Irene *English literature educator*
Thomson, Virginia Winbourn *humanities educator, writer*
Thorson, Connie Capers *library educator*
Tison-Braun, Micheline Lucie *French language educator*
Tollison, Courtney L. *history professor*
Tong, Rosemarie *humanities educator, philosopher*
Trejos, Charlotte Marie *humanities educator, consultant*
Turczyn, Christine Lilian *English literature and writing educator*
Turk, Eleanor Louise *history professor*
Upson, Helen Rena *retired history educator*
Van Ausdal, Vivian Garrison *retired language educator*
Vaz, Katherine Anne *language educator, writer*
Vitt-Maucher, Gisela Maria *German educator*
Walker, Ruth Charlotta *language educator, real estate broker*
Walton, Ann Thorson *art historian, writer, curator, educator*
Warman, Linda K. *retired language educator, retired art educator*
Weisert, Mary Carol *language educator*
West, Donna J. *language arts educator*
Westby, Marcia *language educator*
Westwater, Martha Elizabeth *language educator*
Wiebenson, Dora Louise *architectural historian, editor, writer*
Wright, Josephine Rosa Beatrice *musicologist, educator*
Wych, Amy *interpreter, educator*
Zidovec, Mirta Rosa *Spanish language professional*

HUMANITIES: LIBRARIES

UNITED STATES

ALABAMA

Athens
Kemp, Ann *retired librarian*

Auburn University
MacEwan, Bonnie *librarian, dean*

Birmingham
Murrell, Susan DeBrecht *librarian*

Jacksonville
Merrill, Martha *library and information scientist*

Mobile
Bahr, Alice Harrison *librarian*

Montgomery
Brown, June Iris *retired librarian, artist*
McClain, Juanita *library director*

ARIZONA

Avondale
Gillen, Katherine Elizabeth *librarian*

Camp Verde
Pastine, Maureen Diane *librarian*

Payson
Potvin, Barbara Dirks *librarian*

Phoenix
Anderson, Vicki *retired librarian*
Roof, Sally Jean-Marie *library and information scientist, educator*
Wells, GladysAnn *library director*

Saddlebrooke
Schoepf, Virginia Anne *retired librarian*

Scottsdale
Dalton, Phyllis Irene *library consultant*
Meyer, Madeline Anna *librarian*

Sun City
Crisman, Mary Frances Borden *librarian*

Surprise
Telban, Ethel *retired librarian*

Tempe
Schmidt, Sherrie *library director, dean*

Tucson
Altman, Ellen *librarian, educator*
Griffen, Agnes Marthe *retired library administrator*
James, Ruby May *retired librarian*
Pintozzi, Chestalene *librarian*
Swerdlove, Dorothy Louise *librarian, consultant*

ARKANSAS

Clarendon
Meacham, Dolores Ann (Sissy Meacham) *elementary librarian*

Little Rock
Berry, Janet Claire *librarian*
Pennington, Melinda Snider *librarian*

Stuttgart
Ashley-Iverson, Mary E. *retired librarian*

CALIFORNIA

Alhambra
Birch, Tobeylynn *librarian*

Anaheim
Miller, Jean Ruth *retired librarian*

Antioch
Chan, Patty G. *librarian*

Auburn
Sanborn, Dorothy Chappell *retired librarian*

Berkeley
Cochran, Myrtis *librarian*
Minudri, Regina Ursula *librarian, consultant*
Torykian, Joan Marie *archivist*

Beverly Hills
Ramser, Wanda Tene *librarian, educator*

Capitola
Hawes, Grace Maxcy *archivist, retired writer*

Chico
Mathans, Sharron Hitt *retired librarian*

Costa Mesa
Epstein, Susan Baerg *librarian, consultant*

Davis
Franco, Elaine Adele *librarian*
Sharrow, Marilyn Jane *library administrator*

Downey
Todd, Margaret Donnellan *librarian, director*

El Cerrito
Alldredge, Noreen S. *librarian*
Kao, Yasuko Watanabe *retired library director*

Fremont
Wood, Linda May *librarian*

Fullerton
Johnson, Carolyn Elizabeth *librarian*

Glendale
Michelson, Lillian *librarian, researcher*
Woolls, Esther Blanche *library science educator*

Gustine
Ramirez, Nola Marie *librarian*

Hemet
Carr, Pamela *librarian*

Joshua Tree
Goudelock, Carol V. *library consultant*

La Jolla
Mirsky, Phyllis Simon *librarian*

Long Beach
Proust, Joycelyn Ann *retired librarian*

Los Altos
Rees, Marian Janet *librarian*

Los Angeles
Bates, Marcia Jeanne *information scientist educator*
Ciccone, Amy Navratil *art librarian*
Coolbaugh, Carrie Weaver *librarian*
Holmes, Fontayne *city librarian*
Patron, Susan Hall *librarian, writer*
Robinson, Barbara Jon *librarian*

Monterey
Reneker, Maxine Hohman *librarian*

Monterey Park
Wilson, Linda *librarian*

Moss Landing
Parker, Joan M. *librarian*

Mountain View
Di Muccio, Mary-Jo *retired librarian*

Northridge
Duran, Karin Jeanine *librarian*

Oakland
Ford, Gail *library administrator*
Hafter, Ruth Anne *library director, educator*
Lee, Ella Louise *librarian, educator*
Linden, Margaret Joanne *librarian, foundation administrator*
Rubin, Rhea Joyce *library consultant*
Woodbury, Marda Liggett *librarian, writer*

Orinda
Lorensen, Gunnhildur S. *librarian*

Palm Desert
Alpert, Shirley Marcia *librarian*

Pasadena
Sanders, Jan W. *librarian*

Pollock Pines
Rickard, Margaret Lynn *library director, consultant*

San Diego
Brown, Barbara Sproul *retired librarian, consultant, writer*
Tatár, Anna *library director*
Winn, Jade G. *library science educator*

San Francisco
Bocobo-Balunsat, Dalisay *librarian, journalist*
McQuown, Eloise *librarian*
Romanello, Marguerite Marie *retired librarian*
Thacker-Estrada, Elizabeth Lorelei *librarian, historian*

San Jacinto
Smith, Diane Jans *librarian, educator*

San Jose
Light, Jane Ellen *librarian*

San Luis Obispo
Graham, Priscilla Mann *librarian*

San Marcos
Ciurczak, Alexis *librarian*

San Marino
Robertson, Mary Louise *archivist, historian*

Santa Barbara
Higgins, Isabelle Jeanette *retired librarian*
Larsgaard, Mary Lynette *librarian, writer*

Santa Clara
Hopkinson, Shirley Lois *library and information scientist, educator*

Santa Cruz
Ripma, Mary *librarian*
Welborn, Victoria Lee *science librarian, educator*

Saratoga
Chisholm, Margaret Elizabeth *retired library director*

Spring Valley
Heinecke, Margaret Theresa *librarian*

Stanford
Derksen, Charlotte Ruth Meynink *librarian*

Tujunga
Pozzo, Mary Lou *retired librarian, writer*

Ventura
Kreissman, Starrett *librarian*

Whittier
Weismiller, Eleanor Kovacs *library director*

Woodland Hills
Zeitlin, Eugenia Pawlik *librarian, educator, writer*

COLORADO

Aurora
Miller, Dorothea Helen *librarian, educator*
Miller, Sarah Pearl *librarian*

Bailey
Hoganson, Mary Margaret *librarian*

Boulder
Wertheimer, Marilyn Lou *librarian, educator*

Canon City
Cochran, Susan Mills *research librarian*

Colorado Springs
Meese, Frances Mildred *library administrator*

Denver
Creamer, Deborah *library director, educator*
Garcia, June Marie *librarian*
Phillips, Dorothy Reid *retired medical library technician*
Smith, Sallye Wrye *librarian*
White, Joyce Louise *librarian*

Edwards
Chambers, Joan Louise *retired librarian, retired dean*

Morrison
Neumann, Stephanie Tower *retired librarian*

Pueblo
Jones, Donna Ruth *librarian*
Puls, Elaine Allison *retired librarian*

CONNECTICUT

Bridgeport
Johmann, Nancy *librarian*
Sheridan, Eileen *librarian*

Chester
Harwood, Eleanor Cash *retired librarian*

Fairfield
Bryan, Barbara Day *retired librarian*
Turetsky, Judith *librarian, researcher*

Meriden
Trotta, Marcia Marie *librarian, consultant, education educator*

New Britain
Sohn, Jeanne *librarian*

New Haven
Lorkovic, Tatjana *librarian*
Okerson, Ann Shumelda Lillian *librarian*
Peterson, Sandra Kay *librarian*

New London
Daragan, Patricia Ann *librarian*

Simsbury
Roberts, Celia Ann *librarian*

Storrs Mansfield
Kline, Nancy Mattoon *librarian*

Westport
Campbell, Marta Smith *librarian*

Wilton
Poundstone, Sally Hill *library director*

DISTRICT OF COLUMBIA

Washington
Baum, Ingeborg Ruth *librarian*
Broering, Naomi Cordero *librarian*
Chin, Cecilia Hui-Hsin *librarian*
Chute, Mary L. *library director*
Cooper, Ginnie *library director*
Fifer Canby, Susan Melinda *library administrator*
Gillen, Adrienne Kosciusko *librarian*
Goldstein, Doris Mueller *librarian, researcher*
Harlem, Susan Lynn *librarian*
Hedges, Kamla King *library director*
Hirons, Jean Louise *librarian*
Holt, Helen *librarian, consultant, former government official*
Jacobson, Sabina *library administrator*
Kadis, Averil Jordan *retired librarian*
Knezo, Genevieve Johanna *science and technology policy researcher*
Lyons, Grace Jean *librarian*
Marcum, Deanna Bowling *library administrator*
Martin, Kathleen Suzanne *librarian*
Meyer, Margaret Vaughan *librarian, educator*
Mikel, Sarah Ann *librarian*
Player, Thelma B. *librarian*
Reynolds, Regina Romano *librarian*
Rovelstad, Mathilde V(erner) *retired library and information scientist, educator*
Share, Ellen *librarian*
Toledo, Bridget Marie *librarian*
Vogelsong, Diana Louise *librarian*
Wand, Patricia Ann *librarian*
Wasserman, Krystyna *librarian, art historian*
Watts, Doris Earlene *retired librarian*
Wright, Arthuree Rosemille McLaughlin *library director*

FLORIDA

Clearwater
Werner, Elizabeth Helen *librarian, language educator*

Cocoa Beach
Weston, Janice Leah Colmer *librarian*

Deerfield Beach
Bethel, Marilyn Joyce *librarian*

Deland
Caccamise, Genevra Louise Ball (Mrs. Alfred E. Caccamise) *retired librarian*

Destin
Deel, Frances Quinn *retired librarian*

Fort Lauderdale
Hershenson, Miriam Hannah Ratner *librarian*
Stewart, Linda Berenfield *librarian*

Gainesville
Canelas, Dale Brunelle *library director*
Stipek, Kathleen *reference librarian*

Holmes Beach
Ehde, Ava Louise *librarian, educator*

Jacksonville
Cohen, Kathleen Francis *librarian*
Gubbin, Barbara Ashley Brendon *library director*

Madison
Hiss, Sheila Mary *librarian*

Maitland
Mansson, Joan *librarian, consultant*

Melbourne
Helmstetter, Wendy Lee *librarian*

Miami
Rourke, Diane McLaughlin *librarian*

Naples
Hall, Beverly Barton *librarian*

Orlando
Allison, Anne Marie *retired librarian*

Ormond Beach
von Fettweis, Yvonne Caché *archivist, historian*

Panama City
McCain, Lenda Haynes *librarian*

Pensacola
Demars, Bonnie Macon *librarian*

Sanibel
Allen, Patricia J. *library director*
Hamilton, Jeanne Marie *retired librarian*

Sarasota
Hummel, Dana D. Mallett *librarian*
Retzer, Mary Elizabeth Helm *retired librarian*

Tallahassee
Thompson, Jean Tanner *retired librarian*
Zachert, Martha Jane *retired librarian*

Tampa
Harkness, Mary Lou *librarian*
McCook, Kathleen de la Peña *librarian, educator*

Venice
Crowe, Virginia Mary *retired librarian*

Winter Park
Bloodworth, Velda Jean *librarian, educator*
Craig, Susan Lyons *library director*

GEORGIA

Americus
Tietjen, Mildred Campbell *librarian, college official*

Atlanta
McDavid, Sara June *librarian*
Miller, Rosalind Elaine *librarian, educator*
Smith, Marjorie Hagans *retired librarian*
Wallace, Gladys Baldwin *librarian*
Yates, Ella Gaines *librarian, consultant*

Decatur
Cravey, Pamela J. *librarian*

Marietta
Rogers, Gail Elizabeth *library director*

Rome
Mosley, Mary Mac *retired librarian*

Savannah
Ball, Ardella Patricia *librarian, educator*

Statesboro
Hamilton, Ann Hollingsworth *library director*

Unadilla
Bartlett, Rhonda Woodward *library manager*

Valdosta
Montgomery, Denise Lynne *librarian, researcher*

Warner Robins
Merk, P. Evelyn *librarian*

HAWAII

Hilo
golian-Lui, Linda Marie *librarian*

Honolulu
Flynn, Joan Mayhew *librarian*
Perushek, Diane *university librarian*
Schindler, Jo Ann *librarian, director*

Kahului
Tolliver, Dorothy *librarian*

IDAHO

Plummer
Harp, Diane Christine *librarian, educator*

Rexburg
Lankard Dewey, Judith Margaret *library director, lawyer*

ILLINOIS

Arlington Heights
Giannini, Evelyn Louise *retired library consultant*

Bloomington
Olson, Rue Eileen *retired librarian*

Carbondale
Bauner, Ruth Elizabeth *library director*
Koch, Loretta Peterson *librarian, educator*

Caseyville
Stanford, Diana L. *librarian*

Chicago
Bentley, Carol Ligon *retired library and information scientist*
Butta, Deena Celeste *librarian*
Choldin, Marianna Tax *librarian, educator*
Davis, Mary Ellen K. *library director*
Funk, Carla Jean *library association director*
Hanrath, Linda Carol *librarian, archivist*
Heidkamp, Patricia Jean *librarian*
Parr, Virginia Helen *retired librarian*
Sullivan, Peggy *librarian, consultant*

Downers Grove
Saricks, Joyce Goering *librarian*

Edwardsville
Johnson, Charlotte Lee *librarian*

Elkhart
Cunningham, Donna Lynn *library director*

Evanston
Bjorncrantz, Leslie Benton *librarian*
Cates, Jo Ann *library director*
Crawford, Susan *library director, educator, editor, writer*
Pritchard, Sarah Margaret *library director*
Whiteley, Sandra Marie *librarian, editor*

Freeport
Vogt, Lorna Corrine *retired librarian, small business owner*

Glen Ellyn
Hoornbeek, Lynda Ruth Couch *librarian, educator*

Libertyville
Cunningham, Elizabeth Ann *librarian*

Moline
Curry, Kathleen Bridget *retired librarian*

Peoria
Frey, Yvonne Amar *librarian*

River Forest
Bodi, Sonia Ellen *library director, educator*

River Grove
LaGon, Cynthia Bostic *librarian*

Riverside
Van Cura, Joyce Bennett *librarian*

Schaumburg
Adrianopoli, Barbara Catherine *librarian*

Skokie
Anthony, Carolyn Additon *librarian*
Breckel, Alvina Hefeli *librarian*

South Holland
Connolly, Carla Marie *librarian*

Springfield
Kaige, Alice Tubb *retired librarian*

Urbana
Davis, Elisabeth Bachman *librarian, library administration educator*
Kaufman, Paula T. *librarian*
O'Brien, Nancy Patricia *librarian, educator*
Watson, Paula D. *retired librarian*

Wheaton
Tucker, Beverly Sowers *library and information scientist*

Wheeling
Long, Sarah Ann *librarian*

Woodstock
Koehler, Jane Ellen *librarian*

INDIANA

Bloomington
Jagodzinski, Cecile Marie *librarian*

Evansville
Tannenbaum, Karen Jean *library services supervisor*

Fort Wayne
Raifsnider, Lauretta Jane *librarian*

Indianapolis
Fischler, Barbara Brand *librarian*
Huehls, Frances A. *librarian*

Kokomo
MacKay, Gail *librarian*

Lafayette
McKowen, Dorothy Keeton *librarian, educator*
Mobley, Emily Ruth *library director, educator, dean*

New Harmony
Feiner, Arlene Marie *librarian, researcher, consultant*

Notre Dame
Stevenson, Marsha Joan *librarian*

Valparaiso
Katich, Janet *librarian*

West Lafayette
Andrews, Theodora Anne *retired librarian, educator*
Markee, Katherine Madigan *librarian, educator*
Nixon, Judith May *librarian*

IOWA

Alta Vista
Sweeney, Eileen Mary *librarian, director*

Ames
Hill, Fay Gish *retired librarian*

Cedar Rapids
Alderson, Karen Ann *librarian, private investigator*

Clinton
Lowe, Flora Lester *librarian*

Des Moines
Runge, Kay Kretschmar *library director*

Iowa City
Baker, Nancy L. *university librarian, educator*

Mason City
Iverson, Carol Jean *retired library media specialist*

West Branch
Mather, Mildred Eunice *retired archivist*

KANSAS

Burr Oak
Underwood, Deanna Kay *librarian*

Claflin
Wondra, Judy Ann *librarian, director*

Clay Center
Bachand, Alice Jeanne *school library media specialist*

Emporia
Hale, Martha Larsen *librarian*

Lawrence
Craig, Susan Virginia *librarian*
Fredrickson, Karen Loraine *librarian*
Haricombe, Lorraine *library director, dean*

Overland Park
Carmack, Mona *library administrator*
Childers, Martha Patton *librarian*
Kempf, Andrea Caron *librarian, educator*

Shawnee Mission
McLeod, Debra Ann *librarian, mail order book company executive*

Topeka
Baldwin, Janet Sue *library media specialist*
Monroe, Virginia Marie *library media specialist, educator*

Wichita
Berner Harris, Cynthia Kay *librarian*

KENTUCKY

Corbin
Bruce, Verna Lee Smith Hickey *media specialist, librarian*

Cynthiana
Ellis, E. Susan *library director, lay minister*

La Grange
Morgan, Mary Dan *librarian*

Lexington
Birchfield, Martha *librarian*
Diedrichs, Carol Pitts *librarian, dean*
McQueen, Sharon *library and information scientist, educator*
Rogers, JoAnn Vedder *library and information science educator*

Louisville
Poston, Janice Lynn *librarian*

Marion
Henley, Darl Heathcott *librarian, educator*

Morehead
Nutter, Carol Angell *academic librarian*

LOUISIANA

Baton Rouge
Cargill, Jennifer S. *librarian, dean, educator*
Hayward, Olga Loretta Hines (Mrs. Samuel Ellsworth Hayward) *retired librarian*
Lane, Margaret Beynon Taylor *librarian*
Lusk, Glenna Rae Knight (Mrs. Edwin Bruce Lusk) *librarian*
Wald, Ingeborg *librarian, translator*

Chalmette
Wheeler, Genevieve Stutes *library administrator, educator*

Covington
Stahr, Beth A. *librarian*

Ferriday
Bowman, Sarah *librarian*

Jeanerette
Garcia, Susan Breaux *multi-media specialist, consultant*

Kenner
Duplessis, Sandra Walsh *librarian, educator*

Lake Charles
Curol, Helen Ruth *librarian, English language educator*

New Orleans
Hagedorn, Dorothy Louise *librarian*
Jumonville, Florence M. *librarian, historian*

Shreveport
Brazile, Orella Ramsey *library director*

Thibodaux
Tonn, Anke *library and information scientist, researcher*

MAINE

Bangor
Rea, Ann W. *librarian*

MARYLAND

Baltimore
Allen, Norma Ann *librarian, educator*
Bradley, Wanda Louise *librarian*
Brown, Florence S. *librarian, administrator*
Hayden, Carla Diane *library director, educator*
Leonard, Angela Michele *librarian, educator*
Magnuson, Nancy *librarian*
White, Libby Kramer *librarian*

Bel Alton
Quesada-Embid, Mary Regina Chamberlain *library media specialist*

Beltsville
Andre, Pamela Q. J. *library director*
Frank, Robyn Claire *librarian*

Bethesda
Conger, Lucinda *retired librarian*
Humphreys, Betsy L. *librarian*

Boonsboro
Butler, Naomi Witmer *librarian, educator*

Bowie
Wardrip, Elizabeth Jane *retired librarian*

Chestertown
Rather, Lucia Porcher Johnson *library administrator*

Chevy Chase
Basa, Enikö Molnár *retired librarian*

Columbia
Klein, Sami Weiner *librarian*

Greenbelt
Moore, Virginia Bradley *librarian*

Rockville
Hamilton, Parker *library director*
Kohlhorst, Gail Lewis *librarian*
Renninger, Mary Karen *retired librarian*

Silver Spring
Null, Elisabeth Higgins *librarian, editor*

Springdale
Keith, Patricia *multi-media specialist*

Takoma Park
von Hake, Margaret Joan *librarian*

Upper Marlboro
Rough, Marianne Christina *librarian, educator*

MASSACHUSETTS

Amesbury
Dowd, Frances Connelly *retired librarian*

Boston
Allen, Nancy Schuster *librarian, director information resources*
Christopher, Irene *librarian, consultant*
Desnoyers, Megan Floyd *archivist, educator*
Hebard, Barbara Adams *conservator*

Cambridge
Callahan, Barbara Ann *librarian*
Cole, Heather Ellen *librarian*
Coleman, Sandra Sloan *librarian, academic dean*
Flannery, Susan Marie *library administrator*
Koepp, Donna Pauline Petersen *librarian*
Mitchell, Barbara Anne *librarian*
Schoon, Marion Else *librarian*
Wolpert, Ann J. *library director*

Canton
Kelley, Irene W. *retired librarian, musician, artist*

East Orleans
Natale, Barbara Gustafson *retired librarian*

Fall River
Sullivan, Ruth Anne *librarian*

Gloucester
Cheves, Vera Louisa *retired librarian*

Lexington
Miller, Inabeth *educational administrator, librarian, technology consultant*

Marstons Mills
Martin, Susan Katherine *librarian*

Medford
Michalak, Jo-Ann *library director*

Mill River
Jaffe, Katharine Weisman *retired librarian*

Newton
Glick-Weil, Kathy *library director*

North Easton
Bundy, Annalee Marshall *library director*

Springfield
Stack, May Elizabeth *retired library director*

West Newton
Sarna, Helen Horowitz *retired librarian, educator*

Weymouth
Lamothe, Joanne Lewis *library director, consultant*

Woburn
O'Doherty, Kathleen Marie *library director*
Preve, Roberta Jean *librarian, researcher*

Worcester
Dunlap, Ellen S. *library administrator*
Johnson, Penelope B. *librarian*
Kuklinski, Joan Lindsey *librarian*

MICHIGAN

Allendale
Murray, Diane Elizabeth *librarian*

Ann Arbor
Beaubien, Anne Kathleen *librarian*
Daub, Peggy Ellen *library administrator*
Dede, Bonnie Aileen *librarian, educator*
Didier, Elaine K. *library director, educator*
Dunlap, Connie *librarian*
Johnson, Brenda L. *university librarian*

Battle Creek
Lincoln, Margaret *library media specialist*

Birch Run
Schluckebier, Carol J. *librarian*

Bloomfield Hills
Papai, Beverly Daffern *retired library director*

Clinton
Scott, Sharon Ann *retired librarian, archivist*

Clinton Township
Hage, Christine Lind *library administrator*

Davisburg
Forst, Catherine Phillips *library director*

Detroit
Ashley, Lois A. *retired university reference librarian*
Audia, Christina *librarian*
Field, Judith Judy *librarian*
Frenette, Geraldine Gloria *librarian*
Klont, Barbara Anne *librarian*
Skowronski, Nancy *library director*

Flint
Heymoss, Jennifer Marie *librarian*

Grand Rapids
Hoskins, Debbie Stewart *librarian, artist*

Holt
Smith, Betty W. *librarian*

Interlochen
Tacke, Eleanor *archivist*

Kalamazoo
Grotzinger, Laurel Ann *librarian, educator*
Pinkham, Eleanor Humphrey *retired university librarian*

Marquette
Becker, Amy Salminen *librarian*
Henderson, Roberta Marie *librarian, educator*

Owosso
Bentley, Margaret Ann *librarian*

Plymouth
Berry, Charlene Helen *librarian, musician*

Port Huron
Miller, Theresa L. *library director*

Redford
Karpinski, Huberta *library trustee*

Southfield
Naber, Faith *retired librarian, educator*

Ypsilanti
Beiting, Sarah Louise *library director*

MINNESOTA

Breezy Point
Anderson, Gail Marie *retired librarian*

Eagan
Byrne, Roseanne *library director*

Hopkins
Young, Margaret Labash *librarian, information consultant, editor*

Minneapolis
Dengler, Eartha (Erdmuth) *librarian, archivist*
Johnson, Margaret Ann (Peggy) *library administrator*
Lougee, Wendy Pradt *library director, educator*

Roseville
Miller, Suzanne Marie *library director, educator*

Saint Paul
Wagner, Mary Margaret *library and information scientist, educator*
Zietlow, Ruth Ann *reference librarian*

Thief River Falls
Jauquet-Kalinoski, Barbara *library director*

Winona
Sullivan, Kathryn Ann *librarian, educator*

Zumbrota
Post, Diana Constance *retired librarian*

MISSISSIPPI

Columbus
Nawrocki, Susan Jean *librarian*

Jackson
Dunaway, Charjean Laughlin *librarian*
Smith, Sharman Bridges *state librarian*

Mississippi State
Delgado, Marica LaDonne *librarian, educator*

Natchez
McLemore, Joan Meadows *librarian, consultant*

MISSOURI

Chesterfield
Kohnen, Carol Ann *librarian*
Landram, Christina Louella *librarian*

Columbia
Pinkerton, Marjorie Jean *librarian, educator*

Fredericktown
Stephenson, Jane Phillips *librarian*

Greenwood
Zeller, Marilynn Kay *retired librarian*

Independence
Schultz, Janice Elaine *librarian*

Kansas City
Nelson, Freda Nell Hein *librarian*

Kirksville
Teter, Patricia Ann *librarian*

Lees Summit
Usher, Elizabeth Reuter (Mrs. William A. Scar) *retired librarian*

Parkville
Schultis, Gail Ann *library director*

Saint Charles
Reed, Warlene Patricia *retired librarian*

Saint Joseph
Schneider, Julia *library director*

Saint Louis
Brown, Bettye *librarian, educator*
Carleton, Patricia Ann *librarian*
Christiansen, Bernyce LeeAnn *librarian*
Holt, Leslie Edmonds *librarian*
Lauenstein, Ann Gail *librarian*
McDonald, Brenda Denise *librarian*

Springfield
Busch, Annie *library director*
Horny, Karen Louise *library administrator*

MONTANA

Great Falls
Schmidt, Rita *librarian, retired media specialist*

Helena
Fitzpatrick, Lois Ann *library administrator*

NEBRASKA

Boys Town
DiBacco, Nadine Louise *retired library director, photographer, writer*

Lincoln
Giesecke, Joan Ruth *librarian, dean*

NEVADA

Carson City
Jones, Sara Sue Fisher *librarian*

Henderson
Derner, Carol A. *retired librarian*

Las Vegas
Gray, Phyllis Anne *librarian*
Honsa, Vlasta *retired librarian*
Ramsey, Inez Linn *librarian, educator*
Richardson, Jane *retired librarian*

NEW HAMPSHIRE

Berlin
Doherty, Katherine Mann *librarian, writer*

Concord
Scheckter, Stella Josephine *retired librarian*

Exeter
Thomas, Jacquelyn May *librarian*

Hanover
Otto, Margaret Amelia *librarian*

Londonderry
Ballard, Susan Doyon *library director*

Nashua
Ferrigno, Helen Frances *librarian, educator*

Temple
Weston, Priscilla Atwood *library director*

NEW JERSEY

Caldwell
Alito, Martha-Ann B. *librarian*

Cliffside Park
Chelariu, Ana Radu *library director*

East Orange
Amadei, Deborah Lisa *librarian*

Edgewater
Berliner, Barbara *retired librarian, consultant*

Flanders
Hilbert, Rita L. *librarian*

Glassboro
Willett, Holly Geneva *librarian, educator*

Glen Rock
Savoie, Brietta Dolores *retired librarian*

Haledon
Dougherty, June Eileen *librarian*

Highland Park
Kheel, Susan Talmadge *retired reference services manager*

Hopewell
Baeckler, Virginia Van Wynen *librarian*

Lakewood
Herbert, Barbara Rae *librarian, educational media specialist*

Lambertville
Cusworth, Christyl J. *conservator, artist*

Laurel Springs
Cleveland, Susan Elizabeth *library administrator, researcher*

Lindenwold
Clarke, Betty Ann *librarian, minister*

Livingston
Sikora, Barbara Jean *library director*

Montclair
Cass, Mary Louise *librarian*

New Brunswick
Gaunt, Marianne I. *university librarian*
House, Renee S. *theological librarian, minister*
Turock, Betty Jane *library and information science professor*

Palisades Park
McColl, Terrie Lee *library director*

Point Pleasant
Greene, Ellin *library service educator*

Princeton
Fisher, Heidi Alice *librarian*
Trainer, Karin A. *librarian*

Secaucus
Grazioli, Margaret *librarian*

Sewell
Crocker, Jane Lopes *library director*

Toms River
Matteo, Christine E. *librarian*

Trenton
Russell, Joyce Anne Rogers *retired librarian*

Union
Darden, Barbara S. *library director*
Rogge, Rena Wolcott *librarian*

West Milford
Hannon, Patricia Ann *library director*

Whiting
Randall, Lynn Ellen *librarian*

NEW MEXICO

Albuquerque
Freeman, Patricia Elizabeth *multi-media specialist, educational consultant*
Lewis, Linda Kathryn *librarian*
Snell, Patricia Poldervaart *librarian, consultant*
Wilkinson, Frances Catherine *librarian, educator*

Carlsbad
Regan Gossage, Muriel *librarian*

Gallup
Fellin, Octavia Antoinette *retired librarian, historical researcher*

Los Alamos
Ramsey, Margie *librarian*

Silver City
Gadberry, Vicki Lynn Himes *librarian*

NEW YORK

Albany
Roberson, Suzanne *librarian, researcher*
Sharke, Ingrid *librarian*

Alfred
Johnson, Carla Conrad *library dean*

Astoria
Lekus, Diana Rose *librarian*

Aurora
Vargo, Jeri *librarian*

Beechhurst
Wingate, Constance Blandy *retired librarian*

Brightwaters
Kavanagh, Eileen J. *librarian*

Brockport
Safran, Franciska Kuharovits *retired librarian, curator*

Bronx
Ostrow, Rona Lynn *retired librarian, educator*
Skurdenis, Juliann Veronica *librarian, educator, writer, editor*

Brooklyn
Hill, Leda Katherine *librarian*
Hill, Victoria Ruth *librarian*
Lawrence, Deirdre Elizabeth *librarian*
Mack-Harvin, Dionne *library director*
Stevenson, Gale *librarian*
Stukes, Geraldine Hargro *library and information scientist, educator*
Thomas, Lucille Cole *librarian*

Buffalo
Camhi, Rebecca Ann *librarian, writer*
Kreizman-Reczek, Karen Ingrid *librarian*

Chautauqua
Yurth, Helene Louise *librarian*

Flushing
Cooper, Marianne (Abonyi Cooper) *librarian, educator*

Franklin Square
Henry, Clarice Ruth *librarian*

Great Neck
Rieff, Harriet Lillian *librarian*

Hempstead
Freese, Melanie Louise *librarian, educator*

Hyde Park
Koch, Cynthia M. *library director*

Ithaca
Perry, Margaret *librarian, writer*
Thomas, Sarah E. *librarian*

Jamaica
Becker, Nancy Jane *information science educator*
Lin, Shu-Fang Hsia *librarian*

Jamestown
Disbro, Megan Benner *librarian*

Liverpool
Wightman, Sharon Leilani *librarian*

Long Lake
Waagner, Sharon Flannery *library media specialist*

Mamaroneck
Merskey-Zeger, Marie Gertrude Fine *retired librarian*

Mineola
Hammer, Deborah Marie *librarian, paralegal*

New Paltz
Nyquist, Corinne Elaine *librarian*
Young, Marjorie Ann *librarian*

New York
Ashton, Jean Willoughby *library director*
Berger, Pearl *library director*
Brewer, Karen *librarian*
Bristah, Pamela Jean *librarian*
Browar, Lisa Muriel *librarian*
Cohen, Madeleine L. *library and information scientist*
Cohen, Selma *librarian, researcher*
Giral, Angela *librarian*
Glickstein, Eileen Agard *librarian, consultant*
Goodkind, Joan Carol *librarian*
Harris, Carolyn Louise *librarian*
Hewitt, Vivian Ann Davidson (Mrs. John Hamilton Hewitt Jr.) *retired librarian*
Kagan, Ilse Echt *librarian, researcher, historian*
Kent, Susan *library director, consultant*
LoSchiavo, Linda Bosco *library director*
Lubetski, Edith Esther *librarian*
Mack, Phyllis Green *retired librarian*
Mackey, Patricia Elaine *university librarian*
Mandel, Carol *librarian*
Margalith, Helen Margaret *retired librarian*
Miller, Barbara Kenton *retired librarian*
Moscatt, Angeline Alice *librarian*
Root, Nina J. *librarian, writer*
Slawsky, Donna Susan *librarian, singer*
Stern, Madeleine Bettina *rare book dealer, writer*
Thomas, Dorothy *indexing consultant, writer*

Northville
Fox, Patricia Ann *school librarian, media specialist*

Norwood
Musante, Patricia W. *library director*

Oceanside
Kaikow, Rita Ellen *library media specialist*

Queens Village
Heckman, Lucy T. *librarian*

Rochester
Swanton, Susan Irene *retired library director*

Roslyn
Siahpoosh, Farideh Tamaddon *librarian*

Rye
Harrington, Diane *librarian, writer*

Saratoga Springs
Ratzer, Mary Boyd *librarian, language educator*

Stony Brook
Dole, Wanda Victoria *librarian*

Voorheesville
Sacco, Gail Alter *librarian*

White Plains
Scott-Williams, Wendy Lee *library and information scientist*

Woodside
Sfiroudis, Gloria Tides *library and information scientist, educator*

NORTH CAROLINA

Chapel Hill
Moran, Barbara Burns *librarian, educator*

Charlotte
Welch, Jeanie Maxine *librarian*

Columbus
Wetherby, Ivor Lois *librarian*

Cove City
Hawkins, Elinor Dixon (Mrs. Carroll Woodard Hawkins) *retired librarian*

Denton
Zwiebel, Marie Bee *retired librarian*

Durham
Canada, Mary Whitfield *retired librarian*
Krugman, Marian G. *retired librarian*
Lewis, Margaret Shively *retired librarian*

Gastonia
Burns, Judith O'Dell *library assistant, educator*

Greensboro
Kovacs, Beatrice *library studies educator*

Hillsborough
Stephens, Brenda Wilson *librarian*

New Bern
White, Rhea Amelia *library and information scientist*

Pembroke
Sexton, Jean Elizabeth *librarian*

Pittsboro
Flowers, Helen Foote *librarian, educator*

Raleigh
Freeman, Janet L. *librarian*
Nutter, Susan K. *librarian, academic administrator*

Winston Salem
Sutton, Lynn Sorensen *librarian*
Weavil, Vicki Lemp *library director*

Winton
Williams, Sue Darden *library director*

NORTH DAKOTA

Bismarck
Ott, Doris Ann *librarian*

Mayville
Karaim, Betty June *retired librarian*

Wahpeton
Dohman, Gloria Ann *librarian*

OHIO

Cadiz
Thompson, Sandra Lee *library administrator*

Canton
Cave, Yvonne S. *retired librarian*
Kilcullen, Maureen *librarian, educator*

Cincinnati
Abate, Anne Katherine *librarian, consultant, educator*
Bestehorn, Ute Wiltrud *retired librarian*
Brestel, Mary Beth *librarian*
Church, Sonia Jane Shutter *librarian*
Everson, Jean Watkins Dolores *librarian, media consultant, educator*
Fender, Kimber L. *library director*
Montavon, Victoria A. *university librarian, dean*
Schutzius, Lucy Jean *retired librarian*
Stoms, Donna Sue *librarian*
Wellington, Jean Susorney *librarian*

Cleveland
Gapen, Delores Kaye *librarian, educator*
Siess, Judith Ann *librarian*

Columbus
Meredith, Meri Hill *reference librarian, educator*
Olson, Carol Ann *retired librarian*
Sawyers, Elizabeth Joan *librarian, director*

Dayton
Klinck, Cynthia Anne *library director*

Delaware
Schlichting, Catherine Fletcher Nicholson *librarian, educator*

Hubbard
Trucksis, Theresa A. *retired library director*

Lima
Johnson, Patricia Joseph *librarian*

Lucasville
Crotty, Ladonna Deane *librarian*

Lyndhurst
Packer, Diana *retired reference librarian*

Marietta
Fry, Mildred Covey *regional library executive director*

Marion
Blankenship, Betsy Lee *library director*

Middleburg Heights
Maciuszko, Kathleen Lynn *librarian, educator*

Northfield
Sleeman, Mary (Mrs. John Paul Sleeman) *retired librarian*
Stavole, Janet M. *librarian, director*

Oberlin
Moore, Jane Ross *librarian, educator*

Oregon
Poad, Flora Virginia *retired librarian, retired elementary school educator*

Oxford
Presnell, Jenny Lynn *librarian*
Sessions, Judith Ann *librarian, university library dean*

Parma
Feldman, Sari *library director*

Pepper Pike
Wilkenfeld, Polly *librarian*

South Euclid
Zoller, Karen Ann *library and art gallery director*

Tiffin
Harner, Willa Jean *librarian*
Hillmer, Margaret Patricia *library director*

Wickliffe
Fisher, Nancy DeButts *library director*

Xenia
Vaughan, Doris Celestine Walker *retired librarian, educator*

Zanesville
Danford, Ardath Anne *retired librarian*

OKLAHOMA

Blanchard
Kimbrough, Janie *library director*

Hodgen
Brower, Janice Kathleen *library and information scientist*

Lawton
Bonnell-Mihalis, Pamela Gay Scoggins *library director*
Kroll, Connie Rae *librarian, information services consultant*

Norman
Lester, June *library and information scientist, educator*
Sherman, Mary Angus *public library administrator*

Tulsa
Clement, Evelyn Geer *librarian, educator*
Neal, Marilyn Young *librarian*

OREGON

Beaverton
Burson-Dyer, Lorraine *library executive*
Pond, Patricia Brown *library and information scientist, educator*

Corvallis
Landers, Teresa Price *librarian*

Eugene
Stirling, Isabel Ann *science librarian*

Salem
Weide, Janice Lee *librarian*

PENNSYLVANIA

Allentown
Sacks, Patricia Ann *librarian, consultant*

Berwyn
Langford, Linda Kosmin *library consultant*

Bryn Mawr
Fletcher, Marjorie Amos *librarian*

Butler
Day, Margaret Ann *research librarian, information specialist*

Chambersburg
Stillman, Mary Elizabeth *librarian, administrator, educator*

Clarion
Miller, Andrea Lynn *library science educator*

Danielsville
Pagotto, Sarah Louise *retired library and information scientist*

Doylestown
Waite, Frances W. *librarian, genealogist*

Du Bois
Morris, Trisha Ann *librarian*

Factoryville
Elliott, Carolyn Sayre *librarian, educator*

Greensburg
Duck, Patricia Mary *librarian*

Hazleton
Dougherty, Jane *librarian*

Kingsley
McNabb, Corrine Radtke *librarian*

Mansfield
Donahue, Martha *retired librarian*

Monroeville
Kennedy, Kathy Kay *library director*

New Holland
Fanus, Pauline Rife *librarian*

New Wilmington
Bolger, Dorita Yvonne Ferguson *librarian*

Philadelphia
Davidoff, Joanne Malatesta *multi-media specialist*
Gendron, Michèle Marguerite Madeleine *librarian*
Long, Nina P. *library director, archivist*
Mancall, Jacqueline Cooper *library and information scientist, educator*
Schaeffer-Young, Judith *library director*

Pittsburgh
Johnson-Houston, Debbie *librarian, educator*
St. Clair, Gloriana Strange *librarian, dean*

Punxsutawney
Dinsmore, Roberta Joan Maier *library director*

Riegelsville
Banko, Ruth Caroline *retired library director*

University Park
Cline, Nancy M. *librarian, department chairman*
Eaton, Nancy Ruth Linton *librarian, dean*
Hamburger, Susan *librarian*
Kellerman, Lydia Suzanne (Sue) *librarian*

Villanova
Olsen, Judith Johnson *reference librarian*

Wynnewood
Grenen, Judie Sann *librarian*

RHODE ISLAND

Kingston
Caldwell, Naomi Rachel *library and information scientist, educator, writer*

Providence
Hemmasi, Harriette Ann *university librarian*

Riverside
Schwegler, Nancy Ann *librarian, writer*

Wakefield
Alexander, Jacqueline Peterson *retired librarian*

Warwick
Charette, Sharon Juliette *library administrator*

SOUTH CAROLINA

Beaufort
Moussatos, Martha Ann Tyree *librarian*

Bluffton
Cann, Sharon Lee *retired health science librarian*

Columbia
Paulson-Crawford, Carol *conservator, educator*
Rawlinson, Helen Ann *librarian*
Washington, Nancy Jane Hayes *librarian*
Wilson, Olive Fuller *librarian*
Zimmerman, Nancy Picciano *library and information scientist, educator*

Georgetown
Bazemore, Trudy McConnell *librarian*

Hardeeville
Kadar, Karin Patricia *librarian*

Orangeburg
Thompson, Marguerite Myrtle Graming (Mrs. Ralph B. Thompson) *librarian*

SOUTH DAKOTA

Aberdeen
Hornaman, Elaine Verna *librarian*

Freeman
Koller, Berneda Joleen *library administrator*

Mitchell
Langland, Laurie Lynne *archivist, director, educator*

Sioux Falls
Thompson, Ronelle Kay Hildebrandt *library director*

TENNESSEE

Camden
Tippitt, Rhonda Clement *library director*

Chattanooga
McFarland, Jane Elizabeth *librarian*

Collegedale
Bennett, Peggy Elizabeth *librarian, library director, educator*

Franklin
Douglass, Dorris Callicott *librarian, historian, genealogist*

Gray
Slagle, Lusetta *librarian*

Hermitage
Lyle, Virginia Reavis *retired archivist, genealogist*

Jackson
Hazlewood, Judith Evans *retired librarian*
Hoyle, Shetina Yevette *librarian*

Knoxville
Cottrell, Jeannette Elizabeth *retired librarian*
Dewey, Barbara I. *librarian, dean*
Drumheller, Janet Louise *librarian*
Earl, Martha Frances *librarian, researcher*
Felder-Hoehne, Felicia Harris *librarian, researcher*

Memphis
Drescher, Judith Altman *library director*

Murfreesboro
Vesper, Virginia Ann *librarian*

Nashville
Perry, Glenda Lee *health science librarian*
Radcliff, Joyce B. *librarian*
Wilson, Carolyn Taylor *librarian*

Sewanee
Watson, Gail H. *retired librarian*

Sparta
Young, Olivia Knowles *retired librarian*

Strawberry Plains
Snodderly, Louise Davis *librarian*

TEXAS

Abilene
Alexander, Shirley Birdsall *retired librarian*

Austin
Ardis, Susan Barber *librarian, educator*
Flowers, Betty Sue *library director, educator*
Morrow, Sandra Kay *librarian*

Bovina
Ayers, Kathy Venita Moore *librarian*

Brownwood
Weeks, Patsy Ann Landry *librarian, educator*

Canyon Lake
Bowden, Virginia Massey *librarian*

Cedar Hill
Hickman, Traphene Parramore *retired library director, consultant*

Cedar Park
Lam, Pauline Poha *library director*

Channing
Brian, Mary H. *librarian*

College Station
Cook, C. Colleen *librarian, dean*

Dallas
Evans, Laurie *library director*
Howell, Bradley Sue *retired librarian*

Denton
Nichols, Margaret Irby *librarian, educator, library and information scientist*
Poole, Eva Duraine *librarian*
Simpson, Carol Mann *librarian, educator, editor*
Snapp, Elizabeth *librarian, educator*

El Paso
Gardner, Kerry Ann *librarian*

Fort Worth
Ford, Jeanette White *archivist, educator*
Miller, Carol Lynn *librarian*
Scholl, Belinda K. *librarian*

Grand Prairie
Ritterhouse, Kathy Lee *librarian*

Houston
Hornak, Anna Frances *library administrator*
Lawson, Rhea Brown *library director*
Miller, Sabrina Wares *librarian*
Romero, Annette Louise *multi-media specialist, educator*
Scarbrough, Sara Eunice *librarian, archivist, consultant*
Shapiro, Beth Janet *librarian*
Walshak, Mary Lynn *academic librarian*

Huntsville
Hickey, Lady Jane *librarian, minister*

Irving
Sherlock, Jo Anne C. *librarian*

Kingsville
Beach, Regina Lee *librarian*

Laredo
Weber, Janice Ann *library director, grant writer*

Marshall
Magrill, Rose Mary *library director*
Peterson, Cynthia Lynn *library director, educator*

Odessa
Rocha, Osbelia Maria Juarez *librarian, principal*

Pecos
Purcell, Bonnie Lou *librarian*

San Angelo
Chatfield, Mary Van Abshoven *librarian*

San Antonio
Bivens, Lydia Ruth *librarian*
Gruenbeck, Laurie *librarian*
Hood, Sandra Dale *librarian*
LeFevre, Geraldine *librarian*
Nance, Betty Love *librarian*
Newton, Virginia *archivist, historian, librarian*

Sweetwater
Taylor, Martha Sue *librarian*

Tyler
Cleveland, Mary Louise *librarian, media specialist*

Van Alstyne
Hazelton, Juanita Louise *librarian*

Waco
Roberts, Betty Jo *retired librarian, speech therapist*

Weslaco
Fogarty, Elizabeth Rummans *retired librarian, researcher*

Wichita Falls
Parker, Eva Annette *librarian*

UTAH

Salt Lake City
Love, April Gaye McLean *librarian*
Ogburn, Joyce *library director*
Owen, Amy *library director*

VERMONT

Burlington
Ewins, Maxie Staedtler *librarian*
Kascus, Marie Annette *librarian*
Martin, Rebecca Reist *librarian*

VIRGINIA

Alexandria
Berger, Patricia Wilson *retired librarian*
Budde, Mitzi Marie Jarrett *librarian*
Cross, Dorothy Abigail *retired librarian*
Lockett, Barbara Ann *librarian*
Plitt, Jeanne Given *librarian*

Assawoman
Holley, Pamela Spencer *retired librarian*

Falls Church
Yoshimura, Yoshiko *librarian*

Harrisonburg
Swope, Frances Alderson *retired librarian*

Hudgins
Story, Martha vanBeuren *retired librarian*

Lynchburg
Schwedt, Rachel Elaine *librarian*

Norfolk
Duncan, Cynthia Beryl *university library administrator*
Hilliard-Bradley, Yvonne *library administrator*

Poquoson
Tai, Elizabeth Shi-Jue Lee *library director*

Portsmouth
Monroe, Evelyn Jones *retired librarian*

Richmond
Burner, Clara Miller *librarian*
Henderson, Harriet *librarian, director*
Martin, Ann McCarthy *library-media specialist*
Van Neste, Karen Lane *librarian, editor*

Spotsylvania
Thomas, Sue Ann Appleton *librarian, reading consultant*
Todd, Deborah Kathleen *library media specialist*

Springfield
Heise, Dorothy Hilbert *retired librarian, retired government agency administrator*

Staunton
Arnold, Ruth Southgate *librarian*

Suffolk
Burd, Joyce Ann *librarian*

Washington
Arbelbide, C(indy) L(ea) *librarian, historian, author*

WASHINGTON

College Place
Gaskell, Carolyn Suzanne *librarian*

Everett
Souza, Blase Camacho *librarian, educator*

Kirkland
Sorenson, Lynette Evelyn *librarian*

Lummi Island
Hanson, Polly (Pauline) Mae Early *librarian*

Olympia
Boland, Winnifred Joan *retired librarian*
Hutchins, Diane Elizabeth Rider *librarian*
Zussy, Nancy Louise *librarian*

Seattle
Bishop, Virginia Wakeman *retired librarian, retired humanities educator*
Blase, Nancy Gross *librarian*
Mason, Marilyn Gell *library administrator, writer, consultant*

Spokane
Bender, Betty Wion *librarian*

Tacoma
Fischer, Karen A. *librarian*

Walla Walla
Hagan, Dalia Lapatinskas *library director*

WEST VIRGINIA

Bluefield
Turnbull, Margaret Coombs *librarian*

Huntington
Pratt, Mary Louise *librarian, writer*

Morgantown
Landreth, Barbara Bugg *librarian*

Shepherdstown
Elliott, Jean Ann *retired library director*

WISCONSIN

Bloomer
Kane, Lucile M. *retired archivist, historian*

Eau Claire
Tiefel, Virginia May *librarian*

Green Bay
LaViolette, Catherine Patricia *librarian*

Laona
Sturzl, Alice A. *school library administrator*

Madison
Blankenburg, Julie J. *librarian*
Hawkinson, Lorraine A. *librarian*

Milwaukee
Huston, Kathleen Marie *library administrator*
Kiely, Paula *city librarian*
McKinney, Venora Ware *librarian*

Rhinelander
Wendt, Kristine Adams *librarian*

Rice Lake
Sampson, Zora J. *librarian*

WYOMING

Cheyenne
LeBarron, Suzanne Jane *librarian*

Worland
Overcast, Vickie L. *librarian*

TERRITORIES OF THE UNITED STATES

AMERICAN SAMOA

Pago Pago
Fung-Chen-Pen, Emma Talauna Solaita *librarian, director*

PUERTO RICO

San Juan
González Echevarria, Amelia L. *librarian, counseling administrator*
Muñoz-Solá, Haydeé Socorro *library administrator*

MILITARY ADDRESSES OF THE UNITED STATES

EUROPE

APO
Sokolowski, Denise Georgia *librarian, academic administrator*

CANADA

BRITISH COLUMBIA

Coquitlam
Hainsworth, Melody May *library and information scientist, researcher*

Vancouver
Piternick, Anne Brearley *librarian, educator*

ONTARIO

Ottawa
Scott, Marianne Florence *retired librarian, educator*

Toronto
Bryant, Josephine Harriet *library executive*
Moore, Carole Irene *librarian*

SASKATCHEWAN

Saskatoon
Kennedy, Marjorie Ellen *librarian*

CZECH REPUBLIC

Prague
Turková, Helga *librarian*

WEST INDIES

Commonwealth Dominica
Sullivan, Marilyn Bobette *librarian, consultant*

ADDRESS UNPUBLISHED

Abid, Ann B. *art librarian*
Allen, Victoria Taylor *archivist*
Anderson, Mary Jane *library director, consultant*
Anderson, Rachael Keller (Rachael Keller) *retired library director*
Baker, Carolyn Simmons *library director, consultant, researcher*
Ball, Joyce *retired university librarian and dean*
Bart, Muriel *library educator*
Battin, Patricia Meyer *librarian*
Berman, Miriam Naomi *librarian*
Berson, Bella Zevitovsky *librarian*
Blackburn, Joy Martin *retired librarian*
Blalock, Louise *librarian, public administrator*
Bowen, Jean *retired librarian, consultant*
Brady, Jean Stein *retired librarian*
Bromwell, Linda Anne *librarian, writer*
Brooks Shoemaker, Virginia Lee *librarian*
Brown, Carol Ann *librarian, director*
Brown, Carolyn P. *retired librarian*
Bulmer, Connie J. *film librarian*
Burkhardt, Joanna Marie *librarian*
Bzdell, Susan Rosenblum *archivist, educator*
Cabaniss, Charlotte Jones *library services director*
Cammack, Ann *librarian, secondary school educator*
Cannon, Patricia Althen *librarian, writer*
Carpenter, Janella Ann *retired librarian*
Carr, E. Barbara *librarian*
Cassell, Kay Ann *librarian*
Chirico-Elkins, Ursula *retired librarian*
Chu, Ellin Resnick *librarian, consultant*
Clement, Hope Elizabeth Anna *retired librarian*
Conaway, Margaret Grimes (Peggy Conaway) *library administrator*
Crabb, Virginia Geany Ruth *librarian*
Crahan, Elizabeth Schmidt *librarian*
Crawford, Sheila Jane *librarian, reading specialist*
Daffron, MaryEllen *retired librarian*
Dickinson, Gail Krepps *library science educator*
Drake, Miriam Anna *retired librarian, educator, writer, consultant*
Dykstra Lynch, Mary Elizabeth *library and information scientist, educator*
Eaton, Katherine Girton *retired library educator*
Edmonds, Anne Carey *librarian*
Elder, Mary Louise *librarian*
Ellington, Mildred L. *librarian*
Else, Carolyn Joan *retired library director*
Elwood-Akers, Virginia Edythe *librarian, retired archivist*
Erwin, Linda McIntosh *retired librarian*
Estes, Elaine Rose Graham *retired librarian*
Euster, Joanne Reed *retired librarian*
Everett, Karen Joan *retired librarian, genealogist, educator*
Fasick, Adele Mongan *library and information scientist, educator*
Felsted, Carla Martindell *librarian, writer, editor*
Ford, Barbara Jean *librarian, educator*
Forester, Jean Martha Brouillette *retired librarian, educator, innkeeper*
Foster, Joy Via *retired library media specialist*
Garoogian, Rhoda *librarian*
Gaulke, Mary Florence *retired library administrator*
Gelfand, Julia Maureen *librarian*
Giebel, Miriam Catherine *librarian, genealogist*
Giles, Audrey Elizabeth *reference librarian*
Goldschmidt, Eva *librarian*
Goodwyn, Betty Ruth *librarian*
Gould, Martha Bernice *retired librarian*
Gramling, Audrey *library media specialist, educator*
Gray, Gloria Meador *librarian*
Gray, Patricia B. *retired librarian, information specialist*
Greenberg, Hinda Feige *library director*
Greenwood, Anna Starbuck *librarian*
Gregor, Dorothy Deborah *retired librarian*
Gross, Dorothy-Ellen *library director, educator*
Gustafson-Haigh, Marjorie Ann *retired librarian*
Hashim, Elinor Marie *librarian*
Headley, Lunetta Forsyth *retired librarian*
Heanue, Anne Allen *retired librarian*
Hebert, Mary Olivia *retired librarian*
Hempleman, Barbara Florence *archivist*
Henri, Janine Jacqueline *librarian*
Hewitt, Ruth Price *librarian, educator*
Hogensen, Margaret Hiner *retired librarian, consultant*
Hoke, Sheila Wilder *retired librarian*
Holleman, Marian Isabel *librarian, educator*
Holliday, Barbara Joyce *reference librarian, minister*
Hughes, Sue Margaret *retired librarian*
Jacob, Rosamond Tryon *librarian*
Jameson, Patricia Madoline *science librarian*
Johnson, Carolyn M. *librarian, writer*
Jones-Eddy, Julie Margaret *retired librarian*
Kerby, Ramona Anne *librarian*
Ketchum, Irene Frances *library supporter*
Kirby, Marcia Karen *library and information scientist*
Klein, Susan Elaine *librarian*
Knudsen, Helen Ewing Zollars *librarian*
Korenic, Lynette Marie *librarian*
Kreitzburg, Marilyn June *academic librarian*
Landry, Abbie Vestal *librarian*
LaPolt, Margaret *librarian*
Lathrop, Ann *retired librarian, educator*
Lau, Christina Sielck *librarian*
Lehner-Quam, Alison Lynn *library administrator*
Liu, Rhonda Louise *librarian*
Loewenstein, Lenore Cecile *retired school librarian*
Lofaro, Nanette *information services administrator*
Lovelace, Julianne *former library director*
Lowell, Virginia Lee *retired librarian*
Malone, Nancy J. *librarian*
Marker, Rhonda Joyce *librarian*
McDonald, Arlys Lorraine *retired librarian*
McGrath, Anna Fields *retired librarian*
McIntyre, Elizabeth Jones *retired multi-media specialist, educator*
Meyer, Ursula *retired library director*
Miller, Jacqueline Winslow *library director*
Miller, Marilyn Lea *library and information scientist, educator*
Moody, Marilyn Dallas *retired librarian*
Moore, Beverly Ann *retired librarian*
Moore, Julie L. *bibliographer, librarian*
Morgan, Jane Hale *retired library director*
Naulty, Susan Louise *archivist*
Neeley, Kathleen Louise *librarian*
Nix, Patricia Perry *retired librarian*
Noah, Julia Jeanine *retired librarian*
Notley, Thelma A. *retired librarian, educator*
Ortego, Gilda Baeza *library director, educator*
Parker, Sara Ann *librarian, consultant*
Penny, Laura Jean *librarian*
Peri, Linda Carol *librarian*
Pierik, Marilyn Anne *retired librarian, piano teacher*
Pond, Peggy Ann *librarian*
Potter, Corinne Jean *retired librarian*
Primack, Alice Lefler *retired librarian*
Razoharinoro, *archivist, historian, researcher*
Renfro, Patricia Elise *library director, academic administrator*
Repinski, Sara *library director*
Roark, Barbara Ann *librarian*
Robbins, Jane Borsch *library and information science professor*
Roberts, Judith Marie *librarian, educator*
Robinson, Verna Cotten *retired librarian, real estate manager*
Rusaw, Sally Ellen *librarian*
Sandy, Catherine Ellen *librarian*
Scheiberg, Susan L. *librarian*
Schlesinger, Deborah Lee *retired librarian*
Schlosser, Anne Griffin *librarian*
Schneider, Sherri *library clerk*
Scott, Catherine Dorothy *librarian, library and information scientist, consultant*
Seagraves, Helen Leonard *librarian*
Segal, JoAn Smyth *library consultant, small business owner*
Settles, Jeanne Dobson *retired librarian*
Sheldon, Brooke Earle *librarian, educator*
Shultz, Linda Joyce *retired library director*
Siefert-Kazanjian, Donna *corporate librarian*
Simpson, Zelma Alene *retired librarian*
Smelser, June *librarian*
Soules, Aline *librarian, writer*
Sprince, Leila Joy *retired librarian*
Stewart, Dorothy K. *librarian*
Stickney, Lorraine Phyllis Osberg *retired librarian*
Stoesser, Susan Alice (Susan Alice Lange) *retired librarian, educator, media generalist*
Stoyan, Hortensia Rodríguez-Sánchez *library administrator*
Strait, Viola Edwina Washington *librarian*
Summers, Lorraine Dey Schaeffer *retired librarian*
Taraki, Shirlee *librarian*
Thiele, Gloria Day *librarian, small business owner*
Tolbert, Nina Dianne *library and information scientist*
Triipan, Maive *library director*
VanMeter, Vandelia L. *retired library director*
Van Orden, Phyllis Jeanne *librarian, educator*
Varner, Joyce Ehrhardt *retired librarian*
Vernerder, Gloria Jean *retired librarian*
Vittitow, Susan *librarian, writer*
Walton, Kathleen Endres *librarian*
Warnken, Paula Neuman *university library director, educator*
Watkins, Karen J. *librarian*
Weaver, Barbara Frances *librarian, consultant*
Weikert, Barbara Ruth *librarian*
Weingand, Darlene Erna *librarian, educator*
Whitmore, Menandra M. *librarian*
Wik, Jean Marie (Jean Marie Beck) *librarian, media specialist*
Williams, Mildred Jane *librarian*
Willson, Doris *librarian*
Wilson, Patricia Potter *library and information scientist, educator*
Wingate, Bettye Faye *librarian, educator*
Wong, Suzanne Crawbuck *librarian*
Woodrum, Patricia Ann *librarian*
Woods, Phyllis Michalik *librarian*
Wulff, Lois Yvonne *retired librarian*
Yiotis, Gayle *archivist, researcher, anthropologist, writer*

Young, Susan Babson *retired library director*

HUMANITIES: MUSEUMS

UNITED STATES

ALABAMA

Anniston
Bragg, Cheryl *museum director*

Birmingham
Trechsel, Gail Andrews *museum director*

Florence
Wright, Mildred Anne (Milly Wright) *conservator, researcher*

Mc Calla
Kes, Vicki *museum director*

Montgomery
Belt, Jean Rainer *art gallery owner*

ALASKA

Anchorage
Wolf, Patricia B. *museum director*

ARIZONA

Glendale
Almstead, Sheila Louise *art gallery owner*

Scottsdale
Krane, Susan *museum director, curator*

Tempe
Zeitlin, Marilyn Audrey *museum director*

Tubac
Roseman, Kim *gallery director*

Tucson
Rufe, Laurie J. *museum director*

CALIFORNIA

Berkeley
Day, Lucille Lang *museum administrator, educator, writer*
Efimova, Alla *curator*
Grossman, Bonnie *art gallery director*

Carson
Zimmerer, Kathy Louise *museum director*

Fresno
Monaghan, Kathleen M. *art museum director*

La Jolla
Beebe, Mary Livingstone *curator*

Long Beach
Glenn, Constance White *art museum director, educator, consultant*

Los Angeles
Barron, Stephanie *curator*
Hirano, Irene Ann Yasutake *museum director*
Komaroff, Linda *curator*
Philbin, Ann *art facility director*
Rich, Andrea Louise *museum administrator*
Zelevansky, Lynn *curator*

Montara
Wall, Glennie Murray *historic preservation professional*

Riverside
Warren, Katherine Virginia *art gallery director*

Sacramento
Jones, Lial A. *museum director*

San Diego
Longenecker, Martha W. *museum director*

San Francisco
Sano, Emily Joy *museum director*

San Jose
Hernandez, Jo Farb *museum director, consultant*

The Sea Ranch
Baas, Jacquelynn *museum director, art historian*

COLORADO

Colorado Springs
LeMieux, Linda Dailey *museum director*

Denver
Daley, Ann Scarlett *curator*
Payton, Cydney *museum director, curator*

Vail
Logan, Vicki *art collector*

CONNECTICUT

New Haven
Kane, Patricia Ellen *museum curator*
Meyers, Amy *museum director*
Sorkin, Jenni *curator, critic*

Vogel, Susan Mullin *museum director, art and archaeology professor*

DISTRICT OF COLUMBIA

Washington
Behrensmeyer, Anna K. *curator, research scientist*
Bloomfield, Sara J. *museum director*
Bredhoff, Stacey Anne *curator*
Bretzfelder, Deborah May *retired museum staff member*
Buhler, Leslie Lynn *museum director*
Carr, Carolyn Kinder *art gallery director*
Dwyer Southern, Kathy *museum administrator*
Foster, Mercedes S. *curator, research scientist*
Halpern, Nora R. *museum director, curator*
Harvey, Eleanor Jones *museum curator*
Larson, Judy L. *museum director, curator*
Legro, Patrice *museum director*
Noe, Adrianne *museum administrator*
Patton, Sharon F. *museum director*
Radice, Anne-Imelda Marino *museum director, former federal agency administrator*
Sant, Victoria P. *museum administrator*
Stevenson, Frances Kellogg *retired museum program director*
Stevenson, Nancy Nelson *museum director*
Wolanin, Barbara Ann Boese *curator, art historian*

FLORIDA

Boynton Beach
Waldman, Gloria *art gallery owner, artist*

Coral Gables
Miller, Virginia Irene *fine art galleries executive*

Fort Lauderdale
Cavendish, Kim L. Maher *museum administrator*

Jacksonville
Dundon, Margo Elaine *museum director*

Key West
Pennington, Claudia *museum director*

Miami
Delehanty, Suzanne *museum director*
Morgan, Dahlia *museum director, art educator*

Miami Beach
Camber, Diane Woolfe *museum director*

Orlando
Morrisey, Marena Grant *art museum administrator*

Saint Petersburg
Gordon-Harris, Cassandra I. *curator, educator*
Weaver, F. Louise Beazley *curator, director*

Tallahassee
Palladino-Craig, Allys *museum director, educator*

Vero Beach
Gedeon, Lucinda Heyel *museum director*

West Palm Beach
Orr-Cahall, Anona Christina *museum director, art historian*

GEORGIA

Atlanta
King, Linda Orr *museum director, consultant*

Kathleen
Wills, Lois Elaine *art gallery owner, religious education educator*

Savannah
Lesko, Diane *museum director, curator*

HAWAII

Hilo
King, Codie Mary *art center director, artist*

IDAHO

Coeur D' Alene
Dahlgren, Dorothy *museum director*

ILLINOIS

Chicago
Alexander, Karen *museum staff member*
Dittmer, Frances R. *curator*
Sheehy, Carolyn Aranka *curator*
Smith, Elizabeth Angele Taft *curator*
Terrassa, Jacqueline *museum director*
Von Klan, Laurene *museum administrator*
Wright, Antoinette D. *museum administrator*

Glenview
Kohl, Dolores *museum director, educator*

Mahomet
Kennedy, Cheryl Lynn *museum director*

Princeton
Collins, N. Dana *art gallery owner, consultant, retired art educator*

Springfield
Witter, Karen Ackerman *museum administrator*

INDIANA

Bloomington
Calinescu, Adriana Gabriela *curator, art historian*

Elkhart
Burns, B(illye) Jane *museum director*

Indianapolis
Easter, Jeanmarie *conservator*
Tandy, Kisha Renee *curator*

IOWA

Ames
Pohlman, Lynette *museum director, curator*

KANSAS

Lawrence
Hardy, Saralyn Reece *museum director*
Norris, Andrea Spaulding *art museum director*

KENTUCKY

Lexington
Walsh-Piper, Kathleen A. *museum director*

Louisville
Becker, Gail Roselyn *museum director*

Owensboro
Hood, Mary Bryan *museum director, painter*

LOUISIANA

Deridder
Mallory, Patricia Jody *museum curator*

MAINE

Brunswick
Kline, Katy *museum director*

Lamoine
Schmidt, Christine Alice *art gallery owner*

MARYLAND

Baltimore
Bolger, Doreen *museum director*
Hofmann, Irene E. *art museum director*
Lanier, Jacqueline Ruth *curator, artist*

Bethesda
Fraser, Catriona Trafford *art gallery director, photographer*

Friendship
Clagett, Diana Wharton Sinkler *museum docent*

Landover
Grasselli, Margaret Morgan *curator*

Mitchellville
Marsh, Caryl Amsterdam *retired curator, retired psychologist*

MASSACHUSETTS

Boston
Cronin, Bonnie Kathryn Lamb *museum director*
Curran, Emily Katherine *museum director*
Emerson, Anne Devereux *museum administrator*
Hawley, Anne *museum director*
Hills, Patricia Gorton Schulze *curator, art historian*
Medvedow, Jill *museum director*
Zannieri, Nina *museum director*

Cambridge
Farver, Jane *museum director*
Watson, Rubie S. *museum director*

Chestnut Hill
Netzer, Nancy *museum director, art historian, educator*

Milton
Randall, Lilian Maria Charlotte *museum curator*

Needham
Palmerio, Elvira Castano *art gallery director, art historian*

Northampton
Fabing, Suzannah *museum director*

Sudbury
Pitman, Ursula Wall *curator, educator*

Williamstown
Corrin, Lisa G. *museum director*

Winchester
Fitch, Blake *museum director, photographer, curator*

MICHIGAN

Detroit
Terry, Robin *museum director*

East Lansing
Bandes, Susan Jane *museum director, educator*

MINNESOTA

Minneapolis
Halbreich, Kathy *museum director*
King, Lyndel Irene Saunders *museum director*

Saint Paul
Archabal, Nina M(archetti) *historic site director*

MISSISSIPPI

Jackson
Bradley, Betsy *museum director*

Washington
Branyan, Cheryl Munyer *museum administrator*

MISSOURI

Columbia
McVicker, Mary Ellen Harshbarger *museum director, art educator*

Fredericktown
Sudmeyer, Alice Jean *art gallery owner*

Independence
Potts, Barbara Joyce *retired historic site director*

Kansas City
Cozad, Rachael Blackburn *museum director*
Scott, Deborah Emont *curator*
Svadlenak, Jean Hayden *museum director, consultant*

Saint Louis
Eyerman, Charlotte *curator, art historian*

NEBRASKA

Chadron
Lecher, Belvadine (Belvadine Reeves) *museum curator*

NEVADA

Carson City
Stewart, Phillis *museum official*

Las Vegas
Herridge, Elizabeth *museum director*

NEW HAMPSHIRE

Meredith
Lane, Sophia *art gallery director*

Portsmouth
Nylander, Jane Louise *museum director, educator, writer*

NEW JERSEY

Newark
Price, Mary Sue Sweeney *museum director*
Reynolds, Valrae *museum curator*

Princeton
Taylor, Susan M. *museum director*

Ridgewood
Fox, Ingrid *curator*

Summit
Call, Denise Hodgins *curator, artist, freelance/self-employed writer*

Wayne
Einreinhofer, Nancy Anne *art gallery director*

NEW MEXICO

Albuquerque
Baker, Laura Kay *art gallery owner, writer*

Silver City
Bettison, Cynthia Ann *museum director, archaeologist*

NEW YORK

Albany
Miles, Christine Marie *museum director*

Bronx
Block, Holly *museum director*

Buffalo
Bayles, Jennifer Lucene *museum program director, educator*

Corning
Spillman, Jane Shadel *curator, writer, researcher*

Corona
Smith, Valerie *curator*

East Hampton
Vered, Ruth *art gallery director, owner*

Jamestown
Reale, Sara Jane *museum education director*

Long Island City
Heiss, Alanna *museum director*
Lloyd, Kenita *museum administrator*

Mount Kisco
Bithoney, Carmen C. D'Amborsio *artistic director*

New Kingston
Chase, Linda *curator, writer*

New York
Barnett, Vivian Endicott *curator*
Basquin, Mary Smyth (Kit Basquin) *museum administrator*
Beck, Martha Ann *curator, director*
Brooks, Diana B. *former auction house executive*
Carr, Claudia *art gallery director, artist, art gallery owner*
Chatfield-Taylor, Adele *historic site director*
Dennison, Lisa *museum director*
Desai, Vishakha N. *museum director, professional society administrator*
Ferber, Linda S. *museum director*
Futter, Ellen Victoria *museum administrator*
Globus, Dorothy Twining *museum director*
Golden, Thelma *curator*
Goodman, Susan *curator*
Gumpert, Lynn *gallery director*
Gund, Agnes *retired museum administrator*
Haskell, Barbara *curator*
Hoffman, Nancy *art gallery director*
Hotchner, Holly *museum director, curator, conservator*
Ilse-Neuman, Ursula *curator*
Kallir, Jane Katherine *art gallery director, author*
Kardon, Janet *museum director*
Kramer, Linda Konheim *curator, art historian*
Kujawski, Elizabeth Szancer *art curator, consultant*
Leff, Sandra H. *art gallery director, consultant*
Lynch, Florence *art gallery director*
Martin, Mary-Anne *art gallery owner*
Mertens, Joan R. *museum curator, art historian*
Mitchell, Patricia Edenfield *broadcast museum administrator*
O'Brien, Catherine Louise *museum administrator*
Pesner, Carole Manishin *art gallery owner*
Poulet, Anne Litle *museum director, art historian*
Rafferty, Emily Kernan *museum administrator*
Rosenbaum, Joan Hannah *museum director*
Rosenthal, Nan *curator, educator, author*
Sims, Lowery Stokes *museum curator, museum administrator, writer, educator,*
Singer, Debra *curator*
Subotnick, Ali *curator, writer*
Sutton, Karen E. *museum director*
Tisch Sussman, Laurie *art gallery director*
Tobach, Ethel *retired curator*
Toll, Barbara Elizabeth *art gallery director*

Sands Point
Olian, JoAnne Constance *curator, art historian*

Stony Brook
Stone, Gaynell *museum director, educator*

Stuyvesant
Tripp, Susan Gerwe *museum director*

Syracuse
Trop, Sandra *museum director*

NORTH CAROLINA

Durham
Rorschach, Kimberly *museum director*

Wilmington
Seapker, Janet Kay *museum administrator, historic site director, consultant*

OHIO

Cincinnati
DeWitt, Katharine Cramer *museum administrator*
Shearer, Linda *museum director*
Spangenberg, Kristin Louise *curator*
Timpano, Anne *museum director, art historian*

Cleveland
Snyder, Jill *museum director*

Toledo
Grant, Peggy (Margaret Mary Grant) *art gallery administrator, artist, consultant*

OREGON

Milwaukie
Eichenger, Marilynne Katzen *museum administrator*

Portland
Taylor, J. Mary (Jocelyn Mary Taylor) *museum director, educator, zoologist*

PENNSYLVANIA

Harrisburg
Franco, Barbara Alice *museum director*

Philadelphia
d'Harnoncourt, Anne *museum director, museum administrator*
Gould, Claudia *museum director*
Shoemaker, Innis Howe *art museum curator*

Pittsburgh
Dawson, Mary Ruth *curator, educator*
Jaffe, Gwen Daner *museum program director, educator*
King, Elaine A. *curator, art historian, critic*

University Park
Muhlert, Jan Keene *art museum director*

Wynnewood
Camp, Kimberly N. *museum administrator, artist*

RHODE ISLAND

Newport
Tinney, Harle Hope Hanson *museum administrator*

SOUTH CAROLINA

Columbia
Brosius, Karen *museum director*

Greenville
Davis, Joan Carroll *retired museum director*

Pawleys Island
Matelic, Candace Tangorra *museum director, educator*

TENNESSEE

Memphis
Feldman, Kaywin *museum director, curator*

TEXAS

Dallas
Hoffman, Marguerite Steed *former art gallery director*

Fort Worth
Davis, Carol Lyn *museum administrator*
Loud, Patricia Cummings *curator*
Price, Marla *museum director, curator*

Fredericksburg
Manhart, Marcia Y(ockey) *art museum director*

Frisco
Meadows, Patricia Blachly *curator, civic worker*

Houston
Lee, Janie C. *curator*
Mayo, Marti *museum director, curator*
Ramirez, Mari Carmen *curator*
Tucker, Anne Wilkes *curator, historian, photographer, critic*

Post
Neff, Marie Taylor *museum director, artist*

VIRGINIA

Ashburn
Glick, Paula Florence *art historian, author, lecturer*

Charlottesville
Hartz, Jill *museum director*
Holmes, Carolyn Coggin *museum director*

Keswick
Nosanow, Barbara Shissler *museum program director, curator*

Richmond
Koch, Aimee Helen *art gallery director, photographer*

Virginia Beach
Paqet, Shawna Lee *museum director*

Williamsburg
Christison, Muriel Branham *retired museum director, art history educator*

WASHINGTON

Bellingham
Clark-Langager, Sarah Ann *curator, academic administrator*

Renton
O'Dell, Patsy June *art gallery director*

Seattle
Gates, Mimi Gardner *museum director*

WISCONSIN

Madison
Pillaert, E(dna) Elizabeth *museum curator*

Milwaukee
Peltz, Cissie Jean *art gallery director, cartoonist*

WYOMING

Laramie
Moldenhauer, Susan *museum director, curator*

CANADA

ONTARIO

London
Poole, Nancy Geddes *art gallery curator, writer*

ADDRESS UNPUBLISHED

Adams, Margaret Bernice *retired museum official*
Belkov, Meredith Ann *landmark administrator*
Black, Ruth Idella *museum curator*
Booker, Nana Laurel *art gallery owner, honorary consul*
Brown, Julia *museum director*
Collischan, Judy Kay *art gallery director, museum director, critic, artist*
Damon, Shirley Stockton *art gallery owner*
Decatur, Raylene *former museum director*
Deutschman, Louise Tolliver *curator*
de Zegher, Catherine *museum director, curator*
Doyle, Christine Ellen *museum researcher, educator*
Faunce, Sarah Cushing *retired curator*
Feisthammel, Audrey Marie *museum director, educator*
Godbille, Lara *museum director*
Greenwald, Alice Marian *museum director*
Hess, Wendy K. *curator, researcher, writer*
Ives, Colta Feller *museum curator, educator*
Jacobowitz, Ellen Sue *curator, museum administrator*
Jerger, Holly Anne *museum staff member, artist*
Jones, Charlott Ann *retired museum director, art educator*
Kelm, Bonnie G. *art museum director, educator, art appraiser, consultant*
Ketcham, Sally Ann *historic site staff member, consultant*
Knowles, Elizabeth Pringle *museum director*
Lane, Lilly Katherine *museum staff member*
Liman, Ellen *art gallery owner, painter*
Longstreth-Brown, Kathryn *retired museum administrator*
McCracken, Ursula E. *museum director*
Mercuri, Joan B. *museum administrator*
Meyer, Ruth Krueger *museum director, educator, art historian*
Moore, Rosemary Kuulei *art gallery owner*
Moss, Lynda Bourque *museum director*
Mulryan, Lenore Hoag *art curator, writer*
Pilgrim, Dianne Hauserman *retired museum director*
Plehaty, Phyllis Juliette *retired curator*
Reid, Katharine Lee *museum director*
Reid, Katherine Lee *retired museum director, curator*
Schneider, Janet M. *museum administrator, painter, curator*
Shaw, Nancy Rivard *museum curator, art historian, consultant*
Steinhauser, Janice Maureen *arts administrator, educator, artist*
Towe, A. Ruth *retired museum director*
Trutor, Genevieve Williamson *museum director*
Van Buren, Kari *museum director*
White, Katharine Stone *museum administrator*
Wilson, Karen Lee *museum staff member, researcher*
Yarlow, Loretta *art museum director*

INDUSTRY: MANUFACTURING
See also **FINANCE: FINANCIAL SERVICES**

UNITED STATES

ALABAMA

Athens
Newton, Janet Gail *office manager*

Birmingham
Cohen-DeMarco, Gale Maureen *pharmaceutical executive*

Prattville
Lambert, Meg Stringer *construction executive, architect, interior designer*

ARIZONA

Tucson
Francesconi, Louise L. *defense equipment manufacturing company executive*

ARKANSAS

Little Rock
Johananoff, Pamela *jewelry designer, gemologist*

North Little Rock
Harrison, Angela Eve *manufacturing executive*

Springdale
Beach, Jean Mrha *food products executive*
Dunn, Jeri R. *food products executive*
Earl, Heather Jo *food company professional*

CALIFORNIA

Berry Creek
Montaño, Tiffany Dunhill *aerospace production control specialist*

Bishop
Naso, Valerie Joan *automotive dealership executive, travel company executive*

Burbank
Joseff, Joan Castle *manufacturing executive*

Colusa
Carter, Jane Foster *agricultural industry executive*

Cypress
Garrett, Sharon *health services company executive*
Kosecoff, Jacqueline Barbara *health care company executive*

Lodi
Puerta, Christy L. *construction executive*

Long Beach
Shiffman, Leslie Brown *retired apparel executive*

Los Alamitos
Caplan, Karen B. *food products executive*

Los Altos
Beer, Clara Louise Johnson *retired electronics executive*

Los Angeles
Campanella, Yvette Lynn *cosmetics executive*
Serena, Monique *apparel executive*

Palo Alto
Church, Katrina J. *pharmaceutical executive*
Fenney, Linda *pharmaceutical executive*
Kincaid, Judith Wells *electronics company executive*
Smith, Julie Ann *pharmaceutical executive*

Redwood City
Chow, Irene A. *biopharmaceutical company executive*

Rescue
Ackerly, Wendy Saunders *construction company executive*

San Carlos
Pollack, Betty Gillespie *retired health care services executive*

San Diego
Gillespie, Deirdre Y. *pharmaceutical executive*
Graham, Ginger L. *pharmaceutical executive*

San Francisco
Hudson, Suncerray Ann *research and development company executive*
Morris-Tyndall, Lucy *construction executive*
Ross, Ivy *apparel executive, artist*
Seeger, Laureen E. *health products executive*

San Mateo
Burzik, Catherine M. *pharmaceutical executive*

Santa Clara
Dorchak, Glenda *electronics company executive*
Murray, Patricia *electronics company executive*

South San Francisco
Desmond-Hellmann, Susan *medical products manufacturing executive*
Potter, Myrtle S. *research and development company executive*

Ukiah
Newell, Barbara Ann *coatings company executive*

Willits
Handley, Margie Lee *manufacturing executive*

COLORADO

Denver
Alvarado, Linda G. *construction executive*

Englewood
Rheney, Susan O. *paper company executive*

Jefferson
Maatsch, Deborah Joan *manufacturing executive*

CONNECTICUT

Danbury
Good, Jennifer L. *pharmaceutical executive*

Fairfield
Daley, Pamela *diversified services, technology and manufacturing company executive*
Reif, Deborah *manufacturing executive*

New Haven
Jacob, Deirdre Ann Bradbury *manufacturing executive, finance educator, consultant*

Stamford
Parrs, Marianne M. *paper and lumber company executive*

Wilton
Oberstar, Helen Elizabeth *retired cosmetics company executive*

DELAWARE

Greenville
Walker, Sally Barbara *retired glass company executive*

Newark
Gantzer, Mary Lou *medical products executive*

Wilmington
Gulyas, Diane H. *manufacturing executive*
Kullman, Ellen Jamison *chemicals executive*
McLeer, Laureen Dorothy *drug development and pharmaceutical professional*
Vary, Eva Maros *retired chemicals executive*

DISTRICT OF COLUMBIA

Washington
Buto, Kathleen A. *health products executive*
Mathews, Jessica Tuchman *research executive, federal official, newswriter*
Smith, Madeleine T. *medical products executive*

FLORIDA

Coral Gables
Burini, Sonia Montes de Oca *apparel manufacturing executive, public relations executive*
Jackson, Yvonne Ruth *former pharmaceutical executive*

Delray Beach
Force, Elizabeth Elma *retired pharmaceutical executive*
Mayer, Marilyn Gooder *steel company executive*

Hialeah
Engler, Eva Kay *dental and veterinary products company executive*

Marco Island
Moore, Faye Halfacre *jewelry manufacturer*

Naples
Sekowski, Cynthia Jean *health products executive, medical consultant, contact lens specialist*

New Port Richey
Sebring, Marjorie Marie Allison *former home furnishings company executive*

Reddick
Corwin, Joyce Elizabeth Stedman *construction company executive*

GEORGIA

Atlanta
Camac, Margaret Victoria *construction company executive*
Francis, Julie *beverage company executive*
Isaac, Yvonne Renee *construction executive*
Johnson, Carrie Clements *pharmaceutical executive*
Jones, Ingrid Saunders *food products executive*
Lemos, Gloria Elliott *soft drink company executive*
Minnick, Mary E. *beverage company executive*
Palmer, Vicki R. *food products executive*
Tilley, Tana Marie *pharmaceutical executive*
Young, Joyce L. *chemicals executive*

Fort Mcpherson
Karpinski, Janis Leigh *security manager*

Norcross
Moreno, Veronica *food products executive*

Rossville
Anderson, Kristie *construction company executive*

HAWAII

Kamuela
Stephenson, Nancy Louise *medical products company professional*

IDAHO

Boise
Elg, Annette *food products executive*

Post Falls
Hasalone, Annette Leona *research and development company executive*

ILLINOIS

Abbott Park
Flynn, Gary L. *pharmaceutical executive*

Arlington Heights
Johnson, Margaret H. *welding company executive*

Aurora
Belcher, La Jeune *automotive executive*

Blue Island
Hackenast, Sherri *race track owner, former race car driver*
Heckenast, Sherri *auto parts executive, sports association executive*

Champaign
Stotler, Edith Ann *retired grain company executive*

Chicago
Barnes, Brenda C. *food products executive*
Ferguson, Diana S. *food products executive*
Geraghty, Elizabeth *food products executive*
Gordon, Ellen Rubin *candy company executive*
Tryloff, Robin S. *food products executive*

Decatur
Madding, Claudia *agricultural products executive*
Woertz, Patricia Ann *agricultural company executive, retired oil company executive*

Deerfield
Adams, Jennifer *medical products executive*

Elmhurst
Nedza, Sandra Louise *manufacturing executive*

Gurnee
Hagins, Barbara J. *pharmaceutical consultant*

Melrose Park
Lavin, Bernice E. *cosmetics executive*
Wechter, Clari Ann *manufacturing executive*

Niles
Schyvinck, Christine *electronics executive*

Northfield
Lynch, Kirsten *food products executive*
Rosenfeld, Irene B. *food products company executive*
Sneed, Paula Ann *food products executive*

Tinley Park
Leeson, Janet Caroline Tollefson *cake specialties company executive*

West Chicago
Deaver, Barbara Jean *manufacturing executive*

West Dundee
Plunkett, Melba Kathleen *manufacturing executive*

INDIANA

Indianapolis
Connelly, Deirdre P. *pharmaceutical executive*
Lorell, Beverly H. *medical products executive*

Mishawaka
Rubenstein, Pamela Silver *manufacturing executive*

IOWA

Bettendorf
Collins, Kathleen Elizabeth *pharmaceutical company official*

Marshalltown
Foote, Sherrill Lynne *retired manufacturing company technician*

Pella
Dout, Anne Jacqueline *manufacturing and sales company executive*

KANSAS

Overland Park
Schmidt, Shelley Rae *cosmetics executive, educator*

KENTUCKY

Lexington
Gornik, Kathy *electronics executive*

Louisville
Herron, Beckie Lee *health service executive*
Margulis, Heidi *health products executive*
Wood, Phoebe A. *food products executive*

Newport
Taliaferro, Elizabeth W. *manufacturing executive*

MAINE

Bath
Simone, Gail Elisabeth *manufacturing executive*

MARYLAND

Baltimore
Lucas, Barbara B. *electrical equipment manufacturing executive*

Bethesda
Spector, Eleanor Ruth *manufacturing executive*

Columbia
Warren, Rita Simpson *manufacturing executive*

Davidsonville
Bowles, Liza K. *construction executive*

Hanover
Turner, Valarie English *electronics company administrator*

Reisterstown
Bart, Polly Turner *construction executive*

MASSACHUSETTS

Brookline
Assens, Nathalie *construction executive*

Cambridge
Dunsire, Deborah *pharmaceutical executive*
Matsui, Connie L. *pharmaceutical executive*

Needham
Kolb, Gloria Ro *medical products executive*

Pittsfield
Begley, Charlene *electronics executive*

Roxbury
Cruthird, Brandy K. *gym owner and fitness instructor*

Springfield
Winn, Janice Gail *food products administrator*

MICHIGAN

Auburn Hills
Niekamp, Cynthia Ann *automotive executive*
Unger, Susan J. *automotive executive*

Battle Creek
Banks, Donna Jo *food products executive*

Benton Harbor
Tennant-Snyder, Nancy *appliance company executive*

Bloomfield Hills
Lapadot, Sonee Spinner *retired automobile manufacturing company official*

Dearborn
Buckingham, Lorie *automotive executive*

Detroit
Barclay, Kathleen S. *automotive executive*
Kantrowitz, Jean *health products executive*
Kempston Darkes, V. Maureen *automotive executive*
Owen, Karen Michelle *manufacturing executive*

Grosse Pointe Farms
Obolensky, Marilyn Wall (Mrs. Serge Obolensky) *metals company executive*

Midland
Burns, Stephanie A. *chemicals executive*
Holder, Julie Fasone *chemicals executive*

Novi
Ligocki, Kathleen A. *auto parts company executive*

Portage
Farrand, Lois Barbara *pharmaceutical company administrator*

Troy
Healy, Karen *automotive executive*
Mahone, Barbara Jean *automotive executive*
Walker, Bette *automotive executive*

MINNESOTA

Lindstrom
Messin, Marlene Ann *plastics company executive*

Minneapolis
Bader, Kathleen M. *chemicals executive*
Pletcher, Carol H. *chemicals executive*

MISSOURI

Fenton
Hughes, Barbara Bradford *manufacturing executive, community health nurse*

Saint Louis
Brown, JoBeth Goode *food products executive, lawyer*
Filbert-Zacher, Laura Margaret *research and development company executive*
Weldon, Virginia V. *retired food products executive, retired pediatrician*

NEVADA

Las Vegas
Strahan, Julia Celestine *electronics company executive*

NEW HAMPSHIRE

Keene
Miller, Rita *die-casting company executive, personnel consultant*

NEW JERSEY

Bedminster
Yannuzzi, Elaine Victoria *food and home products executive*

Camden
Reardon, Nancy Anne *food products executive*

Colts Neck
Schmalz, Elizabeth Moody *cosmetics company executive*

Kenilworth
Cox, Carrie *pharmaceutical executive*

Little Falls
Varis, Agnes *pharmaceutical executive*

New Brunswick
Foster-Cheek, Kaye I. *health products executive*
Goggins, Colleen A. *health products executive*
Liao, Mei-June *pharmaceutical executive, researcher*
Poon, Christine A. *pharmaceutical company executive*

Oakland
Manheimer, Heidi *cosmetics company executive*

Paramus
Forman, Beth Rosalyne *specialty food trade executive*

Ridgefield
Riggs, Rory B. *pharmaceutical executive*

Whitehouse Station
Avedon, Marcia J. *pharmaceutical executive*
Lewent, Judy Carol *pharmaceutical executive*
McGlynn, Margaret G. *pharmaceutical executive*
Yarno, Wendy *pharmaceutical executive*

NEW YORK

Bay Shore
Shreve, Sue Ann Gardner *retired health products company administrator*

Brooklyn
Avino-Barracato, Kathleen *construction executive, consultant*

East Syracuse
Lamphere, Barbara L. *construction executive*

Huntington Station
Yacobian, Sonia Simone *metals company executive*

Mahopac
Vigliotti, Patricia Noreen *metal products executive, sculptor*

New Hyde Park
Neal, Elaine Zirli *health products executive*

New Rochelle
Goodman, Joan Frances *avionics manufacturing executive*
Tassone, Gelsomina (Gessie Tassone) *metal products executive*

New York
Azrielant, Aya *jewelry manufacturing executive*
Barnes, Jhane Elizabeth *fashion design company executive, designer*
Binder, Susan A. *chemical company executive*
Burns, Robin *cosmetics company executive*
Ewing-Mulligan, Mary *food products executive*
Goodale, Toni Krissel *research and development company executive*
Howson, Tamar D. *pharmaceutical executive*
Juliber, Lois D. *manufacturing executive*
Jung, Andrea *cosmetics company executive*
Krill, Kay (Katherine Lawther Krill) *apparel executive*
Kropf, Susan J. *retired cosmetics executive*
Lauder, Aerin *cosmetics executive*
Lauder, Evelyn H. *cosmetics executive*
McFadden, Mary Josephine *fashion industry executive*
Montero, Sylvia *pharmaceutical executive*
Moran, Juliette M. *retired chemicals executive*
Mosbacher, Georgette Paulsin *cosmetics executive*
Natori, Josie Cruz (Josefina Almeda Cruz Natori) *apparel executive*
Nelson, Alison *food products executive*
Pollard, Veronica *automotive executive*
Slavin, Rosanne Singer *textile converter*
Sullivan, Trudy F. *apparel executive*

Purchase
Finnerty, Louise Hoppe *food products executive*
Nooyi, Indra K. *food products executive*

Rochester
Friauf, Katherine Elizabeth *metal company executive*

Webster
Curtis, Deana A. *electronics executive, small business owner*

West Harrison
Reichelderfer, Brenda L. *manufacturing executive*

Westbury
Bonazinga, Marie Therese *manufacturing executive*

Williamsville
Krzyzan, Judy Lynn *automotive executive*

NORTH CAROLINA

Greensboro
Chilton, Mary-Dell Matchett *chemical company executive*

OHIO

Canton
Peters, Judy Gale *manufacturing executive, educator*

Cincinnati
Kendle, Candace *pharmaceutical executive*

Columbus
Wexner, Abigail *apparel executive*

Dayton
Jerome, Dolores *retired electronics executive*

Tipp City
Tighe-Moore, Barbara Jeanne *electronics executive*

OKLAHOMA

Tulsa
Marshall-Chapman, Paula *food products executive*

OREGON

Eugene
Woolley, Donna Pearl *lumber company executive*

Portland
Boyle, Gertrude *sportswear company executive*

PENNSYLVANIA

Bensalem
Bern, Dorrit J. *apparel executive*

Eighty Four
Magerko, Margaret Hardy (Maggie Magerko) *lumber company executive*

Gap
Beiler, Anne F. *food company executive*

Halifax
Stauffer, Joanne Rogan *steel company official*

Hershey
Thomas, Andrea B. *food products executive*

Horsham
Christian, Mildred Stoehr *health products executive*

King Of Prussia
McCairns, Regina Carfagno *pharmaceutical executive*

Philadelphia
Payne, Deborah Anne *retired medical company officer*
Sohn, Catherine Angell *pharmaceutical executive, pharmacist*

Pittsburgh
Stein, Laura *food products executive*

Wyomissing
Stevens, Anne L. *metal products executive, retired automotive executive*
Tarnoski, Lori M. *apparel executive*

SOUTH CAROLINA

Clemson
Petzel, Florence Eloise *textiles educator*

Columbia
Duggan, Carol Cook *research and development company executive*

Fort Mill
Bowles, Crandall Close *textiles executive*

TENNESSEE

Collierville
O'Neill Tate, Frances *construction executive*
Smith, Vickie M. *chemicals executive*

Kingsport
Lee, Theresa K. *chemicals executive*

Lafayette
Oliver, Barbara Ann *retired apparel executive*

TEXAS

Austin
Duke, Carol Michiels *health products executive*
Lang, Roberta Lynn *food products company executive, lawyer*

Conroe
Steed, Theresa Jean *manufacturing executive*

Coppell
Minyard, Liz *food products executive*
Williams, Gretchen Minyard *food store executive*

Dallas
Lovett, Melendy *semiconductor company executive*
Sammons, Elaine D. *manufacturing executive*
Tyson, Lisa N. *food products executive*
West, Teresa L. (Terri West) *semiconductor company executive*

Forney
Pick, Mary Frances *manufacturing executive*

Garland
Brumit, Jo Ann *sheet metal manufacturing executive*

Houston
Chang, Nancy T. *pharmaceutical executive*
James, Virginia Lynn *contracts executive*
Kornbleet, Lynda Mae *insulation, fireproofing and acoustical contractor*
Long, Suzanne Lynn *apparel executive*
Merrill, Connie Lange *chemical company executive*
Snowden, Bernice Rives *former construction company executive*
Thompson-Draper, Cheryl L. *electronics executive, real estate executive*

Port Lavaca
Fisher, Jewel Tanner (Mary Fisher) *retired construction company executive*

Richardson
Goodspeed, Linda A. *manufacturing executive*

Santa Fe
Lambert, Willie Lee Bell *mobile equipment company owner, educator*

VIRGINIA

Alexandria
Slutsky, Bernice *agricultural products executive*

Arlington
Rabbitt, Linda *construction executive*

Lynchburg
DePew, Carol Ann *pharmaceutical sales representative*

Mc Lean
Mars, Jacqueline Badger *food products executive*

WASHINGTON

Bellevue
Nowik, Dorothy Adam *medical equipment company executive*
Van Natter, Gayl Price *residential construction company administrator*

Federal Way
Ballard, Ernesta *lumber company executive*

Hoquiam
Lamb, Isabelle Smith *manufacturing executive*

Naches
Assink, Nellie Grace *agricultural executive*

WISCONSIN

Oconomowoc
Peebles, Allene Kay *manufactured housing company executive*

WYOMING

Casper
Osborne, Gayle Ann *manufacturing executive*

CANADA

ONTARIO

Ottawa
Beare-Rogers, Joyce Louise *retired research and development executive*

ENGLAND

London
Bravo, Rose Marie *apparel executive*
Ahrendts, Angela J. *apparel executive*

ADDRESS UNPUBLISHED

Amadio, Bari Ann *metal fabrication executive, retired nurse*
Amsterdam, Millicent *manufacturing executive*
Anastole, Dorothy Jean *retired electronics company executive*
Anderegg, Karen Klok *business executive*
Bellantoni, Maureen Blanchfield *manufacturing and retail executive*
Bergman, Janet Eisenstein *food industry executive*
Blum, Betty Ann *footwear company executive*
Carver, Juanita Ash *inventor*
Congdon, Sarah-Braeme Bird *medical equipment company executive*
Danziger, Gertrude Seelig *retired metal fabricating executive*
DiGregorio, Amanda Elizabeth *medical products executive*
Doyle, Irene Elizabeth *electronic sales executive, nurse*
Dworin, Micki (Maxine Dworin) *automobile dealership executive*
Gates, Martina Marie *food products company executive*
Goldberg, Lee Winicki *furniture company executive*
Greaser, Constance Udean *retired automotive executive*
Green, Sonia Maria *automotive executive*
Grenz, M. Kay *manufacturing executive*
Heuser, Michelle S. *manufacturing executive*
Hill, Emma *apparel executive*
Holden, Betsy D. *former food products company executive*
Hudson, Katherine Mary *manufacturing executive*
Ivanchenko, Lauren Margaret Dowd *pharmaceutical executive*
Jackson, Robbi Jo *agricultural products executive, lawyer*
Jones, Christine Massey *retired furniture company executive*
Katen, Karen L. *pharmaceutical company executive*
King, Susan Bennett *retired glass company executive*
Krise, Patricia Love *automotive industry executive*
Krominga, Lynn *cosmetics executive, lawyer*
Kulik, Rosalyn Franta *food company executive, consultant*
Lewis, Rita Hoffman *plastic products manufacturing company executive*
Liberati, Maria Theresa *lifestyle company executive, cooking expert, writer*
Litzenberger, Lesley Margaret *textiles executive*
Maarbjerg, Mary Penzold *retired office equipment company executive*
Meilan, Celia *food products executive*
Mintz, Susan Ashinoff *apparel manufacturing company executive*
Moore, Shanna La'Von *chemical company executive*
Noe, Elnora (Ellie Noe) *retired chemicals executive*
Pacheco, Susan *automotive executive*
Perkins, Cheryl A. *paper company executive*
Porter, Leah LeEarle *food products executive*
Ray, Jane Zimrude *retired machine shop executive*
Roberson, Janet L. *manufacturing executive*
Rosen, Ana Beatriz *electronics executive*
Sherman, Patsy O'Connell *retired manufacturing executive, chemist*
Simmons, Marguerite Saffold *pharmaceutical sales professional*
Tallett, Elizabeth Edith *biopharmaceutical company executive*
Tane, Susan Jaffe *retired manufacturing company executive*
Thomas-Graham, Pamela *apparel executive*
Tran, Alice *automotive executive*
Turczyn-Toles, Doreen Marie *pharmaceutical consultant*
Vanaltenburg, Betty Marie *lumber company executive*
Vanzura, Liz (Elizabeth K. Vanzura) *automotive executive*
Wachner, Linda Joy *former apparel marketing and manufacturing executive*
Watts, Wendy Hazel *wine consultant*
Williams, Dorothy Standridge *retired food products manager, civic worker*
Yenchko, Suzanne *research and development company executive*

INDUSTRY: SERVICE

UNITED STATES

ALABAMA

Athens
Lafevor, Kimberly Ann *human resources specialist, educator*

Centre
Ellis, Joanne Hammonds *computer consultant*

Huntsville
McIntyre-Ivy, Joan Carol *data processing executive*

Montgomery
Luna, Patricia Adele *marketing executive*

ALASKA

Anchorage
Britton, Emily Maddox *sales executive*
Schmitt, Nancy Cain *retired public and corporate relations executive, writer*

ARIZONA

Chandler
Brunello-McCay, Rosanne *sales executive*

Fort Huachuca
Szymeczek, Peggy Lee *contract specialist*

Gilbert
Hill, Maralyn Dennis *management consultant*

Glendale
Fisher, Debra A. *communications executive, educator*

Green Valley
Gilliam, Mary *travel company executive*

Peoria
Gould, Dorothy Mae *executive secretary, soprano*

Phoenix
Hutchinson, Ann *management consultant*
White, Annette Irene *marketing professional*

Prescott
Haverland, Muriel Jean *speaker, career management consultant*

Scottsdale
Lavenson, Susan Barker *hotel corporate executive, consultant*
MacKinnon, Sally Anne *retired fast food company executive*
Milanovich, Norma JoAnne *training services executive*
Prellberg, Joanne Marie *office manager*

Sun City
Davis, Virginia *trade show producer*

Sun City West
Forti, Lenore Steimle *business consultant*

Tempe
Jefferson, Myra LaVerne Tull *sales executive*

Tucson
Click, Carrie *public relations executive*
Cooper, Corinne *communications consultant, lawyer*
Davis, Megan J. *consulting firm executive*
Flores, Candace *special events director*
Hasselmo, Ann Hayes Die *executive recruiter, consultant, psychologist, educator, retired academic administrator*
Kennedy, Lydia *human resources specialist*
Pedersen, Arlene *web design company executive*
Reinius, Michele Reed *executive recruiter*
Sohnen-Moe, Cherie Marilyn *business consultant*

ARKANSAS

Bella Vista
Anton, Cheryl L. *sales executive*

Fayetteville
Kester, Cheryl L. *management consultant*

Little Rock
McCaleb, Annette Watts *executive secretary*

Monticello
Webster, Linda Jean *communications executive, media consultant*

West Memphis
Howell, Kathy Aileen *advertising executive*

CALIFORNIA

Alameda
Potash, Jeremy Warner *public relations executive*

Aliso Viejo
Harder, Wendy Wetzel *communications executive*

Beverly Hills
McKenzie-Swarts, Molly *human resources specialist, hotel executive*

Brentwood
Fridley, Saundra Lynn *private investigator*

Burbank
Frank, Amélie Lorraine *marketing professional*

Calistoga
Lochanko, Elizabeth Alexandra *communications executive*

Camarillo
Cobb, Shirley Ann Dodson *public relations consultant, journalist*

Carlsbad
Ritchie, Doris Lee *executive secretary*

Chino Hills
Nash, Sylvia Dotseth *management consultant*

Corona
White, Joy Mieko *retired communications executive*

Coyote
Keeshen, Kathleen Kearney *public relations consultant*

Culver City
Boonshaft, Hope Judith *public relations executive*
Van Galder, Valerie *marketing executive*

Cupertino
Johnson, Allison *corporate communications specialist, marketing executive*

Daly City
Hargrave, Sarah Quesenberry *consulting company executive, public relations executive*

El Segundo
McCarty, Shirley Carolyn *consumer products company executive*

Encino
Wald, Donna Gene *advertising executive*

Fremont
Sanchez, Marla Rena *communications executive*

Fresno
Ganulin, Judy *public relations professional*
McGough, MaryLee *marketing professional*

Glendale
Stewart, Julia A. *food service executive*

Granite Bay
Holtz, Sara *marketing consultant*

Half Moon Bay
Fennell, Diane Marie *marketing professional, process engineer*
Hinthorn, Micky Terzagian *retired executive secretary, volunteer*

Hermosa Beach
LaBouff, Jackie Pearson *retired personal care industry executive*

Irvine
Keele, Lucy Anne McCandlish *communications executive, consultant*

La Jolla
Bardwick, Judith Marcia *management consultant*
Jennings, Jan Noreus *public relations executive, writer*

La Quinta
Connerly, Dianna Jean *business official*
Eversole, Barbara Louise *administrative assistant*

La Verne
Jalbert, Janelle Jennifer *executive recruiter, secondary school educator*

Laguna Niguel
Greenberg, Lenore *public relations professional*

Los Angeles
Bianchi, Carisa *advertising company executive*
Bohle, Sue *public relations executive*
Chun, Jennifer *communications executive*
Coleman Smith, Salaam *communications executive*
Coots, Laurie *advertising executive*
Cora, Cat *chef*
Davidson, Judi *public relations executive*
Doll, Lynne Marie *public relations agency executive*
Giffin, Margaret Ethel (Peggy Giffin) *management consultant*
Hartsough, Gayla Anne Kraetsch *management consultant*
Hill, Bonnie Guiton *consulting company executive*
Jacobs, Alicia Melvina *account executive*
Kozberg, Joanne Corday *public affairs consultant*
LeMaster, Susan M. *marketing executive, writer*
Macalister, Kim Porter *advertising executive*
Mathias, Alice Irene *business management consultant*
Rice, Regina Kelly *marketing executive*
Stern, Susan Toy *human resources specialist*
Torres, Cynthia Ann *marketing professional*

Malibu
Tellem, Susan Mary *public relations executive*

Manhattan Beach
McMullen, Melinda Kae *public relations executive*

Marina Del Rey
Gold, Carol Sapin *international management consultant, speaker, writer*

Moreno Valley
Calley, Tranquil Hudson *travel consultant, educator*
Guerrero, Donna Marie *sales executive*

Mountain View
Allen, Vicky *sales and marketing professional*

Newport Beach
Hancock, Ellen Marie *communications executive*

Oakland
Kane, Jacqueline *human resources specialist*
Parker, Melissa Bernice *advertising executive*
Williams, Carol H. *advertising executive*

Palo Alto
Dunn, Debra L. *computer company executive*
Estrin, Judith *computer company executive*
Halloran, Jean M. *human resources specialist*
Lyons, Cathy *computer company executive*
Perez de Alonso, Marcela *human resources specialist, information technology executive*
Spohn, Nor Rae *computer company executive*

Palos Verdes Estates
McNeill, Susan *marketing professional, real estate professional, sales professional*

Pasadena
Wilson, Mary Ellen *retired project administrator*

Rancho Cucamonga
Gavin, Mary Ellen *marketing professional, consultant*

Rancho Palos Verdes
Curtis, Carole Ortale *executive recruiter, consultant*

Rancho Santa Margarita
Newton, Michelle Marie *sales executive*

Redondo Beach
Mackenzie, Linda Alice *media company executive, radio personality, writer, hypnotherapist*

Redwood City
Sharpnack, Rayona *management consultant*

Richmond
Poulos, Paige M. *public relations executive*

San Bernardino
Roberts, Katharine Adair *retired bookkeeper*

San Diego
Amos, Theresa Ann *marketing professional*
Canales, Viola *management consulting executive, writer*
Cline, Stephanie E. *food service executive*
Lang, Linda A. *food service executive*
Ryan, Sherry Lynn *executive administrator*

San Francisco
Bancel, Marilyn *fund raising management consultant*
Bierly, Shirley Adelaide *communications executive*
Bonetti, Susanna *administrative director*
Brady, Lauren Jean *corporate communications specialist*
Broadway, Nancy Ruth *landscape company executive, consultant, model, actress*
Calvin, Dorothy Ver Strate *computer company executive*
Crawford, Carol Anne *marketing professional*
Everett-Thorp, Kate *digital marketing executive*
Henderson, Nancy Grace *marketing executive, technical documentation executive*
Hernandez, Aileen C(larke) *urban consultant*
Hirata, Rhonda Gay *advertising executive*
Kunz, Heidi *healthcare company executive*
Martin-O'Neill, Mary Evelyn *advertising executive, management consultant, marketing professional, consultant, educator*
Molland, Maria U. *Internet company executive*
Murphy, Kathleen Anne Foley *communications executive*
Parker, Diana Lynne *restaurant manager, special events director*
Saeger, Rebecca *advertising executive*
Tom, Cynthia *sales executive, consultant*
Torme, Margaret Anne *public relations executive, management consultant*
Wernick, Sandra Margot *advertising and public relations executive*
Winkler, Agnieszka M. *marketing executive*

San Jose
Bostrom, Susan L. *marketing executive*
Connors, Mary Jean *communications executive*
Lawrence, Deborah Jean *quality assurance professional*
Monia, Joan *retired management consultant*
Whitman, Margaret C. (Meg Whitman) *Internet company executive*

San Mateo
Leong, Carol Jean *electrologist*
Reider, Suzie *Internet company executive, marketing professional*

San Rafael
Bartz, Carol A. *computer software company executive*

San Ramon
Cronin, Patricia Romero *computer company executive*

Santa Ana
Hope, Kathryn Mary *management consultant*
Torrez, Caroline Herminia *human resources specialist, director, actress, musician, singer, dancer*

Santa Barbara
McKee, Kathryn Dian Grant *human resources consultant*

Santa Clara
Jones, Kim *computer company executive*
Shavers, Cheryl L. *technology and business consultant*

Santa Monica
Feniger, Susan *chef, television personality, writer*
Milliken, Mary Sue *chef, television personality, writer*

Sonora
Mathias, Betty Jane *communications and community affairs consultant, editor, educator, writer*
McClymonds, Jean Ellen *marketing professional*

South Lake Tahoe
Nason, Rochelle *conservation organization administrator*

Stockton
Hackley, Carol Ann *public relations educator, consultant*
Jacobs, Marian *advertising executive*

Studio City
Chambers, Clytia Montllor *retired public relations consultant*
Mc Donald, Meg *public relations executive*
Moseley, Chris Rosser *marketing executive*

Sunnyvale
Castro, Christine *Internet company executive*
Decker, Sue (Susan L. Decker) *Internet company executive*
Dunaway, Cammie *marketing executive*
Sartain, Libby *human resources specialist*
Schneider, Hilary A. *Internet company executive*

Sutter Creek
Sanders, Elizabeth Anne Weaver (Betsy Sanders) *management consultant, writer*

Tracy
Kiggins, Mildred L. *marketing professional*

Universal City
Press, Terry *marketing executive*

Victorville
Yochem, Barbara June (Runyan) *sales executive, lecturer*

West Hills
Parisio, Tamara Lynn *marketing professional*

West Hollywood
Goin, Suzanne *chef*
Kingsley, Patricia *public relations executive*

Westlake Village
Troxell, Lucy Davis *management consultant*

Woodland Hills
Stahlecker, Barbara Jean *marketing professional, consultant*

Yreka
Fiock, Shari Lee *marketing professional, consultant*

COLORADO

Black Hawk
Jones, Linda May *tour guide, writer*

Castle Rock
Broer, Eileen Dennery *management consultant*

Colorado Springs
Hyden, Dorothy Louise *consulting company owner*

Denver
Barr, Lois Faye *public relations executive, freelance/self-employed writer*
Dabbs Riley, Jeanne Kernodle *retired public relations executive*
Dickerson, Cynthia Rowe *marketing executive, consultant*
Dunham, Joan Roberts *administrative assistant*
Gleason, Cynthia S. *public relations executive, educator*
Johnston, Gwinavere Adams *public relations consultant*
Kurtz, Maxine *personnel director, writer, lawyer*
Lundy, Barbara Jean *training services executive*
O'Sullivan, Blythe Ann *marketing executive*
Taylor, Teresa *communications executive*
Ullery, Patricia Anne *marketing professional*
Walker, Joan H. *marketing and communications executive*
Williams, Marcia Putnam *human resources specialist*

Englewood
Miles, Amy E. *recreational facility executive*

Fort Collins
Clark, Claudia Ann *business development manager*
Honaker, Stevie Lee *career counselor, consultant*

Golden
Olson, Marian Katherine *management consultant*
Van Dusen, Donna Bayne *communications consultant, educator, researcher*

Grand Junction
Hall, Kathryn H. *public relations executive*

Greeley
Miller, Diane Wilmarth *retired human resources director*

Greenwood Village
Gold, Christina A. *data processing company executive*
Wittman, Vanessa Ames *communications executive*

Littleton
Clark, Julie *consumer products company executive*
Treybig, Edwina Hall *sales executive*

Louisville
Tyson, Charlotte Rose *software development manager*

Niwot
Farrington, Helen Agnes *personnel director*

Pagosa Springs
Howard, Carole Margaret Munroe *retired public relations executive*

Superior
Reagan, Melodie A. *communications executive*

Westminster
Stoian, Cristina *sales executive, real estate broker, mortgage company executive, tax specialist*

CONNECTICUT

Andover
Quint, Dawn Dunaway *personnel executive*

Cromwell
Izzo, Lucille Anne *sales representative*

East Haddam
Clarke, Cordelia Kay Knight Mazuy *management consultant, artist*

Fairfield
Orris-Modugno, Michele Marie *public relations, marketing and advertising consultant*
Peters, Susan P. *human resources specialist*

Greenwich
Lewis, Audrey Gersh *marketing professional, public relations executive, consultant*
Perless, Ellen *advertising executive*
Scott, Mariette A. *marketing executive*

Hamden
Balogh, Anne Marceline *personnel consultant*

Kent
Friedman, Frances *public relations executive*

Norfolk
O'Malley, Margaret Parlin *marketing administrator*

Norwalk
Mintz, Lenore Chaice (Lea Mintz) *consultant*

Ridgefield
Priest, Alexia Z. *purchasing agent*

Riverside
Mallin, Jennifer *Internet company executive, writer*

Shelton
Mariotti, Margaret *executive secretary*

Sherman
Cohn, Jane Shapiro *public relations executive*

Simsbury
Moran, Linda *management consultant, researcher*

Southington
Carrington, Virginia Gail (Vee Carrington) *marketing professional, consultant*

Stamford
Aceto, Lisa M. *management consultant*
Burns, Ursula M. *printing company executive*
Elizondo, Patricia *sales executive*
Mulcahy, Anne Marie *printing company executive*
Nazemetz, Patricia *human resources specialist*
Pappas, Alceste Thetis *consulting company executive, educator*
Vandebroek, Sophie Verdonckt *printing company executive*

Stratford
Vlahac, Mary Ann Rita *marketing executive*

West Hartford
Karotkin, Rose A. *marketing professional*

Westport
Lewis, Margaret Mary *marketing professional*

Wilton
Flesher, Margaret Covington *communications consultant, writer*

DELAWARE

Wilmington
Davis, Mary Kathryn *marketing professional*
Stoker, Penny S. *human resources specialist*
Weisenfeld, Carol Ann Trimble *marketing executive, consultant*

DISTRICT OF COLUMBIA

Washington
Aikens, Martha Brunette *park service administrator*
Balfour, Ana Maria *office manager*
Berman, Ellen Sue *energy and telecommunications executive, theatre producer*
Boza, Clara Brizeida *marketing executive*
Browner, Carol M. *management consultant, former federal agency administrator*
Cafritz, Peggy Cooper *communications executive*
Cashion, Ann *food service executive*
Chittum, Heather *chef*
Comerford, Cristeta *chef*
Cook, Frances D. *management consultant*
Cope, Jeannette Naylor *executive search consultant*
Friedman, Elizabeth Ann *training services executive*
Garvey, Jane *public relations executive*
Gest, Kathryn Waters *public relations executive*
Griffin, Kelly Ann *public relations executive, consultant*
Grigsby, Sharlyn Ann *human resources specialist*
Hagen, Wendy W. *public relations executive*
Hirshberg, Jennefer *public affairs executive*
Jones, A. Elizabeth *corporate communications specialist, former federal agency administrator*
Jordan, Samantha Kristine *communications director*
Jordan, Sandra *public relations professional*
Kennedy, Deborah *communications executive, writer, editor*
Kraus, Margery *management consultant, communications company executive*
Lambert, Deborah Ketchum *public relations executive*
Lassen-Feldman, Wendy Anne *sales executive, lawyer*
Lawson, Kelli *communications executive*
Lisboa-Farrow, Elizabeth Oliver *public and government relations consultant*
Louison, Deborah Finley *global public affairs consultant*
Lovelace, Gail T. *human resources specialist*
Lubic, Benita Joan Alk *travel company executive*
Marshall, Maryann Chorba *executive secretary*
McMeans, Sarah Dornin Wilkinson *communications regulatory specialist*
Mederos, Carolina Luisa *public policy consultant*
Medvidovich, Suzanne F. *human resources specialist*
Melton, Carol A. *communications executive*
Oliver-Simon, Gloria Craig *human resources advisor, consultant, lawyer*
Othello, Maryann Ceclilia *quality improvement specialist*
Patterson, Sally Jane *communications executive, consultant*
Pouillon, Nora Emanuela *food service executive, chef*
Rainey, Jean Osgood *public relations executive*
Rice, Lois Dickson *retired computer company executive*
Richwine, Heather *technology support manager*
Sara, Elizabeth Clorinda *marketing professional*
Seats, Peggy Chisolm *public affairs executive*
Shear, Natalie Pickus *conference and event management executive*
Shreve, Elizabeth Steward *public relations executive, former publishing executive*
Smith, Nancy Lee *communications official*
Stuart, Sandra Kaplan *public policy consultant*
Swain, Susan Marie *communications executive*
Tate, Sheila Burke *public relations executive*
Van Allen, Barbara Martz *marketing professional*
Villarreal, June Patricia *retired sales executive*
Vose, Kathryn Kahler *marketing executive, communications executive*
Whittlesey, Judith Holloway *public relations executive*

FLORIDA

Bartow
Bentley, Joyce Elaine *customer service officer*

Boca Raton
Brunell, Kateri Tabler *performance excellence executive, consultant*
Turner, Lisa Phillips *human resources executive*
Yoder, Patricia Doherty *public relations executive*

Bonita Springs
Hauserman, Jacquita Knight *management consultant*

Cape Coral
Andert, Darlene (Darlene Andert-Schmidt) *management consultant*
Nightingale, Suzanne M. *management consultant*

Celebration
Renard, Meredith Anne *marketing and advertising professional*

Clearwater
Baker-Bowens, Helen L. *administrative assistant, genealogy researcher*
Bazzone, Theresa (Terry) A. *sales executive*

Coral Gables
Gould, Taffy *Internet company executive, real estate executive*

Daytona Beach
Bivens, Carolyn Vesper *former advertising executive, golf association commissioner-elect*
Schauer, Catharine Guberman *public affairs specialist*

Delray Beach
Ehrlich, Geraldine Elizabeth *management consultant*

Estero
MacDougall, Frances Kay *marketing consultant*

Fort Lauderdale
Ambrose, Judith Ann *wedding planner*
Castillo, Carmen *staffing company executive*
Koch, Katherine Rose *communications executive*

Fort Myers
Aron, Eve Glicka Serenson *personal care industry executive*
Goyak, Elizabeth Fairbairn *retired public relations executive*
Jaye, Karen A. *human resources specialist*

Havana
Beare, Muriel Anita Nikki *public relations executive, author*

Jacksonville Beach
Saltzman, Irene Cameron *consumer products company executive*

Key Colony Beach
Crenshaw, Patricia Shryack *sales executive, consultant*

Lakeland
Zucco, Ronda Kay *planning and marketing professional*

Lantana
Gorman, Marcie Sothern *personal care industry executive*

Longwood
Sisselsky, Sharon Lee *travel company executive, secondary school educator*

Lutz
Miller, Bonnie Sewell *marketing professional, writer*

Maitland
Stephens, Patricia Ann *marketing professional*

Miami
Amos, Betty Giles *food service executive, accountant*
Chwat, Anne *food service executive*
Mustelier, Alina Olga *travel consultant, music educator*

Miami Beach
Membiela, Roymi Victoria *marketing professional, consultant*

Mount Dora
Mayek, Helen Cecilia *executive secretary*

North Fort Myers
Callanan, Kathleen Joan *Internet company executive, retired electrical engineer*

North Palm Beach
Wright, Donna Lake *retired marketing professional, volunteer*

Opa Locka
Wright, Jeanne Elizabeth Jason *advertising executive*

Ormond Beach
Graf, Dorothy Ann *human resources specialist*

Palm Bay
Kelley, Patricia *marketing representative*

Palm Beach Gardens
Burgeson, Joyce Ann *travel company executive*

Port Charlotte
Reynolds, Helen Elizabeth *management consultant*

Port Orange
Hensinger, Margaret Elizabeth *real estate, horticultural and agricultural advertising and marketing executive*

Punta Gorda
Van Pelt, Frances Evelyn *management consultant*

Sarasota
Burrell, Lynne *credit manager*
Holcomb, Constance L. *sales and marketing management executive*
Honner Sutherland, B. Joan *advertising executive*
Lee, Nancy Ranck *management consultant*
Schafer, Amy Elisabeth *public relations executive*

Singer Island
Dixson, J. B. *communications executive*

Stuart
Donohue, Edith M. *human resources specialist, educator*

Tallahassee
Crook, Wendy P. *management consultant, educator*
Spooner, Donna *management consultant*

Tampa
Ferree, Patricia Ann *quality assurance professional*

Tarpon Springs
Crismond, Linda Fry *public relations executive*

Terra Ceia
Roehl, Nancy Leary *marketing professional, educator*

Titusville
Horn, Flora Leola *retired administrative assistant*

University Park
Le Count, Virginia G. *communications company executive*

Venice
Bluhm, Barbara Jean *communications agency executive*

Windermere
DeRubertis, Patricia Uhl *software company executive*

Winter Park
Halladay, Laurie Ann *public relations consultant, food products executive*

GEORGIA

Alpharetta
Reed, Wendy *management consultant company executive, information technology executive*

Atlanta
Anderson, Marcie *communications executive*
Barnard, Patricia A. *human resources specialist*
Battista, Bobbie *public relations executive, former television news anchorperson*
Brown-Olmstead, Amanda *public relations executive*
Calhoun, Sabrina *communications executive*
Faulkner, Kristine *communications executive*
Good, Billie B. *sales executive, athletic trainer*
Gordon, Helen Tate *program assistant*
Hines, Alida N. *marketing professional, researcher*
Jerden, Alison D. *human resources consultant*
McKenzie, Kay Branch *public relations executive*
Perez, Beatriz *marketing executive*
Soupata, Lea N. *human resources specialist*
Tome, Carol B. *consumer home products company executive*
Weidman, Sheila *marketing professional*
Winograd, Audrey Lesser *retired advertising executive*

Augusta
Nevins, Frances (Frankie) Rush *tourism professional*

Bainbridge
Burkhalter, Myra Sheram *retired marketing professional*

Ball Ground
Spare, Melanie Kim *management consultant*

Decatur
Barnett, Rebecca Lynn *communications executive*
Breckenridge, Betty Gayle *management development consultant*
Terry, Elizabeth Hudson *personal care industry executive, realtor*

Fairburn
Bobo, Genelle Tant (Nell Bobo) *retired office administrator*

Gainesville
Davis, Connie Waters *public relations executive, marketing professional*

Glennville
Craft, Mary Faye *public relations executive, consultant, television producer, poet*

Lagrange
Nixon, Juana Lynn Whitley *advertising executive*

Lilburn
Magnan, Sarah E. *court reporter*

Marietta
Dobrzyn, Janet Elaine *quality assurance professional*

Nashville
Gaskins, Anne Carson *retired human resources specialist*

Norcross
Herron, Bonnie L. *management consulting company executive*
Robinson, Karen Ann *marketing executive*

Oakwood
Jondahl, Terri Elise *importing and distribution company executive*

Savannah
LaSalle, Diana Margaret *consulting company executive, author*

HAWAII

Kailua
Grimmer, Beverley Sue *consumer products company executive*

Kailua Kona
Leonardo, Ann Adamson *marketing and sales consultant*

Kapaau
Ralston, Joanne Smoot *public relations executive*

IDAHO

Boise
Thornton, Felicia D. *food service company executive*

Idaho Falls
Barbe, Betty Catherine *marketing professional, retired financial analyst*

Kamiah
Mills, Carol Margaret *public relations executive, consultant*

ILLINOIS

Addison
Christopher, Doris K. *consumer products company executive*

Arlington Heights
Fields, Sara A. *travel company executive*

Aurora
Dillitzer, Dianne René *sales executive*

Bannockburn
Daube, Lorrie O. *sales executive*

Bloomington
Daily, Jean A. *marketing executive*

Bradley
White, Cheryl Louise *administrative assistant*

Burr Ridge
Zaccone, Suzanne Maria *sales executive*

Champaign
Follett, Deborah Elaine *sales executive, director, radio director*

Chicago
Allen, Belle *management consulting firm executive, communications executive*
Bergstrom, Betty Howard *consulting executive, foundation administrator*
Beugen, Joan Beth *communications executive*
Bradley, Vanessa Lynn *management consultant*
Diederichs, Janet Wood *public relations executive*
Doetsch, Virginia Lamb *former advertising executive, writer*
Dragonette, Rita Hoey *public relations executive*
Friedlander, Patricia Ann *marketing professional, writer*
Furth, Yvonne *advertising executive*
Gadsby, Monica M. *marketing executive*
Gand, Gale *chef, restaurateur*
Green, RuthAnn *marketing and management consultant*
Healy, Sondra Anita *consumer products company executive*
Hobor, Nancy Allen *communications executive*
Huggins, Lois M. *human resources specialist, consumer products company executive*
LaVelle, Avis *consulting firm executive*
Leadbetter, Tiffany *hotel executive*
McCann, Renetta *advertising executive*
McKay, Melinda *hotel executive*
Mosley-McCall, Jeraldine *funeral director*
Moster, Mary Clare *public relations executive*
Posner, Kathy Robin *retired communications executive*
Prather, Susan Lynn *public relations executive*
Radomski, Robyn L. *marketing executive*
Redmond, Andrea *executive recruiter*
Rich, S. Judith *public relations executive*
Schindler, Judi(th) (Judith Kay Schindler) *public relations executive, marketing professional, consultant*
Seebert, Kathleen Anne *international sales and marketing executive*
Serlin, Marsha *waste management service administrator*
Singer, Emel *staffing industry executive*
Sive, Rebecca Anne *public relations executive*
Strubel, Ella Doyle *advertising executive, public relations executive*
Talbot, Pamela *public relations executive*
Thompson, Jayne Carr *public relations and communications executive, lawyer*

Deerfield
Lezak, Carol Spielman *communications executive, editor, writer, design consultant, medical librarian*
Prete, Gayle Compton *advertising and marketing executive*

Des Plaines
Drake, Ann M. *consumer products company executive*

Edwardsville
Dietrich, Suzanne Claire *communications consultant, researcher*

Elmhurst
Malo, Michele Lee *marketing professional*

Evanston
Blair, Virginia Ann *public relations executive*

Glen Ellyn
Schmidt, Karen Lee *marketing professional, sales executive*

Glenview
Franklin, Lynne *corporate communications specialist, writer*

Grayslake
Vaughn, Connie Marie *marketing professional, writer, consultant*

Hanover Park
Carter, Eleanor Elizabeth *account executive*

Highland Park
Axelrod, Leah Joy *tour company executive*
Burman, Diane Berger *career management and organization development consultant*

Joliet
McMiller, Anita Williams *leasing company executive*
Starner, Barbara Kazmark *marketing, advertising and export sales executive*
Williams, Jennifer Ann *public relations executive*

Kenilworth
Weaver, Donna Rae *winery executive*

Lake Bluff
Scott, Karen Bondurant *consumer catalog company executive*

Lake Forest
Chieger, Kathryn Jean *recreational facility executive*
Goldstein, Marsha Feder *tour company executive*
Rand, Kathy Sue *public relations executive, consultant*

Lansing
Kaplan, Huette Myra *training services executive, consultant*

Libertyville
Devine, Barbara Armstrong *risk manager*

Macomb
Gates, Janice Sue *management consultant, educator*

Melrose Park
Bernick, Carol Lavin *consumer products company executive*

Morton Grove
Smolyansky, Julie *consumer products company executive*

Northbrook
Crockett, Joan M. *human resources executive*
Fettner, Marilyn *management consultant*
Ross, Debra Benita *marketing executive, jewelry designer*
Sprieser, Judith A. *former software company executive*
Sudbrink, Jane Marie *sales and marketing executive*

Northfield
Grimes, Sally *marketing professional*
Vilim, Nancy Catherine *advertising executive*

Oak Brook
Fields, Janice L. *food service executive*
Johnson, Shirley Elaine *management consultant*

Oakbrook Terrace
Hegenderfer, Jonita Susan *public relations executive*

Rockford
Albert, Janyce Louise *human resources specialist, retired business educator, banker, consultant*
Hendershott Love, Arles June *marketing professional*

Rosemont
Le Menager, Lois M. *incentive merchandise and travel company executive*

Saint Charles
Griffin, Sheila MB *strategic marketing executive*
O'Shea, Lynne Edeen *management consultant, educator*

Schaumburg
Fattori, Ruth A. *human resources specialist, electronics executive*
Warrior, Padmasree *communications executive*

Wauconda
Meehan, Jean Marie Ross *human resources, occupational health and safety management consultant*

Westchester
Abbinante, Vita *sales executive, administrator*

Winnetka
Cole, Kathleen Ann *advertising executive, social worker*

INDIANA

Anderson
Perry, Jane A. *customer service administrator*

Bloomington
Spiro, Rosann Lee *marketing professional, educator*

Evansville
Cliff, Karissa *consumer researcher, recruiter*

Fort Wayne
Taritas, Karen Joyce *customer service administrator*

Indianapolis
Ayars, Patti *human resources specialist, health products executive*
Harden, Annette C. *recreation director*

IOWA

Atlantic
Johnson, Joan (Jan) Hope Voss *communications executive, photojournalist, public relations executive*

Des Moines
Amendt, Marilyn Joan *personnel director*

George
Symens, Maxine Brinkert Tanner *retired marketing professional*

Manilla
Stammer, Nancy A. *travel company executive*

KANSAS

Colby
Baldwin, Irene S. *hotel executive, real estate developer*

Great Bend
Siebert-Freund, Deborah Ann *public relations and marketing executive*

Leavenworth
Franklin, Shirley Marie *marketing consultant*

Leawood
King, Barbara Sackheim *travel company executive*

Mission
Alexander, Anne A. *sales consultant*

Topeka
Sipes, Karen Kay *communications executive*

KENTUCKY

Benton
Glass, Mary Jean *management executive*

Bowling Green
Garrison, Geneva *retired administrative assistant*

Louisville
Byerlein, Anne P. *human resources specialist, food products executive*
Topcik, Deborah Fay *marketing executive*

Nicholasville
Bender, Betty Barbee *food service professional*

LOUISIANA

Covington
Doody, Barbara Pettett *computer specialist*

Metairie
Nix, Linda Anne Bean *public relations executive*

Monroe
Puckett, Karen *communications executive*

New Orleans
Creppel, Claire Binet *hotel owner*
Davis, Pamela Marie *administrative analyst*
Tahir, Mary Elizabeth (Liz Tahir) *marketing professional, consultant, writer*

Pineville
Cummings, Karen Sue *retired corrections classification administrator*

Shreveport
Giles, Katharine Emily (J. K. Piper) *retired administrative assistant, writer*

MAINE

Falmouth
Winton, Linda *international trainer, consultant*

MARYLAND

Annapolis
Ryan, Michele King *marketing professional*

Baltimore
Brotman, Phyllis Block *advertising executive, public relations executive*
Clarizio, Lynda M. *advertising executive, lawyer*
Dickinson, Jane W. *retired executive secretary, volunteer*
Friedman, Maria Andre *public relations executive*
Fulton, Judith P. *management consultant*
Kim, Lillian G. Lee *retired administrative assistant*
Robinson, Florine Samantha *marketing executive*
Rosen, Wendy Workman *advertising executive*

Bethesda
Coe, Judith Lynn *retired automobile manufacturing company administrator*

Cambridge
Spahr, Elizabeth *environmental research administrator*

Catonsville
Diggs, Carol Beth *marketing professional*

Chestertown
Docksteader, Karen Kemp *marketing professional*

Chevy Chase
Greenspoon, Irma Naiman *travel company executive*

Cockeysville Hunt Valley
Elkin, Lois Shanman *business systems company executive*

Ellicott City
Estin-Klein, Libbyada *advertising executive, writer*

Fort Washington
Fielding, Elizabeth M(ay) *public relations executive, writer*

Frederick
Schricker, Ethel Killingsworth *retired business management consultant*

Gaithersburg
Kress, Jill Clancy *human resources professional, consultant*

Hagerstown
Higgins, M. Eileen *management consultant, educator*

Hanover
Henderson Hall, Brenda Ford *computer company executive*

Reisterstown
Singer, Paula M. *management consultant*

Riverdale
Bernard, Cathy S. *management corporation executive*

Severna Park
Humphreys Troy, Patricia *communications executive*

Silver Spring
Altschul, B. J. *public relations counselor*
Burke, Margaret Ann *computer company executive, communications executive*
Carter-Johnson, Jean Evelyn *management consultant*
Compton, Mary Beatrice Brown (Mrs. Ralph Theodore Compton) *public relations executive, writer*
Fields, Daisy Bresley *human resources specialist, writer*
Lett, Cynthia Ellen Wein *customer service administrator*
Montalvo, Eileen *communications executive*
Rice, Michelle *communications executive*

Towson
Chase, Jacquelyn Veronica *marketing professional*
Nicolosi, Gianna Ruth *marketing professional*

University Park
Holder, Sallie Lou *training and meeting management consultant, coach*

West River
Bower, Catherine Downes *management consultant*
Pratt, Katherine Merrick *environmental consulting company executive*

MASSACHUSETTS

Boston
Cone, Carol Lynn *public relations executive*
Coville, Andrea *public relations executive*
Finucane, Anne M. *communications executive, marketing executive*
Kim, Hazel *public relations executive*
Lerner, Linda Joyce *human resources executive*
McArdle, Patricia Anne *security company executive*
McGovern, Lore Harp *communications executive, philanthropist*
Peirce, Georgia Wilson *public relations executive*
Warren, Susan Hanke Murphy *international marketing business development executive*

Cambridge
Bloom, Kathryn Ruth *public relations executive*
de Monteiro, Nadsa *chef*
Kilpatrick, Maureen *food service executive*
Sortun, Ana *food service executive*

Chestnut Hill
Addis, Deborah Jane *management consultant*

Dedham
Redstone, Shari E. *amusement company executive*

Foxboro
Ferron, Jennifer *marketing executive*
Furtado-Lavoie, Julia *sales executive*

Framingham
Hillman, Carol Barbara *communications executive, consultant*
Wulf, Sharon Ann *management consultant*

Housatonic
Kelsey, Christine J. *innkeeper, chef*

Kingston
Scalese, Ellen Renee *hotel executive*

Leominster
Lyons, Beryl Barton Anfindsen *advertising executive*

Natick
Stabin, Alice Marie *administrative assistant*

Newton
Benner, Mary Wright *freelance/self-employed conference director*

Springfield
Vincensi, Avis A. *sales executive, medical educator*

Sterling
Lundgren, Ruth Williamson Wood (Ruth Lundgren Williamson Wood) *public relations executive, writer*

Townsend
Smith, Denise Groleau *data processing professional*

Wayland
Caristo-Verrill, Janet Rose *international management consultant*

Wellesley Hills
Imbrescia, Marcia *landscape company executive*

Williamstown
Driscoll, Genevieve Bosson (Jeanne Bosson Driscoll) *management and organization development consultant*

Wilmington
D'Alene, Alixandria Frances *human resources professional*

MICHIGAN

Allen Park
Bizon, Emma Djafar *management consultant*

Ann Arbor
Lindsay, June Campbell McKee *communications executive*
Mitchell, Anna-Marie Rajala *quality/outcomes analyst*

Auburn Hills
Rae, Nancy A. *human resources specialist, automotive executive*

Detroit
Bassett, Tina *communications executive*
Duncan-White, Dynah Naomi Juliette *marketing professional*
McCracken, Caron Francis *information technology consultant*
Salter, Linda Lee *security officer*
Topacio, Angela *marketing executive*

Grand Rapids
Bolhuis, Doreen *recreational facility executive, physical education educator*
Purchase-Owens, Francena *marketing professional, consultant, educator*
Williams, Janice H. *business executive*

Keego Harbor
Gee, Sharon Lynn *funeral director, educator*

Marquette
Earle, Mary Margaret *marketing executive*

Romeo
Matthews Ellis, Bonnie *management consultant*

Saline
Low, Louise Anderson *consulting company executive*

Southfield
Barnett, Marilyn *advertising executive*
Hudson, Cheryl L. *communications executive*

Three Rivers
Pierce, Sue *sales executive*

Troy
Meyers, Christine Laine *marketing and media executive, consultant*

Warren
Zoubareff, Kathy Olga *administrative assistant*

West Bloomfield
Smith, Nancy Hohendorf *sales executive, marketing professional*

MINNESOTA

Bloomington
Taylor, Susan S. *performance consultant*

Glencoe
Delagardelle, Linda *food executive*

Hastings
Avent, Sharon L. Hoffman *manufacturing company executive*

Hibbing
Williams, Jojo Macasaet *office administrator*

Minneapolis
Brooks, Gladys Sinclair *retired public affairs consultant*
deBruin Sample, Anne *human resources specialist*
Hill, Tessa *non profit environmental group executive*
Johnson, Lola Norine *retired advertising and public relations executive, educator*
Moore, Tanna Lynn *marketing professional*

Minnetonka
Nelson, Marilyn Carlson *hotel executive, travel company executive*

Northfield
Immel, Cynthia Luanne *medical sales specialist*

Rochester
Grosset, Jessica Ariane *computer executive*
Hiniker, LuAnn *management consultant, educator, researcher, grants consultant*

MISSISSIPPI

Dublin
Flowers, Judith Ann *marketing and public relations director*

Port Gibson
Alford, Constance Keith *recreational facility executive, artist*

MISSOURI

Ballwin
Corno, Donna A. *retired public relations executive, consultant*

Columbia
Beedle, Dawn Danene *marketing professional*

Independence
Booz, Gretchen Arlene *marketing executive*
Evans, Margaret Ann *human resources administrator, business owner*
Peake, Candice K. Loper *data processing executive*

Kansas City
Belzer, Ellen J. *negotiations and communications trainer, consultant*
Benedict, Stephanie Michelle *purchasing agent, sales consultant*
Courson, Marna B.P. *public relations executive*
Donovan, Ann Burcham *medical office administrator*
James, Claudia Ann *public speaker, corporate trainer, writer*
Solberg, Elizabeth Transou *public relations executive*

Saint Louis
Bellville, Margaret (Maggie Bellville) *communications executive*
Bradley, Marilynne Gail *advertising executive, educator*
Diekemper, Rita Garbs *landscape company executive*
Wright, Diane *procurement manager*

MONTANA

Butte
Ouellette, Debra Lee *administrative assistant, consultant*

Helena
Manuel, Vivian *public relations executive*

NEBRASKA

Beatrice
Garrett, Amy J. *parks director, educational coordinator*

Lincoln
Hawley, Kimra *computer company executive*

Omaha
Ryan, Shelli Ann *public relations executive*
Vieregger, Susan Waynette *marketing professional, educator*

NEVADA

Henderson
Absher, Robin Dawn *security firm executive, private investigator*
Bruno, Cathy Eileen *management consultant, former state official, social sciences educator*

Las Vegas
Brock, Holly Melinda *marketing professional*
Goodwin, Nancy Lee *computer company executive*
Huston, Joyce A. *web site design company executive*
Mataseje, Veronica Julia *sales executive*
Safford, Florence Viray Sunga *travel agent, consultant*
Shively, Judith Carolyn (Judy Shively) *administrative assistant*

Reno
Ford, Victoria *retired public relations executive, writer, oral historian*
Frank, Lillian Gorman *human resources executive, management consultant*

NEW HAMPSHIRE

Bedford
Hall, Pamela S. *environmental services administrator*

Gorham
Langlois, Lori A. *human resources specialist*

Manchester
Cusson-Cail, Kathleen *consulting company executive*

Merrimack
Gallup, Patricia *computer company executive*

Nashua
Hansen, Michele Simone *communications executive*

Portsmouth
Brink, Marion Alice *retired human resources specialist*

NEW JERSEY

Allendale
Repole, Maria *public relations executive*

Basking Ridge
Moden, Joleen *communications executive*

Bedminster
Dabney, Michelle Sheila *administrative assistant*
Graddick-Weir, Mirian *human resources specialist*

Bergenfield
Caramico, Lydia Frances *meeting planner*

Boonton
Ward, Solveig Maria *marketing professional*

Chester
Maddalena, Lucille Ann *management consultant*

Clifton
Bronkesh, Annette Cylia *public relations executive*

Dover
Derr, Debra Hulse *advertising executive, writer*

East Hanover
Nelson, Barbara Kasztan *marketing professional*

Edison
Haberman, Louise Shelly *consulting company executive*

Englewood
Fay, Toni Georgette *communications executive*

Florham Park
Fischer, Pamela Shadel *public relations executive*

Gladstone
Kenny, Jane M. *management consulting executive*

Glenwood
Greilich, Audrey *administrative assistant*

Guttenberg
Pozniakoff, Rita Oppenheim *education software consultant*

Hillsborough
Butcher, Deborah *public relations and communications consultant*

Jersey City
Dupey, Michele Mary *communications specialist*
Windo, Pamela Ann *administrative assistant, writer*

Lawrenceville
Cox, Teri Polack *public relations executive*

Long Branch
Mindnich, Ellen *sales executive*

Madison
O'Brien, Mary Devon *communications executive, consultant*

Mahwah
Wagner, Susan Jane *sales and marketing consulting company executive*

Manalapan
Reisman, Joan Ann *executive secretary*

Maplewood
Hamburger, Mary Ann *management consultant*
Safian, Gail Robyn *public relations executive*

Marlton
Farwell, Nancy Larraine *public relations executive*
O'Connor, Genevieve *marketing executive*

Middletown
Heng, Siang Gek *communications executive*

Mine Hill
Gasperini, Elizabeth Carmela (Lisa Gasperini) *marketing professional*

Monroe Township
Cushman, Helen Merle Baker *retired management consultant*

Montclair
Dubrow, Marsha Ann *management consultant, musicologist*

Morganville
Marder, Carol *advertising specialist and premium firm executive*

Mountainside
Bertsch, Patricia Ann *nature center director*
Lipton, Bronna Jane *marketing communications executive*

New Brunswick
Bradley, Dondeena G. *consumer products company executive*

New Providence
Del Tiempo, Sandra Kay *sales executive*

Newark
Timko, Kathleen *communications executive*

North Arlington
Borowski, Jennifer Lucile *corporate administrator*

North Plainfield
Dunbar, Holly Jean *communications executive, public relations executive*

Parsippany
Azzarone, Carol Ann *marketing executive*

Pennington
Czach, Gabriela Bozena *personal care industry executive*

Perth Amboy
(Carlson)Reno, Arletta Lou *administrative assistant*

Plainsboro
Spiegel, Phyllis *public relations consultant, journalist*

Princeton
Crossley, Helen Martha *public opinion analyst, research consultant*
Siegel, Laurie *human resources specialist*

Randolph
Greenberger, Marsha Moses *sales executive*
Sandidge, Kanita Durice *retired communications executive, consultant*

Ringoes
Tema-Lyn, Laurie *management consultant*

Rochelle Park
Sinis, Elaine M. *personnel director*

Roseland
Steidl, Mary Catherine *food service executive*

Roselle Park
Loredo, Linda S. *marketing executive*

Scotch Plains
Johnsen, Karen Kennedy *marketing professional*

Somerville
Grey, Ruthann E. *corporate communications specialist, director*

Stone Harbor
Hurd, Diane Finore *marketing executive, publisher*

Toms River
Schockaert, Barbara Ann *marketing professional*

Verona
Poor, Suzanne Donaldson *advertising and public relations executive*

West Orange
Bogstahl, Deborah Marcelle *marketing executive*
Kyle, Corinne Silverman *management consultant*

Westfield
Burton, Barbara *marketing executive*

NEW MEXICO

Albuquerque
Myers, Carol McClary *retired sales administrator, editor*
Ortiz, Kathleen Lucille *travel consultant*
Torres, Barbara Wood *technical services professional*

Farmington
Ogilvie, Donna Lee *retired marketing professional, retired journalist*

Placitas
McElhinney, Susan Kay (Kate Echeverria) (Kate McElhinney) *executive assistant*

Portales
Edwards, Carolyn Mullenax *public relations executive*

NEW YORK

Albany
Clifford, Lisa Mary *marketing and sales professional*
Jonquières, Lynne *travel agent*
Lustenader, Barbara Diane *human resources specialist*
Menges, Susan Debra Favreau *management consultant, retired protective services official*

Annandale On Hudson
Darrow, Emily M. *public relations executive, writer*

Armonk
Azua, Maria *computer company executive, computer engineer*
Kohnstamm, Abby E. *marketing executive*

Bellport
Hendrie, Elaine *public relations executive*

Bethpage
Mahony, Sheila Anne *retired communications executive*

Brooklyn
Carswell, Lois Malakoff *botanical garden executive, consultant*
Greenwood, Monique *innkeeper, writer, restaurant owner*
Hendra, Barbara Jane *public relations executive*
Ogunkoya, Andrea *marketing executive*
Quamina, Joyce *management consultant*
Rike, Susan *public relations executive*

Buffalo
Daley, Ruth Margaret *advertising agency administrator*

Candor
Musgrave, Eva Mae *innkeeper, educator*

Delmar
Button, Rena Pritsker *public relations executive*

Dobbs Ferry
Kalvin-Stiefel, Judy *public relations executive*

East Syracuse
Houde, Carmen Milagro *hotel executive*

Elmont
Butera, Ann Michele *consulting company executive*

Farmingdale
Colella, Cathleen *waste management administrator*

Forest Hills
Dessylas, Ann Atsaves *human resources and office management executive*
Spiegel, Andrea *marketing executive*

Garden City
Doucette, Mary-Alyce *computer company executive*
Nelkin Miller, Cathy *hotel executive*

Great Neck
Helstein, Ivy Rae *communications executive, psychotherapist, writer*

Hartsdale
Greenawalt, Peggy Freed Tomarkin *advertising executive*

Hawthorne
Wen, Sheree *computer company executive*

Hempstead
Connolly, Melissa Kane *public relations executive*

Huntington Station
Cannistraci, Diane Frances *sales executive*

Ilion
Nemyier, Margaret Gertrude *sales executive*

Islandia
Cooper, Nancy E. *computer software company executive*

Larchmont
Greenwald, Carol Schiro *professional services marketing research executive*

Loudonville
Burstein, Sharon Ann *corporate communications specialist, apparel designer*

Manlius
der Boghosian, Paula *computer business consultant*

Middle Island
Andrews, Gaylen *public relations executive*

Miller Place
Callahan, Jean M. *personnel administrator*

Montauk
Hartsough, Cheryl Marie *recreation director, nutritionist*

New York
Allen, Alice *communications and marketing executive*
Alston, Alyce *diamond company executive*
Antonacci, Lori (Loretta Marie Antonacci) *marketing executive, consultant*
Appel, Gloria *advertising executive*
Axthelm, Nancy *advertising executive*
Bachrach, Nancy *retired advertising executive*
Baglivo, Mary L. *advertising executive*
Baird, Lisa P. *marketing executive*
Baron, Sheri *advertising agency executive*
Bartow, Diane Grace *marketing professional, sales executive*
Bastianich, Lidia Matticchio *chef, food service executive*
Bauman, Susan *communications executive*
Becker, Susan Kaplan *management and marketing communication consultant, educator*
Berman, Mira *advertising agency executive*
Bishopric, Susan Ehrlich *public relations executive*
Bloomgarden, Kathy Finn *public relations executive*
Borhi, Carol *data processing executive, finance company executive*
Brady, Adelaide Burks *public relations agency executive, giftware catalog executive*
Brisman, Jennifer *event planning executive*
Brooke, Linda Hundley *human resources specialist*
Brooks, Anita Helen *public relations executive*
Bruesewitz-LoPinto, Gail C. *marketing professional*
Bruno, Antoinette *food service executive*
Burton, Peggy *advertising and marketing executive*
Buryk, Alexis *advertising executive*
Busquet, Anne M. *Internet company executive*
Byrd, Eva Wilson *communications executive*
Calabrese, Rosalie Sue *management consultant, writer*
Carter, Carolyn Houchin *advertising agency executive*
Caserta, Jennifer *communications executive*
Chierchia, Madeline Carmella *management consulting company executive*
Comstock, Beth (Elizabeth J. Comstock) *marketing executive*
Craig, Pamela J. *management consulting firm executive*
Daly, Cheryl *communications executive, broadcast executive*
Danielides, Joannie C. *public relations executive*
Dayson, Diane Harris *parks director, cultural organization administrator*
DeMonte, Cynthia Maria *investor relations and management consultant*
DeVard, Jerri *marketing professional*
de Vries, Madeline *public relations executive*
Diamond, Heidi Janice *marketing professional*
Dienstag, Eleanor Foa *corporate communications consultant*
Dolan, Regina A. *security firm executive*
Driscoll, Karen *communications executive*
Dubuc, Nancy *communications executive*
Eisler, Susan Krawetz *advertising executive*
Farinelli, Jean L. *management consultant*
Fili-Krushel, Patricia *media company executive*
Fine, Deborah *Internet company executive, former apparel executive*
Flaherty, Tina Santi *corporate communications specialist, writer*
Friedman, Caitlin *public relations executive*
Fudge, Ann Marie *advertising executive*
Fung, Mina Hsu *advertising executive*
Gerard-Sharp, Monica Fleur *communications executive*
Gerberg, Judith Levine *management consultant*
Gianinno, Susan McManama *advertising executive*
Gill, Linda A. *advertising executive*
Girard, Andrea Eaton *communications executive, consultant*
Goldwater, Edna M. *retired public relations executive*
Greene, Adele S. *management consultant*
Haddad, Colleen *marketing executive*
Hammond, Lou Rena Charlotte *public relations executive*
Hrubec, Jane M. *advertising executive*
Hudes, Nana Brenda *marketing professional*
Hynes, Aedhmar *public relations executive*
Jean-Baptiste, Tricia *public relations executive*
Johnson, Verdia E. *marketing professional*
Josell, Jessica (Jessica Wechsler) *public relations executive*
Just, Gemma Rivoli *retired advertising executive*
Kassel, Terry *human resources specialist*
Kotuk, Andrea Mikotajuk *public relations executive, writer*
Kraus, Norma Jean *human resources executive*
Kugelman, Stephanie *advertising executive*
Kyriakou, Linda Grace *communications executive*
LaNicca Albanese, Ellen *public relations executive*
Larrick, Pamela Maphis *marketing executive*
Lategno-Nicholas, Cristyne *travel company executive*
Lazarus, Shelly (Rochelle Braff Lazarus) *advertising executive*
Lipton, Joan Elaine *advertising executive*
Lorber, Barbara Heyman *communications executive, event producer*
Martínez-López, Carmen Leonor *management consultant, educator*
Mayer, Eve Orlans *marketing professional, writer*
McAveney, Mary Susan *marketing executive*
McCabe, Mary F. *marketing professional*
McCarthy, Lisa *communications executive*
McCaslin, Teresa Eve *human resources specialist*
Mortimer, Ann O. *executive secretary*
Moulton, Sara *chef, magazine editor*
Murphy, Elva Glenn *executive assistant*
Nadler-Hurvich, Hedda Carol *public relations executive*
Naughton, Eileen *Internet company executive*
Newman, Geraldine Anne *advertising executive*
Ogden, Peggy A. *retired personnel director*
Olinger, Carla D(ragan) *medical advertising executive*
Paladino, Jeannette E. *advertising executive, public relations executive*
Parkes, Jacqueline *marketing executive*
Pollock-O'Brien, Louise Mary *public relations executive*
Quinlan, Mary Lou *former advertising executive, consultant*
Ray, Rachael *chef, television personality*
Reals Ellig, Janice *marketing professional, human resources specialist*
Reges, Marianna Alice *marketing executive*
Renna, Cathy *communications executive, activist*
Richardson, Grace Elizabeth *consumer products company executive*
Rose, Joanne W. *rating service executive*
Ross, Jo Ann *media buyer*
Rossi, Norma M. *management consultant*
St. Jean, Catherine Avery *advertising executive*
Saxton, Catherine Patricia *public relations executive*
Schiller, Vivian *Internet company executive*
Schoonover, Jean Way *public relations consultant*
Shepard, Sarah *public relations company executive*
Sheridan, Virginia *public relations executive*
Siegel, Lucy Boswell *public relations executive*
Sinclair, Daisy *communications executive*
Smith, Barbara *food service executive, model*
Stanton, Amy *marketing executive*
Stautberg, Susan Schiffer *communications executive*
Steves, Gale C. *marketing professional, writer, editor-in-chief, publishing executive*
Stewart, Jennifer *advertising executive*
Summer, Sharon *marketing professional, former publisher*
Tanaka, Patrice Aiko *public relations executive*
Thaler, Linda Kaplan *advertising executive*
Underwood, Joanna DeHaven *environmental services administrator*
Vermeer, Maureen Dorothy *sales executive*
Volk, Kristin *advertising agency executive*
von Baillou, Astrid *executive search consultant*
Weinstein, Sharon Schlein *corporate communications executive, educator*
Weiss, Myrna Grace *management consultant*
Wijnberg, Sandra S. *professional services company executive*
Willett, Roslyn Leonore *public relations executive, food service consultant, writer, editor*
Yeo, Patricia *chef*
Yorio, Kimberly *public relations executive*
Yrizarry, Magda N. *communications executive*

Newark
Hemmings, Madeleine Blanchet *management consultant, not-for-profit administrator, media consultant*

Niagara Falls
Jones, Suzanne P. *public relations executive*

Northport
Johnson, Samira El-Chehabi *marketing professional*

Ossining
Gilbert, Joan Stulman *retired public relations executive*

Pawling
Light, Sybil Elizabeth *executive secretary*

Poughkeepsie
VanBuren, Denise Doring *corporate communications executive*

Purchase
Hudson, Dawn Emily *food service company executive*
Moore, Margaret D. *human resources specialist*
Nicholson, Cie (Cynthia Nicholson) *marketing executive, beverage company executive*

Rochester
Harris, Diane Carol *merger and acquisition consulting firm executive*
Wegman, Colleen *food service executive*

Rockville Centre
Beyer, Suzanne *advertising agency executive*

Rye
McDonnell, Mary Theresa *travel company executive*

Schenectady
Sacklow, Harriette Lynn *advertising agency executive*

Syosset
Ruthchild, Geraldine Quietlake *training and development consultant, writer, poet*

Tappan
Fox, Muriel *retired public relations executive*

Tarrytown
Kirsch, Abigail *culinary productions executive*

Westhampton Beach
Maas, Jane Brown *advertising executive*

White Plains
Kovac, Caroline (Carol Kovac) *computer company executive*
Vernon, Lillian *mail order company executive*

Woodhaven
Bolster, Jacqueline Neben (Mrs. John A. Bolster) *communications consultant*

Yonkers
Capodilupo, Elizabeth Jeanne Hatton *public relations executive*
Pickover, Betty Abravanel *retired executive legal secretary, civic volunteer*

Youngstown
Askins, Nancy Ellen Paulsen *training services executive*

NORTH CAROLINA

Canton
Dixon, Shirley Juanita *retired restaurant owner*

Charlotte
Carino, Linda Susan *business consultant*
Hoskie, Lorraine *consumer products representative, poet*
Lyerly, Elaine Myrick *advertising executive*
Mickle, Deloris B. *retired credit manager, artist*
Moore, Bealer Gwen *transcription company executive*

Garner
Barbour, Charlene *management firm executive*

Greensboro
Stone, Theresa M. *communications executive*

Lake Toxaway
Raynolds, Elaine Spalding *sales executive, photojournalist*

Mooresville
Dow, Leslie Wright *communications company executive, photographer, writer*

North Wilkesboro
Parsons, Irene Adelaide *management consultant*

Raleigh
Rauch, Kathleen *computer executive*

Research Triangle Park
Bronstein, Lois Helene *marketing professional*

Roxboro
Hollingsworth, Brenda Jackson *employment consultant*

Sanford
Brown, Eva Everlean *business executive*

Wilson
Woods, Deborah Lynn *recruiter*

Winston Salem
Ivey, Susan M. *tobacco company executive*

NORTH DAKOTA

Dickinson
Nelson, Debra L. *non-profit organization consultant*

OHIO

Akron
Geier, Kathleen T. *human resources specialist*

Chagrin Falls
Kuby, Barbara Eleanor *personnel director, management consultant*

Chardon
Mihalik, Phyllis Ann *management consultant, systems analyst, educator*

Cincinnati
Arnold, Susan E. *consumer products company executive*
Bateman, Sharon Louise *public relations executive*
Brown, Dale Patrick *retired advertising executive*
Goodman, Phyllis L. *public relations executive*
Henretta, Deborah A. *consumer products company executive*
Kotchka, Claudia B. *consumer products company executive, accountant*
Morris, Margaret Elizabeth *marketing professional, small business owner*
Otto, Charlotte R. *consumer products company executive*
Wall, Della *human resources specialist, manufacturing executive*

Cleveland
Cook, Susan J. *human resources specialist, manufacturing executive*
Dougherty, Ursel Thielbeule *communications executive, marketing executive*
Dunbar, Mary Asmundson *communications executive, public information officer, consultant, investor*
Hamilton, Nancy Beth *data processing executive*
Mucha, Mary Ann K. *quality assurance professional*

Dublin
Anderson, Kerrii B. *food service executive*
Bird, Shelley *communications executive*
Watkins, Carole S. *human resources specialist, medical products executive*

Elyria
Nakonecznyj, Nadia *marketing professional*
Pucko, Diane Bowles *public relations executive*

Fostoria
Howard, Kathleen *computer company executive*

Lebanon
Bennett, Alison Mercedes *human resources specialist*

Solon
Johnson, Madeline Mitchell *retired administrative assistant*

Thornville
Coe, Linda Marlene Wolfe *retired marketing professional, freelance photographer*

Xenia
Nutter, Zoe Dell Lantis *retired public relations executive*

OKLAHOMA

Cleveland
Henry, Kathleen Marie *marketing executive*

Enid
Marquardt, Shirley Marie *retired management consultant*

Mustang
Laurent, Jerry Suzanna *communications executive*

Oklahoma City
Jones, Brenda Kaye *public relations executive*
LaMotte, Janet Allison *retired management consultant*

OREGON

Albany
Haralson, Linda Jane *communications executive*

Eugene
Cawood, Elizabeth Jean *public relations executive*

Lake Oswego
Zorkin, Melissa Waggener *public relations executive*

Pendleton
Bedford, Amy Aldrich *public relations executive*

Portland
Kirk, Jill *management consultant*

Salem
Milbrath, Mary Merrill Lemke *quality assurance professional*

Talent
Meyers, Sharon May *sales executive*

PENNSYLVANIA

Allentown
Borger, Ann Work *communications professional, webmaster*

Ardmore
Lockett-Egan, Marian Workman *advertising executive*

Bala Cynwyd
Culp, Dorie *marketing executive*

Bethlehem
Dorward, Judith A. *retired business ordering customer service representative*
Felix, Patricia Jean *retired steel company purchasing professional*

Bryn Mawr
Eiser, Barbara J.A. *management consultant*

Camp Hill
Crist, Christine Myers *consulting executive*

Center Valley
Regnier, Sophie Anne Michelle *business research consultant*

Conshohocken
Thompson, Pamela Padwick *public relations executive*

Doylestown
McCafferty, Barbara Jean (BJ McCafferty) *sales executive*

Fort Washington
Fulton, Cheryl L. *customer service administrator*

Grantville
Sudor, Cynthia Ann *sales and marketing professional*

Indiana
Ruddock, Ellen Sylves *management consultant*

Lancaster
Taylor, Ann *human resources specialist, educator*

Levittown
Camer, Mary Martha *retired secretary*

Lewisburg
Brill, Marilyn *community-based collaboration consultant*
Rote, Nelle Fairchild Hefty *management consultant*

Mechanicsburg
Harper, Diane Marie *retired corporate communications specialist*

Philadelphia
Breslow, Tina *public relations executive*
Brown, Delores Russell *health management company official*
Burns, Marian Law *human resources specialist, legal association administrator*
Coulson, Zoe Elizabeth *retired consumer marketing executive*
Dougherty Buchholz, Karen *communications executive*
Field, Charlotte *communications executive*
Gaillard, Margaret *communications executive*
Lenhard, Sarah *advertising executive*
Logue-Kinder, Joan *public relations consultant*
McKee, Lynn B. *human resources specialist*
Mitchell, Brenda King *training services executive*
Schreur, Lynne Elizabeth *advertising executive*
Scott-Williams, Mildred P. *food service specialist*

Pittsburgh
Anderson, Catherine M. *consulting company executive*
Paugh, Patricia Lou *business consultant*
Peterman, Donna Cole *communications executive*
Rathke, Sheila Wells *marketing professional, consultant*
Reichblum, Audrey Rosenthal *public relations executive, publishing executive*

Plymouth Meeting
Blessing, Carole Anne *human resources manager*

Reading
Hackenberg, Barbara Jean Collar *retired advertising and public relations executive*

Sadsburyville
Gellman, Gloria Gae Seeburger Schick *marketing professional*

Scranton
Williams, Holly Thomas *retired business executive*

Sewickley
Woody, Carol Clayman *data processing executive*

Steelton
Zimmerman, Connie Ann *public administrator*

Wallingford
Adamiec, Jean Kraus *retired advertising executive*

Warrior Run
Scott, Deborah Kathleen *private investigator*

Waynesboro
Pflager, Ruth Wood *retired communications executive*

West Conshohocken
Mullen, Eileen Anne *human resources executive*

Wyomissing
Williams-Wennell, Kathi *human resources specialist*

Yardley
Newsom, Carolyn Cardall *management consultant*

York
Livingston, Pamela A. *corporate image and marketing management consultant*
Snyder, Jan Louise *administrative aide*

RHODE ISLAND

Cumberland
Rush, Lee A. *marketing executive*

Pawtucket
Ferland, Darlene Frances *management consultant*

Woonsocket
Frappier, Pearl Peters *retired bookkeeper*

SOUTH CAROLINA

Charleston
Ballard, Mary Melinda *corporate communications specialist, consumer products company executive*
Dupree, Nathalie *chef, television personality, writer*
Winter-Switz, Cheryl Donna *travel company executive*

Columbia
Barnum, Mary Ann Mook *information management manager*

Greenville
Beattie, Stephanie Shannon *human resources specialist*

Seneca
Strong-Tidman, Virginia Adele *marketing professional*

Spartanburg
Smithart-Oglesby, Debra Lynn *food service executive*
Steinmayer, Janet L. *food service executive, lawyer*

TENNESSEE

Brentwood
Byars, Leisa *marketing professional, music company executive*

Franklin
Power, Elizabeth Henry *marketing professional, consultant*

Knoxville
Cox, Anna Lee *retired administrative assistant*
Herndon, Anne Harkness *sales executive*

Madison
Cage, Allie M. *communications executive*

Memphis
Bollheimer, (Cecilia) Denise *marketing professional, finance company executive*
Edwards, Doris Porter *computer specialist*
Kelley, Linda Rose *human resources specialist*

Nashville
Reynolds, Doris Elizabeth *management consultant, poet*
Sheffield, Stephanie S. *portfolio and marketing management consultant*
Short, Sallie Lee *physical plant service worker*

Sevierville
Etherton, Jane *retired sales executive, marketing professional*

TEXAS

Abilene
Freeman, Carol Lyn *business administrator*

Arlington
Butte, Norine *marketing executive*
English, Marlene Cabral *management consultant*
Sawyer, Dolores *motel chain executive*

Austin
Blackwell, Cara Lynn *printing company executive*
Cunningham, Isabella Clara Mantovani *advertising executive, educator*
Curle, Robin Lea *computer company executive*
Davis, Merrill *public relations executive*
Engle, Sandra Louise *management consultant*
Green, Shirley Moore *retired communications executive, public information officer*
Mathis, Marsha Debra *customer service administrator*
Qunell, Kerri Wynn *marketing professional*
Vandel, Diana Geis *management consultant*

Bedford
Horvat, Vashti *online marketing consultant*

Brownsville
Halaby, Margarita Gonzalez *marketing professional, communications executive*
Trujillo, Anna *food company administrator, city official*

Burleson
Buford, Evelyn Claudene Shilling *retired consumer products company executive*

Carrollton
Odem, Joyce Marie *human resources specialist*

Coppell
Owen, Cynthia Carol *sales executive*

Dallas
Byas, Teresa Ann Uranga *customer service administrator, interior designer, consultant*
Coomer, Donna R. *communications executive*
Dinkins, Jane Poling *management consultant, application developer*
Dykeman, Alice Marie *public relations executive*
Fairbairn, Ursula Farrell *human resources executive*
Loveless, Kathy Lynne *client services executive*
Robertson, Jane Ryding *marketing executive*
Robles, Diana M *administrative assistant*
Zeitlin, Laurie *printing company executive, information technology executive*

Denton
Ryan, Melbagene T. *retired food service and nutrition director*

Fairview
Hansen, Elizabeth (Beth) Stevens *human resources consultant*

Flower Mound
Ross, Lesa Moore *quality assurance professional*

Fort Worth
Newbern, Dianna J. *management consultant, educator*

Grand Prairie
McMillan, Helen Berneice *sales executive*

Houston
Burnett, Susan Walk *personnel service company owner*
Curtis, Barbara *consumer products company professional*
Day, Twila M. *food service executive*
Golan, Yvette Y. *consumer products company executive, lawyer*
Jones, Sonia Josephine *advertising executive*
Mampre, Virginia Elizabeth *communications executive*
McCollam, Marion Andrus *consulting firm executive, educator*
Noland, Mary Richerson *retired management consultant*
Saizan, Paula Theresa *business consultant*
Sweet, Portia Ann *retired human resources specialist*

Junction
Evans, Jo Burt *communications executive, rancher*

Kingsville
Stanford, (Frances) Jane Herring *management consultant, educator, writer*

Leander
Witt, Doreen Marie *sales executive*

Llano
Zachary, Jean *personnel director*

New Caney
Hayes, Ann Carson *computer company executive*

Plainview
Ticer, Terri Jean *sales executive*

Plano
Sivinski, Tina M. *human resources specialist*

Port Lavaca
Boyd, Ann Fisher *office administrator*

Round Rock
Goodman, Kim *marketing professional, computer company executive*
Sheskey, Susan E. *computer company executive*

San Antonio
Edson, Marian Louise *communications executive*
Jennings, Karen *human resources specialist, telecommunications industry executive*
Nava, Carmen P. *communications executive*

San Marcos
Martin, Jerri Whan *public relations executive*

Southlake
Peluso, Michelle *Internet company executive*
Sorge, Karen Lee *printing company executive, consultant*

Stafford
Cahilly, Karen L. *quality assurance professional*

The Woodlands
Jones, Susan Chafin *management consultant*

Tyler
Resnik, Linda Ilene *marketing and information executive, writer, publisher, consultant*

Wellington
Sims, Lennie Coleman *public relations consultant*

VIRGINIA

Abingdon
Ramos-Cano, Hazel Balatero *caterer, chef, innkeeper, restaurateur, entrepreneur*

Alexandria
Coons, Barbara Lynn *public relations executive, librarian*
Daly, Kay R. *public relations professional*
Fosdick, Cora Prifold (Cora Prifold Beebe) *management consultant*
Gallagher, Anne Porter *communications executive*
Lightner, Candy (Candace Lynne Lightner) *non-profit management consultant, advocate*
Meisinger, Susan *human resources specialist*
Paulson, Gwen O. Gampel *government relations consultant, life and leadership coach*
Stone, Ann Elizabeth *marketing agency executive, consultant, entrepreneur, volunteer*
Stone, Ann E.W. *marketing executive*

Arlington
Claussen, Eileen Barbara *environmental services administrator, former federal agency administrator*
Johnson, Rosemary Wrucke *personnel management specialist*
Lieber, Carole Marguerite Renee *human resources specialist, consultant*
Nash, Cathy L. *meeting planner*
Wise, Kathryn E *marketing professional*

Ashburn
Trent, Grace Chen *communications executive*

Chantilly
Bergman, Nomi *communications executive*
Sullivan, Penelope Dietz *computer software development company executive*

Charlottesville
Bly-Monnen, April M. *quality assurance professional*
MacIlwaine, Mary Jarratt *public relations executive*

Dulles
Balis, Janet *Internet company executive*
Rollé, Janet Lydia *Internet company executive*

Fairfax
Bohan, Gloria *travel company executive*

Falls Church
Cianciolo-Carney, Rossana *investigative analyst*
Jones, Linda R. Wolf *consulting company executive*

Fredericksburg
Harrod, Audrey Hunter *retired executive secretary*
Hickman, Margaret Capellini *advertising executive*

Herndon
Alicudo, Lynda *management consultant*
Harris, Shelley Follansbee *business development professional*

Mc Lean
Rose, Susan Porter *management and governmental affairs consultant*
Webber, Diana L. *management consultant executive, engineering educator*

Oakton
Terzian, Grace Paine *communications executive*

Reston
Brooker, Susan Gay *employment consulting firm executive*
Miller, Lynne Marie *environmental services administrator*
Posey, Ada Louise *human resources specialist*
Sarreals, Sonia *data processing executive, consultant*
Witt, Ruth Hutt *management consultant*

Richmond
Bohannon, Sarah Virginia *personnel professional*
Brown, Patricia A. *customer service representative*
Joynes, Barbara Cole *marketing executive*

Seaford
Jenkins, Margaret Bunting *human resources executive*

Springfield
Edwards-LeBoeuf, Renee Camille *public relations executive, protective services official*

Vienna
Miller, Christine Marie *marketing executive, public relations executive*

Winchester
Vaughan, Stephanie Ruth *water aerobics business owner, consultant*

WASHINGTON

Bothell
Kraft, Elaine Joy *community relations and communications official*

Federal Way
Muzyka-McGuire, Amy *marketing professional, nutritionist, consultant*

Gig Harbor
Wissmann, Carol Reneé *sales executive*

Parkland
Johnson, LuAn K. *disaster management consultant*

Port Ludlow
Pappas, Shirley Ann *sales executive*

Redmond
Ambrose, Adele D. *communications executive*
Bradford, Joanne K. *computer software company executive*
Butler, Jannette Sue *human resources professional*

Seattle
Hannaford, Janet Kirtley *software administrative manager*
Patton, Jody *management company executive*
Reis, Jean Stevenson *administrative secretary*
Rowe, Katherine L. *former computer company executive*
Townsend, Wendy *retired marketing executive*

Spokane
Gilpatrick, Janet *public relations executive, consultant*

Tacoma
Bartlett, Norma Thyra *retired administrative assistant*

Vancouver
Ogden, Valeria Munson *management consultant, state representative*

WEST VIRGINIA

Charleston
Offutt, Rebecca Sue *business and sales executive*

South Charleston
Steinberg, Beth Aileen *employee assistance manager*

WISCONSIN

Kohler
Kohler, Laura E. *human resources executive*

La Crosse
Anderson, Gwyn C. *computer company executive*

Lake Geneva
O'Reilly, Sarah M. *sales executive*

Menasha
Streeter, Stephanie Anne *printing company executive*

Milwaukee
Davis, Susan F. *human resources specialist*
Mueller, Marylin *graphic supply company executive*
Rivera-Velazquez, Maria *marketing professional*

Monroe
Bean, Virginia Ann (Ginny Bean) *marketing executive*

Oregon
Glodowski, Shelley Jean *administrator, writer, musician*

Pittsville
Normington, Norma Shotwell *secretary*

Racine
Johnson-Leipold, Helen P. *outdoor recreation company executive*
Johnson-Marquart, Winnie *consumer products company executive*
Klein, Gabriella Sonja *retired communications executive*

CANADA

ONTARIO

Toronto
Taylor, Kathleen P. *hotel executive*

QUEBEC

Rosemere
Hopper, Carol *incentive program administrator, trade association administrator*

Whistler
Rae, Barbara Joyce *employee placement company executive*

ADDRESS UNPUBLISHED

Abraham, Francine Dinneen *sales executive, banker*
Abramson, Stephanie W. *retired advertising executive, lawyer*
Agee, Claudia *executive secretary, tax specialist*
Alexander, Faith Dorothy *retired training services executive*
Alexander, Icie Mae *communications executive*
Allen, Elizabeth Maresca *marketing executive, telecommunications industry executive*
Altschuler, Marjorie *advertising executive*
Anthony, Wilma Tylinda *retired customer service administrator*
Appell, Louise Sophia *retired consulting company executive*
Armstrong Squall, Paula Estelle *executive secretary*
Arnold, Catherine Anderson *communications executive*
Atkins, Candi *management consultant, small business owner*
Atlee, Debbie Gayle *sales consultant, medical educator*
Avrett, Roz (Rosalind Case) *writer*
Bainbridge, Dona Bardelli *marketing professional*
Barad, Jill Elikann *former family products company executive*
Barca, Kathleen *marketing executive*
Barrett, Paulette Singer *public relations executive*
Batory, Joan Anne *solid waste and environmental administrator*
Bauer, Barbara Ann *marketing consultant*
Baugh, Terry *marketing professional*
Baxter, Barbara Morgan *Internet service provider executive, educator*
Beasley, Barbara Starin *sales executive, marketing professional*
Beider, Marlys Anna *hotel executive, writer*
Berman, Cheryl R. *advertising company executive*
Berman, Sandra Rita *retired personnel director*
Binder, Amy Finn *public relations company executive*
Bisconti, Ann Stouffer *public opinion research company executive*
Blatz, Linda Jeanne *sales manager*
Bledsoe, Cynthia Wyrick *sales executive, consultant*
Boatwright, Charlotte Jeanne *marketing professional, public relations executive*
Bottari, Marianna Teresa *public relations executive*
Bowick, Susan D. *retired computer company executive*
Boysen, Jonea Gene *marketing executive, copywriter*
Bradford, Susan Anne *management consultant, writer*
Brady, Donna Elizabeth *sales executive, marketing executive, performing company executive*
Brand, Donna J. *career consultant, mental health counselor*
Brandon, Michelle Marie *marketing executive*
Brannick, Ellen Marie *retired management consultant*
Brecht, Sally Ann *quality assurance executive*
Brennan, Donna Lesley *public relations company executive*
Broaddus, Andrea Lynn *environmental services administrator*
Broderson, Thelma Sylvia *retired marketing professional*
Brown, Hollace Ann Holly *advertising executive*
Buck, Linda Dee *executive recruiting company executive*
Bugbee, Joan Barthelme *retired corporate communications executive*
Burnett, Iris Jacobson *corporate communications specialist*
Butter, Andrea *marketing executive, consultant*
Cairns, Anne Marie *public relations executive*
Caldwell, Judy Carol *advertising executive, consultant, writer*
Cantor, Susan *advertising executive*
Cantu, Delia *training services executive*
Caplin, Jo Ann *communications company executive*
Carpenter, Candice *writer, former media executive*
Carpenter-Mason, Beverly Nadine *quality assurance professional, medical/surgical nurse, pediatric nurse practitioner, consultant, writer*
Carter, Jaine M(arie) *human resources specialist, director*
Cartwright, Talula Elizabeth *management consultant, educator*
Cervantez, Michelle *marketing professional*
Chandler, Kathleen *retired executive secretary*
Chapman, Linda Lee *computer company executive, consultant*
Cheney, Mary Claire *Internet company executive*
Chiavario, Nancy Anne *business and community relations executive*
Chicklis, Barbara Karen Burak *retired data processing executive*
Chin, Janet Sau-Ying *data processing executive, consultant*
Chung, Caroline *marketing professional*
Clarke, Janet Morrison *marketing executive*
Coleman, Claire Kohn *public relations executive*
Cone, Frances McFadden *data processing consultant*
Connell, Shirley Hudgins *public relations professional*
Conover, Pamela C. *cruise line executive*
Constantinople, Alexandra *communications executive*
Cooper, Doris Jean *market research executive*
Corbi, Lana *communications executive*
Covey, Norma Scott *travel service executive*
Cowen, Jean *employee benefits consultant*
Criswell, Kimberly Ann *executive coach, communications consultant, performance artist*
Crittendon, Donna Elizabeth *customer service administrator*
Cruver, Suzanne Lee *communications executive, writer*
Curry, Catharine Terrill *marketing executive, health facility administrator, sales executive*
Cutter Modlin, Beverly Wright *management consultant*
Dandeneau, Billie Jo *retired data processing executive*
D'Antonio, Cynthia Maria *sales and marketing executive*
Davis, Nicole D. *executive secretary, entrepreneur*
Dennick, Lori Ann (L. Anne Carrington) *publicist*
Diamond, Susan Zee *management consultant*
Dillon, Terri L. *consulting firm executive*
Dimopoulos, Linda J. *food service executive*
Dispensa-Rhoads, Jaclyn Marisa *environmental services administrator*
Doan, Mary Frances *advertising executive*
Doherty, Evelyn Marie *data processing consultant*
Doll, Patricia Marie *marketing professional, consultant*
Douglas, Victoria Jean *marketing professional, communications executive, educator*
Dozier, Eleanor Cameron *computer company executive, writer*
Drake, Carolyn A. *administrative assistant*
Drake, Patti Linn *retired consumer products company executive*
Duke, Robin Chandler Tippett *retired public relations executive, former ambassador*
Dunn Kelly, Ruth Emma *management consultant*
East, Janette Diane *marketing consultant*
Echols, Mary Evelyn *training services executive, writer*
Ecton, Donna R. *business executive*
Edwards, Ann Concetta *human resources director*
Emerling, Carol G. *management consultant*
Evans, Charlotte Mortimer *communications consultant, writer*
Evans, Patricia Marie *sales executive*
Faron, Fay Cheryl *private investigator, writer*
Feigin, Barbara Sommer *marketing consultant*
Feld, Carole Leslie *marketing executive*
Fidler, Susan *recreation director*
Fiorina, Carly (Cara Carleton Sneed Fiorina) *former computer company executive*
Frappia, Linda Ann *medical administrator*
Freeman, Chanda *executive secretary, elementary school educator*
Fuller, Kathryn Scott *former environmental services administrator*
Gadiesh, Orit *management consulting executive*
Gaither, Ann Heafner *sales executive*
Gallup, Janet Louise *management consultant*
Gary, Kathleen Noland *public relations executive*
Gaskins, Karen D. *management consultant, research scientist*
Geltzer, Sheila Simon *public relations executive*
George, Sonya Carol *customer service administrator, educator*
Glacel, Barbara Pate *management consultant*
Goetsch, Lara *marketing professional, director*
Goldfarb, Muriel Bernice *marketing consultant, advertising consultant*
Goldschmidt, Amanda (Amy) O'Connell *food service executive*
Goodrich Harwood, Gail Lee *management consultant*
Goss, Martha Clark *consulting company executive*
Grace, Marcia Bell *advertising executive*
Grant, Nancy Marie *marketing professional, journalist*
Green, Linda Gail *retired international healthcare and management consultant, nursing educator*
Green, Rhonda Beverly *management consultant*
Griego, Angelic *marketing professional*
Grindal, Mary Ann *former sales professional*
Gross, Laura Ann *marketing and communications professional, herbalist, acupuncturist*
Gross, Leslie Pamela *sales executive, consultant*
Grosso, Doreen Elliott *management consultant*
Guiliano, Mireille *consumer products company executive*
Hale, Cheryl Wright *marketing professional*
Hall, Adrienne A. *international marketing communications executive, consultant, life balance coach*
Hallman, Cinda A. *management consultant*
Hamlin, Sonya B. *communications specialist*
Hanes, Darlene Marie *marketing professional*
Harr, Lucy Loraine *public relations executive*
Harrison, Judith Anne *human resources executive*
Hartger, Barbara J. *marketing professional*
Hartsock, Linda Sue *retired management consultant*
Hauser, Joyce Roberta *marketing professional*
Hausman, Harriet Seceley *administrator*
Haver-Allen, Ann *communications director*
Hayes, Janet Gray *retired management consultant, retired mayor*
Heagy, Lorraine Mary *office manager*
Heise, Marilyn Beardsley *public relations company executive, publishing company executive*
Hergenhan, Joyce *public relations executive*
Hernandez, Maria *Internet company executive*
Herz, Irene Laurel *web site design company executive, librarian*

Heuer, Margaret B. *retired microcomputer laboratory coordinator*
Hickman, Terrie Taylor *administrator, elementary school educator*
Higbee, Beth *communications executive*
Hilliard, Lil *sales executive*
Hillman, Sandra Schwartz *public relations executive, marketing professional*
Hines, Amy Christine *business analyst*
Hochschild, Carroll Shepherd *computer company and medical equipment executive, educator*
Hollis, Robbie Smagula *marketing communications executive, advertising executive*
Houghtaling, Pamela Ann *communications professional, writer*
Hudson, Sharon Marie *communications executive*
Hunt, Martha *sales executive, researcher*
Hunter, Barbara Way *public relations consultant*
Infante-Ogbac, Daisy Inocentes *sales executive, real estate agent, marketing professional*
Jack, Nancy Rayford *retired supplemental resource company executive, consultant*
Johansen, Karen Lee *retired sales executive*
Johnson, Camille *media executive*
Jones, Dale Cherner *marketing executive, consultant*
Jurman-Shulman, Claudia Lynne *sales executive*
Kane, Karen Marie *public affairs consultant*
Kanuk, Leslie Lazar *management consultant, educator*
Kapner, Lori *marketing professional*
Kassewitz, Ruth Eileen Blower *retired public relations executive*
Kay, Bonnie Kathryn *management consultant*
Kelley, Sheila Seymour *public relations consultant*
Kelly, Carol A. *travel company executive*
Kennedy, Debra Joyce *marketing professional*
Kennedy, Jerrie Ann Preston *public relations executive*
Kennedy, Karen Syence *advertising agency executive*
Kenny, Deborah *marketing professional, finance educator*
Kent, Lisa Barnett *marketing executive, small business owner*
Klages, Constance Warner *management consultant*
Klein, Charlotte Conrad *public relations executive*
Knox, Gertie R. *compliance executive, accountant*
Koelmel, Lorna Lee *data processing executive*
Korologos, Ann McLaughlin *communications executive*
Kramer, Lora L. *executive assistant*
Kraus, Jill Gansman *former jewelry industry marketing executive*
Krohley-Gatt, Patricia Anne *marketing professional, sales executive*
Krumholz, Mimi *human resources administrator*
Lami, Judith Irene *advertising executive*
LaMotta, Connie Frances *public relations executive*
Lampert, Eleanor Verna *retired human resources specialist*
Lee, Daphne Patrice *special events coordinator, academic administrator*
Lee, Jeanne Kit Yew *retired administrative officer*
Lee, Linda M. *technical recruiter*
Leff, Ilene J(afnel) *corporate executive, federal official*
Leinfellner, Ruth *strategic planner*
Lepore, Dawn Gould *Internet company executive*
Livengood, Charlotte Louise *retired human resources specialist*
Livermore, Ann Martinelli *computer company executive*
Livingstone, Susan Morrisey *management consultant, former federal agency administrator*
Loewenthal, Nessa Parker *intercultural communications consultant*
Longaberger, Tami *home decor accessories company executive*
Lotas, Judith Patton *advertising executive*
Luce, Priscilla Mark *public relations executive*
Luciano, Roselle Patricia *advertising executive, editor*
Lynch, Charlotte Andrews *retired communications executive, consultant*
Madden, Glenda Gail *sales professional*
Madison, Anne Conway *marketing professional, public relations professional*
Maeda, J. A. *data processing executive, consultant*
Mainwaring, Susan Adams *recreational facility executive*
Maio, Elsie Regina *communications consultant*
Mallo-Garrido, Josephine Ann *advertising executive*
Malone, Claudine Berkeley *management consultant*
Maneker, Roberta S(ue) *public relations executive*
Marez, Trinnie Marie *marketing professional*
Marlar, Janet Cummings *retired public relations officer*
Martin, Christy *communications executive*
Martin, Renee Cohen *forensic document examiner, author, expert witness*
Marvin, D. Jane *consumer products company executive*
Mascheroni, Eleanor Earle *marketing communications executive*
Matthew, Lyn *sales executive, consultant, marketing professional*
Maxfield, Louisa Fonda Gribble *executive secretary*
McAteer, Deborah Grace *travel company executive*
McCandless, Carolyn Keller *retired human resources specialist*
McCoy, Debra Marlene Black *sales executive*
McElwreath, Sally Chin *corporate communications executive*
McMinn, Virginia Ann *human resources consulting company executive*
McVeigh-Pettigrew, Sharon Christine *communications consultant*
Meade, Patricia Sue *marketing professional*
Meis, Nancy Ruth *marketing executive*
Melicia, Kitty *human resources administrator, foundation administrator*
Menck, J Claire *chef, consultant*
Menconi, Marguerite L. *customer service logistics*
Mikiewicz, Anna Daniella *marketing and international business export manager*
Miles, Laveda Ann *advertising executive*
Miles, Mary Ellen *retired human resources specialist*
Miller, Ellen S. *marketing executive*
Mitchell, Carolyn Cochran *administrative assistant*
Moffat, MaryBeth *consulting company executive*
Moseley, Carol June *security supervisor, small business owner*
Murdock, Pamela Ervilla *travel and advertising company executive*
Nagys, Elizabeth Ann *environmental services administrator, educator*
Nason, Dolores Irene *computer company executive, social welfare administrator, minister*
Neel, Judy Murphy *management consultant*
Nelson, Kimberly Terese *computer software company executive, former federal agency administrator*
Newman, Suzanne Dinkes *web site design company executive*
Nickles-Murray, Elizabeth *advertising executive, writer*
Noonan, Susan Abert *public relations executive*
O'Connor, Betty Lou *retired hotel executive, food service executive*
Odom, Judy *software company executive*
O'Hare, Virginia Lewis *human resources administrator*
Otero-Smart, Ingrid Amarillys *advertising executive*
Pascoe, Clara P. *public relations executive, property manager*
Pate, Jacqueline Hail *retired data processing company executive*
Penrod, Marian Penuel *personnel consultant, retired school librarian*
Peretti, Marilyn Gay Woerner *human services professional*
Perlmutter, Barbara S. *retired advertising executive*
Perlmutter, Diane F. *marketing executive*
Perlov, Dadie *management consultant*
Perraud, Pamela Brooks *human resources professional*
Pervall, Stephanie Joy *management consultant*
Phelan, Mary Michenfelder *public relations executive, writer*
Phillips, Jean Brown *public relations executive, consultant*
Phillips, Joyce Martha *human resources executive*
Plank, Betsy (Mrs. Sherman V. Rosenfield) *public relations counsel*
Plumb, Pamela Pelton *consulting company executive, retired mayor*
Pomeroy, Heather Aline *sales executive, marketing executive*
Pope, Lena Elizabeth *human resources specialist*
Potok, Nancy Ann Fagenson *management consultant*
Pressler, Ciara Nicole Frey *marketing executive, consultant*
Proctor, Barbara Gardner *advertising agency executive, writer*
Pruett-Lawson, Jo Ann *marketing professional, special events coordinator*
Radkowsky, Karen *advertising research specialist*
Railsback, Sherrie Lee *management consultant, educator*
Reed, Anne F. Thomson *management consultant*
Reisman, Judith Ann Gelernter *media communications executive, educator*
Richards, Carmeleete A. *computer company executive, network administrator, consultant*
Richards, Lynn *company training executive, consultant*
Riley-Davis, Shirley Merle *advertising agency executive, marketing consultant, writer*
Robertson, Sara Stewart *private investigator, entrepreneur*
Robinson, Linda Gosden *communications executive*
Roffé, Sarina *public relations executive*
Rook, Vicki Lynn *safety specialist*
Rowland, Pleasant T. *toy company executive, publisher*
Russell, Jacqueline Annette *recreation director*
Rypczyk, Candice Leigh *employee relations executive*
Sacks, Temi J. *public relations executive*
Safian, Shelley Carole *advertising executive*
Sandage-Mussey, Elizabeth Anthea *retired market research executive*
Schubert, Helen Celia *public relations executive*
Seiger, Marilyn Sandra *public relations executive*
Shaffer, Judy Ann *retired data processing professional, educator*
Sharples, Ruth Lissak *communications executive*
Shaw, Cecelia *retired chef*
Shimokubo, Janice Teruko *marketing professional*
Shugart, Anita Carol *research and development cosmetologist*
Shumick, Diana Lynn *retired computer executive*
Silva, Albertina *computer company executive*
Simecka, Betty Jean *marketing executive*
Simmons, Sylvia (Sylvia Simmons Neumann) *advertising executive, writer*
Simpson, Andrea Lynn *communications executive*
Somerville, Virginia Pauline Winters *executive assistant*
Sorstokke, Ellen Kathleen *marketing executive, educator*
Spirn, Michele Sobel *communications professional, writer*
Spivak, Joan Carol *communications executive*
Squazzo, Mildred Katherine (Mildred Katherine Oetting) *corporate executive*
Stadler, Katherine Loy *advertising executive, consultant*
Staniar, Linda Burton *retired communications executive*
Stark, Diana *public relations executive*
Stathakopoulos, Melissa *recreation director*
Steger, Donna Ann *printing company executive, broker*
Stenz, Jessica Lynn *administrative associate*
Stern, S(eesa) Beatrice *executive secretary, medical/surgical nurse*
Stone, Linda *former computer company executive, consultant, speaker, writer*
Stott, Terri Jeuan *residential facility administrator*
Streeter, Carol *technology marketing executive*
Strength, Janis Grace *retired management executive, educator*
Sugra, Cynthia Mariel *marketing executive*
Sutlin, Vivian *advertising executive*
Taylor, Michelle Y. *human resources consultant*
Teater, Tricia L. *human resources specialist*
Tegge, Patricia Ann *retired administrative assistant*
Tersine, Brenda L. *funeral director*
Thomas, Angela M. *marketing professional*
Thomas, Maryellen *public relations executive*
Thurner, Agnes H. *retired administrative secretary*
Timmerman, Anne N. *retired public relations executive*
Tompkins, Julie Lynberg *market research consultant*
Torrence, Margaret Ann Johnson *data processing executive, writer*
Triplett, Arlene Ann *management consultant*
Tripp, Marian Barlow Loofe *retired public relations executive*
Tuft, Mary Ann *executive search firm executive*
Ussery, Luanne *retired communications consultant*
Van Houten, Elizabeth Ann *corporate communications executive, painter*
Vauclair, Marguerite Renée *communications and sales promotion executive*
Vaughndorf, Betty Rachel *executive secretary, artist*
Venables, Norinne *administrative assistant, dancer, educator*
Viscelli, Therese Rauth *materials management consultant*
Wakeman, Olivia Van Horn *marketing professional*
Walk, Barbra Denise *customer service administrator, tutor*
Wallington, Patricia McDevitt *computer company executive*
Walter, Carmel Monica *security firm executive, writer*
Wangsness, Genna Stead *retired hotel executive, innkeeper*
Warrick, Lola June *management consultant*
Water, Linda Gail *public relations executive*
Watson, Rebecca Elaine *human resources specialist, consultant*
Watson, Renée *marketing professional, consultant*
Weaver, Kitra K. *sales and marketing executive*
Webb, Doris McIntosh *human resources specialist*
Weil, Lynne Amy *communications executive, writer*
Westheimer, Ruth Welling *retired management consultant*
Weston, Joan Spencer *communications executive*
Wheeler, Barbara J. *management consultant*
Whitaker, Shirley Ann *retired communications executive*
White, Bonnie Yvonne *management consultant, retired educator*
Williams, Freda Berry *administrative assistant*
Williams, Terrie Michelle *public relations executive*
Wilson-Stewart, Marilyn Lucille *retired human resources leader*
Winter, Nancy Fitz *retired media and public relations executive*
Wolf, Linda S. *retired advertising executive*
Wood, Frances Diane *medical secretary, artist*
Wozniak, Joyce Marie *sales executive*
Wyse, Lois *advertising executive, writer*
Yaeger, Therese F. *management professional*
Yee, Nancy W. *travel consultant*
Yopconka, Natalie Ann Catherine *executive secretary, computer specialist, educator, entrepreneur, small business owner*
Yost, Jean Marie *administrative assistant*

INDUSTRY: TRADE

UNITED STATES

ALABAMA

Jasper
Argo, Betty Earnest *business owner*

Madison
Bogard, Eileen Judith *investor, retired small business owner, retired education administrator*

Montgomery
Moseley, Laurice Culp *small business owner*

Stevenson
Grider Watson, Mary Elizabeth *small business owner*

ALASKA

Salcha
Alsip, Cheryl Ann *small business owner*

Wrangell
Smith, Kimmie Christine *small business owner*

ARIZONA

Clarkdale
Tod, Martha Ann *retired small business owner*

Fountain Hills
Blatt, Melanie Judith *small business owner*

Goodyear
McBride, Janet Marie *small business owner*

Scottsdale
Blair, Karen Elaine *small business owner, social psychology researcher, psychiatric consultant*
Williams-De Silva, Lisa Annette *small business owner, adult nurse practitioner*

Sun City
Thompson, Betty Jane *retired small business owner*

Tempe
Lemmon, Nicolette *small business owner, marketing professional*

Tucson
Fay, Mary Anne *retail executive*

ARKANSAS

Bentonville
Chambers, Susan (M. Susan Chambers) *retail executive*
Curran, Patricia A. *retail executive*
Dillman, Linda M. *retail executive*
Swanson, Celia *retail executive*
Watts, Claire A. *retail executive*
Weir, Rita Mary *retail executive*

CALIFORNIA

Bodega Bay
Freeman, Donna Cook *small business owner*

Chino Hills
Sorenson, Sandra Louise *retired retail executive*

Escondido
Young, Gladys *business owner*

Exeter
Pescosolido, Pamela Jane *graphics designer*

Fountain Valley
Mount, Cindy Kay *small business owner*

Fremont
Buswell, Debra Sue *small business owner, computer technician, financial analyst*
Wilson, Judy *small business owner*

Hanford
Neos, Peri Fitch *small business owner*

Lake Elsinore
Austin, Berit Synnove *retired small business owner, quality assurance professional*

Lancaster
Dalrymple, Marilyn Anita *small business owner, photographer*

Lockeford
Walker, Nancy Anne *small business owner, history and art educator*

Long Beach
Shoji, June Midori *import and export trading executive*

Los Altos
Orr, Susan Packard *small business owner, foundation administrator*

Los Angeles
Massino, Laura Angela *small business owner*

Malibu
Field, Barbara Stephenson *small business owner*

Manhattan Beach
King, Sharon Marie *consulting company executive*

Novato
Podd, Marsha Dianne *small business owner, nurse*

Orange
Busby, Nita June *small business owner*

Pasadena
Olson, Diana Craft *image and etiquette consultant*

Petaluma
Gervais, Cherie Nadine *small business owner*

Pleasanton
Renda, Larree M. *retail executive*

Quartz Hill
Noble, Sunny A. *business owner*

Riverside
White, Clara Jo *small business owner, consultant*

San Diego
Shields, Patricia Allene *retail executive*

San Francisco
Fisher, Doris *retail executive*
Harriss, Cynthia Therese (Cynthia Therese Clarke) *retail executive*
Johnson, Abigail Ridley *tour/travel and performing arts executive*
McCollam, Sharon L. *retail executive*
Robertson, Dawn H. *retail executive*
Sage-Gavin, Eva Marie *retail executive*

Santa Rosa
Jones, Doris (Anna Doris Vogel) *retail buyer*
Monk, Diana Charla *small business owner*

Sonoma
Weinberger, Lilla Gilbrech *bookseller*

Stockton
Blodgett, Elsie Grace *small business owner, property manager*

Walnut Creek
Van Noy, Christine Ann *restaurateur*

West Hollywood
Geddes, Ann *talent agency director*

West Sacramento
Teel, Joyce Raley *retail executive*

COLORADO

Colorado Springs
Buehner, Andrea Ruth *small business owner*
Johnson, Stephanie L. B. *small business owner, office manager*
Varoglu, Mary *wholesale distribution executive*

Denver
Maul, Carol Elaine *small business owner*
Newberry, Elizabeth Carter *greenhouse and floral company owner*

Dolores
Robertson, Virginia Marie *small business owner, publisher*

Golden
Brainerd, Mary *small business owner*

Loveland
Rodman, Sue A. *wholesale company executive, artist, writer*

Vail
Kelley Fitchett, Christine Ruth *business owner, consultant*

CONNECTICUT

Avon
Kling, Phradie (Phradie Kling Gold) *small business owner, educator*

Chaplin
Bruckerhoff, Theresa *business owner, educational researcher*

Greenwich
Rudy, Kathleen Vermeulen *small business owner*

New London
Johnson, Diana Atwood *business owner, innkeeper*

Norwich
Buddington, Olive Joyce *shop owner, retired education educator*

DISTRICT OF COLUMBIA

Washington
Carr, Marie Pinak *book distribution company executive, publishing executive*
Chalkley, Jacqueline Ann *retail company executive*
Fletcher, Keyana James *small business owner, performing company executive*
Malcolm, Ellen Reighley *small business owner*
Pelavin, Diane Christine *small business owner*
Stern, Paula *international trade consultant*
Tetelman, Alice Fran *small business owner*
Wides, Louise D. *small business owner, consultant*

FLORIDA

Altamonte Springs
Homayssi, Ruby Lee *small business owner*

Casselberry
Renee, Lisabeth Mary *small business owner, art designer*

Clearwater
Henderson, Janet Lynn *small business owner*

Cocoa Beach
Taylor, Nancy Alice *mechandiser, buyer*

Delray Beach
Campbell, Cynthia *retail executive*
Carter-Miller, Jocelyn *retail executive*
Luechtefeld, Monica *retail executive*

Gainesville
Hollien, Patricia Ann *small business owner, researcher*

Jacksonville
Constantini, JoAnn M. *small business owner, systems administrator, consultant*

Key Biscayne
de la Cruz, Carlos *wholesale distribution executive*

Key West
Armendariz, Alma Delia *small business owner, researcher*

Lakeland
Wilson, Micheline *small business owner*

Merritt Island
Fischer, Linda DeMoss *small business owner*

Miami
Liebes, Raquel *retired import/export company executive*
Richards-Vital, Claudia *small business owner, recreational facility executive*

North Fort Myers
Ranney, Mary Elizabeth *small business owner*

Orlando
Arlt, Devon Taylor *small business owner*
Smetanka, Sally S. *small business owner*

Panama City Beach
Jenkins, Frances Owens *retired small business owner*

Parrish
Corey, Kay Janis *small business owner, apparel designer, nurse*

Pembroke Pines
Feldman, Jacqueline *retired small business owner*
Schaefer, Bonnie (E. Bonnie Schaefer) *retail executive*
Schaefer, Marla L. *retail executive*

Saint Augustine
Bishop, Claire DeArment *small business owner, retired librarian*

Saint Petersburg
Despanza-Sprenger, Lynette Charlie *small business owner*
Thompson, Dayle Ann *small business owner, consultant*

Tampa
Eddy, Colette Ann *aerial photography studio owner, photographer*

Vero Beach
Murphy, Susan (Jane Murphy) *small business owner, real estate broker*

GEORGIA

Acworth
Hussey, Shelley *graphic design company owner*

Alpharetta
Greene, Melinda Jean *retail maintenance analyst*

Atlanta
Dayhoff, Diane *retail executive*
Landey, Faye Hite *small business owner*
Malcolm, Gloria J. *small business owner*
Parr, Sandra Hardy *small business owner*

Bainbridge
Palmer, Roslyn Wolffe *small business co-owner*

Columbus
Ballard, Laura Clay *small business owner*

Cumming
Pruitt-Streetman, Shirley Irene *small business owner*

Douglasville
Howard, Karen S. *retail executive*

Lagrange
Merrill, Judith Allyn *small business owner*

Marietta
Short-Mayfield, Patricia Ahlene *business owner*
Younker, Pamela Godfrey *business owner, consultant, accountant*

Statesboro
Bacon, Martha Brantley *small business owner*

IDAHO

Boise
Herbert, Kathy J. *retail executive*

ILLINOIS

Burr Ridge
Jones, Shirley Joyce *small business owner, fashion designer*

Charleston
Ball-Saret, Jayne Adams *small business owner*

Chicago
Deli, Anne Tynion *retail executive*
Hunt, Holly *small business owner*
Ziegler, Ann E. *retail executive*

Dixon
Hansen, Linda Marie *small business owner*

Evergreen Park
Arcieri, Sandy Lee *professional collector*

Hoffman Estates
Barraza, Lupe *retail executive*
Meads, Mindy *merchandising and design executive*

Hoopeston
Hicks, Carol Ann *small business owner, educator*

Kenilworth
Owens, Donna Lee *small business owner, consultant*

Kewanee
Grant, Linda Kay (Linda Kay Scott) *small business owner, sales executive*

Lake Forest
Stirling, Ellen Adair *retail executive*
Ysasi-Diaz, Gloria *wholesale distribution executive*

Melrose Park
Kloster, Carol Good *wholesale distribution executive*

Mount Vernon
Kendrick-Hopgood, Debra Jo *small business owner*

Northbrook
Warchol, Judith Marie *small business owner*

Plainfield
Bennett-Hammerberg, Janie Marie *small business owner, writer, consultant, administrative assistant*

Saint Charles
LaHood, Julie Ann *small business owner*

Westchester
Pudelek, Sherry Charlene *small business owner*

INDIANA

Columbus
Jorgensen, Virginia Dyer *antique dealer, museum consultant*

Evansville
Blesch, K(athy) Suzann *small business owner*

Fort Wayne
Cast, Anita Hursh *small business owner*

IOWA

Ankeny
Tomb, Carol E. *retail executive*

Davenport
Sievert, Mary Elizabeth *small business owner, retired secondary school educator*

Des Moines
Barnhart, Dorothy May Kohrs *small business owner*

Fairfield
Drees, Dorothy E. *small business owner, real estate manager*

Waverly
Ahrens, Mary Ann Painovich *small business owner*

West Union
Hansen, Ruth Lucille Hofer *business owner, consultant*

KANSAS

Auburn
Barr, Ginger *business owner, former state legislator*

Shawnee Mission
Mindlin, Susan W. *small business owner, educator*

Wichita
Moore, Peggy Sue *small business owner*

KENTUCKY

Lexington
Jones, Bonnie Quantrell *automobile dealer*

Owensboro
Thomas-Löwe, Christine L. *small business owner*

LOUISIANA

Baton Rouge
Kelley, Nanette Noland *business owner, entrepreneur*

Lafayette
Menutis, Ruth Ann *small business owner*

New Orleans
DeFelice, Frances Radosta *restaurateur*

MAINE

Cumberland
Jamison, Elizabeth Alease *drafting and design business owner*

Portland
Nectowak, Tillian *small business owner*

MARYLAND

Baltimore
Carper, Gertrude Esther *small business owner, real estate developer*
Yellin, Judith *small business owner*

Brandywine
Guiffre, Jean Ellen *shopping service company executive*
Johnson, Madge Richards *business owner, fundraiser, consultant*

Cockeysville Hunt Valley
Roeder Vaughan, Mimi *small business owner*

Forest Hill
Klein, Shirley Snyderman *retail executive*

Ocean City
Showell, Ann Lockhart *small business owner*

Potomac
Carper, Fern Gayle *small business owner, writer*

Salisbury
Loar, Sheila Rae *small business owner*

Silver Spring
Miller, Kendra Danette *art services business owner, consultant*
Wormack, Karen Elise *small business owner, poet*

MASSACHUSETTS

Canton
Bentas, Lily Haseotes *retail executive*

Framingham
Meyrowitz, Carol *retail executive*

Quincy
Conley, Olga L. *retail executive*

Taunton
Messaline, Wendy Jean *retail chain official*
Richardson, Marilyn Goff *small business owner, artist*

MICHIGAN

Ann Arbor
Mouzon, Margaret Walker *information services executive*

Armada
Price, Linda K. *small business owner*

Bath
Wildt, Janeth Kae *small business owner*

Battle Creek
Siano, Jonna Teen *small business owner*
Stuever, Anita Carol *small business owner, secondary school educator*

Bingham Farms
Krevsky, Margery Brown *talent agency executive*

Grand Rapids
DeLapa, Judith Anne *business owner*

Lansing
Stanaway, Loretta Susan *small business owner*

Okemos
Sliker, Shirley J. Brocker *bookseller*

Oscoda
Shackleton, Mary Jane *small business owner*

Portage
Dobler, Janis Dolores *small business owner*

Southfield
Primo, Joan Erwina *retail and real estate consulting business owner*

Troy
Austin, Karen *retail executive*
Elder, Irma *retail executive*

MINNESOTA

Eden Prairie
Knous, Pamela K. *wholesale distribution executive*

Edina
Emmerich, Karol Denise *foundation executive, daylily hybridizer, former retail executive*

Minneapolis
Ahlers, Linda L. *retail executive*
Gralnek, Minda *retail executive*
Logan-Hudson, Veryle *retail executive, realtor*

MISSISSIPPI

Greenwood
Jones, Carolyn Ellis *retired employment agency owner*

MISSOURI

Creve Coeur
Kemper, Christina *small business owner, respiratory therapist, elementary school educator*

Independence
Lundy, Sadie Allen *small business owner*

Joplin
Logsdon, Cindy Ann *small business owner*

Kansas City
Baker, Sharlynn Ruth *livery and limousine service owner*
Jimenez, Bettie Eileen *retired small business owner*
Minkoff, Jill S. *small business owner, educator, entrepreneur*
Olson, Elizabeth Ann *small business owner*

Overland
Clark, Maxine *retail executive*

Saint Louis
Bean, Joan Nona *merchant, consultant*
Novak, Camille *small business owner, consultant*
Rudd, Susan *retail executive*

Unionville
Stottlemyre, Donna Mae *retired small business owner*

MONTANA

Libby
Comeau, Tracy Lynne *small business owner, tax specialist*

NEBRASKA

Lincoln
Rawley, Ann Keyser *small business owner, picture framer*

Omaha
Cappellano, Rosemarie Zaccone *small business owner*

NEVADA

Baker
Koyle, Denys Marie *motel and restaurant executive*

Las Vegas
Vilardo, Carole *retired small business owner, research association administrator*

Wellington
Compston, Marion F. *small business owner*

NEW HAMPSHIRE

Campton
Benton, Geraldine Ann *preschool owner, director*

Concord
Sprague, Marcia Scovel *small business owner*

NEW JERSEY

Avalon
Johnson, Adele Cunningham *small business owner*

East Orange
Teetsell, Janice Marie Newman *business owner, lawyer*

Edison
Kijowski, Rosemary Joan *small business owner, retired music educator*

Hoboken
Capotorto, Rosette *small business owner, printing company executive, writer*

Leonia
Luhrs, Joyce Ann *business owner, consultant, communications and management consultant, writer*

Montclair
Murphy, Betty Jagoda *small business owner*

Newark
Ausley, Geneva Gardner *cosmetologist, foundation executive*

North Brunswick
Shaw, Roslyn Lee *small business owner, retired elementary school educator*

Park Ridge
Ciannella, Joeen Moore *small business owner*

Princeton
Campbell, Mildred Corum *business owner, nurse*

Ship Bottom
Clark, Bonnie A. *small business owner, real estate agent*

Vineland
Middleton, Denise *restaurant owner, real estate agent, educator*

Wayne
Brockett, Francesca L. *retail executive*
Derby, Deborah *retail executive*

NEW MEXICO

Clovis
Brown, Linda Currene *small business executive*

Elephant Butte
Anton, Carol J. *small business owner, writer*

Las Cruces
Arnett, Rita Ann *business executive*

Santa Fe
Caplan, Jessica Marie *small business owner, artist*

Taos
Winslow, Bette Killingsworth *dance studio owner*

NEW YORK

Bellport
Regalmuto, Nancy Marie *small business owner, consultant*

East Setauket
Kefalas, Jessie Ae *visual merchandiser, artist*

New York
Campagnolo, Ann-Casey *retail executive*
Castagna, Vanessa J. *retail executive*
Connors, Cornelia Kathleen *marketing services company executive*
Friedman, Rachelle *music retail executive*
Hughes, Julie *casting director, owner*
Jeanbart-Lorenzotti, Eva *retail executive*
Karp, Roberta Schuhalter *retail executive, lawyer*
Klein, Nancy Lynn *fine jewelry company owner, consultant*
Lazarus, Adrienne *retail executive*
Mello, Dawn *retail executive*
Michelson, Gertrude Geraldine *retired retail executive*
Noce, Donna *retail executive*
Norell, Judith Regina *small business owner, musician, political administrator*
Obler, Geri *small business owner, artist, educator*
Randel, Jane Ann *retail executive*
Safro, Millicent *small business owner, decorative arts scholar, writer*
Toulantis, Marie J. *retail executive*
Vander Heyden, Marsha Ann *business owner*
Washburn, Joan Thomas *small business owner*

Red Hook
Rovigo, Connie Brigitta *jewelry and fine arts retailer*

Rensselaerville
Hanson, Peg *gemstone dealer, psychic, graphic designer, writer*

Riverhead
Carpenter, Angie M. *small business owner, editor, county legislator*

Sag Harbor
Barry, Nada Davies *retail business owner*

Sands Point
Cohen, Ida Bogin (Mrs. Savin Cohen) *import/export company executive*

Skaneateles
Filkins, Susan Esther *small business owner*

Tannersville
Byrne, Patricia Curran *small business owner*

Tarrytown
Amenta, Caroline *small business owner*

NORTH CAROLINA

Carthage
Manning, Patricia Anne *small business owner*

Charlotte
Gambrell, Sarah Belk *retail executive*
Graham, Sylvia Angelenia *wholesale distribution executive, retail buyer*

Greenville
Tripp, Linda A. Lynn *small business owner*

Wilkesboro
Anderson, Theresa A. *retail executive*

NORTH DAKOTA

Bismarck
McCallum, Janet Ann Anderson *retired hardware store owner*

OHIO

Ashland
Finnerty, Madeline Frances *consulting firm owner*

Avon Lake
Parke, M(argaret) Jean *retired business owner, editor*

Bainbridge
Brizius, Janice Jane *producer, owner*

Beachwood
Fufuka, Natika Njeri Yaa *retail executive*

Bexley
Unverferth, Barbara Patten *small business owner*

Centerburg
Comstock-Jones, Janis Lou *business owner, consultant*

Chesterland
Aster, Ruth Marie Rhydderch *business owner*

Cincinnati
Hoguet, Karen M. *retail executive*
Sewell, Phyllis Shapiro *retail chain executive*

Cleveland
Fugo, Denise Marie *small business executive*

Columbus
Hailey, V. Ann *retail executive*
Hollis-Allbritton, Cheryl Dawn *retail paper supply store executive*
Holman-Rao, Marie *retail executive*
Holtz, Diane *retail executive*
Prieto, Emily J. *small business owner, consultant*
Turney, Sharon Jester *retail executive*

Fairlawn
Brubaker, Karen Sue *small business owner*

Pickerington
Callander, Kay Eileen Paisley *business owner, retired education educator, writer*

Reynoldsburg
Neal, Diane L. *retail executive*
Nichols, Grace A. *retail executive*

Toledo
Grundish, Lee Anne *small business owner, writer*

Youngstown
Catoline-Ackerman, Pauline Dessie *small business owner*

OKLAHOMA

Chelsea
Geyer, Kathy Van Ness *retailer*

Newcastle
Howeth, Lynda Carol *small business owner*

Oklahoma City
Gilmore, Joan Elizabeth *small business owner, newspaper columnist*

OREGON

Ashland
Titus, Karen J. *small business owner*

Beaverton
DeBerry, Donna *retail executive*

Eugene
Gillespie, Penny Hannig *business owner*

Forest Grove
Fuiten, Helen Lorraine *small business owner*

Salem
Robertson, Marian Ella (Marian Ella Hall) *small business owner, handwriting analyst*
Winters, Jackie F. *small business owner, foundation administrator*

PENNSYLVANIA

Bala Cynwyd
Armani, Aida Mary *small business owner*

Camp Hill
Sammons, Mary F. *retail executive*

Charleroi
Strauser, Carol Ann *small business owner*

Hatfield
Reast, Deborah Stanek *small business owner*

Johnstown
Borkow, Mary P. *small business owner, consultant*

Lewistown
Wimsatt, Anne Mosher *retail bookstore owner*

Mercer
DaCosta, Caroline Lee *small business owner*

Mount Bethel
LaRussa, Luann *small business owner*

Philadelphia
Payne, Jamila *retail executive, entrepreneur*

Silverdale
Carney, Shannon Maureen *small business owner, educator*

State College
Johnson, Ruth *small business owner*

Upper Black Eddy
McIntyre, Linnea Andren *small business owner*

Villanova
Vander Veer, Suzanne *aupair business executive*

RHODE ISLAND

North Kingstown
Kilguss, Elsie Schaich *small business owner, educator*

Providence
Killeen, Johanne *small business owner*

SOUTH CAROLINA

Hilton Head Island
Davis, Mary Martha (Marty Davis) *small business owner, consultant*

Isle Of Palms
McKinley, Debra Lynn McKinney *small business owner, dog show judge, real estate agent, artist*

Mount Pleasant
Falkowski, Brenda Lisle *retail buyer, director*

TENNESSEE

Collierville
Hays, Louise Stovall *retail fashion executive*

Hermitage
Reid, Donna Joyce *small business owner*

Johnson City
Sell, Joan Isobel *mobile home company owner*

Lafayette
Crowder, Bonnie Walton *small business owner, composer*

Nashville
Latendresse, Chessy Nakamoto *small business owner*

TEXAS

Beaumont
Alter, Shirley Jacobs *jewelry store owner*

Bedford
Newell, Karin Barnes *small business owner*

Brenham
Lubbock, Mildred Marcelle (Midge Lubbock) *former small business owner*

Carrollton
Yarborough, Judith Ann *bookstore owner, librarian, academic administrator*

Carthage
Cooke, Walta Pippen *automobile dealership owner*

Dallas
Augur, Marilyn Hussman *distribution executive*

El Paso
Korth, Charlotte Williams *retail executive*
Miller, Deane Guynes *salon and cosmetic studio owner*

Euless
Gibson, Karen Yvette *small business owner*

Fort Worth
Brister, Gloria Nugent *small business owner, elementary school educator*
Sitterly, Connie S. *small business owner, writer, management consultant*
Thompson, Sue Wanda *small business owner*
West, Sylvia Wandell *small business owner, director, educator, researcher*

Houston
Gaucher, Jane Montgomery *retail executive*
Nesbitt, DeEtte DuPree *small business owner, investor*
Wike, D. Elaine *small business owner*

Hutto
Sanders, Sarah Lynne *small business owner, director*

Irving
Burton, Betsey (Mary Elizabeth Burton) *retail executive*

Jasper
Nolen, Darlene Elizabeth *small business owner*

Muleshoe
Logsdon, Judith Kay *merchandiser, small business owner, apparel designer*

Plano
Samford, Karen Elaine *small business owner, consultant*
West, Catherine G. *retail executive*

Powell
Emerson, Harriett Anne *small business owner*

San Antonio
Condrill, Jo Ellaresa *freelance/self-employed small business owner, writer, consultant*
Jary, Mary Canales *business owner*
Keck, Judith Marie Burke *business owner, retired career officer*
Williams, Docia Schultz *small business owner*

Snyder
Gray, Donna Lea *small business owner*

Vernon
Mikkelsen, Barbara Berry *retired retail executive, rancher*

Weatherford
Pyle, Carol Lynn Horsley *small business owner, educational association administrator*

UTAH

Salt Lake City
Fields, Debbi (Debra Fields Rose) *cookie franchise executive*

VERMONT

Colchester
Lawton, Lorilee Ann *small business owner, accountant*

Putney
Loring, Honey *small business owner*

VIRGINIA

Fairfax
Solomon, Ellen Joan *business owner, consultant*

Falls Church
Fink, Cathy DeVito *small business owner*

Newport News
Williams, Cynthia Ann *small business owner, pediatrics nurse, writer*

Purcellville
Taylor, Carolyn Roberts *small business owner, chef*

Richmond
Austin-Stephens, Ann-Marie *retail executive*
Casini, Jane Sloan *wholesale distribution executive*
Dias, Fiona P. *retail executive*

Upperville
Powell Gebhard, Joy Lee (Bok Sin Lee) *small business owner*

Woodbridge
Austin, Sandra J. *small business owner*

WASHINGTON

Bellingham
Hendricks, Marilyn Louise *small business owner*

Camano Island
Petrakis, Julia Ward *small business owner*

Everett
Olsen-Estie, Jeanne Lindell *golf course owner*

Graham
Christensen, Doris Ann *antique dealer, researcher, writer*

Monroe
Kirwan, Katharyn Grace (Mrs. Gerald Bourke Kirwan Jr.) *retired small business owner*

Seattle
Leale, Olivia Mason *small business owner, import marketing executive*

Silverdale
Balcomb, Mary Nelson *small business owner*

Spokane
Chamberlain, Barbara Kaye *small business owner, communications executive*

Woodway
Kent, Aimee Bernice Petersen *small business owner, interior designer, landscape architect, artist*

Yakima
Newland, Ruth Laura *small business owner*

WEST VIRGINIA

Fairmont
Martin, Evelyn G. *small business owner*

Martinsburg
Ayers, Anne Louise *small business owner, consultant, counselor*

WISCONSIN

Beaver Dam
Brandenburg, Annabel June *retired small business owner*

Delafield
Welsh, Christine Marie *small business owner, dance educator*

La Crosse
Oswalt, Sally Hundt *small business owner*

Madison
Lucas, Patricia Whittlinger *small business owner*

Mequon
Kopfmann, Beverly Jean *small business owner*

Peshtigo
Prudhomme, Shirley Mae *small business owner*

Stoughton
Winter, Shawne Nanisdilda *small business owner*

Warrens
Potter, June Anita *small business owner*

WYOMING

Jackson
Law, Clarene Alta *small business owner, retired state legislator*

CANADA

ONTARIO

Ottawa
Wendling, Louise *wholesale company executive*

ADDRESS UNPUBLISHED

Artl, Karen Ann *business owner, author*
Babrowski, Claire Harbeck *retail executive*
Barrett, Judith Ann *salon owner*
Bernstein, Ellen *business owner*
Binder, Madeline Dotti *retail executive*
Bird, Patricia Coleen *business owner*
Blagden, Susan Lowndes *retired small business owner*
Blizard, Marjorie Claire *small business owner*
Boberg, Laron Capbarat *importer, retailer*
Bowe, Mary Ann *small business owner, art educator*
Brabec, Rosemary Jean *retail executive*
Busch, Joyce Ida *small business owner*
Carlson-Rukavina, Patricia Ann *small business owner*
Castro, Teresa Jacira *small business owner*
Claus, Carol Jean *small business owner*
Connolly, Violette M. *small business owner*
Corwin, Vera-Anne Versfelt *small business owner, consultant*
Cothren, Evangeline (Mrs. J.C.) *retail store owner*
Cox, Joy Dean *small business owner*
Crombie, Pamela Gasparin *restaurant and commercial property owner*
Cummings, Edith Jean *small business owner*
Delaney, Marion Patricia *retail executive*
Demou, Doris Beck *small business owner, civic leader*
Deschamp, Gloria J. *retail liquor store owner*
deVille, Vicki Lynne *jewelry manufacturer, commercial real estate broker*
DeVivo, Ange *retired small business owner*
Dunbar, Shirley Eugenia-Doris *small business owner, writer*
Dunkins, Betty *small business owner, publishing executive*
Dusenbury, Ruth Ellen Cole *business owner*
Dyer, Arlene Thelma *retail company owner*
Edwards, Patricia Burr *small business owner, consultant*
Ellis, Patricia Weathers *retired small business owner, computer technician*
Eyring, Maxine Louise *small business owner, esthetician*
Farrigan, Julia Ann *retired small business owner, educator*
Feinberg, Glenda Joyce *retail executive*
Follit, Evelyn V. *former retail executive*
Foster, Verna Lavonne *small business owner*
Franzetti, Lillian Angelina *former automobile dealership owner*
Glassman, Judith Dale *chocolate company owner, realtor*
Goldberg, Nancy G. *business owner, community volunteer*
Goldstein, Joyce Esersky *restaurant owner*
Goodman, Gail Busman *small business owner*
Grantham, Joyce Carol *small business owner, music educator*
Gray, Deborah Mary *wine importer*
Gust, Anne Baldwin *former retail apparel company executive*
Guzman, Carole L. *small business owner*
Hach, Phila Rawlings *small business owner, writer*
Hackett, Molly Lynn *small business owner, consultant*
Hawkins, Barbara Jane *small business owner, writer*
Healy, Margaret Mary *retail marketing executive*
Heard, Barbara Muse *business owner*
Hild, Heidi *small business owner*
Huntress, Betty Ann *retired small business owner, retired secondary school educator*
Hyland, Virginia Ling *small business owner*
Jaeger, Ellen Louise *small business owner*
Johnson, Dolores Estelle *retired small business owner*
Kipper, Barbara Levy *wholesale distribution executive*
Kretzschmar, Angelina Genzer *small business owner, paralegal*
LaPorta, Sara *retail executive*
Lilly, Elizabeth Giles *small business owner*
Love, Margaret Marks *business owner*
Lowry, Marilyn Jean *horticultural retail company executive*
Masten, Jacqueline Gwendolyn *small business owner*
McCall, Susan Elizabeth *small business owner*
McGraw, Lavinia Morgan *retired retail executive*
Medaglia, Elizabeth Ellen *small business owner*
Melanson, Susan Chapman *small business owner*
Ming, Jenny J. *former retail executive*
Molinari, Ana Maria *salon owner*
Mortenson, Janice Gayle Mills *business owner, accountant*
Moy, Audrey *retired retail buyer*
Nemiroff, Maxine Celia *small business owner, art historian*
O'Donnell Rich, Dorothy Juanita *small business owner*
Palmer, Gracious Anne *small business owner*
Pham, Lara Bach-Vien *small business owner*
Phillips, Kathleen Gay *small business owner*
Portnoy, Lynn Ann *fashion retailer*
Ramsey, Lucie Avra *small business owner, consultant*
Redican, Lois D. *small business owner*
Roberts, Toni *small business owner, jewelry designer*
Rogaczewski, Sherrie Reece *small business owner, singer*
Rohner, Bonnie-Jean *small business owner, computer scientist, consultant*
Shackelford, Nancy Kay *retail executive*
Simms, Maria Kay *small business owner, writer, artist*
Singh, DeAnn Coates *small business owner, artist, educator*
Snodgrass, Lynn *small business owner, former state legislator*
Starr-Wilson, Carol Ann *small business owner, retired researcher and genealogist*
Szczublewski, Wendy Sue *small business owner, musician, freelance/self-employed writer*
Thayer, Martha Ann *small business owner*
Thibideau, Regina *retail executive, social worker*
Thompson, Mary Koleta *small business owner, not-for-profit developer*
Topolewski-Green, Mary Jo Therese *small business owner*
Tudor, Brenda S. *retail company executive*
Turner, Natalie A. *retired consultant*
Vandenburg, Kathy Helen *small business owner*
Vander Naald Egenes, Joan Elizabeth *retired small business owner, educator*
Wagner, Cheri J. *business owner*
Ward, Nina Gillson *jewelry store executive*
Williams, Leona Rae *small business owner, consultant*
Willingham, Mary Maxine *fashion retailer*
Yanda, Cathy L. *small business owner, counselor, illustrator*

INDUSTRY: TRANSPORTATION

UNITED STATES

ALASKA

Anchorage
Williams, Eleanor Joyce *retired government air traffic control specialist*

ARIZONA

Tucson
Mercker, Mary Alice *aviation school administrator*

ARKANSAS

Bella Vista
Jones, Jo Carol *pilot, educator*

CALIFORNIA

Newbury Park
Lindsey, Joanne M. *flight attendant, poet*

Oakland
Reynolds, Kathleen Diane Foy (KDF Reynolds) *transportation executive*

Pasadena
Kennard, Lydia H. *airport terminal executive*

San Francisco
Royer, Kathleen Rose *pilot*

San Jose
Stapleton, Beverly Cooper *aerospace executive*

San Mateo
Pileggi, Jennifer Wendy *transportation services executive*

Simi Valley
Eberhard-Neveaux, Christine *aviation executive, dispute resolution executive*

Torrance
Brown, Adriane M. *aerospace transportation executive*

CONNECTICUT

Noank
Leeds, Robin Leigh *transportation executive*

DELAWARE

Newark
McNeil, Sue *transportation system educator*

DISTRICT OF COLUMBIA

Washington
Carmody, Carol Jones *transportation executive, former federal agency administrator*

FLORIDA

Jacksonville
Crimmel, Cynthia Eileen *rail transportation executive*

Miami
Krissel, Susan Hinkle *transportation company executive*

Orlando
Kilbourne, Krystal Hewett *retired rail transportation executive*

West Palm Beach
Waters, Lisa Lyle *airport administrator, consultant*

GEORGIA

Atlanta
Bridges, Shirley Walton *air transportation executive*
Glover, Lisa Marie *transportation executive, consultant*
Thoms, Jannet *rapid transit executive*

Savannah
Murray, Mary A. *transportation executive*

ILLINOIS

Chicago
Andolino, Rosemarie S. *airport terminal executive*
Apelbaum, Phyllis L. *delivery messenger service executive*
Koellner, Laurette *aerospace transportation executive*

Lake Forest
Krasnewich, Kathryn *water transportation executive*

INDIANA

Lebanon
Geisler, Kay *transportation executive*

KENTUCKY

Louisville
Carranza, Jovita *delivery service executive*

LOUISIANA

New Orleans
Chetta, Holly Ann *transportation executive*

MARYLAND

Bethesda
Maguire, Joanne M. *aerospace transportation executive*

MASSACHUSETTS

Belmont
Baddour, Anne Bridge *pilot*

MINNESOTA

Saint Paul
Nylander, Patricia Marie *pilot*

NEVADA

Nellis Afb
Malachowski, Nicole *pilot*

NEW JERSEY

Mullica Hill
Rose, Carol Ann *retired air transportation executive*

Newark
Baer, Susan M. *airport executive*

NEW YORK

Delhi
Townsend, Sue Joyce *retired air traffic controller*

Jamaica
Feldman, Arlene Butler *aviation industry executive*

Lindenhurst
Boltz, Mary Ann *aerospace materials company executive, travel company executive*

New York
Moss, Sara E. *delivery service executive, lawyer*
Zabrocky, Lois K. *energy transportation executive*

Oyster Bay
Smith, Pamela Rosevear *air transportation executive*

OHIO

Painesville
Luhta, Caroline Naumann *airport manager, flight educator*

TENNESSEE

Chattanooga
Pate, Lisa M. *transportation services executive, lawyer*

Memphis
Aaholm, Sherry A. *delivery service executive*
Price, Hollister Anne Cawein *air transportation executive, interior designer, consultant*
Richards, Christine P. *transportation services executive*

Morristown
Johnson, Evelyn Bryan *airport terminal executive*

Nashville
Seddon, Margaret Rhea *retired astronaut, physician, researcher*

TEXAS

Dallas
Barrett, Colleen Crotty *air transportation executive*
Wright, Laura L. *air transportation executive*

Fort Worth
Oliver, Susan M. *air transportation executive*

Horseshoe Bay
Sommer, Alicia Pine *flight attendant, performing company executive*
Strang, Sandra Lee *airline official*

Houston
Baker, Ellen Shulman *astronaut, physician*

Higginbotham, Joan E. *astronaut*
Hire, Kathryn P. (Kay) *astronaut, military officer*
Ivins, Marcia S. *astronaut*
Lawrence, Wendy B. *astronaut*
Melroy, Pamela Ann *astronaut*
Morgan, Barbara R. *astronaut*
Mukai, Chiaki *astronaut*
Nowak, Lisa M. *astronaut, military officer*
Ochoa, Ellen *astronaut*
Stefanyshyn-Piper, Heidemarie M. *astronaut*
Whitson, Peggy Annette *astronaut, biochemist*
Williams, Sunita L. *astronaut*
Wilson, Stephanie D. *astronaut*

UTAH

Salt Lake City
Courtney-Wilds, Noreen *air transportation executive*

VIRGINIA

Arlington
Beier, Anita P. *air transportation executive*
Binkowski, Sylvia Julia *water transportation executive, consultant*

Hampton
Daniels, Cindy Lou *aerospace transportation executive*

Vienna
Beyer, Barbara Lynn *transportation executive, consultant*

WASHINGTON

Seattle
Strombom, Cathy Jean *transportation planner, consultant*
Tunnell, Clida Diane *air transportation specialist*

Tacoma
Pribble, Elizabeth J. *retired airline administrator*

ADDRESS UNPUBLISHED

Collins, Eileen Marie *astronaut*
Escarra, Vicki B. *retired airline company executive*
Ferguson McGinnis, Kathryn Joan (Kathy Ferguson McGinnis) *flight attendant*
Hahn, Virginia Lynn *reservations agent*
Howell, Saralee Fisher *retired pilot*
Johnson, Linda Arlene *transportation executive*
Mitchell, Pamela Ann *airline pilot*
Purvis, Rebecca C. *transportation executive*
Savitz, Maxine Lazarus *aerospace transportation executive*
Schaupp, Joan Pomprowitz *trucking executive, writer*
Stienmier, Saundra Kay Young *aviation educator*
Warner, Emily Hanrahan Howell *retired pilot, writer*

INDUSTRY: UTILITIES, ENERGY, RESOURCES

UNITED STATES

ARIZONA

Sierra Vista
Gignac, Judith Ann *retired utilities executive, land developer*

Tucson
Bryant, Marian Alanna *electric company consultant*

CALIFORNIA

Del Mar
Gray-Bussard, Dolly H. *energy company executive*

Elk Grove
Romano, Sheila June *telecommunications industry professional, writer, artist*

Los Angeles
Reyes, Susana Marie *utilities executive, environmentalist*

Rosemead
Collins, Jodi M. *utilities executive*
Featherstone, Diane L. *utilities executive*
Parsky, Barbara *utilities executive*
Ryder, Beverly *utilities executive*
Yazdi, Mahvash *utilities executive*

San Jose
Bodensteiner, Lisa M. *utilities executive, lawyer*
Curtis, Ann B. *utilities executive*
Tabbut, Loreen M. *power industry executive*

San Ramon
Yarrington, Patricia *oil industry executive*
Zygocki, Rhonda I. *oil industry executive*

COLORADO

Centennial
Haskell, Cheryl Mona *telecommunications industry executive*

Denver
Kruger, Paula *telecommunications industry executive*
Pollard, Marilyn Bergkamp *retired utility company executive*

CONNECTICUT

Fairfield
Cassidy, Katherine *energy executive*

Stratford
Sahagian, Lucille Bedrosian *gasoline company executive*

DISTRICT OF COLUMBIA

Washington
King, Gwendolyn S. *retired utility company executive, retired federal official*
Miller, Susan M. *telecommunications industry executive*

FLORIDA

Jacksonville
Schlette, Sharon Elizabeth *utility company executive*

Orlando
Gouvellis, Mary C. *utilities executive*

Parkland
Garcia, Laura Catherine *utilities executive*

GEORGIA

Atlanta
Dowling, Kathy *telecommunications industry executive*
Fuller, S(heri) Marce *energy executive*
Reynolds, Paula Rosput *energy executive*

HAWAII

Honolulu
Lau, Constance H. (Connnie Lau) *electric power industry executive*

ILLINOIS

Bloomington
Beeler, Charlotte Jean *oil and supply company executive, interior design business executive*

Chicago
Hightman, Carrie J. *telecommunications industry executive, lawyer*
Strobel, Pamela B. *energy executive*

Naperville
Burken, Ruth Marie *utilities executive*

INDIANA

Indianapolis
Koch, Linda Brown *utility administrator*

KANSAS

Overland Park
Strandjord, M. Jeannine *telecommunications industry executive*
Walker, Kathryn A. *telecommunications industry executive*

KENTUCKY

Glasgow
Duvo, Mechelle Louise *oil company executive, consultant*

LOUISIANA

New Orleans
Taylor, Phyllis Miller *energy executive*

MARYLAND

Baltimore
Chagnoni, Kathleen *energy executive*
Goldberg, Linda *utilities executive, professional society administrator*

Sykesville
Perry, Nancy Trotter *retired telecommunications company executive*

MASSACHUSETTS

Westborough
Bok, Joan Toland *utilities executive*

MICHIGAN

Detroit
Ellyn, Lynne *energy executive*

NEVADA

Reno
Brennan, Susan Mallick *utilities executive*

Winnemucca
Hesse, Martha O. *gas industry executive*

NEW HAMPSHIRE

Warner
Wingfield, Susan *energy executive*

NEW JERSEY

Bedminster
Flaherty, Kathleen Ruth *telecommunications industry executive*

Morristown
Martine, Cathy *telecommunications industry executive*

Murray Hill
Christy, Cindy *telecommunications industry executive*
Davidson, Janet G. *telecommunications industry executive*

New Providence
Russo, Patricia F. *telecommunications company executive*
Spector, Magaly *telecommunications industry executive*

Randolph
Rathore, Uma Pandey *utilities executive*

NEW MEXICO

Albuquerque
Finley, Susie Quanstrom *energy executive, retired elementary school educator*

NEW YORK

Bayside
Burton, Barbara Anne *plumbing and heating company executive*

New York
Bardin, Mary Beth *telecommunications company executive*
Boden, Katherine L. *utilities executive*
Freilich, Joan Sherman *utilities executive*
Kelly, Anastasia D. (Stasia Kelly) *telecommunications industry executive, lawyer*
Loren, Pamela *telecommunications executive*
Ruesterholz, Virginia P. *telecommunications industry executive*
Swittenberg, Michelle Minus *telecommunications industry executive*
Toben, Doreen A. *telecommunications industry executive*
Webster, Catherine T. *telecommunications industry executive*
Zoffer, Rachelle *telecommunications industry executive*

Rochester
VanderLinden, Camilla Denice Dunn *telecommunications industry executive*

Syracuse
Kerr, Darlene Dixon *electric power company executive*

NORTH CAROLINA

Charlotte
Shaw, Ruth G. *energy company executive*

Mount Olive
Johnson, Josephine Powell *power and light company district manager*

OHIO

Columbus
Koeppel, Holly Keller *electric power industry executive*
Tomasky, Susan *electric power industry executive*

PENNSYLVANIA

Philadelphia
Fretz, Deborah McDermott *oil industry executive*
Mulé, Ann C. *oil industry executive*

Presto
Moeller, Audrey Carolyn *retired energy company executive, retired corporate secretary*

TEXAS

Dallas
Harless, Katherine J. *telecommunications industry executive*

Gainesville
McCormack, Lowell Ray *oil industry executive, corporate financial executive, consultant*

Houston
Bartling, Phyllis McGinness *oil company executive*
Campbell, Eileen M. *oil industry executive*
Knickel, Carin S. *oil industry executive*
Kupiec, Suzanne L. *utilities executive*
Mitcham, Carla J. *utilities executive*

Irving
Cavanaugh, Lucille J. *oil industry executive*

Midland
Grover, Rosalind Redfern *oil and gas company executive*

San Antonio
Bagin, Katherine *telecommunications industry executive*
Brown, Mary Rose *energy executive*
Pawel, Nancy Emma Ray *oil industry executive, educator, artist*
Titzman, Donna M. *energy executive*
Wiskocil, Angiolina *telecommunications industry executive*

VIRGINIA

Arlington
Harker, Victoria D. *electric power industry executive*

Ashburn
Bishop, Carol *oil industry executive*

Richmond
Alewine, Betty *retired telecommunications executive*

CANADA

ONTARIO

Toronto
Clark, Maura J. *oil and gas industry executive*

ENGLAND

London
Carroll, Cynthia B. *mining executive*

NETHERLANDS

The Hague
Cook, Linda Z. *utilities executive*
Hodge, Susan *oil industry executive*

ADDRESS UNPUBLISHED

Adams, Valencia I. *telecommunications industry executive*
Bernard, Betsy J. *former telecommunications industry executive*
Blackman, Ghita Waucheta *natural energy consultant*
Brewer, Lynn *energy executive*
Clemons, Julie Payne *telephone company manager*
Coffin, Bertha Louise *retired telecommunications industry executive*
Dunn, Rebecca M. *telecommunications industry executive*
Ford, Judith Ann Tudor *retired natural gas distribution company executive*
Funderburg, Jan *telecommunications industry executive*
Greene, Margaret H. *telecommunications industry executive*
Halloran, Kathleen L. *retired gas industry executive, accountant*
Hughes, Jennifer *utilities executive, photographer*
Lambert, Christina *telecommunications executive*
Lee, Donna A. *telecommunications industry executive*
Mills, Gloria Adams *energy executive, consultant*
Pierce, Lisa Margaret *telecommunications industry executive, marketing professional, educator*
Quirk, Kathleen L. *mining executive*
Sammartino Frese, Jennifer M. *telecommunications industry executive*
Sullivan, Kathryn Meara *telecommunications industry executive*
Wentworth, Lynn A. *telecommunications industry executive*
Wessner, Deborah Marie *telecommunications industry executive, consultant*

INFORMATION TECHNOLOGY

See also SCIENCE: MATHEMATICS AND COMPUTER SCIENCE

UNITED STATES

ARIZONA

Tucson
Karson, Catherine June *systems administrator*

CALIFORNIA

Irvine
Tsao, Janie *information technology executive*

Menlo Park
Steiger, Bettie Alexander *information industry specialist*

Moffett Field
Jackson, Lenore *computer technician*
Jarmann, Janet *systems administrator, systems analyst*

Mountain View
Baker, Mitchell *computer software development foundation administrator*
Brown, Shona *information technology executive*
Cassidy, Sukhinder Singh *information technology executive*
Lucas, Catherine *biotechnology company executive*
Mayer, Marissa Ann *information technology executive*
Rivera, Miriam *information technology executive, lawyer*
Sandberg, Sheryl *information technology executive*
Singh, Sangita *information technology and marketing executive*

Newport Beach
Allen, Karen Alfstad *information technology executive*

Palo Alto
Denzel, Nora *information technology executive*
Greene, Diane *information technology executive*

Redwood City
Catz, Safra *computer software company executive*
Davidson, Mary Ann *information technology executive*
Minton, Jennifer *information technology executive*
Smith, Nancy L. *information technology executive*

Sacramento
Doyel, Cindy M. *information technology specialist*

San Diego
Jaworski, Lisa *information technology executive*

San Francisco
Pure, Pamela J. *information technology executive*
Trott, Mena *application developer*

San Mateo
Infante, Beatriz V. *information technology executive*

Santa Ana
Salem, Karen E. *information technology executive*

Santa Clara
Dai, Weili *information technology executive*
Peterson, Marissa *information technology executive*

Sunnyvale
Perdikou, Kim *information technology executive*

COLORADO

Boulder
Kenney, Belinda Jill Forseman *information technology executive*

Colorado Springs
Coulter, Carolyn Kay *information technology executive*

Denver
Heppler, Robin Lee *project manager*

CONNECTICUT

Fairfield
Fash, Victoria R. *business executive*

New Britain
Margiotta, Mary-Lou Ann *application developer*

Stamford
Perna, Janet *application developer*
Wilderotter, Maggie (Mary Agnes Wilderotter) *software company executive, former cable television executive*

DISTRICT OF COLUMBIA

Washington
Dale, Adrianne Marie *information technology executive, consultant*
McCaleb, Margaret Anne Sheehan *application developer*
McGervey, Teresa Ann *technical information specialist*
Wertheim, Mitzi Mallina *information technology executive*

FLORIDA

Gainesville
Lucas, Michelle Denise *information technology manager*

Miami
Clemence, Cheryl Lynn *systems administrator*

New Port Richey
Cessna, Janice Lynn *systems administrator, information technology manager*

Saint Petersburg
Metzger, Kathleen Ann *computer systems specialist*

Tamarac
Marged, Judith Michele *network technician, educator*

Venice
Kleinlein, Kathy Lynn *training and development executive*

GEORGIA

Alpharetta
Herbig, Joan E. *information technology executive*
Neff, Dianah L. *information technology executive*

Atlanta
Miller, Sue *information technology executive*
Norman, Elaine Mitchell *information technology executive*
Powers, Susan J. *information technology executive*

Marietta
Guentner, Gail Marie *software engineer*

Norcross
Mangum, Mylle Bell *information technology executive*

Savannah
Palanca, Terilyn *software industry analyst*

ILLINOIS

Abbott Park
Burke, Sandra E. *information technology executive*

Bethalto
Talbott, Janet K. *information technology executive*

Centralia
Davidson, Karen Sue *computer software designer*

Chicago
Drewry, June E. *information technology executive*
Garzolini, Judith A. *information technology manager*
Larson, Nancy Celeste *information technology manager*
Scott, Nancy L. *information technology manager, health facility administrator, consultant*

Oak Brook
Marcus, Carol A. *information technology manager*

Schaumburg
Morrison, Patricia B. *information technology executive*

Vernon Hills
Klein, Barbara A. *information technology executive*
Leahy, Christine A. *information technology executive*

INDIANA

Bloomington
Henson, Jane Elizabeth *information management professional, adult education educator*

Columbus
Farnsley, Gail *information technology executive*

Fort Wayne
Carroll, Betty Jean *retired application developer*

Indianapolis
Niederberger, Jane *information technology executive*

IOWA

Des Moines
Ellis, Mary Louise Helgeson *information technology company executive*

KENTUCKY

Lexington
Canales, Denise Niles *software company executive*

LOUISIANA

Baton Rouge
Stockwell, Mary Diamond *information technology manager*

MARYLAND

Baltimore
Gourley, Jacquelyn Elise *information technology manager, researcher*
Park, Mary Woodfill *information consultant, librarian, writer*

Cockeysville Hunt Valley
Worthington, Joan Marie *information technology executive*

Gaithersburg
Kemmerer, Sharon Jean *computer systems analyst*

Germantown
Brunett, Miranda Jo *systems administrator*

Rockville
MacArthur, Diana Taylor *advanced technology executive*
Solomon, Deborah *application developer, educator, lawyer*

MASSACHUSETTS

Boston
Lane, Kathy S. *information technology executive, consumer products company executive*
Masi, Dale A. *project director, social sciences educator, research and development company executive*

Cambridge
Cooper, Mary Campbell *information services executive*

Wakefield
Singleton, Shirley *software development executive*

Waltham
Heystee, Susan *information technology executive*
O'Donnell, Rhonda *software company executive*

MICHIGAN

Auburn Hills
Suravajjala, Mamatha *information technology manager*
Young, Stacy A. *information technology manager*

Dearborn
McKeage, Alice Jane *computer programmer*

Detroit
Kruse, Ronia *information technology executive*

Kalamazoo
Morris, Martha Josephine *information services administrator*

Southfield
Wheeland, Joyce A. *information technology executive*

MINNESOTA

Excelsior
Henke, Janice Carine *educational software developer, marketing professional*

Minneapolis
Marinello, Kathryn V. *information technology executive*

Waite Park
Prins, LaVonne Kay *programmer analyst*

MISSOURI

Chesterfield
Morrison, Ann Hess *systems administrator*

Kansas City
Thompson, Mary Elizabeth *application developer*

Saint Louis
Elliott, Susan Spoehrer *information technology executive*

MONTANA

Bozeman
VanDyken, Nancy A. *information technology executive, web site designer*

NEBRASKA

Omaha
Dufner, Donna Kane *management information systems, project management educator*

NEVADA

Reno
Mullarkey, Maureen T. *game company executive*
Ragavan, Anpalaki Jeyabalasinkham *software developer, researcher*

NEW HAMPSHIRE

Weare
White, Karen Ruth Jones *information systems executive*

NEW JERSEY

Mountain Lakes
Shand, Kimberly *information technology consultant company executive*

Murray Hill
Bruch, Ruth E. *information technology executive*

Neshanic Station
Castellon, Christine New *information systems specialist, real estate agent*

New Providence
Hackenson, Elizabeth *information technology executive, telecommunications industry executive*

Newark
Nash, Alicia *application developer, physicist*

Pompton Plains
Guida, Pat *information broker, literature chemist*

Raritan
Weaver, Sylvia *information technology executive*

Rochelle Park
Olzerowicz, Sharon *information technology executive*

Roseland
Graham, Patricia *information technology executive*

NEW MEXICO

Albuquerque
Alexis, Tracy L. *project manager, project specialist, information technology manager, small business owner*

NEW YORK

Armonk
Villar, Maria *information technology executive*

Brooklyn
Gilmore, Jennifer A.W. *computer specialist, educator*

Buffalo
Overton, Nicole Yolanda *program analyst*

Greenwich
Edsforth, Maureen McGill *instructional technology specialist*

Hawthorne
Yoffa, Ellen J. *information technology executive*

Ithaca
Howell, Debra Lynne *information technology executive*

Massapequa
Batt, Alyse Schwartz *application developer*

Melville
Webber, Pamela D. *information technology executive*

New York
Boyer, Aurelia G. *information technology executive*
Caponnetto, Marianne *information technology executive*
Chang, Mona Mei-Hsuan *computer programmer, analyst*
Iqbal, Syma U. *information technology executive*
Kozik, Susan S. *information technology executive*
Ross, Karen *information technology executive*

Poughkeepsie
Jacobi, Kerry Lee *information systems specialist*

Rochester
VanGelder, Kim E. *information technology executive*

Somers
Sanford, Linda S. *information technology executive*

Webster
Cusick, Patricia A. *information technology executive*

West Harrison
Wieck, Marie L. *information technology executive*

White Plains
Rometty, Ginny (Virginia M. Rometty) *information technology executive*

NORTH CAROLINA

Cary
Gordon, Suzanne *information technology executive*

OHIO

Cincinnati
Laney, Sandra Eileen *information technology executive*

Cleveland
McCormick, Maureen Olivea *computer systems programmer*

Columbus
Roeder, Rebecca Emily *software engineer*
Taylor, Celianna Isley *information systems specialist*

Dayton
Grant, Colleen *information systems specialist*

Dublin
Davids, Jody R. *information technology executive*

Marion
Rowe, Lisa Dawn *computer programmer/analyst, computer consultant*

Van Wert
Huffman, Laura Christine *computer programmer, educator*

OKLAHOMA

Ada
Baker, Judith Ann *retired computer technician*

PENNSYLVANIA

Clarks Summit
Weiss, Tammy Lee *information technology manager*

Gladwyne
Stick, Alyce Cushing *systems administrator, consultant*

King Of Prussia
Swank, Annette Marie *software designer*

Philadelphia
Wilms, Anne M. *information technology executive*
Woods, Deirdre *information technology executive*

Swarthmore
Kaufman, Antoinette Dolores *information technology manager*

SOUTH CAROLINA

Camden
Koestner, Carol Ann *information technology manager, consultant*

Charleston
Nordquist, Sonya Lynn *information technology executive*

Columbia
Hudson, Carolyn Brauer *application developer, educator*

Hopkins
Daniels, Carla Lee *information technology specialist*

TEXAS

Dallas
Kruse, Ann Gray *computer programmer*

Fort Hood
Anderson, Nanci Louise *computer analyst*

Hempstead
Propst, Catherine Lamb *biotechnology company executive, pharmaceutical company executive*

Houston
Wejman, Janet P. *information technology executive, air transportation executive*

Plano
Ansari, Anousheh *digital home and multimedia management technology company executive, first female civilian space traveler*
Gordon, Storrow Moss *information technology executive, lawyer*

San Antonio
Hyman, Betty Harpole *technology executive*

Sugar Land
Forbes, Sharon Elizabeth *software engineer*

The Woodlands
Welch, Kathy Jane *information technology executive*

Waco
Cisneros, Deborah Kathleen *technology educator*

VIRGINIA

Alexandria
Davis, Ruth Margaret (Mrs. Benjamin Franklin Lohr) *information technology executive*
Nodeen, Janey Price *information technology executive*

Falls Church
Gosnell, Nanci Little *information technology executive, nurse*

Herndon
Lovejoy, Kristin Gallina *information technology executive*

Mc Lean
Berdine, Linda *information technology executive*
Neumann, Eva *information technology executive*

Richmond
McDermid, Margaret E. *information technology executive, engineer*

Rosslyn
Agosta, Susan Marie *web site designer*

WASHINGTON

Bellevue
Skredsvig, Janice B. *information technology executive*

Federal Way
Mersereau, Susan *information systems company executive, data processing executive*

Seattle
McConney, Mary E. *information technology executive*

WISCONSIN

Conrath
Bentley, Linda Diane *application developer, artist*

De Pere
Molnar, Kathleen Kay *management information systems educator*

Hales Corners
Holmes, Leigh Ann *web technician*

Milwaukee
Kraut, Joanne Lenora *computer programmer, analyst*

WYOMING

Casper
Davis, Lois Ann *computer specialist, educator*

CANADA

NOVA SCOTIA

Halifax
LeValliant, Debbie *information technology executive*

AUSTRALIA

Altona
Daniel-Dreyfus, Susan B. Russe *information technology executive*

ADDRESS UNPUBLISHED

Aguilar, Miriam Rebecca *technology project manager*
Alexander, Nancy A. *information technology manager, consultant*
Allen, Renee Annette *application developer*
Anania, Andrea *information technology executive*
Bauer, Barbara *information technology executive*
Becker, Karla Lynn *information technology manager, consultant*
Behnke, Doleen *computer and environmental specialist, consultant*
Bluitt, Karen *information technology executive*
Bramhall, Debra A. *information technology manager, consultant*
Bratzler, Mary Kathryn *web services manager*
Creswell, Dorothy Anne *computer consultant*
Culleeney, Maureen Ann *information technology executive, educator*
Davis, Suzanne Spiegel *retired information specialist*
Dawson, Martha Bromley *retired software developer*
Donohue, Anne Emlen *software engineer*
Downing, Sarah Linn *application developer*
Elkins, Jeni L. McIntosh *systems support specialist*
Etheridge, Diana Carol *internet business executive*
Fuller, Cassandra Miller *applications specialist*
Gibbs, Johnie Elizabeth *information technology manager, educator, consultant*
Hariton, Lorraine Jill *information technology executive*
Heck, Debra Upchurch *information technology, procurement professional*
Hughes-Tebo, Jacqueline Emma *regional coordinator*
Jones, Gwenyth Ellen *information technology executive*
Kelley, Mary Elizabeth (Mary LaGrone) *information technology specialist*
Kessler, Jean S. *clinical data manager*
Kramp, Suzan Marie *systems programmer*
LaPierre, Eileen Marie *technical services manager*
Larson, Janice Talley *application developer*
Latimer, Helen *retired information resource manager, writer, researcher*
Levinson, Marina *information technology executive*
Levy, Leslie Ann *application developer*
Maclean, Rhonda *information technology executive*
Maisner, Suzanne *technology consultant, educator*
Maruoka, Jo Ann Elizabeth *retired information systems manager*
McCaffrey, Cindy *information technology executive*
McCoy, Diann L. *information technology acquisition executive*
Morgan, M. Jane *computer systems consultant*
Musser, Cherri M. *information technology executive*
Nelson, Sandra E. *information technology executive*
Nicols, Angela C. *software engineer, consultant*
Nolff, Susan D. *web site designer, small business owner*
Papathomas, Georgia Nikolakopoulou *technology executive*
Pariag, Haimwattie Ramkistodas *information management administrator*
Pearson, Harriet D. *information technology executive*
Porch, Kathy M. *information technology executive, educator*
Raley, Beverly Spickelmier *systems administrator, educator, writer*
Roberts, Marie Dyer *retired computer systems specialist*
Russell, Clara B. *information technology manager*
Sheppard, Gayle Teresa *software executive*
Slater, Lori Annette *project manager*
Spence, Dianna Jeannene *software engineer, educator*
Staley, Mindi K. *information technology manager, educator*
Terrell, Karenann *information technology executive*
Thompson, Joyce Lurine *retired information systems specialist*
Trapani, Gina *web programmer, writer*
Visocki, Nancy Gayle *information services consultant*
Weigle, Peggy *information technology executive*
Westrich, Kate Ann *web site editor, writer*
Wilhelmi, Cynthia Joy *information technology manager, information scientist, consultant*
Wilkins, Rita Denise *product development, research and technology director*
Young, Virginia McLain *information technology consulting executive*

INTERNET *See* INFORMATION TECHNOLOGY

LAW: JUDICIAL ADMINISTRATION

UNITED STATES

ALABAMA

Birmingham
Privett, Caryl Penney *judge*

Mobile
Granade, Callie Virginia Smith *federal judge*

Montgomery
Brown, Jean Williams *former state supreme court justice*
McPherson, Vanzetta Penn *magistrate judge*
Smith, Patricia M. (Patti Smith) *state supreme court justice*
Stuart, Jacquelyn L. *state supreme court justice*

ALASKA

Anchorage
Fabe, Dana Anderson *state supreme court justice*

ARIZONA

Phoenix
Berch, Rebecca White *state supreme court justice, lawyer*
Hicks, Bethany Gribben *judge, lawyer*
McGregor, Ruth Van Roekel *state supreme court justice*
Schroeder, Mary Murphy *federal judge*
Silver, Roslyn Olson *federal judge*

ARKANSAS

Little Rock
Dickey, Betty C. *state supreme court justice*
Imber, Annabelle Clinton *state supreme court justice*
Wright, Susan Webber *federal judge*

CALIFORNIA

Los Angeles
Collins, Audrey B. *judge*
Fischer, Dale Susan *judge*
Manella, Nora Margaret *judge*
Marshall, Consuelo Bland *federal judge*
Zelon, Laurie Dee *judge*

Oakland
Wilken, Claudia *judge*

Pasadena
Hall, Cynthia Holcomb *federal judge*
Nelson, Dorothy Wright (Mrs. James F. Nelson) *federal judge*
Rymer, Pamela Ann *federal judge*
Wardlaw, Kim A. McLane *federal judge*

Sacramento
Callahan, Consuelo Maria *federal judge*

San Diego
Aaron, Cynthia G. *judge*
Adler, Louise DeCarl *judge*
Gonzalez, Irma Elsa *federal judge*
McKeown, Mary Margaret *federal judge*
Porter, Louisa S. *federal judge*

San Francisco
Berzon, Marsha S. *federal judge*
Corrigan, Carol A. *state supreme court justice*
Ikuta, Sandra Segal *federal judge*
Kennard, Joyce L. *state supreme court justice*
Werdegar, Kathryn Mickle *state supreme court justice*

Santa Ana
Moore, Eileen C. *judge, prosecutor*
Stotler, Alicemarie Huber *federal judge*

Ventura
White, Colleen Toy *judge*

Woodland Hills
Mund, Geraldine *judge*

COLORADO

Denver
Coan, Patricia A. *judge*
Krieger, Marcia Smith *federal judge*
Mullarkey, Mary J. *state supreme court chief justice*
Rice, Nancy E. *state supreme court justice*

CONNECTICUT

Hartford
Katz, Joette *state supreme court justice*
Martinez, Donna F. *federal judge*
Peters, Ellen Ash *retired judge*
Vertefeuille, Christine Siegrist *state supreme court justice*

New Haven
Arterton, Janet Bond *federal judge*
Burns, Ellen Bree *federal judge*

DELAWARE

Wilmington
Berger, Carolyn *state supreme court justice*
Robinson, Sue L(ewis) *federal judge*
Roth, Jane Richards *federal judge*

DISTRICT OF COLUMBIA

Washington
Bacon, Sylvia *judge, law educator*
Bartnoff, Judith *judge*
Blackburne-Rigsby, Anna *judge*
Brown, Janice Rogers *federal judge, former state supreme court justice*
Chiechi, Carolyn Phyllis *federal judge*
Cohen, Mary Ann *federal judge*
Crawford, Susan Jean *federal judge*
Ginsburg, Ruth Bader (Joan Ruth Bader Ginsburg) *United States Supreme Court Justice*
Green, Joyce Hens *federal judge*
Henderson, Karen LeCraft *federal judge*
Hewitt, Emily Clark *federal judge, minister*
Horn, Marian Blank *federal judge*
Kessler, Gladys *federal judge*
Kollar-Kotelly, Colleen *federal judge*
Kramer, Noël Anketell *judge*
Kroupa, Diane Lynn *federal judge*
Mack, Julia Cooper *retired judge*
Marvel, L. Paige *federal judge*
Miller, Christine Odell Cook *federal judge*
Moore, Kimberly Ann *federal judge, law educator*
Newman, Pauline *federal judge*
Prost, Sharon *federal judge*
Queen, Evelyn E. Crawford *retired judge*
Rogers, Judith Ann Wilson *federal judge*
Rothstein, Barbara Jacobs *federal judge*
Ruiz, Vanessa *judge*
Schoelen, Mary Jeanette *federal judge*
Sweeney, Margaret Mary *federal judge*
Thompson, Phyllis D. *judge, lawyer*
Wagner, Annice McBryde *judge*
Wald, Patricia McGowan *retired federal judge*
Williams, Mary Ellen Coster *federal judge*

FLORIDA

Miami
Barkett, Rosemary *federal judge*
Cooke, Marcia Gail *federal judge, lawyer*
Lando, Maxine Cohen *circuit judge*
Miller Udell, Bronwyn *judge*
Seitz, Patricia Ann *judge*

Orlando
Fawsett, Patricia Combs *federal judge*
Thorpe, Janet Claire *judge*

Tallahassee
Pariente, Barbara J. *state supreme court justice*
Quince, Peggy A. *judge*

Tampa
Jenkins, Elizabeth Ann *federal judge*

GEORGIA

Atlanta
Bihary, Joyce *federal judge*
Carnes, Julie Elizabeth *judge*
Evans, Orinda D. *federal judge*
Hull, Frank Mays *federal judge*
Hunstein, Carol *state supreme court justice*
Kravitch, Phyllis A. *federal judge*
Sears, Leah Ward *state supreme court chief justice*

HAWAII

Honolulu
Gillmor, Helen *federal judge*
Nakayama, Paula Aiko *state supreme court justice*

IDAHO

Boise
Trout, Linda Copple *state supreme court justice*

ILLINOIS

Chicago
Bucklo, Elaine Edwards *United States district court judge*
Burke, Anne M. *state supreme court justice*
Conlon, Suzanne B. *federal judge*
Garman, Rita B. *state supreme court justice*
Gillis, Susan Fox *judge*
Gottschall, Joan B. *judge*
Lefkow, Joan Humphrey *federal judge*
O'Malley, Denise Margaret *judge*
Pallmeyer, Rebecca Ruth *judge*
Rovner, Ilana Kara Diamond *federal judge*
Sonderby, Susan Pierson *federal judge*
Williams, Ann Claire *federal judge*
Wood, Diane Pamela *federal judge*

Edwardsville
Crowder, Barbara Lynn *judge*

INDIANA

Indianapolis
Barker, Sarah Evans *judge*
Carlisle, Sheila A. *judge*

New Albany
Orth, Susan Lynn *judge*

IOWA

Des Moines
Bremer, Celeste F. *judge*
Ternus, Marsha K. *state supreme court chief justice*

KANSAS

Kansas City
Vratil, Kathryn Hoefer *federal judge*

Lawrence
Briscoe, Mary Beck *federal judge*
Tacha, Deanell Reece *federal judge*

Topeka
Beier, Carol Ann *state supreme court justice*
Luckert, Marla Jo *state supreme court justice*
Marquardt, Christel Elisabeth *judge*
McFarland, Kay Eleanor *state supreme court chief justice*
Robinson, Julie Ann *judge*

KENTUCKY

Lexington
Coffman, Jennifer Burcham *judge*
Varellas, Sandra Motte *judge*

LOUISIANA

Baton Rouge
Noland, Christine A. *judge*

New Orleans
Berrigan, Helen Ginger *federal judge*
Clement, Edith Brown *federal judge*
Johnson, Bernette Joshua *state supreme court justice*
Kimball, Catherine D. *state supreme court justice*
Knoll, Jeannette Theriot *state supreme court justice*

MAINE

Portland
Calkins, Susan W. *state supreme court justice*
Glassman, Caroline Duby *state supreme court justice*
Saufley, Leigh Ingalls *state supreme court chief justice*

MARYLAND

Annapolis
Battaglia, Lynne Ann *judge*
Nolan, Theresa A. *retired judge, mediator, arbitrator*

Baltimore
Blake, Catherine C. *judge*
Gauvey, Susan Kathryn *judge*
Motz, Diana Gribbon *federal judge*

Rockville
Raker, Irma S. *judge*

MASSACHUSETTS

Boston
Bowler, Marianne Bianca *federal judge*
Cowin, Judith Arnold *state supreme court justice*
Dreben, Raya Spiegel *judge*
Feeney, Joan N. *judge*
Lynch, Sandra Lea *federal judge*
Marshall, Margaret Hilary *state supreme court chief justice*
Saris, Patti Barbara *federal judge*
Sosman, Martha B. *state supreme court justice*
Zobel, Rya Weickert *federal judge*

MICHIGAN

Detroit
Corrigan, Maura Denise *state supreme court justice*
Edmunds, Nancy Garlock *federal judge*
Kelly, Marilyn *state supreme court justice*
Kennedy, Cornelia Groefsema *federal judge*
Morgan, Virginia Mattison *judge*
Taylor, Anna Diggs *federal judge*

Grand Rapids
Stevenson, Jo Ann C. *federal bankruptcy judge*

Traverse City
Weaver, Elizabeth A. *state supreme court justice*

MINNESOTA

Lake Elmo
Tomljanovich, Esther M. *retired judge*

Minneapolis
Montgomery, Ann D. *federal judge, educator*
Murphy, Diana E. *federal judge*

Saint Paul
Lancaster, Joan Ericksen *judge*
Meyer, Helen M. *state supreme court justice*

MISSISSIPPI

Jackson
Cobb, Kay Beevers *state supreme court justice, retired state senator*
Owens, Denise *judge*

MISSOURI

High Ridge
Karll, Jo Ann *retired judge, lawyer*

Jefferson City
Russell, Mary Rhodes *state supreme court justice*
Stith, Laura Denvir *state supreme court justice*

Saint Louis
Hamilton, Jean Constance *judge*
Jackson, Carol E. *federal judge*
Medler, Mary Ann L. *federal judge*

MONTANA

Helena
Cotter, Patricia O'Brien *state supreme court justice*
Gray, Karla Marie *state supreme court justice*

NEBRASKA

Lincoln
Miller-Lerman, Lindsey *state supreme court justice*

NEVADA

Carson City
Agosti, Deborah Ann *retired senior justice*

Las Vegas
Becker, Nancy Anne *state supreme court justice*
Rawlinson, Johnnie Blakeney *federal judge*

Owyhee
Shane, Virginia *tribal court judge, lawyer*

NEW JERSEY

Jersey City
Curran, Barbara A. *superior court judge*

Newark
Barry, Maryanne Trump *federal judge*
Hochberg, Faith S. *US district court judge*

Trenton
Cooper, Mary Little *judge*
Hoens, Helen E. *state supreme court justice*
LaVecchia, Jaynee *state supreme court justice*
Long, Virginia *state supreme court justice*
Thompson, Anne Elise *federal judge*

NEW MEXICO

Albuquerque
Baca, Theresa M. *judge*

Santa Fe
Maes, Petra Jimenez *state supreme court justice*
Minzner, Pamela Burgy *state supreme court justice*
Vázquez, Martha Alicia *federal judge*
Yalman, Ann *judge, lawyer*

NEW YORK

Albany
Kaye, Judith Smith *state appeals court judge*
Read, Susan Phillips *state appeals court judge*

Brooklyn
Amon, Carol Bagley *federal judge*
Azrack, Joan M. *judge*
Gershon, Nina *federal judge*
Go, Marilyn Dolan *federal judge*
Irizarry, Dora L. *federal judge*
Mann, Roanne L. *federal judge*
Matsumoto, Kiyo A. *federal judge*
Pollak, Cheryl L. *federal judge*
Raggi, Reena *federal judge*
Ross, Allyne R. *federal judge*
Townes, Sandra L. *federal judge*

Central Islip
Cyganowski, Melanie L. *bankruptcy judge*
Eisenberg, Dorothy *federal judge*
Feuerstein, Sandra Jeanne *judge*
Lindsay, Arlene Rosario *federal judge*
Seybert, Joanna *federal judge*

New York
Barzilay, Judith Morgenstern *federal judge*
Batts, Deborah A. *federal judge*
Brozman, Tina L. *federal judge*
Cedarbaum, Miriam Goldman *federal judge*
Ciparick, Carmen Beauchamp *state appeals court judge*
Cote, Denise Louise *federal judge*
Freedman, Helen E. *judge*
Freeman, Debra *federal judge*
Jones, Barbara S. *federal judge*
Kearse, Amalya Lyle *federal judge*
Kram, Shirley Wohl *federal judge*
Marks, Leah Ruth *judge*
Nelson, Barbara Anne *judge*
O'Connor, Sandra Day *retired United States Supreme Court Justice*
Preska, Loretta A. *federal judge*
Restani, Jane A. *federal judge*
Ridgway, Delissa Anne *federal judge*
Santaella, Irma Vidal *retired state supreme court justice*
Scheindlin, Shira A. *federal judge*
Sotomayor, Sonia *federal judge*
Swain, Laura Taylor *federal judge*
Wood, Kimba M. *federal judge*

Riverhead
Molia, Denise F. *judge*

Slingerlands
Baker, Providence *judge*

Syracuse
Pooler, Rosemary S. *federal judge*

West Seneca
Siegel, Carolyn Augusta *judge, lawyer, social worker*

White Plains
McMahon, Colleen *federal judge*
Smith, Lisa Margaret *federal judge*

NORTH CAROLINA

Raleigh
Duncan, Allyson K. *federal judge*
McGee, Linda Mace *judge, lawyer*
Parker, Sarah Elizabeth *state supreme court chief justice*

Randleman
Jordan, Lillian B. *judge*

Statesville
Gullett, Julia Shuping *judge*

NORTH DAKOTA

Bismarck
Kapsner, Carol Ronning *state supreme court justice*
Maring, Mary Muehlen *state supreme court justice*

OHIO

Akron
Shea-Stonum, Marilyn *federal bankruptcy judge*

Cincinnati
Beckwith, Sandra Shank *federal judge*
Cook, Deborah L. *federal judge, former state supreme court justice*
Dlott, Susan Judy *judge, lawyer*

Cleveland
Aldrich, Ann *judge*
Burke, Lillian Walker *retired judge*
Moore, Karen Nelson *judge*
O'Malley, Kathleen M. *federal judge*
Wells, Lesley *federal judge*

Columbus
King, Norah McCann *federal judge*
Lanzinger, Judith Ann *state supreme court justice*
O'Connor, Maureen *state supreme court justice*
Resnick, Alice Robie *state supreme court justice*
Sellers, Barbara Jackson *federal judge*
Stratton, Evelyn Lundberg *state supreme court justice*

Lisbon
Dailey, Coleen Hall *magistrate*

Youngstown
Bond, Christina M. *judge*

OKLAHOMA

Oklahoma City
Cauthron, Robin J. *federal judge*
Kauger, Yvonne *state supreme court justice*
Miles-La Grange, Vicki *judge*

Tulsa
Seymour, Stephanie Kulp *federal judge*

OREGON

Portland
Graber, Susan P. *federal judge*
Rosenblum, Ellen F. *judge*
Stewart, Janice Mae *federal judge*

PENNSYLVANIA

Harrisburg
Rambo, Sylvia H. *federal judge*

Philadelphia
Angell, Mary Faith *federal magistrate judge*
Pratter, Gene E. K. *federal judge, lawyer*
Rendell, Marjorie O. *federal judge*
Shapiro, Norma Sondra Levy *federal judge*
Sigmund, Diane Weiss *judge*
Sloviter, Dolores Korman *federal judge*

Pittsburgh
Ambrose, Donetta W. *federal judge*
Conti, Joy Flowers *judge*
Fitzgerald, Judith Klaswick *federal judge*
Ross, Eunice Latshaw *retired judge*
Sensenich, Ila Jeanne *judge*

West Conshohocken
Newman, Sandra Schultz *state supreme court justice*

RHODE ISLAND

Providence
Goldberg, Maureen McKenna *state supreme court justice*
Lisi, Mary M. *federal judge*

SOUTH CAROLINA

Columbia
Toal, Jean Hoefer *state supreme court chief justice*

SOUTH DAKOTA

Pierre
Meierhenry, Judith Knittel *state supreme court justice*

Rapid City
Schreier, Karen Elizabeth *judge*

TENNESSEE

Greeneville
Parsons, Marcia Phillips *judge*

Memphis
Donald, Bernice B. *judge*
Gibbons, Julia Smith *federal judge*
Holder, Janice Marie *state supreme court justice*

Nashville
Daughtrey, Martha Craig *federal judge*
Trauger, Aleta Arthur *judge*

TEXAS

Amarillo
Robinson, Mary Lou *federal judge*

Austin
O'Neill, Harriet *state supreme court justice*
Owen, Priscilla Richman *federal judge, former state supreme court justice*
Williams, Mary Pearl *judge*

Corpus Christi
Jack, Janis Graham *judge*

Dallas
Boyle, Jane J. *federal judge, lawyer*
Lang-Miers, Elizabeth Ann *judge*

Houston
Atlas, Nancy Friedman *judge*
Brown, Karen Kennedy *judge*
Jones, Edith Hollan *federal judge*
King, Carolyn Dineen *federal judge*
Sondock, Ruby Kless *retired judge*

Tyler
Guthrie, Judith K. *federal judge*

Victoria
Weiser, Laura Ann *judge*

UTAH

Salt Lake City
Durham, Christine Meaders *state supreme court chief justice*
Parrish, Jill Niederhauser *state supreme court justice*

VERMONT

Montpelier
Johnson, Denise Reinka *state supreme court justice*
Skoglund, Marilyn *state supreme court justice*

VIRGINIA

Chesterfield
Davis, Bonnie Christell *judge*

Falls Church
Cooper, Jean Saralee *judge*

Richmond
Keenan, Barbara Milano *state supreme court justice*
Kinser, Cynthia D. *state supreme court justice*
Lacy, Elizabeth Bermingham *state supreme court justice*
Williams, Karen Johnson *federal judge*

WASHINGTON

Olympia
Bridge, Bobbe Jean *state supreme court justice*
Fairhurst, Mary E. *state supreme court justice*
Madsen, Barbara A. *state supreme court justice*
Owens, Susan *state supreme court justice*

Seattle
Dimmick, Carolyn Reaber *federal judge*
Fletcher, Betty Binns *federal judge*
Overstreet, Karen A. *federal bankruptcy judge*

Spokane
Imbrogno, Cynthia *judge*

WEST VIRGINIA

Charleston
Davis, Robin Jean *state supreme court chief justice*
Stanley, Mary Elizabeth *judge*

Clarksburg
Keeley, Irene Patricia Murphy *federal judge*

WISCONSIN

Madison
Abrahamson, Shirley Schlanger *state supreme court chief justice*
Bradley, Ann Walsh *state supreme court justice*
Crabb, Barbara Brandriff *federal judge*
Roggensack, Patience Drake *state supreme court justice*

Milwaukee
Kessler, Joan F. *judge, lawyer*
Sykes, Diane S. *federal judge, former state supreme court justice*

WYOMING

Cheyenne
Kite, Marilyn S. *state supreme court justice, lawyer*

TERRITORIES OF THE UNITED STATES

GUAM

Hagatna
Tydingco-Gatewood, Frances Marie *judge*
Weeks, Janet Healy *retired supreme court justice*

PUERTO RICO

San Juan
Fiol Matta, Liana *judge*
Rodriguez, Annabelle *judge, former attorney general*

CANADA

NOVA SCOTIA

Halifax
Glube, Constance Rachelle *retired judge*

ONTARIO

Ottawa
McLachlin, Beverley *Canadian supreme court chief justice*

ADDRESS UNPUBLISHED

Aboussie, Marilyn *retired judge*
Batchelder, Alice M. *federal judge*
Black, Susan Harrell *federal judge*
Blatz, Kathleen Anne *former state supreme court justice*
Brady, M. Jane (Muriel Jane Brady) *judge, former state attorney general*
Brown, L. Elizabeth *judge*
Buchanan, Theresa Carroll *judge*
Buchwald, Naomi Reice *federal judge*
Bush, Lynn Jeanne *federal judge*
Dal Santo, Diane *retired judge, writer, arbitrator, mediator*
Firestone, Nancy B. *federal judge*
Flanagan, Louise W. *federal judge*
Frye, Helen Jackson *federal judge*
Goldstein, Debra Holly *judge*
Gorence, Patricia Josetta *judge*
Grant, Isabella Horton *retired judge*
Harris, Dale Hutter *retired judge*
Jones, Phyllis Gene *judge*
Jordan, Michelle Denise *judge*
Krupansky, Blanche Ethel *retired judge*
Lynaugh, Barbara *judge*
Manglona, Ramona V. *judge, former attorney general*
March, Kathleen Patricia *judge*
McMorrow, Mary Ann Grohwin *retired state supreme court justice*
Neuman, Linda Kinney *retired state supreme court justice, lawyer*
Payne, Mary Libby *retired judge*
Pokras, Sheila Frances *retired judge*
Poritz, Deborah Tobias *retired state supreme court justice, former state attorney general*
Prather, Lenore Loving *former State Supreme Court Chief Justice*
Senechal, Alice R. *federal magistrate judge, lawyer*
Shearing, Miriam *retired state supreme court chief justice*
Smith, Fern M. *judge*
Spector, Rose *former state supreme court justice*
Stewart, Annette *judge*
Sypolt, Diane Gilbert *retired judge*

LAW: LAW PRACTICE AND ADMINISTRATION

UNITED STATES

ALABAMA

Birmingham
Corliss, Deane Kenworthy *lawyer*
Long, Deborah Joyce *lawyer*

Mobile
Rhodes, Deborah J. *prosecutor*

Montgomery
Campbell, Maria Bouchelle *lawyer, consultant*
Canary, Leura Garrett *prosecutor*

Tuscaloosa
Cook, Camille Wright *retired law educator*

Tuscumbia
Linville, Kimberly E. *lawyer*

ALASKA

Anchorage
Fortenberry, Nichole Audrey *paralegal, small business owner*
Foster, Rosemary Alice *lawyer, artist*
Grahame, Heather H. *lawyer*
Hughes, Mary Katherine *lawyer*

Bethel
Owen, Lauri J. *lawyer*

Fairbanks
Bodwell, Lori *lawyer*

ARIZONA

Bisbee
Moreno, Patricia Frazier *lawyer*

Phoenix
Grimwood, Helen Perry *lawyer*
Le, Viet V. *lawyer*
Loftin, Nancy Carol *lawyer, utilities executive*
McBride, Melanie Grace *lawyer*
McCormick, Kathryn Ellen *prosecutor*
Phanthourath, Anoma T. *lawyer*
Refo, Patricia Lee *lawyer*
Siegenthaler, Denise L. *lawyer*

Scottsdale
Betts, Janet Gniadek *lawyer*
Bullerdick, Kim H. *lawyer, petroleum executive*

Sun City
Keesling, Karen Ruth *lawyer*

Surprise
Fennelly, Jane Corey *lawyer*

Tempe
Dhillon, Janet L. *lawyer*

Tucson
Betteridge, Frances Carpenter *retired lawyer, mediator*
Froman, Sandra Sue *lawyer*
Jones, Ronnell Andersen *lawyer, educator*
Kuklin, Susan Beverly *law librarian, lawyer*
Rose, Carol Marguerite *law educator*
Samet, Dee-Dee *lawyer*
Simmons, Sarah R. *lawyer*
Spaeth, Jan Mills *jury consultant*
Treadwell-Rubin, Pamela A. *lawyer*
Wrae, Natasha *lawyer*

ARKANSAS

Benton
Krueger, Marlo Bush *retired lawyer*

Little Rock
Casey, Paula Jean *former prosecutor*
Cherry, Sandra Wilson *lawyer*
Greenwood, Sarah Elizabeth *lawyer*
Lemke, Judith A. *lawyer*
Stockburger, Jean Dawson *lawyer*
Witherspoon, Carolyn Brack *lawyer*

North Little Rock
Betty-Singleton, Charmaine Elizabeth *lawyer, military officer*

CALIFORNIA

Alameda
Johnson, Beverly J. *lawyer, congressman*

Arcadia
Abramson, Leslie Hope *lawyer*

Atascadero
Colamarino, Katrin Belenky *lawyer*

Bakersfield
Gong, Gloria Margaret *lawyer, pharmacist*

Berkeley
Arguedas, Cristina Claypoole *lawyer*
Ginger, Ann Fagan *lawyer*
Joseph, Anne M. *lawyer, law educator*
Kay, Herma Hill *law educator*
Meyer, Roberta *mediator, communication consultant*
Moran, Rachel *law educator*
Samuelson, Pamela Ann *law educator*

Beverly Hills
Amado, Honey Kessler *lawyer*
Brockovich-Ellis, Erin *legal researcher*
Kalawski, Eva *lawyer*
Kleiner, Madeleine A. *lawyer*
Opri, Debra A. *lawyer*

Bodega Bay
Sorensen, Linda *lawyer*

Burbank
Brandis, Bernardine *lawyer*
Wise, Helena Sunny *lawyer*

Carmichael
Betts, Barbara Lang *lawyer, real estate agent, rancher*

Costa Mesa
Caldwell, Courtney Lynn *lawyer, real estate consultant*
Grogan, Virginia S. *lawyer*
Marshall, Ellen Ruth *lawyer*
Scheuneman, Christine A. *lawyer*

Culver City
Weil, Leah *lawyer*

Davis
Bruch, Carol Sophie *law educator*

East Palo Alto
Dillon, Carol K. *lawyer*

El Segundo
Willis, Judy Ann *lawyer*

Emeryville
Bartels, Ursula Brennan *lawyer*

Encino
Smith, Selma Moidel *lawyer, composer*

Escondido
Godone-Maresca, Lillian *lawyer*

Glendale
Halaby, Noelle M. *lawyer*
Kendrick, Katherine *lawyer*

Huntington Beach
Garrels, Sherry Ann *lawyer*

Inverness
Ciani, Judith Elaine *retired lawyer*

Irvine
Crawford, Denise F. *lawyer*
Harpen, Shawn M. *lawyer*
Huang, Wendy Wan-Juoh *lawyer*
Keller, Jennifer L. *lawyer*
Lowe, Kathlene Winn *lawyer*
Narayan, Ash *lawyer*

La Jolla
Wilson, Bonnie Jean *lawyer, educator, investor*

Laguna Hills
Reinglass, Michelle Annette *lawyer*

Laguna Niguel
Tjandraswita, Maria C. Inawati *lawyer*

Long Beach
Helwick, Christine *lawyer*

Los Altos
Justice-Moore, Kathleen E. *lawyer*

Los Angeles
Abell, Nancy L. *lawyer*
Allred, Gloria Rachel *lawyer*
Aronoff, Vera *law librarian*
Azad, Susan Stott *lawyer*
Barrett, Jane Hayes *lawyer*
Beezy, Miriam Claire *lawyer*
Bendix, Helen Irene *lawyer*
Bertero, Karen E. *lawyer*
Blendell, Elizabeth A. *lawyer*
Blumberg, Grace Ganz *lawyer, educator*
Boras, Kim *lawyer*
Bryan, Karen Smith *lawyer*
Burke, Yvonne Watson Brathwaite (Mrs. William A. Burke) *lawyer*
Byrd, Christine Waterman Swent *lawyer*
Caruso, Joanne E. *lawyer*
Cate, Jan Harris *lawyer*
Chapman Holley, Shawn Snider *lawyer*
Cheung, Sheri T. *lawyer*
Christ, Roxanne E. *lawyer*
Chung, Christina *lawyer*
Cohen, Cynthia Marylyn *lawyer*
Cook, Melanie K. *lawyer*
Crenshaw, Kimberle Williams *law educator*
D'Angelo Melby, Donna Marie *lawyer*
Diaz, Maria G. *lawyer*
Dodd, Jan Eve *lawyer*
Drummy, Kathleen H. *lawyer*
Dudziak, Mary Louise *law educator*
Fenning, Lisa Hill *lawyer, mediator, retired judge*
Garrett, Elizabeth *law educator, academic administrator*
Graves, Anna Marie *lawyer*
Grode, Susan A. *lawyer*
Handler, Carole Enid *lawyer, city planner*
Harkness, Nancy P. *lawyer*
Hemminger, Pamela Lynn *lawyer*
Hoye, Maria Pilar *lawyer*
Hufstedler, Shirley Mount *lawyer, former federal judge*
Husar, Linda S. *lawyer*
Hyman, Ursula H. *lawyer*
Iredale, Nancy Louise *lawyer*
Jeffrey, Sheri *lawyer*
Johnstone, Kathryn I. *lawyer*
Jordan, Martha B. *lawyer*
Kanoff, Mary Ellen *lawyer*
Kessler, Joan Blumenstein *lawyer*
Keville, Terri Donna *lawyer*
Kim, Sabrina S. *lawyer*
Kirwan, Betty-Jane *lawyer*
Klinger, Marilyn Sydney *lawyer*
Lawler, Jean Marie *lawyer*
Lesser, Joan L. *lawyer*
Levenson, Laurie L. *law educator*
Lewis, Marjorie Ehrich *lawyer*
Marmorstein, Victoria E. *lawyer*
Marshall-Daniels, Meryl *mediator, executive coach*
Melby, Donna D. *lawyer*
Mersel, Marjorie Kathryn Pedersen *lawyer*
Meyer, Catherine Dieffenbach *lawyer*
Neely, Sally Schultz *lawyer*
Nobumoto, Karen S. *prosecutor*
Oh, Angela E. *lawyer*
Olsen, Frances Elisabeth *law educator, theorist*
Ordin, Andrea Sheridan *lawyer*
Palmer, Pamela S. *lawyer*
Perez, Edith R. *lawyer*
Peterson, Linda S. *lawyer*
Petroff, Laura R. *lawyer*
Phillips, Stacy D. *lawyer*
Porter, Verna Louise *lawyer*
Posner, Harriet S. *lawyer*
Pruetz, Adrian Mary *lawyer*
Raeder, Myrna Sharon *lawyer, educator*
Reeves, Barbara Ann *lawyer*
Reisman, Ellen Kelly *lawyer*
Ressler, Alison S. *lawyer*
Rice, Constance LaMay *lawyer*
Rodriguez, Denise Rios *lawyer*
Rotell, Cynthia A. *lawyer*
Ruhl, Mary B. *lawyer*
Rustand, Kay *lawyer*
Sanders, Kathryn A. *lawyer*
Saxe, Deborah Crandall *lawyer*
Shanks, Patricia L. *lawyer*
Sloan, Judy Beckner *law educator*
Starrett, Lucinda *lawyer*
Stein, Sheryl E. *lawyer*
Strickland, Julia B. *lawyer*
Title, Gail Migdal *lawyer*
Von Eschen, Lisa A. *lawyer*
Wasser, Laura Allison *lawyer*
Westhoff, Pamela Lynne *lawyer*
Yang, Debra Wong *lawyer, former prosecutor*
Young, Naomi *lawyer*
Youngblood, Juliette Carolina *lawyer*
Yu, Susan C. (Susan Chung-Mi Yu) *lawyer*

Menlo Park
Fisher, Ora T. *lawyer*
Hermle, Lynne C. *lawyer*

Monterey
Gaver, Frances Rouse *lawyer*

Mountain View
Fuller, Jennifer L. *lawyer*
Wildman, Iris J. *retired law librarian*

Newport Beach
Cano, Kristin Maria *lawyer*

Northridge
Runquist, Lisa A. *lawyer*

Oakland
Banke, Kathy M. *lawyer*
Davies, Colleen T. *lawyer*
Weaver, Pauline Anne *lawyer*

Oxnard
Sands, Velma Ahda *lawyer*

Palo Alto
Chang, Carmen *lawyer*
Fordis, Jean Burke *lawyer*
Frankle, Diane Holt *lawyer*
Kaile, Davina K. *lawyer*
Kosacz, Barbara A. *lawyer*
McCall, Jennifer Jordan *lawyer*
Monroy, Gladys H. *lawyer*
Park, Marina H. *lawyer*
Petkanics, Donna M. *lawyer*
Sterling St. John, Vicki Lynn *lawyer*
Summers, Debra S. *lawyer*
Walker, Ann Yvonne *lawyer*

Palos Verdes Estates
Brigden, Ann Schwartz *mediator, educator*

Pasadena
Mosher, Sally Ekenberg *lawyer, musician*

Pittsburg
Williscroft-Barcus, Beverly Ruth *retired lawyer*

Pleasanton
Fine, Marjorie Lynn *lawyer*

Portola Valley
Nycum, Susan Hubbell *lawyer*

Rancho Cordova
Hall-Barron, Deborah *lawyer*

Redwood City
Sullivan, Kathleen Marie *lawyer, educator, former dean*

Riverside
Carney, Jane W. *lawyer*
Lobb, Cynthia Jean Hocking *lawyer*

Sacramento
Shapiro, Lara Ruth *lawyer*
Smith, Judith A. *legal analyst*
Thiltgen, Christine *law educator*
Willis, Dawn Louise *legal assistant, small business owner*
Wong, Alice *lawyer*

San Clemente
Geyser, Lynne M. *lawyer, writer*

San Diego
Brierton, Cheryl Lynn *lawyer*
Brooks, Juanita Rose *lawyer*
Cohn, Marjorie F. *law educator, legal association administrator*
Cummins, Patricia Ann *lawyer, educator*
Dollarhide, Mary C. *lawyer*
Haile, Lisa A. *lawyer*
Kinsbruner Bush, Jennifer *lawyer*
Lam, Carol C. *prosecutor, lawyer*
McCoy, Lilys D. *lawyer*
Mebane, Julie S. *lawyer*
Morris, Sandra Joan *lawyer*
Mullins, Angela *lawyer*
Naughton, Pamela J. *lawyer*
Shippey, Sandra Lee *lawyer*

San Francisco
Alexis, Geraldine M. *lawyer*
Alioto, Angela Mia *lawyer*
Allecta, Julie *lawyer*
Auwers, Linda S. *lawyer*
Bailey-Wells, Deborah *lawyer*
Baysinger, Kara *lawyer*
Belaga, Debra S. *lawyer*
Brothers, Lynda Lee *lawyer*
Broyles, Deborah J. *lawyer*
Cabraser, Elizabeth Joan *lawyer*
Chun, A. Marisa *lawyer*
Chung, Amy Teresa *lawyer, property manager*
Coleman, Kathryn Anne *lawyer*
Collins, Mary Ann *lawyer*
Corash, Michèle B. *lawyer*
Cranston, Mary Bailey *lawyer*
Cregan, Nora C. *lawyer*
Dwyer, Carrie Elizabeth *lawyer*
Edmonson, Tracy K. *lawyer*
Edwards, Robin Morse *lawyer*
Garvey, Joanne Marie *lawyer*
Gibson, Virginia Lee *lawyer*
Gillette, Patricia K. *lawyer*
Hane, Laurie S. *lawyer*
Harris, Kamala D. *prosecutor*
Hewlett, Clothilde *lawyer*
Hurst, Annette L. *lawyer*
Johnson, Michelle L. *lawyer*
Knutzen, Martha Lorraine *lawyer*
Krane, Hilary K. *lawyer*
Krevans, Rachel *lawyer*
MacGowan, Eugenia *lawyer*
Mao, Dora *lawyer*
Miller, Ann G. *lawyer*
Paterson, Eva *legal association director, educator*
Pope, Marcia L. *lawyer*
Reed, Pamela J. *lawyer*
Richey, Mary Ellen *lawyer*
Sanger, Priya Seshachari *lawyer*
Schechter, Lori A. *lawyer*
Shanahan, Lauri M. *lawyer*
Soberon, Presentacion Zablan *state bar administrator*
Stewart, Terry *lawyer*
Story, Joan H. *lawyer*
Studley, Jamienne Shayne *lawyer, educator*
Sung, Audrey L. *lawyer*
Veaco, Kristina *lawyer*
Waltz, Judith A. *lawyer*
Weber, Paula M. *lawyer*
Welborn, Caryl Bartelman *lawyer*
White, Wilda L. *lawyer*
Williams, Linda C. *lawyer*
Winner, Sonya D. *lawyer*
Wirum, Andrea A. *lawyer*
Zeldin, Kim S. *lawyer*

San Jose
Cottle, Karen Olson *lawyer*
Gallo, Joan Rosenberg *lawyer*

San Rafael
Sterling, Marcia Kemp *lawyer*

Santa Ana
Storer, Maryruth *law librarian*

Santa Clara
Glancy, Dorothy Jean *lawyer, educator*

Sherman Oaks
Levin, Evanne Lynn *lawyer, educator*

Stanford
Alexander, Janet Cooper *law educator*
Babcock, Barbara Allen *lawyer, educator*
Fried, Barbara H. *law educator*
Hensler, Deborah Rosenfield *law educator*
Karlan, Pamela Susan *law educator*
Martinez, Jenny S. *lawyer*
Radin, Margaret Jane *law educator*
Rhode, Deborah Lynn *law educator*
Srikantiah, Jayashri *law educator*

Vista
Cannon, Kathleen *lawyer, educator*

COLORADO

Aurora
Seybert, Janet Rose *lawyer, military officer*

Boulder
Bintliff, Barbara Ann *law educator, library director*
Lacy, Mary T. (Mary Keenan) *prosecutor*

Colorado Springs
Swanson, Victoria Clare Heldman *lawyer*

Denver
Hammerman, Susan Frances Weissfeld *lawyer*
Hanna, Juliet Marie *lawyer*
Krendl, Cathy Stricklin *lawyer*
Mackey, Pamela Robillard *lawyer*
Mathis, Karen J. *lawyer, legal association administrator*
McDowell, Karen Ann *lawyer*
Wunnicke, Brooke *lawyer*

Englewood
Spencer, Margaret Gilliam *lawyer*

Lakewood
Lautigar, Linda L. *lawyer*
Meyer, Lynn Nix *lawyer*

Louisville
Raymond, Dorothy Gill *lawyer*

Snowmass Village
Tester-LaMar, Cynthia Coreyn *lawyer*

CONNECTICUT

Bloomfield
Stravalle-Schmidt, Ann Roberta *lawyer*

Bridgeport
Berman, Renee Caggiano *lawyer*

Danbury
Skolan-Logue, Amanda Nicole *lawyer, consultant*

Derby
McEvoy, Sharlene Ann *law educator*

Farmington
Comerford, Jane Deirdre *lawyer*

Hartford
Harkin, Ruth R. *lawyer*
Sullivan, Katherine McGurk *lawyer*
Valentine, Debra A. *lawyer*

New Britain
Pearl, Helen Zalkan *lawyer*

New Haven
Brilmayer, R. Lea *lawyer, educator*
Chua, Amy *law educator*
Cole, Elsa Kircher *lawyer*
Jolls, Christine Margaret *law educator*
Peters, Jean Koh *law educator*
Resnik, Judith *law educator*
Robinson, Dorothy K. *lawyer*
Rose-Ackerman, Susan *law and political economy educator*
Siegel, Reva *law educator*
Stith-Cabranes, Kate *law educator*

Stamford
Mayes, Michele Coleman *lawyer*
McDonald, Cassandra Burns *lawyer*
Staab, Diane D. *lawyer*
Weinstein, Ruth Joseph *lawyer*

Stratford
DiCicco, Margaret C. *lawyer*

Weston
Meyerson, Amy Lin *lawyer*

Westport
Heyman, Ronnie Feuerstein *lawyer*

DELAWARE

New Castle
Mullen, Regina Marie *lawyer*

Wilmington
Jolles, Janet K. Pilling *lawyer*
McIntyre, Megan D. *lawyer*
Meitner, Pamela *lawyer, educator*
Petrilli, Michelle Leslie *lawyer*
Winslow, Helen Littell *lawyer*

DISTRICT OF COLUMBIA

Washington
Abernathy, Kathleen Quinn *lawyer, former commissioner*
Abrecht, Mary Ellen Benson *lawyer*
Adams, Frances Grant, II, *lawyer*
Allen, Bertrand-Marc *lawyer*
Amron, Cory M. *lawyer*
Anderson, M. Jean *lawyer*
Archibald, Jeanne S. *lawyer*
Armen, Margaret Meis *lawyer*
Arnold, Deborah J. *lawyer*
Arnwine, Barbara Ruth *lawyer*
Auberger, Marcia A. *lawyer*
Ayres, Margaret M. *lawyer*
Bachrach, Eve Elizabeth *lawyer*
Bailey, Patricia Price *lawyer, former government official*
Baker, P. Jean *lawyer, mediator*
Barnett, Helaine M. *lawyer*
Barron, Myra Hymovich *lawyer*
Barshefsky, Charlene *lawyer, former diplomat*
Batts, Alicia J. *lawyer*
Baumann, Linda Adriene *lawyer*
Bear, Dinah *lawyer*
Bea Roberts, Barbara Ann *legal secretary*
Behan, Kathleen A. (Kitty Behan) *lawyer*
Beiro Farabow, Sara *lawyer*
Bello, Judith Hippler *lawyer, trade association administrator*
Benitez, Brigida *lawyer*
Berg, Gracia M. *lawyer*
Bergner, Jane Cohen *lawyer*
Bernabei, Lynne Ann *lawyer*
Bertram, Connie N. *lawyer*
Billauer, Barbara Pfeffer *lawyer, educator*
Birnbaum, S. Elizabeth *lawyer*
Blazek-White, Doris *lawyer*
Bloch, Susan Low *law educator*
Bondareff, Joan M. *lawyer, retired government agency administrator*
Born, Brooksley Elizabeth *retired lawyer*
Bosch, Michele C. *lawyer*
Bosco, Mary Beth *lawyer*
Brannan, Patricia A. *lawyer*
Bresnahan, Pamela Anne *lawyer, mediator, arbitrator*
Brooks, Sharon Diane *lawyer*
Brown, Barbara Berish *lawyer*
Brown Weiss, Edith *law educator*
Bruce, Carol Elder *lawyer*
Brueckner, Leslie A. *lawyer*
Buc, Nancy Lillian *lawyer*
Bumpus, Jeanne *lawyer*
Burke, Beverly J. *lawyer, utilities executive*
Burrous, Beth A. *lawyer*
Bush, Karen Lee *lawyer*
Butcher, Karen A. *lawyer*
Butler, Mary K. *prosecutor*
Campbell, Nancy Duff *lawyer*
Caproni, Valerie E. *lawyer, federal agency administrator*
Carder-Thompson, Elizabeth B. *lawyer*
Carey, Sarah Collins *lawyer*
Carlisle, Linda Elizabeth *lawyer*
Carpenter, Sheila Jane *lawyer*
Cavalier, Gina M. *lawyer*
Cavendish, Elizabeth A. (Betsy Cavendish) *lawyer*
Charytan, Lynn R. *lawyer*
Christian, Betty Jo *lawyer*
Christian, Claudette Marie *lawyer*
Cinciotta, Linda Ann *lawyer*
Clayton, Carol A. *lawyer*
Coffield, Shirley Ann *lawyer, educator*
Colson, David A. *lawyer*
Corrigan, Dara A. *lawyer, former federal agency administrator*
Cowan, Joyce A. *lawyer*
Cox, M. Carolyn *lawyer*
Cross, Meredith B. *lawyer*
Crowley, Juanita A. *lawyer*
Crown, Michele Fleurette *lawyer*
Curtiss, Catherine *lawyer*
Dana, Jane T. *lawyer*
Daniels, Diana M. *lawyer, publishing executive*
Dargan, Catherine Janine *lawyer*
Darr, Carol C. *lawyer*
Deal, Jill B. *lawyer*
Deese, Pamela McCarthy *lawyer*
de Leon, Sylvia A. *lawyer*
Denny, Judith Ann *retired lawyer*
Dewey, Elizabeth R. *lawyer*
Doria, Marilyn L. *lawyer*
DuBelle, Molyneau *legal consultant*
Dwyer, Maureen Ellen *lawyer*
Ebert, Carey Dalton *lawyer*
Edlavitch, Susan T. *lawyer*
Efros, Ellen Ann *lawyer*
Elcano, Mary S. *lawyer*
Engh, Anna P. *lawyer*
Esserman, Susan Gayle *lawyer*
Fahmy Hudome, Randa *lawyer*
Fales, Lisa Jose *lawyer*
Farquhar, Michele C. *lawyer*
Feldman, Clarice Rochelle *lawyer*
Fenton, Kathryn Marie *lawyer*
Ferrell, Elizabeth Ann *lawyer*
Field, Andrea Bear *lawyer*
Fields, Wendy Lynn *lawyer*
Flannery, Ellen Joanne *lawyer*
Flowe, Carol Connor *lawyer*
Ford, Ann K. *lawyer*
Foscarinis, Maria *lawyer*
Foster, Hope S. *lawyer*
Gallozzi, Marialuisa S. *lawyer*
Garr, Sally D. *lawyer*
Gerber, Melanie K. *lawyer*
Gilfoyle, Nathalie Floyd Preston *lawyer*
Gillan, Kayla J. *lawyer*
Gilligan, Courtney *lawyer*
Gleason, Kathryn L. *lawyer*
Goldberg, Jolande Elisabeth *law librarian, lawyer*
Gonzalez, Cecelia *lawyer*
Gorelick, Jamie Shona *lawyer*
Gorman, Joyce J(ohanna) *lawyer*
Grainger, Amanda R. *lawyer*
Gray, Carolyn Doppelt *lawyer*
Greenberger, Marcia Devins *lawyer*
Griggs, Linda L. *lawyer*
Grossman, Joanne Barbara *lawyer*
Grunberg, Nancy R. *lawyer*
Haines, Martha Mahan *lawyer*
Harvey, Sheila McCafferty *lawyer*
Henderson, Frances J. *lawyer*
Hennessy, Ellen Anne *lawyer, financial analyst, educator*
Hills, Carla Anderson *lawyer, former secretary of housing and urban development*
Hobbs, Ann S. *lawyer*
Hollis, Sheila Slocum *lawyer*
Hollman, K. Hollyn *lawyer*
Howell, Beryl A. *lawyer*
Hughes, Elizabeth R. (Beth) *lawyer*
Hughes, Marija Matich *law librarian*
Jennings, Deborah E. *lawyer*
Jones, Erika Ziebarth *lawyer*
Katzen, Sally *lawyer, educator*
Kemnitz, D'Arcy *lawyer, gay lesbian association executive*
Kiko, Colleen Duffy *lawyer*
King, Patricia Ann *law educator*
Kiser, Chérie R. *lawyer*
Klee, Ann Renee *lawyer*
Knapp, Rosalind Ann *lawyer*
Kruger, Leondra R. *lawyer*
Kutler, Alison L. *lawyer*
Lamm, Carolyn Beth *lawyer*
Lardent, Esther Ferster *lawyer, consultant*
Latham, Patricia Horan *lawyer*
Latimer, Allie B. *retired lawyer*
Latimer, Katharine Ruth *lawyer*
Leiter, Amanda C. *lawyer*
Lew, Ginger *lawyer*
Lewis, Eleanor Roberts *lawyer*
Lichtenbaum, Greta L.H. *lawyer*
Lichtenstein, Elissa Charlene *legal association executive*
Little, Kathleen C. *lawyer*
Locklear, Arlinda Faye *lawyer*
Loepere, Carol Colborn *lawyer*
Lopatto, Mary A. *lawyer*
Lott, Cindy M. *lawyer*
Luque, Nancy *lawyer*
Lurensky, Marcia Adele *lawyer*
Luxton, Jane Charlotte *lawyer*
Lyons, Mona *lawyer*
Marlette, Cynthia *lawyer*
Mason, Rosanna Marie *lawyer*
Mays, Janice Ann *lawyer*
Mazzaferri, Katherine Aquino *lawyer, bar association executive*
McDavid, Janet Louise *lawyer*
McDowell, Barbara *lawyer*
McDowell, Heather L. *lawyer*
McGrath, Kathryn Bradley *lawyer*
McGuan, Kathleen H. *lawyer*
McGuirl, Marlene Dana Callis *law librarian, educator*
Medaglia, Mary-Elizabeth *lawyer*
Meers, Elizabeth Blossom *lawyer*
Meloy, Sybil Piskur *retired lawyer*
Mendoza, Julie C. *lawyer*
Menkel-Meadow, Carrie Joan *law educator*
Meshulam, Deborah R. *lawyer*
Meyer, Katherine Anne *lawyer*
Meyer, Lindsay Beardsworth *lawyer*
Minardi, Ann Segura *lawyer, musician*
Mirvahabi, Farin *lawyer*
Moler, Elizabeth Anne *lawyer*
Mooney, Marilyn *lawyer*
Moore, Amy Norwood *lawyer*
Moran, Anne E. *lawyer*
Murphy, Betty Southard (Mrs. Cornelius F. Murphy) *lawyer*
Naegle, LaDawn *lawyer*
Norwood, Deborah Anne *law librarian*
Olson, Pamela Faith *lawyer, former federal agency administrator*
Onel, Suzan *lawyer*
Padgett, Nancy Weeks *law librarian, consultant, lawyer*
Pearson, Rebecca E. *lawyer*
Pensabene, Judith K. *lawyer*
Perkins, Nancy Leeds *lawyer*
Petruzzelli, Julie A. *lawyer*
Pfeiffer, Margaret Kolodny *lawyer*
Pittman, Lisa *lawyer*
Plaine, Lloyd Leva *lawyer*
Porges, Amelia *lawyer*
Powers, Mary Ellen *lawyer*
Price, Mary Kathleen *law librarian, lawyer*
Reade, Claire Elizabeth *lawyer*
Reback, Joyce Ellen *lawyer*
Rehnquist, Janet *lawyer, former federal agency administrator*
Reichs, Kerry E. *lawyer*
Reid, Inez Smith *lawyer, educator, judge*
Remington, Kristi *lawyer*
Richards, Suzanne V. *lawyer*
Richmond, Marilyn Susan *lawyer*
Rickard, Lisa Ann *lawyer*
Roberts, Michele A. *lawyer*
Rothenberg, Pamela V. *lawyer*
St. Amand, Janet G. *government relations lawyer*
St. Martin, Jo-Marie *lawyer*
Sandza, Elizabeth Barry *lawyer*
Satterthwaite, Janet F. *lawyer*
Saunders, Mary Jane *lawyer*
Schiff, Janis Boyarsky *lawyer*
Schiffer, Lois Jane *lawyer*
Schneider, Pauline A. *lawyer*
Schneller, Marina Velentgas *lawyer*
Scott, Portia Adele *paralegal*
Sears, Mary Helen *lawyer*
Sharma, Tina *lawyer*
Simmons, Gail Lindsay *lawyer*
Simon, Karla W. *law educator*
Slater, Valerie A. *lawyer*
Sparacino, Joann *lawyer, consultant*
Sprague, Mary Gabrielle *lawyer*
Stein, Cheryl Denise *lawyer*
Strand, Margaret N. *lawyer*
Strong, Rachel Lisa *lawyer*
Stuart, Pamela Bruce *lawyer*
Suffredini, Kara S. *lawyer*
Sussman, Monica Hilton *lawyer*
Taylor, Nancy Elizabeth *lawyer*
Topelius, Kathleen Ellis *lawyer*
Tsacoumis, Stephanie *lawyer*
Tucker, Marna S. *lawyer*
Tyler, Peggy Lynne Bailey *lawyer*
Tyner, Lee Reichelderfer *lawyer*
Unger, Laura Simone *lawyer, commissioner*
Vanison, Denise A. *lawyer*
Vaughn, Christine L. *lawyer*
Vickery, Ann Morgan *lawyer*
Vikander, Laura A. *lawyer*
Wagner, Martha Jo *lawyer*
Waite, Barbara L. (Pixie) *lawyer*
Walker, Mary L. *lawyer*
Walsh, Alexandra M. *lawyer*
Walter, Sheryl Lynn *lawyer*
Ward, Erica Anne *lawyer, educator*
Waters, Jennifer Nash *lawyer*
Watkin, Virginia Guild *retired lawyer*
Wedgwood, Ruth *law educator, international affairs expert*
West, Gail Berry *lawyer*
White, Sharman Lynell *lawyer*
Wilcox, Justine Elizabeth *lawyer*
Wilkinson, Beth A. *lawyer*
Williams, E. Faye *lawyer, political organization executive, health products executive*
Williams, Karen Hastie *lawyer*
Winston, Judith Ann *lawyer*
Wise, Joan S. *lawyer*
Wiss, Marcia A. *lawyer*
Worthy, Patricia Morris *lawyer, educator*
Ziegler, Janice H. *lawyer*
Zollar, Carolyn Catherine *lawyer*

FLORIDA

Bonita Springs
Hastings, Vivien N. *lawyer*

Brandon
England, Lynne Lipton *lawyer, pathologist*

Clearwater
Dougall-Sides, Leslie K. *lawyer*

Coral Gables
Gustafson, Anne-Lise Dirks *lawyer, consul*
Touby, Kathleen Anita *lawyer*

Fort Lauderdale
Coleman, Phyllis *law educator*
Iglesias, Lisa G. *lawyer*
Richmond, Gail Levin *law educator*

Gainesville
Maurer, Virginia Gallaher *law educator*
Taylor, Grace Elizabeth Woodall (Betty Taylor) *law educator, library administrator*

Hallandale Beach
Engel, Tala *lawyer*

Homestead
Ireland, Patricia *lawyer*

Jacksonville
Kelso, Linda Yayoi *lawyer*
Weaver, Dianne Jay *lawyer*

Lake Mary
Shanahan, Rebecca M. *lawyer*

Longwood
Tomasulo, Virginia Merrills *retired lawyer*

Medley
O'Meara, Vicki A. *lawyer*

Miami
Arsht, Adrienne *lawyer, broadcast executive, bank executive*
Bass, Hilarie *lawyer*
Campos-Orrego, Nora Patricia *lawyer, consultant*
Dienstag, Cynthia Jill *lawyer*
Holifield, Marilyn J. *lawyer*
Hrinak, Donna Jean *lawyer, former ambassador*
Korchin, Judith Miriam *lawyer*
Long, Maxine Master *lawyer*
Mehta, Eileen Rose *lawyer*
Menendez Cambo, Patricia *lawyer*
O'Connor, Kathleen Mary *lawyer*
Osman, Edith Gabriella *lawyer*
Poston, Rebekah Jane *lawyer*
Skolnick, Holly R. *lawyer*
Stanley, Sherry A. *lawyer*
Stratos, Kimarie Rose *lawyer, sports association executive*
Vento, M. Thérèse *lawyer*
Weems, Lori K. *lawyer*

Naples
Blumenthal, Ronnie *lawyer*
Fishbein, Estelle Ackerman *lawyer*
McCaffrey, Judith Elizabeth *lawyer*
Norton, Elizabeth Wychgel *lawyer*
Rawson, Marjorie Jean *lawyer*

Orlando
Eiffert, Crystal L. *lawyer*
Shives, Paula J. *lawyer*

Ormond Beach
Logan, Sharon Brooks *lawyer*

Palm Beach
Canary, Nancy Halliday *lawyer*

Panama City
Carroll, Susan Victoria *lawyer*

Plantation
Berger, Nancy *lawyer*
Tannen, Ricki Lewis *lawyer, psychologist, educator*

Pompano Beach
Gude, Nancy Carlson *lawyer*
Kory, Marianne Greene *lawyer*
Potash, Vella Rosenthal *lawyer, educator*

Saint Petersburg
Bairstow, Frances Kanevsky *arbitrator, mediator, educator*
McKeown, H. Mary *lawyer, law educator*
Moody, Lizabeth Ann *lawyer, educator*

Sarasota
Tachna, Ruth C. *retired lawyer*

Tallahassee
Barnett, Martha Walters *lawyer*
Bassett, Debra Lyn *lawyer, educator*
Johnson, Kelly Overstreet *lawyer*
Reid, Sue Titus *law educator*
Walker, Karen D. *lawyer*

Tampa
Black, Caroline Kapusta *lawyer*
Diehr, Beverly Hunt *lawyer*
Humphries, Celene *lawyer*
Lane, Robin *lawyer*
McDevitt, Sheila Marie *lawyer, energy executive*
Stiles, Mary Ann *lawyer, writer, lobbyist*
Young, Gwynne A. *lawyer*

Vero Beach
Haight, Carol Barbara *lawyer*

West Palm Beach
Cooper, Margaret Leslie *lawyer*
Vilchez, Victoria Anne *lawyer*

Winter Park
DeMarco-Miller, Marie Lisa *lawyer*

GEORGIA

Athens
Hill, Janet Elizabeth *lawyer*
Puckett, Elizabeth Ann *law librarian, educator*

Atlanta
Allen, Pinney L. *lawyer*
Bergeson, Donna Potts *lawyer*
Borders, Sarah Robinson *lawyer*
Brown, Janine *lawyer*
Cahoon, Susan Alice *lawyer*
Cavin, Kristine Smith *lawyer*
Cohen, Lori G. *lawyer*
Deming, N. Karen *lawyer*
DiSantis, Linda Katherine *lawyer*
Feese, Suzanne *lawyer*
Frederick, Paula J. *lawyer*
Girth, Marjorie Louisa *lawyer, educator*
Heit, Marny *lawyer*
Jordan, Katherine D. (Kate Jordan) *lawyer*
Knowles, Marjorie Fine *law educator, dean*
Lawson, Corliss Scroggins *lawyer*
Mason, Karol V. *lawyer*
McClure, Teri Plummer *lawyer*
McDonald, Kristen *lawyer*
Mills-Schreiber, Robin Kate *law librarian*
Noe, Elizabeth Hardy *lawyer*
Oakley, Mary Ann Bryant *lawyer*
Owens, Laura Lewis *lawyer*
Pelypenko, Elizabeth *lawyer*
Price, Elizabeth Anne *lawyer*
Rafuse, Nancy E. *lawyer, director*
Roseborough, Teresa Wynn *lawyer*
Salo, Ann Sexton Distler *lawyer*
Thomas, Lizanne *lawyer*
Thorpe, Jane Fugate *lawyer*
Varner, Chilton Davis *lawyer*
Yip, Bettina W. *lawyer*
Zealey, Sharon Janine *lawyer*

Braselton
Romer, Denise Patrice *lawyer*

Columbus
Cook, Kate Sievert *lawyer*

Dalton
Kirkland, Cindy D. *paralegal*

Decatur
Williams, Rita Tucker *lawyer*

Macon
Dantzler, Deryl Daugherty *lawyer, educator, dean*

Savannah
Wood, Lisa Godbey *prosecutor*

Tucker
Lacey, Ruthann P. *lawyer*

Valdosta
Coons-Long, Brittney Leigh *defender*

HAWAII

Honolulu
Akiba, Lorraine Hiroko *lawyer*
Carson, Ellen Godbey *lawyer*
Mau-Shimizu, Patricia Ann *lawyer*

IDAHO

Boise
Minnich, Diane Kay *legal association administrator*
Moen, Monica Balk *lawyer, real estate developer*
Richardson, Betty H. *lawyer, former prosecutor*
Silak, Cathy R. *lawyer, former state supreme court justice*

Princeton
Severns, Karen S. *family court services administrator*

ILLINOIS

Bloomington
Kennett, Christie Shih *lawyer*

Calumet City
Scullion, Annette Murphy *lawyer, educator*

Chicago
Acker, Ann E. *lawyer*
Albright, Christine L. *lawyer*
Allen, Gemma B. *lawyer*
Allen, Julie O'Donnell *lawyer*
Anderson, Cathy C. *lawyer*
Appel, Nina Schick *law educator, dean, academic administrator*
Aronson, Virginia L. *lawyer*
Badel, Julie *lawyer*
Baker, Pamela *lawyer*
Barner, Sharon R. *lawyer*
Bart, Susan Therese *lawyer*
Bauer, Julie A. *lawyer*
Bellows, Laurel Gordon *business lawyer*
Berman, Debbie L. *lawyer*
Bernstein, Lisa E. *law educator*
Bertagnolli, Leslie A. *lawyer*
Bettman, Suzanne *lawyer*
Boggs, Catherine J. *lawyer*
Bomchill, Fern Cheryl *lawyer*
Bowman, Cynthia Grant *law educator*
Brennan, Noelle C. *lawyer*
Bro, Ruth Hill *lawyer*
Brogan, Lisa S. *lawyer*
Burke, Carol A. *lawyer*
Burke, Michelle C. *lawyer*
Busey, Roxane C. *lawyer*
Buss, Emily *law educator*
Canty, Dawn M. *lawyer*
Case, Mary Anne *law educator*
Ceko, Theresa C. *law educator, lawyer*
Cohen, Melanie Rovner *lawyer*
Cox, Julia Diamond *lawyer*
Crane, Charlotte *law educator*
Cronin, Kathleen M. *lawyer*
Cummings, Andrea J. *lawyer*
Daley, Susan Jean *lawyer*
Dandridge, LeNor *paralegal*
de Hoyos, Debora M. *lawyer*
Diamond, Shari Seidman *law professor, psychology professor*
Dickstein, Beth J. *lawyer, accountant*
Dohrn, Bernardine *law educator, advocate*
Dunlop, Karen Owen *lawyer*
Easton, Lory Barsdate *lawyer*
Eaton, Maja Campbell *lawyer*
Eisner, Rebecca Suzanne *lawyer*
Fontaine, Mary C. *lawyer*
Friedli, Helen Russell *lawyer*
Friedman, Roselyn L. *lawyer, mediator*
Geraghty, Diane C. *law educator*
Gerske, Janet Fay *lawyer*
Getz, Bettina *lawyer*
Gianos, Diane *lawyer*
Gibbons, Kathleen Marie *lawyer*
Gorman, Maureen J. *lawyer*
Grange, Janet Lenore *lawyer, accountant, consultant*
Gullikson, Rosemary *lawyer*
Hablutzel, Nancy Zimmerman *lawyer, educator*
Harmon, Teresa Wilton *lawyer*
Harrington, Carol A. *lawyer*
Harris, Beth A. *lawyer*
Harris, Susan V. *lawyer*
Harrison, Holly A. *lawyer*
Henderson, Janet E. E. *lawyer*
Hesse, Carolyn Sue *lawyer*
Hitselberger, Carol A. *lawyer*
Hoffman, Valerie Jane *lawyer*
Hubbard, Elizabeth Louise *lawyer*
Huber, Anne Marrs *lawyer*
Hughes, Joyce Anne *law educator*
Jachino, Daneen L. *legal administrator*
Jacobs, Caryn Leslie *lawyer, former prosecutor*
Jacobson, Marian Slutz *lawyer*
Kelley, Lydia R.B. *lawyer*
Kellman, Sandra Y. *lawyer*
King, Sharon Louise *lawyer*
Kramer, Andrea S. *lawyer*
Krasny, Paula J. *lawyer*
Landow-Esser, Janine Marise *lawyer*
Landsberg, Jill Warren *lawyer, educator, arbitrator*
Lefco, Kathy Nan *law librarian*
Leonard, Laura L. *lawyer*
Lona, Marie A. *lawyer*
Macaulay, Susan Jane *lawyer, law educator*
Majers, Elizabeth Louise *lawyer*
Mansfield, Karen Lee *lawyer*
Marshall, Juli Wilson *lawyer*
Martin, Laura Keidan *lawyer*
Matlin, Susanne Summer *lawyer*
McBreen, Maura Ann *lawyer*
McCue, Judith W. *lawyer*
McKinley, Anne C. *lawyer*
Meares, Tracey Louise *law educator*
Mihelic, Tracey L. *lawyer*
Mims, Joyce Elaine *lawyer*
Morency, Paula J. *lawyer*
Morgan, Betsy Stelle *lawyer*
Morgan, Donna Evensen *lawyer*
Morrison, Portia Owen *lawyer*
Mudd, Anne Chestney *mediator, law educator, real estate broker*
Murphy, Kathleen M. *lawyer*
Neely, Ellen J. *lawyer*
Newman, Terry E. *lawyer*
Nicastro, Tracey A. *lawyer*
Nicklin, Emily *lawyer*
Nicolaides, Mary *lawyer*
Niehaus, Mary C. *lawyer*
Nijman, Jennifer T. *lawyer, department chairman*
Niro, Cheryl *lawyer*
Odorizzi, Michele L. *lawyer*
O'Meara, Anna M. *lawyer*
O'Neill, Bridget R. *lawyer*
Panich, Danuta Bembenista *lawyer*
Parkhurst, Beverly Susler *lawyer, administrative law judge*
Pengra, R. Rene *lawyer*
Pesch, Ellen P. *lawyer*
Polaski, Anne Spencer *lawyer*
Ponder, Anita J. *lawyer*
Preece, Lynn Sylvia *lawyer*
Rea, Anne E. *lawyer*
Reategui, Lisa J. *lawyer*
Reis, Leslie Ann *law educator, lawyer*
Rich, Nancy Jean *lawyer*
Richardson-Lowry, Mary *lawyer*
Richman, Joan M. *lawyer*
Roach, Kathleen Lynn *lawyer*
Robbins, Ellen Sue *lawyer*
Roberts, Dorothy E. *law educator*
Robinson, Jennifer Jean *lawyer*
Roin, Julie *law educator*
Rosenblum, Judith A. *law educator*
Ross, Nancy G. *lawyer*
Ruiz, Michele Ilene *lawyer*
Ryan, Priscilla E. *lawyer*
Scharf, Stephanie A. *lawyer*
Seegers, Lori C. *lawyer*
Sessions, Barbara C. *lawyer*
Shapo, Helene S. *law educator*
Sher, Susan *lawyer*
Skinner, Mary Jacobs *lawyer*
Smith, Leslie M. *lawyer*
Stevens, Linda K. *lawyer*
Stillman, Nina Gidden *lawyer*
Stone, Susan A. *lawyer*
Sullivan, Marcia Waite *lawyer*
Swiger, Elinor Porter *lawyer*
Treston, Sherry S. *lawyer*
Trost, Eileen Bannon *lawyer*
Utecht, Andrea E. *lawyer*
Van Demark, Ruth Elaine *lawyer*
Weber, Susan A. *lawyer*
Weinstein, Margo *lawyer*
White, Linda Diane *lawyer*
Wine-Banks, Jill Susan *lawyer*
Wright, Judith Margaret *law librarian, educator, dean*
Yuracko, Kimberly *law educator*
Zagel, Margaret Maxwell *lawyer*
Zemm, Sandra Phyllis *lawyer*
Zhao, Jia *lawyer*

Crystal Lake
Thoms, Jeannine Aumond *lawyer*

Deerfield
Green, Dana I. *lawyer, human resources specialist*
Pearson, Louise S. *lawyer*
Persky, Marla Susan *lawyer*

Des Plaines
Gold, Deidra D. *lawyer*

Dunlap
Traicoff, Sandra M. *lawyer*

Geneseo
Brown, Mabel Welton *lawyer*

Hoffman Estates
Zopp, Andrea Lynne *lawyer, retail executive*

Lake Forest
Palmer, Ann Therese Darin *lawyer*

Naperville
Corvino, Beth Byster *lawyer*

Northbrook
McGinn, Mary J. *lawyer, insurance company executive*

Oak Brook
Barnes, Karen Kay *lawyer*
Congalton, Susan Tichenor *lawyer*
Santona, Gloria *lawyer*
Sherman, Jennifer L. *lawyer*

Park Ridge
Naker, Mary Leslie *legal firm executive*

Rolling Meadows
Nicol, Nancy J. *lawyer*

Warrenville
Smith, Michele *lawyer*

Westchester
Castellano, Christine Marie *lawyer*
Doane, Marcia E. *lawyer, food products executive*

INDIANA

Columbus
Rose, Marya Mernitz *lawyer*

Danville
Baldwin, Patricia Ann *lawyer*

Fishers
Marcus, Cynthia Ann *lawyer*

Indianapolis
Braly, Angela F. *lawyer, insurance company executive*
Brooks, Susan W. *prosecutor*
Fruehwald, Kristin Gail *lawyer*
Huffman, Rosemary Adams *lawyer, corporate executive*
Kinney, Eleanor De Arman *law educator*
Kleiman, Mary Margaret *lawyer*
Koch, Edna Mae *lawyer, nurse*
Lamkin, Martha Dampf *lawyer, foundation administrator*
Lisher, Mary Katherine *lawyer*
Otero, Lettice Margarita *lawyer*
Pence, Linda Lee *lawyer*
Pilgrim, Jill *lawyer, consultant*
Thurston, Kathy Lynn *paralegal*

Lagrange
Glick, Cynthia Susan *lawyer*

IOWA

Des Moines
Conlin, Roxanne Barton *lawyer*
Mattsson, Lisa Miller *lawyer, social worker*
Rodgers Smith, Kimberly Jeanne *lawyer*
Shaff, Karen E. *lawyer, insurance company executive*

Iowa City
Gittler, Josephine *law educator*
Wing, Adrien Katherine *law educator*

Ottumwa
Krafka, Mary Baird *lawyer*

KANSAS

Girard
Beezley, Sara Sue *lawyer*

Grantville
Hodges, Edna (Lee) Elizabeth *lawyer, educator*

Leavenworth
Crow, Martha Ellen *lawyer*

Salina
Angell, Samantha *lawyer, educator*

Topeka
Elrod, Linda Diane Henry *lawyer, educator*

Wichita
Foulston, Nola Tedesco *lawyer*
Hoefer, Gladys *lawyer*

KENTUCKY

Bowling Green
Stuart, Flora Templeton *prosecutor*

Catlettsburg
Nixon, Ronda Lynn *paralegal*

Covington
Schaeffer, Andrew *lawyer*

Louisville
Faller, Rhoda *lawyer*
Lyndrup, Peggy B. *lawyer*
Riedman, Mary Suzanne *lawyer*

Prospect
Willenbrink, Rose Ann *retired lawyer*

LOUISIANA

Baton Rouge
Duval, Anne-Gwin *lawyer*
Wisbar, Rebecca Kittok *lawyer*

Hammond
Huszar, Angelia *lawyer*

Mandeville
Ewen, Pamela Binnings *retired lawyer*

Napoleonville
Triche, Jane M. *lawyer*

New Orleans
Benjamin, Adelaide Wisdom *retired lawyer, community volunteer and activist*
Chessin, Cathy E. *lawyer*
Fraiche, Donna DiMartino *lawyer*
Garcia, Patricia A. *lawyer*
Landry, Sherry S. *lawyer*
Longwell, Kelly (A. Kelton Longwell) *lawyer*
Neff, Carole Cukell *lawyer*
Perlis, Sharon A. *lawyer*
Smith, Juanita Bérard *lawyer, artist*

Plaquemine
Engolio, Elizabeth Ann *lawyer*

MAINE

Bangor
Bickford, Meris J. *lawyer, bank executive*

Bernard
Marchetti-Ponte, Karin *lawyer, land conservation consultant*

Boothbay Harbor
Carpenter, Elizabeth Jane *mediator*

Portland
McDaniel, Sarah A. *lawyer*
Mitchell, Carol L. *lawyer*
Silsby, Paula D. *prosecutor*

Yarmouth
McHold, Sharon Lawrence *lawyer, mediator*

MARYLAND

Annapolis
Powers, Eileen Elizabeth *lawyer, mediator*
Sagner, Dianne R. *lawyer*
Shapiro, Susan Stobbart *lawyer*

Baltimore
Babb, Barbara A. *lawyer, educator*
Baker, Constance H. *lawyer*
Capute, Courtney G. *lawyer*
Carnell, Teresa Burt *lawyer*
Chaplin, Peggy Louie *lawyer*
Chesshire, Mary Claire *lawyer*
Ciccolo, Angela *lawyer*
de Soto, Lisa *lawyer*
Devan, Deborah Hunt *lawyer*
Eveleth, Janet Stidman *law association administrator*
Gonzales, Louise Michaux *lawyer*
Guben, Jan K. *lawyer*
Katz, Martha Lessman *lawyer*
Kenney, Brigid E. *lawyer*
Nussbaum, Paul M. *lawyer*
Pollak, Joanne Elizabeth *lawyer*
Schlaff, Barbara E. *lawyer*
Somer-Greif, Penny Lynn *lawyer*
Strachan, Nell B. *lawyer*
Warren, Melissa Allison *lawyer*
White, Pamela Janice *lawyer*

Bethesda
Abdoo, Elizabeth A. *lawyer*
Block, Marian S. *lawyer*
Hagberg, Viola Wilgus *lawyer*

Chevy Chase
Groner, Beverly Anne *retired lawyer*

Columbia
Said, Naima *lawyer*

Frederick
Hogan, Ilona Modly *lawyer*

Hunt Valley
Downs, Mary Alane *lawyer*

Lanham
Eckard Vilardo, Linda J. *lawyer*

Lutherville Timonium
Brown, Ellyn L. *lawyer, consultant*

Odenton
Lundy, Sheila Edwards *lawyer*

Pikesville
Putzel, Constance Kellner *lawyer*

Rockville
Boetticher, Helene *retired lawyer*
Cheston, Sheila Carol *lawyer*

Silver Spring
Becker, Sandra Neiman Hammer *lawyer*

Towson
Koetter, Cornelia M. *lawyer*

MASSACHUSETTS

Boston
Abbott, Susan L. *lawyer*
Adams, Lisa *lawyer*
Agajanian, Anita Shakeh *lawyer*
Allen, Rosemary M. *lawyer*
Amatangel, Lisa *lawyer*
Arrowood, Lisa Gayle *lawyer*
Bachman, Katharine Elizabeth *lawyer*
Baker, Adrienne Marie *lawyer*
Baker, Hollie L. *lawyer*
Bapooji Ryan, Anita B. *lawyer*
Barnard, Deborah E. *lawyer*
Barnett, Jessica Vincent *lawyer*
Basil, Michelle L. *lawyer*
Bassil, Janice *lawyer*
Berliner, Wendy Alissa *lawyer*
Bhatt, Manisha Hemendra *lawyer*
Bierman, Aimee Elizabeth *lawyer*
Bills, Jennifer Leah *lawyer*
Boehs, Sarah Teachworh *lawyer*
Bonauto, Mary *lawyer*
Browne, Marijane Leila Benner *lawyer*
Bucci, Mary D. *lawyer*
Burnett, Elizabeth B. *lawyer*
Burns, Catherine L. *lawyer*
Caldeira, Charlene A. *lawyer*
Candela, Vanessa English *lawyer*
Caperna, Lisa Maria *lawyer*
Carr, Lisa Diane *lawyer*
Carson, Jeniffer A.P. *lawyer*
Casal, Eileen *lawyer*
Cazabon, Rebecca Maria *lawyer*
Chang, Hemmie *lawyer*
Chapon, Eunice Kim *lawyer*
Cherry, Sarah Kathryn *lawyer*
Chu, Sylvia *lawyer*
Chunias, Jennifer Lynn *lawyer*
Connolly, Sarah Thiemann *lawyer*
Costello, Katharine Pacella *lawyer*
Daniels, Cara J. *lawyer*
Daum, Caryn Lynn *lawyer*
DeJuneas, Patricia Ann *lawyer*
Dohoney, Michaela S. *lawyer*
Edwards, MJ *lawyer*
Egan, Jan Wenning *lawyer*
Epstein, Elaine May *lawyer*
Fergus, Katherine Young *lawyer*
Ferrera, Vinita *lawyer*
Fiacco, Barbara A. *lawyer*
Fleming, Darien K.S. *lawyer*
Fletcher, Carrie J. *lawyer*
Flynn, Gina Perez *lawyer*
Flynn-Poppey, Elissa *lawyer*
Fremont-Smith, Marion R. *lawyer*
Furey, Jennifer B. *lawyer*
Furnald, Lisa Anne *lawyer*
Gagan, Sarah K. *lawyer*
Galligan, Lynda T. *lawyer*
Garcia, Grace V. Bacon *lawyer*
Garvin, Michele M. *lawyer*
Gerlovin, Samantha Leigh *lawyer*
Gibbs, Laura Elizabeth *lawyer*
Giner, A. Silvana *lawyer*
Glasgow, Jordana Berkowitz *lawyer*
Goldberg, Lena G. *lawyer, investment company executive*
Goldstein, Jane D. *lawyer*
Gordon, Cecelia T. *lawyer*
Greaney, Jennifer Ellen *lawyer*
Green, Karen F. *lawyer*
Haddad, Lisa R. *lawyer*
Haight, Geri L. *lawyer*
Hamel, Suzanne Patrice *lawyer*
Hardy, Jennifer Beth *lawyer*
Harris, Kari K. *lawyer*
Harris, Maia H. *lawyer*
Hedges, Jessica Diane *lawyer*
Henry, Kathleen Cloherty *lawyer*
Herlihy, Jennifer Boyd *lawyer*
Herman, Kimberly B. *lawyer*
Hertel, Jaime S. *lawyer*
Hertz, Jennifer L. *lawyer*
Hesse, Julia Rush *lawyer*
Hoey, Laura Gaffney *lawyer*
Hogan, Julie A. *lawyer*
Holt, Amanda C. *lawyer*
Howard, Sheryl Andrea *lawyer*
Howe, Janice W. *lawyer*
Howitt-Easton, Deborah *lawyer*
Janos, Ellen L. *lawyer*
Jarrell, Brenda Herschbach *lawyer*
Johnston, Susan A. *lawyer*
Jurgensen LaCivita, Mary R. *lawyer*
Kearns, Ellen Cecelia *lawyer*
Klieman, Rikki Jo *lawyer, legal analyst*
Lange, Maggie A. *lawyer*
LeBlanc, Marianne Camille *lawyer*
Lee, Grace H. *lawyer*
Lukey, Joan A. *lawyer*
McChesney, S. Elaine *lawyer*
McPhee, Joan *lawyer*
Messing, Ellen Jean *lawyer*
Michon, Katherine J. *lawyer*
Miller, Michelle D. *lawyer*
Montgomery, Susan Barbieri *lawyer*
Mulvey, Elizabeth N. *lawyer*
Murley, Susan W. *lawyer*
O'Connell, Mary-Kathleen *lawyer*
O'Donnell, Kathleen Marie *lawyer*
Pisa, Regina Marie *lawyer*
Plimpton, Leslie Kloville *lawyer*
Richmond, Alice Elenor *lawyer*
Robinson, Andrea J. *lawyer*
Ropple, Lisa M. *lawyer*
Rudavsky, Dahlia C. *lawyer*
Shapiro, Sandra *lawyer*
Shilepsky, Nancy Sue *lawyer*
Steinberg, Laura *lawyer*
Tearney, Melissa Bayer *lawyer*
Tse, Marian A. *lawyer*
White, Anne J. *lawyer*
Whitley, L. Tracee *lawyer*

Brockton
Belinsky, Ilene Beth *lawyer*

Cambridge
Bartholet, Elizabeth *law educator*
Desan, Christine *law educator*
Field, Martha Amanda *law educator*
Glendon, Mary Ann *law educator*
Guinier, Lani *law educator*
Halley, Janet E. *law educator*
Minow, Martha Louise *law educator*
Riley, Lynne F. *lawyer*
Steiker, Carol S. *law educator*
Warren, Elizabeth A. *law educator*
White, Lucie E. *law educator*
Wise, Virginia Jo *law educator, librarian*

Cohasset
Chenault Minot, Marilyn *legal executive*

East Boston
Crawford, Linda Sibery *lawyer, educator*

Edgartown
Gatting, Carlene J. *lawyer*

Framingham
McCauley, Ann *lawyer*

Lowell
O'Donnell, Kathleen Marie *lawyer*

Natick
Walker, Kellye L. *lawyer*

Newton
Isselbacher, Rhoda Solin *lawyer*
Krintzman, B. J. *lawyer, real estate broker, television show host*
Metzer, Patricia Ann *lawyer*

Newton Center
Parker, Jacqueline Yvonne *lawyer, educator*

Springfield
Rooke, Michele A. *lawyer*
Susse, Sandra Slone *lawyer*

Waltham
Hill, Anita Faye *law educator*

Wellesley
Pike, Judith Robyn *lawyer*

MICHIGAN

Ann Arbor
Darlow, Julia Donovan *lawyer*
Garcia, Elisa Dolores *lawyer*
Katz, Ellen D. *law educator*
Kramer, Barbara H. *lawyer*
Leary, Margaret A. *law librarian, library director*
MacKinnon, Catharine Alice *lawyer, educator, writer*
Mendelson, Nina *law educator*
Payton, Sallyanne *law educator*
Scott, Rebecca J. *law educator*
Sullivan, Teresa Ann *law and sociology educator, academic administrator*
Whitman, Christina Brooks *law educator*

Auburn Hills
Greenfield, Susan L. *lawyer*
Horiszny, Laurene Helen *lawyer*

Bloomfield Hills
Banas, C(hristine) Leslie *lawyer*
Bogas, Kathleen Laura L. *lawyer*
Simon, Evelyn *lawyer*

Dearborn
Fox, Stacy L. *lawyer*

Detroit
Dannin, Ellen Jean *lawyer*
Diehl, Nancy J. *lawyer*
Felt, Julia Kay *lawyer*
Rozof, Phyllis Claire *lawyer*
Shannon, Margaret Anne *lawyer*
Sikula, Christine Lynn *legal association administrator, education educator*
White, Katherine E. *law educator*

Farmington Hills
Baughman, Leonora Knoblock *lawyer*
Fershtman, Julie Ilene *lawyer*

Grand Rapids
Chiara, Margaret M. *prosecutor, lawyer*

Lansing
Linder, Iris Kay *lawyer*
Tombers, Evelyn Charlotte *lawyer, educator*

Rochester
Pope, Melissa Lopez *law educator*

Southfield
Bingaman, Anne K. *lawyer*
Davis-Yancey, Gwendolyn *lawyer*

Sylvan Lake
Derdarian, Christine Anne *lawyer*

Troy
Navarro, Monica *lawyer*

MINNESOTA

Duluth
Amberg, Deborah Ann *lawyer*

Eagan
Dulas, DeAnne L. *lawyer*

Eden Prairie
Feuss, Linda Anne Upsall *lawyer*

Edina
Davidson, Ann D. *lawyer, aerospace transportation executive*
Schaibley, Ann M. *lawyer*

Medina
McConnell, Mary Patricia *lawyer*

Minneapolis
Anderson, Leslie J. *lawyer*
Benson, Beverly J. *lawyer*
Buckingham, Elizabeth C. *lawyer*
Constantine, Katherine A. *lawyer*
Dale, Candace L. *lawyer*
Deach, Jana Aune *lawyer*
DeVries Smith, Kate *lawyer*
Eng, Holly S.A. *lawyer*
Fisher, Michele Renee *lawyer*
Forneris, Jeanne M. *lawyer*
Hansen, Robyn L. *lawyer*
Heins, Dianne C. *lawyer*
Helsene, Amy L. *lawyer*
Holden, Susan M. *lawyer*
Howland, Joan Sidney *law librarian, educator*
Hunt, Kay Nord *lawyer*
Jacobson, Carrie Isabelle *lawyer*
Jameson, Jennifer A. *lawyer*
Kirtley, Jane Elizabeth *law educator*
Loucks, Kathleen Margaret *lawyer*
Marshall, Siri Swenson *lawyer*
McDermott, Kathleen E. *lawyer*
Meier, Lisa M. *lawyer*
Nelson, Julie Loftus *lawyer*
Ort, Shannon *lawyer*
Paulose, Rachel *prosecutor*
Platt, Nina *law librarian*
Rasmussen, Teresa J. *lawyer, insurance company executive*
Saksena, Marian E. *lawyer*
Santana, Lymari Jeanette *lawyer*
Schneider, Elaine Carol *lawyer, researcher, writer*
Schulkers, Joan M. *lawyer*
Short, Marianne Dolores *lawyer*
Struthers, Margo S. *lawyer*
Van Dyk, Suzanne B. *lawyer*
Weber, Gail Mary *lawyer*
Wille, Karin L. *lawyer*
Younger, Judith Tess *law educator*

Northfield
Lundergan, Barbara Keough *lawyer*

Owatonna
Birk, Peg J. *lawyer*

Roseville
Fisher, Rebecca Rhoda *lawyer*
Fullerton, Denise S.S. *lawyer*

Saint Paul
Arnold, Valerie Downing *lawyer*
Cyr, Lisa Watson *lawyer*
Lebedoff, Randy Miller *lawyer*

MISSISSIPPI

Brandon
Haralson, Keri Temple *prosecutor*

Gulfport
Phillips, Joy Lambert *lawyer, banker*

Jackson
Barnes, Andréa Reneé *lawyer*
Jones, Christy D. *lawyer*

Laurel
Ladner, April C. *lawyer*

Rosedale
Thomas, Aelicia *lawyer*

MISSOURI

Chesterfield
Goldman, Teri B. *lawyer*
Rifkind, Irene Glassman *legal secretary*

Kahoka
Jones, Mary D. *court clerk*

Kansas City
Cannezzaro, Nikki Eckland *lawyer*
Clegg, Karen Kohler *lawyer*
Epps, Mischa Buford *lawyer*
Levings, Theresa Lawrence *lawyer*
Plax, Karen Ann *lawyer*
Roush, Nancy Schmidt *lawyer*
Satterlee, Terry Jean *lawyer*
Sexton, Jacqueline Madeline *lawyer*
Shomin, Janet L. *paralegal*
Whittaker, Judith Ann Cameron *lawyer*

Lexington
Ritchie, Kellie Wingate *lawyer*

Osage Beach
Troutwine, Gayle Leone *lawyer*

Saint Charles
Dorsey, Mary Elizabeth *lawyer*

Saint Louis
Atwood, Hollye Stolz *lawyer*
Boggs, Beth Clemens *lawyer*
Bonacorsi, Ellen E. *lawyer*
Bonacorsi, Mary Catherine *lawyer*
Covington, Ann K. *lawyer, former state supreme court justice*
Hanaway, Catherine Lucille *prosecutor*
Johnson, Sandra Hanneken *law educator*
Joley, Lisa Annette *lawyer*
Martin, Lisa Demet *lawyer*
Perotti, Rose Norma *lawyer*
Searls, Eileen Haughey *retired lawyer, law librarian, educator*
Sherby, Kathleen Reilly *lawyer*
Stratmann, Gayle G. *lawyer, consumer products company executive*
Van Fleet, Lisa A. *lawyer*
Walker Tucker, Dana *lawyer*
Wilson, Margaret Bush *lawyer*

Saint Peters
Dreyer, Shelly C. *lawyer, judge*

Springfield
Shantz, Debra Mallonee *lawyer*

MONTANA

Bozeman
Pape, Rebecca Hogan *lawyer*

Helena
Meadows, Judith Adams *law librarian, educator*

Kalispell
Kortum-Managhan, Santana Natasha *lawyer*

NEBRASKA

Lincoln
Frobom, LeAnn Larson *lawyer*
Ogle, Robbin Sue *criminal justice educator*
Robak, Kim M. *lawyer*

Omaha
Chesterman, Melany Sue *lawyer*
Koplow, Ellen *lawyer, brokerage house executive*

NEVADA

Carson City
McCarthy, Ann Price *lawyer*

Las Vegas
Anderson-Fintak, Heather *lawyer*
Bersi, Ann *lawyer*
Hill, Judith Deegan *retired lawyer*
Kennedy, Margaret Alexis *law educator, researcher*
Landau, Yvette E. *lawyer, resort company executive*

North Las Vegas
Maresso-Newell, Dee *arbitrator, educator*

NEW HAMPSHIRE

Concord
Young, Sherilyn Burnett *lawyer*

Newport
Stamatakis, Carol Marie *lawyer, former state legislator*

Plainfield
Brown, Judith Olans *retired lawyer, educator*

Stratham
Wineberg, Danette *lawyer, apparel executive*

NEW JERSEY

Basking Ridge
Craven, Pamela F. *lawyer*

Bedminster
Marrero, Teresa *lawyer*

Brick
Norgaard, Veronica R. *real estate lawyer*

Camden
Kaden, Ellen Oran *lawyer, consumer products company executive*

East Brunswick
Zaun, Anne Marie *lawyer*

Flemington
Meagher, Deirdra M. *lawyer*

Fort Lee
Weiss, Simona *retired paralegal*

Franklin Lakes
Healy, Bridget M. *lawyer*

Hackensack
Bronson, Meridith J. *lawyer*

Hackettstown
Mulligan, Elinor Patterson *lawyer*

Haddonfield
Chiulli, E. Antoinette *lawyer*

Hopewell
Lester, Pamela Robin *lawyer*

Lavallette
Donato, Michele Roseanne *lawyer, educator*

Montvale
Nachtigal, Patricia *lawyer*

Morristown
Sherman, Sandra Brown *lawyer*

New Brunswick
Miller, Lynn Fieldman *lawyer*
Yorke, Marianne *lawyer, real estate executive*

New Milford
Spiegel, Edna Z. *lawyer*

New Providence
Reinsdorf, Judith A. *lawyer*

Newark
Amalfe, Christine A. *lawyer*
Bizub, Johanna Catherine *law librarian*
Defeis, Elizabeth Frances *law educator, lawyer*
Fox, Jeanne Marie *lawyer*
Henry, Rolanne *law educator*
Mason, Joyce J. *lawyer, telecommunications industry executive*
Rothschild, Gita F. *lawyer*
Storch, Susan Borowski *lawyer*
Van Deusen, Lois M. *lawyer*

Oakland
Schwager, Linda Helen *lawyer*

Passaic
Johnson, Sakinah *paralegal*

Piscataway
Gustafsson, Mary Beth *lawyer*
Lee, Barbara Anne *law educator, dean*

Pomona
Latourette, Audrey Wolfson *law educator*

Princeton
Beidler, Marsha Wolf *lawyer*
Frenier, Diane M. *lawyer*
Greenman, Jane Friedlieb *lawyer, human resources executive*
Kaplowitz, Karen (Jill) *lawyer, consultant*
Rose, Edith Sprung *retired lawyer*
Sullivan, Diane P. *lawyer*

Ridgewood
Harris, Micalyn Shafer *lawyer, educator, arbitrator, consultant, mediator*

Saddle Brook
White, H. Katherine *lawyer*

Somerville
Gross, Carol Ann *lawyer*

Sparta
McMeen, Sheila Taenzler *retired lawyer*

Trenton
Levin, Susan Bass *lawyer*

Wall
Harden, Oleta J. *lawyer, utilities executive*

Warren
Brundage, Maureen *lawyer*

Wildwood
Callinan, Patricia Ann *legal secretary*

Woodbridge
Babineau, Anne Serzan *lawyer*

NEW MEXICO

Albuquerque
Goldberg, Catherine T. *lawyer*
Neerken, Julie P. *lawyer*
Ramo, Roberta Cooper *lawyer*

Corrales
Campion, Kathleen Francis *lawyer, gifted and talented educator*

Santa Fe
Moll, Deborah Adelaide *lawyer*
Nixon, Sunny Jeanne *lawyer*

NEW YORK

Albany
Helmer, Nicole M. *lawyer*
Sandhaas, Jill T. *lawyer*

Amherst
Ifandis, Anastasia *lawyer*

Ballston Spa
Brown, Ifigenia Theodore *lawyer*

Bohemia
Fisher, Irene B. *lawyer*

Briarcliff Manor
Bernstein, Nadia Jacqueline *lawyer*

Brooklyn
Berger, Margaret Adlersberg *law educator*
Fairstein, Linda A. *prosecutor, writer*
Karmel, Roberta Segal *lawyer, educator*
Kerwick, Colleen *lawyer, artist*
Mauskopf, Roslynn R. *prosecutor*
Moran, Marissa J. *law educator*
Murphy, Kathleen Mary *former law firm executive, alternative healing professional*
Roth, Pamela Susan *lawyer*

Buffalo
Freedman, Maryann Saccomando *lawyer*
Mather, Lynn *law educator, political science professor*
O'Donnell, Denise Ellen *lawyer, former prosecutor*
O'Loughlin, Sandra S. *lawyer*

Chappaqua
Hurford, Carol *retired lawyer*

Corning
Hauselt, Denise Ann *lawyer*

Dobbs Ferry
Maiocchi, Christine *lawyer*

Farmingdale
O'Brien, Joan Susan *lawyer, educator*

Flushing
Rivera, Jenny *law educator*
Schwartz, Estar Alma *lawyer*

Garden City
Caputo, Kathryn Mary *paralegal*
Meng, M. Kathryn *lawyer*

Hawthorne
Lieberman, Meryl Robin *lawyer*

Huntington
German, June Resnick *lawyer*
Munson, Nancy K. *lawyer*

Ithaca
Germain, Claire Madeleine *law librarian, educator, lawyer*

Jamesville
DeCrow, Karen *lawyer, educator, writer*

Jericho
Beal, Carol Ann *lawyer*

Latham
Catalano, Jane Donna *lawyer*

Melville
Friedrich, Jennifer *lawyer*

Mineola
Cardo, Marianne *lawyer*
Vogel, Jennifer Lyn *lawyer*

New York
Abatemarco, Tracy J. *lawyer*
Aciman, Carole V. *lawyer*
Adler, Amy M. *law educator*
Almon, Lorie *lawyer*
Alter, Eleanor Breitel *lawyer*
Appelbaum, Ann Harriet *lawyer*
Arabatzis, Constance Elaine *lawyer*
Ash, Karen Artz *lawyer*
Baird, Zoë *lawyer*
Bancroft, Margaret Armstrong *lawyer*
Bansal, Preeta D. *lawyer*
Bateman, Maureen Scannell *lawyer*
Becker, Barbara Lynn *lawyer*
Been, Vicki Lynn *law educator*
Beerbower, Cynthia Gibson *lawyer*
Beeson, Ann *lawyer*
Beinecke, Candace Krugman *lawyer*
Ben-Ami, Leora *lawyer*
Berg, Madelaine R. *lawyer*
Bergman, Arlene *lawyer*
Bergman, Michelle D. *lawyer*
Berkery, Rosemary T. *lawyer, investment company executive*
Berrien, Jacqueline A. *lawyer*
Beshar, Christine *lawyer*
Beshar, Sarah E. *lawyer*
Birnbaum, Sheila L. *lawyer, educator*
Bjorklund, Victoria B. *lawyer*
Black, Barbara Aronstein *legal history educator*
Blanchard, Kimberly Staggers *lawyer, educator*
Blassberg, Franci J. *lawyer*
Bloom, Lisa Read *lawyer*
Boast, Molly Shryer *lawyer*
Boisseau, Jane *lawyer*
Bowen, Sharon Y. *lawyer*
Breslow, Stephanie R. *lawyer*
Bristor, Katherine M. *lawyer*
Buckley, Susan *lawyer*
Burgess, Lynne A *lawyer*
Burgman, Dierdre Ann *lawyer*
Burns, Sarah Ellen *law educator*
Burton, Eve B. *lawyer*
Caldwell, Leslie Ragon *lawyer, former prosecutor*
Caldwell, Paulette M. *law educator*
Camp, Alida Diane *mediator, arbitrator, law educator*
Cendali, Dale Margaret *lawyer*
Cesare, Christine B. *lawyer*
Chaitman, Helen Davis *lawyer*
Champion, Sara Stewart *lawyer*
Chase, Beverly Fanger *lawyer*
Chell, Beverly C. *lawyer*
Chin, Sylvia Fung *lawyer*
Chromow, Sheri P. *lawyer*
Church, Pamela T. *lawyer*
Clark, Carolyn Cochran *lawyer*
Coan, Rachel B. *lawyer*
Cohen, Robin L. *lawyer*
Comfrey, Kathleen Marie *lawyer*
Corello, Sara A. *lawyer*
Corrales, Carmen Amalia *lawyer*
Creenan, Katherine Heras *lawyer*
Crost, Katharine I. *lawyer*
Cundiff, Victoria Anne *lawyer*
Curtis, Susan M. *lawyer*
Czarniak, Julia A. *lawyer*
Damrosch, Lori Fisler *law educator*
Darrow, Jill E(llen) *lawyer*
Davenport, Margaret Andrews *lawyer*
Davidson, Sheila Kearney *lawyer, insurance company executive*
Davis, Florence Ann *lawyer*
Davis, Lisa E. *lawyer*
Davis, Martha Frances *lawyer*
Davis, Peggy Cooper *law educator*
DeCaro, Shana *lawyer*
DeFelice, Laura A. *lawyer*
Degener, Carol M. *lawyer*
DeMasi, Karin A. *lawyer*
Donovan, Maureen Driscoll *lawyer*
Drechsler, Beatrice Krain *lawyer*
Dreizen, Alison M. *lawyer*
Dreyfuss, Rochelle Cooper *law educator*
Duncan, Patricia *lawyer, broadcast executive*
Eisen, LizabethAnn R. *lawyer*
Eisenberg, Barbara Anne K. *lawyer*
Elkin, Judith *lawyer*
Estlund, Cynthia *law educator*
Evans, Julie Robin *lawyer*
Feldman, Elise *lawyer*
Feltenstein, Martha *lawyer*
Fisher, Ann Bailen *lawyer*
Flanagan, Deborah Mary *lawyer*
Flesher, Gail A. *lawyer*
Fodor, Susanna Serena *lawyer*
Forrest, Katherine B. *lawyer*
Franke, Katherine M. *law educator*
Freyer, Dana Hartman *lawyer*
Freyre, Angela Mariana *lawyer*
Friedman, Elaine Florence *lawyer*
Fry, Elizabeth H. W. *lawyer*
Garcia, Angela G. *lawyer*
Garland, Sylvia Dillof *lawyer*
Gelb, Judith Anne *lawyer*
Geoghegan, Patricia *lawyer*
Gill, E. Ann *lawyer*
Glick, Anna H. *lawyer*
Gluck, Abbe R. *lawyer*
Goldbard, Laura E. *lawyer*
Goldstein, Marcia Landweber *lawyer*
Goldstein, Sandra Cara *lawyer*
Grayer, Elizabeth L. *lawyer*
Greenman, Paula S. *lawyer*
Greenzang, Katherine *lawyer, insurance company executive*
Gregory, Robin N. *lawyer*
Gross, Karen Charal *lawyer*
Grossman, Elizabeth *lawyer*
Grubin, Sharon Ellen *lawyer, former federal judge*
Hagberg, Karen L. *lawyer*
Halberstam, Malvina *law educator, lawyer*
Hallingby, Jo Davis *arbitrator*
Handley, Siobhan A. *lawyer*
Hanson, Jean Elizabeth *lawyer*
Harlow, Ruth *lawyer*
Harris, Arlene *lawyer*
Harris, Theresa *lawyer*
Hart, Mary T. *lawyer*
Hauser, Rita Eleanore Abrams *lawyer*
Hayman, Linda C. *lawyer*
Head, Elizabeth *lawyer, arbitrator, mediator*
Heinzelman, Kris F. *lawyer*
Hengen, Nancy L. *lawyer*
Henry, Sally McDonald *lawyer*
Hershkoff, Helen *law educator*
Herzeca, Lois Friedman *lawyer*
Higgins, Tara A. *lawyer*
Hoffmann, Elinor R. *lawyer*
Holtzman, Elizabeth *lawyer*
Huttner, Constance S. *lawyer*
Hynes, Patricia M. *lawyer*
Ivanick, Carol W. Trencher *lawyer*
Jacob, Valerie Ford *lawyer*
Jaffe, Helene D. *lawyer*
Jordan, Nora Margaret *lawyer*
Kalik, Mildred *lawyer*
Kambour, Annaliese Spofford *lawyer, media company executive*
Kamm, Linda Heller *lawyer*
Kanter, Stacy J. *lawyer*
Kaplan, Cathy M. *lawyer*
Kaplan, Madeline *legal administrator*
Kaplan, Roberta A. *lawyer*
Karmali, Rashida Alimahomed *lawyer*
Katz, Sharon *lawyer*
Keefer, Elizabeth J. *lawyer*
Keneally, Kathryn Marie *lawyer*
Kimber, Karen Beecher *law educator*
King, Alison *lawyer*
Kohlmann, Susan J. *lawyer*
Koopersmith, Kim *lawyer*
Korff, Phyllis G. *lawyer*
Korry, Alexandra D. *lawyer*
Kraemer, Lillian Elizabeth *lawyer*
Kuck, Lea Haber *lawyer*
Lambert, Judith A. Ungar *lawyer*
Law, Sylvia A. *law educator*
Lemos, Margaret H. *lawyer*
Lesk, Ann Berger *lawyer*
Lieberman, Nancy Ann *lawyer*
Liebman, Carol Bensinger *lawyer, educator*
Lindblom, Marjorie Press *lawyer*
Livingston, Debra A. *law educator*
Loss, Margaret Ruth *lawyer*
Lowry, Marcia Robinson *legal association administrator*
Luria, Mary Mercer *lawyer*
Lynch, Loretta E. *lawyer, former prosecutor*
Malamud, Deborah C. *law educator*
Malfa, Frances *lawyer*
Malman, Laurie L. *law educator*
Marafioti, Kayalyn A. *lawyer*
Marcus, Maria Lenhoff *lawyer, educator*
Marshall, Sheila Hermes *lawyer*
Martone, Patricia Ann *lawyer*
Marzigliano, Tammy *lawyer*
Mayerson, Sandra Elaine *lawyer*
McCaffrey, Carlyn Sundberg *lawyer*
McGarry, Martha E. *lawyer*
McGowen, Lorraine S. *lawyer*
McHale, Catherine A. *lawyer*
Meeropol, Rachel *lawyer*
Meili, Barbara *lawyer*
Mendelson, Barbara R. *lawyer*
Menkes, Sheryl R. *lawyer*
Menton, Tanya Lia *lawyer, educator*
Merrill, Susan L. *lawyer*
Meyer, Janis M. *lawyer*
Mikumo, Akiko *lawyer*
Moran, Patricia *lawyer*
Nearing, Vivienne W. *lawyer*
Neugebauer, Cynthia A. *lawyer*
Neuner, Lynn K. *lawyer*
Newstead, Jennifer G. *lawyer*
North, Julie A. *lawyer*
Northup, Nancy Jean *lawyer*
Nusbacher, Gloria Weinberg *lawyer*
Oberly, Kathryn Anne *lawyer, diversified financial services company executive*
O'Brien, Clare *lawyer*
Olivier, Jeanne C. *lawyer*
Olshan, Regina *lawyer*
O'Neill, Judith D. *lawyer*
Ottombrino, Lois Kathryn *lawyer*
Palma, Laura *lawyer*
Palmer, Catherine E. *lawyer*
Parker, Kelley D. *lawyer*
Phillips, Pamela Kim *lawyer*
Pineda, Patricia Salas *lawyer*
Pines, Lori L. *lawyer*
Pistor, Katharina *law educator*
Plevan, Bettina B. *lawyer*
Podolsky, Andrea G. *lawyer*
Polevoy, Nancy Tally *lawyer, social worker, genealogist*
Pollack, Jessica Glass *lawyer*
Quinn, Yvonne Susan *lawyer*
Ranney-Marinelli, Alesia *lawyer*
Rappaport, Linda Ellen *lawyer*

Reisman, Sharyl A. *lawyer*
Reynard, Muriel Joyce *lawyer*
Richard, Virginia Rynne *lawyer*
Ritter, Ann L. *lawyer*
Ritter, Jodi Gottesfeld *lawyer*
Robb, Kathy McCleskey *lawyer*
Robfogel, Susan Salitan *lawyer*
Robinson, Barbara Paul *lawyer*
Rockas, Anastasia T. *lawyer*
Rocklen, Kathy Hellenbrand *lawyer*
Rodgers, Kathy *lawyer*
Rodin, Rita Angela *lawyer*
Roer, Ricki E. *lawyer*
Rosenberg, Jill L. *lawyer*
Roth, Judith Shulman *lawyer*
Rothenberg, Laraine S. *lawyer*
Sackmann, Pamela Jayne *lawyer*
Saeed, Faiza J. *lawyer*
Saltzstein, Susan L. *lawyer*
Sanchez, Karla G. *lawyer*
Sanger, Carol *law educator*
Schair, Robin A. *lawyer*
Schatz, Barbara A. *law educator*
Schenk, Deborah Huffman *law educator*
Schlain, Barbara Ellen *lawyer*
Schneider, Willys Hope *lawyer*
Schneirov, Allison R. *lawyer*
Schofield, Lorna Gail *lawyer*
Schwartz, Carol Vivian *lawyer*
Schwartz, Renee Gerstler *lawyer*
Scott, Helen S. *law educator*
Semaya, Francine Levitt *lawyer*
Semlies, Lori R. *lawyer*
Serota, Susan Perlstadt *lawyer, educator*
Seymour, Karen Patton *lawyer, former prosecutor*
Shainwald, Sybil *lawyer*
Shane, Penny *lawyer*
Sharkey, Catherine Moira *law educator*
Shientag, Florence Perlow *lawyer*
Shoss, Cynthia Renée *lawyer*
Sigmond, Carol Ann *lawyer*
Silberman, Linda Joy *law educator*
Simms, Marsha E. *lawyer*
Sirgado, Jo Anne E. *lawyer*
Skaistis, Rachel G. *lawyer*
Sklyar, Adelina M. *lawyer*
Smith, Karen A. *lawyer*
Snyder, Leslie Crocker *lawyer*
Sokoloff, Audrey L. *lawyer*
Sorell Stehr, Deborah K. *lawyer*
Soyster, Margaret Blair *lawyer*
Spellman Sweet, Julia T. *lawyer*
Spinak, Jane M. *law educator*
Stein, Jane Wallison *lawyer*
Steinberg, Debra Brown *lawyer*
Strossen, Nadine *legal association administrator, law educator*
Stuart, Alice Melissa *lawyer*
Sturm, Susan P. *law educator*
Suk, Jeannie *lawyer*
Sullivan, Irene A. *lawyer*
Sutherland, Susan J. *lawyer*
Thoyer, Judith Reinhardt *lawyer*
Thurston, Sally A. *lawyer*
Tiano, Linda V. *lawyer*
Tracy, Janet Ruth *law educator, law librarian, director*
Urda Kassis, Cynthia E. *lawyer*
Vale, Eleanor P. *lawyer*
Vladeck, Judith Pomarlen *lawyer*
Vollweiler, Cheryl P. *lawyer*
Vyskocil, Mary Kay *lawyer*
Walker, Kim A. *lawyer*
Wallace, Nora Ann *lawyer*
Ward, Sarah M. *lawyer*
Warshauer, Irene C. *lawyer*
Waybourn, Kathleen Ann *lawyer, consultant*
Webster, Susan *lawyer*
Weiksner, Sandra S. *lawyer*
Weinroth, Lois L. *lawyer*
Weiss, Lisa Ann *lawyer*
Wenig, Cindy L. *lawyer*
Wesely, Marissa Celeste *lawyer*
Whelchel, Betty Anne *lawyer*
White, Mary Jo *lawyer, former prosecutor*
Williams, Patricia J. *law educator*
Wolff, Margaret Louise *lawyer*
Yablon, Heather D. *lawyer*
Yelenick, Mary Therese *lawyer*
Young, Alice *lawyer*
Young, Nancy *lawyer*
Zagorin, Janet Susan *legal firm administrator, marketing professional*
Zimmerman, Diane Leenheer *law educator*
Zulack, Mary Marsh *law educator*

Poughkeepsie
Teal, Arabella W. *lawyer, former state attorney general*

Rochester
Frazee, Evelyn *lawyer, educator*
Gootnick, Margery Fischbein *lawyer*
Kunkel, Barbara J. *law firm executive*
McCreary, Jean Hutchinson *lawyer*
Morrison, Patrice Burgert *lawyer*
Stewart, Sue S. *lawyer*
Stiller, Sharon Paula *lawyer*

Rosedale
Charrington, Karen Hillary *lawyer, consultant*

Scarsdale
Callaghan, Georgann Mary *lawyer*

Somers
McGuire, Pamela Cottam *lawyer*

Syracuse
Richardson, M. Catherine *lawyer*
Simmons, Doreen Anne *lawyer*

Uniondale
Camelo, Dianne M. *lawyer*

Utica
Stormer, Nancy Rose *lawyer*

Wading River
Budd, Bernadette Smith *lawyer, newspaper executive, public relations consultant*

White Plains
Hattar, Jacqueline *lawyer*
Jacobson, Sandra W. *lawyer*
Pirro, Jeanine Ferris *prosecutor*

Williamsville
Ciprich, Paula Marie *lawyer, gas industry executive*

NORTH CAROLINA

Chapel Hill
Gasaway, Laura Nell *law librarian, educator*
Gervais-Gruen, Elizabeth *lawyer*
Wegner, Judith Welch *lawyer, educator, dean*

Charlotte
Barber, Martha Gayle *lawyer*
Kelley, Janet Godsey *lawyer*
Shappert, Gretchen C. F. (Gretchen Cecilia Frances Shappert) *prosecutor, lawyer*
Withrow, Shawanna Nicole *paralegal, entrepreneur*

Durham
Bernard, Pamela Jenks *lawyer*
Demott, Deborah Ann *law educator*
Fisk, Catherine Laura *law educator, lawyer*
Holder, Angela Roddey *law educator*

Greensboro
Wagoner, Anna Mills S. *prosecutor*

Hendersonville
Consilio, Barbara Ann *legal association administrator, management consultant*

Hertford
Cole, Janice McKenzie *former prosecutor*

Morganton
Pritchard, Michelle C. *lawyer*

Raleigh
Bar, Roselyn R. *legal association administrator, lawyer, executive secretary*
Bellamy, Kristi Michelle *prosecutor*
Carter, Jean Gordon *lawyer*
McNish, Susan Kirk *retired lawyer*
Rudinger, Jennifer Irene *legal association administrator*
Rusher, Mary Nash Kelly *lawyer*

Rocky Mount
Edelman, Betsy A. (Elizabeth Edelman) *lawyer*

Willow Spring
Valvo, Barbara-Ann *lawyer, surgeon*

Wilmington
Robinson, Robin Wicks *lawyer*

Winston Salem
Gregg, Ellen M. *lawyer*
Lambeth, Judy (E. Julia Lambeth) *lawyer*
Oliver, Patricia *lawyer*
Quick, Elizabeth L. *lawyer*

NORTH DAKOTA

Bismarck
Moore, Sherry Mills *lawyer*

Fargo
Herman, Sarah Andrews *lawyer*
Johnson Aldrich, Leslie Deborah *lawyer*

OHIO

Akron
Bishop, Christy B. *lawyer*
Oldfield, Joy Malek *lawyer*
Taylor, E. Jane *lawyer*

Avon Lake
Shiba, Wendy C. *lawyer*

Chagrin Falls
Smith, Barbara Jean *lawyer*

Cincinnati
Anstaett, Jennifer Griffin *lawyer*
Auttonberry, Sheri E. *lawyer*
Bride, Nancy J. *lawyer*
Bruvold, Kathleen Parker *retired lawyer*
Burke, Rachel E. *lawyer*
Childs, Erin C. *lawyer*
Cors, Jeanne Marie *lawyer*
Eckner, Shannon F. *lawyer*
Ellerman, Paige L. *lawyer*
Erhart, Sue A. *lawyer*
Faller, Susan Grogan *lawyer*
Faulkner, Laura R. *lawyer*
Fitzsimmons, Becky Barlow *lawyer*
Garfinkel, Jane E. *lawyer*
Gaunt, Karen Kreider *lawyer*
Hinegardner, Laura A. *lawyer*
Levin, Debbe Ann *lawyer*
Levy, Charlotte Lois *law librarian, educator, lawyer*
Love, Lisa A. *lawyer*
Mason, Rachel J. *lawyer*
Meyers, Karen Diane *lawyer, educator*
Meyers, Pamela Sue *lawyer*
Tankersley, Sarah *lawyer*

Cleveland
Bixenstine, Kim Fenton *lawyer*
Brennan, Maureen *lawyer*
Burke, Kathleen B. *lawyer*
Carrick, Kathleen Michele *law librarian*
Cudak, Gail Linda *lawyer*
DiSilvio, Marilena *lawyer*
Fischer, Michelle K. *lawyer*
Hastings, Susan C. *lawyer*
Jorgenson, Mary Ann *lawyer*
Kilbane, Catherine M. *lawyer*
Kryshtalowych, Helen Zwenyslawa *lawyer*
Lennox, Heather *lawyer*
Leukart, Barbara J. J. *lawyer*
Maloney, Mary D. *lawyer*
Mast, Bernadette Mihalic *lawyer*
Monihan, Mary Elizabeth *lawyer*
Pietrzen, Julie Lynn *lawyer*
Rawson, Rachel L. *lawyer*
Rickert, Jeanne Martin M. *lawyer*
Roberts-Mamone, Lisa A. *lawyer*
Striefsky, Linda A(nn) *lawyer*
Thimmig, Diana Marie *lawyer*
Thomas, Dynda A. *lawyer*
Wong, Margaret Wai *lawyer*

Columbus
Berndt, Ellen German *lawyer*
Crowder, Marjorie Briggs *lawyer*
Davis, Julia A. *lawyer, retail executive*
Grotenrath, Mary Jo *lawyer, writer*
Harwood, Sandra Stabile *lawyer, state representative*
Hatler, Patricia Ruth *lawyer*
Hill, Kathleen Blickenstaff *lawyer, nursing educator, mental health nurse*
Nissl, Colleen Kaye *lawyer*
Rector, Susan Darnell *lawyer*
Sowald, Heather Gay *lawyer*

Dayton
Cramblit, Miggie E. *lawyer*
Vaughn, Noel Wyandt *lawyer*
Wightman, Ann *lawyer*

Dublin
Tenuta, Luigia *lawyer*

Elyria
Miller, Bridget A. *lawyer*

Fairfield
Crane, Debra K. *lawyer*

Hudson
Gentile Sachs, Valerie Ann *lawyer*

Maumee
McBride, Beverly Jean *lawyer*

Mayfield Heights
Vanderwist, Kathryn K. *lawyer*

Newark
Mencer, Jetta *lawyer*

Norwalk
Fresch, Marie Beth *court reporting company executive*

Orrville
Harlan, M. Ann *lawyer*

Westerville
Moss, Judith Dorothy *lawyer, consultant, lecturer*

OKLAHOMA

Edmond
Loving, Susan Brimer *lawyer, former state official*
Wilson, Julia Ann Yother *lawyer*

Eufaula
Dawson, Cindy Marie *lawyer*

Norman
Petersen, Catherine Holland *lawyer*

Oklahoma City
Askins, Jari *lawyer, department chairman, state representative*
Marcussen, Carin Leigh *lawyer*
Mather, Stephanie June *lawyer*
Pain, Betsy M. *lawyer*
Wood, Paula Davidson *lawyer*
Zevnik-Sawatzky, Donna Dee *retired litigation coordinator*

Tulsa
Dexter, Deirdre O'Neil Elizabeth *lawyer*
Gottschalk, Debbra J. *lawyer*
Vaniman, Vicki *lawyer*

OREGON

Beaverton
Vardavas, Stephanie J. *lawyer*

Central Point
Ingraham, Laura *lawyer, political commentator*

Corvallis
Achterman, Gail Louise *lawyer*

Eugene
Aldave, Barbara Bader *lawyer, educator*
McCrea, Shaun S. *lawyer*

Keizer
Stevens, Sharon Cox *lawyer*

Madras
Weires, Sally L. *paralegal*

Portland
Chevis, Cheryl Ann *lawyer*
Cook, Nena *lawyer*
Dailey, Dianne K. *lawyer*
Helmer, M(artha) Christie *lawyer*
Immergut, Karin J. *prosecutor*
Rosenbaum, Lois Omenn *lawyer*
Swenson, Constance Rae *lawyer*
Teller, Susan Elaine *lawyer*

Salem
Gangle, Sandra Smith *arbitrator, mediator*

PENNSYLVANIA

Allentown
Rankin, Jean F. *lawyer*

Bala Cynwyd
Kane-Vanni, Patricia Ruth *lawyer, paleontologist, educator*
Leibman, Faith H. *lawyer, psychologist*

Bethlehem
Rambo, Kelly Clifford *lawyer*

Blue Bell
Sundheim, Nancy Straus *lawyer*

Chadds Ford
Manogue, Caroline B. *lawyer*

Danville
Gubbiotti, Christine M. *lawyer*

Etters
Steps, Barbara Jill *lawyer*

Exton
Segal, Jacqueline Gale *lawyer*

Harrisburg
Adams, Barbara *lawyer*
Kane, Yvette *lawyer, judge*
Meilton, Sandra L. *lawyer*
Miller, Leslie Anne *lawyer*
Pacuska, M. Abbegael *lawyer*

Haverford
Stiller, Jennifer Anne *lawyer*

Kennett Square
Coggins, Eileen M. *lawyer*

King Of Prussia
Schneider, Pam Horvitz *lawyer*

Kittanning
Krzton, Nancy L. *lawyer, writer*

Lancaster
Burns, Erin Cathleen *lawyer*
Whare, Wanda Snyder *lawyer*

Mount Gretna
Warshaw, Roberta Sue *lawyer*

Murrysville
Ferri, Karen Lynn *lawyer*

Natrona Heights
Maleski, Cynthia Maria *lawyer*

Norristown
Casale, Helen E. *lawyer*
Gold-Bikin, Lynne Z. *lawyer*
Rivera Matos, Carmen Lourdes *lawyer*

Oakdale
Feather, Nancy Joanne *lawyer, educator*

Paoli
Laubenstein, Kathleen Marie *lawyer*

Philadelphia
Abraham, Lynne M. *district attorney*
Angel, Marina *law educator*
Austin, Regina *law educator*
Barnett, Bonnie Allyn *lawyer*
Beck, Phyllis Whitman *lawyer, retired judge*
Bergmann, Renee F. *lawyer*
Berkley, Emily Carolan *lawyer*
Boss, Amelia Helen *lawyer, educator*
Brandt, Jennifer Anne *lawyer*
Brier, Bonnie Susan *lawyer*
Chan, Ashely Michelle *lawyer*
Comisky, Hope A. *lawyer*
Connelly, Kori Ann *lawyer*
Fickler, Arlene *lawyer*
Finkelstein, Claire *law educator*
Finken, Tracy Ann *lawyer*
Foley, Regina M. *lawyer*
Fournaris, Christina Mesires *lawyer*
Frampton, J. Paige *lawyer*
Gordon, Sarah Barringer *law educator*
Gupta, Mona *lawyer*
Gussack, Nina M. *lawyer*
Harris, Judith E. *lawyer*
Henderson, Erin F. *lawyer*
Henry, Deborah Epstein *lawyer*
James, Jennifer DuFault *lawyer*
Jones, Donna Lee *lawyer*
Kaiser, Linda Susan *lawyer*
Koc, Lorraine K(iessling) *lawyer*
Lasher, Lori L. *lawyer*
Laupheimer, Ann B. *lawyer*
Leister, Kelly M. *lawyer*
Levering, Kathryn H. *lawyer*
Levin, Shanon S. (Shanon Levin Lehman) *lawyer*
Liebenberg, Roberta D. *lawyer*
Lillie, Charisse Ranielle *lawyer, educator*
Megerian, Talene *lawyer*
Melby, Barbara Murphy *lawyer*
Miller, Camille M. *lawyer*
Peck, Julianne L. *lawyer*
Ramsey, Natalie D. *lawyer*
Resnick, Stephanie *lawyer*
Rhodes, Alice Graham *lawyer, not-for-profit developer, consultant*
Roomberg, Lila Goldstein *lawyer*
Russakoff, Nina L. *lawyer*
Safier, Regan S. *lawyer*
Scheppele, Kim Lane *law educator*
Stern, Joan Naomi *lawyer*
Traynor, Tami Lee *lawyer*
Wax, Amy Laura *law educator*
Wolff, Deborah H(orowitz) *lawyer*

Pittsburgh
Anderson, Lea E. *lawyer*
Bissoon, Cathy *lawyer*
Blum, Eva Tansky *lawyer*

Buchanan, Mary Beth *prosecutor*
Cahouet, Ann P. *lawyer*
Candris, Laura A. *lawyer*
Ellsworth, Laura E. *lawyer*
Fischer, Nora Barry *lawyer*
Hackett, Mary J. *lawyer*
Keane, Margaret A. *lawyer*
Kikel, Suzanne *patent agent*
Litman, Roslyn Margolis *lawyer*
Pudlin, Helen Pomerantz *lawyer*

Pittston
Pollick, Cynthia *lawyer*

Scranton
Handley, Tillian Marie Rose *lawyer*

Sewickley
Jackson, Velma Louise *lawyer*

Towanda
Rockefeller, Shirley E. *court clerk*

West Pittston
Gelb, Lesa S. *lawyer*

Willow Grove
Moses, Bonnie Smith *lawyer, educator*

York
Davis, Jane G. *lawyer*

RHODE ISLAND

Cranston
Alston, Jametta O. *lawyer*

Pawtucket
Belliveau, Kathrin Pagonis *lawyer*

Providence
Coletta, Andria *lawyer*
Farrell, Margaret Dawson *lawyer*
McCann, Gail Elizabeth *lawyer*
Rocha, Patricia Kennedy *lawyer*

SOUTH CAROLINA

Aiken
Rudnick, Irene Krugman *lawyer, educator, former state legislator*

Columbia
Gray, Elizabeth Van Doren *lawyer*

Florence
Chewning, Rangeley Bailey *lawyer*

Greenville
Williams, Martha Garrison *lawyer*

Johns Island
Carter, Mary Andrews *paralegal*

Mount Pleasant
Bernard, Caroline A. *lawyer*

SOUTH DAKOTA

Mission
Shabazz, Frances *lawyer*

Pierre
Johnson, Julie Marie *lawyer, lobbyist, judge*

Sioux Falls
Tapken, Michelle G. *prosecutor*

TENNESSEE

Brentwood
Seifert, Rachel A. *lawyer*
Vance, Kim *lawyer*

Goodlettsville
Lanigan, Susan S. *lawyer*

Knoxville
Dunn, Maureen H. *lawyer*
Kennedy, Deseriee *law educator*
Roberts, Esther Lois *lawyer, music educator, composer, writer*

Maryville
Livesay, Tracie Lynn *paralegal*

Memphis
Smith, Maura Abeln *lawyer, paper company executive*
Steinhauer, Gillian *lawyer*

Murfreesboro
Kendrick, Kimpi King *lawyer*

Nashville
Mayden, Barbara Mendel *lawyer*

TEXAS

Abilene
Trimble, Celia Denise *lawyer*

Addison
Epstein, Brooke C. *lawyer*
McKinney, Melissa A. *lawyer*

Arlington
Stewart, Patricia Kimbriel *retired legal assistant*

Austin
Bartoli, Catherine P. *legal assistant*
Cantú, Norma V. *law educator, former federal official*
Cunningham, Judy Marie *lawyer*
Dahmus, Teresa A. *lawyer*
Garcia, Sara Kruger *lawyer*
Gehm, Amy K. *lawyer*
Giblin, Pamela M. *lawyer*
Hamilton, Dagmar Strandberg *lawyer, educator*
McDaniel, Myra Atwell *lawyer, former state official*
Mullenix, Linda Susan *law educator*
Weddington, Sarah Ragle *lawyer, educator*
Weinberg, Louise *law educator, writer*

Carrollton
Rodriguez, Elaine Flud *lawyer*

Cleveland
Campbell, Selaura Joy *lawyer*

Corsicana
McSpadden, Jody Sodd *lawyer*

Dallas
Ackerman, Deborah *lawyer*
Aldous, Charla G. *lawyer*
Anderson, Barbara McComas *lawyer*
Bergner, John F. *lawyer*
Blue, Lisa A. *lawyer, psychologist*
Brainin, Stacy L. *lawyer*
Burke, Carla Michelle *lawyer*
Burris, Kelly L. *lawyer*
Casada, Hilaree A. *lawyer*
Clancy, Denyse Finn *lawyer*
Crain, Gayla Campbell *lawyer*
Daly, Gail M. *law librarian, educator*
Davis, Clarice McDonald *lawyer*
Demarest, Sylvia M. *lawyer*
Dutton, Diana Cheryl *lawyer*
Farris, Erin Anderson *lawyer*
Fenner, Suzan Ellen *lawyer*
Flood, Joan Moore *paralegal*
Franze, Laura Marie *lawyer*
Freytag, Sharon Nelson *lawyer*
Gray, Amy Castle *lawyer*
Hensley, Noel M. B. *lawyer*
Hirschman, Karen L. *lawyer*
Hurtwitz, Ann *lawyer*
Hurwitz, Ann *lawyer*
Huston, Angela C. *lawyer*
Jayson, Melinda Gayle *lawyer*
Knott, Jennifer W. *lawyer*
Lesmes, Stephanie Brooks *lawyer*
Long, Sarah Holley *lawyer*
McCurley, Mary Johanna *lawyer*
McDole, Sydney Bosworth *lawyer*
Melançon, Renée M. *lawyer*
Moore, Cheryl Jerome (Cheryl Milkes Jerome) *lawyer*
Murphy, Kathryn J. *lawyer*
Nelson, Elaine Edwards *lawyer*
Parker, Emily *lawyer*
Pennington, Karen Harder *lawyer*
Raggio, Louise Ballerstedt *lawyer*
Sharry, Janice Vyn *lawyer*
Turley, Linda *lawyer*
Villareal, Patricia J. *lawyer*
Villarreal, Christie M. *lawyer*
Wansbrough, Ann *legal assistant*
Warman, Lynnette R. *lawyer*
West, Susan D. *lawyer*
Whitaker, Elizabeth D. *lawyer*
Wu, Kathleen J. *lawyer*
Yung, Patsy P. *lawyer*

Fort Worth
Cagle, Karin Knowles *lawyer*
Keith, Courtney S. *lawyer*
Reade, Kathleen Margaret *paralegal, author, educator*

Houston
Addison, Linda Leuchter *lawyer, writer, commentator, columnist*
Aguirre, Sarah K. *lawyer*
Anderson, Doris Ehlinger *lawyer*
Andrews, Sally S. *lawyer*
Asselin, Heather E. *lawyer*
Backus, Marcia Ellen *lawyer*
Bankhead, Sherry L. *lawyer*
Berg, Amie G. *lawyer*
Biery, Evelyn Hudson *lawyer*
Boyce, Maria Wyckoff *lawyer*
Chapman, Cynthia B. *lawyer*
Cline, Vivian Melinda *lawyer*
Dinkins, Carol Eggert *lawyer*
Donnelly, Rosemarie *lawyer*
Farenthold, Frances Tarlton *lawyer*
Galvin, Kerry A. *lawyer*
Gillmore, Kathleen Cory *lawyer*
Goode, Coralyn *lawyer*
Greenberg, Angela Barmby *lawyer*
Heeg, Peggy A. *lawyer, former gas industry executive*
Higgins, Pauline Edwards *lawyer*
Hinton, Paula Weems *lawyer*
Hollingsworth, Lara Hudgins *lawyer*
Jacobs, Tonya A. *lawyer*
Johnson, Alisa B. *lawyer, energy company executive*
Joiner, Jamie A. *lawyer*
Lacy, Terri *lawyer*
Lake, Kathleen Cooper *lawyer*
Liberato, Lynne *lawyer*
Maloney, Marilyn C. *lawyer*
Mathers, Paula Janecek *lawyer*
Mattox, Sharon M. *lawyer*
McFarland, Marcie Allred *lawyer*
McMahon, Catherine Driscoll *lawyer*
Moroney, Linda L.S. (Muffie) *lawyer, educator*
Nacol, Mae *lawyer*
Nelson, Joelle Grace Kenney *lawyer*
Oglesby, GeorgAnn Hedlesten *lawyer*
Pector, Michelle D. *lawyer*
Pennington, Lisa H. *lawyer*
Peterson, Terry Norris *lawyer*
Pilibosian, Michele Mason *lawyer*
Rapoport, Nancy B. *law educator*
Rusnak, Cyndi Moss *lawyer*
Rustay, Jennifer Beth *lawyer*
Shannon, Margaret Barrett *lawyer*
Smith, Alison Leigh *lawyer*
Smith, Martha Lee *lawyer*
Thompson, Sandra Guerra *lawyer, educator*
Tripp, Karen Bryant *lawyer*
Vance, Vanessa L. *lawyer*
Vogel, Jennifer *lawyer*
Wagner, Leslie *lawyer*
Wirz, Melody *lawyer*
Wyrsch, Martha B. *lawyer, energy executive*
Yeates, Marie R. *lawyer*

Irving
Lang, Laura Smith *lawyer*
Molay, Hilary S. *lawyer*
Wenetschlaeger, Patty Strader *lawyer*

Laredo
Goodman, N. Jane *law librarian*

Mc Kinney
Albano, Christine Grace *lawyer*

Midland
Rowe, Mary R. *lawyer*

Plano
Bober, Joanne L. *lawyer*
Weeks, Tresi Lea *lawyer*

Pottsboro
Thomas, Ann Van Wynen *retired law educator*

Richardson
Austin, Ann Sheree *lawyer*

San Antonio
Bowers, Kim *lawyer, energy executive*
Emery, Nancy Beth *lawyer*
Johnson, Anne Stuckly *retired lawyer*
Labenz-Hough, Marlene *mediator*
Pitluk, Ellen Eidelbach *lawyer, mediator*
Reed, Susan D. *prosecutor*
Schuk, Linda Lee *legal assistant, business educator*
Spears, Sally *lawyer*

Sealy
Stevens, Rhea Christina *lawyer*

The Woodlands
Ripley, Charlene A. *lawyer*

Wichita Falls
Farris, Charlye Ola *lawyer*

UTAH

Orem
Jasperson, Jill O. *law educator*

Salt Lake City
Emery, Dawn Webber *lawyer*
Peterson, Kami L. *lawyer*
Smith, Janet Hugie *lawyer*
Threedy, Debora Lynn *law educator*

VERMONT

Montpelier
Errecart, Joyce *lawyer*

VIRGINIA

Alexandria
Blue, Catherine Anne *lawyer*
Ginsberg, Nina *lawyer*
Goodman, Sherri Wasserman *lawyer*
Higgins, Mary Celeste *lawyer, researcher*
Kelly, Nancy Frieda Wolicki *lawyer*
Lewin, Cynthia M. *lawyer*
Sturtevant, Brereton *retired lawyer, retired federal official*
Winzer, P.J. *lawyer*

Arlington
Dalglish, Lucy Ann *lawyer, organization executive*
Lanier, Elizabeth K. *lawyer*
Lauderdale, Katherine Sue *lawyer*
Mullett, Jennifer Anne *lawyer*
O'Sullivan, Lynda Troutman *lawyer*
Swenson, Diane Kay *legal association administrator*

Bristol
Wade, Thelma J. *lawyer, mental health nurse*

Charlottesville
Andrews, Minerva Wilson *retired lawyer*
Armacost, Barbara Ellen *law educator*
BeVier, Lillian Riemer *law educator*
Buck, D. Ruth *legal research and writing educator*
Coughlin, Anne M. *law educator*
Fitchett, Taylor *law librarian*
Hurwitz, Deena R. *law educator*
Magill, M(ary) Elizabeth *law educator*
Mahoney, Julia Delong *law educator*
Riley, Margaret Foster (Mimi Riley) *law educator*
Robinson, Mildred Wigfall *law educator*
Scott, Elizabeth S. *law educator*
Woolhandler, Ann *law educator*

Clarksville
Kyte, Susan Janet *lawyer, consultant*

Fairfax
Susko, Carol Lynne *lawyer, accountant, educator*

Falls Church
Barnes, Jennifer J. *lawyer*
Elderkin, Helaine Grace *lawyer*
Espenoza, Cecelia M. *lawyer, law educator*
Honigberg, Carol Crossman *lawyer*
Keller, Mary Beth *lawyer*
Piccotti, Carolyn M. *lawyer*
Pomeranz, Sharon Jane *lawyer*
Rothwarf, Marta *lawyer*
Van Cleve, Ruth Gill *retired lawyer*

Glen Allen
den Hartog, Grace Robinson *lawyer*
Weaver, Mollie Little *lawyer*

Great Falls
Shay-Byrne, Olivia *lawyer*

Lynchburg
Packert, G(ayla) Beth *retired lawyer*

Mc Lean
Brown, Margaret Ann *lawyer*
Glassman, M. Melissa *lawyer*
LeSourd, Nancy Susan Oliver *lawyer, writer*
Price, Ilene Rosenberg *lawyer*
Reiff, Laura Foote *lawyer*
Saunders, Danielle *lawyer, telecommunications industry executive*
Wall, Barbara Wartelle *lawyer*
Yinger, Emily M. *lawyer*

Norfolk
Diaz, Marla J. *lawyer*
Poston, Anita Owings *lawyer*
Spence, Fay Frances *lawyer, educator*

Petersburg
Burns, Cassandra Stroud *prosecutor*
Everitt, Alice Lubin *labor arbitrator*

Reston
Bredehoft, Elaine Charlson *lawyer*
Butler, Katherine E. *lawyer*
Keler, Marianne Martha *lawyer*
Spander, Deborah L. *lawyer*

Richmond
Brissette, Martha Blevins *lawyer*
Carpi, Janice E. *lawyer*
Gluck, Michelle H. *lawyer*
Hackney, Virginia Howitz *lawyer*
Kiely, Christy E. *lawyer*
Rick, Roseleen P. *lawyer*
Rigsby, Linda Flory *lawyer*
Schwarzschild, Jane L. *lawyer*
Stone, Jacquelyn Elois *lawyer*
Williams, Amy McDaniel *lawyer*
Williams, Christine Alicia *lawyer*

Roanoke
Taylor, Janet Droke *judicial assistant*

Vienna
Artz, Cherie B. *lawyer*
Maguire, Margaret Louise *lawyer*

Virginia Beach
Christiansen, Margaret Louise *law librarian, lawyer*
Lawson, Beth Ann Reid *lawyer, strategic planner*

WASHINGTON

Bellevue
Pinney, Alesia L. *lawyer*
Tee, Virginia *lawyer*

Everett
Ostergaard, Joni Hammersla *lawyer*

Kennewick
Sullivan-Schwebke, Karen Jane *lawyer*

Olympia
Isaki, Lucy Power Slyngstad *lawyer*

Seattle
Boggs, Paula Elaine *lawyer*
Chapman, Fay L. *lawyer*
Char, Patricia Helen *lawyer*
Cunningham, Janis Ann *lawyer*
Glover, Karen Elaine *lawyer*
Hazelton, Penny Ann *law librarian, educator*
Johnsen, Lisa L. *lawyer*
Jones, Susan Delanty *lawyer*
Marchese, Lisa Marie *lawyer, educator*
Niemi, Janice *retired lawyer, retired state legislator*
Osenbaugh, Kimberly W. *lawyer*
Parks, Patricia Jean *lawyer*
Stokke, Diane Rees *lawyer*
Takenaka, Toshiko *lawyer, educator*
Vestal, Josephine Burnet *lawyer*
Wechsler, Mary Heyrman *lawyer*
Williams, Nancy *lawyer*
Wilson, L. Michelle *lawyer*

Selah
Ring, Lucile Wiley *lawyer*

Spokane
Clarke, Judy *lawyer*

WEST VIRGINIA

Beckley
Rhoades, Marye Frances *paralegal*

Charleston
Betts, Rebecca A. *lawyer*

Morgantown
Scudiere, Debra Hodges *lawyer*

Wellsburg
Viderman, Linda Jean *legal assistant, corporate financial executive*

Wheeling
Valdrini, Rita *prosecutor*

WISCONSIN

Eau Claire
Sands, Dawn M. *lawyer*

Greendale
Vinent-Cantoral, Aida R. *mediator*

Hales Corners
Case, Karen Ann *lawyer*

Kenosha
Marrinan, Susan Faye *lawyer*

Madison
Baldwin, Janice Murphy *lawyer*
Barnick, Helen *retired judicial clerk*
Behnke, Michelle A. *lawyer*
Bochert, Linda H. *lawyer*
Braden, Betty Jane *legal association administrator*
Charo, Robin Alta *law educator*
McCallum, Laurie Riach *state government lawyer*
Melli, Marygold Shire *law educator*
Steingass, Susan R. *lawyer*
Swan, Barbara J. *lawyer*

Milwaukee
Ballman, Patricia Kling *lawyer*
Benfield, Linda E. *lawyer*
Geske, Janine Patricia *law educator*
Lione, Gail Ann *lawyer*
McGinnity, Maureen Annell *lawyer*
Neubauer, Lisa S. *lawyer*
Sennett, Nancy J. *lawyer*
Shapiro, Robyn Sue *lawyer, educator*
Walsh, Kathleen *lawyer*

Ripon
Prissel, Barbara Ann *paralegal, law educator*

Sturgeon Bay
Korb, Joan *prosecutor*

Sturtevant
Brandes, Jo Anne *lawyer*

WYOMING

Cheyenne
Carlson, Kathleen Bussart *law librarian*

Laramie
Kinney, Lisa Frances *lawyer*

Powell
Dean, Patricea Louise *lawyer, law educator, small business owner*

TERRITORIES OF THE UNITED STATES

PUERTO RICO

San Juan
Rodriguez-Velez, Rosa *prosecutor*
Santos de Alvarez, Brunilda *lawyer*

CANADA

Toronto
Stanley, Deirdre *lawyer*

CHINA

Shanghai
Lin, Maria C. H. *lawyer*

FRANCE

Draguignan
Frame, Nancy Davis *lawyer*

JAPAN

Tokyo
Dixon, Bonnie Lynn *lawyer*

SWITZERLAND

Geneva
McDougall, Gay *lawyer*

ADDRESS UNPUBLISHED

Allen, Toni K. *lawyer*
Areen, Judith Carol *law educator, dean*
Arnold, Alanna S. Welling *lawyer*
Arnold, Charlotte S. *criminal justice agency executive, activist*
Arrowood, Catharine Biggs *lawyer*
Ashkin, Roberta Ellen *lawyer*
Askew, Kim Juanita *lawyer*
Aune, Debra Bjurquist *lawyer*
Bamberger, Phylis Skloot *lawyer, educator, retired judge*
Baskins, Ann O. *lawyer, former computer company executive*
Bencivengo, Cathy Ann *lawyer*
Benfield, Ann Kolb *retired lawyer*
Benningfield, Carol Ann *lawyer*
Benshoof, Janet Lee *lawyer, association executive*
Bergenfeld, Jennifer Rebekah Lynn *lawyer*
Berman, Lori Beth *lawyer*
Berquist, Katherine Pauline *lawyer*
Boda, Veronica Constance *lawyer*
Booher, Alice Ann *lawyer*
Boulanger, Carol Seabrook *lawyer*
Bower, Jean Ramsay *lawyer, writer*
Bowers, Christi C. *mediator, lawyer, educator, writer, poet*
Bowman, Patricia Lynn *lawyer*
Bradford, Barbara Reed *retired lawyer*
Bradford, Mary Rosen *lawyer*
Brown, Geraldine Reed *lawyer, management consultant*
Brown, Jennifer Kay *lawyer*
Brown, Margaret deBeers *lawyer*
Burke, Linda Beerbower *lawyer, mining executive, metal products executive*
Call, Whitney L. *paralegal*
Cannon, Gayle Elizabeth *lawyer*
Carey, Jana Howard *lawyer*
Carmack, Mildred Jean *retired lawyer*
Carpenter, Susan Karen *defender*
Carter, Jeanne Wilmot *lawyer, publishing executive*
Cazalas, Mary Rebecca Williams *lawyer, nurse*
Chave, Carol *arbitrator, retired lawyer*
Chen, Del-Min Amy *lawyer*
Christensen, Karen Kay *lawyer*
Citron, Beatrice Sally *law librarian, lawyer, educator*
Citron, Diane *lawyer*
Clark, Beverly Ann *retired lawyer*
Clark, Karen Heath *lawyer*
Coffinas, Eleni *lawyer*
Connelly, Sharon Rudolph *lawyer*
Cornish, Jeannette Carter *lawyer*
Crawford, Carol Tallman *law educator*
Crawford, Muriel Laura *lawyer, educator, writer*
Crocker, Saone Baron *lawyer*
Crown, Nancy Elizabeth *lawyer*
Cunningham, Alice Welt *law and mathematics educator*
Curtis, Susan Grace *lawyer*
Dacey, Kathleen Ryan *lawyer, former federal judge*
D'Agusto, Karen Rose *lawyer*
Daley, Linda *lawyer*
Daniel, Marilyn S. *lawyer*
Davidson, Anne Stowell *lawyer*
Davis, Joanne Fatse *lawyer*
Davis, Wanda Rose *lawyer*
Dawson, Mary E. *lawyer*
Dawson, Suzanne Stockus *lawyer*
Dembrow, Dana Lee *lawyer*
DeMitchell, Terri Ann *law educator*
Dennis, Patricia Diaz *lawyer*
DeVore, Daun Aline *lawyer*
Diamond, Helen *arbitrator, freelance/self-employed mediator*
Dickerson, Claire Moore *lawyer, educator*
Diehl, Deborah Hilda *lawyer*
Donoghue, Joan E. *lawyer*
Dowben, Carla Lurie *lawyer, educator*
Driscoll, Kimberlee Marie *lawyer*
Drost, Marianne *lawyer*
Dryden, Mary Elizabeth *law librarian, writer, actress*
DuFresne, Elizabeth Jamison *retired lawyer*
Dunst, Isabel Paula *lawyer*
Durgin, Diane *arbitrator, lawyer, mediator*
Durgom-Powers, Jane Ellyn *lawyer*
Effel, Laura *lawyer*
Elbery, Kathleen Marie *lawyer, accountant, cartoonist*
Ellis, Carolyn Terry *lawyer*
Erlebacher, Arlene Cernik *retired lawyer*
Evans, Carrie L. *state legislative lawyer*
Farmer, Cornelia Griffin *lawyer, consultant, county hearings official*
Ferraro, Geraldine Anne *lawyer, former congresswoman*
Fowler, Flora Daun *retired lawyer*
Fox, Eleanor Mae Cohen *lawyer, educator, writer*
Fulmer, Amy M. *lawyer*
Gay, Faith E. *lawyer, educator*
George, Gay *lawyer*
George, Joyce Jackson *lawyer, writer, retired judge*
George, Katie *lawyer*
Georges, Mara Stacy *lawyer*
Getzendanner, Susan *lawyer*
Gibb, Roberta Louise *lawyer, artist*
Glaser, Patricia L. *lawyer*
Glickman, Gladys *lawyer, writer*
Goldschmidt, Lynn Harvey *lawyer*
Gomez, Melissa Mordell *trial consultant*
Goodman, Elizabeth Ann *retired lawyer*
Gourley, Sara J. *lawyer*
Grant, Paula DiMeo *lawyer, nursing educator, mediator*
Green, Carol H. *lawyer, educator*
Green, Carole L. *lawyer*
Grieb, Elizabeth *lawyer*
Grodsky, Jamie Anne *law educator*
Grutman, Jewel Humphrey *lawyer, writer*
Hackel-Sims, Stella Bloomberg *lawyer, former government official*
Handschu, Barbara Ellen *lawyer*
Haratani, Joan Mei *lawyer*
Harris, Tomika Tantrice *lawyer*
Hasko, Judith Ann *lawyer*
Hatcher, Barbara A. *lawyer*
Hauver, Constance Longshore *lawyer*
Henkel, Kathryn Gundy *lawyer*
Heppe, Karol Virginia *lawyer, educator*
Herringer, Maryellen Cattani *lawyer*
Hester, Julia A. *lawyer*
Heywood, Harriett *lawyer, consultant*
Holbrook, Connie C. *lawyer*
Holt, Marjorie Sewell *lawyer, retired congresswoman*
Hyman, Gayle M. *lawyer*
Jameson, Paula Ann *retired lawyer*
Johnson, Barbara Elizabeth *lawyer*
Johnson, Karen A. *legal association administrator*
Jones, Elaine R. *former legal association administrator, civil rights advocate*
Jones, Mary Gardiner *lawyer, educator, consumer products company executive*
Jordan, Saskia A. *lawyer*
Kantrowitz, Susan Lee *lawyer*
Kaplan, Elaine D. *lawyer*
Kaplan, Helene Lois *lawyer*
Karczewski, Lisa A. *lawyer*
Kaster, Laura A. *lawyer*
Kelehear, Carole Marchbanks Spann *legal assistant*
Kelly, Pamela B. *lawyer*
Kienitz, LaDonna Trapp *lawyer, librarian, municipal official*
Kolbert, Kathryn *lawyer, educator*
Kotcher, Shirley J.W. *lawyer*
Kreindler, Marla J. *lawyer*
Lanam, Linda Lee *lawyer*
Landy, Lisa Anne *lawyer*
LaRobardier, Genevieve Krause *lawyer*
Laudone, Anita Helene *lawyer*
Lee, Carol Frances *lawyer*
Levine, Marilyn Markovich *lawyer, arbitrator*
Libbin, Anne Edna *lawyer*
Liebeler, Susan Wittenberg *lawyer*
Linde, Maxine Helen *lawyer, corporate financial executive, investor*
Logstrom, Bridget A. *lawyer*
Lopo, Diana M. *lawyer*
Lovisone, Sylvia Ruth *lawyer*
Lufkin, Martha B.G. *lawyer, legal writer, art law correspondent*
Maher, Francesca Marciniak *lawyer, former air transportation executive*
Marshall, Kathryn Sue *lawyer*
Martin, Alice Howze *prosecutor*
Mater, Maud *lawyer*
Matthews, Barbara Caridad *lawyer*
McAllister, Singleton Beryl *lawyer*
McCarey, Wilma Ruth *retired lawyer*
McCubbin, Susan Brubeck *lawyer, advertising executive*
McFadden, Rosemary Theresa *retired lawyer, financial services executive*
McIntosh, Terrie Tuckett *lawyer*
McLendon, Susan Michelle *lawyer*
Mehltretter, Kathleen M. *former prosecutor*
Melamed, Carol Drescher *lawyer*
Mendelson, Joan Rintel *lawyer*
Merritt, Nancy-Jo *lawyer*
Miller, Lisa Ann *lawyer*
Mitchell, Ada Mae Boyd *legal assistant*
Moore, Betty Jo *legal assistant*
Morgan, Timi Sue *lawyer*
Mulligan, Erin Leah *lawyer*
Munsell, Elsie Louise *retired lawyer*
Murphy, Sandra Robison *lawyer*
Murray, Kay *lawyer*
Newman, Carol L. *lawyer*
Newman, Joan Meskiel *lawyer*
Noddings, Sarah Ellen *lawyer*
O'Dell, Joan Elizabeth *lawyer, mediator, consumer products company executive, educator*
O'Dowd, Sarah A. *lawyer*
Orlin, Karen J. *lawyer*
Ornt, Jeanine Arden *lawyer*
Oster, Terri *lawyer*
O'Sullivan, Judith Roberta *lawyer, writer, artist*
Otis, Lee (Sarah) Liberman *lawyer, educator*
Page, Stephanie *lawyer*
Parker, Marietta *prosecutor*
Parode, Ann *lawyer*
Parrish, Debra Marie *lawyer*
Paul, Eve W. *retired lawyer*
Peltz, Paulette Beatrice *corporate lawyer*
Phillips, Dorothy K. *lawyer*
Piazza, Rosanna Joy *paralegal*
Platzer, Cynthia Siemen *lawyer*
Plaza, Eva M. *lawyer*
Poppe, Laurie Catherine *matrimonial lawyer, social worker, real estate executive*
Poppler, Doris Swords *lawyer*
Portnoy, Sara S. *lawyer*
Posner, Sylvie Pérez *lawyer*
Powers, Elizabeth Whitmel *lawyer*
Prinz, Kristie Dawn *lawyer*
Prucino, Diane L. *lawyer*
Pugh, Martha Greenewald *lawyer*
Rabkin, Peggy Ann *retired lawyer*
Reid, Joan Evangeline *lawyer, stockbroker*
Reister, Ruth Alkema *lawyer, finance company executive*
Renegar, Joan Ann *lawyer*
Richardson, Margaret Milner *retired lawyer*
Ring, Renee Etheline *lawyer*
Rivlin, Rachel *lawyer*
Roberson, Linda *lawyer*
Roberts, Kathleen Anne *lawyer, former federal judge*
Roditti, Esther C(laire) *lawyer, writer*
Rodriguez, Carolyn *lawyer*
Rohrbach, Heidi A. *lawyer*
Rosseel-Jones, Mary Louise *lawyer*
Rothenberger, Dolores Jane *legal association administrator, actress, singer*
Rowe, Audrey *paralegal*
Ruemmler, Kathryn H. *prosecutor*
Rush, Sophia *law educator*
Russo, Judith A. *paralegal, writer*
Ryan, Cynthia Rhoades *lawyer*
Sagawa, Shirley Sachi *lawyer*
Saunders, Lonna Jeanne *lawyer, newscaster*
Schwab, Eileen Caulfield *lawyer, educator*
Sciacchetano, Gail Mary *lawyer*
Segal, Phyllis Nichamoff *mediator*
Seidman, Ellen Shapiro *lawyer, government official*
Shattuck, Cathie Ann *lawyer, former government official*
Shaw, Nina L. *lawyer*
Siemer, Deanne Clemence *lawyer*
Silvestri, Gina *lawyer*
Skigen, Patricia Sue *lawyer*
Smith, Carole Dianne *retired lawyer, editor, writer, product developer*
Smith, Sherri Lee *law educator*
Smoot, Natalie Marie *lawyer*
Snyder, Jean Maclean *lawyer*
Sowande, Beverly Folasade *lawyer, educator*
Spanninger, Beth Anne *lawyer*
Specht, Lisa *lawyer*
Steptoe, Mary Lou *lawyer*
Stewart, Candra L. *lawyer*
Stillman, Elinor Hadley *retired lawyer*
Strantz, Nancy Jean *law educator, consultant*
Sulzbach, Christi Rocovich *lawyer*
Sundvall, Sheila A. *lawyer*
Tallman, Ann Marie *lawyer*
Tamen, Harriet *lawyer*
Thomas, Patricia Anne *retired law librarian*
Thompson, Holley Marker *lawyer, consultant, marketing professional*
Tinkelman, Joan *lawyer*
Toensing, Victoria *lawyer*
Vallianos, Carole Wagner *lawyer*
Van Ness, Gretchen *lawyer*
Vedouras, Anna *federal lawyer*
Vila, Adis Maria *lawyer, business government executive*
Walker, Linda Lee *lawyer*
Walkowski, Barbara A. *lawyer*
Wallack, Rina Evelyn *lawyer*
Wallison, Frieda K. *lawyer*
Walters, Bette Jean *lawyer, investor*
White, Jill Carolyn *lawyer*
Whiteman Runs Him, Heather Daphne *prosecutor, artist*
Wiehl, Lis W. *law educator, legal analyst*
Williamson, Brynne Amber *paralegal*
Wise, Sandra Casber *lawyer*
Wriston, Kathryn Dineen *corporate director, consultant*
Wyskowski, Barbara Jean *lawyer*
Young, Marlene Annette *lawyer*
Zarro, Janice Anne *lawyer*
Zimmerman, Jean *lawyer*

MEDICINE *See* HEALTHCARE: MEDICINE

MILITARY

UNITED STATES

ALABAMA

Birmingham
Davis, Gwendolyn Louise *military officer, literature educator*

Huntsville
Gawronski, Elizabeth Ann *retired army officer, artist*

Montgomery
Chamberlain, Kathryn Burns Browning *retired military officer*
Fry, Donna Marie *military officer, educator*
Uzzell-Baggett, Karon Lynette *career officer*

Ranburne
Thompson, Jacqueline *retired military officer*

Redstone Arsenal
Burrows, Shania Kay *civilian military employee*

ARIZONA

Phoenix
Lawlis, Patricia Kite *military officer, computer consultant*

Surprise
Lucchetti, Lynn L. *career officer*

CALIFORNIA

Arroyo Grande
Oseguera, Palma Marie *retired career officer*

San Francisco
Gifford, Fereuza *retired military officer*
Thornton, Ann Murphy *retired military officer*

COLORADO

Colorado Springs
Bowen, Clotilde Marion Dent *retired military officer, psychiatrist*

CONNECTICUT

Waterford
Hinkle, Muriel Ruth Nelson *naval warfare analysis company executive*

DISTRICT OF COLUMBIA

Washington
Brice-O'Hara, Sally *career military officer*
Crawford, Mary Louise Perri *career officer*
Crea, Vivien S. *career military officer*
Etter, Delores M. *civilian military employee*
Payton, Sue C. *civilian military employee*
Potter, Lorraine K. *career military officer*

FLORIDA

MacDill AFB
Collins, Jessica Ann *military officer*

GEORGIA

Forest Park
Grace-Crum, Phyllis Venetia *military officer*

Fort Mcpherson
Emery, Carolyn Vera *civilian military employee, retired non-commissioned officer*

HAWAII

Honolulu
Wellein, Marsha Diane Akau *military educator, director*

MARYLAND

Aberdeen Proving Ground
Halstead, Rebecca S. *career military officer*

MASSACHUSETTS

Cambridge
Johnson, Jennifer Toby *military officer*

MISSOURI

Saint Louis
Shodean, Lisa Diane *military officer*

NEW MEXICO

Belen
Smith, Helen Elizabeth *retired career officer*

OKLAHOMA

Tinker Afb
Velasco, Jodi Marie *military lawyer*

OREGON

Canby
Sundquist, Leah Renata *military officer*

TEXAS

Fort Sam Houston
Williams, Pat L. *military officer*

Mission
Eyre, Pamela Catherine *retired career officer*

San Antonio
Corrigan, Paula Ann *military officer, internist*

VIRGINIA

Alexandria
Gurke, Sharon McCue *career officer*
Tyler, Cecilia Kay *retired military officer*

Arlington
Krusa-Dossin, Mary Ann *military officer*

Fort Belvoir
Clark, Trudy H. *career officer*

Herndon
Biely, Debra Marie *retired military officer*

Quantico
Hodges, Adele E. *military officer*

Woodbridge
Lee, Barbara Mahoney *career officer, educator*

WASHINGTON

Tacoma
Baxter, Sheila R. *career military officer*

ADDRESS UNPUBLISHED

Bartz, Debra Ann *retired military officer, pilot*
Brakebill, Jean Newton *military officer, nurse, educator*
Darnell, Susan Laura Browne *retired air force officer*
Desjarlais, Georgia Kathrine *retired military officer*
DiBattiste, Carol A. *military officer*
Esparza, Kacie Lynne *military officer*
Foote, Evelyn Patricia *retired military officer*
Harris, Marcelite Jordan *retired career officer*
Herbert, Linda R. *military officer*
Johnson, Joyce *retired military officer*
Karl, Kailah Marie *military officer, small business owner*
Keene-Burgess, Ruth Frances *military official*
Lynch, Jessica *military officer*
McConnell, Mary Joan *civilian military employee*
Richard, Diana Marie *retired military officer*
Tillman, Shirley *retired military officer*
Truckenbrodt, Yolanda Bernabe *retired air force officer, consultant*
Watts, Helena Roselle *military analyst*
Williamson, Myrna Hennrich *retired career officer, lecturer, consultant*
Wilson, Frances C. *career military officer*

REAL ESTATE

UNITED STATES

ALABAMA

Hayden
Standridge, Jean *real estate company executive, broker*

Montgomery
Farshee, Marlena W. *title company executive*

Montrose
Haynie, Betty Jo Gillmore *personal property appraiser, antiques dealer*

ALASKA

Anchorage
Kelly, Maxine Ann *retired property developer*

ARIZONA

Sedona
Copeland, Suzanne Johnson *real estate company executive*

Tucson
Carman, Mary Ann *realtor, writer, retired medical/surgical nurse*
Tang, Esther Don *real estate developer, consultant, social worker*

Yuma
Lineberry, Laurie Lawhorn *urban planner*

ARKANSAS

Blytheville
Baker, Carlene Poff *real estate agent, reporter*

CALIFORNIA

Apple Valley
Yule, Caroll Jane *real estate broker*

Berkeley
Grimes, Ruth Elaine *city planner*

Beverly Hills
Bergman, Nancy Palm *real estate investment company executive*
Seeger, Melinda Wayne *realtor*

Copperopolis
White, Marnelle Rosalie *real estate broker*

Cottonwood
Pritchett, Lori L. *real estate broker, secondary school educator*

Fountain Valley
Smith, Marie Edmonds *real estate agent, property manager*

Fresno
Dale, Sharon Kay *real estate broker*
Raven, Patricia Elaine (Penny Raven) *real estate broker, developer, columnist, gas industry executive*

Goleta
Koart, Nellie Hart *real estate investor, real estate company executive*

Granite Bay
Kemper, Dorla Dean Eaton (Dorla Dean Eaton) *real estate broker*

Irvine
Myles, Margaret Jean *real estate appraiser*

Long Beach
Cone, Marla *environmentalist, writer*
Davies, Grace Lucille *real estate educator*
Rosenberg, Jill *realtor, civic leader*

Los Angeles
Swartz, Roslyn Holt *real estate company executive*

Mission Viejo
Harris, Ruby Lee *realtor*

Oakland
Brown, Oral Lee *real estate company executive, entrepreneur*
DiMaggio, Debbi *realtor*
Miller, Connie Joy *assistant real estate officer, real estate broker*

Palm Springs
Coffey, Nancy *real estate broker*

Palo Alto
Moore, Cassandra Chrones *real estate broker*

Penn Valley
Nix, Barbara Lois *real estate broker*

Rancho Santa Fe
Land, Judy M. *real estate broker*

San Diego
Oldham, Maxine Jernigan *real estate broker*

San Fernando
Aguilar, Julia Elizabeth *real estate company executive*

San Francisco
Wang, An-Yi (Anne) Chou *real estate broker*

South Pasadena
Bernal, Harriet Jean Daniels *real estate agent*

Spring Valley
Roberts, Carolyn June *real estate broker*

Thousand Oaks
Helton, Patricia Beth *realtor*

Tulare
Hefflefinger, Clarice Thorpe *retired real estate broker*

COLORADO

Aurora
Martinez-Nemnich, Maricela *realtor*
Wessler, Mary Hraha *real estate company executive*

Colorado Springs
Bowers, Zella Zane *real estate broker*

Fort Collins
Jensen, Margaret *real estate broker*

CONNECTICUT

Greenwich
Griggs, Nina M. *realtor*

New Milford
Smith, Virginia *real estate broker*

Norwalk
Soper, Jeannine *real estate agent*

Old Greenwich
Parris, Sally Nye *real estate agent*

DELAWARE

Dover
Taylor, Suzonne Berry Stewart *real estate broker*

Wilmington
Maley, Patricia Ann *preservation planner*

DISTRICT OF COLUMBIA

Washington
Brooks, Jane K. *real estate agent, educator*
Jones, Susan Dorfman *real estate broker, writer*
Wallace Douglas, Jean *conservationist*

FLORIDA

Boca Raton
Innes-Brown, Georgette Meyer *real estate broker, insurance broker*
Phelps, Annette Failla *realtor*

Daytona Beach
Hastings, Mary Lynn *real estate broker*

Fort Lauderdale
Parrish, Lori Nance *property appraiser*

Fort Myers
Van Vleck, Pamela Kay *real estate company officer*

Hutchinson Island
Welch, Martha Lynn *environmentalist, educator*

Jacksonville
Aleschus, Justine Lawrence *retired real estate broker*
Bodkin, Ruby Pate *real estate broker, educator*

Maitland
Vallee, Judith Delaney *environmentalist, writer, not-for-profit fundraiser*

Miami
Ellner, Ruth H. *realtor*
Nestor Castellano, Brenda Diana *real estate company executive*
Vicente, Rachel *real estate agent*

Miami Beach
Garbe-Morillo, Patricia Ann *preservationist*

Naples
Watson, Dorothy Colette *real estate broker*

Nokomis
Gomber, Mary (Dee) *real estate broker*

Ocala
Booth, Jane Schuele *real estate company officer, real estate broker*

Orlando
Crabtree, Valleri Jayne *real estate company executive, educator, lawyer*

Palm Beach
Bagby, Martha L. Green *real estate holding company executive, writer, publishing executive*
Coudert, Dale Hokin *real estate executive, marketing consultant*

Palm Coast
Barnes, Judith Ann *real estate company executive*

Riviera Beach
Totten, Gloria Jean (Dolly Totten) *real estate company executive, financial consultant*

Safety Harbor
Crafton-Masterson, Adrienne *real estate company executive*

Saint Petersburg
Riley, Nancy J. *real estate broker*

Sarasota
Byron, E. Lee *real estate broker*

Satellite Beach
Miller, Susan Laura *real estate company executive, retired special education educator*

Tallahassee
Campbell, Frances Harvell *real estate developer*
Lisenby, Dorrece Edenfield *realtor*

Tampa
Schild, Nancy Lois *realtor, music educator*

Valrico
Tirelli, Maria Del Carmen S. *retired realtor*

West Palm Beach
Kramer, Eleanor *retired real estate broker, tax specialist, financial consultant*

GEORGIA

Athens
Meyer, Gail Barry *retired real estate broker*

Atlanta
Ossewaarde, Anne Winkler *real estate company executive*

Folkston
Crumbley, Esther Helen Kendrick *retired real estate agent, retired secondary school educator, councilman*

Marietta
Shapiro, Abra Blair *real estate company executive*

Roswell
Vandiegriff, Vicki Alvinda *realtor*

Toccoa
Slate, Mary Elizabeth *real estate agent, medical/surgical nurse*

HAWAII

Honolulu
Baker, Helen Doyle Peil *realtor, contractor*

Koloa
Cobb, Rowena Noelani Blake *real estate broker*

IDAHO

Idaho Falls
Thorsen, Nancy Dain *real estate broker*

ILLINOIS

Chicago
DeWoskin, Margaret Fogarty *real estate company executive*
Eubanks-Pope, Sharon G. *real estate company executive, entrepreneur*
Field, Karen Ann (Karen Ann Schaffner) *real estate broker*
Fox, Leslie B. *real estate company executive*
Jarrett, Valerie Bowman *real estate company executive, stock exchange executive*
Julmy, Camille P. *real estate company executive*
Pacher, Nancy A. *real estate company executive*

East Saint Louis
Thomas, Mary Lee *property manager*

Highland Park
Stein, Paula Jean Anne Barton *hotel real estate company executive, real estate broker*

Naperville
Harvard, Rita Grace *real estate agent, volunteer*

Westmont
Harten, Ann M. *relocation services executive*

INDIANA

Fort Wayne
Glick, Anna Margaret *real estate broker, consultant*

Greenwood
Tomlin, Jeanne Brannon *real estate broker, small business owner*

Terre Haute
Flick, Connie Ruth *real estate agent, real estate broker*

IOWA

Ames
Wendell, Barbara Taylor *retired real estate agent*

Cedar Rapids
Baermann, Donna Lee Roth *real estate property executive, retired insurance analyst*

KANSAS

Leawood
Joslin, Janine Elizabeth *preservationist, consultant*

Topeka
Barnett, Mary Lorene *real estate manager*

Wichita
Curry, Sherrie Donell *real estate agent*

KENTUCKY

Lexington
Elder, Donna Redd *real estate broker*

Louisville
Cafaro, Debra A. *real estate company executive*

Winchester
Cantrell, Georgia Ann *realtor*

LOUISIANA

Covington
Gilman-Anderson, Susan Ellen *real estate company executive, consultant*

Metairie
Myers, Iona Raymer *real estate property manager*

MAINE

Kingfield
Clapp, Millicent Evans *real estate broker*

MARYLAND

Berlin
Passwater, Barbara Gayhart *real estate broker*

Bethesda
Klatzkin, Terri *real estate company executive*

Burtonsville
Kammeyer, Sonia Margaretha *real estate agent*

Gibson Island
Hyde, Diana Caroline *retired real estate agent*

Montgomery Village
Wykes, Mary Maushak *real estate agent*

Mount Airy
Lemke, Jill *city planner*

Potomac
Dickerman, Serafina Poerio *real estate broker, consultant*
Eaves, Maria Perry *realtor*

Rockville
Moses, Cynthia Glass *realtor*

Simpsonville
Altschuler, Ruth Phyllis *realtor, secondary school educator*

Westminster
Erb, Betty Jane *retired real estate agent*

MASSACHUSETTS

Boston
Wiggleworth, Margaret *property manager*

Cambridge
de Marneffe, Barbara Rowe *historic preservationist*
Wylie, Joan Blout *real estate rehabilitator, ceramist, designer*

Fall River
Brion, Norma M. *real estate broker*

Falmouth
Milkman, Marianne Friedenthal *retired city planner*

Malden
Darish, Bernice Steiman *realtor*

Natick
Strauss, Harlee Sue *environmentalist, consultant*

Newton
Havens, Candace Jean *urban planner, consultant*

Rockport
Johnson, Janet Lou *real estate company executive, writer*

Winchester
Blackham, Ann Rosemary (Mrs. J. W. Blackham) *realtor*

MICHIGAN

Bloomfield Hills
Katzman, Charlotte Phyllis *realtor*

Detroit
Edwards, Lora Brunett *retired property manager*

Grosse Ile
Smith, Veronica Latta *real estate company officer*

West Bloomfield
Beron, Gail Laskey *real estate analyst, real estate appraiser, consultant*

MISSOURI

Bucklin
Payne, Flora Fern *real estate broker*

Columbia
Northway, Wanda I. *real estate company executive*

Holden
Martin, Laurabelle *property manager*

Ironton
Sebastian, Phylis Sue (Ingram) *real estate broker, appraiser, antique appraiser*

Kansas City
Dumovich, Loretta *retired real estate company executive, retired transportation executive*

Saint Joseph
Rachow, Sharon Dianne *realtor*

Saint Louis
Sutter, Jane Elizabeth *conservationist, science educator*

Stockton
Jackson, Betty L. Deason *real estate developer*

MONTANA

Billings
Stratton, Betty *realtor*

NEBRASKA

Lincoln
Summers, Jane Pfeifer *realtor*

Omaha
Gallagher, Paula Marie *real estate appraiser*
Neal, Bonnie Jean *real estate agent*

NEVADA

Las Vegas
Egidio, Martha L. *real estate broker and salesman*
Merrill, Lynda Mae *real estate broker*
Sherry, Krystal A. *real estate broker*
Walker, Gwendolyn Kaye *real estate agent*

NEW HAMPSHIRE

Portsmouth
Cunningham, Valerie S. *historic preservationist, researcher*

NEW JERSEY

Cape May Point
Chandler, Marguerite Nella *real estate company executive*

Cherry Hill
Rose, Dori *real estate agent*

Essex Fells
Nevius, Janet Dryden *real estate company executive, government agency administrator*

Flemington
Salamon, Renay *real estate broker*

Princeton
Sayer, Ruth P. *realtor*

Summit
Clynes, Carolann Elizabeth *realtor*

NEW YORK

Albany
Morris, Margretta Elizabeth *conservationist*

Briarcliff Manor
Kepcher, Carolyn *real estate company executive*

Bronx
Carter, Majora *urban planner*
Velasquez, Rose *realtor*

Brooklyn
Markgraf, Rosemarie *real estate broker*

Clifton Springs
DeRuyter, Marilyn *real estate broker*

Corona
Maruca, Rita *real estate company executive, real estate broker*

Fresh Meadows
Yang, Susan Xia *real estate consultant, recreational therapist*

Hillsdale
Kersten, Mary Lou *real estate broker*

Howard Beach
Chwalek, Constance *real estate broker, mortgage broker*

Huntington
Petersen, Patricia J. *real estate company executive*

Mohegan Lake
Charney, Lena London *property manager, historian, poet*

New York
Beinecke, Frances G. *environmentalist*
Bodini, Daniele Damaso *real estate company executive*
Consolo, Faith Hope *real estate broker*
Corcoran, Barbara *real estate company executive*
Crowley, Cynthia Wetmore *real estate broker*
Farley, Katherine G. *real estate company executive*
Grau, Marcy Beinish *real estate broker, former investment banker*
Herman, Dorothy *real estate broker*
Hernstadt, Judith Filenbaum *city planner, real estate executive, broadcast executive*
Himmel, Leslie Wohlman *real estate manager*
Lachman, Marguerite Leanne *real estate investment advisor*
Lavori, Nora *real estate executive, lawyer*
Lenz, Dolly (Idaliz Dolly Lenz) *real estate broker*
Mogull, Kim *real estate company executive*
Nichols, Edie Diane *real estate broker*
Pearl, Mary Corliss *wildlife conservationist*
Phillips, Karen A. *urban planner*
Rockefeller, Allison Hall W. *conservationist*
Stroer, Rosemary Ann *real estate broker*
Tighe, Mary Ann *real estate company executive*

Rexford
Schmitt, Claire Kunz *environmentalist, writer*

Southampton
Sheehy, Betty Jo *real estate company executive, investment advisor*

Warwick
Griffin, Julia Wallace *real estate broker*

NORTH CAROLINA

Asheville
Cragnolin, Karen Zambella *real estate developer, lawyer*

Chapel Hill
Weiss, Shirley F. *retired urban and regional planner, economist, educator*

Charlotte
House, Robin Christine *real estate agent, art consultant*
Vowell, Evelene C. *retired real estate broker*

Fayetteville
Kem, Katherine Frances *urban planner*

Fort Bragg
Nichols, Carol-Lee *real estate broker, property manager*

Greensboro
Russell, Anne Wrenn *property manager*

Raleigh
Deihl, Susan Galyen *preservationist*

OHIO

Cincinnati
Ten Eyck, Dorothea Fariss *real estate agent*
Winchell, Margaret J. *realtor*

Columbus
Janik, Melinda A. *real estate company executive*

Geneva
Arkkelin, Cora Rink *realtor*

Hebron
Slater, Wanda Marie Worth *property manager*

Pataskala
Honnold, Kathryn S. *real estate agent*

Wilmington
Evans, Elizabeth Ann West *retired real estate agent*

Worthington
Winston, Janet Margaret *real estate agent, volunteer*

OKLAHOMA

Broken Arrow
Baker, Bonnie Marie *real estate broker*

Norman
Zelby, Rachel *realtor*

OREGON

Grants Pass
Comeaux, Katharine Jeanne *realtor*

Lake Oswego
Marietta, Elizabeth Ann *real estate broker*

PENNSYLVANIA

Allentown
Saab, Deanne Keltum *real estate broker, appraiser*

Blue Bell
Deschaine, Barbara Ralph *retired real estate broker*

Harrisburg
Fenstermacher, Joyce Doris *real estate agent, real estate appraiser*

Philadelphia
Kaplan, Barbara Jane *retired city planner*
Seaman, Tanya *urban planner*

West Chester
Knuth Fischer, Cynthia Strout *environmental consultant*

SOUTH CAROLINA

Aiken
Hallman, Cecilia Ann *real estate consultant*

Bluffton
Windham, Melba B. *real estate broker*

Columbia
Sloan, Saundra Jennings *real estate company executive*

Saint Helena Island
Yates-Williams, Linda Snow *real estate broker*

TENNESSEE

Chattanooga
Harrison (Ingle), Bettye (Bettye Ingle) *real estate company executive*

Hendersonville
Spain, Mary Ann *realtor, educator, historian, writer*

Knoxville
Beeler, Sandra Gillespie *realtor*

Loudon
Hicks, Betty Harris *real estate broker, real estate company executive*

TEXAS

Addison
Cotter, Ka *real estate company executive*
Ragusa, Elysia *real estate company executive*

Austin
Anderson, Mo *real estate company executive*

Boerne
Daugherty, Linda Hagaman *real estate company executive*

Conroe
Judge, Dolores Barbara *real estate broker*

Dallas
Marlow, Patricia Bair Bond *realtor*
McInnis, Carolyn Crawford *real estate broker*

Fort Worth
Danilow, Deborah Marie *realtor, vocalist, composer, musician, rancher*

Frisco
Taylor, Teresa Marie *realtor*

Grand Prairie
Mathis, Prudence Marchman *realtor*

Houston
Blackburn, Sadie Gwin Allen *conservation executive*
Schulz, Amanda Jean *real estate consultant, lawyer*

Lubbock
Wall, Betty Jane *real estate consultant*

Port Aransas
Turner, Elizabeth Adams Noble (Betty Turner) *real estate company executive*

San Antonio
Beauchamp, Francis Drake *real estate agent*
Burke, Betty Jane *retired real estate manager*
Condos, Barbara Seale *real estate broker, developer, investor*
Wilson, F. Jill *real estate company executive, internet consultant*

UTAH

Santa Clara
Tolbert, Beth Willden *real estate company executive, broker*

VERMONT

Burlington
Van Raalte, Barbara G. *retired realtor*

Randolph
French, Patsy *property manager, state representative*

VIRGINIA

Abingdon
Humphreys, Lois H. *retired realtor*

Alexandria
Campagna, Dianna Gwin *real estate broker*
Palma, Dolores Patricia *urban planner, consultant, writer*

Burke
Prieto, Nycthia Ophelia M. *realtor*

Chesapeake
Owens, Susan Elizabeth *realtor*

Christiansburg
Thorpe, Devoria D. *real estate agent*

Dumfries
Thrall, Eileen Fowler *real estate broker*

Falls Church
Cazan, Sylvia Marie Buday (Mrs. Matthew John Cazan) *retired real estate executive*

Norfolk
Heaton, Kathleen Hoge *realtor*

Reston
Aaron, Barbara Robinson *real estate broker*

Richmond
Girone, Joan Christine Cruse *realtor, former county official*

Vienna
Slowik, Sharon A. *real estate agent*

WASHINGTON

Seattle
Dillard, Marilyn Dianne *property manager*

WEST VIRGINIA

Bridgeport
Jones, Mary Lou *real estate broker, real estate company executive*

Martinsburg
Braithwaite, Marilyn Jean *realtor*

WISCONSIN

Lake Mills
Lazaris, Pamela Adriane *community planning and development consultant*

Milwaukee
Gondek, Mary Jane (Mary Jane Suchorski) *property manager*
Smith, Lois Ann *real estate company executive*
Stillman, Sharon J. *real estate broker*

Wausau
Prey, Yvonne Mary *real estate broker*

WYOMING

Casper
Elliott, Marian Kay *real estate manager*

ADDRESS UNPUBLISHED

Allen, Gloria Ann *real estate broker, artist*
Anderson, Amy Lee *realtor*
Anderson, Paulette Elizabeth *real estate developer, retired entrepreneur, retired elementary school educator*
Baiman, Gail *real estate broker*
Barrett, Linda L. *real estate consultant*
Beck, Pamela L. *realtor*
Belford, Roz *real estate broker*
Berliner, Ruth Shirley *real estate company executive*
Bland, Eveline Mae *real estate broker, musician, educator*
Bryan, Mary Jo W. *realtor, artist, art educator*
Chamberlain, Patricia Ann *retired land use planner, farmer*
Corkran, Virginia B. *retired real estate agent*
Corradini, Deedee *real estate company executive, former mayor*
Dahlstrom, Patricia Margaret *real estate appraiser*
Darlington, Hilda Walker *real estate company officer*
Davis, Mary Byrd *conservationist, researcher*
DiGiamarino, Marian Eleanor *retired realty administrator*
Dishong, Linda S. *estate planner*
Edwards, Kathleen *real estate broker, former educator*
Fleming, Cheryl Diane *realtor*
Gasper, Ruth Eileen *real estate executive*
Ghebrhiwet, Freweiny Wendy *real estate broker, consultant*
Goddess, Lynn Barbara *real estate investor*
Hakala, Karen Louise *retired real estate specialist*
Hietala, Valerie Grace *realtor, environmentalist, educator*
Holleb, Doris B. *urban planner, economist*
Ingberman, Sima *real estate company officer*
Johnson, Kay Durbahn *real estate manager, consultant*
Karriem, Fatima *real estate broker*
Kremer, Honor Frances (Noreen Kremer) *real estate broker, small business owner*
Lehman, Joan Alice *real estate company executive*
Lopez-Munoz, Maria Rosa P. *real estate development company executive*
Lowe, Patricia McLaughlin *real estate company executive*
Mazzarelli, Debra Jean *real estate broker*
McGinn, Mary Lyn *real estate company executive*
Mercer, Dorothy May *real estate company executive*
Page, Patricia (Patty) Newton *real estate broker, real estate company executive*
Painter, Diana Jean *urban planner, artist, historian*
Pence, Jean Virginia (Jean Pence) *retired real estate broker*
Penniman, Linda Simmons *retired real estate agent*
Polk, Emily DeSpain *conservationist, writer*
Roth, Pamela Jeanne *intellectual property asset management consultant*
Sassen, Saskia *urban planner, educator*
Smith, Mary Louise *real estate broker*
Sopkin, Carole A. *realtor*
Spadora, Hope Georgeanne *real estate company executive*
Stefanik-Brandt, Janet Ruth *retired realtor*
Toshach, Clarice Oversby *real estate developer, retired computer company executive*
Vella, Ruth Ann *real estate executive*
Walker, Helen Smith *retired real estate broker*
White, Lani Nyla *real estate developer, real estate broker*
Williams, Phyllis Cutforth *retired realtor*
Woods, Sandra Kay *real estate executive*

RELIGION

UNITED STATES

ALABAMA

Bessemer
Collins, Patricia Ann *pastor, pastoral counselor*

Greenville
Longmire, Venus DeLoyse *minister*

Montgomery
Bullard, Mary Ellen *retired religious organization administrator*

ARIZONA

Phoenix
Schenkel, Barbara Ann *minister, nurse, social worker*
Shelton, Rose E. *minister, retired tax specialist*

Sun City
Randall, Claire *retired religious organization administrator*

Tucson
Waterbury, Deborah Kay *minister*

ARKANSAS

Arkadelphia
Pemberton, Barbara Butler *religious studies educator*

Blytheville
Estes, Pamela Jean *pastor*

Morrilton
Crawford-Larson, Kris *minister*

CALIFORNIA

Altadena
Willans, Jean Stone *bishop, religious organization administrator*

Atascadero
Jones, Kathryn Cherie *pastor*

Auburn
Moore, Billie Jo *minister*

Bakersfield
Frazier, Jo Frances *religious organization administrator, writer*
Johnson, Deborah Valerie Germaine *parish administrator*

Berkeley
Farina, Marianne *theology studies educator, consultant*
Massie, Betsy McPherson *clergywoman*

Bermuda Dunes
McCarthy, Kathleen Marie *priest, nurse*

Corona
Wood, Brenda Jean *pastor, evangelist*

Escondido
Linzey, Verna May *minister, writer*

Gold River
Davidson, Diane (Marie Davidson) *publisher*

Happy Camp
Black, Barbara Ann *publisher*

Hollywood
Schuster, Peggy Lindner (Pravrajika Brahmaprana) *sister, nun*

Los Angeles
Daya Mata, Sri (Faye Wright) *clergywoman*

Midway City
Allen, Frances Michael *publisher*

Newport Beach
Ortlund, Anne (Elizabeth Anne Ortlund) *writer, musician*

Palm Desert
Ponder, Catherine *clergywoman*

San Diego
Olson, Linda Ann Salmonson *minister*

Sonora
Jones, Georgia Ann *publisher*

Temecula
Bauer, Judy Marie *minister*

COLORADO

Bennett
Unger Young, Elizabeth (Betty) *hospital chaplain*

Pueblo
Nimmo, Charlene *minister*

Wheat Ridge
Wilcox, Mary Marks *retired Christian education consultant, educator*

CONNECTICUT

Branford
Anderson, Marjo Elizabeth *minister*

Colchester
Nikirk, (Silva) Susan *minister, writer, dancer*

Hartford
Winter, Miriam Therese (Gloria Frances Winter) *nun, religious studies educator*

New London
Clarke, Florence Dorothy *minister, educator*

Storrs Mansfield
Baldwin, Carlita Rose *minister*

DELAWARE

Wilmington
Butcher, Diane *chaplain, bereavement facilitator*
Linderman, Jeanne Herron *priest*

DISTRICT OF COLUMBIA

Washington
Graves, Ruth Elaine *minister, educator*
Harvey, Jane Hull *church administrator*
Jones, Coletta L. *senior pastor*
Leckey, Dolores R. *religious organization administrator, writer*
Outlaw, Wanda Cecelia *priest*
Ross, Annie Lee *minister, counselor*
Ross, Robinette Davis *publisher*
Zikmund, Barbara Brown *minister, religious organization administrator, educator*

FLORIDA

Boca Raton
Eisenberg, Robin Ledgin *religious education administrator*

Coral Gables
Lorber, Charlotte Laura *publisher*

Delray Beach
Wells, Mary Elizabeth Thompson *deacon, chaplain, director*

Fort Lauderdale
McCormick, Queen Esther Williams *clergyman*

Fort Myers
Cummings, Rayann Burnham *minister*
Drushal, Mary Ellen *parish administrator, education educator, former academic administrator*

Fort Walton Beach
Williams, Bethtina Qubré *minister*

Gainesville
Steffee, Nina Dean *publisher*

Jacksonville
Mueller, Cherone *religious organization administrator, writer, minister*

Miami
Gray, Frances Boone *minister*
Weeks, Marta Joan *retired priest*

Ocala
Brown, Sally Day *minister, literature and language educator, pre-school educator*

Palm Bay
Downes, Patricia Ann *minister*

Pompano Beach
Corsello, Lily Joann *minister, counselor, educator*

Saint Augustine
Couture, Sister Diane Rhea *sister, artist, educator*

Saint Petersburg
Petty, M. S. Marty *publisher*

Sarasota
McFarlin, Diane Hooten *publisher*
Towner, Margaret Ellen *retired minister*
Yonteck, Elizabeth Barbara *minister, health care consultant*

Tallahassee
Porterfield, Amanda *religion educator*

Titusville
Rush, Patricia Anne *pastor, music educator*

Winter Haven
Boully, LaJuan Bonnie *minister, religious studies educator*

GEORGIA

Atlanta
Beres, Mary Elizabeth *religious organization administrator*
Farley, Wendy Lee *lay worker, educator*
Hally, Jane Eloise *religious organization administrator, social worker*
King, Barbara Lewis *minister, lecturer*
Rhodes, Lisa Diane *minister*
White, Gayle Colquitt *writer, journalist*

Augusta
Davis, Minnie P. *minister*

Conyers
Henry, Lynn J. *youth church administrator*

Crawford
Spears, Louise Elizabeth *minister, secondary school educator*

Decatur
Daniel, Elinor Perkins (Perky Daniel) *clergywoman*
Hale, Cynthia Lynette *religious organization administrator*

Dublin
Sapp, Peggy G. *pastor, editor, writer, speech professional*

Hinesville
Carter, Georgian L. *minister*

Macon
Good, Estelle M. *minister*

Mc Rae
Allen, Annette *minister*

Perry
Jackson, Rutha Mae *pastor, military reserve officer, secondary school educator*

Stone Mountain
Gary, Julia Thomas *retired minister*

HAWAII

Kahului
Domingo, Cora Maria Corazon Encarnacion *minister*

IDAHO

Nampa
Carrim, Rhonda Lynne *theology studies educator, priest*

ILLINOIS

Chicago
Barbour, Claude Marie *minister, educator*
Carr, Anne Elizabeth *theology studies educator*
Doherty, Sister Barbara *religious institution administrator*
Harris, Mildred Clopton *clergy member, educator*
James, Marie Moody *clergywoman, musician, vocal music educator*
Jegen, Sister Carol Frances *religious studies educator*
Jones, Cordia Cortez *minister*
Lathon, Sheraine *clergyman*
McDonald, Theresa Beatrice Pierce (Mrs. Ollie McDonald) *church official, minister*
Muhammad, Ava *minister and national spokesperson for the Nation of Islam*
Poethig, Eunice Blanchard *clergywoman*
Reece, Beth Pauley *chaplain*
Thistlethwaite, Susan Brooks *religious organization administrator*

Danville
Payne, Paula Marie *minister*

Elgin
Reimer, Judy Mills *pastor, religious executive*

Itasca
Constant, Anita Aurelia *publisher*

Lindenhurst
Blumberg, Sherry Helene *Jewish education educator*

Moline
Johnson, Mary Lou *lay worker, educator*

Naperville
Raccah, Dominique Marcelle *publisher*

Rockford
Gregory, Dola Bell *bishop, customer service administrator*
Schlub, Teresa Rae *minister*

Springfield
Clingan, Wanda Jacqueline *minister*

Wauconda
Gotthardt, Mary Jane *religious studies educator*

West Frankfort
Holley-Gray, Margaret N. *minister*

INDIANA

Fort Wayne
Holzmer, Sister Anita *nun, theology studies educator*

Fortville
Horner, Sylvia Ann *minister, real estate broker*

Greenwood
Knapp, Sylvia Clare *religious studies educator, language educator*

Indianapolis
Hearon, Holly Elizabeth *religious studies educator*
Roger, Janice Lowenstein *cantor*
Waynick, Catherine Elizabeth Maples *bishop*

Muncie
Farr, Barbara F. *minister*

Munster
Taylor, Gloria A. *minister, educator*

Newburgh
McKown, Martha *minister, writer*

Notre Dame
Davis, Stacy Nicole *religious studies educator*

IOWA

Cedar Falls
Balm-Demmel, Darline Dawn *retired minister*

Iowa City
Clark, Dianne Elizabeth *religious studies and reading educator*

Springville
Beals, Karen Marie Downey *pastor*

Waverly
Koob, Kathryn Loraine *religious studies educator*

KANSAS

Clifton
Compton, Doris Martha *lay worker*

Kansas City
Hancock, Melinda Bowne *minister*

Mission
McAleer, Ruth Bresnahan *priest*

Newton
Barrett, Lois Yvonne *minister*

Overland Park
Liston, Helen J. *retired minister*

Topeka
Marney, Brenda Joyce *minister, computer programmer*

KENTUCKY

Hopkinsville
Soberal, Isabel M. *minister, music educator, social worker*

Louisville
Boykin, Gladys *retired religious organization administrator*
Dale, Judy Ries *religious organization administrator, consultant*
Gray, Joan S. *head of religious order*

Middletown
Jones, Doris Moreland *minister, author*

LOUISIANA

Alexandria
Gootee, Christy Beck *minister, educator*

Crowley
Harris, Michelle Reneé *pastor*

Gretna
Doyle, Agnes J *minister*

Ponchatoula
Warden, Waldia Ann *religious center administrator, director*

Shreveport
Flournoy, Linda Wesley *minister, educator*

MAINE

Augusta
Bulba-Carvutto, Susan Dietz *rabbi*

Kingfield
Silver, Sally *minister*

Portland
Knudsen, Chilton Abbie Richardson *bishop*

South Bristol
Lasher, Esther Lu *minister*

Starks
Quimby, Janice Ann *minister*

MARYLAND

Baltimore
Robinson, Carrie *pastor*
Robinson, Sally Shoemaker *lay associate*
Schumann, Jill *religious organization administrator*
Ushry, Roselyn *minister*

Cockeysville
Hager, Louise Alger *retired chaplain*

Columbia
Mills, Ianther Marie *minister*

Frostburg
Weatherford, Hazel Alice *minister*

Hurlock
Shively, Bonnie Lee *pastor*

Lanham Seabrook
Barnes, Margaret Anderson *minister, statistician*

Laurel
Hammond, Deborah Lynn *lay worker*

Owings Mills
Johnson-Cohen, Yevonne B. *minister, counselor*

Rock Hall
Mariner, Linda Ketterman *minister*

Silver Spring
Hunt, Mary Elizabeth *religious studies educator*

MASSACHUSETTS

Auburndale
Gulbrandsen, Natalie Webber *religious association administrator*

Boston
Harris, Gayle Elizabeth *bishop*
Kessler, Diane Cooksey *religious organization administrator, minister*

Brookline
Skeete, Helen Watkins *minister, counselor*

Cambridge
Kujawa-Holbrook, Sheryl *theology studies educator, academic administrator*
Schuessler Fiorenza, Elisabeth *theology studies educator*

Jamaica Plain
White-Hammond, Gloria E. *pastor, pediatrician, human rights advocate*

Marblehead
Tamaren, Michele Carol *spiritual director, writer, retired special education educator, personal coach, presenter*

Medford
Penick, Ann Clarisse *minister, counselor*

Newton
Tannenwald, Leslie Keiter *rabbi, justice of peace, educational association administrator, chaplain*

North Andover
Kimball, Virginia Marie *theology studies educator, writer*

Shelburne Falls
Evelyn, Phyllis *minister*

Somerville
Corso, Susan Falk *minister*
Ragsdale, Katherine Hancock *Episcopal priest, political activist*

Sudbury
Deutsch, Judith *clergywoman*

Vineyard Haven
Kimball, Julie Ellis *small press publisher, humorist, writer*

MICHIGAN

Dearborn
Hess, Margaret Johnston *religious writer, educator*

Erie
Jenne, Carole Seegert *minister, marriage and family therapist*

Flint
McClanahan, Connie Dea *pastoral minister*

Grand Rapids
Hollies, Linda Hall *pastor, educator, author*

River Rouge
Myhand, Cheryl *minister, educator*

Traverse City
Burton, Betty June *retired pastor*

Ypsilanti
Stuppard-Byars, Doris J. *minister*

MINNESOTA

Apple Valley
Haaheim, Patricia Jane Dando *pastor, consultant*

Buffalo
Hemish, Carol Marie *liturgist/spiritual director, musician*

Edina
Worthing, Carol Marie *retired minister*

Mentor
Jerdee, Sylvia Ann *minister*

Minneapolis
Battle, Willa Lee Grant *clergywoman, educational administrator*
Chemberlin, Peg *minister, religious organization administrator*

Preston
Schommer, Trudy Marie *minister, religious studies educator*

Roseville
McMillan, Mary Bigelow *retired minister, volunteer*

Saint Paul
McNamee, Sister Catherine *theology studies educator*

Willmar
Crute, Beverly Jean *minister*

MISSISSIPPI

Columbus
Hall, Maxine P. *minister*

Ellisville
McNair, Emma Louise *minister*

Southaven
Wade, Tonya Sue *religious studies educator, small business owner*

MISSOURI

Bridgeton
Hylla, Linda Kay *sister, social worker*

Creve Coeur
Plankenhorn, Sharon A. *chaplain*

Fredericktown
Morris, Virginia Mary *retired minister*

Hollister
Hopper, Ruby Lou *clergy member*

Independence
Bryan, Kay Marie *retired minister*
Mortimer, Anita Louise *minister*

Kansas City
Hebenstreit, Jean Estill Stark *religion educator, practitioner*
Hoyland, Janet Louise *clergywoman*

Keytesville
McVeigh, Glenna Faye *minister*

Saint Charles
Drury, Mildred Barbara *evangelist, music educator*

Saint Louis
Hoare, Sister Mary Gabriel *nun, educator*
Wilkins, Addi L. *retired lay worker*

Springfield
Gholson, Martha Rachel *religious studies educator*

NEBRASKA

Madison
Westfall, Lois Lorene *retired minister, nurse*

Omaha
Faust, Diana Jean *religious studies educator*
Ward, Vanessa Gayle *religious organization administrator, minister, consultant*

NEVADA

Carson City
Morgan, Elaine Ludlum *minister*

Las Vegas
Freeman-Clark, J. P. Ladyhawk *vicar, underwater exploration, security and transportation executive, educator, model*
Karl, Carol Yvonne *retired minister, religious studies educator, publisher*

NEW HAMPSHIRE

Jaffrey
Van Ness, Patricia Wood *religious studies educator*

Loudon
Moore, Beatrice *religious organization administrator*

Manchester
Ahern, Margaret Ann *nun, nursing educator*

NEW JERSEY

Bloomfield
Glasser, Lynn Schreiber *publisher*

Eatontown
Priesand, Sally Jane *rabbi*

Elizabeth
Blowe, Arnethia *religious studies educator*

Hightstown
Hull, Gretchen Gaebelein *lay worker, writer, lecturer*

Jersey City
Graham, Susan Louise *religious studies educator, consultant*
Katz, Colleen *publisher*

Moorestown
Clark, Maryliz M. *retired minister*

Morristown
Hastings, Mary Jane *minister*

Newark
Moore, Mattie H. *clergy, folk artist, retired educator*
Stephens, B. Consuela *minister, consultant*

Teaneck
Holmes, Miriam H. *publisher*

Toms River
Donaldson, Marcia Jean *lay worker*

NEW MEXICO

Albuquerque
Studdard, Joy *minister*

Moriarty
Moonwalker, Tu *minister, counselor, artist*

Prewitt
Droll, Ruth Lucille *missionary pastor*

NEW YORK

Albany
Kruegler, Catherine A. *sister, parochial school educator*
Lagoy, Mary Elizabeth *sister*

Albion
Allamon, Karen Henn *minister*

Amity Harbor
O'Hanlon, Carol Ann *minister*

Belmont
Lasher, Sandra Lee *minister, artist*

Bronx
Kirmse, Sister Anne-Marie Rose *nun, educator, researcher*
Reeberg, Patricia Aldora *minister, entrepreneur*
Ruffing, Janet Kathryn *spirituality educator*

Brooklyn
McCormick, Mary F. *church administrator*

Buffalo
Smallwood, Sandra Denise *pastor, daycare administrator*

Chautauqua
Campbell, Joan Brown *religious organization executive*

Cicero
Schiess, Betty Bone *priest*

Hempstead
Zagano, Phyllis *religious studies educator*

New York
Balter, Bernice *religious organization administrator*
Berner, Mary *publisher*
Conlon, Peggy Eileen *publisher*
Hirsch, Roseann Conte *publisher*
Holden, Sister Margaret Mary *sister*
Leech, Diane J. *publisher*
Ochs, Carol Rebecca *theologian, writer, theology studies educator, philosopher*
Platzner, Linda *publisher*
Reidy, Carolyn Kroll *publisher*
Rosenberg, Ellen Y. *religious association administrator*
Roskam, Catherine S. *bishop*
Schori, Katharine Jefferts *bishop*
Simpson, Mary Michael *priest, psychotherapist*
Tannenbaum, Bernice Salpeter *national religious organization executive*

Niagara Falls
Douglas, Frances Sonia *minister*

North Syracuse
Williamson, Donna Maria *pastoral counselor*

Nyack
Cozart, Helen Ray *church administrator, educator*

Patchogue
Franck CSJ, Suzanne Elizabeth *religious studies educator, minister*

Rochester
Kelley, Lucille Knight *minister, retired neurology and special duty nurse*
Lacey, Dorothy Ellen *theology studies educator, religious organization administrator*
Tobin, Barbara Kay *minister*

Rye
Kaufman, Shirona *cantor, educator*

Saint Bonaventure
Donovan, Geraldine Ellen *sister*

Scarsdale
Gaeta, Jane *minister*

Syracuse
Jerge, Marie Charlotte *minister*

Uniondale
Stewart, Cynthia Willis *minister*

Unionvale
Berry, Maryann Paradiso *minister*

Yorktown Heights
Braddock, Nonnie Clarke *religious organization administrator*

NORTH CAROLINA

Charlotte
McKay-Wilkinson, Julie Ann *minister, marriage and family therapist*

Davidson
Cathey, Mary Ellen Jackson *religious studies educator*

Drexel
McCall, Maxine Cooper *publisher, minister, educator, writer*

Fayetteville
Batts, Dorothy Marie *clergywoman, educator, writer*

Greenville
Faircloth, Mary Williams *minister, educator*

Lumberton
Johnson, Judy Van *minister, educator*
Tolar, Anne Melton *minister, music educator*

Monroe
Wallace, Patricia Ellen *evangelist, minister*

Mount Olive
Day, Tyanna Yonkers *religious studies educator, minister*

Raleigh
Henderson, Shirley Elizabeth *minister*

Rocky Mount
Dickens, Alice McKnight *minister*

Snow Hill
Stevens, JoAnn A. *textile, political leader, author, minister*

Wentworth
Lumpkin, Vicki G. *minister*

Wilmington
Walters, Doris Lavonne *retired religious organization administrator, human services manager*

Winston Salem
Caldwell, Toni Marie *religious organization administrator*
Hatcher, Beverly J. *pastor*
Hunt, Ellen *minister, evangelist*
Jenkins, Barbara Alexander *pastor, overseer*
Ludolf, Marilyn Marie Keaton *lay worker*

NORTH DAKOTA

Bismarck
Reinert, Agnes Frances *chaplain, educator*

OHIO

Akron
Graham, DeBorah Denise *minister, educator*

Canton
Wolf, Teresa Ann *minister, educator, nun*

Cincinnati
Anderson, Joan Balyeat *theology studies educator, minister*
Duffy, Virginia *minister*

Cleveland
Borchert, Catherine Glennan *minister*

Columbus
Boyd, Hazel *minister*
Smith, Marcia J. *pastor*

Lakeside
Stephens-Rich, Barbara E. *religious studies educator*

Londonderry
Lindsey, Bonnie Lou *minister*

North Canton
Edwards, Sharon Marie *minister, educator*

Wauseon
Stutzman, Donna J. *minister*

West Farmington
Guyette, Diana *minister*

Westlake
Loehr, Marla *chaplain*

Youngstown
Beasley-Martin, Monica Rachael *minister, director*
Dunlap, Catherine Mary *clergywoman*

OKLAHOMA

Del City
Wallace, Fannie Margaret *minister, religious organization administrator*

Lawton
Ellenbrook, Carolyn Kay *religious organization administrator*

Oklahoma City
Hampton, Carol McDonald *priest, educator, historian*
Ridley, Betty Ann *theology studies educator*

Shawnee
McGuire, Anne C. *theology studies educator*

Tulsa
Gottschalk, Sister Mary Therese *nun, hospital administrator*
Saurer, Mary Marcelle *minister*

Vinita
Wright, Jo Anne *priest*

OREGON

Beaverton
Mitchell, Bettie Phaenon *religious organization administrator*

Eugene
Graziano, Margaret A. *chaplain, recreational therapist, educational consultant, volunteer*

Portland
Bryant, Carmen Julia *missionary, educator*
Simmons, Laura *religious studies educator*

PENNSYLVANIA

Akron
Dickinson, Margery Elsie *missionary, clinical psychologist*

Altoona
Anthony, Bertha M. *minister*

Blairsville
Stiffler, Erma Delores *minister, retired elementary school educator*

Clarion
Grejda, Gail Fulton *dean*

Clinton
Talbot, Mary Lee *minister*

Collegeville
Butz, Geneva Mae *pastor*

Cranberry Township
Tiller, Olive Marie *retired church worker*

Farrell
Patton-Newell, Janet Lavelle *minister*

Friedens
Shaffer, Brenda Joyce *minister*

Havertown
Koenig, Norma Evans *retired religious studies educator*

Lafayette Hill
Miller, Nancy Lois *senior pastor*

Lancaster
Aronowicz, Annette *theology studies educator*
Daugherty, Ruth Alice *religious association consultant*

New Wilmington
Cushman, Beverly White *religious studies educator*

Philadelphia
Marple, Dorothy Jane *retired church executive*

Pittsburgh
Collins, Rose Ann *minister*
Mason-Hipkins, Patricia *minister*
Muto, Susan Annette *theology studies educator, academic administrator*
Schaub, Marilyn McNamara *theology studies educator*

Sayre
Bentley, Dianne H. Glover *minister, consultant*

Stroudsburg
Brown, Carol Sue *minister*

Swarthmore
Field, Dorothy Maslin *minister*

Washington
Vande Kappelle, Susan Elizabeth *minister*

Wayne
Rabii, Patricia Berg *church administrator*

RHODE ISLAND

Barrington
Henry, Kathleen Sue *minister*

Providence
Spoolstra, Linda Carol *minister, educator, religious organization administrator*
Wolf, Geralyn *bishop*

Woonsocket
Morris, Mary Elizabeth *pastor*

SOUTH CAROLINA

Anderson
Williford, Velma Jean *minister*
Wisler, Darla Lee *pastor*

Summerville
Cook, Jurena Reneé *pastor*

Taylors
Hager, Beulah Elizabeth *lay worker*

TENNESSEE

Chattanooga
Mohney, Nell Webb *religion educator, speaker, author*

Crossville
Ralstin, Betty Lou *religious organization administrator*

Franklin
Wilharm, Sharon Lynette *religious studies educator, comedienne*

Germantown
Cohen, Diane A. *rabbi*

Greeneville
Wilhite, Nancy Jane *evangelist*

Loudon
Hallstrand, Sarah Laymon *denomination executive*

Madison
Collins, Joyce A.P. *minister, librarian, educator, realtor*

Nashville
Archibald, Chestina Mitchell *minister*
Bigham, Wanda Durrett *religious organization administrator*
Melvin, Mary Belle *religious studies educator, director*
Moore, Elise Lucille *Christian Science practitioner, educator*
Skeen, Judy L. *religious studies educator*

TEXAS

Abilene
Pigott, Susan M. *religious studies educator*

Austin
Hitchcock, Joanna *publisher*

Conroe
Hinson, Cynthia Thomas *minister*

Dallas
Austin-Thorn, Cynthia Kay *religious organization administrator, poet*
Gross, Harriet P. Marcus *religious studies and writing educator*
Pauley, Shirley Stewart *religious organization executive*

Fort Worth
Austin, Linda LaRue *clergyperson*
Yaites, LilliAnn *minister*

Houston
Cooper, Valerie Gail *minister*
Foger, Frances Murchison *minister*
Funk, Edith Kay *minister, consultant, social worker*
Keating, Sister Kevina *nun, education educator*
Lewis, Martha Nell *Christian educator, lay minister, expressive arts therapist*

Lufkin
Harmon, Jacqueline Baas *minister*

Mineola
McCann, Evelyn Louise Johnson *retired minister, retired counselor*

Paris
Proctor, June *retired religious organization administrator, writer*

Plano
Newman, Deborah Rae *minister*

San Antonio
Evans, Betty Vaughn *minister*
Welch, Muriel Ruth *religious organization administrator*

Shamrock
Hervey, Nina Fern *retired church administrator, minister*

Waco
Stratton, Margaret Anne *minister*

UTAH

Ogden
Harrington, Mary Evelina Paulson (Polly Harrington) *writer, educator*

Salt Lake City
Irish, Carolyn Tanner *bishop*

VERMONT

White River Junction
Rutter, Frances Tompson *retired publisher*

VIRGINIA

Arlington
Earl, Sister Patricia Helene *religious studies educator, director*

Charlottesvle
Walker, Beverly Ann *minister, health facility administrator*

Dinwiddie
McCray, Doris Raines *minister*

Falls Church
Bankson, Marjory Zoet *former religious association administrator*

Kents Store
Brown, Nan Marie *retired minister*

Norfolk
Finney, Fannie D. *minister, educator*
Gallagher, Carol Joy *bishop*

Richmond
Aigner, Emily Burke *Christian lay minister*
Robertson, LaVerne *minister*

Roanoke
Schumm, Darla Yzonne *religious studies educator*

WASHINGTON

Edgewood
Martin, Iris Weber *retired minister*

Lakewood
Borgford, Norma Jeanne *minister*

Seattle
Burrows, Elizabeth MacDonald *religious organization executive, educator*
Fluke, Lyla Schram (Mrs. John M. (Lyla) Fluke Sr.) *publisher*
Rivera, Bavi Edna (Nedi Rivera) *bishop*
Stanovsky, Elaine J.W. *minister, church organization administrator*

WEST VIRGINIA

Fayetteville
Seay-Bell, Margaretta *pastoral counselor*

Wheeling
Thurston, Bonnie Bowman *religious studies educator, minister, poet*

WISCONSIN

Baileys Harbor
Zimmerman, Irena Agnes *nun, poet, educator*

Eau Claire
Klink, JoAnn Marie *clergywoman*

Madison
Deming, Joan *clergy*

Merrill
Goessl, Celine *head of religious order*

Middleton
McDermott, Molly *lay minister*

Neenah
Brehm-Gruber, Therese Frances *minister, consulting psychologist*

WYOMING

Cody
Grimes, Daphne Buchanan *priest, artist*

Rock Springs
Jackman Dabb, Holly Pieper *publisher*

CANADA

BRITISH COLUMBIA

Prince George
Kerr, Nancy Karolyn *pastor, mental health services professional*

ONTARIO

Toronto
McWilliam, Joanne Elizabeth *retired theology studies educator*

INDIA

Kollum
Devi, Amritanandamayi (Sri Mata Amritanandamayi Devi, Amma) *spiritual leader*

SINGAPORE

Singapore
Berkram, Patricia Clarke *religious studies educator*

ADDRESS UNPUBLISHED

AdamS, Sharon Butler *minister, philosopher, researcher*
Ambers, Ann *bishop, educator*
Baldwin, Leah Zavin *minister, writer, interior designer, educator*
Banks, Deirdre Margaret *retired church organization administrator*
Barbey, Adélaïde *publisher*
Barragan, Linda Diane *religious organization administrator*
Bickford, Margaret Wyatt *minister*
Born, Ethel Wolfe *religious writer*
Braddy, Carolyn Morton *pastor*
Brown, Deborah Eleanor *priest*
Browne, Bonnie Esther *minister*
Burris-Schnur, Catherine *minister, pastoral psychotherapist, medical/surgical nurse, educator*
Carlson, Natalie Traylor *publisher*
Cash, Mary Frances *minister, retired civilian military employee*
Chapman, Amy L. *religious studies educator*
Clemetson, Cheryl Price *minister, consultant*
Crabtree, Davida Foy *minister*
Cyford, Janet Irene *Spiritualist medium, meditation consultant*
Delaney, Mary Anne *retired theology studies educator*
Dockstader, Deborah Ruth *minister*
Douglass, Jane Dempsey *retired theology educator*
Droste, Catherine Joseph *sister*
Eucharista, Sister Mary *sister, educational association administrator, secondary school educator*
Ewing, Elisabeth Anne Rooney *priest*
Fazio, Evelyn M. *publisher, writer, agent, editor*
Finnegan, Sara Anne (Sara F. Lycett) *publisher*
Flye, Carolyn Marie *minister*
Ford, Irene Elaine *pastor*
Frankson-Kendrick, Sarah Jane *publisher*
Frazier, Eloise M. *minister*
Frost, Linda Gail *clergyman, hospital chaplain*
Fry, Hedy *Member of Parliament*
Fullard, Henrietta *minister*
Giles, Judith Margaret *minister, educator, real estate broker*
Glenn, Sara *religious studies educator, director*
Grady, Sandra C. *minister, counselor*
Hanson, Norma Halmagyi *priest*
Harper, Marsha Wilson *retired religious organization administrator*
Harris, Virginia Sydness *religious organization administrator, publisher*
Helm, Judith *retired clergywoman*
Henderson, Alma *religious studies educator*
Holleman, Sandy Lee *religious organization administrator*
Holyfield-Vega, Doretta Joyce *religious studies educator*
Hughes, Cheryl Dempsey *theology studies educator*
Hunter, Georgia L. *clergywoman*
Hunter, Juanita Walters *minister*
Ingram, Barbara Averett *minister*
Jabs, Aura Lee *minister, educator*
Jacober, Amy Elizabeth *theology studies educator*
James, Melissa Marie *religious studies educator*
Jean-Baptiste, Jean *minister*
Joye, Afrie Songco *minister*
Kester, Helen Mary *minister*
Kirchmeier, Emmalou Handford *minister, writer*
LaVerdiere, Claudette Marie *nun, head of religious order*
Lazovsky, Lorna Deane *minister*
Leasor, Jane *religious studies educator, humanities educator, musician*
Levy, Valery *publisher*
Lopez, Patricia Nell *minister, educator*
Lufty, JoyBeth *minister*
Martin, Helen Loene *minister*
Mayes, Ila Laverne *minister*
McCann, Margaret Ann *sister, educator*
McClurg, Patricia A. *minister*
McDermott, Lucinda Mary *ecumenical minister, educator, psychologist, poet, philosopher*
McDonald, Vivian *minister*
McKinley, Ellen Bacon *priest*
McMaster, Belle Miller *religious organization administrator*
Milligan, Sister Mary *theology studies educator, consultant*
Moore, Alma Donst *writer, lyricist*
Muhammad, Claudette Marie *religious organization administrator*
Normann, Margaret Ella *deacon, educator*
Nunes, Winifred O. *minister, educator*
Owen-Towle, Carolyn Sheets *clergywoman*
Pagels, Elaine Hiesey *theology studies educator, writer*
Ramey, Eudora Malois *minister*
Reece, Belynda M. *minister, consultant, military officer*
Reed, Cynthia Kay *minister*
Ridlen, Judith Elaine *minister*
Roche, Barbara Anne *retired minister, editor*
Rock, Caro *publisher*
Rosenbaum, Belle Sara *religious studies educator, religious organization administrator*
Seckel, Carol Ann *Methodist minister*
Seplowin, Judith *cantor*
Siegmund, Mary Kay *priest, counselor, marriage and family therapist*
Singletary, Patricia Ann *minister*
Skavlem, Melissa Kline *publisher*
Sledge, Lela Bell *minister*
Smith, D(aisy) Mullett *publisher*
Smith, Joan Addison *priest*
Spalding, Almut Marianne *minister*
Staggers, Mary E. *minister*
Stewart, Barbara Lynn *church administrator*
Taylor, June Ruth *retired minister*
Topolewski, Nancy Eleanor *minister*
Tumio, Vera Ann *Reiki master priest*
Turley, Susan Gwen *minister*
Walker, E. Ann *minister, writer, pastoral counselor, consultant*
Ware, Sandra Marie *minister, music educator, composer*
Weber, Gloria Richie *retired minister, retired state legislator*
Weihmuller, Patricia Ann *minister, artist, retired executive secretary*
Weinkauf, Mary Louise Stanley *retired clergywoman, educator*
Wharton, Margaret Mary *nun, educator*
Wilson, Lois M. *minister*
Wisehart, Mary Ruth *retired religious organization administrator*
Wolford, Kathryn Frances *religious organization administrator*
Wong, Corinne Hong Sling *minister, theologian*
Wooten, Joan Hedrich *minister*
Zirbes, Mary Kenneth *retired minister*

SCIENCE: LIFE SCIENCE

UNITED STATES

ALABAMA

Anniston
Howell, Laura Clark *biologist, educator, small business owner*

Birmingham
Elgavish, Ada *molecular and cellular biologist*
Finley, Sara Crews *medical geneticist, educator*
Jackson, Davida Janae *science educator*

Eva
Hudson, Rhonda Ann *science educator*

Florence
Greenlee, Michelle Jayne Ory *science educator*

Homewood
Nance, Marione E. *biology educator*

Huntsville
Bishop, Amy *biology professor*
Richardson-Weninegar, Loretta Lynne *biologist, educator*

Livingston
Duckworth, Tracy Wells *research scientist, educator, biotechnologist*

Millbrook
Roy, Nancy Lou *science educator*

Mobile
French, Elizabeth Irene *biology professor, musician*
Nicholson, Yvette Renee *science educator*

Monroeville
Loyd, Martha Rose *forester*

Montgomery
Graham, Louvenia Dorsey *science educator*

Muscle Shoals
King, Amanda Wilhite *science educator*

Talladega
Schwinghamer, Mary Denise *veterinarian*

ALASKA

Anchorage
Nielsen, Jennifer Lee *molecular ecologist, researcher*

Fairbanks
Kessel, Brina *ornithologist, educator, researcher*
Mellish, Jo-Anne Elizabeth *marine biologist, researcher*

ARIZONA

Flagstaff
Cortner, Hanna Joan *retired research scientist, political scientist*
Wilcoxson-Ueckert, Catherine Ann *science educator, consultant*

Glendale
Milne, Karen Louise *science educator*

Mesa
Seibert, Barbara *science educator*

Phoenix
Davey, Eleanor Ellen *science educator*

Scottsdale
Shirk, Marianne Eileen *veterinarian*

Taylor
Kerr, Barbara Prosser *research scientist, educator*

Tucson
Bernstein, Carol *molecular biologist*
Bittel, Kirstin Alicia *science educator*
Kolchens, Silvia *science educator*
Lai, LiWen *geneticist, educator*
Macys, Sonja *science association director*
Moran, Nancy A. *ecologist, educator*
Vandiver, Pamela Bowren *science educator*
Zou, Changping *research scientist, educator*

ARKANSAS

Cabot
Daugherty, Debra L. *science educator*

Dover
Kanady, Janet *science educator*

Little Rock
Abercrombie, Eydie L. *physiologist, consultant*
Tarasenko, Olga *biologist, educator*
Wight, Patricia Anne *neuroscience educator*

Magnolia
Hamilton, Barbara Denise *computer science educator*

Mountainburg
Richmond, Daphne Kay *science educator*

Pocahontas
Moss, Linda Elaine *science educator*

Walnut Ridge
Wheeless, Charlotte Ann *science educator*

Ward
Rudy, Janet Faye Walker *science educator*

CALIFORNIA

Alhambra
Malonek, Jennie Sue *science educator*

Bakersfield
Kreber, Lisa Ann *neuroscientist, psychologist*

Berkeley
Burnside, Mary Beth *biology professor, researcher*
Chen, Lu *neurobiologist, biology professor*
Fleiszig, Suzanne Mariane Janete *optometry educator*
Fung, Inez Y. *science educator*
King, Nicole *molecular biologist, educator*
Koehl, Mimi R. *integrative biology professor*
Kohwi-Shigematsu, Terumi *research scientist*
Scott, Eugenie Carol *science foundation director, anthropologist*
Wake, Marvalee Hendricks *biology professor*

Carlsbad
Parshall, B. Lynne *science administrator*

Carmel
Pasten, Laura Jean *veterinarian*

Chico
Dorsey-Tyler, April Melody *science educator*

Danville
Gilcrist, Tracy Ann *science educator*

Davis
Horwitz, Barbara Ann *physiologist, educator, consultant*
Keen, Susan Lynn *biology professor*
Kuhl, Tonya L. *science educator*
Meyer, Margaret Eleanor *retired microbiologist*
Ronald, Pamela C. *plant pathologist, educator*

Del Mar
Farquhar, Marilyn Gist *cell biologist, pathologist, educator*

El Cajon
Higginson, Jane *environmental educator, biologist, conservationist*

Escondido
Sloan, Anne Elizabeth *food scientist, writer*

Fresno
Waters, Rosemary R. *biology professor*

Fullerton
Dickson, Kathryn *science educator*
Woyski, Margaret Skillman *retired geology educator*

Hermosa Beach
Chi, Lois Wang *retired biology professor, research scientist*

Huntington Park
Gaines-Page, Rena L. *science educator*

Irvine
Riley, Sally Jean *science educator*

Kelseyville
Sandmeyer, E. E. *toxicologist, consultant*

La Habra
Enochs, Lori M. *science educator, department chairman*

La Jolla
Alvariño De Leira, Angeles (Angeles Alvariño) *biologist, oceanographer*
Baldridge, Kim *science educator*
Forsburg, Susan Louise *molecular geneticist*
Rahman, Yueh-Erh *biologist*

Los Alamitos
Njavro, E. Randelle *science educator*

Los Angeles
Connor-Dominguez, Billie Marie *science information professional*
Cox, Cathleen Ruth *zoologist, educator*
Craft, Cheryl Mae *neurobiologist, anatomist, researcher*
Gasson, Judith C. *research scientist*
Ghez, Andrea Mia *astronomy educator, physics educator*
Simmons, Donna Marie *neuroscientist, histotechnologist, neuroendocrine anatomist, researcher*
Szego, Clara Marian *cell biologist, educator*
Wright, Sandra *science administrator*

Lynwood
Trousdale, Margaret Mary *science educator*

Malibu
Hunt, Valerie Virginia *electrophysiologist, educator*

Montebello
Pasinato, Yvonne Louise *science educator*

Monterey
Packard, Julie *aquarium administrator*
Packard Burnett, Nancy *biologist*

Mountain View
Cabrol, Nathalie Agnes *research scientist*
Tarter, Jill Cornell *science foundation director, astronomer, researcher*

Oakland
Earle, Sylvia Alice *research biologist, oceanographer*

Palm Desert
Sausman, Karen *zoological park administrator*

Pasadena
Huang, Alice Shih-hou *biologist, educator, virologist*
Trendler, Teresa Ann *science educator*

Riverside
Talbot, Prue *biology professor*

Sacramento
Elizabeth, Mary *science educator, consultant*
Gluckmann, Ema *science educator*

San Diego
Crutchfield, Susan Ramsey *neurophysiologist*
Roeder, Phoebe Elizabeth *science educator*
Rovniak, Liza S. *research scientist, educator*
Swenson, Christine Erica *microbiologist*

San Francisco
Bargmann, Cornelia I. *neuroscientist, science educator*
Baxter-Lowe, Lee Ann *science educator*
Blackburn, Elizabeth Helen *molecular biologist*
Guo, Su *science educator*
Likova Mineva, Lora T. *research scientist*
Márquez-Magaña, Leticia Maria *biology professor*
Pera, Renee Reijo *biology professor*
Tlsty, Thea Dorothy *research scientist, educator*
Vidwans, Smruti Jayant *microbiologist*

San Jacinto
Stange, Sharon (Sherri) *science educator*

San Juan Capistrano
White, Beverly Jane *cytogeneticist*

San Luis Obispo
Waldo, Anna Lee *retired science educator, writer*

San Marcos
Dowey, Ana L. *microbiologist, educator*
Fabry, Victoria Joan *biology professor*

Santa Barbara
Tucker, Shirley Lois Cotter *botanist, educator*

Santa Cruz
Langenheim, Jean Harmon *biologist, educator*

Solana Beach
Culley, Deborah Anita *science educator*

Stanford
Arvin, Ann Margaret *microbiology and immunology educator, researcher*
Daily, Gretchen Cara *ecologist, environmental services administrator*
Francke, Uta *geneticist, educator*
Shapiro, Lucy *molecular biology educator*
Theriot, Julie *microbiologist, medical educator*

Stockton
Ford, Shirley Griffin *science educator, pharmacist*
Lin-Cereghino, Joan *science educator*
Magness, Rhonda Ann *retired microbiologist*

Sylmar
Faye, Thalia Garin *retired microbiologist, educator*

Tulare
Vickrey, Herta M. *microbiologist*

Union City
Baker, Vicki L. *science educator*

Walnut
Anderson, Cynthia Boot *biological science educator*

Walnut Creek
Elliott, Margaret S. *science educator*

Williams
Knight, Katherine Ellen *science educator, mathematics educator*

COLORADO

Aurora
Horwitz, Kathryn Bloch *molecular biologist, educator, breast cancer researcher*
Neville, Margaret Cobb *physiologist, educator*

Boulder
Fifkova, Eva *behavioral neuroscience educator*
Meier, Beverly Joyce Loeffler *science educator, educational consultant*

Carbondale
Cowgill, Ursula Moser *biologist, educator, environmental consultant*

Colorado Springs
Apodaca, Christy McCormick *exercise physiologist, athletic trainer*
Comstock, Diane Elaine *science educator, consultant*

Denver
Ehret, Josephine Mary *microbiologist, researcher*
Hays, Clare A. *veterinarian, biologist, educator*
Regensteiner, Judith Gail *science educator, research scientist*
Stephens, Kathryn J. *science educator*

Grand Junction
Childers, Margaret Anne *science educator*

Greeley
Green, Lynn Tesson *science educator, secondary school educator*

Northglenn
Hemlock, Roberta Leigh *veterinary technician*

Sterling
Zink, Brenda Lee *biology professor*

Yuma
Sinclair, Lisa *science educator*

CONNECTICUT

Cheshire
Beitler, Karen Ann *biology professor, technologist*

Coventry
Hayes, Julia Moriarty *retired science educator*

Fairfield
Earls, Christine Ross *biology professor*

Hamden
Adair, Eleanor Reed *environmental biologist*

Mystic
Hutchison, Dorris Jeannette *retired microbiologist, educator*

New Canaan
Donnelly, Laura Jean *science educator*
Grace, Julianne Alice *retired biotechnologist*

New Haven
Dunleavy, Mara Anne *science educator*

New London
Tassinari, Melissa Sherman *reproductive toxicologist*

New Milford
Behan, Sandra Holloway *science educator*

Newtown
Babbitt, Martha E. *science educator*

Rocky Hill
Kahn, Carolyn R. *biotechnology executive*

Trumbull
D'Addario, Jody Ann *science educator*

West Hartford
Dickie, Florence *science educator*

DELAWARE

Wilmington
Sippel-Wetmore, Frances Marie *microbiologist, retired business owner*

DISTRICT OF COLUMBIA

Washington
Berg, Patricia Elene *molecular biologist*
Chotin, Elizabeth Ettlinger *science foundation director*
Falk, Diane M. *research information specialist, librarian, writer, editor, director*
Harding, Fann *retired science administrator*
Jackson, Margaret Elizabeth *science educator*
Malcom, Shirley Mahaley *science association executive*
Neita, Marguerite Elaine *science educator*
Nightingale, Elena Ottolenghi *pediatric geneticist, academic administrator, educator*
Ridenour, Amy Moritz *research center administrator*
Soloway, Rose Ann Gould *clinical toxicologist*
Spelman, Lucy H. *zoological park administrator*
Tidball, M. Elizabeth Peters *physiologist, educator*
Torrey, Barbara Boyle *research council administrator*

FLORIDA

Altamonte Springs
Nieto, Shirley L. *science educator*

Boca Raton
More, Kane Jean *science educator*

Cape Coral
Minich, Jacqueline Hutton *science educator*

Clermont
Hicks, Debra Carter *biology professor*

Coral Springs
McFarlane, Dana B. *science educator, secondary school educator*

Crestview
Howard, Kelli Michelle *science educator*

Eatonville
Ebert, Tracy *science educator*

Fort Pierce
Rice, Mary Esther *biologist*
Widder, Edith Anne *biologist*

Gainesville
Green, Eleanor Myers *veterinarian, educator*
Grobman, Hulda Gross (Mrs. Arnold B. Grobman) *health science educator*
Hoy, Marjorie Ann *entomology educator*
Schmidt-Nielsen, Bodil Mimi (Mrs. Roger G. Chagnon) *retired physiologist, educator*

Jacksonville
Carson, Ellen Kathleen *biology professor*
Murphy, Jeanne M. *science educator*

Lakeland
Chapman, Angela Marie *science educator*
Pospichal, Marcie W. *neuroscientist, psychologist, educator*

Loxahatchee
Slygh, Carolyn V. *biologist, educator*

Macclenny
Hobbs, Brita Spence *science educator*

Melbourne
Storrs, Eleanor Emerett *science administrator, consultant*

Miami
Rodriguez, Irmina Bestard *science educator*

Mount Dora
Moreau, Patricia D. *science educator*

Orlando
DeNoon, Patricia Y'Vette *science educator, consultant*
Foster-Henningham, Shari M. *science educator*
Klein, Jenny Lynn *neuroscientist, researcher*
Knowles, Patricia Marie *science educator*
Lindner, Catherine Patricia *science educator*

Pensacola
Ables, Linda Bomberger *biology professor*
Kuhl, Judith Annette *retired science educator*

Plantation
Wyse-Feders, Mary *science educator*

Ruskin
Briscoe, Anne M. *retired science educator*

Saint Augustine
Kehoe, Kathryn J. *science educator, researcher*

Sarasota
Clark, Eugenie *zoologist, educator*

Spring Hill
Rothenberg, Linda Ann *science educator*

Tallahassee
Anderson, Theresa Ann *science educator*

Tampa
Hinsch, Gertrude Wilma *biology professor*
Pisaneschi, Dena Marie *science educator*

Tavernier
Engler, Deanna K. *science educator*

West Palm Beach
Browning, Sara Louise *science educator*

GEORGIA

Adairsville
Dobson, Suzanne *science educator*

Albany
Marshall, Cindy Lou *science educator, social studies educator*

Athens
Meyer, Judy L. *science educator, director*

Atlanta
Cox, Nancy Jane *microbiologist*
Day, Diane Elaine *science educator, researcher*
DuBose, Patricia Chapman *science educator, consultant*

Augusta
Kutlar, Ferdane *genetics educator, researcher*

Calhoun
Haygood, Theresa *science educator, medical technician*

Cave Spring
Willis, Heather Nicole *science educator*

Columbus
Spenard, Patricia Ann *science educator*

Cornelia
Franks, Jane Woodall *science educator*

Duluth
Pratt, Bonnie *science educator*

Elberton
McCarty, Dixie Rayle *science educator*

Fort Oglethorpe
Mobley, Brooke Michelle *science educator*

Lovejoy
Burchfield, Ella Loggins *science educator*

Marietta
Tucker, Rebecca Denise *science educator*

Mcdonough
Norby, Rena Faye *science educator*

Newnan
Culbreth, Lucretia Joy *science educator*

Sharpsburg
Crosby, Letitia Jordan *science educator*

Statesboro
Leege, Lissa Maria *biology professor*

Stone Mountain
Antoine, Alissa Quiana *science educator*

Tifton
Heidt, Amy R. *science educator*

HAWAII

Honolulu
Abbott, Isabella Aiona *retired biology educator*
Fok, Agnes Kwan *retired cell biologist, educator*
Uchida, Janice Yukiko *plant pathologist/mycologist, researcher*

Lihue
Ortiz, Joni Lynne *science educator*

IDAHO

Boise
Woods, Jean Frahm *science educator*

Horseshoe Bend
Haley, Jenifer Jo *science educator*

Lewiston
Finan, Jane *zoologist, educator*

ILLINOIS

Aurora
Elgar, Sharon Kay *science educator*
Lach, Elizabeth *science educator*

Belleville
Burch, Julie S. *science educator*

Carbondale
Achenbach, Laurie A. *science educator*

Chicago
Lerman, Zafra Margolin *science educator, public policy professor*
McClintock, Martha K. *biologist, educator*
Olopade, Olufunmilayo Falusi (Funmi Olopade) *geneticist, educator, oncologist, hematologist*
Overton, Jane Vincent Harper *biology professor*
Straus, Lorna Puttkammer *biology professor*

Coal City
DiGiusto, Elaine Bessie *science educator*

Dolton
McNamara, Kimberly Diane *science educator, department chairman*

Downers Grove
MacArtney, Lisa Lani *science educator, consultant*

Dundee
Hernandez, Peggy Sue *science educator*

Dupo
Kautzer, Susan Ann *science educator*

Elgin
Deichstetter, Peggy Ann *science educator*
Garcia, Donna M. *science educator*

Evanston
Enroth-Cugell, Christina Alma Elisabeth *neurophysiologist, educator*

Glen Ellyn
Anderson, Barbara Jean *biology professor*
Persky, Karen Rae *biologist, educator*

Heyworth
Gregory, M. Christine *science educator*

Highland Park
Miller, Maureen Chertow *science educator*

Machesney Park
Brewer, Valerie D. *science educator, secondary school educator*

Macomb
Barclay, Martha Jane *science educator, research scientist*
Barden, Laura Marie *science educator*

Mattoon
Horton, Lucinda *biology professor*

Naperville
Armstrong, Patricia Kay *ecologist*

Normal
Davis, Janet R. Beach *science educator*

Northbrook
Garcia, Mary Frances *science educator*

Orland Park
Burfeind, Betty Ruth *science educator*

Plainfield
Matlock, B. Jane *science educator*

River Grove
Gardner, Sandi B. *biology professor*

Robinson
Mallard, Carrie Charlene *science educator*

Romeoville
Vander Vliet, Valerie Jeanne *biology educator*

Saint Charles
Leppert, Andrea *science educator*

Taylorville
Turner, Cynthia M. *science educator*

Urbana
Berenbaum, May Roberta *entomology educator*
Goodrum, Shanda S. *science educator*
Ridgway, Marcella Davies *veterinarian*
Williams, Martha Ethelyn *information science educator*

Westchester
Webb, Emily *retired plant morphologist*

Woodstock
Dorn, Diane M. *science educator*

INDIANA

Anderson
Harris, Tina *science educator*

Bloomington
Clevenger, Sarah *botanist, consultant*
Ketterson, Ellen D. *biologist, educator*

Carmel
Kundrat, Virginia Lynn *science educator*

Fort Wayne
Beam, Teresa Ann *biology professor*

Gary
Pratt, Diane Ford *science educator*

Hammond
Reinke, Frances Marylou *science educator*

Haubstadt
Elpers, Kimberly Kay *science educator, consultant*

Jasper
Wineinger, Barbara Ann *science educator*

Jeffersonville
Scholes, Janis Wolf *science educator*

Lanesville
Cleveland, Peggy Rose Richey *cytotechnologist*

Lebanon
Hedge, Christine Marle *science educator*

Madison
Grahn, Ann Wagoner *retired science administrator*

New Harmony
Gray, Lois Mittino *biologist, educator*

Notre Dame
Shrader-Frechette, Kristin *science educator*

Pittsboro
Swango, Colleen Jill *science educator*

Scottsburg
Kendall, Susan Carol *science educator*

West Lafayette
Creech, Rebecca J. *science educator*
Mason, Sally Kay Frost *biology professor, academic administrator*

West Terre Haute
Adams, Diedre Shook *science educator*

IOWA

Des Moines
Spencer, Melissa Fischer *science educator*
Weeks, Randi Montag *science educator*

Iowa City
Eichenberger Gilmore, Julie Mae *research scientist*
Maxson, Linda Ellen *biologist, educator*
Stay, Barbara *zoologist, educator*

Marion
Van Nest, Ann Marie *science educator*

Parkersburg
Lievens, Rebecca S.A. *science educator*

Pocahontas
Jarvis, Sue Kay *science educator*

KANSAS

Arkansas City
Moscript, Barbara Ann *science educator*
Neal, Melinda K. *science educator*

Isabel
Brant, Dorris Ellen Stapleton *bacteriologist, music educator*

Kansas City
Hodison, Patricia Mary Kathleen *science educator*

NEW HAMPSHIRE

Alton
Sweezy, Vicky Lynn *science educator, emergency medical technician*

Goffstown
Seastream, Doris *science educator*

Hanover
Burchenal, Joan Riley *science educator*
Guerinot, Mary Lou *biology professor*
Spiegel, Evelyn Sclufer *biology professor*

Lebanon
Mc Cann, Frances Veronica *physiologist, educator*

Manchester
Bruno, Sherrie L. *science educator*

Raymond
Gospodarek, Angela M *science educator*

Sanbornton
Weiant, Elizabeth Abbott *retired biology professor*

NEW JERSEY

Bayonne
Levin, Holly J. *science educator*

East Brunswick
Dombrowski, Anne Wesseling *retired microbiologist*
Strapko, Irene *science educator*

Glen Ridge
Roethlin, Mary Jane *science educator*

Kenilworth
Kravec, Cynthia Vallen *microbiologist*

Livingston
Scott, Jane Vicroy *microbiologist*

Moorestown
Collins, Angelo *science educator*

Mountain Lakes
Wallace, MaryJean Elizabeth *science educator*

New Brunswick
Mabb, Karen Terri *ornithologist*

Newark
Cheng, Mei-Fang *psychobiology educator, neuroscientist*
Weis, Judith Shulman *biology professor*

Old Tappan
Lovitch, Joan *science educator, coach*

Paterson
Kelder, Dorothy Mae *science educator*
Tanis, Barbara Ann *science educator*

Perth Amboy
Daily, Anna Wilkins *science educator*

Piscataway
Ferstandig Arnold, Gail *research scientist, educator*
Witz, Gisela *research scientist, educator*

Princeton
Altmann, Jeanne *zoologist, educator*
Drakeman, Lisa N. *biotechnologist*
Grant, Barbara Rosemary *science educator, researcher*
Marshall, Carol Joyce *science administrator*
Witkin, Evelyn Maisel *retired geneticist*

Rahway
Strack, Alison Merwin *neurobiologist*

Ridgewood
Kuiken, Diane (Dee) Marie *science educator*

Scotch Plains
Levins, Mary Clare *science educator*

Shrewsbury
Westerman, Liane Marie *research scientist executive*

Sussex
Carter, Joy T. *science educator*

Toms River
Kudryasheva, Aleksandra A. *microbiologist, nutritionist*

Wallington
Safira, Barabara *science educator*

Wayne
Desroches, Danielle *biology professor, researcher*

Wyckoff
Chen, Loris Jean *science educator*
Cropper, Susan Peggy *veterinarian*

NEW MEXICO

Albuquerque
Henderson, Rogene Faulkner *toxicologist, researcher*
Jones, Patricia A. *science educator*
Sanchez, Victoria Wagner *science educator*
Woodward, Joan B. *science association director*

Carlsbad
Angell, Carye Lou *science educator*

Santa Fe
Harding, Marie *ecological executive, artist*

Socorro
Boston, Penelope J. *science educator, researcher*

NEW YORK

Albany
Stewart, Margaret McBride *biology professor, researcher*

Astoria
Sagiani, Frederica *science educator*

Auburn
Coye, Judy *science educator*

Aurora
Wahl, Christina M. *biology professor, researcher*

Bronx
Brown, Lucy L. *neurology and neuroscience professor, researcher*

Brooklyn
Altura, Bella T. *physiologist, educator*
Bucolo, Gail Ann *biotechnologist*
Jacobson, Leslie Sari *biologist, educator*
Schwartz-Giblin, Susan Toby *neuroscientist, educator, dean*

Buffalo
Rodriguez, Gloria E. *science educator*

Canton
Bodensteiner, Karin Johanna *biology professor, researcher*

Cedarhurst
Peel, Barbara Jean *science educator*

Clarence
Furlano, Joanne Elizabeth *science educator*

Copenhagen
O'Shaughnessy, Nadine M. *science educator*

Cortlandt Manor
Traille, Joy Myra *microbiologist, eldercare service provider*

Dryden
Morris, Carol E. *biologist, educator*

Flushing
Schnall, Edith Lea *microbiologist, educator*

Fulton
Noel, Karen Ann *science educator*

Garden City
Burkett, Janice Mayo *science educator*
Podwall, Kathryn Stanley *biology professor*
Ver Pault, Carolyn *science educator*

Ithaca
Henry, Susan Armstrong *biology professor, dean*
Nasrallah, June *plant pathologist, department chairman*

Mamaroneck
McCormick, Margaret C. *science educator*

Montgomery
Belgiovene, Melanie C. *science educator*

Mount Sinai
Sill, Linda DeHart *science educator*

Mount Vernon
Young, Paula Eva *animal shelter director*

Neponsit
Nicastri, Ann Gilbert *science educator*

New Hyde Park
Ashtari, Manzar *neuroscientist*

New Rochelle
Winstead, Melody *science educator*

New York
Buckley, Nancy Margaret *retired research scientist*
Calame, Kathryn Lee *microbiologist, educator*
Carlson, Marian Bille *geneticist, researcher, educator*
Chan, Siu-Wai *materials science educator*
Davis, Jessica G. *geneticist*
de Lange, Titia *research scientist, educator*
Dobrof, Rose Wiesman *gerontology educator*
Eckhardt, Laurel Ann *biologist, researcher, educator*
Fuchs, Elaine V. *molecular biologist, educator*
Garcia, Minerva A.F. *microbiologist, research and clinical laboratory scientist*
Hirschhorn, Rochelle *genetics educator*
Kelley, Darcy B. *biology professor*
Korsten, Susan Snyder *science educator*
Perez, Wilma *microbiologist, researcher*
Prives, Carol *biologist, educator*
Shapiro, Anna *microbiologist, researcher*
Willner, Judith P. *clinical geneticist, pediatrician, educator*

Newburgh
Garey, Velma Kay *science foundation director, educator*

North Collins
Brosnick, Lisa A. *science educator*

Orchard Park
Urbanski, Jane F. *retired microbiologist*

Port Chester
Brescia, Alicia *science educator, vice principal*

Purchase
Ehrman, Lee *geneticist, educator*

Red Hook
Beam, Deborah Ann *science educator*

Rochester
Rodgers, Suzanne Hooker *physiologist, consultant*

Rome
Ramos, Maria *science educator*

Roslyn
Shubin, Joanna *science educator*

Rye
Sales, Mitzi S. *science educator*

Schuylerville
Rechak, Ivy Maria *science educator*

Seaford
Degnan, Keri-Jene *science educator*
Pellegrino, Roseann *science educator*

Sinclairville
Martin, Amy H. *science educator*

Suffern
Stritmater, Colleen Leigh *science educator*

Tuxedo Park
Rossman, Toby Gale *molecular and genetic toxicology educator, researcher*

Yorktown Heights
Smith, Cheryl A. *science educator*

NORTH CAROLINA

Chapel Hill
Farber, Rosann Alexander *geneticist, educator*
Mueller, Nancy Schneider *retired biology professor*
Sharpe, Karen L. *science association director*

Charlotte
Stone, Katherine Smith *science educator*

Claremont
Elmore, Beth Robinson *science educator*

Dunn
Norris, Wanda Payne *science educator*

Durham
Hogan, Brigid L.M. *molecular biologist*
Nwosu, Veronica C. *microbiologist, science educator, medical researcher*
Rouse, Doris Jane *physiologist, research scientist*

Fayetteville
Squire, Sheri Marie *science educator*

Hickory
Whiteley, Emily C. *biology professor*

Kill Devil Hills
Blonder, Barbara Irene *biologist*

Knightdale
Rhodes, Rhonda Cockrell *science educator*

Laurinburg
Williams, Kathryn Vandervoort *science educator*

Mount Olive
Mason Foster, Angela Marie *biology professor*

Research Triangle Park
Bond, Enriqueta Carter *science administrator*
Fought, Lorianne *plant pathologist*
Haynes, Victoria F. *science administrator*

Statesville
Crosby, Jane Watts *science educator*
Harris, Crystal Stone *science educator, coach*

Wilmington
Desjardins, Betty Lee *histologist*
Kelley, Patricia Hagelin *geology educator*

NORTH DAKOTA

Bisbee
Keller, Michelle R. *science educator*

Bismarck
Niksic, Gwen M. *biology professor*

Fargo
Richman, Rachel L. *food scientist, microbiologist, educator*

Lisbon
Taylor, Ardis *science educator*

OHIO

Bellbrook
Mann, Rebecca Ann *science educator, secondary school educator*

Bowling Green
Clark, Eloise Elizabeth *biologist, educator*

Brunswick
Sadd, Wendy Marie *science educator*
Timco, Melanie Suzanne *science educator*

Canton
Bernstein, Penny L. *biologist, educator*

Chillicothe
Metzger, Jamie B. *science educator*

Cincinnati
Perna, Belinda A. *science educator*
Walters, Bridget C. *science educator*

Cleveland
Beard, Lydia Jean *research scientist, educator*
Manes, Andrea M. *science educator*

Columbus
Henkin, Tina M. *science educator, researcher*
Knotts, Maureen Mary *science educator*

Copley
Galang, Monica Lynn *science educator, department chairman*

Dayton
Hollebeke, Norma L. *biologist, educator*

Elyria
Thompson, Janis Grocock *biology professor*

Fairview Park
Leickly, Portia Elaine *science educator*

Findlay
McIntosh, Julie Dean *science educator*

Highland Hills
Kharina, Nina Yurievna *science educator, dental assistant*

Howard
Dixon, Carmen Sue *science educator*

Twinsburg
Murphy, Kathleen S. *science educator*

Wellston
Hockman, Lori Lynn *biologist, educator*

West Carrollton
Bebout, Jennifer Lucille *science educator*

Whitehall
Falcon, Kimberly Sue *science educator*

Wooster
Saif, Linda J. *veterinary scientist, virologist, immunologist*

OKLAHOMA

Ada
Benson, Jade *science educator*

Ardmore
Fisher, Linda R. *science educator, department chairman*

Durant
Dixon, Diane Marie *biology professor*

Elgin
McMasters, Glenetta G. *science educator*

Eufaula
Flud, Sherrie Mae *science educator*

Gore
Chair, Lisa *science educator*

Guthrie
Allen, Lori Ann *science educator*

Muskogee
Helwick, Amber *science educator*

Oklahoma City
Ousley, Amy Michelle *science educator*

Park Hill
Yeager, Debra Lyn *science educator*

Stilwell
Doyle, Rhonda Gail *science educator*

Tulsa
Stewart, Mary Tomlinson *science educator, researcher*
Vincent, Suzanne Sawyer *physiologist, educator*

OREGON

Bend
McDermott, Mary Katheryn *science educator*

Corvallis
Cope, Rhian Brianna *toxicologist, educator*

Pendleton
Klepper, Elizabeth Lee *retired physiologist*

Portland
Balkowiec, Agnieszka Zofia *science educator, researcher*
Cady, Sherry L. *astrobiologist, educator*
Ozawa, Connie Patricia *science educator*

PENNSYLVANIA

Allentown
Shaffer-Shriver, Julie Renée *science educator*

Annville
Verhoek, Susan Elizabeth *botany educator*

Bangor
Steele, Kathleen Patricia *science educator*

Barto
Kirk, Kathryn A. *science educator*

Bensalem
Kline, Sharon Elaine *science educator*

Bradford
Robbins, Andrea M. *science educator*

Bryn Mawr
Crawford, Maria Luisa Buse *geology educator*

Camp Hill
Sweeney, Susan Lynn *science educator*

Du Bois
Burkett, Julie Ann *science educator*

Elizabethtown
Marjorie, Reed L. *science educator*

Erie
Mackowski, Pamela Anne *science educator*
Voss, Margaret A. *biology professor*

Fairview
Ruud, Ruth Marie *science educator*

Greensburg
Kuznik, Rachelle Lee *science educator, writer*

Halifax
Fasnacht, Judy Ann *science educator, small business owner*

Haverford
DiBerardino, Marie Antoinette *developmental biologist, educator*

Hershey
Blosky, Elizabeth Anne *science educator*
Hopper, Anita Klein *molecular genetics educator*

Midland
Katich, Eleanor Patience *retired science educator*

Philadelphia
Eisenstein, Toby K. *microbiology professor*
Patrick, Ruth (Mrs. Ruth Hodge Van Dusen) *botany educator, curator*
Siegman, Marion Joyce *physiologist, educator*

Phoenixville
Hanlon, Barbara Jean *family and consumer sciences educator*

Pittsburgh
Amara, Susan *neuroscientist*
Frost, Laura Lynn *microbiology educator*
Gollin, Susanne Merle *cell biologist, researcher*
Karenbauer, Jacalynn *science educator*
Marazita, Mary Louise *genetics researcher*

Reading
Chinni, Rosemarie Catherine *science educator*

Robesonia
Kissling, Phleane M. *science educator*

Swarthmore
Sawyers, Claire Elyce *arboretum administrator*

University Park
Brenchley, Jean Elnora *microbiologist, researcher, science administrator*
Fedoroff, Nina Vsevolod *research scientist, consultant, educator*
Roy, Della Martin *materials science educator, researcher*

Verona
McWilliams, Betty Jane *science administrator, speech pathology/audiology services professional, educator*

West Chester
Flood, Dorothy Garnett *neuroscientist*

Wilkes Barre
Coffin, Joan M. *neuroscience educator*

Williamsport
Buckman, Debra Ann *science educator*

RHODE ISLAND

Kingston
Hufnagel, Linda Ann *biology professor, researcher*

Providence
Gerbi, Susan Alexandra *biology professor*
Schmitt, Johanna Marie *plant population biologist, educator*

SOUTH CAROLINA

Anderson
Rhoe, Wilhelmina Robinson *retired science educator*
Spigener, Susan Arnold *science educator*

Beaufort
Jones, Sarah Ann *science educator*

Cayce
Bouknight, Fran Shoolbred *science educator*

Charleston
Machowski, Liisa Ervin Sharpes *science educator*

Clemson
Minor, V. Christine Mahaffey *science educator*

Columbia
Aelion, C. Marjorie *science educator*
McAlpine, Lisa K. *science educator*
Smith, Theresa Joanne *research scientist, educator*
Wideman, Ida Devlin *science educator*

Conway
Gilman, Sharon Larimer *biology professor*

Florence
Price, Stacy D. *science educator*

Greenville
Cureton, Claudette Hazel Chapman *biology professor*
Leavitt, Beth Meade *science educator, department chairman*

Greenwood
Lutz, Laura Elise *science educator*

Mc Cormick
Soni, Jayshri *science educator, director*

North Augusta
Rodriguez, Doris Jones *retired science educator*

TENNESSEE

Brentwood
James, Elizabeth Jeanette Thompson *science educator*

Denmark
Lipscomb, Carol Matthews *science educator*

Dyersburg
Rose, Wendy Michelle *science educator*

Harrison
Sellers, Donna Northcutt *science educator*

Hendersonville
McPherson, Mona Sue *science educator, department chairman*

Huntingdon
King, Tracy Lynn *science educator*

Jacksboro
King, Shelley B. *science educator*

Johnson City
Robertson, Laura Elizabeth *science educator*

Knoxville
Anderson, Ilse Janell *clinical geneticist*

Maryville
Swann, Jerilyn Mitchell *science educator*

Mc Minnville
Shockley, Penny Michelle *science educator*

Memphis
Benstein, Barbara DuBray *cytotechnologist, educator*
Harris, Cora Lee *science educator, small business owner*
Howe, Martha Morgan *microbiologist, educator*
Pruitt, Rosalyn Jolena *science educator*

Nashville
Fanning, Ellen *biology professor, research scientist*
Orgebin-Crist, Marie-Claire *retired biology professor, department chairman*

South Pittsburg
Lawhorn, Shannon Hibbs *science educator*

TEXAS

Aransas Pass
Flores, Robin Kay *science educator*

Arlington
Huse, Regina Marie *biologist, educator*
Sierra, Regina Aurelia *science educator*

Austin
Drummond Borg, Lesley Margaret *geneticist*
Fryxell, Greta Albrecht *marine botany educator, oceanographer*
Meyers, Lauren Ancel *biologist*
Mikels, Jo *science educator*
Ramirez Garza, Elizabeth Ann *biology professor, researcher*
Simpson, Beryl Brintnall *botany educator*

Brooks City-Base
Miller, Carolyn Lyons *microbiologist, military officer*

Clarksville
Smith, Roberta Hawkins *plant physiologist*

College Station
Beaver, Bonnie Veryle *veterinarian, educator*
Fechhelm, Janice *science educator, researcher, illustrator*
Foster, Andrea Susan *science educator*

Dallas
Robinson, Debra JoAnn *science educator*
Tanous, Melissa Lynn *science educator*
Vitetta, Ellen S. *microbiologist, educator, immunologist*

Denton
Coogan, Melinda Ann Strank *biology professor, chemistry professor*

El Paso
Santiago, Irma *science educator, department chairman*

Floresville
Tieken, Lisa Marie *science educator*

Fort Worth
de Schweinitz, Jean Howard *biology professor*
Holcomb, Anna Louise *physical science educator*

Houston
Durham, Susan K. *research scientist*
Estes, Mary K. *virologist*
Garay, Dolores Lollie *science educator*
Harris, Deborah Ann *science educator*
Roberts, Janet Lynn Lekowski *science educator*
Seaton, Alberta Jones *biologist, educator, consultant*
Sisson, Virginia Baker *geology educator*
Strong, Louise Connally *geneticist*

Hurst
Jacaruso, Diana *biology professor*
Lindsey, Jerri Kay *biologist, educator*

Lewisville
Jones, Pamela Walsh *science educator*
Whitney, Sharry Jan *science educator*

Longview
Berry, Keysha Roshawn *science educator*

Lubbock
Edwards, Shannon J. *science educator*
Pitcock, Michelle Marie *science educator*
Reed, Teresa F. *science educator, elementary school educator*

Lufkin
Randell, Stephanie McMillan *biology professor*

Midland
Faught, Brenda Dorman *health sciences educator*
Welch, Lisa Renea *biology professor*

New Braunfels
Ortiz, Denise M. *science educator*

Plano
Jacoby, Teresa Michelle *zoologist, consultant, small business owner, entrepreneur*

Royse City
Atkins, Janet Necette *science educator, department chairman*

San Angelo
Furlong, Ebba Von *science educator*

San Antonio
Ghinaudo, Penny Alicia *science educator, department chairman*
Robinson, Joyce Elaine *science educator*
Turner, Judy C. *research scientist*
Wang, Yufeng *science educator*

Selma
Sharp, Bridget Marie *science educator*

Stafford
Wiersema, Donna Sanders *science educator*

Temple
Yarbrough, Jennifer Gay *science educator*

Terrell
Bracken, Mary Parker *biologist, educator*

Van Alstyne
Smith, Carol Lee *science educator*

Victoria
Venneman, Sandy S. *biology professor*

Wills Point
Sherrard, Harriett *science educator*

UTAH

Centerville
Schwartz, Heidi K. *science educator*

VERMONT

Middlebury
Spatafora, Grace Ann *biology professor*

Morrisville
Lechevalier, Mary Pfeil *retired microbiologist, educator*

Richmond
Fary, Sandra Suzanne *science educator*

South Duxbury
Villemaire, Diane Davis *science educator*

VIRGINIA

Alexandria
Vosbeck, Elizabeth Just *retired geneticist*
Woolley, Mary Elizabeth *science administrator, advocate*

Amissville
Hunter, Beverly Claire *research scientist, educator*

Appomattox
Pickrel, Felicia Renee *science educator*

Arlington
Boesz, Christine C. *science foundation administrator*
Cehelsky, Marta *scientific organization executive*
Markessini, Joan *research scientist, psychologist*
Olsen, Kathie Lynn *science foundation director*
Vasquez, Jo Anne *retired science educator*
Whyte, Nancy Gooch *microbiologist*

Burke
Barrile, Judith *science educator, consultant*

Chester
Carr, Carol Elaine *biology professor*

Christiansburg
Shelton, Sylvia Lawson *science educator*

Dublin
Linzey, Juanita Bird *biology professor*

Falls Church
Bryan, Billie Marie (Mrs. James A. Mackey) *retired biologist*

Farmville
Alvarez, Consuelo Jackeline *science educator, researcher*

Fincastle
Sprinkle, Denise L. *science educator*

Gloucester
Pace, Sandra McMillen *science educator*

Gloucester Point
Bush, Elizabeth Olney *marine lab technician*

Hampton
Kelley, Mary E. *science educator*
Tominack, Debra Dillard *science educator*

Hopewell
Arbogast, Sally S. *science educator*

Lansdowne
Miller, Dorothy Anne Smith *retired cytogenetics educator*

Mc Lean
DeGiovanni-Donnelly, Rosalie Frances *biologist, educator*

Midlothian
Ameen, Betsy Harrison *science educator, department chairman*

Norfolk
Rivera, Caroline Clark *biologist, educator*
Xu, Xiaohong Nancy *chemistry and biomedical science educator*

Orange
Gore, Rebecca Estes *science educator*

Richmond
Boadle-Biber, Margaret Clare *physiologist, educator*
Gregory, Jean Winfrey *ecologist, educator*

Salem
Secor, Margaret J. *science educator*

Sterling
Gulden, Linda Lober *science educator*

Vienna
Davis, Lauren Alexis *science educator*

Virginia Beach
Hyman, Pamela Dronette *science educator*
Young, Dell *science educator*

Woodbridge
St. Clair, Miriam Macleod *biology professor*
Taylor, Jane Bartlett *biology professor, educational consultant*

WASHINGTON

Bellingham
Ross, June Rosa Pitt *biologist, educator*

Bothell
Flynn-James, Stephanie *biologist, educator*

Lopez Island
Brownstein, Barbara Lavin *geneticist, educator, director*

Pullman
Sprunger, Lisa Karen *physiologist, educator*
Thomashow, Linda Suzanne *microbiologist*

Richland
Chou, Charissa J. *staff scientist*

Seattle
Boersma, P. Dee *marine biologist, educator*
Fidel, Raya *information science educator*
King, Mary-Claire *geneticist, educator*
Kuhl, Patricia K. *science educator*
Riddiford, Lynn Moorhead *biologist, educator*
Szkody, Paula *astronomy educator, researcher*
Wilson-McNamara, Pamela *microbiologist, educator*

WEST VIRGINIA

Huntington
Fike, Dorothy Jean *science educator*

Morgantown
Wenger, Sharon Louise *cytogeneticist, researcher, educator*

WISCONSIN

Clintonville
Primmer, Lillian Juanda *science educator*

Madison
Beyer-Mears, Annette *physiologist*
Dierauf, Leslie Ann *wildlife veterinarian, conservation biologist, consultant*
Handelsman, Jo *plant pathologist, educator*
Marrett, Cora B. *science educator*
Turner, Monica Goigel *ecologist*

Menomonee Falls
Janzen, Norine Madelyn Quinlan *clinical laboratory scientist*

Milwaukee
Estrin, Alejandra Audrey *science educator*

Verona
Hawkins, Peggy Anne *veterinarian*

Wilmot
Volden, Stephanie Kay *science educator*

WYOMING

Casper
Jacobs, Carolyn Dianne Crouch *science educator*

Cheyenne
Zumo, Billie Thomas *retired biologist*

TERRITORIES OF THE UNITED STATES

PUERTO RICO

Ponce
Smith, Maria Carmen *retired science educator*

CANADA

BRITISH COLUMBIA

Sidney
Bigelow, Margaret Elizabeth Barr (M.E. Barr) *retired botany educator*

ONTARIO

Ottawa
Adams, Gabrielle *biologist*

QUEBEC

Montreal
Gibbs, Sarah Preble *biologist, educator*

Pointe-Claire
Lapointe, Lucie *research institute executive*

AFGHANISTAN

Strongsville
Grumbach, Katherine Elizabeth *science educator*

AUSTRALIA

Melbourne
Bishop, Ruth Frances *microbiologist, research scientist, educator*

ADDRESS UNPUBLISHED

Addor, Lina Al Kaissy *science educator*
Ah Soon, Melanie Frances Kawamoto *science educator*
Alanazi, Jessica Lane *science educator*
Anderson, Elaine Janet *science educator*
Anderson, Melissa Ann *science educator*
Andre, Angela Renee *science educator*
Armani, Donna *science educator*
Baca, Joy *science educator*
Barnes-Kempton, Isabel Janet *retired microbiologist, dean*
Bartlett, Denise Margaret *science educator*
Bednar-Stanley, Monica Mary *science educator, educational consultant*
Berman Robinson, Sherry H. *science educator, consultant*
Bertino, Patricia Nolan *science educator*
Bethune, Nikki *science educator*
Bick, Katherine Livingstone *neuroscientist, educator, researcher*
Bland, Deborah Elaine *science educator*
Branch, Laura Michelle *science educator*
Browning, Emily Rose *science educator*
Burdett, Barbra Elaine *biology professor*
Bushong Whitehead, Pat J. *science educator, consultant*
Cannizzaro, Linda Ann *geneticist, researcher*
Champey, Elaine *science foundation director*
Clark, Mary Etta *science writing consultant*
Cobb, Delores Massey *science educator*
Cole, Rachel P. *science educator*
Colwell, Rita Rossi *microbiologist, former federal agency administrator, medical educator*
Conway, Jaime J. *science educator*
Cooper, Lynne Marie *veterinarian, educator*
Coyle, Marie Bridget *retired microbiologist, retired lab administrator*
Craig, Linda (Teri) Carol *science educator*
Crudup, Pamela Tracy Parham *science educator, writer*
Currier, Patty *physiologist*
DaSilva, Dina Patricia *science educator*
DeBakey, Lois *science administrator, educator*
de Limantour, Clarice Barr *food scientist*
Del Villar, Aurora *science educator*
Doman, Elvira *retired science administrator*
Dominguez, Andrea Hope *science educator*
Donegan, Teresa E. *pharmaceutical educator*
Donovan, Kierston Foley *science educator*
Durham Norman, Thena Monts *microbiologist, researcher, health facility administrator*
Dybowski, Jane *science educator*
Edwards, Julie Ann *science researcher*
Evans, Robyn V. *science educator*
Federman, Cindy B. *science educator, retail executive*
Feir, Dorothy Jean *entomologist, educator, physiologist*
Finnegan, Jennifer Michelle *veterinarian*
Florence, Melanie Anne *biologist, writer*
Ford, Carol *science educator*
Fotopoulos, Sophia Stathopoulos *medical research scientist, administrator*
Frank, Linda Maria *science educator*
Frossard, Janice L. *science educator*
Gabor-Hotchkiss, Magda *research scientist, librarian*
Gerritsen, Mary Ellen *vascular and cell biologist*
Gibson, Tracie M. *biology professor*
Glasner, Cristin Anne *science educator*
Goodall, Jane *zoologist*
Green, Karen Marie *science educator, gifted and talented educator*
Habermann, Helen Margaret *botanist, educator*
Hamil, Burnette Wolf *science educator*
Harlin, Marilyn Miler *marine botany educator, researcher, consultant*
Hatch, Sally *science educator*
Held, Karen Lee *science educator*
Hemmingsen, Barbara Bruff *retired microbiologist*
Heyer, Stephanie *science educator*
Hicks, Debra Lee *science educator*
Hildebrand, Verna Lee *human ecology educator*
Hitchcock, Karen Ruth *biology professor, dean, academic administrator*
Hlawaty, Heide *science educator, researcher*
Hoffman, Linda S. *science educator, special education educator*
Holland, Branti Latessa *science educator*
Honour, Lynda Charmaine *research scientist, psychotherapist, educator*
Houseknecht, Karen L. *research scientist, educator*
Howard-Peebles, Patricia Nell *clinical cytogeneticist*
Howell, Kimberly Lynne *science educator*
Huffman, Amie Michelle Breaud *science educator*
Hughes, Susan Michele *science educator, researcher*
Huie, Carol P. *information science educator*
Jackson, Dana Lee *science educator*
Jalbert, Amy *science educator*
Jensvold, Mary Lee Abshire *research scientist*
Kaiser, Bonnie L. *science educator, educator*
Katz, Anne Harris *biologist, educator, writer*
Kerr, Janet Spence *physiologist, pharmacologist, researcher*
Kirchner, Ursula Schwebs *science educator*
Kleven, Laura *science educator*
Koenig, Maureen Catherine *science educator*
Kolasa, Kathryn Marianne *food and nutrition educator, consultant*
Kreider, Louisa J. *biologist, librarian*
Lafferty, Christine Elizabeth *science educator*
LaMere, Melissa Jo *biomechanics educator*
LaRochelle, Wanda Carlene *science educator*
Lee, Marvina Sue *science educator*
Leventhal, Ruth *retired parasitology educator, university official*
Lindley, Suzanne Evers *biology professor, researcher*
Lingle, Sarah Elizabeth *research scientist*
Litz, Claudia *science educator*
Locklear, Tina Michelle *science educator*
Lustyk, Mary Kathleen *neuroscientist, educator*
MacWilliam, Barb *science educator*
Madison, Rachel Christine *science educator*
Mancini, Lorraine *science educator*
Marino, Deirdre J. *science educator*
Mark, Hon Fong Louie *cytogeneticist*
Maroni, Donna Farolino *biologist, researcher*
Mars, Cheri Higdon *science educator*
Martin, Marcia D. *science educator*
Massagli, Jennifer Ann *science educator*
Mayhugh, Tiffany *science educator*
McAuliffe, Maureen *science educator*
McCarthy, Aimee Lamar *science educator*
McDowell, Elizabeth Mary *retired pathology educator*
McQuarrie, Megan *science educator*
Melton, Amanda Louise *science educator*
Messerly, Jennifer *science educator*
Miekka, Jeanette Ann *retired science educator*
Milligan, Margaret Erin *science educator*
Minahan, Janice Terry *science educator*
Mitchell, Margaret Yvonne *forester*
Monzingo, Agnes Yvonne *veterinary technician*
Moon, Karen Robin *science educator*
Neumark, Gertrude Fanny *materials science educator*
Nichols, Christine Carolyn *science educator*
Nighswonger, Linda *science educator*
Nix, Rachel Ann Hackmann *science educator*
Norflus, Fran *biology professor*
O'Brien, Kathleen Anne *science educator*
Ochsner, Carol M. *science educator*
Owens, Mary Bentley *science educator, mathematics educator*
Parrott, Annette Michele *science educator, consultant*
Parsons, Marilee Benore *science educator*
Peaslee, Margaret Mae Hermanek *zoology educator*
Peeples, Mary Anne Baumann *science educator*
Peitsmeyer, Natalie Mary *science educator*
Pennington, Valerie J. *biology professor, dancer*
Penwell, Rebecca Ann *science educator*
Perez-Orozco, Jacqueline *science educator*
Phillips, Cynthia Ann *science educator*
Phillips, Peggy V. *former biotechnology company executive*
Pittman, Rachel Doby *science educator*
Pitts, Amy Kathleen *science educator*
Player, Audrey Nell *research scientist*
Pollack, Sylvia Byrne *retired science educator, researcher, counselor*
Porto, Vicki A. *science educator*
Prazak, Bessmarie Lillian *science educator*
Rain, Kathleen Marie *science educator*
Ray, Raegan L. *science educator*
Readie, Colleen Beth *microbiologist*
Reaves, Lisa Golden *science educator*
Reynolds, Charlotte N. *science educator*
Riccio, Angela *science educator*
Ridley, Julie A. *biologist, educator*
Rivera, Yelissa Marie *science educator, coach*
Rogers, Ruth Frances *retired microbiologist*
Ryan, Rita Marie *science educator*
Samuels, Linda S. *science administrator, consultant*
Schaal, Barbara Anna *evolutionary biologist, educator*
Schmeer, Arline Catherine *research scientist*
Schweitzer-Morris, Nancy N. *retired science educator, writer*
Scruggs, Teresa Eileen *science educator*
Servedio, Maria R. *science educator*
Setser, Carole Sue *food scientist, educator*
Shannon, Marilyn McCusker *biologist, educator*
Shaw, Helen Lester Anderson *nutrition educator, researcher, retired dean*
Sheild, Carolyn Jean *science educator*
Shepard, Katherine *science educator, consultant*
Sherman, Sherry Wiggins *science educator*
Sklenarik, Denise Lauren *science educator*
Slatter, Michele Denise *science educator*
Slayman, Carolyn Walch *geneticist, educator*
Smith, Catherine Marie *science educator*
Smith, Lynda Mitchell *science educator*
Stark, Nellie May *forester, ecologist, educator*
Stein, Dawn Marie *science educator*
Stiles, Carol M. *plant pathologist, educator*
Sturtevant, Kristen Amy *science educator*
Sullivan, Margaret M. *biologist, educator*
Thomas, Teresa Ann *microbiologist, educator*
Toole, Christine R. *science educator*
Topolski, Catherine *science educator*
Trammel, Denise *science educator*
Trane, Leslie *science educator*
Travaille, Madelaine *science educator*
Turner-Reid, Marsha Marie *science educator*
Tytler, Linda Jean *science administrator, retired state legislator*
Ulgen, Ayse *statistical geneticist, educator*
Vann, Esther Martinez *science educator*
Villa-Komaroff, Lydia *molecular biologist, educator, academic administrator*
Von Gizycki, Alkistis Romanoff *research scientist, writer*
Walsh, Alana Joy *science educator*
Westrich, Kathleen Maureen *science educator*
Willson, Mary Frances *ecology researcher, educator*
Worrel, Connie Rae *science educator*
Wright, Georgette L. *science educator*
Young, Judith Anne *animal conservationist*
Zeigler, Bekki LarissA *biology professor*
Zuk, Judith *retired botanist, director*

SCIENCE: MATHEMATICS AND COMPUTER SCIENCE *See also* INFORMATION TECHNOLOGY

UNITED STATES

ALABAMA

Athens
Gasbarro, Dottie Fuller *mathematics professor*

Attalla
Saffels, Anna Wayne Brothers *retired mathematician, educator*

Huntsville
Pruitt, Alice Fay *mathematician, engineer*

ARIZONA

Phoenix
Doto, Irene Louise *statistician*

Sierra Vista
Smith, Barbara Jane *computer scientist, educator*

ARKANSAS

Fort Smith
Smith-Leins, Terri L. *mathematics instructor*

Helena
Stroope, Kay *mathematician, educator*

CALIFORNIA

Berkeley
Agogino, Alice Merner *computer scientist, mechanical engineer, educator*
Bajcsy, Ruzena Kucerova *computer science educator*
Graham, Susan Lois *computer scientist, consultant*

Davis
Thompson, Abigail *mathematics professor*

Fullerton
Ikeda, Nancy *mathematician, educator*

Grass Valley
Molitor, Kelley Marie *mathematics professor*

Huntington Beach
Sward, Andrea Jeanne *information and computer scientist, musician*

Irvine
Jitomirskaya, Svetlana *mathematics professor*

La Jolla
Terras, Audrey Anne *mathematics professor*

Laguna Hills
Green, Millie Ann *mathematician, educator*

Menifee
Levasseur, Janice Thoni *mathematician, educator*

Moffett Field
Munoz, Christine *systems analyst*

Newport Beach
Duvall, Florence Marie *software engineer*

Rancho Santa Margarita
Berta, Melissa Rose *mathematics professor*

Redondo Beach
Woike, Lynne Ann *computer scientist*

San Bernardino
Ellis, Yvonne *mathematics professor*

San Francisco
Asher, Shoshana Chana *mathematics professor*
Goldberg, Adele J. *computer scientist*

San Jose
Ho, Yinhsin *retired mathematician, artist*
Selinger, Patricia Griffiths *computer science professional*

San Luis Obispo
McQuaid, Patricia A. *information systems educator*

San Rafael
Barker, Celeste Arlette *computer scientist*

Stanford
Koller, Daphne *computer scientist*
Whittemore, Alice *biostatistician*

Stockton
Bickford, Melissa A. *computer scientist*

Walnut
Sholars, Joan Dianne *mathematics professor*

COLORADO

Boulder
Farsi, Carla Emilia *mathematics professor*

Carbondale
Williams, Natasha Bondareva *information scientist, educator*

Fort Collins
Menzel, Barbara Edwina *systems analyst*

CONNECTICUT

Bridgeport
Anderson, Sheila K. *mathematics professor*

Danbury
Wright, Marie Anne *management information systems educator*

Fairfield
Shaffer, Dorothy Browne *retired mathematician, educator*

Farmington
Nash, Judith Kluck *mathematics professor*

New Haven
Feigenbaum, Joan *computer scientist, mathematician*

Stratford
Monda, Marilyn *statistician, quality assurance professional*

DELAWARE

Dover
Lott, Dawn Alisha *mathematics professor*

DISTRICT OF COLUMBIA

Washington
Bailey, Judy Long *outreach and education specialist, social worker*
Baran, Christine *systems analyst*
Gray, Mary Wheat *statistician, lawyer*
Kahlow, Barbara Fenvessy *statistician*
Nesbitt, Veronica A. *program support analyst*
Raphael, Louise Arakelian *mathematician, educator*
Young, Heather A. *statistician, researcher*

FLORIDA

Boca Raton
Kewley, Sharon Lynn *systems analyst, consultant*

Fort Lauderdale
Littman, Marlyn Kemper *information scientist, educator*

Fort Myers
Faith, Ruth L. *retired mathematician*

Fort Pierce
Lindsay, Rita Carol *mathematics professor*

Jacksonville
Collins, Carlita Raulerson *mathematician, educator*

Miami
Dimitriou, Dolores Ennis *computer consultant*
Lawton, Thelma Cuttino *mathematics professor, consultant*

Naples
Bland, Iris C. *retired mathematics professor*

Niceville
Stallworth-Allen, Elizabeth Ann *business and computer science educator*

Saint Augustine
Jurgens, Julie Graham *mathematics professor*

Titusville
Wilkinson, MaryE *mathematics educator*

GEORGIA

Atlanta
Falcones, Etta Z. *mathematician, math and computer science education and administration*
Wilding, Diane *computer scientist, consultant*

Augusta
Craig, Cynthia Mae *mathematics professor*

Carrollton
Sifton, Karen Marie *mathematics professor*

East Point
Jackson, Julie Ann *mathematics professor*

Marietta
Rutherfoord, Rebecca Hudson *computer scientist, educator*

Milledgeville
Sargent, Jane Diane Robertson *mathematician, educator*

Statesboro
Lanier, Susie Mae *mathematics professor*
Mitra, Aditi *mathematician, educator*

Valdosta
Moch, Peggy L. *mathematics professor*

Woodstock
Dowdy, Elizabeth Ann *mathematician, educator*

HAWAII

Hilo
Gersting, Judith Lee *computer scientist, educator, researcher*

ILLINOIS

Chicago
Kirkpatrick, Anne Saunders *systems analyst*

Dekalb
Sons, Linda Ruth *mathematician, educator*

Glen Ellyn
Cook, Joann Catherine *computer professor*
Nunamaker, Susan Sun *mathematics professor*

La Grange Park
Butler, Margaret Kampschaefer *retired computer scientist*

Lisle
Bazik, Edna Frances *mathematician, educator*

Mc Gaw Park
Risen-White, Angela Lorri *systems analyst*

River Forest
Helwig, Janet *computer science educator*
Weedermann, Marion *mathematics professor*

Urbana
Liebman, Judith Rae Stenzel *retired operations research specialist*

INDIANA

Evansville
Mohr, Doris Jean *mathematics professor*

Indianapolis
Cliff, Johnnie Marie *mathematics and chemistry professor*

Marion
Personette, Louise Metzger (Sister Mary Roger Metzger) *mathematics professor*

IOWA

Denison
Withhart, Carol Joyce *mathematician, educator*

Des Moines
Wilson, Sal *systems analyst*

Pella
Weber, Wendy A. *mathematics professor*

KANSAS

El Dorado
Choate, Melody Lynn *mathematics professor*

Emporia
Yanik, Elizabeth Greenwell *mathematics professor*

Kansas City
Davis, Kathy E. *information analyst*

Pittsburg
Woodburn, Cynthia J. *mathematics professor*

Wichita
Palmer, Ada Margaret *systems analyst, consultant*

KENTUCKY

Campbellsville
Miller, Janet Lutz *mathematics professor, department chairman*

Cynthiana
Florence, Joyce Fritz *mathematics professor*

Hazard
Cory, Cynthia Strong *mathematics professor*

LOUISIANA

Bossier City
Phillips, Staci Davis *mathematics professor, director*

Eunice
Hernandez, Gloria *mathematician, educator*

Lafayette
Cain, Judith Sharp *mathematics professor, consultant*

Lake Charles
Andrus, Tiffany Shantel *mathematics professor*

Ruston
Carpenter, Jenna Price *mathematics professor, academic administrator*

MARYLAND

Baltimore
Koch, Gretchen Ann *mathematics and computer science professor*
Lidtke, Doris Keefe *retired computer science educator*

Bethesda
Lipkin, Bernice Sacks *computer scientist, educator*
Tilley, Carolyn Bittner *information scientist*

Columbia
Gregorie, Corazon Arzalem *operations research specialist*

Gaithersburg
Rosenblatt, Joan Raup *mathematical statistician*

Perryville
Dunne, Judith Doyle *information scientist, educator*

Potomac
Medin, Julia Adele *mathematics professor, researcher*
Peters, Carol Beattie Taylor (Mrs. Frank Albert Peters) *mathematician*

Rockville
Massie, Tammy Jeanne Parliment *statistician*

Savage
Hicks, Karen T. *mathematician*

Silver Spring
Sammet, Jean E. *computer scientist*

MASSACHUSETTS

Boston
Kopell, Nancy *mathematician, education educator*
Schribman, Shelley Iris *database engineer, consultant*

Cambridge
Goldwasser, Shafrira *computer scientist*
Lipson, Pamela *information scientist*
Lynch, Nancy Ann *computer scientist, educator*
Merseth, Katherine K. *mathematician, education educator*
Roberts, Nancy *computer scientist, educator*

Lexington
Schafer, Alice Turner *retired mathematics professor*

Medford
Perrone, Lisa *mathematics professor*
Ruskai, Mary Beth *mathematics professor*

Springfield
Murphy, Eileen Bridget *retired mathematics professor*

MICHIGAN

Ann Arbor
Conway, Lynn *computer scientist, electrical engineer, educator*
Gilbert, Anna *mathematics professor*
Perez, Laura R. *mathematics professor*
Shure, Patricia D. *mathematician, education educator*
Smith, Karen E. *mathematician, educator*

Kalamazoo
Hollar, Susan Steffens *mathematics professor*

Manistique
Jeffcott, Janet Bruhn *statistician, consultant*

Roscommon
Balbach, Lisa Jean *information scientist, educator*

Southfield
Miller, Nancy Ellen *computer scientist, consultant*

Ypsilanti
Warner, Jo F. *mathematics instructor*

MINNESOTA

Circle Pines
Roden, Mary Jane *mathematician, educator*

Minneapolis
Adlis, Susan Annette *biostatistician*
Pour-El, Marian Boykan *mathematician, educator*

Shakopee
Eliason, Arlene F. *mathematician, educator*

MISSISSIPPI

Clinton
Gann, Melinda Denise *mathematics professor*

Meridian
Russell, Joy R. *computer scientist, educator*

MISSOURI

Columbia
Flournoy, Nancy *statistician, educator*

Earth City
Kiry-Ryan, Rita Irene *computer scientist, educator*

Nevada
Callahan, Susan Lane *mathematics professor*

Saint Louis
Deutsch, Jennifer Loren *mathematics professor*

Union
Boehmer, Ann *mathematics professor*

University City
Collins, Nancy Lee *mathematician, educator*

Warrensburg
McKee, Rhonda Louise *mathematics professor*
McLaughlin, Phoebe *mathematics professor*

Winona
Marshall, Lucille Ruth *retired mathematics professor*

MONTANA

Butte
Van Dyne, Michele Miley *information engineer*

NEBRASKA

Lincoln
Wiegand, Sylvia Margaret *mathematician, educator*

NEVADA

Las Vegas
Blattner, Meera McCuaig *computer scientist, educator*

NEW HAMPSHIRE

Nashua
Lerch, Carol M. *mathematics professor*

Plymouth
Vinogradova, Natalya *mathematician, educator*

NEW JERSEY

Highlands
Dann, Emily *mathematics educator*

Jersey City
Metallo, Frances Rosebell *mathematics professor*
Poiani, Eileen Louise *mathematician, academic administrator*

Lincroft
Ventola, Frances Ann *mathematics professor*

New Brunswick
Scanlon, Jane Cronin *mathematics professor*

Ocean City
Culbertson, Jane Young *statistician*

Princeton
Chang, Sun-Yung Alice *mathematics professor*

Somerset
Becker, Phyllis *systems analyst*

NEW MEXICO

Farmington
Doig, Beverly Irene *retired systems specialist*

Las Cruces
Selden, Annie *mathematics professor*

Roswell
Martinez, Cheryl A. *mathematics professor*

Santa Fe
Tokheim, Sara Ann *writer, information technology professional*
White, Denise *mathematics professor, department chairman*

NEW YORK

Baldwinsville
Lotano, Denise Arlene *mathematician, educator*

Batavia
Rigerman, Ruth Underhill *mathematics professor*

Brewster
Dominicus, Adele Marilyn *mathematician, educator*

Bronx
Miller, Elizabeth J. *mathematician, educator*
Prabhu, Vrunda P. *mathematics professor*
Tyler, Helene Renée *mathematics professor*

Brooklyn
Grinstein Richman, Louise Sonia *mathematics professor*
Siegel, Stephanie S. *mathematics professor*

Buffalo
Seitz, Mary Lee *mathematics professor*

Depew
Mercuri, Theresa B. *mathematician, educator*

Dix Hills
Blumstein, Reneé J. *educational research and evaluation consultant*

Ithaca
Hockett, Shirley O. *mathematics professor, writer*

Jamaica
DeBello, Joan Elizabeth *mathematics professor*

New York
Chichilnisky, Graciela *mathematician, educator, economist, writer*
Friedman, Linda Weiser *operations researcher, educator*
Kirnos, Dina *technology support professional*
Morawetz, Cathleen Synge *mathematician*
Taylor, Jean Ellen *mathematics professor, researcher*
Wright, Margaret Hagen *computer scientist, administrator*

Orangeburg
Siegel, Carole Ethel *mathematician*

Orchard Park
Landrigan, Cynthia Scheer *mathematician, educator*

Rochester
Kuby, Patricia J. *mathematics professor*

Selden
Cook, Lisa Marie *mathematics professor, mathematics learning center coordinator*

Syracuse
Doucette, Michelle Anne *mathematics professor*
Lutz, Heather *information scientist, researcher*

Tarrytown
Maun, Mary Ellen *computer consultant*

Troy
Kutryb, Susan L. *mathematician, educator*
Schoonmaker, Doris *mathematics professor*

NORTH CAROLINA

Durham
Hankins, Sherlene LaSalle *mathematician, educator*

Greenville
Khuri, Soumaya Makdissi *mathematics professor*

Hickory
Touchette, Collette W. *mathematics professor*

NORTH DAKOTA

Mayville
Champion, Kathleen Ann *mathematics professor*

Trenton
Folkestad, Ruth L. *mathematics professor*

OHIO

Ashland
Van Dresar, Vickie Janette *mathematician, educator*

Gambier
Holdener, Judy Ann *mathematics professor, researcher*

Newark
Sharrock (Wrentmore), Anita Kay *information technology specialist*

OKLAHOMA

Edmond
Loman, Mary LaVerne *retired mathematics professor*

Norman
Bethel, Joann D. *computer programmer, analyst*

Tulsa
O'Sullivan, Cindy Marie *mathematics professor*

OREGON

Eugene
Lary, Lynn M. *computer scientist, educator*

PENNSYLVANIA

Bethlehem
King, Jane Connell *mathematics professor*
Schattschneider, Doris Jean *retired mathematics professor*

Blue Bell
Halas, Cynthia Ann *business information specialist*

Bryn Mawr
Hughes, Rhonda J. *mathematics professor*

Philadelphia
Wallowicz, Marcella Louise *mathematics professor*

Pittsburgh
Blum, Lenore *mathematician, computer scientist, educator*
Carbo, Toni (Toni Carbo Bearman) *information scientist, educator*
Knox, Lori Brickner *mathematician, educator*
Shaw, Mary M. *computer scientist, educator*

Schnecksville
Labbiento, Julianne Marie *mathematics professor*

SOUTH CAROLINA

Clemson
Hare, Eleanor O'Meara *computer scientist, educator*

SOUTH DAKOTA

Rapid City
Geary, Laura Alma *mathematics professor*

TENNESSEE

Covington
Smith, Melody Kennon *mathematics professor*

Hermitage
Castner, Catherine S. *information technology administrator*

Kingsport
Fanslow, Mary Frances *information scientist*

Knoxville
Lenhart, Suzanne *mathematician, education educator*

Nashville
Tallon, Becky Jo *computer scientist, educator*

TEXAS

Austin
Hunter, Dorothy Evelyn *mathematician, educator*
Pickett, Sandra *information scientist*

Brenham
Anglin, Karen Locher *mathematics professor*

Conroe
Sharman, Diane Lee *mathematics professor*

Cypress
Gamber, Heather Anne *mathematics professor, statistician, consultant*

Denton
Hays, Edith H. *mathematics professor*
Thompson, Frances McBroom *mathematics professor, writer*

El Paso
Smith, Sarah Seelig *mathematics professor*

Fort Sam Houston
Wojcik, Barbara Elzbieta *statistician, researcher*

Houston
Fenn, Sandra Ann *programmer, analyst*
Kavraki, Lydia *computer scientist, educator*
Leveille, Nancy Anne *mathematics professor*
Morrison, Stacey *information scientist*

Irving
Cherri, Mona Y. *computer scientist, educator, computer scientist, consultant*

Prairie View
Barber-Freeman, Pamela Telia *mathematician, educator, researcher*

San Antonio
Roy, Anuradha *statistician, educator, researcher*

Stephenville
Bane, Alma Lynn *computer scientist, educator, director*

Waco
Maddox, Amy B. *statistician, educator*

UTAH

Park City
Vance, Dianne Sanchez *mathematician, educator*

Salt Lake City
Horn, Susan Dadakis *statistician, educator*

VIRGINIA

Alexandria
Greer, Frances Ellen DuBois, Jr., (Nancy Greer Jr., Nancy Greer Hamilton) *retired statistician, volunteer*

Blacksburg
Hovakimyan, Naira *mathematician, educator*

Charlottesville
Parshall, Karen Virginia Hunger *mathematician*

Clifton
Hoffman, Karla Leigh *mathematician, educator*

Fairfax
Mulvaney, Mary Frederica *systems analyst*

Fredericksburg
Chiang, Yuan Jen *mathematics professor*

Gainesville
Bendig, Judith Joan *information systems specialist, computer company executive*

Heathsville
Stubbs, Susan Conklin *retired statistician*

Herndon
Hollis, Katherine Mary *information scientist, consultant*

Norfolk
Marshall, Deborah Kay *instructional technology resource specialist*

Radford
Carter, Edith Houston *statistician, educator*

Roanoke
Wallace, Linda Kay *mathematics professor*

Sweet Briar
Kirkwood, Bessie Hershberger *mathematics professor*

Vienna
Gardenier, Turkan Kumbaraci *statistician, researcher*

WASHINGTON

Carlsborg
Scairpon, Sharon Cecilia *retired information scientist*

Redmond
Oliver, Nuria *computer scientist*

WISCONSIN

Whitewater
Baica, Malvina Florica *mathematician, educator, researcher*

MILITARY ADDRESSES OF THE UNITED STATES

EUROPE

APO
Simpson, Sandra Kay *operations research specialist*

ADDRESS UNPUBLISHED

Adiletta, Debra Jean Olson *mathematics professor*
Albrecht, Rebekah S. *mathematician, educator*
Allen, Frances Elizabeth *computer scientist*
Bailar, Barbara Ann *retired statistician*
Barrett, Lida Kittrell *mathematics professor*
Barto, Rebecca Lynn *systems analyst*
Bender, Virginia Best *computer scientist, educator*
Benoit, Leilani *computer scientist, educator*
Brasoveanu Tarpy, Alexandra *mathematics professor*
Caroleo, Linn E. *mathematician, writer*
Corbett, Lenora Meade *mathematician, community college educator*
Cotmans, Sharon Jenkins *computer scientist, educator*
De Both, Tanya *statistician*
Downey, Deborah Ann *systems specialist*
Esselstein, Rachel *mathematician, educator*
Fabry, Marilyn Sue *mathematician, educator*
Faulkner, Martye Leanne *mathematician, educator*
Gifford, Marjorie Fitting *mathematician, educator, consultant*
Goodwin, Danielle Marie *mathematician*
Grasserbauer, Doris *computer scientist, mathematician, educator*
Gross, Kathy Aldrich *mathematics professor*
Ham, Jill Marie *mathematician, educator*
Harnedy, Joan Catherine Holland *retired systems analyst*
Head, Rebecca Ann *mathematics professor*
Henderson, Dona Lee *mathematics educator*
Hollis, Deborah D. *systems analyst, application developer*
Hudachek-Buswell, Mary R. *mathematics professor*
Hunte, Beryl Eleanor *mathematics professor*
Johnson, Sheila Lynn *mathematician, educator*
Jones, Anita Katherine *computer scientist, educator*
Keala, Betty Ann Lyman *computer scientist*
Keating, Regina G. *computer analyst consultant*
King, Amy Cathryne Patterson *retired mathamatics educator, researcher*
Leppard, Stephanie Jean *systems analyst, artist*
Libert, Cleo Patricia *computer scientist, consultant*
Mansfield, Lois Edna *mathematics professor, researcher*
Merritt, Susan Mary *computer science educator, dean*
Michaelis, Gabrielle deMonceau *mathematics professor*
Natarajan, Uma *mathematician, educator*
Natsuyama, Harriet Hatsune Kagiwada *mathematician, educator*
Neagoy, Monica Maria Martha *mathematician, consultant*
Nelson, Martine Levy *mathematics professor*
Newbury, Kirsten Rae *computer scientist, educator*
Padberg, Harriet Ann *mathematician, educator*
Pendleton, Joan Marie *microprocessor designer*
Pickle, Linda Williams *biostatistician*
Pollock, Karen Anne *computer analyst*
Pritchard, Lucille Kramer *mathematics professor, department chairman*
Reece, Julia Ruth *systems analyst, entrepreneur*
Risser, Hilary S. *mathematician, educator*
Rivera, Georgina Pereira *mathematician, educator*
Robinson, Molly Jahnige *statistician, educator*
Roitman, Judith *mathematician, educator*
Scarbrough-Clay, Linda Kathleen *mathematician, educator*
Sheppard, Lenora Gertrude *mathematics professor*
Shier, Gloria Bulan *mathematics professor*
Smith, Elizabeth Turner *mathematician, educator*
Stern, Nancy Fortgang *mathematics and computer science, educator*
Stuart, Sandra Joyce *computer information scientist*
Stulpin, Cynthia Louise *mathematics professor, real estate appraiser*
Ternovitz, Ruth *mathematics and computer educator*
Tobiassen, Barbara Sue *systems analyst, consultant, volunteer*
Torkzadeh, Rita *health information scientist*
Tyler, Eiko Nakayama *mathematician, educator*
Ullman, Nelly Szabo *statistician, educator*
Urban, Carrie *computer specialist*
Watkins, Ann Esther *mathematics professor*
Wayne, Sharon H. *mathematics professor*
Wechsler, Susan Linda *business operations director, research and development software manager*
Weisbart, Jennifer Rachel *mathematician, educator*
Welna, Cecilia *retired mathematics professor, dean*
Yntema, Mary Katherine *retired mathematics educator*
Young, Lai-Sang *mathematician, educator*
Zalila-Mili, Rym *computer scientist, educator*
Zyroff, Ellen Slotoroff *information scientist, classicist, educator*

SCIENCE: PHYSICAL SCIENCE

UNITED STATES

ALABAMA

Birmingham
Nikles, Jacqueline Amine *chemistry professor*

Gurley
Patrick, Laura Daphene Layman *retired physicist*

Montgomery
Jones, Kathy W. *research scientist, educator*

ALASKA

Anchorage
Keffer, Maria Jean *environmental scientist*

Fairbanks
Cahill, Catherine Frances *environmental scientist, educator*

Saint Paul Island
Lestenkof, Aquilina Debbie *environmental advocate*

ARIZONA

Flagstaff
Barlow, Nadine Gail *planetary geoscientist*
Shoemaker, Carolyn Spellman *planetary astronomer*

Tempe
Narayanan, Radha *chemist, researcher*
Wyckoff, Susan *astronomy researcher*

Tucson
Neugebauer, Marcia *physicist, researcher*
Roemer, Elizabeth *retired astronomer, educator*
Sprague, Ann Louise *aerospace scientist*
Vilas, Faith *aerospace scientist*
Weeks, Wendy L. *chemistry professor, consultant*
Wolff, Sidney Carne *astronomer, science administrator*

CALIFORNIA

Altadena
Mkryan, Sonya *geophysicist, educator, research scientist*

Berkeley
Gaillard, Mary Katharine *physicist, educator*
Hellman, Frances *physics professor*
Hoffman, Darleane Christian *chemistry professor*
Klinman, Judith Pollock *biochemist, educator*
Shapiro, Marjorie D. *physics professor*

Chico
Mejia, Barbara Oviedo *retired chemistry professor*

China Lake
Bennett, Jean Louise McPherson *physicist, research scientist*

El Granada
Heere, Karen R. *astrophysicist*

Emeryville
Bibel, Debra Jan *public health scientist, editor*

Fullerton
Fearn, Heidi *physicist, researcher*

Irvine
Finlayson-Pitts, Barbara Jean *chemistry professor*

La Jolla
Burbidge, E. Margaret *astronomer, educator*
Ride, Sally Kristen *physics professor, research scientist, retired astronaut*
Taylor, Susan Serota *biochemist, researcher*

Los Angeles
Byers, Nina *physics professor*
Horn, Cindy Harrell *environmental advocate*
Kivelson, Margaret Galland *physicist*
Kobe, Lan *medical physicist*
Neufeld, Elizabeth Fondal *biochemist, educator*

Menlo Park
Drell, Persis *physicist*

Monterey
Blair, Cynthia *meteorologist, oceanographer, researcher*

Moss Landing
McNutt, Marcia Kemper *geophysicist*

Pasadena
Freedman, Wendy Laurel *astronomer, educator*
Lopes, Rosaly Mutel Crocce *astronomer, planetary geologist*
Sargent, Anneila Isabel *astrophysicist*
Spilker, Linda Joyce *aerospace scientist*
Syvertson, Marguerite *geologist*

Pomona
Starkey, Laurie Shaffer *chemistry professor*

Rancho Santa Margarita
Hoppe, Dorothe Anna *chemistry professor*

Redlands
Van Engelen, Debra Lynn *chemistry educator*

Redondo Beach
Martin, Melissa Carol *radiological physicist*

San Francisco
Archer, Cristina Lozej *meteorologist*
Hale, Victoria G. *chemist, pharmaceutical executive*

Santa Cruz
Faber, Sandra Moore *astronomer, educator*
Max, Claire Ellen *physicist*

Santa Monica
Intriligator, Devrie Shapiro *physicist*
Kline, Margaret *chemistry professor*

South San Francisco
Ruggles, Sandra Waugh *biophysicist*

Stanford
Keren, Kinneret *biophysicist*
Matson, Pamela Anne *environmental scientist, science educator*

COLORADO

Boulder
Foland, Sara *geologist, association executive*
Hill, Mary C. *hydrologist*
LeMone, Margaret Anne *atmospheric scientist*

Denver
Gries, Robbie Rice *geologist, gas and petroleum company executive*
Landon, Susan Melinda *petroleum geologist*

Fort Collins
Ladanyi, Branka Maria *chemist, educator*

CONNECTICUT

Farmington
Osborn, Mary Jane Merten *biochemist, educator*

New Haven
Curran, Lisa M. *environmental scientist, educator*
Ramirez, Ainissa *materials scientist*
Schepartz, Alanna *biochemist, educator*
Skinner, Helen Catherine Wild *biomineralogist*
Steitz, Joan Argetsinger *biochemistry professor*

West Haven
Onton, Ann Louise Reuther *chemist*

Winsted
Jassen, Alison P. *chemistry professor, biology professor*

DELAWARE

Wilmington
Marcali, Jean Gregory *retired chemist*
Petrucci-Samija, Maria *chemist*

DISTRICT OF COLUMBIA

Washington
Bakowski, Nancy *chemist*
Donohue, Joyce Morrissey *biochemist, toxicologist, dietician, educator*
Esfandiary, Mary S. *physicial scientist, operations consultant*
Karle, Isabella L. *chemist*
Kimble, Melinda Louise *environmental administrator*
Oran, Elaine Surick *physicist*
Ram, Bonnie *environmental scientist, consultant*
Singer, Maxine Frank *retired biochemist, science association director*
Uria, Adriana C. Ocampo *geologist*

FLORIDA

Brooksville
McBride, Tamera Shawn Dew *geologist*

Coral Gables
Van Vliet, Carolyn Marina *physicist, researcher*

Daytona Beach
David, Valentina S. *physics professor*

Fort Myers
Lewton, Betsy *chemistry professor*

Lithia
Kulkarni, Kavita-Vibha Arun *chemist*

Miami
Fine, Rana Arnold *chemical and physical oceanographer*
Kowalska, Maria Teresa *research scientist, educator*

Tallahassee
Clayson, Carol Anne *meteorologist, educator*
Gilmer, Penny Jane *biochemist, educator*
Hanley, Deborah Elizabeth *meteorologist, wildland firefighter*
Moulton, Grace Charbonnet *retired physicist*

GEORGIA

Athens
Black, Marsha C. *environmental scientist*
Yager, Patricia Lynn *oceanographer, educator*

Atlanta
Anderson, Gloria Long *chemistry professor*
Goetz, Betty Barrett *physicist*
Hicks, Heraline Elaine *environmental health scientist, educator*
Zeng, Fanxing *chemist*

Milledgeville
Metzker, Julia *chemistry professor*

Morrow
Todebush, Patricia Metthe *chemistry professor*

HAWAII

Honolulu
Kong, Laura S. L. *geophysicist*

IDAHO

Moscow
Shreeve, Jean'ne Marie *chemist, educator*

ILLINOIS

Argonne
Jonkouski, Jill Ellen *materials scientist, ceramics engineer, educator*

Bolingbrook
Sabau, Carmen Sybile *retired chemist*

Chicago
Gerber, Cecilia Elena *physics professor, researcher*
Harvey, Allison Charmaine *chemist*
Herzenberg, Caroline Stuart Littlejohn *physicist*

Evanston
Cao, Hui *physics and astronomy professor*
Godwin, Hilary A. *chemistry professor, research scientist*
Odom, Teri Wang *chemist*

Jacksonville
Beal, Deborah L. *environmental scientist, educator*

Lombard
McCoy, Jeanie Shearer *analytical chemist, consultant*

Naperville
Sherren, Anne Terry *chemistry professor*

North Chicago
Loga, Sanda *physicist, researcher*

Peoria
Hojilla-Evangelista, Milagros Parker *research chemist, research scientist*

Rockford
Walhout, Justine Simon *chemistry professor*

Urbana
Makri, Nancy *chemistry professor*

INDIANA

Bloomington
Easton, Susan Dawn *biochemist, educator*

Elkhart
Free, Helen Murray *chemist, consultant*

Greenfield
Kallman, Mary Jeanne *research scientist*

Indianapolis
Ritchie, Ingrid Maria *environmental scientist, educator*
Wilson, Anne Marie *chemistry professor*

Notre Dame
Feigl, Dorothy Marie *chemistry professor, academic administrator*
Maurice, Patricia Ann *geochemist, educator*

West Lafayette
Arns, Laura *research scientist*

IOWA

Ames
Hong, Mei *chemistry professor*

KANSAS

Lawrence
Dreschhoff, Gisela Auguste Marie *physicist, researcher*

Topeka
Barton, Janice Sweeny *chemistry professor*

KENTUCKY

Lexington
Brock, Carolyn Pratt *chemist, educator*
Hojahmat, Marhaba *research scientist*
Penn, Lynn Sharon *materials scientist, educator*

Louisville
Dietrich, Ruth Robinson *chemist, researcher, genealogist*

LOUISIANA

Baton Rouge
Garno, Jayne C. *chemistry professor*

Walker
Michel, Jacqueline *geochemist*

MARYLAND

Baltimore
Jones, Hendree Evelyn *research scientist, psychologist*

Bel Air
Cash, LaVerne (Cynthia Cash) *physicist*

Beltsville
Johnson, Phyllis Elaine *chemist, researcher*

Bethesda
Vaughan, Martha *biochemist, educator*
Wickner, Sue Hengren *biochemist*
Zoon, Kathryn Christine *biochemist*

College Park
Fenselau, Catherine Clarke *chemistry professor*
Lubkin, Gloria Becker *physicist*

Derwood
Stadtman, Thressa Campbell *biochemist*

Frederick
Henderson, Madeline Mary (Berry Henderson) *chemist, researcher, consultant*
Smith, Sharron Williams *chemistry professor*

Gaithersburg
Jacox, Marilyn Esther *chemist*
Sengers, Johanna M. H. Levelt *physicist*

Germantown
Foulke, Judith Diane *health physicist*

Greenbelt
Maynard, Nancy Gray *biological oceanographer*
Simpson, Joanne Malkus *meteorologist*

Hagerstown
Corbett, Helen A. *chemist, chemical engineer*

Laytonsville
Holland, Christie Anna *biochemist, virologist*

Mount Airy
Johnston, Josephine Rose *chemist*

MASSACHUSETTS

Bourne
Fantozzi, Peggy Ryone *geologist, environmental planner*

Cambridge
Ceyer, Sylvia T. *chemistry professor, department chairman*
Chisholm, Sallie Watson *biological oceanography educator, researcher*
Dresselhaus, Mildred Spiewak *physics professor, engineering educator*
Friend, Cynthia M. *chemist, educator*
Geller, Margaret Joan *astrophysicist, educator*
Marvin, Ursula Bailey *retired geologist*
Randall, Lisa *physics professor*
Zuber, Maria T. *geophysicist, educator*

Chestnut Hill
Kelley, Shana O. *biochemist*

Framingham
Dawicki, Doloretta Diane *analytical chemist, research biochemist, educator*

Roxbury
Simons, Elizabeth R(eiman) *biochemist, educator*

South Hadley
Ewing Browne, Sheila *chemistry professor, physical organic chemist*

Waltham
Lees, Marjorie Berman *biochemist, neuroscientist*

Weston
Lin, Alice Lee Lan *physicist, researcher, educator*

MICHIGAN

Ann Arbor
Aller, Margo Friedel *astronomer*
Ludwig, Martha *biochemist, educator*

Carrollton
Talik (Logan), Rebecca Lyn *chemistry professor*

Monroe
Bean, Lori J. *chemistry professor*

Okemos
Burnett, Jean B. (Mrs. James R. Burnett) *biochemist, educator*

MINNESOTA

Moorhead
Strong, Judith Ann *chemist, educator*

MISSOURI

Columbia
Plummer, Patricia Lynne Moore *chemist, educator*
Randall, Linda Lea *biochemist, educator*

Kansas City
Kloth, Carolyn *meteorologist*

Rolla
Sotiriou-Leventis, Chariklia *chemist, educator, researcher*

MONTANA

Billings
Paul, Bessie Margrette *retired weather forecaster*

NEBRASKA

Crete
Holmes, Andrea *chemistry professor, researcher*

Omaha
Myers, Sara A. *research scientist*

NEVADA

Genoa
Dix, Loraine H. *chemist*

NEW HAMPSHIRE

Litchfield
Miller, Dawn Marie *retired meteorologist*

NEW JERSEY

Annandale
Baugh, Lisa Saunders (Lisa Saunders Boffa) *chemist, researcher*

Edgewater
Zhou, Yan *chemist*

Mountainside
Vice, Susan F. *medicinal chemist*

New Providence
Sivco, Deborah Lee *materials scientist, researcher*

Oaklyn
Miranda, Minda *chemist, pharmacy technologist*

Piscataway
Champe, Pamela Chambers *biochemistry professor, writer*

Princeton
Bahcall, Neta Assaf *astrophysicist*
Carter, Emily Ann *physical chemist, researcher, educator*
Finn, Frances Mary *biochemist, researcher*
Ward, Bess B. *oceanographer, educator*

Rahway
Chen, Liya *chemist*
Garcia, Maria Luisa *biochemist, researcher*

Skillman
Diaz, Teresita Perez *chemist*

NEW MEXICO

Los Alamos
Korber, Bette Tina Marie *chemist*
Lu, Ningping *environmental chemist*

NEW YORK

Amityville
Citrano-Cummiskey, Debra Moira *chemist, network technician*

Bronx
Hartil, Kirsten *research scientist*
Yalow, Rosalyn Sussman *biophysicist*

Brooklyn
Mook, Sarah *retired chemist*
Shcherbakova, Estella *chemist, mathematician, educator*

Buffalo
Andersen, Martha S. *biophysicist, researcher*

Hawthorne
Batstone, Joanna Louise *physicist*

Manhasset
Spetsieris, Phoebe George *physicist, application developer, researcher*

Manlius
O'Reilly, Mary *environmental scientist, educator*

New York
Breslow, Esther May Greenberg *biochemistry professor, researcher*
Chapman, Sally *chemistry professor*
Hoffman, Linda M. *chemist, educator*
Levin, Janna J. *physicist, educator*
Russell, Charlotte Sananes *biochemistry professor, researcher*
St. Germain, Jean Mary *medical physicist*
Sarachik, Myriam Paula Morgenstein *physics professor, condensed matter physicist*
Sidran, Miriam *retired physicist*

Palisades
Goddard, Lisa *meteorologist*

Rochester
Bren, Kara L. *chemistry professor*
Conwell, Esther Marly *physicist, researcher*
Houde-Walter, Susan *optics scientist, educator*

Syracuse
Senecah, Susan Louise *environmental scientist, educator, state government policy analyst*

Troy
Krause, Sonja *chemistry professor*

Upton
Fowler, Joanna S. *chemist*
Setlow, Jane Kellock *biophysicist*

White Plains
Flanigen, Edith Marie *materials scientist, consultant*

NORTH CAROLINA

Chapel Hill
Dolan, Louise Ann *physicist*

Durham
Moss, Marcia Lynn *retired biochemist*
Watkins, Melynda *chemist, researcher*

Wilmington
Kinney, Robin Smith *chemist, educator*

Wingate
Sunderland, Deborah P. *chemist, educator*

OHIO

Akron
Piirma, Irja *chemist, educator*
Ramsey, Sally Judith Weine *chemist, research and development company executive*

Batavia
Lewis, Joan Carol *chemist, educator*

Bolwing Green
Snavely, Deanne Lynn *chemistry professor*

Cincinnati
Briskin, Madeleine *oceanographer, paleontologist*
Meal, Larie *chemistry professor, researcher, consultant*

Delaware
Fryer, Karen Helene *geologist, educator*

Kent
Tuan, Debbie Fu-Tai *chemist, educator*

Liberty Township
Conditt, Margaret Karen *research scientist*

Middletown
Marine, Susan Sonchik *analytical chemist, educator*

Wickliffe
Krause, Marjorie N. *biochemist*

Youngstown
Clymer, Janis E. *physics professor*

OKLAHOMA

Bartlesville
Yao, Jianhua *chemist, researcher*

Oklahoma City
Zhu, Hua *biochemist, researcher*

OREGON

Corvallis
Shoemaker, Clara Brink *retired chemistry professor, researcher*

Eugene
Richmond, Geraldine Lee *chemist, educator*

PENNSYLVANIA

Abington
Schuster, Ingeborg Ida *chemistry professor*

Bryn Mawr
Riihimaki, Catherine Anne *geologist*

Loretto
Clark, Rose Ann *chemist, educator*

Media
Whittington, Cathy Dee *chemist*

Philadelphia
Ajzenberg-Selove, Fay *physicist, researcher*
Cohn, Mildred *retired biochemist, retired educator*
Farren, Ann Louise *chemist, information scientist, educator*
Glusker, Jenny Pickworth *chemist*
Lester, Marsha I. *chemistry professor*
Yang, Shu *materials scientist*

South Park
Lotze, Barbara *retired physicist*

University Park
Garrison, Barbara Jane *chemistry professor*
Ross, A. Catharine *biochemist, educator*

Waynesburg
Maguire, Mildred May *chemistry professor, researcher*

RHODE ISLAND

Westerly
Hindle, Marguerita Cecelia *textile chemist, consultant*

SOUTH CAROLINA

Aiken
Paviet-Hartmann, Patricia *chemist, researcher*

Charleston
Zuraw, Lisa Ann *chemistry professor, department chairman*

Columbia
Samuel, May Linda *environmental scientist*

Due West
Bruce, Chrystal Dawn *chemistry professor*

Greenville
Belanger, Laura Hewlette *environmental scientist, consultant*

TENNESSEE

Clinton
Hutchens, Gail R. *chemist*

Kingsport
Sass, Candace Elaine *chemist, researcher*

Memphis
Cook, Mary Phelps *chemistry professor*
Crane, Laura Jane *retired chemist*
Pourmotabbed, Tayebeh *biochemist*

Murfreesboro
Weller, Martha Riherd *physics and astronomy professor, consultant*

TEXAS

Amarillo
Barker, Sheila *chemist, educator*
Stovich, Joy *chemistry professor*

Arlington
Willoughby, Sarah-Margaret C. *retired chemist, educator, chemical engineer, consultant*

Austin
DeWitt-Morette, Cécile *physicist*
Lindsay, Lynda *research scientist*

Calvert
Alemán, Marthanne Payne *environmental scientist, consultant*

Canyon
Brasher, Treasure Ann Kees *physics professor*

Denton
Wilson, Angela K. *chemistry professor*

Houston
Caldwell, Tracy Ellen *surface chemist, researcher*
Jeevarajan, Judith A. *chemist*
Kasi, Leela Peshkar *pharmaceutical chemist*
Lucid, Shannon W. *biochemist, astronaut*
Reiff, Patricia Hofer *space physicist, educator*

San Antonio
Masters, Bettie Sue Siler *biochemist, educator*

VIRGINIA

Blacksburg
Schmittmann, Beate *physics professor*

Charlottesville
Gaskin, Felicia *biochemist, educator*

Chester
Smetana, Kristine Samaria *chemistry professor, consultant*

Farmville
Parry, Michelle *physics professor*

Poquoson
Berg, Lillian Douglas *chemistry professor*

Reston
Naeser, Nancy Dearien *geologist, researcher*
Pozun Watson, Heather Dawn *environmental scientist, educator*
Revesz, Kinga *chemist, isotope geochemist, researcher*

WASHINGTON

East Wenatchee
Kissler, Cynthia Eloise *geologist, consultant*

Ellensburg
Rosell, Sharon Lynn *physics and chemistry professor*

Seattle
Beckmann, M. Patricia *biochemist*
Deming, Jody Wheeler *oceanography educator*
El-Moslimany, Ann Paxton *paleoecologist, educator, writer*
Olmstead, Marjorie Ann *physics professor*

WEST VIRGINIA

Charleston
Meschke, Debra JoAnn *polymer chemist*

Fairmont
Swiger, Elizabeth Davis *chemist, educator*

Morgantown
Beattie, Diana Scott *biochemistry professor*

WISCONSIN

Kenosha
Kolb, Vera M. *chemist, educator*

Madison
Coppersmith, Susan Nan *physicist*

Whitewater
Kumpaty, Hephzibah J. *chemistry professor*

CANADA

NOVA SCOTIA

Tatamagouche
Roach, Margot Ruth *retired biophysicist, educator*

ONTARIO

Toronto
Packham, Marian Aitchison *biochemistry professor*

ENGLAND

London
Wallace, Bonnie Ann *biochemist, biophysicist, educator*

TURKEY

Mersin
Yalin, Serap *biochemist, educator*

ADDRESS UNPUBLISHED

Ancker-Johnson, Betsy *physicist, engineer, retired automotive executive*
Bajura, Rita A. *research scientist*
Brienza, Paula Kenah *retired chemist*
Broers, Brenda Ann *chemistry professor*
Brown, Rhonda Rochelle *chemist, health facility administrator, lawyer*
Bunyan, Ellen Lackey Spotz *retired chemist*
Cai, Ming Zhi *chemist, researcher, film producer*
Campbell, Mary Stinecipher *retired chemist*
Cartwright, Katharine Aileen *geologist*
Cathou, Renata Egone *chemist, consultant*
Ceulemans, Sophia *biochemist*
Chiu, Bella Chao *astrophysicist, writer*
Ciocan, Eugenia *physicist, educator*
Colmenares, Leticia *chemistry professor*
de Planque, E. Gail *physicist*
Detert, Miriam Anne *chemical analyst*
Devine, Katherine *environmental scientist, educator*
Di Iorio, Daniela *oceanographer, researcher*
Donaldson, Eva G. *chemist, writer*
Drahos, Sandra P. *retired chemist*
Evans, Susan A. *chemist*
Franz, Judy R. *physics professor*
French, Julia McAllister (Judy McAllister French) *environmental consultant*
Gabel, Connie *chemist, educator*
Galloway, Eilene Marie *space and astronautics consultant*
Garmany, Catharine Doremus *astronomer*
Hirsch, Phyllis Sinman *biochemist, researcher*
Hoffleit, Ellen Dorrit *astronomer*
Ivey, Elizabeth Spencer *retired physicist, educator*
Jackson, Dionne Broxton *chemist*
Keiser, Nanette Marie *research scientist*
Kistiakowsky, Vera *physical researcher, educator*
Kisvarsanyi, Eva Bognar *retired geologist*
Korn, Jessica Susan *research scientist, educator*
Kraus, Naomi *retired biochemist*
Krebs, Martha *physicist, federal science agency administrator*
Kuhlmann-Wilsdorf, Doris *materials scientist, inventor, retired educator*
Latham, Tamara Beryl *chemist, researcher*
Lean, Judith *physicist, researcher*
Levi, Barbara Goss *physicist, editor*
Li, Lijuan *chemistry professor*
Li, Mary J. *scientist, educator*
McPherson, Renee *meteorologist*
Oesterlin, Lovye Gwendolyn *retired chemist, educator, retired educational consultant*
Pytlewski, Laura Jean *chemistry professor*
Quinn, Helen Rhoda Arnold *physicist*
Reichmanis, Elsa *chemist*
Roman, Nancy Grace *astronomer, consultant*
Rubin, Vera Cooper *astronomer, researcher*
Saleh, Farida Yousry *chemistry professor*
Schwartz, Lisa M. (Lisa Shepard) *research and development chemist*
Schwartz, Shirley E. *retired chemist, researcher*
Shands, Gail Maxine *environmental scientist*
Sheinin, Rose *biochemist, educator*
Shoemaker, Deirdre Marie *physics professor*
Sprague, Elizabeth Anne *chemistry professor, researcher*
Sullivan, Kathryn D. *geologist, former astronaut, former science association executive*
Tabazadeh, Azadeh *environmental scientist, researcher*
Taylor, Kathleen (Christine Taylor) *physical chemist, researcher*
Thompson, Mary Eileen *chemistry professor*
Thornton, Rita Louise *environmental scientist, lawyer*
Townsend, Katheryn Estelle *chemistry professor*
Wallace, Jane House *retired geologist*
Wallach-Levy, Wendee Esther *astronomer*
Weisburger, Elizabeth Kreiser *retired chemist*
Wilson, Peggy Mayfield *retired chemist*

SOCIAL SCIENCE

UNITED STATES

ALABAMA

Auburn
Clark, Janet Eileen *political science professor*

Auburn University
Frieda-Siepmann, Elaina M. *psychology professor*

Birmingham
Cormier, Loretta A. *anthropologist*
Daniels-Rogers, LaTausha *social sciences educator, entrepreneur*

Dothan
Kogelschatz, Joan Lee *psychologist, psychotherapist*

Hoover
Fineburg, Amy C. *social studies educator*

Jacksonville
Chargois, Deborah Majeau *psychology professor, researcher*
Dunaway, Carolyn Bennett *retired sociology professor*
Eyre, Heidi L. *psychology professor*

Normal
Lane, Rosalie Middleton *extension specialist*

Tuscaloosa
Fish, Mary Martha *economics professor*

ALASKA

Anchorage
Obermeyer, Theresa Nangle *sociology educator*

Fairbanks
Shier, Juliet Marie *social studies educator*

ARIZONA

Buckeye
Privette, Louise Judith *school psychologist*

Chandler
Newman, Phyllis *retired counselor, therapist, hypnotist*

Flagstaff
Lusk, Della S. *psychologist*

Green Valley
Foley, Teresa A. *psychologist*

Mesa
Taylor, Patti Ann *psychologist, educator*
Yates, Cheryl Ann *home economist, educator*

Phoenix
Fishgrab, Barbara Jeanne *school psychologist, mental health services professional*
Fontes, Bianca Michelle *social studies educator*
Rees, Sarah Lynn *school psychologist*
Smith, Barbara Gail *economist*
Wolf, Irna Lynn *psychologist*

Prescott
Walker, Winnetta Dorrean *social studies educator*
Zabukovec, Jamie Jo *clinical psychologist*

Scottsdale
Roberts, Joan Ila *psychologist, educator*

Tempe
Caterino, Linda Claire *psychologist*
Menjivar, Cecilia *social sciences educator*
Rowley, Beverley Davies *sociologist*

Tucson
Dobyns, Susan Dianne *anthropologist, sociologist, educator*
Hill, Jane H. *anthropologist, educator*
Ingram, Helen Moyer *political science professor*
Larwood, Laurie *psychologist*
Montero, Leticia *social studies educator*
Norrander, Barbara *political science professor*
Parra, Elena Batriz-Guadalupe *psychologist, educator*
Serido, Joyce *psychologist, researcher*
Underwood, Jane Hainline Hammons *anthropologist, educator*

Yuma
Anderson, Stacey Ann *school psychologist*
McCarthy, Sherri Nevada *psychologist, educator, educational consultant*

ARKANSAS

Arkadelphia
Sandford, Juanita Dadisman *sociologist, educator, writer*

Little Rock
Coleman, Marshia Adams *social sciences educator*
Murray-Norman, Natasha J. *political science professor, pastor*

Pine Bluff
Engle, Carole Ruth *aquaculture economics professor*

Searcy
Thompson, Linda Ruth *psychology educator, university administrator*

Wheatley
Gehring, Elizabeth A. *social studies educator*

Winslow
Wright, Mary E. (Mary E. Guen) *clinical psychologist*

CALIFORNIA

Alameda
Troll, Lillian Ellman *psychologist, educator*
Trufant, Carol Ann *psychologist, consultant*

Altadena
Miller, Karen *clinical psychologist, neuropsychologist*

Atascadero
Thacker, Stacy Leigh *psychologist*

Azusa
Miyake, Stephanie Ann *psychology professor, director, marriage and family therapist*

Bakersfield
Granskog, Jane Ellen *anthropologist, educator*
Kemp, Donna Renee *public administration educator, public policy educator, academic administrator*
Osterkamp, Dalene May *psychology educator, artist*
Rienzi, Beth Ann Menees *psychologist, educator, director*

Berkeley
Baumrind, Diana *research psychologist*
Canfield, Judy S. *psychologist*
Crawford, Charlotte Joanne *psychologist, psychoanalyst, psychological anthropologist*
Edelman, Lauren B. *sociologist, law educator*
Gibbs, Jewelle Taylor *clinical psychologist*
Joyce, Rosemary Alexandria *anthropology educator, department chairman*
Luker, Kristin *sociology educator*
Maslach, Christina *psychology professor*
Nader, Laura *anthropologist, educator*
Nathanson, Marjorie Ann *psychologist*
Nemeth, Charlan Jeanne *psychology educator*
Petiet, Carole Anne *psychologist*
Stewart, Patricia Rhodes *former clinical psychologist, researcher*

Beverly Hills
Arutt, Cheryl *clinical and forensic psychologist, educator*
Blakeley, Linda *psychologist, speaker, consultant, writer*
Pomeroy, Eleanor Lisa Beyea *psychologist, psychoanalyst*

Yaryan, Ruby Bell *psychologist*

Big Pine
Reynaud-Roepke, Suzanne *psychologist*

Bonita
Deane, Debbe *psychologist, journalist, editor, consultant*

Camarillo
Meyer, Barbara *psychologist*

Carson
Hurtado-Ortiz, Maria T. *psychology professor*
Palmer, Beverly Blazey *psychologist, educator*

Chico
Monges, Miriam M. *social studies educator*
Smith, Valene Lucy *anthropologist, educator*
Transchel, Kate *social sciences educator*

Chino Hills
Fisher, Teresa Marie *psychologist, forensic specialist*

Citrus Heights
Mart, Joann *social sciences educator*

Claremont
Albaum, Jean Stirling *psychologist, educator*
Halpern, Diane F. *psychology educator, professional association executive*
Lipman-Blumen, Jean *public policy and organizational behavior educator*
Morgan, Ann Marie *psychologist*
Vajk, Fiona *psychologist, educator*

Compton
Drew, Sharon Lee *sociologist*

Del Mar
Ceren, Sandra Levy *psychologist, writer*
Quinn, Katherine Sarah *psychologist*

El Monte
Merrill Warner, Veronique *psychologist*

Encinitas
Lougeay, Denruth Colleen *clinical psychologist, educator*

Encino
Davis, Berta *psychologist*

Fullerton
Segal, Nancy Lee *psychology professor, researcher*

Garden Grove
Greenslade, Cindy Louise *psychologist*

Grass Valley
Phillips-Jones, Linda *consulting psychologist*

Hayward
Meyer, Ann Jane *human development educator*

Hemet
Levine, Elaine Prado *psychologist, music educator, artist, small business owner*

Hermosa Beach
Wickwire, Patricia Joanne Nellor *psychologist, educator*

Hollister
Harris, Wendy Take *psychologist, educator*

Huntington Beach
Ogata, Susan Naomi *psychologist*

Indian Wells
McGraw, Phyllis Mae *psychologist, geriatric specialist*

Inglewood
Marks, Laura B. *psychologist*

Irvine
Feldman, Martha Sue *political scientist, educator*
Greenberger, Ellen *psychologist, educator*
Treas, Judith Kay *sociology educator*

La Jolla
Coburn, Marjorie Foster *psychologist, educator*
Cox, Barbara Joanne *psychologist, consultant*
Mandler, Jean Matter *psychologist, educator*
Margolin, Frances Mongin *clinical psychologist, educator*
White, Michelle Jo *economics professor*

Laguna Beach
Heussenstamm, Frances Kovacs *psychologist, artist*

Lake Forest
Smoot, Skipi Lundquist *psychologist*

Lancaster
Holley, Susan L. *psychologist*

Long Beach
Solovei, Marion *clinical psychologist*

Los Altos Hills
Gibbs, Patricia Leigh *social sciences educator, researcher*

Los Angeles
Akhavanhaidary, Sepideh *psychologist, educator*
Anawalt, Patricia Rieff *anthropologist, researcher*
Archuleta, Randi Lisa *psychologist*
Currie, Janet M. *economics professor*
Dennis, Jessica Michele *psychology professor*
Gunn, Karen Sue *psychologist, educator*
Kalish-Weiss, Beth Isaacs *psychologist, psychoanalyst, consultant*
Kenyon, Geraldine Mona *psychologist, consultant*
Lear, Lyn Davis *psychologist*
Mahmoudi, Homa *psychologist*
Montoya, Velma *economist, consultant*
Reznick, Charlotte *educational psychologist, consultant*
Riffkind, Randi Jan *psychologist*
Taylor, Shelley E. *psychology researcher, educator*
Telles, Cynthia Ann *psychologist*
Tickner, Judith Ann *political science educator*
Tonick, Illene *clinical psychologist*
Van Tilburg, JoAnne *archaeologist, educator, foundation administrator*
Watson, Sharon Gitin *psychologist*
Whitney, Constance Clein *psychologist, educator, consultant*
Wood, Nancy Elizabeth *psychologist, educator*

Los Gatos
Ohanjanian, Ruzanna *clinical psychologist*

Malibu
Barnett, Ola Wilma *psychology educator*
Miller-Perrin, Cindy Lou *psychology professor*

Mill Valley
Vaughan, Frances Elizabeth *psychologist*

Moffett Field
Clearwater, Yvonne A. *psychologist*

Napa
Geca, Monique *psychologist*

Northridge
Butler, Karla *psychologist, educator*
Reagan, Janet Thompson *psychologist, educator*

Novato
Codoner, Sheila Dowds *psychologist*
Criswell, Eleanor Camp *psychologist*
Weedn, Sonnee D. *psychologist*

Oakland
Bobino, Rita Florencia *psychologist*
Hsu, Helen Hua *psychologist, consultant*
Neeley, Beverly Evon *sociologist, consultant*
Preston, Elizabeth A. *psychologist*

Oceanside
Hertweck, Alma Louise *sociology and child development educator*

Orange
Carty, Victoria Louise *sociologist, educator*
Stevens, Cherita Wyman *social sciences educator, writer*

Palm Desert
Bantz, Jody Lenore *psychologist*

Palo Alto
Bystritsky, Marina *psychologist*
Lewis, Virginia Marie *psychologist*
Scitovsky, Anne Aickelin *economist, researcher*
Sherlock, Phyllis Krafft *psychologist*

Palos Verdes Peninsula
Skorka, Darlene McDonald *psychologist*

Paramount
Landes, Geraldine Steinberg *psychologist*

Redding
Drake, Patricia Evelyn *psychologist*

Redondo Beach
McWilliams, Margaret Ann *home economist, educator, writer*

Riverside
Bridges, Lisa Jane *psychology educator*
Lyubomirsky, Sonja *psychology professor*
Mancilla, Faustina Ramirez *retired psychologist*
Winter, Patricia Lea *psychologist, researcher*

Sacramento
Krebs, Nina Boyd *psychologist*
Lindahl, Kathleen Ann *archaeologist*
Senna, Doborah Jean *psychology professor*
Stolba, Soheir Sukkary *anthropologist, educator*
Wilcox, Lynn E. *psychology educator*

San Bernardino
Griffiths, Barbara Lorraine *psychologist, writer, marriage and family therapist*

San Clemente
Fox, Lorraine Esther *psychologist, human services consultant*

San Diego
Blade, Melinda Kim *archaeologist, educator, research scientist*
Boesky, Lisa *child/adolescent psychologist, writer, speaker, consultant*
Brien, Lois Ann *psychologist, educator*
Brown, Sandra Ann *psychology educator*
Fernandes, Kathleen *scientist*
Hoston, Germaine Annette *political science professor*
Lane, Sylvia *economist, educator*
Maheu, Marlene Muriel *psychologist*
Saltman, Juliet A. *retired sociology educator*
Sheldon-Morris, Tiffini Anne *clinical psychologist, consultative examiner*
Sundayo, Judy *psychologist, educator*

San Francisco
Adamson, Mary Anne *geographer, systems engineer, consultant*
Chase, Alexandra Nin *psychologist, writer*
Estes, Carroll Lynn *sociologist, educator*
Fields, Laurie *psychologist, educator*
Giraudo, Suzanne McDonnell *psychologist*
Hudson, Patricia Ann Siegel *psychologist*
Loewy, Becky White *psychologist, educator*
Mirabal, Nancy Raquel *social sciences educator, researcher*
Ratum, Cecilia Bangloy *retired psychologist*
Rice, Dorothy Pechman (Mrs. John Donald Rice) *medical economist*
Roy, Beth *sociologist, mediator*
Saunders, Virginia Fox *psychology educator*
Sedway, Lynn Massel *real estate economist*
Soh, Chunghee Sarah *anthropology educator*
Tsoh, Janice Yusze *clinical psychologist, researcher*
Wells, Gertrude Beverly *psychologist*

San Jose
Fiedler, Lois Jean *psychologist, educator*
McDowell, Jennifer *sociologist, composer, playwright*
Weiss, Elizabeth *anthropologist, educator*

San Luis Obispo
Holder, Elaine Edith *psychologist, educator*

San Marino
Martin, Olivia Jean *social studies educator*
Medici, Rochelle *psychologist, brain researcher*

San Rafael
Yates, Margaret Marlene *psychologist*

Santa Ana
Klassen, Margreta *clinical psychologist, educator*

Santa Barbara
Harwick, Betty Corinne Burns *sociology educator*
Mack, Judith Cole Schrim *retired political scientist*
Nyborg, Vanessa Marie *psychologist, researcher, educator*
Weidemann, Celia Jean *social sciences educator, management consultant, financial consultant*

Santa Clara
Bell, Genevieve *anthropologist*
Gilbert, Lucia Albino *psychology professor*
Talbot, Nyna Lucille *psychologist, writer*

Santa Clarita
Earnest-Rahman, Michelle L. *psychologist*

Santa Cruz
Roby, Pamela Ann *sociologist, educator*

Santa Monica
Ellickson, Phyllis Lynn *political scientist*
Gray, Laura B. *psychology professor, counselor*
Lehman, Ellen J. *psychologist*
Malmstrom Lakeman, Dorothy E. *psychologist*

Santa Rosa
Jandrey, Becky Lee *psychologist*
Rogers, Natalie *psychologist*

Sherman Oaks
Gross, Sharon Ruth *forensic psychologist, researcher*

Sonora
Clarke, Paula Katherine *anthropologist, researcher, social studies educator*

Stanford
Maccoby, Eleanor Emmons *psychology professor*
Martin, Joanne *social sciences educator*
Ricardo-Campbell, Rita *economist, educator*

Stockton
McCarty, Lois Leone *retired sociologist*
Roll, Renée F. *retired psychologist, publishing executive*

Taft
Lose, Cynthia A. *psychologist, educator*

Temecula
Arban, Diana Marie *social sciences educator*

Trabuco Canyon
Addy, Jo Alison Phears *economist*

Venice
Greenfield, Patricia Ann Marks *psychology educator*

Vista
Savage, Linda Eileen *psychologist*

Watsonville
West, Karrie L. *school psychologist*

Whittier
McKenna, Jeanette Ann *archaeologist*

Woodland Hills
Pollock, Vicki Eileen *psychologist*
Thomsen, Mary Joan Margaret *psychology educator*

COLORADO

Aspen
Newman, Ruth Gallert *psychologist*

Aurora
Doze, Maureen Adele (Maureen Adele Mee) *social studies educator*
Warnell, Rebecca E. *social studies educator*

Boulder
Edwards, Donna Hohmann *psychologist*
Healy, Alice Fenvessy *psychology professor, researcher*
Joyce, Janet S. *psychologist*
Menken, Jane Ava *demographer, educator*

Centennial
Dineen, Bonnie R. *social studies educator*
Messer, Bonnie Jeanne *psychologist*

Colorado Springs
Farrer, Claire Anne Rafferty *anthropologist, educator*
Weir, Catherine Grant *psychology educator*

Denver
Hamm, Suzanne Margaret *psychologist*
Heitler, Susan McCrensky *clinical psychologist*
Hoffman, Elizabeth *economics professor*
Nelson, Sarah Milledge *archaeology educator*
Post, Robin Dee *psychologist*
Swain, Nicole Falvo *psychologist*

Fort Collins
Sedei Rodden, Pamela Jean *psychologist, director*

Grand Junction
Godsman, Katherine *retired psychologist, educator*

Greeley
Ackerman, Joyce Shohet *psychologist*
Blake, Margaret Tate *psychologist, educator*
Hawthorne, Barbara L. *anthropologist, educator*

Lakewood
Stoloff, Carolyn Ruth *clinical psychologist*

Limon
Richards, Ann Adair *psychologist*

Littleton
Lohman, Loretta Cecelia *social scientist, consultant*

Loveland
Kasenberg, Darlene Frances *psychologist*

Northglenn
Nucci, Sunni Lynn *social studies educator*

Pueblo
Alt, Betty L. *sociology educator*
Gardner, Tracy A. *social studies educator*

U S A F Academy
Caldwell, Jo Lynn *research psychologist*

Wheat Ridge
Civish, Gayle Ann *psychologist*

Wiggins
Midcap, Linda Luree *social studies educator*

CONNECTICUT

Bolton
Toomey, Laura Carolyn *psychologist*

Bridgeport
Coba-Loh, Claudine Jean *psychology professor*

Derby
Brassil, Jean Ella *psychologist*

Fairfield
Morehouse, Sarah McCally *retired political science professor*

Guilford
Shelton, Darlene *psychologist, consultant*

Higganum
de Brigard, Emilie *anthropologist, consultant*

Lisbon
Powell, Diane Marie *psychologist*

Manchester
Fitzgerald, Mary Irene *retired school psychologist*

Meriden
Losada-Zarate, Gloria *psychologist*

Middletown
Blume, Ginger Elaine *psychologist*
Corrao, Angela M. *psychologist*

Milford
Boyer, Carolyn Merwin *school psychologist*
Krall, Vita *psychologist*

New Canaan
Thomas, Marianne Gregory *school psychologist*

New Haven
Chevalier, Judith A. *economics professor, finance professor*
Ember, Carol R. *anthropology educator, writer*
Kaufman, Nadeen Laurie *clinical psychology educator, writer*
Nelson, Alondra R. *social sciences educator*
Speicher, Hilda *psychologist, educator*
Wynn, Karen *psychologist, educator, researcher*

Norwalk
Timlin-Scalera, Rebecca Mary *neuropsychologist*

Plainville
Perkins- Banas, Melissa Veronica *psychologist*

Stamford
Halligan, Fredrica Rose *clinical psychologist*
Teeters, Nancy Hays *economist, director*

Voluntown
Thevenet, Patricia Confrey *social studies educator*

Waterbury
Andonucci-Hill, Heather L. *psychologist*
Stella, Robin Lynn *psychologist*

Waterford
Hinkle, Janet *psychologist*

West Hartford
Lawrence, Sarah Anne *social studies educator*
Rhinehart, Elizabeth D. *psychologist*

Westport
Lee, Janet Mentore *psychologist, educator*
Levy, Wendy *psychologist*

Willimantic
Clifford, Maryanne Theresa *economics professor, researcher*
Free, Rhona Campbell *economics professor*

DELAWARE

Dover
Bugglin, Carol Stephanie *clinical psychologist, psychotherapist*

Wilmington
Graham, Frances Keesler (Mrs. David Tredway Graham) *psychologist, educator*

DISTRICT OF COLUMBIA

Washington
Ashmore-Hudson, Anne *psychologist, writer, consultant*
Becker, Mary Louise *political scientist*
Bergmann, Barbara Rose *economics professor*
Bloom-Feshbach, Sally *psychologist, educator*
Bowes, Rosemary Tofalo *psychologist, consultant*
Brautigam, Deborah Anne *political science professor*
Brooks, Renana Esther *clinical psychologist, consultant, researcher*
Burk, Martha Gertrude *political psychologist*
Cole, Angela P. *psychologist, educator*
Egan, Michelle D. *social sciences educator*
Flattau, Pamela Ebert *research psychologist, consultant*
Fusillo, Alice Elbert *retired sociologist, sculptor*
Garfinkel, Renée Efra *psychologist*
Gonzalez-Hermosillo, Brenda *economist, researcher*
Grapin, Jacqueline G. *economist*
Green, Karen Ina Margulies *psychologist*
Hillsman, Sally T. *sociologist*
Jones, Barbara Pendleton *psychologist, educator*
Kirkpatrick, Jeane Duane Jordan *political scientist, federal official*
Kravis, Marie-Josee Drouin *economist*
Krokos, Kelley Joan *psychologist, consultant*
Krueger, Anne *economist*
Krulfeld, Ruth Marilyn *anthropologist, educator*
Kuh, Charlotte Virginia *economist*
Kuhn, Harriet Lurensky *school psychologist*
Kybal, Elba Gómez del Rey *economist, not-for-profit developer*
Marcuss, Rosemary Daly *economist*
Martin, Linda Gaye *demographer, economist*
Martinez, Herminia S. *economist, banker*
McGoldrick, Jane R. *psychologist, writer, editor*
Meggers, Betty Jane *anthropologist, researcher*
Mezoughem, Claire Virginia *economist*
Miller, Margery *psychologist, educator, speech pathology/audiology services professional, mental health services professional*
O'Connor, Karen *political science professor, researcher, writer*
Penn, Jennifer *psychologist, consultant*
Phillips, Karen Borlaug *economist, rail transportation executive*
Rivlin, Alice Mitchell *economics professor, former federal official*
Rodriguez, Rita Maria *economist*
Sawhill, Isabel Van Devanter *economist*
Schorr, Lisbeth Bamberger *sociologist, researcher*
Scott, Charneta Claudetta *psychologist, educator*
Scrivner, Ellen M. *psychologist*
Solomon, Elinor Harris *economics professor*
Utgoff, Kathleen Platt *economist, pension fund administrator*
Weinhold, Linda Lillian *psychologist, researcher*
Wilensky, Gail Roggin *economist, researcher*
Willner, Ann Ruth *political scientist, educator*
Willner, Dorothy *anthropologist, educator*

FLORIDA

Aventura
Krop, Lois Pulver *psychologist*

Baker
Fjelsted, Mae Francis *retired psychologist*

Boca Raton
Aiken, Lisa Anne *psychologist, author, lecturer*
Klasfield, Ilene *psychologist*
Shalom, Galit *psychologist*

Clearwater
Holbrook, Taryl Ann *psychological consultant*

Coral Gables
Humphries, Joan Ropes *psychologist, educator*

Davie
Ross, Kathryn Amie *psychologist*

Englewood
Ness, Sharon L. *social studies educator, coach*

Fort Lauderdale
Bartelstone, Rona Sue *gerontologist*
McGreevy, Mary Sharron *former psychology educator*
Segal, Marilyn Mailman *psychologist, educator*

Gainesville
Abrams, Julie Marie *counseling psychologist*
Harrison, Faye Venetia *anthropologist, educator, writer*
Sackellares, Dalma Kalogjera *psychologist*
Wass, Hannelore Lina *educational psychology educator*
West, Robin Lea *psychology educator*
White, Susie Mae *school psychologist*

Glen Saint Mary
Richerson, Kristina Marie *social studies educator*

Hollywood
Valdes, Jacqueline Chehebar *psychologist, consultant, researcher*

Jacksonville
O'Donnell, Elisabeth Pallant *social studies educator*
Scheck, Elizabeth A. *sociologist, educator*
Scott, Kamela Koon *psychologist, educator*

Key West
Post-Gorden, Joan Carolyn *retired psychology educator*

Lake Worth
Gilbert, Lisa Marie *social studies educator*

Land O Lakes
Wilkinson, Denise V. *psychologist*

Lutz
Ellis, Leslie Elaine *psychologist*
Garcia, Sandra Joanne Anderson *law and psychology educator*

Miami
Arango, Penelope Corey *psychologist, consultant*
Bruel, Iris Barbara *psychologist*
Field, Julia Allen *futurist, strategist, environmentalist*
Huysman, Arlene Weiss *psychologist, educator, writer*
Linoff-Thornton, Marian Gottlieb *retired psychologist*
Muniz, Diane Virginia *psychologist*
Silverman, Wendy K. *psychologist, educator*

Miami Beach
Freshwater, Shawna Marie *neuropsychologist, clinical psychologist, cognitive neuroscientist*
Kalsner-Silver, Lydia *psychologist*

North Miami Beach
Girden, Ellen Robinson *retired psychology educator*

Ocala
Blalock, Carol Douglass *psychologist, educator*

Odessa
Diemer, Madeline Ann (Madeline DeMer) *psychology educator*

Orlando
Ashe, Diane Davis *psychology professor, sport psychology consultant*
Fine, Terri Susan *political science professor*
Jung, Nicole P *psychologist*

Palm Harbor
Diamond, Linda Mann *social studies educator*

Panama City
Brown, Greta Kay *psychologist*
Kline, Kelley Knapp *psychology professor*

Pensacola
Privette, P(atricia) Gayle *psychology educator, psychotherapist*
Stanny, Claudia J. *psychology professor*
Wilcox, Krysta *social studies educator*

Plantation
Ackerman, Helen Ruth Penner *psychologist*

Pompano Beach
Gelske, Andrea Janna *psychologist*
Pigott, Melissa Ann *social psychologist*

Port Richey
Mueller, Lois M. *psychologist*

Saint Augustine
Henderson, Hazel *economist, writer*

Saint Petersburg
Kesler, Bonnie L. *psychology professor*
Khosh, Mary Sivert *psychologist*
Rosenblum, Zina Michelle Zarin *psychology professor, marketing professional, researcher*

Sarasota
Elmendorf-Langdraf, Mary Lindsay *retired anthropologist*
Watson, Joyce Morrissa *forensic and clinical psychologist*

South Miami
Villacian, Vanessa Luisa *psychologist*

St Augustine
Cremona, Rachel Karen *political science professor*

Stuart
Whichello, Carol *political scientist, educator, writer*

Sun City Center
Petersen, Carolyn Ashcraft *psychologist*

Tallahassee
Hull, Elaine Mangelsdorf *psychology professor*
Johnson, Suzanne Bennett *psychologist*

Tampa
Berne, Patricia Higgins *psychologist, writer, educator*
Cimino, Cynthia R. *neuropsychologist, education educator*
Genshaft, Judy Lynn *psychologist, educator*
Kimmel, Ellen Bishop *psychologist, educator*
MacManus, Susan Ann *political science professor, researcher*
Mulloy, Jean Marie *psychologist, human services administrator*
Musante, Linda *psychologist*

Winter Park
Cook, Jo Ann Likins *psychologist*
Harvey, Joan Carol *psychologist*

GEORGIA

Atlanta
Davis, Aimee Slaughter *social studies educator*
Dierickx, Constance Ricker *psychologist, management consultant*
Garland, LaRetta Matthews *psychologist, nursing educator*
Kelley, Linda Elaine Spadafora *school psychologist, educator*
Kerr, Nancy Helen *psychology educator*
Miller, Patricia Hackney *psychology educator*
Speckhart, Dawn Seidner *bone marrow transplant/leukemia psychologist*
Winkler, Rebecca B. *psychologist*

Auburn
Reuter, Helen Hyde *psychologist*

Bainbridge
Dixon, Lugenia *psychology educator*

Blairsville
Jones, Mary Emma B. *psychologist*

Carrollton
Holland, Laurel Long *sociologist, educator*
Stone, Sandra Smith *sociologist, researcher, academic administrator*

Demorest
Vance, Cynthia Lynn *psychology educator*

Evans
Zachert, Virginia *retired psychologist*

Fayetteville
Furbee, Amy H. *social studies educator*
Ward, Connie Michele *psychologist, educator, environmentalist*

Fort Stewart
McCarthy, Dorothy A. (Landers) *social studies educator*

Gainesville
Frank, Mary Lou Bryant *psychologist, educator*

Griffin
Shockley, Carol Frances *psychologist, psychotherapist*

Hiram
Moyer, Dianna Kay *social studies educator*

Hoschton
Keyes, Maria Vega *social studies educator*

Jesup
Terradas, Shirley Arnold *clinical psychologist*

Lawrenceville
Mayfield, Peggy Jordan *psychologist, minister*

Macon
Cook, Charlotte C. *psychologist*
Lewis, Sandra Combs *research psychologist, writer*

Marietta
Hirsch, Kerri Ann *social studies educator*

Mcdonough
Gale, Michelle Sue *retired clinical psychologist*

Milledgeville
Moses, Catherine *political science professor*

Powder Springs
Roberson-Brown, Linda Marie *social studies educator*

Ringgold
Hayes Gladson, Laura Joanna *psychologist*

Savannah
Martin, Grace Burkett *psychologist*
Rozantine, Gayle Stubbs *psychologist*
Traylor, Jessica Stephens *psychologist*

Social Circle
Archibald, Claudia Jane *parapsychologist, counselor, consultant*

Statesboro
Lloyd, Margaret Ann *psychologist, educator*
Nettles, Saundra R. Murray *psychologist, writer, educator*

Stone Mountain
Farngalo, Rosemarie Merritt *school psychologist*

Toccoa Falls
Brock, Dorothy Dixon *psychologist, psychology professor*

HAWAII

Holualoa
Scarr, Sandra Wood *retired psychology educator, researcher*

Honolulu
Finucane, Melissa Lucille *psychologist, researcher*
Hatfield, Elaine Catherine *psychology professor*
Ishikawa-Fullmer, Janet Satomi *psychologist, educator*
Kennedy, Reneau Charlene Ufford *forensic psychologist, consultant*
O'Brien, Kendra Allen *psychologist, researcher*

Kailua
Fine, Virginia O. *psychologist*
Stamper, Ewa Szumotalska *psychologist*
Tavares, Samantha *psychologist, educator*

Kamuela
Richards, Phyllis Anderson *psychologist*

Kaneohe
Coberly, Margaret *psychologist, educator*

Lahaina
Hill, Ruth Elaine *social studies educator, department chairman*

Wahiawa
Kiyota, Heide P. *psychologist*

IDAHO

Boise
Sterling, Lisa Anne *psychologist*

Garden Valley
Bellamy, Joan Elizabeth *psychologist, consultant*

Moscow
Wyatt, Carolyn J. *psychologist*

Twin Falls
Wright, Frances Jane *educational psychologist*

ILLINOIS

Arlington Heights
Greenburg, Sharon Louise *psychologist*
Griffin, Jean Latz *political strategist, writer, publisher*
Lewin, Pearl Goldman *psychologist*
McEvers, Allison H. *psychologist*
Witt, Sally Eleanor *psychologist, educator*

Aurora
Franuik, Ranae *psychology professor*
Herrera, Bethany Sara *social studies educator*

Barrington
Sherman, Beth Marie *psychologist*
Wood, Andrée Robitaille *archaeologist, researcher*

Bourbonnais
Mills, Bethany S. *psychologist, educator*

Calumet City
Pickel, Joyce Kiley *psychologist*

Carbondale
DiLalla, Lisabeth Anne Fisher *developmental psychology researcher, educator*
Fuller, Janet McCray *anthropologist, educator*

Cary
Monti, Laura Anne *psychology researcher, educator*

Champaign
Allen, Deborah Rudisill *clinical psychologist, educator*
Jacobson, Elaine Zeporah *clinical psychologist*
Juraska, Janice Marie *psychology professor*
Osgood, Judy Kay *clinical psychologist, educator, consultant*

Chicago
Bae, Sue Hyun *psychologist, educator*
Bajich, Milena Tatic *psychologist*
Baum, Cynthia Gail *psychologist, educator, association administrator*
Carney, Jean Kathryn *psychologist*
Comella, Cynthia Louise *psychologist, neurologist, sociologist, educator*
Connors, Mary Eileen *psychologist*
Dawdy, Shannon Lee *archaeologist, historical anthropologist*
Elshtain, Jean Bethke *social sciences educator*
Epstein, Lee Joan *political science professor, law educator*
Freeman, Susan Tax *anthropologist, educator, culinary historian*
Gannon, Sister Ann Ida *retired philosophy educator*
Graber, Doris Appel *political scientist, writer, editor*
Harris, Betty Jean *social sciences educator*
Hoogenboom, Carol Annette *clinical neuropsychologist*
Lake, Constance Williams *psychologist, public health administrator*
Levy, Jerre Marie *psychobiology educator*
Lowe, Sandra Elveta *psychologist*
Nissenson, Norma *clinical psychologist*
Rogalski, Carol Jean *clinical psychologist, educator*
Sanders, Jacquelyn Seevak *psychologist, educator*
Schanzenbach, Diane Whitmore *economist*
Simons, Helen *school psychologist, psychotherapist, educator*
Tsiang, Grace Renjuei *economist, educator*
Weed, Mary Theophilos *psychology educator*
Zoloth, Laurie Susan *bioethicist*

Deerfield
Parent, Miriam Stark *psychology educator*

Dekalb
Weisenthal, Rebecca G. *clinical psychologist*

Evanston
Eisen, Marlene Ruth *psychologist, educator*
Gentner, Dedre *psychology professor*
Hurd, Elizabeth Shakman *social studies educator*
Koenigsberg, Judy Z. Nulman *psychologist*
Mineka, Susan *psychology professor*
Richeson, Jennifer Anne *psychology professor, researcher*
Thompson, Leigh Lassiter *psychologist, educator*

Glen Ellyn
Alberti, Jean Mae Claire *clinical psychologist*
Benzies, Bonnie Jeanne *clinical and addictions psychologist*

Grayslake
Fout, Jeanine Marie *social studies educator*
Landry, Tracey Katherine *social studies educator*

Hillside
Kapsalis, Frances Hinos *psychologist, educator*

Indian Head Park
Beck, Ariadne Plumis *psychologist, psychotherapist, management consultant*

Lake Barrington
Black, Kathryn N. *psychologist, educator*

Libertyville
Pollina, Kristen Mittl *child and adolescent psychologist*

Lindenhurst
Eron, Madeline Marcus *psychologist*

Maryville
Stark, Patricia Ann *psychologist*

Milford
Beall, Pamela Honn *psychologist, consultant*

Moline
Sausedo, Sasha A. *social studies educator*

Naperville
Cowlishaw, Mary Lou *government educator*
Gaeth, Roxanne *school psychologist*
Galvan, Mary Theresa *economics professor*
Rebeck, Pamela Joan *psychologist*

Northbrook
Costello, Joan *psychologist*
Warren, Elizabeth Curran *retired political science professor*

Oak Lawn
Peczkowski, Kristin Marie *social sciences educator, coach*

Oak Park
Lare, Jane Cameron *school psychologist*

Peoria
Mariani, Theresa Lynn *sociologist, educator*

Rock Island
Johnson, Ruth Ann Craig Goswick *psychology educator*

Rockford
Fisher, Erin *psychology professor*

Rolling Meadows
Burger, Mary Louise *psychologist, educator*

Saint Charles
Patten, Maurine Diane *psychologist*

Skokie
Baehr, Elsa Telser *clinical psychologist, neurotherapist*
Sheban, Lynne Rosenzweig *psychologist*
Yogev, Sara *psychologist*

University Park
Johnson, Elizabeth Jean *psychology professor*

Urbana
Warren, Pamela A. *psychologist*

Villa Park
Fitzgerald, Christine Elizabeth *school psychologist*

Waukegan
Conolly-Wilson, Christina *psychologist*

Western Springs
Zamora, Marjorie Dixon *retired political science professor*

Wheaton
Riley, Betty Anne *psychologist, educator*

Winnetka
Krueger, Deborah A. Blake *school psychologist, consultant*

Woodstock
Wertheimer-Sexton, Willa Renee *clinical psychologist*

INDIANA

Bloomington
Brehm, Sharon Stephens *psychology professor, former academic administrator*
Ostrom, Elinor *political science professor, researcher*
Thorelli, Sarah V. *economist, researcher*

Columbus
Johnson, Jane *school psychologist*

Elkhart
Strong, Nena L. *social studies educator*

Indianapolis
Cardwell, Sue Webb *psychology professor*
Plascak-Craig, Faye Dene *psychology educator, researcher*

Mishawaka
Hossler, Elizabeth *psychology professor, department chairman, institutional researcher, director*

Muncie
Maine, Kathryn Lew *social studies educator*
Woodward, Lucinda Emily *psychology professor*

New Albany
Crump, Claudia *geographer, educator*

New Haven
Moran, Donna Marie *school psychologist, counselor, educator*

North Judson
Miller, Kimberly M. *social studies educator*

Notre Dame
Hallinan, Maureen Theresa *sociologist, educator*

South Bend
Zegiob-Devereaux, Leslie Elaine *clinical psychologist*

Terre Haute
Anderson, Veanne Nixon *psychology educator, researcher*
Clouse, Bonnidell *psychology educator*

West Lafayette
Jagacinski, Carolyn Mary *psychology professor*

IOWA

Ames
Flora, Cornelia Butler *sociologist, educator*
Roskey, Carol Boyd *social studies educator, dean, director*

Cedar Rapids
Pike, Shirley *school psychologist*

Grinnell
Gibson, Janet Marie *psychology educator*

Iowa City
Lopes, Lola Lynn *psychologist, educator*

Mount Vernon
Astley, Suzette Lynn *psychology educator, researcher*

Oskaloosa
Anderson, Roxanna Marion *psychology professor*

Pella
Baker-Roelofs, Mina Marie *retired home economist, educator*

Sioux City
Hatfield, Susan William *school psychologist*

KANSAS

Bern
Dassel-Stuke, Donna Jane *psychologist, educator*

Emporia
Karr, Sharon Kay *psychology educator*
Mallein, Darla J. *social studies educator*

Kansas City
Baggett, Kathleen M. *psychologist, research scientist*
Carlson-Jukes, Holly Ann *social studies educator*

Oxford
Patterson, Sandra May *school psychologist*

Prairie Village
Lyon, Joanne B. *psychologist*

Shawnee Mission
Gaar, Marilyn Audrey Wiegraffe *political scientist, educator, property manager*

Topeka
Altman, Joanne D. *psychology professor*
Altus, Deborah Elaine *social sciences educator*

Wichita
Hawley, Suzanne *psychologist, researcher*

KENTUCKY

Bowling Green
Merryman-Marr, Melissa Jo *social studies educator*
Onyekwuluje, Anne Bernice *sociology educator*

Covington
Littleton, Nan Elizabeth Feldkamp *psychologist, educator*

Lexington
Marczinski, Cecile Anne *psychologist, researcher*
Shurling, Anne Marlowe *psychology educator, consultant*
Worell, Judith P. *psychologist, educator*

Louisville
Gulati, Geetanjali *psychologist*
Titus, Donna G. *psychologist*

Paducah
Machanic, Mindy Robin *artist, photographer, educator, consultant, writer*

Richmond
Adams, Constance Ewing *school psychologist, art therapist*
Callahan, Connie J. *psychologist, educator*
Mercer, Dorothy L. *psychology educator, consultant*
Pogatshnik, Lee Wolfram *psychologist, educator*

Shelbyville
Scheidt, Rebecca Lynnell *psychologist, educator*

Williamsburg
Weaver, Susan Jeanne *sociology educator*

LOUISIANA

Baton Rouge
Geiselman, Paula Jeanne *psychologist, educator*
Myers, Valerie Harwell *psychologist*
Schechter, Lynn Renee *psychologist*

Bossier City
Paris, Norma Jean *psychologist, educator*

Lafayette
Lynch, Cheryl Stelly *psychology educator*

Mandeville
Dempsey, Margaret Theresa *psychologist*

Metairie
Falco, Maria Josephine *political scientist*

Monroe
Fouts, Elizabeth Browne *psychologist, metals company executive*
Smith, Pamela LaTrice *school psychologist*

New Orleans
Moely, Barbara E. *psychologist, educator*
Tesvich, Lisa Kay *industrial and organizational psychologist*

Shreveport
Street, Jeanne *psychologist*

MAINE

Bath
Galleher, Gay *psychologist*

Belfast
Hughes, Helen Elizabeth *psychologist*

Eliot
Mahar, Carol *psychologist, consultant*

Surry
Pickett, Betty Horenstein *psychologist*

Waterville
Gilkes, Cheryl Louise Townsend *sociologist, educator, minister*

Wells
Lahar, Cindy J. *psychologist, educator*

Winslow
Bourgoin, Mary Beth Nivison *social studies educator*
Gillman, Karen Lee *clinical psychologist*

Yarmouth
McCoy, Carol P. *psychologist, training executive*

MARYLAND

Annapolis
Connolly, Janet Elizabeth *retired sociologist, retired criminal justice educator*

Baltimore
Bright, Margaret *sociologist*
Ensminger, Margaret E. *sociologist, researcher*
Franklin, Paula Anne *artist, writer, psychologist*
Lyles, Barbara Diggs *retired human development educator*
Puglisi, Mary Joanna *psychologist*
Samuelson, Emily Meg *psychologist*
Wasik, Barbara Ann *psychologist, researcher*
Weldon, Linda Jean *psychology educator*

Bethesda
de Vries, Margaret Garritsen *economist*
Haugan, Gertrude M. *clinical psychologist*
Kelty, Miriam Carol *psychologist, health science administrator*
Lystad, Mary Hanemann (Mrs. Robert Lystad) *sociologist, writer*
Ruttenberg, Ruth A. *economist*
Wood, Barbara Louise *psychologist*

Chevy Chase
Norwood, Janet Lippe *economist*

College Park
Gratz, Kim L. *psychologist, researcher*
Hill, Clara Edith *psychologist, educator*
MacKenzie, Doris Layton *psychologist, educator, researcher, criminologist*
Presser, Harriet Betty *social studies educator*
Sorenson, Georgia Lynn Jones *political science professor*

Columbia
Knapp, Patricia Ann *psychologist, educator*

Davidsonville
Blaxall, Martha Ossoff *economist*

Ellicott City
Robison, Susan Miller *psychologist, speaker, consultant*

Gaithersburg
Celotta, Beverly Kay *psychologist*

Ijamsville
Thompson, Jaime Lynn *social studies educator*

Lanham Seabrook
Corrothers, Helen Gladys *criminal justice official*

Lutherville
Smith, Michelle Sun *psychologist*

Lutherville Timonium
Richmond, Lee Joyce *psychologist, educator*

Mitchellville
Grier Wallen, Mary Elizabeth *retired psychologist*

Potomac
Rotberg, Iris Comens *social scientist*
Vadus, Gloria A. *scientific document examiner*

Princess Anne
Brockett, Ramona *criminologist, educator*

Reisterstown
Holley-Allen, Lauren Allana *psychologist*

Rockville
Niewiaroski, Trudi Osmers (Gertrude Niewiaroski) *social studies educator*
Shields, Julie Seligson *psychologist, entrepreneur*

Rosedale
Stearns, Ann Kaiser *psychologist, educator, writer*

Royal Oak
Israel, Lesley Lowe *retired political scientist*

Saint Marys City
Williams, Elizabeth Nutt *psychologist, educator*

Silver Spring
Bate, Marilyn Anne *psychologist*
Mohr, Christina *retired economist*
Moon, Marilyn Lee *economist*
Rayburn, Carole Ann (Mary Aida) *psychologist, researcher, writer, consultant*
Rivera-Sinclair, Elsa *psychologist, consultant, researcher*

Towson
McCartney, Alison Rios Millett *political science professor*
Williams, Tara Lyn *psychologist*

Upper Marlboro
Greene, Monica Lynn Banks *psychologist*

MASSACHUSETTS

Abington
Delaplain, Laura Zuleme *psychologist*

Amherst
Aizen, Rachel K. *clinical psychologist*
Keen, Rachel *psychology professor*
Mac Donald, Marian Louise *psychologist, educator*
Mills, Patricia Jagentowicz *philosophy scholar, educator, writer*
Romney, Patricia Ann *psychologist, educator*
Rossi, Alice S. *sociology educator, writer*
Strickland, Bonnie Ruth *psychologist, educator*

Auburn
Allard, Marvel June *psychology educator, researcher*

Bedford
Ryser, Carol Pierson *psychologist*

Belmont
Levine, Sarah Loewenberg *developmental psychologist, school director*

Boston
Abraham, Melissa E. *psychologist*
Allinson, Deborah Louise *economist*
Dimmitt, Cornelia *psychologist, educator*
Gleason, Jean Berko *psychology professor*
Grossman, Frances Kaplan *psychologist*
Harvey, Virginia Smith *psychologist, educator*
Herzlinger, Regina *economist, educator, writer*
King, Lynda Anne Whitlow *psychologist, educator*
O'Hern, Jane Susan *psychologist, educator*

Braintree
Salloway, Josephine Plovnick *psychologist, educator, marriage and family therapist, mental health counselor*

Bridgewater
Krauss, Jamie Gail *psychologist*
Seide, Janet H. *psychologist*

Brookline
Baumrind, Lydia *psychologist*
Buchin, Jacqueline Chase *psychologist*
Cromwell, Adelaide M. *sociology educator*
Doherty, Patricia McGinn *psychologist*
Goodwin, Rhoda Sherman *psychologist*
Miller, Debra Lynn *political scientist*
Mountford, Alison Leigh *psychologist*

Cambridge
Bailyn, Lotte *psychologist, educator*
Bar-Yam, Miriam *psychologist, consultant, researcher*
Daley, Barbara Sabin *clinical psychologist*
Forbes, Kristin J. *economics professor, former federal official*
Frisch, Rose Epstein *population sciences researcher*
Kellerman, Barbara *political science professor, writer*
Langer, Ellen Jane *psychologist, educator, writer, artist*
Mansbridge, Jane Jebb *political scientist, educator*
Moore, Sally Falk *anthropology educator*
Parlee, Mary Brown *psychology educator*
Power, Samantha J. *public policy educator, writer*
Rosenblum, Nancy Lipton *political science professor*
Toft, Monica Duffy *economics professor*
Waters, Mary Catherine *sociology educator*
Zinberg, Dorothy Shore *sociologist, educator*

Chestnut Hill
Kanin, Doris May *political scientist, consultant*
Munnell, Alicia Haydock *economist*

Dartmouth
Sweeney, Shawna Elizabeth *political science professor, researcher*

Dorchester
Medeiros, Jennifer Lynn *school psychologist, consultant*

Fitchburg
Levine, Sara Pollak *psychology professor*

Framingham
Coiner, Maryrose C. *psychologist*

Lexington
Jordan, Judith Victoria *clinical psychologist, educator*
Levine, Janice R. *clinical psychologist*
Shapiro, Marian Kaplun *psychologist*

Lowell
Galizzi, Monica *economics professor*

Marshfield
Goode, Cynthia A. *social studies educator, secondary school educator*

Medford
Ambady, Nalini *social psychologist, educator, researcher*
Kanarek, Robin Beth *psychology educator, nutrition educator, researcher*

Milton
Raelin, Abby Phyllis *school psychologist*

Needham
Boulding, Elise Marie *sociologist, educator*
Silverstein, Judith Lynn *clinical psychologist*

Newburyport
Keller, Clare Graham Marrow *psychologist*

Newton
Burlage, Dorothy Dawson *clinical psychologist*
Rebelsky, Freda Ethel Gould *psychologist*

Northampton
Dean, Dorothy G. *psychologist, social sciences educator, researcher*

Orleans
Rappaport, Margaret Mary Williams Ewing *psychologist, physician, writer, pilot, consultant*

Plymouth
Lashley, Barbara Theresa *psychologist, educator, mental health counselor*
Leonard-Zabel, Ann Marie T. *psychologist, educator*

Roxbury Crossing
Berger, Ellen Tessman *psychologist*

Sandwich
Podbros, Linda Zoe *neuropsychologist, consultant*

Shrewsbury
Smith, Carolyn J(ane) Hostetter *psychologist, educator*

South Hadley
Tatum, Beverly Daniel *psychology and education educator*

South Natick
Cantor, Pamela Corliss *psychologist*

Springfield
Harnois, Veronica *psychologist, educator*

Truro
Kelley, Maryellen R. *economist, management consultant*

Waban
Javitch, Anki Wolf (Ann Louise Wolf Javitch) *psychologist*

Waltham
Adams, Marilyn Jager *developmental psychologist*
McCulloch, Rachel *economist, educator*
Thorne, Eva Treneice *political science professor*
Unger, Rhoda Kesler *psychology educator*

Watertown
Weingarten, Kaethe *clinical psychologist*

Wellesley
Miller, Linda B. *political scientist*

West Springfield
Anderson, Rita McKenzie *psychologist*
McKenzie-Anderson, Rita Lynn *psychologist*

Westborough
Staffier, Pamela Moorman *psychologist*

Williamstown
Cramer, Phebe *psychologist*

Worcester
Dyer-Cole, Pauline *school psychologist, educator*
Falmagne, Rachel Joffe *psychologist, educator*
Ott, Attiat Farag *economist, educator*
Upshur, Carole Christof *psychologist, educator*

MICHIGAN

Ann Arbor
Agresta, Diane Marie *psychologist*
Apperson, Jean *psychologist*
Arlinghaus, Sandra Judith Lach *mathematical geographer, educator*
Barbour, Carol Goodwin *psychoanalyst*
Dominguez, Kathryn Mary *economist, educator*
Eccles, Jacquelynne S. *psychology educator*
Ellsworth, Phoebe Clemencia *psychology professor*
Kaplan, Rachel *environmental psychologist, educator*
Marcus, Joyce (Joyce Marcus Flannery) *anthropology educator*
Markel, Geraldine *educational psychologist, consultant*
Shatz, Marilyn Joyce *psychologist, educator*
Singer, Eleanor *sociologist, editor*
Waltz, Susan *political scientist, educator*
Warren, Jane Carol *psychologist*
Whitman, Marina Von Neumann *economist, educator*

Auburn Hills
Etefia, Florence Victoria *retired school psychologist*

Berrien Springs
Hamel, Lorie Ann *psychologist*

Beverly Hills
Harms, Deborah Gayle *psychologist*

Canton
Schulz, Karen Alice *psychologist, medical psychotherapist, medical and vocational case manager*

Clifford
Staples, Lynne Livingston Mills *retired psychologist, educator, consultant*

Detroit
Galovich, Beverly Lucille *psychologist*
McCrae, Jocelyn Diane *psychologist*
Morrow, Kathy Ann *psychologist, social worker*

East Lansing
Crewe, Nancy Moe *retired psychologist*
Kalof, Linda Henry *sociologist, educator*
McKinley, Camille Dombrowski *psychologist*

Farmington Hills
Robinson, Amorie Alexia *psychologist, educator*

Grosse Pointe Farms
Kerns, Gertrude Yvonne *psychologist*

Kalamazoo
Buskirk, Phyllis Richardson *retired economist*
Walcott, Delores Deborah *psychologist, educator*

Livonia
Juenemann, Julie Ann *psychologist, educator*

Okemos
Berkman, Claire Fleet *psychologist*

Rochester
Cordes, Mary Kenrick *psychologist, retired*

Saint Clair Shores
Vogel, Sally Thomas *psychologist, social worker, educator*

Southfield
Giles, Lynda Fern *clinical psychologist*
Siegel-Hinson, Robyn Lee *psychologist, consultant, clinic director*
Weiner, Karen Colby (Karen Lynn Colby) *psychologist, lawyer*

Sterling Heights
Forche, Jennifer Roth *clinical psychologist*

Traverse City
Leuenberger, Betty Lou *psychologist, educator*

Wayne
Drake, Patricia Ann Glasscock *psychologist*

Whitmore Lake
White, Susan Rochelle *psychologist, investor*

MINNESOTA

Bloomington
vanReken, Mary K. *psychologist*

Chaska
Affinito, Mona Gustafson *psychologist*

Duluth
Stoddard, Patricia Florence Coulter *retired psychologist*

Eden Prairie
Schaeffer, Brenda Mae *psychologist, author*

Forest Lake
Skrip, Cathy Lee *psychologist*

Inver Grove Heights
Ochman, Janet *psychology professor*

Mankato
Purscell, Helen Duncan *sociologist, educator*

Maple Grove
Ones, Deniz S. *psychologist, educator*

Minneapolis
Bancroft, Ann E. *polar explorer*
Berscheid, Ellen S. *psychology professor, writer, researcher*
Corcoran, Mary Elizabeth *educational psychology professor emeritus*
Dyrud, Grace Beatrice *psychology professor*
Hansen, Jo-Ida Charlotte *psychology professor, researcher*
Horton, Stephanie McNeill *psychologist*
May, Elaine Tyler *social sciences educator, history professor*
Perry, Julia Nichole *psychologist*
Trout, Deborah Lee *clinical psychologist, healthcare executive, consultant, director*
Williams, Carolyn Lillian *psychology educator*

Minnetonka
Hartzler, Belinda Sue *social studies educator*
Thomas, Heidi Janet Krueger *social studies educator*

Morris
Benson, Katherine Alice *psychology educator*

Saint Cloud
Hoffman, Patricia Patrick *retired psychologist*

Saint Louis Park
Mills-Novoa, Beverly A. *psychologist, consultant*

Saint Paul
Barnwell, Adrienne Knox *pediatric psychologist*
Johnson, Badri Nahvi *social studies educator, real estate company officer*
Meissner, Ann Loring *psychologist, educator*

Waconia
Aarsvold-Indrelie, Judith *psychologist*

Winona
Holm, Joy Alice *goldsmith, psychology professor, artist, art educator*

MISSISSIPPI

Brandon
Fargason, Patricia J. *psychologist*

Decatur
Pouncey, Alice Gertrude Moore *psychology professor, educator, home economics professor*

Grenada
Harville, Myra M. *psychologist, educator*

Jackson
Thompson, Judith Geoffriau *psychometrician, consultant*

Meridian
Murphey, Jeannette Windham *psychology professor*

Mississippi State
Henington, Carlen *psychologist, educator*
Wall, Diane Eve *political science professor*

Whitfield
Swann, Melissa Lynne *psychologist*

MISSOURI

Cape Girardeau
Overbey, Gail Ann Urhahn *psychology professor*

Chesterfield
Falk, Barbara Marie *psychologist*

Columbia
Bank, Barbara J. *sociology educator*
McGavock, Brenda Weishaar *clinical psychologist*

Edwards
Findley, Kathryn E.C. *psychologist*

Holden
Wagoner, Deborah Anne *social studies educator*

Kansas City
Nagle, Jean Susan Karabacz *retired sociologist, psychologist*
Nielson, Constance Jo *psychologist, educator*
Wilson, Susan Bernadette *psychologist*

Kirkwood
Pierroutsakos, Sophia L. *psychology professor*

Parkville
Mandernach, Beryl Jean *psychologist, educator*

Richmond
Bartlett, D. Jane *retired psychology educator*

Rock Port
Ross, Becky L *social studies educator*

Saint Louis
Beck, Lois Grant *anthropologist, educator, author*
De Voe, Pamela Ann *anthropologist, educator*
Dick, Danielle Marie *psychology professor, psychiatrist, educator*
Dodd, Kristen L *social studies educator*
Kinney, Nancy Theresa *political science professor*
Loevinger, Jane *psychologist, educator*
Ozawa, Martha Naoko *social work educator*
Shine, Katina Lynniece Wilbon *neuropsychologist, consultant*
Storandt, Martha *psychologist*
Swiener, Rita Rochelle *psychologist, educator*
Telowitz, Marilyn Marie *English and social studies educator*
Todorova-Moreno, Ilina *psychologist, educator*

Sedalia
Frazelle, Rhonda J. *psychology professor, counselor*

Springfield
Branstetter, Ann Dyche *psychology professor*
Corcoran, Deborah B. *geographer, educator*
Gill, Angela Sue *clinical psychologist*
Hart, Nan Susan *counselor*
Hasty, Jennifer Eleanor *anthropologist, educator*

Urbana
Frey, Lucille Pauline *social studies educator, consultant*

MONTANA

Billings
Scott, Linda Preston *psychologist, educator*

Helena
Seiler, Karen Peake *organizational psychologist*

Kalispell
Gallagher-Dalton, Tonya Marie *family support specialist*

Missoula
Ammons, Carol Hamrick *psychologist, editor*
Cummings, Kelli Dawn *psychology professor*
McKeown, Ashley *biological anthropologist, educator*
Wollersheim, Janet Puccinelli *psychology professor*

NEBRASKA

Chadron
Gaudet, Laura Latta *psychologist, educator*

Crete
Conway, Mary Margaret *social studies educator*

Lincoln
Braymen-Lawyer, Rebecca Kay *psychologist*
Sullivan, Mary Ann *retired school psychologist*

Omaha
Jones-Thurman, Rosanna Marie *psychologist*
Kahn, Ronni M. *psychologist*

NEVADA

Ely
Alderman, Minnis Amelia *psychologist, educator, small business owner*

Las Vegas
Cole, Ann Harriet *psychologist, consultant*
Lerman, Hannah *psychologist*
Shelton, Samantha *psychologist*
Shenassa, Cheryl Renée *psychologist, mediator*

Reno
Berger, Laura Patricia *psychologist*
Collier, Helen Vandivort *psychologist*
Leland, Joy Hanson *retired anthropologist, researcher*

NEW HAMPSHIRE

Alton
Corriveau, Heather M., II, *social studies educator*

Bedford
Collins, Diana Josephine *psychologist*

Exeter
Schubart, Caren Nelson *psychologist*

Greenfield
Lewicke, Bette *psychologist, writer*

Henniker
Braiterman, Thea Gilda *economics professor, state legislator*

Lebanon
Emery, Virginia Olga Beattie *psychologist, researcher*

Rochester
Hegger, Samantha Lynn *social studies educator*

NEW JERSEY

Allenwood
Carbone, Diane M. *psychologist, consultant*

Bergenfield
Aguado, Sandra *social studies educator*

Berkeley Heights
Hansburg, Freda B. *psychologist, mental health consultant*

Califon
Jeffers, Victoria Wilkinson *psychologist*

Deptford
Kelly, Barbara Sue *psychologist*

Englewood
Choi, Namhong Lee *retired psychologist*

Englewood Cliffs
Farrell, Patricia Ann *psychologist, educator, writer*

Ewing
Kirnan, Jean Powell *psychology educator*

Florham Park
Brodkin, Adele Ruth Meyer *psychologist*

Gillette
Pfafflin, Sheila Murphy *psychologist*

Hamburg
Hagin, Rosa A. *psychologist, educator*

Holmdel
Zupkus, Ellen Ciccone *clinical psychologist, consultant*

Jersey City
Urso, Ida *psychologist*

Lakewood
Katz, Sally Norma *psychologist*

Lawrenceville
Stein, Sandra Lou *educational psychology professor*

Linwood
Cohen, Diana Louise *psychologist, educator, consultant*

Morristown
Thomas, Nina K. *psychologist*

Mount Laurel
Giampetro, Kathleen A. *school psychologist*

Mountain Lakes
Loomis, Rebecca C. *psychologist*

New Brunswick
Clauss-Ehlers, Caroline S. *psychologist, educator, journalist*
Russell, Louise Bennett *economist, educator*

Newark
Adler, Freda Schaffer (Mrs. G. O. W. Mueller) *criminologist, educator*
Hiltz, Starr Roxanne *sociologist, educator, writer, consultant, computer scientist*

Newfoundland
Vandenburg, Mary Lou *psychologist*

Paramus
Hochberg, Lois J. *school psychologist*
Perkins-Munn, Tiffany Sabrena *psychologist, researcher*

Parsippany
Anselmi, Elvira *psychologist, researcher*

Piscataway
Gelman, Rochel *psychology professor*
Goss, Mary E. Weber *sociology educator*
McCrady, Barbara Sachs *psychologist, educator*

Princeton
Bogan, Elizabeth Chapin *economist, educator*
Browning, Charlotte Elisabeth *social studies educator*
Christian, Carole Ann *psychologist, academic administrator*
DeKlyen, Michelle *psychologist*
Girgus, Joan Stern *psychologist, educator, director*
Keller, Suzanne *sociologist, psychotherapist*
Neimark, Edith Deborah *psychologist, educator*
Tienda, Marta *demographer, educator*

Randolph
Goldman, Phyllis E. *psychology educator*

Red Bank
McWhinney, Madeline H. (Mrs. John Denny Dale) *economist, director*

Ridgefield Park
Magdosko, Paula *school psychologist*

Ridgewood
Le May, Moira Kathleen *retired psychology educator*

Roselle
Tanner-Oliphant, Karen M. *family and consumer science educator*

Rutherford
Dahse, Linda Jewell *social studies educator*

Saddle River
Lasser, Gail Maria *psychologist, educator*

Somerset
Selkow, Paula *psychologist*

South Orange
Steiner, Gloria Litwin *psychologist*

Springfield
O'Desky, Ilyse Hope *psychologist, educator*

Summit
Dorlen, Rosalind *clinical psychologist, psychoanalyst, medical researcher, educator*
Hall, Pamela Elizabeth *psychologist*
Lovett, Juanita Pelletier *clinical psychologist*

Teaneck
Brudner, Helen Gross *social sciences educator*

Tenafly
Blank, Marion Sue *psychologist, educator*

Tinton Falls
Butler, Nancy Taylor *gender equity specialist, religious program administrator*
Day, Mary Carol *human factors psychologist*

Toms River
Serrao, Susan *social studies educator*

Towaco
Olimpio, Suzanne M. *psychologist*

Union
Norward, Josephine Norma *social work educator, consultant*

Warren
Feldman, Janie Lynn *psychologist*

NEW MEXICO

Albuquerque
Condie, Carol Joy *anthropologist, science administrator*
Grossetete, Ginger Lee *retired gerontology administrator, consultant*
Owens, Georgia Katherine *social sciences educator, consultant*
Williams, Enid Roberta (Enid W. Troll) *psychologist, nurse*

Carlsbad
Tackitt, Karen Ann *social sciences educator*

El Prado
Reading, Margery Schrock *psychology professor, artist*

Los Alamos
Thompson, Lois Jean Heidke Ore *psychologist*

Placitas
Frantzve, Jerri Lyn *psychologist, educator, consultant*

Roswell
Daugherty, Lynn Bayliss *psychologist, consultant*

Santa Fe
Perry, Elisabeth Scherf *psychologist*

Silver City
Gilbert, Kathie Simon *economist, educator*
Lopez, Linda Carol *social sciences educator*

NEW YORK

Albany
Capaldi, Elizabeth Ann Deutsch *psychological sciences professor*
McCarthy, Denise Eileen *clinical psychologist*
Pezzulo, Jacqueline *psychologist, researcher*

Baldwin
Johnston, Kimberly Anne *social studies educator*

Bay Shore
Murphy, Kelly Ann *psychologist*

Bellmore
Dacek, Joanne Carole *psychologist*

Bellport
Moeller, Mary Ella *retired home economist, retired educator, radio personality*

Brentwood
Liebert, Lynn Langenbach *psychologist, educator*

Bridgehampton
Kothera, Lynne Maxine *psychologist*

Brockport
Anselm, Cherie Ann *social sciences educator*

Bronx
Durglishvili, Nana Z. *psychologist, language educator*
Macklin, Ruth *bioethics educator*
Muller, Katherine Lynn *clinical psychologist*
Procidano, Mary Elizabeth *psychologist, educator*
Yorburg, Betty (Mrs. Leon Yorburg) *sociology educator*

Bronxville
Doyle, Charlotte Lackner (Mrs. James J. Doyle) *psychology educator, writer*

Brooklyn
Pines, Beverly Irene *retired clinical psychologist*
Reinisch, June Machover *psychologist, educator*
Rothenberg, Mira Kowarski *clinical psychologist, psychotherapist*
Sesin, Maria Carmen *psychologist, researcher*
Somers, Marion *gerontologist, family therapist*
Thacher, Barbara Burrall *psychologist, educator*
Weinstein, Marie Pastore *psychologist*
Weinstock, Deborah *psychologist*

Buffalo
Friedman, Gloria Landsman (Mrs. Daniel A. Roblin Jr.) *psychologist, educator*
Hulicka, Irene M. *psychologist, educator*
Marinaccio, Bridget C. *social sciences educator*
O'Quin, Karen *psychology professor, dean*

Canandaigua
Ristuccia, Lavern K. Cole *psychologist, consultant*

Canton
Auster, Nancy Eileen Ross *economics professor*

Carmel
Huckabee, Carol Brooks *psychologist*

Commack
Nilson, Patricia *clinical psychologist*

Cortland
McGuire, Mary Patricia *political science professor*

Cortlandt Manor
Lupiani, Jennifer Lynne *school psychologist*

Dobbs Ferry
Kraetzer, Mary C. *sociologist, educator, consultant*

Eastchester
Caine, Edye *social studies educator*

Fishkill
Stein, Paula Nancy *psychologist, educator*

Flushing
Jones, Tina Moreau *psychology educator*
Reuder, Mary E(ileen) *retired psychology professor, retired statistician*

Franklin Square
Bergen, Jeannine Evelyn *psychologist*

Fredonia
Kenney, Dolores Theresa *home economist*
Marshall, Jill Galley *social studies educator*

Freeport
Ferentino, Sheila Connolly *psychologist, consultant*

Garden City
Cashin, Maura Dennehy *psychologist, music educator*
Steil, Janice M. *social psychology educator*

Glen Head
Heath-Psyd, Pamela B. Wasserman *psychologist*

Glen Oaks
Smith, Heather Lee *psychologist*

Great Neck
Aronson, Margaret Rupp *school psychologist*
Natalucci-Hall, Carla *psychologist*
Soleymani, Nancy *psychologist, researcher*

Harrison
Krigsman, Naomi *psychologist, consultant, photographer*

Hempstead
Bose, Meena *political science professor*

Hopewell Junction
Lemy, Marie Edith *psychologist, educator*

Huntington
Kanner, Ellen Barbara *clinical psychologist*

Ithaca
Adkins-Regan, Elizabeth Kocher *biological psychology educator*
Assie-Lumumba, N'Dri T. *Africana studies educator*
Beneria, Lourdes *economist, educator*
Blau, Francine Dee *economics professor*
Mueller, Betty Jeanne *social work educator*
Pelto, Gretel H. *nutritional anthropologist, educator*
Starer, Ruana Maxine *freelance/self-employed psychologist*

Jamaica
Wick, Erika Elisabeth *psychologist, educator, researcher*
Zak, Dorothy Zerykier *psychologist*

Kingston
Dougherty, Andrea M. *social studies educator*

Lewiston
Preston, Joan Muriel *psychology professor, communications educator*

Lindenhurst
Kaufman, Susan Shiffman *psychologist*

Liverpool
Brooks, Janet Pfohl *social studies educator, department chairman*

Manhasset
Pitta, Patricia Joyce *psychologist*
Savage, Clare Leavy *school psychologist*

Montrose
Guadagno, Christine Ellen *social studies educator*

Nesconset
Burns-Riviello, Michaela Aileen *social studies educator*

New Paltz
Freeman, Phyllis Risë *psychology educator*

New Rochelle
Grimes, Tresmaine Judith Rubain *psychology educator*
Rutstein, Eleanor H. *psychologist*

New York
Aiello, Theresa *social sciences educator*
Andersen, Marianne Singer *psychologist*
Andersen, Susan Marie *psychologist, educator, director*
Bachant, Janet Lee *psychologist*
Bardach, Joan Lucile *clinical psychologist*
Barrish, Carol Lampert *psychologist*
Baten, Amanda Zoe *psychologist*
Baumrind, Rosalyn Muriel Greenwald *psychologist*
Bird, Sharlene *psychologist*
Bowers, Patricia Eleanor Fritz *economist*
Browne, Joy *psychologist, radio personality*
Brunswick, Ann Finkenberg *social psychologist, health researcher*
Buck, Louise Zierdt *psychologist*
Case, Nan Barkin *psychologist*
Castro, Rosa *drug counselor*
Chamson, Sandra Potkorony *psychologist*
Chelstrom, Marilyn Ann *political science educator, consultant*
Clamar, Aphrodite J. *psychologist*
Cohen, Lisa Janet *psychologist, educator*
Denmark, Florence Harriet Levin *psychology professor*
Difede, JoAnn *psychologist*
Doyle, Kristene Anne *psychologist, educator*
Drago-Severson, Eleanor Elizabeth E. *developmental psychologist, educator, researcher*
Elto, Erin K. *psychologist*
Epstein, Cynthia Fuchs *sociology educator, writer*
Fischbach, Ruth Linda *ethics educator, social scientist, researcher*
Fodor, Iris Elaine *clinical psychologist, educator, psychotherapist*
Fosler, Gail D. *economist*
Frost, Ellen Elizabeth *psychologist*
Geller, Ethell A. *consulting clinical psychologist*
Gerber, Gwendolyn Loretta *psychologist, educator*
Gilligan, Carol *psychologist, writer*
Greene Oster, Selmaree *medical anthropologist, researcher*
Grody, Deborah *psychologist, director*
Habachy, Suzan Salwa Saba *economist, not-for-profit developer*
Hamilton, Linda Helen *psychologist*
Heyde, Martha Bennett *psychologist*
Hill, Marjorie Jean *psychologist, association executive*
Hunter, Patricia O. *psychologist*
Jasso, Guillermina *sociologist, educator*
Jonas, Ruth Haber *psychologist*
Kavaler-Adler, Susan *clinical psychologist, psychoanalyst*
Kouffman, Paulette *psychologist*
Krawitz, Rhoda Nayor *clinical psychologist, psychoanalyst*
Kurzweil, Edith *social sciences educator, editor*
Laughlin, Linda R. *psychoanalyst, psychotherapist*
Lerner, Harriet Goldhor *psychologist, writer*
Magee-Egan, Pauline Cecilia *psychology professor, management educator*
Maldonado-Bear, Rita Marinita *economist, educator*
Marks, Lillian Shapiro *retired secretarial studies educator, writer, editor*
Marshall, Simone Verniere *psychologist, psychoanalyst*
Mechaneck, Ruth Sara *clinical psychologist*
Meed, Rita Goldwasser *clinical psychologist*
Miller, Lisa Friedman *psychology educator*
Miller, Ruby Sills *retired gerontologist*
Nakhle, Djenane *psychologist*
O'Neill, June Ellenoff *economist*
Oppenheim, Sara E. *psychologist*
Panken, Shirley *psychologist*
Pappas, Eva *psychologist, psychoanalyst*
Park, Cynthia *sociology educator, consultant*
Persell, Caroline Hodges *sociologist, educator, author, researcher, consultant*
Piven, Frances Fox *political scientist, educator*
Potash, Marlin Sue *psychologist, educator*
Ravdin, Lisa Dawn *neuropsychologist*
Richman, Sophia *psychologist*
Robbins, Lillian Cukier *psychology educator*
Rosman, Paula *anthropologist, educator*
Rothman, Barbara Katz *sociology educator*
Sandy, Sandra V. *psychologist*
Sang, Barbara Ellen *psychologist*
Schwartz, Anna Jacobson *economist*
Scott, Nancy Ellen *psychologist*
Shamberg, Barbara A(nn) *psychologist*
Shapiro, Sandra M. *psychologist, psychoanalyst, educator*
Sheldon, Eleanor Harriet Bernert *sociologist, writer*
Shell, (Peterson) Juanita *psychologist, educator*
Silvestri, Heather L. *psychologist*
Simon, Jacqueline Albert *political scientist, writer*
Solanto, Mary Victoria *psychologist*
Tallmer, Margot Sallop *psychologist, gerontologist, psychoanalyst*
Terris, Lillian Dick *psychologist, health facility administrator*
Tuccillo, Elaine *psychologist, educator*
Wade, Estelle B. *psychologist, psychoanalyst*
Weisberg-Samuels, Janet S. *psychologist*
Welkowitz, Joan *psychology educator*
Westheimer, Ruth Siegel (Karola Westheimer) *psychologist, television personality*
Zunino, Natalia *psychologist*

Newburgh
Fallon, Rae Mary *psychology professor, educational consultant*

Northport
Donenfeld, Sharon Etta *psychologist*

Oneonta
Holleran, Paula Rizzo *psychology and counseling educator, researcher, consultant*

Orchard Park
Orser, Janet Christine *psychologist*

Oyster Bay
Landrón, Ana *school psychologist*

Palisades
Balstad, Roberta *social scientist*

Pleasant Valley
Marshall, Natalie Junemann *economics professor*

Purchase
Newton, Esther Mary *anthropologist, educator*

Riverdale
Dytell, Rita Scher *health psychology educator, researcher, administra*

Rochester
Berger, Audrey Marilyn *psychologist*
Buckingham, Barbara Rae *social studies educator*
Freeman, Leslie Jean *neuropsychologist, researcher*
McDaniel, Susan Holmes *psychologist*
Newport, Elissa L. *psychology professor*

Roslyn Heights
Schwartzberg, Neala Spiegel *psychologist, writer*

Rye
Buchsbaum, Betty Cynthia *clinical psychologist*

Saratoga Springs
Miller, Anita Diane *psychologist*

Scarsdale
Wolfzahn, Annabelle Forsmith *psychologist*

Shoreham
Fontana, Barbara *psychologist*

Staten Island
Lewis, Carla Susan *psychology educator*

Stony Brook
Squires, Nancy *psychology professor*
Stone, Elizabeth Cecilia *anthropology educator*
Tanur, Judith Mark *sociologist, educator*

Syracuse
Fiske, Sandra Rappaport *psychologist, educator*
Smith, Corinne Roth *psychologist*
Wadley, Susan Snow *anthropologist*

Wilkinson, Louise Cherry *psychology professor, dean*

Tarrytown
Tower, Roni Beth *psychologist*

Tonawanda
Cavanaugh, Maxine Cornell *clinical psychologist*

Valhalla
Dornbush, Rhea L. *psychologist, educator*
Urban, Diane *psychologist, educator*

Valley Stream
Margolies, Allison *clinical psychologist*

Wappingers Falls
Sucich, Diana Catherine *retired marriage, family, and child psychologist, counselor*

West Babylon
Prohaske, Donna D. *social studies educator, department chairman*

West Brentwood
Gazdag, Gail Elizabeth *psychology associate*

Woodbury
Maltin, Marjorie Solomon *psychologist, psychoanalyst*

Woodstock
Lieberman, Josefa Nina *psychologist, educator, writer*

NORTH CAROLINA

Andrews
Marta, Dawn Reneé *psychologist*

Boiling Springs
Wright, Bonnie McLean *psychology educator*

Boone
Miller, Geraldine Alice *psychologist, educator*

Chapel Hill
Bayen, Ute Johanna *psychology professor, researcher*
Campbell, Frances Alexander *psychologist*
Gil, Karen M. *psychology professor*
Gray, Virginia Hickman *political science professor*
Gray-Little, Bernadette *psychologist, educator*
Vachudova, Milada Anna *political science professor*
Wasik, Barbara Hanna *psychologist, educator*

Charlotte
Brazeal, Donna Smith *psychologist*
Fretwell, Dorrie Shearer *retired psychologist*
Goolkasian, Paula A. *psychologist, educator*
Gross, Patricia Louise *neuropsychologist*
Hicks-Ray, Denyse *psychologist, commentator*
Vazquez Rivera, Ornela Amliv *psychologist*

Durham
McClain, Paula Denice *political scientist, educator*
Schiffman, Susan Stolte *medical psychologist, educator*
Stevens, Jane Sexton *psychologist*

Elon
Wilmshurst, Linda Anne *psychologist, writer*

Greensboro
Chandler, Austin Grace *psychologist*
Gill, Diane Louise *psychology professor, dean*
Helms-VanStone, Mary Wallace *anthropology educator*
Smith, Rebecca McCulloch *social sciences educator*
Tinsley, Karen Mccoy *psychology professor*

Greenville
Bjorkman, Sylvia Johnson *psychologist*

Kernersville
McGuire, Andrea Bullard *social studies educator*

Laurinburg
Hamby, Sherry Lynne *psychologist, researcher*

Pilot Mountain
Sawyers, Lorrie Brown *social studies educator*

Raleigh
Brooks, Jackie Daniel *social studies educator*
Fantz, Janet Nelsen *school psychologist*
Goldwasser, Shirley Whiteman *educational psychologist*
Hiday, Virginia Aldigé *sociologist, educator*
Johnson, Melissa Ramirez *psychologist*
Lamarque, Natalie Ghisslaine *psychologist*
Occhetti, Dianne *psychologist, writer*

Research Triangle Park
Karg, Rhonda Suzanne *psychologist, researcher*

Sanford
Lloyd, Jennifer Leigh *psychology professor*

Shallotte
Weaver, Lyn Ann Simmons *psychologist*

Wilmington
Bomhan, Ruth Walker *social studies educator*
Foglia, Michelle Lynn *psychologist*

NORTH DAKOTA

Grand Forks
Hume, Wendelin M. *criminologist, educator*
Mikulak, Marcia Lee *anthropologist, educator*
Tiemann, Kathleen Anne *sociologist, educator*

Minot
Olson, Deborah J. *psychologist, educator*

Ray
Anderson, Denise W. *psychologist, writer, musician*

Williston
Long, Amelia Rose *psychologist*

OHIO

Akron
Franck, Ardath Amond *psychologist, educator*
Garbrandt, Gail Elaine *political science professor, consultant*
Smith, Priscilla R. *social sciences educator*
Subich, Linda Mezydlo *counseling psychology educator*

Ashland
Ford, Lucille Garber *economist, educator*

Athens
Heaton, Jeanne Albronda *psychologist*

Bowling Green
Krane, Vikki *psychology educator*
Krebs, Marjori Maddox *social studies educator, consultant*

Brunswick
Harr, Gale Ann *school psychologist*

Canton
Lowery-O'Connell, Susan Ellen *psychologist*

Centerville
Kauffold, Ruth Elizabeth *psychologist*

Chillicothe
Matyi, Cindy Lou *psychology professor, consultant*

Cincinnati
Ashley, Lynn *social sciences educator, consultant*
Bluestein, Venus Weller *retired psychologist, educator*
Burklow, Kathleen Ann *psychologist*
Dember, Cynthia Fox *retired clinical psychologist*
Repka, Fran Ann, Sr. *psychologist*

Circleville
Southward, Patricia Ann *school psychologist*

Cleveland
Beall, Cynthia *anthropologist, educator*

Cleveland Heights
Hefter, Shoshana *psychologist*

Columbus
Bradley, Betty Hunt *psychologist, consultant*
Brewer, Marilynn B. *psychology professor*
Everhart, Velma Vizedom *retired home economics educator, retired real estate agent*
Green, Lennis Harris *psychologist*
Huber, Joan Althaus *sociology educator*
Johnson, Martha (Marty) Junk (Marty Johnson) *psychology professor*
Kiecolt-Glaser, Janice Kay *psychologist*
Peterson, Ruth D. *sociologist*

Cuyahoga Falls
Bultrowicz, Tara Lynn *school psychologist*

Dayton
Calhoun, Gloria Lynn *experimental psychologist*
Sowald, Debra Kay *psychologist*

Gambier
Payne, Tabitha Wynn *psychologist, educator, researcher*

Gates Mills
Fesler, Elizabeth *educator, psychologist*

Granville
Buker, Eloise Ann *political science educator*
Hutson-Comeaux, Sarah Louise *psychology professor, department chairman*
Knox, Trudy *publisher, consultant, retired psychologist*

Huron
Strong, Kay Elaine *economics professor*

Kent
Khol, Charel L. *psychologist*

Lima
Bonifas, Jane Marie *psychologist*

Lorain
Giannuzzi, Judy L. *psychologist*

Lyndhurst
Dellas, Marie C. *retired psychology educator, consultant*

Medina
Doyle, Heather Sue *psychologist*
Moll, Sara H. *psychologist, volunteer*

Middletown
Gilmore, June Ellen *psychologist*

North Olmsted
Rimm, Sylvia Barkan *psychologist, media personality educator*

Novelty
Cutujian, Paulette Sue *school psychologist*

Pepper Pike
Seaton, Jean Robarts *psychology educator*

Sandusky
Yunghans, Eleanor Janice *social studies educator*

Toledo
Heintz, Carolinea Cabaniss *retired home economist, retired educator*
Mihura, Joni Lynn *psychologist, educator*

Warren
Ross, Karen Lee Hromyak *retired school psychologist*

Wooster
McClure, Carolyn F. *psychologist*

Youngstown
Thomas, Julie Elizabeth *clinical psychologist, educator*

OKLAHOMA

Broken Arrow
Biggs, Ruth Ann *social studies educator*

Edmond
Dedmon, Angela Marie Maxine *psychologist*
Necco, Edna Joanne *school psychologist*

Norman
Affleck, Marilyn *retired sociology educator*

Oklahoma City
Allbright, Karan Elizabeth *psychologist, consultant*

Woodward
Fisher, Deena Kaye *social studies education administrator*

Wynnewood
Watrous, Naoma Dickson *retired clinical psychologist*

OREGON

Canby
Walsh, Erin Kathleen *social studies educator*

Corvallis
Aldwin, Carolyn Magdalen *behavioral science educator*

Eugene
Beickel, Sharon Lynne *psychologist*
Freyd, Jennifer Joy *psychology professor*
Hunt, Elizabeth Hope *psychologist*
Peterson, Donna Rae *gerontologist*
Porter, Catherine (Kay Porter) *therapist, business consultant*
Taylor, Marjorie *psychology professor*

Gresham
Davidson, Joan Elizabeth Gather *psychologist*

La Grande
Thompson, Joan (Jo) *anthropologist*

Lake Oswego
Finley, Patricia Ann *psychologist, artist*

Newberg
Gathercoal, Kathleen Kleiner *psychology educator*
Warford, Patricia *psychologist*

Oregon City
White, Deborah Lee *psychologist*

Portland
Kelly, Carol Rowden *psychologist*
Matarazzo, Ruth Gadbois *retired psychologist, educator*
Mersereau, Susan S. *clinical psychologist*

Roseburg
Young, Susan Mark *psychologist*

Salem
Warnath, Maxine Ammer *psychologist, arbitrator*

PENNSYLVANIA

Allentown
Panfile, Patricia McCloskey *psychologist*

Bloomsburg
Holloway, Sybil Lymorise *psychologist, writer*

Bryn Mawr
Porter, Judith Deborah Revitch *sociologist*

Canonsburg
McMaster, Janet Lynn *psychologist*

Coraopolis
Stage, Ginger Rooks *psychologist*

Doylestown
Dimond, Roberta Ralston *psychology and sociology educator*

East Stroudsburg
Hodge, Donna Lynn *psychologist, educator*

Erie
Pawlowski, Janet M. *psychologist*

Friendsville
Bjick, Suzanne Carter *psychologist*

Gettysburg
Schein, Virginia Ellen *psychologist, editor*

Glenside
Jones, Elaine F. *psychologist, educator*
Miserandino, Marianne *psychology educator*

Greensburg
Conlin, Kathryn Marie *social studies educator*

Gwynedd
LeFevre, Carol Baumann *psychologist, educator*

Haverford
Henle, Mary *retired psychology educator*
Widseth, Jane Christina *psychologist, psychotherapist*

Hershey
Butterfield, Andrea Christine *psychology educator, educational association administrator*

Indiana
Mabry, J. Beth *sociologist, educator*
Reynolds, Virginia Edith *sociologist, anthropologist, educator, artist*

Jenkintown
Goldman, Janice Goldin *psychologist, educator*
Hankin, Elaine Krieger *psychologist, researcher*

Kennett Square
Smith, Virginia Eleanore *psychologist, educator*

Lafayette Hill
Klein, Carol Lynne *psychologist*

Lancaster
Kay, Margaret J. *psychologist*

Langhorne
Dorfman, Lorraine M. *clinical psychologist, consultant*

Lewisburg
Morin, Karen M. *geographer, educator*

Malvern
Gillespie, Mary Krempa *psychologist, consultant*
Hochberg, Marcia Gail *psychologist*

Mc Murray
Cmar, Janice Butko *home economist, educator*

Mifflintown
Sieber, Angela R. *social studies educator*

New Alexandria
Sehring, Hope Hutchison *library science educator*

Philadelphia
Bailey, Elizabeth Ellery *economics professor*
Chambless, Dianne L. *psychology professor*
Chapman, Judith Griffin *psychologist, educator, academic administrator*
Coché, Judith *psychologist, educator*
Coons, Helen L. *clinical psychologist*
Cunningham, Jacqueline Lemmé *psychologist, educator, researcher*
Dean-Zubritsky, Cynthia Marian *psychologist, researcher*
Dennehy, Mary Nora *psychologist*
Fox, Renée Claire *sociology educator*
Frankel, Francine Ruth *political science professor*
Gershenfeld, Matti Kibrick *psychologist*
Jemmott, Loretta Sweet *HIV/AIDS researcher, nursing educator*
Kane, Pamela *psychologist*
Lydick, Nancy M. *psychologist*
Meredith, Lisa Ann Marie *social studies educator, consultant*
Miller, Arlyn Hochberg *psychologist*
Newcombe, Nora *psychology professor*
Okoniewski, Lisa Anne *psychologist*
Orne, Emily Carota *psychologist, researcher*
Orr, Nancy A. *educational psychologist*
Rima, Ingrid Hahne *economics professor*
Shure, Myrna Beth *psychologist, educator*
Thomas, Janet Y. *political science professor, researcher*
Zubernis, Lynn Smith *psychologist, counselor*

Phoenixville
Smith-McLaughlin, Amy Elizabeth *psychologist*

Pittsburgh
Barack, Robin Sheffman *psychologist*
Cunningham, Karla *political scientist, researcher*
Curry, Nancy Ellen *psychologist, psychoanalyst, educator*
Donini, Dina A. *social studies educator*
Keairns, Yvonne Ewing *psychologist*
Lave, Judith Rice *economics professor*
Schorr-Ribera, Hilda Keren *psychologist*
Sikora, Gloria Jean *social studies educator, department chairman*
Strick, Sadie Elaine *psychologist*
Work, Jane Allen *psychologist*

Radnor
Sicoli, Mary Louise Corbin *psychologist, educator*

Royersford
Krell-Morris, Cheri Lee *psychologist*

State College
Isenberg, Ann Marie *psychologist*
Kirchner, Elizabeth Parsons *clinical psychologist*

Swarthmore
Berger, Dianne Gwynne *family life educator, consultant*
Keith, Jennie *anthropology educator, academic administrator, writer*
Marecek, Jeanne *psychologist, educator*

Throop
Kozloski, Lisa Marie *psychologist, director*

Titusville
Altomare, Erica Von Scheven *psychologist*

University Park
Conway, Anne Marie *psychologist, social worker*

Warrington
Pfeffer, Judith Stadlen *psychologist, consultant*

Weatherly
Moore, Cathleen Turner *retired psychology professor*

West Grove
Loveland, Christine Frances *psychologist*

Wilkes Barre
Baloga, Lucille Wujcik *psychologist*

Wyomissing
Genieser-DeRosa, Anya *psychologist*

York
Bitzer, Joan Louise *psychologist*

RHODE ISLAND

Kingston
Newman, Barbara Miller *psychologist, educator*

Newport
Wachs, Caryn Lee *psychologist, researcher*

Portsmouth
Dennis, Lorraine Bradt *psychology educator*

Providence
Azarian, Anait *psychologist, researcher*
Goldscheider, Frances K. *sociologist, educator*
Goulder, Caroljean Hempstead *retired psychologist, consultant*
Wetle, Terrie Fox *gerontologist, educator, dean*

Smithfield
Morahan-Martin, Janet May *psychologist, educator*

Warwick
DeCollibus, Paula (DiLuglio) *psychologist*

SOUTH CAROLINA

Ballentine
Bayless, Alice Paige *psychologist*

Boiling Springs
Rucker, Margaret Rickenbacker *psychologist, special education educator*

Chapin
Freitag, Carol Wilma *political scientist*

Charleston
Doughty, Shannon Sue *behavior analyst*
Libet, Alice Quante *clinical psychologist*
Lovinger, Sophie Lehner *child psychologist*
Swickert, Rhonda J. *psychology professor*

Columbia
Della, Teresa Brisbon *social studies educator*
Glad, Betty *political scientist, educator*
Logan, Sandra Jean *retired economics professor, retired business educator*
Manning, Sandra Chapman *psychologist, consultant*
Shea, Mary Elizabeth Craig *psychologist, educator*
Wandersman, Lois Pall *psychologist*

Greenville
Harris-Lewis, Tamela Suzette *social studies educator, tax specialist*
Westrope, Martha Randolph *psychologist, consultant*

Hartsville
McClerklin-Motley, Shirley *social sciences educator*

Moore
Darby, Shannon Smith *social studies educator*

Orangeburg
Shuler, Caroletta Alexis *psychologist, educator*

Rock Hill
Kedrowski, Karen Marie *political science professor*
Manetta, Ameda Avrill *social sciences educator*

Spartanburg
Baker, Susan Himber *school psychologist*
Newman, Barbara Tate *retired social studies educator*

Williamston
Hawkins-Sneed, Janet Lynn *school psychologist, human resources administrator, small business owner*

York
Jonas, Cynthia *social studies educator*

SOUTH DAKOTA

Madison
Johnson, Viki *sociology professor*

Rapid City
Kennedy, Judith Mary *school psychologist*

Redfield
Schoen, Jill F. *psychologist, educator*

Sioux Falls
Kuntz, Carol B. *psychologist, educator, marriage and family therapist*

TENNESSEE

Cookeville
Asanbe, Comfort Bola *psychologist, educator*

Gleason
Freeman, Stacie Drerup *sociologist, educator*

Johnson City
Zimmern-Reed, Annette Wacks *psychologist*

Kingsport
Abbott, Verna Ruth *social studies educator*

Knoxville
Bateman, Veda Mae *industrial psychologist, management consultant*
Harper, Janice *anthropologist, educator*
Harris, Diana Koffman *sociologist, educator*
Infante, Isa Maria *political scientist, educator, lawyer, writer*
Pulsipher, Lydia Mihelic *geographer, educator*
Rocha, Cynthia J. *social sciences educator, consultant*
Wilson, K. Shannon *psychologist*

Memphis
Geter, Jennifer L. *psychologist*

Nashville
Ascencao, Erlete Malveira *psychologist, educator*
Blair, Margaret Mendenhall *economist, consultant, law educator*
Morton-Young, Tommie *psychology professor, writer*

Oak Ridge
Wurth, Patsy Ann *geographic information systems specialist*

TEXAS

Abilene
Bertrand, Tina Louise *political science professor*
Crowell, Sherry Diegel *psychologist*

Arlington
Buckner, Joyce *psychologist, educator*

Austin
Allen, Barbara Rothschild *retired psychology professor*
Bost, Jane Morgan *psychologist*
Brinkley, Edna *psychologist, consultant*
Ehrenberg, Sara Jean *psychologist*
Eldridge, Linda *psychologist*
Johnson, Jo-Ann Hunter *psychologist*
Lowry, Alaire Howard *psychologist*
MacLachlan, Patricia Lynn *political science professor*
Rostow, Elspeth Davies *political science professor*
Walter, Virginia Lee *psychologist, educator*

Bedford
Deal, Marci Smith *social studies educator, consultant*

Big Spring
Edgemon, Connie Kay *director, information management, hospital administrator*

Brenham
Spears, Julia Buckner *psychologist*

Bryan
Kimbrough, Frances Harriett *psychologist*

Canyon
Bigham, Marsha Ellis *social studies educator, department chairman*
Parker, Mary E. *educational psychology educator*

Cedar Park
Nader, Kathleen Olympia *psychotherapist, consultant in childhood trauma*

College Station
Ory, Marcia Gail *social science researcher*

Dallas
Betts, Dianne Connally *economist, educator*
Castillo, Christine Lynn *pediatric neuropsychologist*
Free, Mary Moore *biological and medical anthropologist*
Gibby, Mabel Enid Kunce *psychologist*
Johnson, Berit Bailey *psychologist, consultant*
Oualline, Viola Jackson *psychologist, consultant*
Patterson, Carole A. *psychologist, educator*
Stearns, Linda Brewster *sociologist, educator*
Williams, Martha Spring *psychologist*

Denison
Arthur, Susan Helene *social studies educator*

Denton
Cogan, Karen Diane *psychologist educator*

El Paso
Morales, Maria Cristina *social sciences educator*

Fort Worth
Colaluca, Beth *pediatric neurpsychologist*
Dees, Sandra Kay Martin *psychologist, research scientist*
Strother McKeown, Dora Dougherty *retired aviation psychologist, pilot*

Friendswood
Sutter, Emily May Geeseman *retired psychologist, educator*

Galveston
Rosenthal, Susan Leslie *psychologist*

Hereford
Stewart, Tracy Flood *social studies educator*

Houston
Black, Donna Lord *psychologist*
Burks, Robin J. *psychologist*
Condit, Linda Faulkner *retired economist*
Demouy, Alyson M. *social studies educator*
Dybell, Elizabeth Anne Sledden *psychologist*
Feigin, Judith Zobel *educational psychologist*
Gibson, Kathleen Rita *anatomy and anthropology educator*
Greco, Janice Teresa *psychology educator*
Grossett, Deborah Lou *psychologist, consultant*
Haensly, Patricia Anastacia *psychology professor*
Landers, Susan Mae *psychotherapist, professional counselor*
McMahon, Susanna Rosemary *clinical psychologist, author*
Miller, Janel Howell *psychologist*
Rogers, Virginia Marie Buxton *industrial psychologist*
Salomon, Lauren Manning *psychologist*
Woodward, Natalie E. *social studies educator*

Humble
Schindler, Gail Lewis *psychologist*

Katy
Haymond, Paula J. *psychologist, diagnostician, hypnotherapist*

Kerrville
Abney, Denise Ann Cardin *psychologist, researcher*

Lackland Afb
Neal-Walden, Tracy A. *psychologist*

Laredo
Riggs, William W. *social sciences educator*

Lewisville
Netz, Deborah Rudder *psychologist*

Mc Kinney
Anderson-Bruess, Judith *social studies educator*

Mesquite
Byrd, Kathryn Susan *psychologist, educator*

Midland
Sherpa, Fran Magruder *geography educator*

Pasadena
Kotecki, Dawn Marie *social studies educator*

Prairie View
Prestage, Jewel Limar *political science professor*

San Antonio
Anderson, Anita L. *psychology professor*
Austin, Lola Houston *psychologist*
Callihan, D. Jeanne *psychologist, educator*
Case, Elizabeth Joy *psychology and educational assessment director*
Celmer, Virginia *psychologist*
Cusack, Regina M. *psychology professor, lawyer*
Hancock, Kathleen J. *political science professor*

Stafford
Krenek, Mary Louise *political scientist, researcher*

Sugar Land
Lankford, Janna Louise *social studies educator*

UTAH

Brigham City
Halterman, Karen Annie *psychologist*

Logan
Van Dusen, Lani Marie *psychologist*

Ogden
Lang, Anna Joyce *geography professor*

Park City
Brandon, Kathleen Virginia *social studies educator*

Provo
Ballif-Spanvill, Bonnie *psychologist, educator*

Salt Lake City
Benjamin, Lorna Smith *psychologist*
Cole, Sally J. (Sarah Jewell Cole) *archaeologist, researcher*
Livne, Nava Levia *psychologist, researcher*

Sandy
Durham, Lynn Ellen *school psychologist*
Snell, Marilyn Nelson *psychologist, researcher*

Springville
Leek, Priscilla *social sciences educator*

VERMONT

Burlington
Jacobs, Genevieve M. *psychology professor, communications educator*
Longmaid, Kate Jessamyn *psychologist*

Colchester
Whitney, Carolyn *psychology professor*

East Calais
Elliott, Susan Auguste *psychologist, psychotherapist, consultant*

Essex Junction
Dietzel, Louise Alverta *psychologist*

Lyndonville
Werdenschlag, Lori B. *psychologist, educator*

Middlebury
Lamberti, Marjorie *retired social studies educator*

Montgomery Center
Oktavec, Eileen M. *anthropologist, artist*

VIRGINIA

Alexandria
Matalin, Mary *political consultant*
Tarr, Linda Haas *psychologist*

Annandale
Carvalho, Julie Ann *psychologist*

Arlington
Davis, Lynn Etheridge *political scientist, educator*
Durham, Mary Sherrill *psychologist, writer*
Gramm, Wendy Lee *economics professor, retired government agency administrator*
Siddayao, Corazón Morales *economist, educator, consultant*

Ashburn
Gross, Linda Armani *social studies educator*

Ashland
Polce-Lynch, Mary Elise *psychologist*

Catawba
Bartizal, Denise *psychologist*

Charlottesville
Friedman, Susan Lynn Bell *economist*
Hanft, Ruth S. Samuels *economist, consultant*
Hetherington, Eileen Mavis *psychologist, educator*
Lanham, Betty Bailey *anthropologist, educator*
Moreno, Zerka Toeman *psychodrama educator*

Chesterfield
Wilczewski, Lynn Cheryl *social studies educator, department chairman*

Claremont
Seward, Troilen Gainey *retired psychologist*

Colonial Heights
Huff, Rebecca Suzette *psychologist*

Eastville
Williams, Ida Jones *consumer and home economics educator, writer*

Fairfax
Kitsantas, Anastasia *educational psychologist*
Tolchin, Susan Jane *political science professor, writer*

Falls Church
Calkins, Susannah Eby *retired economist*
Roussel, Lee Dennison *economist*

Fort Belvoir
O'Kane, Barbara Lynn *research psychologist*

Fredericksburg
Rampersad, Peggy A. Snellings *sociologist, consultant*

Hampton
Duncan, Nancy Carol *psychology professor*
Johnson, Leona Melissa *psychology professor, researcher*

Harrisonburg
Ferraiolo, Kathleen Mary *political science professor*
Finney, Sara Jane *psychologist, educator*

Lancaster
Beane, Judith Mae *retired psychologist*

Lansdowne
Stanley, Lila Gail *political science professor, art appraiser*

Lynchburg
Payne, Pauleta Polly *psychologist*

Mathews
Gillikin, Lynn *retired psychologist*

Mc Lean
Auerbach, Anita L. *psychologist*

Mechanicsville
Wells, Mary Julia *psychologist*

Newington
Robertson, Jean Elizabeth *sociology educator*

Norfolk
Doumas, Judith *psychologist, educator*
Leitch, Sally Lynn *social studies educator*
Neumann, Serina Ann Louise *psychologist, researcher*

Oakton
Trifoli-Cunniff, Laura Catherine *psychologist, consultant*

Portsmouth
Ojeda, Ana Maria *therapist, clinical caseworker*

Radford
Lips, Hilary Margaret *psychology educator, writer*

Richmond
Cooper, Deborah Kay *forensic psychologist*
Radecki, Catherine *psychologist*

Salem
LaRocco, Theresa M. *social studies educator*

Sterling
Hill-Wagner, Aimee Elizabeth *social studies educator*

Stuart
Belcher, Lisa Roop *social studies educator*

White Stone
Graves, Pirkko Maija-Leena *clinical psychologist, psychoanalyst*

Williamsburg
Kerns, Virginia B. *anthropologist, writer*
Peterson, Susan *political science professor, dean*

Winchester
Chen, Yvonne *economics professor*

Yorktown
Pagels, Carrie Fancett *psychologist*

WASHINGTON

Bellingham
Collamer, Barbara Ellen *social sciences educator*
Lois, Jennifer M. *sociologist, educator*

Colville
Culton, Sarah Alexander *psychologist, educator*

Ellensburg
Miller, Maxine Lynch *retired home economist, retired interior designer, educator*

Everett
Van Ry, Ginger Lee *school psychologist*

Federal Way
Ruddell, Alysa Ann *clinical psychologist*

Hansville
Blalock, Ann Bonar *evaluation researcher*

Issaquah
Drazdoff, Nola Gay *psychologist*

Marysville
Adams, Julie Karen *psychologist*

Mercer Island
Carey, Susan M. *psychologist*
Kessler, Gale Suzanne *psychologist, educator*

Olympia
Jun, Heesoon *psychology professor*

Pullman
McSweeney, Frances Kaye *psychology professor*

Seattle
Burchfield, Susan *psychologist*
Coffman, Sandra Jeanne *psychologist*
Cote, Charlotte June *social sciences educator, consultant*
Green, G. Dorsey *psychologist, author*
Hayes, Camela Paige *psychologist*
Look, Janet K. *psychologist*
Martin, Joan Callaham *psychologist, educator*
Robinson, Nancy Mayer *psychology educator*
Schwartz, Pepper Judith *sociologist, educator*
Teller, Davida Young *psychology, physiology and biophysics educator*

Spokane
Fritts, Anna Nicole *psychologist*

Tacoma
Don, Audrey *clinical psychologist, neuropsychologist, violist, artist*
Forrest, Kelly Alexandra *psychology professor*
Harris, Marian S. *social work educator*

Toppenish
Alexander, Judith Elaine *psychologist*

WEST VIRGINIA

Morgantown
Peterson, Sophia *political scientist, educator*
Waller, Stacey *psychologist*

WISCONSIN

Cascade
Baumann, Carol Edler *retired political scientist*

Deerfield
Bazan, Angela Lynn *social studies educator*

Dodgeville
Filardo, Tamra L. *social studies educator*

Eau Claire
Hugo, Miriam Jeanne *counseling psychologist, educator*

Fennimore
Croft, Candace Ann *psychology professor, academic administrator, small business owner*

Kenosha
Cassiday, Karen Lynn *psychologist*

La Crosse
Seebach, Elizabeth Emily *psychologist, educator*

Madison
McDonald, Susan B. *psychologist*
Rice, Joy Katharine *psychologist, education educator*
Sherman, Julia Ann *psychologist*
Strier, Karen Barbara *anthropologist, educator*
Vandell, Deborah Lowe *educational psychology educator*
Wolfe, Barbara L. *economics professor, researcher*

Milwaukee
Carter, Charlene Ann *psychologist*
Fouad, Nadya A. *psychology professor*
Kupst, Mary Jo *psychologist, researcher*
Nielson, Kristy Ann *psychology educator, researcher*

New Berlin
Bielke, Patricia Ann *psychologist*
Marsh, Clare Teitgen *retired school psychologist*

Racine
Zimmel, Tammy Lynn *psychologist*

Stevens Point
Doherty, Patricia Anne *psychologist*

Superior
Taylor, Winnifred Jane *psychologist*

Thiensville
Franciosi, L. Patt *psychologist, mental health services professional, consultant*

Waukesha
Parsons, Virginia Mae *psychology educator*

WYOMING

Laramie
Williams, Martha Jane Shipe *psychologist, retired educator*

Thermopolis
Gear, Kathleen O'Neal *archaeologist, writer*

TERRITORIES OF THE UNITED STATES

PUERTO RICO

Ponce
Veray, Brunilda *psychologist, educator*

San Juan
Folch-Serrano, Karen D. *psychologist, consultant*
Mejia, Migdalia Teresa *psychologist, performing arts educator*
Roca de Torres, Irma Eneida *retired psychology professor*

Toa Baja
Almeida, Michelle Kathleen *psychologist, educator*

MILITARY ADDRESSES OF THE UNITED STATES

ATLANTIC

APO
Sosa, Rita Sladen *social sciences educator*

CANADA

BRITISH COLUMBIA

Burnaby
Kimura, Doreen *psychology professor, researcher*

Vancouver
Marchak, Maureen Patricia *anthropology and sociology educator, academic administrator*

NOVA SCOTIA

Chester Basin
Parr-Johnston, Elizabeth *economist, consultant*

ONTARIO

Hamilton
Ryan, Ellen Bouchard *psychology professor, gerontologist*

Toronto
Dobson, Wendy Kathleen *economics professor*

QUEBEC

Montreal
Ikawa-Smith, Fumiko *anthropologist, educator*
Steinberg, Blema *political science professor*

BERMUDA

Saint Georges
Jackson, Hermoine Prestine *psychologist*

EGYPT

Cairo
Lesch, Ann Mosely *political scientist, educator*

ENGLAND

London
Junz, Helen B. *economist*

GERMANY

Mannheim
Flor, Herta *psychology professor*

ITALY

Rome
Masini, Eleonora Barbieri *futurist*

SCOTLAND

Saint Andrews
Tanner, Joanne Elizabeth *psychologist, researcher*

ADDRESS UNPUBLISHED

Abu-Lughod, Janet Lippman *sociologist, educator*
Adam, Justine E. *psychologist*
Albagli, Louise Martha *psychologist*
Alberti-Chappell, Roxana Dearing *psychologist*
Alexander, Ascencion (Cency) H. *school psychologist, educator*
Allen, Leatrice Delorice *psychologist*
Allen, Pamela Smith *retired psychologist, writer*
Altemara, Maria Christi Staley *anthropologist, sociologist, educator*
Alvarez-Corona, Marti *school psychologist, educator*
Amar, Paula Bram *psychologist, consultant*
Ancoli-Israel, Sonia *psychologist, researcher*
Andrews, Pat R. *political science professor*
Ansevics, Nancy Leah *mental health services administrator*
Anthony-Perez, Bobbie Cotton Murphy *retired psychology professor*
Aviles, Alice Alers *psychologist*
Baba, Marietta Lynn *anthropologist, academic administrator*
Babcock-Lumish, Terry Lynne *economic geographer*
Babladelis, Georgia *retired psychology educator*
Bailey, Catherine Suzanne *psychologist*
Baker, Andrea J. *sociologist, educator*
Bateson, Mary Catherine *retired anthropology educator*
Bearden, Amy Jean *social studies educator, department chairman*
Beca, Monique *psychologist*
Beckett, Faye Trumbo *school psychologist*
Bell, Linda Green *psychology educator, therapist*
Benoit, Jo *psychologist, consultant*
Bernstein, Phyliss Louise *psychologist*
Best, Judith A. *political science professor*
Bethea, Elizabeth *social sciences educator, psychologist, minister*
Bhatia, Sonia Singh *psychologist*
Bilich, Marion Yellin *psychologist, writer*
Birdsall, Nancy *economist*
Blank, Rebecca Margaret *economist*
Bluth, B. J. (Elizabeth Jean Catherine Bluth) *sociologist, aerospace technologist*
Blystone, Debra A. *social studies educator*
Bohen, Barbara Elizabeth *archaeologist, retired museum director*
Bolla, Karen Irene *neuropsychologist, educator*
Boltuck, Mary A. *retired psychologist, educator*
Bomboy, Jennifer Marie *social studies educator, coach*
Bonnell, Victoria Eileen *sociologist, educator*
Bornstein, Barbara Markey *psychologist*
Boumenot, Stacy Leah *school psychologist*
Bourguignon, Erika Eichhorn *anthropologist, educator*
Breitbart, Barbara Renee *psychologist, administrator, writer*
Bricker, Victoria Reifler *anthropologist, educator*
Bronzaft, Arline L. *psychology consultant*
Brooks, Lynda Barbara *psychologist*
Brown, Amira Khalila *neuropsychologist, researcher*
Buck, Jane Louise *retired psychology professor*
Bullard, Judith Eve *psychologist, systems engineer*
Burns, Marcelline *retired psychologist, researcher*
Burnside, Mary Ardis *psychologist*
Bush, Rebecca R. *psychologist*
Buttel, Stacey Jeanne *social studies educator*
Carlsen, Mary Baird *clinical psychologist*
Carlson, Janet Frances *psychologist, educator*
Carrillo, Juanita *gerontological services consultant*
Carton, Lonnie Caming *educational psychologist*
Cartwright, Lillian *psychologist, researcher, artist*
Cavin, Susan Elizabeth *sociologist, writer*
Chapman, Hope Horan *psychologist*
Chatterji, Angana P. *anthropologist*
Cohen, Lois Jean *developmental psychologist, retired*
Colip, Olga Shearin *retired home economist, volunteer*
Collarini Schlossberg, Antoinette Marie *psychologist*
Corno, Lyn *psychology educator*
Cotten, Annie Laura *psychologist, educator*
Crisci, Pat Devita *retired psychology educator*
Crozier, Prudence Slitor *economist*
Damrosch, Shirley Patchel *social psychologist, educator*
Daniels, Arlene Kaplan *sociology educator*
Day, Joyce Cerejo *school psychologist*
Devany Serio, Catherine *clinical psychologist*
DeVaris, Jeannette Mary *psychologist*
DiCiacco, Janis Annette *psychologist*
DiGiovanni, Joan Fimbel *psychology educator*
Dillon, Kerris *social studies educator*
Dixon, Carrie J. *social studies educator*
Dore, Patricia Ann *psychologist*
Dotterweich, Lisa Josette *political science professor, researcher*
Durell, Viviane G. *psychologist, small business owner*
Eberly, Raina Elaine *retired psychologist, educator*
Ehrenberg, Miriam Colbert *psychologist*
Ellington, Jane Elizabeth *experimental psychologist*
Emerson, Alice Frey *political scientist, educator emerita*
End, Laurel Jean *psychologist, educator*
Espiritu, Antonina *economics professor*
Estés, Clarissa Pinkola *psychoanalyst, poet, writer*
Estevez, Anne-Marie *psychologist, lawyer*
Farnham-Diggory, Sylvia *psychologist, educator*
Fennell, Teresa Ann *psychologist*
Feshbach, Norma Deitch *psychologist, educator*
Filippelli Marandola, Linda Patricia *school psychologist*
Finnberg, Elaine Agnes *psychologist, editor*
Fletcher, Rita R. *social studies educator*
Follingstad, Carol C. *psychologist, consultant, educator*
Fontes, Patricia J. *psychologist*
Frankel, Judith Jennifer Mariasha *clinical psychologist, consultant*
Franklin, Margery Bodansky *psychology professor, researcher*
Frawley-O'Dea, Mary Gail *clinical psychologist, psychoanalyst, educator*
Friedman, Nicole *psychologist, consultant*
Friedman, Sofia *social sciences educator, nutritionist, educator*
Frontani, Heidi Glaesel *geographer, educator*
Frost, Ellen Louise *political economist*
Fury, Sara Jo *social studies educator, coach*
Gallucci-Breithaupt, Adrianne *psychologist, social worker*
Gandhi, Purvi B. *psychologist*
Garzarelli, Elaine Marie *economist*
Gashaw-Gant, Gebaynesh Gelila *psychologist, consultant*
Gaskin-Butler, Vikki Twynette *clinical psychologist*
Gawkowski, Spring Page *social sciences educator, social worker*
Geertz, Hildred Storey *anthropology educator*
Genia, Vicky *psychologist*
Genis, Alice Singer *psychologist*
Gibson, Janice Thorne *developmental psychology educator, author, academic administrator*
Giele, Janet Zollinger *sociologist, educator*
Gilbert, Anita Rae *psychologist, educator*
Giomi, Thelma Anne *clinical psychologist*
Glick, Myrna Joan *psychologist*
Golomb, Claire *psychology educator*
Golub, Sharon Bramson *retired psychologist, educator*
Goren, Judith Ann *retired psychologist*
Goron, Mara J. *social studies educator, assistant principal*
Gottsegen, Gloria *psychologist, educator*
Grant, Carmen Hill *psychologist, psychotherapist*
Greenwood, Janet Kae Daly *psychologist, academic administrator, marketing professional*
Gross, Amber Savage *social sciences educator*
Guinn, Janet Martin *psychologist, consultant*
Haining, Jeane *psychologist*
Hall, Ella Taylor *clinical school psychologist*
Hamlett, Tiffany *psychologist, educator*
Hammel, Sabrina Irene *political scientist, educator*
Harari, Zaraleya Kurzweil *psychologist, psychotherapist*
Hartzell, Irene Janofsky *retired psychologist*
Hattery, Angela Jean *sociologist, educator*
Hawes, Bess Lomax *retired folklorist*
Hawkins, DaLana Marie *social studies educator*
Haynes, Patricia L. *psychologist, researcher*
Hefferan, Colien Joan *economist*
Henry, Lois Hollender *psychologist*
Heyse, Patricia Lynn *school psychologist*
Hidden-Dodson, Nancy *retired psychologist, consultant, educator*
Higa, Charmaine Keala *psychologist*
Hilsabeck, Kristine *social studies educator*
Honig, Alice Sterling *psychologist*
Hoopes, Margaret Howard *educator, psychologist, marriage and family therapist*
Hopkins, Brenda Luvenia *social sciences educator, minister*
Horai, Joann *psychologist*
Htun, Mala *political science professor*
Huckstead, Charlotte Van Horn *retired home economist, artist*
Hughes, Ann Hightower *retired economist, trade association administrator*
Hughes, Deanna Elma *psychologist*
Hughes, Teresa Mead *psychologist*
Izawa, Chizuko *psychologist, researcher*
Jackson, Kelly Sue *social studies educator*
Jacobs, Marianne *anthropologist, educator, medical/surgical nurse*
Jacobs, Marion Kramer *psychologist*
James, Estelle *economist, educator*
Jellison, Jenny Lynne *psychology professor*
Jern, Donna L. *social studies educator*
Johnson, Crystal Duane *psychologist*
Johnson, J(anet) Susan *psychologist*
Johnston, Janis Clark *psychologist, consultant*
Johnston, Mary Hollis *clinical psychologist*
Jones, Cynthia R. *social studies educator*
Jones, Joan Megan *anthropologist*
Joyce, Diana *psychologist, education educator*
Kahana, Eva Frost *sociology educator*
Kamenske, Gloria L. *retired psychologist*
Kaminsky, Irene *psychologist*
Karabinus, Cynthia Julie Ann *psychology and sociology educator*
Karayan, Ani A. *psychologist, consultant*
Kaslow, Florence Whiteman *psychologist, educator, family business consultant*
Katz, Phyllis Alberts *developmental research psychologist*
Kaye, Janet Miriam *psychologist, educator*
Keeney, Marisa Gesina *psychologist*
Keim, Katherine I. *psychologist*
Kellums, Karen J. *psychologist*
Kennedy, Marla Catherine *psychologist*
Kennedy, Muriel *psychologist, consultant, educator*
Keohane, Nannerl Overholser *political scientist, academic administrator*
King, Rosalyn Mercita *social sciences educator, researcher, psychologist*
Kinget, G. Marian *educator, psychologist*
Kirschman, Ellen Freeman *psychologist*
Kirschner-Bromley, Victoria Ann *clinical counselor*
Kist-Tahmasian, Candace Lynee *psychologist*
Kocel, Katherine Merle *psychology professor, researcher*
Komechak, Marilyn Gilbert *psychologist, educator*
Kornrich, Rhoda *psychologist*
Kos, Nirvana Gabriela *psychologist*
Kosisky, Shelley Ann *psychologist*
Koss, Mary Lyndon Pease *psychology educator, researcher*

Kramer, Karen Sue *psychologist, educator*
Kronenberg, Mindy Ellen *psychologist, psychology professor*
Lacher, Miriam Browner *neuropsychologist*
LaGanke, Allyson Ann *psychologist*
Lancaster, Kirsten Kezar *psychologist*
Landvogt, Penny Lucille *psychotherapist, educator*
Lapp, Kathryn S. *social studies educator*
Lautzenhiser, Niann Kay *psychologist, real estate broker*
Lawrence, Janice Fletcher *psychologist*
Leblanc, Jeanne Marie *psychologist, educator*
Lee, Tabia (T. Lee) *social studies educator*
Legendre, Jaclyn *psychologist*
Leith, Karen Pezza *psychologist, educator*
Leonard, Jo Ann Warner *social sciences educator*
Lertora, Joanne Marie *psychologist*
Leventer, Terri *psychologist*
Levermore, Monique A. *psychologist, educator*
Liebman, Nina R. *economic developer*
Loveman, Aurelia Leffler *psychologist, writer*
Lovick, Norma McGinnis *social studies educator*
Lowe, Patricia A. *psychologist, educator*
Lu, May *psychologist, counselor, writer, watercolorist*
Lynton, Sandra M. *psychologist*
MacLennan, Beryce Winifred *psychologist*
Magana, Melanie G *psychologist, consultant*
Malik, Josie M. Meza *psychologist*
Manis, Laura Glance *retired psychology educator*
Marcus, Kelly Stein *psychologist, health science association administrator*
Matyas, Cindy Susanne *psychologist, educator*
Mc Clellan, Catharine *anthropologist, educator*
McDunn, Adrienne *human behavior consultant*
McPherson, Mary E. *social studies educator*
Mederich, Amy Marie *social studies educator*
Meek, Carroll Lee Larson *psychologist, graphic designer*
Meit, Heather Tonia *psychologist*
Menlove, Frances Lee *psychologist*
Messé, Madelyn Renée *clinical psychologist, consultant*
Meyers, May Lou *retired psychologist, educational consultant*
Michalek, Tina A. *social studies educator*
Miksis, Christina Barbara *psychologist*
Miller, Geraldine *clinical psychologist*
Miller, Lillian May *psychologist*
Miller, Monica Lisa *social studies educator*
Mockler, Jennifer Lynn *psychologist, education educator*
Moevs, Maria Teresa Marabini *archaeologist*
Moore, Erin M. *social studies educator*
Morse, Gayle Skawennio *psychologist, consultant*
Mowrer-Reynolds, Elizabeth Louise *educational psychology educator*
Muhn, Judy Ann *psychologist, genealogist, trainer*
Muller, Frederica Daniela *psychology educator*
Murphy, Evelyn Frances *economist*
Nabuda, Janice Ann *social studies educator*
Naviaux, LaRee DeVee *retired psychologist, academic administrator, director*
Neibert, Betsy Lyn *psychologist*
Newcomb, Rachel *anthropologist, educator*
Newton, Niles Rumely *psychologist, educator*
Ng, Ming T. *psychologist*
Oksas, Joan Kay *economist, educator*
Okun, Barbara Frank *psychologist, educator*
Orr, Amy J. *sociologist, educator*
Ortiz, Mayra Zoe *psychologist*
Osowiec, Darlene Ann *clinical psychologist, educator, consultant*
Ouyang, Norma M. *psychologist*
Packert, Ginger E. *social studies educator, education educator*
Palmer, April Marie *social studies educator*
Palmer, Linda K. *psychology educator, writer, editor*
Papaioannou, Evangelia-Lilly *psychologist, researcher*
Patino-Brandfon, Sylvia *retired psychologist*
Pauley, Elsa P. *psychologist, educator*
Peattie, Lisa Redfield *retired urban anthropology educator*
Pelcyger, Elaine *school psychologist*
Pelcyger, Gwynne Ellice *school psychologist*
Pepper, Joline Romano *psychologist, educator*
Pepper, Pamela Poe *psychologist*
Peretti, Terri L. *political science professor, department chairman*
Perez, Luz Lillian *psychologist*
Perry, Misty J. *social studies educator*
Pezeshk, Violet *psychologist, educator*
Pope, Lillie *psychologist, educator, writer, consultant*
Popoff, Edna Spieler *psychologist, consultant*
Potts, Latonya G. *social studies educator*
Power, Mary Susan *political scientist, educator*
Punnett, Audrey Frances *clinical psychologist, educator*
Recker, Stacy *social studies educator*
Reed, Diane Marie *retired psychologist*
Reichs, Kathy Joan *forensic anthropologist, educator, writer*
Reitan, Ann *psychologist, writer*
Revere, Virginia Lehr *psychologist*
Richardson, Laurel Walum *sociology educator*
Richstone, Beverly June *psychologist, writer*
Rickel, Annette Urso *psychology and psychiatry researcher, educator*
Robinson, Marguerite Stern *anthropologist, educator, consultant*
Rogers, Audrey Patricia *social studies educator, consultant*
Romanucci-Ross, Lola *anthropologist, educator*
Romer, Ann Elizabeth *school psychologist*
Rosicki, Maria Trzetrzewinska-Trett *clinical psychologist*
Ross, Jeanne Nmi *psychologist*
Rudd, Ann Talton *psychologist, artist*
Runyon, Melissa K. *psychologist, educator*
Russell, Deborah Louise *psychologist, researcher*
Rustgi, Eileen Boyle *clinical psychologist*
Salzman, Anne Meyersburg *retired psychologist*
Sanders, Linda E. *psychologist, educator*
Santamaria, Joanne C. *psychologist*
Santana, Niurka Maribel *neuropsychologist, educator*
Sarris, Jean Adams *retired psychologist*
Saunders, Antoinette Mercier *psychologist, educator*
Saunders, Mari Pittman *psychologist*
Schafer, Lorraine *psychologist, researcher*
Schaffer, Bonnie Lynn *psychologist*
Scheinman, Nancy Jane *psychologist*
Schmandt-Besserat, Denise *archaeologist, educator*
Schmeidler, Gertrude Raffel *psychology educator*
Schneider, Greta *economist, writer, speaker, efficiency expert, security consultant, public administration expert*
Schneider Vaulman, Sharon Kay *neuropsychologist, educator*
Schnorr, Janet Kay *psychology educator, researcher*
Schwartz, Beth Meryl *psychology professor*
Schwartz, Susan Evalyn *psychologist*
Schwendinger, Julia Rosalind Siegel *sociology researcher*
Selders, Jean E. *retired psychology professor*
Seltzer, Vivian Center *psychologist, educator*
Seymour, Pearl M. *retired psychologist*
Shaffer, Dorothy Tien *clinical psychologist*
Sharma, Martha Bridges *geography educator*
Sharp, Kay Frances *psychologist*
Shea, M. *psychology professor*
Shillinglaw, Regina D. *psychologist*
Shutter, Christine *psychologist*
Siegel, Erika Janet *psychologist*
Silverman, Sydel Finfer *anthropologist*
Simon, Norma Plavnick *psychologist*
Sisk, Jane Elizabeth *economist, educator*
Sisley, Emily Lucretia *psychologist, writer*
Smith, Karen Gil *social studies educator*
Smith, Susannah *clinical and organizational development consulting psychologist*
Smith, Vme Edom (Verna Mae Edom Smith) *social sciences educator, freelance photographer, freelance writer*
Smith Brinton, Marcia *psychologist, consultant*
Snyder, Andrea Jill *psychologist*
Sosnick, Amanda Joy *social studies educator*
Spangler, Edra Mildred *psychologist*
Spooner, Susan Elizabeth *counseling psychologist, educator*
Staheli, Linda Anne *social science executive*
Sterling, Sarah L. *archaeologist, educator*
Stevenson, Joyce R.L. *psychologist*
Stewart, Bonnie Louise *psychologist*
Stokey, Nancy L. *economist, educator*
Strong, Sara Dougherty *psychologist, family therapist, custody mediator*
Styer, Denise Marie *psychologist*
Suberri, Keren Chansky *psychologist, educator, marriage and family therapist*
Suh, Eun Jung *psychologist, researcher*
Sumter, Joni Lynn *political science professor*
Sussman, Janet I. *social sciences educator*
Swaner, Paula Margetts *clinical psychologist*
Swearingen, Lucinda Ellen *retired psychologist*
Swift, Patricia Anne *school psychologist*
Szeliga, Victoria I. *social studies educator*
Taranto, Maria Antoinette *psychology researcher, educator*
Tepe, Victoria *research psychologist, women's health care advocate*
Terris, Kathleen Elizabeth *social studies educator*
Thayer, Jane Hillis *psychologist*
Thompson, Vetta Lynn Sanders *psychologist, educator*
Tonello-Stuart, Enrica Maria *political scientist, economist*
Torney-Purta, Judith Vollmar *developmental psychologist*
Torok, Sarah E. *psychology professor*
Tripp, Aili Mari *political scientist, educator*
Troiani, Maryann Victoria *psychologist*
Trujillo, Stephanie N. *social sciences educator*
Tufo Jarnagin, Kelli *social studies educator*
van Assendelft, Laura Anne *political science professor*
Vanderhost, Leonette Louise *psychologist*
Vaughan, Nadine *psychologist*
Veit, Clairice Gene Tipton *measurement psychologist*
Von Braunsberg, Mary Jane *clinical psychologist*
Wagner, Angela Dawn *social studies educator*
Ward, Jeannette Poole *retired psychologist, educator*
Washburn, Patricia Cheyne *retired psychologist, environmental scientist, conservationist*
Watson, Patty Jo *anthropology educator*
Watton, Rhonda Kay *social studies educator*
Weiner, Ferne *psychologist*
Wents, Doris Roberta *psychologist*
Werner-Jacobsen, Emmy Elisabeth *developmental psychologist*
Whitehead, Tanya Dianne Grubbs *psychologist, educator, researcher*
Wiesenberg, Jacqueline Leonardi *social sciences educator*
Wilcox, Diane Marie *educational psychologist, software designer*
Wilkinson, Doris *medical sociology educator*
Williams, Cecelia Peay *retired psychologist*
Wilson, Shauna B. *psychologist, researcher*
Woods, Merilyn Baron *psychologist, consultant*
Wyner, Ethel Schiff *psychologist, director*
Yali, Ann Marie *psychology professor*
Yancey, Elizabeth Stilphen *political scientist*
Yates, Kimberly Nicole *school psychologist*
Yoder, Nanci Sue *retired psychologist*
York, Joan Elizabeth Smith *psychologist*
Zanjani, Sally *political science educator, author*
Zilberberg, Barbara *psychologist*
Zuckerman, Harriet *sociologist, educator*